**"EASILY THE MOST COM
ITS KIND ANYWHERE.
EVERY TV AND VCR IN EV**

"LEONARD MALTIN REMAINS . . . THE FATHER OF WHAT HAS BECOME THE SINGLE MOST IMPORTANT REFERENCE BOOK IN EVERY AMERICAN HOME."—*Esquire*

Summer blockbusters and independent sleepers . . . the masterworks of John Ford, Alfred Hitchcock, and Frank Capra . . . the timeless comedy of the Marx Brothers and Buster Keaton . . . the animated classics of Walt Disney . . . the greatest foreign films ever made. . . . This 2001 edition is packed with the films you can't afford to miss—and those you can—from box-office smashes to cult classics to forgotten gems to forgettable bombs. They're all listed here alphabetically, complete with all the essential information you could ask for:

- Date of release, running time, director, stars, MPAA rating, color or black and white
- Concise summary, capsule review, and four-star-to-BOMB rating system
- Notes on computer-colorized films and those shot in widescreen format and best viewed in letterbox format
- Symbols for videocassette, DVD, and laserdisc releases
- Completely updated index of leading actors
- Updated source list for buying and renting videocassettes, DVDs, and laserdiscs

Leonard Maltin's

MOVIE AND VIDEO GUIDE

"INCH FOR INCH, DOLLAR FOR DOLLAR, MALTIN'S BOOK GIVES YOU THE MOST." —*Boston Sunday Herald*

"MALTIN'S FILM GUIDE STILL ****" —*USA Today*

"THE BEST OF THE BUNCH." —*San Francisco Examiner & Chronicle*

"THE BEST ALL-PURPOSE VIDEO GUIDE . . . THE MOST UP-TO-DATE." —*New York Daily News*

"I RECOMMEND LEONARD MALTIN'S GUIDE, WHICH HAS BECOME STANDARD." —*Roger Ebert's Video Companion*

LEONARD MALTIN'S

MOVIE & VIDEO GUIDE

2001 Edition

Edited by Leonard Maltin

MANAGING EDITOR
Cathleen Anderson

ASSOCIATE EDITOR
Luke Sader

CONTRIBUTING EDITORS
Mike Clark
Rob Edelman
Spencer Green
Alvin H. Marill
Michael Scheinfeld
Bill Warren

VIDEO EDITOR
Casey St. Charnez

CONTRIBUTORS
Jerry Beck
Pete Hammond
Kevin Maynard

PENGUIN BOOKS

PENGUIN BOOKS

Published by the Penguin Group
Penguin Books Ltd, 27 Wrights Lane, London W8 5TZ, England
Penguin Putnam Inc., 375 Hudson Street, New York, New York 10014, USA
Penguin Books Australia Ltd, Ringwood, Victoria, Australia
Penguin Books Canada Ltd, 10 Alcorn Avenue, Toronto, Ontario, Canada M4V 3B2
Penguin Books India (P) Ltd, 11 Community Centre, Panchsheel Park, New Delhi – 110 017, India
Penguin Books (NZ) Ltd, Cnr Rosedale and Airborne Roads, Albany, Auckland, New Zealand
Penguin Books (South Africa) (Pty) Ltd, 5 Watkins Street, Denver Ext 4, Johannesburg 2094, South Africa

Registered Offices: Harmondsworth, Middlesex, England

First published in the United States of America by Signet 2000
Published in Great Britain by Penguin Books 2000
1

Printed in England by Clays Ltd, St Ives plc

LEONARD MALTIN is one of the country's most respected film historians. After establishing himself with a series of definitive books (on topics ranging from Hollywood cameramen to the history of animated cartoons), he became known to an even wider audience as the film critic and historian on television's popular syndicated program *Entertainment Tonight*, where he has worked since 1982. In the summer of 1998 he was named film critic for *Playboy* magazine. He also hosts a daily syndicated radio program, *Leonard Maltin's Video View*, provides regular commentary for the cable TV service Encore, and hosts *Leonard Maltin Presents* on Odyssey. His books include *The Great American Broadcast*, *Of Mice and Magic: A History of American Animated Cartoons*, *The Great Movie Comedians*, *The Disney Films*, *The Art of the Cinematographer*, *Movie Comedy Teams*, *Selected Short Subjects (The Great Movie Shorts)*, *The Whole Film Sourcebook*, *Leonard Maltin's Movie Encyclopedia*, and (as coauthor) *The Little Rascals: The Life and Times of Our Gang*. He teaches at the University of Southern California, in the Cinema-Television Department, and served for two years as president of the Los Angeles Film Critics Association. As a member of the National Film Preservation Board, he votes on the twenty-five films named each year to join the Library of Congress' National Film Registry. For nine years he was the editor and publisher of *Film Fan Monthly* magazine; his articles have appeared in the *New York Times*, the *Los Angeles Times*, *Smithsonian*, *TV Guide*, *Variety*, *Esquire*, *Disney Magazine*, *Film Comment*, and *American Film*. He lectures on film subjects around the country, and for nine years was a member of the faculty of the New School for Social Research in New York City. In 1976 he served as guest programmer for the Museum of Modern Art's Bicentennial Salute to American Film Comedy and returned in 1985 to organize a tribute to Warner Bros. Cartoons. He has written a number of television specials, including *Fantasia: The Creation of a Disney Classic*. He has also produced, written, and hosted such original cable TV and home-video programs as *Cartoon Madness: The Fantastic Max Fleischer Cartoons*, *Young Duke: The Making of a Movie Star* (which debuted on A&E's *Biography*), *Cliffhangers: Adventures from the Thrill Factory*, *The Making of "The Quiet Man," The Making of "High Noon," The Lost Stooges*, and *Cartoons for Big Kids*. He and his wife, Alice, are the proud parents of Jessica Bennett Maltin, who wrote the entry for *Deuce Bigelow: Male Gigolo* in this edition.

About the Editors

Luke Sader was introduced to old movies by his father, then really got hooked watching vintage Hollywood and foreign films while at college. He majored in English at Johns Hopkins University, then went backpacking abroad for a year, catching movies everywhere from Helsinki to Cairo. His association with this book was foreshadowed by the capsulized reviews he provided for cinema screenings during a stay on an Israeli kibbutz. He has worked at CBS Cable, CBS News in New York, and on *Entertainment Tonight* in Los Angeles. He is currently Coordinating Producer for Entertainment News at CNN on the West Coast. In 1994 he served as co-editor of *Leonard Maltin's Movie Encyclopedia.*

Mike Clark is currently senior film critic and writer of the Friday Home Viewing page for *USA Today*, but he first came to prominence in 1958, as a ten-year-old, when he won $16,000 answering movie questions on the television quiz show *The $64,000 Question*. Since then he has attended NYU's Graduate School of Cinema, been the film critic for the *Detroit Free Press*, and conceived approximately 150 thematic film series as Director and Program Planner of the American Film Institute Theater of the John F. Kennedy Center for the Performing Arts in Washington, D.C. He is a weekly contributor to "Critical Mass" in *Entertainment Weekly*'s Movies section, writes the "Best Bets" column for *Satellite Direct*, and has appeared on HBO, Cinemax, *Entertainment Tonight*, *E! Entertainment*, CNN's *Reliable Sources*, and Turner Classic Movies. He is a member of the National Society of Film Critics.

Rob Edelman is the author of *Great Baseball Films* and *Baseball on the Web* (which Amazon.com cited as one of the Top 10 Internet books of 1998). He is co-author (with his wife, Audrey Kupferberg) of *Angela Lansbury: A Life on Stage and Screen*, *The John Travolta Scrapbook*, and *Meet the Mertzes*, a dual biography of Vivian Vance and William Frawley. He is the director of programming of Home Film Festival, offers film commentary on WAMC (Northeast) Public Radio, and is a contributing editor of *Leonard Maltin's Family Film Guide* and *Leonard Maltin's Movie Encyclopedia*. His byline has appeared in the *New Haven Register* (where he was film critic), many reference books (including *A Political Companion to American Film*, *Total Baseball*, *International Directory of Films and Filmmakers*, *The Total Baseball Catalog*, and *Women Filmmakers and Their Films*), and dozens of periodicals (from *American Film* to *Variety* and the *Washington Post*). He has programmed film series at the American Film Institute and taught/lectured at Iona College, Sacred Heart University, The School of Visual Arts, and the University at Albany (SUNY).

Alvin H. Marill is the author of the definitive reference work *Movies Made for Television* and served for many years as Television Editor of *Films in Review* magazine. Among his many books are *Samuel Goldwyn Presents*, *The Complete Films of Edward G. Robinson*, *Robert*

Mitchum on the Screen, *More Theatre: Stage to Screen to Television*, *The Ultimate John Wayne Trivia Book*, *Keeping Score: The Movie Composer*, and *The Films of Tommy Lee Jones*. He is an editor for the mystery/horror bi-monthly *Scarlet Street* and an editorial consultant for a number of publishing houses.

Bill Warren is the author of the two-volume *Keep Watching the Skies*, which has been called "one of the rare reference works that combines genuine entertainment with impeccable information," and wrote *Set Visits*, about visiting movie sets, and *The Evil Dead Companion* about that film trilogy. He has also written for such magazines as *Starlog*, *Fangoria*, *American Film*, *Video Watchdog*, and *Galaxy Online*. He contributed to *The New Encyclopedia of Science Fiction*, two volumes on Stephen King, and the annual Science Fiction Writers of America Nebula volumes. Without being able to speak more French than *auteur* and *pommes frites*, he was the Hollywood correspondent for the French television show *Destination Series*.

Casey St. Charnez waltzes in the New Mexico mountains with strawberry blonde Lisa Suzanne Harris, his fiancée of twenty-three years and counting. Many moons ago, he and Leonard Maltin attended New York University, where he earned an M.A. in cinema studies and a Ph.D. in movie musicals (he also holds degrees in English literature and comparative mythology). A former publicity associate with Paramount and Fox, he has written for *Film Fan Monthly*, *The Hollywood Reporter*, and *American Film*, and is the author of *The Complete Films of Steve McQueen*. Recently, he contributed an endword about Greer Garson to the omnibus history *100 Years: A Celebration of Filmmaking in New Mexico*. Casey's mom Linda used to work for a Hollywood law firm, and one time she answered the phone and it was Cary Grant.

Cathleen Anderson is.

Spencer Green recently escaped from prison by wishing himself into a cornfield outside of Titusville, Florida. Now, he and wife Emily Watson travel across country in a van, solving mysteries and entertaining transients with their unique blend of folk songs, pantomime, and pre-ban black market firearms. He has written for *In Living Color*, *AAAHH!!! Real Monsters*, *Duckman*, and *Mad TV*, and was a co-editor of *Leonard Maltin's Movie Encyclopedia*. Mr. Green also sees dead people and they look surprisingly just like chicken.

Michael Scheinfeld is a Senior Writer for *TV Guide* and has also written reviews for the tvguide.com Movie Database. He served as a contributing editor of *Leonard Maltin's Family Film Guide* and writes reviews for the children's video website familywonder.com. He has also written reviews and articles for *The Motion Picture Guide*, *Films in Review*, *Laserviews*, and the National Board of Review's book *The 500 Best British and Foreign Films*. Additionally, he has worked for American Movie Classics and MTV Films, and has produced and programmed film series for cable systems in New York City and Philadelphia.

Key to This Book

Alphabetization: Articles of speech—A, An, The—are eliminated. (*The Mouthpiece* is listed under *Mouthpiece, The.*) Aside from that, film titles are listed in strict letter-by-letter spelling sequence. Separation of words and punctuation is ignored; everything hinges on the letters. So, *Roberta* is listed before *Rob Roy*, because "e" comes before "r." Titles that begin with *Mister* or *Doctor* will come before titles abbreviated *Mr.* or *Dr.* Let the alphabet be your guide, letter-by-letter, and you'll find the title you're looking for.

Each entry lists title and year of release. The letter "C" before a running time indicates that the film was made in color. "D:" indicates the name of the director. This is followed by a listing of the principal cast members. Alternate titles (if any) are noted at the end of the entry.

Ratings range from ★★★★, for the very best, to ★½, for the very worst. There is no ★ rating; instead, for these bottom-of-the-barrel movies, we use the citation BOMB.

Made-for-TV movies receive no star rating. They are indicated by the abbreviation TVM, and evaluated at the end of each entry as being Above average, Average, or Below average.

▼ This symbol indicates the title is available on videocassette;
● indicates laserdisc availability;
◗ indicates DVD (digital video disc) availability.

(These symbols indicate that a film has been released on video; we cannot guarantee current availability.)

The MPAA rates with the following symbols:

G	General Audiences: All ages admitted.
PG	Parental Guidance Suggested: Some material may not be suitable for children.
PG-13	Parents Strongly Cautioned: Some material may be inappropriate for children under 13.
R	Restricted: Children under 17 require accompanying parent or adult guardian.
NC-17	No Children Under 17 Admitted (age may vary in certain areas).

The rating symbols GP, M, and X are no longer used to classify films.

Introduction to 2001 Edition

I remember seeing Stanley Kubrick's *2001: A Space Odyssey* when it was new, in 1968, and thinking that the year 2001 seemed a long way off. The following year the first edition of this book was published; I never dreamed it would have such a long life, or that one day it would bear the name of the year that for several decades had relevance only as the title of a seminal science-fiction film.

Fittingly, futurist Kubrick lived to see the development of cable and satellite television, and digital video discs, or DVDs, but he chose not to tamper with his films for the newest means of watching movies at home. He even frustrated technophiles by insisting that some of his films be released in full-screen, monaural editions.

As usual, Kubrick was swimming against the tide. Nowadays, directors with only a fraction of his talent and an iota of his perfectionism are providing full-length commentaries about their work on DVD, and offering deleted scenes, outtakes, storyboards, and additional material related to their movies. But I'm not sure we need to see additional scenes for movies that were too long to begin with, or hear about the modus operandi of filmmakers who haven't yet established a track record, let alone a personal stamp.

It's almost become a cliché when directors, on the eve of their films' theatrical releases, promise that scenes they cut will turn up on the DVD. What, then, are we paying eight bucks to see on that theater screen—a rough draft?

On the other hand, when studios go back to original materials to improve the picture and sound quality, and when archivists can offer the best available versions of genuine classics like *Lost Horizon*, *The Wizard of Oz*, and *City Lights*, it's cause for celebration. Or when the medium affords us the opportunity to see two different versions of Howard Hawks' *The Big Sleep*, that's a boon for film buffs and scholars around the world.

Video and cable TV have created another phenomenon: the original, theatrical versions of some high-profile movies, from the Judy Garland version of *A Star Is Born* to Orson Welles' *Touch of Evil* to the studio-sanctioned version of Sam Peckinpah's *Pat Garrett & Billy the Kid*, are now moribund, replaced in all existing media by recent restorations. (This will only add to the challenges of film study in years to come.)

The flood of director's editions on DVD has kept us busy making notations in this book. Our concern is not outtakes or cut scenes, but when the director presents a new or alternate version of the film, be it Michael Mann's recut of *The Last of the Mohicans* or Richard Donner's revision of the first three *Lethal Weapon* movies. (Did anyone think they needed revising?)

The video world has also given shelf life to a number of worthwhile movies that can't make their way in the theatrical marketplace. I don't think there's anything more satisfying than being given the opportunity to steer people toward some of these unsung films, like *Kabloonak*, the story of Robert Flaherty's challenge in making his pioneer Eskimo documentary *Nanook of the North*, with Charles Dance in the leading role . . . or Sarah Kernochan's very entertaining *All I Wanna Do* (formerly known as

Strike!), a well-observed story of life at a girls' school in the early 1960s, starring Kirsten Dunst and Rachael Leigh Cook, which had only perfunctory release . . . or Bill Plympton's delightfully wacky handmade animated feature *I Married a Strange Person!*

Films like these, made with passion and purpose, so outweigh the weekly accumulation of formula-bound direct-to-video fodder that they easily earn a place in these pages.

Then, too, we sometimes realize we've given short shrift to a film that's already listed here and feel the need to revise its rating and review. I would call your attention to *Eden*, a genuinely original and provocative film written and directed by Howard Goldberg.

Of course, it's fun to play our annual game of find-the-future-star. Did you know it was Heather Graham who gave birth to the title characters played (as adults) by Arnold Schwarzenegger and Danny DeVito in *Twins*? Or that Haley Joel Osment had a part in Nora Ephron's 1994 comedy *Mixed Nuts*?

We've added early credits for a rather wide variety of actors this year, including Richard Farnsworth, Jennifer Lopez, Janet McTeer, Cherry Jones, Julia Stiles, Lucy Liu, Shawn Hatosy, Philip Seymour Hoffman, Michael Clarke Duncan, Mena Suvari, Judi Dench, Ving Rhames, and Tobey Maguire. It's a source of never-ending fascination to us that some of these performers have gone from almost complete obscurity to worldwide recognition—and even Oscar nominations—in as little as one to two years' time.

The other constant in our annual endeavor is the amount of time and effort required to find reliable information about brand-new movies! Even the screen credits themselves aren't infallible. (Meat Loaf is billed as such in the opening credits of *Fight Club*, but listed as Meat Loaf Aday in the closing crawl!)

Thank goodness for my team of colleagues, stalwarts all who delight in ferreting out those often-elusive details: Cathleen Anderson, Luke Sader, Mike Clark, Rob Edelman, Spencer Green, Alvin H. Marill, Bill Warren, Casey St. Charnez, Jerry Beck, Pete Hammond, Kevin Maynard, and Michael Scheinfeld. Thanks, too, go to our eagle-eyed friends Tom Weaver and Jan Willemsen.

My beneficent editior Hugh Rawson continues to steer me toward the right decisions all year long, and Bill Harris, Arthur Maisel, Ken May, and Kathy Murray navigate the book through its annual obstacle course of production with unfailing good cheer and dedication.

I am grateful, too, to our readers for their continuing input and encouragement, as well as their corrections. To the ones who write nasty, vituperative letters, I wish a cable channel with endless reruns of *In the Army Now*, *Transylvania 6-5000*, and *Maximum Overdrive*.

Watching movies is fun, but sharing them with my wife, Alice, and daughter, Jessie, is even better. They are very much a part of this book.

Working on a reference volume such as this, one can drown in a sea of minutiae, but having the support of loving family, good friends, enthusiastic colleagues, and loyal readers keeps me afloat. In fact, by the time you read this, we'll have already set sail for the next edition.

—LEONARD MALTIN

100+ Recommended Family Films

No two families are alike; choosing a film that's appropriate for your kids is ultimately up to you. Older films often contain material that isn't politically correct by today's standards, but that can be a springboard for positive family discussion. One good film leads to another, so use this list as a starting point to discover the many worthwhile films you can enjoy together, as a family.

Comedies. The Kid; The General; The Kid Brother; The Circus; Horse Feathers; A Night at the Opera; Modern Times; Way Out West; The Three Musketeers (1939); Abbott and Costello Meet Frankenstein; The Long, Long Trailer; The Court Jester; You're Never Too Young

Adventure and Fantasy. King Kong (1933); The Prisoner of Zenda (1937); The Adventures of Robin Hood (1938); Gunga Din; The Wizard of Oz; The Thief of Bagdad (1940); The Mark of Zorro (1940); The Jungle Book (1942); Mighty Joe Young; Treasure Island (1950); The Story of Robin Hood; The Day the Earth Stood Still; 20,000 Leagues Under the Sea; 7th Voyage of Sinbad; The Time Machine; The Golden Voyage of Sinbad; Star Wars; The Empire Strikes Back; Return of the Jedi; Superman; Raiders of the Lost Ark; E.T. the Extra-Terrestrial

Musicals. March of the Wooden Soldiers (Babes in Toyland); Follow the Fleet; Poor Little Rich Girl; Yankee Doodle Dandy; Meet Me in St. Louis; Hans Christian Andersen; Singin' in the Rain; Calamity Jane; Seven Brides for Seven Brothers; Oklahoma!; Carousel; The King and I; The Pajama Game; Li'l Abner; The Sound of Music

Great stories. Little Women (1933 and 1994); David Copperfield (1935); The Prince and the Pauper (1937); The Adventures of Tom Sawyer (1938); Huckleberry Finn (1939); Lassie Come Home; National Velvet; Pollyanna; Sounder; Black Beauty (1994); A Little Princess (1995)

Favorites, old . . . The Little Colonel; Mr. Deeds Goes to Town; Here Comes Mr. Jordan; The Pride of the Yankees; It's a Wonderful Life; Miracle on 34th Street (1947); She Wore a Yellow Ribbon; 3 Godfathers (1948); It Happens Every Spring; Harvey; The Greatest Show on Earth; Angels in the Outfield (1951); Shane

. . . and new. The Karate Kid; Honey, I Shrunk the Kids; Wild Hearts Can't Be Broken; Honey, I Blew Up the Kid; FernGully: The Last Rainforest; Homeward Bound: The Incredible Journey; Rookie of the Year; Little Giants; Cool Runnings; Princess Caraboo; The Santa Clause; I.Q.; Babe (1995); Toy Story; Fairy Tale: A True Story; A Bug's Life; Toy Story 2; My Dog Skip; Stuart Little

Disney. *All* the cartoon classics; So Dear to My Heart; Davy Crockett, King of the Wild Frontier; Johnny Tremain; Old Yeller; Third Man on the Mountain; Darby O'Gill and the Little People; Swiss Family Robinson; The Absent Minded Professor; The Parent Trap; Mary Poppins; The Gnome-Mobile; The Love Bug; Bedknobs and Broomsticks

Mail-Order Sources for Video

Here are some of the name-brand companies who sell and/or rent copyrighted and/or public domain titles by mail in the U.S., from the vintage format Beta, through the current industry standard VHS, and on to the digital future with DVD. There are also several companies that feature the international PAL and SECAM cassette alternatives.

Our movie reviews show video availability with a ▼ for tape, a ● for laser, and/or a ◗ for DVD. Movies without these symbols have yet to appear in home media. Be aware, too, that movies on video disappear from the marketplace very quickly; even the biggest distributor can't send you a movie that's been out-of-print for years.

Each entry has the following information (as applicable): company name and address, order line and fax phone numbers, website, e-mail address, a brief description of the house library, and catalog, if any.

While most places deal solely with mail-order collectors, many also invite video store accounts (use your company letterhead). Often, schools, libraries, and churches can order as well. When ordering, ask about shipping and handling rates, plus guarantees and product return policies, and make a dated copy of the order. If you're asked to include a SASE, that's a Self-Addressed Stamped Envelope.

Please bear in mind that this information is provided as a service to our readers, not as endorsement but as assessment.

Further, by dint of space, clearly this list can't be all-inclusive. With hundreds of video businesses out there, and ever-increasing numbers in cyberspace, instead we seek to offer an overview, recognizing not only the great mass-marketeer behemoths (like Critics' Choice, Movies Unlimited, and PBS) but also the indies (like one fellow here who installs air-conditioners by day and devotedly distributes silent cinema on video by night).

And although this year we note with regret the passing of industry stalwart Video Yesteryear, visible in these pages for the last decade, we must also congratulate other charter ''Mail-Order Sources''—independents such as Captain Bijou, Discount, Eddie Brandt's, Festival Films, Home Film Festival, Loonic, and Sinister, who continue to maintain strong presences in a monstrously competitive marketplace.

Finally, all data were correct at press time, but of course terms and services are always subject to change—not to mention addresses and phone numbers. In any case, we sincerely hope we help you find what you want. Happy hunting!

Absolute Beta Format Videos, POB 130, Remington, VA 22734
fax 540-439-9780; www.absolutebeta.com Betamax videos, Beta VCRs, Beta accessories. Club dues: $9/yr., includes discounts and bi-monthly catalog. Sales to U.S. consumers only. *Catalog:* free sample with SASE.

Asymmetrical Entertainment Inc., 110 Remsen St. #1A, Brooklyn Heights, NY 11201; info/fax 718-237-6031;
www.asymmetricalvideo.com; info@asymmetricalvideo.com Film fans tailor personalized purchases for other film fans. All films in circulation available. *Catalog:* by mail or online.

Best Video, 1842 Whitney Ave., Hamden, CT 06517
Sales: 203-230-5951, fax 203-230-0030
Rents: 800-727-3843, 203-287-9286, fax 203-248-4910
www.bestvideo.com; staff@bestvideo.com Large choice of hard-to-find movies for rental or purchase. *Catalog:* none.

Beta Library, POB 836224, Richardson, TX 75083-6224
972-233-4552, fax 972-233-6329; www.Betalab.org/Betalib;
Betalib@Betalab.org Special format tapes. New/used prerecorded Beta. Machine-certified Beta & Hi8 blanks. Please send your alphabetized want/sell lists. *Catalog:* free (include SASE).
Captain Bijou, POB 87, Toney, AL 35773-0087
256-837-0049, fax 256-837-8393; www.captainbijou.com;
captbijo@hiwaay.net Monster collection of scary movies, serials, B-pics, Westerns, Golden Age TV. Also sells posters, autographs, photos. *Catalog:* $5.
Cinemacabre Video, POB 10005, Baltimore, MD 21285-0005
Genre trailers, old tube, short subjects, off-center flicks, music featurettes, all $19.95 or lower. No phone, mail only. *Catalog:* $1.
Cinema Classics, 332 E. 11th St., New York, NY 10003
212-677-6309, fax 212-675-6594; www.cinemaclassics.com;
cclassics@cinemaclassics.com Comprehensive, often weird collection housed in NYC's only cafe/repertory theater. *Catalog:* $5 ($8 overseas) or free with any purchase; *DVD catalog:* $10.
Critics' Choice, POB 749, Itasca, IL 60143-0749
800-367-7765, fax 630-775-3355; www.ccvideo.com;
vcatalog@ccvideo.com The land of 10,000 movies: classic, Western, British, comedy, more. Sale products, exclusives, Spanish/TDD order lines. *Catalog:* free.
Culture Q Connection, 405 E. Wetmore Rd. #117-PMB516, Tucson, AZ 85705-1700
888-542-5421, 520-622-2900, fax 520-622-2992;
www.cultureqconnection.com; glvideos@cultureqconnection.com
First stop for serious gay/lesbian video collectors. *Catalog:* free.
Dave's Video, The Laser Place, 12144 Ventura Blvd., Studio City, CA 91604
818-760-3472, 800-736-1659 (outside L.A. County), fax 818-760-3818; davesvideo@earthlink.net Mecca for Hollywood DVD & laser buffs. Great discounts with great service. *Catalog:* yes.
Eddie Brandt's Saturday Matinee, 5006 Vineland Ave., N. Hollywood, CA 91601
818-506-4242, -7722, fax 818-506-5649 The forefather of all L.A. video stores is a well-stocked rental outlet run by people who love movies and TV. Also has bunches of movie stills for sale. Family owned and operated since 1968. *Catalog:* $3.
Facets, 1517 W. Fullerton Ave., Chicago, IL 60614
800-331-6197, fax 773-929-5437; www.facets.org; sales@facets.org
Sales/rentals of film/art/buff titles from a film-knowledgeable organization. Also distributes Whole Toon Catalog. *Catalog:* $9.95 (with six updates, $14.95).
Festival Films, 6115 Chestnut Terr., Shorewood, MN 55331
info/fax 612-470-2172; www.hometown.aol.com/fesfilms/ VHS/DVD connoisseur's collection of wide-ranging international titles, run by lifelong film buffs who will answer all domestic and foreign inquiries. *Catalog:* in cyberspace.
Hollywood's Attic/Discount Video Tapes, POB 7122, Burbank, CA 91510
818-843-3366, fax 818-843-3821; www.hollywoodsattic.com;
wwwjr@hollywoodsattic.com Classics, Westerns, black artists, serials, sci-fi, TV, silents, foreign. *Catalog:* free sample.
Home Film Festival, POB 2032, Scranton, PA 18501
800-258-3456, fax 570-344-3810; www.homefilmfestival.com;
homefilm@scranton.com Notable foreign, American indie, documentary

sales/rentals. Seasonal specials. Gift certificates. Club dues: $15. *Catalog:* members only, but call for free info pack/title list.
International Film & Video Center, 989 First Ave., New York, NY 10022
212-826-8848, fax 212-750-8846; www.IFVC.com; IFVC@IFVC.com
Sales/rentals from around the world, dealing with individuals, corporations, schools. Finder's service. Multi-index database searches. *Catalog:* none.
Ken Crane's DVD Planet, 15251 Beach Blvd., Westminster, CA 92683
800-624-3078, 714-892-2283, fax 714-892-8369; www.dvdplanet.com; discs-@kencranes.com DVD mail-order/retail store. All titles discounted. *Catalog:* free.
Kim's Video, 6 St. Mark's Place, New York, NY 10003
800-617-5467, fax 212-995-5586; www.kimsvideo.com;
info@kimsvideo.com A true film buff's paradise: classic/contemporary cult, foreign, laser, DVD, books, OOP, art-house, anime. *Catalog:* $5.
Loonic Video, POB 2052, El Cerrito, CA 94530
info/fax 510-526-5681; loonicvideo@worldnet.att.net "Making the odd and forgotten films of the past available again," and it's true, even to the stocking of antique British serials. Questions by phone, orders by mail only. *Catalog:* $1.
A Million and One World-Wide Videos, POB 349, Orchard Hill, GA 30266
800-849-7309, 770-227-7309, faxes 800-849-0873 & 770-227-0873;
www.wwvideos.com; barbara@wwvideos.com Lost, rare or out-of-prints exclusively. Free searches. *Catalog:* call for free info pack.
Movies Unlimited, 3015 Darnell Rd., Philadelphia, PA 19154
800-466-8437, 215-637-4444, fax 215-637-2350;
www.moviesunlimited.com; movies@moviesunlimited.com America's largest video dispenser by volume, accessing 70,000+ titles, inc. hard-to-finds and exclusives. *Catalog:* $11.95 (it's huge).
NetFlix.com Inc., 750 University Ave., Los Gatos, CA 95032-7606
408-399-3700; www.netflix.com Internet homevideo's first DVD rental store, with thousands of discs available for short or long-term lease. Well-organized website has absorbing features and must-read columns. *Catalog:* by e-mail.
PBS Home Video, 1320 Braddock Pl., Alexandria, VA 22314-1698
800-645-4727, fax 703-739-8131; www.shoppbs.com Interesting assortment of exactly what one expects. *Catalog:* free.
Peter Kavel Video, 1123 Ohio Ave., Alamogordo, NM 88310
www.netmdc.com/~pkavel; pkavel@netmdc.com Unique silent/sound titles, foreign and domestic, truly unavailable elsewhere. *Catalog:* $1 (refundable with first order).
The Picture Palace, POB 281, Caldwell, NJ 07006
info/fax 800-261-0906; www.picpal.com/; picpal@picpal.com Industry's first web-only video store. Interactive online catalog updated weekly. *Catalog:* free online (print updates $7/yr.).
The Right Stuf International, POB 71309, Des Moines, IA 50325
800-338-6827, fax 515-252-0555; www.rightstuf.com;
info@rightstuf.com Japanese animation tapes, discs, related merchandise. *Catalog:* $3 (refundable with first order).
Science Fiction Continuum, 1701 E. Second St., Scotch Plains, NJ 07067
908-322-2010, fax 908-322-5501; www.sfcontinuum.com;
sfcsu@aol.com SF, fantasy, horror, Hong Kong, anime, esoteric fantastica. New: toys, t-shirts, other odd stuff. *Catalog:* only onsite.

Sinister Cinema, POB 4369, Medford, OR 97501-0168
541-773-6860, fax 541-779-8650; www.sinistercinema.com;
info@sinistercinema.com Terrific selection of nostalgic sci-fi, horror, B-westerns, etc., with 1,700+ offbeat offerings for $11.95–$16.95. *Catalog:* free.

Something Weird Video, POB 33664, Seattle, WA 98133
206-361-3759, fax 206-364-7526; www.somethingweird.com;
questions@somethingweird.com An unparalleled collection of exquisite trash. *Catalog:* $5 (over 18 only).

TLA Video, 234 Market St., Philadelphia, PA 19106
800-333-8521, 215-733-0608; www.tlavideo.com;
sales@tlavideo.com A large, opinionated sales library for discriminating, opinionated VHS and/or DVD viewers. *Catalog:* $15.95.

The Video Catalog, POB 64267, St. Paul, MN 55164-0267
800-733-2232, fax 651-645-7092 A video-only relative of Signals (''A Catalog for Fans & Friends of Public TV'') and Wireless (''. . . Public Radio''). *Catalog:* free (call 800-793-0672).

Video Dimensions, 208 W. 30th St., New York, NY 10001
info 212-216-9628, fax 630-604-8791; www.cultvideo.com;
video@cultvideo.com Classics, world cinema, animation, nostalgia. Naughty little sister company (**Mondo Movies, info/fax 212-894-3707 ext. 9173; mondo@-cultvideo.com**) has softcore exploitation, schlock, tasty sleaze. Each business is mail-order only. *Catalog:* both free.

Video Discounters, P.O. Box 1448, Jensen Beach, FL 34958-1448
561-334-4386, fax 561-334-6296; www.video-discounters.com;
videodiscounts@juno.com Off-the-market titles located. Current releases discounted. *Catalog:* none (ask for inventory price list).

VideoFinders 800-343-4727 ''The ultimate source for quality entertainment,'' they describe themselves. Public TV members get 10% off. New and hard-to-finds. *Catalog:* none.

Video Library, 7157 Germantown Ave., Philadelphia, PA 19119
800-669-7157, fax 215-248-5627; www.vlibrary.com;
rentals@vlibrary.com Rent-by-mail from 18,000+ titles. Strong foreign, vintage, out-of-print holdings. No membership fee. *Catalog:* free.

Video Oyster, 137 W. 12th St., Box 663, New York, NY 10011
212-989-3300, fax 212-989-3533; www.videooyster.com;
video@videooyster.com Prehistoric videos from a curator of rare VHS. Website auctions at www.bideo.com; streaming site at www.isontv.com; books, music etc. at www.rarestore.com. *Catalog:* two sample back issues, $5, free online.

Video Search of Miami, POB 16-1917, Miami, FL 33116
888-279-9773, fax 303-598-5265; www.vsom.com;
vsom@aol.com Members-only service ($10 lifetime dues) imports contemporary European and Asian fare in versions otherwise unavailable in U.S. *Catalog:* free.

Video Specialists International, 182-LM Jackson St., Dallas, PA 18612
570-675-0227 Uncommon curios from a vendor that boasts ''We've got what the others don't'' . . . and he's right. Emphasis on once-vanished films in all genres, mainly 1900–1960s, many exclusive, starting at $9.95. *Catalog:* $3.

Video Vault, 323 S. Washington St., Alexandria, VA 22314
800-828-5866, 703-549-8848, fax 703-836-5720; www.videovault.com/; flix@videovault.com Sales/rentals from extensive alternative store. Wide letterboxed selection. Free searches. *Catalog:* $3.

Widescreen Glossary

An aspect ratio is the relationship between the width and height of a screen image. Virtually all sound films until 1953 were 1.37 to 1, that is, slightly wider than they were tall—a modest rectangle. Since television screen size is 1.33:1, little is lost when an older movie is shown on TV. (Even films in the later standard 1.66:1 don't suffer *too* badly.)

In the 1950s, however, Hollywood's attempt to lure people away from TV and back into theaters led to a battle of screen sizes, beginning with CinemaScope, more than twice as wide as it was high.

Today, most films are 1.85:1; since this has become the norm, they are no longer thought of as "widescreen." Our listings only cite films in special widescreen processes, such as the ones below:

Actionscope—2.35:1 (same as Toeiscope)
Agascope—2.35:1 (Sweden/Hungary)
Arriscope—2.35:1 (Arriflex cameras/lenses)
ArriVision—2.35:1 (in 3-D)
Cinepanormique—2.35:1 (France)
CinemaScope—2.35:1 (some early titles 2.66:1 and 2.55:1)
CinemaScope 55—2.35:1 (55mm)
Cinerama—2.6:1 to 2.8:1
Cinescope—2.35:1 (Italy)
Clairmont-Scope—2.35:1 (Clairmont cameras/lenses)
Colorscope—AIP studios' umbrella name for various ratios
Cromoscope—2.35:1 (same as Techniscope)
Daieiscope—2.35:1 (Japan)
Dimension 150—2.2:1 (70mm)
Dimensionscope—2.35:1 (in 3-D)
Duo-Vision—2.35:1 (split-screen)
Dyaliscope—2.35:1 (France)
Euroscope—2.35:1
Franscope—2.35:1 (France)
Grandeur—2:1 approx. (70mm)
Grandscope—2.35:1 (Japan)
Hammerscope—2.35:1 (England)
J-D-C Scope—2.35:1
Megascope—2.35:1 (England)
Metroscope—1.66:1 to 2:1 (hard-matted prints or negative)
MGM Camera 65—2.75:1 (70mm; same as Ultra Panavision)
Multi(ple)-Screen—2.35:1 (split screen)
Natural Vision—2:1 approx. (63.5mm)
Naturama—2.35:1 (Republic studios)
Nikkatsu Scope—2.35:1 (Japan)
Panascope—2:1
Panavision—2.35:1 (2.4:1 from 1971)
Panavision Super 70—2.2:1 (70mm); 2.35:1 (35mm)
Panoramic(a)—1.85:1 to 2.35:1 (Italy)
Part Widescreen—some scenes in 2.35:1 format
Realife—2:1 approx. (70mm)
Regalscope—2.35:1
RKO-Scope—2.35:1 (same as SuperScope 235)
Scanoscope—2.35:1
Shawscope—2.35:1 (Hong Kong)
Sovscoope/Sovscope 70—2.35:1 (U.S.S.R.)
Space-Vision—2.35:1 (in 3-D)
Spectrascope—2.35:1
StereoScope—2.35:1 (in 3-D)
Superama—2.35:1 (same as Super 35)
SuperCinescope—2.35:1 (Italy)
Superpanorama 70—2.2:1 (70mm)
Super Panavision 70—2.2:1 (70mm); 2.35:1 (35mm)
SuperScope—2:1
SuperScope 235—2.35:1 (origin of Super 35)
Super Technirama 70—2.2:1 (70 mm)
Super Techniscope—1.85:1 to 2.35:1 (same as Super 35)
Super 35—1.85:1 to 2.35:1
SuperTotalscope—2.35:1 (Italy)
System 35—1.85:1 to 2.35:1 (same as Super 35)
Technirama—2.35:1
Techniscope—2.35:1
Technovision—2.35:1 (Italy)
Todd-AO—2.2:1 (70mm)
Todd-AO 35—2.35:1 (35mm)
Toeiscope—2.35:1 (Japan)
Tohoscope—2.35:1 (Japan)
Totalscope—2.35:1 (Italy/France)
Totalvision—2.35:1
2.35 Research PLC—2.35:1
Ultra Panavision 70—2.76:1 (70mm)
Ultrascope—2.35:1 (Germany)
Vistarama—2.35:1
Vistascope—2.35:1
VistaVision—1.66:1 to 2:1 (1.85:1 recommended)
Vistascope—2:1 approx. (65mm)
WarnerScope—2.35:1
Warwickscope—2.35:1 (England)
"Widescreen" means uncredited or undetermined process

Aaron Loves Angela (1975) **C-98m.** *** D: Gordon Parks, Jr. Kevin Hooks, Irene Cara, Moses Gunn, Robert Hooks, Ernestine Jackson, José Feliciano. New York-made variation on Romeo and Juliet set in Harlem, with black boy (Kevin) in love with Puerto Rican girl (Cara). OK combination of comedy, drama, violence, and Feliciano's music. [R] ▼

Aaron Slick From Punkin Crick (1952) **C-95m.** ** D: Claude Binyon. Alan Young, Dinah Shore, Adele Jergens, Robert Merrill, Minerva Urecal, Veda Ann Borg. Innocuous musical of dreamy farm widow Shore, obsessed with moving to the city; she's courted by shy-bumpkin neighbor Young, and is taken by on-the-lam crooks Merrill and Jergens. Based on a 1919 play—and it shows. Unmemorable score.

Aaron's Magic Village (1995-French-German) **C-78m.** ** D: Albert Hanan Kaminski. Voices of Tommy Michaels, Ronn Carroll, Tovah Feldshuh, Steven Newman, Ivy Austin, Harry Goz, Lee Wilkof, Chip Zien, Lewis J. Stadlen; narrated by Fyvush Finkel. Animated adaptation of four fables by Isaac Bashevis Singer features an orphan, a talking goat, and an amnesiac elf trying to save a Moldavian town from sorcery and its own foolishness. Earnest but rather flat cartoon picks up near the end, with a computer-assisted golem attack. Forgettable Michel Legrand–Sheldon Harnick songs. Additional animation by Buzz Potamkin. [G]▼

Abandoned (1949) **79m.** *½ D: Joe Newman. Gale Storm, Dennis O'Keefe, Raymond Burr, Marjorie Rambeau, Jeff Chandler. Lukewarm tale of newspaperman O'Keefe helping Storm find her sister's illegitimate baby, and becoming involved with adoption racket.

Abandon Ship (1957-British) **100m.** *** D: Richard Sale. Tyrone Power, Mai Zetterling, Lloyd Nolan, Stephen Boyd, Moira Lister, James Hayter. Tyrone is officer suddenly in command of lifeboat holding survivors from sunken luxury liner. Tense, exciting study of people fighting to stay alive while exposed to savage seas and each other. British title: SEVEN WAVES AWAY.▼

Abbott and Costello Go to Mars (1953) **77m.** *½ D: Charles Lamont. Robert Paige, Mari Blanchard, Martha Hyer, Horace McMahon. Unimaginative vehicle has Bud and Lou sailing through space with escaped gangsters, landing on Venus—despite the film's title. Look quickly for Anita Ekberg.▼

Abbott and Costello in Hollywood (1945) **83m.** ** D: S. Sylvan Simon. Frances Rafferty, Robert Stanton, Jean Porter, Warner Anderson, Dean Stockwell. Uneven comedy with A&C as barber and porter in Tinseltown. A few peeks behind the scenes at MGM with Rags Ragland, Lucille Ball, Preston Foster, Butch Jenkins, and director Robert Z. Leonard. Officially titled BUD ABBOTT AND LOU COSTELLO IN HOLLYWOOD.▼●

Abbott and Costello in the Foreign Legion (1950) **80m.** ** D: Charles Lamont. Patricia Medina, Walter Slezak, Douglass Dumbrille. Unexceptional vehicle pitting A&C against nasty sergeant Slezak. Best scene involves mirages in the desert. ▼◗

Abbott and Costello in the Navy SEE: **In the Navy**

Abbott and Costello Meet Captain Kidd (1952) **C-70m.** ** D: Charles Lamont. Charles Laughton, Hillary Brooke, Fran Warren, Bill Shirley, Leif Erickson. Middling pirate spoof with too many lousy songs, worth catching to see Laughton having the time of his life in atypical low comedy.▼

Abbott and Costello Meet Dr. Jekyll and Mr. Hyde (1953) **77m.** ** D: Charles Lamont. Boris Karloff, Craig Stevens, Reginald Denny, Helen Westcott, John Dierkes. Disappointing attempt to mix A&C with Jekyll (Karloff) and Hyde (stuntman Eddie Parker), with too few funny scenes. Special effects are film's main asset.▼●

Abbott and Costello Meet Frankenstein (1948) **83m.** ***½ D: Charles Barton. Lon Chaney, Jr., Bela Lugosi, Lenore Aubert, Jane Randolph, Glenn Strange, Frank Ferguson. Dracula (Lugosi) plans to put Lou's brain in Frankenstein's monster; werewolf Larry Talbot (Chaney) has his paws full convincing the boys they're in danger. All-time great horror-comedy still works beautifully, mainly because the monsters play it straight. Yes, that *is* Vincent Price's voice at the end. ▼●

Abbott and Costello Meet the Invisible Man (1951) **82m.** *** D: Charles Lamont. Nancy Guild, Arthur Franz, Adele Jergens, Sheldon Leonard. One of the team's best vehicles, with Bud and Lou as detectives helping boxer (Franz) who's been framed to

trap mobster Leonard, with aid of invisibility formula. The effects are top-notch.▼●
Abbott and Costello Meet the Keystone Kops (1955) **79m.** ** D: Charles Lamont. Fred Clark, Lynn Bari, Mack Sennett, Maxie Rosenbloom, Frank Wilcox, Henry Kulky, Sam Flint. Low-budget comedy could have been better. Clark is fine as conniving producer in this synthetic period-piece of silent-movie days.▼
Abbott and Costello Meet the Killer Boris Karloff (1949) **84m.** **½ D: Charles Barton. Lenore Aubert, Gar Moore, Donna Martell, Alan Mowbray, James Flavin. Pleasant blend of comedy and whodunit with bodies hanging in closets perplexing hotel dick Abbott, and phony mystic Karloff trying to do away with klutzy bellboy Costello.▼●
Abbott and Costello Meet the Mummy (1955) **79m.** **½ D: Charles Lamont. Marie Windsor, Michael Ansara, Dan Seymour, Kurt Katch, Richard Deacon. Amusing adventure with A&C mixed up with villainess Windsor, a valuable tomb, and a mummy who's still alive. ▼●
Abby (1974) **C-92m.** **½ D: William Girdler. Carol Speed, William Marshall, Terry Carter, Austin Stoker, Juanita Moore. Not-bad black variation on THE EXORCIST. Speed, wife of minister Carter and daughter-in-law of minister Marshall, is the possessed Abby. Out of circulation for years because of a lawsuit that claimed it was a ripoff of THE EXORCIST.
ABC Murders, The SEE: **Alphabet Murders, The**
Abdication, The (1974-British) **C-103m.** ** D: Anthony Harvey. Peter Finch, Liv Ullmann, Cyril Cusack, Paul Rogers, Michael Dunn. Plodding historical drama of what happened to Sweden's Queen Christina when she abdicated to convert to Catholicism. Finch is the cardinal who must test her sincerity and with whom she falls in love. [PG]
Abduction (1975) **C-100m.** *½ D: Joseph Zito. Gregory Rozakis, Judith-Marie Bergan, David Pendleton, Leif Erickson, Dorothy Malone, Lawrence Tierney. Wealthy California coed is kidnapped by a group of leftists. Could be retitled "The Patty Hearst Story," though based on a novel (Harrison James's *Black Abductors*) written before the Hearst kidnapping. [R]▼
Abductors, The (1957) **80m.** *½ D: Andrew McLaglen. Victor McLaglen, George Macready, Fay Spain, Gavin Muir. Boring account of McLaglen and Macready's scheme to steal and hold for ransom the remains of Abraham Lincoln; based on fact. Director McLaglen is the star's son. Regalscope.
Abe Lincoln in Illinois (1940) **110m.** **** D: John Cromwell. Raymond Massey, Gene Lockhart, Ruth Gordon, Mary Howard, Dorothy Tree, Minor Watson, Alan Baxter, Howard da Silva. First-rate Americana; sincere story of Lincoln's life and career is beautifully acted by Massey, with top support from Gordon as Mary Todd. Based on Robert Sherwood's Pulitzer Prize-winning play.▼
Abe Lincoln of Ninth Avenue, The SEE: **Streets of New York**
Abie's Irish Rose (1946) **96m.** BOMB D: A. Edward Sutherland. Joanne Dru, Richard Norris, Michael Chekhov, Eric Blore, Art Baker. Outmoded remake of the legendary, long-running 1920s Broadway comedy about an ethnic culture clash when a Jewish boy wants to marry an Irish girl. Filmed before in 1929. Produced by Bing Crosby.
Abigail: Wanted SEE: **Stingray** (1978)
Abilene Town (1946) **89m.** *** D: Edwin L. Marin. Randolph Scott, Ann Dvorak, Edgar Buchanan, Rhonda Fleming, Lloyd Bridges. Above-average Scott vehicle as patient sheriff tries to straighten out homesteader conflict out West after the Civil War. Also shown in computer-colored version.▼
Abominable Dr. Phibes, The (1971-British) **C-94m.** *** D: Robert Fuest. Vincent Price, Joseph Cotten, Peter Jeffrey, Hugh Griffith, Terry-Thomas, Virginia North. Above average camp horror film in which Price, disfigured in a car wreck, seeks revenge on those he believes responsible for the death of his wife. Sequel: DR. PHIBES RISES AGAIN!▼●
Abominable Snowman of the Himalayas, The (1957-British) **90m.** **½ D: Val Guest. Forrest Tucker, Peter Cushing, Richard Wattis, Maureen Connell, Robert Brown. Intelligent tale of good man (Cushing) and corrupt man (Tucker) seeking the elusive title creature, with surprising results. Aka THE ABOMINABLE SNOWMAN. Original U.S. running time 85m. Widescreen Hammerscope. ▼●
About Face (1952) **C-94m.** *½ D: Roy Del Ruth. Gordon MacRae, Eddie Bracken, Dick Wesson, Phyllis Kirk, Joel Grey. Dull comedy-musical remake of BROTHER RAT, about three friends in military academy, one of them secretly married. Grey's film debut.
About Last Night . . . (1986) **C-113m.** ** D: Edward Zwick. Rob Lowe, Demi Moore, James Belushi, Elizabeth Perkins, George DiCenzo, Michael Alldredge, Robin Thomas. True-to-life look at problems faced by a young couple fleeing the singles scene, biggest problem being his inability to make genuine emotional commitment to her. True-to-life doesn't make it terribly *interesting,* however. Expanded (and diluted) from David Mamet's one-act play *Sexual Perversity in Chicago.* Coscenarist Tim Kazurinsky appears briefly. [R] ▼●◗
About Mrs. Leslie (1954) **104m.** *** D: Daniel Mann. Shirley Booth, Robert Ryan, Marjie Millar, Alex Nicol, Sammy White, James Bell, Eilene Janssen, Henry (Harry)

Morgan, Gale Page, Ellen Corby, Amanda Blake, Joan Shawlee, Benny Rubin, Jack Larson, Jerry Paris. Flashbacks reveal romance between chanteuse (Booth) and mysterious, lonely magnate (Ryan). Well-acted soaper; forgivable illogical coupling of stars.

Above and Beyond (1952) **122m.** *** D: Melvin Frank, Norman Panama. Robert Taylor, Eleanor Parker, James Whitmore, Jim Backus. Meaningful account of U.S. pilot who flew over Hiroshima with first atomic bomb; film focuses on his training and its effect on his personal life. Tibbets' story also told in 1980 TV movie ENOLA GAY.▼

Above Suspicion (1943) **90m.** *** D: Richard Thorpe. Joan Crawford, Fred MacMurray, Conrad Veidt, Basil Rathbone, Reginald Owen, Richard Ainley. Crawford and MacMurray asked to do spy mission during European honeymoon on the eve of WW2. Pure escapism, with Joan more than a match for the Nazis.▼

Above the Law (1988) **C-99m.** ** D: Andrew Davis. Steven Seagal, Pam Grier, Sharon Stone, Henry Silva, Ron Dean, Daniel Faraldo, Thalmus Rasulala. Chicago cop doesn't hesitate to use his martial arts skills as he battles police corruption and drug dealing. Seagal's film debut reveals the real-life Aikido master to be more of the Chucknorrisian than the Stanislavskian school of acting. Seagal also cowrote and coproduced; slick but stupid actioner. [R] ▼●◗

Above the Rim (1994) **C-93m.** **½ D: Jeff Pollack. Duane Martin, Leon, Tupac Shakur, David Bailey, Tonya Pinkins, Marlon Wayans, Bernie Mac. By-the-numbers tale of a promising high school basketball player (Martin) and his conflicting relationships with two very different brothers: one a drug dealer (Shakur), the other a troubled ex-scholastic hoop star (Leon) employed as a school security guard. Despite insightful moments, film wallows in clichés and plot contrivances. Pollack coscripted and coproduced. [R] ▼●

Above Us the Waves (1956-British) **92m.** *** D: Ralph Thomas. John Mills, John Gregson, Donald Sinden, James Robertson Justice. Utilizing documentary style, film relates account of unrelenting British attempt to destroy Nazi warship. Fine cast in exciting submarine drama.▼

Abraham Lincoln (1930) **97m.** **½ D: D. W. Griffith. Walter Huston, Una Merkel, Edgar Dearing, Russell Simpson, Cameron Prud'homme, Oscar Apfel, Henry B. Walthall. Huston is excellent in this sincere but static biography of Lincoln; can't match Griffith's silent masterpieces. ▼●

A Brivele der Mamen (1938-Polish) **100m.** ** D: Joseph Green. Lucy Gehrman, Misha Gehrman, Max Bozyk, Edmund Zayenda, Alexander Stein. Overly sentimental Yiddish-language soaper that examines the effect of immigration on the family; the scenario focuses on a Polish-Jewish mother and son, and what happens when the latter heads off to America. The title's English translation is A LETTER TO MOTHER; also known as THE ETERNAL SONG.▼

Abroad With Two Yanks (1944) **80m.** **½ D: Allan Dwan. William Bendix, Helen Walker, Dennis O'Keefe, John Loder, John Abbott. Bendix and O'Keefe are marines on the loose in Australia, both chasing Walker; breezy comedy.▼

Absence of Malice (1981) **C-116m.** *** D: Sydney Pollack. Paul Newman, Sally Field, Bob Balaban, Melinda Dillon, Luther Adler, Barry Primus, Josef Sommer, John Harkins, Don Hood, Wilford Brimley. A reporter (Field) is duped by a scheming government investigator into printing a story that discredits innocent Newman; while she hides behind the privilege of the press, he determines to get even. Absorbing drama by former reporter Kurt Luedtke with two charismatic star performances. Filmed in Miami. [PG] ▼●◗

Absent Minded Professor, The (1961) **97m.** *** D: Robert Stevenson. Fred MacMurray, Nancy Olson, Keenan Wynn, Tommy Kirk, Ed Wynn, Leon Ames, Elliott Reid. MacMurray discovers flubber (flying rubber) in this Disney audience-pleaser, but no one will believe him except Keenan Wynn, who tries to steal the substance. Broad comedy and bright special effects make this a lot of fun. Also shown in computer-colored version. Sequel: SON OF FLUBBER. Remade in 1995 (as a TVM) and in 1997 as FLUBBER.▼●

Absinthe SEE: **Madame X** (1929)

Absolute Beginners (1986-British) **C-107m.** **½ D: Julien Temple. Eddie O'Connell, Patsy Kensit, David Bowie, James Fox, Ray Davies, Ege Ferret, Anita Morris, Lionel Blair, Steven Berkoff, Mandy Rice-Davies, Sade Adu. Energetic, original musical set in London, 1958, when teenagers first came into their own. Highly stylized film (directed by music-video veteran Temple) suffers from two-dimensional characters and a misguided attempt to add substance by dealing with the rise of racism in England . . . but its virtues *almost* outweigh its shortcomings. Pulsating score supervised by jazz great Gil Evans; musical highlights from Sade (''Killer Blow'') and jazz veteran Slim Gaillard (''Selling Out''). And don't miss that incredible opening shot! Adapted from Colin MacInnes' 1959 novel. Super Techniscope. [PG-13] ▼●

Absolute Power (1997) **C-120m.** ** D: Clint Eastwood. Clint Eastwood, Gene Hackman, Ed Harris, Laura Linney, Judy Davis, E. G. Marshall, Scott Glenn, Dennis Haysbert, Melora Hardin. Aging thief pulls off one valedictory jewel heist, but along the way accidentally witnesses a sexual assault and murder involving none other than the President of the United States (Hackman). Barely credible (and fatally diluted) adaptation of David Baldacci's best-seller by William Goldman. Eastwood and Harris (as a wily cop) play a fun game of cat and mouse, but Hackman is over the top, and the whole thing runs aground in the second half. Panavision. [R]▼●◗

Absolute Strangers (1991) **C-100m. TVM** D: Gilbert Cates. Henry Winkler, Karl Malden, Richard Kiley, Patty Duke, Audra Lindley, Jennifer Hetrick, Mitchell Laurance. A husband struggles to keep his comatose wife alive by allowing the termination of her pregnancy, while pro-lifers mount a legal campaign to gain custody of the unborn fetus. Thoughtful script by playwright Robert Anderson and earnest performance by Winkler give impetus to this fact-based drama. Above average.

Absolution (1981-British) **C-105m.** **½ D: Anthony Page. Richard Burton, Dominic Guard, Dai Bradley, Billy Connolly, Andrew Keir, Willoughby Gray. Burton gives a commanding performance as a humorless, by-the-book priest who teaches at a boys' school, and falls victim to a snowballing practical joke played upon him by his pet student. Straightforward melodrama loses credibility toward the end. Written by Anthony Shaffer. Filmed in 1978, unreleased in the U.S. until 1988, four years after Burton's death. [R] ▼●

Abyss, The (1989) **C-145m.** *** D: James Cameron. Ed Harris, Mary Elizabeth Mastrantonio, Michael Biehn, Leo Burmester, Todd Graff, John Bedford Lloyd, J.C. Quinn, Kimberly Scott, Jimmie Ray Weeks, Chris Elliott. Spectacular underwater saga about an oil-rig crew that gets involved in a perilous mission to rescue a sunken nuclear sub. Better as underwater adventure than futuristic sci-fi, with a couple of crises too many, but still a fascinating, one-of-a-kind experience. Great score by Alan Silvestri; Oscar winner for Visual Effects. Special edition on laserdisc includes 27m. of extra footage, some of it all-too-obviously cut from theatrical release. It fleshes out characters, amplifies plot points, and includes some spectacular special effects—but "literalizes" the other-worldly finale. Super 35. [PG-13] ▼●◗

Acapulco Gold (1978) **C-105m.** ** D: Burt Brinckerhoff. Marjoe Gortner, Robert Lansing, Ed Nelson, John Harkins, Randi Oakes. Ordinary drug-smuggling tale benefits from attractive location shooting on Hawaiian island of Kauai. [PG]▼

Accatone (1961-Italian) **120m.** *** D: Pier Paolo Pasolini. Franco Citti, Franca Pasut, Roberto Scaringella, Adele Cambria, Paolo Guidi, Silvana Corsini. Pasolini's first film is a vivid, unsentimental look at the desperate (and depressing) existence of pimps and petty thieves living in the slums of Rome. Bernardo Bertolucci was one of the assistant directors. Released in the U.S. in 1968.▼●

Accent on Youth (1935) **77m.** **½ D: Wesley Ruggles. Sylvia Sidney, Herbert Marshall, Phillip Reed, Holmes Herbert, Catharine Doucet, Astrid Allwyn. Trim comedy from Samson Raphaelson's play about middle-aged playwright pursued by his young secretary. A bit talky by modern standards, but quite watchable. Remade as MR. MUSIC and BUT NOT FOR ME.

Accident (1967-British) **C-105m.** ***½ D: Joseph Losey. Dirk Bogarde, Stanley Baker, Jacqueline Sassard, Delphine Seyrig, Alexander Knox, Michael York, Vivien Merchant, Harold Pinter, Freddie Jones. Complex, thought-provoking script by Harold Pinter uses story (about Oxford professor who falls in love with a student) as just a foundation for examination of characters' thoughts and actions. A challenging film that operates on many levels; entire cast superb, including York in his first major film role. Based on a novel by Nicholas Mosley, who plays Don. Pinter is amusing as a TV producer.▼

Accidental Death (1963-British) **57m.** **½ D: Geoffrey Nethercott. John Carson, Jacqueline Ellis, Derrick Sherwin, Richard Vernon. Edgar Wallace suspenser with gimmick of letting the viewer guess the identity of the murderer in question.

Accidental Tourist, The (1988) **C-121m.** *** D: Lawrence Kasdan. William Hurt, Kathleen Turner, Geena Davis, Amy Wright, Bill Pullman, Robert Gorman, David Ogden Stiers, Ed Begley, Jr. Hurt gives an exquisite performance as a man shattered by the death of his son, who comes out of his shell when he meets a kooky, aggressive young woman (Oscar winner Davis) who couldn't be less his type. Finely wrought, extremely faithful adaptation of Anne Tyler's novel dares to take its time; may be too slow and quiet for some viewers, but offers many rewards. Panavision. [PG] ▼●

Accidents (1988-Australian) **C-90m.** **½ D: Gideon Amir. Edward Albert, Leigh Taylor-Young, Jon Cypher, Ian Yule, Candice Hillebrand. "Think tank" chief Cypher steals scientist Albert's electronic brain-surgery device, turns it into a weapon he plans to sell to terrorists, and frames Albert for murders he's committed. Not-bad little thriller; likable performances by Albert and Taylor-Young help compensate for some gaps in the story. [R]▼

Accidents Will Happen (1939) **62m.** **½ D: William Clemens. Ronald Reagan, Gloria Blondell, Sheila Bromley, Dick Purcell, Addison Richards. Good little "B" picture about a young go-getting insurance claims adjuster who tries to blow the whistle on a phony-accident racket.

Accompanist, The (1992-French) **C-111m.** ** D: Claude Miller. Richard Bohringer, Elena Safonova, Romaine Bohringer, Samuel Labarthe, Bernard Verley. Somber drama of deceit (toward oneself and one's country) set during WW2. An unworldly young woman (Bohringer) is hired as accompanist to a famous Parisian singer who, with her husband, has been collaborating with the enemy. Potentially potent story but the result is too often bland and forgettable.▼

Accomplices, The (1959-Italian) **93m.** *½ D: Gianni Vernuccio. Sandro Luporini, Sandro Fizzotro, Annabella Incontrera, Jeannie. Lurid, minor film of love triangle, with resulting murder; unconvincing and pat.

Accursed, The (1958-British) **78m.** *½ D: Michael McCarthy. Donald Wolfit, Robert Bray, Jane Griffiths, Anton Diffring, Christopher Lee. Tepid whodunit involving the extinction of veterans of British military unit, and survivors' attempt to find killer.

Accused, The (1948) **101m.** *** D: William Dieterle. Loretta Young, Robert Cummings, Wendell Corey, Sam Jaffe, Douglas Dick. Loretta accidentally becomes a murderess in this taut thriller of a woman on the run; good support from Cummings.

Accused (1957) SEE: **Mark of the Hawk, The**

Accused, The (1988) **C-110m.** *** D: Jonathan Kaplan. Kelly McGillis, Jodie Foster, Bernie Coulson, Leo Rossi, Ann Hearn, Carmen Argenziano, Steve Antin, Tom O'Brien, Peter Van Norden. Public prosecutor McGillis deals with a gang-rape case in cut-and-dried fashion, until the victim demands full retribution for what she has suffered. Compelling drama inspired by a notorious real-life case and propelled by Foster's powerhouse, Oscar-winning performance as the provocative, foul-mouthed woman who gets her day in court. Only quibble: Was the climactic reenactment really necessary? [R] ▼●

Accused of Murder (1956) **C-74m.** ** D: Joseph Kane. David Brian, Vera Ralston, Sidney Blackmer, Virginia Grey. Bland handling of police detective Brian, entranced with singer Ralston, involved in underworld killing. Naturama.

Ace, The SEE: **Great Santini, The**

Ace Eli and Rodger of the Skies (1973) **C-92m.** ** D: Bill Sampson (John Erman). Cliff Robertson, Pamela Franklin, Eric Shea, Rosemary Murphy, Bernadette Peters, Alice Ghostley. Tepid tale of 1920s stunt flyer and son who tags along. Muddled film sat on shelf a long time; doctoring didn't help. Story by Steven Spielberg. Peters' film debut. Panavision. [PG]

Ace High (1969-Italian) **C-123m.** ** D: Giuseppe Colizzi. Eli Wallach, Terence Hill, Bud Spencer, Brock Peters, Kevin McCarthy, Steffen Zacharias. Awkwardly dubbed spaghetti Western tries to imitate Clint Eastwood-Sergio Leone epics, but director Colizzi lacks Leone's style. Hill plays a character named Cat Stevens, but there are no rock songs here. Techniscope. [M] ▼

Ace in the Hole SEE: **Big Carnival, The**

Ace of Aces (1933) **76m.** ** D: J. Walter Ruben. Richard Dix, Elizabeth Allan, Ralph Bellamy, Theodore Newton, Frank Conroy, William Cagney. Sculptor Dix has no use for flagwaving as America enters WW1; after being admonished by girlfriend Allan, he becomes a fighter pilot . . . and undergoes a personality change. Sincere anti-war tract, but far too melodramatic. Co-scripted by John Monk Saunders. ▼

Aces High (1976-British) **C-104m.** *** D: Jack Gold. Malcolm McDowell, Christopher Plummer, Simon Ward, Peter Firth. Strong antiwar statement focusing on indoctrination of WW1 pilot Firth and his disillusioned squadron leader (McDowell). Solid cast (with cameos by John Gielgud, Ray Milland, Trevor Howard, and Richard Johnson) and exciting aerial dogfights highlight this remake of R. C. Sherriff's JOURNEY'S END. [PG]

Aces: Iron Eagle III (1992) **C-93m.** *½ D: John Glen. Louis Gossett, Jr., Rachel McLish, Christopher Cazenove, Horst Buchholz, Sonny Chiba. This time, maverick pilot Gossett and a group of WW2 veteran pilots stage an air raid on a Peruvian cocaine factory (having run out of targets in the Middle East). Unsatisfying mélange of flyboy machismo, unintentional slapstick, and inane action—with novelty of female bodybuilder McLish in cast. [R]▼

Ace Ventura, Pet Detective (1994) **C-86m.** ** D: Tom Shadyac. Jim Carrey, Courteney Cox, Sean Young, Tone Lōc, Dan Marino, Noble Willingham, Troy Evans, Randall "Tex" Cobb. Miami-based "pet detective" is hired to find the kidnapped mascot of the Dolphins football team. No-brainer comedy/whodunit was the breakout role for hyperkinetic, rubber-faced Carrey, who mugs non-stop (and we mean non-stop). Some good gags, but runs out of steam—which Carrey never does. Real-life members of the Miami Dolphins appear, with quarterback Marino in featured role. A minute of new footage added for video. Followed by a sequel and an animated TV series. [PG-13]▼●◗

Ace Ventura: When Nature Calls (1995) **C-105m.** ** D: Steve Oedekerk. Jim Carrey, Ian McNeice, Simon Callow, Maynard Eziashi, Bob Gunton, Sophie Okonedo, Tommy Davidson. Sloppy assemblage of gags (with most of the good ones weighted near the beginning) ostensibly about Ace's anti-p.c. hijinks with battling African tribes while trying to locate a rare white bat. A clever opening spoof of CLIFFHANGER and a funny sight gag involving asparagus; otherwise this is the kind of lazily conceived box-office smash that can belatedly rebound on a performer when audiences finally figure out that they've been used. Super 35. [PG-13] ▼●◗

Across 110th Street (1972) **C-102m.** *** D: Barry Shear. Anthony Quinn, Yaphet Kotto, Anthony Franciosa, Richard Ward, Paul Benjamin, Ed Bernard, Antonio Fargas, Norma Donaldson, Gilbert Lewis. N.Y.C. police race the mobs to catch three blacks who, disguised as cops, stole $300,000 from a Mafia-controlled bank; mutual distrust of both black and Italian hoods is mirrored by differences between cops Quinn and Kotto. Exciting, well-paced, and extremely violent, with fine use of Harlem locations. Quinn was also coexecutive producer. [R] ▼

Across the Bridge (1957-British) **103m.** **½ D: Ken Annakin. Rod Steiger, David Knight, Bernard Lee, Eric Pohlmann. Agreeable study of panicky businessman Steiger on the run from authorities for stealing a fortune; taut performances.▼

Across the Great Divide (1977) **C-100m.** **½ D: Stewart Raffill. Robert Logan, Heather Rattray, Mark Edward Hall, George "Buck" Flower. Innocuous tale of conman Logan and reluctant orphans Rattray and Hall, intent on traveling across the west to Oregon. Lots of horses, bears, deer, pretty scenery. From the makers of the WILDERNESS FAMILY films. [G] ▼

Across the Pacific (1942) **97m.** **½ D: John Huston. Humphrey Bogart, Mary Astor, Sydney Greenstreet, Victor Sen Yung, Keye Luke, Richard Loo. Three MALTESE FALCON leads reteamed for enjoyable WW2 adventure. Bogart trails spies to Panama, has running battle of wits with Greenstreet, while romancing enticing Astor. Despite title, the movie never gets to the Pacific, much less across it. Also shown in computer-colored version.▼●

Across the Tracks (1991) **C-101m.** **½ D: Sandy Tung. Rick Schroder, Brad Pitt, Carrie Snodgress, David Anthony Marshall. Reasonably compelling teen sports drama with Schroder returning from reform school stint to compete on high school track team and outperforming straight-A track star brother (Pitt). Realistic portrayal of teen problems and aspirations make this best suited for young people, although the R rating (for normal raunchy high school language) may make this film inaccessible to its key audience. [R]▼●

Across the Wide Missouri (1951) **C-78m.** **½ D: William Wellman. Clark Gable, Ricardo Montalban, John Hodiak, Adolphe Menjou, Maria Elena Marques, J. Carrol Naish, Jack Holt, Alan Napier, George Chandler, Richard Anderson. Location filming helps pedestrian frontier adventure about explorer Gable and other pathfinders moving westward in 19th century.▼

Acting on Impulse (1993) **C-93m. TVM** D: Sam Irvin. Linda Fiorentino, C. Thomas Howell, Nancy Allen, Judith Hoag, Paul Bartel, Isaac Hayes, Patrick Bauchau, Mary Woronov, Dick Sargent, Miles O'Keeffe, Cassandra Peterson. Seriocomic movie-on-movies thriller about a slasher star on the lam after her overbearing producer is found cut up. Loaded with film old-timers as well as one-time TV names like Peter Lupus (*Mission: Impossible*) as an intrepid reporter and Don Most (*Happy Days*) as a house dick. Made for cable. Average.▼

Action for Slander (1938-British) **83m.** **½ D: Tim Whelan. Clive Brook, Ann Todd, Margaretta Scott, Arthur Margetson, Ronald Squire, Athole Stewart, Percy Marmont, Francis L. Sullivan, Felix Alymer, Googie Withers. Adequate drama about suave, stiff-upper-lip cavalry officer Brook, who feels his life is ruined when he's falsely accused of cheating at cards. Sparked by Sullivan's forceful presence as Brook's lawyer.▼

Action in Arabia (1944) **72m.** **½ D: Leonide Moguy. George Sanders, Virginia Bruce, Gene Lockhart, Robert Armstrong, Lenore Aubert, H. B. Warner, Alan Napier, Marcel Dalio, Michael Ansara. OK drama in which troubleshooting reporter Sanders tangles with assorted characters in Damascus, where Nazis and Allies are jockeying for Arab support on the eve of WW2. Desert footage was shot by Merian C. Cooper and Ernest B. Schoedsack for an unmade film. ▼

Action in the North Atlantic (1943) **127m.** *** D: Lloyd Bacon. Humphrey Bogart, Raymond Massey, Alan Hale, Julie Bishop, Ruth Gordon, Sam Levene, Dane Clark. Rousing tribute to WW2 merchant marine, with officers Bogart and Massey, seamen Hale and Levene, usual hothead Clark, and Gordon as Massey's wife. Also shown in computer-colored version.▼

Action Jackson (1988) **C-95m.** ** D: Craig R. Baxley. Carl Weathers, Craig T. Nelson, Vanity, Sharon Stone, Thomas F. Wilson, Bill Duke, Robert Davi, Jack Thibeau. Strictly standard B movie fare pitting good guy Weathers (a cop) vs. bad guy Nelson. Plenty of explosions, car chases, corpses and noise. [R] ▼●◗

Action of the Tiger (1957-British) **C-94m.** **½ D: Terence Young. Van Johnson, Martine Carol, Herbert Lom, Anna Gerber, Sean Connery. Action packed, clichéd adventure story with Johnson the virile American rescuing pro-Western refugees from Albania. CinemaScope.

Act of Love (1953) **108m.** **½ D: Anatole Litvak. Kirk Douglas, Dany Robin, Barbara Laage, Robert Strauss, Gabrielle

Dorziat, Serge Reggiani, Brigitte Bardot. Entertaining if unremarkable chronicle of the romance between lonely American soldier Douglas and down-and-out French girl Robin in Paris. Scripted by Irwin Shaw, based on Alfred Hayes' novel *The Girl on the Via Flaminia.*

Act of Murder, An (1948) **91m.** *** D: Michael Gordon. Fredric March, Florence Eldridge, Edmond O'Brien, Geraldine Brooks. March is excellent as strict judge who must judge himself for saving his wife the anguish of illness by killing her; absorbing drama.

Act of the Heart, The (1970-Canadian) **C-103m.** *** D: Paul Almond. Genevieve Bujold, Donald Sutherland, Bill Mitchell, Monique Leyrac. Fascinating study of religious fanaticism manifesting itself in one young woman and her love for a Catholic priest. Beautifully atmospheric but ending deeply hurts film. [PG]

Act of Vengeance (1974) SEE: **Rape Squad**

Act of Vengeance (1986) **C-96m. TVM** D: John Mackenzie. Charles Bronson, Ellen Burstyn, Wilford Brimley, Hoyt Axton, Robert Schenkkan, Ellen Barkin, Keanu Reeves. Bronson, sans mustache, in a rare television performance, is Jock Yablonski, the United Mine Workers official whose challenge to incumbent president Tony Boyle (Brimley) led to his and his family's murder. Passionless based-on-fact drama scripted by Scott Spencer. Made for cable. Average.▼

Act of Violence (1949) **82m.** *** D: Fred Zinnemann. Van Heflin, Robert Ryan, Janet Leigh, Mary Astor, Phyllis Thaxter, Berry Kroeger, Taylor Holmes. Stark, well-acted drama, with crippled, embittered Ryan stalking former senior officer Heflin, who betrayed his men while a POW. Fine vignette by Astor as a sympathetic call girl.

Act One (1963) **110m.** **½ D: Dore Schary. George Hamilton, Jason Robards, George Segal, Eli Wallach, Sam Levene, Ruth Ford, Jack Klugman. Interesting for oddball cast, this fabrication of writer Moss Hart's autobiography lacks finesse or any sense of reality, but Robards is ideally cast as George S. Kaufman.

Actors and Sin (1952) **82m.** **½ D: Ben Hecht, Lee Garmes. Edward G. Robinson, Eddie Albert, Marsha Hunt, Alan Reed, Dan O'Herlihy, Tracey Roberts, Rudolph Anders, Paul Guilfoyle, Jenny Hecht, John Crawford. Uneven two-part film: the overly melodramatic "Actor's Blood" concerns has-been thespian Robinson and his hard-hearted (and murdered) Broadway star daughter Hunt; the more successful "Woman of Sin" details the plight of agent Albert, whose newest client is a 9-year-old (Hecht, Ben's daughter), who's penned a lascivious book.▼

Actor's Revenge, An (1963-Japanese) **C-114m.** **½ D: Kon Ichikawa. Kazuo Hasegawa, Ayako Wakao, Fujiko Yamamoto, Ganjiro Nakamura, Raizo Ichikawa. Confusing tale of Kabuki actor Hasagawa getting back at a lord (Nakamura) responsible for the demise of his parents. Unevenly directed. Aka THE REVENGE OF UKENO-JO. Daieiscope.▼

Actress, The (1953) **91m.** **½ D: George Cukor. Spencer Tracy, Jean Simmons, Teresa Wright, Anthony Perkins, Mary Wickes. Flavorful account based on Ruth Gordon's experiences as a teenager in early 20th-century Massachusetts, determined to become an acting star; Tracy is the irascible father. Perkins' film debut.

Ada (1961) **C-109m.** *** D: Daniel Mann. Susan Hayward, Dean Martin, Wilfrid Hyde-White, Martin Balsam. Rags-to-riches soaper of poor Hayward maneuvering easy-going Martin to governor's mansion, using hellbent stamina to overcome political corruption. Hayward vs. Hyde-White in state senate is highlight. CinemaScope.

Adalen 31 (1969-Swedish) **C-115m.** *** D: Bo Widerberg. Peter Schildt, Kerstin Tidelius, Roland Hedlund, Stefan Feierbach. Strikers in a Swedish paper mill disagree over whether or not to make their case with violence; matters are further complicated when a striker's son falls in love with—and impregnates—the factory manager's daughter. Generally appealing mix of romance and history, though no one will ever mistake Widerberg (the director of ELVIRA MADIGAN) for a gritty filmmaker of social realism. Techniscope. [X]

Adam (1983) **C-100m. TVM** D: Michael Tuchner. Daniel J. Travanti, JoBeth Williams, Martha Scott, Richard Masur, Paul Regina, Mason Adams. Compelling drama of true-life couple who, after the kidnap and murder of their child, lobby Congress to permit parents to use the FBI's national crime computer to help locate missing children. Script by Allan Leicht. Followed by sequel ADAM: HIS SONG CONTINUES in 1986. Above average.▼

Adam and Evalyn (1949-British) **92m.** **½ D: Harold French. Jean Simmons, Stewart Granger, Wilfrid Hyde-White, Helen Cherry, Raymond Young. Pleasant but ordinary tale of gambler Granger and the daughter he adopts when a friend dies. British title: ADAM AND EVELYNE.▼

Adam at 6 A.M. (1970) **C-100m.** *** D: Robert Scheerer. Michael Douglas, Lee Purcell, Joe Don Baker, Grayson Hall, Charles Aidman, Meg Foster. Underrated film about young college professor from California who spends summer in Missouri working as a laborer. Authentic location footage and good performances by Purcell and Baker give rare, genuine feeling for the Midwest. [PG]▼

Adam Had Four Sons (1941) **81m.** **½

D: Gregory Ratoff. Ingrid Bergman, Warner Baxter, Susan Hayward, Fay Wray, Richard Denning, Johnny Downs, June Lockhart. Handsome but predictable family saga about French governess Bergman watching over Baxter's household after his wife's death. Bergman gives warm performance, and Hayward plays bad girl to the hilt.▼

Adam's Rib (1949) **100m.** **** D: George Cukor. Spencer Tracy, Katharine Hepburn, Judy Holliday, Tom Ewell, David Wayne, Jean Hagen, Hope Emerson, Polly Moran, Marvin Kaplan, Paula Raymond, Tommy Noonan. Smart, sophisticated comedy (by Ruth Gordon and Garson Kanin) about husband and wife lawyers on opposing sides of the same murder case. One of Hollywood's greatest comedies about the battle of the sexes, with peerless Tracy and Hepburn supported by movie newcomers Holliday, Ewell, Hagen, and Wayne. Cole Porter contributed the song "Farewell, Amanda." Remade in Bulgaria in 1956 (in this version the heroine rebels against tradition as a result of her conversion to Marxism-Leninism!). Later a TV series. Also shown in computer-colored version. ▼●◗

Adam's Woman (1970-U.S.-Australian) **C-116m.** **½ D: Philip Leacock. Beau Bridges, John Mills, Jane Merrow, James Booth, Andrew Keir, Tracy Reed. Interesting if not altogether successful story of innocent Bridges suffering in 19th-century Australian penal colony. Although put on probation, he's still determined to escape. Panavision. [M]

Addams Family, The (1991) **C-101m.** *** D: Barry Sonnenfeld. Anjelica Huston, Raul Julia, Christopher Lloyd, Dan Hedaya, Elizabeth Wilson, Judith Malina, Carel Struycken, Dana Ivey, Paul Benedict, Christina Ricci, Jimmy Workman. Piquant comedy based on Charles Addams' macabre cartoon family (later popularized on the same-named TV series), whose greedy lawyer tries to plunder their fortune by planting an impostor in the household who claims to be their long-lost Uncle Fester. Huston and Julia are absolutely perfect as Morticia and Gomez, and manage to maintain a light touch while dispensing their gleefully ghoulish black humor. Impressive directorial debut for talented cinematographer Sonnenfeld. Followed by two sequels. [PG-13]▼●◗

Addams Family Values (1993) **C-93m.** *** D: Barry Sonnenfeld. Anjelica Huston, Raul Julia, Christopher Lloyd, Joan Cusack, Christina Ricci, Carol Kane, Jimmy Workman, Carel Struycken, Dana Ivey, Peter MacNicol, Christine Baranski, Mercedes McNab, Nathan Lane, Peter Graves, Tony Shalhoub, David Hyde Pierce. Funny follow-up to the 1991 hit has scheming Cusack invading the Addams household, plotting to marry Fester for his money, then bump him off. Full of hilarious one-liners (delivered with gusto by Julia, as Gomez, and Lloyd, as Fester), but the real star is young Ricci as the stone-faced Wednesday, who finally exacts her revenge for being sent to a summer camp run by a pair of bland and giddy grownups (MacNicol and Baranski). Runs out of steam toward the end. Direct-to-video sequel: ADDAMS FAMILY REUNION. [PG-13] ▼●◗

Addict SEE: **Born to Win**

Addicted to Love (1997) **C-100m.** ** D: Griffin Dunne. Meg Ryan, Matthew Broderick, Kelly Preston, Tcheky Karyo, Maureen Stapleton, Nesbitt Blaisdell, Remak Ramsay. Jilted lover Broderick settles in an abandoned N.Y.C. building across the street from his ex-girlfriend's apartment so he can watch her and her new lover. Then he's joined by the lover's ex-g.f., whose agenda is even more extreme: she wants revenge. Dark, twisted comedy has its moments, and a likable cast, but Ryan's seriously disturbed character makes it hard to "root" for her, and renders the inevitable fadeout scene less than ideal. Feature directing debut for actor-producer Dunne; his famous father, author Dominick Dunne, plays a restaurant critic. [R]▼●◗

Addiction, The (1995) **82m.** *** D: Abel Ferrara. Lili Taylor, Christopher Walken, Annabella Sciorra, Edie Falco, Paul Calderon, Kathryn Erbe, Michael Imperioli, Fredro Starr. Intelligent, allegorical vampire movie, shot in beautiful black-and-white, about a New York University philosophy student (well played by Taylor), a decent human being who is horrified by the atrocities of history. Her good intentions do not protect her from evil, as she is bitten by a vampiress and goes on to crave the blood of any- and everyone she meets. Not nearly as bloody and outrageous as some of Ferrara's earlier films; this one says the only hope for mankind is in spirituality. An interesting companion piece to Ferrara's KING OF NEW YORK and BAD LIEUTENANT. ▼●

Adding Machine, The (1969-U.S.-British) **C-100m.** **½ D: Jerome Epstein. Milo O'Shea, Phyllis Diller, Billie Whitelaw, Sydney Chaplin, Julian Glover. Accountant becomes desperate upon learning he's to be replaced by a computer. This Elmer Rice comedy-fantasy is flawed but interesting. Diller has unusual straight role as harridan. [M/PG]

Address Unknown (1944) **72m.** ** D: William Cameron Menzies. Paul Lukas, Mady Christians, Morris Carnovsky, Carl Esmond, K.T. Stevens, Peter Van Eyck. Longtime American resident Lukas returns to his native Germany, and is all too easily swept up by Naziism. Offbeat visual style of director Menzies doesn't alleviate hollowness of this heavy-handed parable.

Adele Hasn't Had Her Supper Yet SEE: **Dinner for Adele**

Adios Amigo (1975) **C-87m.** ** D: Fred Williamson. Fred Williamson, Richard Pryor, Thalmus Rasulala, James Brown, Robert Phillips, Mike Henry. Offbeat Western comedy, written, produced, and directed by Williamson, who plays perennial patsy to con man Pryor. No sex or violence in this innocuous film; too bad it doesn't pull together. Panavision. [PG] ▼

Adios, Sabata (1971-Italian-Spanish) **C-104m.** *½ D: Frank Kramer (Gianfranco Parolini). Yul Brynner, Dean Reed, Pedro Sanchez (Ignazio Spalla), Gerard Herter. Gunslinger gets involved with Mexican revolutionaries, helping himself to a cache of gold along the way. Ersatz sequel to SABATA (with Brynner instead of Lee Van Cleef) was titled INDIGO BLACK until dubbed and retitled for U.S. release. Genuine sequel, THE RETURN OF SABATA, showed up in 1972. Techniscope. [PG]

Adjuster, The (1991-Canadian) **C-102m.** *** D: Atom Egoyan. Elias Koteas, Arsinee Khanjian, Maury Chaykin, Gabrielle Rose, Jennifer Dale, David Hemblen, Don McKellar. Audacious, provocative examination of voyeurism and the power of images. Among the characters are an insurance adjuster (Koteas) who plays peekaboo with the lives of those he deals with professionally and his wife (Khanjian), a censor who secretly tapes the pornographic material she's classifying. Panavision. [R]▼

Admirable Crichton, The (1957-British) **C-94m.** ** D: Lewis Gilbert. Kenneth More, Diane Cilento, Cecil Parker, Sally Ann Howes, Martita Hunt. Oft-filmed James Barrie classic wears thin: impeccable servant proves to be most resourceful when he and his aristocratic employers are ship-wrecked on an island. Retitled: PARADISE LAGOON. VistaVision.▼

Admiral Was a Lady, The (1950) **87m.** ** D: Albert Rogell. Edmond O'Brien, Wanda Hendrix, Rudy Vallee, Steve Brodie. Ex-Wave Hendrix encounters quartet of fun-loving, work-hating men, all interested in courting her; weak.▼

Adolescent, The SEE: **L'Adolescente**

Adorable Creatures (1956-French) **108m.** ** D: Christian-Jaque. Daniel Gelin, Martine Carol, Edwige Feuillère, Danielle Darrieux, Marilyn Buferd, Louis Seigner. Saucy, inconsequential study of life and love in Gallic country, focusing on bedroom romances.

Adorable Julia (1962-French-Austrian) **94m.** *** D: Alfred Weidenmann. Lilli Palmer, Charles Boyer, Jean Sorel, Thomas Fritsch. Charming rendering of Somerset Maugham's novel *Theatre,* and the play of the same title he penned with Guy Bolton. Palmer is an aging stage star who becomes the mistress of young Sorel (despite being wed to director-producer Boyer). Bolton also cowrote the script.▼

Adulteress, The (1973) **C-85m.** BOMB D: Norbert Meisel. Eric Braeden, Greg Morton, Tyne Daly, Lynn Roth. Pro actors stuck in amateurish film that has stud Braeden servicing impotent old Morton's young wife Daly at her husband's request. Embarrassing, especially when the director tries for touches of Ingmar Bergman.▼

Advance to the Rear (1964) **97m.** **½ D: George Marshall. Glenn Ford, Stella Stevens, Melvyn Douglas, Joan Blondell, Jim Backus, Andrew Prine. During Civil War, Northern soldier rejects are sent to Western territory. Stevens as Reb spy and Blondell as saucy worldly woman add only spice to predictable slapstick comedy. Panavision.

Adventure (1945) **125m.** ** D: Victor Fleming. Clark Gable, Greer Garson, Joan Blondell, Thomas Mitchell, Tom Tully, John Qualen, Richard Haydn. Gable's back, Garson's got him; they both sink in cumbersome comedy of seagoing roustabout and meek librarian. Not even breezy Blondell can save it.▼

Adventure, The SEE: **L'Avventura**

Adventure for Two SEE: **Demi-Paradise, The**

Adventure in Baltimore (1949) **89m.** ** D: Richard Wallace. Shirley Temple, John Agar, Robert Young, Josephine Hutchinson. Mild (and, some might say, reactionary) comedy, set in the horse-and-buggy era. Temple plays a spunky miss whose independent spirit and feminist leanings are depicted as youthful folly. Young, auditioning for *Father Knows Best,* plays Shirley's understanding pastor-father.

Adventure in Diamonds (1940) **76m.** ** D: George Fitzmaurice. George Brent, Isa Miranda, John Loder, Nigel Bruce. Tepid formula programmer dealing with jewel robberies in Africa.

Adventure in Manhattan (1936) **73m.** **½ D: Edward Ludwig. Jean Arthur, Joel McCrea, Reginald Owen, Thomas Mitchell, Herman Bing. Bizarre blend of comedy and melodrama with the stars foiling planned bank robbery. Doesn't always work, but interesting.

Adventure in Washington (1941) **84m.** ** D: Alfred E. Green. Herbert Marshall, Virginia Bruce, Gene Reynolds, Samuel S. Hinds, Ralph Morgan. Misleading title for tame account of Senator Marshall and his attempts to reform a delinquent youth who is working as a Senate page boy.

Adventure Island (1947) **C-66m.** ** D: Peter Stewart (Sam Newfield). Rory Calhoun, Rhonda Fleming, Paul Kelly, John Abbott, Alan Napier. Too much talk and too little action sink this weak remake of EBB TIDE, about three men and a woman who find themselves marooned on a tropical island ruled by maniacal Napier.▼

Adventure of Sherlock Holmes' Smarter Brother, The (1975) **C-91m.** **½ D: Gene Wilder. Gene Wilder, Madeline Kahn, Marty Feldman, Dom DeLuise, Leo McKern,

Roy Kinnear, John LeMesurier. Wilder's first film as writer-director-star is mild spoof of Sherlockian adventures, as Sigerson Holmes becomes involved with music-hall songstress Kahn, a damsel in distress. DeLuise, as hammy opera star, adds film's liveliest moments. Made in England. [PG]▼

Adventurers, The (1952) SEE: **Fortune in Diamonds**

Adventurers, The (1970) **C-171m.** BOMB D: Lewis Gilbert. Bekim Fehmiu, Candice Bergen, Ernest Borgnine, Olivia de Havilland, Leigh Taylor-Young, Thommy Berggren, Rossano Brazzi, Jaclyn Smith. Three-hour challenge to the kidneys based on Harold Robbins' best-seller about fictional South American republic that has a new revolution every two minutes. Incredible mess wastes attractive cast. Panavision. [PG—edited from original R rating]▼

Adventures at Rugby SEE: **Tom Brown's School Days** (1940)

Adventures in Babysitting (1987) **C-99m.** ** D: Chris Columbus. Elisabeth Shue, Maia Brewton, Keith Coogan, Anthony Rapp, Calvin Levels, Vincent Phillip D'Onofrio, Penelope Ann Miller, Albert Collins, George Newbern, John Ford Noonan, Lolita David (Davidovich). Shue, extremely winning in her first lead role, plays a teenager who takes her two babysitting charges into downtown Chicago to help get a friend out of a jam—and winds up in a snowballing series of wild adventures, à la FERRIS BUELLER'S DAY OFF. Young teens might go for it, but it's mediocre at best. Screenwriter Columbus' directing debut. [PG-13] ▼●◗

Adventures of a Taxi Driver (1976-British) **C-89m.** BOMB D: Stanley Long. Barry Evans, Judy Geeson, Adrienne Posta, Diana Dors, Liz Fraser. Tasteless, unfunny comedy about put-upon young cabdriver, his sexual exploits, and his involvement with jewel thieves.▼

Adventures of a Young Man SEE: **Hemingway's Adventures of a Young Man**

Adventures of Baron Munchausen, The (1989) **C-126m.** *** D: Terry Gilliam. John Neville, Eric Idle, Sarah Polley, Oliver Reed, Charles McKeown, Winston Dennis, Jack Purvis, Valentina Cortese, Jonathan Pryce, Bill Paterson, Peter Jeffrey, Uma Thurman, Alison Steadman, Sting, Robin Williams. The legendary tale spinner returns in a new interpretation of his exploits by director-cowriter Gilliam. Breathtaking special effects go hand in hand with Gilliam's outlandishly funny and far-out ideas; a visual feast that's worth staying with through its occasional lulls. The Baron's exploits were previously filmed in 1943 and (as THE FABULOUS BARON MUNCHAUSEN) in 1961. [PG] ▼●◗

Adventures of Barry McKenzie, The (1972-Australian) **C-114m.** **½ D: Bruce Beresford. Barry Crocker, Barry Humphries, Peter Cook, Spike Milligan. Melbournian Crocker, not particularly fond of the British, finds himself displaced in England. Broad, gross comedy, overlong, and a bit much for American audiences. Beresford's first film, from a cartoon strip by Humphries and Nicholas Garland. Sequel: BARRY MCKENZIE HOLDS HIS OWN.

Adventures of Buckaroo Banzai Across the Eighth Dimension, The (1984) **C-103m.** ** D: W. D. Richter. Peter Weller, John Lithgow, Ellen Barkin, Jeff Goldblum, Christopher Lloyd. Off-the-wall pulp fiction by Earl Mac Rauch about a hero who's a neurosurgeon, physicist, rocket-car driver, rock singer, and government troubleshooter. Should be fun, but it's incoherent, like coming in at the *second* chapter of a Saturday matinee serial. Still, it has a fervent following. Aka BUCKAROO BANZAI. Panavision. [PG] ▼●

Adventures of Bullwhip Griffin, The (1967) **C-110m.** *** D: James Neilson. Roddy McDowall, Suzanne Pleshette, Karl Malden, Harry Guardino, Richard Haydn, Hermione Baddeley, Bryan Russell. Bright Disney spoof of gold-rush sagas, with McDowall as Bostonian butler who learns to fend for himself in the wild and woolly West. Clever comic ideas and visual gimmickry make this fun.▼

Adventures of Captain Fabian (1951) **100m.** *½ D: William Marshall. Errol Flynn, Micheline Presle, Agnes Moorehead, Vincent Price. Soggy sea yarn has Flynn involved with accused murderess.▼

Adventures of Casanova (1948) **83m.** ** D: Roberto Gavaldon. Arturo de Cordova, Lucille Bremer, Turhan Bey, John Sutton. Very ordinary swashbuckler of Casanova de Cordova leading the oppressed people of Sicily against tyrannical rule; this one cries for color.

Adventures of Curley and His Gang, The SEE: **Curley**

Adventures of Don Juan (1948) **C-110m.** *** D: Vincent Sherman. Errol Flynn, Viveca Lindfors, Robert Douglas, Alan Hale, Ann Rutherford, Raymond Burr. Handsome tongue-in-cheek swashbuckler has Errol stringing along countless maidens and even enticing the Queen (Lindfors); Oscar winner for Best Costumes.▼●

Adventures of Elmo in Grouchland, The (1999) **C-73m.** **½ D: Gary Halvorson. Mandy Patinkin, Vanessa L. Williams; voices of Kevin Clash, Fran Brill, Stephanie D'Abruzzo, Jerry Nelson, Carol Spinney, Frank Oz, Steve Whitmire. TV's Elmo (the red, furry three-year-old monster from *Sesame Street*) loses his precious blanket and his search leads him to Grouchland, where he tangles with the villainous Huxley (Patinkin). Fine fare for young fans, but little else for older viewers. Elmo, Patinkin and Williams seem to be having fun. [G]▼◗

Adventures of Ford Fairlane, The (1990) **C-96m.** *½ D: Renny Harlin. Andrew Dice Clay, Wayne Newton, Priscilla Presley, Morris Day, Lauren Holly, Maddie Corman, Gilbert Gottfried, David Patrick Kelly, Brandon Call, Robert Englund, Ed O'Neill, Tone Loc, Sheila E. Controversial standup comic Clay's first starring vehicle is an old-time private-eye yarn transplanted to the contemporary world of rock 'n' roll. Clay's got what it takes, but the film is clumsy, crude, and immature (just like his character). For rabid Clay fans only. Panavision. [R] ▼●

Adventures of Gallant Bess (1948) **C-73m.** ** D: Lew Landers. Cameron Mitchell, Audrey Long, Fuzzy Knight, James Millican. Mitchell is torn between his girl and his horse in this colorful but routine equestrian drama.▼

Adventures of Gerard, The (1970-British-Italian-Swiss) **C-91m.** BOMB D: Jerzy Skolimowski. Peter McEnery, Claudia Cardinale, Eli Wallach, Jack Hawkins, John Neville. Clumsy farce from Arthur Conan Doyle story about cocky but stupid officer who becomes fall guy for Napoleon's (Wallach) wartime strategy. Panavision.

Adventures of Hajji Baba, The (1954) **C-94m.** **½ D: Don Weis. John Derek, Elaine Stewart, Thomas Gomez, Amanda Blake. Derek adds spark to OK desert tale of his romancing sheik's daughter, who's out to marry heir of rival kingdom. CinemaScope.

Adventures of Hercules, The SEE: **Hercules II**

Adventures of Huck Finn, The (1993) **C-108m.** ** D: Stephen Sommers. Elijah Wood, Courtney B. Vance, Robbie Coltrane, Jason Robards, Ron Perlman, Dana Ivey, Anne Heche, James Gammon, Paxton Whitehead, Tom Aldredge, Curtis Armstrong, Mary Louise Wilson, Frances Conroy. Utterly unimaginative rendering of Mark Twain's perennial, which should remain off-limits to Hollywood from this point on unless Robert Altman wants to take a crack. As Huck, young Wood looks and acts too contemporary by decades, while Vance (as Jim) seems too young. Early scenes involving Huck's brutal father may be too intense for very young children . . . and this a Disney release! [PG]▼●

Adventures of Huckleberry Finn, The (1960) **C-107m.** *** D: Michael Curtiz. Tony Randall, Eddie Hodges, Archie Moore, Patty McCormack, Neville Brand. Good version of Twain's story with an appealing Hodges (Huck) and excellent Archie Moore (Jim). Assorted characters played by veterans Buster Keaton, Andy Devine, Judy Canova, John Carradine, Mickey Shaughnessy, and Sterling Holloway. CinemaScope.▼

Adventures of Huckleberry Finn (1985) **C-105m.** *** D: Peter H. Hunt. Patrick Day, Jim Dale, Frederic Forrest, Lillian Gish, Barnard Hughes, Richard Kiley, Geraldine Page, Sada Thompson, Samm-Art Williams, Butterfly McQueen. Literate, enjoyable version of the Twain classic, with Day a smart, energetic Huck. Centers mostly on his relationship with Jim, the runaway slave (Williams); as richly rewarding for adults as for kids. Edited down from 240m. version, broadcast on PBS's *American Playhouse.*▼

Adventures of Ichabod and Mr. Toad, The (1949) **C-68m.** *** D: Jack Kinney, Clyde Geronimi, James Algar. Voices of Eric Blore, Pat O'Malley, John Ployardt, Colin Campbell, Claude Allister, The Rhythmaires. Very entertaining animated doubleheader from Disney: a witty adaptation of Kenneth Grahame's *The Wind in the Willows,* about the puckish residents of Toad Hall centering on Toad's infatuation with motorcars, narrated by Basil Rathbone; and a broad, cartoony version of Washington Irving's *The Legend of Sleepy Hollow,* with a genuinely scary climax, narrated (and sung) by Bing Crosby.▼●

Adventures of Jack London, The SEE: **Jack London**

Adventures of Marco Polo, The (1938) **100m.** **½ D: Archie Mayo. Gary Cooper, Sigrid Gurie, Basil Rathbone, George Barbier, Binnie Barnes, Ernest Truex, Alan Hale. Lighthearted approach to famed explorer's life doesn't always work, but Cooper is pleasant and Rathbone's a good villain; sumptuous production. Look for Lana Turner as one of the handmaidens.▼

Adventures of Mark Twain, The (1944) **130m.** *** D: Irving Rapper. Fredric March, Alexis Smith, Donald Crisp, Alan Hale, C. Aubrey Smith, John Carradine, Percy Kilbride. This Hollywoodized story of Samuel Clemens' colorful life may not be great biography, but it's consistently entertaining—despite some biopic clichés. March is fine in title role. Filmed in 1942. ▼

Adventures of Mark Twain, The (1985) **C-90m.** ** D: Will Vinton. Voices of James Whitmore, Chris Ritchie, Gary Krug, Michele Mariana. Tom Sawyer, Huck Finn, and Becky Thatcher stow away on Mark Twain's amazing flying machine, heading for Halley's Comet in this clay-figure animated feature. Strangely disjointed and ineffectual, incorporating pieces of Twain stories with interesting (but unsettling) look at darker side of his personality. Still, impressive use of Claymation technique. [G] ▼●

Adventures of Martin Eden, The (1942) **87m.** *** D: Sidney Salkow. Glenn Ford, Claire Trevor, Evelyn Keyes, Stuart Erwin, Dickie Moore. Sturdy Jack London tale of seaman aboard terror of a ship, writing account of sailing, fighting for literary recognition.

Adventures of Milo and Otis, The (1989-Japanese) **C-76m.** **½ D: Masanori Hata. Narrated by Dudley Moore. Cute film for kids about a dog and a cat who venture away from their farm and experience a variety of adventures. Not very strong on story but buoyed (in the U.S. release version) by Moore's delightful narration. Original version, released in 1986, ran 90m. [G] ▼●◗

Adventures of Picasso, The (1978-Swedish) **C-92m.** **½ D: Tage Danielsson. Gosta Ekman, Hans Alfredson, Margaretha Krook, Bernard Cribbins, Wilfred Brambell, Per Oscarsson, Lena Nyman, Lennart Nyman, Lena Olin. Frantic slapstick, with actors impersonating the likes of Picasso, Dali, Apollinaire, Gertrude Stein, and Alice B. Toklas (the last two played by Cribbins and Brambell); often funny but misses the mark. ▼

Adventures of Pinocchio, The (1996-British-French-German) **C-96m.** *** D: Steve Barron. Martin Landau, Jonathan Taylor Thomas, Genevieve Bujold, Udo Kier, Bebe Neuwirth, Rob Schneider, Corey Carrier, John Sessions, voice of David Doyle. Appealing live-action rendition of the Collodi fable about a wood-carver who creates the magical, mischievous marionette Pinocchio . . . who wants only to be a real boy. Some variations from the Disney version, but gentle of spirit and enjoyable throughout. Only adults are likely to question the variety of accents (American, British, German, Italian) in a story supposedly set in Italy. Panavision. [G]▼●◗

Adventures of Priscilla, Queen of the Desert, The (1994-Australian) **C-102m.** *** D: Stephan Elliott. Terence Stamp, Hugo Weaving, Guy Pearce, Bill Hunter, Sarah Chadwick, Mark Holmes. Cheerfully outrageous comedy about three flamboyant lip-sync performers—two drag queens and a transsexual—who journey to a remote desert gig on a converted schoolbus named Priscilla. Diverting, if you can get past the bitchy banter, and anchored by Stamp as the transsexual. A must for ABBA fans. Oscar winner for Costume Design. Arriscope (and Dragarama). [R]▼●◗

Adventures of Rin Tin Tin, The SEE: **Return of Rin Tin, Tin, The**

Adventures of Robin Hood, The (1938) **C-102m.** **** D: Michael Curtiz, William Keighley. Errol Flynn, Olivia de Havilland, Basil Rathbone, Claude Rains, Patric Knowles, Eugene Pallette, Alan Hale, Herbert Mundin, Una O'Connor, Melville Cooper, Ian Hunter, Montagu Love. Dashing Flynn in the definitive swashbuckler, winning hand of de Havilland (never lovelier as Maid Marian), foiling evil prince Rains, dueling wicked Rathbone. Erich Wolfgang Korngold's outstanding score earned an Oscar, as did the art direction and editing. Scripted by Norman Reilly Raine and Seton I. Miller. Arguably Flynn's greatest role. ▼●

Adventures of Robinson Crusoe (1952-Mexican) **C-90m.** ***½ D: Luis Buñuel. Dan O'Herlihy, Jaime Fernandez. Colorful, entertaining adaptation of Daniel Defoe's classic story about a resourceful shipwreck victim, with some distinctive Buñuel touches; vivid performance by O'Herlihy, who got an Oscar nomination when film was given U.S. release in 1954. Screenplay by Philip Ansell Roll (Hugo Butler) and Buñuel. Excellent music score by Anthony Collins. Main title on film is ROBINSON CRUSOE.

Adventures of Sadie, The (1954-British) **C-88m.** **½ D: Noel Langley. Joan Collins, George Cole, Kenneth More, Robertson Hare, Hermione Gingold, Walter Fitzgerald, Hattie Jacques. Obvious sex satire relying on premise of Collins stuck on desert isle with love-hungry men. From an Ernest K. Gann novel. Original British title: OUR GIRL FRIDAY.▼

Adventures of Sebastian Cole, The (1999) **C-104m.** *** D: Tod Williams. Adrian Grenier, Clark Gregg, Aleska Palladino, Margaret Colin, John Shea, Marni Lustig, Joan Copeland, Tom Lacy, Rory Cochrane, Levon Helm, Famke Janssen. Compassionate coming-of-age story about an introverted adolescent and the impact on him and his family when his stepfather (Gregg) announces he is planning a sex-change operation. Despite this offbeat premise, the film is more true to life than many other teen-angst tales. [R]▼◗

Adventures of Sherlock Holmes, The (1939) **85m.** ***½ D: Alfred Werker. Basil Rathbone, Nigel Bruce, Ida Lupino, Alan Marshal, Terry Kilburn, George Zucco, E. E. Clive, Mary Gordon. The master sleuth faces one of his greatest challenges when the nefarious Professor Moriarty (Zucco) plots to steal the Crown Jewels. The second and last of Fox's excellent Rathbone-Bruce period pieces which led to Universal's entertaining modern series.▼●

Adventures of Sherlock Holmes' Smarter Brother, The SEE: **Adventure of Sherlock Holmes' Smarter Brother, The**

Adventures of Tartu, The (1943-British) **103m.** *** D: Harold S. Bucquet. Robert Donat, Valerie Hobson, Walter Rilla, Phyllis Morris, Glynis Johns. Well-turned spy drama with intrepid British soldier Donat dispatched incognito into Nazi-occupied Czechoslovakia to blow up a German poison gas plant. Donat's lively performance makes this one worth watching. Retitled: TARTU. ▼

Adventures of the Great Mouse Detective, The SEE: **Great Mouse Detective, The**

Adventures of the Wilderness Family, The (1975) **C-100m.** *** D: Stewart Raffill. Robert F. Logan, Susan Damante Shaw, Hollye Holmes, Ham Larsen, Buck Flower, William Cornford. Good human-interest drama. Modern couple with two children forsake big city for life in magnificent but sometimes dangerous Rocky Mountain region. Followed by two look-alike sequels. [G]▼

Adventures of Tom Sawyer, The (1938) **C-77m.** ***½ D: Norman Taurog. Tommy Kelly, Jackie Moran, Ann Gillis, May Robson, Walter Brennan, Victor Jory, Spring Byington, Margaret Hamilton. Entertaining David O. Selznick production of Mark Twain classic with more slapstick than Twain may have had in mind. Cave sequence with Injun Joe is unforgettable. Original running time 93m. Previously filmed in 1930, and again in 1973 (twice that year)—all under the title TOM SAWYER. Refilmed in 1995 as TOM AND HUCK.▼●

Adventuress, The (1946-British) **98m.** *** D: Frank Launder. Deborah Kerr, Trevor Howard, Raymond Huntley, Liam Redmond, Harry Webster. A feisty Irish lass is persuaded to help a German agent during WW2—because it will hurt her sworn enemies, the British. Well-made, low-key film with touches of droll humor. British prints were originally 114m., which explains some abruptness in exposition. British title: I SEE A DARK STRANGER.▼

Adventurous Blonde (1937) **60m.** **½ D: Frank McDonald. Glenda Farrell, Barton MacLane, Anne Nagel, Tom Kennedy, George E. Stone, Natalie Moorhead, William Hopper. One of the better *Torchy Blane* entries, with sardonic crime reporter Farrell interrupting her wedding to cantankerous cop MacLane in order to probe the murder of a publicity-seeking actor.

Advice to the Lovelorn (1933) **62m.** **½ D: Alfred Werker. Lee Tracy, Sally Blane, Sterling Holloway, Jean Adair, Paul Harvey. Engaging comedy-drama capitalizing on Tracy's success in BLESSED EVENT; here he parlays a lonelyhearts column into business enterprise, with unexpected results. Loosely based on Nathanael West's *Miss Lonelyhearts*. Holloway excellent in key supporting role. Filmed again as LONELYHEARTS.

Advise & Consent (1962) **139m.** *** D: Otto Preminger. Henry Fonda, Don Murray, Charles Laughton, Walter Pidgeon, Peter Lawford, Gene Tierney, Franchot Tone, Lew Ayres, Burgess Meredith, Paul Ford, George Grizzard, Betty White. Long but engrossing drama of Washington wheeling and dealing, from Allen Drury novel. Cast is fine, with effective underplaying by Ayres and Tone standing out among more flamboyant performances by Laughton (his last film) and Grizzard. Also shown in computer-colored version. Panavision. ▼●◗

Advocate, The (1994-British) **C-101m.** *** D: Leslie Megahey. Colin Firth, Amina Annabi, Jim Carter, Donald Pleasence, Ian Holm, Nicol Williamson, Lysette Anthony. Lawyer Firth abandons the bustle of 15th-century Paris for the supposedly more pastoral pace of rural France, only to get involved in a murder-cover-up that culminates in his defending a pig—back when animals actually used to stand trial. Very offbeat but very accessible drama of courtroom intrigue with vivid characterizations. Aka HOUR OF THE PIG. [R]▼

Aerial Gunner (1943) **78m.** ** D: William H. Pine. Richard Arlen, Chester Morris, Lita Ward, Jimmy Lydon, Keith Richards, Dick Purcell. Formula WW2 action propaganda, pitting old rivals Arlen and Morris during basic training and competing for Ward's love. Partially salvaged by some energetic combat scenes. Look quick for Robert Mitchum.▼

Affair, The (1973) **C-74m. TVM** D: Gilbert Cates. Natalie Wood, Robert Wagner, Bruce Davison, Jamie Smith Jackson, Kent Smith, Frances Reid, Pat Harrington. Sensitive, careful handling of 30-ish female songwriter with polio (Wood) experiencing first love affair with lawyer (Wagner). Excellent cast, expert script by Barbara Turner. Above average.▼●

Affair, The (1995) **C-110m. TVM** D: Paul Seed. Courtney B. Vance, Kerry Fox, Leland Gantt, Beatie Edney, Ciaran Hinds, Bill Nunn, Ned Beatty. Bittersweet story of forbidden love between a black G.I. and a lonely, married Englishwoman in WW2, and the tragic consequences when the secret affair is discovered. Vance's strong performance propels this surprisingly honest British-made racial drama inspired by true stories. Written by Pablo Fenjves and Bryan Goluboff from a story by Fenjves and Walter Bernstein. Harry Belafonte executive produced. Made for cable. Above average.▼●

Affair in Havana (1957) **77m.** *½ D: Laslo Benedek. John Cassavetes, Raymond Burr, Sara Shane, Lila Lazo. Unexciting tale of songwriter in love with crippled man's wife. Filmed in Cuba.

Affair in Monte Carlo (1953-British) **C-75m.** ** D: Victor Saville. Merle Oberon, Richard Todd, Leo Genn, Peter Illing. Rich widow tries to convince gambler that romance is more rewarding than roulette. Monte Carlo backgrounds don't help.

Affair in Reno (1957) **75m.** *½ D: R. G. Springsteen. John Lund, John Archer, Doris Singleton, Alan Hale. Inoffensive little film about detective Singleton falling in love with PR-man Lund. Naturama.

Affair in Trinidad (1952) **98m.** **½ D: Vincent Sherman. Rita Hayworth, Glenn Ford, Alexander Scourby, Torin Thatcher, Juanita Moore, Steven Geray. Hayworth and Ford sparkle as cafe singer and brother-in-law seeking her husband's murderer. Hayworth is most enticing.▼●

Affair of Love, An (1999-French-Belgian) **C-80m.** *** D: Frédéric Fonteyne. Nathalie Baye, Sergi Lopez. Provocative and interesting film about a woman who places an ad in a magazine to find a man who will participate in her sexual fantasy. Soon the couple is meeting on a weekly basis, but she is reluctant to take the next step and get to know him as a person. French title is UNE LIAISON PORNOGRAPHIQUE (A PORNOGRAPHIC AFFAIR), which refers to Baye's definition of their relationship; the film itself is fairly discreet. ▼

Affairs in Versailles SEE: **Royal Affairs in Versailles**

Affairs of Annabel, The (1938) **68m.** **½ D: Ben Stoloff. Jack Oakie, Lucille Ball, Ruth Donnelly, Bradley Page, Fritz Feld, Thurston Hall. Fair film industry satire, with Ball scoring as an actress and Oakie her scheming press agent whose publicity gimmicks always backfire. Followed by ANNABEL TAKES A TOUR. ▼●

Affairs of Cellini (1934) **80m.** *** D: Gregory La Cava. Constance Bennett, Fredric March, Frank Morgan, Fay Wray, Jessie Ralph. March is excellent as roguish Renaissance artist who falls in love with Duchess. Lavish production, fine cast make this most entertaining. Lucille Ball plays a lady in waiting.

Affairs of Dobie Gillis, The (1953) **74m.** *** D: Don Weis. Debbie Reynolds, Bobby Van, Hans Conried, Lurene Tuttle, Bob Fosse. Entertaining musicomedy based on Max Shulman's book of college kids. Debbie and Van make a cute couple; Conried is their dour professor. Later a TV series. ▼

Affairs of Susan, The (1945) **110m.** **½ D: William A. Seiter. Joan Fontaine, George Brent, Dennis O'Keefe, Don DeFore, Rita Johnson, Walter Abel. Fairly entertaining comedy of actress Fontaine who does more acting for her beaus than she does onstage.

Affair to Remember, An (1957) **C-115m.** **½ D: Leo McCarey. Cary Grant, Deborah Kerr, Richard Denning, Neva Patterson, Cathleen Nesbitt, Robert Q. Lewis, Charles Watts, Fortunio Bonanova. Middling remake of McCarey's LOVE AFFAIR. Bubbling shipboard comedy in first half, overshadowed by draggy soap-opera clichés and unnecessary musical numbers in N.Y.C. finale. Vic Damone croons title tune on soundtrack. Film was to turn up decades later as a major plot device in 1993 hit SLEEPLESS IN SEATTLE. Remade again as LOVE AFFAIR in 1994. CinemaScope. ▼●◗

Affair With a Stranger (1953) **89m.** ** D: Roy Rowland. Jean Simmons, Victor Mature, Mary Jo Tarola, Monica Lewis, Jane Darwell, Dabbs Greer, Olive Carey. Bland romantic drama, mostly told in flashback, chronicling relationship between struggling playwright Mature (who is sorely miscast) and model Simmons.

Affectionately Yours (1941) **90m.** ** D: Lloyd Bacon. Merle Oberon, Dennis Morgan, Rita Hayworth, Ralph Bellamy, George Tobias. Attractive triangle flounders in weak comedy of Morgan trying to win back wife Oberon, with interference from Hayworth. Bellamy is the poor sap again.

Affliction (1998) **C-114m.** ** D: Paul Schrader. Nick Nolte, Sissy Spacek, James Coburn, Willem Dafoe, Mary Beth Hurt, Marian Seldes, Jim True. Portrait of a man whose screwed-up life—and mental imbalance—can be laid at the feet of his abusive father; the son (Nolte) tries to stay afloat, as traffic cop/jack-of-all-trades (and miserable part-time dad) in a small, wintry New Hampshire town. Bleak in the extreme, with no light or hope for any of its principal characters, but extremely well acted; Coburn won a Best Supporting Oscar. Schrader adapted Russell Banks's novel. [R] ▼●◗

Afraid of the Dark (1991-British-French) **C-92m.** **½ D: Mark Peploe. James Fox, Fanny Ardant, Paul McGann, Clare Holman, Robert Stephens, David Thewlis, Susan Wooldridge, Ben Keyworth. Offbeat psychological thriller, loaded with plot twists, about imaginative boy (Keyworth) whose father is a cop and whose mother is blind. The latter is at risk during a killing spree in which the victims are sightless females. Result is alternately gripping and ponderous. Feature directing debut for co-writer Peploe (THE LAST EMPEROR). [R] ▼●

Africa Addio (1966-Italian) **C-122m.** *** D: Gualtiero Jacopetti, Franco Prosperi. Intriguing survey of contemporary Africa focusing on racial differences and variant tribal customs on the continent; gruesome at times. Recut and retitled AFRICA BLOOD AND GUTS. Techniscope. ▼

Africa Blood and Guts SEE: **Africa Addio**

African Elephant, The (1972) **C-92m.** *** D: Simon Trevor. Excellent documentary on African wildlife centering on elephants and their sometimes strange habits. Released theatrically as KING ELEPHANT. Panavision.

African Lion, The (1955) **C-75m.** ***½ D: James Algar. Narrated by Winston Hibler. Outstanding True-Life documentary is perhaps Disney's best. Naturalists Alfred and Elma Milotte filmed the African lion in his native habitat through a year's cycle of seasons. Filled with drama, excitement, color, humor. A gem.

African Queen, The (1951) **C-105m.** **** D: John Huston. Katharine Hepburn, Humphrey Bogart, Robert Morley, Peter Bull, Theodore Bikel, Walter Gotell. Superb combination of souse Bogart (who won an Oscar) and spinster Hepburn traveling downriver in Africa during WW1, combating the elements and the Germans, and each other. Script by James Agee and director Huston from C. S. Forester's novel; gorgeously filmed on location in the Belgian Congo by Jack Cardiff. ▼●

African Rage SEE: **Target of an Assassin**

African Treasure (1952) **70m.** *½ D:

Ford Beebe. Johnny Sheffield, Laurette Luez, Lyle Talbot, Arthur Space, Martin Garralaga, Robert "Smoki" Whitfield, Leonard Mudie. Bomba the Jungle Boy vs. diamond smugglers posing as geologists. Formulaic jungle intrigue. Look for Woody Strode as a native mailman.

Africa Screams (1949) **79m.** *** D: Charles Barton. Bud Abbott, Lou Costello, Hillary Brooke, Max Baer, Clyde Beatty, Frank Buck, Shemp Howard, Joe Besser. A&C go on safari in this funny outing full of wheezy but often hilarious gags and routines. Also shown in computer-colored version. ▼●◗

Africa—Texas Style! (1967) **C-106m.** **½ D: Andrew Marton. Hugh O'Brian, John Mills, Nigel Green, Tom Nardini, Adrienne Corri. Feature (which later spun off a TV series, *Cowboy in Africa*) doesn't offer much excitement, with O'Brian helping Mills preserve wild game in the dark continent. ▼

Afterburn (1992) **C-105m. TVM** D: Robert Markowitz. Laura Dern, Robert Loggia, Victor Spano, Michael Rooker, Richard Jenkins, Andy Romano. Downed pilot's wife goes after the big corporation guys who might have sent him up in an unsafe jet. Dern is unflinching as real-life crusader Janet Harduvel in Elizabeth Chandler's hard-edged script. Made for cable. Above average. ▼

After Dark, My Sweet (1990) **C-114m.** **½ D: James Foley. Jason Patric, Rachel Ward, Bruce Dern, George Dickerson, James Cotton, Rocky Giordani, Corey Carrier. Piquant modern-day film noir based on a Jim Thompson novel, about a drifter who becomes involved with a beautiful but troubled woman and her criminally scheming friend. Interesting at first, but eventually you catch on that it's heading nowhere—10 miles per hour, at that. Both Patric and Dern are excellent. Super 35. [R] ▼●◗

Afterglow (1997-U.S.-Canadian) **C-113m.** **½ D: Alan Rudolph. Nick Nolte, Julie Christie, Lara Flynn Boyle, Jonny Lee Miller, Jay Underwood, Domini Blythe, Yves Corbeil. Typically odd Rudolph fare, set in Montreal: longtime marrieds Nolte and Christie have hit an emotional roadblock; he's a handyman (named Lucky) who cats around while she seeks to relive her days as a movie actress. Meanwhile, businessman Miller has given his young, beautiful wife the cold shoulder—leaving her vulnerable to the charms of Nolte. Dense, slow, not entirely satisfying, but Christie is impressive as a woman who's drowning in sorrow and doesn't know how to save herself. Written by Rudolph, produced by Robert Altman. [R] ▼●

After Hours (1985) **C-97m.** **½ D: Martin Scorsese. Griffin Dunne, Rosanna Arquette, Verna Bloom, Thomas Chong, Linda Fiorentino, Teri Garr, John Heard, Cheech Marin, Catherine O'Hara, Dick Miller, Bronson Pinchot. Ordinary guy goes through a series of bizarre experiences during one incredible night in N.Y.C. How much you enjoy this comic nightmare will depend on how closely you identify with Dunne—the only normal person in the picture! [R] ▼●

After Life (1998-Japanese) **C-118m.** ***½ D: Kore-eda Hirokazu. Aarata, Erika Oda, Susuma Terajima, Taketoshi Naito, Kyoko Kagawa, Kei Tani, Takashi Naito, Yusuke Iseya. Beautifully told story of caseworkers at a way station between heaven and earth, who help the recently deceased choose a single moment from their pasts to live inside for the rest of eternity. Quiet, poetic examination of life, death, and memory, filled with gentle humor and blessedly free of any feel-good bromides. A plea to Hollywood: *do not* remake this. Written by the director.

After Midnight (1989) **C-90m.** *½ D: Ken and Jim Wheat. Jillian McWhirter, Pamela Segall, Ramy Zade, Nadine Van Der Velde, Marc McClure, Marg Helgenberger, Billy Ray Sharkey. Four coeds take turns telling the scariest story they know in this weak and predictable horror anthology . . . with a high violence quotient. This got limited theatrical release before heading to videoland. [R] ▼

After Midnight With Boston Blackie (1943) **64m.** **½ D: Lew Landers. Chester Morris, Ann Savage, George E. Stone, Richard Lane, Cy Kendall, George McKay, Walter Sande, Lloyd Corrigan. Blackie helps a jailbird's daughter retrieve some hidden diamonds and winds up being accused of the old man's murder. Minor but quite enjoyable entry.

After Office Hours (1935) **75m.** ** D: Robert Z. Leonard. Constance Bennett, Clark Gable, Stuart Erwin, Billie Burke, Harvey Stephens, Henry Travers, William Demarest, Katherine Alexander. Editor Gable tries to manipulate society girl Bennett while investigating shady Stephens. Gable's charm cannot overcome forgettable script (written by Herman J. Mankiewicz).

After the Fox (1966-British-Italian) **C-103m.** **½ D: Vittorio De Sica. Peter Sellers, Victor Mature, Britt Ekland, Martin Balsam. Not always successful comedy of Italian con man Sellers, who poses as a movie director. A must-see for Mature's performance as a fading romantic star with tremendous ego. Script by Neil Simon. Panavision. ▼●

After the Rehearsal (1984-Swedish) **C-72m.** *** D: Ingmar Bergman. Erland Josephson, Ingrid Thulin, Lena Olin, Nadja Palmstjerna-Weiss, Bertil Guve. While staging the production of a Strindberg play a womanizing director is browbeaten by the actress daughter of an old lover, then a middle-aged actress/ex-lover who has fallen on tougher times. Short running time or not, you can exhaust yourself trying to figure out the relationships here. Small-screen viewing should make this original telefilm easier to take than it was in theatrical screenings. Fine acting. [R]▼

After the Thin Man (1936) **113m.** ★★★½ D: W. S. Van Dyke II. William Powell, Myrna Loy, James Stewart, Elissa Landi, Joseph Calleia, Jessie Ralph, Alan Marshal, Penny Singleton, William Law, Sam Levene, George Zucco. Delightful second entry in the series finds the urbane Charleses in San Francisco and, when not inordinately inebriated, investigating murder charges brought against Loy's unstable cousin (Landi). Slightly overlong but first rate, with a truly surprising culprit and a cute finale involving Asta. Also shown in computer-colored version.▼●

Afurika Monogatari (1981-Japanese) **C-120m.** BOMB D: Susumu Hani. James Stewart, Philip Sayer, Kathy, Eleanora Vallone, Heekura Simba. Pilot Sayer crashes plane in wilds of Africa, comes upon game preserve occupied by Stewart and granddaughter. Even old Jimmy is boring. Filmed in Kenya. Aka A TALE OF AFRICA and THE GREEN HORIZON. ▼

Against a Crooked Sky (1975) **C-89m.** ★★ D: Earl Bellamy. Richard Boone, Stewart Peterson, Geoffrey Land, Jewel Blanch, Henry Wilcoxon, Clint Ritchie. A boy searches for his sister, who's been kidnapped by Indians; simplistic, old-fashioned family western. Todd-AO 35. [G] ▼

Against All Flags (1952) **C-83m.** ★★½ D: George Sherman. Errol Flynn, Maureen O'Hara, Anthony Quinn, Mildred Natwick. Flynn found his forte again as dashing British soldier who maneuvers way into pirate fortress, while managing to flirt with O'Hara. Although not Flynn's final swashbuckler, this was his last *good* entry in that genre. Remade as THE KING'S PIRATE.▼●

Against All Odds (1968) SEE: **Blood of Fu Manchu, The**

Against All Odds (1984) **C-128m.** ★★½ D: Taylor Hackford. Rachel Ward, Jeff Bridges, James Woods, Alex Karras, Jane Greer, Richard Widmark, Dorian Harewood, Swoosie Kurtz, Saul Rubinek, Pat Corley, Bill McKinney, Kid Creole and the Coconuts. Unemployed jock accepts a job from a sleazy ex-teammate to find his girlfriend, who's run off to Mexico. The plot thickens, in several directions, in this loose remake of OUT OF THE PAST (with Greer playing the mother of her character in the original). Good stab at film noir feeling, but script is plot-heavy and unsatisfying. Best scene—a hair-raising race along Sunset Boulevard—is completely out of step with the rest of the film. An interesting misfire. Haunting title song by Phil Collins. [R] ▼●◗

Against the Wall (1994) **C-110m. TVM** D: John Frankenheimer. Kyle MacLachlan, Samuel L. Jackson, Clarence Williams III, Frederic Forrest, Philip Bosco, Tom Bower, David Ackroyd, Harry Dean Stanton, Anne Heche. The 1971 Attica prison riot redux. Violent, profane, but underneath it all, just another B prison pic, with the name of Frankenheimer (returning to his TV stomping grounds) attached. Made for cable. Average. ▼

Against the Wind (1948-British) **96m.** ★★★ D: Charles Crichton. Robert Beatty, Simone Signoret, Jack Warner, Gordon Jackson, Paul Dupuis, James Robertson Justice. Taut, engrossing tale of British spies trained for mission inside occupied France during WW2. Documentary-style training scenes complement the dramatic story of resistance fighters.▼

Agatha (1979) **C-98m.** ★★★ D: Michael Apted. Dustin Hoffman, Vanessa Redgrave, Timothy Dalton, Helen Morse, Celia Gregory, Paul Brooke. Fictional speculation on writer Agatha Christie's famous 11-day disappearance in 1926; Redgrave is superb in this absorbing yarn, Hoffman oddly miscast as smooth American reporter who tracks her down. [PG] ▼●

Agatha Christie's Endless Night SEE: **Endless Night**

Agatha Christie's Murder with Mirrors SEE: **Murder with Mirrors**

Age Isn't Everything (1991) **C-88m.** ★½ D: Douglas Katz. Jonathan Silverman, Robert Prosky, Rita Moreno, Paul Sorvino, Rita Karin, Robert Cicchini, Brian Williams, Dee Hoty. Limp, leaden-paced fantasy/comedy/message movie about a young man who abandons his dream of becoming an astronaut-explorer for a job in business—and finds himself transformed overnight into a little old man. Well meaning, but unsubtle and unfunny. [R]▼

Agency (1981-Canadian) **C-94m.** ★½ D: George Kaczender. Robert Mitchum, Lee Majors, Valerie Perrine, Saul Rubinek, Alexandra Stewart. Shifty Mitchum plots to gain political clout via information transmitted subliminally in television ads. Fascinating idea, but result is dull and unconvincing. Aka MIND GAMES. [R] ▼

Agent 8¾ (1964-British) **C-98m.** ★★★ D: Ralph Thomas. Dirk Bogarde, Sylva Koscina, Leo McKern, Robert Morley, Roger Delgado, John LeMesurier. Released at height of James Bond craze, this spoof features Bogarde as a bumbling secret agent working in Czechoslovakia. Sometimes witty, bright comedy. Originally released in U.S. at 77m. Original British title: HOT ENOUGH FOR JUNE.

Agent for H.A.R.M. (1966) **C-84m.** ★½ D: Gerd Oswald. Mark Richman, Wendell

Corey, Carl Esmond, Barbara Bouchet, Martin Kosleck, Rafael Campos, Alizia Gur. Yet another secret agent adventure, definitely a lesser one, about investigation of scientist who is trying to combat spores that turn people into fungi. Shot as a TV pilot, but released to theaters instead.

Age of Consent (1969-Australian) **C-103m.** **½ D: Michael Powell. James Mason, Helen Mirren, Jack MacGowran, Neva Carr-Glyn, Frank Thring. A put-upon artist escapes to the quietude of Australia's Great Barrier Reef, where he's inspired by a feisty young girl whom he persuades to pose (often nude) for him. General amiability and pretty scenery help make up for clumsy comedy relief and gaps in story and characterization. Based on life of Norman Lindsay, later the subject of SIRENS. [R]

Age of Innocence, The (1934) **81m.** **½ D: Philip Moeller. Irene Dunne, John Boles, Lionel Atwill, Helen Westley, Laura Hope Crews, Julie Haydon. Modest but effective version of Edith Wharton's novel about a thwarted romance between an engaged attorney and a divorcée, in rigid 1870s Manhattan society. Starts off with a terrific Jazz Age montage prologue, then gets bogged down in static, stagy treatment as elderly Boles relates the story of his ill-fated affair to his grandson. Still, Dunne gives a luminous and touching performance, Westley is a hoot as Granny Mingott, and the themes of repressed feelings and self-sacrifice amid hypocritical "social distinctions" remain valid today. Remade in 1993.

Age of Innocence, The (1993) **C-133m.** **½ D: Martin Scorsese. Daniel Day-Lewis, Michelle Pfeiffer, Winona Ryder, Richard E. Grant, Alec McCowen, Geraldine Chaplin, Mary Beth Hurt, Miriam Margolyes, Sian Phillips, Michael Gough, Alexis Smith, Norman Lloyd, Jonathan Pryce, Robert Sean Leonard, Carolyn Farina, narrated by Joanne Woodward. In 1870s N.Y. society, well-bred young man (Day-Lewis), engaged to marry well-bred young woman (Ryder), is smitten by notorious beauty (Pfeiffer) with a somewhat scandalous background and an independent spirit. Sumptuous adaptation of Edith Wharton's Pulitzer Prize-winning novel about repressed emotions in a convention-bound society, but amidst the meticulous detail and opulent settings, it's hard to connect with these characters on an emotional level. Oscar-winner for Costume Design. Filmed previously in 1924 and 1934. Super 35. [PG]▼●

Age-Old Friends (1989) **C-85m. TVM** D: Allan Kroeker. Hume Cronyn, Vincent Gardenia, Tandy Cronyn, Michele Scarabelli, Esther Rolle. Poignant tale of a sprightly nursing-home resident and his crotchety buddy (who's drifting into senility) who try to exert their independence. Cronyn is aces, as usual, in this sentimental adaptation by Bob Larby of his play, *A Month of Sundays.* Cronyn and Gardenia both won Emmy awards. Made for cable. Above average.▼

Agnes Browne (1999-U.S.-Irish) **C-92m.** **½ D: Anjelica Huston. Anjelica Huston, Marion O'Dwyer, Ray Winstone, Arno Chevrier, Gerard McSorley, Tom Jones. Good-natured film about a working-class stiff in late 1960s Dublin whose husband has just died, leaving her to raise seven children on her own. Fortunately, her best friend (O'Dwyer) is always there to lend a hand. Comedy is rich in atmosphere but pat, with a subplot involving singer Tom Jones pushing things a bit too far. [R]▼

Agnes of God (1985) **C-98m.** ***½ D: Norman Jewison. Jane Fonda, Anne Bancroft, Meg Tilly, Anne Pitoniak, Winston Reckert, Gratien Gelinas. A young nun apparently became pregnant, then murdered the baby in the cloistered atmosphere of a convent, but court-appointed psychiatrist finds no easy explanations. Disturbing, not always satisfying, but electrified by three lead performances, and beautifully photographed by Sven Nykvist. Screenplay by John Pielmeier, from his play. [PG-13] ▼●

Agony and the Ecstasy, The (1965) **C-140m.** **½ D: Carol Reed. Charlton Heston, Rex Harrison, Diane Cilento, Harry Andrews, Adolfo Celi. Huge spectacle of Michelangelo's artistic conflicts with Pope Julius II has adequate acting overshadowed by meticulous production. Short documentary on artist's work precedes fragmentary drama based on bits of Irving Stone's novel. Todd-AO. ▼●

Aguirre: The Wrath of God (1972-German) **C-94m.** ***½ D: Werner Herzog. Klaus Kinski, Ruy Guerra, Del Negro, Helena Rojo, Cecilia Rivera, Peter Berling. Powerful, hypnotic tale of deluded conquistador who leads a group of men away from Pizarro's 1560 South American expedition in search of seven cities of gold. Dreamlike film was shot on location in remote Amazon jungles; Kinski is perfect as the mad Aguirre. Filmed in both German- and English-language versions; try to avoid the latter.▼

A-Haunting We Will Go (1942) **68m.** *½ D: Alfred Werker. Stan Laurel, Oliver Hardy, Dante the Magician, Sheila Ryan, John Shelton, Don Costello, Elisha Cook, Jr. One of Stan and Ollie's poorest films, involving them with gangsters, a troublesome coffin, and a hokey stage magician. No magic in this turkey.

Ah, Wilderness! (1935) **101m.** ***½ D: Clarence Brown. Wallace Beery, Lionel Barrymore, Aline MacMahon, Eric Linden, Cecilia Parker, Mickey Rooney, Frank Albertson, Bonita Granville. Rich Americana in this adaptation of Eugene O'Neill play about turn-of-the-century small-town life, focusing on boy facing problems of adolescence. Rooney, playing younger brother, took the lead in musical remake SUMMER HOLIDAY. Screenplay by Albert Hackett and Frances Goodrich. ▼

Aida (1953-Italian) **C-96m.** **½ D: Clemente Fracassi. Sophia Loren, Lois Maxwell, Luciano Della Marra, Afro Poli, Antonio Cassinelli. Medium adaptation of the Verdi opera, of interest mostly for casting of Loren, in one of her earlier screen appearances, as the tragic Ethiopian princess. Her singing is dubbed by Renata Tebaldi.

Aileen Wuornos: The Selling of a Serial Killer (1992-British) **C-87m.** *** D: Nick Broomfield. Graphic, soul-rattling documentary about "America's first female serial killer," sentenced to death for murdering seven men in Florida, and how her story is shamelessly exploited by those eager to profit from the tragedy. While Wuornos is far from likable, she comes off as the most sympathetic figure in the story . . . which is quite a feat! Wuornos' case was also recounted in the TV movie OVERKILL (the production of which is one of the central issues dealt with here). ▼

Ain't Misbehavin' (1955) **C-82m.** **½ D: Edward Buzzell. Rory Calhoun, Piper Laurie, Jack Carson, Mamie Van Doren, Reginald Gardiner, Barbara Britton. Pleasant musical fluff about rowdy Laurie crashing high society when wealthy Calhoun falls in love with her.

Air America (1990) **C-112m.** ** D: Roger Spottiswoode. Mel Gibson, Robert Downey, Jr., Nancy Travis, David Marshall Grant, Lane Smith, Ken Jenkins, Burt Kwouk, Art La Fleur, Tim Thomerson. Pilots Mel and Bob are part of the C.I.A.'s smuggling operation in Laos during the Vietnam War. They crate anything and anyone anywhere—too bad they couldn't fly in a script doctor. Alleged action-comedy has few laughs and makes little sense. Even Gibson's patented swagger can't keep this one airborne. No relation to the 1998 TV series. Super 35. [R] ▼●◗

Airborne (1993) **C-91m.** *½ D: Rob Bowman. Shane McDermott, Seth Green, Brittney Powell, Edie McClurg, Patrick O'Brien, Chris Conrad. Pedestrian teen film about a surfer who's shipped off to Cincinnati, where, away from the waves, he seeks to gain respect through his amazing skill on rollerblades. Tough skating for anyone but kids; some truly spectacular rollerblading stunts are the film's sole grace. [PG] ▼●

Air Bud (1997) **C-97m.** **½ D: Charles Martin Smith. Kevin Zegers, Michael Jeter, Wendy Makkena, Bill Cobbs, Eric Christmas. Innocuous Disney kiddie film about a new boy in town who befriends a lovable stray dog with the uncanny ability to shoot hoops. Jeter is malevolent fun as Bud's former owner, a terrible children's party clown who tries to cash in on the dog's celebrity. Little here that would usurp Benji or Lassie as top movie dog, but still mildly entertaining. Director Smith starred in NEVER CRY WOLF, a much superior Disney film about animals. Followed by a sequel. [PG] ▼●◗

Air Bud: Golden Receiver (1998) **C-90m.** **½ D: Richard Martin. Kevin Zegers, Gregory Harrison, Shayn Solberg, Cynthia Stevenson, Nora Dunn, Perry Anzilotti, Robert Costanzo, Tim Conway, Dick Martin. Here, the title canine catches pigskins rather than shoots hoops. He and his young owner (Zegers, the lone cast member from the original) join the school football team—plus, a pair of Boris and Natasha–like villains plot to abduct the pooch for their traveling circus. Predictable but harmless fun. [G] ▼●◗

Air Cadet (1951) **94m.** ** D: Joseph Pevney. Stephen McNally, Gail Russell, Alex Nicol, Richard Long, Charles Drake, Robert Arthur, Rock Hudson, Peggie Castle, James Best, Parley Baer. Familiar account of Air Force recruits training to become fighter pilots; McNally plays their tough but troubled flight commander. It's fun to see Hudson barking orders at the recruits.

Air Force (1943) **124m.** *** D: Howard Hawks. John Garfield, John Ridgely, Gig Young, Arthur Kennedy, Charles Drake, Harry Carey, George Tobias, Faye Emerson. Archetypal WW2 movie, focusing on archetypal bomber crew. Tough to stomach at times ("Fried Jap going down," chimes Tobias after scoring a hit), but generally exciting, well-done. ▼●

Air Force One (1997) **C-124m.** *** D: Wolfgang Petersen. Harrison Ford, Gary Oldman, Glenn Close, Dean Stockwell, Wendy Crewson, Paul Guilfoyle, William H. Macy, Liesel Matthews, Xander Berkeley, Bill Smitrovich, Elya Baskin, Jürgen Prochnow. Supercharged thriller about brutal Kazakhstani terrorists taking over *Air Force One* and holding the President, his family and his entourage hostage in midair. Intense, violent, edge-of-your-seat popcorn fodder, anchored by Ford as a two-fisted president who's not afraid to fight. Requires the usual suspension of disbelief, but pays back in spades. Thundering score by Jerry Goldsmith. Super 35. [R] ▼●◗

Airheads (1994) **C-91m.** ** D: Michael Lehmann. Brendan Fraser, Joe Mantegna, Steve Buscemi, Adam Sandler, Chris Farley, Michael McKean, Judd Nelson, Ernie Hudson, Amy Locane, Nina Siemaszko. Three metalheads with toy guns reluctantly take a rock radio station hostage, hoping to get play for their one existent demo tape. Not exactly the toughest subject to satirize, but the script is dull-witted anyway; fairly energetic direction and compact running time help a bit. [PG-13] ▼●

Airmail (1932) **83m.** *** D: John Ford.

Pat O'Brien, Ralph Bellamy, Russell Hopton, Slim Summerville, Frank Albertson, Gloria Stuart. Routine story of pioneer airmail pilots supercharged by fine aerial scenes and good cast. First-rate. From a Frank "Spig" Wead story.

Airplane! (1980) **C-86m.** *** D: Jim Abrahams, David Zucker, Jerry Zucker. Robert Hays, Julie Hagerty, Robert Stack, Lloyd Bridges, Peter Graves, Kareem Abdul-Jabbar, Leslie Nielsen, Lorna Patterson, Stephen Stucker. Very funny spoof of AIRPORT-type pictures (and Arthur Hailey's ZERO HOUR in particular), with a nonstop string of gags that holds up almost to the end (why carp?). Our favorite: the strange plight of Lt. Hurwitz. Stay tuned through final credits. Followed by a sequel. [PG]▼●

Airplane II: The Sequel (1982) **C-85m.** **½ D: Ken Finkleman. Robert Hays, Julie Hagerty, Lloyd Bridges, Peter Graves, William Shatner, Chad Everett, David Paymer. Mildly funny rehash of AIRPLANE (by a new writer-director), but can't match the quantity, or quality, of laughs in the original. Many cameos include Raymond Burr, Chuck Connors, Sonny Bono, Rip Torn. [PG]▼●

Airport (1970) **C-137m.** ***½ D: George Seaton. Burt Lancaster, Dean Martin, George Kennedy, Helen Hayes, Jean Seberg, Jacqueline Bisset, Van Heflin, Maureen Stapleton, Barry Nelson, Dana Wynter, Lloyd Nolan, Barbara Hale, Gary Collins. GRAND HOTEL plot formula reaches latter-day zenith in ultraslick, old-fashioned movie that entertains in spite of itself, detailing hectic winter night at metropolitan airport. Plastic performances dominate, with down-to-earth Kennedy, touching Stapleton, and nervous Heflin standing out. Helen Hayes won Oscar as impish stowaway. Based on the Arthur Hailey bestseller; followed by three sequels—so far. Todd-AO. [G]▼●◗

Airport 1975 (1974) **C-106m.** *½ D: Jack Smight. Charlton Heston, Karen Black, George Kennedy, Efrem Zimbalist, Jr., Susan Clark, Helen Reddy, Gloria Swanson, Linda Blair, Dana Andrews, Sid Caesar, Myrna Loy, Nancy Olson, Roy Thinnes, Martha Scott. Yet another jetliner disaster epic, not worth your time unless you get your kicks watching a *Hollywood Squares*-type cast that includes Helen Reddy as a (singing) nun. Swanson plays herself in her final film. Look quickly for Sharon Gless. Panavision. [PG]▼●◗

Airport '77 (1977) **C-113m.** **½ D: Jerry Jameson. Jack Lemmon, Lee Grant, Brenda Vaccaro, George Kennedy, James Stewart, Joseph Cotten, Olivia de Havilland, Darren McGavin, Christopher Lee, Robert Foxworth, Robert Hooks, Monte Markham, Kathleen Quinlan, Gil Gerard, Pamela Bellwood, Arlene Golonka, M. Emmet Walsh, Chris Lemmon. All the clichés and stock characters are trucked out for another made-to-order disaster epic, not bad as these things go: Stewart's private luxury jet is sabotaged and sinks in the ocean, forcing daring rescue attempt. Lemmon brings conviction to his role as dedicated pilot. New footage added for network showing. Panavision. [PG] ▼●◗

Airport '79 SEE: **Concorde, The—Airport '79**

Air Raid Wardens (1943) **67m.** ** D: Edward Sedgwick. Stan Laurel, Oliver Hardy, Edgar Kennedy, Jacqueline White, Horace (Stephen) McNally, Donald Meek. Weak, later Laurel and Hardy comedy. One potentially good scene with slow-burn expert Kennedy doesn't meet expectations.▼

Air Up There, The (1994) **C-102m.** ** D: Paul M. Glaser. Kevin Bacon, Charles Gitonga Maina, Yolanda Vazquez, Winston Ntshona, Mabutho "Kid" Sithole, Sean McCann, Dennis Patrick. Brash ex-hoopster with college coaching aspirations journeys to Africa in search of the perfect prospect, leading to the standard culture-clashing situations one might expect. As affably minor as director Glaser's previous THE CUTTING EDGE, but not as deftly put together. [PG]▼●

A.K.A. Cassius Clay (1970) **C-85m.** **½ D: Jim Jacobs. Narrated by Richard Kiley. Interesting documentary about the controversial heavyweight champion. [PG]

Akira (1988-Japanese) **C-124m.** *** D: Katsuhiro Otomo. Voices of Jimmy Flanders, Drew Thomas, Lewis Lemay, Barbara Larsen, Stanley Gurd, Jr. Bloody and violent animated science-fiction feature based on Japanese comic-book novel. A group of motorcycle-riding teenagers living in post-apocalyptic Neo-Tokyo tries to stop one of the gang who has run amok after becoming empowered with telekinetic powers in a government experiment. Technically spectacular, with colorful animation somewhat derailed by confusing storytelling and a cryptic ending. A must-see for adult animation buffs.▼●

Akira Kurosawa's Dreams (1990-Japanese) **C-120m.** *** D: Akira Kurosawa. Akira Terao, Mitsuko Baisho, Mieko Harada, Chishu Ryu, Hisashi Igawa, Mitsunori Isaki, Toshihiko Nakano, Yoshitaka Zushi, Toshie Negishi, Martin Scorsese. Eight vignettes—increasingly apocalyptic—as "dreamt" by an 80-year-old widely regarded as the greatest living filmmaker of the era. Results vary in quality, though any three viewers are likely to rate the episodes in widely shuffled order. At least one—mountain climbers caught in an all-consuming blizzard—is vintage "K." Scorsese portrays Van Gogh in one segment. (Do you detect any Burt Lancaster in his speech patterns?) [PG]▼●

Aku Aku (1961) **C-86m.** **½ No director credited. Documentary of anthropologist

Thor Heyerdahl's trip to Easter Island and his encounters with the natives.

Aladdin (1992) **C-90m.** *** D: John Musker, Ron Clements. Voices of Scott Weinger, Robin Williams, Linda Larkin, Jonathan Freeman, Frank Welker, Gilbert Gottfried, Douglas Seale; singing voices of Brad Kane, Lea Salonga. Disney's animated Arabian Nights tale is filtered through the sensibility of an old Warner Bros. cartoon, as Aladdin conjures up a Genie who's bursting with shtick. Williams' hilarious rapid-fire patter (with equally rapid-fire animation by Eric Goldberg) forms the centerpiece of this otherwise conventional story, colorfully (and tunefully) presented. Music and lyrics by Alan Menken, Howard Ashman, and Tim Rice; Oscar winner for Best Music Score (Menken) and Best Song ("A Whole New World," by Menken and Rice). Followed by direct-to-video sequels, THE RETURN OF JAFAR, ALADDIN AND THE KING OF THIEVES, and an animated TV series. [G]▼●

Aladdin and His Lamp (1952) **C-67m.** *½ D: Lew Landers. Patricia Medina, Richard Erdman, John Sands, Noreen Nash. Poppycock, based on the juvenile fable, that will bore even the least discriminating children.

Aladdin and the King of Thieves (1996) **C-82m.** **½ D: Tad Stones. Voices of Robin Williams, Val Bettin, Jim Cummings, Gilbert Gottfried, Linda Larkin, Jerry Orbach, John Rhys-Davies, Scott Weinger, Frank Welker, Corey Burton. Williams has fun returning to the role of the big blue Genie in this second made-for-video sequel to Disney's ALADDIN. Bright, lightly enjoyable cartoon feature, in which Aladdin risks everything to infiltrate the 40 Thieves and find his long-lost father. Nowhere in the same league as the Disney theatrical films, but pleasant and well made, with five original songs. A decided improvement over its predecessor, THE RETURN OF JAFAR.▼●

Alakazam the Great (1961) **C-84m.** **½ Voices of Jonathan Winters, Frankie Avalon, Arnold Stang, Sterling Holloway. Japanese-made cartoon is good children's entertainment; story centers on magical monkey's ambitious adventures, from bullfight in the pit of a volcano to an epic battle with Hercules. Toeiscope. ▼●

Alambrista! (1977) **C-110m.** ***½ D: Robert M. Young. Domingo Ambriz, Trinidad Silva, Linda Gillin, Ned Beatty, Julius Harris, Paul Berrones, Edward James Olmos. Boyish, naive Ambriz illegally crosses the U.S.-Mexican border and is exploited as he seeks work to support his family. Touching, fresh, insightful; director Young's first feature.

Alamo, The (1960) **C-161m.** *** D: John Wayne. John Wayne, Richard Widmark, Laurence Harvey, Richard Boone, Carlos Arruza, Frankie Avalon, Pat Wayne, Linda Cristal, Chill Wills, Ken Curtis, Hank Worden, Denver Pyle, Olive Carey, Veda Ann Borg, John Dierkes, Guinn "Big Boy" Williams. Long, and long-winded, saga of the Alamo, with plenty of historical name-dropping and speechifying. Worthwhile for final attack, a truly memorable movie spectacle. Fine score by Dimitri Tiomkin includes popular "The Green Leaves of Summer." Filmed on location in Brackettville, Texas. Cut by 26m. after its L.A. premiere; restored for 1992 tape and laser reissues. Todd-AO.▼●

Alamo Bay (1985) **C-98m.** **½ D: Louis Malle. Amy Madigan, Ed Harris, Ho Nguyen, Donald Moffat, Truyer V. Tran, Rudy Young. Well-made but strangely uninvolving film based on real-life conflict between Vietnamese immigrants and American fishermen on the Texas Gulf Coast. [R]▼●

À la Mode (1994-French) **C-82m.** ** D: Remy Duchemin. Ken Higelin, Jean Yanne, Francois Hautesserre, Florence Darel. Lighthearted French comedy of a teenage orphan who becomes apprentice to a small village's tailor, only to break into the fashion world of the 60s. If the rest of the film were as witty as the clothing there might be more to recommend. Harmless fluff. Original French title: FAUSTO. [R]▼

Alamo: 13 Days to Glory, The (1987) **C-145m. TVM** D: Burt Kennedy. James Arness, Brian Keith, Raul Julia, Alec Baldwin, Lorne Greene, Isela Vega, Gene Evans, David Ogden Stiers, Ethan Wayne. Clichéd rehash of the last days of Jim Bowie (Arness), Davy Crockett (Keith), Col. William Travis (Baldwin) and the valiant band of doomed Texans at the Alamo, with Lorne Greene doing a throwaway as Sam Houston. Raul Julia's flamboyant performance as Santa Anna and robust battle scenes filmed by John Elsenbach are on the plus side in this adaptation of J. Lon Tinkle's book, *Thirteen Days to Glory.* Average.▼

Alan & Naomi (1992) **C-96m.** **½ D: Sterling VanWagenen. Lukas Haas, Vanessa Zaoui, Michael Gross, Amy Aquino, Kevin Connolly, Zohra Lampert. Jewish teen Haas tries to befriend a young, catatonic neighbor (Zaoui) whose father was murdered by Nazis right before her eyes. Good performances help this slow-moving, stage-bound film set in 1944 Brooklyn. [PG]▼

Alan Smithee Film: Burn Hollywood Burn, An (1998) **C-86m.** BOMB D: Alan Smithee. Ryan O'Neal, Eric Idle, Coolio, Chuck D, Richard Jeni, Leslie Stefanson, Sandra Bernhard, Harvey Weinstein, Sylvester Stallone, Whoopi Goldberg, Jackie Chan. Any film with Robert Evans and Billy Barty in its cast can't be ignored—but this leaden, sophomoric Hollywood satire ought to be. Idle plays a filmmaker named Alan Smithee—but since that's also the pseudonym directors must use when they don't want screen credit, he's stuck when he wants to disown his latest movie. As one character says of the film-within-a-film, "It's worse than SHOWGIRLS." The ultimate irony: this film's director, Arthur Hiller, removed *his* name after squabbling with writer-producer Joe Eszterhas. [R]▼●

Alarmist, The (1998) **C-93m.** ** D: Evan Dunsky. David Arquette, Stanley Tucci, Kate Capshaw, Mary McCormack, Ryan Reynolds, Tricia Vessey, Michael Learned. Offbeat but uneven black comedy about a novice door-to-door security alarm salesman (Arquette) who discovers that his boss and self-styled mentor (Tucci) actually breaks into people's homes to stir up business. Then the young man falls in love with his first customer (Capshaw). Adapted by Dunsky from Keith Reddin's play *Life During Wartime,* this is never the sharp satire on modern paranoia it strives to be, though Tucci is terrific. Arquette's father Lewis and brother Richmond appear as his onscreen family. [R]▼●◗

Alaska (1996) **C-110m.** **½ D: Fraser C. Heston. Thora Birch, Vincent Kartheiser, Dirk Benedict, Charlton Heston, Duncan Fraser, Gordon Tootoosis. Juvenile adventure yarn on a grand scale, as a brother and sister take off in search of their father and his downed airplane. Plotted like an old grade-B melodrama, but carried out with conviction against magnificent, snowy scenery . . . and featuring an irresistible polar bear who befriends the young people. Heston (whose son directed the picture) plays a mean, wily bad guy. Super 35. [PG]▼●

Alaska Seas (1954) **78m.** ** D: Jerry Hopper. Robert Ryan, Jan Sterling, Brian Keith, Gene Barry, Ross Bagdasarian. Crooks will be crooks, in insipid tale of north-country salmon canner who regrets rehiring former partner, now an ex-con. Remake of SPAWN OF THE NORTH.

Albino Alligator (1997) **C-97m.** ** D: Kevin Spacey. Matt Dillon, Faye Dunaway, Gary Sinise, William Fichtner, Viggo Mortensen, John Spencer, Skeet Ulrich, M. Emmet Walsh, Joe Mantegna, Frankie Faison, Melinda McGraw. Disappointing chamber piece about a trio of dysfunctional criminals who hide out in a basement bar in New Orleans, inadvertently initiating a hostage siege. Meanwhile, the Feds gather outside, thinking a much more dangerous (and wanted) criminal is holed up inside. Spacey's directorial debut presents a good cast and gets off to a good start, but it sputters to a dramatic halt halfway through. Super 35. [R]▼●◗

Albuquerque (1948) **C-89m.** ** D: Ray Enright. Randolph Scott, Barbara Britton, Gabby Hayes, Lon Chaney (Jr.), Russell Hayden. Good Western for Scott fans, with young man finally rebelling against overly strict uncle.

Al Capone (1959) **105m.** **½ D: Richard Wilson. Rod Steiger, Fay Spain, James Gregory, Martin Balsam, Nehemiah Persoff, Murvyn Vye. Good latter-day gangster biography with Steiger tirading as scarfaced Capone; good supporting cast, bringing back memories of Cagney-Robinson-Bogart films of the 30s.▼

Alchemist, The (1985) **C-84m.** *½ D: James Amante (Charles Band). Robert Ginty, Lucinda Dooling, John Sanderford, Viola Kate Stimpson, Robert Glaudini. Minor rural horror flick is set in 1955. Ginty was cursed a century ago by Glaudini to live as an animal; he's ultimately saved by lovely Dooling, a lookalike of the 19th-century woman who came between the two men. Filmed in 1981. [R]▼

Alexander (1968-French) **C-89m.** *** D: Yves Robert. Philippe Noiret, Francoise Brion, Marlene Jobert, Jean Carmet, Pierre Richard. Entertaining comedy about overworked, hilariously henpecked farmer Noiret and how he earns his liberation—not without the help of a cute, bright little dog. Occasionally silly but frequently inspired. [G]

Alexander Hamilton (1931) **73m.** **½ D: John Adolfi. George Arliss, Doris Kenyon, Montagu Love, Dudley Digges, June Collyer, Alan Mowbray. Arliss cowrote the story for this vehicle that focuses on one crucial period in the political (and personal) life of the American patriot, who refuses to surrender his ideals, and thinks only of his country. Typical Arliss theatrics, and enjoyable.

Alexander Nevsky (1938-Russian) **107m.** **** D: Sergei Eisenstein. Nikolai Cherkassov, Nikolai Okhlopkov, Alexander Abrikossov, Dmitri Orlov, Vassily Novikov. Epic tale of Cherkassov and Russian army repelling German invasion during the 13th century, a disturbing parallel to world situation at time of production. Magnificently visualized battle sequences, wonderful Prokofiev score. A masterpiece.▼●◗

Alexander's Ragtime Band (1938) **105m.** *** D: Henry King. Tyrone Power, Alice Faye, Don Ameche, Ethel Merman, Jack Haley, Jean Hersholt, Helen Westley, John Carradine. Corny but entertaining musical chronicling the professional and romantic ups and downs of hot-headed aristocrat bandleader Power, nice-guy pianist-composer Ameche, and tough-but-vulnerable singer Faye (in one of her best performances). Sparked by such Irving Berlin songs, "Blue Skies," "Easter Parade," and the title tune.▼●

Alexander the Great (1956) **C-141m.** *** D: Robert Rossen. Richard Burton, Fredric March, Claire Bloom, Danielle Darrieux, Harry Andrews, Stanley Baker, Peter Cushing, Michael Hordern, Helmut Dantine. Remarkable cast, intelligent acting, but a static epic, lacking essential sweep to make tale of Greek conqueror moving. CinemaScope.▼●

Alex and the Gypsy (1976) **C-99m.** **½ D: John Korty. Jack Lemmon, Genevieve Bujold, James Woods, Gino Ardito, Robert Emhardt, Titos Vandis. Meandering story of romance between bailbondsman Lemmon and gypsy Bujold who's accused of attempted murder. Some interesting ideas lost in the muddle of an indecisive film. [PG—originally rated R]

Alex in Wonderland (1970) **C-109m.** ** D: Paul Mazursky. Donald Sutherland, Ellen Burstyn, Viola Spolin, Federico Fellini, Jeanne Moreau. Camera follows young film director Sutherland through tedium of his everyday life. Self-indulgent imitation of Fellini (who appears briefly) caused some wags to dub this film *1½*. Burstyn stands out as Sutherland's wife. [R]▼

Alfie (1966-British) **C-114m.** ***½ D: Lewis Gilbert. Michael Caine, Shelley Winters, Millicent Martin, Julia Foster, Jane Asher, Shirley Anne Field, Vivien Merchant, Eleanor Bron, Denholm Elliott, Alfie Bass, Graham Stark, Murray Melvin. Well-turned version of Bill Naughton play (he also scripted). Caine is superb as philandering Cockney playboy who can't decide if bachelor life is so bloody marvelous. Cher sings title tune. Followed by ALFIE DARLING. Techniscope. ▼●

Alfie Darling (1975-British) **C-102m.** ** D: Ken Hughes. Alan Price, Jill Townsend, Joan Collins, Annie Ross, Sheila White, Rula Lenska. Forgettable sequel to ALFIE, with Price a most inadequate replacement for Michael Caine. This time around our hero falls for a chic magazine editor. Video title: OH, ALFIE.▼

Alfredo, Alfredo (1972-Italian) **C-98m.** *½ D: Pietro Germi. Dustin Hoffman, Stefania Sandrelli, Carla Gravina, Clara Colosimo, Daniele Patella, Duilio Del Prete. All-too-typical Italian comedy about a milquetoast who wins and weds a sexy woman, only to regret his conquest. Sole interest is observing Hoffman in this unusual setting (with a dubbed voice!). Originally 110m. [R]▼

Alfred the Great (1969-British) **C-122m.** ** D: Clive Donner. David Hemmings, Michael York, Prunella Ransome, Colin Blakely, Julian Glover, Ian McKellen. Story of young leader of 9th-century England can't decide if it's a serious historical chronicle or broad swashbuckler; succeeds in neither department. Only highlight is series of meticulously filmed battle scenes; otherwise, ambitious script is boring. McKellen's film debut. Panavision. [M/PG]

Algiers (1938) **95m.** *** D: John Cromwell. Charles Boyer, Sigrid Gurie, Hedy Lamarr, Joseph Calleia. Alan Hale, Gene Lockhart, Johnny Downs, Paul Harvey. Boyer as Pepe Le Moko falls in love with alluring Lamarr visiting Casbah district of Algiers: Calleia as police official, Lockhart as informer, stand out in well-cast romance. Remake of French PEPE LE MOKO, remade as CASBAH.▼

Alias a Gentleman (1948) **76m.** ** D: Harry Beaumont. Wallace Beery, Tom Drake, Dorothy Patrick, Gladys George, Leon Ames. Minor saga of an aging jailbird (Beery) who doesn't want to see his daughter involved with shady characters like himself.

Alias Boston Blackie (1942) **67m.** **½ D: Lew Landers. Chester Morris, Adele Mara, Richard Lane, George E. Stone, Lloyd Corrigan, Walter Sande, Larry Parks, George McKay, Cy Kendall. When Blackie stages a magic act as part of a prison Christmas show, an innocent con (Parks) escapes to track down the men who framed him. (Incidentally, Morris was a magic enthusiast in real life.) Look fast for Lloyd Bridges as a bus driver.

Alias Bulldog Drummond SEE: **Bulldog Jack**

Alias Jesse James (1959) **C-92m.** *** D: Norman McLeod. Bob Hope, Rhonda Fleming, Wendell Corey, Jim Davis, Gloria Talbott. One of Hope's funniest has him an insurance salesman out West, mistaken for sharpshooter. Fleming is a lovely Western belle; the two do a cute song together. Many guests appear at the climax.▼●

Alias Nick Beal (1949) **93m.** *** D: John Farrow. Ray Milland, Audrey Totter, Thomas Mitchell, George Macready, Fred Clark. Allegory of Devil (Milland) corrupting honest politician Mitchell with help of trollop Totter. Interesting drama with unusually sinister Milland.

Ali Baba and the Forty Thieves (1944) **C-87m.** **½ D: Arthur Lubin. Maria Montez, Jon Hall, Scotty Beckett, Turhan Bey, Kurt Katch, Andy Devine, Frank Puglia. Colorful escapism with rightful-prince Hall battling evil man who put him out of the way years ago; much footage reused in SWORD OF ALI BABA. Devine speaking in flowery "Arabian Nights" dialogue may put off all but his staunchest fans.▼●

Ali Baba Goes to Town (1937) **81m.** *** D: David Butler. Eddie Cantor, Tony Martin, Roland Young, June Lang, John Carradine, Louise Hovick (Gypsy Rose Lee). Entertaining musical comedy sends Cantor back in time but retains topical jokes of 1937; nice production with Cantor in top form. Ends with modern-day movie premiere and glimpses of many stars, from Shirley Temple to Tyrone Power.

Alibi (1929) **84m.** ** D: Roland West. Chester Morris, Harry Stubbs, Mae Busch, Eleanor Griffith, Irma Harrison, Regis Toomey, Al Hill. Creaky, early-talkie gangster melodrama about a hood (Morris), just released from jail, who feigns honesty, weds a police sergeant's daughter, and then is suspected of killing a cop. Highly regarded in its time—this earned Oscar nominations for Best Picture and Actor—it pales beside such bona-fide classics as THE PUBLIC ENEMY and LITTLE CAESAR. Still, it's of note for its striking visuals and sets.▼

Alibi Ike (1935) **73m.** *** D: Ray Enright. Joe E. Brown, Olivia de Havilland, William Frawley, Ruth Donnelly, Roscoe Karns. Brown is aces as the title character, a brash Chicago Cubs rookie hurler who's always ready with excuses for his mistakes. He becomes involved with pretty de Havilland, and tangles with gamblers who try to bribe him. Based on a story by Ring Lardner; the last of Brown's baseball trilogy, following FIREMAN, SAVE MY CHILD and ELMER THE GREAT.

Alice (1990) **C-106m.** ** D: Woody Allen. Mia Farrow, Alec Baldwin, Blythe Danner, Judy Davis, William Hurt, Keye Luke, Joe Mantegna, Bernadette Peters, Cybill Shepherd, Gwen Verdon, Patrick O'Neal, Julie Kavner, Caroline Aaron, Holland Taylor, Robin Bartlett, Bob Balaban, Elle Macpherson. One of Woody's "chamber films" with Farrow as the mousy, pampered wife of wealthy Hurt, trying to find herself, and contemplating the unthinkable—an extramarital affair. With that cast, it's certainly watchable, but the whimsy seems forced, the story overly familiar. Even Allen's usually infallible choice of soundtrack music is heavy-handed. Nice screen farewell for character actor Keye Luke, however. Judith Ivey has an unbilled cameo. [PG-13]▼●

Alice Adams (1935) **99m.** ***½ D: George Stevens. Katharine Hepburn, Fred MacMurray, Fred Stone, Evelyn Venable, Ann Shoemaker, Frank Albertson, Hattie McDaniel, Charlie Grapewin, Grady Sutton, Hedda Hopper. Excellent small-town Americana with social-climbing girl finally finding love in person of unpretentious MacMurray. Booth Tarkington's Pulitzer Prize-winning novel becomes fine film, if not altogether credible. The dinner-table scene is unforgettable. Screenplay by Dorothy Yost, Mortimer Offner, and Jane Murfin. Filmed before in 1923, with Florence Vidor.▼●

Alice Doesn't Live Here Anymore (1974) **C-113m.** ***½ D: Martin Scorsese. Ellen Burstyn, Kris Kristofferson, Billy Green Bush, Alfred Lutter, Diane Ladd, Jodie Foster, Harvey Keitel, Vic Tayback, Valerie Curtin. Excellent look at a woman's odyssey to find herself and some measure of happiness after her husband dies, leaving her and a young son penniless. Kristofferson is gentle, well-meaning man who tries to win her love. Burstyn won well-deserved Oscar for Best Actress. Rich screenplay by Robert Getchell. Look very carefully in the final diner scene for Ladd's daughter Laura Dern eating ice cream cone at counter. Later reworked into a long-running TV sitcom called *Alice*. [PG]▼●

Alice in the Cities (1974-German) **110m.** *** D: Wim Wenders. Rudiger Vogler, Yella Rottlander, Lisa Kreuzer, Chuck Berry. After wandering aimlessly across America, alienated journalist Vogler meets a woman—and finds himself saddled with her nine-year-old daughter when she mysteriously disappears. Intelligent, often hypnotic film reflects on the effect of American pop culture on post-war Europeans. The first in Wenders' "road movie" trilogy, followed by WRONG MOVE and KINGS OF THE ROAD.▼

Alice in Wonderland (1933) **77m.** ** D: Norman Z. McLeod. Charlotte Henry, Richard Arlen, Gary Cooper, W.C. Fields, Cary Grant, Edward Everett Horton, Baby LeRoy, Edna May Oliver, Jack Oakie, many others. Top Paramount stars appear, disguised as Lewis Carroll characters, in this slow-moving adaptation of the classic story. Fascinating for its casting—Cooper as White Knight, Fields as Humpty Dumpty, Grant as Mock Turtle—but, overall, a bore. Screenplay by Joseph L. Mankiewicz and William Cameron Menzies.

Alice in Wonderland (1950-British) **C-83m.** ** D: Dallas Bower. Carol Marsh, Stephen Murray, Pamela Brown, Felix Aylmer, Ernest Milton. Static adaptation of Lewis Carroll classic with gimmick of mixing live action and puppets; most of the wit and charm are missing.▼

Alice in Wonderland (1951) **C-75m.** *** D: Clyde Geronimi, Hamilton Luske, Wilfred Jackson. Voices of Kathryn Beaumont, Ed Wynn, Richard Haydn, Sterling Holloway, Jerry Colonna, Verna Felton, Bill Thompson. Entertaining, if somewhat aloof, rendering of Lewis Carroll's classic, with the Walt Disney animation team at its best bringing the Cheshire Cat, the Queen of Hearts, and the Mad Hatter to life. Episodic film is given major boost by strong personalities of Wynn, Colonna, Holloway, et al, and such tunes as "I'm Late" and "The Unbirthday Song." ▼●

Alice's Adventures in Wonderland (1972) **C-96m.** *½ D: William Sterling. Fiona Fullerton, Michael Crawford, Ralph Richardson, Flora Robson, Peter Sellers, Dudley Moore, Michael Jayston. Tedious British film version of Lewis Carroll's classic proves Americans don't have a monopoly on making bad children's musicals. Waste of a good cast. Todd-AO 35.[G]▼

Alice's Restaurant (1969) **C-111m.** *** D: Arthur Penn. Arlo Guthrie, Pat Quinn, James Broderick, Michael McClanathan, Geoff Outlaw, Tina Chen. Guthrie's popular record inspired this odd blend of satire, whimsy, melodrama, and social commentary. Generally fun, with quizzically downbeat ending, showing freeform life-style of group of friends headed by Broderick and Quinn (as Alice). [PG—edited from original R rating]▼

Alice, Sweet Alice SEE: **Holy Terror**

Alien (1979) **C-117m.** **½ D: Ridley Scott. Tom Skerritt, Sigourney Weaver, John Hurt, Ian Holm, Harry Dean Stanton, Yaphet Kotto, Veronica Cartwright. Commercial spacecraft unwittingly takes on an alien being that wreaks merciless havoc on the crew. Space-age horror film reverts to 1950s formula, but adds stomach-churning violence, slime, and shocks. Still, some people's idea of a good time. Oscar-winning effects. Inspired by IT! THE TERROR FROM BEYOND SPACE. Followed by ALIENS. Panavision. [R]▼●◗

Alienator (1989) **C-92m.** ** D: Fred Olen Ray. Jan-Michael Vincent, John Phillip Law, Ross Hagen, Teagan, Dyann Ortelli, Jesse Dabson, Dawn Wildsmith, P. J. Soles, Robert Clarke, Richard Wiley, Leo V. Gordon, Robert Quarry. Gimlet-eyed Vincent, a cruel alien prison warden, sends unstoppable, Amazonian ''hunter unit'' Teagan after fugitive Hagen, who's crash-landed on Earth. OK sci-fi from the prolific Ray, with a great B movie cast, but looks like two movies overlapping. [R]▼●

Alien From L.A. (1987) **C-87m.** *½ D: Albert Pyun. Kathy Ireland, Thom Matthews, William R. Moses, Don Michael Paul, Richard Haines, Linda Kerridge, Janie du Plessis. California Valley Girl falls down hole, finds herself in the lost city of Atlantis. As silly as it sounds. [PG]▼●

Alien Nation (1988) **C-94m.** **½ D: Graham Baker. James Caan, Mandy Patinkin, Terence Stamp, Kevin Major Howard, Leslie Bevins. In the near future, a race of odd-looking aliens is slowly (and grudgingly) being integrated into society. World-weary L.A. cop Caan agrees to take one on as his partner, so he can track down the alien who killed his former sidekick. A great concept that doesn't quite pay off, despite many clever touches and terrific performances by Caan and Patinkin. Followed by a TV series and three made-for-TV movies. Super 35. [R]▼●

Alien Predator (1987) **C-90m.** BOMB D: Deran Sarafian. Dennis Christopher, Martin Hewitt, Lynn-Holly Johnson, Luis Prendes, J.O. Bosso. Idiotic horror film is an imitation of THE ANDROMEDA STRAIN, with three teens vacationing in Spain, beset by monsters created by microbes from Skylab (which fell to Earth there in 1979). Cast and special effects are terrible. Filmed in 1984. [R] ▼

Alien Resurrection (1997) **C-108m.** ** D: Jean-Pierre Jeunet. Sigourney Weaver, Winona Ryder, Dominique Pinon, Ron Perlman, Gary Dourdan, Michael Wincott, Kim Flowers, Dan Hedaya, J. E. Freeman, Brad Dourif. Two hundred years after ALIEN^3, Ripley (Weaver) is cloned aboard a spaceship with a touch of alien in her makeup, and more aliens to battle with the help of a band of space pirates. Clumsy sequel with crummy logic, fair effects and far too many wisecracks; a few good action scenes, but otherwise strictly for series fans. Super 35. [R]▼●◗

Aliens (1986) **C-137m.** ***½ D: James Cameron. Sigourney Weaver, Carrie Henn, Michael Biehn, Paul Reiser, Lance Henriksen, Bill Paxton, Jenette Goldstein. Weaver, the sole human survivor from ALIEN, returns to planet that spawned the yukky creatures with a Marine squadron that's ready to wipe them out. Intense, exciting sequel directed by Cameron the same way he did THE TERMINATOR—once it gets going there's just no letup! Weaver is sensational in compelling lead role. The special effects won an Oscar. ''Director's cut'' version runs 154m. Followed by ALIEN^3. [R]▼●◗

Alien's Return, The SEE: **Return, The**

Alien Terror SEE: **Sinister Invasion**

Alien^3 (1992) **C-115m.** ** D: David Fincher. Sigourney Weaver, Charles S. Dutton, Charles Dance, Paul McGann, Brian Glover, Ralph Brown, Danny Webb, Christopher John Fields, Holt McCallany, Lance Henriksen, Pete Postlethwaite. More-of-the-same sequel has Weaver and other survivors of ALIENS on isolated prison planet where (you guessed it) the alien regenerates itself and runs amok. Good performances, some scares, but a definite feeling of déjà vu hangs over the proceedings. Followed by ALIEN RESURRECTION. Panavision. [R]▼●◗

Alien Thunder (1973-Canadian) **C-90m.** ** D: Claude Fournier. Donald Sutherland, Kevin McCarthy, Chief Dan George, Jean Duceppe, Jack Creely, Francine Racette. Mountie Sutherland chases Cree Indian accused of a sergeant's murder in this handsome but tedious actioner. Video title: DAN CANDY'S LAW. [PG]▼

Ali—Fear Eats the Soul (1974-German) **C-94m.** *** D: Rainer Werner Fassbinder. Brigitte Mira, El Hedi Ben Salem, Barbara Valentin, Irm Hermann, Rainer Werner Fassbinder. Widow Mira, in her 60s, falls in love with and marries an Arab 30 years her junior. Interesting, quietly effective Fassbinder film, a remake of Douglas Sirk's ALL THAT HEAVEN ALLOWS.▼

Alive (1993) **C-125m.** *** D: Frank Marshall. Ethan Hawke, Vincent Spano, Josh Hamilton, Bruce Ramsay, John Haymes Newton, David Kriegel, Kevin Breznahan, Sam Behrens, Illeana Douglas, Jack Noseworthy. Queasy movie about the rugby team that survived 72 days in the Andes

Mountains when their plane crashed on its way from Uruguay to Chile. A half-good movie encumbered by clunky dialogue (or its delivery)—but physically impressive beyond the astonishing particulars of its story (which involves cannibalism). Unquestionably the most chilling portrayal of a plane crash in movie history. Scripted by John Patrick Shanley, from the book by Piers Paul Read. Same story previously filmed as SURVIVE! [R]▼●

Alive and Kicking (1997-British) **C-98m.** *** D: Nancy Meckler. Jason Flemyng, Antony Sher, Dorothy Tutin, Anthony Higgins, Bill Nighy, Philip Voss, Diane Parish. Martin Sherman (author of the play *Bent*) scripted this touching drama about a self-involved gay dancer (Flemyng) who refuses to let the fact that he is afflicted with AIDS disrupt his career; he also becomes romantically involved with a therapist (Sher) who treats HIV-positive patients. The scenario may be familiar, but it's sincere and extremely well acted, and the world of dance is nicely rendered. Original British title: INDIAN SUMMER. [R]▼

Al Jennings of Oklahoma (1951) **C-79m.** ** D: Ray Nazarro. Dan Duryea, Gale Storm, Dick Foran, Gloria Henry. Modest Western enhanced by Duryea in title role of gangster who serves his time and goes straight; sporadic action.

All About Eve (1950) **138m.** **** D: Joseph L. Mankiewicz. Bette Davis, Anne Baxter, George Sanders, Celeste Holm, Gary Merrill, Thelma Ritter, Marilyn Monroe, Hugh Marlowe, Gregory Ratoff. Brilliantly sophisticated (and cynical) look at life in and around the theater, with a heaven-sent script by director Mankiewicz (based on the story "The Wisdom of Eve" by Mary Orr). Davis is absolutely perfect as an aging star who takes in an adoring fan (Baxter) and soon discovers that the young woman is taking over her life. Witty dialogue to spare, especially great when spoken by Sanders and Ritter. Six Oscars include Best Picture, Director, Screenplay, and Supporting Actor (Sanders). Later musicalized on Broadway as *Applause*.▼●◗

All About My Mother (1999-Spanish-French) **C-101m.** ***½ D: Pedro Almodóvar. Cecilia Roth, Marisa Paredes, Penélope Cruz, Antonia San Juan, Candela Peña, Rosa Maria Sardá, Eloy Azorin. When a woman loses her son, she returns to Barcelona, rekindles a dormant friendship with a transvestite pal, and becomes involved with a stage actress her son admired. Almodóvar's most moving film—more serious than most, but not without his trademark humor—and distinguished by exceptional performances all around. A paean to women, in real life and on stage and film. Oscar winner for Best Foreign Film. Panavision. [R]▼◗

All American (1953) **83m.** ** D: Jesse Hibbs. Tony Curtis, Lori Nelson, Richard Long, Mamie Van Doren, Gregg Palmer, Stuart Whitman. Ordinary drama in which college football hero Curtis gives up the game after his parents' death, and accepts an architecture scholarship at a snooty Ivy League–type school. Of note for appearances of several all-Americans (including Frank Gifford). Look fast for football great Tom Harmon in the announcing booth.

All-American Boy, The (1973) **C-118m.** ** D: Charles Eastman. Jon Voight, E. J. Peaker, Ned Glass, Anne Archer, Carol Androsky. Muddled drama about Olympic hopeful Voight's attempt to succeed as a boxer; striking locations of northern California, but that's all. Panavision. [R]▼

All-American Murder (1992) **C-93m.** ** D: Anson Williams. Christopher Walken, Charlie Schlatter, Josie Bissett, Joanna Cassidy, Richard Kind, Woody Watson, J. C. Quinn. Rebellious college student Schlatter is suspected of murdering the virginal girl he loved, but cop Walken's not so sure. Highly guessable plot studded with slasher-movie murders cheats viewers; frequent tilted camera angles may make you seasick. [R]▼●

Allan Quatermain and the Lost City of Gold (1987) **C-99m.** BOMB D: Gary Nelson (additional scenes: Newt Arnold). Richard Chamberlain, Sharon Stone, James Earl Jones, Henry Silva, Robert Donner, Doghmi Larbi, Cassandra Peterson. Cheapjack followup to 1985 version of KING SOLOMON'S MINES with the same stars; Chamberlain returns to Africa in search of his brother, who's been tracking a lost white tribe. Post-production patchups are all too obvious—and they don't much help. Remake of the 1977 KING SOLOMON'S TREASURE. J-D-C Scope. [PG]▼

All Ashore (1953) **C-80m.** *½ D: Richard Quine. Mickey Rooney, Dick Haymes, Peggy Ryan, Ray MacDonald. Musical yarn of three gobs on shore leave finding gals, sinks despite Rooney's sprite spirit.

All at Sea (1957-British) **87m.** *** D: Charles Frend. Alec Guinness, Irene Browne, Percy Herbert, Harold Goodwin. Robust comedy that holds its own throughout. Guinness is admirable as seaman who can't bear sight of water but buys rundown house-laden pier, turning it into an amusement palace. Original title: BARNACLE BILL.

All Creatures Great and Small (1974-U.S.-British) **C-92m. TVM** D: Claude Whatham. Simon Ward, Anthony Hopkins, Lisa Harrow, Brian Stirner, Freddie Jones, T. P. McKenna. Gentle drama about rural English life, taken from James Herriot's autobiographical best-sellers (*If Only They Could Talk* and *It Shouldn't Happen to a Vet*). Ward plays the author in his younger days as apprentice to an eccentric veterinarian, wonderfully acted by Hopkins. Rich period piece. Script by Hugh Whitemore. Followed by a British TV series. Sequel: ALL THINGS BRIGHT AND BEAUTIFUL. Above average.▼

All Dogs Go to Heaven (1989) **C-85m.** *½ D: Don Bluth. Voices of Burt Reynolds, Loni Anderson, Judith Barsi, Dom DeLuise, Vic Tayback, Charles Nelson Reilly, Melba Moore. Bluth's colorful animation is only saving grace of this downbeat musical cartoon about an orphan "adopted" by an unlovable mutt (Reynolds) who has returned from heaven to do a good deed. Misguided film has some good moments (a musical sequence with a Cajun alligator), but hurt by unappealing characters, confused storytelling, and forgettable songs. Followed by three sequels and an animated TV series. [G]▼●

All Dogs Go to Heaven 2 (1996-U.S.-British) **C-84m.** **½ D: Paul Sebella, Larry Leker. Voices of Charlie Sheen, Sheena Easton, Dom DeLuise, Ernest Borgnine, George Hearn, Bebe Neuwirth, Adam Wylie, Dan Castellaneta, Wallace Shawn, Pat Corley, Bobby DiCicco, Jim Cummings, Maurice La Marche. Cartoon canine Charlie Barkin (Sheen), bored with life in heaven, volunteers a return to earth in an effort to retrieve Gabriel's horn, which was stolen by evil dog Carface (Borgnine). There, he falls in love, befriends a boy who needs him, and does battle with a devilish cat. Big improvement over the first picture in terms of story and music, but fails to match the original's lush animation production. Followed by two direct-to-video sequels. [G]▼●

Allegheny Uprising (1939) **81m.** *** D: William Seiter. John Wayne, Claire Trevor, George Sanders, Brian Donlevy, Robert Barrat, Moroni Olsen, Chill Wills. Wayne leads band of brave men against crooked Donlevy, tyrannical British captain Sanders in pre-Revolutionary colonies. Fine, unpretentious film; Trevor appealing as girl who goes after Wayne. Also shown in computer-colored version.▼●

Allegro Non Troppo (1976-Italian) **C-75m.** *** D: Bruno Bozzetto. Animator Bozzetto's answer to Disney's FANTASIA is an uneven but imaginative collection of vignettes set to music by Debussy, Dvorak, Vivaldi, Stravinsky, and others, framed by heavy-handed live-action slapstick featuring an oafish orchestra-conductor. Best sequences: Sibelius' "Valse Triste," with a melancholy cat, and a chronicle of evolution set to Ravel's "Bolero."▼●

All Fall Down (1962) **110m.** *** D: John Frankenheimer. Warren Beatty, Eva Marie Saint, Karl Malden, Angela Lansbury, Brandon de Wilde. Improbable but absorbing William Inge script about narcissistic young man (Beatty), his admiring younger brother (de Wilde), indulgent parents (Lansbury and Malden), and the older woman (Saint) with whom he becomes involved. Fine performances. Also shown in computer-colored version.▼

All Hands on Deck (1961) **C-98m.** ** D: Norman Taurog. Pat Boone, Buddy Hackett, Dennis O'Keefe, Barbara Eden. Innocuous musical comedy of free-wheeling sailors, Boone and Hackett, is lightweight entertainment. CinemaScope.

All I Desire (1953) **79m.** **½ D: Douglas Sirk. Barbara Stanwyck, Richard Carlson, Lyle Bettger, Lori Nelson, Maureen O'Sullivan. Family togetherness and home-town approval is answer to title, in period-piece uplifted by Stanwyck's valiant performance as erring mother of three who returns to her husband.▼

Alligator (1980) **C-94m.** *** D: Lewis Teague. Robert Forster, Robin Riker, Michael Gazzo, Perry Lang, Jack Carter, Henry Silva, Bart Braverman, Dean Jagger, Angel Tompkins, Sue Lyon, Pat Petersen. If you've got to make a film about a giant alligator that's terrorizing Chicago, this is the way to do it—with a sense of fun to balance the expected violence and genuine scares. The knowing screenplay is by John Sayles; Silva does a hilarious self-parody as an egomaniacal Great White Hunter. Don't miss the graffiti in the final scene. Followed by a sequel. [R]▼

Alligator II: The Mutation (1991) **C-92m.** BOMB D: Jon Hess. Joseph Bologna, Dee Wallace Stone, Richard Lynch, Woody Brown, Holly Gagnier, Bill Dailey, Steve Railsback, Brock Peters, Julian Reyes. Another big alligator menaces another big city, with only cops Bologna and Brown, plus Cajun alligator hunter Lynch, to stop it from gobbling up the revelers at a lake. Astonishingly lame-brained and dreary. [PG-13]▼

Alligator Eyes (1990) **C-101m.** ** D: John Feldman. Annabelle Larsen, Roger Kabler, Mary McLain, Allen McCullough. Three friends on vacation in North Carolina pick up a mysterious young blind woman who alters the course of their journey, leading them into trouble. Independently made psychological thriller introduces a fine group of promising actors to the screen, but its plot is sometimes hard to take. Larsen, in particular, stands out. [R]▼●

Alligator Named Daisy, An (1957-British) **C-88m.** **½ D: J. Lee Thompson. Diana Dors, Donald Sinden, Stanley Holloway, Roland Culver, Margaret Rutherford, Stephen Boyd. Dors reveals pleasing comic talent in fabricated account of salesman who mistakenly picks up someone else's alligator suitcase, leading to complications. VistaVision.

Alligator People, The (1959) **74m.** **½ D: Roy Del Ruth. Beverly Garland, George Macready, Lon Chaney (Jr.), Richard Crane, Frieda Inescort, Bruce Bennett. Garland searches for runaway husband and finds him at his family's Southern mansion—partly transformed into an alligator! Strictly routine. CinemaScope.▼

Alligator Shoes (1981-Canadian) **C-98m.** **½ D: Clay Borris. Garry Borris, Ronalda Jones, Clay Borris, Rose Maltais-Borris, Len Perry. Clever but uneven fictionalized drama about the director's family, focusing on brother Garry's hustling and conning. Excellent use of working class Toronto locations.▼

All in a Night's Work (1961) **C-94m.** **½ D: Joseph Anthony. Dean Martin, Shirley MacLaine, Charlie Ruggles, Cliff Robertson. Featherweight (and often featherbrained) comedy about innocent office worker caught in compromising position with big-business exec, leading to a series of misunderstandings. Filled with familiar character actors (Gale Gordon, Jerome Cowan, Jack Weston, Norma Crane, et al). ▼

All I Wanna Do (1998) **C-97m.** *** D: Sarah Kernochan. Kirsten Dunst, Gaby Hoffmann, Lynn Redgrave, Rachael Leigh Cook, Thomas Guiry, Vincent Kartheiser, Monica Keena, Matthew Lawrence, Heather Matarazzo. Clever, funny comedy with serious undertones about a girls' boarding school in 1963—in the years just before women's lib—where newcomer Hoffmann bonds with a group of mischief-makers. Good showcase for its talented young cast, though somehow this never got a wide theatrical release. Written by the director. Originally screened as STRIKE! [PG-13]▼

All I Want for Christmas (1991) **C-92m.** *½ D: Robert Lieberman. Harley Jane Kozak, Jamey Sheridan, Ethan Randall (Embry), Kevin Nealon, Thora Birch, Leslie Nielsen, Lauren Bacall. Slapdash tale of kids' efforts to get their divorced parents back together for the title holiday. A feel-good movie whose emotion seems as authentic as a plastic Christmas tree. A waste of time for all concerned (including Bacall, as the children's grandmother). [G]▼●

All Mine to Give (1957) **C-102m.** **½ D: Allen Reisner. Cameron Mitchell, Glynis Johns, Patty McCormack, Hope Emerson. Often touching story of pioneer family in Wisconsin determined to overcome all obstacles.▼

All My Sons (1948) **94m.** *** D: Irving Reis. Edward G. Robinson, Burt Lancaster, Mady Christians, Louisa Horton, Howard Duff, Arlene Francis, Lloyd Gough, Henry (Harry) Morgan. Arthur Miller's compelling drama of returning soldier (Lancaster) discovering that his father (Robinson) cheated on a war matériel order, with tragic results. Post-WW2 drama is well acted, but verbose and preachy.▼

Allnighter, The (1987) **C-108m.** BOMB D: Tamar Simon Hoffs. Susanna Hoffs, Dedee Pfeiffer, Joan Cusack, Michael Ontkean, John Terlesky, James Anthony Shanta, Pam Grier, Meshach Taylor. Three female airheads stumble through assorted sexual hijinks during the final senior weekend at a Pacific party college. Grotesque in the AIDS era, though it would be a stinker anytime. Director Hoffs is the mother of the star, a member of The Bangles rock group. [PG-13]▼◗

All Night Long (1961-British) **95m.** **½ D: Basil Dearden. Patrick McGoohan, Marti Stevens, Betsy Blair, Keith Michell, Richard Attenborough. Fair updating of *Othello,* about an interracial couple, a white singer and black bandleader, and their Iago, a drummer (amusingly played by McGoohan). Guest musicians include Dave Brubeck, Charlie Mingus, John Dankworth.

All Night Long (1981) **C-88m.** ***½ D: Jean-Claude Tramont. Gene Hackman, Barbra Streisand, Diane Ladd, Dennis Quaid, Kevin Dobson, William Daniels, Ann Doran. Married Hackman takes up with neighbor's wife Streisand after he's demoted to managing a downtown all-night drugstore, the clientele of which has torridly high weirdo quotient. Streisand is badly, if rather endearingly, miscast (she replaced Lisa Eichhorn after film was already in production), but Hackman is at the peak of his charm in this gentle, underrated comedy. [R]▼

All of Me (1934) **75m.** ** D: James Flood. Fredric March, Miriam Hopkins, George Raft, Helen Mack, Blanche Frederici. Ineffectual melodrama of professor March yearning for open spaces and lover Hopkins learning about true devotion from gun moll Mack.

All of Me (1984) **C-93m.** *** D: Carl Reiner. Steve Martin, Lily Tomlin, Victoria Tennant, Madolyn Smith, Richard Libertini, Dana Elcar, Jason Bernard, Selma Diamond. The soul and spirit of a crotchety millionairess (Tomlin) enter the body of a young, idealistic lawyer (Martin) with often hilarious results. Uneven comedy-fantasy actually gets better as it goes along, and characters become more endearing. Martin's performance is a comic tour-de force. [PG]▼●◗

Allotment Wives (1945) **83m.** ** D: William Nigh. Kay Francis, Paul Kelly, Otto Kruger, Gertrude Michael, Teala Loring. Mild sensationalism involving women who marry servicemen to collect their military pay; not one of Francis' better films.

All Over Me (1997) **C-90m.** *** D: Alex Sichel. Alison Folland, Tara Subkoff, Wilson Cruz, Cole Hauser, Ann Dowd, Pat Briggs, Leisha Hailey, Shawn Hatosy. Dark, brooding but absorbing coming-of-age drama about two girls—one gay, one straight—

whose friendship unravels after a fatal gay-bashing in their Hell's Kitchen neighborhood. The whole cast is excellent, but Folland as the shy budding lesbian is the emotional center. Powered by a terrific soundtrack featuring Patti Smith and Ani DiFranco, among others. Film's costars are also indie rockers: Briggs is the frontman of Psychotica, Hailey sings with The Murmurs. Written by director Sichel's sister, Sylvia. [R]▼●

All Over Town (1937) **62m.** **½ D: James W. Horne. Ole Olsen, Chic Johnson, Mary Howard, Harry Stockwell, Franklin Pangborn, James Finlayson. Low-budget shenanigans, with Olsen and Johnson trying to stage a show in a "jinxed" theater. Spotty, but has some funny moments.▼

All Quiet on the Western Front (1930) **133m.** **** D: Lewis Milestone. Lew Ayres, Louis Wolheim, John Wray, Slim Summerville, Russell Gleason, Ben Alexander, Beryl Mercer. Vivid, moving adaptation of Erich Maria Remarque's eloquent pacifist novel about German boys' experiences as soldiers during WW1. Time hasn't dimmed its power, or its poignancy, one bit. Scripted by Milestone, Maxwell Anderson, Del Andrews, and George Abbott. Academy Award winner for Best Picture and Director. Originally shown at 140m., then cut many times over the years; restored in 1998. It's 130m. on home video. Sequel: THE ROAD BACK. Remade for TV a half century later.▼●◗

All Quiet on the Western Front (1979) **C-150m. TVM** D: Delbert Mann. Richard Thomas, Ernest Borgnine, Patricia Neal, Ian Holm, Donald Pleasence. Solid remake of the vintage classic about young German soldiers in WW1 and the grizzled veteran who teaches them to grow up fast in the trenches. Borgnine and Neal received Emmy nominations as did the film itself, adapted by Paul Monash from the Remarque novel. Above average.▼

All Screwed Up (1974-Italian) **C-105m.** *** D: Lina Wertmuller. Luigi Diberti, Nino Bignamini, Lina Polito, Sara Rapisarda. Appealing tragicomedy of various young working-class men and women, and what happens when they move into a Milan apartment. Released in the U.S. in 1976. [PG]▼

All's Fair (1989) **C-89m.** BOMB D: Rocky Lane. George Segal, Sally Kellerman, Robert Carradine, Jennifer Edwards, Jane Kaczmarek, John Kapelos, Lou Ferrigno. Dreadful comedy about some good-old-boy executives who spend their weekends playing macho war games, and end up taking on their wives and female counterparts in "battle." It'd be hard to find a comedy as unfunny as this. [PG-13]▼●

All That Heaven Allows (1955) **C-89m.** *** D: Douglas Sirk. Jane Wyman, Rock Hudson, Agnes Moorehead, Conrad Nagel, Virginia Grey, Gloria Talbott, William Reynolds, Charles Drake, Merry Anders. When middle-class widow Wyman allows gardener Hudson—a younger man—to romance her, she faces the ire of her children, friends, and society. Typically sleek Sirk soaper. Remade by Rainer Werner Fassbinder as ALI—FEAR EATS THE SOUL.▼

All That Jazz (1979) **C-123m.** **½ D: Bob Fosse. Roy Scheider, Jessica Lange, Ann Reinking, Leland Palmer, Cliff Gorman, Ben Vereen, Erzsebet Foldi, Sandahl Bergman, John Lithgow, Keith Gordon, Ben Masters, Nicole Fosse, Theresa Merritt, Wallace Shawn. Director-choreographer Fosse's own **8½** casts a self-indulgent and largely negative look at his life; great show biz moments and wonderful dancing are eventually buried in pretensions, and an interminable finale which leaves a bad taste for the whole film. But that opening number (set to George Benson's recording of "On Broadway") is a wow! [R]▼●

All That Money Can Buy SEE: **Devil and Daniel Webster, The**

All the Brothers Were Valiant (1953) **C-101m.** **½ D: Richard Thorpe. Robert Taylor, Stewart Granger, Ann Blyth, Keenan Wynn, James Whitmore, Lewis Stone. Water-logged adventurer based on Ben Ames Williams' novel. Taylor and Granger lack conviction as New Bedford whalers having career and romantic conflicts.▼

All the Fine Young Cannibals (1960) **C-112m.** *½ D: Michael Anderson. Robert Wagner, Natalie Wood, Susan Kohner, George Hamilton, Pearl Bailey, Anne Seymour. Clichés abound in this romantic soap opera that was actually inspired by the life of jazz trumpeter Chet Baker (whose role is played here, somewhat improbably, by Wagner). British music group Fine Young Cannibals took its name from this film. CinemaScope.

All the King's Horses (1934) **87m.** ** D: Frank Tuttle. Carl Brisson, Mary Ellis, Edward Everett Horton, Katherine DeMille, Eugene Pallette. Mediocre musical about movie star who exchanges places with lookalike king, causing complications for both men, especially where l'amour is concerned.

All the King's Men (1949) **109m.** **** D: Robert Rossen. Broderick Crawford, Joanne Dru, John Ireland, Mercedes McCambridge, John Derek, Shepperd Strudwick, Anne Seymour. Brilliant adaptation (by director Rossen) of Robert Penn Warren's Pulitzer Prize-winning novel about the rise and fall of a Huey Long-like senator, played by Crawford in the performance of his career. He and McCambridge (in her first film) won well-deserved Oscars, as did the film, for Best Picture. Campaign montages directed by Don Siegel. ▼●

. . . All the Marbles (1981) **C-113m.** *** D: Robert Aldrich. Peter Falk, Vicki Frederick, Laurene Landon, Burt Young, Tracy Reed, Ursaline Bryant-King, Claudette Nevins, Richard Jaeckel. There's no reason why this sloppily constructed, shallowly written movie—about a pair of beautiful female wrestlers and their two-bit manager—should be so entertaining, but it is. The climactic championship bout is a real audience-rouser. Retitled THE CALIFORNIA DOLLS. Aldrich's final film. [R]▼

All the Mornings of the World SEE: **Tous les Matins du Monde**

All the President's Men (1976) **C-138m.** **** D: Alan J. Pakula. Robert Redford, Dustin Hoffman, Jason Robards, Jack Warden, Martin Balsam, Hal Holbrook, Jane Alexander, Stephen Collins, Meredith Baxter, Ned Beatty, Robert Walden, Polly Holliday, F. Murray Abraham, Lindsay Ann Crouse. Redford and Hoffman play real-life *Washington Post* reporters Bob Woodward and Carl Bernstein, who persevered in their investigation of Watergate break-in that led to earthshaking scandal. Best elements of newspaper pictures, detective stories, and thrillers rolled into one superb movie. Won Oscars for Supporting Actor (Robards), Screenplay (William Goldman), Art Direction, and Sound. [PG] ▼●

All the Right Moves (1983) **C-91m.** **½ D: Michael Chapman. Tom Cruise, Craig T. Nelson, Lea Thompson, Charles Cioffi, Paul Carafotes, Christopher Penn. Amiable youth film about a goal-oriented high-school football player (Cruise) who runs afoul of his hotheaded—and equally ambitious—coach (Nelson). Location filming in Johnstown, Pa., adds flavor. [R]▼●

All These Women (1964-Swedish) **C-80m.** **½ D: Ingmar Bergman. Jarl Kulle, Harriet Andersson, Bibi Andersson, Allan Edwall. Satirical frolic involving woman-chasing cellist. He bargains with music critic to have biography written by agreeing to play writer's composition. Notable only as Bergman's first film in color. Aka NOW ABOUT ALL THESE WOMEN.

All the Vermeers in New York (1990) **C-87m.** *** D: Jon Jost. Emmanuelle Chaulet, Stephen Lack, Grace Phillips, Laurel Lee Kiefer, Gordon Joseph Weiss, Katherine Bean, Gracie Mansion, Roger Ruffin. Provocative drama with a singular cinematic sensibility, about a stressed-out Wall Street wheeler-dealer (Lack); while at the Metropolitan Museum, he meets a beautiful, mysterious French actress (Chaulet) who resembles a Vermeer portrait. Loaded with lingering shots, carefully composed images, and improvised dialogue; the scenario examines the relationship between art and commerce, and the hypocrisy beneath the surface of N.Y.C.'s high-powered art and financial worlds. "Conceived, photographed, directed, and edited" by avant-garde filmmaker Jost.▼●

All the Way SEE: **Joker Is Wild, The**

All the Way, Boys (1973-Italian) **C-105m.** *½ D: Giuseppe Colizzi. Terence Hill, Bud Spencer, Cyril Cusack, Michele Antoine, Rene Koldehoff. Big comedown for the TRINITY boys; soggy comedy has them operating a ramshackle airplane in the Andes. Pathos overwhelms the slapstick, and it works about as well here as it did in Jerry Lewis' films. Widescreen. [PG]▼

All the Way Home (1963) **97m.** ***½ D: Alex Segal. Jean Simmons, Robert Preston, Aline MacMahon, Pat Hingle, Michael Kearney, John Cullum, Thomas Chalmers. Outstanding filmization of the Tad Mosel play, set in 1915 Tennessee, an adaptation of James Agee's *A Death in the Family*. Preston is subdued in the pivotal role of a father and husband who is accidentally killed, leaving his loved ones to interpret the meaning of their lives before and after his death. Beautifully done, with Simmons offering an award-caliber performance as Preston's wife. Fine script by Philip Reisman, Jr.

All the Way, Trinity SEE: **Trinity Is STILL My Name!**

All the Young Men (1960) **87m.** **½ D: Hall Bartlett. Alan Ladd, Sidney Poitier, James Darren, Glenn Corbett, Mort Sahl. Hackneyed Korean war story with all the stereotypes present, mouthing the same old platitudes.▼

All Things Bright and Beautiful (1979-British) **C-94m.** **½ D: Eric Till. John Alderton, Lisa Harrow, Colin Blakely, Bill Maynard, Richard Pearson, Paul Shelley. Pleasant, inoffensive film for kids who like animals and can appreciate an entertainment devoid of car crashes. Kind-hearted veterinarian James Herriot (Alderton) tends to under-the-weather animals in Yorkshire at the end of the '30s. Based on two of Herriot's books, *Let Sleeping Vets Lie* and *Vet in Harness,* published in the U.S. as *All Things Bright and Beautiful.* A sequel to ALL CREATURES GREAT AND SMALL, made for American television. Aka IT SHOULDN'T HAPPEN TO A VET. [G]

All Things Fair (1995-Swedish-Danish) **C-128m.** ***½ D: Bo Widerberg. Johan Widerberg, Marika Lagercrantz, Tomas Von Brömssen, Karin Huldt, Nina Gunke, Bjorn Kjellman, Kenneth Milldoff. In 1943 Sweden a recently transferred high school student falls for his attractive new teacher; their subsequent affair is both passionate and deceitful on many levels. Extremely well made film is exquisitely performed by the two leads (young Johan Widerberg is the director's son) and Swedish star Von Brömssen is equally adept in the role of

an unorthodox cuckolded husband. Director Widerberg (of ELVIRA MADIGAN fame) also wrote the screenplay and edited the film. This can stand alongside the best coming-of-age films.
All This, and Heaven Too (1940) **143m.** *** D: Anatole Litvak. Bette Davis, Charles Boyer, Jeffrey Lynn, Barbara O'Neil, Virginia Weidler, Helen Westley, Walter Hampden, Henry Daniell, June Lockhart. Nobleman Boyer falls in love with governess Davis, causing scandal and death; stars do very well in elaborate filmization of Rachel Field book set in 19th-century France.▼
All This and World War II (1976) **C-88m.** ** D: Susan Winslow. Unusual documentary traces chronology of WW2 with Movietone newsreels and 20th Century-Fox feature film footage, all set to Beatles music! Not as bad as it sounds, but not particularly good either, because there is no point—or point of view. [PG]
All Through the Night (1942) **107m.** *** D: Vincent Sherman. Humphrey Bogart, Conrad Veidt, Kaaren Verne, Jane Darwell, Frank McHugh, Peter Lorre, Judith Anderson, William Demarest, Jackie Gleason, Phil Silvers, Barton MacLane, Martin Kosleck. Bogart's gang tracks down Fifth Columnists (Veidt, Lorre, Anderson) in WW2 N.Y.C. Interesting blend of spy, gangster, and comedy genres, with memorable double-talk and auction scenes.▼●
Almost a Bride SEE: **Kiss For Corliss, A**
Almost an Angel (1990) **C-95m.** ** D: John Cornell. Paul Hogan, Elias Koteas, Linda Kozlowski, Charlton Heston, Doreen Lang, Joe Dallesandro, David Alan Grier, Stephanie Hodge. Hokey, paper-thin afterlife fantasy with Hogan a thief who turns do-gooder after an otherworldly confrontation with God (Heston, naturally). Hogan's effortless charisma cannot salvage it. He also scripted and executive produced. Super 35. [PG]▼●
Almost Angels (1962) **C-93m.** **½ D: Steve Previn. Peter Weck, Hans Holt, Fritz Eckhardt, Bruni Lobel, Vincent Winter, Sean Scully. Schmaltzy but entertaining Disney film about two youngsters who become friends in the Vienna Boys Choir. Pleasant story, fine music.▼
Almost Heroes (1998) **C-90m.** *½ D: Christopher Guest. Chris Farley, Matthew Perry, Eugene Levy, Kevin Dunn, Lisa Barbuscia, Bokeem Woodbine, Steve M. Porter, David Packer, Hamilton Camp, Lewis Arquette; narrated by Harry Shearer. A would-be explorer hires a rowdy tracker in the hope of beating Lewis and Clark to the Pacific Ocean in 1804. Farley (in his last starring film, shot in 1996 and released six months after his death) is as bombastic as ever, but the gags are either flat or nonexistent in this misbegotten comedy. Levy and Dunn have all the best moments, in colorful supporting roles. [PG-13]▼●
Almost Human (1974-Italian) **C-92m.** BOMB D: Umberto Lenzi. Tomas Milian, Henry Silva, Anita Strindberg, Raymond Lovelock, Laura Belli. Sadistic punk Milian versus tired cop Silva. Not another gory horror film, just another clichéd crime melodrama. Originally titled THE KIDNAP OF MARY LOU. [R]▼
Almost Perfect Affair, An (1979) **C-93m.** **½ D: Michael Ritchie. Keith Carradine, Monica Vitti, Raf Vallone, Christian De Sica, Dick Anthony Williams. Romantic comedy-drama about affair between naive American filmmaker and worldly wife of film producer; set against whirring backdrop of Cannes Film Festival, it will appeal mostly to film buffs and insiders. [PG]▼
Almost Summer (1978) **C-88m.** *½ D: Martin Davidson. Bruno Kirby, Lee Purcell, John Friedrich, Didi Conn, Thomas Carter, Tim Matheson. End-of-term frolics, and a cutthroat school election, are presented here in much the same fashion as BEACH BLANKET BINGO. [PG]
Almost You (1984) **C-96m.** *½ D: Adam Brooks. Brooke Adams, Griffin Dunne, Karen Young, Marty Watt, Christine Estabrook, Josh Mostel, Laura Dean, Dana Delany, Miguel Pinero, Joe Silver, Joe Leon, Spalding Gray. Muddled, overlong, self-satisfied "romantic comedy" about Dunne's attempts to break out of his plodding existence with wife Adams in N.Y.C. Originally shown at 110m, which only made matters worse. [R]▼
aloha, bobby and rose (1975) **C-88m.** ** D: Floyd Mutrux. Paul LeMat, Dianne Hull, Tim McIntire, Leigh French, Martine Bartlett, Robert Carradine, Eddie (Edward James) Olmos. OK melodrama follows predictable pattern as auto mechanic LeMat and girlfriend Hull are inadvertently drawn into crime, causing them to take it on the lam with the law in pursuit. [PG]▼◗
Aloha Summer (1988) **C-98m.** ** D: Tommy Lee Wallace. Chris Makepeace, Yuji Okumoto, Don Michael Paul, Tia Carrere, Andy Bumatai, Lorie Griffin, Sho Kosugi. Well-meaning but bland story about six young American, Japanese, and Hawaiian boys coming of age on surfboards in Waikiki during the summer of 1959. There's nothing fresh here; the whole thing looks and feels as if it were made in 1959. The waves, however, are outtasight. [PG] ▼●
Aloma of the South Seas (1941) **C-77m.** ** D: Alfred Santell. Dorothy Lamour, Jon Hall, Lynne Overman, Philip Reed, Katherine DeMille. Still another sarong saga with native Hall sent to U.S. for education, returning when father dies to stop revolution on once peaceful island. Filmed before in 1927, with Gilda Gray.

Alone in the Dark (1982) **C-92m.** *½ D: Jack Sholder. Jack Palance, Donald Pleasence, Martin Landau, Dwight Schultz, Erland van Lidth de Jeude, Deborah Hedwall. Mental patients escape from a lunatic asylum and go on a rampage. If your IQ is 15, you might enjoy this. [R]▼

Alone on the Pacific (1963-Japanese) **C-100m.** *** D: Kon Ichikawa. Yujiro Ishihara, Kinuyo Tanaka, Masayuki Mori, Ruriko Asaoka, Hajime Hara. Stirring tale of youth (Ishihara) sailing the Pacific from Osaka to San Francisco by himself. Based on a true story. Original running-time: 104m. Aka MY ENEMY, THE SEA. CinemaScope.

Along Came Jones (1945) **90m.** *** D: Stuart Heisler. Gary Cooper, Loretta Young, William Demarest, Dan Duryea, Frank Sully, Russell Simpson. Three stars are most ingratiating in very low-key, leisurely Western spoof, with Cooper (who also produced) mistaken for notorious outlaw Duryea.▼

Along the Great Divide (1951) **88m.** **½ D: Raoul Walsh. Kirk Douglas, Virginia Mayo, John Agar, Walter Brennan. Douglas is appropriately tight-lipped as lawman determined to bring in his man, despite desert storm; some spectacular scenery.▼

Alphabet City (1984) **C-98m.** ** D: Amos Poe. Vincent Spano, Kate Vernon, Michael Winslow, Zohra Lampert, Jami Gertz, Raymond Serra. Slick, arty but shallow and almost plotless portrait of teenage hood Spano and his life on N.Y.C.'s Lower East Side. All imagery, no content. [R]▼

Alphabet Murders, The (1966-British) **90m.** **½ D: Frank Tashlin. Tony Randall, Anita Ekberg, Robert Morley, Guy Rolfe, James Villiers. Odd adaptation of Agatha Christie's *The ABC Murders* (the film's original British title), with Hercule Poirot after a killer who seems to be doing in his victims in alphabetical order. Strange casting of Randall as the Belgian sleuth and a little too much slapstick make this more a curiosity than anything else. Margaret Rutherford makes a gag appearance as Miss Marple.▼

Alphaville (1965-French) **95m.** ** D: Jean-Luc Godard. Eddie Constantine, Anna Karina, Akim Tamiroff, Howard Vernon. Constantine, as super private-eye Lemmy Caution, is sent to futuristic city run by electronic brain to rescue scientist trapped there. Jumbled Godard epic, recommended for New Wave disciples only.▼●◗

Alsino and the Condor (1982-Nicaraguan-Mexican-Cuban-Costa Rican) **C-89m.** *** D: Miguel Littin. Dean Stockwell, Alan Esquivel, Carmen Bunster, Alejandro Parodi, Delia Casanova. Idealistic young peasant (Esquivel) jumps out of a tree in the hope of flying; he becomes a hunchback, but learns to stand tall when he joins guerillas fighting in a Central American country. Certainly unsubtle, but far from uninteresting allegory, filmed in Nicaragua. [R]▼●

Altered States (1980) **C-102m.** **½ D: Ken Russell. William Hurt, Blair Brown, Bob Balaban, Charles Haid, Thaao Penghlis, Dori Brenner, George Gaynes, Drew Barrymore. A scientist (Hurt, in his film debut) becomes involved with primal research, using himself as guinea pig with mind-bending results. Talky and cerebral at first, then turns into a cross between THE WOLF MAN and THE TIME MACHINE, using state-of-the-art special effects. More successful as an assault on the senses than as a film, with thoroughly unappealing protagonists and a ludicrous story resolution. Paddy Chayefsky disowned his adaptation of his novel, and the script is now credited to his given name, "Sidney Aaron." Barrymore's film debut. Look for John Larroquette as an X-ray technician. [R]▼●◗

Alvarez Kelly (1966) **C-116m.** **½ D: Edward Dmytryk. William Holden, Richard Widmark, Janice Rule, Victoria Shaw, Patrick O'Neal. Slow-moving Civil War tale. Holden is cattle driver who sells herd to Yankees, then is kidnapped by Reb Widmark who wants him to steal cattle for the South; incongruous love scenes thrown in. Panavision. ▼●◗

Always (1985) **C-105m.** *** D: Henry Jaglom. Henry Jaglom, Patrice Townsend, Joanna Frank, Alan Rachins, Melissa Leo, Jonathan Kaufer, Bob Rafelson, Michael Emil, Andre Gregory. Often hilarious, but also insightful, comedy about what it means to be a couple. A trio of them—one about to get divorced, one about to get married, one solidly married—spend a July 4th weekend together. The first is played by the director and Townsend, his own ex-wife. Like all of Jaglom's stream-of-consciousness films, this one's not for all tastes. [R]▼●

Always (1989) **C-121m.** **½ D: Steven Spielberg. Richard Dreyfuss, Holly Hunter, John Goodman, Brad Johnson, Audrey Hepburn, Roberts Blossom, Keith David, Marg Helgenberger. Slick remake of 1943's A GUY NAMED JOE, with Dreyfuss as a cocky pilot who specializes in dousing forest fires from the air, and Hunter as the dispatcher who loves him—and fears for his life. When he does in fact die, he returns in spirit form to guide a young pilot (Johnson) who wants to pursue the same career and the same woman. Certainly entertaining but suffers from a serious case of The Cutes. Hepburn, in her final film appearance, plays an angel. [PG]▼●◗

Always a Bride (1954-British) **83m.** ** D: Ralph Smart. Peggy Cummins, Terence Morgan, Ronald Squire, James Hayter. Mild comedy of treasury officer romancing girl, aiding her dad to fleece others.

Always Goodbye (1938) **75m.** **½ D: Sidney Lanfield. Barbara Stanwyck, Herbert Marshall, Ian Hunter, Cesar Romero, Lynn Bari, Binnie Barnes. Still another sacrificing mother tale—specifically, a remake of GALLANT LADY. Stanwyck is forced to give up her illicit child. Nicely done, but the same old story.

Always in My Heart (1942) **92m.** *½ D: Jo Graham. Kay Francis, Walter Huston, Gloria Warren, Una O'Connor, Sidney Blackmer. Soaper of convict Huston returning to find wife Francis about to marry Blackmer and a daughter (Warren) who doesn't know him.

Always Leave Them Laughing (1949) **116m.** **½ D: Roy Del Ruth. Milton Berle, Virginia Mayo, Ruth Roman, Bert Lahr, Alan Hale. Berle is at home in tale of cocky comedian's ups and downs. Unfortunately, zesty opening leads into soggy drama. Lahr does his classic "stop in the name of the stationhouse" routine.

Always Together (1948) **78m.** **½ D: Frederick de Cordova. Robert Hutton, Joyce Reynolds, Cecil Kellaway, Ernest Truex; guests Humphrey Bogart, Jack Carson, Dennis Morgan, Janis Paige, Alexis Smith. Innocuous fluff of dying millionaire Kellaway giving money to young Reynolds, then discovering he's quite healthy. Worthwhile only for amusing cameos by many Warner Bros. stars throughout film.

Amadeus (1984) **C-158m.** **½ D: Milos Forman. F. Murray Abraham, Tom Hulce, Elizabeth Berridge, Simon Callow, Roy Dotrice, Christine Ebersole, Jeffrey Jones. Abraham won well-deserved Oscar as composer Salieri, whose music never surpasses mediocrity, while a hedonistic young boor named Mozart expresses musical genius almost without trying! Literate, intelligent, exquisitely filmed (in Prague, by Miroslav Ondricek) . . . but fatally overlong and missing dramatic fire that distinguished Peter Shaffer's play (Shaffer rethought and rewrote it for the screen). Worth noting: Jones' wonderful performance as musical dilettante Emperor Joseph II. Winner of seven other Oscars, including Best Picture, Director, Screenplay, Art Direction. Panavision. [PG]▼●◗

Amarcord (1974-Italian) **C-127m.** ***½ D: Federico Fellini. Magali Noel, Bruno Zanin, Pupella Maggio, Armando Brancia, Giuseppe Lanigro, Josiane Tanzilli. Fellini's nostalgia trip to the Italy of his youth in the 1930s; warm, funny, poignant, bawdy episodes about love, sex, politics, family life, and growing up. Academy Award winner as Best Foreign Film. [R] ▼●◗

Amateur, The (1982-Canadian) **C-111m.** BOMB D: Charles Jarrott. John Savage, Christopher Plummer, Marthe Keller, Arthur Hill, Ed Lauter, Nicholas Campbell, Graham Jarvis, John Marley. Savage is grossly miscast as a CIA computer whiz who hunts down the terrorists who seized the American Consulate in Munich and murdered his girlfriend. Complex and ultimately ridiculous spy thriller. [R]▼

Amateur (1994-U.S.-French) **C-105m.** **½ D: Hal Hartley. Isabelle Huppert, Martin Donovan, Elina Lowensohn, Damian Young, Chuck Montgomery, David Simonds, Parker Posey. Typically quirky Hartley tale about an ex-nun (Huppert) who writes pornographic fiction (!) and hooks up with a seemingly harmless amnesiac (Donovan) with a disturbing past. As in all of the director's films, this one is filled with offbeat characters who do and say the weirdest things; among them are a pair of hit men who look like Wall Street yuppies. Interesting stuff, but most decidedly not for all tastes. An *American Playhouse* coproduction. [R]▼

Amazing Adventure (1936-British) **70m.** **½ D: Alfred Zeisler. Cary Grant, Mary Brian, Henry Kendall, Leon M. Lion, Garry Marsh, John Turnbull. Grant inherits a fortune and, feeling guilty, sets out to earn his living instead. One of those The-Poor-Are-Smarter comedies typical of the era, and a rare opportunity to see Cary working on his home turf. Originally titled THE AMAZING QUEST OF ERNEST BLISS in Britain, ROMANCE AND RICHES in the U.S. E. Phillips Oppenheim's novel filmed before in England in 1920.▼

Amazing Colossal Man, The (1957) **80m.** **½ D: Bert I. Gordon. Glenn Langan, Cathy Downs, James Seay, Larry Thor. Army officer who survives an atomic explosion starts growing; at sixty feet he attacks Las Vegas! Starts well but ends up as your standard monster-on-the-loose flick. Sequel: WAR OF THE COLOSSAL BEAST.▼

Amazing Dobermans, The (1976) **C-94m.** **½ D: David and Byron Chudnow. James Franciscus, Barbara Eden, Fred Astaire, Jack Carter, Billy Barty. Engaging action comedy that has Bible-quoting ex-con-man Astaire's five remarkable Doberman pinschers helping treasury agent Franciscus thwart a racketeer and his gang. Higher-budgeted sequel to THE DOBERMAN GANG and THE DARING DOBERMANS, aided by offbeat casting of Astaire. [PG—edited from original R rating]▼

Amazing Dr. Clitterhouse, The (1938) **87m.** *** D: Anatole Litvak. Edward G. Robinson, Claire Trevor, Humphrey Bogart, Allen Jenkins, Donald Crisp, Gale Page. Amusing film of "method doctor" Robinson trying to discover what makes a crook tick; he joins Bogart's gang and becomes addicted.▼

Amazing Grace (1974) **C-99m.** ** D:

Stan Lathan. Moms Mabley, Slappy White, Moses Gunn, Rosalind Cash, Dolph Sweet. A few laughs in Philadelphia-made comedy about an elderly busybody who disrupts corrupt Baltimore politics. Mabley's only starring film; cameos by Butterfly McQueen, unrecognizable Stepin Fetchit. [G]▼

Amazing Grace and Chuck (1987) **C-115m.** *½ D: Mike Newell. Jamie Lee Curtis, Alex English, Gregory Peck, William L. Petersen, Joshua Zuehlke, Dennis Lipscomb, Lee Richardson. A 12-year-old Little League whiz decides to stop playing baseball until the world agrees to complete nuclear disarmament . . . and soon, other athletes around the world follow suit, as the protest escalates. Producer-writer David Field's Capraesque wish-fufillment fantasy is one of those films you either swallow wholeheartedly, or don't. It's dripping with good intentions. [PG] ▼●

Amazing Mr. Blunden, The (1972-British) **C-99m.** *** D: Lionel Jeffries. Laurence Naismith, Lynne Frederick, Garry Miller, Rosalyn Landor, Marc Granger, Diana Dors, James Villiers. Dickensian fantasy about a genial ghost who takes two children back in time to help two mistreated tots. Colorful family film whose only liability is somewhat muddled storyline. [G]▼

Amazing Mrs. Holliday, The (1943) **96m.** **½ D: Bruce Manning. Deanna Durbin, Edmond O'Brien, Barry Fitzgerald, Arthur Treacher, Frieda Inescort. Lukewarm WW2 comedy-drama about dedicated missionary Durbin trying to sneak Chinese orphans into U.S. Deanna's song interludes offer respite from silly plot. Much of this was directed by Jean Renoir, but his and Durbin's plans for the film went awry.▼

Amazing Mr. Williams (1939) **80m.** **½ D: Alexander Hall. Melvyn Douglas, Joan Blondell, Clarence Kolb, Ruth Donnelly. Douglas holds up his marriage to investigate murder in this satisfying comedy-mystery.

Amazing Mr. X, The (1948) **78m.** **½ D: Bernard Vorhaus. Turhan Bey, Lynn Bari, Cathy O'Donnell, Richard Carlson, Donald Curtis, Virginia Gregg. Intriguing little chiller in which wealthy, vulnerable widow Bari desperately misses her late husband. Will she be able to contact him via the powers of psychic Bey? Aka THE SPIRITUALIST. ▼●

Amazing Panda Adventure, The (1995-U.S.-China) **C-85m.** **½ D: Christopher Cain. Ryan Slater, Stephen Lang, Yi Ding, Huang Fei, Zhou Jiugou, Yao Erga. Time-honored "boy and his dog" story, except in this case it's a boy and his panda. Ten-year-old American boy and a Chinese girl trek through China in order to rescue the cub from poachers. Too predictable for adult viewers, but the spectacular Chinese scenery makes it worthwhile. Slater is Christian's younger brother. [PG]▼●

Amazing Quest of Ernest Bliss, The SEE: **Amazing Adventure**

Amazing Transparent Man, The (1960) **58m.** BOMB D: Edgar G. Ulmer. Douglas Kennedy, Marguerite Chapman, James Griffith, Ivan Triesault. Tawdry cheapie in which a mad scientist makes a convict invisible to steal radioactive materials for him, but the subject is more interested in testing his new power on a nearby bank. Disappointed Ulmer fans will wish they had the formula themselves.▼●◗

Amazon Women on the Moon (1987) **C/B&W-85m.** *½ D: Joe Dante, Carl Gottlieb, Peter Horton, John Landis, Robert K. Weiss. Rosanna Arquette, Ralph Bellamy, Carrie Fisher, Griffin Dunne, Steve Guttenberg, Michelle Pfeiffer, Peter Horton, Sybil Danning, Ed Begley, Jr., Henny Youngman, Paul Bartel, Lou Jacobi, Howard Hesseman, B.B. King, Steve Allen, Steve Forrest, Russ Meyer, Arsenio (Hall), Phil Hartman, Joe Pantoliano, Rip Taylor, David Alan Grier, Angel Tompkins, Kelly Preston, Andrew Dice Clay, Mike Mazurki, Corinne Wahl. Series of unrelated skits in the KENTUCKY FRIED MOVIE vein, most of them astonishingly unfunny. Parody of CAT WOMEN OF THE MOON that punctuates the film is so exact that you might as well watch the original—it's just as funny. Best of all is the 1930s sex-film spoof with Bartel and Fisher, but that comes at the very end. [R]▼●◗

Ambassador, The (1984) **C-90m.** *** D: J. Lee Thompson. Robert Mitchum, Ellen Burstyn, Rock Hudson, Fabio Testi, Donald Pleasence, Michal Bat-Adam. Intelligent, entertaining thriller of American ambassador Mitchum, his adulterous wife Burstyn, and his attempts to peacefully mediate the Israeli-Palestinian crisis. Based on Elmore Leonard's novel *52 Pick-Up*, and remade just two years later under that name. Hudson's final theatrical film. [R]▼

Ambassador Bill (1931) **68m.** **½ D: Sam Taylor. Will Rogers, Greta Nissen, Marguerite Churchill, Tad Alexander, Ray Milland, Gustav von Seyffertitz. Tailor-made Rogers vehicle about a U.S. ambassador who's dispatched to a country torn by civil strife and conspiracy; he makes friends with the boy-king who will eventually rule the kingdom and teaches him to be a "regular guy."▼

Ambassador's Daughter, The (1956) **C-102m.** **½ D: Norman Krasna. Olivia de Havilland, John Forsythe, Myrna Loy, Adolphe Menjou, Edward Arnold, Francis Lederer, Tommy Noonan, Minor Watson. Oomph is missing even though stars give all to uplift sagging comedy of de Havilland out for a fling in Paris, romanced by soldier Forsythe. CinemaScope.▼

Ambition (1991) **C-100m.** BOMB D: Scott D. Goldstein. Lou Diamond Phillips, Clancy Brown, Cecilia Peck, Richard Bradford, Willard Pugh, Grace Zabriskie, Katherine Armstrong, J. D. Cullum, Haing S. Ngor. Awful thriller about a writer who becomes totally obsessed with his subject—a man who happens to be a convicted murderer. Phillips makes his screenwriting debut here but he's bitten off more than he can type. A bust! [R]▼●

Ambulance, The (1990) **C-95m.** ** D: Larry Cohen. Eric Roberts, James Earl Jones, Megan Gallagher, Richard Bright, Janine Turner, Eric Braeden, Red Buttons, Nicholas Chinlund. Muddled thriller which tells the story of what happens when innocent people begin disappearing off the streets of N.Y. Routine stuff, but look for an especially fine performance by Buttons. Roberts plays a comic book artist, and Marvel Comics editor Stan Lee appears as himself. [R]▼●

Ambush (1949) **89m.** **½ D: Sam Wood. Robert Taylor, John Hodiak, Arlene Dahl, Don Taylor, Jean Hagen, Bruce Cowling, Leon Ames, John McIntire, Chief Thundercloud. Formula Western with Apaches vs. cavalry.

Ambush at Cimarron Pass (1958) **73m.** ** D: Jodie Copelan. Scott Brady, Margia Dean, Clint Eastwood, Baynes Barron, William Vaughn. Stranded cowboys and cavalrymen try to protect shipment of guns from Indians—though they disagree strongly on strategy. Post–Civil War Western features young Eastwood, who continually flies into a white-hot rage whenever he hears the word "Yankee." Regalscope.

Ambush at Tomahawk Gap (1953) **C-73m.** *½ D: Fred F. Sears. John Hodiak, John Derek, David Brian, Percy Helton, Maria Elena Marques. Standard oater has quartet of ex-convicts caught by Indian attack. One is left alive; he rides into sunset with newly-found squaw.▼

Ambush Bay (1966) **C-109m.** **½ D: Ron Winston. Hugh O'Brian, Mickey Rooney, James Mitchum, Harry Lauter. Lackluster adventures of marine group on Jap-held island during WW2 trying to help partisans—good cast wasted.

Ambushers, The (1968) **C-102m.** BOMB D: Henry Levin. Dean Martin, Senta Berger, Janice Rule, James Gregory, Albert Salmi, Kurt Kasznar, Beverly Adams. Do you really care that the first U.S. flying saucer will be sabotaged in space unless Matt Helm comes to the rescue? Third entry in the series may be the weakest, but few film scholars will want to take time making certain. Sequel: THE WRECKING CREW. ▼●

Amelia Earhart: The Final Flight (1994) **C-100m. TVM** D: Yves Simoneau. Diane Keaton, Rutger Hauer, Bruce Dern, Paul Guilfoyle, Denis Arndt, David Carpenter, Diana Bellamy. Keaton's single-minded Earhart is the center of this stunningly photographed, beautifully appointed, though indifferently acted bio, an episodic recreation of the aviatrix's lifelong fascination with aviation ending with her luckless last flight in 1937. Dern does a nice turn as publisher G. P. Putnam, her impresario husband/manager/press agent. Earhart's story was tackled before as a similarly titled TVM in 1976 with Susan Clark. Made for cable. Average.▼●

America (1924) **93m.** *** D: D.W. Griffith. Neil Hamilton, Carol Dempster, Erville Alderson, Charles Emmett Mack, Lee Beggs, Frank McGlynn, Lionel Barrymore, Louis Wolheim. Impressive silent-film treatment of Revolutionary War, with fine battle scenes, period flavor, marred somewhat by silly love story; florid villainy by Barrymore. Still quite good. ▼●◗

America (1986) **C-83m.** BOMB D: Robert Downey. Zack Norman, Tammy Grimes, Michael J. Pollard, Monroe Arnold, Richard Belzer, Liz Torres, Howard Thomashefsky, Laura Ashton. Downey lamely attempts to recapture the freewheeling satires of the 1960s (such as his classic PUTNEY SWOPE) with this amateurish tale of the loonies at a N.Y. cable TV station, whose signal is accidentally bounced off the moon, bringing them worldwide fame. Hopelessly dated; filmed in 1982. [R]▼

America, America (1963) **168m.** **** D: Elia Kazan. Stathis Giallelis, Frank Wolff, Elena Karam, Lou Antonio, John Marley, Estelle Hemsley. The dream of passage to America—as it unfolded for late 19th-century immigrants—is movingly captured by writer-director Kazan in this long, absorbing film, based on his uncle's experiences. Heartfelt and heart-rending, with impressive Oscar-winning art direction/set decoration by Gene Callahan.▼●

America at the Movies (1976) **C/B&W-116m.** ** No director credited. Mindlessly amusing but ultimately pointless potpourri of clips from 83 American movies (YANKEE DOODLE DANDY, THE GRAPES OF WRATH, GIANT, etc.), originally produced by the American Film Institute as a Bicentennial project. Can anyone explain how FIVE EASY PIECES—which takes place in California oil fields and Puget Sound—shows up in a section devoted to "The Cities"? A similar lack of direction pervades throughout. [PG]▼

Americana (1981) **C-91m.** **½ D: David Carradine. David Carradine, Barbara Hershey, Michael Greene. Vietnam veteran Carradine attempts to rebuild a merry-go-round in rural Kansas town. Odd, thoughtful little drama, adequately directed by its star. Filmed in 1973. Panavision. [PG]▼

American Anthem (1986) **C-100m.** *½ D: Albert Magnoli. Mitch Gaylord, Janet

Jones, Michelle Phillips, R.J. Williams, Michael Pataki, Patrice Donnelly. Supremely corny, badly written tale of a gymnast with family problems which keep him from fulfilling his destiny. Inauspicious movie debut for Olympic gymnast Gaylord is strangely reminiscent of PURPLE RAIN, with the same music video approach to drama; Magnoli directed them both. [PG-13]▼●
American Beauty (1999) **C-121m.** ***½ D: Sam Mendes. Kevin Spacey, Annette Bening, Thora Birch, Wes Bentley, Mena Suvari, Chris Cooper, Peter Gallagher, Allison Janney, Scott Bakula, Sam Robards. Exceptional and original look at the American Dream gone sour. Spacey is having a midlife crisis, and decides to throw caution to the winds; his wife, Bening, who's forsaken him for her real estate career, seeks sexual fulfillment elsewhere. And their alienated teenage daughter is attracted to a strange young man next door. Amusing, bittersweet, and insightful script by Alan Ball is perfectly realized by a superb cast and first-time film director. Oscar winner for Best Picture, Director, Screenwriter, Actor (Spacey), and Cinematography (Conrad L. Hall). Super 35. [R]▼◗
American Boyfriends (1989-Canadian) **C-90m.** ** D: Sandy Wilson. Margaret Langrick, John Wildman, Jason Blicker, Liisa Repo Martell, Michael Bardeaux, Delia Brett. Dull, overly sentimental followup to MY AMERICAN COUSIN. It's now the 1960's and the heroine of the earlier film (Langrick) is a teenybopper who heads off to Oregon for American cousin Wildman's wedding. Lacks the spark of the original. [PG-13]▼●
American Buffalo (1996) **C-87m.** *** D: Michael Corrente. Dustin Hoffman, Dennis Franz, Sean Nelson. Arresting film version of David Mamet's profane, provocative three-character play. Hoffman plays Teach, a self-enobled world expert who horns in on the plans of his friend, junk shop owner Don (Franz), to commit a robbery with the help of a teenaged protégé (Nelson). A simple character study, with perfectly cast actors bringing Mamet's own screen adaptation to life. One of the rare photographed stage plays that works. [R]▼●
American Clock, The SEE: **Arthur Miller's "The American Clock"**
American Commandos (1985) **C-88m.** BOMB D: Bobby A. Suarez. Christopher Mitchum, John Phillip Law, Franco Guerrero, Willie Williams, Ken Metcalfe. Poorly made action film about Vietnam war vets who go to the Golden Triangle in Southeast Asia on an anti-narcotics mission. Opening scenes set in California are ridiculously simulated on Filipino locations. Original title: HITMAN. [R]▼
American Dream, An (1966) **C-103m.** **½ D: Robert Gist. Stuart Whitman, Janet Leigh, Eleanor Parker, Barry Sullivan, Lloyd Nolan, Murray Hamilton, J. D. Cannon, Les Crane, Paul Mantee, Harold Gould, George Takei. Distorted, watered-down Norman Mailer novel, dealing superficially with TV commentator wanted by underworld and police for murdering his wife; nightmare sequences are sterile.
American Dream (1989) **C-100m.** ***½ D: Barbara Kopple. Gripping, Academy Award-winning documentary about the hows, whats and whys of a labor strike at the Hormel meat plant in the small town of Austin, Minnesota. It's the story of a profitable company attempting to reduce wages and break a union just for the sake of doing so. This is the stuff of high drama.▼●
American Dreamer (1984) **C-105m.** ** D: Rick Rosenthal. JoBeth Williams, Tom Conti, Giancarlo Giannini, Coral Browne, James Staley, Huckleberry Fox, C.B. Barnes. Misguided, miscast comedy-adventure yarn about a housewife who wins trip to Paris and (through circumstance) believes herself to be the daring heroine of a series of adventure thrillers. Cute idea (not dissimilar to ROMANCING THE STONE) that an otherwise able cast can't pull off. [PG]▼
American Empire (1942) **82m.** **½ D: William McGann. Richard Dix, Leo Carrillo, Preston Foster, Frances Gifford, Guinn Williams. Dix and Foster join forces to develop cattle empire in Texas after Civil War, but not without problems. Pretty good outdoor actioner.▼
Americaner Schadchen (1940) **87m.** ** D: Edgar G. Ulmer. Leo Fuchs, Judith Abarbanel, Yudel Dubinsky, Wolf Mercur, Rosetta Bialis. Slight romantic satire about a movie star (Fuchs) whose fiancées keep breaking their engagements, and who opens a marriage bureau. The last of four Yiddish-language features made by cult director Ulmer. Aka AMERICAN MATCHMAKER. ▼
American Flyers (1985) **C-114m.** *** D: John Badham. Kevin Costner, David Grant, Rae Dawn Chong, Alexandra Paul, Janice Rule, Luca Bercovici, Robert Townsend, John Amos, Jennifer Grey. Two brothers—one of whom is dying—enter a grueling bicycle race marathon. Likable, sweet-natured, root-for-the-good-guys film, if a bit too pat and manipulative at times. Written by Steve Tesich, whose cycle theme fared even better in BREAKING AWAY. Panavision. [PG-13]▼●◗
American Friend, The (1977-U.S.-French-German) **C-127m.** *** D: Wim Wenders. Dennis Hopper, Bruno Ganz, Lisa Kreuzer, Gerard Blain, Jean Eustache, Sam Fuller, Nicholas Ray. Vague but suspenseful statement about American gangster films and the Americanization of European cinema and lifestyles, centering on a young

German picture-framer (Ganz) hired to assassinate a mobster. Hopper is the title character, a mystery man; film directors Ray and Fuller appear as heavies. Based on Patricia Highsmith's *Ripley's Game*. Hopper's character, Tom Ripley, also appears in PURPLE NOON and its remake, THE TALENTED MR. RIPLEY.▼●

American Friends (1991-British) **C-95m.** **½ D: Tristram Powell. Michael Palin, Trini Alvarado, Connie Booth, Alfred Molina, David Calder, Simon Jones, Robert Eddison, Alun Armstrong. A very proper (and very repressed) senior tutor at Oxford chances to meet a young American girl during a holiday in the Swiss Alps and finds his outlook on life undergoing some dramatic changes. Slight, slowly paced, but diverting; Palin coscripted the film, based on journals left behind by his great-grandfather. ▼

American Gigolo (1980) **C-117m.** BOMB D: Paul Schrader. Richard Gere, Lauren Hutton, Hector Elizondo, Nina Van Pallandt, Frances Bergen, Bill Duke. Schrader presents his weakest variation yet on his favorite theme, the seamy side of American life. Feeble morality play, posing as a thriller, is further undermined by neurasthenic acting and some of the unsexiest sex scenes ever. [R]▼●◗

American Gothic (1988) **C-90m.** BOMB D: John Hough. Rod Steiger, Yvonne De Carlo, Michael J. Pollard, Fiona Hutchison, Sarah Torgov, Mark Lindsay Chapman. Three couples off for an island weekend off the Seattle coast are forced to land at an unknown island dominated by murderous Ma and Pa (DeCarlo and Steiger) and their "kids" (grownups who've been kept mentally adolescent by their backward, backwoods parents). Populated exclusively by obnoxious characters; even Steiger can't help this one. [R]▼●

American Graffiti (1973) **C-110m.** ***½ D: George Lucas. Richard Dreyfuss, Ronny Howard, Paul LeMat, Charlie Martin Smith, Cindy Williams, Candy Clark, Mackenzie Phillips, Wolfman Jack, Harrison Ford, Bo Hopkins, Kathy Quinlan, Suzanne Somers, Joe Spano, Debralee Scott. Highly entertaining, insightful mosaic about youngsters "coming of age" after high school graduation in 1962. Often hilarious, always on-target, this film made Dreyfuss a star and boosted many other careers. Reedited to 112m. for 1978 reissue to play up latter-day stars. Look fast for Kay Lenz at the dance. Sequel: MORE AMERICAN GRAFFITI. Techniscope. [PG]▼●◗

American Guerilla in the Philippines (1950) **C-105m.** **½ D: Fritz Lang. Tyrone Power, Micheline Prelle (Presle), Tom Ewell, Bob Patten, Tommy Cook, Jack Elam. Interesting but flawed account of resistance to Japanese after the fall of the Philippines during WW2, focusing on the activities of American naval officer Power. Marred by clichéd, jingoistic script, predictable romantic subplot involving Prelle. On-location filming adds authentic flavor. Based on Ira Wolfert's novel.

American Heart (1993) **C-113m.** *** D: Martin Bell. Jeff Bridges, Edward Furlong, Lucinda Jenney, Tracey Kapisky, Don Harvey, Maggie Welsh. Sobering, sometimes brilliant drama of gruff ex-con who is reunited with his son, an alienated teen in desperate need of a dad. Jarring, credible portrait of lost souls in urban America, with riveting performances by its stars. First fiction feature for Bell, who directed the documentary STREETWISE. Bridges also coproduced. [R]▼

American History X (1998) **C/B&W-118m.** *** D: Tony Kaye. Edward Norton, Edward Furlong, Fairuza Balk, Beverly D'Angelo, Avery Brooks, Stacy Keach, Jennifer Lien, Elliott Gould, William Russ, Joe Cortese. Hard-hitting drama of a young man who's seduced into a white supremacy movement in Venice, California, goes to prison after committing a heinous crime, and has his head straightened out. When he's released, his only thought is to steer his younger brother away from that same existence. Frighteningly powerful—and believable—performance by Norton sparks this intense drama of a family torn apart. [R] ▼●◗

American Hot Wax (1978) **C-91m.** *** D: Floyd Mutrux. Tim McIntire, Fran Drescher, Jay Leno, John Lehne, Laraine Newman, Jeff Altman, Chuck Berry, Jerry Lee Lewis, Screamin' Jay Hawkins. Rose-colored story of controversial 1950s disc jockey Alan Freed. Uneven dramatically, but McIntire is excellent, period flavor is strong, and the original rock 'n' roll acts are fun to see. Freed's life also is chronicled in MR. ROCK AND ROLL (in which the DJ plays himself) and the TVM MR. ROCK 'N' ROLL: THE ALAN FREED STORY. [PG]▼

American in Paris, An (1951) **C-115m.** ***½ D: Vincente Minnelli. Gene Kelly, Leslie Caron, Oscar Levant, Georges Guetary, Nina Foch. Joyous, original musical built around Gershwin score; dazzling in color. Plot of artist Kelly torn between gamine Caron and wealthy Foch is creaky, but the songs, dances, production are superb. Oscars include Best Picture, Story and Screenplay (Alan Jay Lerner), Cinematography (Alfred Gilks and John Alton), Scoring (Johnny Green and Saul Chaplin), Art Direction, Costume Design, and a special citation to Kelly. Look fast for Noel Neill as an art student. ▼●◗

Americanization of Emily, The (1964) **117m.** ***½ D: Arthur Hiller. James Garner, Julie Andrews, Melvyn Douglas, James Coburn, Joyce Grenfell, Keenan Wynn,

Judy Carne, Liz Fraser, Edward Binns, William Windom, Alan Sues. Garner is fall guy for U.S. admiral's master plan to have American naval officer first Normandy invasion victim, with predictable results. Cynical Garner-Andrews romance blends well with realistic view of life among U.S. military brass. Script by Paddy Chayefsky, from William Bradford Huie's novel. Also shown in computer-colored version.▼●

American Justice SEE: **Jackals**

American Madness (1932) **81m.** *** D: Frank Capra. Walter Huston, Pat O'Brien, Kay Johnson, Constance Cummings, Gavin Gordon. Huston is dynamic as a put-upon bank president in the depths of the Great Depression; vivid, upbeat film marred only by idiotic romantic subplot.▼

American Matchmaker SEE: **Americaner Schadchen**

American Me (1992) **C-126m.** **½ D: Edward James Olmos. Edward James Olmos, William Forsythe, Pepe Serna, Danny De La Paz, Evelina Fernandez, Sal Lopez, Daniel Villarreal, Cary Hiroyuki Tagawa. Ambitious look at the so-called "Mexican Mafia" reflected through the life of a crime lord (Olmos), and the cycle of gang violence which extends from prison to the Southwest's Hispanic barrio communities. Attempts to be epic in scope and subject, but is too unfocused to really score, despite many tough, powerful moments. Olmos—who made his directorial debut here—and Forsythe stand out in the large cast. The prison scenes at Folsom were actually shot there. [R]▼●

American Movie (1999) **C-104m.** ***½ D: Chris Smith. Thoroughly engaging documentary about Mark Borchardt, an obsessive independent filmmaker whose aspirations clearly outweigh his talent. Unable to fund his most recent project, he sets out to complete the cheesy horror film he started but abandoned years earlier. Funny and revealing, but director Smith is never condescending toward his subject's dreams and desire for acknowledgment. [R]▼◗

American Ninja (1986) **C-95m.** *½ D: Sam Firstenberg. Michael Dudikoff, Steve James, Judie Aronson, Guich Koock, John Fujioka, Don Stewart, John LaMotta. Low-grade martial-arts entry series set at U.S. Army base in Philippines, with beefy Dudikoff as a soldier who finds ample reason to use his deadly skills. James comes off well as Dudikoff's equally proficient Army pal. Followed by several sequels. [R]▼

American Ninja 2: The Confrontation (1987) **C-89m.** *½ D: Sam Firstenberg. Michael Dudikoff, Steve James, Larry Poindexter, Gary Conway, Jeff Weston, Michelle Botes. Slight improvement over AMERICAN NINJA benefits from screen rapport of Dudikoff and James, as G.I. hunks who investigate disappearance of Marines on Caribbean island—where local druglord is training them for his own evil purposes. Bad guy Conway coscripted the film with actor James Booth. [R]▼●

American Ninja 3: Blood Hunt (1989) **C-90m.** BOMB D: Cedric Sundstrom. David Bradley, Steve James, Marjoe Gortner, Michele Chan, Calvin Jung. Tiresome entry in the series, with Bradley (replacing Michael Dudikoff as the hero) battling dastardly Gortner. Even martial arts fans will be bored. [R]▼●

American Ninja 4: The Annihilation (1991) **C-95m.** *½ D: Cedric Sundstrom. Michael Dudikoff, David Bradley, James Booth, Dwayne Alexandre. Dull, wooden, chopsocky effort is so bad that starring head-basher Dudikoff doesn't even appear until the film is half over. Tired story has good ninjas rescuing commandoes from the clutches of bad ninja army and attempting to foil terrorist plot centering around lap-top nuclear weapon. Followed by AMERICAN NINJA 5. [R]▼●

Americano, The (1955) **C-85m.** **½ D: William Castle. Glenn Ford, Cesar Romero, Frank Lovejoy, Ursula Thiess, Abbe Lane. Good-guy Ford meets Brazilian badguys in standard Western, with change of scenery as major asset.▼

American Pie (1999) **C-95m.** *** D: Paul Weitz. Jason Biggs, Shannon Elizabeth, Alyson Hannigan, Chris Klein, Natasha Lyonne, Thomas Ian Nicholas, Tara Reid, Seann W. Scott, Eugene Levy, Lawrence Pressman, Mena Suvari. Good-natured teen comedy about four guys who vow to lose their virginity by the night of the high school prom. Raunchy gags gave this film its reputation, but they grow honestly out of its believable characters and situations. In fact, its values are old-fashioned, even if its sense of humor is not. Also available in unrated version. [R]▼●◗

American Pop (1981) **C-97m.** **½ D: Ralph Bakshi. Voices of Ron Thompson, Marya Small, Jerry Holland, Lisa Jane Persky, Roz Kelly. Ambitious animated film, which follows 20th-century American music through pivotal characters in four generations. Bold graphics and a challenging narrative keep this interesting, if not always successful; animation buffs may wince at awkward rotoscoping (tracing from live action). Ultimate dilemma: the culmination of this heavily dramatic, multigenerational saga is the creation of punk rock! [R]▼●◗

American President, The (1995) **C-115m.** *** D: Rob Reiner. Michael Douglas, Annette Bening, Martin Sheen, Michael J. Fox, Anna Deavere Smith, John Mahoney, Samantha Mathis, Shawna Waldron, David Paymer, Anne Haney, Richard Dreyfuss, Nina Siemaszko, Wendie Malick, Gail Strickland. Slick, entertaining Hollywood concoction about a widowed president who's attracted to a lobbyist and decides to pursue her—naively ignoring the political impact this liaison may have during an election year. Appealing performances and a bright screenplay (by Aaron Sorkin) help this likable movie glide along past its considerable gaps in credibility. This is the ultimate wish-fulfillment movie, with a president who's handsome, funny, forthright, decisive, and honest. If only! Panavision. [PG-13]▼●◗

American Psycho (2000) **C-97m.** *½ D: Mary Harron. Christian Bale, Willem Dafoe, Jared Leto, Reese Witherspoon, Samantha Mathis, Chloë Sevigny, Justin Theroux, Guinevere Turner, Matt Ross. A 1980s Wall Street yuppie has all the trappings of success—and the need to fit in—but also has an uncontrollable drive to kill people. Intense adaptation of Bret Easton Ellis' 1991 novel makes its satiric points early on, then has nothing to add. Bale gives a dynamic performance in this turgid film. Super 35. [R]▼◗

American Romance, An (1944) **C-122m.** **½ D: King Vidor. Brian Donlevy, Ann Richards, Walter Abel, John Qualen, Stephen McNally. Long, flavorful story of immigrant steelworker's rise to wealth and power. Might have been a better film with someone more magnetic than Donlevy in the lead. Originally released at 151m.

American Roulette (1988-British-Australian) **C-102m.** BOMB D: Maurice Hatton. Andy Garcia, Kitty Aldridge, Robert Stephens, Al Matthews, Susannah York. Dreadful political thriller about the president of a Latin American country (Garcia), who also doubles as a poet, and his plight as he's hunted by a death squad while in exile in London. Poorly directed and crammed with plot holes; padded with scenes of Garcia racing through the London Underground, yet it's unclear as to who's chasing him. [R]▼●

American Soldier, The (1970-German) **80m.** **½ D: Rainer Werner Fassbinder. Karl Scheydt, Elga Sorbas, Jan George, Margarethe von Trotta, Hark Bohm, Ingrid Caven, Kurt Raab. Fassbinder sacrifices believability for mood in this dour film noir about a Vietnam vet (Scheydt) who becomes a hired assassin in the Munich underworld. Not so much an ode to the celluloid American gangster or allegory about the Vietnam war as a character study, loaded with in-jokes and absurdist references (such as the duplicitous moll named Rosa von Praunheim). Fassbinder also scripted.▼

American Success SEE: **American Success Company, The**

American Success Company, The (1979) **C-94m.** ** D: William Richert. Jeff Bridges, Belinda Bauer, Ned Beatty, Steven Keats, Bianca Jagger, John Glover. A contemporary fable about a young loser—in business and marriage—who decides to change his luck by emulating a macho prince. Offbeat in the extreme, often funny, but decidedly uneven. Filmed in Germany; based on a story by Larry Cohen. Richert has twice reedited and reissued the film: in 1981 as AMERICAN SUCCESS, then in 1983 simply as SUCCESS. [PG]

American Tail, An (1986) **C-80m.** **½ D: Don Bluth. Voices of Dom DeLuise, Christopher Plummer, Nehemiah Persoff, Madeline Kahn, Phillip Glasser, John Finnegan, Cathianne Blore, Will Ryan. A young Russian mouse is separated from his family as they're about to arrive at their new homeland, America, in the late 19th century. Handsome, occasionally heart-tugging cartoon feature with a cute main character—but serious story flaws (why are there *three* climaxes?). Producer Steven Spielberg's first foray into animation. Followed by three sequels and an animated TV series, *Fievel's American Tails.* [G]▼●

American Tail: Fievel Goes West, An (1991) **C-74m.** **½ D: Phil Nibbelink, Simon Wells. Voices of Philip Glasser, James Stewart, Erica Yohn, Cathy Cavadini, Nehemiah Persoff, Dom DeLuise, Amy Irving, John Cleese, Jon Lovitz. Pleasant-enough animated feature for small fry follows immigrant Fievel the mouse and his family on a trek to the American West. Mediocre songs and uninspired character animation make it less than memorable—but Stewart's performance as over-the-hill sheriff Wylie Burp is a treat. Followed by two direct-to-video sequels. [G]▼●

American Tragedy, An (1931) **95m.** ** D: Josef von Sternberg. Phillips Holmes, Sylvia Sidney, Frances Dee, Irving Pichel, Frederick Burton, Claire McDowell. Straightforward telling of Theodore Dreiser story about weak young man torn between poor girlfriend and beautiful, wealthy girl who falls in love with him. Sidney is ideally cast, but film is cold and uninvolving; certainly not as florid as remake A PLACE IN THE SUN.

American Way, The SEE: **Riders of the Storm**

American Werewolf in London, An (1981) **C-97m.** *** D: John Landis. David Naughton, Jenny Agutter, Griffin Dunne, John Woodvine, Brian Glover. A young man is bitten by a wolf on the British moors, with terrifying results. Not a spoof, but a full-blooded horror film that happens to have a sharp sense of humor—as well as a reverence for horror films past. Dynamite direction and script by Landis, startling Oscar-winning makeup effects by Rick Baker. Followed by an in-name-only sequel. [R] ▼●◗

American Werewolf in Paris, An (1997-British-U.S.-Luxembourgian-Dutch-French) **C-97m.** *½ D: Anthony Waller. Tom Everett Scott, Julie Delpy, Vince Vieluf, Phil Buckman, Julie Bowen, Pierre Cosso, Tom Novembre, Thierry Lhermitte. Thrill-seeking American Scott falls for Parisienne Delpy, but she's a werewolf, and soon he's one, too, pitted against a group of leering lycanthropes bent on wiping out the unfit—such as American tourists. Begins well, but soon goes awry, with too much comedy and romance, and too much plot; the werewolf effects are plentiful but second-rate at best. No plot connections to the superior John Landis original. [R]▼●◗

Americathon (1979) **C-86m.** BOMB D: Neil Israel. Harvey Korman, John Ritter, Nancy Morgan, Peter Riegert, Fred Willard, Zane Buzby, Richard Schaal, Elvis Costello, Chief Dan George, Tommy Lasorda, Jay Leno, Peter Marshall, Meat Loaf, Howard Hesseman. Unfunny comedy wastes great premise: in 1998, America must hold a telethon in order to raise money to save itself. Only spark is set by Buzby as Vietnamese punk-rocker. Narrated by George Carlin. [PG]▼

Amin—The Rise and Fall (1981-Kenya) **C-101m.** *½ D: Sharad Patel. Joseph Olita, Geoffrey Keen, Denis Hills, Leonard Trolley, Diane Mercier. Superficial, bloody potboiler chronicling the atrocities committed by Uganda dictator Idi Amin, played by look-alike Olita. [R]▼

Amistad (1997) **C-152m.** *** D: Steven Spielberg. Morgan Freeman, Anthony Hopkins, Matthew McConaughey, Nigel Hawthorne, Djimon Hounsou, David Paymer, Pete Postlethwaite, Stellan Skarsgård, Anna Paquin, Tomas Milian, Austin Pendleton, Allan Rich, Paul Guilfoyle, Peter Firth, Xander Berkeley, Jeremy Northam. Little-known saga of the Spanish slave ship *La Amistad,* whose "cargo" broke their chains in 1839—and wound up in a U.S. courtroom, ultimately attracting the attention of ex-president John Quincy Adams (Hopkins). A good film that's frustratingly uneven: the slave ship scenes are wrenching (and unavoidably reminiscent of Spielberg's SCHINDLER'S LIST), and Adams' final summation is a showcase speech. But the film is long, and the dramatic gaps too many. Hounsou offers a powerful presence as Cinque, the leader of the slave revolt. Arliss Howard appears unbilled. [R]▼●◗

Amityville: A New Generation (1993) **C-92m.** ** D: John Murlowski. Ross Partridge, Julia Nickson-Soul, Lala Sloatman, David Naughton, Barbara Howard, Jack R. Orend, Richard Roundtree, Terry O'Quinn. A demonic mirror from the original house haunts the illegitimate son of the man whose slaughter of his family started it all, and drives other tenants in his artists' loft apartment to suicide. Better acted and written than others in this series, but hampered by slow pace and ragged editing. [R]▼

Amityville Curse, The (1990-Canadian-U.S.) **C-91m.** *½ D: Tom Berry. Kim Coates, Dawna Wightman, Helen Hughes, David Stein, Anthony Dean Rubes, Cassandra Gava, Jan Rubes. Attempt to cash in on the Amityville name with a strictly ho-hum story (based on Hans Holzer's book) about the house with a life of its own. Without interesting special effects there's no point to this one at all. Released directly to video. [R]▼●

Amityville Horror, The (1979) **C-117m.** *½ D: Stuart Rosenberg. James Brolin, Margot Kidder, Rod Steiger, Don Stroud, Murray Hamilton, Michael Sacks, Helen Shaver, Natasha Ryan, Val Avery, John Larch, Amy Wright, James Tolkan. Family moves into supposedly haunted Long Island home, finds that "supposedly" is inoperative. Based on Jay Anson's (supposedly) nonfiction best-seller, film is yawn-inducing rehash of all the old schticks; not even good for laughs, with Steiger mercilessly hamming it up as local priest. Followed by a prequel, AMITYVILLE II: THE POSSESSION, a TV movie, and several so called sequels. [R]▼●

Amityville II: The Possession (1982) **C-104m.** BOMB D: Damiano Damiani. Burt Young, Rutanya Alda, James Olson, Jack Magner, Diane Franklin, Andrew Prine, Ted Ross, Moses Gunn. Officially a prequel to THE AMITYVILLE HORROR, but actually just a ripoff. A loathsome lout (Young) moves into notorious Long Island house with his troubled family and all hell breaks loose. Alternately dull and disgusting. [R]▼●

Amityville: The Demon SEE: **Amityville 3-D**

Amityville 3-D (1983) **C-105m.** **½ D: Richard Fleischer. Tony Roberts, Tess Harper, Robert Joy, Candy Clark, John Beal, Leora Dana, John Harkins, Lori Loughlin, Meg Ryan. Thoroughly familiar retread of spirit-in-the-house formula, with Roberts as a Doubting Thomas who buys the dreaded Amityville house (seen in two otherwise unrelated films). Competence at every level keeps this from being trash; excellent 3-D effects too. Shown on TV as AMITYVILLE: THE DEMON; followed by TV movie AMITYVILLE 4: THE EVIL ESCAPES. ArriVision. [PG]▼●

Amityville 4: The Evil Escapes (1989) **C-100m. TVM** D: Sandor Stern. Patty Duke, Jane Wyatt, Frederic Lehne, Norman Lloyd, Brandy Gold, Aron Eisenberg. Fourth in the series based on John G. Jones' horror thrillers is about par for the (TV) course, bringing into the "don't go in the attic/basement/pantry/front hall closet" genre a couple of frantic exorcists trying to save Duke & dodos. Video title: THE AMITYVILLE HORROR: THE EVIL ESCAPES—PART IV. Average. ▼●

Amityville 1992: It's About Time (1992) **C-95m.** *½ D: Tony Randel. Stephen Macht, Shawn Weatherly, Megan Ward, Damon Martin, Jonathan Penner, Nita Talbot, Dick Miller. All the trouble in Amityville, we now learn, was due to the mantel clock of 15th-century child-killer Gilles de Rais. Now the fiendish timepiece is in a different town, causing the usual problems for a new family. Ranges from imaginative to crudely obvious, sometimes in the same scene. Made for video. [R]▼●

Among Giants (1998-British) **C-96m.** **½ D: Sam Miller. Pete Postlethwaite, Rachel Griffiths, James Thornton, Lennie James, Andy Serkis, Rob Jarvis, Alan Williams. A rough-hewn contractor hires a rowdy lot to paint the huge electric pylons that dot the British countryside. They become a sort of outlaw family, and are joined by an adventurous Aussie woman who likes heights. Good performances and rich atmosphere help, but it's a less successful dip into working-class life by the writer of THE FULL MONTY, Simon Beaufoy. [R] ▼

Amongst Friends (1993) **C-86m.** **½ D: Rob Weiss. Joseph Lindsey, Patrick McGaw, Steve Parlavecchio, Mira Sorvino, Brett Lambson, Michael Artura. Superficial (and, by now, all-too-familiar) tale of young male punks coming of age on America's mean streets, only these are suburban rather than urban and the boys are wealthy instead of working-class. Well made and not uninteresting, but Martin Scorsese did it—and did it better—twenty years earlier. Weiss also scripted. [R]▼

Among the Living (1941) **68m.** **½ D: Stuart Heisler. Albert Dekker, Susan Hayward, Frances Farmer, Harry Carey, Gordon Jones. Intriguing little B film about a deranged man, one of twins, kept isolated for years, who breaks loose and stirs up trouble. Some great moments, but film is a little too hurried and simplistic; Dekker is excellent in dual role.

Amor Bandido (1979-Brazilian) **C-95m.** *** D: Bruno Barreto. Paulo Gracindo, Cristina Ache, Paulo Guarnieri, Ligia Diniz, Flavio Sao Thiago. Tough drama of 17-year-old dancer-hooker Ache, estranged from cop father Gracindo, who takes up with baby-faced killer Guarnieri. Uncompromis-ing and, ultimately, sad; based on one of Brazil's most notorious criminal cases.▼●

Amorous Adventures of Moll Flanders, The (1965-British) **C-126m.** **½ D: Terence Young. Kim Novak, Richard Johnson, Angela Lansbury, George Sanders, Vittorio De Sica, Lilli Palmer, Leo McKern, Cecil Parker. Billed as female Tom Jones, Moll is far from thrilling. Fine cast romps through 18th-century England from bedroom to boudoir, but film needs more spice than Novak can muster. The two leads were married briefly in real life. Panavision. ▼●

Amorous Mister Prawn (1962-British) **89m.** **½ D: Anthony Kimmins. Joan Greenwood, Cecil Parker, Ian Carmichael, Robert Beatty. Diverting fluff finds wife (Greenwood) of general (Parker) devising a scheme to obtain badly needed money so they can retire in style.

Amos (1985) **C-100m. TVM** D: Michael Tuchner. Kirk Douglas, Elizabeth Montgomery, Dorothy McGuire, Pat Morita, James Sloyan, Ray Walston. One-time baseball coach, now in his late seventies, finds himself confined to a nursing home against his will and crossing swords with the steely head nurse in this drama that shares many similarities with ONE FLEW OVER THE CUCKOO'S NEST (in which Douglas starred on Broadway). Peter Douglas (Kirk's son) produced, and Montgomery here plays a rare heavy. Average.▼

Amos & Andrew (1993) **C-94m.** BOMB D: E. Max Frye. Nicolas Cage, Samuel L. Jackson, Dabney Coleman, Brad Dourif, Michael Lerner, Margaret Colin, Chelcie Ross, I. M. Hobson, Jodi Long, Giancarlo Esposito, Loretta Devine, Bob Balaban, Tracey Walter. Agonizing comedy about a professionally distinguished black man who moves into a new home, only to be harassed by white neighbors who assume he's a prowler. Intended social satire is as broadly silly as a '60s Disney comedy; maybe they should have called this THAT DARN AFRO-AMERICAN. [PG-13]▼●

Amsterdam Affair (1968-British) **C-91m.** **½ D: Gerry O'Hara. Wolfgang Kieling, William Marlowe, Catherine von Schell, Pamela Ann Davy. Inspector believes there's more to young woman's murder than supposed open-and-shut case against her lover would indicate. Passable thriller, pleasing Amsterdam locations.

Amsterdam Kill, The (1977) **C-90m.** **½ D: Robert Clouse. Robert Mitchum, Bradford Dillman, Richard Egan, Leslie Nielsen, Keye Luke. Tired drug bust movie gets a shot from Mitchum's presence as a retired narc who's lured back by a former colleague suspected of being part of an international dope ring. Panavision. [R]▼●

Amsterdamned (1988-Dutch) **C-113m.** ** D: Dick Maas. Huub Stapel, Monique van de Ven, Serge-Henre Valcke, Hidde Maas, Wim Zomer. Elusive killer emerges by night from Amsterdam's canals to murder people at random; he's hunted by a police detective as determined as he is. Unusual setting and sleekness of production help disguise the fact that it's just another urban cop thriller, with slasher-movie overtones. Director Maas also wrote the script. [R]▼●

Amuck (1972-Italian) **C-85m.** **½ D: Silvio Amadio. Farley Granger, Barbara Bouchet, Rosalba Neri. Solid suspense thriller set in

Venice with Granger as a mystery writer; new secretary Bouchet tries to find out what happened to her missing friend, his former secretary. Originally titled REPLICA OF A CRIME; unreleased in the U.S. until 1978.

Amy (1981) **C-100m.** *** D: Vincent McEveety. Jenny Agutter, Barry Newman, Kathleen Nolan, Chris Robinson, Lou Fant, Margaret O'Brien, Nanette Fabray, Lance LeGault, Lucille Benson. Sincere, entertaining Disney tale of Agutter leaving her husband in the early 1900s, teaching at a school for the handicapped. Though the film is targeted at kids, parents won't be bored. Made for TV, released to theaters instead. [G]▼

Anaconda (1997) **C-90m.** ** D: Luis Llosa. Jennifer Lopez, Ice Cube, Jon Voight, Eric Stoltz, Jonathan Hyde, Kari Wuhrer, Owen Wilson, Vincent Castellanos. Documentary film crew adrift on the Amazon is besieged by a giant killer snake. Hokey special effects and an expositionless script detract, but there's campy fun in the form of Voight's demonic snake poacher, who speaks with a bad Brandoesque drawl and strangles human victims between his knees. Film makes most of beautiful Brazilian rainforest locale, yet the big serpentine climax looks strangely like deepest, darkest Arcadia. (In fact, it's the Arboretum in L.A. County.) Super 35. [PG-13]▼●◗

Analyze This (1999) **C-103m.** *** D: Harold Ramis. Robert De Niro, Billy Crystal, Lisa Kudrow, Joe Viterelli, Chazz Palminteri, Bill Macy, Leo Rossi, Max Casella, Molly Shannon, Pat Cooper, Elizabeth Bracco. Amusing comedy about a mob boss who's losing his grip and is persuaded to talk to a psychiatrist—which causes him great embarrassment. A small idea stretched out too far but made worthwhile by De Niro's wonderful comic performance as the foulmouthed mobster who feels "conflicted." [R]▼●◗

Anastasia (1956) **C-105m.** **** D: Anatole Litvak. Ingrid Bergman, Yul Brynner, Helen Hayes, Akim Tamiroff, Martita Hunt, Felix Aylmer, Natalie Schafer, Ivan Desny. Inspired casting makes this film exceptional. Bergman won Oscar as amnesiac refugee selected by Brynner to impersonate surviving daughter of Russia's last czar. Confrontation scene in which Hayes as grand duchess must determine if girl is her relative is grand. Screenplay by Arthur Laurents based on Marcelle Maurette's play. CinemaScope.▼●

Anastasia (1997) **C-88m.** **½ D: Don Bluth, Gary Goldman. Voices of Meg Ryan, John Cusack, Kelsey Grammer, Angela Lansbury, Christopher Lloyd, Hank Azaria, Bernadette Peters, Kirsten Dunst, Andrea Martin, Jim Cummings, Liz Callaway, Lacey Chabert, Jonathan Dokuchitz. Elaborate but uneven cartoon musical about the daughter of Nicholas and Alexandra, who supposedly survived in Russia in 1917 only to reappear in Paris a decade later—where two schemers try to collect part of her inheritance from her grandmother, the Dowager Empress. Innocuous enough for kids, but adults may question the 90s American dialogue (and readings). Animation style is also inconsistent—some of it realistic, some of it wildly fanciful. Loosely based on the 1956 movie. Followed in 1999 by a direct-to-video sequel: BARTOK THE MAGNIFICENT. CinemaScope. [G]▼●◗

Anastasia: The Mystery of Anna (1986) **C-200m. TVM** D: Marvin J. Chomsky. Amy Irving, Olivia de Havilland, Omar Sharif, Jan Niklas, Claire Bloom, Edward Fox, Elke Sommer, Susan Lucci, Nicolas Surovy, Rex Harrison. Sumptuous retelling of the story of Anna Anderson, who claimed to have been the surviving daughter of Czarist Russia's Nicholas and Alexandra (played by Sharif and Bloom). James Goldman's literate script was based not on the familiar stage and screen tale of Anastasia of the 1950s but on Peter Kurth's book *Anastasia: The Riddle of Anna Anderson.* Originally shown in two parts. Above average.▼

Anatomist, The (1961-British) **73m.** ** D: Leonard William. Alastair Sim, George Cole, Jill Bennett, Margaret Gordon. Respected surgeon encourages corpse-stealing for experiments, causing rash of murders. Sim is wry in tame spooker.▼

Anatomy of a Marriage (1964-French) **193m.** **½ D: André Cayatte. Comprised of: "My Days with Jean-Marc" and "My Nights with Françoise." Jacques Charrier, Marie-Jose Nat, Georges Rivière, Macha Meril. Well-intentioned film which through its two parts attempts to analyze problems of young married couple from each one's point of view; becomes repetitious. Franscope.

Anatomy of a Murder (1959) **160m.** **** D: Otto Preminger. James Stewart, Lee Remick, Ben Gazzara, Arthur O'Connell, Eve Arden, Kathryn Grant (Crosby), George C. Scott, Orson Bean, Murray Hamilton. Long, exciting courtroom drama; daring when released, tamer now. Large cast is fine: O'Connell as drunken lawyer aroused by Stewart, Joseph Welch as judge (Welch was the famous Army-McCarthy hearings lawyer who later became a judge in real life), Scott as prosecuting attorney. Stewart towers over all as witty, easygoing, but cagy defense lawyer. Script by Wendell Mayes, from novel by Robert Traver (Judge John D. Voelker). Duke Ellington composed the score and also appears onscreen.▼●

Anatomy of a Syndicate SEE: **Big Operator, The**

Anchors Aweigh (1945) **C-140m.** **½ D: George Sidney. Frank Sinatra, Kathryn Grayson, Gene Kelly, Jose Iturbi, Dean Stockwell, Pamela Britton. Popular '40s musical of sailors on leave doesn't hold up storywise, but musical numbers still good: Sinatra's "I Fall in Love Too Easily," Kelly's irresistible dance with Jerry the cartoon mouse.▼●◗

And Baby Makes Three (1949) **84m.** ** D: Henry Levin. Robert Young, Barbara Hale, Robert Hutton, Billie Burke, Melville Cooper. OK comedy has Hale about to marry for second time, only to discover she's pregnant, and she really does want to stay married to Hubby #1 (Young).

Anderson Platoon, The (1967-French) **65m.** ***½ D: Pierre Schoendorffer. Superior chronicle of soldiers in American Army platoon fighting, living, and dying in Vietnam. Vivid, striking images, photographed at the front line. A Best Documentary Academy Award winner.▼

Anderson's Angels SEE: **Chesty Anderson, USN**

Anderson Tapes, The (1971) **C-98m.** *** D: Sidney Lumet. Sean Connery, Dyan Cannon, Martin Balsam, Ralph Meeker, Alan King, Margaret Hamilton, Christopher Walken, Garrett Morris. Fast-paced thriller of ex-con's master holdup plan, and strange electronic surveillances that have tracked him since he left prison. Climax is particularly exciting. Fine Quincy Jones score; Walken's debut. [PG]▼●

Andersonville (1996) **C-168m. TVM** D: John Frankenheimer. Jarrod Emick, Frederic Forrest, Ted Marcoux, Tom Aldredge, Carmen Argenziano, Jayce Bartok, Frederick Coffin, Cliff De Young, William H. Macy, Justin Henry, Jan Triska, William Sanderson. Ambitious Civil War saga, focusing on the notorious Confederate POW camp where nearly 13,000 prisoners died in 1864. Unremittingly grim, and too long by a third. Triska gives an over-the-top performance as Wirtz, the crazed camp commandant. (Diehards might want to search out a 1970 PBS tape of *The Andersonville Trial* with Richard Basehart as Wirtz, and an all-star cast.) Written and produced by David W. Rintels. Made for cable; originally shown in two parts. Average.▼●

. . . And God Created Woman (1956-French) **C-92m.** **½ D: Roger Vadim. Brigitte Bardot, Curt Jurgens, Jean-Louis Trintignant, Christian Marquand, Georges Poujouly, Jean Tissier. Location shooting (at St. Tropez) and famous Bardot figure on display in simple tale of man-teaser finding it hard to resist temptation. Great cast clicks in Brigitte's best-known vehicle. Beware edited prints. Remade (in name only) by Vadim in the U.S. in 1987. CinemaScope. ▼●

And God Created Woman (1987) **C-100m.** *½ D: Roger Vadim. Rebecca De Mornay, Vincent Spano, Frank Langella, Donovan Leitch, Judith Chapman, Jaime McEnnan, Benjamin Mouton, David Shelley. Surprisingly tepid "variation" on director Vadim's one-time *scandale internationale* (see above). Luscious De Mornay marries carpenter Spano merely to secure her release from prison, then keeps him panting as she frolics with gubernatorial candidate Langella. Not all *that* different from Goldie Hawn's OVERBOARD; beware rock 'n' roll subplot. [R]▼●◗

. . . And God Spoke (the making of . . .) (1993) **C-83m.** *** D: Arthur Borman. Michael Riley, Stephen Rappaport, Lou Ferrigno, Soupy Sales, Eve Plumb, Fred Kaz, Michael Medved. Occasionally clever satire in the THIS IS SPINAL TAP mold, only the subject here is the casting and production of a numbingly awful multi-million-dollar biblical epic. After one day the production is behind schedule. Lou (*The Incredible Hulk*) Ferrigno plays Cain; Eve (*The Brady Bunch*) Plumb is Mrs. Noah; and Soupy Sales is Moses! You don't have to be in the movie business to enjoy this amusing little sleeper.▼

And Hope to Die (1972-French) **C-99m.** *** D: René Clement. Robert Ryan, Tisa Farrow, Jean-Louis Trintignant, Lea Massari, Aldo Ray. Above-average caper with offbeat touches; gang hired to kidnap girl goes through with scheme even though she's already dead. [PG]▼

. . . And Justice for All (1979) **C-117m.** **½ D: Norman Jewison. Al Pacino, Jack Warden, John Forsythe, Lee Strasberg, Jeffrey Tambor, Christine Lahti, Sam Levene, Craig T. Nelson, Joe Morton. Lawyer Pacino single-handedly battles Maryland's judicial system. Outrageous satire mixes uncomfortably with painfully sad moments, in attempt to make biting statement on buying and selling of justice. Strong performances and good location photography cannot overcome weak script. Written by Barry Levinson and Valerie Curtin. Lahti's feature debut. [R] ▼●

And Millions Will Die (1973) **C-96m.** ** D: Leslie Martinson. Richard Basehart, Susan Strasberg, Leslie Nielsen, Tony Wager, Peter Sumner. Environmental crisis expert Basehart is called in when it's discovered that a madman has buried a time bomb filled with deadly nerve gas beneath the streets of Hong Kong. Lackluster suspense story.

And Nothing But the Truth (1982-British) **C-90m.** **½ D: Karl Francis. Glenda Jackson, Jon Finch, Kenneth Colley, James Donnelly, Emrys James, Karen Archer. An examination of the role and responsibility of the media, focusing on documentary filmmaker Jackson and reporter Finch at work on a TV magazine show. Earnest, not without merit, but ordinary; originally titled GIRO CITY, and released at 102m.▼

And Now For Something Completely Different (1971-British) **C-89m.** *** D: Ian McNaughton. Graham Chapman, John

Cleese, Eric Idle, Terry Gilliam, Terry Jones, Michael Palin, Carol Cleveland, Connie Booth. First feature by the Monty Python troupe is a kind of "Greatest Hits" album, with some of the most popular sketches and animated bits from their long-running TV series. Fine introduction to their peculiar brand of humor includes Dead Parrot, The World's Deadliest Joke, Upper-Class Twit of the Year, and memorable Lumberjack Song. [PG]▼◗

And Now Miguel (1966) **C-95m.** *** D: James Clark. Pat Cardi, Michael Ansara, Guy Stockwell, Joe De Santis. Flavorful, leisurely paced account of young boy who wants to join his father on his summer mountain trip to graze sheep; set in Southwest. Produced by Robert Radnitz. Techniscope.

And Now My Love (1975-French) **C-121m.** ***½ D: Claude Lelouch. Marthe Keller, Andre Dussollier, Charles Denner, Carla Gravina, Gilbert Becaud, Charles Gerard. A what'll-he-do-next kind of extravaganza, in which Lelouch salutes life, love and the 20th century, using comedy, drama, and music to bring wealthy Keller and ne'er-do-well Dussollier together for the fadeout. Opens in b&w. [PG]▼

And Now the Screaming Starts! (1973-British) **C-87m.** ** D: Roy Ward Baker. Peter Cushing, Stephanie Beacham, Herbert Lom, Patrick Magee, Ian Ogilvy. Beacham weds Ogilvy and finds that she's living in a house that has been under a curse for years; OK horror drama with a good cast. [R]▼

And Now Tomorrow (1944) **85m.** **½ D: Irving Pichel. Alan Ladd, Loretta Young, Susan Hayward, Barry Sullivan, Beulah Bondi, Cecil Kellaway. Poor doctor Ladd falls in love with deaf socialite patient Young in this Rachel Field romance; sticky going at times.

And Quiet Flows the Don (1957-Russian) **C-107m.** *** D: Sergei Gerasimov. Ellina Bystritskaya, Pyotr Glebov, Zinaida Kirienko, Danilo Ilchenko. Faithful realization of Mikhail Sholokhov's novel revolving around life of small village family during WW1 and after. Absorbing study of social upheavals caused by revolution and war. Originally a multi-part film; only one segment was released in the West.

Andre (1994) **C-94m.** *** D: George Miller. Keith Carradine, Tina Majorino, Chelsea Field, Aidan Pendleton, Shane Meier, Keith Szarabajka, Joshua Jackson. Agreeably old-fashioned family film, set in a coastal town in Maine in the early 1960s, about an animal-loving clan who adopts a baby seal that adopts them in return, and refuses to leave. Aimed at children, but amiable enough for parents to enjoy as well, with a soundtrack full of 1960s pop music. Based on a true story; watch that vintage home-movie footage of Andre during the closing credits. Clairmont-Scope. [PG]▼●

Andrei Roublev (1966-Russian) **C/B&W-185m.** **** D: Andrei Tarkovsky. Anatoli Solonitzine, Ivan Lapikov, Nikolai Grinko, Nikolai Sergueiev. Brilliantly devised and directed account of the famous 15th-century icon painter, focusing on an age-old conflict: should an artist participate in the political and social upheavals of the time, or should he simply record history with his brush? This magnificent film is worthy of comparison with the best of Eisenstein's historical dramas. Scripted by Tarkovsky and Andrei Milchakov-Konchalovsky; shelved by the Soviet authorities, and unseen until 1971. Sovscope. ▼●◗

Androcles and the Lion (1952) **98m.** *** D: Chester Erskine. Jean Simmons, Alan Young, Victor Mature, Maurice Evans, Elsa Lanchester, Robert Newton. Shaw's amusing satire of ancient Rome can't be dampened by dull production retelling fable of Christian and lion he befriends. ▼

Android (1982) **C-80m.** *** D: Aaron Lipstadt. Klaus Kinski, Don Opper, Brie Howard, Norbert Weisser, Crofton Hardester, Kendra Kirchner. Entertaining sci-fi story about an almost-human android who's been working as assistant to mad scientist Kinski on a remote space station and learns he is about to be put out of commission. Charming, quirky ultra-low-budget film made on leftover sets from Roger Corman's BATTLE BEYOND THE STARS. Opper, who plays Max 404, also cowrote screenplay. [PG]▼●

Andromeda Strain, The (1971) **C-130m.** **½ D: Robert Wise. Arthur Hill, David Wayne, James Olson, Kate Reid, Paula Kelly. Overlong sci-fi thriller in which small team of superscientists tries to isolate deadly strain of virus from outer space, racing against time and nuclear detonation. From Michael Crichton's novel. Panavision. [G] ▼●◗

And Soon the Darkness (1970-British) **C-98m.** ** D: Robert Fuest. Pamela Franklin, Michele Dotrice, Sandor Eles, John Nettleton, Clare Kelly. Moody thriller with sexual undertones. Franklin is one of two vacationing British nurses bicycling through rural France, menaced by mysterious sex murderer. [PG]▼

And So They Were Married (1936) **74m.** **½ D: Elliott Nugent. Melvyn Douglas, Mary Astor, Edith Fellows, Dorothy Stickney, Jackie Moran, Donald Meek. Predictable but amusing little comedy with good co-stars.

And So They Were Married (1944) SEE: **Johnny Doesn't Live Here Any More**

And Suddenly It's Murder! (1964-Italian) **90m.** **½ D: Mario Camerini. Alberto Sordi, Vittorio Gassman, Silvana Mangano. Frail but frantic minor comedy satire revolving around trip of couples on the Riviera, each suspected of murder. Also known as CRIMINALS. CinemaScope.

And the Angels Sing (1944) **96m.** **½ D: George Marshall. Dorothy Lamour, Fred MacMurray, Betty Hutton, Diana Lynn, Raymond Walburn, Eddie Foy, Jr. Agreeable musical of singing sister act trying to make it big; MacMurray gives them their break. Brassy Hutton tries to steal the show.

And the Band Played On (1993) **C-155m. TVM** D: Roger Spottiswoode. Matthew Modine, Alan Alda, Richard Gere, Lily Tomlin, Steve Martin, Anjelica Huston, Swoosie Kurtz, Ian McKellen, Bud Cort, Phil Collins, David Dukes, Glenne Headly. Respectable if uninspired all-star dramatization by Arnold Schulman of the Randy Shilts best-seller about the early years of the AIDS epidemic. Particularly noteworthy are Gere, in a heartfelt turn as a dying dance director (based on Michael Bennett); Martin, who's nearly unrecognizable in one scene; McKellen, as a victim; and Tomlin, as a San Francisco public health doctor. Well done, but doesn't deliver the emotional wallop many viewers were expecting from this much-anticipated production. Made for cable. Average.▼●

And Then There Were None (1945) **98m.** **** D: René Clair. Barry Fitzgerald, Walter Huston, Louis Hayward, Roland Young, June Duprez, C. Aubrey Smith, Judith Anderson, Mischa Auer, Richard Haydn. Highly suspenseful Agatha Christie yarn of ten people invited to lonely island where one by one they're murdered. Great script by Dudley Nichols complemented by superb visual ideas. Remade three times as TEN LITTLE INDIANS.▼●◗

And the Ship Sails On (1984-Italian) **C-138m.** *** D: Federico Fellini. Freddie Jones, Barbara Jefford, Victor Poletti, Peter Cellier, Janet Suzman, Elisa Mai Nardi, Norma West, Paolo Paoloni. Uniquely Felliniesque ocean voyage, circa 1914, with an earnest journalist (Jones) acting as our "host" and introducing us to a variety of celebrated guests who have gathered for funeral voyage of great opera star. Flagrantly unrealistic, deliciously absurd, and somewhat uneven, but full of striking images and those indelible Fellini faces . . . plus an opening sequence that's absolutely mesmerizing. [PG]▼◗

Andy (1965) **86m.** *** D: Richard C. Sarafian. Norman Alden, Tamara Daykarhonova, Zvee Scooler, Murvyn Vye. Touching insight into existence of retarded middle-aged man and his unique problems in N.Y.C. slum life.

Andy Hardy One of the most popular series of all time, the Hardy family first appeared in A FAMILY AFFAIR (1937) with Lionel Barrymore and Mickey Rooney as father and son. In 1938, YOU'RE ONLY YOUNG ONCE began the official series in the town of Carvel, with Rooney as Andy Hardy, typical American teen-ager, interested in cars and girls, Lewis Stone as Judge James Hardy, a stern but understanding father, Fay Holden as his "swell" mother, Cecilia Parker as Marian, his older sister striving to be a young lady, Sara Haden as Aunt Millie, and Ann Rutherford as Polly, the girlfriend who was often neglected for other prospects but to whom Andy always returned; George B. Seitz directed most entries in the series. Testament to the series' great appeal was the special 1942 Oscar given MGM "for its achievement in representing the American Way of Life." MGM used the films to springboard young starlets such as Judy Garland, Lana Turner, Esther Williams, Kathryn Grayson, and Donna Reed. The Andy Hardy films do not always wear well; they serve mainly as reminders of an era in Hollywood and in America that is long gone. Indeed, when the cast, except Stone, was reunited, in 1958 for ANDY HARDY COMES HOME, the formula just didn't jell.

ANDY HARDY

A Family Affair (1937)
You're Only Young Once (1938)
Judge Hardy's Children (1938)
Love Finds Andy Hardy (1938)
Out West With the Hardys (1938)
The Hardys Ride High (1939)
Andy Hardy Gets Spring Fever (1939)
Judge Hardy and Son (1939)
Andy Hardy Meets Debutante (1940)
Andy Hardy's Private Secretary (1941)
Life Begins for Andy Hardy (1941)
The Courtship of Andy Hardy (1942)
Andy Hardy's Double Life (1942)
Andy Hardy's Blonde Trouble (1944)
Love Laughs at Andy Hardy (1946)
Andy Hardy Comes Home (1958)

Andy Hardy Comes Home (1958) **80m.** ** D: Howard W. Koch. Mickey Rooney, Patricia Breslin, Fay Holden, Cecilia Parker, Sara Haden, Joey Forman, Jerry Colonna. Andy, now a middle-aged married man with children, returns to Carvel on business and gets involved in local politics. Belated, undistinguished reunion for the Hardy clan, with a conspicuously absent Lewis Stone. Teddy Rooney, Mickey's son, plays Andy Hardy, Jr.

Andy Hardy Gets Spring Fever (1939) **85m.** **½ D: W. S. Van Dyke II. Lewis Stone, Mickey Rooney, Cecilia Parker, Fay Holden, Ann Rutherford, Sara Haden, Helen Gilbert, Terry Kilburn, Sidney Miller. Amusing series entry as Andy falls for his high school drama teacher and writes a play for himself to star in.▼

Andy Hardy Meets Debutante (1940) **89m.** ★★½ D: George B. Seitz. Mickey Rooney, Lewis Stone, Fay Holden, Cecilia Parker, Judy Garland, Sara Haden, Ann Rutherford, Tom Neal, Diana Lewis. Heartache and disillusionment result when Andy is smitten by a Manhattan socialite. Garland sings "Alone" and "I'm Nobody's Baby."▼●

Andy Hardy's Blonde Trouble (1944) **107m.** ★★½ D: George B. Seitz. Mickey Rooney, Lewis Stone, Fay Holden, Sara Haden, Bonita Granville, Jean Porter, Keye Luke, Herbert Marshall. Starting college, Andy has his hands full with precocious twins (Lee and Lyn Wilde). Well-produced but overlong entry.

Andy Hardy's Double Life (1942) **92m.** ★★½ D: George B. Seitz. Mickey Rooney, Lewis Stone, Cecilia Parker, Ann Rutherford, Sara Haden, Esther Williams, William Lundigan, Susan Peters. Andy, finished with high school, turns his attention to girls, including the aquatic charms of Williams. Look for Bobby (Robert) Blake in a small role.▼

Andy Hardy's Private Secretary (1941) **101m.** ★★½ D: George B. Seitz. Mickey Rooney, Lewis Stone, Fay Holden, Ian Hunter, Sara Haden, Kathryn Grayson, Todd Karns, Gene Reynolds. As he's about to graduate from high school, Andy gets a swelled head and hires Grayson (who gets to sing Strauss's "Voices of Spring") to be his social secretary.▼●

And You Thought Your Parents Were Weird (1991) **C-92m.** ★★½ D: Tony Cookson. Joshua Miller, Edan Gross, Marcia Strassman, Susan Gibney, John Quade, Eric Walker, Gustav Vintas, voice of Alan Thicke. Kids of deceased inventor help mom meet expenses by completing Dad's robot prototype. After some dubious doings at a teen séance, Dad's spirit (and voice) now inhabit the robot! Innocuous low-budget film isn't in the same league as HONEY, I SHRUNK THE KIDS—though it would like to be! [PG]▼

Andy Warhol's Bad (1977) **C-100m.** ★★½ D: Jed Johnson. Carroll Baker, Perry King, Susan Tyrrell, Stefania Cassini, Cyrinda Foxe. Queens housewife supplements her facial-hair-removal business by running a murder-for-hire concern specializing in children and animals. Goes without saying that Warhol's most expensive film is in execrable taste, but it frequently succeeds as a sick joke; Baker, at least, seems to be having a good time. [R]▼●

Andy Warhol's Dracula (1974-Italian-French) **C-93m.** ★★ D: Paul Morrissey. Udo Kier, Joe Dallesandro, Arno Juerging, Vittorio De Sica, Maxime McKendry, Roman Polanski. Dracula (Kier) learns he must have blood of virgins (pronounced "where-gins") in order to survive. Companion piece to ANDY WARHOL'S FRANKENSTEIN is far less bloody and has some amusing bits . . . but a long way from LOVE AT FIRST BITE. Originally released at 106m.; aka BLOOD FOR DRACULA and YOUNG DRACULA. [R—edited from original X rating] ▼●◗

Andy Warhol's Frankenstein (1974-Italian-German-French) **C-94m.** BOMB D: Paul Morrissey. Joe Dallesandro, Monique Van Vooren, Udo Kier, Srdjan Zelenovic, Dalila di Lazzaro. Mad baron Kier clones body-beautiful monsters out of bloody human innards. Campy and disgusting, with severed heads and hands galore. Originally shown in 3-D. Aka FLESH FOR FRANKENSTEIN. [R—edited from original X rating.] Space-Vision. ▼●◗

Andy Warhol Superstar SEE: **Superstar**

Angel (1937) **91m.** ★★ D: Ernst Lubitsch. Marlene Dietrich, Herbert Marshall, Melvyn Douglas, Edward Everett Horton, Laura Hope Crews. Disappointing film for Dietrich-Lubitsch team about Marlene leaving husband Marshall for vacation, falling in love with Douglas. Not worthy of star trio.▼●

Angel (1982) SEE: **Danny Boy**

Angel (1984) **C-92m.** ★½ D: Robert Vincent O'Neil. Cliff Gorman, Susan Tyrrell, Dick Shawn, Rory Calhoun, John Diehl, Donna Wilkes. Wilkes is a straight-A high school student by day, Hollywood hooker by night—but despite "colorful" characters like drag queen Shawn, film goes nowhere, and remains inexplicably tame in terms of what it shows. Sequel: AVENGING ANGEL. [R]▼●

Angela (1955) **81m.** ★★ D: Dennis O'Keefe. Dennis O'Keefe, Mara Lane, Rossano Brazzi, Arnold Foa, Nino Crisman. Poor man's DOUBLE INDEMNITY has O'Keefe drawn into murder and double-dealing by seductive Lane. Standard programmer, filmed in Italy. O'Keefe also scripted.

Angela (1984-Canadian) **C-100m.** ★★ D: Boris Sagal. Sophia Loren, Steve Railsback, John Huston, John Vernon. Dreary story of the relationship between a woman and a younger man who turns out to be her son. Made in 1978.▼

Angela (1995) **C-103m.** ★★½ D: Rebecca Miller. Anna Thomson, John Ventimiglia, Miranda Stuart-Rhyne, Charlotte Blythe. A ten-year-old girl (Stuart-Rhyne) becomes convinced that if she purifies her soul of sin, she can cure her mentally ill mother, a faded, Marilyn Monroe–esque starlet. Creepy, evocative, but protracted exploration of childhood directed by Arthur Miller's actress daughter. Slow pace and heavy-handed allusions to Christianity redeemed somewhat by Ellen Kuras' lush and earthy cinematography.

Angel and the Badman (1947) **100m.** *** D: James Edward Grant. John Wayne, Gail Russell, Harry Carey, Irene Rich, Bruce Cabot. First-rate Western with Russell humanizing gunfighter Wayne; predictable plot is extremely well handled. Also shown in computer-colored version. ▼●◗

Angel, Angel, Down We Go (1969) **C-103m.** *½ D: Robert Thom. Jennifer Jones, Jordan Christopher, Holly Near, Roddy McDowall, Lou Rawls, Charles Aidman. Awesomely dated tale of corruption, sex, drugs, and fame. Overweight teenager (Near) is distraught when her rock 'n' roll lover (Christopher) begins an affair with her jewelry-obsessed mother (Jones). Dismal attempt by American-International Pictures to go straight. Reissued as CULT OF THE DAMNED. [R]

Angela's Ashes (1999) **C-145m.** **½ D: Alan Parker. Emily Watson, Robert Carlyle, Joe Breen, Ciaran Owens, Michael Legge, Ronnie Masterson, Pauline McLynn, Eanna Macliam, Gerard McSorley, Eammon Owens; narrated by Andrew Bennett. Competent but uninspired adaptation of Frank McCourt's hugely popular, Pulitzer Prize-winning memoir about growing up in the dire poverty of Dublin in the 1930s and 40s, with a large family, a ne'er-do-well father, and an indomitable mother. Has the right look and feel, but lacks resonance and humor. [R]▼◗

Angel at My Table, An (1990-New Zealand) **C-158m.** ***½ D: Jane Campion. Kerry Fox, Alexia Keogh, Karen Fergusson, Iris Churn, K.J. Wilson, Martyn Sanderson. Stunning, biting autobiography of Janet Frame, a roly-poly, repressed little girl who grew up to become New Zealand's most famous novelist/poet—but not before being misdiagnosed a schizophrenic, spending eight years in a mental hospital. Campion beautifully portrays the various stages of Frame's life, and captures the writer's inner world. Fox is riveting as the adult Janet. Scripted by Laura Jones; adapted from a trio of Frame's autobiographies. Originally produced as a three-part television series.▼●

Angel Baby (1961) **97m.** *** D: Paul Wendkos, Hubert Cornfield. George Hamilton, Salome Jens, Mercedes McCambridge, Joan Blondell, Henry Jones, Burt Reynolds. Penetrating exposé of evangelistic circuit plying backwood country; Jens in title role, Hamilton the promoter, McCambridge his shrewish wife—marvelous cameos by Blondell and Jones. Reynolds's film debut.▼

Angel Baby (1995-Australian) **C-105m.** **½ D: Michael Rymer. John Lynch, Jacqueline MacKenzie, Colin Friels, Deborra Lee Furness. Lynch and MacKenzie play an emotionally fragile Melbourne couple who meet and fall in love in a rehabilitation center, throwing his family for a loop when she gets pregnant and can't subject the fetus to her medication. Well-acted but overelaborate treatment of the subject matter; won Australian Film Institute awards for Best Picture, Actor, Actress, Director, Screenplay, Cinematography, and Editing.▼●

Angel Face (1953) **91m.** **½ D: Otto Preminger. Robert Mitchum, Jean Simmons, Herbert Marshall, Mona Freeman, Leon Ames, Barbara O'Neil, Jim Backus. Title figure (Simmons) in slowly paced film revealed as angel of death causing demise of those who love her.

Angel From Texas, An (1940) **69m.** **½ D: Ray Enright. Eddie Albert, Wayne Morris, Rosemary Lane, Jane Wyman, Ronald Reagan, Ruth Terry, John Litel. Producers Morris and Reagan con innocent Albert into backing their show. Pleasant farce, nicely acted by the stars of BROTHER RAT. Based on George S. Kaufman's *The Butter and Egg Man,* filmed many times under different titles.

Angel Heart (1987) **C-113m.** **½ D: Alan Parker. Mickey Rourke, Robert De Niro, Lisa Bonet, Charlotte Rampling, Stocker Fountelieu, Brownie McGhee, Michael Higgins, Charles Gordone, Kathleen Wilhoite, Pruitt Taylor Vince. Two-bit private eye Rourke is hired by mysterious De Niro to track down a missing man, which leads him into a serpentine investigation—and a kind of emotional quicksand. An American Gothic yarn, full of striking, sensual, and frightening images, though after a while it bogs down. Intriguing, if not terribly appealing. Script by director Parker, based on the novel *Falling Angel* by William Hjortsberg. A steamy sex scene was snipped (by seconds) to avoid an X-rating in the U.S.; it's restored on video. [R] ▼●◗

Angel in a Taxi (1959-Italian) **95m.** **½ D: Antonio Leonviola. Vera Cecova, Vittorio De Sica, Marietto, Gabriele Ferzetti, Roberto Risso. Marietto is the whole show in this cute if predictable comedy-fantasy of a six-year-old orphan who sees a photo of pretty ballerina Cecova—and decides that she's his mother. De Sica appears in three small but important roles.▼

Angel in Exile (1948) **90m.** **½ D: Allan Dwan, Philip Ford. John Carroll, Adele Mara, Thomas Gomez, Barton MacLane, Alfonso Bedoya. Carroll heads for Arizona gold mine upon release from jail but has a change of heart when he's hailed as a religious figure by simple Mexican villagers. Unusual Republic semi-Western.

Angel in My Pocket (1969) **C-105m.** ** D: Alan Rafkin. Andy Griffith, Lee Meriwether, Jerry Van Dyke, Kay Medford, Edgar Buchanan, Gary Collins. Fans of Griffith's TV series may enjoy homespun story of young minister trying to win confidence of new small-town parish. Predictable situations, cliché dialogue, with Van

Dyke intolerable as obnoxious brother-in-law. Techniscope. [G]

Angel Levine, The (1970) **C-104m.** ***½ D: Jan Kadar. Zero Mostel, Harry Belafonte, Ida Kaminska, Milo O'Shea, Eli Wallach, Anne Jackson, Gloria Foster. Touching, humorous, and sad. Black angel named Levine, on the outs in Heaven, tries to help poor old Morris Mishkin. A tale often told—seldom this well. Based on a story by Bernard Malamud; script by Bill Gunn and Ronald Ribman. [PG]

Angel of Vengeance SEE: **Ms. 45**

Angelo, My Love (1983) **C-115m.** *** D: Robert Duvall. Angelo Evans, Michael Evans, Steve "Patalay" Tsigonoff, Millie Tsigonoff, Cathy Kitchen. Fascinating journey into world of modern-day gypsies, with "story" loosely wrapped around precocious Angelo Evans, a remarkable young street hustler. Surprisingly successful attempt by Duvall to weave fictional story into real settings with nonprofessional cast. Incidentally, the two men who sing "Golden Days" in a restaurant scene are Duvall's brothers. [R]▼●

Angel on My Shoulder (1946) **101m.** *** D: Archie Mayo. Paul Muni, Anne Baxter, Claude Rains, George Cleveland, Onslow Stevens. Entertaining fantasy of murdered convict Muni sent to earth by Devil as respected judge, and his efforts to outwit Satan while still in mortal form. Remade for TV in 1980 with Peter Strauss and Richard Kiley.▼●

Angel on the Amazon (1948) **86m.** *½ D: John H. Auer. George Brent, Vera Ralston, Constance Bennett, Brian Aherne, Fortunio Bonanova. Ludicrous "romance" with Vera in a state of eternal youth; good cast can't rescue clumsy story.

Angels SEE: **Angels Hard as They Come**

Angels' Alley (1948) **67m.** ** D: William Beaudine. Leo Gorcey, Huntz Hall, Gabriel Dell, Billy Benedict, David Gorcey, Frankie Darro, Nestor Paiva, Rosemary La Planche, Bennie Bartlett. Slip's ex-con cousin (Darro) comes to visit and gets the Bowery Boys into predictable scrapes with the law.

Angels and Insects (1995-U.S.-British) **C-116m.** *** D: Philip Haas. Mark Rylance, Kristin Scott Thomas, Patsy Kensit, Jeremy Kemp, Douglas Henshall, Saskia Wickham, Chris Larkin, Annette Badland, Anna Massey. Fascinating, mature drama, set in Victorian England, with impoverished naturalist Rylance taken in by Kemp's wealthy family and falling for his lovely, soft-spoken daughter (Kensit). While the man of science studies the social order of the insect world, the humans around him appear increasingly eccentric. Film methodically builds to devastating conclusion; Scott Thomas (playing a poor relation assisting Rylance with his work) delivers an award-caliber performance. A. S. Byatt's novella *Morpho Eugenia* was adapted by the director and his wife, Belinda Haas. A PBS *American Playhouse* presentation. [R] ▼●

Angels' Brigade (1979) **C-87m.** ** D: Greydon Clark. Jack Palance, Neville Brand, Jim Backus, Pat Buttram, Alan Hale, Jr., Peter Lawford, Jacqueline Cole, Susan Kiger, Sylvia Anderson. Mindless entertainment about seven young women who team up and outfit a "super-van" to combat drug dealing. Lots of action. Aka ANGELS' REVENGE. [PG]▼

Angels Die Hard (1970) **C-86m.** ** D: Richard Compton. Tom Baker, William Smith, Connie Nelson, R. G. Armstrong, Beach Dickerson, Rita Murray, Dan Haggerty, Bambi Allen, Michael Stringer, Gary Littlejohn. Average biker picture has Angels turning out to be good guys for a change as they save people in a mine disaster. Boasts an impressive cast of regulars from this genre. [R]▼

Angels From Hell (1968) **C-86m.** *½ D: Bruce Kessler. Tom Stern, Arlene Martel, Ted Markland, Stephen Oliver, Paul Bertoya. Violent time-waster with Vietnam war hero Stern coming home to start a new motorcycle gang, tangling with rival bikers and police. [R]▼

Angels Hard as They Come (1971) **C-90m.** *½ D: Joe Viola. James Iglehart, Gilda Texter, Gary Busey, Charles Dierkop, Gary Littlejohn, Larry Tucker, Sharon Peckinpah, Scott Glenn. Loosely structured road movie satirizes the format, but can't escape the clichés. Produced and cowritten by Jonathan Demme (who claims it's a biker version of RASHOMON); Busey's film debut. Aka ANGELS. [R]▼

Angels in Disguise (1949) **63m.** ** D: Jean Yarbrough. Leo Gorcey, Huntz Hall, Billy Benedict, David Gorcey, Gabriel Dell, Bennie Bartlett, Mickey Knox, Jean Dean, Bernard Gorcey. The Bowery Boys go undercover to help catch some Runyonesque gangsters.

Angels in the Outfield (1951) **102m.** *** D: Clarence Brown. Paul Douglas, Janet Leigh, Keenan Wynn, Donna Corcoran, Spring Byington, Ellen Corby, Lewis Stone, Bruce Bennett, voice of James Whitmore. Cute comedy-fantasy with Douglas ideally cast as the Pittsburgh Pirates' hot-tempered, foul-mouthed manager, whose hard-luck team goes on a winning streak thanks to some heavenly intervention. Amusing cameos from the worlds of baseball and show business. Remade in 1994. ▼●

Angels in the Outfield (1994) **C-102m.** **½ D: William Dear. Danny Glover, Tony Danza, Brenda Fricker, Ben Johnson, Joseph Gordon-Levitt, Milton Davis, Jr., Christopher Lloyd, Jay O. Sanders, Taylor Negron, Matthew McConaughey, Dermot

Mulroney, Adrien Brody. Inoffensive remake, with the last-place Pittsburgh Pirates of the original now the last-place California Angels. Glover replaces Paul Douglas as the team's scowling manager; the invisible angels of the original are now depicted with glitzy special effects; and the prayers of a boy (Gordon-Levitt), rather than a girl, result in the title miracle. A satisfactory entertainment for kids, but the original was better. Followed by two TV sequels: ANGELS IN THE ENDZONE and ANGELS IN THE INFIELD. [PG]▼●

Angels of Darkness (1953-Italian) **84m.** ** D: Giuseppe Amato. Linda Darnell, Anthony Quinn, Valentina Cortese, Lea Padovani. Aimless account of life and love among unhappy inhabitants of Rome—waste of stars' abilities.

Angels One Five (1954-British) **98m.** ** D: George More O'Ferrall. Jack Hawkins, Michael Denison, Dulcie Gray, John Gregson. Grounded for accidental plane mishap, British war pilot rebels against officers and friends, seeking to fly again.

Angels Over Broadway (1940) **80m.** **½ D: Ben Hecht, Lee Garmes. Douglas Fairbanks, Jr., Rita Hayworth, Thomas Mitchell, John Qualen, George Watts. Mordant, ahead-of-its-time black comedy in which hustler Fairbanks decides to do "one good deed"—rescuing suicidal embezzler Qualen—aided by chorus girl Hayworth and boozy Mitchell (who spouts reams of sardonic dialogue in a bravura performance). Hecht buffs will undoubtedly rate this higher, but despite impeccable production, it's just too offbeat (and pleased with itself about it) for most viewers.▼●

Angels' Revenge SEE **Angels' Brigade**

Angel Street SEE: **Gaslight** (1940)

Angels Wash Their Faces, The (1939) **84m.** **½ D: Ray Enright. Ann Sheridan, Dead End Kids, Frankie Thomas, Bonita Granville, Ronald Reagan, Margaret Hamilton, Marjorie Main, Eduardo Ciannelli. Protective sister Sheridan tries to clear brother Thomas' police record, but he joins Dead End Kids for more trouble. OK juvenile delinquent drama.

Angels With Dirty Faces (1938) **97m.** ***½ D: Michael Curtiz. James Cagney, Pat O'Brien, Humphrey Bogart, Ann Sheridan, George Bancroft, Billy Halop, Leo Gorcey, Huntz Hall, Gabe Dell, Bobby Jordan, Bernard Punsley. Superior cast in archetypal tale of two playmates; one (Cagney) becomes a gangster, the other (O'Brien) a priest. The Dead End Kids idolize Cagney, much to O'Brien's chagrin. Rowland Brown's story was scripted by John Wexley and Warren Duff. Quintessential Warner Bros. melodrama, a favorite of parodists for decades. Also shown in computer-colored version. ▼●

Angel Unchained (1970) **C-92m.** ** D: Lee Madden. Don Stroud, Luke Askew, Larry Bishop, Tyne Daly, Aldo Ray, Bill McKinney. Biker Stroud joins a hippie commune. Dune buggy-riding cowboys don't like hippies, so it's Stroud's ex-buddies to the rescue. Anyway, the cast is interesting. [PG]▼

Angel Who Pawned Her Harp, The (1954-British) **76m.** ** D: Alan Bromly. Felix Aylmer, Diane Cilento, Jerry Desmonde, Joe Linnane, Alfie Bass, David Kossoff, Sheila Sweet. Cilento, in her film debut, stars as an angel who visits earth and becomes involved in various people's lives. Slight, forgettable fare.

Angel Wore Red, The (1960) **99m.** **½ D: Nunnally Johnson. Ava Gardner, Dirk Bogarde, Joseph Cotten, Vittorio De Sica. Sometimes engrossing tale of clergyman who joins the Spanish loyalist cause and his romance with a good-natured entertainer.

Angie (1994) **C-107m.** *** D: Martha Coolidge. Geena Davis, Stephen Rea, James Gandolfini, Aida Turturro, Philip Bosco, Jenny O'Hara, Michael Rispoli, Betty Miller, Charlaine Woodard, Bibi Osterwald. Davis shines in this star vehicle about an Italian-American from Brooklyn who's always marched to her own drum, and finds—when she's on the verge of marriage and motherhood—that something significant is missing from her life. Todd Graff's script runs the gamut from romantic comedy to melodrama, but Davis' character—both assertive and vulnerable—has the glue to keep it all together. She's surrounded by a fine supporting cast. Panavision. [R]▼●

Angry Breed, The (1969) **C-89m.** BOMB D: David Commons. Jan Sterling, James MacArthur, William Windom, Jan Murray, Murray McLeod, Lori Martin, Melody Patterson. Vietnam veteran comes to Hollywood after discharge, gets mixed up with a group of motorcyclists. Twelfth-rate in all departments. [PG]▼

Angry Harvest (1985-West German) **C-102m.** *** D: Agnieszka Holland. Armin Mueller-Stahl, Elisabeth Trissenaar, Kathe Jaenicke, Hans Beerhenke, Isa Haller, Margit Carstensen, Wojtech Pszoniak, Kurt Raab. Discerning drama, set during WW2, highlighting the intricacies in the relationship between a working-class Polish farmer (Stahl, who is outstanding) and the upper-class Viennese Jewish refugee (Trissenaar) he shelters. Scripted by director Holland (who later made EUROPA, EUROPA).▼

Angry Hills, The (1959) **105m.** **½ D: Robert Aldrich. Robert Mitchum, Elisabeth Mueller, Stanley Baker, Gia Scala, Theodore Bikel, Sebastian Cabot. Mitchum shows vim in WW2 actioner as war correspondent plotting escape from Greece with valuable data for Allies.

Angry Red Planet, The (1959) **C-83m.**

** D: Ib Melchior. Gerald Mohr, Nora Hayden, Les Tremayne, Jack Kruschen, Paul Hahn. Martians sic incredible monsters on first Earth expedition to Mars. Lots of wild-eyed effects have given this film cult status. Filmed in odd "Cinemagic" process, which mostly turns everything pink.▼●

Angry Silence, The (1960-British) **95m.** *** D: Guy Green. Richard Attenborough, Pier Angeli, Michael Craig, Bernard Lee, Geoffrey Keen, Oliver Reed. Rewarding, unheralded film about brave stand by a simple Britisher who refuses to join wildcat strike, the repercussions he endures.

Anguish (1987-Spanish) **C-89m.** **½ D: Bigas Luna. Zelda Rubinstein, Michael Lerner, Talia Paul, Clara Pastor. Imaginative but overly violent horror film turns the action in on itself, as a mad-killer film unspools inside a theater where another mad killer is loose in the audience. Theatrical release carried warnings regarding use of subliminal effects on soundtrack. Well-recorded English dialogue. J-D-C Scope. [R]▼●

Angus (1995) **C-89m.** ** D: Patrick Read Johnson. Charlie Talbert, George C. Scott, Kathy Bates, Ariana Richards, Chris Owen, James Van Der Beek, Lawrence Pressman, Rita Moreno. Ostensibly well-meaning—but obvious and superficial—film about an overweight teenager with low self-esteem and a lifelong crush on a cute blond schoolmate. Amidst its upbeat, self-affirming messages, however, we get too many crude jokes and incompetently staged comic scenes that deflate film's impact. Scott's chess-playing partner is played by veteran director Irvin Kershner. [PG-13] ▼●

Animal Behavior (1989) **C-88m.** BOMB D: H. Anne Riley. Karen Allen, Armand Assante, Holly Hunter, Josh Mostel, Richard Libertini, Alexa Kenin, Jon Matthews, Nan Martin. A man, a woman, a chimp, a campus—and let us all be thankful that Bonzo didn't live to see this. Allen, as a monkey researcher sweating out funding, delivers a most discomforting lemme-outa-here performance. Director's name is a pseudonym; Jenny Bowen started the picture in 1984; producer Kjehl Rasmussen finished it. [PG]▼●

Animal Crackers (1930) **98m.** *** D: Victor Heerman. Groucho, Harpo, Chico, and Zeppo Marx, Margaret Dumont, Lillian Roth, Louis Sorin, Hal Thompson, Robert Greig. Marx Brothers' second movie, adapted from Broadway success, suffers from staginess and musical comedy plotting, but gives the zany foursome plenty of comic elbowroom. "Story" has to do with stolen painting, but never mind: Groucho performs "Hooray for Captain Spaulding," Chico and Harpo play bridge, Groucho shoots an elephant in his pajamas, etc.▼●◗

Animal Farm (1955-British) **C-75m.** *** D: John Halas, Joy Batchelor. Good straightforward animated-feature version of George Orwell's political satire. Ending changed from original to make it more upbeat, but trenchant views of government still hold fast. Not a kiddie film. Remade for cable TV in 1999. ▼●

Animal House SEE: **National Lampoon's Animal House**

Animal Kingdom, The (1932) **85m.** *** D: Edward H. Griffith. Ann Harding, Leslie Howard, Myrna Loy, William Gargan, Neil Hamilton, Ilka Chase, Henry Stephenson. Publisher Howard, undergoing a crisis in values, has had a relationship with free-spirited artist Harding but marries manipulative, middle-class Loy. Sophisticated entertainment, still adult by today's standards, adapted from the Philip Barry play. Remade as ONE MORE TOMORROW.▼

Animals, The (1970) **C-86m.** *½ D: Ron Joy. Henry Silva, Keenan Wynn, Michele Carey, John Anderson, Joseph Turkel. Sadistic Western with routine performances and stereotyped plot. Pretty schoolteacher vows revenge on five brutes who raped and humiliated her after holding up her stagecoach. Similar to the later HANNIE CAULDER. Techniscope. [R]

Animalympics (1979) **C-80m.** ** D: Steven Lisberger. Voices of Gilda Radner, Billy Crystal, Harry Shearer, Michael Fremer. Animated spoof of Olympics events and ubiquitous TV coverage by various anthropomorphic characters. Enough clever, funny material for a good short subject, but stretched to feature length. Cut to 48m. for network showings.▼

Anna (1951-Italian) **95m.** **½ D: Alberto Lattuada. Silvana Mangano, Raf Vallone, Vittorio Gassman, Gaby Morlay. Thoughtful study of confused young woman who enters convent to avoid deciding which man she really loves; fate forces her to decide. Look quick for Sophia Loren.▼

Anna (1987) **C-100m.** **½ D: Yurek Bogayevicz. Sally Kirkland, Paulina Porizkova, Robert Fields, Ruth Maleczech, Stefan Schnabel, Larry Pine. Middle-aged Czech actress, once a star in her native country but now struggling to survive in N.Y.C., takes in an impoverished young immigrant and teaches her the ropes—only to see her succeed where she has failed. Intriguing little film misses the bull's-eye but still has much to offer, especially a riveting and heart-rending performance by Kirkland (who is *not* Czech). Supermodel Porizkova (who is) makes an impressive screen debut. [PG-13]▼●

Anna and the King (1999) **C-147m.** **½ D: Andy Tennant. Jodie Foster, Chow Yun-Fat, Bai Ling, Tom Felton, Syed Alwi, Randall Duk Kim, Deanna Yusoff, Geoffrey Palmer. Lavish remake of the now-familiar story (memorably musicalized as THE KING AND I) about a young British widow who travels to Siam in 1862 to work as schoolteacher for the King's fifty-eight children. Put off at first, she and the imperious monarch soon develop an understanding and an unspoken attraction. Unfortunately, film goes on too long, with at least one subplot too many and a terribly contrived action climax. Foster and Yun-Fat are fine. Panavision. [PG-13]▼◗

Anna and the King of Siam (1946) **128m.** ***½ D: John Cromwell. Irene Dunne, Rex Harrison, Linda Darnell, Lee J. Cobb, Gale Sondergaard, Mikhail Rasumny. Sumptuous production chronicling the experiences of a British governess in 19th-century Thailand, and her battle of wits with strong-willed ruler. Based on Margaret Landon's book about real-life Anna Leonowens (renamed Anna L. Owens in the movie). Dunne and Harrison (in his Hollywood debut) are superb; won Oscars for Cinematography (Arthur Miller) and Art Direction/Set Decoration (then known as "Interior Decoration"). Screenplay by Talbot Jennings and Sally Benson. Later musicalized as THE KING AND I; remade as ANNA AND THE KING.▼

Annabel Takes a Tour (1938) **67m.** ** D: Lew Landers. Lucille Ball, Jack Oakie, Ruth Donnelly, Bradley Page, Ralph Forbes, Frances Mercer, Donald MacBride. Disappointing follow-up to THE AFFAIRS OF ANNABEL, with actress Ball going on tour with press agent Oakie. Second and last entry in series.▼

Anna Christie (1930) **90m.** *** D: Clarence Brown. Greta Garbo, Charles Bickford, Marie Dressler, Lee Phelps, George Marion. Garbo is effective in her first talkie as girl with shady past finding love with seaman Bickford. Film itself is rather static. From the play by Eugene O'Neill. Beware of 74m. prints. Filmed simultaneously in a German-language version, with Garbo and a different supporting cast. Some people actually find this version to be superior; it was directed by Jacques Feyder, and runs 82m. Filmed before in 1923, with Blanche Sweet. ▼●

Anna Karenina (1935) **95m.** **** D: Clarence Brown. Greta Garbo, Fredric March, Freddie Bartholomew, Maureen O'Sullivan, May Robson, Basil Rathbone. Tolstoy's tragic love chronicle makes excellent Garbo vehicle, with fine support from March as her lover, Rathbone her husband, and Bartholomew, her adoring son. Filmed before with Garbo as LOVE; remade three times.▼●

Anna Karenina (1948-British) **123m.** **½ D: Julien Duvivier. Vivien Leigh, Ralph Richardson, Kieron Moore, Sally Ann Howes, Niall MacGinnis, Martita Hunt, Marie Lohr, Michael Gough. Despite its stellar cast, this is a mostly turgid adaptation of the Tolstoy classic about a woman married to stodgy bureaucrat, who falls in love with a dashing army officer. Duvivier and Jean Anouilh were among the scriptwriters. ▼●◗

Anna Karenina (1985) **C-150m. TVM** D: Simon Langton. Jacqueline Bisset, Christopher Reeve, Paul Scofield, Ian Ogilvy, Anna Massey, Judi Bowker. Glossy but overlong remake of Tolstoy classic with Scofield (as Karenin, Anna's dispassionate husband) acting rings around his co-stars. Average.▼●

Anna Karenina (1997) SEE: **Leo Tolstoy's Anna Karenina**

Anna Lucasta (1949) **C-86m.** ** D: Irving Rapper. Paulette Goddard, William Bishop, Oscar Homolka, John Ireland, Broderick Crawford, Will Geer, Gale Page, Mary Wickes, Whit Bissell. Sluggish, watered-down version of Philip Yordan's Broadway play (which featured an all-black cast, as does the 1958 remake). Goddard plays the title role, a woman of the Brooklyn streets who was tossed out of her home by her alcoholic father; her oppressive brother-in-law tries to marry her off, in a money-making scheme. Scripted by Yordan (who also produced) and Arthur Laurents.

Anna Lucasta (1958) **97m.** ** D: Arnold Laven. Eartha Kitt, Sammy Davis, Jr., Frederick O'Neal, Henry Scott, Rex Ingram. Tepid remake of Philip Yordan's play about a prostitute who tries to leave her past behind. Kitt doesn't so much act as pose, but Ingram is excellent as her father.

Annapolis Story, An (1955) **C-81m.** ** D: Don Siegel. John Derek, Diana Lynn, Kevin McCarthy, Pat Conway. Uninspired reuse of old service-school formula with Derek and McCarthy undergoing rigid training, both romancing Lynn.▼

Anna to the Infinite Power (1983) **C-101m.** ** D: Robert Wiemer. Dina Merrill, Martha Byrne, Jack Gilford, Mark Patton, Donna Mitchell. Bright kid discovers that she is the result of a cloning experiment and tries to find her "sisters," connected by telepathy. Mild science fiction drama aimed at youngsters.▼

Anne Frank Remembered (1995-British) **C/B&W-117m.** ***½ D: Jon Blair. Narrated by Kenneth Branagh; diary read by Glenn Close. Deeply moving documentary on the young Jewish girl whose diary became an international best-seller. The filmmakers interview many who knew Anne and even turn up a brief home-movie scene of the girl herself. Perhaps the greatest impression is made by Miep Gies, the matter-of-fact Dutch woman who helped hide the Franks, and who found the diary. Oscar winner for Best Documentary. [PG]▼

Anne of Avonlea (1987-Canadian) **C-227m. TVM** D: Kevin Sullivan. Megan Follows, Colleen Dewhurst, Frank Converse, Schuyler Grant, Jonathan Crombie, Patricia Hamilton, Rosemary Dunsmore. Rare case of a sequel matching the original in near-perfection, focusing on Anne Shirley (Follows) at 18 as a teacher at Avonlea and dreaming of meeting her ideal man. Adapted by Sullivan from three Lucy Maud Montgomery books bringing the title character into adulthood: *Anne of Avonlea, Anne of the Island* and *Anne of Windy Poplars.* Originally shown in two parts. Also called ANNE OF GREEN GABLES: THE SEQUEL. Above average.▼●

Anne of Green Gables (1934) **79m.** *** D: George Nicholls, Jr. Anne Shirley, Tom Brown, O. P. Heggie, Helen Westley, Sara Haden. Utterly charming adaptation of L. M. Montgomery's book (filmed before in 1919) about a spirited orphan with a vivid imagination who endears herself to the older couple who take her in . . . and everyone else around her. Only the conclusion seems hurried and contrived. Anne Shirley took her professional name from the character she played in this film (until then she was known as Dawn O'Day). Followed by ANNE OF WINDY POPLARS. Remade for TV.▼

Anne of Green Gables (1985 Canadian) **C-195m. TVM** D: Kevin Sullivan. Megan Follows, Colleen Dewhurst, Patricia Hamilton, Marilyn Lightstone, Charmion King, Rosemary Radcliffe, Jackie Burroughs, Richard Farnsworth. Lovely adaptation of the classic children's story chronicling young life of title character (Follows), from her adoption by bachelor farmer Matthew Cuthbert and his sister Marilla to her blossoming love for Gilbert Blythe. Shown in two parts, as ANNE OF GREEN GABLES: A NEW HOME and ANNE OF GREEN GABLES: A BEND IN THE ROAD. Followed by ANNE OF AVONLEA. Remade for TV. Above average.▼●

Anne of Green Gables: The Sequel SEE: **Anne of Avonlea**

Anne of the Indies (1951) **C-81m.** **½ D: Jacques Tourneur. Jean Peters, Louis Jourdan, Debra Paget, Herbert Marshall. Peters isn't always believable as swaggering pirate, but surrounded by professionals and good production, actioner moves along.

Anne of the Thousand Days (1969) **C-145m.** *** D: Charles Jarrott. Richard Burton, Genevieve Bujold, Irene Papas, Anthony Quayle, Peter Jeffrey. Often inaccurate but totally engrossing, well-acted historical drama centering on Anne Boleyn and King Henry VIII. Lovely scenery, brilliant performance by Bujold, and Oscar-winning costumes by Margaret Furse. Panavision. [M/PG]▼●

Anne of Windy Poplars (1940) **88m.** ** D: Jack Hively. Anne Shirley, James Ellison, Henry Travers, Patric Knowles, Slim Summerville, Elizabeth Patterson, Marcia Mae Jones. Uninspired sequel to ANNE OF GREEN GABLES. Anne has grown up and become a dedicated, kind-hearted schoolteacher, but has to contend with local politics and hypocrisy in the small town where she lives and works. Remade for TV.

Annie (1982) **C-128m.** **½ D: John Huston. Albert Finney, Carol Burnett, Aileen Quinn, Bernadette Peters, Tim Curry, Ann Reinking, Geoffrey Holder, Edward Herrmann. Overblown adaptation of the Broadway musical hit about the Depression's most famous foundling (based on Harold Gray's "Little Orphan Annie" comic strip). Appealing performances by Quinn, as Annie, and Finney, as Daddy Warbucks, help buoy an uninspired—and curiously claustrophobic—production. Followed by made-for-TV sequel, ANNIE: A ROYAL ADVENTURE! Remade for TV in 1999. Panavision. [PG]▼●

Annie Get Your Gun (1950) **C-107m.** *** D: George Sidney. Betty Hutton, Howard Keel, Louis Calhern, Edward Arnold, Keenan Wynn, Benay Venuta, J. Carrol Naish. Lively filming of Irving Berlin's Wild West show musical about Annie Oakley getting her man—sharpshooter Frank Butler. Songs include "Anything You Can Do," "Doin' What Comes Naturally," "There's No Business Like Show Business."

Annie Hall (1977) **C-94m.** **** D: Woody Allen. Woody Allen, Diane Keaton, Tony Roberts, Paul Simon, Shelley Duvall, Carol Kane, Colleen Dewhurst, Christopher Walken, Janet Margolin, John Glover. Woody's best film, an autobiographical love story with incisive Allenisms on romance, relationships, fame, N.Y.C. vs. L.A., and sundry other topics. Warm, witty, intelligent Oscar winner for Best Picture, Actress, Direction, Screenplay (Allen and Marshall Brickman). Look sharp and you'll spot future stars Jeff Goldblum (at the L.A. party), Shelley Hack (on the street), Beverly D'Angelo (on a TV monitor), and Sigourney Weaver (as Woody's date seen in extreme long-shot near the end of the picture). [PG]▼●◗

Annie Oakley (1935) **88m.** *** D: George Stevens. Barbara Stanwyck, Preston Foster, Melvyn Douglas, Pert Kelton, Andy Clyde. Lively biography of female sharpshooter Stanwyck and her on-again off-again romance with fellow-performer Foster. Tight direction within episodic scenes gives believable flavor of late 19th-century America. Moroni Olsen plays Buffalo Bill. Also shown in computer-colored version.▼

Annie's Coming Out SEE: **Test of Love, A**

Annihilators, The (1985) **C-84m.** BOMB D: Charles E. Sellier, Jr. Christopher Stone, Andy Wood, Lawrence Hilton-Jacobs, Gerrit Graham, Dennis Redfield, Paul Koslo. Formula vigilante tale of neighborhood folks in southern town who hire a bunch of Vietnam vets to protect them from local youth gangs. Nasty film with repellant violence. [R]▼

Anniversary, The (1968-British) **C-95m.** **½ D: Roy Ward Baker. Bette Davis, Sheila Hancock, Jack Hedley, James Cossins, Christian Roberts, Elaine Taylor. Human monster Davis uses date of wedding anniversary as excuse to reunite family, continue her stranglehold on them. Adapted from MacIlwraith stage play, black comedy emerges as vehicle for Davis' hammy performance.▼

Ann Vickers (1933) **72m.** **½ D: John Cromwell. Irene Dunne, Walter Huston, Bruce Cabot, Edna May Oliver, Conrad Nagel, Sam Hardy, Mitchell Lewis. Feminist–social worker–prison reformer Dunne has an affair with heel Cabot, eventually finds love with charismatic, controversial judge Huston. Leads are fine in this cut-down adaptation of the Sinclair Lewis novel; more episodic than any movie has a right to be.▼

À Nos Amours (1984-French) **C-102m.** *** D: Maurice Pialat. Sandrine Bonnaire, Dominique Besnehard, Maurice Pialat, Evelyne Ker, Anne-Sophie Maille, Christophe Odent. A 15-year-old's casual promiscuity runs her family through the ringer, but they've got problems of their own—Pop's moving out, Mom's a screaming neurotic, and Brother's embraces are too hearty to be healthy. Dramatically uneven and somewhat of a downer, but Bonnaire creates a full-blooded, memorable character. Winner of France's César. [R]▼

Another Country (1984-British) **C-90m.** **½ D: Marek Kanievska. Rupert Everett, Colin Firth, Michael Jenn, Robert Addie, Cary Elwes, Anna Massey, Betsy Brantley. Faithful adaptation of Julian Mitchell's hit London play that speculates about the 1930s private-school experiences of Guy Burgess and Donald Maclean, who twenty years later were found to be spying for the Russians. Arguably more meaningful to British audiences, this examination of an oppressive existence that shuns any nonconformity makes for a pretty oppressive movie. [PG]▼●

Another Dawn (1937) **73m.** **½ D: William Dieterle. Kay Francis, Errol Flynn, Ian Hunter, Frieda Inescort, Mary Forbes. Francis is torn between devotion to husband Hunter and officer Flynn in well-paced adventure story set at British army post in African desert.

Another Day in Paradise (1998) **C-100m.** *** D: Larry Clark. James Woods, Melanie Griffith, Vincent Kartheiser, Natasha Gregson Wagner, James Otis, Paul Hipp, Brent Briscoe, Clarence Carter, Peter Sarsgaard. Arresting drama about a teenage junkie/thief who, with his girlfriend, goes on the road with a slick, experienced criminal and becomes part of his extended family. Woods is dynamite as the frighteningly intense, mood-swinging crime daddy, and Griffith is equally good as his nurturing girlfriend. Clark invests the film with a sense of immediacy and truth, even as its emotional peaks grow larger than life. Lou Diamond Phillips appears unbilled. [R]▼●◗

Another 48 HRS (1990) **C-95m.** ** D: Walter Hill. Eddie Murphy, Nick Nolte, Brion James, Kevin Tighe, Ed O'Ross, David Anthony Marshall, Bernie Casey. Strictly by-the-numbers rehash of the first film, without its spontaneity, pizzazz, or humor: Nolte is forced to turn to Murphy (who's just being sprung from jail) to help him solve a case and save his police career. Watchable, but not terribly invigorating; must set some sort of record, however, for breaking more panes of glass than any movie in history. [R]▼●◗

Another Language (1933) **77m.** *** D: Edward H. Griffith. Helen Hayes, Robert Montgomery, Louise Closser Hale, John Beal, Margaret Hamilton, Henry Travers. Vivid, devastating picture of American family life (based on Rose Franken's play), with Hayes as an outsider who marries Montgomery and faces hostility from matriarch Hale and her gossipy offspring.

Another Man, Another Chance (1977-French-U.S.) **C-132m.** **½ D: Claude Lelouch. James Caan, Genevieve Bujold, Francis Huster, Jennifer Warren, Susan Tyrrell, Richard Farnsworth. Virtual remake of Lelouch's A MAN AND A WOMAN, with late-1800s Western setting; Bujold and Caan are widow and widower who fall in love after losing their spouses. Mild-mannered to the point of distraction, and much too long. [PG]▼

Another Man's Poison (1951-British) **89m.** **½ D: Irving Rapper. Bette Davis, Gary Merrill, Emlyn Williams, Anthony Steel, Barbara Murray, Reginald Beckwith. Bette is feisty, man-hungry novelist on isolated Yorkshire farm who won't let her criminal husband, or his crony Merrill, get in her way. Well-paced melodrama can't hide its stage origins, but Davis wrings every drop out of a showy role. Coproduced by Douglas Fairbanks, Jr.▼◗

Another Part of the Forest (1948) **107m.** *** D: Michael Gordon. Fredric March, Dan Duryea, Edmond O'Brien, Ann Blyth, Florence Eldridge, John Dall. Lillian Hellman's story predates THE LITTLE FOXES by tracing the Hubbard family's ruthlessness; unpleasant but well-acted movie.

Another Stakeout (1993) **C-109m.** **½ D: John Badham. Richard Dreyfuss, Emilio Estevez, Rosie O'Donnell, Dennis Farina, Marcia Strassman, Cathy Moriarty, John Rubinstein, Miguel Ferrer, Dan Lauria, Sharon Maughan. Lots of fun here for fans of the first STAKEOUT, but little for anyone seeking substance or Shavian wit. The inept cop partners return to track down no-good Moriarty, but are saddled with assistant D.A. O'Donnell and her dog, who are both along for the ride. Highlight: dinner party that goes from bad to worse to hysterical. Madeleine Stowe (costar of the original film) briefly re-creates her role but takes no billing. Panavision. [PG-13]▼●

Another Thin Man (1939) **105m.** *** D: W. S. Van Dyke II. William Powell, Myrna Loy, C. Aubrey Smith, Otto Kruger, Nat Pendleton, Virginia Grey, Tom Neal, Marjorie Main, Ruth Hussey, Sheldon Leonard. Murder strikes at a Long Island estate and the screen's favorite lush-detective couple (along with Asta and newborn son Nick, Jr.) move in to solve it, although motherhood has slowed down Nora's drinking a bit. Enjoyable third entry in the series and the last to be based on a Dashiell Hammett story.▼●

Another Time, Another Place (1958) **98m.** **½ D: Lewis Allen. Lana Turner, Barry Sullivan, Glynis Johns, Sean Connery. Unconvincing melodrama; Turner suffers nervous breakdown when her lover is killed during WW2. Filmed in England. VistaVision. ▼●

Another Woman (1988) **C-84m.** ***½ D: Woody Allen. Gena Rowlands, Mia Farrow, Ian Holm, Blythe Danner, Gene Hackman, Betty Buckley, Martha Plimpton, John Houseman, Sandy Dennis, David Ogden Stiers, Philip Bosco, Harris Yulin, Frances Conroy. Woody ventures into Bergman territory again (with Ingmar's cameraman, Sven Nykvist, no less) with tremendous success. Rowlands plays a woman who has managed to live her life shielding herself from all emotions, until a series of incidents force her to take stock. Searing, adult drama with a magnificent cast and many memorable moments . . . though like Allen's other dramas, it's not to everyone's taste. [PG]▼●

Another You (1991) **C-98m.** *½ D: Maurice Phillips. Richard Pryor, Gene Wilder, Mercedes Ruehl, Stephen Lang, Vanessa Williams, Phil Rubenstein, Peter Michael Goetz, Kevin Pollak, Vincent Schiavelli. Compulsive liar Wilder is released from a sanitarium into the care of parolee Pryor, a street hustler who's got to perform community service; together they become embroiled in an elaborate scam. Anemic comedy relies entirely on its stars to support third-rate material. Sadly, Pryor's real-life health problems are all too apparent. [R]▼●

À Nous la Liberte (1931-French) **97m.** **** D: René Clair. Raymond Cordy, Henri Marchand, Rolla France, Paul Olivier, Jacques Shelly, Andre Michaud. Classic satire on machinery and industrialization centering on the adventures of escaped prisoner Cordy, who becomes owner of a phonograph factory, and his former jail friend (Marchand), now a vagrant. Predates and equals MODERN TIMES in poignancy, with groundbreaking use of music. Arguably, Clair's masterpiece.▼

Anthony Adverse (1936) **141m.** ***½ D: Mervyn LeRoy. Fredric March, Olivia de Havilland, Donald Woods, Anita Louise, Edmund Gwenn, Claude Rains, Louis Hayward, Gale Sondergaard, Akim Tamiroff, Billy Mauch, Ralph Morgan, Henry O'Neill, Scotty Beckett, Luis Alberni. Blockbuster filmization of Hervey Allen bestseller (scripted by Sheridan Gibney) of young man gaining maturity through adventures in various parts of early 19th-century Europe, Cuba, and Africa. Sondergaard won Oscar as Best Supporting Actress in her film debut; rousing musical score by Erich Wolfgang Korngold and Tony Gaudio's cinematography also won. ▼●

Antonia & Jane (1991-British) **C-77m.** *** D: Beeban Kidron. Saskia Reeves, Imelda Staunton, Brenda Bruce, Bill Nighy, Lila Kaye, Alfred Marks, Richard Hope. Pleasingly quirky, clever chronicle of the relationship between two friends from school. Antonia (Reeves) is attractive and arrogant; Jane (Staunton) is plump, but adventuresome. They share mutual envy (as well as the same therapist) . . . and Antonia's husband is Jane's ex-boyfriend. Very funny little sleeper made for British television.▼

Antonia: A Portrait of the Woman (1974) **C-58m.** ***½ D: Judy Collins, Jill Godmilow. Heartfelt documentary about conductor Antonia Brico and her struggle to triumph over sexual prejudice within the symphonic community. Inspiring.▼

Antonia's Line (1995-Dutch-Belgian-British) **C-105m.** *** D: Marleen Gorris. Willeke van Ammelrooy, Els Dottermans, Jan Decleir, Mil Seghers, Marina de Graaf, Jan Steen, Veerle Van Overloop, Elsie de Brauw, Thyrza Ravesteijn, Wimie Wilhelm. Spirited woman returns to her provincial Dutch village after WW2 and takes up residence there with her daughter. Then, over a span of years, she raises not only her own child but an extended family which comes under the shelter (and aura) of this unusual woman who defies convention. Disarmingly unpredictable comedy-drama is a treat from start to finish. Oscar winner as Best Foreign Film. [R]▼●◗

Antonio (1973) **C-81m.** ** D: Claudio Guzman. Trini Lopez, Larry Hagman, Noemi Guerrero, Pedro Becker, Marvin Walkenstein. South American village potter's life gets complicated after an eccentric Texas oilman gives him a car, so he sets out to return it. Good-hearted if empty-headed version of city mouse-country mouse fable. Hagman hams it up in pre-*Dallas* oilman role.▼

Antony and Cleopatra (1973) **C-160m.** *½ D: Charlton Heston. Charlton Heston, Hildegard Neil, Eric Porter, John Castle, Fernando Rey. Labor-of-love undertaking by Heston results in sluggish treatment of Shakespearean play, hampered by severe budgetary limitations. Todd-AO 35. ▼

Antz (1998) **C-83m.** *** D: Eric Darnell, Tim Johnson. Voices of Woody Allen, Sharon Stone, Sylvester Stallone, Gene Hackman, Christopher Walken, Anne Bancroft, Dan Aykroyd, Jane Curtin, Danny Glover, Jennifer Lopez, John Mahoney, Paul Mazursky. Entertaining computer-animated feature about an ant named Z (with the voice and personality of Woody Allen) who doesn't respond well to regimentation—especially after he's smitten with the queen ant's daughter, Princess Bala. Meanwhile, the colony is threatened, not only by termites but by a megalomaniacal general with his own agenda. Clever and enjoyable (all the more so for Woodyphiles), but too sophisticated and violent for young kids. [PG] ▼●◗

Any Given Sunday (1999) **C-162m.** ** D: Oliver Stone. Al Pacino, Cameron Diaz, Dennis Quaid, James Woods, Jamie Foxx, LL Cool J, Charlton Heston, Matthew Modine, Jim Brown, Ann-Margret, Aaron Eckhart, John C. McGinley, Lauren Holly, Lela Rochon, Lawrence Taylor, Bill Bellamy, James Karen, Elizabeth Berkley. Strident, one-note concoction about the world of pro football, on and off the field. Pacino is an aging coach who's given his all to the game, Diaz a demanding, mercurial team owner, Foxx an up-and-coming quarterback who gets a big head. Loud and obvious from the word go. Various sports figures play themselves; Stone appears as a booth announcer. Super 35. [R]▼●◗

Any Gun Can Play (1967-Italian-Spanish) **C-103m.** BOMB D: Enzo G. Castellari. Edd Byrnes, Gilbert Roland, George Hilton, Kareen O'Hara, Pedro Sanchez, Gerard Herter. Bounty hunter Hilton, bandit Roland and bank official Byrnes vie for gold treasure. Silly spaghetti Western, filmed in Spain. Aka FOR A FEW BULLETS MORE. Techniscope. ▼

Any Man's Death (1990) **C-110m.** *½ D: Tom Clegg. John Savage, William Hickey, Mia Sara, Ernest Borgnine, Michael Lerner, James Ryan. Stultifying tale of a reporter who stumbles onto a Nazi war criminal in Africa, and has to deal with the issues raised by his discovery. Pretty interesting cast, but nothing else to recommend in this hollow moralistic drama. [R]▼●

Any Number Can Play (1949) **112m.** ** D: Mervyn LeRoy. Clark Gable, Alexis Smith, Wendell Corey, Audrey Totter, Mary Astor, Lewis Stone, Marjorie Rambeau, Darryl Hickman. Low-key drama of gambling-house owner Gable, estranged from wife Smith and son Hickman. Good character roles breathe life into film.▼

Any Number Can Win (1963-French) **108m.** **½ D: Henri Verneuil. Jean Gabin, Alain Delon, Viviane Romance, Carla Marlier. Gabin leads bank robbery in Riviera resort. Comedy and suspense blend in "perfect crime" attempt. Dyaliscope.◗

Anyone Can Play (1968-Italian-French) **C-88m.** ** D: Luigi Zampa. Ursula Andress, Virna Lisi, Claudine Auger, Marisa Mell, Brett Halsey, Jean-Pierre Cassel. Aside from obvious good looks of four leading actresses, tale of adultery in Italy is not one of that country's better farces. [R]

Anything Can Happen (1952) **107m.** ** D: George Seaton. Jose Ferrer, Kim Hunter, Kurt Kasznar, Eugenie Leontovich, Oscar Beregi, Nick Dennis. Intriguingly awful comedy/propaganda piece with Ferrer as a wide-eyed Russian who emigrates to the U.S. Very much a product of its time.

Anything for Love SEE: **11 Harrowhouse**

Anything Goes (1936) **92m.** **½ D: Lewis Milestone. Bing Crosby, Ethel Merman, Charlie Ruggles, Ida Lupino, Grace Bradley, Arthur Treacher. Pleasant Crosby shipboard musical retains Merman from the cast of the Broadway show, but scuttles much of the plot and most of Cole Porter's songs (except "You're the Top" and "I Get a Kick Out of You"). Remade (again with Bing) in 1956. Retitled for TV: TOPS IS THE LIMIT.

Anything Goes (1956) **C-106m.** ** D: Robert Lewis. Bing Crosby, Jeanmaire, Donald O'Connor, Mitzi Gaynor, Phil Harris, Kurt Kasznar. Flat musical involving show business partners Crosby and O'Connor each signing a performer for the leading role in their next show. Sidney Sheldon's script bears little resemblance to the original Broadway show, though some Cole Porter songs remain. Crosby fared better in the 1936 film. VistaVision.

Any Wednesday (1966) **C-109m.** *** D: Robert Ellis Miller. Jane Fonda, Jason Robards, Dean Jones, Rosemary Murphy. Bedroom farce of N.Y.C. executive using his mistress' apartment for business deductions. Fonda is appropriately addled in unstagy sex comedy.▼

Anywhere But Here (1999) **C-114m.** ** D: Wayne Wang. Susan Sarandon, Natalie Portman, Hart Bochner, Shawn Hatosy, Bonnie Bedelia, John Diehl, Paul Guilfoyle, Caroline Aaron. Optimistic single mom who can still turn heads and a wearily-seen-it-all adolescent daughter leave small-town Wisconsin to seek a new beginning in Beverly Hills, commencing a series of episodic adventures that never take emotional hold. Sizzleless adaptation of Mona Simpson's best-seller pales not only next to ALICE DOESN'T LIVE HERE ANYMORE and MEN DON'T LEAVE, but to the low-budget indie TUMBLEWEEDS, which stole this slicker entry's thunder. Super 35. [PG-13]▼◗

Any Which Way You Can (1980) **C-116m.** **½ D: Buddy Van Horn. Clint Eastwood, Sondra Locke, Geoffrey Lewis, William Smith, Harry Guardino, Ruth Gordon, Glen Campbell, Anne Ramsey, Logan Ramsey, Barry Corbin, James Gammon. This sequel to EVERY WHICH WAY BUT LOOSE is funnier, if no more intelligent. Clint's climactic bare-fisted fight with Smith is a highlight, but the filmmakers wisely gave most of the laughs to the star's orangutan friend, Clyde. [PG]▼●

Anzio (1968-French-Italian-Spanish) **C-117m.** ** D: Edward Dmytryk. Robert Mitchum, Peter Falk, Robert Ryan, Earl Holliman, Mark Damon, Arthur Kennedy, Reni Santoni, Patrick Magee. Undistinguished retelling of Allied invasion of Anzio; all-star cast, large-scale action, but nothing memorable. Aka THE BATTLE FOR ANZIO. Panavision. [M/PG]▼

Apache (1954) **C-91m.** ** D: Robert Aldrich. Burt Lancaster, Jean Peters, John McIntire, Charles (Bronson) Buchinsky. Pacifist Indian (Lancaster) learns might makes right from U.S. cavalry; turns to fighting one man crusade for his tribe's rights. Overacted and improbable (though based on fact).▼●

Apache Drums (1951) **C-74m.** **½ D: Hugo Fregonese. Stephen McNally, Coleen Gray, Willard Parker, Arthur Shields, James Griffith, Georgia Backus, James Best, Clarence Muse. Zesty little Western in which gambler "Sam Slick" (McNally) is kicked out of the town of Spanish Boot. What will happen to him when he returns to warn its citizens of an impending Apache attack?

Apache Gold (1965-German) **C-91m.** **½ D: Harald Reinl. Lex Barker, Mario Adorf, Pierre Brice, Marie Versini. A sort of Eastern-Western has good Indian atmosphere, plenty of action. Ultrascope.

Apache Massacre SEE: **Cry for Me, Billy**

Apache Rifles (1964) **C-92m.** **½ D: William Witney. Audie Murphy, Michael Dante, Linda Lawson, John Archer, J. Pat O'Malley. Audie is stalwart cavalry captain assigned to corral renegading Apaches. Stock footage and plot mar potentials of actioner.

Apache Territory (1958) **C-75m.** *½ D: Ray Nazarro. Rory Calhoun, Barbara Bates, John Dehner, Carolyn Craig. Calhoun almost single-handedly routs rampaging Apaches and rescues defenseless Bates.

Apache Uprising (1966) **C-90m.** *½ D: R. G. Springsteen. Rory Calhoun, Corinne Calvet, John Russell, Lon Chaney (Jr.), Gene Evans, Richard Arlen, Arthur Hunnicutt, DeForest Kelley, Johnny Mack Brown, Jean Parker, Don "Red" Barry. No production values, but cast of familiar names may make it possible for some to sit through standard Western where Rory fights both Indians and outlaws. Techniscope.▼●

Apache Warrior (1957) **74m.** ** D: Elmo Williams. Keith Larsen, Jim Davis, Michael Carr, Eddie Little. When an Indian leader's brother is killed, Apaches go on the warpath. Nothing new. Regalscope.

Apache War Smoke (1952) **67m.** *½ D: Harold F. Kress. Gilbert Roland, Robert Horton, Glenda Farrell, Gene Lockhart, Bobby (Robert) Blake. Pat Western involving stagecoach robbery and Indian attack on stage-line station. Good supporting cast wasted.

Apache Woman (1955) **C-83m.** BOMB D: Roger Corman. Lloyd Bridges, Joan Taylor, Lance Fuller, Morgan Jones, Paul Birch, Dick Miller, Chester Conklin. Government affairs expert Bridges attempts to ease tension between Apaches and whites, tangles with hellcat halfbreed Taylor. Sometimes hilariously bad, but mostly a bore.▼

Aparajito (1956-Indian) **108m.** ***½ D: Satyajit Ray. Pinaki Sen Gupta, Smaran Ghosal, Karuna Banerji, Kanu Banerji, Ramani Sen Gupta. The second of Ray's Apu trilogy is a moving, beautifully filmed story of life and death in a poor Indian family, with the son, Apu (Ghosal), trekking off to college in Calcutta. Aka THE UNVANQUISHED.▼

Apartment, The (1960) **125m.** **** D: Billy Wilder. Jack Lemmon, Shirley MacLaine, Fred MacMurray, Ray Walston, Jack Kruschen, Edie Adams, David Lewis, Joan Shawlee. Superb comedy-drama that manages to embrace both sentiment and cynicism. Lemmon attempts to climb corporate ladder by loaning his apartment key to various executives for their extramarital trysts, but it backfires when he falls for his boss's latest girlfriend. Fine performances all around, including MacMurray as an uncharacteristic heel. Oscar winner for Best Picture, Director, Screenplay (Wilder and I.A.L. Diamond), Editing (Daniel Mandell), Art Direction-Set Decoration (Alexander Trauner, Edward G. Boyle). Later a Broadway musical, *Promises, Promises.* Panavision. ▼●

Apartment for Peggy (1948) **C-99m.** *** D: George Seaton. Jeanne Crain, William Holden, Edmund Gwenn, Gene Lockhart. Breezy story of newlyweds trying to live on college campus; old pros Gwenn and Lockhart steal film from young lovers.

Apartment Zero (1988-British) **C-124m.** *** D: Martin Donovan. Colin Firth, Hart Bochner, Dora Bryan, Liz Smith, Fabrizio Bentivoglio. Odd, intriguing psychological drama with political, moral, and sexual overtones. Fastidious film buff Firth's life is profoundly altered when he takes in freewheeling—and mysterious—Bochner as a boarder. Not for all tastes but extremely well acted and definitely worth a look. Set in Buenos Aires; scripted by Donovan and David Koepp. Shortened by eight minutes for video by director. [R]▼●

Ape, The (1940) **62m.** ** D: William Nigh. Boris Karloff, Gertrude W. Hoffman, Henry Hall, Maris Wrixon. Low-budget shocker with mad doctor Karloff donning pelt of slain circus ape so he can kill his neighbors for their spinal fluid.▼◗

Ape Man, The (1943) **64m.** ** D: William Beaudine. Bela Lugosi, Louise Currie, Wallace Ford, Henry Hall, Minerva Urecal. Minor horror effort with Lugosi and cast overacting in story of scientist injecting himself to attain power of simian relatives. Followed by non-sequel, RETURN OF THE APE MAN.▼

Apex (1994) **C-103m.** ** D: Phillip J. Roth. Richard Keats, Mitchell Cox, Lisa Ann Russell, Marcus Aurelius, Adam Lawson, David Jean Thomas, Anna B. Choi, Kristin Norton. A misfired time excursion from 2073 to 1973 creates a diseased, ruined future overrun with killer robots—and only one man knows what's happened. Pokey but mildly engrossing low-budgeter plays with time-paradox ideas in comic book fashion (lots of gunfire and explosions, little real action). [R]▼●

Apocalypse Now (1979) **C-150m.** ***½ D: Francis Coppola. Marlon Brando, Robert Duvall, Martin Sheen, Frederic Forrest, Albert Hall, Sam Bottoms, Larry Fishburne, Dennis Hopper, G. D. Spradlin, Harrison Ford, Scott Glenn, Tom Mason, Colleen Camp. Coppola's controversial Vietnam war epic, based on Joseph Conrad's *Heart of Darkness.* Special agent Sheen journeys upriver into Cambodia with orders to find and kill errant officer Brando, leading him (and viewer) on a mesmerizing odyssey of turbulent, often surreal encounters. Unfortunately, film's conclusion—when he does find Brando—is cerebral and murky. Still, a great movie experience most of the way, with staggering, Oscar-winning photography by Vittorio Storaro. The documentary HEARTS OF DARKNESS: A FILMMAKER'S APOCALYPSE chronicles the film's production. Technovision. [R]▼●

Apollo 13 (1995) **C-139m.** ***½ D: Ron Howard. Tom Hanks, Bill Paxton, Kevin Bacon, Gary Sinise, Ed Harris, Kathleen Quinlan, Miko Hughes, David Andrews, Chris Ellis, Joe Spano, Xander Berkeley, Marc McClure, Tracy Reiner, Brett Cullen; opening narration by Walter Cronkite. Exhilarating story of ill-fated Apollo 13 moon mission, and how the heroic work of astronaut Jim Lovell and his crew, combined with the dogged persistence of the NASA team in Houston, averted tragedy. A rare instance where special effects actually serve the story and help make it completely credible; perfect 1970s period detail is another asset. Screenplay by William Broyles, Jr., and Al Reinert, from the book *Lost Moon* by Lovell and Jeffrey Kluger. Director Howard's brother Clint has a good role as one of the Houston eggheads; father, Rance, plays a priest; and mother, Jean, is a treat as Jim Lovell's mom. The real Lovell appears as an officer on the aircraft carrier in the final sequence. Winner of Oscars for Film Editing and Sound. Super 35. [PG]▼●◗

Apostle, The (1997) **C-134m.** *** D: Robert Duvall. Robert Duvall, Farrah Fawcett, Miranda Richardson, Billy Bob Thornton, June Carter Cash, Todd Allen, John Beasley, Billy Joe Shaver. Duvall—in an obvious labor of love as writer, director, producer, and star—is superb as a womanizing Pentecostal minister who is forced to leave his Texas home (and church) after committing a violent act. Fascinating study of a wayward man's journey to understand his life, and the many people who help him find his way. Wonderful small-town Southern atmosphere. Lags a bit, but the performances by Duvall and his supporting cast make up for it. James Gammon appears unbilled. [PG-13]▼●◗

Appaloosa, The (1966) **C-98m.** **½ D: Sidney J. Furie. Marlon Brando, Anjanette Comer, John Saxon, Alex Montoya, Frank Silvera. Brooding Western set in 1870s with Brando trying to recover horse stolen from him by Mexican bandit; slowly paced, well photographed by Russell Metty. Techniscope. ▼●

Applause (1929) **78m.** **½ D. Rouben Mamoulian. Helen Morgan, Joan Peers, Fuller Mellish, Jr., Henry Wadsworth, Dorothy Cumming. Revolutionary early talkie may seem awfully hokey to modern audiences (Morgan plays a fading burlesque queen with a two-timing boyfriend and an innocent young daughter just out of a convent), but Morgan's heart-rending performance, and innovative use of camera and sound by Mamoulian (in his film directing debut), make it a must for buffs.▼

Apple, The (1980) **C-90m.** BOMB D: Menahem Golan. Catherine Mary Stewart, Allan Love, George Gilmour, Grace Kennedy, Joss Ackland, Vladek Sheybal. Futuristic musical set in 1994, when a young couple's entry in songwriting contest is sabotaged by devilish Mr. Boogalow. As bad as it sounds—possibly worse. Panavision. [PG]▼

Apple Dumpling Gang, The (1975) **C-100m.** ** D: Norman Tokar. Bill Bixby, Susan Clark, Don Knotts, Tim Conway, David Wayne, Slim Pickens, Harry Morgan. Disney Western comedy with gambler Bixby inheriting three children. Predictable doings sparked by Knotts and Conway as bumbling crooks. [G]▼●

Apple Dumpling Gang Rides Again, The (1979) **C-88m.** ** D: Vincent McEveety. Tim Conway, Don Knotts, Tim Matheson, Kenneth Mars, Elyssa Davalos, Jack Elam, Robert Pine, Harry Morgan, Ruth Buzzi. More of the same, with Knotts and Conway as bumbling outlaws in the Old West; usual Disney slapstick, without much zip or originality. [G]▼

Applegates, The SEE: **Meet the Applegates**

Appointment, The (1969) **C-100m.** **½ D: Sidney Lumet. Omar Sharif, Anouk Aimée, Lotte Lenya. Brilliant attorney falls in love with a girl who eventually ruins him. Soapy and long. [R]

Appointment for Love (1941) **89m.** **½ D: William Seiter. Charles Boyer, Margaret Sullavan, Rita Johnson, Reginald Denny, Ruth Terry, Eugene Pallette. Frothy comedy showcasing delightful stars: husband and wife with careers find happy marriage almost impossible.

Appointment in Berlin (1943) **77m.** **½ D: Alfred E. Green. George Sanders, Marguerite Chapman, Onslow Stevens, Gale Sondergaard, Alan Napier. Another WW2 intrigue film, better than most, with Sanders joining Nazi radio staff to learn secret plans.

Appointment in Honduras (1953) **C-79m.** **½ D: Jacques Tourneur. Ann Sheridan, Glenn Ford, Zachary Scott, Jack Elam. Idealistic American (Ford) out to save Latin-American country, corrals villainous companions into helping crusade. Sheridan is not focal point, and a pity.▼

Appointment in London (1953-British) **96m.** *** D: Philip Leacock. Dirk Bogarde, Ian Hunter, Dinah Sheridan, William Sylvester, Walter Fitzgerald, Bryan Forbes. Engrossing story of British bomber squadron in WW2, and high-pressured officer Bogarde who insists on flying dangerous mission in spite of orders to the contrary.

Appointment With a Shadow (1958) **73m.** ** D: Richard Carlson. George Nader, Joanna Moore, Brian Keith, Virginia Field, Frank De Kova. Former ace reporter swears off alcohol and scoops big story. CinemaScope.

Appointment With Danger (1951) **89m.** *** D: Lewis Allen. Alan Ladd, Phyllis Calvert, Paul Stewart, Jan Sterling, Jack Webb, Harry Morgan. Ladd is a U.S. postal inspector aided by nun Calvert in cracking a case. Forget that part of the story; Webb and Morgan are the *villains* here, and *Dragnet* fans will be extremely amused. Best bit: Ladd "dropping" Webb on a handball court.

Appointment With Death (1988) **C-108m.** *½ D: Michael Winner. Peter Ustinov, Lauren Bacall, Carrie Fisher, John Gielgud, Piper Laurie, Hayley Mills, Jenny Seagrove, David Soul. Ustinov returns yet again as Agatha Christie's detective Hercule Poirot in this obvious, depressingly unsuspenseful mystery. It seems that greedy Laurie wants her late husband's money all for herself. How soon will she be murdered? And how soon will Poirot name her killer? Another loser from Winner; scripted by Anthony Shaffer, Peter Buckman and the director. [PG]▼●

Appointment With Murder (1948) **67m.** *½ D: Jack Bernhard. John Calvert, Catherine Craig, Jack Reitzen, Lyle Talbot, Robert Conte. Appointment with boredom is more like it in this quickie *Falcon* mystery centering on international art thieves.

Apprenticeship of Duddy Kravitz, The (1974-Canadian) **C-121m.** ***½ D: Ted Kotcheff. Richard Dreyfuss, Micheline Lanctot, Jack Warden, Randy Quaid, Joseph Wiseman, Denholm Elliott, Joe Silver. Mordecai Richler's vivid comedy-drama of an ambitious kid from Montreal's Jewish ghetto in the 1940s, determined to make good no matter how many toes he steps on. Pretentious bar mitzvah movie made by Duddy's "client," artsy director Elliott, is just one comic highlight. Panavision. [PG]▼

Apprentice to Murder (1988) **C-94m.** ** D: R. L. Thomas. Donald Sutherland, Chad Lowe, Mia Sara, Knut Husebo, Rutanya Alda. Odd, affected, fact-based account of a practitioner of medieval medicine (Sutherland, in a disappointing performance), and his complex relationship with young Lowe. Filmed in Norway. [PG-13]▼●

April Fools, The (1969) **C-95m.** ** D: Stuart Rosenberg. Jack Lemmon, Catherine Deneuve, Peter Lawford, Harvey Korman, Sally Kellerman, Myrna Loy, Charles Boyer, Melinda Dillon, Kenneth Mars, Jack Weston, David Doyle. Attempt at old-fashioned romantic comedy is forced, unbelievable, unfunny. Lemmon is married businessman who decides to chuck it all to run away with Deneuve, who's wasted, along with Loy and Boyer. Panavision. [M/PG]▼

April Fool's Day (1986) **C-88m.** ** D: Fred Walton. Deborah Foreman, Griffin O'Neal, Clayton Rohner, Thomas F. Wilson, Deborah Goodrich. Practical joker (Foreman) invites college pals to spend a weekend in her family's mansion on an off-coast island; one by one they're threatened and killed. Attempt to bring humor to FRIDAY THE 13TH formula isn't a total washout but doesn't quite click, either. Panavision. [R]▼●

April in Paris (1952) **C-101m.** **½ D: David Butler. Doris Day, Ray Bolger, Claude Dauphin, Eve Miller, George Givot, Paul Harvey. Diplomatic corps bureaucrat who's trying to boost Franco-American relations falls in love with a showgirl who's mistakenly been chosen to appear in the "April in Paris" show he's staging. Mediocre Warner Bros. musical buoyed by the personalities of Day and Bolger—who make an unconvincing romantic couple.▼●

April Love (1957) **C-97m.** **½ D: Henry Levin. Pat Boone, Shirley Jones, Dolores Michaels, Arthur O'Connell, Matt Crowley. Engaging musical with wholesome Boone visiting relatives' Kentucky farm, falling in love with neighbor Jones. Pat had a hit with the title tune. Previously filmed as HOME IN INDIANA. CinemaScope.

April Morning (1988) **C-100m. TVM** D: Delbert Mann. Tommy Lee Jones, Robert Urich, Chad Lowe, Susan Blakely, Rip Torn, Meredith Salenger. A teenage boy's coming of age on the eve of the American Revolution when the Colonists make their stand on the Lexington green. Well-crafted adaptation by James Lee Barrett of Howard Fast's 1961 novel. Above average.▼

April Showers (1948) **94m.** ** D: James V. Kern. Jack Carson, Ann Sothern, Robert Alda, S. Z. Sakall, Robert Ellis. Hackneyed backstage vaudeville yarn with Carson-Sothern teaming, splitting, re-teaming, etc.

Apt Pupil (1998) **C-111m.** *½ D: Bryan Singer. Ian McKellen, Brad Renfro, Bruce Davison, Elias Koteas, Joe Morton, Jan Triska, Michael Byrne, Heather McComb, David Schwimmer, Joshua Jackson, James Karen. A student studying the Holocaust becomes overly absorbed in the subject. When he spots an old man on the bus and realizes that he's a former Nazi war criminal, he cultivates a curious "friendship" with the unrepentant elder. Fascinating premise, from a Stephen King novella, soon grows untenable—and doesn't know when to quit. Good performances by McKellen and Renfro can't save this extremely unpleasant film. Super 35. [R]▼●◗

Arab Conspiracy, The SEE: **Next Man, The**

Arabella (1969-Italian) **C-91m.** *½ D: Adriano Barocco. Virna Lisi, James Fox, Margaret Rutherford, Terry-Thomas. Silly drawing-room black comedy in which Thomas plays four different roles, as various victims of Lisi's larceny. Filmed in widescreen Panoramica. [M/PG]

Arabesque (1966) **C-105m.** *** D: Stanley Donen. Sophia Loren, Gregory Peck, Alan Badel, Kieron Moore, George Coulouris. Modern secret-agent escapism as Peck is drawn into espionage with Sophia, who was never more beautiful. Exciting, beautifully photographed, minus any message or deep thought. Panavision. ▼

Arabian Adventure, An (1979-British) **C-98m.** **½ D: Kevin Connor. Christopher Lee, Milo O'Shea, Puneet Sira, Oliver Tobias, Emma Samms, Peter Cushing, Mickey Rooney, Capucine, John Ratzenberger. Just what the title says; colorful enough to entertain kids, with enough effects gimmicks and cameo performances to intrigue older viewers as well. [G]

Arabian Knight (1995) **C-72m.** ** D: Richard Williams. Voices of Vincent Price, Matthew Broderick, Jennifer Beals, Eric Bogosian, Toni Collette, Jonathan Winters, Bobbi Page, Clive Revill, Kevin Dorsey, Kenneth Williams. Colorful but disappointing (and ultimately, boring) yarn of a lowly cobbler who falls in love with a princess and does battle with a wily wizard named Zig Zag. Some engaging and amusing scenes for kids, with exceptionally interesting graphics and color schemes, but the story is too fragmented to really take hold; the songs are instantly forgettable. This film shows the scars of major production woes; it was begun by Williams in 1968(!), then taken out of his hands in the early 1990s. Retitled THE THIEF AND THE COBBLER (the film's original name while in production) for video. Panavision. [G]▼●

Arabian Nights (1942) **C-86m.** **½ D: John Rawlins. Jon Hall, Maria Montez, Sabu, Leif Erickson, Turhan Bey, Billy Gilbert, Shemp Howard, John Qualen, Thomas Gomez. Colorful, corny escapist stuff—beautifully mounted in Technicolor—about a dashing hero, an enslaved Sheherazade, and an evil caliph. Shemp also memorable as a retired Sinbad the Sailor. First teaming of Montez, Hall, and Sabu. ▼●

Arabian Nights (1974-Italian-French) **C-128m.** *** D: Pier Paolo Pasolini. Ninetto Davoli, Ines Pellegrini, Franco Citti, Tessa Bouche, Margarethe Clementi, Franco Merli. Several *Thousand and One Nights* tales are framed by the story of slave-girl Pellegrini, who becomes "king" of a great city. Dreamlike, exotic; the last and best of Pasolini's medieval trilogy. Running-time originally 155m., then 130m.▼●◗

Arachnophobia (1990) **C-109m.** *** D: Frank Marshall. Jeff Daniels, Harley Jane Kozak, John Goodman, Julian Sands, Stuart Pankin, Brian McNamara, Mark L. Taylor, Henry Jones, Peter Jason, James Handy. Fear of spiders is taken to extremes in this slick comic thriller from Steven Spielberg and Co. Small-town doctor Daniels (who hates spiders) and family play host to a wayward tropical arachnid that promptly sets up web in the barn out back. Essentially Grade Z movie fodder is socked across here by a big budget and spirited performances. Directorial debut of longtime Spielberg producer Marshall. Not recommended for anyone who's *ever* covered their eyes during a movie. [PG-13]▼●◗

Arch of Triumph (1948) **114m.** **½ D: Lewis Milestone. Ingrid Bergman, Charles Boyer, Charles Laughton, Louis Calhern. Sluggish drama of refugee Boyer falling in love with Bergman in WW2 France, based on Erich Maria Remarque's novel. Archivally restored to 131m. Remade for TV in

1985 with Anthony Hopkins and Lesley-Anne Down.▼

archy and mehitabel SEE: **shinbone alley**

Are Husbands Necessary? (1942) **79m.** ** D: Norman Taurog. Ray Milland, Betty Field, Patricia Morison, Eugene Pallette, Cecil Kellaway. And what about this film?

Arena (1953) **C-83m.** ** D: Richard Fleischer. Gig Young, Jean Hagen, Polly Bergen, Henry (Harry) Morgan, Barbara Lawrence, Lee Aaker. Sappy, soapy story of rodeo star (Young) whose marriage is on the skids; film's only value is in realistic rodeo scenes, filmed on location in Arizona. Originally shown in 3-D.

Arena, The (1973) **C-83m.** ** D: Steve Carver. Pam Grier, Margaret Markov, Lucretia Love, Paul Muller. Lavish (by Roger Corman standards) spectacle set in an ancient Rome in which all the gladiators are women. Rather surprisingly pro-feminist point of view, but Grier's and Markov's physiques remain the chief attractions. Retitled NAKED WARRIORS. Techniscope. [R]▼◗

Are Parents People? (1925) **60m.** **½ D: Malcolm St. Clair. Betty Bronson, Adolphe Menjou, Florence Vidor, Lawrence Gray. Enjoyable silent with good cast; innocuous story of young Bronson bringing her estranged parents together.

Are You With It? (1948) **90m.** **½ D: Jack Hively. Donald O'Connor, Olga San Juan, Martha Stewart, Lew Parker. Bright little musical of math-whiz O'Connor joining a carnival.

Argentine Nights (1940) **74m.** **½ D: Albert S. Rogell. Ritz Brothers, Andrews Sisters, Constance Moore, George Reeves, Peggy Moran, Anne Nagel. Boisterous musical comedy with the Ritzes fleeing the U.S., hooking up with troupe of entertainers in Argentina. Incoherent plotwise, but diverting.

Aria (1987-British) **C-90m.** BOMB D: Bill Bryden, Nicolas Roeg, Charles Sturridge, Jean-Luc Godard, Julien Temple, Bruce Beresford, Robert Altman, Franc Roddam, Ken Russell, Derek Jarman. John Hurt, Theresa Russell, Nicola Swain, Jack Kayle, Buck Henry, Anita Morris, Beverly D'Angelo, Elizabeth Hurley, Peter Birch, Julie Hagerty, Genevieve Page, Bridget Fonda, Tilda Swinton, Spencer Leigh, Amy Johnson. Godawful collection of short films, each one supposedly inspired by an operatic aria. Precious few make sense, or even seem to match the music; some are downright embarrassing. Roddam's bittersweet Las Vegas fable (set to *Tristan und Isolde*), Beresford's sweet and simple rendering of Erich Wolfgang Korngold's *Die Totestadt* are among the better segments—relatively speaking. A pitiful waste of talent. Fonda's first film. [R]▼●◗

Ariel (1988-Finnish) **C-74m.** *** D: Aki Kaurismaki. Turo Pajala, Susanna Haavisto, Matti Pellonpää. Surreal, dryly hilarious road movie from one of the most talented directors to emerge on the international film scene in the late 1980s. The scenario chronicles the plight of a mine worker (Pajala) who loses his job, and sets out on a cross-country odyssey.▼

Arise, My Love (1940) **113m.** **½ D: Mitchell Leisen. Claudette Colbert, Ray Milland, Walter Abel, Dennis O'Keefe, Dick Purcell. Reporter Colbert rescues flyer Milland from a Spanish firing squad in the days before WW2 breaks out in Europe. Bright stars make Billy Wilder–Charles Brackett script seem better than it is; Benjamin Glazer and John S. Toldy received Oscars for their original story.

Aristocats, The (1970) **C-78m.** *** D: Wolfgang Reitherman. Voices of Eva Gabor, Phil Harris, Sterling Holloway, Scatman Crothers, Paul Winchell, Lord Tim Hudson, Vito Scotti, Thurl Ravenscroft, Nancy Kulp, Pat Buttram, George Lindsey, Monica Evans, Carole Shelley. A cat and her offspring will inherit a fortune from their mistress, which makes them prime targets for her scheming butler, who'll collect the money if they're out of the picture. Enter Thomas O'Malley Cat (voiced by the inimitable Phil Harris) to the rescue. Derivative of earlier Disney animated features but entertaining just the same. [G]▼●◗

Arizona (1940) **127m.** **½ D: Wesley Ruggles. Jean Arthur, William Holden, Warren William, Porter Hall, Paul Harvey. Lively story of determined woman battling corruption and plundering while trying to settle in new Arizona territory. Well done, but seems to go on forever.▼●

Arizona Bushwhackers (1968) **C-86m.** *½ D: Lesley Selander. Howard Keel, Yvonne De Carlo, John Ireland, Marilyn Maxwell, Scott Brady, Brian Donlevy, Roy Rogers, Jr., James Craig. Confederate spy Keel takes job as sheriff in Arizona and routs Brady, who has been selling weapons to Apaches. Routine Western. Narration by James Cagney. Techniscope.▼●

Arizona Dream (1993-French-U.S.) **C-119m.** **½ D: Emir Kusturica. Johnny Depp, Jerry Lewis, Faye Dunaway, Lili Taylor, Paulina Porizkova, Vincent Gallo, Michael J. Pollard. Odd but intriguing film about a young dreamer (Depp) who's shanghaied into a trip to Arizona, where he catches up with a favorite uncle (Lewis) who wants him to settle down, and falls madly in love with an emotionally frail, childlike woman (Dunaway). European-styled film (from the Yugoslav director of WHEN FATHER WAS AWAY ON BUSINESS) boasts exceptionally good performances—one of Dunaway's best in years, one of Lewis' most impressive—though the often pathetic characters wear out their welcome after a while. Filmed in 1991; 142m. European version earned a brief U.S. theat-

rical release in 1995; shorter version is available on video. [R]▼
Arizona Mission SEE: **Gun the Man Down**
Arizona Raiders (1965) **C-88m.** **½ D: William Witney. Audie Murphy, Michael Dante, Ben Cooper, Buster Crabbe, Gloria Talbott. Murphy is Confederate army officer heading Arizona rangers after Civil War, battling Quantrill's raiders. Techniscope. ▼
Arizona to Broadway (1933) **66m.** ** D: James Tinling. James Dunn, Joan Bennett, Herbert Mundin, Sammy Cohen, Theodore von Eltz, J. Carrol Naish. Joan enlists carnival con-man Dunn's help in reclaiming money lost to gang of swindlers; predictable tale, remade as JITTERBUGS.
Arizonian, The (1935) **75m.** **½ D: Charles Vidor. Richard Dix, Margot Grahame, Preston Foster, Louis Calhern, James Bush, Willie Best, Joseph Sauers (Sawyer), Ray Mayer, Francis Ford. Entertaining B-plus Western programmer with marshal Dix teaming with outlaw Foster to rid town of corrupt Calhern. Script by Dudley Nichols.
Arkansas Traveler, The (1938) **85m.** ** D: Alfred Santell. Bob Burns, Fay Bainter, Jean Parker, Irvin S. Cobb, John Beal, Lyle Talbot, Dickie Moore, Porter Hall. Burns rambles into small town, keeps the local paper afloat, and plays Cupid. Pleasant entertainment relies on the charm of Bazooka Bob.
Arlington Road (1999) **C-119m.** ** D: Mark Pellington. Jeff Bridges, Tim Robbins, Joan Cusack, Hope Davis, Robert Gossett, Spencer Treat Clark, Mason Gamble. Labored conspiracy thriller about a history professor (Bridges) haunted by his wife's death, who becomes suspicious of his new neighbor (Robbins) and starts investigating his curious past. Obvious and overdone. Panavision. [R]▼●◗
Armageddon (1998) **C-151m.** ** D: Michael Bay. Bruce Willis, Billy Bob Thornton, Liv Tyler, Ben Affleck, Will Patton, Peter Stormare, Keith David, Steve Buscemi, Owen Wilson, William Fichtner, Udo Kier, Michael (Clarke) Duncan; narrated by Charlton Heston. Opens with a bang, and sets up an exciting (if improbable) story about NASA and the U.S. government turning to a veteran oil-well driller and his motley team to save humanity by flying to an asteroid and planting a nuclear bomb. After a while it becomes so routine, so predictable, and so redundant that all the fun is drained away. Unrated director's cut runs 153m. Panavision. [PG-13]▼●◗
Armed and Dangerous (1986) **C-88m.** *½ D: Mark L. Lester. John Candy, Eugene Levy, Robert Loggia, Kenneth McMillan, Meg Ryan, Brion James, Jonathan Banks, Don Stroud, Steve Railsback. Lame comedy sticks talented costars with unappealing script about two bozos who wind up working for an armed security company—and tangling with a gangland boss (Loggia, wasted in a stereotype role). Even the chase finale is weak. [PG-13]▼●
Armed Response (1986) **C-85m.** ** D: Fred Olen Ray. David Carradine, Lee Van Cleef, Mako, Lois Hamilton, Ross Hagen, Brent Huff, Laurene Landon, Dick Miller, Michael Berryman. Modest actioner of Carradine and family becoming involved in a Chinatown war over a stolen jade art object. Cheapie benefits from a solid cast of both new and old B-movie favorites. [R]▼●
Armored Attack SEE: **North Star, The**
Armored Car Robbery (1950) **68m.** *** D: Richard Fleischer. Charles McGraw, Adele Jergens, William Talman, Steve Brodie, Douglas Fowley, Don McGuire, Gene Evans. Crackerjack crime drama in which Talman masterminds the title theft; he and his gang are pursued by determined cop McGraw.▼
Armored Command (1961) **99m.** ** D: Byron Haskin. Howard Keel, Tina Louise, Warner Anderson, Burt Reynolds. Bland war film with stars merely going through their paces.▼
Armour of God (1986-Hong Kong) **C-94m.** **½ D: Jackie Chan. Jackie Chan, Rosamund Kwan, Alan Tam, Lola Forna, Maria Dolores. Jackie plays an Indiana Jones—style adventurer who must find legendary suit of armor to rescue his girlfriend from a cult. Enjoyable film marred by slow spots and obviously cheated final stunt. Fight with four leather-clad women is a blast. Watch the outtakes at the end to see the mishap that nearly killed Chan. Followed by a sequel.
Armour of God 2: Operation Condor (1991-Hong Kong) **C-112m.** *** D: Jackie Chan. Jackie Chan, Carol (Dodo) Cheng, Eva Cobo deGarcia, Ikeda Shoko, Aldo Sanchez, Ken Lo. Lavish adventure epic sends Chan off to Europe and Africa in search of huge Nazi gold cache, with three female companions in tow. Crackerjack comedy-adventure filled with great fights, stunts, and slapstick; final battle in a wind tunnel is a knockout. One of Jackie's best. Recut, dubbed, and trimmed to 89m. for 1997 U.S. release as OPERATION CONDOR—which isn't as good as the original. Technovision. [PG-13]▼●
Army of Darkness (1993) **C-81m.** ** D: Sam Raimi. Bruce Campbell, Embeth Davidtz, Marcus Gilbert, Ian Abercrombie, Richard Grove, Michael Earl Reid, Timothy Patrick Quill, Bridget Fonda, Patricia Tallman, Theodore Raimi, Ivan Raimi. Mark Twain's Connecticut Yankee is crossed here with Bob Vila, as a hardware store employee is transported back (with his '73 Olds and a chainsaw) to King Arthur's 14th-century turf. Chiseled-grin Campbell's comic book features serve this movie well, as do a few witty bits and an army of skeletons obvi-

ously inspired by JASON AND THE ARGONAUTS. Doldrums set in when nifty special effects and verbal exchanges are out grabbing a smoke. Campbell also coproduced. Third in the EVIL DEAD series. [R]▼●◗

Arnelo Affair, The (1947) **86m.** ** D: Arch Oboler. John Hodiak, George Murphy, Frances Gifford, Dean Stockwell, Eve Arden. Neglected wife drawn hypnotically to husband's client finally learns of his involvement in girl's murder.

Arnold (1973) **C-100m.** **½ D: Georg Fenady. Stella Stevens, Roddy McDowall, Elsa Lanchester, Shani Wallis, Farley Granger, Victor Buono, John McGiver, Patric Knowles. Bizarre horror comedy features novel deaths and offbeat humor, centering around luscious Stevens' marriage to corpse Norman Stuart. [PG]▼

Around the World (1943) **79m.** ** D: Allan Dwan. Kay Kyser and His Band, Mischa Auer, Joan Davis, Marcy McGuire, Wally Brown, Georgia Carroll, Alan Carney, Ish Kabibble, Robert Armstrong, Barbara Hale, Rosemary La Planche. Hokey fare with Kyser and band traveling the globe, putting on shows for soldiers (and, in a silly subplot, battling Nazis).▼●

Around the World in Eighty Days (1956) **C-167m.** *** D: Michael Anderson. David Niven, Cantinflas, Shirley MacLaine, Robert Newton, Buster Keaton, Jose Greco, John Gielgud, Robert Morley, Marlene Dietrich, all-star cast. Oscar-winning favorite has lost much of its charm over the years, but even so, Mike Todd's version of the Jules Verne tale offers plenty of entertainment, and more than forty cameo appearances offer plenty of star-gazing for buffs. Great Victor Young score was also an Oscar-winner, as was the screenplay (James Poe, John Farrow, S. J. Perelman), cinematography (Lionel Lindon) and editing (Gene Ruggiero, Paul Weatherwax). Remade as a TV miniseries. Todd-AO. ▼●

Around the World in 80 Ways (1986-Australian) **C-90m.** **½ D: Stephen MacLean. Philip Quast, Allan Penney, Diana Davidson, Kelly Dingwall, Gosia Dobrowolska. Off-center Aussie farce about two brothers who contrive to spring their aging dad from his stultifying rest home and take him on an imaginary trip around the world. Wacky, and more than a bit crude at times, but likable throughout. [R]▼●

Around the World Under the Sea (1966) **C-117m.** ** D: Andrew Marton. Lloyd Bridges, Shirley Eaton, David McCallum, Brian Kelly, Keenan Wynn, Marshall Thompson. Several TV personalities appear in this undistinguished underwater tour about testing earthquake warnings. Panavision. ▼

Arousers, The (1970) **C-90m.** *** D: Curtis Hanson. Tab Hunter, Nadyne Turney, Roberta Collins, Isabel Jewell. Little-known, case-history B movie with topnotch performance by Hunter as lonely Venice, California, psychopath who can't make love to women, so he ends up killing them. Unsung thriller packs a wallop; worth searching out. Originally released as SWEET KILL; aka A KISS FROM EDDIE.▼

Arrangement, The (1969) **C-120m.** BOMB D: Elia Kazan. Kirk Douglas, Faye Dunaway, Deborah Kerr, Richard Boone, Hume Cronyn. Muddled, unpleasant film from Kazan's own novel about man fed up with Madison Avenue rat-race who suddenly goes berserk, reevaluates his life, family, surroundings. Good cast down the drain; Kerr's role is particularly demeaning. Panavision. [R]▼

Arrest Bulldog Drummond (1939) **57m.** **½ D: James Hogan. John Howard, Heather Angel, H. B. Warner, George Zucco, E. E. Clive, Reginald Denny. Drummond is framed in the murder of a ray-gun inventor and tracks down the real culprits in this zippy entry.▼

Arrival, The (1996) **C-109m.** *** D: David Twohy. Charlie Sheen, Ron Silver, Lindsay Crouse, Teri Polo, Richard Schiff, Tony T. Johnson, Leon Rippy, Buddy Joe Hooker. Radio astronomer is fired when he tells his boss that he's picked up signals proving there's intelligent life in space. Then he learns that the aliens are already here and up to no good. Clever, intelligent sci-fi thriller of the old school, with many bright ideas; suffers from flaccid pacing in the last third but remains fun throughout. Written by the director. Followed by a video sequel. [PG-13]▼●◗

Arrivederci, Baby! (1966) **C-105m.** *½ D: Ken Hughes. Tony Curtis, Rosanna Schiaffino, Lionel Jeffries, Zsa Zsa Gabor, Nancy Kwan. Comic theme about Bluebeard type who murders his wives for their money has been handled more successfully by others. Not very funny. Panavision. ▼

Arrowhead (1953) **C-105m.** **½ D: Charles Marquis Warren. Charlton Heston, Jack Palance, Katy Jurado, Brian Keith, Milburn Stone. Well-paced account of cavalry scout Heston, who despises Indians, and his response when Apaches return to their reservation and Apache chief Palance arrives on the scene. Watch this, and you will understand why Native Americans have lambasted the manner in which they have been depicted by Hollywood. Keith's first film appearance since his screen debut in 1924, at age three.▼●

Arrow In the Dust (1954) **C-80m.** ** D: Lesley Selander. Sterling Hayden, Coleen Gray, Keith Larsen, Tom Tully. Deserting horse soldier (Hayden) learns sterling virtues when he assumes identity of dead commanding officer, warding off Indian attack on passing wagon train.

Arrowsmith (1931) **99m.** **½ D: John Ford. Ronald Colman, Helen Hayes, Richard Bennett, A. E. Anson, Claude King, Russell Hopton, Myrna Loy, Beulah Bondi, John Qualen. Seriously flawed and illogical adaptation of Sinclair Lewis' novel about a dedicated young research doctor who spends most of his life facing the temptation of selling out. Worth seeing for some fine performances and stirring moments. Screenplay by Sidney Howard (who fared better with Lewis's *Dodsworth*). Originally 110m.; cut to 101m. for reissue, restored in recent years to 99m.▼●

Arruza (1972) **C-75m.** **½ D: Budd Boetticher. Narrated by Anthony Quinn. Interesting documentary, many years in production, about bullfighter Carlos Arruza. Well made, but the impact is nowhere near that of Boetticher's own fictional BULLFIGHTER AND THE LADY. [M/PG]▼

Arsenal Stadium Mystery, The (1939-British) **85m.** *** D: Thorold Dickinson. Leslie Banks, Greta Gynt, Ian MacLean, Liane Linden, Anthony Bushell, Esmond Knight. Who is responsible for the murder of football star Bushell—right in the middle of a game? Eccentric, crackerjack Scotland Yard inspector Banks finds out. Neat little whodunit, and very British.▼

Arsene Lupin (1932) **84m.** *** D: Jack Conway. John Barrymore, Lionel Barrymore, Karen Morley, John Miljan, Henry Armetta, Tully Marshall. Ripe detective yarn set in Paris: John is a gentleman, Lionel a detective, Morley a mystery woman. Which one is the title jewel thief? John and Lionel B. make a marvelous team in their first film together.

Arsenic and Old Lace (1944) **118m.** ***½ D: Frank Capra. Cary Grant, Priscilla Lane, Raymond Massey, Peter Lorre, Jack Carson, Josephine Hull, Jean Adair, James Gleason, Grant Mitchell, John Alexander, Edward Everett Horton. Hilarious adaptation of Joseph Kesselring's hit play (scripted by the Epstein bros.) about two seemingly harmless old ladies who poison lonely gentlemen callers. Frantic cast is excellent, especially Lorre and Massey as unsuspecting murderers holed up in Brooklyn household. Made in 1941. Hull, Adair, and Alexander repeat their Broadway roles. Also shown in computer-colored version.▼●

Artemisia (1997-French-Italian-German) **C-96m.** **½ D: Agnès Merlet. Valentina Cervi, Michel Serrault, Miki Manojlovic, Luca Zingaretti, Emmannuelle Devos, Frederic Pierrot, Yahn Tregouet. Biopic of one of the earliest women painters in history, 17th-century Italian Artemisia Gentileschi. Her desire to express herself is tempered by her relationships with two strong men: her loving but rigid father (Serrault) and her mentor (Manojlovic), whose seduction and rape of his protégée leads to a notorious trial. An accomplished if uninspired depiction of this historical figure, whose fate is still debated by scholars and feminists. [R]▼●◗

Arthur (1981) **C-97m.** ***½ D: Steve Gordon. Dudley Moore, Liza Minnelli, John Gielgud, Geraldine Fitzgerald, Jill Eikenberry, Stephen Elliott, Ted Ross, Barney Martin. Winning 1930s-style comedy, written by first-timer Gordon, who died the following year. Spoiled millionaire must choose between continued wealth (in a planned marriage) and true love (with working-class waitress Minnelli). More genuine laughs than most recent comedies put together, and a memorable, Oscar-winning performance by Gielgud as a protective, acid-tongued valet; title song "Best That You Can Do (Arthur's Theme)" also earned a statuette. Followed by ARTHUR 2: ON THE ROCKS. [PG]▼●◗

Arthur 2: On the Rocks (1988) **C-110m.** ** D: Bud Yorkin. Dudley Moore, Liza Minnelli, John Gielgud, Geraldine Fitzgerald, Stephen Elliott, Paul Benedict, Cynthia Sikes, Kathy Bates, Jack Gilford, Ted Ross, Daniel Greene. Arthur goes broke and his wife wants to adopt a baby. The cast tries, and there are scattered laughs, but this schmaltzy sequel (executive produced by Moore) is a disappointment. Gielgud "appears" briefly as a ghost. That's Dudley's then-wife, Brogan Lane, as Liza's hash-slinging colleague. [PG]▼●◗

Arthur Miller's "The American Clock" (1993) **C-120m. TVM** D: Bob Clark. Roberts Blossom, Eddie Bracken, Jim Dale, Loren Dean, Yaphet Kotto, Mary McDonnell, Darren McGavin, Rebecca Miller, Estelle Parsons, John Randolph, Tony Roberts, Kelly Preston. Impressive cast adds luster to Miller's episodic theatrical piece about the Great Depression, as brought to life through the remembrances of Randolph (who originated his part on stage) and McGavin. An entry in Steven Spielberg and TNT's admirable if eclectic "Screenworks" series. Made for cable. Average.

Arthur the King (1985) **C-150m. TVM** D: Clive Donner. Malcolm McDowell, Candice Bergen, Edward Woodward, Dyan Cannon, Lucy Gutteridge, Rupert Everett, Liam Neeson, Michael Gough, Maryam D'Abo. The Arthurian saga, filtered through Lewis Carroll and a contemporary twist as Cannon tumbles down a rabbit hole into Camelot while wandering around Stonehenge. A bizarre adventure (glom Candice's fright wig!) and an unintentional hoot that sat for nearly three years before initial airing. Video title: MERLIN AND THE SWORD; cut to 94m. Below average.▼

Article 99 (1992) **C-99m.** **½ D: Howard Deutch. Ray Liotta, Kiefer Sutherland, Forest Whitaker, Lea Thompson, John C. McGinley, John Mahoney, Keith David, Kathy Baker, Eli Wallach, Noble Willingham, Julie Bovasso, Troy Evans, Lynne Thigpen, Jeffrey Tambor, Rutanya Alda. Heartfelt but disappointingly one-dimensional, "lighthearted" exposé of Veterans' Administration hospital abuse, focusing on spunky surgeon Liotta and his compatriots, who try to thwart the bureaucracy; Sutherland is the new doc on the block. Hijinks are more reminiscent of DOCTOR IN THE HOUSE than THE HOSPITAL—and that's the problem. [R]▼●

Artists & Models (1937) **97m.** **½ D: Raoul Walsh. Jack Benny, Ida Lupino, Judy Canova, Gail Patrick, Richard Arlen, Martha Raye, Connee Boswell, Ethel Clayton. Lupino pretends to be a socialite in flimsy plot with uncharacteristic Benny and songs "Stop You're Breaking My Heart," "Whispers in the Dark." Vintage fun.

Artists and Models (1955) **C-109m.** *** D: Frank Tashlin. Dean Martin, Jerry Lewis, Shirley MacLaine, Dorothy Malone, Eva Gabor, Anita Ekberg. Cartoonist Martin uses Lewis's far-out dreams as inspiration for his comic strips in this deliciously garish Technicolor outing. VistaVision. ▼●

Artists and Models Abroad (1938) **90m.** *** D: Mitchell Leisen. Jack Benny, Joan Bennett, Mary Boland, Charley Grapewin, Yacht Club Boys, Joyce Compton. Breezy, entertaining froth of musical troupe stranded in Paris, perennially saved by conniving boss Benny. Yacht Club Boys sing incredible song, "You're Broke, You Dope."

Art of Love, The (1965) **C-99m.** ** D: Norman Jewison. James Garner, Dick Van Dyke, Elke Sommer, Angie Dickinson, Ethel Merman, Carl Reiner. Ordinary comedy set in France, with a bemused cast headed by Van Dyke as a struggling artist who fakes death to increase the value of his work. Sommer is his virtuous girl, boisterous Merman a local madam with a yen for singing.

Ascent, The (1994) **C-96m.** ** D: Donald Shebib. Vincent Spano, Ben Cross, Tony Lo Bianco, Rachel Ward, Mark Ingall, John De Veillers. Beautiful scenery cannot save this unexceptional WW2 drama, set in a POW camp where Italian prisoners challenge their British captors to a race in which both sides will scale nearby Mount Kenya. If they win, they will regain a measure of honor; however, freedom-loving prisoner Spano is intent on escaping. Based on a true story. Panavision. [PG]▼

As Good As It Gets (1997) **C-138m.** ***½ D: James L. Brooks. Jack Nicholson, Helen Hunt, Greg Kinnear, Cuba Gooding, Jr., Skeet Ulrich, Shirley Knight, Yeardley Smith, Lupe Ontiveros, Bibi Osterwald, Randall Batinkoff, Brian Doyle-Murray. Professional malcontent (and full-time phobic) Nicholson is unavoidably drawn into the lives of his favorite waitress and his gay next-door neighbor. Gradually, and against his own judgment, he begins to show signs of humanity. Wonderful comedy-drama (written by Mark L. Andrus and Brooks) takes the viewer on an emotional journey, with laughs and tears along the way. Both Nicholson and Hunt won Oscars for their roles. Writer-directors Harold Ramis, Lawrence Kasdan, Shane Black, and Todd Solondz all have small roles. [PG-13]▼●◗

Ashanti (1979) **C-117m.** ** D: Richard Fleischer. Michael Caine, Peter Ustinov, Beverly Johnson, Kabir Bedi, Omar Sharif, Rex Harrison, William Holden. Beautiful wife (Johnson) of missionary-doctor Caine is kidnapped by slave trader Ustinov, prompting hot pursuit through the mideast. Tepid adventure yarn, despite great cast and promising story elements. Aka ASHANTI: LAND OF NO MERCY. Panavision. [R]▼

Ashes and Diamonds (1958-Polish) **96m.** ***½ D: Andrzej Wajda. Zbigniew Cybulski, Ewa Krzyzanowska, Adam Pawlikowski, Bogumil Kobiela, Waclaw Zastrzezynski. Stark, intelligent, perceptive account of the Resistance movement in Poland during the closing days of WW2. Cybulski, the Polish James Dean, came into his own with his portrayal of a young Resistance fighter. The last of Wajda's War trilogy, following A GENERATION and KANAL.▼●

Ash Wednesday (1973) **C-99m.** BOMB D: Larry Peerce. Elizabeth Taylor, Henry Fonda, Helmut Berger, Keith Baxter, Margaret Blye. Liz undergoes a facelift to regain her youth, but she still looks older than Fonda. Sit through this one and you'll need surgery on your posterior. [R]▼

As If It Were Raining (1963-French) **85m.** ** D: Jose Monter. Eddie Constantine, Henri Cogan, Elisa Montes, Jose Nieto, Sylvia Solar. Constantine is at liberty in Spain, enmeshed in an embezzlement scheme; wooden yarn.▼

Ask Any Girl (1959) **C-101m.** *** D: Charles Walters. David Niven, Shirley MacLaine, Gig Young, Rod Taylor, Jim Backus, Elisabeth Fraser. Effervescent gloss of naive MacLaine coming to N.Y., discovering most men have lecherous designs on girls; she wants a husband, however. CinemaScope. ▼

As Long As They're Happy (1957-British) **C-76m.** *½ D: J. Lee Thompson. Janette Scott, Jean Carson, Diana Dors, Hugh McDermott, Jack Buchanan. Mini-musical involving daughter of staid British stockholder who falls for visiting song-and-dance man.

Aspen Extreme (1993) **C-115m.** *½ D: Patrick Hasburgh. Paul Gross, Peter Berg, Finola Hughes, Teri Polo, William Russ, Trevor Eve, Martin Kemp, Stewart Finley-McLennan, Tony Griffin, William McNamara, Andy Mill, Nicolette Scorsese. For two Detroit buddies, the Motown slopes are not enough—so it's off to the Colorado Rockies for sex, tragedy, and skiing success amid the lifestyles of the rich and banal. Satisfactory outdoor scenes, but little else beyond jarring lapses in plot continuity. Hollywood Pictures, which opened this a week after ALIVE, must have gotten a deal on some parkas. [PG-13]▼●

Asphalt Jungle, The (1950) **112m.** ***½ D: John Huston. Sterling Hayden, Louis Calhern, Jean Hagen, James Whitmore, Sam Jaffe, John McIntire, Marc Lawrence, Marilyn Monroe. The plotting of a crime, and the gathering of a gang to pull it off; a taut, realistic film full of fine characterizations (especially Jaffe, and Monroe in a memorable bit). A model of its kind, frequently copied, and remade no less than three times (as THE BADLANDERS, CAIRO, COOL BREEZE). Scripted by Ben Maddow and Huston, from a W. R. Burnett novel. Also shown in computer-colored version.▼●

Asphyx, The (1972-British) **C-99m.** *** D: Peter Newbrook. Robert Stephens, Robert Powell, Jane Lapotaire, Ralph Arliss, Alex Scott. Good fantasy plot has 19th-century scientist Stephens isolating the Asphyx, the spirit of death that appears around a person's body at times of imminent danger. In so doing, he becomes immortal. Lapotaire, who scored internationally on stage in *Piaf*, appears here as Stephens's daughter. Aka SPIRIT OF THE DEAD. Todd-AO 35. [PG]▼◗

Assam Garden, The (1985-British) **C-92m.** *** D: Mary McMurray. Deborah Kerr, Madhur Jaffrey, Alec McCowen, Zia Mohyeddin, Anton Lesser. Quietly rewarding drama with Kerr in her best role in years (and first theatrical release since 1969's THE ARRANGEMENT), as a stuffy, long-repressed, just-widowed woman. While tending her husband's garden and dealing with his memory, she strikes up a curious complex friendship with Indian neighbor Jaffrey.

Assassin, The (1953-British) **90m.** ** D: Ralph Thomas. Richard Todd, Eva Bartok, George Coulouris, Margot Grahame. Todd is detective on manhunt in postwar Venice; usual murders and romance result.

Assassin, The (1961-Italian) **105m.** **½ D: Elio Petri. Marcello Mastroianni, Salvo Randone, Micheline Presle, Cristina Gajoni. Engaging study of scoundrel Mastroianni implicated in a murder, broken by the police, proven innocent, with a wry ending.

Assassin (1973-British) **C-83m.** ** D: Peter Crane. Ian Hendry, Edward Judd, Frank Windsor, Ray Brooks. Routine cold war espionage film, or, the loneliness of the long-distance assassin.

Assassination (1987) **C-88m.** *½ D: Peter Hunt. Charles Bronson, Jill Ireland, Stephen Elliott, Jan Gan Boyd, Randy Brooks, Erik Stern, Michael Ansara, James Staley, Kathryn Leigh Scott. Bronson is a Secret Service bodyguard, Ireland the wife of the President, in this ridiculous, slapdash political thriller with more explosions than anything else. The First Lady is referred to here as One Mama! [PG-13]▼●

Assassination Bureau, The (1969-British) **C-110m.** *** D: Basil Dearden. Oliver Reed, Diana Rigg, Telly Savalas, Curt Jurgens, Clive Revill. Fun tale based on Jack London story of secret club that eliminates unworthy people, until greed more than dedication begins to cloud the operation. [M]▼●

Assassination of Trotsky, The (1972-French-Italian-British) **C-103m.** **½ D: Joseph Losey. Richard Burton, Alain Delon, Romy Schneider, Valentina Cortese. Last days of Russian rebel make for uneven melodrama of hunters and hunted. Burton's performance is strong but unconvincing. [R]▼●

Assassin of Youth (1937) **80m.** *½ D: Elmer Clifton. Luana Walters, Arthur Gardner, Dorothy Short, Earl Dwire, Fern Emmett. Another hokey marijuana exposé (this one a notch above the rest), about some fun-loving teens who smoke one too many reefers at one too many reefer parties. An intrepid investigative reporter poses as a soda jerk to expose their decadence. The short film within a film, THE MARIJUANA MENACE, is a hoot.▼

Assassins (1995) **C-132m.** ** D: Richard Donner. Sylvester Stallone, Antonio Banderas, Julianne Moore, Anatoly Davydov. World's number one paid hit man is dogged at every turn by a young rival. Then he (inexplicably) falls in love with a female "mark." Stallone is in good form, but this big-scale action yarn/star vehicle suffers from rampant stupidity. [R]▼●◗

Assault (1971) SEE: **In the Devil's Garden**

Assault, The (1986-Dutch) **C-149m.** ***½ D: Fons Rademakers. Derek de Lint, Marc van Uchelen, Monique van de Ven, John Kraaykamp, Huub van der Lubbe, Elly Weller. A 12-year-old's family is liquidated in the final days of WW2, and he represses his memories and feelings while growing into manhood. Evocative performances and fine direction enhance a story that is both truthful and heartbreaking. Long, but suspenseful, with many thought-provoking moments. Screenplay by Gerard Soeteman based on a novel by Harry Mulisch. Winner of the Best Foreign Language Film Oscar. A film not easy to forget. [PG]▼

Assault Force SEE: **ffolkes**

Assault of the Rebel Girls SEE: **Cuban Rebel Girls**

Assault on Agathon (1975-British-Greek) **C-96m.** **½ D: Laslo Benedek. Nico Minardos, Nina van Pallandt, Marianne Faithfull, John Woodvine. Tepid drug-dealing thriller with spectacular Greek sce-

nery overshadowing CIA man Minardos' efforts to nab Mr. Big. [PG]▼
Assault on a Queen (1966) **C-106m.** **½ D: Jack Donohue. Frank Sinatra, Virna Lisi, Tony Franciosa, Richard Conte, Alf Kjellin, Errol John, Murray Matheson, Reginald Denny. Sloppy Sinatra vehicle about big heist of H.M.S. *Queen Mary*'s vault. Script by Rod Serling from novel by Jack Finney. Panavision. ▼
Assault on Precinct 13 (1976) **C-90m.** ***½ D: John Carpenter. Austin Stoker, Darwin Joston, Laurie Zimmer, Martin West, Tony Burton, Nancy Loomis, Kim Richards, Henry Brandon. A nearly deserted L.A. police station finds itself under a state of siege by a youth gang in this riveting thriller, a modern-day paraphrase of Howard Hawks' RIO BRAVO. Writer-director Carpenter also did the eerie music score for this knockout. Panavision. [R] ▼●◗
Assignment, The (1977-Swedish) **C-94m.** **½ D: Mats Arehn. Christopher Plummer, Thomas Hellberg, Carolyn Seymour, Fernando Rey, Per Oscarsson, Walter Gotell. Modest drama of Swedish diplomat sent to mediate turbulent political situation in Latin American country.▼
Assignment, The (1997) **C-115m.** **½ D: Christian Duguay. Aidan Quinn, Donald Sutherland, Ben Kingsley, Liliana Komorowska, Céline Bonnier, Claudia Ferri, Vlasta Vrana, Von Flores, Al Waxman. Well-directed, violent thriller with Quinn in a dual role as notorious terrorist Carlos the Jackal and a lookalike U.S. naval officer recruited to participate in an elaborate scheme to capture the terrorist. Sutherland is the CIA man who is obsessed with nabbing Carlos. [R]▼●◗
Assignment In Brittany (1943) **96m.** ** D: Jack Conway. Pierre (Jean-Pierre) Aumont, Susan Peters, Richard Whorf, Margaret Wycherly, Signe Hasso, Reginald Owen. Aumont is lookalike for Nazi leader, uses this to his advantage working for French underground; patriotic WW2 melodrama.
Assignment K (1968-British) **97m.** *½ D: Val Guest. Stephen Boyd, Camilla Sparv, Michael Redgrave, Leo McKern, Jeremy Kemp, Robert Hoffman. Still another spy drama—this one a dull story about secret agent's disillusionment upon discovering that his girl and seemingly everyone he knows is a double agent. Techniscope.
Assignment: Kill Castro SEE: **Cuba Crossing**
Assignment—Paris (1952) **85m.** ** D: Robert Parrish. Dana Andrews, Marta Toren, George Sanders, Audrey Totter. Fitfully entertaining drama of reporter Andrews trying to link together threads of plot between Communist countries against the West. Filmed in Paris.
Assignment Redhead SEE: **Million Dollar Manhunt**
Assignment Terror (1970-Spanish-German-Italian) **C-86m.** BOMB D: Tulio Demicheli. Michael Rennie, Karin Dor, Craig Hill, Paul Naschy, Patty Shepard. Alien invader Rennie revives various earth monsters (including ersatz Frankenstein, Dracula, and Mummy) but socially conscious werewolf (Naschy) helps to combat his evil forces. Unwatchable stupidity. Aka DRACULA VS. FRANKENSTEIN. Techniscope.▼
Assignment to Kill (1968) **C-102m.** ** D: Sheldon Reynolds. Patrick O'Neal, Joan Hackett, John Gielgud, Herbert Lom, Eric Portman, Peter Van Eyck, Oscar Homolka. Private eye checks out shady corporation in Switzerland in this unrewarding thriller from the writer-director of TV's *Foreign Intrigue* series. Panavision.
Assisi Underground, The (1985) **C-115m.** ** D: Alexander Ramati. Ben Cross, James Mason, Irene Papas, Maximilian Schell, Edmund Purdom, Karl Heinz Hackl, Delia Boccardo, Riccardo Cucciolla. Good cast is wasted in this overblown thriller, with a based-on-fact scenario. Cross plays a courageous young minister in charge of disguising Jews in Assisi, Italy, during WW2. Mason's last film. Originally released at 178m. [PG]▼
Associate, The (1996) **C-114m.** **½ D: Donald Petrie. Whoopi Goldberg, Dianne Wiest, Eli Wallach, Tim Daly, Bebe Neuwirth, Austin Pendleton, Lainie Kazan, Colleen Camp Wilson. Wall St. whiz Whoopi has hit the glass ceiling at her company, so she breaks off on her own, but can't make it without inventing a white male partner. Designed as a comedy, but laughs are few. Still, it's an interesting look at corporate America and the obstacles and slights that women and minorities endure. Wiest is terrific. Remake of the 1979 French film L'ASSOCIE; based on the novel *El Socio.* [PG-13]▼●◗
As Summers Die (1986) **C-87m. TVM** D: Jean-Claude Tramont. Scott Glenn, Jamie Lee Curtis, Bette Davis, John Randolph, Penny Fuller, Beah Richards, Ron O'Neal, John McIntire. Louisiana, 1959. Smalltown lawyer Glenn clashes with powerful local family when he tries to help a destitute black woman save her property. He finds unlikely allies in an eccentric old lady and her niece, both members of the greedy clan. Leisurely adaptation of Winston Groom's novel. The old Davis fire returns in her few scenes. Average.▼
As the Sea Rages (1960) **74m.** ** D: Horst Haechler. Maria Schell, Cliff Robertson, Cameron Mitchell. Seaman Robertson arrives in Greece planning a sponge-diving business and meets resistance from townfolk and the elements; muddled script.
Astonished Heart, The (1950-British) **92m.**

**½ D: Terence Fisher, Anthony Darnborough. Noel Coward, Celia Johnson, Margaret Leighton, Joyce Carey. Drawing-room melodrama about a married psychiatrist who succumbs to the wiles of another woman—an old schoolmate of his wife's—with unhappy results. One of Coward's lesser stories.

Astounding She-Monster, The (1958) **60m.** BOMB D: Ronnie Ashcroft. Robert Clarke, Kenne Duncan, Shirley Kilpatrick, Marilyn Harvey, Jeanne Tatum, Ewing Brown. Awesomely cheap little film about an apparently evil female alien who kills with a touch, interacting with kidnappers and the kidnappees out in the woods. Has developed a kind of perverse fan following. ALIENATOR is a semi-remake.▼

Astronaut's Wife, The (1999) **C-109m.** *½ D: Rand Ravich. Johnny Depp, Charlize Theron, Joe Morton, Clea DuVall, Donna Murphy, Nick Cassavetes, Samantha Eggar, Gary Grubbs, Blair Brown, Tom Noonan. Happily married astronaut has a strange experience during a space mission. Has he changed somehow, or is it his young wife's imagination? ROSEMARY'S BABY-style thriller is just a big tease; sluggish and unsatisfying, with an especially stupid finale. [R]▼●◗

Astro-Zombies (1967) **C-83m.** BOMB D: Ted V. Mikels. Wendell Corey, John Carradine, Tom Pace, Joan Patrick, Rafael Campos. Demented Carradine creates title monsters in yet another nominee for worst picture of all time. Script by Mikels and Wayne Rogers (the same). [PG] ▼

Asylum (1972-British) **C-92m.** *** D: Roy Ward Baker. Barbara Parkins, Sylvia Syms, Richard Todd, Peter Cushing, Robert Powell, Barry Morse, Britt Ekland, Herbert Lom, Patrick Magee, Charlotte Rampling. Four fun chillers by Robert Bloch woven into puzzle that is solved at the conclusion of the fourth tale. Reissued in 1980 as HOUSE OF CRAZIES, trimmed to 86m. [PG]▼●

As You Desire Me (1932) **71m.** **½ D: George Fitzmaurice. Greta Garbo, Melvyn Douglas, Erich von Stroheim, Hedda Hopper, Owen Moore. OK version of Pirandello play about amnesiac (Garbo) returning to husband she doesn't really remember. Never as compelling as it should be.▼

As You Like It (1936-British) **96m.** *** D: Paul Czinner. Elisabeth Bergner, Laurence Olivier, Sophie Stewart, Henry Ainley, Leon Quartermaine, Felix Aylmer. Olivier is solid (and handsome) as Orlando in his first attempt at the Bard on celluloid, but Bergner's Rosalind is more a matter of taste. Overall, an enjoyable production of this Shakespeare comedy. ▼●◗

As Young As You Feel (1951) **77m.** **½ D: Harmon Jones. Monty Woolley, Thelma Ritter, David Wayne, Jean Peters, Constance Bennett, Marilyn Monroe, Allyn Joslyn, Albert Dekker. Printing company employee Woolley is "retired" when he turns 65, and he just won't sit still for it. Amiable satire of corporate bureaucracy, with a first-rate cast, based on a story by Paddy Chayefsky.▼

At Close Range (1986) **C-115m.** **½ D: James Foley. Sean Penn, Christopher Walken, Christopher Penn, Mary Stuart Masterson, Millie Perkins, Eileen Ryan, Alan Autry, Candy Clark, Tracey Walter, David Strathairn, Crispin Glover, Kiefer Sutherland. Brooding, but curiously unmoving, story about teenage half-brothers who first get to know their no-account father, and come to realize what a dangerous person he is. Downbeat drama is marked by good acting, thoughtful filmmaking, but emotional impact is muted. Based on a true incident. Super 35. [R]▼●

At First Sight (1998) **C-128m.** **½ D: Irwin Winkler. Val Kilmer, Mira Sorvino, Kelly McGillis, Steven Weber, Bruce Davison, Nathan Lane, Ken Howard, Diana Krall. Driven N.Y.C. career woman falls in love with a self-reliant blind man. Then she finds a doctor who can restore his sight—but is this necessarily a good thing? Overtly soapy romantic drama doesn't pretend to be anything but what it is, and the stars are likable . . . but it goes on too long. Based on a true story chronicled by Dr. Oliver Sacks (AWAKENINGS). Having a George Shearing cut on the soundtrack is a nice touch. [PG-13]▼●◗

At Gunpoint (1955) **C-81m.** **½ D: Alfred L. Werker. Fred MacMurray, Dorothy Malone, Walter Brennan, Tommy Rettig, Jack Lambert. MacMurray is well suited to role of peace-loving man drawn into gunplay by taunting outlaws. CinemaScope.▼

Athena (1954) **C-96m.** **½ D: Richard Thorpe. Jane Powell, Debbie Reynolds, Edmund Purdom, Vic Damone, Louis Calhern, Evelyn Varden, Steve Reeves, Linda Christian. Back Bay lawyer (Purdom) and singer (Damone) romance two sisters living with eccentric grandparents. Wispy plot, average tunes.▼●

Atlantic City (1944) **87m.** **½ D: Ray McCarey. Brad Taylor (Stanley Brown), Constance Moore, Charley Grapewin, Jerry Colonna, Adele Mara, Paul Whiteman & Orchestra, Louis Armstrong & Orchestra, Buck and Bubbles, Belle Baker, Dorothy Dandridge, Joe Frisco. Plethora of good musical numbers compensates for unoriginal plot about promoter who turns the Atlantic City pier into "the playground of America," starting pre-WW1. Taylor, who took his name from this (he was Stanley Brown at Columbia), and Moore are Republic Pictures' John Payne-Alice Faye counterparts.

Atlantic City (1980-Canadian-French)

C-104m. **** D: Louis Malle. Burt Lancaster, Susan Sarandon, Kate Reid, Michel Piccoli, Hollis McLaren, Robert Joy, Al Waxman, Wally Shawn. Rich character study of a city in transition, focusing on small-time losers who've stayed there too long and big-time dreamers who are just arriving. European in its ambience and storytelling approach, though its setting is an American resort. Lancaster gives one of his finest performances as an aging two-bit hood who's all style and no substance. Screenplay by John Guare. First shown abroad with the title ATLANTIC CITY, U.S.A. [R]▼●

Atlantis, the Lost Continent (1961) **C-90m.** *½ D: George Pal. Anthony Hall, Joyce Taylor, John Dall, Frank de Kova. Famed sci-fi producer George Pal's worst film is set on the island of Atlantis, in the time of ancient Greece. Heroic young fisherman becomes involved in tedious intrigue before, finally, the place sinks. Lots of stock footage, poor effects. Occasionally funny—but not on purpose. ▼●

Atlas (1961) **C-80m.** ** D: Roger Corman. Michael Forest, Frank Wolff, Barboura Morris, Walter Maslow, Christos Exarchos. Praximedes convinces Olympic champion Atlas to represent him in battle, but Atlas eventually fights for the common folk. Slightly hilarious low-budget nonsense, filmed in Greece. VistaScope. ▼

At Long Last Love (1975) **C-118m.** *½ D: Peter Bogdanovich. Burt Reynolds, Cybill Shepherd, Madeline Kahn, Duilio Del Prete, Eileen Brennan, John Hillerman, Mildred Natwick. Burt and Cybill are no Fred and Ginger. Bogdanovich's homage to 1930s Hollywood musicals has everything money can buy—including lavish sets and a Cole Porter score—but lacks the proper stars to put it over. Reedited (and ostensibly improved) for TV by the director; that version runs 115m. [G]

Atoll K SEE: **Utopia**

Atomic Brain, The SEE: **Monstrosity**

Atomic Cafe, The (1982) **88m.** *** D: Kevin Rafferty, Jayne Loader, Pierce Rafferty. Consistently chilling, occasionally hilarious, arguably monotonal compilation of U.S. government and "educational" propaganda shows how Americans of the 1950s Learned to Stop Worrying and Love the Bomb. One-of-a-kind is undeniably provocative, to say nothing of topical, but argues its point a little longer than necessary.▼

Atomic City, The (1952) **85m.** **½ D: Jerry Hopper. Gene Barry, Nancy Gates, Lydia Clarke, Lee Aaker. Tightly knit caper involving kidnapping of atomic scientist's son, well played by young Aaker.▼

Atomic Kid, The (1954) **86m.** *½ D: Leslie Martinson. Mickey Rooney, Robert Strauss, Elaine Davis, Bill Goodwin. Rooney survives desert atomic blast, discovering he's radioactive. Slight spy comedy. Davis was Mrs. Rooney at the time. Story by Blake Edwards.▼

Atomic Man, The (1955-British) **78m.** ** D: Ken Hughes. Gene Nelson, Faith Domergue, Joseph Tomelty, Peter Arne. Bland narrative of reporter and girlfriend involved in a mystery in which title character's experiments with radioactive materials have put him a few seconds into the future (allowing him to answer questions before they are asked). Still, this is basically a spy melodrama.▼

Atomic Monster SEE: **Man-Made Monster**

Atomic Submarine, The (1959) **72m.** ** D: Spencer Bennet. Arthur Franz, Dick Foran, Brett Halsey, Tom Conway, Bob Steele, Victor Varconi, Joi Lansing. In the near future, title sub investigates mysterious goings-on in the Arctic Circle. The culprit is an underwater flying saucer piloted by an alien! Typical Alex Gordon production, boasting lots of familiar character actors, is appealing and atmospheric. For diehard buffs.▼●◗

Atonement of Gosta Berling, The (1924-Swedish) **91m.** *** D: Mauritz Stiller. Lars Hanson, Greta Garbo, Ellen Cederstrom, Mona Martenson, Jenny Hasselquist, Gerda Lundequist. Memorable drama, from the Selma Lagerlof novel, about a defrocked priest (Hanson) and his love for a young married woman (a pleasingly plump Garbo, in the role which brought her to world attention). Stiller was, of course, Garbo's discoverer and mentor. Several longer versions run between 105m. and 165m. Aka GOSTA BERLING'S SAGA, THE SAGA OF GOSTA BERLING, THE LEGEND OF GOSTA BERLING, and THE STORY OF GOSTA BERLING.▼

Ator, the Fighting Eagle (1983) **C-100m.** BOMB D: David Hills. Miles O'Keeffe, Sabrina Siani, Ritza Brown, Edmund Purdom, Laura Gemser. Ridiculous Italian-made imitation of CONAN THE BARBARIAN has muscular O'Keeffe as the mythical title warrior, with beautiful blonde Siani along for the ride on his trek against evil. Followed by 2 sequels: THE BLADE MASTER and ATOR III: THE FIGHTING EAGLE aka QUEST FOR THE MIGHTY SWORD. [PG]▼

Ator the Invincible SEE: **Blade Master, The**

At Play in the Fields of the Lord (1991) **C-187m.** *** D: Hector Babenco. Tom Berenger, Aidan Quinn, Kathy Bates, John Lithgow, Daryl Hannah, Tom Waits, Stenio Garcia, Nelson Xavier. Long, at first lumbering, but ultimately powerful rainforest epic of two Protestant missionaries (one a charlatan, one sincere) who end up doing about equal damage to the jungle Indians they are supposed to serve. Faithful, well-cast film of Peter Mathiessen's great (though admittedly difficult) novel; pace picks up a lot in the second half, leading to memorable finale. [R]▼●

Atragon (1963-Japanese) **96m.** ** D: Ishiro Honda. Tadao Takashima, Yoko Fujiyama, Yu Fujiki, Horisho Koizumi. World is threatened by undersea kingdom in this juvenile sci-fi adventure, with enjoyable (if not believable) special effects. Title refers to giant submarine rather than a monster. Tohoscope.

At Sword's Point (1952) **C-81m.** **½ D: Lewis Allen. Cornel Wilde, Maureen O'Hara, Robert Douglas, Dan O'Herlihy, Alan Hale Jr., Blanche Yurka. Silly but likable variation on THE THREE MUSKETEERS with energetic cast, vivid technicolor settings.▼●

Attack (1956) **107m.** *** D: Robert Aldrich. Jack Palance, Eddie Albert, Lee Marvin, Robert Strauss, Richard Jaeckel, Buddy Ebsen, William Smithers. Reenactment of the Battle of the Bulge, emphasizing a group of American soldiers "led" by cowardly captain Albert; tightly directed, avoids war movie clichés. ●

Attack and Retreat SEE: **Italiano Brava Gente**

Attack Force Z (1981-Australian-Taiwanese) **C-84m.** **½ D: Tim Burstall. John Phillip Law, Sam Neill, Mel Gibson, Chris Haywood, John Waters. Taut little war drama: commandos set out to rescue survivors of a plane crash on a Japanese-held island during WW2.▼

Attack of the Crab Monsters (1957) **68m.** ** D: Roger Corman. Richard Garland, Pamela Duncan, Russell Johnson, Leslie Bradley, Mel Welles, Ed Nelson. People are trapped on a shrinking island by intelligent, brain-eating giant crabs. Interesting early Corman thriller is hampered by a low budget—and some very silly monsters—but Charles B. Griffith's script has many ingenious ideas.▼

Attack of the 50 Ft. Woman (1958) **66m.** BOMB D: Nathan Juran. Allison Hayes, William Hudson, Yvette Vickers, Roy Gordon. A harridan with a philandering husband has an alien encounter and grows to mammoth proportions. Hilariously awful sci-fi with some of the funniest special effects of all time. Remade for TV in 1993 with Daryl Hannah.▼●

Attack of the Giant Leeches (1959) **62m.** *½ D: Bernard L. Kowalski. Ken Clark, Yvette Vickers, Jan Shepard, Michael Emmet, Gene Roth, Bruno Ve Sota. Giant leeches in back waters of a Southern swamp take prisoners and suck their blood. Ludicrous hybrid of white trash and monster genres; screenplay by actor Leo Gordon. Aka THE GIANT LEECHES.▼

Attack of the Killer Tomatoes! (1980) **C-87m.** *½ D: John De Bello. David Miller, Sharon Taylor, George Wilson, Jack Riley, Rock Peace, The San Diego Chicken. Title and opening credits are the funniest things in this low-budget spoof of low-budget science-fiction, which cracks its one joke and then beats it to death for another eighty-five minutes. A staple at Worst Film Festivals, but nowhere nearly as hilarious as movies that aren't supposed to be. Followed by RETURN OF THE KILLER TOMATOES!, KILLER TOMATOES STRIKE BACK, KILLER TOMATOES EAT FRANCE!, and an animated TV series. [PG]▼●

Attack of the Mayan Mummy (1963) **77m.** BOMB D: Jerry Warren. Richard Webb, Nina Knight, John Burton, Steve Conte. Scientist gets patient to revert to former life and reveal site of ancient tomb in this grade-Z outing, comprised largely of Mexican horror-film footage.▼

Attack of the Puppet People (1958) **78m.** *½ D: Bert I. Gordon. John Agar, John Hoyt, June Kenney, Scott Peters. Low-class shocker about mad scientist who shrinks people; good performance by Hoyt, otherwise predictable and amateurish.▼

Attack of the Rebel Girls SEE: **Cuban Rebel Girls**

Attack on the Iron Coast (1968) **C-89m.** **½ D: Paul Wendkos. Lloyd Bridges, Andrew Keir, Sue Lloyd, Mark Eden, Maurice Denham. Canadian officer Bridges leads commando attack on German naval base in France during WW2. Capable if unsurprising action film, made in England. [G]

Attempt to Kill (1961-British) **57m.** ** D: Royston Morley. Derek Farr, Tony Wright, Richard Pearson, Freda Jackson. Mild Edgar Wallace entry, salvaged by superior cast in predictable Scotland Yard manhunt caper.

Attention Bandits SEE: **Bandits**▼

At the Circus (1939) **87m.** **½ D: Edward Buzzell. Groucho, Chico and Harpo Marx, Margaret Dumont, Eve Arden, Nat Pendleton, Kenny Baker, Fritz Feld, Florence Rice. Not top-grade Marx Brothers, but some good scenes as they save circus from bankruptcy. Highlight: Groucho singing "Lydia the Tattooed Lady."▼●

At the Earth's Core (1976-British) **C-90m.** **½ D: Kevin Connor. Doug McClure, Peter Cushing, Caroline Munro, Cy Grant, Godfrey James, Sean Lynch. Colorful fantasy-adventure based on Edgar Rice Burroughs' novel. Inventor Cushing and protégé McClure bore their way from Victorian England to the center of the earth and encounter a lost world of prehistoric beasts and subhuman warriors. Competent special effects make this yarn palatable. [PG]▼

Attic, The (1979) **C-97m.** **½ D: George Edwards. Carrie Snodgress, Ray Milland, Rosemary Murphy, Ruth Cox, Francis Bay,

Marjorie Eaton. Good cast helps this psychological thriller about a sheltered spinster's revolt against her tyrannical invalid father. A notch or two above routine. [PG]▼

Attica (1980) **C-100m. TVM** D: Marvin J. Chomsky. Charles Durning, George Grizzard, Glynn Turman, Anthony Zerbe, Henry Darrow, Joel Fabiani, Roger E. Mosley, Morgan Freeman. Gripping dramatization by James Henerson of the harrowing Attica Prison uprising of 1971. Taken from Tom Wicker's best-selling account, *A Time to Die*. Above average.▼

Attic: The Hiding of Anne Frank, The (1988) **C-100m. TVM** D: John Erman. Mary Steenburgen, Paul Scofield, Huub Stapel, Eleanor Bron, Miriam Karlin, Lisa Jacobs, Ronald Pickup. Steenburgen shines in her TV-movie debut as Miep Gies, the courageous Dutch woman who chose to hide her employer, Otto Frank, and his family from the Nazis. The Anne Frank story, told from a different perspective, artfully adapted by William Hanley from Gies' book, *Anne Frank Remembered*. Beautifully crafted production made by top-of-the-line talent. Above average.▼

Attila (1954-Italian-French) **C-83m.** *½ D: Pietro Francisci. Anthony Quinn, Sophia Loren, Henri Vidal, Irene Papas. Inept spectacle with ridiculous script of Attila readying to conquer Rome.▼

At War with the Army (1950) **93m.** **½ D: Hal Walker. Dean Martin, Jerry Lewis, Polly Bergen, Angela Greene, Mike Kellin. In their first starring feature, Dean and Jerry are in the service, with some funny sequences, including memorable soda machine gag.▼●◗

Audrey Rose (1977) **C-113m.** **½ D: Robert Wise. Marsha Mason, John Beck, Anthony Hopkins, Susan Swift, Norman Lloyd, John Hillerman. Overlong, underplayed reincarnation thriller. Mason and Beck are happily married couple until a stranger (Hopkins) tells them that their 12-year-old girl is his dead daughter returned to life. Script by Frank DeFelitta, from his novel. [PG]▼

August (1996-British) **C-90m.** *½ D: Anthony Hopkins. Anthony Hopkins, Kate Burton, Gawn Grainger, Rhian Morgan, Rhoda Lewis. *Uncle Vanya* comes to Wales in yet another version of the oft-adapted Chekhov play, with real-life Welshman Hopkins (in his directorial debut) misdirecting himself in the lead. Boring rendition with inaccessible characters about whom we do not care. Incidentally, Hopkins also composed the score. [PG]▼●

Auntie Mame (1958) **C-143m.** ***½ D: Morton DaCosta. Rosalind Russell, Forrest Tucker, Coral Browne, Fred Clark, Roger Smith, Patric Knowles, Peggy Cass, Joanna Barnes, Pippa Scott, Lee Patrick, Willard Waterman, Connie Gilchrist. Colorful film version of Patrick Dennis' novel about his eccentric aunt, who believes that "life is a banquet, and most poor suckers are starving to death." Episodic but highly entertaining, sparked by Russell's tour-de-force performance. Betty Comden–Adolph Green script was adapted from the Jerome Lawrence–Robert E. Lee Broadway play. Musicalized as MAME. Technirama. ▼●

Au Revoir, Les Enfants (1987-French) **C-103m.** ***½ D: Louis Malle. Gaspard Manesse, Raphael Fejto, Francine Racette, Stanislas Carre de Malberg, Philippe Morier-Genoud, Francois Berleand, Irène Jacob. Deeply felt film based on an incident from Malle's youth, during WW2, when the headmaster of his Catholic boarding school decided to shield several Jewish children in the midst of Nazi-occupied France. Filled with telling details, the story unfolds at a deliberate pace, leading up to an emotionally devastating finale. [PG]▼●

Austin Powers: International Man of Mystery (1997) **C-89m.** ** D: Jay Roach. Mike Myers, Elizabeth Hurley, Michael York, Mimi Rogers, Robert Wagner, Seth Green, Fabiana Udenio, Charles Napier. Swinging '60s spy is cryogenically frozen, then thawed out in the '90s to do battle with megalomaniac Dr. Evil—but he can't quite shake his mod '60s style or argot ("Groovy, baby!"). Myers (who also wrote and coproduced) is fun, especially as Dr. Evil, but this one-joke premise is stretched far beyond its limits. Carrie Fisher and Tom Arnold appear in unfunny cameos. Coproduced by Demi Moore. Followed by a sequel. Super 35. [PG-13]▼●◗

Austin Powers: The Spy Who Shagged Me (1999) **C-92m.** **½ D: Jay Roach. Mike Myers, Heather Graham, Rob Lowe, Michael York, Elizabeth Hurley, Robert Wagner, Gia Carides, Seth Green, Verne Troyer, Mindy Sterling, Kristen Johnson, Will Ferrell, Fred Willard, Charles Napier. More swingin' '60s lunacy as Dr. Evil returns to Earth with a time-travel machine and goes back to 1969 to steal Austin's mojo. More laughs than the original—and more than enough gross-out gags—though it's still spotty. Several star cameos, though Troyer, as Mini-Me, steals the film. Myers cowrote and coproduced; Demi Moore coproduced. Super 35. [PG-13]▼●◗

Author! Author! (1982) **C-110m.** *** D: Arthur Hiller. Al Pacino, Dyan Cannon, Tuesday Weld, Eric Gurry, Alan King, Bob Dishy, Bob Elliott, Ray Goulding, Andre Gregory, Ari Meyers. Pacino's flaky wife walks out on him and their kids (most from her previous marriages) just as his play is about to open on Broadway. Slight but winning little comedy; likable performances all around. Written by playwright Israel Horovitz. [PG]▼

Autobiography of a Princess (1975-British)

C-60m. **½ D: James Ivory. James Mason, Madhur Jaffrey, Keith Varnier, Diane Fletcher, Timothy Bateson. Uneven (but not uninteresting) little film about an exiled Indian princess (Jaffrey) and an Englishman (Mason), who come together once a year to sip tea and watch home movies of their life in feudal India. Notable as a look at a time and place that no longer exist, but too often bogged down in talk. Scripted by Ruth Prawer Jhabvala.▼●

Autobiography of Miss Jane Pittman, The (1974) **C-110m. TVM** D: John Korty. Cicely Tyson, Barbara Chaney, Richard Dysart, Katherine Helmond, Michael Murphy, Odetta, Thalmus Rasulala. Acclaimed drama from Ernest J. Gaines' epic novel covering, through the memories of a fictional 110-year-old slave (Tyson), the black experience from the Civil War to the civil rights movement. Tyson's tour-de-force performance, Korty's subtle direction, and Tracy Keenan Wynn's intelligent script received three of the film's nine Emmy Awards. One of TV's all-time best. Above average.▼

Autumn Afternoon, An (1962-Japanese) **C-115m.** *** D: Yasujiro Ozu. Chishu Ryu, Shima Iwashita, Shinichiro Mikami, Keiji Sada, Mariko Okada. Contemplative study of loneliness and the fleeting nature of life, about a middle-class widower (Ryu) who dutifully arranges the marriage of his daughter. A series of subplots focus on various characters who are in some way connected to the nuptials. Ozu's final film.▼

Autumn Leaves (1956) **108m.** **½ D: Robert Aldrich. Joan Crawford, Cliff Robertson, Vera Miles, Lorne Greene. Middle-aged typist marries younger man (Robertson), only to discover he is mentally disturbed and already married. Stalwart performance by Crawford as troubled woman.▼

Autumn Sonata (1978-Swedish) **C-97m.** *** D: Ingmar Bergman. Ingrid Bergman, Liv Ullmann, Lena Nyman, Halvar Bjork, Gunnar Bjornstrand. Ingrid, a famed concert pianist, locks horns with daughter Ullmann when they visit for the first time in seven years. Director Bergman's drama is full of déjà vu, but Ingrid (in her final theatrical film) keeps it on the track most of the time. Sven Nykvist's photography is peerless. [PG]▼●◗

Autumn Tale (1998-French) **C-112m.** ***½ D: Eric Rohmer. Marie Rivière, Béatrice Romand, Alain Libolt, Didier Sandre, Alexia Portal, Stéphane Darmon. Delicious adult comedy dealing with two lifelong female friends, now in their 40s: one is happily married and would like to see her friend (a moody, independent vineyard owner) settle down, so she places a personals ad in the paper and "auditions" a proper suitor. Meanwhile, the younger generation gets involved providing comic complications. This is Rohmer at his best; glorious fun with a most appealing cast. [PG]▼◗

Avalanche (1946) **70m.** *½ D: Irving Allen. Bruce Cabot, Roscoe Karns, Helen Mowery, Veda Ann Borg. Programmer tale of murder and suspense at an isolated ski lodge; shoddy production.

Avalanche (1978) **C-91m.** ** D: Corey Allen. Rock Hudson, Mia Farrow, Robert Forster, Jeanette Nolan, Rick Moses, Barry Primus. Disaster at the newly opened ski resort where hard-driving tycoon Hudson is determined to double his not insubstantial investment while his ex-wife Mia is making whoopee with one of the locals championing ecology. Stodgy performances almost outweighed by special effects. [PG]▼

Avalanche Express (1979) **C-88m.** BOMB D: Mark Robson. Lee Marvin, Robert Shaw, Linda Evans, Maximilian Schell, Joe Namath, Mike Connors, Horst Buchholz. KGB head Shaw tries to defect on a Dutch train that's threatened by lots and lots of falling snow. Cast has enough stiffs in it to resemble audition time at the Hollywood Wax Museum. Sadly, final film for both Shaw and director Robson; in fact, most of Shaw's dialogue had to be dubbed by a mimic. Panavision. [PG]▼

Avalon (1990) **C-126m.** *** D: Barry Levinson. Aidan Quinn, Elizabeth Perkins, Armin Mueller-Stahl, Joan Plowright, Lou Jacobi, Leo Fuchs, Eve Gordon, Kevin Pollak, Israel Rubinek, Elijah Wood, Grant Gelt, Bernard Hiller. Deeply felt, personal story by writer-director Levinson of an immigrant's life and times in Baltimore, and the changes the years bring to his large and boisterous family. Long, deliberately paced, and not always successful, but filled with telling moments and loving visual reminders of a way of life that's disappeared from our midst. The third of Levinson's Baltimore chronicles, following DINER and TIN MEN. Melancholy and evocative score by Randy Newman. [PG]▼●

Avanti! (1972) **C-144m.** ***½ D: Billy Wilder. Jack Lemmon, Juliet Mills, Clive Revill, Edward Andrews, Gianfranco Barra, Franco Angrisano. Sadly underrated comedy about stuffy Baltimore millionaire who falls in love with daughter of his late father's mistress when he comes to Italy to claim the old man's body. Closer to LOVE IN THE AFTERNOON than Wilder's satirical comedies; lovely scenery, wonderful performances by all, especially Revill as crafty hotel manager. [R]▼●

Avenger, The (1960-German) **102m.** **½ D: Karl Anton. Ingrid Van Bergen, Heinz Drache, Ina Duscha, Maria Litto. Above-par shocker based on Edgar Wallace tale of bestial villain beheading several people, mailing them to appropriate recipients.▼

Avengers, The (1942) SEE: **Day Will Dawn, The**

Avengers, The (1998) **C-89m.** ** D: Jeremiah Chechik. Ralph Fiennes, Uma Thurman, Sean Connery, Jim Broadbent, Fiona Shaw, Eddie Izzard, Eileen Atkins, John Wood. Retread of the popular British TV show of the '60s about two saucy secret agents tries in vain to capture its stylishness and insouciance—but Fiennes is woefully miscast, Connery gives a one-note performance as a bad guy who wants to control the earth's weather, and a fine supporting cast is wasted. Thurman is likable enough, but the film is utterly flat. Patrick Macnee, star of the original series, has an amusing voice-only cameo. [PG-13]▼●◗

Avenging Angel (1985) **C-93m.** BOMB D: Robert Vincent O'Neil. Betsy Russell, Rory Calhoun, Susan Tyrrell, Robert F. Lyons, Ossie Davis. Ex–teen prostitute, now college material, recruits pal Calhoun (still acting like the valedictorian at the Gabby Hayes Academy of Dramatic Arts) and takes to the street as an undercover cop. Follow-up to ANGEL proves conclusively that HEAVEN'S GATE is the only '80s film that can't rate a sequel. Followed by ANGEL III: THE FINAL CHAPTER. [R]▼●

Avenging Angel, The (1995) **C-100m. TVM** D: Craig R. Baxley. Tom Berenger, Charlton Heston, James Coburn, Fay Masterson, Kevin Tighe, Jeffrey Jones, Tom Bower, Leslie Hope, Daniel Quinn, Andrew Prine, Lisa Banes. Little-known fact-based tale about a Mormon loner who makes it his cause to protect Brigham Young (Heston) and other church leaders from assassination by their enemies. Part intriguing look at a relatively closed society, part historical drama, part Western, and part murder mystery–thriller. Coproduced by Berenger. Made for cable. Average.▼

Avenging Force (1986) **C-103m.** **½ D: Sam Firstenberg. Michael Dudikoff, Steve James, John P. Ryan, James Booth, Bill Wallace, Karl Johnson. Dudikoff is retired secret agent Matt Hunter, who's forced into action when his one-time comrade (James), a black man running for office, is threatened by a right-wing terrorist group called Pentangle. A cut above the norm for the action/revenge genre, with exciting climax, and a truly heinous villain (well played by Ryan). Screenwriter James Booth also plays Dudikoff's former boss. [R]▼●

Avenging Spirit SEE: **Dominique**

Aviator, The (1985) **C-98m.** ** D: George Miller. Christopher Reeve, Rosanna Arquette, Jack Warden, Sam Wanamaker, Scott Wilson, Tyne Daly, Marcia Strassman. Pioneer pilot Reeve crash-lands in the middle of some 1928 nowhere with whiny adolescent Arquette. Dull Ernest Gann story barely made it (and understandably so) to theaters; director is the MAN FROM SNOWY RIVER—not MAD MAX—George Miller. [PG]▼

Aviator's Wife, The (1981-French) **C-104m.** ***½ D: Eric Rohmer. Philippe Marlaud, Marie Riviere, Anne-Laure Meury, Matthieu Carriere. Melancholy but charming story of young man's unhappy involvement with title character being interrupted by happy encounter with stranger in the park. Lovers of MAUD, CLAIRE, and CHLOE will be happy to find Rohmer in near-peak form after long layoff. [PG]▼◗

Awakening, The (1980) **C-102m.** *½ D: Mike Newell. Charlton Heston, Susannah York, Jill Townsend, Stephanie Zimbalist. Archeologist Heston enters the tomb of Egyptian Queen Kara, whose spirit enters the body of his newborn daughter. Need we continue? From a novel by Bram Stoker, filmed before as BLOOD FROM THE MUMMY'S TOMB. [R]▼●

Awakenings (1990) **C-121m.** ***½ D: Penny Marshall. Robert De Niro, Robin Williams, Julie Kavner, Ruth Nelson, John Heard, Penelope Ann Miller, Max von Sydow, Alice Drummond, Mary Alice, Anne Meara, Richard Libertini, Dexter Gordon. Powerfully affecting true-life story of a painfully shy research doctor who takes a job at a Bronx hospital's chronic care ward in 1969—and discovers that his comatose patients still have life inside them. Williams is superb as the doctor, and De Niro is his match as a patient who awakens from a thirty-year coma to deal with life as an adult for the first time. Steven Zaillian's screenplay is based on the book (and experiences of) Dr. Oliver Sacks. [PG-13]▼●◗

Away All Boats (1956) **C-114m.** **½ D: Joseph Pevney. Jeff Chandler, George Nader, Julie Adams, Lex Barker, Keith Andes, Richard Boone, David Janssen. Strict, aloof captain Chandler must ignite spark of fighting spirit among inexperienced crew aboard WW2 attack transport *Belinda*. Exciting, inspiring story of battle action in Pacific Theater. Look fast for Clint Eastwood as a medical orderly near film's end. VistaVision. ▼◗

Awful Dr. Orloff, The (1961-Spanish) **95m.** ** D: Jess Franco. Howard Vernon, Conrado Sanmartin, Diana Lorys, Ricardo Valle, Perla Cristal. Medium spooker about deranged surgeon operating on a series of women, trying to find spare parts to revitalize his disfigured daughter. A long, disjointed Orloff series followed.▼

Awfully Big Adventure, An (1995-British-Irish) **C-101m.** **½ D: Mike Newell. Hugh Grant, Alan Rickman, Georgina Cates, Rita Tushingham, Peter Firth, Alan Cox, Prunella Scales. Grant's reunion with his FOUR WEDDINGS director is an ill-focused though rarely boring drama about a capriciously cruel stage director who browbeats a Liverpool rep company in the late 1940s. The screenplay, from Beryl Bainbridge's novel, is by Charles Wood, who cowrote HELP! for the Beatles. The photography—more stylized bleakness from NAKED's Dick Pope—is a plus. [R]▼●

Awful Truth, The (1937) **92m.** ***½ D: Leo McCarey. Irene Dunne, Cary Grant, Ralph Bellamy, Cecil Cunningham, Mary Forbes, Alex D'Arcy, Joyce Compton. Hilarious screwball comedy; Cary and Irene divorce, she to marry hayseed Bellamy, he to wed aristocratic Molly Lamont. Each does his best to spoil the other's plans. McCarey won an Oscar for his inspired direction. Screenplay by Vina Delmar. Based on a play by Arthur Richman previously filmed in 1925 and 1929; remade in 1953 as the musical LET'S DO IT AGAIN.▼●

A.W.O.L. SEE: **Lionheart** (1991)▼●

Ay, Carmela! (1990-Spanish) **C-103m.** ***½ D: Carlos Saura. Carmen Maura, Andres Pajares, Gabino Diego, Maurizio di Razza, Miguel A. Rellan. Maura shines in this clever, rapier-witted farce as a vaudevillian who entertains the partisans during the Spanish Civil War. The story chronicles her plight after she, her husband, and their mute assistant find themselves trapped behind enemy lines. Both funny and poignant.▼●

Ayn Rand—A Sense of Life (1998) **C/B&W-145m.** **½ D: Michael Paxton. Narrated by Sharon Gless. Examination of the popular author, screenwriter, and philosopher, tracing her historic roots in the Soviet Union, her years in Hollywood, her talk show appearances expounding her controversial theories of Objectivism and individual rights, and her testimony before the House Un-American Activities Committee. Also incorporates dramatizations of her works and sequences illustrating her life. Too long—and pedantic—for some viewers, but a must for Rand enthusiasts.

Babar The Movie (1989-Canadian-French) **C-70m.** *** D: Alan Bunce. Voices of Gordon Pinsent, Gavin Magrath, Elizabeth Hanna, Sarah Polley, Chris Wiggins. Entertaining feature-length cartoon based on the classic children's books by Jean and Laurent de Brunhoff. Strictly serviceable (and uninspired) animation is made up for by an engaging story line that's sure to appeal to young children. [G]▼●

Babbitt (1934) **74m.** **½ D: William Keighley. Guy Kibbee, Aline MacMahon, Claire Dodd, Maxine Doyle, Minor Watson, Minna Gombell, Alan Hale, Berton Churchill. Sinclair Lewis' indictment of business class blowhards is transformed into a typical vehicle for blustery Kibbee and tower-of-strength MacMahon. Amusing but forgettable—bears only nominal resemblance to Lewis' novel. Previously filmed in 1924.

Babe (1975) **C-100m. TVM** D: Buzz Kulik. Susan Clark, Alex Karras, Slim Pickens, Jeanette Nolan, Ellen Geer, Ford Rainey. Rich, absorbing film biography of Babe Didrickson Zaharias, America's foremost woman athlete, beautifully played by Clark (who won an Emmy). Ex-football star Karras offers a sensitive portrayal of her wrestler husband George, under Kulik's imaginative direction. The courageous Babe's tragic story leaves not a dry eye in the house, but secret ingredient here is taste. Adapted by Joanna Lee from the athlete's autobiography, *This Life I've Led.* Above average.

Babe, The (1992) **C-115m.** *** D: Arthur Hiller. John Goodman, Kelly McGillis, Trini Alvarado, Bruce Boxleitner, Peter Donat, James Cromwell, J. C. Quinn, Joe Ragno, Bernard Kates, Michael McGrady, Stephen Caffrey. Agreeably sentimental, old-fashioned bio of the great Babe Ruth is largely a vehicle for Goodman, who's terrific in the lead. Though facts are tampered with and often ignored, the essence of this larger-than-life character (and his genuine love of baseball) still comes through. [PG]▼●

Babe (1995-U.S.-Australian) **C-92m.** ***½ D: Chris Noonan. James Cromwell, Magda Szubanski; voices of Christine Cavanaugh, Miriam Margolyes, Danny Mann, Hugo Weaving, Miriam Flynn, Russi Taylor, Evelyn Krape; narrated by Roscoe Lee Browne. Delightful, disarming family fodder about an orphaned pig taken in by a quietly eccentric farmer who develops a strong attachment to the little fellow. The farmyard animals all converse with one another in this endearing (and often very funny) tale, based on the book *The Sheep-Pig* by Dick King-Smith. The Oscar-winning special effects, combining real animals, animatronic doubles, and computer technology, are both seamless and convincing. This is one "family film" that adults can enjoy right along with their kids. Followed by a sequel. [G]▼●◗

Babe: Pig in the City (1998-U.S.-Australian) **C-95m.** **½ D: George Miller. Magda Szubanski, James Cromwell, Mickey Rooney; voices of E. G. Daily, Danny Mann, Glenne Headly, Steven Wright, Stanley Ralph Ross, Russi Taylor; narrated by Roscoe Lee Browne. Disappointing (and superfluous) sequel puts Babe and everyone around him, human and animal, in almost continual peril, as the pig is taken to America by Mrs. Hoggett. Overblown, with unpleasant images unsuitable for the youngest children, but rescued somewhat by the indomitable Babe, who's as endearing as ever, and those three singing mice, whose choice of material is quite funny. [G] ▼●◗

Babe Ruth Story, The (1948) **106m.** BOMB D: Roy Del Ruth. William Bendix, Claire Trevor, Charles Bickford, Sam Levene, William Frawley, Mark Koenig, Mel Allen, Harry Wismer, H. V. Kaltenborn. Perfectly dreadful bio of the Sultan of Swat is sugar-coated beyond recognition; the Babe is depicted as an overgrown child whose behavior is constantly misunderstood. Bendix is badly miscast, and the finale is not to be believed. ▼

Babes in Arms (1939) **96m.** **½ D: Busby Berkeley. Mickey Rooney, Judy Garland, Charles Winninger, Guy Kibbee, June Preisser, Douglas McPhail. Rodgers and Hart's musical, minus most of their songs, and one that's left, "Where or When," is trammeled to death. What remains is energetic but standard putting-on-a-show vehicle for Mickey and Judy. Dated fun. Original ending, "My Day," was a production number spoofing Mr. and Mrs. Franklin D. Roosevelt, which was later removed for a 1948 reissue and later restored by Turner. Also shown in computer-colored version. ▼●

Babes in Bagdad (1952-U.S.-British-Spanish) **C-79m.** BOMB D: Edgar G. Ulmer. Paulette Goddard, Gypsy Rose Lee, Richard Ney, John Boles, Sebastian Cabot, Christopher Lee. Embarrassing, hokey costumer made even seedier by miscast veteran performers.

Babes in Toyland (1934) **73m.** ***½ D: Gus Meins, Charles R. Rogers. Stan Laurel, Oliver Hardy, Charlotte Henry, Henry Kleinbach (Brandon), Felix Knight, Jean Darling, Johnny Downs, Marie Wilson. L&H version of Victor Herbert operetta looks better all the time, compared to lumbering "family musicals" of recent years. Stan and Ollie are in fine form, and fantasy element of Toyland—especially attack by Bogeymen—is excellent. Video title: MARCH OF THE WOODEN SOLDIERS. Originally released at 79m. Also shown in computer-colored version. ▼●

Babes in Toyland (1961) **C-105m.** **½ D: Jack Donohue. Ray Bolger, Tommy Sands, Annette Funicello, Henry Calvin, Gene Sheldon, Tommy Kirk, Ed Wynn, Ann Jillian. Colorful but contrived Disneyfication of Victor Herbert operetta has no substance or heart; classic songs, visual gimmicks, clowning of Calvin and Sheldon keep it afloat. Remade for TV in 1986.

Babes on Broadway (1941) **118m.** **½ D: Busby Berkeley. Mickey Rooney, Judy Garland, Fay Bainter, Virginia Weidler, Richard Quine, Ray McDonald, Donna Reed. Showcase for Mickey and Judy's talents, with duo doing everything from imitations of Carmen Miranda and Bernhardt to minstrel numbers. Standout is Judy's "F.D.R. Jones." Film debut of Margaret O'Brien. ▼●

Babette Goes to War (1959-French) **C-106m.** **½ D: Christian-Jaque. Brigitte Bardot, Jacques Charrier, Francis Blanche, Ronald Howard. Bardot is not at her forte playing lighthearted comedy. Flimsy WW2 account of French agent Bardot working for British, being sent back to France to kidnap a Nazi bigwig. CinemaScope.

Babette's Feast (1987-Danish) **C-102m.** **** D: Gabriel Axel. Stephane Audran, Jean-Philippe Lafont, Gudmar Wivesson, Jarl Kulle, Bibi Andersson, Birgitte Federspiel, Bodil Kjer. Exquisite, delicately told tale of two beautiful young minister's daughters who pass up love and fame to remain in their small Danish village. They grow old, using religion as a substitute for living life . . . and then take in Parisian refugee Audran, a woman with a very special secret. Subtle, funny and deeply felt, with several wonderful surprises: an instant masterpiece that deservedly earned a Best Foreign Film Academy Award. Axel wrote the screenplay, from an Isak Dinesen short story originally published in the *Ladies Home Journal.* Don't miss this one. [G]▼●

Baby, The (1973) **C-102m.** ** D: Ted Post. Anjanette Comer, Ruth Roman, Marianna Hill. Social worker who gets in too deep with a man-child case, has to kill to keep "baby" at home with her. [PG]▼◗

Baby and the Battleship, The (1956-British) **C-96m.** **½ D: Jay Lewis. John Mills, Richard Attenborough, Andre Morell, Bryan Forbes, Lisa Gastoni, Michael Hordern, Lionel Jeffries, Gordon Jackson. Mildly amusing account of sailor Mills smuggling Italian baby aboard ship and his antics as he tries to keep it hidden from top brass.▼

Baby Blue Marine (1976) **C-90m.** **½ D: John Hancock. Jan-Michael Vincent, Glynnis O'Connor, Katherine Helmond, Dana Elcar, Bert Remsen, Richard Gere, Art Lund. Norman Rockwell's America come to life, in bucolic tale of Marine dropout during WW2 who's mistaken for hero by residents of small town. Too bland to add up. [PG]

Baby Boom (1987) **C-103m.** *** D: Charles Shyer. Diane Keaton, Harold Ramis, Sam Shepard, Sam Wanamaker, James Spader, Pat Hingle, Britt Leach, Mary Gross, Victoria Jackson, Paxton Whitehead, Annie Golden, Dori Brenner, Robin Bartlett, Christopher Noth. Keaton is in top comic form as a supercharged business exec whose life changes dramatically when she "inherits" a baby. Amiable comedy takes well-aimed potshots at 80s yuppie motherdom but remains agreeably sweet-natured start to finish, helping it over an occasional story lull. Written by Shyer and Nancy Meyers. Followed by a TV series. [PG]▼●

Baby Dance, The (1998) **C-92m. TVM** D: Jane Anderson. Stockard Channing, Laura Dern, Richard Lineback, Peter Riegert. A childless, well-to-do California couple comes to claim the soon-to-be-born baby they contracted for from a trailer-park couple in Louisiana, with unforeseen events for both families. Channing and Dern shine as they express second thoughts about the arrangement. Jodie Foster executive-produced; director Anderson adapted her Off-Broadway play. Made for cable. Above average.▼

Baby Doll (1956) **114m.** ***½ D: Elia Kazan. Karl Malden, Carroll Baker, Eli Wallach, Mildred Dunnock, Lonny Chapman, Rip Torn. Starkly photographed on location in Mississippi, story revolves around a child bride, her witless and blustery husband, and a smarmy business rival bent on using both of them. Condemned by Legion of Decency when released, this Tennessee Williams story, although tame by today's standards, still sizzles. Film debuts of Wallach and Torn.▼

Baby Face (1933) **70m.** **½ D: Alfred E. Green. Barbara Stanwyck, George Brent, Donald Cook, Margaret Lindsay, Douglass Dumbrille, John Wayne. Pre-Production Code item has Stanwyck bartending at a speakeasy, then literally sleeping her way floor by floor to the top of a N.Y.C. office building. Great first half gives way to sappily moralistic conclusion. Wayne's coat-and-tie bit—as one of the office help used by the heroine—is a hoot.▼●

Baby Face Harrington (1935) **61m.** **½ D: Raoul Walsh. Charles Butterworth, Una Merkel, Harvey Stephens, Nat Pendleton, Eugene Pallette. Mild-mannered Butterworth gets mixed up with gangsters in this pleasant comedy vehicle that takes its time getting started.

Baby Face Nelson (1957) **85m.** ** D: Don Siegel. Mickey Rooney, Carolyn Jones, Cedric Hardwicke, Jack Elam, Ted De Corsia. Rooney gives flavorful performance in title role of gun-happy gangster in Prohibition-Depression days; low-budget product, but action-filled.

Babyfever (1994) **C-110m.** **½ D: Henry Jaglom. Victoria Foyt, Matt Salinger, Dinah Lenney, Eric Roberts, Frances Fisher, Elaine Kagan. An array of career-women at a Malibu baby shower examine, discuss, and discuss some more their own ticking biological clocks. Meanwhile, one of the guests (Foyt) is awaiting results of her own pregnancy test! Shot in Jaglom's usual vérité style, this is best appreciated by fans of the highly personal filmmaker. With the drubbing that men take here, this is definitely not a ''first date'' film.▼

Baby Geniuses (1999) **C-94m.** BOMB D: Bob Clark. Kathleen Turner, Christopher Lloyd, Peter MacNicol, Kim Cattrall, Dom DeLuise, Ruby Dee. Unless you want to see walking, talking toddlers hypnotizing DeLuise into picking his nose, steer clear of this almost history-making comedy clinker about power-mad child psychologist Turner, who's raising these bright babies in her lab. Technically shoddy and recipient of some of the decade's worst reviews (though people did go to see it). If these kids are such geniuses, why can't they spark even a single laugh? Super 35. [PG] ▼●◗

Baby It's You (1983) **C-105m.** **½ D: John Sayles. Rosanna Arquette, Vincent Spano, Joanna Merlin, Jack Davidson, Nick Ferrari, Dolores Messina, Leora Dana, Sam McMurray, Tracy Pollan, Matthew Modine, Robert Downey, Jr., Caroline Aaron, Fisher Stevens. A middle-class Jewish girl is pursued by a working-class Italian Catholic boy who calls himself The Sheik in this slice-of-life set in 1960s New Jersey. Writer-director Sayles's eye for detail and ear for dialogue give his fine cast a solid foundation—but the script loses momentum after the characters graduate from high school. Story by coproducer Amy Robinson; Modine's film debut. [R]▼●

Baby Maker, The (1970) **C-109m.** ** D: James Bridges. Barbara Hershey, Colin Wilcox-Horne, Sam Groom, Scott Glenn, Jeannie Berlin. Childless couple hires young semi-hippie to have a baby by the husband when wife discovers she is sterile. Made at a time when the notion of surrogate mothers was considered bizarre. [R]▼

Baby's Day Out (1994) **C-98m.** BOMB D: Patrick Read Johnson. Lara Flynn Boyle, Joe Mantegna, Jacob and Adam Worton, Joe Pantoliano, Brian Haley, Cynthia Nixon, Fred Dalton Thompson, John Neville, Eddie Bracken. In a ''plot'' reminiscent of several Swee Pea cartoons, a Chicago baby violently foils kidnappers as he embarks on a parentless Pampers odyssey to Marshall Field's, the zoo, and to the top of a skyscraper building site. A box office flop despite scripter/coproducer John Hughes' cynical HOME ALONE cloning; in standard Hughes fashion, it's full of kicked-and-torched gonads jokes, but all sweetness and light at the end. [PG]▼●

Baby . . . Secret of the Lost Legend (1985) **C-95m.** ** D: B.W.L. Norton. William Katt, Sean Young, Patrick McGoohan, Julian Fellowes, Kyalo Mativo. Old-fashioned yarn about discovery of a dinosaur family follows basic KING KONG outline—and the baby dino is sure to charm kids—but elements of racism, sexism, and much-too-casual violence just about kill it. TV title: DINOSAUR . . . SECRET OF THE LOST LEGEND. Super Techniscope. [PG]▼●

Babysitter, The (1969) **70m.** ** D: Don Henderson. Patricia Wymer, George E. Carey, Ann Bellamy, Cathy Williams, Robert Tessier, James McLarty. Low-budget drive-in fare is dated but still mildly enjoyable; young blonde babysitter seduces the district attorney and hilarity ensues. Lots of double duty on this one: Carey produced, McLarty wrote the script. Followed by nonsequel, WEEKEND WITH THE BABYSITTER. [R]

Babysitter, The (1975-Italian-French-German) **C-111m.** BOMB D: René Clement. Maria Schneider, Sydne Rome, Vic Morrow, Robert Vaughn, Renato Pozzetto, Nadja Tiller, Carl Mohner. In misfired melodrama, Schneider is innocently duped into taking part in a kidnapping by roommate Rome. Schneider's walk-through nonacting is abysmal, as is miscasting of chubby Italian comedian Pozzetto as her boyfriend. Retitled: WANTED: BABYSITTER. Video title: THE RAW EDGE.▼

Babysitter, The (1995) **C-90m.** ** D: Guy Ferland. Alicia Silverstone, Jeremy London, J. T. Walsh, Lee Garlington, Nicky Katt, Lois Chiles, George Segal, Ryan Slater. A beautiful teenager inspires sexual fantasies in the people around her as she babysits for Walsh and his wife. Unimaginative writing (by the director) and slow pace explain why this went straight to video, though it was released in theaters after Silverstone's great success in CLUELESS. [R]▼●

Baby-Sitters Club, The (1995) **C-85m.** **½ D: Melanie Mayron. Schuyler Fisk, Bre Blair, Rachel Leigh Cook, Zelda Harris, Tricia Joe, Larisa Oleynik, Stacey Linn Ramsower, Austin O'Brien, Aaron Metchik, Christian Oliver, Brooke Adams, Peter Horton, Ellen Burstyn, Bruce Davison, Harris Yulin. Kristy (Fisk), founder and leader of the Baby-Sitter's Club, run by seven girls who are best friends, proposes starting a summer camp. Then her long-absent father shows up, and wants to spend time with her—but insists she keep his presence a secret. Good-hearted adaptation of Ann M. Martin's hugely popular books for preteen girls. Low-key, episodic, but agreeable entertainment. Director Mayron can be spotted briefly in the opening sequence. Fisk is the daughter of Sissy Spacek. [PG]▼●

Baby Snakes (1979) **C-166m.** BOMB D: Frank Zappa. Frank Zappa, Ron Delsener, Joey Psychotic, Donna U. Wanna, Frenchy the Poodle, Ms. Pinky's Larger Sister, Angel, Janet the Planet, Diva, John, Chris, Nancy. Excruciatingly overlong ego trip for musical maverick Zappa. In every fifth shot, it seems, Frankie is in close-up or a fan rushes up to him, kisses him, and screeches for joy. Zappa the producer should have fired Zappa the director, but Zappa the editor finally cut it down to 91m. for 1984 reissue. Bruce Bickford's clay animation is film's sole virtue. [R]▼

Baby Take a Bow (1934) **76m.** ** D: Harry Lachman. Shirley Temple, James Dunn, Claire Trevor, Alan Dinehart, Ray Walker. Shirley's first starring vehicle seems one of her weakest today, but helped boost her career nonetheless; in typical little-miss-fixit fashion, she helps her ex-con father beat a bum rap. Also shown in computer-colored version.▼

Baby The Rain Must Fall (1965) **100m.** *** D: Robert Mulligan. Lee Remick, Steve McQueen, Don Murray, Paul Fix, Josephine Hutchinson, Ruth White. Much underrated account of ex-convict McQueen, returning to his wife and daughter, but unable to change his restless ways. Murray is sincere sheriff who tries to help. Screenplay by Horton Foote, from his play *The Traveling Lady*.▼●

Bachelor, The (1991-Italian-Hungarian-British) **C-105m.** *** D: Roberto Faenza. Keith Carradine, Miranda Richardson, Kristin Scott Thomas, Sarah-Jane Fenton, Max von Sydow, Mario Adorf. Subtle, thoughtful story of repressed emotion, about a staid, middle-aged, unmarried doctor and self-described "nomad" (Carradine), and how he responds when his sister and long-time constant companion commits suicide. Richardson, in a dual role, plays the latter, as well as one of a trio of very different women with whom the doctor becomes involved. Based on a novel by Arthur Schnitzler.▼

Bachelor, The (1999) **C-101m.** *½ D: Gary Sinyor. Chris O'Donnell, Renée Zellweger, Hal Holbrook, James Cromwell, Peter Ustinov, Edward Asner, Brooke Shields, Mariah Carey, Artie Lange, Jennifer Esposito. Hapless O'Donnell would do better aping Buster Brown than taking on the Buster Keaton role in a woeful update of the still uproarious 1925 classic SEVEN CHANCES, playing a misdirected 30-year-old youth who must find a wife immediately or forfeit a $100 million inheritance left him by his crotchety grandfather. A mistake from top to bottom. The view of women here might even offend the Rat Pack. [PG-13]▼●◗

Bachelor and the Bobby-Soxer, The (1947) **95m.** *** D: Irving Reis. Cary Grant, Myrna Loy, Shirley Temple, Rudy Vallee, Ray Collins, Harry Davenport. Judge Loy orders playboy Grant to wine and dine her sister Temple, so the teenager will forget her infatuation for him. Breezy entertainment earned Sidney Sheldon an Oscar for his original screenplay. Also shown in computer-colored version.▼●

Bachelor Apartment (1931) **77m.** **½ D: Lowell Sherman. Lowell Sherman, Irene Dunne, Mae Murray, Claudia Dell, Noel Francis, Bess Flowers. Sophisticated comedy about gay-blade Sherman shuffling his various girls back and forth; ancestor of COME BLOW YOUR HORN, etc.▼

Bachelor Father, The (1931) **90m.** **½ D: Robert Z. Leonard. Marion Davies, Ralph Forbes, C. Aubrey Smith, Doris Lloyd, Halliwell Hobbes, Ray Milland.

Once dashing bachelor Smith, now old and lonely, wants to know his three grown children. Staid but enjoyable adaptation of Edward Childs Carpenter's stage play.

Bachelor Flat (1962) C-91m. ** D: Frank Tashlin. Tuesday Weld, Richard Beymer, Celeste Holm, Terry-Thomas. Weld visits her mother's beach house and finds scientist Thomas at work; she moves in anyway and creates eventual havoc. Thomas has had better material; film's entertainment is all in his lap. CinemaScope.

Bachelor in Paradise (1961) C-109m. ** D: Jack Arnold. Bob Hope, Lana Turner, Janis Paige, Jim Hutton, Paula Prentiss, Don Porter, Agnes Moorehead. Hope vehicle about the only bachelor in a community of married couples. Amusing, but not great. Hope has done better; Paige is fun as always. CinemaScope.▼

Bachelor Mother (1939) 81m. ***½ D: Garson Kanin. Ginger Rogers, David Niven, Charles Coburn, Frank Albertson, Ernest Truex. Rogers unwittingly becomes guardian for abandoned baby in this delightful comedy by Norman Krasna. Remade as BUNDLE OF JOY. Also shown in computer-colored version.▼●

Bachelor Party, The (1957) 93m. *** D: Delbert Mann. Don Murray, E. G. Marshall, Jack Warden, Patricia Smith, Carolyn Jones, Larry Blyden, Philip Abbott, Nancy Marchand. Perceptive Paddy Chayefsky drama (originally a TV play) about bachelor party for groom-to-be Abbott, and its emotional effect on other married participants. Jones is exceptional as philosophical nympho.▼

Bachelor Party (1984) C-106m. ** D: Neal Israel. Tom Hanks, Tawny Kitaen, Adrian Zmed, George Grizzard, Robert Prescott. Amiable comedy about preparations for a raunchy bachelor party has real laughs for a while, then gets increasingly desperate and tasteless. [R]▼●

Back at the Front (1952) 87m. **½ D: George Sherman. Tom Ewell, Harvey Lembeck, Mari Blanchard, Richard Long. Follow-up to UP FRONT, with Bill Mauldin's army goof-offs Willie and Joe scampering around post-WW2 Tokyo. Retitled: WILLIE AND JOE BACK AT THE FRONT.

Backbeat (1993-British) C-100m. **½ D: Iain Softley. Stephen Dorff, Sheryl Lee, Ian Hart, Gary Bakewell, Chris O'Neill, Scot Williams, Kai Weisinger, Paul Humpoletz. Stuart Sutcliffe (Dorff) goes along with his pal John Lennon when their rock 'n' roll band tries to establish itself in early 60s Hamburg—but his ambitions lay elsewhere. Initially intriguing true story of the man who deserted the about-to-be-Beatles grows tired after a while, especially when Lennon (as played by the dynamic Hart) seems so much more interesting. The period and its music are well captured, however. [R]▼●

Back Door to Heaven (1939) 85m. **½ D: William K. Howard. Wallace Ford, Aline MacMahon, Stuart Erwin, Patricia Ellis, Bert Frohman, Kent Smith, George Lewis, Billy (William) Redfield, Iris Adrian. Small-town schoolteacher awaits the arrival of former pupils for a reunion, believing they've all succeeded in life—except for the one boy who went to reform school. The truth is much harsher, however. Ambitious social drama doesn't entirely succeed but has enough originality to make you stick with it to the end. James Lydon is impressive in his screen debut. That's director Howard as the prosecuting attorney in the courtroom scene. ▼

Back Door to Hell (1964) 68m. **½ D: Monte Hellman. Jimmie Rodgers, Jack Nicholson, John Hackett, Annabelle Huggins, Conrad Maga. Mildly interesting film about WW2 reconnaissance mission in the Philippines; early collaboration of Nicholson and Hellman, who filmed FLIGHT TO FURY back to back with this.

Backdraft (1991) C-135m. *** D: Ron Howard. Kurt Russell, William Baldwin, Robert De Niro, Donald Sutherland, Jennifer Jason Leigh, Scott Glenn, Rebecca De Mornay, Jason Gedrick, J. T. Walsh, Tony Mockus, Sr., Clint Howard. Two brothers whose father died fighting a fire now spend their time on the force battling each other. A hoary B-movie-type script fired up by square-jawed conviction, and stunning special effects; also the first film to ever explore a sheer fascination with fire. The gifted Leigh fails miserably playing a normal young woman. Footage added for network TV showings. Super 35. [R]▼●◗

Backfire (1950) 91m. ** D: Vincent Sherman. Virginia Mayo, Gordon MacRae, Edmond O'Brien, Viveca Lindfors, Dane Clark, Ed Begley. OK mystery tale has MacRae search for missing friend through maze of murder and romance.

Backfire (1961-British) 59m. ** D: Paul Almond. Alfred Burke, Zena Marshall, Oliver Johnston. Noel Trevarthen is insurance investigator solving arson and murder at a cosmetics firm; adequate programmer based on Edgar Wallace yarn.

Backfire (1987-U.S.-Canadian) C-92m. **½ D: Gilbert Cates. Karen Allen, Keith Carradine, Jeff Fahey, Bernie Casey, Dean Paul Martin, Dinah Manoff, Virginia Capers, Philip Sterling. Complicated plot with several surprises is best not revealed here, but it does involve wealthy, disturbed Vietnam vet Fahey, his wrong-side-of-the-tracks wife Allen, and mysterious drifter Carradine. Familiar story but well acted; builds up a fair amount of suspense. Good use of Canadian locations. [R]▼●

Backfire! (1994) C-89m. *½ D: A. Dean

Bell. Kathy Ireland, Robert Mitchum, Telly Savalas, Shelley Winters, Josh Mosby, Mary McCormack. In the wake of AIRPLANE! and THE NAKED GUN comes this astoundingly unfunny comedy about an inept young man attempting to join an all-female fire department. Mitchum (as a semi-senile fire marshal) and Winters have come a long way since THE NIGHT OF THE HUNTER! [PG-13]▼

Back From Eternity (1956) **97m.** **½ D: John Farrow. Robert Ryan, Anita Ekberg, Rod Steiger, Phyllis Kirk. Moderately engrossing account of victims of plane crash, stranded in South American jungle, and their various reactions to the situation. OK remake of FIVE CAME BACK.▼●

Back From the Dead (1957) **79m.** BOMB D: Charles Marquis Warren. Peggie Castle, Arthur Franz, Marsha Hunt, Evelyn Scott, James Bell. Castle is earnest as wife possessed by will of husband's dead first spouse, but cliché-ridden production makes everything ridiculous. Regalscope.

Background to Danger (1943) **80m.** *** D: Raoul Walsh. George Raft, Brenda Marshall, Sydney Greenstreet, Peter Lorre, Osa Massen, Kurt Katch. Slam-bang WW2 story with Raft swept into Nazi intrigue in Turkey; terrific car chase caps fast-moving tale.▼

Back Home (1990-British) **C-105m. TVM** D: Piers Haggard. Hayley Mills, Hayley Carr, Jean Anderson, Rupert Frazer, Brenda Bruce, Adam Stevenson, George Clark. Sentimental Disney film about a family's reunion, and renewal, in post-WW2 England, when the 12-year-old daughter, who's been living in America for the duration, returns home. Made for cable. Average.

Back in the USSR (1991) **C-87m.** *½ D: Deran Serafian. Frank Whaley, Natalya Negoda, Roman Polanski, Ravil Issyanov, Dey Young, Andrew Divof, Brian Blessed, Harry Ditson. American tourist Whaley gets involved in "the case of the disappearing icon" on a visit to Russia. It's almost impossible to follow this loophole laden script where coincidences abound and the importance of the central object of desire—the icon—is never established.▼●

Backlash (1947) **66m.** ** D: Eugene Forde. Jean Rogers, Richard Travis, Larry Blake, John Eldredge, Leonard Strong, Robert Shayne, Louise Currie, Douglas Fowley. OK programmer of man trying to frame his wife for murder he committed. Also shown in computer-colored version.

Backlash (1956) **C-84m.** **½ D: John Sturges. Richard Widmark, Donna Reed, William Campbell, John McIntire, Barton MacLane, Henry (Harry) Morgan, Edward C. Platt. In the aftermath of an Apache ambush, Widmark (who believes his father was in the doomed party) and Reed (whose husband was killed in the massacre) become involved in a serpentine search for the lone survivor and some missing gold. Plotty Western written by Borden Chase.

Backlash (1986-Australian) **C-88m.** **½ D: Bill Bennett. David Argue, Gia Carides, Lydia Miller, Brian Syron, Anne Smith. Well-meaning but muddled account of a young aborigine barmaid who's sodomized, then charged with the murder of her assailant, and finally treks across the outback in custody of two mindlessly jabbering cops. Bits of snappy dialogue and intriguing commentary on race relations, but far too much is left unexplained. [R]▼

Backroads (1977-Australian) **C-61m.** ***½ D: Phillip Noyce. Bill Hunter, Gary Foley, Zac Martin, Julie McGregor, Terry Camilleri. Aborigine Foley joins with loutish, self-centered white criminal Hunter, with tragic results. Superior drama is an incisive commentary on racism; in private life Foley is a radical black activist. Noyce's feature directorial debut.

Back Roads (1981) **C-94m.** *½ D: Martin Ritt. Sally Field, Tommy Lee Jones, David Keith, Miriam Colon, Michael V. Gazzo, M. Emmet Walsh. Attractive leads are scant consolation for thoroughly unfunny comedy about a hooker and a drifter who find love on the road. Not as enjoyable as Hollywood's 10,000 previous derivations of the same script. Panavision. [R]▼

Backstage at the Kirov (1983) **C-80m.** *** D: Derek Hart. Galina Mezentxseva, Konstantin Zaklinsky, Altyani Assylmuratova, other dancers. Handsome, entertaining look at Leningrad's famed Kirov ballet troupe, behind the scenes and on-stage (performing "Swan Lake").▼

Back Street (1932) **89m.** *** D: John M. Stahl. Irene Dunne, John Boles, George Meeker, ZaSu Pitts, Arlette Duncan, June Clyde, William Bakewell, Doris Lloyd, Jane Darwell. Dunne shines in oft-filmed Fannie Hurst soaper of spirited young woman who becomes the mistress of Boles and must forever remain in the shadows. Dated, to be sure, but still entertaining. Remade in 1941 and 1961.

Back Street (1941) **89m.** *** D: Robert Stevenson. Charles Boyer, Margaret Sullavan, Richard Carlson, Frank McHugh, Tim Holt. Fine team of Boyer and Sullavan breathes life into Fannie Hurst perennial soaper of woman whose love for man doesn't die when he marries another.

Back Street (1961) **C-107m.** **½ D: David Miller. Susan Hayward, John Gavin, Vera Miles, Charles Drake, Virginia Grey, Reginald Gardiner, Natalie Schafer. Lavish, unbelievable third version of Fannie Hurst's story of a woman's love for married man. Doesn't play as well as previous versions but a fashion show for Hayward in Jean Louis designs. Ross Hunter produced.▼

Back to Bataan (1945) **95m.** *** D: Edward Dmytryk. John Wayne, Anthony

Quinn, Beulah Bondi, Fely Franquelli, Richard Loo, Philip Ahn, Lawrence Tierney. Good, sturdy WW2 action film with officer Wayne leading Filipino guerillas to victory in the South Pacific. Also shown in computer-colored version.▼●

Back to God's Country (1953) **C-78m.** **½ D: Joseph Pevney. Rock Hudson, Marcia Henderson, Steve Cochran, Hugh O'Brian, Chubby Johnson. Sea captain Hudson and wife Henderson face rigors of nature and villainy of Cochran in the Canadian wilds. Competent programmer; from James Oliver Curwood's classic story.

Back to School (1986) **C-96m.** *** D: Alan Metter. Rodney Dangerfield, Sally Kellerman, Burt Young, Keith Gordon, Robert Downey, Jr., Paxton Whitehead, Terry Farrell, M. Emmet Walsh, Adrienne Barbeau, Ned Beatty, Severn Darden, Sam Kinison, Robert Picardo, Kurt Vonnegut, Jr., Edie McClurg, Jason Hervey. Bombastic, uneducated, self-made millionaire enrolls in college, in order to encourage his student son. Very entertaining comedy, full of hilarious Dangerfield one-liners, but key to the film's success is that Rodney's character is so likable. Kellerman shines, too, as English professor who becomes the apple of his eye. [PG-13]▼●◗

Back to the Beach (1987) **C-92m.** ** D: Lyndall Hobbs. Frankie Avalon, Annette Funicello, Lori Loughlin, Tommy Hinckley, Connie Stevens, Demian Slade; guest appearances by Don Adams, Bob Denver, Alan Hale, Jerry Mathers, Tony Dow, Barbara Billingsley, Edd Byrnes, Pee-wee Herman (Paul Reubens), Dick Dale and The Del-Tones. Frankie and Annette return to the scene of their youth—older but no wiser—as the parents of teens. The fun wears thin pretty fast in this uninspired comedy—despite the efforts of *six writers* and the presence of 1950s and 60s TV sitcom stars in cameo roles. The songs are dull, too, though Annette's "Jamaica Ska" has its moments. [PG]▼●

Back to the Future (1985) **C-116m.** *** D: Robert Zemeckis. Michael J. Fox, Christopher Lloyd, Crispin Glover, Lea Thompson, Wendie Jo Sperber, Marc McClure, Claudia Wells, Thomas F. Wilson, James Tolkan, Casey Siemaszko, Billy Zane, Jason Hervey. A teenager of the '80s travels back in time to the '50s, where he must arrange for his mismatched parents to meet—or else *he* won't exist! Wonderful, wacked-out time-travel comedy takes its time to get going, but once it does, it's a lot of fun, building to a frantic climax just like other Bob Gale–Robert Zemeckis scripts (USED CARS, I WANNA HOLD YOUR HAND, 1941). Lloyd is a standout as crazed scientist who sets story in motion. Huey Lewis, who sings film's hit song, "The Power of Love," has cameo as a high-school teacher. Produced by Steven Spielberg and company. Followed by two sequels and an animated TV series. [PG]▼●

Back to the Future Part II (1989) **C-107m.** ** D: Robert Zemeckis. Michael J. Fox, Christopher Lloyd, Lea Thompson, Thomas F. Wilson, Harry Waters Jr., Charles Fleischer, Joe Flaherty, Elisabeth Shue, James Tolkan, Casey Siemaszko, Elijah Wood. Joyless, frenetic follow-up to Part 1 which sends mad inventor Lloyd and young Fox back into their time-traveling DeLorean. Considerable ingenuity, but hardly any laughs, and a surprising amount of unpleasantness. Works best toward the end when it creates a parallel existence to the climactic action in Part 1, but then it turns out to be a cliffhanger, advertising the upcoming Part III! Talk about a cheat . . . [PG]▼●

Back to the Future Part III (1990) **C-118m.** ***½ D: Robert Zemeckis. Michael J. Fox, Christopher Lloyd, Mary Steenburgen, Thomas F. Wilson, Lea Thompson, Elisabeth Shue, Matt Clark, Richard Dysart, Pat Buttram, Harry Carey, Jr., Dub Taylor, James Tolkan, ZZ Top. Delightful conclusion to this time-travel trilogy sends Fox back to the Old West, circa 1885, in search of Lloyd—hoping to change history and keep him from being shot in the back by a bad guy. The dormant movie Western gets a major dose of adrenaline from this high-tech, high-powered comic adventure, which offers great fun, dazzling special effects, and imagination to spare. There's real movie magic at work here. [PG]▼●

Back to the Wall (1959-French) **94m.** ** D: Edouard Molinaro. Gerard Oury, Jeanne Moreau, Philippe Nicaud, Claire Maurier, Jean Lefebvre. As the adulterous wife, Moreau spins entertaining web of extortion and murder; satisfactory suspenser.▼

Backtrack (1969) **C-95m.** ** D: Earl Bellamy. Neville Brand, James Drury, Doug McClure, Peter Brown, Ida Lupino, Rhonda Fleming, Fernando Lamas. Maverick cowboy on the range. No more than an elongated version of a 1965 *Virginian* TV episode (which served as a pilot for the subsequent *Laredo* series). [G]

Backtrack (1989) **C-98m.** **½ D: Dennis Hopper. Dennis Hopper, Jodie Foster, Dean Stockwell, Vincent Price, John Turturro, Fred Ward, Charlie Sheen, G. Anthony Sirico, Julie Adams, Sy Richardson, Frank Gio, Helena Kallianiotes, Bob Dylan. Contemporary melodrama about a hit man hired to rub out murder eyewitness Foster—but falling in love and taking it on the lam with her instead. Although film isn't particularly distinguished, it *is* entertaining—especially with that Who's Who cast. (Joe Pesci, despite a substantial role, appears unbilled.) Released first in Europe as CATCHFIRE; Hopper disowned that version.

Restored to his cut (116m.) for U.S. release on cable and video in 1991. [R]▼

Backwoods Massacre SEE: **Midnight** (1981)

Bad and the Beautiful, The (1952) **118m.** ***½ D: Vincente Minnelli. Kirk Douglas, Lana Turner, Dick Powell, Gloria Grahame, Barry Sullivan, Walter Pidgeon, Gilbert Roland. Captivating Hollywood story of ambitious producer (Douglas) told via relationships with actress Turner, writer Powell, director Sullivan. Solid, insightful, witty, with Lana's best performance ever. Five Oscars include Supporting Actress (Grahame), Screenplay (Charles Schnee). David Raksin's wonderful score is another asset. Minnelli and Douglas followed this a decade later with TWO WEEKS IN ANOTHER TOWN. Also shown in computer-colored version.▼●

Bad Bascomb (1946) **110m.** ** D: S. Sylvan Simon. Wallace Beery, Margaret O'Brien, Marjorie Main, J. Carrol Naish, Marshall Thompson. Overlong Western with fine action scenes, overshadowed by incredibly syrupy ones with Beery and O'Brien.

Bad Behavior (1993-British) **C-103m.** **½ D: Les Blair. Stephen Rea, Sinead Cusack, Philip Jackson, Clare Higgins, Phil Daniels, Mary Jo Randle, Saira Todd, Amanda Boxer. Amusing comedy with Rea and Cusack as a couple whose marital complacency is challenged by their friends, their jobs, and a bathroom renovation. A quietly quirky slant on domestic life in the Mike Leigh mold (the actors improvised from director Blair's story outline) which rambles along nicely without ever really catching fire. Rea and Cusack are charming in the lead roles.▼

Bad Blood (1981-New Zealand-British) **C-104m.** *** D: Mike Newell. Jack Thompson, Carol Burns, Denis Lill, Donna Akersten, Martyn Sanderson, Marshall Napier. Set during WW2, this provocative drama is a fact-based account of a backwoods farmer (Thompson) who shoots several people and is hunted in the New Zealand bush. The incident ends up being exploited by Lord Haw-Haw, the notorious Nazi propagandist.▼

Bad Blood (1987-French) **C-128m.** ** D: Leos Carax. Michel Piccoli, Denis Lavant, Juliette Binoche, Hans Meyer, Julie Delpy, Carroll Brooks, Serge Reggiani. Occasionally interesting but too often pretentious account of plot to pilfer a serum that's an antidote for an AIDS-like disease. Shot mostly in close-ups of faces, legs, etc., which eventually grows tiresome. [R]▼

Bad Blood (1989) **C-104m.** ** D: Chuck Vincent. Gregory Patrick, Ruth Raymond, Linda Blair, Troy Donahue, Carolyn Van Bellinghen. Overlong, low-budget thriller with OK plot (reminiscent of Stephen King's *Misery*) about Patrick learning he's the long-lost son of eccentric, possessive millionairess Raymond; Blair is his victimized wife. Some good ideas, many bad ones—occasional scenes go on for minutes without cuts. [R]▼

Bad Boy (1949) **86m.** **½ D: Kurt Neumann. Lloyd Nolan, Jane Wyatt, Audie Murphy, James Gleason, Martha Vickers, Stanley Clements, Rhys Williams, James Lydon, Dickie Moore, Selena Royle, Tommy Cook. Slight BOYS TOWN variation in which Murphy, in his first starring role, plays a supposedly incorrigible teen destined to straighten out during his stay at the Variety Clubs Boys Ranch. Also known as THE STORY OF DANNY LESTER.▼

Bad Boys (1983) **C-123m.** *** D: Rick Rosenthal. Sean Penn, Reni Santoni, Esai Morales, Eric Gurry, Jim Moody, Ally Sheedy, Clancy Brown, Alan Ruck. Tough urban melodrama about juvenile prison, and a personal vendetta that reaches its peak within prison walls. Criticized by some as being amoral—and not always credible—but certainly scores on an emotional level. Sheedy's feature film debut. [R]▼●◗

Bad Boys (1995) **C-126m.** **½ D: Michael Bay. Martin Lawrence, Will Smith, Téa Leoni, Theresa Randall, Tcheky Karyo, Marg Helgenberger, Anna Thomson. Highly formulaic but not altogether disposable Miami actioner about two cops—one married with kids, the other equipped with a bachelor apartment—who are forced to switch roles after they're mistaken for each other during a drug-murder case. A return by producers Don Simpson and Jerry Bruckheimer to the kind of corpse-littered escapism that established them in the '80s; wildly uneven comedy is aided by the spin Leoni puts on her role as a material witness who's hiding undercover with the heroes. A robust half hour padded into two hours. [R]▼●◗

Bad Channels (1992) **C-88m.** BOMB D: Ted Nicolaou. Paul Hipp, Martha Quinn, Aaron Lustig, Ian Patrick Williams, Michael Huddleston, Victor Rogers, Charlie Spradling, Melissa Behr. An alien resembling a two-legged, metallic blue cauliflower takes over a radio station and begins shrinking girls who have rock video visions. Confused, silly mess of a movie; rotten channels is more like it. Sequel: DOLLMAN VS. THE DEMONIC TOYS (1993). From Full Moon. [R]▼

Bad Company (1931) **75m.** **½ D: Tay Garnett. Ricardo Cortez, Helen Twelvetrees, John Garrick, Paul Hurst, Frank Conroy, Frank McHugh, Kenneth Thomson, Harry Carey. Fair curio with hood Cortez arranging for lawyer underling Garrick to wed naive Twelvetrees, sister of his rival. Deservedly not as famous as the other gangster pictures of its day.▼●

Bad Company (1972) **C-93m.** ***½ D: Robert Benton. Jeff Bridges, Barry Brown, Jim Davis, David Huddleston, John Savage,

Jerry Houser. Highly entertaining sleeper about two young drifters of wildly differing temperaments who rob their way West during the Civil War; aided immeasurably by Gordon Willis' subdued photography, Harvey Schmidt's piano score. Written by Benton and David Newman; Benton's directorial debut. [PG]▼

Bad Company (1995) **C-108m.** *½ D: Damian Harris. Ellen Barkin, Laurence Fishburne, Frank Langella, Michael Beach, Gia Carides, David Ogden Stiers, Daniel Hugh Kelly, Spalding Gray, James Hong. Ex-CIA staffer is recruited to join a private firm specializing in "covert operations"—like blackmail and murder—but there's more than meets the eye at every twist and turn. Never-ending series of double-crosses leads to a "who cares?" finale. Only some hot-and-heavy sex scenes stand out. Michael Murphy appears unbilled as Smitty. Panavision. [R]▼●

Bad Day at Black Rock (1955) **C-81m.** ***½ D: John Sturges. Spencer Tracy, Robert Ryan, Anne Francis, Dean Jagger, Walter Brennan, John Ericson, Ernest Borgnine, Lee Marvin. Powerhouse cast in yarn of one-armed man (Tracy) uncovering skeleton in Western town's closet. Borgnine memorable as slimy heavy. Millard Kaufman expertly adapted Howard Breslin's story "Bad Time at Hondo." Excellent use of CinemaScope is lost on TV.▼●

Bad Dreams (1988) **C-84m.** BOMB D: Andrew Fleming. Jennifer Rubin, Bruce Abbott, Richard Lynch, Harris Yulin, Dean Cameron, Susan Barnes, E.G. Daily, Sy Richardson, Susan Ruttan, Charles Fleischer. Imitative horror flick about Rubin awakening as an adult after thirteen years in a coma (following her scrape with death as part of a suicide pact enacted by cult leader Lynch). Members of her therapy group are murdered one by one and she thinks Lynch's ghost is responsible. Chintzy effects, poor script and direction sink this one. [R]▼●

Bad For Each Other (1953) **83m.** **½ D: Irving Rapper. Charlton Heston, Lizabeth Scott, Dianne Foster, Mildred Dunnock, Marjorie Rambeau. Idealistic doctor Heston finds Pennsylvania mining town has more worthy patients than idle social set. Pouty Scott and wise Rambeau are good.

Badge of the Assassin (1985) **C-100m. TVM** D: Mel Damski. James Woods, Yaphet Kotto, Alex Rocco, David Harris, Steven Keats, Larry Riley, Pam Grier, Rae Dawn Chong, Richard Bradford. Bristling police drama about real-life Manhattan assistant D.A. who directed campaign to locate a pair of cop killers of the '70s. Based by Lawrence Roman on the bestseller by Robert K. Tanenbaum (played with nervous intensity by Woods) and Philip Rosenberg. Above average.▼●

Badge 373 (1973) **C-116m.** *½ D: Howard W. Koch. Robert Duvall, Verna Bloom, Henry Darrow, Eddie Egan, Felipe Luciano, Tina Christiana. Very minor follow-up to THE FRENCH CONNECTION. Policeman Duvall tries to fight crime syndicate single-handedly in N.Y.C. Dull. [R]▼

Bad Girl (1956-British) **100m.** ** D: Herbert Wilcox. Anna Neagle, Sylvia Syms, Kenneth Haigh, Norman Wooland, Wilfrid Hyde-White, Helen Haye, Julia Lockwood. Widowed mom Neagle becomes distraught when 17-year-old daughter Syms takes up with creep Haigh. Cornball curio which serves as proof that not all bad 1950s movies about teenagers were made in the U.S. Video title: TEENAGE BAD GIRL. Original British title: MY TEENAGE DAUGHTER.▼

Bad Girls (1994) **C-99m.** *½ D: Jonathan Kaplan. Madeleine Stowe, Mary Stuart Masterson, Andie MacDowell, Drew Barrymore, Dermot Mulroney, James Russo, Robert Loggia, Jim Beaver, Cooper Huckabee. Stowe and three other prostitutes go on the lam after a brothel shooting, eventually hooking up with a male outlaw from her past. Troubled production is an uneasy combination of feminist statement, homage to (or rip-off of) THE WILD BUNCH's finale, and an advertisement for good-looking Western duds. A collectible poster in search of a movie. Unrated video version available. [R]▼●

Bad Guys (1986) **C-86m.** BOMB D: Joel Silberg. Adam Baldwin, Mike Jolly, Michelle Nicastro, Ruth Buzzi, James Booth, Gene LeBell, Norman Burton. Shamelessly inane comedy about a pair of moronic young cops who become wrestlers after receiving their walking papers from the force. Predictably, a ringful of popular wrestlers also appear. Yecch! [PG]▼

Bad Influence (1990) **C-99m.** **½ D: Curtis Hanson. Rob Lowe, James Spader, Lisa Zane, Christian Clemenson, Kathleen Wilhoite, Tony Maggio, David Duchovny. Spader befriends Lowe after the latter gets him out of a tense barroom confrontation, then finds this psychopathic leech calling the shots in his romantic—and professional—life. Slick, high-tech variation on STRANGERS ON A TRAIN knows which buttons to push. Lowe is passable, but he's no Robert Walker. [R]▼●

Bad Jim (1990) **C-90m.** ** D: Clyde Ware. James Brolin, Richard Roundtree, John Clark Gable, Harry Carey, Jr., Rory Calhoun, Ty Hardin, Pepe Serna, Bruce Kirby. Not-bad Western has three good/bad men purchasing Billy the Kid's horse—and using it to pass themselves off as Billy's gang. Nice locations and welcome cast of veterans help make up for leisurely pace and lack of real action. Screen debut for Clark Gable's son, as the youngest of the bandit trio. [PG]▼●

Badlanders, The (1958) **C-83m.** *** D: Delmer Daves. Alan Ladd, Ernest Borgnine, Katy Jurado, Claire Kelly. Turn-of-the-century Western set in Arizona with Ladd and Borgnine planning gold robbery, each trying to outsmart the other; nicely handled by all. Remake of THE ASPHALT JUNGLE. CinemaScope. ▼

Bad Lands (1939) **70m.** **½ D: Lew Landers. Noah Beery, Jr., Robert Barrat, Guinn Williams, Douglas Walton, Andy Clyde, Addison Richards, Robert Coote, Paul Hurst. Thinly disguised Western remake of THE LOST PATROL, about a posse stranded in the Arizona wilderness and trapped by Apaches. Painless and forgettable.▼

Badlands (1973) **C-95m.** **½ D: Terrence Malick. Martin Sheen, Sissy Spacek, Warren Oates, Ramon Bieri, Alan Vint. Stark, moody, moderately successful thriller inspired by the Starkweather-Fugate killing spree in the 50s. Well-cast film has cult following. [PG]▼●◗

Badlands of Dakota (1941) **74m.** **½ D: Alfred E. Green. Robert Stack, Ann Rutherford, Richard Dix, Frances Farmer, Broderick Crawford, Hugh Herbert. Brothers Crawford and Stack fight over Rutherford, while Wild Bill Hickok (Dix) does fighting of another kind.

Badlands of Montana (1957) **75m.** *½ D: Daniel B. Ullman. Rex Reason, Beverly Garland, Keith Larsen, Jack Kruschen. Unimaginative oater leading up to inevitable climax of former buddies, sheriff and gunslinger, having shoot-out. Regalscope.

Bad Lieutenant (1992) **C-98m.** ** D: Abel Ferrara. Harvey Keitel, Frankie Thorn, Paul Hipp, Victor Argo, Paul Calderone, Leonard Thomas. Also bad husband, bad substance abuser, all-around bad dude. Over-the-top Catholic guilt movie about a cop who starts to pull himself out of the abyss when he investigates the rape of a nun who refuses to press charges. More pretentious than Ferrara's earlier work, though film has substantial critical and cult following. Featured player Zoe Lund (who also coscripted with Ferrara) was formerly Zoe Tamerlis, star of Ferrara's MS. 45. At the very least, this is the first movie that offers full-frontal Keitel and a cameo by Jesus. [NC-17]▼●◗

Bad Lord Byron (1951-British) **85m.** **½ D: David Macdonald. Dennis Price, Joan Greenwood, Mai Zetterling, Sonia Holm. Potentially exciting but static retelling of the life of 19th-century poet and lover, focusing on his many romances.▼

Bad Love (1992) **C-94m.** BOMB D: Jill Goldman. Tom Sizemore, Pamela Gidley, Seymour Cassel, Richard Edson, Debi Mazar, Jennifer O'Neill, Margaux Hemingway, Joe Dallesandro. BAD MOVIE would be a more appropriate title. Perfectly dreadful drama about hot-tempered, two-bit hustler Sizemore and pretty loser Gidley who commence a hot-and-heavy, ill-fated romance. Poor direction and a laughable script do this one in. [R]▼◗

Bad Man, The (1941) **70m.** **½ D: Richard Thorpe. Wallace Beery, Lionel Barrymore, Laraine Day, Ronald Reagan, Henry Travers. Fairly good co-starring vehicle for Beery, as Western outlaw, and Barrymore, as former friend who depends on the bad man's loyalty.

Bad Manners (1998) **C-90m.** *** D: Jonathan Kaufer. David Strathairn, Bonnie Bedelia, Saul Rubinek, Caroleen Feeney, Julie Harris. An egotistical musicologist and his companion spend the weekend with his ex-lover, who's now married to a college professor. Sparks fly from the start as the four flinty personalities collide; an exercise in sexual and psychological gamesmanship reminiscent of WHO'S AFRAID OF VIRGINIA WOOLF?, and splendidly acted all around. Adapted by David Gilman from his play *Ghost in the Machine*. [R]▼

Bad Man of Brimstone (1938) **90m.** ** D: J. Walter Ruben. Wallace Beery, Virginia Bruce, Dennis O'Keefe, Joseph Calleia, Lewis Stone, Guy Kibbee, Bruce Cabot. Low-grade Western vehicle is for Beery fans, with star as outlaw who is reformed by family revelation.

Badman's Country (1958) **68m.** **½ D: Fred F. Sears. George Montgomery, Buster Crabbe, Neville Brand, Malcolm Atterbury. Fictionalized Western history with name-dropping cast of characters. Sheriff Pat Garrett (Montgomery) joins with Wyatt Earp (Crabbe) and Buffalo Bill (Atterbury) for showdown with Butch Cassidy (Brand).

Bad Man's River (1972-Italian-Spanish) **C-89m.** ** D: Gene (Eugenio) Martin. Lee Van Cleef, James Mason, Gina Lollobrigida, Simon Andreu, Diana Lorys. Van Cleef is head of an outlaw gang repeatedly out-smarted by devilish Lollobrigida in this pallid comedy-Western made in Spain. Franscope. [PG]▼●◗

Badman's Territory (1946) **97m.** *** D: Tim Whelan. Randolph Scott, Ann Richards, George "Gabby" Hayes, Ray Collins, James Warren, Morgan Conway, Virginia Sale, Chief Thundercloud, Lawrence Tierney, Steve Brodie, Isabel Jewell. Solid Western in which a sheriff (Scott, at his stalwart best) is forced to ride into an outlaws' haven, setting off non-stop fireworks. Rich characterizations, with Hayes fun as the Coyote Kid. Also shown in computer-colored version.▼

Bad Medicine (1985) **C-96m.** BOMB D: Harvey Miller. Steve Guttenberg, Alan Arkin, Julie Hagerty, Bill Macy, Curtis Armstrong, Julie Kavner, Joe Grifasi, Robert Romanus, Taylor Negron, Gilbert Gottfried. Guttenberg can't get into any domestic medical schools, so he's forced to attend a dubious Central American institution run by Arkin. Cheap jokes and ethnic putdowns abound. Our prescription: skip it. [PG-13]▼

Bad Men of Missouri (1941) **74m.** *** D: Ray Enright. Dennis Morgan, Jane Wyman, Wayne Morris, Arthur Kennedy, Victor Jory, Alan Baxter. Younger brothers, enraged by Southern carpetbaggers, turn to lawless life in fictional Western, with good cast.

Bad Moon (1996) **C-79m.** ** D: Eric Red. Mariel Hemingway, Michael Paré, Mason Gamble, Ken Pogue, Hrothgar Mathews. Hemingway is glad when her brother comes to live with her and her young son Gamble; only the family German shepherd knows that Paré is really the werewolf that has been killing locals in the Northwest woods. Good-looking horror movie with a strong performance from Paré is underpopulated and predictable, though the dog's great. From the novel *Thor* by Wayne Smith. Clairmont-Scope. [R]▼●

Bad News Bears, The (1976) **C-102m.** *** D: Michael Ritchie. Walter Matthau, Tatum O'Neal, Vic Morrow, Joyce Van Patten, Jackie Earle Haley, Alfred W. Lutter. Bright comedy about hopeless Little League baseball team that scores with an unlikely combination: a beer-guzzling coach (Matthau) and a female star pitcher (O'Neal). Some of film's major appeal—young kids spouting four-letter words—may be lost on TV. Clever use of Bizet's music from *Carmen*. Followed by two sequels and a TV series. [PG]▼●

Bad News Bears Go To Japan, The (1978) **C-91m.** ** D: John Berry. Tony Curtis, Jackie Earle Haley, Tomisaburo Wakayama, George Wyner, Lonny Chapman. Curtis is good as a small-time hustler who sees money-making opportunity in the now-familiar baseball team. Third film was the kids' last, and it's easy to see why. [PG]▼●

Bad News Bears in Breaking Training, The (1977) **C-100m.** **½ D: Michael Pressman. William Devane, Jackie Earle Haley, Jimmy Baio, Clifton James, Chris Barnes. Sentimental sequel to 1976 hit, with dirty talk largely absent. Star of the kids' baseball team, Haley heads for the Houston Astrodome and enlists the aid of estranged father Devane in coaching the misfits. Sporadically funny. [PG]▼●

Bad Seed, The (1956) **129m.** *** D: Mervyn LeRoy. Nancy Kelly, Patty McCormack, Henry Jones, Eileen Heckart, Evelyn Varden, William Hopper. Stagy but spellbinding account of malicious child McCormack whose inherited evil "causes" deaths of several people. Fine performances; Maxwell Anderson's Broadway play was adapted by John Lee Mahin, with Kelly, McCormack, Jones, and Heckart recreating their stage roles. The corny "Hollywoodized" postscript is often cut but remains intact on the videocassette. Remade for TV in 1985. McCormack later played a bad seed grown up in MOMMY.▼●

Bad Sleep Well, The (1960-Japanese) **135m.** *** D: Akira Kurosawa. Toshiro Mifune, Takeshi Kato, Masayuki Mori, Takashi Shimura, Akira Nishimura. Kurosawa effectively captures the spirit of 1940s Warner Bros. crime dramas in this engrossing tale of rising executive Mifune and corruption in the corporate world. Actually, it's a variation on *Hamlet*. Original version runs 151m. Tohoscope. ▼●

Bad Taste (1988-New Zealand) **C-90m.** **½ D: Peter Jackson. Peter Jackson, Pete O'Herne, Mike Minett, Terry Potter, Craig Smith, Doug Wren, Dean Lawrie. Title is absolutely accurate in describing this gory comedy about callous alien fast-food entrepreneurs, here to harvest humanity, and battling it out with government hit squad. Quirky, fragmented direction matches subject matter and acting styles. Director Jackson also acted, wrote, edited, produced, and did the uneven but occasionally excellent makeup. A cult hit worldwide.▼●

Bad Timing: A Sensual Obsession (1980-British) **C-129m.** ***½ D: Nicolas Roeg. Art Garfunkel, Theresa Russell, Harvey Keitel, Denholm Elliott, Daniel Massey. Mesmerizing melodrama triumphs over badly miscast male leads and occasional pretentiousness. Roeg's kinetic style brings the necessary passion to oddball story of a psychiatrist sexually engulfed by a self-destructive tramp. Russell is simply great, as is knockout background music from The Who, Keith Jarrett, and Billie Holiday. Technovision. [R—originally rated X]

Bagdad (1949) **C-82m.** ** D: Charles Lamont. Maureen O'Hara, Paul Christian, Vincent Price, John Sutton. Costume hijinks with O'Hara fetching if not believable as native chieftain's daughter seeking revenge for father's death in old Turkey.▼

Bagdad Cafe (1988-West German) **C-108m.** **½ D: Percy Adlon. Marianne Sägebrecht, CCH Pounder, Jack Palance, Christine Kaufmann, Monica Calhoun, Darron Flagg. Nearly plotless charmer from the director and star of SUGARBABY has Sägebrecht stranded in the California desert, making friends with the kooky folks who hang out at Pounder's roadside cafe. Palance provides a special treat portraying an ex-Hollywood set decorator who becomes obsessed with painting Sägebrecht's portrait. German version runs twenty minutes longer. Later a TV series. [PG]▼●

Bahama Passage (1941) **C-83m.** **½ D: Edward Griffith. Madeleine Carroll, Sterling Hayden, Flora Robson, Leo G. Carroll, Mary Anderson. Scenery is chief asset of routine tale of lovely Madeleine meeting handsome Sterling in beautiful Bahama, with much hamming by Carroll and Robson. The stars later married in real life.

Bailiff, The SEE: **Sansho the Bailiff**

Bailout at 43,000 (1957) **78m.** ** D: Francis D. Lyon. John Payne, Karen Steele, Paul Kelly, Richard Eyer, Constance Ford. Dilemma of air force pilot Payne whose relief at not having to test new safety device is outweighed by coward-guilt complex. Routine material is not enhanced by flight sequences or romantic relief.▼

Bait (1954) **79m.** *½ D: Hugo Haas. Cleo Moore, Hugo Haas, John Agar, Emmett Lynn. A mining-camp ménage à trois. Heavy-handed Haas at his worst, despite intriguing pre-credit prologue with Cedric Hardwicke as the Devil.

Baja Oklahoma (1988) **C-105m. TVM** D: Bobby Roth. Lesley Ann Warren, Peter Coyote, Swoosie Kurtz, Billy Vera, Anthony Zerbe, William Forsythe, Julia Roberts, Willie Nelson, Emmylou Harris, Alice Krige, Bob Wills, Jr. Lively adaptation of Dan Jenkins' funny novel of a smalltown Texas barmaid who is juggling her dreams of becoming a songwriter with her rocky romances. Loaded with local color and music stars like Billy Vera (of Billy and the Beaters), Willie Nelson (who cowrote the title song with Jenkins), Emmylou Harris, Bob Wills, Jr. (as his dad), plus South African actress Alice Krige as Patsy Cline. Written by Jenkins and director Roth. Made for cable, but also briefly released to theaters. Above average.▼●

Baker's Hawk (1976) **C-98m.** *** D: Lyman D. Dayton. Clint Walker, Burl Ives, Diane Baker, Lee H. Montgomery, Alan Young, Taylor Lacher. Fine family drama about young boy (Montgomery) who befriends hermitlike Ives, and comes of age as he participates in parents' struggle against vigilante forces. Beautifully filmed on location in Utah. [G]▼◗

Baker's Wife, The (1938-French) **124m.** ***½ D: Marcel Pagnol. Raimu, Ginette Leclerc, Charles Moulin, Robert Vattier, Robert Brassac, Charpin. Abandoned by his wife for a shepherd, baker Raimu is unable to function; villagers, who love his bread as much as he loves his wife, bring back the wayward woman. Hilarious.▼

Balalaika (1939) **102m.** ** D: Reinhold Schunzel. Nelson Eddy, Ilona Massey, Charles Ruggles, Frank Morgan, Lionel Atwill, George Tobias. Plodding operetta of Russian revolution with little to recommend it.▼

Balboa (1986) **C-91m.** **½ D: James Polakof. Tony Curtis, Carol Lynley, Jennifer Chase, Chuck Connors, Lupita Ferrer, Sonny Bono, Catherine Campbell, Cassandra Peterson, Martine Beswicke, Henry Jones, Steve Kanaly. Road company version of TV soap *Dallas,* replete with guest star Kanaly, is enjoyably silly. Curtis is the hissable tycoon in Balboa, out to pull off a real estate scam while everybody's sleeping with everyone else's mate. Episodic structure (narrated by Beswicke) is the result of film being edited down from original (unsold) miniseries. Filmed in 1982.▼

Balcony, The (1963) **84m.** ** D: Joseph Strick. Shelley Winters, Peter Falk, Lee Grant, Ruby Dee, Peter Brocco, Kent Smith, Jeff Corey, Leonard Nimoy. Low-budget, none-too-successful attempt to adapt Jean Genet play to the screen, with Winters as madam who maintains her brothel during a revolution. Grant stands out as Winters' lesbian confidante.▼●

Ballad in Blue SEE: **Blues for Lovers**

Ballad of a Soldier (1959-Russian) **89m.** *** D: Grigori Chukrai. Vladimir Ivashov, Shanna Prokhorenko, Antonina Maximova, Nikolai Kruchkov. Effectively simple, poetic love story chronicling the plight of Russian soldier who falls in love with country girl while on leave during WW2. Works both as a romantic drama and an allegory about the sadness and stupidity of war.▼●

Ballad of Cable Hogue, The (1970) **C-121m.** *** D: Sam Peckinpah. Jason Robards, Stella Stevens, David Warner, Strother Martin, Slim Pickens, L. Q. Jones, R.G. Armstrong. Peckinpah's lyrical, wholly enjoyable fable of loner who builds a life for himself in remote part of the Old West. Stevens has one of her best roles as whore who joins Cable Hogue in quest for the good life. Overlong. [R]▼●

Ballad of Gregorio Cortez, The (1982) **C-99m.** **½ D: Robert M. Young. Edward James Olmos, James Gammon, Tom Bower, Bruce McGill, Brion James, Alan Vint, Rosana DeSoto, Pepe Serna, William Sanderson, Barry Corbin, Tim Scott. True story, told from several points of view, of 1901 incident in which a young Mexican killed an American sheriff, then managed to elude a 600-man posse for nearly two weeks! Authentic to the core—almost like being in a time capsule, in fact—but too subdued, especially in its portrayal of Cortez, whose plight isn't fully explained until the end of the film. A PBS *American Playhouse* presentation. [PG]▼●

Ballad of Josie, The (1967) **C-102m.** **½ D: Andrew McLaglen. Doris Day, Peter Graves, George Kennedy, Andy Devine, William Talman, David Hartman, Don Stroud. Uninspired Western spoof with widow Day running a ranch and trying to lead the good life. Techniscope.

Ballad of Little Jo, The (1993) **C-120m.** *** D: Maggie Greenwald. Suzy Amis, Bo Hopkins, Ian McKellen, David Chung, Carrie Snodgress, Rene Auberjonois, Heather Graham, Sam Robards, Ruth Malaczech, Anthony Heald, Melissa Leo. Fascinating tale of a genteel young woman in 1866 who, disgraced by having a child out of wedlock, flees to the American West and quickly learns that the only way to survive on her own is to pretend that she's a man. Writer-director Greenwald hits all the right notes in this convincing and well-crafted piece of fiction (inspired by a real-life woman), with a first-rate cast making the most of every incident. Amis is a revelation in the leading role. Flavorful music score composed and performed by David Mansfield. [R]▼●

Ballad of Tam Lin, The (1971) **C-107m.** ** D: Roddy McDowall. Ava Gardner, Ian McShane, Stephanie Beacham, Cyril Cusack, Richard Wattis, Sinead Cusack, Joanna Lumley. A wealthy, beautiful woman gathers hedonistic young people around her—and seeks to control their destinies. Based (believe it or not) on a Robert Burns poem, reset in England in the Swingin' Sixties. McDowall's only directorial effort is ambitious and unusual, but unsatisfying. Shot in 1969, recut and released under various titles including TAM LIN and THE DEVIL'S WIDOW. Panavision. [PG]▼

Ballad of the Sad Cafe, The (1991) **C-101m.** *½ D: Simon Callow. Vanessa Redgrave, Keith Carradine, Rod Steiger, Cork Hubbert, Austin Pendleton, Beth Dixon, Lanny Flaherty. Truly odd stab at filming Depression-era tale of Southerner Redgrave, a loner who rules rural hamlet like a despot—until hunchback Hubbert and ex-con husband Carradine appear. Far too theatrical in its look, tone, and pacing; Redgrave's performance may interest drama students, but nothing in film really works. Based on Carson McCullers' novella (and its stage adaptation by Edward Albee). Film directing debut of British actor/stage director Callow.▼

Ball of Fire (1941) **111m.** ***½ D: Howard Hawks. Gary Cooper, Barbara Stanwyck, Oscar Homolka, Dana Andrews, Dan Duryea, S. Z. Sakall, Richard Haydn, Henry Travers, Tully Marshall, Gene Krupa. Burlesque dancer moves in with eight prissy professors (led by Cooper) to explain "slang" for their new encyclopedia; delightful twist on *Snow White and the Seven Dwarfs* by screenwriters Billy Wilder and Charles Brackett. Remade (by same director) as A SONG IS BORN.▼●◗

Baltimore Bullet, The (1980) **C-103m.** **½ D: Robert Ellis Miller. James Coburn, Omar Sharif, Bruce Boxleitner, Ronee Blakley, Jack O'Halloran, Calvin Lockhart. Pleasant enough film about major-league pool hustlers Coburn and Boxleitner, and their buildup to a high noon showdown with smoothie Sharif. [PG]▼

Balto (1995) **C-77m.** **½ D: Simon Wells. Voices of Kevin Bacon, Bob Hoskins, Bridget Fonda, Jim Cummings, Phil Collins, Miriam Margolyes, Lola Bates-Campbell. Loosely based on a true story of the 1920s, Balto is a half-dog, half-wolf who overcomes his outcast past to guide a sled carrying urgent medical supplies to a town full of sick children in Alaska. Wholesome, lovingly told, and well animated, this offers humor, romance, villainy, warmth, and gives its young viewers something to think about. You could do a lot worse. Executive-produced by Steven Spielberg. [G]▼●

Bambi (1942) **C-69m.** **** D: David Hand. Walt Disney's moving and exquisitely detailed animated feature about a deer, and how the phases of its life parallel the cycle of seasons in the forest. An extraordinary achievement, with the memorably endearing character of Thumper stealing every scene he's in.▼●

Bambole! (1965-Italian) **111m.** ** D: Dino Risi. Luigi Comencini, Franco Rossi, Mauro Bolognini, Virna Lisi, Nino Manfredi, Elke Sommer, Monica Vitti, Gina Lollobrigida, Akim Tamiroff, Jean Sorel. Quartet of stories on Italian life that never sparkles. "The Phone Call," "Treatise on Eugenics," "The Soup," "Monsignor Cupid." Retitled: FOUR KINDS OF LOVE.

Bamboo Prison, The (1954) **80m.** ** D: Lewis Seiler. Robert Francis, Dianne Foster, Brian Keith, Jerome Courtland, E. G. Marshall, Earle Hyman. Superficial handling of loyal American soldier Francis posing as informer in North Korean P.O.W. camp to outwit enemy.

Bamboo Saucer, The (1968) **C-100m.** **½ D: Frank Telford. Dan Duryea, John Ericson, Lois Nettleton, Nan Leslie, Bob Hastings. Better-than-average low-budget sci-fier about American and USSR teams investigating a UFO spotting in mainland China. Nettleton's tongue-in-cheek portrayal of a Russian scientist aids considerably. Duryea's last film. Aka COLLISION COURSE. [PG]▼

Banana Monster, The SEE: **Schlock**

Banana Peel (1964-French) **97m.** *** D: Marcel Ophuls. Jeanne Moreau, Jean-Paul Belmondo, Gert Frobe. Rogues cheat millionaire out of a small fortune in this engaging comedy. Franscope.

Bananas (1971) **C-82m.** **** D: Woody Allen. Woody Allen, Louise Lasser, Carlos Montalban, Howard Cosell, Rene Enriquez, Charlotte Rae, Conrad Bain. Hilarious; the usual assortment of good jokes, bad jokes, bizarre ideas built around unlikely premise of Woody becoming involved in revolution south of the border. Funny score by Marvin Hamlisch; look for Sylvester Stallone as hoodlum, Allen Garfield as man on cross. [PG]▼●

Bananas Boat, The (1974-British) **C-82m.** BOMB D: Sidney Hayers. Doug McClure, Hayley Mills, Lionel Jeffries, Warren Mitchell, Dilys Hamlett. Heavy-handed farce about young boob's attempts to escape from troubled banana republic by piloting boat out of its harbor. Originally titled WHAT CHANGED CHARLEY FARTHING, running-time 101m.▼

Bandido (1956) **C-92m.** *** D: Richard Fleischer. Robert Mitchum, Zachary Scott,

Ursula Thiess, Gilbert Roland, Rodolfo Acosta. Mitchum is gun supplier who tries to play both sides during 1916 Mexican rebellion; constant action, endless cat-and-mouse twists with rival Scott keep this one humming. CinemaScope.

Bandit of Sherwood Forest, The (1946) **C-86m.** **½ D: George Sherman, Henry Levin. Cornel Wilde, Anita Louise, Jill Esmond, Edgar Buchanan. Colorful but standard swashbuckler with Wilde as son of Robin Hood carrying on in faithful tradition with the Merry Men.

Bandit of Zhobe, The (1959-British) **C-80m.** **½ D: John Gilling. Victor Mature, Anthony Newley, Norman Wooland, Anne Aubrey, Walter Gotell, Sean Kelly. Moderate actioner set in 19th-century India with Mature as native chief turned outlaw combatting the British. CinemaScope.

Bandit Queen (1994-Indian) **C-119m.** *** D: Shekhar Kapur. Seema Biswas, Nirmal Pandey, Manoj Bajpai, Rajesh Vivek, Raghuvir Yadav, Govind Namdeo. Action-packed, fact-based adventure/drama/character study of the notorious female Indian outlaw Phoolan Devi (Biswas), who emerged from a life of poverty and ritual brutalization to be charged with numerous kidnappings, robberies, and killings. Yet she remains beloved by many of her country's poor as a Robin Hood–like legend. The film was as controversial as its subject; while based in part on diaries authored by Devi while in jail, she eventually repudiated the material. ▼●◗

Bandits, The (1967-Mexican) **C-89m.** ** D: Robert Conrad, Alfredo Zacharias. Robert Conrad, Jan-Michael Vincent, Roy Jenson, Pedro Armendariz, Jr., Manuel Lopez Ochoa. Ordinary Western about three cowboys, saved from the hangman's noose, who accompany their Mexican rescuer on various adventures south of the border. Unreleased here until 1979. ▼

Bandits (1986-French) **C-98m.** ** D: Claude Lelouch. Jean Yanne, Marie-Sophie L. (Lelouch), Patrick Bruel, Corinne Marchand, Charles Gerard. Yanne is a criminal, just released from prison, who's out to revenge his wife's murder and become reunited with daughter Marie-Sophie L. (director Lelouch's real-life wife). Sentimental drama downplays the thrills in favor of a nostalgic approach similar to Lelouch's superior HAPPY NEW YEAR, in which Gerard played virtually an identical sidekick role. Striking widescreen photography suffers on TV. CinemaScope. ▼

Bandits of Corsica, The (1953) **81m.** ** D: Ray Nazarro. Richard Greene, Paula Raymond, Raymond Burr, Lee Van Cleef. Pat costumer with Greene championing cause of the righteous.

Band of Angels (1957) **C-127m.** **½ D: Raoul Walsh. Clark Gable, Yvonne De Carlo, Sidney Poitier, Efrem Zimbalist, Jr., Patric Knowles. Flat costume epic from Robert Penn Warren's Civil War novel; Gable is Southern gentleman with shady past, in love with high-toned De Carlo who discovers she has Negro ancestors. Poitier is resolute educated slave. ▼●

Band of Outsiders (1964-French) **97m.** *** D: Jean-Luc Godard. Anna Karina, Sami Frey, Claude Brasseur, Louisa Colpeyn. Karina enlists the aid of two male hoods to swipe her aunt's stash, but as usual the supposed plot is only a jumping-off point for Godard's commentary on Hollywood melodramas and other twentieth-century artifacts. Among the more entertaining of the director's output; looks delightfully mellow today. ▼

Band of the Hand (1986) **C-109m.** BOMB D: Paul Michael Glaser. Stephen Lang, Michael Carmine, Lauren Holly, John Cameron Mitchell, James Remar, Daniele Quinn, Gerrit Graham. Five Miami punks are whipped into shape by a Vietnam vet, then form a vigilante unit to wipe out drug dealers. Moronic, way overlong junk from the creators of *Miami Vice*; Bob Dylan (*why,* Bob?) sings the title tune. [R] ▼●

Bandolero! (1968) **C-106m.** **½ D: Andrew V. McLaglen. James Stewart, Dean Martin, Raquel Welch, George Kennedy, Andrew Prine, Will Geer. Jimmy and Dino play outlaw brothers whose gang flees across Mexican border with Raquel as hostage. Not exactly like real life, but nice outdoor photography makes it passable escapism. Panavision. [PG] ▼

Band Wagon, The (1953) **C-112m.** **** D: Vincente Minnelli. Fred Astaire, Cyd Charisse, Oscar Levant, Nanette Fabray, Jack Buchanan. Sophisticated backstage musical improves with each viewing. Astaire plays a "washed-up" movie star who tries his luck on Broadway, under the direction of maniacal genius Buchanan. Musical highlights include "Dancing in the Dark," "Shine on Your Shoes," and "That's Entertainment" (all by Howard Dietz and Arthur Schwartz) and Astaire's Mickey Spillane spoof "The Girl Hunt." ▼●

Bang (1997) **C-98m.** *** D: Ash. Darling Narita, Peter Greene, Michael Newland, Luis Guzar, Lucy Liu. A desperate, unemployed actress (Narita) finds personal meaning and empowerment when she masquerades as a policewoman for a day. She also gets much more than she bargains for. Provocative look at L.A. on the brink. Film's shoestring budget and handheld camera work to brutally powerful effect despite uneven performances. ▼●◗

Bang-Bang Kid, The (1968-Spanish-Italian) **C-90m.** **½ D: Stanley Prager. Guy Madison, Tom Bosley, Sandra Milo, Riccardo Garrone, Jose Caffaral. Offbeat lighthearted turn-of-the-century Western that pits an iron-handed sheriff against an unassuming bumbler and a gun-toting robot called The Bang-Bang Kid. Aka BANG BANG.▼

Bang, Bang, You're Dead! (1966-British) **C-92m.** **½ D: Don Sharp. Tony Randall, Senta Berger, Terry-Thomas, Herbert Lom, Wilfrid Hyde-White. Unsuspecting Randall gets involved with Moroccan gangsters in OK spoof; good location shooting. Shown on TV as BANG BANG!▼

Bang the Drum Slowly (1973) **C-97m.** ***½ D: John Hancock. Michael Moriarty, Robert De Niro, Vincent Gardenia, Phil Foster, Ann Wedgeworth, Patrick McVey, Heather MacRae, Selma Diamond, Barbara Babcock, Tom Ligon, Nicolas Surovy, Danny Aiello. Touching study of two professional baseball players on fictional N.Y. team drawn to each other under unusual circumstances. Outstanding performances by two leads (Moriarty as hustling star pitcher, De Niro as simpleton catcher) in slightly longish, episodic script. Screenplay by Mark Harris, based on his 1956 novel; first dramatized on TV, with Paul Newman. Aiello's film debut. [PG] ▼●

Bang You're Dead SEE: **Game of Danger**

Banjo (1947) **67m.** **½ D: Richard Fleischer. Sharyn Moffett, Jacqueline White, Walter Reed, Una O'Connor, Herbert Evans, Louise Beavers. Warm little girl-and-her-dog tale, with young Moffett as a Southern orphan who loses her beloved pet when she has to move up to Boston and live with her snooty aunt. Formula stuff, well handled.

Banjo on My Knee (1936) **96m.** *** D: John Cromwell. Barbara Stanwyck, Joel McCrea, Walter Brennan, Buddy Ebsen, Helen Westley, Walter Catlett, Tony Martin. Stanwyck's the whole show in riverboat saga, singing with Martin, dancing with Ebsen, scrapping with Katherine DeMille.

Bank Dick, The (1940) **74m.** **** D: Eddie Cline. W. C. Fields, Cora Witherspoon, Una Merkel, Evelyn Del Rio, Jessie Ralph, Grady Sutton, Franklin Pangborn, Shemp Howard, Russell Hicks, Reed Hadley. Classic of insane humor loosely wound about a no-account who becomes a bank guard; Sutton as nitwit prospective son-in-law, Pangborn as bank examiner match the shenanigans of Fields. Screenplay by "Mahatma Kane Jeeves."▼●

Banker, The (1989) **C-95m.** *½ D: William Webb. Robert Forster, Duncan Regehr, Shanna Reed, Jeff Conaway, Leif Garrett, Richard Roundtree, Deborah Richter. Title character (Regehr) is murdering and mutilating prostitutes; police sergeant Forster sets out to trap him. By-the-book programmer. [R]▼●

Bank Robber (1993) **C-94m.** BOMB D: Nick Mead. Patrick Dempsey, Lisa Bonet, Olivia d'Abo, Forest Whitaker, Judge Reinhold, Michael Jeter, Joe Alaskey. If you want to kill time, this film beats it to death . . . slowly and painfully. Dempsey plays a robber who pulls one last job and ends up hiding out in a seedy hotel where his anonymity comes at a price. Whitaker and Reinhold are "sensitive" officers looking for him; Bonet plays the good-hearted prostitute who falls for the robber. Video version trimmed for R rating. [NC-17]▼●

Bank Shot (1974) **C-83m.** *** D: Gower Champion. George C. Scott, Joanna Cassidy, Sorrell Booke, G. Wood, Clifton James, Bob Balaban, Bibi Osterwald. Fast-paced, engagingly nutty comedy with criminal mastermind Scott planning a literal bank robbery—making off with the entire building! Based on the novel by Donald Westlake, a sequel to THE HOT ROCK (with Scott in the role played by Robert Redford in the film version of that book). Panavision. [PG]▼

Bannerline (1951) **88m.** ** D: Don Weis. Keefe Brasselle, Sally Forrest, Lionel Barrymore, Lewis Stone. Brasselle is optimistic fledgling reporter who sparks civic pride into town fighting corruption; film marred by typecasting and clichéd plotline.

Banning (1967) **C-102m.** *** D: Ron Winston. Robert Wagner, Anjanette Comer, Jill St. John, Guy Stockwell, James Farentino, Susan Clark, Howard St. John, Mike Kellin, Gene Hackman, Sean Garrison, Logan Ramsey. Entertaining soap opera about corruption and infidelity in and about a swank L.A. golf club. Wagner is the pro with a past, St. John a love-hungry young woman. Music score by Quincy Jones. Techniscope.

B*A*P*S (1997) **C-91m.** *½ D: Robert Townsend. Halle Berry, Natalie Desselle, Ian Richardson, Martin Landau, Luigi Amodeo, Jonathan Fried. With a dream of earning $10,000, waitresses Berry and Desselle (Black American Princesses) head for L.A. where, in contrived movie fashion, they wind up living in the mansion of fabulously wealthy Landau. This silly, fairy-tale-ish spin on the fish-out-of-water comedy formula falls flat on its face. Various sports and music personalities show up in cameos. [PG-13]▼●

Barabbas (1961) **C-134m.** *** D: Richard Fleischer. Anthony Quinn, Silvana Mangano, Arthur Kennedy, Jack Palance, Ernest Borgnine, Katy Jurado. Lavish production, coupled with good script (based on Lagerkvist's novel) and generally fine acting by large cast make for engrossing, literate experience. Overly long. Super Technirama 70. ▼

Baraka (1992) **C-96m.** *** D: Ron Fricke. Strikingly visual, insightful *National Geographic* issue come to life, which tells the story of the evolution of Earth and Mankind, and the manner in which man relates to his environment. Shot on location in 24 countries. There's no dialogue, only sounds and images; this will lose much of its effect on the small screen. Todd-AO 70mm. ▼◗

Barbados Quest SEE: **Murder on Approval**

Barbarella (1968-French-Italian) **C-98m.** **½ D. Roger Vadim. Jane Fonda, John Phillip Law, Anita Pallenberg, Milo O' Shea, David Hemmings, Marcel Marceau, Claude Dauphin, Ugo Tognazzi. Midnight-movie favorite based on popular French comic strip about sexy 41st-century space adventuress. Not especially funny, but watchable, with Fonda's strip-tease during opening credits the principal reason for its cult status. Trivia footnote: rock group Duran Duran took its name from O'Shea's character. Aka BARBARELLA, QUEEN OF THE GALAXY. Panavision. [PG]▼●◗

Barbarian, The (1933) **82m.** ** D: Sam Wood. Ramon Novarro, Myrna Loy, Reginald Denny, Louise Closser Hale, C. Aubrey Smith, Edward Arnold, Hedda Hopper. Overbaked account of sleazy, superficially charming Arab guide Novarro, who persistently pursues tourist Loy. Set in Egypt; lots of Myrna on display here—including a nude bathing scene. Screenplay by Anita Loos and Elmer Harris.

Barbarian and the Geisha, The (1958) **C-105m.** **½ D: John Huston. John Wayne, Eiko Ando, Sam Jaffe, So Yamamura. Twisting of 19th-century history allows Wayne as Ambassador Townsend Harris to romance Japanese beauty (Ando). Miscasting of Wayne is ludicrous, throwing costumer amuck. CinemaScope.▼

Barbarian and the Lady, The SEE: **Rebel Son, The**

Barbarians, The (1987) **C-87m.** *½ D: Ruggero Deodato. David Paul, Peter Paul, Richard Lynch, Eva La Rue, Virginia Bryant, Sheeba Alahani, Michael Berryman. Staggeringly silly sword-and-sorcery saga starring two awesome-looking bodybuilders (brothers in real life), whose main achievement is keeping a straight face while mouthing their dialogue. [R]▼●

Barbarians at the Gate (1993) **C-120m. TVM** D: Glenn Jordan. James Garner, Jonathan Pryce, Peter Riegert, Joanna Cassidy, Fred Dalton Thompson, Leilani Ferrer, Matt Clark, Jeffrey DeMunn, David Rasche, Tom Aldredge, Graham Beckel, Peter Dvorsky, Peter Frechette, Rita Wilson. Dynamite seriocomedy based on the true story of the leveraged buyout of the giant conglomerate RJR-Nabisco in the greedy '80s. Scripter Larry Gelbart and director Jordan amazingly turn corporate and financial politics into the stuff of great entertainment. Garner is ideal as F. Ross Johnson, the salesman/charmer who bites off more than he can chew. Based on the best-selling book by Bryan Burrough and John Helyar. Above average.▼●

Barbaric Beast of Boggy Creek, The, Part II (1985) **C-91m.** ** D: Charles B. Pierce. Charles B. Pierce, Cindy Butler, Serene Hedin, Chuck Pierce, Jimmy Clem. Slight, forgettable story of anthropology professor Pierce, who leads an expedition to find the Boggy Creek monster. Although titled "Part II," this is the third journey to Boggy Creek, following THE LEGEND OF . . . and RETURN TO . . . Filmed in 1983. Formerly titled BOGGY CREEK II. [PG]▼●

Barbarosa (1982) **C-90m.** *** D: Fred Schepisi. Willie Nelson, Gary Busey, Isela Vega, Gilbert Roland, Danny De La Paz, George Voskovec. Nelson is fine as legendary, free-spirited outlaw constantly on the lam, with able support from Busey as country boy who becomes his protégé. Solid Western, flavorfully directed by Schepisi. Panavision. [PG]▼●

Barbary Coast (1935) **90m.** ***½ D: Howard Hawks. Miriam Hopkins, Edward G. Robinson, Joel McCrea, Walter Brennan, Frank Craven, Brian Donlevy. Lusty tale of San Francisco in the late 19th century with dance-hall queen Hopkins running head-on into big-shot Robinson. David Niven can be glimpsed as an extra.▼●

Barbary Coast Gent (1944) **87m.** ** D: Roy Del Ruth. Wallace Beery, Binnie Barnes, John Carradine, Noah Beery, Sr., Frances Rafferty, Chill Wills, Donald Meek. Typical Beery vehicle, with good supporting cast, about smooth-talking bandit who goes straight.

Barb Wire (1996) **C-90m.** ** D: David Hogan. Pamela Anderson Lee, Temuera Morrison, Victoria Rowell, Jack Noseworthy, Steve Railsback. In 2017, the U.S. is run by a fascist dictatorship. Lee is a bounty hunter and nightclub owner living in a city on the fringe of freedom. Her former lover asks her to help him spirit his wife into Canada to help the rebellion. Lots of gaudy but uninvolving action; surly, pneumatic Lee is no actress, just a 15-year-old boy's fantasy figure. Actually rips off the plot of CASABLANCA! Also available in unrated video version. [R]▼●◗

Barcelona (1994) **C-100m.** **½ D: Whit Stillman. Taylor Nichols, Chris Eigeman, Tushka Bergen, Mira Sorvino, Pep Munne, Nuria Badia, Hellena Schmied, Francis Creighton, Thomas Gibson, Jack Gilpin. Young, nerdy American businessman (Nichols) living in Spain is joined by his Naval officer cousin (Eigeman); the two woo a variety of women and debate anti-American attitudes and actions that prevail among the local populace. Set in the concluding months of the Cold War, film's theme is admirably original, and often amusing, if not always compelling. Writer-director Stillman's second offbeat talkfest (following METROPOLITAN) isn't quite as focused as the first, though reteaming of male costars is a plus.▼●

Barefoot Contessa, The (1954) **C-128m.** *** D: Joseph L. Mankiewicz. Humphrey Bogart, Ava Gardner, Edmond O'Brien, Marius Goring, Rossano Brazzi, Valentina Cortesa, Elizabeth Sellars, Warren Stevens. Cynical tale of beautiful Spanish dancer Gardner and how director Bogart makes her a Hollywood star. Mankiewicz's script is full of juicy dialogue, as usual. O'Brien won an Oscar as the press agent. ▼●

Barefoot Executive, The (1971) **C-96m.** ** D: Robert Butler. Kurt Russell, Joe Flynn, Harry Morgan, Wally Cox, Heather North, Alan Hewitt, John Ritter. Russell discovers chimp with ability to pick top-rated TV shows, and becomes vice-president of a network. Routine Disney slapstick. Remade for TV in 1995. [G]▼

Barefoot in the Park (1967) **C-105m.** *** D: Gene Saks. Robert Redford, Jane Fonda, Charles Boyer, Mildred Natwick, Herb Edelman, Mabel Albertson, Fritz Feld, Doris Roberts. Plotless, entertaining Neil Simon comedy finds Fonda and Redford newlyweds in five-story walkup apartment. Running gag about climbing stairs grows thin, but film doesn't. Redford and Natwick recreate their Broadway roles; Saks' screen directing debut. Later, briefly a TV series with an all-black cast. ▼●

Barefoot Mailman, The (1951) **C-83m.** ** D: Earl McEvoy. Robert Cummings, Terry Moore, Jerome Courtland, Will Geer. Potentially engaging story of a first postal route in Florida bogs down in tale of former con-man (Cummings) tempted to fleece citizens of Miami with phony railroad stock; Moore is pert leading lady.

Barfly (1987) **C-97m.** *** D: Barbet Schroeder. Mickey Rourke, Faye Dunaway, Alice Krige, Jack Nance, J.C. Quinn, Frank Stallone. Surprisingly enjoyable portrait of L.A. lowlife, and a boozy, foolishly macho writer played with comic bravado by Rourke. Dunaway is exceptional as his alcoholic soulmate. Based on the autobiographical writings of cult favorite Charles Bukowski, who can be glimpsed on one of the bar stools. Veteran character actor Fritz Feld has a lovely bit as a bum who gives Dunaway a light. [R]▼●

Bar Girls (1994) **C-95m.** **½ D: Marita Giovanni. Nancy Allison Wolfe, Liza D'Agostino, Camila Griggs, Justine Slater, Lisa Parker, Pam Raines. Amiable (if flawed) romantic comedy with a twist: all of its major characters are lesbians who congregate at L.A.'s Girl Bar. The main character is obsessive, wryly funny Loretta (Wolfe), a female Woody Allen who is forever seeking a perfect significant other while not quite understanding what it means to truly and completely love another person. The film's shortcomings are compensated for by clever dialogue and believable characters. Adapted for the screen by Lauran Hoffman from her play. [R]▼●

Barkleys of Broadway, The (1949) **C-109m.** *** D: Charles Walters. Fred Astaire, Ginger Rogers, Oscar Levant, Billie Burke, Gale Robbins. Astaire and Rogers reteamed after ten years in this witty Comden-Green script about show biz couple who split, then make up. Songs include "You'd Be Hard to Replace," "They Can't Take That Away from Me." Ginger reading "La Marseillaise" is a definite low point.▼●

Barnacle Bill (1941) **98m.** ** D: Richard Thorpe. Wallace Beery, Marjorie Main, Leo Carrillo, Virginia Weidler, Donald Meek, Barton MacLane. Beery and Main support basically run-of-the-mill material as old salt and woman trying to snare him into marriage.

Barnacle Bill (1957) SEE: **All at Sea**

Barney's Great Adventure (1997) **C-75m.** ** D: Steve Gomer. George Hearn, Shirley Douglas, Trevor Morgan, Kyla Pratt, Diana Rice, David Joyner, Jeff Ayres. Preschoolers who cannot get enough of TV's Big Purple Dinosaur will take to this, Barney's first feature, in which he mixes with some kids on a farm; together, they set off on an adventure in search of a missing egg. Inoffensive, to be sure, but for anyone over five it's a real yawn. [G]▼●◗

Baron Blood (1972-Italian) **C-90m.** **½ D: Mario Bava. Joseph Cotten, Elke Sommer, Massimo Girotti, Rada Rassimov, Antonio Cantafora, Alan Collins. Descendant of evil nobleman attempts "novel" rejuvenation principles. Standard plot livened by unusual settings and lighting. Aka THE TORTURE CHAMBER OF BARON BLOOD. Original Italian version runs longer. [PG]▼●◗

Baroness and the Butler, The (1938) **75m.** ** D: Walter Lang. William Powell, Annabella, Helen Westley, Henry Stephenson, Joseph Schildkraut, J. Edward Bromberg. Powell leads double life as Annabella's butler and member of parliament. He's fine as usual but script is rather thin.

Baron Müenchhausen (1943-German) **C-110m.** *** D: Josef von Baky. Hans Albers, Brigitte Horney, Wilhelm Bendow, Leo Slezak, Ferdinand Marian. Lavish, impressive curio which tells of the legendary, free-spirited Baron, his exploits in Russia, Turkey, Venice, and elsewhere, and his quest for beautiful princesses and empresses. While ostensibly an escapist entertainment, the Baron is an heroic German: noble, shrewd, and ever loyal to the Fatherland. Produced on the order of Goebbels, Hitler's Minister of Propaganda and Public Enlightenment, to mark the 25th anniversary of UFA, the German production studio. This would make a fascinating (if overlong) double bill with

Terry Gilliam's THE ADVENTURES OF BARON MUNCHAUSEN.▼

Baron of Arizona, The (1950) **96m.** **½ D: Samuel Fuller. Vincent Price, Ellen Drew, Beulah Bondi, Reed Hadley. Price has field day as landgrabbing scoundrel who almost gains control of Arizona in the 19th century.▼

Barquero (1970) **C-115m.** *½ D: Gordon Douglas. Lee Van Cleef, Warren Oates, Forrest Tucker, Kerwin Mathews, Mariette Hartley. Bad-guy Oates, on the run after wiping out a town, has to deal with Van Cleef, a feisty ferry operator, in order to escape. [PG]

Barracuda (1978) **C-90m.** ** D: Harry Kerwin. Wayne-David Crawford, Jason Evers, Bert Freed, Roberta Leighton, Cliff Emmich. Chemical dumping affects fish and then people in small Florida community. Predictable formula film. Aka THE LUCIFER PROJECT.▼

Barretts of Wimpole Street, The (1934) **110m.** *** D: Sidney Franklin. Norma Shearer, Fredric March, Charles Laughton, Maureen O'Sullivan, Katherine Alexander, Una O'Connor, Ian Wolfe. Handsome, well-acted, and most entertaining MGM production of classic romance between Elizabeth Barrett and Robert Browning in 19th century England. Director Franklin remade this two decades later. Retitled for TV: FORBIDDEN ALLIANCE.▼●

Barretts of Wimpole Street, The (1957-U.S.-British) **C-105m.** **½ D: Sidney Franklin. Jennifer Jones, John Gielgud, Bill Travers, Virginia McKenna. Tame interpretation of the lilting romance between poets Browning, Barrett, with actors bogged down in prettified fluff. Director Franklin fared better with this material in 1934. CinemaScope. ▼●

Barricade (1939) **71m.** ** D: Gregory Ratoff. Alice Faye, Warner Baxter, Charles Winninger, Arthur Treacher, Keye Luke. Faye and Baxter are trapped in Chinese embassy and fall in love; rather tame.

Barricade (1950) **C-75m.** ** D: Peter Godfrey. Dane Clark, Ruth Roman, Raymond Massey, Robert Douglas. Clark pitted against Massey in gold-mining-camp Western lends a spark to usual battle of good vs. evil. Mild rehash of THE SEA WOLF.

Barrier (1966-Polish) **84m.** **½ D: Jerzy Skolimowski. Joanna Szczerbic, Jan Nowicki, Tadeusz Lomnicki, Maria Malicka. Interesting view of youthful attitudes in Poland, combining reportage with fantasy elements. Not a total success, but still intriguing.

Barry Lyndon (1975-British) **C-183m.** ***½ D: Stanley Kubrick. Ryan O'Neal, Marisa Berenson. Patrick Magee, Hardy Kruger, Steven Berkoff, Gay Hamilton, Murray Melvin, Frank Middlemass, Andre Morell, Leonard Rossiter, Marie Kean, narrated by Michael Hordern. Exquisite, meticulously detailed period piece stars O'Neal as Thackeray's 18th-century Irish rogue-hero who covets success but lets it go to his head. Long, deliberately paced but never boring. Won Oscars for John Alcott's photography, Leonard Rosenman's adaptation of period music, Art Direction–Set Decoration, and Costume Design. Screenplay by Kubrick. [PG]▼●◗

Barry McKenzie Holds His Own (1974-Australian) **C-93m.** *½ D: Bruce Beresford. Barry Crocker, Barry Humphries, Donald Pleasence, Dick Bentley, Louis Negin. Idiotic follow-up to THE ADVENTURES OF BARRY MCKENZIE, about oafish title character, his twin brother (both played by Crocker), and one Edna Everage (Humphries, in drag), who is kidnapped and taken to Transylvania. Panavision. ▼

Bar Sinister SEE: **It's a Dog's Life**

Bartleby (1972-British) **C-78m.** **½ D: Anthony Friedmann. Paul Scofield, John McEnery, Thorley Walters, Colin Jeavons, Raymond Mason. Herman Melville's great short story about 19th-century auditing clerk who refuses to leave job after he is fired is admirably attempted in modern-day update, even though story doesn't really lend itself to filming; Scofield is fine as bewildered but sympathetic boss.▼●

Barton Fink (1991) **C-117m.** **½ D: Joel Coen. John Turturro, John Goodman, Judy Davis, Michael Lerner, John Mahoney, Tony Shalhoub, Jon Polito, Steve Buscemi, David Warrilow, Richard Portnow, Christopher Murney. Self-important N.Y. playwright Turturro comes to Hollywood in 1941 to write a screenplay, and finds it a living hell—in more ways than one. Barbed look at vintage Hollywood, filled with incredible detail and amazing scenes; told in Joel and Ethan Coen's typically flamboyant visual style. BUT, at a crucial point the film takes a sharp left turn toward the bizarre, and never returns. Great performances all around. [R]▼●

BASEketball (1998) **C-103m.** ** D: David Zucker. Trey Parker, Matt Stone, Yasmine Bleeth, Jenny McCarthy, Robert Vaughn, Ernest Borgnine, Dian Bachar, Trevor Einhorn, Bob Costas, Al Michaels, Robert Stack. Sporadically funny gross-out comedy about two goofballs who invent a driveway basketball game that soon sweeps the country—and turns them into professional athletes. Some funny gags, but a surprisingly pedestrian storyline makes it sag. Starring (but not written by) the creators of TV's *South Park.* Recommended for anyone eager to see Borgnine sing "I'm Too Sexy for My Shirt." [R]▼●◗

Bashful Elephant, The (1962-German) **82m.** BOMB D: Dorrell McGowan, Stuart E. McGowan. Molly Mack, Helmut Schmid, Kai Fischer, Buddy Baer. Supposedly a family film, this import spends more time on an elephant trainer's divorce than anything else. Not worth your time.

Basic Instinct (1992) **C-127m.** ★★★ D: Paul Verhoeven. Michael Douglas, Sharon Stone, George Dzundza, Jeanne Tripplehorn, Denis Arndt, Leilani Sarelle, Bruce A. Young, Chelcie Ross, Dorothy Malone, Wayne Knight, Stephen Tobolowsky. In-your-face sex thriller, with Douglas as a San Francisco cop who's fatally attracted to a key suspect in an ice-pick murder: brazenly sexy (and manipulative) Stone. Audacious, erotic, and larger-than-life—with an ending that falls short of real satisfaction. Released overseas in an unrated version that's even *more* sexually explicit! Both versions are available on video. The notorious eight shots of erotic grappling totaling 42 seconds were restored to 1993 laser and tape editions. Panavision. [R] ▼●◗

Basic Training (1985) **C-88m.** ★½ D: Andrew Sugerman. Ann Dusenberry, Rhonda Shear, Angela Aames, Will Nye, Walter Gotell. Lamebrained raunch comedy about young woman who overcomes sexual harassment in the Pentagon by turning the tables on the lechers who surround her and her buxom colleagues. Pretty rank. Filmed in 1983. [R]▼

Basil (1998) **C-102m.** ★★ D: Rhada Bharadwaj. Jared Leto, Christian Slater, Claire Forlani, Derek Jacobi, Rachel Pickup, David Ross. Turn-of-the-20th-century tale about a young aristocrat who (with the help of a mysterious friend) becomes entangled with a beautiful but selfish temptress. Murky slice of Gothic suffers from sluggish pacing and lack of passion. Leto struggles with his British accent and the lovely Forlani has one haughty facial expression for every emotion. Based on a Wilkie Collins novel. Never theatrically released. [R]▼

Basileus Quartet (1982-French-Italian) **C-118m.** ★★★ D: Fabio Carpi. Pierre Malet, Hector Alterio, Omero Antonutti, Michel Vitold, Alain Cuny, Gabriele Ferzetti, Lisa Kreuzer. A violinist suddenly dies and his colleagues, who have lived only for music, must get on with their lives—which are profoundly altered by the young replacement for the deceased. Stark, quietly absorbing, beautifully realized.▼●

Basketball Diaries, The (1995) **C-100m.** ★★ D: Scott Kalvert. Leonardo DiCaprio, Lorraine Bracco, Bruno Kirby, Marilyn Sokol, Mark Wahlberg, James Modio, Ernie Hudson. Drably downbeat and none-too-stylish rendering of poet-musician Jim Carroll's 60s recollections of heroin abuse and on-court prowess at a N.Y.C. Catholic school. DiCaprio is well cast in role intended for River Phoenix, but imprecise updating from Carroll's very specific time frame leads to a fuzzy point of view. [R]▼●◗

Basket Case (1982) **C-91m.** ★★½ D: Frank Henenlotter. Kevin Van Hentenryck, Terri Susan Smith, Beverly Bonner, Robert Vogel, Diana Browne. Extremely self-conscious but intriguing tongue-in-cheek low-budget horror film about a twin who arrives in N.Y.C. from a small town carrying his deformed telepathic mutant brother in a basket. Some interesting animated sequences in this John Waters-ish film that boasts some effective horror moments. Followed by several sequels. [R]▼●◗

Basket Case 2 (1990) **C-89m.** BOMB D: Frank Henenlotter. Kevin Van Hentenryck, Annie Ross, Jason Evers, Kathryn Meisle, Heather Rattray, Ted Sorel. Van Hentenryck and his monstrously deformed twin brother take refuge in a house of freaks, but are tracked down by tabloid reporter. Arch, pseudo-hip film totally lacks the conviction of the first; icy cold. [R]▼●

Basket Case 3 (1992) **C-90m.** ★½ D: Frank Henenlotter. Kevin Van Hentenryck, Annie Ross, Gil Roper, Tina Louise Hilbert, Dan Biggers, Jim O'Doherty. Van Hentenryck is separated from his deformed brother, who fathers a set of duodectuplets when the house of freaks from previous entry moves to Georgia. Flatly photographed, with a meandering, uninvolving plot. More serious than previous entry, but still strains for laughs. [R]▼●

Basquiat (1996) **C-108m.** ★★½ D: Julian Schnabel. Jeffrey Wright, David Bowie, Dennis Hopper, Gary Oldman, Willem Dafoe, Michael Wincott, Benicio Del Toro, Claire Forlani, Parker Posey, Christopher Walken, Courtney Love, Tatum O'Neal, Paul Bartel. Meandering though not uninteresting bio of controversial black artist Jean-Michel Basquiat, who went from unknown graffiti practitioner to spent comet between 1981 and 1987. The movie doesn't capture the presumed intensity of a rapid career ascent before death from heroin at 28. Yet the supporting cast is rich, topped by Bowie's portrayal of Andy Warhol, which is precise even down to the pasty skin. Look carefully at the chic party guests Basquiat spies through the gallery window, and you'll spot Isabella Rossellini. Directorial debut for artist Schnabel, who also scripted. [R]▼●

Bastard Out of Carolina (1996) **C-97m. TVM** D: Anjelica Huston. Jennifer Jason Leigh, Ron Eldard, Jena Malone, Glenne Headly, Dermot Mulroney, Diana Scarwid, Lyle Lovett, Michael Rooker, Grace Zabriskie, Pat Hingle, Christina Ricci; narrated by Laura Dern. Compelling drama set in the '50s South about a preteen (Malone) who suffers emotional, physical, and sexual abuse at the hands of her stepfather as white-trash mom Leigh looks the other way, afraid of losing her brutal, no-good husband (Eldard). Huston made her directorial debut with this quite violent film of Dorothy Allison's autobiographical bestseller (adapted by Anne Meredith). Made for cable. Video version is 4m. longer. Above average. ▼●◗

Bat, The (1959) **80m.** ★★½ D: Crane Wilbur. Vincent Price, Agnes Moorehead, Gavin Gordon, John Sutton, Lenita Lane, Elaine Edwards, Darla Hood. Faithful filming of the Mary Roberts Rinehart–Avery Hopwood play, with mystery writer Moorehead renting an eerie mansion for the summer; she and her maid soon are plagued by the title fiend. Filmed before in 1915, 1927 and (as THE BAT WHISPERS) in 1930.▼●◗

Bataan (1943) **114m.** *** D: Tay Garnett. Robert Taylor, George Murphy, Thomas Mitchell, Lloyd Nolan, Lee Bowman, Robert Walker, Desi Arnaz, Barry Nelson. Realistically made drama of famous WW2 incident on Pacific Island; good combat scenes. Also shown in computer-colored version.▼●◗

Bathing Beauty (1944) **C-101m.** **½ D: George Sidney. Red Skelton, Esther Williams, Basil Rathbone, Ethel Smith, Xavier Cugat, Lina Romay, Harry James and His Orchestra. Esther's first starring vehicle gives Skelton and musical guest stars the spotlight most of the way, but does have a spectacular aquatic finale. Silly script, thankless role for Rathbone.▼●

Batman (1966) **C-105m.** ** D: Leslie Martinson. Adam West, Burt Ward, Burgess Meredith, Cesar Romero, Frank Gorshin, Lee Meriwether, Neil Hamilton, Madge Blake, Reginald Denny. Quickly made feature to cash in on then-hot TV series pulls out all stops, features the Joker, Riddler, Penguin, and Catwoman trying to undo the caped crusader. Really misses the mark; the campy humor worked better in the TV series. ▼●

Batman (1989) **C-126m.** **½ D: Tim Burton. Jack Nicholson, Michael Keaton, Kim Basinger, Robert Wuhl, Pat Hingle, Billy Dee Williams, Michael Gough, Jack Palance, Jerry Hall, Tracey Walter, Lee Wallace. There's razzle-dazzle to spare in this dark, intense variation on Bob Kane's comic book creation—but there's also something askew when the villain (a particularly psychotic villain, played overboard by Nicholson) is so much more potent than the hero! Still, lots to grab your attention, including Anton Furst's Oscar-winning production design and Danny Elfman's terrific score. Prince contributes several songs. Followed by BATMAN RETURNS. [PG-13]▼●◗

Batman & Robin (1997) **C-130m.** **½ D: Joel Schumacher. Arnold Schwarzenegger, George Clooney, Chris O'Donnell, Uma Thurman, Alicia Silverstone, Michael Gough, Pat Hingle, John Glover, Elle Macpherson, Vivica A. Fox, Vendela K. Thommessen, Elizabeth Sanders, Jeep Swenson, Coolio. Batman #4 spotlights two colorful villains, Schwarzenegger's lusty Mr. Freeze, and Thurman's deliciously nasty Poison Ivy, who (for different reasons) want to destroy Gotham City, but even their antics can't sustain an overlong, episodic film in which the "story" often makes no sense. Clooney is OK but unremarkable as Bruce Wayne/Batman, ditto for Silverstone as the new Batgirl. The action and effects are loud, gargantuan, and ultimately numbing. [PG-13] ▼●◗

Batman Forever (1995) **C-121m.** *** D: Joel Schumacher. Val Kilmer, Tommy Lee Jones, Jim Carrey, Nicole Kidman, Chris O'Donnell, Michael Gough, Pat Hingle, Drew Barrymore, Debi Mazar, Rene Auberjonois, Joe Grifasi. Kilmer makes the role of Batman/Bruce Wayne his own in this well-written sequel in which the Caped Crusader battles Two-Face (Jones) and The Riddler (Carrey) while attempting—at least for a while—to resist the advances of a sexy psychologist (Kidman). He also acquires a partner in O'Donnell (as Robin), and it's this aspect of the film—the character relationships—that give it solidity. The loud, razzle-dazzle special effects are overkill. Ed Begley, Jr., appears unbilled. Followed by BATMAN & ROBIN. [PG-13]▼●◗

Batman: Mask of the Phantasm (1993) **C-76m.** **½ D: Eric Radomski, Bruce W. Timm. Voices: Kevin Conway, Dana Delany, Hart Bochner, Mark Hamill, Stacy Keach, Jr., Efrem Zimbalist, Jr., Abe Vigoda, Dick Miller, John P. Ryan. Batman battles a mysterious figure who's killing the great gangsters of Gotham City, while, as Bruce Wayne, he romances his college sweetheart, just returned to town. Then the Joker turns up. . . . Excellent design (inspired by the 1940s Superman cartoons) is hampered by mediocre animation, but the story isn't bad, and the dialogue is better than you'd expect. This spinoff from the animated *Batman* TV series was originally intended for videotape release only, but went to theaters instead. [PG]▼●◗

Batman Returns (1992) **C-126m.** ** D: Tim Burton. Michael Keaton, Danny DeVito, Michelle Pfeiffer, Christopher Walken, Michael Gough, Michael Murphy, Cristi Conaway, Andrew Bryniarski, Pat Hingle, Vincent Schiavelli, Jan Hooks, Paul Reubens. Nasty, nihilistic nightmare movie about an abandoned freak baby who grows up to be The Penguin—a deadly threat to Gotham City, especially when he teams up with megalomaniac Max Schreck (Walken). Meanwhile, Batman finds a more personal enemy in Catwoman. Rich performances, dazzling production design, and occasional cleverness can't make up for a dark, mean-spirited (and often incoherent) screenplay. Followed by Keatonless BATMAN FOREVER. [PG-13]▼●◗

Baton Rouge (1988-Spanish) **C-98m.** ** D: Rafael Moleon. Antonio Banderas, Victoria Abril, Carmen Maura, Andres Lopez, Laura Cepeda. Gigolo Banderas preys on a sexually dysfunctional wealthy woman, and winds up in a scam with her psychiatrist. Interesting sex scenes and suspense can't make up for utterly confusing plot twists. Another "adorable Antonio" film taken off the shelf after he became well known in the U.S. [R]▼

Bat People (1974) **C-95m.** *½ D: Jerry Jameson. Stewart Moss, Marianne McAndrew, Michael Pataki, Paul Carr, Arthur Space. A doctor is bitten by a bat while on his honeymoon, with expected results. Paltry horror entry from AIP, originally titled IT LIVES BY NIGHT.▼

Bats (1999) **C-91m.** BOMB D: Louis Morneau. Lou Diamond Phillips, Dina Meyer, Bob Gunton, Leon, Carlos Jacott, David McConnell. Hordes of mutated killer bats attack a Southwestern community. That's all the plot the movie has, but it does feature a top-of-the-line motivation for its mad scientist (Gunton): he creates the bats, he says, because he *can*. Deplorable. Clairmont-Scope. [R]▼◗

***batteries not included** (1987) **C-106m.** ** D: Matthew Robbins. Hume Cronyn, Jessica Tandy, Frank McRae, Elizabeth Pena, Michael Carmine, Dennis Boutsikaris. Steven Spielberg's Amblin Productions has gone to the same well once too often. Cloying sci-fi fantasy has a "family" of small alien spacecrafts arrive to assist New Yorkers whose tenement is about to be demolished. Cronyn and Tandy do far more for the film than it does for them. [PG]▼●◗

Battle at Apache Pass, The (1952) **C-85m.** **½ D: George Sherman. Jeff Chandler, John Lund, Beverly Tyler, Richard Egan, Hugh O'Brian, Jay Silverheels. Chandler reprises his BROKEN ARROW role as Cochise, who tries to prevent Indian wars but doesn't quite succeed.

Battle at Bloody Beach (1961) **83m.** **½ D: Herbert Coleman. Audie Murphy, Gary Crosby, Dolores Michaels, Alejandro Rey. Sporadically exciting WW2 action with soldier Murphy locating his wife on a Pacific Island, involved with partisan cause and its leader. CinemaScope.

Battleaxe, The (1962-British) **66m.** ** D: Godfrey Grayson. Jill Ireland, Francis Matthews, Joan Haythorne, Michael Beint. Obvious sex farce with Matthews suing Ireland for breach of promise, Haythorne in title role supplying expected gags.

Battle Beneath the Earth (1967-British) **C-91m.** **½ D: Montgomery Tully. Kerwin Mathews, Viviane Ventura, Robert Ayres, Peter Arne, Al Mulock, Martin Benson. Silly but enjoyable pulp fantasy about Chinese plan to invade U.S. through network of tunnels.▼

Battle Beyond the Stars (1980) **C-104m.** **½ D: Jimmy T. Murakami. Richard Thomas, John Saxon, Robert Vaughn, Darlanne Fleugel, George Peppard, Sybil Danning, Sam Jaffe, Morgan Woodward, Jeff Corey, Julia Duffy. Not-bad space saga from Roger Corman, with good special effects and a John Sayles script that uses the reliable SEVEN SAMURAI/MAGNIFICENT SEVEN formula (with Vaughn from the SEVEN cast). Sets and special effects were reused for countless subsequent Corman cheapies. [PG]▼●

Battle Beyond the Sun (1963) **C-75m.** ** D: Thomas Colchart. Edd Perry, Arla Powell, Andy Stewart, Bruce Hunter. Soviet sci-fi film NEBO ZOVYOT (1959) is refashioned into so-so American product by producer Roger Corman; story deals with rival space missions to Mars. The names of the director and actors are all pseudonyms; Francis Ford Coppola, credited as Associate Producer, oversaw the English adaptation. His father Carmine (billed as "Carmen" Coppola) wrote the music.▼

Battle Circus (1953) **90m.** **½ D: Richard Brooks. Humphrey Bogart, June Allyson, Keenan Wynn, Robert Keith, Philip Ahn. OK tale of MASH unit during Korean War is well acted, and occasionally exciting, but hampered by too much emphasis on the romance between surgeon Bogart and nurse Allyson. Surprisingly ordinary, coming from writer-director Brooks.▼

Battle Cry (1955) **C-149m.** *** D: Raoul Walsh. Van Heflin, Aldo Ray, Mona Freeman, Nancy Olson, James Whitmore, Raymond Massey, Tab Hunter, Dorothy Malone, Anne Francis, William Campbell, John Lupton, Fess Parker, Rhys Williams, Allyn (Ann) McLerie. Entertaining version of Leon Uris WW2 Marine novel, with much barracks profanity removed for film, focusing on servicemen in training, wartime romance, and frustrating battle assignments—with Heflin striving to get his men the tough combat action they yearn for. Hunter as wholesome soldier and Malone a love-hungry Navy wife stand out in episodic actioner. Ray gives good performance as rough-hewn gyrene who falls in love with "nice girl" Olson. Film debut of Justus McQueen, who thereafter acted under the name of his character, L.Q. Jones. Musical score by Max Steiner. Screenplay by Uris. CinemaScope. ▼●

Battlefield Earth (2000) **C-117m.** BOMB D: Roger Christian. John Travolta, Barry Pepper, Forest Whitaker, Kim Coates, Richard Tyson, Sabine Karsenti, Michael MacRae, Kelly Preston. Psychlos (business-minded aliens) conquered Earth a century ago; what remains of humanity are slaves or ignorant savages. Gold-greedy Psychlo security chief Travolta educates bright human Pepper, hoping "man animals" can mine the metal for him. Big mistake. . . . So is the movie, based on the novel by L. Ron Hubbard. Clumsy plot, misplaced satire, unbelievable coincidences and a leaden pace trample Travolta's weird but amusing performance. Super 35. [PG-13]

Battle Flame (1959) **78m.** *½ D: R. G. Springsteen. Scott Brady, Elaine Edwards, Robert Blake, Gordon Jones, Wayne Heffley, Richard Harrison. Programmer about

Korean War and soldier Brady's romance with nurse Edwards.

Battle for Anzio, The SEE: **Anzio**

Battle Force SEE: **Great Battle, The**

Battle for the Planet of the Apes (1973) **C-92m.** ** D: J. Lee Thompson. Roddy McDowall, Natalie Trundy, Severn Darden, Paul Williams, Claude Akins, John Huston. Substandard; fifth (and last) apes installment attempts to bring entire series full-cycle. Good footage from earlier films helps, but not much. A TV series followed. Panavision. [G]▼●

Battleground (1949) **118m.** *** D: William Wellman. Van Johnson, John Hodiak, Ricardo Montalban, George Murphy, Marshall Thompson, Denise Darcel, Don Taylor, Richard Jaeckel, James Whitmore, James Arness, Scotty Beckett. Star-studded replay of Battle of the Bulge: division of American troops, their problems and reactions to war. Robert Pirosh's slick script, which was awarded an Oscar, lacks genuine insight into the characters; Paul C. Vogel also earned a statuette for his cinematography. Also shown in computer-colored version.▼●

Battle Hymn (1957) **C-108m.** *** D: Douglas Sirk. Rock Hudson, Martha Hyer, Anna Kashfi, Dan Duryea, Don DeFore. Hudson gives convincing performance as clergyman who returns to military duty in Korean War to train fighter pilots; expansive production values. CinemaScope. ▼

Battle in Outer Space (1959-Japanese) **C-74m.** *½ D: Ishiro Honda. Ryo Ikebe, Kyoko Anzai, Leonard Stanford, Harold Conway. Unexciting sci-fi as Earth prepares for attack from outer space. Plenty of special effects. Tohoscope.

Battle of Algiers, The (1965-Italian-Algerian) **123m.** *** D: Gillo Pontecorvo. Yacef Saadi, Jean Martin, Brahim Haggiag, Tommaso Neri, Samia Kerbash. Straightforward drama about revolt against the French by Algerians from 1954–1962. Winner of many awards, but the objective, pseudo-documentary fashion in which it was filmed somewhat limits its dramatic power. Nonetheless, a good film. ▼●

Battle of Austerlitz, The (1960-French-Italian-Yugoslavian-Lichtensteiner) **C-123m.** *½ D: Abel Gance. Claudia Cardinale, Martine Carol, Leslie Caron, Vittorio De Sica, Jean Marais, Ettore Manni, Jack Palance, Orson Welles. International cast reenacts the epic of Napoleon's greatest battle in stultifying fashion. Drastic cutting from original 166m. and terrible dubbing doom it. Originally titled AUSTERLITZ. Dyaliscope. ▼

Battle of Britain (1969-British) **C-132m.** ** D: Guy Hamilton. Harry Andrews, Michael Caine, Trevor Howard, Curt Jurgens, Kenneth More, Laurence Olivier, Christopher Plummer, Michael Redgrave, Ralph Richardson, Robert Shaw, Susannah York. Superb widescreen aerial sequences, which will suffer on TV, hardly redeem yet another "spot-the-star" WW2 epic, this time about British airmen who prevented threatened Nazi invasion. Panavision. [G]▼●

Battle of El Alamein (1968-Italian-French) **C-105m.** ** D: Calvin Jackson Padget (Giorgio Ferroni). Frederick Stafford, Ettore Manni, Robert Hossein, Michael Rennie, George Hilton, Ira Furstenberg. Plenty of action as Italians and Germans, partners in an uneasy alliance, fight the British in the North African desert in 1942. Hossein plays Rommel, and Rennie does an unsympathetic Field Marshal Montgomery (the British are the villains in this one). Cromoscope. [PG]▼

Battle of Mareth, The SEE: **Greatest Battle, The**

Battle of Neretva, The (1970-Yugoslavian-U.S.-Italian-German) **C-102m.** ** D: Veljko Bulajic. Yul Brynner, Sergei Bondarchuk, Curt Jurgens, Sylva Koscina, Hardy Kruger, Franco Nero, Orson Welles. Originally an Oscar nominee for Best Foreign Film, but when this $12 million spectacle about Nazi invasion of Yugoslavia was cut down from nearly three hours, it lost most of its coherency. Too bad. Panavision. [G]▼

Battle of Rogue River (1954) **C-71m.** ** D: William Castle. George Montgomery, Richard Denning, Martha Hyer, John Crawford. Much needed action sequence never comes in lopsided Western of Montgomery negotiating Indian truce as settlers seek statehood for Oregon in 1850s.

Battle of the Bulge (1965) **C-163m.** ** D: Ken Annakin. Henry Fonda, Robert Shaw, Robert Ryan, Telly Savalas, Dana Andrews, George Montgomery, Ty Hardin, Pier Angeli, Charles Bronson. Originally presented in Cinerama, this overinflated war drama about an important event cannot triumph over banal script. Read a good book on the subject instead. Ultra Panavision 70.▼●

Battle of the Commandos (1969-Italian) **C-94m.** ** D: Umberto Lenzi. Jack Palance, Curt Jurgens, Tomas Hunter, Diana Lorys, Wolfgang Preiss. Palance leads a small band of commandos on an assault on a powerful German cannon that has to be destroyed before the D-Day invasion. Aka LEGION OF THE DAMNED.▼

Battle of the Coral Sea (1959) **80m.** **½ D: Paul Wendkos. Cliff Robertson, Gia Scala, Teru Shimada, Patricia Cutts, Gene Blakely, Gordon Jones. Staunch Robertson is submarine captain on Japanese-held island during WW2, seeking to send vital data to U.S. fleet.

Battle of the River Plate, The SEE: **Pursuit of the Graf Spee**

Battle of the Sexes, The (1959-British) **84m.** *** D: Charles Crichton. Peter Sellers, Robert Morley, Constance Cummings, Jameson Clark. Sparkling British comedy with macabre overtones; Sellers is elderly Scotsman contemplating murder. Supporting cast keeps this moving.▼

Battle of the Villa Fiorita, The (1965-British) **C-111m.** ★★½ D: Delmer Daves. Maureen O'Hara, Rossano Brazzi, Richard Todd, Phyllis Calvert, Martin Stephens. Unconvincing soaper with O'Hara running off to Italy to carry on with widower Brazzi; predictable interference from each's children. Panavision.

Battle of the Worlds (1961-Italian) **C-84m.** ★½ D: Anthony Dawson (Antonio Margheriti). Claude Rains, Maya Brent, Bill Carter, Umberto Orsini, Jacqueline Derval. Rains adds some weight to this English-dubbed cheapie about scientists' frantic efforts to stop alien planet from colliding with Earth. Eerie atmosphere also helps a little.▼

Battleship Potemkin SEE: **Potemkin**

Battle Shock SEE: **Woman's Devotion, A**

Battlestar: Galactica (1979) **C-125m.** ★★½ D: Richard A. Colla. Richard Hatch, Dirk Benedict, Lorne Greene, Ray Milland, John Colicos, Patrick Macnee, Lew Ayres, Jane Seymour, Laurette Spang, Terry Carter. Feature cut down from first and fifth episodes of short-lived TV series; Greene is commander of starship taking survivors of doomed planet in search of new home. Belongs on small screen, where it's moderately interesting and John Dykstra's special effects come off best. Premiere originally telecast at 148m. [PG]▼●◗

Battle Stations (1956) **81m.** ★½ D: Lewis Seiler. John Lund, William Bendix, Keefe Brasselle, Richard Boone, James Lydon, Claude Akins. Rehash about crew in WW2 Pacific and their preparation for fighting the Japanese.

Battle Stripe SEE: **Men, The**

Battle Taxi (1955) **82m.** ★★ D: Herbert L. Strock. Sterling Hayden, Arthur Franz, Marshall Thompson, Joel Marston, Leo Needham. Ordinary tale of Korean War missions; strictly pedestrian.

Battletruck SEE: **Warlords of the 21st Century**

Battle Zone (1952) **82m.** ★★ D: Lesley Selander. John Hodiak, Linda Christian, Stephen McNally, Philip Ahn. Hodiak vies with McNally for Christian, with brief time out to fight Commies in static Korean War film.

Battling Bellhop SEE: **Kid Galahad** (1937)

Battling Butler (1926) **71m.** ★★½ D: Buster Keaton. Buster Keaton, Sally O'Neil, Snitz Edwards, Francis McDonald, Mary O'Brien, Tom Wilson, Eddie Borden. Pampered young millionaire falls in love with a girl during a camping trip, and then has to pretend he's actually a champion prizefighter. One of Buster's weaker silent features still has its share of funny moments. Based on a stage play. ▼●◗

Battling Hoofer SEE: **Something to Sing About**

Bat*21 (1988) **C-105m.** ★★★ D: Peter Markle. Gene Hackman, Danny Glover, Jerry Reed, David Marshall Grant, Clayton Rohner, Erich Anderson, Joe Dorsey. Air Force Colonel and strategist Hackman has only seen the war from 30,000 feet, until he's shot down behind enemy lines. Now it's up to Glover to get him out before the Viet Cong get him, and before his own forces carpet-bomb the area. Taut, compelling film, based on a true story, with fine acting all around. Costar Reed was executive producer and wrote some of the songs for the soundtrack. [R]▼●◗

Bat Whispers, The (1930) **84m.** ★½ D: Roland West. Chester Morris, Una Merkel, Chance Ward, Richard Tucker, DeWitt Jennings, Maude Eburne, Spencer Charters, William Bakewell, Gustav von Seyffertitz. Excruciatingly archaic "old dark house" thriller about the search for a mysterious killer known as The Bat. Of interest to buffs for its striking visuals, including some eye-popping miniature sets. Remake of THE BAT (1926), itself remade in 1959. Simultaneously filmed in experimental 70mm widescreen process called Magnifilm. ▼●◗

Bawdy Adventures of Tom Jones, The (1976-British) **C-94m.** ★★ D: Cliff Owen. Nicky Henson, Trevor Howard, Joan Collins, Terry-Thomas, Arthur Lowe, Georgia Brown. Mild doings, based on London stage musical, can't hold a candle to 1963 classic (TOM JONES). This time, Tom's amorous adventures are pat and predictable, with Collins, as highwaywoman Black Bess, adding only zing. [R]▼

Baxter (1973) **C-100m.** ★★★ D: Lionel Jeffries. Patricia Neal, Scott Jacoby, Jean-Pierre Cassel, Lynn Carlin, Britt Ekland, Sally Thomsett, Paul Eddington. Well acted drama about young Jacoby's emotional problems and his relationship with speech therapist Neal, who tries to correct his lisp. [PG]

Baxter (1991-French) **C-82m.** ★★★ D: Jerome Boivin. Lise Delamare, Jean Mercure, Jacques Spiesser, Catherine Ferran, Jean-Paul Roussillon. Illuminating observation of the human condition as perceived through the unlikeliest of eyes: the title canine, a bull terrier who thinks and feels, and reveals what's on his mind. The most disturbing of his various masters: a seemingly average young boy who turns out to be a fascist-in-training. Boivin coscripted.▼●

Bay Boy, The (1984-Canadian-French) **C-107m.** ★★ D: Daniel Petrie. Liv Ullmann, Kiefer Sutherland, Peter Donat, Mathieu Carriere, Isabelle Mejias, Alan Scarfe, Chris Wiggins, Leah Pinsent. Well-meaning but hopelessly predictable portrayal of a teenager (Sutherland, son of Donald), and his coming of age in rural Canadian community during 1930s. You've seen this one many times before; Ullmann in partic-

ular is one-dimensional as Sutherland's hardworking mother. [R]▼●
Bay of Blood SEE: **Twitch of the Death Nerve**
Bay of Saint Michel, The (1963-British) **73m.** ** D: John Ainsworth. Keenan Wynn, Mai Zetterling, Ronald Howard, Rona Anderson, Trader Faulkner. Adequate actioner of ex-WW2 commandos (one of whom is a woman) working to recover a Nazi general's plundered loot. Retitled: OPERATION MERMAID. Video title: PATTERN FOR PLUNDER.▼
Beach, The (2000) **C-120m.** **½ D: Danny Boyle. Leonardo DiCaprio, Tilda Swinton, Virginie Ledoyen, Guillaume Canet, Paterson Joseph, Robert Carlyle, Peter Youngblood Hills. Young American looking for "something different" goes to Bangkok, hooks up with a French couple, and together they follow a map to an elusive and secluded island beach . . . but paradise is not all it's cracked up to be. Consistently interesting if sometimes muddled adaptation of Alex Garland's novel is naive at times and leans toward purplish prose in DiCaprio's narration. Super 35. [R]▼◗
Beach Ball (1965) **C-83m.** ** D: Lennie Weinrib. Edd Byrnes, Chris Noel, Robert Logan, Gale Gilmore, Aron Kincaid. Different group tries a beach picture, but it's essentially the same. Pretty girls, surfing, Edd in drag, and performances by The Supremes, Four Seasons, Righteous Bros., Hondells, Walker Bros.
Beach Blanket Bingo (1965) **C-98m.** *** D: William Asher. Frankie Avalon, Annette Funicello, Paul Lynde, Harvey Lembeck, Don Rickles, Linda Evans, Jody McCrea, Marta Kristen, John Ashley, Deborah Walley, Buster Keaton, Bobbi Shaw, Timothy Carey. Fifth BEACH PARTY movie is the best (and best known); amid various plot entanglements (parachuting, kidnapped singing idol Evans, mermaid Kristen), Lynde sneers at everybody, Rickles insults everybody, and Lembeck gets to sing before being cut into two halves by Carey's buzzsaw. For those so inclined, the ultimate wallow in '60s surfing nostalgia. Sequel: HOW TO STUFF A WILD BIKINI. Panavision. ▼●
Beach Boys: An American Band, The (1985) **C-103m.** ** D: Malcolm Leo. Ineffectual "authorized" bio of the Boys lacks focus and peters out after a delightful opening half hour. High points: numbers long excised from THE T.A.M.I SHOW, hilarious clip from THE GIRLS ON THE BEACH, wild TV appearance on a Bob Hope special. [PG-13]▼●
Beachcomber, The (1938-British) **92m.** *** D: Erich Pommer. Charles Laughton, Elsa Lanchester, Tyrone Guthrie, Robert Newton, Dolly Mollinger. Disheveled bum Laughton, living on island paradise, is reformed by missionary Lanchester. Two stars (married in real life) delightful in filmization of W. Somerset Maugham story originally titled VESSEL OF WRATH. The sole directorial outing of esteemed German producer (and Laughton partner) Pommer. Remade in 1955.▼
Beachcomber, The (1955-British) **C-82m.** *** D: Muriel Box. Glynis Johns, Robert Newton, Donald Sinden, Michael Hordern, Donald Pleasence. Remake of Somerset Maugham tale of South Sea island bum entangled with strait-laced sister of missionary is still flavorful.
Beaches (1988) **C-123m.** **½ D: Garry Marshall. Bette Midler, Barbara Hershey, John Heard, Spalding Gray, Lainie Kazan, James Read, Grace Johnston, Mayim Bialik, Marcie Leeds. Bittersweet saga of a thirty-year friendship that begins when two girls—one rich and pampered, the other poor and driven to show-biz success—meet on the beach at Atlantic City. OK as soap opera (not much depth to the characters and their motives, and at least two endings too many) but as a vehicle for Midler it's dynamite, and she even gets to sing. Based on a novel by Iris Rainer Dart; Midler coproduced. Director Marshall features his on-screen "regulars" in a variety of cameo roles, including Hector Elizondo as a justice of the peace. [PG-13]▼●
Beachhead (1954) **C-89m.** *** D: Stuart Heisler. Tony Curtis, Frank Lovejoy, Mary Murphy, Eduard Franz, Skip Homeier. Nicely handled action of marine quartet on dangerous mission in WW2.
Beach Party (1963) **C-101m.** ** D: William Asher. Frankie Avalon, Annette Funicello, Bob Cummings, Dorothy Malone, Harvey Lembeck, Jody McCrea, John Ashley, Morey Amsterdam, Candy Johnson, Eva Six. Anthropologist Cummings studies teenagers' "wild" behavior, but comes to learn they aren't so bad after all. First in long-running series is typical blend of slapstick and forgettable songs, as well as introduction of Lembeck's dopey Brando-biker takeoff, Eric Von Zipper. Sequel: MUSCLE BEACH PARTY. Panavision. ▼
Beach Red (1967) **C-105m.** *** D: Cornel Wilde. Cornel Wilde, Rip Torn, Burr De Benning, Patrick Wolfe, Jean Wallace. Hard look at military life in South Pacific attempts to show ugly side of war. Likely to be watered down for TV.
Bean (1997-British) **C-90m.** *** D: Mel Smith. Rowan Atkinson, Peter MacNicol, Pamela Reed, Harris Yulin, Burt Reynolds, John Mills. Mr. Bean, featured in a series of TV skits and specials, makes his feature-film debut as a guard at the National Gallery of Art in London who's sent to America, posing as a noted art expert, to accompany "Whistler's Mother" as it is unveiled at a California museum. Never quite as wonderful

as you'd like it to be, but often very funny. Bean's misadventures are reminiscent of silent film comedy, and largely dependent on the winning silliness of Atkinson himself. [PG-13] ▼●◗

Beans of Egypt, Maine, The (1994) **C-100m.** **½ D: Jennifer Warren. Martha Plimpton, Kelly Lynch, Rutger Hauer, Patrick McGaw, Richard Sanders, Michael MacRae. Episodic, mildly interesting account of the Beans, a large, rough-and-tumble backwoods clan, and the most notorious residents of Egypt, Maine (pop. 729). Film centers on the relationship, sexual and otherwise, between Beal Bean (McGaw), a hot, prideful young stud, and the Beans' neighbor (Plimpton). Based on the best-selling novel by Carolyn Chute. An *American Playhouse* coproduction. Retitled FORBIDDEN CHOICES for video. [R]▼●

Bear, The (1984) **C-112m.** ** D: Richard Sarafian. Gary Busey, Cynthia Leake, Harry Dean Stanton, Jon-Erik Hexum, Carmen Thomas, Cary Guffey, D'Urville Martin. Incredibly corny, old-fashioned Hollywood bio of famed Alabama collegiate football coach Paul "Bear" Bryant. Busey's sincere, gravel-voiced portrayal can't compensate for episodic, repetitive, and undramatic script. [PG]

Bear, The (1989-French) **C-93m.** *** D: Jean-Jacques Annaud. Bart, Douce, Jack Wallace, Tcheky Karyo, Andre Lacombe. Captivating and unusual film about a bear cub who is orphaned and forced to fend for itself, until it finds a new protector in a giant Kodiak—the tempting target for a pair of hunters. Filmed with utmost respect for animals and a real sense of nature's magnificence, though manipulative, to be sure. Based on *The Grizzly King,* a 1917 novel by James Oliver Curwood. Panavision. [PG]▼●

Bear Island (1979-British-Canadian) **C-118m.** *½ D: Don Sharp. Donald Sutherland, Vanessa Redgrave, Richard Widmark, Christopher Lee, Barbara Parkins, Lloyd Bridges, Lawrence Dane. One of Alistair MacLean's best novels became one of his worst films, mixing murder, intrigue and stolen bullion near the top of the world. Strong cast, capable director and scenic locations come to naught. Barely released to theatres. Panavision. [PG]▼

Bears and I, The (1974) **C-89m.** *½ D: Bernard McEveety. Patrick Wayne, Chief Dan George, Andrew Duggan, Michael Ansara. Vietnam vet Wayne tries to soothe relations in North Woods between Indians and white bigots. Mild Disney film. [G]▼◗

Beast, The (1971) SEE: **Equinox**

Beast, The (1988) **C-109m.** ** D: Kevin Reynolds. Jason Patric, Steven Bauer, George Dzundza, Stephen Baldwin, Don Harvey, Kabir Bedi, Erick Avari, Haim Gerafi. Soviet tank, cut off from its battalion in Afghan desert, tries to reach safety, while pursued by vengeful Afghan rebels. Eventually, a peace-minded Russian from the tank, left to die by his brutal commander, joins the rebels himself. Serviceable (if predictable) plot is undermined by ponderous pace and stereotyped characters. Filmed in Israel. [R]▼

Beast From Haunted Cave (1960) **64m.** ** D: Monte Hellman. Michael Forest, Sheila Carol, Frank Wolff, Richard Sinatra, Wally Campo. Economically shot (to say the least) by Roger Corman's company on scenic locations near Deadwood, South Dakota, this pits fleeing robbers against a mysterious, spiderlike monster. Charles B. Griffith script has some good dialogue, and Sinatra (Frank's nephew) and Carol showed promise. Monster created and played by actor Chris Robinson. Remake of NAKED PARADISE, with monster added.▼

Beast From 20,000 Fathoms, The (1953) **80m.** ** D: Eugene Lourie. Paul Christian, Paula Raymond, Cecil Kellaway, Kenneth Tobey, Donald Woods, Lee Van Cleef, Ross Elliott. Prehistoric rhedosaurus wreaks havoc when thawed after an atom-bomb blast. Good Ray Harryhausen special effects, especially in amusement park finale. Suggested by the Ray Bradbury short story "The Fog Horn."▼●

Beast in the Cellar, The (1971-British) **C-87m.** ** D: James Kelly. Beryl Reid, Flora Robson, John Hamill, T. P. McKenna, Tessa Wyatt. Two sisters hide their maniac brother in the cellar; performances of Reid and Robson bring movie to average level. British running time was 101m.▼

Beastmaster, The (1982) **C-118m.** ** D: Don Coscarelli. Marc Singer, Tanya Roberts, Rip Torn, John Amos, Rod Loomis. Yet another sword and sandal fantasy with Conan/Tarzan-clone hero who communicates with animals (including, believe it or not, some comedic ferrets), falls in love with slave girl Roberts and seeks revenge against evil priest (Torn) who killed his father. Cinematography by John Alcott (BARRY LYNDON). Followed by several sequels. [PG]▼●

Beastmaster 2: Through the Portal of Time (1991) **C-107m.** *½ D: Sylvio Tabet. Marc Singer, Kari Wuhrer, Sarah Douglas, Wings Hauser, James Avery, Robert Fieldsteel, Arthur Malet, Robert Z'Dar, Michael Berryman, Larry Dobkin. Hero Dar returns (belatedly) to battle another evil wizard (Hauser)—this time, thanks to magician Douglas, in the streets of modern-day L.A. Some cleverness, but cheaply made and contrived. *Nine* writers are credited. Followed by a TV sequel.▼●

Beast Must Die, The (1974-British) **C-93m.** *** D: Paul Annett. Calvin Lockhart, Peter Cushing, Charles Gray, Marlene Clark, Anton Diffring. New twists on the old werewolf theme make the difference. Millionaire sportsman Lockhart invites guests to his electronically bugged mansion, knowing one of them is a werewolf. Lockhart is overly mannered, while Cushing gains sympathy in his usual quiet but effective way. Like TEN LITTLE INDIANS, this movie gives audience a minute to guess killer's identity. From story "There Shall Be No Darkness" by James Blish. Video title: BLACK WEREWOLF. [PG]▼●

Beast of Blood SEE: **Beast of the Dead**

Beast of Budapest, The (1958) **72m.** *½ D: Harmon Jones. Gerald Milton, John Hoyt, Greta Thyssen, Michael Mills, John Banner, Robert Blake. Trite rendering of father vs. son conflict over politics, resolved when elder's death awakens son to truth about life in Communist Hungary.

Beast of Hollow Mountain, The (1956-Mexican-U.S.) **C-80m.** **½ D: Edward Nassour, Ismael Rodriguez. Guy Madison, Patricia Medina, Eduardo Noriega, Carlos Rivas. Unusual combination of Western and monster-on-the-loose formula works well, with clever ending. From screen story by Willis O'Brien. Filmed in Mexico. CinemaScope.●

Beast of the City, The (1932) **87m.** *** D: Charles Brabin. Walter Huston, Jean Harlow, Wallace Ford, Jean Hersholt, Dorothy Peterson, Tully Marshall, John Miljan, Mickey Rooney. "Instead of the glorification of gangsters, we need the glorification of policemen," reads President Hoover's opening statement, and this film delivers, in W. R. Burnett's solid, surprisingly gritty story, a sort of early DIRTY HARRY with a downbeat ending. Harlow is incredibly sexy as a gang moll.

Beast of the Dead (1970) **C-90m.** BOMB D: Eddie Romero. John Ashley, Eddie Garcia, Beverly Miller, Celeste Yarnall. Sequel to MAD DOCTOR OF BLOOD ISLAND, with that film's headless monster stalking natives on Pacific island while mad doctor plans new head transplant. Filmed in the Philippines. Originally titled BEAST OF BLOOD. [PG]▼

Beast of Yucca Flats, The (1961) **60m.** BOMB D: Coleman Francis. Douglas Mellor, Tor Johnson, Barbara Francis. Johnson becomes a disfigured monster as a result of exposure to an A-bomb test. One of the worst films ever made, presented as a virtual silent film with voice-over narration. Subplot of a succession of voluptuous women being strangled bears little relation to the main story.▼

Beasts SEE: **Twilight People**

Beast with Five Fingers, The (1946) **88m.** **½ D: Robert Florey. Robert Alda, Andrea King, Peter Lorre, Victor Francen, J. Carrol Naish. Intriguing if not entirely successful mood-piece about aging pianist and strange doings in his household. Lorre's confrontation with disembodied hand a horror highlight.▼●

Beast Within, The (1982) **C-90m.** BOMB D: Philippe Mora. Ronny Cox, Bibi Besch, Paul Clemens, Don Gordon, R. G. Armstrong, L. Q. Jones, Meshach Taylor. Besch was raped by hairy-legged "thing" while on honeymoon; her son (Clemens), now a teenager, commences killing, and killing, and killing. Oh, yes, he changes into a monster at one point, if you care. Panavision. [R]▼

Beat, The (1988) **C-98m.** *½ D: Paul Mones. John Savage, David Jacobson, Kara Glover, William McNamara, Jeffrey Horowitz. Well-meaning but painfully gauche drama of new kid Jacobson at a N.Y.C. high school dominated by gangs. He brings poetry and mystical fantasy into his classmates' lives. Earnest cast but treatment of generation gap issues is old hat. [R]▼●

Beat Generation, The (1959) **95m.** *½ D: Charles Haas. Steve Cochran, Mamie Van Doren, Ray Danton, Fay Spain, Louis Armstrong, Maggie Hayes, Jackie Coogan, Ray Anthony, Maxie Rosenbloom, Irish McCalla, Vampira. Exploitation-type story of detective Cochran tracking down insane sexual assaulter; vivid sequences marred by hokey script. Retitled THIS REBEL AGE. CinemaScope.●

Beat Girl SEE: **Wild for Kicks**

Beatlemania (1981) **C-86m.** BOMB D: Joseph Manduke. Mitch Weissman, Ralph Castelli, David Leon, Tom Teeley. Awful, pretentious musical based on the equally awful, pretentious stage show, with look-alikes impersonating John, Paul, George, and Ringo. Turn off the tube and dust off your old copy of *Abbey Road.* Aka BEATLEMANIA, THE MOVIE. [PG]▼

Beatrice (1988-French) **C-128m.** *** D: Bertrand Tavernier. Bernard Pierre Donnadieu, Julie Delpy, Nils Tavernier, Monique Chaumette, Robert Dhery, Michele Gleizer. Moody and well-mounted, if essentially ugly saga of the Hundred Years War; a father returns home from the front to bully his weakling son and engage his tougher (and beautiful) daughter in incest. Extremely violent and not for all tastes, but obviously the work of an outstanding filmmaker; try reconciling this with Tavernier's A SUNDAY IN THE COUNTRY. Video title: THE PASSION OF BEATRICE. [R]▼●

Beat Street (1984) **C-106m.** **½ D: Stan Lathan. Rae Dawn Chong, Guy Davis, Jon Chardiet, Leon W. Grant, Saundra Santiago, Robert Taylor. Urban ghetto kids find creative outlets in painting graffiti, breakdancing, rapping, and developing new disco d.j. routines. A slicker version of WILD STYLE that places the old Mickey & Judy "let's put on a show" formula into a more realistic contemporary setting. In-

nocuous trend piece, coproduced by Harry Belafonte. [PG]▼●
Beat the Devil (1954) **89m.** *** D: John Huston. Humphrey Bogart, Jennifer Jones, Gina Lollobrigida, Robert Morley, Peter Lorre, Edward Underdown. Huston and Truman Capote concocted this offbeat, very funny satire of MALTESE FALCON-ish movies on location in Italy. Low-key nature of comedy eluded many people in 1954 and it immediately became a cult favorite, which it remains today.▼●◗
Beau Brummell (1954-U.S.-British) **C-113m.** **½ D: Curtis Bernhardt. Stewart Granger, Elizabeth Taylor, Peter Ustinov, Robert Morley. Handsome cast in lavish production from Granger's rash of costume epics. Here, he's the famous 19th-century British Casanova-fop (played by John Barrymore in the 1924 version). ▼
Beau Geste (1939) **114m.** *** D: William Wellman. Gary Cooper, Ray Milland, Robert Preston, Brian Donlevy, Susan Hayward, J. Carrol Naish, Albert Dekker, Broderick Crawford, Donald O'Connor. Scene-for-scene remake of famous 1926 silent film (with Ronald Colman) isn't quite as good but faithfully retells story of three devoted brothers serving in the Foreign Legion and battling sadistic martinet commander (Donlevy). Nothing can top that opening sequence! Based on the novel by P.C. Wren. Remade in 1966.▼●
Beau Geste (1966) **C-103m.** ** D: Douglas Heyes. Telly Savalas, Guy Stockwell, Doug McClure, Leslie Nielsen. The third version of Christopher Wren's adventure about honor in the French Foreign Legion is barely adequate, with brothers battling rampaging Arabs and sadistic commander Savalas. Techniscope.
Beau James (1957) **C-105m.** *** D: Melville Shavelson. Bob Hope, Vera Miles, Paul Douglas, Alexis Smith, Darren McGavin; narrated by Walter Winchell. Flavorful recreation of the political career of Mayor Jimmy Walker in 1920s N.Y.C., based on Gene Fowler's book. Hope is fine in basically noncomic performance. Guest appearances by Jimmy Durante, Jack Benny, George Jessel, Walter Catlett. VistaVision.
Beaumarchais the Scoundrel (1996-French) **C-100m.** *** D: Edouard Molinaro. Fabrice Luchini, Manuel Blanc, Sandrine Kiberlain, Jacques Weber, Florence Thomassin, Jean Yanne, Michel Piccoli, Michel Serrault, Jean-Claude Brialy. Luchini gives a marvelous performance as the 18th-century playwright, wit, and defender of human rights in this episodic biopic that encompasses everything from backstage theatrical drama and royal intrigue to gun-running for the American Revolution. As light and insubstantial as a soufflé, but beautifully crafted and always entertaining. Panavision.▼
Beau Père (1981-French) **C-120m.** ***½ D: Bertrand Blier. Patrick Dewaere, Ariel Besse, Maurice Ronet, Nicole Garcia, Nathalie Baye, Maurice Risch, Macha Meril. Piano player Dewaere is seduced by his determined stepdaughter, a 14-year-old child-woman (Besse), after the death of her mother. Thoughtful comedy-drama is sensitively, not exploitively, handled by director Blier. Panavision. ▼◗
Beautician and the Beast, The (1997) **C-105m.** *½ D: Ken Kwapis. Fran Drescher, Timothy Dalton, Ian McNeice, Patrick Malahide, Lisa Jakub, Michael Lerner, Phyllis Newman. Stuck in the salon with her TV aspirations going nowhere, a Queens beautician readily accepts when she's hired (on a blunder) to tutor the emotionally deprived children of Slovetzia's widowed dictator. No nun sings "Climb Ev'ry Mountain," but this comedy can be taken as a warped variation on THE SOUND OF MUSIC. Drescher's beguiling loopiness carries it for a while, but the already limited chuckles halt with a full half-hour to go. [PG]▼●
Beauties of the Night (1954-French) **84m.** **½ D: René Clair. Gérard Philipe, Martine Carol, Gina Lollobrigida, Magali Vendeuil. Diverting fantasy involving aspiring composer Philipe with penchant for dreams wandering through various eras of history. ▼
Beautiful Blonde From Bashful Bend, The (1949) **C-77m.** **½ D: Preston Sturges. Betty Grable, Cesar Romero, Rudy Vallee, Olga San Juan, Porter Hall, Sterling Holloway, El Brendel. Film was major flop in 1949, looks somewhat better today; broad Western farce has Grable a gun-toting saloon girl mistaken for schoolmarm in hick town. Hugh Herbert hilarious as nearsighted doctor.▼●
Beautiful but Deadly SEE: **Don Is Dead, The**
Beautiful Dreamers (1990-Canadian) **C-107m.** **½ D: John Kent Harrison. Colm Feore, Rip Torn, Wendel Meldrum, Sheila McCarthy. Free-spirited American poet Walt Whitman (Torn) befriends Dr. Maurice Bucke (Feore), intrigued by his progressive treatment of the mentally retarded. Their combined roguish idealism confounds their peers and sets Victorian sensibilities askew. Trite handling of interesting story, with outstanding performances by Torn and Feore. [PG-13]▼●
Beautiful Girls (1996) **C-107m.** *** D: Ted Demme. Timothy Hutton, Matt Dillon, Noah Emmerich, Annabeth Gish, Lauren Holly, Rosie O'Donnell, Max Perlich, Martha Plimpton, Natalie Portman, Michael Rapaport, Mira Sorvino, Uma Thurman, Pruitt Taylor Vince, Anne Bobby, Richard Bright, Sam Robards, David Arquette. Hutton, on the verge of marrying his girlfriend but unsure of himself, goes back to his Massachusetts hometown and hangs out with his pals

from high school, whose lives—and relationships with women—haven't changed a bit. Well-observed and well-cast slice of life about the continuity of small-town working-class existence and the ruts both men and women can find themselves in. Some great moments for precocious Portman, smart-mouthed O'Donnell, and others in the ensemble. [R]▼●◗

Beautiful People (1999-British) **C-109m.** *** D: Jasmin Dizdar. Charlotte Coleman, Charles Kay, Rosalind Ayres, Roger Sloman, Heather Tobias, Danny Nussbaum, Siobhan Redmond, Gilbert Martin, Edin Dzandzanovic. Sharply observed film about various people—mostly Brits and Bosnians—caught in England's contemporary melting pot, but told with a sense of humor and hope in its heart instead of despair. A striking and believable film from writer-director Dizdar. [R]▼

Beautiful Stranger SEE: **Twist of Fate** (1954)

Beautiful Thing (1996-British) **C-89m.** *** D: Hettie Macdonald. Glen Berry, Linda Henry, Scott Neal, Tameka Empson, Ben Daniels, Martin Walsh. Amiable and insightful tale of two working-class adolescent boys (Berry and Neal), neighbors with very different home lives, who become sexually and romantically involved. Sharp bits of humor and the blue-collar setting add punch to the proceedings, resulting in a winning coming-out/coming-of-age story. Love that Mama Cass sound track! Scripted by Jonathan Harvey, based on his play. [R]▼

Beauty and the Beast (1946-French) **95m.** **** D: Jean Cocteau. Jean Marais, Josette Day, Marcel André. Cocteau's hauntingly beautiful, visually dazzling masterpiece, detailing what happens when, to save her father, Beauty (Day) gives herself to the Beast (Marais). Great fantasy, great filmmaking—beguiling on any level.▼●◗

Beauty and the Beast (1963) **C-77m.** *½ D: Edward L. Cahn. Joyce Taylor, Mark Damon, Eduard Franz, Michael Pate, Merry Anders, Dayton Lummis, Walter Burke. Curse turns handsome prince into werewolf-like beast every night; princess defends him, while a usurper seeks his throne. Colorful but turgid rewrite of the famous tale, set in knights-and-castles period. Makeup by the fabled Jack P. Pierce.▼

Beauty and the Beast (1991) **C-85m.** ***½ D: Gary Trousdale, Kirk Wise. Voices of Paige O'Hara, Robby Benson, Jerry Orbach, Angela Lansbury, Richard White, David Ogden Stiers, Jesse Corti, Rex Everhart, Bradley Michael Pierce, Jo Anne Worley, Kimmy Robertson. Classic Disney cartoon version of the classic tale, with bookish Belle and a ferocious Beast learning to love one another after he makes her prisoner in his desolate castle (where the only signs of life come from humanized household fixtures). Cannily presented in the style of a Broadway musical, with a fine-tuned script by Linda Woolverton, and a rousing, Oscar-winning score by Alan Menken (with another Oscar for Menken and Howard Ashman's title tune). The first animated feature to earn an Oscar nomination as Best Picture. Followed by a Broadway musical, a TV series, and two direct-to-video sequels. [G]▼●

Beauty and the Robot, The SEE: **Sex Kittens Go to College**

Beauty for Sale (1933) **87m.** *** D: Richard Boleslawsky. Madge Evans, Alice Brady, Otto Kruger, Una Merkel, May Robson, Phillips Holmes, Eddie Nugent, Hedda Hopper, Florine McKinney, Isabel Jewell, Charles Grapewin. Entertaining soaper about girl whose job at high-society beauty salon leads to liaison with husband of wealthy customer. Evans never looked more beautiful, photographed here by James Wong Howe. Based on a Faith Baldwin story.

Beauty for the Asking (1939) **68m.** **½ D: Glenn Tryon. Lucille Ball, Patric Knowles, Frieda Inescort, Donald Woods, Inez Courtney, Leona Maricle. Working girl Ball is jilted by money-hungry Knowles; he comes crawling back after she invents an exclusive beauty cream. Watchable programmer, with an interesting feminist viewpoint and good early Ball performance.▼

Beavis and Butt-head Do America (1996) **C-80m.** **½ D: Mike Judge. Voices of Mike Judge, Robert Stack, Cloris Leachman, Eric Bogosian, Richard Linklater. The unabashedly ignorant, flagrantly antisocial, hormonally charged duo from MTV's animated series find themselves on a cross-country odyssey that begins when someone steals their all-important TV set. Alternately stupid, gross, and hilarious, this modest cartoon feature is certainly true to itself and certain to please *B&B* fans. Bruce Willis, Demi Moore, and David Letterman contribute unbilled voices, but best of all is the casting of Stack as a hard-nosed Federal agent. Huh-huh-huh. [PG-13]▼●◗

Bebe's Kids (1992) **C-74m.** **½ D: Bruce Smith. Voices of Faizon Love, Nell Carter, Myra J., Vanessa Bell Calloway, Tone Loc, Wayne Collins, Jonell Green, Marques Houston. Raucous animated feature based on a routine by the late comedian Robin Harris (voiced here by Faizon Love) whose date with an attractive woman turns into a nightmare when she brings along her son—and three brats she's looking after. The first animated feature aimed squarely at a black audience is lively, often funny—but a bit protracted. [PG-13]▼●

Be Beautiful but Shut Up (1957-French) **94m.** ** D: Henri Verneuil. Mylene Demongeot, Henri Vidal, Isabelle Miranda. Unremarkable study of young hoods involved with smuggling and carefree living.▼

Bebo's Girl (1964-Italian) **106m.** **½ D: Luigi Comencini. Claudia Cardinale, George Chakiris, Mario Lupi, Dany Paris. At times memorable love story spotlighting Cardinale's decision to leave her new lover in order to reaffirm her attachment with first love, now serving a prison term.

Because He's My Friend (1978-Australian) **C-93m. TVM** D: Ralph Nelson. Karen Black, Keir Dullea, Jack Thompson, Tom Oliver, Don Reid, Barbara Stephens. Sensitive drama about the plight of parents with a retarded child and the effect on their marriage. The youngster is especially well-played by Australian actor Warwick Poulsen. Above average.

Because of Him (1946) **88m.** **½ D: Richard Wallace. Deanna Durbin, Franchot Tone, Charles Laughton, Helen Broderick, Donald Meek. Contrived comedy recalls Deanna's earlier (and better) vehicles as she schemes to become the protégée of Broadway star Laughton, with interference from playwright Tone. A few songs are shoehorned into the film as arbitrarily as most of the story elements.▼

Because of You (1952) **95m.** ** D: Joseph Pevney. Loretta Young, Jeff Chandler, Alex Nicol, Frances Dee, Mae Clarke, Alexander Scourby. Loretta weds Jeff—but fails to inform him that she's a parolee; then she takes up with her ex-boyfriend, a drug smuggler. Trite and forgettable.▼

Because They're Young (1960) **102m.** **½ D: Paul Wendkos. Dick Clark, Michael Callan, Tuesday Weld, Victoria Shaw, Doug McClure, James Darren, Warren Berlinger, Roberta Shore, Duane Eddy and The Rebels. Clark made his screen acting debut—if you really must know—in this ho-hum adaptation of John Farris' *Harrison High*. Mr. American Bandstand stars as an understanding do-gooder teacher, who attempts to help his troubled students.

Because You're Mine (1952) **C-103m.** ** D: Alexander Hall. Mario Lanza, James Whitmore, Doretta Morrow, Dean Miller, Paula Corday, Jeff Donnell, Spring Byington, Don Porter, Eduard Franz, Bobby Van. Opera star Lanza is drafted and falls in love with Morrow, the sister of his top sergeant (Whitmore). For Lanza fans only.▼

Becket (1964) **C-148m.** **** D: Peter Glenville. Richard Burton, Peter O'Toole, John Gielgud, Donald Wolfit, Martita Hunt, Pamela Brown, Felix Aylmer. Stunning film, adapted by Edward Anhalt (who won an Oscar) from the Jean Anouilh play, centers on stormy friendship between Archbishop of Canterbury Thomas à Becket and his English King, Henry II. Superbly acted and magnificently photographed (by Geoffrey Unsworth) on location in England. Panavision. ▼●

Becky Sharp (1935) **C-83m.** **½ D: Rouben Mamoulian. Miriam Hopkins, Frances Dee, Cedric Hardwicke, Billie Burke, Alison Skipworth, Nigel Bruce. Witty but sometimes ponderous adaptation of Thackeray's *Vanity Fair* with Hopkins as self-reliant girl whose sole concern is herself. Historically important as first full-Technicolor (3-color) feature, designed by Robert Edmond Jones (and photographed by Ray Rennahan). Long available to TV only in inferior 67m. Cinecolor reissue prints; archivally restored in 1985. Previously filmed (as VANITY FAIR) in 1923 and 1932.▼

Becoming Colette (1992-U.S.-German) **C-97m.** *½ D: Danny Huston. Klaus Maria Brandauer, Mathilda May, Virginia Madsen, Paul Rhys, John van Dreelen, Jean-Pierre Aumont. Ridiculous tale of the famed French writer Colette (May), depicted as an inexperienced country girl who weds publisher Brandauer. He prints her writing under his name, and sets up a threesome with Madsen (but becomes outraged when the women fall in love). The director is the son of John Huston, but may as well be the protégé of Zalman King. [R]▼

Bed and Board (1970-French) **C-97m.** ***½ D: François Truffaut. Jean-Pierre Léaud, Claude Jade, Hiroko Berghauer, Daniel Ceccaldi, Claire Duhamel. Chapter Four of the Antoine Doinel story. Here, Doinel (Léaud) is married to Christine (Jade); he is confused, immature, becomes a father, and has an affair with Berghauer. Lovingly directed by Truffaut; Jacques Tati has an amusing cameo as M. Hulot. Followed by LOVE ON THE RUN. [PG]◗

Bed and Breakfast (1992) **C-98m.** **½ D: Robert Ellis Miller. Roger Moore, Talia Shire, Colleen Dewhurst, Nina Siemaszko, Ford Rainey, Stephen Root, Jamie Walters, Victor Slezak. A debonair stranger makes his impact on a houseful of women, who span several generations. First-rate performances, and a gorgeous setting on the Maine coast, make this modest film worth seeing, especially on the small screen; filmed in 1989. [PG-13]▼●

Bedazzled (1967-British) **C-107m.** *** D: Stanley Donen. Peter Cook, Dudley Moore, Eleanor Bron, Raquel Welch, Alba, Barry Humphries. Cult film updating Faust legend is as sacrilegious as THE SINGING NUN and usually funnier. The laughs aren't always consistent, but the Cook-Moore team is terrific and Donen's direction stylish. And remember the magic words: "Julie Andrews!" Panavision. ▼●

Bedelia (1946-British) **92m.** **½ D: Lance Comfort. Margaret Lockwood, Ian Hunter, Barry K. Barnes, Anne Crawford, Jill Esmond. Naive Hunter marries a woman with a past, including (it turns out) several husbands who met mysterious ends. Absorbing but not terribly suspenseful. Based on a Vera Caspary novel.

Bedevilled (1955) **C-85m.** ** D: Mitchell Leisen. Anne Baxter, Steve Forrest, Simone Renant, Victor Francen. Bizarre yarn of chanteuse Baxter fleeing from murder scene, protected by Forrest, who's studying for priesthood; filmed in Paris. CinemaScope.

Bedford Incident, The (1965) **102m.** *** D: James B. Harris. Richard Widmark, Sidney Poitier, James MacArthur, Martin Balsam, Wally Cox, Eric Portman, Donald Sutherland. Strong Cold War story of authoritarian Navy captain (Widmark) scouting Russian subs near Greenland and the mental conflicts that develop on his ship. Poitier is reporter too good to be true, Balsam a sympathetic doctor disliked by Widmark. Cast excels in intriguing battle of wits.▼

Bedknobs and Broomsticks (1971) **C-117m.** *** D: Robert Stevenson. Angela Lansbury, David Tomlinson, Roddy McDowall, Sam Jaffe, Roy Snart, Cindy O'Callaghan, Ian Weighill. Elaborate Disney musical fantasy about amateur witch who helps British cause in WW2; no MARY POPPINS, but quite enjoyable, with Oscar-winning special effects and delightful animated cartoon sequences directed by Ward Kimball. Reissued at 98m. 141 min. archival edition assembled in 1996, with more (and longer) songs, clearer plot, and more of a part for McDowall. [G]▼●

Bedlam (1946) **79m.** *** D: Mark Robson. Boris Karloff, Anna Lee, Ian Wolfe, Richard Fraser, Billy House, Jason Robards, Sr. Atmospheric Val Lewton chiller of courageous Lee trying to expose inadequate conditions at insane asylum, committed to one by institution head Karloff. Set in 18th-century London. Robert Clarke appears unbilled.▼●

Bed of Roses (1933) **67m.** *** D: Gregory La Cava. Constance Bennett, Joel McCrea, Pert Kelton, John Halliday, Samuel S. Hinds, Franklin Pangborn. Smart pre-Code comedy-drama with Bennett and Kelton released from reform school and on the make for plenty of 'umpchays with ashcay,' that is, until Bennett falls for riverboat skipper McCrea. Kelton is hilarious as a slinky, no-holds-barred "bad girl" with an acid tongue.

Bed of Roses (1996) **C-87m.** ** D: Michael Goldenberg. Christian Slater, Mary Stuart Masterson, Pamela Segall, Josh Brolin, Ally Walker, Debra Monk. Business exec Masterson is courted by florist Slater (a young widower), but her past troubled relationships prevent her from committing to him. Attempt at a serious romantic film is emotionally off the mark, though the performers try their best. [PG]▼●◗

Bedroom Window, The (1987) **C-112m.** *** D: Curtis Hanson. Steve Guttenberg, Elizabeth McGovern, Isabelle Huppert, Paul Shenar, Carl Lumbly, Wallace Shawn, Frederick Coffin, Brad Greenquist. An innocent man offers to alibi for his boss' sexy wife, who witnessed an assault from his bedroom window after they made love. This apparently simple gesture snowballs into a web of crime and duplicity, in this attractive, sexy, and suspenseful Hitchcock homage. Guttenberg is no Cary Grant (or James Stewart), but the film is consistently enjoyable—if not always absolutely believable. J-D-C Scope. [R]▼●◗

Bedside Manner (1945) **72m.** ** D: Andrew L. Stone. Ruth Hussey, John Carroll, Charles Ruggles, Ann Rutherford, Claudia Drake, Renee Godfrey, Esther Dale. Carroll is pilot being treated by woman doctor Hussey; guess what happens? Routine, inoffensive romantic-comedy. Aka HER FAVORITE PATIENT. ▼

Bed Sitting Room, The (1969-British) **C-91m.** **½ D: Richard Lester. Rita Tushingham, Ralph Richardson, Peter Cook, Dudley Moore, Harry Secombe, Arthur Lowe, Roy Kinnear, Spike Milligan, Michael Hordern, Mona Washbourne. Moderately successful black-comedy look at distorted devastated England three years after nuclear war. A few funny bits, great cast, but film doesn't click. Marty Feldman makes his film debut in a brief bit.

Bedtime for Bonzo (1951) **83m.** **½ D: Frederick de Cordova. Ronald Reagan, Diana Lynn, Walter Slezak, Jesse White, Lucille Barkley. Often cited as the pinnacle of absurdity in Reagan's career, but in fact it's a cute, harmless little comedy about a professor who treats a chimp as his child for a heredity experiment. Reagan did not appear in the sequel, BONZO GOES TO COLLEGE.▼

Bedtime Story, A (1933) **87m.** **½ D: Norman Taurog. Maurice Chevalier, Helen Twelvetrees, Baby LeRoy, Adrienne Ames, Edward Everett Horton. Breezy Chevalier musical vehicle with Parisian playboy playing father to abandoned baby who interferes with his romancing.

Bedtime Story (1941) **85m.** *** D: Alexander Hall. Fredric March, Loretta Young, Robert Benchley, Allyn Joslyn, Eve Arden. Fine cast in sparkling comedy of playwright March trying to stop wife Young from retiring so she can star in his next play.

Bedtime Story (1964) **C-99m.** **½ D: Ralph Levy. Marlon Brando, David Niven, Shirley Jones, Dody Goodman, Marie Windsor. Offbeat casting of stars provides chief interest in lackluster comedy of con men Brando and Niven competing for Jones' affection. Remade as DIRTY ROTTEN SCOUNDRELS.▼

Been Down So Long It Looks Like Up to Me (1971) **C-90m.** *½ D: Jeffrey Young. Barry Primus, Linda DeCoff, David Browning, Susan Tyrrell, Philip Shafer, Bruce Davison, Raul Julia. Bland, dated film version of Richard Fariña's novel about hip

1960s type trying to endure life on a 1958 campus. [R]

Beer (1985) **C-82m.** *½ D: Patrick Kelly. Loretta Swit, Rip Torn, Kenneth Mars, David Alan Grier, William Russ, Saul Stein, Dick Shawn. Unimaginative, ultimately tasteless spoof of Madison Avenue hype, with Swit as an ad-agency executive who devises a highly successful commercial campaign to sell beer. Not so far from reality—and not terribly funny. [R]▼

Bees, The (1978) **C-83m.** *½ D: Alfredo Zacharias. John Saxon, Angel Tompkins, John Carradine, Claudio Brook, Alicia Encinias. After THE SWARM, if you sincerely want to see this low-budget disaster film about killer bees, you get what you deserve. Filmed in Mexico. [PG]▼

Beethoven (1992) **C-87m.** **½ D: Brian Levant. Charles Grodin, Bonnie Hunt, Dean Jones, Oliver Platt, Stanley Tucci, Nicholle Tom, Christopher Castile, Sarah Rose Karr, David Duchovny, Patricia Heaton, Laurel Cronin, and Chris. Innocuous family comedy about an uptight Dad (Grodin) whose family talks him into keeping a runaway puppy that grows into a big, slobbering St. Bernard. It's fun to watch all-American, clean-cut Jones playing a slimy, raspy-voiced villain here. Followed by BEETHOVEN'S 2ND and a direct-to-video sequel. [PG]▼●◗

Beethoven's Great Love (1936-French) **116m.** ***½ D: Abel Gance. Harry Baur, Jean-Louis Barrault, Marcel Dalio, Jany Holt, Annie Ducaux, Jean Debucourt, Sylvie Gance. The life of the great composer told with titanic verve. Beethoven's artistic triumphs and his tragic struggle with deafness are portrayed against the backdrop of his compositions. Gance's bravura use of images and expressionistic use of sound make this a worthy companion piece to his silent masterpiece NAPOLEON. American titles: BEETHOVEN and THE LIFE AND LOVES OF BEETHOVEN.▼

Beethoven's 2nd (1993) **C-86m.** **½ D: Rod Daniel. Charles Grodin, Bonnie Hunt, Nicholle Tom, Christopher Castile, Sarah Rose Karr, Debi Mazar, Chris Penn, Ashley Hamilton, Maury Chaykin, Jeff Corey, Virginia Capers, and Beethoven. Painless sequel, on par with its predecessor, which charts the various complications when Grodin's kids raise St. Bernard Beethoven's puppies on the sly. If you liked the original . . . Followed by a direct-to-video sequel. [PG]▼●◗

Beetle Juice (1988) **C-92m.** *** D: Tim Burton. Michael Keaton, Alec Baldwin, Geena Davis, Jeffrey Jones, Catherine O'Hara, Winona Ryder, Sylvia Sidney, Robert Goulet, Glenn Shadix, Dick Cavett, Annie McEnroe. Newly deceased couple in need of help coping with the afterlife, and obnoxious family who's moved into their home, get it in the form of renegade spirit Betelgeuse (Keaton, who pulls out all the stops). Fantastic special effects make this a sort of live-action cartoon. Added treat: Sylvia Sidney as harried case worker in the hereafter. Great fun, and surprisingly good-natured in spirit. Music by Danny Elfman, with a strong assist from Harry Belafonte. Academy Award winner for makeup. Followed by an animated TV series. [PG]▼●◗

Before and After (1996) **C-107m.** *** D: Barbet Schroeder. Meryl Streep, Liam Neeson, Edward Furlong, Alfred Molina, Julia Weldon, Daniel von Bargen, John Heard, Ann Magnuson, Larry Pine, Wesley Addy. Sober tale of a New England family torn apart—and ostracized—when the son is accused of murdering a teenage girl and then disappears. The father is willing to cover the boy's tracks, while mother and daughter want to tell the truth, in spite of the consequences. Absorbing and believable story (written by Ted Tally). [PG-13]▼●

Before I Hang (1940) **71m.** **½ D: Nick Grinde. Boris Karloff, Evelyn Keyes, Bruce Bennett, Pedro de Cordoba, Edward Van Sloan. Contrived but intriguing tale of prison scientist Karloff having youth serum backfire on him, driving him mad at odd moments.▼●

Before I Wake SEE: **Shadow of Fear**

Before Sunrise (1995) **C-101m.** **½ D: Richard Linklater. Ethan Hawke, Julie Delpy. Young American strikes up a conversation with a fellow train passenger and persuades her to get off in Vienna and share his last night in Europe; they do, in fact, spend the entire night talking and falling in love. A somewhat daring idea for the '90s, buoyed by two engaging performers; it is (unavoidably) awfully talky, but it's also undeniably romantic. [R]▼●◗

Before the Rain (1994-Macedonian-British-French) **C-114m.** *** D: Milcho Manchevski. Katrin Cartlidge, Rade Serbedzija, Gregoire Colin, Labina Mitevska. Fascinating look at several intertwining lives in the newly independent, and strife-torn, Republic of Macedonia (formerly Yugoslavia), where rural poverty and violent rage are prevalent. Story links a young monk, a globetrotting photojournalist, and a stylish young woman in London who is at a crossroads in her personal life. Film's structure resembles PULP FICTION, which debuted almost simultaneously. A strong statement that unfolds slowly; stick with this one. Technovision.▼

Before the Revolution (1964-Italian) **115m.** *** D: Bernardo Bertolucci. Adriana Asti, Francisco Barilli, Alain Midgette, Morando Morandini, Domenico Alpi. Bertolucci's second feature (which he wrote when he was 22 years old) dramatizes the dilemma of young, middle-class Barilli. Will he embrace a life of social and political radicalism, or submit to the bourgeois status quo? Revealing 1960s time capsule, loaded with topical ideas, references, and fervor.▼

Before Winter Comes (1969-British) **C-102m.** **½ D: J. Lee Thompson. David Niven, Topol, Anna Karina, John Hurt, Anthony Quayle, Ori Levy. Topol is interpreter for British officer Niven in displaced persons' camp following WW2. Uneven comedy-drama with many touching moments, capturing plight of refugees. Topol's warmth shines in winning performance. [M/PG]

Beggar's Opera, The (1953-British) **C-94m.** *** D: Peter Brook. Laurence Olivier, Stanley Holloway, Dorothy Tutin, Daphne Anderson, Mary Clare, Hugh Griffith, Laurence Naismith. Celebrated stage director Brook made his film debut with this vivid, energetic version of John Gay's opera. Coproducer and star Olivier is somewhat miscast but more than makes up for it with his sly portrayal of a jailed highwayman who exaggerates his exploits into a musical revue.

Beginner's Luck (1983) **C-85m.** *** D: Frank Mouris. Sam Rush, Riley Steiner, Charles Homet, Kate Talbot, Mickey Coburn. Charming, refreshingly original little comedy about uptight, virginal law student Rush and his lusty upstairs neighbors (Steiner, Homet), with their friendship culminating in a zany ménage à trois. A trifle silly at times but often funny and attractively performed. [R]▼

Beginning of the End (1957) **73m.** *½ D: Bert I. Gordon. Peggie Castle, Peter Graves, Morris Ankrum, Thomas Browne Henry. Awful sci-fi outing about giant grasshoppers (thanks to radiation) on the rampage; at the climax, they invade Chicago—but none too convincingly.▼

Beginning or the End, The (1947) **112m.** *** D: Norman Taurog. Brian Donlevy, Robert Walker, Beverly Tyler, Audrey Totter, Hume Cronyn. Engrossing account of atomic bomb development, depicting both human and spectacular aspects.

Beguiled, The (1971) **C-109m.** *** D: Don Siegel. Clint Eastwood, Geraldine Page, Elizabeth Hartman, Jo Ann Harris, Darleen Carr, Pamelyn Ferdin. Offbeat, methodically paced story set in Civil War South. Wounded Eastwood brought to girls' school to recuperate; he becomes catalyst for flurry of jealousy and hatred. Unusual Eastwood fare, but for patient viewers, a rich, rewarding film. [R]▼●◗

Behave Yourself (1951) **81m.** ** D: George Beck. Farley Granger, Shelley Winters, William Demarest, Francis L. Sullivan, Margalo Gilmore, Lon Chaney, Jr., Sheldon Leonard, Marvin Kaplan, Glenn Anders, Allen Jenkins, Elisha Cook, Jr., Hans Conried. Loud, limp black comedy with Granger and Winters miscast as young marrieds who take in a dog trained to act as a link between two gangs in a smuggling scheme. Good supporting cast is wasted. The title song was cowritten by Buddy Ebsen!▼

Behind Enemy Lines (1986) SEE: **P.O.W. The Escape**

Behind Locked Doors (1948) **62m.** ** D: Oscar (Budd) Boetticher. Lucille Bremer, Richard Carlson, Douglas Fowley, Tom Browne Henry. Mishmash of judge on the lam seeking refuge in an insane asylum, and the reporter who tracks him down for the story. Aka THE HUMAN GORILLA. ▼

Behind That Curtain (1929) **90m.** *½ D: Irving Cummings. Warner Baxter, Lois Moran, Gilbert Emery, Claude King, Philip Strange, Boris Karloff, E. L. Park. Exceedingly stilted and old-fashioned early-talkie melodrama about heiress Moran victimized by her scoundrel of a husband, fleeing to arms of lover Baxter. Noteworthy only as the first sound film appearance of Charlie Chan (Park), albeit in an irrelevant five-minute part near the end. Long considered lost, this is one "treasure" that could have stayed buried.▼

Behind the Door SEE: **Man with Nine Lives, The**

Behind the Eight Ball (1942) **60m.** ** D: Edward F. Cline. Ritz Brothers, Carol Bruce, Grace McDonald, Dick Foran, William Demarest, Johnny Downs. Entertainers get tangled in murder whodunit, with Demarest as determined detective. Typical nonsense plot squeezed in between musical numbers.

Behind the Front (1926) **60m.** **½ D: A. Edward Sutherland. Wallace Beery, Mary Brian, Raymond Hatton, Richard Arlen, Tom Kennedy, Chester Conklin, Gertrude Astor. Entertaining silent army comedy, broadly played by buddies Beery and Hatton. Many devices have been reused countless times, but they're handled smoothly here.▼

Behind the High Wall (1956) **85m.** ** D: Abner Biberman. Tom Tully, Sylvia Sidney, Betty Lynn, John Gavin. Intertwining yarn of grasping prison warden, his crippled wife (nicely played by Sidney), hidden money, and convict escape plan. Remake of THE BIG GUY.

Behind the Iron Curtain SEE: **Iron Curtain, The**

Behind the Lines SEE: **Regeneration** (1997-British-Canadian)

Behind the Mask (1932) **70m.** ** D: John Francis Dillon. Jack Holt, Constance Cummings, Boris Karloff, Edward Van Sloan, Claude King. Secret-service man Holt tries to expose mysterious head of dope ring in this okay thriller, not a horror film despite presence of Karloff and Van Sloan.

Behind the Rising Sun (1943) **89m.** **½ D: Edward Dmytryk. Margo, Tom Neal, J. Carrol Naish, Robert Ryan, Gloria Holden, Don Douglas, George Givot. Japanese man (Naish) urges his Americanized son (Neal) to become involved in Sino-Japanese war during 1930s, but doesn't like what happens as a result. Interesting for WW2-era point of view.▼

Behold a Pale Horse (1964) **118m.** **½ D: Fred Zinnemann. Gregory Peck, Anthony Quinn, Omar Sharif, Mildred Dunnock, Christian Marquand, Raymond Pellegrin. Peck and Quinn wage an ideological battle in post–Spanish Civil War story of politics and violence that loses focus, becoming confused and talky. Valiant try by all.▼

Behold My Wife (1935) **78m.** ** D: Mitchell Leisen. Sylvia Sidney, Gene Raymond, Juliette Compton, Laura Hope Crews, Ann Sheridan. Raymond's snobbish family objects to his love for Indian maiden Sidney. Predictable wrong-side-of-the-reservation romance.

Being, The (1983) **C-79m.** *½ D: Jackie Kong. Martin Landau, Jose Ferrer, Dorothy Malone, Ruth Buzzi, Marianne Gordon Rogers, Murray Langston, Kinky Friedman, Johnny Dark. Creature spawned by nuclear waste terrorizes Idaho community. Humor is film's saving grace, but it isn't enough to overcome grade-Z script and production. Producer William Osco (Kong's then-husband) also costars under the name Rexx Coltrane. Filmed in 1980; briefly shown as EASTER SUNDAY. [R]▼

Being at Home With Claude (1992-Canadian) **C/B&W-85m.** **½ D: Jean Beaudin. Roy Dupuis, Jacques Godin, Jean-Francois Pichette, Gaston Lepage, Hugo Dube. Thoughtful but stagy, occasionally overwrought psychological drama about a gay hustler (Dupuis) who has committed murder during a sexual encounter and then turned himself in; he's interrogated by a cop (Godin), who is determined to learn the motive.▼

Being Human (1994-British-U.S.) **C-122m.** **½ D: Bill Forsyth. Robin Williams, John Turturro, Anna Galiena, Vincent D'Onofrio, Hector Elizondo, Lorraine Bracco, Lindsay Crouse, Grace Mahlaba, Dave Jones, Jonathan Hyde, Lizzy McInnerny, William H. Macy, Helen Miller, Charles Miller. Narrated by Theresa Russell. Queer duck of a movie with Williams as five different men—through five periods of time (spanning 10,000 years)—who are cosmically related. All of them are struggling and striving, without much success, to find happiness. If you can get past the off-putting narration, it's intermittently intriguing, a definite original from writer-director Forsyth. The always watchable Williams makes this journey worthwhile. [PG-13]▼●

Being John Malkovich (1999) **C-112m.** ***½ D: Spike Jonze. John Cusack, John Malkovich, Cameron Diaz, Catherine Keener, Orson Bean, Mary Kay Place, Charlie Sheen. Remarkable, audaciously original black comedy/fantasy about an iconoclastic puppeteer (Cusack) who discovers a portal into the mind of actor John Malkovich, and decides to exploit its possibilities. A far-out premise (by writer Charlie Kaufman) is ingeniously developed into a full-blown story and acted with pizzazz. Malkovich is a marvel in an especially sly, nuanced performance. Other stars make gag cameos. Feature debut for commercial and music video director Jonze. [R]▼●◗

Being There (1979) **C-130m.** **½ D: Hal Ashby. Peter Sellers, Shirley MacLaine, Melvyn Douglas, Jack Warden, Richard Dysart, Richard Basehart, James Noble, David Clennon, Ruth Attaway. A childlike man (Sellers) chances to meet important, powerful people who interpret his bewildered silence as brilliance. Low-keyed black humor, full of savagely witty comments on American life in the television age, but fatally overlong. Adapted by Jerzy Kosinski from his own story. Douglas won Oscar as political kingmaker. [PG]▼●

Bela Lugosi Meets a Brooklyn Gorilla (1952) **74m.** BOMB D: William Beaudine. Bela Lugosi, Duke Mitchell, Sammy Petrillo, Charlita, Muriel Landers, Ramona the Chimp. One of the all-time greats. Mitchell and Petrillo (the very poor man's Martin and Lewis) are stranded on a jungle island, where Lugosi is conducting strange experiments. Proceed at your own risk. Aka THE BOYS FROM BROOKLYN. ▼

Believe in Me (1971) **C-90m.** ** D: Stuart Hagmann. Michael Sarrazin, Jacqueline Bisset, Jon Cypher, Allen Garfield, Kurt Dodenhoff. Still another 70s film about drug addiction, and none too good; clean-cut career girl Bisset becomes addicted to speed in the East Village. Performers do their best. [R]

Believers, The (1987) **C-114m.** **½ D: John Schlesinger. Martin Sheen, Helen Shaver, Harley Cross, Robert Loggia, Elizabeth Wilson, Lee Richardson, Harris Yulin, Richard Masur, Carla Pinza, Jimmy Smits. Gripping, genuinely frightening story of widower and son who move to N.Y.C. and become involved (in more ways than one) with cultish religion of Santeria, which believes in the sacrifice of children. Well-crafted film knows how to manipulate its audience but shows no mercy, either: a boy sees his mother electrocuted in the very first scene! [R]▼●

Belizaire the Cajun (1986) **C-100m.** **½ D: Glen Pitre. Armand Assante, Gail Youngs, Michael Schoeffling, Stephen McHattie, Will Patton, Nancy Barrett. Assante is well cast as a charismatic herbal dealer in love with the Cajun wife of a wealthy Anglo in this uneven and somewhat predictable drama about Anglo prejudice and violence against Cajuns in 19th-century Louisiana. Made with obvious enthusiasm on a low budget. Robert Duvall, credited as creative consultant, appears briefly as a preacher. [PG]▼

Bell' Antonio (1960-Italian-French) **101m.** **½ D: Mauro Bolognini. Marcello Mastroianni, Claudia Cardinale, Pierre Brasseur, Rina Morelli. OK seriocomedy of what happens when Mastroianni is unable to consummate his marriage to Cardinale. Coscripted by Pier Paolo Pasolini. Video title: IL BELL' ANTONIO.▼

Bell, Book and Candle (1958) **C-103m.** **½ D: Richard Quine. James Stewart, Kim Novak, Jack Lemmon, Janice Rule, Ernie Kovacs, Hermione Gingold. John Van Druten play becomes so-so vehicle to showcase Novak as fetching witch who charms about-to-be-married publisher Stewart. Kovacs and Gingold supply their brands of humor.▼●◗

Bellboy, The (1960) **72m.** *** D: Jerry Lewis. Jerry Lewis, Alex Gerry, Bob Clayton, Sonny Sands. Amusing series of blackouts with Jerry as a bellboy at Fontainebleau in Miami Beach. No plot but a lot of funny gags. Milton Berle and Walter Winchell have guest appearances. Lewis's directorial debut.▼●

Belle de Jour (1967-French-Italian) **C-100m.** **** D: Luis Buñuel. Catherine Deneuve, Jean Sorel, Michel Piccoli, Genevieve Page, Francisco Rabal, Pierre Clementi, George Marchal, Françoise Fabian. Buñuel's wry and disturbing tale of a virginal newlywed who works the day shift in a high-class Parisian brothel, unbeknownst to her patient husband. Buñuel's straight-faced treatment of shocking subject matter belies the sharp wit of his script (cowritten with Jean-Claude Carrière). Deneuve's finest, most enigmatic performance. [R]▼●

Belle Epoque (1992-Spanish) **C-108m.** *** D: Fernando Trueba. Fernando Fernan Gomez, Jorge Sanz, Maribel Verdu, Ariadna Gil, Miriam Diaz-Aroca, Penelope Cruz, Mary Carmen Ramirez, Michel Galabru, Gabino Diego. Set in 1931, a time of promise and optimism in pre-Franco Spain, this delightfully earthy, cheerful comedy tells of a hearty young army deserter (Sanz) who's befriended by an elderly recluse, and enchanted by his four beautiful daughters. A multi-award winner in Spain; won Best Foreign Film Oscar. Panavision.▼●

Belle Le Grand (1951) **90m.** *½ D: Allan Dwan. Vera Ralston, John Carroll, William Ching, Muriel Lawrence. Weak Ralston vehicle has her a Western lady gambler willing to play any stakes to win back rambunctious Carroll. Look for James Arness in the fire scene.

Belle of New York, The (1952) **C-82m.** **½ D: Charles Walters. Fred Astaire, Vera-Ellen, Marjorie Main, Keenan Wynn, Alice Pearce. Uninspired musical set in Gay 90s N.Y.C. with Astaire a rich playboy chasing mission worker Vera-Ellen; Pearce adds comic touches. Songs include "Let A Little Love Come In."▼●

Belle of the Nineties (1934) **73m.** *** D: Leo McCarey. Mae West, Roger Pryor, Johnny Mack Brown, Warren Hymer, Duke Ellington Orchestra. Mae struts, sings "My Old Flame," and heats up a gallery of admirers in amusing example of Western humor.▼●◗

Belle of the Yukon (1944) **C-84m.** **½ D: William Seiter. Randolph Scott, Gypsy Rose Lee, Bob Burns, Dinah Shore, Charles Winninger, William Marshall, Guinn "Big Boy" Williams, Robert Armstrong, Florence Bates. Minor musical of saloon-owner Scott going straight at insistence of his girl (Lee); fast-moving, forgettable. Technicolor is film's best feature.

Belles of St. Trinians, The (1954-British) **90m.** ***½ D: Frank Launder. Alastair Sim, Joyce Grenfell, George Cole, Hermione Baddeley, Beryl Reid. Hilarious filmization of Ronald Searle's cartoons about completely crazy school for girls, run by dotty headmistress whose brother, a bookie, wants to use school to his advantage. Sim plays dual role in delightful madcap farce which spawned several sequels.▼

Belles on Their Toes (1952) **C-89m.** *** D: Henry Levin. Myrna Loy, Jeanne Crain, Debra Paget, Jeffrey Hunter, Edward Arnold, Hoagy Carmichael, Barbara Bates, Robert Arthur, Verna Felton, Martin Milner. Pleasing follow-up to CHEAPER BY THE DOZEN, with a potent feminist point-of-view. Here, widowed engineer Loy must struggle to support (as well as raise) her maturing brood. 20th Century-Fox backlot seen at its best in recapturing 1900s America. Clifton Webb makes a brief appearance at the finale. Scripted by Henry and Phoebe Ephron.

Belle Starr (1941) **C-87m.** **½ D: Irving Cummings. Randolph Scott, Gene Tierney, Dana Andrews, John Sheppard (Shepperd Strudwick), Elizabeth Patterson. Sophisticated Tierney miscast as notorious female outlaw in slowly paced account of her criminal career. Remade for TV in 1980 with Elizabeth Montgomery.

Belle Starr's Daughter (1948) **86m.** ** D: Lesley Selander. George Montgomery, Rod Cameron, Ruth Roman, Wallace Ford, Isabel Jewell. Roman is title character, coming to rough Western town to avenge her mother's murder; fair Western.

Bell for Adano, A (1945) **103m.** ***½ D: Henry King. Gene Tierney, John Hodiak, William Bendix, Glenn Langan, Richard Conte, Stanley Prager, Henry (Harry) Morgan, Hugo Haas, Fortunio Bonanova, Henry Armetta, Luis Alberni, Eduardo Ciannelli, Grady Sutton. John Hersey's moving narrative of American WW2 occupation of small Italian village; Hodiak is sincere commander, Bendix his aide, blonde Tierney the local girl he is attracted to. Scripted by Lamar Trotti (who also coproduced) and Norman Reilly Raine.

Bellissima (1951-Italian) **112m.** ** D: Luchino Visconti. Anna Magnani, Walter Chiari, Tina Apicella, Gastone Renzelli, Alessandro Blasetti. Obvious drama about pushy, patronizing stage mother Magnani, obsessed to the point of hysteria with getting her cute, obedient little daughter into the movies. Loud when it should be tender, and ultimately tiresome.▼

Bell Jar, The (1979) **C-107m.** **½ D: Larry Peerce. Marilyn Hassett, Julie Harris, Anne Jackson, Barbara Barrie, Robert Klein, Donna Mitchell, Jameson Parker, Thaao Penghlis. Sylvia Plath's virtually unfilmable novel about the crack-up of an over-achiever in the 50s has a few powerful scenes and a good supporting performance by Barrie, but doesn't really come off. Hassett is well cast but fails to deliver the truly bravura performance this film needs. [R]▼

Bellman & True (1988-British) **C-112m.** **½ D: Richard Loncraine. Bernard Hill, Kieran O'Brien, Richard Hope, Frances Tomelty, Derek Newark, John Kavanagh, Ken Bones. Meek computer programmer is drawn into an elaborate bank heist scheme, without ever realizing just how dangerous the people he's associating with can be. More a character study than a caper film, very low-key and very drawn-out, but with a number of rewarding moments and vignettes. Original running time 122m. [R]▼

Bells SEE: **Murder by Phone**

Bells Are Ringing (1960) **C-127m.** *** D: Vincente Minnelli. Judy Holliday, Dean Martin, Fred Clark, Eddie Foy, Jr., Jean Stapleton, Ruth Storey, Frank Gorshin, Gerry Mulligan. Sprightly adaptation of Broadway musical hit by Betty Comden, Adolph Green, and Jule Styne, with Holliday recreating her starring role as an answering-service operator who falls in love with the man she's known only as a voice on the telephone. Songs include "Just in Time," "The Party's Over." Sadly, Holliday's last film. CinemaScope. ▼●

Bells of St. Mary's, The (1945) **126m.** *** D: Leo McCarey. Bing Crosby, Ingrid Bergman, Henry Travers, William Gargan, Ruth Donnelly, Joan Carroll, Martha Sleeper, Rhys Williams. Amiable if meandering sequel to GOING MY WAY, with Father O'Malley assigned to a run-down parish where Bergman is the Sister Superior. Bing introduces the song "Aren't You Glad You're You?" Also shown in computer-colored version.▼●◗

Belly (1998) **C-95m.** *½ D: Hype Williams. Nas, DMX, Taral Hicks, Tionne "T-Boz" Watkins, Method Man. Hyper-stylized, pretentious "gangsta" melodrama about two lifelong buddies (rappers Nas and DMX) whose friendship is violently tested when they get involved in dealing Jamaican heroin. Features some of hip-hop's finest; too bad they can't act. Clichéd script doesn't help. Film debut of music video director Williams isn't much of a movie, just an extended montage. [R]▼●◗

Belly of an Architect, The (1987-British-Italian) **C-108m.** **½ D: Peter Greenaway. Brian Dennehy, Chloe Webb, Lambert Wilson, Sergio Fantoni, Stephania Cassini, Vanni Corbellini. Highly personalized chronicle of an architect (Dennehy) and his wife (Webb), who arrive in Rome where he's to curate an exhibition. It's about architecture and art, obsession and omens, immortality and mortality; crammed with symbolism, striking visuals and beautiful cinematography by Sacha Vierny. Some will find it pretentious; others will be fascinated. [R]▼●

Beloved (1998) **C-171m.** ** D: Jonathan Demme. Oprah Winfrey, Danny Glover, Kimberly Elise, Thandie Newton, Beah Richards, Lisa Gay Hamilton, Irma P. Hall, Albert Hall, Tracey Walter, Thelma Houston, Jason Robards, Wes Bentley. Excruciating (if well-crafted) adaptation of Toni Morrison's Pulitzer Prize–winning novel about a woman who's made her way from slavery to a free life in Ohio in 1873, and will do anything—anything—to protect her children. Filled with mysticism and mumbo jumbo, the story demands a leap of faith but doesn't reward the viewer in kind; its lead character isn't sympathetic enough to earn our empathy, even though we understand that she has suffered. Tough going, in more ways than one. Winfrey also produced with Demme. [R]▼●◗

Beloved Enemy (1936) **86m.** *** D: H. C. Potter. Merle Oberon, Brian Aherne, Karen Morley, Henry Stephenson, Jerome Cowan, David Niven, Donald Crisp. High-class love story set during Irish Rebellion with Britisher Oberon in love with rebel leader Aherne.▼●

Beloved Infidel (1959) **C-123m.** ** D: Henry King. Gregory Peck, Deborah Kerr, Eddie Albert, Philip Ober, Herbert Rudley, John Sutton, Karin Booth, Ken Scott. Ill-conceived casting of Peck as F. Scott Fitzgerald makes romance with Hollywood columnist Sheilah Graham (Kerr) in late 1930s more ludicrous than real; lush photography is only virtue of blunt look at cinema capital. CinemaScope.▼

Beloved Rogue, The (1927) **99m.** ***½ D: Alan Crosland. John Barrymore, Conrad Veidt, Marceline Day, Henry Victor, Lawson Butt, Mack Swain, Slim Summerville. Rousing, stunningly filmed story of poet-adventurer François Villon, his battle of wits with Louis XI (Veidt) and his swashbuckling romance with a damsel in distress. Not history, just an eye-filling, spirited, tongue-in-cheek costume tale with Barrymore in great form.▼●

Below the Belt (1980) **C-98m.** ★★★ D: Robert Fowler. Regina Baff, Mildred Burke, John C. Becher, Annie McGreevey, Jane O'Brien, Shirley Stoler, Dolph Sweet. Waitress Baff seeks fortune and fame as a lady wrestler. Low-budget drama, filmed mostly in 1974; a sometimes fascinating portrait of people eking out existence on the edge of society. Based on a novel by Rosalyn Drexler. [R]▼

Be My Guest (1965-British) **82m.** ★½ D: Lance Comfort. David Hemmings, Stephen Marriot, Andrea Monet, Avril Angers, Joyce Blair, Jerry Lee Lewis, Nashville Teens. Young Hemmings uncovers attempt to mount a phony music contest, while his family takes over a seaside guest house. Trifling musical.

Ben (1972) **C-95m.** ★½ D: Phil Karlson. Lee Harcourt Montgomery, Joseph Campanella, Arthur O'Connell, Rosemary Murphy, Meredith Baxter. WILLARD sequel finds sick youth befriended by Ben the rat. Title song (sung by young Michael Jackson) summed up situation but spared gory visuals that make this film so bad. [PG]▼

Bend of the River (1952) **C-91m.** ★★★ D: Anthony Mann. James Stewart, Arthur Kennedy, Julia (Julie) Adams, Rock Hudson, Jay C. Flippen, Lori Nelson, Stepin Fetchit, Henry (Harry) Morgan, Frances Bavier, Royal Dano. Compelling Western of 1840s Oregon, with bristling conflict between Stewart, outlaw turned wagon-train scout, and Kennedy, his one-time comrade who hijacks settlers' supplies for profit.▼●

Beneath the Planet of the Apes (1970) **C-95m.** ★★½ D: Ted Post. James Franciscus, Kim Hunter, Maurice Evans, Linda Harrison, Charlton Heston, Victor Buono, Thomas Gomez. Second APES film still has great sets, makeup and ideas, but somebody let it get away as Apes battle human mutants who survived a nuclear blast many years before. Followed by ESCAPE FROM . . . Panavision. [G] ▼●

Beneath the 12 Mile Reef (1953) **C-102m.** ★★½ D: Robert Webb. Robert Wagner, Terry Moore, Gilbert Roland, J. Carrol Naish, Richard Boone, Peter Graves. Romeo-and-Juliet-ish tale of sponge-diving families on Key West, Florida. Scenery outshines all. One of the first CinemaScope films.▼●◗

Benefit of the Doubt, The (1967-British) **C-70m.** ★★½ D: Peter Whitehead. Eric Allan, Mary Allen, Jeremy Anthony, Noel Collins. Documentary shows British view of Vietnam War, featuring scenes from Peter Brook play *US* (Royal Shakespeare Company); thought-provoking at times. Retitled: US.

Benefit of the Doubt (1993) **C-90m.** ★½ D: Jonathan Heape. Donald Sutherland, Amy Irving, Rider Strong, Christopher McDonald, Graham Greene, Theodore Bikel, Gisele Kovach. Flat thriller in which ex-con Sutherland, jailed for murdering his wife, disrupts the life of daughter Irving (whose testimony helped convict him two decades earlier). With a bit of imagination, this could have been first rate. [R]▼

Bengal Brigade (1954) **C-87m.** ★★ D: Laslo Benedek. Rock Hudson, Arlene Dahl, Ursula Thiess, Torin Thatcher, Arnold Moss, Dan O'Herlihy, Michael Ansara. Low-level costumer with Hudson badly miscast as a British army officer working to thwart a Sepoy rebellion in India.

Bengazi (1955) **78m.** ★½ D: John Brahm. Richard Conte, Victor McLaglen, Richard Carlson, Mala Powers. Lackluster adventure of Powers and trio of men entrapped in desert shrine by marauding natives. SuperScope.

Ben-Hur (1925) **141m.** ★★★ D: Fred Niblo. Ramon Novarro, Francis X. Bushman, May McAvoy, Betty Bronson, Claire McDowell, Carmel Myers, Nigel de Brulier. Biggest of all silent spectacles holds up quite well against talkie remake, particularly the exciting chariot race and sea battle (both directed by B. Reeves Eason); Novarro (as Judah) and Bushman (as Messala) give the performances of their careers. Trouble-plagued film was years in production, at a then-record cost of $4,000,000, but final result, despite a slow second half, is worth it. Some sequences filmed in two-color Technicolor. Filmed once before (in one reel!) in 1907.▼●

Ben-Hur (1959) **C-212m.** ★★★½ D: William Wyler. Charlton Heston, Jack Hawkins, Stephen Boyd, Haya Harareet, Hugh Griffith, Martha Scott, Sam Jaffe, Cathy O'Donnell, Finlay Currie. Epic-scale rendering of Gen. Lew Wallace's "tale of the Christ." Heston and Boyd are well matched as the proud Jew Ben-Hur and his boyhood friend Messala, whose blind allegiance to Rome turns him into a bitter enemy. Poky at times, but redeemed by the strength of its convictions. Some of the special effects show their age, though the galley-slave sequence, and climactic chariot race (directed by Andrew Marton and staged by the legendary stunt expert Yakima Canutt) are still great. Won a record 11 Oscars for Best Picture, Director, Actor (Heston), Supporting Actor (Griffith), Cinematography (Robert L. Surtees), Music Score (Miklos Rozsa), Art Direction, Film Editing, Sound, Costume Design, and Special Effects. Some TV prints expand to widescreen format for the 15-minute chariot race sequence only. MGM Camera 65.▼●

Beniker Gang, The (1985) **C-87m.** ★★½ D: Ken Kwapis. Andrew McCarthy, Jennifer Dundas, Charles Fields, Jeff Alan-Lee, Danny Pintauro. Orphaned teen McCarthy takes action when his younger friends go up for adoption, threatening their extended family. Warm-hearted little film is perfect for pre-teens. [G]▼

Benjamin (1968-French) **C-100m.** BOMB D: Michel Deville. Catherine Deneuve, Michele Morgan, Pierre Clementi, Michel Piccoli, Francine Berge, Anna Gael. Beautiful Deneuve, Morgan, cinematography; otherwise, boring tale of country boy Clementi's initiation into upper-class immorality. Also shown at 105m. and 108m. [X]

Benji (1974) **C-86m.** ***½ D: Joe Camp. Peter Breck, Deborah Walley, Edgar Buchanan, Frances Bavier, Patsy Garrett. Instant classic of a remarkable dog (played by Higgins) who thwarts the kidnappers of two small children. Texas-made feature is ideal for family viewing. Sequel: FOR THE LOVE OF BENJI. [G]▼◗

Benji the Hunted (1987) **C-88m.** *½ D: Joe Camp. Benji, Red Steagall, Frank Inn. Every dog has his day, but this talented canine deserves a better movie vehicle. Humans are incidental in this story of Benji surviving in the mountain wilds, and it looks as if they were incidental in making the film as well. [G]▼●

Benny & Joon (1993) **C-98m.** *** D: Jeremiah Chechik. Johnny Depp, Mary Stuart Masterson, Aidan Quinn, Julianne Moore, Oliver Platt, CCH Pounder, Dan Hedaya, Joe Grifasi, William H. Macy, Eileen Ryan. Sweet-natured film about put-upon auto mechanic Quinn, who tries to look after his mentally ill sister. Almost accidentally he stumbles onto the perfect companion for her: a male misfit who sees himself as a reincarnation of Buster Keaton. Endearing performances put over this fable, which otherwise would strain all credibility. Depp is impressive as he re-creates silent-comedy routines by Chaplin, Keaton, et al. [PG]▼●

Benny Goodman Story, The (1955) **C-116m.** **½ D: Valentine Davies. Steve Allen, Donna Reed, Herbert Anderson, Hy Averback, Berta Gersten, Robert F. Simon, Sammy Davis, Sr., Gene Krupa, Lionel Hampton, Teddy Wilson. Typical Hollywood gloss about the bandleader's rise to fame and his romance with Reed; not 100% factual, with cliché dialogue to spare, but the music is great. Additional guest performers include Harry James, Ziggy Elman and Martha Tilton. Goodman himself dubbed Allen's clarinet playing.▼

Benson Murder Case (1930) **69m.** **½ D: Frank Tuttle. William Powell, Natalie Moorhead, Eugene Pallette, Paul Lukas, William Boyd, E. H. Calvert, May Beatty, Mischa Auer. An unscrupulous stockbroker is killed at his country estate and Philo Vance (Powell) is on hand to solve whodunit. Neat mystery, but slowly paced, and bearing no relationship whatsoever to the original Van Dine novel.

Bent (1997-British) **C-104m.** **½ D: Sean Mathias. Lothaire Bluteau, Clive Owen, Brian Webber, Ian McKellen, Mick Jagger, Nikolaj Waldau, Jude Law, Gresby Nash, Rupert Graves, Charlie Watts. Raw drama following the plight of a brash, manipulative gay German (Owen) under Hitler, and his eventual internment in Dachau with fellow prisoner Bluteau. Stagy film, with undeniably powerful scenes, but not the formidable depiction of Nazi-era homosexuals it might have been. Scripted by Martin Sherman, from his groundbreaking 1979 play. [NC-17]▼●

Bequest to the Nation, A SEE: **Nelson Affair, The**

Berkeley Square (1933) **84m.** *** D: Frank Lloyd. Leslie Howard, Heather Angel, Irene Browne, Beryl Mercer, Samuel S. Hinds. Intriguing fantasy of young American Howard finding himself in 18th-century London, living completely different life. Remade as I'LL NEVER FORGET YOU.

Berlin Affair, The (1985-Italian-West German) **C-96m.** BOMB D: Liliana Cavani. Gudrun Landgrebe, Kevin McNally, Mio Takaki, Massimo Girotti, Philippe Leroy, Hanns Zischler, William Berger. English-language misfire adapts Junichiro Tanizuki's novel *The Buddhist Cross.* Director Cavani (of THE NIGHT PORTER) is slumming in Nazi Germany again for a tale of a lesbian love affair between Landgrebe and ambassador's daughter Takaki. Lifeless film isn't even sexy, quite surprising in view of the casting of A WOMAN IN FLAMES star Landgrebe. Original European running time was 115m. [R]▼

Berlin Alexanderplatz (1980-German) **C-931m.** **** D: Rainer Werner Fassbinder. Gunter Lamprecht, Hanna Schygulla, Barbara Sukowa, Gottfried John, Elisabeth Trissenaar, Brigitte Mira, Karin Baal, Ivan Desny. Monumental adaptation of Alfred Doblin's novel about German life in the late 1920s, focusing on a simple Everyman (Lamprecht), who has just been released from prison. He yearns for respectability but is led like a sheep by forces beyond his control into criminality and insanity. An epic if there ever was one, with stunning performances, cinematography (by Xaver Schwarzenberger), and direction. Originally produced for television in fourteen episodes. Filmed before in 1931.▼

Berlin Correspondent (1942) **70m.** **½ D: Eugene Forde. Virginia Gilmore, Dana Andrews, Mona Maris, Martin Kosleck, Sig Ruman. American reporter risks life so that his sweetheart and her professor father can escape Nazi Germany.

Berlin Express (1948) **86m.** *** D: Jacques Tourneur. Merle Oberon, Robert Ryan, Charles Korvin, Paul Lukas, Robert Coote. Taut, suspenseful spy story set in post

WW2 Europe. Members of several nations combine efforts to save German statesman kidnapped by Nazi underground.▼●
Bermuda Mystery (1944) **65m.** ** D: Benjamin Stoloff. Preston Foster, Ann Rutherford, Charles Butterworth, Helene Reynolds. Mild account of strange murder and dead man's heirs' pursuit of criminal.
Bernadette of Lourdes (1961-French) **90m.** **½ D: Robert Darene. Daniele Ajoret, Nadine Alari, Robert Arnoux, Blanchette Brunoy. Straightforward account of the peasant girl who saw a vision and was elevated to sainthood; unpretentious.
Bernardine (1957) **C-95m.** ** D: Henry Levin. Pat Boone, Terry Moore, Janet Gaynor, Dean Jagger, Walter Abel. Very weak look at teen-age life (all different now) marked return of Janet Gaynor to films after twenty years. Wholesome Pat Boone (in his film debut) sings and sings and sings. Eh! CinemaScope.
Berserk (1967-British) **C-96m.** ** D: Jim O'Connolly. Joan Crawford, Ty Hardin, Diana Dors, Michael Gough, Judy Geeson. Sadistic shocker with Crawford the shapely owner of a British circus, haunted by series of brutal murders. Supporting cast lacks verve.▼●
Bert Rigby, You're a Fool (1989) **C-94m.** ** D: Carl Reiner. Robert Lindsay, Robbie Coltrane, Anne Bancroft, Corbin Bernsen, Cathryn Bradshaw, Bruno Kirby, Jackie Gayle. Writer-director Reiner conceived this deliberately old-fashioned musical comedy strictly as a showcase for the talents of Lindsay (who scored such a smash on stage in *Me and My Girl*), and that's its only value. He's a delight to watch—singing, dancing, and clowning as a jaunty British coal miner who wants to break into show business—but the well-meaning film is silly and contrived. [R]▼●
Besieged (1998-Italian-British) **C-94m.** *** D: Bernardo Bertolucci. Thandie Newton, David Thewlis, Claudio Santamaria. Provocative film about an African immigrant who works as housemaid for a reclusive English pianist in Rome. She's intrigued by his mysterious ways, while he is infatuated with her and determines to find a way to prove his love. Sinuous and surprising, with fine performances by the two leads; written by Bertolucci and Clare Peploe, from a story by James Lasdun. Originally made for Italian TV. [R]▼◗
Best Boy (1979) **C-111m.** **** D: Ira Wohl. Poignant, beautifully filmed documentary about Wohl's 52-year-old mentally retarded cousin Philly and his family's struggle as he learns to relate to the outside world. Sequences related to his father's death and his visit backstage with Zero Mostel—together they sing "If I Were a Rich Man"—are especially moving. A Best Documentary Academy Award winner. Sequel: BEST MAN: 'BEST BOY' AND ALL OF US TWENTY YEARS LATER.▼●
Best Defense (1984) **C-94m.** *½ D: Willard Huyck. Dudley Moore, Eddie Murphy, Kate Capshaw, George Dzundza, Helen Shaver, David Rasche. Unpleasant and unfunny comedy about defense-industry designer who inadvertently acquires blueprint sought by the KGB. "Strategic Guest Star" Murphy is no help. [R]▼●
Best Foot Forward (1943) **C-95m.** *** D: Edward Buzzell. Lucille Ball, William Gaxton, Virginia Weidler, Tommy Dix, Nancy Walker, Gloria De Haven, June Allyson. Entertaining film of Broadway musical about movie star Ball visiting small-town school for a lark; score includes "Buckle Down Winsockie." Harry James and his band do definitive "Two O'Clock Jump." Walker, as dynamic plain-Jane, and Allyson make their feature film debuts recreating their stage roles. Future filmmaker Stanley Donen can be glimpsed in "The Three B's" number, holding De Haven's legs.▼●
Best Friends (1982) **C-116m.** ** D: Norman Jewison. Burt Reynolds, Goldie Hawn, Jessica Tandy, Barnard Hughes, Audra Lindley, Keenan Wynn, Ron Silver, Carol Locatell. Lackluster comedy vehicle for two top stars, as screenwriters who function better as lovers than as husband and wife. Some funny vignettes with fine supporting cast (including Richard Libertini as Mexican justice-of-the-peace), but the lead characters aren't terribly interesting. Indulgent script by real-life "best friends" Barry Levinson and Valerie Curtin. [PG]▼●
Best House in London, The (1969-British) **C-105m.** BOMB D: Philip Saville. David Hemmings, Joanna Pettet, George Sanders, Dany Robin, Warren Mitchell. Boring comedy about group of government officials in London who sponsor official bawdy house. Film didn't deserve "X" rating it got at the time. Look for John Cleese in a bit part. [X]
Best Intentions, The (1992-Swedish) **C-182m.** *** D: Bille August. Samuel Froler, Pernilla August, Max von Sydow, Ghita Norby, Lennart Hjulstrom, Mona Malm, Lena Endre, Anita Bjork. Ingmar Bergman scripted this ambitious epic tale of the courtship and subsequent marriage of his own parents. Henrik Bergman (Froler) starts out as a poor theology student, and wife Anna (August, the director's wife) comes from a wealthy, bourgeois family; their fundamental differences—and stormy relationship—form the crux of the film. A six-hour version was made for Swedish television. A follow-up to FANNY AND ALEXANDER; followed by SUNDAY'S CHILDREN and PRIVATE CONFESSIONS. ▼
Best Laid Plans (1999) **C-92m.** **½ D: Mike Barker. Alessandro Nivola, Reese

Witherspoon, Josh Brolin, Rocky Carroll, Michael G. Hagerty, Terrence Howard. When an old pal comes back to town, a broke local and his girlfriend find themselves caught up in a web of blackmail and deceit. Convoluted film noir plays like a Gen-X USUAL SUSPECTS, but the problem is too many twists, and after a while this gimmicky thriller runs out of steam. Good acting, especially by Nivola in his first lead role. [R]▼◗

Best Little Whorehouse in Texas, The (1982) **C-114m.** ** D: Colin Higgins. Burt Reynolds, Dolly Parton, Dom DeLuise, Charles Durning, Jim Nabors, Robert Mandan, Lois Nettleton, Theresa Merritt, Noah Beery, Jr., Barry Corbin. Flashy but unsatisfying musical (based on Broadway hit) about pressures brought to bear on sheriff (Reynolds) to close a popular establishment called The Chicken Ranch—run by his ladyfriend. Dolly's a delight, Durning has a showstopping number as the Governor, but occasionally film actually tries to get serious and screeches to a halt. Dolly's hit song "I Will Always Love You" (which she also wrote) had been #1 in 1974—and would be an even bigger hit for Whitney Houston in 1992's THE BODYGUARD. Panavision. [R]▼●

Best Man, The (1964) **102m.** *** D: Franklin Schaffner. Henry Fonda, Cliff Robertson, Edie Adams, Margaret Leighton, Kevin McCarthy, Shelley Berman, Lee Tracy, Ann Sothern, Gene Raymond, Richard Arlen, Mahalia Jackson. Sharp filmization of Gore Vidal's play about political conventioning with several determined presidential candidates seeking important endorsement at any cost; brittle, engrossing drama. Screenplay by Vidal.▼●

Best Man, The (1998-Italian) **C-106m.** *** D: Pupi Avati. Diego Abatantuono, Inès Sastre, Dario Cantarelli, Cinzia Mascoli, Valeria D'Obici. Warm, wildly romantic comedy of manners set in a small Italian town on December 31, 1899, about a young woman who rebels against her arranged marriage to a wealthy businessman and falls in love with his best man during the wedding party. Slight but charming and evocative allegory, symbolically set on the eve of the 20th century. Written by the director. [PG]▼●

Best Man, The (1999) **C-120m.** **½ D: Malcolm D. Lee. Taye Diggs, Nia Long, Morris Chestnut, Harold Perrineau, Terrence Howard, Monica Calhoun. Galley proofs are circulating for a new novel full of thinly disguised characters, causing no shortage of problems for author Diggs, who has to contend with a slew of offended participants. Overlong feature debut for Spike Lee's writer/director cousin adds nothing new to the wedding-comedy genre, but attractive characters carry it for a while. The end-credits sequence, with spiffily dressed dancers, tries to convince you that you've had a better time than you've had. [R] ▼●◗

Best of Enemies, The (1961-British-Italian) **C-104m.** *** D: Guy Hamilton. David Niven, Michael Wilding, Harry Andrews, Alberto Sordi, Noel Harrison, Amedeo Nazzari, David Opatoshu. Nice counterplay between Niven and Sordi, as British and Italian officers who constantly, comically cross each other's paths during WW2. Their growing relationship serves to mirror the idiocy of war. Technirama.

Best of Everything, The (1959) **C-121m.** *** D: Jean Negulesco. Hope Lange, Stephen Boyd, Suzy Parker, Diane Baker, Martha Hyer, Joan Crawford, Brian Aherne, Robert Evans, Louis Jourdan. Multifaceted fabrication about women seeking success and love in the publishing jungles of N.Y.C., highlighted by Crawford's performance as tough executive with empty heart of gold; from superficial Rona Jaffe novel. CinemaScope.▼

Best of the Badmen (1951) **C-84m.** **½ D: William D. Russell. Robert Ryan, Claire Trevor, Robert Preston, Jack Buetel, Walter Brennan, Bruce Cabot. Band of outlaws (including James and Younger brothers) help former Union colonel Ryan in vendetta against detective Preston. Offbeat Western has more talk than action.▼

Best of the Best (1989) **C-97m.** BOMB D: Bob Radler. Eric Roberts, James Earl Jones, Sally Kirkland, Christopher Penn, Louise Fletcher, Phillip Rhee, John Dye. Yet another ROCKY-style rip-off in which five young men must overcome differences before they can unite as the U.S. Karate Team and compete in an international match. Top-drawer cast appallingly wasted. Followed by three sequels. [PG-13]▼●

Best of the Best 2 (1993) **C-101m.** ** D: Robert Radler. Eric Roberts, Phillip Rhee, Christopher Penn, Edan Gross, Ralph Moeller, Meg Foster, Sonny Landham, Wayne Newton. Sequel to the original flop bucks the odds and actually improves on its lame predecessor. Two former U.S. Karate Team members set out to avenge the death of their friend who was killed during a shady competition. Roberts has actually said he made this film to make up for the first one. What a considerate guy! [R]▼●

Best of Times, The (1986) **C-104m.** **½ D: Roger Spottiswoode. Robin Williams, Kurt Russell, Pamela Reed, Holly Palance, Donald Moffat, Margaret Whitton, M. Emmet Walsh, Donovan Scott, R. G. Armstrong, Kirk Cameron. Williams has never lived down the moment he dropped winning pass in a high-school football game—so, twenty years later he fires up former teammate (Russell), the rival team, and his entire home town for a rematch. Some quirky, offbeat touches highlight Ron Shelton's script, and the wives (Reed, Palance) are a treat but seemingly surefire film becomes too strident (and too exaggerated) to really score. [PG-13]▼●◗

Best Seller (1987) **C-110m.** ** D: John Flynn. James Woods, Brian Dennehy, Victoria Tennant, Allison Balson, Paul Shenar, George Coe, Anne Pitoniak. Dennehy, a cop-turned-author (à la Joseph Wambaugh), is approached by Woods to write the story of his former life as hit man for prominent businessman (Shenar) whose underworld tactics have long been covered up. Despite teaming of two terrific actors, film never quite cuts it, due to many holes in Larry Cohen's script—and Woods' largely unappealing character. [R]▼●

Best Things in Life Are Free, The (1956) **C-104m.** **½ D: Michael Curtiz. Gordon MacRae, Dan Dailey, Ernest Borgnine, Sheree North, Tommy Noonan, Murvyn Vye. Typical of the antiseptic 1950s musicals, this film "recreates" the careers of Tin Pan Alley writers DeSylva, Brown, and Henderson. Highlight: North and Jacques D'Amboise dancing to "The Birth of the Blues." CinemaScope.

Best Years of Our Lives, The (1946) **172m.** **** D: William Wyler. Fredric March, Myrna Loy, Teresa Wright, Dana Andrews, Virginia Mayo, Harold Russell, Hoagy Carmichael, Gladys George, Roman Bohnen, Steve Cochran. American classic of three veterans returning home after WW2, readjusting to civilian life. Robert Sherwood's script from MacKinlay Kantor's book perfectly captured mood of postwar U.S.; still powerful today. Seven Oscars include Best Picture, Wyler, March, Russell, Sherwood, Daniel Mandell's editing, Hugo Friedhofer's score. Russell, an actual veteran who lost his hands, also took home a second Oscar, a special award for bringing hope and courage to other veterans. Remade as 1975 TVM, RETURNING HOME, with Tom Selleck and Dabney Coleman.▼●◗

Bethune (1977-Canadian) **C-88m.** *** D: Eric Till. Donald Sutherland, Kate Nelligan, David Gardner, James Hong. Thoughtful biography with Sutherland fine as Dr. Norman Bethune, the controversial, humanistic Canadian doctor who, most intriguingly, aided Mao Tse-tung's army during its famous march. Made for Canadian television; Sutherland also played the character in Phillip Borsos' BETHUNE: THE MAKING OF A HERO, a 1990 feature (which was released in the U.S. in 1993 as DR. BETHUNE).▼

Betrayal (1983-British) **C-95m.** *½ D: David Jones. Jeremy Irons, Ben Kingsley, Patricia Hodge. Harold Pinter's fascinating play about a triangle relationship—progressing *backward* in time—falls flat on screen, despite a powerhouse cast. [R]▼

Betrayal From the East (1945) **82m.** ** D: William Berke. Lee Tracy, Nancy Kelly, Richard Loo, Abner Biberman, Regis Toomey, Philip Ahn. Americans vs. Japanese in usual flag-waving espionage film, no better or worse than most.▼

Betrayed (1944) SEE: **When Strangers Marry**

Betrayed (1954) **C-108m.** ** D: Gottfried Reinhardt. Clark Gable, Lana Turner, Victor Mature, Louis Calhern, O.E. Hasse, Wilfrid Hyde-White, Ian Carmichael. Colonel Gable falls for Dutch Resistance member Turner, who's suspected of being in cahoots with the Nazis. Ho-hum WW2 melodrama, with some nice on-location filming in The Netherlands. Clark and Lana's fourth and final teaming.▼●

Betrayed (1988) **C-127m.** *½ D: Costa-Gavras. Debra Winger, Tom Berenger, John Heard, Betsy Blair, John Mahoney, Ted Levine, Jeffrey DeMunn, Albert Hall, David Clennon, Richard Libertini. Appalling botch of a film about the stupidest FBI undercover agent in movie history who's sent to sniff out white supremacists in America's heartland—but falls in love with her target instead. Important and genuinely upsetting subject matter is dealt with in pedantic terms. Even the moments of straight suspense are muffed! Winger's performance is virtually the only saving grace. Timothy Hutton can be seen fleetingly at the fairgrounds. [R]▼●◗

Betrayed Women (1955) **70m.** *½ D: Edward L. Cahn. Carole Mathews, Beverly Michaels, Peggy Knudsen, Tom Drake, Sara Haden. Low-key filming of potentially volatile subject, sadistic treatment of inmates in women's prison.

Betsy, The (1978) **C-125m.** **½ D: Daniel Petrie. Laurence Olivier, Robert Duvall, Katharine Ross, Tommy Lee Jones, Jane Alexander, Lesley-Anne Down, Kathleen Beller, Edward Herrmann. Moderately enjoyable trash, adapted from Harold Robbins' novel about the multigenerational wheelings and dealings between an auto company patriarch and his family. Olivier's hamminess and Down's loveliness are the pluses here. [R]▼●◗

Betsy's Wedding (1990) **C-94m.** *** D: Alan Alda. Alan Alda, Joey Bishop, Madeline Kahn, Anthony LaPaglia, Catherine O'Hara, Joe Pesci, Molly Ringwald, Ally Sheedy, Burt Young, Julie Bovasso, Nicolas Coster, Bibi Besch, Dylan Walsh. Amusing social comedy about the plans, preparations, and events surrounding Ringwald's wedding—especially as they affect her father. One of writer-director-star Alda's better outings, a bit cluttered (and occasionally clumsy) but filled with enough truthful observations to strike a great many familiar chords. [R]▼●

Better Late Than Never (1982) **C-95m.** *½ D: Bryan Forbes. David Niven, Art Carney, Maggie Smith, Kimberly Partridge,

Catherine Hicks, Melissa Prophet. Two ne'er-do-wells vie for acceptance by a 10-year-old heiress, who's a granddaughter to one of them. Nice locations in the South of France can't compensate for lightheaded script and waste of star talent. [PG]▼

Better Off Dead (1985) **C-98m.** **½ D: Savage Steve Holland. John Cusack, David Ogden Stiers, Kim Darby, Demian Slade, Scooter Stevens, Diane Franklin, Curtis Armstrong. Off-kilter comedy about teenage boy who's just lost the girl of his dreams. Frustrating film starts off with lots of funny, original gags—it even has a terrific "hamburger video" by clay-animation specialist Jimmy Picker—then it settles into much-too-conventional story and goes down the drain. Feature debut for writer-director Holland. [PG]▼●

Better Off Dead (1993) **C-100m. TVM** D: M. Neema Bernette. Mare Winningham, Tyra Ferrell, Kevin Tighe, Don Harvey, Reed McCants, Marilyn Coleman. Winningham gives a sizzling performance as a longtime loser who winds up on death row and insists that the state pull the switch. Unusually meaty TV movie tackles a range of subjects—not just capital punishment—with fire and intelligence. Coproduced by Gloria Steinem, written by Marlane X. Meyers. Made for cable. Above average. ▼

Better Than Chocolate (1999-Canadian) **C-101m.** *** D: Anne Wheeler. Wendy Crewson, Karyn Dwyer, Christina Cox, Anne-Marie MacDonald, Peter Outerbridge, Marya Delver, Kevin Mundy. Engaging adult comedy about the evolving, hot-and-heavy relationship between college dropout/wannabe writer Dwyer and artist/drifter Cox. Loaded with wit, well-drawn characters, and perceptive commentary on such hot-button issues as censorship, and more personal ones, such as self-acceptance. Outerbridge is a standout as a transgendered lesbian. Unrated version runs 102m. [R]▼◗

Better Tomorrow, A (1986-Hong Kong) **C-95m.** *** D: John Woo. Chow Yun-Fat, Ti Lung, Leslie Cheung, Waise Lee. Exciting action thriller about a gangster (Lung) who wants to go straight and his brother (Cheung), a dedicated police inspector who blames him for their father's death. Woo's breakthrough film (which became one of Hong Kong's highest grossers ever and gained international attention) is not as assured as his later work, but still has explosive set pieces and a terrific performance by Chow as a mob enforcer. Woo also coscripted. Followed by two sequels. ▼◗

Betty (1992-French) **C-100m.** **½ D: Claude Chabrol. Marie Trintignant, Stephane Audran, Jean-Francois Garreaud, Yves Lambrecht, Christiane Minazolli. Boozy Betty, 28 and long since banished from home, is taken in by an older widow (who also enjoys the grape) in the posh hotel she owns. So-so character study is not one of Chabrol's stronger works; juggling of flashbacks will either keep you on your toes or zone you out into slumber. Adapted from a Georges Simenon novel.▼

Betty Blue (1986-French) **C-120m.** **½ D: Jean-Jacques Beineix. Jean-Hugues Anglade, Beatrice Dalle, Gerard Darmon, Consuelo de Havilland, Clementine Celarie, Jaques Mathou, Vincent Lindon. Handyman and dangerously schizoid sexpot map-hop France practically waiting for her to crack up; when it finally happens, the grisly violence doesn't quite mesh with the light tone of what's come before. Well-photographed and sometimes quite funny, but ultimately much ado about nothing. If you're watching this for sex, don't miss the opening five minutes. Director's cut of 192m. available on video.▼●

Between Friends (1983) **C-100m. TVM** D: Lou Antonio. Elizabeth Taylor, Carol Burnett, Barbara Bush, Stephen Young, Henry Ramer, Bruce Grey, Charles Shamata. Two middle-aged divorcees from totally different backgrounds run into each other—literally—and become fast friends. Tour-de-force performances by the two leads, though it's stretching credibility that Carol is the desirable sex object and Liz has trouble getting guys. Adapted by producers Shelley List and Jonathan Estrin from List's novel, *Nobody Makes Me Cry*. Made for cable. Above average.▼

Between Heaven and Hell (1956) **C-94m.** ** D: Richard Fleischer. Robert Wagner, Terry Moore, Broderick Crawford, Buddy Ebsen, Robert Keith, Brad Dexter, Mark Damon, Harvey Lembeck, Skip Homeier, L.Q. Jones, Carl Switzer, Frank Gorshin. Disjointed psychological drama about thoughtless Southerner Wagner, and how he is changed by his experiences in WW2 (especially while under the command of psycho Crawford). CinemaScope▼

Between Midnight and Dawn (1950) **89m.** ** D: Gordon Douglas. Mark Stevens, Edmond O'Brien, Gale Storm, Donald Buka, Gale Robbins, Anthony Ross, Roland Winters. Overly familiar crime drama in which sector-car cops bust thug Buka, leading to tragedy. Storm is the woman whom both lawmen love.

Between the Lines (1977) **C-101m.** ***½ D: Joan Micklin Silver. John Heard, Lindsay Crouse, Jeff Goldblum, Jill Eikenberry, Bruno Kirby, Gwen Welles, Stephen Collins, Michael J. Pollard, Lane Smith, Marilu Henner, Joe Morton, Southside Johnny & The Asbury Jukes. Thoroughly enjoyable sleeper about the emotional problems of the staff of a Boston underground newspaper which is about to be purchased by a print tycoon. The performances by a then-unknown cast are first rate all the way. Story by Fred

Barron and David M. Helpern, Jr.; screenplay by Fred Barron. [R]▼

Between Time and Eternity (1960-German) **C-98m.** ★★½ D: Arthur Maria Rabenalt. Lilli Palmer, Willy Birgel, Ellen Schwiers, Carlos Thompson. Palmer makes tear-jerker believable in story of middle-aged woman dying of rare disease, seeking romance and fun while she can.

Between Two Women (1944) **83m.** ★★ D: Willis Goldbeck. Van Johnson, Lionel Barrymore, Gloria DeHaven, Keenan Wynn, Marilyn Maxwell, Keye Luke, Alma Kruger, Walter Kingsford, Marie Blake, Nell Craig. Dr. Adams (Johnson) gets more screen time than Gillespie himself (Barrymore) in this mild triangle tale involving Johnson, Maxwell, and DeHaven (who finds time to sing "I'm in the Mood for Love"). Late Dr. Kildare series entry.

Between Two Worlds (1944) **112m.** ★★½ D: Edward A. Blatt. John Garfield, Eleanor Parker, Sydney Greenstreet, Faye Emerson, Paul Henreid, Sara Allgood, Isobel Elsom, George Tobias, Edmund Gwenn. Updated remake of OUTWARD BOUND, with various deceased individuals aboard a ship that will take each one to heaven or hell. Flawed, but good acting by Warner Bros. star stock company makes it worthwhile.

Between Us Girls (1942) **89m.** ★★ D: Henry Koster. Kay Francis, Diana Barrymore, Robert Cummings, Andy Devine, John Boles, Scotty Beckett. Chic Francis and daughter Barrymore have romances at the same time in this OK comedy.

Beverly Hillbillies, The (1993) **C-93m.** ★½ D: Penelope Spheeris. Jim Varney, Diedrich Bader, Erika Eleniak, Cloris Leachman, Lily Tomlin, Dabney Coleman, Lea Thompson, Rob Schneider, Penny Fuller, Dolly Parton, Buddy Ebsen, Zsa Zsa Gabor. Big-screen rehash of the corny 1960s TV series, with the backwoods Clampett clan striking oil and moving to Beverly Hills, where they're prey for sharpie Schneider and his girlfriend (Thompson). The actors are earnest and enjoyable, but the script (by four writers—count 'em—four) is more lamebrained than the sitcom ever was, with smarmy sex jokes thrown in for good measure. Even worse, director Spheeris doesn't know how to stage a gag. [PG]▼●

Beverly Hills Brats (1989) **C-90m.** ★½ D: Dimitri Sotirakis. Peter Billingsley, Martin Sheen, Terry Moore, Burt Young, Ramon Estevez. Annoying, pretentious so-called satire, in which a wealthy but lonely boy arranges his own kidnapping so that parents will give him attention. This one was a family affair: associate producer is Janet (daughter of Martin) Sheen; Estevez is Sheen's son. Moore coproduced, and coauthored the original story. [PG-13]▼●

Beverly Hills Cop (1984) **C-105m.** ★★★½ D: Martin Brest. Eddie Murphy, Judge Reinhold, John Ashton, Lisa Eilbacher, Ronny Cox, Steven Berkoff, James Russo, Jonathan Banks, Stephen Elliott, Paul Reiser, Damon Wayans. Smart-mouthed Detroit cop, who never plays by the rules, goes to L.A. to track down an old friend's killers. Sassy, tough, and very funny vehicle for Murphy, who's in peak form as a guy who's never caught off guard. Deft blend of comedy and violent action, extremely well cast, with terrific song score. Script by Daniel Petrie, Jr. Bronson Pinchot has hilarious scene-stealing role as gay art gallery worker. Followed by two sequels. [R] ▼●

Beverly Hills Cop II (1987) **C-102m.** ★★ D: Tony Scott. Eddie Murphy, Judge Reinhold, Jürgen Prochnow, Ronny Cox, John Ashton, Brigitte Nielsen, Allen Garfield, Dean Stockwell, Paul Reiser, Gil Hill, Robert Ridgley, Chris Rock. Contrived, cold-hearted (and misogynistic) sequel has few laughs, mediocre music, and a ridiculous story: it manages to coast as far as it does on the strength of Murphy alone. All credibility goes out the window at the start when B.H. Captain Cox is seen talking to Murphy about a fishing trip. Are these the same characters we saw in the first film? Super 35. [R]▼●

Beverly Hills Cop III (1994) **C-100m.** ★★½ D: John Landis. Eddie Murphy, Judge Reinhold, Hector Elizondo, Theresa Randle, Bronson Pinchot, Timothy Carhart, John Saxon, Alan Young, Stephen McHattie, Al Green. Detroiter Murphy goes back to L.A., site of a theme park whose in-house security cops have hatched a counterfeiting ring—right under the nose of the sweet old gramps figure (Young) who's nominally in charge. Fast pace and inspired setting can't camouflage the bankruptcy of the concept. Gags are subordinate to action here—which, given the gags, may not have been such a bad idea. As usual, Landis features a number of prominent directors (including George Lucas, Joe Dante, Martha Coolidge, Arthur Hiller, Ray Harryhausen, Peter Medak, George Schaefer, Barbet Schroeder, and John Singleton) in cameo roles. Pinchot makes a welcome return from the original COP movie as Serge. [R]▼●

Beverly Hills Ninja (1997) **C-88m.** ★½ D: Dennis Dugan. Chris Farley, Nicollette Sheridan, Robin Shou, Nathaniel Parker, Soon-Tek Oh, Keith Cookie Hirabayashi, Chris Rock. Baby Farley is washed ashore Moses style in Japan, whereupon he spends a klutzy lifetime being schooled in combat (and apparently, object breakage). Sheridan then hires him for an assignment back in Beverly Hills, where the two become (just as we know they would in real life) romantically involved. Sub-routine comedy. [PG-13]▼●◗

Beverly Hills Vamp (1989) **C-89m.** ★★½ D: Fred Olen Ray. Eddie Deezen, Britt

Ekland, Tim Conway, Jr., Jay Richardson, Michelle Bauer, Robert Quarry, Dawn Wildsmith, Pat McCormick. Cheerfully cheap little film effectively spoofs itself while also being an entertaining vampire comedy. Jerry Lewis-oid Deezen is pitted against vampire madam Ekland and her three bloodsucking hookers. [R]▼

Beware, My Lovely (1952) **77m.** **½ D: Harry Horner. Ida Lupino, Robert Ryan, Taylor Holmes, O. Z. Whitehead, Barbara Whiting. Widow Lupino hires Ryan as handyman, discovers he is psychopath; brooding and atmospheric.▼●

Beware of Blondie (1950) **66m.** ** D: Edward Bernds. Penny Singleton, Arthur Lake, Larry Simms, Marjorie Kent, Adele Jergens, Dick Wessel, Jack Rice, Emory Parnell, Isabel Withers, Danny Mummert. Mr. Dithers makes the biggest mistake of his life when he takes a vacation and puts Dagwood in charge of the office. Edward Earle plays Dithers in this final series entry, which also features the Bumsteads' comic strip neighbors the Woodleys.▼

Beware of Children (1961-British) **80m.** *½ D: Gerald Thomas. Leslie Phillips, Geraldine McEwan, Julia Lockwood, Noel Purcell. Young married couple transforms an inheritance of land into summer camp for all sorts of children, focusing on tedious, predictable pranks of youngsters.

Beware of Pity (1946-British) **102m.** **½ D: Maurice Elvey. Lilli Palmer, Albert Lieven, Cedric Hardwicke, Gladys Cooper, Linden Travers, Ernest Thesiger. Maudlin but effective drama of young Austrian lieutenant Lieven, who allows himself to become involved with crippled baron's daughter Palmer. Based on a novel by Stefan Zweig.▼

Beware, Spooks! (1939) **68m.** ** D: Edward Sedgwick. Joe E. Brown, Mary Carlisle, Clarence Kolb, Marc Lawrence. Good fun as Brown solves mystery and becomes hero in Coney Island fun house.▼

Beware! The Blob (1972) **C-88m.** *½ D: Larry Hagman. Robert Walker, Richard Stahl, Godfrey Cambridge, Carol Lynley, Larry Hagman, Cindy Williams, Shelley Berman, Marlene Clark, Gerrit Graham, Dick Van Patten. They should have left it frozen in the Arctic. Weak comedy-sequel finds the gooey mess doing its thing once again. Aka SON OF BLOB; reissued in 1982 with the tag line, "The Film That J.R. Shot!" [PG]▼

Bewitched (1945) **65m.** ** D: Arch Oboler. Phyllis Thaxter, Edmund Gwenn, Horace (Stephen) McNally, Henry H. Daniels, Jr., Addison Richards, Kathleen Lockhart, Minor Watson. Ambitious B film based on Oboler's radio play "Alter Ego," about a woman tormented by a second personality locked inside her. Interesting idea, especially for its time, but heavy-handed.

Beyond, The (1981-Italian) **C-87m.** ** D: Lucio Fulci. Katherine (Catriona) MacColl, David Warbeck, Sarah Keller (Cinzia Monreale), Antoine Saint John (Antoine Domingo), Veronica Lazar. A woman inherits a hotel in Louisiana situated on one of the seven gates to Hell, where it's host to an army of zombies (definitely not good for tourism.) Ultra-gory Italian splatter film has developed a cult, but it's just one bloody set-piece after another, with outlandishly gruesome makeup effects (including crucifixions, acid poured onto faces, etc.). Aka SEVEN DOORS OF DEATH, which runs 82m. Techniscope.

Beyond a Reasonable Doubt (1956) **80m.** **½ D: Fritz Lang. Dana Andrews, Joan Fontaine, Sidney Blackmer, Philip Bourneuf, Barbara Nichols. Far-fetched tale of man who pretends to be guilty of murder to get first-hand view of justice system, unable to prove himself innocent later on. Pale production values. Intriguing idea doesn't hold up.▼

Beyond Atlantis (1973-U.S.-Filipino) **C-89m.** *½ D: Eddie Romero. Patrick Wayne, John Ashley, Leigh Christian, Lenore Stevens, George Nader, Sid Haig, Eddie Garcia, Vic Diaz. Low-budget fantasy about lost civilization, represented by amphibious humanoids; combines feminist subplot with philosophizing about modern extinction of cultures. [PG]▼

Beyond Evil (1980) **C-94m.** ** D: Herb Freed. John Saxon, Lynda Day George, Michael Dante, Mario Milano, Janice Lynde, David Opatoshu. Saxon and George move into an old house occupied by the spirit of a 100-year-old woman, who does not like this intrusion into her privacy. OK of its kind. [R]▼

Beyond Forty SEE: **Over Forty**

Beyond Glory (1948) **82m.** **½ D: John Farrow. Alan Ladd, Donna Reed, George Macready, George Coulouris. Predictable account of West Point captain Ladd, a WW2 veteran, on trial for misconduct. Audie Murphy's first film.

Beyond Justice (1992) **C-113m.** *½ D: Duccio Tessari. Rutger Hauer, Carol Alt, Omar Sharif, Elliott Gould, Kabir Bedi, Brett Halsey, Peter Sands. Preposterous action-adventure story of Chairman of the Board Alt, who employs hired-gun Hauer to retrieve her kidnapped son from his Arab grandfather, Emir Omar. Amid the machine-gun fire we often don't know who is being shot at—nor do we care. [R]▼●

Beyond Mombasa (1956-U.S.-British) **C-90m.** ** D: George Marshall. Cornel Wilde, Donna Reed, Leo Genn, Ron Randell, Christopher Lee. Tame African adventure tale with Wilde seeking mysterious killers of his brother and clues to hidden uranium mine.

Beyond Obsession SEE: **Beyond the Door** (1982)

Beyond Rangoon (1995) **C-99m.** **½ D: John Boorman. Patricia Arquette, Frances McDormand, Spalding Gray, U Aung Ko, Adele Lutz, Victor Slezak. Emotionally troubled American tourist puts herself at risk during a trip to Burma in 1988. She's soon fleeing from the military and heading to the Thai border with a former university professor who's now a wanted man. Hollow at times, and heavy-handed in its effort to promote awareness of the political situation in Burma (now Myanmar). Biggest problem is Arquette, who just doesn't register. Still, a fairly interesting story from an always-committed filmmaker. Panavision. [R]▼●

Beyond Reason (1977) **C-83m.** *½ D: Telly Savalas. Telly Savalas, Laura Johnson, Diana Muldaur, Marvin Laird, Bob Basso, Biff Elliot. Savalas made his writing-directing debut with this film about a psychologist who's going off the deep end. Never released theatrically, and it's easy to see why. Priscilla Barnes was replaced as leading lady but still turns up in several shots. [PG]▼

Beyond Reasonable Doubt (1980-New Zealand) **C-127m.** **½ D: John Laing. David Hemmings, John Hargreaves, Martyn Sanderson, Grant Tilly, Diana Rowan. Adequate docudrama chronicling the conviction on trumped-up charges of innocent farmer Arthur Thomas (Hargreaves) for a double murder. Hemmings is good as the hard-boiled cop who plants evidence that leads to Thomas's downfall. Screenplay by David Yallop, from his book. Panavision. ▼

Beyond Silence (1996-German-Swiss) **C-105m.** *** D: Caroline Link. Sylvie Testud, Tatjana Trieb, Howie Seago, Emmanuelle Laborit, Sibylle Canonica. An eight-year-old German girl serves as the speaking voice (and a sometimes sly interpreter) for her deaf parents. When she matures and becomes a talented clarinetist, she considers heading for a Berlin conservatory, amid the repercussions of possibly leaving the nest. Nicely turned emotional tale of familial love and forgiveness, and a girl's growing pains. [PG-13]▼

Beyond the Blue Horizon (1942) **C-76m.** ** D: Alfred Santell. Dorothy Lamour, Richard Denning, Jack Haley, Walter Abel, Elizabeth Patterson, Abner Biberman, Patricia Morison. Sarong queen Lamour turns out to be heiress to great fortune; witless film wastes more talent than usual.

Beyond the Call (1996) **C-95m. TVM** D: Tony Bill. Sissy Spacek, Arliss Howard, David Strathairn, Janet Wright, Lindsay Murrell, Les Carlson. Happily married woman goes to the aid of the high school sweetheart she hasn't seen for twenty years after learning he's a convict on death row for killing a cop. A trio of terrific performances, but this earnest film becomes overly talky. Made for cable. Average.▼

Beyond the Door (1974-U.S.-Italian) **C-94m.** BOMB D: Oliver Hellman (Ovidio Assonitis). Juliet Mills, Richard Johnson, Elizabeth Turner, David Colin, Jr. Mills becomes pregnant with a fetus possessed by the Devil. Vulgar EXORCIST ripoff, complete with pea-green regurgitation, head spins, and Mercedes McCambridge-like voice. Warner Bros. even took legal action against the film. Followed by the inevitable BEYOND THE DOOR II. [R]▼

Beyond the Door II (1979-Italian) **C-92m.** *½ D: Mario Bava. Daria Nicolodi, John Steiner, David Colin, Jr., Ivan Rassimov. Corpse of dead man possesses his son, seeks vengeance on his wife. Nice directorial touches cannot save confusing, needlessly bloody EXORCIST clone; only resemblances to first film are actor Colin and "possession" plot line. [R]▼

Beyond the Door (1982-Italian) **C-116m.** ** D: Liliana Cavani. Marcello Mastroianni, Tom Berenger, Eleonora Giorgi, Michel Piccoli. Overbaked melodrama centering on complex relationship between jailed father Mastroianni and daughter Giorgi, complicated by arrival of American engineer Berenger. Also known as BEYOND OBSESSION.▼

Beyond the Fog SEE: **Horror on Snape Island**

Beyond the Forest (1949) **96m.** ** D: King Vidor. Bette Davis, Joseph Cotten, David Brian, Ruth Roman, Dona Drake, Regis Toomey. Muddled murder story of grasping Davis, her small-town doctor husband (Cotten), and wealthy neighbor (Brian). Davis' overly mannered performance doesn't help. This is the film in which she utters the immortal line, "What a dump!"▼

Beyond the Law (1968-Italian) **C-91m.** ** D: Giorgio Stegani. Lee Van Cleef, Antonio Sabato, Lionel Stander, Bud Spencer, Gordon Mitchell, Ann Smyrner. Formula Western with a whole lot of Van Cleef and almost as much humor. Bad guy turns good guy, becomes sheriff long enough to get his hands on a shipment of silver, and then splits. Aka BLOODSILVER, THE GOOD DIE FIRST. Techniscope. ▼

Beyond the Law (1992) **C-108m.** **½ D: Larry Ferguson. Charlie Sheen, Linda Fiorentino, Michael Madsen, Courtney B. Vance, Leon Rippy, Dennis Burkley, Rip Torn. Traumatized cop Sheen—he was abused as a child—has just been fired by his corrupt boss. Recruited to work undercover, he joins a band of scuzzy, drug-dealing bikers. Not bad of its type, with an unusually high level of character development, but the often illogical scenario eventually does it in. Based on a true story. [R]▼

Beyond the Limit (1983) **C-103m.** *½ D: John Mackenzie. Michael Caine, Richard Gere, Bob Hoskins, Elpidia Carrillo, Joaquim De Almeida, A Martinez. Muddled adaptation of Graham Greene's *The Honorary Consul* with Gere miscast as Britishdoctor who becomes involved with revolutionaries in South American country—and sexually involved with the ex-prostitute wife of boozy diplomat (well played by Caine). Slow, murky, completely uninvolving. [R]▼

Beyond the Living (1978) **C-88m.** ** D: Al Adamson. Jill Jacobson, Geoffrey Land, Marilyn Joi, Mary Kay Pass. OK horrorpic in the CARRIE vein. Nurse is possessed by the spirit of a patient who died during surgery and begins killing the doctors who performed the operation. Best scene takes place in a foundry. Released to theaters as NURSE SHERRI. Video titles: HOSPITAL OF TERROR, HANDS OF DEATH, KILLER'S CURSE, G.I. BRO, and TERROR HOSPITAL.▼

Beyond the Mat (1999) **C-102m.** *** D: Barry Blaustein. Screenwriter Blaustein (best known for his work with Eddie Murphy) indulges his lifelong passion for professional wrestling in this absorbing documentary, which tries to put a human face on the often circus-like sport. Among his subjects: Mankind (aka Mick Foley), a WWF superstar who's nothing like his ring persona; an aging but still potent Terry Funk; and a very troubled Jake the Snake (Jack Roberts). Compelling viewing even for non–wrestling fans. [R]▼◗

Beyond the Poseidon Adventure (1979) **C-122m.** *½ D: Irwin Allen. Michael Caine, Sally Field, Telly Savalas, Peter Boyle, Jack Warden, Shirley Knight, Slim Pickens, Shirley Jones, Karl Malden, Mark Harmon, Veronica Hamel. Following THE SWARM, Caine teamed up with Irwin Allen for another career killer—a needless sequel about attempts to loot the vessel before it sinks. Panavision. [G]▼

Beyond Therapy (1987) **C-93m.** BOMB D: Robert Altman. Julie Hagerty, Jeff Goldblum, Glenda Jackson, Tom Conti, Christopher Guest, Genevieve Page, Cris Campion, Sandrine Dumas. Dreadful adaptation of Christopher Durang's paper-thin comic play about neurotic singles and their psychiatrists. Given the director and cast, it's hard to believe how awful this is—until you see for yourself! Filmed in Paris, though set in N.Y.C. [R]▼

Beyond the Reef (1981) **C-91m.** ** D: Frank C. Clark. Dayton Ka'ne, Maren Jensen, Kathleen Swan, Keahi Farden, Joseph Ka'ne. In the wake of THE HURRICANE, Dino De Laurentiis produced this innocuous South Seas romance with two attractive leads. Old fashioned, to say the least. Completed in 1979. Aka SHARK BOY OF BORA BORA and SEA KILLER. [PG]

Beyond the Stars (1989) **C-87m.** *½ D: David Saperstein. Martin Sheen, Christian Slater, Robert Foxworth, Sharon Stone, Olivia d'Abo, F. Murray Abraham. Excruciatingly slow story of former astronaut Sheen who once walked on the moon. Would-be astronaut Slater idolizes him, to the consternation of his ex-NASA employee dad (Foxworth). Top cast cannot rise above a poor script. [PG]▼

Beyond the Time Barrier (1960) **75m.** ** D: Edgar G. Ulmer. Robert Clarke, Darlene Tompkins, Arianne Arden, Vladimir Sokoloff. Test pilot zooms into the future to find society decimated by plague. Cheap film shot in Texas has a few blinks of inspiration.▼

Beyond the Valley of the Dolls (1970) **C-109m.** *** D: Russ Meyer. Dolly Read, Cynthia Myers, Marcia McBroom, David Gurian, John LaZar, Michael Blodgett, Edy Williams, Erica Gavin, Phyllis Davis, Charles Napier, Strawberry Alarm Clock. Female rock trio attempts to make it (and make it and make it) in Hollywood. Time has been kind to raunchy in-name-only sequel to (and spoof of) VALLEY OF THE DOLLS. Screenplay by Roger Ebert, story by Meyer and Ebert, and picked by two prominent critics as one of the 10 best U.S. films 1968–78. Panavision. [NC-17—originally rated X]▼●

Beyond the Walls (1984-Israeli) **C-103m.** ** D: Uri Barbash. Arnon Zadok, Muhamad Bakri, Assi Dayan, Rami Danon, Boaz Sharambi. This potentially powerful drama about life in an Israeli prison, centering on the explosive relationship between Jewish and Arab convicts, is just a standard, predictable, noisy men-in-the-big-house yarn. Incredibly, it earned a Best Foreign Film Oscar nomination. [R]▼

Beyond Tomorrow (1940) **84m.** **½ D: A. Edward Sutherland. Richard Carlson, Jean Parker, Harry Carey, C. Aubrey Smith, Charles Winninger, Maria Ouspenskaya, Rod LaRocque. Sensitive little drama of three wealthy men sharing Christmas with down-and-out Carlson and Parker, who fall in love.▼

Be Yourself! (1930) **77m.** ** D: Thornton Freeland. Fanny Brice, Robert Armstrong, Harry Green, Gertrude Astor, Pat Collins. Contrived vehicle for Fanny as nightclub entertainer who falls in love with punchy prizefighter (Armstrong); silly story, overdose of sentiment leave too few moments for star to be herself.▼

B. F.'s Daughter (1948) **108m.** *½ D: Robert Z. Leonard. Barbara Stanwyck, Van Heflin, Charles Coburn, Richard Hart, Keenan Wynn, Margaret Lindsay. Disastrous film of J. P. Marquand novel, with Stanwyck the domineering girl ruining marriage to professor Heflin.

Bhowani Junction (1956-U.S.-British) **C-110m.** **½ D: George Cukor. Ava Gardner, Stewart Granger, Bill Travers, Abraham Sofaer. Set in post WW2 India; Gardner is half-caste torn between love of country and love for a British colonel. Based on John Masters novel; strikingly shot on location. CinemaScope. ▼●

Bible, The (1966-Italian) **C-174m.** BOMB D: John Huston. Michael Parks, Ulla Bergryd, Richard Harris, John Huston, Stephen Boyd, George C. Scott, Ava Gardner, Peter O'Toole, Franco Nero. Narrated by Huston. Unsuccessful epic dealing with Adam and Eve, Cain and Abel, Noah and the Flood, etc. (first 22 chapters of Genesis). Only Huston himself as Noah escapes heavy-handedness. Definitely one time you should read the Book instead. Dimension 150. ▼●

Bicentennial Man (1999) **C-130m.** **½ D: Chris Columbus. Robin Williams, Sam Neill, Embeth Davidtz, Wendy Crewson, Hallie Kate Eisenberg, Stephen Root, Lynne Thigpen, Kiersten Warren, Oliver Platt. In the near future, a family buys an all-purpose robot, which turns out to have human emotions. His interactions with the family and their descendants are followed over the next 200 years. Sincere, sentimental, but goes for the jokes too often. Williams is good as the robot, too familiar when he becomes human. From a short story by Isaac Asimov and a novel by Asimov and Robert Silverberg. [PG]▼◗

Bicycle Thief, The (1947-Italian) **90m.** **** D: Vittorio De Sica. Lamberto Maggiorani, Lianella Carell, Enzo Staiola, Elena Altieri. Simple, realistic tale of workingman whose job depends on his bicycle, and the shattering week he spends with his young son after it is stolen. An honest, beautiful film that deservedly earned a special Academy Award (before foreign films had a category of their own); one of the all-time classics.▼●◗

Big (1988) **C-102m.** ***½ D: Penny Marshall. Tom Hanks, Elizabeth Perkins, John Heard, Jared Rushton, Robert Loggia, David Moscow, Jon Lovitz, Mercedes Ruehl, Josh Clark, Tracy Reiner. A 12-year-old boy wishes he were "big"—and gets his wish, waking up the next morning as a 30-year-old man! Charming fantasy tackles a rare modern-day subject—innocence—and pulls it off thanks to Hanks' superb, seemingly guileless performance, and Marshall's surefooted direction. A real treat. Written by coproducers Gary Ross and Anne Spielberg. Later a Broadway musical. [PG]▼●◗

Bigamist, The (1953) **80m.** *** D: Ida Lupino. Edmond O'Brien, Joan Fontaine, Ida Lupino, Edmund Gwenn, Jane Darwell, Kenneth Tobey. Compassionate look at lonely man who finds himself married to (and in love with) two different women. Extremely well acted; one of Lupino's best directorial efforts and the only time she ever directed herself.▼

Big Bad John (1990) **C-92m.** ** D: Burt Kennedy. Ned Beatty, Jack Elam, Bo Hopkins, Jimmy Dean, John Dennis Johnston, Jeff Osterhage, Ned Vaughn, Buck Taylor, Anne Lockhart. Dumb movie based on the long-ago hit song by costar Dean. Here, he plays a former Southern sheriff driving crosscountry to rescue his daughter—with the title character on his tail. The record was better. [PG-13]▼●

Big Bad Mama (1974) **C-83m.** *** D: Steve Carver. Angie Dickinson, Tom Skerritt, William Shatner, Susan Sennett, Robbie Lee, Dick Miller, Joan Prather, Royal Dano, Sally Kirkland. Sexy knock-off of BONNIE AND CLYDE has Angie and her two teen daughters spending as much time fooling around with partners Shatner and Skerritt as they do robbing banks. Angie's nude scenes make this a cable-TV favorite (and led to a sequel thirteen years later!). Flavorful score by David Grisman. [R]▼

Big Bad Mama II (1987) **C-83m.** *½ D: Jim Wynorski. Angie Dickinson, Robert Culp, Danielle Brisebois, Julie McCullough, Bruce Glover. In this loosely linked sequel (more like a remake), Angie and her two daughters again shoot up rural, Depression-era America, robbing banks to avenge her husband's murder. Culp provides brief love interest. *Archie Bunker's Place* alumna Brisebois does a surprising topless scene. [R]▼

Big Bang, The (1990) **C-81m.** *** D: James Toback. Fascinating documentary in which Toback poses some basic philosophical questions—why were we born? who are we? and where are we going?—to a variety of people, from boxer/author José Torres to astronomer Fred Hess, basketball player Darryl Dawkins to film producer Don Simpson. Most amusing are the comments of an ex-mobster, and most sobering are those of an Auschwitz survivor. We even see Toback on camera, trying to finance the film. [R]▼

Big Beat, The (1958) **C-81m.** ** D: Will Cowan. William Reynolds, Andra Martin, Gogi Grant, Rose Marie, Hans Conried, Jeffrey Stone, The Del Vikings, Fats Domino, The Diamonds, The Four Aces, Harry James, Mills Brothers. Reynolds is a record exec, Martin his secretary. The Big Bore—except for the vintage performances of Domino ("I'm Walking"), The Diamonds ("Little Darling") and company.

Big Bird Cage, The (1972) **C-88m.** **½ D: Jack Hill. Pam Grier, Anitra Ford, Sid Haig, Candice Roman, Vic Diaz, Carol Speed. Amusing spoof of Filipino prison films has pleasant team of Grier and Haig as thieving mercenaries who engineer a prison break from the outside. A follow-up to THE BIG DOLL HOUSE. Aka WOMEN'S PENITENTIARY II. [R]▼

Big Blockade, The (1942-British) **77m.** ** D: Charles Frend. Michael Redgrave, Leslie Banks, Will Hay, John Mills, Frank Cellier, Robert Morley, Alfred Drayton,

Bernard Miles, Marius Goring, Michael Rennie, Michael Wilding. Dated propaganda chronicling Britain's economic blockade of Nazi Germany.

Big Blue, The (1988-U.S.-French) **C-119m.** ** D: Luc Besson. Rosanna Arquette, Jean-Marc Barr, Jean Reno, Paul Shenar, Sergio Castellito, Marc Duret, Griffin Dunne. Waterlogged chronicle of famed free diver Jacques Mayol (Barr), with Arquette redoing her DESPERATELY SEEKING SUSAN performance as a ditsy insurance investigator who falls for him. As much a psychological study as a drama of athletic competition—but who cares? Underwater photography is the main attraction here. CinemaScope. [PG]▼●

Big Bluff, The (1955) **70m.** ** D: W. Lee Wilder. John Bromfield, Martha Vickers. Robert Hutton, Rosemarie Bowe, Eve Miller. Ordinary melodrama about suave conman Bromfield, who sets his sights on a wealthy young widow (Vickers) with a short time to live.▼

Big Boodle, The (1957) **83m.** *½ D: Richard Wilson. Errol Flynn, Pedro Armendariz, Rossana Rory, Jacques Aubuchon. Tame caper of gangsters and counterfeit money, set in Havana. Seedy programmer emphasizing Flynn's career decline.

Big Boss, The SEE: **Fists of Fury**

Big Bounce, The (1969) **C-102m.** ** D: Alex March. Ryan O'Neal, Leigh Taylor-Young, James Daly, Robert Webber, Lee Grant, Van Heflin. Muddle-headed tale of drifter O'Neal becoming involved with vixenish Taylor-Young, who has strange ideas of what to do for kicks. Panavision. [PG—edited from original R rating]

Big Boy (1930) **69m.** **½ D: Alan Crosland. Al Jolson, Claudia Dell, Louise Closser Hale, Lloyd Hughes, Eddie Phillips, John Harron, Noah Beery. Jolson energetically recreates his 1925 stage success as Gus, black stable boy who hopes to ride the title horse in the Kentucky Derby. Jolie appears in blackface until the conclusion, when he sings "Tomorrow Is Another Day." A real curio, extremely dated, but fascinating nonetheless.●

Big Brass Ring, The (1999) **C-104m.** ** D: George Hickenlooper. William Hurt, Miranda Richardson, Nigel Hawthorne, Irène Jacob, Ewan Stewart, Gregg Henry, Ron Livingston. Independent politician running for governor of Missouri—with his wife's money—is unnerved when his former mentor threatens to unveil a skeleton in his closet, with an eager investigative reporter waiting to pounce. Strong cast and impressive pedigree (based on an unproduced screenplay by Orson Welles and Oja Kodar) can't change the fact that the film sinks under its own weight. After a while the characters are simply boring. Made for theaters; debuted on cable. [R]▼◗

Big Brawl, The (1980) **C-95m.** **½ D: Robert Clouse. Jackie Chan, Jose Ferrer, Kristine DeBell, Mako, Ron Max. The martial arts are applied to '30s gangster movie set in Chicago. Appealing cast, lots of comedy, along with director and some of the production staff from ENTER THE DRAGON, make this a moderately successful chop-socky. Panavision. [R]▼

Big Broadcast, The (1932) **87m.** *** D: Frank Tuttle. Bing Crosby, Kate Smith, George Burns, Gracie Allen, Stuart Erwin, Leila Hyams, Cab Calloway, Mills Brothers, Boswell Sisters. Failing radio station owned by Burns is taken over by millionaire Erwin, who presents an all-star show featuring Bing and many radio stars. Many offbeat, bizarre touches in standard love-triangle story make this a delight. Bing sings "Please," "Here Lies Love."

Big Broadcast of 1936, The (1935) **97m.** **½ D: Norman Taurog. Jack Oakie, George Burns, Gracie Allen, Lyda Roberti, Henry Wadsworth, Wendy Barrie, C. Henry Gordon, Ethel Merman, Charlie Ruggles, Mary Boland, Bill "Bojangles" Robinson, The Nicholas Brothers. Curious muddle of specialty acts and nonsensical "plot" involving radio station owner Oakie. Vignettes feature everyone from radio's original Amos 'n' Andy (Freeman Gosden and Charles Correll, in blackface) to the Vienna Boys Choir. Bing Crosby sings lovely "I Wished on the Moon."

Big Broadcast of 1937, The (1936) **102m.** *** D: Mitchell Leisen. Jack Benny, George Burns, Gracie Allen, Bob Burns, Martha Raye, Shirley Ross, Ray Milland. Another plotless but enjoyable variety romp with many stars, plus guests Benny Goodman, Leopold Stokowski, Larry Adler, etc. Songs such as: "Here's Love In Your Eye," "La Bomba," "Night In Manhattan."

Big Broadcast of 1938, The (1938) **90m.** ** D: Mitchell Leisen. W. C. Fields, Martha Raye, Dorothy Lamour, Shirley Ross, Lynne Overman, Bob Hope, Ben Blue, Leif Erickson. Hodgepodge of bad musical numbers from Tito Guizar to Kirsten Flagstad, notable only for Fields' few scenes, Hope and Ross's rendition of Oscar-winning "Thanks For The Memory." Hope's first feature.▼

Big Brown Eyes (1936) **77m.** **½ D: Raoul Walsh. Joan Bennett, Cary Grant, Walter Pidgeon, Isabel Jewell, Lloyd Nolan. Bennett helps detective Grant trap a gang of thieves in pleasing romantic mystery.

Big Bully (1996) **C-97m.** *½ D: Steve Miner. Rick Moranis, Tom Arnold, Julianne Phillips, Carol Kane, Jeffrey Tambor, Curtis Armstrong, Faith Prince, Tony Pierce, Don Knotts, Stuart Pankin. Having parlayed his newly published book into an offer to teach a course at his old school, author Moranis is horrified to discover that his long unseen childhood tormentor is now the shop instructor. Comedy is so dull in the opening childhood flashbacks that it's already d.o.a. by the time Moranis and Arnold show up. Phillips disappears abruptly in the film's second half—lucky for her. [PG]▼●◗

Big Bus, The (1976) **C-88m.** **½ D: James Frawley. Joseph Bologna, Stockard Channing, John Beck, Lynn Redgrave, Jose Ferrer, Ruth Gordon, Richard B. Shull, Sally Kellerman, Ned Beatty, Bob Dishy, Stuart Margolin, Richard Mulligan, Larry Hagman, Howard Hesseman, Harold Gould. Funny spoof of disaster films, using a super-duper Trailways bus; all expected clichés come in for ribbing, but film doesn't sustain its promising idea. Murphy Dunne hilarious as inane cocktail pianist. Panavision. [PG]▼

Big Business (1988) **C-97m.** **½ D: Jim Abrahams. Bette Midler, Lily Tomlin, Fred Ward, Edward Herrmann, Michele Placido, Daniel Gerroll, Barry Primus, Michael Gross, Joe Grifasi, Mary Gross. Two sets of twins are mismatched and separated at birth; years later the girls who've grown up in the boonies come to N.Y.C. for a showdown with the conglomerate that's going to wipe out their little town, hardly dreaming that the corporation is run by their identical twins! Agreeable farce never really catches fire, though Bette is terrific and the effects are remarkable. [PG] ▼●

Big Business Girl (1931) **75m.** ** D: William A. Seiter. Loretta Young, Ricardo Cortez, Frank Albertson, Joan Blondell, Frank Darien. Young is cute and perky as a career-minded woman on her way up the corporate ladder, trying to help her singer-boyfriend and keep her amorous boss at arm's length.▼

Big Cage, The (1933) **82m.** **½ D: Kurt Neumann. Clyde Beatty, Anita Page, Mickey Rooney, Andy Devine, Vince Barnett, Raymond Hatton, Wallace Ford. Beatty plays himself in silly but watchable circus story; sappy love angle doesn't help, but supporting cast does, including Mickey as youngster who wants to be Just Like Beatty. Exciting animal footage was reused in countless films.

Big Caper, The (1957) **84m.** **½ D: Robert Stevens. Rory Calhoun, Mary Costa, James Gregory, Robert Harris. Well-done account of Calhoun and Costa posing as married couple in small town in order to set up gang caper; realities of life reform them.

Big Carnival, The (1951) **112m.** *** D: Billy Wilder. Kirk Douglas, Jan Sterling, Bob Arthur, Porter Hall, Frank Cady, Richard Benedict, Ray Teal, Gene Evans. An embittered reporter looking for the elusive brass ring finds it when he stumbles onto a story of a man trapped in an ancient Indian ruin. Unrelentingly cynical (yet mostly believable) tale of how the reporter exploits the "human interest story" for his own benefit—and how the potential tragedy turns into a three-ring circus—has a peculiarly contemporary ring to it. Biting and extremely well acted. Originally titled ACE IN THE HOLE.

Big Chill, The (1983) **C-103m.** *** D: Lawrence Kasdan. Tom Berenger, Glenn Close, Jeff Goldblum, William Hurt, Kevin Kline, Mary Kay Place, Meg Tilly, JoBeth Williams, Don Galloway. Entertaining, surface-level look at a group of former college-radical friends who've dropped back into Society. Wonderful acting ensemble, irresistible soundtrack of 60s hits help camouflage weaknesses of script—which bears more than passing resemblance to John Sayles' RETURN OF THE SECAUCUS SEVEN. (Trivia note: the deceased friend was played by Kevin Costner, whose scenes were cut from the finished film. But that's still him being dressed for his funeral under the main titles!) [R]▼●◗

Big Circus, The (1959) **C-108m.** **½ D: Joseph M. Newman. Victor Mature, Red Buttons, Rhonda Fleming, Kathryn Grant, Vincent Price, Peter Lorre, David Nelson, Gilbert Roland, Howard McNear, Steve Allen. Corny and predictable, but still entertaining hokum under the big top, with Lorre as a sardonic clown and Roland tightrope-walking over Niagara Falls. And what a cast! CinemaScope.▼

Big City, The (1937) **80m.** **½ D: Frank Borzage. Spencer Tracy, Luise Rainer, Eddie Quillan, William Demarest, Regis Toomey, Charley Grapewin, Victor Varconi. Cabdriver Tracy and wife Rainer are pitted against crooked taxi bosses in well-acted but average film. Retitled: SKYSCRAPER WILDERNESS.

Big City, The (1948) **103m.** **½ D: Norman Taurog. Margaret O'Brien, Robert Preston, Danny Thomas, George Murphy, Betty Garrett. Priest Preston, cantor Thomas, and cop Murphy "adopt" little O'Brien in this maudlin drama.

Big City, The (1963-Indian) **122m.** *** D: Satyajit Ray. Madhabi Mukherjee, Anil Chatterjee, Haradhan Banarjee, Vicky Redwood, Jaya Bhaduri, Shephalika Devi. Unassuming tale of domestic life in Calcutta projects modern attitudes in story of a man who is forced to let his wife work and finds that she soon becomes the only one of the two with a job. Interesting portrait of Indian society; originally released at 133m.

Big City Blues (1932) **65m.** **½ D: Mervyn LeRoy. Joan Blondell, Eric Linden, Inez Courtney, Evalyn Knapp, Guy Kibbee, Humphrey Bogart, Ned Sparks. Polished Warner Bros. programmer of hayseed Linden encountering disillusionment and love in N.Y.C.

Big Clock, The (1948) **95m.** *** D: John Farrow. Ray Milland, Charles Laughton, Maureen O'Sullivan, George Macready, Rita Johnson, Dan Tobin, Henry (Harry) Morgan. Tyrannical publisher of crime magazine (Laughton) commits murder; his editor (Milland) tries to solve case and finds all the clues pointing to himself. Vibrant melodrama; taut script by Jonathan Latimer from Kenneth Fearing novel. Elsa Lanchester has hilarious vignette as eccentric artist. Remade as NO WAY OUT (1987).▼

Big Combo, The (1955) **89m.** *** D: Joseph (H.) Lewis. Cornel Wilde, Jean Wallace, Brian Donlevy, Richard Conte, Lee Van Cleef, Robert Middleton, Earl Holliman, Helen Walker. Raw, violent film noir about persistent cop Wilde going up against cunning, sadistic racketeer Conte. A cult item, stylishly directed; Donlevy's demise is a highlight.▼◗

Big Country, The (1958) **C-166m.** *** D: William Wyler. Gregory Peck, Burl Ives, Jean Simmons, Carroll Baker, Charlton Heston, Chuck Connors, Charles Bickford. Overblown Western has ex-sea captain Peck arrive to marry Baker, but forced to take sides in battle against Ives and sons over water rights. Heston as quick-tempered ranch foreman and Ives (who won an Oscar) as burly patriarch stand out in energetic cast. Jerome Moross' score has become a classic. Technirama. ▼●

Big Cube, The (1969) **C-98m.** *½ D: Tito Davison. Lana Turner, George Chakiris, Richard Egan, Dan O'Herlihy, Karin Mossberg. Absurd drama about relationship between beautiful young girl, her gigolo boyfriend, and her actress-mother at least offers some unintentional laughs. For camp followers only. [M/PG]

Big Daddy (1999) **C-95m.** **½ D: Dennis Dugan. Adam Sandler, Joey Lauren Adams, Rob Schneider, Jon Stewart, Leslie Mann, Josh Mostel, Joseph Bologna, Kristy Swanson, Steve Buscemi, Cole and Dylan Sprouse. An overgrown, irresponsible slacker tries to look after a young boy who's been dumped on his doorstep; naturally, he becomes attached to the youngster, and vice versa. Tailor-made Sandler vehicle is utterly contrived but delivers expected laughs; the courtroom climax is too silly for words. That's director Dugan as the man who won't cooperate on Halloween. [PG-13] ▼◗

Big Day, The SEE: **Jour De Fete**

Big Deal on Madonna Street (1958-Italian) **91m.** ***½ D: Mario Monicelli. Vittorio Gassman, Marcello Mastroianni, Renato Salvatori, Rossana Rory, Carla Gravina, Toto. Classic account of misadventures of amateurish crooks attempting to rob a store; hilarious satire on all burglary capers. Retitled: BIG DEAL; remade as CRACKERS, and followed by a sequel, BIG DEAL ON MADONNA STREET . . . 20 YEARS LATER, which was actually released 30 years later! Also adapted for Broadway—unsuccessfully.▼●

Big Doll House, The (1971) **C-93m.** **½ D: Jack Hill. Judy Brown, Roberta Collins, Pam Grier, Brooke Mills, Pat Woodell, Sid Haig. Fast paced, tongue-in-cheek adventure shot in Philippines mixes sex, comedy, and violence in confrontation between sadistic warden and female prisoners. One of the earliest, most successful and influential of women-in-prison exploitation films. Followed by THE BIG BIRD CAGE. Aka WOMEN'S PENITENTIARY I. [R]▼◗

Big Easy, The (1987) **C-108m.** *** D: Jim McBride. Dennis Quaid, Ellen Barkin, Ned Beatty, John Goodman, Ebbe Roe Smith, Lisa Jane Persky, Charles Ludlam, Tom O'Brien, Grace Zabriskie, Marc Lawrence, Solomon Burke, Jim Garrison. Highly original crime yarn with steamy romance and unique New Orleans atmosphere. A stylish homicide detective (Quaid) runs afoul of the new, uptight assistant D.A. (Barkin) while investigating a local mob murder; soon they're romantically involved, even while they're at odds professionally. Sassy and sexy, with terrific Cajun music score. Written by Daniel Petrie, Jr. Later a cable TV series. [R]▼●◗

Big Fisherman, The (1959) **C-149m.** **½ D: Frank Borzage. Howard Keel, John Saxon, Susan Kohner, Herbert Lom, Martha Hyer, Ray Stricklyn, Alexander Scourby. Sprawling religious epic, from Lloyd Douglas' book about the life of St. Peter; seldom dull, but not terribly inspiring. Borzage's last film. Originally 184m., then cut to 164m. Super Panavision 70.

Big Fix, The (1978) **C-108m.** *** D: Jeremy Paul Kagan. Richard Dreyfuss, Susan Anspach, Bonnie Bedelia, John Lithgow, F. Murray Abraham, Ofelia Medina, Fritz Weaver. Good vehicle for now-familiar Dreyfuss personality as 1960s-campus-radical-turned-private-eye Moses Wine, who becomes involved in tangled whodunit in which a former hippie cult leader figures prominently. Screenplay by Roger L. Simon, based on his novel. Look fast for Mandy Patinkin as a pool cleaner. Leon Redbone's "I Want to Be Seduced" is not in video version. [PG]▼

Big Gamble, The (1961) **C-100m.** **½ D: Richard Fleischer. Stephen Boyd, Juliette Greco, David Wayne, Sybil Thorndike. Not-too-convincing account of Irish adventurer and bride Greco who dally on the African Ivory Coast seeking to build their future the easy way. CinemaScope.

Bigger Than Life (1956) **C-95m.** *** D: Nicholas Ray. James Mason, Barbara Rush, Walter Matthau, Robert Simon, Roland Winters. Compelling drama of teacher Mason who becomes hooked on drugs, and its devastating effects on him and his family. Mason also produced the film. Quite bold for its time. CinemaScope.

Biggest Battle, The SEE: **Greatest Battle, The**

Biggest Bundle of Them All, The (1968) **C-110m.** *½ D: Ken Annakin. Robert

Wagner, Raquel Welch, Vittorio De Sica, Edward G. Robinson, Godfrey Cambridge. Supposedly a comedy, film is slapdash tale of amateur criminals who try to kidnap American gangster. Filmed in France and Italy. Panavision.▼

Big Girls Don't Cry . . . They Get Even (1992) **C-96m.** ** D: Joan Micklin Silver. Hillary Wolf, David Strathairn, Margaret Whitton, Griffin Dunne, Patricia Kalember, Adrienne Shelly, Dan Futterman, Ben Savage. The product of a mélange of multiple divorces and remarriages, teenager Wolf, fed up with various stepparents and half-siblings, hightails it during her current family's vacation. Bittersweet comedy is too superficial (and predictable) to say anything meaningful on a subject relevant to many teens. [PG]▼●

Biggles: Adventures in Time (1986-British) **C-108m.** ** D: John Hough. Neil Dickson, Alex Hyde-White, Fiona Hutchinson, Peter Cushing, Marcus Gilbert. Curious, occasionally entertaining sci-fi adventure with Hyde-White inexplicably traveling through time from 1986 N.Y.C. to WW1 Europe . . . where he assists British flyboy Dickson. Based on characters created by Capt. W. E. Johns. Original British title: BIGGLES. [PG]▼●

Big Green, The (1995) **C-100m.** ** D: Holly Goldberg Sloan. Steve Guttenberg, Olivia d'Abo, Jay O. Sanders, John Terry, Chauncey Leopardi, Patrick Renna, Anthony Esquivel, Bug Hall. Slight Disney fare chronicling the plight of the "Bad News Bears" and the "Mighty Ducks" of soccer teams in a depressed Texas town. Overly familiar but inoffensive; OK for less discriminating children. [PG]▼●

Big Guns SEE: **No Way Out** (1972)

Big Guy, The (1939) **78m.** **½ D: Arthur Lubin. Jackie Cooper, Victor McLaglen, Ona Munson, Peggy Moran, Edward Brophy. Fairly interesting story of warden McLaglen given choice between wealth and saving innocent man on death row. Remade as BEHIND THE HIGH WALL.

Big Hand for the Little Lady, A (1966) **C-95m.** *** D: Fielder Cook. Henry Fonda, Joanne Woodward, Jason Robards, Charles Bickford, Burgess Meredith. Excellent comedy centering on poker game in old West. Outstanding roster of character actors includes John Qualen, Paul Ford, and Robert Middleton. There's a neat surprise ending, too.▼

Big Hangover, The (1950) **82m.** ** D: Norman Krasna. Van Johnson, Elizabeth Taylor, Leon Ames, Edgar Buchanan, Rosemary DeCamp, Gene Lockhart. Ambitious but noble war veteran Johnson, whose allergy to alcohol makes him drunk at inopportune moments, joins a staid law firm. How long will he remain there? And will he hook up with wealthy Taylor? Predictable, as well as silly and boring.▼

Big Heat, The (1953) **90m.** *** D: Fritz Lang. Glenn Ford, Gloria Grahame, Jocelyn Brando, Alexander Scourby, Lee Marvin, Carolyn Jones, Jeanette Nolan. Time has taken the edge off once-searing story of cop determined to bust city crime ring; famous coffee-hurling scene still jolts, and Grahame is excellent as bad girl who helps Ford.▼●

Big Hit, The (1998) **C-99m.** *** D: Che-Kirk Wong. Mark Wahlberg, Lou Diamond Phillips, Christina Applegate, China Chow, Avery Brooks, Bokeem Woodbine, Antonio Sabato, Jr., Lainie Kazan, Elliott Gould, Sab Shimono, Lela Rochon. Expert hit man Wahlberg is beset by insecurity, a confusing romantic life, and a treacherous partner (Phillips). The result is gunfire, car chases, explosions, and martial arts galore. Unique action comedy with Hong Kong flavors doesn't always work, but the cast is lively and the stunt work awesome, fueled by a blazing pace. [R] ▼●◗

Big House, The (1930) **86m.** *** D: George Hill. Wallace Beery, Chester Morris, Robert Montgomery, Lewis Stone, Karl Dane, Leila Hyams. The original prison drama, this set the pattern for all later copies; it's still good, hard-bitten stuff with one of Beery's best tough-guy roles. Won Oscars for Writing (Frances Marion) and Sound Recording.▼

Big House, U.S.A. (1955) **82m.** **½ D: Howard W. Koch. Broderick Crawford, Ralph Meeker, Reed Hadley, Charles Bronson, Lon Chaney, Jr. Brutal account of a kidnapper/extortionist, and the FBI agents sent to track him down.

Big Jack (1949) **85m.** ** D: Richard Thorpe. Wallace Beery, Marjorie Main, Edward Arnold, Richard Conte, Vanessa Brown. Beery's last film, rather flat; he and Main are vagabond thieves in colonial America, Conte a moralistic doctor.

Big Jake (1971) **C-110m.** *** D: George Sherman. John Wayne, Richard Boone, Maureen O'Hara, Patrick Wayne, Chris Mitchum, Bobby Vinton, Bruce Cabot. Tough Westerner is called back by estranged wife to rescue their grandson from a gang of kidnappers headed by Boone (who's especially good). Underrated turn-of-the-century Western; well paced, handsomely shot. Wayne's fifth and final pairing with O'Hara; Chris Mitchum and the Duke's son Patrick play his sons. Panavision. [PG]▼●

Big Jim McLain (1952) **90m.** **½ D: Edward Ludwig. John Wayne, Nancy Olsen, James Arness, Alan Napier, Veda Ann Borg, Hans Conried. Wayne and Arness are HUAC investigators who go commie-hunting in Hawaii. One of the Duke's few dull films, but fascinating as a relic of its era.▼●

Big Kahuna, The (2000) **C-90m.** **½ D: John Swanbeck. Kevin Spacey, Danny DeVito, Peter Facinelli. Absorbing adaptation of Roger Rueff's play *Hospitality Suite,* essentially a three-character piece about two world-weary salesmen and a naive young colleague at an out-of-town convention. Their criticism clashes with the young man's religious fervor as they wait for an important customer to show up at their hotel suite. As photographed plays go this one is pretty good, with top-notch performances, but it never quite becomes a movie. Coproduced by Spacey. [R]▼

Big Knife, The (1955) **111m.** *** D: Robert Aldrich. Jack Palance, Ida Lupino, Shelley Winters, Rod Steiger, Ilka Chase, Wendell Corey. Clifford Odets' cynical view of Hollywood comes across well in hard-punching film, with fine portrayals that almost overcome stereotypes.●

Big Land, The (1957) **C-92m.** **½ D: Gordon Douglas. Alan Ladd, Virginia Mayo, Edmond O'Brien, Julie Bishop. Cattle owners and grain farmers join together to bring railroad link to Texas; easygoing, familiar.

Big Leaguer (1953) **70m.** **½ D: Robert Aldrich. Edward G. Robinson, Vera-Ellen, Jeff Richards, Richard Jaeckel, William Campbell, Carl Hubbell, Paul Layton, Al Campanis. Robinson uplifts this standard baseball tale as real-life ex-major-leaguer John B. "Hans" Lobert, who runs a baseball tryout camp. The scenario follows a group of hopefuls who dream of professional stardom under his watchful eye.

Big Lebowski, The (1998) **C-117m.** **½ D: Joel Coen. Jeff Bridges, John Goodman, Julianne Moore, Steve Buscemi, Peter Stormare, David Huddleston, Philip Seymour Hoffman, Flea, Sam Elliott, John Turturro, David Thewlis, Ben Gazzara. One big shaggy-dog joke, courtesy of the Coen brothers, about a slacker who's mistaken for a crime bigwig of the same name—and then gets hired by the guy to pay off a ransom. Mostly an excuse for off-the-wall character vignettes, some of which are amusing, some of which are just . . . strange. Minor Coen concoction with a most agreeable cast. Turturro is a standout as Jesus the bowler. [R]▼●◗

Big Lift, The (1950) **120m.** **½ D: George Seaton. Montgomery Clift, Paul Douglas, Cornell Borchers, O. E. Hasse. GI flight technicians involved in post-WW2 Berlin airlift and romance with German women. More interesting for on-location photography than uneven story line.▼◗

Big Lobby, The SEE: **Rosebud Beach Hotel, The**

Big Man, The SEE: **Crossing the Line**

Big Mo SEE: **Maurie**

Big Mouth, The (1967) **C-107m.** **½ D: Jerry Lewis. Jerry Lewis, Harold Stone, Susan Bay, Buddy Lester, Del Moore, Paul Lambert. Typical Lewis effort, with Jerry involved in murder and search for missing treasure in California. ▼

Big Night, The (1951) **75m.** **½ D: Joseph Losey. John Barrymore, Jr., Preston Foster, Howland Chamberlain, Joan Lorring, Dorothy Comingore, Howard St. John. Brooding account of rebellious teenager Barrymore's emotional flare-up with humanity at large; well done.

Big Night (1996) **C-107m.** **½ D: Stanley Tucci, Campbell Scott. Stanley Tucci, Minnie Driver, Tony Shalhoub, Ian Holm, Isabella Rossellini, Campbell Scott, Allison Janney, Caroline Aaron. Endearing story of Italian immigrant brothers trying to survive as restaurateurs in 1950s America; one is an artist in the kitchen, the other a would-be businessman. Their bombastic rival (Holm) gives them a shot at the brass ring by inviting Louis Prima to be their guest one night. Finely tuned performances, amusing vignettes and observations make this small endeavor worthwhile, but it's too slow and quiet for its own good. Tucci also co-scripted; codirector Scott has a small but funny part as a Cadillac salesman. The feast on-screen is mouthwatering! [R] ▼●◗

Big Noise, The (1944) **74m.** BOMB D: Malcolm St. Clair. Stan Laurel, Oliver Hardy, Arthur Space, Veda Ann Borg, Bobby (Robert) Blake, Jack Norton. L&H's worst film, about them delivering a bomb . . . and they do.▼

Big One, The (1998-U.S.-British) **C-96m.** **½ D: Michael Moore. Puckish pest Moore chronicles the real-life events that occur (mostly at his own instigation) while on a book tour to promote his best-selling *Downsize This!* Self-aggrandizing documentary is sometimes smarmy, sometimes as invasive as anything on *Candid Camera* . . . but it's also fast and consistently funny, as Moore routinely shows up at someone's corporate headquarters to launch some mischief. One example: presenting a downsizing company's chairman with an 80-cent check to cover the first hourly wage for some new worker—in a less developed country. [PG-13]▼●

Big Operator, The (1959) **91m.** ** D: Charles Haas. Mickey Rooney, Steve Cochran, Mamie Van Doren, Mel Torme, Ray Danton, Jim Backus. Ray Anthony, Jackie Coogan. Rooney tries to add vim and vigor to title role as tough hood who goes on violent rampage when federal agents investigate his business activities. Paul Gallico story filmed before as JOE SMITH, AMERICAN. Retitled: ANATOMY OF A SYNDICATE. CinemaScope.

Big Parade, The (1925) **141m.** **** D: King Vidor. John Gilbert, Renee Adoree, Hobart Bosworth, Claire McDowell, Claire Adams, Karl Dane, Tom O'Brien. One of the best WW1 films ever; clean-shaven Gilbert a wonderful hero, Adoree an unforgettable heroine. Filled with memorable vignettes, and some of the most harrowingly realistic battle scenes ever filmed. A gem.▼●

Big Parade of Comedy SEE: **MGM's Big Parade of Comedy**

Big Payoff, The SEE: **Win, Place, or Steal**

Big Picture, The (1989) **C-100m.** **½ D: Christopher Guest. Kevin Bacon, Emily Longstreth, J. T. Walsh, Jennifer Jason Leigh, Michael McKean, Kim Miyori, Teri Hatcher, Dan Schneider, Jason Gould, Tracy Brooks Swope. Slight but good-natured comedy about Hollywood wheeling and dealing. Bacon is a naive student filmmaker courted by a movie studio exec and swallowed whole into The System. Lots of inside jokes for Hollywood audiences. Very funny performance by Leigh as an arty dingbat, and many amusing cameos, including unbilled Martin Short as an agent. Guest's first feature directing (he also scripted with costar McKean and Michael Varhol). [PG-13]▼●

Big Pond, The (1930) **75m.** **½ D: Hobart Henley. Maurice Chevalier, Claudette Colbert, George Barbier, Nat Pendleton. Claudette brings Maurice to America, where to make good he works in chewing gum factory. Chevalier charm overcomes trivia, song: "You Brought A New Kind Of Love To Me." Dialogue by Preston Sturges.

Big Punch, The (1948) **80m.** ** D: Sherry Shourds. Wayne Morris, Gordon MacRae, Lois Maxwell, Mary Stuart, Jimmy Ames, Anthony Warde. Boxer MacRae is falsely accused of murder, finds refuge with Morris, who has spurned ring for the pulpit. Serviceable melodrama.

Big Red (1962) **C-89m.** *** D: Norman Tokar. Walter Pidgeon, Gilles Payant, Emile Genest, Janette Bertrand, Doris Lussier. Charming, understated Disney drama of young boy who goes to work for wealthy dog fancier (Pidgeon) and becomes devoted to prize Irish setter. Fine family fare. Filmed in Canada. From popular novel by Jim Kjelgaard.▼◗

Big Red One, The (1980) **C-113m.** ***½ D: Samuel Fuller. Lee Marvin, Mark Hamill, Robert Carradine, Bobby Di Cicco, Kelly Ward, Siegfried Rauch, Stephane Audran. Fuller returned to filmmaking after a long hiatus with this vivid, autobiographical account of a special infantry squadron and its intrepid sergeant during WW2. Hard to believe one film could pack so much into its narrative; a rich, moving, realistic, and poetic film. [PG]▼●◗

Big Risk, The (1960-French) **111m.** ** D: Claude Sautet. Jean-Paul Belmondo, Lino Ventura, Marcel Dalio, Sandra Milo. Too-leisurely-paced account of criminal on the lam, who for sake of his family gives himself up to police.

Big Scam, The SEE: **Nightingale Sang in Berkeley Square, A**

Big Score, The (1983) **C-85m.** ** D: Fred Williamson. Fred Williamson, John Saxon, Richard Roundtree, Nancy Wilson, Ed Lauter, D'Urville Martin, Michael Dante, Joe Spinell. Barely adequate DIRTY HARRY clone with narc Williamson ignoring the rules and taking on thug Spinell. (In fact, this script was originally commissioned by Clint Eastwood for a Dirty Harry vehicle that never got made.) [R]▼

Big Search, The SEE: **East of Kilimanjaro**

Big Shakedown, The (1934) **64m.** ** D: John Francis Dillon. Bette Davis, Ricardo Cortez, Glenda Farrell, Charles Farrell, Adrian Morris. Inconsequential tale. Davis rejects husband Farrell when he joins forces with mobster Cortez in cosmetic fraud.

Big Shot, The (1942) **82m.** **½ D: Lewis Seiler. Humphrey Bogart, Irene Manning, Susan Peters, Minor Watson, Chick Chandler, Richard Travis, Stanley Ridges, Howard Da Silva. OK grade-B gangster yarn with Bogey a three-time loser involved in robbery frameup and prison break.

Big Shots (1987) **C-90m.** **½ D: Robert Mandel. Ricky Busker, Darius McCrary, Robert Joy, Robert Prosky, Jerzy Skolimowski, Paul Winfield. So-so juvenile adventure about an inexperienced white boy and streetwise urban black who come together and become involved with dead bodies, hired killers and other mayhem. Panavision. [PG-13]▼●

Big Show, The (1961) **C-113m.** **½ D: James B. Clark. Esther Williams, Cliff Robertson, Nehemiah Persoff, Robert Vaughn. Drama of family conflict, similar to 1949's HOUSE OF STRANGERS, somehow set in a circus with Williams in a rare dramatic rôle. Glug! CinemaScope.

Big Sky, The (1952) **122m.** *** D: Howard Hawks. Kirk Douglas, Dewey Martin, Elizabeth Threatt, Arthur Hunnicutt, Buddy Baer, Steven Geray, Hank Worden, Jim Davis. Camaraderie and conflict as fur-trapper Douglas leads expedition up the Missouri River. Eventful, evocative film adapted from A. B. Guthrie, Jr., book by Dudley Nichols; well-directed by Hawks. Originally released at 141m. Also shown in computer-colored version.▼

Big Sleep, The (1946) **114m.** **** D: Howard Hawks. Humphrey Bogart, Lauren Bacall, John Ridgely, Martha Vickers, Louis Jean Heydt, Regis Toomey, Peggy Knudsen, Dorothy Malone, Bob Steele, Elisha Cook, Jr. Classic mystery thriller from Raymond Chandler's first novel; detective Philip Marlowe (Bogart) becomes involved with wealthy Bacall and her uncontrollable little sister Vickers. So convoluted even Chandler didn't know who committed one murder, but so incredibly entertaining that no one has ever cared. Powerhouse direction, unforgettable dialogue; script by William Faulkner, Jules Furthman and Leigh Brackett. Pre-release version (shown to Armed Forces overseas in 1945) runs 116m., with

18m. of scenes reshot or unused in the official release. This version has less of Bogie and Bacall and a more linear plot, but is somehow less exotic and interesting. Also shown in computer-colored version. ▼●◗

Big Sleep, The (1978-British) **C-100m.** ** D: Michael Winner. Robert Mitchum, Sarah Miles, Candy Clark, Oliver Reed, Richard Boone, James Stewart, Joan Collins, Edward Fox, John Mills, Harry Andrews, Richard Todd, Colin Blakely. Follow-up to FAREWELL, MY LOVELY is less a remake of the Hawks classic than a more faithful rendering of the Chandler novel, albeit updated and set in London. If you can get by that, it's tolerable, with a strong cast, fresh locations, and thankful lack of camp. [R]▼

Big Squeeze, The (1996) **C-98m.** *½ D: Marcus De Leon. Lara Flynn Boyle, Peter Dobson, Danny Nucci, Luca Bercovici, Teresa Despina, Michael Chieffo. Boyle works in a bar to support her injured ballplayer husband (Bercovici)—then learns he's neglected to inform her of a $130,000 settlement he's received, so she enlists a drifter-hustler (a miscast Dobson) to get the money. Pretty poor. Video version is 7 minutes longer, if you care. Aka BODY OF A WOMAN. [R]▼●◗

Big Steal, The (1949) **71m.** *** D: Don Siegel. Robert Mitchum, Jane Greer, William Bendix, Patric Knowles, Ramon Novarro. Mitchum is on the trail of Army payroll thief Knowles; he in turn is chased by Bendix, and becomes involved with enticing Greer. Well-made robbery caper, set in Mexico and shot on location, is full of terrific plot twists.▼●

Big Store, The (1941) **80m.** ** D: Charles Riesner. Groucho, Chico and Harpo Marx, Tony Martin, Virginia Grey, Margaret Dumont, Douglass Dumbrille, Henry Armetta. Big comedown for Marxes in weak film of detective Groucho investigating crooked Dumbrille's department store. Low spot is Martin's "The Tenement Symphony."▼●

Big Street, The (1942) **88m.** **½ D: Irving Reis. Henry Fonda, Lucille Ball, Barton MacLane, Eugene Pallette, Agnes Moorehead, Sam Levene, Ray Collins, Hans Conried, Ozzie Nelson and Orchestra. Damon Runyon produced this treacly adaptation of his own *Collier's* magazine story "Little Pinks," about a timid busboy who devotes himself to a self-centered nightclub singer. Odd (and oddly watchable), with very unconventional roles for both Fonda and Ball.▼●

Big Tease, The (2000) **C-83m.** **½ D: Kevin Allen. Craig Ferguson, Frances Fisher, Mary McCormack, David Rasche, Chris Langham, Sara Gilbert, John Pankow, Donal Logue, Charles Napier, Larry Miller, Ted McGinley. Scottish hairdresser mistakenly thinks he's been invited to L.A. to take part in the World Freestyle Hairdressing Championship, but won't be deterred from competing for the Platinum Scissors award. Amusing if lightweight romp through the tresses of Tinseltown. Drew Carey (Ferguson's costar on TV's *The Drew Carey Show*) is among a handful of celebrity cameos. Cowritten by Ferguson. [R]▼

Big Time (1988) **C-87m.** *** D: Chris Blum. Tom Waits. Concert footage filmed at L.A.'s Wiltern Theater is combined with scenes of the chameleonlike Waits as various and sundry characters: you'll see Waits the sleazy lounge lizard, Waits the gravel-voiced crooner, and Waits the truly amazing performer. For Tom Waits fans, this is the next best thing to seeing him live. [PG]▼

Big Tip Off, The (1955) **79m.** *½ D: Frank McDonald. Richard Conte, Constance Smith, Bruce Bennett, Cathy Downs, James Millican, Dick Benedict. Forgettable programmer about newspaper columnist Conte and his dealings with hood Bennett and a fund-raising scam.

Big T.N.T. Show, The (1966) **93m.** ** D: Larry Peerce. David McCallum, Roger Miller, Joan Baez, Ike and Tina Turner, Bo Diddley, The Ronettes, Ray Charles, The Lovin' Spoonful. Follow-up to THE T.A.M.I. SHOW casts a wider musical net, with lesser results, but Diddley, Tina Turner, and Ronnie Spector keep it pumping. Shot on tape, transferred to film; footage reused in THAT WAS ROCK.

Big Top Pee-wee (1988) **C-90m.** **½ D: Randal Kleiser. Pee-wee Herman, Penelope Ann Miller, Kris Kristofferson, Valeria Golino, Susan Tyrrell, Albert Henderson, Kevin Peter Hall, Kenneth Tobey, Stephanie Hodge, Benicio Del Toro, voice of Wayne White. Farmer Pee-wee allows a traveling circus to stay on his property, and quickly develops circus fever—as well as a romance with the pretty trapeze artist (Golino). Quirky if overly bland comedy (cowritten and produced by Pee-wee's alter ego, Paul Reubens) has many clever moments, along with some curious ones. Ought to please kids and family audiences. [PG]▼●

Big Town (1947) **60m.** ** D: William C. Thomas. Philip Reed, Hillary Brooke, Veda Ann Borg, Robert Lowery, Byron Barr, Charles Arnt, Nana Bryant, Frank Fenton. Suave but overly aggressive newspaper editor (Reed) goes on a crime crusade to boost circulation—but soon gets carried away. First in the short-lived *Big Town* series, based on the popular radio program. Retitled: GUILTY ASSIGNMENT.▼

Big Town, The (1987) **C-109m.** ** D: Ben Bolt. Matt Dillon, Diane Lane, Tommy Lee Jones, Tom Skerritt, Lee Grant, Bruce Dern, Suzy Amis, David Marshall Grant, Lolita David (Davidovich), Cherry Jones, Gary Farmer, Sarah Polley. Small-town crapshooter with a "golden arm" comes to Chicago in the 1950s to become a big-time gambler, but still has a lot to learn. With that cast (and Lane as a stripper) it's easy to watch . . . but just as easy to forget. [R]▼●

Big Town After Dark (1947) **69m.** **½ D: William C. Thomas. Philip Reed, Hillary Brooke, Richard Travis, Anne Gillis, Vince Barnett, Joe Sawyer. OK follow-up to BIG TOWN. Niece of a newspaper publisher inadvertently leads editor Reed and police reporter Brooke on the trail of mobsters in a gambling racket. Retitled: UNDERWORLD AFTER DARK.▼

Big Trail, The (1930) **121m.** *** D: Raoul Walsh. John Wayne, Marguerite Churchill, El Brendel, Tully Marshall, Tyrone Power Sr., David Rollins, Ian Keith. Epic Western may seem creaky to some viewers, but remains one of the most impressive early talkies, with its grand sweep and naturalistic use of sound. John Wayne was "discovered" for starring role, and already shows easygoing charm. Originally filmed in pioneer 70mm widescreen process called Grandeur. ▼

Big Trees, The (1952) **C-89m.** ** D: Felix Feist. Kirk Douglas, Eve Miller, Patrice Wymore, Edgar Buchanan, John Archer, Alan Hale, Jr., Roy Roberts, Ellen Corby. Brutally ambitious lumberman Douglas runs afoul of a religious sect—and practically everybody else around him—in this cornball outdoor melodrama. A remake of VALLEY OF THE GIANTS with stock footage from that earlier color movie. ▼●◗

Big Trouble (1985) **C-93m.** ** D: John Cassavetes. Peter Falk, Alan Arkin, Beverly D'Angelo, Charles Durning, Robert Stack, Paul Dooley, Valerie Curtin, Richard Libertini. Harried insurance salesman Arkin needs money to put his three sons through Yale, so he becomes involved with ditsy D'Angelo in a plot to kill her loony husband (Falk). Pretty silly stuff, although the sardine-flavored liqueur does provide a couple of chuckles. Reteaming of talents from THE IN-LAWS had a troubled production, and barely received theatrical release. Andrew Bergman wrote the script under the name Warren Bogle. [R]▼●

Big Trouble in Little China (1986) **C-99m.** *½ D: John Carpenter. Kurt Russell, Kim Cattrall, Dennis Dun, James Hong, Victor Wong, Kate Burton, Suzee Pai. Blowhard trucker Russell finds himself knee-deep in Chinatown intrigue (and mumbo-jumbo) when a friend's fiancée is kidnapped right in front of his eyes. High-tech INDIANA JONES-style adventure has heavy tongue-in-cheek attitude, but everything else about it is heavy, too . . . including Russell's John Wayne-ish swagger. Good electronic music score by director Carpenter. Panavision. [PG-13]▼●

Big Wave, The (1960-Japanese) **60m.** *½ D: Tad Danielewski. Sessue Hayakawa, Ichizo Itami, Mickey Curtis, Koji Shitara. Slowly paced account from Pearl Buck novel involving two boys who are childhood friends but later in life clash over their love for a local girl.

Big Wednesday (1978) **C-120m.** **½ D: John Milius. Jan-Michael Vincent, William Katt, Gary Busey, Lee Purcell, Patti D'Arbanville, Sam Melville, Robert Englund, Barbara Hale, Reb Brown, Steve Kanaly, Michael Talbott, Charlene Tilton. Half of a good flick on surfing, Pacific Coast-style, early 60s. Up to midway point, a ridiculous comedy about macho Vincent and his fun-loving, destructive ways. As he and buddies Katt and Busey get older and action is brought up to 70s, dramatic content improves. Hale (who plays Mrs. Barlow) and Katt are real-life mother and son. Milius recut to 104m. for pay-TV release. Retitled SUMMER OF INNOCENCE for TV. Panavision. [PG]▼●

Big Wheel, The (1949) **92m.** **½ D: Edward Ludwig. Mickey Rooney, Thomas Mitchell, Spring Byington, Mary Hatcher, Allen Jenkins, Michael O'Shea. Rooney is determined race-car driver following in father's footsteps despite dad's death on track; familiar plot well done.▼

Big Zapper (1973-British) **C-94m.** *½ D: Lindsay Shonteff. Linda Marlowe, Gary Hope, Sean Hewitt, Richard Monette, Penny Irving. Tough blonde Marlowe is well cast in this low-grade comic strip adventure as a violent private eye with a trusty (and masochistic) sidekick named Rock. [R]▼

Bikini Beach (1964) **C-100m.** **½ D: William Asher. Frankie Avalon, Annette Funicello, Keenan Wynn, Martha Hyer, Harvey Lembeck, Don Rickles, John Ashley, Jody McCrea, Meredith MacRae, Donna Loren, Candy Johnson, Timothy Carey, "Little" Stevie Wonder, Michael Nader. Third BEACH PARTY movie is second best, with Avalon in dual role as Frankie and a British singing rage called "The Potato Bug" (get it?). Relic of bygone era. Followed by PAJAMA PARTY. Panavision. ▼

Bilitis (1977-French) **C-95m.** ** D: David Hamilton. Patti D'Arbanville, Mona Kristensen, Bernard Giraudeau, Mathieu Carriere, Gilles Kohler. Superficial story of young student D'Arbanville and her first romance. All imagery, no substance. Director Hamilton is better-known for his lush coffee-table photo books of nude women. [R]▼

Bill and Coo (1947) **C-61m.** *** D: Dean Riesner. Produced and narrated by Ken Murray. Charming, unique live-action film using trained birds in a story situation. A special Oscar winner, later reedited with new introductory material by Murray.▼

Bill & Ted's Bogus Journey (1991) **C-98m.** **½ D: Peter Hewitt. Keanu Reeves, Alex Winter, William Sadler, Joss Ackland, George Carlin, Hal Landon, Jr.,

Pam Grier, Amy Stock-Poynton, Sarah Trigger. In this sequel, the dimwitted duo travel to Heaven, Hell, and points in between as they duel with an evil pair of robots who are posing as Bill and Ted. Along the way they meet (among others) Albert Einstein, the Easter Bunny, and the Grim Reaper! Special effects almost take over in this outing, but B&T are even dumber here than in the original film. One more sequel and they qualify as the Hope and Crosby of the '90s, dudes! [PG]▼●

Bill & Ted's Excellent Adventure (1989) **C-90m.** ** D: Stephen Herek. Keanu Reeves, Alex Winter, George Carlin, Bernie Casey, Amy Stock-Poynton, Terry Camilleri, Dan Shor, Ted Steedman. Inseparable teenage airheads, who are about to flunk their history course, are given the opportunity to go traveling through time to meet (and round up) such historical figures as Napoleon, Joan of Arc, and Abraham Lincoln. Radical! Reeves and Winter are great fun as Bill and Ted, but this goofy comedy never takes off as it should. Followed by an animated TV series, a live-action TV series, and BILL & TED'S BOGUS JOURNEY. Panavision. [PG]▼●

Bill Cosby—"Himself" (1982) **C-105m.** **½ D: Bill Cosby. Likable in-concert film, featuring Cosby on the subjects of child rearing, human nature, family life. Pleasant but hardly "an event." [PG]▼●

Billie (1965) **C-87m.** **½ D: Don Weis. Patty Duke, Warren Berlinger, Jim Backus, Jane Greer, Billy DeWolfe, Charles Lane, Dick Sargent. Airy comedy of tomboyish Duke and her athletic aspirations. Backus and Greer are her perplexed parents, Berlinger her boyfriend. Duke sings, runs, prances. Techniscope. ▼●

Billion Dollar Brain (1967-British) **C-111m.** *** D: Ken Russell. Michael Caine, Karl Malden, Ed Begley, Oscar Homolka, Françoise Dorleac. Third in series that began with THE IPCRESS FILE finds Harry Palmer (Caine) again up to his neck in exciting espionage, this time in Scandinavia. Based on Len Deighton's novel. Followed thirty years later by a pair of cable TV sequels. Panavision.

Billion Dollar Hobo, The (1978) **C-96m.** *½ D: Stuart E. McGowan. Tim Conway, Will Geer, Eric Weston, Sydney Lassick, John Myhers, Frank Sivero. Dreary comedy about bumbling Conway becoming a hobo to qualify for inheritance. [G]▼

Bill of Divorcement, A (1932) **69m.** *** D: George Cukor. John Barrymore, Katharine Hepburn, Billie Burke, David Manners, Henry Stephenson. Barrymore gives sensitive performance as man released from mental institution who returns to wife Burke and gets to know his daughter for the first time. Dated but worth seeing; notable as Hepburn's screen debut. Originally released at 75m. Remade in 1940.▼●

Bill of Divorcement, A (1940) **74m.** **½ D: John Farrow. Maureen O'Hara, Adolphe Menjou, Fay Bainter, Herbert Marshall, Dame May Whitty, C. Aubrey Smith, Patric Knowles. Adequate remake with Menjou as mentally ill man who suddenly regains his sanity and returns home, with resulting dramatic fireworks. Scripted by Dalton Trumbo. Retitled NEVER TO LOVE.

Billy Bathgate (1991) **C-106m.** **½ D: Robert Benton. Dustin Hoffman, Nicole Kidman, Loren Dean, Bruce Willis, Steven Hill, Steve Buscemi, Billy Jaye, John Costelloe, Tim Jerome, Stanley Tucci, Mike Starr, Katharine Houghton, Rachel York, Moira Kelly. Absorbing, exceptionally good-looking adaptation of E. L. Doctorow's fanciful novel about young man who hooks up with gangster Dutch Schultz in the waning days of his crime career in the 1930s. Hoffman's commanding performance makes this flawed film worth watching, though the story's momentum erodes toward the end. Photographed by Nestor Almendros, with remarkable production design by Patrizia von Brandenstein. Screenplay by Tom Stoppard. [R]▼●

Billy Budd (1962-U.S.-British) **122m.** ***½ D: Peter Ustinov. Robert Ryan, Peter Ustinov, Melvyn Douglas, Terence Stamp, Paul Rogers, David McCallum. Melville's classic good vs. evil novella set in British Navy, 1797. Naive, incorruptible seaman is court-martialed for murder of sadistic master-at-arms. Film deals simply with heavier issues of morality. Sterling performances by all. Ustinov also produced and coscripted with DeWitt Bodeen. Stamp's film debut. CinemaScope.▼

Billy Galvin (1986) **C-95m.** **½ D: John Gray. Karl Malden, Lenny Von Dohlen, Joyce Van Patten, Toni Kalem, Keith Szarabajka, Alan North, Paul Guilfoyle, Barton Heyman. Well-meaning, fairly effective meat-and-potatos drama about title character (Von Dohlen), who wants to be a construction worker like his old man (Malden), a tough, obstinate codger who does everything to discourage him. Not without its share of moments, but also a bit too obvious. Good performances. An *American Playhouse* presentation. [PG]▼

Billy in the Lowlands (1979) **C-88m.** *** D: Jan Egleson. Henry Tomaszewski, Paul Benedict, David Morton, David Clennon, Ernie Loew. Diverting tale of young, working class Tomaszewski struggling for an identity, breaking out of jail to meet his estranged father. Filmed independently, in Boston; followed by thematically similar THE DARK END OF THE STREET.

Billy Jack (1971) **C-114m.** *½ D: T. C. Frank (Tom Laughlin). Tom Laughlin, Delores Taylor, Clark Howat, Kenneth Tobey, Bert Freed, Julie Webb. Half-breed karate expert protects a free school imperiled by reactionary townspeople in this grass-roots hit.

Its politics are highly questionable, and its "message" of peace ridiculous, considering the amount of violence in the film. Memorable title sequence depicting slaughter of wild mustangs introduced hit song "One Tin Soldier" by Coven. Preceded by BORN LOSERS; followed by THE TRIAL OF BILLY JACK and BILLY JACK GOES TO WASHINGTON. [PG]▼●◗

Billy Jack Goes to Washington (1977) **C-155m.** ** D: Tom Laughlin. Tom Laughlin, Delores Taylor, Sam Wanamaker, Lucie Arnaz, E. G. Marshall, Pat O'Brien. Contrived update of MR. SMITH GOES TO WASHINGTON, with writer-director-star Laughlin, a supposed "everyman," fighting big-time corruption in the Senate. Basic story is still good, but it goes on forever. Panavision.▼

Billy Liar (1963-British) **98m.** ***½ D: John Schlesinger. Tom Courtenay, Julie Christie, Wilfred Pickles, Mona Washbourne, Ethel Griffies, Finlay Currie, Leonard Rossiter. Cast excels in story of ambitious but lazy young man caught in dull job routine who escapes into fantasy world, offering some poignant vignettes of middleclass life. Based on Keith Waterhouse novel and play; scripted by Waterhouse and Willis Hall (who also cowrote stage version). CinemaScope.▼

Billy Madison (1995) **C-89m.** *½ D: Tamra Davis. Adam Sandler, Darren McGavin, Bridgette Wilson, Bradley Whitford, Josh Mostel, Norm Macdonald, Mark Beltzman, Larry Hankin, Theresa Merritt. Another comic celebration of infantilism and crudity, as spoiled rich kid Sandler must repeat grades 1–12 in order to take over his millionaire father's business. A little of this goes a long way. Sandler (who can be funny and endearing when he wants to be) also cowrote the script. His *Saturday Night Live* castmate Chris Farley and Steve Buscemi appear unbilled. [PG-13]▼●◗

Billy Rose's Diamond Horseshoe SEE: **Diamond Horseshoe**

Billy Rose's Jumbo (1962) **C-125m.** *** D: Charles Walters. Doris Day, Stephen Boyd, Jimmy Durante, Martha Raye, Dean Jagger. OK circus picture, at best during Rodgers and Hart songs, well-staged by Busby Berkeley. Durante (who had starred in the 1935 Broadway production) and Raye are marvelous. Songs include "The Most Beautiful Girl in the World," "My Romance," "This Can't Be Love." Aka JUMBO. Panavision. ▼●

Billy's Hollywood Screen Kiss (1998) **C-92m.** **½ D: Tommy O'Haver. Sean P. Hayes, Brad Rowe, Richard Ganoung, Meredith Scott Lynn, Paul Bartel, Armando Valdes-Kennedy, Annabelle Gurwitch, Holly Woodlawn. Unemployed L.A. photographer Billy (Hayes) decides to re-create a series of classic movie kisses from Hollywood's golden age, utilizing drag queens and other gay pals. He immediately gets sidetracked upon meeting gorgeous Gabriel (Rowe). Flashy low-budget effort that manages to be both humorous and sensitive, though the writer-director isn't kidding when he calls it "A Tom O'Haver Trifle." He says his inspiration came from the ambiguity of the Clift–de Havilland romance in THE HEIRESS! Panavision. [R]▼●◗

Billy the Kid (1930) **90m.** **½ D: King Vidor. Johnny Mack Brown, Wallace Beery, Kay Johnson, Karl Dane, Roscoe Ates. Realistic early talkie Western with marshal Beery trying to capture outlaw Brown; some performances seem badly dated today. Retitled: THE HIGHWAYMAN RIDES. Originally shown in early Realife 70 mm. widescreen process.

Billy the Kid (1941) **C-95m.** **½ D: David Miller. Robert Taylor, Brian Donlevy, Ian Hunter, Mary Howard, Gene Lockhart, Lon Chaney, Jr. Cast looks uncomfortable in remake of 1930 Western, but plot is sturdy enough for OK viewing, with Taylor in title role and Donlevy as marshal.▼

Billy the Kid vs. Dracula (1966) **C-74m.** ** D: William Beaudine. Chuck Courtney, John Carradine, Melinda Plowman, Virginia Christine, Walter Janovitz, Bing Russell, Olive Carey, Harry Carey, Jr. Famed outlaw decides it's time to get married—but doesn't realize that his bride's "uncle" is a vampire. Campy nonsense.▼

Billy Two Hats (1974) **C-99m.** **½ D: Ted Kotcheff. Gregory Peck, Desi Arnaz, Jr., Jack Warden, Sian Barbara Allen, David Huddleston. Offbeat Western filmed in Israel, about a middle-aged Scot and a young half-Indian pursued by the law for bank robbery. Peck is appealing in unusual character role. Retitled THE LADY AND THE OUTLAW. [PG]▼

Biloxi Blues (1988) **C-106m.** *** D: Mike Nichols. Matthew Broderick, Christopher Walken, Matt Mulhern, Corey Parker, Casey Siemaszko, Markus Flanagan, Michael Dolan, Penelope Ann Miller, Park Overall. The further adventures of Eugene Jerome, Neil Simon's youthful alter ego introduced in BRIGHTON BEACH MEMOIRS. Here, WW2 is winding down, and Eugene (Broderick) forsakes Brooklyn for Biloxi, Miss., and ten grueling weeks of army basic training, where he comes that much closer to manhood. Quite wonderful, in its best moments. Followed by TV movie BROADWAY BOUND. Super 35. [PG-13] ▼●

Bingo (1991) **C-87m.** *½ D: Matthew Robbins. Cindy Williams, David Rasche, Robert J. Steinmiller, Jr., David French, Kurt Fuller, Joe Guzaldo, Glenn Shadix. Basic update of the "boy wants a dog, boy can't have a dog, boy finds a dog who has

run away from the circus, boy hides the dog from his parents, boy must move out of town and leave the dog behind, boy finds dog again" genre. Kids might like it, but it's a real bow-wow. [PG]▼●
Bingo Long Traveling All-Stars & Motor Kings, The (1976) **C-110m.** *** D: John Badham. Billy Dee Williams, James Earl Jones, Richard Pryor, Ted Ross, DeWayne Jessie, Stan Shaw. Bright, original comedy about baseball player Williams trying to buck owners of Negro National League in 1939 by starting his own razzle-dazzle team. Williams' character is modeled after Satchel Paige, while Jones' is based on Josh Gibson. [PG]▼●
Bio-Dome (1996) **C-95m.** BOMB D: Jason Bloom. Pauly Shore, Stephen Baldwin, William Atherton, Joey (Lauren) Adams, Teresa Hill, Henry Gibson, Kevin West, Dara Tomanovich, Denise Dowse, Kylie Minogue, Patricia Hearst, Roger Clinton, Rose McGowan. Two layabouts from Tucson are sealed up for a year inside a Biosphere-like experimental habitat and drive the scientists in charge bonkers. A good comedy premise is trashed through crude writing, inept plotting, and having as heroes two worthless jerks we're supposed to find lovable. [PG-13]▼●
Biography of a Bachelor Girl (1935) **82m.** *½ D: Edward Griffith. Ann Harding, Robert Montgomery, Edward Everett Horton, Edward Arnold, Una Merkel. A notorious woman is persuaded to write her memoirs by an aggressive magazine editor—who falls in love with her in spite of the fact that she represents everything he loathes. Dreary, endlessly talky adaptation of S. N. Behrman play.
Birch Interval (1977) **C-104m.** *** D: Delbert Mann. Eddie Albert, Rip Torn, Ann Wedgeworth, Susan McClung, Brian Part. Eleven-year-old girl, sent to live with relatives in Amish country, finds out about life, love, suffering and compassion. Beautiful, sensitive film. [PG]▼
Bird (1988) **C-160m.** **½ D: Clint Eastwood. Forest Whitaker, Diane Venora, Michael Zelniker, Samuel E. Wright, Keith David, Michael McGuire, James Handy. Heartfelt but overlong biography of legendary saxophonist Charlie Parker, who revolutionized jazz music in the 1940s. While there's much music on hand, this is mostly the story of one man's drug addiction and self-destructive life. Fails to balance its story with any explanation of Parker's influence in the world of music. Excellent and believable performances help. Parker plays on the soundtrack, though all accompanying music was rerecorded in 1988. (The film won an Oscar for sound recording.) [R]▼●
birdcage, The (1996) **C-119m.** **½ D: Mike Nichols. Robin Williams, Gene Hackman, Nathan Lane, Dianne Wiest, Hank Azaria, Christine Baranski, Dan Futterman, Calista Flockhart, Tom McGowan, Grant Heslov, Kirby Mitchell. Polished if obvious remake of LA CAGE AUX FOLLES will please anyone who hasn't seen or doesn't remember the original: Williams is fairly subdued as a South Beach, Miami, nightclub owner who's forced to ask his high-strung, drag-queen performer/partner (Lane) to hide away while his son brings his prospective in-laws—an ultra-conservative couple—to dinner. Screenplay by Elaine May, who added fresh lines to the foolproof blueprint of the original. [R]▼●◗
Birdman of Alcatraz (1962) **143m.** *** D: John Frankenheimer. Burt Lancaster, Karl Malden, Thelma Ritter, Betty Field, Neville Brand, Edmond O'Brien, Hugh Marlowe, Telly Savalas. Pensive study of prisoner Robert Stroud who during his many years in jail became a world-renowned bird authority. Film becomes static despite imaginative sidelights to enlarge scope of action. 148m. version used for overseas release now turning up here.▼●
Bird of Paradise (1932) **80m.** ** D: King Vidor. Joel McCrea, Dolores Del Rio, John Halliday, Skeets Gallagher, Lon Chaney, Jr. Exotic but empty South Seas romance with McCrea as adventurer who falls in love with native-girl Del Rio. Handsome but unmoving; remade in 1951.▼
Bird of Paradise (1951) **C-100m.** ** D: Delmer Daves. Louis Jourdan, Debra Paget, Jeff Chandler, Everett Sloane. Jourdan's marriage to South Sea isle chief's daughter causes native uprising in grandly filmed but vapid tale. Remake of 1932 film.
Bird of Prey (1996-U.S.-Bulgarian) **C-101m.** BOMB D: Temistocles Lopez. Jennifer Tilly, Boyan Milushev, Richard Chamberlain, Lenny Von Dohlen, Robert Carradine, Lesley Ann Warren. Preposterous thriller about a Bulgarian dissenter and an American photojournalist who unite to battle a slimy businessman. Tilly, playing Chamberlain's daughter (and Milushev's love interest), seems to be in another movie. It took four writers to concoct this clinker, which barely earned a theatrical release. [R]▼
Bird on a Wire (1990) **C-110m.** ** D: John Badham. Mel Gibson, Goldie Hawn, David Carradine, Bill Duke, Stephen Tobolowsky, Joan Severance, Jeff Corey. Star power is about all this lame action-comedy has going for it, as drug-running murderers force Mel, who's been hiding in the F.B.I. witness relocation program, and Goldie, his onetime sweetheart, to take it on the lam. Script on a shoestring. Super 35. [PG-13]▼●◗
Birds, The (1963) **C-120m.** ***½ D: Alfred Hitchcock. Rod Taylor, Tippi Hedren, Jessica Tandy, Suzanne Pleshette, Veronica Cartwright, Ethel Griffies, Charles

McGraw, Joe Mantell, Elizabeth Wilson, Doodles Weaver, Richard Deacon, Suzanne Cupito (Morgan Brittany). Hitchcock's classic about a woman (Hedren) and mass bird attacks that follow her around isolated coastal California community. Not for the squeamish; a delight for those who are game. Hold on to something and watch. Script by Evan Hunter, loosely based on Daphne du Maurier's story. Followed by a terrible TV sequel in 1994. ▼●◗

Birds and the Bees, The (1956) **C-94m.** ** D: Norman Taurog. George Gobel, Mitzi Gaynor, David Niven, Reginald Gardiner, Fred Clark, Hans Conried. Bland remake of THE LADY EVE about rich playboy who breaks off romance with cardshark girlfriend, but later decides he still loves her. Screenplay by Sidney Sheldon (and Preston Sturges). VistaVision. ▼

Birds Do It (1966) **C-95m.** ** D: Andrew Marton. Soupy Sales, Tab Hunter, Arthur O'Connell, Edward Andrews, Beverly Adams, Frank Nastasi. Soupy's first starring vehicle has him under the spell of serum that enables him to fly. Fairly entertaining for kids.

Birds, The Bees and the Italians, The (1966-Italian-French) **115m.** *** D: Pietro Germi. Virna Lisi, Gastone Moschin, Nora Ricci, Alberto Lionello, Franco Fabrizi. Very funny bedroom farce chronicling the sexual and romantic exploits of various residents in a small Italian town.

Bird With the Crystal Plumage, The (1969-Italian-West German) **C-98m.** **½ D: Dario Argento. Tony Musante, Suzy Kendall, Eva Renzi, Enrico Maria Salerno, Mario Adorf, Renato Romano, Umberto Rano, Werner Peters. American writer living in Rome witnesses attempted murder in gallery; he and his mistress become involved in case. Uneven; best viewed on large screen. Reissued as THE PHANTOM OF TERROR. Cromoscope. [PG]▼●◗

Birdy (1984) **C-120m.** ***½ D: Alan Parker. Matthew Modine, Nicolas Cage, John Harkins, Sandy Baron, Karen Young, Bruno Kirby. Cage, reunited with schizophrenically silent Modine in an army hospital, flashes back to their adolescence in working-class Philadelphia and on Modine's lifelong desire to be a bird. William Wharton's allegorical novel, updated from WW2 to Vietnam, makes a surprisingly workable movie despite a weak "gag" ending. Terrific performances, with Modine a standout in a tricky, physically demanding role. Screenplay by Sandy Kroopf and Jack Behr. [R]▼●◗

Birgit Haas Must Be Killed (1981-French) **C-105m.** **½ D: Laurent Heynemann. Philippe Noiret, Jean Rochefort, Lisa Kreuzer, Bernard Le Coq. Unscrupulous police officer Noiret dupes innocent Rochefort into romancing former left-wing terrorist Kreuzer, intending to have her assassinated and hang the blame on Rochefort! Intriguing idea never really catches fire, despite honorable efforts; might have worked better if the two male stars had switched roles.▼

Birthday Party, The (1968-British) **C-127m.** *** D: William Friedkin. Robert Shaw, Patrick Magee, Dandy Nichols, Sydney Tafler, Moultrie Kelsall, Helen Fraser. Uncinematic film version of Harold Pinter's play about boarding house and its mysterious tenant (Shaw) is helped by good acting and playwright's usual superior dialogue. [G]

Birth of a Nation, The (1915) **186m.** **** D: D. W. Griffith. Lillian Gish, Mae Marsh, Henry B. Walthall, Miriam Cooper, Robert Harron, Wallace Reid, Joseph Henabery. The landmark of American motion pictures. Griffith's epic story of two families during Civil War and Reconstruction is still fascinating. Sometimes the drama survives intact; other times, one must watch in a more historical perspective. Griffith's portrayal of Ku Klux Klan in heroic role has kept this film a center of controversy to the present day. Running time varies from print to print. ▼●◗

Birth of the Blues (1941) **85m.** *** D: Victor Schertzinger. Bing Crosby, Brian Donlevy, Carolyn Lee, Eddie (Rochester) Anderson, Mary Martin. Fiction about Crosby organizing jazz band in New Orleans has great music like "St. Louis Blues," "St. James Infirmary," "Melancholy Baby" and title tune to uplift fair story.▼

Biscuit Eater, The (1940) **83m.** *** D: Stuart Heisler. Billy Lee, Cordell Hickman, Helene Millard, Richard Lane, Lester Matthews. Warm, winning adaptation of James Street story about two boys—one white, one black—who take unwanted dog from litter and try to turn him into champion bird dog. A B-picture that was regarded as the sleeper of the year. Remade in 1972.

Biscuit Eater, The (1972) **C-90m.** **½ D: Vincent McEveety. Earl Holliman, Lew Ayres, Godfrey Cambridge, Patricia Crowley, Beah Richards, Johnny Whitaker, George Spell. Wholesome, uninspired Disney remake with Whitaker and Spell as the young friends who devote themselves to training a champion bird dog. [G]

Bishop Misbehaves, The (1935) **86m.** **½ D: E. A. Dupont. Edmund Gwenn, Maureen O'Sullivan, Norman Foster, Lucile Watson, Reginald Owen, Dudley Digges, Lillian Bond, Melville Cooper. Tongue-in-cheek mystery with Gwenn (in his first American film) as an English Bishop with a taste for detective stories who gets mixed up in a real jewel heist. Enjoyable but slow paced.

Bishop Murder Case (1930) **91m.** ** D: Nick Grinde. Basil Rathbone, Leila Hyams, Roland Young, George T. Marion, Alec

B. Francis, Zelda Sears, Bodil Rosing, Carroll Nye, Delmer Daves. Philo Vance investigates a crafty killer whose murders are patterned after Mother Goose nursery rhymes. Rathbone is disappointingly ordinary as Vance, and while the story itself is clever, it moves at a snail's pace.

Bishop's Wife, The (1947) **108m.** *** D: Henry Koster. Cary Grant, Loretta Young, David Niven, Monty Woolley, James Gleason, Gladys Cooper, Elsa Lanchester. Christmas fantasy of suave angel (Grant) coming to earth to help Bishop Niven and wife Young raise money for new church. Engaging performances by all—and fun to see children from IT'S A WONDERFUL LIFE, Karolyn Grimes and Bobby Anderson, appearing together. Also shown in computer-colored version. Remade as THE PREACHER'S WIFE.▼●◗

Bitch, The (1979-British) **C-93m.** BOMB D: Gerry O'Hara. Joan Collins, Kenneth Haigh, Michael Coby, Ian Hendry, Carolyn Seymour, Sue Lloyd, John Ratzenberger. Weak entry in the Bimbo Chic genre, a follow-up to THE STUD, based on a book by Joan's sister, Jackie Collins. Joan gets involved in everything from smuggling to fixed horse racing in attempts to save her failing London disco, but who cares? And, yes, there is a title song. [R]▼

Bite the Bullet (1975) **C-131m.** **** D: Richard Brooks. Gene Hackman, Candice Bergen, James Coburn, Ben Johnson, Ian Bannen, Jan-Michael Vincent, Robert Donner, Paul Stewart, Dabney Coleman, Sally Kirkland. Grand adventure in the classic tradition. Disparate types compete in a grueling, 600-mile horse race at the turn of the century; the finalists develop a grudging—and growing—respect for each other. Script by director Brooks. Beautifully filmed on magnificent locations by Harry Stradling, Jr., in Panavision. [PG]▼●

Bitter Creek (1954) **74m.** *½ D: Thomas Carr. Bill Elliott, Carleton Young, Beverly Garland, Claude Akins, Jim Hayward. Tame happenings as Elliott seeks revenge for his brother's untimely death in the old West.

Bitter Moon (1992-French-British) **C-139m.** **½ D: Roman Polanski. Peter Coyote, Emmanuelle Seigner, Hugh Grant, Kristin Scott Thomas, Victor Banerjee, Sophie Patel. Deliciously trashy tale of wealthy, wheelchair-bound jerk Coyote, a failed American writer who's been living in Paris with voluptuous French wife Seigner. Once they were ecstatically in love, but their relationship has taken on a bizarre, sadistic bent; they go on an ocean voyage, and beguile a very proper British couple (Grant, Scott Thomas). Often overwrought, with laughable dialogue and not-to-be-believed sex scenes. A guilty pleasure, to be sure. Polanski also produced and coscripted. Stockard Channing appears unbilled. [R]▼●

Bitter Rice (1948-Italian) **107m.** *** D: Giuseppe De Santis. Silvana Mangano, Vittorio Gassman, Raf Vallone, Doris Dowling, Lia Corelli. Effective portrayal of the dreary, backbreaking existence of women toiling in the Po Valley rice fields, exploited by the rice growers and their go-betweens. The seductive Mangano, as a worker who betrays her comrades, became an international star.▼

Bitter Sweet (1933-British) **93m.** *** D: Herbert Wilcox. Anna Neagle, Fernand Graavey (Gravet), Miles Mander, Clifford Heatherley, Esme Percy, Ivy St. Helier, Pat Paterson, Kay Hammond. Noel Coward's first major work as a composer, filmed by the team of Wilcox-Neagle. Sentimental operetta creaks a bit, but the story of young love in 1880 Vienna is a must for musical theater buffs. Lovely score includes "If Love Were All" and "I'll See You Again." St. Helier vividly recreates her London stage role of Manon la Crevette, written for her by Coward. Remade in 1940.▼

Bitter Sweet (1940) **C-92m.** *** D: W.S. Van Dyke II. Jeanette MacDonald, Nelson Eddy, George Sanders, Felix Bressart, Lynne Carver, Ian Hunter, Sig Ruman. Ignore plot, enjoy Noel Coward's songs in lavishly filmed operetta. Wonderful Herman Bing provides funniest scene as shopkeeper who hires Nelson and Jeanette to give his daughter music lessons.▼

Bittersweet Love (1976) **C-92m.** *½ D: David Miller. Lana Turner, Robert Lansing, Celeste Holm, Robert Alda, Scott Hylands, Meredith Baxter Birney. Excellent cast wasted on improbable story of young married couple (expecting a baby) suddenly discovering they are half-brother and sister. Termination of pregnancy and marriage are then talked to death. [PG]▼

Bitter Tea of General Yen, The (1933) **89m.** ***½ D: Frank Capra. Barbara Stanwyck, Nils Asther, Gavin Gordon, Toshia Mori, Richard Loo, Lucien Littlefield, Clara Blandick, Walter Connolly. May seem antiquated to modern audiences, but Capra's sensuous story of American woman's strange fascination with a Chinese warlord is still dazzling. A moody, beautifully atmospheric, sensitively performed film.▼

Bitter Tears of Petra Von Kant, The (1973-German) **C-119m.** ** D: Rainer Werner Fassbinder. Margit Carstensen, Hanna Schygulla, Irm Hermann, Eva Mattes, Karin Schaake, Gisela Fackelday. Wealthy lesbian fashion designer Petra Von Kant (Carstensen) worries over habits of inconsistent lover Schygulla and unmercifully bosses secretary Hermann. The action is limited to Petra's apartment, and the pace is annoyingly slow. Based on a Fassbinder play; overrated by some.▼

Bitter Vengeance (1994) **C-90m.** ** D: Stuart Cooper. Virginia Madsen, Bruce

Greenwood, Kristen Hocking, Eddie Velez, Gordon Jump, Carlos Gomez, Tim Russ. Disappointing thriller about a self-pitying bank security guard (Greenwood) who takes out his anger on his supportive wife (Madsen). He eventually begins cheating on her, and concocts a robbery scheme in which his mate will take the fall. Holds your interest for a while, but eventually becomes much too implausible. [R]▼

Bitter Victory (1957-French) **82m.** *** D: Nicholas Ray. Richard Burton, Curt Jurgens, Ruth Roman, Raymond Pellegrin, Anthony Bushell, Christopher Lee. Strong WW2 story with Jurgens as unfit commander who receives undeserved citation for mission against Rommel's desert headquarters; Roman is his wife who's had prior affair with officer Burton. 103m. versions now in circulation are from British release of this film. CinemaScope.

Bix: An Interpretation of a Legend (1990-Italian) **C-100m.** **½ D: Pupi Avati. Bryant Weeks, Emile Levisetti, Sally Groth, Mark Collver, Ray Edelstein, Julia Ewing, Barbara Wilder, Romano Luccio Orzari. Fragmented bio of 1920s jazz legend Bix Beiderbecke, who skyrocketed to fame—and burned out just as fast. Dramatically uneven, but enhanced by loving recreation of the period (using many authentic locations in and around Bix's home town of Davenport, Iowa) and great reproductions of his music by Bob Wilber and some first-class musicians. Originally 20m. longer.▼

Black Abbot, The (1963-German) **95m.** *½ D: F. J. Gottlieb. Joachim Berger (Fuchsberger), Dieter Borsche, Grit Bottcher, Eva Ingeborg Scholtz, Werner Peters, Klaus Kinski. Talky, boring Edgar Wallace yarn about mysterious goings-on at a country mansion, where various greedy characters conspire to purloin some hidden treasure.▼

Black and White (2000) **C-100m.** *** D: James Toback. Bijou Phillips, Brooke Shields, Robert Downey, Jr., Allan Houston, Ben Stiller, Claudia Schiffer, Stacy Edwards, Gaby Hoffmann, Elijah Wood, Scott Caan, Jared Leto, Marla Maples, Method Man, Power, Raekwon, Joe Pantoliano, James Toback, Mike Tyson. Edgy N.Y.C. slice-of-life about social and sexual interaction between blacks and whites of various backgrounds, including a white teen hipster (Phillips) who hangs out in Harlem with an ambitious rap artist, a basketball player (real-life hoop star Houston) who's manipulated by his beautiful white girlfriend (Schiffer) and a documentary filmmaker (Shields) who's shooting a film on why white kids are so fascinated by hip-hop culture. Crammed with interesting ideas and observations. Toback also scripted. Super 35. [R]▼◗

Black and White in Color (1977-French-African) **C-90m.** ***½ D: Jean-Jacques Annaud. Jean Carmet, Jacques Dufilho, Catherine Rouvel, Jacques Spiesser, Dora Doll. Unusual and witty story of self-satisfied Frenchmen at remote African trading post who are fired by sudden patriotism at outbreak of WW1, and decide to attack nearby German fort. Oscar winner as Best Foreign Film. [PG]▼●

Black Angel (1946) **80m.** *** D: Roy William Neill. Dan Duryea, June Vincent, Peter Lorre, Broderick Crawford, Wallace Ford. First-rate whodunit (by Cornell Woolrich) of Vincent trying to clear husband of charge that he murdered Duryea's wife. Imaginative film will have you glued to the screen all the way.▼

Black Arrow, The (1948) **76m.** *** D: Gordon Douglas. Louis Hayward, Janet Blair, George Macready, Edgar Buchanan, Paul Cavanagh. Superior swashbuckler with dashing knight Hayward, lovely heroine Blair, and villain Macready. Truly exciting finale with hero vs. villain in jousting tournament. Based on a Robert Louis Stevenson novel. Remade for TV in 1985.▼

Black Bart (1948) **C-80m.** **½ D: George Sherman. Yvonne De Carlo, Dan Duryea, Jeffrey Lynn, Percy Kilbride. Enticing De Carlo steps between outlaws Duryea and Lynn, foiling their attempt to overthrow Wells Fargo company.

Blackbeard's Ghost (1968) **C-107m.** *** D: Robert Stevenson. Peter Ustinov, Dean Jones, Suzanne Pleshette, Elsa Lanchester, Joby Baker, Elliott Reid, Richard Deacon. Jones conjures up title character (Ustinov) who helps protect his descendants' home from being taken over by racketeers who want to make it a casino. Engaging slapstick comedy from Disney.▼●

Blackbeard, the Pirate (1952) **C-99m.** ** D: Raoul Walsh. Robert Newton, Linda Darnell, William Bendix, Keith Andes, Richard Egan, Irene Ryan. Newton is rambunctious as 17th-century buccaneer, with lovely Darnell his captive; fun for a while, but Newton's hamming soon grows tiresome.▼●

Black Beauty (1946) **74m.** **½ D: Max Nosseck. Mona Freeman, Richard Denning, Evelyn Ankers, Terry Kilburn, Arthur Space, J. M. Kerrigan. Second sound version of Anna Sewell's tale of little girl and her love for her horse is decent if unspectacular, with pleasing Dimitri Tiomkin score. Remade in 1971 and 1994.▼

Black Beauty (1971-British) **C-106m.** **½ D: James Hill. Mark Lester, Walter Slezak, Peter Lee Lawrence, Ursula Glas. The story of a horse who passes from owner to owner; fails to capture the qualities that make Anna Sewell's novel a classic, but it's not bad. [G]▼●

Black Beauty (1994) **C-85m.** *** D: Caroline Thompson. Sean Bean, David Thewlis, Jim Carter, Peter Davison, Alun Armstrong, John McEnery, Eleanor Bron, Peter Cook, Andrew Knott, voice of Alan Cumming.

Handsome remake of the Anna Sewell family classic about a horse's trials and tribulations as it passes from one owner to another in 19th-century England, experiencing everything from benevolent guardianship to ignorant abuse. Narrated, quite engagingly, by the horse itself. Evocative score by Danny Elfman. Screenwriter Thompson's directing debut. Made in England. [G]▼●◗

Black Belly of the Tarantula (1972-Italian) **C-88m.** *½ D: Paolo Cavara. Giancarlo Giannini, Stefania Sandrelli, Barbara Bouchet. Folks are being murdered in mysterious ways at health and beauty salon; none too exciting. Cromoscope. [R]

Black Belt Jones (1974) **C-87m.** **½ D: Robert Clouse. Jim Kelly, Gloria Hendry, Scatman Crothers, Alan Weeks, Nate Esformes. Black-oriented kung-fu mayhem from the team that made ENTER THE DRAGON. Kelly battles the Mafia to save his school of self-defense in Watts area of L.A. No gore, but lots of action and comedy. [R]▼

Black Bird, The (1975) **C-98m.** BOMB D: David Giler. George Segal, Stephane Audran, Lionel Stander, Lee Patrick, Elisha Cook Jr., Felix Silla, Signe Hasso. Horrendously bad, unfunny takeoff on THE MALTESE FALCON, with Segal as Sam Spade, Jr., not saved by the presence of Patrick and Cook from the '41 cast. [PG]▼

Blackboard Jungle (1955) **101m.** ***½ D: Richard Brooks. Glenn Ford, Anne Francis, Vic Morrow, Louis Calhern, Sidney Poitier, Richard Kiley, Warner Anderson, Margaret Hayes, Emile Meyer, John Hoyt, Rafael Campos, Paul Mazursky. Excellent adaptation of Evan Hunter's novel (scripted by the director) of a teacher's harrowing experiences in N.Y.C. school system. Poitier memorable as a troubled youth. Hard-hitting entertainment. This was the first film to feature rock music—Bill Haley's "Rock Around the Clock" is played over the opening credits. Look for a young Jamie Farr (billed as Jameel Farah). Also shown in computer-colored version.▼●

Black Book, The SEE: **Reign of Terror**

Black Bounty Killer, The SEE: **Boss Nigger**

Black Caesar (1973) **C-96m.** **½ D: Larry Cohen. Fred Williamson, Art Lund, Julius W. Harris, Gloria Hendry, D'Urville Martin. Better-than-average gangster film follows rise to the top of shrewd, bloodthirsty black baddie. Sequel: HELL UP IN HARLEM. [R]▼●

Black Camel, The (1931) **71m.** **½ D: Hamilton MacFadden. Warner Oland, Sally Eilers, Bela Lugosi, Dorothy Revier, Victor Varconi, Robert Young, Dwight Frye, Marjorie White, C. Henry Gordon, Mary Gordon. Interesting early-talkie *Charlie Chan* whodunit, with Oland probing the murders of an actress and a beachcomber on his home turf of Hawaii, with cute scenes of his domestic life with ten kids. Picturesque locations and exceptional cast highlight this entry, based on Earl Derr Biggers novel.

Black Castle, The (1952) **81m.** ** D: Nathan Juran. Richard Greene, Boris Karloff, Stephen McNally, Paula Corday, Lon Chaney, Jr., John Hoyt. Uninspired gothic melodrama has Greene investigating disappearance of two friends who were guests of sinister Austrian count (McNally). Karloff reduced to colorless supporting role.▼

Black Cat, The (1934) **65m.** ***½ D: Edgar G. Ulmer. Boris Karloff, Bela Lugosi, David Manners, Jacqueline Wells (Julie Bishop), Lucille Lund, Henry Armetta, Harry Cording. Polished horror film with bizarre sets, even more bizarre plot. Confrontation of architect/devil-worshiper Karloff and doctor Lugosi is still fascinating. The first of Boris and Bela's many teamings. Look fast for John Carradine as an organist at Satanic Mass. Film bears absolutely no resemblance to eponymous Edgar Allan Poe tale.▼●

Black Cat, The (1941) **70m.** **½ D: Albert S. Rogell. Basil Rathbone, Hugh Herbert, Broderick Crawford, Bela Lugosi, Gale Sondergaard, Anne Gwynne, Gladys Cooper. Herbert and Crawford provide laughs, the others provide chills, in lively comedy-mystery not to be confused with earlier horror film. Look for Alan Ladd in a small role. Atmospheric photography by Stanley Cortez.▼

Black Cat, White Cat (1998-Yugoslavian-French-German) **C-129m.** *** D: Emir Kusturica. Bajram Severdzan (Doctor Kolja), Florijan Ajdini, Jas'ar Destani, Adnan Bekir, Zabit Mehmedovski, Sabri Sulejmani. Dizzying farce about gypsy families who live on the Danube and a bitter rivalry between two elders whose offspring cause them no end of headaches. Kusturica (who also coscripted) builds to a crescendo of slapstick action in this exuberant film that reminds us how much we all have in common, regardless of nationality. [R]▼

Black Cauldron, The (1985) **C-80m.** **½ D: Ted Berman, Richard Rich. Voices of Grant Bardsley, Susan Sheridan, Freddie Jones, John Byner, John Hurt. Disney's expensive, ambitious animated feature is a pretty good but unmemorable sword-and-sorcery tale about a young boy who must find powerful black cauldron before it falls into the hands of evil Horned King. Good storytelling for kids, with impressive effects animation for buffs. Supporting characters Gurgi (a good guy) and Creeper (a baddie) have all the best moments. Super Technirama 70. [PG]▼●

Black Christmas (1975-Canadian) **C-98m.** **½ D: Bob Clark. Olivia Hussey, Keir Dullea, Margot Kidder, John Saxon, Art Hindle, Douglas McGrath, Andrea Martin. Bizarre horror thriller about warped murderer in sorority house on Christmas Eve and two days following. Not bad; Kidder steals it as a nasty, foul-mouthed sorority sister. Aka SILENT NIGHT, EVIL NIGHT and STRANGER IN THE HOUSE. [R]▼●

Black Cross (1960-Polish) **C-175m.** ** D: Aleksander Ford. Urszula Modrzynska, Grazyna Staniszewska, Andrzej Szalawski, Henryk Borowski. Unremarkable account of Teutonic knights raiding Poland; notable only for detailed medieval settings; sterile presentation. Dyaliscope.

Black Dakotas, The (1954) **C-65m.** ** D: Ray Nazarro. Gary Merrill, Wanda Hendrix, John Bromfield, Noah Beery, Jr. Bland oater of greedy men who try to outwit the redskins and incite a war.

Black Devils of Kali, The SEE: **Mystery of the Black Jungle**

Black Dog (1998) **C-88m.** *½ D: Kevin Hooks. Patrick Swayze, Randy Travis, Meat Loaf, Gabriel Casseus, Brian Vincent, Brenda Strong, Stephen Tobolowsky, Charles S. Dutton. An ex-con trucker with a suspended license makes one last run to avoid foreclosure, and his rig turns out to be full of concealed assault weapons that his corrupt boss is planning to sell. There's no dirty dancing for Swayze here but lots of dirty driving. Heavier on crashes than coherency. Super 35. [PG-13]▼●◗

Black Dragons (1942) **61m.** *½ D: William Nigh. Bela Lugosi, Joan Barclay, Clayton Moore, George Pembroke, Robert Frazer. Nazi doctor Lugosi has been altering the faces of some Japanese, to make them pass as Americans. Then topical chiller is now a sleep-inducing bore.▼

Black Eagle (1988) **C-93m.** **½ D: Eric Karson. Sho Kosugi, Jean-Claude Van Damme, Vladimir Skontarovsky, Doran Clark, Bruce French, William H. Bassett. Standard martial arts adventure. Kosugi's the secret-agent hero, Van Damme's the Russian villain, and there's plenty of action. Kosugi's real-life children, Kane and Shane, appear in cameos as his screen character's kids. [R]▼◗

Black Evil SEE: **Demons of the Mind**

Black Eye (1974) **C-98m.** ** D: Jack Arnold. Fred Williamson, Rosemary Forsyth, Richard Anderson, Teresa Graves, Cyril Delevanti. Involved action-mystery has black private detective Williamson investigating murders connected with a dope ring in Venice, Cal. Bret Morrison, radio's "The Shadow," plays a porno moviemaker. Standard fare. [PG]▼

Black Fist (1976) **C-105m.** **½ D: Timothy Galfas, Richard Kaye. Richard Lawson, Philip Michael Thomas, Annazette Chase, Dabney Coleman, Robert Burr. Coleman's gritty performance as a crooked cop elevates this standard blaxploitation drama about tough Lawson, hired by a crime boss as a streetfighter. Aka THE BLACK STREETFIGHTER and HOMEBOY. [R]▼

Black Fox, The (1962) **89m.** ***½ D: Louis Clyde Stoumen. Narrated by Marlene Dietrich. Exceedingly taut, grim documentary tracing the rise and fall of Adolph Hitler, focusing on his use of power during Third Reich. Academy Award winner as Best Documentary Feature.▼

Black Friday (1940) **70m.** **½ D: Arthur Lubin. Boris Karloff, Bela Lugosi, Stanley Ridges, Anne Nagel, Anne Gwynne, Virginia Brissac. Well-made little chiller with Karloff putting gangster's brain into a professor's body. Jekyll-Hyde results are fascinating; Ridges excellent as victim. Lugosi has small, thankless role as gangster.▼

Black Fury (1935) **92m.** *** D: Michael Curtiz. Paul Muni, Karen Morley, William Gargan, Barton MacLane, John Qualen, J. Carrol Naish, Vince Barnett. Hard-hitting Warner Bros. melodrama about union manipulation of coal miners, with Muni as robust "bohunk" who gets in over his head. Realistic, strikingly filmed, if a bit uneven dramatically. Muni's accent makes it tough to understand him at times. Based on a true story.▼

Black Girl (1972) **C-97m.** *** D: Ossie Davis. Brock Peters, Leslie Uggams, Claudia McNeil, Louise Stubbs, Gloria Edwards, Peggy Pettitt, Ruby Dee. One of the best black-oriented films of the 1970s spotlights the complex relationship between the title character (Pettitt), an aspiring dancer, and her emotionally clueless mother (Stubbs). Well acted by the entire cast; scripted by J. E. Franklin, and based on her play. [PG]

Black Gold (1947) **C-92m.** **½ D: Phil Karlson. Anthony Quinn, Katherine DeMille, Elyse Knox, Ducky Louie, Kane Richmond, Moroni Olsen, Raymond Hatton, Thurston Hall, Darryl Hickman. Effective, if sentimental, tale of Indian Quinn who discovers oil on his land and trains a Chinese orphan (Louie) to be the jockey for his beloved thoroughbred. Low-budget, but warmly acted, with excellent use of Cinecolor process. Quinn and DeMille were then husband and wife.▼

Black Gold (1963) **98m.** ** D: Leslie Martinson. Philip Carey, Diane McBain, James Best, Claude Akins, Iron Eyes Cody. Predictable search for oil set in Oklahoma, with standard villain and supposedly ironic outcome.

Black Gunn (1972) **C-98m.** ** D: Robert Hartford-Davis. Jim Brown, Martin Landau, Brenda Sykes, Luciana Paluzzi. Black nightclub owner goes after the Man when his brother is killed. Routine black actioner. [R]▼

Black Hand (1950) **93m.** **½ D: Richard Thorpe. Gene Kelly, J. Carrol Naish, Teresa Celli, Marc Lawrence, Frank Puglia. If you can buy Kelly as an Italian immigrant (circa 1908), you'll probably go along with this naive but entertaining story about a young man's attempt to avenge his father's murder by the infamous—and seemingly unstoppable—Italian crime syndicate known as the Black Hand, in N.Y.C. ▼

Black Hole, The (1979) **C-97m.** **½ D: Gary Nelson. Maximilian Schell, Anthony Perkins, Robert Forster, Joseph Bottoms, Yvette Mimieux, Ernest Borgnine. U.S. expedition finds long-lost madman in space about to explore a "black hole." Disney studios' ambitious sci-fi effort is a throwback to 1957 Saturday matinee fodder, with thin story, cardboard characters. OK on that level—with great special effects—but should have been much better. Technovision. [PG—Disney's first] ▼●◗

Black Horse Canyon (1954) **C-81m.** **½ D: Jesse Hibbs. Joel McCrea, Mari Blanchard, Race Gentry, Murvyn Vye. Diverting, gentle Western about rebellious black stallion and those who recapture him.

Black Ice (1992-Canadian) **C-90m.** ** D: Neill Fearnley. Michael Nouri, Michael Ironside, Joanna Pacula, Mickey Jones, Brent Heale, Arne Olsen, Rick Skene. Following the accidental death of her politician lover, Pacula has philosophical cabbie Nouri drive her from Detroit to Seattle during the winter; they're pursued by murderous Ironside. Good performances, and handsome wintry landscapes, can't overcome a complicated plot—and its unsatisfactory resolution. Unrated video version runs 92m. [R]▼●

Black Jack SEE: **Wild in the Sky**

Blackjack Ketchum, Desperado (1956) **76m.** *½ D: Earl Bellamy. Howard Duff, Victor Jory, Maggie Mahoney, Angela Stevens. Former gunslinger must endure another shoot-out before returning to a peaceful way of life.

Black Knight, The (1954-U.S.-British) **C-85m.** **½ D: Tay Garnett. Alan Ladd, Patricia Medina, Andre Morell, Harry Andrews, Peter Cushing. Ladd lends some bounce to small budgeter about mysterious horseman championing King Arthur's cause in merry old England.

Black Lancers, The SEE: **Charge of the Black Lancers**

Black Legion (1936) **83m.** *** D: Archie Mayo. Humphrey Bogart, Erin O'Brien-Moore, Dick Foran, Ann Sheridan, Joe Sauers (Sawyer), Helen Flint, Dickie Jones, Henry Brandon. Factory worker Bogart, disappointed at losing a promotion to a coworker named "Dombrowski," becomes involved with a Ku Klux Klanish group. Powerful, still-relevant social drama, compactly told.▼

Black Like Me (1964) **107m.** *** D: Carl Lerner. James Whitmore, Roscoe Lee Browne, Lenka Petersen, Sorrell Booke, Will Geer, Al Freeman, Jr., Dan Priest, Raymond St. Jacques. Strong drama based on actual history of reporter who took drugs that allowed him to pass for black so he could experience racial prejudice firsthand. Some aspects of presentation are dated, but themes are still timely.▼●

Black Magic (1944) **67m.** *½ D: Phil Rosen. Sidney Toler, Mantan Moreland, Frances Chan, Jacqueline de Wit, Claudia Dell, Edward Earle, Joseph Crehan. Minor *Charlie Chan* mystery involving phony fortune tellers and murder at a seance. Aka MEETING AT MIDNIGHT.▼●

Black Magic (1949) **105m.** **½ D: Gregory Ratoff. Orson Welles, Akim Tamiroff, Nancy Guild, Raymond Burr, Frank Latimore. Welles is predictably florid in chronicle of famous charlatan Cagliostro who seeks to rise to power in 18th century Italy. (He codirected this handsome film, uncredited.)▼●

Blackmail (1929-British) **86m.** *** D: Alfred Hitchcock. Anny Ondra, Sara Allgood, John Longden, Charles Paton, Donald Calthrop, Cyril Ritchard. Young woman kills man who tries to rape her, then finds herself caught between investigating detective (who happens to be her boyfriend) and a blackmailer. Hitchcock's—and England's—first talking picture is still exciting, especially for fans and students of the director's work. Originally shot as a silent; that version, running 75m., also exists (and is significantly better). Leading lady Ondra had a heavy accent, so her voice was dubbed for the talkie.▼●◗

Blackmail (1939) **81m.** **½ D: H. C. Potter. Edward G. Robinson, Gene Lockhart, Guinn Williams, Ruth Hussey, Esther Dale. Robinson is freed after serving stretch for crime he didn't commit; guilty Lockhart blackmails him in taut drama.

Black Mama, White Mama (1972-U.S.-Filipino) **C-87m.** ** D: Eddie Romero. Pam Grier, Margaret Markov, Sid Haig, Lynn Borden. Clichéd, violent female rehash of THE DEFIANT ONES, as blonde Markov and black Grier escape chained together from a Filipino prison camp. Haig is hammy in cowboy costume. Story cowritten by Jonathan Demme. [R]▼

Black Marble, The (1980) **C-113m.** **½ D: Harold Becker. Robert Foxworth, Paula Prentiss, Harry Dean Stanton, Barbara Babcock, John Hancock, Raleigh Bond, Judy Landers, James Woods, Michael Dudikoff, Anne Ramsey, Christopher Lloyd. Insightful but curiously unmemorable love story about sexy cop Prentiss and her new partner (Foxworth), an alcoholic romantic drowning in the reality of his job. Misses much of the humor that marked Joseph Wambaugh's novel. Panavision. [PG]▼

Black Mask (1997-Hong Kong) **C-96m.** *** D: Danny Lee. Jet Li, Karen Mok, Françoise Yip, Lau Ching Wan, Patrick Lung Kang, Anthony Wong. Biologically engineered super-soldier Li has to give up a peaceful life to battle his equally enhanced former comrades, who are trying to take over the Hong Kong drug rackets. Smart, stylish, and lightning-paced thriller is an ideal showcase for the dazzling skills of its star (who, in his disguise, resembles the Green Hornet's Kato). Recut and revised from 106m. Hong Kong version. [R]▼●◗

Black Moon (1934) **68m.** **½ D: Roy William Neill. Jack Holt, Fay Wray, Dorothy Burgess, Cora Sue Collins, Arnold Korff, Clarence Muse. N.Y. businessman takes his family to the West Indies, where his wife becomes immersed in sacrificial voodoo rituals. Very odd, dark, downbeat film is too sluggish to have the impact it promises early on, but still interesting. Moodily photographed by Joseph August.

Black Moon Rising (1986) **C-100m.** BOMB D: Harley Cokliss. Tommy Lee Jones, Linda Hamilton, Robert Vaughn, Richard Jaeckel, Bubba Smith, Lee Ving, William Sanderson. Vaughn's hot-car ring steals the Black Moon, one of those zoom-across-the-salt-flats dream machines no taller than a munchkin's shin; high-tech thief Jones pursues. Punk-rocker-turned-actor Ving wears a coat and tie, but that's about it for novelty value; this one deserves to get a Big Moon Rising. From a story by John Carpenter. [R]▼●

Black Narcissus (1947-British) **C-99m.** **** D: Michael Powell, Emeric Pressburger. Deborah Kerr, David Farrar, Sabu, Jean Simmons, Kathleen Byron, Flora Robson, Esmond Knight. Visually sumptuous, dramatically charged movie, from Rumer Godden novel, about nuns trying to establish a mission in a remote Himalayan outpost amid formidable physical and emotional challenges. One of the most breathtaking color films ever made (winning Oscars for cinematographer Jack Cardiff and art director Alfred Junge). Scenes in which Sister Superior Kerr recalls her former life, a key plot element, were originally censored from American prints.▼●

Black Oak Conspiracy (1977) **C-92m.** **½ D: Bob Kelljan. Jesse Vint, Karen Carlson, Albert Salmi, Seymour Cassel, Robert F. Lyons. Predictable action drama pitting an "average Joe" (Vint) against a crooked sheriff and unscrupulous land grabbers. Situations and dialogue are written to formula. [R]▼

Black Orchid, The (1959) **96m.** **½ D: Martin Ritt. Sophia Loren, Anthony Quinn, Ina Balin, Jimmie Baird, (Peter) Mark Richman, Naomi Stevens, Frank Puglia. Fabricated soaper of bumbling businessman (Quinn) romancing criminal's widow (Loren) and the problem of convincing their children that marriage will make all their lives better. VistaVision. ▼

Black Orpheus (1959-French-Brazilian) **C-103m.** ***½ D: Marcel Camus. Breno Mello, Marpessa Dawn, Lea Garcia, Adhemar Da Silva, Lourdes De Oliveira. Street-car conductor Mello and country-girl Dawn fall in love in Rio de Janeiro during Carnival. Lyrical updating of the Orpheus and Eurydice legend is beautifully acted and directed. Oscar winner for Best Foreign Film; rhythmic score by Luis Bonfa and Antonio Carlos Jobim.▼●◗

Blackout (1954-British) **87m.** ** D: Terence Fisher. Dane Clark, Belinda Lee, Betty Ann Davies, Eleanor Summerfield. Clark, down on his luck, makes some fast money by agreeing to marry a pretty blonde—and then finds himself the patsy in a murder case. Ordinary programmer. Original British title: MURDER BY PROXY.

Blackout (1978-Canadian-French) **C-89m.** ** D: Eddy Matalon. Jim Mitchum, Robert Carradine, Belinda Montgomery, June Allyson, Jean-Pierre Aumont, Ray Milland. Violent story of criminals who terrorize apartment dwellers during N.Y.'s 1977 power blackout. Balanced with black comedy for so-so results. [R]▼

Black Patch (1957) **83m.** BOMB D: Allen H. Miner. George Montgomery, Diane Brewster, Leo Gordon, Sebastian Cabot. Inconsequential trivia with Montgomery as gun-toting sheriff out to clear his name.

Black Pirate, The (1926) **C-85m.** *** D: Albert Parker. Douglas Fairbanks, Sr., Billie Dove, Anders Randolf, Donald Crisp, Tempe Piggott, Sam De Grasse. Robust silent swashbuckler with Fairbanks a nobleman who turns pirate after being victimized by cutthroats. Filmed in early Technicolor process, but some extant prints are b&w.▼●◗

Black Pirates, The (1954-Mexican) **C-72m.** **½ D: Allen H. Miner. Anthony Dexter, Martha Roth, Lon Chaney (Jr.), Robert Clarke. Uninspired account of pirates searching for gold.▼

Black Rain (1989) **C-126m.** **½ D: Ridley Scott. Michael Douglas, Andy Garcia, Ken Takakura, Kate Capshaw, Yusaku Matsuda, Shigeru Koyama, John Spencer. Tough, violent, foulmouthed action yarn about street-worn N.Y.C. cop and his partner who are supposed to deliver a Japanese mobster to cops in Osaka—then wind up pursuing him on his own turf. Too long, too predictable at times, but slick and entertaining. Super 35. [R]▼●◗

Black Rain (1989-Japanese) **123m.** *** D: Shohei Imamura. Yoshiko Tanaka, Kazuo Kitamura, Etsuko Ichihara, Shoichi Ozawa, Norihei Miki, Keisuke Ishida. Somber, restrained, and very moving story detailing five years in the life of a family which survived Hiroshima, and the ways their bodies and souls are poisoned by the fallout—or "black rain." A quietly observant character study with a number of haunting black and white images. ▼●◗

Black Rainbow (1991-British) **C-100m.** *** D: Mike Hodges. Rosanna Arquette, Jason Robards, Tom Hulce, Mark Joy, Ron Rosenthal, John Bennes, Linda Pierce. Offbeat, intriguing psychological drama-chiller with Arquette impressive as a medium who offers public exhibitions of her abilities. During one of them, she "sees" a murder and the killer—just before the crime is committed. Robards is her besotted father, a character worthy of Eugene O'Neill. Occasionally loses its way, but there's more than enough originality and good acting to compensate. Hodges also scripted; filmed in North Carolina. [R]▼

Black Raven, The (1943) **64m.** *½ D: Sam Newfield. George Zucco, Wanda McKay, Noel Madison, Bob Randall (Bob Livingston), Byron Foulger. Paltry (and obvious) whodunit, with various people stranded at Zucco's inn during a storm. Glenn Strange is the comedy relief!▼

Black Rebels, The SEE: **This Rebel Breed**

Black Rider, The SEE: **Joshua**

Black Robe (1991-Canadian-Australian) **C-101m.** **½ D: Bruce Beresford. Lothaire Bluteau, August Schellenberg, Aden Young, Sandrine Holt, Tantoo Cardinal. Epic look at a 17th-century Jesuit priest who goes to Quebec to colonize the "Indian" tribes. Director Beresford travels much the same territory as DANCES WITH WOLVES, but paints a much bleaker picture. Beautifully photographed (by Peter James) but graphically violent, this flawed, fascinating film is for demanding viewers. [R] ▼●◗

Black Rodeo (1972) **C-87m.** **½ D: Jeff Kanew. Archie Wycoff, Clarence Gonzalez, Pete Knight, Marval Rogers, Reuben Heura. Offbeat, frequently interesting documentary about a rodeo that takes place largely in Harlem; background music is performed by such stars as B.B. King, Ray Charles, Dee Dee Sharpe. [G]

Black Room, The (1935) **67m.** *** D: Roy William Neill. Boris Karloff, Marian Marsh, Robert Allen, Katherine DeMille, John Buckler, Thurston Hall. Excellent, understated thriller of twin brothers (Karloff) and the ancient curse that dominates their lives. Features one of Karloff's best performances.▼●

Black Rose, The (1950) **C-120m.** ** D: Henry Hathaway. Tyrone Power, Cecile Aubry, Orson Welles, Jack Hawkins, Michael Rennie, Herbert Lom, James Robertson Justice, Finlay Currie, Bobby (Robert) Blake, Laurence Harvey. Sweeping pageantry follows Norman-hating Power on Oriental adventures during 1200s; plodding film only somewhat redeemed by dynamic action scenes. Filmed in England and North Africa by Jack Cardiff.

Black Sabbath (1963-Italian) **C-99m.** **½ D: Mario Bava. Boris Karloff, Mark Damon, Suzy Anderson, Jacqueline Pierreux. Italian three-part film hosted by Karloff, who appears in final episode about a vampire controlling an entire family. Other sequences are good, atmospheric.▼●

Black Scorpion, The (1957) **88m.** *½ D: Edward Ludwig. Richard Denning, Carlos Rivas, Mara Corday, Mario Navarro. Outstanding animation by KING KONG's Willis O'Brien is the highlight of this sci-fi thriller about giant arachnids popping out of a volcanic fissure in Mexico. Basically a remake of the superior THEM!▼●

Black Sheep (1996) **C-87m.** BOMB D: Penelope Spheeris. Chris Farley, David Spade, Tim Matheson, Christine Ebersole, Gary Busey, Grant Heslov, Timothy Carhart, Bruce McGill. Gubernatorial candidate Matheson needs to keep his bumbling brother (Farley) out of the public eye, and Spade volunteers for the job. Insulting "comedy" reunites the stars of TOMMY BOY for virtually the same movie, which attempts to mine all the humor it can out of Farley's mugging and endless pratfalls, plus Spade's sarcasm. Pitiful and shameless. [PG-13]▼●

Black Shield of Falworth, The (1954) **C-99m.** **½ D: Rudolph Maté. Tony Curtis, Janet Leigh, David Farrar, Barbara Rush, Herbert Marshall. Juvenile version of Howard Pyle novel, *Men of Iron*; Curtis unconvincing as nobility rising through ranks to knighthood in medieval England. Settings, supporting cast bolster production. CinemaScope.▼

Black Sleep, The (1956) **81m.** *½ D: Reginald LeBorg. Basil Rathbone, Akim Tamiroff, Lon Chaney (Jr.), John Carradine, Bela Lugosi, Tor Johnson, Herbert Rudley. Big horror cast cannot save dull, unatmospheric tale of doctor doing brain transplants in remote castle. Laughable. Reissued as DR. CADMAN'S SECRET. ▼

Black Spurs (1965) **C-81m.** *½ D: R. G. Springsteen. Rory Calhoun, Terry Moore, Linda Darnell, Scott Brady, Lon Chaney (Jr.), Bruce Cabot, Richard Arlen, Patricia Owens, James Best, Jerome Courtland, DeForest Kelley. Ordinary Western with attraction of one-time movie stars including Darnell (her last film). Standard horse opera. Techniscope.

Black Stallion, The (1979) **C-118m.** *** D: Carroll Ballard. Kelly Reno, Mickey Rooney, Teri Garr, Clarence Muse, Hoyt Axton, Michael Higgins. Exquisitely filmed story of a young boy's adventures with a magnificent black stallion—from a dramatic shipwreck to a racing championship. Too slow at times, but still worthwhile, with many precious moments, stunning cinematography by Caleb Deschanel, Rooney's lovely performance as veteran horse trainer. Based on classic children's novel by Walter

Farley. Followed by 1983 sequel, and TV series (with Rooney). [G] ▼●◗

Black Stallion Returns, The (1983) **C-93m.** **½ D: Robert Dalva. Kelly Reno, Vincent Spano, Allen Goorwitz (Garfield), Woody Strode, Ferdinand Mayne, Jodi Thelen, Teri Garr. Fair action sequel with Reno, now a teenager, searching the Sahara for his Arabian horse. Those expecting the magic of the original will be disappointed. First-time director Dalva edited the 1979 film. [PG]▼●

Black Streetfighter, The SEE: **Black Fist**

Black Sunday (1961-Italian) **83m.** **½ D: Mario Bava. Barbara Steele, John Richardson, Ivo Garrani, Andrea Checchi. Intriguing story of the one day each century when Satan roams the earth. Steele is a witch who swears vengeance on the descendants of those who killed her hundreds of years ago. Beautifully atmospheric.▼●◗

Black Sunday (1977) **C-143m.** *** D: John Frankenheimer. Robert Shaw, Bruce Dern, Marthe Keller, Fritz Weaver, Steven Keats, Bekim Fehmiu, Michael V. Gazzo, William Daniels. International terrorist organization plots to blow up the Super Bowl, enlists the aid of former Vietnam POW Dern, who pilots the TV blimp. Generally compelling adaptation (by Ernest Lehman, Kenneth Ross, Ivan Moffat) of the Thomas Harris bestseller, with Dern at his unhinged best. Splendid aerial photography. Panavision. [R]▼●

Black Swan, The (1942) **C-85m.** *** D: Henry King. Tyrone Power, Maureen O'Hara, Laird Cregar, Thomas Mitchell, George Sanders, Anthony Quinn. Power makes a dashing pirate in this colorful swashbuckler, fighting Sanders and Quinn, rescuing O'Hara from their clutches. Leon Shamroy's cinematography deservedly earned him an Oscar.▼

Black Tent, The (1957-British) **C-93m.** ** D: Brian Hurst. Anthony Steel, Donald Sinden, Anna Maria Sandri, Donald Pleasence. Passable mixture of romance and action in the African desert as British soldier Steel romances native chief's daughter, helps tribe fight off Nazi attack. VistaVision. ▼

Black Tights (1960-French) **C-120m.** *** D: Terence Young. Cyd Charisse, Moira Shearer, Zizi Jeanmaire, Dirk Sanders, Roland Petit. Narrated by Maurice Chevalier. Ballet fans will feast on this quartet of stunning performances, featuring some of the era's top dance talent. Our favorite: the ballet of Rostand's *Cyrano de Bergerac,* with Shearer a lovely Roxanne. Super Technirama 70.▼

Black Tuesday (1954) **80m.** *** D: Hugo Fregonese. Edward G. Robinson, Peter Graves, Jean Parker, Milburn Stone. Throwback to 1930-ish gangster films, with Robinson and Graves as escaped convicts being hunted by cops—nice gunplay, with Parker good as the moll.

Blackwell's Island (1939) **71m.** **½ D: William McGann. John Garfield, Rosemary Lane, Dick Purcell, Victor Jory, Stanley Fields, Peggy Shannon, Leon Ames, Milburn Stone. Peppy little based-on-fact gangster film with crusading reporter Garfield attempting to nail tough but dimwitted mobster Fields.

Black Werewolf (1974) SEE: **Beast Must Die, The**

Black Whip, The (1956) **77m.** *½ D: Charles Marquis Warren. Hugh Marlowe, Coleen Gray, Angie Dickinson, Sheb Wooley. Only spice to this oater is bevy of beautiful girls who are rescued by Marlowe. Regalscope.

Black Widow (1954) **C-95m.** ** D: Nunnally Johnson. Ginger Rogers, Van Heflin, Gene Tierney, George Raft, Peggy Ann Garner, Reginald Gardiner, Virginia Leith, Otto Kruger, Cathleen Nesbitt, Skip Homeier. Broadway producer Heflin takes young writer Garner under his wing, is naturally suspected when she turns up dead in his apartment. Glossy but dull adaptation of Patrick Quentin mystery, with remarkably poor performances by Rogers as bitchy star and Raft as dogged detective. Johnson also produced and wrote the screenplay. CinemaScope.

Black Widow (1987) **C-103m.** **½ D: Bob Rafelson. Debra Winger, Theresa Russell, Sami Frey, Dennis Hopper, Nicol Williamson, Terry O'Quinn, D. W. Moffett, Lois Smith, Mary Woronov, Rutanya Alda, James Hong, Diane Ladd. Female investigator for the Justice Dept. becomes intrigued—then obsessed—by young woman who seduces, marries, and murders wealthy men. Handsome, stylishly crafted yarn, loaded with sexual tension, that stops just short of hitting the mark. Winger and Russell are both terrific. Photographed by Conrad Hall; effective music score by Michael Small. Amusing cameo by playwright David Mamet as one of Winger's poker-playing colleagues. [R]▼●

Black Windmill, The (1974-British) **C-106m.** **½ D: Don Siegel. Michael Caine, Joseph O'Conor, Donald Pleasence, John Vernon, Janet Suzman, Delphine Seyrig. Slick, craftsmanlike but generally undistinguished thriller, as espionage agent Caine tries to locate his son's kidnappers. Siegel has done better. Aka DRABBLE. Panavision. [PG]▼

Black Zoo (1963) **88m.** *½ D: Robert Gordon. Michael Gough, Virginia Grey, Jerome Cowan, Elisha Cook, Jeanne Cooper. Gough, head of private zoo, doubles as leader of cult of animal worshipers. Good cast flounders, but film has a moment or two. From the man who gave you I WAS A TEEN-AGE WEREWOLF. Panavision.

Blacula (1972) **C-92m.** *** D: William Crain. William Marshall, Denise Nicholas, Vonetta McGee, Thalmus Rasulala, Ketty Lester, Elisha Cook, Jr., Gordon Pinsent. Dracula bit a Black Prince and now black vampire is stalking the streets of L.A. Some terrific shocks, and some very lively dialogue. Sequel: SCREAM, BLACULA, SCREAM. [PG] ▼●

Blade (1973) **C-90m.** **½ D: Ernest Pintoff. John Marley, Jon Cypher, Kathryn Walker, William Prince, John Schuck, Rue McClanahan, Morgan Freeman. N.Y.-made actioner about female-hating Cypher, who indulges in violent killings, and tough policeman Marley, who tracks him down. A bit pretentious and involved; fairly absorbing. [R]▼

Blade (1998) **C-123m.** **½ D: Stephen Norrington. Wesley Snipes, Stephen Dorff, Kris Kristofferson, N'bushe Wright, Donal Logue, Udo Kier, Arly Jover, Traci Lords, Tim Guinee. If you think you've seen bloody urban-vigilante pics before . . . well, you haven't. Snipes is part human and part vampire, which means he's the perfect warrior to combat a megalomaniacal bloodsucker who's plotting world domination. A potentially rousing 90-minute gorefest bloated by a half hour, film never tops its spectacularly gross opening set-piece in a vampire disco. Snipes coproduced. Based on the character created for Marvel Comics by Marv Wolfman. Clairmont-Scope. [R] ▼●◗

Blade Master, The (1984-Italian) **C-92m.** *½ D: David Hills. Miles O'Keeffe, Lisa Foster (Lisa Raines), Charles Borromel, David Cain Haughton, Chen Wong. Silly sequel to ATOR THE FIGHTING EAGLE has O'Keeffe as the prehistoric warrior on a quest to protect the Earth from a primitive atomic bomb called the "Geometric Nucleus." As in TARZAN, THE APE MAN, O'Keeffe wrestles with an oversize rubber snake, but silliest scene has him hang-gliding to storm an enemy castle. Original title: ATOR THE INVINCIBLE. TV title: CAVE DWELLERS. [PG]▼

Blade Runner (1982) **C-118m.** *½ D: Ridley Scott. Harrison Ford, Rutger Hauer, Sean Young, Edward James Olmos, William Sanderson, Daryl Hannah, Joe Turkel, Joanna Cassidy, Brion James. In 21st-century L.A., a former cop (Ford) is recruited to track down androids who have mutinied in space and made their way to Earth. A triumph of production design, defeated by a muddled script and main characters with no appeal whatsoever. However, the film has a fervent following. Loosely based on Philip K. Dick's novel *Do Androids Dream of Electric Sheep?* Futuristic stylings by Syd Mead and Lawrence G. Paull. At least 2 alternate versions have been released since the original, followed in 1993 by the "director's cut," which the film's champions hail as a vast improvement: Ford's voice-over has been dropped, footage has been added, and the ending has changed. It runs 117m. Panavision. [R]▼●◗

Blair Witch Project, The (1999) **C/B&W-87m.** **½ D: Daniel Myrick, Eduardo Sanchez. Heather Donahue, Michael Williams, Joshua Leonard. Young woman hires a film crew to accompany her into the Maryland woods to chronicle local, age-old yarns and superstitions about witchcraft. Soon the threesome get lost, and with each day grow more desperate as spooky goings-on at night begin to frazzle their nerves. Largely ad-libbed, this comes off more as a student exercise than a movie, but by the end does create an atmosphere of fear and anxiety. [R]▼●◗

Blame It on Rio (1984) **C-100m.** **½ D: Stanley Donen. Michael Caine, Joseph Bologna, Valerie Harper, Michelle Johnson, Demi Moore, Jose Lewgoy. Caine has a fling with his best friend's sexy teenage daughter while vacationing in Rio de Janeiro. Caine's terrific, Johnson is voluptuous, Demi is obviously intimidated in topless beach scenes, and the script is kind of a sniggering TV sitcom, with a heavy-handed music score of too-familiar records. Written by Charlie Peters and Larry Gelbart. Remake of the French film ONE WILD MOMENT. [R]▼●

Blame It on the Bellboy (1991-British) **C-78m.** ** D: Mark Herman. Dudley Moore, Bryan Brown, Richard Griffiths, Andreas Katsulas, Patsy Kensit, Alison Steadman, Bronson Pinchot, Lindsay Anderson. Behind the dynamic title lies an old-fashioned farce: three guys, named Orton, Lawton, and Horton, check into a Venice hotel, leading to the expected mix-ups after bellboy Pinchot confuses their messages. Brown (as a hit man) and the short running time keep this sometimes sleazy comedy from being a complete ordeal; even at 78m., though, you can feel the padding. [PG-13]▼●

Blame It on the Night (1984) **C-85m.** *½ D: Gene Taft. Nick Mancuso, Byron Thames, Leslie Ackerman, Dick Bakalyan, Merry Clayton, Billy Preston, Ollie E. Brown. Plodding tale of rock star Mancuso, who attempts to buy the love of his ultrastraight, illegitimate, military cadet son. Based on a story by Taft and Mick Jagger. [PG-13]▼

Blanche Fury (1948-British) **C-95m.** *** D: Marc Allegret. Stewart Granger, Valerie Hobson, Walter Fitzgerald, Michael Gough, Maurice Denham. Beautifully mounted gothic melodrama about a governess who marries into wealthy family, and the headstrong steward (Granger) who aspires to run the estate.▼

Blank Check (1994) **C-93m.** *½ D: Rupert Wainwright. Brian Bonsall, Karen Duffy, Miguel Ferrer, Michael Lerner, James Rebhorn, Jayne Atkinson, Michael Faustino, Chris Demetral, Tone Loc, Rick Ducommun, Debbie Allen, Lu Leonard. Comedy for blank minds shamelessly rips off HOME ALONE. 11-year-old manages to cash thug Ferrer's check for a million dollars, parlaying it into such life necessities as a dishy grownup girlfriend and a backyard water slide. Hard to swallow even on its own slumming-Disney level, but likely to hit very young children where they live. [PG]▼●

Blankman (1994) **C-92m.** *½ D: Mike Binder. Damon Wayans, David Alan Grier, Robin Givens, Christopher Lawford, Lynne Thigpen, Jon Polito, Jason Alexander. Shrill, witless comedy in which Wayans becomes a crimefighting superman in a crime-ridden metropolis. He has no super powers; he's aided instead by his own homemade contraptions. Might have some appeal to less-discriminating five-year-old boys. Wayans coscripted. [PG-13]▼●

Blast From the Past (1999) **C-111m.** **½ D: Hugh Wilson. Brendan Fraser, Alicia Silverstone, Christopher Walken, Sissy Spacek, Dave Foley, Jenifer Lewis, Rex Linn. Young man emerges after spending his entire 35 years in a fallout shelter with his loving parents, only to find that contemporary life in L.A. is not the way he pictured it to be. Cute-enough comedy benefits from Fraser's enthusiasm, but Silverstone's character is fuzzily defined at best. Spacek and especially Walken are wonderful as the early '60s parents who remain in a time warp. Super 35. [PG-13]▼●◗

Blast-Off SEE: **Those Fantastic Flying Fools**

Blaze (1989) **C-119m.** **½ D: Ron Shelton. Paul Newman, Lolita Davidovich, Jerry Hardin, Gailard Sartain, Jeffrey DeMunn, Garland Bunting, Richard Jenkins, Robert Wuhl. Newman gives a flashy, uninhibited performance as Earl Long, the flamboyant governor of Louisiana in the 1950s who fell headlong in love with stripper Blaze Starr (Davidovich, in her first lead role). Seemingly surefire story, peppered with colorful characters and incidents, falls alarmingly flat after a while and never recovers. Real-life Blaze Starr appears fleetingly as Lily, the stripper whose shoulder Newman kisses backstage. [R]▼●

Blaze of Noon (1947) **91m.** **½ D: John Farrow. Anne Baxter, William Holden, Sonny Tufts, William Bendix, Sterling Hayden. Hokey story of Holden torn between his wife (Baxter) and true love, flying.

Blazing Forest, The (1952) **C-90m.** *½ D: Edward Ludwig. John Payne, Agnes Moorehead, Richard Arlen, William Demarest, Susan Morrow. Felling trees and romancing Moorehead's niece (Morrow) occupies Payne till big fire diverts him, but not the bored viewer.

Blazing Magnums SEE: **Strange Shadows in an Empty Room**

Blazing Saddles (1974) **C-93m.** ***½ D: Mel Brooks. Cleavon Little, Gene Wilder, Harvey Korman, Madeline Kahn, Slim Pickens, David Huddleston, Alex Karras, Burton Gilliam, Mel Brooks, John Hillerman, Liam Dunn, Carol Arthur, Dom DeLuise, Robert Ridgely, George Furth. Brooks's first hit movie is a riotous Western spoof, with Little an unlikely sheriff, Korman as villainous Hedley Lamarr, and Kahn as a Dietrich-like chanteuse. None of Brooks's later films have topped this one for sheer belly laughs. Scripted by Brooks, Andrew Bergman, Richard Pryor, Norman Steinberg, and Alan Uger; story by Bergman. Title song sung by Frankie Laine. Network TV version substitutes cutting-room-floor footage for some of the raunchier gags. Panavision. [R]▼●◗

Bleak Moments (1971-British) **C-111m.** *** D: Mike Leigh. Anne Raitt, Sarah Stephenson, Eric Allan, Joolia Cappleman, Mike Bradwell, Liz Smith. Leigh's debut feature is a potent, deeply human drama, which charts the plight of a lonesome officeworker (Raitt) who looks after her mentally retarded sister and hopes that her relationship with a schoolteacher will lead to marriage. Leigh (who also scripted) offers knowing insight into his characters.▼

Blessed Event (1932) **83m.** *** D: Roy Del Ruth. Lee Tracy, Mary Brian, Dick Powell, Emma Dunn, Frank McHugh, Allen Jenkins, Ned Sparks, Ruth Donnelly. Tracy's most famous role has him a Walter Winchell prototype whose spicy column makes him famous but also gets him in hot water; Powell makes film debut as crooner. Fast-moving, delightful.▼●

Bless the Beasts and Children (1972) **C-109m.** *** D: Stanley Kramer. Billy Mumy, Barry Robins, Miles Chapin, Ken Swofford, Jesse White, Vanessa Brown. Exciting and well-intentioned, if repetitious, story of six young misfit boys, campers at a ranch, who attempt to free a captive herd of buffalo scheduled for slaughter. The Barry DeVorzon–Perry Botkin music that later became known as "Nadia's Theme" and the *Young and the Restless* theme originated here. [PG]▼

Blind Alley (1939) **71m.** **½ D: Charles Vidor. Chester Morris, Ralph Bellamy, Ann Dvorak, Joan Perry, Melville Cooper, Rose Stradner, John Eldredge. One of Hollywood's first attempts to illustrate psychological ideas. Morris is troubled gangster who holds psychiatrist Bellamy prisoner, and allows himself to be analyzed. Dated but interesting. Remade as THE DARK PAST.

Blind Alley (1984) SEE: **Perfect Strangers**

Blind Date (1934) **71m.** **½ D: Roy William Neill. Ann Sothern, Paul Kelly, Neil Hamilton, Mickey Rooney, Jane Darwell, Joan

Gale. Sothern has her hands full choosing between mechanic Kelly and wealthy Hamilton in this pleasant little domestic comedy.

Blind Date (1959) SEE: **Chance Meeting**

Blind Date (1984) **C-100m.** **½ D: Nico Mastorakis. Joseph Bottoms, Kirstie Alley, James Daughton, Lana Clarkson, Keir Dullea. Dr. Dullea tests a portable machine that stimulates vision on blind Bottoms, causing Bottoms to become obsessed with capturing a psycho killer who's on the loose. Solid cast perks up a contrived thriller, filmed in Greece. [R]▼

Blind Date (1987) **C-93m.** *½ D: Blake Edwards. Kim Basinger, Bruce Willis, John Larroquette, William Daniels, Phil Hartman, Stephanie Faracy, Joyce Van Patten, Alice Hirson, George Coe, Mark Blum, Graham Stark. Tiresome retread of all-too-familiar farcical material by Blake Edwards. Yuppie Willis takes Basinger out on a blind date, warned that she can't tolerate alcohol—and immediately gives her champagne. Alternately boring and grating. This was Willis' starring debut; guitarist Stanley Jordan makes a musical appearance. Panavision. [PG-13]▼●

Blind Faith (1998) **C-107m.** **½ D: Ernest Dickerson. Courtney B. Vance, Charles S. Dutton, Kadeem Hardison, Lonette McKee, Garland Whitt. Two brothers, one a police captain and the other a defense attorney, find their relationship—and their own sense of self-worth as black men in 1950s America—turned upside down when the captain's son is accused of murder. Hard-hitting drama, which opens in the late '80s, focuses on the racial divide and unjust justice system. Solid performances all around, especially from the two leads. Released theatrically (at 118m.) after debut on U.S. cable TV. [R]▼●

Blindfold (1966) **C-102m.** **½ D: Philip Dunne. Rock Hudson, Claudia Cardinale, Jack Warden, Guy Stockwell, Anne Seymour. Attractive cast falters in film that wavers from comedy to mystery. Slapstick scenes seem incongruous as Hudson engages in international espionage with a noted scientist. Panavision.

Blind Fury (1990) **C-86m.** **½ D: Phillip Noyce. Rutger Hauer, Terrance (Terry) O'Quinn, Brandon Call, Lisa Blount, Randall "Tex" Cobb, Noble Willingham, Meg Foster, Sho Kosugi, Nick Cassavetes, Charles Cooper, Rick Overton. Smiling, sword-wielding, *blind* Vietnam vet Hauer carves up bad guys, saves a kid, and even duels with his mentor in this brash, lively (but failed) attempt to Americanize Japanese "Zato-ichi" movies. Hauer is perfectly cast, and the film is amusingly tongue-in-cheek, but it doesn't altogether work. [R]▼●◗

Blindman (1972-Italian) **C-105m.** ** D: Ferdinando Baldi. Tony Anthony, Ringo Starr, Agneta Eckemyr, Lloyd Batista. Blindman (Anthony) seeks revenge on man who stole fifty mail-order brides. Mindless entertainment, though any movie with Ringo as a slimy Mexican bandit can't be *all* bad. Techniscope. [R]

Blind Man's Bluff SEE: **Cauldron of Blood**

Blind Rage (1978-Philippine) **C-80m.** *½ D: Efren C. Pinon. D'Urville Martin, Leo Fong, Tony Ferrer, Fred Williamson, Dick Adair. Five blind men attempt to rip off a bank. Bright idea for an action-adventure spoof, but poorly handled. [R]▼

Blind Side (1993) **C-100m. TVM** D: Geoff Murphy. Rutger Hauer, Rebecca De Mornay, Ron Silver, Jonathan Banks, Mariska Hargitay, Tamara Clatterbuck. Thriller about an upscale American couple involved in a fatal hit-and-run on a trip to Mexico. Later, they're blackmailed by a charming but dangerous stranger who turns up at their doorstep back home. Made for cable. Above average.▼

Blind Spot (1947) **73m.** *** D: Robert Gordon. Chester Morris, Constance Dowling, Steven Geray, Sid Tomack. Mystery writer Morris has to extricate himself from charge of murdering his publisher in this tight little mystery.

Blind Spot (1993) **C-100m. TVM** D: Michael Toshiyuki Uno. Joanne Woodward, Laura Linney, Reed Diamond, Fritz Weaver, Patti D'Arbanville. Woodward (who coproduced) was Emmy-nominated for her gritty portrayal of an ambitious congresswoman whose life is affected by drug addiction in her family. Good script by Nina Shengold. Above average.▼

Blink (1994) **C-106m.** **½ D: Michael Apted. Madeleine Stowe, Aidan Quinn, Laurie Metcalf, James Remar, Peter Friedman, Bruce A. Young, Matt Roth, Paul Dillon. Did she or didn't she see a murderer leaving the scene of the crime? That's the central question when beautiful, strong-willed musician Stowe, blind since childhood, has her sight restored. Story relies on viewer's acceptance of screenwriter's gimmick of "retroactive vision," a post-surgery delayed reaction. Best thing in film is Stowe; otherwise this treads on too familiar blind-woman-in-jeopardy territory. Alternative Irish-American band The Drovers appear as themselves. Super 35. [R]▼●

Bliss (1985-Australian) **C-111m.** *½ D: Ray Lawrence. Barry Otto, Lynette Curran, Helen Jones, Miles Buchanan, Gia Carides, Tim Robertson. High-powered businessman has a major heart attack, sees himself dying, then revives—which changes his entire outlook on life. After a dynamic opening this stylized satire slows to a snail's pace and loses its thrust. Nevertheless, it was an Australian Academy Award winner and an international film festival favorite, so judge for yourself. [R]▼●

Bliss (1997) **C-103m.** **½ D: Lance Young. Craig Sheffer, Terence Stamp,

Sheryl Lee, Spalding Gray, Casey Siemaszko, Ken Camroux, Pamela Perry, Leigh Taylor-Young, Lois Chiles, Theresa Saldana, Molly Parker. Unusual film about a young married couple's emotional journey into sexual awakening with the help of a sex therapist. Stamp excels as teacher and mentor to the husband, who unwittingly unlocks the door to his wife's forgotten past. Melodramatic story gets in the way of some genuinely interesting and even educational dialogue, though it's almost too clinical at times. Actress Taylor-Young is the sister of the writer-director. Filmed in 1995. [R]▼●

Bliss of Mrs. Blossom, The (1968-U.S.-British) **C-93m.** *** D: Joe McGrath. Shirley MacLaine, Richard Attenborough, James Booth, Freddie Jones, Bob Monkhouse, John Cleese. Oddball, original comedy with delicious performances. Wife of brassiere manufacturer keeps a lover in their attic for five years. Bogs down toward the end, but for the most part a delight. [M/PG]▼●

Blithe Spirit (1945-British) **C-96m.** ***½ D: David Lean. Rex Harrison, Constance Cummings, Kay Hammond, Margaret Rutherford, Hugh Wakefield, Joyce Carey. Delicious adaptation of Noel Coward's comedy-fantasy about a man whose long-dead first wife appears to haunt—and taunt—him in his newly married life. Rutherford is wonderful as Madame Arcati, the spiritual medium; this earned an Oscar for its special effects. Scripted by the director, the producer (Anthony Havelock-Allan), and the cinematographer (Ronald Neame).▼●◗

Blob, The (1958) **C-86m.** ** D: Irvin S. Yeaworth, Jr. Steven McQueen, Aneta Corseaut, Earl Rowe, Olin Howlin. Endearingly campy classic of cheap 50s sci-fi has "Steven" (in his first starring role) leading teenagers into battle to save their small town from being swallowed up by giant glop of cherry Jell-O from outer space. Not really all that good, but how can you hate a film like this? (Especially when Burt Bacharach composed the title song.) Sequel: BEWARE! THE BLOB. Remade thirty years later.▼●

Blob, The (1988) **C-95m.** ** D: Chuck Russell. Shawnee Smith, Donovan Leitch, Ricky Paull Goldin, Kevin Dillon, Billy Beck, Candy Clark, Joe Seneca. Needless, if undeniably gooey, remake about a man-made what's-it that wipes out the standard number of vagrants and oversexed teenagers on its way to enveloping a small town. Showstopper finds a restaurant employee getting pulled head first down a kitchen drain after foolishly attempting to "plunge" the Blob. [R] ▼●

Blockade (1938) **85m.** *** D: William Dieterle. Madeleine Carroll, Henry Fonda, Leo Carrillo, John Halliday, Vladimir Sokoloff, Reginald Denny. Vivid romance drama of Spanish Civil War with globe-trotting Carroll falling in love with fighting Fonda.

Block Busters (1944) **60m.** ** D: Wallace Fox. Leo Gorcey, Huntz Hall, Gabriel Dell, Jimmy Strand, Minerva Urecal, Noah Beery, Sr., Billy Benedict, Bernard Gorcey. Muggs fights a new French kid in town, but all is forgiven when he helps the East Side Kids win the big baseball game. Raucous comedy; a sad comedown for silent clown Harry Langdon in a bit part.

Block-Heads (1938) **55m.** *** D: John G. Blystone. Stan Laurel, Oliver Hardy, Patricia Ellis, Minna Gombell, Billy Gilbert, James Finlayson. Stan's been marching in a trench for twenty years—nobody told him WW1 was over! Ollie brings him home to find he hasn't changed. Top L&H. Also shown in computer-colored version. ▼

Blockhouse, The (1973-British) **C-90m.** *½ D: Clive Rees. Peter Sellers, Charles Aznavour, Per Oscarsson, Peter Vaughan, Jeremy Kemp, Alfred Lynch. Dismal, downbeat story of laborers trapped in underground bunker when the Allies land at Normandy on D-Day. Panavision. ▼

Blonde Bait (1956-British) **70m.** ** D: Elmo Williams. Beverly Michaels, Jim Davis, Joan Rice, Richard Travis, Paul Cavanagh, Thora Hird, Avril Angers, Gordon Jackson. Cheap, toothy blond bombshell Michaels excels as a Yank showgirl breaking out of a sedate British prison for women. British film, originally titled WOMEN WITHOUT MEN, was retitled, reedited, and reshot (with Davis, Travis, and Cavanagh added to cast) for U.S. release.

Blonde Bombshell SEE: **Bombshell**

Blonde Crazy (1931) **79m.** **½ D: Roy Del Ruth. James Cagney, Joan Blondell, Louis Calhern, Ray Milland, Polly Walters, Nat Pendleton. Dated fun with Cagney as small-time con-man who plays cat-and-mouse with big-time sharpie Calhern. Young Milland appears as businessman who marries Jimmy's girlfriend, Blondell. ▼●

Blonde Dynamite (1950) **66m.** ** D: William Beaudine. Leo Gorcey, Huntz Hall, Gabriel Dell, Adele Jergens, Harry Lewis, Murray Alper, Bernard Gorcey, Billy Benedict, David Gorcey, Jody Gilbert. The Bowery Boys go into the escort service business and predictably get mixed up with crooks.

Blonde Fever (1944) **69m.** ** D: Richard Whorf. Philip Dorn, Mary Astor, Felix Bressart, Gloria Grahame, Marshall Thompson. Astor lends class to this mild account of married woman whose husband (Dorn) is vamped by sultry Grahame. Based on a play by Ferenc Molnar. Look for Ava Gardner in a bit. And yes, that's Jessica Tandy and Hume Cronyn, appearing briefly (without billing).

Blonde for a Day (1946) **67m.** *½ D: Sam Newfield. Hugh Beaumont, Kathryn Adams, Cy Kendall, Marjorie Hoshelle, Richard Fraser, Paul Bryar. Negligible *Michael Shayne* murder mystery, centering on a female crime reporter targeted for death by the crooks she's exposing.

Blonde From Peking, The SEE: **Peking Blonde**

Blonde in a White Car SEE: **Nude in a White Car**

Blondes at Work (1938) **63m.** ** D: Frank McDonald. Glenda Farrell, Barton MacLane, Tom Kennedy, Rosella Towne, Donald Briggs, John Ridgely, Carole Landis. Farrell is back as indefatigable reporter Torchy Blane, confounding her colleagues with scoops stolen directly from her cop boyfriend MacLane. Reworking of the 1935 Bette Davis FRONT PAGE WOMAN.

Blonde Venus (1932) **97m.** *** D: Josef von Sternberg. Marlene Dietrich, Herbert Marshall, Cary Grant, Dickie Moore, Sidney Toler. Episodic story of notorious Dietrich leading unsavory life to support herself and child. A triumph of style over content; this is the film where Marlene appears in an ape suit to sing "Hot Voodoo"! Most TV prints are missing opening sequence of Dietrich skinny-dipping when Marshall happens along.▼●

Blondie With a vast audience already familiar with the Chic Young comic strip (which had made its debut in 1930), a Blondie movie series seemed like a shoo-in in 1938—and it was. Penny Singleton, the former Dorothy McNulty, bleached her hair blonde and was a perfect choice to play the title character. Arthur Lake found the role of a lifetime as bumbling Dagwood Bumstead. Larry Simms was cast as Baby Dumpling, and an endearing pooch was found to play Daisy. Character actor Jonathan Hale was an inspired choice for Dagwood's irascible boss, J. C. Dithers. Inquisitive Alvin Fuddle was played by Danny Mummert, with Fay Helm as his mother. The series prospered for twelve years and twenty-eight episodes. The first ones were the best—fresh and original, with many clever touches belying the fact that they were low-budget films. By the mid-1940s, however, a formula set in; the films became more predictable, and the humor more contrived. One plus for the series was that there was some continuity from one episode to the next, with Baby Dumpling growing up, starting school in the fourth film, taking the name of Alexander in the eleventh. Cookie is also born in the eleventh film, and Daisy has pups in the following one. Another bonus derives from the fact that Columbia used the series as a proving ground for some of its fledgling stars, including Rita Hayworth in BLONDIE ON A BUDGET, Glenn Ford in BLONDIE PLAYS CUPID, and Larry Parks and Janet Blair in BLONDIE GOES TO COLLEGE. Other future "names" like Lloyd Bridges and Robert Sterling turn up in bit parts. The films were a particular field day for familiar-faced character actors, including Irving Bacon, who created the role of the harassed mailman (later played by Eddie Acuff and then Dick Wessel), Jerome Cowan (who replaced Jonathan Hale as Dagwood's boss), and Jack Rice (best-remembered as Edgar Kennedy's obnoxious brother-in-law, playing a not dissimilar role in Dagwood's office).

BLONDIE

Blondie (1938)
Blondie Meets the Boss (1939)
Blondie Takes a Vacation (1939)
Blondie Brings Up Baby (1939)
Blondie on a Budget (1940)
Blondie Has Servant Trouble (1940)
Blondie Plays Cupid (1940)
Blondie Goes Latin (1941)
Blondie in Society (1941)
Blondie Goes to College (1942)
Blondie's Blessed Event (1942)
Blondie for Victory (1942)
It's a Great Life (1943)
Footlight Glamour (1943)
Leave It to Blondie (1945)
Life With Blondie (1946)
Blondie's Lucky Day (1946)
Blondie Knows Best (1946)
Blondie's Big Moment (1947)
Blondie's Holiday (1947)
Blondie in the Dough (1947)
Blondie's Anniversary (1947)
Blondie's Reward (1948)
Blondie's Secret (1948)
Blondie's Big Deal (1949)
Blondie Hits the Jackpot (1949)
Blondie's Hero (1950)
Beware of Blondie (1950)

Blondie (1938) **68m.** *** D: Frank Strayer. Penny Singleton, Arthur Lake, Larry Simms, Gene Lockhart, Ann Doran, Jonathan Hale, Gordon Oliver, Danny Mummert, Irving Bacon, Fay Helm. First in the series of 28 *Blondie* films, introducing the farcical Bumstead family with a typically amusing plot: Dagwood is sacked from his job and Blondie thinks he's running around on her on the eve of their fifth anniversary.▼

Blondie and Dagwood—It's a Great Life SEE: **It's a Great Life**

Blondie Brings Up Baby (1939) **67m.** **½ D: Frank Strayer. Penny Singleton, Arthur Lake, Larry Simms, Danny Mummert, Jonathan Hale, Fay Helm, Peggy Ann Garner, Helen Jerome Eddy, Irving Bacon. Standard screwball antics when Baby Dumpling starts school and promptly disappears, sending bumbling Dagwood in hot pursuit. Future leading men Robert Sterling and Bruce Bennett have bits.▼

Blondie for Victory (1942) **70m.** ** D: Frank Strayer. Penny Singleton, Arthur Lake, Larry Simms, Majelle White, Stuart Erwin, Jonathan Hale, Danny Mummert,

Edward Gargan, Renie Riano, Irving Bacon. Dagwood and the other neighborhood husbands suffer when Blondie organizes a housewives' war effort. Cast strains for laughs in this topical series entry.▼

Blondie Goes Latin (1941) **69m.** **½ D: Frank Strayer. Penny Singleton, Arthur Lake, Larry Simms, Tito Guizar, Ruth Terry, Jonathan Hale, Danny Mummert, Irving Bacon, Janet Burston. Silliness on a South American cruise as Dagwood joins Tito Guizar's conga band and Blondie cuts loose in some song-and-dance routines. Look for future "Sky King" Kirby Grant in a small role as a band singer.▼

Blondie Goes to College (1942) **74m.** ** D: Frank Strayer. Penny Singleton, Arthur Lake, Larry Simms, Jonathan Hale, Danny Mummert, Larry Parks, Janet Blair, Lloyd Bridges, Esther Dale, Adele Mara. Predictable complications occur when the Bumsteads go back to school (where most of the students are Columbia's young contract players) and pretend they're not married.▼

Blondie Has Servant Trouble (1940) **70m.** **½ D: Frank Strayer. Penny Singleton, Arthur Lake, Larry Simms, Danny Mummert, Jonathan Hale, Arthur Hohl, Esther Dale, Irving Bacon, Fay Helm. Enjoyable haunted-house comedy, as the Bumsteads stay in a creepy mansion replete with strange servants and "ghosts."▼

Blondie Hits the Jackpot (1949) **66m.** *½ D: Edward Bernds. Penny Singleton, Arthur Lake, Larry Simms, Jerome Cowan, Lloyd Corrigan, Ann Carter, George Humbert, David Sharpe, Danny Mummert, James Flavin, Dick Wessel. Dagwood is rescued from manual labor at a construction company when Blondie wins a radio quiz show in this threadbare entry.▼

Blondie in Society (1941) **75m.** **½ D: Frank Strayer. Penny Singleton, Arthur Lake, Larry Simms, Jonathan Hale, Danny Mummert, William Frawley, Edgar Kennedy, Chick Chandler, Irving Bacon, Robert Mitchell Boys Choir. Blondie enters a pedigreed Great Dane in a dog show but gets Dagwood into trouble with a client who also has a dog in the running. Pretty funny entry with the added bonus of old pros Frawley and Kennedy.▼

Blondie in the Dough (1947) **69m.** ** D: Abby Berlin. Penny Singleton, Arthur Lake, Larry Simms, Marjorie Kent, Jerome Cowan, Hugh Herbert, Clarence Kolb, Danny Mummert, Eddie Acuff. Blondie's in the dough up to her neck when she starts a baking business which attracts the attention of a cookie tycoon (Herbert).▼

Blondie Johnson (1933) **67m.** **½ D: Ray Enright. Joan Blondell, Chester Morris, Allen Jenkins, Claire Dodd, Earle Foxe, Arthur Vinton, Sterling Holloway, Mae Busch. Pretty good story of Depression victim Blondell vowing to stop at nothing to get ahead, working her way into a position of power in the underworld. Keeps shifting tone, from light to heavy, and doesn't quite pay off, but still entertaining.

Blondie Knows Best (1946) **69m.** ** D: Abby Berlin. Penny Singleton, Arthur Lake, Larry Simms, Marjorie Kent, Steven Geray, Shemp Howard, Ludwig Donath, Jerome Cowan, Danny Mummert, Jack Rice. Dagwood pretends to be his boss, Mr. Dithers, causing predictable complications in this minor entry enlivened by Shemp as a myopic process server.▼

Blondie Meets the Boss (1939) **75m.** **½ D: Frank Strayer. Penny Singleton, Arthur Lake, Larry Simms, Dorothy Moore, Jonathan Hale, Stanley Brown, Inez Courtney, Don Beddoe, Danny Mummert, Irving Bacon. Second entry in the series has Blondie taking over at the office for Dagwood when he goes on a fishing trip. Look for James Craig and Robert Sterling in bits.▼

Blondie of the Follies (1932) **90m.** **½ D: Edmund Goulding. Marion Davies, Robert Montgomery, Billie Dove, Jimmy Durante, ZaSu Pitts, Sidney Toler, Louise Carter. Davies and Dove vie for the affection of Montgomery, while ascending to stardom in the Follies. Dramatically wobbly, but the musical numbers are fun. James Gleason fine as Marion's dad. Best are Davies and Durante spoofing Garbo and Barrymore in GRAND HOTEL.

Blondie on a Budget (1940) **73m.** **½ D: Frank Strayer. Penny Singleton, Arthur Lake, Rita Hayworth, Larry Simms, Danny Mummert, Don Beddoe, John Qualen, Fay Helm, Irving Bacon, Thurston Hall. Columbia ingenue Hayworth drops by as Dagwood's ex-sweetheart, which not surprisingly makes Blondie jealous. Lovely Rita helps perk up this entry.

Blondie Plays Cupid (1940) **68m.** **½ D: Frank Strayer. Penny Singleton, Arthur Lake, Glenn Ford, Larry Simms, Danny Mummert, Jonathan Hale, Irving Bacon, Luana Walters. Blondie helps a young couple elope, but the course of true love does not run smoothly. Cute entry notable for early appearance by Ford.▼

Blondie's Anniversary (1947) **75m.** ** D: Abby Berlin. Penny Singleton, Arthur Lake, Larry Simms, Marjorie Kent, Adele Jergens, Jerome Cowan, Grant Mitchell, William Frawley, Jack Rice, Eddie Acuff. Dagwood brings home a fancy watch for a client's wife, which Blondie naturally believes is her anniversary gift.▼

Blondie's Big Deal (1949) **66m.** ** D: Edward Bernds. Penny Singleton, Arthur Lake, Larry Simms, Jerome Cowan, Marjorie Kent, Collette Lyons, Ray Walker, Eddie Acuff, Jack Rice, Danny Mummert. Dagwood gets a shellacking when he invents a nonflammable paint and tests it out on his boss's house. Naturally, unscrupulous competitors switch the paint.▼

Blondie's Big Moment (1947) **69m.** ** D: Abby Berlin. Penny Singleton, Arthur Lake, Larry Simms, Marjorie Kent, Jerome Cowan, Anita Louise, Danny Mummert, Jack Rice, Eddie Acuff. Dagwood gets into trouble with his new boss, throwing the whole Bumstead household into chaos. Nothing new.▼

Blondie's Blessed Event (1942) **69m.** **½ D: Frank Strayer. Penny Singleton, Arthur Lake, Larry Simms, Norma Jean Wayne, Jonathan Hale, Danny Mummert, Hans Conried, Mary Wickes, Stanley Brown, Irving Bacon. Dagwood wreaks havoc at a convention while Baby Dumpling gets a new sister, Cookie, in this typically frantic series entry. Look for a young Arthur O'Connell as an intern.▼

Blondie's Hero (1950) **67m.** ** D: Edward Bernds. Penny Singleton, Arthur Lake, Larry Simms, Marjorie Kent, William Frawley, Danny Mummert, Joe Sawyer, Teddy Infuhr, Alyn Lockwood, Frank Jenks, Iris Adrian, Edward Earle, Dick Wessel. Penultimate series entry is a stock service farce, as Dagwood accidentally joins the Army reserve.▼

Blondie's Holiday (1947) **67m.** ** D: Abby Berlin. Penny Singleton, Arthur Lake, Larry Simms, Marjorie Kent, Jerome Cowan, Grant Mitchell, Sid Tomack, Jeff York, Alyn Lockwood, Jack Rice, Eddie Acuff. Dagwood gets involved with gamblers and winds up in jail when he decides to play the ponies for some quick money. Bobby Larson replaced Danny Mummert as Alvin for this one entry.▼

Blondie's Lucky Day (1946) **75m.** ** D: Abby Berlin. Penny Singleton, Arthur Lake, Larry Simms, Marjorie Kent, Robert Stanton, Angelyn Orr, Frank Jenks, Paul Harvey, Charles Arnt, Jack Rice, Frank Orth. Dagwood gets fired (again), and decides to go into business with the help of a WAC, which naturally makes Blondie nervous.▼

Blondie's Reward (1948) **67m.** ** D: Abby Singer. Penny Singleton, Arthur Lake, Larry Simms, Marjorie Kent, Jerome Cowan, Gay Nelson, Ross Ford, Danny Mummert, Paul Harvey, Frank Jenks, Chick Chandler, Jack Rice, Eddie Acuff, Alyn Lockwood. Dagwood the bonehead is demoted to office boy when he purchases the wrong real estate property. Very mild entry with the gags (and all concerned) showing their age.▼

Blondie's Secret (1948) **68m.** ** D: Edward Bernds. Penny Singleton, Arthur Lake, Larry Simms, Marjorie Kent, Jerome Cowan, Thurston Hall, Jack Rice, Danny Mummert, Frank Orth, Alyn Lockwood, Eddie Acuff. Dagwood's boss doesn't want him to take a vacation, so he hires some bumbling crooks to steal the Bumsteads' luggage. Trivial fluff, with the tired series coming into the home stretch.▼

Blondie Takes a Vacation (1939) **68m.** **½ D: Frank Strayer. Penny Singleton, Arthur Lake, Larry Simms, Danny Mummert, Donald Meek, Donald MacBride, Elizabeth Dunne, Irving Bacon. Blondie and family take over a mountain lodge to save it from bankruptcy and get into plenty of hot water in this diverting entry.▼

Blood Alley (1955) **C-115m.** **½ D: William Wellman. John Wayne, Lauren Bacall, Paul Fix, Mike Mazurki, Anita Ekberg. Enjoyable escapism with Wayne, Bacall, and assorted Chinese escaping down river to Hong Kong pursued by Communists. CinemaScope.▼●

Blood and Black Lace (1964-Italian-French-German) **C-88m.** *½ D: Mario Bava. Cameron Mitchell, Eva Bartok, Mary Arden. Gruesome thriller about a sex murderer doing in fashion models. Wooden script and performances don't help. Fans of the genre will at least enjoy Bava's imaginative direction.▼●

Blood and Concrete (1991) **C-97m.** **½ D: Jeffrey Reiner. Billy Zane, Jennifer Beals, Darren McGavin, James Le Gros, Nicholas Worth, William Bastiani, Harry Shearer. Offbeat but way overbaked comic thriller about third-rate car thief Zane and troubled singer Beals, who fall in love and become involved in murder and mayhem. Tries to be hip and stylish, and occasionally succeeds, but too self-conscious for its own good. The full title is BLOOD AND CONCRETE, A LOVE STORY. [R]▼●

Blood & Donuts (1995-Canadian) **C-89m.** *** D: Holly Dale. Gordon Currie, Justin Louis, Helene Clarkson, Fiona Reid, Frank Moore, David Cronenberg. Reluctant vampire Currie crawls into his bag when man first walks on the moon, reemerging in contemporary Toronto, where he holes up in a 24-hour donut shop. Characterful comedy/drama plays colloquially, like DINER, but at night and with fangs. Cronenberg plays a gangster. [R]▼

Blood & Guts (1978-Canadian) **C-93m.** ** D: Paul Lynch. William Smith, Micheline Lanctot, Henry Beckman, Brian Clark. Predictable film about wrestling troupe and the young tyro who joins it. [PG]▼

Blood and Lace (1971) **C-87m.** BOMB D: Philip Gilbert. Gloria Grahame, Melody Patterson, Milton Selzer, Len Lesser, Vic Tayback. Rock-bottom cheapie about murders tied in to corrupt orphanage. Don't bother. [PG]▼

Blood and Roses (1961-Italian) **C-74m.** **½ D: Roger Vadim. Mel Ferrer, Elsa Martinelli, Annette Vadim, Marc Allegret. This story of a jealous girl's obsession with her family's history of vampirism was based on Sheridan Le Fanu's *Carmilla.*

Despite effective moments, film does not succeed. Same story refilmed as THE VAMPIRE LOVERS and THE BLOOD-SPATTERED BRIDE. Technirama.▼

Blood and Sand (1922) **80m.** **½ D: Fred Niblo. Rudolph Valentino, Lila Lee, Nita Naldi, George Field, Walter Long, Leo White. Dated but still absorbing story of bullfighter Valentino torn between good-girl Lee and vampish Naldi. Scenes of hero being seduced are laughable, but bull-fight material holds up well. Remade in 1941 and 1989.▼●

Blood and Sand (1941) **C-123m.** *** D: Rouben Mamoulian. Tyrone Power, Linda Darnell, Rita Hayworth, Nazimova, Anthony Quinn, J. Carrol Naish, John Carradine, George Reeves. Pastel remake of Valentino's silent film about naive bull-fighter who ignores true-love (Darnell) for temptress (Hayworth). Slow-paced romance uplifted by Nazimova's knowing performance as Power's mother; beautiful color production earned cinematographers Ernest Palmer and Ray Rennahan Oscars.▼

Blood and Sand (1989-Spanish) **C-95m.** ** D: Javier Elorrieta. Chris Rydell, Sharon Stone, Ana Torrent, Guillermo Montesinus, Albert Vidal, Simon Andreu, Antonio Glez Flores. Cocky young bullfighter achieves success in the arena and forsakes his loving wife for a sexy siren. Authentic Spanish locations and good bullfighting footage compensate for predictability of this drama; hot sex scenes are what distinguish it from the earlier versions.▼●

Blood and Wine (1997) **C-98m.** *** D: Bob Rafelson. Jack Nicholson, Michael Caine, Judy Davis, Stephen Dorff, Jennifer Lopez, Harold Perrineau, Jr. Juicy film noir about a Florida no-good with an embittered wife, a resentful stepson, and a sexy Cuban mistress, who takes on an unlikely partner (an oily, consumptive Caine) for a high-risk jewel robbery. Delicious detail fills this well-thought-out melodrama; only fault is that it goes on a bit too long. Nicholson and Caine make a marvelous team. [R]▼●

Blood Arrow (1958) **75m.** *½ D: Charles Marquis Warren. Scott Brady, Paul Richards, Phyllis Coates, Don Haggerty. Uninspired tale of Mormon girl Coates trudging through Indian territory to obtain medicine, with usual Indian attacks. Regalscope.

Blood Barrier (1979-British) **C-86m.** **½ D: Christopher Leitch. Telly Savalas, Danny De La Paz, Eddie Albert, Michael Gazzo, Cecilia Camacho. Savalas plays a maverick border-patrolman who hates slimy Gazzo's exploitation of poor Mexicans, illegally trucked by Gazzo to California to be day laborers. Interesting drama isn't fully developed and suffers from pointless finale. Exteriors filmed in Mexico. Originally titled THE BORDER. [R]▼

Blood Bath (1966) **80m.** *½ D: Stephanie Rothman, Jack Hill. William Campbell, Jonathan Haze, Sid Haig, Marissa Mathes, Lori Saunders, Sandra Knight. Another AIP paste-job, with half an hour from a Yugoslavian vampire film worked into tale of California artist who murders his models. Eerie atmosphere, some occasional frissons, but overall a mishmash. Shown on TV as TRACK OF THE VAMPIRE.▼

Blood Beach (1981) **C-89m.** ** D: Jeffrey Bloom. John Saxon, David Huffman, Mariana Hill, Otis Young, Stefan Gierasch, Burt Young. People are mysteriously disappearing into the sand at the local beach. Not very bloody, thank heavens, but not very good either. [R]▼

Blood Beast from Outer Space SEE: **Night Caller from Outer Space**

Bloodbrothers (1978) **C-116m.** **½ D: Robert Mulligan. Richard Gere, Paul Sorvino, Tony Lo Bianco, Lelia Goldoni, Yvonne Wilder, Kenneth McMillan, Marilu Henner, Danny Aiello. Interesting if somewhat overblown drama about big-city construction workers. Best when actors have opportunity to underplay, e.g., Sorvino's touching story of baby son's death, Gere's interplay with young hospital patients. Gere stands out as son who wants to break away from family tradition. Recut to 98m. by Mulligan for pay-TV release; retitled A FATHER'S LOVE for network TV. [R]▼

Blood Creature SEE: **Terror Is a Man**

Blood Demon, The SEE: **Torture Chamber of Dr. Sadism, The**

Blood Evil SEE: **Demons of the Mind**

Blood Feud (1979-Italian) **C-112m.** ** D: Lina Wertmuller. Sophia Loren, Marcello Mastroianni, Giancarlo Giannini, Turi Ferro. Lawyer Mastroianni and hood Giannini both love Sicilian widow Loren, and she returns their favors. Loud, overblown, ineffective; set during the Fascist '20s. Also known as REVENGE, cut to 99m. [R]▼

Blood Fiend SEE: **Theatre of Death**

Bloodfist (1989) **C-85m.** *½ D: Terence H. Winkless. Don "The Dragon" Wilson, Joe Marie Avellana, Michael Shaner, Riley Bowman, Rob Kaman. Any action film with opening credits more exciting than the balance of the movie is bound to be a disappointment. Virtually the same plot as KICKBOXER, this one has violence aplenty, as kicker Wilson puts the foot to the bad guys who killed his brother. Followed by six sequels, all with Wilson. [R]▼

Blood for Dracula SEE: **Andy Warhol's Dracula**

Blood From the Mummy's Tomb (1972-British) **C-94m.** *** D: Seth Holt, Michael Carreras. Andrew Keir, Valerie Leon, James Villiers, Hugh Burden. Surprisingly satisfying chiller dealing with attempt at reincarnating ancient Egyptian high priestess. Based on Bram Stoker's *Jewel of the*

Seven Stars. Remade as THE AWAKENING. [PG]
Bloodhounds of Broadway (1952) **C-90m.** **½ D: Harmon Jones. Mitzi Gaynor, Scott Brady, Mitzi Green, Michael O'Shea, Marguerite Chapman, Charles Buchinski (Bronson). Hick Gaynor becomes slick gal in N.Y.C., involved with pseudo-Damon Runyon folk; funny Green has too small a role. Songs include "I Wish I Knew." Runyon stories used as basis for 1989 film of the same name.
Bloodhounds of Broadway (1989) **C-93m.** ** D: Howard Brookner. Matt Dillon, Madonna, Jennifer Grey, Rutger Hauer, Randy Quaid, Julie Hagerty, Esai Morales, Anita Morris, Madeleine Potter, Ethan Phillips, Steve Buscemi, Michael Wincott. Bland Damon Runyon tale chronicling the escapades of a gallery of gangsters, gamblers, and showgirl types on the Great White Way during New Year's Eve, 1928. The cast is game and there are some funny bits, but it's mostly a snooze. Documentary director Brookner's sole fiction feature; he died prior to its release. William Burroughs—the subject of one of his earlier films—appears in a small role as a butler. A PBS *American Playhouse* theatrical production. [PG]▼●
Blood Hunt SEE: **Thirsty Dead, The**
Blood In Blood Out SEE: **Bound By Honor**
Blood Island SEE: **Shuttered Room, The**
Blood Legacy (1971) **C-90m.** ** D: Carl Monson. John Carradine, Faith Domergue, John Russell, Merry Anders, Jeff Morrow, Richard Davalos. To claim inheritance, heirs to a fortune must spend a night in a "haunted" house. Awfully familiar stuff, helped by a few good scenes, and a familiar cast of veterans. Aka LEGACY OF BLOOD. [R]▼
Bloodline (1979) **C-116m.** BOMB D: Terence Young. Audrey Hepburn, Ben Gazzara, James Mason, Michelle Phillips, Omar Sharif, Romy Schneider, Irene Papas, Gert Frobe, Beatrice Straight, Maurice Ronet. Hepburn finds her life endangered after inheriting a Zurich-based pharmaceutical company. Unbearable adaptation of Sidney Sheldon's novel (one of those best-sellers California blondes read on the beach when no one wants to play volleyball). Nearly forty minutes of footage added for network showing. Officially released as SIDNEY SHELDON'S BLOODLINE. [R]▼
Blood Mania (1970) **88m.** BOMB D: Robert O'Neil. Peter Carpenter, Maria De Aragon, Vicki Peters, Reagan Wilson, Alex Rocco. Avaricious woman kills her surgeon father—only to find her sister is the beneficiary in his will. Low-budget sleaze. [R]▼
Blood Money (1933) **65m.** *** D: Rowland Brown. George Bancroft, Frances Dee, Judith Anderson, Chick Chandler, Blossom Seeley. Lively, implausible story of underworld bail-bondsman Bancroft falling for thrill-a-minute socialite Dee, causing friction with Bancroft's female cohort (played by Anderson in incongruously gutsy, glamorous role). Dee's closing scene is a knockout. Look fast for Lucille Ball as Chandler's girlfriend at the racetrack.▼
Blood Money (1988) SEE: **Clinton and Nadine**
Blood of a Poet, The (1930) **52m.** *** D: Jean Cocteau. Lee Miller, Pauline Carton, Odette Talazac, Enrique Rivero, Jean Desbordes. Cocteau's first feature is a highly personal, poetic, symbolic fantasy, which supposedly transpires in a split second: the time it takes for a chimney to crumble and land. Imaginative, dreamlike, and still a visual delight. The commentary is spoken by Cocteau.▼
Blood of Dracula (1957) **68m.** *½ D: Herbert L. Strock. Sandra Harrison, Gail Ganley, Jerry Blaine, Louise Lewis. Inoffensive programmer about girl being hypnotized into a life of vampirism.▼
Blood of Dracula's Castle (1967) **C-84m.** BOMB D: Al Adamson. John Carradine, Paula Raymond, Alex D'Arcy, Robert Dix, Barbara Bishop. Tacky low-budget mixture of vampirism and kinky sex, with Dracula and his bride "collecting" girls and chaining them up. [M]▼
Blood of Fu Manchu, The (1968) **C-91m.** ** D: Jesus Franco. Christopher Lee, Richard Greene, Gotz George, Howard Marion Crawford, Shirley Eaton, Maria Rohm. Fourth in Lee's international FU MANCHU series, several pegs below its predecessors, finds him in the heart of the Amazon, injecting ten beautiful girls with a deadly potion and dispatching them to give the kiss of death to his enemies in various capitals. Aka KISS AND KILL and AGAINST ALL ODDS. Sequel: THE CASTLE OF FU MANCHU. Released theatrically in the U.S. in b&w. Video title: KISS OF DEATH. Widescreen. [M/PG]▼
Blood of Ghastly Horror (1972) **C-87m.** BOMB D: Al Adamson. John Carradine, Kent Taylor, Tommy Kirk, Regina Carrol. Carradine stars as Dr. Van Ard, whose brain-transplant experiments lead to murder and mayhem. Ghastly indeed! Made in 1969; also known as THE FIEND WITH THE ATOMIC BRAIN, PSYCHO A GO-GO!, THE LOVE MANIAC, THE MAN WITH THE SYNTHETIC BRAIN, and THE FIEND WITH THE ELECTRONIC BRAIN. Techniscope. ▼
Blood of Heroes, The (1990-Australian-U.S.) **C-90m.** *½ D: David Peoples. Rutger Hauer, Joan Chen, Vincent Phillip D'Onofrio, Anna Katarina, Delroy Lindo. In the usual desolate post-nuclear war world one-eyed Hauer and apprentice Chen are specialists at "juggers"—a kind of futuristic

rugby where the scorer places a dog's skull atop a vertical stick on the opposing team's goal line. Stick to *Home Run Derby* reruns on ESPN instead; this may be the grimiest movie since C.H.U.D., which did, after all, take place in a sewer. Australian title: SALUTE OF THE JUGGER. [R]▼●

Blood of the Vampire (1958-British) **C-87m.** ** D: Henry Cass. Donald Wolfit, Barbara Shelley, Vincent Ball, Victor Maddern. Potentially vivid horror film weakened by slack production: doctor sent to prison hospital finds the warden is an anemic mad scientist (need more be said?). Wolfit is made up to resemble Bela Lugosi.▼

Blood on Satan's Claw, The (1971-British) **C-93m.** *** D: Piers Haggard. Patrick Wymark, Linda Hayden, Barry Andrews, Michele Dotrice, Tamara Ustinov. In 17th-century Britain a demon is unearthed which a group of evil farm children begin worshipping, sacrificing other children to it. Richly atmospheric horror film with erotic undertones, somewhat gruesome at times. Original title: SATAN'S SKIN, running 100m. Retitled SATAN'S CLAW. [R]▼

Blood on the Arrow (1964) **C-91m.** *½ D: Sidney Salkow. Dale Robertson, Martha Hyer, Wendell Corey, Elisha Cook, Ted de Corsia. Humdrum Western dealing with Apache massacre and survivors' attempt to rescue son who is held captive.

Blood on the Moon (1948) **88m.** *** D: Robert Wise. Robert Mitchum, Barbara Bel Geddes, Robert Preston, Walter Brennan, Phyllis Thaxter, Frank Faylen, Tom Tully, Charles McGraw, Tom Tyler. Straightforward Western tale (from a novel by Luke Short) about a drifter who's hired by his former partner to help him bilk some naive landowners. Mitchum sizes up the situation and decides he doesn't like it; Preston is an unrepentant villain. Watch for that great confrontation scene in a darkened barroom. Also shown in computer-colored version.▼●

Blood on the Sun (1945) **98m.** *** D: Frank Lloyd. James Cagney, Sylvia Sidney, Wallace Ford, Rosemary DeCamp, Robert Armstrong. Cagney, in Japan during the 1930s, smells trouble coming but is virtually helpless; good melodrama. Also shown in computer-colored version.▼●◗

Blood Red (1988) **C-91m.** BOMB D: Peter Masterson. Eric Roberts, Giancarlo Giannini, Dennis Hopper, Burt Young, Carlin Glynn, Lara Harris, Joseph Running Fox, Al Ruscio, Michael Madsen, Elias Koteas, Marc Lawrence, Frank Campanella, Aldo Ray, Susan Anspach, Horton Foote, Jr., Julia Roberts. Ruthless, Irish-born Hopper wants to build his railroad through the land of Sicilian immigrant Giannini and his fellow wine-growers in 1890s California. Dreadful film, with lots of explosions; huge, good cast can't save it. Julia Roberts, Eric's kid sister, makes her screen debut as his sibling (and Giannini's daughter). [R]▼

Blood Relatives (1978-French-Canadian) **C-100m.** *** D: Claude Chabrol. Donald Sutherland, Aude Landry, Lisa Langlois, Laurent Malet, Micheline Lanctot, Stephane Audran, Donald Pleasence, David Hemmings. Barely released thriller about a secret, incestuous relationship with deadly consequences. Interesting cast and Chabrol's cold, scientifically masterful direction make this less unpleasant and gory than it might have been. Not released until 1981 in U.S. [R]▼

Blood Salvage (1990) **C-98m.** ** D: Tucker Johnston. Danny Nelson, Lori Birdsong, John Saxon, Ray Walston, Evander Holyfield. Grisly gorefest (with humorous touches splattered throughout) has religious nutso Nelson running a body parts junkyard and preying on waylaid tourists. Not for the weak-stomached. Coexecutive producer of film, heavyweight boxer Evander Holyfield, challenged his pugilist peers to sit through this one without flinching; he reportedly had no takers. [R]▼●

Bloodsilver SEE: **Beyond the Law**

Blood Simple (1984) **C-97m.** *** D: Joel Coen. John Getz, Frances McDormand, Dan Hedaya, Samm-Art Williams, M. Emmet Walsh. Flamboyant homage to film noir made on a shoestring by brothers Joel and Ethan Coen in Texas. A cuckolded husband hires slimy character to kill his wife and her boyfriend . . . but that's just the beginning of this serpentine story. A visual delight, full of show-offy stylistics; just a bit "cold around the heart," to quote an earlier noir classic. McDormand's film debut. Recut, remixed, restored and reissued in 2000 with a new 5m. introduction. [R]▼●

Blood-Spattered Bride, The (1969-Spanish) **C-83m.** *½ D: Vicente Aranda. Maribel Martin, Simon Andreu, Alexandra Bastedo, Dean Selmier, Montserrat Julio. Newlyweds in secluded mansion are terrorized by a strange guest, the reincarnation of a murderess dead 200 years. Based on LeFanu's *Carmila,* but poorly done. Aka TIL DEATH DO US PART. [R]▼

Bloodsport (1987) **C-92m.** ** D: Newt Arnold. Jean-Claude Van Damme, Donald Gibb, Leah Ayres, Norman Burton, Forest Whitaker, Bolo Yeung. Belgian-born Van Damme joins the movie macho brigade in this story (based on true events) of American Ninja Frank Dux, the first westerner to win the Kumite, an international martial arts competition that tests its participants to their limits. Violent, low-budget action film has its moments. Followed by three direct-to-video sequels. [R]▼●

Blood Suckers, The (1967) SEE: **Return from the Past**

Bloodsuckers (1970-British) **C-87m.** *½ D: Robert Hartford-Davis. Patrick Macnee, Peter Cushing, Alex Davion, Patrick Mower, Johnny Sekka, Medeline Hinde, Imogen Hassall, Edward Woodward. Confusing horror yarn about ancient vampire cult on Greek island of Hydra, somehow linked to sinister Oxford dons. Mishmash includes many narrated silent sequences and other evidence of considerable post-production tampering. Aka INCENSE FOR THE DAMNED and DOCTORS WEAR SCARLET. [R]▼

Blood, Sweat and Fear (1975-Italian) **C-90m.** *½ D: Stevio Massi. Lee J. Cobb, Franco Gasparri, Giorgia Albertazzi, Sora Sperati. Plodding action drama involving a cat-and-mouse game between Cobb, as the brains behind a grand-scale drug operation, and Gasparri, as an ambitious young narcotics agent. [R]

Blood Thirst SEE: **Salem's Lot**

Blood Tide (1982) **C-82m.** *½ D: Richard Jeffries. James Earl Jones, José Ferrer, Lila Kedrova, Mary Louise Weller, Martin Kove, Deborah Shelton. Lovely Greek scenery is the only distinction of this substandard programmer in which a monster from the deep is unleashed, causing predictable mayhem. Good cast shamelessly wasted. Aka THE RED TIDE. [R]▼

Blood Ties (1986-Italian) **C-120m.** *** D: Giacomo Battiato. Brad Davis, Tony Lo Bianco, Vincent Spano, Barbara De Rossi, Delia Boccardo, Ricky Tognazzi, Maria Conchita Alonso, Michael Gazzo. Uncompromising crime actioner about an innocent American (Davis), coerced by the mob into assassinating his Sicilian cousin (Lo Bianco), who's been investigating Mafia activities. Good job all around. Originally a four-hour television movie; video version runs 98m.▼

Blood Wedding (1981-U.S.) SEE: **He Knows You're Alone**

Blood Wedding (1981-Spanish) **C-72m.** *** D: Carlos Saura. Antonio Gades, Cristina Hoyos, Juan Antonio Jimenez, Pilar Cardenas, Carmen Villena. Gades' adaptation for ballet of Federico Garcia Lorca's classic tragedy, performed in full costume in a bare rehearsal hall. Saura's direction is best described as intimate in this happy union of dance and film. ▼●

Bloody Birthday (1986) **C-85m.** ** D: Ed Hunt. Susan Strasberg, Jose Ferrer, Lori Lethin, Melinda Cordell, Julie Brown, Joe Penny, Billy Jacoby, Michael Dudikoff. Three 10-year-old killer kids go on a rampage; they were born during a lunar eclipse. Formula horror fare "boasts" very tasteless premise but lapses into the usual killing spree. Filmed in 1980. [R]▼

Bloody Brood, The (1959-Canadian) **80m.** ** D: Julian Roffman. Jack Betts, Barbara Lord, Peter Falk, Robert Christie, Ronald Hartmann. Mind-boggling time capsule with Falk most impressive in his second screen role as Nico, a deranged "beatnik" who gets his kicks by feeding a hamburger laced with broken glass to an unsuspecting kid! Laughable, thoroughly cynical depiction of the Beat Generation.▼

Bloody Dead, The SEE: **Creature With the Blue Hand**

Bloody Mama (1970) **C-90m.** *½ D: Roger Corman. Shelley Winters, Don Stroud, Pat Hingle, Robert De Niro, Clint Kimbrough, Robert Walden, Diane Varsi, Bruce Dern, Pamela Dunlap. Excellent performances cannot save sordid story of Ma Barker and her ugly brood. Film unsuccessfully mixes action narrative with psychological study. [R]▼●

Blossoms In the Dust (1941) **C-100m.** *** D: Mervyn LeRoy. Greer Garson, Walter Pidgeon, Felix Bressart, Marsha Hunt, Fay Holden, Samuel S. Hinds. Slick tear-jerker of Texas orphanage founded by Garson when she loses her own child; tastefully acted.▼

Blowing Wild (1953) **90m.** ** D: Hugo Fregonese. Gary Cooper, Barbara Stanwyck, Ruth Roman, Anthony Quinn, Ward Bond. Tempestuous Stanwyck is married to oil tycoon Quinn, but sets her sights on wildcatter Cooper, who's fully recovered from their one-time affair. Heated emotions can't warm up this plodding story, filmed in Mexico.▼●

Blown Away (1994) **C-121m.** ** D: Stephen Hopkins. Jeff Bridges, Tommy Lee Jones, Lloyd Bridges, Forest Whitaker, Suzy Amis, John Finn, Stephi Lineburg, Loyd Catlett, Caitlin Clarke, Chris De Oni, Ruben Santiago-Hudson. Dreary action thriller with Irish wacko Jones targeting Boston's bomb removal squad—and one member in particular (Bridges, a former IRA crony)—with his insidious explosions. Irish accents come and go, and so does story interest, which trods on all-too-familiar turf. Bridges Sr. is fun to watch as a wily old son of Eire. Super 35. [R]▼●◗

Blow Out (1981) **C-107m.** **½ D: Brian De Palma. John Travolta, Nancy Allen, John Lithgow, Dennis Franz, Peter Boyden. Intriguing variation on Antonioni's BLOWUP (with a similar title, no less!) set in Philadelphia, about a sound-effects man who records a car accident that turns out to be a politically motivated murder. Absorbing most of the way, but weakened by show-off camerawork and logic loopholes. Panavision. [R]▼●

Blowup (1966-British-Italian) **C-111m.** ***½ D: Michelangelo Antonioni. Vanessa Redgrave, David Hemmings, Sarah Miles, Jill Kennington, Verushka, Peter Bowles, Jane Birkin, Gillian Hills, The Yardbirds. Writer-director Antonioni's hypnotic pop-culture parable of photographer caught in passive lifestyle. Arresting, provocative film, rich in color symbolism, many-layered meanings. Music by Herbie Hancock.▼●

Blue (1968) **C-113m.** *½ D: Silvio Narizzano. Terence Stamp, Joanna Pettet, Karl Malden, Ricardo Montalban, Joe DeSantis, Sally Kirkland. Undistinguished, poorly written Western about American-born, Mexican-raised boy who trusts no one until bullet wounds force him to trust a woman. See also: FADE-IN. Panavision. ▼●

Blue (1993-French) **C-100m.** **½ D: Krzysztof Kieslowski. Juliette Binoche, Benoit Regent, Florence Pernel, Charlotte Very, Helene Vincent, Philippe Volter, Hugues Quester, Emmanuelle Riva, Julie Delpy. Binoche loses her family in a tragic accident and decides to radically change her world; she leaves behind any memories of her husband, a renowned composer, and moves into a Paris flat to contemplate life. Slow-moving drama is borderline interesting but remains more a showcase for its leading lady than anything else. First of Polish director Kieslowski's "Three Colors" trilogy probing life in contemporary Europe: BLUE/"Liberty"; WHITE/"Equality"; RED/"Fraternity."▼●

Blue Angel, The (1930-German) **103m.** ***½ D: Josef von Sternberg. Marlene Dietrich, Emil Jannings, Kurt Gerron, Rosa Valetti, Hans Albers. Ever-fascinating film classic with Jannings as stuffy professor who falls blindly in love with cabaret entertainer Lola-Lola (Dietrich), who ruins his life. Dietrich introduces "Falling in Love Again"; this role made her an international star. Robert Liebman scripted, from Heinrich Mann's novel *Professor Unrath*. Simultaneously shot in German and English versions; the former is obviously superior. Remade in 1959. Restored on video and laserdisc to 106m.▼●

Blue Angel, The (1959) **C-107m.** *½ D: Edward Dmytryk. Curt Jurgens, May Britt, Theodore Bikel, John Banner, Ludwig Stossel, Fabrizio Mioni. Disastrous remake of Josef von Sternberg-Marlene Dietrich classic, from Heinrich Mann's novel of precise professor won over by tawdry nightclub singer. CinemaScope.

Bluebeard (1944) **73m.** *** D: Edgar G. Ulmer. Jean Parker, John Carradine, Nils Asther, Ludwig Stossel, Iris Adrian, Emmett Lynn. Surprisingly effective story of incurable strangler Carradine, who falls for smart-girl Parker who senses that something is wrong.▼

Bluebeard (1962-French-Italian) **C-114m.** **½ D: Claude Chabrol. Charles Denner, Michele Morgan, Danielle Darrieux, Hildegarde Neff, Stephane Audran, Catherine Rouvel, Françoise Lugagne. Retelling of life of French wife-killer, far less witty than Chaplin's MONSIEUR VERDOUX. Original French title: LANDRU.▼

Bluebeard (1972) **C-125m.** ** D: Edward Dmytryk. Richard Burton, Raquel Welch, Virna Lisi, Joey Heatherton, Nathalie Delon, Karin Schubert. Burton doesn't make much of an impression as world's most famous ladykiller. Women are all beautiful, but script gives them little to do. International production. [R]▼

Bluebeard's Eighth Wife (1938) **80m.** ** D: Ernst Lubitsch. Claudette Colbert, Gary Cooper, David Niven, Edward Everett Horton, Elizabeth Patterson, Herman Bing. Contrived comedy about a woman determined to gain the upper hand over an oft-married millionaire. One of Lubitsch's weakest films, notable mainly for the way its two stars "meet cute." Script by Billy Wilder and Charles Brackett. Previously filmed in 1923.▼

Bluebeard's Ten Honeymoons (1960-British) **93m.** ** D: W. Lee Wilder. George Sanders, Corinne Calvet, Jean Kent, Patricia Roc. Sanders enlivens OK chronicle of fortune hunter who decides that marrying and murdering a series of women is the key to financial success.

Blue Bird, The (1940) **C-88m.** ** D: Walter Lang. Shirley Temple, Spring Byington, Nigel Bruce, Gale Sondergaard, Eddie Collins, Sybil Jason. Released one year after THE WIZARD OF OZ, this lavish Technicolor fantasy (based on the famous play by Maurice Maeterlinck) has everything but charm. Even Shirley seems stiff. Filmed before in 1918, remade in 1976.▼

Blue Bird, The (1976-Russian-U.S.) **C-99m.** ** D: George Cukor. Todd Lookinland, Patsy Kensit, Elizabeth Taylor, Jane Fonda, Ava Gardner, Cicely Tyson George Cole, Will Geer, Robert Morley, Harry Andrews. Posh, star-studded but heavy-handed fantasy based on Maeterlinck's play about children seeking the bluebird of happiness. First coproduction between U.S. and Russia is unbelievably draggy. [G]

Blue Blood (1951) **C-72m.** *½ D: Lew Landers. Bill Williams, Jane Nigh, Arthur Shields, Audrey Long. Lackluster racehorse story with a few good moments by Shields as elderly trainer seeking comeback.

Blue Chips (1994) **C-101m.** **½ D: William Friedkin. Nick Nolte, Mary McDonnell, J. T. Walsh, Ed O'Neill, Alfre Woodard, Bob Cousy, Shaquille O'Neal, Anfernee "Penny" Hardaway, Matt Nover, Anthony C. Hall, Robert Wuhl, Jerry Tarkanian, Bobby Knight, Richard Pitino, George Raveling. After his first losing season, hard-driving collegiate basketball coach Nolte agrees to look the other way while fat-cat recruiters bribe new talent to join his team. Reasonably compelling at first, then all too obvious and predictable.

Written by Ron Shelton. Towering NBA superstar O'Neal is engaging as one of the recruits; other hoop stars like Larry Bird have small parts, while legendary champion Cousy plays the college athletic director. Louis Gossett, Jr., appears unbilled. [PG-13]▼●

Blue City (1986) **C-83m.** BOMB D: Michelle Manning. Judd Nelson, Ally Sheedy, David Caruso, Paul Winfield, Scott Wilson, Anita Morris. Perfectly awful film about wiseguy kid who returns to Florida hometown after five years, discovers that his father was killed, and vows to avenge (and solve) his murder. Senseless and stupid; Nelson's unappealing character seems to possess a one-word vocabulary, and the word *isn't* fudge. Based on a good book by Ross Macdonald. [R]▼●

Blue Collar (1978) **C-114m.** ***½ D: Paul Schrader. Richard Pryor, Harvey Keitel, Yaphet Kotto, Ed Begley, Jr., Harry Bellaver, George Memmoli. Punchy, muckraking exposé melodrama with Pryor, Keitel, and Kotto delivering strong performances as auto workers who find that it isn't just management ripping them off—it's their own union. Schrader's directing debut. [R]▼●◗

Blue Dahlia, The (1946) **99m.** *** D: George Marshall. Alan Ladd, Veronica Lake, William Bendix, Howard da Silva, Hugh Beaumont, Doris Dowling. Exciting Raymond Chandler–scripted melodrama has Ladd returning from military service to find wife unfaithful. She's murdered, he's suspected in well-turned film. Produced by John Houseman. ▼

Blue Denim (1959) **89m.** *** D: Philip Dunne. Carol Lynley, Brandon de Wilde, Macdonald Carey, Marsha Hunt, Warren Berlinger, Roberta Shore. De Wilde and Lynley are striking as teen-agers faced with Carol's pregnancy. Generation gap problem and youths' naiveté date story, but believable performances make it worthwhile. CinemaScope.

Blue Fin (1978-Australian) **C-90m.** ** D: Carl Schultz. Hardy Kruger, Greg Rowe, Elspeth Ballantyne, Liddy Clark, John Jarratt. Mild (but scenic) family outing about a father and son, not on the best of terms, who sail together in search of elusive tuna catch off Australia's southern coast. [PG]▼

Blue Gardenia, The (1953) **90m.** *** D: Fritz Lang. Anne Baxter, Richard Conte, Ann Sothern, Raymond Burr, Jeff Donnell, George Reeves, Nat King Cole. Engaging murder caper with 1940s flavor. Baxter is accused of murdering wolfish Burr, decides to take columnist Conte's offer of help. Solid film with twist ending. ▼◗

Blue Grass of Kentucky (1950) **C-71m.** ** D: William Beaudine. Bill Williams, Jane Nigh, Ralph Morgan. Routine account of horse-breeding families, their rivalry and eventual healing of old wounds when romance blooms between the younger generations.

Blue Hawaii (1961) **C-101m.** **½ D: Norman Taurog. Elvis Presley, Joan Blackman, Angela Lansbury, Roland Winters, Iris Adrian. Agreeable Presley vehicle bolstered by Lansbury's presence as mother of ex-G.I. (Presley) returning to islands and working with tourist agency. Elvis performs one of his prettiest hits, "Can't Help Falling in Love." Panavision. ▼●◗

Blue Ice (1992-British-U.S.) **C-105m.** **½ D: Russell Mulcahy. Michael Caine, Sean Young, Ian Holm, Bobby Short, Alun Armstrong, Sam Kelly, Jack Shepherd. Retired British agent Caine is dragged out of his beloved jazz club and back into service to help crack an illegal arms ring. Cabaret legend Bobby Short has an acting role here, and unbilled Bob Hoskins turns up briefly as Caine's chum from the old days. Premiered on cable in the U.S. at 100m.▼●

Blue Iguana, The (1988) **C-88m.** BOMB D: John Lafia. Dylan McDermott, Jessica Harper, James Russo, Pamela Gidley, Tovah Feldshuh, Dean Stockwell, Yano Anaya, Flea, Michele Seipp. Amateurish spoof is a hybrid of B Western and film noir, with a down-and-out bounty hunter on a suicide mission to recover $20 million in contraband money from a gaggle of bad guys south of the border. This turkey barely made it to theaters; even an amusing cameo by Stockwell can't save it. [R]▼●

Blue in the Face (1995) **C-84m.** *½ D: Wayne Wang, Paul Auster. Harvey Keitel, Lou Reed, Michael J. Fox, Roseanne, Mel Gorham, Jim Jarmusch, Lily Tomlin, Jared Harris, Giancarlo Esposito, Jose Zuniga, Victor Argo, Madonna, Mira Sorvino, Keith David, RuPaul. Meandering, overindulgent mess of a movie filmed immediately after SMOKE and improvised from sketches developed by Wang and Auster in collaboration with the actors. Set mostly in and around the Brooklyn cigar store managed by Keitel. In desperate need of a script. [R]▼●

Blue Juice (1995-British) **C-99m.** ** D: Carl Prechezer. Sean Pertwee, Catherine Zeta-Jones, Steven Mackintosh, Peter Gunn, Ewan McGregor, Heathcote Williams, Colette Brown, Jenny Agutter. Low-octane tale of aging, self-absorbed surfer boy Pertwee, who's constantly putting off practical-minded (and increasingly flustered) girlfriend Zeta-Jones to hang with his mates. Superficial and predictable to an extreme; of note only for the early-career presence of Zeta-Jones and McGregor (as an obnoxious, pathetic slacker/drug dealer). [R] ▼◗

Blue Kite, The (1993-Chinese) **C-140m.** *** D: Tian Zhuangzhuang. Yi Tian, Zhang

Wenyao, Chen Xiaoman, Lu Liping, Pu Quanxin, Li Xuejian. Absorbing, uncompromising saga of the life and times of—and emotional upheaval within—one Chinese family during the tumultuous 1950s and 60s, told from the point of view of a child. An unsubtle condemnation of blind revolution and the political system in Communist China. It was (unsurprisingly) highly controversial back home; at one point its filming was halted because of the scenario's "political leanings."▼●

Blue Lagoon, The (1949-British) **C-101m.** *** D: Frank Launder. Jean Simmons, Donald Houston, Noel Purcell, Cyril Cusack, Maurice Denham. Idyllic romance of Simmons and Houston, shipwrecked on tropic isle, falling in love as they grow to maturity; slowly paced but refreshing. Remade in 1980.

Blue Lagoon, The (1980) **C-104m.** *½ D: Randal Kleiser. Brooke Shields, Christopher Atkins, Leo McKern, William Daniels. Remake of the 1949 film is little more than softcore cinema for the heavy-petting set, as two children become sexually aware of each other after being shipwrecked on an island for several years. Nestor Almendros' photography can't save it. Followed over a decade later by RETURN TO THE BLUE LAGOON. [R]▼●◗

Blue Lamp, The (1950-British) **84m.** *** D: Basil Dearden. Jack Warner, Jimmy Hanley, Dirk Bogarde, Robert Flemyng, Bernard Lee, Peggy Evans, Patric Doonan, Gladys Henson, Meredith Edwards. Crackerjack manhunt thriller about Scotland Yard's search for murderer of policeman. Unpretentious and exciting—a key British postwar film. Music hall star Tessie O'Shea appears as herself.▼

Blue Light, The (1932-German) **77m.** ** D: Leni Riefenstahl. Leni Riefenstahl, Mathias Weimann, Beni Fuhrer, Max Holzboer. Mysterious mountain-maiden Riefenstahl is loved and destroyed by artist Weimann. Slow, pretentious fable, also produced and cowritten by Riefenstahl. She recut film in 1952, and it is this version that's usually shown today.▼

Blue Manhattan SEE: **Hi, Mom!**

Blue Max, The (1966) **C-156m.** **½ D: John Guillermin. George Peppard, James Mason, Ursula Andress, Jeremy Kemp, Carl Schell. Fantastic aerial photography and memorable Jerry Goldsmith score are the assets of this silly drama, taken from German point of view, about dogfighting in WW1. Steamy Peppard-Andress love scenes aren't bad either. CinemaScope.▼●

Blue Monkey (1987) **C-98m.** BOMB D: William Fruet. Steve Railsback, Gwynyth Walsh, Susan Anspach, John Vernon, Joe Flaherty, Robin Duke, Sarah Polley. Silly monster film set at hospital that's quarantined after a monster escapes. Poorly filmed in semi-darkness. Title is meaningless and randomly selected; it was originally called GREEN MONKEY! Laser title: INSECT. [R]▼●

Blue Murder at St. Trinian's (1957-British) **86m.** **½ D: Frank Launder. Terry-Thomas, George Cole, Joyce Grenfell, Lionel Jeffries, Eric Barker, Lisa Gastoni, Ferdy Mayne, Alastair Sim. OK entry in the series of farces set at the St. Trinian's School for Girls. Ever-mischievous students win a trip to the continent and become immersed in various hijinks. Sim appears too briefly (in drag) as Miss Amelia Fritton, the school's headmistress.▼

Blueprint for Murder, A (1953) **76m.** **½ D: Andrew L. Stone. Joseph Cotten, Jean Peters, Gary Merrill, Jack Kruschen, Mae Marsh. Whodunit has Peters as prime suspect of poison killings, with Cotten seeking the truth.

Blueprint for Robbery (1961) **87m.** **½ D: Jerry Hopper. J. Pat O'Malley, Robert Wilke, Robert Gist, Romo Vincent, Tom Duggan. Deliberately offbeat, low-key film of heist engineered by old-timer O'Malley; good moments put this above average, but overall result is unmemorable.

Blues Brothers, The (1980) **C-130m.** *** D: John Landis. John Belushi, Dan Aykroyd, The Blues Brothers Band, Cab Calloway, John Candy, Henry Gibson, Carrie Fisher, Charles Napier, Jeff Morris, Ray Charles, Aretha Franklin, James Brown, Kathleen Freeman. Engagingly nutty comedy about the title characters (deadpan musical performers introduced on TV's *Saturday Night Live*) trying to raise money to save their orphanage by reuniting their old band—and nearly destroying Chicago in the process. Off the wall from start to finish, with some fine music woven in, including wonderful numbers by Franklin and Calloway. Numerous cameos include Steven Spielberg, Frank Oz, Steve Lawrence, John Lee Hooker, Twiggy, and Paul Reubens (Pee-wee Herman). Special edition runs 147m. Followed by a sequel. [R]▼●◗

Blues Brothers 2000 (1998) **C-123m.** **½ D: John Landis. Dan Aykroyd, John Goodman, Joe Morton, Nia Peeples, Kathleen Freeman, J. Evan Bonifant, Frank Oz, Steve Lawrence, Darrell Hammond, Erykah Badu. Just sprung from prison, Elwood Blues reunites his old band (minus brother Jake—the late John Belushi), with a young orphan (Bonifant) in tow. Silly "plot" goes on too long, but high spirits prevail, especially during infectious music numbers like "634-5789" and Aretha Franklin's "Respect." Incredible lineup of guest musicians includes B.B. King, James Brown, Junior Wells, Isaac Hayes, Eric Clapton, Dr. John, Wilson Pickett, Bo Diddley, Eddie Floyd, Jonny Lang, Billy Preston, Travis Tritt, and music supervisor Paul Shaffer. Aykroyd and Landis co-produced and scripted. [PG-13]▼●◗

Blues Busters (1950) **67m.** **½ D: William Beaudine. Leo Gorcey, Huntz Hall, Adele Jergens, Gabriel Dell, Craig Stevens, Phyllis Coates, Billy Benedict, Bernard Gorcey, David Gorcey. Louie's Sweet Shop is turned into a nightclub when Sach's tonsillectomy turns him into a swooning crooner. Amusing *Bowery Boys* comedy, with Hall a standout.▼

Blues for Lovers (1966-British) **89m.** ** D: Paul Henreid. Ray Charles, Tom Bell, Mary Peach, Dawn Addams, Piers Bishop, Betty McDowall. Story of Charles (playing himself) and blind child is maudlin, but fans will like generous footage devoted to Ray's song hits, including "I Got a Woman" and "What'd I Say?" Aka BALLAD IN BLUE.▼

Blues in the Night (1941) **88m.** **½ D: Anatole Litvak. Priscilla Lane, Richard Whorf, Betty Field, Lloyd Nolan, Jack Carson, Elia Kazan, Wallace Ford, Billy Halop, Peter Whitney. Intriguing musical drama abandons early promise for soapy, silly melodramatics, in story of self-destructive musician (Whorf) and his band (young Kazan is featured as clarinetist). Good moments, wonderful Warner Bros. montages, but the great title song is never played once in its entirety!

Blue Skies (1946) **C-104m.** *** D: Stuart Heisler. Fred Astaire, Bing Crosby, Joan Caulfield, Billy De Wolfe, Olga San Juan, Frank Faylen. Astaire and Crosby play onetime show-biz partners and rivals in this paper-thin vehicle kept aloft by lots and lots of Irving Berlin songs. Highlights: Astaire's terrific "Puttin' on the Ritz," star duo's "A Couple of Song and Dance Men."▼●

Blue Skies Again (1983) **C-90m.** **½ D: Richard Michaels. Harry Hamlin, Robyn Barto, Mimi Rogers, Kenneth McMillan, Dana Elcar, Andy Garcia, Marcos Gonzales. Friendly, well-meaning but ultimately minor-league chronicle of a young woman (Barto) attempting to play professional baseball. [PG]▼

Blue Sky (1994) **C-101m.** **½ D: Tony Richardson. Jessica Lange, Tommy Lee Jones, Powers Boothe, Carrie Snodgress, Amy Locane, Chris O'Donnell, Mitchell Ryan, Dale Dye, Tim Scott, Annie Ross, Anna Klemp. A dedicated military man endures continual embarrassment by his teasingly sexy (and emotionally unstable) wife, for one simple reason: he loves her. Intelligent and compassionate drama, set in the early 1960s, loses its way as it gets involved in a nuclear cover-up subplot, but rates as a must-see for anyone who admires its stars: both Jones and Lange (in an Oscar-winning performance) are extraordinarily good. Shot in 1990; director Richardson died the following year. Timothy Bottoms appears unbilled. [PG-13]▼●

Blue Steel (1990) **C-102m.** *½ D: Kathryn Bigelow. Jamie Lee Curtis, Ron Silver, Clancy Brown, Elizabeth Pena, Louise Fletcher, Philip Bosco. Stupid thriller with Curtis as a rookie cop stalked by a slick psycho (Silver) in N.Y.C. Laughably ludicrous dialogue is matched by preposterous story turns. [R]▼●

Blue Streak (1999) **C-94m.** ** D: Les Mayfield. Martin Lawrence, Luke Wilson, Dave Chappelle, William Forsythe, Nicole Ari Parker, Peter Greene. Loud boilerplate action comedy casts Lawrence as a so-called master thief who has socked away a stolen jewel in the innards of a construction site—only to discover, upon his release from jail, that the completed structure is a police precinct. The solution is to become a cop, just as the solution for Lawrence might be to stay away from moldy scripts like this. [PG-13]▼◗

Blue Sunshine (1976) **C-97m.** **½ D: Jeff Lieberman. Zalman King, Deborah Winters, Mark Goddard, Robert Walden, Charles Siebert. Young man accused of murders eludes cops, discovers that apparently "random" killings derive from delayed drug reactions of ten-year-old college class. Offbeat psychological thriller, quite violent at times. [R]▼

Blue Thunder (1983) **C-108m.** ** D: John Badham. Roy Scheider, Malcolm McDowell, Candy Clark, Daniel Stern, Warren Oates, Paul Roebling, Joe Santos. Slick action film built around L.A.'s police helicopter surveillance team. Fun at first, but gets stupider (and crueler) as film goes on—with villainous McDowell character especially ludicrous. Even escapist fare has to be believable on its own terms. Later a TV series. Panavision. [R]▼●◗

Blue Veil, The (1951) **113m.** *** D: Curtis Bernhardt. Jane Wyman, Charles Laughton, Joan Blondell, Richard Carlson, Agnes Moorehead, Don Taylor, Audrey Totter, Everett Sloane, Cyril Cusack, Natalie Wood, Warner Anderson, Vivian Vance, Philip Ober. Wyman is self-sacrificing nursemaid whose life story is chronicled with intertwined episodes of her charges and their families. Well done.

Blue Velvet (1986) **C-120m.** ** D: David Lynch. Kyle MacLachlan, Isabella Rossellini, Dennis Hopper, Laura Dern, Hope Lange, Dean Stockwell, Jack Nance, Brad Dourif. Terminally weird, though flamboyantly original film about a young man's involvement in a small-town mystery involving a kinky nightclub singer, a sadistic kidnapper/drug dealer, and other swell folks. A highly individual look at the bizarre elements just behind the facade of a picture-perfect American town. Too audacious to be easily dismissed, but too strange to be easily enjoyed . . . yet this was one of the most critically praised movies of 1986! Lynch's use of widescreen will suffer on TV; the director also wrote this one. J-D-C Scope. [R]▼●◗

Blue Water, White Death (1971) **C-99m.** *** D: Peter Gimbel, James Lipscomb. Vivid documentary on one of the sea's most voracious and feared predators, the great white shark; terrifying underwater scenes but somewhat overstated. Techniscope. [G]

Blue, White and Perfect (1941) **73m.** **½ D: Herbert I. Leeds. Lloyd Nolan, Mary Beth Hughes, Helene Reynolds, George Reeves, Steven Geray, Curt Bois. Slick espionage action, with tough shamus Michael Shayne (Nolan) turning patriotic to catch enemy agents trying to smuggle industrial diamonds to their countries. Reeves is notable as glib mystery man who may or may not be the ringleader.

Bluff SEE: **Con Artists**

Blume in Love (1973) **C-117m.** **½ D: Paul Mazursky. George Segal, Susan Anspach, Kris Kristofferson, Marsha Mason, Shelley Winters, Paul Mazursky. Self-indulgent film about divorce-lawyer Segal refusing to accept fact that his wife (Anspach) has walked out on him, determining to win her back. Good look at modern marriages, but overlong, rambling; Kristofferson delightful as man who moves in with Anspach. [R]▼

B. Monkey (1999-British-U.S.) **C-90m.** ** D: Michael Radford. Asia Argento, Jared Harris, Jonathan Rhys Meyers, Rupert Everett, Tim Woodward, Ian Hart. Superficial fluff about a mild-mannered British schoolteacher who falls for a sultry bank robber trying to leave her criminal past behind. Radford's first film since IL POSTINO is a disappointment, particularly since most of it reportedly ended up on the cutting room floor. Still watchable, with a smoldering central performance from Argento, daughter of horrormeister Dario Argento. Completed in 1996. [R]▼◗

Boarding School (1977-German) **C-98m.** *½ D: Andre Farwagi. Nastassja Kinski, Gerry Sundquist, Kurt Raab, Sean Chapman. Sex comedy with Kinski in one of her first starring roles, as an American girl in an exclusive Swiss boarding school, circa 1956. She devises a ruse of the girls pretending to be prostitutes in order to seduce cute guys at nearby boys' school. Original title: THE PASSION FLOWER HOTEL. ▼

Boardwalk (1979) **C-98m.** **½ D: Stephen Verona. Ruth Gordon, Lee Strasberg, Janet Leigh, Joe Silver, Eli Mintz, Eddie Barth. Poignant view of elderly couple struggling to survive in decaying neighborhood missteps into DEATH WISH melodramatics for its finale. Fine performances, including Leigh as duty-bound daughter.

Boat, The SEE: **Das Boot**

Boat People (1983-Hong Kong-Chinese) **C-106m.** ***½ D: Ann Hui. Lam Chi-Cheung, Cora Miao, Season Ma, Andy Lau, Paul Ching. Harrowing, heartbreaking, highly provocative account of Japanese photojournalist Chi-Cheung's experiences in Vietnam after Liberation, particularly his friendship with 14-year-old Ma and her family. [R]

Bob & Carol & Ted & Alice (1969) **C-104m.** *** D: Paul Mazursky. Natalie Wood, Robert Culp, Elliott Gould, Dyan Cannon, Horst Ebersberg, Greg Mullavey, Lee Bergere. Glossy look at modern lifestyles; ultrasophisticated couple (Wood & Culp) try to modernize thinking of their best friends (Gould & Cannon) about sexual freedom. Sharp observations, fine performances, marred by silly, pretentious finale. Written by Mazursky and Larry Tucker; Mazursky's directorial debut. Later a short-lived TV series. [R]▼●

Bobbie Jo and the Outlaw (1976) **C-89m.** ** D: Mark L. Lester. Marjoe Gortner, Lynda Carter, Jesse Vint, Merrie Lynn Ross, Belinda Balaski, Peggy Stewart. Competent but excessively violent drive-in fare; bored carhop Carter hooks up with Marjoe and his gang for a robbing and killing spree. Noteworthy for a couple of glimpses of Lynda's left breast and the occasional film-buff in-joke (e.g., a tobacco-chewing deputy named Abel Gance), courtesy scripter Vernon Zimmerman. [R]▼

Bobbikins (1960-British) **89m.** ** D: Robert Day. Max Bygraves, Shirley Jones, Steven Stocker, Billie Whitelaw. Gimmicky comedy with British singer Bygraves and Jones the parents of an infant who talks like an adult. Not bad . . . but that awful title! CinemaScope.

Bobby Deerfield (1977) **C-124m.** BOMB D: Sydney Pollack. Al Pacino, Marthe Keller, Anny Duperey, Walter McGinn, Romolo Valli, Stephen Meldegg. Grand Prix race-car driver Pacino romances Florentine aristocrat Keller, who is dying of that unnamed disease that seems disproportionately to afflict movie heroines. Her suffering is nothing compared to the audience's; even Pacino is deadening. Recut to 99m. by Pollack for cable TV release. Panavision. [PG]▼

Bobby Ware Is Missing (1955) **67m.** *½ D: Thomas Carr. Neville Brand, Arthur Franz, Jean Willes, Walter Reed. Tedious boy-hunt as his parents and sheriff track down kidnappers.

Bob Le Flambeur (1955-French) **102m.** *** D: Jean-Pierre Melville. Roger Duchesne, Isabel Corey, Daniel Cauchy, Guy Decomble, Andre Garet, Gerard Buhr, Howard Vernon. Witty inversion of THE ASPHALT JUNGLE: hard-luck gambler

Duchesne enlists pals in intricate plan to knock over Deauville casino, but everything is so stacked against them that we almost hope he'll call it off. Clever and atmospheric, blessed with eerily sexy Corey and a great closing line. Unreleased in the U.S. until 1982. [PG]▼●

Bob Mathias Story, The (1954) **80m.** *** D: Francis D. Lyon. Bob Mathias, Ward Bond, Melba Mathias, Paul Bryar, Ann Doran. Agreeable biography of olympic star athlete, his sports career, military duty, family life. Mathias turns in an engaging portrayal of himself.

Bobo, The (1967-British) **C-105m.** ** D: Robert Parrish. Peter Sellers, Britt Ekland, Rossano Brazzi, Adolfo Celi, Ferdy Mayne. Misfire comedy casts Sellers as aspiring singing matador who's promised a booking if he can seduce Ekland, the most desirable woman in Barcelona, within three days. Filmed in Spain and Rome.▼●

Bob Roberts (1992) **C-101m.** *** D: Tim Robbins. Tim Robbins, Giancarlo Esposito, Ray Wise, Rebecca Jenkins, Harry J. Lennix, John Ottavino, Robert Stanton, Alan Rickman, Gore Vidal, Brian Murray, Anita Gillette, David Strathairn. Smart, funny political satire about a right-wing, folk-singing Senatorial candidate who knows how to manipulate an audience—and the media. Turns into a political polemic near the end, using speechifying instead of incident and dialogue to make its points. Still, a stimulating ride, and an impressive writing-directing debut for Robbins, who also composed the songs with his brother David. Funny cameos by a variety of famous actors as air-headed TV news anchors and reporters; Bob Balaban and John Cusack add verisimilitude to a pseudo-*Saturday Night Live* sequence. [R]▼●

Boccaccio '70 (1962-Italian) **C-165m.** *** D: Vittorio De Sica, Luchino Visconti, Federico Fellini. Anita Ekberg, Sophia Loren, Romy Schneider, Peppino De Filippo, Dante Maggio, Tomas Milian. Trio of episodes: "The Raffle"—timid soul wins a liaison with a girl as prize; "The Job"—aristocrat's wife takes a job as her husband's mistress; "The Temptation of Dr. Antonio"—fantasy of puritanical fanatic and a voluptuous poster picture which comes alive. A fourth episode, directed by Mario Monicelli, was dropped for U.S. release.▼

Bodies, Rest & Motion (1993) **C-93m.** **½ D: Michael Steinberg. Phoebe Cates, Bridget Fonda, Tim Roth, Eric Stoltz, Alicia Witt, Rich Wheeler. Low-key vignette about four young people trying to connect with each other—and with their own feelings—in a bleak Arizona town. Too obviously based on a stage play (by Roger Hedden), this laid-back film is often inert, but appealing performances—especially by Fonda and Stoltz—give it some spark. Amusing cameo by Bridget's father Peter Fonda. Stoltz also coproduced. [R]▼●

Body and Soul (1947) **104m.** **** D: Robert Rossen. John Garfield, Lilli Palmer, Hazel Brooks, Anne Revere, William Conrad, Joseph Pevney, Canada Lee. Most boxing films pale next to this classic (written by Abraham Polonsky) of Garfield working his way up by devious means, becoming famous champ. Superb photography by James Wong Howe, and Oscar-winning editing by Francis Lyon and Robert Parrish. Remade in 1981 and for TV in 1998.▼●

Body and Soul (1981) **C-100m.** *½ D: George Bowers. Leon Isaac Kennedy, Jayne Kennedy, Peter Lawford, Michael V. Gazzo, Perry Lang, Kim Hamilton. Poor remake of the 1947 classic, with welterweight boxer Kennedy shunning corruption and becoming champion. Leon tries, but is defeated by his paper-thin screenplay. Muhammad Ali appears briefly as himself. [R]▼

Body Count (1998) **C-80m.** BOMB D: Robert Patton-Spruill. David Caruso, Ving Rhames, Linda Fiorentino, John Leguizamo, Donnie Wahlberg, Forest Whitaker. Good cast in an irredeemably awful film that (understandably) didn't make it to theaters in the U.S. A daring museum heist goes bad, leaving the volatile partners to drive to Miami to make their dropoff—if they can avoid killing each other along the way. A more despicable bunch of characters would be hard to imagine. [R]▼●

Body Disappears, The (1941) **72m.** ** D: Ross Lederman. Jeffrey Lynn, Jane Wyman, Edward Everett Horton, Marguerite Chapman. Not a very inspired mixture of comedy, suspense, and sci-fi, as Lynn is involved in invisible-making formula causing havoc with the police.

Body Double (1984) **C-109m.** *½ D: Brian De Palma. Craig Wasson, Gregg Henry, Melanie Griffith, Deborah Shelton, Guy Boyd, Dennis Franz. Gullible (and brainless) actor Wasson becomes obsessed with beautiful woman he's been eyeing through telescope and soon finds himself embroiled in labyrinthine murder plot. Another sleazy fetish film from De Palma, who not only rips off Hitchcock (again) but even himself (OBSESSION, DRESSED TO KILL, BLOW OUT). Some clever moments amid the sleaze, and a good performance by Griffith as porno actress. [R]▼●◗

Bodyguard (1948) **62m.** **½ D: Richard Fleischer. Lawrence Tierney, Priscilla Lane, Philip Reed, June Clayworth, Elizabeth Risdon, Steve Brodie. Hard-boiled homicide cop Tierney is suspended; he reluctantly takes a job as a bodyguard and is promptly framed on a murder rap. Solid little B film, strikingly directed. Based on a story coauthored by 23-year-old Robert Altman!

Bodyguard, The (1992) **C-129m.** **½ D:

Mick Jackson. Kevin Costner, Whitney Houston, Gary Kemp, Bill Cobbs, Ralph Waite, Tomas Arana, Michele Lamar Richards, Mike Starr, DeVaughn Nixon, Robert Wuhl, Bert Remsen, Stephen Shellen, Debbie Reynolds. Cold-as-steel professional bodyguard signs on to protect a music superstar (against his better judgment)—then falls in love with her. Overblown dual-star vehicle makes no sense, but has many crowd-pleasing ingredients—as well as moments of high kitsch. Solid film debut for Houston, who's most effective singing Dolly Parton's old song "I Will Always Love You." Lawrence Kasdan's screenplay was written years earlier—reportedly as a Steve McQueen vehicle. [R]▼●◗

Body Heat (1981) **C-113m.** *** D: Lawrence Kasdan. William Hurt, Kathleen Turner, Richard Crenna, Ted Danson, J. A. Preston, Mickey Rourke. Hurt is a Florida lawyer whose brains work at half speed; Turner is a married socialite who turns on the heat and inspires him to bump off her husband. Over-derivative of 1940s melodramas at first, then goes off on its own path and scores. Turner's first film; Kasdan's directorial debut. [R]▼●◗

Bodyhold (1949) **63m.** *½ D: Seymour Friedman. Willard Parker, Lola Albright, Hillary Brooke, Allen Jenkins, Gordon Jones. Programmer of wrestler and girlfriend seeking to clean up fight game corruption.

Body of a Woman SEE: **Big Squeeze, The**

Body of Evidence (1993) **C-99m.** ** D: Uli Edel. Madonna, Willem Dafoe, Joe Mantegna, Anne Archer, Jürgen Prochnow, Julianne Moore, Frank Langella, Stan Shaw, Charles Hallahan, Lillian Lehman. Lawyer Dafoe—the kind of guy you don't want handling *your* case—falls under the spell of his client (Madonna), who's accused of killing her wealthy lover with too much rough sex. One-note melodrama with "hot" lovemaking scenes that inspire more discomfort than titillation. Also released in unrated version and an explicit NC-17 edition. [R]▼●

Body Parts (1991) **C-88m.** *½ D: Eric Red. Jeff Fahey, Lindsay Duncan, Kim Delaney, Brad Dourif, Zakes Mokae, John Walsh, Paul Benevictor. Attempt at a hyperkinetic sci-fi/horror shocker is just another variation on the same old "Hands of Orlac" plot: this time, *several* key body parts of a killer are grafted onto people, with violent results. Escalating plot also escalates viewer's disbelief. Panavision. [R]▼●

Body Rock (1984) **C-93m.** *½ D: Marcelo Epstein. Lorenzo Lamas, Vicki Frederick, Cameron Dye, Ray Sharkey, Michelle Nicastro. Formula break-dancing movie (shot by the great Robby Muller!) casts beefy Lamas as hero/heel who dumps his best friend, his bf's quietly voluptuous sis, and other pals when he's hired to emcee a chic uptown club. Watching L.L. clomp to the beat is like watching Victor Mature boogaloo. [PG-13]▼

Body Shots (1999) **C-105m.** BOMB D: Michael Cristofer. Sean Patrick Flanery, Jerry O'Connell, Amanda Peet, Tara Reid, Ron Livingston, Emily Procter, Brad Rowe, Sybil Tamchen. Trying to shed light on the state of sex and dating in the 1990s, film follows eight twentysomethings as they explore the wild L.A. nightlife. Dark, dreary and derivative attempt to say something "important" about relationships. If this is truly where the world is heading, it's time to get off! Super 35. [R]▼

Body Slam (1987) **C-89m.** **½ D: Hal Needham. Dirk Benedict, Tanya Roberts, Roddy Piper, Capt. Lou Albano, Barry Gordon, Charles Nelson Reilly, Billy Barty, John Astin. Barely-released comedy, based on the successful rock 'n' roll/wrestling connection of the early 1980s, deserved better. Benedict is charming as an unscrupulous music promoter who latches onto wrestling as his meal ticket; "Rowdy" Roddy makes an engaging screen debut. Watch for cameos by many grapplers, including the Wild Samoans, Ric Flair and Bruno Sammartino. [PG]▼

Body Snatcher, The (1945) **77m.** ***½ D: Robert Wise. Boris Karloff, Bela Lugosi, Henry Daniell, Edith Atwater, Russell Wade, Rita Corday. Fine, atmospheric tale from Robert Louis Stevenson short story of doctor (Daniell) who is forced to deal with scurrilous character (Karloff) in order to get cadavers for experiments. Last film to team Karloff and Lugosi, their scenes together are eerie and compelling. One of the classic Val Lewton thrillers. Screenplay by Philip MacDonald and Carlos Keith (Lewton).▼●

Body Snatchers (1994) **C-87m.** **½ D: Abel Ferrara. Gabrielle Anwar, Meg Tilly, Forest Whitaker, Terry Kinney, Billy Wirth, Reilly Murphy, Christine Elise, R. Lee Ermey. Teenage Anwar moves to a military base with her family and soon discovers that pods from outer space are duplicating and replacing everyone there. Third version of Jack Finney's eerie novel is the least satisfactory; impatience, rather than tension, is aroused, and the horror is diminished because it's strangers who are being replaced. (Setting the story at a military base—where everyone is *supposed* to act alike—may not have been a good idea, either.) Both earlier versions titled INVASION OF THE BODY SNATCHERS. Arriscope. [R]▼●◗

Body Stealers, The SEE: **Thin Air**

Boeing Boeing (1965) **C-102m.** *** D: John Rich. Jerry Lewis, Tony Curtis, Dany Saval, Christiane Schmidtmer, Suzanna Leigh, Thelma Ritter. A surprisingly subdued Lewis is paired with Curtis in story of American newspaperman who runs swinging pad in Paris, constantly stocked with stewardesses, to the chagrin of housekeeper Ritter. Amusing.▼●

Bofors Gun, The (1968) **C-106m.** *** D: Jack Gold. Nicol Williamson, Ian Holm, David Warner, Peter Vaughn, John Thaw, Richard O'Callaghan, Barry Jackson, Donald Gee, Barbara Jefford. British soldier, on the eve of his return home in 1950s, comes tragically face-to-face with a rebellious Irish gunner. Engrossing, well acted.

Bog (1984) **C-87m.** BOMB D: Don Keeslar. Gloria De Haven, Aldo Ray, Marshall Thompson, Leo Gordon, Glen Voros, Rojay North, Ed Clark. Man in monster suit rises from bottom of lake and goes on rampage, sucking the blood from his victims. Ultra-cheap, ultra-bad time-killer. Filmed in Wisconsin in 1978. De Haven displays her versatility by appearing in a dual role.▼

Boggy Creek II SEE: **Barbaric Beast of Boggy Creek, The, Part II**

Bogus (1996) **C-111m.** ** D: Norman Jewison. Whoopi Goldberg, Gérard Depardieu, Haley Joel Osment, Nancy Travis, Denis Mercier, Andrea Martin, Ute Lemper, Sheryl Lee Ralph, Al Waxman, Don Francks, Mo Gaffney. Curious fable about a boy whose single mom dies in an accident; his closest relative, a foster aunt (Goldberg), turns out to be an uptight businesswoman with no motherly instincts whatsoever. So he invents a friend, Bogus (Depardieu), who cheers him up and sticks by his side. Odd, melancholy, and vaguely unsatisfying—not to mention long and slow. [PG] ▼●

Bogus Bandits SEE: **Devil's Brother, The**

Bohemian Girl, The (1936) **70m.** *** D: James Horne, Charles R. Rogers. Stan Laurel, Oliver Hardy, Thelma Todd, Antonio Moreno, Darla Hood, Jacqueline Wells (Julie Bishop), Mae Busch. Nifty comic opera with Stan and Ollie part of gypsy caravan. They adopt abandoned girl who turns out to be a princess.▼●

Boiler Room (2000) **C-117m.** *** D: Ben Younger. Giovanni Ribisi, Nia Long, Vin Diesel, Ben Affleck, Ron Rifkin, Tom Everett Scott, Scott Caan, Jamie Kennedy, Nicky Katt, Taylor Nichols. Young man — like most of his generation, to hear him tell it—wants success without having to work for it. This puts him at odds with his judgmental father (who happens to be a judge) until he signs on at a maverick brokerage house where the money flows freely . . . *too* freely. Naive at times, but entertaining. Tyro writer-director Younger makes disarming reference to WALL STREET and GLENGARRY GLEN ROSS, which this movie echoes in certain ways. [R]▼◗

Boiling Point (1993) **C-92m.** ** D: James B. Harris. Wesley Snipes, Dennis Hopper, Lolita Davidovich, Viggo Mortensen, Dan Hedaya, Seymour Cassel, Jonathan Banks, Christine Elise, Tony LoBianco, Valerie Perrine, James Tolkan, Paul Gleason. Snipes plays a federal agent determined to nail the man responsible for killing his colleague and friend during a sting operation. Misnamed crime yarn is tepid at best, but well shot on L.A. locations, and filled with familiar faces. [R]▼●◗

Bold and the Brave, The (1956) **87m.** *** D: Lewis R. Foster. Wendell Corey, Mickey Rooney, Don Taylor, Nicole Maurey. Routine WW2 study of soldiers fighting in Italy, greatly uplifted by unstereotyped performances; Rooney is outstanding. SuperScope.

Bolero (1934) **83m.** **½ D: Wesley Ruggles. George Raft, Carole Lombard, Sally Rand, Gertrude Michael, William Frawley, Ray Milland. Silly, protracted story of cocky dancer's rise to fame is made fun by good stars and production values; dance sequences are first-rate, although much of Raft and Lombard's footwork is "doubled" by professionals. Rand, in a rare film appearance, performs her famous fan dance. Raft and Lombard reteamed for RUMBA.

Bolero (1981-French) **C-173m.** *½ D: Claude Lelouch. James Caan, Geraldine Chaplin, Robert Hossein, Nicole Garcia, Daniel Olbrychski, Evelyne Bouix. Boring tale of various characters of different nationalities and their love of music, set during a 50-year time span. The actors play more than one character, and the result is confusion.▼

Bolero (1984) **C-104m.** BOMB D: John Derek. Bo Derek, George Kennedy, Andrea Occipiniti, Ana Obregon, Olivia d'Abo. Colossally boring sexual drama, for Bo-peepers only . . . though even voyeurs will be yawning during long stretches between nude scenes. Bo also produced the picture. [R]▼●

Bomba the Jungle Boy In 1949 producer Walter Mirisch, who has gone on to far greater things, decided to produce a series of low-budget adventure films based on Roy Rockwood's series of popular juvenile books from the 1920s about a boy who grew up in the jungle. For this road-company Tarzan series he hired Johnny Sheffield, who had played Boy in the Tarzan films, and veteran serial and B-picture director Ford Beebe, an expert at making something out of nothing. With a small studio backlot, and access to the 1930 documentary film AFRICA SPEAKS for stock footage, BOMBA THE JUNGLE BOY emerged, a not-bad little adventure, with talented Peggy Ann Garner playing opposite Sheffield. The subsequent ten films in the series, however, worked their way into a standard formula that quickly wore thin. Bomba was made for younger audiences, who may still respond to the formula plots.

BOMBA THE JUNGLE BOY

Bomba, The Jungle Boy (1949)
Bomba on Panther Island (1949)
The Lost Volcano (1950)
The Hidden City (1950), AKA: Bomba and the Hidden City
Bomba and the Elephant Stampede (1951), AKA: The Elephant Stampede
African Treasure (1952)
Bomba and the Jungle Girl (1952)
Safari Drums (1953)
The Golden Idol (1954)
Killer Leopard (1954)
Lord of the Jungle (1955)

Bomba and the Elephant Stampede (1951) **71m.** ** D: Ford Beebe. Johnny Sheffield, Donna Martell, Edith Evanson, Martin Wilkins, Myron Healey, Leonard Mudie. A politically correct Bomba the Jungle Boy combats ivory poachers who are slaughtering elephants. One of the most bearable of this minor series. Also known as ELEPHANT STAMPEDE.
Bomba and the Hidden City SEE: **Hidden City, The**
Bomba and the Jungle Girl (1952) **70m.** *½ D: Ford Beebe. Johnny Sheffield, Karen Sharpe, Walter Sande, Suzette Harbin, Martin Wilkins, Leonard Mudie. Jungle Boy meets Jungle Girl (Sharpe) and Jungle chimp (Kimba) on a quest to discover the true identity of Bomba's parents.
Bomba and the Lost Volcano SEE: **Lost Volcano, The**
Bomba on Panther Island (1949) **76m.** *½ D: Ford Beebe. Johnny Sheffield, Allene Roberts, Lita Baron, Charles Irwin, Smoki Whitfield. Bomba battles a deadly black panther and superstitious natives in this trite entry.
Bombardier (1943) **99m.** *** D: Richard Wallace. Pat O'Brien, Randolph Scott, Anne Shirley, Eddie Albert, Walter Reed, Robert Ryan, Barton MacLane. Familiar framework of fliers being trained during WW2 comes off well with fast-moving script. Also shown in computer-colored version.▼
Bomba, The Jungle Boy (1949) **70m.** ** D: Ford Beebe. Johnny Sheffield, Peggy Ann Garner, Smoki Whitfield, Onslow Stevens, Charles Irwin. First in the series has Bomba helping a photographer and his daughter on a perilous safari.
Bomb at 10:10 (1966-Yugoslavian) **C-86m.** ** D: Charles Damic. George Montgomery, Rada Popovic, Peter Banicevic, Branko Plesa. Thrown-together mishmash with Montgomery escaping from Nazi P.O.W. camp, plotting to help partisans and destroy prison leaders.▼
Bombay Talkie (1970-Indian) **C-105m.** **½ D: James Ivory. Shashi Kapoor, Jennifer Kendal, Zia Mohyeddin, Aparna Sen, Updal Dutt. A bored, pleasure-seeking British writer (Kendal) becomes romantically involved with an Indian movie actor (Kapoor). The subject—the interaction between different cultures—has been a staple in Ivory's films, but the presentation here is less than memorable. Scripted by Ivory and Ruth Prawer Jhabvala. [PG]▼
Bombers B-52 (1957) **C-106m.** **½ D: Gordon Douglas. Natalie Wood, Karl Malden, Marsha Hunt, Efrem Zimbalist, Jr., Dean Jagger. Ordinary love story between army pilot Zimbalist and Wood, with latter's sergeant father objecting, intertwined with good aerial footage of jet plane maneuvers. CinemaScope.▼
Bomb in the High Street (1964-British) **60m.** **½ D: Terence Bishop. Ronald Howard, Terry Palmer, Suzanna Leigh. Unpretentious robbery caper involving phony bomb scare to divert authorities from site of crime.
Bombshell (1933) **95m.** ***½ D: Victor Fleming. Jean Harlow, Lee Tracy, Frank Morgan, Franchot Tone, Una Merkel, Pat O'Brien, C. Aubrey Smith, Ted Healy, Isabel Jewell. Devastating satire of 1930s Hollywood, with Harlow a much-abused star, Tracy an incredibly unscrupulous publicity director making her life hell. No holds barred. Scripted by John Lee Mahin and Jules Furthman, from a play by Caroline Francke and Mack Crane. Retitled BLONDE BOMBSHELL.▼●
Bombs Over Burma (1942) **62m.** ** D: Joseph H. Lewis. Anna May Wong, Noel Madison, Dan Seymour, Richard Loo, Nedrick Young. Grade-B wartime saga of devoted Wong risking life for sake of China on espionage mission.
Bone Collector, The (1999) **C-117m.** *** D: Phillip Noyce. Denzel Washington, Angelina Jolie, Queen Latifah, Michael Rooker, Mike McGlone, Luis Guzman, Leland Orser, John Benjamin Hickey, Ed O'Neill. The NYPD's leading forensics expert, now a bedridden quadriplegic, enlists the help of a reluctant cop (Jolie) to be his eyes and ears in tracking down a games-playing serial killer. First-rate suspense thriller/whodunit, based on a novel by Jeffery Deaver. Not for the squeamish. Super 35. [R] ▼●◗
Bonfire of the Vanities, The (1990) **C-125m.** BOMB D: Brian De Palma. Tom Hanks, Bruce Willis, Melanie Griffith, Kim Cattrall, Saul Rubinek, Morgan Freeman, John Hancock, Kevin Dunn, Clifton James, Louis Giambalvo, Barton Heyman, Donald Moffat, Alan King, Mary Alice, Andre Gregory, Richard Libertini, Robert Stephens, Kirsten Dunst, Rita Wilson, Malachy McCourt, Camryn Manheim, Richard

Belzer. Appallingly heavy-handed "comedy" about a cocky Wall Street wheeler-dealer whose well-insulated life begins to crumble when his wife learns he's fooling around, and he and his paramour are involved in a hit-and-run accident. With all the power—and nuance—of Tom Wolfe's novel removed, and all the characters turned into caricatures (racist and otherwise), what's left is a pointless charade, and a pitiful waste of money and talent. F. Murray Abraham appears unbilled as the Bronx D.A. Super 35. [R]▼●◗

Bonjour Tristesse (1958) **C-94m.** *** D: Otto Preminger. Deborah Kerr, David Niven, Jean Seberg, Geoffrey Horne, Mylene Demongeot. Teen-ager does her best to break up romance between playboy widowed father and his mistress, with tragic results. Francoise Sagan's philosophy seeps through glossy production; Kerr exceptionally fine in soaper set on French Riviera. CinemaScope. ▼

Bonnie and Clyde (1967) **C-111m.** **** D: Arthur Penn. Warren Beatty, Faye Dunaway, Michael J. Pollard, Gene Hackman, Estelle Parsons, Denver Pyle, Gene Wilder, Dub Taylor. Trend-setting film about unlikely heroes of 1930s bank-robbing team has spawned many imitators but still leads the pack. Veering from comedy to melodrama and social commentary, it remains vivid, stylish throughout. When released, violent conclusion was extremely controversial. Screenplay by David Newman and Robert Benton. Parsons and cinematographer Burnett Guffey were Oscar winners. Wilder's first film.▼●◗

Bonnie Parker Story, The (1958) **81m.** **½ D: William Witney. Dorothy Provine, Jack Hogan, Richard Bakalyan, Joseph Turkel. With the success of BONNIE AND CLYDE, this film takes on added luster, recounting the lurid criminal life of the female crook (Provine)—though Clyde Barrow isn't even mentioned in this low-budget saga. Superama.

Bonnie Prince Charlie (1948-British) **C-118m.** ** D: Anthony Kimmins. David Niven, Margaret Leighton, Jack Hawkins, Judy Campbell, Morland Graham, Finlay Currie. Niven is Prince Charles of 18th-century Scotland in this draggy, overlong historical drama. The battle scenes are well staged and the photography of Robert Krasker is excellent, but when film was first released in England, it was considered a total disaster. Released at 140m., then cut to 118m. U.S. TV prints run 100m. and are in black and white.▼

Bonnie Scotland (1935) **80m.** **½ D: James Horne. Stan Laurel, Oliver Hardy, June Lang, William Janney, Anne Grey, Vernon Steele, James Finlayson. Plot sometimes gets in the way of L&H, but their material is well up to par; Stan and Ollie inadvertently join a Scottish military regiment stationed in the desert.▼●

Bon Voyage! (1962) **C-130m.** *½ D: James Neilson. Fred MacMurray, Jane Wyman, Michael Callan, Deborah Walley, Tommy Kirk, Kevin Corcoran. Slow, drawn-out Disney comedy about "typical" American family's misadventures on trip to Europe. Aimed more at adults than kids, but too draggy and simple-minded for anyone.▼

Bon Voyage Charlie Brown (and Don't Come Back!) (1980) **C-75m.** *** D: Bill Melendez. Voices of Daniel Anderson, Casey Carlson, Patricia Patts, Arrin Skelley. Charlie Brown and company travel to France as exchange students. Cute animated entertainment for Peanuts devotees. [G]▼●

Bonzo Goes to College (1952) **80m.** ** D: Frederick de Cordova. Maureen O'Sullivan, Charles Drake, Edmund Gwenn, Gigi Perreau, Gene Lockhart, Irene Ryan, David Janssen. Follow-up to BEDTIME FOR BONZO has brainy chimp lead college football team to victory; good cast takes back seat to monkey-shines.

Boogens, The (1981) **C-95m.** BOMB D: James L. Conway. Rebecca Balding, Fred McCarren, Anne-Marie Martin, Jeff Harlan, John Crawford, Med Flory. The Boogens are scaly monsters who do away with character after character when a Colorado silver mine is reopened. As unappealing as its title. [R]▼

Boogeyman, The (1980) **C-86m.** *** D: Ulli Lommel. Suzanna Love, Ron James, Michael Love, John Carradine, Raymond Boyden. Shards of mirror that "witnessed" horrible murder cause gruesome deaths. German art film actor-director Lommel lends unconventional angle to this combination of THE EXORCIST and HALLOWEEN. Effects are quite colorful, if somewhat hokey. Followed by BOOGEYMAN II. [R]▼●◗

Boogeyman II (1983) **C-79m.** BOMB D: Bruce Starr. Suzanna Love, Shana Hall, Ulli Lommel. Survivor of BOOGEYMAN goes to Hollywood to live with producer who is going to turn her life story into a movie. Moronic slasher film depends mostly on footage from BOOGEYMAN, amply used in flashbacks. Almost laughable.▼

Boogie Man Will Get You, The (1942) **66m.** **½ D: Lew Landers. Boris Karloff, Peter Lorre, Jeff Donnell, Larry Parks, Slapsy Maxie Rosenbloom, Maude Eburne, Don Beddoe, Frank Puglia. Good cast in lightweight cash-in on ARSENIC AND OLD LACE. Karloff is dotty scientist attempting to make supermen out of traveling salesmen while Donnell tries to turn his home into Colonial tourist trap; Lorre is screwy doctor/sheriff/notary/loan shark. No great shakes, but pleasant.

Boogie Nights (1997) **C-152m.** ***½ D: Paul Thomas Anderson. Mark Wahlberg, Burt Reynolds, Julianne Moore, John C. Reilly, Don Cheadle, Heather Graham, Luis Guzman, Philip Seymour Hoffman, William H. Macy, Alfred Molina, Philip Baker Hall, Robert Ridgely, Ricky Jay, Jack Riley, Joanna Gleason. Extraordinary, intense re-creation of life among a ''family'' of pornographers in the San Fernando Valley, from the late 1970s through the early 1980s. Wahlberg plays a disaffected 17-year-old with no brains but a formidable sex organ who becomes a porn-movie sensation; Reynolds is perfect as the director/paterfamilias who makes him a star. Writer-director Anderson doesn't judge his characters, but makes them—and their actions—seem utterly real. Tough going at times, but gripping and funny as well. Panavision. [R] ▼●◗

Book of Love (1990) **C-82m.** *½ D: Robert Shaye. Chris Young, Keith Coogan, Aeryk Egan, Josie Bissett, Tricia Leigh Fisher, Michael McKean, Danny Nucci, John Cameron Mitchell. Offensively inconsequential '50s teen romance about the usual clichés: James Dean, dilapidated cars, and greasy hair dressings. Standard anachronisms abound, starting with the use of the title oldie (a 1958 hit) in a film set in 1956. Inauspicious directorial debut for New Line Cinema's founder/CEO. Fisher (daughter of Connie Stevens and Eddie Fisher) is the sole standout as a tough girl with a soft heart. [PG-13]▼●

Book of Numbers (1973) **C-80m.** **½ D: Raymond St. Jacques. Raymond St. Jacques, Phillip Thomas, Freda Payne, Hope Clarke, D'Urville Martin, Gilbert Green. Uneven but sometimes enjoyable story of a black numbers-racket operation in a rural town during the Depression. [R]▼

Boom! (1968-U.S.-British) **C-113m.** ** D: Joseph Losey. Elizabeth Taylor, Richard Burton, Noel Coward, Joanna Shimkus, Michael Dunn. Thud: Only film buffs who admire Losey's very original directorial style are likely to appreciate fuzzy adaptation of Tennessee Williams' *The Milk Train Doesn't Stop Here Anymore*. Fine location photography in Sardinia and Rome; good performance by Shimkus can't save this. Panavision. [M/PG]

Boomerang! (1947) **88m.** ***½ D: Elia Kazan. Dana Andrews, Jane Wyatt, Lee J. Cobb, Arthur Kennedy, Sam Levene, Robert Keith, Taylor Holmes, Ed Begley, Karl Malden, Cara Williams, Barry Kelley. Minister's murder brings rapid arrest of an innocent man; prosecuting attorney determines to hunt out real facts. Brilliant drama in all respects. Richard Murphy's taut screenplay, from Anthony Abbott's article ''The Perfect Case,'' is based on a factual incident. Playwright Arthur Miller appears as one of the line-up suspects.▼

Boomerang (1992) **C-118m.** ** D: Reginald Hudlin. Eddie Murphy, Halle Berry, Robin Givens, David Alan Grier, Martin Lawrence, Grace Jones, Geoffrey Holder, Eartha Kitt, Chris Rock, Tisha Campbell, John Witherspoon, Melvin Van Peebles. Murphy makes a lumpy transition from comic to leading man, as a lifelong womanizer who finally meets his counterpart in his new boss (Givens). The women are fun to watch, but the humor is surprisingly crude at times, and the story is virtually nonexistent. A mixed bag at best, ridiculously padded out to two hours. [R]▼●

Boom in the Moon (1946-Mexican) **C-83m.** BOMB D: Jaime Salvador. Buster Keaton, Angel Garasa, Virginia Serret, Fernando Soto, Luis Barreiro. Rock-bottom ''comedy'' vehicle for poor Buster as an innocent thought to be a modern-day Bluebeard, who then gets shanghaied to fly a rocketship to the moon. Filmed as A MODERN BLUEBEARD, and barely seen until its video release in the 1980s. ▼

Boom Town (1940) **118m.** *** D: Jack Conway. Clark Gable, Spencer Tracy, Claudette Colbert, Hedy Lamarr, Frank Morgan, Lionel Atwill, Chill Wills. No surprises in tale of get-rich-quick drilling for oil, but star-studded cast gives it life. Also shown in computer-colored version.▼●

Boondock Saints (1999) **C-110m.** ** D: Troy Duffy. Willem Dafoe, Sean Patrick Flanery, Norman Reedus, David Della Rocco, Billy Connolly, Ron Jeremy Hyatt, David Ferry. Ultra-violent, low-budget Tarantino wannabe focuses on two Irish-American brothers who decide to rub out what they perceive to be evil forces in Boston. With off-the-wall humor and Dafoe's loony, gay FBI agent thrown in for good measure, this ain't no Tea Party. A hit-or-miss affair. [R]▼

Boost, The (1988) **C-95m.** *½ D: Harold Becker. James Woods, Sean Young, John Kapelos, Steven Hill, Kelle Kerr, John Rothman, Amanda Blake, Grace Zabriskie. An anti-drug movie that's on the screen nearly an hour before you even realize it *is* an anti-drug movie. Woods is the hotshot salesman who goes to hell (and bankruptcy) via cocaine, with Young the sometime user who tries to stand by him. As with Jack Nicholson in THE SHINING, it's difficult to distinguish the ''before'' Woods from the ''after'' in this misfire. [R]▼●

Boot Hill (1969-Italian) **C-87m.** ** D: Giuseppe Colizzi. Terence Hill, Bud Spencer, Woody Strode, Victor Buono, Lionel Stander, Eduardo Ciannelli. Western ravioli representing another of the traditional teamings of blue-eyed, rock-jawed Hill and his bear of a sidekick Spencer. Uneven pasta of violence and comedy. Aka TRINITY RIDES AGAIN. Techniscope. [PG]▼

Bootleggers (1974) **C-101m.** ** D: Charles B. Pierce. Paul Koslo, Dennis Fimple, Slim Pickens, Jaclyn Smith, Chuck Pierce, Jr. Typical yahoo action comedy set in 1930s Arkansas with Koslo and Fimple trying to outsmart and outdo rival moonshining family while running their supplies to Memphis. Retitled BOOTLEGGERS' ANGEL to capitalize on Smith's later TV stardom. Todd-AO 35. [PG]

Boots Malone (1952) **103m.** *** D: William Dieterle. William Holden, Johnny Stewart, Ed Begley, Harry Morgan, Whit Bissell. Holden comes alive in role of shady character who reforms when he trains Stewart to become a jockey.▼

Booty Call (1997) **C-77m.** ** D: Jeff Pollack. Jamie Foxx, Tommy Davidson, Vivica A. Fox, Tamala Jones, Scott LaRose, Kam Ray Chan, Ric Young. Or, Two Guys in Search of Condoms. Raunchy comedy is definitely PC (politically correct and pro-condom) as these two hapless souls just can't seem to please their hot-to-trot girlfriends until they find the perfect latex helper. Just a couple of genuinely funny scenes in this broad, lowbrow comedy. [R]▼●◗

Bop Girl (1957) **79m.** *½ D: Howard W. Koch. Judy Tyler, Bobby Troup, Margo Woode, Lucien Littlefield, Mary Kaye Trio, Nino Tempo. Psychologist Troup predicts that rock 'n' roll will lose its popularity to calypso. He was wrong. Aka BOP GIRL GOES CALYPSO.

Bop Girl Goes Calypso SEE: **Bop Girl**

Bopha! (1993) **C-120m.** *** D: Morgan Freeman. Danny Glover, Malcolm McDowell, Alfre Woodard, Marius Weyers, Maynard Eziashi, Malick Bowens, Grace Mahlaba. Tense, involving drama with Glover and Woodard (who played Nelson and Winnie Mandela in the TV movie MANDELA) starring as a married couple residing in a peaceful South African township. He's a police officer who upholds the status quo; their world is sure to crumble when their son (Eziashi) takes part in a rebellion against the discipline and curriculum of the local white-run school. Freeman's directorial debut; Arsenio Hall executive produced. [PG-13] ▼●

Bordello of Blood (1996) **C-87m.** ** D: Gilbert Adler. Dennis Miller, Erika Eleniak, Angie Everhart, Chris Sarandon, Corey Feldman, William Sadler, Aubrey Morris. Private eye Miller tries to locate Eleniak's brother, who's wound up at a mortuary brothel staffed by gorgeous vampires and run by Everhart. Fitfully amusing juvenile horror comedy with a heavy t&a quotient; Miller created much of his wise-guy dialogue. Whoopi Goldberg has a cameo. On-screen title: *TALES FROM THE CRYPT* PRESENTS BORDELLO OF BLOOD. [R]▼●

Border, The (1982) **C-107m.** **½ D: Tony Richardson. Jack Nicholson, Harvey Keitel, Valerie Perrine, Warren Oates, Elpidia Carrillo. Border patrolman Nicholson, spurred on by money-hungry spouse Perrine, begins taking payoffs from illegal Mexican aliens he's supposed to be arresting, eventually becomes emotionally involved with young mother Carrillo. Cast and storyline beg for Sam Peckinpah in his prime; mildly interesting, but never really takes off. Nice music by Ry Cooder. Panavision. [R]▼●

Border Incident (1949) **92m.** *** D: Anthony Mann. Ricardo Montalban, George Murphy, Howard da Silva, Teresa Celli, Charles McGraw. Tension-packed story of U.S. agents cracking down on smuggling of immigrants across Texas-Mexico border. Well directed, and uncompromisingly violent.

Borderline (1950) **88m.** ** D: William A. Seiter. Fred MacMurray, Claire Trevor, Raymond Burr, Jose Torvay, Morris Ankrum, Roy Roberts. Odd thriller-comedy in which L.A. cop Trevor attempts to gather evidence against wily drug smuggler Burr while mixing with tough guy MacMurray in Mexico. Starts out promisingly, but soon bogs down in silliness. Burr makes a vivid villain.▼●

Borderline (1980) **C-105m.** ** D: Jerrold Freedman. Charles Bronson, Bruno Kirby, Bert Remsen, Michael Lerner, Kenneth McMillan, Ed Harris, Wilford Brimley. Bronson, minus Jill Ireland this time, is a Border Patrol officer searching for a killer. Undistinguished formula vehicle for Old Stone Face. [PG]▼

Border River (1954) **C-80m.** ** D: George Sherman. Joel McCrea, Yvonne De Carlo, Pedro Armendariz, Howard Petrie. Mildly intriguing Western about Rebel officer McCrea's mission to buy much-needed weapons from Mexicans to continue fight against Yankees.

Border Shootout (1990) **C-110m.** *½ D: C. J. McIntyre. Cody Glenn, Jeff Kaake, Glenn Ford, Lizabeth Rohovit, Michael Horse, Russell Todd, Michael Ansara, Michael Forrest. Naive rancher is made deputy in Arizona border town that's fed up with aging sheriff Ford, but the townspeople's lynching of alleged rustlers brings about immediate conflict. Good Western plot (from Elmore Leonard novel) ruined by amateurish production. Ford seems to be walking through his role.▼

Bordertown (1935) **90m.** *** D: Archie Mayo. Paul Muni, Bette Davis, Eugene Pallette, Margaret Lindsay. Fine drama of unusual triangle in bordertown cafe, with Davis as flirtatious wife of Pallette with designs on lawyer Muni; her overwrought scene on the witness stand is not easily forgotten. Used as basis for later THEY DRIVE BY

NIGHT, but more serious in tone. Also shown in computer-colored version.

Boris and Natasha: The Movie (1992) **C-88m.** ** D: Charles Martin Smith. Sally Kellerman, David Thomas, Paxton Whitehead, Andrea Martin, Alex Rocco, Larry Cedar, Arye Gross, Christopher Neame, Anthony Newley. Silly live-action version of the fondly remembered "Rocky and Bullwinkle" cartoon series with our dastardly (but dated) Russian spies up to no good as usual. Spirited, but not enough. John Candy, John Travolta, and director Smith pop up in cameos. Made as a theatrical feature in 1988 (when the Cold War was still topical). It debuted on cable TV instead. [PG]▼●

B.O.R.N. (1989) **C-92m.** ** D: Ross Hagen. Ross Hagen, Hoke Howell, P. J. Soles, William Smith, Russ Tamblyn, Amanda Blake, Rance Howard, Clint Howard, Claire Hagen, Dawn Wildsmith. Someone is kidnapping young people from the streets of L.A. to cut up as involuntary organ donors, but they didn't reckon with hero Hagen and his ex-cop pal Howell. Wild-eyed, bizarre action thriller has too many characters and too much gunfire but has its moments too. Title refers to "Body Organ Replacement Network." [R]▼

Born Again (1978) **C-110m.** *½ D: Irving Rapper. Dean Jones, Anne Francis, Jay Robinson, Dana Andrews, Raymond St. Jacques, George Brent. If one is inspired by the religious rebirth of Pres. Nixon's Special Counsel (Charles Colson) after his Washington skullduggery, one might be absorbed by this one-dimensional film account. Others beware! [PG]▼

Born American (1986-U.S.-Finnish) **C-95m.** ** D: Renny Harlin. Mike Norris, Steve Durham, David Coburn, Thalmus Rasulala, Albert Salmi. The Cold War lives on as three young Americans vacationing in Finland accidentally cross the border into Russia, where they fight it out with the local troops. OK action scenes and personable young cast sugarcoat the heavy-handed political overtones. [R]▼

Born Free (1966-British) **C-96m.** ***½ D: James Hill. Virginia McKenna, Bill Travers, Geoffrey Keen, Peter Lukoye. Exceptional adaptation of Joy Adamson's book about Elsa the lioness, who was raised as a pet by two Kenya game wardens (played by real-life couple McKenna and Travers). Sincere, engrossing film, a must for family viewing. Oscars for Best Original Score (John Barry) and Title Song (Barry and Don Black). Screenplay by Gerald L.C. Copley (Lester Cole). Followed by a sequel (LIVING FREE) and a brief TV series. Remade for TV in 1996. Story is continued in TO WALK WITH LIONS (1999). Panavision. ▼●

Born in East L.A. (1987) **C-87m.** *½ D: Cheech Marin. Cheech Marin, Daniel Stern, Paul Rodriguez, Jan-Michael Vincent, Kamala Lopez, Alma Martinez, Tony Plana. Third-generation American Hispanic gets caught in an immigration raid minus I.D. and is deported to Tijuana; it takes a tiresome hour and a half of screen time to get back. Nothing offensive but also nothing special; Rodriguez's dim-witted comedy relief is a particular drag. Based on Marin's popular Bruce Springsteen parody record. Expanded to 93m. for TV. [R]▼●◗

Born Innocent (1974) **C-100m. TVM** D: Donald Wrye. Linda Blair, Joanna Miles, Kim Hunter, Richard Jaeckel, Mary Murphy, Allyn Ann McLerie, Mitch Vogel. Graphic story of teenage girl's struggle to adjust to rigors of tough juvenile detention home. Uncompromising film, achieved notoriety in its original showing by a realistic rape of Blair by her fellow inmates (now cut from film). Otherwise, played for the sensational. Average.▼

Born Losers, The (1967) **C-112m.** **½ D: T. C. Frank (Tom Laughlin). Tom Laughlin, Elizabeth James, Jeremy Slate, William Wellman, Jr., Robert Tessier. What seemed at the time just another biker film gained new interest in the 70s as the introduction of Billy Jack; he helps free young dropout James from the clutches of Slate's gang. Good action scenes, but Laughlin's use of violence as *an indictment of* violence is already present. Jane Russell makes a guest appearance as a mother. Followed by BILLY JACK. [PG]▼

Born on the Fourth of July (1989) **C-144m.** ***½ D: Oliver Stone. Tom Cruise, Willem Dafoe, Raymond J. Barry, Caroline Kava, Kyra Sedgwick, Bryan Larkin, Jerry Levine, Josh Evans, Frank Whaley, Stephen Baldwin, John Getz, Lili Taylor, Tom Berenger, Abbie Hoffman, Jason Gedrick, Ed Lauter, Michael Wincott, Tom Sizemore, Mike Starr, James Le Gros, John C. McGinley, Wayne Knight, Bob Gunton. Relentlessly realistic and powerful saga of real-life Vietnam vet Ron Kovic, who joined the Marines as a gung-ho recruit in the 1960s and came home paralyzed from the chest down—only to endure an even greater ordeal of physical and mental rehabilitation before emerging as an antiwar activist. Stone cowrote the screenplay with Kovic, and spares us nothing in recreating some of America's most painful years. Stone's finest film to date. Cruise delivers a top-notch performance; enhanced by a great John Williams score. Kovic can be seen in opening parade scene; Stone plays a TV reporter. Oscar winner for Best Director and Film Editing. Panavision. [R]▼●◗

Born Reckless (1959) **79m.** *½ D: Howard W. Koch. Mamie Van Doren, Jeff Richards, Arthur Hunnicutt, Carol Ohmart,

Tom Duggan, Jeanne Carmen. Rodeo star Richards divides his time between busting broncos and busting heads of lecherous old cowpokes trying to paw Mamie. Not bad enough to be really funny, but it has its moments; Mamie sings five of film's eight songs, including unforgettable "I'm Just a Nice, Sweet, Home-Type of Girl."

Born to Be Bad (1950) **94m.** **½ D: Nicholas Ray. Joan Fontaine, Robert Ryan, Zachary Scott, Joan Leslie, Mel Ferrer, Harold Vermilyea. "Little fake" Fontaine, despite attraction to writer Ryan, schemes to win wealthy Scott away from fiancée Leslie. And that's just for openers. Good cast in somewhat overwrought, predictable drama. ▼●

Born to Be Loved (1959) **82m.** ** D: Hugo Haas. Carol Morris, Vera Vague (Barbara Jo Allen), Hugo Haas, Dick Kallman, Jacqueline Fontaine. Low-key yarn of poor-but-honest Morris and rich widow Vague seeking romance, helped by elderly music instructor Haas.

Born to Be Wild (1995) **C-100m.** ** D: John Gray. Will Horneff, Helen Shaver, Peter Boyle, Jean Marie Barnwell, John C. McGinley, Marvin J. McIntyre. OK family film grafts a gorilla onto the FREE WILLY formula: a teenage boy forms a bond with an ape on the lam in Seattle, helping her in quest for freedom. Kids might go for it, even if they figure out that the lead "actor" is just an animatronic thespian passing for the real thing. [PG]▼●

Born to Dance (1936) **105m.** *** D: Roy Del Ruth. Eleanor Powell, James Stewart, Virginia Bruce, Una Merkel, Sid Silvers, Frances Langford, Raymond Walburn, Buddy Ebsen, Reginald Gardiner. Powell bears out title in good Cole Porter musical with sensational footwork and fine songs: "Easy To Love," "I've Got You Under My Skin."▼●

Born to Kill (1947) **92m.** *** D: Robert Wise. Claire Trevor, Lawrence Tierney, Walter Slezak, Audrey Long, Elisha Cook, Jr., Philip Terry. Murderer Tierney marries insecure Long, but can't stay away from her divorced sister Trevor. Supertough film noir is uncharacteristically mean-spirited for director Wise, but is well put together nonetheless. A cult item.▼

Born to Kill (1974) SEE: **Cockfighter**

Born to Race (1988) **C-98m.** BOMB D: James Fargo. Joseph Bottoms, Marc Singer, George Kennedy, Marla Heasley, Antonio Sabato, Robert F. Logan, Dirk Blocker, Michael McGrady. Silly tripe set against backdrop of North Carolina stock car races, where Heasley has brought her revolutionary prototype engine, and the "bad guys" set out to steal her blueprints. [R]▼

Born to Rock: The T.A.M.I. Show SEE: **That Was Rock**

Born to Win (1971) **C-90m.** **½ D: Ivan Passer. George Segal, Karen Black, Paula Prentiss, Jay Fletcher, Hector Elizondo, Robert De Niro. Unjustly neglected, but not altogether successful comedy-drama about ex-hairdresser in N.Y.C. and his $100-a-day heroin habit. Very well acted, particularly by Segal. Aka ADDICT. [R]▼◗

Born Wild (1994) **C-98m.** ** D: Duncan McLachlan. Brooke Shields, John Varty, Martin Sheen, David Keith, Elmon Mhlongo, Norman Ansty, Thembe Ndaba, Renee Estevez. The story of real-life conservationist Varty, who plays himself, and his multi-year relationship with a family of leopards. When documentarian Shields wants to make a film of his experiences, her efforts are predictably sabotaged by jealous colleagues and corrupt game wardens. Set in South Africa, Kenya, and Zambia; extraordinary footage of animals in the wild is trivialized by the Hollywoodization of the movie within the movie. [PG]▼●

Born Yesterday (1950) **103m.** ***½ D: George Cukor. Judy Holliday, William Holden, Broderick Crawford, Howard St. John. Junk-dealer-made-good Crawford wants girlfriend (Holliday) culturefied, hires Holden to teach her in hilarious Garson Kanin comedy set in Washington, D.C. Priceless Judy repeated Broadway triumph and won Oscar for playing quintessential dumb blonde. Remade in 1993. ▼●◗

Born Yesterday (1993) **C-101m.** **½ D: Luis Mandoki. Melanie Griffith, John Goodman, Don Johnson, Edward Herrmann, Max Perlich, Michael Ensign, Benjamin C. Bradlee, Sally Quinn, William Frankfather, Fred Dalton Thompson, Celeste Yarnall, Nora Dunn. Amiable remake of Garson Kanin comedy, set in Washington, D.C., about boorish tycoon who hires bookish reporter to give his mistress some education and couth. The three leads are well cast, but the movie sags after a while, losing its comic punch. [PG]▼●

Borrower, The (1991) **C-97m.** **½ D: John McNaughton. Rae Dawn Chong, Don Gordon, Tom Towles, Antonio Fargas, Neil Giuntoli, Larry Pennell, Tony Amendola, Pam Gordon, Mädchen Amick, Stuart Cornfeld. An alien criminal is "devolved" to human shape and exiled on Earth; when his head explodes, he starts ripping the heads off human beings (and others) and donning them until they go bad, too. Understandably confused cops Chong and Gordon are on his trail. Gleefully outrageous horror premise supported by strong, stylish direction and a well-written script. [R]▼

Borrowers, The (1997-British) **C-83m.** **½ D: Peter Hewitt. John Goodman, Jim Broadbent, Mark Williams, Hugh Laurie, Bradley Pierce, Flora Newbigin, Tom Felton, Celia Imrie, Ruby Wax. Just OK rendering of Mary Norton's children's novels about a household of tiny human pilferers who reduce baddie Goodman to rubble after he cheats a nice family out of their inherited house. Actors acting against oversized sets remains an irresistible concept, but the movie won't make anyone forget THE INCREDIBLE SHRINKING MAN or the wonderful fantasy scenes in Nicolas Roeg's THE WITCHES. A bit too much HOME ALONE–style slapstick violence, but the short running time helps. Filmed before as a British miniseries in 1993. [PG]▼●◗

Borsalino (1970-French) **C-125m.** *** D: Jacques Deray. Jean-Paul Belmondo, Alain Delon, Michel Bouquet, Catherine Rouvel, Francoise Christophe. PUBLIC ENEMY, French-style; delightful seriocomic film of two likable hoods who become gangland chieftains in 1930s Marseilles. Stars in top form; Claude Bolling's infectious music helps. Sequel: BORSALINO & CO. [PG]▼

Boss, The (1956) **89m.** *** D: Byron Haskin. John Payne, William Bishop, Gloria McGhee, Doe Avedon, Joe Flynn. Effective study of WW1 veteran returning to St. Louis and combatting corruption and crime; one of Payne's best performances as the city's underworld boss.

Boss SEE: **Boss Nigger**

Bossa Nova (1999-Brazilian-U.S.) **C-95m.** ** D: Bruno Barreto. Amy Irving, Antonio Fagundes, Alexandre Borges, Débora Bloch, Drica Moraes, Giovanna Antonelli, Alberto de Mendoza, Stephen Tobolowsky. Airy romantic comedy-of-errors involving Brazilian-based widow and English tutor (Irving), the successful older businessman who falls in love with her (Fagundes), and a variety of friends and family members whose love lives crisscross around them. Pleasant enough, with attractive scenery, but resolutely ordinary. Super 35. [R]

Boss Nigger (1975) **C-92m.** ** D: Jack Arnold. Fred Williamson, D'Urville Martin, R. G. Armstrong, William Smith, Barbara Leigh, Carmen Hayworth. Clichéd blaxploitation Western with Williamson as a bounty hunter who predictably outhustles every white man in sight. In spite of its title, not as offensive as others of the genre (mainly because there's no graphic violence). Williamson scripted; also known as BOSS and THE BLACK BOUNTY KILLER. Todd-AO 35. [PG]▼

Boss's Son, The (1978) **C-97m.** *** D: Bobby Roth. Asher Brauner, Rudy Solari, Rita Moreno, Henry G. Sanders, James Darren, Richie Havens, Piper Laurie, Elena Verdugo. Good little independent feature by writer-director Roth about a young man reluctantly going into his father's carpet factory business. Credible, engaging.▼

Boss' Wife, The (1986) **C-83m.** *½ D: Ziggy Steinberg. Daniel Stern, Arielle Dombasle, Fisher Stevens, Melanie Mayron, Lou Jacobi, Martin Mull, Christopher Plummer, Thalmus Rasulala, Robert Costanzo. Interesting cast falters in this tepid will-he-or-won't-he comedy about an ambitious young stockbroker (Stern) and the title lady (Dombasle), who's out to seduce him. [R]▼

Boston Blackie Over a span of nine years, Chester Morris starred in fourteen films as Boston Blackie, a former thief now on the right side of the law but preferring to work for himself rather than for the police. He brought to the role a delightful offhand manner and sense of humor that kept the films fresh even when the scripts weren't. (He even got to pursue his hobby—performing magic—in a couple of episodes.) From MEET BOSTON BLACKIE (1941) to BOSTON BLACKIE'S CHINESE VENTURE (1949), Morris was Blackie. Regulars included Richard Lane as a frustrated police detective convinced that Blackie was up to no good, but always one step behind him; George E. Stone as Blackie's talkative, dim-witted buddy; and Lloyd Corrigan as a dizzy millionaire pal who'd do anything for a lark. Top-flight directors Robert Florey and Edward Dmytryk got the series started, and when the films fell into less capable hands, Morris and company came to the rescue with consistently ingratiating performances. While no classics, the Boston Blackie films offer a great deal of fun.

BOSTON BLACKIE

Meet Boston Blackie (1941)
Confessions of Boston Blackie (1941)
Alias Boston Blackie (1942)
Boston Blackie Goes Hollywood (1942)
After Midnight With Boston Blackie (1943)
The Chance of a Lifetime (1943)
One Mysterious Night (1944)
Boston Blackie Booked on Suspicion (1945)
Boston Blackie's Rendezvous (1945)
A Close Call for Boston Blackie (1946)
The Phantom Thief (1946)
Boston Blackie and the Law (1946)
Trapped by Boston Blackie (1948)
Boston Blackie's Chinese Venture (1949)

Boston Blackie and the Law (1946) **70m.** ** D: D. Ross Lederman. Chester Morris, Trudy Marshall, Constance Dowling, Richard Lane, George E. Stone, Frank Sully. Blackie uses his skill at prestidigitation to catch a killer who escaped from a women's prison during one of his magic shows. Mediocre entry utilizing a distaff version of the ALIAS BOSTON BLACKIE plot.

Boston Blackie Booked on Suspicion (1945) **66m.** **½ D: Arthur Dreifuss. Chester Morris, Lynn Merrick, Richard Lane, Frank Sully, Steve Cochran, George E. Stone, Lloyd Corrigan. Blackie becomes a

prime suspect when he helps out an auctioneer friend and discovers counterfeit rare books—and murder. Fair mystery brightened by jaunty playing.
Boston Blackie Goes Hollywood (1942) **68m.** *** D: Michael Gordon. Chester Morris, George E. Stone, Richard Lane, Forrest Tucker, Constance Worth, William Wright, Lloyd Corrigan, Walter Sande. Classy entry with the nimble Blackie transporting $60,000 for a friend to California. The cops follow him in hope of finding the lost Monterey diamond.
Boston Blackie's Appointment With Death SEE: **One Mysterious Night**
Boston Blackie's Chinese Venture (1949) **59m.** ** D: Seymour Friedman. Chester Morris, Joan Woodbury, Maylia, Richard Lane, Don McGuire, Sid Tomack, Frank Sully, Charles Arnt, Philip Ahn, Benson Fong. Last, and least, of the Blackie mysteries finds our hero probing Chinatown murders, which he's naturally been accused of. George E. Stone is sorely missed as sidekick "Runt," replaced by Tomack for this final entry.
Boston Blackie's Rendezvous (1945) **64m.** **½ D: Arthur Dreifuss. Chester Morris, Nina Foch, Steve Cochran, Richard Lane, George E. Stone, Frank Sully, Iris Adrian, Harry Hayden. Fairly tense entry, with Blackie on the trail of Cochran, a psycho killer who escapes from an asylum and goes on a murder spree.
Bostonians, The (1984) **C-120m.** ** D: James Ivory. Christopher Reeve, Vanessa Redgrave, Madeleine Potter, Jessica Tandy, Nancy Marchand, Wesley Addy, Linda Hunt, Wallace Shawn. Redgrave is perfectly cast as Henry James's 19th-century feminist heroine in this careful adaptation of his novel by Ruth Prawer Jhabvala . . . but the film itself, for all its period detail, is deadly slow and uninvolving. Reeve is in over his head as Redgrave's contrary cousin. ▼●◗
Boston Strangler, The (1968) **C-120m.** *** D: Richard Fleischer. Tony Curtis, Henry Fonda, George Kennedy, Mike Kellin, Hurd Hatfield, Murray Hamilton, Jeff Corey, Sally Kellerman, William Marshall, George Voskovec, William Hickey, James Brolin. Absorbing drama, semi-documentary-style, detailing rise, manhunt, capture, prosecution of notorious criminal. Curtis gives startling performance as killer. Complex multi-image technique may be lost on TV screen. Panavision. [R]▼
Botany Bay (1953) **C-94m.** **½ D: John Farrow. Alan Ladd, James Mason, Patricia Medina, Cedric Hardwicke. Based on Charles Nordhoff novel set in 1790s, picturesque yarn tells of convict ship bound for Australia, focusing on conflict between prisoner Ladd and sadistic skipper Mason, with Medina as Ladd's love interest.▼
Both Sides of the Law (1954-British) **94m.** *** D: Muriel Box. Peggy Cummins, Terence Morgan, Anne Crawford, Rosamund John. Documentary-style account of London policewomen and their daily activity. Unpretentious production allows for good natural performances.
Bottle Rocket (1996) **C-95m.** **½ D: Wes Anderson. Owen C. Wilson, Luke Wilson, Robert Musgrave, Andrew Wilson, Lumi Cavazos, James Caan, Teddy Wilson, Jim Ponds. Original, low-key comedy about two young friends—and chronic screw-ups—who attempt to embark on a life of crime. Engaging performances by Owen C. Wilson (who cowrote the film), as Dignan, and his real-life brother Luke, as Anthony, stand out. (A third brother, Andrew, plays their friend's bullying older sibling.) Expanded from a 13m. short subject. [R]▼●◗
Bottom of the Bottle, The (1956) **C-88m.** **½ D: Henry Hathaway. Van Johnson, Joseph Cotten, Ruth Roman, Jack Carson, Margaret Hayes, Bruce Bennett, Brad Dexter, Jim Davis, Margaret Lindsay, Henry (Harry) Morgan. Hot-and-heavy soaper detailing fireworks after alcoholic fugitive Johnson appears on the doorstep of his respectable lawyer-rancher brother (Cotten). Based on a novel by Georges Simenon. CinemaScope.
Boudu Saved From Drowning (1932-French) **87m.** *** D: Jean Renoir. Michel Simon, Charles Granval, Marcelle Hania, Severine Lerczynska. Title tramp is rescued from the Seine and taken home by well-meaning book dealer; he eventually takes over household, then seduces both the wife and maid. Classic attack on complacency still holds up, with ratty-bearded Simon giving the performance of a lifetime. U.S. remake: DOWN AND OUT IN BEVERLY HILLS.▼●
Boulevard Nights (1979) **C-102m.** ** D: Michael Pressman. Richard Yniguez, Marta Du Bois, Danny De La Paz, Betty Carvalho, Carmen Zapata, James Victor, Victor Millan. Sincere but uninspiring story of Chicano youth who yearns to move away from street-gang life, but drawn back because of hot-blooded young brother. Filmed in the barrios of L.A. [R]▼
Bound (1996) **C-109m.** *** D: The Wachowski Brothers (Larry, Andy). Jennifer Tilly, Gina Gershon, Joe Pantoliano, John Ryan, Christopher Meloni, Richard C. Sarafian. Sexy, stylishly violent noir with a Sapphic twist, about a handywoman (Gershon) and a gangster's moll (Tilly) who conspire to run off together with a suitcase containing two million bucks. The women have chemistry to burn, but Pantoliano steals the movie as the mobster caught in the middle. Impressive directorial debut from the screenwriting-brother duo who wrote ASSASSINS. Lesbian-erotica author Susie Bright appears in the film, and served as technical

adviser to make sure the bedroom action was appropriately steamy. [R]▼●◗

Bound and Gagged: A Love Story (1993) **C-101m.** *½ D: Daniel Appleby. Ginger Lynn Allen, Karen Black, Chris Denton, Elizabeth Saltarrelli, Mary Ella Ross, Chris Mulkey. Yet another road movie; this one explores the sexual trials and tribulations of two bisexual women and a rather confused straight guy who's despondent over the breakup of his marriage. Quirky, rather than interesting. Was supposed to usher ex–porn queen Allen into a mainstream movie career. Better luck next time. [R]▼●◗

Bound by Honor (1993) **C-180m.** ** D: Taylor Hackford. Damian Chapa, Jesse Borrego, Benjamin Bratt, Enrique Castillo, Victor Rivers, Delroy Lindo, Tom Towles, Carlos Carrasco, Teddy Wilson, Raymond Cruz, Lanny Flaherty, Billy Bob Thornton, Natalija Nogulich, Ving Rhames. Ambitious look at Chicano gang life concerns two half-brothers and a half-white cousin who evolve into a drug-addicted artist, a narcotics detective, and a repeat-offender prisoner. Despite lots of screen time (and a passable beginning), this violent film gives top-heavy emphasis to the cellblock portion of the saga. Script was predominantly written, with shared credit, by acclaimed poet Jimmy Santiago Baca. Video title: BLOOD IN BLOOD OUT. [R]▼●◗

Bound for Glory (1976) **C-147m.** ***½ D: Hal Ashby. David Carradine, Ronny Cox, Melinda Dillon, Gail Strickland, John Lehne, Ji-Tu Cumbuka, Randy Quaid, M. Emmet Walsh. Life of folk singer-composer Woody Guthrie, superbly played by Carradine, with great feeling for 1936–40 period as Guthrie travels the country fighting and singing for the underdogs, victims of the Great Depression. Haskell Wexler's Oscar-winning photography is tops throughout, as is Leonard Rosenman's score adaptation (also an Oscar-winner). Beware of shorter prints. [PG]▼●◗

Bounty, The (1984) **C-130m.** *** D: Roger Donaldson. Mel Gibson, Anthony Hopkins, Laurence Olivier, Edward Fox, Daniel Day-Lewis, Bernard Hill, Liam Neeson. Handsome, well made retelling of history's most famous mutiny (*not* based on the Nordhoff-Hall book) paints Bligh as repressed and stubborn, not mad, and Christian as a dilettante with no real substance. Interesting all the way, but emotionally aloof. Great use of widescreen will suffer badly on TV. J-D-C Scope. [PG]▼●

Bounty Hunter, The (1954) **C-79m.** **½ D: Andre de Toth. Randolph Scott, Dolores Dorn, Marie Windsor, Howard Petrie. Scott is on his horse again, this time tracking down three murderers.

Bounty Killer, The (1965) **C-92m.** **½ D: Spencer G. Bennet. Dan Duryea, Rod Cameron, Audrey Dalton, Richard Arlen, Buster Crabbe, Fuzzy Knight, Johnny Mack Brown, Bob Steele, Bronco Billy Anderson. Chief interest is cast of old-timers from Hollywood Westerns. Unlike their previous vehicles, this is adult, low-key, and minus happy ending. Interesting on both counts. Techniscope. ▼

Bourne Identity, The (1988) **C-200m. TVM** D: Roger Young. Richard Chamberlain, Jaclyn Smith, Anthony Quayle, Donald Moffat, Yorgo Voyagis, Denholm Elliott. An amnesiac spy runs all over Europe with a woman he's kidnapped trying to prove to the assassins dogging his footsteps that he's not really the man he appears to be. Exciting although somewhat convoluted adaptation by Carol Sobieski of Robert Ludlum's best-seller, with Tony Pierce Roberts' evocative photography helping immensely. Originally shown in two parts. Above average.▼

Bowery, The (1933) **90m.** *** D: Raoul Walsh. Wallace Beery, George Raft, Jackie Cooper, Fay Wray, Pert Kelton, Herman Bing. Raft is Steve Brodie, Beery a notorious saloon owner, Cooper his young nemesis in rowdy story of N.Y.C.'s Bowery during the Gay 90s. Kelton is marvelous as Beery's saloon soubrette.

Bowery at Midnight (1942) **63m.** ** D: Wallace Fox. Bela Lugosi, John Archer, Wanda McKay, Tom Neal, Dave O'Brien. Lugosi is kindly psychiatrist who leads double life as criminal mastermind in the Bowery. Also involves reviving the dead. Mild but atmospheric.▼

Bowery Battalion (1951) **69m.** ** D: William Beaudine. Leo Gorcey, Huntz Hall, Donald MacBride, Virginia Hewitt, Russell Hicks, William (Billy) Benedict, Bernard Gorcey, David Gorcey. Serviceable service romp, as the Bowery Boys join the Army to catch some spies.

Bowery Blitzkrieg (1941) **62m.** *½ D: Wallace Fox. Leo Gorcey, Bobby Jordan, Huntz Hall, Sunshine Sammy Morrison, Donald Haines, David Gorcey, Warren Hull, Charlotte Henry, Keye Luke, Bobby Stone, Dennis Moore. Cliché-ridden *East Side Kids* entry about good kid Jordan torn between boxing and school, mixed up with the requisite gangsters.▼

Bowery Bombshell (1946) **65m.** **½ D: Phil Karlson. Leo Gorcey, Huntz Hall, Bobby Jordan, Warren Hull, Billy Benedict, David Gorcey, Teala Loring, James Burke, Sheldon Leonard, Bernard Gorcey. The boys track down some bank robbers when Sach becomes a suspect in this amusing entry with perennial nightclub gangster Leonard in fine form.

The Bowery Boys Sidney Kingsley's Broadway play *Dead End* was a superior drama that cast a critical eye on big-city tenement slums. When Samuel Goldwyn brought it to the screen, he retained the services of the young performers who'd played the street kids on stage: Billy Halop, Bobby Jordan, Gabriel Dell, Huntz Hall, Leo Gorcey, and Bernard Punsley. Though Kingsley never intended to glorify hoodlums, these young actors made a tremendous impact on audiences, much as gangster antiheroes had earlier in the decade . . . and before long, The "Dead End Kids" were stars! Warner Bros. featured them in six films over the next few years with such costars as James Cagney (ANGELS WITH DIRTY FACES), Humphrey Bogart (CRIME SCHOOL), and John Garfield (THEY MADE ME A CRIMINAL). Most of these films maintained the *Dead End* stance of portraying these juvenile delinquents as victims of society, though some of this posturing rang hollow considering their shenanigans. Some of the gang also found work at Universal; a B-picture called LITTLE TOUGH GUY launched a series of "Dead End Kids and Little Tough Guys" films, which included both original kids and newcomers. These vehicles were a motley and uneven bunch randomly integrating action, melodrama, and juvenile comedy. Not only wasn't there the pointedness of *Dead End*; there was often no point at all. Universal even featured the group in three Saturday matinee serials, JUNIOR G-MEN, SEA RAIDERS and JUNIOR G-MEN OF THE AIR. Then, in 1940, producer Sam Katzman launched a low-budget series called *The East Side Kids* for Monogram Pictures, featuring Leo Gorcey and Bobby Jordan, who were later joined by fellow Dead Enders Huntz Hall and Gabriel Dell. These low-budget films stressed (grade-B) drama as much as comedy. Gamblers, boxers, and Nazis figured prominently, along with Bela Lugosi, who costarred in SPOOKS RUN WILD and GHOSTS ON THE LOOSE. The cast members began to hit their stride in these films, developing the camaraderie that was to make them enduringly popular. In 1946, Leo Gorcey took a hand in revamping the films, assumed the official starring role of Slip Mahoney, with Huntz Hall as his sidekick Sach Jones, and the series was rechristened *The Bowery Boys.* For several years' time these films flirted with drama, as in HARD BOILED MAHONEY, IN FAST COMPANY, and JINX MONEY, but then decided to go all-out with broad juvenile comedy. Audiences enjoyed the results, and The Bowery Boys experienced a healthy run right into the 1950s. Leo Gorcey's father, Bernard, played Louie Dumbrowski, proprietor of the gang's ice-cream parlor hangout, and when he died in 1956, Gorcey left the series. Stanley Clements was brought in to replace him, for seven more generally lackluster comedies (HOT SHOTS, HOLD THAT HYPNOTIST, UP IN SMOKE, etc.) before the series finally breathed its last in 1958.

THE BOWERY BOYS

The Dead End Kids
Dead End (1937)
Crime School (1938)
Angels With Dirty Faces (1938)
They Made Me a Criminal (1939)
Hell's Kitchen (1939)
Angels Wash Their Faces, The (1939)
On Dress Parade (1939)

The Dead End Kids and Little Tough Guys
Little Tough Guy (1938)
Call a Messenger (1939)
You're Not So Tough (1940)
Give Us Wings (1940)
Hit the Road (1941)
Mob Town (1941)
Tough as They Come (1942)
Mug Town (1943)
Keep 'Em Slugging (1943)

East Side Kids
East Side Kids (1940)
Boys of the City (1940)
That Gang of Mine (1940)
Pride of the Bowery (1941)
Flying Wild (1941)
Bowery Blitzkrieg (1941)
Spooks Run Wild (1941)
Mr. Wise Guy (1942)
Let's Get Tough! (1942)
Smart Alecks (1942)
'Neath Brooklyn Bridge (1942)
Kid Dynamite (1943)
Clancy Street Boys (1943)
Ghosts on the Loose (1943)
Mr. Muggs Steps Out (1943)
Million Dollar Kid (1944)
Follow the Leader (1944)
Block Busters (1944)
Bowery Champs (1944)
Docks of New York, The (1945)
Mr. Muggs Rides Again (1945)
Come Out Fighting (1945)

Bowery Boys
Live Wires (1946)
In Fast Company (1946)
Bowery Bombshell (1946)
Spook Busters (1946)
Mr. Hex (1946)
Hard Boiled Mahoney (1947)
News Hounds (1947)
Bowery Buckaroos (1947)
Angels' Alley (1948)
Jinx Money (1948)
Smugglers' Cove (1948)
Trouble Makers (1948)
Fighting Fools (1949)
Hold That Baby! (1949)
Angels in Disguise (1949)

Master Minds (1949)
Blonde Dynamite (1950)
Lucky Losers (1950)
Triple Trouble (1950)
Blues Busters (1950)
Bowery Battalion (1951)
Ghost Chasers (1951)
Let's Go Navy! (1951)
Crazy Over Horses (1951)
Hold That Line (1952)
Here Come the Marines (1952)
Feudin' Fools (1952)
No Holds Barred (1952)
Jalopy (1953)
Loose in London (1953)
Clipped Wings (1953)
Private Eyes (1953)
Paris Playboys (1954)
The Bowery Boys Meet the Monsters (1954)
Jungle Gents (1954)
Bowery to Bagdad (1954)
High Society (1955)
Spy Chasers (1955)
Jail Busters (1955)
Dig That Uranium (1956)
Crashing Las Vegas (1956)
Fighting Trouble (1956)
Hot Shots (1956)
Hold That Hypnotist (1957)
Spook Chasers (1957)
Looking for Danger (1957)
Up in Smoke (1957)
In the Money (1958)

Bowery Boys Meet the Monsters, The (1954) **65m.** **½ D: Edward Bernds. Leo Gorcey, Huntz Hall, Bernard Gorcey, Bennie Bartlett, Lloyd Corrigan, Ellen Corby, John Dehner, Paul Wexler. Efficient blend of laughs and chills as the gang gets mixed up with a family of transplant-happy mad scientists.

Bowery Buckaroos (1947) **66m.** ** D: William Beaudine. Leo Gorcey, Huntz Hall, Bobby Jordan, Gabriel Dell, Billy Benedict, David Gorcey, Julie Gibson, Bernard Gorcey, Minerva Urecal, Russell Simpson, Iron Eyes Cody. Mild spoof, with the boys getting into all sorts of trouble out West in Hangman's Hollow.▼

Bowery Champs (1944) **62m.** ** D: William Beaudine. Leo Gorcey, Huntz Hall, Billy Benedict, Jimmy Strand, Bud Gorman, Gabriel Dell, Anne Sterling, Evelyn Brent, Ian Keith. Newshound Muggs (Gorcey) gets embroiled in a murder investigation in this frantic *East Side Kids* outing. Former costar Bobby Jordan appears as himself in an amusing running gag.

Bowery to Bagdad (1954) **64m.** ** D: Edward Bernds. Leo Gorcey, Huntz Hall, David Gorcey, Bennie Bartlett, Bernard Gorcey, Joan Shawlee, Eric Blore, Robert Bice, Rick Vallin, Jean Willes. As if there wasn't enough turmoil in the Middle East, the Bowery Boys find Aladdin's lamp and are whisked away to Iraq. Unsubtle, to say the least. Veteran scene-stealer Blore appears as the genie!

Bowery to Broadway (1944) **94m.** **½ D: Charles Lamont. Jack Oakie, Donald Cook, Maria Montez, Louise Allbritton, Susanna Foster, Turhan Bey, Andy Devine, Rosemary DeCamp, Frank McHugh, Ann Blyth, Leo Carrillo, Evelyn Ankers, Peggy Ryan, Donald O'Connor. Film depends solely on its many guest stars for what entertainment it has; limp story of rival theatrical producers (Oakie, Cook) doesn't make it.

Bowfinger (1999) **C-97m.** **½ D: Frank Oz. Steve Martin, Eddie Murphy, Heather Graham, Christine Baranski, Jamie Kennedy, Robert Downey, Jr., Terence Stamp, Adam Alexi-Malle, Barry Newman. Desperate, down-and-out filmmaker Bobby Bowfinger (Martin) schemes to make a movie with the top action star in Hollywood (Murphy)—without bothering to tell him that he's in the picture! Likable costars carry this comedy a long way; there are some good laughs throughout, but it's never as satisfying as you'd like it to be. Murphy has fun playing a doofus look-alike for the action hero. Written by Martin. [PG-13]▼●◗

Boxcar Bertha (1972) **C-88m.** **½ D: Martin Scorsese. Barbara Hershey, David Carradine, Barry Primus, Bernie Casey, John Carradine. Scorsese's first studio film is yet another BONNIE AND CLYDE cash-in, with small-town girl Hershey falling in with Carradine and his band of train robbers. Good of its kind, but buffs looking for embryonic Scorsese stylistics may be a little let down . . . although there *are* two minor characters named Michael Powell and Emeric Pressburger! [R]▼●

Boxer, The (1971) SEE: **Ripped Off**

Boxer, The (1997-U.S.-Irish) **C-113m.** *** D: Jim Sheridan. Daniel Day-Lewis, Emily Watson, Brian Cox, Ken Stott, Gerard McSorley, Eleanor Methven, Ciaran Fitzgerald, Kenneth Cranham. Powerful, straightforward story of a boxer and former IRA member released from prison after 14 years, trying to rebuild his life in troubled Belfast and becoming involved with his old sweetheart, who's married to a political prisoner. Third teaming of Day-Lewis and director/cowriter Sheridan lacks the complexity and resonance of MY LEFT FOOT and IN THE NAME OF THE FATHER, but is still compelling human drama, anchored by Day-Lewis and the luminous Watson. Stunningly filmed by Chris Menges in Dublin. [R]▼●◗

Boxing Helena (1993) **C-107m.** *½ D: Jennifer Chambers Lynch. Julian Sands, Sherilyn Fenn, Bill Paxton, Art Garfunkel, Kurtwood Smith, Betsy Clark, Nicolette Scorsese. Perfectly dreadful debut feature from the 24-year-old daughter of David Lynch, about an esteemed surgeon (Sands) whose obsession with sexpot Fenn leads to a most bizarre set of circumstances. Tries to be provocative and shocking, but the result is unintentional laughter (when it's not boring). Originally NC-17, re-rated after appeal. Super 35.▼●

Box of Moonlight (1997) **C-107m.** **½ D: Tom DiCillo. John Turturro, Sam Rockwell, Catherine Keener, Lisa Blount, Annie Corley, Dermot Mulroney. A very slight slice of whimsy about an uptight engineer, supervising a construction project out of town, who quite by chance falls in with a free spirit who lives in the woods . . . and finds that he feels liberated as he spends time away from the precision of his normal life. Turturro is excellent, as always, and so is Rockwell as Kid, but the story has few surprises, and its charms are stretched pretty thin. DiCillo also scripted. [R] ▼●◗

Boy and His Dog, A (1975) **C-87m.** **½ D: L. Q. Jones. Don Johnson, Susanne Benton, Jason Robards, Alvy Moore, Helene Winston, Charles McGraw, Tiger, voice of Tim McIntire. Cult black comedy is definitely not a kiddie movie, despite its title. In the post-holocaust future, young punk Johnson, aided by his telepathic (and much smarter) dog, forages for food and women, is eventually lured into bizarre underground civilization. Faithful adaptation of Harlan Ellison's novella. Revised in 1982 to include a 1m. prologue. Techniscope. [R] ▼●◗

Boy and the Pirates, The (1960) **C-82m.** **½ D: Bert I. Gordon. Charles Herbert, Susan Gordon, Murvyn Vye, Paul Guilfoyle. OK fantasy-adventure for kids about a boy who is magically transported back to the days of pirates on the high seas. Vye is well cast as the main cutthroat.

Boy Cried Murder, The (1966-British) **C-86m.** **½ D: George Breakston. Veronica Hurst, Phil Brown, Beba Loncar, Frazer MacIntosh, Tim Barrett. A reworking of THE WINDOW set in Adriatic resort town. Youngster noted for his fabrications witnesses a murder; no one but the killer believes him.

Boy, Did I Get a Wrong Number! (1966) **C-99m.** BOMB D: George Marshall. Bob Hope, Elke Sommer, Phyllis Diller, Cesare Danova, Marjorie Lord. They sure did; result is worthless film that should be avoided. Absolutely painful.▼

Boy Friend, The (1971-British) **C-135m.** *** D: Ken Russell. Twiggy, Christopher Gable, Moyra Fraser, Max Adrian, Vladek Sheybal, Georgina Hale, Tommy Tune; cameo by Glenda Jackson. Director Russell's homage to Hollywood musicals works on several levels, from tacky matinee performance of a show to fantasy-world conception of same material, all loosely tied to Sandy Wilson's cunning spoof of 1920s musical shows. Busby Berkeley-ish numbers (choreographed by Gable) come amazingly close to spirit and execution of the Master himself. Originally released in U.S. at 110m. Panavision. [G]▼●

Boyfriends and Girlfriends (1987-French) **C-102m.** *** D: Eric Rohmer. Emmanuelle Chaulet, Sophie Renoir, Anne-Laure Meury, Eric Viellard, Francois-Eric Gendron. The sixth of Rohmer's "Comedies and Proverbs" is a typically witty, perceptive, ironic account of two very different young women who strike up a friendship . . . and commence playing romantic musical chairs with a couple of men. Nobody can direct characters who are forever falling in and out of love quite like Eric Rohmer. Originally shown as MY GIRLFRIEND'S BOYFRIEND. [PG]▼●◗

Boy From Indiana (1950) **66m.** ** D: John Rawlins. Lon McCallister, Lois Butler, Billie Burke, George Cleveland. Modest horseracing yarn, with McCallister grooming his beloved horse while romancing Butler.

Boy From Oklahoma, The (1954) **C-88m.** **½ D: Michael Curtiz. Will Rogers, Jr., Nancy Olson, Lon Chaney (Jr.), Anthony Caruso, Wallace Ford, Merv Griffin. Quiet Western film with Rogers as pacifist sheriff who manages to keep the town intact and romance Olson; good production values. Spun off as TV series *Sugarfoot*.

Boy in Blue, The (1986-Canadian) **C-98m.** ** D: Charles Jarrott. Nicolas Cage, Cynthia Dale, Christopher Plummer, David Naughton, Sean Sullivan, Melody Anderson. Humdrum tale of real-life 19th-century Canadian rowing champ Ned Hanlan; filled with stock characters, from faithful manager to "unattainable" love interest. Barely stays afloat. [R]▼

Boy in the Plastic Bubble, The (1976) **C-100m. TVM** D: Randal Kleiser. John Travolta, Glynnis O'Connor, Robert Reed, Diana Hyland, Ralph Bellamy, Karen Morrow, John Friedrich, Buzz Aldrin, Anne Ramsey. Travolta is forced to live in an isolation bubble because he's been born without immunities. Engrossing look at a boy's coming of age under unusual—and challenging—circumstances. Script by Douglas Day Stewart, from his and Joseph Morgenstern's story. Hyland won a posthumous Emmy. Above average.▼◗

Boy Meets Girl (1938) **86m.** **½ D: Lloyd Bacon. James Cagney, Pat O'Brien, Marie Wilson, Ralph Bellamy, Frank McHugh, Dick Foran, Penny Singleton, Ronald Reagan. Screwball spoof of Hollywood sometimes pushes too hard, but has enough sharp dialogue, good satire in tale of two sharpster screenwriters to make it worthwhile. Script by Samuel and Bella Spewack, from their Broadway play.▼

Boy Named Charlie Brown, A (1969) **C-85m.** *** D: Bill Melendez. Voices of Peter Robbins, Pamelyn Ferdin, Glenn Gilger, Andy Pforsich. *Peanuts* gang makes surprisingly successful feature-film debut, with ingenious visual ideas adding to usual fun. Only debit: Rod McKuen's absurd songs. [G]▼●

Boy of the Streets (1937) **75m.** **½ D: William Nigh. Jackie Cooper, Maureen O'Connor, Kathleen Burke, Robert Emmett O'Connor, Marjorie Main, George Cleveland. Atmospheric little programmer with Cooper a cocky young punk who hero-worships his dad, a slimy political hack. Awfully sentimental at times.▼

Boy on a Dolphin (1957) **C-111m.** **½ D: Jean Negulesco. Alan Ladd, Clifton Webb, Sophia Loren, Laurence Naismith. Grecian isles are backdrop to pedestrian sunken-treasure yarn. Loren, in U.S. film debut, cast as skindiver helping Ladd. CinemaScope.▼

Boys, The (1961-British) **123m.** *** D: Sidney J. Furie. Richard Todd, Robert Morley, Felix Aylmer, Wilfred Brambell. Engrossing study of attorney who tries to uncover motives for crimes allegedly committed by four teenagers. CinemaScope.

Boys, The (1991) **C-100m. TVM** D: Glenn Jordan. James Woods, John Lithgow, Joanna Gleason, Eve Gordon, Alan Rosenberg, Jon Vickery. Off-center black comedy about two lifelong friends, pranksters and Hollywood writing partners, who learn that one is terminally ill from breathing the other's cigarette smoke for years. Written by William Link, inspired apparently by the death of his longtime pal and colleague Richard Levinson. Average.

Boys (1996) **C-88m.** ** D: Stacy Cochran. Winona Ryder, Lukas Haas, John C. Reilly, James LeGros, Skeet Ulrich, Wiley Wiggins, Russell Young, Chris Cooper, Jessica Harper, Catherine Keener. Moody but muddled coming-of-age story about a prep school boy (Haas) who helps a woman (Ryder) after an accident and then becomes entangled in her mysterious past. Frustrating plot takes time getting started, but has no real story to tell. Attractive New England locations and good performance by Haas can't make up for lapses in logic . . . and a tacked-on happy ending. This sat on the shelf for over a year. [PG-13]▼●

Boys Don't Cry (1999) **C-119m.** **½ D: Kimberly Peirce. Hilary Swank, Chloë Sevigny, Peter Sarsgaard, Brendan Sexton III, Alison Folland, Alicia Goranson, Jeannetta Arnette. Searing drama based on the 1993 case of Brandon Teena (Swank, in an Oscar-winning performance), a girl who passes herself off as a boy in rural Nebraska. Moving to a new town, she/he finds a soul mate who deliberately doesn't ask too many questions . . . but infuriates the girl's trailer-trash friends and family. Well made in every respect, but fails to get inside the characters' heads; the violent conclusion is almost unbearable to watch. Same material explored in the documentary THE BRANDON TEENA STORY. [R]▼◗

Boys From Brazil, The (1978) **C-123m.** **½ D: Franklin J. Schaffner. Gregory Peck, Laurence Olivier, James Mason, Lilli Palmer, Uta Hagen, John Dehner, Rosemary Harris, Anne Meara, John Rubinstein, Denholm Elliott, Steven Guttenberg, David Hurst, Jeremy Black, Bruno Ganz, Walter Gotell, Michael Gough, Prunella Scales. Former Nazi chieftain Dr. Josef Mengele (Peck) has insidious plan to breed new race of Hitlers. Interesting but ultimately silly and unbelievable; worth watching, though, for Olivier's brilliant, credible performance as aging Jewish Nazi-hunter. Based on Ira Levin novel. [R]▼●◗

Boys From Brooklyn, The SEE: **Bela Lugosi Meets a Brooklyn Gorilla**

Boys From Syracuse, The (1940) **73m.** **½ D: A. Edward Sutherland. Allan Jones, Joe Penner, Martha Raye, Rosemary Lane, Irene Hervey, Eric Blore. Disappointingly ordinary adaptation of Rodgers & Hart's Broadway musical based on Shakespeare's *Comedy of Errors*, but set in ancient Greece. Songs: "This Can't Be Love," "Falling In Love With Love."

Boys in Company C, The (1978) **C-127m.** *** D: Sidney J. Furie. Stan Shaw, Andrew Stevens, James Canning, Michael Lembeck, Craig Wasson, Scott Hylands, James Whitmore, Jr., Lee Ermey. Shaw (in a standout performance) whips a bunch of green Marine recruits into shape for combat in Vietnam; good, tough film focuses on stupidity of military brass and demoralization of the soldiers. Panavision. [R]▼●

Boys in the Band, The (1970) **C-119m.** ***½ D: William Friedkin. Kenneth Nelson, Peter White, Leonard Frey, Cliff Gorman, Frederick Combs, Laurence Luckinbill, Keith Prentice, Robert LaTourneaux, Reuben Greene. Excellent filmization of Mart Crowley's landmark play about nine men at a birthday party: eight are gay, the ninth insists he's not. Often hilarious, frequently sad, but always thought provoking, and sensationally acted by the original stage cast; a rare case where a single, claustrophobic set is actually an asset. Avoid the shredded 108m. version released to commercial TV. [R]▼●

Boys Next Door, The (1985) **C-88m.** ** D: Penelope Spheeris. Maxwell Caulfield, Charlie Sheen, Christopher McDonald, Hank Garrett, Patti D'Arbanville, Moon Zappa. Alienated teens Caulfield and Sheen, just about to graduate high school, go on a murder spree. A not-uninteresting portrait of desperation and hopelessness that ultimately fails because there's no real insight into the boys' behavior. [R]▼●

Boys Next Door, The (1996) **C-100m. TVM** D: John Erman. Nathan Lane, Robert

Sean Leonard, Tony Goldwyn, Michael Jeter, Courtney B. Vance, Mare Winningham, Elizabeth Wilson, Lynne Thigpen, Jenny Robertson. Poignant and comic ensemble piece about four mentally challenged men in an urban group home and their devoted social worker, whose decision to move on will change the lives of "the boys." Take special note of Winningham in a small part as a backward plain Jane who meets one of the boys at a dance. Adapted by William Blinn from Tom Griffin's off-Broadway play. Above average.▼●

Boys' Night Out (1962) **C-115m.** *** D: Michael Gordon. Kim Novak, James Garner, Tony Randall, Howard Duff, Janet Blair, Patti Page, Zsa Zsa Gabor, Howard Morris. Trio of married men and bachelor Garner decide to set up an apartment equipped with Novak. Some interesting innuendos, with comic relief from Blair, Page, and Gabor. CinemaScope.▼

Boys of Paul Street, The (1969-Hungarian-U.S.) **C-108m.** *** D: Zoltan Fabri. Anthony Kemp, Robert Efford, Gary O'Brien, Mark Colleano, John Moulder Brown. Allegory of children's battle for control of vacant lot in Budapest, from Ferenc Molnar's novel; eloquent statement on war. Filmed before in Hollywood as NO GREATER GLORY. Agascope. [G]

Boys of the City (1940) **65m.** ** D: Joseph H. Lewis. Leo Gorcey, Bobby Jordan, Sunshine Sammy Morrison, David Gorcey, Dave O'Brien, Vince Barnett, Dennis Moore, Donald Haines, Hally Chester, Frankie Burke. Muggs (Gorcey) and his gang are sent to the country where they get mixed up with murder in a "haunted" house. OK follow-up to EAST SIDE KIDS and the first official entry in the series.▼

Boys on the Side (1995) **C-117m.** *** D: Herbert Ross. Whoopi Goldberg, Mary-Louise Parker, Drew Barrymore, Matthew McConaughey, James Remar, Billy Wirth, Anita Gillette, Estelle Parsons, Dennis Boutsikaris, Gedde Watanabe. Extremely likable film about three disparate women who travel cross-country and become involved in each other's lives. Any film incorporating physical abuse, premarital pregnancy, AIDS, and lesbianism has got its work cut out for it; three strong, appealing performances make up for story contrivances (and credibility gaps). Super 35. [R]▼●◗

Boys Town (1938) **96m.** *** D: Norman Taurog. Spencer Tracy, Mickey Rooney, Henry Hull, Gene Reynolds, Leslie Fenton, Addison Richards, Edward Norris, Sidney Miller, Bobs Watson, Frankie Thomas. Tracy won Oscar as Father Flanagan, who develops school for juvenile delinquents; Rooney is his toughest enrolee. Syrupy but well-done; Eleanore Griffin and Dore Schary also earned Oscars for their original story. Sequel: MEN OF BOYS TOWN. Almost 60 years later, Rooney played Father Flanagan in the direct-to-video feature THE ROAD HOME. Also shown in computer-colored version. ▼●

Boy Ten Feet Tall, A (1963-British) **C-118m.** *** D: Alexander Mackendrick. Edward G. Robinson, Fergus McClelland, Constance Cummings, Harry H. Corbett. Colorful, charming film about orphaned boy traveling through Africa alone to reach his aunt, who lives in Durban. Cut to 88m. for American release, footage was restored for TV print. Originally titled SAMMY GOING SOUTH. CinemaScope.

Boy! What a Girl (1946) **70m.** *** D: Arthur Leonard. Tim Moore, Duke Williams, Elwood Smith, Sheila Guyse, Betti Mays, Deek Watson and His Brown Dots, Big Sid Catlett, International Jitterbugs, Slam Stewart, Ann Cornell. Wonderfully entertaining musical comedy featuring all-black cast (with the exception of Gene Krupa). Scenario centers around a couple of producers attempting to win backing for their show. Moore is funny in drag; the jitterbugging is quite X-rated for 1946.▼

Boy Who Caught a Crook (1961) **72m.** ** D: Edward L. Cahn. Wanda Hendrix, Roger Mobley, Don Beddoe, Richard Crane, Johnny Seven. Newsboy is menaced by bank robber who thinks the boy has the lost loot. Title tells rest.

Boy Who Could Fly, The (1986) **C-114m.** **½ D: Nick Castle. Lucy Deakins, Jay Underwood, Bonnie Bedelia, Fred Savage, Colleen Dewhurst, Fred Gwynne, Louise Fletcher, Jason Priestley. Sensitive girl moves to a new neighborhood and befriends an autistic (and mysterious) boy next door. Warm, well-intentioned film moves very slowly and makes uncomfortable turn from believable drama to fantasy—undermining much of its effectiveness. Good feelings and good performances (especially Bedelia and newcomer Deakins) help keep it aloft. Written by director Castle. [PG]▼●

Boy Who Cried Bitch, The (1991) **C-101m.** *** D: Juan Jose Campanella. Harley Cross, Karen Young, Dennis Boutsikaris, Adrien Brody, Gene Canfield, Moira Kelly, Jesse Bradford, J. D. Daniels, Kario Salem, Samuel Wright. Thoughtful, unsettling drama about violent, psychotic 12-year-old Cross, whose mother hasn't given him proper parental attention, and whose psychiatric care is inadequate at best. Well made, extremely well acted, but be forewarned: it's unrelentingly grim and sad.

Boy Who Cried Werewolf, The (1973) **C-93m.** ** D: Nathan Juran. Kerwin Mathews, Elaine Devry, Scott Sealey, Robert J. Wilke, Susan Foster. Boy discovers his own father has become a werewolf and is on the prowl. More like an adventure thriller than a horror movie, but not much good as anything. Odd werewolf makeup. [PG]

Boy Who Had Everything, The (1984-Australian) **C-94m.** ** D: Stephen Wallace. Jason Connery, Diane Cilento, Laura Williams, Lewis Fitz-Gerald, Ian Gilmour. Uneven, inconsequential account of sensitive first-year university student Connery, his relationships with his mother and girlfriend, and his growing pains. Jason is the son of Sean Connery and Diane Cilento (who plays his mom here). [R]

Boy Who Stole a Million, The (1960-British) **64m.** ** D: Charles Crichton. Maurice Reyna, Virgilio Texera, Marianne Benet, Harold Kasket. Family-type film of youth who gets involved in bank theft to help father with oppressive debts.

Boy With Green Hair, The (1948) **C-82m.** *** D: Joseph Losey. Pat O'Brien, Robert Ryan, Barbara Hale, Dean Stockwell, Dwayne Hickman. Thought-provoking allegory of war orphan Stockwell, who becomes a social outcast when his hair changes color. Controversial on its release because of its pacifistic point of view. Dale Robertson and Russ Tamblyn appear uncredited.▼●

Boyz N the Hood (1991) **C-107m.** *** D: John Singleton. Larry Fishburne, Ice Cube, Cuba Gooding, Jr., Nia Long, Morris Chestnut, Tyra Ferrell, Angela Bassett, Whitman Mayo. Sober, thoughtful look at life in the black section of South Central L.A. A divorced father strives to raise his son with values—and steer him away from the ignorance and aimlessness that has led to an epidemic of senseless violence in the neighborhood. Impressive debut for 23-year-old writer-director Singleton; longish, and not always on-the-money, but overall quite potent and effective. Singleton has a bit part as a mailman. [R]▼●◗

Braddock: Missing in Action III (1988) **C-101m.** BOMB D: Aaron Norris. Chuck Norris, Aki Aleong, Roland Harrah III, Miki King. Dreary comic book sequel with Colonel Norris returning to Vietnam yet again, this time to look for his wife. Chuck even coscripted, with brother Aaron serving as director. [R]▼●

Brady Bunch Movie, The (1995) **C-90m.** **½ D: Betty Thomas. Shelley Long, Gary Cole, Michael McKean, Jean Smart, Henriette Mantel, Christopher Daniel Barnes, Christine Taylor, Paul Sutera, Jennifer Elise Cox, Jesse Lee, Olivia Hack, Reni Santoni. Dead-on parody of the enduringly popular early '70s TV sitcom, with America's favorite white-bread family unaware that values and mores have changed all around them. Long and Cole are a hoot as the parents, but if you're not a series devotee, many of the gags and story references will have no meaning whatsoever. Predictably, there are cameos by veterans of the original show. Followed by A VERY BRADY SEQUEL. [PG-13]▼●

Brady's Escape (1984-U.S.-Hungarian) **C-96m.** ** D: Pal Gabor. John Savage, Kelly Reno, Ildiko Bansagi, Laszlo Mensaros, Ferenc Bacs. Bland adventure yarn about a flier (Savage) shot down over Hungary during WW2, and how some Magyar cowboys help him to elude the Nazis. ▼●

Brain, The (1962-British-German) **85m.** *** D: Freddie Francis. Anne Heywood, Peter Van Eyck, Cecil Parker, Bernard Lee, Maxine Audley, Jeremy Spenser, Jack MacGowran. Good remake of DONOVAN'S BRAIN, about scientist overtaken by the brain of a vengeance-seeking dead man that is being kept "alive" in his laboratory. Original British title: VENGEANCE.▼

Brain, The (1969-French) **C-100m.** ** D: Gerard Oury. David Niven, Jean-Paul Belmondo, Bourvil, Eli Wallach, Silvia Monti, Fernand Valois. Fine international cast in OK caper comedy about a train heist masterminded by Niven. Franscope. [G]▼

Brain Candy (1996) **C-88m.** **½ D: Kelly Makin. David Foley, Bruce McCulloch, Kevin McDonald, Mark McKinney, Scott Thompson, Kathryn Greenwood, Janeane Garofalo. New wonder drug that cures depression has devastating side effect on the population now addicted to the product. This premise intertwines the lives of over thirty characters played by Kids in the Hall, the Canadian TV sketch troupe in their feature-film debut. Funny sequences and bizarre characters don't add up to a satisfying whole, but the cast is energetic in many original and unusual guises, often in drag. Standout moment has Thompson "coming out" in splashy Hollywood musical production number. Brendan Fraser appears unbilled. Onscreen title is KIDS IN THE HALL BRAIN CANDY. [R]▼●

Brain Damage (1988) **C-94m.** *** D: Frank Henenlotter. Rick Herbst, Gordon MacDonald, Jennifer Lowry, Theo Barnes, Lucille Saint-Peter, Vicki Darnell. Extremely strange, oddly effective horror film about Herbst and a monster parasite that gives him psychedelic "highs" by injecting fluid into his brain. And that's not the half of it! Clever parable about drug addiction features a funny cameo by the star of Henenlotter's first film, BASKET CASE. [R]▼◗

Brain Donors (1992) **C-80m.** ** D: Dennis Dugan. John Turturro, Bob Nelson, Mel Smith, Nancy Marchand, John Savident, George De La Pena, Juli Donald, Spike Alexander, Teri Copley. Three social misfits team up to bilk a wealthy matron who wants to establish her own ballet company. Full-bore attempt to recreate an old-time movie comedy, officially "suggested" by A NIGHT AT THE OPERA, with Turturro as Groucho, Nelson as Harpo,

Smith as Chico, and Marchand as Margaret Dumont. Scores high marks for good intentions but pretty much falls flat. Great Claymation title sequence by Will Vinton's studio. Written by Pat Proft. [PG]▼●

Brain Eaters, The (1958) **60m.** ** D: Bruno Ve Sota. Joanna Lee, Jody Fair, Edwin Nelson, Alan Frost. Loosely based on Robert Heinlein's *Puppet Masters*, this has spongy brain creatures boring up from inner earth in a ship, attaching themselves to people's heads and turning them into mindless zombies. Some mildly scary moments. Look for early Leonard Nimoy cameo.▼

Brain From Planet Arous, The (1958) **70m.** ** D: Nathan Juran. John Agar, Joyce Meadows, Robert Fuller, Henry Travis, Morris Ankrum, Tom Browne Henry. Giant floating brain (with eyes) takes over the body of scientist Agar as its first step in conquering Earth; meanwhile, policeman brain hides out in Agar's dog while waiting for the right moment to make the arrest. As you can see, this is not Kubrick's 2001 we're talking here, but it *is* fun in an idiotic sort of way, and Agar is pretty good under the circumstances.▼●

Brain Machine, The (1956-British) **72m.** ** D: Ken Hughes. Patrick Barr, Elizabeth Allan, Maxwell Reed, Vanda Godsell. Average yarn about drug smuggling and those involved, one of them as the result of mind-shattering machine.

Brainscan (1994-U.S.-Canadian) **C-95m.** ** D: John Flynn. Edward Furlong, Frank Langella, T Rider-Smith, Amy Hargreaves, Jamie Marsh, Victor Ertmanis, David Hemblen. Teenaged Furlong has few friends, still grieves over the accident that killed his mother, and is obsessed by horror movies and computer games. All of which makes him ripe for the new game, Brainscan—which seems to be turning him into an unwitting murderer. A good cast and director do what they can with mediocre material. Fantasy character, Trickster (who emerges from the game), is a transparent bid for a Freddy Krueger–like franchise, but lacks appeal. [R]▼●

Brain Smasher . . . A Love Story (1993) **C-88m.** *½ D: Albert Pyun. Andrew Dice Clay, Teri Hatcher, Yuji Okumoto, Deborah Van Valkenburgh, Brion James, Tim Thomerson, Charles Rocket, Nicholas Guest. One night in Portland, Oregon, nightclub bouncer Clay helps model Hatcher combat a mob of evil Chinese monks who are after the Red Lotus of Ultimate Power. Failed attempt to turn Clay into a Stallone-like action star is a slow, foggy bore. Hatcher is cute in hot pants, though. [PG-13]▼●

Brainstorm (1965) **114m.** ** D: William Conrad. Jeff Hunter, Anne Francis, Dana Andrews, Viveca Lindfors, Stacy Harris, Kathie Brown. Fair thriller about a determined man (Hunter) who attempts the perfect crime in order to eliminate Andrews and marry Francis. Contrived. Panavision.

Brainstorm (1983) **C-106m.** *** D: Douglas Trumbull. Christopher Walken, Natalie Wood, Louise Fletcher, Cliff Robertson, Joe Dorsey, Jordan Christopher. Research scientists Walken and Fletcher perfect a sensory experience device—in the form of a headset—with explosive potential. Entertainingly old-fashioned "mad scientist" type tale brought up to date, though it's best not to examine story too closely. Fletcher gives film's standout performance, but Wood, in her last film (she died during production in 1981) has a basically thankless role. Sure to lose most of its impact on TV, since Trumbull's state-of-the-art visual effects were designed for 70mm Super Panavision. [PG]▼●◗

Brain That Wouldn't Die, The (1963) **81m.** *½ D: Joseph Green. Herb (Jason) Evers, Virginia Leith, Adele Lamont, Leslie Daniel, Paula Maurice. Poorly produced tale of surgeon trying to find body to attach to fiancée's head (she was decapitated but still lives). Beware of shorter version, which eliminates most of the gore.▼

Brainwash SEE: **Circle of Power**

Brainwashed (1961-German) **102m.** ** D: Gerd Oswald. Curt Jurgens, Claire Bloom, Hansjorg Felmy, Albert Lieven. Austrian Jurgens' struggle to retain sanity while undergoing intense Nazi interrogation is basis of this psychological drama. Strong performances but weak story mars film.

BrainWaves (1982) **C-80m.** ** D: Ulli Lommel. Keir Dullea, Suzanna Love, Tony Curtis, Vera Miles, Percy Rodrigues, Paul Willson. Young woman, injured in an accident, receives the brain (and brainwaves) of a murdered girl and then is stalked by her killer. A glum-looking Tony Curtis is the modern-day Dr. Frankenstein in this pedestrian thriller. [PG—edited from original R rating]▼

Bramble Bush, The (1960) **C-105m.** **½ D: Daniel Petrie. Richard Burton, Barbara Rush, Jack Carson, Angie Dickinson. Charles Mergendahl's potboiler becomes superficial gloss with Burton, totally ill at ease, playing New England doctor returning to Cape Cod, where he falls in love with his dying friend's wife.▼

Bram Stoker's Dracula (1992) **C-123m.** ***½ D: Francis Ford Coppola. Gary Oldman, Winona Ryder, Anthony Hopkins, Keanu Reeves, Richard E. Grant, Cary Elwes, Bill Campbell, Sadie Frost, Tom Waits, Jay Robinson. Sumptuous retelling of the Dracula legend as originally conceived by Stoker in his 1897 novel. Avenging the death of his beloved wife, a 15th-century Romanian warrior lives on through the ages . . . and sets his sights on

Victorian London. Sexual, sinuous, exquisitely realized (using every movie artifice imaginable); occasionally let down by story lags . . . but always has one more goodie up its sleeve. Written by James Victor Hart. Kudos to Thomas Sanders' production design, Michael Ballhaus' cinematography, and Wojciech Kilar's powerful music. Won Oscars for makeup, sound effects editing, and costume design. [R]▼●◗

Branded (1950) **C-95m.** **½ D: Rudolph Maté. Alan Ladd, Mona Freeman, Charles Bickford, Joseph Calleia, Milburn Stone. Outlaws use carefree Ladd to impersonate rancher Bickford's long-missing son, leading to much different outcome than anticipated; action and love scenes balanced OK.▼●

Brannigan (1975-British) **C-111m.** **½ D: Douglas Hickox. John Wayne, Richard Attenborough, Judy Geeson, John Vernon, Mel Ferrer, Ralph Meeker, Lesley-Anne Down. A criminal flees to London to avoid extradition, and Chicago cop Wayne pursues him. Overlong, but change of locale serves Duke well; highlight is amusing brawl in pub. Panavision. [PG]▼●

Brasher Doubloon, The (1947) **72m.** ** D: John Brahm. George Montgomery, Nancy Guild, Conrad Janis, Roy Roberts, Fritz Kortner. Rare coin seems to be object of several murders in very uneven version of Philip Marlowe detective mystery. Filmed before as TIME TO KILL.

Brass Bottle, The (1964) **C-89m.** ** D: Harry Keller. Tony Randall, Burl Ives, Barbara Eden, Edward Andrews, Ann Doran. Juvenile comedy-fantasy about genie Ives coming out of magic bottle to serve Randall. Leading lady Eden fared better when she went into a lamp herself on TV. ▼

Brassed Off (1996-British-U.S.) **C-109m.** *** D: Mark Herman. Pete Postlethwaite, Tara Fitzgerald, Ewan McGregor, Stephen Tompkinson, Jim Carter, Philip Jackson, Peter Martin, Sonue Johnston, Mary Healey, Lill Roughley. Yorkshire mine workers eke out a living but find solace as members of an amateur, all-male brass band. They are threatened by the not unrelated factors of (a) the mining pit's possible closure and (b) a young woman invading their territory. Seriocomic drama provides an emotional tour de force for Postlethwaite as dogged bandleader, and also for Tompkinson as his beleaguered son. Those are the real-life musicians—members of the Grimethorpe Colliery Band—on the soundtrack. [R]▼●◗

Brass Legend, The (1956) **79m.** *½ D: Gerd Oswald. Hugh O'Brian, Nancy Gates, Raymond Burr, Reba Tassell. Routine Western uplifted by Burr's villain role.

Brass Target (1978) **C-111m.** ** D: John Hough. John Cassavetes, Sophia Loren, George Kennedy, Max von Sydow, Robert Vaughn, Bruce Davison, Patrick McGoohan. Rambling thriller speculates that Gen. Patton (Kennedy) was assassinated just after WW2 because of major gold heist perpetrated by his subordinates. Unfocused storyline is major liability; von Sydow is major asset as the killer. Panavision. [PG] ▼●

Bravados, The (1958) **C-98m.** *** D: Henry King. Gregory Peck, Joan Collins, Stephen Boyd, Albert Salmi. Compelling Western starring Peck, seeking four men who raped and killed his wife, discovering that he has become no better than those he hunts. Joe De Rita (later Curly Joe of The Three Stooges) plays the hangman. CinemaScope. ▼

Brave Bulls, The (1951) **108m.** *** D: Robert Rossen. Mel Ferrer, Miroslava, Anthony Quinn, Eugene Iglesias. Flavorful account of public and private life of a matador, based on Tom Lea book. Film admirably captures atmosphere of bullfighting. Some prints now available run 114m., with bullfight footage originally deemed too gruesome for U.S. audiences.

Braveheart (1995) **C 177m.** ***½ D: Mel Gibson. Mel Gibson, Sophie Marceau, Patrick McGoohan, Catherine McCormack, Brendan Gleeson, James Cosmo, David O'Hara, Angus McFadyen, Peter Henly, James Robinson, Alun Armstrong, Ian Bannen. Big, booming, epic tale of 13th-century Scottish rebel warrior William Wallace, who builds a grass-roots resistance to the tyranny of English King Edward I (McGoohan). Manages to tell a gripping personal story that grows in scale through a series of eye-popping (and bloody) battle scenes. Only the denouement starts to drag. A powerful, passionate film about a powerful, passionate man. Winner of Academy Awards for Best Picture, Director, Cinematography (John Toll), Makeup, and Sound Effects Editing. Panavision. [R] ▼●

Brave Little Toaster, The (1987) **C-90m.** *** D: Jerry Rees. Voices of Jon Lovitz, Tim Stack, Timothy E. Day, Thurl Ravenscroft, Deanna Oliver, Phil Hartman. Entertaining animated feature about a group of humanized household appliances who embark on a perilous journey to find their young master. A welcome throwback to the cartoons of yore, with equal doses of heart and hip humor to please both kids and their parents. Some nice songs by Van Dyke Parks, too. Based on the novel by Thomas M. Disch. Followed by two direct-to-video sequels. ▼●

Brave One, The (1956) **C-100m.** *** D: Irving Rapper. Michel Ray, Rodolfo Hoyos, Fermin Rivera, Elsa Cardenas, Carlos Navarro, Joi Lansing. Predictable but charming tale of peasant-boy Ray and his love for Gitano, a valiant bull destined to meet his fate in the arena. Filmed in Mexico. "Robert Rich" (a pseudonym for blacklisted Dalton Trumbo) received a Best Original Story Academy Award, which went unclaimed until 1975. CinemaScope. ▼●◗

Brave Warrior (1952) **C-73m.** *½ D: Spencer G. Bennet. Jon Hall, Jay Silverheels, Michael Ansara, Christine Larson. Inept yarn, set in 1800s Indiana, has Hall preventing Indian hostilities.

Brazil (1985) **C-131m.** *** D: Terry Gilliam. Jonathan Pryce, Kim Greist, Robert De Niro, Katherine Helmond, Ian Holm, Bob Hoskins, Michael Palin, Ian Richardson, Peter Vaughan. Dazzlingly different look at bleak future society (kind of a cross between 1984 and A CLOCKWORK ORANGE) where one hapless clerk (Pryce) clings to his ideals and dreams, including his Dream Girl (Greist). A triumph of imagination and production design, full of incredible black comedy . . . but also a relentless film that doesn't know when to quit: second half is often redundant and ineffectual. Gilliam cut film from 142m. for American release. Screenplay by Gilliam, Tom Stoppard, and Charles McKeown. [R]▼●◗

Bread and Chocolate (1978-Italian) **C-107m.** ***½ D: Franco Brusati. Nino Manfredi, Anna Karina, Johnny Dorelli, Paolo Turco, Max Delys. Manfredi is marvelous as a Chaplinesque everyman, an optimistic lower-class worker who treks to Switzerland to make his fortune yet remains the eternal outsider. Memorable sequence in a chicken coop. Original running time: 111m.▼

Bread, Love and Dreams (1954-Italian) **90m.** *** D: Luigi Comencini. Vittorio De Sica, Gina Lollobrigida, Marisa Merlini, Roberto Risso. Peppery comedy with spicy Gina vying for attention of town official De Sica.▼

Break, The (1998-British-Irish-German-Japanese) **C-96m.** **½ D: Robert Dornhelm. Stephen Rea, Alfred Molina, Rosana Pastor, Brendan Gleeson, Jorge Sanz, Pruitt Taylor Vince. Rea is excellent, as usual, as an IRA terrorist who unexpectedly becomes part of a Belfast prison break. Before long he's living in N.Y.C., where his long-ago training finds a new outlet as he becomes involved with Guatemalan immigrants. Engrossing if not terribly inspired film based on an idea by Rea. [R]

Breakdown (1997) **C-93m.** *** D: Jonathan Mostow. Kurt Russell, J. T. Walsh, Kathleen Quinlan, M. C. Gainey, Jack Noseworthy, Rex Linn, Ritch Brinkley. Married couple moving west have car trouble in the midst of the wide open spaces; a trucker picks up the wife so she can phone for help, but that's the last her husband sees of her . . . and no one seems willing or able to help. Superior thriller delivers the goods with airtight plot and all-too-believable situations. Hang on! Cowritten by director Mostow. Super 35. [R]▼●◗

Breaker! Breaker! (1977) **C-86m.** BOMB D: Don Hulette. Chuck Norris, George Murdock, Terry O'Connor, Don Gentry. Cheap, stupid actioner with some (occasional) intentional comedy. Little made of the CB craze as trucker Norris searches for kid brother Michael Augenstein in corrupt judge Murdock's speedtrap town. [PG]▼

'Breaker' Morant (1979-Australian) **C-107m.** ***½ D: Bruce Beresford. Edward Woodward, Jack Thompson, John Waters, Bryan Brown, Charles Tingwell, Vincent Ball, Lewis Fitz-Gerald. Potent drama based on the true story of three soldiers whose actions during the Boer War are used as fodder for a trumped-up court martial—in order to satisfy the political plans of the British Empire. Based on a play by Kenneth G. Ross. Winner of several Australian Academy Awards. [PG]▼●◗

Breakfast at Tiffany's (1961) **C-115m.** ***½ D: Blake Edwards. Audrey Hepburn, George Peppard, Patricia Neal, Buddy Ebsen, Mickey Rooney, Martin Balsam, John McGiver. Charming film from Truman Capote's story, with Hepburn as Holly Golightly, backwoods girl who goes mod in N.Y.C. Dated trappings don't detract from high comedy and winning romance. Screenplay by George Axelrod. Oscar-winner for Score (Henry Mancini) and Song, "Moon River" (Mancini and Johnny Mercer).▼●

Breakfast Club, The (1985) **C-97m.** **½ D: John Hughes. Emilio Estevez, Judd Nelson, Molly Ringwald, Anthony Michael Hall, Ally Sheedy, Paul Gleason. A bold experiment in the era of teen raunch movies (written and directed by a man who's made more than his share): five kids sit and talk about themselves, during day-long detention. Alternately poignant, predictable, and self-important, but filled with moments of truth and perception. [R]▼●◗

Breakfast in Hollywood (1946) **91m.** *½ D: Harold Schuster. Tom Breneman, Bonita Granville, Beulah Bondi, Edward Ryan, Raymond Walburn, ZaSu Pitts, Billie Burke, Hedda Hopper. Uninspired film derived from radio series of the same name; romantic plot offset by musical numbers with Spike Jones, The (Nat) King Cole Trio, and others.▼

Breakfast in Paris (1982-Australian) **C-86m.** *½ D: John Lamond. Barbara Parkins, Rod Mullinar, Jack Lenoir, Elspeth Ballantyne, Jeremy Higgins, Graham Stanley. Schlocky romance, with obnoxious fashion designer Parkins pursued by klutzy photographer Mullinar. The best thing about this is its title.▼

Breakfast of Champions (1999) **C-110m.** *½ D: Alan Rudolph. Bruce Willis, Albert Finney, Nick Nolte, Barbara Hershey,

Glenne Headly, Lukas Haas, Omar Epps, Buck Henry, Vicki Lewis, Jake Johannsen, Will Patton, Owen Wilson, Chip Zien, Alison Eastwood. Lives in confusion: Car dealer Willis is suicidal, his salesman Nolte is a secret transvestite, and obscure sci-fi writer Kilgore Trout (Finney) is hitching cross-country to be honored for the first time. Rudolph's go-for-broke, in-your-face style does no favors to Kurt Vonnegut, Jr.'s already bizarre novel, which Rudolph adapted and Willis self-financed as a labor of love. Haas and Hershey are excellent. Vonnegut briefly appears. [R]▼◗

Breakheart Pass (1976) **C-95m.** *** D: Tom Gries. Charles Bronson, Ben Johnson, Richard Crenna, Jill Ireland, Charles Durning, Ed Lauter, Roy Jenson, Bill McKinney, Sally Kirkland, Casey Tibbs. Slam-bang action Western, with second unit work by Yakima Canutt. Based on Alistair MacLean novel and set mainly on a train, it has Bronson as an undercover agent seeking gun runners and confronting a false epidemic. Highlight: incredible fight between Bronson and former boxing champ Archie Moore. [PG]▼●

Break In SEE: **Loophole** (1980)

Breakin' (1984) **C-90m.** ** D: Joel Silberg. Lucinda Dickey, Adolfo (Shabba-Doo) Quinones, Michael (Boogaloo Shrimp) Chambers, Ben Lokey, Christopher McDonald, Phineas Newborn 3rd, Ice-T. Harmless FLASHDANCE clone, but with the emphasis on breakdancing. Here, heroine Dickey waitresses rather than welds. Look for Jean-Claude Van Damme as an extra at the beach. A sequel followed before the year was out. [PG] ▼●

Breakin' 2: Electric Boogaloo (1984) **C-94m.** *½ D: Sam Firstenberg. Lucinda Dickey, Adolfo (Shabba-Doo) Quinones, Michael (Boogaloo Shrimp) Chambers, Susie Bono. Two worthy adversaries—a toothy WASP developer who could rate a centerfold in *Forbes* and a young urban black whose earring is longer than a bola—clash when the former tries to bulldoze a community rec center. The 18 breakdancing standards include "Do Your Thang" and "Oye Mamacita." [PG]▼●

Breaking Away (1979) **C-100m.** ***½ D: Peter Yates. Dennis Christopher, Dennis Quaid, Daniel Stern, Jackie Earle Haley, Barbara Barrie, Paul Dooley, Robyn Douglass, Hart Bochner, Amy Wright, John Ashton, Pamela Jayne (P.J.) Soles. Winning, unpretentious film about four college-age friends in Bloomington, Indiana, who don't know what to do with their lives; Dooley stands out in first-rate cast as Christopher's bewildered father. This sleeper hit really comes to life with an audience, may not play as well on TV. Steve Tesich's original screenplay won well-deserved Oscar; later spawned a brief TV series. [PG]▼●

Breaking Glass (1980-British) **C-104m.** **½ D: Brian Gibson. Phil Daniels, Hazel O'Connor, Jon Finch, Jonathan Pryce, Peter-Hugo Daly, Mark Wingett. Rocker O'Connor rises from playing small London clubs to superstardom, finds success isn't everything. Good performances by O'Connor, Daniels (as her youthful manager), Pryce (as a junkie saxophone player) offset predictable story line. Panavision. [PG]▼

Breaking Home Ties SEE: **Norman Rockwell's Breaking Home Ties**

Breaking In (1989) **C-91m.** **½ D: Bill Forsyth. Burt Reynolds, Casey Siemaszko, Sheila Kelley, Lorraine Toussaint, Albert Salmi, Harry Carey, Maury Chaykin, Steve Tobolowsky, David Frishberg. Low-key, off-center comedy about an aging safecracker who takes on a young protégé who's got a lot to learn about life, as well as his new profession. John Sayles' script, as interpreted by director Forsyth, is inventive and often quite funny . . . but not enough to keep this wispy film afloat. Reynolds is extremely good in his first character role. [R]▼●

Breaking Point, The (1950) **97m.** ***½ D: Michael Curtiz. John Garfield, Patricia Neal, Phyllis Thaxter, Wallace Ford, Sherry Jackson. High-voltage refilming of Hemingway's TO HAVE AND HAVE NOT, with Garfield as skipper so desperate for money he takes on illegal cargo. Garfield and mate Juano Hernandez give superb interpretations. Screenplay by Ranald MacDougall. Remade again as THE GUN RUNNERS.

Breaking Point (1976-Canadian) **C-92m.** BOMB D: Bob Clark. Bo Svenson, Robert Culp, John Colicos, Belinda J. Montgomery, Stephen Young, Linda Sorenson. Svenson is pursued by Mafiosos after he testifies against them in court. Nothing new here. [R]▼

Breaking Point (1993-Canadian) **C-96m.** ** D: Paul Ziller. Gary Busey, Kim Cattrall, Darlanne Fluegel, Jeff Griggs. After a serial killer known as "The Surgeon" strikes close to home, haunted cop Busey is asked to capture him. This grisly and erotic thriller is titillating, mildly surprising at first, but ultimately predictable. [R]▼●

Breaking the Rules (1992) **C-100m.** *½ D: Neal Israel. Jason Bateman, C. Thomas Howell, Jonathan Silverman, Annie Potts, Kent Bateman, Shawn Phelan. Yet another road movie in which two friends take their dying buddy on one last "journey of life." The story is meant to make you laugh and cry, but it's so manipulative it only induces yawns. Potts is the single standout, as a free-spirited waitress. Filmed in 1989. [PG-13]▼●

Breaking the Sound Barrier (1952-British) **109m.** ***½ D: David Lean. Ralph Richardson, Ann Todd, Nigel Patrick, John Justin, Dinah Sheridan, Denholm Elliott. Grade-A documentary-style story of early days of jet planes, and men who tested them; Richardson particularly good. Originally shown in England as THE SOUND BARRIER at 118m.

Breaking the Waves (1996-Danish) **C-156m.** ***½ D: Lars von Trier. Emily Watson, Stellan Skarsgård, Adrian Rawlins, Katrin Cartlidge, Jean-Marc Barr, Jonathan Hackett, Sandra Voe, Udo Kier. Extraordinary story of a young, simple-minded, God-fearing Scottish woman who willingly takes lovers in the belief that it will cure her paralyzed husband. A bold, often unsettling examination of love and faith, given immediacy and power by von Trier's documentarylike approach and cinematographer Robby Müller's faded visual scheme, which root the miraculous in the everyday world. Watson, in her film debut, is absolutely unforgettable in the lead role. Von Trier also wrote the screenplay. Super 35. [R] ▼●

Breaking Up (1997) **C-90m.** *½ D: Robert Greenwald. Salma Hayek, Russell Crowe. Tiresome treatise on love in the 90s, showing how many times two self-centered adults can break up, reunite, and break up again. They can't stand each other, and we can't stand *them*! Screenplay by Michael Cristofer, from his play. Filmed in 1995. [R]▼●

Break in the Circle (1957-British) **C-69m.** *½ D: Val Guest. Forrest Tucker, Eva Bartok, Marius Goring, Guy Middleton, Eric Pohlman. Unexciting chase tale has Tucker a brash adventurer hired by greedy Goring to smuggle a Polish physicist out of East Germany.▼

Break of Hearts (1935) **80m.** ** D: Philip Moeller. Katharine Hepburn, Charles Boyer, John Beal, Jean Hersholt, Sam Hardy, Susan Fleming, Jean Howard. Temperamental orchestra conductor Boyer, who has been spoiled by success, weds unknown composer Hepburn . . . then there are complications. Stars try hard but can do nothing with sappy, sub-par material. ▼●

Breakout (1959-British) **99m.** **½ D: Don Chaffey. Richard Todd, Richard Attenborough, Michael Wilding, Dennis Price, Bernard Lee, Donald Houston, Michael Caine. Although format is now familiar, this remains an exciting story of British P.O.W.s attempting escapes from Axis prison camp during WW2. Fine performances all around. Original title: DANGER WITHIN.

Breakout (1975) **C-96m.** *** D: Tom Gries. Charles Bronson, Robert Duvall, Jill Ireland, John Huston, Sheree North, Randy Quaid. Crisp action film generously laced with comedy touches has devil-may-care bush pilot Bronson taking on the job of spiriting Duvall, framed for murder, from a seedy Mexican prison. Awfully violent, though. Panavision. [PG]▼●

Breakthrough (1950) **91m.** **½ D: Lewis Seiler. David Brian, John Agar, Frank Lovejoy, Paul Picerni, William Self. Saga of men training for combat, their days of fighting and romancing; stark and satisfactory.▼

Breakthrough (1978-West German) **C-115m.** *½ D: Andrew V. McLaglen. Richard Burton, Robert Mitchum, Rod Steiger, Curt Jurgens, Klaus Loewitsch, Helmut Griem, Michael Parks. Superficial sequel to CROSS OF IRON, with the focus on the western front during WW2. German sergeant Burton becomes entangled in anti-Hitler conspiracy, saves the life of U.S. colonel Mitchum. Particularly disappointing, considering cast. Also known as SERGEANT STEINER. [PG]▼

Break to Freedom (1955-British) **88m.** ** D: Lewis Gilbert. Anthony Steel, Jack Warner, Robert Beatty, William Sylvester, Michael Balfour. Typical P.O.W.s escape-from-German-camp, uplifted by restrained acting.

Breathing Lessons (1994) **C-100m. TVM** D: John Erman. Joanne Woodward, James Garner, Kathryn Erbe, Joyce Van Patten, Eileen Heckart, Paul Winfield, Henry Jones, Tim Guinee. Wry, nicely paced road movie following an often bickering middle-aged couple on their one-day detour-filled odyssey to a friend's funeral. Adapted by Robert Lenski from Anne Tyler's Pulitzer Prize–winning novel. Above average.▼

Breathing Room (1996) **C-90m.** **½ D: Jon Sherman. Susan Floyd, Dan Futterman, Nadia Dajani, Edie Falco, Saverio Guerra, David Thornton. Sweet film of contemporary N.Y.C. couple deciding on their future together by separating between Thanksgiving and Christmas. The issue of commitment is honestly explored and feels universal. A "date" movie with more food for thought than might be comfortable for unmarried couples.▼

Breathless (1959-French) **89m.** ***½ D: Jean-Luc Godard. Jean Seberg, Jean-Paul Belmondo, Daniel Boulanger, Liliane David. Belmondo is ideally cast as a Parisian hood who, accompanied by American girl (Seberg), is chased by police after stealing a car and killing a cop. Groundbreaking, influential New Wave tale with a classic romanticized gangster-hero and great candid shots of Paris life. Dedicated to Monogram Pictures, with a story by François Truffaut. Remade in 1983. ▼●

Breathless (1983) **C-100m.** ** D: Jim McBride. Richard Gere, Valerie Kaprisky, Art Metrano, John P. Ryan, William Tepper, Gary Goodrow. Remake of landmark 1959 Godard film follows basic outline of the original—an amoral punk on the lam from police—but lacks its sociological potency. Gere's kinetic performance is something to see, but his character, hooked on Jerry Lee Lewis music and "Silver Surfer" comics, soon grows tiresome. [R]▼●◗

Breath of Life (1992-Italian) **C-96m.** ** D: Beppe Cino. Franco Nero, Vanessa Redgrave, Fernando Rey, Lucrezia Rovere, Salvatore Cascio. Grim, episodic psychological study of the wounded lives of a group of Italians in a post-WW2 sanitarium. Nero gives a solid performance as a tubercular professor in love with a mentally troubled ballerina (Rovere). Unfortunately he has little to do with Redgrave here—his former CAMELOT costar and one-time real-life lover.

Breath of Scandal, A (1960) **C-98m.** ** D: Michael Curtiz. Sophia Loren, John Gavin, Maurice Chevalier, Isabel Jeans, Angela Lansbury. Molnar's play *Olympia* is limp costume vehicle for Loren, playing a princess romanced by American Gavin. Chevalier and Lansbury vainly try to pump some life into proceedings.▼

Breed Apart, A (1984) **C-101m.** ** D: Philippe Mora. Rutger Hauer, Powers Boothe, Kathleen Turner, Donald Pleasence, John Dennis Johnston, Brion James. Picturesque but illogical, uninvolving tale of famed mountain climber Boothe, hired to pilfer specimens of a new bald-eagle breed, and his entanglement with conservationist Hauer and fishing-supply store owner Turner. [R]▼

Breezy (1973) **C-108m.** ** D: Clint Eastwood. William Holden, Kay Lenz, Roger C. Carmel, Marj Dusay, Shelley Morrison, Joan Hotchkis. Jaded middle-ager finds Truth with a teen-aged hippie in sappy romance. Fine performances by the leads only help up to a point. [R]▼

Brenda Starr (1992) **C-87m.** *½ D: Robert Ellis Miller. Brooke Shields, Tony Peck, Timothy Dalton, Diana Scarwid, Jeffrey Tambor, June Gable, Nestor Serrano, Kathleen Wilhoite, Charles Durning, Eddie Albert, Henry Gibson, Ed Nelson. This fiasco, based on Dale Messick's comic strip, sat on the shelf for years, and no wonder. Artist Peck enters the strip to talk Brenda out of quitting the paper, is drawn into her adventuresome life. Aimless and uninvolving. The creators have contempt for their source, always deadly in films like this. Filmed in 1986. [PG]▼◗

Brewster McCloud (1970) **C-101m.** *** D: Robert Altman. Bud Cort, Sally Kellerman, Michael Murphy, William Windom, Shelley Duvall, Rene Auberjonois, Stacy Keach, John Schuck, Margaret Hamilton. Patently indescribable movie following exploits of owlish boy (Cort) whose ambition is to take wing and fly inside Houston Astrodome. Extremely bizarre; for certain tastes, extremely funny. Altman fans have head start. Panavision. [R]▼●

Brewster's Millions (1945) **79m.** **½ D: Allan Dwan. Dennis O'Keefe, Helen Walker, Eddie "Rochester" Anderson, June Havoc, Gail Patrick, Mischa Auer, Joe Sawyer, Herbert Rudley. Bright, energetic filming of venerable George Barr McCutcheon comedy about ordinary guy (this time, a returning G.I.) who must spend $1 million in a month's time in order to receive major inheritance. First filmed in 1914; remade in 1985.▼

Brewster's Millions (1985) **C-97m.** ** D: Walter Hill. Richard Pryor, John Candy, Lonette McKee, Stephen Collins, Jerry Orbach, Pat Hingle, Tovah Feldshuh, Joe Grifasi, Hume Cronyn. Seventh film version of venerable novel and play; here baseball player Pryor has one month to spend $30 million. Surefire premise squelched by unfunny script and wooden direction. When Pryor and Candy can't make it work, you know there's something wrong. [PG] ▼●◗

Brian's Song (1971) **C-73m. TVM** D: Buzz Kulik. Billy Dee Williams, James Caan, Jack Warden, Judy Pace, Shelley Fabares. Exceptional film relating real-life relationship between Chicago Bears football players Brian Piccolo (Caan) and Gale Sayers (Williams), and tragedy which affects entire team when Piccolo develops cancer. Outstanding teleplay by William Blinn from Sayers' *I Am Third.* Beautiful score by Michel Legrand. A milestone of excellence in made-for-TV movies. Above average. [G]▼●

Bribe, The (1949) **98m.** ** D: Robert Z. Leonard. Robert Taylor, Ava Gardner, Charles Laughton, Vincent Price, John Hodiak. Taylor looks uncomfortable playing federal man who almost sacrifices all for sultry singer Gardner.

Bridal Path, The (1959-Scottish) **C-95m.** ***½ D: Frank Launder. Bill Travers, Bernadette O'Farrell, Alex MacKenzie, Eric Woodburn, Jack Lambert, John Rae. Charming film of young islander who goes to Scottish mainland in search of a wife. Enhanced by beautiful scenery in color.

Bride, The (1974) SEE: **House That Cried Murder, The**

Bride, The (1985) **C-118m.** **½ D: Franc Roddam. Sting, Jennifer Beals, Clancy Brown, David Rappaport, Geraldine Page, Anthony Higgins, Veruschka, Quentin Crisp, Cary Elwes. Revisionist remake of BRIDE OF FRANKENSTEIN brilliantly captures look and feel of a great gothic horror film—but fails to deliver on its promise of enlightened psychological approach to the story. Both Sting and Beals give one-note performances. Film is easily stolen by Rappaport, as dwarf who befriends Dr. Frankenstein's male monster (Brown); their sequences make film worth watching. [PG-13]▼●

Bride and the Beast, The (1958) **78m.** BOMB D: Adrian Weiss. Charlotte Austin, Lance Fuller, Johnny Roth, Steve

Calvert. A gorilla fancies the wife of an explorer. Screenplay by Edward D. Wood, Jr.; aka QUEEN OF THE GORILLAS.

Bride Came C.O.D., The (1941) **92m.** **½ D: William Keighley. James Cagney, Bette Davis, Stuart Erwin, Eugene Pallette, Jack Carson, George Tobias. Unlikely comedy team in vehicle made enjoyable only by their terrific personalities; he's a flier, she's an abducted bride.▼●

Bride Comes Home, The (1935) **82m.** **½ D: Wesley Ruggles. Claudette Colbert, Fred MacMurray, Robert Young, William Collier, Sr., Edgar Kennedy. Breezy fluff with wealthy Young competing against roughneck MacMurray for Claudette's affections in vintage comedy.

Bride Comes to Yellow Sky, The SEE: **Face to Face** (1952)

Bride for Sale (1949) **87m.** **½ D: William D. Russell. Claudette Colbert, Robert Young, George Brent, Max Baer. Veteran star trio carries on despite thin story of female tax expert (Colbert) seeking wealthy spouse.

Bride Goes Wild, The (1948) **98m.** **½ D: Norman Taurog. Van Johnson, June Allyson, Butch Jenkins, Hume Cronyn, Una Merkel, Arlene Dahl. Silly, sometimes funny tale of Johnson pretending to be Jenkins' father in order to woo Allyson; nice cast does its best.

Bride Is Much Too Beautiful, The (1956-French) **85m.** ** D: Pierre Gaspard-Huit. Louis Jourdan, Brigitte Bardot, Micheline Presle, Marcel Amont, Jean-Francois Calve. Paper-thin sex farce with Bardot a country girl who becomes a famous model, finds herself the "bride" in a fake marriage. Aka HER BRIDAL NIGHT.▼

Bride of Chucky (1998) **C-89m.** ** D: Ronny Yu. Jennifer Tilly, Katherine Heigl, Nick Stabile, John Ritter, Alexis Arquette, Gordon Michael Woolvett, Kathy Najimy, voice of Brad Dourif. Wicked trailer trash Tilly works voodoo to revive Chucky (the killer doll from three earlier CHILD'S PLAY movies), and ends up a literal living doll herself. Innocent bystanders get caught up in Chucky's plans to become human again. Better than you'd expect, with good lines and an impressively raunchy performance by Tilly, it's let down by clumsy plotting; director Yu can't seem to figure out what to do with the dolls. [R] ▼●◗

Bride of Frankenstein (1935) **75m.** **** D: James Whale. Boris Karloff, Colin Clive, Valerie Hobson, Ernest Thesiger, Elsa Lanchester, Una O'Connor, E. E. Clive, Gavin Gordon, Douglas Walton, O. P. Heggie, Dwight Frye, John Carradine. Eye-filling sequel to FRANKENSTEIN is even better, with rich vein of dry wit running through the chills. Inimitable Thesiger plays weird doctor who compels Frankenstein into making a mate for his creation; Lanchester plays both the "bride" and, in amusing prologue, Mary Shelley. Pastoral interlude with blind hermit and final, riotous creation scene are highlights of this truly classic movie. Scripted by John L. Balderston and William Hurlbut. Marvelous Franz Waxman score, reused for many subsequent films. Followed by SON OF FRANKENSTEIN; reworked in 1985 as THE BRIDE.▼●

Bride of Re-Animator (1990) **C-99m.** ** D: Brian Yuzna. Jeffrey Combs, Bruce Abbott, Claude Earl Jones, Fabiana Udenio, David Gale, Kathleen Kinmont. Followup to RE-ANIMATOR with more gory fun from that wacky pair of Dr. Frankenstein wannabes, Combs and Abbott. Strong stuff, with much splicing of bloodied body parts; wait till you see the crawling eyeball! This sort-of homage to BRIDE OF FRANKENSTEIN isn't nearly as successful as original RE-ANIMATOR. Nominally based on H. P. Lovecraft's *Herbert West—Re-Animator.* [R]▼●

Bride of the Gorilla (1951) **76m.** ** D: Curt Siodmak. Raymond Burr, Barbara Payton, Lon Chaney, Jr., Tom Conway, Paul Cavanagh. Surprisingly watchable trash movie set on a jungle plantation, where hulking Burr marries sexy Payton—only to find himself the victim of a voodoo curse. Terrible but fun.▼

Bride of the Monster (1955) **69m.** BOMB D: Edward D. Wood, Jr. Bela Lugosi, Tor Johnson, Tony McCoy, Loretta King, Harvey B. Dunn, George Becwar, Don Nagel, Bud Osborne. A dissipated Lugosi creates giant rubber octopus that terrorizes woodland stream. Huge Swedish wrestler Johnson provides added laughs as hulking manservant Lobo. Another hilariously inept Grade Z movie from the king of bad cinema. Sequel: NIGHT OF THE GHOULS.▼●◗

Bride of Vengeance (1949) **91m.** ** D: Mitchell Leisen. Paulette Goddard, John Lund, Macdonald Carey, Raymond Burr, Albert Dekker, Rose Hobart. Medium-warm costumer of medieval Italy with Goddard as a Borgia sent to do mischief but instead falling in love.

Brides of Dracula, The (1960-British) **C-85m.** **½ D: Terence Fisher. Peter Cushing, Martita Hunt, Yvonne Monlaur, Freda Jackson, David Peel. Above-average entry in Hammer horror series, with the famed vampire's disciple (Peel) seeking female victims. ▼●

Brides of Fu Manchu, The (1966-British) **C-94m.** **½ D: Don Sharp. Christopher Lee, Douglas Wilmer, Marie Versini, Tsai Chin. Fu doesn't give up easily, still bent on conquering the world by forcing scientists to develop powerful ray gun. Sequel to FACE OF FU MANCHU, not as good, still diverting; followed by VENGEANCE OF FU MANCHU.▼

Bride Walks Out, The (1936) **81m.** ** D: Leigh Jason. Barbara Stanwyck, Gene Raymond, Robert Young, Ned Sparks, Helen Broderick, Hattie McDaniel. Flat comedy of model Stanwyck who, against her better instincts, goes domestic and weds brash, struggling engineer Raymond. Buffs will enjoy spotting Ward Bond as a taxi cab-driving extra in the "Fifth Avenue and 45th Street" scene.▼

Bride With White Hair, The (1993-Hong Kong) **C-89m.** *** D: Ronny Yu. Brigitte Lin, Leslie Cheung, Ng Chun-yu, Elaine Lui, Nam Kit-ying. Beautifully made tale based on a famous Chinese fable about rival Ming Dynasty clans and a forbidden love affair between a swordsman and a "wolf girl" who possesses supernatural powers. Highly effective blend of myth, romance and super-stylized violence, plus elegant use of color and widescreen, puts this a cut above the usual Hong Kong actioner. Panavision.▼●◗

Bride Wore Black, The (1968 French) **C-107m.** ***½ D: François Truffaut. Jeanne Moreau, Claude Rich, Jean-Claude Brialy, Michel Bouquet, Michel Lonsdale, Charles Denner. Hitchcockian suspenser about Moreau tracking down and killing the quintet of men who accidentally killed her husband on their wedding day. Exciting, entertaining homage to The Master, right down to the Bernard Herrmann score (although Truffaut omitted the twist ending of the novel by William Irish, aka Cornell Woolrich).▼●

Bride Wore Boots, The (1946) **86m.** ** D: Irving Pichel. Barbara Stanwyck, Robert Cummings, Diana Lynn, Peggy Wood, Robert Benchley, Natalie Wood, Willie Best. Witless comedy of horse-loving Stanwyck saddled by Cummings, who does his best to win her total affection; they all try but script is weak.

Bride Wore Red, The (1937) **103m.** ** D: Dorothy Arzner. Joan Crawford, Franchot Tone, Robert Young, Billie Burke, Reginald Owen. More fashion show than plot in this glossy Crawford soaper of girl who works her way up society ladder. ▼

Bridge, The (1960-German) **100m.** *** D: Bernhard Wicki. Folker Bohnet, Fritz Wepper, Michael Hinz, Frank Glaubrecht. Unrelenting account of teen-age boys drafted into the German army in 1945, as last resort effort to stem Allied invasion.▼

Bridge at Remagen, The (1969) **C-115m.** **½ D: John Guillermin. George Segal, Robert Vaughn, Ben Gazzara, Bradford Dillman, E.G. Marshall, Peter Van Eyck. Well-acted film about group of Allies defending bridge toward the end of WW2 can't quite overcome familiar plot line; lots of good explosions for those who care. Panavision. [M/PG]▼◗

Bridge of San Luis Rey, The (1944) **89m.** ** D: Rowland V. Lee. Lynn Bari, Nazimova, Louis Calhern, Akim Tamiroff, Francis Lederer, Blanche Yurka, Donald Woods. Thornton Wilder's moody, unusual story of five people meeting doom on a rickety bridge makes a slow-moving film. Previously filmed in 1929.▼●◗

Bridge on the River Kwai, The (1957-British) **C-161m.** **** D: David Lean. William Holden, Alec Guinness, Jack Hawkins, Sessue Hayakawa, Geoffrey Horne, James Donald, Andre Morell, Ann Sears. British soldiers in Japanese prison camp build a bridge as a morale exercise—under single-minded leadership of British colonel Guinness—as Holden and Hawkins plot to destroy it. Psychological battle of wills combined with high-powered action sequences make this a blockbuster. Seven Oscars include Picture, Director, Actor (Guinness), Cinematography (Jack Hildyard), Editing (Peter Taylor), Scoring (Malcolm Arnold—who used the famous WWI whistling tune "Colonel Bogey March"), and Screenplay (by Carl Foreman and Michael Wilson, based on Pierre Boulle's novel). The writers were blacklisted, so Boulle—who spoke no English—was credited with the script! Filmed in Ceylon. CinemaScope. ▼●

Bridges at Toko-Ri, The (1954) **C-103m.** ***½ D: Mark Robson. William Holden, Grace Kelly, Fredric March, Mickey Rooney, Robert Strauss, Earl Holliman. Powerful, thoughtful drama, based on the James Michener best-seller, focusing on the conflicts and exploits of lawyer Holden after he is recalled by the Navy to fly jets in Korea. While the flying sequences are exciting—the special effects earned an Oscar—the ultimate futility of Korean War is in no way deemphasized.▼●

Bridges of Madison County, The (1995) **C-135m.** *** D: Clint Eastwood. Clint Eastwood, Meryl Streep, Annie Corley, Victor Slezak, Jim Haynie. In the 1960s, an itinerant *National Geographic* photographer comes to Iowa to shoot covered bridges and chances to meet a woman who's vaguely dissatisfied with life as farm-bound wife and mother. Modern spin on BRIEF ENCOUNTER (based on Robert James Waller's hugely popular book) features a winning and vulnerable Eastwood and a wondrous Streep as an unlikely but convincing couple. A satisfying and romantic film, if a bit long and slow at times. That bass player in the blues band who gets a closeup is Eastwood's son, Kyle. [PG-13]▼●◗

Bridge to Nowhere (1986-New Zealand) **C-86m.** *½ D: Ian Mune. Bruno Lawrence, Alison Routledge, Philip Gordon, Margaret Umbers, Stephen Judd, Shelley Luxford, Matthew Hunter. Kiwi variation on a familiar theme: backpacking kids raise the ire of hermit Lawrence, causing a war for survival. Well made but trite; features a solid role for Lawrence, the ubiquitous star of New Zealand films.▼

Bridge Too Far, A (1977-British) **C-175m.** ** D: Richard Attenborough. Dirk Bogarde, James Caan, Michael Caine, Sean Connery, Edward Fox, Elliott Gould, Gene Hackman, Anthony Hopkins, Hardy Kruger, Laurence Olivier, Ryan O'Neal, Robert Redford, Maximilian Schell, Liv Ullmann, Arthur Hill, John Ratzenberger. Lifeless, overproduced version of the fine Cornelius Ryan book about disastrous 1944 Allied airdrop behind German lines in Holland. Some prints run 158m. Panavision. [PG] ▼●◗

Bridge to the Sun (1961-U.S.-French) **113m.** *** D: Etienne Perier. Carroll Baker, James Shigeta, James Yagi. Well-intentioned telling of Southern girl Baker who marries Japanese diplomat Shigeta and moves to Japan at outbreak of WW2. Based on Gwen Terasaki's autobiography.

Brief Encounter (1945-British) **85m.** **** D: David Lean. Celia Johnson, Trevor Howard, Stanley Holloway, Cyril Raymond, Joyce Carey. Two ordinary strangers, both married, meet at a train station and find themselves drawn into a short but poignant romance. Intense and unforgettable, underscored by perfect use of Rachmaninoff's *Second Piano Concerto.* Adapted by Noel Coward from his one-act play "Still Life" (from *Tonight at Eight-thirty*); screenplay by director Lean and Ronald Neame. A truly wonderful film. Remade as a TV movie in 1974 with Richard Burton and Sophia Loren.▼●

Brief History of Time, A (1992-U.S.-British) **C-84m.** ***½ D: Errol Morris. Another outstanding documentary from Morris (GATES OF HEAVEN, THE THIN BLUE LINE), this one a portrait of cosmologist Stephen Hawking, who's afflicted with amyotrophic lateral sclerosis and communicates verbally with a voice synthesizer. In Hawking's best-selling book, for which the film is named, he explains the nature of the universe in layman's terms; even those who are bored or perplexed by science will enjoy this unique film.▼

Brief Vacation, A (1973-Italian) **C-106m.** *** D: Vittorio De Sica. Florinda Bolkan, Renato Salvatori, Daniel Quenaud, Jose Maria Prada, Teresa Gimpera. Poorly educated woman leaves terrible job, despicable in-laws, and callous husband for a comparatively pleasant stay in a TB sanitorium. De Sica's sure-handed direction and Bolkan's knowing performance make this worth watching. [PG]

Brigadoon (1954) **C-108m.** *** D: Vincente Minnelli. Gene Kelly, Van Johnson, Cyd Charisse, Elaine Stewart, Barry Jones, Hugh Laing. Americans Kelly and Johnson discover magical Scottish village in this entertaining filmization of Lerner & Loewe Broadway hit. Overlooked among 1950s musicals, it may lack innovations but has its own quiet charm, and lovely score, including "I'll Go Home with Bonnie Jean." CinemaScope. ▼●◗

Brigand, The (1952) **C-94m.** ** D: Phil Karlson. Anthony Dexter, Anthony Quinn, Gale Robbins, Jody Lawrance. Dexter is lookalike for king and becomes involved with court intrigue; flat costumer.

Brigand of Kandahar, The (1965-British) **C-81m.** **½ D: John Gilling. Ronald Lewis, Oliver Reed, Duncan Lamont, Yvonne Romain, Catherine Woodville. Nonsense set on British outpost in 1850s India with rampaging natives. CinemaScope.

Brigham Young (1940) **114m.** ** D: Henry Hathaway. Tyrone Power, Linda Darnell, Dean Jagger, Brian Donlevy, John Carradine, Jane Darwell, Jean Rogers, Mary Astor, Vincent Price. Well-intentioned but ludicrous depiction of Mormon leader with Jagger nominally in the lead, focus shifting to tepid romance between Power and Darnell; Astor all wrong as homespun wife. ▼

Bright Angel (1991) **C-94m.** **½ D: Michael Fields. Dermot Mulroney, Lili Taylor, Sam Shepard, Burt Young, Valerie Perrine, Bill Pullman, Mary Kay Place, Kevin Tighe, Sheila McCarthy, Delroy Lindo, Benjamin Bratt. Teenaged Montana boy, shaken by events at home, agrees to take a runaway girl to Wyoming so she can bail her brother out of jail. Uneven, sometimes affecting slice of life, with a very stylized script by novelist Richard Ford and a cast full of familiar faces. Mulroney is first-rate in the lead. [R]▼

Bright Eyes (1934) **83m.** **½ D: David Butler. Shirley Temple, James Dunn, Judith Allen, Jane Withers, Lois Wilson, Charles Sellon. Early Shirley, and pretty good, with juvenile villainy from Withers in tale of custody battle over recently orphaned Temple. Includes "On the Good Ship Lollipop." Also shown in computer-colored version.▼

Bright Leaf (1950) **110m.** **½ D: Michael Curtiz. Gary Cooper, Lauren Bacall, Patricia Neal, Jack Carson, Donald Crisp. Loose chronicle of 19th-century tobacco farmer (Cooper) building successful cigarette empire, seeking revenge on old enemies and finding romance.

Bright Lights (1935) **83m.** ** D: Busby Berkeley. Joe E. Brown, Ann Dvorak, Patricia Ellis, William Gargan, Joseph Cawthorn, Arthur Treacher. Rags-to-riches show business tale of husband and wife separating while trying to hit it big. Entertaining, but full of clichés.

Bright Lights, Big City (1988) **C-110m.** **½ D: James Bridges. Michael J. Fox, Kiefer Sutherland, Phoebe Cates, Swoosie

Kurtz, Frances Sternhagen, Tracy Pollan, John Houseman, Charlie Schlatter, Jason Robards, Dianne Wiest, William Hickey, Kelly Lynch, David Hyde Pierce. Everyone gets an A for effort on this adaptation of Jay McInerney's popular novel. Fox gives a good performance as the young Midwesterner whose life has started coming apart at the seams in N.Y.C., where he gets caught up in an endless cycle of drugs and nightlife. But the more cerebral aspects of the book (and some of its purple prose) don't translate to film . . . and it takes a long time to develop any real sympathy for Fox and his plight. Sutherland is convincingly smarmy as his druggie pal. [R] ▼●

Brighton Beach Memoirs (1986) **C-110m.** ★★½ D: Gene Saks. Blythe Danner, Bob Dishy, Jonathan Silverman, Brian Drillinger, Stacey Glick, Judith Ivey, Lisa Waltz, Jason Alexander, Steven Hill, Fyvush Finkel. Pleasant, if mostly undistinguished, adaptation of Neil Simon's celebrated autobiographical play about two families living under the same roof in 1937 Brooklyn. Oddly cast—Danner and Ivey play Jewish sisters—with attractive production design; Dishy underplays nicely as narrator Silverman's father. Followed by BILOXI BLUES and (on TV) BROADWAY BOUND. [PG-13]▼●◗

Brighton Rock (1947-British) **86m.** ★★★ D: John Boulting. Richard Attenborough, Carol Marsh, Hermione Baddeley, William Hartnell, Harcourt Williams, Nigel Stock. Tour-de-force role for young Attenborough as loathsome, baby-faced gangster who finally gets his comeuppance. Notable for incredibly cynical trick ending. Screenplay by Terence Rattigan and Graham Greene from Greene's novel. U.S. title: YOUNG SCARFACE.▼

Brighton Strangler, The (1945) **67m.** ★★½ D: Max Nosseck. John Loder, June Duprez, Michael St. Angel, Miles Mander, Rose Hobart, Gilbert Emery. Eerie little thriller, similar to A DOUBLE LIFE, set in WW2 England. Actor Loder has made a hit as "The Brighton Strangler" on the stage, but when he's conked on the head during an air raid, he begins to live the part.▼

Bright Road (1953) **69m.** ★★ D: Gerald Mayer. Dorothy Dandridge, Harry Belafonte, Robert Horton, Philip Hepburn. Well-intentioned but labored tale of black teacher in small Southern town trying to solve her young pupils' problems. Belafonte's film debut.

Bright Shining Lie, A (1998) **C-115m. TVM** D: Terry George. Bill Paxton, Amy Madigan, Vivian Wu, Donal Logue, Eric Bogosian, Kurtwood Smith, Ed Lauter, Harve Presnell, James Rebhorn. The odyssey of John Paul Vann, one of the first senior U.S. military advisers sent to Vietnam, a brilliant militarist turned skeptic who wound up violently anti-war. Based on Neil Sheehan's 1988 Pulitzer Prize–winning book. Made for cable. Average.▼●◗

Bright Victory (1951) **97m.** ★★★ D: Mark Robson. Arthur Kennedy, Peggy Dow, Julia (Julie) Adams, James Edwards, Will Geer, Nana Bryant, Jim Backus, Murray Hamilton, Richard Egan. Touching account of blinded ex-soldier who slowly readjusts to civilian life, even finding love. Potentially sticky subject handled well, with Kennedy excellent in lead role. Rock Hudson can be glimpsed as a soldier.

Brighty of the Grand Canyon (1967) **C-89m.** ★★½ D: Norman Foster. Joseph Cotten, Pat Conway, Karl Swensen, Dick Foran, Jason Clark. Harmless tale of a burro in the title locale; best for the kids.▼

Brilliant Lies (1996-Australian) **C-93m.** ★★★ D: Richard Franklin. Anthony LaPaglia, Gia Carides, Zoe Carides, Ray Barrett, Michael Veitch, Catherine Wilkin, Neil Melville, Grant Tilly. As testimony is given in a woman's sexual harassment suit, her boss is shown to be a chauvinist pig . . . but she's revealed as promiscuous gold digger whose own sister doubts her. The ultimate truth proves to be more complicated than it appears. Absorbing, well-acted adaptation of David Williamson's play about the subjective nature of truth, which unfolds in fragmented flashbacks as each party gives their side of the story, and broadens its scope to deal with filial conflicts as well. LaPaglia and Gia Carides are a couple in real life. ▼

Brimstone (1949) **C-90m.** ★★ D: Joseph Kane. Rod Cameron, Walter Brennan, Adrian Booth, Forrest Tucker, Jack Holt. Usual account of cattle-rustling and law enforcer who brings outlaws to justice.▼

Brimstone & Treacle (1982-British) **C-85m.** ★★½ D: Richard Loncraine. Sting, Denholm Elliott, Joan Plowright, Suzanna Hamilton. Strange, intriguing (but often unpleasant) film about a young man who worms his way into the lives of a vulnerable middle-class couple, whose daughter lies in a coma. Good performance by Sting. [R]▼

Bring 'Em Back Alive (1932) **65m.** ★★½ D: Clyde Elliott. Frank Buck plays Great White Hunter (and narrator) in this documentary curio, a great hit in its day and still interesting for its exciting jungle footage, as well as its often blatant phoniness. The inspiration for a same-named TV series fifty years later.▼

Bringing Out the Dead (1999) **C-120m.** ★★★ D: Martin Scorsese. Nicolas Cage, Patricia Arquette, John Goodman, Ving Rhames, Tom Sizemore, Marc Anthony, Mary Beth Hurt, Cliff Curtis, Aida Turturro. Life on the N.Y.C. streets from the point of view of a paramedic: a surreal, episodic film about a burnout case whose only hope for sanity and salvation is to save someone's life. Based on the book by former EMS driver Joe Connelly, told in harrowing and visually arresting fashion. Script by Paul Schrader; remarkable cinematography by Robert Richardson. Panavision. [R]▼●◗

Bringing Up Baby (1938) **102m.** **** D: Howard Hawks. Cary Grant, Katharine Hepburn, Charlie Ruggles, May Robson, Barry Fitzgerald, Walter Catlett, Fritz Feld, Ward Bond. In her sole venture into slapstick, Hepburn plays a madcap heiress—"Baby" is her pet leopard—who sets her sights on absentminded zoologist Grant and inadvertently (?) proceeds to make a shambles of his life. Not a hit when first released, this is now considered the definitive screwball comedy and one of the fastest, funniest films ever made; grand performances by all. Screenplay by Dudley Nichols and Hagar Wilde, from Wilde's original story. More or less remade as WHAT'S UP, DOC? Also shown in computer-colored version.▼●

Bring Me the Head of Alfredo Garcia (1974) **C-112m.** ** D: Sam Peckinpah. Warren Oates, Isela Vega, Gig Young, Robert Webber, Helmut Dantine, Emilio Fernandez, Kris Kristofferson. American piano player in Mexico gets involved with a smorgasbord of psychos; sub-par bloodbath doesn't even have the usual Peckinpah fast pace. [R]▼●

Bring On the Girls (1945) **C-92m.** ** D: Sidney Lanfield. Veronica Lake, Sonny Tufts, Eddie Bracken, Marjorie Reynolds, Alan Mowbray, Grant Mitchell, Frank Faylen, Huntz Hall. Wealthy Bracken is unable to find a girl who isn't a golddigger, so he joins the Navy. Slight comedy, with music; best are numbers by dancer Johnny Coy and Spike Jones and His City Slickers. That's Yvonne De Carlo as the hatcheck girl.

Bring On the Night (1985-British) **C-97m.** *** D: Michael Apted. Sting, Omar Hakim, Darryl Jones, Kenny Kirkland, Branford Marsalis, Dolette McDonald, Janice Pendarvis, Trudie Styler, Miles Copeland. First-rate musical documentary about the formation of Sting's rock-jazz band, culminating in their first concert performance (performing the serious, often politically oriented material on the *Dream of the Blue Turtles* album). More than just a concert movie, thanks in large part to director Apted. Handsomely photographed by Ralf Bode. [PG-13]▼●

Bring Your Smile Along (1955) **C-83m.** ** D: Blake Edwards. Frankie Laine, Keefe Brasselle, Constance Towers, Lucy Marlow, William Leslie, Jack Albertson. Thin musical comedy of schoolteacher/songwriter Towers coming to N.Y.C. and hooking up with Brasselle both professionally and romantically. Laine records their songs, and he perks up the proceedings. This was Edwards' directing debut; he also wrote the script.

Brink of Life (1958-Swedish) **84m.** **½ D: Ingmar Bergman. Eva Dahlbeck, Ingrid Thulin, Bibi Andersson, Barbro Hiort af Ornas, Erland Josephson, Max von Sydow, Gunnar Sjoberg. Realistic, almost documentary-like chronicle of the lives of three women in a maternity ward. Meticulously filmed, but also gloomy and static; one of Bergman's lesser efforts.▼

Brink's Job, The (1978) **C-103m.** *** D: William Friedkin. Peter Falk, Peter Boyle, Allen Goorwitz (Garfield), Warren Oates, Gena Rowlands, Paul Sorvino, Sheldon Leonard. Entertaining, comically oriented account of the infamous 1950 Boston heist, masterminded by Falk and motley gang of accomplices. Excellent period and location flavor. [PG]▼

Britannia Hospital (1982-British) **C-115m.** **½ D: Lindsay Anderson. Leonard Rossiter, Graham Crowden, Malcolm McDowell, Joan Plowright, Jill Bennett, Marsha Hunt, Frank Grimes, Roland Culver, Fulton Mackay, Vivian Pickles, Mark Hamill, Liz Smith, Alan Bates, Arthur Lowe. Absurdist comedy about a hospital beleaguered by labor woes, protest groups, impatient patients, a resident mad doctor, and an impending visit by the Queen Mother. Heavy-handed satire, but entertaining nonetheless, with some actors in continuing roles from Anderson's IF . . . and O LUCKY MAN! Written by David Sherwin. [R]▼

Britannia Mews SEE: **Forbidden Street, The**

British Agent (1934) **81m.** *½ D: Michael Curtiz. Kay Francis, Leslie Howard, William Gargan, Philip Reed, J. Carrol Naish, Cesar Romero. British diplomat Howard falls for staunch Soviet Francis in 1917 Russia; a trite script sinks this turkey, which tries to combine romance and international intrigue.

British Intelligence (1940) **62m.** **½ D: Terry Morse. Boris Karloff, Margaret Lindsay, Maris Wrixon, Holmes Herbert, Leonard Mudie. Not-bad programmer gives Karloff a good part as Valdar, a butler who works for a British cabinet minister during WW1, and who may just be a spy. He tangles with alluring secret agent Lindsay—who may just be a double agent. Remake of THREE FACES EAST (1930).▼●

Broadcast News (1987) **C-131m.** *** D: James L. Brooks. William Hurt, Albert Brooks, Holly Hunter, Robert Prosky, Lois Chiles, Joan Cusack, Peter Hackes, Jack Nicholson. Appealing and intelligent comedy about a highly charged, neurotic woman who's a successful TV news producer, and her attraction to a pretty-boy anchorman who joins her network—and represents everything she hates about TV news. All three stars are fine, but Brooks is a special standout as an ace reporter, and Hunter's best friend, who's really in love with her. Nicholson contributes a funny unbilled performance as the network's star anchorman.

Written by the director; set and filmed in Washington, D.C. [R]▼●◗

Broadminded (1931) **72m.** **½ D: Mervyn LeRoy. Joe E. Brown, William Collier, Jr., Margaret Livingston, Thelma Todd, Bela Lugosi, Ona Munson, Holmes Herbert. Pleasant Brown comedy with added spice of lovely Todd and hilarious cameo by Lugosi as man whose hot dog was stolen.

Broadway (1942) **91m.** *** D: William A. Seiter. George Raft, Pat O'Brien, Janet Blair, Broderick Crawford, Marjorie Rambeau, S.Z. Sakall. Raft recalls his days as a nightclub hoofer in this Prohibition yarn (remake of 1929 film), full of colorful characters and incidents but without an eye toward believability. O'Brien is tough copper, Crawford a ruthless gangster.

Broadway Bad (1933) **61m.** **½ D: Sidney Lanfield. Joan Blondell, Ricardo Cortez, Ginger Rogers, Adrienne Ames. Chorus girl Blondell is unjustly maligned by husband, decides to milk bad publicity for all it's worth. A 1930s soap given first-class treatment.

Broadway Bill (1934) **102m.** *** D; Frank Capra. Warner Baxter, Myrna Loy, Walter Connolly, Helen Vinson, Lynne Overman, Raymond Walburn, Clarence Muse, Douglass Dumbrille, Charles Lane, Ward Bond, Margaret Hamilton, Clara Blandick, Frankie Darro, Jason Robards (Sr.), and Broadway Bill. Baxter, who's "sold out" and married money, risks his marriage and his future on a racehorse; Loy, his wife's sister, seems to be the only one who believes in him. The unremitting good cheer of this Capra concoction overcomes its flaws. Script by Robert Riskin, from the Mark Hellinger story "On the Nose." Remade (by Capra) in 1950 as RIDING HIGH—using some of the same actors, and even some of the same footage. Look fast for a young, blonde Lucille Ball as a telephone operator.▼●

Broadway Bound SEE: **Neil Simon's "Broadway Bound"**

Broadway Danny Rose (1984) **86m.** *** D: Woody Allen. Woody Allen, Mia Farrow, Nick Apollo Forte, Sandy Baron, Corbett Monica, Morty Gunty, Will Jordan, Milton Berle, Joe Franklin. Allen is wonderful as pathetic small-time manager who tries to boost career of over-the-hill singer Forte. Terrific casting, funny show-biz jokes but eventually wears a bit thin; a slight but amusing film. [PG]▼●

Broadway Gondolier (1935) **98m.** **½ D: Lloyd Bacon. Dick Powell, Joan Blondell, Adolphe Menjou, Louise Fazenda, William Gargan, Grant Mitchell. Powell goes globetrotting so he'll be discovered by famous producer. Songs include: "Lulu's Back in Town."

Broadway Limited (1941) **74m.** ** D: Gordon Douglas. Dennis O'Keefe, Victor McLaglen, Marjorie Woodworth, ZaSu Pitts, Patsy Kelly, George E. Stone, Leonid Kinskey. Considering cast, a big disappointment, though innocuous entertainment: florid director Kinskey makes his new star (Woodworth) the center of publicity stunt that backfires.▼

Broadway Melody, The (1929) **100m.** **½ D: Harry Beaumont. Bessie Love, Anita Page, Charles King, Jed Prouty, Kenneth Thomson, Edward Dillon, Mary Doran. Early talkie musical curio about a pair of stage-struck sisters who seek fame on the Great White Way and fall for a charming song-and-dance man. This was the first musical to win a Best Picture Academy Award. Awfully dated today, but there's still a good score by Arthur Freed and Nacio Herb Brown: Title tune, "You Were Meant for Me," and "The Wedding of the Painted Doll." Some sequences originally in Technicolor; remade as TWO GIRLS ON BROADWAY.▼●

Broadway Melody of 1936 (1935) **101m.** *** D: Roy Del Ruth. Jack Benny, Eleanor Powell, Robert Taylor, Una Merkel, Sid Silvers, Buddy Ebsen. Pleasant musicomedy with Winchell-like columnist Benny trying to frame producer Taylor via dancer Powell, whose solo spots are pure delight. Arthur Freed-Nacio Herb Brown songs: "You Are My Lucky Star," "Broadway Rhythm," "I've Got A Feelin' You're Foolin,' " (which earned an Oscar for Dave Gould's dance direction).▼●

Broadway Melody of 1938 (1937) **110m.** **½ D: Roy Del Ruth. Robert Taylor, Eleanor Powell, George Murphy, Binnie Barnes, Buddy Ebsen, Judy Garland, Sophie Tucker, Charles Igor Gorin, Raymond Walburn, Robert Benchley, Willie Howard, Billy Gilbert. Not up to 1936 MELODY, with tuneful but forgettable songs, overbearing Tucker, and elephantine finale. Powell's dancing is great and Garland sings "Dear Mr. Gable." ▼●

Broadway Melody of 1940 (1940) **102m.** *** D: Norman Taurog. Fred Astaire, Eleanor Powell, George Murphy, Frank Morgan, Ian Hunter, Florence Rice, Lynne Carver, Ann Morriss. Friendship and rivalry between dance partners Astaire and Murphy spark delightful, underrated MGM musical, with hilarious vignettes, fine performance from Astaire, outstanding Cole Porter songs, and matchless Astaire-Powell numbers like "Begin the Beguine" (danced *twice* in the finale). If only they'd tie up the plot a bit sooner. Douglas McPhail (unbilled) introduces the Porter standard "I Concentrate On You." ▼●

Broadway Musketeers (1938) **62m.** **½ D: John Farrow. Margaret Lindsay, Ann Sheridan, Marie Wilson, John Litel, Janet Chapman, Richard Bond. Three women who grew up together in an orphanage meet again as adults, having taken very different paths in life. Snappy remake of the melodramatic THREE ON A MATCH with some interesting plot variations, and a couple of songs from Sheridan.

Broadway Rhythm (1944) **C-114m.** ** D: Roy Del Ruth. George Murphy, Ginny Simms, Charles Winninger, Gloria De Haven, Nancy Walker, Ben Blue, Tommy Dorsey and Orch. Tedious, overlong MGM musical with plot (ex-vaudevillian Winninger at odds with producer-son Murphy) getting in the way of good songs like "Amor," "All the Things You Are."▼

Broadway Serenade (1939) **114m.** ** D: Robert Z. Leonard. Jeanette MacDonald, Lew Ayres, Ian Hunter, Frank Morgan, Rita Johnson, Virginia Grey, William Gargan, Katharine Alexander. Mediocre musical of songwriter Ayres and wife, singer MacDonald, having careers split up their marriage.▼

Broadway to Hollywood (1933) **85m.** ** D: Willard Mack. Alice Brady, Frank Morgan, Jackie Cooper, Russell Hardie, Madge Evans, Mickey Rooney, Eddie Quillan. Three generations of show biz (Cooper grows up to be Hardie, whose son, Rooney, grows up to be Quillan) in a story that's for the birds—but the acting is good, and some of the production numbers (lifted from MGM's famous 1930 extravaganza THE MARCH OF TIME) interesting to see.

Brokedown Palace (1999) **C-100m.** ** D: Jonathan Kaplan. Claire Danes, Kate Beckinsale, Bill Pullman, Jacqueline Kim, Lou Diamond Phillips, Daniel Lapaine, Tom Amandes, Aimee Graham, John Doe. By-the-numbers cautionary melodrama in which naive best pals Danes and Beckinsale, on a trip to Thailand to celebrate their high school graduation, are set up by a drug smuggler and tossed into prison. Done in by its sheer predictability—and lack of chemistry between the stars. Super 35. [PG-13]▼◗

Broken Arrow (1950) **C-93m.** *** D: Delmer Daves. James Stewart, Jeff Chandler, Debra Paget, Will Geer, Jay Silverheels. Authentic study of 1870s Apache Chief Cochise (Chandler) and ex-Army man (Stewart) trying to seek accord between feuding Indians and settlers. Flavorful and effective; good action sequences. Screenplay, credited to Michael Blankfort, was actually written by Albert Maltz, then a blacklistee. Chandler played Cochise again in THE BATTLE AT APACHE PASS. Later a TV series.▼

Broken Arrow (1996) **C-108m.** ** D: John Woo. John Travolta, Christian Slater, Samantha Mathis, Delroy Lindo, Bob Gunton, Frank Whaley, Howie Long, Vondie Curtis-Hall, Jack Thompson, Kurtwood Smith, Daniel von Bargen. Extraordinarily stupid action movie about a high-security, high-tech Air Force pilot who deliberately crash-lands a U.S. plane in the midst of Utah and plans to hold its nuclear weapons for ransom. He doesn't reckon with his younger copilot (Slater) or the U.S. park ranger (Mathis) who join in a determined pursuit to thwart him. Packed with director Woo's expected action set pieces and stunts, but Travolta's over-the-top bad guy is fairly monotonous, and story continuity/credibility is almost nonexistent. Did it have to be *this* dumb? Super 35. [R]▼●◗

Broken Blossoms (1919) **95m.** *** D: D. W. Griffith. Lillian Gish, Richard Barthelmess, Donald Crisp, Arthur Howard, Edward Piel. Dated but lovely film of Chinaman Barthelmess protecting frail Gish from clutches of brutal father Crisp; still creates a mood sustained by sensitive performances. One of Griffith's more modest, and more successful, films. Remade in England in 1936.▼●◗

Broken Chain, The (1993) **C-100m. TVM** D: Lamont Johnson. Eric Schweig, Wes Studi, Buffy Sainte-Marie, Pierce Brosnan, Graham Greene, J.C. White Shirt, Floyd Red Crow Westerman, Nathan Chasing His Horse. Striking and vastly entertaining history lesson about one of the lesser-known chapters of American history: the tearing apart of the Iroquois Confederacy in the Northeast during the French and Indian Wars of the 1700s. Told through the splintered friendship of two Mohawk braves, this second entry in Ted Turner's "Native Americans" series improved on the earlier GERONIMO. Made for cable. Above average.▼●

Broken English (1996-New Zealand) **C-92m.** *** D: Gregor Nicholas. Aleksandra Vujcic, Julian Arahanga, Rade Serbedzija, Marton Csokas, Madeline McNamara. A Croatian tyrant living in New Zealand goes ballistic when his daughter becomes romantically involved with a hunkish Maori cook. Consistently absorbing drama—and an interesting thematic companion piece to ONCE WERE WARRIORS—gets its surprising NC-17 rating from an exuberant bed-breaking scene of young lovers in love. Seconds were shaved for R version available on video. [NC-17]▼

Broken Lance (1954) **C-96m.** ***½ D: Edward Dmytryk. Spencer Tracy, Robert Wagner, Jean Peters, Richard Widmark, Katy Jurado, Hugh O'Brian, Eduard Franz, Earl Holliman, E.G. Marshall. Tracy is superlative in tight-knit script (by Richard Murphy, from an Oscar-winning Philip Yordan story) about patriarchal rancher who finds he's losing control of his cattle empire and his family is fragmenting into warring factions. Remake of HOUSE OF STRANGERS (although it owes more to *King Lear*!). CinemaScope.▼●

Broken Land, The (1962) **C-60m.** ** D: John Bushelman. Kent Taylor, Dianna

Darrin, Jody McCrea, Robert Sampson, Jack Nicholson. Routine low-budget Western about a sadistic sheriff (Taylor) who browbeats just about everybody, including his deputy (McCrea) and the harmless son (Nicholson) of a notorious gunman. CinemaScope.

Broken Lullaby (1932) **77m.** *** D: Ernst Lubitsch. Lionel Barrymore, Nancy Carroll, Phillips Holmes, ZaSu Pitts, Lucien Littlefield, Emma Dunn. Excellent drama of French soldier who feels guilty for killing German during war, then falls in love with dead man's sweetheart. Retitled: THE MAN I KILLED.

Broken Rainbow (1985) **C/B&W-70m.** *** D: Maria Florio, Victoria Mudd. Narrator: Martin Sheen. Historical voices: Burgess Meredith. Translator: Buffy Sainte-Marie. Touching, biting, appropriately one-sided, yet sometimes unnecessarily romanticized documentary about the relocation—and resistance—of Navajo Indians in Arizona. A Best Documentary Academy Award-winner.

Broken Sky (1982-Swedish) **C-96m.** **½ D: Ingrid Thulin. Susanna Kall, Thommy Berggren, Agneta Eckemyr, Margaretha Krook. Ambitious but uneven account of 13-year-old Kall, in the process of breaking free from her childhood, and her relationships with various family members. Thulin also wrote the script.

Broken Trust (1995) **C-100m. TVM** D: Geoffrey Sax. Tom Selleck, Elizabeth McGovern, Marsha Mason, Charles Haid, William Atherton, Fritz Weaver, Nicholas Pryor, Cynthia Martells. Upright, bespectacled judge Selleck discovers he's a pawn after being recruited by the feds to help ferret out corrupt members of the bench. Offbeat but lethargic good guys/bad guys tale adapted by the estimable Joan Didion and John Gregory Dunne from William Wood's crackling novel *Court of Honor*. Made for cable. Average.▼●

Bronco Billy (1980) **C-119m.** *** D: Clint Eastwood. Clint Eastwood, Sondra Locke, Geoffrey Lewis, Scatman Crothers, Bill McKinney, Sam Bottoms, Dan Vadis, Sierra Pecheur, Juliette Lewis. Enjoyable yarn about self-styled cowboy hero who runs a fly-by-night Wild West show and the spoiled heiress who joins his entourage of escapees from reality. Locke's rich-bitch character is a bit hard to take, but neither she nor some superfluous subplots can sour the charm of this film. Look fast for Hank Worden! [PG]▼●

Bronco Buster (1952) **C-81m.** **½ D: Budd Boetticher. John Lund, Scott Brady, Joyce Holden, Chill Wills, Casey Tibbs. Minor story of rodeo star Lund helping Brady learn the ropes, forced to fight him for Holden's love. Good rodeo action.

Brontë (1983-Irish-U.S.) **C-88m.** *** D: Delbert Mann. Julie Harris. Engrossing performance by Harris portraying Charlotte Brontë in one-woman show recounting her life and family troubles via intimate, first-person monologues. Unusual, literate film benefits from all-location filming in Ireland. Scripted by William Luce from his radio play based on Brontë's own writings.

Brontë Sisters, The (1979-French) **C-115m.** **½ D: André Téchiné. Isabelle Adjani, Marie-France Pisier, Isabelle Huppert, Pascal Gregory, Patrick Magee. Well-mounted but slightly sluggish portrait of the famous literary sisters and their repressed lives. Worth a look mainly to see three of France's most appealing actresses in one film. Also shot in English-language version, which doesn't play as well.

Bronx Tale, A (1993) **C-122m.** ***½ D: Robert De Niro. Robert De Niro, Chazz Palminteri, Lillo Brancato, Francis Capra, Taral Hicks, Kathrine Narducci, Clem Caserta, Alfred Sauchelli, Jr., Frank Pietrangolare, Joe Pesci. Longish but well-observed slice of life, as a boy grows up with two heroes of conflicting nature and beliefs—his loving, hard-working father, and the neighborhood capo, who takes him as a personal protégé. Written by Palminteri, and based on his play; an impressive directorial debut for De Niro, who brings a keen eye and equally strong sensibility to this potent (but ultimately upbeat) material. Incidentally, to re-create the Bronx of the 1960s, De Niro had to shoot this in Brooklyn and Queens! [R]▼●◗

Bronx War, The (1990) **C-91m.** ** D: Joseph B. Vasquez. Joseph, Fabio Urena, Charmaine Cruz, Andre Brown, Marlene Forte, Frances Colon, Miguel Sierra, Kim West. Ambitious, gritty but annoyingly uneven actioner chronicling the plight of Tito Sunshine (Joseph), a product of the mean streets of The Bronx, whose good intentions are obscured by the fact that he's a crack dealer. Dramatically overwrought, unrelentingly violent and profane, but not without its moments. Available on video in R and unrated versions.▼

Brood, The (1979-Canadian) **C-90m.** BOMB D: David Cronenberg. Oliver Reed, Samantha Eggar, Art Hindle, Cindy Hinds, Nuala Fitzgerald, Susan Hogan. Eggar eats her own afterbirth while midget clones beat grandparents and lovely young schoolteachers to death with mallets. It's a big, wide, wonderful world we live in! [R]▼●

Brother Can You Spare a Dime (1975) **103m.** **½ D: Philippe Mora. Documentary on 1930s has fuzzy point of view, and no narration to tie footage together; it also mixes newsreels and Hollywood clips. If you know and like the period, the footage will speak for itself and provide a certain measure of entertainment. [PG]▼◗

Brother From Another Planet, The (1984) **C-104m.** *** D: John Sayles. Joe Morton, Darryl Edwards, Steve James, Leonard Jackson, Maggie Renzi, Rosetta Le Noire, David Strathairn, Bill Cobbs. Amiable, ingenious contemporary fantasy, filmed on a shoestring, about a black visitor from another planet who (like Chance in BEING THERE) impresses most of the people he meets because he doesn't say a word—and lets them do all the talking! Falls apart toward the end with a subplot about drug dealers; but still worthwhile. Fine dialogue by writer-director Sayles, who, as usual, gives himself a funny role (as one of the Brother's outer-space pursuers). ▼

Brotherhood, The (1968) **C-98m.** *** D: Martin Ritt. Kirk Douglas, Alex Cord, Irene Papas, Luther Adler, Susan Strasberg, Murray Hamilton. Excellent story of Mafia in changing times; tradition-bound Douglas clashes with younger brother Cord who feels no ties to old-fashioned dictates. Pre-GODFATHER, but in the same league. [M]▼●

Brotherhood of Satan (1971) **C-92m.** **½ D: Bernard McEveety. Strother Martin, L. Q. Jones, Charles Bateman, Ahna Capri, Charles Robinson. Witches' coven takes over town in this horrifying little terror tale. Techniscope. [PG]▼

Brotherhood of the Yakuza SEE: **Yakuza, The**

Brother John (1972) **C-94m.** *** D: James Goldstone. Sidney Poitier, Will Geer, Bradford Dillman, Beverly Todd, Ramon Bieri, Warren J. Kemmerling, Lincoln Kilpatrick, Paul Winfield. Highly entertaining tale of the Messiah's return—only no one knows that he's come, and that he's black. [PG]▼

Brotherly Love (1970-British) **C-112m.** *** D: J. Lee Thompson. Peter O'Toole, Susannah York, Michael Craig, Harry Andrews, Cyril Cusack, Judy Cornwell, Brian Blessed. Very funny study of relationships in upper-class British household. O'Toole and York are delightful. Original British title: COUNTRY DANCE. [R]

Brother Orchid (1940) **91m.** *** D: Lloyd Bacon. Edward G. Robinson, Ann Sothern, Humphrey Bogart, Ralph Bellamy, Donald Crisp, Allen Jenkins. Farfetched but entertaining yarn of racketeer Robinson who seeks "the real class" in life. When he tries to rejoin his old mob, they throw him out and Robinson joins a monastery to plot his next move! Sothern delightful as his ever-faithful girlfriend.▼●

Brother Rat (1938) **90m.** *** D: William Keighley. Priscilla Lane, Wayne Morris, Johnnie Davis, Jane Bryan, Eddie Albert, Ronald Reagan, Jane Wyman, William Tracy. Comedy of three pals at Virginia Military Institute isn't as fresh as it was in the 1930s, but still remains entertaining, with enthusiastic performances by all. Albert stands out in his screen debut, in a role he played on the stage. Sequel: BROTHER RAT AND A BABY. Remade as ABOUT FACE.

Brother Rat and a Baby (1940) **87m.** **½ D: Ray Enright. Priscilla Lane, Wayne Morris, Eddie Albert, Jane Bryan, Ronald Reagan, Jane Wyman. Sassy follow-up to BROTHER RAT is not the same success, but is still fun. Morris, Reagan, and Albert have graduated the Virginia Military Institute; the first two come to the latter's aid when he's up for VMI baseball coach job. Look quickly for Alan Ladd as a cadet.

Brothers (1977) **C-104m.** **½ D: Arthur Barron. Bernie Casey, Vonetta McGee, Ron O'Neal, Renny Roker, Stu Gilliam, John Lehne. Well-intentioned story based on relationship between militant professor Angela Davis and literate black convict George Jackson during 1960s. Sloppy filmmaking and awkward scripting diminish impact of film's better moments. [R]

Brothers in Arms (1989) **C-94m.** *½ D: George Jay Bloom III. Todd Allen, Charles Grant, Jack Starrett, Dedee Pfeiffer, Mitch Pileggi, Dan Bell, Shannon Norfleet. Uninteresting variation on DELIVERANCE pits estranged brothers against family of murderous religious fanatics in modern-day Rockies. Competent but unpleasant, and it goes on and on and on. [R]▼●

Brothers in Law, The (1957-British) **94m.** **½ D: Roy Boulting. Richard Attenborough, Ian Carmichael, Terry-Thomas, Jill Adams, Miles Malleson, Raymond Huntley. Misadventures of a young lawyer (Carmichael) fill this amiable British comedy.▼

Brother's Justice, A SEE: **Gleaming the Cube**

Brothers Karamazov, The (1958) **C-146m.** *** D: Richard Brooks. Yul Brynner, Maria Schell, Claire Bloom, Lee J. Cobb, Richard Basehart, William Shatner, Albert Salmi. Set in 19th-century Russia, film version of Dostoyevsky's tragedy revolving about death of a dominating father (Cobb) and effect on his sons: fun-seeking Brynner, scholarly Basehart, religious Shatner, and epileptic Salmi. Exceptionally well scripted by Brooks. William Shatner's first film. ▼

Brother's Keeper (1992) **C-104m.** ***½ D: Joe Berlinger, Bruce Sinofsky. Exceptional documentary/slice-of-life which offers a portrait of backwoods America rarely seen in mainstream movies. It's the story of Delbert Ward, a reserved, uneducated upstate New York farmer who was thrown into jail after being accused of murdering his sickly brother. When he goes on trial, his neighbors, who barely know him, rally to his defense. An intriguing treatise on human nature and a telling look at how the media plays a role in a controversial case like this.▼●

Brother's Kiss, A (1997) **C-92m.** *** D: Seth Zvi Rosenfeld. Nick Chinlund, Michael Raynor, Talent Harris, John Leguizamo, Cathy Moriarty, Adrian Pasdar, Rosie Perez, Justin Pierce, Marisa Tomei, Michael Rapaport, Joshua Danowsky. Raw, riveting drama depicting the complex relationship between brothers, Lex (Chinlund) and Mick (Raynor), who came of age on the mean streets of N.Y.'s East Harlem. Mick, the younger, has become a cop, while Lex, who's never been able to catch a break, is a drug addict. Flashbacks to the brothers' childhood are especially effective—and heartbreaking. Based on Rosenfeld's stage play. [R]▼●

Brothers McMullen, The (1995) **C-97m.** **½ D: Edward Burns. Jack Mulcahy, Mike McGlone, Edward Burns, Shari Albert, Maxine Bahns, Connie Britton, Jennifer Jostyn, Elizabeth P. McKay, Catherine Bolz. Three brothers are temporarily living together under one roof; the married one is tempted to stray, the one who's involved with a woman has Catholic guilt about sinning, and the third wears his cynicism about relationships on his sleeve—even after he falls in love. Made on a minuscule budget, this modest film grows more compelling as it goes along, with two assets missing from slicker Hollywood movies: The actors are appealing and their conversations are totally believable. First-time director Burns also wrote the script and costars. [R]▼●

Brothers O'Toole, The (1973) **C-90m.** ** D: Richard Erdman. John Astin, Steve Carlson, Pat Carroll, Hans Conried, Lee Meriwether, Allyn Joslyn, Jesse White. Strictly for the kids is this comedy Western. Actor turned director Erdman has a bit. [G]▼

Brothers Rico, The (1957) **92m.** **½ D: Phil Karlson. Richard Conte, Dianne Foster, Kathryn Grant (Crosby), Larry Gates, James Darren. Incisive gangster yarn; Conte comes to N.Y.C. to counteract nationwide criminal gang's plot to eliminate his two brothers. Based on Georges Simenon novel; remade for TV as THE FAMILY RICO in 1972.

Brother Sun, Sister Moon (1973-Italian-British) **C-121m.** **½ D: Franco Zeffirelli. Graham Faulkner, Judi Bowker, Leigh Lawson, Alec Guinness, Valentina Cortese, Kenneth Cranham. Zeffirelli's wide-eyed youth-oriented slant on Francis of Assisi story runs hot and cold; some delicate, lovely scenes, but other ideas don't always come across. Songs by Donovan. [PG]▼

Broth of a Boy (1959-Irish) **77m.** **½ D: George Pollock. Barry Fitzgerald, Harry Brogan, Tony Wright, June Thorburn, Eddie Golden. British TV producer hits upon scheme of filming birthday celebration of oldest man in the world, Irish villager Fitzgerald. The latter's battle to get cut of the pie is vehicle for study of human nature; quietly effective.▼

Browning Version, The (1951-British) **90m.** ***½ D: Anthony Asquith. Michael Redgrave, Jean Kent, Nigel Patrick, Brian Smith, Wilfrid Hyde-White, Ronald Howard, Bill Travers. Redgrave is superb as middle-aged boarding school teacher who realizes he's a failure, with an unfaithful wife and a new teaching position he doesn't want. Cast does full justice to the play by Terence Rattigan; he also scripted. Remade in 1994.▼

Browning Version, The (1994-U.S.-British) **C-97m.** **½ D: Mike Figgis. Albert Finney, Greta Scacchi, Matthew Modine, Julian Sands, Michael Gambon, Ben Silverstone, Maryam D'Abo, David Lever. Well-mounted, though stodgy, remake of Terence Rattigan's play of retiring schoolmaster whose dedication is unappreciated and whose marriage is unraveling. Finney is good as man out of step with the times, Scacchi is fine (if oddly cast). Touching and tragic, but it's hard to beat Michael Redgrave's performance in 1951 version. Panavision. [R]▼●

Brubaker (1980) **C-132m.** **½ D: Stuart Rosenberg. Robert Redford, Yaphet Kotto, Jane Alexander, Murray Hamilton, David Keith, Morgan Freeman, Matt Clark, Tim McIntire, Linda Haynes, M. Emmet Walsh, Richard Ward, Albert Salmi, John McMartin, Wilford Brimley, Joe Spinell, Lee Richardson, Harry Groener, John Glover. Earnest but predictable prison drama based on true story of reform-minded warden who dares to uncover skeletons in corrupt Southern prison system. [R]▼●

Bruce Lee's Game of Death SEE: **Game of Death**

Brute, The SEE: **El Bruto**

Brute Force (1947) **98m.** ***½ D: Jules Dassin. Burt Lancaster, Hume Cronyn, Charles Bickford, Yvonne De Carlo, Ann Blyth, Ella Raines, Howard Duff, Whit Bissell, Jeff Corey, Sam Levene, Roman Bohnen, John Hoyt, Anita Colby. Tingling, hard-bitten prison film with its few clichés punched across solidly. Brutal captain Cronyn is utterly despicable, but you *know* he's going to get it in the end. Scripted by Richard Brooks, from Robert Patterson's story. Duff's film debut. ▼●◗

Brute Man (1946) **60m.** *½ D: Jean Yarbrough. Tom Neal, Rondo Hatton, Jane Adams, Peter Whitney, Jan Wiley. Loosely based on Hatton's own tragic life (handsome as a youth, he became disfigured by acromegaly), this deals with a disfigured man who becomes a mad killer. ▼●◗

Brylcreem Boys, The (1996-British) **C-105m.** ** D: Terence Ryan. Bill Campbell,

William McNamara, Angus Macfadyen, Gabriel Byrne, Jean Butler, John Gordon Sinclair, Oliver Tobias. Allied airmen of WW2, shot down over Ireland, are astonished to learn that they are to be held in a POW camp, right alongside German prisoners—a quintessentially curious way for Ireland to maintain and enforce its official neutrality during the war. Intriguing premise gets mediocre treatment in this superficial and disappointing film.▼●

B.S. I Love You (1971) **C-99m.** *½ D: Steven Hilliard Stern. Peter Kastner, Joanna Cameron, Louise Sorel, Gary Burghoff, Richard B. Shull, Joanna Barnes. Stale "youth" comedy about young ad-man who makes it with both mother and daughter is only for those who haven't seen THE GRADUATE or YOU'RE A BIG BOY NOW. [R]

Bubble, The SEE: **Fantastic Invasion of Planet Earth**

Buccaneer, The (1938) **124m.** *** D: Cecil B. DeMille. Fredric March, Franciska Gaal, Margot Grahame, Akim Tamiroff, Walter Brennan, Anthony Quinn. Typically entertaining epic-scale saga from DeMille, with florid performance by March as pirate-hero Jean Lafitte, who aids American cause during Battle of New Orleans. Good storytelling, and good fun. Remade in 1958.

Buccaneer, The (1958) **C-121m.** *** D: Anthony Quinn. Yul Brynner, Charlton Heston, Claire Bloom, Charles Boyer, Inger Stevens, Henry Hull, E. G. Marshall, Lorne Greene, Fran Jeffries, Woodrow (Woody) Strode. Starchy swashbuckler retelling events during Battle of New Orleans when Andrew Jackson (Heston) is forced to rely on buccaneer Lafitte (Brynner) to stem the British invasion; action is spotty but splashy. Quinn's only film as director; executive produced by his then-father-in-law Cecil B. DeMille, who directed the 1938 original, and whose last film this was. VistaVision. ▼●

Buccaneer's Girl (1950) **C-77m.** ** D: Frederick de Cordova. Yvonne De Carlo, Philip Friend, Elsa Lanchester, Andrea King, Henry Daniell. Pure escapism with De Carlo cavorting as New Orleans singer and later helping to free pirate-friend from prison.

Buchanan Rides Alone (1958) **C-78m.** *** D: Budd Boetticher. Randolph Scott, Craig Stevens, Barry Kelley, Tol Avery, Peter Whitney, Manuel Rojas. Scott runs afoul of corrupt family in control of border town; taut B Western never runs out of plot twists.

Buck and the Preacher (1972) **C-102m.** **½ D: Sidney Poitier. Sidney Poitier, Harry Belafonte, Ruby Dee, Cameron Mitchell, Nita Talbot. Black-oriented Western of "hustler" preacher is long on getting to the action and short on staying with it. Good characterizations are major point of interest. Music by Benny Carter. Poitier's directorial debut. [PG]▼◗

Buckaroo Banzai SEE: **Adventures of Buckaroo Banzai Across the Eighth Dimension, The**

Buck Benny Rides Again (1940) **82m.** *** D: Mark Sandrich. Jack Benny, Ellen Drew, Andy Devine, Phil Harris, Virginia Dale, Dennis Day, Eddie "Rochester" Anderson. Amusing Western spoof with Jack trying to convince Drew that he's a 100% cowboy. Radio colleagues help out, with Rochester supplying steady flow of funny dialogue.

Bucket of Blood, A (1959) **66m.** *** D: Roger Corman. Dick Miller, Barboura Morris, Antony Carbone, Julian Burton, Ed Nelson, Bert Convy. Wimpy busboy impresses his coffeehouse betters with amazingly lifelike "sculptures." Writer Charles Griffith's predecessor to THE LITTLE SHOP OF HORRORS is nifty semi-spoof of dead-bodies-in-the-wax-museum genre. Nicely captures spirit of beatnik era; cult actor Miller's finest hour (he's reused his character's name, Walter Paisley, several times since). Remade for TV as THE DEATH ARTIST in 1996. ▼

Buck Privates (1941) **84m.** **½ D: Arthur Lubin. Bud Abbott, Lou Costello, Lee Bowman, Alan Curtis, Andrews Sisters, Jane Frazee, Nat Pendleton, Shemp Howard. Dated but engaging Army opus with Bud and Lou accidentally enlisting. Brassy songs (including Andrews Sisters' "Boogie Woogie Bugle Boy") and subplots get in the way, but A&C's routines are among their best; their first starring film.▼●◗

Buck Privates Come Home (1947) **77m.** *** D: Charles Barton. Bud Abbott, Lou Costello, Tom Brown, Joan Fulton (Shawlee), Nat Pendleton, Beverly Simmons, Don Beddoe. One of A&C's most enjoyable romps has boys returning to civilian life and trying to smuggle a young European orphan into this country. Climactic chase a highlight.▼●◗

Buck Rogers SEE: **Destination Saturn**

Buck Rogers in the 25th Century (1979) **C-89m.** ** D: Daniel Haller. Gil Gerard, Pamela Hensley, Erin Gray, Tim O'Connor, Henry Silva, Joseph Wiseman, Felix Silla, voice of Mel Blanc. The legendary space hero returns, decked out in contemporary glibness, trying to prove he's not in league with intergalactic pirates. Much of the hardware and gadgetry (along with some footage) is from TV's expensive dud, BATTLESTAR GALACTICA, turned out by the same producers. Pilot for the TV series; released theatrically first. [PG]▼

Buckskin (1968) **C-97m.** *½ D: Michael Moore. Barry Sullivan, Joan Caulfield, Wendell Corey, Lon Chaney, John Russell, Barbara Hale, Barton MacLane, Leo Gordon. Land-baron Corey tries to force homesteaders out of territory, but Marshal Sullivan is there to stop him. [G]▼●

Buckskin Frontier (1943) **74m.** ** D: Lesley Selander. Richard Dix, Jane Wyatt, Albert Dekker, Lee J. Cobb, Victor Jory, Lola Lane, Max Baer, Joe Sawyer, George Reeves. Unusual cast adds interest to this otherwise standard Western about railroad man Dix and his conflicts with proud Cobb (who fears for the demise of his freight company) and slimy Jory. Cobb, who's exactly the same age as Wyatt, is cast here as her father!▼

Bucktown (1975) **C-94m.** *½ D: Arthur Marks. Fred Williamson, Pam Grier, Thalmus Rasulala, Tony King, Bernie Hamilton, Art Lund. Repellent blaxploitation picture about war between whites and blacks in corruption-filled Southern town, which intensifies when blacks get into office and make things even worse. [R]▼

Bud Abbott and Lou Costello in Hollywood SEE: **Abbott and Costello in Hollywood**

Bud and Lou (1978) **C-100m. TVM** D: Robert C. Thompson. Harvey Korman, Buddy Hackett, Michele Lee, Arte Johnson, Robert Reed. Major intent of this hackneyed biopic on Abbott and Costello is portraying Lou as an s.o.b, but its fatal flaw is Hackett and Korman's painfully unfunny renderings of classic A&C routines. Below average.▼●

Buddy (1997) **C-84m.** **½ D: Caroline Thompson. Rene Russo, Robbie Coltrane, Alan Cumming, Irma P. Hall, Paul Reubens, John Aylward, Mimi Kennedy. Sweet-natured film about a most unusual woman, real-life Gertrude Lintz, who in the 1920s kept an incredible menagerie of animals on her Long Island estate. Her greatest challenge: raising a gorilla from infancy and treating him almost like a human child. Russo is excellent, and the film has much charm, but it's too leisurely and likely to make kids squirm in their seats. Panavision. [PG]▼●

Buddy Buddy (1981) **C-96m.** *** D: Billy Wilder. Jack Lemmon, Walter Matthau, Paula Prentiss, Klaus Kinski, Dana Elcar, Miles Chapin, Joan Shawlee. Modest black comedy about a hit man whose current job is mucked up by an intrusive stranger. A simple farce, played to perfection by Lemmon and Matthau, adapted by Wilder and I.A.L. Diamond from the French film A PAIN IN THE A—. Panavision. [R]▼

Buddy Holly Story, The (1978) **C-113m.** ***½ D: Steve Rash. Gary Busey, Charles Martin Smith, Don Stroud, Maria Richwine, Amy Johnston, Conrad Janis, Dick O'Neill, William Jordan, Will Jordan (they're different actors), Fred Travalena, "Stymie" Beard. Busey gives an electrifying performance as the rock 'n' roll legend in this long but very satisfying musical drama, not quite the usual glossy Hollywood biography. Busey, Smith and Stroud sing and play "live," giving an extra dimension to Holly's hit songs; Joe Renzetti won an Oscar for Score Adaptation. [PG]▼●◗

Buddy System, The (1984) **C-110m.** **½ D: Glenn Jordan. Richard Dreyfuss, Susan Sarandon, Nancy Allen, Jean Stapleton, Wil Wheaton, Edward Winter, Keene Curtis. Lonely kid tries to play matchmaker between his single mom and a grown-up friend, would-be novelist and gadget inventor Dreyfuss, but there are emotional complications. Nicely played but overly familiar (and overlong) romantic comedy. [PG]▼

Buena Vista Social Club (1999-U.S.-German-French-Cuban) **C-105m.** *** D: Wim Wenders. Seductive documentary about the title group, composed of veteran Havana musicians and singers brought together by American guitarist Ry Cooder after years in obscurity. Two years after cutting a top-selling, award-winning record, they are filmed by Wenders at a recording session, in concert, and reminiscing about their music and their lives. Some are in their 80s (and even 90s), but their music is timeless and musicianship invigorating. [G]▼◗

Buffalo Bill (1944) **C-90m.** **½ D: William Wellman. Joel McCrea, Maureen O'Hara, Linda Darnell, Thomas Mitchell, Anthony Quinn, Edgar Buchanan, Chief Thundercloud, Sidney Blackmer. Colorful biography of legendary Westerner should have been much better, but still provides some fun and has good cast.▼

Buffalo Bill and the Indians, or Sitting Bull's History Lesson (1976) **C-120m.** ** D: Robert Altman. Paul Newman, Joel Grey, Kevin McCarthy, Burt Lancaster, Geraldine Chaplin, Harvey Keitel, Frank Kaquitts, Will Sampson. Altman makes the point that Buffalo Bill was a flamboyant fraud, then belabors it for two hours. Not without interest, but still one of the director's duller movies. Panavision. [PG]▼●

Buffalo 66 (1998) **C-112m.** ** D: Vincent Gallo. Vincent Gallo, Christina Ricci, Anjelica Huston, Ben Gazzara, Kevin Corrigan, Mickey Rourke, Rosanna Arquette, Jan-Michael Vincent. Director-star Gallo plays a convict just released from prison who kidnaps a teenage girl (Ricci) and demands that she pose as his wife to impress his parents. Their evolving relationship makes up the bulk of this sincere, rambling film, which has its moments but confuses grittiness and endless repetition with integrity and truth, and fails to create much interest in the characters. Gallo, whose directing debut this is, also cowrote the screenplay and composed the music. ▼●◗

Buffalo Soldiers (1997) **C-100m. TVM** D: Charles Haid. Danny Glover, Timothy Busfield, Bob Gunton, Carl Lumbly, Clifton Powell, Glynn Turman, Michael Warren, Mykelti Williamson, Tom Bower. Full-blooded, often violent, if fictionalized, version of the post–Civil War black cavalry corps (under racist white officers), and their place in the winning of the West. Powerful, well-acted tale written by Frank Military, Susan Rhinehart, and Jonathan Klein. Glover also executive-produced. Made for cable. Above average.▼●

Buffet Froid (1979-French) **C-95m.** ***½ D: Bertrand Blier. Gérard Depardieu, Bernard Blier, Jean Carmet, Genevieve Page, Denise Gence, Carole Bouquet, Jean Benguigui, Michel Serrault. Strange, surreal, outrageously funny black comedy detailing the misadventures of hapless murderers Depardieu, Carmet, and Blier (the director's father). Brilliantly acted and directed; a treat.▼●◗

Buffy the Vampire Slayer (1992) **C-86m.** **½ D: Fran Rubel Kuzui. Kristy Swanson, Donald Sutherland, Paul Reubens, Rutger Hauer, Luke Perry, Michele Abrams, Hilary Swank, Paris Vaughan, David Arquette, Randall Batinkoff, Candy Clark, Natasha Gregson Wagner. Cute variation on vampire sagas, with high school Valley Girl Swanson turning out to be "the chosen one" of her generation to kill roaming vampires. Sutherland is ideal as her mentor and guide, and Reubens (the former Pee-wee Herman) is fun as one of the fanged menaces . . . but Hauer is an utter disappointment as vampire Uno. Natasha Gregson Wagner, who plays Cassandra, is the daughter of Natalie Wood. Look for Ben Affleck as a basketball player. Ricki Lake appears unbilled. Later a TV series. [PG-13]▼●

Bug (1975) **C-100m.** ** D: Jeannot Szwarc. Bradford Dillman, Joanna Miles, Richard Gilliland, Jamie Smith Jackson, Alan Fudge, Patricia McCormack, Jesse Vint. Earthquake releases a disgusting variety of beetle from the earth, capable of setting people, animals, and objects on fire. Spray your set with Raid after watching this one. Produced by William Castle, whose last film this was. [PG]▼

Bugles in the Afternoon (1952) **C-85m.** **½ D: Roy Rowland. Ray Milland, Forrest Tucker, George Reeves, Helena Carter, Gertrude Michael. Standard tale of man branded coward (Milland) during Civil War, with Little Bighorn finale.▼

Bugle Sounds, The (1941) **101m.** ** D: S. Sylvan Simon. Wallace Beery, Marjorie Main, Lewis Stone, George Bancroft, Henry O'Neill, Donna Reed. Old-time sergeant Beery objects to progress in the army, bails cavalry out of trouble in finale.

Bugs Bunny/Road Runner Movie, The (1979) **C-92m.** **½ D: Chuck Jones, Phil Monroe. New footage of Bugs Bunny surrounds this compilation of some of Chuck Jones' best Warner Bros. cartoon shorts. Not the best way to see these wonderful films, as the repetition grows tiresome, but still worthwhile. First shown in theaters as THE GREAT AMERICAN CHASE. Cut to 78m. for pay TV, and 48m. for network TV. Followed by THE LOONEY, LOONEY, LOONEY BUGS BUNNY MOVIE. [G]▼●

Bugs Bunny's 3rd Movie: 1001 Rabbit Tales (1982) **C-76m.** **½ D: David Detiege, Art Davis, Bill Perez. Yet another compilation of Warner Bros. cartoons, with better-than-average linking material. Some good episodes with Daffy Duck, Tweety and Sylvester, et al., plus Chuck Jones' classic "One Froggy Evening" (minus the punchline), but these are still better seen as individual shorts, and not as an ersatz feature film. Produced by Friz Freleng. Followed by DAFFY DUCK'S MOVIE: FANTASTIC ISLAND. [G]▼

Bugs Bunny Superstar (1975) **C-91m.** *** D: Larry Jackson. Narrated by Orson Welles. Modestly produced compilation of 1940's Warner Bros. cartoons features interviews with the men who created some of the greatest animated films ever made—Bob Clampett, Friz Freleng, and Tex Avery—along with priceless home movies and behind-the-scenes material, as well as nine complete shorts, including A WILD HARE (the first real Bugs Bunny cartoon), CORNY CONCERTO, THE OLD GREY HARE, MY FAVORITE DUCK, and WHAT'S COOKIN' DOC?▼●

bug's life, a (1998) **C-94m.** ***½ D: John Lasseter, Andrew Stanton. Voices of Dave Foley, Julia Louis-Dreyfus, Kevin Spacey, Phyllis Diller, David Hyde Pierce, Denis Leary, Richard Kind, John Ratzenberger, Roddy McDowall, Madeline Kahn, Bonnie Hunt, Edie McClurg, Alex Rocco. Terrific computer-animated feature from Pixar studio (of TOY STORY fame), about a well-meaning ant named Flik who tries to help his beleaguered colony from the plundering of Hopper and his grasshopper cronies. Meaning to hire tough insects to fight them off, he unwittingly recruits a circus troupe instead! Consistently clever and funny; in fact, overflowing with gags and visual ideas. A treat for young and old alike. Screenplay by Stanton, Donald McEnery, and Bob Shaw, from a story by Lasseter, Stanton, and Joe Ranft. Music by Randy Newman. Digital Widescreen. [G] ▼●◗

Bugsy (1991) **C-135m.** *** D: Barry Levinson. Warren Beatty, Annette Bening,

Harvey Keitel, Ben Kingsley, Elliott Gould, Joe Mantegna, Richard Sarafian, Bebe Neuwirth, Wendy Phillips, Robert Beltran, Bill Graham, Lewis Van Bergen, Debrah Farentino. Beatty gives the most forceful performance of his career as Benjamin "Bugsy" Siegel, the fabled crackpot gangster who helped build Las Vegas. Long but well-told tale manages to dodge gangster clichés. Beatty and Bening set off sparks together (just as they did in real life), and a strong supporting cast fleshes out James Toback's intelligent script (though Mantegna, as George Raft, is wasted). Keitel, cast as Mickey Cohen, played Siegel in the TV movie THE VIRGINIA HILL STORY. Oscar winner for Art Direction–Set Decoration and Costume Design. [R]▼●◗

Bugsy Malone (1976-British) **C-93m.** **½ D: Alan Parker. Scott Baio, Florrie Dugger, Jodie Foster, John Cassisi, Martin Lev. Unique musical spoof of Prohibition-era gangster films with all-kiddie cast; script clichés are intact, but the machine-guns shoot whipped cream instead of bullets. Beautiful production cannot escape coyness and doesn't hold up; plastic rendition of Paul Williams' score doesn't help. [G]▼●

Bulldog Drummond Hugh "Bulldog" Drummond, an ex-British army officer who yearned for adventure, was created in 1919 by "Sapper" (Herman Cyril McNeile); the character's film possibilities were realized and Drummond was the subject of several silent films. The definitive BULLDOG DRUMMOND was made in 1929 with dashing Ronald Colman in the lead and Claud Allister as his constant companion Algy; Colman also starred in a delightful sequel, BULLDOG DRUMMOND STRIKES BACK, which unfortunately is not available to TV. No one ever approached Colman's charm—or the wittiness of these first two scripts—in subsequent efforts (though the British spoof called BULLDOG JACK scored a bull's-eye in its own comic way, and other Britishers like Jack Buchanan and Ralph Richardson had a go at the role—like the second Colman film, these interesting-sounding entries cannot be seen on TV). The major series was made in the late 1930s by Paramount, with John Howard as Drummond, John Barrymore as Inspector Neilson of Scotland Yard, Reginald Denny as Algy, and E. E. Clive as the butler Tenny. These were brief (around one hour), entertaining mysteries with such formidable villains as J. Carrol Naish, Anthony Quinn, George Zucco, and Eduardo Ciannelli. In the late 1940s Ron Randell and Tom Conway did two Drummonds each, which weren't bad but didn't catch on. The last one was CALLING BULLDOG DRUMMOND, a 1951 film with Walter Pidgeon in the lead and David Tomlinson as Algy. (One attempt to revive the character was a flop: DEADLIER THAN THE MALE and SOME GIRLS DO, both with Richard Johnson.) Other older films that still pop up include such Drummonds as John Lodge and Ray Milland.

BULLDOG DRUMMOND

Bulldog Drummond (1929)
The Return of Bulldog Drummond (1934)
Bulldog Jack (1934)
Bulldog Drummond Escapes (1937)
Bulldog Drummond at Bay (1937)
Bulldog Drummond Comes Back (1937)
Bulldog Drummond's Revenge (1937)
Bulldog Drummond's Peril (1938)
Bulldog Drummond in Africa (1938)
Bulldog Drummond's Secret Police (1939)
Bulldog Drummond's Bride (1939)
Arrest Bulldog Drummond (1939)
Bulldog Drummond at Bay (1947)
Bulldog Drummond Strikes Back (1947)
The Challenge (1948)
13 Lead Soldiers (1948)
Calling Bulldog Drummond (1951)
Deadlier Than the Male (1967)
Some Girls Do (1969)

Bulldog Drummond (1929) **89m.** ***½ D: F. Richard Jones. Ronald Colman, Joan Bennett, Lilyan Tashman, Montagu Love, Lawrence Grant, Claud Allister. Colman is a delight (in his first talking picture) as the bored ex-British Army officer who comes to the rescue of a wealthy American (Bennett) whose uncle is being held captive in an asylum by a sadistic doctor. Sidney Howard's polished script, Gregg Toland and George Barnes' stylish photography, and William Cameron Menzies' stylish sets help make this a classy and sophisticated romp.▼●

Bulldog Drummond at Bay (1937-British) **62m.** **½ D: Norman Lee. John Lodge, Dorothy Mackaill, Victor Jory, Claud Allister, Hugh Miller, Marie O'Neill. Innocuous British "quota-quickie" has Drummond (Lodge) battling foreign agents trying to steal plans for a top-secret British aircraft. Most faithful screen adaptation of character as created by H. C. McNeile.▼

Bulldog Drummond at Bay (1947) **70m.** *½ D: Sidney Salkow. Ron Randell, Anita Louise, Pat O'Moore, Terry Kilburn, Holmes Herbert. Quickie entry with Drummond, now portrayed by Australian Randell, after a murderous diamond thief.▼

Bulldog Drummond Comes Back (1937) **64m.** **½ D: Louis King. John Barrymore, John Howard, Louise Campbell, Reginald Denny, E. E. Clive, J. Carrol Naish, John Sutton. Naish and his gang kidnap Drummond's fiancée and are pursued by the adventurer and his friend Colonel Nielson. Howard makes an urbane, if bland Drummond, but Barrymore is a hoot as his master-of-disguise pal from Scotland Yard. Adapted from McNeile's *The Female of the Species.*▼

Bulldog Drummond Escapes (1937) **65m.** ** D: James Hogan. Ray Milland, Guy Standing, Heather Angel, Porter Hall, Reginald Denny, E. E. Clive, Fay Holden. Drummond falls for the pretty heiress (Angel) he's been hired to protect from spies. Milland had his one shot at portraying Drummond in this lightweight programmer.▼

Bulldog Drummond in Africa (1938) **60m.** **½ D: Louis King. John Howard, Heather Angel, H. B. Warner, J. Carrol Naish, Reginald Denny, Anthony Quinn, Michael Brooke. Scotland Yard Inspector Nielson (Warner, replacing John Barrymore) is abducted, sending Drummond on a deadly trek into the wilds of the jungle. Atmospheric entry with a formidable supporting cast.▼

Bulldog Drummond's Bride (1939) **55m.** **½ D: James Hogan. John Howard, Heather Angel, H. B. Warner, Reginald Denny, Eduardo Ciannelli, Elizabeth Patterson. Bulldog and his fiancée have their wedding plans in France interrupted when Bulldog takes off after villainous Ciannelli and his gang of bank robbers in this high-speed entry.▼

Bulldog Drummond's Peril (1938) **66m.** **½ D: James Hogan. John Barrymore, John Howard, Louise Campbell, Reginald Denny, E. E. Clive, Porter Hall, Nydia Westman. Drummond's wedding is interrupted by murder, sending the sleuth off on an adventure involving synthetic diamonds. Pleasing, swift-moving series entry.▼

Bulldog Drummond's Revenge (1937) **60m.** **½ D: Louis King. John Barrymore, John Howard, Louise Campbell, Reginald Denny, E. E. Clive, Nydia Westman, Lucien Littlefield. Drummond (Howard) tracks down a gang of spies after a secret bomb formula in this lean entry. ▼

Bulldog Drummond's Secret Police (1939) **56m.** **½ D: James Hogan. John Howard, Heather Angel, H. B. Warner, Reginald Denny, Leo G. Carroll, Elizabeth Patterson. Pared-down entry features a mad scientist, torture chambers and an eerie old castle, with Carroll excellent in three villainous roles. Lengthy dream sequence incorporates footage from earlier series episodes.▼

Bulldog Drummond Strikes Back (1947) **65m.** *½ D: Frank McDonald. Ron Randell, Gloria Henry, Pat O'Moore, Anabel Shaw, Terry Kilburn. Pedestrian entry built around a favorite plot of mystery series writers: the old one about a phony heiress trying to pick up an inheritance.

Bulldog Jack (1934-British) **73m.** *** D: Walter Forde. Jack Hulbert, Ralph Richardson, Fay Wray, Claude Hulbert, Athole Fleming. British comedian Hulbert finds himself taking the place of ailing Bulldog Drummond on a sinister case. Fast and funny with some first-rate suspense as well; memorable climax set in the London underground system. Originally shown in the U.S. as ALIAS BULLDOG DRUMMOND, with all the comedy cut out!▼

Bull Durham (1988) **C-108m.** *** D: Ron Shelton. Kevin Costner, Susan Sarandon, Tim Robbins, Trey Wilson, Robert Wuhl, Jenny Robertson, Max Patkin. Smart, sassy film about minor-league North Carolina baseball team and its attentive, intelligent groupie (Sarandon) who feels it is her mission to live with one young player per season and help him mature. Costner is a hardened young veteran of the game whose job is to help one particular player—cocky, undisciplined, but talented pitcher Robbins. Literate and funny, if a bit sluggish at times, with some seriously sexy scenes near the end. [R]▼●◗

Bullet for a Badman (1964) **C-80m.** **½ D: R. G. Springsteen. Audie Murphy, Darren McGavin, Ruta Lee, Skip Homeier, George Tobias, Bob Steele. Another revenge tale involving outlaw, his ex-wife, and a friend who married her.

Bullet for Joey, A (1955) **85m.** **½ D: Lewis Allen. Edward G. Robinson, George Raft, Audrey Totter, Peter Van Eyck. Veteran cast improves caper about Communist agent attempting to kidnap U.S. nuclear scientist.▼

Bullet for Sandoval, A (1970-Italian-Spanish) **C-91m.** ** D: Julio Buchs. Ernest Borgnine, George Hilton, Alberto De Mendoza, Gustavo Rojo, Leo Anchoriz, Annabella Incontrera. Average foreign oater, with lots of action. Ex-Confederate Hilton plots revenge on don Borgnine, grandfather of Hilton's illegitimate son, for indirectly causing the baby's death. Cromoscope. [PG]▼

Bullet for Stefano (1950-Italian) **96m.** ** D: Duilio Coletti. Rossano Brazzi, Valentina Cortese, Carlo Campanini, Lillian Laine. Carefree young man (Brazzi) falls into life of crime and finds it pleasant; cast is engaging.

Bullet for the General, A (1967-Italian) **C-115m.** ** D: Damiano Damiani. Gian-Maria Volonté, Lou Castel, Klaus Kinski, Martine Beswick. Blond gringo joins marauding guerrillas and contributes to gory bloodletting. Not bad for the genre. Techniscope.▼

Bullet in the Head (1990-Hong Kong) **C-136m.** *** D: John Woo. Tony Leung, Jacky Cheung, Waise Lee, Simon Yam, Fennie Yeun, Yolinda Yan. Intense, highly charged story of three friends who leave Hong Kong to reap profits in war-torn 1967

Saigon and get caught up in a whirlwind of troubles that tests their loyalty. An epic film, emotional and overwrought, with action footage and confrontations (particularly a long sequence in a POW camp) that are as bold as anything Woo has attempted onscreen. Woo cowrote the screenplay and also edited. Running time is the full-length director's cut; most American prints run 100m.●◗

Bullet Is Waiting, A (1954) **C-82m.** **½ D: John Farrow. Jean Simmons, Rory Calhoun, Stephen McNally, Brian Aherne. Interesting human nature study hinging on sheriff's discovery that his prisoner is really innocent; nice desert locale.▼

Bulletproof (1988) **C-94m.** BOMB D: Steve Carver. Gary Busey, Darlanne Fluegel, Henry Silva, L.Q. Jones, R.G. Armstrong, Juan Fernandez, Rene Enriquez. L.A. cop Busey, who keeps the 39 bullets his body has taken in a bathroom mason jar, kamikazes across the Mexican border to rescue kidnapped army personnel (ex-love Fluegel included) from Silva's Soviet stooge. Preposterous, but you have to admire Silva for having kept the same act going for so many years; peroxided hair is simply not to Busey's advantage. [R]▼●

Bulletproof (1996) **C-85m.** BOMB D: Ernest Dickerson. Adam Sandler, Damon Wayans, James Caan, Kristen Wilson, James Farentino, Bill Nunn, Jeep Swenson. A racial inversion of 48HRS. without the redeeming craft. Undercover cop Wayans teams up with Sandler, the crook he's trying to bust. Their fortunes and ambitions are unified—often acrimoniously—by a vindictive drug kingpin/car dealer played by a pitifully hammy Caan. Once great cinematographer Dickerson squanders his talent here directing a sociopathic mix of graphic violence and slapstick. A catastrophe of continuity to boot. Super 35. [R]▼●◗

Bulletproof Heart (1994) **C-100m.** ** D: Mark Malone. Anthony LaPaglia, Mimi Rogers, Peter Boyle, Matt Craven, Joseph Maher. Prosperous hit man LaPaglia gets a gig he's not quite prepared for: rub out a well-connected knockout who actually *wants* to die. Four well-shaped, well-played characters—including Boyle's shady mobster and Craven's dimwit sidekick—don't add up to a satisfying whole. The slim story could have used some serious fleshing out. Two pluses: an intriguingly steamy sex scene, and another incisive performance from Rogers. Played the film festival circuit as KILLER. [R]▼●

Bullets or Ballots (1936) **81m.** *** D: William Keighley. Edward G. Robinson, Joan Blondell, Barton MacLane, Humphrey Bogart, Frank McHugh. Cop Robinson pretends to leave police force to crack citywide mob ring run by MacLane. Good, tough gangster film.▼●

Bullets Over Broadway (1994) **C-99m.** *** D: Woody Allen. John Cusack, Dianne Wiest, Jennifer Tilly, Chazz Palminteri, Mary-Louise Parker, Jack Warden, Joe Viterelli, Rob Reiner, Tracey Ullman, Jim Broadbent, Harvey Fierstein, Stacey Nelkin. Delightful Woody Allen bauble about a self-serious 1920s playwright who quickly sells out when he's offered a chance to direct his latest work on Broadway—with a gangster's moll in a key role, and an intoxicatingly seductive star in the lead. An actors' field day, with particularly juicy parts for Wiest (who won an Oscar) as the flamboyant actress, Palminteri, as a thug with an unexpected gift, and Tilly as the ditsy moll. The period detail is so rich and right it all seems stunningly real. Allen coscripted with Douglas McGrath. [R]▼●◗

Bullfighter and the Lady (1951) **87m.** ***½ D: Budd Boetticher. Robert Stack, Joy Page, Gilbert Roland, Katy Jurado, Virginia Grey, John Hubbard. Cocky American visiting Mexico decides that he wants to tackle bullfighting and enlists the aid of the country's leading matador with tragic results. The movies' best treatment of this subject, a fine, mature drama with unforgettable bullfighting scenes and an appealing love story as well. Roland has never been better; only the second leads (Grey, Hubbard) are a detriment. Produced by John Wayne. Boetticher's version, running 124m., has been restored, and it's even better than the shorter print. ▼●

Bullfighters, The (1945) **61m.** ** D: Mal St. Clair. Stan Laurel, Oliver Hardy, Margo Woode, Richard Lane, Carol Andrews, Diosa Costello. One of better L&H later works, involving mistaken identity (Stan is lookalike for famous matador), subsequent nonsense in bull ring.▼

Bullies (1986-Canadian) **C-96m.** BOMB D: Paul Lynch. Jonathan Crombie, Janet Laine Green, Stephen B. Hunter, Dehl Berti, Olivia D'Abo, Bill Croft. Mindlessly violent garbage about a family of sadistic, booze-guzzling rednecks who terrorize a small town. [R]▼●

Bullitt (1968) **C-113m.** ***½ D: Peter Yates. Steve McQueen, Robert Vaughn, Jacqueline Bisset, Don Gordon, Robert Duvall, Simon Oakland, Norman Fell, Victor (Vic) Tayback. Definitive McQueen antihero: police detective who senses something fishy behind assignment to guard criminal witness. Taut action-film makes great use of San Francisco locations, especially in now-classic car chase, one of the screen's all-time best; Oscar-winning editing by Frank Keller. Scripted by Alan R. Trustman and Harry Kleiner, from Robert L. Pike's novel *Mute Witness*. [M/PG] ▼●◗

Bullseye! (1989) **C-89m.** BOMB D: Michael Winner. Michael Caine, Roger Moore, Sally Kirkland, Lee Patterson, Deborah Barrymore, Mark Burns, Debra Lang, Lynn

Nesbitt, Steffanie Pitt, Patsy Kensit, Alexandra Pigg, Jenny Seagrove. Deadly nonsense which completely wastes Caine and Moore as criminals who are dead ringers for a couple of nuclear scientists (up to no good themselves). Confusing story complications and heavyhanded humor make this a dog. Barrymore is Moore's real-life daughter; John Cleese has an unbilled cameo near the end. Released direct to video. [PG-13]▼

Bullshot (1983-British) **C-85m.** **½ D: Dick Clement. Alan Shearman, Diz White, Ron House, Frances Tomelty, Michael Aldridge, Ron Pember, Billy Connolly. Occasionally funny Monty Python-ish parody, with Shearman cast as one Captain Hugh "Bullshot" Crummond, a Bulldog Drummond caricature. Plenty of one-liners and slapstick, some humorous and some silly. The screenplay was adapted by Shearman, White, and House, from their stage play. [PG]▼

Bullwhip (1958) **C-80m.** ** D: Harmon Jones. Guy Madison, Rhonda Fleming, James Griffith, Don Beddoe. Madison is offered the choice of marrying Fleming or being hanged on phony murder charge; expected results. CinemaScope.▼

Bulworth (1998) **C-107m.** ***½ D: Warren Beatty. Warren Beatty, Halle Berry, Don Cheadle, Oliver Platt, Paul Sorvino, Jack Warden, Isaiah Washington, Joshua Malina, Christine Baranski, Amiri Baraka, Sean Astin, Laurie Metcalf, Richard Sarafian, Nora Dunn, Jackie Gayle, Michael Clarke Duncan. Audacious political satire about a California senator, running for reelection in 1996, who solves his crisis of conscience by telling the truth—and embracing the black community. Unsettling at times—as it's meant to be—with trenchant observations on the political process and the plight of the poor. One of Beatty's best films—as actor, director, cowriter (with Jeremy Pikser). William Baldwin and Paul Mazursky appear unbilled. [R]▼●◗

Bundle of Joy (1956) **C-98m.** ** D: Norman Taurog. Eddie Fisher, Debbie Reynolds, Adolphe Menjou, Tommy Noonan. Labored musical remake of BACHELOR MOTHER has Reynolds as salesgirl who takes custody of a baby, causing scandal that boyfriend Fisher (in starring debut) is child's father. Made when Debbie and Eddie were America's favorite couple. ▼

Bunker, The (1981) **C-150m. TVM** D: George Schaefer. Anthony Hopkins, Piper Laurie, Richard Jordan, Susan Blakely, Cliff Gorman, James Naughton, Michael Lonsdale. Hopkins won an Emmy for his chilling portrayal of Adolf Hitler in this adaptation by John Gay of the James P. O'Donnell book depicting the Third Reich's final days. Piper Laurie was nominated for an Emmy Award for her performance as Magda Goebbels. Above average.▼

Bunny Caper, The (1974-British) **C-85m.** *½ D: Jack Arnold. Christina Hart, Jane Anthony, Drina Pavlovic, Jill Damas, Ed Bishop. Subpar sex comedy satirizing political intrigue during the Nixon/Kissinger era. An off-day assignment for noted sci-fi director Arnold. Aka GAMES GIRLS PLAY and SEX PLAY. [R]▼

Bunny Lake Is Missing (1965) **107m.** ** D: Otto Preminger. Laurence Olivier, Carol Lynley, Keir Dullea, Noel Coward, Martita Hunt, Finlay Currie, The Zombies. Aimless story of Lynley's child being kidnapped, subsequent investigation among several homosexual characters and assorted oddballs; pretty dreary going. Made in England. Panavision.

Bunny O'Hare (1972) **C-91m.** *½ D: Gerd Oswald. Bette Davis, Ernest Borgnine, Jack Cassidy, Joan Delaney, Reva Rose, John Astin. Bizarre, totally inept tale of bank robbers who look like hippies but are actually Davis and Borgnine. Don't bother watching. [PG]

Buona Sera, Mrs. Campbell (1969) **C-113m.** *** D: Melvin Frank. Gina Lollobrigida, Peter Lawford, Shelley Winters, Phil Silvers, Telly Savalas, Lee Grant, Janet Margolin. Bright comedy about Italian woman who's accepted money from three American men who all think they fathered her child during WW2. Now they're all coming back to Italy for Army reunion and "Mrs. Campbell" is in a state of panic. Good fun with top cast. [M/PG]▼●

'burbs, The (1989) **C-103m.** ** D: Joe Dante. Tom Hanks, Bruce Dern, Carrie Fisher, Rick Ducommun, Corey Feldman, Wendy Schaal, Henry Gibson, Brother Theodore, Courtney Gains, Gale Gordon, Dick Miller. Strange new neighbors set a neighborhood abuzz, and lead several slightly cracked compadres to extreme measures so they can learn just what's going on behind closed doors. Comically warped view of suburban life takes far too much time to play out its paper-thin premise, and leads to (mostly) predictable results. [PG] ▼●◗

Burden of Dreams (1982) **C-94m.** ***½ D: Les Blank. Werner Herzog, Klaus Kinski, Claudia Cardinale, Jason Robards, Mick Jagger. Extraordinary documentary of the filming of Herzog's FITZCARRALDO in the Peruvian Amazon. Despite the filmmaker's high technology, his dream of completing the film is constantly thwarted by nature and clashing cultures. Some find this more compelling than FITZCARRALDO itself.▼

Bureau of Missing Persons (1933) **75m.** **½ D: Roy Del Ruth. Bette Davis, Lewis S. Stone, Pat O'Brien, Allen Jenkins, Ruth Donnelly, Hugh Herbert, Glenda Farrell, Alan Dinehart, George Chandler. Typically fast-paced—but strange—Warner Bros. programmer about big-city bureau of missing persons, where benevolent Stone plays God with the losers and hard-luck cases that come before him. Hip-shooting cop O'Brien is transferred there in hopes he'll mellow out, and we'll bet you a dollar six bits he doesn't. Davis is a mystery woman with whom he gets involved.▼

Burglar, The (1956) **90m.** **½ D: Paul Wendkos. Dan Duryea, Jayne Mansfield, Martha Vickers, Peter Capell, Mickey Shaughnessy, Phoebe Mackay. Odd little film noir about burglars Duryea and Mansfield, who've grown up together, and their unpredictable accomplices in a bizarre burglary. Remade in 1972.

Burglar (1987) **C-102m.** *½ D: Hugh Wilson. Whoopi Goldberg, Bob Goldthwait, G.W. Bailey, Lesley Ann Warren, James Handy, Anne DeSalvo, John Goodman. Whoopi plays a cat burglar who accidentally witnesses a murder—and then tries to solve the crime, in order to clear herself. Unfunny, unsuspenseful, and completely unappealing comedy/mystery, with a superfluous, built-up secondary role for Goldthwait (who has a few good moments). Another waste of Whoopi's talent. [R]▼●◗

Burglars, The (1972-French) **C-117m.** **½ D: Henri Verneuil. Jean-Paul Belmondo, Omar Sharif, Dyan Cannon, Robert Hossein. Routine crime film set against lush Greek backdrop, with good cast. One good chase and it's all over. Remake of THE BURGLAR. Panavision. [PG]

Buried Alive (1990) **C-91m.** *½ D: Gerard Kikoine. Robert Vaughn, Donald Pleasence, Karen Witter, John Carradine, Nia Long, Ginger Lynn Allen. Murky thriller about a mansion where "doctor" Vaughn imprisons young women. Story uses elements from several Edgar Allan Poe stories, but juices them up with sex and gore. Filmed in South Africa. Carradine's last feature film. [R]▼●

Buried Alive (1990) **C-100m. TVM** D: Frank Darabont. Jennifer Jason Leigh, Tim Matheson, William Atherton, Hoyt Axton. Well-turned horror tale of a man waking up alive in his grave and going after the mercenary wife who poisoned him and ran off with her doctor-lover. Written by Mark Patrick Carducci. Made for cable. Sequel: BURIED ALIVE II. Above average.▼

Burke and Wills (1986-Australian) **C-140m.** *** D: Graeme Clifford. Jack Thompson, Nigel Havers, Greta Scacchi, Matthew Fargher, Ralph Cotterill, Drew Forsythe, Chris Haywood. Impressive, larger-than-life historical drama chronicling the title characters' expedition through 1860 Australia, the first two men to cross the continent. Thompson is especially fine as Burke; another version of the saga was made the same year, titled WILLS AND BURKE. Panavision. [PG-13]▼●

Burma Convoy (1941) **72m.** **½ D: Noel Smith. Charles Bickford, Evelyn Ankers, Frank Albertson, Cecil Kellaway, Keye Luke, Turhan Bey. Neat little actioner of conflicting trucking interests involved in carrying needed supplies over the Burma Road during hectic days of WW2.

Burmese Harp, The (1956-Japanese) **116m.** ***½ D: Kon Ichikawa. Rentaro Mikuni, Shoji Yasui, Tatsuya Mihashi, Tanie Kitabayashi, Yunosuke Ito. Private Yasui volunteers to persuade a group of mountain fighters to surrender at the end of WW2 and undergoes a religious experience, becoming obsessed with desire to bury war casualties. Extraordinary antiwar drama is affecting and memorable if a bit overlong. Also known as HARP OF BURMA; remade by Ichikawa in 1985.▼●

Burn! (1969-Italian-French) **C-112m.** *** D: Gillo Pontecorvo. Marlon Brando, Evaristo Marquez, Renato Salvatori, Tom Lyons, Norman Hill. Egomaniacal Sir William Walker (Brando) is sent by the British to instigate a slave revolt on a Portuguese-controlled sugar-producing Caribbean island. This political drama is visually striking but muddled, with a strong Brando performance. Ed Harris plays the same role in WALKER. Cut by 20m. before its U.S. release. Aka QUEMADA! [PG]▼●

Burndown (1989) **C-87m.** *½ D: James Allen. Peter Firth, Cathy Moriarty, Michael McCabe, Hal Orlandini, Hugh Rouse. A murderous *and* radioactive rapist is stalking a Southern town, tracked by Sheriff Firth and his reporter/lover Moriarty. Bizarre accents, a slow pace, a dull plot, and an inconclusive ending obliterate interesting work by the actors. [R] ▼●

Burning, The (1981) **C-90m.** BOMB D: Tony Maylam. Brian Matthews, Leah Ayres, Brian Backer, Larry Joshua, Lou David, Jason Alexander, Fisher Stevens. Awful FRIDAY THE 13TH ripoff (with Tom Savini's bloody makeup effects) about an old caretaker at a summer camp who takes his revenge in the usual way. Holly Hunter's screen debut. [R]▼

Burning Bed, The (1984) **C-100m. TVM** D: Robert Greenwald. Farrah Fawcett, Paul LeMat, Richard Masur, Grace Zabriskie, Penelope Milford, James Callahan. In a surprisingly effective performance Fawcett shows substance as a battered wife who sets her ex-husband on fire one night after living with his beatings and humiliations for years. Emmy nominations went to, among others, Fawcett and writer Rose Leiman Goldemberg, who based her script on Faith McNulty's book. One of the highest rated TV movies of all time. Above average.▼

Burning Cross, The SEE: **Klansman, The**

Burning Hills, The (1956) **C-94m** ** D: Stuart Heisler. Tab Hunter, Natalie Wood, Skip Homeier, Eduard Franz, Earl Holliman, Claude Akins. Passive Hunter can't spark life into tired script based on a Louis L'Amour novel. Man on run from cattle thieves is sheltered by Wood, miscast as a half-breed Mexican girl. CinemaScope.▼

Burning Man, The SEE: **Dangerous Summer, A**

Burning Season, The (1994) **C-127m. TVM** D: John Frankenheimer. Raul Julia, Sonia Braga, Edward James Olmos, Kamala Dawson, Luis Guzman, Nigel Havers, Tomas Milian, Esai Morales. Julia gives a passionate performance as real-life Chico Mendes, an activist murdered while fighting to protect his people in the Amazon rain forest. A bull's-eye for Julia (in one of his last films) and director Frankenheimer, who both won Emmys. Screenplay by Michael Tolkin, Ron Hutchinson, and William Mastrosimone from his story and two separate novels. Made for cable. Above average.▼

Burning Secret (1988-U.S.-British-German) **C-106m.** **½ D: Andrew Birkin. Faye Dunaway, Klaus Maria Brandauer, David Eberts, Ian Richardson. Brandauer offers a splendid performance (as usual) as a charming, amoral baron, a WW1 vet who's nursing a bayonet wound at a sanitarium. In order to get to Dunaway, he initiates a friendship with her impressionable, asthmatic 12-year-old son (Eberts). Generally compelling, and lushly filmed in Prague and Marienbad; however, Dunaway is miscast, and there are several key moments that simply don't work. Based on a Stefan Zweig short story; originally made in Germany in 1933 by Robert Siodmak, as BRENNENDES GEHEIMNIS. [PG]▼●

Burnt by the Sun (1994-Russian-French) **C-135m.** *** D: Nikita Mikhalkov. Nikita Mikhalkov, Ingeborga Dapkounaite, Oleg Menchikov, Nadia Mikhalkov, Andre Oumansky. The year is 1936, and Sergei Kotov (played by director Mikhalkov) is an aging hero of the Bolshevik Revolution whose eyes are closed to the present-day tyranny of Josef Stalin. All of this is about to change upon the arrival of his wife's ex-lover, who is employed by Stalin's governmental police. Provocative, moving meditation on the political and social realities of life in Stalinist Russia deservedly earned a Best Foreign Film Oscar. Sergei's daughter, Nadia, who has a key role in the story, is played by Mikhalkov's real-life daughter, Nadia. ▼●

Burnt Offerings (1976) **C-115m.** ** D: Dan Curtis. Karen Black, Oliver Reed, Burgess Meredith, Eileen Heckart, Lee Montgomery, Dub Taylor, Bette Davis, Anthony James. Ordinary couple, with young son and aunt in tow, rent an old mansion as summer home, unaware that it's haunted. Strange occurrences lead to totally predictable "surprise" ending. A big buildup to nothing. From Robert Marasco's novel. [PG]▼●

Burn, Witch, Burn! (1962-British) **90m.** *** D: Sidney Hayers. Janet Blair, Peter Wyngarde, Margaret Johnston, Anthony Nicholls. Story of witchcraft entering lives of schoolteacher and his wife builds to shattering suspense, genuinely frightening climax. Fritz Leiber's novel *Conjure Wife* was filmed before as WEIRD WOMAN; this version scripted by Charles Beaumont and Richard Matheson. Later spoofed in WITCHES' BREW. Original British title: NIGHT OF THE EAGLE. ●

Bury Me an Angel (1971) **C-86m.** **½ D: Barbara Peeters. Dixie Peabody, Terry Mace, Joanne Jordan, Clyde Ventura, Dan Haggerty, Stephen Whittaker, Gary Littlejohn, Beach Dickerson. Tautly directed biker film, told from the woman's point-of-view; heroine sets out on the road, toting a shotgun and meaning business, to avenge her brother's murder. Haggerty is effective in small role as struggling artist. [R]▼

Bush Christmas (1947-Australian) **76m.** *** D: Ralph Smart. Chips Rafferty, John Fernside, Stan Tolhurst, Pat Penny, Thelma Grigg. Solid little adventure about some children who set out across the Australian bush in pursuit of horse thieves. Holds up quite nicely; kids should enjoy it. Remade in 1983.

Bushido Blade, The (1979-Japanese) **C-104m.** **½ D: Tom Kotani. Richard Boone, Frank Converse, James Earl Jones, Toshiro Mifune, Mako, Sonny Chiba, Laura Gemser. 19th-century Kung Fu action in Japan as Cmdr. Matthew Perry (Boone) leads a band of his men in the recovery of a treasured sword. Of note: Boone's last role; Mifune plays the Shogun, as he did in later TV miniseries. Aka THE BLOODY BUSHIDO BLADE. [R]▼

Bushwhacked (1995) **C-90m.** *½ D: Greg Beeman. Daniel Stern, Jon Polito, Brad Sullivan, Ann Dowd, Anthony Heald, Tom Wood, Blake Bashoff, Corey Carrier, Michael Galeota, Max Goldblatt. On the lam for a murder he didn't commit, a delivery man "hides out" by posing as the leader of a Ranger Scout troop that embarks on a wilderness adventure neither he nor they will ever forget. Unfortunately, all of us will. Stern is way over the top in this familiar fish-out-of-water premise that draws on two of his past triumphs, CITY SLICKERS and HOME ALONE. For younger kids only. Clairmont-Scope. [PG-13] ▼●

Bushwackers, The (1952) **70m.** ** D: Rod Amateau. John Ireland, Wayne Morris, Lawrence Tierney, Dorothy Malone, Lon Chaney, Jr., Myrna Dell, Jack Elam. Standard oater of peace-loving Civil War vet Ireland, who heads west and predictably finds that he must dust off his gun to fight corruption. Of interest mostly for the sermonizing in Amateau and Tom Gries' script, which offers parallels to the political climate in America during the post-Civil War and post-World II eras.▼

Business As Usual (1987-British) **C-89m.** **½ D: Lezli-An Barrett. Glenda Jackson, John Thaw, Cathy Tyson, Mark McGann,

Eamon Boland, James Hazeldine, Buki Armstrong, Stephen McGann. Passionate but didactic pro-labor drama with Jackson as a Liverpool boutique manager whose arbitrary firing (after she's lodged a complaint about sexual harassment on behalf of an employee) escalates into a national cause celebre. One of the angry anti-Thatcher films of the late 80s; written by first-time feature director Barrett. Excellent performances help a one-sided script. [PG]▼

Busman's Honeymoon SEE: **Haunted Honeymoon** (1940)

Bus Riley's Back in Town (1965) **C-93m.** **½ D: Harvey Hart. Ann-Margret, Michael Parks, Janet Margolin, Brad Dexter, Kim Darby, Jocelyn Brando, Larry Storch, David Carradine. Muddled William Inge script of folksy people in the Midwest. Parks, ex-sailor, returns home, torn by faltering ambitions and taunted by wealthy ex-girlfriend Ann-Margret. Character cameos make the film worthwhile.▼

Bus Stop (1956) **C-96m.** ***½ D: Joshua Logan. Marilyn Monroe, Don Murray, Arthur O'Connell, Betty Field, Eileen Heckart, Hope Lange, Hans Conried, Casey Adams. The film that finally proved Monroe really could act; excellent comedy-drama about innocent cowboy (Murray) who falls for saloon singer and decides to marry her—without bothering to ask. Fine performances by all, with MM's famed rendition of "(That Old) Black Magic" a highlight; adapted by George Axelrod from the William Inge play. Film debuts of Murray and Lange (who subsequently married). Some older TV prints are titled THE WRONG KIND OF GIRL. Later a brief TV series. CinemaScope.▼●

Buster (1988-British) **C-102m.** **½ D: David Green. Phil Collins, Julie Walters, Larry Lamb, Stephanie Lawrence, Ellen Beaven, Michael Atwell, Ralph Brown, Christopher Ellison, Sheila Hancock, Martin Jarvis, Anthony Quayle. Buster Edwards, one of the men behind Britain's all-time biggest robbery, turns out to have been just a working-class stiff with big dreams and a bad track record of success, who wanted the good life for his wife and child. Singer Collins' starring film debut is a diverting (if forgettable) yarn, with Walters a good match as his loving, long-suffering spouse. Great soundtrack includes Collins' performances of "Two Hearts (One Mind)" and "Groovy Kind of Love." [R]▼●

Buster and Billie (1974) **C-100m.** *½ D: Daniel Petrie. Jan-Michael Vincent, Joan Goodfellow, Pamela Sue Martin, Clifton James, Robert Englund. Blubbery account of high school romance in 1948 rural Georgia (the loosest girl in class is redeemed by love) can't overcome clichéd premise. [R]▼

Buster Keaton Story, The (1957) **91m.** *½ D: Sidney Sheldon. Donald O'Connor, Ann Blyth, Rhonda Fleming, Peter Lorre, Larry Keating. Weak fiction ignores the facts about silent-star Keaton, making up its own. More private life than on-screen moments are detailed with Blyth as his true love and Fleming as a siren. Little comedy in this tale of a great comedian. VistaVision.

Busting (1974) **C-92m.** **½ D: Peter Hyams. Elliott Gould, Robert Blake, Allen Garfield, Antonio Fargas, Michael Lerner, Sid Haig, Cornelia Sharpe. Realistic if empty comedy-action-drama with Gould and Blake as unorthodox L.A. vice cops. Gay activists complained about film's few minutes of homosexual caricatures. Hyams, once a CBS-TV newsman, also did script. [R]▼

Bustin' Loose (1981) **C-94m** *** D: Oz Scott. Richard Pryor, Cicely Tyson, Robert Christian, Alphonso Alexander, Janet Wong. Despite the (expected) street language, this is at heart a family picture about an ex-convict who shepherds teacher Tyson and a busload of emotionally and physically handicapped youngsters to a new life. Best scene: a KKK band becomes putty in Pryor's hands. Filmed mostly in 1979, but not completed until 1981 because of Pryor's near fatal accident. Film debut for Broadway director Scott; Pryor coproduced and wrote the story. Later a TV series. [R]▼●◗

Busy Body, The (1967) **C-90m.** **½ D: William Castle. Sid Caesar, Robert Ryan, Anne Baxter, Kay Medford, Jan Murray, Richard Pryor, Dom DeLuise, Godfrey Cambridge, Marty Ingels, Bill Dana, George Jessel. Broad, forced comedy involving gangsters and corpses, with Caesar as the patsy for Ryan's underworld gang. Supporting comics give film its funniest moments. Pryor's film debut. Techniscope.

Butch and Sundance: The Early Days (1979) **C-110m.** **½ D: Richard Lester. William Katt, Tom Berenger, Jeff Corey, John Schuck, Michael C. Gwynne, Brian Dennehy, Jill Eikenberry, Peter Weller, Arthur Hill. Prequel to BUTCH CASSIDY AND THE SUNDANCE KID has everything going for it—engaging performances, beautiful atmosphere and location photography—except a story. Pleasant enough but ultimately disappointing. [PG]▼

Butch Cassidy and the Sundance Kid (1969) **C-112m.** **** D: George Roy Hill. Paul Newman, Robert Redford, Katharine Ross, Strother Martin, Henry Jones, Jeff Corey, George Furth, Cloris Leachman, Ted Cassidy, Kenneth Mars, Christopher Lloyd. Delightful seriocomic character study masquerading as a Western; outlaws Newman and Redford are pursued by relentless but remote sheriff's posse. Many memorable vignettes. Won Oscars for Cinematography (Conrad Hall), Original Score (Burt Bacharach), Song, "Raindrops Keep Fallin' On My

Head'' (Bacharach and Hal David), and William Goldman's original screenplay, which brims over with sharp dialogue. Look for Sam Elliott as a card player. Followed a decade later by a prequel, BUTCH AND SUNDANCE: THE EARLY DAYS. Then in 1976 Ross returned as Etta Place in TVM WANTED: THE SUNDANCE WOMAN (aka MRS. SUNDANCE RIDES AGAIN). Panavision. [PG]▼●◗

Butcher, The SEE: **Le Boucher**

Butcher Boy, The (1997-U.S.-Irish) **C-106m.** ***½ D: Neil Jordan. Stephen Rea, Fiona Shaw, Eamonn Owens, Alan Boyle, Andrew Fullerton, Aisling O'Sullivan, Ian Hart, Sinéad O'Connor, Milo O'Shea, Brendan Gleeson. Arresting film about an Irish boy who doesn't have a chance in life: his father is a perpetual drunk, his mother a mentally fragile soul. Yet he greets the world with bravado and the gift of gab; the only problem is, he's deranged. Bold, darkly (even absurdly) comic, hallucinatory at times, hiding its heartrending truths behind a glib facade—just like its hero. A true original. Written by Jordan and Patrick McCabe, from the latter's novel; McCabe also appears as the town drunk, Jimmy the Skite. [R]▼●

Butcher's Wife, The (1991) **C-105m.** ** D: Terry Hughes. Demi Moore, Jeff Daniels, George Dzundza, Mary Steenburgen, Frances McDormand, Margaret Colin, Max Perlich, Miriam Margolyes, Christopher Durang, Diane Salinger. North Carolina clairvoyant marries a Greenwich Village butcher, then begins dispensing advice: to a lesbian boutique owner, a spinsterish choir director, a soap opera actress and more. So strange—starting with Moore's goldilocks—that it almost compels a glance. Only Steenburgen, though, seems thoroughly in the swing of this comedy's intended whimsy. [PG-13]▼●

Butley (1974-British) **C-127m.** **** D: Harold Pinter. Alan Bates, Jessica Tandy, Richard O'Callaghan, Susan Engel, Georgina Hale. Bates is superb in American Film Theatre presentation, recreating his 1971 London stage role as a teacher with sexual and other problems. Playwright Pinter made his film directing debut with this outrageous comedy by Simon Gray. [R]▼

But Not for Me (1959) **105m.** *** D: Walter Lang. Clark Gable, Carroll Baker, Lilli Palmer, Barry Coe, Lee J. Cobb, Thomas Gomez, Charles Lane. Chic remake of Samson Raphaelson's ACCENT ON YOUTH. 22-year-old secretary/aspiring actress Baker falls for her has-been theatrical-producer boss (Gable), who won't admit he's on the dark side of 50. Palmer is his wily ex-wife, Cobb a faded playwright. VistaVision.▼

Buttercup Chain, The (1971-British) **C-95m.** BOMB D: Robert Ellis Miller. Hywel Bennett, Leigh Taylor-Young, Jane Asher, Sven-Bertil Taube, Clive Revill, Michael Elphick. Cousins are raised together and find they needn't stop at kissing. Beautifully photographed in Spain, Sweden, and London; otherwise, an atrocity. Panavision. [R]

Butterfield 8 (1960) **C-109m.** **½ D: Daniel Mann. Elizabeth Taylor, Laurence Harvey, Eddie Fisher, Dina Merrill, Mildred Dunnock, Susan Oliver, Betty Field, Jeffrey Lynn, Kay Medford. Adaptation of O'Hara novel substitutes clichéd ending in tale of high-class prostitute wanting to go straight, convincing herself she's found Mr. Right. Film's major assets: great supporting cast and old-style performance by Taylor, who won Oscar. CinemaScope. ▼●

Butterflies Are Free (1972) **C-109m.** *** D: Milton Katselas. Goldie Hawn, Edward Albert, Eileen Heckart, Mike Warren, Paul Michael Glaser. Filmization of Leonard Gershe's Broadway play detailing blind boy's romance with kookie next-door neighbor (Hawn) and inevitable showdown with his overpossessive mother. Good light entertainment; Heckart won Best Supporting Actress Oscar. [PG] ▼●

Butterfly (1981-U.S.-Canadian) **C-107m.** ** D: Matt Cimber. Stacy Keach, Pia Zadora, Orson Welles, Lois Nettleton, Edward Albert, James Franciscus, Stuart Whitman, Ed McMahon, June Lockhart, Paul Hampton. Trashy soap opera, based on James M. Cain's novel, with gold-digging sex-kitten Zadora seducing Keach, who is supposed to be her dad. Welles steals the film—not difficult—as a judge. [R]▼●

Butterfly Affair, The (1970-French-Italian) **C-100m.** ** D: Jean Herman. Claudia Cardinale, Stanley Baker, Henri Charriere, Georges Arminel, Leroy Haynes, Joannin Hansen. Charriere (PAPILLON) wrote this diamond heist double cross story; he also co-stars as the mastermind, but his performance, like the picture, is routine. Claudia, at her sexiest, adds some bright moments. Original title: POPSY POP. [PG]▼

Buy & Cell (1989) **C-95m.** *½ D: Robert Boris. Robert Carradine, Michael Winslow, Malcolm McDowell, Lise Cutter, Randall "Tex" Cobb, Roddy Piper, Ben Vereen, Fred Travalena, Tony Plana, Michael Goodwin. Uninteresting would-be comedy set in prison, where a framed stockbroker secretly sets up a multi-million-dollar business with the help of stereotyped inmates. Shot in Italy, set in U.S. [R]▼●

Buy Me That Town (1941) **70m.** **½ D: Eugene Forde. Lloyd Nolan, Constance Moore, Albert Dekker, Sheldon Leonard, Barbara Allen (Vera Vague), Warren Hymer, Edward Brophy, Horace MacMahon, Russell Hicks. Clever little "B" comedy-drama about gangster (Nolan) who actually buys a bankrupt little village; he plans to use it as a hideout for law-breaker pals, but eventually becomes more civic-minded. Amusing and observant, with great cast full of veteran tough guys.

Bwana Devil (1952) **C-79m.** *½ D: Arch Oboler. Robert Stack, Barbara Britton, Nigel Bruce, Paul McVey. Dud actioner was sparked theatrically as first commercial 3-D feature; man-eating lions set their teeth on railway workers in Africa.

By Candlelight (1934) **70m.** ** D: James Whale. Paul Lukas, Elissa Landi, Nils Asther, Dorothy Revier, Lawrence Grant, Esther Ralston. Typical Continental fluff about valet who poses as his master to woo woman he believes is a countess. Leaden Lukas is so wrong for the part that he almost sinks the film, but a few Whale touches make it watchable; buffs may find it more to taste.

By Dawn's Early Light (1990) **C-100m. TVM** D: Jack Sholder. Powers Boothe, Rebecca De Mornay, James Earl Jones, Martin Landau, Darren McGavin, Rip Torn, Peter MacNicol. Cold War thriller (one of the last) about the political and military debate as the button is about to be pushed initiating nuclear war: an unidentified missile detonates over a Russian city causing the USSR to launch an attack against the U.S. Taut adaptation (by Bruce Gilbert) of William Prochnau's novel, *Trinity's Child.* Made for cable. Above average.▼●

By Design (1981-Canadian) **C-88m** ** D: Claude Jutra. Patty Duke Astin, Sara Botsford, Saul Rubinek, Sonia Zimmer. Lesbian fashion designer Astin decides she wants to be a mother. Potentially interesting subject matter is awkwardly handled; one of Astin's few bad performances.▼

Bye Bye Birdie (1963) **C-112m.** *** D: George Sidney. Janet Leigh, Dick Van Dyke, Ann-Margret, Maureen Stapleton, Paul Lynde, Jesse Pearson, Bobby Rydell, Ed Sullivan. Entertaining version of Broadway musical about drafted rock 'n' roll idol coming to small town to give "one last kiss" to one of his adoring fans. Lynde stands out as Ann-Margret's father. Remade for TV in 1995 with Jason Alexander and Vanessa Williams. Panavision. ▼●

Bye Bye Blues (1989-Canadian) **C-116m.** *** D: Anne Wheeler. Rebecca Jenkins, Luke Reilly, Stuart Margolin, Kate Reid, Michael Ontkean, Wayne Robson, Robyn Stevan. Affectionate WW2 drama of Jenkins, proper, protected, and pregnant, who's stationed with her doctor-husband in India. Intensely moving story of how war affects the lives of those on the home front; if this doesn't give your tear ducts a workout, nothing will. Loosely based on the life of Wheeler's mother and a nice companion piece to her short documentary-drama, A WAR STORY. [PG]▼

Bye Bye Braverman (1968) **C-109m.** **½ D: Sidney Lumet. George Segal, Jack Warden, Joseph Wiseman, Sorrell Booke, Jessica Walter, Phyllis Newman, Zohra Lampert, Godfrey Cambridge, Alan King. To paraphrase one of the characters, in the sum of its many parts this yields pleasure of a kind; but fuzzy, unresolved story of four Jewish intellectuals on their way to a friend's funeral is ultimately disappointing.

Bye Bye Brazil (1980-Brazil) **C-110m.** *** D: Carlos Diegues. Jose Wilker, Betty Faria, Fabio Junior, Zaira Zambelli. Bawdy comedy-drama about a troupe of traveling entertainers is really a travelogue of the country, from jungles to honky-tonk port towns. Not quite the total sensual pleasure of DONA FLOR AND HER TWO HUSBANDS, but still one of the best Brazilian imports. [R]▼●

Bye Bye, Love (1995) **C-106m.** ** D: Sam Weisman. Matthew Modine, Randy Quaid, Paul Reiser, Janeane Garofalo, Rob Reiner, Amy Brenneman, Eliza Dushku, Ed Flanders, Maria Pitillo, Lindsay Crouse, Johnny Whitworth, Ross Malinger, Pamela Dillman, Brad Hall. Mediocre seriocomedy about three dads, devoted to their kids, trying to make their way through divorcehood. Some sincere moments and occasional comic insights are washed away in a sea of sappiness. Garofalo, as Quaid's hilarious date from hell, almost makes the film worth watching. [PG-13]▼●

Bye Bye Monkey (1978-French-Italian) **C-114m.** BOMB D: Marco Ferreri. Gérard Depardieu, Marcello Mastroianni, Gail Lawrence (Abigail Clayton), James Coco, Geraldine Fitzgerald, Mimsy Farmer, Clarence Muse. Sardonic, bleak comedy about a group of misfits in a decrepit area of Manhattan where rats seem about to displace humanity in all the buildings. Depardieu, irresistible to women as always, prefers the company of a chimpanzee he finds near the carcass of a giant ape, presumably left over from the remake of KING KONG. Good cast is wasted, including Fitzgerald, who also has a love scene with Depardieu. Filmed in English in N.Y.C.▼●◗

By Love Possessed (1961) **C-115m.** **½ D: John Sturges. Lana Turner, Efrem Zimbalist, Jr., Jason Robards, Jr., George Hamilton, Thomas Mitchell, Susan Kohner, Barbara Bel Geddes, Everett Sloane, Carroll O'Connor. Ultraglossy, well-cast but empty soaper, in which neurotic Turner commences an affair with Zimbalist, the law partner of her impotent husband (Robards). Based on—but not true to—the James Gould Cozzens novel.▼●

By the Book SEE: **Renaissance Man**

By the Light of the Silvery Moon (1953) **C-102m.** **½ D: David Butler. Doris Day, Gordon MacRae, Leon Ames, Rosemary DeCamp, Mary Wickes, Billy Gray. Set in post WW1, this Booth Tarkington story finds returning soldier MacRae and fiancée

Day readjusting to life. Ames wonderful as father thought to be romancing French actress, and Wickes delightful as family maid. Merv Griffin pops up in the closing scene. This old-fashioned musical was a sequel to ON MOONLIGHT BAY.▼●

By the Sword (1993) **C-91m.** *½ D: Jeremy Kagan, John McDonald. F. Murray Abraham, Eric Roberts, Mia Sara, Chris Rydell, Elaine Kagan, Brett Cullen, Doug Wert, Stoney Jackson. By-the-numbers revenge story set in the world of competitive fencing. Roberts is intense as usual, but the story isn't. If it's fencing you want, rent an Errol Flynn movie. Super 35. [R]▼

Cabaret (1972) **C-128m.** ***½ D: Bob Fosse. Liza Minnelli, Michael York, Helmut Griem, Joel Grey, Fritz Wepper, Marisa Berenson. Stylish film based on Fred Ebb-John Kander Broadway musical, from John van Druten's play *I Am a Camera* (filmed before in 1955), now more a vehicle for Minnelli in her Oscar-winning performance as Sally Bowles, American girl caught up in phony glitter of pre-war Berlin. Song numbers counterpoint dramatic narrative, including newly written "The Money Song," great duet for Minnelli and Oscar-winner Grey. Screenplay by Jay Presson Allen; the story's genesis was Christopher Isherwood's book *Goodbye to Berlin*. Won eight Academy Awards in all, including Director, Cinematography (Geoffrey Unsworth) and Score Adaptation (Ralph Burns). [PG]▼●◗

Cabaret Balkan (1998-Yugoslavian-French) **C-102m.** **½ D: Goran Paskaljevic. Miki Manojlovic, Sergei Trifunovic, Mirjana Jokovic, Lazar Ristovski. In the strife-torn city of Belgrade, all sense of logic and order has evaporated, leaving a society so desperate and stressed-out that even a casual encounter may lead to violence. Powerful series of vignettes—sometimes grim, sometimes absurdly funny—but the film goes on a while after it's made its point. Originally shown in Europe as THE POWDER KEG.▼

Cabin Boy (1994) **C-80m.** **½ D: Adam Resnick. Chris Elliott, Ritch Brinkley, James Gammon, Brian Doyle-Murray, Brion James, Melora Walters, Ann Magnuson, Russ Tamblyn, Ricki Lake, Andy Richter. Strange, fitfully amusing comedy of snobby "Fancy Lad" Elliott who accidentally boards a fishing boat with hard-nosed seamen . . . and becomes a man. Film's success depends largely on your tolerance for Elliott's obnoxious comic persona, but there are many clever jokes and an endearingly (and intentionally) tacky visual approach. Several good cameos, particularly one from Elliott's former boss David Letterman—billed as Earl Hofert. Elliott cowrote the film's story. Produced by Tim Burton. [PG-13]▼●

Cabinet of Caligari, The (1962) **104m.** **½ D: Roger Kay. Dan O'Herlihy, Glynis Johns, Richard Davalos, Lawrence Dobkin, Estelle Winwood, J. Pat O'Malley. Unimaginative remake of the 1919 German classic, removing all the mystery-exotic appeal; Johns tries hard as lady in ornate modern home confronted by O'Herlihy's sinister Caligari; many bizarre scenes. Written by Robert Bloch. CinemaScope.

Cabinet of Dr. Caligari, The (1919-German) **69m.** ***½ D: Robert Wiene. Werner Krauss, Conrad Veidt, Lil Dagover. Somewhat stiff but still fascinating German Expressionist film about "magician" Caligari and hypnotic victim who carries out his evil bidding. Landmark film still impresses audiences today.▼●◗

Cabin in the Cotton, The (1932) **77m.** **½ D: Michael Curtiz. Richard Barthelmess, Dorothy Jordan, Bette Davis, Hardie Albright, David Landau, Berton Churchill, Henry B. Walthall, Tully Marshall. Dated melodrama of sharecroppers, with earnest Barthelmess almost led to ruin by Southern belle Davis; exaggerated, but interesting. Bette's immortal line: "Ah'd like to kiss ya, but Ah jes' washed mah hair."▼

Cabin in the Sky (1943) **100m.** *** D: Vincente Minnelli. Eddie "Rochester" Anderson, Lena Horne, Ethel Waters, Louis Armstrong, Rex Ingram, Duke Ellington and His Orchestra, The Hall Johnson Choir. Stellar black cast in winning (if somewhat racist) musical fable about forces of good and evil vying for the soul of Little Joe (Anderson). John Bubbles' dancing, Waters singing "Happiness Is a Thing Called Joe" (written for the film) among musical highlights. First feature for Minnelli (who, with Waters and Ingram, came from the Broadway production). ▼●

Cabiria (1914-Italian) **148m.** ***½ D: Piero Fosco (Giovanni Pastrone). Italia Almirante Manzini, Lidia Quaranta, Bartolomeo Pagano, Umberto Mozzato, Vitale de Stefano. Still-impressive silent epic, a landmark film for its use of lighting and camera movement, as well as its sheer spectacle. The story chronicles the plight of the title character (Quaranta), a Sicilian slave girl, during the Second Punic War. Pastrone coscripted with poet Gabriele D'Annunzio, who penned those lushly composed intertitles. This also served as an inspiration to D. W. Griffith, particularly for the Babylonian sequence of INTOLERANCE.▼●

Cable Guy, The (1996) **C-94m.** **½ D: Ben Stiller. Jim Carrey, Matthew Broderick, Leslie Mann, George Segal, Diane Baker, Jack Black, Eric Roberts, Janeane Garofalo, Andy Dick, Charles Napier. Black comedy about a cable TV installer who forces his friendship onto a vulnerable customer who's just moved out of his girlfriend's apartment. Many clever, funny scenes, but film wavers between comedy and a darker, more serious tone, which—while also interesting—keeps us off-balance. Repeated digs at TV are among the brightest moments; director Stiller has a funny recurring cameo. Super 35. [PG-13]▼●◗

Caboblanco (1980) **C-87m.** ** D: J. Lee Thompson. Charles Bronson, Jason Robards, Dominique Sanda, Fernando Rey, Simon MacCorkindale, Camilla Sparv, Gilbert Roland, Denny Miller. Murky ripoff of CASABLANCA, with Bronson a barkeeper in Peru. Robards plays a Nazi, Rey a police captain, Sanda a Frenchwoman searching for her lover. Panavision. [R]▼◗

Cactus (1986-Australian) **C-93m.** **½ D: Paul Cox. Isabelle Huppert, Robert Menzies, Norman Kaye, Monica Maughan, Banduk Marika. Slow, deliberately paced story of Huppert's agony when her sight is impaired in an auto mishap and her growing relationship with blind Menzies. Of interest only when it sticks to the story, which isn't often enough.▼

Cactus Flower (1969) **C-103m.** **½ D: Gene Saks. Walter Matthau, Ingrid Bergman, Goldie Hawn, Jack Weston, Rick Lenz, Vito Scotti, Irene Hervey. Glossy comedy was pretty thin for Broadway, even thinner on film, with Bergman as prim nurse to dentist Matthau who blossoms when she realizes she's in love with him. Best moments belong to Hawn, who won Oscar for her first big role. [M/PG]▼●

Caddie (1976-Australian) **C-107m.** **½ D: Donald Crombie. Helen Morse, Takis Emmanuel, Jack Thompson, Jacki Weaver, Melissa Jaffer. Adaptation of a popular Australian autobiography set in the late '20s and early '30s, telling story of an independent-minded young woman determined to succeed on her own, despite the pressure of having two children to raise. Moments of insight and originality give way too often to cliché and overriding blandness. Morse is fine in lead. ▼

Caddy, The (1953) **95m.** *½ D: Norman Taurog. Dean Martin, Jerry Lewis, Donna Reed, Fred Clark, Barbara Bates, Joseph Calleia. Weak Martin & Lewis vehicle about golf-nut Jerry coaching Dean to be a champion player. Dean sings "That's Amore." ▼

Caddyshack (1980) **C-98m.** ** D: Harold Ramis. Chevy Chase, Rodney Dangerfield, Ted Knight, Michael O'Keefe, Bill Murray, Cindy Morgan, Sarah Holcomb, Scott Colomby, Brian Doyle-Murray, Chuck E. Rodent. ANIMAL HOUSE-type hijinks at a posh country club; another comedy where irreverence and destruction are a substitute for humor. Saving grace is Dangerfield, whose opening scenes are sidesplittingly funny. Followed by a sequel. [R]▼●◗

Caddyshack II (1988) **C-99m.** ** D: Allan Arkush. Jackie Mason, Dyan Cannon, Robert Stack, Dina Merrill, Chevy Chase, Dan Aykroyd, Randy Quaid, Jessica Lundy, Jonathan Silverman, Chynna Phillips, Brian McNamara. In-name-only sequel to 1980 hit gets a big boost from Mason, extremely winning in the role of a plain-talking, self-made millionaire whose daughter wants acceptance by the snooty crowd at a local country club. Unfortunately, film runs out of script (and laughs) after a half hour. [PG]▼●◗

Cadence (1991) **C-97m.** *½ D: Martin Sheen. Charlie Sheen, Martin Sheen, Larry Fishburne, Michael Beach, Ramon Estevez, John Toles-Bey, Blu Mankuma, Harry Stewart, James Marshall. U.S. soldier Charlie lands in a West German brig, the lone white among a group of black prisoners; conflict, however, centers on warden Martin, who's slowly coming apart at the seams. Sheen family enterprise is overwrought and insignificant, with just one compelling scene: the brigmates march in jivey cadence to their own rendition of Sam Cooke's "Chain Gang." Would Ernie Borgnine's Fatso Judson have allowed this in FROM HERE TO ETERNITY? [PG-13]▼●

Cadillac Man (1990) **C-97m.** **½ D: Roger Donaldson. Robin Williams, Tim Robbins, Pamela Reed, Fran Drescher, Zack Norman, Annabella Sciorra, Lori Petty, Paul Guilfoyle, Bill Nelson, Eddie Jones, Judith Hoag. Williams is terrific, as usual, playing an aggressive car salesman who may lose his job, his mistress, his other girlfriend, his Mafioso protector, and his daughter all during one eventful weekend. Wildly uneven film swings from comedy to melodrama, dragging and then picking up again. Elaine Stritch appears unbilled as a grieving widow. [R]▼●

Cadillac Ranch (1996) **C-95m.** **½ D: Lisa Gottlieb. Suzy Amis, Renee Humphrey, Caroleen Feeney, Linden Ashby, Christopher Lloyd, Jim Metzler. Amiable tale of three sisters who, despite some long-time friction, band together to find a cache of money left behind by their Daddy when they were just kids . . . tracked, all the while, by bad guy Lloyd. Likable performances by the female trio boost this modest Texas-made production. Panavision. [R]▼

Caesar and Cleopatra (1946-British) **C-134m.** ** D: Gabriel Pascal. Claude Rains, Vivien Leigh, Stewart Granger, Flora Robson, Francis L. Sullivan, Cecil Parker. Two fine stars suffer through static, boring rendition of George Bernard Shaw's play, which seems to go on forever. Occasional wit and intrigue can't keep this afloat.▼

Cafe au Lait (1994-French) **C-94m.** *** D: Mathieu Kassovitz. Julie Mauduech, Hubert Kounde, Mathieu Kassovitz. Kassovitz' first feature is the SHE'S GOTTA HAVE IT/JULES AND JIM-like story of a young, pregnant Parisian (Mauduech) who is uncertain which of her boyfriends is the father. Is it the African Muslim law student (Kounde)? Or the Jewish bicycle messenger (played by the director)? Sweetly funny, and a heartening look at contemporary relations between the races. Kassovitz also scripted.▼

Cafe Express (1981-Italian) **C-89m.** **½ D: Nanni Loy. Nino Manfredi, Adolfo Celi, Vittorio Mezzogiorno, Luigi Basagaluppi, Silvio Spaccesi. Manfredi, virtually repeating his characterization in BREAD AND CHOCOLATE, is a Neapolitan working man illegally selling coffee on the Milan to Naples train. Sometimes funny and profound, more often trite. Manfredi, as usual, is fine. Originally ran 105m.▼

Cafe Metropole (1937) **84m.** **½ D: Edward H. Griffith. Loretta Young, Tyrone Power, Adolphe Menjou, Gregory Ratoff, Charles Winninger, Helen Westley. Young is courted by penniless playboy Power, who's passing bad checks and posing as a Russian prince. OK comedy, from a story by Ratoff.

Cafe Society (1939) **83m.** **½ D: Edward H. Griffith. Madeleine Carroll, Fred MacMurray, Shirley Ross, Jessie Ralph, Claude Gillingwater. This time around Carroll chases MacMurray to win husband on a bet; chic fluff.

Cafe Society (1995) **C/B&W-107m.** *** D: Raymond De Felitta. Frank Whaley, Peter Gallagher, Lara Flynn Boyle, John Spencer, Anna Thomson, David Patrick Kelly, Christopher Murney, Richard B. Shull, Paul Guilfoyle, Alan North, Kelly Bishop, Zach Grenier. Atmospheric, fact-based account, set in 1952, about Mickey Jelke (Whaley), a poor little rich boy set to inherit $5 million. Jelke hobnobs with N.Y.C. cafe society, and thinks nothing of pimping, just for the fun of it. Gallagher is the vice cop who's determined to nail him; Boyle (who makes a great noir heroine) is the woman with whom Jelke becomes involved, on several levels. De Felitta, working with a low budget, nonetheless creates an impressive and authentic period feel. [R]▼

Cage, The (1978) SEE: **Mafu Cage, The**

Cage (1989) **C-101m.** BOMB D: Lang Elliott. Lou Ferrigno, Reb Brown, Michael Dante, Mike Moroff, Marilyn Tokuda, James Shigeta, Al Ruscio. Pointless, violent film provides viewers with the human equivalent of a cockfight as Ferrigno and Brown go at it in the Asian "sport" of cage fighting. A better title might have been THE INCREDIBLE HOKUM. [R]▼●

Caged (1950) **96m.** *** D: John Cromwell. Eleanor Parker, Agnes Moorehead, Ellen Corby, Hope Emerson, Jan Sterling, Jane Darwell, Gertrude Michael. Remarkable performances in stark record of Parker going to prison and becoming hardened criminal after exposure to brutal jail life. Remade as HOUSE OF WOMEN.

Caged Fury (1948) **60m.** ** D: William Berke. Richard Denning, Sheila Ryan, Mary Beth Hughes, Buster Crabbe. Not bad low-budgeter about mad killer on the loose in a circus.▼

Caged Heat (1974) **C-84m.** **½ D: Jonathan Demme. Juanita Brown, Erica Gavin, Roberta Collins, Rainbeaux Smith, Barbara Steele, Toby Carr-Rafelson. Demme's first feature is tongue-in-cheek but otherwise typical women's prison flick, chiefly novel for being set in the U.S. instead of some banana republic, plus neat turn by Steele as wheelchair-bound warden. Has a sizable cult following. Aka RENEGADE GIRLS. [R]▼

Cage of Gold (1950-British) **83m.** **½ D: Basil Dearden. Jean Simmons, David Farrar, James Donald, Madeleine Lebeau, Herbert Lom, Bernard Lee. Fair suspense yarn with sleazy Farrar, supposedly dead in a plane crash, attempting to blackmail wife Simmons, now remarried to doctor Donald.

Cahill—United States Marshal (1973) **C-103m.** ** D: Andrew V. McLaglen. John Wayne, George Kennedy, Gary Grimes, Neville Brand, Marie Windsor, Harry Carey, Jr. Marshal Wayne's law enforcement duties are complicated as one of his sons threatens to enter a life of crime; routine, violent Western suffers from the same kind of sermonizing that plagued most of the Duke's later films. Panavision. [PG]▼●

Cain and Mabel (1936) **90m.** ** D: Lloyd Bacon. Marion Davies, Clark Gable, David Carlyle (Robert Paige), Allen Jenkins, Roscoe Karns, Walter Catlett, Hobart Cavanaugh, Ruth Donnelly, Pert Kelton. Publicist concocts phony romance between Broadway star Davies (who's miscast) and heavyweight champ Gable—who happen to despise one another. Gargantuan production numbers add nothing to stale plot. Rescued somewhat by the snappy one-liners delivered by the supporting cast.

Caine Mutiny, The (1954) **C-125m.** **** D: Edward Dmytryk. Humphrey Bogart, Jose Ferrer, Van Johnson, Robert Francis, May Wynn, Fred MacMurray, E.G. Marshall, Lee Marvin, Tom Tully, Claude Akins. Naval officers Johnson and Francis mutiny against paranoid, unpopular Capt. Queeg (Bogart) and are court-martialed in this exciting adaptation (by Stanley Roberts) of Herman Wouk's Pulitzer Prize novel. Wartime mutiny scene during typhoon still packs a wallop. Followed by a TVM in 1988.▼●◗

Caine Mutiny Court-Martial, The (1988) **C-100m. TVM** D: Robert Altman. Eric Bogosian, Jeff Daniels, Brad Davis, Peter Gallagher, Michael Murphy, Kevin J.

O'Connor, Daniel Jenkins. Fine restaging of Herman Wouk's 1953 play, the heart of his Pulitzer Prize novel. Bogosian and Davis stand out in a fine ensemble as Defense Attorney Barney Greenwald and Lt. Cmdr. Phillip Queeg. Kudos to director Altman. Above average.▼●

Cairo (1942) **101m.** ** D: W.S. Van Dyke II. Jeanette MacDonald, Robert Young, Ethel Waters, Reginald Owen, Lionel Atwill, Dooley Wilson. Musi-comedy spoof of WW2 spy films is strained, although stars are pleasant and production is well-mounted.▼

Cairo (1963-British) **91m.** **½ D: Wolf Rilla. George Sanders, Richard Johnson, Faten Hamama, John Meillon, Eric Pohlmann, Walter Rilla. Mediocre remake of THE ASPHALT JUNGLE with the "surefire" caper aiming to steal King Tut's treasures from the Cairo Museum.

Cal (1984-British) **C-102m.** *** D: Pat O'Connor. Helen Mirren, John Lynch, Donal McCann, John Kavanagh, Ray McAnally, Stevan Rimkus, Kitty Gibson. Intelligent drama of modern-day Northern Ireland, with Lynch, 19, falling for older widow Mirren—despite his IRA involvement with her husband's murder. Strong performances, especially by Mirren; produced by David Puttnam. [R]▼

Calaboose SEE: **Dudes Are Pretty People**

Calamity Jane (1953) **C-101m.** *** D: David Butler. Doris Day, Howard Keel, Allyn (Ann) McLerie, Philip Carey, Gale Robbins, Dick Wesson, Paul Harvey. Doris is irresistible as the bombastic, rootin'-tootin' title character in this lively musical, with Keel as Wild Bill Hickok, who only begins to realize his feelings for her when she makes a stab at becoming more "feminine." Sammy Fain–Paul Francis Webster score includes the Oscar-winning "Secret Love." Jane Alexander later played Calamity in a 1984 TV movie. ▼●

Calamity Jane and Sam Bass (1949) **C-85m.** *½ D: George Sherman. Yvonne De Carlo, Howard Duff, Dorothy Hart, Lloyd Bridges, Milburn Stone. Tattered retelling of 19th-century cowgirl and Texas outlaw, with De Carlo and Duff a disinterested duo.

Calcutta (1947) **83m.** **½ D: John Farrow. Alan Ladd, Gail Russell, William Bendix, June Duprez, Lowell Gilmore. Standard actioner with pilot Ladd avenging friend's murder.

Calendar (1993-Canadian-Armenian) **C-75m.** ** D: Atom Egoyan. Arsinée Khanjian, Ashot Adamian, Atom Egoyan. A photographer (Egoyan) and his wife (Khanjian) travel from Canada to Armenia to shoot photos of historical churches for inclusion on a wall calendar; as he looks through his lens, his marriage falls apart before his eyes as his mate comes in touch with her roots and falls for their guide. Some intriguing ideas are at work here, but the film is much like an out-of-focus snapshot and too loosely structured to be effective. Egoyan and Khanjian are married off screen.▼

Calendar Girl (1993) **C-90m.** ** D: John Whitesell. Jason Priestley, Gabriel Olds, Jerry O'Connell, Joe Pantoliano, Steve Railsback, Kurt Fuller, Stephen Tobolowsky, Emily Warfield, Maxwell Caulfield, Stephanie Anderson, Chubby Checker. Pat, overly familiar coming-of-age tale of three high school grads who head off to L.A. in 1962 to seek out their idol, Marilyn Monroe. Ultimately harmless, but you've seen it a million times before. One of the executive producers was Penny Marshall. [PG-13] ▼●

California (1946) **C-97m.** **½ D: John Farrow. Barbara Stanwyck, Ray Milland, Barry Fitzgerald, Albert Dekker, Anthony Quinn, Julia Faye, George Coulouris. Ray is a wagonmaster with a past, Stanwyck a shady gal who makes good in this elaborately ordinary Western.

California Conquest (1952) **C-79m.** **½ D. Lew Landers. Cornel Wilde, Teresa Wright, John Dehner, Hank Patterson. Film deals with sidelight of American history. Californian Wilde et al. under Spanish control help their ally against Russian attempt to confiscate the territory.

California Dolls, The SEE: **... All the Marbles**

California Dreaming (1979) **C-92m.** **½ D: John Hancock. Dennis Christopher, Glynnis O'Connor, Seymour Cassel, Dorothy Tristan, John Calvin, Tanya Roberts, Todd Susman, Alice Playten, Ned Wynn, Jimmy Van Patten, Stacey Nelkin, Marshall Efron. Revisionist beach party movie finds nerd Christopher trying desperately to fit in with the surfing crowd, blind to the fact that their lives are even emptier than his. Strong drama sometimes bites off more than it can chew, but overall fairly compelling and surprisingly erotic; Wynn also wrote the screenplay. [R]▼

California Split (1974) **C-108m.** **½ D: Robert Altman. George Segal, Elliott Gould, Ann Prentiss, Gwen Welles, Joseph Walsh, Bert Remsen, Jeff Goldblum. Realistic but rambling look at two compulsive gamblers, their strange lifestyles, and the emptiness of winning. Altman's multi-channel soundtrack only adds to the muddle. Panavision. [R]

California Straight Ahead (1937) **67m.** ** D: Arthur Lubin. John Wayne, Louise Latimer, Robert McWade, Theodore Von Eltz, Tully Marshall. Good little actioner with Wayne competing in cross-country race between trucks and train.

California Suite (1978) **C-103m.** *** D: Herbert Ross. Jane Fonda, Alan Alda, Maggie Smith, Michael Caine, Walter Matthau, Elaine May, Richard Pryor, Bill

Cosby, Gloria Gifford, Sheila Frazier, Herb Edelman, Denise Galik. Four Neil Simon skits set at the Beverly Hills Hotel (and adapted from his Broadway hit). Oscar-winning Smith and husband Caine as gently bickering Britishers in town for Academy Awards come off best; Pryor and Cosby as unfunnily combative "friends" are the worst. Pleasant time-filler, with nice jazz score by Claude Bolling. [PG] ▼●

Caligula (1980) **C-156m.** *½ D: Tinto Brass. Malcolm McDowell, Peter O'Toole, Teresa Ann Savoy, Helen Mirren, John Gielgud, Guido Mannari. Filmdom's first $15 million porno (to say nothing of home) movie, produced by *Penthouse* and set in Rome in the 1st century A.G. (After Guccione), follows ruthless ruler through endless series of decapitations and disembowelings. Chutzpah and six minutes of not-bad hard-core footage earn this half a star for the faithful, but most viewers will be rightfully repelled. And besides, Jay Robinson does much better by the title character in THE ROBE and DEMETRIUS AND THE GLADIATORS. Reissued in 105m., R-rated version—which is considerably changed. [R—edited from original unrated version] ▼●◗

Call a Messenger (1939) **65m.** ** D: Arthur Lubin. Billy Halop, Huntz Hall, William Benedict, David Gorcey, Robert Armstrong, Buster Crabbe, Anne Nagel, Victor Jory, El Brendel, Mary Carlisle. Well-cast *Little Tough Guys* outing. Halop gets a job as a junior mailman and tangles with gangsters in this typical crime yarn. Crabbe makes an impressive heavy, complete with mustache.

Callan (1974-British) **C-106m.** **½ D: Don Sharp. Edward Woodward, Eric Porter, Carl Mohner, Catherine Schell, Peter Egan. Adequate drama of aging secret agent Woodward, demoted because he cares too much about his adversaries, assigned to kill a German businessman. Woodward had previously played same role on British TV. Video title: THE NEUTRALIZER.▼

Callaway Went Thataway (1951) **81m.** **½ D: Norman Panama, Melvin Frank. Fred MacMurray, Dorothy McGuire, Howard Keel, Jesse White, Fay Roope, Natalie Schafer, Stan Freberg. Gentle spoof of early-TV "Hopalong Cassidy" craze, with Keel as lookalike who impersonates veteran cowboy star for promotional purposes; good fun until it starts getting serious. Several MGM stars make cameo appearances.

Caller, The (1989) **C-97m.** ** D: Arthur Allan Seidelman. Malcolm McDowell, Madolyn Smith. Strange two-character mystery set mostly in an isolated cabin in the woods; the verbal sparring partners are not what they seem to be. Partly effective, but goes on much too long; might have worked as a *Twilight Zone* episode. Shot in Italy in 1987. [R]▼

Call Her Savage (1932) **88m.** **½ D: John Francis Dillon. Clara Bow, Gilbert Roland, Thelma Todd, Monroe Owsley, Estelle Taylor, Russell Simpson, Margaret Livingston. Wild comeback vehicle for indefatigable Clara Bow ranges from sharp comedy to teary-eyed soap opera, but it's never dull. Bow is amazingly sensual throughout, matched in brief confrontations with Todd; great fun.

Call Him Mr. Shatter (1974-British) **C-90m.** *½ D: Michael Carreras. Stuart Whitman, Ti Lung, Lily Li, Peter Cushing, Anton Diffring. Hammer's entry into the Kung Fu market, begun by Monte Hellman, stars Whitman as a burned-out hit man on assignment in Hong Kong. Plenty of action, but nothing to hold it together; presence of three cinematographers is a tip-off to extensive production woes. Aka SHATTER. [R]▼●

Calling Bulldog Drummond (1951-U.S.-British) **80m.** **½ D: Victor Saville. Walter Pidgeon, Margaret Leighton, Robert Beatty, David Tomlinson, Peggy Evans, Charles Victor, Bernard Lee. Pidgeon makes a satisfactory Drummond as the sleuth is called out of retirement to help Scotland Yard nab a gang of sophisticated thieves armed with military hardware. Starts well but bogs down in talk.

Calling Dr. Death (1943) **63m.** ** D: Reginald LeBorg. Lon Chaney, Jr., Ramsay Ames, Patricia Morison, J. Carrol Naish, David Bruce. Ultra-low-budget mystery about a neurologist who is tormented by the realization that he may have killed his unfaithful wife during a moment of madness. First of the *Inner Sanctum* series.▼

Calling Dr. Gillespie (1942) **84m.** **½ D: Harold S. Bucquet. Lionel Barrymore, Philip Dorn, Donna Reed, Phil Brown, Nat Pendleton, Alma Kruger, Mary Nash, Walter Kingsford, Charles Dingle, Nell Craig, Marie Blake, Jonathan Hale. With Lew Ayres gone, the series continues with Gillespie getting a new assistant (Dorn), while the crusty old sawbones himself is the target of a homicidal maniac. Enjoyable melodrama; look sharp for Ava Gardner.

Calling Dr. Kildare (1939) **86m.** **½ D: Harold S. Bucquet. Lew Ayres, Lionel Barrymore, Laraine Day, Lana Turner, Lynne Carver, Nat Pendleton, Samuel S. Hinds, Emma Dunn, Walter Kingsford, Marie Blake, Donald Barry. Efficient second entry in the series has Kildare in trouble with the police for treating a gangster and getting involved with the hood's cute sister (Turner).

Calling Homicide (1956) **61m.** *½ D: Edward Bernds. Bill Elliott, Don Haggerty, Kathleen Case, Myron Healey. Low-key detective yarn following detective Elliott's search for cop-killer.

Calling Northside 777 SEE: **Call Northside 777**

Calling Philo Vance (1940) **62m.** ** D: William Clemens. James Stephenson, Margot Stevenson, Henry O'Neill, Edward Brophy, Ralph Forbes, Martin Kosleck. Stephenson makes a refined (if sinister) Philo Vance, investigating the death of an aircraft manufacturer by foreign agents. Minor, but watchable, entry is virtually a scene-for-scene remake of THE KENNEL MURDER CASE, updated to wartime.

Call It a Day (1937) **89m.** ** D: Archie Mayo. Olivia de Havilland, Ian Hunter, Alice Brady, Anita Louise, Peggy Wood, Frieda Inescort, Roland Young, Bonita Granville. Tiresome trivia about a British family's comic trials and tribulations during the course of an average day.

Call It Murder SEE: **Midnight** (1934)

Call Me (1988) **C-96m.** **½ D: Sollace Mitchell. Patricia Charbonneau, Patti D'Arbanville, Sam Freed, Boyd Gaines, Stephen McHattie, Steve Buscemi, John Seitz, David Strathairn. Horny reporter saddled with a lackluster boyfriend begins receiving obscene phone calls, and almost finds herself enjoying the experience. Very well-acted by Charbonneau, but too many of the supporting roles are weakly cast; excessive melodrama detracts from what could have been a more compelling psychological study. [R]▼●

Call Me Bwana (1963) **C-103m.** ** D: Gordon Douglas. Bob Hope, Anita Ekberg, Edie Adams, Lionel Jeffries, Arnold Palmer. Hope and Adams on jungle safari encounter Ekberg and Jeffries and nothing much happens. The ladies are lovely.▼●

Call Me Madam (1953) **C-117m.** *** D: Walter Lang. Ethel Merman, Donald O'Connor, George Sanders, Vera-Ellen, Billy DeWolfe, Walter Slezak, Lilia Skala. Often stagy musical from Irving Berlin tuner based on Perle Mesta's life as Washington, D.C., hostess and Liechtenstein ambassadress. Merman is blowsy delight. Songs include "The Best Thing For You," "It's A Lovely Day Today," "You're Just in Love."

Call Me Mister (1951) **C-95m.** **½ D: Lloyd Bacon. Betty Grable, Dan Dailey, Danny Thomas, Dale Robertson, Benay Venuta, Richard Boone, Frank Fontaine, Jeffrey Hunter. Acceptable plot line helps buoy this musical. Soldier Dailey, based in Japan, goes AWOL to patch up marriage with Grable traveling with USO troupe. Bears little resemblance to the Broadway revue on which it's supposedly based. An unbilled Bobby Short sings "Going Home Train."

Call Northside 777 (1948) **111m.** ***½ D: Henry Hathaway. James Stewart, Richard Conte, Lee J. Cobb, Helen Walker, Moroni Olsen, E.G. Marshall. Absorbing drama of reporter Stewart convinced that convicted killer is innocent, trying to prove it; handled in semi-documentary style. Retitled: CALLING NORTHSIDE 777.▼●

Call of the Wild, The (1935) **81m.** *** D: William Wellman. Clark Gable, Loretta Young, Jack Oakie, Reginald Owen, Frank Conroy. More Hollywood than Jack London, this Yukon adventure/romance is lots of fun, and Owen a fine snarling villain. Original release was 95m. Remade in 1972 and as a TV movie in 1976, 1993, and 1997.

Call of the Wild (1972) **C-100m.** **½ D: Ken Annakin. Charlton Heston, Michele Mercier, Maria Rohm, Rik Battaglia. Lackluster version of the Jack London adventure classic, produced by a multinational film combine and wasting the talents of a diverse cast. One redeeming quality: the striking Finnish scenery. [PG]▼

Call of the Wild, The (1976) **C-100m. TVM** D: Jerry Jameson. John Beck, Bernard Fresson, John McLiam, Donald Moffat, Michael Pataki, Billy Green Bush, Penelope Windust, Johnny Tillotson. Stark but quite graphic remake of Jack London's 1903 tale of gold fever and adventure in the Klondike. Beck is eager greenhorn, Fresson is veteran prospector, but the star is sled dog named Buck, who faces the hazards of man as well as nature. Script by James Dickey. Above average.▼

Call of the Wild (1997) SEE: **Jack London's Call of the Wild**

Call Out the Marines (1942) **67m.** ** D: Frank Ryan, William Hamilton. Edmund Lowe, Victor McLaglen, Binnie Barnes, Paul Kelly, Dorothy Lovett, Franklin Pangborn. Tepid comedy, Lowe and McLaglen's last starring film together. The boys tangle with waterfront seductress Barnes while on the trail of spies. Several forgettable tunes (like "Zana Zaranda") to boot.▼

Call the Cops! SEE: **Find the Lady**

Call to Remember (1997) **C-100m. TVM** D: Jack Bender. Blythe Danner, Joe Mantegna, David Lascher, Kevin Segers, Joe Spano, Rita Zohar. Moving drama about two Holocaust survivors (not exactly typecast, one must admit) who found each other in America—and then learn, in the 1960s, that the woman's older son may have survived the death camps. Written by Max Eisenberg, based on his experience as the son of Holocaust survivors. Above average.▼

Caltiki, the Immortal Monster (1959-Italian) **76m.** ** D: Robert Hampton (Riccardo Freda). John Merivale, Didi Sullivan, Gerard Herter, Daniela Rocca. Set in Mexico, sci-fi has blob-ish fiend pursuing members of scientific expedition; poorly conceived but amusing. Photographed by Mario Bava.

Calypso Heat Wave (1957) **86m.** ** D: Fred F. Sears. Johnny Desmond, Merry Anders, Paul Langton, Michael Granger,

Meg Myles, Joel Grey, The Treniers, The Tarriers, The Hi-Lo's, Maya Angelou, Darla Hood. Trite plot—crooked Granger takes over Langton's record company—takes a back seat to performances by Desmond, Grey, Hi-Lo's, etc. A once-in-a-lifetime cast. Alan Arkin is one of The Tarriers.

Calypso Joe (1957) **76m.** *½ D: Edward Dein. Herb Jeffries, Angie Dickinson, Edward Kemmer, Stephen Bekassy, Laurie Mitchell, Lord Flea and His Calypsonians. Thin programmer about stewardess Dickinson and TV star Kemmer quarreling and making-up in a South American setting. Jeffries sings seven songs.

Camelot (1967) **C-178m.** *½ D: Joshua Logan. Richard Harris, Vanessa Redgrave, Franco Nero, David Hemmings, Lionel Jeffries. Appalling film version of Lerner-Loewe musical has only good orchestrations and sporadically good acting to recommend it; no one can sing and production looks cheap, in spite of big budget. This did, however, win Oscars for Costumes, Scoring, and Art Direction/Set Decoration. Film's nonstop use of close-ups may help it on TV. Panavision. ▼●◗

Cameraman, The (1928) **69m.** *** D: Edward Sedgwick. Buster Keaton, Marceline Day, Harold Goodwin, Sidney Bracy, Harry Gribbon, Edward Brophy. Buster plays a lovesick would-be newsreel cameraman in this entertaining silent comedy, a cut below his masterpieces but still brimming with invention, ingenious set-pieces, and big laughs. Remade with Red Skelton as WATCH THE BIRDIE.▼●

Cameron's Closet (1989) **C-86m.** *½ D: Armand Mastroianni. Cotter Smith, Mel Harris, Scott Curtis, Chuck McCann, Leigh McCloskey, Kim Lankford, Tab Hunter. Pointlessly cluttered horror tale of a father whose constant mind experiments on his son have created an actual monster in the boy's closet. Lumbering in every way, with a dull monster created by Carlo Rambaldi. [R]▼●

Camila (1984-Argentine) **C-105m.** **½ D: Maria Luisa Bemberg. Susu Pecoraro, Imanol Arias, Hector Alterio. Shades of ELVIRA MADIGAN, in a story based on 19th-century Argentine fact, about a Jesuit priest and a young Catholic socialite who commit love on the lam as the authorities stalk them for 500 miles. Interesting, but never altogether compelling.▼

Camilla (1994-Canadian-British) **C-95m.** **½ D: Deepa Mehta. Jessica Tandy, Bridget Fonda, Hume Cronyn, Elias Koteas, Maury Chaykin, Graham Greene, Ranjit Chowdhry, Atom Egoyan, Don McKellar. Tandy, in her final film, is the sole reason to see this otherwise so-so road movie about the budding friendship between a young would-be singer-songwriter (Fonda) and an elderly, eccentric (and high-spirited) former concert violinist. Cronyn plays Tandy's former lover, and their on-screen time together is something special. [PG-13]▼◗

Camille (1937) **108m.** ***½ D: George Cukor. Greta Garbo, Robert Taylor, Lionel Barrymore, Elizabeth Allan, Laura Hope Crews, Henry Daniell, Joan Brodel (Leslie). Beautiful MGM production; in one of her most famous roles, Garbo is Dumas' tragic heroine who must sacrifice her own happiness in order to prove her love. Taylor is a bit stiff as Armand, but Daniell is a superb villain. Filmed before in 1915 (with Clara Kimball Young), 1917 (Theda Bara), and 1921 (Nazimova, with Rudolph Valentino as Armand). Remade for TV in 1984 with Greta Scacchi. Also shown in computer-colored version.▼●

Camille Claudel (1988-French) **C-149m.** ** D: Bruno Nuytten. Isabelle Adjani, Gérard Depardieu, Laurent Grevill, Alain Cuny, Madeleine Robinson, Katrine Boorman. Overblown biography of the French sculptress (Adjani), who has a "madness of mud" and who single-mindedly pursues her art; Depardieu plays Auguste Rodin, with whom she has a complex, turbulent relationship. Potentially provocative story is emotionally uninvolving, with an astonishing lack of depth. Wonderful production values and period detail, but all for naught. Cinematographer Nuytten's directorial debut. Original French running time 173m. Panavision. [R]▼●

Camorra (1986-Italian) **C-115m.** **½ D: Lina Wertmuller. Angela Molina, Harvey Keitel, Daniel Ezralow, Francisco Rabal, Paolo Bonacelli, Isa Danieli, Lorraine Bracco. Complex tale of drug traffic, murder, and mayhem, focusing on the trials of ex-prostitute Molina; well-meaning in its depiction of how preteens are used and abused by drug kingpins. Generally better than the director's later work, but miles below her gems of the 1970s. [R]▼

Camouflage (1977-Polish) **C-106m.** ***½ D: Krzysztof Zanussi. Piotr Garlicki, Zbignieu Zapasiewicz, Christine Paul, Mariusz Dmochowski. Arrogant tenured professor Zapasiewicz challenges the independence of idealistic teaching assistant Garlicki at a summer school-camp for linguists. Pungently funny satire about conformity, the Communist hierarchy.

Campbell's Kingdom (1957-British) **C-102m.** ** D: Ralph Thomas. Dirk Bogarde, Stanley Baker, Michael Craig, Barbara Murray. Set in Canadian Rockies, big-budget adventure film focuses on landowner Bogarde's conflict with Baker et al, when latter seeks to build large dam near his property.

Camp Nowhere (1994) **C-96m.** *½ D: Jonathan Prince. Jonathan Jackson, Andrew Keegan, Marne Patterson, Melody Kay,

Christopher Lloyd, M. Emmet Walsh, Wendy Makkena, Kate Mulgrew, Burgess Meredith, Peter Scolari, Romy Walthall, Peter Onorati, Nathan Cavaleri. Computer geeks, show biz wannabes, kid commandos, and other neighborhood cast-offs band together to form their own communal summer camp, supervised by token adult Lloyd, who has somehow managed to convince parents he's a responsible authority figure. Assembly-line, end-of-summer release occasionally has a wittier gag than expected. [PG]▼●

Camp on Blood Island, The (1958-British) **81m.** ** D: Val Guest. Andre Morell, Carl Mohner, Walter Fitzgerald, Edward Underdown. So-so gore as inhabitants rebel against brutal commander of prison compound. Followed by THE SECRET OF BLOOD ISLAND. Megascope.

Campus Man (1987) **C-94m.** ** D: Ron Casden. John Dye, Steve Lyon, Morgan Fairchild, Kim Delaney, Kathleen Wilhoite, Miles O'Keeffe. Glossy but vacuous teen comedy of collegiate entrepreneur (*i.e.* hustler) who publishes a male beefcake calendar featuring his roommate, a hunky diver, and spawning all kinds of complications. Based on story of Arizona State University alumnus Todd Headlee (the film's associate producer), whose ASU calendar launched the nationwide craze. [PG]▼●

Canadian Bacon (1995) **C-91m.** **½ D: Michael Moore. Alan Alda, John Candy, Rhea Perlman, Kevin Pollak, Rip Torn, Kevin J. O'Connor, Bill Nunn, G. D. Spradlin, Steven Wright, James Belushi, Brad Sullivan. In order to gain a strong platform for re-election, the president of the United States does the unthinkable and declares war on our neighbor to the north, Canada. Moore stumbles with his second film after the terrific ROGER & ME. A top cast is wasted in this one-joke premise which lacks the satiric edge it needs. [PG] ▼●

Canadian Pacific (1949) **C-95m.** **½ D: Edwin L. Marin. Randolph Scott, Jane Wyatt, J. Carrol Naish, Victor Jory, Nancy Olson. Scott is railroad surveyor helping with construction of train link, fighting Indians while romancing Wyatt and Olson.

Canadians, The (1961) **C-85m.** ** D: Burt Kennedy. Robert Ryan, John Dehner, Torin Thatcher, John Sutton, Teresa Stratas. Cornball nonsense about Mounties who pacify war-happy Sioux. Film features Metropolitan Opera singer Stratas to no advantage. Filmed in Canada; Kennedy's first feature as director. CinemaScope.

Canaris Master Spy (1954-German) **92m.** ** D: Alfred Weidenmann. O. E. Hasse, Martin Held, Barbara Rutting, Adrian Hoven. Potentially interesting account of German Intelligence leader during 1930s who tried to depose Hitler; meandering.

Canary Murder Case (1929) **81m.** **½ D: Malcolm St. Clair. William Powell, Louise Brooks, James Hall, Jean Arthur, Charles Lane. Stilted but interesting and well-cast early talkie (originally shot as a silent) with Powell debuting as urbane sleuth Philo Vance, probing the death of scheming nightclub singer Brooks. (She made this right before her classic German films with G. W. Pabst. When she refused to return for retakes she was doubled, fairly obviously in some scenes, by Margaret Livingston.)

Can-Can (1960) **C-131m.** **½ D: Walter Lang. Frank Sinatra, Shirley MacLaine, Maurice Chevalier, Louis Jourdan, Juliet Prowse. Lackluster version of Cole Porter musical of 1890s Paris involving lawyer Sinatra defending MacLaine's right to perform "daring" dance in her nightclub. Chevalier and Jourdan try to inject charm, but Sinatra is blasé and MacLaine shrill. Songs: "C'est Magnifique," "I Love Paris," "Let's Do It," "Just One of Those Things." Todd-AO. ▼●

Cancel My Reservation (1972) **C-99m.** BOMB D: Paul Bogart. Bob Hope, Eva Marie Saint, Ralph Bellamy, Forrest Tucker, Anne Archer, Keenan Wynn, Ned Beatty, Chief Dan George. Hope should have canceled this movie, a time-wasting turkey about a troubled talk-show host who gets involved in a murder case in Arizona. Based on a Louis L'Amour novel! [G]▼

Candidate, The (1972) **C-109m.** *** D: Michael Ritchie. Robert Redford, Peter Boyle, Don Porter, Allen Garfield, Karen Carlson, Melvyn Douglas, Quinn Redeker, Michael Lerner, Kenneth Tobey. Keen-eyed political satire doesn't stray far from reality. Redford is idealist talked into running for Senate with promise of absolute integrity in campaign, since he's bound to lose—or is he? Oscar-winning screenplay by Jeremy Larner. [PG]▼●◗

Candidate for Murder (1962-British) **60m.** **½ D: David Villiers. Michael Gough, Erika Remberg, Hans Barsody, John Justin. Gough is deranged husband of actress Remberg, out to kill her; nicely told Edgar Wallace suspenser.

Candleshoe (1978) **C-101m.** *** D: Norman Tokar. David Niven, Jodie Foster, Helen Hayes, Leo McKern, Veronica Quilligan, Ian Sharrock, Vivian Pickles. Con man McKern tries to pass off orphan Foster as Hayes' heiress in order to locate hidden family treasure. Entertaining Disney comedy filmed in England, with Niven as disguise-laden butler. [G]▼●◗

Candy (1968-U.S.-Italian-French) **C-115m.** ** D: Christian Marquand. Ewa Aulin, Richard Burton, Marlon Brando, Charles Aznavour, James Coburn, John Huston, Walter Matthau, Ringo Starr, John Astin. Strained sexual satire about a nubile blonde who is attacked by every man she meets.

Fair share of funny moments and bright performances (particularly by Burton and Astin), but not enough to sustain 115m. Adapted from Terry Southern and Mason Hoffenberg's book by Buck Henry. [R]

Candy Man, The (1969) **98m.** ** D: Herbert J. Leder. George Sanders, Leslie Parrish, Gina Ronan, Carlos Cortez. Routine kidnap drama filmed in Mexico City involving world-weary British drug pusher and American film star. [G]▼

Candyman (1992) **C-93m.** *** D: Bernard Rose. Virginia Madsen, Tony Todd, Xander Berkeley, Kasi Lemmons, Vanessa Williams, DeJuan Guy, Michael Culkin. Effectively eerie psychological chiller, filled with clever, unusual touches, about an academic (Madsen) who begins researching the legend of a mysterious serial killer named Candyman (Todd); this leads her to Chicago's crime-infested Cabrini-Green public housing project. Rose (who plays the role of "Archie Walsh") also scripted, from Clive Barker's novel *The Forbidden* (which is set in Liverpool). Followed by two sequels. [R]▼●◗

Candyman: Farewell to the Flesh (1995) **C-94m.** ** D: Bill Condon. Tony Todd, Kelly Rowan, Timothy Carhart, Veronica Cartwright, William O'Leary, Fay Hauser, Bill Nunn, Matt Clark. Title avenger is resurrected in mediocre sequel to terrorize an aristocratic New Orleans family just in time for Mardi Gras. Good production values, including some convincing local color, are undermined by obvious plotting and nondescript supporting cast. Bland but for the menacing Todd in the title role. Followed by a direct-to-video sequel. [R]▼●

Candy Mountain (1987-Canadian-French-Swiss) **C-91m.** ** D: Robert Frank, Rudy Wurlitzer. Kevin J. O'Connor, Harris Yulin, Tom Waits, Bulle Ogier, Roberts Blossom, Leon Redbone, Dr. John, Joe Strummer, David Johansen (Buster Poindexter). Uneven account of has-been rocker O'Connor and his trip through America and Canada in search of elusive guitarmaker Yulin. Intriguing collaboration between photographer/filmmaker Frank, screenwriter Wurlitzer, and an eclectic cast . . . but the results are too often dull. [R]▼

Candy Stripe Nurses (1974) **C-80m.** *½ D: Allan Holleb. Candice Rialson, Robin Mattson, Maria Rojo, Kimberly Hyde, Dick Miller, Stanley Ralph Ross, Monte Landis, Tom Baker. Last of Roger Corman's five "nurse" pictures is tired sex comedy, focusing on antics of pretty volunteers; kept afloat by cast full of old hands at this sort of thing. Aka SWEET CANDY. [R]▼

Can Hieronymus Merkin Ever Forget Mercy Humppe and Find True Happiness? (1969-British) **C-106m.** *½ D: Anthony Newley. Anthony Newley, Joan Collins, Milton Berle, Connie Kreski, George Jessel, Stubby Kaye. Fellini-influenced mess about song-and-dance man who reviews his debauched past. Low-grade in all departments, though Connie reveals why she was "Playmate of the Year." Newley and Collins were then real-life husband and wife. [R—edited from original X rating]

Can I Do It . . . Til I Need Glasses? (1977) **C-72m.** BOMB D: I. Robert Levy. Victor Dunlap, Moose Carlson, Walter Olkewicz, Joey Camen, Ann Kellogg, Robin Williams. Sophomoric series of sex-related skits, most of which would bore immature 11-year-olds. Williams appears very briefly, in footage tacked on after the film's premiere (and after his *Mork and Mindy* stardom). [R]▼

Cannery Row (1982) **C-120m.** **½ D: David S. Ward. Nick Nolte, Debra Winger, Audra Lindley, Frank McRae, M. Emmet Walsh, Sunshine Parker, Santos Morales, narrated by John Huston. Entertaining tug-of-war romance between baseball-player-turned-marine-biologist Nolte and drifter-turned-floozie Winger is hampered by sloppy, self-conscious direction, awkward continuity. Attractive performances by Nolte and Winger; great set design by Richard MacDonald. Based on John Steinbeck's *Cannery Row* and *Sweet Thursday*. Ward's directorial debut. [PG]▼●

Cannibal Attack (1954) **69m.** *½ D: Lee Sholem. Johnny Weissmuller, Judy Walsh, David Bruce, Bruce Cowling. Weissmuller dropped the *Jungle Jim* monicker and used his own name in this juvenile yarn about enemy agents who disguise themselves as crocodiles(!?) to steal cobalt.▼

Cannibal Girls (1973-Canadian) **C-84m.** ** D: Ivan Reitman. Eugene Levy, Andrea Martin, Ronald Ulrich, Randall Carpenter, Bonnie Neison. Confused, convoluted low-budget Canadian import, an early effort by young talents Reitman, Levy, and Martin, has funny first half about a couple stranded in eerie town where there's a rather strange restaurant. Second half falls apart. Warning buzzer precedes gore scenes (which aren't much), and doorbell-like sound announces they're over. [R]

Cannibal! The Musical (1998) **C-92m.** **½ D: Trey Parker. Juan Schwartz (Trey Parker), Dian Bachar, Ian Hardin, John Hegel, Matt Stone, Toddy Walters. Wacky, low-budget musical based on real-life story of Alferd Packer, who led an expedition that degenerated into cannibalism in the Colorado Rockies, circa 1874. Gross-out gags alternate for screen time with some pretty good songs; our favorite is "Shpadoinkle." First feature for the SOUTH PARK team of Parker and Stone. Made in 1993. [R]▼

Cannonball (1976) **C-93m.** ** D: Paul Bartel. David Carradine, Veronica Hamel, Bill McKinney, Gerrit Graham, Robert

Carradine, Belinda Balaski, Judy Canova, Carl Gottlieb. Comic account of cross-country road race first depicted in THE GUMBALL RALLY. Funny moments are muted by unpleasant characters and inept stuntwork. As usual, many of Bartel's pals and coworkers appear in bits, including Sylvester Stallone, Roger Corman, and directors Martin Scorsese, Jonathan Kaplan, and Joe Dante. [PG]▼

Cannonball Run, The (1981) **C-95m.** BOMB D: Hal Needham. Burt Reynolds, Roger Moore, Farrah Fawcett, Dom DeLuise, Dean Martin, Sammy Davis, Jr., Terry Bradshaw, Jackie Chan, Bert Convy, Jamie Farr, Peter Fonda, Bianca Jagger, Molly Picon, Jimmy "The Greek" Snyder, Mel Tillis. Just what civilization needs—more Reynolds car-chase silliness, inspired by the same cross-country road race depicted in THE GUMBALL RALLY and CANNONBALL. Pretty unendurable, despite unusual cast; rumor has it that the one responsible for casting Dino and Sammy as priests is still doing his Hail Marys. Followed by a sequel. [PG]▼●

Cannonball Run II (1984) **C-108m.** BOMB D: Hal Needham. Burt Reynolds, Dom DeLuise, Shirley MacLaine, Marilu Henner, Dean Martin, Sammy Davis, Jr., Susan Anton, Catherine Bach, Ricardo Montalban, Jim Nabors, Charles Nelson Reilly, Telly Savalas, Jamie Farr, Jack Elam, Frank Sinatra, Sid Caesar, and many others. Sequel to 1981 box-office hit looks like someone's bad home movies. Amateurish action comedy with tons of tacky guest-star cameos. What a waste! Final film roles for Martin and Sinatra. [PG] ▼●◗

Cannon for Cordoba (1970) **C-104m.** **½ D: Paul Wendkos. George Peppard, Giovanna Ralli, Raf Vallone, Peter Duel, Don Gordon, John Russell. Peppard leads a band of soldiers against Mexican bandits on the Texas border ca. 1912, and tries to destroy stolen cannons. Standard action fare with a familiar ring. Panavision.

Canon City (1948) **82m.** *** D: Crane Wilbur. Scott Brady, Jeff Corey, Whit Bissell, Stanley Clements, DeForest Kelley. Solid crime thriller follows members of a prison break from a Colorado State jail in semidocumentary style. Strong and violent with excellent photography by John Alton.

Can She Bake a Cherry Pie? (1983) **C-90m.** *½ D: Henry Jaglom. Karen Black, Michael Emil, Michael Margotta, Frances Fisher, Martin Harvey Friedberg. Neurotic, unpredictable Black, whose husband has just left her, takes up with Emil, who never seems to stop talking. A couple of chuckles, but all the rest is rambling, superficial. [R]▼

Can't Buy Me Love (1987) **C-94m.** **½ D: Steve Rash. Patrick Dempsey, Amanda Peterson, Courtney Gains, Tina Caspary, Seth Green, Sharon Farrell. Known as BOY RENTS GIRL during production, story has nerdy Dempsey paying senior heartthrob Peterson a hard-earned grand to pose as his girlfriend, correctly surmising his own stock will rise. Sentimental rendering of a terrific high school comedy premise. Peterson is excellent, Dempsey just adequate. [PG-13]▼●

Canterbury Tale, A (1944-British) **124m.** *** D: Michael Powell, Emeric Pressburger. Eric Portman, Sheila Sim, John Sweet, Dennis Price, Esmond Knight, Charles Hawtrey, Hay Petrie. Curious and disarming film from the Powell–Pressburger writing-and-directing team draws on British eccentricities—and provincial flavor—to flesh out its simple story about three people whose lives cross in a small English village during the war. There's only the slightest tangent with the Chaucer work from which it draws its title. American version with added footage of Kim Hunter runs 95m. and doesn't retain the charm of the original.▼

Canterbury Tales, The (1971-Italian-French) **C-109m.** BOMB D: Pier Paolo Pasolini. Laura Betti, Ninetto Davoli, Pier Paolo Pasolini, Hugh Griffith, Josephine Chaplin, Michael Balfour, Jenny Runacre. Travelers recount four Chaucer stories—which, unfortunately, are enacted for the viewer. Tiresome, offensive, graphically sadistic, with Pasolini appearing as Chaucer. Italian-English cast; the second of the director's medieval trilogy.▼●◗

Canterville Ghost, The (1944) **96m.** *** D: Jules Dassin. Charles Laughton, Robert Young, Margaret O'Brien, William Gargan, Reginald Owen, Rags Ragland, Una O'Connor, Mike Mazurki, Peter Lawford. Enjoyable fantasy, loosely adapted from Oscar Wilde's short story, of 17th-century ghost Laughton, spellbound until descendant Young helps him perform heroic deed. Remade for TV in 1986 (with John Gielgud) and 1996 (with Patrick Stewart). ▼●

Can't Hardly Wait (1998) **C-98m.** ** D: Deborah Kaplan, Harry Elfont. Jennifer Love Hewitt, Ethan Embry, Charlie Korsmo, Lauren Ambrose, Peter Facinelli, Seth Green, Michelle Brookhurst. On high school graduation night, Embry tries to work up the nerve to express his long-pent-up feelings for Hewitt—who's just broken up with the class jock. Set in and around a wild house party, this cheerful but predictable teen comedy comes off as a poor relation to AMERICAN GRAFFITI aimed at teens of the 1990s. Jenna Elfman, Melissa Joan Hart, and Jerry O'Connell appear unbilled. [PG-13]▼●◗

Can't Help Singing (1944) **C-89m.** **½ D: Frank Ryan. Deanna Durbin, Robert Paige, Akim Tamiroff, Ray Collins, Thomas Gomez. Durbin goes West to find her roaming lover; despite good cast and Jerome Kern songs, it's nothing much. ▼●

Can't Stop the Music (1980) **C-118m.** ** D: Nancy Walker. The Village People, Valerie Perrine, Bruce Jenner, Steve Guttenberg, Paul Sand, Tammy Grimes, June Havoc, Barbara Rush, Jack Weston, Leigh Taylor-Young. One or two catchy production numbers aren't enough to salvage otherwise stiff comedy about the music-publishing biz, though some will feel they *have* to see what V. People and Jenner are doing in same film. Gay subtext abounds, despite eye-boggling profile shots of Perrine. Panavision. [PG]▼

Canyon Crossroads (1955) **83m.** **½ D: Alfred L. Werker. Richard Basehart, Russell Collins, Phyllis Kirk, Stephen Elliott. On-location filming in Colorado highlights this tale of uranium hunt, with Basehart quite convincing.

Canyon Passage (1946) **C-92m.** *** D: Jacques Tourneur. Dana Andrews, Brian Donlevy, Susan Hayward, Ward Bond, Andy Devine, Lloyd Bridges. Plotty, colorful Western mixing action, beautiful scenery, heated love relationships, and Hoagy Carmichael singing "Ole Buttermilk Sky." Well made and entertaining.▼

Canyon River (1956) **C-80m.** *½ D: Harmon Jones. George Montgomery, Marcia Henderson, Peter Graves, Richard Eyer. Trite Western of Indian and rustler attacks on cattle drive. CinemaScope.

Cape Canaveral Monsters (1960) **69m.** BOMB D: Phil Tucker. Scott Peters, Linda Connell, Jason Johnson, Katherine Victor, Gary Travis. Aliens, who possess no form of their own, inhabit slowly decomposing corpses in order to shoot down U.S. rockets; science student Peters, using wallet inserts and Pig Latin, combats the invaders. Astonishing film is almost the equal of writer-director Tucker's legendarily awful ROBOT MONSTER.▼

Cape Fear (1962) **105m.** *** D: J. Lee Thompson. Gregory Peck, Robert Mitchum, Polly Bergen, Martin Balsam, Lori Martin, Jack Kruschen, Telly Savalas, Barrie Chase, Edward Platt. Mitchum is memorably (and believably) creepy as a wily Southern ex-con who blames lawyer Peck for his incarceration, and plots an insidious revenge on his family. Dated only in its lack of explicitness, but still daring for its time. Based on John D. MacDonald's novel *The Executioners.* Musical score by Bernard Herrmann is reminiscent of his best work with Hitchcock. Remade in 1991.▼●

Cape Fear (1991) **C-128m.** **½ D: Martin Scorsese. Robert De Niro, Nick Nolte, Jessica Lange, Juliette Lewis, Joe Don Baker, Robert Mitchum, Gregory Peck, Martin Balsam, Illeana Douglas, Fred Dalton Thompson. Released from prison after 14 years, a self-educated wacko vows to make a living hell for the lawyer who sent him up. Remake of the 1962 thriller fleshes out its characters, and adds fascinating psychological layers—but turns a gripping, realistic story into an overblown, unbelievable horror film: CAPE FEAR for the Freddy Krueger generation. Scorsese's brilliant command of the medium is squandered on severely unpleasant material (with an A-list of collaborators, including cinematographer Freddie Francis and composer Elmer Bernstein, adapting Bernard Herrmann's original score). Major asset: exceptionally good performances (including amusingly cast cameos by Mitchum, Peck, and Balsam, who starred in the '62 movie). Panavision. [R]▼●

Caper of the Golden Bulls, The (1967) **C-104m.** BOMB D: Russell Rouse. Stephen Boyd, Yvette Mimieux, Giovanna Ralli, Walter Slezak, Vito Scotti. Lots of bull but not much gold in this unendurable "thriller" about bank heist in Pamplona.▼

Cape Town Affair, The (1967) **C-103m.** ** D: Robert D. Webb. Claire Trevor, James Brolin, Jacqueline Bisset, Bob Courtney, Jon Whiteley, Gordon Milholland. Pedestrian remake of PICKUP ON SOUTH STREET, made in South Africa. Interest here is seeing Bisset and Brolin at the beginnings of their careers and Trevor making something different of the old Thelma Ritter role. Story deals with a Communist spy ring in Cape Town and an elusive envelope containing top secret microfilm.▼

Capitaine Conan (1996-French) **C-132m.** *** D: Bertrand Tavernier. Philippe Torreton, Samuel Le Bihan, Bernard Le Coq, Catherine Rich, François Berleand, Pierre Val. Powerful indictment of militarism and false heroism, centering on reckless title character, who leads French troops in a secret war in the Balkans following the end of WW1, but pays a heavy price for his valor. Torreton won a French César award for his forceful performance, as did Tavernier for his virtuoso direction. Super 35.▼

Capone (1975) **C-101m.** BOMB D: Steve Carver. Ben Gazzara, Susan Blakely, Harry Guardino, John Cassavetes, Sylvester Stallone, Frank Campanella. Gazzara has cotton in his jowls and a cigar in his mouth, making most of the dialogue in this gangster saga incomprehensible—but that's OK, you've heard it all before. One big shootout is stock footage from THE ST. VALENTINE'S DAY MASSACRE. [R]

Caprice (1967) **C-98m.** BOMB D: Frank Tashlin. Doris Day, Richard Harris, Ray Walston, Jack Kruschen, Edward Mulhare, Lilia Skala, Irene Tsu, Michael J. Pollard. Terrible vehicle for Doris as industrial spy plunged into international intrigue with fellow-agent Harris. Muddled, unfunny, straining to be "mod." CinemaScope.

Capricorn One (1978) **C-124m.** *** D: Peter Hyams. Elliott Gould, James Brolin, Hal Holbrook, Sam Waterston, Karen Black, O. J. Simpson, Telly Savalas, Brenda Vaccaro, Denise Nicholas, David Huddleston, Robert Walden, David Doyle. Whirlwind contemporary adventure plays like a condensed Republic serial. First manned flight to Mars turns out to be a hoax, and when capsule supposedly burns up in re-entry, the astronauts suddenly realize they're expendable. Lots of great chases punctuated by Hyams' witty dialogue; not always plausible, but who cares? Panavision. [PG]▼●◗

Captain America (1990) **C-103m.** *½ D: Albert Pyun. Matt Salinger, Ronny Cox, Ned Beatty, Darren McGavin, Scott Paulin, Michael Nouri, Kim Gillingham, Melinda Dillon, Billy Mumy. Dismayingly awful adaptation of the great Joe Simon–Jack Kirby comic book. Cap (Salinger) barely gets in one failed WW2 adventure pitted against Red Skull (Paulin), before being frozen in Alaska ice. Thawed out 50 years later, he spends too long in civvies before facing the Skull again. Clumsy, synthetic direction, actionless plot, boring opponents overwhelm the sincerity of Salinger's performance. Never released theatrically in the U.S.▼

Captain Apache (1971) **C-94m.** ** D: Alexander Singer. Lee Van Cleef, Carroll Baker, Stuart Whitman, Percy Herbert. Violence in Old West laid on with a trowel. Filled with stereotypes. Franscope. [PG]▼

Captain Blackjack (1951-U.S.-French) **90m.** ** D: Julien Duvivier. George Sanders, Herbert Marshall, Patricia Roc, Agnes Moorehead, Marcel Dalio. Tacky tale of derelict ship purchased by suave Sanders to use for drug-smuggling, and what happens when all those on board mysteriously die. Moorehead is good as a villainess. Filmed in Spain; released in France at 105m.▼

Captain Blood (1935) **119m.** ***½ D: Michael Curtiz. Errol Flynn, Olivia de Havilland, Lionel Atwill, Basil Rathbone, Ross Alexander, Guy Kibbee, Henry Stephenson, Robert Barrat, Donald Meek, J. Carrol Naish. Flynn's first swashbuckler, based on Rafael Sabatini's novel, scores a broadside. He plays Irish physician Peter Blood who is forced to become a pirate, teaming for short spell with French cutthroat Rathbone, but paying more attention to proper young lady de Havilland. Vivid combination of exciting sea battles, fencing duels, and tempestuous romance provides Flynn with a literally star-making vehicle. First original film score for Erich Wolfgang Korngold. Beware of 99m. reissue version. Also shown in computer-colored version. ▼●

Captain Blood (1960-French) **C-95m.** ** D: Andre Hunebelle. Jean Marais, Elsa Martinelli, Arnold Foa, Bourvil, Pierrette Bruno. Set in 17th-century France, this juvenile costumer deals with plot to overthrow throne of Louis XIII. Dyaliscope.

Captain Boycott (1947-British) **92m.** **½ D: Frank Launder. Stewart Granger, Kathleen Ryan, Cecil Parker, Mervyn Johns, Alastair Sim. Poor Irish farmers band together to combat the abuses of their landlords in early 19th century; interesting but dramatically uneven, with misplaced components of humor and romance. Robert Donat appears briefly as Charles Parnell; Parker has title role.▼

Captain Carey, U.S.A. (1950) **83m.** *** D: Mitchell Leisen. Alan Ladd, Wanda Hendrix, Francis Lederer, Russ Tamblyn. Nicely turned account of ex-military officer Ladd returning to Italy to uncover informer who cost lives of villagers. Theme song "Mona Lisa" won an Oscar.

Captain Caution (1940) **85m.** ** D: Richard Wallace. Victor Mature, Louise Platt, Leo Carrillo, Bruce Cabot, Vivienne Osborne, Robert Barrat. OK action film of spunky Platt commandeering her father's ship into war; no messages, just fast-moving narrative. Look for Alan Ladd as a sailor.▼

Captain China (1949) **97m.** ** D: Lewis R. Foster. John Payne, Gail Russell, Jeffrey Lynn, Lon Chaney (Jr.), Edgar Bergen. Often listless sea yarn of Payne, seeking out persons responsible for his losing his ship's command.

Captain Clegg SEE: **Night Creatures**

Captain Eddie (1945) **107m.** **½ D: Lloyd Bacon. Fred MacMurray, Lynn Bari, Charles Bickford, Thomas Mitchell, Lloyd Nolan, James Gleason. Routine aviation film doesn't do justice to exciting life of Eddie Rickenbacker; it's standard stuff.

Captain From Castile (1947) **C-140m.** *** D: Henry King. Tyrone Power, Jean Peters, Cesar Romero, Lee J. Cobb, John Sutton, Antonio Moreno. Power, driven to avenge the cruel treatment of his family by Spanish Inquisitor (Sutton), eventually serves with Cortez (Romero) during his conquest of Mexico. Color and romance; magnificent location photography by Charles Clarke and Arthur E. Arling; Alfred Newman's magnificent score ranks with Hollywood's very best. Peters' film debut.▼●

Captain Fury (1939) **91m.** *** D: Hal Roach. Brian Aherne, Victor McLaglen, Paul Lukas, June Lang, John Carradine, George Zucco, Douglass Dumbrille, Charles Middleton. Australia serves as background in story of illustrious adventurer fighting evil land baron.

Captain Hates the Sea, The (1934) **93m.** ** D: Lewis Milestone. Victor McLaglen, John Gilbert, Walter Connolly, Wynne Gibson, Helen Vinson, Alison Skipworth, Leon Errol, Walter Catlett, Akim Tamir-

off, Donald Meek, Arthur Treacher, The Three Stooges. Bizarre, seagoing GRAND HOTEL, with accent on comedy; romances and intrigues carry on under bored eye of disgruntled skipper Connolly. Once-in-a-lifetime cast does its best with mediocre script; Gilbert (ironically cast as a heavy drinker) gives a solid performance in his final film.
Captain Horatio Hornblower (1951-British) **C-117m.** *** D: Raoul Walsh. Gregory Peck, Virginia Mayo, Robert Beatty, Denis O'Dea, Christopher Lee, Stanley Baker, James Robertson Justice. Exciting, well-produced sea epic based on C. S. Forester's British naval hero of the Napoleonic wars. ▼●
Captain Is a Lady, The (1940) **63m.** ** D: Robert B. Sinclair. Charles Coburn, Beulah Bondi, Virginia Grey, Helen Broderick, Billie Burke, Dan Dailey. Thin little comedy of Coburn pretending to be a woman to accompany wife Bondi to old ladies' home.
Captain January (1936) **75m.** **½ D: David Butler. Shirley Temple, Guy Kibbee, Slim Summerville, Buddy Ebsen, June Lang, Sara Haden. Straightforward, sentimental tale of orphaned Shirley, and the new truant officer who tries to separate her from her adoptive father, lighthouse keeper Kibbee. Short and sweet. Shirley and Ebsen sing and dance "At the Codfish Ball."▼
Captain John Smith and Pocahontas (1953) **C-75m.** *½ D: Lew Landers. Anthony Dexter, Jody Lawrance, Alan Hale, Jr., Douglass Dumbrille. Title tells all in pedestrian tale set in colonial America.
Captain Kidd (1945) **89m.** ** D: Rowland V. Lee. Charles Laughton, Randolph Scott, Barbara Britton, Reginald Owen, John Carradine, Gilbert Roland, Sheldon Leonard. Even with Laughton, this is slow-going low-budget stuff.▼
Captain Kidd and the Slave Girl (1954) **C-83m.** ** D: Lew Landers. Anthony Dexter, Eva Gabor, Alan Hale, Jr., James Seay. Modest costumer has Dexter and Gabor in title roles romping the seas to find treasure for their benefactor.
Captain Kronos: Vampire Hunter (1974-British) **C-91m.** *** D: Brian Clemens. Horst Janson, John Carson, Caroline Munro, Shane Briant, John Cater, Lois Diane, Ian Hendry. Unique blend of horror and swashbuckler genres follows sword-wielding stranger as he stalks new breed of vampire across European countryside. Artsy, exciting, almost intoxicatingly atmospheric chiller has developed considerable following; one of the best (and least typical) Hammer productions. Released in Britain as simply KRONOS. [R]▼
Captain Lightfoot (1955) **C-91m.** *** D: Douglas Sirk. Rock Hudson, Barbara Rush, Jeff Morrow, Finlay Currie, Kathleen Ryan. Fine, flavorful costume adventure about 19th-century Irish rebellion and one of its dashing heroes. Beautifully filmed on location in Ireland in CinemaScope.
Captain Nemo and the Underwater City (1970) **C-105m.** **½ D: James Hill. Robert Ryan, Chuck Connors, Nanette Newman, Luciana Paluzzi. Average undersea fantasy centered on Captain Nemo who lives in an underwater fortress. Panavision. [G]
Captain Newman, M.D. (1963) **C-126m.** *** D: David Miller. Gregory Peck, Angie Dickinson, Tony Curtis, Eddie Albert, Jane Withers, Bobby Darin, Larry Storch, Bethel Leslie, Robert Duvall. Provocative, well-acted comedy-drama about dedicated Army psychiatrist Peck, battling bureaucracy and the macho military mentality on a stateside air base during WW2. Darin is particularly good as a troubled, ill-fated corporal. Based on Leo Rosten's best-selling novel.▼
Captain Pirate (1952) **C-85m.** **½ D: Ralph Murphy. Louis Hayward, Patricia Medina, John Sutton, Charles Irwin, George Givot, Ted de Corsia. Reformed pirate must return to his renegade ways in order to expose the imposter who is using his name; good-enough programmer based on Sabatini's *Captain Blood Returns.*
Captain Ron (1992) **C-100m.** BOMB D: Thom Eberhardt. Kurt Russell, Martin Short, Mary Kay Place, Benjamin Salisbury, Meadow Sisto, Emannuel Logrono, Jorge Luis Ramos, J. A. Preston, Tanya Soler, John Scott Clough. Yuppies Get Away From It All by taking an inherited sailboat into the Caribbean, with eye-patched Russell (the very poor man's Robert Newton) at the helm. Dreadful time-waster establishes its comic credentials by giving Russell the funny role and Short the straight one; pirates and multiple falls into the drink are a given. Paul Anka (you tell *us* why) plays a boat salesman. [PG-13]▼●
Captain Scarlett (1953) **C-75m.** *½ D: Thomas Carr. Richard Greene, Leonora Amar, Nedrick Young, Edourado Noriega. Acceptable costumer with Greene properly dashing.▼
Captains Courageous (1937) **116m.** **** D: Victor Fleming. Freddie Bartholomew, Spencer Tracy, Lionel Barrymore, Melvyn Douglas, Charley Grapewin, John Carradine, Mickey Rooney, Walter Kingsford. Spoiled rich-boy Bartholomew falls off cruise ship, rescued by Portuguese fisherman Tracy (who won Oscar for role). Boy learns to love seafaring on crusty Barrymore's fishing vessel. Enthusiastic cast in this splendid production of Kipling's story. Scripted by John Lee Mahin, Marc Connelly, and Dale Van Every. Remade as a TV movie in 1977 (with Karl Malden and Ricardo Montalban) and 1996 (with Robert

Urich). Also shown in computer-colored version.▼●

Captain Sindbad (1963) **C-85m.** **½ D: Byron Haskin. Guy Williams, Heidi Bruhl, Pedro Armendariz, Abraham Sofaer, Bernie Hamilton. Guy Williams is an energetic Sindbad in this elaborate, effects-filled but ponderous European fantasy.▼

Captain Sirocco SEE: **Pirates of Capri, The**

Captains of the Clouds (1942) **C-113m.** *** D: Michael Curtiz. James Cagney, Dennis Morgan, Alan Hale, Brenda Marshall, George Tobias. Cagney and company join Canadian air force as a lark, but prove their worth under fire. Colorful war-time drama.▼

Captain's Paradise, The (1953-British) **77m.** *** D: Anthony Kimmins. Alec Guinness, Yvonne De Carlo, Celia Johnson, Bill Fraser. Guinness has field day as carefree skipper who shuttles back and forth between wives in opposite ports. De Carlo and Johnson make a good contrast as the two women. Original British running time: 86m.▼●

Captain's Table, The (1960-British) **C-90m.** ** D: Jack Lee. John Gregson, Peggy Cummins, Donald Sinden, Nadia Gray. Satisfactory comedy involving skipper of cargo vessel (Gregson) who is given trial command of luxury liner, and the chaos ensuing trying to keep order among crew and passengers.▼

Captain Tugboat Annie (1945) **60m.** ** D: Phil Rosen. Jane Darwell, Edgar Kennedy, Charles Gordon, Mantan Moreland, Pamela Blake, Hardie Albright, H.B. Warner. Annie sails again in low-budget epic which depends entirely on its stars, Darwell and Kennedy, for its flavor.

Captive City, The (1952) **90m.** *** D: Robert Wise. John Forsythe, Joan Camden, Harold J. Kennedy, Marjorie Crosland, Victor Sutherland, Ray Teal, Martin Milner. Small-city newspaper editor Forsythe gradually learns that the Mafia has taken over bookie operations formerly run by corrupt local businessmen. Based-on-fact drama is earnest and intelligent, with fine noir-style photography by Lee Garmes. Sen. Estes Kefauver provides an afterword.

Captive Girl (1950) **73m.** ** D: William Berke. Johnny Weissmuller, Buster Crabbe, Anita Lhoest, Rick Vallin, John Dehner. More *Jungle Jim* hokum, this time he's trying to save young Lhoest from a witch doctor, while battling treasure hunter Crabbe. Interesting primarily for pitting two former Tarzans against each other.

Captive Heart, The (1946-British) **108m.** ***½ D: Basil Dearden. Michael Redgrave, Mervyn Johns, Basil Radford, Jack Warner, Jimmy Hanley, Gordon Jackson, Ralph Michael, Rachel Kempson. Compelling examination of British P.O.W.s during WW2 and their German captors with controlled, flawless performance by Redgrave and excellent supporting cast. Patrick Kirwan's story was scripted by Angus MacPhail and Guy Morgan. Original British running time: 98m.▼

Captive Hearts (1987) **C-97m.** ** D: Paul Almond. Noriyuki (Pat) Morita, Chris Makepeace, Mari Sato, Michael Sarrazin, Seth Sakai. American soldier shot down and taken prisoner in Japan during WW2 falls in love with a Japanese woman. If that sounds familiar, or simplistic, wait till you see the film! Easy to see why this barely made it to theaters. [PG]▼

Captives (1995-U.S.-British) **C-99m.** **½ D: Angela Pope. Tim Roth, Julia Ormond, Colin Salmon, Keith Allen, Siobhan Redmond, Peter Capaldi. Unusual drama set in a contemporary London prison where a lonely female dentist ends up in a deadly game of blackmail when she falls for one of her convict patients. Some melodramatic silliness aside (including scenes of dental foreplay), this is a showcase for two highly skilled actors, Roth and Ormond. [R]▼●

Captive Wild Woman (1943) **61m.** **½ D: Edward Dmytryk. John Carradine, Evelyn Ankers, Milburn Stone, Acquanetta, Martha MacVicar (Vickers), Lloyd Corrigan. Carradine turns an orangutan into beautiful woman (Acquanetta), who goes berserk with unrequited love. Good fun; Stone's animal-training scenes are stock footage of Clyde Beatty from THE BIG CAGE. Sequels: JUNGLE WOMAN, JUNGLE CAPTIVE.▼

Capture, The (1950) **91m.** **½ D: John Sturges. Lew Ayres, Teresa Wright, Victor Jory, Jacqueline White, Jimmy Hunt, Barry Kelley, Duncan Renaldo. Oil field supervisor Ayres begins to ponder whether the payroll robber he shot really was an innocent man. Straightforward, well-acted, but slow at times.▼

Captured (1933) **72m.** **½ D: Roy Del Ruth. Leslie Howard, Douglas Fairbanks, Jr., Paul Lukas, Margaret Lindsay. Fair story of honor and love, switching WW1 story from German prison camp, to warfront, to society England. Good cast major asset of production.

Car, The (1977) **C-95m.** *½ D: Elliot Silverstein. James Brolin, Kathleen Lloyd, John Marley, Ronny Cox, R.G. Armstrong, John Rubinstein. Hokey thriller about a killer car demonically running down most of the cast. *Twilight Zone* once did a tidier, quite similar job in one third the time. Panavision. [PG]▼●◗

Caravan (1934) **101m.** **½ D: Erik Charrell. Loretta Young, Charles Boyer, Jean Parker, Phillips Holmes, Louise Fazenda. Offbeat musical of royal Loretta forced to marry vagabond Boyer; main interest is curiosity in this not altogether successful film.

Caravans (1978-U.S.-Iranian) **C-123m.** **½ D: James Fargo. Anthony Quinn, Jennifer O'Neill, Michael Sarrazin, Christopher Lee, Joseph Cotten, Barry Sullivan. Expensive-looking version of James Michener's contemporary desert epic about a search through the Middle East for the daughter (O'Neill) of a U.S. senator. Won't fool those who recognize it as just another updated version of THE SEARCHERS. Panavision. [PG]

Carbine Williams (1952) **91m.** *** D: Richard Thorpe. James Stewart, Jean Hagen, Wendell Corey, Paul Stewart, James Arness. Sturdy history of the inventor of famed rifle, his problems with the law, and his simple family life. Stewart is most convincing in title role. Also shown in computer-colored version.

Carbon Copy (1981) **C-92m.** ** D: Michael Schultz. George Segal, Susan Saint James, Denzel Washington, Jack Warden, Paul Winfield, Dick Martin, Tom Poston. Segal has hidden his identity as a Jew and become a successful corporate executive—until the arrival of his illegitimate 17-year-old son (Washington, in film debut), who is black. Silly, uneven, but not uninteresting blend of comedy and social drama. Written by Stanley Shapiro. Panavision. [PG]▼●

Card, The SEE: **Promoter, The**

Cardiac Arrest (1980) **C-90m.** ** D: Murray Mintz. Garry Goodrow, Mike Chan, Maxwell Gail, Susan O'Connell, Ray Reinhardt. Murderer is terrorizing San Francisco, removing the hearts of his victims, and the cops are stumped. [PG]▼◗

Cardinal, The (1963) **C-175m.** **½ D: Otto Preminger. Tom Tryon, John Huston, Romy Schneider, Carol Lynley, Jill Haworth, Raf Vallone, Joseph Meinrad, Burgess Meredith, Ossie Davis, John Saxon, Robert Morse, Dorothy Gish, Tullio Carminati, Maggie McNamara, Bill Hayes, Cecil Kellaway, Murray Hamilton, Patrick O'Neal, Chill Wills, Arthur Hunnicutt. Long, long story of an Irish-American's rise from priesthood to the College of Cardinals. Has some outstanding vignettes by old pros like Meredith, but emerges as an uneven, occasionally worthwhile film. Panavision.▼●

Cardinal Richelieu (1935) **83m.** **½ D: Rowland V. Lee. George Arliss, Maureen O'Sullivan, Edward Arnold, Cesar Romero. Arliss etches another historical portrayal of France's unscrupulous cardinal who controlled Louis XIII (Arnold). Good cast supports star.

Care Bears Adventure in Wonderland!, The (1987-Canadian) **C-75m.** ** D: Raymond Jafelice. Voices of Bob Dermer, Eva Almos, Dan Hennessy, Jim Henshaw, Colin Fox. The Care Bears follow Alice through the looking glass in this typically bland kiddie outing, with music by John Sebastian. [G]▼●

Care Bears Movie, The (1985-Canadian) **C-75m.** ** D: Arna Selznick. Voices of Mickey Rooney, Georgia Engel. Songs by Carole King, John Sebastian. Animated feature based on heavily merchandised characters is strictly for toddlers, tough sledding for anyone older. Produced by Canadian Nelvana animation studio. Followed by two sequels and a TV series. [G]▼

Care Bears Movie II, The: A New Generation (1986) **C-77m.** BOMB D: Dale Schott. Voices of Maxine Miller, Pam Hyatt, Hadley Kay. Your kids deserve better entertainment than this treacly stuff about the Kingdom of Caring. Prefab animation from the era of toy merchandising tie-ins. [G]▼

Career (1959) **105m.** *** D: Joseph Anthony. Dean Martin, Anthony Franciosa, Shirley MacLaine, Carolyn Jones, Joan Blackman, Robert Middleton, Donna Douglas. Occasionally shrill, generally forceful presentation of an actor's (Franciosa's) tribulations in seeking Broadway fame; Jones is excellent as lonely talent agent.▼●

Career Girl (1959) **C-61m.** *½ D: Harold David. June Wilkinson, Charles Robert Keane, Lisa Barrie, Joe Sullivan. Sloppy account of Wilkinson going to Hollywood, seeking screen career; sleazy production values.

Career Girls (1997-British) **C-87m.** ***½ D: Mike Leigh. Katrin Cartlidge, Lynda Steadman, Kate Byers, Mark Benton, Joe Tucker. Another satisfying (and unpredictable) slice of life from writer-director Leigh, about two former roommates reunited after six years. Flashbacks reveal how much they've changed and matured from their uncertain college years, when Cartlidge was a mass of tics and Steadman was, in her friend's words, "a walking open wound." Remarkable performances from both actresses. Music by Tony Remy and Marianne Jean-Baptiste (costar of Leigh's previous film, SECRETS & LIES). [R]▼●

Career Opportunities (1991) **C-84m.** *½ D: Bryan Gordon. Frank Whaley, Jennifer Connelly, Dermot Mulroney, Kieran Mulroney, John M. Jackson, Jenny O'Hara, Noble Willingham, Barry Corbin, Denise Galik, William Forsythe. Otherwise unemployable teen gets the night watchman job at an all-purpose department store; his first night is an idyllic round-the-clocker with a girl who's hiding out inside, and who just happens to be the town's no. 1 rich dish. Typical ode to arrested development from writer-producer John Hughes, a 10m. idea stretched into a feature. Tolerable only for John Candy's unbilled cameo, and as a showcase for gorgeous Connelly. Panavision. [PG-13] ▼●◗

Carefree (1938) **80m.** *** D: Mark Sandrich. Fred Astaire, Ginger Rogers, Ralph Bellamy, Luella Gear, Jack Carson, Franklin Pangborn. Madcap Rogers is sent to psychiatrist Astaire, and romance naturally blossoms; Fred and Ginger's most comic outing, wacky and offbeat, with good Irving Berlin score including "Change Partners," "I Used to Be Color Blind."▼●

Careful, He Might Hear You (1983-Australian) **C-116m.** ***½ D: Carl Schultz. Wendy Hughes, Robyn Nevin, Nicholas Gledhill, John Hargreaves, Geraldine Turner. Involving drama about Depression-era custody battle between wealthy Hughes and working-class sister Nevin for their nephew, whose mother is dead and father has abandoned him. Manages to be credible yet larger-than-life at the same time, with wonderful shadings and observations. Effectiveness of its wide-screen camerawork will be lost on TV, alas. Michael Jenkins scripted, from a novel by Sumner Locke Elliott. Panavision. [PG]▼

Caretaker, The SEE: **Guest, The**

Caretakers, The (1963) **97m.** *** D: Hall Bartlett. Robert Stack, Joan Crawford, Polly Bergen, Susan Oliver, Janis Paige, Constance Ford, Barbara Barrie, Herbert Marshall. At times incisive view of a West Coast mental hospital, marred by flimsy script and poor editing. Good characterizations by Crawford and Ford as nurses, Bergen and Paige as patients.▼

Carey Treatment, The (1972) **C-101m.** *** D: Blake Edwards. James Coburn, Jennifer O'Neill, Pat Hingle, Skye Aubrey, Elizabeth Allen, Alex Dreier. Good solid whodunit set in hospital, where doctor Coburn is determined to clear colleague of murder charge. O'Neill provides love interest in complicated but satisfying mystery, shot in Boston. Based on the novel *A Case of Need* by Michael Crichton. Panavision. [PG]

Car 54, Where Are You? (1994) **C-89m.** *½ D: Bill Fishman. David Johansen, John C. McGinley, Al Lewis, Fran Drescher, Nipsey Russell, Rosie O'Donnell, Daniel Baldwin, Jeremy Piven, Bobby Collins, Louis Di Bianco, Penn & Teller, Tone Loc. This retread of the hilarious 1960s TV show about N.Y.C. cops with a hefty Keystone quotient is a woefully embarrassing assemblage of gags that would bring up the rear in POLICE ACADEMY. O'Donnell (her screen debut), Drescher, and Piven acquit themselves well, under the circumstances. Despite presence of Al Lewis—reprising his Schnauzer role from the original Nat Hiken series—this turkey sat on the shelf after completion in 1991. [PG-13]▼●

Cargo to Capetown (1950) **80m.** *½ D: Earl McEvoy. Broderick Crawford, John Ireland, Ellen Drew, Edgar Buchanan. Tramp steamer is setting for mild love triangle as Crawford and Ireland vie for Drew.

Caribbean (1952) **C-97m.** ** D: Edward Ludwig. John Payne, Arlene Dahl, Cedric Hardwicke, Francis L. Sullivan, Woody Strode. 18th-century costume vehicle allows Payne to battle pirates and flirt with Dahl.

Cariboo Trail (1950) **C-81m.** **½ D: Edwin L. Marin. Randolph Scott, George "Gabby" Hayes, Bill Williams, Karin Booth, Victor Jory, Jim Davis, Dale Robertson. Standard telling of conflict between cattlemen and settlers bringing civilization obliterating the grazing lands.▼●

Carla's Song (1996-British-Spanish) **C-125m.** *** D: Ken Loach. Robert Carlyle, Oyanka Cabezas, Scott Glenn, Salvador Espinoza, Louise Goodall. Unusual political drama/love story set in 1987 with Glasgow bus driver Carlyle becoming involved with beautiful but deeply troubled Nicaraguan refugee Cabezas. It's difficult to navigate the Scottish accents at first, but the final part of the story, set in the Nicaraguan war zone, is poignant and heartbreaking.▼●◗

Carlito's Way (1993) **C-144m.** *** D: Brian De Palma. Al Pacino, Sean Penn, Penelope Ann Miller, Luis Guzman, John Leguizamo, Ingrid Rogers, James Rebhorn, Joseph Siravo, Viggo Mortensen, Richard Foronjy, Jorge Porcel, Adrian Pasdar. Street-wise Puerto Rican Pacino winds up a five-year jail term and tries to go straight, but loyalty to his sleazy lawyer (Penn), and his inability to accept the fact that "the street" has changed, seal his doom. Flawed but still compelling; based on two Edwin Torres novels about a man with an outmoded code of honor. Pacino is arresting as always; so is an almost unrecognizable Penn. Director Paul Mazursky has a terrific cameo as a judge at the beginning of the story. Panavision. [R]▼●◗

Carlton-Browne of the F.O. SEE: **Man in a Cocked Hat**

Carmen (1983-Spanish) **C-102m.** *** D: Carlos Saura. Antonio Gades, Laura Del Sol, Paco de Lucia, Cristina Hoyos, Juan Antonio Jimenez, Sebastian Moreno. Choreographer prepares dance production of Bizet's opera, but falls under spell of real-life Carmen he casts in leading role. Choreographer/star Gades and sensual Del Sol are superb, though dramatic impact dissipates somewhat during second half. A must for dance buffs. [R]▼●

Carmen (1984-French-Italian) **C-152m.** ** D: Francesco Rosi. Julia Migenes-Johnson, Placido Domingo, Ruggero Raimondi, Faith Esham, Jean-Philippe Lafont, Gerard Garino. Disappointing filmization of the Bizet opera is overbaked and unbelievably inept. Still, opera buffs will enjoy the music—if they close their eyes. Panavision. [PG]▼●

Carmen Jones (1954) **C-105m.** ***½ D: Otto Preminger. Dorothy Dandridge, Harry Belafonte, Pearl Bailey, Roy Glenn, Diahann Carroll, Brock Peters. Powerful melodrama adapted from Bizet's opera by Oscar Hammerstein II, with exciting music and equally exciting Dandridge as the ultimate femme fatale. Stars' singing voices are all dubbed—Dandridge's by opera star Marilyn Horne. Film debuts of Carroll and Peters. CinemaScope. ▼●

Carmen Miranda: Bananas Is My Business (1994-U.S.-Brazilian) **C/B&W-91m.** *** D: Helena Solberg. Savvy exploration of the Brazilian Bombshell's life and times, chronicling the sad transition from revered musical artist in her homeland to caricatured cliché in Hollywood. Filmmaker Solberg's lifelong fascination with Miranda is expressed through film clips, revealing interviews with Brazilian and American colleagues and family, and strikingly, re-creations of moments in her life using a female impersonator! ▼◗

Carnage SEE: **Twitch of the Death Nerve**

Carnal Knowledge (1971) **C-96m.** *** D: Mike Nichols. Jack Nicholson, Candice Bergen, Arthur Garfunkel, Ann-Margret, Rita Moreno, Cynthia O'Neal, Carol Kane. Thought-provoking (if depressing) look at the sexual attitudes and obsessions of two male friends, from college through middle age. Ann-Margret won acclaim for performance as Nicholson's kittenish mistress. Jules Feiffer originally wrote this as a play, then adapted it as a screenplay instead; in 1990 it was staged off-Broadway. Kane's film debut. Panavision. [R]▼●◗

Carnegie Hall (1947) **134m.** **½ D: Edgar G. Ulmer. Marsha Hunt, William Prince, Frank McHugh, Martha O'Driscoll. Lame story about a pushy mother and her pianist son links magnificent concert performances by the cream of the classical music world: Artur Rubinstein, Leopold Stokowski, Jascha Heifetz, Rise Stevens, Lily Pons, Ezio Pinza, Jan Peerce, Gregor Piatigorsky, Bruno Walter and The New York Philharmonic. Some mediocre pop tunes are shoehorned into the proceedings, along with Vaughn Monroe and Harry James.▼

Carnet de Bal SEE: **Un Carnet de Bal**

Carnival in Costa Rica (1947) **C-95m.** ** D: Gregory Ratoff. Dick Haymes, Vera-Ellen, Cesar Romero, Celeste Holm, Anne Revere, J. Carrol Naish. Despite fair cast, boring musical of trip to Costa Rica and the shenanigans of newlyweds and their quarreling parents.

Carnival of Souls (1962) **83m.** **½ D: Herk Harvey. Candace Hilligoss, Sidney Berger, Frances Feist, Herk Harvey, Stan Levitt, Art Ellison. Eerie little film of "phantom figure" pursuing Hilligoss after she has seemingly drowned. Imaginative low-budget effort. Filmed mostly in Lawrence, Kansas. Has developed a strong cult reputation in recent years. Original running time: 91m. Remade in 1998. ▼●◗

Carnival Rock (1957) **75m.** ** D: Roger Corman. Susan Cabot, Dick Miller, Brian Hutton, The Platters, David Houston, David J. Stewart. Stewart, owner of a dilapidated nightclub, loves singer Cabot, who in turn loves gambler Hutton. Forgettable melodrama with The Platters, Houston, and others in musical cameos.▼

Carnival Story (1954) **C-95m.** ** D: Kurt Neumann. Anne Baxter, Steve Cochran, Lyle Bettger, George Nader, Jay C. Flippen. Hardened Baxter is involved with sleazy Cochran. "Nice guy" high diver Bettger takes her on as a protégée, and there are complications. When this romantic melodrama is not trashy, it's sluggish. Set in Germany, and not unlike E.A. Dupont's classic, VARIETY. A German version was also filmed, with Eva Bartok, Bernhard Wicki, and Curt Jurgens.▼

Carnosaur (1993) **C-82m.** ** D: Adam Simon. Diane Ladd, Raphael Sbarge, Jennifer Runyon, Harrison Page, Ned Bellamy, Clint Howard. Brilliant geneticist Ladd hatches man-eating dinosaurs from virus-infected chicken eggs and lets them run amok in an unsuspecting Midwestern city. Roger Corman produced this forgettable film, whose only notoriety will be its legacy as 1993's "other" dinosaur movie (which starred Ladd's daughter, Laura Dern). Followed by two sequels. [R]▼●◗

Carny (1980) **C-107m.** *** D: Robert Kaylor. Gary Busey, Jodie Foster, Robbie Robertson, Meg Foster, Bert Remsen, Kenneth McMillan, John Lehne, Elisha Cook, Craig Wasson. Striking, atmospheric film about a symbiotic pair of carnival hustlers and the teenage runaway who joins them on the road. Candid, intimate (and somewhat voyeuristic) look at seamy midway life, hurt by unsatisfying and abrupt conclusion. Rock star Robertson also produced and cowrote the film. Wonderful score by Alex North. [R]▼

Caro Diario (1994-Italian-French) **C-100m.** *** D: Nanni Moretti. Nanni Moretti, Renato Carpentieri, Antonio Neiwiller, Carlo Mazzacurati, Claudia Della Seta, Jennifer Beals, Alexandre Rockwell. Witty, thoughtful, three-part feature from Moretti, one of the most acclaimed contemporary Italian film director–comedians. He appears in each as himself. First he romps around Rome on a Vespa. Next he goes island-hopping in southern Italy, where he wryly examines Europeans' obsession with American pop culture. Lastly, and most soberly, he recounts his own cancer treatment.▼●

Carolina Cannonball (1955) **74m.** *½ D: Charles Lamont. Judy Canova, Andy Clyde, Jack Kruschen, Ross Elliott. Hicksville hokum with Canova involved with enemy

agents and a missile that lands in her backyard.
Caroline? (1990) **C-100m. TVM** D: Joseph Sargent. Stephanie Zimbalist, Pamela Reed, George Grizzard, Patricia Neal, Dorothy McGuire, Shawn Phelan, Jenny Jacobs. Tense suspenser about a woman, long presumed dead, returning to claim the family inheritance, though there are doubts about her identity. Emmy winner as Outstanding Drama with another Emmy going to director Sargent. Adapted by Michael de Guzman from E. L. Konigsburg's *Father's Arcane Daughter.* Above average. ▼●
Carousel (1956) **C-128m.** ***½ D: Henry King. Gordon MacRae, Shirley Jones, Cameron Mitchell, Barbara Ruick, Claramae Turner, Robert Rounseville, Gene Lockhart. Excellent filmization of Rodgers & Hammerstein's memorable adaptation of Ferenc Molnar's *Liliom*, with MacRae as rowdy carousel barker Billy Bigelow, who tries to change for the better when he falls in love with Jones. Excitement of widescreen location filming will be minimized on TV, but moving characters, timeless songs remain. Script by Phoebe and Henry Ephron. Filmed before as LILIOM in 1930 and 1934. CinemaScope 55.▼●◗
Carpetbaggers, The (1964) **C-150m.** **½ D: Edward Dmytryk. George Peppard, Carroll Baker, Alan Ladd, Bob Cummings, Martha Hyer, Elizabeth Ashley, Lew Ayres, Martin Balsam, Ralph Taeger, Archie Moore, Leif Erickson, Tom Tully, Audrey Totter. Blowsy claptrap based on Harold Robbins novel of millionaire plane manufacturer (Peppard) dabbling in movies and lovemaking à la Howard Hughes. Set in 1920s-30s; sexploitational values are tame. Ladd's last film; followed by prequel, NEVADA SMITH. Panavision.▼●
Carpool (1996) **C-119m.** **½ D: Arthur Hiller. Tom Arnold, David Paymer, Rhea Perlman, Rachael Leigh Cook, Rod Steiger, Kim Coates, Micah Gardener, Mikey Kovar, Colleen Rennison, Jordan Warkov. A desperate down-on-his-luck carnival owner (Arnold) botches his first holdup attempt and takes a harried carpool dad (Paymer) and his young passengers hostage. Some laughs in this likable but uneven comedy. Perlman is wasted. [PG]▼●
Carrie (1952) **118m.** **½ D: William Wyler. Jennifer Jones, Laurence Olivier, Miriam Hopkins, Eddie Albert, Mary Murphy, William Reynolds. Jones passively plays the title role in this uneven turn-of-the-century soaper of poor farm girl who comes to Chicago, eventually links up with unhappily married restaurant manager Olivier (who is excellent). David Raksin's score is a plus. Based on Theodore Dreiser's *Sister Carrie*.▼●
Carrie (1976) **C-97m.** **½ D: Brian De Palma. Sissy Spacek, Piper Laurie, William Katt, John Travolta, Amy Irving, Nancy Allen, Betty Buckley, P.J. Soles, Priscilla Pointer. Evocative story of high school misfit degenerates into cheap, gory melodrama when Spacek unleashes telekinetic powers in revenge against those who have mocked her. De Palma borrows much from Hitchcock, but has little of The Master's wit or subtlety. Screenplay by Lawrence D. Cohen, from Stephen King's novel. Debut film for Irving, Buckley and Soles. Later a stage musical. Followed by THE RAGE: CARRIE 2. [R]▼●◗
Carried Away (1996) **C-107m.** **½ D: Bruno Barreto. Dennis Hopper, Amy Irving, Amy Locane, Julie Harris, Gary Busey, Hal Holbrook, Priscilla Pointer. Hopper gives a thoughtful performance in an unusual role: a small-town Midwestern farmer/teacher who keeps putting off marrying his fiancée (Irving), and then is not unwillingly seduced by teen vamp Locane. Abundant nudity may grab attention. Based on a novel by Jim Harrison. Barreto is Irving's husband, and Pointer is her mother. [R]▼●
Carrier, The (1988) **C-99m.** *** D: Nathan J. White. Gregory Fortescue, Stevie Lee, Steve Dixon, N. Paul Silverman, Paul Urbanski, Patrick Butler. Allegorical, Stephen King–inspired indie, shot in Michigan, about mysterious dissolving disease striking a small town. Unknown to all, disease is carried by a persecuted young man. Well-acted, inexpensive film is confident and aware of its own absurdities, though it falters at the very end. [R]▼
Carrington (1995-British-French) **C-122m.** *** D: Christopher Hampton. Emma Thompson, Jonathan Pryce, Steven Waddington, Rufus Sewell, Samuel West, Penelope Wilton, Janet McTeer, Peter Blythe, Jeremy Northam. Gifted English painter Dora Carrington is afraid of her own sexuality, until she meets eccentric (and homosexual) writer Lytton Strachey and experiences love for the first time. What's more, he feels the same way . . . except they're never able to resolve their hesitancy about a full commitment. Compelling character study is slowly paced and perhaps redundant at times, but made fascinating by the leads' superb portrayals. Playwright/screenwriter Hampton's directing debut. [R]▼●
Carrington, V. C. SEE: **Court Martial**
Carry On Admiral SEE: **Ship Was Loaded, The**
Carry On Camping (1972-British) **C-89m.** ** D: Gerald Thomas. Sidney James, Kenneth Williams, Joan Sims, Barbara Windsor, Bernard Bresslaw, Terry Scott. The gang encounters hippie types at weekend campsite; usual double-entendre jokes in entry from never-ending series. [R]▼
Carry On Cleo (1965-British) **C-92m.** **½ D: Gerald Thomas. Amanda Barrie, Sid-

ney James, Kenneth Williams, Joan Sims, Kenneth Connor, Charles Hawtrey. Diverting reworking of ancient history to serve as amusing satire on CLEOPATRA epic, sufficiently laced with hijinks by perennial misfits. Also on tape as CALIGULA'S FUNNIEST HOME VIDEOS. ▼

Carry On Doctor (1968-British) **C-95m.** ** D: Gerald Thomas. Frankie Howerd, Kenneth Williams, Jim Dale, Barbara Windsor. Madcap group takes on medical profession. As usual, interest wanes after an hour and the amount of laughter varies quite a bit. [PG]▼

Carry On Henry VIII (1972-British) **C-90m.** ** D: Gerald Thomas. Sidney James, Kenneth Williams, Joan Sims, Charles Hawtrey, Barbara Windsor. Lecherous king, ribald times perfect milieu for "Carry On" gang's brand of farce; for fans only. [PG]▼

Carry On Nurse (1959-British) **90m.** **½ D: Gerald Thomas. Kenneth Connor, Shirley Eaton, Charles Hawtrey, Hattie Jacques, Terence Longdon, Leslie Phillips, Joan Sims, Kenneth Williams, Wilfrid Hyde-White, Joan Hickson, Jill Ireland, Michael Medwin. Occasionally funny but too often silly farce detailing the various hijinks in a hospital ward. Typical entry in the series is crammed with lowbrow humor.▼

Carry On Sergeant (1959-British) **88m.** ** D: Gerald Thomas. William Hartnell, Bob Monkhouse, Shirley Eaton, Eric Barker, Dora Bryan, Bill Owen, Kenneth Connor. This time around prankish misfits are the bane of Army officer's existence, who swears he'll make these recruits spiffy soldiers or bust.

Carry On Spying (1965-British) **88m.** **½ D: Gerald Thomas. Kenneth Williams, Barbara Windsor, Bernard Cribbins, Charles Hawtrey, Eric Barker, Victor Maddern. Acceptable James Bond spoof with daffy novice spy-catchers on the hunt for enemy agents who stole secret formula.

Carson City (1952) **C-87m.** ** D: Andre De Toth. Randolph Scott, Lucille Norman, Raymond Massey, Don Beddoe, Richard Webb, James Millican, Larry Keating, George Cleveland. Opposing forces clash when construction engineer Scott commences building a railroad through Nevada in the 1870s. OK of its type.

Cars That Ate Paris, The (1974-Australian) **C-91m.** **½ D: Peter Weir. Terry Camilleri, John Meillon, Melissa Jaffa, Kevin Miles. The poor people of Paris (Paris, Australia, that is) keep the economy going by inducing traffic accidents and selling the spare parts/scrap metal. Iffy black comedy has its moments; must viewing for those who've followed Weir's directorial career step-by-step into the big leagues. Originally released in the U.S. at 74m, retitled THE CARS THAT EAT PEOPLE; full-length version finally made it here in 1984. Panavision. [PG]▼

Cars That Eat People, The SEE: **Cars That Ate Paris, The**

Carthage in Flames (1959-Italian) **C-96m.** ** D: Carmine Gallone. Jose Suarez, Pierre Brasseur, Anne Heywood, Illaria Occhini. Unremarkable mixture of love and intrigue set against backdrop of Rome-Carthage war of 2nd century B.C.; spirited action scenes. Super Technirama 70.▼

Cartouche (1964-French-Italian) **C-115m.** ***½ D: Philippe De Broca. Jean-Paul Belmondo, Claudia Cardinale, Odile Versois, Jess Hahn, Jean Rochefort, Philippe Lemaire, Marcel Dalio, Noel Roquevert. Colorful, exciting exploits of 18th-century French Robin Hood who takes over a Parisian crime syndicate. Belmondo is dashing as Cartouche and Cardinale is ravishing as Venus, his gypsy-mistress, in this rousing action-comedy. Dyaliscope.▼

Car Trouble (1985-British) **C-93m.** *** D: David Green. Julie Walters, Ian Charleson, Vincenzo Ricotta, Stratford Johns, Hazel O'Connor, Dave Hill. Low-key farce about a hilariously hideous couple whose Bickerson-like marriage is put to the ultimate test when he buys his dream car, and she goes for a fateful spin. Walters and Charleson are ideal, and the film offers some genuine belly laughs. [R]▼

Carve Her Name With Pride (1958-British) **119m.** *** D: Lewis Gilbert. Virginia McKenna, Paul Scofield, Jack Warner, Maurice Ronet, Bill Owen, Denise Grey, Billie Whitelaw, Michael Caine. McKenna, widowed during WW2, becomes a courageous British secret agent. Solid and inspiring; based on a true story.▼

Car Wash (1976) **C-97m.** **½ D: Michael Schultz. Richard Pryor, Franklin Ajaye, Sully Boyar, Ivan Dixon, George Carlin, Irwin Corey, Melanie Mayron, The Pointer Sisters, Garrett Morris, Antonio Fargas, Brooke Adams. Boisterous look at L.A. car-wash is light excuse for barely connected comedy set-pieces, involving various and sundry characters, and pulsating soul music performed by Rose Royce. Often very funny, but no awards for good taste; written by Joel Schumacher. [PG]▼●◗

Casablanca (1942) **102m.** **** D: Michael Curtiz. Humphrey Bogart, Ingrid Bergman, Paul Henreid, Claude Rains, Conrad Veidt, Peter Lorre, Sydney Greenstreet, Dooley Wilson, Marcel Dalio, S.Z. Sakall, Joy Page, Helmut Dantine, Curt Bois. Everything is right in this WW2 classic of war-torn Morocco with elusive nightclub owner Rick (Bogart) finding old flame (Bergman) and her husband, underground leader Henreid, among skeletons in his closet. Rains is marvelous as dapper police chief, and nobody sings "As Time Goes By" like Dooley Wilson. Three Oscars include Picture, Director, and Screenplay (Julius & Philip Epstein and Howard Koch). Our candidate for the best Hollywood movie of all time. Spawned short-lived TV series in the 1950s and the 1980s. Also shown in computer-colored version.▼●◗

Casanova & Co. (1976-Austrian-Italian-French-German) **C-88m.** *½ D: Franz Antel. Tony Curtis, Marisa Berenson, Sylva Koscina, Hugh Griffith, Britt Ekland, Marisa Mell, Umberto Orsini, Andrea Ferreol, Victor Spinetti, Lillian Muller. Misfired slapstick romp debunks the legend with Curtis playing dual roles of Casanova and a lookalike commoner. Diverse female cast (including former *Playboy* Playmates) disrobes at will, while Tony in drag explicitly mocks his classic SOME LIKE IT HOT role. Video titles: SEX ON THE RUN and SOME LIKE IT COOL.▼

Casanova Brown (1944) **94m.** **½ D: Sam Wood. Gary Cooper, Teresa Wright, Frank Morgan, Anita Louise, Isobel Elsom. Cooper has divorced Wright, but now she's pregnant; entertaining little comedy with stars outshining material. Filmed in 1930 and 1939 as LITTLE ACCIDENT. ▼

Casanova in Burlesque (1944) **74m.** **½ D: Leslie Goodwins. Joe E. Brown, June Havoc, Dale Evans, Lucien Littlefield, Ian Keith. Shakespearean professor leads double life as burlesque clown; spirited little comedy with Brown in good form.

Casanova's Big Night (1954) **C-86m.** *** D: Norman Z. McLeod. Bob Hope, Joan Fontaine, Audrey Dalton, Basil Rathbone, Raymond Burr, Vincent Price. Lavish costumed fun with Bob masquerading as Casanova (Price) in Venice and wooing lovely Fontaine.▼●

Casanova '70 (1965-French-Italian) **C-113m.** **½ D: Mario Monicelli. Marcello Mastroianni, Virna Lisi, Michele Mercier, Marisa Mell, Marco Ferreri, Enrico Maria Salerno. Dashing Major Mastroianni is only interested in seducing women when there is an element of danger involved. Modest, though amusing.▼

Casa Ricordi SEE: **House of Ricordi**

Casbah (1948) **94m.** *** D: John Berry. Tony Martin, Yvonne de Carlo, Peter Lorre, Marta Toren, Hugo Haas, Thomas Gomez, Douglas Dick, Katherine Dunham, Herbert Rudley, Virginia Gregg. If you can accept singer Martin as slippery thief Pepe Le Moko (he's actually quite good) you'll enjoy this musical remake of ALGIERS. It's stylishly directed and designed, and features Lorre in one of his best performances as the crafty inspector determined to nail Le Moko. Fine score by Harold Arlen and Leo Robin includes "For Every Man There's a Woman" and "Hooray for Love." Look fast and you'll spot Eartha Kitt, then one of the Katherine Dunham dance troupe. Martin also produced the film.▼

Case Against Brooklyn, The (1958) **82m.** *½ D: Paul Wendkos. Darren McGavin, Maggie Hayes, Warren Stevens, Peggy McCay. Unexciting little exposé yarn involves fledgling cop McGavin combatting gambling syndicate in title borough.

Case Against Mrs. Ames, The (1936) **85m.** **½ D: William Seiter. Madeleine Carroll, George Brent, Arthur Treacher, Alan Baxter, Beulah Bondi. D.A. Brent finds himself falling in love with beautiful Carroll, suspected of murdering her husband.

Case of Dr. Laurent, The (1958-French) **91m.** ** D: Jean-Paul le Chanois. Jean Gabin, Nicole Courcel, Sylvia Monfort, Michel Barbey. Film was exploited theatrically for its frank birth sequence, only small logical sequence in recounting life of country doctor Gabin who advocates natural childbirth.▼

Case of Jonathan Drew, The SEE: **Lodger, The** (1926)

Case of Mrs. Loring, The SEE: **Question of Adultery, A**

Case of the Black Cat, The (1936) **65m.** **½ D: William McGann. Ricardo Cortez, June Travis, Jane Bryan, Craig Reynolds, Harry Davenport. A trio of murders, a treasure hunt and a shrieking feline are the ingredients of this enjoyable *Perry Mason* mystery, with Cortez quite adequate in his only crack at the role.

Case of the Curious Bride, The (1935) **80m.** ** D: Michael Curtiz. Warren William, Margaret Lindsay, Donald Woods, Claire Dodd, Allen Jenkins, Wini Shaw. Shrill Perry Mason film takes offhanded approach to murder mystery with large doses of humor; Perry (William) is more interested in gourmet food than he is in the case! Errol Flynn has small role as the victim in his second Hollywood film.

Case of the Howling Dog, The (1934) **75m.** ** D: Alan Crosland. Warren William, Mary Astor, Helen Trenholme, Allen Jenkins, Grant Mitchell, Dorothy Tree. First of the *Perry Mason* series is probably the least interesting, centering on the case of feuding neighbors who both claim they're married to the same woman.

Case of the Lucky Legs, The (1935) **76m.** **½ D: Archie Mayo. Warren William, Genevieve Tobin, Patricia Ellis, Lyle Talbot, Allen Jenkins, Barton MacLane. Stylish *Perry Mason* whodunit centering on the murder of a sleazy beauty contest promoter. A dose of humor is added by having bon vivant Perry struggling to stay on the wagon.▼

Case of the Red Monkey (1955-British) **73m.** ** D: Ken Hughes. Richard Conte, Rona Anderson, Colin Gordon, Russell Napier. Acceptable police-on-the-case fare, tracking down murderers of atomic scientists.

Case of the Stuttering Bishop, The (1937) **70m.** ** D: William Clemens. Donald

Woods, Ann Dvorak, Anne Nagel, Linda Perry, Craig Stevens. Woods is a bland Perry Mason in this last series entry, concerning a phony heiress.
Case of the Velvet Claws, The (1936) **60m.** ** D: William Clemens. Warren William, Claire Dodd, Winifred Shaw, Gordon (William) Elliott, Joseph King. Perry Mason (William) finally weds Della Street, but the honeymoon is interrupted by the case of a murdered scandal sheet publisher. Brisk entry marked William's final appearance in the role.
Casey's Shadow (1978) **C-117m.** **½ D: Martin Ritt. Walter Matthau, Alexis Smith, Robert Webber, Murray Hamilton, Andrew A. Rubin, Stephen Burns. Lackadaisical family film about a ne'er-do-well horse trainer who has to raise three sons after his wife leaves him. Generally satisfactory, but should have been better. Panavision. [PG]▼
Cash (1933-British) **73m.** *½ D: Zoltan Korda. Robert Donat, Wendy Barrie, Edmund Gwenn, Clifford Heatherley, Morris Harvey. Dull, disappointing comedy about ex-rich boy Donat, now working for a living, who becomes involved with pretty Barrie and scheming father Gwenn. The U.S. title was FOR LOVE OR MONEY; aka IF I WERE RICH.▼
Cash McCall (1959) **C-102m.** **½ D: Joseph Pevney. James Garner, Natalie Wood, Nina Foch, Dean Jagger, E.G. Marshall, Henry Jones, Otto Kruger, Roland Winters. Garner is just right as business tycoon who adopts new set of values as he romances daughter (Wood) of failing businessman Jagger. Superficial film from Cameron Hawley novel.▼
Cash on Delivery (1956-British) **82m.** ** D: Muriel Box. Shelley Winters, John Gregson, Peggy Cummins, Wilfrid Hyde-White. Story with a twist suffers from sloppy execution. Winters seeks to earn inheritance by preventing ex-husband's wife from having a child. Original title: TO DOROTHY A SON.
Casino (1995) **C-182m.** ** D: Martin Scorsese. Robert De Niro, Sharon Stone, Joe Pesci, James Woods, Don Rickles, Alan King, Kevin Pollak, L. Q. Jones, Dick Smothers, Frank Vincent, Melissa Prophet, John Bloom (Joe Bob Briggs). Long, tedious tale of a numbers-obsessed gambler sent to Las Vegas by the mob to run a casino in the 1970s. Problem is, neither he nor his loose-cannon pal, who follows him, nor the hustler he decides to marry has any idea how to hold on to what they've got. Disappointing reteaming of Scorsese and writer Nicholas Pileggi, who scored big with GOODFELLAS; this time, their story is overlong, repetitive, and aloof. Stone makes her mark amidst a heavyweight cast with a full-blown dramatic performance. Super 35. [R]▼●◗
Casino Murder Case (1935) **85m.** ** D: Edwin L. Marin. Paul Lukas, Alison Skipworth, Donald Cook, Rosalind Russell, Arthur Byron, Ted Healy, Eric Blore, Leo G. Carroll, William Demarest. Polished but perfunctory *Philo Vance* mystery about a series of murders at the mansion of eccentric old lady Skipworth, with Healy and Blore around for comic relief. Stolid, thickly accented Lukas is not very effective as Vance.
Casino Royale (1967-British) **C-130m.** **½ D: John Huston, Ken Hughes, Robert Parrish, Joe McGrath, Val Guest. Peter Sellers, Ursula Andress, David Niven, Orson Welles, Joanna Pettet, Woody Allen, Deborah Kerr, William Holden, Charles Boyer, John Huston, George Raft, Jean-Paul Belmondo, Jackie (Jacqueline) Bisset. Gigantic, overdone spoof of James Bond films with Niven as the aging secret agent who relinquishes his position to nephew Allen and host of others. Money, money everywhere, but film is terribly uneven—sometimes funny, often not. Good score by Burt Bacharach, including hit song "The Look of Love." Panavision.▼●
Casper (1995) **C-100m.** BOMB D: Brad Silberling. Christina Ricci, Bill Pullman, Cathy Moriarty, Eric Idle, Amy Brenneman, Ben Stein, Don Novello, voices of Malachi Pearson, Joe Nipote, Joe Alaskey, Brad Garrett. High-tech Hollywood "product" takes the vintage cartoon character—a friendly ghost—and literalizes him in this story of *a dead boy* whose haunted house is invaded by a widowed paranormalist (and daughter) seeking the spirit of his dead wife. Talk about family fun! Absolutely dreadful, wrong-headed movie is strictly for families who are already dead from the neck up. A handful of surprise Hollywood cameos add a few fleeting laughs. Followed by two direct-to-video sequels. [PG]▼●◗
Cassandra Crossing, The (1977-British) **C-127m.** *** D: George Pan Cosmatos. Richard Harris, Sophia Loren, Burt Lancaster, Ava Gardner, Martin Sheen, O.J. Simpson, John Phillip Law, Ingrid Thulin, Alida Valli, Lionel Stander. Entertaining disaster epic as train carrying plague approaches a weakened bridge. Filmed in France and Italy. [R]▼◗
Cass Timberlane (1947) **119m.** **½ D: George Sidney. Spencer Tracy, Lana Turner, Zachary Scott, Tom Drake, Mary Astor, Albert Dekker. Overblown adaptation of Sinclair Lewis novel of esteemed judge trying to keep pace with new young wife; not Tracy's cup of tea.▼
Cast a Dark Shadow (1955-British) **84m.** *** D: Lewis Gilbert. Dirk Bogarde, Margaret Lockwood, Kathleen Harrison, Kay Walsh, Robert Flemyng, Mona Washbourne. Tense suspenser with Bogarde in fine form as a psychotic Bluebeard who murders rich, aging mate Washbourne.

Lockwood and Walsh won't be such easy prey, however.▼

Cast a Giant Shadow (1966) **C-142m.** ** D: Melville Shavelson. Kirk Douglas, John Wayne, Frank Sinatra, Yul Brynner, Senta Berger, Angie Dickinson, James Donald, Luther Adler, (Chaim) Topol. Hokey bio of Arab-Israeli war hero Mickey Marcus has Kirk leaving Angie's bed to join Senta and several other less sexy freedom fighters. Guest roles by big names make film seem even sillier. Panavision.▼●

Cast a Long Shadow (1959) **82m.** *½ D: Thomas Carr. Audie Murphy, Terry Moore, John Dehner, James Best, Rita Lynn, Denver Pyle, Ann Doran. Murphy, troubled by shady past, is reformed by being given a ranch and building a new future; plodding oater.

Castaway (1987) **C-117m.** **½ D: Nicolas Roeg. Oliver Reed, Amanda Donohoe, Tony Rickards, Todd Rippon, Georgina Hale, Frances Barber. Scruffy Reed advertises for a "wife" to join him for a year on a desert island; Donohoe is the incongruously vavavoomish adventure seeker who answers it. Visually splendid adaptation of Lucy Irvine's best-seller seems unlikely *as told*, though it remains a visceral experience, particularly for Roeg fans. Eventually overplays its hand. [R]▼

Castaway Cowboy, The (1974) **C-91m.** ** D: Vincent McEveety. James Garner, Vera Miles, Robert Culp, Eric Shea, Elizabeth Smith, Gregory Sierra. Cowboy Garner is shipwrecked on Hawaiian island, runs into pretty widow and bad-guy Culp who wants her land. Old B-Western plot, Disney-fied on Hawaiian locations. [G]▼◗

Castilian, The (1963-Spanish) **C-129m.** **½ D: Javier Seto. Cesar Romero, Alida Valli, Frankie Avalon, Broderick Crawford, Spartaco Santoni. Strange grouping of actors are given little support by sticky script in costumer of nobleman leading his people against invaders.▼

Castle, The (1968-German-Swiss) **C-93m.** *** D: Rudolf Noelte. Maximilian Schell, Cordula Trantow, Trudik Daniel, Helmut Qualtinger. Appropriately vague filmization of Kafka's novel: "K" (Schell), a land surveyor, is called to a castle for work but is unable to gain admittance.▼

Castle, The (1997-Australian) **C-84m.** *** D: Rob Sitch. Michael Caton, Anne Tenney, Stephen Curry, Anthony Simcoe, Sophie Lee, Wayne Hope, Tiriel Mora, Charles (Bud) Tingwell. Winning low-budget comedy of the unsophisticated Kerrigan family, whose home sits atop a toxic landfill—adjacent to an airport runway! When Dad (Caton) decides to fight the government to keep their ramshackle abode, watch out. Equal parts Capraesque, goofy, and heartfelt. Conceived by several Australian radio and TV comedy hands; a smash in its native country. [R]▼

Castle in the Desert (1942) **62m.** *** D: Harry Lachman. Sidney Toler, Arleen Whelan, Richard Derr, Douglass Dumbrille, Henry Daniell, Edmund MacDonald, Victor Sen Yung, Ethel Griffies. Twentieth Century-Fox's last *Charlie Chan* entry is a first-rate mystery set in a spooky mansion in the Mojave, where mysterious deaths are occurring.▼

Castle Keep (1969) **C-105m.** *½ D: Sydney Pollack. Burt Lancaster, Peter Falk, Patrick O'Neal, Jean-Pierre Aumont, Scott Wilson, Al Freeman, Jr., Tony Bill, Bruce Dern, Astrid Heeren, Michael Conrad. Pretentious adaptation of William Eastlake's novel about eight soldiers on French border in WW2. Good cast, but film has no coherency. Panavision. [R]

Castle of Blood SEE: **Castle of Terror, The**

Castle of Evil (1966) **C-81m.** BOMB D: Francis D. Lyon. Scott Brady, Virginia Mayo, David Brian, Lisa Gaye, Hugh Marlowe. Electronic man belonging to dead chemist becomes unprogrammed at the reading of his master's will and starts killing the survivors. Producers should have taken the film's production costs and bought a candy bar instead.▼

Castle of Fu Manchu, The (1970) **92m.** BOMB D: Jess Franco. Christopher Lee, Richard Greene, Maria Perschy, Gunther Stoll, Howard Marion Crawford. Lee buries Fu Manchu with this one—the pits—experimenting with more deadly potions in his castle near Istanbul and parrying with his perennial adversary, Nayland Smith (Greene) of Britain's Home Office. Originally released in the U.S. as ASSIGNMENT ISTANBUL. Widescreen. [PG]▼

Castle of Terror, The (1964-Italian-French) **85m.** ** D: Anthony Dawson (Antonio Margheriti). Barbara Steele, George Riviere, Margrete Robsahm, Henry Kruger, Montgomery Glenn, Sylvia Sorente. On a wager, poet spends the night in haunted castle. Atmospheric chiller. Remade by the same director as WEB OF THE SPIDER.▼

Castle of the Living Dead (1963-Italian-French) **90m.** ** D: Herbert Wise (Luciano Ricci). Christopher Lee, Gala Germani, Philippe Leroy, Jacques Stanislawski, Donald Sutherland. Lee is suitably cast as sinister Count Drago, who mummifies visitors to his gothic castle. Unexceptional horror fare, notable mainly as Sutherland's film debut in two roles—one an old lady.▼

Castle of the Walking Dead SEE: **Torture Chamber of Dr. Sadism, The**

Castle on the Hudson (1940) **77m.** *** D: Anatole Litvak. John Garfield, Pat O'Brien, Ann Sheridan, Burgess Meredith, Jerome Cowan, Henry O'Neill, Guinn "Big

Boy'' Williams, John Litel. Faithful but familiar remake of 20,000 YEARS IN SING SING, with tough, stubborn hood Garfield going up against dedicated, reform-minded warden O'Brien.

Castles in the Sky SEE: **Yidl Mitn Fidl**

Casual Sex? (1988) **C-97m.** **½ D: Genevieve Robert. Lea Thompson, Victoria Jackson, Stephen Shellen, Jerry Levine, Andrew (Dice) Clay, Mary Gross. Lightweight look at two young women who are looking for something more than a one-night stand—especially in these cautious times—and try their luck at a health and fitness spa. Slight but engaging contemporary comedy from young women's point of view, adapted from the play by Wendy Goldman and Judy Toll. [R]▼●◗

Casualties of War (1989) **C-113m.** ** D: Brian De Palma. Michael J. Fox, Sean Penn, Don Harvey, John C. Reilly, John Leguizamo, Thuy Thu Le, Erik King, Sam Robards, Ving Rhames. Vietnam War picture focusing on one patrol, led by off-the-wall Penn, and its inhumane treatment of an innocent Vietnamese girl. As the Voice of Reason, Fox is well cast, but his clean-cut decency gets to be a bit much; Penn and Thu Le (the victim) are more effective. For all its good intentions, film has a jumbled, detached feel to it (though it's scripted by playwright David Rabe, a Vietnam veteran and author of *Sticks and Bones* and *Streamers*). Based on a real incident detailed in Daniel Lang's *New Yorker* article, later published as a book. Panavision. [R]▼●

Catalina Caper (1967) **C-84m.** *½ D: Lee Sholem. Tommy Kirk, Del Moore, Peter Duryea, Robert Donner, Ulla Stromstedt, Brian Cutler, Little Richard, The Cascades. There's little to recommend—not even Little Richard—in this forgettable beach-party item about college boys Kirk and Cutler on the trail of art thieves. Aka NEVER STEAL ANYTHING WET. [G]

Catamount Killing, The (1974-German) **C-93m.** ** D: Krzysztof Zanussi. Horst Buchholz, Ann Wedgeworth, Chip Taylor, Louise Clark, Patricia Joyce, Polly Holliday. German film made in Vermont with Polish director. Passably interesting story of two small-town people who try to pull off bank heist and then come to grips with themselves as criminals.▼

Cat and Mouse (1974) SEE: **Mousey**

Cat and Mouse (1975-French) **C-107m.** ***½ D: Claude Lelouch. Michele Morgan, Serge Reggiani, Philippe Leotard, Jean-Pierre Aumont, Valerie Lagrange. Anyone could've killed wealthy Aumont, philandering husband of Morgan, and Inspector Reggiani finds out who and why. Denouement is only letdown in this delightful comedy mystery, written, directed, and produced by master Lelouch. Dazzling views of Paris and the countryside. Released here in 1978. [PG]▼

Cat and the Canary, The (1927) **74m.** *** D: Paul Leni. Laura LaPlante, Tully Marshall, Flora Finch, Creighton Hale, Gertrude Astor, Lucien Littlefield. Delightful silent classic, the forerunner of all ''old dark house'' mysteries, with nice touch of humor throughout as heiress LaPlante and nervous group spend night in haunted house. Remade several times.▼●

Cat and the Canary, The (1939) **74m.** *** D: Elliott Nugent. Bob Hope, Paulette Goddard, Gale Sondergaard, John Beal, Douglass Montgomery, Nydia Westman, Elizabeth Patterson, George Zucco. Entertaining remake of the venerable ''old dark house'' chiller, spiced with Hope's brand of humor. This film cemented his movie stardom and led to the even more successful scare comedy THE GHOST BREAKERS. Remade again in 1978.

Cat and the Canary, The (1978-British) **C-90m.** **½ D: Radley Metzger. Honor Blackman, Michael Callan, Edward Fox, Wendy Hiller, Olivia Hussey, Carol Lynley, Peter McEnery, Wilfrid Hyde-White. Entertaining remake of the old-dark-house staple, with a likable cast; reasonably faithful to the original, with the nicest twist being Hyde-White's method of communicating with his heirs. [PG]▼●◗

Cat and the Fiddle, The (1934) **90m.** *** D: William K. Howard. Jeanette MacDonald, Ramon Novarro, Frank Morgan, Charles Butterworth, Jean Hersholt. Delightful Jerome Kern-Oscar Hammerstein operetta, filled with sly comedy and clever ideas. Novarro is a struggling composer who forces his attentions on MacDonald; Morgan is ''benefactor'' who comes between them. Songs include ''The Night Was Made for Love,'' ''She Didn't Say Yes.'' Final sequence is in color.▼

Cat Ballou (1965) **C-96m.** ***½ D: Elliot Silverstein. Jane Fonda, Lee Marvin, Michael Callan, Dwayne Hickman, Tom Nardini, John Marley, Reginald Denny, Jay C. Flippen, Arthur Hunnicutt, Bruce Cabot. Funny Western spoof, with Fonda as Cat Ballou, notorious school-teacher-turned-outlaw. Marvin copped an Oscar for his dual role as a drunken gunman and his twin, a desperado with an artificial nose. Nat King Cole and Stubby Kaye appear as strolling minstrels. Roy Chanslor's novel was adapted by Walter Newman and Frank R. Pierson.▼●

Cat Chaser (1989) **C-90m.** **½ D: Abel Ferrara. Kelly McGillis, Peter Weller, Frederic Forrest, Charles Durning, Tomas Milian, Juan Fernandez. Wordy political thriller based on Elmore Leonard's novel about an ex-soldier reuniting with old flame whose husband happens to be the head of the secret police in Santo Domingo. Some

decent performances, but film is often confusing and dull. Never released theatrically. Alternate, unrated version runs 92m. [R]▼
Catch Me a Spy SEE: **To Catch a Spy**
Catch My Soul (1974) **C-95m.** *½ D: Patrick McGoohan. Richie Havens, Lance LeGault, Season Hubley, Tony Joe White, Susan Tyrrell, Delaney and Bonnie Bramlett. Jack Good's rock-opera adaptation of Shakespeare's *Othello*, with Havens as sanctimonious preacher and LeGault as his Iago is uninvolving, heavy-handed stuff. Some good music, but if the play's the thing, this one doesn't make it. Retitled: SANTA FE SATAN. [PG]
Catch-22 (1970) **C-121m.** **½ D: Mike Nichols. Alan Arkin, Martin Balsam, Richard Benjamin, Arthur (Art) Garfunkel, Jack Gilford, Buck Henry, Bob Newhart, Anthony Perkins, Paula Prentiss, Martin Sheen, Jon Voight, Orson Welles, Bob Balaban, Marcel Dalio, Norman Fell, Charles Grodin, Austin Pendleton, Peter Bonerz, Elizabeth Wilson. Long, labored, expensive film of Joseph Heller's book halfway succeeds in capturing surrealist insanity of WW2 Army life. Heavy-handedness spoils potential; good cast tries its best. Script by costar Henry. Panavision. [R]▼●
Catch Us If You Can SEE: **Having a Wild Weekend**
Cat Creature, The (1973) **C-72m. TVM** D: Curtis Harrington. Meredith Baxter, David Hedison, Gale Sondergaard, Stuart Whitman, Keye Luke, John Carradine, Peter Lorre, Jr. Script by Robert Bloch and good direction combine in unusual horror tale of cat goddess possessing victims to gain access to gold amulet. Good suspense. Above average.
Cat Creeps, The (1946) **58m.** BOMB D: Erle C. Kenton. Noah Beery, Jr., Lois Collier, Paul Kelly, Douglass Dumbrille, Rose Hobart. Lowest of low-grade horrors, with cat possessing dead girl's soul.
Catered Affair, The (1956) **93m.** *** D: Richard Brooks. Bette Davis, Ernest Borgnine, Debbie Reynolds, Barry Fitzgerald, Rod Taylor. Davis sheds all glamour as Bronx taxi driver's wife wanting to give daughter ritzy wedding. Gore Vidal's script based on Paddy Chayefsky TV play. Also shown in computer-colored version.▼
Cat From Outer Space, The (1978) **C-104m.** **½ D: Norman Tokar. Ken Berry, Sandy Duncan, McLean Stevenson, Harry Morgan, Roddy McDowall, Ronnie Schell. Kids will probably like this Disney fantasy-comedy, though it holds few surprises: cat from another world seeks help from U.S. scientists to repair his spaceship, but military protocol and enemy spying get in the way. Ironically, plot has many similarities to later E.T.! [G] ▼●◗
Cat Girl (1957-British) **69m.** *½ D: Alfred Shaughnessy. Barbara Shelley, Robert Ayres, Kay Callard, Paddy Webster. Shelley is possessed by family curse which gives her a psychic link with ferocious leopard; rash of murders ensues. Pacing and low production values spoil it.▼
Catherine & Co. (1975-French-Italian) **C-99m.** ** D: Michel Boisrond. Jane Birkin, Patrick Dewaere, Jean-Pierre Aumont, Vittorio Caprioli, Jean-Claude Brialy. Slight sexual comedy about young girl who becomes prostitute and decides to incorporate herself. TV prints run 84m. [R]▼
Catherine the Great (1934-British) **92m.** **½ D: Paul Czinner. Douglas Fairbanks, Jr., Elisabeth Bergner, Flora Robson, Joan Gardner, Gerald Du Maurier. Lavish historical drama of Russian czarina whose life is spoiled by rigidly planned marriage. Slow-moving but interesting. Also known as THE RISE OF CATHERINE THE GREAT.▼●
Catholics (1973) **C-78m. TVM** D: Jack Gold. Trevor Howard, Martin Sheen, Raf Vallone, Cyril Cusack, Andrew Keir, Michael Gambon, Leon Vitale. Powerful futuristic religious drama pitting strong-willed abbot Howard against emissary-of-change Sheen, sent by the Vatican to his secluded monastery. Wordy but thought-provoking; adapted by Brian Moore from his novel. Video title: THE CONFLICT. Above average.▼
Cathy Tippel SEE: **Keetje Tippel**
Catlow (1971) **C-103m.** **½ D: Sam Wanamaker. Yul Brynner, Richard Crenna, Leonard Nimoy, Daliah Lavi, Jo Ann Pflug, Jeff Corey. Outlaw tries to avoid interference on his way to $2 million gold robbery. Basically a comedy, with a surprisingly ebullient Brynner. Based on a Louis L'Amour novel. [PG]▼
Cat on a Hot Tin Roof (1958) **C-108m.** ***½ D: Richard Brooks. Elizabeth Taylor, Paul Newman, Burl Ives, Jack Carson, Judith Anderson, Madeleine Sherwood, Larry Gates. Southern patriarch Ives learns he is dying; his greedy family, except for son Newman, falls all over itself sucking up to him. Tennessee Williams' classic study of "mendacity" comes to the screen somewhat laundered but still packing a wallop; entire cast is sensational. Adaptation by Brooks and James Poe.▼●◗
Cat o' Nine Tails, The (1971-Italian-German-French) **C-112m.** BOMB D: Dario Argento. Karl Malden, James Franciscus, Catherine Spaak, Cinzia De Carolis, Carlo Alighiero. Former newsman Malden, now blind, teams with reporter Franciscus to track down psycho killer in this gruesome murder mystery; graphic gore and sex, and badly dubbed, to boot. Techniscope.[PG]▼
Cat People (1942) **73m.** *** D: Jacques Tourneur. Simone Simon, Kent Smith, Tom Conway, Jack Holt, Jane Randolph. Storyline and plot elements don't hold up, but moments of shock and terror are undiminished in the first of producer Val

Lewton's famous horror films. Smith falls in love with strange, shy woman (Simon) who fears ancient curse of the panther inside her. Followed by CURSE OF THE CAT PEOPLE. Remade in 1982.▼●

Cat People (1982) **C-118m.** ** D: Paul Schrader. Nastassia Kinski, Malcolm McDowell, John Heard, Annette O'Toole, Ruby Dee, Ed Begley, Jr., Scott Paulin, John Larroquette. Virginal Kinski moves in with brother McDowell, a "cat man," and falls in love with zoo curator Heard as a black panther rampages through community. Sexy, bloody, technically well crafted, but uneven and ultimately unsatisfying; Schrader seems more concerned with camera angles and nudity than coherent storyline. Loosely based on the 1942 film. [R]▼●◗

Cats Don't Dance (1997) **C-75m.** *½ D: Mark Dindal. Voices of Scott Bakula, Jasmine Guy, Natalie Cole, Ashley Peldon, Kathy Najimy, John Rhys-Davies, George Kennedy, Rene Auberjonois, Hal Holbrook, Don Knotts, Betty Lou Gerson. Fairly dreary cartoon feature about a wide-eyed cat from Kokomo who goes to Hollywood to star in musical movies, circa 1939. What he finds instead is a town full of cynics and broken dreams. The villain is a hyper-bratty child star who hates animals. That's entertainment? Unmemorable songs by Randy Newman. Gene Kelly served as a choreography consultant. [G]▼●

Cat's Eye (1985) **C-93m.** *½ D: Lewis Teague. Drew Barrymore, James Woods, Alan King, Kenneth McMillan, Robert Hays, Candy Clark, James Naughton, Patricia Kalember, Charles Dutton. Trio of heavy-handed Stephen King stories, short on irony, long on mean-spiritedness. J-D-C Scope. [PG-13]▼●

Cat's-Paw, The (1934) **98m.** **½ D: Sam Taylor. Harold Lloyd, Una Merkel, George Barbier, Alan Dinehart, Grace Bradley, Nat Pendleton. Harold is a missionary's son, raised in China; he comes to U.S. a babe in the woods, is duped into running for mayor in big city by corrupt politicos who regard him as perfect patsy. Odd Capraesque comedy ends with strange denouement where Lloyd takes law into his own hands. A real curio. Edited for TV.

Cattle Annie and Little Britches (1980) **C-95m.** *** D: Lamont Johnson. Burt Lancaster, Rod Steiger, Amanda Plummer, Diane Lane, John Savage, Scott Glenn, Michael Conrad. Very pleasant little Western, which was thrown away by its distributor, Universal. In 1893, Eastern girls Plummer (Annie) and Lane (Britches) join remnants of the Doolin-Dalton gang and inspire them to pull a few more jobs. Winning cast, including Plummer in film debut. Based on Robert Ward's novel. [PG]

Cattle Drive (1951) **C-77m.** **½ D: Kurt Neumann. Joel McCrea, Dean Stockwell, Leon Ames, Chill Wills. Stockwell does well in role of bratty teen-ager who learns a sense of values from veteran cowhand McCrea on arduous cow drive.

Cattle Empire (1958) **C-83m.** ** D: Charles Marquis Warren. Joel McCrea, Gloria Talbott, Don Haggerty, Phyllis Coates. McCrea agrees to lead cattle drive, planning revenge on cattle owners who sent him to jail; OK Western. CinemaScope.

Cattle King (1963) **C-88m.** ** D: Tay Garnett. Robert Taylor, Joan Caulfield, Robert Loggia, Robert Middleton, Larry Gates, Malcolm Atterbury. Control of grazing land subject of standard Western confrontation saga, Taylor and Middleton squaring off in forgettable drama. Metroscope.

Cattle Queen of Montana (1954) **C-88m.** **½ D: Allan Dwan. Barbara Stanwyck, Ronald Reagan, Gene Evans, Lance Fuller, Anthony Caruso, Jack Elam. Stanwyck battles to protect her livestock and property from plundering by Indians—and a ruthless villain (Evans). Reagan plays second fiddle to feisty Stanwyck here—but they're both done in by mediocre script. Beautiful scenery helps.▼●

Cattle Town (1952) **71m.** ** D: Noel Smith. Dennis Morgan, Philip Carey, Amanda Blake, Rita Moreno, Sheb Wooley, Merv Griffin. Both Warner Bros. and Morgan were at low points when this sad echo of a slick Western was churned out.

Cat Women of the Moon (1954) **64m.** *½ D: Arthur Hilton. Sonny Tufts, Victor Jory, Marie Windsor, Bill Phipps, Douglas Fowley, Susan Morrow. All-star cast in tacky sci-fi entry about a moon expedition that discovers female civilization and its underground empire. Originally shown in 3-D; aka ROCKET TO THE MOON. Remade as MISSILE TO THE MOON.▼

Caught (1949) **88m.** *** D: Max Ophuls. James Mason, Barbara Bel Geddes, Robert Ryan, Frank Ferguson, Curt Bois, Natalie Schafer. Compelling, intelligent story of young girl who marries powerful millionaire, tries to escape her shallow existence with him. Fine performances, skilled direction by Ophuls.▼

Caught (1996) **C-109m.** *** D: Robert M. Young. Edward James Olmos, Maria Conchita Alonso, Arie Verveen, Bitty Schram, Steven Schub. Tension-packed, if somewhat familiar, film noir about long-married couple whose relationship is disrupted when a drifter (Verveen) comes to live with the couple and work in their fish store; then their married son (Schub) arrives on the scene. This POSTMAN ALWAYS RINGS TWICE variation has atmosphere to spare; sharply acted and scripted (by Edward Pomerantz, based on his novel *Into It*). [R]▼●

Caught in the Draft (1941) **82m.** *** D: David Butler. Bob Hope, Dorothy Lamour, Lynne Overman, Eddie Bracken. The last thing movie star Hope wants is to get drafted, but he accidentally enlists himself. Very funny service comedy.▼

Caught Up (1998) **C-95m.** BOMB D: Darin Scott. Bokeem Woodbine, Cynda Williams, Jeffrey Combs, Tony Todd, Snoop Doggy Dogg, LL Cool J, Michael (Clarke) Duncan. Witless blaxploitation/film noir about an ex-con (Woodbine) who falls back into L.A.'s underworld when he gets involved with a sexy psychic (Williams) who's a dead ringer for his ex-wife (also Williams). Marked by convoluted plotting, gross stereotypes, and cameos by star rappers (Snoop plays a drug courier named Cool Kitty Kat—get it?). That's CANDYMAN's Tony Todd as a malevolent parole officer and RE-ANIMATOR's Jeffrey Combs as a Shakespeare-quoting eunuch security guard. [R] ▼●◗

Cauldron of Blood (1967-Spanish-U.S.) **C-95m.** *½ D: Edward Mann (Santos Alcocer). Boris Karloff, Viveca Lindfors, Jean-Pierre Aumont, Jacqui Speed, Rosenda Monteros. Sordid, sleep-inducing tale of blind sculptor (Karloff) whose skeletal models are actually victims of his murdering wife. Also known as BLIND MAN'S BLUFF. Filmed in widescreen Panoramica. [PG]▼

Cause for Alarm (1951) **74m.** *** D: Tay Garnett. Loretta Young, Barry Sullivan, Bruce Cowling, Margalo Gillmore, Carl Switzer, Richard Anderson. Simple, effective thriller with Young registering as the panic-stricken wife of psychotic Sullivan. Tension builds, and there's a neat plot twist.▼●◗

Cavalcade (1933) **110m.** **** D: Frank Lloyd. Diana Wynyard, Clive Brook, Herbert Mundin, Ursula Jeans, Margaret Lindsay, Beryl Mercer, Una O'Connor, Billy Bevan, Frank Lawton. Lavish Hollywood adaptation of Noel Coward's London stage success (which may remind many of TV's *Upstairs, Downstairs*) chronicling two families from eve of the 20th century to early 1930s. Nostalgic, richly atmospheric, but also sharply critical of war and the aftershocks that brought an end to a wonderful way of life. Oscar winner for Best Picture, Best Director, and "Interior Decoration" (it *is* handsome).▼

Cavalry Charge SEE: **Last Outpost, The** (1951)

Cavalry Scout (1951) **C-78m.** ** D: Lesley Selander. Rod Cameron, Audrey Long, Jim Davis, James Millican, James Arness. Routine Western of scout Cameron tracking down stolen army goods and romancing Long.▼

Cave Dwellers SEE: **Blade Master, The**

Caveman (1981) **C-92m.** **½ D: Carl Gottlieb. Ringo Starr, Barbara Bach, John Matuszak, Shelley Long, Dennis Quaid, Avery Schreiber, Jack Gilford. Stoned-age spoof follows prehistoric Starr's adventures in One Zillion B.C. as a misfit who forms his own tribe, which is composed of outcasts from other caves. Dum-dum comedy saved by fantastic (and funny) special-effects dinosaurs created by Jim Danforth and David Allen. [PG]▼●

Cave of Outlaws (1951) **C-75m.** ** D: William Castle. Macdonald Carey, Alexis Smith, Edgar Buchanan, Victor Jory. Search for stolen gold leads ex-con, lawman, miner, et al. to title situation; Smith is wasted.

Cavern, The (1966) **94m.** **½ D: Edgar G. Ulmer. Rosanna Schiaffino, John Saxon, Brian Aherne, Peter L. Marshall, Larry Hagman, Hans Von Borsody. Six soldiers are trapped for over a year in a cavern with Schiaffino, but plot contrivance isn't handled badly in above-average programmer. The prolific director's swan song.

CB4 (1993) **C-88m.** ** D: Tamra Davis. Chris Rock, Allen Payne, Deezer D, Chris Elliott, Phil Hartman, Charlie Murphy, Khandi Alexander, Arthur Evans, Theresa Randle, Willard E. Pugh, Stoney Jackson, La Wanda Page. Group of middle-class guys, led by Rock (who also cowrote the film), takes on a tough, prison-like persona to form a rap group called Cell Block 4—which leads to complications when they get mistaken for the real thing. Mildly amusing satirical look at the world of Gangsta Rap—is no THIS IS SPINAL TAP. [R]▼●

C.C. and Company (1970) **C-88m.** *½ D: Seymour Robbie. Joe Namath, Ann-Margret, William Smith, Jennifer Billingsley, Teda Bracci, Greg Mullavey, Sid Haig, Bruce Glover, Wayne Cochran & The C.C. Riders. Broadway Joe gets sacked in his first starring role as a motorcyclist who tangles with Smith's biker gang while trying (not very hard) to fight off Ann-Margret's advances. Bracci's comedy relief is principal virtue, but the big laughs are unintentional. Produced by Roger Smith (who also wrote the screenplay) and Allan Carr. Aka CHROME HEARTS. [PG—edited from original R rating] ▼

Cease Fire (1985) **C-97m.** **½ D: David Nutter. Don Johnson, Lisa Blount, Robert F. Lyons, Richard Chaves, Rick Richards, Chris Noel. Earnest drama about Vietnam vet who's still haunted by his experiences fifteen years later and unwilling to acknowledge that he has a problem. Sincere, poignant at times, but dramatically uneven. George Fernandez adapted script from his one-act play. [R]▼

Ceiling Zero (1936) **95m.** *** D: Howard Hawks. James Cagney, Pat O'Brien, June Travis, Stuart Erwin, Barton MacLane, Isabel Jewell. Irresponsible mail flier Cagney causes no end of grief for old pal (and boss) O'Brien, especially when he sets his sights on young pilot Travis. Typically machine-gun-paced Hawks drama belies its stage origins; one of the best Cagney-O'Brien vehicles. Based on the play by Frank "Spig" Wead; remade as INTERNATIONAL SQUADRON.▼

Celebration, The (1998-Danish) **C-101m.** ***½ D: Thomas Vinterberg. Ulrich Thomsen, Henning Moritzen, Thomas Bo Larsen, Paprika Steen, Birthe Neumann, Trine Dyrholm. A prodigal son's return for his prosperous father's sixtieth birthday party sets the stage for a dysfunctional family reunion in the Danish countryside. Harsh, sardonically humorous look at the dark side of relationships—and hidden skeletons. Strongly scripted by the director (who also has a bit as a cab driver) and Mogens Rukov, under the "pure cinema" rules of Dogma 95. [R]▼

Celebration at Big Sur (1971) **C-82m.** ** D: Baird Bryant, Johanna Demetrakas. Joan Baez, Crosby, Stills, Nash and Young, Joni Mitchell, John Sebastian, Mimi Fariña. Lesser folk-rock documentary, filmed at 1969 Big Sur Festival, suffers from poor production values. Baez is highlighted, singing "I Shall Be Released," "Song for David," etc. [PG]

Celebrity (1998) **114m.** ** D: Woody Allen. Kenneth Branagh, Judy Davis, Joe Mantegna, Leonardo DiCaprio, Winona Ryder, Charlize Theron, Hank Azaria, Melanie Griffith, Famke Janssen, Michael Lerner, Bebe Neuwirth, Larry Pine, Marian Seldes, Andre Gregory, Gretchen Mol, Dylan Baker, Sam Rockwell, Allison Janney, Celia Weston, Aida Turturro, Kate Burton, Patti D'Arbanville, Debra Messing, Donna Hanover, Karen Duffy. Branagh becomes Woody Allen in this rambling look at a neurotic N.Y. magazine writer, his messed-up love life and career. Allen is coasting here, with an attractive cast, some amusing moments, but nothing much to say. Davis is, as always, incredibly good. Shot in black-and-white by Sven Nykvist. [R] ▼●◗

Celeste (1981-German) **C-107m.** *** D: Percy Adlon. Eva Mattes, Jurgen Arndt, Norbert Wartha, Wolf Euba, Leo Bardischewski. Slow-moving but stunningly photographed and detailed account of the relationship between Marcel Proust (Arndt) and his devoted housekeeper (Mattes). Based on the real Celeste's memoirs.▼

Celine and Julie Go Boating (1974-French) **C-193m.** ***½ D: Jacques Rivette. Juliet Berto, Dominique Labourier, Bulle Ogier, Marie-France Pisier, Barbet Schroeder, Nathalie Ansar. Librarian Julie (Labourier) strikes up a friendship with magician Celine (Berto), who tells her of a mythical haunted house, which the two visit; they eventually become involved in the "lives" of the ghosts who reside there. Eerie, thoroughly entrancing (if a bit overlong) comedy-drama-fantasy. Scripted by Berto, Labourier, Ogier, Pisier, Rivette, and Eduardo de Gregorio, based on short stories by Henry James.▼

Cell 2455, Death Row (1955) **77m.** ** D: Fred F. Sears. William Campbell, Kathryn Grant, Vince Edwards, Marian Carr. Unsensational retracing of life of sex-offender Caryl Chessman and his bouts, while in prison, for retrials. Alan Alda later played Chessman in KILL ME IF YOU CAN.

Celluloid Closet, The (1995) **C-102m.** *** D: Rob Epstein, Jeffrey Friedman. Narrated by Lily Tomlin. Entertaining, insightful look at homosexuality as reflected in movies. Well-chosen clips are sandwiched by interviews with many actors and filmmakers (Whoopi Goldberg, Tony Curtis, Harvey Fierstein, Arthur Laurents, Shirley MacLaine, Tom Hanks, Susan Sarandon, Mart Crowley, John Schlesinger). One highlight: Gore Vidal revealing the gay subtext in his screenplay for BEN-HUR. Tomlin coexecutive-produced. [R]▼●

Celtic Pride (1996) **C-91m.** BOMB D: Tom De Cerchio. Damon Wayans, Daniel Stern, Dan Aykroyd, Gail O'Grady, Adam Hendershott, Paul Guilfoyle, Deion Sanders, Christopher McDonald. Two obsessed Boston Celtics fans drunkenly kidnap the arrogant star of the rival basketball team to ensure that theirs wins the championship. Might have worked as a wild farce, but in this "realistic" comic mode, it's a disaster, with repellent characters, leaden pacing, and no laughs. [PG-13]▼●

Cement Garden, The (1992-German-British-French) **C-105m.** **½ D: Andrew Birkin. Charlotte Gainsbourg, Andrew Robertson, Sinead Cusack, Hanns Zischler, Alice Coulthard, Ned Birkin, Jochen Horst. Strange, complex account of the way four young siblings react to the death of their parents (and go about hiding the demise of their mom)—with youthful bewilderment, erotic anxiety, and clandestine yearning. Vivid, but also terribly affected. The director (who scripted, from Ian McEwan's novel) is Gainsbourg's uncle, and Ned Birkin's father.▼

Cemetery Club, The (1992) **C-106m.** **½ D: Bill Duke. Ellen Burstyn, Olympia Dukakis, Diane Ladd, Danny Aiello, Lainie Kazan, Jeff Howell, Christina Ricci, Bernie Casey, Robert Costanzo, Wallace Shawn, Louis Guss. The friendship of three women (all Jewish, all played—none too persuasively—by Gentiles) is underscored by the loss of their husbands, until one of them enters into a tentative relationship with a man. Burstyn is a joy to watch, but Dukakis' and Ladd's caricatured performances throw modestly entertaining film off-balance. Ivan Menchell adapted his own play, though comic writer Marshall Brickman has "production consultant" credit. Jerry Orbach and Lee Richardson appear unbilled as husbands. [PG-13] ▼●

Cemetery Girls SEE: **Velvet Vampire, The**

Cemetery Man (1995-U.S.-Italian) **C-100m.** ** D: Michele Soavi. Rupert Everett,

Francois Hadji-Lazaro, Anna Falchi, Stefano Masciarelli, Mickey Knox. Zombies rise from the dead a week after their demise, and it's "Cemetery Man's" job to kill them again, with the assistance of a grotesque mute companion. Based on an Italian comic book series, *Dylan Dog,* a promising concept becomes overwhelming and repetitive. At times outrageous, funny, sexy, and disgusting, with a startlingly enigmatic and fascinating ending. [R]▼●

Centennial Summer (1946) C-102m. **½ D: Otto Preminger. Jeanne Crain, Cornel Wilde, Linda Darnell, William Eythe, Walter Brennan, Constance Bennett, Dorothy Gish. Leisurely, plush musical of Philadelphia Exposition of 1876, with sisters Crain and Darnell both after handsome Wilde; nice Jerome Kern score helps.

Centerfold Girls, The (1974) C-93m. *½ D: John Peyser. Andrew Prine, Tiffany Bolling, Aldo Ray, Ray Danton, Francine York, Jeremy Slate, Mike Mazurki, Dan Seymour. Fine cast of familiar faces helps routine tale of psycho Prine killing pinup girls. [R]▼

Center of the Web (1992) C-88m. ** D: David A. Prior. Robert Davi, Charlene Tilton, Ted Prior, Tony Curtis, Bo Hopkins, William Zipp, Graham Timbes, Eric Stenson, Charles Napier. Hired killer is murdered, and government agents force a man who looks just like him to pose as the dead bad-guy. Or is that what's really going on? Complicated plot, smoothly directed, but of no real distinction. [R]▼●

Center Stage (2000) C-113m. ** D: Nicholas Hytner. Amanda Schull, Zoë Saldana, Susan May Pratt, Peter Gallagher, Donna Murphy, Debra Monk, Ethan Stiefel, Sascha Radetsky, Shakiem Evans. Routine backstage soaper about young students at a prestigious N.Y.C. ballet company, focusing on a plucky starlet's infatuation with the company's cocky male lead (American Ballet Theater star Stiefel). Lots of Broadway pedigree behind the scenes, including choreography by Tony Award-winner Susan Stroman, but this plays like *Dawson's Creek* in Capezios. Only a couple of the dance set-pieces really fly. Fun cameo from ex-*Chorus Line* hoofer Priscilla Lopez. Super 35. [PG-13]▼

Central Airport (1933) 75m. **½ D: William A. Wellman. Richard Barthelmess, Sally Eilers, Tom Brown, Glenda Farrell, Harold Huber, Grant Mitchell, Willard Robertson. Film's title has nothing to do with its story, a romantic rivalry between pilot brothers Barthelmess and Brown. Some great aerial stunts and impressive miniature special effects help make up for underdeveloped script. Blink and you'll miss John Wayne in a bit part as Brown's copilot in the climactic sequence.

Central Park (1932) 61m. **½ D: John Adolfi. Joan Blondell, Guy Kibbee, Wallace Ford, Henry B. Walthall, Patricia Ellis, Charles Sellon. Blondell and Ford uplift this programmer as a pair of small-town kids making their way in the big city who inadvertently become involved with gangsters. Set entirely in N.Y.C.'s Central Park.

Central Station (1998-Brazilian-French) C-107m. *** D: Walter Salles. Fernanda Montenegro, Vinicius de Oliveira, Marilia Pêra, Sôia Lira, Othon Bastos, Otávio Augusto, Stela Freitas. A woman who writes letters for the illiterate at Rio de Janeiro's central train station feels obliged to help a 9-year-old boy whose mother has just been killed. The two form an unlikely bond and journey to a remote area of Brazil to try to find his father. Predictable on one level, but extremely well done, with a shining performance by Montenegro (one of Brazil's leading actresses) and newcomer de Oliveira. Super 35. [R]▼◗

Century (1994-British) C-112m. ** D: Stephen Poliakoff. Charles Dance, Miranda Richardson, Clive Owen, Robert Stephens, Lena Headey, Neil Stuke, Joan Hickson, Fiona Walker. Romantic drama set in turn-of-the-century London examines the relationships of three very different people as the Victorian era dissolves into the 20th century and the world becomes a different place. Mildly involving period piece, but top-notch cast can't breathe life into a premise that doesn't quite come off.▼

Ceremony, The (1963) 105m. **½ D: Laurence Harvey. Laurence Harvey, Sarah Miles, Robert Walker, Jr., John Ireland, Ross Martin, Lee Patterson, Noel Purcell. Mishmash about convicted killer rescued by brother who demands liaison with sister-in-law as reward.

Certain Fury (1985) C-87m. BOMB D: Stephen Gyllenhaal. Tatum O'Neal, Irene Cara, Nicholas Campbell, George Murdock, Moses Gunn, Peter Fonda. Atrocious film about two girls on the lam, featuring a pair of Academy Award winners (as the ads proclaimed) giving two of the worst performances in recent memory. Made in Canada. [R]▼●

Certain Sacrifice, A (1985) C-60m. BOMB D: Stephen Jon Lewicki. Madonna Ciccone, Jeremy Pattnosh. The Material Girl's "screen debut" is dreadful, bargain-basement junk. She's cast as a streetwise teen who manages to get herself raped. Filmed during 1978–1981, and never released theatrically. Madonna was allegedly paid $100 for working in this; it's no wonder she sued (unsuccessfully) to halt its video release.▼

Certain Smile, A (1958) C-106m. **½ D: Jean Negulesco. Rossano Brazzi, Joan Fontaine, Bradford Dillman, Christine Carere. Françoise Sagan's novella becomes overblown soap opera. Romance between Parisian students Dillman (in film debut) and Carere interrupted when she is beguiled by roué Brazzi; chic Fontaine is wasted. CinemaScope.

Cervantes SEE: **Young Rebel**

Cesar (1936-French) **170m.** ***½ D: Marcel Pagnol. Raimu, Pierre Fresnay, Orane Demazis, Charpin, Andre Fouche, Alida Rouffe. Fanny's son (Fouche), now grown, learns that his father is Marius (Fresnay), not Panisse (Charpin). Raimu steals the film in the title role, particularly when he gives a poignant discourse on death. Third of Pagnol's trilogy, preceded by MARIUS and FANNY. All three were the basis of the play and movie FANNY (1961).▼●

César and Rosalie (1972-French-Italian-German) **C-104m.** *** D: Claude Sautet. Yves Montand, Romy Schneider, Sami Frey, Umberto Orsini, Eva Marie Meineke, Isabelle Huppert. Appealing stars in typically French story of a menage à trois relationship (a woman and her two lovers) and how it changes over the years. [R]▼●

Ces Dames Preferent le Mambo SEE: **Dishonorable Discharge**

C'est la Vie (1990-French) **C-97m.** *** D: Diane Kurys. Nathalie Baye, Julie Bataille, Candice Lefranc, Richard Berry, Jean-Pierre Bacri, Zabou. Autobiographical coming-of-age chronicle, strikingly similar to Kurys' PEPPERMINT SODA, about a 13-year-old girl (Bataille) and her experiences one long-ago summer at a beach resort. Despite the familiarity of theme, the film is provocative and charming. A sequel—or, more precisely, companion piece—to ENTRE NOUS, which must be seen to fully appreciate the character of the girl's mother (here Nathalie Baye, in ENTRE NOUS, Isabelle Huppert). Panavision.

Chad Hanna (1940) **C-86m.** ** D: Henry King. Henry Fonda, Dorothy Lamour, Linda Darnell, Guy Kibbee, Jane Darwell, John Carradine. Rather flat circus drama set in 19th-century New York; colorful but empty.

Chained (1934) **76m.** **½ D: Clarence Brown. Joan Crawford, Clark Gable, Otto Kruger, Stuart Erwin, Una O'Connor, Akim Tamiroff. Chic formula MGM love triangle with Crawford torn between love for Gable and married lover Kruger. Watch for Mickey Rooney splashing in a swimming pool.▼

Chained Heat (1983-U.S.-German) **C-95m.** BOMB D: Paul Nicolas. Linda Blair, John Vernon, Sybil Danning, Tamara Dobson, Stella Stevens, Louisa Moritz, Nita Talbot, Michael Callan, Henry Silva, Edy Williams. Innocent Blair finds herself in a prison where the warden has a hot tub in his office. Strictly for the grind-house crowd on 42nd Street. Followed by CHAINED HEAT 2. [R]▼●

Chain Lightning (1950) **94m.** ** D: Stuart Heisler. Humphrey Bogart, Eleanor Parker, Raymond Massey, Richard Whorf. After WW2, bomber pilot Bogart becomes a test pilot for jet manufacturer Massey. Some romantic rivalry over Parker with inventor Whorf is as low-key as the rest of this bland, uninvolving movie.▼●

Chain of Desire (1992) **C-107m.** *½ D: Temistocles Lopez. Malcolm McDowell, Linda Fiorentino, Kevin Conroy, Seymour Cassel, Assumpta Serna, Elias Koteas, Angel Aviles, Patrick Bauchau, Grace Zabriskie, Tim Guinee, Jamie Harrold. Pompous reworking of LA RONDE, set in the era of AIDS and chronicling various out-of-the-ordinary sexual encounters among a group of shallow, jaded Manhattanites. Almost unbearably bad at times.▼

Chain of Evidence (1957) **64m.** *½ D: Paul Landres. Bill Elliott, Don Haggerty, James Lydon, Claudia Barrett. Programmer has dedicated cop Elliott track down real killer of businessman.

Chain Reaction (1980-Australian) **C-87m.** **½ D: Ian Barry. Steve Bisley, Arna-Maria Winchester, Ross Thompson, Ralph Cotterill, Patrick Ward. OK thriller chronicling the repercussions of a nuclear plant accident on a contaminated employee (Thompson) and an innocent couple (Bisley, Winchester) forced to contend with Big Brother. Look quickly for Mel Gibson as a bearded car mechanic. Video title: NUCLEAR RUN. ▼●

Chain Reaction (1996) **C-106m.** *½ D: Andrew Davis. Keanu Reeves, Morgan Freeman, Rachel Weisz, Fred Ward, Kevin Dunn, Brian Cox, Joanna Cassidy, Nicholas Rudall. Machinist working on hydrogen-energy project is blamed for a devastating explosion and takes it on the lam along with a female physicist on the project. What's really behind all this skulduggery? Uninspired, ultimately ludicrous blend of action, chase, and political thriller genres has barely a believable moment. [PG-13]▼●

Chains of Gold (1991) **C-95m.** ** D: Rod Holcomb. John Travolta, Marilu Henner, Joey Lawrence, Bernie Casey, Ramon Franco, Hector Elizondo, Benjamin Bratt, Conchata Ferrell, Tammy Lauren. A dedicated social worker (Travolta) transforms himself into a Stallone clone as he sets out to rescue a young friend caught up with a gang of crack dealers. Ludicrous actioner is yet another of Travolta's grade-D pre–PULP FICTION efforts (although he co-wrote this one!). Made for theatrical release in 1989, but debuted on cable TV. [R]▼◗

Chairman, The (1969) **C-102m.** **½ D: J. Lee Thompson. Gregory Peck, Anne Heywood, Arthur Hill, Alan Dobie, Conrad Yama. Lots of talk but little action in story of American scientist sent to Communist China on super-secret espionage mission. Panavision. [M/PG]

Chairman of the Board (1998) **C-95m.** BOMB D: Alex Zamm. Carrot Top, Courtney Thorne-Smith, Larry Miller, Raquel

Welch, Jack Warden, M. Emmet Walsh, Estelle Harris, Bill Erwin, Little Richard, Taylor Negron, Butterbean. Excruciatingly stupid story of inventor/beach bum Carrot Top, who inherits a major corporation from a complete stranger, to the vexation of sleazy corporate nephew Miller. Harris hits the film's low point as his landlady, a woman with a laryngectomy who ceaselessly curses. Someone thought this was funny? [PG-13] ▼●◗

Chalk Garden, The (1964-British) **C-106m.** *** D: Ronald Neame. Deborah Kerr, Hayley Mills, John Mills, Edith Evans, Felix Aylmer, Elizabeth Sellars. Very-high-class soap opera with good cast supporting story of teenager set on right path by governess Kerr; colorful production, quite entertaining. From Enid Bagnold play.▼

Challenge, The (1948) **68m.** ** D: Jean Yarbrough. Tom Conway, June Vincent, Richard Stapley, John Newland, Eily Malyon, Terry Kilburn, Stanley Logan. Conway easily slides into the role of Bulldog Drummond in this fair mystery about a murdered sea captain who knew the whereabouts of hidden gold.

Challenge, The (1960) SEE: **It Takes a Thief**

Challenge (1974) **C-84m.** BOMB D: Martin Beck. Earl Owensby, William Hicks, Katheryn Thompson, Johnny Popwell. North Carolina-based Owensby's first film (which he also produced) amateurishly goes through the usual vengeance-for-killing-my-family paces. Opening printed crawl celebrates this as return of "clean, decent entertainment," followed by Owensby causing the deaths of various badguys. But don't worry—none of his victims is naked. Dreadful. [PG]▼

Challenge, The (1982) **C-112m.** **½ D: John Frankenheimer. Scott Glenn, Toshiro Mifune, Donna Kei Benz, Atsuo Nakamura, Calvin Young. Entertaining but sometimes pretentious actioner, with American boxer Glenn becoming involved in conflict between brothers Mifune and Nakamura over rights to family swords. Scripted by John Sayles and Richard Maxwell. Exteriors shot mostly in Kyoto. Completely recut for TV release as SWORD OF THE NINJA, running 97m. [R]▼

Challenge for Robin Hood, A (1968-British) **C-85m.** ** D: C. M. Pennington-Richards. Barrie Ingham, James Hayter, Leon Greene, Peter Blythe, Gay Hamilton, Alfie Bass. Hammer Films produced this inoffensive but undistinguished adventure yarn, which is of little interest except to children. Originally 96m. [G]▼

Challenge To Be Free (1976) **C-88m.** **½ D: Tay Garnett. Mike Mazurki, Vic Christy, Jimmy Kane, Fritz Ford. Fur trapper is pursued by the law in Arctic surroundings; simple and simple-minded, best for younger viewers. Made in 1972 as MAD TRAPPER OF THE YUKON, this marked last film for veteran director Garnett, who appears briefly as Marshal McGee. [G]▼

Challenge to Lassie (1949) **C-76m.** **½ D: Richard Thorpe. Edmund Gwenn, Donald Crisp, Geraldine Brooks, Reginald Owen, Alan Webb, Ross Ford, Henry Stephenson, Alan Napier, Sara Allgood, Arthur Shields. Based-on-fact story, set in 19th-century Edinburgh, about a dog (actually a Skye terrier but played here by Lassie), who keeps returning to a churchyard where its master (Crisp) is buried. Pleasant film, with a fine character actor cast. Remade as GREYFRIARS BOBBY, which also features Crisp (as the cemetery caretaker). ▼

Challenge to White Fang SEE: **White Fang** (1972)

Chamber, The (1996) **C-110m.** ** D: James Foley. Chris O'Donnell, Gene Hackman, Faye Dunaway, Robert Prosky, Raymond Barry, Lela Rochon, Harve Presnell, Bo Jackson. Young lawyer feels impelled to defend a Mississippi death row inmate, convicted of a racist/terrorist bombing years ago, because the man is his grandfather. Reopening this volatile case causes pain and hardship for all involved. Curiously unmoving (and talky) adaptation of the John Grisham best-seller. O'Donnell is earnest but unconvincing; Hackman never successfully disappears into the role of a racist pig. Panavision. [R]▼●◗

Chambermaid on the Titanic, The (1997-French-Spanish-Italian) **C-96m.** *** D: Bigas Luna. Olivier Martinez, Romane Bohringer, Aitana Sánchez Gijón, Didier Bezace, Aldo Maccione. Utterly original and beautifully filmed fable about fantasy, desire and storytelling, centering on a French foundry worker who wins a trip to watch the launch of the *Titanic* in England and becomes obsessed with a woman he meets there. When he returns home, he becomes famous for spinning fantastical tales—which may or may not be true—about his wild night of passion with the woman. Unpredictable, unexpectedly moving film from the usually outrageous Luna (JAMÓN JAMÓN). Aka THE CHAMBERMAID. Cinecam-Scope.▼

Chamber of Horrors (1940-British) **80m.** **½ D: Norman Lee. Leslie Banks, Lilli Palmer, Romilly Lunge, Gina Malo, Richard Bird, Cathleen Nesbitt. Low-budget horror comes over fairly well, with dastardly Banks making his house a mass morgue, menacing lovely Palmer. Based on Edgar Wallace story. Original title: THE DOOR WITH SEVEN LOCKS.▼●

Chamber of Horrors (1966) **C-99m.** *½ D: Hy Averback. Patrick O'Neal, Cesare Danova, Wilfrid Hyde-White, Patrice Wymore, Suzy Parker, Marie Windsor, Tony Curtis, Wayne Rogers. Wax museum provides setting for uneven mystery

about mad killer on the loose. Intended for TV, it has mark of low-budget film plus two gimmicks: the "Horror Horn" and the "Fear Flasher."
Chameleon Street (1991) **C-95m.** *** D: Wendell B. Harris, Jr. Wendell B. Harris, Jr., Angela Leslie, Amina Fakir. Knowing sleeper based on true story of William Douglas Street, Jr. (played by director-writer Harris), a black man whose uncanny ability to intuit other people's needs enables him to successfully impersonate a reporter, a surgeon, an exchange student, and an attorney. Ingratiating film with a biting comic edge, and something to say about the way a black man struggles to make it in a white man's world. [R]▼
Champ, The (1931) **87m.** ***½ D: King Vidor. Wallace Beery, Jackie Cooper, Irene Rich, Roscoe Ates, Edward Brophy, Hale Hamilton. Superb tearjerker about a washed-up prizefighter and his adoring son, played to perfection by Beery and Cooper (in the first of their several teamings). Simple, sentimental in the extreme, but extremely effective. Beery won an Oscar for his performance, as did Frances Marion for her original story. Remade in 1953 (as THE CLOWN) and 1979.▼●
Champ, The (1979) **C-121m.** *½ D: Franco Zeffirelli. Jon Voight, Faye Dunaway, Ricky Schroder, Jack Warden, Arthur Hill, Strother Martin, Joan Blondell, Elisha Cook. Voight is too intelligent to convince as a dumb pug, and Dunaway, as a loving mother, looks as if she wants to bed down with her kid in hopeless remake of the 1931 sudser. Young Schroder cries (and cries) convincingly. [PG]▼●
Champagne (1928-British) **93m.** **½ D: Alfred Hitchcock. Betty Balfour, Jean Bradin, Gordon Harker, Ferdinand von Alten, Clifford Heatherley, Jack Trevor. Romantic escapades of irresponsible socialite Balfour whose father pretends he's broke to teach her a lesson. Overlong silent Hitch is moderately entertaining with the usual quota of striking visuals.▼
Champagne Charlie (1944) **107m.** **½ D: Cavalcanti. Tommy Trinder, Betty Warren, Stanley Holloway, Austin Trevor, Jean Kent, Guy Middleton. Splendid evocation of British music halls of the 1860s and their robust entertainers simply hasn't got enough story to last 107m. The songs are still great fun. Look for young Kay Kendall.
Champagne for Caesar (1950) **99m.** *** D: Richard Whorf. Ronald Colman, Celeste Holm, Vincent Price, Barbara Britton, Art Linkletter. Genius Colman becomes national celebrity on TV quiz show; sponsor Price sends temptress Holm to distract big winner. Enjoyable spoof; Price hilarious as neurotic soap manufacturer. ▼●
Champagne Murders, The (1967-French) **C-98m.** *** D: Claude Chabrol. Anthony Perkins, Maurice Ronet, Stephane Audran, Yvonne Furneaux, Suzanne Lloyd, Catherine Sola. Sale of champagne company to U.S. conglomerate manipulated by various weird, competing types, complicated by murders which point to playboy (Ronet). Murder-mystery narrative backdrop for odd psychological drama; one-of-a-kind film was shot in both English and French-language versions. Techniscope.
Champagne Waltz (1937) **87m.** ** D: A. Edward Sutherland. Gladys Swarthout, Fred MacMurray, Jack Oakie, Herman Bing, Vivienne Osborne. Flyweight musical about rivalry between Vienna waltz palace and American jazz band next door gets sillier as it goes along; operatic Swarthout is saddled with mediocre songs, as well. Oakie's comedy relief most welcome.
Champ for a Day (1953) **90m.** ** D: William Seiter. Alex Nicol, Audrey Totter, Charles Winninger, Hope Emerson, Henry (Harry) Morgan. Brooklyn boxer tracks down friend's murderer. Standard.
Champion (1949) **99m.** ***½ D: Mark Robson. Kirk Douglas, Marilyn Maxwell, Arthur Kennedy, Ruth Roman, Paul Stewart, Lola Albright. Unscrupulous boxer punches his way to the top, thrusting aside everybody and everything. Douglas perfectly cast in title role; gripping film, with Harry Gerstad's Oscar-winning editing. Also shown in computer-colored version. ▼●
Champions (1983-British) **C-115m.** **½ D: John Irvin. John Hurt, Edward Woodward, Jan Francis, Ben Johnson, Kirstie Alley, Peter Barkworth, Ann Bell, Judy Parfitt. Formula drama of determined jockey Hurt battling cancer and hoping to make a comeback in the Grand National Steeplechase. The opening is reminiscent of CHARIOTS OF FIRE, the finale of ROCKY; however, the scenes with Hurt and his niece, and Hurt among children undergoing cancer treatment, are quite moving. Based on a true story. [PG]▼●
Champions Forever (1989) **C-87m.** *** D: Dimitri Logothetis. Fascinating, insightful look back at the careers of five modern heavyweight boxing legends: Muhammad Ali, Joe Frazier, George Foreman, Larry Holmes, and Ken Norton. Interviews with each fighter are juxtaposed with classic footage of their ring battles with Ali the dominant presence throughout. Candor and a subtle pathos make the interviews as poignant as the boxing scenes are exciting. Though sobering to see the once verbose Ali reduced to a whispering giant, news clips of poetry-spouting Cassius Clay *are* the greatest. ▼●
Chance at Heaven (1933) **70m.** ** D: William Seiter. Ginger Rogers, Joel McCrea, Marian Nixon, Andy Devine, Ann Shoemaker, Betty Furness. Honest, hardworking McCrea leaves fiancée Ginger for spoiled

society brat Nixon. Sincere performances and realistic small-town atmosphere are only virtues of this humdrum film.

Chance Meeting (1959-British) **96m.** **½ D: Joseph Losey. Hardy Kruger, Stanley Baker, Micheline Presle, Robert Flemyng, Gordon Jackson. Kafkaesque story of painter framed for girlfriend's murder. Intriguing little mystery becomes talky, loses initial momentum. British title: BLIND DATE.

Chance of a Lifetime, The (1943) **65m.** **½ D: William Castle. Chester Morris, Eric Rolf, Jeanne Bates, Richard Lane, George E. Stone, Lloyd Corrigan, Walter Sande, Douglas Fowley, Cy Kendall. Director Castle made his debut with this proficient *Boston Blackie* episode about a group of prisoners who are paroled to Blackie's care to work in a war plant—but some of them have larceny and not patriotism in mind.

Chance of a Lifetime (1950-British) **89m.** *** D: Bernard Miles, Alan Osbiston. Basil Radford, Niall MacGinnis, Bernard Miles, Geoffrey Keen, Kenneth More, Julien Mitchell, Hattie Jacques. Nearly a landmark film by actor-director Miles, blending comedy and drama when a fed-up factory owner (Radford) agrees to turn over all management duties to his workers. Laborers, led by Miles and More, eventually learn how difficult it is to run a business. Outstanding performances and realistic location filming.

Chances (1931) **72m.** *** D: Allan Dwan. Douglas Fairbanks, Jr., Rose Hobart, Anthony Bushell, Mary Forbes, William Austin. Entertaining, neatly acted drama of love and war, with soldier-brothers Fairbanks and Bushell both falling for Hobart. Fairbanks in particular is a standout.

Chances Are (1989) **C-108m.** *** D: Emile Ardolino. Cybill Shepherd, Robert Downey, Jr., Ryan O'Neal, Mary Stuart Masterson, Christopher McDonald, Josef Sommer, Joe Grifasi, Susan Ruttan, Fran Ryan, James Noble. A woman remains devoted to her husband years after his death . . . and then, one day, his spirit returns in the body of a much younger man. Surprisingly skillful blend of fantasy and romantic comedy manages to maintain its sweet-natured tone from start to finish. Appealing stars are supported by a gallery of top character actors. Written by Perry Howze and Randy Howze. [PG]▼●◗

Chandler (1972) **C-88m.** *½ D: Paul Magwood. Warren Oates, Leslie Caron, Alex Dreier, Gloria Grahame, Mitchell Ryan. Private-eye falls in love with ex-mistress of racketeer. Substandard yarn. Panavision. [PG]

Chandu the Magician (1932) **70m.** *½ D: William Cameron Menzies, Marcel Varnel. Edmund Lowe, Bela Lugosi, Irene Ware, Henry B. Walthall, Herbert Mundin. Spiritualist Chandu battles madman whose death ray threatens to destroy world; not as good as most serials of this genre, and even sillier. Disappointing.

Chanel Solitaire (1981-U.S.-French) **C-120m.** ** D: George Kaczender. Marie-France Pisier, Timothy Dalton, Rutger Hauer, Karen Black, Brigitte Fossey. Stylish but cliché-ridden biography of designer Coco Chanel, covering her first 38 years and focusing on her love life. [R]▼●

Chang (1927) **67m.** ***½ D: Merian C. Cooper, Ernest B. Schoedsack. Kru, Chantui, Nah, Ladah, Bimbo. Set in the jungle of Siam (Thailand), this fascinating ethnographic documentary/narrative tells the story of Kru and his family, and their daily struggle for survival amid wild animals and cruel forces of nature—particularly a herd of *chang* (the Siamese word for "elephant"). Some of the shots of animals are truly amazing. The Cooper-Schoedsack team later made KING KONG. ▼●

Changeling, The (1979-Canadian) **C-109m.** *** D: Peter Medak. George C. Scott, Trish Van Devere, Melvyn Douglas, John Colicos, Jean Marsh, Madeleine Thornton-Sherwood. Good, scary ghost story with Scott as recently widowed musician who moves into old house inhabited by spirit of a child who lived there 70 years ago. [R]▼●

Change of Habit (1969) **C-93m.** ** D: William Graham. Elvis Presley, Mary Tyler Moore, Barbara McNair, Jane Elliot, Leora Dana, Edward Asner, Doro Merande, Regis Toomey. Moore, a nun, is forced to choose between Dr. Presley and the church in substandard drama that at least represents slight change from typical Elvis fare. Presley's last screen role. [G]▼

Change of Heart (1943) **90m.** ** D: Albert S. Rogell. John Carroll, Susan Hayward, Gail Patrick, Eve Arden, Melville Cooper, Walter Catlett, Dorothy Dandridge, Count Basie & Orchestra, Freddy Martin & Orchestra. Forgettable musical numbers abound in this romantic trifle of Carroll stealing songwriter Hayward's work. Of course, they fall in love. Originally titled HIT PARADE OF 1943.

Change of Mind (1969) **C-103m.** **½ D: Robert Stevens. Raymond St. Jacques, Susan Oliver, Janet MacLachlan, Leslie Nielsen, Donnelly Rhodes, David Bailey. In an emergency operation, the brain of a white district attorney is successfully transplanted into the body of a black man (St. Jacques). Racial-protest sci-fi thriller is contrived, to say the least. Filmed in Canada. [R]

Change of Seasons, A (1980) **C-102m.** **½ D: Richard Lang. Shirley MacLaine, Anthony Hopkins, Bo Derek, Michael Brandon, Mary Beth Hurt, Ed Winter. College professor Hopkins, drowning in male menopause, has an affair with student Derek, so wife MacLaine decides to take a lover of her own. One of the better midlife crisis films of this period, though many thought its major asset was opening sequence of Bo bouncing in a hot tub. Cowritten by Erich Segal. [R]▼

Chan Is Missing (1982) **80m.** *** D: Wayne Wang. Wood Moy, Marc Hayashi, Laureen Chew, Judy Mihei, Peter Wang, Presco Tabios. Wry, low-key comedy of cabdrivers Moy and Hayashi tracking down the mysterious Mr. Chan Hung, who absconded with their $4,000. Independently produced on shoestring budget and shot in San Francisco's Chinatown.▼

Chantilly Lace (1993) **C-102m. TVM** D: Linda Yellen. Lindsay Crouse, Jill Eikenberry, Martha Plimpton, Ally Sheedy, Talia Shire, Helen Slater, JoBeth Williams. Eikenberry hosts three off-beat, biting reunions among seven women at a retreat over the course of a year, involving celebrations and sadness and some incisive conversation that was said to be totally improvised (although the pseudonymous Gisela Birnice gets obligatory writer credit). Made for cable. Above average.▼

Chant of Jimmie Blacksmith, The (1978-Australian) **C-124m.** ***½ D: Fred Schepisi. Tommy Lewis, Freddy Reynolds, Angela Punch, Ray Barrett, Jack Thompson, Peter Carroll, Bryan Brown. Half-white aborigine Lewis, brought up by Methodist pastor, is caught between two cultures and exploited, with tragic results. Harrowing indictment of racism, a problem certainly not unique to U.S. Based on fact. Director Schepisi's screenplay was adapted from a Thomas Keneally novel (Keneally also plays the role of Cook). Most U.S. prints run 108m. Panavision.

Chaplin (1992-British-U.S.) **C-144m.** **½ D: Richard Attenborough. Robert Downey, Jr., Dan Aykroyd, Geraldine Chaplin, Kevin Dunn, Anthony Hopkins, Milla Jovovich, Moira Kelly, Kevin Kline, Diane Lane, Penelope Ann Miller, Paul Rhys, John Thaw, Marisa Tomei, Nancy Travis, James Woods, David Duchovny, Deborah Maria Moore, Bill Paterson, John Standing, Robert Stephens. Reverent, lovingly detailed bio of Charlie Chaplin—from his squalid childhood in London to early moviemaking days with Mack Sennett, to international stardom, celebrity, and scandal. Downey is astonishingly good as Charlie and the film starts out great, but flattens midway through and tries to cover too much ground. Geraldine Chaplin plays her own grandmother, Charlie's severely neurotic mom. [PG-13]▼●◗

Chaplin Revue, The (1958) **119m.** ***½ D: Charles Chaplin. Charlie Chaplin, Edna Purviance, Sydney Chaplin, Mack Swain. Three of Chaplin's best shorts strung together with his own music, narration, and behind-the-scenes footage: A DOG'S LIFE (1918), one of his loveliest films; SHOULDER ARMS (1918), a classic WW1 comedy; and THE PILGRIM (1923), his underrated gem about a convict who disguises himself as a minister.▼

Chapman Report, The (1962) **C-125m.** **½ D: George Cukor. Efrem Zimbalist, Jr., Shelley Winters, Jane Fonda, Claire Bloom, Glynis Johns, Ray Danton, Ty Hardin, Andrew Duggan, John Dehner, Harold J. Stone, Corey Allen, Cloris Leachman, Chad Everett, Henry Daniell, Jack Cassidy. Slick, empty yarn about Kinsey-like sex researchers coming to suburban community to get statistical survey, with repercussions on assorted females. Potboiler material elevated by good performances and direction.

Chappaqua (1966) **C/B&W-92m.** ** D: Conrad Rooks. Jean-Louis Barrault, Conrad Rooks, William S. Burroughs, Allen Ginsburg, Ravi Shankar, Paula Pritchett, Ornette Coleman. Rooks, an alcoholic heroin addict, travels to Paris for a sleep cure and hallucinates while withdrawing. Autobiographical—and vague, surreal, phony. Prints of 82m. and 75m. also exist.▼◗

Chapter Two (1979) **C-124m.** ** D: Robert Moore. James Caan, Marsha Mason, Valerie Harper, Joseph Bologna. Neil Simon's autobiographical comedy-drama—one of his best Broadway plays—gets lost in screen translation. Caan is miscast as sharp-minded writer who's drawn into new romance (with Mason) before he's really recovered from death of his wife. Long, plastic, and unmoving. [PG]▼●

Character (1997-Dutch) **C-125m.** *** D: Mike van Diem. Fedja van Huet, Jan Decleir, Betty Schuurman, Victor Low, Tamar van den Dop, Hans Kesting, Lou Landre, Bernhard Droog. Oscar-winning, powerful story of a virtuous young man (van Huet), in 1920s Rotterdam, caught in a web of financial entanglements with his estranged, malevolent father (Decleir). Assured feature directorial debut by van Diem feels Dickensian, but moves like wildfire. Strong performances by a cast of stage actors, save Belgian film stalwart Decleir; young lead van Huet is a dead ringer for Robert Downey, Jr. Based on a popular 1938 Dutch novel by Ferdinand Bordewijk and filmed throughout Europe. [R]▼

Charade (1963) **C-114m.** ***½ D: Stanley Donen. Cary Grant, Audrey Hepburn, Walter Matthau, James Coburn, George Kennedy, Ned Glass, Jacques Marin. Suave comedy-mystery in Hitchcock vein, with Grant aiding widow Hepburn to recover fortune secreted by husband, being sought by trio of sinister crooks; set in Paris. Excellent screenplay by Peter Stone, score by Henry Mancini.▼◗

Charge at Feather River, The (1953) **C-96m.** **½ D: Gordon Douglas. Guy Madison, Vera Miles, Frank Lovejoy, Helen

Westcott, Ron Hagerthy. One of many Westerns which literally threw action at viewers to utilize 3-D in its original release; now, just standard.

Charge of the Black Lancers (1961-Italian) **C-97m.** **½ D: Giacomo Gentilomo. Mel Ferrer, Yvonne Furneaux, Jean Claudio, Leticia Roman. Well-mounted and fast-paced costumer. Claudio is traitor to country with his brother (Ferrer) leading patriots in defense of homeland. Cinescope.▼

Charge of the Lancers (1954) **C-74m.** ** D: William Castle. Paulette Goddard, Jean-Pierre Aumont, Richard Stapley, Karin Booth, Charles Irwin. Stilted affair of gypsy Goddard and British officer Aumont finding romance in midst of Crimean War.

Charge of the Light Brigade, The (1936) **116m.** *** D: Michael Curtiz. Errol Flynn, Olivia de Havilland, Patric Knowles, Henry Stephenson, Nigel Bruce, Donald Crisp, David Niven, C. Henry Gordon, Robert Barrat, Spring Byington, J. Carrol Naish. Thundering action based on Tennyson's poem, with immortal charge into the valley of death by British 27th Lancers cavalry. Lavish production values accent romantic tale of Flynn and de Havilland at army post in India. Max Steiner's first musical score for Warner Brothers is superb. Balaklava Heights charge directed by action specialist B. Reeves Eason. Also shown in computer-colored version.▼●

Charge of the Light Brigade, The (1968-British) **C-130m.** **½ D: Tony Richardson. David Hemmings, Vanessa Redgrave, John Gielgud, Harry Andrews, Trevor Howard, Jill Bennett, Mark Burns. Exquisitely made, but ultimately disappointing drama of events leading up to British involvement in Crimean War. Stunning battle sequence cannot make up for dramatic loopholes in this story of military minds gone mad. Clever animated segments by Richard Williams. Redgrave and Richardson's young daughters Natasha and Joely are members of the wedding party. Panavision. [M/PG]▼●

Charge of the Model Ts, The (1979) **C-94m.** *½ D: Jim McCullough. John David Carson, Louis Nye, Arte Johnson, Herb Edelman, Carol Bagdasarian. Deplorable family-oriented comedy, filmed in Texas, about a German spy who tries to infiltrate the U.S. during WW1 with a specially equipped weapon-bearing automobile. Made in 1977. Panavision. [G]▼

Chariots of Fire (1981-British) **C-123m.** ***½ D: Hugh Hudson. Ben Cross, Ian Charleson, Nigel Havers, Nick Farrell, Alice Krige, Cheryl Campbell, Ian Holm, John Gielgud, Lindsay Anderson, Patrick Magee, Nigel Davenport, Dennis Christopher, Brad Davis. Absorbing and unusual drama based on true story of two men—devout Scottish missionary Eric Liddell, driven Jewish Cambridge student Harold Abrahams—who run in the 1924 Olympics. Fascinating probe of their motives, challenges, and problems, and a case study of repressed emotions even in the midst of exultation. Feature debut for director Hudson. Oscars for Best Picture, Colin Welland's script, Vangelis' excellent score, and Milena Canonero's costumes. [PG]▼●◗

Chariots of the Gods? (1974) **C-98m.** *** D: Harald Reinl. First of too many speculative documentaries about ancient visitors from outer space who helped advance mankind's knowledge centuries ago. Well-made and filled with many natural beauties. Based on Erich Von Daniken's book. [G] ▼●◗

Charleston (1978-Italian) **C-91m.** ** D: Marcello Fondato. Bud Spencer, James Coco, Herbert Lom. Title refers not to the dance and not to the city but to beefy Italian superstar Spencer as a flashy conman who supports his expensive tastes by parting rich American gangster Coco from his ill-gotten gains.

Charley and the Angel (1973) **C-93m.** **½ D: Vincent McEveety. Fred MacMurray, Cloris Leachman, Harry Morgan, Kurt Russell, Vincent Van Patten, Kathleen Cody. MacMurray learns he has only a short time left on earth from helpful angel (Morgan) and changes his hard ways with family. Lightly amusing Disney film, but the warmth and nostalgia seem artificial this time around. [G]▼

Charley One-Eye (1973) **C-107m.** ** D: Don Chaffey. Richard Roundtree, Roy Thinnes, Nigel Davenport, Jill Pearson. Basically two-man show. Black Union Army deserter (Roundtree) and outcast Indian (Thinnes) thrown together in desert wasteland; gradual tragic relationship develops when outside forces interfere. Far too long; should've been a TV movie. [R]

Charley's Aunt (1930) **88m.** **½ D: Al Christie. Charles Ruggles, June Collyer, Hugh Williams, Doris Lloyd, Halliwell Hobbes. Ruggles shines in this amusing (if occasionally creaky) version of the Brandon Thomas farce. He's a twit who impersonates the title relative and chaperones for a couple of his pals and their girlfriends. Originally filmed in 1925 (with Sydney Chaplin); remade in 1941.▼

Charley's Aunt (1941) **81m.** **½ D: Archie Mayo. Jack Benny, Kay Francis, James Ellison, Anne Baxter, Edmund Gwenn, Reginald Owen. Broad but surefire filming of Brandon Thomas play about Oxford student posing as maiden aunt, joke getting out of hand. Previously filmed six other times! Remade as musical WHERE'S CHARLEY?

Charley Varrick (1973) **C-111m.** ***½ D: Don Siegel. Walter Matthau, Joe Don Baker, Felicia Farr, John Vernon, Andy Robinson, Jacqueline Scott, Sheree North,

Norman Fell, Woodrow Parfrey. Neatly contrived thriller with Matthau as a bank robber who discovers that his small-town take is actually laundered Mafia money. On target all the way, with a particularly satisfying wrap-up. [PG]▼●

Charlie Bubbles (1968) **C-91m.** **½ D: Albert Finney. Albert Finney, Colin Blakely, Billie Whitelaw, Liza Minnelli. Finney's first directing attempt concerns itself with married writer who begins affair with his secretary. Not especially moving, but Minnelli's screen debut adds quite a bit of sparkle to film.

Charlie Chan Earl Derr Biggers enjoyed great success with a series of novels featuring Charlie Chan, an Oriental detective on the Honolulu police force. The character first appeared on screen in 1926, but did not make an impression until Warner Oland took over the role in 1931's CHARLIE CHAN CARRIES ON (one of four early Chan films which, sad to say, no longer exist for us to see—the others being CHARLIE CHAN'S CHANCE, CHARLIE CHAN'S COURAGE, and CHARLIE CHAN'S GREATEST CASE). Swedish-born Oland seemed born to play the Mandarin-like sleuth, but the series really hit its stride when Keye Luke was cast as his youthful, Americanized "Number One Son" Lee in CHARLIE CHAN IN PARIS; their good-natured parrying gave the series a uniquely human, and humorous, foundation that made them more than mere whodunits. Oland's death in 1937 might have spelled the end of the series, but 20th Century-Fox decided to continue, and found another actor well suited to the part, Sidney Toler. He was soon joined by (Victor) Sen Yung, who was cast as Jimmy Chan, Charlie's Number Two Son. The series became more formularized, but still benefited from good writing and the best array of character actors in Hollywood to play the various red herrings. Fox retired the series in 1942, but two years later, low-budget Monogram Pictures decided to revive it, with Toler in the lead. These potboilers have little to recommend them. In 1947, after Toler's death, Roland Winters took on the role for a final round before the series expired in 1949. The vintage Chan movies, from the mid-1930s to the early 1940s, remain highly enjoyable today, deftly blending crime solving and comedy, and always punctuated by Charlie's wise sayings, like: "Insignificant molehill sometimes more important than conspicuous mountain."

CHARLIE CHAN

Behind That Curtain (1929)
The Black Camel (1931)
Charlie Chan in London (1934)
Charlie Chan in Paris (1935)
Charlie Chan in Egypt (1935)
Charlie Chan in Shanghai (1935)
Charlie Chan's Secret (1936)
Charlie Chan at the Circus (1936)
Charlie Chan at the Race Track (1936)
Charlie Chan at the Opera (1936)
Charlie Chan at the Olympics (1937)
Charlie Chan on Broadway (1937)
Charlie Chan at Monte Carlo (1938)
Charlie Chan in Honolulu (1938)
Charlie Chan in Reno (1939)
Charlie Chan at Treasure Island (1939)
Charlie Chan in City in Darkness (1939)
Charlie Chan in Panama (1940)
Charlie Chan's Murder Cruise (1940)
Charlie Chan at the Wax Museum (1940)
Murder Over New York (1940)
Dead Men Tell (1941)
Charlie Chan in Rio (1941)
Castle in the Desert (1942)
Charlie Chan in the Secret Service (1944)
The Chinese Cat (1944)
Black Magic (1944); AKA: Meeting at Midnight
The Jade Mask (1945)
The Scarlet Clue (1945)
The Shanghai Cobra (1945)
The Red Dragon (1945)
Dark Alibi (1946)
Shadows Over Chinatown (1946)
Dangerous Money (1946)
The Trap (1947)
The Chinese Ring (1947)
Docks of New Orleans (1948)
The Shanghai Chest (1948)
The Golden Eye (1948)
The Feathered Serpent (1948)
The Sky Dragon (1949)

Charlie Chan and the Curse of the Dragon Queen (1981) **C-97m.** *½ D: Clive Donner. Peter Ustinov, Lee Grant, Angie Dickinson, Richard Hatch, Brian Keith, Michelle Pfeiffer, Roddy McDowall, Rachel Roberts, Paul Ryan, Johnny Sekka. Boring comedy wastes its talented cast. Ustinov is badly miscast, gives one of the worst performances of his career. Hatch is his clumsy half-Jewish, half-Oriental grandson. Paging Warner Oland. [PG]▼

Charlie Chan and the Golden Eye SEE: **Golden Eye, The**

Charlie Chan at Monte Carlo (1938) **71m.** ** D: Eugene Forde. Warner Oland, Keye Luke, Virginia Field, Sidney Blackmer, Harold Huber, Kay Linaker, Robert Kent. A casino vacation on the Riviera turns into a murder investigation for the inscrutable detective. Oland's final appearance as Chan is not one of his best.

Charlie Chan at the Circus (1936) **72m.** **½ D: Harry Lachman. Warner Oland, Keye Luke, George and Olive Brasno, Francis Ford, Maxine Reiner, John McGuire, Shirley Deane, J. Carrol Naish. Murder strikes under the big top, with

Charlie and his twelve kids on hand to investigate. Pleasing entry.

Charlie Chan at the Olympics (1937) **71m.** **½ D: H. Bruce Humberstone. Warner Oland, Keye Luke, Katherine DeMille, Pauline Moore, Allan Lane, C. Henry Gordon, Jonathan Hale, Morgan Wallace, Layne Tom, Jr., John Eldredge, Frederick Vogeding. Spies converge on the 1936 Berlin games and kidnap Number One Son Luke from the American swim team. Neat entry featuring well-integrated Olympic newsreel footage, and amusing byplay with plucky Charlie Chan, Jr. (Tom).

Charlie Chan at the Opera (1936) **66m.** *** D: H. Bruce Humberstone. Warner Oland, Boris Karloff, Keye Luke, Charlotte Henry, Thomas Beck, Margaret Irving, Gregory Gaye, Nedda Harrigan, Frank Conroy, William Demarest. The series at its peak, a stylish blend of murder and music, with Karloff as the leading suspect, Demarest as a skeptical cop, and a bogus opera written for the film by Oscar Levant. ▼●

Charlie Chan at the Race Track (1936) **70m.** **½ D: H. Bruce Humberstone. Warner Oland, Keye Luke, Helen Wood, Thomas Beck, Alan Dinehart, Gavin Muir, Gloria Roy, Jonathan Hale, Junior Coghlan, Frankie Darro. Chan corrals some crooked gamblers during the investigation of a horse owner's murder, with Number One Son Luke starting to become a regular participant in the series.

Charlie Chan at the Wax Museum (1940) **63m.** **½ D: Lynn Shores. Sidney Toler, Sen Yung, C. Henry Gordon, Marc Lawrence, Joan Valerie, Marguerite Chapman, Ted Osborn, Michael Visaroff. A gangster put away by Chan escapes and swears vengeance, hiding out at a wax museum run by a madman. Atmospheric entry with an appropriately creepy milieu, and a handful of surprises. ▼●

Charlie Chan at Treasure Island (1939) **75m.** *** D: Norman Foster. Sidney Toler, Cesar Romero, Pauline Moore, Sen Yung, Douglas Fowley, June Gale, Sally Blane, Wally Vernon, Donald MacBride, Douglass Dumbrille. One of the best Toler entries, with Charlie getting help from magician Romero in his attempt to prove that a phony psychic was behind the mysterious suicide of his friend. Tight script by John Larkin.

Charlie Chan in Black Magic SEE: **Black Magic** (1944)

Charlie Chan in City in Darkness (1939) **75m.** ** D: Herbert I. Leeds. Sidney Toler, Lynn Bari, Richard Clarke, Harold Huber, Pedro de Cordoba, Dorothy Tree, C. Henry Gordon, Douglass Dumbrille, Noel Madison, Lon Chaney, Jr., Leo G. Carroll, Frederick Vogeding. In Paris, Chan takes on an arms dealer who's supplying weapons to the Germans. Mediocre entry with a topical angle.

Charlie Chan in Dangerous Money SEE: **Dangerous Money**

Charlie Chan in Egypt (1935) **72m.** *** D: Louis King. Warner Oland, "Pat" Paterson, Thomas Beck, Rita Cansino (Hayworth), Jameson Thomas, Frank Conroy, Nigel de Brulier, Paul Porcasi, Stepin Fetchit. Highly enjoyable mystery about the search for a mummified archeologist in the land of the pyramids. Many horror-movie trappings in this one, including music lifted from CHANDU THE MAGICIAN (1932).

Charlie Chan in Honolulu (1938) **68m.** **½ D: H. Bruce Humberstone. Sidney Toler, Phyllis Brooks, Sen Yung, Eddie Collins, John King, Claire Dodd, George Zucco, Robert Barrat, Marc Lawrence, Richard Lane, Philip Ahn. Toler makes a serviceable Chan in his first outing (with Yung also debuting as Number Two Son Jimmy), probing murder on a ship docked in Hawaii while his daughter is about to give birth to his number one grandchild. Layne Tom, Jr., is fun as the daring young Charlie Chan, Jr.

Charlie Chan in London (1934) **79m.** *** D: Eugene Forde. Warner Oland, Drue Leyton, Douglas Walton, Alan Mowbray, Mona Barrie, Raymond (Ray) Milland, George Barraud, David Torrence, Madge Bellamy, Murray Kinnell, E. E. Clive. Charlie tries to solve a murder during a foxhunt weekend at a British country estate—while dodging death-dealing darts and interpreting mysterious notes. Solid entry is helped by good portrayal of gentried British types . . . including a young Ray Milland.

Charlie Chan in Meeting at Midnight SEE: **Black Magic** (1944)

Charlie Chan in Panama (1940) **67m.** **½ D: Norman Foster. Sidney Toler, Jean Rogers, Kane Richmond, Lionel Atwill, Mary Nash, Sen Yung, Chris-Pin Martin, Jack La Rue. They really started to play up the WW2 angle with this one, a slick entry about saboteurs planning to attack Navy ships in the Panama Canal. Strong cast helps.

Charlie Chan in Paris (1935) **72m.** **½ D: Lewis Seiler. Warner Oland, Mary Brian, Thomas Beck, Erik Rhodes, John Miljan, Ruth Peterson, Minor Watson, Murray Kinnell, John Qualen, Keye Luke, Henry Kolker. Compact early entry has Chan rounding up counterfeiters with the help of Number One Son Luke, making his first appearance as Lee. ▼●

Charlie Chan in Reno (1939) **70m.** **½ D: Norman Foster. Sidney Toler, Ricardo Cortez, Phyllis Brooks, Pauline Moore, Slim Summerville, Kane Richmond, Sen Yung, Robert Lowery, Eddie Collins, Kay Linaker, Morgan Conway. Chan heads for the divorce capital to defend a fellow Hawaiian on murder charges in this trim episode.

Charlie Chan in Rio (1941) **61m.** **½ D:

Harry Lachman. Sidney Toler, Mary Beth Hughes, Cobina Wright, Jr., Ted (Michael) North, Victor Jory, Harold Huber, Victor Sen Yung, Richard Derr, Kay Linaker. Picturesque Brazil is the backdrop for this entertaining murder mystery, with Chan joining the local police to solve a double homicide. A reworking of THE BLACK CAMEL (1931), which was directed by Hamilton MacFadden, who appears in this film as Bill Kellogg.▼●

Charlie Chan in Shanghai (1935) **70m.** **½ D: James Tinling. Warner Oland, Irene Hervey, Russell Hicks, Keye Luke, Halliwell Hobbes, Charles Locher (Jon Hall), Frederick Vogeding. Charlie tracks down murderous opium smugglers in this one. More physical action than usual.

Charlie Chan in the Secret Service (1944) **63m.** ** D: Phil Rosen. Sidney Toler, Mantan Moreland, Gwen Kenyon, Benson Fong, Arthur Loft, Marianne Quon. The Oriental sleuth probes the murder of an inventor in this initial *Charlie Chan* film for low-budget Monogram studios, which resulted in an obvious drop in production quality and the addition of Moreland in the stereotyped role of Birmingham, a frightened cab driver.▼●

Charlie Chan on Broadway (1937) **68m.** *** D: Eugene Forde. Warner Oland, Keye Luke, Joan Marsh, J. Edward Bromberg, Leon Ames, Joan Woodbury, Douglas Fowley, Louise Henry, Donald Woods, Harold Huber, Marc Lawrence. Slangy entry about a shady chanteuse who's murdered for her little black book containing the names and misdeeds of some highly placed criminals. Try to solve this one—and look fast for Lon Chaney, Jr.

Charlie Chan's Murder Cruise (1940) **75m.** ** D: Eugene Forde. Sidney Toler, Sen Yung, Marjorie Weaver, Lionel Atwill, Robert Lowery, Don Beddoe, Leo G. Carroll, Cora Witherspoon, Kay Linaker, Harlan Briggs, Charles Middleton, Layne Tom, Jr. Overly familiar shipboard whodunit centering on the murder of a Scotland Yard inspector. Remake of CHARLIE CHAN CARRIES ON (1931), which no longer exists.

Charlie Chan's Secret (1936) **71m.** ** D: Gordon Wiles. Warner Oland, Rosina Lawrence, Charles Quigley, Henrietta Crosman, Edward Trevor, Astrid Allwyn, Herbert Mundin. Hollow mystery about a missing heir believed drowned who turns up alive, only to be killed during a seance. Number One Son is sorely missed.▼

Charlie Chaplin Carnival (1938) **100m.** **** Four vintage comedies from Chaplin's 1916-17 peak period: BEHIND THE SCREEN, THE COUNT, THE FIREMAN, THE VAGABOND. First one is best, with leading lady Edna Purviance and oversized villain Eric Campbell. Some prints run 75m.▼

Charlie Chaplin Cavalcade (1938) **75m.** **** More priceless gems from 1916-17 period: ONE A.M. (Chaplin's famous solo film), THE RINK, THE PAWNSHOP, THE FLOORWALKER. All great.▼

Charlie Chaplin Festival (1938) **96m.** **** Best of the Chaplin compilations, which all suffer from obtrusive sound effects and music: THE ADVENTURER, THE CURE, EASY STREET, THE IMMIGRANT. Four of the greatest comedies ever made— don't miss them. Some prints run 75m.▼

Charlie McCarthy, Detective (1939) **65m.** **½ D: Frank Tuttle. Edgar Bergen, Charlie McCarthy, Constance Moore, Robert Cummings, Louis Calhern, John Sutton, Harold Huber, Edgar Kennedy. Good comedy-whodunit with Bergen & McCarthy rivaling Inspector Kennedy's investigation.

Charlie Muffin (1979-British) **C-109m. TVM** D: Jack Gold. David Hemmings, Sam Wanamaker, Jennie Linden, Ian Richardson, Ralph Richardson, Pinkas Braun, Shane Rimmer. Literate, extremely entertaining tale of a shrewd, crafty—and very human—British espionage operative who lives by his own rules and is in disfavor with his stuffy superiors, and his involvement with an ''alleged'' Soviet defector. The finale is a stunner. Above average.

Charlie's Ghost Story (1994) **C-88m.** ** D: Anthony Edwards. Cheech Marin, Anthony Edwards, Linda Fiorentino, Trenton Knight, Charles Rocket, J. T. Walsh, Daphne Zuniga. Occasionally funny story of the ghost of explorer Coronado haunting people to get his bones properly buried so he can finally rest in peace. Actually, it's a rather sad story of child neglect. Archeologist/dad Edwards is so enthralled with his discovery of Coronado's cave, he completely ignores his son, who is the target of the ''haunting.'' Fiorentino is wasted in the thankless role of the family maid. Based on a story by Mark Twain. [PG]▼

Charlie, the Lonesome Cougar (1968) **C-75m.** **½ No director credited. Narrated by Rex Allen. Ron Brown, Brian Russell, Linda Wallace, Jim Wilson. Average Disney animal adventure-comedy about a friendly cougar who lives in a lumber camp.▼◗

Charlotte's Web (1973) **C-93m.** *** D: Charles A. Nichols, Iwao Takamoto. Voices of Debbie Reynolds, Henry Gibson, Paul Lynde, Agnes Moorehead, Charles Nelson Reilly. Narrated by Rex Allen. Charming animated feature based on E. B. White classic of barnyard spider who befriends shy piglet. Above average for Hanna-Barbera cartoon studio. Songs by Richard M. and Robert B. Sherman. [G]▼●

Charly (1968) **C-103m.** ***½ D: Ralph Nelson. Cliff Robertson, Claire Bloom,

Lilia Skala, Leon Janney, Dick Van Patten. Robertson won Oscar for fine work as retarded man turned into super-brain in scientific experiment (a role he first tackled on TV's *U.S. Steel Hour* in 1961). Bloom is sympathetic caseworker who becomes attached to Charly. Based on Daniel Keyes' *Flowers for Algernon* (and remade for TV in 2000 under that title). First rate. Techniscope. [M/PG]▼●

Charming Sinners (1929) **85m.** *½ D: Robert Milton. Ruth Chatterton, Clive Brook, William Powell, Mary Nolan, Laura Hope Crews, Florence Eldridge. Obvious, creaky marital drama of Chatterton, whose philandering husband (Brook) has taken up with her best friend. To pique his jealousy, she pretends to become involved with former boyfriend Powell. Based on Somerset Maugham's *The Constant Wife.*

Charro! (1969) **C-98m.** BOMB D: Charles Marquis Warren. Elvis Presley, Ina Balin, Victor French, Lynn Kellogg, Barbara Werle, Paul Brinegar. Attempt to change Presley's image by casting him in straight Western is total failure. Elvis sings only one song. Panavision. [G]▼

Chartroose Caboose (1960) **C-75m.** ** D: William "Red" Reynolds. Molly Bee, Ben Cooper, Edgar Buchanan, Mike McGreevey. Buchanan, an eccentric retired train conductor, shelters a young couple in his strange house, a converted caboose. Panavision.

Chase, The (1946) **86m.** **½ D: Arthur D. Ripley. Robert Cummings, Michele Morgan, Steve Cochran, Peter Lorre, Lloyd Corrigan, Jack Holt, Don Wilson, James Westerfield. Mildly diverting melodrama with luckless vet Cummings becoming involved with a ruthless racketeer (well played by Cochran) and his melancholy wife (Morgan). Scripted by Philip Yordan, based on a book by Cornell Woolrich.▼

Chase, The (1966) **C-135m.** **½ D: Arthur Penn. Marlon Brando, Jane Fonda, Robert Redford, Angie Dickinson, Janice Rule, James Fox, Robert Duvall, E.G. Marshall, Miriam Hopkins, Martha Hyer. Intriguing, unsubtle drama of how prison escape by local boy (Redford) affects worthless Texas town and its sheriff (Brando). Based on a novel by Horton Foote. Notorious for behind-the-scenes conflicts with director Penn, screenwriter Lillian Hellman, and producer Sam Spiegel, it's not surprising that finished product misses the mark. Panavision. ▼●

Chase, The (1994) **C-94m.** *½ D: Adam Rifkin. Charlie Sheen, Kristy Swanson, Henry Rollins, Josh Mostel, Wayne Grace, Rocky Carroll, Miles Dougal, Ray Wise, Claudia Christian, Natalija Nogulich, Flea, Anthony Kiedis, Cary Elwes, Cassian Elwes. Falsely accused prison escapee is forced to kidnap the daughter of California's version of Donald Trump, setting off a movie-length pursuit by police and a TV news helicopter. Why bother? [PG-13]▼●

Chase a Crooked Shadow (1958-British) **87m.** *** D: Michael Anderson. Richard Todd, Anne Baxter, Herbert Lom, Alexander Knox. Heiress Baxter doubts her sanity when allegedly dead brother Todd appears to claim inheritance; exciting, Hitchcock-like melodrama.

Chase for the Golden Needles, The SEE: **Golden Needles**

Chase Me Charlie (1932) **61m.** ** Narrated by Teddy Bergman. Charlie Chaplin, Edna Purviance, Ben Turpin. Inept attempt to string early Chaplin shorts into story line—1914 material used is often weak.

Chasers (1994) **C-101m.** *½ D: Dennis Hopper. Tom Berenger, Erika Eleniak, William McNamara, Crispin Glover, Matthew Glave, Dean Stockwell, Gary Busey, Seymour Cassel, Frederic Forrest, Marilu Henner. Two Navy men are assigned to prisoner-escort duty only to discover that the dangerous criminal they are escorting is—gulp!—a beautiful sexpot. That's as close as this misfire gets to the far superior THE LAST DETAIL. Lowbrow comedy has little to recommend it, even for fans of t&a. Many of Hopper's acting cronies appear in small roles, and Hopper himself turns up as a perverted underwear salesman. [R]▼●

Chasing Amy (1997) **C-111m.** ***½ D: Kevin Smith. Ben Affleck, Joey Lauren Adams, Jason Lee, Dwight Ewell, Jason Mewes, Kevin Smith, Matt Damon, Casey Affleck. Winning, original comedy-drama about a comic book artist who lives with his dour work partner—until he meets an attractive up-and-coming female artist with a dynamite personality. He's seriously smitten—and stays that way even after learning that she's gay. Writer-director Smith hits all the right notes in this honest and appealing film, which refuses to take the easy way out (just like its lead character) right to the end. Affleck and Adams are perfect. Smith and Mewes reprise their Silent Bob and Jay characters from CLERKS and MALLRATS. [R] ▼●◗

Chasing Dreams (1982) **C-105m.** *½ D: Sean Roche, Therese Conte. David G. Brown, John Fife, Jim Shane, Matthew Clark, Lisa Kingston, Claudia Carroll, Kevin Costner. Hopelessly hokey soaper of insecure, self-conscious farmboy Brown, who "finds" himself by playing college baseball. Of interest solely for early, brief appearance of Costner as Brown's older, medical-student brother. [PG]▼

Chastity (1969) **C-98m.** ** D: Alessio de Paola. Cher, Barbara London, Tom Nolan, Stephen Whittaker. Interesting story of girl who takes to the highway to find life of her own. Cher in solo acting debut is surprisingly good. [PG—originally rated R]

Chastity Belt, The SEE: **On My Way to the Crusades, I Met a Girl Who . . .**

Chato's Land (1972-Spanish-British) **C-110m.** **½ D: Michael Winner. Charles Bronson, Jack Palance, Richard Basehart, Ralph Waite, Richard Jordan, Victor French, Jill Ireland. Posse seeks Indian Bronson in connection with marshal's murder; usual quota of blood in lengthy film. [PG]▼

Chattahoochee (1990) **C-98m.** ** D: Mick Jackson. Gary Oldman, Dennis Hopper, Frances McDormand, Pamela Reed, Ned Beatty, M. Emmet Walsh, William De Acutis, Lee Wilkof, Matt Craven, Gary Klar. Enervatingly straightforward account of man (Oldman) whose mental breakdown (actually post-Korea combat stress) wrongfully landed him in a Karloff-caliber Florida institution. Standard "reform" drama—though based on fact—with Hopper's role (as a fellow patient) a glorified cameo; McDormand and Reed do all right as, respectively, Oldman's wife and crusading sister. [R] ▼●

Chattanooga Choo Choo (1984) **C-102m.** ** D: Bruce Bilson. Barbara Eden, George Kennedy, Melissa Sue Anderson, Joe Namath, Bridget Hanley, Clu Gulager, Christopher McDonald, Davis Roberts, Tony Azito, Parley Baer. In order to collect inheritance, goofball Kennedy must restore the famous train and make one final 24-hour run from Pennsylvania Station. Spirited cast in a sitcom-level script. Rubber-limbed Azito is amazing as waiter who's never dropped a tray. [PG]▼

Chatterbox (1943) **76m.** **½ D: Joseph Santley. Joe E. Brown, Judy Canova, Rosemary Lane, John Hubbard, Gus Schilling, Chester Clute, Anne Jeffreys. Entertaining comedy of radio-cowboy Brown (not much of a hero in real life) visiting dude ranch for publicity purposes.

Che! (1969) **C-96m.** BOMB D: Richard Fleischer. Omar Sharif, Jack Palance, Cesare Danova, Robert Loggia, Woody Strode. Comic-book treatment of famed revolutionary became one of the biggest film jokes of 1960s. However, you haven't lived until you see Palance play Fidel Castro. Panavision. [PG]▼

Cheap Detective, The (1978) **C-92m.** *** D: Robert Moore. Peter Falk, Ann-Margret, Eileen Brennan, Sid Caesar, Stockard Channing, James Coco, Dom DeLuise, Louise Fletcher, John Houseman, Madeline Kahn, Fernando Lamas, Marsha Mason, Phil Silvers, Vic Tayback, Abe Vigoda, Paul Williams, Nicol Williamson, David Ogden Stiers. For Neil Simon and Peter Falk to parody Bogart movies like MALTESE FALCON is an easy task, but it's still pretty funny when not resorting to the obvious. Panavision. [PG]▼●

Cheaper by the Dozen (1950) **C-85m.** *** D: Walter Lang. Clifton Webb, Myrna Loy, Jeanne Crain, Mildred Natwick, Edgar Buchanan. Charming turn-of-the-century story of the Gilbreth children, twelve strong, their exacting father (well played by Webb) and mother (Loy). From the Gilbreth-Carey novel. Sequel: BELLES ON THEIR TOES.▼

Cheaper to Keep Her (1980) **C-92m.** BOMB D: Ken Annakin. Mac Davis, Tovah Feldshuh, Art Metrano, Ian McShane, Priscilla Lopez, Rose Marie, Jack Gilford, J. Pat O'Malley. Detective Davis is hired by lawyer Feldshuh to check out McShane and Gilford, who have been lax in their alimony checks. Sexist, racist, and obnoxious. [R]▼

Cheat, The (1915) **59m.** *** D: Cecil B. DeMille. Fannie Ward, Sessue Hayakawa, Jack Dean, James Neill. Once audacious melodrama remains an engrossing curio about a proper, upper-class Long Island lady (Ward) who is exploited by a licentious Asian (Hayakawa). Watch this, and you'll see why Hayakawa was one of the most popular screen actors of the time.▼●

Cheaters, The (1945) **87m.** *** D: Joseph Kane. Joseph Schildkraut, Billie Burke, Eugene Pallette, Ona Munson, Raymond Walburn, Ruth Terry. Excellent cast in enjoyable tale of wealthy family of snobs humanized by downtrodden actor they invite for Christmas dinner. Aka THE CASTAWAY.

Cheatin' Hearts (1993) **C-90m.** ** D: Rod McCall. Sally Kirkland, James Brolin, Kris Kristofferson, Pamela Gidley, Laura Johnson, Michael Moore, Renee Estevez. Very ordinary love story set in New Mexico, involving romantic relationships in a sleepy little town. Stars are all attractive, but story is just too thin to hold much interest. Kirkland and Brolin executive produced. [R]▼

Check and Double Check (1930) **80m.** BOMB D: Melville Brown. Freeman Gosden, Charles Correll, Sue Carol, Charles Morton, Ralf Harolde, Duke Ellington and His Band. Movie debut for radio's Amos 'n' Andy is a leaden-paced early talkie with stale script and precious little comedy; not nearly as good as a sample radio (or later TV) episode of the show.▼●

Checkered Flag or Crash (1977) **C-95m.** ** D: Alan Gibson. Joe Don Baker, Susan Sarandon, Larry Hagman, Alan Vint, Parnelli Jones, Logan Clark. A 1,000 mile off-road race in the Philippines is the focal point of this unmemorable programmer; for car-action fans only. Panavision. [PG]

Checking Out (1989-U.S.-British) **C-96m.** *½ D: David Leland. Jeff Daniels, Melanie Mayron, Michael Tucker, Kathleen York, Ann Magnuson, Allan Havey, Jo Harvey Allen, Felton Perry, Alan Wolfe. When Daniels' best friend dies of a heart attack he suddenly turns into a raging hypochondriac, convinced the same thing will happen to him. After 90 minutes of this overblown black comedy you pray that it will. Panavision. [R]▼●

Check Is in the Mail, The (1986) **C-91m.** ** D: Joan Darling. Brian Dennehy, Anne Archer, Hallie Todd, Chris Herbert, Michael Bowen, Nita Talbot, Dick Shawn. Ineffectual comedy about a beleaguered family man who decides to beat the system by making his home self-sufficient. Episodic, slow-paced film wears out its sometimes likable ingredients. [R]▼

Cheech & Chong's Next Movie (1980) **C-99m.** *½ D: Thomas Chong. Cheech Marin, Thomas Chong, Evelyn Guerrero, Betty Kennedy, Sy Kramer, Rikki Marin. After an auspicious debut in UP IN SMOKE, the pothead, put-on comic duo go seriously awry in this crude, incoherent film, which offers only sporadic laughs. [R]▼●

Cheech & Chong's Nice Dreams (1981) **C-89m.** ** D: Thomas Chong. Cheech Marin, Thomas Chong, Evelyn Guerrero, Paul Reubens (Pee-wee Herman), Stacy Keach, Dr. Timothy Leary, Sandra Bernhard. Episodic, generally below par C&C comedy finds them as owners of an ice-cream truck that fronts for more lucrative grass trade. Some hilarity involving a sexually jealous biker; Guerrero once again an apt comic foil. [R] ▼●

Cheech & Chong's The Corsican Brothers (1984) **C-90m.** BOMB D: Thomas Chong. Cheech Marin, Thomas Chong, Roy Dotrice, Shelby Fiddis, Rikki Marin, Edie McClurg, Rae Dawn Chong, Robbi Chong. The boys (in three roles each) and their families (in one role each) star in their first non-drug (but still tasteless) comedy, an inept parody which seems all the more empty because of its magnificent French locations. Staggeringly unfunny even by C&C standards; the *previews* for START THE REVOLUTION WITHOUT ME have more laughs. [PG]▼●

Cheers for Miss Bishop (1941) **95m.** *** D: Tay Garnett. Martha Scott, William Gargan, Edmund Gwenn, Sterling Holloway, Sidney Blackmer, Mary Anderson, Dorothy Peterson. Sentimental story of Scott devoting her life to teaching in small Midwestern town. Nicely done.▼

Cheetah (1989) **C-84m.** *** D: Jeff Blyth. Keith Coogan, Lucy Deakins, Collin Mothupi, Timothy Landfield, Breon Gorman, Ka Vundia, Kuldeep Bhakoo, Paul Onsongo. Two Southern California kids join their parents for several months in Kenya, make friends with a young Masai, and adopt an orphaned cheetah, which they raise as a pet. Simple story line is aimed squarely at kids, but it's believable and entertaining and teaches good lessons about tolerance and respect for the wild. A Disney release. [G]▼●

Chef in Love, A (1996-French-Russian) **C-100m.** **½ D: Nana Djordjadze. Pierre Richard, Nino Kirtadze, Micheline Presle, Timur Kamkhadze, Jean-Yves Gautier, Ramaz Chkhikvadze, Danielle Darrieux. Yet another film which equates food with love and sex. Richard, a fabled French chef, comes to live in Georgia just before the Russian Revolution, where he romances a princess (Kirtadze) and opens a restaurant; his life is irrevocably altered upon the arrival of the Red Army. Despite some mouth-watering scenery (and food), the result is annoyingly uneven. [PG-13]▼

Cherokee Strip (1940) **86m.** **½ D: Lesley Selander. Richard Dix, Florence Rice, Victor Jory, William Henry, Andy Clyde, George E. Stone. Solid if unsurprising little Western with quiet but determined Dix becoming marshal of small town, hoping to get the goods on crooked Jory and his gang.

Cherry 2000 (1988) **C-93m.** **½ D: Steve DeJarnatt. Melanie Griffith, Ben Johnson, Harry Carey, Jr., David Andrews, Tim Thomerson, Pamela Gidley, Jennifer Mayo. Post-MAD MAX adventure about a female mercenary hired to bust into a 21st-century robot warehouse operated by psychos in what used to be the American Southwest. Derivative, but a bit more fun than its limited theatrical release might lead you to believe; Johnson and Carey are worth their combined weights in audience goodwill. Filmed in 1986. [PG-13]▼●

Chesty Anderson, USN (1976) **C-88m.** ** D: Ed Forsyth. Shari Eubank, Rosanne Katon, Dorri Thomson, Marcie Barkin, Timothy Carey, Scatman Crothers, Frank Campanella, Fred Willard, Betty Thomas. Sexploitation comedy about female naval recruits is so timid that it keeps its lovely cast clothed even during physical exams! Retitled ANDERSON'S ANGELS for TV. [R]▼

Chevy Van SEE: **Van, The** (1976)

Cheyenne (1947) **100m.** ** D: Raoul Walsh. Dennis Morgan, Jane Wyman, Janis Paige, Bruce Bennett, Alan Hale, Arthur Kennedy, Barton MacLane. Standard Western as gambler attempts to capture outlaw—instead spends time with outlaw's wife. Later a TV series. Retitled THE WYOMING KID.

Cheyenne Autumn (1964) **C-145m.** *** D: John Ford. Richard Widmark, Carroll Baker, Karl Malden, Dolores Del Rio, Sal Mineo, Edward G. Robinson, James Stewart, Ricardo Montalban, Gilbert Roland, Arthur Kennedy, Patrick Wayne, Elizabeth Allen, Victor Jory, John Carradine, Mike Mazurki, John Qualen, George O'-Brien. Sprawling, uneven, but entertaining John Ford Western (his last) about Cheyenne Indian tribe and its eventful journey back to original settlement after being relocated by the government. Director Ford's last film in Monument Valley. Dodge City sequence (with Stewart as Wyatt Earp) was cut after premiere engagements;

restored to 154m. on video. Super Panavision 70. ▼●

Cheyenne Social Club, The (1970) **C-103m.** ★★½ D: Gene Kelly. Henry Fonda, James Stewart, Shirley Jones, Sue Ane Langdon, Elaine Devry. Jimmy inherits and runs a bawdy house in the Old West. Lots of laughs, but clichés run throughout. Panavision. [PG]▼

Cheyenne Warrior (1994) **C-86m.** ★★★ D: Mark Griffiths. Kelly Preston, Pato Hoffmann, Bo Hopkins, Rick Dean, Clint Howard, Charles Powell, Dan Clark, Winterhawk, Dan Haggerty. Modest but engrossing Western character study about the growing bond between a proud Indian warrior and a naive white woman who loses her husband while heading west in the 1800s. Well cast, and well written (by Michael B. Druxman). [PG]▼◗

Chicago Calling (1951) **74m.** ★★ D: John Reinhardt. Dan Duryea, Mary Anderson, Gordon Gebert, Ross Elliott. Slim premise has Duryea sitting by telephone awaiting news of estranged family injured in car accident; mild tour de force.

Chicago Confidential (1957) **73m.** ★★½ D: Sidney Salkow. Brian Keith, Beverly Garland, Dick Foran, Beverly Tyler, Elisha Cook. Keith and Garland make good protagonists in their crusade to clean up corruption and crime amid the labor unions of the Windy City.

Chicago Deadline (1949) **87m.** ★★½ D: Lewis Allen. Alan Ladd, Donna Reed, June Havoc, Irene Hervey, Arthur Kennedy, Shepperd Strudwick. Potentially topnotch actioner bogs down in clichés, with Ladd as crusading reporter in corruption-filled city. Remade as FAME IS THE NAME OF THE GAME.

Chicago Joe and the Showgirl (1990-British) **C-103m.** ★★½ D: Bernard Rose. Kiefer Sutherland, Emily Lloyd, Patsy Kensit, Keith Allen, Liz Fraser, Alexandra Pigg, Ralph Nossek, Colin Bruce, John Lahr. Yank soldier-hood Sutherland, stationed in London during WW2, joins a self-deluded British tart (Lloyd) in committing petty crimes that escalate into murder. Famed British tabloid fodder gets the low-budget "period" treatment. Mildly interesting account never quite jells, though some of the violence offers surprisingly stylized jolts. Lloyd is a lot more interesting than her costar here. [R]▼●

Chicago Syndicate (1955) **83m.** ★★ D: Fred F. Sears. Dennis O'Keefe, Abbe Lane, Paul Stewart, Xavier Cugat. Passable exposé film involving cleanup of Windy City rackets.▼

Chicken Chronicles, The (1977) **C-95m.** ★½ D: Francis Simon. Steven Guttenberg, Ed Lauter, Lisa Reeves, Meridith Baer, Branscombe Richmond, Gino Baffa, Phil Silvers. Lowjinks of a high school senior, circa 1969, whose principal preoccupation is bedding the girl of his dreams. Guttenberg's film debut. [PG]▼

Chicken Every Sunday (1948) **91m.** ★★½ D: George Seaton. Dan Dailey, Celeste Holm, Colleen Townsend, Alan Young, Natalie Wood. Easygoing turn-of-the-century Americana about get-rich-quick schemer Dailey and understanding wife Holm.

Chief Crazy Horse (1955) **C-86m.** ★★½ D: George Sherman. Victor Mature, Suzan Ball, John Lund, Ray Danton, Keith Larsen, Paul Guilfoyle, David Janssen, Dennis Weaver. Intelligent if slow-moving Western with Mature perfectly cast as the proud, idealistic Sioux chief who unites the indian tribes (and defeats Custer at Little Big Horn). CinemaScope.

Chikamatsu Monogatari SEE: **Crucified Lovers, The**

Child Is Born, A (1940) **79m.** ★★★ D: Lloyd Bacon. Geraldine Fitzgerald, Jeffrey Lynn, Gladys George, Gale Page, Spring Byington, Eve Arden. Smooth, touching remake of LIFE BEGINS about everyday life in maternity ward, involving prisoner Fitzgerald sent to hospital to have her child.

Childish Things SEE: **Confessions of Tom Harris**

Child Is Waiting, A (1963) **102m.** ★★★ D: John Cassavetes. Burt Lancaster, Judy Garland, Gena Rowlands, Steven Hill, Bruce Ritchey. Poignant story of Lancaster's attempts to treat retarded children with the help of overly sympathetic Garland. Sensitive subject handled with honesty and candor.▼●

Child of Satan SEE: **To The Devil—A Daughter**

Children, The (1980) **C-89m.** ★½ D: Max Kalmanowicz. Martin Shakar, Gil Rogers, Gale Garnett, Jesse Abrams, Tracy Griswold, Joy Glacum. When mysterious gas from nuclear plant contaminates school bus, kids become radioactive and burn up whoever they hug. Dull movie with a few laughs and no suspense at all. [R]▼

Children, The (1990-British-West German) **C-115m.** ★★ D: Tony Palmer. Ben Kingsley, Kim Novak, Siri Neal, Geraldine Chaplin, Joe Don Baker, Britt Ekland, Donald Sinden, Karen Black, Robert Stephens, Rupert Graves. Kingsley's plans to marry recently widowed Novak are thrown askew by his involvement with the ill-cared-for children of an old college friend . . . and his gradual infatuation with the eldest teenage daughter. Based on an Edith Wharton novel filmed in 1929 as THE MARRIAGE PLAYGROUND. Kingsley and Novak are excellent, but film is irritating and slow, with tiresome use of steadicam. Filmed in Venice and Switzerland.▼

Children of a Lesser God (1986) **C-110m.** ★★★ D: Randa Haines. William Hurt, Marlee Matlin, Piper Laurie, Philip Bosco, Alison Gompf, John F. Cleary, John Basinger.

New teacher at school for the deaf is intrigued by an obviously intelligent but isolated young woman who works there as a janitor. The warmth of Hurt's performance, and the credibility of Matlin's, shine through this moving and unusual love story . . . though it lacks the edge and bite of Mark Medoff's play, on which it's based. An impressive feature-film directing debut for Haines. Matlin, also making her film debut, won an Oscar. Filmed in New Brunswick. [R]▼●

Children of An Lac, The (1980) **C-100m. TVM** D: John Llewellyn Moxey. Shirley Jones, Ina Balin, Beulah Quo, Alan Fudge, Ben Piazza, Lee Paul, Kieu Chinh, Vic Diaz. The story of three women (among them Ina Balin in her own real-life role) who try to evacuate hundreds of Vietnamese orphans just before the fall of Saigon. Lovely performance by veteran actress Quo. Blanche Hanalis wrote the teleplay from Balin's story. Above average.▼

Children of Heaven (1997-Iranian) **C-88m.** *** D: Majid Majidi. Amir Naji, Mir Farrokh Hashemian, Bahareh Seddigi, Nafiseh Jafar Mohammadi, Fereshteh Sarabandi. Poignant story of a young boy trying to replace his sister's newly repaired pink shoes. This became Iran's first Oscar contender for Best Foreign Language Film, and deservedly so. Simple tale shows the importance of family, perseverance and honor, as we follow an eight-year-old's seemingly impossible quest to make up for his single misdeed. Well worth watching for children and adults alike. [PG]▼

Children of Paradise (1945-French) **195m.** **** D: Marcel Carné. Jean-Louis Barrault, Arletty, Pierre Brasseur, Albert Remy, Maria Casarés, Leon Larive, Marcel Herrand, Pierre Renoir. Timeless masterpiece of filmmaking (and storytelling), focusing on a rough-and-tumble theatrical troupe in 19th-century France. Barrault plays the mime whose unfulfilled passion for free-spirited Arletty dominates his life, even as he achieves great fame on stage. Wise, witty, and completely captivating. Written by Jacques Prévert. Filming began in 1943 in Nazi-occupied France, but wasn't completed until 1945.▼●

Children of Sanchez, The (1978-U.S.-Mexican) **C-117m.** *½ D: Hall Bartlett. Anthony Quinn, Dolores Del Rio, Melanie Farrar, Katy Jurado, Stathis Giallelis, Lucia Mendez, Duncan Quinn. Quinn is a widowed Mexico City worker who has several common-law wives, and refuses to show affection for his children. Well-meaning look at the folly of machismo, but it's leaden-paced and often excruciating. Chuck Mangione's popular pop-jazz score too often seems to belong to another film. [R]▼

Children of Theatre Street, The (1977) **C-92m.** ***½ D: Robert Dornhelm, Earle Mack. Narrated by Princess Grace (Grace Kelly). Outstanding documentary about Leningrad's famed Kirov Ballet School, among whose graduates are Baryshnikov, Nureyev, Balanchine, and Nijinsky. The focus is on a trio of students, and the rigorous training they undergo. A must for balletomanes, and especially recommended as an introduction to the art of ballet for children. [G]▼

Children of the Corn (1984) **C-93m.** *½ D: Fritz Kiersch. Peter Horton, Linda Hamilton, R. G. Armstrong, John Franklin, Courtney Gains, Robby Kiger. Laughable adaptation of Stephen King short-short story about young couple who stumble onto Iowa town that's been taken over by sinister juvenile cultists—and then, like all stupid couples in movies like this, fail to get out while the getting is good. Pretty tacky. Look for a young Charlize Theron being dragged underground. Followed by four sequels. [R]▼●

Children of the Corn II—The Final Sacrifice (1993) **C-94m.** *½ D: David F. Price. Terence Knox, Paul Scherrer, Rosalind Allen, Christie Clark, Ned Romero. Barely based on the Stephen King story. Once again, the kids of an isolated Nebraska farming community are killing the adults and nobody knows why. Nobody knows the reason for this movie's existence either. Followed by three more "sequels"! [R]▼●

Children of the Damned (1964-British) **90m.** **½ D: Anton Leader. Ian Hendry, Alan Badel, Barbara Ferris, Patrick White, Bessie Love. Follow-up to VILLAGE OF THE DAMNED suffers from unimaginative account of precocious deadly children and their quest for power.▼●

Children of the Night (1992) **C-92m.** *½ D: Tony Randel. Karen Black, Peter DeLuise, Ami Dolenz, Evan MacKenzie, Maya McLaughlin, Josette DiCarlo, David Sawyer, Garrett Morris. Vampires take over a small town in this low-rent variation on SALEM'S LOT. Peculiar deviation from vampire mythology—they sleep underwater with their lungs floating on the surface—is the only novelty, unless you count the highly variable acting. [R]▼

Children of the Revolution (1996-Australian) **C-101m.** **½ D: Peter Duncan. Judy Davis, Sam Neill, F. Murray Abraham, Geoffrey Rush, Richard Roxburgh, Rachel Griffiths, Russell Kiefel, John Gaden. Fervent Stalinist (Davis) ends up secretly pregnant with the famed leader's son, then watches as he grows up mirroring his father's revolutionary behavior. Australian black comedy tackles the collapse of communism blending humor and tragedy, fact and fiction, but the pacing is uneven and the satire often heavy-handed. Worth seeing for two knockout performances, from the always reliable Davis and from Griffiths, as her policewoman daughter-in-law. [R] ▼●

Children Shouldn't Play With Dead Things (1972) **C-85m.** *½ D: Benjamin (Bob) Clark. Alan Ormsby, Anya Ormsby, Valerie Mauches, Jane Daly, Jeffrey Gillen. Young, kinky movie-makers take over a rural graveyard and unwittingly resurrect the evil dead. Weird. [PG]▼●◗

Children's Hour, The (1961) **107m.** **½ D: William Wyler. Audrey Hepburn, Shirley MacLaine, James Garner, Miriam Hopkins, Fay Bainter, Karen Balkin, Veronica Cartwright. Updated version of Lillian Hellman's play is more explicit in its various themes, including lesbianism, than original THESE THREE (also made by Wyler), but not half as good. Impact is missing, despite MacLaine and Hepburn as two teachers, Hopkins as meddling aunt, Bainter as questioning grandmother.▼●

Child's Play (1972) **C-100m.** **½ D: Sidney Lumet. James Mason, Robert Preston, Beau Bridges, Ronald Weyand, Charles White, David Rounds, Kate Harrington, Jamie Alexander. Well-acted but somber and confusing account of rivalry between Catholic school professors Mason and Preston, and the seemingly senseless acts of violence perpetrated by some of their students. From the Robert Marasco play. [PG]

Child's Play (1988) **C-87m.** *** D: Tom Holland. Catherine Hicks, Chris Sarandon, Alex Vincent, Brad Dourif, Dinah Manoff, Tommy Swerdlow, Jack Colvin. Scary and clever horror thriller in which only young Vincent knows his new Chucky doll is really a monster, possessed with the spirit of dead murderer Dourif. His mom (Hicks) and the cop on the case (Sarandon) finally believe him but not before several deaths. Sleeper hit packs a wallop, with excellent special effects bringing the doll to life. Followed by three sequels. [R]▼●◗

Child's Play 2 (1990) **C-84m.** *½ D: John Lafia. Alex Vincent, Jenny Agutter, Gerrit Graham, Christine Elise, Grace Zabriskie, Peter Haskell, Beth Grant, voice of Brad Dourif. Traumatized by Chucky's 1988 antics, affected youngster begins boarding with foster parents. Agutter and Graham ought to be anyone's couple-of-the-month, but the film is utterly worthless until the finale: 15 minutes of doll-factory yuck (with a particular nod to conveyor belts); its unexpected stylishness saves this d.o.a. from a BOMB rating. [R]▼●◗

Child's Play 3 (1991) **C-90m.** BOMB D: Jack Bender. Justin Whalin, Perrey Reeves, Jeremy Sylvers, Peter Haskell, Dakin Matthews, Andrew Robinson, voice of Brad Dourif. It's been eight years since Chucky first terrorized young Andy Barclay (Whalin), and now the kid is a screwed-up loner of 16 in a military school; to make things worse, the prez of the Play Pals Toy Company is about to put the "C" doll back into production. An amusement park finale is desperately contrived, even by the standards of this junk. Followed by BRIDE OF CHUCKY. [R]▼●

Child Under a Leaf (1974-Canadian) **C-88m.** ** D: George Bloomfield. Dyan Cannon, Joseph Campanella, Donald Pilon. Boring drama about an unhappily married woman who feels she cannot leave her husband for her lover. [R]

Chill Factor (1999) **C-101m.** ** D: Hugh Johnson. Cuba Gooding, Jr., Skeet Ulrich, Peter Firth, David Paymer, Hudson Leick, Daniel Hugh Kelly, Kevin J. O'Connor. Convenience store clerk Ulrich and ice cream truck driver Gooding reluctantly team up to keep an explosive, safe as long as it's cold, from falling into the hands of terrorist Firth. Routine, predictable action movie helped by the likable (if miscast) leads. Panavision. [R]▼●◗

Chilling, The (1989) **C-95m.** BOMB D: Deland Nuse and Jack A. Sunseri. Linda Blair, Dan Haggerty, Troy Donahue, Jack A. De Rieux, Ron Vincent. Amateurism, familiarity, and too many plot elements doom this ultracheap, Kansas City–made tale of cryogenic corpses turned into (yawn) cannibalistic zombies. At one point we see the shambling corpse of the Ayatollah Khomeni, surely some kind of first—but not a good kind.▼

Chilly Scenes of Winter SEE: **Head Over Heels**

Chimes at Midnight (1966-Spanish-Swiss) **115m.** *** D: Orson Welles. Orson Welles, Jeanne Moreau, Margaret Rutherford, John Gielgud, Marina Vlady, Keith Baxter; narrated by Ralph Richardson. Welles combined parts of five Shakespeare plays with mixed results, with his own portrayal of Falstaff the most interesting aspect. Well cast, but limited budget hurt the effort. Aka FALSTAFF.▼

China (1943) **79m.** ** D: John Farrow. Loretta Young, Alan Ladd, William Bendix, Philip Ahn, Iris Wong, Sen Yung. Pat wartime tale of mercenary Ladd who suddenly realizes his true allegiance while helping enemy.▼

China Clipper (1936) **85m.** **½ D: Ray Enright. Pat O'Brien, Beverly Roberts, Ross Alexander, Humphrey Bogart, Marie Wilson, Henry B. Walthall. O'Brien stars as man determined to develop trans-Pacific flights; usual plot of initial failure, grim determination, and neglected wife; fairly well done.

China Corsair (1951) **67m.** *½ D: Ray Nazzaro. Jon Hall, Lisa Ferraday, Ron Randell, Douglas Kennedy, Ernest Borgnine. Tinsel-like adventure of Hall's romancing, combating crooks aboard title ship. Borgnine's film debut.

China Doll (1958) **88m.** *½ D: Frank

Borzage. Victor Mature, Li Li Hua, Bob Mathias, Stuart Whitman. Bizarre story line can't boost dull film of Mature accidentally buying Oriental wife whom he grows to love. When they are killed, daughter comes to U.S.A.

China Gate (1957) **97m.** *** D: Samuel Fuller. Gene Barry, Angie Dickinson, Nat King Cole, Paul Dubov, Lee Van Cleef, George Givot, Marcel Dalio. International soldiers under French command attack Communist munitions dumps in Indochina. Interesting subplots flesh out Fuller's dynamic action story, with early view of Vietnam's internal strife. CinemaScope.▼

China Girl (1942) **95m.** ** D: Henry Hathaway. Gene Tierney, George Montgomery, Lynn Bari, Victor McLaglen, Sig Ruman, Bobby (Robert) Blake, Ann Pennington, Philip Ahn. American photographer in mysterious Orient during WW2 is background for unbelievable adventure yarn; Bari best item in film.

China Girl (1987) **C-88m.** **½ D: Abel Ferrara. James Russo, Richard Panebianco, Sari Chang, David Caruso, Russell Wong. Atmospheric romantic thriller about warring Chinese and Italian youth gangs in N.Y.C., with Panebianco and Chang as star-crossed lovers. Director Ferrara provides tremendous energy and some over-the-top violence. [R]▼●

China Moon (1994) **C-99m.** ** D: John Bailey. Ed Harris, Madeleine Stowe, Charles Dance, Benicio Del Toro, Pruitt Taylor Vince, Roger Aaron Brown, Patricia Healy. Small-town cop Harris lusts after unhappily married Stowe in this moody film noir. A couple of neat twists, but production is more than a bit reminiscent of (the superior) BODY HEAT—down to the Florida locale. Directorial debut for Bailey, better known as a top cinematographer (ORDINARY PEOPLE, IN THE LINE OF FIRE). Filmed in 1991. Panavision. [R]▼●

China 9, Liberty 37 (1978) **C-102m.** **½ D: Monte Hellman. Warren Oates, Fabio Testi, Jenny Agutter, Sam Peckinpah. Sluggish, mythicized Western in which railroad barons save a man from gallows in exchange for killing former gunfighter; gunfighter's wife falls for killer and helps do his dirty work. Title refers to signpost giving distance to two nearby towns. Video title: GUNFIRE. Technovision. [R]▼

China Seas (1935) **90m.** *** D: Tay Garnett. Clark Gable, Jean Harlow, Wallace Beery, Lewis Stone, Rosalind Russell, Dudley Digges, Robert Benchley, C. Aubrey Smith, Hattie McDaniel. Impossible to dislike film with that cast, even if the story—about mysterious goings-on and relationships on Gable's Singapore-bound ship—is ludicrous. Also shown in computer-colored version.▼●

China Sky (1945) **78m.** ** D: Ray Enright. Randolph Scott, Ruth Warrick, Ellen Drew, Anthony Quinn, Carol Thurston, Richard Loo. Slow-moving Pearl Buck story of dedicated doctor Scott fighting Japanese with Chinese comrades during WW2.▼●

China's Little Devils (1945) **74m.** ** D: Monta Bell. Harry Carey, Paul Kelly, Ducky Louie, Hayward Soo Hoo, Gloria Ann Chew. Patriotic yarn of Chinese waifs helping downed American pilots get going again.

China Syndrome, The (1979) **C-123m.** **** D: James Bridges. Jane Fonda, Jack Lemmon, Michael Douglas, Scott Brady, James Hampton, Peter Donat, Wilford Brimley, James Karen. Heartpounding drama about attempted cover-up of accident at California nuclear plant is as much a probe of television news as it is a story of nuclear power— and it scores bullseye on both fronts. There is no music score; story tension propels film by itself, along with solid performances by Fonda as TV reporter, Douglas (who also produced film) as radical cameraman, and especially Lemmon as dedicated plant exec. Screenplay by Mike Gray, T.S. Cook, and Bridges. [PG]▼●◗

Chinatown (1974) **C-131m.** **** D: Roman Polanski. Jack Nicholson, Faye Dunaway, John Huston, Perry Lopez, John Hillerman, Roy Jenson, Dick Bakalyan, Joe Mantell, Bruce Glover, James Hong, Noble Willingham, Burt Young. Bizarre, fascinating mystery in the Hammett-Chandler tradition (and set in the 1930s) with Nicholson as L.A. private eye led into a complex, volatile case by femme fatale Dunaway. Director Polanski appears briefly as the hood who knifes Nicholson. Oscar for Best Original Screenplay (Robert Towne). Sequel: THE TWO JAKES. Panavision. [R]▼●◗

China Venture (1953) **83m.** **½ D: Don Siegel. Edmond O'Brien, Barry Sullivan, Jocelyn Brando, Richard Loo, Philip Ahn. Exciting WW2 adventure film of marine group on mission to capture Japanese naval commander wanted by U.S. interrogation department.

Chinchero SEE: **Last Movie, The**

Chinese Box (1997-Japanese-French-U.S.) **C-100m.** ** D: Wayne Wang. Jeremy Irons, Gong Li, Maggie Cheung, Michael Hui, Ruben Blades. Murky drama set in the final six months of Great Britain's rule over Hong Kong, with the smell of change in the air as China prepares to take over. Irons plays a jaded journalist whose own life is at a crossroads. Li is not well showcased in her first English-language film, as a woman "with a past" whom Irons adores but cannot have. Heavy-handed allegory was conceived by Wang, Paul Theroux, and Jean-Claude Carrière. [R]▼●◗

Chinese Cat, The (1944) **65m.** ** D: Phil Rosen. Sidney Toler, Benson Fong, Joan Woodbury, Mantan Moreland, Weldon

Heyburn, Ian Keith, John Davidson, Betty Blythe. Formula *Charlie Chan* programmer, with usual assortment of villains literally dying to get their hands on statue containing an uncut diamond. ▼●

Chinese Connection, The (1972-Hong Kong) **C-107m.** *** D: Lo Wei. Bruce Lee, Miao Ker Hsiu, James Tien, Robert Baker. Violent Kung Fu film has Lee in Shanghai in early 1900s seeking vengeance on the murderers of his teacher. Graceful, powerful, humorous, and charismatic; Lee at his best. Original title: FIST OF FURY. Aka THE IRON HAND. Shawscope. [R] ▼●◗

Chinese Ring, The (1947) **65m.** *½ D: William Beaudine. Roland Winters, Warren Douglas, Victor Sen Yung, Mantan Moreland, Philip Ahn, Louise Currie, Byron Foulger. Charlie Chan probes the murder of a Chinese princess, with Winters debuting as the great detective. Routine entry indistinguishable from the other Monogram cheapies.▼

Chinese Roulette (1976-German) **C-86m.** *** D: Rainer Werner Fassbinder. Margit Carstensen, Ulli Lommel, Anna Karina, Macha Meril, Brigitte Mira, Andrea Schober, Volker Spengler. Intense, biting comedy about a disabled girl (Schober), who plots to have her parents and their lovers visit a country house on the same weekend. Perceptive—but potentially off-putting—film is recommended mainly for Fassbinder fans.▼●

Chino (1973-Italian) **C-98m.** **½ D: John Sturges. Charles Bronson, Jill Ireland, Vincent Van Patten, Marcel Bozzuffi, Fausto Tozzi, Melissa Chimenti. Offbeat Western that barely received theatrical release here in 1976; Bronson plays halfbreed whose attempts to maintain his horse ranch in peace are short-lived. Aka THE VALDEZ HORSES. [PG]▼◗

Chip Off the Old Block (1944) **82m.** ** D: Charles Lamont. Donald O'Connor, Peggy Ryan, Ann Blyth, Helen Vinson, Helen Broderick, Arthur Treacher, Patric Knowles, Ernest Truex. Innocuous wartime musical of misunderstandings, climaxing in teenage romance and musical show.

Chips, the War Dog (1990) **C-90m. TVM** D: Ed Kaplan. Brandon Douglas, Ned Vaughn, Paxton Whitehead, Ellie Cornell, Robert Miranda, William Devane. Amiable Disney tale of a WW2 Army recruit, deathly afraid of dogs, who's assigned to be the handler of a German shepherd. Made for cable. Average.▼

Chisum (1970) **C-111m.** **½ D: Andrew V. McLaglen. John Wayne, Geoffrey Deuel, Forrest Tucker, Christopher George, Ben Johnson, Glenn Corbett, Bruce Cabot, Patric Knowles, Lynda Day, Richard Jaeckel. Wayne is the real-life cattle baron of the title, but takes a back seat to Billy the Kid (Deuel) in this routine but handsome Western. It's about the efforts of good ranchers like Wayne and Knowles to prevent the takeover of Lincoln County, New Mexico, by corrupt Tucker. One of very few Wayne Westerns based on historical events. Panavision. [G]▼●

Chitty Chitty Bang Bang (1968) **C-142m.** *½ D: Ken Hughes. Dick Van Dyke, Sally Ann Howes, Lionel Jeffries, Gert Frobe, Anna Quayle, Benny Hill. Children's musical about flying car is one big Edsel itself, with totally forgettable score and some of the shoddiest special effects ever. Loosely based on book by Ian Fleming. Super Panavision 70. [G]▼●◗

Chloe in the Afternoon (1972-French) **C-97m.** ***½ D: Eric Rohmer. Bernard Verley, Zouzou, Francoise Verley, Daniel Ceccaldi. No. 6 of Rohmer's "Six Moral Tales" depicts married man's fascination with kooky girl during daylight hours. As Chloe, Zouzou becomes more alluring as film unwinds. [R]▼●◗

Chocolat (1988-French-German-Camaroon) **C-105m.** *** D: Claire Denis. Isaach de Bankolé, Giulia Boschi, François Cluzet, Cécile Ducasse, Jean-Claude Adelin, Jacques Denis, Mireille Perrier. Subtle, slowly paced slice-of-life about a young woman's memories of her childhood in French West Africa, where whites are masters and most blacks are servants. This very personal, autobiographical film (which first-time director Denis coscripted) is quietly rewarding. [PG-13]▼●

Chocolate Soldier, The (1941) **102m.** ** D: Roy Del Ruth. Nelson Eddy, Rise Stevens, Nigel Bruce, Florence Bates, Dorothy Gilmore, Nydia Westman. Not the Oscar Straus operetta, but rather a remake of Molnar's THE GUARDSMAN. Eddy and Stevens are husband-wife opera stars; to test her fidelity, he disguises himself as a Cossack and woos her. Much too talky, and not enough music; remade as LILY IN LOVE.▼

Chocolate War, The (1988) **C-103m.** *** D: Keith Gordon. John Glover, Ilan Mitchell-Smith, Wally Ward, Bud Cort, Adam Baldwin, Jenny Wright, Doug Hutchinson. A Catholic boys school is divided by a power struggle between an idealistic student and a dictatorial acting headmaster, as each tries to deal with The Vigils, a secret society of schoolboys out for control. Chilling and impressive, well directed on a low budget by actor Gordon, who also adapted Robert Cormier's novel. Glover is wonderfully wicked. [R]▼●

Choice of Arms (1981-French) **C-117m.** *** D: Alain Corneau. Yves Montand, Catherine Deneuve, Gerard Depardieu, Michel Galabru, Gerard Lanvin. Well-directed drama about retired gangster Montand forced into antagonistic relationship with young punk Depardieu, leading to reciprocal violence. Despite hostility, both men come to understand how similar they are. Good performances by excellent cast, especially Depardieu. Original French running time 135m. Panavision.▼

Choice of Weapons SEE: **Dirty Knight's Work**

Choices (1981) **C-90m.** **½ D: Silvio Narizzano. Paul Carafotes, Victor French, Lelia Goldoni, Val Avery, Dennis Patrick, Demi Moore, Billy Moses, Pat Buttram. Partially deaf teenager Carafotes becomes alienated when prevented from playing football because of his handicap. Well-intentioned but obvious drama is helped by fine performances. Moore's film debut.▼

Choirboys, The (1977) **C-119m.** BOMB D: Robert Aldrich. Charles Durning, Louis Gossett, Jr., Perry King, Clyde Kusatsu, Stephen Macht, Tim McIntire, Randy Quaid, Chuck Sacci, Don Stroud, James Woods, Burt Young, Robert Webber, Jeanie Bell, Blair Brown, Michele Carey, Charles Haid, Joe Kapp, Barbara Rhoades, Jim Davis, Phyllis Davis, Jack DeLeon, David Spielberg, Vic Tayback, Michael Wills, George DiCenzo. Supposedly comic escapades of L.A. cops who relieve work pressures by raunchy doings. Foul-mouthed, foul-minded, heavy-handed film from book by Joseph Wambaugh, who disavowed this turkey. [R]▼

Choke Canyon (1986) **C-94m.** **½ D: Chuck Bail. Stephen Collins, Janet Julian, Lance Henriksen, Bo Svenson, Victoria Racimo, Nicholas Pryor. Fun sci-fi about stubborn cowboy physicist (!) who fights off corrupt industrialist's henchmen, trying to protect the environment against nuclear waste dumping on the eve of Halley's Comet's visit near Earth. Terrific aerial stuntwork. Widescreen. [PG]▼

C.H.O.M.P.S. (1979) **C-89m.** *½ D: Don Chaffey. Wesley Eure, Valerie Bertinelli, Conrad Bain, Chuck McCann, Red Buttons, Larry Bishop, Hermione Baddeley, Jim Backus. Cartoon-makers Hanna & Barbera struck out with this Disneyesque comedy about a young inventor (Eure) and his mechanical dog. Originally rated PG for mild profanities voiced by *another* dog in the film—then redubbed for kids' sake. Title is acronym for Canine HOMe Protection System. [G]▼

Choose Me (1984) **C-106m.** ***½ D: Alan Rudolph. Genevieve Bujold, Keith Carradine, Lesley Ann Warren, Rae Dawn Chong, Patrick Bauchau, John Larroquette, John Considine. Outrageously inventive tale of the various relationships, truths, and lies that link radio sex-talk-show hostess Bujold, bar owner Warren, and mental hospital escapee Carradine, among others. This comedy-drama about the different roles that people play in life is a real kick, with a wonderful from-midnight-till-dawn feel and good performances by all. Evocative use of L.A. locations and Teddy Pendergrass songs. A companion piece to Rudolph's WELCOME TO L.A. and REMEMBER MY NAME. [R]▼●

Chopping Mall (1986) **C-76m.** *½ D: Jim Wynorski. Kelli Maroney, Tony O'Dell, John Terlesky, Russell Todd, Paul Bartel, Mary Woronov, Dick Miller, Karrie Emerson, Barbara Crampton, Suzee Slater, Gerrit Graham, Mel Welles. Eight teenagers are trapped overnight in a shopping mall where three malfunctioning guard robots go on a killing spree. Endless injokes and cameo roles (including Bartel and Woronov in their EATING RAOUL characters) fail to save a story that lapses into clichés. Originally titled: KILLBOTS. [R]▼

Chorus Line, A (1985) **C-113m.** ** D: Richard Attenborough. Michael Douglas, Terrence Mann, Alyson Reed, Cameron English, Vicki Frederick, Audrey Landers, Gregg Burge, Nicole Fosse, Janet Jones. Auditionees for Broadway chorus line reveal their innermost thoughts and emotions in song and dance before a hard-boiled director (Douglas). Thoroughly uninspired, unmemorable filming of the landmark Broadway musical; watchable, especially if you never saw the play, but what can you say about a musical in which all the singing and all the dancing is mediocre? And the show's biggest number, "What I Did for Love," is treated as a throwaway! Panavision. [PG-13]▼●

Chorus of Disapproval, A (1988-British) **C-100m.** ** D: Michael Winner. Jeremy Irons, Anthony Hopkins, Prunella Scales, Sylvia Syms, Lionel Jeffries, Gareth Hunt, Patsy Kensit, Alexandra Pigg, Jenny Seagrove. Shy, simple-minded widower moves to a seaside town and joins an amateur theatrical troupe, in which romantic intrigues abound. Some pearly performances (especially Hopkins, as the director, and Scales, as his wife) can't overcome the slightness of the material and its faltering execution. Adapted from Alan Ayckbourn's play by the author and Winner. [PG]▼●

Chosen, The (1978-Italian-British) **C-105m.** BOMB D: Alberto De Martino. Kirk Douglas, Agostina Belli, Simon Ward, Anthony Quayle, Virginia McKenna, Alexander Knox. Nuclear power exec Douglas slowly realizes that his son (Ward) is the Antichrist, who plans to use nuclear power to bring on world destruction. There! We just saved you 105 minutes. Originally titled HOLOCAUST 2000. Technovision. [PG]▼

Chosen, The (1981) **C-108m.** ***½ D: Jeremy Paul Kagan. Maximilian Schell, Rod Steiger, Robby Benson, Barry Miller, Hildy Brooks, Ron Rifkin, Val Avery. Excellent adaptation of Chaim Potok's novel, centering on friendship between Americanized Jew Miller and Hassidic Benson.

Steiger, as Benson's rabbi father, gives his best performance in years, and even Robby isn't bad. Set in 1940s Brooklyn; later made into a Broadway musical. [PG]▼

Chosen Survivors (1974) **C-99m.** ** D: Sutton Roley. Jackie Cooper, Alex Cord, Richard Jaeckel, Bradford Dillman, Pedro Armendariz, Jr., Diana Muldaur, Barbara Babcock. Good cast in formula nonsense about group of people "selected" to survive future holocaust in underground shelter. Just one hitch: the shelter is invaded by vampire bats. Dialogue and characterizations from grade-Z movies of the past. [PG]

Christiane F. (1981-German) **C-124m.** **½ D: Ulrich Edel. Nadja Brunkhorst, Thomas Haustein, Jens Kuphal, Reiner Wolk. Grim, gruesome account of bored teenager Brunkhorst falling in with crowd of junkie-hustler Haustein. Well-meaning but uneven; based on a true story. Features unmemorable David Bowie concert sequence. [R]▼

Christian Licorice Store, The (1971) **C-90m.** ** D: James Frawley. Beau Bridges, Maud Adams, Gilbert Roland, Anne Randall, Allen Arbus, McLean Stevenson. Quirky, dated comic study of tennis player Bridges looking for meaning in life. Loads of cameos, including directors Jean Renoir, Monte Hellman, Theodore J. Flicker, and James B. Harris. Filmed in 1969. [PG]

Christian the Lion (1976-British) **C-89m.** **½ D: Bill Travers, James Hill. Bill Travers, Virginia McKenna, George Adamson, Anthony Bourke. Pleasant docudrama about the efforts of BORN FREE stars—and real-life wildlife expert George Adamson, whom Travers portrayed in earlier film—to return a lion born in London Zoo to its native habitat in Kenya. Expanded from 1971's THE LION AT WORLD'S END. [G]▼

Christina (1974) **C-98m.** ** D: Paul Krasny. Barbara Parkins, Peter Haskell, James McEachin, Marlyn Mason, Barbara Gordon. Beautiful woman offers unemployed man $25,000 to marry her—in name only. Just as he's falling in love with her, she disappears. Murky thriller shot in Canada. [PG]▼

Christine (1983) **C-111m.** ** D: John Carpenter. Keith Gordon, John Stockwell, Alexandra Paul, Robert Prosky, Harry Dean Stanton, Christine Belford, Roberts Blossom, Kelly Preston. Stephen King bestseller about a '58 Plymouth with demonic powers never hits bull's-eye, despite a promising start that captures teenage life quite nicely. Panavision. [R]▼●◗

Christine Jorgensen Story, The (1970) **C-89m.** BOMB D: Irving Rapper. John Hansen, Joan Tompkins, Quinn Redeker, John W. Hines, Ellen Clark. Ludicrous biography of famed 50s phenomenon is not exactly an in-depth study; one problem is that actor Hansen looks more masculine as female Christine and vice versa. [R]

Christmas Box, The (1995) **C-100m. TVM** D: Marcus Cole. Richard Thomas, Maureen O'Hara, Annette O'Toole, Kelsey Mulrooney, Robert Curtis-Brown, Michael Ensign. O'Hara returns to television after 23 years as a rich elderly widow who takes in a goal-oriented yuppie and his family to care for her and teaches them the true meaning of Christmas. O'Hara is graying but still feisty in the flip side of MIRACLE ON 34TH STREET, adding charm to Greg Taylor's adaptation of the sentimental best-seller by Richard Paul Evans (played here by Thomas). Average.▼

Christmas Carol, A (1938) **69m.** *** D: Edwin L. Marin. Reginald Owen, Gene Lockhart, Kathleen Lockhart, Terry Kilburn, Barry MacKay, Lynne Carver, Leo G. Carroll, Ann Rutherford. Nicely done adaptation of Dickens' classic with Owen a well-modulated Scrooge, surrounded by good MGM players and period settings. Young June Lockhart makes her screen debut. Also shown in computer-colored version. ▼●

Christmas Carol, A (1951-British) **86m.** **** D: Brian Desmond-Hurst. Alastair Sim, Jack Warner, Kathleen Harrison, Mervyn Johns, Hermione Baddeley, Clifford Mollison, Michael Hordern, George Cole, Carol Marsh, Miles Malleson, Ernest Thesiger, Hattie Jacques, Peter Bull, Hugh Dempster. Superb film is too good to be shown only at Christmastime; always delightful Sim makes Scrooge a three-dimensional character in this faithful, heart-warming rendition of the Dickens classic. Screenplay by Noel Langley. Patrick Macnee plays young Marley. Original British title: SCROOGE. Also shown in computer-colored version. ▼●◗

Christmas Carol, A (1984) **C-100m. TVM** D: Clive Donner. George C. Scott, Nigel Davenport, Frank Finlay, Edward Woodward, Lucy Gutteridge, Angela Pleasence, Roger Rees, David Warner, Susannah York, Anthony Walters, Joanne Whalley. Beautifully staged retelling of the Dickens classic with a memorable interpretation of Scrooge by Scott, by George! Handsomely filmed in Shrewsbury, England. Script by Roger O. Hirson. Above average.▼◗

Christmas Eve (1947) **90m.** *½ D: Edwin L. Marin. George Brent, George Raft, Randolph Scott, Joan Blondell, Virginia Field, Ann Harding, Reginald Denny. Slow-moving mixture of comedy and drama as foster sons discover evil intentions of relations to victimize Harding. Retitled: SINNER'S HOLIDAY.

Christmas Evil SEE: **You Better Watch Out**

Christmas Holiday (1944) **92m.** *** D: Robert Siodmak. Deanna Durbin, Gene Kelly, Gale Sondergaard, Gladys George, Richard Whorf. Somerset Maugham novel reset in America. Crime story with Durbin gone wrong to help killer-hubby Kelly;

songs include "Spring Will Be A Little Late This Year."

Christmas in Connecticut (1945) **101m.** ★★½ D: Peter Godfrey. Barbara Stanwyck, Dennis Morgan, Sydney Greenstreet, Reginald Gardiner, S.Z. Sakall, Robert Shayne, Una O'Connor. Airy fluff with Stanwyck, a chic magazine writer who's supposed to be an expert homemaker, forced to entertain a war veteran (Morgan) and her boss (Greenstreet) for the holidays. Standard studio corn it may be, but a wonderful treat for late-night viewing on Christmas Eve. Remade for cable TV in 1992. Also shown in computer-colored version.▼●

Christmas in Connecticut (1992) **C-100m. TVM** D: Arnold Schwarzenegger. Dyan Cannon, Kris Kristofferson, Tony Curtis, Richard Roundtree, Kelly Cinnante, Gene Lithgow, Vivian Bonnell. Terminally chipper Dyan, never-say-die Tony, and game Arnie's movie directing debut are the selling points of this pointless remake of the 1945 romantic comedy, filmed on location —not in Connecticut but Grand Teton National Park (with fake snow). Made for cable. Average.▼●

Christmas in July (1940) **67m.** ★★★½ D: Preston Sturges. Dick Powell, Ellen Drew, Raymond Walburn, William Demarest, Ernest Truex, Franklin Pangborn. Top Sturges comedy about Powell going on shopping spree after mistakenly believing he has won big contest. Walburn and Demarest are at their best.▼●

Christmas Kid, The (1968-Spanish) **C-89m.** ★★ D: Sidney Pink. Jeffrey Hunter, Louis Hayward, Gustavo Rojo, Perla Cristal, Luis Prendes. Average frijole Western about saddletramp's search for his true identity. ▼

Christmas Lilies of the Field (1979) **C-100m. TVM** D: Ralph Nelson. Billy Dee Williams, Maria Schell, Fay Hauser, Judith Piquet, Hanna Hertelendy, Lisa Mann. Joyous followup to Nelson's Oscar-winning original of 16 years earlier, with Homer Smith turning up at the chapel he built in the Arizona desert and being conned once again by Mother Maria—this time to put up an orphanage and kindergarten. Above average.▼

Christmas Mountain (1980) **C-90m.** ★★ D: Pierre Moro. Slim Pickens, Mark Miller, Barbara Stanger, Fran Ryan, Tina Minard, John Hart. An old cowboy finds the living spirit of Christmas with widow and her family in midst of blizzard of '88 out West. Minor holiday fare.

Christmas Story, A (1983) **C-98m.** ★★★½ D: Bob Clark. Peter Billingsley, Darren McGavin, Melinda Dillon, Ian Petrella, Scott Schwartz, Tedde Moore. Humorist Jean Shepherd's delightful memoir of growing up in the 1940s and wanting nothing so much as a Red Ryder BB gun for Christmas. Shepherd narrates in the first person, and Billingsley portrays him (delightfully) as a boy. Truly funny for kids and grownups alike; wonderful period flavor. Based on a portion of *In God We Trust, All Others Pay Cash.* Shepherd appears unbilled as a department store customer. Followed by IT RUNS IN MY FAMILY. [PG]▼●◗

Christmas That Almost Wasn't, The (1966-Italian-U.S.) **C-95m.** ★½ D: Rossano Brazzi. Rossano Brazzi, Paul Tripp, Lidia Brazzi, Sonny Fox, Mischa Auer. Santa Claus hijack makes for weak kiddie fare, none too thrilling for grownups either. [G]▼

Christmas to Remember, A (1978) **C-100m. TVM** D: George Englund. Jason Robards, Eva Marie Saint, Joanne Woodward, George Perry, Bryan Englund. Sentimental Depression-era tale about an elderly farm couple who take in their city-bred adolescent grandson for the holidays. High-powered star cast elevates this already satisfying adaptation by Stewart Stern of Glendon Swarthout's novel, *The Melodeon.* Above average.▼

Christmas Tree, The (1969) **110m.** ★½ D: Terence Young. William Holden, Virna Lisi, Bourvil, Brook Fuller, Madeleine Damien. Sappy tear-jerker about relationship between young boy and his wealthy father when the latter learns his son's death is imminent. Cast is divided between those who overact and those who don't seem to care one way or the other. Aka WHEN WOLVES CRY. [G]▼

Christmas Tree, The (1996) **C-100m. TVM** D: Sally Field. Julie Harris, Andrew McCarthy, Trini Alvarado, Jessica Hecht, Shannon Holt, Betty Aberlin, Anne Pitoniak. Onetime flying nun Field coexecutive-produced, cowrote, and made her directing debut with this gentle Yuletide tale of an unworldly nonflying nun (Harris), a harried young man, and a pet Norwegian Spruce. Adapted from the delightful novel by Julie Salamon and Jill Weber. Average.

Christmas Visitor, The (1987-Australian) **C-98m. TVM** D: George Miller. Dee Wallace Stone, John Waters, Charles Tingwell, Bill Kerr, Andrew Ferguson. Well-crafted holiday tale set in the drought-ridden Australian outback of the 1890s. Initially a coproduction with the Disney people for cable and known alternately (Down Under, at least) as BUSHFIRE MOON. Above average.

Christmas Wife, The (1988) **C-73m. TVM** D: David Jones. Jason Robards, Julie Harris, Don Francks, James Eckhouse, Patricia Hamilton, Deborah Grover. Sturdy character study of lonely widower who "hires" a woman to be his companion for a Christmas vacation at his comfortable mountain cabin. Reminiscent of the great "Golden Age of TV" dramas adapted from

Helen Norris' short story by Katherine Ann Jones. Made for cable. Above average.▼

Christopher Columbus (1949-British) **C-104m.** *** D: David Macdonald. Fredric March, Florence Eldridge, Francis L. Sullivan, Linden Travers, Kathleen Ryan, Derek Bond, James Robertson Justice, Felix Aylmer, Nora Swinburne, Abraham Sofaer. Stark, slowly paced biography of explorer, with earnest portrayal by March in title role; good period setting.▼●

Christopher Columbus—the Discovery (1992-U.S.-Spanish) **C-120m.** BOMB D: John Glen. Marlon Brando, Tom Selleck, George Corraface, Rachel Ward, Robert Davi, Benicio Del Toro, Catherine Zeta Jones, Oliver Cotton, Mathieu Carriere, Nigel Terry. "In nineteen-hundred-and-ninety-two, Columbus sailed two screen boo-boos." Corraface plays the explorer in this one, which beat 1492: CONQUEST OF PARADISE to the big screen, bringing an infectious smile and notably heavy beard follicles to an extremely complex historical character. Brando has a cameo as Spanish Inquisitor Tomas de Torquemada (his dullest performance since DESIREE), while Selleck dresses up as King Ferdinand—the guy with three ships and a lady. Not ripe for *re*discovery. Panavision. [PG-13]▼●

Christopher Strong (1933) **77m.** **½ D: Dorothy Arzner. Katharine Hepburn, Colin Clive, Billie Burke, Helen Chandler, Jack LaRue. Hepburn's an aviatrix in love with married Clive. Dated film intriguing for star's performance as headstrong, individualistic woman—and dig that silver lamé costume.▼●

Christ Stopped at Eboli SEE: **Eboli**

Chrome and Hot Leather (1971) **C-91m.** BOMB D: Lee Frost. William Smith, Tony Young, Michael Haynes, Peter Brown, Marvin Gaye. Lurid time-waster about some motorcycle thugs responsible for woman's death and her Green Beret fiancé (Young) who seeks revenge. [PG]▼

Chrome Hearts SEE: **C.C. and Company**

Chubasco (1968) **C-100m.** **½ D: Allen H. Miner. Richard Egan, Christopher Jones, Susan Strasberg, Ann Sothern, Simon Oakland, Audrey Totter, Preston Foster. Young man working on tuna boat gets along with the skipper until he learns the boy has married his daughter; overlong but likable programmer. Jones and Strasberg were then married in real life. Panavision.

Chu Chu and the Philly Flash (1981) **C-100m.** BOMB D: David Lowell Rich. Alan Arkin, Carol Burnett, Jack Warden, Danny Aiello, Adam Arkin, Danny Glover, Sid Haig, Ruth Buzzi, Vito Scotti, Lou Jacobi. Maddeningly moronic comedy revolving around bum Arkin, show-biz failure Burnett, and a briefcase filled with secret government papers. A low point in the careers of its stars; Burnett isn't even funny in Carmen Miranda getup. Scripted by Barbara Dana (Mrs. Arkin). [PG]▼

Chuck Berry Hail! Hail! Rock 'n' Roll (1987) **C-120m.** ***½ D: Taylor Hackford. Chuck Berry, Keith Richards, Eric Clapton, Robert Cray, Etta James, Julian Lennon, Linda Ronstadt. Two delights in one: an overview of rock legend Chuck Berry's career—sparked by interviews with Richards, Clapton, Bo Diddley, Little Richard, Roy Orbison, The Everly Brothers, Willie Dixon, Bruce Springsteen, and the subject himself—and a climactic 60th birthday Berry concert held in his hometown of St. Louis. Whitewashes Berry's womanizing and early 1960s jail term, but his hot temper is much in evidence during some amusing skirmishes with concert producer Richards. Worthy of its title . . . if slightly overlong. [PG]▼

Chuck Norris Vs. The Karate Cop SEE: **Slaughter in San Francisco**

C.H.U.D. (1984) **C-90m.** BOMB D: Douglas Cheek. John Heard, Daniel Stern, Kim Greist, Brenda Currin, Justin Hall, Christopher Curry, Michael O'Hare, Sam McMurray, Patricia Richardson, Raymond Baker, Peter Michael Goetz, John Bedford Lloyd, John Goodman, Jay Thomas. That's Cannibalistic Humanoid Underground Dwellers, folks—a band of ragtag derelicts who come up to street level at night to munch on human flesh. Greist made this before BRAZIL—but what are Heard and Stern doing in this film? Grimy on all levels. Followed by a sequel. [R] ▼●

C.H.U.D. II—Bud the Chud (1989) **C-84m.** BOMB D: David Irving. Brian Robbins, Bill Calvert, Gerrit Graham, Tricia Leigh Fisher, Robert Vaughn, Larry Cedar, Bianca Jagger, Larry Linville, Jack Riley, Norman Fell, June Lockhart. Teenagers swipe a corpse (Graham), unaware that it is a cannibalistic CHUD that passes on its tendencies to anyone it bites. Comedy sequel to straight original is far worse, but Graham is genuinely funny as the monster. Script credited to "M. Kane Jeeves." [R]▼●

Chuka (1967) **C-105m.** ** D: Gordon Douglas. Rod Taylor, John Mills, Ernest Borgnine, Luciana Paluzzi, James Whitmore, Angela Dorian, Louis Hayward. Good cast is wasted in routine Western about grizzled gunfighter who tries to promote peace between Indians and some undisciplined soldiers guarding nearby fort.▼

Chump at Oxford, A (1940) **63m.** **½ D: Alfred Goulding. Stan Laurel, Oliver Hardy, Wilfred Lucas, Forrester Harvey, James Finlayson, Anita Garvin. So-called feature is more like a series of barely related shorts; film is nearly half over before L&H even get to Oxford. Still quite funny, especially when they settle down in the Dean's quarters. A young Peter Cushing plays one of the boys' tormentors.

Also shown in computer-colored version. ▼●

Chungking Express (1994-Hong Kong) **C-103m.** **½ D: Wong Kar-Wai. Brigitte Lin, Takeshi Kaneshiro, Tony Leung, Faye Wang, Valerie Chow, "Piggy" Chan. Two tangentially related stories of lovesickness, obsession, and the peccadilloes of relationships in a modern world. The catalyst for both liaisons, involving young Hong Kong policemen, is the proprietor of a fast-food establishment. Light, funny, and offbeat, though the second tale goes on far too long. Quentin Tarantino's Rolling Thunder company acquired this for U.S. release, and many critics applauded its postmodern approach and stylistics. [PG-13]▼●

Chushingura (1962-Japanese) **C-108m.** ***½ D: Hiroshi Inagaki. Koshiro Matsumoto, Yuzo Kayama, Chusha Ichikawa, Toshiro Mifune, Yoko Tsukasa. Young lord Kayama is forced to commit hara kiri by corrupt feudal lord Ichikawa, and his forty-seven samurai retainers (or ronin) seek vengeance. A version of an oft-filmed story, based on a real life event. Sprawling, episodic, exquisitely beautiful, if a bit slow. Sometimes referred to as the GONE WITH THE WIND of Japanese cinema. Originally released in Japan in two parts, running 204m. Tohoscope.●◗

Ciao! Manhattan (1972) **C/B&W-84m.** ** D: John Palmer, David Weisman. Edie Sedgwick, Isabel Jewell, Roger Vadim, Baby Jane Holzer, Viva, Wesley Hayes, Paul America. Pasted-together documentary portrait of Edie Sedgwick, who quite literally overdosed (in 1971, at age 28) on her fifteen minutes of celebrity as one of Andy Warhol's 1960s "Superstars." A mess of a movie that some will nonetheless find fascinating, but most will wish to avoid. Aka EDIE IN CIAO! MANHATTAN. [R]▼●

Ciao, Professore! (1992-Italian) **C-91m.** ** D: Lina Wertmuller. Paolo Villaggio, Isa Danieli, Gigio Morra, Sergio Solli, Esterina Carloni, Paolo Bonacelli. A middle-aged elementary school teacher from an upper-class section of Italy is mistakenly transferred to a run-down school in a decaying town near Naples. Naturally, both he and his students wind up learning a lot from each other. Wertmuller's attempt to comment on her country's educational system, this Italian TO SIR, WITH LOVE is a mostly labored lesson. [R]▼●

Cider House Rules, The (1999) **C-125m.** **** D: Lasse Hallström. Tobey Maguire, Charlize Theron, Michael Caine, Delroy Lindo, Paul Rudd, Kathy Baker, Jane Alexander, Kieran Culkin, Erykah Badu, Kate Nelligan, Heavy D., K. Todd Freeman. Loving adaptation of John Irving's novel (by the author), telescoped from the sprawling story about a boy raised in a Maine orphanage (and abortion clinic) by an eccentric doctor who treats him like his own son—and begrudges the boy's decision to go out and see the world once he comes of age in the 1940s. Well cast, beautifully crafted; filmed on perfect locations throughout New England. Beautiful score by Rachel Portman and cinematography by Oliver Stapleton. Oscar winner for Best Screenplay and Supporting Actor (Caine). Super 35. [PG-13]▼◗

Cimarron (1931) **124m.** **½ D: Wesley Ruggles. Richard Dix, Irene Dunne, Estelle Taylor, Nance O'Neil, William Collier, Jr., Roscoe Ates. Edna Ferber's saga about an American family and the effect of empire building on the American West, 1890–1915. Oscar winner for Best Picture and Best Screenplay (Howard Estabrook), it dates badly, particularly Dix's overripe performance—but it's still worth seeing. Remade in 1960.▼

Cimarron (1960) **C-147m.** **½ D: Anthony Mann. Glenn Ford, Maria Schell, Anne Baxter, Arthur O'Connell, Russ Tamblyn, Mercedes McCambridge, Vic Morrow, Charles McGraw, Henry (Harry) Morgan, Edgar Buchanan, Robert Keith, Aline MacMahon, David Opatoshu, Mary Wickes. Edna Ferber's chronicle of frontier life in Oklahoma between 1890 and 1915 becomes an indifferent sprawling soap opera unsalvaged by a few spectacular scenes. CinemaScope.▼●

Cimarron Kid, The (1951) **C-84m.** ** D: Budd Boetticher. Audie Murphy, Beverly Tyler, James Best, Yvette Dugay, Hugh O'Brian, Rand Brooks. Uninspired formula Western with Murphy in title role, persuaded to give up his criminal life by his sweetheart.

Cincinnati Kid, The (1965) **C-113m.** **½ D: Norman Jewison. Steve McQueen, Ann-Margret, Edward G. Robinson, Karl Malden, Tuesday Weld, Joan Blondell, Rip Torn, Jack Weston, Cab Calloway. Roving card-sharks get together in New Orleans for big poker game; side episodes of meaningless romance. Robinson, Blondell, and Malden come off best as vivid members of the playing profession. Script by Ring Lardner, Jr., and Terry Southern; Jewison replaced Sam Peckinpah as director.▼●

Cinderella (1950) **C-74m.** ***½ D: Wilfred Jackson, Hamilton Luske, Clyde Geronimi. Voices of Ilene Woods, William Phipps, Eleanor Audley, Rhoda Williams, Lucille Bliss, Verna Felton. One of Walt Disney's best animated fairy tales spins the traditional story with some delightful comic embellishments, including a couple of mice named Gus and Jaq who befriend the put-upon heroine. Tuneful score includes "A Dream Is a Wish Your Heart Makes" and "Bibbidi Bobbidi Boo."▼●

Cinderella Jones (1946) **88m.** ** D: Busby Berkeley. Joan Leslie, Robert Alda, S.Z.

Sakall, Edward Everett Horton, Ruth Donnelly, Elisha Cook. Silly comedy of girl who must marry brainy husband to collect inheritance; good cast defeated by trivial script.

Cinderella Liberty (1973) **C-117m.** ***½ D: Mark Rydell. James Caan, Marsha Mason, Eli Wallach, Kirk Calloway, Burt Young, Bruce Kirby, Jr. (Bruno Kirby), Allyn Ann McLerie, Dabney Coleman, Sally Kirkland. Sensitive, original story by Darryl Ponicsan (based on his novel) about romance between simple, good-hearted sailor and a hooker with an illegitimate black son. Artfully mixes romance and realism, with sterling performances by Caan and Mason. Panavision. [R]▼

Cinderfella (1960) **C-91m.** **½ D: Frank Tashlin. Jerry Lewis, Ed Wynn, Judith Anderson, Anna Maria Alberghetti, Henry Silva, Count Basie. Jerry is the poor stepson turned into a handsome prince for a night by fairy godfather Wynn. Fairy tale classic revamped as a pretentious Lewis vehicle, with talky interludes and ineffectual musical sequences.▼

Cindy (1978) **C-100m. TVM** D: William A. Graham. Clifton Davis, Charlaine Woodard, Scoey Mitchlll, Mae Mercer, Nell-Ruth Carter, Alaina Reed. Original musical updates Cinderella story to Harlem during WW2; delightful concoction with multi-talented black cast. Above average.

Cinema Paradiso (1988-Italian-French) **C-123m.** ***½ D: Giuseppe Tornatore. Philippe Noiret, Jacques Perrin, Salvatore Cascio, Mario Leonardi, Agnese Nano, Leopoldo Trieste. A young boy is mesmerized by the movie theater in his small Italian town (in the years following WW2), and pursues a friendship with its crusty but warm-hearted projectionist. Captivating, bittersweet film, with a perfect finale; Noiret and the boy (Cascio) are wonderful. Written by the director. After abortive Italian release in 1988 (at 155m.), film was shortened by a half-hour and awarded a Special Jury Prize at the 1989 Cannes Film Festival; it went on to win the Best Foreign Film Oscar. [PG]▼●◗

Circle, The (1959-British) **84m.** **½ D: Gerald Thomas. John Mills, Derek Farr, Roland Culver, Wilfrid Hyde-White. Well-acted, neatly paced murder yarn involving London medico. Retitled: THE VICIOUS CIRCLE.

Circle of Children, A (1977) **C-100m. TVM** D: Don Taylor. Jane Alexander, Rachel Roberts, David Ogden Stiers, Nan Martin, Matthew Laborteaux. Beautifully acted drama about affluent suburbanite whose volunteer work with emotionally disturbed children fills the void in her life. Mary MacCracken's autobiographical novel served as the basis for this sensitive, intelligent, surprisingly unsentimental film. Alexander's superb performance is matched by Roberts as a gifted, demanding teacher. Script by Steven Gethers. Sequel: LOVEY: A CIRCLE OF CHILDREN, PART II. Above average.

Circle of Danger (1951-British) **86m.** **½ D: Jacques Tourneur. Ray Milland, Patricia Roc, Marius Goring, Hugh Sinclair. Straightforward account of Milland returning to England to ferret out brother's killers. ▼

Circle of Deceit (1981-French-German) **C-108m.** **** D: Volker Schlöndorff. Bruno Ganz, Hanna Schygulla, Jean Carmet, Jerzy Skolimowski, Gila von Weitershausen. Thoughtful, chilling, unrelentingly sober account of German journalist Ganz covering a Lebanese civil war, focusing on how he is affected by his experiences and his relationship with widow Schygulla. Actually filmed in Beirut against a backdrop of political turmoil; a superior film in every respect. Originally shown as FALSE WITNESS. [R]

Circle of Deception, A (1961-British) **100m.** **½ D: Jack Lee. Bradford Dillman, Suzy Parker, Harry Andrews, Robert Stephens, Paul Rogers. At times engaging psychological yarn of WW2 espionage agent Dillman who breaks under Axis torture; ironic climax. Dillman and Parker later married in real life. CinemaScope.

Circle of Friends (1995-U.S.-Irish) **C-96m.** *** D: Pat O'Connor. Chris O'Donnell, Minnie Driver, Geraldine O'Rawe, Saffron Burrows, Alan Cumming, Colin Firth, Aidan Gillen. Spirited and individualistic young woman leaves her Irish village to attend university in Dublin and falls madly in love with a handsome lad. He loves her, too, but their relationship is impeded by chance and circumstance. Perhaps more ado than necessary for such a simple tale, but still satisfying; anchored by Driver's irresistible performance as Benny. Adapted from Maeve Binchy's novel and set in the 1950s. [PG-13]▼●◗

Circle of Iron (1979) **C-102m.** **½ D: Richard Moore. David Carradine, Jeff Cooper, Roddy McDowall, Eli Wallach, Erica Creer, Christopher Lee. Strange, sometimes silly, but watchable blend of martial arts action and Zen philosophy; from an idea concocted by James Coburn and Bruce Lee. Cooper (looking like a California surfer) must pass rites of trial to find secret book of knowledge. Carradine plays four roles in this Stirling Silliphant-scripted fantasy, filmed in Israel as THE SILENT FLUTE.[R]▼

Circle of Love (1964-French-Italian) **C-105m.** *½ D: Roger Vadim. Jane Fonda, Jean-Claude Brialy, Maurice Ronet, Jean Sorel, Catherine Spaak, Anna Karina, Marie Dubois, Claude Giraud, Françoise Dorléac. Undistinguished remake of Ophuls' classic LA RONDE: A seduces B, B makes love to C, C has an affair with D—circling all the way back to A. Screenplay by Jean Anouilh; original running time: 110m. Franscope.▼

Circle of Power (1983) **C-103m.** **½ D: Bobby Roth. Yvette Mimieux, Christopher Allport, Cindy Pickett, John Considine, Julius Harris, Scott Marlowe, Fran Ryan, Walter Olkewicz, Danny Dayton, Denny Miller, Terence Knox. Intriguing—and disquieting—tale of businessmen and their wives who undergo EDT (Executive Development Training), which, as administered by Mimieux, turns out to be a horrifying and humiliating series of rituals. Based on actual events, believe it or not. Originally released as MYSTIQUE; also known as BRAINWASH and THE NAKED WEEKEND. [R]▼

Circle of Two (1980-Canadian) **C-105m.** ** D: Jules Dassin. Richard Burton, Tatum O'Neal, Nuala FitzGerald, Robin Gammell, Patricia Collins, Kate Reid. Sixty-year-old artist has romantic but platonic relationship with 16-year-old student. Burton is OK, and Dassin does not go for the cheap thrill, but the result is slight and forgettable. [PG]▼

Circumstantial Evidence (1945) **68m.** **½ D: John Larkin. Michael O'Shea, Lloyd Nolan, Trudy Marshall, Billy Cummings, Ruth Ford, Reed Hadley, Roy Roberts, Scotty Beckett. Thoughtful, engaging programmer of O'Shea fighting with a grocer, who is accidentally killed; he then finds himself accused of murder and convicted on the testimony of eyewitnesses who think they saw him commit the crime.

Circus, The (1928) **72m.** ***½ D: Charles Chaplin. Charlie Chaplin, Merna Kennedy, Allan Garcia, Betty Morrissey, Harry Crocker. Not the "masterpiece" of THE GOLD RUSH or CITY LIGHTS, but still a gem; story has Charlie accidentally joining traveling circus, falling in love with bareback rider. Hilarious comedy, with memorable finale. Chaplin won a special Academy Award for "versatility and genius in writing, acting, directing and producing" this.▼●◗

Circus Clown, The (1934) **63m.** ** D: Ray Enright. Joe E. Brown, Dorothy Burgess, Patricia Ellis, Lee Moran, Tom Dugan, William Demarest. Brown mixes comedy and drama in account of circus star whose father objects to his work.

Circus of Fear SEE: **Psycho-Circus**

Circus of Horrors (1960-British) **C-89m.** **½ D: Sidney Hayers. Anton Diffring, Erika Remberg, Yvonne Monlaur, Donald Pleasence. A most unethical plastic surgeon and nurse join bizarre circus to escape deformed patient threatening their lives; rousing horror film.▼●

Circus World (1964) **C-135m.** **½ D: Henry Hathaway. John Wayne, Rita Hayworth, Claudia Cardinale, John Smith, Lloyd Nolan, Richard Conte. Made in Spain, film has nothing new to offer, but rehashes usual circus formula quite nicely with the Duke as Big Top boss trying to pull his three-ring wild west show through various perils during European tour. Climactic fire sequence is truly spectacular. Super Technirama 70.▼●

Cisco Kid, The (1994) **C-100m. TVM** D: Luis Valdez. Jimmy Smits, Cheech Marin, Bruce Payne, Ron Perlman, Tony Amendola, Pedro Armendariz, Jr., Tim Thomerson, Sadie Frost. Amiable (if forgettable) redo of the oft-filmed tale of a couple of happily footloose do-good amigos by way of O. Henry. For contemporary audiences there's Cheech singing the title theme written by rock group War. But "Hey Ceesco! Hey Pancho!"—bring back Duncan Renaldo and Leo Carrillo. Made for cable. Average. ▼●

Cisco Pike (1972) **C-94m.** *** D: B. W. L. Norton. Kris Kristofferson, Karen Black, Gene Hackman, Viva!, Roscoe Lee Browne, Harry Dean Stanton. Surprisingly good drama about crooked cop Hackman getting mixed up with drug dealing, and blackmailing ex-rock star Kristofferson (among Kris's songs is "Lovin' Her Was Easier"). [R]

Citadel, The (1938-U.S.-British) **112m.** ***½ D: King Vidor. Robert Donat, Rosalind Russell, Ralph Richardson, Rex Harrison, Emlyn Williams, Penelope Dudley-Ward, Francis L. Sullivan. Superb adaptation of A. J. Cronin novel of impoverished doctor Donat eschewing ideals for wealthy life of treating rich hypochondriacs, neglecting wife and friends in the process; tragedy opens his eyes. Weak ending, but fine acting makes up for it. Frank "Spig" Wead, Emlyn Williams, Ian Dalrymple, Elizabeth Hill, and John Van Druten all contributed to the script. Remade in Britain as a TV miniseries.▼

Citizen Cohn (1992) **C-115m. TVM** D: Frank Pierson. James Woods, Joe Don Baker, Joseph Bologna, Ed Flanders, Frederic Forrest, Lee Grant, Pat Hingle, John McMartin, Josef Sommer, Tovah Feldshuh, Frances Foster, Allen Garfield. Woods craftily worms his way through the life of Roy Cohn, the opportunistic lawyer who became Senator Joseph McCarthy's right hand in the fifties. David Franzoni's incisive adaptation of Nicholas von Hoffman's best-seller tells the stream-of-consciousness story as Cohn hallucinates in a hospital bed while dying of AIDS in 1988. Forrest reprises his role as Dashiell Hammett from the 1983 film HAMMETT. Made for cable. Above average.▼●

Citizen Kane (1941) **119m.** **** D: Orson Welles. Orson Welles, Joseph Cotten, Everett Sloane, Agnes Moorehead, Dorothy Comingore, Ray Collins, George Coulouris, Ruth Warrick, William Alland, Paul Stewart, Erskine Sanford. Welles' first and best, a film that broke all the rules and invented some new ones, with fascinating story of Hearst-like publisher's rise to power. The cinematography (by Gregg Toland), music score (by Bernard Herrmann), and Oscar-winning screenplay (by Welles and Herman J. Mankiewicz) are all first-rate. A stunning film in every way . . . and Welles was only 25 when he made it! Incidentally, the reporter with a pipe is Alan Ladd; Arthur O'Connell is another one of the reporters.▼●

Citizen Ruth (1996) **C-109m.** *** D: Alexander Payne. Laura Dern, Swoosie Kurtz, Mary Kay Place, Kurtwood Smith, Kelly Preston, M. C. Gainey, Kenneth Mars, Burt Reynolds, Alicia Witt, Tippi Hedren, Kathleen Noone. Dern is a pregnant chemical-inhaling homeless woman who inadvertently becomes the center of a pro-life vs. pro-choice struggle over her unborn child. A stinging satire of fanaticism, with many funny scenes, though it peters out a bit toward the end; well played by a devoted cast. Diane Ladd has a raunchy unbilled cameo. [R]▼●

Citizens Band SEE: **Handle With Care** (1977)

Citizen X (1995) **C-105m. TVM** D: Chris Gerolmo. Stephen Rea, Donald Sutherland, Jeffrey DeMunn, Joss Ackland, John Wood, Max von Sydow. Dogged Russian detective spends eight years pursuing an elusive serial killer who murdered fifty-two people between 1982 and 1990. Real-life events, chronicled in Robert Cullen's book *The Killer Department* and adapted by director Gerolmo, provide an unusual glimpse into the workings of the Russian police state during changing times. Acted by an international (almost all non-Russian) cast in Hungary. Made for cable. Above average. ▼●

City, The (1999) **88m.** ***½ D: David Riker. Fernando Reyes, Marcos Martinez Garcia, Moises Garcia, Anthony Rivera, Cipriano Garcia. Striking neorealist-style film offers four vignettes about Latino immigrants and their struggle for survival in N.Y.C. Alternately poignant, amusing, and heartbreaking, these living portraits are enacted with a keen eye for detail and an overwhelming amount of empathy. Writer-director Riker and cinematographer Harlan Bosmajian shot their film (in black & white) with non-professional actors over six years' time. Aka LA CIUDAD.▼

City Across the River (1949) **90m.** **½ D: Maxwell Shane. Stephen McNally, Thelma Ritter, Luis Van Rooten, Jeff Corey, Anthony (Tony) Curtis, Richard Jaeckel. Watered-down version of Irving Shulman's novel *The Amboy Dukes*, involving tough life in Brooklyn slums, with predictable hoods et al.

City After Midnight (1957-British) **84m.** *½ D: Compton Bennett. Phyllis Kirk, Dan O'Herlihy, Petula Clark, Wilfrid Hyde-White, Jack Watling. Tame detective film of private eye O'Herlihy investigating death of antique dealer. British title: THAT WOMAN OPPOSITE.

City Beneath the Sea (1953) **C-87m.** **½ D: Budd Boetticher. Robert Ryan, Mala Powers, Anthony Quinn, Suzan Ball, Woody Strode. Inconsequential underwater yarn invigorated by Ryan and Quinn as deep-sea divers hunting treasure off Jamaican coast.

City for Conquest (1940) **101m.** *** D: Anatole Litvak. James Cagney, Ann Sheridan, Frank Craven, Arthur Kennedy, Donald Crisp, Frank McHugh, George Tobias, Elia Kazan, Anthony Quinn. Cagney makes this a must as boxer devoted to younger brother Kennedy. Beautiful production overshadows film's pretentious faults. A rare chance to see young Kazan in an acting role, as a neighborhood pal turned gangster.▼●

City Girl, The (1984-U.S.-Canadian) **C-85m.** *** D: Martha Coolidge. Laura Harrington, Joe Mastroianni, Carole McGill, Peter Riegert, Colleen Camp, Jim Carrington, Geraldine Baron. Solid, uncompromising tale of a young woman (expertly played by Harrington) attempting to advance her career as a photographer, and her various, unsatisfactory relationships with men. Refreshingly realistic, and even funny; a winner. Peter Bogdanovich was executive producer.

City Hall (1996) **C-111m.** **½ D: Harold Becker. Al Pacino, John Cusack, Bridget Fonda, Danny Aiello, Martin Landau, David Paymer, Anthony Franciosa, Richard Schiff, Lindsay Duncan, Nestor Serrano, Mel Winkler, Roberta Peters. N.Y.C. deputy mayor Cusack selflessly serves his mayor, a superb politician who really cares about his constituents. When a shootout involving a cop, a drug dealer, and an innocent child escalates into a citywide scandal, however, Cusack finds that the pathway to the truth is a political minefield. Snappy behind-the-scenes-of-urban-politics story pulls you in, then veers toward melodrama, with a finale that's pretty hard to swallow. This was the work of a real-life deputy mayor, Ken Lipper, and no fewer than three top screenwriters (Bo Goldman, Paul Schrader, Nicholas Pileggi)! [R]▼●◗

City Heat (1984) **C-97m.** ** D: Richard Benjamin. Clint Eastwood, Burt Reynolds, Jane Alexander, Madeline Kahn, Rip Torn, Irene Cara, Richard Roundtree, Tony Lo Bianco, William Sanderson, Robert Davi. Two macho stars do caricatures of themselves in this 1930s gangster/detective yarn that takes turns trying to be funny and serious (when they pour gasoline on a guy and set him on fire we're apparently supposed to find it funny). For diehard fans of Clint and Burt only. [PG]▼●

City in Darkness SEE: **Charlie Chan in City in Darkness**

City Lights (1931) **86m.** **** D: Charles

Chaplin. Charlie Chaplin, Virginia Cherrill, Harry Myers, Hank Mann. Chaplin's masterpiece tells story of his love for blind flower girl, and his hot-and-cold friendship with a drunken millionaire. Eloquent, moving, and funny. One of the all-time greats. ▼●◗

City Limits (1985) **C-85m.** BOMB D: Aaron Lipstadt. Darrell Larson, John Stockwell, Kim Cattrall, Rae Dawn Chong, John Diehl, Don Opper, James Earl Jones, Robby Benson, Danny De La Paz, Norbert Weisser. Disastrous sci-fi followup by the team that made ANDROID, an incoherent mess set 15 years in the future after a plague has devastated the planet, leaving roving youth gangs warring in MAD MAX fashion. Even a strong cast can't save this one, with most of the plot expressed in tacked-on narration by Jones. [PG-13]▼

City of Angels (1998) **C-117m.** **½ D: Brad Silberling. Nicolas Cage, Meg Ryan, Andre Braugher, Dennis Franz, Colm Feore, Robin Bartlett, Joanna Merlin, Sarah Dampf. An angel, who longs to know more about human beings and finds himself attracted to a hard-working female doctor, decides to sacrifice his heavenly status and fall to earth so he can experience love. Americanization of Wim Wenders' haunting WINGS OF DESIRE is—by the very nature of American movie conventions—less ethereal than the original film, but still intriguing and in its own way romantic. Only the climax seems routine and therefore disappointing. Panavision. [PG-13]▼●◗

City of Bad Men (1953) **C-82m.** ** D: Harmon Jones. Jeanne Crain, Dale Robertson, Richard Boone, Lloyd Bridges, Carl Betz. Robbers attempt to steal prizefight proceeds in 1890s Nevada; film combines Western with recreation of Jim Corbett–Bob Fitzsimmons fight bout.

City of Fear (1959) **81m.** *½ D: Irving Lerner. Vince Edwards, Lyle Talbot, John Archer, Steven Ritch, Patricia Blair. Programmer involving escaped convict Edwards sought by police and health officials; container he stole is filled with radioactive material, not money.

City of Fear (1966-British) **90m.** *½ D: Peter Bezencenet. Paul Maxwell, Terry Moore, Marisa Mell, Albert Lieven, Pinkas Braun. Tedious caper involving news reporter and refugee going to Hungary to smuggle out pro-Westerners.

City of Hope (1991) **C-129m.** **½ D: John Sayles. Vincent Spano, Tony Lo Bianco, Joe Morton, John Sayles, Angela Bassett, David Strathairn, Maggie Renzi, Anthony John Denison, Kevin Tighe, Barbara Williams, Chris Cooper, Jace Alexander, Todd Graff, Frankie Faison, Gloria Foster, Tom Wright, Michael Mantell, Josh Mostel, Joe Grifasi, Louis Zorich, Gina Gershon, Rose Gregorio, Bill Raymond, Lawrence Tierney, Maeve Kinkead, Ray Aranha. Ambitious multi-character drama about a strife-torn inner city and the people whose lives intersect within it. Writer-director-editor Sayles (who wrote himself a good part, as the slimy Carl) brings vivid and believable characters to life, and makes some pungent comments about contemporary society, but loses his momentum somewhere along the way. Might have been more effective if trimmed a bit. Panavision. [R] ▼●

City of Industry (1997) **C-97m.** *½ D: John Irvin. Harvey Keitel, Stephen Dorff, Famke Janssen, Timothy Hutton, Wade Dominguez, Michael Jai White, Reno Wilson, Lucy Alexis Liu. Depressing story of robbery, deceit, murder, and revenge, set in current-day L.A. Keitel seems like a caricature of himself and Hutton is unconvincing as a sleaze, even with that scruffy beard. Elliott Gould appears unbilled. [R]▼●

City of Joy (1992-British-French) **C-134m.** **½ D: Roland Joffé. Patrick Swayze, Pauline Collins, Om Puri, Shabana Azmi, Ayesha Dharker, Santu Chowdury, Imran Badsah Khan, Art Malik, Shyamanand Jalan. Aimless, cynical American surgeon Swayze, living in Calcutta, "finds" himself after becoming involved with a health clinic for the poor, taking on the local mafia, and befriending hardworking but poverty-stricken Puri. Well-intentioned but pretentious film scripted by Mark Medoff from Dominique Lapierre's book. Swayze tries his best, but is outshone by supporting cast; similar territory is covered better in SALAAM BOMBAY! Sam Wanamaker appears unbilled as Swayze's father. [PG-13]▼●

City of Lost Children, The (1995-French-Spanish-German) **C-112m.** *** D: Jean-Pierre Jeunet, Marc Caro. Ron Perlman, Joseph Lucien, Daniel Emilfork, Mireille Mosse, Judith Vittet, Dominique Pinon. Provocative fantasy about a wicked scientist (Emilfork) who is unable to dream, and who goes about purloining children—with the help of remarkable "cloned" henchmen—and invading their dreams. Although dramatically uneven, this mix of *Oliver Twist* and BRAZIL is a marvel of production design, with sumptuous visuals and painstaking invention. The voice of Irvin, the disembodied brain, is provided by Jean-Louis Trintignant. From the directors of DELICATESSEN. [R]▼●

City of Shadows (1955) **70m.** *½ D: William Witney. Victor McLaglen, John Baer, Kathleen Crowley, Anthony Caruso. Mild happenings about crafty newsboys involved with derelict racketeer McLaglen.

City of the Dead, The SEE: **Horror Hotel** (1960-British)

City of the Walking Dead (1983-Spanish-Italian) **C-92m.** *½ D: Umberto Lenzi. Mel Ferrer, Hugo Stiglitz, Laura Trotter, Francisco Rabal, Maria Rosaria Omaggio. Zombie-like monsters are on the prowl. If you've seen one . . . Filmed in 1980;

originally titled NIGHTMARE CITY. [R]▼

City of Women (1980-Italian) **C-139m.** *** D: Federico Fellini. Marcello Mastroianni, Anna Prucnal, Bernice Stegers, Iole Silvani, Donatella Damiani. Marcello falls asleep on a train, dreams he has stumbled into an all-female society. Lavish fantasy could only have been made by one filmmaker; a Fellini feast or déjà vu o.d., depending on your mood and stamina. Technovision. [R]▼

City on a Hunt SEE: **No Escape** (1953)

City on Fire (1979-Canadian) **C-101m.** *½ D: Alvin Rakoff. Barry Newman, Henry Fonda, Ava Gardner, Shelley Winters, Susan Clark, Leslie Nielsen, James Franciscus, Jonathan Welsh. Dull, fill-in-the-blanks disaster film about citywide fire torched by a disgruntled ex-employee of local oil refinery. Good cast wasted. For pyromaniacs only. [R]▼◗

City Slickers (1991) **C-112m.** *** D: Ron Underwood. Billy Crystal, Daniel Stern, Bruno Kirby, Patricia Wettig, Helen Slater, Jack Palance, Noble Willingham, Tracey Walter, Josh Mostel, David Paymer, Bill Henderson, Jeffrey Tambor, Phill Lewis, Kyle Secor. Three friends who are going through various degrees of mid-life crisis sign up for a two-week cattle drive, to clear their minds and set them back on-course. Enjoyable comedy, whose generous array of funny lines and good moments makes up for its "serious" pretensions and flaws. Palance won Best Supporting Actor Oscar for his role as the leathery trail boss. Followed by a sequel. [PG-13]▼●

City Slickers: The Legend of Curly's Gold (1994) **C-116m.** **½ D: Paul Weiland. Billy Crystal, Daniel Stern, Jon Lovitz, Jack Palance, Patricia Wettig, Pruitt Taylor Vince, Bill McKinney, Noble Willingham, David Paymer, Josh Mostel. A contrived sequel if there ever was one, with Crystal and Stern going back West (with Billy's screw-up brother Lovitz) to locate gold from a treasure map Palance (from the first film) left behind. Lack of plot and purpose are balanced by magnificent Moab, Utah, scenery—and a lot of genuine laughs, in the script by Crystal, Lowell Ganz, and Babaloo Mandel. Crystal also produced. [PG-13]▼●

City Streets (1931) **82m.** *** D: Rouben Mamoulian. Gary Cooper, Sylvia Sidney, Paul Lukas, Wynne Gibson, Guy Kibbee, Stanley Fields. Cooper is an unambitious carnival worker who's drawn into the underworld by his love for racketeer's daughter (Sidney). Stylish melodrama is more interesting for Mamoulian's innovative presentation (and the stunning camerawork of Lee Garmes) than for its predictable plot. Lukas and Kibbee stand out in unusually smarmy characterizations. Notable, too, as Dashiell Hammett's only original screen story.

City Streets (1938) **68m.** ** D: Albert S. Rogell. Edith Fellows, Leo Carrillo, Tommy Bond, Mary Gordon, Helen Jerome Eddy. Painless programmer with kindly Carrillo fighting for the interests of crippled orphan Fellows. Likable performances by the leads.

City That Never Sleeps (1953) **90m.** *** D: John H. Auer. Gig Young, Mala Powers, William Talman, Edward Arnold, Chill Wills, Marie Windsor, Paula Raymond, Otto Hulett, Wally Cassell, Tom Poston. Film noir about one night in the life of Chicago cop Young, who plans to quit his job and leave his wife for nightclub singer Powers. Events centering on criminal Talman and crooked lawyer Arnold interfere. Tense and ethically complex in the noir manner, and well photographed on location. Main misstep: Wills plays Chicago, the city itself, in human form.▼

City Under the Sea, The SEE: **War Gods of the Deep**

City Without Men (1943) **75m.** *½ D: Sidney Salkow. Linda Darnell, Michael Duane, Sara Allgood, Edgar Buchanan, Glenda Farrell, Leslie Brooks, Margaret Hamilton, Sheldon Leonard, Rosemary DeCamp. Very routine lower-berth item about a boardinghouse near a prison where the women wait for their men to get out.▼

Civil Action, A (1998) **C-115m.** ***½ D: Steven Zaillian. John Travolta, Robert Duvall, Tony Shalhoub, William H. Macy, Željko Ivanek, Bruce Norris, John Lithgow, Kathleen Quinlan, Peter Jacobson, Sydney Pollack, Dan Hedaya, James Gandolfini. Slick Boston injury lawyer gets in over his head when he takes a case against two industrial giants whose alleged pollution of a river caused the deaths of children in Woburn, Mass. Engrossing, literate, well-observed film (adapted by the director from Jonathan Harr's best-seller) explores the foibles of American justice—and how pride, human frailty, and emotions can affect a case. Based on a true story. Kathy Bates appears unbilled. [PG-13]▼●◗

Civilization (1916) **86m.** **½ D: Thomas H. Ince, Raymond B. West, Reginald Barker. Howard Hickman, Enid Markey, Herschel Mayall, Lola May, George Fisher, J. Frank Burke. Intriguing if drawn-out epic set in a fictitious kingdom, portraying its destiny in time of war. Of interest mostly for historical reasons, as a humanistic, anti-war morality tale intended to champion the foreign policy of President Woodrow Wilson (before America became involved in WW1).▼●

Clair de Femme (1979-French) **C-103m.** ** D: Costa-Gavras. Yves Montand, Romy Schneider, Romolo Valli, Lila Kedrova, Heinz Bennent, Roberto Benigni, Jean Reno. Slow-moving chronicle of the relationship between traumatized widower Montand and Schneider, who has been scarred by the death of her young daughter in an auto accident. Characters are one-dimensional, and film is gloomy, gloomy, gloomy. Based on novel by Romain Gary.

Claire of the Moon (1992) **C-105m.** ** D: Nicole Conn. Trisha Todd, Karen Trumbo, Faith McDevitt, Damon Craig. Heterosexual, self-destructive author Todd and lesbian therapist Trumbo share a cabin at a woman writers' retreat; they spar intellectually, and become friends and lovers. Awkward, self-conscious and predictable drama. ▼◗

Claire's Knee (1971-French) **C-103m.** ***½ D: Eric Rohmer. Jean-Claude Brialy, Aurora Cornu, Beatrice Romand, Laurence De Monaghan, Michele Montel. No. 5 of Rohmer's "Six Moral Tales" has widest appeal. Young man about to be married is obsessed with a girl he doesn't even like, his attention focusing on her knee. Full of delicious relationships, but too talky for some viewers. [PG]▼●◗

Clairvoyant, The (1934-British) **80m.** **½ D: Maurice Elvey. Claude Rains, Fay Wray, Jane Baxter, Mary Clare, Athole Stewart, Felix Aylmer, Donald Calthrop. A phony music hall mind-reader suddenly acquires clairvoyant powers—and soon discovers they're more of a curse than a blessing. Intriguing storyline doesn't hold up to the end, though Rains is fine as always. Also known as THE EVIL MIND.▼●

Clambake (1967) **C-97m.** *½ D: Arthur Nadel. Elvis Presley, Shelley Fabares, Will Hutchins, Bill Bixby, Gary Merrill, James Gregory. Elvis is a millionaire's son who wants to make it on his own, so he trades places with water-skiing instructor Hutchins in Miami. One of Presley's weakest. Techniscope.▼

Clancy Street Boys (1943) **66m.** **½ D: William Beaudine. Leo Gorcey, Huntz Hall, Bobby Jordan, Sunshine Sammy Morrison, Noah Beery, Sr., Amelita Ward, Bennie Bartlett, Rick Vallin, Billy Benedict. Farcical *East Side Kids* yarn, with Muggs (Gorcey) enlisting the boys to be his siblings for benefit of uncle Beery. Hall in drag is a comic highlight.▼

Clan of the Cave Bear, The (1986) **C-98m.** *½ D: Michael Chapman. Daryl Hannah, Pamela Reed, James Remar, Thomas G. Waites, John Doolittle, Curtis Armstrong. World's first feminist caveman movie, minus the anthropological detail of Jean Auel's popular book. Hannah is perfectly cast as outsider who joins band of nomadic Neanderthals, but the story (such as it is) is alternately boring and unintentionally funny. Subtitles translate cave people's primitive tongue. Screenplay by John Sayles. Technovision. [R]▼●◗

Clara's Heart (1988) **C-108m.** *½ D: Robert Mulligan. Whoopi Goldberg, Michael Ontkean, Kathleen Quinlan, Neil Patrick Harris, Spalding Gray, Beverly Todd. Whoopi plays a Jamaican domestic (think of Shirley Booth's *Hazel* with a reggae bias), a soft-spoken know-it-all who works for insufferable Maryland yuppies and their young, impressionable son (well played by Harris). The kind of movie best described as "nice" by undiscriminating viewers in search of blandness—and seemingly edited with a chainsaw. [PG-13]▼●

Clarence and Angel (1980) **C-75m.** *** D: Robert Gardner. Darren Brown, Mark Cardova, Cynthia McPherson, Louis Mike, Leroy Smith, Lola Langley, Lolita Lewis. Aggressive, kung-fu-mad Angel (Cardova) befriends his new schoolmate, shy, illiterate Clarence (Brown), who has recently arrived in Harlem from South Carolina, and teaches him to read. Technically crude, but funny and touching; sequence in principal's office, in which Clarence's mother fakes reading a test score, is a gem.▼

Clarence, the Cross-Eyed Lion (1965) **C-98m.** **½ D: Andrew Marton. Marshall Thompson, Betsy Drake, Cheryl Miller, Richard Haydn, Alan Caillou. Basis for *Daktari* TV show is good family entertainment set in Africa with adventure and wholesome comedy well blended.▼

Clash by Night (1952) **105m.** *** D: Fritz Lang. Barbara Stanwyck, Paul Douglas, Robert Ryan, Marilyn Monroe, Keith Andes, J. Carrol Naish. Moody, well-acted Clifford Odets story of drifter Stanwyck settling down, marrying good-natured fisherman Douglas. Cynical friend Ryan senses that she's not happy, tries to take advantage. Andes and Monroe provide secondary love interest.▼●

Clash of Steel (1962-French) **C-79m.** **½ D: Bernard Borderie. Gerard Barray, Gianna Maria Canale, Michele Grellier, Jean Topart. Thin plot involving overthrow of French king, Henry of Navarre, boosted by lively production and zesty swordplay. Franscope.

Clash of the Titans (1981-British) **C-118m.** **½ D: Desmond Davis. Laurence Olivier, Harry Hamlin, Judi Bowker, Burgess Meredith, Sian Phillips, Maggie Smith, Claire Bloom, Ursula Andress, Tim Pigott-Smith. Juvenile fantasy-adventure based on Greek mythology. Olivier is Zeus, and Hamlin is his mortal son Perseus, who must face a variety of awesome challenges in pursuit of his destiny. Long and episodic, with some fine elements (the taming of Pegasus, the threat of Medusa—who can turn men into stone with one glance), but not enough guts or vigor. As is, mainly for kids. Special effects by Ray Harryhausen. [PG]▼●

Class (1983) **C-98m.** ** D: Lewis John Carlino. Rob Lowe, Jacqueline Bisset, Andrew McCarthy, Stuart Margolin, Cliff Robertson, John Cusack, Alan Ruck, Remak Ramsay, Virginia Madsen, Casey Siemaszko, Anna Maria Horsford, Joan Cusack. Naive prep-school boy stumbles (almost literally) into affair with beautiful older woman, unaware of her identity.

Slick but uneven mix of romance, comedy, and drama with one-dimensional characters and a lack of credibility. Some good moments lost in the shuffle. [R]▼●

Class Act (1992) **C-98m.** **½ D: Randall Miller. Christopher Reid, Christopher Martin, Meshach Taylor, Karyn Parsons, Doug E. Doug, Rick Ducommun, Lamont Johnson, Rhea Perlman. Straight-A student (Reid) and street-wise juvenile delinquent (Martin) switch identities when they both transfer to a new high school; complications ensue when they find it tough sledding in their new environs. Broad, cartoony comedy is nothing special; neither is the obligatory anti-drug rap song at the end of the film. [PG-13]▼●

Class Action (1991) **C-109m.** *** D: Michael Apted. Gene Hackman, Mary Elizabeth Mastrantonio, Colin Friels, Joanna Merlin, Larry Fishburne, Donald Moffat, Jan Rubes, Matt Clark, Fred Dalton Thompson, Jonathan Silverman, Dan Hicks. Crusading lawyer takes on a class-action suit against a negligent auto company—while his feisty daughter represents the other side. Crackling performances by the two stars, as the long-embattled father and daughter, make this well worth seeing, even though the story becomes obvious at the climactic turn. [R]▼●

Class of '44 (1973) **C-95m.** **½ D: Paul Bogart. Gary Grimes, Jerry Houser, Oliver Conant, Deborah Winters, William Atherton, Sam Bottoms, John Candy. Sequel to SUMMER OF '42 is less ambitious, lightly entertaining story, with Grimes going to college, falling in love, growing up. Good period atmosphere. Panavision. [PG]▼

Class of Miss MacMichael, The (1978-British) **C-99m.** *½ D: Silvio Narizzano. Glenda Jackson, Oliver Reed, Michael Murphy, Rosalind Cash, John Standing, Riba Akabusi, Phil Daniels. Echoes of TO SIR, WITH LOVE don't flatter this shrill comedy-drama of a dedicated teacher with a class full of social misfits. [R]▼

Class of 1984 (1982) **C-93m.** ** D: Mark L. Lester. Perry King, Merrie Lynn Ross, Roddy McDowall, Timothy Van Patten, Stefan Arngrim, Al Waxman, Michael J. Fox, Lisa Langlois. Unpleasant, calculatedly campy melodrama about the harassment of high school teacher King by psychotic student Van Patten—with more than a few echoes of BLACKBOARD JUNGLE. As revenge movies go, the buzz-saw finale is not bad. Followed by CLASS OF 1999. [R]▼●

Class of 1999 (1990) **C-98m.** *½ D: Mark L. Lester. Bradley Gregg, Traci Lind, Malcolm McDowell, Stacy Keach, Patrick Kilpatrick, Pam Grier, John P. Ryan, Darren E. Burrows, Joshua Miller. Followup to CLASS OF 1984 pictures high school of the near-future as Hell on Earth, with ultraviolent gang members meeting their match in a trio of robots recruited as teachers. Heavy-handed film wavers between high camp and taking itself seriously as a message movie! Keach goes overboard as a maniacal robot operator. Unrated video version also available. 1993 sequel: CLASS OF 1999 II: THE SUBSTITUTE. [R]▼

Class of Nuke 'Em High (1986) **C-81m.** BOMB D: Richard Haines, Samuel Weil. Janelle Brady, Gilbert Brenton, Robert Prichard, R. L. Ryan. Obnoxious horror comedy about a New Jersey high school near a nuclear waste spill that creates monsters and disgustingly transforms model teens Brady and Brenton. Dehumanizing, sadistic gags masquerade as lowbrow entertainment. Followed by two sequels. [R]▼●◗

Claudelle Inglish (1961) **99m.** **½ D: Gordon Douglas. Diane McBain, Arthur Kennedy, Will Hutchins, Constance Ford, Claude Akins, Chad Everett, Robert Logan. Trite soaper derived from Erskine Caldwell tale of Southern farm gal who gives all to find excitement, with predictable consequences.

Claudia (1943) **91m.** *** D: Edmund Goulding. Dorothy McGuire, Robert Young, Ina Claire, Reginald Gardiner, Olga Baclanova, Jean Howard. Warm comedy of young Claudia suddenly marrying, facing adult problems, learning a lot about life in short period; beautifully acted. McGuire, in film debut, recreates her Broadway role. Sequel: CLAUDIA AND DAVID.

Claudia and David (1946) **78m.** *** D: Walter Lang. Dorothy McGuire, Robert Young, Mary Astor, John Sutton, Gail Patrick, Florence Bates. Enjoyable follow-up to CLAUDIA with McGuire and Young having a baby, adjusting to suburban life; engaging, well acted.

Claudine (1974) **C-92m.** **½ D: John Berry. Diahann Carroll, James Earl Jones, Lawrence Hilton-Jacobs, Tamu, David Kruger, Adam Wade. Slice-of-life comedy with a serious edge: Romance between garbage-man Jones and young ghetto mother Carroll is charming and credible, but the problems of dealing with her six kids, and their collective poverty, can't be treated so lightly. "Upbeat" finale just doesn't ring true. [PG]

Clay Pigeon, The (1949) **63m.** **½ D: Richard O. Fleischer. Bill Williams, Barbara Hale, Richard Loo, Richard Quine, Frank Fenton, Martha Hyer. Neat little actioner with Williams, a seaman accused of treason and of responsibility in the death of his friend, on the trail of the real culprit, a Japanese prison guard. Written by Carl Foreman, based on a true incident. ▼

Clay Pigeon (1971) **C-97m.** *½ D: Tom Stern, Lane Slate. Tom Stern, Telly Savalas, Robert Vaughn, John Marley, Burgess Meredith, Ivan Dixon. Good cast in dull crime melodrama of Vietnam vet settling into

drug scene who experiences change of heart and goes after big-league pusher. [R]
Clay Pigeons (1998) **C-104m.** **½ D: David Dobkin. Joaquin Phoenix, Vince Vaughn, Janeane Garofalo, Georgina Cates, Scott Wilson, Vince Vieluf, Phil Morris. Clever film noir set in a small town out west. A patsy falls prey first to his best friend, then the friend's slatternly wife, and finally to a mysterious stranger just passing through, whose actions bring a cynical big-city FBI agent (Garofalo) to town. Twisty black comedy has much to enjoy but leaves the viewer less than completely satisfied. Overemphatic use of source music is a debit; its greatest asset is a grabber of an opening. [R]▼●◗
Clean and Sober (1988) **C-125m.** *** D: Glenn Gordon Caron. Michael Keaton, Kathy Baker, Morgan Freeman, M. Emmet Walsh, Tate Donovan, Henry Judd Baker, Luca Bercovici, Claudia Christian, Pat Quinn, Ben Piazza. A young hustler enrolls in a drug rehabilitation program in order to duck out of sight for a while, refusing to admit to himself that he's an addict, too. Powerful drama showcases Keaton in an utterly believable performance, though the film's relentlessness makes it tough to watch. [R]▼●◗
Clean, Shaven (1993) **C-80m.** *** D: Lodge Kerrigan. Peter Greene, Robert Albert, Jennifer MacDonald, Megan Owen. Unusual, subtly chilling psychological drama about Peter (Greene), a schizophrenic released from an institution who is grasping for a human connection. Meanwhile, his young daughter has been put up for adoption by her mother, a cop, who's investigating the brutal murder of another child and becomes convinced Peter is the culprit. A meditation on deep feelings of loss and alienation; not always easy to follow, but challenging and in its own way, haunting.▼
Clean Slate (1981) SEE: **Coup de Torchon**
Clean Slate (1994) **C-107m.** ** D: Mick Jackson. Dana Carvey, Valeria Golino, James Earl Jones, Kevin Pollak, Michael Gambon, Michael Murphy, Olivia d'Abo, Tim Scott, Angela Paton, Jayne Brook, Gailard Sartain, Phil Leeds. Carvey plays a detective who awakens each morning with no memory whatsoever. Did somebody say GROUNDHOG DAY? It's D.O.A. all the way, though there are some mildly amusing gags involving a klutzy terrier named Barkley who hasn't any depth perception. [PG-13] ▼●
Clear All Wires (1933) **78m.** **½ D: George Hill. Lee Tracy, Benita Hume, Una Merkel, James Gleason, Alan Edwards. Tracy enlivens this so-so story of a manipulative, globe-trotting journalist, who creates as much news as he covers; highlighted are his escapades while in Russia. Script by Bella and Sam Spewack, from their play.
Clear and Present Danger (1994) **C-141m.** **½ D: Phillip Noyce. Harrison Ford, Willem Dafoe, Anne Archer, Joaquim de Almeida, James Earl Jones, Henry Czerny, Harris Yulin, Donald Moffat, Miguel Sandoval, Benjamin Bratt, Raymond Cruz, Dean Jones, Thora Birch, Ann Magnuson, Hope Lange. CIA whiz Jack Ryan (Ford) finds himself waist-deep in highest-level Washington politics when his ailing mentor (Jones) names him as his replacement. Soon he's caught in the middle of double-dealing with a Colombian druglord. The always watchable Ford plays more a symbol than a character here, and the action climax seems somehow pat. Still, it's an intelligent and entertaining sequel to PATRIOT GAMES. Panavision. [PG-13] ▼●◗
Clearcut (1991-Canadian) **C-98m.** **½ D: Richard Bugajski. Ron Lea, Graham Greene, Michael Hogan, Floyd (Red Crow) Westerman, Rebecca Jenkins. Multileveled drama about Indian activist Greene (who kidnaps the boss of a sawmill company responsible for cutting down forests) and naively liberal laywer Lea (who's failed to halt the destruction in the courts). Presence of graphic violence in the midst of a thought-provoking drama is jarring, to say the least, but the subject, and Greene's performance, make it worthwhile. [R]▼
Cleo From 5 to 7 (1962-French) **90m.** *** D: Agnés Varda. Corinne Marchand, Antoine Bourseiller, Dorothée Blanck, Michel Legrand, Anna Karina, Eddie Constantine, Jean-Luc Godard. Intelligent, fluid account of Parisian songstress forced to reevaluate her life while awaiting vital medical report on her physical condition.▼●◗
Cleopatra (1934) **100m.** ***½ D: Cecil B. DeMille. Claudette Colbert, Warren William, Henry Wilcoxon, Gertrude Michael, Joseph Schildkraut, C. Aubrey Smith, Claudia Dell, Robert Warwick. Opulent DeMille version of Cleopatra doesn't date badly, stands out as one of his most intelligent films, thanks in large part to fine performances by all. Top entertainment, with Oscar-winning cinematography by Victor Milner.▼●
Cleopatra (1963) **C-243m.** ** D: Joseph L. Mankiewicz. Elizabeth Taylor, Richard Burton, Rex Harrison, Pamela Brown, George Cole, Hume Cronyn, Cesare Danova, Kenneth Haigh, Andrew Keir, Martin Landau, Roddy McDowall, Robert Stephens, Francesca Annis, Herbert Berghof, Michael Hordern, John Hoyt, Carroll O'Connor. Saga of the Nile goes on and on and on. Definitely a curiosity item, but you'll be satisfied after an hour. Good acting, especially by Harrison and McDowall, but it's lost in this flat, four-hour misfire. Nevertheless earned Oscars for cinematography, art direc-

tion–set decoration, costumes, special effects. Released to TV at 194m. Todd-AO.▼●

Cleopatra Jones (1973) **C-89m.** ** D: Jack Starrett. Tamara Dobson, Bernie Casey, Shelley Winters, Brenda Sykes, Antonio Fargas, Bill McKinney, Esther Rolle. Black bubblegum stuff with Dobson as karate-chopping government agent chasing drug kingpins. Lots of action and violence. Panavision. [PG]▼◗

Cleopatra Jones and the Casino of Gold (1975) **C-96m.** **½ D: Chuck Bail. Tamara Dobson, Stella Stevens, Tanny, Norman Fell, Albert Popwell, Caro Kenyatta, Christopher Hunt. Wild, woolly, sexy, violent sequel to CLEOPATRA JONES. Stevens plays "The Dragon Lady," a tip-off on what to expect. Panavision. [R]▼

Cleopatra's Daughter (1960-Italian) **C-102m.** ** D: Richard McNamara. Debra Paget, Ettore Manni, Erno Crisa, Robert Alda, Corrado Panni. American actors are lost in this costumer, more intent on playing up sadistic sequences; intrigue at Egyptian court the highlight. Ultrascope.▼

Clerks (1994) **89m.** *** D: Kevin Smith. Brian O'Halloran, Jeff Anderson, Marilyn Ghigliotti, Lisa Spoonauer, Jason Mewes, Kevin Smith. Black and white, $27,000 wonder by first-time filmmaker Kevin Smith is a brash, foul-mouthed, often very funny look at a day in the lives of a New Jersey convenience-store clerk and his abrasive pal, who mans the video place next door—when he feels like it. Well written and well acted; certainly more provocative and entertaining than many glossy Hollywood movies of the 90s. Later an animated series. [R]▼●◗

Client, The (1994) **C-122m.** *** D: Joel Schumacher. Susan Sarandon, Tommy Lee Jones, Brad Renfro, Mary-Louise Parker, Anthony LaPaglia, Ossie Davis, Bradley Whitford, Anthony Edwards, J.T. Walsh, Walter Olkewicz, Will Patton, Anthony Heald, William H. Macy. Top-flight adaptation of John Grisham's best-seller about an 11-year-old boy who finds himself in hot water with both the Feds (led by Jones) and the Mob when he learns too much from a Mafia lawyer who's about to kill himself. Sarandon is the lawyer who takes the kid's case. Suspense is neatly woven with character development; really satisfying entertainment. Later a TV series. Panavision. [PG-13]▼●◗

Cliffhanger (1993-U.S.-French) **C-118m.** *** D: Renny Harlin. Sylvester Stallone, John Lithgow, Michael Rooker, Janine Turner, Paul Winfield, Ralph Waite, Rex Linn, Caroline Goodall, Leon, Craig Fairbrass, Michelle Joyner, Max Perlich. Self-doubting mountain rescue expert Sly is pitted against really rotten Lithgow and his gang, who are after $100 million lost in the Rockies. Eye-popping photography (by Alex Thomson), white-knuckle stunts, a swift pace, and entertaining characters add up to what a well-made action film should be: tons of fun. Story is thin, though. Italy's Dolomites stand in for the Rockies. Panavision. [R]▼●◗

Clifford (1994) **C-89m.** *½ D: Paul Flaherty. Martin Short, Charles Grodin, Mary Steenburgen, Dabney Coleman, G. D. Spradlin, Anne Jeffreys, Richard Kind, Jennifer Savidge, Ben Savage. Moronic comedy in the (unfortunate) mold of PROBLEM CHILD, with Short uninspiringly cast as a cloyingly obnoxious ten-year-old who makes life pure hell for his uncle (Grodin). Short's playing a child is a gimmick which quickly proves tiresome. Completed in 1991, this could have stayed on the shelf. [PG]▼●

Climate for Killing, A (1990) **C-103m.** *** D: J. S. Cardone. John Beck, Steven Bauer, Mia Sara, Katharine Ross, John Diehl, Phil Brock, Dedee Pfeiffer, Lu Leonard, Jack Dodson, Eloy Casados. A grisly murder confronts, and confounds, small-time Arizona cop Beck; he's joined by big city evaluator Bauer, who questions his approach to law enforcement while becoming involved with his daughter (Sara). Solid, engrossing mystery-drama. [R]▼●

Climax, The (1944) **C-86m.** **½ D: George Waggner. Boris Karloff, Gale Sondergaard, Susanna Foster, Turhan Bey, Thomas Gomez, Scotty Beckett, George Dolenz, Jane Farrar, June Vincent, Ludwig Stossel. Technicolor tale of suave but sinister physician to the Vienna Opera House who takes an unnatural interest in their newest soprano (Foster)—just as he did another singer who disappeared ten years ago. No surprises here, but slickly done. ▼●

Clinging Vine, The (1926) **71m.** **½ D: Paul Sloane. Leatrice Joy, Tom Moore, Toby Claude, Robert Edeson, Dell Henderson. Handsome fluff about unfeminine executive (Joy) who becomes involved in business swindle, and falls in love.▼

Clinic, The (1982-Australian) **C-92m.** **½ D: David Stevens. Chris Haywood, Simon Burke, Rona McLeod, Gerda Nicolson, Suzanne Roylance, Veronica Lang, Pat Evison. Straightforward but much too obvious comedy-drama about the goings-on in a VD clinic operated by doctor Haywood.▼

Clinton and Nadine (1988) **C-110m. TVM** D: Jerry Schatzberg. Andy Garcia, Ellen Barkin, Morgan Freeman, Michael Lombard, John C. McGinley, Alan North, Brad Sullivan. Erotic, fast-paced drama about a small-time smuggler and high-class hooker who get mixed up in a plot to run guns to the Nicaraguan contras. Writer Robert Foster had his name removed at the last minute, with credit going to pseudonymous "Willard Walpole." Made for cable. Aka BLOOD MONEY. Average.▼●

Clipped Wings (1953) **65m.** **½ D: Edward Bernds. Leo Gorcey, Huntz Hall, Bernard Gorcey, David (Gorcey) Condon,

Bennie Bartlett, Renie Riano, Todd Karns, June Vincent, Mary Treen, Philip Van Zandt. Sach and Slip join the Air Force in a fast and funny *Bowery Boys* entry.▼

Clive of India (1935) **90m.** **½ D: Richard Boleslawski. Ronald Colman, Loretta Young, Colin Clive, Francis Lister, C. Aubrey Smith, Cesar Romero, Montagu Love, Leo G. Carroll, Don Ameche. Colman is ideally cast as Robert Clive, the "man of destiny" who secured British rule in India at the sacrifice of his own personal happiness. More fanciful than factual, but entertaining and lavishly produced.

Cloak and Dagger (1946) **106m.** **½ D: Fritz Lang. Gary Cooper, Lilli Palmer, Robert Alda, Vladimir Sokoloff, Ludwig Stossel. Professor Cooper becomes a secret agent on his trip to Germany; Lang intrigue is not among his best, but still slick.▼●

Cloak & Dagger (1984) **C-101m.** *** D: Richard Franklin. Henry Thomas, Dabney Coleman, Michael Murphy, John McIntire, Jeanette Nolan, Christine Nigra. Young Thomas gets involved with murderous espionage—but no one will believe him. Flawed but enjoyable reworking of THE WINDOW. Coleman's a delight in dual role as his father and his make-believe hero. [PG]▼●

Cloak Without Dagger SEE: **Operation Conspiracy**

Clock, The (1945) **90m.** ***½ D: Vincente Minnelli. Judy Garland, Robert Walker, James Gleason, Keenan Wynn, Marshall Thompson, Lucille Gleason. Soldier Walker has two-day leave in N.Y.C., meets office worker Judy; they spend the day falling in love, encountering friendly milkman Gleason, drunk Wynn; charming little love story with beguiling Garland. Also shown in computer-colored version.▼●

Clockers (1995) **C-129m.** *** D: Spike Lee. Harvey Keitel, John Turturro, Delroy Lindo, Mekhi Phifer, Isaiah Washington, Keith David, Pee Wee Love, Regina Taylor, Tom Byrd, Sticky Fingaz, Mike Starr, Spike Lee. The night manager of a fast-food restaurant is murdered, but a no-nonsense Brooklyn cop doesn't believe that the young man who confessed to the crime is really guilty. He's got his eye on the suspect's brother (Phifer), who works for the neighborhood drug czar. A penetrating, multilayered look at the reality of life on the street and in "the projects," and a challenging treatise on personal responsibility. It's tough to decipher the street lingo and dialect in the opening scenes, but once the story kicks in, it's dynamite. Richard Price adapted his novel with Lee; a fortuitous merging of two distinctive talents. Coproduced by Martin Scorsese. [R]▼●◗

Clockmaker, The (1973-French) **C-105m.** ***½ D: Bertrand Tavernier. Philippe Noiret, Jean Rochefort, Jacques Denis, Julien Bertheau. Noiret is superb as a watchmaker who is forced to reevaluate his life after his son is arrested for murder. Meticulously directed; based on a novel by Georges Simenon. Tavernier's feature directing debut. ▼

Clockwatchers (1997) **C-105m.** ** D: Jill Sprecher. Toni Collette, Parker Posey, Lisa Kudrow, Alanna Ubach, Helen Fitzgerald, Stanley DeSantis, Jamie Kennedy, Kevin Cooney, Paul Dooley, Bob Balaban. Four office temps in corporate hell form a fast friendship that ultimately jeopardizes their attempts at careers. Indie spin on NINE TO FIVE captures working-week tedium hilariously for a while, then gets bogged down in tedious Kafkaesque second half. Posey's bitchy comic flair throughout gives the film its only real juice. [PG-13]▼●◗

Clockwise (1986-British) **C-96m.** **½ D: Christopher Morahan. John Cleese, Penelope Wilton, Alison Steadman, Stephen Moore, Sharon Maiden, Joan Hickson. Cleese is a school headmaster, obsessed with punctuality, en route to make a speech at a convention and constantly getting into trouble. A tour de force role that is a must for Cleese fans; others will be disappointed with the thinness of playwright Michael Frayn's script. [PG] ▼●

Clockwork Orange, A (1971) **C-137m.** ***½ D: Stanley Kubrick. Malcolm McDowell, Patrick Magee, Michael Bates, Adrienne Corri, Aubrey Morris, James Marcus, Steven Berkoff, David Prowse. A scathing satire on a society in the not so distant future, with an excellent performance by McDowell as a prime misfit. Kubrick's vivid adaptation of Anthony Burgess's novel was too strong for some to stomach in 1971, and it remains potent today. [R—edited from original X rating] ▼●◗

Clonus Horror, The SEE: **Parts: The Clonus Horror**

Close Call for Boston Blackie, A (1946) **60m.** ** D: Lew Landers. Chester Morris, Lynn Merrick, Richard Lane, Frank Sully, George E. Stone, Claire Carleton, Erik Rolf, Charles Lane. Blackie is framed for murder by a femme fatale in this disappointing entry with a plethora of comedy.

Close Call for Ellery Queen (1942) **65m.** *½ D: James Hogan. William Gargan, Margaret Lindsay, Charley Grapewin, Ralph Morgan, Kay Linaker, Edward Norris, James Burke, Addison Richards. Gargan picks up the role of Queen in this dreary entry about a missing heirs racket.

Close Encounters of the Third Kind (1977) **C-135m.** **** D: Steven Spielberg. Richard Dreyfuss, François Truffaut, Teri Garr, Melinda Dillon, Cary Guffey, Bob Balaban. Superb, intelligent sci-fi (written by Spielberg) about UFO mystery that leads to first contact with alien beings. Dreyfuss is perfect Everyman struggling with frustrating enigma that finally becomes clear. Powerhouse special effects throughout, plus John Williams' evocative score. Vilmos Zsigmond's impressive cinematography won an Oscar. Reedited by Spielberg to tighten midsection and add alien-encounter material to finale and reissued in 1980 at 132m. as THE SPECIAL EDITION. (Then, for network showings, *all* existing footage was used!) Reedited yet again by Spielberg in 1998 to 137m. for a Collectors Edition. Panavision. [PG]▼●

Closely Watched Trains (1966-Czech) **89m.** ★★★ D: Jiri Menzel. Vaclav Neckar, Jitka Bendova, Vladimir Valenta, Libuse Havelkova, Josef Somr. Enjoyable but slightly overrated tragicomedy about naive apprentice train-dispatcher Neckar's attempts at sexual initiation during the German Occupation. Academy Award winner as Best Foreign Film.▼●

Close My Eyes (1991-British) **C-109m.** ★★★ D: Stephen Poliakoff. Alan Rickman, Clive Owen, Saskia Reeves, Karl Johnson, Lesley Sharp, Kate Gartside. Vaguely unhappy woman makes sexual overtures to her brother, which explode into full-fledged incest five years later when she's married and living in a mansion by the Thames. Film is a bit haphazard setting up the basic situation, but soon becomes a riveting view. Extremely well acted, with confident performances by Owen and Reeves (as the taboo-flaunting siblings) and Rickman, in a supporting role as the husband. [R]▼

Closer, The (1990) **C-86m.** ★½ D: Dimitri Logothetis. Danny Aiello, Michael Paré, Joe Cortese, Justine Bateman, Diane Baker, James Karen, Michael Lerner. Highly successful businessman is forced to retire and creates a tension-filled night of competition in order to pick his successor. Aiello is compelling as always, but this would-be *Death of a Salesman* never gets out of the gate. Aiello originated the role on Broadway in 1976; Louis La Russo II's play was titled *Wheelbarrow Closers.* [R]▼●

Closer You Get, The (2000-Irish-British) **C-90m.** ★★½ D: Aileen Ritchie. Ian Hart, Sean McGinley, Niamh Cusack, Ruth McCabe, Ewan Stewart, Pat Shortt, Cathleen Bradley, Sean McDonagh. Flyweight comedy about a remote Irish island village where the young men decide to do something about the lack of eligible, attractive females: they take a want ad in a Miami newspaper, inviting sexy, athletic, marriage-minded American women to come on over. Self-consciously cute and padded out, but still amusing. [PG-13]▼

Closet Land (1991) **C-89m.** ★½ D: Radha Bharadwaj. Madeleine Stowe, Alan Rickman. Among the oddest of early '90s films: a two-character drama about the political interrogation of an allegedly subversive children's author by one of a totalitarian society's finest. Like a bad play that never went beyond workshop status, though no one can accuse the filmmakers of taking the easy way out. Well performed, under the circumstances. Coproduced by Ron Howard! [R]▼

Close to Eden (1992-Russian) **C-106m.** ★★★ D: Nikita Mikhalkov. Badema, Byaertu, Vladimir Gostukhin, Babushka, Larissa Kuznetsova, Jon Bochinski, Bao Yongyan. Russian truckdriver accidentally comes into the lives of a Mongol family, adroitly raising the question of who's "civilized" and who isn't. Beautifully filmed in the Mongolian steppe region of inner China by the acclaimed director of DARK EYES. Worth seeing.▼

Close to My Heart (1951) **90m.** ★★★ D: William Keighley. Ray Milland, Gene Tierney, Fay Bainter, Howard St. John. Superior soaper; Tierney attaches herself to waif in Bainter's orphanage, but husband Milland won't allow adoption until child's background is traced.

Cloudburst (1951-British) **83m.** ★★½ D: Francis Searle. Robert Preston, Elizabeth Sellars, Harold Lang, Noel Howlett. Impressive little film of Preston, WW2 veteran working in British Foreign Office, seeking his wife's murderers.

Cloud Dancer (1980) **C-108m.** ★★½ D: Barry Brown. David Carradine, Jennifer O'Neill, Joseph Bottoms, Colleen Camp, Albert Salmi, Salome Jens, Nina Van Pallandt. Uneven tale of aerobatic-obsessed Carradine and his relationship with O'Neill. Nice—if too many—flying sequences, hokey melodramatics. Filmed in 1978. [PG]▼

Clouded Yellow, The (1950-British) **85m.** ★★½ D: Ralph Thomas. Jean Simmons, Trevor Howard, Sonia Dresdel, Barry Jones, Kenneth More, Geoffrey Keen, Andre Morell, Maxwell Reed. Moderately entertaining psychological drama/mystery/chase film in which ex-secret serviceman Howard takes a job cataloguing butterflies, and becomes involved with a strange, fragile young girl (Simmons)—and murder.▼

Clouds Over Europe SEE: **Q Planes**

Clown, The (1953) **91m.** ★★½ D: Robert Z. Leonard. Red Skelton, Tim Considine, Jane Greer, Loring Smith, Philip Ober. Sentimental remake of THE CHAMP about a washed-up, self-destructive comic with a devoted son who looks out for him. Skelton's not bad in rare dramatic role; Considine is so good he overcomes some of the hokiness of script. Charles Bronson has a bit role in dice game scene.▼

Clown Murders, The (1975-Canadian) **C-96m.** ★½ D: Martyn Burke. Stephen Young, Susan Keller, Lawrence Dane, John Candy, Gary Reineke, Al Waxman, Cec Linder. Melodrama set among the idle rich at a Halloween party where envious pals stage a fake kidnapping to botch pompous Dane's real-estate deal. Clumsy thriller boasts comic Candy in early dramatic role (with his weight problem a running gag).▼

Clowns, The (1971-Italian) **C-90m.** ***½ D: Federico Fellini. Fellini's homage to circus clowns is itself a clownish spoof of documentaries, a funny, fully entertaining piece of fluff from this great director, even making fun of himself. Made for Italian TV. [G]▼

Club, The (1980-Australian) **C-99m.** *** D: Bruce Beresford. Jack Thompson, Graham Kennedy, Frank Wilson, Harold Hopkins, John Howard. Thompson is excellent as a football coach in this searing drama about off-the-field politics in a football club. Script by David Williamson, based on his play. Aka PLAYERS. Panavision. ▼

Club Dead SEE: **Terror at Red Wolf Inn**

Club Extinction (1990-German-Italian-French) **C-112m.** ** D: Claude Chabrol. Alan Bates, Jennifer Beals, Jan Niklas, Hans Zischler, Benoit Regent, Peter Fitz, Andrew McCarthy, Wolfgang Preiss, Isolde Barth. A wave of suicides shocks near-future Berlin; police investigator Niklas begins to suspect involvement of Beals, spokesperson for an Eden-like resort, who's linked to media baron Dr. Marsfeldt (Bates). Chabrol's attempt at updating Dr. Mabuse (film credits Norbert Jacques' original novel, *Mabuse der Spieler*) misfires; Bates is miscast, and film lacks any thematic resonances. Still, an interesting curiosity. European title: DR. M. Shot in English. [R]▼●

Club Havana (1945) **62m.** ** D: Edgar G. Ulmer. Tom Neal, Margaret Lindsay, Don Douglas, Gertrude Michael, Isabelita (Lita Baron), Dorothy Morris, Ernest Truex. Roadshow GRAND HOTEL is very cheap production with little of interest.▼

Clubland (1999) **C-94m.** ** D: Mary Lambert. Jimmy Tuckett, Lori Petty, Brad Hunt, Heather Stephens, Rodney Eastman, Buddy Quaid, Terence Trent D'Arby, Alexis Arquette, Steven Tyler. Young man and his buddies are determined to make it big in the music world by performing at a trendy club on L.A.'s Sunset Strip, but they have to deal with sleazy promoters and personality problems within the band. Contemporary music and trappings can't disguise, or overcome, a soggy story that might have been made as a 1930s B movie. Written by successful music producer Glen Ballard. [R]▼

Club Life (1985) **C-92m.** **½ D: Norman Thaddeus Vane. Tony Curtis, Tom Parsekian, Dee Wallace, Michael Parks, Jamie Barrett, Ron Kuhlman, Yana Nirvana, Pat Ast. Hunk Parsekian arrives in Hollywood with stars in his eyes, hoping for a movie career; instead, he finds himself toiling as a bouncer in Curtis' bar. Nicely stylized and acted (if all-too-familiar) tale of Tinseltown decadence. How could you not like a film in which Ast appears as a lesbian bar owner named Butch? Vane also produced and scripted.▼

Club Paradise (1986) **C-104m.** ** D: Harold Ramis. Robin Williams, Peter O'Toole, Rick Moranis, Jimmy Cliff, Twiggy, Adolph Caesar, Eugene Levy, Joanna Cassidy, Andrea Martin, Robin Duke, Mary Gross, Simon Jones, Carey Lowell. Pleasant cast in pleasant surroundings, lacking only a script and a few more laughs. Williams plays Chicago fireman who retires to West Indian island, goes halfies with native Cliff on turning ramshackle beachfront property into vacation resort. Writers even try to shoehorn a "serious" subplot about exploitation of the natives into the proceedings! Best of all is Cliff's almost nonstop music; his performance isn't bad, either. [PG-13]▼●

Clue (1985) **C-87m.** **½ D: Jonathan Lynn. Eileen Brennan, Tim Curry, Madeline Kahn, Christopher Lloyd, Michael McKean, Martin Mull, Lesley Ann Warren, Colleen Camp, Lee Ving, Bill Henderson, Howard Hesseman. Silly comic whodunit based on the popular board game of the same name with all the familiar characters (Mrs. Peacock, Colonel Mustard, Miss Scarlet, et al) gathered for a murderous night in a Victorian mansion. Everyone tries very hard—*too* hard, since the script, by first-time feature director Lynn, is so slim; addle-brained Brennan and puckish butler Curry come off best. When this played theatrically, audiences saw one of three alternate endings. Video has all three in a row to total 96m. [PG]▼●

Clueless (1995) **C-97m.** *** D: Amy Heckerling. Alicia Silverstone, Stacey Dash, Brittany Murphy, Paul Rudd, Donald Faison, Breckin Meyer, Jeremy Sisto, Justin Walker, Elisa Donovan, Dan Hedaya, Wallace Shawn, Twink Caplan, Julie Brown. Sharp, funny, original take on Beverly Hills high school teens of the 90s, by the director of FAST TIMES AT RIDGEMONT HIGH (and based—believe it or not—on Jane Austen's *Emma*). Silverstone is perfect as Cher, who with her best friend Dionne—they're both named after famous pop singers—knows everything about being gorgeous, popular, and always in vogue. This laugh-out-loud satire is never mean, which is a big part of its charm; it also introduces wonderfully funny vernacular, which we won't spoil by reciting here. As if! Heckerling also scripted. Later a TV series. [PG-13] ▼●

Clue of the New Pin (1960-British) **58m.** *½ D: Allan Davis. Paul Daneman, Bernard Archard, James Villiers, Catherine Woodville, Clive Morton. Old-fashioned Edgar Wallace yarn about "perfect crime," with Villiers a TV interviewer who tangles with murderer; ponderous.

Clue of the Silver Key (1961-British) **59m.** **½ D: Gerald Glaister. Bernard Lee, Lyndon Brook, Finlay Currie, Jennifer Daniels. Above-par Edgar Wallace yarn, highlighted by Lee's performance as de-

termined Scotland Yard inspector unraveling series of murders.
Cluny Brown (1946) **100m.** ***½ D: Ernst Lubitsch. Charles Boyer, Jennifer Jones, Peter Lawford, Helen Walker, Reginald Gardiner, C. Aubrey Smith, Reginald Owen, Richard Haydn, Sara Allgood, Ernest Cossart, Una O'Connor, Florence Bates, Christopher Severn. Delightful comedy which charts the evolving relationship between orphan Jones and penniless Czech refugee professor Boyer in pre–WW2 England. Takes hilarious pot-shots at the British class system, with the help of a sterling cast of character actors. Screenplay by Samuel Hoffenstein and Elizabeth Reinhardt, from Marjorie Sharp's novel.
"C" Man (1949) **75m.** **½ D: Joseph Lerner. Dean Jagger, John Carradine, Harry Landers, Lottie Elwen, Rene Paul. Spunky little programmer in which U.S. Customs agent Jagger sets out to track a stolen necklace and find the killer of another agent, his longtime friend.▼
C'mon, Let's Live a Little (1967) **C-85m.** BOMB D: David Butler. Bobby Vee, Jackie De Shannon, Eddie Hodges, John Ireland, Jr., Suzie Kaye, Bo Belinsky, Patsy Kelly, Kim Carnes. Folk singer Vee enrolls in college, romances De Shannon, is manipulated by student radical Ireland. Perfectly awful. Techniscope.
Coach (1978) **C-100m.** ** D: Bud Townsend. Cathy Lee Crosby, Michael Biehn, Keenan Wynn, Steve Nevil, Channing Clarkson, Sydney Wicks. Olympic gold medal winner Crosby is accidentally hired as a high school basketball coach for boys. Exploitation film that turns out disappointingly tame and predictable. [PG]▼
Coal Miner's Daughter (1980) **C-125m.** ***½ D: Michael Apted. Sissy Spacek, Tommy Lee Jones, Beverly D'Angelo, Levon Helm, Phyllis Boyens, Ernest Tubb. Rags-to-riches story of country singer Loretta Lynn is among the best musical bios ever made, though final quarter does slide over some "down side" details. Spacek won well-deserved Oscar (and did her own singing), but Jones, D'Angelo, and Helm (drummer for The Band) are just as good. Screenplay by Tom Rickman. [PG]▼●
Coast Guard (1939) **72m.** ** D: Edward Ludwig. Randolph Scott, Frances Dee, Ralph Bellamy, Walter Connolly, Warren Hymer, Robert Middlemass, Stanley Andrews. Scott and Bellamy are hard-loving, hard-fighting guardsmen in love with Dee. When one of them is stranded in the snow after a plane crash, the other must decide whether to help or not. Routine but action-filled hokum with similarities to Capra's DIRIGIBLE.
Coast of Skeletons (1964-British) **C-91m.** ** D: Robert Lynn. Richard Todd, Dale Robertson, Heinz Drache, Marianne Koch, Elga Andersen, Derek Nimmo. Edgar Wallace's *Sanders of the River* is basis for largely rewritten tale of ex-officer hired to investigate scuttling of American tycoon's African diamond operation. Todd repeats role he played in SANDERS (DEATH DRUMS ALONG THE RIVER). Techniscope.
Coast of Terror SEE: **Summer City**
Coast to Coast (1980) **C-95m.** ** D: Joseph Sargent. Dyan Cannon, Robert Blake, Quinn Redeker, Michael Lerner, Maxine Stuart, Bill Lucking. A nutty woman (who's been institutionalized by her divorce-seeking husband) escapes from a sanitarium and travels cross-country with trucker Blake, who's got problems of his own. Strained road comedy, often abrasive, with occasional laughs. [PG]▼●
Cobb (1994) **C-128m.** **½ D: Ron Shelton. Tommy Lee Jones, Robert Wuhl, Lolita Davidovich, Lou Myers, Stephen Mendillo, William Utay, J. Kenneth Campbell. Portrait of Ty Cobb—widely regarded as the greatest baseball player of all time—as an old, eccentric, embittered man, determined to tell his sanitized life story to sportswriter Al Stump (Wuhl). Perhaps a Hollywood first: a biopic that reveals its subject as the meanest sonofabitch who ever lived, with no redeeming qualities whatever. Fascinating for a while, but gets redundant. Worth seeing for Jones' commanding performance. Panavision. [R]▼●
Cobra (1925) **75m.** *** D: Joseph Henabery. Rudolph Valentino, Nita Naldi, Gertrude Olmstead, Casson Ferguson, Henry Barrows, Lillian Langdon. Valentino produced Martin Brown's play about an aristocratic seducer held in thrall by a female serpent. The star shows acting muscle his peers never noticed in a three-dimensional role as tailor-made for him as a fine Italian suit. Pluses: gowns by MGM's Adrian and handsome art deco direction by William Cameron Menzies.▼◗
Cobra (1986) **C-87m.** *½ D: George P. Cosmatos. Sylvester Stallone, Brigitte Nielsen, Reni Santoni, Andrew Robinson, Lee Garlington, John Herzfeld, Art Le Fleur, Brian Thompson, David Rasche, Val Avery. Once more, Stallone wraps himself in the American flag and fights for the greater glory of mankind by going after criminal vermin; this time, he's a cop. Typical low-grade action fare, where all the other cops are stubborn dummies, and all the bad guys are repellent creeps. Some good action sequences. [R]▼●◗
Cobra Woman (1944) **C-70m.** *** D: Robert Siodmak. Maria Montez, Jon Hall, Sabu, Lon Chaney (Jr.), Edgar Barrier, Lois Collier, Mary Nash. Camp classic, with island beauty Montez, set to wed Hall, finding herself kidnapped and discovering she has an evil twin sister. Sabu plays Hall's faithful

(and ever-so-goofy) companion Kado. Co-scripted by Richard Brooks!
Cobweb, The (1955) **C-124m.** ** D: Vincente Minnelli. Richard Widmark, Lauren Bacall, Gloria Grahame, Charles Boyer, Lillian Gish, John Kerr, Susan Strasberg, Oscar Levant, Tommy Rettig, Paul Stewart, Adele Jergens. Good cast in static soaper detailing the goings-on in psychiatric clinic headed by Dr. Widmark; of course, some of the personnel are more unbalanced than the patients. Scripted by John Paxton, produced by John Houseman. Film debuts of Strasberg and Kerr. CinemaScope.●
Coca-Cola Kid, The (1985-Australian) **C-94m.** **½ D: Dusan Makavejev. Eric Roberts, Greta Scacchi, Bill Kerr, Chris Haywood, Kris McQuade, Max Gilles, Rebecca Smart. Droll, sometimes wacky comedy about a hotshot Coca-Cola sales exec sent on mission to Australia, leading to various misadventures. Roberts' performance strictly a matter of taste, as is this offbeat, mildly satiric film. Sexy Scacchi is the best thing in the picture. [R]▼●
Cocaine Cowboys (1979) **C-87m.** BOMB D: Ulli Lommel. Jack Palance, Tom Sullivan, Andy Warhol, Suzanna Love, Pete Huckabee. Dreadful film about rock group that supports itself "between engagements" by dope smuggling; filmed at Warhol's Montauk home, where this film should have remained. [R]▼
Cocaine Fiends, The (1936) **68m.** BOMB D: William A. O'Connor. Noel Madison, Lois January, Sheila Manners, Dean Benton, Lois Lindsay, Eddie Phillips. Dope peddler and mob front man, on the lam from the law, turns a young girl on to cocaine (which she believes is "headache powder") . . . and she's hopelessly addicted. Then her brother is taken "on a sleigh ride with some snow birds." Tawdry, hilariously awful and, in its way, a bit depressing; from the REEFER MADNESS school of filmmaking. Originally shown as THE PACE THAT KILLS.▼
Cockeyed Cavaliers (1934) **72m.** *** D: Mark Sandrich. Bert Wheeler, Robert Woolsey, Thelma Todd, Dorothy Lee, Noah Beery, Franklin Pangborn. Colorful costume comedy with Wheeler & Woolsey trying to crash into society by posing as the King's physicians; lively mix of slapstick, puns, and music.▼
Cockeyed Cowboys of Calico County (1970) **C-99m.** ** D: Ranald MacDougall. Dan Blocker, Nanette Fabray, Jim Backus, Wally Cox, Jack Elam, Stubby Kaye, Mickey Rooney, Noah Beery, Marge Champion, Jack Cassidy. Great cast and waste of a movie. Turn-of-the-century progress in the Old West, but villains, varmints and saloons still remain. Made for TV, but released to theaters instead. [G]
Cockeyed Miracle, The (1946) **81m.** ** D: S. Sylvan Simon. Frank Morgan, Keenan Wynn, Cecil Kellaway, Audrey Totter, Marshall Thompson. Good cast carries weak material. Morgan returns from heaven to make up for financial error he made involving family.
Cockeyed World, The (1929) **118m.** *½ D: Raoul Walsh. Victor McLaglen, Edmund Lowe, Lily Damita, El Brendel, Lelia Karnelly, Stuart Erwin. Sequel to WHAT PRICE GLORY? with McLaglen and Lowe as battling Marines Flagg and Quirt sent to South Sea island where fiery Damita captures their attention. Smash hit in 1929, it moves like molasses today, and is no match for GLORY.
Cockfighter (1974) **C-83m.** *** D: Monte Hellman. Warren Oates, Richard B. Shull, Harry Dean Stanton, Troy Donahue, Millie Perkins. Offbeat, violent but interesting drama of a man who trains fighting cocks in Georgia. Oates is silent until the very end, his thoughts serving as narration. Filmed in Georgia. Aka BORN TO KILL, WILD DRIFTER, GAMBLIN' MAN [R]▼
Cockleshell Heroes, The (1955-British) **C-97m.** ** D: Jose Ferrer. Jose Ferrer, Trevor Howard, Dora Bryan, Anthony Newley, Victor Maddern, Christopher Lee. Special task force is trained in the use of kayaks for WW2 mission. Film never gels. CinemaScope.
Cocktail (1988) **C-100m.** ** D: Roger Donaldson. Tom Cruise, Bryan Brown, Elisabeth Shue, Lisa Banes, Laurence Luckinbill, Kelly Lynch, Gina Gershon, Ron Dean, Paul Benedict. Young hotshot comes to N.Y.C. to make his fortune, but winds up becoming a "hot" bartender instead, under the tutelage of self-styled barman/philosopher Brown. Cruise flashes his smile, Shue is cute, but that can't redeem the junior-high-school-level dramatics. [R]▼●
Cocktail Molotov (1980-French) **C-100m.** *** D: Diane Kurys. Elise Caron, Philippe Lebas, Francois Cluzet, Genevieve Fontanel, Henri Garcin, Michel Puterflam. Pleasant follow-up to PEPPERMINT SODA, with a trio of teenagers wandering through Europe at the time of the '68 student rebellion. Caron, Lebas, and Cluzet are attractive as the youngsters testing their wings. [R]▼
Cocoanut Grove (1938) **85m.** ** D: Alfred Santell. Fred MacMurray, Harriet Hilliard (Nelson), Yacht Club Boys, Ben Blue, Rufe Davis, Billy Lee, Eve Arden. MacMurray's band just has to make good at Cocoanut Grove audition in flimsy musical with nine songs you'll never hear again.
Cocoanuts, The (1929) **96m.** *** D: Joseph Santley, Robert Florey. Groucho, Harpo, Chico, Zeppo Marx, Kay Francis, Oscar Shaw, Mary Eaton, Margaret Dumont. The Marxes' first film suffers from stagy filming and stale musical subplot, but

when the brothers have scenes to themselves it's a riot; highlights include hilarious auction, classic ''viaduct'' routine.▼●◗

Cocoon (1985) **C-117m.** ***½ D: Ron Howard. Don Ameche, Wilford Brimley, Hume Cronyn, Brian Dennehy, Jack Gilford, Steve Guttenberg, Maureen Stapleton, Jessica Tandy, Gwen Verdon, Herta Ware, Tahnee Welch, Barret Oliver, Linda Harrison, Tyrone Power, Jr., Clint Howard. Florida senior citizens discover an actual fountain of youth in this warm, humanistic fantasy-drama, marred only by derivative and too literal science-fiction finale. What a pleasure to watch this cast at work! (Ameche won Best Supporting Actor Oscar.) Screenplay by Tom Benedek, from David Saperstein's novel; another impressive directing job by Howard. Followed by a sequel. [PG-13]▼●

Cocoon: The Return (1988) **C-116m.** ** D: Daniel Petrie. Don Ameche, Jack Gilford, Gwen Verdon, Maureen Stapleton, Steve Guttenberg, Hume Cronyn, Jessica Tandy, Wilford Brimley, Elaine Stritch, Tahnee Welch, Courteney Cox. Disappointing follow-up in which the elderly earthlings return for a visit to their home planet. Most of the magic and warmth of the original are missing; while it's always a joy to see Ameche and company on screen, the actors are unable to transcend their material. [PG]▼●

Code, The SEE: **Farewell, Friend**

Code Name: Emerald (1985) **C-95m.** ** D: Jonathan Sanger. Ed Harris, Max von Sydow, Horst Buchholz, Helmut Berger, Cyrielle Claire, Eric Stoltz, Patrick Stewart, Graham Crowden. Old-fashioned WW2 espionage tale has Harris as a double agent in plot to capture an Overlord (person with information on the plans for the D-Day invasion). Credibility is undermined by miscasting of Stoltz, who looks way too young to be an intelligence lieutenant and the target Overlord. [PG]▼●

Code Name, Red Roses (1969-Italian) **C-97m.** **½ D: Fernando Di Leo. James Daly, Pier Angeli, Michael Wilding, Peter Van Eyck. The old ''American saboteur behind enemy lines'' plot reenacted by a pretty fair cast. Also called RED ROSES FOR THE FUEHRER. Dyaliscope.

Code Name: Trixie SEE: **Crazies, The**

Codename: Wildgeese (1986-German-Italian) **C-101m.** ** D: Anthony M. Dawson (Antonio Margheriti). Lewis Collins, Lee Van Cleef, Ernest Borgnine, Klaus Kinski, Mimsy Farmer. Action footage redeems this cornball commando film of Collins and mercenary troops sent to wipe out a Far East drug stronghold. No relation to THE WILD GEESE or its sequel. Widescreen. [R]▼

Code of Scotland Yard (1946-British) **90m.** *** D: George King. Oscar Homolka, Derek Farr, Muriel Pavlov, Kenneth Griffith, Manning Whiley, Kathleen Harrison, Diana Dors. Entertaining melodrama with Homolka most effective as a seemingly respectable London antique dealer who's really an escapee from Devil's Island; Griffith matches him as his slimy assistant. Original British title: THE SHOP AT SLY CORNER.▼

Code of Silence (1985) **C-101m.** **½ D: Andy Davis. Chuck Norris, Henry Silva, Bert Remsen, Molly Hagan, Joseph Guzaldo, Mike Genovese, Dennis Farina. Norris plays a loner on Chicago police force who makes his own rules in dealing with violent gang war. In other words, it's ''Dirty Chuckie.'' Formula action film, and not bad. [R]▼●

Code of the Secret Service (1939) **58m.** *½ D: Noel Smith. Ronald Reagan, Rosella Towne, Eddie Foy, Jr., Moroni Olsen, Edgar Edwards, Jack Mower. Limp actioner with Lt. Brass Bancroft (Reagan) tangling with counterfeiters in Mexico. Second of a series, following SECRET SERVICE OF THE AIR.

Code 7 Victim 5 (1964-British) **C-88m.** **½ D: Robert Lynn. Lex Barker, Ronald Fraser, Walter Rilla, Dietmar Schonherr. Moderate actioner with Barker investigating murder in South Africa; nicely paced. Techniscope.

Code Two (1953) **69m.** ** D: Fred Wilcox. Ralph Meeker, Sally Forrest, Keenan Wynn, Robert Horton, Jeff Richards. Three recruits on L.A. motorcycle police force face occupational hazards; when Richards is killed, Meeker et al. seek to capture those responsible.

Coffy (1973) **C-90m.** **½ D: Jack Hill. Pam Grier, Booker Bradshaw, Robert DoQui, William Elliott, Allan Arbus, Sid Haig. Fast-moving, generally agreeable trash about nurse who goes after junkies who turned her young sister into an addict; lots of nudity in Grier's biggest hit. [R]▼●

Cohen and Tate (1989) **C-85m.** *½ D: Eric Red. Roy Scheider, Adam Baldwin, Harley Cross, Cooper Huckabee. In this grim variation on O. Henry's ''Ransom of Red Chief,'' Scheider and Baldwin, the hit men of the title, murderously kidnap young Cross, sole witness to a gang killing; story takes place almost entirely in their car. Clumsy irony, theatrical style, leaden illogic sink the film early. Scheider tries hard. [R]▼●

Cold Around the Heart (1997) **C-96m.** ** D: John Ridley. David Caruso, Kelly Lynch, Stacey Dash, Chris Noth, John Spencer, Pruitt Taylor-Vince, Richard Kind. Barely released and highly derivative thieves-fall-out crime drama. Grungy-looking Caruso is out for revenge against ruthless femme fatale Lynch when she double-crosses him after a jewel heist. Decent cast helps, but it's nothing you haven't seen done better about a million times before. Super 35. [R]▼

Coldblooded (1995) **C-91m.** ** D: M. Wallace Wolodarsky. Jason Priestley, Peter Riegert, Kimberly Williams, Janeane Garofalo, Robert Loggia, Josh Charles. Black comedy about a nerdy young bookkeeper for the mob who finally gets a chance to become a full-fledged hit man—and adapts to the job better than he ever dreamed. Love soon complicates the picture, and also bogs down what could have been a clever, if twisted, story. This ''hit'' is a miss. Look for Michael J. Fox (who coproduced the film) in a cameo. [R]▼

Cold Comfort Farm (1995-British) **C-95m.** *** D: John Schlesinger. Eileen Atkins, Kate Beckinsale, Sheila Burrell, Stephen Fry, Freddie Jones, Joanna Lumley, Ian McKellen, Miriam Margolyes, Rufus Sewell. Deliciously eccentric comedy about a well-bred young woman who goes to live with distant relatives at their spooky old farm, which is dominated by a dotty grandmother living in the attic. Our heroine then implacably sets about reordering their lives! Good fun, based on a 1932 novel by Stella Gibbons. Made for British TV. [PG]▼●

Cold Feet (1984) **C-96m.** ** D: Bruce van Dusen. Griffin Dunne, Marissa Chibas, Blanche Baker, Mark Cronogue, Joseph Leon, Marcia Jean Kurtz. A couple of chuckles are not enough to save this sluggish comedy about the courtship of Dunne and Chibas, who've been unlucky in love before. Baker steals the film as Dunne's flaky ex-wife. [PG]▼

Cold Feet (1989) **C-94m.** *½ D: Robert Dornhelm. Keith Carradine, Sally Kirkland, Tom Waits, Rip Torn, Bill Pullman, Kathleen York, Vincent Schiavelli. Carradine and Waits (the latter near-psychotic) squabble for hundreds of miles over a horse; marriage-hungry Kirkland is the flake who rounds out the threesome. Reminiscent in tone of coscripter Thomas McGuane's RANCHO DELUXE (which pops up on a theater marquee here)—but without the laughs; RANCHO'S Jeff Bridges is unbilled as a smalltown bartender. [R]▼●

Cold Fever (1995-U.S.-Iceland) **C-82m.** *** D: Fridrik Thor Fridriksson. Masatoshi Nagase, Lili Taylor, Fisher Stevens, Gisli Halldorsson, Laura Hughes, Seijun Suzuki. Amiable, Jarmusch-like comic road movie that charts the adventures of Atsushi (Nagase), a Japanese businessman who decides to go to Iceland and trek to the site where his parents died, so their souls can rest in peace. In Iceland, there is plenty of snow, ice, and cold, and Atsushi is most definitely a stranger in a strange land. Coscripted by the director and Jim Stark, the producer of several Jim Jarmusch films. Panavision.▼

Cold Heaven (1992) **C-105m.** ** D: Nicolas Roeg. Theresa Russell, Mark Harmon, James Russo, Talia Shire, Will Patton, Richard Bradford. Adulterous wife (Russell) is on the verge of telling her husband (Harmon) that she is dumping him when he is killed in a gruesome vacation boating accident—or is he? Russell's guilt and paranoia bring on a host of ponderous *sturm und drang* encounters and experiences. Lifeless and confusing. [R]▼

Colditz Story, The (1957-British) **97m.** ***½ D: Guy Hamilton. John Mills, Eric Portman, Christopher Rhodes, Lionel Jeffries, Bryan Forbes, Ian Carmichael, Richard Wattis, Anton Diffring, Theodore Bikel. Super-solid P.O.W. saga set in Germany's Colditz Castle, supposedly ''escape-proof'' but challenged by various European prisoners, and a hardy British group in particular.▼

Cold Sassy Tree (1989) **C-100m. TVM** D: Joan Tewkesbury. Faye Dunaway, Richard Widmark, Neil Patrick Harris, Frances Fisher, Lee Garlington, John Jackson. Handsome May-December romantic drama set in a sleepy Southern town at the turn of the century. An independent lady from up North causes a scandal when she decides to wed the local general-store owner just three weeks after he's been widowed. Dunaway and Widmark are a delight in this adaptation of Olive Ann Burns's novel (by director Tewkesbury). Made for cable. Above average.▼●

Cold Steel (1987) **C-90m.** ** D: Dorothy Ann Puzo. Brad Davis, Sharon Stone, Jonathan Banks, Jay Acovone, Adam Ant, Eddie Egan. Standard actioner about cop Davis, his father murdered by disfigured psychotic Banks; he seeks revenge, natch. [R]▼

Cold Sweat (1971-French-Italian) **C-94m.** ** D: Terence Young. Charles Bronson, Liv Ullmann, James Mason, Jill Ireland, Michel Constantin, Gabriele Ferzetti. Richard Matheson's thriller *Ride the Nightmare* has been converted into a predictable action movie with Bronson as American expatriate in France forced into the drug trade by crime czar Mason. [PG]▼●◗

Cold Turkey (1971) **C-99m.** *** D: Norman Lear. Dick Van Dyke, Pippa Scott, Tom Poston, Bob Newhart, Vincent Gardenia, Barnard Hughes, Edward Everett Horton, Jean Stapleton, Graham Jarvis. Bittersweet satire of contemporary America; minister Van Dyke leads township crusade to stop smoking, in order to win mammoth contest. Trenchant finale doesn't entirely gibe with rest of film: still worthwhile, with Bob & Ray hilarious as newscasters. Fine score by Randy Newman; Horton's last film. Made in 1969. [PG]▼●

Cold Wind in August, A (1961) **80m.** **½ D: Alexander Singer. Lola Albright, Scott Marlowe, Herschel Bernardi, Joe De Santis. Offbeat account of tenement boy

Marlowe having affair with stripper Albright; frank, flavorful tale.
Cole Younger, Gunfighter (1958) **C-78m.** ** D: R. G. Springsteen. Frank Lovejoy, James Best, Abby Dalton, Jan Merlin. Modest actioner has gunfights to perk up trite account of 1870s Texas. CinemaScope.
Colin Nutley's House of Angels SEE: **House of Angels**
Collector, The (1965) **C-119m.** *** D: William Wyler. Terence Stamp, Samantha Eggar, Maurice Dallimore, Mona Washbourne. Disturbing story of man who collects more than just butterflies, which is where Eggar fits in. Chilling, if not altogether believable. Based on the novel by John Fowles.▼●
Collector, The (1975) SEE: **Death Collector**
Colleen (1936) **89m.** *** D: Alfred E. Green. Dick Powell, Ruby Keeler, Jack Oakie, Joan Blondell, Hugh Herbert, Paul Draper, Louise Fazenda, Marie Wilson. Neglected Warner Bros. musical is quite good, with usual boy-meets-girl plot framing tasteful musical numbers. Includes perhaps-definitive Hugh Herbert performance.
College (1927) **65m.** *** D: James W. Horne. Buster Keaton, Anne Cornwall, Flora Bramley, Harold Goodwin, Grant Withers, Snitz Edwards. Highbrow student Buster has to become an all-star athlete to please his girlfriend; episodic gag structure makes this less impressive than other Keaton features, but it's awfully funny.▼●◗
College Coach (1933) **75m.** **½ D: William Wellman. Dick Powell, Ann Dvorak, Pat O'Brien, Hugh Herbert, Herman Bing, Lyle Talbot. Well-paced tale of ruthless football coach O'Brien, neglected wife Dvorak, star player Powell who also likes chemistry. Look for John Wayne in a bit part.
College Confidential (1960) **91m.** *½ D: Albert Zugsmith. Steve Allen, Jayne Meadows, Mamie Van Doren, Walter Winchell, Herbert Marshall, Cathy Crosby, Conway Twitty, Ziva Rodann, Mickey Shaughnessy. Idiocy involving sociology professor Allen and what happens when he surveys the sexual activities of his students. "Special Guests" include Rocky Marciano, Sheilah Graham, Pamela Mason, and Earl Wilson.
College Holiday (1936) **88m.** **½ D: Frank Tuttle. Jack Benny, George Burns, Gracie Allen, Mary Boland, Martha Raye, Marsha Hunt, Eleanore Whitney. Silly musicomedy about college types coming to bankrupt hotel where Boland is doing sex experiments.
College Humor (1933) **80m.** *** D: Wesley Ruggles. Bing Crosby, Jack Oakie, Burns and Allen, Richard Arlen, Mary Carlisle, Mary Kornman, Joseph Sauers (Sawyer). College was never like this. Hokey, entertaining rah-rah musical with Bing a professor (!), Arlen and Oakie football stars; Carlisle and Kornman provide love interest. Songs: "Learn to Croon," "Down the Old Ox Road," among others.
College Rhythm (1934) **75m.** **½ D: Norman Taurog. Jack Oakie, Joe Penner, Lanny Ross, Helen Mack, Lyda Roberti, Mary Brian, George Barbier, Franklin Pangborn, Dean Jagger. Brash Oakie, All-American football player and "cupid's gift to coeds," finds himself unemployed and humbled upon graduation; however, you know he will get to redeem himself. Silly but enjoyable musical/comedy/romance with Mack Gordon–Harry Revel songs. Penner and his duck are even tolerable here.
College Swing (1938) **86m.** *** D: Raoul Walsh. George Burns, Gracie Allen, Martha Raye, Bob Hope, Edward Everett Horton, Florence George, Ben Blue, Betty Grable, John Payne, Robert Cummings, Jerry Colonna. Gracie hasn't been able to graduate from school in this entertaining collegiate musicomedy with top cast, forgettable songs. Preston Sturges worked (uncredited) on the script.▼
Collision Course (1968) SEE: **Bamboo Saucer, The**
Collision Course (1987) **C-96m.** ** D: Lewis Teague. Jay Leno, Pat Morita, Chris Sarandon, Ernie Hudson, John Hancock, Al Waxman, Randall "Tex" Cobb, Soon-Teck Oh. Cops Morita (from Japan) and Leno (from Detroit) link up on a case. Harmless, occasionally funny, instantly forgettable buddy-movie. Leno's only starring role to date. [PG]▼●
Colonel Blimp SEE: **Life and Death of Colonel Blimp, The**
Colonel Chabert (1994-French) **C-110m.** **½ D: Yves Angelou. Gérard Depardieu, Fanny Ardant, Andre Dussollier, Fabrice Luchini, Daniel Prevost, Olivier Saladin, Claude Rich, Albert Delpy, Romane Bohringer, Julie Depardieu. Respectable costumer, adapted from a Balzac novel, about the belated return of an officer supposedly killed in the Napoleonic wars and the effect it has on his so-called widow (who's using his inheritance to boost husband no. 2's career). Well acted and well mounted, but the laundry put in extra starch; debuting director Angelou is the esteemed cinematographer of TOUT LES MATINS DU MONDE and UN COEUR EN HIVER. Julie Depardieu is the actor's daughter. ▼
Colonel Effingham's Raid (1945) **70m.** **½ D: Irving Pichel. Charles Coburn, Joan Bennett, William Eythe, Allyn Joslyn, Elizabeth Patterson, Donald Meek. Entertaining little comedy of ex-officer Coburn fighting to save town's historical landmark; cast supports fair material.▼
Colonel Redl (1985-German-Hungarian-Austrian) **C-149m.** *** D: Istvan Szabo. Klaus Maria Brandauer, Armin Muller-Stahl, Gudrun Landgrebe, Jan Niklas, Hans-

Christian Blech, Laszlo Mensaros, Andras Balint. Complex, fascinating account—inspired by John Osborne's *A Patriot for Me* as well as by actual historical evidence—of an ambitious, homosexual career soldier, whose ordinary family background does not hinder his rise to a position of high military rank in the Austro-Hungarian Empire prior to WW1. An incisive examination of the politics of power, highlighted by a superb Brandauer performance. Second in a trilogy, after MEPHISTO and followed by HANUSSEN. [R]▼●

Colorado Territory (1949) **94m.** *** D: Raoul Walsh. Joel McCrea, Virginia Mayo, Dorothy Malone, Henry Hull, John Archer, Frank Puglia. Strong, fast-moving Western with McCrea an outlaw on the lam; remake of director Walsh's HIGH SIERRA, later remade as I DIED A THOUSAND TIMES. Also shown in computer-colored version.

Color Me Dead (1969-U.S.-Australian) **C-97m.** ** D: Eddie Davis. Tom Tryon, Carolyn Jones, Rick Jason, Patricia Connolly, Tony Ward. Story of a slowly poisoned man spending his last days tracking down his own murderer was done better as D.O.A. in 1950. Aka D.O.A. II. [R]▼

Color of Money, The (1986) **C-119m.** *** D: Martin Scorsese. Paul Newman, Tom Cruise, Mary Elizabeth Mastrantonio, Helen Shaver, John Turturro, Bill Cobbs, Robert Agins, Forest Whitaker. Sharply made, nicely textured sequel to THE HUSTLER, with Newman's Fast Eddie Felson finding a younger, greener version of himself in small-time pool hotshot Cruise, whom he decides to promote for another shot at the big time. Hardboiled script by Richard Price, flashy direction by Scorsese, flamboyant camerawork by Michael Ballhaus, and top-notch performances by Cruise and especially Newman make this a must-see . . . though film's second half is protracted and disappointing, with a hoped-for climax that never occurs. Newman finally picked up an Academy Award for his fine work here. [R]▼●

Color of Night (1994) **C-125m.** BOMB D: Richard Rush. Bruce Willis, Jane March, Ruben Blades, Lesley Ann Warren, Scott Bakula, Brad Dourif, Lance Henriksen, Kevin J. O'Connor, Andrew Lowery, Eriq La Salle, Jeff Corey, Kathleen Wilhoite, Shirley Knight. Ludicrous thriller in which weirded-out therapist Willis (whose patient has just committed suicide before his eyes) heads to L.A. for a breather; he immediately finds himself immersed in a murder mystery, and involved with mysterious March. Much-publicized sex scenes aren't very sexy; this garnered hype for the editing of Willis' full frontal nudity to earn an R rating. Also on video in an "R-rated director's cut," with 17m. of extra footage, including more of Bruce-in-the-buff and some sexy scenes with Warren and March. Rush's first feature since THE STUNT MAN (1980). [R]▼●◗

Color Purple, The (1985) **C-152m.** ***½ D: Steven Spielberg. Danny Glover, Whoopi Goldberg, Margaret Avery, Oprah Winfrey, Willard Pugh, Akosua Busia, Desreta Jackson, Adolph Caesar, Rae Dawn Chong, Dana Ivey, Larry Fishburne. A black girl's life and hard times in the South, spanning some forty years: a sprawling saga of characters both frustrated and fulfilled, and at the center a Survivor. Spielberg's controversial interpretation of Alice Walker's Pulitzer Prize-winning book will either grab you emotionally (in which case you'll overlook its flaws) or leave you cold. Masterfully filmed from Menno Meyjes's script, with striking cinematography by Allen Daviau, moving music score by Quincy Jones (who also coproduced). Rich performances include screen debut for Winfrey. (Avery's singing was dubbed, by the way.) [PG-13]▼●◗

Colors (1988) **C-120m.** *** D: Dennis Hopper. Sean Penn, Robert Duvall, Maria Conchita Alonso, Randy Brooks, Grand Bush, Don Cheadle, Rudy Ramos, Trinidad Silva, Damon Wayans, Glenn Plummer. Penn and Duvall are well matched as street cops assigned to gang detail in L.A. Their conflicts and experiences play out against the backdrop of nihilistic gang life in this realistic if unexceptional slice of life. Only serious flaw: unbelievable and unnecessary subplot with female lead Alonso. Hopper's 127m. version, altered by the theatrical distributor, is available on video. [R]▼●

Colors Straight Up (1998) **C-95m.** *** D: Michele Ohayon. Heartfelt, powerful documentary about an L.A. inner-city after-school drama program that gives at-risk Black and Latino teens a chance to strut their stuff onstage. Simply and beautifully done, with some truly amazing young subjects at its center. One teacher tells the group they must learn to "function in disaster and finish with style," and they do exactly that. Guaranteed to move you to tears.▼

Colossus of New York, The (1958) **70m.** ** D: Eugene Lourie. John Baragrey, Mala Powers, Otto Kruger, Robert Hutton, Ross Martin. Doctor implants dead son's brain into oversized robot with predictable chaos.

Colossus of Rhodes, The (1960-Italian) **C-128m.** **½ D: Sergio Leone. Rory Calhoun, Lea Massari, Georges Marchal, Conrado Sanmartin, Angel Aranda, Mabel Karr. Big-budget sword-and-sandal spectacular about a slave revolt against the corrupt leaders of ancient Rhodes. Though Calhoun looks mighty uncomfortable in a toga and the dubbing is poor, Leone's directorial debut is notable for some well-staged battle scenes and impressive sets, including the title edifice. SuperTotalscope.

Colossus: The Forbin Project (1970) **C-100m.** *** D: Joseph Sargent. Eric Braeden, Susan Clark, Gordon Pinsent, William Schallert. Well-directed suspense thriller. Computer runs amok and uses its superior intelligence to sabotage man at every turn. Chilling and believable. Aka THE FORBIN PROJECT. Panavision.▼●

Colt .45 (1950) **C-74m.** **½ D: Edwin L. Marin. Randolph Scott, Zachary Scott, Ruth Roman, Lloyd Bridges, Chief Thundercloud. The renowned title gun is star of this sometimes action-filled Western. Retitled: THUNDERCLOUD.

Column South (1953) **C-85m.** ** D: Frederick de Cordova. Audie Murphy, Joan Evans, Robert Sterling, Ray Collins. OK mixture of Civil War and Indian fighting, as Union officer Murphy champions underdog Indians to prevent hostilities.

Coma (1978) **C-113m.** *** D: Michael Crichton. Genevieve Bujold, Michael Douglas, Elizabeth Ashley, Rip Torn, Richard Widmark, Lance LeGault, Lois Chiles. Someone is killing and stealing patients from a big-city hospital, and a woman doctor bucks male superiors to pursue her suspicions. Bujold and Widmark are well-matched adversaries in original suspenser that combines best of hospital pictures and mystery thrillers; scripted by director Crichton from Robin Cook's novel. Look for Tom Selleck as Murphy, Ed Harris as a pathology resident. [PG]▼●◗

Comanche (1956) **C-87m.** ** D: George Sherman. Dana Andrews, Kent Smith, Linda Cristal, Nestor Paiva, Henry Brandon. Andrews is staunch as Indian scout seeking to patch Indian-cavalry hostilities in this pat Western. CinemaScope.

Comancheros, The (1961) **C-107m.** *** D: Michael Curtiz. John Wayne, Stuart Whitman, Lee Marvin, Ina Balin, Bruce Cabot, Nehemiah Persoff. Well-paced actioner with Duke a Texas Ranger out to bring in gang supplying liquor and firearms to the Comanches. Curtiz' last film. CinemaScope.▼●

Comanche Station (1960) **C-74m.** **½ D: Budd Boetticher. Randolph Scott, Nancy Gates, Claude Akins, Skip Homeier, Richard Rust, Rand Brooks. Scott rescues a woman from Indian capture, then runs into an old nemesis who wants to turn her in himself—for a fat reward. Typically interesting Boetticher/Scott Western, with a Burt Kennedy script. CinemaScope.▼

Comanche Territory (1950) **C-76m.** **½ D: George Sherman. Maureen O'Hara, Macdonald Carey, Will Geer, Charles Drake, Pedro de Cordoba, James Best. So-so Western in which Jim Bowie (Carey) tangles with fiery bar owner O'Hara as he aids the Comanches, whose treaty with the U.S. government is about to expire.▼

Combat Squad (1953) **72m.** *½ D: Cy Roth. John Ireland, Lon McCallister, Hal March, Tris Coffin. Weak study of men in war; this time Korea.

Combination Platter (1993) **C-84m.** *** D: Tony Chan. Jeff Lau, Colleen O'Brien, Lester (Chit-Man) Chan, Colin Mitchell, Kenneth Lu. A young illegal immigrant from Hong Kong (Lau) toils in a Queens, N.Y., Chinese restaurant, and covets U.S. citizenship—but learns that this may mean having to marry an American, the thought of which staggers him. Hong Kong–born director-cowriter Chan, himself an immigrant, knowingly captures the experience of the foreigner in America. This marks the 23-year-old's directing debut.▼

Come and Get It (1936) **99m.** *** D: Howard Hawks, William Wyler. Edward Arnold, Joel McCrea, Frances Farmer, Walter Brennan, Andrea Leeds, Frank Shields, Mady Christians, Mary Nash. Arnold plays a self-made empire-builder who fights his way to the top in Wisconsin lumber business, sacrificing the one love of his life. Farmer has best screen showcase of her career, in dual role, as a saloon entertainer and (years later) her own daughter; Brennan won his first Best Supporting Actor Oscar playing Arnold's simple Swedish pal. Typically plotty, two-generation Edna Ferber saga. Reissued as ROARING TIMBER. ▼●◗

Come and See (1985-Russian) **C-142m.** ***½ D: Elem Klimov. Alexei Kravchenko, Olga Mironova, Lubomiras Lauciavicus. Thoroughly mesmerizing chronicle of the initiation of a young teen (impressively played by Kravchenko) into the horror and insanity of war, as the Nazis maraud through northwestern Russia in 1943. An extraordinary film about the need to maintain one's humanity and dignity no matter what the situation. Don't miss this one.▼

Comeback SEE: **Love Is Forever**

Comeback, The (1978-British) **C-100m.** BOMB D: Pete Walker. Jack Jones, Pamela Stephenson, David Doyle, Bill Owen, Sheila Keith, Richard Johnson. Gruesome story of American singer trying for showbiz comeback in England, drawn instead into a chain of gory murders. Aka THE DAY THE SCREAMING STOPPED and ENCORE (1978). ▼

Come Back, Charleston Blue (1972) **C-100m.** ** D: Mark Warren. Raymond St. Jacques, Godfrey Cambridge, Jonelle Allen, Adam Wade, Peter DeAnda. Further adventures of Gravedigger and Coffin on their Harlem police beat. Loads of violence, no comedy; not nearly as good as original, COTTON COMES TO HARLEM. Fine Donny Hathaway score. [PG]▼

Come Back, Little Sheba (1952) **99m.** ***½ D: Daniel Mann. Burt Lancaster,

Shirley Booth, Terry Moore, Richard Jaeckel, Philip Ober. William Inge play is emotional tour de force for Booth (who won an Oscar recreating her Tony Award–winning stage role) as slovenly housewife coping with drunken ex-chiropractor husband (Lancaster) and boarder Moore, whose curiosity about her landlords sets drama in motion. Screenplay by Ketti Frings. ▼●

Come Back to the 5 & Dime Jimmy Dean, Jimmy Dean (1982) **C-110m.** ★★½ D: Robert Altman. Sandy Dennis, Cher, Karen Black, Sudie Bond, Kathy Bates, Marta Heflin. Girlfriends hold twenty-year reunion of a James Dean fan club they formed when he was filming GIANT in a nearby Texas town; the get-together becomes an occasion for personal and painful revelations. Strong performances, and Altman's lively approach to filming Ed Graczyk's Broadway play, can't completely hide the fact that this is second-rate material. Cher's first film since CHASTITY in 1969. [PG]▼●

Comeback Trail, The (1974) **C-80m.** ★½ D: Harry Hurwitz. Chuck McCann, Buster Crabbe, Robert Staats, Ina Balin, Jara Kahout. Two-bit movie czar McCann stars faded cowboy hero Crabbe in a film, hoping the resulting disaster will salvage his studio. Dismal comedy, with occasional film buff in-jokes, and guest appearances by Henny Youngman, Irwin Corey, Hugh Hefner, Joe Franklin, and Monte Rock III. Never released theatrically.

Come Blow Your Horn (1963) **C-112m.** ★★★ D: Bud Yorkin. Frank Sinatra, Lee J. Cobb, Molly Picon, Barbara Rush, Jill St. John, Tony Bill. Sinatra is good as a free-swinging bachelor with wall-to-wall girls and a nagging father (Cobb). He also sings the title song, and teaches kid brother (Bill) the ropes. From Neil Simon play. Panavision.▼

Come Dance With Me! (1959-French) **C-91m.** ★★½ D: Michel Boisrond. Brigitte Bardot, Henri Vidal, Dawn Addams, Noel Roquevert, Dario Moreno, Philippe Nicaud, Serge Gainsbourg. Sometimes amusing mystery-comedy with Bardot a pert dentist's wife who plays detective when her husband is suspected of murder. Video title: DO YOU WANT TO DANCE WITH ME?▼◗

Comedians, The (1967) **C-148m.** ★★½ D: Peter Glenville. Elizabeth Taylor, Richard Burton, Alec Guinness, Peter Ustinov, Paul Ford, Lillian Gish, Raymond St. Jacques, Zakes Mokae, Roscoe Lee Browne, Gloria Foster, Georg Stanford Brown, James Earl Jones, Cicely Tyson. Excellent cast in uninspired adaptation of Graham Greene's novel about political intrigue in Haiti, although film is more interesting today, since the departure of Duvalier. Beware 130m. prints. Panavision.▼

Comedy of Terrors, The (1963) **C-84m.** ★★½ D: Jacques Tourneur. Vincent Price, Peter Lorre, Boris Karloff, Basil Rathbone, Joe E. Brown, Joyce Jameson. Medium horror spoof with undertaker Price trying to hasten customers' demise, "helped" by bumbling assistant Lorre. Great cast; Richard Matheson wrote the screenplay. Panavision.▼●

Come Fill the Cup (1951) **113m.** ★★½ D: Gordon Douglas. James Cagney, Phyllis Thaxter, Raymond Massey, James Gleason, Gig Young. Cagney is quite restrained as ex-newspaperman seeking to conquer alcoholism. Fine performance by Gleason as helpful ex-drunk and by Young as drunken playboy.

Come Fly With Me (1963) **C-109m.** ★★½ D: Henry Levin. Hugh O'Brian, Pamela Tiffin, Dolores Hart, Karl Boehm, Lois Nettleton, Karl Malden. Flighty fluff of three stewardesses trying to catch husbands, becoming involved with three men on a trans-Atlantic flight. Glossy, easy to take. Panavision.

Come Live With Me (1941) **86m.** ★★★ D: Clarence Brown. James Stewart, Hedy Lamarr, Ian Hunter, Verree Teasdale, Donald Meek, Barton MacLane, Adeline de Walt Reynolds. Charming romantic comedy with starving writer Stewart marrying Lamarr so she won't be deported. Strong supporting cast, with Reynolds fine as Stewart's grandmother.

Come Next Spring (1956) **C-92m.** ★★★ D: R. G. Springsteen. Ann Sheridan, Steve Cochran, Walter Brennan, Sherry Jackson, Richard Eyer, Edgar Buchanan, Sonny Tufts, Mae Clarke, Roscoe Ates, James Best. Charming slice of Americana, set in 1920s Arkansas. Cochran walked out on his wife and kids nine years ago; now he returns, cold sober and determined to make good (and try to make up for his past transgressions). Appealing performances and a nice feel for the material distinguish this modest film, which Cochran also produced.

Come 'n' Get It SEE: **Lunch Wagon**

Come-On, The (1956) **83m.** ★★ D: Russell Birdwell. Anne Baxter, Sterling Hayden, John Hoyt, Jesse White. Baxter is dramatically fine as unscrupulous con woman involved with murder, but the story is hackneyed. SuperScope.

Come Out Fighting (1945) **62m.** ★½ D: William Beaudine. Leo Gorcey, Huntz Hall, Billy Benedict, Gabriel Dell, Mende Koenig, Bud Gorman, Johnny Duncan, Amelita Ward, June Carlson. The police commissioner asks the East Side Kids to toughen up his wimpy son in this grating entry. Last in the series before it was revamped and rechristened *The Bowery Boys.*

Comes a Horseman (1978) **C-118m.** ★★½ D: Alan J. Pakula. Jane Fonda, James Caan, Jason Robards, George Grizzard,

Richard Farnsworth, Jim Davis, Mark Harmon. Starkly simple Western story (set in 1940s) about rival ranch owners whose roots are in the land. Low-key to the point of catatonia, but offers some beautiful tableaux and moving scenes. Panavision. [PG]▼●

Come See The Paradise (1990) **C-138m.** ** D: Alan Parker. Dennis Quaid, Tamlyn Tomita, Sab Shimono, Shizuko Hoshi, Stan Egi, Ronald Yamamoto, Akemi Nishino, Naomi Nakano, Brady Tsurutani, Pruitt Taylor Vince. Hotheaded union organizer Quaid falls in love with Tomita in L.A.'s Little Tokyo in the late 1930s; after the bombing of Pearl Harbor, he is separated from his wife and family when they are sent to a Japanese internment camp. Curiously aloof and unmoving story fashioned around one of the bleaker chapters of American history; should have been much stronger. Written by director Parker. [R]▼●

Come September (1961) **C-112m.** *** D: Robert Mulligan. Rock Hudson, Gina Lollobrigida, Sandra Dee, Bobby Darin, Walter Slezak, Joel Grey. Frothy comedy about the younger generation (Darin and Dee) vs. the "older" folks (Hudson and Lollobrigida) at an Italian villa. Good fun, with some dated Darin vocals. CinemaScope.▼

Come Spy With Me (1967) **C-85m.** *½ D: Marshall Stone. Troy Donahue, Andrea Dromm, Albert Dekker, Mart Hulswit, Valerie Allen, Dan Ferrone. Except for those who want to tell their friends they actually saw a film called COME SPY WITH ME starring Troy Donahue, this secret-agent film about blond Dromm's attempts to solve murders of two Americans in the Caribbean isn't worth anyone's time. Smokey Robinson sings the title song!

Come to the Stable (1949) **94m.** *** D: Henry Koster. Loretta Young, Celeste Holm, Hugh Marlowe, Elsa Lanchester, Regis Toomey, Mike Mazurki. Young and Holm register well as French nuns living in New England, seeking aid from a variety of local characters in building a children's dispensary. Warm, sentimental comedy-drama. Story by Clare Boothe Luce. ▼

Comet Over Broadway (1938) **69m.** *½ D: Busby Berkeley. Kay Francis, Ian Hunter, John Litel, Donald Crisp, Minna Gombell, Melville Cooper. Sappy, dated soap opera tells risible story of stage star Francis and the tragedy caused by her burning ambition. Not even a musical number to save it.

Comfort and Joy (1984-British) **C-105m.** *** D: Bill Forsyth. Bill Paterson, Eleanor David, C. P. Grogan, Alex Norton, Patrick Malahide, Rikki Fulton, Roberto Bernardi. Another quirky comedy from writer-director Forsyth (GREGORY'S GIRL, LOCAL HERO), though this one isn't as potent or consistent. Paterson plays a popular Scottish disc jockey who's going through some difficult changes in his personal life, then finds himself caught between two underworld families fighting for territorial rights to ice-cream vans! Entertaining and offbeat, though never as on-target as one might like it to be; Paterson is a delight. [PG]▼

Comfort of Strangers, The (1991-Italian-U.S.) **C-105m.** *½ D: Paul Schrader. Christopher Walken, Natasha Richardson, Rupert Everett, Helen Mirren. Unmarried couple is befriended by a mysterious local while vacationing in Venice. Shaggy-dog lead-up to an "oh, come on" finale. As murky as canal sewage, offering sharply contrasting male acting styles: Everett is a posturing male mannequin, while Walken is a titan of twitch. Screenplay by Harold Pinter, from Ian McEwan's novel. [R]▼●

Comic, The (1969) **C-94m.** **½ D: Carl Reiner. Dick Van Dyke, Michele Lee, Mickey Rooney, Cornel Wilde, Nina Wayne, Pert Kelton, Steve Allen, Carl Reiner, Jeannine Riley. Sincere seriocomedy about a silent-movie clown with a destructive ego. Artificial trappings surround truthful portrait (a composite of several real comics) by Van Dyke. Best of all: vivid recreations of silent comedies. Uneven; of interest mainly to film buffs. [M/PG]▼●

Comic Book Confidential (1989-U.S.-Canadian) **C-90m.** *** D: Ron Mann. R. Crumb, Will Eisner, Jack Kirby, William M. Gaines, Harvey Kurtzman, Stan Lee, Harvey Pekar, Lynda Barry, Frank Miller. Good introduction to the genuine art to be found in comic books, featuring interviews with many of the top talents of yesterday and today. Marred by too much effort to be "cinematic"; also demonstrates a bias against standard commercial comics.▼●

Comin At Ya! (1981-Italian) **C-91m.** BOMB D: Ferdinando Baldi. Tony Anthony, Gene Quintano, Victoria Abril, Ricardo Palacios, Gordon Lewis. 3-D spaghetti Western take-off features rats, bats, and blood, all hugged to death by the camera (and often in slow motion!). No redeeming sense of humor, either. It's films like this that killed 3-D the first time around. Dimensionscope. [R]

Coming Apart (1969) **110m.** *½ D: Milton Moses Ginsberg. Rip Torn, Viveca Lindfors, Megan McCormick, Lois Markle, Sally Kirkland. Fascinatingly bad drama about psychiatrist who sets up concealed movie camera in his apartment to record the messed-up lives of himself and women who visit him. Kirkland's most substantial screen role prior to ANNA in 1987.▼

Coming Attractions SEE: **Loose Shoes**

Coming Home (1978) **C-127m.** ***½ D: Hal Ashby. Jane Fonda, Jon Voight, Bruce Dern, Robert Carradine, Robert Ginty, Penelope Milford, David Clennon. Powerful look at the effect of Vietnam war on people at home. Fonda falls in love with paraplegic Voight while her husband (Dern) is overseas. Mature, gripping film, marred only by lapses into melodrama. Academy Awards went to Fonda, Voight, and writers Waldo Salt, Robert C. Jones, and Nancy Dowd. [R]▼●

Coming-Out Party (1934) **79m.** *½ D: John G. Blystone. Frances Dee, Gene Raymond, Alison Skipworth, Nigel Bruce, Harry Green. Tired tale of young socialite Dee in love with jazz musician, fighting her mother's ambitions for her to marry within social class.

Coming-Out Party (1961-British) **100m.** **½ D: Ken Annakin. James Robertson Justice, Leslie Phillips, Stanley Baxter, Eric Sykes, Richard Wattis. P.O.W. comedy with prisoner Baxter impersonating lookalike Nazi commandant to help peevish scientist Justice escape camp. Original title: VERY IMPORTANT PERSON.

Coming Out Under Fire (1994) **C/B&W-71m.** *** D: Arthur Dong. Narrated by Salome Jens. A tough ex-Marine, a WAC, a black, a heavily Dixie-toned Southerner, and a N.Y. Jew are among those who recall what it was like to be very, very quietly gay during WW2 and, in the most abjectly humiliating cases, to be mustered out of the service upon detection. A fresh and contemporary documentary despite recalling events that took place half a century earlier; in a clip from one of the era's official army sex education films, 1950s song-and-dance man Keefe Brasselle plays a G.I. with condoms on his mind.▼

Coming Through (1985-British) **C-80m.** ** D: Peter Barber-Fleming. Kenneth Branagh, Helen Mirren, Alison Steadman, Philip Martin Brown, Norman Rodway. Static tale of young D. H. Lawrence (Branagh), and his relationship with Frieda von Richthofen (Mirren), awkwardly paralleled with present-day story of young man who completely misses the point of Lawrence's writing. Sorely lacking the author's own fire and intensity.▼

Coming to America (1988) **C-116m.** *** D: John Landis. Eddie Murphy, Arsenio Hall, James Earl Jones, John Amos, Madge Sinclair, Shari Headley, Paul Bates, Allison Dean, Eriq La Salle, Louie Anderson, Calvin Lockhart, Samuel L. Jackson, Cuba Gooding, Jr., Vanessa Bell (Calloway), Frankie Faison, Vondie Curtis-Hall. Cute change-of-pace film for Murphy, as the genteel prince of an African royal family who wants to choose his own wife, and decides that he will find her in America. Old-fashioned romantic comedy peppered with director Landis' in-jokes (including an update of TRADING PLACES, in which Murphy starred) and some surprise cameos. Subsequent litigation awarded columnist Art Buchwald with original story credit. [R]▼●◗

Coming Up Roses (1986-British) **C-93m.** ** D: Stephen Bayly. Dafydd Hywel, Iola Gregory, Olive Michael, Mari Emlyn. Whimsical Welsh-language comedy concerns a group of townsfolk who band together to save a local cinema by growing mushrooms in the darkness of the empty theatre. Cute, but lacks the wit and sharp ensemble acting of the hilarious British comedies of the 1940s and 1950s. [PG]▼

Comin' Round the Mountain (1951) **77m.** *½ D: Charles Lamont. Bud Abbott, Lou Costello, Dorothy Shay, Kirby Grant, Joe Sawyer, Glenn Strange. Bud and Lou invade hillbilly country in this substandard comedy, with far too much footage of singing Shay.▼

Command, The (1954) **C-88m.** ** D: David Butler. Guy Madison, Joan Weldon, James Whitmore, Carl Benton Reid. Madison unflinchingly copes with smallpox epidemic and rampaging Indians as he leads troops and civilians through Wyoming. Filmed (but not released) in 3-D. CinemaScope.

Command Decision (1948) **112m.** ***½ D: Sam Wood. Clark Gable, Walter Pidgeon, Van Johnson, Brian Donlevy, Charles Bickford, John Hodiak, Edward Arnold, Marshall Thompson, Richard Quine, Cameron Mitchell, John McIntire. Taut, engrossing adaptation of the William Wister Haines stage hit, with Gable a Flight Commander who knows that, to win the war, he must send his men on suicide missions over Germany. Intriguing look at behind-the-scenes politics of the U.S. war effort. Screenplay by William Laidlaw and George Froeshel. Also shown in computer-colored version.▼●

Commandments (1997) **C-86m.** ** D: Daniel Taplitz. Aidan Quinn, Courteney Cox, Anthony LaPaglia, Louis Zorich, Pamela Gray, Pat McNamara, Tom Aldredge, Alice Drummond, Jack Gilpin. When a man's life hits rock bottom he decides to test the whole concept of spirituality by breaking each of the Ten Commandments. Uneven black comedy shifts in tone from light to dark, losing its meaning along the way. Quinn is effective, but this must have looked a lot better on paper. [R]▼

Commando (1964-Italian) **90m.** **½ D: Frank Wisbar. Stewart Granger, Dorian Gray, Fausto Tozzi, Carlos Casaravilla. Granger leads mission to rescue Algerian rebel leader, later learning ironic political significance. Satisfactory actioner.

Commando (1985) **C-88m.** ** D: Mark L. Lester. Arnold Schwarzenegger, Rae Dawn Chong, Dan Hedaya, Vernon Wells, David Patrick Kelly, Alyssa Milano, James Olson, Bill Duke, Bill Paxton. Exceptionally noisy comic-book yarn about retired special agent Schwarzenegger, who's forced to go back into action when vengeful goons kidnap his daughter. Film's sense of humor (courtesy scripter Steven E. de Souza) is largely obliterated by all the noise and mindless violence. [R]▼●◗

Commandos (1968-Italian-German) **C-89m.** ** D: Armando Crispino. Lee Van Cleef, Jack Kelly, Giampiero Albertini, Marino Masé, Pierre Paulo Capponi, Duilio Del Prete. Cliché-filled war drama with familiar plot; Italian commandos, led by a couple of stalwart Americans, must secure an important oasis in North African desert in advance of Allied landings. Cromoscope. [PG]▼

Commando Squad (1987) **C-89m.** BOMB D: Fred Olen Ray. Brian Thompson, Kathy Shower, William Smith, Sid Haig, Ross Hagen, Robert Quarry, Mel Welles. Thompson and Shower (former *Playboy* Playmate of the Year) are government agents sent to Mexico to wipe out Smith's cocaine factory. Tiresome film features numerous screen veterans, including Marie Windsor and Russ Tamblyn. [R]▼

Commandos Strike at Dawn (1942) **96m.** **½ D: John Farrow. Paul Muni, Anna Lee, Lillian Gish, Cedric Hardwicke, Robert Coote, Ray Collins, Rosemary DeCamp, Alexander Knox. Well-intentioned drama of Norwegian Muni aiding British commandos in attack on Nazis who have invaded Norway. Dated propaganda angle lessens impact today.▼

Commitments, The (1991-British-Irish) **C-117m.** ***½ D: Alan Parker. Robert Arkins, Michael Aherne, Angeline Ball, Maria Doyle, Dave Finnegan, Bronagh Gallagher, Félim Gormley, Glen Hansard, Dick Massey, Johnny Murphy, Kenneth McCluskey, Andrew Strong, Colm Meaney. Enormously satisfying tale of an ambitious young Dubliner who takes on the challenge of assembling and managing a band made up of other working-class Dubliners who sing '60s-style soul music! Disarmingly engaging from the word go, with charismatic cast of unknowns; filled with irresistible music. A real treat. Written by Dick Clement, Ian La Frenais, and Roddy Doyle; the first of Doyle's Barrytown trilogy, followed by THE SNAPPER and THE VAN. [R] ▼●◗

Committed (2000) **C-98m.** ** D: Lisa Krueger. Heather Graham, Casey Affleck, Luke Wilson, Goran Visnjic, Alfonso Arau, Patricia Velazquez, Mark Ruffalo, Clea DuVall, Summer Phoenix, Mary Kay Place, Art Alexakis, Jon Stewart, Dylan Baker, Carlin Glynn. Young N.Y.C. club manager believes in commitment at work and in her marriage (though she's surrounded by slacker friends), so she's thrown for a loop when her husband (Wilson) bolts to "find himself." Graham is the whole show here, but she's stuck in a lightweight road-movie/culture-clash tale. If this is screwball romance for the new millennium, we're in trouble. [R]▼◗

Common Threads: Stories From the Quilt (1989) **C/B&W-75m.** *** D: Robert Epstein, Jeffrey Friedman. Narrated by Dustin Hoffman. Compassionate documentary focusing on five individuals afflicted with AIDS: a former Olympic athlete, a retired U.S. Navy commander, an 11-year-old hemophiliac, a N.Y. writer and gay activist, and an I.V. drug user. Title refers to AIDS Memorial Quilt, consisting of thousands of panels, each dedicated to an AIDS victim. Produced by HBO; a worthy Best Documentary Academy Award winner.▼●

Communion (1977) SEE: **Holy Terror**

Communion (1989) **C-107m.** **½ D: Philippe Mora. Christopher Walken, Lindsay Crouse, Frances Sternhagen, Andreas Katsulas, Terri Hanauer, Joel Carlson, Basil Hoffman. Psychological thriller with Walken well cast as writer Whitley Strieber, who finds himself visited by strange creatures. Does he need a psychiatrist or an exorcist? A bit overlong, and the dramatic scenes between Walken and wife Crouse don't quite work, but still effectively scary while never gratuitously gory. Strieber adapted his own best-selling book, which he claims is true. Super 35. [R]▼●

Companeros! (1971-Italian-Spanish-German) **C-105m.** ** D: Sergio Corbucci. Franco Nero, Tomas Milian, Jack Palance, Fernando Rey, Iris Berben, Karin Schubert. Swedish mercenary (Nero) seeks his fortune by running guns in revolution-racked Mexico at the turn of the century. Violent western fare. Techniscope. [R]▼

Company Business (1991) **C-98m.** *½ D: Nicholas Meyer. Gene Hackman, Mikhail Baryshnikov, Kurtwood Smith, Terry O'Quinn, Daniel Von Bargen, Oleg Rudnick, Geraldine Danon. When a planned spy swap comes unglued, two aging agents (one CIA, one KGB) become unlikely allies as the old cold-war espionage rules they once lived by melt away. Interesting premise goes awry in this dumb spy comedy. [PG-13]▼●

Company of Killers (1970) **C-88m.** ** D: Jerry Thorpe. Van Johnson, Ray Milland, John Saxon, Brian Kelly, Fritz Weaver, Clu Gulager, Susan Oliver, Diana Lynn, Robert Middleton. Gunman (Saxon) working for Murder, Inc. becomes target for his employers and big city police department after patrolman is shot down. Bites off more than it can chew. Video title: THE HIT TEAM. [G]▼

Company of Wolves, The (1984-British) **C-95m.** ** D: Neil Jordan. Angela Lansbury, David Warner, Stephen Rea, Tusse Silberg, Sarah Patterson, Graham Crowden. Freudian, adult version of "Little Red Riding Hood," based on the premise that a wolf may not be what he seems. Intriguing idea mired in murky presentation, encompassing several different stories; strange, slow, and unsatisfying. [R]▼●

Company She Keeps, The (1950) **83m.** **½ D: John Cromwell. Lizabeth Scott, Jane Greer, Dennis O'Keefe, Fay Baker, John Hoyt, Don Beddoe. Satisfactory tale of ex-con Greer, who's determined to go straight. She yearns for companionship and makes a play for O'Keefe, the boyfriend of her parole officer (Scott). Produced by John Houseman. Jeff Bridges' screen debut; he's the baby in Greer's arms.

Competition, The (1980) **C-129m.** *** D: Joel Oliansky. Richard Dreyfuss, Amy Irving, Lee Remick, Sam Wanamaker, Joseph Cali, Ty Henderson, Priscilla Pointer, James B. Sikking. Two young pianists, competing for the same prize, fall in love. Nothing much more than that, but smoothly done, with some excellent piano "faking." Screenwriter Oliansky's directing debut. [PG]▼●

Compleat Beatles, The (1982) **C-120m.** *** D: Patrick Montgomery. Narrated by Malcolm McDowell. Absorbing chronicle of The Beatles and how they reflected (and often triggered) changes in society in the 1960s and '70s. Filled with great Beatles songs, on the soundtrack and in performance. Intensely nostalgic and bittersweet for anyone who lived through that time. Produced for home video. ▼●

Compromising Positions (1985) **C-98m.** **½ D: Frank Perry. Susan Sarandon, Raul Julia, Edward Herrmann, Judith Ivey, Mary Beth Hurt, Joe Mantegna, Josh Mostel, Anne De Salvo, Joan Allen. Long Island housewife becomes fascinated with the murder of a local dentist who (it turns out) was also an incredible womanizer. When it sticks to black comedy, the film is sharp and funny, but its other elements (male chauvinism, mystery, romance) don't pan out. Ivey has scene-stealing role as Sarandon's acid-tongued best friend. Screenplay by Susan Isaacs, from her novel. [R]▼●

Compulsion (1959) **103m.** ***½ D: Richard Fleischer. Orson Welles, Diane Varsi, Dean Stockwell, Bradford Dillman, E.G. Marshall, Martin Milner. Hard-hitting version of Leopold-Loeb thrill murder case of 1920s Chicago. Good characterizations, period decor, and well-edited courtroom scenes. Story also told in earlier ROPE and later SWOON. CinemaScope.▼●

Computer Wore Tennis Shoes, The (1970) **C-91m.** ** D: Robert Butler. Kurt Russell, Cesar Romero, Joe Flynn, William Schallert, Alan Hewitt, Richard Bakalyan. The first of Disney's carbon-copy comedies with young Russell as the college whiz injected with a computer-brain, which poses threat to local gangster Romero. Standard slapstick. Followed by NOW YOU SEE HIM, NOW YOU DON'T. Remade as a TVM in 1995. [G]▼

Comrades of Summer, The (1992) **C-110m. TVM** D: Tommy Lee Wallace. Joe Mantegna, Natalya Negoda, Mark Rolston, John Fleck, Eric Allan Kramer, Ian Tracey, Michael Lerner. Winning baseball comedy has arrogant but newly fired big league manager finding himself whipping a gaggle of Russian athletes (not a ballplayer among them) into diamond contention for the summer Olympics back in the States. Trenchant Robert Rodat script and loopy Mantegna portrayal knock this saga—partially filmed in Moscow—over the fence. Made for cable. Above average.▼●

Comrade X (1940) **90m.** **½ D: King Vidor. Clark Gable, Hedy Lamarr, Felix Bressart, Oscar Homolka, Eve Arden, Sig Ruman. NINOTCHKA-esque plot with American Gable warming up icy Russian Lamarr (a streetcar conductor). Synthetic romance tale never convinces; Bressart has great closing line, though.▼

Conagher (1991) **C-100m. TVM** D: Reynaldo Villalobos. Sam Elliott, Katharine Ross, Barry Corbin, Billy Green Bush, Ken Curtis, Buck Taylor, Dub Taylor, Daniel Quinn, Anndi McAfee. Beautifully realized Louis L'Amour Western (adapted by Elliott and Ross, along with Jeffrey M. Meyer) with Sam a weathered cowpoke who stops off to help Katharine, the lonely frontier woman running a stagecoach waystop while waiting in vain for her husband to return from a cattle-buying expedition. And then the Indians attack. Poetic directing debut by ace cinematographer Villalobos. Made for cable. Above average.▼●

Con Air (1997) **C-115m.** ** D: Simon West. Nicolas Cage, John Cusack, John Malkovich, Steve Buscemi, Ving Rhames, Colm Meaney, Mykelti Williamson, Rachel Ticotin, Nick Chinlund, M. C. Gainey, Brendan Kelly, Danny Trejo, Dave Chappelle. Megastupid megamovie about a federal marshals' plane carrying a cargo of heinous criminals—and a handful of parolees, including Cage, who was unfairly imprisoned in the first place. Once the plane is aloft, the bad guys quickly foil security and take over. Good actors can only do so much with a script this dumb, and dozens of explosions and stunts don't make enough of a difference. Panavision. [R]▼●◗

Conan the Barbarian (1982) **C-129m.** **½ D: John Milius. Arnold Schwarzenegger, Sandahl Bergman, James Earl Jones, Gerry Lopez, Mako, Ben Davidson, Sven Ole Thorsen, Max von Sydow, Valerie Quennessen, Cassandra Gaviola, William Smith. The sword-wielding warrior seeks vengeance on the cult leader who enslaved him and massacred his village in this full-blooded (and bloody) adventure epic based on Robert E. Howard's pulp tales. Ron Cobb's spectacular production design and

Basil Poledouris' vibrant score help make this superior to the many low-grade imitations it spawned. Written by Milius and Oliver Stone. Also shown at 115m. and 123m. Sequel: CONAN THE DESTROYER. Todd-AO 35. [R]▼●◗

Conan the Destroyer (1984) **C-103m.** *½ D: Richard Fleischer. Arnold Schwarzenegger, Grace Jones, Wilt Chamberlain, Mako, Tracey Walter, Sarah Douglas, Olivia D'Abo. Lumbering attempt to pit Robert E. Howard's Hyborian Age hero against very derivative special effects—leading to ridiculous climax. J-D-C Scope. [PG]▼●◗

Con Artists, The (1977-Italian) **C-87m.** ** D: Sergio Corbucci. Anthony Quinn, Corinne Clery, Capucine, Adriano Celentano. Con man Quinn, recently sprung from prison, and his protégé Celentano, try to outwit the deadly Capucine. THE STING it ain't. Aka BLUFF and THE SWITCH. ▼◗

Conceiving Ada (1999) **C-85m.** ** D: Lynn Hershman Leeson. Tilda Swinton, Timothy Leary, Karen Black, Francesca Faridany, John O'Keefe, J. D. Wolfe. Clichéd fantasy that contrasts the lives of Emmy (Faridany), a contemporary computer genius, and Ada Byron King (Swinton), the daughter of Lord Byron, who in the mid–19th century helped conceive the Analytic Engine, the forerunner of the computer. Using some digital instruments she has invented, Emmy reconstructs Ada's life and determines to communicate with her. Premise is intriguing, but result is obvious and far too preachy. ▼◗

Concorde, The—Airport '79 (1979) **C-123m.** BOMB D: David Lowell Rich. Alain Delon, Susan Blakely, Robert Wagner, Sylvia Kristel, George Kennedy, Eddie Albert, Bibi Andersson, John Davidson, Andrea Marcovicci, Martha Raye, Cicely Tyson, Jimmie Walker, David Warner, Mercedes McCambridge. Wagner is a brilliant scientist, Kennedy and Andersson make love by the fire, Davidson's hair stays in place when the plane turns upside down, and McCambridge is a Russian gymnastics coach. Thank goodness Charo is around for credibility. Aka AIRPORT '79. Nineteen minutes of footage was added for network TV. [PG]▼

Concrete Jungle, The (1960-British) **86m.** *** D: Joseph Losey. Stanley Baker, Margit Saad, Sam Wanamaker, Gregoire Aslan, Jill Bennett, Laurence Naismith, Edward Judd, Patrick Magee. Baker shines in this intense, stunningly directed account of a criminal who must contend with jailer Magee and, most tellingly, hood Wanamaker (with whom he robs a racetrack). More than just a crime drama, it's a story of how greed and lust for money can result in alienation, and the destruction of the spirit. Original title: THE CRIMINAL, released at 97m.

Concrete Jungle, The (1982) **C-99m.** *½ D: Tom DeSimone. Jill St. John, Tracy Bregman, Barbara Luna, Peter Brown, Aimee Eccles, Nita Talbot, Sondra Currie. Bregman's heel boyfriend gets her wrongly busted for drugs, leading to standard women's prison melodrama with St. John the kind of movie warden who is given glasses to show how uptight she is. Luna's performance as a hard-bitten prison vet is a cut above the others'. Followed by CHAINED HEAT. [R]▼

Condemned (1929) **86m.** ** D: Wesley Ruggles. Ronald Colman, Ann Harding, Louis Wolheim, Dudley Digges, William Elmer. Suave thief Colman is sent to Devil's Island, where he becomes romantically involved with the wife of sadistic warden Digges. Stiff early-talkie melodrama, which attempts to depict social evils of the infamous penal colony. Scripted by Sidney Howard.

Condemned of Altona, The (1962-Italian) **114m.** **½ D: Vittorio De Sica. Sophia Loren, Fredric March, Robert Wagner, Maximilian Schell, Francoise Prevost. Sluggish pseudo-intellectual version of Jean-Paul Sartre play about post-WW2 Germany involving dying magnate (March), his two sons—one a playboy (Wagner) with an actress wife (Loren); the other an insane Nazi war criminal (Schell). CinemaScope.

Condemned Women (1938) **77m.** **½ D: Lew Landers. Louis Hayward, Anne Shirley, Sally Eilers, Esther Dale, Lee Patrick, Leona Roberts, George Irving. Blunt little women-in-prison drama, a precursor of CAGED, with embittered prisoner Eilers becoming romantically linked to penitentiary psychiatrist Hayward. There's a ruthless matron, a naive inmate who's taken the rap for her boyfriend, a prison break. . . .

Condition Red (1995-U.S.-Finnish) **C-86m.** ** D: Mika Kaurismaki. James Russo, Cynda Williams, Paul Calderon, Victor Argo, Dierdre Lewis. Grittily realistic but ever-so-obvious thriller in which alienated, deeply troubled prison guard Russo becomes involved in a volatile sexual relationship with tough convict Williams, a singer doing jail time to protect her slimy boyfriend. Too many lapses in logic, though the performances are fine. [R]▼

Condorman (1981-British) **C-90m.** ** D: Charles Jarrott. Michael Crawford, Oliver Reed, James Hampton, Barbara Carrera, Jean-Pierre Kalfon, Dana Elcar. Cartoonist Crawford is transformed into Condorman, a comic book superhero who assists Soviet spy Carrera in her efforts to defect. Silly Disney film for only the most undiscriminating children. Panavision. [PG]▼◗

Conductor, The SEE: **Orchestra Conductor, The**

Conduct Unbecoming (1975-British) **C-107m.** **½ D: Michael Anderson. Michael York, Richard Attenborough, Trevor Howard, Stacy Keach, Susannah York, Christopher Plummer. Quaintly old-fashioned drama of honor and outrage among the Bengal Lancers, where an officer's widow (York) is sexually attacked. Too stuffy to be fun, yet too modern in other ways to be an antique; star performances are saving grace. [PG]▼

Coneheads (1993) **C-88m.** *** D: Steve Barron. Dan Aykroyd, Jane Curtin, Michelle Burke, Michael McKean, Jason Alexander, Lisa Jane Persky, Chris Farley, David Spade, Phil Hartman, Dave Thomas, Sinbad, Jan Hooks, Michael Richards, Jon Lovitz, Kevin Nealon, Adam Sandler, Garrett Morris, Laraine Newman, Tim Meadows, Julia Sweeney, Ellen DeGeneres, Parker Posey, Joey Lauren Adams. Unexpectedly benign (and good-natured) comedy based on the 1970s *Saturday Night Live* skits. The Coneheads (from the planet Remulak) land on earth in a botched mission and, to their own surprise, adapt to middle-class suburban life. A most enjoyable family film that combines silliness with some sly and unexpected gags. Amusing cameos by a gaggle of past and present *SNL* cast members. Watch for Drew Carey in a taxi. Aykroyd also cowrote the film. [PG]▼●

Coney Island (1943) **C-96m.** *** D: Walter Lang. Betty Grable, George Montgomery, Cesar Romero, Charles Winninger, Phil Silvers, Matt Briggs. Breezy, enjoyable turn-of-the-century musical of saloon entertainer Grable turned into famous musical star by hustling Montgomery. Remade with Grable seven years later as WABASH AVENUE.

Confess, Dr. Corda (1958-German) **81m.** ** D: Josef von Baky. Hardy Kruger, Elisabeth Mueller, Lucie Mannheim, Hans Nielsen. Tedious handling of story of Kruger circumstantially involved in death of his mistress, with his attempt to prove innocence at trial.

Confession (1937) **86m.** *** D: Joe May. Kay Francis, Basil Rathbone, Ian Hunter, Donald Crisp, Jane Bryan, Dorothy Peterson, Laura Hope Crews, Veda Ann Borg, Robert Barrat. Extremely stylish, well-acted soap opera in the MADAME X vein, with singer Francis recounting events leading up to her murder of oily Rathbone. Visually arresting, this looks more like a 1920s German film than a late 1930s Hollywood product; in fact, director May was a German émigré. Based very closely on the 1935 German film MAZURKA (which starred Pola Negri).

Confession, The (1970) **C-138m.** **½ D: Costa-Gavras. Yves Montand, Simone Signoret, Gabriele Ferzetti, Michel Vitold, Jean Bouise. True story of Czechoslovakian Communist Arthur London and his unjustified 1951 purge trial for treason; interesting tale well acted by Montand, but film is as talky and overrated as many of Costa-Gavras' other efforts. [PG]

Confessional, The (1975-British) **C-104m.** *½ D: Pete Walker. Anthony Sharp, Susan Penhaligon, Stephanie Beacham, Norman Eshley, Sheila Keith. Lurid melodrama about a deranged priest. You've been warned. Originally titled HOUSE OF MORTAL SIN. [R]▼

Confessions of a Nazi Spy (1939) **102m.** **½ D: Anatole Litvak. Edward G. Robinson, Francis Lederer, George Sanders, Paul Lukas, Henry O'Neill, James Stephenson, Sig Rumann, Dorothy Tree, Lya Lys, Joe Sawyer. Fast-paced but obvious drama of FBI agent Robinson investigating vast Nazi spy ring operating in the U.S. Of interest mainly as a reflection of its era; Lukas, as a German-American Bund leader, clearly patterns his mannerisms and speeches on those of Hitler.

Confessions of an Opium Eater (1962) **85m.** *½ D: Albert Zugsmith. Vincent Price, Linda Ho, Richard Loo, June Kim, Philip Ahn, Victor Sen Yung. Bizarre low-budgeter. Price is hammy in tale of slave girls brought to San Francisco and the adventurer who aids them. Retitled: SOULS FOR SALE.▼

Confessions of a Peeping John SEE: **Hi, Mom!**

Confessions of a Police Captain (1971-Italian) **C-102m.** **½ D: Damiano Damiani. Martin Balsam, Franco Nero, Marilu Tolo, Claudio Gora. Interesting, sometimes ponderous drama of dedicated cop Balsam caught up in suffocating big-city corruption, as he tries to bring in an elusive criminal. Techniscope. [PG]▼

Confessions of a Sorority Girl (1994) **C-83m. TVM** D: Uli Edel. Jamie Luner, Alyssa Milano, Brian Bloom, Sadie Kratzig, Natalija Nogulich, Peter Simmons, Danni Wheeler, David Brisbin, Lorinne Dills-Vozoff, Judson Mills. 1958: Gorgeous but troubled Sabrina arrives at a new college determined to make herself queen of her sorority, whatever it takes. Exceptional example of this kind of thing, with good acting and direction, and an enjoyably bold use of color. One of Showtime's "Rebel Highway" entries based on old American-International pictures, this a remake of SORORITY GIRL (1957). Above average.

Confessions of a Window Cleaner (1974-British) **C-90m.** ** D: Val Guest. Robin Askwith, Anthony Booth, Linda Hayden, Bill Maynard, Dandy Nichols. British sex farce about voyeuristic window cleaner was dated when it came out; too obvious to be terribly funny. Followed by other CONFESSIONS films. [R]

Confessions of Boston Blackie (1941) **65m.** *** D: Edward Dmytryk. Chester Morris, Harriet Hilliard (Nelson), Richard Lane, George E. Stone, Lloyd Corrigan,

Joan Woodbury, Walter Sande. Delightful second entry in the series finds Blackie, trying to smash a murderous art forgery racket, being chased by the killers as well as the relentless Inspector Farraday. George E. Stone joins the cast as Blackie's sidekick "Runt" (replacing Charles Wagenheim), providing ample comic relief.

Confessions of Felix Krull, The (1958-German) **107m.** **½ D: Kurt Hoffman. Horst Buchholz, Lilo Pulver, Ingrid Andree, Susi Nicoletti. Waggish chronicle of charming rascal Buchholz rising in rank as Parisian hotel employee; based on Thomas Mann novel.▼

Confessions of Tom Harris (1972) **C-98m.** ** D: John Derek and David Nelson. Don Murray, Linda Evans, David Brian, Gary Clarke, Logan Ramsey. Offbeat, gritty study of a corrupt, amoral prizefighter, played by Murray, who also produced and wrote the story. Derek also photographed it. Filmed in 1966. First released in 1969 as CHILDISH THINGS. [PG]▼

Confidence (1979-Hungarian) **C-117m.** ***½ D: Istvan Szabo. Ildiko Bansagi, Peter Andorai, O. Gombik, Karoly Csaki, Ildiko Kishonti. Bansagi and Andorai, each separately married, fall in love while posing as husband and wife to elude the Germans during WW2. Striking, involving tale of trust and survival.

Confidential (1935) **67m.** **½ D: Edward L. Cahn. Donald Cook, Evalyn Knapp, Warren Hymer, J. Carrol Naish, Herbert Rawlinson, Theodore von Eltz, Morgan Wallace, Kane Richmond, Reed Howes. Fast-moving gangster programmer with G-man Cook going undercover to bust open a crime syndicate. Knapp is a sassy blonde; Hymer a dumb lug with Brooklyn accent; Naish a cold-blooded killer. Good fun.▼

Confidential Agent (1945) **118m.** *** D: Herman Shumlin. Charles Boyer, Lauren Bacall, Katina Paxinou, Peter Lorre, Victor Francen, George Coulouris, Wanda Hendrix, John Warburton. Boyer is Graham Greene's hero in engrossing spy yarn of Spanish Civil War; he meets Bacall along the way; they battle enemy agents Lorre and Paxinou.

Confidentially Connie (1953) **74m.** **½ D: Edward Buzzell. Van Johnson, Janet Leigh, Louis Calhern, Walter Slezak, Gene Lockhart. Mild chuckles as pregnant wife Leigh schemes to get underpaid professor hubby (Johnson) to leave academic circles. Calhern as Van's rich Texan father is amusing.

Confidentially Yours (1982-French) **111m.** *** D: François Truffaut. Fanny Ardant, Jean-Louis Trintignant, Philippe Laudenbach, Caroline Sihol, Philippe Morier-Genoud, Xavier Saint Macary. Businessman is wanted for murder, and his secretary takes on job of finding real killer while he hides out from the cops. Truffaut's final feature is airy mystery-comedy in the Hitchcock mold, based on an American novel (*The Long Saturday Night* by Charles Williams); beautifully shot in black & white by Nestor Almendros. No depth whatsoever, but lightly entertaining; Ardant is delightful. French title: VIVEMENT DIMANCHE! [PG]▼●◗

Confidential Report SEE: **Mr. Arkadin**

Confirm or Deny (1941) **73m.** **½ D: Archie Mayo. Don Ameche, Joan Bennett, Roddy McDowall, John Loder, Raymond Walburn. Love in an air-raid shelter with Ameche and Bennett as reporter and wireless operator; pleasant romance.

Conflagration SEE: **Enjo**

Conflict (1945) **86m.** **½ D: Curtis Bernhardt. Humphrey Bogart, Alexis Smith, Sydney Greenstreet, Rose Hobart, Charles Drake, Grant Mitchell. Far-fetched story of husband (Bogart) plotting to murder wife (Hobart) to marry her sister (Smith). Unconvincing plot not salvaged by good cast.▼

Conflict (1966) SEE: **Judith**

Conformist, The (1971-Italian-French-West German) **C-115m.** ***½ D: Bernardo Bertolucci. Jean-Louis Trintignant, Stefania Sandrelli, Dominique Sanda, Pierre Clementi, Pasquale Fortunato, Gastone Moschin. Disturbing blend of character study and historical context of 1930s. Repressing homosexual drives, Marcello Clerici strives for "acceptable" life as member of Italian Fascist secret service, and middle-class would-be wife chaser, until odd series of events make him a willing murderer. Film's overall mood uniquely tense. Cut by 5m. for American release; the missing "Dance of the Blind" sequence was restored for 1994 reissue. [R]▼●

Congo (1995) **C-108m.** ** D: Frank Marshall. Laura Linney, Ernie Hudson, Tim Curry, Grant Heslov, Dylan Walsh, Joe Don Baker, Stuart Pankin, Mary Ellen Trainor, James Karen. Clumsily written Saturday-matinee nonsense about a gorilla expert who goes on a trouble-laden expedition to Africa with a Roumanian fortune hunter and a high-tech communications expert who's searching for her ex-fiancé. Sort of watchable, but poky pacing, unappealing characters, and senseless script sink it. The big special-effects climax is as unconvincing as Amy, the costarring gorilla. Michael Crichton's novel was adapted by—of all people—John Patrick Shanley (MOONSTRUCK). Joe Pantoliano appears unbilled. [PG-13]▼●◗

Congo Crossing (1956) **C-87m.** ** D: Joseph Pevney. Virginia Mayo, George Nader, Peter Lorre, Michael Pate, Rex Ingram. OK adventure yarn set in Africa, involving wanted criminals and construction engineer's attempt to civilize the Congo territory.

Congo Maisie (1940) **70m.** **½ D: H. C. Potter. Ann Sothern, John Carroll, Shepperd Strudwick, Rita Johnson, J. M. Kerrigan, E. E. Clive. Second *Maisie* entry, in which Brooklyn chorus girl Sothern finds herself involved with doctor Carroll in the middle of an African native revolt.

Conjugal Bed, The (1963-French-Italian) **90m.** *** D: Marco Ferreri. Ugo Tognazzi, Marina Vlady, Walter Giller, Linda Sini. Tognazzi is admirably suited to the role of a middle-aged bachelor who weds beautiful young Vlady and must cope with her sexual demands as she desires to become pregnant. A funny, entertaining sex comedy.

Con Men, The SEE: **Con Artists, The**

Connecticut Yankee, A (1931) **78m.** *** D: David Butler. Will Rogers, Maureen O'Sullivan, Myrna Loy, Frank Albertson, William Farnum. Mark Twain's classic story of a man who travels back in time to King Arthur's court, rewritten to suit Rogers' genial personality. Full of contemporary wisecracks and funny ideas, though the script gets a bit silly.▼

Connecticut Yankee in King Arthur's Court, A (1949) **C-107m.** **½ D: Tay Garnett. Bing Crosby, Rhonda Fleming, William Bendix, Cedric Hardwicke, Henry Wilcoxon, Murvyn Vye, Virginia Field. Mark Twain's story becomes carefree Crosby musical, with Bing transported into past, branded a wizard. No great songs, but colorful production. Previously filmed in 1921 and 1931 (with Will Rogers); remade in 1979 (as UNIDENTIFIED FLYING ODDBALL); TVMs in 1989 and 1995. ▼●

Connecting Rooms (1969-British) **C-103m.** ** D: Franklin Gollings. Bette Davis, Michael Redgrave, Alexis Kanner, Kay Walsh, Olga Georges-Picot, Leo Genn. Muddled melodrama of relationships in a rooming house. Davis is a street musician, Redgrave a former schoolmaster, and Kanner the rebellious youth who disrupts their equilibrium.

Connection, The (1961) **103m.** ***½ D: Shirley Clarke. William Redfield, Warren Finnerty, Garry Goodrow, Jerome Raphael, James Anderson, Carl Lee, Roscoe Lee Browne, Jackie McLean. Searing, admirably acted drama of junkies awaiting arrival of their "connection" with heroin, and a documentary filmmaker (Redfield) filming them. Independently produced, based on Jack Gelber's stage play. Original running time 110m.; some prints run 93m.▼

Conquered City, The (1962-Italian) **C-87m.** **½ D: Joseph Anthony. David Niven, Ben Gazzara, Michael Craig, Martin Balsam, Lea Massari, Daniela Rocca. Niven and disparate international group are holed up in Athens hotel under siege in waning days of WW2; not-bad programmer released overseas as THE CAPTIVE CITY at 108m.

Conqueror, The (1956) **C-111m.** ** D: Dick Powell. John Wayne, Susan Hayward, Pedro Armendariz, Agnes Moorehead, Thomas Gomez, John Hoyt, William Conrad. Mongols vs. Tartars, and John Wayne vs. the silliest role of his career, Genghis Khan. Expensive epic has camp dialogue to spare. The film had a sobering real-life aftermath, however: it was shot on location in Utah near an atomic test site, and an alarming number of its cast and crew (including the stars) were later stricken by cancer. CinemaScope.▼◗

Conquerors, The (1932) **86m.** ** D: William Wellman. Richard Dix, Ann Harding, Edna May Oliver, Guy Kibbee, Julie Haydon, Donald Cook. Unabashed rip-off of CIMARRON with Dix and Harding as newlyweds who go West to make their fortune, and build a banking empire that spans fifty years of ups and downs. Some good scenes lost in clichés in this epic saga. Retitled PIONEER BUILDERS.

Conqueror Worm (1968-British) **C-98m.** *** D: Michael Reeves. Vincent Price, Ian Ogilvy, Hilary Dwyer, Rupert Davies, Robert Russell, Patrick Wymark, Wilfred Brambell. As Matthew Hopkins, real-life witch-hunter during era of Cromwell, Price gives excellent nonhammy performance in underrated low-budget (and bloody) period thriller. Literate, balanced script pits him against young sympathetic lovers Ogilvy and Dwyer. Original British title: THE WITCHFINDER GENERAL.▼●

Conquest (1937) **112m.** *** D: Clarence Brown. Greta Garbo, Charles Boyer, Reginald Owen, Alan Marshal, Henry Stephenson, Leif Erickson, Dame May Whitty, Maria Ouspenskaya, Vladimir Sokoloff, Scotty Beckett. Boyer as Napoleon and Garbo as Polish countess Walewska in fairly interesting costumer with fine performances making up for not-always-thrilling script.▼

Conquest of Cochise (1953) **C-70m.** ** D: William Castle. John Hodiak, Robert Stack, Joy Page, John Crawford. Unspectacular Indian vs. cavalry, set in 1850s Southwest, as Stack and troops try to calm Cochise's (Hodiak) rampaging braves.▼

Conquest of Everest, The (1953-British) **C-78m.** *** No director credited. Outstanding, Oscar-nominated documentary chronicle of Edmund Hillary and company's successful expedition to the summit of Mount Everest. As dramatic as the most complexly plotted fiction; breathtaking photography by Thomas Stobart and George Love. ▼

Conquest of Space (1955) **C-80m.** **½ D: Byron Haskin. Eric Fleming, William Hopper, Ross Martin, Walter Brooke, Joan Shawlee. Despite some good special effects, this George Pal production about the first trip to Mars is hampered by a pedestrian script and an inappropriate emphasis on religion. A disappointment, based on Werner von Braun's book *The Mars Project*.▼

Conquest of the Planet of the Apes (1972) **C-87m.** **½ D: J. Lee Thompson. Roddy McDowall, Don Murray, Ricardo Montalban, Natalie Trundy, Severn Darden. Fourth APES feature shows how apes came to rebel and subsequently vanquish man. Loosely acted and often trite, but still interesting. Followed by BATTLE FOR THE PLANET OF THE APES. Todd-AO 35. [PG]▼●

Conrack (1974) **C-107m.** *** D: Martin Ritt. Jon Voight, Paul Winfield, Hume Cronyn, Madge Sinclair, Tina Andrews, Antonio Fargas, Ruth Attaway. Pleasant film based on Pat Conroy's *The Water Is Wide*, about his attempts to bring common-sense education to backward black school on island off South Carolina. Subplot with hermit-like Winfield doesn't work, unfortunately. Panavision. [PG]▼

Conseil de Famille SEE: **Family Business** (1986-French)

Consenting Adults (1992) **C-100m.** *½ D: Alan J. Pakula. Kevin Kline, Mary Elizabeth Mastrantonio, Kevin Spacey, Rebecca Miller, Forest Whitaker, E. G. Marshall, Kimberly McCullough, Billie Neal. There's Hell in Suburbia when Kline becomes morally polluted by a leechy neighbor who proposes a wife-swapping pact. Incredible lapses in logic for a director of Pakula's caliber, though Spacey is creepily credible as the murderer-next-door. Unintentional laughs help. [R]▼●

Consolation Marriage (1931) **82m.** ** D: Paul Sloane. Irene Dunne, Pat O'Brien, John Halliday, Myrna Loy, Matt Moore, Lester Vail. Dunne and O'Brien are married after they're both jilted by their respective mates but years later must decide what to do when the former lovers return. Standard marital melodrama uplifted by considerably charming cast.▼

Conspiracy (1939) **58m.** **½ D: Lew Landers. Allan Lane, Linda Hayes, Robert Barrat, Charley Foy, Lionel Royce, J. Farrell MacDonald, Lester Matthews, Henry Brandon. Taut little B thriller about a ship's radio operator (Lane), who finds himself immersed in intrigue when his craft pulls into port in a fascist country. Jerome Chodorov's unsubtle script mirrors the world situation at the time of the film's release.

Conspiracy of Hearts (1960-British) **116m.** *** D: Ralph Thomas. Lilli Palmer, Sylvia Syms, Yvonne Mitchell, Ronald Lewis. Despite familiar situation of nuns sheltering refugee Jewish youths in Northern Italy, this film is both suspenseful and moving.▼

Conspiracy Theory (1997) **C-135m.** *** D: Richard Donner. Mel Gibson, Julia Roberts, Patrick Stewart, Cylk Cozart, Stephen Kahan, Terry Alexander. Lumpy but entertaining story about a half-crazed N.Y.C. cabdriver who lives a life of paranoia, obsessed with a woman who works for the Justice Department. One day, however, he comes to her with a story that seems to make sense about a conspiracy and cover-up; soon, they're both embroiled in a situation bigger than they ever imagined. The script isn't airtight, but it's enjoyable, with Gibson's edgy performance right on target. Panavision. [R]▼●◗

Conspirator (1949-British) **85m.** **½ D: Victor Saville. Robert Taylor, Elizabeth Taylor, Honor Blackman, Wilfrid Hyde-White. Elizabeth is confronted by the fact that British husband Taylor is a Communist agent; story often better than stars.▼

Conspirators, The (1944) **101m.** **½ D: Jean Negulesco. Hedy Lamarr, Paul Henreid, Sydney Greenstreet, Peter Lorre, Victor Francen, Vladimir Sokoloff, George Macready, Monte Blue, Joseph Calleia. WW2 intrigue in Lisbon, with echoes of CASABLANCA; this one's no classic, but with that cast (and Hedy at her most beautiful) how bad can it be?

Constance (1984-New Zealand) **C-104m.** ** D: Bruce Morrison. Donogh Rees, Shane Briant, Judie Douglass, Martin Vaughan, Donald MacDonald, Mark Wignall. Muddled, forgettable tale of an ambitious, beautiful teacher (Rees), whose fantasy life is influenced by images from the Hollywood films she loves.

Constans SEE: **Constant Factor, The**

Constant Factor, The (1980-Polish) **C-96m.** *** D: Krzysztof Zanussi. Tadeusz Bradecki, Zofia Mrozowska, Malgorzata Zajaczkowska, Cezary Morawska. Idealistic mountain climber Bradecki refuses to kowtow to a hypocritical bureaucracy and winds up a window cleaner. Incisive, but not top-drawer Zanussi; filmed simultaneously with the director's CONTRACT.▼

Constant Husband, The (1955-British) **C-88m.** *** D: Sidney Gilliat. Rex Harrison, Margaret Leighton, Kay Kendall, Cecil Parker, Nicole Maurey, George Cole, Raymond Huntley, Michael Hordern, Robert Coote, Eric Pohlmann. Harrison, recovering from amnesia, realizes he's wed to more than one woman. Entertaining comedy, with sexy Rexy ideally cast (opposite real-life wife Kendall).

Constantine and the Cross (1962-Italian) **C-120m.** *** D: Lionello de Felice. Cornel Wilde, Christine Kaufmann, Belinda Lee, Elisa Cegani, Massimo Serato. Intelligent interpretation of 4th century A.D. Emperor (Wilde) battling Romans for Christianity. Good action. Totalscope.▼

Constant Nymph, The (1943) **112m.** ***½ D: Edmund Goulding. Charles Boyer, Joan Fontaine, Alexis Smith, Brenda Marshall, Charles Coburn, Dame May Whitty, Peter Lorre, Joyce Reynolds, Jean Muir, Montague Love, Edward (Eduardo) Ciannelli. Intensely romantic story of a Belgian gamine (Fontaine) who's madly in love with a self-serious and self-absorbed composer (Boyer). He marries a socialite (Smith) without ever realizing the depth of his own feelings for the younger girl. Touching, intelligent, and beautifully realized, with sweeping music by Erich Wolfgang

Korngold. Margaret Kennedy's novel and play were adapted by Kathryn Scola. Filmed before in 1928 and 1934.

Consuming Passions (1988-U.S.-British) **C-98m.** *½ D: Giles Foster. Vanessa Redgrave, Jonathan Pryce, Tyler Butterworth, Freddie Jones, Sammi Davis, Prunella Scales, Thora Hird. Dumb dud of a satire about what happens when three men are accidentally shoved into a vat of chocolate in a candy factory . . . and chocolate lovers favor the resulting confections. Sounds a lot more promising than it plays; based on a play by Michael Palin and Terry Jones. [R]▼●

Contact (1997) **C-150m.** *** D: Robert Zemeckis. Jodie Foster, Matthew McConaughey, James Woods, John Hurt, Tom Skerritt, William Fichtner, David Morse, Angela Bassett, Geoffrey Blake, Rob Lowe, Jake Busey. A woman who has devoted her life to studying the stars—believing there's life Out There—is ostracized by her superior at the National Science Foundation, and eventually cut off, until she actually receives a message from space. Intensely involving story in which we're drawn into Foster's obsession and share her odyssey into the unknown. Passionate and intelligent, this film manages to inspire a feeling of awe and wonder, which makes up for its overlength and false endings. Foster is simply sensational. Based on the novel by Carl Sagan. Panavision. [PG]▼●◗

Contempt (1963-French-Italian) **C-103m.** ***½ D: Jean-Luc Godard. Brigitte Bardot, Jack Palance, Michel Piccoli, Giorgia Moll, Fritz Lang. Perversely funny look at international moviemaking with Piccoli as a dramatist of integrity who gets mixed up with a vulgar producer (Palance) and director (Lang—playing himself) in a film version of *The Odyssey*. Producer Joseph E. Levine didn't seem to understand that Godard, who appears here as Lang's assistant, held *him* in contempt, making this film a highly amusing "in" joke. Bardot's appearance only adds to the fun. Franscope.▼●

Contest Girl (1966-British) **C-82m.** **½ D: Val Guest. Ian Hendry, Janette Scott, Ronald Fraser, Edmund Purdom, Linda Christian. Film well conveys glamorous and seamy sides of beauty-contest world. Purdom gives effective performance. CinemaScope.

Continental Divide (1981) **C-103m.** ** D: Michael Apted. John Belushi, Blair Brown, Allen Goorwitz (Garfield), Carlin Glynn, Tony Ganios, Val Avery, Tim Kazurinsky. One of those "concept" movies that's all premise, no payoff: Belushi's a hard-hitting Chicago newspaper columnist, Brown's a self-reliant naturalist at home observing eagles in the Rockies. Can this romance survive? Interesting mainly to see Belushi playing such a "normal" and likable character. Written by Lawrence Kasdan, who obviously couldn't come up with a finish. Steven Spielberg was executive producer. [PG]▼●

Continental Twist, The SEE: **Twist All Night**

Contraband (1940-British) **92m.** ***½ D: Michael Powell. Conrad Veidt, Valerie Hobson, Hay Petrie, Joss Ambler, Raymond Lovell, Esmond Knight, Peter Bull, Leo Genn. Superior spy yarn from the team of Michael Powell and Emeric Pressburger that's very much in the Hitchcock vein. Veidt is a Danish merchant sea captain, Hobson an enigmatic passenger—both get caught up with London spy ring. Though set in 1939, film hardly seems dated at all! That's Bernard Miles as a disgruntled smoker. Powell and Brock Williams adapted Pressburger's story. P&P had teamed up with Veidt and Hobson the previous year for THE SPY IN BLACK. Original U.S. title: BLACKOUT.▼

Contract (1980-Polish) **C-114m.** ***½ D: Krzysztof Zanussi. Leslie Caron, Maja Komorowska, Tadeusz Lomnicki, Magda Jaroszowna. Superb laced-in-acid comedy-satire centering on a wedding between the career-oriented son of a wealthy doctor and his none-too-eager bride. Zanussi incisively chides corrupt politicians and businessmen; Caron is memorable as a kleptomaniacal ballerina. Filmed simultaneously with the director's CONSTANS (THE CONSTANT FACTOR).▼

Contract on Cherry Street (1977) **C-150m. TVM** D: William A. Graham. Frank Sinatra, Harry Guardino, Martin Balsam, Henry Silva, Verna Bloom, Michael Nouri, Martin Gabel. Sinatra's only TV-movie (and first role after his seven-year "retirement") has him well cast as N.Y.C. police officer who takes on organized crime in his own fashion after his partner is gunned down. Aces to this fine thriller, adapted by Edward Anhalt from Philip Rosenberg's book. Above average.

Convent, The (1995-Portuguese-French) **C-90m.** ** D: Manoel de Oliveira. Catherine Deneuve, John Malkovich, Duarte D'Almeida, Luis Miguel Cintra, Heloisa Miranda, Leonor Silveira. A professor (Malkovich) is attempting to prove that Shakespeare is of Spanish descent. To further his research, he and his wife (Deneuve) travel to an ancient convent, where there are eerie and mysterious goings-on. Languid tale made by the well-respected Portuguese writer-director de Oliveira (who was 86 years old when this was released!).▼

Conversation, The (1974) **C-113m.** **** D: Francis Ford Coppola. Gene Hackman, John Cazale, Allen Garfield, Frederic Forrest, Cindy Williams, Michael Higgins, Elizabeth MacRae, Teri Garr, Harrison Ford, Robert Shields. Brilliant film about obsessive surveillance expert (Hackman) who makes professional mistake of becoming involved in a case, and finds himself entangled in murder and high-level power plays. Coppola's top-notch, disturbing script makes larger statements about privacy and personal responsibility. An unbilled Robert Duvall has a cameo. One of the best films of the 1970s. [PG]▼●

Conversation Piece (1975-Italian) **C-122m.** ** D: Luchino Visconti. Burt Lancaster, Silvana Mangano, Helmut Berger, Claudia Marsani, Claudia Cardinale. Ponderous story of aging, aloof professor Lancaster who becomes involved with matron Mangano's hedonistic children and her young lover, Berger. All talk. Filmed in both English and Italian-language versions. Todd-AO 35. [R]▼

Convict Cowboy (1995) **C-98m. TVM** D: Rod Holcomb. Jon Voight, Kyle Chandler, Marcia Gay Harden, Stephen McHattie, Glenn Plummer, Ben Gazzara, Blu Mankuma. Convict lifer Voight, a onetime rodeo champion, runs a prison ranch and takes a hotshot short-termer with promise under his wing. Their goal: to get the younger man in shape for an upcoming riding contest with another lockup. Voight's world-weary appearance suits the leading role of this sturdy little modern-day Western. Made for cable. Average.▼

Convicted (1950) **91m.** **½ D: Henry Levin. Glenn Ford, Broderick Crawford, Dorothy Malone, Roland Winters, Ed Begley. Sincere account of prison warden's efforts to help unjustly convicted man, and those on the outside seeking actual killer. Remake of THE CRIMINAL CODE.

Convicts (1991) **C-95m.** *** D: Peter Masterson. Robert Duvall, Lukas Haas, James Earl Jones, Starletta DuPois. A young boy (Haas) comes of age observing the violent scenes on a Texas Gulf Coast canefield in 1902—even as life seems to be cycling to an end for imposing plantation boss (Duvall) who survives by using convict labor to work in his fields. A towering performance by Duvall and stark, authentic dialogue by Horton Foote (based on his nine-play cycle *The Orphan's Home*) are the strengths in this poignant elegy. ▼●

Convicts 4 (1962) **105m.** *** D: Millard Kaufman. Ben Gazzara, Stuart Whitman, Ray Walston, Vincent Price, Rod Steiger, Broderick Crawford, Sammy Davis, Jr., Jack Kruschen. Gazzara gives sincere portrayal as long-term prisoner who becomes professional artist. Oddball supporting cast. Retitled: REPRIEVE. ▼

Convoy (1978) **C-110m.** ** D: Sam Peckinpah. Kris Kristofferson, Ali MacGraw, Ernest Borgnine, Burt Young, Madge Sinclair, Franklyn Ajaye, Cassie Yates. Amiable comic-book movie based on the hit song about an independent trucker who leads protesting colleagues on a trek through the Southwest. Stupid script and blah acting redeemed somewhat by Peckinpah's punchy directorial style. Panavision. [PG]▼

Coogan's Bluff (1968) **C-100m.** *** D: Don Siegel. Clint Eastwood, Lee J. Cobb, Susan Clark, Tisha Sterling, Don Stroud, Betty Field, Tom Tully. Arizona lawman Eastwood comes to N.Y.C. to show city cops a thing or two about tracking down a wanted man. Stylish action film, good location work. Sterling enjoyable as hippie. Later evolved into the *McCloud* TV series. [R]▼●

Cookie (1989) **C-93m.** *** D: Susan Seidelman. Peter Falk, Dianne Wiest, Emily Lloyd, Michael V. Gazzo, Brenda Vaccaro, Adrian Pasdar, Lionel Stander, Jerry Lewis, Bob Gunton, Ricki Lake. Droll comedy about a sassy teenager who gets to meet her mobster dad for the first time when he's sprung from prison after a long stretch. No fireworks here, but the performances are great fun to watch, especially Wiest as Falk's breathless mistress (and Lloyd's mother). Written by Nora Ephron and Alice Arlen. [R]▼●

Cookie's Fortune (1999) **C-118m.** *** D: Robert Altman. Glenn Close, Julianne Moore, Liv Tyler, Chris O'Donnell, Charles S. Dutton, Patricia Neal, Ned Beatty, Courtney B. Vance, Donald Moffat, Lyle Lovett, Danny Durst, Matt Malloy. Picaresque yarn spun in a small Southern town where an eccentric woman's death sets in motion a series of events revealing the true nature—both good-hearted and greedy—of various relatives and friends. Colorful characters abound in this easygoing, fanciful film, sparked by Dutton's wonderful performance. [PG-13]▼

Cook, The Thief, His Wife & Her Lover, The (1989-French-Dutch) **C-124m.** *** D: Peter Greenaway. Helen Mirren, Michael Gambon, Tim Roth, Richard Bohringer, Alan Howard. Another stylish, challenging piece of cinema from Greenaway that's set in a plush gourmet restaurant and details the various relationships between the title characters. This parable about love, revenge, and, most of all, greed is both funny and horrifying—and right on target. However, those who do not appreciate Greenaway's cinematic sensibility may be put off. Sacha Vierny's cinematography is an asset. Technovision. [NC-17 and R-rated versions are available]▼●

Cool and the Crazy, The (1958) **78m.** *** D: William Witney. Scott Marlowe, Gigi Perreau, Dick Bakalyan, Dick Jones. Fifties equivalent of REEFER MADNESS is a great unsung j.d. melodrama; reform school veteran introduces thirtyish-looking high schoolers to grass, turns them into psychotics. On-location Kansas City photography gives this one an authentic feel.

Cool and the Crazy (1994) **C-84m. TVM** D: Ralph Bakshi. Jennifer Blanc, Matthew Flint, Jared Leto, Alicia Silverstone, Bradford Tatum, Christine Harnos, Tuesday Knight, John Kapelos. The 1950s: A bored young mother starts an affair, infuriating her husband. Dreary and unimaginative, this stale concoction trots out L.A. location names, but it was obviously originally written to take place in N.Y.C. One of Showtime's "Rebel Highway" entries, all based on old American-International pictures, but the plot here is original. Below average.

Cool as Ice (1991) **C-100m.** BOMB D: David Kellogg. Vanilla Ice, Kristin Minter, Michael Gross, Candy Clark, Sydney Lassick, Dody Goodman, Naomi Campbell, Bobby Brown. The Sealtest man's rap numbers frame seemingly unreleasable "wandering cyclist" yarn about a numbskull who manages to romance the town's SAT standard-bearer. Oh, did we mention that her father is in the government's witness relocation program? Ice's parlance ("Drop that zero/get with the hero") in his first starring film does not rekindle fond memories of Ronald Colman. [PG]▼●

Cool Breeze (1972) **C-101m.** *½ D: Barry Pollack. Thalmus Rasulala, Judy Pace, Jim Watkins, Lincoln Kilpatrick, Sam Laws, Margaret Avery, Raymond St. Jacques. Routine remake of THE ASPHALT JUNGLE with plot line updated so that diamond robbery proceeds will go to set up a black people's bank.[R]

Cool, Dry Place, A (1999) **C-97m.** **½ D: John N. Smith. Vince Vaughn, Joey Lauren Adams, Monica Potter, Devon Sawa, Bobby Moat, Todd Louiso. Hotshot lawyer is raising his five-year-old son since his wife walked out on them. Having lost his job, he tries to build a new life in Texas and meets a woman he likes . . . then the plot thickens. Believable story, if predictable at times; benefits from good performances. [PG-13]▼◗

Cooler Climate, A (1999) **C-100m. TVM** D: Susan Seidelman. Sally Field, Judy Davis, Winston Rekert, Jerry Wasserman, Carly Pope. Impoverished divorcée Field becomes housekeeper to snobbish matron Davis in a small resort town, but a turn of events, and terrific chemistry, make the two lonely women bosom buddies. Playwright Marsha Norman adapted Zena Collier's novel with insight and humor. Made for cable. Above average.▼

Cooley High (1975) **C-107m.** *** D: Michael Schultz. Glynn Turman, Lawrence Hilton-Jacobs, Garrett Morris, Cynthia Davis, Corin Rogers, Maurice Leon Havis. Inner-city rip-off of AMERICAN GRAFFITI (set in Chicago, 1964) is nonetheless pleasing on its own terms, though only on the level of a good TV show. Lots of laughs. Look fast for Robert Townsend. Later evolved into the *What's Happening!!* TV series. [PG]▼●◗

Cool Hand Luke (1967) **C-126m.** ***½ D: Stuart Rosenberg. Paul Newman, George Kennedy, J.D. Cannon, Lou Antonio, Robert Drivas, Strother Martin, Jo Van Fleet, Wayne Rogers, Anthony Zerbe, Ralph Waite, Harry Dean Stanton, Dennis Hopper, Richard Davalos, Warren Finnerty, Morgan Woodward, Clifton James, Joe Don Baker. Modern slant on prison camps shows little change since Paul Muni; more irreverent, however, with memorably funny egg-eating contest. Top-notch film with Kennedy's Oscar-winning performance as prisoner. Panavision.▼●◗

Cool Ones, The (1967) **C-95m.** BOMB D: Gene Nelson. Roddy McDowall, Debbie Watson, Gil Peterson, Phil Harris, Robert Coote, Glen Campbell, Mrs. Miller. Inane "musical" comedy spoofing trendy music business. Embarrassing on all counts, with broad performances. If you turn up your volume, you might hear a faint laugh track. Panavision.

Cool Runnings (1993) **C-97m.** *** D: Jon Turtletaub. Leon, Doug E. Doug, John Candy, Rawle D. Lewis, Malik Yoba, Raymond J. Barry. Family-oriented feel-good movie from Disney—based on a true story—about the unlikely formation of a Jamaican bobsled team to compete in the 1988 Winter Olympics. (The participants have never even seen snow, let alone a bobsled!) Candy is well cast as a disgraced former Olympian who redeems himself. [PG]▼●◗

Cool World (1992) **C-101m.** *½ D: Ralph Bakshi. Gabriel Byrne, Kim Basinger, Brad Pitt, Frank Sinatra, Jr. Pointless live-action/animation feature from Bakshi, who's covered this ground before, much more successfully. Ex-con comic-book artist Byrne discovers his cartoon creations are real, and live in a parallel universe called Cool World. After sexy "doodle" Holli (Basinger) has sex with Byrne, she becomes human and escapes to real world, with detective Pitt in tow. Too serious to be fun, too goofy to take seriously; lead characters unlikable and unappealing. Looks like a Roger Corman version of ROGER RABBIT. [PG-13]▼●

Coonskin (1975) **C-83m.** **½ D: Ralph Bakshi. Barry White, Charles Gordone, Scatman Crothers, Philip (Michael) Thomas. Outrageous, original film about the status of blacks in America is told with live-action and animation vignettes, the best of which are sly parodies of the stories from Disney and Uncle Remus' SONG OF THE SOUTH. Very much in the Bakshi vein; uneven but worth a look. Video title: STREET FIGHT. [R]▼

Cooperstown (1993) **C-100m. TVM** D:

Charles Haid. Alan Arkin, Graham Greene, Hope Lange, Ed Begley, Jr., Josh Charles, Paul Dooley, Charles Haid, Maria Pitillo, Ann Wedgeworth. Arkin is terrific as a one-time big league pitcher stewing for thirty years over, among other things, being bypassed by the Baseball Hall of Fame; he finally decides to do something about it, with the ghost of long-estranged best friend Greene, who was elected on the eve of his death. Multiple vignettes help make this picaresque comedy-drama a winner. Written by playwright Lee Blessing. Made for cable. Above average.

Cop (1987) **C-110m.** **½ D: James B. Harris. James Woods, Lesley Ann Warren, Charles Durning, Charles Haid, Raymond J. Barry, Randi Brooks, Annie McEnroe, Vicki Wauchope. Woods is excellent as usual in this otherwise familiar drama about a dedicated cop, his troubled marriage, and the difficulties he encounters while on a murder case. Woods and Harris coproduced. [R]▼●

Copacabana (1947) **92m.** ** D: Alfred E. Green. Groucho Marx, Carmen Miranda, Andy Russell, Steve Cochran, Gloria Jean, Louis Sobol, Abel Green, Earl Wilson. Potentially intriguing Marx–Miranda casting can't save this unengrossing musical comedy. Groucho is a Broadway agent attempting to promote Carmen, his only client, resulting in her being hired for two jobs (in two different guises) at the same nightclub. This was Groucho's first film without his brothers. Also shown in computer-colored version. ▼●

Cop & ½ (1993) **C-93m.** BOMB D: Henry Winkler. Burt Reynolds, Norman D. Golden II, Ruby Dee, Holland Taylor, Ray Sharkey, Sammy Hernandez, Frank Sivero. And a hemorrhoid-and-a-half to anyone who sits all the way through it. Circumstances (read: scriptwriter's contrivance) dictate that a cop-addicted black kid become the new partner of a white detective who's trying to crack a drug punk. Abjectly painful comedy. Low point: a urination bonding scene with Reynolds in which the youngster wants to "make swords." [PG]▼●◗

Cop au Vin (1984-French) **C-110m.** ***½ D: Claude Chabrol. Jean Poiret, Stephane Audran, Michel Bouquet, Jean Topart, Lucas Belvaux, Pauline Lafont. Chabrol is in fine form in this diverting, neatly paced thriller about a young mail boy, his widowed, invalid mother, and a greedy trio who attempt to evict them from their home. Murder brings a shrewd cop on the scene to investigate. Followed by a sequel, INSPECTEUR LAVARDIN.

Cop Killers SEE: **Corrupt**

Cop Land (1997) **C-105m.** **½ D: James Mangold. Sylvester Stallone, Harvey Keitel, Ray Liotta, Robert De Niro, Peter Berg, Janeane Garofalo, Robert Patrick, Michael Rapaport, Annabella Sciorra, Noah Emmerich, Cathy Moriarty, John Spencer, Frank Vincent, Malik Yoba, Bruce Altman. Stallone plays a sheriff who's eaten a few too many donuts and is responsible for looking the other way in a New Jersey town inhabited almost exclusively by N.Y.C. cops who exist, it seems, above the law. Keitel is their ringleader, De Niro an Internal Affairs officer on his trail. A solid premise, and a riveting start, give way to increasingly conventional (and predictable) plotting by writer-director Mangold. [R]▼●◗

Cop-Out (1967-British) **C-95m.** **½ D: Pierre Rouve. James Mason, Geraldine Chaplin, Bobby Darin, Paul Bertoya, Ian Ogilvy, Bryan Stanton. OK murder mystery with dated generation-gap overtones. Reclusive lawyer Mason comes out of retirement to defend his daughter's boyfriend on trumped-up murder charge. Remake of 1942 French film STRANGER IN THE HOUSE.

Copper Canyon (1950) **C-83m.** **½ D: John Farrow. Ray Milland, Hedy Lamarr, Macdonald Carey, Mona Freeman, Harry Carey, Jr., Frank Faylen, Hope Emerson, Percy Helton. OK Western of post-Civil War days, with Confederate vet Milland faced with decision to assist fellow Southerners who are being harassed as they attempt to mine copper. Lamarr plays the femme fatale.▼●

Cops and Robbers (1973) **C-89m.** *** D: Aram Avakian. Cliff Gorman, Joseph Bologna, Dick Ward, Shepperd Strudwick, John P. Ryan, Ellen Holly, Dolph Sweet, Joe Spinell. Enjoyable Donald Westlake tale about two policemen who pull a million-dollar caper on Wall Street. Funny and exciting, with good location photography by David L. Quaid. [PG]▼

Cops and Robbersons (1994) **C-93m.** ** D: Michael Ritchie. Chevy Chase, Jack Palance, Dianne Wiest, Robert Davi, David Barry Gray, Jason James Richter, Fay Masterson, Mike Hughes, Richard Romanus. Veteran cop Palance and a young cohort need to borrow Chase's house to stake out a lowlife who's living next door; this, it turns out, is a dream come true for Chevy, who's addicted to TV cop shows and fancies himself a hero. Premise of a baby boomer living out his pop-culture fantasies echoes CITY SLICKERS (Palance included) but isn't nearly as good. [PG]▼●

Copycat (1995) **C-125m.** *** D: Jon Amiel. Sigourney Weaver, Holly Hunter, Dermot Mulroney, Harry Connick, Jr., William McNamara, Will Patton, John Rothman, J. E. Freeman. Psychiatrist (Weaver) who's an expert on serial killers—and now traumatized into an agoraphobic existence—joins forces with dedicated cops Hunter and Mulroney to track down the latest (and smartest) murderer in San Francisco. Slickly made, tense and entertaining, although it, like the concurrent SE7EN, forces us to get to know a sick mind better than we might care to. And like many visceral thrillers, it will not stand up to intense scrutiny. Panavision. [R]▼●◗

Coquette (1929) **75m.** ** D: Sam Taylor. Mary Pickford, John Mack Brown, Matt Moore, John Sainpolis, William Janney, Henry Kolker, George Irving, Louise Beavers. Pickford's first talkie, for which she won an Oscar playing an ill-tempered flapper who becomes involved with a man who is beneath her station, resulting in tragedy. This stilted, artificial melodrama is a curio at best, notable as a showcase for Pickford's "new," modern screen personality. Based on a play which was a famous vehicle for Helen Hayes.▼

Corky (1972) **C-88m.** **½ D: Leonard Horn. Robert Blake, Charlotte Rampling, Patrick O'Neal, Christopher Connelly, Ben Johnson, Laurence Luckinbill. Blake's obsession for stock-car racing shuts out everything else in his life, including wife and friends. Good racing sequences, fairly absorbing character study. Originally titled LOOKIN' GOOD. Panavision. [PG]

Cornbread, Earl and Me (1975) **C-95m.** **½ D: Joe Manduke. Moses Gunn, Bernie Casey, Rosalind Cash, Madge Sinclair, Keith Wilkes, Tierre Turner, Larry Fishburne. Well-intentioned but overly melodramatic account of a black youth, on his way out of the ghetto on a basketball scholarship, who is innocently gunned down by police bullets. Fine performances and warm sense of black life evaporate in TV clichés. Fishburne's film debut. [PG]▼

Cornered (1945) **102m.** *** D: Edward Dmytryk. Dick Powell, Walter Slezak, Micheline Cheirel, Nina Vale, Morris Carnovsky, Luther Adler. High-tension drama with determined Canadian flyer Powell in Buenos Aires, tracking down the man responsible for the death of his French bride during WW2. Powell is in peak form. Also shown in computer-colored version. ▼●

Corn Is Green, The (1945) **114m.** ***½ D: Irving Rapper. Bette Davis, Nigel Bruce, John Dall, Joan Lorring, Rhys Williams, Rosalind Ivan, Mildred Dunnock. Thoughtful acting in this story of devoted middle-aged teacher Davis in Welsh mining town coming to terms with her prize pupil. Emlyn Williams' play was adapted by Casey Robinson and Frank Cavett. Remade, beautifully, for TV with Katharine Hepburn in 1979.▼

Coronado (1935) **77m.** **½ D: Norman Z. McLeod. Johnny Downs, Betty Burgess, Jack Haley, Andy Devine, Leon Errol, Jacqueline Wells (Julie Bishop), Alice White, Eddy Duchin with His Orchestra. Unspectacular but pleasant B musical about wealthy, brash songwriter Downs, and his romantic escapades with singer Burgess one summer at a resort hotel. Haley and Devine lend support as a couple of hapless sailors.

Coroner Creek (1948) **C-93m.** *** D: Ray Enright. Randolph Scott, Marguerite Chapman, George Macready, Sally Eilers, Edgar Buchanan, Barbara Reed, Wallace Ford, Forrest Tucker, William Bishop. Single-minded Scott seeks vengeance against the seemingly respectable man responsible for the events leading to a mysterious death. Solid little Western, based on a Luke Short novel; Scott's fisticuffs with henchman Tucker are a highlight. ▼

Corporate Affairs (1990) **C-82m.** *½ Terence Winkless. Peter Scolari, Mary Crosby, Chris Lemmon, Ken Kercheval, Richard Herd, Lisa Moncure, Kim Gillingham. Doomed attempt to cross-pollinate WEEKEND AT BERNIE'S with WORKING GIRL. Scolari takes advantage of former lover Crosby when she gives CEO Kercheval a heart attack during a tryst. But is he really dead? Somehow enormous amounts of T&A are shown to advantage in a concurrent office orgy. [R]▼

Corpse Came C.O.D., The (1947) **87m.** ** D: Henry Levin. George Brent, Joan Blondell, Adele Jergens, Jim Bannon, Leslie Brooks, Grant Mitchell, Una O'Connor, Marvin Miller. Rival reporters Brent and Blondell attempt to solve the mystery of why movie star Jergens has received a dead body. Passable comedy-mystery, with too much emphasis on the former.

Corpse Vanishes, The (1942) **64m.** ** D: Wallace Fox. Bela Lugosi, Luana Walters, Tristram Coffin, Elizabeth Russell, Vince Barnett, Joan Barclay, Angelo Rossitto. A cut above the average low-grade thrillers Lugosi made for producer Sam Katzman. Bela is a scientist who kidnaps brides for the purpose of using their body fluids to rejuvenate wife Russell, an elderly countess.▼◗

Corregidor (1943) **73m.** ** D: William Nigh. Otto Kruger, Elissa Landi, Donald Woods, Frank Jenks, Rick Vallin, Wanda McKay, Ian Keith. Routine WW2 melodrama focusing not so much on the American military's courageous stand against the Japanese at the title locale but on a corny love triangle involving a trio of doctors (one of whom is a woman). Unintentionally funny at times; Eddie Hall and Charles Jordan play characters named "Brooklyn" and "Bronx." Coscripted by Edgar Ulmer.▼

Corridor of Mirrors (1948-British) **105m.** *** D: Terence Young. Eric Portman, Edana Romney, Barbara Mullen, Hugh Sinclair, Joan Maude, Lois Maxwell, Christopher Lee. Underrated "art" film, similar to Jean Cocteau's work of this period, has Portman well cast as an artist who lives in the past, surrounding himself with Renaissance-era objects. Beauteous Romney (whose acting is not so hot) is the woman he falls in love with. Stunning sets, photography, and musical score.▼

Corridors of Blood (1962-British) **86m.** **½ D: Robert Day. Boris Karloff, Betta St. John, Finlay Currie, Christopher Lee, Francis Matthews, Adrienne Corri, Nigel Green. Middling account of 19th-century British doctor who experiments with anesthetics, becomes addicted to the narcotics, and winds up a grave-robber to continue his experiments. Unreleased until the early 1960s, at which time Lee received higher billing than his supporting role warranted. Filmed in 1958. Originally titled THE DOCTOR FROM SEVEN DIALS.▼●◗

Corrina, Corrina (1994) **C-114m.** *** D: Jessie Nelson. Whoopi Goldberg, Ray Liotta, Tina Majorino, Don Ameche, Wendy Crewson, Larry Miller, Erica Yohn, Jenifer Lewis, Joan Cusack, Harold Sylvester, Steven Williams, Patrika Darbo, Lucy Webb. Sweet-natured film about a young widower who hires a housekeeper to help take care of his daughter—little dreaming how important she'll become to both of them. As a document of social mores in the late 1950s this has its ups and downs, but endearing performances and upbeat point of view make it good entertainment. Written by the director. [PG]▼●

Corrupt (1983-Italian) **C-99m.** *** D: Roberto Faenza. Harvey Keitel, Nicole Garcia, Leonard Mann, John Lydon, Sylvia Sidney. Intriguing, entertaining psychological thriller about N.Y.C. policeman Keitel, his victimization by mysterious Lydon, and a hunt for a cop killer. Lydon used to be known as Johnny Rotten (of the punk rock group, The Sex Pistols). Fine performances; originally titled ORDER OF DEATH, with a 113m. running time, and also known as COP KILLERS and CORRUPT LIEUTENANT. [R]▼

Corruption (1968-British) **C-91m.** ** D: Robert Hartford-Davis. Peter Cushing, Sue Lloyd, Noel Trevarthen, David Lodge, Kate O'Mara. Famed surgeon Cushing slowly becomes insane as he stops at nothing, including murder, to restore the disfigured face of his fashion model fiancée (Lloyd). Predictable, formulaic horror opus. [R]

Corrupt Lieutenant SEE: **Corrupt**

Corrupt Ones, The (1966-French-Italian-West German) **C-92m.** **½ D: James Hill. Robert Stack, Elke Sommer, Nancy Kwan, Christian Marquand, Werner Peters. Knock-about photographer Stack is befriended by stranger who gives him key (literally!) to ancient Chinese emperor's treasure. With better dialogue for its many grotesque characters, film could've been a knockout. Techniscope.▼

Corruptor, The (1999) **C-110m.** ** D: James Foley. Chow Yun-Fat, Mark Wahlberg, Ric Young, Paul Ben-Victor, Jon Kit Lee, Andrew Pang, Brian Cox, Elizabeth Lindsey, Byron Mann, Kim Chan, Tovah Feldshuh. Wahlberg is assigned to the otherwise all-Chinese NYPD Asian gang unit and gradually wins the trust of Yun-Fat, leader of the task force. However, not everyone is as honest as they seem. Routine cop action film enlivened—but not enough—by Yun-Fat's sizzling star performance and Wahlberg's solid work. Lee is both silky and slimy in the title role. Super 35. [R] ▼●◗

Corsican Brothers, The (1941) **112m.** *** D: Gregory Ratoff. Douglas Fairbanks Jr., Ruth Warrick, Akim Tamiroff, J. Carrol Naish, H. B. Warner, Henry Wilcoxon. Entertaining swashbuckler from Dumas story of twins who are separated, but remain spiritually tied. Fairbanks excellent in the dual lead, with strong support, ingenious photographic effects. Remade for TV in 1985.▼

Corvette K-225 (1943) **99m.** *** D: Richard Rosson. Randolph Scott, James Brown, Ella Raines, Barry Fitzgerald, Andy Devine, Walter Sande, Richard Lane. First-rate war film with Canadian officer Scott fighting to save prominent navy destroyer from enemy attack; realistic actioner produced by Howard Hawks. Look quickly for Robert Mitchum.

Corvette Summer (1978) **C-105m.** ** D: Matthew Robbins. Mark Hamill, Annie Potts, Eugene Roche, Kim Milford, Richard McKenzie, William Bryant. High schooler Hamill falls for aspiring hooker Potts while in Vegas tracking down the person who stole the sports car restored by his shop class. Bland comedy drama offers Potts' disarmingly off-the-wall performance to keep your attention. [PG]▼

Così (1996-Australian) **C-100m.** ** D: Mark Joffe. Ben Mendelsohn, Barry Otto, Toni Collette, Rachel Griffiths, Aden Young, Colin Friels, Greta Scacchi, Paul Mercurio. Professionally unfulfilled drifter with a stable law school girlfriend makes a desperate career move when he agrees to stage Mozart's *Così Fan Tutte* as part of a therapy session for Sydney mental inmates. Unusual but eventually tiresome comedy, from Louis Nowra's play, features lots of familiar faces (to fans of Australian cinema) in supporting roles. [R]▼●

Cosmic Eye, The (1985) **C-76m.** *** D: Faith Hubley. Voices of Maureen Stapleton, Dizzy Gillespie, Sam Hubley, Linda Atkinson. Wonderfully imaginative, life-affirming animated feature about the needs, rights, and struggles of mankind, most especially children, around the world. A tapestry that includes pieces of earlier animated shorts by John and Faith Hubley, with music by such notables as Dizzy Gillespie, Benny Carter, and Elizabeth Swados.▼●

Cosmic Man, The (1959) **72m.** *½ D: Herbert Greene. Bruce Bennett, John

Carradine, Angela Greene, Paul Langton, Scotty Morrow. Mediocre sci-fi, a pale imitation of THE DAY THE EARTH STOOD STILL, in which the title creature (Carradine) arrives on earth. The military wants to destroy it, while scientists argue that this would result in dire consequences. Well-intentioned message regarding abuse of atomic energy is lost in poorly made film.▼

Cosmic Monster, The (1958-British) **75m.** *½ D: Gilbert Gunn. Forrest Tucker, Gaby Andre, Martin Benson, Alec Mango, Wyndham Goldie, Hugh Latimer. Britain's only Giant Bug movie is talky tale of a mad scientist whose magnetism experiments punch a hole in the ionosphere, letting in cosmic rays which enlarge insects in the woods. Gleefully ghoulish at times. Original British title: THE STRANGE WORLD OF PLANET X.▼

Cossacks, The (1959-Italian) **C-113m.** ** D: Giorgio Rivalta. Edmund Purdom, John Drew Barrymore, Giorgia Moll, Massimo Girotti. Heavy-handed historical tale set in 1850s Russia; Cossack Purdom and son Barrymore clash in loyalties to Czar Alexander II. Totalscope.

Costa Azzura SEE: **Wild Cats on the Beach**

Cottage to Let (1941-British) **90m.** ** D: Anthony Asquith. Alastair Sim, John Mills, Leslie Banks, Michael Wilding, Carla Lehmann, Catherine Lacey, George Cole. Good cast is wasted in this disappointing thriller about Nazi spies attempting to pilfer the plans for inventor Banks's secret bomb sight.▼

Cotter (1973) **C-94m.** **½ D: Paul Stanley. Don Murray, Carol Lynley, Rip Torn, Sherry Jackson. After tragic rodeo incident, unhappy Indian clown (Murray) struggles to reestablish himself in home town. Good cast in fair script that fares best in creating small-town atmosphere.▼

Cotton Club, The (1984) **C-127m.** **½ D: Francis Coppola. Richard Gere, Gregory Hines, Diane Lane, Lonette McKee, Bob Hoskins, James Remar, Nicolas Cage, Allen Garfield, Fred Gwynne, Gwen Verdon, Maurice Hines, Joe Dallesandro, Julian Beck, Jennifer Grey, Lisa Jane Persky, Tom Waits, Diane Venora, Woody Strode, Charles "Honi" Coles, Larry Fishburne, James Russo, Giancarlo Esposito. Homage to the days of colorful gangsters and Harlem nightlife has style to spare and a wonderful soundtrack full of Duke Ellington music (Gere plays his own cornet solos); all it needs is a story and characters whose relationships make some sense. Visually striking with good scenes scattered about. In any case, the movie isn't nearly as interesting as the published stories about its tumultuous production! [R]▼●

Cotton Comes to Harlem (1970) **C-97m.** *** D: Ossie Davis. Godfrey Cambridge, Raymond St. Jacques, Calvin Lockhart, Judy Pace, Redd Foxx, Emily Yancy, Cleavon Little. St. Jacques is Coffin Ed Johnson, Cambridge is Gravedigger Jones, black cops who suspect preacher Lockhart's back-to-Africa campaign is a swindle. Neatly combines action and comedy, with fine use of Harlem locales; from Chester Himes' novel. Sequel: COME BACK, CHARLESTON BLUE. [R]▼

Cotton Mary (1999-French-British-U.S.) **C-124m.** *½ D: Ismail Merchant. Greta Scacchi, Madhur Jaffrey, James Wilby, Sakina Jaffrey, Neena Gupta, Prayag Raaj, Laura Lumley, Gemma Jones, Sarah Badel. Stultifying drama, set in India in 1954, in which the Anglo-Indian title character manipulates her way into a British household and causes all sorts of tumult. Potentially interesting story of the clash between British and Indian cultures is full of obvious symbolism; a real snooze. Madhur Jaffrey (who plays Cotton Mary) is listed in the credits as "co-director." [R]

Couch, The (1962) **100m.** **½ D: Owen Crump. Shirley Knight, Grant Williams, Onslow Stevens, William Leslie. Bizarre yarn of psychopathic killer on the prowl while under analysis. Script by Robert Bloch from screen story cowritten by Blake Edwards.

Couch in New York, A (1996-Belgian-French-German) **C-105m.** *½ D: Chantal Akerman. Juliette Binoche, William Hurt, Stephanie Buttle, Barbara Garrick, Paul Guilfoyle, Richard Jenkins, Kent Broadhurst. N.Y.C. therapist Hurt, in desperate need of a change of scenery, switches apartments with Parisian dancer Binoche. Flat, uninspired romantic comedy. [R]▼●

Couch Trip, The (1988) **C-97m.** **½ D: Michael Ritchie. Dan Aykroyd, Walter Matthau, Charles Grodin, Donna Dixon, Richard Romanus, Arye Gross, David Clennon, Mary Gross. Amusing, if somewhat lackluster, comedy about a mental institution escapee who masquerades as a successful Beverly Hills psychiatrist and radio adviser. Some good laughs, served by a solid cast, but the story is pretty thin. [R]▼●

Counsellor-at-Law (1933) **82m.** **** D: William Wyler. John Barrymore, Bebe Daniels, Doris Kenyon, Onslow Stevens, Isabel Jewell, Melvyn Douglas, Thelma Todd, John Qualen, Mayo Methot, Vincent Sherman. Vivid adaptation of Elmer Rice play about rags-to-riches Jewish lawyer who can't escape his background—and begins to question his success when he learns his wife has been unfaithful. Barrymore gives one of his greatest performances in meaty, colorful role; Wyler keeps this comedy-drama moving at breakneck pace. Scripted by Rice.

Countdown (1968) **C-101m.** ***½ D: Robert Altman. James Caan, Joanna Moore, Robert Duvall, Barbara Baxley, Charles Aidman, Steve Ihnat, Michael Murphy, Ted

Knight. Near-flawless depiction of real-life trials and concerns of American astronauts, their wives, co-workers, leading to first flight to moon. Excellent ensemble performances, intelligent script by Loring Mandel, based on Hank Searls' novel. Dated technology only liability. An early gem from Altman. Panavision.▼

Countdown at Kusini (1976-Nigerian) **C-101m.** ** D: Ossie Davis. Ruby Dee, Ossie Davis, Greg Morris, Tom Aldredge, Michael Ebert, Thomas Baptiste. Well-meaning treatment of liberation of fictional African country, "Fahari." Action and ideas are constantly swallowed up by romantic subplot. Financed by DST Telecommunications, subsidiary of Delta Sigma Theta, world's largest black sorority. [PG]▼

Count Dracula (1970-Italian-Spanish-German) **C-98m.** **½ D: Jess Franco. Christopher Lee, Herbert Lom, Klaus Kinski, Frederick Williams, Maria Rohm, Soledad Miranda. Flawed but interesting low-budget adaptation of Bram Stoker novel which sticks close to its source; Lee turns in remarkably low-key performance. TV prints run 90m. Techniscope. [PG]▼

Count Dracula and His Vampire Bride (1973-British) **C-84m.** *½ D: Alan Gibson. Christopher Lee, Peter Cushing, Michael Coles, William Franklyn, Freddie Jones, Joanna Lumley. Last of the Hammer Films Dracula series is awfully tired, despite modern-day setting; the Count gets hold of a plague virus that can destroy mankind. Cut for U.S. release from original 88m. version called SATANIC RITES OF DRACULA. Video title: THE RITES OF DRACULA. [R]▼●◗

Counter-Attack (1945) **90m.** **½ D: Zoltan Korda. Paul Muni, Marguerite Chapman, Larry Parks, Philip Van Zandt, George Macready, Roman Bohnen. Satisfactory WW2 movie of Allied fighters going behind enemy lines to sabotage German positions; no classic, but good.

Counter-Espionage (1942) **73m.** **½ D: Edward Dmytryk. Warren William, Eric Blore, Hillary Brooke, Thurston Hall, Fred Kelsey, Forrest Tucker. Deftly handled *Lone Wolf* series entry pits the sleuth against Nazi spies in London amidst the brutal German bombing blitz.

Counterfeit Commandos SEE: **Inglorious Bastards**

Counterfeiters (1948) **73m.** **½ D: Peter Stewart (Sam Newfield). John Sutton, Doris Merrick, Hugh Beaumont, Lon Chaney (Jr.), George O'Hanlon, Herbert Rawlinson. Not bad little actioner with Scotland Yard cop Sutton going undercover to nab counterfeiter Beaumont and his gang.

Counterfeit Killer, The (1968) **C-95m.** ** D: Josef Leytes. Jack Lord, Shirley Knight, Jack Weston, Charles Drake, Joseph Wiseman, Don Hanmer. Adapted from TV film THE FACELESS MAN, meandering actioner has Lord a secret service man infiltrating a counterfeit syndicate, with predictable results. Video title: CRACKSHOT.▼

Counterfeit Plan, The (1957-British) **80m.** ** D: Montgomery Tully. Zachary Scott, Peggie Castle, Mervyn Johns, Sydney Tafler. Scott is appropriately nasty as escaped murderer who sets up international counterfeit syndicate.

Counterfeit Traitor, The (1962) **C-140m.** ***½ D: George Seaton. William Holden, Lilli Palmer, Hugh Griffith, Erica Beer, Werner Peters, Eva Dahlbeck. Holden is a double agent during WW2, falls in love with Palmer between various dangerous missions. Authentic backgrounds and fine cast. Based on true story.▼●

Counterplot (1959) **76m.** ** D: Kurt Neumann. Forrest Tucker, Allison Hayes, Gerald Milton, Edmundo Rivera Alvarez. Mundane hide-and-seeker set in Puerto Rico where Tucker is hiding out from police and his double-dealing attorney.

Counterpoint (1968) **C-107m.** *½ D: Ralph Nelson. Charlton Heston, Maximilian Schell, Kathryn Hays, Leslie Nielsen, Anton Diffring. Absurd WW2 melodrama about symphony conductor captured by Nazi general, forced to put on private concert; Heston looks comfortable because he doesn't have to change facial expressions while conducting. Techniscope.

Counter Punch SEE: **Ripped Off**

Counter Tenors, The SEE: **White Voices, The**

Countess Dracula (1972-British) **C-94m.** ** D: Peter Sasdy. Ingrid Pitt, Nigel Green, Peter Jeffrey, Lesley-Anne Down. Countess masquerades as her own daughter, needs blood to maintain facade of youth. OK shocker. Based on historical figure Elisabeth Bathory; has nothing to do with Dracula.▼●

Countess From Hong Kong, A (1967-British) **C-108m.** *½ D: Charles Chaplin. Marlon Brando, Sophia Loren, Sydney Chaplin, Tippi Hedren, Patrick Cargill, Margaret Rutherford. Director-writer-composer (and bit-part actor) Chaplin's attempt to make old-fashioned romantic comedy sinks fast, though everybody tries hard. Sophia stows away in shipboard stateroom of diplomat Brando. Badly shot, badly timed, badly scored. A pity, particularly because this is Chaplin's cinematic swan song.▼

Countess of Monte Cristo, The (1948) **77m.** ** D: Frederick de Cordova. Sonja Henie, Olga San Juan, Dorothy Hart, Michael Kirby, Arthur Treacher. Sonja and Olga pretend to be royal visitors in this limp costume comedy.

Count Five and Die (1958-British) **92m.** **½ D: Victor Vicas. Jeffrey Hunter, Nigel Patrick, Ann-Marie Duringer, David Kossoff. WW2 espionage flick has Hunter an

American agent working with British to mislead Nazis about Allied landing site. CinemaScope.

Count of Monte Cristo, The (1934) **119m.** ***½ D: Rowland V. Lee. Robert Donat, Elissa Landi, Louis Calhern, Sidney Blackmer, Raymond Walburn, O.P. Heggie, Luis Alberni, Irene Hervey. Superb filmization of classic story of Edmond Dantes, who spends years in prison unjustly but escapes to seek revenge on enemies who framed him. Donat leads excellent cast in rousing classic from Dumas' story.▼

Count of Monte Cristo, The (1954-French) **C-97m.** **½ D: Robert Vernay. Jean Marais, Lia Amanda, Roger Piquat. Serviceable rendition of Alexandre Dumas costume classic.

Count of Monte Cristo, The (1961-French) **C-90m.** **½ D: Claude Autant-Lara. Louis Jourdan, Yvonne Furneaux, Pierre Mondy, Bernard Dheran. Faithful adaptation of Dumas novel, but Jourdan hasn't the zest that Robert Donat gave the role in 1934. Originally 120m. Dyaliscope.

Count of Monte Cristo, The (1975) **C-100m. TVM** D: David Greene. Richard Chamberlain, Tony Curtis, Trevor Howard, Louis Jourdan, Donald Pleasence, Taryn Power, Kate Nelligan. Lavish costume drama with Chamberlain quite all right as a swashbuckling Edmond Dantes and Curtis as the villainous Mondego. Sidney Carroll's adaptation of Dumas holds its own against its many predecessors. Average.▼

Country (1984) **C-109m.** *** D: Richard Pearce. Jessica Lange, Sam Shepard, Wilford Brimley, Matt Clark, Therese Graham, Levi L. Knebel. Penetrating, believable look at modern farming family torn apart when government threatens to foreclose on loan and take their land away. It's the woman whose strength holds things together (and it's Lange who coproduced the film); all performances are first-rate, and William D. Wittliff's script neatly avoids clichés. [PG]▼●

Country Dance SEE: **Brotherly Love** (1969)

Country Gentlemen (1936) **66m.** ** D: Ralph Staub. Ole Olsen, Chic Johnson, Joyce Compton, Lila Lee, Pierre Watkin, Donald Kirke, Ray Corrigan. Slight Olsen & Johnson comedy, with the boys cast as fast-talking conmen involved in a variety of shenanigans.▼

Country Girl, The (1954) **104m.** ***½ D: George Seaton. Bing Crosby, Grace Kelly, William Holden, Anthony Ross. Kelly won an Oscar as wife of alcoholic singer (Crosby) trying for comeback via help of director (Holden). Crosby excels in one of his finest roles. Writer-director Seaton also won Academy Award for adaptation of Clifford Odets play.▼

Country Life (1995-Australian) **C-107m.** *** D: Michael Blakemore. Sam Neill, Greta Scacchi, John Hargreaves, Kerry Fox, Michael Blakemore, Googie Withers, Maurie Fields, Robyn Cruze, Ron Blanchard. Chekhov's *Uncle Vanya* is transposed to an Australian sheep farm, circa WW1, and the result is absolutely delightful. Colonial Aussies simultaneously crave and clash with European sensibilities, especially when the enigmatic paterfamilias Alexander (a wickedly fun role, played by writer-director Blakemore) returns from London with the stunning Scacchi in tow. Subtle comedy, high drama, and a great deal of aroused passions ensue. And, yes, that's Britain's Googie Withers (longtime resident of Australia) as Hannah the maid—stealing every scene she's in. [PG-13]▼●

Country Music Holiday (1958) **81m.** ** D: Alvin Ganzer. Ferlin Husky, Zsa Zsa Gabor, Jesse White, Rocky Graziano, Cliff Norton, Clyde Woods, June Carter, The Jordanaires, Drifting Johnny Miller. A hillbilly's rise to fame; lots of songs and specialties dominate this curio.

Country Music Murders, The SEE: **Murder in Music City**

Count the Hours (1953) **76m.** ** D: Don Siegel. Teresa Wright, Macdonald Carey, Dolores Moran, Adele Mara, Jack Elam. Lawyer Carey takes case of migrant worker falsely accused of a double murder. Trim, well-directed (if implausible) story; Elam is at his slimiest as an alcoholic psycho.

Count Three and Pray (1955) **C-102m.** **½ D: George Sherman. Van Heflin, Joanne Woodward, Raymond Burr, Nancy Kulp. Atmospheric rural Americana in post-Civil War days, with Heflin exerting influence on townfolk as new pastor with reckless past. Woodward (making film debut) as strong-willed orphan lass and Burr, the perennial villain, are fine. CinemaScope.

Count Yorga, Vampire (1970) **C-91m.** *** D: Bob Kelljan. Robert Quarry, Roger Perry, Donna Anders, Michael Murphy, Michael Macready. Sophisticated, clever vampire (Quarry) establishes coven in modern-day Southern California. Fast-paced and convincing. Sequel: THE RETURN OF COUNT YORGA. [PG]▼●

Count Your Blessings (1959) **C-102m.** ** D: Jean Negulesco. Deborah Kerr, Rossano Brazzi, Maurice Chevalier, Martin Stephens, Tom Helmore, Patricia Medina. Unfunny comedy that even Chevalier's smile can't help. Kerr marries French playboy Brazzi during WW2; he goes off philandering for years. Their child conspires to bring them together again. CinemaScope.

Count Your Bullets SEE: **Cry For Me, Billy**

Coup de Foudre SEE: **Entre Nous**

Coup de Grace (1976-French-German) **C-96m.** ** D: Volker Schlöndorff. Margarethe von Trotta, Matthias Habich, Rudiger Kirschstein, Valeska Gert. Disappointing tale of a self-destructive countess (von Trotta, wife of the director), who wastes her life because the officer she loves does not reciprocate her feelings. Bleak, sometimes confusing film, not as emotional or involving as it should be.▼

Coup de Torchon (1981-French) **C-128m.** ***½ D: Bertrand Tavernier. Philippe Noiret, Isabelle Huppert, Stephane Audran, Irene Skobline, Eddy Mitchell, Jean-Pierre Marielle, Guy Marchand. Strong, disturbing black comedy, based on a novel by American Jim Thompson but reset in 1936 Equatorial Africa. Easygoing police chief (Noiret) of small colonial town is a doormat for everyone in sight, especially his wife; he gradually realizes he can use his position to gain vengeance with impunity. Fascinating film eventually overplays its hand, but enthralling most of the way, with marvelously shaded performance by Noiret. Aka CLEAN SLATE. ▼●

Coupe de Ville (1990) **C-99m.** ** D: Joe Roth. Patrick Dempsey, Arye Gross, Daniel Stern, Alan Arkin, Annabeth Gish, Rita Taggart, Joseph Bologna, James Gammon. Obvious, forgettable formula tale of three warring brothers forced to deal with their feelings as they drive dad Arkin's car from Detroit to Florida. Set in 1963 and—guess what?—there are oldies on the soundtrack. Still, the sequence in which the boys debate the origin of, and words to, "Louie, Louie" is almost worth the price of admission. Super 35. [PG-13]▼●

Courage (1984) **C-90m.** BOMB D: Robert L. Rosen. Ronny Cox, Lois Chiles, Art Hindle, M. Emmet Walsh, Tim Maier, Lisa Sutton. Perfectly horrendous thriller about a trio of marathon runners taken prisoner by a citizen army in the New Mexico desert. Jog on. Also known as RAW COURAGE. [R]▼

Courage (1986) **C-150m. TVM** D: Jeremy Kagan. Sophia Loren, Billy Dee Williams, Hector Elizondo, Val Avery, Ron Rifkin, Jose Perez, Dan Hedaya. Crackerjack drama about a real-life wife and mother who, heartbroken to discover her eldest son a drug addict, becomes an undercover operative for the Drug Enforcement Agency. Loren admirably dresses down to play a Queens, N.Y., housefrau for her gritty portrayal. E. Jack Neuman's solid screenplay is based on Michael Daly's 1984 *New York* Magazine piece, "Mother Courage." Above average.▼

Courage Mountain (1989-U.S.-French) **C-98m.** **½ D: Christopher Leitch. Juliette Caton, Charlie Sheen, Leslie Caron, Joanna Clarke, Nicola Stapleton, Jade Magri, Kathryn Ludlow, Jan Rubes, Yorgo Voyagis. Implausible though inoffensive updating of Johanna Spyri's *Heidi*, detailing what happens when the teenage girl is sent off to boarding school at the outset of WW1. Sheen is sorely miscast as Peter, her ever-loyal beau. [PG]▼●

Courage of Black Beauty (1957) **C-77m.** ** D: Harold Schuster. John Crawford, Diane Brewster, J. Pat O'Malley, John Bryant. Wholesome programmer of Crawford and colt he is given.▼

Courage of Lassie (1946) **C-92m.** **½ D: Fred Wilcox. Elizabeth Taylor, Frank Morgan, Tom Drake, Selena Royle, George Cleveland, Carl (Alfalfa) Switzer. Third of the MGM Lassie movies has a radiant Taylor trying to rehabilitate the collie after his combat experiences during WW2. Despite title, the dog in question is called Bill, not Lassie, though played by the same collie who starred in the other studio films. Filmed on beautiful locations in Canada.▼

Courageous Dr. Christian (1940) **67m.** ** D: Bernard Vorhaus. Jean Hersholt, Dorothy Lovett, Robert Baldwin, Tom Neal, Maude Eburne. The good doctor battles a town's indifference to its homeless and an epidemic that breaks out in shantytown. Typical entry in Hersholt's B picture series.▼

Courageous Mr. Penn (1941-British) **79m.** ** D: Lance Comfort. Clifford Evans, Deborah Kerr, Dennis Arundell, Aubrey Mallalieu, D. J. Williams. Repetition overwhelms this sometimes intelligent—but mostly dull—biography of Quaker William Penn, his trial for religious freedom and founding of the Pennsylvania colony. Original British title: PENN OF PENNSYLVANIA. ▼

Courage Under Fire (1996) **C-115m.** ***½ D: Edward Zwick. Denzel Washington, Meg Ryan, Lou Diamond Phillips, Michael Moriarty, Sean Astin, Matt Damon, Seth Gilliam, Tim Guinee, Scott Glenn, Bronson Pinchot, Kathleen Widdoes, Diane Baker. Compelling tale of a career Army officer, troubled by Persian Gulf War incident in which he was involved in an accidental death. Now he's assigned to investigate the death of a female Captain (Ryan) nominated for the Medal of Honor. In RASHOMON-like flashbacks, we learn that there's more to her story than meets the eye. Intelligent, multilayered story (by Patrick Sheane Duncan) about integrity, personal honor, and public hypocrisy. [R]▼●

Court Jester, The (1956) **C-101m.** **** D: Norman Panama, Melvin Frank. Danny Kaye, Glynis Johns, Basil Rathbone, Angela Lansbury, Cecil Parker, Mildred Natwick, Robert Middleton, John Carradine. One of the best comedies ever made has Danny as phony jester who finds himself involved in romance, court intrigue, and a deadly joust. Delightfully complicated comic situations (scripted by the directors), superbly performed. And re-

member: the pellet with the poison's in the vessel with the pestle. VistaVision.▼●◗
Court Martial (1955-British) **105m.** *** D: Anthony Asquith. David Niven, Margaret Leighton, Victor Maddern, Maurice Denham. Tense courtroom story of officer Niven accused of stealing military funds. The trial reveals provocations of grasping wife. A solid drama. Originally released as CARRINGTON, V.C.▼
Court-Martial of Billy Mitchell, The (1955) **C-100m.** *** D: Otto Preminger. Gary Cooper, Charles Bickford, Ralph Bellamy, Rod Steiger, Elizabeth Montgomery, Fred Clark, James Daly, Jack Lord, Peter Graves, Darren McGavin. Low-key drama about trial of military pioneer who in 1925 predicted Japanese attack on U.S. Steiger adds spark to slowly paced film as wily attorney; Montgomery made her movie debut here. CinemaScope.▼●
Court-Martial of Jackie Robinson, The (1990) **C-100m. TVM** D: Larry Peerce. Andre Braugher, Daniel Stern, Ruby Dee, Stan Shaw, Kasi Lemmons, Paul Dooley, Bruce Dern. Intriguing drama about a little-known event in the future baseball great's life, when he faced bigotry as a G.I. Hits a homer, thanks to Braugher's forceful performance. Ruby Dee, who played Robinson's wife in the 1950 THE JACKIE ROBINSON STORY, plays his mother here. Made for cable. Above average.▼●
Courtney Affair, The (1947-British) **112m.** **½ D: Herbert Wilcox. Anna Neagle, Michael Wilding, Gladys Young, Coral Browne, Michael Medwin. Wealthy young man marries housemaid in this family saga tracing the years 1900–1945; amiable but soapy, this was a big hit in England. Originally ran 120m. Original title: THE COURTNEYS OF CURZON STREET.▼
Courtneys of Curzon Street, The SEE: **Courtney Affair, The**
Courtship of Andy Hardy, The (1942) **93m.** ** D: George B. Seitz. Mickey Rooney, Lewis Stone, Fay Holden, Cecilia Parker, Ann Rutherford, Sara Haden, Donna Reed, William Lundigan. While Judge Hardy handles a divorce case, Andy romances the couple's withdrawn daughter (Reed). Sticky series entry.
Courtship of Eddie's Father, The (1963) **C-117m.** *** D: Vincente Minnelli. Glenn Ford, Ronny Howard, Shirley Jones, Stella Stevens, Dina Merrill, Roberta Sherwood, Jerry Van Dyke. Cute family comedy with Howard trying to find wife for widower father Ford. Look sharp for Lee Meriwether as Glenn's assistant. Later a TV series. Panavision. ▼●
Cousin Bette (1998) **C-108m.** **½ D: Des McAnuff. Jessica Lange, Bob Hoskins, Elisabeth Shue, Hugh Laurie, Aden Young, Geraldine Chaplin, Laura Fraser, Toby Stephens, Kelly Macdonald, Janie Hargreaves, John Sessions, John Benfield. Lange sees her chance for revenge after a lifetime of mistreatment when her beautiful, pampered cousin dies and Lange becomes part of the cousin's household. But her plans go awry as each person in her scheme pursues his or her own selfish agenda. Venomously witty black comedy from the Balzac novel, set in 1840s Paris, dulls its impact by taking a few turns too many. Shue is ideal as a sexy, self-absorbed soubrette. Panavision. [R]▼●◗
Cousin Bobby (1991) **C-70m.** ***½ D: Jonathan Demme. Highly personal, intelligent documentary about director Demme looking up his cousin after many years, and learning about his work. The Reverend Robert Castle is a Harlem priest who is steadfastly devoted to his parishioners, and long committed to radical political activism. A fascinating portrait of a complex individual, and of his evolving relationship with his filmmaker cousin.▼
Cousin, Cousine (1975-French) **C-95m.** *** D: Jean-Charles Tacchella. Marie-Christine Barrault, Victor Lanoux, Marie-France Pisier, Guy Marchand, Ginette Garcin, Sybil Maas. Barrault and Lanoux, married to others, become cousins by marriage and decide to go way beyond the kissing stage. Mild, easy-to-take comedy that became a surprise box-office sensation in U.S.—where it was later remade as COUSINS. [R]▼●
Cousins, The (1959-French) **112m.** ***½ D: Claude Chabrol. Jean-Claude Brialy, Gerard Blain, Juliette Mayniel, Claude Cerval, Genevieve Cluny. Complex, depressing, ultimately haunting tale of youthful disillusion, with decadent city boy Brialy and provincial cousin Blain competing for the affection of beauty Mayniel. Superbly directed by Chabrol.▼
Cousins (1989) **C-110m.** *** D: Joel Schumacher. Ted Danson, Isabella Rossellini, Sean Young, William Petersen, Lloyd Bridges, Norma Aleandro, George Coe, Keith Coogan, Gina de Angelis. A big family wedding sets the stage for romantic intrigues within two colorful clans. Highly enjoyable Americanization of the French hit COUSIN, COUSINE with charming performances by Danson, as a free-spirited soul, and Rossellini, as the married cousin to whom he's attracted. [PG-13]▼●
Covenant with Death, A (1967) **C-97m.** ** D: Lamont Johnson. George Maharis, Laura Devon, Katy Jurado, Earl Holliman, Sidney Blackmer, Gene Hackman. Unjustly convicted murderer kills his hangman and is then found to be innocent of the first offense; what now? Interesting idea is handled too melodramatically to be effective.
Covered Wagon, The (1923) **98m.** **½ D: James Cruze. J. Warren Kerrigan, Lois Wilson, Alan Hale, Ernest Torrence. Slow-paced silent forerunner of Western epics,

following a wagon train as it combats Indians and the elements; beautifully photographed, but rather tame today.▼●

Cover Girl (1944) **C-107m.** *** D: Charles Vidor. Rita Hayworth, Gene Kelly, Lee Bowman, Phil Silvers, Jinx Falkenburg, Eve Arden, Otto Kruger, Anita Colby. Incredibly clichéd plot is overcome by loveliness of Rita, fine Jerome Kern-Ira Gershwin musical score (including "Long Ago and Far Away"), and especially Kelly's solo numbers. Silvers adds some laughs, but Eve Arden steals the film as Kruger's wisecracking assistant.▼●

Cover Me Babe (1970) **C-89m.** BOMB D: Noel Black. Robert Forster, Sondra Locke, Susanne Benton, Robert S. Fields, Ken Kercheval, Sam Waterston, Regis Toomey. Depressingly bad movie about student filmmaker who lets nothing stand in the way of gaining a contract. [PG—edited from original R rating]

Covert Action (1978-Italian) **C-95m.** *½ D: Romolo Guerrieri. David Janssen, Arthur Kennedy, Corinne Clery, Maurizio Merli, Stefano Satta Flores. Janssen is former CIA man whose life is imperiled after he writes a book about his experiences. Filmed in Greece.

Cow and I (1961-French) **98m.** *** D: Henri Verneuil. Fernandel, Rene Havard, Albert Remy, Bernard Musson. Country-style humor bolstered by Fernandel as peasant escaped from German farm prison, assisted by loyal cow.

Cowboy (1958) **C-92m.** *** D: Delmer Daves. Glenn Ford, Jack Lemmon, Anna Kashfi, Brian Donlevy, Dick York. Intelligent, atmospheric Western based on Frank Harris' reminiscences as a tenderfoot. Lemmon is Harris, with Ford as his stern boss on eventful cattle roundup.▼

Cowboy and the Lady, The (1938) **91m.** **½ D: H. C. Potter. Gary Cooper, Merle Oberon, Patsy Kelly, Walter Brennan, Fuzzy Knight, Harry Davenport, Henry Kolker. Bored, aristocratic Oberon, whose father is a presidential aspirant, goes slumming at a rodeo and falls for reluctant cowpuncher Cooper. Slight (if sometimes overly cute) comedy. Leo McCarey cowrote the story; the script had contributions from Anita Loos and Dorothy Parker!▼●

Cowboy From Brooklyn, The (1938) **80m.** **½ D: Lloyd Bacon. Dick Powell, Pat O'Brien, Priscilla Lane, Dick Foran, Ann Sheridan, Johnnie Davis, Ronald Reagan, Emma Dunn. Powell can only get radio job if he proves he's an authentic cowhand. Silly musicomedy includes songs "Ride Tenderfoot Ride," title tune. Remade as TWO GUYS FROM TEXAS.

Cowboys, The (1972) **C-128m.** ** D: Mark Rydell. John Wayne, Roscoe Lee Browne, Bruce Dern, Colleen Dewhurst, Slim Pickens, Lonny Chapman, A Martinez, Robert Carradine, Allyn Ann McLerie, Richard Farnsworth. Well-produced but sluggish Western about aging rancher forced to take 11 youngsters with him on cattle drive; disappointing film whose message seems to be that violent revenge is good. Carradine's first film. Later a short-lived TV series. Panavision. [PG] ▼●◗

Cowboy Way, The (1994) **C-102m.** ** D: Gregg Champion. Woody Harrelson, Kiefer Sutherland, Ernie Hudson, Dylan McDermott, Tomas Milian, Marg Helgenberger, Luis Guzman, Travis Tritt, Christopher Durang. Two rodeo pals from New Mexico come to N.Y.C. to see what's happened to a Cuban friend who disappeared there—and soon find themselves caught in underworld crossfire. Needlessly ugly, pointlessly unrealistic; only the good-natured performances of the two leads to carry it. [PG-13]▼●◗

Cow Country (1953) **82m.** ** D: Lesley Selander, Curtis Bishop. Edmond O'Brien, Helen Westcott, Peggie Castle, Raymond Hatton. Earnest Western of 1880s Texas, with debt-ridden ranchers overcoming all.

Cracker Factory, The (1979) **C-100m. TVM** D: Burt Brinckeroff. Natalie Wood, Perry King, Peter Haskell, Vivian Blaine, Juliet Mills, Marian Mercer, Shelley Long. Wood shines as a suicidal suburban housewife who's in and out of the asylum throughout this Richard Shapiro adaptation of Joyce Rebeta-Burditt's novel. Above average.▼

Crackers (1984) **C-92m.** ** D: Louis Malle. Donald Sutherland, Jack Warden, Sean Penn, Wallace Shawn, Trinidad Silva, Larry Riley, Christine Baranski, Charlaine Woodard, Irwin Corey. Remake of the classic caper comedy BIG DEAL ON MADONNA STREET, set in San Francisco, strives for the offbeat (in its motley collection of misfit characters) but forgets to go for the laughs, too. [PG]▼●

Cracking Up (1983) **C-83m.** ** D: Jerry Lewis. Jerry (Who Else?), Herb Edelman, Zane Buzby, Dick Butkus, Milton Berle, Sammy Davis, Jr., Foster Brooks, Buddy Lester. Jerry plays various characters in vignettes loosely tied to suicidal klutz seeking help from shrink Edelman. There are funny moments (some mildly risqué), but Jerry refuses to believe that Less Is More. Originally titled SMORGASBORD; shelved after test engagements. [PG]▼

Crack in the Mirror (1960) **97m.** *** D: Richard Fleischer. Orson Welles, Juliette Greco, Bradford Dillman, Alexander Knox. Welles, Greco, and Dillman enact contrasting dual roles in intertwining love triangles set in contemporary Paris, involving murder, courtroom trial, and illicit love; novelty eventually wears thin, marring Grade-A effort. CinemaScope.

Crack in the World (1965) **C-96m.** **½ D: Andrew Marton. Dana Andrews, Janette Scott, Kieron Moore, Alexander Knox,

Peter Damon. Believable sci-fi about scientists trying to harness earth's inner energy but almost causing destruction of the world; realistic special effects.
Crackshot SEE: **Counterfeit Killer, The**
Crack-Up (1937) **71m.** **½ D: Malcolm St. Clair. Peter Lorre, Brian Donlevy, Helen Wood, Ralph Morgan, Thomas Beck, Kay Linaker. Not-bad espionage tale, with Lorre highly amusing as a spy trying to secure plans for experimental airplane; Donlevy's the test pilot he tries to bribe.
Crack-Up (1946) **93m.** *** D: Irving Reis. Pat O'Brien, Claire Trevor, Herbert Marshall, Wallace Ford, Ray Collins. Art critic O'Brien remembers surviving a train wreck that never took place; it's just the first incident in a growing web of intrigue and murder. Tense, fast-paced Hitchcockian thriller with many imaginative touches. ▼●
Cradle Will Rock (1999) **C-134m.** ***½ D: Tim Robbins. Hank Azaria, Ruben Blades, Joan Cusack, John Cusack, Cary Elwes, Philip Baker Hall, Cherry Jones, Angus Macfadyen, Bill Murray, Vanessa Redgrave, Susan Sarandon, Jamey Sheridan, John Turturro, Emily Watson, Bob Balaban, Paul Giamatti, Harris Yulin, Barnard Hughes, John Carpenter, Gretchen Mol, Audra McDonald, Stephen Spinella, Jack Black. Sprawling, invigorating concoction uses Orson Welles and John Houseman's legendary stage production of Marc Blitzstein's *The Cradle Will Rock* as a springboard for looking at 1930s art, culture, politics, and big business. Writer-director Robbins takes liberties with the facts but creates a fascinating patchwork of personalities, ideas, and ideals. Aims high and succeeds amazingly well. Super 35. [R]▼◗
Craft, The (1996) **C-100m.** *** D: Andrew Fleming. Robin Tunney, Fairuza Balk, Neve Campbell, Rachel True, Christine Taylor, Skeet Ulrich, Assumpta Serna, Cliff De Young, Helen Shaver. Four teenage girls, students at a private L.A. school, dabble in witchcraft. At first, they're gleeful about their powers, but eventually things get out of hand. Surprisingly witty, intelligent movie handles this goofy premise better than you'd think but goes too far at the end. [R]▼●◗
Craig's Wife (1936) **75m.** *** D: Dorothy Arzner. Rosalind Russell, John Boles, Billie Burke, Jane Darwell, Dorothy Wilson, Alma Kruger, Thomas Mitchell. Russell scored first big success as domineering wife who thinks more of material objects than of her husband. Based on George Kelly play, remade as HARRIET CRAIG. ▼
Cranes Are Flying, The (1957-Russian) **94m.** ***½ D: Mikhail Kalatozov. Tatyana Samoilova, Alexei Batalov, Vasili Merkuriev, A. Shvorin. Lilting love story set in WW2 Russia. Doctor's son (Batalov) leaves his sweetheart (Samoilova) to join the army. She is seduced by his cousin, marries him, and from subsequent tragedies tries to rebuild her life.▼●
Crash, The (1932) **58m.** ** D: William Dieterle. George Brent, Ruth Chatterton, Paul Cavanagh, Barbara Leonard, Henry Kolker, Lois Wilson. Chatterton is fine in this otherwise plodding drama about a self-centered, materialistic woman whose stockbroker husband (Brent) loses his fortune.
Crash! (1977) **C-85m.** *½ D: Charles Band. Jose Ferrer, Sue Lyon, John Ericson, Leslie Parrish, John Carradine. Strange, unbelievable mixture of occult and car chase. Jealous invalid-husband Ferrer tries to kill wife Lyon, who uses demonic device to cause mayhem on her own. Panavision. [PG]
Crash (1996-Canadian) **C-100m.** *½ D: David Cronenberg. James Spader, Holly Hunter, Elias Koteas, Rosanna Arquette, Deborah Kara Unger, Peter MacNeil. Steely-cold look at alienated people who find sexual excitement in automobile crashes. Filled with explicit sex as well as fetishistic scenes involving car accidents. Curiosity seekers may find it intriguing for a while, but it's awfully hard to take. Cronenberg adapted this fatally unpleasant film from J. G. Ballard's novel. Creeps along at the pace of a Yugo. R-rated version cut by 10m. [NC-17]▼●◗
Crash and Burn (1990) **C-85m.** ** D: Charles Band. Paul Ganus, Megan Ward, Ralph Waite, Bill Moseley, Eva Larue, Jack McGee, Elizabeth MacLellan. In the year 2030, a group isolated in a desert installation is menaced by one of them, secretly a killer android. A mix of ideas from THE THING, THE TERMINATOR, and ALIEN is occasionally effective, but too slow and familiar. Some good if brief David Allen effects involving a giant robot turn up at the end. From Full Moon. [R]▼
Crash Dive (1943) **C-105m.** **½ D: Archie Mayo. Tyrone Power, Anne Baxter, Dana Andrews, James Gleason, Dame May Whitty, Henry (Harry) Morgan. Submarine battleground just backdrop for love story; Power and Andrews both love young Baxter. Oscar-winner for special effects, film's main asset.▼
Crashing Las Vegas (1956) **62m.** ** D: Jean Yarbrough. Leo Gorcey, Huntz Hall, Jimmy Murphy, David (Gorcey) Condon, Mary Castle, Nicky Blair. An electric shock enables Sach to predict numbers in this flat *Bowery Boys* entry. A noticeably inebriated Gorcey threw in the towel after this one, claiming he couldn't go on after the death of his father Bernard, who played "Louie Dumbrowski" in the series.
Crash Landing (1958) **76m.** *½ D: Fred F. Sears. Gary Merrill, Nancy Davis (Reagan), Irene Hervey, Roger Smith. Insipid revelations of passengers aboard plane facing possible crash landing into the ocean.

Crash of Silence (1953-British) **93m.** *** D: Alexander Mackendrick. Phyllis Calvert, Jack Hawkins, Terence Morgan, Mandy Miller. Honest drama of young deaf girl (Miller) and her mother's dilemma: keep her at home or send her to a special school. Originally titled MANDY.▼

Crashout (1955) **90m.** **½ D: Lewis R. Foster. William Bendix, Arthur Kennedy, Luther Adler, William Talman. Low-budget but interesting story of prison break headed by Bendix. Kennedy as humane gang member is fine.▼

Crater Lake Monster, The (1977) **C-74m.** BOMB D: William R. Stromberg. Richard Cardella, Glenn Roberts, Mark Siegel, Kacey Cobb. Amateurish tale of carnivorous critter from Crater Lake (not the National Park) is climaxed by fine stop-motion animation of the menace, a plesiosaur. Too little too late, of interest to genre buffs only. [PG]▼

Crawling Eye, The (1958-British) **85m.** **½ D: Quentin Lawrence. Forrest Tucker, Laurence Payne, Janet Munro, Jennifer Jayne, Warren Mitchell. OK, if predictable, tale (adapted by Jimmy Sangster from British TV series *The Trollenberg Terror*) about cloud hiding alien invaders on mountaintop. Hampered by low-grade special effects. ▼●

Crawling Hand, The (1963) **89m.** *½ D: Herbert L. Strock. Peter Breck, Kent Taylor, Rod Lauren, Arline Judge, Richard Arlen, Allison Hayes, Alan Hale. Astronaut's disembodied hand instigates rash of stranglings in this amateurish rehash of THE BEAST WITH FIVE FINGERS. Good for a few (unintended) laughs, anyway.▼

Crawling Monster, The SEE: **Creeping Terror, The**

Crawlspace (1986) **C-82m.** BOMB D: David Schmoeller. Klaus Kinski, Talia Balsam, Sally Brown, Barbara Whinnery. Shameless imitation of PEEPING TOM, as Kinski spies on young women from his apartment's hidden crawlspace area and then kills them, the legacy of his father having been a Nazi war criminal. [R]▼

Craze (1974-British) **C-96m.** *½ D: Freddie Francis. Jack Palance, Diana Dors, Julie Ege, Trevor Howard, Suzy Kendall, Michael Jayston, Dame Edith Evans. More laughs than horror as antique dealer Palance makes human sacrifices to African idol. Hugh Griffith and Howard wisely kid the material. British title: THE INFERNAL IDOL; aka THE DEMON MASTER. [R]▼

Crazies, The (1973) **C-103m.** ** D: George Romero. Lane Carroll, W.G. McMillan, Harold Wayne Jones, Lloyd Hollar, Lynn Lowry. Biological plague hits small Pennsylvania town. The Army is called in to contain it; townspeople rebel, defy soldiers. Gory but exciting. Aka CODE NAME: TRIXIE. [R]▼

Crazy Desire (1964-Italian) **108m.** ***½ D: Luciano Salce. Ugo Tognazzi, Catherine Spaak, Gianni Garko, Beatrice Altariba. Disarming fluff of Tognazzi enamoured of young funseekers, and Spaak in particular. Totalscope.

Crazy From the Heart (1991) **C-94m. TVM** D: Thomas Schlamme. Christine Lahti, Ruben Blades, William Russ, Louise Latham, Tommy Muniz, Kamala Lopez, Bibi Besch, Robyn Lively. Refreshing romantic comedy about a spinsterish small-town Texas teacher who raises eyebrows when she takes up with the school's life-embracing Mexican janitor. Lahti glows under husband Schlamme's direction. Written by Linda Voorhees. Made for cable. Above average.▼●

Crazy Horse SEE: **Friends, Lovers, & Lunatics**

Crazy House (1943) **80m.** *** D: Edward F. Cline. Ole Olsen, Chic Johnson, Martha O'Driscoll, Patric Knowles, Cass Daley, Percy Kilbride. Olsen & Johnson take over film studio to make epic in frantic musicomedy with guests galore: Basil Rathbone, Count Basie, Allan Jones, Edgar Kennedy, Billy Gilbert, Andy Devine, etc.

Crazy House (1973-British) **C-90m.** ** D: Peter Sykes. Ray Milland, Frankie Howerd, Rosalie Crutchley, Kenneth Griffith, Elizabeth McClennan. Horror spoof that fails as comedy but succeeds with the chills. Overage entertainer Howerd finds he's related to Milland's greedy family, which is being killed off for an inheritance. U.S. title: NIGHT OF THE LAUGHING DEAD. Video title: HOUSE IN NIGHTMARE PARK. [PG]▼

Crazy in Alabama (1999) **C-104m.** **½ D: Antonio Banderas. Melanie Griffith, David Morse, Lucas Black, Cathy Moriarty, Meat Loaf Aday, Rod Steiger, Richard Schiff, John Beasley, Robert Wagner, Paul Mazursky, Elizabeth Perkins, Noah Emmerich, Fannie Flagg. Picaresque tale of the mid-1960s South: abused Griffith chops off her husband's head, leaves her seven kids, and goes to Hollywood seeking fame and fortune, toting hubby's head in a hatbox. Meanwhile, her oldest son comes face to face with racism. Doesn't succeed in tying its parallel stories together but holds your interest. Creditable directing debut for Banderas, whose wife is well cast. Super 35. [PG-13]▼◗

Crazy in Love (1992) **C-100m. TVM** D: Martha Coolidge. Holly Hunter, Gena Rowlands, Bill Pullman, Julian Sands, Herta Ware, Frances McDormand, Joanne Baron. Cozy tale of a three-generation family of women living on Washington state's Puget Sound and the feckless men in their lives.

Rowlands steals it. Pungent script by Gerald Ayres, based on Luanne Rice novel. Made for cable. Above average.▼

Crazy Jack and the Boy SEE: **Silence**

Crazy Joe (1974-Italian-U.S.) **C-100m.** **½ D: Carlo Lizzani. Peter Boyle, Rip Torn, Fred Williamson, Eli Wallach, Paula Prentiss, Luther Adler. Crime drama based on the bloody career of New York racketeer Crazy Joe Gallo is tolerable, due to its cast. Henry Winkler can be seen as a mustached hoodlum. [R]▼

Crazylegs (1953) **87m.** *½ D: Francis D. Lyon. Elroy Hirsch, Lloyd Nolan, Joan Vohs, Louise Lorimer. Inconclusive fiction based on the football escapades of Elroy "Crazylegs" Hirsch with gridiron star playing himself.

Crazy Mama (1975) **C-82m.** *** D: Jonathan Demme. Cloris Leachman, Stuart Whitman, Ann Sothern, Jim Backus, Donny Most, Linda Purl, Bryan Englund, Merie Earle, Sally Kirkland. Joyous, unrelentingly kitschy celebration of '50s America (opportunity, rock 'n' roll, and the road), made during Demme's exploitation days, follows three generations of women (Sothern, Leachman, Purl) and the men they pick up, on an absurdist crime spree from California to family homestead in Arkansas. Rough in places; overall a gem. Dennis Quaid has bit part in film debut. [PG] ▼

Crazy Moon (1986-Canadian) **C-87m.** *** D: Allan Eastman. Kiefer Sutherland, Peter Spence, Vanessa Vaughan, Ken Pogue, Eve Napier. Occasionally clichéd, but still warm, winning little story of wealthy, alienated teen Sutherland and his romance with bright, independent—and deaf—salesgirl Vaughan. Originally titled HUGGERS. [PG-13]▼●

Crazy Over Horses (1951) **65m.** ** D: William Beaudine. Leo Gorcey, Huntz Hall, William (Billy) Benedict, Bernard Gorcey, David Gorcey, Bennie Bartlett, Ted de Corsia, Allen Jenkins. The Bowery Boys get mixed up with a race horse (again) and some crooked gamblers (again).

Crazy People (1990) **C-90m.** ** D: Tony Bill. Dudley Moore, Daryl Hannah, Paul Reiser, Mercedes Ruehl, J.T. Walsh, Bill Smitrovich, Alan North, David Paymer, Dick Cusack, Ben Hammer. Stressed-out ad exec Moore devises a series of brutally honest (and very funny) advertisements, which prompt his partner to place him in a mental institution. Then, to everyone's amazement, the ads are a sensational success. Though the mock ads are quite funny, film is bland, even dull. Everlikable Dudley chalks up a few extra points. [R]▼●

Crazy-Quilt, The (1966) **75m.** *** D: John Korty. Ina Mela, Tom Rosqui, David Winters, Ellen Frye. Korty's first feature is almost a home movie, featuring arresting images but diffuse, whimsical (ultimately pompous) story of girl's various romantic liaisons while her exterminator husband sits around and mopes. Filmed silent, with awkward post-synched dialogue; relies heavily upon Burgess Meredith's narration, unusual score by Peter Schickele.

Crazy Stranger SEE: **Gadjo Dilo**

Crazy Streets SEE: **Forever, Lulu**

Crazy World of Julius Vrooder, The (1974) **C-89m.** **½ D: Arthur Hiller. Timothy Bottoms, Barbara Hershey, George Marshall, Albert Salmi, Lawrence Pressman. Nobody likes this offbeat comedy of a confused Vietnam vet who acts insane to cope with a crazy world, but it has a certain charm. Veteran director Marshall returned to acting here shortly before his death. [PG]

Crazy World of Laurel and Hardy, The (1967) **83m.** **½ Narrated by Garry Moore. Unlike most L&H compilations, this one uses talkie material as well as silent footage; some good routines are fragmented, with too much lumped together, but Stan and Ollie survive nicely.

Created to Kill SEE: **Embryo**

Creation of the Humanoids (1962) **C-75m.** BOMB D: Wesley E. Barry. Don Megowan, Frances McCann, Erica Elliott, Don Doolittle. Years after an atomic war, human beings are about to be outnumbered by their subservient robots; anti-robot Megowan discovers a plot to replace people with robot duplicates. Andy Warhol loved this slow, stagy cheapie.▼

Creator (1985) **C-107m.** ** D: Ivan Passer. Peter O'Toole, Mariel Hemingway, Vincent Spano, Virginia Madsen, David Ogden Stiers, John Dehner, Jeff Corey. O'Toole once again plays a Lovable Eccentric (which he does to perfection), this time a university-based scientist who's trying to revive his long-dead wife and who serves as mentor for impressionable student Spano. Amiable but aimless adaptation of Jeremy Leven's novel, redeemed only by O'Toole's magnetism. [R]▼●◗

Creature (1985) **C-97m.** ** D: William Malone. Stan Ivar, Wendy Schaal, Lyman Ward, Robert Jaffe, Diane Salinger, Annette McCarthy, Klaus Kinski. Imitation of ALIEN set on Saturn's moon Titan has nondescript cast investigating life forms discovered (fatally) by a previous mission. Guest star Kinski is funny, whether spouting gibberish or munching nonchalantly on a sandwich during otherwise tense scenes. Originally titled TITAN FIND. [R]▼●

Creature From Black Lake (1976) **C-97m.** ** D: Joy Houck, Jr. Jack Elam, Dub Taylor, Dennis Fimple, John David Carson, Bill Thurman, Catherine McClenny. Two young men venture into Louisiana swamps, only to run smack into Bigfoot; not-bad low-budgeter follows familiar formula, with typically amusing performance

by Elam. McClenny is Morgan Fairchild's sister. Todd-AO 35. [PG]▼
Creature From the Black Lagoon (1954) **79m.** *** D: Jack Arnold. Richard Carlson, Julia (Julie) Adams, Richard Denning, Antonio Moreno, Whit Bissell, Nestor Paiva, Ricou Browning, Ben Chapman. Archetypal 50s monster movie has been copied so often that some of the edge is gone, but story of Amazon expedition encountering deadly Gill-Man is still entertaining, with juicy atmosphere, luminous underwater photography sequences directed by James C. Havens. Originally in 3-D, but just as good without it. Two sequels: REVENGE OF THE CREATURE and THE CREATURE WALKS AMONG US.▼●
Creature From the Haunted Sea (1961) **74m.** *½ D: Roger Corman. Antony Carbone, Betsy Jones-Moreland, Edward Wain, E. R. Alvarez, Robert Bean. Gangster tries to cover crime wave by creating panic with story of sea monster . . . then real sea monster shows up. Roger Corman quickie comedy is not as freakish as his others. Costar Wain is actually Oscar-winning screenwriter Robert Towne. Remake of NAKED PARADISE.▼
Creature of Destruction (1968) **C-80m.** BOMB D: Larry Buchanan. Les Tremayne, Pat Delaney, Aron Kincaid, Scotty McKay. Mysterious hypnotist Tremayne and pretty assistant predict murders at a country club; murders are committed by title monster, which rises from a lake. Excruciating, with hilariously illogical musical interludes. Remake of THE SHE CREATURE.▼
Creature of the Walking Dead (1965) **74m.** *½ D: Frederic Corte (Fernando Cortes). Rock Madison, Ann Wells, George Todd, Willard Gross, Bruno Ve Sota. Mad scientist brings his equally mad grandfather back to life, with Frankenstein-ish results, in this impoverished horror quickie. Made in Mexico in 1960, then "expanded" with new footage for American release by Jerry Warren.▼
Creatures SEE: **From Beyond the Grave**
Creatures of the Prehistoric Planet SEE: **Vampire Men of the Lost Planet**
Creatures the World Forgot (1971-British) **C-94m.** *½ D: Don Chaffey. Julie Ege, Tony Bonner, Robert John, Sue Wilson, Rosalie Crutchley. Hammer Films gives us another prehistoric movie with no dinosaurs and little credibility. [PG]▼
Creature Walks Among Us, The (1956) **78m.** ** D: John Sherwood. Jeff Morrow, Rex Reason, Leigh Snowden, Gregg Palmer. Sequel to REVENGE OF THE CREATURE has Gill-man caged by humans, subjected to plastic surgery in hopes of humanizing him, returning to the ocean after a few mild tantrums.▼●
Creature Wasn't Nice, The (1981) **C-88m.** *½ D: Bruce Kimmel. Cindy Williams, Bruce Kimmel, Leslie Nielsen, Gerrit Graham, Patrick Macnee, Ron Kurowski. Silly monster-loose-in-spaceship parody: Nielsen is the firm but obtuse commander, Macnee the loony scientist, Williams the only woman on board, etc. Believe it or not, this is a musical (one song is titled "I Want to Eat Your Face"). Video titles: SPACESHIP and NAKED SPACE. [PG]▼
Creature With the Atom Brain (1955) **70m.** ** D: Edward L. Cahn. Richard Denning, Angela Stevens, Gregory Gaye, Tristram Coffin. Passable hokum: scientist revives the dead via high-charged brain tissue, and these robots are used by gangster seeking revenge.
Creature With the Blue Hand (1970-German) **C-74m.** ** D: Alfred Vohrer. Klaus Kinski, Diana Kerner, Carl Lang, Ilse Page, Harold Leopold. OK Edgar Wallace story has innocent man accused of murders perpetrated by title creature. Aka THE BLOODY DEAD. [PG]▼
Creeper, The (1948) **64m.** ** D: Jean Yarbrough. Onslow Stevens, Eduardo Ciannelli, June Vincent, Ralph Morgan, Janis Wilson. Stevens is mad doctor whose serum turns man into catlike killer.▼
Creeper, The (1978) SEE: **Rituals**
Creepers, The (1971) SEE: **In the Devil's Garden**
Creepers (1984-Italian) **C-82m.** *** D: Dario Argento. Jennifer Connelly, Donald Pleasence, Daria Nicolodi, Dalila Di Lazzaro, Patrick Bauchau, Fiore Argento. Typically stylish, bizarre Argento horror opus whose premise—a mad killer running amok at a Swiss girls' school—serves as a framework for some cleverly weird goings-on. For openers, Connelly plays a girl who has a most unusual relationship with insects. Don't say you weren't warned! Aka PHENOMENA. Original running time: 110m. [R]▼◗
Creeping Flesh, The (1973-British) **C-94m.** *** D: Freddie Francis. Peter Cushing, Christopher Lee, Lorna Heilbron, George Benson. Well-intentioned, old-fashioned monster film on reincarnation of ancient evil spirit. Cushing and Lee play rival brothers competing over ancient skeleton that slowly returns to life. Numerous subplots add to the fun. [PG]▼●
Creeping Terror, The (1964) **75m.** BOMB D: Art J. Nelson. Vic Savage, Shannon O'Neill, William Thourlby, Louise Lawson, Robin James. Awful horror movie, poor on every conceivable (and inconceivable) level. Monster aptly described as a giant carpet absorbs humans into its body. When it's destroyed, another takes its place. Badly shot on Lake Tahoe. Aka THE CRAWLING MONSTER.▼
Creeping Unknown, The (1956-British) **82m.** *** D: Val Guest. Brian Donlevy, Margia Dean, Jack Warner, Richard Words-

worth. A spaceship returns to earth with only one man left on board; infested by an alien entity, he gradually transforms into a hideous monster. Tense, imaginative, adult; well acted by all concerned. Based on hit BBC-TV serial by Nigel Kneale. Also known under original British title, THE QUATERMASS XPERIMENT. Followed by three sequels, beginning with ENEMY FROM SPACE.▼●

Creepshow (1982) C-120m. ** D: George Romero. Hal Holbrook, Adrienne Barbeau, Fritz Weaver, Leslie Nielsen, Carrie Nye, E. G. Marshall, Viveca Lindfors, Ed Harris, Ted Danson, Gaylen Ross. Romero nicely captures the look of a comic book in this homage to 1950s E.C. Comics, but Stephen King's five ''fantastic tales'' of revenge and just desserts are transparent and heavy-handed (King himself stars in the second episode, as an ill-fated rube). Finale has hundreds of cockroaches bursting through the stomach of a man with an insect phobia (Marshall). If that's your cup of tea, tune in. Followed by a sequel. [R]▼●◗

Creepshow 2 (1987) C-89m. *½ D: Michael Gornick. Lois Chiles, George Kennedy, Dorothy Lamour, Tom Savini, Domenick John, Frank S. Salsedo, Holt McCallany, David Holbrook, Page Hannah. George A. Romero scripted this trio of Stephen King short stories, but their combined reputations can't lift this cheap-looking movie out of the muck. As in the much slicker CREEPSHOW, all the stories are juvenile and heavy-handed (a wooden Indian comes to life, a hitchhiker run over by a motorist lives on to terrorize her, etc.). King appears briefly as a truck driver. [R]▼●

Crescendo (1972-British) C-83m. *½ D: Alan Gibson. Stefanie Powers, James Olson, Margaretta Scott, Jane Lapotaire, Joss Ackland. Tiresome chiller has grad student Powers traveling to France for some research on a dead composer, becoming involved with his crazy family. [PG—edited from original R rating]

Crest of the Wave (1954-British) 90m. **½ D: John Boulting, Roy Boulting. Gene Kelly, John Justin, Bernard Lee, Jeff Richards. Static account of navy officer Kelly joining British research group to supervise demolition experiments.

Cries and Whispers (1972-Swedish) C-106m. *** D: Ingmar Bergman. Harriet Andersson, Liv Ullmann, Ingrid Thulin, Kari Sylwan, Erland Josephson, George Arlin, Henning Moritzen. Beautifully photographed and acted drama about lives of a dying woman, her sisters and a servant girl was tremendous critical success, but may be too talky for some. Cinematographer Sven Nykvist won an Oscar. [R]▼●

Cries in the Night SEE: Funeral Home▼

Crime Against Joe (1956) 69m. ** D: Lee Sholem. John Bromfield, Julie London, Henry Calvin, Patricia Blake. Standard find-the-actual-murderer fare.

Crime and Passion (1976) C-92m. *½ D: Ivan Passer. Omar Sharif, Karen Black, Joseph Bottoms, Bernhard Wicki. Bizarre comedy-thriller set in Austrian Alps. Sharif is international financier who persuades secretary-mistress Black to wed industrialist Wicki for his money, then finds they are both marked for death by the husband. [R]▼

Crime and Punishment (1935) 88m. **½ D: Josef von Sternberg. Edward Arnold, Peter Lorre, Marian Marsh, Tala Birell, Elisabeth Risdon. Fascinating Hollywoodization of Dostoyevsky's novel about man haunted by murder he committed. Low-budget but full of inventive ideas by von Sternberg.▼●

Crime and Punishment (1958-French) 108m. *** D: Georges Lampin. Jean Gabin, Marina Vlady, Ulla Jacobsson, Bernard Blier. Perceptive updating of Dostoyevsky novel set in Paris. Retitled: THE MOST DANGEROUS SIN.

Crime & Punishment, USA (1959) 78m. **½ D: Denis Sanders. George Hamilton, Mary Murphy, Frank Silvera, Marian Seldes, John Harding, Wayne Heffley. Trim, updated version of Dostoyevsky novel has Hamilton (film debut) a law student who becomes involved in robbery and murder.

Crime Boss (1972-Italian) C-93m. *½ D: Albert DeMartino. Telly Savalas, Antonio Sabato, Paola Tedesca. Crime czar Savalas takes on a young protege and lives to regret it. One of Telly's numerous Mafioso roles before sticking a lollipop in his mouth and a gold NYPD badge on his chest. Plodding and formula-bound. [R]

Crimebroker (1993) C-99m. *½ D: Ian Barry. Jacqueline Bisset, Masaya Kato, Peter Boswell, John Bach, Ralph Cotterill, Gary Day, Victoria Longley. A respected judge (Bisset) leads a double life as a criminal mastermind planning robberies. Kato is a criminologist who discovers her secret and joins her in the scheme. Intriguing premise is underdeveloped and the characters are never more than caricatures. [R] ▼◗

Crime Busters (1980-Italian) C-98m. *½ D: E. B. Clucher (Enzo Barboni). Terence Hill, Bud Spencer, Laura Gemser, Luciana Catenacci. Filmed in Miami, this cop-movie parody is a hair better than other Hill-Spencer efforts, but not a patch on the Trinity films; chief novelty derives from watching them go through their paces in a contemporary American setting. Bad dubbing doesn't help. Filmed in 1976 as TWO SUPERCOPS. Originally 115m. [PG]▼

Crime By Night (1944) 72m. **½ D: William Clemens. Jane Wyman, Jerome Cowan, Faye Emerson, Eleanor Parker, Creighton Hale. Good little murder mystery with detective Cowan unwittingly walking into murder case.

Crime Doctor In 1943 Columbia Pictures took Max Marcin's successful radio show CRIME DOCTOR and initiated a film series of that name with Warner Baxter in the lead. The first film set the premise of an amnesia victim named Dr. Ordway becoming the country's leading criminal psychologist, later discovering that he was a gang leader himself before a blow clouded his memory. This idea served as the basis for ten fairly respectable, enjoyable mysteries. Most of the films followed a standard whodunit formula, but were well acted and directed (by such people as William Castle and George Archainbaud), with competent players rounded up from Columbia's contract list. The films moved along briskly, most of them running barely over an hour.

CRIME DOCTOR

Crime Doctor (1943)
Crime Doctor's Strangest Case (1943)
Shadows in the Night (1944)
Crime Doctor's Courage (1945)
Crime Doctor's Warning (1945)
Crime Doctor's Man Hunt (1946)
Just Before Dawn (1946)
The Millerson Case (1947)
Crime Doctor's Gamble (1947)
Crime Doctor's Diary (1949)

Crime Doctor (1943) **66m.** **½ D: Michael Gordon. Warner Baxter, Margaret Lindsay, John Litel, Ray Collins, Harold Huber, Don Costello, Leon Ames. Ex-gang leader Baxter loses his memory and becomes a criminal psychologist, only to stand trial when his past is revealed. Slow-starting, but fairly good initial entry. Remake of THE MAN WHO LIVED TWICE, remade in 1953 as MAN IN THE DARK.

Crime Doctor's Courage (1945) **70m.** **½ D: George Sherman. Warner Baxter, Hillary Brooke, Jerome Cowan, Robert Scott, Lloyd Corrigan, Emory Parnell, Stephen Crane. Dr. Ordway probes the murder of a man whose first two wives died mysteriously in this OK entry.

Crime Doctor's Diary (1949) **61m.** ** D: Seymour Friedman. Warner Baxter, Lois Maxwell, Adele Jergens, Robert Armstrong. The Crime Doctor's final case, with a lethargic Baxter trying to prove his patient was framed on arson charges.

Crime Doctor's Gamble (1947) **66m.** **½ D: William Castle. Warner Baxter, Micheline Cheirel, Roger Dann, Steven Geray, Marcel Journet. The doc's vacation in gay Paris is interrupted by murder that involves a case of art theft and a colorful chase across Europe.

Crime Doctor's Man Hunt (1946) **61m.** **½ D: William Castle. Warner Baxter, Ellen Drew, William Frawley, Frank Sully, Claire Carleton, Bernard Nedell. An amnesiac soldier is murdered and Ordway is led into a web of deceit by the man's fiancée in this lively episode with a good script by Leigh Brackett and welcome wisecracks by cop Frawley.

Crime Doctor's Strangest Case (1943) **68m.** ** D: Eugene J. Forde. Warner Baxter, Lynn Merrick, Lloyd Bridges, Reginald Denny, Barton MacLane, Jerome Cowan, Rose Hobart. Dr. Ordway analyzes an old lady's dreams which hold the key to a murder in this sluggish entry.

Crime Doctor's Warning (1945) **70m.** **½ D: William Castle. Warner Baxter, John Litel, Dusty Anderson, Coulter Irwin, Miles Mander, John Abbott. Engrossing entry, as Dr. Ordway gets involved in the case of an emotionally unstable artist who suffers from blackouts and is suspected of murder when his models start turning up dead.

Crime Does Not Pay (1962-French) **159m.** **½ D: Gerard Oury. Pierre Brasseur, Gino Cervi, Danielle Darrieux, Gabriele Ferzetti, Annie Girardot, Michele Morgan, Richard Todd. Interesting gimmick for three-part film—would-be-wife-killer goes to cinema showing trio of stories on murder: "The Spider's Web," "The Fenyrou Case," and "The Mask." Retitled: GENTLE ART OF MURDER. Dyaliscope.

Crime, Inc. SEE: **Gangs, Inc.**

Crime in the Streets (1956) **91m.** **½ D: Donald Siegel. James Whitmore, John Cassavetes, Sal Mineo, Mark Rydell, Virginia Gregg, Denise Alexander, Will Kuluva, Peter Votrian, Malcolm Atterbury. Incisive if overlong drama of angry, alienated teen Cassavetes, who conspires to commit murder. Good performances by Cassavetes, Mineo and future director Rydell as his cronies, and Whitmore as an idealistic social worker. Adapted by Reginald Rose from his 1955 teleplay; Cassavetes, Rydell, and Kuluva repeat their TV performances.▼

Crime of Dr. Crespi, The (1935) **63m.** ** D: John H. Auer. Erich von Stroheim, Dwight Frye, Paul Guilfoyle, Harriett Russell, John Bohn. Von Stroheim gets even with man who loves his girl by planning unspeakable torture for him. Low-grade chiller. Allegedly based on "The Premature Burial" by Edgar Allan Poe.▼

Crime of Dr. Hallet, The (1938) **68m.** *½ D: S. Sylvan Simon. Ralph Bellamy, William Gargan, Josephine Hutchinson, Barbara Read, John King. Tedious story of jungle doctor working on fever cure who assumes assistant's identity when the latter dies in experiment. Remade as STRANGE CONQUEST.

Crime of Monsieur Lange, The (1936-French) **90m.** *** D: Jean Renoir. Rene Lefevre, Jules Berry, Florelle, Nadia

Sibirskaia, Sylvia Bataille, Jean Daste. Clever (if a bit too talky) tale of an exploited publishing house clerk (Lefevre), who pens stories in his spare time, his evil, lecherous boss (Berry), and a host of complications. Scripted by Jacques Prévert, with a pointed anti-capitalist message.▼●

Crime of Passion (1957) **84m.** **½ D: Gerd Oswald. Barbara Stanwyck, Sterling Hayden, Raymond Burr, Fay Wray, Royal Dano, Virginia Grey. Stanwyck is rough and tough as grasping wife who'll do anything to forward hubby's career.▼

Crime of the Century (1996) **C-115m. TVM** D: Mark Rydell. Stephen Rea, Isabella Rossellini, J. T. Walsh, Michael Moriarty, David Paymer, Allen Garfield, Gerald S. O'Loughlin, Barry Primus, John Harkins, Bert Remsen, Jay Acavone. Rea's performance as Bruno Hauptmann, convicted and executed for the 1932 kidnapping and murder of the Lindbergh baby, and particularly Rossellini's as his trusting wife, Anna, anchor this murkily photographed docudrama told, by William Nicholson, as one of the great miscarriages of American justice. Based on Sir Ludovic Kennedy's 1965 book *The Airman and the Carpenter.* Acting students might compare Rea's Hauptmann with Anthony Hopkins' in THE LINDBERGH KIDNAPPING CASE (1976). Made for cable. Above average.▼●

Crimes and Misdemeanors (1989) **C-104m.** ***½ D: Woody Allen. Caroline Aaron, Alan Alda, Woody Allen, Claire Bloom, Mia Farrow, Joanna Gleason, Anjelica Huston, Martin Landau, Jenny Nichols, Jerry Orbach, Sam Waterston. Film's title indicates the themes of two separate stories, which are neatly tied up in the final scene. Landau plays a married man who is desperate to cut off an adulterous relationship in this somberly tragic tale. Allen is an unhappy documentary filmmaker who's wooing attractive Farrow while making a film about insufferably self-centered TV producer Alda, in a hilariously bittersweet story. Arguably Woody's most ambitious film, playing heavy drama against often uproarious comedy, and certainly one of his most passionately debated; a one-of-a-kind effort that only he could pull off. Daryl Hannah has an unbilled cameo as one of Alda's chippies. [PG-13]▼●◗

Crimes at the Dark House (1940-British) **69m.** *** D: George King. Tod Slaughter, Sylvia Marriott, Hilary Eaves, Geoffrey Wardell, Hay Petrie. Slaughter is at his lip-smacking best in this adaptation of Wilkie Collins' *The Woman in White.* Old-fashioned melodrama without a whiff of condescension is not to all tastes, but for those with a liking for this rip-snorting stuff, this is one of the best. Typical line: "I'll feed your entrails to the pigs!"▼

Crime School (1938) **86m.** **½ D: Lewis Seiler. Dead End Kids (Billy Halop, Bobby Jordan, Huntz Hall, Leo Gorcey, Bernard Punsley, Gabriel Dell), Humphrey Bogart, Gale Page. Bogart sets out to improve a reform school, but meets his match in the Dead End Kids. OK reworking of THE MAYOR OF HELL, weakened by the Kids' disreputable personalities and Bogart's unlikely casting as a do-gooder. Story rehashed again as HELL'S KITCHEN.

Crimes of Dr. Mabuse, The SEE: **Testament of Dr. Mabuse, The**

Crimes of Passion (1984) **C-101m.** ** D: Ken Russell. Kathleen Turner, Anthony Perkins, John Laughlin, Annie Potts, Bruce Davison. Laughlin, trapped in a stale marriage, takes up with mysterious Turner—fashion designer by day, hooker by night. Watchable mess is, given the subject matter, less out of control than other Russell movies. Turner actually gives a performance; Perkins amuses in one of his standard nutso roles. One of the two homevideo versions has several minutes of kinky footage originally seen only in Europe. [R] ▼●◗

Crimes of Stephen Hawke, The (1936-British) **69m.** **½ D: George King. Tod Slaughter, Marjorie Taylor, D. J. Williams, Eric Portman, Ben Soutten. Florid melodrama with Slaughter deliciously ripe as kindly moneylender Hawke, secretly the murderous fiend known as Spine Breaker. Stodgy direction, in this case, seems appropriate. Lower the rating if you can't stand barnstorming thrillers. Aka STRANGLER'S MORGUE. ▼

Crimes of the Heart (1986) **C-105m.** **½ D: Bruce Beresford. Diane Keaton, Jessica Lange, Sissy Spacek, Sam Shepard, Tess Harper, David Carpenter, Hurd Hatfield. Three Southern sisters, who are equally off-center, share their various woes and idiosyncrasies (along with pent-up jealousies and resentments) during a fateful reunion. Superior performances can't make a really good film out of Beth Henley's Pulitzer Prize-winning play, even though Henley wrote the screenplay herself. [PG-13]▼●

Crime Wave (1954) **74m.** **½ D: Andre De Toth. Sterling Hayden, Gene Nelson, Phyllis Kirk, Ted de Corsia, Charles Buchinsky (Bronson), Jay Novello, James Bell, Dub Taylor, Timothy Carey. Neat little B-picture about some escaped cons who try to involve a former prisonmate (who's now gone straight) in their latest heist. Actuality-style filming on L.A. locations gives this an extra boost.

Crimewave (1985) **C-83m.** **½ D: Sam Raimi. Louise Lasser, Paul L. Smith, Brion James, Sheree J. Wilson, Bruce Campbell, Reed Birney, Edward R. Pressman, Julius Harris. After a successful debut with EVIL DEAD, director Raimi pays tribute to slapstick comedy with this weird, almost incoherent crime story set in Detroit.

Smith and James are well cast as grotesque goons on a robbery/killing spree. This exercise in style was cowritten by Raimi's pals, Joel and Ethan Coen. [PG-13]▼

Crime Without Passion (1934) **72m.** *** D: Ben Hecht, Charles MacArthur. Claude Rains, Margo, Whitney Bourne, Stanley Ridges, Esther Dale, Leslie Adams. Bizarre, fascinating melodrama of callous lawyer Rains, jealous of Margo's escorts, who must establish false alibi after shooting her in lovers' quarrel. Helen Hayes (Mrs. Charles MacArthur) and Fanny Brice have brief cameos in hotel lobby scene, and directors Hecht and MacArthur play reporters! Slavko Vorkapich contributed that incredible opening montage depicting The Furies in night flight over N.Y.C.

Crime Zone (1988) **C-93m.** **½ D: Luis Llosa. David Carradine, Peter Nelson, Sherilyn Fenn, Michael Shaner, Orlando Sacha. Moody sci-fi set in repressive, stratified future society. Upper-caste Carradine recruits young lovers to commit crimes for a surprising reason. Profane, satiric, well-crafted low-budgeter, but loses its way before the finish. Shot in Peru! [R]▼

Criminal, The SEE: **Concrete Jungle, The** (1960)

Criminal Behavior (1992) **C-100m. TVM** D: Michael Miller. Farrah Fawcett, A Martinez, Morgan Stevens, Dakin Matthews, John Hancock, Cliff DeYoung, Andrew Robinson, James Gammon. Tough lady lawyer is pursued by a killer in this sweaty thriller adapted by veteran Wendell Mayes from Ross MacDonald's detective novel *The Ferguson Affair.* Above average.

Criminal Code, The (1931) **95m.** **½ D: Howard Hawks. Walter Huston, Phillips Holmes, Constance Cummings, Mary Doran, Boris Karloff, De Witt Jennings. Warden Huston—tough but essentially fair—faces a dilemma when his daughter falls in love with prisoner Holmes. Creaky in parts, lively in others, but cast and director make this a must for buffs. Remade as PENITENTIARY in 1938 and CONVICTED in 1950.▼

Criminal Court (1946) **63m.** ** D: Robert Wise. Tom Conway, Martha O'Driscoll, Robert Armstrong, Addison Richards, June Clayworth, Pat Gleason, Steve Brodie. Disappointingly routine programmer finds O'Driscoll charged with murder of blackmailer Armstrong, defended by wily attorney Conway who is the real killer (by accident). Confusing mystery tale. ▼

Criminal Justice (1990) **C-90m. TVM** D: Andy Wolk. Forest Whitaker, Jennifer Grey, Rosie Perez, Tony Todd, Anthony LaPaglia. Powerhouse drama by Wolk about an angry black ex-con who has lost all faith in the system, and the young white woman who prosecutes him for assaulting a prostitute. Made for cable. Above average.▼

Criminal Law (1989) **C-117m.** *½ D: Martin Campbell. Gary Oldman, Kevin Bacon, Karen Young, Joe Don Baker, Tess Harper, Elizabeth Sheppard. Weak suspense film, done in by an unsatisfying script and unbelievable story. Slick attorney Oldman (playing an American—and quite well) matches wits with wealthy psychopath Bacon in tale of serial murders in Boston. Unnecessarily pretentious, unintentionally funny, and, unfortunately, filmed nowhere near Boston. [R]▼●

Criminal Lawyer (1951) **74m.** *½ D: Seymour Friedman. Pat O'Brien, Jane Wyatt, Carl Benton Reid, Mary Castle. Alcoholic attorney O'Brien sobers up to defend friend saddled with homicide charge.

Criminal Life of Archibaldo de la Cruz, The (1955-Mexican) **91m.** ** D: Luis Buñuel. Ernesto Alonso, Miroslava Stern, Rita Macedo, Ariadna Welter, Rodolfo Landa, Andrea Palma. Very minor psychological drama from Buñuel. As a boy, Archibaldo witnesses his governess' death and is fascinated by what he feels; as a man, he's obsessed with murder and dying. Much too talky; it sounds far more interesting than it plays.▼

Crimson Altar, The SEE: **Crimson Cult, The**

Crimson Blade, The (1963-British) **C-82m.** **½ D: John Gilling. Lionel Jeffries, Oliver Reed, Jack Hedley, June Thorburn, Duncan Lamont. OK swashbuckler features romance between two young people on opposite side of Cromwell's struggle for power in 17th century; good-looking Hammer production. Originally titled THE SCARLET BLADE. Megascope.

Crimson Canary, The (1945) **64m.** **½ D: John Hoffman. Noah Beery Jr., Lois Collier, Danny Morton, John Litel, Claudia Drake, Steven Geray. Offbeat murder mystery with nightclub musicians the suspects, nicely done.

Crimson Circle, The SEE: **Red Circle, The**

Crimson Cult, The (1968-British) **C-87m.** ** D: Vernon Sewell. Mark Eden, Virginia Wetherell, Christopher Lee, Boris Karloff, Michael Gough, Barbara Steele. Lackluster script and pacing major flaws in standard witchcraft thriller featuring aging Karloff as expert on black magic, Steele (in green makeup) as 300-year-old witch. Original British titles: CURSE OF THE CRIMSON ALTAR and THE CRIMSON ALTAR. [M/PG]▼●

Crimson Kimono, The (1959) **82m.** ** D: Samuel Fuller. Victoria Shaw, Glenn Corbett, James Shigeta, Anna Lee, Paul Dubov, Jaclynne Greene, Gloria Pall. Two L.A. detectives investigate a stripper's murder in this offbeat little film; more interesting for Sam Fuller buffs than general viewers, who may find story and treatment too low-key and meandering.

Crimson Pirate, The (1952) **C-104m.** ***½ D: Robert Siodmak. Burt Lancaster,

Nick Cravat, Eva Bartok, Torin Thatcher, Christopher Lee. Lancaster and Cravat swashbuckle their way across the Mediterranean in one of the great genre classics of all time. Cult film offers loads of thrills and laughs to both children and adults.▼●

Crimson Romance (1934) **72m.** *** D: David Howard. Ben Lyon, Sari Maritza, Erich von Stroheim, Hardie Albright, James Bush, William Bakewell, Herman Bing, Jason Robards, Sr. Provocative drama of impetuous American test pilot Lyon, whose German-born pal returns to the Fatherland during WW1—before America's involvement in the fracas. He joins his friend in the German military, and finds himself at odds with a sadistic commandant (who else but von Stroheim?).▼

Crimson Tide (1995) **C-115m.** *** D: Tony Scott. Denzel Washington, Gene Hackman, Matt Craven, George Dzundza, Viggo Mortensen, James Gandolfini, Rocky Carroll, Jaime P. Gomez, Michael Milhoan, Scott Burkholder, Danny Nucci, Lillo Brancato, Jr., Rick Schroder, Vanessa Bell Calloway, Steve Zahn, Ryan Phillippe. The producer-director team that brought you TOP GUN fashioned this macho power-play saga aboard a Navy nuclear submarine. Tensions run high when the U.S. is pushed to the brink of war with Russia, especially when veteran sub commander Hackman starts showing Capt. Queeg tendencies and his new lieutenant (Washington) tries to assert himself. Obvious, to be sure, with a foregone conclusion, but highly entertaining just the same. Jason Robards appears unbilled. Hip dialogue added (without credit) by Quentin Tarantino. Panavision. [R] ▼●◗

Cripple Creek (1952) **C-78m.** **½ D: Ray Nazarro. George Montgomery, Karin Booth, Jerome Courtland, Richard Egan. Government agents Montgomery and Courtland track down mining crooks by joining gang in this OK Western.

Crisis (1950) **95m.** **½ D: Richard Brooks. Cary Grant, Jose Ferrer, Paula Raymond, Signe Hasso, Ramon Novarro, Antonio Moreno, Leon Ames, Gilbert Roland. Melodrama of American doctor (Grant) held in South American country to treat ailing dictator (Ferrer); intriguing but slow. Brooks's first film as director. Also shown in computer-colored version.

Criss Cross (1949) **87m.** *** D: Robert Siodmak. Burt Lancaster, Yvonne De Carlo, Dan Duryea, Stephen McNally. Lancaster returns to hometown, where he crosses path of ex-wife De Carlo, who's taken up with gangster Duryea. Potent film noir look (by cinematographer Franz Planer) and music (by Miklos Rozsa) help compensate for Lancaster's miscasting as an easily manipulated husband. Tony Curtis' screen debut; he's briefly seen as De Carlo's dance partner. Remade in 1995 as THE UNDERNEATH.▼●

CrissCross (1992) **C-100m.** ** D: Chris Menges. Goldie Hawn, Arliss Howard, James Gammon, David Arnott, Keith Carradine, J. C. Quinn, Steve Buscemi, Paul Calderon. Good intentions abound in this low-key drama set in Key West, Florida in 1969. A 12-year-old boy lives with his mom, trying to survive since his Dad (a messed-up Vietnam vet) deserted them three years ago. The boy's rootlessness and (eventual) moral dilemma are delineated in credible but much too leisurely fashion, making this potential sleeper a yawner instead. [R]▼●

Critical Care (1997) **C-109m.** **½ D: Sidney Lumet. James Spader, Helen Mirren, Kyra Sedgwick, Albert Brooks, Anne Bancroft, Wallace Shawn, Philip Bosco, Jeffrey Wright, Margo Martindale, Colm Feore, Edward Herrmann. A young resident, already cynical about the medical system and his career, is drawn into a controversy over a patient who's on a life support system, and whose two daughters disagree about his future. Satire of modern medicine (from the director of NETWORK) is heavy-handed and obvious at times, but redeems itself with a satisfying conclusion. Brooks is fun as the aged, once-brilliant doctor whose memory is now shot. And it's hard to dislike any film that begins with the Delta Rhythm Boys singing "Dry Bones." [R]▼●◗

Critical Condition (1987) **C-107m.** BOMB D: Michael Apted. Richard Pryor, Rachel Ticotin, Ruben Blades, Joe Mantegna, Bob Dishy, Sylvia Miles, Joe Dallesandro, Bob Saget, Randall "Tex" Cobb, Garrett Morris. Pryor is a con artist who takes charge at a prison hospital, with predictable results. He's in good form, but the material just isn't there; its semi-serious and sentimental threads don't work at all, and the comedy is pretty anemic. [R]▼●

Critic's Choice (1963) **C-100m.** **½ D: Don Weis. Bob Hope, Lucille Ball, Marilyn Maxwell, Rip Torn, Jessie Royce Landis, Marie Windsor, John Dehner. An in-joke Broadway play diluted for movie audience consumption. Lucy as a novice playwright outshines Hope who plays her drama critic hubby. Film emerges as tired, predictable comedy, with best moments contributed by supporting players. Based on a play by Ira Levin. Panavision.▼

Critters (1986) **C-86m.** **½ D: Stephen Herek. Dee Wallace Stone, M. Emmet Walsh, Billy Green Bush, Scott Grimes, Nadine Van Der Velde, Terrence Mann, Billy Zane. GREMLINS-inspired aliens roll along like tumbleweeds, gobbling everything in sight while chuckling to themselves—until they're menaced by critter-hunters from space. Pretty good little thriller with comic overtones. Followed by three sequels. [PG-13]▼●

Critters 2: The Main Course (1988) **C-87m.** ** D: Mick Garris. Scott Grimes, Liane Curtis, Don Opper, Barry Corbin, Tom Hodges, Sam Anderson, Lindsay Parker, Herta Ware, Terrence Mann, Roxanne Kernohan. The big-mouthed, quill-shooting nasties take on an entire town. Nothing special. [PG-13]▼●

Critters 3 (1992) **C-86m.** **½ D: Kristine Peterson. Aimee Brooks, John Calvin, Katherine Cortez, Leonardo DiCaprio, Geoffrey Blake, Don Opper, Diana Bellamy, Terrence Mann. In this low-budget DIE HARD-with-Critters, the fanged furballs invade a cheap L.A. apartment house. Not quite enough Critters action, but OK of its kind, with better characters than usual. Ends with a setup for CRITTERS 4; they were filmed back-to-back for video release. [PG-13]▼●

Critters 4 (1992) **C-95m.** ** D: Rupert Harvey. Don Opper, Brad Dourif, Paul Whitthorne, Angela Bassett, Anders Hove, Eric DaRe, Terrence Mann, Anne Elizabeth Ramsay, voice of Martine Beswicke. Series leaps to the future with the fanged fuzzballs menacing the crew of a spaceship. Peculiarly paced, with not enough Critter stuff, but OK of its kind. Dourif gives another interesting but weird performance. Made for video. [PG-13]▼●

"Crocodile" Dundee (1986-Australian) **C-98m.** *** D: Peter Faiman. Paul Hogan, Linda Kozlowski, John Meillon, David Gulpilil, Mark Blum, Michael Lombard, Irving Metzman. Amiable, laid-back Aussie comedy (that became an enormous worldwide hit) about an adventurer who shows a pretty American reporter around the bush country, then accompanies her to the equally strange terrain of New York City. Irresistibly simple and old-fashioned, with a sweetness that's rare in modern comedies. Hogan, making his movie debut, also cowrote the screenplay (reportedly inspired by TARZAN'S NEW YORK ADVENTURE). For American release quotation marks were added around CROCODILE—lest anyone think it was about a reptile! Followed by a sequel. Panavision. [PG-13]▼●

"Crocodile" Dundee II (1988-U.S.-Australian) **C-110m.** **½ D: John Cornell. Paul Hogan, Linda Kozlowski, John Meillon, Ernie Dingo, Hechter Ubarry, Juan Fernandez, Charles Dutton, Kenneth Welsh. Pleasant followup to the runaway hit reverses the original by opening in N.Y.C. and winding up in the bush country of Australia. This time the unflappable tracker runs afoul of an international drug kingpin. So leisurely that after a while you wish they'd get on with it—especially when all suspense about the outcome is eliminated. Hogan's charisma carries this almost singlehandedly. Written by Hogan and his son Brett. Panavision. [PG]▼●

Cromwell (1970-British) **C-145m.** ** D: Ken Hughes. Richard Harris, Alec Guinness, Robert Morley, Dorothy Tutin, Frank Finlay, Timothy Dalton, Patrick Wymark, Patrick Magee, Nigel Stock, Charles Gray, Michael Jayston, Geoffrey Keen. Turgid historical epic has everything money can buy, but no human feeling underneath. Harris is coldly unsympathetic as 17th-century Briton determined to rid England of tyrannical rule; one feels more sympathy for King Charles I (Guinness), which is not the idea. Great battle scenes, great cinematography and Oscar-winning costume design, hampered by Harris and amateurish music score. Panavision. [G]▼●

Cronos (1992-Mexican) **C-92m.** *** D: Guillermo Del Toro. Federico Luppi, Ron Perlman, Claudio Brook, Margarita Isabel, Tamara Shanath, Daniel Cacho, Mario Martinez, Juan Colombo, Farnesio DeBernal. An elderly, kindly antique dealer accidentally activates the Cronos Device, an instrument that grants eternal life—but at a great price: it turns the person who uses it into a (non-traditional) vampire. Howard Hughes–like billionaire Brook sends his chuckling nephew Perlman after the gadget. Inventive, entertaining film blends wit, horror, tragedy, and suspense in about equal doses, adding lots of oddball character details.▼

Crook, The (1971-French) **C-120m.** *** D: Claude Lelouch. Jean-Louis Trintignant, Daniele Delorme, Charles Denner, Christine Lelouch. Very funny pop-art caper film of incurable thief, his successes and failures. [G]

Crooked Hearts (1991) **C-112m.** *** D: Michael Bortman. Vincent D'Onofrio, Jennifer Jason Leigh, Pete Berg, Cindy Pickett, Peter Coyote, Juliette Lewis, Noah Wyle, Marg Helgenberger, Wendy Gazelle. Engaging, multileveled domestic drama showing how husband/father Coyote's indiscretion affects the various members of his family. A thoughtful, well-acted sleeper. Bortman also scripted, from Robert Boswell's novel. [R]▼●

Crooked Road, The (1965-British) **86m.** **½ D: Don Chaffey. Robert Ryan, Stewart Granger, Nadia Gray, Marius Goring, George Coulouris. OK battle of wits between dictator Granger and newspaperman Ryan, who's got the goods on him.

Crooked Way, The (1949) **90m.** ** D: Robert Florey. John Payne, Sonny Tufts, Ellen Drew, Rhys Williams. Military hero Payne recovers from shellshock to be confronted by criminal past and his old gang seeking to eliminate him.

Crooked Web, The (1955) **77m.** *½ D: Nathan Juran. Frank Lovejoy, Mari Blanchard, Richard Denning, Richard Emory. Ponderous unspinning of government officer's ensnaring prime suspect to return to Germany, scene of the crime.

Crooklyn (1994) **C-132m.** **½ D: Spike

Lee. Alfre Woodard, Delroy Lindo, David Patrick Kelly, Zelda Harris, Carlton Williams, Sharif Rashed, Tse-Mach Washington, Christopher Knowings, Jose Zuniga, Spike Lee, Frances Foster, Norman Matlock, Joie Susannah Lee, Vondie Curtis-Hall, RuPaul. At times abrasive, at times embracing comedy-drama about a family's life and times in 1970s Brooklyn, focusing on young Troy (Harris), who has a special relationship with her fiery mother and warmhearted father—and little use for her four raucous brothers. Vivid; semi-autobiographical film, written by Lee with his brother and sister, has strong performances and many fine moments, but it seems aimless at first and goes on for quite some time. One long sequence is shot in a deliberately distorted format. [PG-13]▼●◗

Crooks and Coronets (1969-British) **C-106m.** ** D: Jim O'Connolly. Telly Savalas, Edith Evans, Warren Oates, Cesar Romero, Harry H. Corbett. Crooks Savalas and Oates are hired to rob Evans' estate, but can't bring themselves to do it once they get to know her. Amiable but ordinary heist comedy. Aka SOPHIE'S PLACE. [M/PG]▼

Crooks Anonymous (1962-British) **87m.** *½ D: Ken Annakin. Leslie Phillips, Stanley Baxter, Wilfrid Hyde-White, James Robertson Justice, Julie Christie. Cornball comedy with thief Phillips enrolling in Alcoholics Anonymous-type organization for hoods. Christie, in her film debut, plays Babette La Vern, a stripper.

Crosby Case, The (1934) **60m.** **½ D: Edwin L. Marin. Wynne Gibson, Alan Dinehart, Onslow Stevens, Warren Hymer, Skeets Gallagher. Former lovers have to clear themselves when police suspect them of murder. Good whodunit with interesting plot point—a hint of abortion.

Cross and the Switchblade, The (1972) **C-106m.** *½ D: Don Murray. Pat Boone, Erik Estrada, Jackie Giroux, Jo-Ann Robinson. Crusading minister Boone winds up in New York street-gang rumbles. Uneven, uninteresting, though sincere attempt at uplifting, moralistic filmmaking. [PG]▼

Cross Creek (1983) **C-122m.** *** D: Martin Ritt. Mary Steenburgen, Rip Torn, Peter Coyote, Dana Hill, Alfre Woodard, Joanna Miles, Ike Eisenmann, Cary Guffey. Leisurely paced but rewarding drama of writer Marjorie Kinnan Rawlings's endeavor to "find herself" by moving to remote Florida backwoods home—and dealing with the simple people around her. Wonderful performances and regional flavor—though Dalene Young's script takes more than a few liberties with the facts. Steenburgen's then real-life husband Malcolm McDowell has cameo as famed editor Maxwell Perkins. [PG]▼

Crossed Swords (1954-Italian) **C-86m.** *½ D: Milton Krims. Errol Flynn, Gina Lollobrigida, Cesare Danova, Nadia Gray. Unsuccessful attempt to recapture flavor of swashbucklers of 1930s; set in 16th-century Italy with Flynn out to save Gina and her father's kingdom.

Crossed Swords (1978) **C-113m.** ** D: Richard Fleischer. Mark Lester, Oliver Reed, Raquel Welch, Ernest Borgnine, George C. Scott, Rex Harrison, Charlton Heston. Lester is too old for his dual role in well-acted but flat version of Mark Twain's *The Prince and the Pauper*. Lavish sets, costumes, and Jack Cardiff's photography will suffer on TV. Also known as THE PRINCE AND THE PAUPER. Panavision. [PG]▼

Crossfire (1947) **86m.** ***½ D: Edward Dmytryk. Robert Young, Robert Mitchum, Robert Ryan, Gloria Grahame, Paul Kelly, Richard Benedict, Sam Levene, Jacqueline White, Steve Brodie, Lex Barker. Engrossing film of insane ex-soldier leading city police in murderous chase. Anti-Semitic issue handled with taste, intelligence. Script by John Paxton, from Richard Brooks' novel *The Brick Foxhole*. Also shown in computer-colored version.▼●

Crossing Delancey (1988) **C-97m.** *** D: Joan Micklin Silver. Amy Irving, Reizl Bozyk, Peter Riegert, Jeroen Krabbe, Sylvia Miles, Suzzy Roche, George Martin, John Bedford Lloyd, Claudia Silver, Rosemary Harris, Amy Wright, David (Hyde) Pierce. Charming comedy about a self-reliant young N.Y.C. woman whose Jewish grandmother arranges for her to meet an eligible bachelor through the services of a marriage broker . . . much to her chagrin. Amusing, sometimes wistful look at the clash between old-world traditions and our modern way of life. Adapted by Susan Sandler, from her play. [PG]▼●

Crossing Guard, The (1995) **C-114m.** ** D: Sean Penn. Jack Nicholson, David Morse, Anjelica Huston, Robin Wright, Piper Laurie, Richard Bradford, Robbie Robertson, John Savage, Priscilla Barnes, Kari Wuhrer, Richard Sarafian. Introspective mood piece about a man's inability to deal with the drunk-driving death of his young daughter six years earlier, and his pursuit of the killer, who's just been released from prison. Sober and somber, but heavy-handed and never terribly moving. Penn wrote the original screenplay; his mother, Eileen Ryan, plays a jewelry store customer, and his father, Leo Penn, plays the skipper of a fishing boat. [R]▼●

Crossing the Bridge (1992) **C-103m.** **½ D: Mike Binder. Josh Charles, Jason Gedrick, Stephen Baldwin, Cheryl Pollak, Jeffrey Tambor, Rita Taggart, Hy Anzell, Richard Edson, Ken Jenkins, David Schwimmer. Modest memory movie, set in the 1960s, about Detroit teens tempted to cross the bridge into Windsor, Canada—to transport hashish back into the States. Nothing special, but certainly nothing disgraceful, either. Stephen Baldwin gets a good showcase here. [R]▼

Crossing the Line (1991-U.S.-English-Scottish) **C-93m.** **½ D: David Leland. Liam Neeson, Joanne Whalley-Kilmer, Ian Bannen, Billy Connolly, Hugh Grant, Maurice Roeves, Rab Affleck. Two-fisted mine worker who's been blackballed out of work accepts an offer from a mysterious millionaire to fight bare-knuckled, but begins to worry that he's abandoned his principles for some quick cash. Serious-minded film has pretensions of eloquence and import, but doesn't really deliver; solid performances and canny filmmaking help. Connolly is a standout as Neeson's cheerfully sleazy friend. Based on William McIlvanney's novel *The Big Man* (also its video title). [R]▼

Cross My Heart (1946) **83m.** ** D: John Berry. Betty Hutton, Sonny Tufts, Rhys Williams, Ruth Donnelly, Iris Adrian, Michael Chekhov. Compulsive liar Hutton claims she's a killer so scrupulously honest lawyer husband Tufts can clear her and earn a reputation. Almost as bad as the comedy it's a remake of, TRUE CONFESSION.

Cross My Heart (1987) **C-90m.** ** D: Armyan Bernstein. Martin Short, Annette O'Toole, Paul Reiser, Joanna Kerns. The story of a date where everything goes wrong, mainly because both the man and the woman refuse to act natural and be themselves. Winning costars bring out the truthful observations in this comic script (by director Bernstein and Gail Parent), but it's just too slight, and too slow. [R]▼

Cross of Iron (1977-British-West German) **C-119m.** *** D: Sam Peckinpah. James Coburn, Maximilian Schell, James Mason, David Warner, Senta Berger, Klaus Lowitsch. Peckinpah's only war film, told from the viewpoint of Germans on the Russian front in 1943, is compelling without being particularly distinguished. The standard Peckinpah action scenes are excitingly done. European version runs 130m. Sequel: BREAKTHROUGH. [R]▼

Cross of Lorraine, The (1943) **90m.** ***½ D: Tay Garnett. Jean-Pierre Aumont, Gene Kelly, Cedric Hardwicke, Richard Whorf, Joseph Calleia, Peter Lorre, Hume Cronyn. High-grade propaganda of WW2 POW camp with hero Aumont rousing defeated Kelly to battle; Whorf is dedicated doctor, Lorre a despicable Nazi, Cronyn a fickle informer.

Crossover SEE: **Mr. Patman**

Crossover Dreams (1985) **C-86m.** ** D: Leon Ichaso. Ruben Blades, Shawn Elliot, Tom Signorelli, Elizabeth Pena, Frank Robles, Joel Diamond. Salsa performer Blades starts shafting his pals, enjoying the good life, when he thinks his upcoming album is going to make him a smash with mainstream audiences . . . then the record flops. Standard backstage drama offers nothing beyond novel ethnicity, though Blades has real presence on camera.▼

Crossroads (1942) **82m.** *** D: Jack Conway. William Powell, Hedy Lamarr, Claire Trevor, Basil Rathbone, Margaret Wycherly, Felix Bressart, Reginald Owen, Sig Ruman, H. B. Warner. Smooth, clever tale of respected diplomat Powell, who was once a victim of amnesia; he is accused by an extortionist of having a previous identity as a sly petty crook, causing much grief for him and his new wife (Lamarr).

Crossroads (1986) **C-96m.** **½ D: Walter Hill. Ralph Macchio, Joe Seneca, Jami Gertz, Joe Morton, Robert Judd, Harry Carey, Jr. Cocky young musician tracks down legendary bluesman in a Harlem hospital and agrees to bring him back to his Mississippi home in return for some long-lost songs. Promising idea turns into contrived formula film (with undeveloped subplot about the old-timer having sold his soul to the devil). Gets a shot in the arm from Ry Cooder's music score and Seneca's flavorful performance as the cranky old bluesman. [R]▼●

Crosstrap (1961-British) **62m.** *½ D: Robert Hartford-Davis. Laurence Payne, Jill Adams, Gary Cockrell, Zena Marshall. Juvenile thriller involving rival gangs of jewel thieves and murder.

Crosswinds (1951) **C-93m.** ** D: Lewis R. Foster. John Payne, Rhonda Fleming, Forrest Tucker, Robert Lowery. Payne tries to retrieve cargo of gold from plane that crashed in New Guinea, encountering headhunters, crooks, and gorgeous Fleming.

Croupier (1999-British-German) **C-91m.** ***½ D: Mike Hodges. Clive Owen, Gina McKee, Alex Kingston, Alexander Morton, Kate Hardie, Paul Reynolds, Nick Reding, Nicholas Ball. Highly original film about a young man who, while pursuing his goal to become a published author, takes a job as croupier in a London casino—but never stops observing those around him, or remarking on his own behavior. Tough, smart script by Paul Mayersberg.

Crow, The (1994) **C-100m.** *** D: Alex Proyas. Brandon Lee, Ernie Hudson, Michael Wincott, David Patrick Kelly, Angel David, Rochelle Davis, Bai Ling, Tony Todd, Jon Polito. A year after his murder and that of his fiancée by inner-city hoodlums, a young rock musician rises from the grave, seeking vengeance; he's guided by a spectral crow. Dark, rainy, and violent, the film's familiar revenge plot is offset by a strong style and an aura of tragic melancholy. Great urban-hell production design, good performances. Lee died shortly before filming was complete; digital movie magic enabled him to appear in the rest of the picture. From James O'Barr's black and white comic book. Followed by a sequel and TV series. [R]▼●◗

Crow: City of Angels, The (1996) **C-84m.** BOMB D: Tim Pope. Vincent Perez, Mia Kirshner, Richard Brooks, Iggy Pop,

Thomas Jane, Vincent Castellanos, Thuy Trang. Anemic follow-up to THE CROW, concerning a murdered man who returns to life in order to seek revenge on those who killed him and his cute young son. If you last to the end of the film, you'll be wishing he stayed six feet under. Perez is as grating as the nonstop soundtrack. [R] ▼●◗

Crowd, The (1928) **104m.** **** D: King Vidor. Eleanor Boardman, James Murray, Bert Roach, Daniel G. Tomlinson, Dell Henderson, Lucy Beaumont. Classic drama about a few happy and many not-so-happy days in the marriage of hard-luck couple. One of the greatest silent films; holds up beautifully. Written by Harry Behn, John V.A. Weaver, and director Vidor, from the latter's original story.▼●

Crowded Sky, The (1960) **C-105m.** **½ D: Joseph Pevney. Dana Andrews, Rhonda Fleming, Efrem Zimbalist, Jr., John Kerr, Troy Donahue, Keenan Wynn, Joe Mantell, Donald May, Louis Quinn, Edward Kemmer, Jean Willes, Patsy Kelly. Slick film focusing on emotional problems aboard jet liner and navy plane bound for fateful collision; superficial but diverting.

Crowd Roars, The (1932) **70m.** **½ D: Howard Hawks. James Cagney, Joan Blondell, Ann Dvorak, Eric Linden, Guy Kibbee, Frank McHugh. Exciting racing-driver tale with Cagney in typically cocky role, familiar plot devices, but well done by Warner Bros. stock company. Remade as INDIANAPOLIS SPEEDWAY.

Crowd Roars, The (1938) **92m.** **½ D: Richard Thorpe. Robert Taylor, Edward Arnold, Frank Morgan, Maureen O'Sullivan, William Gargan, Lionel Stander, Jane Wyman. Tippling Morgan gets son Taylor into fighting game, and involved with underworld chief Arnold in well-handled yarn. Remade as KILLER McCOY.

Crucible, The (1956-French-East German) **140m.** *** D: Raymond Rouleau. Simone Signoret, Yves Montand, Mylene Demongeot, Jean Debucourt, Raymond Rouleau. Successful French translation of Arthur Miller's stirring play about the Salem witchcraft trials of the 17th century. Signoret and Montand are excellent, re-creating their stage performances in the leading roles. Adaptation by Jean-Paul Sartre. Originally titled THE WITCHES OF SALEM. Remade in 1996.▼

Crucible, The (1996) **C-123m.** *** D: Nicholas Hytner. Daniel Day-Lewis, Winona Ryder, Joan Allen, Paul Scofield, Bruce Davison, Rob Campbell, Jeffrey Jones, George Gaynes. Caught performing a "sinful" dance, a group of New England girls, led by Ryder, claim they were overtaken by the Devil; soon their village is caught in a frenzy of accusations, naming various citizens as witches without so much as a shred of evidence. First American film rendering of Arthur Miller's classic 1953 play about parallels between Salem witch-hunts of the 1600s and Communist witch-hunts of the 1940s and '50s. Gets off to a shaky start, but finds its voice as the story deepens, and hits its stride with the arrival of Scofield, who's brilliant as the judge and inquisitor. Miller himself wrote the screenplay. [PG-13]▼●

Crucible of Horror (1971-British) **C-91m.** ** D: Viktors Ritelis. Michael Gough, Sharon Gurney, Yvonne Mitchell. Murdered man returns to haunt the living. Nothing new here. [PG]▼

Crucifer of Blood, The (1991-British) **C-131m. TVM** D: Fraser C. Heston. Charlton Heston, Richard Johnson, Susanna Harker, John Castle, Clive Wood, Simon Callow, Edward Fox. Heston and Johnson put their stamp on Holmes and Watson in this smartly turned adaptation by Heston fils of Paul Giovanni's 1978 Sherlock Holmes play (loosely based on Conan Doyle's "The Sign of the Four"), lovingly photographed by Robin Vidgeon. A jolly good show made for cable. Above average.▼●

Crucified Lovers, The (1954-Japanese) **100m.** ***½ D: Kenji Mizoguchi. Kazuo Hasegawa, Kyoko Kagawa, Yoko Minamida, Eitaro Shindo, Sakae Ozawa. Timid scroll-maker Hasegawa loves his master's wife (Kagawa), with tragic results. Superior performances, stunning direction; originally a marionette play written in 1715. Better known by its original Japanese title, CHIKAMATSU MONOGATARI.▼

Cruel Intentions (1999) **C-97m.** ** D: Roger Kumble. Ryan Phillippe, Sarah Michelle Gellar, Reese Witherspoon, Selma Blair, Joshua Jackson, Eric Mabius, Christine Baranski, Swoosie Kurtz, Louise Fletcher. Contemporary telling of Choderlos de Laclos' 18th-century novel *Les Liaisons Dangereuses* . . . with teenagers! Wealthy, jaded stepsiblings Phillippe and Gellar bet on whether he can seduce virgin Witherspoon. The cast is good, story is interesting, but sexual decadence among the young is sometimes hard to watch. Filmed before as DANGEROUS LIAISONS 1960, DANGEROUS LIAISONS, and VALMONT. [R]▼●◗

Cruel Sea, The (1953-British) **121m.** ***½ D: Charles Frend. Jack Hawkins, Donald Sinden, Denholm Elliott, Stanley Baker, John Stratton, Virginia McKenna, Alec McCowen. Well-conceived documentary-style account of British warship during WW2 and its crew. Original British running time 126m.▼

Cruel Swamp SEE: **Swamp Women**

Cruel Tower, The (1956) **79m.** **½ D: Lew Landers. John Ericson, Mari Blanchard, Charles McGraw, Steve Brodie, Peter Whitney, Alan Hale Jr. Friendship, loyalty, jealousy, and fighting among a crew of highriggers; standard stuff, well done.

Cruising (1980) **C-106m.** *½ D: William Friedkin. Al Pacino, Paul Sorvino, Karen Allen, Richard Cox, Don Scardino, Ed O'Neil, voice of James Sutorius. Cop Pacino goes underground to ferret out bloody killer of homosexuals in this distasteful, badly scripted film. Gay world presented as sick, degrading, and ritualistic. Filmed on authentic N.Y.C. locations. [R]▼

Crumb (1994) **C-119m.** ***½ D: Terry Zwigoff. Extraordinarily intimate portrait of underground comic artist (and cult hero) Robert Crumb, creator of "Keep on Truckin' " and Fritz the Cat. Zwigoff traces his career and celebrates his works while exploring the cultural influences that shaped him. By the time we meet Crumb's dysfunctional brothers, we realize that he survived a horrific upbringing and found a way to channel his own demons through his art. Perhaps this documentary's greatest achievement is enabling almost any viewer to feel better about his own family! [R] ▼●◗

Crusades, The (1935) **123m.** *** D: Cecil B. DeMille. Loretta Young, Henry Wilcoxon, Ian Keith, C. Aubrey Smith, Katherine DeMille, Joseph Schildkraut, Alan Hale, C. Henry Gordon, J. Carrol Naish. Love, action, and great big siege machines in DeMille version of medieval era Holy Crusades spectacle that's good for fun, with Young a luminous queen who's kidnapped by infidels; Wilcoxon as Richard the Lion-Hearted must rescue her. Look fast for Ann Sheridan as a Christian girl.▼

Crush (1992-New Zealand) **C-97m.** **½ D: Alison Maclean. Marcia Gay Harden, Donough Rees, Caitlin Bossley, William Zappa. Intriguing, multi-layered (if occasionally overbaked) tale of seduction, betrayal, jealousy and revenge, in which Harden impersonates her friend, literary critic Rees (who's just been injured in a car crash), and becomes involved in the lives of a writer and his teen daughter. Director-coscripter Maclean's feature debut is crammed with offbeat touches, hidden meanings, and agendas; at its best when exploring the complex relationship of the three female characters.▼

Crush, The (1993) **C-89m.** *½ D: Alan Shapiro. Cary Elwes, Alicia Silverstone, Jennifer Rubin, Amber Benson, Kurtwood Smith, Gwynyth Walsh. Ridiculous thriller about a thick-witted, twentysomething journalist (Elwes) who becomes the target of a pretty, obsessive fourteen-year-old Lolita (Silverstone). A completely unnecessary FATAL ATTRACTION/HAND THAT ROCKS THE CRADLE/SINGLE WHITE FEMALE clone; for a perceptive, non-exploitive look at the same subject, see the 1981 French film BEAU PÈRE. [R]▼●◗

Crusoe (1988) **C-91m.** *** D: Caleb Deschanel. Aidan Quinn, Ade Sapara, Warren Clark, Hepburn Grahame, Jimmy Nail, Tim Spall, Michael Higgins, Shane Rimmer, Oliver Platt. Solid version of the oft-filmed Defoe classic, with Quinn cast as the title character, a slave trader who's shipwrecked on a deserted isle, where he must deal with loneliness, isolation, survival; most intriguing of all is his evolving relationship with black warrior Sapara. Strikingly photographed by Tom Pinter, mostly in the Seychelles. [PG-13]▼

Cry-Baby (1990) **C-85m.** **½ D: John Waters. Johnny Depp, Amy Locane, Susan Tyrrell, Polly Bergen, Iggy Pop, Ricki Lake, Traci Lords, Kim McGuire, Troy Donahue, Mink Stole, Joe Dallesandro, Joey Heatherton, David Nelson, Patricia Hearst, Willem Dafoe. Baltimore, 1954, and good-girl Locane is torn between her pristine roots and kids in black leather—especially the Elvis type (Depp) who'd love her to mount his cycle. More polished than Waters' previous HAIRSPRAY, but not as well focused, though performed with gusto. Uneven and exhausting; a few set pieces really deliver. [PG-13]▼●

Cry Baby Killer, The (1958) **62m.** *½ D: Jus Addiss. Harry Lauter, Jack Nicholson, Carolyn Mitchell, Brett Halsey, Lynn Cartwright, Ed Nelson. Nicholson's film debut is a Roger Corman quickie about juvenile delinquent who panics when he thinks he's committed murder. A curio at best, with coscripter Leo Gordon and Corman himself in bit parts. TV print runs 60m.

Cry Blood, Apache (1970) **C-82m.** BOMB D: Jack Starrett. Jody McCrea, Dan Kemp, Marie Gahua, Robert Tessier, Joel McCrea. Boring Western about some sadistic cowboys who look like hippies and lust after gold. The elder McCrea is wasted. Also on tape as MACHISMO. [R]▼

Cry Danger (1951) **79m.** *** D: Robert Parrish. Dick Powell, Rhonda Fleming, Richard Erdman, Regis Toomey, William Conrad. Effective revenge yarn; ex-con Powell hunts down those responsible for his prison term.▼

Cry for Happy (1961) **C-110m.** **½ D: George Marshall. Glenn Ford, Donald O'Connor, Miiko Taka, Myoshi Umeki. Poor man's TEAHOUSE OF THE AUGUST MOON, involving Navy photography team in Tokyo using a geisha house for their home. CinemaScope.

Cry for Me, Billy (1972) **C-93m.** ** D: William A. Graham. Cliff Potts, Xochitl, Harry Dean Stanton, Don Wilbanks. Drifter falls in love with Indian girl, with tragic consequences, in this violent Western. Its title (and alleged year of release) keeps changing, but the film doesn't get any better. Aka FACE TO THE WIND, COUNT YOUR BULLETS, APACHE MASSA-

CRE, and THE LONG TOMORROW. Panavision. [R]▼

Cry Freedom (1987-British) **C-157m.** *** D: Richard Attenborough. Kevin Kline, Penelope Wilton, Denzel Washington, Kevin McNally, John Thaw, Timothy West, Juanita Waterman, John Hargreaves, Alec McCowen, Zakes Mokae, Ian Richardson. Sweeping and compassionate film about South African activist Steve Biko (well played by Washington) and his friendship with crusading newspaper editor Donald Woods (Kline). Unfortunately second half of film, minus the Biko character, loses momentum as it spends too much time on Kline and his family's escape from South Africa, but cannily injects flashbacks of Biko to steer it back on course. Screenplay by John Briley. Expanded by 23m. to fill a two-part TV time slot. Panavision. [PG]▼●◗

Cry From the Streets, A (1959-British) **99m.** *** D: Lewis Gilbert. Max Bygraves, Barbara Murray, Colin Peterson, Dana Wilson. Kathleen Harrison. Poignant handling of story about homeless London children and social workers who attempt to rehabilitate them; plot is forgivably diffuse and episodic.▼

Cry "Havoc" (1943) **97m.** *** D: Richard Thorpe. Margaret Sullavan, Joan Blondell, Ann Sothern, Fay Bainter, Marsha Hunt, Ella Raines, Frances Gifford, Diana Lewis, Heather Angel. Female volunteers join some overworked American nurses on beleaguered island of Bataan during WW2. Reveals its stage origins and incorporates expected clichés, but also presents pretty honest picture of war. Robert Mitchum has a bit part as a dying soldier.

Crying Game, The (1992-British) **C-112m.** ***½ D: Neil Jordan. Stephen Rea, Miranda Richardson, Forest Whitaker, Jim Broadbent, Ralph Brown, Adrian Dunbar, Jaye Davidson. Strikingly original and adult story with Rea as an IRA volunteer who helps capture a British soldier (Whitaker) only to befriend him and later become involved with his lover. What begins as a thriller unexpectedly turns into a poignant and ironic love story, with plot twists that deepen the film's almost dreamlike power. Stunningly acted by Rea, Richardson, and Whitaker, with an amazing debut by Davidson, as Dil. A unique, seductive film that writer/director Jordan pulls off with poetic ease; he earned an Oscar for his screenplay. Panavision. [R]▼●◗

Cry in the Dark, A (1988-U.S.-Australian) **C-121m.** ***½ D: Fred Schepisi. Meryl Streep, Sam Neill, Bruce Myles, Charles Tingwell, Nick Tate, Neil Fitzpatrick, Maurie Fields, Lewis Fitzgerald. Astonishing true story of Lindy Chamberlain, an Australian woman accused of murdering her baby, despite her claims that the child was carried off by a dingo (wild dog). Writer-director Schepisi tells his story with almost documentary-like reality, eloquently attacking the process of trial by rumor that made Chamberlain and her husband the most maligned couple in Australia. Streep and Neill are heartbreakingly good. Australian title: EVIL ANGELS. Panavision. [PG-13]▼●◗

Cry in the Night, A (1956) **75m.** ** D: Frank Tuttle. Edmond O'Brien, Brian Donlevy, Natalie Wood, Raymond Burr, Richard Anderson. Why is mysterious, psychotic Burr spying on Wood and her boyfriend? And what happens after he kidnaps her? Overwrought drama, but fascinating as a time capsule of its era, and then prevalent attitudes toward cops and victims. Burr is quite good.

Cry of Battle (1963) **99m.** **½ D: Irving Lerner. Van Heflin, Rita Moreno, James MacArthur, Leopoldo Salcedo. Uneven actioner set in Philippines with MacArthur as son of wealthy businessman who joins partisan cause, finding romance and sense of maturity.▼

Cry of the Banshee (1970-British) **C-87m.** **½ D: Gordon Hessler. Vincent Price, Elisabeth Bergner, Essy Persson, Hugh Griffith, Hilary Dwyer, Sally Geeson, Patrick Mower. Witch Oona (Bergner) summons servant of Satan to avenge nobleman (Price)'s bloody reign of witch-hunting. Confusion sets in midway. [PG]▼●

Cry of the City (1948) **95m.** **½ D: Robert Siodmak. Victor Mature, Richard Conte, Fred Clark, Shelley Winters, Betty Garde, Debra Paget, Hope Emerson. Rehash of MANHATTAN MELODRAMA about childhood pals, one who becomes a cop, the other a criminal—slick but predictable.

Cry of the Hunted (1953) **80m.** ** D: Joseph H. Lewis. Vittorio Gassman, Barry Sullivan, Polly Bergen, William Conrad. Unnoteworthy chase film involving escaped convict Gassman being sought by lawman Sullivan, with a few atmospheric sequences set in Louisiana marshland.

Cry of the Penguins (1971-British) **C-101m.** ** D: Al Viola. John Hurt, Hayley Mills, Dudley Sutton, Tony Britton, Thorley Walters, Judy Campbell. Can a womanizing young biologist find true happiness and redemption among an Antarctic colony of penguins? Do you care? Similar to later NEVER CRY WOLF—except in interest. Famed documentary filmmaker Arne Sucksdorff shot the fascinating but horrifying scenes of life and death among a penguin colony; an uncredited Roy Boulting reportedly directed the scenes with Hayley Mills. Original British title: MR. FORBUSH AND THE PENGUINS.

Cry of the Werewolf (1944) **63m.** ** D: Henry Levin. Nina Foch, Stephen Crane, Osa Massen, Blanche Yurka, Fritz Leiber, John Abbott. Young woman raised by gypsies is the daughter of a werewolf and becomes one herself, killing those who have found her out. OK low-grade thriller.▼

Crystal Ball, The (1943) **81m.** ** D: Elliott Nugent. Paulette Goddard, Ray Milland, Virginia Field, Gladys George, William Bendix, Ernest Truex. Weak comedy of beauty-contest loser who becomes fortune-teller; good players left stranded by stale material.

Crystal Heart (1987) **C-102m.** ** D: Gil Bettman. Tawny Kitaen, Lee Curreri, Lloyd Bochner, Simon Andreu, May Heatherly, Marina Saura. Young man who must live his life like the "boy in a bubble," confined to a controlled environment, develops a relationship with a sexy rock singer with whom he's fallen in love long-distance. Mild, predictable outing with music video segments from Kitaen. [R]▼

Cry Terror (1958) **96m.** *** D: Andrew L. Stone. James Mason, Rod Steiger, Inger Stevens, Neville Brand, Angie Dickinson, Jack Klugman. Tight pacing conceals implausibilities in caper of psychopath Steiger forcing Mason to aid him in master extortion plot, filmed on N.Y.C. locations. Stevens good as Mason's frightened but resourceful wife. Also shown in computer-colored version.

Cry, the Beloved Country (1951-British) **111m.** ***½ D: Zoltan Korda. Canada Lee, Charles Carson, Sidney Poitier, Geoffrey Keen, Reginald Ngeabo, Joyce Carey. Simple back-country minister journeys to Johannesburg in search of his son, while fate links his path with that of a wealthy, bigoted white landowner. Heart-rending story chronicles racial divisiveness (and its roots) in South Africa without resorting to preachiness. Alan Paton's book was also basis for stage and film musical LOST IN THE STARS. Some TV prints run 96m. Remade in 1995.▼●

Cry, the Beloved Country (1995-U.S.-British-South African) **C-120m.** *** D: Darrell James Roodt. Richard Harris, James Earl Jones, Charles S. Dutton, Vusi Kunene, Leleti Khumalo, Ian Roberts, Dambisa Kente, Eric Miyeni. Moving remake of the 1951 film based on Alan Paton's celebrated novel, about a backwoods minister (Jones) who, in 1946, makes his first-ever trip to the city of Johannesburg in search of his errant son, while wealthy landowner Harris travels there to claim the body of *his* son, who has just been killed. Excellent performances by Jones, Harris, and a largely unfamiliar supporting cast. Not as understated as the original, but effective in its own way. Screenplay by Ronald Harwood. [PG-13]▼●

Cry Tough (1959) **83m.** ** D: Paul Stanley. John Saxon, Linda Cristal, Joseph Calleia, Arthur Batanides, Joe De Santis, Barbara Luna, Frank Puglia. Saxon emotes well as Puerto Rican ex-con tempted back into criminal life by environment and his old gang. Torrid love scenes shot for foreign markets gave film initial publicity.

Cry Uncle! (1971) **C-87m.** **½ D: John G. Avildsen. Allen Garfield, Madeleine de la Roux, Devin Goldenberg, David Kirk, Sean Walsh, Nancy Salmon. Private detective gets involved with murder, sex and blackmail in spoof of questionable taste; frequently hilarious, however. [R]▼◗

Cry Vengeance (1954) **83m.** **½ D: Mark Stevens. Mark Stevens, Martha Hyer, Skip Homeier, Joan Vohs. Stevens lives up to title as innocent ex-con seeking gangsters who sent him to prison.▼

Cry Wolf (1947) **83m.** ** D: Peter Godfrey. Barbara Stanwyck, Errol Flynn, Geraldine Brooks, Richard Basehart, Jerome Cowan. Static adventure-mystery of Stanwyck attempting to untangle family secrets at late husband's estate.▼

Cuba (1979) **C-121m.** *** D: Richard Lester. Sean Connery, Brooke Adams, Jack Weston, Hector Elizondo, Denholm Elliott, Chris Sarandon, Lonette McKee. Entertaining adventure film/love story has mercenary Connery renewing an old affair with factory manager Adams, set against the fall of Batista in late '59. Director Lester is in pretty good form, with most scenes punctuated by memorable throwaway bits. [R]▼

Cuba Crossing (1980) **C-90m.** BOMB D: Chuck Workman. Stuart Whitman, Robert Vaughn, Caren Kaye, Raymond St. Jacques, Woody Strode, Sybil Danning, Albert Salmi, Michael Gazzo. Tough Whitman becomes embroiled in a plot to kill Fidel Castro. Filmed in Key West, Florida, and at least the scenery is pretty. Retitled KILL CASTRO and ASSIGNMENT: KILL CASTRO. Video titles: THE MERCENARIES and SWEET VIOLENT TONY. [R]▼

Cuban Love Song, The (1931) **80m.** **½ D: W.S. Van Dyke. Lawrence Tibbett, Lupe Velez, Ernest Torrence, Jimmy Durante, Karen Morley, Hale Hamilton, Louise Fazenda. Generally enjoyable, if slow-moving, musical-romance with fun-loving marine Tibbett (surprisingly effective as a romantic lead) tangling amorously with hot-tempered peanut vendor Velez in Havana—a cue for the song "The Peanut Vendor." Torrence and Durante are Tibbett's rowdy sidekicks.

Cuban Rebel Girls (1959) **68m.** BOMB D: Barry Mahon. Errol Flynn, Beverly Aadland, John McKay, Marie Edmund, Jackie Jackler. Flynn's last film is an embarrassment: playing himself, he aids Fidel Castro in his overthrow of Batista. Shot on location during the Castro revolution. Of interest only to see Flynn teamed with his final girlfriend, 16-year-old Aadland. Aka ASSAULT OF THE REBEL GIRLS. Video title: ATTACK OF THE REBEL GIRLS.▼

Cube (1998-Canadian) **C-90m.** ** D:

Vincenzo Natali. Maurice Dean Wint, Nicole deBoer, Nicky Guadagni, David Hewlett, Andrew Miller, Julian Richings, Wayne Robson. Or, six characters in search of an exit, from a giant cube with countless compartments—many of them booby-trapped. How and why are they there—and how can they escape? Nerves start to wear thin, which may also apply to the audience, as this intriguing film becomes highly unpleasant . . . with an unsatisfying conclusion. Cowritten by the director. [R]▼●◗

Cuckoos, The (1930) **97m.** ** D: Paul Sloane. Bert Wheeler, Robert Woolsey, June Clyde, Hugh Trevor, Dorothy Lee, Ivan Lebedeff, Marguerita Padula, Mitchell Lewis, Jobyna Howland. Following their success in RIO RITA, RKO quickly reteamed Wheeler and Woolsey for this similar musical comedy about the adventures of two phony fortune tellers who get mixed up with gypsies. Pretty creaky, like a photographed stage play, though W&W are funny and Wheeler has one good song, "I Love You So Much." Some sequences in two-strip Technicolor.

Cujo (1983) **C-91m.** *** D: Lewis Teague. Dee Wallace, Danny Pintauro, Daniel Hugh-Kelly, Christopher Stone, Ed Lauter, Mills Watson. Genuinely frightening adaptation of Stephen King thriller about a woman and her son terrorized by a rabid St. Bernard dog. Builds slowly but surely to terrifying (but not gory) climax. Not for children. [R]▼●

Cul-De-Sac (1966-British) **111m.** *** D: Roman Polanski. Donald Pleasence, Françoise Dorléac, Lionel Stander, Jack MacGowran, Iain Quarrier, Jacqueline Bisset. Macabre comedy about two wounded gangsters who terrorize middle-aged milquetoast and his beautiful young wife. Not a total success, but good cast and stylish direction make it a winner. Some prints cut to 103m.▼

Culpepper Cattle Company, The (1972) **C-92m.** **½ D: Dick Richards. Gary Grimes, Billy "Green" Bush, Luke Askew, Bo Hopkins, Geoffrey Lewis, Wayne Sutherlin. A 16-year-old persuades trail boss to take him along on cattle drive, becomes a man in the process. Fair but excessively violent Western. [R]▼

Cult of the Cobra (1955) **82m.** **½ D: Francis D. Lyon. Faith Domergue, Richard Long, Marshall Thompson, Jack Kelly, David Janssen. Minor camp masterpiece involves ex-servicemen being killed by exotic serpent lady Domergue.▼

Cult of the Damned SEE: **Angel, Angel, Down We Go**

Cult of the Dead SEE: **Snake People**

Cup, The (1999-Bhutanese) **C-93m.** *** D: Khyentse Norbu. Jamyang Lodro, Orgyen Tobgyal, Neten Chokling, Lama Chonjor, Godu Lama, Thinley Nudi. Sweet, funny comedy in which an adolescent, soccer-obsessed Tibetan monk-in-training (Lodro) schemes to win permission to watch the 1998 World Cup final between France and Brazil on television. Slowly paced but still winning, with an insightful subtext examining spirituality, modernity, consumerism, and Tibet's endless political struggle against China. Writer-director Norbu is himself a Bhutanese high lama. [G]▼

Curdled (1996) **C-94m.** *½ D: Reb Braddock. William Baldwin, Angela Jones, Bruce Ramsay, Lois Chiles, Barry Corbin, Mel Gorham, Daisy Fuentes, Kelly Preston, Carmen Lopez. Grisly black comedy about young woman obsessed with the how's and why's of violent crimes, who gets a job scrubbing up after them on the Post-Forensic Cleaning Service. Only for viewers with the darkest sense of humor. Executive-produced by none other than Quentin Tarantino. [R]▼●

Cure, The (1995) **C-99m.** **½ D: Peter Horton. Joseph Mazzello, Brad Renfro, Annabella Sciorra, Diana Scarwid, Bruce Davison, Nicky Katt, Aeryk Egan, Renee Humphrey. Imperfect but often moving story about two small-town, pre-teen outsiders who become fast friends: new-kid-in-town Renfro and AIDS-stricken Mazzello, who contracted the HIV virus during a blood transfusion. At its best when focusing on the boys' evolving relationship; the title refers to a miracle AIDS cure which plays a key role in the story. [PG-13]▼●

Curley (1947) **C-54m.** *½ D: Bernard Carr. Frances Rafferty, Larry Olsen, Gerald Perreau, Eilene Janssen, Dale Belding, Kathleen Howard. Producer Hal Roach's feeble attempt to revive Our Gang finds these unappealing little rascals tormenting their new schoolteacher (Rafferty). Almost unwatchable. Followed by WHO KILLED DOC ROBBIN? Reissued as part of HAL ROACH'S COMEDY CARNIVAL. Later retitled THE ADVENTURES OF CURLEY AND HIS GANG for TV.▼

Curley and His Gang in the Haunted Mansion SEE: **Who Killed Doc Robbin?**

Curly Sue (1991) **C-101m.** *½ D: John Hughes. James Belushi, Kelly Lynch, Alisan Porter, John Getz, Fred Dalton Thompson, Cameron Thor, Edie McClurg. Homeless con-artist and his adopted waif leech onto a tightly wound dish of an attorney. She, in turn, determines that this four-flushing twosome is just what she needs to enrich her life. A John Hughes formula movie where the formula doesn't work, though if there's such a thing as "quintessential James Belushi" this is it. Lynch's obvious discomfort suggests she may have seen the rushes. [PG]▼●

Curly Top (1935) **75m.** **½ D: Irving Cummings. Shirley Temple, John Boles, Rochelle Hudson, Jane Darwell, Rafaela

Ottiano, Arthur Treacher. Shirley sings "Animal Crackers In My Soup" as she plays Cupid again, this time for sister Hudson and handsome Boles. Based on Jean Webster's DADDY LONG LEGS. Also shown in computer-colored version.▼

Curse, The (1987) **C-90m.** BOMB D: David Keith. Wil Wheaton, Claude Akins, Cooper Huckabee, John Schneider, Amy Wheaton. Actor Keith steps behind the camera to direct this down-home horror movie: a deadly meteorite lands on a Tennessee farm, literally driving the folks crazy after contaminating their food. Loosely based on H. P. Lovecraft's novella *The Color Out of Space*, previously filmed as DIE, MONSTER, DIE! Aka THE FARM. Followed by three unrelated "sequels." [R]▼●

Curse of Bigfoot, The (1972) **C-87m.** BOMB D: Don Fields. William Simonsen, Robert Clymire, Ruth Ann Mannella. Students unearth a dormant beast in this docudrama-style, low-budget waste of time. Aka TEENAGERS BATTLE THE THING.▼

Curse of Dracula, The SEE: **Return of Dracula, The**

Curse of Frankenstein, The (1957-British) **C-83m.** **½ D: Terence Fisher. Peter Cushing, Christopher Lee, Hazel Court, Robert Urquhart, Valerie Gaunt, Noel Hood. OK retelling of original Shelley tale, with Cushing as Baron von Frankenstein, whose experimentation with creation of life becomes an obsession. First of Hammer Films' long-running horror series, and itself followed by six sequels, starting with REVENGE OF FRANKENSTEIN.▼●

Curse of the Cat People, The (1944) **70m.** *** D: Gunther von Fritsch, Robert Wise. Simone Simon, Kent Smith, Jane Randolph, Elizabeth Russell, Ann Carter, Julia Dean. Follow-up to CAT PEOPLE creates wonderful atmosphere in story of lonely little girl who conjures up vision of Simon, her father's mysterious first wife. Despite title, not a horror film but a fine, moody fantasy. Produced by Val Lewton, written by DeWitt Bodeen. Wise's directing debut. Also available in computer-colored version.▼●

Curse of the Crimson Altar SEE: **Crimson Cult, The**

Curse of the Demon (1958-British) **83m.** ***½ D: Jacques Tourneur. Dana Andrews, Peggy Cummins, Niall MacGinnis, Maurice Denham, Athene Seyler. Andrews is a stuffily cynical psychologist who doesn't believe that series of deaths have been caused by ancient curse, but film convinces audience right off the bat and never lets up. Charles Bennett and producer Hal E. Chester adapted Montague R. James's story "Casting the Runes." Exceptional shocker, originally called NIGHT OF THE DEMON. Original British version available on tape and laser runs 95m. ▼●

Curse of the Faceless Man (1958) **66m.** BOMB D: Edward L. Cahn. Richard Anderson, Elaine Edwards, Adele Mara, Luis Van Rooten. Silly sci-fi horror as gladiator encased in lava by eruption of Pompeii (yes, the hero has no face) comes back to life thinking he still has to rescue the woman he loves, conveniently reincarnated as the heroine.●

Curse of the Fly, The (1965-British) **86m.** *½ D: Don Sharp. Brian Donlevy, Carole Gray, George Baker, Michael Graham, Jeremy Wilkins, Charles Carson. In the third and last of original THE FLY series, young escapee from a mental institution winds up involved with the Delambre family, still doggedly trying to make their teleportation machine work. Highly inadequate makeup, weak script, but very atmospheric direction produce oddly mixed results. CinemaScope.

Curse of the Living Corpse (1964) **84m.** ** D: Del Tenney. Helen Warren, Roy R. Sheider (Scheider), Margo Hartman, Hugh Franklin, Candace Hilligoss. Tepid old-dark-house murder mystery with dead man supposedly returning to "life" and committing series of killings. Scheider's film debut.▼

Curse of the Living Dead SEE: **Kill Baby Kill**

Curse of the Mummy's Tomb, The (1964-British) **C-81m.** ** D: Michael Carreras. Terence Morgan, Ronald Howard, Fred Clark, Jeanne Roland, George Pastell, Jack Gwillim, Dickie Owen (as the Mummy). Handsomely photographed but routine Hammer thriller featuring vengeful mummy at large in Victorian London, killing the usual profaners of the tomb in foggy surroundings. Most unusual twist: The (human) villain is in fact the Mummy's brother. Follow-up, not sequel, to THE MUMMY (1959). Techniscope.

Curse of the Pink Panther (1983) **C-109m.** *½ D: Blake Edwards. Ted Wass, David Niven, Robert Wagner, Herbert Lom, Joanna Lumley, Capucine, Robert Loggia, Harvey Korman, Burt Kwouk, Leslie Ash, Andre Maranne. Writer-director Edwards' pointless attempt to keep the Pink Panther series alive despite Peter Sellers' death—by putting Wass through Sellers' sight-gag paces, and surrounding him with costars of earlier Panther films, who (all too obviously) shot their cameos at the same time as TRAIL OF THE PINK PANTHER. What a waste! Niven's final film (with his voice dubbed by Rich Little). Panavision. [PG]▼

Curse of the Starving Class (1995) **C-102m. TVM** D: J. Michael McClary. James Woods, Kathy Bates, Randy Quaid, Henry Thomas, Kristin Fiorella, Louis Gossett, Jr. Executive producer Bruce Beresford's adaptation of Sam Shepard's coming-of-age play about a dirt-poor Depression-era farm family. Dad's a foul-mouthed, falling-down drunk, Mom's in despair trying to save what's left of them, and their teenage son (Thomas) hungers for a better life. Well acted but relatively depressing. Made for cable. Average. ▼●

Curse of the Stone Hand (1965) **72m.** BOMB D: Jerry Warren, Carl Schlieppe. John Carradine, Sheila Bon, Ernest Walch, Katherine Victor, Lloyd Nelson. Americanized version of 1959 Mexican film tries to interweave two separate story elements with incoherent results.▼

Curse of the Swamp Creature (1966) **C-80m.** BOMB D: Larry Buchanan. John Agar, Francine York, Shirley McLine, Bill Thurman, Jeff Alexander. A geological expedition stumbles onto a mad doctor who's trying to evolve a man-monster. Low-budget junk.▼

Curse of the Undead (1959) **79m.** ** D: Edward Dein. Eric Fleming, Michael Pate, Kathleen Crowley, John Hoyt, Bruce Gordon, Edward Binns. Once-novel mixture of horror-Western tale hasn't much zing. Mysterious stranger has vampirish designs on Crowley.▼

Curse of the Voodoo (1965-British) **77m.** *½ D: Lindsay Shonteff. Bryant Halliday, Dennis Price, Lisa Daniely, Mary Kerridge. Modest film promises some exotic native black magic hi-jinks, but nothing worthwhile occurs.◗

Curse of the Werewolf, The (1961-British) **C-91m.** **½ D: Terence Fisher. Clifford Evans, Oliver Reed, Yvonne Romain, Anthony Dawson. Reed has wolf's blood and struggles to control the monster within him; it finally erupts when he is denied his girl's love. Eerie atmosphere pervades this good chiller. Loosely based on novel *The Werewolf of Paris* by Guy Endore.▼●

Curse of the Yellow Snake, The (1963-German) **98m.** **½ D: Franz Gottlieb. Joachim Fuchsberger, Eddi Arent, Brigitte Grothum, Charles Regnier, Werner Peters, Claus Holm. Edgar Wallace yarn dealing with anti-Western uprising by fanatic Oriental cult; eerie and atmospheric.▼

Curse III: Blood Sacrifice (1990) **C-91m.** *½ D: Sean Barton. Christopher Lee, Jennilee Harrison, Henry Cole, Andre Jacobs, Zoe Randall, Olivia Dyer. 1950, East Africa. Tribal magic produces murderous demon-like monster (unseen until the end) slaughtering mostly whites. Drearily routine; one would-be "tense" scene (with no payoff) after another. Lee looks very serious. Original title: PANGA. [R]▼

Curtain Call (1998) **C-94m.** ** D: Peter Yates. James Spader, Polly Walker, Maggie Smith, Michael Caine, Buck Henry, Sam Shepard, Marcia Gay Harden, Frances Sternhagen, Frank Whaley. Fine cast in fluffy fantasy about marriage-phobic book publisher Spader who's afraid to propose to his longtime girlfriend, then moves into a Manhattan brownstone that's haunted by the ghosts of a famous old theatrical couple who teach him about love and commitment. Curious, slowly paced blend of supernatural whimsy, romantic comedy and relationship drama never really gels. Made for theaters, this debuted on cable. Valerie Perrine appears unbilled. [PG-13]▼◗

Curtain Call at Cactus Creek (1950) **C-86m.** **½ D: Charles Lamont. Donald O'Connor, Gale Storm, Vincent Price, Walter Brennan, Eve Arden. Sometimes foolish slapstick as O'Connor, touring with road show, gets involved with bank robbers and irate citizens of Arizona.

Curtain Up (1952-British) **85m.** **½ D: Ralph Smart. Robert Morley, Margaret Rutherford, Kay Kendall, Olive Sloane, Joan Rice, Michael Medwin, Charlotte Mitchell, Liam Gaffney. Mild but amusing look at a repertory troupe in the British provinces that suffers a minor crisis when the amateur playwright of its latest show turns up on the first day of rehearsals. Morley (as the director) and Rutherford (as the playwright) are great fun to watch.

Curucu, Beast of the Amazon (1956) **C-76m.** *½ D: Curt Siodmak. John Bromfield, Beverly Garland, Tom Payne, Harvey Chalk. One of the most infamous disappointments (for monster-loving kids) of the 1950s. Bromfield and Garland go after title monster, discover it is merely disguised Indian trying to scare people away. Boo hiss.

Custer of the West (1968-U.S.-Spanish) **C-140m.** **½ D: Robert Siodmak. Robert Shaw, Mary Ure, Jeffrey Hunter, Robert Ryan, Ty Hardin, Charles Stalnaker, Robert Hall, Lawrence Tierney. Fairly ambitious bio of famed general suffers from script that doesn't quite know how to characterize him. Some prints run 120m. Super Technirama 70. [G]◗

Cutter and Bone SEE: **Cutter's Way**

Cutter's Way (1981) **C-105m.** **½ D: Ivan Passer. Jeff Bridges, John Heard, Lisa Eichhorn, Ann Dusenberry, Stephen Elliott, Nina Van Pallandt, Julia Duffy. Intriguing if not always satisfying film about a boozy, belligerent Vietnam vet (Heard) who prods his aimless friend (Bridges) into action after he's seen a man who may be a murderer. Low-key, sometimes enervating adaptation of Newton Thornburg's novel *Cutter and Bone* (this film's original title), enhanced by director Passer's eye for interesting detail. [R]▼●

Cutthroat Island (1995-U.S.-French) **C-**

123m. ** D: Renny Harlin. Geena Davis, Matthew Modine, Frank Langella, Maury Chaykin, Patrick Malahide, Stan Shaw, Harris Yulin, Rex Linn, Paul Dillon, Chris Masterson, Jimmie F. Skaggs. Pirate Davis must join forces with roguish Modine to avenge her father's death, find a treasure map and battle her ferocious pirate uncle, Dawg (Langella). Or something like that. Hapless movie has special effects and stunts to spare, but nothing to get you involved. The actors do their best in cardboard roles. Where's Robert Newton when you really need him? Arrrr! Panavision and Technovision. [PG-13]▼●◗

Cutting Class (1989) **C-91m.** *½ D: Rospo Pallenberg. Donovan Leitch, Jill Schoelen, Roddy McDowall, Brad Pitt, Martin Mull. A slasher is running amok at a high school. This one's only if your idea of a four-star movie is FRIDAY THE 13TH. [R]▼●

Cutting Edge, The (1992) **C-101m.** **½ D: Paul M. Glaser. D. B. Sweeney, Moira Kelly, Roy Dotrice, Terry O'Quinn, Dwier Brown. Bitchy ice skater Kelly is paired with banged-up hockey player Sweeney in a last-ditch attempt to score an Olympic gold medal in paired figure skating. Cute, if predictable, comedy with Sweeney and Kelly building believable sexual tension as they're forced to work together, sniping all the way. [PG]▼

Cyborg (1989) **C-86m.** BOMB D: Albert Pyun. Jean-Claude Van Damme, Deborah Richter, Vincent Klyn, Alex Daniels, Dayle Haddon, Blaise Loong, Rolf Muller. Van Damme plays a savior battling evil gangs who seem to enjoy various plagues and finding gruesome ways to murder people. Even for a post-apocalyptic trash movie, this plumbs new depths. Repulsive. Followed by two unrelated sequels. [R]▼●◗

Cyborg 2087 (1966) **C-86m.** ** D: Franklin Adreon. Michael Rennie, Wendell Corey, Eduard Franz, Karen Steele, Warren Stevens. Future Earth civilization sends cyborg—part machine, part human—back in time to 1960s so future can be changed. Good idea all but ruined due to unconvincing script and TV-style production.

Cycle Savages, The (1969) **C-82m.** BOMB D: Bill Brame. Bruce Dern, Melody Patterson, Chris Robinson, Maray Ayres, Scott Brady. Psychotic biker/white slaver Dern is displeased when artist Robinson opens his sketch pad, so he plans to crush the budding Rembrandt's hands. Sadism and torture galore; coproduced by deejay Casey Kasem and record exec Mike Curb, later the lieutenant governor of California. [R]

Cyclone (1987) **C-83m.** ** D: Fred Olen Ray. Heather Thomas, Jeffrey Combs, Ashley Ferrare, Dar Robinson, Martine Beswicke, Robert Quarry, Martin Landau. TV star Thomas plays second fiddle to a high-tech motorcycle that's stolen by Landau's henchmen. Watch for numerous cameos including Huntz Hall, Troy Donahue, Russ Tamblyn and Michael Reagan. [R]▼●

Cyclone Z SEE: **Dragons Forever**

Cyclops, The (1957) **75m.** ** D: Bert I. Gordon. James Craig, Gloria Talbott, Lon Chaney, Jr., Tom Drake. Expedition scours Mexico in search of Talbott's lost fiancé, discovers that radiation has transformed him into an enormous monster. Nothing much in this cheapie.▼

Cynara (1932) **78m.** ** D: King Vidor. Ronald Colman, Kay Francis, Henry Stephenson, Phyllis Barry, Paul Porcasi. Badly dated film about British lawyer who has interlude with working girl while wife is away; Colman is good as usual.

Cynthia (1947) **98m.** *½ D: Robert Z. Leonard. Elizabeth Taylor, George Murphy, S. Z. Sakall, Mary Astor, Gene Lockhart, Spring Byington, Jimmy Lydon. Sugary film of sickly girl Taylor finding outlet in music; good cast wasted.

Cyrano de Bergerac (1950) **112m.** ***½ D: Michael Gordon. Jose Ferrer, Mala Powers, William Prince, Morris Carnovsky, Elena Verdugo. Ferrer received an Oscar for portraying the tragic 17th-century wit, renowned for his nose but longing for love of a beautiful lady. From Edmond Rostand's play. Later modernized as ROXANNE; remade in France in 1990. Also shown in computer-colored version. ▼●

Cyrano de Bergerac (1990-French) **C-138m.** ***½ D: Jean-Paul Rappeneau. Gérard Depardieu, Anne Brochet, Vincent Perez, Jacques Weber, Roland Bertin, Philippe Morier-Genoud. Likely to remain the definitive screen version of the Edmond Rostand perennial (depending on your personal passion for Steve Martin's ROXANNE). Quite visceral, and frequently inspired (vide the decision to stage the balcony scene during a mild rainstorm), faltering only a little during the finale, which is overextended. Jean-Claude Carrière and director Rappeneau scripted; English subtitles by Anthony Burgess. [PG]▼●

Da (1988) **C-102m.** **½ D: Matt Clark. Barnard Hughes, Martin Sheen, Karl Hayden, Doreen Hepburn, William Hickey, Hugh O'Conor, Ingrid Craigie. Sheen returns to his native Ireland for his father's funeral, which triggers a series of remembrances of his irascible "da." Hugh Leonard's adaptation of his autobiographical stage comedy doesn't work as well on the screen, but remains a touching account of a father-son relationship that isn't interrupted by death. Hughes beautifully recreates his Tony-winning performance, and Sheen is equally good. Hepburn is marvelous as Hughes' pesky wife; Leonard appears briefly as a pallbearer. Filmed mostly on location in Ireland. [PG]▼●

Dad (1989) **C-117m.** ** D: Gary David Goldberg. Jack Lemmon, Ted Danson, Olympia Dukakis, Kathy Baker, Kevin Spacey, Ethan Hawke, Zakes Mokae, J. T. Walsh. Busy, distracted executive learns his father may be dying; he winds up becoming his dad's caretaker and companion, and they grow closer than they've ever been. Genuinely affecting tearjerker turns sappy and "cute" at the midway point, almost negating Lemmon's fine performance. Why couldn't they have quit while they were ahead? Feature directing debut for TV sitcom producer Goldberg. [PG]▼●

Daddy (1987) **C-100m. TVM** D: John Herzfeld. Dermot Mulroney, Patricia Arquette, John Karlen, Tess Harper, Trey Adams, Danny Aiello. Thoughtful "children having children" drama about two high schoolers unprepared for the reality of parenthood. Incisively written by director Herzfeld. Above average.

Daddy Long Legs (1955) **C-126m.** **½ D: Jean Negulesco. Fred Astaire, Leslie Caron, Thelma Ritter, Fred Clark, Terry Moore, Larry Keating. Overlong musical remake of oft-filmed story about playboy (Astaire) anonymously sponsoring waif's education—then she falls in love with him. Some good dance numbers, and Johnny Mercer score highlighted by "Something's Got to Give." Previously filmed in 1919, 1931, and (as CURLY TOP) in 1935. CinemaScope.▼●

Daddy Nostalgia (1990-French) **C-105m.** **½ D: Bertrand Tavernier. Dirk Bogarde, Jane Birkin, Odette Laure. Birkin rushes to the Cote d'Azur to be at the side of her father, who may be dying; during her extended stay she tries to sort out her relationship with him, and understand the life he's led. Utterly believable, but not always compelling; Bogarde's charming (and commanding) screen presence makes it well worth seeing. Panavision. [PG]▼

Daddy-O (1959) **74m.** BOMB D: Lou Place. Dick Contino, Sandra Giles, Bruno VeSota, Gloria Victor, Ron McNeil. Thugs recruit truck driver-singer Contino to drive a getaway car. Like wow, man, this flick's for squares. Aka OUT ON PROBATION. ▼

Daddy's Dyin' . . . Who's Got the Will? (1990) **C-95m.** **½ D: Jack Fisk. Beau Bridges, Keith Carradine, Beverly D'Angelo, Tess Harper, Judge Reinhold, Amy Wright, Patrika Darbo, Molly McClure, Bert Remsen. Affection, reminiscence, avarice, and hostility intermingle as a family of memorable oddballs gathers at the old Texas homestead to wait for their father to die and to find out what's in the will. Del Shores adapted his own stage play, and the results run from flat and predictable to sharp and funny; a terrific cast punches everything across. [PG-13]▼●

Daddy's Gone A-Hunting (1969) **C-108m.** *** D: Mark Robson. Carol White, Paul Burke, Scott Hylands, Rachel Ames, Mala Powers, James B. Sikking. Happily married and pregnant, White is horrified when her previous lover turns up, demanding she kill her baby to atone for having aborted his child. Though contrived, story becomes increasingly tense, with nail-biting climax; shot in San Francisco. [M/PG]▼

Daffodil Killer SEE: **Devil's Daffodil, The**

Daffy Duck's Movie: Fantastic Island (1983) **C-78m.** *½ D: Friz Freleng. Fourth and weakest of Warner Bros.' cartoon compilations. Linking material (spoofing TV's *Fantasy Island*) is flat, and few of the ten cartoon shorts included are better than average. Hardly Daffy's finest hour. [G]▼●

Daffy Duck's Quackbusters (1989) **C-79m.** *** D: Greg Ford, Terry Lennon. Voice of Mel Blanc. Perhaps the most watchable of the Warner cartoon-compilation films, with a clever bridging story incorporating the studio's many vintage horror-movie spoofs. Daffy Duck inherits a fortune and sets up a "ghost-busting" service with pals Bugs Bunny and Porky Pig. Contains the new short THE DUXORCIST and a cameo appearance by Egghead. [G]▼●

Daggers of Blood SEE: **With Fire and Sword**

Daisies in December (1995-British) **C-95m. TVM** D: Mark Haber. Jean Simmons, Joss Ackland, Pippa Guard, Barbara Lott, Judith Barker, Muriel Pavlow, Wolfe Morris. Endearing December-December romance involving two elderly tourists, a standoffish widowed stockbroker who hates being around old folks and a kindly librarian with a full heart. They find a spark at a seaside resort hotel, and spring in the middle of winter. Eloquent, leisurely paced gem, written by John Kane. Above average.

Daisy Kenyon (1947) **99m.** **½ D: Otto Preminger. Joan Crawford, Dana Andrews, Henry Fonda, Ruth Warrick, Martha Stewart, Peggy Ann Garner, Connie Marshall. Love triangle starts intelligently, bogs down halfway into typical soapy histrionics (with a plot thread about child abuse surprising for its time). Good performances; handsomely filmed. Look sharp in the Stork Club scene for Walter Winchell, John Garfield, and Leonard Lyons.

Daisy Miller (1974) **C-91m.** **½ D: Peter Bogdanovich. Cybill Shepherd, Barry Brown, Cloris Leachman, Mildred Natwick, Eileen Brennan, Duilio Del Prete. Handsome, intelligent adaptation of Henry James' story misses the mark; the tone is cold, and Shepherd's hollow performance as a naive American courting European society in the late 1800s nearly sinks the film. Filmed in Italy. [G]▼

Dakota (1945) **82m.** ** D: Joseph Kane. John Wayne, Vera Ralston, Walter Brennan, Ward Bond, Ona Munson, Hugo Haas. Sprawling Wayne vehicle with Duke involved in pioneer railroad territory dispute; Vera is his lovely wife!▼●

Dakota (1988) **C-97m.** ** D: Fred Holmes. Lou Diamond Phillips, Eli Cummins, DeeDee Norton, Jordan Burton, Steve Ruge, John Hawkes. Well-meaning but slight, independently produced drama about a youth on the run (Phillips), who works on a Texas ranch and interrelates with various characters. Phillips, who served as associate producer, is the sole interest here; he made the film prior to attaining stardom in LA BAMBA. [PG]▼●

Dakota Incident (1956) **C-88m.** **½ D: Lewis R. Foster. Linda Darnell, Dale Robertson, John Lund, Ward Bond. Indians attack stagecoach, leading to fight to the finish.▼

Dakota Lil (1950) **C-88m.** ** D: Lesley Selander. George Montgomery, Marie Windsor, Rod Cameron, Marion Martin, Wallace Ford. Pedestrian Western saved by Windsor's vitality in title role as crook who helps lawmen trap railroad thieves.

Daleks—Invasion Earth 2150 A.D. (1966-British) **C-84m.** **½ D: Gordon Flemyng. Peter Cushing, Bernard Cribbins, Andrew Keir, Ray Brooks, Jill Curzon, Roberta Tovey. Agreeable sequel to DR. WHO AND THE DALEKS, with the Earth threatened by Dalek aggressors. Retitled INVASION EARTH 2150 A.D. Techniscope.▼

Dallas (1950) **C-94m.** **½ D: Stuart Heisler. Gary Cooper, Ruth Roman, Steve Cochran, Raymond Massey, Antonio Moreno. Cooper returns to Big D. of post-Civil War days seeking revenge; finds love with Roman and gunplay from Cochran and other intended victims.▼

Damage (1992-British) **C-111m.** **½ D: Louis Malle. Jeremy Irons, Juliette Binoche, Miranda Richardson, Rupert Graves, Ian Bannen, Leslie Caron, Peter Stormare, Gemma Clark. Arch-to-a-fault adaptation of Josephine Hart's minimalist best-seller, about a middle-aged Brit politician who squanders his career and family by embarking a hot-sex affair with his son's mysterious girlfriend. Binoche is frigidly one-note as the latter, sinking what in some ways is dispassionately accomplished filmmaking. Richardson is spectacularly good as Irons' spurned wife. Screenplay by David Hare. Fine score by Zbigniew Preisner. Unrated version available. [R]▼●◗

Damaged Lives (1937) **61m.** ** D: Edgar G. Ulmer. Diane Sinclair, Lyman Williams, Cecilia Parker, George Irving, Almeda Fowler, Jason Robards, Sr. Earnest melodrama preaching against the perils of extramarital flings which, in this case, leads to venereal disease. Definitely low-budget, but not the exploitation "camp" one would assume. Originally followed by a half-hour medical lecture on VD. Made in 1933, but unreleased for four years.▼

Dam Busters, The (1954-British) **102m.** ***½ D: Michael Anderson. Richard Todd, Michael Redgrave, Ursula Jeans, Basil Sydney. During WW2, British devise an ingenious plan to blow up Germans' Ruhr dam. Exciting and intelligent film. Original British running time: 119m.▼

Dames (1934) **90m.** *** D: Ray Enright. Joan Blondell, Dick Powell, Ruby Keeler, ZaSu Pitts, Hugh Herbert, Guy Kibbee, Phil Regan. Short on plot (let's-back-a-Broadway-musical) but has top Busby Berkeley production ensembles like "I Only Have Eyes For You." Other songs include "When You Were A Smile On Your Mother's Lips And A Twinkle In Your Daddy's Eye," and classic title tune.▼●

Damien—Omen II (1978) **C-107m.** **½ D: Don Taylor. William Holden, Lee Grant, Lew Ayres, Sylvia Sidney, Robert Foxworth, Jonathan Scott-Taylor, Leo McKern, Meshach Taylor. Sequel to huge hit of 1976 is less effective, still has shock value from grisly murders, plus good work by Holden. Best scene is Ayres' death under an icy lake. Scott-Taylor is the demon child; Holden and Grant his stupidly unsuspecting kin. Taylor took over directing from Michael Hodges, who worked on screenplay. Followed by THE FINAL CONFLICT. Panavision. [R]▼●

Damnation Alley (1977) **C-91m.** *½ D: Jack Smight. Jan-Michael Vincent, George Peppard, Dominique Sanda, Paul Winfield, Jackie Earle Haley. Five survivors of nuclear wipeout travel cross-country in search of civilization. Futuristic van in which they travel is more interesting than story or characters in this uninspiring sci-fi saga. Distantly related to the Roger Zelazny novel. Panavision. [PG]▼

Damn Citizen (1958) **88m.** **½ D: Robert Gordon. Keith Andes, Maggie Hayes, Gene Evans, Lynn Bari. Realistically told account of WW2 veteran (Andes) hired to wipe out corruption in state police.

Damned, The (1962) SEE: **These Are the Damned**

Damned, The (1969-Italian-West German) **C-155m.** *** D: Luchino Visconti. Dirk Bogarde, Ingrid Thulin, Helmut Griem, Helmut Berger, Charlotte Rampling, Florinda Bolkan. Grim drama depicting the plight of a family of German industrialists during the 1930s; their decline parallels the rise of Hitler. Violent, melodramatic, and controversial, but undeniably illuminating. [X]▼

Damned Don't Cry, The (1950) **103m.** **½ D: Vincent Sherman. Joan Crawford,

David Brian, Steve Cochran, Kent Smith, Richard Egan. Follow-up to FLAMINGO ROAD formula; Crawford is well cast as lower-class gal rising to wealth via wit and looks, discovering too late that a gangster's moll has no right to love and happiness.

Damned in the USA (1991-British) **C-76m.** **½ D: Paul Yule. Adequate documentary about the debate over censorship and public funding on the American arts scene, that was itself the object of controversy when Donald Wildmon, the conservative activist who is interviewed in the film, attempted to have it legally suppressed. He lost his case, and the film opened theatrically in late 1992, a booking it may not have received without the publicity surrounding the lawsuit. Originally produced for British television.▼

Damn the Defiant! (1962-British) **C-101m.** *** D: Lewis Gilbert. Alec Guinness, Dirk Bogarde, Maurice Denham, Nigel Stock, Richard Carpenter, Anthony Quayle. Bogarde vs. Guinness in stalwart tale of British warship during Napoleonic campaign. Production shows great attention to historic detail. CinemaScope.▼●

Damn Yankees (1958) **C-110m.** *** D: George Abbott, Stanley Donen. Tab Hunter, Gwen Verdon, Ray Walston, Russ Brown, Jimmie Komack, Jean Stapleton, Nathaniel Frey. Aging, frustrated Washington Senators baseball fan says he'd sell his soul to see the club get one good hitter; a devilish Mr. Applegate appears to fulfill his wish, and transforms *him* into the club's new star. Faithful translation of hit Broadway musical (with Walston, Verdon, and others repeating their original roles) loses something along the way, and has a particularly weak finale, but it's still quite entertaining. Songs include "(You Gotta Have) Heart," "Whatever Lola Wants," and a mambo memorably danced by Verdon and choreographer Bob Fosse.▼●

Damon and Pythias (1962-Italian) **C-99m.** ** D: Curtis Bernhardt. Guy Williams, Don Burnett, Ilaria Occhini, Liana Orfei, Arnoldo Foa. Title reveals all in this routine costumer making legendary figures juvenile cardboard heroes.

Damsel in Distress, A (1937) **101m.** *** D: George Stevens. Fred Astaire, George Burns, Gracie Allen, Joan Fontaine, Constance Collier, Reginald Gardiner, Montagu Love. Bright Gershwin musical set in London, with dancing star Astaire pursuing aristocratic heiress Fontaine. Burns and Allen have never been better—they even get to sing and dance. Songs include "Foggy Day in London Town," "Nice Work If You Can Get It." The clever "Fun House" sequence won an Oscar for Hermes Pan's dance direction.▼●

Dan Candy's Law SEE: **Alien Thunder**

Dance, Fools, Dance (1931) **81m.** **½ D: Harry Beaumont. Joan Crawford, Cliff Edwards, Clark Gable, Earl Foxe, Lester Vail, Natalie Moorhead. Crawford, alone in the world, becomes reporter out to expose mobster Gable by winning him over. Interesting for early Gable-Crawford teaming; brisk pre-Code drama.▼

Dance, Girl, Dance (1940) **90m.** **½ D: Dorothy Arzner. Maureen O'Hara, Louis Hayward, Lucille Ball, Virginia Field, Ralph Bellamy, Maria Ouspenskaya, Mary Carlisle, Walter Abel, Edward Brophy. Innocent young girl (O'Hara) aspires to be a ballerina, but self-centered Ball steers her toward burlesque instead. Film has won latter-day acclaim for feminist angles, especially for O'Hara's burlesque-hall speech; unfortunately, it's not as good as one would like. Lucy is terrific as Bubbles.▼●

Dance Goes On, The (1991-Canadian) **C-103m.** ** D: Paul Almond. Matthew James Almond, James Keach, Genevieve Bujold, Bryan Hennessey, Louise Marleau, Leslie Hope, Cary Lawrence, Deborah Freeland. Young Almond, who's insensitive and money-hungry (because he has grown up in L.A.), arrives in Quebec where he's inherited his uncle's farm. Will he get in touch with his roots, and experience "real life"? Ever-so-predictable (not to mention boring) drama. Actor Almond is the son of Bujold and director Almond (who also produced and scripted).▼

Dance Hall (1941) **74m.** *½ D: Irving Pichel. Carole Landis, Cesar Romero, William Henry, June Storey. Mild romantic musical with Romero, who runs a dance hall, falling in love with worker Landis.▼

Dance Hall (1950-British) **78m.** ** D: Charles Crichton. Natasha Parry, Jane Hylton, Diana Dors, Petula Clark, Donald Houston, Bonar Colleano, Sydney Tafler, Kay Kendall, Geraldo, Ted Heath Band. Episodic tale of four factory girls' encounters and adventures at local dance hall. Nothing much.▼

Dance Hall Racket (1953) **60m.** *½ D: Phil Tucker. Lenny Bruce, Honey Harlowe, Timothy Farrell, Sally Marr. This one could be retitled *All in the* (Dysfunctional) *Family*: Lenny plays a hood, real-life wife Harlowe is a bimbo who shows off her cleavage, and mom Marr is along for laughs. Scripted by Bruce; it would make a classy double bill with Tucker's ROBOT MONSTER.▼

Dance Little Lady (1955-British) **C-87m.** **½ D: Val Guest. Mai Zetterling, Terence Morgan, Guy Rolfe, Mandy Miller, Eunice Gayson, Reginald Beckwith. Prima ballerina Zetterling is married to heel Morgan; after a car accident ends her career, he exploits the dancing talent of their daughter (Miller). Corny drama is aided by pleasant dance sequences.▼

Dancemaker (1999) **C-98m.** ***½ D: Matthew Diamond. Fascinating study of choreographer Paul Taylor and the endless difficulties managing his company and its dancers. Footage of his dance creations is artfully interspersed with preparations for the troupe's engagement in India. Film provides an insider's look at what it takes to be a dancer—and a dancemaker. A feast for dance buffs.

Dance of Death (1969-British) **C-138m.** ★★★ D: David Giles. Laurence Olivier, Geraldine McEwan, Robert Lang, Malcolm Reynolds, Janina Faye, Carolyn Jones. Film version of National Theatre production of August Strindberg's angst-laden play about an aging sea captain, notable chiefly for Olivier's fiery performance. Unreleased in U.S. until 1979. [PG—originally rated G]

Dance of Death (1971) SEE: **House of Evil**

Dance of the Damned (1988) **C-83m.** ★★½ D: Katt Shea Ruben. Cyril O'Reilly, Starr Andreef, Deborah Ann Nassar, Maria Ford, Athena Worthy, Tom Ruben. Eerie, fascinating, very low-budget horror drama, in which a vampire selects an intelligent, troubled stripper as his next victim, but first insists she tell him what daylight is like. Slow to get started, but ambitious and mature, with good characterizations and acting. [R]▼●

Dance of the Dwarfs (1983) **C-93m.** ★½ D: Gus Trikonis. Peter Fonda, Deborah Raffin, John Amos, Carlos Palomino. Female anthropologist (Raffin) searching for lost pygmy tribe in jungle hooks up with drunken helicopter pilot (Fonda) in this stupid AFRICAN QUEENish adventure shot in Philippines. They encounter strange creatures, audience encounters boredom. Video title: JUNGLE HEAT. [PG]▼

Dance of the Vampires SEE: **Fearless Vampire Killers or: Pardon Me, But Your Teeth Are in My Neck, The**

Dancers (1987) **C-99m.** ★½ D: Herbert Ross. Mikhail Baryshnikov, Alessandra Ferri, Leslie Browne, Thomas Rall, Lynn Seymour, Victor Barbee, Mariangela Melato, Julie Kent. Trite, inexplicably bad movie about a ballet star/lothario (Baryshnikov, ideally cast) who's rehearsing a screen version of "Giselle," and becomes infatuated with an innocent young dancer. A waste of time. Baryshnikov, Browne and Ross collaborated ten years earlier on THE TURNING POINT. [PG]▼●

Dancers in the Dark (1932) **60m.** ★★½ D: David Burton. Miriam Hopkins, Jack Oakie, George Raft, William Collier, Jr., Eugene Pallette, Lyda Roberti. Bandleader Oakie tries to kindle romance with taxi-dancer Hopkins, by sending her boyfriend (Collier) out of town, but doesn't reckon with gangster Raft falling for her too. Good stars help murky drama.

Dancer, Texas Pop. 81 (1998) **C-95m.** ★★½ D: Tim McCanlies. Ethan Embry, Breckin Meyer, Peter Facinelli, Eddie Mills, Ashley Johnson, Patricia Wettig, Michael O'Neill. Slight but pleasant LAST PICTURE SHOW–lite tale of four small-town teenage buddies facing life after high school and wondering whether they should make good on a childhood pact to move to L.A. Appealing performances by the male leads make up for their schematic roles. Promising debut for writer-director McCanlies. [PG]▼●◗

Dances With Wolves (1990) **C-181m.** ★★★★ D: Kevin Costner. Kevin Costner, Mary McDonnell, Graham Greene, Rodney A. Grant, Floyd Red Crow Westerman, Tantoo Cardinal, Robert Pastorelli, Charles Rocket, Maury Chaykin, Larry Joshua, Wes Studi. Altogether extraordinary film (all the more so for being Costner's directing debut) about an idealistic young Civil War soldier who makes friends with a Sioux Indian tribe and, eventually, becomes one of them. Simply and eloquently told, with every element falling into place (on breathtaking South Dakota locations). A triumph in every respect. Oscar winner for Best Picture, Director, Screenplay (Michael Blake, from his novel), Original Score (John Barry), Cinematography (Dean Semler), Editing (Neil Travis), and Sound Recording. Costner has also prepared a 237m. "special edition" that expands the story and characterizations. Both versions are on video. Panavision. [PG-13]▼●◗

Dance With a Stranger (1985-British) **C-101m.** ★★★½ D: Mike Newell. Miranda Richardson, Rupert Everett, Ian Holm, Matthew Carroll, Tom Chadbon, Joanne Whalley, Jane Bertish. Stylish, trenchant study of romantic self-destruction based on the true story of Ruth Ellis, who in 1955 became the last woman ever executed in Britain. Peaks with about a half hour to go, but Richardson, her leading men, and a haunting atmosphere more than compensate. Ellis' story was earlier told in YIELD TO THE NIGHT (BLONDE SINNER), with Diana Dors. [R]▼●

Dance With Me (1998) **C-126m.** ★★½ D: Randa Haines. Vanessa L. Williams, Chayanne, Kris Kristofferson, Joan Plowright, Jane Krakowski, Beth Grant. Likable if formulaic (and overlong) film about a Houston dance instructor (Williams) who learns a thing or two from a Cuban émigré who's come to work at the dance studio. What the studio owner (Kristofferson) doesn't know is that the handsome young man is his son. Appealing cast and terrific dance sequences—including a knockout at a Latin dance club—give this life, and Plowright steals most of her scenes as a matronly but enthusiastic student. [PG]▼●◗

Dance With Me Henry (1956) **79m.** ★½ D: Charles Barton. Lou Costello, Bud Abbott, Gigi Perreau, Rusty Hamer. Low-grade Abbott and Costello involving the duo's ownership of run-down amusement park and two kids they've adopted; their last film together.▼

Dancing at Lughnasa (1998-U.S.-British-Irish) **C-92m.** *** D: Pat O'Connor. Meryl Streep, Michael Gambon, Catherine McCormack, Kathy Burke, Sophie Thompson, Brid Brennan, Rhys Ifans, Darrell Johnston, narrated by Gerard McSorley. Flavorful filmization of Brian Friel's play about a close-knit rural Irish family—five unmarried sisters—in the 1930s and the return of their brother, Jack (a priest), from his post in Africa. No strong story here but a rich feel for time, place, atmosphere, and character, with fine performances all around. [PG] ▼●◗

Dancing in the Dark (1949) **C-92m.** **½ D: Irving Reis. William Powell, Betsy Drake, Mark Stevens, Adolphe Menjou, Walter Catlett. Occasionally bubbly musical comedy with Powell hoping to cement good relations with film company by signing Broadway star; he becomes intrigued with talents of unknown girl, who turns out to be his daughter.

Dancing in the Dark (1986-Canadian) **C-98m.** ** D: Leon Marr. Martha Henry, Neil Munro, Rosemary Dunsmore, Richard Manette. Henry is impressive in this otherwise obvious, predictable account of a perfect, devoted wife, a meticulously controlled woman, and how she comes to have a mental breakdown. [PG-13]▼

Dancing Lady (1933) **94m.** **½ D: Robert Z. Leonard. Joan Crawford, Clark Gable, Franchot Tone, May Robson, Nelson Eddy, Fred Astaire, Robert Benchley, Ted Healy and his Stooges. Glossy backstage romance is best remembered for Astaire's film debut (he plays himself), dancing opposite a less-than-inspired Crawford. Show-biz story, three-cornered romance are strictly standard, but cast and MGM gloss add points. Funniest moments belong to the Three Stooges. Look fast for a young Eve Arden.▼●

Dancing Masters, The (1943) **63m.** *½ D: Mal St. Clair. Oliver Hardy, Stan Laurel, Trudy Marshall, Robert Bailey, Matt Briggs, Margaret Dumont. L&H overcome by routine material, special effects that look phony. Robert Mitchum has bit as a hood.

Dancing Mothers (1926) **60m.** **½ D: Herbert Brenon. Clara Bow, Alice Joyce, Dorothy Cumming, Norman Trevor. Sprightly account of Flapper Bow defying conventions as prototype of the Jazz Age. Silent film has simple plot but enthusiastic performances.▼

Dancing on a Dime (1940) **74m.** **½ D: Joseph Santley. Grace McDonald, Robert Paige, Virginia Dale, Peter Lind Hayes. Programmer musical with wispy plot allowing for McDonald et al. to do some dancing and vocalizing, such as "I Hear Music" and title tune. Not bad.

Dandy in Aspic, A (1968-British) **C-107m.** ** D: Anthony Mann. Laurence Harvey, Tom Courtenay, Mia Farrow, Lionel Stander, Harry Andrews, Peter Cook. Wooden spy melodrama in which principals keep switching sides so rapidly it becomes impossible to follow. Mann died during filming; Harvey completed director's chores. Panavision. [R]▼●

Danger: Diabolik (1967-Italian-French) **C-100m.** *** D: Mario Bava. John Phillip Law, Marisa Mell, Michel Piccoli, Adolfo Celi, Terry-Thomas, Claudio Gora. Entertaining, tongue-in-cheek exploits of super-criminal Diabolik (Law), with wonderfully outré sets and costumes, stylish photography, and a bizarre psychedelic score by Ennio Morricone. An indelible 60s time-capsule based on the European comic-strip character. Originally released as DIABOLIK, at 105m. Panoramica.▼●

Danger in the Skies SEE: **Pilot, The**

Danger Island SEE: **Mr. Moto in Danger Island**

Danger Lights (1930) **73m.** ** D: George B. Seitz. Louis Wolheim, Jean Arthur, Robert Armstrong, Hugh Herbert, Robert Edeson. Tough but kindhearted railroad supervisor Wolheim is engaged to marry Arthur, but she falls for younger, handsomer tramp turned engineer Armstrong. Predictable, with race-against-the-clock finale. Natural Vision 70mm.▼

Danger—Love at Work (1937) **81m.** **½ D: Otto Preminger. Ann Sothern, Jack Haley, Mary Boland, John Carradine, Edward Everett Horton, E. E. Clive, Stanley Fields. Wacky comedy of family headed by nutty Boland involved in shotgun wedding of Sothern and Haley.

Dangerous (1935) **78m.** **½ D: Alfred E. Green. Bette Davis, Franchot Tone, Margaret Lindsay, Alison Skipworth, John Eldredge, Dick Foran. Former star Davis, on the skids, is rehabilitated by Tone in good but syrupy tale, with flamboyant Oscar-winning performance by Davis. Remade as SINGAPORE WOMAN.▼●

Dangerous Beauty (1998) **C-114m.** **½ D: Marshall Herskovitz. Catherine McCormack, Rufus Sewell, Jacqueline Bisset, Oliver Platt, Moira Kelly, Fred Ward, Jeroen Krabbé, Joanna Cassidy. Chronicle of a fascinating woman in 16th-century Venice, where women had no rights and no education—but courtesans did. Sacrificing her one true love, she becomes the most notorious, outspoken, and desired woman in Venice. McCormack is superb in the leading role, and Bisset is ideal as her mother, but the story takes a sharp turn toward the end (incorporating the plague and the Inquisition) and loses its dramatic grip. Still a good-looking and, for the most part, absorbing tale, based on a true story. Super 35. [R]▼●◗

Dangerous Break SEE: **Special Delivery** (1976)

Dangerous Corner (1934) **66m.** **½ D: Phil Rosen. Virginia Bruce, Conrad Nagel, Melvyn Douglas, Erin O'Brien Moore, Ian Keith, Betty Furness, Doris Lloyd. Interesting, well-acted adaptation of J. B. Priestley's play about a group of friends whose after-dinner conversation reveals the truth about an alleged suicide and theft committed years before; unique flashback structure and trick ending hold up.

Dangerous Crossing (1953) **75m.** **½ D: Joseph M. Newman. Jeanne Crain, Michael Rennie, Casey Adams, Carl Betz, Mary Anderson, Willis Bouchey. Well-acted suspenser has Crain a bride on ocean liner whose husband mysteriously disappears. Based on a John Dickson Carr story. Remade for cable TV in 1992 as TREACHEROUS CROSSING.

Dangerous Exile (1958-British) **C-90m.** ** D: Brian Desmond Hurst. Louis Jourdan, Belinda Lee, Keith Michell, Richard O'Sullivan. Jourdan is properly dashing in OK adventurer in which he saves royalty from execution during French revolution, aided by English lass (Lee). VistaVision.

Dangerous Female SEE: **Maltese Falcon, The** (1931)

Dangerous Friend, A SEE: **Todd Killings, The**

Dangerous Game (1993) **C-105m.** BOMB D: Abel Ferrara. Harvey Keitel, Madonna, James Russo, Nancy Ferrara, Reilly Murphy, Victor Argo, Leonard Thomas, Christina Futon. Humiliatingly banal Madonna career-killer about filmmaker whose latest project begins to reflect his own life—or is it the other way around? Barely released, and surprisingly tame, given Ferrara's previous movies, and Madonna's inclination to hang it all out. Working title was SNAKE EYES, which is what the studio rolled when it bankrolled this one. [R]▼●

Dangerous Ground (1997) **C-95m.** *½ D: Darrell James Roodt. Ice Cube, Elizabeth Hurley, Ving Rhames, Sechaba Morajele, Eric Miyeni. Dangerous, and silly, too. Back in rural South Africa for a funeral several years after his apartheid-imposed flight to the U.S., literature major Cube fulfills a promise to mom by tracking down his fugitive younger brother who's involved in a drug ring. Despite broad plot parallels, don't look for the solemn tone director Roodt brought to his remake of CRY, THE BELOVED COUNTRY. Hurley, in harsh makeup, is cast as the wayward brother's girlfriend. [R]▼●◗

Dangerous Liaisons (1988) **C-120m.** ***½ D: Stephen Frears. Glenn Close, John Malkovich, Michelle Pfeiffer, Swoosie Kurtz, Keanu Reeves, Mildred Natwick, Uma Thurman, Peter Capaldi. In 18th-century France, an unscrupulous woman manipulates the lives of those around her, just for amusement, with the help of a like-minded count. Excellent adaptation of Christopher Hampton's play *Les Liaisons Dangereuses,* based on the famous period novel. Close is magnificent, Malkovich good (though miscast). Hampton's screenplay won an Oscar, as did the art direction and costumes. Same story filmed in 1959 (as DANGEROUS LIAISONS 1960), 1989 (as VALMONT), and 1999 (as CRUEL INTENTIONS). [R] ▼●◗

Dangerous Liaisons 1960 (1959-French) **106m.** *** D: Roger Vadim. Gérard Philipe, Jeanne Moreau, Jeanne Valérie, Annette (Stroyberg) Vadim, Simone Renant, Jean-Louis Trintignant. Modern-dress version of the 18th-century novel of sexcapades among the debauched . . . and who better to film it than Vadim? Faithful in spirit to its origins, though the leads here are a *married* couple, cavorting in Paris and the Alps. Lots of fun, with gorgeous actors and jazz soundtrack by Thelonious Monk, Art Blakey, and Duke Jordan, who also appear. Don't miss Vadim's priceless prologue, shot for 1961 American audiences. French title: LES LIAISONS DANGEREUSES. ▼●

Dangerously Close (1986) **C-95m.** *½ D: Albert Pyun. John Stockwell, J. Eddie Peck, Carey Lowell, Bradford Bancroft, Don Michael Paul, Thom Mathews, Jerry Dinome (Gerard Christopher), Madison Mason. Annoyingly muddled account of some rich, clean-cut young fascists who sadistically bully those in their school who are of the "wrong element." Slickly edited and photographed, and there's the germ of a serious theme, but the result is sloppily plotted and laughably predictable. [R]▼

Dangerously They Live (1942) **77m.** **½ D: Robert Florey. John Garfield, Nancy Coleman, Raymond Massey, Moroni Olsen, Lee Patrick. When spy Coleman is captured by Nazis, doctor Garfield comes to her aid. Tried-and-true WW2 spy tale.

Dangerous Minds (1995) **C-99m.** **½ D: John N. Smith. Michelle Pfeiffer, George Dzundza, Courtney B. Vance, Robin Bartlett, Bruklin Harris, Renoly Santiago, Wade Dominguez, Beatrice Winde, Lorraine Toussaint, John Neville. Wide-eyed, inexperienced teacher (and ex-Marine) takes over a class of "unteachable" inner-city kids. She learns that changing their attitude requires a deeper understanding of their hard-knock lives. What might seem like a superficial retread of BLACKBOARD JUNGLE or TO SIR, WITH LOVE is a well-meaning, well-acted film, although some of it just doesn't wash (Pfeiffer seems awfully mousy for an ex-Marine). Followed by a TV series. [R]▼●◗

Dangerous Mission (1954) **C-75m.** *½ D: Louis King. Victor Mature, Piper Laurie, William Bendix, Vincent Price, Betta St. John. Laurie, witness to gang murder, flees N.Y.C. to Glacier National Park. Embarrassingly bad film was apparently edited with a buzz saw; if you must watch, look for Dennis Weaver in Bendix's office.▼

Dangerous Money (1946) **64m.** *½ D: Terry Morse. Sidney Toler, Gloria Warren, Victor Sen Yung, Rick Vallin, Joseph Crehan, Willie Best. Yawnworthy *Charlie Chan* entry about the hunt for a murderer aboard a ship.

Dangerous Moonlight (1941-British) **83m.** *** D: Brian Desmond Hurst. Anton Walbrook, Sally Gray, Derrick de Marney, Keneth Kent. Intelligently presented account of concert pianist who becomes a member of a British fighter squadron during WW2; musical interludes (including Richard Addinsell's well-known "Warsaw Concerto") well handled. Look for Michael Rennie in a small role. Retitled: SUICIDE SQUADRON.▼

Dangerous Moves (1984-Swiss) **C-100m.** *** D: Richard Dembo. Michel Piccoli, Alexandre Arbatt, Leslie Caron, Liv Ullmann, Daniel Olbrychski, Michel Aumont. Absorbing, thought-provoking film about international intrigue surrounding a world chess championship. Academy Award winner for Best Foreign Film.▼

Dangerous Orphans (1986-New Zealand) **C/B&W-94m.** ** D: John Laing. Peter Stevens, Jennifer Ward-Lealand, Michael Hurst, Ross Girven, Peter Bland, Ian Mune, Zac Wallace, Grant Tilly. Slick but standard, bloody actioner about title trio's vendetta against thugs who wrecked their early lives. Plays like a TV episode. [R]▼

Dangerous Partners (1945) **74m.** **½ D: Edward L. Cahn. James Craig, Signe Hasso, Edmund Gwenn, Audrey Totter, Mabel Paige, John Warburton. After surviving a plane crash, a couple tries to unravel the mystery of a fellow passenger who was carrying four wills for a million dollars—with each one naming him the beneficiary. Not-bad grade-B mystery yarn.

Dangerous Profession, A (1949) **79m.** ** D: Ted Tetzlaff. George Raft, Pat O'Brien, Ella Raines, Jim Backus, Roland Winters. Mystery involving ex-bondsman, blackmail, and murder; not bad but standard.

Dangerous Summer, A (1981-Australian) **C-100m.** *½ D: Quentin Masters. Tom Skerritt, Ian Gilmour, James Mason, Wendy Hughes, Ray Barrett, Guy Doleman. Confusing, hilariously unsubtle drama of psychotic arsonist Gilmour trying to torch a summer resort. Good cast looks ill at ease. Originally titled THE BURNING MAN. Video title: FLASH FIRE. Panavision. ▼●◗

Dangerous to Know (1938) **70m.** **½ D: Robert Florey. Akim Tamiroff, Anna May Wong, Gail Patrick, Lloyd Nolan, Harvey Stephens, Anthony Quinn, Roscoe Karns. Slick, class-conscious mobster Tamiroff sets his sights on aristocratic Patrick, while his elegant hostess (Wong) suffers in silence. Interesting B picture never quite delivers.

Dangerous When Wet (1953) **C-95m.** *** D: Charles Walters. Esther Williams, Fernando Lamas, Jack Carson, Charlotte Greenwood, Denise Darcel, William Demarest, Donna Corcoran, Barbara Whiting. Cute musical comedy, one of Esther's best, about a health-conscious family whose leading light tries to swim the English Channel. Williams cavorts underwater with the animated Tom and Jerry in one memorable scene. She later married leading-man Lamas in real life. ▼●

Dangerous Woman, A (1993) **C-99m.** ** D: Stephen Gyllenhaal. Debra Winger, Barbara Hershey, Gabriel Byrne, David Strathairn, Chloe Webb, John Terry, Laurie Metcalf, Jan Hooks, Paul Dooley. Muddled movie of Mary McGarry Morris's acclaimed novel, with Winger the unceasingly frank nebbish niece of wealthy widow Hershey (who's been having an affair with a married politician). Winger is memorable in an unattractive part; Hershey's role is impossible; and Byrne (as the handyman who comes between them) comes off as the Great Stone Face. [R]▼●

Danger Route (1968-British) **C-90m.** ** D: Seth Holt. Richard Johnson, Carol Lynley, Barbara Bouchet, Sylvia Sims, Diana Dors, Harry Andrews, Gordon Jackson, Sam Wanamaker. Appearance (in both senses of the word) of Lynley and Bouchet gives a little boost to typical secret-agent tale with several plot twists. [M/PG]

Danger Signal (1945) **78m.** ** D: Robert Florey. Faye Emerson, Zachary Scott, Rosemary DeCamp, Bruce Bennett, Mona Freeman. No-account Scott comes between Emerson and her family in this routine drama; Scott is a most convincing heel.

Danger Within SEE: **Breakout** (1959)

Daniel (1983) **C-130m.** *** D: Sidney Lumet. Timothy Hutton, Mandy Patinkin, Lindsay Crouse, Edward Asner, Ellen Barkin, Julie Bovasso, Tovah Feldshuh, Joseph Leon, Amanda Plummer, John Rubinstein. Excellent adaptation of E. L. Doctorow's *The Book of Daniel*, about the children of a couple patterned after Julius and Ethel Rosenberg who must confront their painful heritage in order to deal with their own lives in the protest-filled 1960s. Not without its flaws, but overall a provocative and extremely well-made film. [R]▼

Daniel Boone (1936) **75m.** **½ D: David Howard. George O'Brien, Heather Angel, John Carradine, Ralph Forbes, Clarence Muse. OK action adventure detailing a chapter in the life of the legendary pioneer:

his leading some settlers west from North Carolina into Kentucky. O'Brien is well cast in the title role.▼

Daniel Boone, Trail Blazer (1956) **C-76m.** **½ D: Albert C. Gannaway, Ismael Rodriquez. Bruce Bennett, Lon Chaney (Jr.), Faron Young, Kem Dibbs. Generally well-acted low-budget version of life of famous frontier explorer and his skirmishes with Indians. Filmed in Mexico.▼

Danny Boy (1982-Irish-British) **C-92m.** ** D: Neil Jordan. Veronica Quilligan, Stephen Rea, Alan Devlin, Peter Caffrey, Honor Heffernan, Lise-Ann McLaughlin, Donal McCann, Ray McAnally, Marie Kean. Ambitious but pretentious, unrelentingly dreary melodrama of sax player Rea, who exchanges his instrument for a machine gun after witnessing a double murder. Jordan's directorial debut, which he also scripted; he and leading man Rea later reteamed for THE CRYING GAME. Original British title: ANGEL. [R]▼

Dante's Inferno (1935) **88m.** **½ D: Harry Lachman. Spencer Tracy, Claire Trevor, Henry B. Walthall, Alan Dinehart, Scotty Beckett. No Dante in this yarn of carnival owner who gets too big for his own good; just one elaborate sequence showing Satan's paradise in good Tracy vehicle. Young Rita Hayworth dances in one scene.

Dante's Peak (1997) **C-108m.** *** D: Roger Donaldson. Pierce Brosnan, Linda Hamilton, Jamie Renée Smith, Jeremy Foley, Elizabeth Hoffman, Charles Hallahan, Grant Heslov. Formulaic but entertaining disaster movie about a scientist from the U.S. Geological Survey who sniffs around a mountainside town in Washington just below a volcano that he feels is going to blow at any minute. Along the way he falls in love with the town's mayor. Critics dumped on the first of 1997's two volcano movies, but hey—it ain't supposed to be *Henry V*. The characters are likable and the effects are completely convincing. Super 35. [PG-13] ▼●◗

Danton (1982-Polish-French) **C-136m.** **** D: Andrzej Wajda. Gérard Depardieu, Wojciech Pszoniak, Patrice Chereau, Angela Winkler, Boguslaw Linda. Literate, absorbing, knowing drama of Danton, Robespierre, and the Reign of Terror following the French Revolution. A brilliant film, with obvious parallels to contemporary political situation in Poland. Depardieu is magnificent in the title role. [PG]▼●

Danzon (1991-Mexican) **C-103m.** *** D: Maria Novaro. Maria Rojo, Carmen Salinas, Blanca Guerra, Margarita Isabel, Tito Vasconcelos. Arresting feminist tale about a dreary telephone operator (Rojo) who comes alive only when performing a ballroom dance known as the "danzon." Her life undergoes a transformation when her longtime partner mysteriously disappears, and she becomes obsessed with finding him. The scenes with Rojo and Vasconcelos (playing a transvestite nightclub performer) are especially effective. [PG-13]▼

Darby O'Gill and the Little People (1959) **C-90m.** ***½ D: Robert Stevenson. Albert Sharpe, Janet Munro, Sean Connery, Jimmy O'Dea, Kieron Moore, Estelle Winwood. Outstanding Disney fantasy about an Irish caretaker (Sharpe) who spins so many tales that no one believes him when he says he's befriended the King of Leprechauns. An utter delight, with dazzling special effects—and some truly terrifying moments along with the whimsy.▼●

Darby's Rangers (1958) **121m.** **½ D: William Wellman. James Garner, Etchika Choureau, Jack Warden, Edward Byrnes, Venetia Stevenson, Torin Thatcher, Peter Brown, Corey Allen, Stuart Whitman, Murray Hamilton, David Janssen. Garner does well in WW2 actioner as leader of assault troops in North Africa and Italy, focusing on relationships among his command and their shore romances.▼

Daredevil, The (1972) **C-70m.** ** D: Robert W. Stringer. George Montgomery, Terry Moore, Gay Perkins, Cyril Poitier, Bill Kelly. Offbeat, somewhat unappetizing actioner has heel Montgomery, a top racer, as driver for a dope ring. One of the odd twists has Poitier, a black mortician, cast as villain. Music by The Brooklyn Bridge. [PG]

Daring Dobermans, The (1973) **C-90m.** **½ D: Bryon Chudnow. Charles Knox Robinson, Tim Considine, David Moses, Claudio Martinez, Joan Caulfield. Sequel to THE DOBERMAN GANG provides amiable family viewing as the canines are trained for another daring heist by a new gang of crooks. [G]▼

Daring Game (1968) **C-100m.** **½ D: Laslo Benedek. Lloyd Bridges, Nico Minardos, Michael Ansara, Joan Blackman. Not bad adventure tale of underwater expert (guess who?) in search of husband and daughter of his former girlfriend.▼

Daring Young Man (1942) **73m.** ** D: Frank Strayer. Joe E. Brown, Marguerite Chapman, William Wright, Roger Clark. Brown is able to make this formula Nazi spy chase comedy of passable interest; set in N.Y.C.▼

Dark, The (1979) **C-92m.** ** D: John (Bud) Cardos. William Devane, Cathy Lee Crosby, Richard Jaeckel, Keenan Wynn, Jacquelyn Hyde, Biff Elliott, Vivian Blaine. Fairly well made but predictable sci-fier; writer Devane and TV reporter Crosby take on a homicidal alien in a California town. Aka THE MUTILATOR. Panavision. [R]▼

Dark Alibi (1946) **61m.** *½ D: Phil Karlson. Sidney Toler, Benson Fong, Mantan Moreland, Teala Loring, George

Holmes, Edward Earle, Russell Hicks, Joyce Compton. Someone's committing crimes and framing innocents by forging their fingerprints in this tedious *Charlie Chan* outing for Karlson completists only.

Dark Angel, The (1935) **110m.** *** D: Sidney Franklin. Fredric March, Merle Oberon, Herbert Marshall, Janet Beecher, John Halliday. Effective soaper of love, guilt, and fate. The three leads are lifelong friends; March and Oberon are destined to marry, but he and Marshall head off to WW1—and tragedy. Coscripted by Lillian Hellman; based on a play by H. B. Trevelyan (Guy Bolton). Originally filmed in 1925 with Ronald Colman and Vilma Banky.

Dark at the Top of the Stairs, The (1960) **C-123m.** ***½ D: Delbert Mann. Robert Preston, Dorothy McGuire, Eve Arden, Angela Lansbury, Shirley Knight, Lee Kinsolving, Frank Overton, Robert Eyer. Simple, eloquent drama, set in 1920s Oklahoma, with Preston in top form as a traveling salesman caught in a passionless marriage. His relationships with wife McGuire, daughter Knight, and "friend" Lansbury are played out in a series of beautifully acted scenes. Poignant script by Irving Ravetch and Harriet Frank, Jr., from William Inge's Pulitzer Prize–winning play.

Dark Avenger, The SEE: **Warriors, The** (1955)

Dark Backward, The (1991) **C-104m.** *½ D: Adam Rifkin. Judd Nelson, Bill Paxton, Wayne Newton, Lara Flynn Boyle, James Caan, Rob Lowe, King Moody, Claudia Christian. Yes, that's a third arm growing out of Nelson's back—and it's putting the necessary edge on his wide professional reputation as the worst stand-up comic in show-biz history. Contrived in an attempt to be culty, but unsuccessful even on those terms. Still, film has a casting mix one could cherish. Lowe is fitted out with what appears to the untrained eye to be Mr. Hyde's dental work. Director Rifkin appears as Rufus Bing. [R]▼●

Dark City (1950) **98m.** **½ D: William Dieterle. Charlton Heston, Lizabeth Scott, Viveca Lindfors, Dean Jagger, Jack Webb, Don DeFore, Ed Begley, Henry (Harry) Morgan. Moody drama of cynical, alienated Heston, and what happens when he and his cronies take sap DeFore in a card game. It's fun to see Webb and Morgan, both of later *Dragnet* fame, cast as a wiseguy and ex-pug at each other's throat. This was Heston's Hollywood debut.

Dark City (1998) **C-100m.** *** D: Alex Proyas. Rufus Sewell, Kiefer Sutherland, Jennifer Connelly, Richard O'Brien, Ian Richardson, Colin Friels, Bruce Spence, William Hurt. In a city where it is always night, aliens conduct secret experiments to learn what makes us human. Meanwhile, his memory mostly gone, Sewell is suspected of being a serial killer, and finds he now has telekinetic powers. Richly plotted sci-fi has striking set design and excellent use of special effects; complex, with a new surprise every few minutes. Filmed in Australia. Cowritten by the director. Super 35. [R]▼●◗

Dark Command (1940) **94m.** *** D: Raoul Walsh. Claire Trevor, John Wayne, Walter Pidgeon, Roy Rogers, George "Gabby" Hayes, Porter Hall, Marjorie Main. Pidgeon plays character based on 1860s renegade Quantrill, small-town despot who (in this story) launches his terror raids after clashing with new marshal Wayne. Dramatically uneven, but entertaining. Also shown in computer-colored version. ▼

Dark Corner, The (1946) **99m.** *** D: Henry Hathaway. Lucille Ball, Clifton Webb, William Bendix, Mark Stevens, Kurt Kreuger, Cathy Downs, Reed Hadley, Constance Collier. Top-notch mystery with secretary Ball helping moody boss Stevens escape from phony murder charge. Well-acted, exciting film noir. ▼

Dark Crystal, The (1983-British) **C-94m.** *** D: Jim Henson and Frank Oz. Performed by Jim Henson, Kathryn Mullen, Frank Oz, Dave Goelz, Brian Muehl, Jean Pierre Amiel, Kiran Shah. Elaborate fantasy—a cross between Tolkien and the Brothers Grimm—from the Muppets crew, with imaginative (and often grotesque) cast of characters enacting classic quest: a missing piece of the powerful Dark Crystal must be found or evil will take over the world. Takes time to warm up to, but worth the effort. Panavision. [PG]▼●◗

Dark Delusion (1947) **90m.** ** D: Willis Goldbeck. Lionel Barrymore, James Craig, Lucille Bremer, Jayne Meadows, Warner Anderson, Henry Stephenson, Alma Kruger, Keye Luke, Art Baker, Marie Blake, Nell Craig. The *Dr. Kildare/Dr. Gillespie* series came to an end with this blah entry about Gillespie getting a new protégé (Craig) who's assigned to the case of a neurotic socialite whose family wants her committed.

Dark End of the Street, The (1981) **C-90m.** *** D: Jan Egleson. Laura Harrington, Henry Tomaszewski, Michelle Green, Lance Henriksen, Pamela Payton-Wright, Terence Grey. Low-budget independent feature, shot in and around Boston, about white teenagers who witness a black friend's accidental death. Realistic depiction of urban working-class lifestyle and problems. Fine performances, particularly by Harrington and Green (as her best friend).

Darker Than Amber (1970) **C-97m.** **½ D: Robert Clouse. Rod Taylor, Suzy Kendall, Theodore Bikel, Jane Russell, James Booth, Janet MacLachlan. OK action melodrama casts Taylor as John D. MacDonald's detective Travis McGee; he's after thugs who beat up Kendall. Good location photography in Miami and Caribbean. [PG—edited from original R rating]▼

Dark Eyes (1987-Italian) **C-118m.** ***½ D: Nikita Mikhalkov. Marcello Mastroianni, Silvana Mangano, Marthe Keller, Elena Safonova, Pina Cei. Mastroianni gives a tour-de-force performance as a once-young, idealistic, aspiring architect, who settled for a life of wealth and ease after marrying a banker's daughter . . . and proved incapable of holding on to what's important to him. A rich, beautifully detailed, multileveled film that's at once sad, funny, and haunting. Based on short stories by Anton Chekhov (one of which was previously filmed as LADY WITH A DOG).▼●

Dark Eyes of London SEE: **Human Monster, The**

Dark Forces SEE: **Harlequin**

Dark Habits (1984-Spanish) **C-116m.** **½ D: Pedro Almodóvar. Cristina S. Pascual, Carmen Maura, Julieta Serrano, Marisa Paredes. Singer Pascual takes it on the lam after her lover ODs and finds herself in a convent crammed with wacky, free-spirited nuns. Funny, but not up to some of Almodóvar's later work.▼●

Dark Half, The (1993) **C-122m.** ** D: George A. Romero. Timothy Hutton, Amy Madigan, Michael Rooker, Julie Harris, Robert Joy, Kent Broadhurst, Beth Grant, Rutanya Alda, Tom Mardirosian, Glenn Colerider, Chelsea Field, Royal Dano. Another Stephen King movie without a good half. Hutton plays a successful writer, under a pseudonym, who fails when he writes under his own name. When he's threatened with exposure, he announces the death of his alter ego—which causes the "pseudonym," to come to life and embark on a murderous rampage. (King himself published several novels under the pseudonym Richard Bachman before killing him off.) Scripted by Romero. [R]▼●◗

Dark Hazard (1934) **72m.** ** D: Alfred E. Green. Edward G. Robinson, Genevieve Tobin, Glenda Farrell, Henry B. Walthall, Sidney Toler. Robinson is bright spot of programmer about his precarious married life to Tobin, endangered by girlfriend Farrell and urge to gamble.

Dark Horse, The (1932) **75m.** **½ D: Alfred E. Green. Warren William, Bette Davis, Guy Kibbee, Vivienne Osborne, Frank McHugh. Lively political spoof with nitwit Kibbee running for governor with help from campaign manager William and co-worker Davis.▼

Dark Intruder (1965) **59m.** *** D: Harvey Hart. Leslie Nielsen, Judi Meredith, Mark Richman, Werner Klemperer, Gilbert Green, Charles Bolender. Uneven performances major liability in near-flawless supernatural thriller. Occult expert called in by San Francisco police in connection with series of weird murders. Intricate plot and exceptional use of time period blending with suspense make this a one-of-a-kind movie. Busted TV pilot given theatrical release.

Dark Journey (1937-British) **82m.** *** D: Victor Saville. Conrad Veidt, Vivien Leigh, Joan Gardner, Anthony Bushell, Ursula Jeans. Engrossing love story, set in WW1 Stockholm, about dress-shop-owner-double agent Leigh, who gets involved with baron Veidt, head of German Intelligence. Young Vivien is radiant.▼

Darkman (1990) **C-95m.** **½ D: Sam Raimi. Liam Neeson, Frances McDormand, Colin Friels, Larry Drake, Nelson Mashita, Jesse Lawrence Ferguson, Rafael H. Robledo, Danny Hicks, Bruce Campbell. Scientist hot on the trail of a formula for cloning body parts by computer is savagely attacked (and left for dead) by thugs who represent a crooked city developer. Retreating into a shadow world, and seeking revenge, the laboratory genius reinvents himself as Darkman. Grandiose melodramatics, and Raimi's over-the-top approach, are entertaining to a point, but there's a fundamental hollowness to this comic-book script. Old-fashioned laboratory montage and main titles by Pablo Ferro. Jenny Agutter and John Landis appear unbilled. Followed by two video sequels in 1995 and 1996. [R] ▼●◗

Dark Mirror, The (1946) **85m.** *** D: Robert Siodmak. Olivia de Havilland, Lew Ayres, Thomas Mitchell, Richard Long, Charles Evans, Garry Owen. De Havilland plays twin sisters—one good, one disturbed—who are implicated in murder. One of Hollywood's post-WW2 forays into psychological drama; no longer fresh, but still entertaining. Remade for TV in 1984 with Jane Seymour.▼

Dark Night of the Scarecrow (1981) **C-100m. TVM** D: Frank De Felitta. Charles Durning, Robert F. Lyons, Claude Earl Jones, Lane Smith, Tonya Crowe, Larry Drake, Jocelyn Brando. Satisfying if predictable chiller about a young girl's innocent friendship with the town dummy, whose killing by a group of vigilantes leads to a series of inexplicable events. Above average.▼

Dark Obsession (1989-British) **C-87m.** BOMB D: Nicholas Broomfield. Gabriel Byrne, Amanda Donohoe, Michael Hordern, Judy Parfitt, Douglas Hodge, Sadie Frost, Ian Carmichael. Byrne and his regiment buddies run over a chambermaid after a night of drinking—and the only one who feels guilt about the death is the only one who will suffer. Documentary director Broomfield's first fiction feature is an obvious, boring parable about the amorality of the rich and titled. Even Donohoe's frequent nudity quickly becomes dreary. Original British title: DIAMOND SKULLS. Released in U.S. in 1991. Available in both NC-17- (100m.) and R-rated versions. ▼●

Dark of the Night (1985-New Zealand) **C-89m.** *** D: Gaylene Preston. Heather Bolton, David Letch, Gary Stalker, Danny Mulheron, Kate Harcourt, Michael Haigh. Bolton buys a used Jaguar that's seemingly haunted by its previous owner, a woman who was murdered. Entertainingly loopy psychological thriller that's also a keenly observed feminist fable about the frustrations and perils of a woman seeking independence in a "man's world." Original New Zealand title: MR. WRONG. ▼

Dark of the Sun (1968-British) **C-101m.** *** D: Jack Cardiff. Rod Taylor, Yvette Mimieux, Jim Brown, Kenneth More, Peter Carsten, Andre Morell, Calvin Lockhart. Excellent cast in nerve-wracking actioner with Rod the leader of mercenary expedition to retrieve uncut diamonds and besieged refugees in Congo. One of Taylor's best pictures. Panavision. [PG]▼

Dark Passage (1947) **106m.** *** D: Delmer Daves. Humphrey Bogart, Lauren Bacall, Bruce Bennett, Agnes Moorehead. Engrossing caper of escaped convict (Bogart) undergoing plastic surgery, hiding out at Bacall's apartment till his face heals. Stars outshine far-fetched happenings. Also shown in computer-colored version. ▼●

Dark Past, The (1948) **75m.** *** D: Rudolph Maté. William Holden, Nina Foch, Lee J. Cobb, Adele Jergens, Stephen Dunne. Absorbing narrative of mad killer holding psychologist prisoner and latter's attempts to talk sense into the maniac. Remake of BLIND ALLEY.▼

Dark Places (1975-British) **C-91m.** *½ D: Don Sharp. Christopher Lee, Joan Collins, Robert Hardy, Herbert Lom, Jane Birkin, Jean Marsh. Mild horror thriller. Hardy, heir to an insane murderer's estate, is possessed by his spirit, kills those who try to do him out of it. [PG]▼

Dark Sands (1937-British) **77m.** ** D: Thornton Freeland. Paul Robeson, Henry Wilcoxon, Wallace Ford, Princess Kouka, John Laurie. Weak drama with American deserter Robeson joining African desert tribe to avoid corporal punishment. Robeson again defeated by his material. Originally titled JERICHO.▼

Dark Secret of Harvest Home (1978) **C-200m. TVM** D: Leo Penn. Bette Davis, David Ackroyd, Rosanna Arquette, Rene Auberjonois, Norman Lloyd, Michael O'Keefe. Leisurely gothic horror tale set in New England village where Bette and other weirdos maintain ritualistic lifestyle, to the dismay of artist who has moved his family there from Manhattan. Adapted from Thomas Tryon's novel *Harvest Home*; narrated in eerie fashion by Donald Pleasence. Above average.▼

Dark Side of the Sun, The (1997-Canadian) **C-101m.** BOMB D: Bozidar Nikolic. Brad Pitt, Guy Boyd, Cheryl Pollak, Milena Dravic, Constantin Nitchoff. In MEET JOE BLACK, Pitt played Death; here he plays dying. Awful weepie about a young American exile who covers his body from head to toe in leather because of a fatal skin disease. He decides to chuck life for a few days of passion when he meets a traveling actress. Entire film takes place in the Slavic countryside and features an irritating polka score! Even diehard Pitt fans best beware. Made in 1990. ▼

Dark Star (1974) **C-83m.** **½ D: John Carpenter. Dan O'Bannon, Dre Pahich, Brian Narelle. Satiric, spaced-out comedy of weary astronauts whose mission is to blow up unstable planets; one of their sentient bombs gets its own ideas. Enjoyable for sci-fi fans and surfers; stretches its shoestring budget pretty well. Carpenter's first feature, expanded from a college short he wrote with O'Bannon. [G]▼●◗

Darktown Strutters (1975) **C-85m.** *½ D: William Witney. Trina Parks, Edna Richardson, Bettye Sweet, Shirley Washington, Roger E. Mosley, Stan Shaw, Christopher Joy. Poor spoof of black and white stereotypes. Story is about Parks attempting to find her kidnapped mother. Original running time: 90m. Retitled GET DOWN AND BOOGIE. [PG]▼

Dark Tower (1987) **C-91m.** BOMB D: Ken Barnett. Michael Moriarty, Jenny Agutter, Carol Lynley, Anne Lockhart, Theodore Bikel, Kevin McCarthy, Patch Mackenzie. Appallingly bad supernatural thriller about architect Agutter's husband's ghost, which seems to be committing murder during the construction of her skyscraper. Barnett is a pseudonym for Freddie Francis (who's done far better). [R]▼●

Dark Victory (1939) **106m.** ***½ D: Edmund Goulding. Bette Davis, George Brent, Humphrey Bogart, Geraldine Fitzgerald, Ronald Reagan, Cora Witherspoon, Henry Travers. Definitive Davis performance as spoiled socialite whose life is ending; Brent as brain surgeon husband, Fitzgerald as devoted friend register in good soaper. Bogart as Irish stable master seems out of place. Remade as STOLEN HOURS, and for TV in 1976 with Elizabeth Montgomery and Anthony Hopkins. Also shown in computer-colored version. ▼●◗

Dark Waters (1944) **90m.** ** D: Andre de Toth. Merle Oberon, Franchot Tone, Thomas Mitchell, Fay Bainter, Rex Ingram, John Qualen, Elisha Cook, Jr. Cast sinks into the bog (some literally) in confused film of innocent girl staying with peculiar family.▼●◗

Dark Wind, The (1994) **C-111m.** *½ D: Errol Morris. Lou Diamond Phillips, Gary Farmer, Fred Ward, Guy Boyd, John Karlen. Disappointing feature from acclaimed documentarian Morris: a ponderously slow, muddled account of young Navajo cop Phillips, new to his district, who attempts to solve a mystery amid Navajo–Hopi differences. Script by Neal Jimenez and Eric Bergren, based on Tony Hillerman's novel. One of the executive producers was Robert Redford. Filmed in 1991. [R]▼

Darling (1965-British) **122m.** ***½ D: John Schlesinger. Julie Christie, Dirk Bogarde, Laurence Harvey, Roland Curram, Jose Luis de Villalonga, Alex Scott, Basil Henson. Christie won Oscar as girl who rises from commonplace life to marry an Italian noble, with several unsatisfactory love affairs in between. Trendy, influential 60s film—in flashy form and cynical content. Frederic Raphael's script and costume designer Julie Harris also won Oscars.▼●

Darling, How Could You! (1951) **96m.** **½ D: Mitchell Leisen. Joan Fontaine, John Lund, Mona Freeman, Peter Hanson, David Stollery. Doctor Lund and wife Fontaine return from Central America to their three children, with various comical complications. Strictly sitcom stuff, sometimes sweet but mostly silly and stupid. Based on a James M. Barrie play.

Darling Lili (1970) **C-136m.** *** D: Blake Edwards. Julie Andrews, Rock Hudson, Jeremy Kemp, Lance Percival, Jacques Marin, Michael Witney. Critically lambasted when first released, this entertaining spoof has Andrews and Hudson at their best, along with writer/director Edwards, keeping tongue-in-cheek but not becoming coy in telling story of German spy Julie posing as London entertainer during WW1, falling in love with squadron commander Hudson. Great fun, good music, including Johnny Mercer and Henry Mancini's lovely song "Whistling Away the Dark." Two decades after the fact, Edwards prepared an alternative "director's cut" of the film, more serious in tone, for cable TV; it runs 114m. Panavision. [G]

Darwin Adventure, The (1972) **C-91m.** **½ D: Jack Couffer. Nicholas Clay, Susan Macready, Ian Richardson, Christopher Martin. Curious tale focusing on career of Charles Darwin and his theories on evolution of man. [G]

D.A.R.Y.L. (1985) **C-99m.** **½ D: Simon Wincer. Mary Beth Hurt, Michael McKean, Barret Oliver, Kathryn Walker, Colleen Camp, Josef Sommer, Steve Ryan, Danny Corkill. Childless couple adopts a little boy who's really a sophisticated robot. Good premise undermined by incredibly bland presentation; young kids might enjoy it. Panavision. [PG]▼●

Das Boot (1981-German) **C-145m.** ***½ D: Wolfgang Petersen. Jürgen Prochnow, Herbert Gronemeyer, Klaus Wennemann, Hubertus Bengsch, Martin Semmelrogge, Bernd Tauber, Erwin Leder, Martin May. Realistic, meticulously mounted nail-biter chronicling a German U-boat on a mission during WW2, with Prochnow solid as its commander. Manages to embrace an anti-war message, as well. Based on Lothar-Guenther Buchheim's autobiographical novel. Originally shot as a TV miniseries, released in that 211m. form in 1997. Well-dubbed American version is titled THE BOAT. [R]▼●◗

Dash and Lilly (1999) **C-105m. TVM** D: Kathy Bates. Sam Shepard, Judy Davis, Bebe Neuwirth, Laurence Luckinbill, David Paymer, Željko Ivanek. Shepard and Davis shine as literary greats Dashiell Hammett and Lillian Hellman, who launched an often-contentious thirty-year love affair as his career was winding down (into the bottle) and hers was taking off. Neuwirth does a memorable turn as Dorothy Parker. Written by Jerry Ludwig. Bates' TV movie directing debut. Made for cable. Above average. ▼

Date With an Angel (1987) **C-105m.** BOMB D: Tom McLoughlin. Michael E. Knight, Phoebe Cates, Emmanuelle Béart, David Dukes, Phil Brock, Albert Macklin. Aspiring musician Knight, about to be swallowed up by marriage and his future father-in-law's firm, finds salvation with the broken-winged angel who crashes into his pool on the night of his bachelor party. Unbearable comic fantasy despite Beart's appropriately ethereal beauty. J-D-C Scope. [PG]▼●

Date With Death, A SEE: **McGuire Go Home!**

Date With Judy, A (1948) **C-113m.** **½ D: Richard Thorpe. Wallace Beery, Jane Powell, Elizabeth Taylor, Carmen Miranda, Xavier Cugat, Robert Stack, Scotty Beckett. Musicomedy of two teen-agers involved in family shenanigans; highlight is Beery dancing with Miranda. Songs include "It's a Most Unusual Day."▼●

Date With the Falcon, A (1941) **63m.** **½ D: Irving Reis. George Sanders, Wendy Barrie, James Gleason, Allen Jenkins, Mona Maris, Frank Moran, Ed Gargan. Sanders interrupts his wedding plans to find a missing scientist who has invented a synthetic diamond formula. Entertaining second entry in the series, with a good deal of comic relief.

Daughter of Dr. Jekyll (1957) **71m.** *½ D: Edgar G. Ulmer. John Agar, Gloria Talbott, Arthur Shields, John Dierkes. Talbott thinks she is the half-human/half-monster her father was, especially when the village death rate increases. But someone has gotten hold of her daddy's secret formula. Madly scrambles vampire, werewolf, and Jekyll-Hyde story elements.▼

Daughter of Mata Hari SEE: **Mata Hari's Daughter**

Daughter of Rosie O'Grady, The (1950) **C-104m.** **½ D: David Butler. June Haver, Gordon MacRae, Debbie Reynolds, Gene Nelson, James Barton, S. Z. Sakall, Jane Darwell. Formula period musical with Haver in title role singing turn-of-the-century favorites. Talented MacRae is her love interest, and Sakall is forced to give another cuddly stereotype.

Daughter of Shanghai (1937) **63m.** **½ D: Robert Florey. Anna May Wong, Charles Bickford, Buster Crabbe, Cecil Cunningham, J. Carrol Naish, Anthony Quinn, Philip Ahn, Fred Kohler, Evelyn Brent, Frank Sully. Good-girl Wong seeks to expose illegal alien racket in tight-knit B actioner.

Daughter of the Dragon (1931) **72m.** **½ D: Lloyd Corrigan. Warner Oland, Anna May Wong, Sessue Hayakawa, Bramwell Fletcher, Frances Dade, Holmes Herbert. Oland is Dr. Fu Manchu in this entertaining, if familiar, adaptation of a Sax Rohmer story; the good doctor dispatches daughter Wong to commit murder, and she becomes entangled with Scotland Yard sleuth Hayakawa.▼

Daughters Courageous (1939) **107m.** *** D: Michael Curtiz. John Garfield, Claude Rains, Fay Bainter, Priscilla Lane, Rosemary Lane, Lola Lane, Gale Page, May Robson, Donald Crisp, Frank McHugh. Enjoyable reworking of FOUR DAUGHTERS, featuring the same cast and chronicling what happens when wanderer Rains returns to the family he abandoned 20 years before. Garfield is fine as the brash charmer who's romancing Priscilla Lane.

Daughters of Darkness (1971-Belgian-French) **C-87m.** **½ D: Harry Kumel. Delphine Seyrig, Daniele Ouimet, John Karlen, Andrea Rau, Paul Esser, George Jamin, Joris Collet, Fons Rademakers. Sophisticated, witty, but cold tale of honeymooning couple meeting lesbian vampire Elisabeth Bathory (a real historical figure), becoming enmeshed in her schemes. Elegant, but pretentious and slow. Highly regarded by many. Also shown at 96m. Director's cut runs 100m.▼●◗

Daughters of Destiny (1954-French) **94m.** ** D: Marcel Pagliero. Claudette Colbert, Michele Morgan, André Clement, Daniel Ivernel. Over-blown, sluggish trio of tales telling of three famous women of history: Elizabeth I, Lysistrata, Joan of Arc.

Daughters of Satan (1972) **C-96m.** ** D: Hollingsworth Morse. Tom Selleck, Barra Grant, Tani Phelps Guthrie, Paraluman. Witches' curses, mumbo jumbo, and a lot of hokum as young girl is lured into witches' coven. [R]▼

Daughters of the Dust (1991) **C-114m.** **½ D: Julie Dash. Cora Lee Day, Alva Rodgers, Adisa Anderson, Kaycee Moore, Barbara O, Eartha D. Robinson, Bahni Turpin, Cheryl Lynn Bruce. Poetic, turn-of-the-century tale of the Gullah, descendants of slaves who resided on islands near South Carolina and Georgia and maintained their West African heritage. The material is fascinating, and some of the imagery is stunning, but too much of the historical background remains unexplained, and the slow pace weighs it down. Dash also scripted this *American Playhouse* theatrical feature.▼

Dave (1993) **C-105m.** *** D: Ivan Reitman. Kevin Kline, Sigourney Weaver, Frank Langella, Ben Kingsley, Kevin Dunn, Ving Rhames, Charles Grodin, Faith Prince, Laura Linney, Bonnie Hunt, Parley Baer, Stefan Gierasch, Anna Deavere Smith. Shades of PRISONER OF ZENDA! U.S. president, incapacitated by stroke, is replaced by look-alike (and everyman) Kline, who proceeds to win over the press, public, and even the president's estranged wife (Weaver) in this amusing political comedy. Farfetched premise made believable by winning cast and cameos by celebrities, real reporters, and actual U.S. senators! [PG-13]▼●◗

David (1979-German) **C-106m.** ***½ D: Peter Lilienthal. Mario Fischel, Walter Taub, Irene Vrkijan, Torsten Hentes, Eva Mattes. Jewish teenager Fischel manages to survive in Berlin during the Nazi reign of terror. Sometimes hard to follow, but still touching, haunting, powerful in its own quiet way. Based on a novel by Joel Konig.▼

David and Bathsheba (1951) **C-116m.** ** D: Henry King. Gregory Peck, Susan Hayward, Raymond Massey, Kieron Moore, James Robertson Justice, Jayne Meadows, John Sutton, George Zucco. Biblical epic with good production values but generally boring script; only fair performances.▼●

David and Goliath (1960-Italian) **C-95m.** ** D: Richard Pottier, Ferdinando Baldi. Orson Welles, Ivo Payer, Edward Hilton, Eleonora Rossi-Drago, Massimo Serato. Juvenile spectacle based on biblical tale, with wooden script, bad acting, Welles as hefty King Saul. Totalscope.▼

David and Lisa (1962) **94m.** *** D: Frank Perry. Keir Dullea, Janet Margolin, Howard da Silva, Neva Patterson, Clifton James. Independently made film about two disturbed teen-agers is excellent, sensitively played by newcomers Dullea and Margolin. Da Silva is fine as an understanding doctor. Remade for TV in 1998. ▼●◗

David Copperfield (1935) **130m.** **** D: George Cukor. Freddie Bartholomew, Frank Lawton, W.C. Fields, Lionel Barrymore, Madge Evans, Roland Young, Basil Rathbone, Edna May Oliver, Maureen O'Sullivan, Lewis Stone, Lennox Pawle, Elsa Lanchester, Una O'Connor, Arthur Treacher.

Hollywood does right by Dickens in this lavishly mounted, superbly cast production, following David's exploits from youth to young manhood, with such unforgettable characterizations as Fields's Micawber, Rathbone's Mr. Murdstone, Young's Uriah Heep, and Oliver's Aunt Betsey. A treat from start to finish. Screenplay by Howard Estabrook and Hugh Walpole; the latter also portrays the vicar. Also shown in computer-colored version.▼●

David Copperfield (1970) **C-110m. TVM** D: Delbert Mann. Robin Phillips, Susan Hampshire, Edith Evans, Michael Redgrave, Ralph Richardson, Laurence Olivier, Wendy Hiller, Emlyn Williams, Richard Attenborough. Top-drawer cast in moody new version of the classic. Giants of the English theater give what support they can to a rather limp script and an unanimated lead. Average. ▼

David Harum (1934) **83m.** **½ D: James Cruze. Will Rogers, Louise Dresser, Evelyn Venable, Kent Taylor, Stepin Fetchit, Noah Beery, Charles Middleton. Foxy rancher Rogers plays matchmaker for Venable and Taylor, while spinning his own brand of folksy humor. Filmed before in 1915.

David Holzman's Diary (1968) **74m.** ***½ D: Jim McBride. L. M. Kit Carson, Eileen Dietz, Louise Levine, Lorenzo Mans. Superior, perceptively funny cinema verité feature about a serious young filmmaker who seeks truth by making a movie of his life. A classic of its kind.▼

Davy Crockett and the River Pirates (1956) **C-81m.** **½ D: Norman Foster. Fess Parker, Buddy Ebsen, Jeff York, Kenneth Tobey, Clem Bevans, Irvin Ashkenazy. Second CROCKETT feature strung together from two Disney TV shows; first half is comic keelboat race with Mike Fink (York)—self-proclaimed "King of the River," second half is more serious confrontation with Indians. Lightweight fun.▼●

Davy Crockett, Indian Scout (1950) **71m.** ** D: Lew Landers. George Montgomery, Ellen Drew, Philip Reed, Chief Thundercloud. Humdrum wagon train saga which has nothing whatsoever to do with the legend of Davy C. (Montgomery plays one of his descendants.) Retitled INDIAN SCOUT.

Davy Crockett, King of the Wild Frontier (1955) **C-93m.** *** D: Norman Foster. Fess Parker, Buddy Ebsen, Basil Ruysdael, Hans Conried, William Bakewell, Kenneth Tobey. Originally filmed as three segments for Disney's TV show, this created a nationwide phenomenon in 1955; it's still fun today with Parker as famous Indian scout and Ebsen as his pal George Russel, whose adventures take them from Washington, D.C. to the Alamo.▼

Dawn at Socorro (1954) **C-80m.** **½ D: George Sherman. Rory Calhoun, Piper Laurie, David Brian, Kathleen Hughes, Edgar Buchanan, Alex Nicol, Lee Van Cleef, Skip Homeier. Calhoun is gunslinger wishing to reform, but fate forces inevitable shootout.

Dawning, The (1988-British) **C-97m.** **½ D: Robert Knights. Anthony Hopkins, Jean Simmons, Trevor Howard, Rebecca Pidgeon, Hugh Grant, Tara MacGowran. Set in Southern Ireland in 1920, this well-made but curiously ordinary drama chronicles the political turmoil of the time as perceived by a spirited, rapidly maturing 18-year-old girl (Pidgeon) who comes to the aid of a mysterious stranger (Hopkins). Howard's last film; he's cast as her wheelchair-bound grandfather. [PG]▼●

Dawn of the Dead (1978) **C-126m.** ***½ D: George A. Romero. David Emge, Ken Foree, Scott Reiniger, Gaylen Ross, Tom Savini. Sequel-cum-remake of NIGHT OF THE LIVING DEAD is apocalyptic horror masterpiece; as zombie population increases, four people set up quasi-Utopian existence in barricaded shopping mall. Satiric, metaphorically rich adventure jerks viewers' emotions around with stunning ease, as zombies are, by turns, horrifying, heroic, made clownish, and even forgotten. Savini's hideously gory effects are mostly confined to the first and last half hours. Nontheatrical prints run 140m. Followed by DAY OF THE DEAD.▼●◗

Dawn Patrol, The (1930) **82m.** **½ D: Howard Hawks. Richard Barthelmess, Douglas Fairbanks Jr., Neil Hamilton, William Janney, James Finlayson, Clyde Cook. John Monk Saunders's Oscar-winning story of a beleaguered aerial squadron in WW1 France. Devotees of director Hawks prefer this to 1938 remake, but it doesn't hold up as well, particularly the stiff, overdrawn performances. Originally 95m. TV title: FLIGHT COMMANDER.

Dawn Patrol, The (1938) **103m.** ***½ D: Edmund Goulding. Errol Flynn, Basil Rathbone, David Niven, Donald Crisp, Melville Cooper, Barry Fitzgerald. Remake of 1930 classic is fine actioner of WW1 flyers in France; Rathbone as stern officer forced to send up green recruits, Flynn and Niven as pilot buddies, all excellent. Insightful study of wartime camaraderie and grueling pressures of battlefront command.▼●

Day After, The (1983) **C-120m. TVM** D: Nicholas Meyer. Jason Robards, JoBeth Williams, Steve Guttenberg, John Cullum, John Lithgow, Bibi Besch, Lori Lethin, Amy Madigan, Jeff East. Chilling aftereffects of the catastrophic nuclear bombing of Lawrence, Kansas, in a potent drama written by Edward Hume. Probably the most controversial TV movie of its time, with unrelenting grimness, performances ranging from sturdy to overwrought, and a rare musical score by David Raksin, with Virgil Thompson's "The River" interpolated. Foreign theatrical and homevideo tape (but *not* video disc) versions run 126m. Cut by 23m. for network rerun. Above average.▼●

Day and the Hour, The (1963-French-Italian) **115m.** **½ D: René Clement. Simone Signoret, Stuart Whitman, Genevieve Page, Michel Piccoli, Reggie Nalder, Pierre Dux, Billy Kearns. In Nazi-occupied France, Signoret is a widow who becomes involved in the Resistance movement; Whitman is an American paratrooper trying to escape to Spain. Franscope.▼

Day at the Races, A (1937) **111m.** ***½ D: Sam Wood. Groucho, Harpo and Chico Marx, Allan Jones, Maureen O'Sullivan, Esther Muir, Margaret Dumont, Douglass Dumbrille, Sig Ruman. The Marxes wreak havoc at a sanitorium, where wealthy hypochondriac Dumont is the leading patient; often uproarious comedy features some of the trio's funniest set pieces (Chico selling race tips, the seduction scene, etc.). A perfunctory storyline, and unmemorable songs, keep it from topping its immediate predecessor A NIGHT AT THE OPERA . . . but the comedy content is sensational.▼●

Daybreak (1939) SEE: **Le Jour Se Lève**

Daybreak (1946-British) **75m.** ** D: Compton Bennett. Eric Portman, Ann Todd, Maxwell Reed, Edward Rigby, Bill Owen, Jane Hylton. Repressed Portman weds sultry Todd. He's out of town once too often . . . while oily, menacing Reed comes on the scene. Contrived film noir is only modestly entertaining.

Daydreamer, The (1966) **C-98m.** *** D: Jules Bass. Ray Bolger, Jack Gilford, Margaret Hamilton, Paul O'Keefe, voices of Tallulah Bankhead, Boris Karloff, Burl Ives, Victor Borge, Terry-Thomas, Patty Duke. Partly animated story of Hans Christian Andersen as a 13-year-old who meets many of the fairy tale characters he later writes about. Surprisingly pleasant.▼

Day for Night (1973-French) **C-120m.** ***½ D: François Truffaut. Jacqueline Bisset, Jean-Pierre Aumont, Valentina Cortese, François Truffaut, Jean-Pierre Léaud, Alexandra Stewart, Dani, Nathalie Baye. Enjoyable fluff about a motion picture director (Truffaut) and his problems in trying to film a silly love story; bright performances and a loving look into the intricacies of filmmaking. Oscar winner as Best Foreign Film. [PG]▼

Day in October, A (1990-Danish-U.S.) **C-97m.** *** D: Kenneth Madsen. D. B. Sweeney, Kelly Wolf, Daniel Benzali, Tovah Feldshuh, Ole Lemmeke. Gripping, fact-based drama set in WW2 Denmark chronicles the fate of young Jewish woman (Wolf); she brings a stranger—wounded resistance fighter Sweeney—into her home, disrupting the lives of her family. Knowing parable about the need to take sides (and take action) when confronted by evil. Don't miss this sleeper. [PG-13]▼

Day in the Country, A (1946-French) **40m.** **** D: Jean Renoir. Sylvia Bataille, Georges Saint-Saens (Georges Darnoux), Jacques Borel (Jacques Brunius), Jeanne Marken. At a picnic along a river, a bourgeois Parisian mother and daughter find romance while the menfolk try to fish. Nature plays a starring role in this cinematic tone poem about the emotional depth of spiritual love and the sexual high of a romp in the hay. Screenplay by Renoir, from a short story by Guy de Maupassant; among his assistants on this were Yves Allegret, Jacques Becker, Henri Cartier-Bresson, and Luchino Visconti! Renoir cast himself as Poulain the innkeeper. Shot in 1936, only partially completed, and edited in Renoir's absence. Original title: UNE PARTIE DE CAMPAGNE.▼

Day in the Death of Joe Egg, A (1972-British) **C-106m.** ***½ D: Peter Medak. Alan Bates, Janet Suzman, Peter Bowles, Sheila Gish, Joan Hickson. Excellent black comedy about a couple with a child who contemplate mercy-killing. Not a crowd-pleaser, but extremely well done. Peter Nichols adapted his own play. [R]▼

Daylight (1996) **C-114m.** *** D: Rob Cohen. Sylvester Stallone, Amy Brenneman, Viggo Mortensen, Dan Hedaya, Jay O. Sanders, Karen Young, Claire Bloom, Vanessa Bell Calloway, Barry Newman, Stan Shaw, Colin Fox. Good old-fashioned disaster movie, built on a formulaic foundation. Stallone is a disgraced Emergency Medical Services worker who springs into action when a huge explosion cripples a tunnel under N.Y.C.'s Hudson River, with a handful of survivors inside. Great stunts and special effects. That's Sly's son Sage as a cocky young scam artist being taken to prison. [PG-13]▼●◗

Day Mars Invaded Earth, The (1962) **70m.** *½ D: Maury Dexter. Kent Taylor, Marie Windsor, William Mims, Betty Beall, Lowell Brown, Gregg Shank. Martians are exact doubles for scientist Taylor and family as they wreak havoc on pitiful earthlings. Minor sci-fi B pic. CinemaScope.

Day My Parents Ran Away, The (1993) **C-95m.** BOMB D: Martin Nicholson. Matt Frewer, Bobby Jacoby, Brigid Conley Walsh, Blair Brown, Martin Mull. Wimpy, whiny dad Frewer and doting mom Brown literally run away from their horrific, egocentric teenage son and take refuge at a summer camp–like shelter for parents of teens. Try watching this so-called satire and you may do the same. [PG]▼●

Day of Anger (1969-Italian) **C-109m.** *½ D: Tonino Valerii. Lee Van Cleef, Giuliano Gemma, Walter Rilla, Christa Linder, Ennio Balbo. Story of callous gunman and his relationship with young protégé is below par, even for an Italian Western; only for the

Van Cleef cult. Aka DAY OF WRATH. Techniscope. [M/PG]▼

Day of Fury, A (1956) **C-78m.** *** D: Harmon Jones. Dale Robertson, Mara Corday, Jock Mahoney, Carl Benton Reid. Offbeat study of rebellious Robertson who can't cope with conventions of Western town he lives in.

Day of the Animals (1977) **C-98m.** **½ D: William Girdler. Christopher George, Lynda Day George, Leslie Nielsen, Richard Jaeckel, Michael Ansara, Ruth Roman. Fair action thriller in the nature-on-the rampage mold, with back packers in the High Sierras at the mercy of hostile creatures crazed by the sun's radiation after the earth's ozone layer has been destroyed. Final score: Beasts 7, Cast 0 (in acting as well as survival). Aka SOMETHING IS OUT THERE. Todd-AO 35. [PG]▼◗

Day of the Bad Man (1958) **C-81m.** ** D: Harry Keller. Fred MacMurray, Joan Weldon, John Ericson, Robert Middleton. MacMurray is appropriately stiff in tame account of country judge holding off condemned man's brothers so scheduled hanging can occur. CinemaScope.

Day of the Dead (1985) **C-102m.** ** D: George A. Romero. Lori Cardille, Terry Alexander, Joseph Pilato, Jarlath Conroy, Antone DiLeo, Jr., Richard Liberty, Howard Sherman. Romero's creatures trap a female scientist with some army sexists in an underground bunker; she wants to "study" them, but the army balks at being zombie brunch. Third DEAD entry is relentlessly talky for over an hour, but Tom Savini's effects do give this a show-stopping finale. Easily the least of the series. ▼●◗

Day of the Dolphin, The (1973) **C-104m.** ** D: Mike Nichols. George C. Scott, Trish Van Devere, Paul Sorvino, Fritz Weaver, Jon Korkes, Edward Herrmann, John Dehner. Big-budget misfire about scientist Scott using his trained (and talking!) dolphins to foil an assassination plot. A waste of many talents. Scripter Buck Henry also provides the voices for the dolphins. Panavision. [PG]▼●

Day of the Evil Gun (1968) **C-93m.** ** D: Jerry Thorpe. Glenn Ford, Arthur Kennedy, Dean Jagger, John Anderson, Paul Fix, Nico Minardos, Royal Dano, (Harry) Dean Stanton. Very routine Western with Ford and Kennedy going after Indians who abducted the former's wife; Kennedy is smooth in likable-villain role he's played many times. Panavision. [G]

Day of the Jackal, The (1973-British-French) **C-141m.** ***½ D: Fred Zinnemann. Edward Fox, Alan Badel, Tony Britton, Cyril Cusack, Michel Lonsdale, Eric Porter, Delphine Seyrig, Derek Jacobi, Ronald Pickup. Exciting adaptation of Frederick Forsyth's best-seller about plot to assassinate De Gaulle and the painstaking preparations of the assassin. Beautifully filmed throughout Europe with a first-rate cast. Reworked in 1997 as THE JACKAL. [PG]▼●◗

Day of the Locust, The (1975) **C-144m.** ***½ D: John Schlesinger. Donald Sutherland, Karen Black, Burgess Meredith, William Atherton, Geraldine Page, Richard A. Dysart, Bo Hopkins, Pepe Serna, Lelia Goldoni, Billy Barty, Madge Kennedy, Florence Lake, Natalie Schafer, Nita Talbot, Paul Stewart, John Hillerman, Robert Pine, Dennis Dugan, Jackie Earle Haley, David Ladd, Dick Powell, Jr. Excellent adaptation of Nathanael West's sweeping novel about Hollywood's netherworld in 1930s, seen mostly through eyes of a young artist (Atherton) who finds little glamor and a lot of broken-down people in Tinseltown. Disturbing, depressing . . . and absolutely fascinating. Script by Waldo Salt. [R]▼●

Day of the Outlaw (1959) **91m.** *** D: Andre de Toth. Robert Ryan, Burl Ives, Tina Louise, Alan Marshal, Nehemiah Persoff, Venetia Stevenson, David Nelson, Jack Lambert, Elisha Cook. Stark Western melodrama of outlaw Ives and gang taking over isolated Western town.

Day of the Triffids, The (1963-British) **C-95m.** **½ D: Steve Sekely. Howard Keel, Nicole Maurey, Janette Scott, Kieron Moore, Mervyn Johns. Meteor display blinds everyone who watched, while mutating experimental plants into giant, walking maneaters. Based on John Wyndham's classic sci-fi novel. Variable special effects. Remade in 1981 as a British TV miniseries; and in 1997 as a cable TV movie. CinemaScope. ▼●

Day of the Wolves (1973) **C-95m.** **½ D: Ferde Grofe Jr. Richard Egan, Martha Hyer, Rick Jason, Jan Murray. Ex-sheriff Egan tries to thwart bizarre attempt by strange group to isolate his town for three days, in order to pull off "perfect crime." [G]▼

Day of Wrath (1943-Danish) **110m.** ***½ D: Carl Theodor Dreyer. Thorkild Roose, Lisbeth Movin, Sigrid Neiiendam, Preben Lerdorff, Anna Svierker. Strikingly composed drama about an old woman accused of being a witch and the curse that she puts on the pastor who is responsible for her burning. Serious, stark cinema, peerlessly photographed by Carl Andersson. Some prints run 95m.▼

Day One (1989) **C-150m. TVM** D: Joseph Sargent. Brian Dennehy, David Strathairn, Michael Tucker, Hume Cronyn, Richard Dysart, Hal Holbrook, Barnard Hughes, David Ogden Stiers, John McMartin. Strong but somewhat unwieldy drama (due to telescoping of events for time purposes) about the men who made first atomic bomb. Anchored by Dennehy as Gen. Leslie Groves, who supervised the project and wet-nursed the assorted scientists who bickered their way to its culmination.

David Rintels' intelligent script (from Peter Wyden's book) could well have been expanded for another hour. Compare this to the theatrical film FAT MAN AND LITTLE BOY. Above average.▼

Days of Glory (1944) **86m.** **½ D: Jacques Tourneur. Gregory Peck, Alan Reed, Maria Palmer, Lowell Gilmore, Tamara Toumanova. Sincere but plodding WW2 action pitting Russians against Nazis, memorable only as Peck's screen debut.▼

Days of Heaven (1978) **C-95m.** ***½ D: Terrence Malick. Richard Gere, Brooke Adams, Sam Shepard, Linda Manz, Robert Wilke, Jackie Shultis, Stuart Margolin. Exquisite mood-piece about a turbulent love triangle set against midwestern wheat harvests at the turn of the century. Originally shown in 70mm, its visual beauty will be diminished on TV, leaving only the story—which is second priority here. Nestor Almendros won well-deserved Oscar for his cinematography. [PG]▼●◗

Days of Thrills and Laughter (1961) **93m.** **** Compiled by Robert Youngson. Third Youngson silent-film compilation combines comedy clips (with Chaplin, Laurel and Hardy, the Keystone Kops) with serials and action films (featuring Douglas Fairbanks, Pearl White, Harry Houdini). Great fun. ▼

Days of Thunder (1990) **C-107m.** ** D: Tony Scott. Tom Cruise, Robert Duvall, Randy Quaid, Nicole Kidman, Cary Elwes, Michael Rooker, Fred Dalton Thompson, Jerry Molen. Flashy, noisy race-car saga set in the South, by the filmmakers and star of TOP GUN. Viewer can a) savor crew chief Duvall's fine performance, b) revel in neurosurgeon/love interest Kidman's disdain for racing, c) sit back and soak up Cruise's charisma, or d) count the clichés (cooked up by coauthors Cruise and Robert Towne). Gives new meaning to the term Formula One. Panavision. [PG-13]▼●◗

Days of Wine and Roses (1962) **117m.** ***½ D: Blake Edwards. Jack Lemmon, Lee Remick, Charles Bickford, Jack Klugman, Alan Hewitt, Tom Palmer, Jack Albertson. Modern LOST WEEKEND set in San Francisco, with Lemmon marrying Remick and pulling her into state of alcoholism. Realistic direction and uncompromising writing combine for excellent results; poignant score by Henry Mancini, who also earned an Oscar for the title song with Johnny Mercer. Originally a television play, written by JP Miller.▼●

Day That Shook the World, The (1977) **C-111m.** ** D: Veljko Bulajic. Christopher Plummer, Florinda Bolkan, Maximilian Schell. Plodding historical drama surrounding the events leading up to WW1 with the death of Archduke Ferdinand (Plummer) at Sarajevo. Yugoslavian-made with a humorless international cast, resulting in tedious though epic-sized chronicle. [R]▼

Day the Earth Caught Fire, The (1961-British) **99m.** *** D: Val Guest. Edward Judd, Janet Munro, Leo McKern, Michael Goodliffe, Bernard Braden. Intelligent, absorbing sci-fi drama of gradual chaos that follows when atomic explosions start Earth spiraling toward the sun. Judd is the reporter who first breaks the story, with the assistance of Munro (whom he romances). Watch for Michael Caine as a policeman directing traffic! Dyaliscope.▼

Day the Earth Stood Still, The (1951) **92m.** **** D: Robert Wise. Michael Rennie, Patricia Neal, Hugh Marlowe, Sam Jaffe, Billy Gray, Frances Bavier, Lock Martin. Landmark science-fiction drama about dignified alien (Rennie) who comes to Earth to deliver anti-nuclear warning, stays to learn that his peaceful views are shared by most humans—but not all. Brilliantly acted, more timely than ever, with trenchant script by Edmund North, moody score by Bernard Herrmann. And remember: *Klaatu barada nikto!*▼●

Day the Fish Came Out, The (1967-Greek-British) **C-109m.** BOMB D: Michael Cacoyannis. Tom Courtenay, Candice Bergen, Colin Blakely, Sam Wanamaker, Ian Ogilvy. Plot about the loss of two atom bombs over the Aegean Sea provides framework for disastrous comedy about homosexuals; combo of Candy Bergen plus whips, chains, and leather doesn't work.

Day the Hot Line Got Hot, The (1969-French-Spanish) **C-92m.** *½ D: Etienne Perier. Robert Taylor, Charles Boyer, George Chakiris, Dominique Fabre, Gerard Tichy. Hollow attempt at topicality as secret agents mess up Moscow–Washington hot line, causing international crisis. Taylor's final film. Video title: HOT LINE. [M/PG]▼

Day the Screaming Stopped, The SEE: **Comeback, The**

Day the Sky Exploded, The (1958-Italian) **80m.** ** D: Paolo Heusch. Paul Hubschmid, Madeleine Fischer, Fiorella Mari, Ivo Garrani. Film doesn't live up to potential excitement as exploding missile in outer space sends debris to earth, causing chaos.▼

Day the World Ended (1956) **82m.** ** D: Roger Corman. Richard Denning, Lori Nelson, Adele Jergens, Touch (Mike) Connors. Modest sci-fi involving survivors of nuclear war and interplay of human nature that causes friction among the group. And yes, there's a monster. Remade as YEAR 2889. SuperScope.▼

Day They Robbed the Bank of England, The (1960-British) **85m.** *** D: John Guillermin. Aldo Ray, Elizabeth Sellars, Peter O'Toole, Hugh Griffith, Kieron Moore, Albert Sharpe. IRA members plan to rob the Bank of England in this meticulous caper film. Metroscope.

Day Time Ended, The (1980) **C-79m.** ** D: John (Bud) Cardos. Jim Davis, Dorothy Malone, Christopher Mitchum, Marcy Lafferty, Scott Kolden, Natasha Ryan. Sci-fi mishmash about a family living in the desert, who witness strange and terrifying phenomena. Badly scripted, and never really explained. Fine special effects by David Allen. Filmed in 1978 as TIME WARP. Panavision. [PG]▼

Day-Time Wife (1939) **71m.** ** D: Gregory Ratoff. Tyrone Power, Linda Darnell, Warren William, Binnie Barnes, Wendy Barrie, Joan Davis. Power and Darnell make an engaging couple, even in lightweight fare such as this: wife thinks husband is fooling around with his secretary, so she gets an office job to see why bosses are attracted to their help.

Dayton's Devils (1968) **C-107m.** ** D: Jack Shea. Rory Calhoun, Leslie Nielsen, Lainie Kazan, Hans Gudegast (Eric Braeden), Barry Sadler. Another heist film, this time about plot to rob an Air Force base of $2 million; Lainie's rendition of "Sunny" provides only special moment.▼

Daytrippers, The (1996) **C-87m.** *** D: Greg Mottola. Hope Davis, Stanley Tucci, Parker Posey, Liev Schreiber, Anne Meara, Pat McNamara, Campbell Scott, Marcia Gay Harden. Funny, touching first feature about Eliza, a Long Island wife who discovers what appears to be a clandestine love letter written to her husband; she and her family pile into a station wagon and set off on a road trip to (and through) Manhattan to confront him. Mottola also scripted this thoroughly likable, low-budget winner. [R]▼

Day Will Dawn, The (1942-British) **99m.** *** D: Harold French. Hugh Williams, Griffiths Jones, Deborah Kerr, Ralph Richardson, Francis L. Sullivan, Roland Culver, Finlay Currie, Niall MacGinnis, Raymond Huntley, Patricia Medina. Solid WW2 adventure about foreign correspondent Williams and his involvement in destroying a German U-boat base in Norway. Kerr is fine in one of her early roles, as a young Norwegian lass who assists him. Written by Terence Rattigan, Anatole de Grunwald, and Patrick Kirwen. Also known as THE AVENGERS.▼

Dazed and Confused (1993) **C-94m.** *** D: Richard Linklater. Jason London, Wiley Wiggins, Sasha Jenson, Rory Cochrane, Milla Jovovich, Marissa Ribisi, Adam Goldberg, Anthony Rapp, Matthew McConaughey, Ben Affleck, Parker Posey. Diverting, refreshingly unsentimental mid-1970s time capsule from director-screenwriter Linklater (SLACKER), following a varied group of suburban Texas teens on the last day of school in 1976. Characterization outweighs narrative here: Linklater accurately captures teen lifestyles and attitudes at a specific moment in time. Great soundtrack includes carefully selected period music. [R]▼●◗

D.C. Cab (1983) **C-99m.** **½ D: Joel Schumacher. Adam Baldwin, Charlie Barnett, Irene Cara, Anne DeSalvo, Max Gail, Gloria Gifford, DeWayne Jessie, Bill Maher, Whitman Mayo, Mr. T, Paul Rodriguez, Gary Busey, Marsha Warfield. Consistently likable, if loosely wound, comedy about a Washington taxi company staffed by misfits who get their act together when it really counts. After a few trims by TV censors it will be perfect for kids. [R]▼●

D-Day the Sixth of June (1956) **C-106m.** *** D: Henry Koster. Robert Taylor, Richard Todd, Dana Wynter, Edmond O'Brien. Well-executed study of WW2's Normandy invasion, with massive action shots; film focuses on American officer Taylor and British leader Todd, their professional and personal problems. You may like THE LONGEST DAY better. CinemaScope. ▼

Dead, The (1987) **C-83m.** *** D: John Huston. Anjelica Huston, Donal McCann, Rachael Dowling, Cathleen Delany, Helena Carroll, Ingrid Craigie, Dan O'Herlihy, Frank Patterson, Donal Donnelly, Marie Kean, Maria McDermottroe, Sean McClory, Colm Meaney. All-Irish cast helps Huston bring James Joyce's short story (from *Dubliners*) to life, a vignette about a lively holiday dinner party in 1904, followed by a melancholy confrontation between a loveless husband and wife. Not for every taste, this finely embroidered film celebrates time, place, and atmosphere, without much discernible plot, but with a host of marvelous characterizations. Huston's last film as director scripted by his son Tony. [PG]▼●

Dead Again (1991) **C-107m.** **½ D: Kenneth Branagh. Kenneth Branagh, Andy Garcia, Derek Jacobi, Hanna Schygulla, Emma Thompson, Wayne Knight, Campbell Scott, Gregor Hesse, Christine Ebersole, Robin Williams. Unusually constructed film noir thriller about an L.A. gumshoe who tries to help a woman with amnesia, and finds they are both connected—in a strange twist of reincarnation—to a notorious forty-year-old murder. Intriguing, and great fun to see Branagh playing an American, but ultimately the story is too dense, and too artificial, to really work. And talk about artificial—dig that aging makeup for Garcia! Williams appears as one of Branagh's sources. [R]▼●

Dead Alive (1992-New Zealand) **C-97m.** *** D: Peter Jackson. Timothy Balme, Diana Penalver, Liz Moody, Ian Watkin, Brenda Kendall. Pity poor Balme; not only is he in the thrall of his domineering mother, but when the bite of a rat monkey from Skull Island turns her into a hungry zombie, he still has to look after her—and all the other zombies that soon proliferate. Astonishing, vigorous, inventively gruesome comedy is—one hopes—the pinnacle of its kind. Warning: The rating above is *strictly* for those with a tolerance for extreme violence and gore. Original title: BRAIN DEAD. Released in unrated version and 85m. R-rated video version.▼●◗

Dead and Buried (1981) **C-92m.** **½ D: Gary A. Sherman. James Farentino, Melody Anderson, Jack Albertson, Dennis Redfield, Nancy Locke Hauser, Lisa Blount. Bizarre murders in a small New England town seem even stranger when the corpses come back to life. Gory but well-made chiller; from a Dan O'Bannon story. [R]▼

Dead Are Alive, The (1972-Yugoslavian-German-Italian) **C-98m.** *½ D: Armando Crispino. Alex Cord, Samantha Eggar, John Marley, Nadja Tiller, Horst Frank, Enzo Tarascio. Confused, uninteresting suspenser dealing with series of murders that take place while archeologists are studying ancient tombs; Eggar is wasted. [R]

Dead Bang (1989) **C-103m.** *½ D: John Frankenheimer. Don Johnson, Penelope Ann Miller, William Forsythe, Bob Balaban, Tim Reid, Frank Military, Tate Donovan, Michael Higgins, Evans Evans. L.A. detective Johnson tries to forget about his dismal home life by chasing nasty white supremacists around the West. Unpleasant, fact-based action film offers nothing you haven't seen before, except for the hero vomiting on a suspect. [R]▼●◗

Dead Calm (1989-Australian) **C-96m.** *** D: Phillip Noyce. Sam Neill, Nicole Kidman, Billy Zane. A married couple, recovering from a family tragedy by spending some time on their yacht at sea, pick up a stranger who proceeds to terrorize them. Full-blooded thriller is so skillfully acted and directed that it enables you to gloss over its flaws—and forgive its slasher-movie-inspired finale. Based on a novel by Charles Williams. Panavision. [R]▼●◗

Dead Connection (1993) **C-93m.** ** D: Nigel Dick. Michael Madsen, Lisa Bonet, Gary Stretch, Damian Chapa, Tim Russ, Carmen Argenziano, Clarence Landry, Parker Posey. Dedicated L.A. cop goes one-on-one against a psycho/rapist/killer. Sound familiar? Madsen invests far more in the role and film than they deserve. [R]▼

Dead End (1937) **93m.** ***½ D: William Wyler. Sylvia Sidney, Joel McCrea, Humphrey Bogart, Wendy Barrie, Claire Trevor, Marjorie Main, Huntz Hall, Leo Gorcey, Gabriel Dell, Ward Bond, Billy Halop, Bernard Punsley, Allen Jenkins. Grim Sidney Kingsley play of slum life shows vignettes of humanity at breaking point in N.Y.C. tenements; extremely well directed, engrossing. Script by Lillian Hellman; magnificent sets by Richard Day. Introduced the Dead End Kids, who appeared in the original Broadway production (see *Bowery Boys* entry for details).▼●

Dead-End Drive In (1986-Australian) **C-92m.** **½ D: Brian Trenchard-Smith. Ned Manning, Natalie McCurry, Peter Whitford, Wilbur Hide, Dave Gibson. Government authorities lure kids they consider to be problem teens to a drive-in theater, then simply don't let them leave. Nice try at mixing satire with teen action-movie elements, in story set in the near future. Widescreen. [R]▼

Dead End Kids (1986) **C/B&W-90m.** *** D: JoAnne Akalaitis. Ellen McElduff, Ruth Maleczech, George Bartenieff, David Brisbin, Terry O'Reilly. Effective, free-form dramatic narrative of the history of nuclear power—where it comes from and what it does—features some good performances and cohesive direction. Faithfully adapted from the off-Broadway production by Mabou Mines. Original score by David Byrne and additional music by Philip Glass, both of whom appear briefly. The full title is DEAD END KIDS: A STORY OF NUCLEAR POWER.

Deadfall (1968-British) **C-120m.** ** D: Bryan Forbes. Michael Caine, Giovanna Ralli, Eric Portman, Nanette Newman, David Buck. Jewel thief falls in love with beautiful woman who is married to her homosexual father. And you think you have problems? Overdirected film is not as interesting as it sounds. [R]

Deadfall (1993) **C-98m.** BOMB D: Christopher Coppola. Michael Biehn, Sarah Trigger, Nicolas Cage, James Coburn, Peter Fonda, Charlie Sheen, Talia Shire, Michael Constantine, Gigi Rice, Angus Scrimm, Micky Dolenz, Marc Coppola, Renee Estevez, Clarence Williams III. Bargain-basement, cliché-ridden vanity project about con man Biehn, who's always been a team with his dad; his world begins to unravel after he accidentally kills the old man. Almost unbearable at times, with an unrestrained Cage chewing and throwing up the scenery as a coke-snorting thug. Coppola is the nephew of Francis (and Cage's brother); he also coscripted. [R]▼●

Deadhead Miles (1972) **C-93m.** **½ D: Vernon Zimmerman. Alan Arkin, Paul Benedict, Hector Elizondo, Oliver Clark, Charles Durning, Larry Wolf, Barnard Hughes, Loretta Swit, Allen Garfield, Bruce Bennett, John Milius, Ida Lupino, George Raft. Plotless allegory about a trucker's experiences on the road, with unusual cast, loads of in-jokes. Unreleased and unseen for many years. A real curio, written by Zimmerman and Terrence Malick. [R]

Dead Heat (1988) **C-86m.** BOMB D: Mark Goldblatt. Treat Williams, Joe Piscopo, Lindsay Frost, Darren McGavin, Vincent Price, Keye Luke. Moronic, occasionally disgusting turkey with cops Williams and Piscopo confronted by criminals miraculously returning from the dead. [R]▼●

Dead Heat on a Merry-Go-Round (1966) **C-104m.** *** D: Bernard Girard. James Coburn, Camilla Sparv, Aldo Ray, Rose Marie, Severn Darden, Robert Webber. Involved but entertaining crime drama about an intricate plan to rob an airport bank, with a surprise ending. Look quickly for a barely recognizable Harrison Ford, in his film debut, playing a bellhop.

Dead Kids SEE: **Strange Behavior**

Deadlier Than the Male (1957-French) **104m.** ** D: Julien Duvivier. Jean Gabin, Daniele Delorme, Lucienne Bogaert, Gerard Blain. Delorme encamps in ex-stepfather's home, planning to marry and then murder him; Gabin is stodgy as girl's intended victim.

Deadlier Than the Male (1967-British) **C-101m.** **½ D: Ralph Thomas. Richard Johnson, Elke Sommer, Sylva Koscina, Nigel Green, Suzanna Leigh. Standard fare which half-heartedly resurrects Bulldog Drummond, trying to solve whodunit centering around two shapely suspects. Sequel: SOME GIRLS DO. Techniscope.

Deadliest Sin, The (1956-British) **77m.** *½ D: Ken Hughes. Sydney Chaplin, Audrey Dalton, John Bentley, Peter Hammond. Good triumphing over evil is moral of this slight story of thief involved in murder.

Deadline (1987-German) **C-100m.** *½ D: Nathaniel Gutman. Christopher Walken, Hywel Bennett, Marita Marschall, Arnon Zadok, Amos Lavie. Convoluted political thriller with globe-trotting journalist Walken becoming enmeshed in various intrigues and lies in Lebanon. Strictly Grade-D stuff. [R]▼●

Deadline Assault SEE: **Act of Violence** (1979)

Deadline at Dawn (1946) **83m.** **½ D: Harold Clurman. Susan Hayward, Paul Lukas, Bill Williams, Joseph Calleia, Osa Massen, Lola Lane, Jerome Cowan, Steven Geray. Atmospheric but muddled murder mystery, with aspiring actress Hayward attempting to clear naive sailor Williams, who is suspected of murder. Clurman's only film as director. Screenplay by Clifford Odets, from a novel by William Irish (Cornell Woolrich).▼

Deadline U.S.A. (1952) **87m.** *** D: Richard Brooks. Humphrey Bogart, Ethel Barrymore, Kim Hunter, Ed Begley, Warren Stevens, Paul Stewart, Martin Gabel, Joe De Santis, Audrey Christie, Jim Backus. Biting account of newspaper's struggle to survive and maintain civic duty. Bogey is tops as the crusading editor; taut, knowing script by director Brooks. Most enjoyable.

Deadly Affair, The (1967) **C-107m.** *** D: Sidney Lumet. James Mason, Simone Signoret, Maximilian Schell, Harriet Andersson, Harry Andrews, Lynn Redgrave, Kenneth Haigh, Roy Kinnear. Top-notch suspense tale with British agent Mason trying to unravel complicated mystery behind an agency official's suicide. Filmed in England and based on John Le Carre's novel *Call For The Dead.*

Deadly Bees, The (1967-British) **C-85m.** ** D: Freddie Francis. Suzanna Leigh, Guy Doleman, Catherine Finn, Katy Wild, Frank Finlay. High-powered shock scenes involving swarming bees are only worthwhile attraction in dull horror film cowritten by Robert Bloch. Techniscope.

Deadly Blessing (1981) **C-102m.** ** D: Wes Craven. Maren Jensen, Susan Buckner, Sharon Stone, Lois Nettleton, Ernest Borgnine, Jeff East, Lisa Hartman. Following her husband's murder, widow and two friends are terrorized, apparently by nearby repressive sect, headed by the father (Borgnine) of the dead man. Rural horror thriller has some good shocks but becomes confused and ultimately silly, especially the ending. [R]▼

Deadly Companion SEE: **Double Negative**

Deadly Companions, The (1961) **C-90m.** **½ D: Sam Peckinpah. Maureen O'Hara, Brian Keith, Steve Cochran, Chill Wills. Ex-army officer accidentally kills O'Hara's son and he makes amends by escorting the funeral procession through Indian country. Peckinpah's first feature is decent if unspectacular Western. Panavision.▼●

Deadly Desire (1970) SEE: **Maybe I'll Come Home in the Spring**

Deadly Drifter SEE: **Out**

Deadly Encounter SEE: **Meal, The**

Deadly Eyes (1982) **C-93m.** ** D: Robert Clouse. Sam Groom, Sara Botsford, Scatman Crothers, Lisa Langlois, Cec Linder. Overgrown rats on the warpath, with science teacher Groom and health official Botsford to the rescue. You've seen it all before. Originally titled, appropriately enough, THE RATS. [R]▼

Deadly Force (1983) **C-95m.** BOMB D: Paul Aaron. Wings Hauser, Joyce Ingalls, Paul Shenar, Al Ruscio, Arlen Dean Snyder, Lincoln Kilpatrick. Ex-cop Hauser is on the trail of a killer; he's harassed by former colleague Kilpatrick, and trying to start over with estranged wife Ingalls. Rock-bottom DIRTY HARRY clone. [R]▼

Deadly Friend (1986) **C-92m.** **½ D: Wes Craven. Matthew Laborteaux, Kristy Swanson, Anne Twomey, Michael Sharrett, Richard Marcus, Anne Ramsey. Inventive teenager, in love with the girl next door, revives her (à la Frankenstein) after she's killed. More heart, and more actual entertainment, than you'd expect from a Wes Craven horror film . . . though it's probably the only movie ever made in which someone is beheaded by a basketball! [R]▼●

Deadly Games (1982) **C-95m.** **½ D:

Scott Mansfield. Sam Groom, Jo Ann Harris, Steve Railsback, Dick Butkus, Alexandra Morgan, Colleen Camp, Christine Tudor, June Lockhart, Denise Galik. Groom is a cop, Harris a reporter in routine mystery about a slasher on the loose. In-jokes come fast and furious in this very knowing film, keyed to a horror board game played by the principals. Final plot explanation is really stupid. [R]▼

Deadly Hero (1976) **C-102m.** ** D: Ivan Nagy. Don Murray, Diahn Williams, James Earl Jones, Lilia Skala, George S. Irving, Conchata Ferrell, Charles Siebert, Dick A. Williams, Treat Williams, Joshua Mostel. Interesting premise: righteous cop (Murray) saves woman's life by killing her attacker (Jones) . . . but then woman begins to question the cop's motives. Performances outshine violent presentation. Treat Williams' film debut. Danny DeVito is also listed in the closing credits. [R]▼

Deadly Illusion (1987) **C-87m.** **½ D: William Tannen, Larry Cohen. Billy Dee Williams, Vanity, Morgan Fairchild, John Beck, Joseph Cortese, Dennis Hallahan, Joe Spinell. Fair programmer with Williams well cast as a detective framed in murder plot. Some humorous touches add to the proceedings. Cohen wrote the script; aka LOVE YOU TO DEATH. [R]▼●

Deadly Impact (1985-Italian) **C-91m.** *½ D: Larry Ludman (Fabrizio De Angelis). Bo Svenson, Fred Williamson, Marcia Clingan, John Morghen, Vincent Conte. Svenson and Williamson try to enliven unbelievable crime caper in which a computer is used to tap into Las Vegas casinos and predict when slot machines will pay off. Filmed in the U.S.A. in 1983.▼

Deadly Is the Female SEE: **Gun Crazy**

Deadly Mantis, The (1957) **78m.** ** D: Nathan Juran. Craig Stevens, William Hopper, Alix Talton, Donald Randolph. N.Y.C. is threatened again, here by giant insect heading south after Arctic tour de force; obligatory love story interrupts good special effects.▼●

Deadly Ray From Mars, The (1938) **99m.** **½ D: Ford Beebe, Robert Hill. Buster Crabbe, Jean Rogers, Charles Middleton, Frank Shannon, Donald Kerr, Beatrice Roberts. Reedited version of FLASH GORDON'S TRIP TO MARS serial. Flash, Dale Arden, and Dr. Zarkov seek mysterious force which drains nitrogen from earth's atmosphere, eventually discover Ming's behind it all. Uninspired handling of original footage. Aka FLASH GORDON: MARS ATTACKS THE WORLD.▼◗

Deadly Strangers (1974-British) **C-93m.** *** D: Sidney Hayers. Hayley Mills, Simon Ward, Sterling Hayden, Ken Hutchison, Peter Jeffrey. Lurid, exciting thriller about Mills offering a ride to young man, unaware that a violent patient has escaped from a nearby mental hospital.▼

Deadly Thief SEE: **Shalimar**

Deadly Three, The SEE: **Enter the Dragon**

Deadly Tower, The (1975) **C-100m. TVM** D: Jerry Jameson. Kurt Russell, Richard Yniquez, John Forsythe, Ned Beatty, Pernell Roberts, Clifton James, Paul Carr. Fact-based drama about Charles Whitman (Russell), who holed up in University of Texas tower in August, 1966, and fired at all in sight, killing 13 and wounding 33. Authentic, well-made recreation of the fateful event, with acting honors going to Yniquez as Mexican-American police officer and Beatty as passerby who reluctantly agrees to help him. Above average. Video title: SNIPER.▼

Deadly Trackers, The (1973) **C-110m.** BOMB D: Barry Shear. Richard Harris, Rod Taylor, Al Lettieri, Neville Brand, William Smith, Isela Vega. Dreadful, violent Western; Harris, an Irish sheriff of a small Texas town, trails bank robber Taylor and gang to Mexico to avenge the deaths of wife and son. Sam Fuller wrote story and was original director. [PG]▼●

Deadly Trap, The (1971-French-Italian) **C-96m.** BOMB D: René Clement. Faye Dunaway, Frank Langella, Barbara Parkins, Karen Glanguernon, Maurice Ronet. A deadly bore, about an industrious espionage organization that goes after one-time member Langella by harassing his emotionally fragile wife (Dunaway). Retitled DEATH SCREAM. [PG]▼

Deadly Treasure of the Piranha SEE: **Killer Fish**

Deadly Weapon (1989) **C-89m.** *½ D: Michael Miner. Rodney Eastman, Kim Walker, Gary Frank, Michael Horse, Joe Regalbuto, William Sanderson, Ed Nelson. Another put-upon nerd strikes back, with a secret ray-gun weapon he found in an Arizona stream. Clumsy, erratic low-budgeter fails to build sympathy for its protagonist. [PG-13]▼

Dead Man (1996-U.S.-German-Japanese) **120m.** *** D: Jim Jarmusch. Johnny Depp, Gary Farmer, Lance Henriksen, Michael Wincott, Mili Avital, Iggy Pop, Jared Harris, Billy Bob Thornton, Crispin Glover, Eugene Byrd, Gabriel Byrne, John Hurt, Alfred Molina, Robert Mitchum. In 1875, Cleveland accountant Depp heads west for a new job but ends up being pursued as a murderer by bounty hunters. Indian Farmer, who helps him, is convinced that he is the poet William Blake returned to life. One-of-a-kind Western, written by the director, is measured in its pace, full of unusual cameos, and occasionally quite funny though it's not a comedy. Steve Buscemi appears unbilled. [R]▼●

Dead Man on Campus (1998) **C-94m.** BOMB D: Alan Cohn. Tom Everett Scott,

Mark-Paul Gosselaar, Poppy Montgomery, Lochlyn Munro, Randy Pearlstein, Alyson Hannigan. Dead is right. This black comedy hinges on the urban myth that American universities will award 4.0 GPA's to any student whose roommate kills himself. Clean-cut straight arrow and his spoiled preppie pal team up to find a suicidal candidate. Laughless script aspires to be a teen ripoff of THE FORTUNE COOKIE, but these cocky kids are no Lemmon and Matthau. [R]▼●◗

Dead Man Out (1989) **C-86m. TVM** D: Richard Pearce. Danny Glover, Ruben Blades, Tom Atkins, Larry Block, Sam Jackson, Maria Ricossa. Searing drama about a psychiatrist who is hired by the state to "cure" an insane convict in order that the death sentence can be carried out. Gritty confrontational performances that give a contemporary sensibility to Stanley Kramer's PRESSURE POINT of 25 years earlier. Written by Ron Hutchinson. Made for cable. Above average.▼●

Dead Man's Eyes (1944) **64m.** **½ D: Reginald LeBorg. Lon Chaney, Jr., Jean Parker, Paul Kelly, Thomas Gomez, Acquanetta. Interesting *Inner Sanctum* yarn of blind man (Chaney) accused of murdering girlfriend's father, whose announced intention was to bequeath his eyes to Chaney for transplant operation.▼

Dead Man's Float (1980-Australian) **C-75m.** **½ D: Peter Sharp. Sally Boyden, Greg Rowe, Jacqui Gordon, Rick Ireland, Bill Hunter, Sue Jones, John Heywood. Kids tangle with drug-smuggling adults. Unmemorable, though fast-moving and not unentertaining; for younger audiences.

Dead Man Walking (1995) **C-122m.** ***½ D: Tim Robbins. Susan Sarandon, Sean Penn, Robert Prosky, Raymond J. Barry, R. Lee Ermey, Celia Weston, Lois Smith, Scott Wilson, Roberta Maxwell, Margo Martindale, Barton Heyman, Larry Pine, Peter Sarsgaard. Powerful drama based on the true story of a nun in Louisiana who becomes the spiritual advisor to a death row inmate, convicted of the murder of two young adults and awaiting execution. As she tries to redeem his soul, she must also reconcile his needs with the heinousness of the crime and the grief of the murdered children's parents. Strong performances by Sarandon (who won a Best Actress Oscar) and Penn anchor this sobering story which, despite the humanizing of its central character, is not a simple pro– or anti–death penalty treatise. [R]▼●◗

Dead Men Don't Die (1991) **C-94m.** *½ D: Malcolm Marmorstein. Elliott Gould, Melissa (Sue) Anderson, Mark Moses, Mabel King, Jack Betts, Philip Bruns. Ten-cent ripoff of GHOST, with egotistical news anchor Gould murdered, then rising from the dead, with the assistance of medium/cleaning lady King (aping Whoopi Goldberg). A too-obvious parody of how TV news has become show biz. [PG-13]▼

Dead Men Don't Wear Plaid (1982) **89m.** ** D: Carl Reiner. Steve Martin, Rachel Ward, Reni Santoni, Carl Reiner, George Gaynes, Frank McCarthy. A one-joke movie, based on 1940s film noir melodramas, has detective Martin interacting with clips from various vintage films, and a very live client (Ward). Fun at first, but with no story and cardboard characters, it wears thin fast; film buffs will enjoy it more than the average viewer. Dedicated to famed costume designer Edith Head, whose final film this was. [PG]▼●◗

Dead Men Tell (1941) **60m.** **½ D: Harry Lachman. Sidney Toler, Sheila Ryan, Robert Weldon, Sen Yung, Don Douglas, Kay Aldridge, George Reeves, Ethel Griffies. Suspenseful *Charlie Chan* mystery, centering on a treasure hunt for $60 million in pirate booty. Clever direction, moody camerawork overcome claustrophobic setting.

Dead Men Walk (1943) **67m.** ** D: Sam Newfield. George Zucco, Mary Carlisle, Nedrick Young, Dwight Frye, Fern Emmett. Zucco plays brothers, one good, one evil, in this standard low-budget vampire tale—but it's hard to dismiss any film with Dwight Frye as a maniacal assistant.▼◗

Dead of Night (1945-British) **102m.** **** D: Cavalcanti, Basil Dearden, Robert Hamer, Charles Crichton. Mervyn Johns, Roland Culver, Antony Baird, Judy Kelly, Miles Malleson, Sally Ann Howes, Googie Withers, Ralph Michael, Michael Redgrave, Basil Radford, Naunton Wayne, Frederick Valk. Classic chiller of gathering at a country house, where guests trade ghost stories. One of them (Johns) has been having nightmares that now seem to be coming true; all five supernatural tales are good for a shiver—final sequence with Redgrave as a schizophrenic ventriloquist is a knockout. U.S. theatrical version ran 77m.; complete edition has been restored for TV.▼●

Dead of Night (1972) SEE: **Deathdream**

Dead of Winter (1987) **C-100m.** *** D: Arthur Penn. Mary Steenburgen, Roddy McDowall, Jan Rubes, William Russ, Ken Pogue, Wayne Robson. Down-on-her-luck actress is hired for a movie role by an eccentric man who lives in an eerie old mansion; eventually she realizes that she's being held prisoner. Somewhat predictable but extremely well-crafted thriller with crackerjack performances all around. Based, fairly transparently, on the 1940s B movie MY NAME IS JULIA ROSS: a key character name here is Julie Rose. [R]▼●

Dead Pigeon on Beethoven Street (1972-German) **C-102m.** **½ D: Samuel Fuller. Glenn Corbett, Christa Lang, Stephane Audran, Anton Diffring, Alex D'Arcy. Fast-paced, tongue-in-cheek Fuller thriller (financed by German TV) has Corbett on a detective mission, aided by lovely Lang (Mrs. Fuller in real life). [PG]

Dead Poets Society (1989) **C-128m.** *** D: Peter Weir. Robin Williams, Robert Sean Leonard, Ethan Hawke, Josh Charles, Gale Hansen, Dylan Kussman, Allelon Ruggiero, James Waterston, Norman Lloyd, Kurtwood Smith, Lara Flynn Boyle. Williams is a charismatic English teacher at a staid New England prep school in 1959, whose infectious love of poetry—and insistence that each boy "seize the day" and make the most of life—inspires his impressionable students, not always in the right direction. Well made, extremely well acted, but also dramatically obvious and melodramatically one-sided. Nevertheless, Tom Schulman's screenplay won an Oscar. 13m. added for network showings. [PG] ▼●◗

Dead Pool, The (1988) **C-91m.** **½ D: Buddy Van Horn. Clint Eastwood, Patricia Clarkson, Evan C. Kim, Liam Neeson, David Hunt, Michael Currie, James Carrey. Fifth (and final) DIRTY HARRY movie finds Callahan investigating a bizarre death threat list, while becoming involved with a female TV reporter. The story's pretty straightforward—check out Carrey as a druggy rock star—the killing almost cartoonish, and the film surprisingly watchable (if not inspired). Eastwood's charisma makes all the difference. [R]▼●

Dead Presidents (1995) **C-119m.** *** D: The Hughes Brothers. Larenz Tate, Keith David, Chris Tucker, N'Bushe Wright, Freddy Rodriguez, Rose Jackson, Michael Imperioli, David Barry Gray, Jaimz Woolvett, Jenifer Lewis, James Pickens, Jr., Clifton Powell, Bokeem Woodbine. Absorbing and ambitious chronicle of a young black man's odyssey from the late 1960s Bronx, through a tour of duty in Vietnam, then back . . . to a dead-end existence. Tries to cover a broad landscape (with a passing nod to the Black Revolution movement), then winds up as a crime caper. Imperfect, but still a compelling tale of how the brutality of war spilled over onto America's urban streets. Warning: the violence is jarringly (and purposefully) graphic. Scripted by Michael Henry Brown from Allen and Albert Hughes's story. Seymour Cassel and Martin Sheen appear unbilled. Super 35. [R]▼●◗

Dead Reckoning (1947) **100m.** *** D: John Cromwell. Humphrey Bogart, Lizabeth Scott, Morris Carnovsky, William Prince, Wallace Ford. Bogart's fine as tough WW2 veteran solving soldier-buddy's murder. Well-acted drama.▼●

Dead Right SEE: **If He Hollers, Let Him Go**

Dead Ringer (1964) **115m.** **½ D. Paul Henreid. Bette Davis, Karl Malden, Peter Lawford, Jean Hagen, George Macready, Estelle Winwood. A double dose of Davis, playing twin sisters (as she did earlier in A STOLEN LIFE) bearing a long-time grudge over a man, the sinister one trying to get even. Farfetched but fun; Bette's vehicle all the way, directed by her 1940s costar Paul Henreid. Remade for TV as THE KILLER IN THE MIRROR (1986, with Ann Jillian).▼●

Dead Ringers (1988-Canadian) **C-115m.** **½ D: David Cronenberg. Jeremy Irons, Genevieve Bujold, Heidi Von Palleske, Barbara Gordon, Shirley Douglas, Stephen Lack. Fascinating but extremely unpleasant story of twin gynecologists who share each other's lives—and lovers. Notable for a pair of superb performances by Irons, and the attendant trickery that makes us forget, at times, that we're watching one man play both roles. Based (believe it or not) on a true story! [R]▼●◗

Dead Run (1969) **C-92m.** ** D: Christian-Jaque. Peter Lawford, Countess Ira Furstenberg, George Geret. Stolen defense plans in Berlin and Rome. Dull, but Lawford and beautiful on-location filming help a bit. [R]▼

Dead Silence (1989) **C-90m.** **½ D. Harrison Ellenshaw. Clete Keith, Joseph Scott, Craig Fleming, Doris Anne Soyka, James Austin, Leslie Charles, Bruce R. Barrett. Young screenwriter and would-be director finds a backer for his newest movie—a mafioso type. But after taking his money, he learns that this road-company Godfather expects his stumblebum son to get the starring part in the picture! Amiable comedy about the perils of low-budget moviemaking, with a wonderful final twist. Written by Keith, who plays the filmmaker. Directing debut for special effects whiz Ellenshaw. [R]▼

Dead Silence (1997) **C-100m. TVM** D: Daniel Petrie, Jr. James Garner, Marlee Matlin, Kim Coates, Charles Martin Smith, Lolita Davidovich, Kenneth Welsh. Burned-out FBI negotiator matches wits with a vicious band of kidnappers who've snatched a busload of deaf teenagers and their teacher. Taut tale with a tangled twist, adapted by Donald Stewart from Jeffrey Deaver's book *A Maiden's Grave*. Made for cable. Above average.▼●

Dead Solid Perfect (1988) **C-95m. TVM** D: Bobby Roth. Randy Quaid, Kathryn Harrold, Jack Warden, Corinne Bohrer, Larry Riley, DeLane Matthews, Bibi Besch, Brett Cullen. Quirky comedy/drama based on Dan Jenkins' best-seller about life and love on the pro golf circuit. Title refers to how it is when the golfer hits the ball at a perfect angle; film itself isn't quite. Made for cable. Average.▼

Dead Tired SEE: **Grosse Fatigue**

Dead Women in Lingerie (1991) **C-87m.** *½ D: Erica Fox. John Romo, Maura Tierney, June Lockhart, Lyle Waggoner, Jerry Orbach. Amateurish spoof of hard-boiled detective films also tries to provide a look inside the garment industry. Titillating title (just a play on words) indicates a type of t&a film, which this is not.▼

Dead Zone, The (1983) **C-103m.** *** D: David Cronenberg. Christopher Walken, Brooke Adams, Tom Skerritt, Herbert Lom, Anthony Zerbe, Colleen Dewhurst, Martin Sheen, Nicholas Campbell, Jackie Burroughs. Absorbing Stephen King story of young man who emerges from near-fatal accident with the gift (or curse) of second sight—being able to tell a person's fate just by making physical contact. Walken's moving, heartfelt performance is the core of involving, if sometimes meandering movie where (despite reputations of King and Cronenberg) the emphasis is not on blood-and-guts horror. [R] ▼●

Deaf Smith & Johnny Ears (1973-Italian) **C-91m.** *** D: Paolo Cavara. Anthony Quinn, Franco Nero, Pamela Tiffin, Ira Furstenberg. Well-made "buddy Western" teams deaf-mute Quinn with upstart Nero as two common-man bystanders during a time of social upheaval in Texas. Beautifully photographed by Tonino Delli Colli. Originally titled LOS AMIGOS. [PG]

Dealers (1989-British) **C-91m.** **½ D: Colin Bucksey. Paul McGann, Rebecca De Mornay, Derrick O'Connor, John Castle, Paul Guilfoyle. These "dealers" don't sell drugs but trade dollars for a London-based bank. Flashy treatment of unexceptional story with reckless McGann sparring (and falling in love) with De Mornay. Good cast and novel setting help raise it slightly above the routine. [R]▼

Dealing: or The Berkeley-to-Boston Forty-Brick Lost-Bag Blues (1972) **C-99m.** **½ D: Paul Williams. Robert F. Lyons, Barbara Hershey, John Lithgow, Charles Durning, Joy Bang. Dated but still watchable adaptation of Robert and Michael Crichton's lighthearted novel about Harvard law student who runs pot on the side. Lyons is pretty blah, but compensation is provided by Hershey as his free-thinking girlfriend and Lithgow (in film debut) as the head dope. Panavision. [R]

Deal of the Century (1983) **C-99m.** ** D: William Friedkin. Chevy Chase, Sigourney Weaver, Gregory Hines, Vince Edwards, Richard Libertini, William Marquez, Eduardo Ricard, Wallace Shawn. Attempted satire of international weapons merchants. Its leading characters are so cold-blooded and unappealing, and its script (by Paul Brickman) so disjointed, that the results are a mishmash. [PG]▼●

Dean Koontz's Phantoms SEE: **Phantoms**

Dear America: Letters Home From Vietnam (1987) **C/B&W-87m. TVM** D: Bill Couturie. Narration by Robert De Niro, Michael J. Fox, Ellen Burstyn, Kathleen Turner, Tom Berenger, Willem Dafoe, Sean Penn, Matt Dillon, Kevin Dillon, Robin Williams, Howard Rollins, Jr., many others. Extremely moving account of the whos, whens and wheres of Vietnam, told via news footage and letters written by American soldiers. Gut-wrenching human drama that makes excellent use of appropriate music, from 1960s rock classics to Bruce Springsteen's "Born in the U.S.A." HBO production also received theatrical release. Based on the book edited by Bernard Edelman. Above average. ▼

Dear Brat (1951) **82m.** **½ D: William A. Seiter. Mona Freeman, Billy DeWolfe, Edward Arnold, Lyle Bettger. This sequel to DEAR RUTH has Freeman in title role involved with a crook trying to reform.

Dear Brigitte (1965) **C-100m.** **½ D: Henry Koster. James Stewart, Fabian, Glynis Johns, Cindy Carol, Billy Mumy, John Williams, Jack Kruschen, Alice Pearce, Jesse White, Ed Wynn. Guest: Brigitte Bardot. Good cast in OK family farce about an 8-year-old genius (Stewart's son, Mumy) with a crush on Brigitte Bardot (who makes a brief appearance near the end). Tries to be whimsical but is contrived instead. Look fast for James Brolin as student spokesman. CinemaScope.▼

Dear, Dead Delilah (1972) **C-90m.** *½ D: John Farris. Agnes Moorehead, Will Geer, Michael Ansara, Patricia Carmichael, Dennis Patrick. Low-budgeter about grisly competition for $600,000 buried somewhere around home of dying Moorehead. Filmed in Nashville, originally 95m. For axe-murder aficionados only. [R]▼

Dear Detective (1977-French) **C-105m.** **½ D: Philippe De Broca. Annie Girardot, Philippe Noiret, Catherine Alric, Hubert Deschamps, Paulette Dubost. Girardot is fine as woman cop who becomes involved with old flame (pompous professor Noiret) as she hunts a killer. Sometimes funny, more often predictable and pointless. Remade in 1979 as a TV movie. Retitled DEAR INSPECTOR. Sequel: JUPITER'S THIGH. [PG]▼

Dear God (1996) **C-112m.** ** D: Garry Marshall. Greg Kinnear, Laurie Metcalf, Maria Pitillo, Tim Conway, Hector Elizondo, Jon Seda, Roscoe Lee Browne, Anna Maria Horsford, Nancy Marchand, Larry Miller, Rue McClanahan, Jack Sheldon, Coolio, Seth Mumy, Jack Klugman, Ellen Cleghorne. Con man Kinnear gets one last chance to go straight, with a job at the post office. There, in the dead-letter department, he and his motley colleagues make "miracles" happen for needy people who write to God. Whimsical comedy gets off to a good start but loses the one thing it needs most: conviction. Director Marshall has a cameo, along with various celebs (including stars of long-ago Marshall-produced TV series). [PG] ▼●

Dear Heart (1964) **114m.** *** D: Delbert Mann. Glenn Ford, Geraldine Page, Michael Anderson, Jr., Barbara Nichols, Angela Lansbury, Patricia Barry, Charles Drake, Alice Pearce, Mary Wickes. Winning romance with gentlemanly traveling salesman Ford coming to N.Y.C., meeting up with sweetly wacky postmistress Page, who's in town for a convention. Excellent characterizations, with fine comic supporting players.▼

Dear Inspector SEE: **Dear Detective**

Dear Mr. Wonderful (1982-German) **C-115m.** *** D: Peter Lilienthal. Joe Pesci, Karen Ludwig, Evan Handler, Ivy Ray Browning, Frank Vincent, Paul Herman, Tony Martin. Ruby Dennis (Pesci) owns a bowling alley-nightclub in Jersey City, thinks he's on the verge of crashing Las Vegas. The American Jewish working class experience, viewed with a European sensibility, doesn't ring true; still, a thoughtful portrait of a little man who must learn to take what life has to offer. The sequence with Martin is particularly memorable. Video title: RUBY'S DREAM.▼

Dear Murderer (1947-British) **90m.** **½ D: Arthur Crabtree. Eric Portman, Greta Gynt, Dennis Price, Maxwell Reed, Jack Warner, Hazel Court. Husband Portman kills wife's lover. All-too-familiar "perfect crime" melodrama sparked by fine Portman performance.▼

Dear Ruth (1947) **95m.** **½ D: William D. Russell. Joan Caulfield, William Holden, Mona Freeman, Edward Arnold, Billy DeWolfe. Bouncy, naive comedy of errors with young girl pretending to be her older sister to impress soldier she corresponds with. Norman Krasna's Broadway smash was also a Hollywood hit and led to sequels DEAR WIFE and DEAR BRAT.

Dear Wife (1949) **88m.** **½ D: Richard Haydn. Joan Caulfield, William Holden, Edward Arnold, Billy DeWolfe, Mona Freeman. Follow-up to DEAR RUTH focuses on Freeman's antics to get Holden elected to the state senate, although her politician father Arnold is seeking same position.▼

Death and the Maiden (1994) **C-103m.** *** D: Roman Polanski. Sigourney Weaver, Ben Kingsley, Stuart Wilson. Generally fluid filmization of Ariel Dorfman's three-character (and mostly one-room) play about an edgy onetime victim of torture and sexual abuse who gets a chance to exact at-home revenge. Though Weaver's occasionally over-the-top performance contributes to a wobbly midsection, Polanski is pretty much up to the tough claustrophobic challenge. Kingsley is exceptional as a physician who gets the surprise of his life when he drops in to a secluded beach house (presumably in Chile) for a nightcap. [R]▼●

Death Becomes Her (1992) **C-104m.** ** D: Robert Zemeckis. Meryl Streep, Bruce Willis, Goldie Hawn, Isabella Rossellini, Ian Ogilvy, Adam Storke, Nancy Fish, Alaina Reed Hall, Michelle Johnson, Mimi Kennedy, Jonathan Silverman, Fabio. Black comedy about a glamorous, self-absorbed star (Streep) who's obsessed with staying young, and a woman scorned (Hawn) who vows revenge against her—at any price. Effects-laden comedy of absurd extremes is told with too heavy a hand, though Streep is a hoot as the egomaniacal actress. Film director Sydney Pollack is also funny in an unbilled bit as a Beverly Hills doctor. Won Visual Effects Oscar. [PG-13]▼●◗

Deathbed SEE: **Terminal Choice**

Death Before Dishonor (1987) **C-95m.** ** D: Terry J. Leonard. Fred Dryer, Brian Keith, Paul Winfield, Joanna Pacula, Kasey Walker, Rockne Tarkington. Clichéd, by-the-numbers story of Marine gunnery sergeant Dryer (who keeps a picture of John Wayne from SANDS OF IWO JIMA on his wall), who singlehandedly battles Middle Eastern terrorists after they stage a massacre—and kidnap his superior (Keith). Lotsa stunts, little sense. [R]▼●

Death Bite SEE: **Spasms**

Death Collector (1975) **C-85m.** BOMB D: Ralph De Vito. Joseph Cortese, Lou Criscuolo, Joe Pesci, Bobby Alto, Frank Vincent. Poor melodrama about Cortese's involvement with various hoods is of interest solely for early performance by Pesci. Video titles: THE ENFORCER and FAMILY ENFORCER. [R]▼

Death Corps SEE: **Shock Waves**

Deathdream (1972-Canadian) **C-90m.** **½ D: Bob Clark. John Marley, Richard Backus, Lynn Carlin, Henderson Forsythe. Backus is Vietnam vet, thought dead, who returns to his family a virtual stranger with a murderous lust for blood. Grim, fairly shocking. Aka DEAD OF NIGHT.▼

Death Drug (1978) **C-73m.** *½ D: Oscar Williams. Philip-Michael Thomas, Rosalind Cash, Vernee Watson, Frankie Crocker. Clichéd saga of singer-songwriter whose life and career go to pieces after he becomes addicted to "angel dust." Video release of this terrible low-budgeter is framed with new footage of *Miami Vice* star Thomas, including a music video! [PG-13]▼

Death Drums Along the River SEE: **Sanders**

Death Game (1977) **C-89m.** *½ D: Peter S. Traynor. Sondra Locke, Colleen Camp, Seymour Cassel, Beth Brickell. Unpleasant (and ultimately ludicrous) film about two maniacal lesbians who—for no apparent reason—tease, titillate, and torture a man in his own house. Filmed in 1974. Trivia fans: Sissy Spacek was one of the set decorators! Aka THE SEDUCERS. [R]▼

Death Hunt (1981) **C-97m.** ** D: Peter R. Hunt. Charles Bronson, Lee Marvin, Andrew Stevens, Angie Dickinson, Carl

Weathers, Ed Lauter. Tough Mountie Marvin pursues proud, self-reliant trapper Bronson, innocent of a murder charge, across icy Canada. Good action, but not enough of it. Angie is wasted. [R]▼●

Death in Granada SEE: **Disappearance of Garcia Lorca, The**

Death in Small Doses (1957) **79m.** *½ D: Joseph M. Newman. Peter Graves, Mala Powers, Chuck Connors, Merry Anders. Low-budget drama of narcotics use among truck drivers; dull presentation.

Death in Venice (1971-Italian) **C-130m.** ***½ D: Luchino Visconti. Dirk Bogarde, Mark Burns, Marisa Berenson, Bjorn Andresen, Silvana Mangano, Luigi Battaglia. Study of an artist, his loves, his homosexuality, and continuous search for beauty. Thomas Mann's slow-moving classic is splendidly brought to the screen. Music by Gustav Mahler (whom Bogarde is made up to resemble). Panavision. [PG]▼●

Death Kiss, The (1933) **75m.** *** D: Edwin L. Marin. Bela Lugosi, David Manners, Adrienne Ames, John Wray, Vince Barnett, Edward Van Sloan. Minor but entertaining whodunit set inside a movie studio, where an actor is killed filming a scene. Nice atmosphere of studio at work.▼

Deathline SEE: **Raw Meat**

Deathmask (1984) **C-87m.** ** D: Richard Friedman. Farley Granger, Lee Bryant, John McCurry, Arch Johnson, Barbara Bingham, Danny Aiello, Ruth Warrick. Medical investigator Granger, haunted by the accidental drowning of his daughter, attempts to find the identity of a dead four-year-old boy. Might have been a good mystery-chiller, an effective study of a man obsessed, but done in by confusing direction, unnecessary exploitation elements. Video version is 103m.▼

Deathmaster, The (1972) **C-88m.** ** D: Ray Danton. Robert Quarry, Bill Ewing, Brenda Dickson, John Fiedler, Betty Ann Rees, William Jordan. Spellbinding stranger (Quarry) leads on a group of unsuspecting hippies; their "guru" turns out to be a vampire in this bloody, run-of-the-mill outing. [PG]

Death of a Gunfighter (1969) **C-100m.** **½ D: Allen Smithee. Richard Widmark, Lena Horne, John Saxon, Michael McGreevey, Darleen Carr, Carroll O'Connor, Kent Smith. Downbeat but interesting Western drama of unwanted sheriff who refuses to be fired. Horne wasted as Widmark's occasional love interest. Directed by Robert Totten and Don Siegel, credited to fictitious Smithee (his directorial "debut"). [M/PG]▼

Death of a Jew SEE: **Sabra**

Death of an Angel (1985) **C-95m.** ** D: Petru Popescu. Bonnie Bedelia, Nick Mancuso, Pamela Ludwig, Alex Colon, Irma Garcia. Inspirational misfire about newly ordained female priest Bedelia getting involved with Mexican religious charlatan Mancuso after her crippled daughter (Ludwig) runs away to join his flock. Well-meaning, well-acted effort is extremely hokey, with a fantasy ending that is wholly unbelievable. [PG]▼●

Death of a Prophet (1981) **C&B/W-60m.** **½ D: Woodie King, Jr. Morgan Freeman, Yolanda King, Mansoor Najee-ullah, Sam Singleton, Tommie Hicks, Yusef Iman, Sonny Jim Gaines, Ossie Davis. Low-budget but involving drama (with some documentary scenes) about the last day in the life of a black American leader. He's clearly supposed to be Malcolm X, though that name is not mentioned. Freeman is excellent, and the film's documentary style is effective. Yolanda King is the daughter of Martin Luther King, Jr. ▼

Death of a Salesman (1951) **115m.** ***½ D: Laslo Benedek. Fredric March, Mildred Dunnock, Kevin McCarthy, Cameron Mitchell, Howard Smith, Royal Beal, Jesse White. Arthur Miller's Pulitzer Prize-winning social drama of middle-aged man at end of emotional rope is transformed to the screen intact, with stagy flashbacks. March in title role can't fathom why business and family life failed; Dunnock is patient wife; McCarthy and Mitchell are disillusioned sons. Superb. Dunnock, Mitchell, and Smith recreate their Broadway roles; McCarthy, making his film debut, repeats the role he played on the London stage. Remade for TV in 1985.

Death of a Salesman (1985) **C-150m. TVM** D: Volker Schlöndorff. Dustin Hoffman, Kate Reid, John Malkovich, Stephen Lang, Charles Durning, Louis Zorich. Stunning though stylistic remounting of Hoffman's 1984 Broadway revival of classic Arthur Miller play with most of the cast from that production. A landmark of its type. Executive-produced by Hoffman and Miller. Hoffman and Malkovich both won acting Emmys. Above average. ▼●

Death of a Scoundrel (1956) **119m.** **½ D: Charles Martin. George Sanders, Yvonne de Carlo, Zsa Zsa Gabor, Victor Jory. Episodic chronicle of foreigner coming to U.S., ingratiating himself with an assortment of women whom he cons into helping him get ahead. Low-budget but fascinating.▼●

Death of a Soldier (1986-Australian) **C-93m.** ** D: Philippe Mora. James Coburn, Bill Hunter, Maurie Fields, Belinda Davey, Max Fairchild. Yank soldier in 1942 Melbourne is strangling Aussie women; the U.S. Army—which desperately needs Allied help just after MacArthur's arrival there from the Philippines—wants to hang the assailant instead of providing the professional help he really needs. Based on fact, but not as interesting as it sounds;

Coburn is the American MP who gets caught in the middle. Panavision. [R]▼

Death of Her Innocence SEE: **Our Time**

Death on the Diamond (1934) **69m.** ** D: Edward Sedgwick. Robert Young, Madge Evans, Nat Pendleton, Ted Healy, C. Henry Gordon, David Landau, Paul Kelly. Absurd crime tale in which a mystery man is murdering St. Louis Cardinals ballplayers one by one. It'll be up to rookie hurler Young to discover the culprit. Watch for Mickey Rooney as a clubhouse boy, Walter Brennan selling hot dogs, Ward Bond as a cop.

Death on the Nile (1978-British) **C-140m.** **½ D: John Guillermin. Peter Ustinov, Bette Davis, David Niven, Mia Farrow, Angela Lansbury, George Kennedy, Maggie Smith, Jack Warden, Lois Chiles, Olivia Hussey, Simon MacCorkindale, Jane Birkin, Jon Finch, Harry Andrews, I.S. Johar. Visually sumptuous but only marginally engrossing Agatha Christie mystery has Hercule Poirot (Ustinov) faced with a shipload of suspects after the murder of Chiles. A deserving Oscar winner for Anthony Powell's costume design; script by Anthony Shaffer. The first of Ustinov's portrayals of the Belgian detective. [PG]▼●

Death Race 2000 (1975) **C-78m.** **½ D: Paul Bartel. David Carradine, Simone Griffeth, Sylvester Stallone, Louisa Moritz, Mary Woronov, Don Steele, Joyce Jameson, Fred Grandy, Martin Kove, T. R. Sloane, John Landis. Outrageous tongue-in-cheek action film about futuristic society where no-holds-barred auto race is the national sport, and points scored by running down pedestrians. Fast-paced fun, marred by unnecessary gore. Followed by DEATHSPORT. [R]▼●◗

Death Rage (1976-Italian) **C-98m.** *½ D: Anthony M. Dawson (Antonio Margheriti). Yul Brynner, Barbara Bouchet, Martin Balsam, Massimo Ranieri. Brynner plays American hit man duped into agreeing to kill underworld kingpin in Naples. All this film kills is time. TV print runs 90m. [R]▼

Death Rides a Horse (1967-Italian) **C-114m.** ** D: Giulio Petroni. Lee Van Cleef, John Phillip Law, Luigi Pistilli, Anthony Dawson (Antonio Margheretti). Long, drawn-out Italian revenge Western with Law seeking murderers of his family, unaware that his companion (Van Cleef) is one of them. Techniscope. [M]▼

Death Ship (1980-Canadian) **C-91m.** BOMB D: Alvin Rakoff. George Kennedy, Richard Crenna, Nick Mancuso, Sally Ann Howes, Kate Reid, Saul Rubinek. Luxury liner collides with "death ship." Survivors board "death ship." "Death ship" tries to murder survivors. Forget it. [R]▼

Deathsport (1978) **C-82m.** ** D: Henry Suso, Allan Arkush. David Carradine, Claudia Jennings, Richard Lynch, David McLean, Jesse Vint. Follow-up to DEATH RACE 2000 again puts Carradine into future world where he and Jennings battle destructocycles to survive. Not as campy or enjoyable as earlier film, though Claudia unclothed is a visual asset. TV prints run 76m. [R]▼◗

Deathstalker (1984) **C-80m.** BOMB D: John Watson. Richard Hill, Barbi Benton, Richard Brooker, Lana Clarkson, Victor Bo, Bernard Erhard. Tacky sword-and-sorcery opus, good only for unintended laughs and gratuitous female nudity. Filmed in Argentina. Followed by several sequels. [R]▼●

Deathstalker II (1987) **C-77m.** ** D: Jim Wynorski. John Terlesky, Monique Gabrielle, John La Zar, Toni Naples, Maria Socas. Princess in exile (Gabrielle) is trying to regain her throne, with the aid of soldier of fortune Terlesky, in a medieval fantasyland. Filmed on the cheap in Argentina. Voyeurs will appreciate topless scenes by former model Gabrielle (in a dual role, no less). Watch for funny outtakes at the end. Aka DEATHSTALKER II: DUEL OF THE TITANS. [R]▼●

Deathstalker III (1989) **C-86m.** BOMB D: Alfonso Corona. John Allen Nelson, Carla Herd, Terri Treas, Thom Christopher, Aaron Hernan, Roger Cudney, Claudia Inchaurregui. Cheap, boring time-waster, in which Nelson seeks a lost treasure and becomes involved with twin princesses (both played by Herd). Also known as DEATHSTALKER III: THE WARRIORS FROM HELL. Followed by DEATHSTALKER IV: MATCH OF TITANS. [R]▼●

Death Takes a Holiday (1934) **78m.** ***½ D: Mitchell Leisen. Fredric March, Evelyn Venable, Guy Standing, Gail Patrick, Helen Westley, Kent Taylor, Henry Travers, Katherine Alexander. Fascinating allegory about Death (March) entering the human world to discover what makes us tick, and falling in love. Maxwell Anderson, Gladys Lehman, and Walter Ferris adapted Alberto Casella's play. Remade as a TVM in 1971 (with Melvyn Douglas, Myrna Loy, and Monte Markham), and as MEET JOE BLACK in 1998.▼

Death Train (1993-U.S.-British-Yugoslavian) **C-100m. TVM** D: David S. Jackson. Pierce Brosnan, Patrick Stewart, Alexandra Paul, Ted Levine, Christopher Lee. Predictable action thriller involving a stressed-out mercenary who's paid by a renegade Russian general to hijack a train and transport a nuclear bomb across Europe for delivery to Saddam Hussein. Alistair MacLean's name on the title created false expectations in this by-the-numbers story filmed in Serbia. Shown as ALISTAIR MACLEAN'S "DEATH TRAIN." Video title: DETONATOR. Followed by ALISTAIR MACLEAN'S "NIGHT WATCH." Made for cable. Average.▼

Death Trap (1976) SEE: **Eaten Alive!**

Deathtrap (1982) **C-116m.** ** D: Sidney

Lumet. Michael Caine, Christopher Reeve, Dyan Cannon, Irene Worth, Henry Jones, Joe Silver. Playwright Caine, suffering through a series of flops, might just kill to take credit for novice author Reeve's new work; Cannon is Caine's hysterical wife. An overlong, second-rate SLEUTH, adapted by Jay Presson Allen from Ira Levin's hit play. One sequence was added for original network showing. [PG]▼●◗

Death Valley (1982) **C-87m.** *½ D: Dick Richards. Paul Le Mat, Catherine Hicks, Stephen McHattie, A. Wilford Brimley, Peter Billingsley, Edward Herrmann. Young Billingsley, a city boy, visits mom in Arizona, becomes entangled with psychotic criminal McHattie. Pretty bad, with a fine cast wasted. [R]▼

Death Warrant (1990-Canadian) **C-111m.** **½ D: Deran Serafian. Jean-Claude Van Damme, Robert Guillaume, Cynthia Gibb, George Dickerson, Art Le Fleur, Patrick Kilpatrick. Van Damme plays a Royal Canadian Mountie posing as a prisoner to find out who has been offing penitentiary inmates. You guessed it . . . his cover is threatened by incoming transfer of one of his old Mountie foes. Hard to say how Sgt. Preston would have handled this one. Slightly better than most of this genre. [R]▼●

Death Watch (1980-French-German) **C-119m.** *** D: Bertrand Tavernier. Romy Schneider, Harvey Keitel, Harry Dean Stanton, Max von Sydow. Intelligent sci-fi drama. In a future civilization, TV producer Stanton uses Keitel—who has a camera in his brain—to film a documentary on terminally ill Schneider. A biting commentary on media abuse and manipulation, with solid performances, direction. Panavision. [R]▼●

Death Weekend SEE: **House by the Lake**

Death Wheelers, The SEE: **Psychomania** (1971)

Death Wish (1974) **C-93m.** *** D: Michael Winner. Charles Bronson, Hope Lange, Vincent Gardenia, Steven Keats, William Redfield, Stuart Margolin, Stephen Elliott, Olympia Dukakis, Christopher Guest, Paul Dooley, Eric Laneuville. Audience manipulation at its zenith: Businessman Bronson's wife and daughter are savagely raped, and his wife dies, turning mild-mannered liberal Bronson into a vigilante on N.Y.C. streets. Chilling but irresistible; a bastardization of the Brian Garfield novel, in which vigilantism as a deterrent to crime is not a solution but another problem. Music by Herbie Hancock. One of the muggers is played by Jeff Goldblum, in his film debut. Followed by four sequels. [R] ▼●

Death Wish II (1982) **C-93m.** BOMB D: Michael Winner. Charles Bronson, Jill Ireland, Vincent Gardenia, J. D. Cannon, Anthony Franciosa, Ben Frank, Robin Sherwood, Robert F. Lyons, Larry Fishburne. Bronson's back in action, this time bringing his one-man vigilante act to L.A. Made by profiteers, not filmmakers; poorly directed to boot, with Charlie giving a wooden-Indian performance. [R] ▼●

Death Wish 3 (1985) **C-90m.** *½ D: Michael Winner. Charles Bronson, Deborah Raffin, Ed Lauter, Martin Balsam, Gavan O'Herlihy, Kirk Taylor, Alex Winter, Tony Spiridakis, John Gabriel, Marina Sirtis. Same old stuff, except that Bronson's "ordinary guy" vigilante is no longer convincing; his entire immediate family was wiped out in the first two movies! [R]▼●

Death Wish 4: The Crackdown (1987) **C-99m.** BOMB D: J. Lee Thompson. Charles Bronson, Kay Lenz, John P. Ryan, Perry Lopez, George Dickerson, Soon-Teck Oh, Dana Barron. Cheapie entry in this worn-out series has a different director and an L.A. setting. This time vigilante Bronson's mission includes wiping out the gangs supplying crack. [R]▼●

Death Wish V: The Face of Death (1994-Canadian) **C-96m.** BOMB D: Allan A. Goldstein. Charles Bronson, Lesley-Anne Down, Michael Parks, Chuck Shamata, Kevin Lund, Robert Joy, Saul Rubinek, Erica Lancaster. No plot, just a pretext: Bronson's fiancée is murdered on the orders of her mobster ex-husband (Parks), so (yawn) he turns vigilante yet again. Crude, stupid entry in weary series, very badly directed, with an emphasis on torture. [R]▼●◗

Decameron, The (1970-Italian-French-West German) **C-111m.** **½ D: Pier Paolo Pasolini. Franco Citti, Ninetto Davoli, Angela Luce, Patrizia Capparelli, Jovan Jovanovic, Silvana Mangano, Pier Paolo Pasolini. An octet of tales from Boccaccio's *Decameron*, with Pasolini as Giotto, linking them up. Lively, earthy; the first of the director's medieval trilogy. [X]▼●◗

Decameron Nights (1952-British) **C-87m.** ** D: Hugo Fregonese. Joan Fontaine, Louis Jourdan, Binnie Barnes, Joan Collins, Marjorie Rhodes. Boring tale of Boccaccio (Jourdan), on the run after martial law is declared in Florence; he hides out at Fontaine's villa, where in the company of his hostess and her wards a trio of romantic tales are spun (each of which also stars Jourdan and Fontaine).▼

Deceived (1991) **C-103m.** ** D: Damian Harris. Goldie Hawn, John Heard, Robin Bartlett, Ashley Peldon, Tom Irwin, Beatrice Straight, Kate Reid, Maia Filar, Jan Rubes, Amy Wright. In-name-only "thriller" about happily married N.Y. yuppie who discovers her husband's litany of duplicities after the guy is supposedly murdered. Hawn's attempt to play it straight is too derivative (to say nothing of incredible) to carry much clout. [PG-13]▼●

Deceiver (1998) **C-102m.** BOMB D: Jonas Pate, Joshua Pate. Tim Roth, Chris Penn, Michael Rooker, Renée Zellweger, Rosanna Arquette, Ellen Burstyn. Did Roth, a boozy rich kid with temporal lobe epilepsy, hack prostitute Zellweger in two? Pretentious, derivative groaner about Roth's subsequent police interrogation futilely tries to make us care. With its casting—Penn and Rooker as the grilling cops—it's a given that Roth isn't going to be the only one with personal demons. If you must watch, see if you can make sense of Arquette's role as Rooker's sex-starved wife. J-D-C Scope. [R]▼●

Deceivers, The (1988-British-Indian) **C-112m.** BOMB D: Nicholas Meyer. Pierce Brosnan, Saeed Jaffrey, Shashi Kapoor, Helena Mitchell, Keith Michell, David Robb. Limp adventure saga of British officer Brosnan going undercover in colonial India to infiltrate a murderous brotherhood. Intriguing premise, deadening result; Brosnan simply fails to register. Produced, oddly enough, by Ismail Merchant. [PG-13]▼●

December (1991) **C-92m.** ** D: Gabe Torres. Balthazar Getty, Jason London, Brian Krause, Wil Wheaton, Chris Young, Robert Miller, Ann Hartfield. In the wake of the Pearl Harbor bombing in 1941 five young men must decide what to do with their lives. Talky movie takes place mostly in dorm rooms; might have played better on a stage. [PG]▼●

December Bride (1991-British-Irish) **C-90m.** *** D: Thaddeus O'Sullivan. Donal McCann, Saskia Reeves, Ciaran Hinds, Patrick Malahide, Brenda Bruce. Austere but involving romantic drama set in a rural, conservative Irish farm community, in which an independent-minded servant (Reeves) becomes pregnant and refuses to reveal the identity of the father. A story of simple but deeply felt emotion, and an allegory about the constrictions of hell-and-damnation religion. Stunningly directed, and crammed with painterly images.▼

Deception (1946) **112m.** ***½ D: Irving Rapper. Bette Davis, Paul Henreid, Claude Rains, John Abbott, Benson Fong. Acting duel de force by Davis and Rains as pianist and her jealous benefactor, with Henreid overshadowed by star duo.▼

Deception (1993) **C-90m.** **½ D: Graeme Clifford. Andie MacDowell, Liam Neeson, Viggo Mortensen, Jack Thompson, Paul Spencer, Chad Power, Monica Mikala, Jeff Corey, Miriam Reed. Better-than-average mystery follows a determined woman around the world as she sniffs out a trail of bank accounts left by her deceased husband. A pleasant diversion, enhanced by MacDowell and some nice scenery. Filmed as RUBY CAIRO, this languished on the shelf for a while. [PG-13]▼

Decision Against Time (1957-British) **87m.** **½ D: Charles Crichton. Jack Hawkins, Elizabeth Sellars, Eddie Byrne, Lionel Jeffries, Donald Pleasence. Hawkins is effective as test pilot giving all to save troubled craft for boss and to protect job future.

Decision at Sundown (1957) **C-77m.** **½ D: Budd Boetticher. Randolph Scott, John Carroll, Karen Steele, Noah Beery, John Litel. Scott tracks down man supposedly responsible for his wife's suicide in this odd but interesting Western.▼

Decision Before Dawn (1952) **119m.** *** D: Anatole Litvak. Richard Basehart, Gary Merrill, Oskar Werner, Hildegarde Neff, Dominique Blanchar, O. E. Hasse, Wilfried Seyfert. Top-notch WW2 espionage thriller, with Werner an idealistic German medic/P.O.W. who agrees to become a spy for his captors. Outstanding work by Werner, Neff (as a sympathetic bar-girl), and the supporting cast. Look quickly for Klaus Kinski as a whining soldier. Perceptive script by Peter Viertel; Litvak coproduced.

Decision of Christopher Blake, The (1948) **75m.** **½ D: Peter Godfrey. Alexis Smith, Robert Douglas, Cecil Kellaway, Ted Donaldson, John Hoyt. Insipid drama of child suffering from his parents' divorce.

Decks Ran Red, The (1958) **84m.** **½ D: Andrew L. Stone. James Mason, Dorothy Dandridge, Broderick Crawford, Stuart Whitman. Bizarre sea yarn with strange casting involves sailors' attempt to murder freighter captain and use vessel for salvage.

Decline of the American Empire, The (1986-Canadian) **C-101m.** *** D: Denys Arcand. Dominique Michel, Dorothée Berryman, Louise Portal, Geneviève Rioux, Pierre Curzi, Remy Girard, Yves Jacques, Daniel Brière, Gabriel Arcand. Witty, on-target account of how men and women feel about each other, and use each other, in their quests for pleasure and happiness. Focus is on a group of friends: The men prepare a gourmet dinner, while the women exercise in a health club, then they come together. [R]▼

Decline and Fall of a Bird Watcher (1969-British) **C-86m.** ** D: John Krish. Robin Phillips, Colin Blakely, Leo McKern, Genevieve Page, Felix Aylmer, Robert Harris, Donald Wolfit, Patrick Magee. Uneven, often labored satirical farce about a young man who joins faculty of strange boys' school and becomes involved with manipulative older woman (Page). Adapted from Evelyn Waugh's novel. [PG]

Decline of Western Civilization, The (1981) **C-100m.** *** D: Penelope Spheeris. Alice Bag Band, Black Flag, Catholic Discipline, Circle Jerks, Fear, Germs, X. Funny, revealing documentary record of the whos, whats, and whys of the L.A. punk rock scene at the end of the 1970s: the music, performers, dancing, clubs, violence, desperation. An aptly titled chronicle. Much of cast now dead. Followed by a sequel. [R]▼

Decline of Western Civilization Part II: The Metal Years, The (1988) **C-90m.** *** D: Penelope Spheeris. Joe Perry, Steven Tyler, Gene Simmons, Paul Stanley,

Chris Holmes, Lemmy, Ozzy Osbourne, Faster Pussycat, Lizzy Borden, London, Odin, Seduce, Megadeth. Follow-up to definitive punk rock documentary concentrates more heavily on interviews, juxtaposing thoughts of seen-it-all veterans (Osbourne, Simmons, Perry, and Tyler of Aerosmith) with young aspirants bucking odds for success. Sympathetic to its subjects without condoning lifestyle it depicts; probably only chance you'll ever get to see Osbourne cook breakfast. [R]▼

Deconstructing Harry (1997) **C-96m.** ***½ D: Woody Allen. Woody Allen, Richard Benjamin, Kirstie Alley, Billy Crystal, Judy Davis, Bob Balaban, Elisabeth Shue, Demi Moore, Robin Williams, Caroline Aaron, Eric Bogosian, Mariel Hemingway, Amy Irving, Julie Kavner, Eric Lloyd, Julia Louis-Dreyfus, Tobey Maguire, Stanley Tucci, Hazelle Goodman, Gene Saks. A writer uses his life as fodder for his work—infuriating his friends, family, and lovers. Unusually candid (and foul-mouthed) self-examination by Allen, incorporating his various encounters as well as enactments of his fables and fancies; non-fans may think it overly indulgent, but Woodyphiles should find it fascinating and extremely funny. No one writes funnier dialogue—or keeps the spirit of Jewish humor alive so well. [R]▼●◗

Decoration Day (1990) **C-100m. TVM** D: Robert Markowitz. James Garner, Judith Ivey, Ruby Dee, Bill Cobbs, Larry Fishburne, Jo Anderson. Top-notch drama about a retired Georgia judge (Garner) who finds some meaning in life when asked to get his estranged childhood friend (Cobbs), a black WW2 vet, to belatedly accept the Congressional Medal of Honor he's been refusing. Sensitively adapted by Robert W. Lenski from John William Corrington's novella. Above average.▼●

Decoy for Terror (1968-Canadian) **C-85m.** *½ D: Erick Santamaria. William Kerwin, Jean Christopher, Neil Sedaka, Andree Champagne, Mary Lou Collier. Talky low-budget film about an insane painter suspected of murdering his models and a woman set as bait to catch him. Originally titled PLAYGIRL KILLER. ▼

Deep, The (1977) **C-123m.** ** D: Peter Yates. Robert Shaw, Jacqueline Bisset, Nick Nolte, Louis Gossett, Eli Wallach, Robert Tessier. Endless film of Peter Benchley's novel about innocent couple who hit on treasure and drugs while scuba-diving off Bermuda coast. Gratuitous violence and titillation—not to mention unbelievable plot—sink this handsome production. NBC added 53m. for its first network showing. Panavision. [PG]▼●◗

Deep Blue Sea, The (1955-British) **C-99m.** **½ D: Anatole Litvak. Vivien Leigh, Kenneth More, Eric Portman, Emlyn Williams. Terence Rattigan play of marital infidelity and the repercussions on Leigh, frustrated well-married woman; slow-moving, but interesting. CinemaScope.

Deep Blue Sea (1999) **C-105m.** **½ D: Renny Harlin. Thomas Jane, Saffron Burrows, Samuel L. Jackson, Jacqueline McKenzie, Michael Rapaport, Stellan Skarsgård, LL Cool J, Aida Turturro. Floating scientific base is crippled by an unlikely accident, and the super-intelligent sharks developed by researchers ungratefully begin chasing down their creators as the base slowly sinks. Sometimes-exciting combination of JAWS and ALIEN has some surprises, but terrible dialogue and a preposterous premise. Ronny Cox appears unbilled. Super 35. [R] ▼●◗

Deep Cover (1992) **C-112m.** **½ D: Bill Duke. Larry Fishburne, Jeff Goldblum, Victoria Dillard, Charles Martin Smith, Sydney Lassick, Clarence Williams III, Gregory Sierra, Roger Guenveur Smith, Def Jef, Glynn Turman. Fishburne, whose dad was killed during a holdup, grows up to be an undercover narc. Half standard urban action pic—but also half original. Goldblum puts a deliciously eccentric spin on his role as a lawyer who becomes Fishburne's unwitting "partner" in shady drug dealings. Better if taken purely as a genre picture, though there are indications the film wants to be something more; expert action scenes. [R]▼●

Deep Crimson (1996-Mexican-French-Spanish) **C-114m.** *** D: Arturo Ripstein. Regina Orozco, Daniel Gimenez-Cacho, Marisa Paredes, Veronica Merchant, Julieta Egurrola, Patricia Reyes Spindola. Spectacularly unpleasant and disturbing true-life crime story, based on the same "Lonely Hearts" case that inspired THE HONEYMOON KILLERS, about the murderous love affair between an obese nurse and a gigolo who swindle wealthy widows in 1940s Mexico. Extremely well acted and directed study of *l'amour fou* and the banality of evil. Packs a wallop, and pulls no punches in its horrific depiction of the couple's violent descent into madness.▼

Deep End (1970-U.S.-German) **C-88m.** *** D: Jerzy Skolimowski. Jane Asher, John Moulder-Brown, Diana Dors, Karl Michael Vogler. Innocent 15-year-old Moulder-Brown, an attendant in a dreary public bath, falls in love with his 20-ish female counterpart (Asher). Well-made tragedy of obsessive love; set in London, with music by Cat Stevens. [R]▼

Deep End of the Ocean, The (1999) **C-109m.** *** D: Ulu Grosbard. Michelle Pfeiffer, Treat Williams, Whoopi Goldberg, Jonathan Jackson, Ryan Merriman, John Kapelos, Michael Mcelroy. Persuasively acted adaptation of Jacquelyn Mitchard's best-seller about the disappearance of a three-year-old at his mother's high school reunion, and his chance return nine years later. Two-part story is admittedly a whopper, yet it's handled in credible fashion that makes one willing to accept it. Plays like a TV movie at times, but by and large, an exceptional one, with the dynamics between the two newfound brothers ringing true. [PG-13]▼●◗

Deep Impact (1998) **C-120m.** *** D: Mimi Leder. Robert Duvall, Téa Leoni, Elijah Wood, Vanessa Redgrave, Morgan Freeman, Maximilian Schell, James Cromwell, Ron Eldard, Jon Favreau, Laura Innes, Mary McCormack, Richard Schiff, Blair Underwood, Bruce Weitz, Betsy Brantley, Charles Martin Smith, Leelee Sobieski. Exciting yarn about attempts to ward off a comet hurtling toward Earth—and preparations to save as many people as possible if it hits. Freeman is the rock-solid U.S. President, Duvall a veteran astronaut on a space mission to explode the comet; their authoritative presence adds weight to this saga, while Leoni seems a bit of a flyweight by contrast as the ambitious TV newswoman who breaks the story. Super 35. [PG-13]▼●◗

Deep in My Heart (1954) **C-132m.** **½ D: Stanley Donen. Jose Ferrer, Merle Oberon, Helen Traubel, Doe Avedon, Tamara Toumanova, Paul Stewart, Douglas Fowley, Jim Backus; guest stars Walter Pidgeon, Paul Henreid, Rosemary Clooney, Gene and Fred Kelly, Jane Powell, Vic Damone, Ann Miller, Cyd Charisse, Howard Keel, Tony Martin. The life of composer Sigmund Romberg is not the stuff of high drama, but film sparkles in production numbers with MGM guest stars. Highlights include Kelly brothers' only film appearance together, Charisse's exquisite and sensual dance number with James Mitchell, and an incredible number featuring Ferrer performing an entire show himself.▼●

Deep in the Heart (1983-British) **C-101m.** *** D: Tony Garnett. Karen Young, Clayton Day, Suzie Humphreys, Ben Jones. Thought-provoking, if occasionally simplistic, drama about the evolution of a young woman (nicely played by Young) from passivity to violence, resulting from her relationship with macho Texan Day. Originally titled HANDGUN. [R]▼

Deep Red (1975-Italian) **C-98m.** **½ D: Dario Argento. David Hemmings, Daria Nicolodi, Gabriele Lavia, Macha Meril, Glauco Mauri. There's style to burn in senseless horror thriller with Hemmings on trail of sadistic psycho killer. Flashy, bizarre murders set to pounding rock soundtrack. Aka THE HATCHET MURDERS; original Italian version, PROFONDO ROSSO, is 20m. longer and much more violent. Cromoscope. [R]▼◗

Deep Rising (1998) **C-106m.** ** D: Stephen Sommers. Treat Williams, Famke Janssen, Anthony Heald, Wes Studi, Kevin J. O'Connor, Djimon Hounsou, Derrick O'Connor. Skipper-for-hire Williams finds himself in over his head when his current clients (a scummy lot led by heavily armed Studi) attack a luxury liner, unaware that the ship has been under siege by some sort of horrific ocean creatures. High-tech scare movie with a hokey script; some fun on a no-brainer level. Super 35. [R]▼●◗

Deep Six, The (1958) **C-105m.** **½ D: Rudolph Maté. Alan Ladd, Dianne Foster, William Bendix, Keenan Wynn, James Whitmore, Efrem Zimbalist, Jr., Joey Bishop. Ladd is Quaker naval officer during WW2 who compensates for past inaction by heading dangerous shore mission; Bendix gives able support.▼

Deep Space (1987) **C-90m.** **½ D: Fred Olen Ray. Charles Napier, Ann Turkel, Julie Newmar, James Booth, Ron Glass, Anthony Eisley, Bo Svenson, Peter Palmer. An ALIEN-like creature runs amok. Ultra-hokey sci-fi thriller with comic overtones. Napier is perfectly cast as a cop on its trail. Good fun for genre fans. Incidentally, title has nothing to do with the film! [R]▼

DeepStar Six (1989) **C-100m.** *½ D: Sean S. Cunningham. Greg Evigan, Nancy Everhard, Cindy Pickett, Miguel Ferrer, Taurean Blacque, Marius Weyers, Nia Peeples, Matt McCoy, Elya Baskin, Thom Bray. In the near future, an undersea research and missile-installation base is threatened by a carnivorous swimming crustacean. Plodding, familiar story and talky script (not to mention an elaborate but unconvincing monster) sink this. [R]▼●

Deep Valley (1947) **104m.** *** D: Jean Negulesco. Ida Lupino, Dane Clark, Wayne Morris, Fay Bainter, Henry Hull. Into Lupino's humdrum farm life comes a gangster from nearby prison camp; first rate cast in excellent drama.

Deep Waters (1948) **85m.** ** D: Henry King. Dana Andrews, Jean Peters, Cesar Romero, Dean Stockwell, Anne Revere, Ed Begley. Slick, empty tale of fisherman Andrews and landlubber Peters brought together by cute little Stockwell.

Deer Hunter, The (1978) **C-183m.** **** D: Michael Cimino. Robert De Niro, John Cazale, John Savage, Meryl Streep, Christopher Walken, George Dzundza, Chuck Aspegren. Stunning film about young Pennsylvania steelworkers, their lives before, during, and after wartime duty in Vietnam. Long but not overlong, this sensitive, painful, evocative work packs an emotional wallop. Story by Cimino, Deric Washburn, Louis Garfinkle and Quinn Redeker; scripted by Washburn. Five Oscars include Picture, Director, Supporting Actor (Walken), Editing (Peter Zinner). Panavision. [R] ▼●◗

Deerslayer, The (1957) **C-78m.** *½ D: Kurt Neumann. Lex Barker, Forrest Tucker, Rita Moreno, Jay C. Flippen, Cathy O'Donnell, Carlos Rivas. James Fenimore Cooper's Leatherstocking novel is given pedestrian treatment, with virtually all indoor sets and rear-screen projection. Barker links up with Chingachgook (Rivas), his Mohican blood-brother, to rescue an ornery hunter and his two daughters from the Hurons. Filmed before, as early as 1913; remade as a TVM. CinemaScope.

Def by Temptation (1990) **C-95m.** ★★★ D: James Bond III. Cynthia Bond, Kadeem Hardison, James Bond III, Bill Nunn, Melba Moore, Samuel L. Jackson. Southern divinity student visits his older brother in N.Y.C., just in time for the latter to get involved with a seductive succubus who preys on men in bars. All-black sleeper is extremely stylish, aided no end by the photography of Spike Lee's longtime cameraman, Ernest Dickerson. [R]▼●◗

Defcon-4 (1984) **C-89m.** BOMB D: Paul Donovan. Lenore Zann, Maury Chaykin, Kate Lynch, Tim Choate. It sounds like an industrial-strength roach killer, and it could use one. Three astronauts return to a post-holocaust earth run by some truly slimy punks. Next to C.H.U.D., the grimiest-looking movie of its time (at least *that* one took place underground). [R]▼●

Defector, The (1966) **C-106m.** ★★½ D: Raoul Levy. Montgomery Clift, Hardy Kruger, Roddy McDowall, David Opatoshu. Hackneyed Cold War spy trivia filmed in Europe, interesting only as Clift's last film; good cameo by McDowall.

Defence of the Realm (1985-British) **C-96m.** ★★★½ D: David Drury. Gabriel Byrne, Greta Scacchi, Denholm Elliott, Ian Bannen, Bill Paterson, Fulton Mackay. Tough, obsessive journalist Byrne's investigative story causes a British MP to resign—but there's more to the case than he knows. A taut, extremely entertaining political thriller that also touches on the subject of journalistic responsibility and the public's right to know what its government is up to. [PG]▼●

Defending Your Life (1991) **C-111m.** ★★★ D: Albert Brooks. Albert Brooks, Meryl Streep, Rip Torn, Lee Grant, Buck Henry, George D. Wallace, Lillian Lehman, Peter Schuck, Ethan Randall (Embry). Brooks dies in a car crash and finds himself in Judgment City, where Torn is assigned to defend his life before a tribunal . . . and where he falls in love with fellow candidate Streep, who's too good to be true. Imperfect, like all of Brooks' movies, but full of funny ideas and hard to dislike. [PG]▼●

Defenseless (1991) **C-104m.** ★★½ D: Martin Campbell. Barbara Hershey, Sam Shepard, Mary Beth Hurt, J. T. Walsh, Kellie Overbey, Jay O. Sanders, Randy Brooks, John Kapelos, Sheree North. Suspense thriller in which attorney Hershey discovers her client (and lover) murdered—and finds herself not only suspected of the crime, but stalked by a mysterious killer. Not bad, and a good showcase for a first-rate cast, especially Hurt, who chews the scenery in a change-of-pace part. [R]▼●

Defiance (1980) **C-102m.** ★★½ D: John Flynn. Jan-Michael Vincent, Art Carney, Theresa Saldana, Danny Aiello. Fernando Lopez, Rudy Ramos. Gritty little film about rootless blue-collar loner Vincent, who in an attempt to match up his dying youngster's bone marrow with that of single-handedly tames a vicious N.Y.C. street gang. A synthesis of '30s Warner Bros. melodramas, B Westerns, ON THE WATERFRONT, and BOARDWALK, with atmospheric direction and colorful supporting performances. [PG]▼

Defiant, The SEE: **Wild Pack, The**

Defiant Ones, The (1958) **97m.** ★★★★ D: Stanley Kramer. Tony Curtis, Sidney Poitier, Theodore Bikel, Charles McGraw, Cara Williams, Lon Chaney, Jr. Engrossing story of two escaped convicts—one black, one white—shackled together as they flee from police in the South. Fine performances by Williams and Chaney as people they meet along the way. Academy Award-winning screenplay by Harold Jacob Smith and Nathan E. Douglas (blacklisted actor-writer Nedrick Young) and cinematography by Sam Leavitt. Remade for TV in 1986 with Robert Urich and Carl Weathers.▼●

Def Jam's How to Be a Player (1997) **C-94m.** ★½ D: Lionel C. Martin. Bill Bellamy, Natalie Desselle, Lark Voorhies, Mari Morrow, Pierre, Jermaine ''Big Hugg'' Hopkins, A. J. Johnson, Beverly Johnson, Max Julien, Gilbert Gottfried, Bernie Mac, Elise Neal, Amber Smith. Smooth-talking womanizer tries one-upping his sister and her friend after they invite all the ''entries'' in his little black book to the same party. Completely flat comedy is meant to capitalize on TV's no-holds-barred *Def Jam,* but the show seems a lot raunchier than this big-screen trifle. [R]▼●◗

Déja Vu (1985) **C-95m.** ★½ D: Anthony Richmond. Jaclyn Smith, Shelley Winters, Claire Bloom, Nigel Terry. Smith and Terry relive the love affair they experienced in an earlier incarnation . . . then this supernatural thriller becomes a whodunit! Muddled, to say the least, though Smith is quite beautiful in her dual role; her then-husband directed the film. [R]▼

Déja Vu (1998-U.S.-British) **C-116m.** ★★★½ D: Henry Jaglom. Stephen Dillane, Victoria Foyt, Vanessa Redgrave, Glynis Barber, Michael Brandon, Noel Harrison, Rachel Kempson, Aviva Marks. Unusual romance about the inexplicable and profound attraction between an American woman abroad and a London painter. Though already attached to others, at every turn they receive ''cosmic confirmation'' of their belonging together. The acting is so good and story so satisfying that plot contrivances don't matter. Nepotism is a big plus, with Jaglom's wife Foyt in the lead and Redgrave's mother Kempson in their first joint screen appearance. Writer-director Jaglom's best; Foyt coscripted. [PG-13]▼

Delicate Balance, A (1973) **C-132m.** ** D: Tony Richardson. Katharine Hepburn, Paul Scofield, Lee Remick, Kate Reid, Joseph Cotten, Betsy Blair. Edward Albee's Pulitzer Prize-winning play about a neurotic Connecticut family and the old friends who decide to move in with them indefinitely makes for stagy, uninvolving film, extraordinary cast notwithstanding. An American Film Theater Production. [PG]▼

Delicate Delinquent, The (1957) **100m.** *** D: Don McGuire. Jerry Lewis, Martha Hyer, Darren McGavin, Horace McMahon, Milton Frome. Jerry's first solo effort after splitting with Dean Martin has him as delinquent who becomes a cop with McGavin's help. Agreeable blend of sentiment and slapstick. VistaVision.▼●

Delicatessen (1991-French) **C-102m.** ***½ D: Jean-Pierre Jeunet, Marc Caro. Marie-Laure Dougnac, Dominique Pinon, Karin Viard, Jean Claude Dreyfus, Ticky Holgado, Anne Marie Pisani, Edith Ker. Post-apocalyptic comedy about a landlord who slices humans into cutlets for non-vegetarian tenants. At the very least, this is the most original and entertaining comedy about cannibalism made to date. Brown-and-white color schemes, which would ordinarily look like a lab mistake, contribute to the film's trenchant visual style. Codirector Caro plays Fox, one of the Cave Dwellers. "Presented" by Terry Gilliam.▼●

Delicious (1931) **106m.** *½ D: David Butler. Janet Gaynor, Charles Farrell, El Brendel, Raul Roulien, Virginia Cherrill. Insipid romance; Janet as Scottish lassie who falls in love with wealthy Farrell in N.Y.C. Brief highlights in Gershwin score are bizarre dream sequence of Janet's welcome to America, and "New York Rhapsody."

Delightfully Dangerous (1945) **93m.** **½ D: Arthur Lubin. Jane Powell, Ralph Bellamy, Constance Moore, Morton Gould, Arthur Treacher, Louise Beavers. Enjoyable fluff with spunky teen Powell unaware that big sister Moore is a burlesque star. Bellamy is kindly Broadway producer who gets immersed in Powell's shenanigans. ▼

Delinquents, The (1957) **75m.** ** D: Robert Altman. Tom Laughlin, Peter Miller, Richard Bakalyan, Rosemary Howard, Helene Hawley. Intriguingly awful exploitation drama about nice boy who becomes involved with a street gang because girlfriend is too young to go steady. Altman's first film, made in Kansas City, with Julia Lee singing "Dirty Rock Boogie."

Delirious (1991) **C-96m.** *½ D: Tom Mankiewicz. John Candy, Mariel Hemingway, Emma Samms, David Rasche, Charles Rocket, Raymond Burr, Dylan Baker, Jerry Orbach, Renee Taylor. Astonishingly stupid comedy with a neat premise: a beleaguered soap-opera writer gets a conk on the head and dreams that he's stuck in his own story—in a heroic role that enables him to have his way with the woman he worships in real life. Bad writing and ham-handed direction foil a willing cast. [PG]▼●

Deliverance (1972) **C-109m.** **** D: John Boorman. Jon Voight, Burt Reynolds, Ned Beatty, Ronny Cox, Billy McKinney, Herbert "Cowboy" Coward, James Dickey. Superlative recreation of Dickey novel of four Atlanta businessmen who get more than they bargained for during a weekend canoe trip. McKinney and Coward are two of the most terrifying film villains in history; "Dueling Banjos" scene is equally memorable. Film debuts of Beatty and Cox. James Dickey adapted his own novel, and appears in the film as a sheriff; Ed O'Neill appears as a highway patrolman near end of film. The director's son Charley (later star of THE EMERALD FOREST) plays Voight's son here. Panavision. [R]▼●

Delta Factor, The (1970) **C-91m.** ** D: Tay Garnett. Christopher George, Yvette Mimieux, Diane McBain, Ralph Taeger. OK Mickey Spillane tale about a private eye on a CIA mission to rescue a scientist imprisoned on an island. [PG]

Delta Force, The (1986) **C-129m.** **½ D: Menahem Golan. Chuck Norris, Lee Marvin, Martin Balsam, Joey Bishop, Robert Forster, Lainie Kazan, George Kennedy, Hanna Schygulla, Susan Strasberg, Bo Svenson, Robert Vaughn, Shelley Winters, Assaf Dayan. Surprisingly straightforward and straight-faced (considering that cast) account of terrorist plane hijack in the Middle East—until rescue climax when America's special squadron (led by Marvin and Norris) take on bad guys in comic-book style. Uneven, to say the least, but never boring. Filmed in Israel. Followed by several sequels. [R]▼●

Delta Force 2 (1990) **C-110m.** *½ D: Aaron Norris. Chuck Norris, John P. Ryan, Paul Perri, Richard Jaeckel, Begonia Plaza, Mateo Gomez, Hector Mercardo, Billy Drago. Norris leads his Delta Force brigade into Latin America in an effort to snuff out an elusive drug lord. Strictly by-the-numbers. [R]▼●

Delta Fox (1977) **C-92m.** ** D: Beverly and Ferd Sebastian. Richard Lynch, Priscilla Barnes, Stuart Whitman, John Ireland, Richard Jaeckel. Unremarkable action-chase opus about a smuggler on the run from Miami to L.A.▼

Deluge (1933) **70m.** ** D: Felix E. Feist. Sidney Blackmer, Peggy Shannon, Lois Wilson, Matt Moore, Edward Van Sloan, Fred Kohler, Sr. Justly famous for its spectacular special effects sequence of N.Y.C. destroyed by tidal wave; unfortunately, the *rest* of the story (about a handful of survivors) is second-rate melodrama.▼

Delusion (1990) **C-100m.** ★★★ D: Carl Colpaert. Jim Metzler, Jennifer Rubin, Kyle Secor, Robert Costanzo, Tracey Walter, Jerry Orbach. Tough, taut thriller about a yuppie computer executive-embezzler and his plight after happening upon a Las Vegas showgirl and her killer-for-hire boyfriend (Secor, in an eye-opening performance) on a Death Valley highway. Thoroughly entertaining tale of desperation and isolation, with a point-of-view. Super 35. [R]▼

Dementia 13 (1963) **81m.** ★★ D: Francis Ford Coppola. William Campbell, Luana Anders, Bart Patton, Mary Mitchell, Patrick Magee. Gory horror film, set in Ireland, about a series of axe murders. Coppola's directorial debut—excluding his earlier nudie, TONITE FOR SURE—filmed for about 29¢ for Roger Corman; may be worth a look for curiosity's sake.▼●

Demetrius and the Gladiators (1954) **C-101m.** ★★½ D: Delmer Daves. Victor Mature, Susan Hayward, Michael Rennie, Debra Paget, Anne Bancroft, Richard Egan, Ernest Borgnine. Hokey sequel to THE ROBE has Emperor Caligula (Jay Robinson) searching for magic robe of Christ; Mature dallies with royal Hayward. CinemaScope.▼●

Demi-Paradise, The (1943-British) **115m.** ★★★ D: Anthony Asquith. Laurence Olivier, Penelope Dudley Ward, Leslie Henson, Marjorie Fielding, Margaret Rutherford, Felix Aylmer, Edie Martin, Joyce Grenfell, Jack Watling, Miles Malleson, John Laurie, Wilfrid Hyde-White, George Cole. Charming romantic comedy-satire with Olivier intriguingly cast as a Russian engineer who skeptically comes to England . . . and promptly becomes involved with Ward. Perceptive and, in its way, still-topical Anatole de Grunwald script gently chides people's prejudice against "foreigners." Marred only by the predictable finale. U.S. title: ADVENTURE FOR TWO.▼

Demolition Man (1993) **C-115m.** ★★½ D: Marco Brambilla. Sylvester Stallone, Wesley Snipes, Sandra Bullock, Nigel Hawthorne, Benjamin Bratt, Bob Gunton, Glenn Shadix. Ex-cop Stallone is sprung after 36 years of deep-freeze imprisonment for manslaughter when blond Snipes (his long-ago psycho nemesis) escapes from his own government-imposed hibernation; the joke is that the "San Angeles" of 2032 is a pacifistic society that nixes violence and profanity (and where every restaurant is a Taco Bell). Fast, surprisingly funny, bloodletter is still only marginally brainier than Sly's TANGO & CASH. Panavision. [R] ▼●◗

Demon (1977) **C-95m.** ★★½ D: Larry Cohen. Tony Lo Bianco, Sandy Dennis, Sylvia Sidney, Deborah Raffin, Sam Levene, Richard Lynch, Mike Kellin. Weird, confusing shocker in which New York cop Lo Bianco investigates motiveless killings by ordinary people possessed by Christ-like demon. Some good scenes. Originally titled GOD TOLD ME TO. [R]▼●

Demon Barber of Fleet Street, The SEE: **Sweeney Todd, The Demon Barber of Fleet Street**

Demoniaque (1958-French) **97m.** ★★½ D: Luis Saslavsky. Francois Perier, Micheline Presle, Jeanne Moreau, Madeleine Robinson. Perky yarn of French P.O.W. escaping and seeking refuge with girl his dead buddy romanced via the mails; girl believes him to be the letter-writer.

Demon Knight SEE: **Tales From The Crypt Presents Demon Knight**

Demon Master, The SEE: **Craze**

Demonoid, Messenger of Death (1981) **C-78m.** ★½ D: Alfred Zacharias. Samantha Eggar, Stuart Whitman, Roy Cameron Jenson, Erika Carlson, Lew Saunders. Eggar and husband, while working Mexican mine, unearth a hand, which possesses him, wreaking terror and havoc. Insipid direction, a rotten script, and shoddy special effects get in the way of any suspense. Aka MACABRA. [R]▼

Demon Planet, The SEE: **Planet of the Vampires**

Demons (1986-Italian) **C-89m.** ★½ D: Lamberto Bava. Urbano Barberini, Natasha Hovey, Paolo Cozza, Karl Zinny, Fiore Argento, Fabiola Toledo, Nicoletta Elmi. A horror film transforms its audience one by one into drooling, fanged "demons" who attack the remaining humans. Extremely gruesome and violent; no characterization, no logic, no plot. Achieved critical fame in some quarters. Director, who shows some visual style, is son of horror maestro Mario Bava. Cowritten and produced by Dario Argento. Followed by several sequels.▼●◗

Demons 2 (1987-Italian) **C-88m.** ★★ D: Lamberto Bava. David Knight, Nancy Brilli, Coralina Cataldi Tassoni, Bobby Rhodes, Asia Argento, Virginia Bryant. Sequel is improvement on first film but highly derivative of NIGHT OF THE LIVING DEAD and THEY CAME FROM WITHIN. Demonic infection spreads among people in modern apartment building; they transform into fanged, clawed monsters and attack others. Like its predecessor, achieved great acclaim among gore fans. [R]▼●◗

Demon Seed (1977) **C-94m.** ★★★½ D: Donald Cammell. Julie Christie, Fritz Weaver, Gerrit Graham, Berry Kroeger, Lisa Lu. Intelligent futuristic thriller, provocatively written, stylishly directed, and well acted, especially by Christie, the beauty terrorized by an ultra-sophisticated computer (voice of Robert Vaughn) that's decided to take over the world. As riveting as it is bizarre. Adapted by Robert Jaffe and Roger O. Hirson from the Dean Koontz novel. Panavision. [R] ▼●

Demons of the Mind (1971-British) **C-**

89m. *** D: Peter Sykes. Paul Jones, Yvonne Mitchell, Gillian Hills, Robert Hardy, Patrick Magee, Michael Hordern, Shane Briant. A 19th-century baron imprisons his son and daughter, believing they are possessed. Enticingly eerie Hammer horror film. Aka BLACK EVIL and NIGHTMARE OF TERROR. [R]▼

Demon Within, The SEE: **Happiness Cage, The**

Denial (1991) **C-103m.** BOMB D: Erin Dignam. Robin Wright, Jason Patric, Rae Dawn Chong, Barry Primus, Christine Harnos. Muddled, incoherent story of a woman obsessed with the memory of her lost, brooding lover. Flashbacks are virtually indistinguishable from the present-day narrative! This went straight to video. [R]▼

Denise Calls Up (1996) **C-80m.** *** D: Hal Salwen. Tim Daly, Caroleen Feeney, Dan Gunther, Dana Wheeler-Nicholson, Liev Schreiber, Aida Turturro, Alanna Ubach, Sylvia Miles. Nina tries to fix up a friend—no easy task—while Denise (Ubach) surprises Gunther with a phone call he never expected to get. Wickedly funny satire about New Yorkers who never seem to be able to get together and only talk on the phone. A one-joke premise, but writer-director Salwen keeps adding clever twists and touches. [PG-13]▼●

Dennis the Menace (1993) **C-94m.** ** D: Nick Castle. Walter Matthau, Mason Gamble, Joan Plowright, Christopher Lloyd, Lea Thompson, Robert Stanton, Paul Winfield, Amy Sakasitz, Arnold Stang, Ben Stein. Unconscionable, jerry-built ripoff of the HOME ALONEs from John Hughes, based on Hank Ketcham's comic strip, with the blond rascal's skirmishes with cantankerous neighbor Mr. Wilson (Matthau) a mere warmup to the more Culkin-ian climactic punch-out of a robber/derelict (Lloyd). Fun for under-8's and well served by its cast, but still a desperate collection of crotch and flatulence jokes. Followed by a direct-to-video sequel. [PG-13]▼●

Den of Doom SEE: **Glass Cage, The**

Dentist in the Chair (1960-British) **84m.** ** D: Don Chaffey. Peggy Cummins, Bob Monkhouse, Kenneth Connor, Eric Barker. Occasionally amusing shenanigans of dentists involved in crooked dealings, trying to undo their mischievous thefts.▼

Dentist on the Job SEE: **Get On With It**

Denver and Rio Grande, The (1952) **C-89m.** **½ D: Byron Haskin. Edmond O'Brien, Sterling Hayden, Dean Jagger, ZaSu Pitts, J. Carrol Naish, Laura Elliott, Lyle Bettger, Paul Fix. Another railroad rivalry Western as two competing companies battle elements and each other to complete tie-line through title area. Climax features an actual head-on collision between two steam locomotives.▼

Deported (1950) **80m.** **½ D: Robert Siodmak. Marta Toren, Jeff Chandler, Claude Dauphin, Carlo Rizzo. Engaging gangster yarn with Chandler deported to Italy, involved in the black market, but going straight to win Toren's love.

Deranged (1974) **C-82m.** **½ D: Jeff Gillen, Alan Ormsby. Roberts Blossom, Cosette Lee, Leslie Carlson, Robert Warner, Marcia Diamond. Blossom's neat performance uplifts this predictable shocker of a mother-obsessed farmer who preserves the old lady's corpse, then kills and stuffs other women to keep her company. Based on the same real-life case that inspired PSYCHO and THE TEXAS CHAINSAW MASSACRE. [R]▼

Derby (1971) **C-96m.** **½ D: Robert Kaylor. Charlie O'Connell, Eddie Krebs, Mike Snell, Christina Snell, Butch Snell. Documentary about roller derby stars and hopefuls is uneven; some scenes are vivid, others talky and dull. Provides a good look at one segment of Middle America. Filmed in Dayton, Ohio. [PG—edited from original R rating]▼

Derby Day (1952-British) **84m.** **½ D: Herbert Wilcox. Anna Neagle, Michael Wilding, John McCallum, Googie Withers. Diverting study of human nature, as an assortment of people intermingle at Epsom Downs race track. Retitled: FOUR AGAINST FATE.

Der Purimshpiler (1937-Polish) **90m.** *** D: Joseph Green, Jan-Nowina Przybylski. Zygmund Turkow, Miriam Kressyn, Hymie Jacobson, Max Bozyk, Berta Litwina. Amusing Yiddish-language musical fable, set in Galicia, about a wandering vaudeville actor; he falls in love with the pretty daughter of a cobbler, who wants to marry her off into a prominent family. The title's English translation is THE PURIM PLAYER; aka THE JESTER and THE JEWISH JESTER. ▼

Dersu Uzala (1975-Japanese-Russian) **C-140m.** ***½ D: Akira Kurosawa. Maxim Munzuk, Yuri Solomine. Simple, gentle gold hunter-guide Munzuk teaches Russian explorer Solomine the rules of survival in Siberia; they develop mutual respect and friendship. A poignant, poetic examination of contrasting lives. Filmed in Russia; Best Foreign Film Oscar-winner. Sovscope 70. [G]▼●

De Sade (1969-U.S.-West German) **C-92m.** ** D: Cy Endfield. Keir Dullea, Senta Berger, Lilli Palmer, Anna Massey, John Huston. Fictionalized biography of world's most celebrated sexual and physical pervert. If you're expecting something raunchy, forget it. Pretty tepid stuff. Original running time: 113m. [R]

Desert Attack (1960-British) **79m.** *** D: J. Lee Thompson. John Mills, Sylvia Syms, Anthony Quayle, Harry Andrews, Diane Clare. Well-handled psychological drama of British ambulance officer, two nurses, and a German soldier brought together in African desert. Original British version ICE COLD IN ALEX runs 132 m.

Desert Bloom (1986) **C-106m.** ***½ D: Eugene Corr. Jon Voight, JoBeth Williams, Ellen Barkin, Annabeth Gish, Allen Garfield, Jay D. Underwood. Perceptive, exquisitely realized memoir, set in 1951 Nevada—the dawn of the Atomic Age. Heroine is 13-year-old Gish, whose mother (Williams) only sees what she wants to and whose stepfather (solidly acted by Voight) is an embittered, alcoholic WW2 hero reduced to running a gas station. Corr wrote the poignantly precise script from a story by Linda Remy and himself. [PG] ▼●

Desert Blue (1999) **C-93m.** *** D: Morgan J. Freeman. Brendan Sexton III, Kate Hudson, Christina Ricci, Daniel von Bargen, John Heard, Lucinda Jenney, Casey Affleck, Sara Gilbert, Peter Sarsgaard, Michael Ironside. A professor of American culture and his ambitious actress-daughter find themselves stuck in a remote western town, where the young woman bonds with the locals—especially Blue, who is fixated on realizing his late father's dream of building a water park in the desert! Well-drawn characters and a sharp sense of time and place help make this a winner. Written by the director. [R]▼

Desert Desperados (1959) **81m.** *½ D: Steve Sekely. Ruth Roman, Akim Tamiroff, Otello Toso, Gianni Glori. Unsuccessful mishmash of romance and unconvincing intrigue set in Egyptian desert; a waste of Roman's most capable talents. Retitled: THE SINNER.

Deserter, The (1971-Italian-Yugoslavian) **C-99m.** *½ D: Burt Kennedy. Bekim Fehmiu, John Huston, Richard Crenna, Chuck Connors, Ricardo Montalban, Ian Bannen, Brandon de Wilde, Slim Pickens, Woody Strode, Patrick Wayne. Dull cavalry pic about Indian fighting on Mexican border. Cast is capable, except for Fehmiu, who didn't improve after THE ADVENTURERS. Aka RIDE TO GLORY. Panavision. [PG]▼

Desert Fox, The (1951) **88m.** *** D: Henry Hathaway. James Mason, Cedric Hardwicke, Jessica Tandy, Luther Adler, Everett Sloane, Leo G. Carroll, George Macready, Richard Boone, Robert Coote. Mason standout as Field Marshal Rommel in sensitive account of his military defeat in WW2 Africa and disillusioned return to Hitler Germany. Mason repeated role in THE DESERT RATS.▼●

Desert Fury (1947) **C-95m.** **½ D: Lewis Allen. John Hodiak, Lizabeth Scott, Burt Lancaster, Mary Astor, Wendell Corey. Mild drama of love and mystery among gamblers, stolen by Astor in bristling character portrayal.

Desert Hawk, The (1950) **C-77m.** ** D: Frederick de Cordova. Yvonne De Carlo, Richard Greene, Jackie Gleason, Rock Hudson, George Macready, Joe Besser. Pat Arabian desert tale, interesting for Gleason and Hudson in secondary roles.

Desert Hearts (1985) **C-93m.** **½ D: Donna Deitch. Helen Shaver, Patricia Charbonneau, Audra Lindley, Andra Akers, Dean Butler, Jeffrey Tambor. Uptight female professor comes to Reno to get a divorce in the 1950s and is pursued by a young woman who forces her to examine her own sexuality. Debut feature for writer-director Deitch (with a contemporary nod to THE WOMEN) has its moments, but characters are sketchily developed and story moves in fits and starts. [R]▼●

Desert Hell (1958) **82m.** ** D: Charles Marquis Warren. Brian Keith, Barbara Hale, Richard Denning, Johnny Desmond. French Foreign Legion battles warring Arabs to save peace; very little of promised action given to viewer. Regalscope.

Desert Legion (1953) **C-86m.** ** D: Joseph Pevney. Alan Ladd, Richard Conte, Arlene Dahl, Akim Tamiroff. Mild Ladd vehicle of battling French Foreign-Legion in a lost city; cowritten by Irving Wallace.

Desert Patrol (1958-British) **78m.** **½ D: Guy Green. Richard Attenborough, John Gregson, Michael Craig, Vincent Ball. Staunch account of British patrol attempting to blow up Axis fuel dump before pending WW2 battle of El Alamein. Originally titled SEA OF SAND.▼

Desert Rats, The (1953) **88m.** *** D: Robert Wise. Richard Burton, James Mason, Robert Newton, Chips Rafferty. Fine WW2 actioner with Mason convincing as Field Marshal Rommel (repeating his role from THE DESERT FOX); Burton is British commando trying to ward off Germans in North Africa.▼

Desert Song, The (1953) **C-110m.** **½ D: H. Bruce Humberstone. Kathryn Grayson, Gordon MacRae, Steve Cochran, Raymond Massey, William Conrad, Dick Wesson. Third version of Sigmund Romberg operetta set in Africa creaks along on thin plot. American MacRae is secret leader of good natives (Riffs) in battle against evil Arabs. Songs: "The Riff Song," "One Alone." Previously filmed in 1929 and 1944.▼

Designated Mourner, The (1997-British) **C-94m.** ** D: David Hare. Miranda Richardson, Mike Nichols, David de Keyser. Endlessly talky dissertation on the death of culture, set in an unnamed country in what could be the immediate future. Nichols marries into the intellectual upper crust of this mysterious society, which has cast off its artists and rendered them virtual prisoners. Shot in three days, the film (adapted by Wallace Shawn from his play) is a series

of monologues and probably should have remained a theater piece. Nichols makes a long-awaited film acting debut, but perhaps he should have waited just a little while longer. [R]▼◗
Design for Living (1933) **90m.** *** D: Ernst Lubitsch. Fredric March, Gary Cooper, Miriam Hopkins, Edward Everett Horton, Franklin Pangborn, Isabel Jewell, Jane Darwell. Ben Hecht adapted Noel Coward's stage comedy about artist Cooper and playwright March, best friends and Americans in Paris, and what happens when they both fall in love with Hopkins. Most of the witty innuendos are left intact (even if the pacing isn't quite right).●
Design for Scandal (1941) **85m.** **½ D: Norman Taurog. Rosalind Russell, Walter Pidgeon, Edward Arnold, Lee Bowman, Jean Rogers, Mary Beth Hughes, Guy Kibbee. Deft performances in comedy of reporter Pidgeon doing sensational story involving prominent female judge Russell.
Designing Woman (1957) **C-118m.** *** D: Vincente Minnelli. Gregory Peck, Lauren Bacall, Dolores Gray, Sam Levene, Mickey Shaughnessy, Chuck Connors, Ed Platt, Jack Cole. Sportswriter and fashion designer marry and run head-on in this chic comedy reminiscent of the great Hepburn-Tracy vehicles. Bacall and Peck do their best; George Wells won an Oscar for Best Story and Screenplay. CinemaScope. ▼●
Desire (1936) **96m.** *** D: Frank Borzage. Marlene Dietrich, Gary Cooper, John Halliday, William Frawley, Ernest Cossart, Akim Tamiroff, Alan Mowbray, Zeffie Tilbury. American car-designer Cooper falls in love with jewel thief Dietrich. Sophisticated romancer set in Spain; Marlene sings "Awake In a Dream." From the scintillating start to the finish, it bears the stylish stamp of its producer, Ernst Lubitsch.▼
Desire and Hell at Sunset Motel (1992) **C-90m.** *½ D: Allen Castle. Sherilyn Fenn, Whip Hubley, David Hewlett, David Johansen, Paul Bartel. A paranoid salesman and his wife stay at a motel in Anaheim, California, on their way to Disneyland, but get involved in blackmail and murder instead. A "comedy noir" set in 1958, this *very* low-budget effort never quite escapes its stage origins. Fenn does look great, however. [PG-13]▼●
Desiree (1954) **C-110m.** **½ D: Henry Koster. Marlon Brando, Jean Simmons, Merle Oberon, Michael Rennie, Cameron Mitchell, Elizabeth Sellars, Cathleen Nesbitt, Richard Deacon, Carolyn Jones. Tepid, elaborate costumer: Brando plays a confused Napoleon, Simmons his seamstress love who marries another man; Oberon is quite lovely as Empress Josephine. Fiction and fact are muddled backdrop for rise and fall of the Emperor; few action scenes. CinemaScope.▼●
Desire in the Dust (1960) **102m.** **½ D: William F. Claxton. Raymond Burr, Martha Hyer, Joan Bennett, Ken Scott. Good casting carries this turgid soaper of a Southern aristocrat with a yen for politics, who tries to hide the shady past of some family members. CinemaScope.
Desire Me (1947) **91m.** ** D: No director credited. Greer Garson, Robert Mitchum, Richard Hart, George Zucco, Morris Ankrum. Weak melodramatic romance with Garson caught between new love and old husband, presumed dead, who returns to make problems. Familiar story not helped by limp script. Directed mostly by George Cukor, who removed his name after studio tampering; Mervyn LeRoy and Jack Conway also had a hand in it.
Desire Under the Elms (1958) **114m.** **½ D: Delbert Mann. Sophia Loren, Anthony Perkins, Burl Ives, Frank Overton. Eugene O'Neill stage piece about family hatred and greed for land. Loren miscast as Ives' young wife in love with stepson Perkins, but she sparks some life into brooding account of 19th-century New England farm story. VistaVision.▼●
Desk Set (1957) **C-103m.** ***½ D: Walter Lang. Spencer Tracy, Katharine Hepburn, Gig Young, Joan Blondell, Dina Merrill, Sue Randall, Neva Patterson, Diane Jergens, Merry Anders. Broadway play becomes a vehicle for Hepburn and Tracy, a guarantee for top entertainment. He's an efficiency expert automating her research department at a TV network; they clash, argue, and fall in love. Great fun. Scripted by Phoebe and Henry Ephron, from the stage play by William Marchant. Merrill's film debut. CinemaScope.▼●
Despair (1979-West German) **C-119m.** *** D: Rainer Werner Fassbinder. Dirk Bogarde, Andrea Ferreol, Volker Spengler, Klaus Lowitsch. Playwright Tom Stoppard's adaptation of the Nabokov novel concentrates too many of its wittiest lines in the first third, but the film still has its moments. Bogarde is brilliant as the Russian émigré who runs a German chocolate factory as Nazis start to take power.▼
Desperado (1995) **C-106m.** ** D: Robert Rodriguez. Antonio Banderas, Joaquim de Almeida, Salma Hayek, Steve Buscemi, Cheech Marin, Quentin Tarantino, Carlos Gomez, Angel Aviles, Danny Trejo, Tito Larriva. A mysterious stranger arrives in a Mexican town, seeking revenge on the local crime boss. Opens with an amusing shaggy-dog sequence featuring Buscemi and Marin and grabs your attention with its hyperkinetic scenes of gunplay, but soon it becomes clear that the film has no story—and no point. Physical attraction of Banderas and leading lady Hayek provides its only pizazz. This is

Rodriguez's reworking of his inventive debut picture, EL MARIACHI. [R]▼●◗

Desperadoes, The (1943) **C-85m.** *** D: Charles Vidor. Randolph Scott, Glenn Ford, Claire Trevor, Evelyn Keyes, Edgar Buchanan, Raymond Walburn, Guinn Williams. Pretty good Western; bandit Ford goes straight, joins forces with marshal Scott to clean up town.▼

Desperados, The (1969) **C-91m.** **½ D: Henry Levin. Vince Edwards, Jack Palance, George Maharis, Neville Brand, Sylvia Syms. Civil War deserters ravage the West. Not bad. [M]▼

Desperados Are in Town, The (1956) **73m.** *½ D: Kurt Neumann. Robert Arthur, Kathy Nolan, Rhys Williams, Rhodes Reason. Bland oater of young man proving his worth by killing outlaws who murdered his friend. Regalscope.

Desperate (1947) **73m.** **½ D: Anthony Mann. Steve Brodie, Audrey Long, Raymond Burr, Douglas Fowley, William Challee, Jason Robards, Sr. An honest truck driver is victimized by racketeers and forced to flee with his wife. Well-made little film noir, if not as good as director Mann's follow-ups (RAW DEAL, T-MEN, etc.). Also shown in computer-colored version.▼

Desperate Chance for Ellery Queen (1942) **70m.** *½ D: James Hogan. William Gargan, Margaret Lindsay, Charley Grapewin, John Litel, Lillian Bond, James Burke, Jack LaRue, Morgan Conway. Gargan's second shot as Queen is no better than the first; he's hired by a woman to find her husband, a missing banker.

Desperate Characters (1971) **C-88m.** *** D: Frank D. Gilroy. Shirley MacLaine, Kenneth Mars, Gerald O'Loughlin, Sada Thompson, Jack Somack, Rose Gregorio, Carol Kane. Story of the horrors of day-to-day living in N.Y.C. is a bit too theatrical but benefits from excellent acting; one of MacLaine's best performances. [R]▼●

Desperate Hours, The (1955) **112m.** ***½ D: William Wyler. Humphrey Bogart, Fredric March, Arthur Kennedy, Martha Scott, Dewey Martin, Gig Young, Mary Murphy, Robert Middleton. Extremely well acted account of escaped convicts terrorizing family household. From Joseph Hayes' novel and Broadway play, inspired by actual events. Remade in 1990. VistaVision. ▼●

Desperate Hours (1990) **C-105m.** *½ D: Michael Cimino. Mickey Rourke, Anthony Hopkins, Mimi Rogers, Lindsay Crouse, Kelly Lynch, Elias Koteas, David Morse, Shawnee Smith, Danny Gerard, Matt McGrath. Ludicrous remake of the better-than-ever 1955 nailbiter, prison escapees Rourke et al. taking over the Hopkins-Rogers household. No suspense, at times laughable use of music, with daughter-victim you'll beg to see coldcocked. Cimino's unmotivated, kamikaze disrobings of attorney Lynch have already entered the realm of modern movie folklore. [R]▼●

Desperate Journey (1942) **107m.** *** D: Raoul Walsh. Errol Flynn, Raymond Massey, Ronald Reagan, Nancy Coleman, Alan Hale, Arthur Kennedy, Albert Basserman. Spirited WW2 drama of American pilots stranded in Germany, struggling to cross border; forgivable propaganda interludes. Wait till you see Reagan doubletalk Nazi.▼

Desperately Seeking Susan (1985) **C-104m.** *** D: Susan Seidelman. Rosanna Arquette, Madonna, Aidan Quinn, Mark Blum, Robert Joy, Laurie Metcalf, Steven Wright, Richard Hell, Ann Magnuson, Richard Edson, John Lurie, Anne Carlisle, John Turturro. Delightfully offbeat, original comedy about a bored suburban housewife whose fascination with a kooky character she's read about in the personal ads leads to her being mistaken for the woman herself. Sort of an upscale underground film, inventively directed by Seidelman, though it doesn't sustain its buoyancy straight to the end. [PG-13]▼●

Desperate Man, The (1959-British) **57m.** *½ D: Peter Maxwell. Jill Ireland, Conrad Phillips, William Hartnell, Charles Gray. Dull yarn of reporter Phillips and gal (Ireland) involved in tracking down a Sussex crook; photography only virtue.

Desperate Measures (1998) **C-105m.** *½ D: Barbet Schroeder. Michael Keaton, Andy Garcia, Marcia Gay Harden, Brian Cox, Joseph Cross. Offensively stupid thriller about San Francisco cop Garcia and the amount of physical damage he unintentionally causes when he finds a potential bone marrow donor for his dying son: hardened con Keaton. About as bad as a movie can get from a reputable filmmaker. Try to figure out how many charges Garcia would eventually be brought up on in real life! [R]▼●◗

Desperate Moment (1953-British) **88m.** **½ D: Compton Bennett. Dirk Bogarde, Mai Zetterling, Philip Friend, Gerard Heinz. Taut melodrama involving displaced person in post-WW2 Berlin falsely accused of homicide; sensibly acted.

Desperate Ones, The (1968-Italian) **C-104m.** **½ D: Alexander Ramati. Maximilian Schell, Raf Vallone, Irene Papas, Theodore Bikel. Siberian labor camp escapees join Polish army. Okay if nothing else is on.

Desperate Search (1952) **73m.** **½ D: Joseph H. Lewis. Howard Keel, Jane Greer, Patricia Medina, Keenan Wynn. Trim film of two kids stranded in Canadian wastelands after plane crash, and their father's efforts to find them.

Desperate Siege SEE: **Rawhide**

Desperate Trail, The (1994) **C-93m.** *** D: P. J. Pesce. Sam Elliott, Craig Sheffer,

Linda Fiorentino, Bradley Whitford, Frank Whaley, John Furlong, Robin Westphal, Boots Southerland. Tough, original Western saga released direct to video, with Elliott as an unforgiving marshal whose plan to deliver Fiorentino to the hangman goes awry when she flees with genteel outlaw Sheffer. Well-written (and well-acted) Western with interesting characters, some potent violence, and surprises in store to the very end of the trail. [R]▼●

Destination Gobi (1953) **C-89m.** **½ D: Robert Wise. Richard Widmark, Don Taylor, Casey Adams, Murvyn Vye, Darryl Hickman, Martin Milner. Unusual WW2 actioner involving U.S. naval men joining forces with natives against Japanese assaults; nice action sequences.

Destination Inner Space (1966) **C-83m.** ** D: Francis D. Lyon. Sheree North, Scott Brady, Gary Merrill, John Howard. Undersea lab encounters an alien spaceship and a pod that grows into an amphibian monster. Routine but competent.

Destination Moon (1950) **C-91m.** **½ D: Irving Pichel. John Archer, Warner Anderson, Tom Powers, Dick Wesson, Erin O'Brien-Moore. One of the pioneer sci-fi films, modestly mounted but still effective. Won an Oscar for its special effects. Produced by George Pal; coscripted by Robert Heinlein. Woody Woodpecker makes a "guest appearance."▼●◗

Destination Saturn (1939) **91m.** **½ D: Ford Beebe, Saul Goodkind. Buster Crabbe, Constance Moore, Jackie Moran, Jack Mulhall, Anthony Warde. Feature version of BUCK ROGERS serial. Buck and Buddy Wade, revived from suspended animation by future Earth scientists, fight Killer Kane and his supergangsters. Uninspired handling of original footage.▼

Destination 60,000 (1957) **65m.** BOMB D: George Waggner. Preston Foster, Pat Conway, Jeff Donnell, Coleen Gray. Worn-out premise: test pilots zoom through space, families wait nervously on the ground.

Destination Tokyo (1943) **135m.** *** D: Delmer Daves. Cary Grant, John Garfield, Alan Hale, John Ridgely, Dane Clark, Warner Anderson, William Prince. Suspenseful WW2 account of U.S. submarine sent into Japanese waters and interaction among crew. Commander Grant, seamen Garfield and Clark ring true. John Forsythe makes his film debut. Also shown in computer-colored version.▼

Destiny (1944) **65m.** ** D: Reginald LeBorg. Gloria Jean, Alan Curtis, Frank Craven, Grace McDonald. Routine study of man sent to prison on homicide charge, and snowballing effects on his life. Expanded from a 30m. sequence originally shot by Julien Duvivier for FLESH AND FANTASY.

Destiny Turns On the Radio (1995) **C-101m.** BOMB D: Jack Baran. Dylan McDermott, Nancy Travis, Quentin Tarantino, James Belushi, James LeGros, Janet Carroll, David Cross, Richard Edson, Bobcat Goldthwait, Barry "Shabaka" Henley, Lisa Jane Persky, Sarah Trigger, Tracey Walter, Allen Garfield. Escaped convict goes to Las Vegas to reclaim his girlfriend and a stash of loot he left with his partner at the Marilyn Motel. However, Fate—in the form of a mysterious dude named Destiny—has its own agenda. Pseudo-hip script, utterly bereft of wit, is directed with no energy. A complete waste of time. [R]▼●

Destroy All Monsters! (1968-Japanese) **C-88m.** ** D: Ishiro Honda. Akira Kubo, Jun Tazaki, Yoshio Tsuchiya, Kyoko Ai. All-star monster cast (from Toho Studios) teams up to combat alien forces bent on destruction. Godzilla, Mothra, Rodan, and other favorites are on hand in this juvenile epic. Tohoscope. [G]▼◗

Destroyer (1943) **99m.** **½ D: William Seiter. Edward G. Robinson, Glenn Ford, Marguerite Chapman, Edgar Buchanan, Leo Gorcey, Regis Toomey, Ed Brophy. Predictable wartime drama: aging seaman Robinson shown up by novice Ford; of course Eddie comes through in the end. ▼

Destructors, The (1968) **C-97m.** ** D: Francis D. Lyon. Richard Egan, Patricia Owens, John Ericson, Michael Ansara, Joan Blackman, David Brian. Programmer nonsense with federal agent Egan investigating the theft of rubies needed to operate a deadly laser-ray gun. This sat on the shelf for two years before its release.

Destructors, The (1974-British) **C-89m.** *** D: Robert Parrish. Anthony Quinn, Michael Caine, James Mason, Maureen Kerwin, Marcel Bozzufi, Maurice Ronet, Alexandra Stewart. Good Paris-localed crime melodrama with Quinn a U.S. drug agent out to stop kingpin Mason. An animated Caine is fine as a likable assassin. Original title: THE MARSEILLE CONTRACT. [PG]▼

Destry (1954) **C-95m.** **½ D: George Marshall. Audie Murphy, Mari Blanchard, Lyle Bettger, Lori Nelson, Thomas Mitchell, Edgar Buchanan, Wallace Ford. Audie is gun-shy sheriff who tames town and dance-hall girl without violence. The 1939 version—DESTRY RIDES AGAIN—is still unsurpassed. Later a TV series.

Destry Rides Again (1939) **94m.** **** D: George Marshall. James Stewart, Marlene Dietrich, Charles Winninger, Brian Donlevy, Una Merkel, Mischa Auer, Allen Jenkins, Irene Hervey, Jack Carson, Billy Gilbert, Samuel S. Hinds. Slam-bang, action-filled Western satire, with Stewart taming rowdy town without violence and tangling with boisterous dance-hall girl Dietrich. Marlene sings "See What the Boys in the Back Room Will Have" in this Max Brand story, filmed before in 1932, then again in 1950 (as FRENCHIE), and in 1954 (as DESTRY). Screenplay by Felix Jackson, Gertrude Purcell, and Henry Myers. Simply wonderful.▼●

Detective, The (1954-British) **91m.** *** D: Robert Hamer. Alec Guinness, Joan Greenwood, Peter Finch, Cecil Parker, Bernard Lee, Sidney James, Ernest Thesiger. Guinness is in rare form as G. K. Chesterton's clerical sleuth after stolen art treasures; another British gem, superbly cast. British title: FATHER BROWN.▼

Detective, The (1968) **C-114m.** *** D: Gordon Douglas. Frank Sinatra, Lee Remick, Ralph Meeker, Jacqueline Bisset, William Windom, Al Freeman, Tony Musante, Jack Klugman, Robert Duvall. Trashy script, based on Roderick Thorpe's best-selling novel, pits cops against homosexuals; more than redeemed by fast, no-nonsense direction, good acting, particularly by Sinatra and Freeman. Panavision. ▼●

Detective (1985-French) **C-95m.** ** D: Jean-Luc Godard. Claude Brasseur, Nathalie Baye, Johnny Hallyday, Laurent Terzieff, Jean-Pierre Léaud, Alain Cuny, Stephane Ferrara, Julie Delpy. The scenario takes a backseat in this talky, contrived film noir homage about a variety of characters and their business and intrigues in an elegant Paris hotel. The look and feel are uniquely of the director, but it's ultimately annoying, more a concept than a movie. Godard dedicated this to John Cassavetes, Edgar G. Ulmer, and Clint Eastwood!▼

Detective Kitty O'Day (1944) **63m.** ** D: William Beaudine. Jean Parker, Peter Cookson, Tim Ryan, Veda Ann Borg. Parker adds bubbly zest as amateur sleuth who sets out to solve a crime; pleasant fluff on low-budget scale.

Detective Story (1951) **103m.** ***½ D: William Wyler. Kirk Douglas, Eleanor Parker, Horace McMahon, William Bendix, Lee Grant, Craig Hill, Cathy O'Donnell, Bert Freed, George Macready, Joseph Wiseman, Gladys George, Frank Faylen, Luis van Rooten, Warner Anderson. Sidney Kingsley's once-forceful play about life at a N.Y.C. police precinct has lost much of its punch, but is still a fine film. Well cast, with Douglas a bitter detective, Parker his ignored wife, and Bendix, in one of his best roles, a sympathetic colleague. McMahon (the shrewd precinct head), Wiseman (an hysterical thief), and Grant (unforgettable as a frightened shoplifter) recreate their Broadway roles. This was Grant's first film—and also her last—before being blacklisted. Screenplay by Philip Yordan and Robert Wyler (the director's brother).

Deterrence (2000) **C-101m.** *** D: Rod Lurie. Kevin Pollak, Timothy Hutton, Sheryl Lee Ralph, Sean Astin, Bajda Djola, Mark Thompson, Michael Mantell. Absorbing brinkmanship thriller in the vein of FAIL-SAFE, with Pollak (admittedly, an unlikely choice for President of the U.S.) stranded in a Colorado diner during a snowstorm, having to make a tough decision about firing a nuclear weapon, and involving the civilians who happen to be there in the mounting drama. Contrived but exciting; feature writing-directing debut for film critic Lurie. [R]▼

Detonator SEE: **Death Train**

Detour (1945) **69m.** **½ D: Edgar G. Ulmer. Tom Neal, Ann Savage, Claudia Drake, Edmund MacDonald, Tim Ryan, Esther Howard. Intriguing melodrama about hitchhiker Neal, who gets involved with femme fatale Savage, and murder. Ultracheap movie has deserved cult following. Remade in 1992, with Tom Neal, Jr. ▼●

Detroit Heat SEE: **Detroit 9000**

Detroit 9000 (1973) **C-106m.** *½ D: Arthur Marks. Alex Rocco, Hari Rhodes, Vonetta McGee, Ella Edwards, Scatman Crothers. Cops pursue jewel thieves. Bloody blaxploitation entry with an integrated cast. Aka DETROIT HEAT. Panavision. [R]▼●

Detroit Rock City (1999) **C-94m.** **½ D: Adam Rifkin. Edward Furlong, Giuseppe Andrews, James De Bello, Sam Huntington, Lin Shaye, Natasha Lyonne, Shannon Tweed, Joe Flaherty, KISS. Ultra-dopey teen flick about four teenagers trying to scam tickets for a KISS concert, circa 1978. Lots of crude physical comedy and head-banging metal anthems, but that's precisely the point. Plays like a cross between I WANNA HOLD YOUR HAND and an episode of *That '70s Show.* Shaye's a hoot as a bewigged mom on a crusade to stop rock 'n' roll. The original tongue-wagging glam rockers appear only briefly at the end. Super 35. [R]▼◗

Deuce Bigalow: Male Gigolo (1999) **C-88m.** **½ D: Mike Mitchell. Rob Schneider, William Forsythe, Eddie Griffin, Arija Bareikis, Oded Fehr, Gail O'Grady, Richard Riehle, Jacqueline Obradors, Big Boy. Professional fish-tank cleaner breaks an expensive tank, and in order to pay for it becomes a gigolo. (Why not?) Potty humor and outlandish situations abound, but Schneider's character is surprisingly likable in this silly comedy. [R]▼◗

Devil, The SEE: **To Bed . . . Or Not To Bed**

Devil and Daniel Webster, The (1941) **85m.** ***½ D: William Dieterle. Edward Arnold, Walter Huston, James Craig, Anne Shirley, Jane Darwell, Simone Simon, Gene Lockhart, John Qualen, H.B. Warner. Stephen Vincent Benet's story is a visual delight, with Huston's sparkling performance as Mr. Scratch (the Devil) matched by Arnold as the loquacious Webster. Oscar-winning score by Bernard Herrmann, cinematography by Joseph August, and special effects by Vernon L. Walker all superb. Screenplay by the author and Dan Totheroh. Cut for reissue in 1952; restored to 107m. on video and laserdisc, adding interesting material missing from other extant prints. Aka ALL THAT MONEY CAN BUY and DANIEL AND THE DEVIL. ▼●

Devil and Max Devlin, The (1981) **C-96m.** ** D: Steven Hilliard Stern. Elliott Gould, Bill Cosby, Susan Anspach, Adam Rich, Julie Budd, David Knell. Gould returns to life to recruit three innocent souls for devil Cosby. Undistinguished Disney fare. [PG]▼

Devil and Miss Jones, The (1941) **92m.** ***½ D: Sam Wood. Jean Arthur, Robert Cummings, Charles Coburn, Spring Byington, Edmund Gwenn, S.Z. Sakall, William Demarest. Delightful social comedy by Norman Krasna; millionaire Coburn masquerades as clerk in his own department store to investigate employee complaints. A must.▼

Devil and the Deep (1932) **70m.** **½ D: Marion Gering. Tallulah Bankhead, Gary Cooper, Charles Laughton, Cary Grant, Paul Porcasi. Overplayed but lush melodrama of Bankhead, her suitors Grant and Cooper, and jealous husband, submarine commander Laughton.

Devil and the Ten Commandments, The (1962-French) **143m.** **½ D: Julien Duvivier. Michel Simon, Lucien Baroux, Claude Nollier, Dany Saval, Charles Aznavour. Episodic film in ten parts illustrating each of the commandments—too often superficial instead of cynical. Franscope.

Devil at 4 O'Clock, The (1961) **C-126m.** **½ D: Mervyn LeRoy. Spencer Tracy, Frank Sinatra, Jean-Pierre Aumont, Kerwin Mathews, Barbara Luna. Static production, not saved by volcanic eruption climax, involving priest Tracy helping to evacuate children's hospital in midst of lava flow. Stars are lost in weak film.▼●

Devil Bat, The (1941) **69m.** ** D: Jean Yarbrough. Bela Lugosi, Suzanne Kaaren, Dave O'Brien, Guy Usher, Yolande Mallott, Donald Kerr. Lugosi raises bats and trains them to suck victim's blood on cue. One of Lugosi's more notorious pictures, and fairly entertaining. Aka KILLER BATS. Remade as THE FLYING SERPENT. Sequel: DEVIL BAT'S DAUGHTER. ▼●◗

Devil Bat's Daughter (1946) **66m.** ** D: Frank Wisbar. Rosemary La Planche, Molly Lamont, John James, Ed Cassidy. In this sequel to THE DEVIL BAT, La Planche is thought to have inherited the murderous tendencies of her late father, but in a bizarre turn of events, Dad turns out to have been a kindly researcher (contradicting the first film entirely!).▼

Devil Commands, The (1941) **65m.** **½ D: Edward Dmytryk. Boris Karloff, Amanda Duff, Richard Fiske, Anne Revere, Ralph Penny, Dorothy Adams, Kenneth MacDonald. Improbable but intriguing chiller of scientist Karloff obsessed with idea of communicating with dead wife. Predictable but fun. Only debit: the absurd narration.

Devil Dogs of the Air (1935) **86m.** ** D: Lloyd Bacon. James Cagney, Pat O'Brien, Margaret Lindsay, Frank McHugh. Tiresome potboiler with Marine Air Corps rivalry between Cagney and O'Brien. Their personalities, and good stunt-flying scenes, are only saving grace.▼

Devil-Doll, The (1936) **79m.** *** D: Tod Browning. Lionel Barrymore, Maureen O'Sullivan, Frank Lawton, Robert Greig, Lucy Beaumont, Henry B. Walthall, Grace Ford, Rafaela Ottiano. Very entertaining yarn of Devil's Island escapee Barrymore shrinking humans to doll-size to carry out nefarious schemes. Coscripted by Erich von Stroheim.▼●

Devil Doll (1964-British) **80m.** *** D: Lindsay Shonteff. Bryant Halliday, William Sylvester, Yvonne Romain, Philip Ray. Obscure, underrated mystery features an eerily effective Halliday as a hypnotist-ventriloquist trying to transfer Romain's soul into that of a dummy, as he had already done with his onetime assistant. An exquisitely tailored, sharply edited sleeper.▼

Devil Girl From Mars (1954-British) **77m.** *½ D: David MacDonald. Patricia Laffan, Hugh McDermott, Hazel Court, Adrienne Corri, Peter Reynolds, Joseph Tomelty, John Laurie. Clad in black leather, Laffan lands in remote Scotland with her refrigeratorlike robot, hunting for human husbands! Hilariously solemn, high-camp British imitation of U.S. cheapies would be even funnier if it weren't rather dull and set-bound.▼

Devil Goddess (1955) **70m.** *½ D: Spencer Bennet. Johnny Weissmuller, Angela Stevens, Selmer Jackson, William Tannen, Ed Hinton. Weissmuller helps a professor look for an ex-colleague who's set himself up as a "god." The end of the vine for *Jungle Jim* Weissmuller, who retired from the big screen after this.

Devil in a Blue Dress (1995) **C-102m.** **½ D: Carl Franklin. Denzel Washington, Tom Sizemore, Jennifer Beals, Don Cheadle, Maury Chaykin, Terry Kinney, Mel Winkler, Albert Hall, Lisa Nicole Carson, Jernard Burks. It's L.A., 1948; Washington is unemployed and thus easy prey for a hood who needs a favor done. All he has to do is find an elusive white woman, the former fiancée of a mayoral candidate. The film is oozing with atmosphere and period detail, but its look and feel overwhelm the convoluted (and not always compelling) story. Washington is terrific in a tailor-made part as Easy Rawlins; adapted from Walter

Mosley's novel. Black point of view is the film's strong suit, making it unique in the film noir genre. [R] ▼●◗

Devil in Love, The (1966-Italian) **97m.** *½ D: Ettore Scola. Vittorio Gassman, Mickey Rooney, Claudine Auger, Ettore Manni, Annabella Incontrera. Gassman comes up from Hell during the French Renaissance to botch up an impending peace between Rome and Florence, but loses his powers when he falls for Auger. Comedy is both heavy-handed and unfunny.

Devil in the Flesh (1946-French) **110m.** ***½ D: Claude Autant-Lara. Gérard Philipe, Micheline Presle, Denise Grey, Jacques Tati. Exquisitely filmed, compassionate story of WW1 love affair between married woman and sensitive high school student. Controversial in its day because of sensual love scenes and cuckolding of soldier husband. Remade in 1986.▼

Devil in the Flesh (1986-Italian-French) **C-110m.** *** D: Marco Bellocchio. Maruschka Detmers, Federico Pitzalis, Anita Laurenzi, Riccardo De Torrebruna. Director Bellocchio remakes and updates the 1946 French classic as another of his studies of madness. Dutch actress Detmers burns up the screen as the going-nutty beauty torn between her terrorist boyfriend (De Torrebruna) and a handsome young boy (Pitzalis). Reportedly the first mainstream film in which a respected actress was involved in an explicitly pornographic sex scene. Available in both R- and X-rated versions.▼●

Devil in the House of Exorcism SEE: **Lisa and the Devil**

Devil Is a Sissy, The (1936) **92m.** **½ D: W. S. Van Dyke. Freddie Bartholomew, Mickey Rooney, Jackie Cooper, Ian Hunter, Peggy Conklin, Katherine Alexander. Three top juvenile stars outclass their material in this rambling, episodic tale of tenement-district pals and British newcomer (Bartholomew) who tries to join their gang.

Devil Is a Woman, The (1935) **83m.** *** D: Josef von Sternberg. Marlene Dietrich, Lionel Atwill, Cesar Romero, Edward Everett Horton, Alison Skipworth. Sumptuous-looking film about alluring but heartless woman and the men who all but ruin their lives for her, set against backdrop of 19th-century Spanish revolution. Hypnotic, if dramatically shaky; Luis Buñuel used same source material for THAT OBSCURE OBJECT OF DESIRE.▼

Devil Is a Woman, The (1975-Italian) **C-105m.** BOMB D: Damiano Damiani. Glenda Jackson, Adolfo Celi, Lisa Harrow, Claudio Cassinelli, Arnoldo Foa, Francisco Rabal. Ponderous, superficial melodrama: Jackson, the head of a religious hostel, casts spells over its "permanent residents." The convent is more like a psycho ward than a place for religious meditation. Indifferently acted, technically atrocious. Widescreen. [R]▼

Devil Makes Three, The (1952) **96m.** ** D: Andrew Marton. Gene Kelly, Pier Angeli, Richard Egan, Claus Clausen. Kelly (none too convincing in one of his rare nonmusicals) plays a soldier returning to Munich to thank family who helped him during WW2; he becomes involved with daughter Angeli and black market gangs.

Devil on Horseback (1954-British) **89m.** ** D: Cyril Frankel. Googie Withers, John McCallum, Jeremy Spenser, Liam Redmond, Meredith Edwards, Sam Kydd, Vic Wise, George Rose. Inconsequential racing yarn, with talented but cocky teen apprentice jockey Spenser attempting to bully his way to success. Coproduced by John Grierson.▼

Devil Pays Off (1941) **56m.** ** D: John H. Auer. J. Edward Bromberg, Osa Massen, William Wright, Margaret Tallichet. Meager account of one-time navy man trying to redeem his honor by tracking down espionage agents within the naval service.

Devils, The (1971-British) **C-109m.** **½ D: Ken Russell. Oliver Reed, Vanessa Redgrave, Dudley Sutton, Max Adrian, Gemma Jones, Murray Melvin, Michael Gothard. Fine performances save confused mixture of history, comedy, and surrealism in wide-eyed adaptation of Whiting play and Huxley book dealing with witchcraft and politics in 17th-century France. A mad movie, with fiery finale not for the squeamish. Original British version is 12 minutes longer. Panavision. [R—edited from original X version]▼

Devil's Advocate, The (1997) **C-144m.** *** D: Taylor Hackford. Al Pacino, Keanu Reeves, Charlize Theron, Jeffrey Jones, Judith Ivey, Connie Nielsen, Craig T. Nelson, Tamara Tunie, Debra Monk, Heather Matarazzo. Wild, over-the-top movie about a young hotshot lawyer from Florida who's recruited to join a sleek N.Y.C. firm run by a charming megalomaniac (Pacino) who earmarks the newcomer for Big Things. But there are devilish hints that all is not right. Reeves is completely believable, and Pacino gives a delicious, pull-out-the-stops performance as his manipulative mentor. The film goes on too long, but it's spiked with arresting scenes and fine performances. Great showcase, too, for Theron as Reeves' impressionable wife. Delroy Lindo appears unbilled. Panavision. [R]▼●◗

Devil's Angels (1967) **C-84m.** *½ D: Daniel Haller. John Cassavetes, Beverly Adams, Mimsy Farmer, Leo Gordon. Killer cyclists head for outlaw sanctuary breaking everything in their way. Lurid and cheap. Panavision. [PG]▼

Devil's Arithmetic, The (1999) **C-95m.** **TVM** D: Donna Deitch. Kirsten Dunst, Brittany Murphy, Paul Freeman, Mimi Rogers,

Louise Fletcher. Mall-hopping suburban teen Dunst learns a powerful lesson about her Jewish heritage when she's time-warped back from her family's Passover seder table to German-occupied Poland in 1941. There, she discovers friendship and life's meaning in a concentration camp. Adapted by Robert J. Avrech from popular 1988 novel by Jane Yolen that is now standard reading in many high schools. Dustin Hoffman (who isn't in it) and Mimi Rogers (who is) executive produced. Made for cable. Above average. ▼

Devil's Bait (1959-British) **58m.** *½ D: Peter Graham Scott. Geoffrey Keen, Jane Hylton, Gordon Jackson, Dermot Kelly. Intriguing if leisurely paced B film, about baker and his wife who accidentally put poison in their wares, trying to find purchasers.

Devil's Bride, The (1968-British) **C-95m.** *** D: Terence Fisher. Christopher Lee, Charles Gray, Nike Arrighi, Patrick Mower, Sarah Lawson, Paul Eddington. Taut filming of Dennis Wheatley novel. Duc de Richleau (Lee) assists young friend under spell of Mocate, ultra-evil Satanist. Watch out for that climax! British title: THE DEVIL RIDES OUT. [G]▼

Devil's Brigade, The (1968) **C-130m.** ** D: Andrew V. McLaglen. William Holden, Cliff Robertson, Vince Edwards, Michael Rennie, Dana Andrews, Carroll O'Connor, Gretchen Wyler, Andrew Prine, Claude Akins, Richard Jaeckel, Paul Hornung, Patric Knowles, James Craig, Richard Dawson. Standard WW2 fare about reckless recruits fashioned into creditable fighting unit; goes on far too long. Holden is wasted. Panavision.▼●

Devil's Brother, The (1933) **88m.** *** D: Hal Roach, Charles R. Rogers. Stan Laurel, Oliver Hardy, Dennis King, Thelma Todd, James Finlayson, Henry Armetta. L&H adaptation of operetta with King as romantic lead—a famous bandit, the boys as would-be assistants. One of their best. Originally titled FRA DIAVOLO. Aka BOGUS BANDITS.▼●

Devil's Canyon (1953) **C-92m.** ** D: Alfred L. Werker. Virginia Mayo, Dale Robertson, Stephen McNally, Arthur Hunnicutt. Former marshal put in prison for shoot-outs, where he's entangled in prison riot. Photographed in 3-D.▼

Devil's Cargo, The (1948) **61m.** *½ D: John F. Link. John Calvert, Rochelle Hudson, Roscoe Karns, Lyle Talbot, Tom Kennedy, Theodore Von Eltz. Poverty-row continuation of *The Falcon* series; mundane murder mystery showcasing Calvert's magic act skills.▼

Devil's Commandment, The (1957-Italian) **90m.** **½ D: Riccardo Freda. Gianna Maria Canale, Antoine Balpetre, Paul Muller, Carlo Dangelo, Wandisa Guida. A reporter in Paris investigates a string of murders in which women's bodies are drained of blood. This stylish yarn started the trend of gothic Italian horrors of the 1950s and 1960s. Photographed by Mario Bava (who also codirected, sans credit). Beware of 70m. version which inserts bogus footage shot by the American distributor (featuring Al Lewis!). Originally titled I VAMPIRI. CinemaScope.▼

Devil's Daffodil, The (1961-British) **86m.** ** D: Akos Rathony. William Lucas, Penelope Horner, Christopher Lee, Ingrid van Bergen, Albert Lieven. Flabby entry in Edgar Wallace series, involving a rash of murders linked with dope smuggling. Retitled: DAFFODIL KILLER.

Devil's Disciple, The (1959-British) **82m.** ***½ D: Guy Hamilton. Burt Lancaster, Kirk Douglas, Laurence Olivier, Janette Scott, Eva LeGallienne, Harry Andrews, Basil Sydney, George Rose, Neil McCallum, David Horne, Mervyn Johns. Sparkling adaptation of George Bernard Shaw's satire, set during American Revolution, with standout performances by star trio (notably Olivier as General Burgoyne, who serves as Shaw's mouthpiece). Shows how, in Shaw's view, the bumbling British managed to lose their colonies. Screenplay by John Dighton and Roland Kibbee.▼

Devil's Doorway (1950) **84m.** *** D: Anthony Mann. Robert Taylor, Louis Calhern, Paula Raymond, Marshall Thompson, Edgar Buchanan. Well-turned Western with offbeat casting of Taylor as Indian who served in Civil War, returning home to find that he must fight to right the injustices done against his people.

Devil's Eight, The (1969) **C-97m.** ** D: Burt Topper. Christopher George, Fabian, Ralph Meeker, Leslie Parrish. Federal agent helps six convicts escape from road gang to train them to smash moonshine rings. Undistinguished. [M]

Devil's Eye, The (1960-Swedish) **90m.** *** D: Ingmar Bergman. Jarl Kulle, Bibi Andersson, Nils Poppe, Sture Lagerwall. A woman's chastity gives the Devil sty in his eye, so he sends Don Juan back to Earth from Hell to seduce her, but the modern-day woman finds his old-fashioned charm amusing rather than irresistible. Droll Bergman comedy is a bit slow, but witty and playful.▼

Devil's General, The (1956-German) **C-120m.** ***½ D: Helmut Kautner. Curt Jurgens, Marianne Cook (Koch), Victor De Kowa, Karl John, Eva-Ingeborg Scholz, Albert Lieven. Jurgens is outstanding as a German war hero aviator who becomes disenchanted with Hitler and Nazism. Allegedly based on fact.▼

Devil's Hairpin, The (1957) **C-82m.** **½ D: Cornel Wilde. Cornel Wilde, Jean Wallace, Mary Astor, Arthur Franz. Wilde is reckless sports car champion who learns

fair play on the track; obligatory racing scenes are above average. VistaVision.
Devil's Henchman, The (1949) **69m.** ** D: Seymour Friedman. Warner Baxter, Mary Beth Hughes, Mike Mazurki, Harry Shannon. In this programmer, Baxter sets out to capture waterfront gang and becomes involved in murder.
Devil-Ship Pirates (1964-British) **C-89m.** **½ D: Don Sharp, Christopher Lee, Andrew Keir, Michael Ripper, John Cairney. Good little movie of stray Spanish ships conquering English countryside, unaware Armada has been defeated. Megascope.
Devil's Impostor, The SEE: **Pope Joan**
Devil's in Love, The (1933) **71m.** **½ D: William Dieterle. Loretta Young, Victor Jory, Vivienne Osborne, C. Henry Gordon, David Manners, J. Carrol Naish. Very odd, well-made film about doctor falsely accused of murder, efforts to clear his name. Bela Lugosi has good, small role as prosecuting attorney.
Devil's Island (1940) **62m.** **½ D: William Clemens. Boris Karloff, Nedda Harrigan, James Stephenson, Adia Kuznetzoff, Will Stanton, Edward Keane. Above-average Karloff vehicle of innocent doctor exiled to Devil's Island, mistreated by supervisor Stephenson, saved in twist finish.
Devil's Mask, The (1946) **66m.** ** D: Henry Levin. Jim Bannon, Anita Louise, Michael Duane, Mona Barrie, Ludwig Donath, Barton Yarborough. OK entry in short-lived I LOVE A MYSTERY series with Bannon as Jack Packard, Yarborough as Doc Young. Far-fetched story involving shrunken heads and murder is intriguing but spoiled by obvious identity of killer.
Devil's Men, The SEE: **Land of the Minotaur**
Devil's Messenger (1962-U.S.-Swedish) **72m.** *½ D: Curt Siodmak. Lon Chaney (Jr.), Karen Kadler, John Crawford, Michael Hinn. Sultry girl is sent to earth to help Satan carry out master plan that will envelop the world; hazy plot, poor production values. Originally three episodes of unsold TV series *13 Demon Street.*▼
Devil's Own, The (1966-British) **C-90m.** *** D: Cyril Frankel. Joan Fontaine, Kay Walsh, Alec McCowen, Ann Bell, Ingrid Brett, Gwen ffrangcon-Davies. Good Hammer chiller with Fontaine as headmistress of private school who learns that a student is to be sacrificed by a local voodoo cult. British title: THE WITCHES.▼
Devil's Own, The (1997) **C-110m.** **½ D: Alan J. Pakula. Harrison Ford, Brad Pitt, Margaret Colin, Ruben Blades, Treat Williams, George Hearn, Mitchell Ryan, Natascha McElhone, Simon Jones, Julia Stiles. Young Irish terrorist comes to N.Y.C. to broker an arms deal, and gets room and board from a straight-arrow cop who has no idea who he is. Watchable film has two charismatic stars playing deeply committed characters; their separate stories build in intensity, but when their lives finally intersect the story peters out. Panavision. [R] ▼●◗
Devil's Party, The (1938) **65m.** ** D: Ray McCarey. Victor McLaglen, William Gargan, Paul Kelly, Beatrice Roberts, Frank Jenks, Samuel S. Hinds. So-so melodrama of former Hell's Kitchen pals who reunite once a year . . . except this year one of them is murdered.▼
Devil's Playground (1937) **74m.** **½: D. Erle C. Kenton. Richard Dix, Dolores Del Rio, Chester Morris, Pierre Watkin, Ward Bond. Good combination of action and romance with diver Dix discovering wife Del Rio in love with Morris; exciting underwater climax. Remake of 1928 Frank Capra film SUBMARINE.
Devil's Playground, The (1976-Australian) **C-107m.** *** D: Fred Schepisi. Arthur Dignam, Nick Tate, Simon Burke, Charles McCallum, John Frawley, Jonathan Hardy, Gerry Duggan. Young boys reaching puberty act out sexually while boarded at Roman Catholic school; meanwhile, their teachers have problems of their own. Pointed and well made, if a bit predictable.▼
Devil's Rain, The (1975) **C-85m.** **½ D: Robert Feust. Ernest Borgnine, Ida Lupino, William Shatner, Tom Skerritt, Eddie Albert, Keenan Wynn, Joan Prather. Offbeat approach to story of devil worshippers provides some effective horror and also some unintentional humor. Most of the cast melts in a memorable finale. John Travolta makes his debut in a bit part. Todd-AO 35. [PG]▼●◗
Devil's Undead, The SEE: **Nothing but the Night**
Devil's Wanton, The (1949-Swedish) **72m.** **½ D: Ingmar Bergman. Doris Svedlund, Birger Malmsten, Eva Henning, Hasse Ekman. Sober account of desperate girl finding romance with another equally unhappy soul, reaffirming their faith in humanity. Not released in U.S. until 1962.▼
Devil's Widow, The SEE: **Ballad of Tam Lin, The**
Devil Thumbs a Ride, The (1947) **62m.** **½ D: Felix Feist. Lawrence Tierney, Ted North, Nan Leslie, Betty Lawford, Andrew Tombes, Harry Shannon. Tierney, a "slap-happy bird with a gun," commits robbery and murder, then hitches a ride with friendly, tipsy North. Fast-paced B film.▼
Devil Times Five (1974) **90m.** **½ D: Sean McGregor. Gene Evans, Sorrell Booke, Shelley Morrison, Dawn Lyn, Leif Garrett, Taylor Lacher. Five children who escape from state mental institution take refuge in Evans' winter retreat and terrorize its inhabitants. Not bad. Originally released as PEOPLETOYS; aka PEOPLE TOYS and THE HORRIBLE HOUSE ON THE HILL. [R]▼

Devil to Pay, The (1930) **73m.** **½ D: George Fitzmaurice. Ronald Colman, Loretta Young, David Torrence, Myrna Loy, Mary Forbes, Paul Cavanagh. Early talkie shows its age, but Colman is fine in this drawing-room comedy.●

Devil Within Her, The (1975-British) **C-90m.** *½ D: Peter Sasdy. Joan Collins, Eileen Atkins, Donald Pleasence, Ralph Bates, Caroline Munro, Hilary Mason, John Steiner. Collins's newborn baby is possessed. Another idiotic ROSEMARY'S BABY/EXORCIST rip-off. Aka I DON'T WANT TO BE BORN. [R]▼

Devonsville Terror, The (1983) **C-82m.** ** D: Ulli Lommel. Suzanna Love, Robert Walker, Donald Pleasence, Paul Wilson. Love (wife of German director Lommel) is the new teacher in the town of Devonsville, a burg haunted by a witch's curse from 300 years ago. Copycat horror film steals its climax directly from RAIDERS OF THE LOST ARK.▼◗

Devotion (1946) **107m.** **½ D: Curtis Bernhardt. Olivia de Havilland, Ida Lupino, Paul Henreid, Sydney Greenstreet, Nancy Coleman, Arthur Kennedy, Dame May Whitty. Powerful real-life story of Brontë sisters becomes routine love triangle with Henreid in the middle; worthwhile for intense, dramatic performances. Made in 1943.

D. I., The (1957) **106m.** **½ D: Jack Webb. Jack Webb, Don Dubbins, Lin McCarthy, Jackie Loughery, Monica Lewis, Virginia Gregg, Barbara Pepper. Ostensibly realistic account of Marine basic training is today a wonderful exercise in high camp. Webb is emotionally empty sergeant trying to whip his raw recruits (most of them played by actual soldiers) into shape; stubborn Dubbins is the chief thorn in his side. Sequence where soldiers search for a "murdered" sand flea is priceless. Story reused 13 years later (but with a different outcome) for a TVM, TRIBES.▼

Diabolical Dr. Mabuse, The SEE: **Thousand Eyes of Dr. Mabuse, The**

Diabolik SEE **Danger: Diabolik**

Diabolique (1955-French) **114m.** ***½ D: Henri-Georges Clouzot. Simone Signoret, Vera Clouzot, Paul Meurisse, Charles Vanel, Michel Serrault. Tyrannical schoolmaster (Meurisse) is bumped off by his long-suffering wife (Clouzot) and mistress (Signoret). Classic chiller builds slowly, surely to final quarter hour that will drive you right up the wall. A must. Older American prints run 107m. Aka LES DIABOLIQUES; remade for U.S. TV as REFLECTIONS OF MURDER (1974) and HOUSE OF SECRETS (1993), and for theaters in 1996. Rereleased theatrically in 1994 with 9m. of footage edited out of original U.S. theatrical version.▼●◗

Diabolique (1996) **C-107m.** *½ D: Jeremiah Chechik. Sharon Stone, Isabelle Adjani, Chazz Palminteri, Kathy Bates, Spalding Gray, Shirley Knight, Allen Garfield, Adam Hann-Byrd, Clea Lewis. Top-notch cast founders in this amazingly monotonous (not to mention crude and embarrassing) redo of the 1955 classic, with Palminteri cast as the unmerciful schoolmaster, Stone his icy, murderous mistress, and Adjani his more reserved wife. This dreary film thoroughly trashes the memory of the original—and even the made-for-TV remakes! [R]▼●

Diagnosis: Murder (1975-British) **C-95m.** *** D: Sidney Hayers. Christopher Lee, Judy Geeson, Jon Finch, Tony Beckley, Dilys Hamlett, Jane Merrow. Psychiatrist is drawn into bizarre sequence of events when his wife disappears and he is accused of murdering her. Solid little suspenser.

Dial M for Murder (1954) **C-105m.** *** D: Alfred Hitchcock. Ray Milland, Grace Kelly, Robert Cummings, John Williams, Anthony Dawson. Frederick Knott's suspense play of man plotting wife's murder and subsequent police investigation: stagey at times but slick and entertaining. Filmed in 3-D. Remade for TV in 1981 with Angie Dickinson and Christopher Plummer, and in 1998 as A PERFECT MURDER.▼●

Dial 1119 (1950) **75m.** ** D: Gerald Mayer. Marshall Thompson, Virginia Field, Andrea King, Sam Levene, Keefe Brasselle. Modest suspenser hinged on plot of killer holding a group of bar patrons hostage.

Diamond Earrings SEE: **Earrings of Madame de . . . , The**

Diamond Head (1963) **C-107m.** **½ D: Guy Green. Charlton Heston, Yvette Mimieux, George Chakiris, France Nuyen, James Darren, Aline MacMahon, Elizabeth Allen. Soap opera set in Hawaii with Heston the domineering head of his family, whose dictates almost ruin their lives. Panavision.▼●

Diamond Horseshoe (1945) **C-104m.** **½ D: George Seaton. Betty Grable, Dick Haymes, Phil Silvers, William Gaxton, Beatrice Kay, Carmen Cavallaro, Margaret Dumont. Musical performer Grable has to choose between a long-cherished dream of luxury and life with struggling med student-cum-singer Haymes. Colorful escapism, with good Harry Warren–Mack Gordon songs: "The More I See You," "I Wish I Knew." Original title: BILLY ROSE'S DIAMOND HORSESHOE.

Diamond Hunters (1956-French-Mexican) **C-92m.** *** D: Luis Buñuel. Simone Signoret, Georges Marchal, Charles Vanel, Michele Girardon, Michel Piccoli, Tito Junco. Fleeing an unspecified Fascist state, a ragged group—including a prostitute, a miner, and a priest—embark on a surreal trek through the jungles of South America. This may have merely been a "commercial chore" for the great Buñuel, but it's fascinating nonetheless. Originally titled LA

MORT EN CE JARDIN at 97m; also known as GINA and EVIL EDEN.

Diamond Jim (1935) **93m.** *** D: A. Edward Sutherland. Edward Arnold, Jean Arthur, Binnie Barnes, Cesar Romero, Eric Blore. Big-budget biography of eccentric millionaire of 19th century whose appetite for money is only matched by love of food and Lillian Russell; Arthur has dual role in recreation of Gay 90s era. Most entertaining. Screenplay by Preston Sturges.

Diamond Lust SEE: **Kingfisher Caper, The**

Diamond Queen, The (1953) **C-80m.** ** D: John Brahm. Fernando Lamas, Arlene Dahl, Gilbert Roland, Michael Ansara. Dahl is dazzling title figure over whom Lamas and Roland fight in costumer set in India.

Diamonds (1975-Israeli) **C-101m.** ** D: Menahem Golan. Robert Shaw, Richard Roundtree, Shelley Winters, Barbara (Hershey) Seagull, Shai K. Ophir. OK heist movie with Shaw in dual role, as diamond merchant who masterminds break-in at Tel Aviv diamond vault, and twin brother who designed the security system there. Good location work in Tel Aviv and Jerusalem. [PG]▼

Diamonds (1999) **C-91m.** *** D: John Asher. Kirk Douglas, Dan Aykroyd, Corbin Allred, Lauren Bacall, Kurt Fuller, Jenny McCarthy, Mariah O'Brien, John Landis. An elderly ex-boxer goes on a trip with his alienated son and loving grandson that winds up in Reno, where he searches for diamonds he stashed away decades ago. A tailor-made vehicle for Douglas makes excellent use of his macho image, his movie past (through clips from CHAMPION showing him in the ring), and even his real-life stroke in telling its likable, sentimental story. [PG-13]▼◗

Diamonds and Crime SEE: **Hi Diddle Diddle**

Diamonds Are Forever (1971-British) **C-119m.** ***½ D: Guy Hamilton. Sean Connery, Jill St. John, Charles Gray, Lana Wood, Jimmy Dean, Bruce Cabot, Bruce Glover, Putter Smith, Bernard Lee, Lois Maxwell, Desmond Llewelyn, Leonard Barr, Laurence Naismith, Marc Lawrence. After a one-picture hiatus, Connery returned as James Bond in this colorful comic-book adventure set in Las Vegas; closer in spirit to Republic serials than Ian Fleming, but great fun. Panavision. [PG]▼●

Diamond's Edge SEE: **Just Ask for Diamond**

Diamonds for Breakfast (1968-British) **C-102m.** ** D: Christopher Morahan. Marcello Mastroianni, Rita Tushingham, Warren Mitchell, Elaine Taylor, Francisca Tu, Maggie Blye. Son of Russian nobleman tries to steal royal diamonds his father gambled away on the night of his birth. Offbeat comedy caper with fantasy elements just doesn't work, relies heavily on Mastroianni charm. [M/PG]

Diamond Skulls SEE: **Dark Obsession**

Diamonds of the Night (1964-Czech) **71m.** ***½ D: Jan Nemec. Ladislav Jansky, Antonin Kumbera, Ilse Bischofova. Nemec's first feature is a landmark of the ill-fated Czech "New Wave": a haunting, startlingly directed chronicle of two Jewish boys' experiences after escaping from a train heading for a Nazi death camp during WW2. Scripted by Nemec and Arnost Lustig (based on the latter's story).▼

Diamond Wizard, The (1954-British) **83m.** ** D: Dennis O'Keefe. Dennis O'Keefe, Margaret Sheridan, Philip Friend, Alan Wheatley. OK caper of U.S. and British agents tracking down diamond counterfeiters. Filmed in 3-D.

Diane (1956) **C-110m.** **½ D: David Miller. Lana Turner, Pedro Armendariz, Roger Moore, Marisa Pavan, Sir Cedric Hardwicke, Henry Daniell. Although predictable, medieval romance has good cast, gorgeous sets and costumes, and comes off surprisingly well. Lana looks lovely, and Miklos Rozsa's score helps set the mood. CinemaScope. ▼●

Diary of a Bachelor (1964) **88m.** *½ D: Sandy Howard. William Traylor, Dagne Crane, Joe Silver, Chris Noel, Paula Stewart, Arlene Golonka, Dom DeLuise. Meager pickings. Fiancée reads boyfriend's daily ledger and decides he'd better mend his ways; time passes and he has, but she's changed her way of life.

Diary of a Chambermaid (1946) **87m.** ** D: Jean Renoir. Paulette Goddard, Hurd Hatfield, Francis Lederer, Burgess Meredith, Judith Anderson, Irene Ryan, Florence Bates, Reginald Owen. Uneasy attempt at Continental-style romantic melodrama, with blonde Goddard as outspoken maid who arouses all sorts of emotions in her snooty household. Tries hard, but never really sure of what it wants to be. Meredith as nutsy neighbor and Ryan as timid scullery maid do their best; Meredith also coproduced and wrote the screenplay. Remade in 1964. ▼

Diary of a Chambermaid (1964-French) **97m.** ***½ D: Luis Buñuel. Jeanne Moreau, Michel Piccoli, Georges Geret, Francoise Lugagne, Daniel Ivernel, Jean Ozenne. Remake of Jean Renoir's 1946 film concerns fascism in France in 1939 and how the bourgeoisie are viewed by maid Moreau. Sharp, unrelenting film from one of the great directors. Franscope. ▼●

Diary of a Country Priest (1950-French) **120m.** ***½ D: Robert Bresson. Claude Laydu, Nicole Ladmiral, Jean Riveyre, Nicole Maurey, Andre Guibert, Martine Lemaire. The life and death of an unhappy young priest attempting to minister to his first parish in rural France. Slow-moving

but rewarding, with brilliantly stylized direction. Bresson also scripted.▼●
Diary of a Hitman (1992) **C-91m.** *** D: Roy London. Forest Whitaker, John Bedford-Lloyd, James Belushi, Lois Chiles, Sharon Stone, Sherilyn Fenn, Seymour Cassel, Lewis Smith. Assassin-for-hire Whitaker plans to retire after one last job, but his intended victim (Fenn) tries to convince him to spare her. Riveting little thriller is well directed and extremely well acted by all (with kudos to Whitaker and especially Fenn). Scripted by Kenneth Pressman, based on his play *Insider's Price.* [R]▼●
Diary of a Lost Girl (1929-German) **104m.** ***½ D: G. W. Pabst. Louise Brooks, Fritz Rasp, Josef Ravensky, Sybille Schmitz, Valeska Gert. Pabst and Brooks' followup to their PANDORA'S BOX is even more sordid, yet in some ways more intriguing: Louise is, in succession, raped, gives birth, is put in a detention home, then a brothel, inherits money, marries, is widowed . . . and writer Rudolf Leonhardt claims only the first half of his script was filmed. Fascinating nonetheless, with an explicitness that's still surprising; a must for devotees of German stylistics (and of course, Brooks). Fully restored version was reissued in 1984.▼●
Diary of a Mad Housewife (1970) **C-103m.** **½ D: Frank Perry. Richard Benjamin, Frank Langella, Carrie Snodgress, Lorraine Cullen, Frannie Michel, Katherine Meskill. Interesting but pointless story of harried N.Y.C. wife finding much needed release via affair with self-centered Langella. Asinine husband Benjamin would drive anyone mad. Peter Boyle has prominent bit in final scene. Script by Eleanor Perry from Sue Kaufman's novel. "Alternate" version prepared for TV, with different footage, runs 95m. [R]▼
Diary of a Madman (1963) **C-96m.** **½ D: Reginald Le Borg. Vincent Price, Nancy Kovack, Chris Warfield, Ian Wolfe, Nelson Olmstead. 19th-century magistrate Price is possessed by an evil spirit called the Horla, which compels him to murder. Colorful but routine. Based on a story by Guy de Maupassant.▼●
Diary of Anne Frank, The (1959) **156m.** ***½ D: George Stevens. Millie Perkins, Joseph Schildkraut, Shelley Winters, Richard Beymer, Lou Jacobi, Diane Baker, Ed Wynn. Meticulously produced version of Broadway drama dealing with Jewish refugees hiding in WW2 Amsterdam. Unfortunately, Perkins never captures pivotal charm of title character, though Schildkraut is fine as father Frank. Winters won Supporting Actress Oscar as shrill Mrs. Van Daan, ever fearful of Nazi arrest, and the cinematography (William C. Mellor) and art direction-set decoration also earned Academy Awards. Frances Goodrich and Albert Hackett utilized Anne's diary for their stage play and its screen adaptation. Originally released at 170m.; this version now is available on video. Remade as a TV movie in 1980. CinemaScope.▼●
Diary of a Young Comic (1979) **C-67m. TVM** D: Gary Weis. Richard Lewis, Stacy Keach, Dom DeLuise, Nina Van Pallandt, Bill Macy, George Jessel. The title tells all in this at once silly and engaging chronicle of stand-up comic Lewis, and his plight as he abandons N.Y.C. for L.A. Scripted by Lewis and Bennett Tranner; Weis directed many of the short films featured on *Saturday Night Live* (which this preempted for its TV premiere). Average.▼
Diary of Forbidden Dreams SEE: **What?**
Diary of Oharu SEE: **Life of Oharu, The**
Dice Rules (1991) **C-87m.** **½ D: Jay Dubin. Andrew Dice Clay. Film opens with a series of curious and mostly embarrassing blackout skits with Clay imitating Jerry Lewis! Finally it moves on to the standup comic's sold-out Madison Square Garden concert, in which his audience communication is total, and his sex-oriented material is predictably crude, embarrassing, outrageous—and often very funny. [NC-17]▼
Dick (1999) **C-95m.** *** D: Andrew Fleming. Kirsten Dunst, Michelle Williams, Dan Hedaya, Dave Foley, Saul Rubinek, Harry Shearer, Jim Breuer, Will Ferrell, Teri Garr, Bruce McCulloch, Ted McGinley, G.D. Spradlin, Ana Gasteyer, Ryan Reynolds. Clever cross of CLUELESS and ALL THE PRESIDENT'S MEN has two likable teenage airheads (delightfully played by Dunst and Williams) stumbling into all the key players in the Watergate scandal—up to and including President Richard Nixon himself (Hedaya)—but never having an inkling of what is going on. Funny script by Fleming and Sheryl Longin is even more enjoyable if you remember the real-life events of the 1970s. [PG-13]▼◗
Dick Tracy Chester Gould's immortal comic-strip crimefighter first came to movies in a quartet of Republic Pictures Saturday-matinee serials in the late 1930s and early 40s. Except for the first, these cliffhangers were full of action, excitement, and imagination . . . though they bore little resemblance to the newspaper strip. Leading man Ralph Byrd was born to play Gould's jut-jawed hero. In 1945 RKO decided to revive Tracy for a series of grade-B feature films, but the results were mostly mediocre. Morgan Conway played Tracy in the first two, without distinction, then Byrd returned to the role. None of the four RKO features capitalized on the rich lode of material that Gould had provided in his years of daily detective adventures.

DICK TRACY

Dick Tracy (1945) AKA: Dick Tracy, Detective
Dick Tracy Versus Cueball (1946)
Dick Tracy's Dilemma (1947)
Dick Tracy Meets Gruesome (1947)

Dick Tracy (1990) **C-104m.** *** D: Warren Beatty. Warren Beatty, Madonna, Al Pacino, Glenne Headly, Charlie Korsmo, Mandy Patinkin, Charles Durning, Paul Sorvino, William Forsythe, Seymour Cassel, Dustin Hoffman, Dick Van Dyke, Catherine O'Hara, James Caan, Michael J. Pollard, Estelle Parsons, James Tolkan, R.G. Armstrong, Kathy Bates. Colorful, high-style adaptation of the Chester Gould comic strip classic, with Beatty redefining the hawk-nosed, jut-jawed hero. Story is simple in the extreme, but there's so much to take in you really don't mind: a galaxy of guest stars as Gould's grotesque villains, eye-popping, Academy Award-winning make-up and art direction and Madonna singing new Stephen Sondheim songs (if a few too many). One of them, "Sooner or Later (I Always Get My Man)," also won an Oscar. Standout: Pacino's hilarious, over-the-top performance as Big Boy Caprice. Super 35. [PG]▼●

Dick Tracy, Detective (1945) **62m.** ** D: William Berke. Morgan Conway, Anne Jeffreys, Mike Mazurki, Jane Greer. Programmer entry about Chester Gould's square-jawed detective combatting crime; needed production values are lacking. Originally titled DICK TRACY.▼●

Dick Tracy Meets Gruesome (1947) **65m.** ** D: John Rawlins. Boris Karloff, Ralph Byrd, Anne Gwynne, Lyle Latell. Karloff is fun as Gruesome, who uses Dr. A. Tomic's experimental gas (which causes people to freeze in place) to commit daring bank robbery. Silly but watchable. Lex Barker has a bit role as ambulance driver. ▼●

Dick Tracy's Dilemma (1947) **60m.** ** D: John Rawlins. Ralph Byrd, Lyle Latell, Kay Christopher, Jack Lambert, Ian Keith. RKO contract players abound in this Tracy series entry; fast pacing makes predictable crime-solving satisfactory.▼●

Dick Tracy Versus Cueball (1946) **62m.** ** D: Gordon Douglas. Morgan Conway, Anne Jeffreys, Lyle Latell, Rita Corday, Dick Wessel. Ralph Byrd is definitive screen Tracy, but he isn't in this one; Conway does his best in OK entry in the Tracy series.▼●

Dick Turpin (1925) **73m.** *** D: John G. Blystone. Tom Mix, Kathleen Myers, Philo McCullough, Alan Hale, Bull Montana. Mix abandoned cowboy clothes to play famous English highwayman, but retained surefire formula of action and comedy in this enjoyable vehicle.▼

Did You Hear the One About the Traveling Saleslady? (1968) **C-97m.** BOMB D: Don Weis. Phyllis Diller, Bob Denver, Joe Flynn, Eileen Wesson, Jeanette Nolan, Bob Hastings, David Hartman, Charles Lane, Kent McCord. You've all heard it, so why bother watching this dud. For only the most fervent Diller fans. Techniscope . . . Why?

Die! Die! My Darling! (1965-British) **C-97m.** **½ D: Silvio Narizzano. Tallulah Bankhead, Stefanie Powers, Peter Vaughan, Donald Sutherland, Yootha Joyce. Tallulah, in her last film, has field day as weirdo who keeps Powers under lock and key for personal vengeance against the death of her son. Engaging fun, especially for Bankhead devotees. Script by Richard Matheson. Original British title: FANATIC.▼

Die Hard (1988) **C-131m.** *** D: John McTiernan. Bruce Willis, Alan Rickman, Bonnie Bedelia, Alexander Godunov, Reginald VelJohnson, Paul Gleason, De'voreaux White, William Atherton, Hart Bochner, James Shigeta, Lorenzo Caccialanza, Robert Davi, Rick Ducommun, Rebecca Broussard, Vondie Curtis Hall, Don Harvey. Dynamite action yarn about a N.Y.C. cop who just happens to be visiting an L.A. highrise when it's commandeered by terrorist thieves. Great action scenes and stunts, with Richard Edlund's special effects, and a perfect part for Willis, who plays cat-and-mouse with bad guy Rickman. Marred only by overlength and too many needlessly stupid supporting characters. Followed by two sequels. Panavision. [R]▼●◗

Die Hard 2 (1990) **C-124m.** *** D: Renny Harlin. Bruce Willis, Bonnie Bedelia, William Atherton, Reginald VelJohnson, Franco Nero, William Sadler, John Amos, Dennis Franz, Art Evans, Fred Dalton Thompson, Sheila McCarthy, Robert Patrick, John Leguizamo, Robert Costanzo. Stupendously unbelievable—but very entertaining—sequel to the action hit; while waiting for his wife to land at Washington's Dulles Airport, Willis dives head-first into trouble when he gets wind of an impending terrorist-type plot. Lots of violent, large-scale action, and lots of fun—just don't look for lots of logic. Based on Walter Wager's novel *58 Minutes.* Panavision. [R]▼●◗

Die Hard With a Vengeance (1995) **C-128m.** *** D: John McTiernan. Bruce Willis, Jeremy Irons, Samuel L. Jackson, Graham Greene, Colleen Camp, Larry Bryggman, Anthony Peck, Nick Wyman, Sam Phillips. A madman (Irons) holds N.Y.C. hostage with bombings—and threats of more—targeting his demands at ousted cop John McClane (Willis), who inadvertently acquires a partner in hostile Harlem storekeeper Jackson. Logic and motivation take a backseat to big-scale action in this nonstop roller-coaster ride; it's like watching 12 chapters of a high-tech Saturday matinee serial all at once. Panavision. [R]▼●◗

Die Laughing (1980) **C-108m.** BOMB D: Jeff Werner. Robby Benson, Linda Grovenor, Charles Durning, Elsa Lanchester, Bud Cort, Peter Coyote. Benson is star, co-author, coproducer, and composer of this sophomoric black comedy and gives an excruciating performance as a cabbie who accidentally becomes implicated in the murder of a nuclear scientist. Cort is disgustingly oily as fascist villain. [PG]▼

Die, Monster, Die! (1965) **C-80m.** ** D: Daniel Haller. Boris Karloff, Nick Adams, Freda Jackson, Suzan Farmer, Terence de Marney, Patrick Magee. Based on H. P. Lovecraft story, this thriller has Karloff a recluse who discovers a meteor which gives him strange powers. Good premise is not carried out well. Filmed in England. Remade as THE CURSE (1987). Horrifying Colorscope.▼●

Die Nibelungen (1924-German) **186m.** **** D: Fritz Lang. Paul Richter, Margarete Schon, Theodor Loos, Hanna Ralph, Rudolf Klein-Rogge, Georg John. Lang's epic masterpiece of German mythology is told in two parts, each different in style and theme. In SIEGFRIED, the titanic hero achieves virtual immortality by bathing in the blood of a slain dragon (a landmark scene in silent cinema). After his death, Siegfried's widow seeks vengeance in KRIEMHILD'S REVENGE, in which she marries Attila the Hun in order to carry out her plan. A rich treasure trove of folklore and magic, in which Lang creates a mystical geometric universe where the characters play against vast architectural landscapes. A must-see.▼●

Different for Girls (1997-British) **C-92m.** *** D: Richard Spence. Steven Mackintosh, Rupert Graves, Neil Dudgeon, Saskia Reeves. A demure transsexual who writes greeting card verses takes up with a rowdy biker—the same long-ago schoolmate who protected her against adolescent persecutors before the operation that changed her life. One of the more distinctive odd-couple romantic comedies of our time; kept on track by the central performance of Mackintosh, who pulls off a difficult role. [R]▼◗

Different Story, A (1978) **C-108m.** **½ D: Paul Aaron. Perry King, Meg Foster, Valerie Curtin, Peter Donat, Richard Bull, Barbara Collentine. Gays King and Foster get married to prevent his deportation, then fall in love. Sounds terrible, but first half is surprisingly good until film succumbs to conventionality. Foster is terrific. [PG—edited from original R rating]▼

Digby—The Biggest Dog in the World (1974-British) **C-88m.** BOMB D: Joseph McGrath. Jim Dale, Spike Milligan, Milo O'Shea, Angela Douglas, Norman Rossington. Poor comedy-fantasy concerning liquid Project X, which causes sheepdog Digby to grow to huge proportions. Bad special effects, too. Written by Ted Key, creator of "Hazel," strictly for kids. [G]▼

Digger (1994) **C-92m.** ** D: Robert Turner. Adam Hann-Byrd, Joshua Jackson, Barbara Williams, Timothy Bottoms, Olympia Dukakis, Leslie Nielsen, P. Lynn Johnson, Lochlyn Munro. An attractive but depressing film of people dealing with losses in their lives: a couple who have buried a drowned child, a boy dying of leukemia therapy complications, and his friend whose parents are divorcing. Dukakis and Nielsen provide welcome relief as older couple in the throes of romance. Unfortunately, no great insights here. [PG] ▼●

Digging to China (1997) **C-98m.** ** D: Timothy Hutton. Evan Rachel Wood, Kevin Bacon, Mary Stuart Masterson, Cathy Moriarty, Marian Seldes. Sincere but one-note film about the growing friendship between a troubled 10-year-old girl (Wood) and a mentally retarded young man (Bacon). Its offbeat qualities seem a bit too contrived, though the performances can't be faulted. Hutton's feature directing debut. [PG] ▼●◗

Diggstown (1992) **C-97m.** **½ D: Michael Ritchie. James Woods, Louis Gossett, Jr., Bruce Dern, Oliver Platt, Heather Graham, Randall "Tex" Cobb, Thomas Wilson Brown, Duane Davis, Willie Green, George D. Wallace. Amiable yarn about a con-artist just sprung from prison who sets his sights on a high-rolling meanie in a small Georgia town—with boxer Gossett as his lure for big-time bets. The two stars are very watchable, even if the script is contrived. Gossett's then-wife Cyndi plays his spouse on-screen. [R]▼●◗

Dig That Uranium (1956) **61m.** ** D: Edward Bernds. Leo Gorcey, Huntz Hall, Bernard Gorcey, Bennie Bartlett, Mary Beth Hughes, Raymond Hatton, Myron Healey, Harry Lauter. Broad Western spoof, as the Bowery Boys get mixed up with crooks and a phony uranium mine. Look for Carl "Alfalfa" Switzer in a bit.

Dillinger (1945) **70m.** *** D: Max Nosseck. Edmund Lowe, Anne Jeffreys, Lawrence Tierney, Eduardo Ciannelli, Elisha Cook, Jr., Marc Lawrence. Solid gangster yarn written by Philip Yordan, one of the best B movies of its kind (though a key bank robbery is comprised of stock footage lifted from Fritz Lang's YOU ONLY LIVE ONCE).▼

Dillinger (1973) **C-96m.** *** D: John Milius. Warren Oates, Ben Johnson, Cloris Leachman, Michelle Phillips, Richard Dreyfuss, Harry Dean Stanton, Steve Kanaly. Heavily romanticized gangster movie is aided by some rough, violent gun battles. Story follows Dillinger midway through his bank-robbing career up until his death outside the Biograph Theatre. [R]▼●

Dillinger and Capone (1995) **C-94m.** **

D: Jon Purdy. Martin Sheen, F. Murray Abraham, Stephen Davies, Catherine Hicks, Don Stroud, Sasha Jenson, Michael Oliver, Jeffrey Combs, Michael C. Gwynne, Anthony Crivello, Bert Remsen, Clint Howard. 1940: released from prison, Al Capone (Abraham) holds captive the family of John Dillinger (Sheen) who, here at least, wasn't gunned down at the Biograph. Big Al wants the famed bank robber to recover 15 million dollars of Capone's ill-gotten gains from a hotel in Chicago. The clever idea is boosted by slick acting, but it soon slides into a routine heist thriller. [R]▼

Dime With a Halo (1963) **97m.** **½ D: Boris Sagal. Barbara Luna, Roger Mobley, Paul Langton, Rafael Lopez, Manuel Padilla. Five poor Mexican kids steal ten cents from church collection plate and bet on a racehorse. Minor but winning little film.

Dimples (1936) **78m.** **½ D: William Seiter. Shirley Temple, Frank Morgan, Helen Westley, Robert Kent, Stepin Fetchit, Astrid Allwyn. Prime Shirley, with our heroine doing her best to save her destitute father, played by marvelous Morgan. Songs: "Oh Mister Man Up In The Moon," "What Did The Bluebird Say." Also shown in computer-colored version. ▼

Dim Sum: a little bit of heart (1984) **C-89m.** *** D: Wayne Wang. Laureen Chew, Kim Chew, Victor Wong, Ida F.O. Chung, Cora Miao. Occasionally slow—there are one too many shots of empty rooms—but mostly wise, endearing tale of Chinese-Americans in San Francisco, focusing on the dynamics of a mother-daughter relationship. Characters may be distinctively Chinese, but there's a refreshing, knowing universality to this comedy. [PG]▼●

Diner (1982) **C-110m.** *** D: Barry Levinson. Steve Guttenberg, Daniel Stern, Mickey Rourke, Kevin Bacon, Timothy Daly, Ellen Barkin, Paul Reiser, Michael Tucker. Problems of growing up are nicely synthesized by writer-director Levinson in this look at a group of friends who hang out in a Baltimore diner in the 1950s. Obviously made with care and affection; a real sleeper. Levinson's directorial debut and first film of Barkin and Reiser. [R]▼●◗

Dingaka (1965-South African) **C-98m.** **½ D: Jamie Uys. Stanley Baker, Juliet Prowse, Ken Gampu, Siegfried Mynhardt, Bob Courtney. Film focuses on contrasting white-black ways of life and the clashes of the two cultures; production bogs down in stereotypes. CinemaScope.▼

Dingo (1991-Australian-French) **C-108m.** **½ D: Rolf de Heer. Colin Friels, Miles Davis, Helen Buday, Joe Petruzzi, Bernadette Lafont, Bernard Fresson. A chance appearance by jazz trumpeter Billy Cross (Davis) in a boy's rural community inspires him to pursue music himself; now grown up, he still dreams of playing for a living—and winning the approval of his lifelong idol. Amiable but slow-paced story is sparked by Miles Davis' dynamic presence and ingratiating performance. Chuck Findley doubled Friels' trumpeting on the soundtrack. Invigorating score by Michel Legrand and Davis. Panavision.▼

Dinky (1935) **65m.** ** D: D. Ross Lederman, Howard Bretherton. Jackie Cooper, Mary Astor, Roger Pryor, Henry Armetta. Astor is framed, accused of fraud. She tries to keep it from hurting son Cooper in military school. Nothing special.

Dinner at Eight (1933) **113m.** **** D: George Cukor. Marie Dressler, John Barrymore, Wallace Beery, Jean Harlow, Lionel Barrymore, Lee Tracy, Edmund Lowe, Billie Burke, Madge Evans, Jean Hersholt, Karen Morley, Phillips Holmes, May Robson. Vintage MGM constellation of stars portray various strata of society in N.Y.C., invited to dine and shine; Harlow in fine comedy form, but Dressler as dowager steals focus in filmization of George Kaufman-Edna Ferber play. Scripted by three top writers: Herman Mankiewicz, Frances Marion, and Donald Ogden Stewart. Don't miss this one. Remade for cable TV in 1989 with Lauren Bacall.▼●

Dinner at the Ritz (1937-British) **77m.** **½ D: Harold Schuster. Annabella, Paul Lukas, David Niven, Romney Brent. Diverting murder whodunit with Annabella seeking the killer of her father; classy settings spice film.▼

Dinner for Adele (1978-Czech) **C-100m.** **½ D: Oldrich Lipsky. Michal Docolomansky, Rudolf Hrusinsky, Milos Kopecky, Nada Konvalinkova, Ladislav Pesek. Truly off-the-wall film festival favorite finds pulp hero Nick Carter (Docolomansky) in Prague in the year 1900 investigating murder spree that eventually leads to carnivorous plant named Adele. Tongue-in-cheek, gadget-laden film done in the style of a silent melodrama; worthwhile for those seeking the unusual. Originally titled NICK CARTER IN PRAGUE; aka ADELE HASN'T HAD HER SUPPER YET.

Dinner Game, The (1998-French) **C-81m.** ***½ D: Francis Veber. Thierry Lhermitte, Jacques Villeret, Francis Huster, Daniel Prevost, Alexandra Vandernoot, Catherine Frot. Laugh-out-loud farce (from the writer of LA CAGE AUX FOLLES) about a self-centered publisher who participates in a weekly ritual with his friends: to invite the stupidest person they can find to dinner. Lhermitte has found a doozy, civil servant Villeret (who created this part on stage), but the well-meaning oaf intrudes on his life in unexpected ways. Hilariously funny without being cruel—which is no mean feat. Technovision. [PG-13]▼◗

Dino (1957) **94m.** **½ D: Thomas Carr. Sal

Mineo, Brian Keith, Susan Kohner, Joe De Santis, Penny Santon, Frank Faylen, Richard Bakalyan. Mineo at his rebellious best playing juvenile delinquent befriended by a girl (Kohner) and a social worker (Keith). Reginald Rose adapted his acclaimed TV play, and Mineo recreated his starring role.▼
Dinosaur (2000) **C-82m.** *** D: Ralph Zondag, Eric Leighton. Voices of D.B. Sweeney, Alfre Woodard, Ossie Davis, Max Casella, Hayden Panettiers, Samuel E. Wright, Julianna Margulies, Peter Siragusa, Joan Plowright, Della Reese. Disney story of a dinosaur raised by a family of lemurs; when a meteor shower destroys their island home, they flee to another island where they join a tribe of dinosaurs on a desperate trek to safety. On one level, a children's fable about survival and compassion; on another, a dazzling display of computer animation and technology that's almost overwhelming. But the use of modern dialogue for comedy relief ultimately brands the film as kid stuff. [PG]
Dinosaur . . . Secret of the Lost Legend SEE: **Baby . . . Secret of the Lost Legend**
Dinosaurus! (1960) **C-85m.** **½ D: Irvin S. Yeaworth, Jr. Ward Ramsey, Paul Lukather, Kristina Hanson, Alan Roberts. Interesting and amusing story of hazards faced by caveman and two prehistoric monsters who are accidentally unearthed on an isolated tropical island. CinemaScope.▼
Dion Brothers, The SEE: **Gravy Train, The**
Diplomaniacs (1933) **63m.** *** D: William A. Seiter. Bert Wheeler, Robert Woolsey, Marjorie White, Louis Calhern, Edgar Kennedy, Hugh Herbert. Genuinely odd but endearing nonsense musical comedy (cowritten by Joseph L. Mankiewicz!) about barbers from Indian reservation sent to Geneva peace conference. Reminiscent of MILLION DOLLAR LEGS and DUCK SOUP, with memorable comic performances by Herbert—as a Confucius-quoting sage—and Calhern.▼●
Diplomatic Courier (1952) **97m.** *** D: Henry Hathaway. Tyrone Power, Patricia Neal, Stephen McNally, Hildegarde Neff, Karl Malden. Power seeks to avenge friend's death in Trieste, becomes involved in international espionage. Cold War film is exciting, well acted. Look for Lee Marvin, Charles Bronson, and Michael Ansara in small, unbilled roles.▼
Dirigible (1931) **100m.** **½ D: Frank Capra. Jack Holt, Ralph Graves, Fay Wray, Hobart Bosworth, Roscoe Karns. Frank "Spig" Wead story about Navy pilots' experimental use of dirigibles in the Antarctic has plenty of action and guts, but a sappy romantic story to weigh it down. On the whole, an interesting antique.
Dirt Bike Kid, The (1986) **C-90m.** **½ D: Hoite C. Caston. Peter Billingsley, Stuart Pankin, Anne Bloom, Patrick Collins, Sage Parker, Chad Sheets. Strictly formula teen melodrama, with young Billingsley taking on evil banker Pankin and some nasty bikers with the help of a very unusual Yamaha. Harmless and forgettable. [PG]▼●
Dirty Dancing (1987) **C-97m.** **½ D: Emile Ardolino. Jennifer Grey, Patrick Swayze, Jerry Orbach, Cynthia Rhodes, Jack Weston, Jane Brucker, Kelly Bishop, Lonny Price, Charles "Honi" Coles, Wayne Knight. Superficial but audience-pleasing tale of spoiled teenage girl who learns something about real life—as well as a thing or two about dancing—during family vacation at a Catskills, N.Y., resort hotel in the early 1960s. Sparked by some hot dance numbers and charismatic leads. Most of the music is 1980s-style, not 1960s, but it seems to work. For a richer portrait of Catskills life see another 1987 release, SWEET LORRAINE. Oscar winner for best song: "(I've Had) The Time of My Life." Followed by a TV series. [PG-13]▼●◗
Dirty Dingus Magee (1970) **C-90m.** *** D: Burt Kennedy. Frank Sinatra, George Kennedy, Anne Jackson, Lois Nettleton, Michele Carey, Jack Elam, John Dehner, Henry Jones, Harry Carey, Jr., Paul Fix. Broad, bawdy spoof with Sinatra as $10 outlaw whose attempts to make it big are slightly hindered by equally bungling sheriff Kennedy (not to mention assorted whores, Indians, and the U.S. Cavalry). Subtle it's not, but fast-paced and amusing, especially for Western buffs; Nettleton is a delight as Joanne Woodward-ish schoolmarm inappropriately named Prudence. Cowritten by Joseph Heller. TV prints run 79m. Panavision. [PG]▼
Dirty Dishes (1978-French) **C-92m.** **½ D: Joyce Buñuel. Carole Laure, Pierre Santini, Catherine Lachens, Veronique Silver. Entertaining but obvious feminist comedy of Laure rebelling against her duties as a housewife. Director Buñuel is the late Luis Buñuel's daughter-in-law. [R]▼
Dirty Dozen, The (1967) **C-150m.** ***½ D: Robert Aldrich. Lee Marvin, Ernest Borgnine, Jim Brown, John Cassavetes, Robert Ryan, Charles Bronson, Donald Sutherland, George Kennedy, Telly Savalas, Ralph Meeker, Richard Jaeckel, Clint Walker, Trini Lopez. Box-office hit about 12 murderers, rapists, and other prisoners who get a chance to redeem themselves in WW2. Exciting, funny, and well acted, especially by Marvin and Cassavetes. Nunnally Johnson and Lukas Heller scripted from E. M. Nathanson novel. Followed in 1985, 1987, 1988 by trio of inferior TV movies with such original cast members as Marvin, Jaeckel, Savalas, Borgnine; then a short-lived series. Metroscope.▼●◗
Dirty Game, The (1965-Italian) **91m.** **½ D: Terence Young, Christian-Jaque, Carlo Lizzani. Henry Fonda, Vittorio Gassman,

Annie Girardot, Robert Ryan, Peter Van Eyck. Hodgepodge of stories dealing with espionage in post-WW2 era; none of episodes is convincing, stars don't help much.▼

Dirty Hands (1976-French) **C-102m.** ** D: Claude Chabrol. Rod Steiger, Romy Schneider, Paolo Giusti, Jean Rochefort, Hans Christian Blech. Laughable wife-and-lover-conspire-to-murder-husband melodrama; corpses keep turning up alive with boring regularity. However, some striking camera work, eerie sequences. Aka INNOCENTS WITH DIRTY HANDS. [R]▼

Dirty Harry (1972) **C-102m.** ***½ D: Don Siegel. Clint Eastwood, Harry Guardino, Reni Santoni, John Larch, Andy Robinson, and John Vernon as "The Mayor." Riveting action film with Eastwood as iconoclastic cop determined to bring in psychotic serial killer Robinson, even if he has to break some rules. Brilliantly filmed and edited for maximum impact. Jazzy score by Lalo Schifrin. Filmed "in tribute to the police officers of San Francisco who gave their lives in the line of duty." Followed by MAGNUM FORCE, THE ENFORCER, SUDDEN IMPACT, and THE DEAD POOL. Panavision. [R]▼●◗

Dirty Heroes (1969-Italian) **C-105m.** **½ D: Alberto DeMartino. Frederick Stafford, Daniela Bianchi, Curt Jurgens, John Ireland, Adolfo Celi, Michael Constantine. Wartime escape and revenge action drama—a poor man's DIRTY DOZEN—with a gang of ex-cons turned G.I.'s working behind enemy lines in Holland. Techniscope. [G]▼

Dirty Knight's Work (1976-British) **C-88m.** ** D: Kevin Connor. John Mills, Donald Pleasence, Barbara Hershey, David Birney, Margaret Leighton, Peter Cushing. Birney enlists Mills' help in solving his father's murder, zeroes in on strange society of latter-day knights with vigilante tendencies. Offbeat and mildly diverting. Original title: TRIAL BY COMBAT. Video title: CHOICE OF WEAPONS. [PG]▼

Dirty Laundry (1987) **C-79m.** ** D: William Webb. Leigh McCloskey, Jeanne O'Brien, Frankie Valli, Sonny Bono, Nicholas Worth, Robbie Rist, Edy Williams. Odd cast (including Olympic champs Carl Lewis and Greg Louganis) is the only point of interest in this comedy of innocent McCloskey becoming involved with gangsters. [PG-13]▼

Dirty Laundry (1998) **C-86m.** ** D: Michael Normand, Robert Sherwin. Jay Thomas, Tess Harper, Tresa Hughes, Michael Marcus, Stanley Earl Harrison, Erin Underwood, John Driver. Paper-thin romantic comedy about a dry-cleaning business owner (Thomas), mired in a midlife crisis, who is told by his psychiatrist that extramarital sex will add spark to his life. [R]▼

Dirty Little Billy (1972) **C-100m.** *** D: Stan Dragoti. Michael J. Pollard, Lee Purcell, Charles Aidman, Richard Evans. Offbeat story based on early life of Billy the Kid. Grimy, muddy, adventurous; not a normal Western by any stretch of the imagination. Produced by Jack L. Warner! [R]

Dirty Mary Crazy Larry (1974) **C-93m.** *** D: John Hough. Peter Fonda, Susan George, Adam Roarke, Vic Morrow, Roddy McDowall. Very fast action as racing driver Fonda, pickup George and mechanic Roarke demolish every car in sight while escaping with supermarket loot. Hardly a letup, and marred only by downbeat finale. [PG]▼

Dirty Money (1972-French) **C-98m.** **½ D: Jean-Pierre Melville. Alain Delon, Richard Crenna, Catherine Deneuve, Ricardo Cucciolla, Michael Conrad. Pedestrian melodrama of bank robbery and drug trafficking. Delon and Crenna are muscular, Deneuve and the scenery gorgeous.

Dirty Rotten Scoundrels (1988) **C-110m.** **½ D: Frank Oz. Steve Martin, Michael Caine, Glenne Headly, Anton Rodgers, Barbara Harris, Ian McDiarmid, Dana Ivey. A career con artist who fleeces women with great elan in the south of France must find a way to deal with crass new competition, in the person of American Martin. Eventually they decide to compete to see who can dupe wide-eyed Headly first. Extremely pleasant but unremarkable comedy, a remake of the 1964 BEDTIME STORY, filmed on beautiful Riviera locations. [PG]▼●◗

Dirty Tricks (1980-U.S.-Canadian) **C-91m.** *½ D: Alvin Rakoff. Elliott Gould, Kate Jackson, Rich Little, Arthur Hill, Nick Campbell, Angus McInnes. Harvard history professor Gould tussles with baddies over a letter written by George Washington. A comedy-thriller that is neither funny nor thrilling. [PG]

Dirty Work (1998) **C-81m.** *½ D: Bob Saget. Norm Macdonald, Jack Warden, Artie Lange, Traylor Howard, Don Rickles, Christopher McDonald, Chevy Chase, Chris Farley, Gary Coleman, Ken Norton, John Goodman, Adam Sandler, Rebecca Romijn. Crude, mean-spirited comedy vehicle for former *Saturday Night Live* star Macdonald about a shiftless loser who teams up with his best friend to start a "revenge business" for the common man. Potentially clever idea squandered by endless barrage of fat and gay jokes. Lots of comic talent wasted, although Rickles is good as an obnoxious movie theater manager. [PG-13]▼●◗

Disappearance, The (1977-Canadian) **C-88m.** ** D: Stuart Cooper. Donald Sutherland, Francine Racette, David Hemmings, David Warner, Christopher Plummer, John Hurt, Virginia McKenna, Peter Bowles. Slow-moving account of a hit-man's preoccupation with the disappearance of his wife. Strong Sutherland performance is obliterated by confusing script, pretentiously arty direction. Originally 100m. [R]▼

Disappearance of Aimee, The (1976) **C-110m. TVM** D: Anthony Harvey. Faye Dunaway, Bette Davis, James Sloyan, James Woods, John Lehne, Lelia Goldoni, Barry Brown, Severn Darden. Period drama covering, through a courtroom hearing, the sensational disappearance and reappearance of the famed preacher, Aimee Semple McPherson, in 1926. Dunaway is fascinating as Aimee, Davis feisty as her mother in this absorbing, richly atmospheric dramatization. Above average.▼

Disappearance of Garcia Lorca, The (1997-U.S.-Spanish-Puerto Rican) **C-108m.** ** D: Marcos Zurinaga. Andy Garcia, Esai Morales, Edward James Olmos, Jeroen Krabbé, Marcela Wallerstein, Miguel Ferrer, Giancarlo Giannini. Dreary fictionalized account of the mysterious death of the radical Spanish poet-playwright Federico Garcia Lorca at the hands of Franco's Fascists in 1936. Film is good to look at, courtesy Juan Ruiz-Anchia's elegant widescreen photography, but script is hopelessly clichéd and contrived, and fails in its attempts to turn historical speculation into a political thriller. Original title: DEATH IN GRANADA. Panavision. [R]▼

Disaster in Time SEE: **Grand Tour, The**

Disc Jockey Jamboree SEE: **Jamboree**

Disclosure (1994) **C-127m.** *** D: Barry Levinson. Michael Douglas, Demi Moore, Donald Sutherland, Caroline Goodall, Dylan Baker, Roma Maffia, Dennis Miller, Allan Rich, Nicholas Sadler, Rosemary Forsyth. Entertaining corporate thriller based on Michael Crichton's book about a not-so-bright exec (Douglas) in a highly competitive computer company who sues his new, sexy shark of a boss (Moore) for sexual harassment! Plotted like a mystery, with plenty of surprising twists and turns. Only complaint: hasn't Douglas played this same kind of role a bit too often? Panavision. [R]▼●◗

Discreet Charm of the Bourgeoisie, The (1972-French) **C-101m.** **** D: Luis Buñuel. Fernando Rey, Delphine Seyrig, Stephane Audran, Bulle Ogier, Jean-Pierre Cassel, Michel Piccoli. A Buñuel joke on his audience, using friends' attempts to have dinner party as excuse for series of surrealistic sequences. Reality and illusion soon blur into one, with delicious comic results. Oscar-winner as Best Foreign Film. Screenplay by Buñuel and Jean-Claude Carrière. [PG]▼●

Disembodied, The (1957) **65m.** *½ D: Walter Grauman. Paul Burke, Allison Hayes, Eugenia Paul, Robert Christopher. Standard voodoo chiller situated in dark jungle; usual results.▼

Dishonorable Discharge (1958-French) **105m.** ** D: Bernard Borderie. Eddie Constantine, Pascale Roberts, Lino Ventura, Lise Bourdin. Variation on Hemingway's TO HAVE AND HAVE NOT, with Constantine skippering luxury ship loaded with hidden dope; flabby film. Franscope.▼

Dishonored (1931) **91m.** **½ D: Josef von Sternberg. Marlene Dietrich, Victor McLaglen, Lew Cody, Warner Oland, Gustav von Seyffertitz. Alluring Dietrich makes the most of a creaky script starring her as secret agent X-27 during WW1. Worth seeing for her masquerade as peasant girl.▼

Dishonored Lady (1947) **85m.** ** D: Robert Stevenson. Hedy Lamarr, Dennis O'Keefe, John Loder, William Lundigan, Morris Carnovsky, Natalie Schafer, Paul Cavanagh, Douglass Dumbrille, Margaret Hamilton. Adequate drama of glamorous but neurotic magazine art editor Lamarr, who leaves her job and takes on a new identity. She falls in love with nice-guy O'Keefe, and promptly becomes a murder suspect. Lamarr and Loder were married when this was made.▼

Disorderlies (1987) **C-86m.** *½ D: Michael Schultz. The Fat Boys, Ralph Bellamy, Tony Plana, Anthony Geary, Marco Rodriguez, Troy Beyer. Get *down* with Bellamy, as a Palm Beach millionaire about to be murdered for his estate by a conniving nephew and the valet; the title chubs—kind of a rap version of The Three Stooges—come to the rescue. Pretty desperate, but the ultimate in casting curios. [PG]▼●

Disorderly Orderly, The (1964) **C-90m.** *** D: Frank Tashlin. Jerry Lewis, Glenda Farrell, Susan Oliver, Everett Sloane, Jack E. Leonard, Alice Pearce, Kathleen Freeman, Barbara Nichols, Milton Frome. First-rate slapstick and sight gags (including a wild chase finale) mix with cloying sentiment as Jerry runs amuck in a nursing home. Best scene: Jerry's suffering of "sympathy pains" as patient Pearce complains of her ills. Title tune sung by Sammy Davis, Jr.▼

Disorganized Crime (1989) **C-101m.** *½ D: Jim Kouf. Hoyt Axton, Corbin Bernsen, Ruben Blades, Fred Gwynne, Ed O'Neill, Lou Diamond Phillips, Daniel Roebuck, William Russ, Marie Butler Kouf. Witless crime-chase comedy about a quartet of crooks waiting for leader Bernsen, who's plotted the perfect bank heist but has managed to get himself arrested. [R]▼●

Dispatch From Reuters, A (1940) **89m.** **½ D: William Dieterle. Edward G. Robinson, Edna Best, Eddie Albert, Albert Basserman, Gene Lockhart, Nigel Bruce, Otto Kruger. Watchable (if not always inspired) Warner Bros. biography of the man who started famous worldwide news agency by using pigeons to transmit information across the European continent.

Disputed Passage (1939) **87m.** **½ D: Frank Borzage. Dorothy Lamour, Akim Tamiroff, John Howard, Victor Varconi,

Keye Luke. Elisabeth Risdon, Philip Ahn. Average drama of conflict between scientists in their ideals. One believes that there's no place for marriage in science field.
Disraeli (1929) **89m.** *** D: Alfred E. Green. George Arliss, Joan Bennett, Florence Arliss, Anthony Bushell, David Torrence, Ivan Simpson. Somewhat stagy but effective vehicle for Arliss, who won Oscar as cunning British prime minister:—a great statesman, devoted husband, and matchmaker (for Bennett and Bushell). Very much a one-man show.▼
Distance (1975) **C-94m.** **½ D: Anthony Lover. Paul Benjamin, Eija Pokkinen, James Woods, Bibi Besch, Hal Miller, Polly Holliday. Impressive, though flawed, independently made drama detailing the problems of two army couples during the 1950s. Fine performances, particularly by Besch and Woods; Lover and producer George Coe were responsible for the classic short THE DOVE. [R]
Distant Drums (1951) **C-101m.** ** D: Raoul Walsh. Gary Cooper, Mari Aldon, Richard Webb, Ray Teal. Tame actioner of Seminole Indians on warpath in early 19th-century Florida, with Cooper as stalwart swamp fighter. A reworking of the central story idea from director Walsh's WW2 saga OBJECTIVE BURMA.▼●
Distant Harmony (1987) **C-85m.** **½ D: DeWitt Sage. Luciano Pavarotti, Kallen Esperian, Madelyn Renee. Disappointing documentary of opera superstar Pavarotti's 1986 visit to China. Has its moments, but lacks depth and insight . . . and pales beside FROM MAO TO MOZART: ISAAC STERN IN CHINA. Mainly for opera and Pavarotti fans. [G]▼
Distant Thunder (1973-Indian) C-100m. *** D: Satyajit Ray. Soumitra Chatterji, Babita, Sandhya Roy, Gobinda Chakravarty, Romesh Mukerji. Famine strikes Bengal in 1942 and affects the lives of various families in many different ways. Harsh, vividly filmed tale in which one can almost feel the sand and wind blowing across the screen.▼
Distant Thunder (1988-U.S.-Canadian) **C-114m.** ** D: Rick Rosenthal. John Lithgow, Ralph Macchio, Kerrie Keane, Reb Brown, Janet Margolin, Denis Arndt, Jamey Sheridan, Tom Bower. Well-intentioned but gooey soaper about yet one more emotionally troubled Vietnam vet (nicely played by the ever-reliable Lithgow), who lives alone in the wilderness, and whose long-abandoned son (Macchio) sets out to find him. [R]▼●
Distant Trumpet, A (1964) **C-117m.** **½ D: Raoul Walsh. Troy Donahue, Suzanne Pleshette, Kent Smith, Claude Akins, James Gregory. Paul Horgan's novel gets short-circuited in stock presentation of army men in the Old West combatting warring Indians while romancing women on the post; good supporting cast. Panavision.
Distant Voices, Still Lives (1988-British) **C-85m.** *** D: Terence Davies. Freda Dowie, Peter Postlethwaite, Angela Walsh, Diane McBain, Dean Williams, Lorraine Ashbourne. Strikingly visual evocation of England during the 1940s and '50s, a time when the corny, happy lyrics of popular songs can be contrasted to the drab, stultifying lives of the working class. Davies' autobiographical script mirrors the lives of his various family members, each of whom is brutalized by his irrationally cruel father. While there's little narrative structure and no depth to the characters, the haunting imagery makes this most worthwhile. Sequel: THE LONG DAY CLOSES. [PG-13]▼●
Distinguished Gentleman, The (1992) **C-112m.** *** D: Jonathan Lynn. Eddie Murphy, Lane Smith, Sheryl Lee Ralph, Joe Don Baker, Victoria Rowell, Grant Shaud, Kevin McCarthy, Charles S. Dutton, Victor Rivers, Noble Willingham, Gary Frank, Cynthia Harris, James Garner. Florida con artist Murphy realizes that the real con-game is the political scene in Washington, D.C.—and gets himself elected to the House of Representatives. Satirical barbs about the System blend neatly with Eddie's irresistible huckster persona for this ingratiating (if somewhat overlong) comedy, aided by a strong supporting cast. [R]▼●
Disturbed (1991) **C-96m.** *½ D: Charles Winkler. Malcolm McDowell, Geoffrey Lewis, Pamela Gidley, Priscilla Pointer, Irwin Keyes, Peter Murnik. Terrific, funny performance by McDowell can't save this florid thriller set in an insane asylum where what might have been a murder took place 10 years before. Flashy camerawork is merely distracting here; one shot is from the point of view of a penis! [R]▼
Disturbing Behavior (1998-U.S.-Australian) **C-83m.** BOMB D: David Nutter. James Marsden, Katie Holmes, Nick Stahl, William Sadler, Bruce Greenwood, Steve Railsback, Tobias Mehler, Ethan Embry. Teenager Marsden, a newcomer in town, soon realizes there's a sinister plot by the high school guidance counselor to "reform" troubled kids: they become well groomed, love yogurt and freak out when horny. Predictable, coldly calculated and trendy, this is teen-targeted dreck. Give us SCREAM—or at least I WAS A TEEN-AGE WEREWOLF. Director's cut runs 94m. [R]▼●◗
Diva (1982-French) **C-123m.** ***½ D: Jean-Jacques Beineix. Wilhelmenia Wiggins Fernandez, Frederic Andrei, Richard Bohringer, Thuy An Luu, Jacques Fabbri. Music-loving mailman bootleg-tapes the concert of a superstar diva who's never made a recording, finds himself in even hotter water when his possession is mixed up with a second tape that will incriminate

gangsters. High-tech melodrama occasionally rubs your nose in its technique, but still makes for whale of a directorial debut by Beineix. Subway motorcycle chase is an action classic. [R] ▼●◗

Dive Bomber (1941) **C-133m.** *** D: Michael Curtiz. Errol Flynn, Fred MacMurray, Ralph Bellamy, Alexis Smith, Robert Armstrong, Regis Toomey, Craig Stevens. Exciting, well-paced aviation film of experiments to eliminate pilot-blackout. Flynn, MacMurray, and Smith perform well in formula story. ▼●

Divertimento SEE: **La Belle Noiseuse**

Divided Heart, The (1954-British) **89m.** *** D: Charles Crichton. Cornell Borchers, Yvonne Mitchell, Armin Dahlen, Alexander Knox, Michel Ray, Geoffrey Keen, Theodore Bikel. Intelligent study of dilemma faced by parents of foster child when real mother, thought dead, returns to claim her son. Set in Europe after WW2.

Divine Madness! (1980) **C-95m.** **½ D: Michael Ritchie. Bette Midler fanatics would probably up this rating a half star or so, but unevenness and occasional oppressiveness of this concert film may even get to them. Some funny bits, but will someone tell her to quit desecrating rock'n'roll? Panavision. [R] ▼●◗

Divine Nymph, The (1979-Italian) **C-90m.** *½ D: Giuseppe Patroni Griffi. Marcello Mastroianni, Laura Antonelli, Terence Stamp, Michele Placido, Duilio Del Prete, Ettore Manni, Marina Vlady. Poor melodrama chronicling beautiful Antonelli's involvements with marquis Mastroianni and baron Stamp. Of interest only when Laura doffs her duds. ▼

Divorce (1945) **71m.** ** D: William Nigh. Kay Francis, Bruce Cabot, Helen Mack, Craig Reynolds, Larry Olsen, Mary Gordon. Francis is city girl who returns to home town, enticing Cabot away from Mack and family; satisfactory programmer.

Divorce American Style (1967) **C-109m.** *** D: Bud Yorkin. Dick Van Dyke, Debbie Reynolds, Jason Robards, Jean Simmons, Van Johnson, Joe Flynn, Shelley Berman, Martin Gabel, Lee Grant, Pat Collins, Tom Bosley, Eileen Brennan. Highly entertaining comedy of Van Dyke and Reynolds finding more problems than they expected when they get divorced. Stars are unusually good in offbeat roles. Written by Norman Lear. ▼

Divorcee, The (1930) **83m** **½ D: Robert Z. Leonard. Norma Shearer, Chester Morris, Conrad Nagel, Robert Montgomery, Florence Eldridge. Stagy but interesting tale of young wife Shearer who puts up with husband Morris's flirtations until she decides to equal him. Shearer won an Oscar for this performance. ▼

Divorce—Italian Style (1961-Italian) **104m.** ***½ D: Pietro Germi. Marcello Mastroianni, Daniela Rocca, Stefania Sandrelli, Leopoldo Trieste. Marcello can't stomach wife Rocca, so he schemes to wed sexy young Sandrelli. Hilarious, flavorful comedy, which earned an Oscar for its story and screenplay. The twist ending adds a perfect—and most ironic—touch. ▼

Divorce of Lady X, The (1938-British) **C-91m.** **½ D: Tim Whelan. Merle Oberon, Laurence Olivier, Binnie Barnes, Ralph Richardson, Morton Selten. Cute but extremely dated screwball comedy with lawyer Olivier forced to share a hotel room with mischievous Oberon. He becomes convinced he's the cause of her pending divorce—even though she's not married. ▼●

Dixiana (1930) **C/B&W-98m.** **½ D: Luther Reed. Bebe Daniels, Everett Marshall, Bert Wheeler, Robert Woolsey, Joseph Cawthorn, Jobyna Howland, Dorothy Lee, Bill "Bojangles" Robinson. Ambitious but dated early-talkie musical set in 1840s New Orleans, with Daniels as a circus star who falls in love with the scion of a wealthy family (Metropolitan Opera star Marshall). Enlivened by Wheeler and Woolsey's comedy relief, and (in restored prints) a beautiful two-color Technicolor Mardi Gras finale, with a showstopping tap dance solo by Bojangles. Beware TV print which lops off the final color reels—and leaves the story unfinished! ▼◗

Dixie (1943) **C-89m.** *** D: A. Edward Sutherland. Bing Crosby, Dorothy Lamour, Billy DeWolfe, Marjorie Reynolds, Lynne Overman, Raymond Walburn, Eddie Foy, Jr., Grant Mitchell. Atmosphere overshadows plot in this biography of pioneer minstrel Dan Emmett, who wrote title song; Bing also sings "Sunday, Monday or Always."

Dixie Dynamite (1976) **C-89m.** *½ D: Lee Frost. Warren Oates, Christopher George, Jane Anne Johnstone, Kathy McHaley, Wes Bishop, Mark Miller, R. G. Armstrong, Stanley Adams. Johnstone and McHaley wreak havoc on town after they are dispossessed from their farm and their moonshiner father is killed by a trigger-happy deputy. Sound familiar? [PG] ▼

Django (1966-Italian-Spanish) **C-92m.** **½ D: Sergio Corbucci. Franco Nero, Loredano Nusciak, Eduardo Fajardo, Jose Bodalo, Angel Alvarez, Jimmy Douglas. Though not as good as the Leone-Eastwood spaghetti Westerns, this is an above-average example of the genre, with the gimmick of Nero as a ruthless gunfighter who drags around a coffin containing a machine gun wherever he goes. This became a cult film and inspired a slew of European oaters with the name "Django" in their titles. Followed by DJANGO STRIKES AGAIN. ▼◗

D.O.A. (1950) **83m.** ***½ D: Rudolph Maté. Edmond O'Brien, Pamela Britton, Luther Adler, Beverly Campbell (Garland),

Lynn Baggett, William Ching, Henry Hart, Neville Brand. Gripping, original film noir with O'Brien desperately trying to find who has given him a slow-acting poison—and why. Inventively photographed (by Ernest Laszlo) on the streets of San Francisco and L.A. Written by Russell Rouse and Clarence Greene. Music by Dimitri Tiomkin. Remade in 1969 (as COLOR ME DEAD) and 1988. Also shown in computer-colored version.▼●◗

D.O.A. (1981) **C-93m.** *½ D: Lech Kowalski. Sex Pistols, Dead Boys, Rich Kids, Generation X, Terry and the Idiots, X-Ray Spec, Nancy Spungen. Crummy documentary rip-off about the infamous punk rock band Sex Pistols. Of interest only for footage of the pathetic Sid Vicious and girlfriend Nancy Spungen.▼

D.O.A. (1988) **C-100m.** BOMB D: Rocky Morton, Annabel Jankel. Dennis Quaid, Meg Ryan, Daniel Stern, Charlotte Rampling, Jane Kaczmarek, Christopher Neame. Noisy and needless remake of the film noir original, transplanted to academia. Quaid is a college professor fed a slow-acting toxin in a dispute over a prized fiction manuscript; Ryan is an innocent student helping him pursue his "killer." Badly overdirected by the *Max Headroom* creators; obvious red herrings abound. [R] ▼●

D.O.A. II SEE: **Color Me Dead**

Doberman Gang, The (1972) **C-87m.** **½ D: Byron Chudnow. Byron Mabe, Julie Parrish, Hal Reed, Simmy Bow, Jojo D'Amore. Trim low-budget heist movie about a crook's ingenious plan to use six dobermans to pull off bank job. Dogs steal not only the loot but the picture, and starred in two sequels. [G]▼

Doc (1971) **C-96m.** ** D: Frank Perry. Stacy Keach, Harris Yulin, Faye Dunaway, Michael Witney, Denver John Collins, Dan Greenburg. Well-crafted but unpleasant anti-Western, telling the story of Wyatt Earp and Doc Holliday in revisionist terms. Script by Pete Hamill. [PG—edited from original R rating]

Doc Hollywood (1991) **C-104m.** **½ D: Michael Caton-Jones. Michael J. Fox, Julie Warner, Bridget Fonda, Barnard Hughes, Woody Harrelson, David Ogden Stiers, Frances Sternhagen, George Hamilton, Roberts Blossom, Barry Sobel. Fox is on his way to a career in L.A. plastic surgery when he crashes his car in South Carolina's podunk squash capital and is sentenced to perform much-needed medical community service. Agreeably played but nothing special. Warner has a memorable first scene, and there's an amusing star cameo near the end. Director Caton-Jones appears as a maître d'. [PG-13]▼●◗

Dock Brief, The (1962-British) **88m.** **½ D: James Hill. Peter Sellers, Richard Attenborough, Beryl Reid, David Lodge. Sellers is aging barrister who incompetently represents accused killer Attenborough with strange results; pleasant comic satire. John Mortimer adapted his own play. U.S. title: TRIAL AND ERROR. ▼

Docks of New Orleans (1948) **64m.** BOMB D: Derwin Abrahams. Roland Winters, Victor Sen Yung, Mantan Moreland, John Gallaudet, Virginia Dale, Carol Forman, Douglas Fowley. Bottom-of-the-barrel *Charlie Chan* entry about killers trying to get their hands on a chemical shipment.

Docks of New York, The (1928) **76m.** **** D: Josef von Sternberg. George Bancroft, Betty Compson, Olga Baclanova, Mitchell Lewis, Clyde Cook, Gustav von Seyffertitz. Burly ship stoker Bancroft marries the attempted suicide victim he saved from the drink, first taking her for granted, then coming to love her. A rival to SUNRISE as the visual apogee of silent cinema, though the smoky hues of Sternberg's waterfront dive can fully be appreciated only on the big screen. Gaylord Carter's organ score on the videocassette version is a big plus. ▼

Docks of New York, The (1945) **61m.** ** D: Wallace Fox. Leo Gorcey, Huntz Hall, Billy Benedict, Gloria Pope, Carlyle Blackwell, Jr., Bud Gorman, George Meeker. The East Side Kids get mixed up in another murder mystery, this time involving a stolen necklace. Incidentally, Carlyle Blackwell, Jr., is now better known as flamboyant fashion critic Mr. Blackwell.

Doc Savage: The Man of Bronze (1975) **C-100m.** **½ D: Michael Anderson. Ron Ely, Darrell Zwerling, Michael Miller, Pamela Hensley, Paul Wexler, Robyn Hilton, William Lucking, Paul Gleason. Film debut of Kenneth Robeson's pulp hero was sold (and accepted) as camp; in reality, it's a straight-faced period adventure that just came out at the wrong time. Story has Doc (Ely) and his Fabulous Five heading to South America to investigate his father's death, tangling with evil Captain Seas (Wexler). Fun for kids and buffs, with amusing score built around Sousa marches; final film of producer George Pal. [G]▼●

Doctor, The (1991) **C-125m.** *** D: Randa Haines. William Hurt, Christine Lahti, Elizabeth Perkins, Mandy Patinkin, Adam Arkin, Charlie Korsmo, Wendy Crewson, Bill Macy. Successful surgeon is diagnosed with throat cancer—and for the first time in his career, learns what it's like to be a patient at the mercy of cold-blooded doctors and a bureaucratic hospital. Perkins stands out in a showy role as fellow cancer patient. Engrossing, well acted, and utterly believable; based on Dr. Ed Rosenbaum's own experiences, described in his book *A Taste of My Own Medicine*. [PG-13]▼●

Doctor and the Devils, The (1985) **C-93m.** ** D: Freddie Francis. Timothy Dalton,

Jonathan Pryce, Twiggy, Julian Sands, Stephen Rea, Phyllis Logan, Beryl Reid, Patrick Stewart, Sian Phillips. Serious-minded but unsuccessful (and unappealing) Gothic tale of grave robbers who supply a dedicated doctor who's content not to ask too many questions. Based on a 1940s screenplay by Dylan Thomas, revised by Ronald Harwood. Reminiscent of vintage Hammer horror films; no coincidence, with veteran Francis directing. Made in England. J-D-C Scope. [R]▼

Doctor and the Girl, The (1949) **98m.** **½ D: Curtis Bernhardt. Glenn Ford, Charles Coburn, Gloria DeHaven, Janet Leigh, Warner Anderson, Nancy Davis (Reagan). Ford is appropriately sterile as idealistic young doctor who married poor girl and practices medicine in N.Y.C. slum.

Doctor at Large (1957-British) **C-98m.** **½ D: Ralph Thomas. Dirk Bogarde, Muriel Pavlow, Donald Sinden, James Robertson Justice, Shirley Eaton, Derek Farr, Michael Medwin, George Coulouris, Anne Heywood, Lionel Jeffries, Mervyn Johns, Ernest Thesiger. Another entry in pleasing series, with novice doctor Bogarde seeking staff position in wealthy hospital. VistaVision.▼

Doctor At Sea (1955-British) **C-93m.** **½ D: Ralph Thomas. Dirk Bogarde, Brigitte Bardot, Brenda de Banzie, James Robertson Justice, Maurice Denham, Michael Medwin, Raymond Huntley. Preferring the bachelor life, Bogarde signs on as ship's doctor on passenger-carrying freighter, in second entry of this entertaining series. VistaVision.▼

Doctor Blood's Coffin (1961-British) **C-92m.** **½ D: Sidney Furie. Kieron Moore, Hazel Court, Ian Hunter, Fred Johnson. In Cornwall, young scientist holes up in an abandoned tin mine to work on his theory that placing a live heart in a corpse will bring it back to life. He's right, as it turns out, but unfortunately he's also crazy. . . . Crude but lively imitation-Hammer horror opus.▼●

Doctor Death, Seeker of Souls (1973) **C-73m.** *½ D: Eddie Saeta. John Considine, Barry Coe, Cheryl Miller, Florence Marly, Jo Morrow. Cheap horror item about the transferring of souls by 1,000-year-old Considine. Few effective moments include The Three Stooges' Moe Howard in a gag bit. Aka DOCTOR DEATH. [R]▼

Doctor Detroit (1983) **C-89m.** ** D: Michael Pressman. Dan Aykroyd, Howard Hesseman, T. K. Carter, Donna Dixon, Lynn Whitfield, Lydia Lei, Fran Drescher, Kate Murtagh, George Furth, Andrew Duggan, Glenne Headly, James Brown. Wimpy college professor becomes embroiled with pimps, prostitutes, and underworld intrigue, but the results are surprisingly bland, and only sporadically funny. Story by Bruce Jay Friedman. Aykroyd later married costar Dixon. [R]▼●

Doctor Dolittle (1967) **C-144m.** *½ D: Richard Fleischer. Rex Harrison, Samantha Eggar, Anthony Newley, Richard Attenborough, Peter Bull, Geoffrey Holder. Robert Surtees' photography is great, and that's it for this colossal musical dud that almost ruined 20th Century-Fox studios. The charm of Hugh Lofting's stories is gone. One merit: if you have unruly children, it may put them to sleep. Songs by Leslie Bricusse (including the Oscar-winning "Talk to the Animals") and choreography by Herbert Ross. Oscar winner for special visual effects. Originally 152m. Remade in 1998 as DR. DOLITTLE. Todd-AO.▼●

Doctor Faustus (1967-British) **C-93m.** ** D: Richard Burton, Nevill Coghill. Richard Burton, Andreas Teuber, Ian Marter, Elizabeth Taylor. Burton's retelling of Faustus legend lacks everything but a buxom Mrs. Burton in brief sequence as Helen of Troy. Strictly for their fans.▼

Doctor From Seven Dials, The SEE: **Corridors of Blood**

Doctor In Clover (1965-British) **C-101m.** ** D: Ralph Thomas. Leslie Phillips, James Robertson Justice, Shirley Anne Field, John Fraser, Joan Sims. New doctor, same old zany situations in sixth entry of series. Doctor studies nurses more than medicine. Not up to the others' standard.

Doctor In Distress (1963-British) **C-102m.** **½ D: Ralph Thomas. Dirk Bogarde, Samantha Eggar, James Robertson Justice, Mylene Demongeot, Donald Houston, Barbara Murray, Dennis Price, Leo McKern. Pompous chief surgeon falls in love for the first time, and his assistant tries to help the romance along while balancing his own love life. Another entertaining entry in comedy series. Bogarde's last appearance as Dr. Sparrow.▼

Doctor In Love (1960-British) **C-93m.** ** D: Ralph Thomas. Michael Craig, James Robertson Justice, Virginia Maskell, Carole Lesley, Leslie Phillips, Liz Fraser. Craig inherited Bogarde's role in DOCTOR series. This entry centers on young medic's inability to avoid romantic attachments.

Doctor in the House (1954-British) **C-92m.** ***½ D: Ralph Thomas. Dirk Bogarde, Muriel Pavlow, Kenneth More, Donald Sinden, Kay Kendall, James Robertson Justice, Donald Houston, Suzanne Cloutier, Geoffrey Keen, George Coulouris, Shirley Eaton, Joan Hickson, Richard Wattis. Hilarious comedy follows exploits of medical students intent on studying beautiful women and how to become wealthy physicians. This delightful film (from Richard Gordon's stories) spawned six other "Doctor" movies, plus a TV series. Justice memorable as Sir Lancelot Spratt. Scripted by Gordon, Ronald Wilkenson, and costar Nicholas Phipps.▼

Doctor in Trouble (1970-British) **C-90m.** ** D: Ralph Thomas. Leslie Phillips, Harry Secombe, James Robertson Justice, Angela Scoular, Irene Handl, Robert Morley. Fair entry in the on-and-off British comedy series concerns Dr. Phillips' problems when he stows away on ocean liner; good supporting cast help a bit. [R]▼

Doctor Mordrid (1992) **C-89m.** **½ D: Albert and Charles Band. Jeffrey Combs, Yvette Nipar, Brian Thompson, Jay Acovone, Keith Coulouris, Ritch Brinkley, Pearl Shear, Murray Rubin, Jeff Austin, John Apicella. A woman discovers her reclusive neighbor is a powerful sorcerer sworn to save the world from his evil counterpart. Satisfying little movie, confident of its intent, with a sensitive performance by Combs. From Full Moon. [R]▼

Doctor Rhythm (1938) **80m.** **½ D: Frank Tuttle. Bing Crosby, Mary Carlisle, Beatrice Lillie, Andy Devine, Laura Hope Crews, Sterling Holloway. Amiable but second-rate Crosby vehicle about doctor who masquerades as cop and falls in love with woman he's assigned to guard. Lillie adds her distinctive spark.

Doctor's Dilemma (1958-British) **C-99m.** *** D: Anthony Asquith. Leslie Caron, Dirk Bogarde, Alastair Sim, Robert Morley. Bubbly Shaw period play of young wife Caron conniving to convince medical specialists that her scoundrel husband is worth saving.

Doctors Wear Scarlet SEE: **Bloodsuckers** (1970-British)

Doctors' Wives (1971) **C-100m.** *½ D: George Schaefer. Dyan Cannon, Richard Crenna, Gene Hackman, Rachel Roberts, Carroll O'Connor, Janice Rule, Diana Sands, Cara Williams, Ralph Bellamy. Super-sudsy soaper sparked by mysterious murder of cheating wife; glossy garbage. Scripted by a slumming Daniel Taradash. [R]▼

Doctor Syn (1937-British) **80m.** **½ D: Roy William Neill. George Arliss, Margaret Lockwood, John Loder, Roy Emerton, Graham Moffatt. Arliss' final film finds aging star somewhat miscast as English vicar who rides at night as a pirate, but director Neill keeps things moving at his usual pace, and the atmosphere is rich. Remade twice in 1962—as NIGHT CREATURES, and DR. SYN, ALIAS THE SCARECROW.▼

Doctor Takes a Wife, The (1940) **89m.** *** D: Alexander Hall. Ray Milland, Loretta Young, Reginald Gardiner, Gail Patrick, Edmund Gwenn, Frank Sully, Gordon Jones. Milland is mistaken for Young's husband, then forced to pretend he is. Stars and material spark each other at a lively pace.▼

Doctor X (1932) **C-80m.** ** D: Michael Curtiz. Lionel Atwill, Fay Wray, Lee Tracy, Preston Foster, Robert Warwick, Mae Busch. Police have tracked the "full-moon strangler" to Atwill's experimental laboratory. Ludicrous Grand Guignol chiller (Wray's entrance has her screaming—for no reason at all) is a must for horror-film buffs because of its Anton Grot sets, special Max Factor makeup, and rich use of two-color Technicolor (though most TV prints are b&w) . . . but it creaks *badly* and seems much longer than it is.▼●

Doctor, You've Got to Be Kidding (1967) **C-94m.** BOMB D: Peter Tewksbury. Sandra Dee, George Hamilton, Celeste Holm, Bill Bixby, Dick Kallman, Mort Sahl, Dwayne Hickman, Allen Jenkins. Dee would rather marry the boss than pursue singing career. Even *her* singing might have helped this alleged comedy. Panavision.

Doctor Zhivago (1965) **C-197m.** ***½ D: David Lean. Omar Sharif, Julie Christie, Geraldine Chaplin, Tom Courtenay, Alec Guinness, Siobhan McKenna, Ralph Richardson, Rod Steiger, Rita Tushingham, Adrienne Corri, Geoffrey Keen, Jeffrey Rockland, Klaus Kinski, Jack MacGowran, Tarek Sharif. Sumptuous, sprawling epic from Boris Pasternak's acclaimed novel; Sharif is charismatic as Russian poet/doctor Zhivago, an orphan who later marries aristocratic Chaplin but falls in love with politicized nurse Christie. Film spans several decades, including WW1 and Bolshevik Revolution, and features stirring crowd scenes, gorgeous romantic vistas (set to Maurice Jarre's sweeping music) and a powerful exodus sequence on train. Overlong, but with top production values and superb acting in every role. Won Oscars for screenplay (Robert Bolt), cinematography (Freddie Young), art direction–set decoration (John Box and Terry Marsh; Dario Simoni), costume design (Phyllis Dalton), and music score. Reissued at 180m. Epic use of Panavision.▼●◗

Dodes'ka-den (1970-Japanese) **C-140m.** **½ D: Akira Kurosawa. Yoshitaka Zushi, Tomoko Yamazaki, Hiroshi Akutagawa, Noboru Mitani. Episodic chronicle of life in a Tokyo slum; characters include a little boy who feeds himself and derelict dad by scrounging garbage—together, they visualize a dream house; a wan girl who makes artificial flowers to support her alcoholic stepfather; etc. Kurosawa's first film in color. Originally 244m.▼●

Dodge City (1939) **C-105m.** *** D: Michael Curtiz. Errol Flynn, Olivia de Havilland, Ann Sheridan, Bruce Cabot, Frank McHugh, Alan Hale, John Litel, Victor Jory, Ward Bond, Cora Witherspoon. Errol tames the West and de Havilland, in entertaining large-scale Western, with Warner Bros. stock company giving good vignettes, and granddaddy of all barroom brawls. The principal inspiration for BLAZING SADDLES.▼●

Dodsworth (1936) **101m.** **** D: William Wyler. Walter Huston, Ruth Chatterton, Paul Lukas, Mary Astor, David Niven, Gregory Gaye, Maria Ouspenskaya, Spring Byington, Grant Mitchell, Harlan Briggs. Superb adaptation of Sinclair Lewis novel about middle-aged American industrialist who retires, goes to Europe, where he and his wife find differing sets of values, and new relationships. Intelligently written (by Sidney Howard), beautifully filmed, extremely well acted, with Huston recreating his Broadway role. John Payne (billed as John Howard Payne) makes screen debut in small role. Won Oscar for Interior Decoration (Richard Day). Unusually mature Hollywood film, not to be missed. ▼●◗

Dog, a Mouse and a Sputnik, A SEE: **Sputnik**

Dog Day (1983-French) **C-101m.** **½ D: Yves Boisset. Miou Miou, Lee Marvin, Jean Carmet, Victor Lanoux, David Bennent, Bernadette Lafont, Jean-Pierre Kalfon, Pierre Clementi, Tina Louise. Intriguing if gratuitously violent thriller about a tough but doomed American gangster on the lam (Marvin, well cast) who hides out on the farm of a depraved French family. Fairly effective as an ode to the mythical image of the American screen hood.▼

Dog Day Afternoon (1975) **C-130m.** ***½ D: Sidney Lumet. Al Pacino, John Cazale, Charles Durning, James Broderick, Chris Sarandon, Sully Boyar, Penny Allen, Carol Kane, Lance Henriksen, Dick Anthony Williams, Philip Charles Mackenzie. Incredible-but-true story of a loser (Pacino) who holds up a Brooklyn bank to raise money for his lover's sex-change operation, and sees simple heist snowball into a citywide incident. Pacino's performance and Lumet's flavorful N.Y.C. atmosphere obscure the fact that this is much ado about nothing. Frank Pierson won an Oscar for his screenplay (based on an article by P. F. Kluge and Thomas Moore). [R] ▼●◗

Dog Eat Dog (1964-U.S.-Italian-German) **84m.** BOMB D: Gustav Gavrin. Cameron Mitchell, Jayne Mansfield, Dody Heath, Ivor Salter, Isa Miranda, Werner Peters. Unintentionally funny potboiler of lust, greed, and depravity, with various characters intent upon making off with a stolen million dollars. A highlight: Jayne's constant complaining about her need for clean panties. Not released in the U.S. until 1966; various sources list Albert Zugsmith and Ray Nazarro as director.▼

Dogfight (1991) **C-92m.** ***½ D: Nancy Savoca. River Phoenix, Lili Taylor, Richard Panebianco, Anthony Clark, Mitchell Whitfield, Holly Near, E. G. Daily, Brendan Fraser. Title refers to a cruel wager by Vietnam-bound Marines in 1963 San Francisco. Taylor (superb) is a physically plain folkie who becomes an unwitting partner in Phoenix's attempt to bring the ugliest "date" to a party. Original, barely released sleeper is surprisingly unmawkish, thanks to a good script by Bob Comfort, and Savoca's tough direction. Unusually apt use of period music. [R]▼●

Dogma (1999) **C-135m.** **½ D: Kevin Smith. Matt Damon, Ben Affleck, Linda Fiorentino, Alan Rickman, Chris Rock, Salma Hayek, Jason Lee, Kevin Smith, Jason Mewes, George Carlin, Alanis Morissette, Janeane Garofalo, Bud Cort. Ambitious comic fantasy in which age-old battles between outcast angels, Lucifer, and God are played out in modern-day America, as a young woman who's lost her faith (Fiorentino) is chosen to save humanity. Irreverent, to say the least; challenging and clever at times, but also puerile and silly, not to mention long. Smith and Mewes reprise their characters from Smith's earlier films. Smith also scripted. Super 35. [R]▼◗

Dog of Flanders, A (1959) **C-96m.** ** D: James B. Clark. David Ladd, Donald Crisp, Theodore Bikel, Max Croiset, Monique Ahrens. Tear-jerker for children about a boy, his dog, and friends they make. Crisp and Bikel have good character roles. Remade in 1999. CinemaScope.▼

Dog of Flanders, A (1999) **C-100m.** *½ D: Kevin Brodie. Jack Warden, Jeremy James Kissner, Jesse James, Jon Voight, Cheryl Ladd, Steven Hartley, Bruce McGill, Andrew Bicknell. A 19th-century Belgian boy rescues an abandoned dog and uses him to pull a milk-delivery cart for him and his grandfather . . . but the boy really longs to be a painter like the great Reubens. Despite excellent photography of Belgian locations, this adaptation of Ouida's classic children's novel is a joyless, anachronistic, moralistic snoozer. [PG]▼●◗

Dog Park (1999-U.S.-Canadian) **C-91m.** *½ D: Bruce McCulloch. Natasha Henstridge, Luke Wilson, Kathleen Robertson, Janeane Garofalo, Bruce McCulloch, Kristin Lehman, Harland Williams, Mark McKinney. Howlingly bad romantic comedy squanders cute premise about a group of Toronto singles whose lackluster love lives affect their pet pooches. Self-absorbed, unlikable lead characters and meandering subplots don't help. Inauspicious writing-directing debut from *Kids in the Hall* alum McCulloch; film's only laughs come from fellow *Kids* member McKinney as a pet therapist. [R]▼

Dogpound Shuffle (1975) **C-95m.** *** D: Jeffrey Bloom. Ron Moody, David Soul, Pamela McMyler, Ray Stricklyn, Raymond Sutton. Unpretentious little fable about cynical ex-vaudevillian tap-dancer—now a bum—who must raise $30 to rescue his dog from the pound. Funny and wistful, with excellent character performance by Moody. Aka SPOT. [PG]▼

Dogs (1976) **C-90m.** *½ D: Burt Brinckerhoff. David McCallum, George Wyner, Eric Server, Sandra McCabe, Sterling Swanson, Linda Gray. Low-budget yawner about a pack of dogs on the prowl. Get out the flea powder. Video title: SLAUGHTER. [R]▼

Dogs in Space (1986-Australian) **C-105m.** BOMB D: Richard Lowenstein. Michael Hutchence, Saskia Post, Nique Needles, Deanna Bond, Chris Haywood. Noisy film tries to encapsule punk era of the late '70s but is merely a tiresome slice-of-life peek at wayward youth. Title refers to the epochal effect of early space flights, including the Russian missions with dogs. Panavision. [R]▼

Dogs of War, The (1980-British) **C-102m.** *** D: John Irvin. Christopher Walken, Tom Berenger, Colin Blakely, Hugh Millais, Paul Freeman, JoBeth Williams, Ed O'Neill. Appropriately mean if overly somber adaptation of the Frederick Forsyth best-seller about a mercenary who tangles with an Amin-like dictator in an African hell-hole. Will not promote one-worldism, but Walken takes a screen beating nearly as impressively as Brando. British running time 118m. [R]▼●

Dog Soldiers SEE: **Who'll Stop the Rain**

Doing Time (1979-British) **C-95m.** **½ D: Dick Clement. Ronnie Barker, Richard Beckinsale, Fulton Mackay, Brian Wilde, Peter Vaughan. Barker is a delight as a habitual prison inmate who inadvertently escapes—and wants back in! Reportedly not as funny as the TV series on which it's based, but that's usually the case with feature spinoffs. (The show was tried on American TV as *On the Rocks*.) Original British title: PORRIDGE.

Doin' It SEE: **First Time, The** (1983)

Doin' Time (1985) **C-81m.** BOMB D: George Mendeluk. Jeff Altman, Dey Young, Richard Mulligan, John Vernon, Colleen Camp, Melanie Chartoff, Graham Jarvis, Pat McCormick, Eddie Velez, Jimmie Walker, Judy Landers, Mike Mazurki, Muhammad Ali. Shoddy, thoroughly obnoxious POLICE ACADEMY clone, set in the John Dillinger Memorial Penitentiary (yuk, yuk). [R]▼

Doin' Time on Planet Earth (1988) **C-83m.** **½ D: Charles Matthau. Nicholas Strouse, Andrea Thompson, Hugh Gillin, Adam West, Candice Azzara, Hugh O'Brian, Matt Adler, Timothy Patrick Murphy, Roddy McDowall, Maureen Stapleton. Fresh-feeling but thin teen comedy about boy who feels *literally* alienated from his family and their Holiday Inn home: cheerful wackos West and Azzara convince him that he's really an alien born on Earth, destined to lead others back to the stars. Amusingly designed, inventively directed, but aimless. [PG]▼

Dolemite (1975) **C-88m.** *½ D: D'Urville Martin. Rudy Ray Moore, Jerry Jones, Lady Reed. Occasionally funny but amateurish vehicle for standup comedian Moore (who also produced the film), a stout nonactor who combines the personality of Mr. T with a rhyming rap routine. Karate gangster spoof is set in the milieu of black nightclubs where Moore performs. [R]▼◗

$(Dollars) (1971) **C-119m.** ***½ D: Richard Brooks. Warren Beatty, Goldie Hawn, Gert Frobe, Robert Webber, Scott Brady. Top-notch caper thriller (scripted by the director) set in Germany with unusual chase that goes on for more than a fifth of the film. Awfully similar to PERFECT FRIDAY. Bouncy Quincy Jones score. [R]▼●

Doll Face (1945) **80m.** **½ D: Lewis Seiler. Vivian Blaine, Dennis O'Keefe, Perry Como, Carmen Miranda, Martha Stewart, Michael Dunne. Burlesque dancer Blaine makes good in the big time; pleasant musical with Como's hit "Hubba Hubba Hubba."▼

Dollmaker, The (1984) **C-150m. TVM** D: Daniel Petrie. Jane Fonda, Levon Helm, Amanda Plummer, Susan Kingsley, Geraldine Page. Fonda's glowing, Emmy-winning TV-movie debut, as a woman from the Kentucky hills who uproots her kids to follow her husband to a big-city job during WW2 and finds a new way of life using her natural whittling talents. Susan Cooper and Hume Cronyn (who wrote Broadway's *Foxfire*) beautifully adapted Harriette Arnow's novel. Above average.▼

Dollman (1991) **C-86m.** BOMB D: Albert Pyun. Tim Thomerson, Jackie Earl Haley, Kamala Lopez, Humberto Ortiz, Nicholas Guest, Judd Omen. Tough alien cop (from a planet identical to a slightly futuristic Earth) chases a villainous flying head to our planet, but surprise! The cop is only 13 inches tall. Underproduced trifle with poor FX and a deadly slow pace. Followed by DOLLMAN VS. THE DEMONIC TOYS. [R]▼●

Dolls (1987) **C-77m.** ** D: Stuart Gordon. Ian Patrick Williams, Carolyn Purdy-Gordon, Carrie Lorraine, Guy Rolfe, Hilary Mason, Bunty Bailey, Cassie Stuart, Stephen Lee. OK horror from the director of RE-ANIMATOR has unsuspecting people taking shelter from a storm in mansion owned by elderly couple who make murderous dolls. Nothing special here. [R]▼●

Doll's House, A (1973-British) **C-105m.** **½ D: Patrick Garland. Claire Bloom, Anthony Hopkins, Ralph Richardson, Denholm Elliott, Anna Massey, Edith Evans. Bloom and Hopkins give thoughtful performances in this rather stagy filmization of Ibsen's play. Still, the words are there and the play is a strong statement about women's (and all people's) rights to be human beings. [G]▼

Doll's House, A (1973-British) **C-106m.** **½ D: Joseph Losey. Jane Fonda, David Warner, Trevor Howard, Delphine Seyrig, Edward Fox. Moderately successful, cinematic version of Ibsen play, worth a look for Fonda's controversial interpretation of a 19th-century liberated woman. Howard shines as the dying Dr. Rank. [G]▼

Doll Squad, The (1973) **C-101m.** BOMB D: Ted V. Mikels. Michael Ansara, Francine York, Anthony Eisley, John Carter, Rafael Campos, Lisa Todd. Sexy York leads her all-female trio against ex-CIA agent Ansara, out to rule the world. Poorly made and boring, with very little action. Interesting only as a forerunner to *Charlie's Angels*; the smart one's even named Sabrina! Aka HUSTLER SQUAD. [PG]▼

Dolly Sisters, The (1945) **C-114m.** **½ D: Irving Cummings. Betty Grable, John Payne, June Haver, S. Z. Sakall, Reginald Gardiner, Frank Latimore. Sassy hokum about popular vaudeville sister act with two lovely stars and a bevy of old song favorites, plus newly written "I Can't Begin to Tell You."▼●

Dolores Claiborne (1995) **C-131m.** ***½ D: Taylor Hackford. Kathy Bates, Jennifer Jason Leigh, Judy Parfitt, Christopher Plummer, David Strathairn, Eric Bogosian, John C. Reilly, Ellen Muth, Bob Gunton. A Maine woman is accused of murdering her longtime employer, which brings her estranged daughter home for the first time in years. Now, the two women begin to sort out unanswered questions from the past. Gripping adaptation of Stephen King's novel (by Tony Gilroy) holds your interest from start to finish, as the real story unfolds. Bates' performance is a powerhouse, and the rest of the cast is equally fine. Kudos, too, to Hackford's arresting visual treatment. Panavision. [R]▼●◗

Dominick and Eugene (1988) **C-111m.** *** D: Robert M. Young. Tom Hulce, Ray Liotta, Jamie Lee Curtis, Todd Graff, Mimi Cecchini, Robert Levine, Bill Cobbs, David Strathairn. Heartrending story of a bright young intern (Liotta) and his devotion to a childlike twin brother (Hulce) who needs looking after. An overtly sentimental, sometimes melodramatic, but completely affecting story of love, compassion and responsibility. Hulce's performance as the sweet-natured, slow-witted Dominick is superb. [PG-13]▼●◗

Dominique (1978-British) **C-100m.** ** D: Michael Anderson. Cliff Robertson, Jean Simmons, Jenny Agutter, Simon Ward, Ron Moody, Judy Geeson, Michael Jayston, Flora Robson, David Tomlinson, Jack Warner. Great cast tries its best in disappointing melodrama; crippled Simmons believes husband Robertson wants to drive her mad; she dies, but comes back to haunt him. Video titles: DOMINIQUE IS DEAD and AVENGING SPIRIT. [PG]▼

Dominique Is Dead SEE: **Dominique**

Domino Kid, The (1957) **73m.** *½ D: Ray Nazarro. Rory Calhoun, Kristine Miller, Andrew Duggan, Roy Barcroft. Revengeoater with Calhoun returning to Lone Star State to seek killers of his family.

Domino Principle, The (1977) **C-97m.** BOMB D: Stanley Kramer. Gene Hackman, Candice Bergen, Richard Widmark, Mickey Rooney, Edward Albert, Eli Wallach. Muddled thriller about lunkhead Hackman's recruitment by a mysterious organization bent on political assassination. Bergen fails to convince as a lower-middle-class housewife. [R]▼

Dona Flor and Her Two Husbands (1978-Brazilian) **C-106m.** ***½ D: Bruno Barreto. Sonia Braga, Jose Wilker, Mauro Mendoca, Dinorah Brillanti. Braga is torn between giving body and soul to the dead, irresponsible husband who keeps returning to earth, or to the considerate dullard who's become her new mate. Original, very sexy fantasy. Remade as KISS ME GOODBYE. [R]▼●

Dona Herlinda and Her Son (1986-Mexican) **C-91m.** *** D: Jaime Humberto Hermosillo. Arturo Meza, Marco Antonio Trevino, Leticia Lupersio, Guadalupe del Toro, Angelica Guerrero. Amusing, cheerfully subversive comedy about a pair of gay men, one a surgeon and the other a student, who move in with the former's willful mother. Liberating in its depiction of the lovers; a film to be savored regardless of one's sexual preference.▼

Dondi (1961) **100m.** BOMB D: Albert Zugsmith. David Janssen, Patti Page, David Kory, Walter Winchell, Gale Gordon. Adaptation of sentimental comic strip about a cute war orphan trying to get along in the U.S. Goshes! Watch this film and you'll know why Janssen became a fugitive!

Don Is Dead, The (1973) **C-115m.** *½ D: Richard Fleischer. Anthony Quinn, Frederic Forrest, Robert Forster, Al Lettieri, Angel Tompkins, Ina Balin. Mafia wars form the convoluted plot of this trashy, derivative gangster saga. Retitled BEAUTIFUL BUT DEADLY. [R]▼

Don Juan (1926) **111m.** *** D: Alan Crosland. John Barrymore, Mary Astor, Willard Louis, Estelle Taylor, Helene Costello, Warner Oland, Montagu Love, Myrna Loy, Hedda Hopper. Entertaining swashbuckler, with Barrymore at his amorous best, surrounded by a top cast (including Oland as Cesare Borgia and Taylor as the infamous Lucretia) and lavish settings. Notable as the first silent film released with Vitaphone music and sound effects. ▼●

Don Juan DeMarco (1995) **C-97m.** ***

D: Jeremy Leven. Marlon Brando, Johnny Depp, Faye Dunaway, Geraldine Pailhas, Bob Dishy, Rachel Ticotin, Talisa Soto, Richard Sarafian, Tresa Hughes, Franc Luz. Psychotherapist on the verge of retirement becomes entranced with a new patient, a fervent young man who believes he is the world's greatest lover. Fanciful story (by director Leven) is made compulsively watchable by its stars: Brando, compelling as ever, Depp, hypnotically believeable, and Dunaway, a delightful match for Brando, as his wife. Ill-fated Tejano singer Selena appears in the opening scene. [PG-13] ▼●◗

Don Juan Quilligan (1945) **75m.** **½ D: Frank Tuttle. William Bendix, Joan Blondell, Phil Silvers, Anne Revere, B. S. Pully, Mary Treen. Bendix marries two girls at same time; lightweight comedy.

Donkey Skin (1971-French) **C-90m.** *** D: Jacques Demy. Catherine Deneuve, Jacques Perrin, Jean Marais, Delphine Seyrig. Charming adaptation of Charles Perrault's fairy tale about widowed King who vows that his new Queen must be as beautiful as his first. Sumptuous color production, witty script by Demy.▼

Don King: Only in America (1997) **C-110m. TVM** D: John Herzfeld. Ving Rhames, Vondie Curtis Hall, Keith David, Jeremy Piven, Loretta Devine, Lou Rawls, Darius McCrary, Ron Leibman, Brad Garrett. Rhames is magnetic as the outrageous and controversial boxing promoter. Story follows his rise from the streets to the big time, managing the careers of Muhammad Ali, Mike Tyson, George Foreman, and Larry Holmes (and according to this script, stealing from them as well). Rhames not only stars but also plays his own Greek chorus. Adapted by Kario Salem from Jack Newfield's biography. Above average.▼●

Donnie Brasco (1997) **C-121m.** ***½ D: Mike Newell. Al Pacino, Johnny Depp, Michael Madsen, Bruno Kirby, James Russo, Anne Heche, Željko Ivanek, Gerry Becker, Zach Grenier, Brian Tarantina, Val Avery, Gretchen Mol. Fresh, original take on life among the "wiseguys" in N.Y.C.'s Italian crime families, with rich characterizations by Pacino (as a low-level hood in the Mob food chain) and Depp (as an FBI undercover agent who becomes his protégé). Depp's assignment forces him to virtually abandon his wife and children, as he becomes more and more a part of his adoptive Mob family. Rings true start to finish; based on Joseph Pistone's memoir, scripted by Paul Attanasio. Super 35. [R] ▼●◗

Do Not Disturb (1965) **C-102m.** **½ D: Ralph Levy. Doris Day, Rod Taylor, Hermione Baddeley, Sergio Fantoni, Reginald Gardiner, Mike Romanoff, Leon Askin. Mild Day vehicle with Taylor as executive husband who brings her to suburban England. She meets suave Fantoni, enraging jealous hubby. Not up to her earlier fashion romps. CinemaScope.

Donovan's Brain (1953) **83m.** *** D: Felix Feist. Lew Ayres, Gene Evans, Nancy Davis (Reagan), Steve Brodie. Scientist is dominated by brain of dead industrialist, which he's kept alive in his lab; intriguing story by Curt Siodmak; modest, capable production. Filmed before as THE LADY AND THE MONSTER, again as THE BRAIN.▼●

Donovan's Reef (1963) **C-109m.** *** D: John Ford. John Wayne, Lee Marvin, Elizabeth Allen, Jack Warden, Cesar Romero, Dorothy Lamour, Mike Mazurki. Action-comedy bounces along with a good cast. Wayne and his freewheeling friends on a Pacific island are disrupted by Warden's grown daughter (Allen) who comes to visit. Lots of fun in Wayne's last feature film with John Ford. That's Ford's yacht *Araner* in several scenes.▼●

Don Q, Son of Zorro (1925) **110m.** **½ D: Donald Crisp. Douglas Fairbanks, Mary Astor, Jack McDonald, Donald Crisp, Stella De Lanti, Warner Oland, Jean Hersholt, Lottie Pickford Forrest, Charles Stevens. Fairbanks in his element in OK sequel to THE MARK OF ZORRO, as Don Cesar de Vega, who romances lovely Astor, clashes with heinous Crisp (and is falsely accused of murder). Doug is both father and son in the rousing finale. ▼●

Don Quixote (1973) **C-107m.** *** D: Rudolf Nureyev, Robert Helpmann. Nureyev, Helpmann, Lucette Aldous, Australian Ballet. Fine ballet version of Cervantes' classic, choreographed by Nureyev, who plays barber Basilio; Helpmann is the wandering knight. Not just for ballet buffs. [G]▼

Don's Party (1976-Australian) **C-91m.** ***½ D: Bruce Beresford. John Hargreaves, Pat Bishop, Graham Kennedy, Veronica Lang, Candy Raymond, Harold Hopkins. Powerful black comedy chronicling the interaction—sexual and otherwise—among a group of young suburbanites who get together to watch election returns. (Important note: In Australia, the "liberals" are actually the conservative party.) Stunning direction, top performances by all; biting script by David Williamson, from his play.▼◗

Don't Answer the Phone (1980) **C-94m.** BOMB D: Robert Hammer. James Westmoreland, Flo Gerrish, Ben Frank, Nicholas Worth, Stan Haze. Another sadistic killer who's a Vietnam veteran. Don't watch this movie. [R]▼

Don't Be a Menace to South Central While Drinking Your Juice in the Hood (1995) **C-88m.** ** D: Paris Barclay. Shawn Wayans, Marlon Wayans, Keenen Ivory Wayans, Chris Spencer, Suli McCullough, Darrell Heath, Helen Martin, Isaiah Barnes, Craig Wayans, Kim Wayans, Omar Epps, Faizon Love, Antonio Fargas, LaWanda

Page, Damon Wayans. NAKED GUN–like spoof of coming-of-age "hood" pictures is only intermittently successful, despite the presence of more Wayanses than there are in Heaven. Thoroughly predictable. Marlon and Shawn (who also cowrote and coexecutive-produced) are amusing as homies. [R] ▼●◗

Don't Bother to Knock (1952) **76m.** **½ D: Roy (Ward) Baker. Richard Widmark, Marilyn Monroe, Anne Bancroft, Jeanne Cagney, Elisha Cook, Jr., Gloria Blondell. Title has more punch than improbable yarn of mentally disturbed Monroe hired as babysitter in large hotel, saved from killing herself and charge by tough-but-good Widmark. Bancroft's film debut. Remade for TV as THE SITTER.▼

Don't Cry, It's Only Thunder (1982) **C-108m.** *** D: Peter Werner. Dennis Christopher, Susan Saint James, Roger Aaron Brown, Lisa Lu. Dramatically uneven, but moving account of G.I. Christopher and doctor Saint James' involvement with makeshift orphanage in Vietnam. Based on a true incident. [PG]▼

Don't Do It! (1994) **C-90m.** *½ D: Eugene Hess. Alexis Arquette, Balthazar Getty, Heather Graham, James Le Gros, Sheryl Lee, James Marshall, Esai Morales, Sarah Trigger. Talented cast flounders in this confusing, meandering Generation X drama of various couples whose love and sex lives are intertwined. Means to be insightful, but the result is a talky bore.▼◗

Don't Drink the Water (1969) **C-100m.** ** D: Howard Morris. Jackie Gleason, Estelle Parsons, Ted Bessell, Joan Delaney, Michael Constantine, Howard St. John, Avery Schreiber. Uninspired adaptation of Woody Allen play about American family held prisoner in Iron Curtain country of Vulgaria, and their desperate attempts to escape. Cast works hard, with sporadic results. Remade for TV. [G]▼

Don't Drink the Water (1994) **C-100m. TVM** D: Woody Allen. Woody Allen, Michael J. Fox, Mayim Bialik, Dom DeLuise, Julie Kavner, Edward Herrmann, Austin Pendleton, Josef Sommer. Amusing but dated adaptation of Woody's 1966 Broadway farce about innocent American tourists who find themselves stranded behind the (now long gone) Iron Curtain. Of interest as Allen's TV acting and directing debut, a remake of the 1969 film version which Allen found wanting. Average.

Don't Give Up the Ship (1959) **89m.** *** D: Norman Taurog. Jerry Lewis, Dina Merrill, Diana Spencer, Mickey Shaughnessy, Robert Middleton, Gale Gordon, Claude Akins. Top comedy with Jerry as ensign who lost a battleship during war and doesn't remember how. Shaughnessy is pal who helps look for it underwater. One of Lewis' all-time best. VistaVision. ▼

Don't Go Near the Water (1957) **C-107m.** *½ D: Charles Walters. Glenn Ford, Gia Scala, Anne Francis, Fred Clark, Eva Gabor, Earl Holliman, Keenan Wynn, Russ Tamblyn, Jeff Richards, Mickey Shaughnessy, Jack Albertson. Submerged comedy of sailors in the South Pacific of WW2 building a recreation hall. Clark, as a frustrated officer, is best thing in slow film. CinemaScope.▼

Don't Just Stand There (1968) **C-100m.** **½ D: Ron Winston. Robert Wagner, Mary Tyler Moore, Harvey Korman, Glynis Johns, Barbara Rhoades. Frantic comedy with perky stars; Wagner and Moore try to unravel mystery of disappearance of authoress Johns after writing the first half of a new book. Players' vivacity makes script seem better than it is. Techniscope.

Don't Knock the Rock (1956) **84m.** ** D: Fred F. Sears. Bill Haley and His Comets, Alan Freed, Little Richard, Alan Dale, The Treniers, Patricia Hardy. Rock 'n' roll star Dale returns to his hometown, encounters adult hostility. Of course, the elders are cheering the rockers by the finale. Little Richard sings "Long Tall Sally" and "Tutti Frutti."

Don't Knock the Twist (1962) **87m.** BOMB D: Oscar Rudolph. Chubby Checker, Gene Chandler, Vic Dana, Linda Scott, Mari Blanchard, Lang Jeffries. The Dovells. Television producer Jeffries, with Checker's assistance, coordinates a twist show. Chandler, with cape, monocle and top hat, sings "Duke of Earl"; otherwise, you may want to twist your way to your TV set and turn the dial.

Dont Look Back (1967) **96m.** ***½ D: D. A. Pennebaker. Bob Dylan, Joan Baez, Donovan, Alan Price, Albert Grossman, Allen Ginsberg. Candid documentary about Dylan's '65 concert tour of England, highlighted by his pseudo-hip personality, appearances by Baez and Grossman (Dylan's manager). Dylan performs "The Times They Are a Changin'," "Don't Think Twice, It's All Right," "It's All Over Now, Baby Blue," and "Subterranean Homesick Blues."▼●◗

Don't Look in the Basement (1973) **C-95m.** *½ D: S. F. Brownrigg. William McGee, Annie MacAdams, Rosie Holotik, Gene Ross, Jessie Lee Fulton, Camilla Carr. Amateurish horror thriller about inmates of secluded Florida insane asylum who contrive a bloody takeover. [R]▼◗

Don't Look Now (1973-British) **C-110m.** *** D: Nicolas Roeg. Julie Christie, Donald Sutherland, Hilary Mason, Clelia Matania, Massimo Serato. Arty, overindulgent but gripping Daphne du Maurier occult thriller about parents of drowned child and their horror-laden visit to Venice; highlighted by memorably steamy love scene and violent climax. [R]▼●

Don't Make Waves (1967) **C-97m.** *** D: Alexander Mackendrick. Tony Curtis, Claudia Cardinale, Sharon Tate, Robert Webber, Mort Sahl, Jim Backus, Edgar Bergen. The one gem out of nine million bad Tony Curtis comedy vehicles; satire on Southern California has good direction, funny performance by Sharon Tate, and a catchy title song sung by the Byrds. Good fun. Panavision.▼

Don't Raise the Bridge, Lower the River (1968) **C-99m.** ** D: Jerry Paris. Jerry Lewis, Terry-Thomas, Jacqueline Pearce, Bernard Cribbins, Patricia Routledge. Jerry plays American in England whose get-rich-quick schemes have put him on verge of divorce; mild Lewis comedy scripted by Max Wilk, from his novel. [G]▼

Don't Take It to Heart (1945-British) **89m.** *** D: Jeffrey Dell. Richard Greene, Patricia Medina, Richard Bird, Wylie Watson, Ernest Thesiger, Ronald Squire. Pleasant romantic comedy of ghost-ridden castle; Greene helps Medina and her townfolk overcome avaricious landowner.

Don't Tell Her It's Me (1990) **C-101m.** *½ D: Malcolm Mowbray. Steve Guttenberg, Jami Gertz, Shelley Long, Kyle MacLachlan, Kevin Scannell, Madchen Amick, Beth Grant. If you can buy Guttenberg and Long as siblings, or Guttenberg in a skull cap and bloated facial makeup to convey Parkinson's disease radiation treatments, or Guttenberg masquerading as a scruffy New Zealand biker, then maybe you'll find something to like in this romantic comedy of mistaken identity . . . but don't tell her (or him) you did. [PG-13]▼●

Don't Tell Mom the Babysitter's Dead (1991) **C-105m.** ** D: Stephen Herek. Christina Applegate, Joanna Cassidy, John Getz, Keith Coogan, Josh Charles, David Duchovny, Kimmy Robertson, Eda Reiss Merin, Jayne Brook, Cathy Ladman, Christopher Plummer. Superficial comedy about kids whose babysitter dies, leaving them to get along without supervision or money. The core of the film is not as bad as the title might suggest—that is, if you can get past the first fifteen minutes. Cassidy is a standout as Applegate's boss. [PG-13]▼●

Don't Touch the Loot SEE: **Grisbi**

Don't Trust Your Husband SEE: **Innocent Affair, An**

Don't Turn the Other Cheek (1973-Italian) **C-93m.** **½ D: Duccio Tessari. Franco Nero, Lynn Redgrave, Eli Wallach, Marilu Tolo, Horst Janson. Slapstick spaghetti Western detailing exploits of unlikely trio; a fiery, revolution-fomenting Irish journalist (Redgrave), a bogus Russian prince (Nero), and a seedy Mexican bandit (Wallach) with proverbial heart of gold. Aka LONG LIVE YOUR DEATH. Techniscope. [PG]▼

Don't Worry, We'll Think of a Title (1966) **83m.** BOMB D: Harmon Jones. Morey Amsterdam, Rose Marie, Joey Adams, Danny Thomas, Milton Berle, Nick Adams. Grade-Z shambles, despite many guest cameos by big TV and movie stars. Start worrying when you turn it on.

Doolins of Oklahoma, The (1949) **90m.** **½ D: Gordon Douglas. Randolph Scott, George Macready, Louise Allbritton, John Ireland. Action-packed Western with Scott as head of the Doolin gang, who decides to give up his life of crime.▼

Doomed to Die (1940) **57m.** *½ D: William Nigh. Boris Karloff, Grant Withers, Marjorie Reynolds, Melvin Lang, Guy Usher. Fifth entry in the Mr. Wong series, with the detective on the trail of a shipping tycoon's killer, uncovering the whereabouts of some missing contraband bonds.▼◗

Doom Generation, The (1995-U.S.-French) **85m.** *½ D: Gregg Araki. Rose McGowan, James Duval, Johnathon Schaech, Margaret Cho, Lauren Tewes, Christopher Knight, Parker Posey, Amanda Bearse, Heidi Fleiss. Two young lovers turn their lives upside down when they pick up a dangerous drifter who involves them in murder and a sexual triangle. Bleak, bleak view of the younger generation makes KIDS look like THE LITTLE MERMAID. ▼◗

Doomsday Machine, The (1972) **C-88m.** BOMB D: Lee Sholem, Harry Hope. Denny Miller, Mala Powers, Bobby Van, Ruta Lee, Grant Williams, Henry Wilcoxon. Tired cast in lumpy, stultifyingly boring melodrama about scientists on a space voyage who are constantly bickering. Aka ESCAPE FROM PLANET EARTH. ▼

Doomwatch (1972-British) **C-92m.** *** D: Peter Sasdy. Ian Bannen, Judy Geeson, George Sanders, John Paul, Simon Oates, Geoffrey Keen. Dr. Bannen investigates the effects of radioactivity on an island inhabited by a rather odd-acting population. Topical, thought-provoking mystery-thriller, not at all bad of its type. Based on the British TV series of the same name.▼

Doors, The (1991) **C-135m.** **½ D: Oliver Stone. Val Kilmer, Frank Whaley, Kevin Dillon, Meg Ryan, Kyle MacLachlan, Billy Idol, Dennis Burkley, Josh Evans, Michael Madsen, Michael Wincott, Kathleen Quinlan, John Densmore, Will Jordan, Mimi Rogers, Paul Williams, Crispin Glover, Bill Graham, Billy Vera, Bill Kunstler, Wes Studi, Costas Mandylor. Vivid impression of famed rocker Jim Morrison's rise to fame, and eventual undoing. Stone masterfully recreates the late '60s/early '70s rock and drug scene, and Kilmer is perfect in the lead . . . but when it's all over you don't know very much more about Morrison than when the film began. The film's excesses also tend to parallel Morrison's. Stone appears briefly as a UCLA film professor. Panavision. [R]▼●◗

Door-to-Door Maniac (1961) **80m.** *½ D: Bill Karn. Johnny Cash, Donald Woods, Cay Forrester, Pamela Mason, Midge Ware, Victor Tayback, Ronny Howard, Merle Travis. Cash and Tayback plot a bank robbery. Of interest only for the cast; also known as FIVE MINUTES TO LIVE.▼

Doorway to Hell (1930) **78m.** *½ D: Archie L. Mayo. Lew Ayres, Charles Judels, Dorothy Matthews, Leon Janney, Robert Elliott, James Cagney, Kenneth Thomson. Antique, early-talkie gangster saga with Ayres improbably cast as ruthless Chicago underworld biggie and Cagney (billed sixth, in his second film) as his henchman.

Door With Seven Locks, The (1962-German) **96m.** **½ D: Alfred Vohrer. Eddie Arent, Heinz Drache, Klaus Kinski, Adi Berber, Sabina Sesselman. Bizarre account of man who leaves in his will seven keys to treasure vault, with expected friction and murder; from Edgar Wallace story made before as CHAMBER OF HORRORS. ▼●

Doppelganger (1969) SEE: **Journey to the Far Side of the Sun**

Doppelganger: The Evil Within (1992) **C-104m.** BOMB D: Avi Nesher. Drew Barrymore, George Newbern, Dennis Christopher, Leslie Hope, Sally Kellerman, George Maharis, Luana Anders. Screenwriter Newbern's roommate, heiress Barrymore, claims her doppelganger (ghostly double) is killing off her family in this sick, nonsensical, would-be slasher film. Loud (and corny) music renders the dialogue unintelligible, which is actually no loss. Drew's mother, Jaid Barrymore, plays her mom on screen. [R]▼●

Dorian Gray (1970-Italian-German-Lichtensteinian) **C-93m.** *½ D: Massimo Dallamano. Helmut Berger, Richard Todd, Herbert Lom, Marie Liljedahl, Margaret Lee. Trashy, slow-moving filmization of Oscar Wilde's novel, updated to the present: vain, immoral young man (Berger) ceases to grow older—his portrait ages instead. 1945's THE PICTURE OF DORIAN GRAY is vastly superior. Aka THE SECRET OF DORIAN GRAY. [R]▼

Do the Right Thing (1989) **C-120m.** *** D: Spike Lee. Danny Aiello, Ossie Davis, Ruby Dee, Richard Edson, Giancarlo Esposito, Spike Lee, Bill Nunn, John Turturro, Paul Benjamin, Frankie Faison, Robin Harris, John Savage, Sam (Samuel L.) Jackson, Rosie Perez, Martin Lawrence. Idealized, individualistic look at life in the black community of Bedford-Stuyvesant in Brooklyn, where a white-owned pizza parlor flourishes . . . and where circumstance leads to an outbreak of hostilities on a sweltering summer day. Entertaining and provocative, with a much-discussed (and troubling) finale. Writer-director Lee also stars as Mookie, the delivery boy; his real-life sister Joie plays his sister in the film. [R]▼●◗

Double Bunk (1960-British) **92m.** *½ D: C. M. Pennington-Richards. Ian Carmichael, Janette Scott, Sidney James, Liz Fraser. Slapstick account of Carmichael and Scott navigating their houseboat down the Thames, with predictable sight gags.

Double Con SEE: **Trick Baby**

Double Confession (1950-British) **86m.** ** D: Ken Annakin. Derek Farr, Joan Hopkins, Peter Lorre, William Hartnell, Kathleen Harrison, Naunton Wayne. Murky melodrama at a seaside resort: an innocent man tries to set someone else up as a murder suspect in his wife's mysterious death, only to get involved with some real killers.▼

Double Cross (1941) **66m.** *½ D: Albert Kelley. Kane Richmond, Pauline Moore, Wynne Gibson. Mild account of cop seeking to get the goods on criminal gang; nothing unusual.▼

Double Cross (1949-Italian) **77m.** **½ D: Riccardo Freda. Vittorio Gassman, Amedeo Nazzari, Gianna Maria Canale. Acceptable account of two crooks who doublecross each other, with the victim seeking revenge years later.

Double Cross (1956-British) **71m.** ** D: Anthony Squire. Donald Houston, Fay Compton, Anton Diffring, Delphi Lawrence. Mild account of foreign agents involved in typical espionage plot to steal government secrets.

Double Crossbones (1951) **C-75m.** ** D: Charles Barton. Donald O'Connor, Helena Carter, Will Geer, Hope Emerson, Glenn Strange, Rock Hudson. O'Connor is would-be buccaneer who seeks to win his sweetheart and expose crooked city official. Light satire which doesn't quite come off.

Double Deal (1984-Australian) **C-90m.** *½ D: Brian Kavanagh. Louis Jourdan, Angela Punch-McGregor, Diana Craig, Warwick Comber, Peter Cummins. Idiotic drama about bored, married fashion model-designer Punch-McGregor who takes up with drifter Comber. Filmed in 1981. Panavision.▼

Double Dragon (1994) **C-96m.** *½ D: James Yukich. Robert Patrick, Mark Dacascos, Scott Wolf, Julia Nickson, Kristina Malandro Wagner, John Mallory Asher, Leon Russom, Alyssa Milano, Michael Berryman, Vanna White, George Hamilton. In the junky, gang-dominated post-earthquake "New Angeles" of 2007, martial artist brothers Dacascos and Wolf battle evil billionaire Patrick for the possession of a two-part Chinese medallion that grants mystical powers. Sometimes lively but mostly silly and tedious; based on an arcade game. [PG-13]▼●◗

Double Dynamite (1951) **80m.** ** D: Irving Cummings, Jr. Frank Sinatra, Jane Russell, Groucho Marx, Don McGuire. Sinatra plays a bank clerk falsely accused of robbery. Flat comedy marked a career low-point for all three of its stars. Filmed in 1948.▼

Double Edge (1992-U.S.-Israeli) **C-86m.** ★★½ D: Amos Kollek. Faye Dunaway, Amos Kollek, Mohammad Bakri, Makram Khouri, Anat Atzmon. Dunaway is well cast as an overly ambitious American reporter covering the Arab-Israeli conflict in this uneven drama about journalistic objectivity and responsibility. Never quite delivers as it should, but it does effectively mix fiction with fact, as Dunaway interviews Jerusalem mayor Teddy Kollek (the director-actor-screenwriter's father) and other real-life political figures. [PG-13]▼

Double Happiness (1994-Canadian) **C-100m.** ★★★ D: Mina Shum. Sandra Oh, Stephen Chang, Allanah Ong, Frances You, Callum Rennie. Insightful, refreshingly unclichéd tale of a free-thinking young Chinese-Canadian woman (appealingly played by Oh), an aspiring actress whose Old World parents are pressuring her to find a boyfriend and marry. Writer-director Shum does not paint the parents as stodgy villains; they just want what they feel is best for the daughter they love. Bright touches of humor enhance this charming film. [PG-13] ▼●

Double Impact (1991) **C-118m.** ★★ D: Sheldon Lettich. Jean-Claude Van Damme, Geoffrey Lewis, Alan Scarfe, Alonna Shaw, Cory Everson. Identical twins are separated at six months when Hong Kong thugs murder their parents, only to be reunited in revenge a quarter-century later. Van Damme's attempts to delineate two characters (one of them a gruff cigar-chomper) are nearly as goofy as one slow-motion love scene; studio press material, praising this Van Damme career stretch, extolled "the light, charming side of his persona that we haven't seen before." [R]▼●

Double Indemnity (1944) **106m.** ★★★★ D: Billy Wilder. Barbara Stanwyck, Fred MacMurray, Edward G. Robinson, Porter Hall, Fortunio Bonanova, Jean Heather, Bess Flowers. Wilder–Raymond Chandler script (from the James M. Cain novel) packs fireworks in account of insurance salesman MacMurray coerced into murder plot by alluring Stanwyck and subsequent investigation by Fred's colleague Robinson. An American movie classic, with crackling dialogue throughout. Remade for TV in 1973 with Richard Crenna and Samantha Eggar, and the obvious inspiration for Lawrence Kasdan's BODY HEAT.▼●◗

Double Jeopardy (1999) **C-105m.** ★★★ D: Bruce Beresford. Tommy Lee Jones, Ashley Judd, Bruce Greenwood, Annabeth Gish, Roma Maffia, Davenia McFadden. Woman is framed for the murder of her husband; while serving the jail sentence she learns he's alive and vows revenge, especially since she can't be tried twice for the same crime. Slick entertainment gives you pretty much what you'd expect. Panavision. [R]▼●◗

Double Life, A (1947) **104m.** ★★★½ D: George Cukor. Ronald Colman, Signe Hasso, Edmond O'Brien, Shelley Winters, Ray Collins, Millard Mitchell. Colman gives a bravura, Oscar-winning performance as an actor whose stage roles spill over into his life—and now he's about to play Othello. Brilliant melodrama by Ruth Gordon and Garson Kanin, with wonderful New York theater flavor. Miklos Rozsa's fine score also won an Oscar. Watch for playwright Paddy Chayefsky as a crime-scene photographer. ▼

Double Life of Veronique, The (1991-Polish-French) **C-97m.** ★★½ D: Krzysztof Kieslowski. Irène Jacob, Wladyslaw Kowalski, Guillaume de Tonquedec, Philippe Volter. Two women (one Polish, one French, both played by Jacob) subtly affect each other's lives while remaining total strangers. Unfolds like a half-hour teleplay with a supernatural premise stretched to 1½ hours. Film, though, has enough going for it to pick up a cult, for which luminous lead Jacob deserves credit.▼●

Double Man, The (1967-British) **C-105m.** ★★½ D: Franklin Schaffner. Yul Brynner, Britt Ekland, Clive Revill, Anton Diffring, Moira Lister, Lloyd Nolan. Unconvincing spy thriller with Brynner playing both unemotional C.I.A. agent *and* East German lookalike. Excellent photography by Denys Coop will suffer on TV.

Double McGuffin, The (1979) **C-89m.** ★★½ D: Joe Camp. Ernest Borgnine, George Kennedy, Elke Sommer, Rod Browning, Dion Pride, Lisa Whelchel, Jeff Nicholson, Michael Gerard, Vincent Spano. Teenagers stumble onto clues leading to assassination plot, but no one will believe them. Family-oriented thriller from creator of BENJI. Orson Welles explains film's title at the outset, for non-Hitchcock devotees. [PG]▼

Double Negative (1986-Canadian) **C-96m.** ★½ D: George Bloomfield. Michael Sarrazin, Susan Clark, Anthony Perkins, Howard Duff, Kate Reid, Al Waxman, Elizabeth Shepherd. Confusing, annoying thriller with mentally tortured photojournalist Sarrazin attempting to track down his wife's murderer. Sarrazin is his usual bland self; Clark is wasted. Based on Ross Macdonald's *The Three Roads.* Aka DEADLY COMPANION.▼

Double or Nothing (1937) **95m.** ★★½ D: Theodore Reed. Bing Crosby, Martha Raye, Andy Devine, Mary Carlisle, William Frawley, Fay Holden, Frances Faye. Entertaining musical about four people given 30 days to double gifts of $5000. Several good specialty acts thrown in for good measure, and Bing sings "The Moon Got in My Eyes."

Double Team (1997) **C-91m.** ★½ D: Tsui

Hark. Jean-Claude Van Damme, Dennis Rodman, Mickey Rourke, Paul Freeman, Natacha Lindinger, Valeria Cavalli. Mismatched buddy film with Van Damme as a world-class counterterrorist who teams with weapons expert Rodman in a quest to stop Mickey Rourke (not a bad idea). Pointless action thriller from cult Hong Kong director Hark. Scenes in which the hero's baby is placed in constant jeopardy would be hard to stomach even in a coherent film—which this isn't. Super 35. [R]▼●◗

Double Trouble (1962) SEE: **Swingin' Along**

Double Trouble (1967) **C-90m.** ** D: Norman Taurog. Elvis Presley, Annette Day, John Williams, Yvonne Romain, The Wiere Brothers, Chips Rafferty, Michael Murphy. Teen-age heiress falls for pop singer Presley when he's performing in England; usual Elvis fare, but he does sing "Long Legged Girl," one of his best post-Army tunes. Panavision.▼●

Double Wedding (1937) **87m.** *** D: Richard Thorpe. William Powell, Myrna Loy, Florence Rice, Edgar Kennedy, Sidney Toler, Mary Gordon. Wackier than usual for Powell and Loy, as avant-garde painter and dress designer who want Loy's sister Rice to marry, but do it themselves.▼

Doubting Thomas (1935) **78m.** *** D: David Butler. Will Rogers, Billie Burke, Alison Skipworth, Sterling Holloway, Andrew Tombes, Gail Patrick, Frank Albertson, John Qualen. Rogers is at his best dealing with a variety of eccentric and pompous characters when his stagestruck wife Burke joins an amateur theatrical troupe. Often hilarious adaptation of George Kelly's play *The Torch Bearers,* with Skipworth in rare form as the play's directress.▼

Doughboys (1930) **79m.** *½ D: Edward Sedgwick. Buster Keaton, Sally Eilers, Cliff Edwards, Edward Brophy, Victor Potel. One of Buster's worst films; a tiresome Army comedy. Obnoxious sergeant Brophy overrides few comic moments; some bright spots with "Ukulele Ike" Edwards. ▼●

Doughgirls, The (1944) **102m.** **½ D: James V. Kern. Ann Sheridan, Alexis Smith, Jane Wyman, Eve Arden, Jack Carson, Charlie Ruggles, Alan Mowbray, Craig Stevens, Regis Toomey. Brittle comedy, still another variation on crowded situation in wartime Washington, with newlyweds Carson and Wyman on hectic honeymoon. Arden stands out as Russian army officer.

Doug's 1st Movie (1999) **C-77m.** *½ D: Maurice Joyce. Voices of Thomas McHugh, Fred Newman, Chris Phillips, Constance Shulman, Doug Preis, Guy Hadley, Alice Playten. The star of TV's animated *Doug* is featured in this bland, formulaic story, strictly for kids. Mild-mannered preteen Doug Funnie's efforts to save a local endangered "monster" conflict with his desire to take his girlfriend to the school dance. Created as a direct-to-video feature but given theatrical release after the success of THE RUGRATS MOVIE. [G]▼●◗

Dove, The (1974) **C-105m.** **½ D: Charles Jarrott. Joseph Bottoms, Deborah Raffin, John McLiam, Dabney Coleman. Pleasant round-the-world adventure based on true story of 16-year-old who sails to every imaginable port. Produced by Gregory Peck. Filmed on location. Panavision. [PG]▼

Down Among the Sheltering Palms (1953) **C-87m.** ** D: Edmund Goulding. William Lundigan, Jane Greer, Mitzi Gaynor, David Wayne, Gloria DeHaven, Billy Gilbert, Jack Paar. Poor man's SOUTH PACIFIC recounts love problems of two U.S. army officers stationed in Pacific after WW2. Look fast for Lee Marvin.

Down Among the Z Men (1952-British) **70m.** ** D: Maclean Rogers. Harry Secombe, Peter Sellers, Carole Carr, Spike Milligan, Clifford Stanton, Graham Stark, Miriam Karlin. Creaky vehicle for radio's The Goons in story of criminals who visit small town to steal a professor's secret scientific formula. Some good bits, especially Sellers doing impressions of Yank soldiers, but overloaded with dull song-and-dance numbers by a female chorus line.▼●

Down and Out in Beverly Hills (1986) **C-103m.** **½ D: Paul Mazursky. Nick Nolte, Richard Dreyfuss, Bette Midler, Little Richard, Tracy Nelson, Elizabeth Pena, Evan Richards, Valerie Curtin, Barry Primus, Dorothy Tristan, Alexis Arquette, Mike the Dog. Bum moves in with neurotic, nouveau-riche Bev Hills family and takes over their lives. Slick, often funny, but unusually obvious satire for Mazursky (who also appears as one of Dreyfuss's fat-cat friends). Some good performances, though Mike the Dog easily steals the film. A remake of Renoir's BOUDU SAVED FROM DROWNING. Later a TV series. [R]▼●

Down Argentine Way (1940) **C-90m.** *** D: Irving Cummings. Don Ameche, Betty Grable, Carmen Miranda, Charlotte Greenwood, J. Carrol Naish, Henry Stephenson, Leonid Kinskey. Enjoyable 20th Century-Fox musical with Grable (in the movie that boosted her to stardom) falling in love with smooth Argentinian horse breeder Ameche. Miranda is terrific in her first American movie, performing infectious Brazilian songs with her own band . . . and look out for the Nicholas Brothers, who do a dynamite specialty number. Picture-postcard color throughout.▼●

Down by Law (1986) **107m.** **½ D: Jim Jarmusch. Tom Waits, John Lurie, Roberto Benigni, Ellen Barkin, Billie Neal, Rockets Redglare, Vernel Bagneris, Nicoletta Braschi. Third feature by writer-director Jarmusch is intriguing, amusing, and ever so slight, a look at three losers who wind up in jail together—and then make a break for it. Really comes alive when Italian comic Benigni turns up. Slow-moving, strikingly photographed (in black & white) by Robby Müller on location in Louisiana. Costars Lurie and Waits also provide music on the soundtrack. [R]▼●

Down Came a Blackbird (1995) **C-95m. TVM** D: Jonathan Sanger. Raul Julia, Laura Dern, Vanessa Redgrave, Cliff Gorman, Sarita Choudhury, Jeffrey DeMunn, L. Scott Caldwell, Falconer Abraham, Jay O. Sanders. Journalist Dern is drawn to Redgrave's private clinic for former torture victims where, in group sessions, unsettling memories are painfully revived. Harrowing and often graphic scenes accompany disturbing monologues by those intent on repressing the past. Strongly acted by an emaciated Julia (in his final role) as a former professor with a dark past, as well as Dern, Redgrave, Gorman (oddly cast as thick-accented Greek partisan). Written with rage by Kevin Droney. Made for video; debuted on cable. Above average. ▼

Downhill (1927-British) **95m.** **½ D: Alfred Hitchcock. Ivor Novello, Ben Webster, Robin Irvine, Sybil Rhoda, Lillian Braithwaite, Isabel Jeans, Ian Hunter. Schematic silent film charts a man's slide downhill, beginning when, as a schoolboy, he is disowned by his family after an indiscretion with a girl, and later as an adult when his wife fritters away his unexpected inheritance. Major debit: the contrived happy ending. Lesser Hitchcock boasts the master's visual flair. Cowritten by Novello.

Downhill Racer (1969) **C-102m.** *** D: Michael Ritchie. Robert Redford, Gene Hackman, Camilla Sparv, Karl Michael Vogler, Jim McMullan, Christian Doermer, Dabney Coleman. Vivid study of an empty life, with Redford as small-town egotist who joins U.S. Olympic ski team. Basically a character study; problem is an unappealing character. Dazzling ski scenes make lulls worth enduring. Ritchie's feature directorial debut. [M/PG]▼●

Down in the Delta (1998) **C-111m.** **½ D: Maya Angelou. Alfre Woodard, Al Freeman, Jr., Wesley Snipes, Mary Alice, Esther Rolle, Loretta Devine. With her life a mess and virtually no hope of employment, single mom Woodard boards the bus with her two children to spend the summer in the Mississippi Delta, living with relatives and working in their chicken restaurant. Episodic drama recovers from clumsy exposition to win points for sheer likability, though it's put over almost exclusively by its cast. Woodard shines, and Freeman gives one of the best performances of his career. [PG-13]▼●◗

Down Memory Lane (1949) **72m.** *** D: Phil Karlson (new footage). Steve Allen, Franklin Pangborn, Frank Nelson, Mack Sennett; scenes of W. C. Fields, Bing Crosby, others. Allen decides to show old Sennett comedies on his TV show. OK framework for silent clips of Ben Turpin, Gloria Swanson, etc. Fields' classic THE DENTIST and Crosby's BLUE OF THE NIGHT both shown almost in toto, making silly Allen footage worth watching.

Down Periscope (1996) **C-92m.** **½ D: David S. Ward. Kelsey Grammer, Lauren Holly, Bruce Dern, Rob Schneider, Rip Torn, Harry Dean Stanton, William H. Macy, Ken Hudson Campbell, Toby Huss, Duane Martin, Jonathan Penner, Harland Williams. Maverick naval officer is finally given a submarine to command, but it turns out to be a mothballed wreck—with a crew that's not much better. But if he can prove his mettle (and the ship's) in a war game environment, he can graduate to a first-class nuclear sub. Mild comedy follows the misfits-make-good formula fairly well. Surprisingly well-developed plot line but not enough laughs. [PG-13]▼●

Downstairs (1932) **77m.** ***½ D: Monta Bell. John Gilbert, Paul Lukas, Virginia Bruce, Hedda Hopper, Reginald Owen, Olga Baclanova. Crackling, adult drama about a heel who sleeps and cajoles his way from one wealthy household to another—using both the mistresses of the house upstairs, and the servants downstairs. Gilbert delivers an audacious performance that more than any other redeems his maligned reputation as a "talkie" actor; he also gets story credit for the film. Leading lady Bruce was then his wife. Karen Morley appears unbilled in final scene.

Down the Drain (1990) **C-105m.** ** D: Robert C. Hughes. Andrew Stevens, John Matuszak, Don Stroud, Teri Copley, Joseph Campanella, Stella Stevens, Jerry Mathers, Buck Flower, Pedro Gonzalez-Gonzalez, Benny (The Jet) Urquidez. Lawyer Stevens, with the help of his clients, pulls off a bank robbery. Strictly ho-hum. [R]▼●

Down Three Dark Streets (1954) **85m.** **½ D: Arnold Laven. Broderick Crawford, Ruth Roman, Martha Hyer, Marisa Pavan, Casey Adams, Kenneth Tobey, Gene Reynolds, Claude Akins. Smoothly done interweaving episodes, pegged on FBI agent following through on trio of dead buddy's cases; Roman quite effective.

Down to Earth (1932) **73m.** **½ D: David Butler. Will Rogers, Irene Rich, Dorothy Jordan, Mary Carlisle, Matty Kemp. Homer Croy's sequel to THEY HAD TO SEE PARIS has nouveau riche Midwesterner Rogers putting an end to his family's foolish spending by declaring that he's broke. OK Rogers vehicle, but not up to his best film efforts.

Down to Earth (1947) **C-101m.** ** D: Alexander Hall. Rita Hayworth, Larry Parks, Marc Platt, Roland Culver, James Gleason, Edward Everett Horton. Terpsichore, the Goddess of Dance (Hayworth), comes to earth to help Parks with his mythological musical play. Rita's beauty is only asset of this hack musical, which appropriates Gleason, Horton and Culver characters from HERE COMES MR. JORDAN. Remade as XANADU.▼●

Down to the Sea in Ships (1922) **83m.** **½ D: Elmer Clifton. William Walcott, Marguerite Courtot, Clara Bow, Raymond McKee, J. Thornton Baston. Archaic plot line of romantic conflict in a whaling family enhanced by vivid atmosphere of on-location shooting in New England, and on board actual whaling ships at sea. Also notable as Clara Bow's film debut.▼

Down to the Sea in Ships (1949) **120m.** *** D: Henry Hathaway. Richard Widmark, Lionel Barrymore, Dean Stockwell, Cecil Kellaway, Gene Lockhart. Young Stockwell fulfills seafaring goal on crusty Barrymore's whaling ship, under guidance of sailor Widmark. Good atmospheric yarn.

Downtown (1990) **C-96m.** ** D: Richard Benjamin. Anthony Edwards, Forest Whitaker, Joe Pantoliano, David Clennon, Penelope Ann Miller, Kimberly Scott, Art Evans, Rick Aiello. Naive white cop Edwards is transferred from easy suburban precinct to tough downtown area of Philadelphia and teamed with a sad, streetwise loner (Whitaker); together they go after a peculiar stolen-car ring. Uneasy mix of farce, melodrama, and buddy movie looks something like a pilot for a (bad) TV series. [R]▼●

Down to You (2000) **C-91m.** BOMB D: Kris Isacsson. Freddie Prinze, Jr., Julia Stiles, Shawn Hatosy, Selma Blair, Zak Orth, Ashton Kutcher, Rosario Dawson, Henry Winkler, Lucie Arnaz. Prinze and Stiles futilely try chumming us up by speaking directly into the camera, explaining how their once-idyllic college romance went bust (though not as bust as the movie). Somehow, this manages to find room for subplots about a TV cooking show (hosted by Winkler, as Prinze's dad) and a buddy who dabbles as an adult-movie entrepreneur with a kind of bohemian/intellectual porn actress. Numbingly inept comedy. [PG-13]▼◗

Down Twisted (1987) **C-88m.** *½ D: Albert Pyun. Carey Lowell, Charles Rocket, Trudi Dochtermann, Thom Matthews, Norbert Weisser, Linda Kerridge, Nicholas Guest. Unremittingly complicated, and unsatisfying, caper yarn with innocent young woman suddenly caught up in web of intrigue when she's thought to have a priceless artifact the bad guys are after. Echoes of other (better) movies abound.[R]▼

Do You Love Me? (1946) **C-91m.** **½ D: Gregory Ratoff. Maureen O'Hara, Dick Haymes, Harry James, Reginald Gardiner, Alma Kruger. Lightweight musical of band-singer Haymes romancing college dean O'Hara.

Do You Remember Love (1985) **C-100m. TVM** D: Jeff Bleckner. Joanne Woodward, Richard Kiley, Geraldine Fitzgerald, Jim Metzler, Jordan Charney, Rose Gregorio, Susan Ruttan. Masterful performances by Woodward (who won the Emmy) and Kiley distinguish this exceptional drama about the effect on the family of a middle-aged college professor when she contracts Alzheimer's disease. Superb script by first-time author (and Emmy winner) Vickie Patik. Above average.

Do You Want to Dance With Me? SEE: **Come Dance With Me!**

Dozens, The (1981) **C-78m.** **½ D: Christine Dall, Randall Conrad. Debra Margolies, Edward Mason, Marian Taylor, Jessica Hergert, Ethel Michelson, Genevieve Reale. Tough, volatile young woman (Margolies) is released from prison, tries to rebuild her life. Not bad, but not particularly involving. Based on fact, and filmed in Boston.

Drabble SEE: **Black Windmill, The**

Dracula (1931) **75m.** ***½ D: Tod Browning. Bela Lugosi, David Manners, Helen Chandler, Dwight Frye, Edward Van Sloan, Herbert Bunston, Frances Dade. Classic horror film of Transylvanian vampire working his evil spell on perplexed group of Londoners. Lugosi's most famous role with his definitive interpretation of the Count, ditto Frye as looney Renfield and Van Sloan as unflappable Professor Van Helsing. Sequel: DRACULA'S DAUGHTER.▼●◗

Dracula (1931) **103m.** *** D: George Melford. Carlos Villar (Villarias), Lupita Tovar, Pablo Alvarez Rubio, Barry Norton, Eduardo Arozamena, Carmen Guerrero, Manuel Arbo. This scene-for-scene, line-for-line Spanish-language adaptation of the horror classic was filmed simultaneously with the Hollywood version—at night, on the very same sets—but much of the staging and camerawork is actually better! Other major difference: the women are dressed more provocatively. All that's missing is an actor with the charisma of Lugosi in the lead.▼

Dracula (1958) SEE: **Horror of Dracula**

Dracula (1974) **C-100m. TVM** D: Dan Curtis. Jack Palance, Simon Ward, Nigel Davenport, Pamela Brown, Fiona Lewis, Penelope Horner, Murray Brown. The indomitable count of Transylvania lives in the person of Palance, who plays Bram Stoker's vampire king as a slightly pathetic figure, a victim of twisted fate. Sterling cast, Richard Matheson's faithful adaptation, and Oswald Morris' exceptional photography, rich in gothic touches, add to this classy new version of the old chestnut. Above average.▼

Dracula (1979) **C-109m.** *½ D: John Badham. Frank Langella, Laurence Olivier, Donald Pleasence, Kate Nelligan, Trevor Eve, Janine Duvitski, Tony Haygarth. Murky retelling of Bram Stoker classic, with Langella's acclaimed Broadway characterization lost amid trendy horror gimmicks and ill-conceived changes in original story. Filmed in England. Panavision. [R]▼●◗

Dracula (1992) SEE: **Bram Stoker's Dracula**

Dracula A.D. 1972 (1972-British) **C-100m.** ** D: Alan Gibson. Peter Cushing, Christopher Lee, Stephanie Beacham, Michael Coles, Christopher Neame, Caroline Munro. Farfetched, confusing tale of modern-day descendant of Dr. Van Helsing (Cushing) battling recently revived vampire (Lee). Somewhat jarring to see Dracula amid 1970s youth setting. Aka DRACULA TODAY. Followed by THE SATANIC RITES OF DRACULA. [PG]▼

Dracula and Son (1979-French) **C-78m.** *½ D: Eduard Molinaro. Christopher Lee, Bernard Menez, Marie-Helene Breillat, Catherine Breillat, Jack Boudet. Limp horror satire chronicling the comic misadventures of the title vampire (Lee) and his bumbling offspring (Menez); they become rivals for the pretty heroine. Virtually destroyed by grotesquely inappropriate English dubbing. Aka DRACULA, FATHER AND SON and DRACULA PERE ET FILS. [PG]▼

Dracula: Dead and Loving It (1995) **C-90m.** ** D: Mel Brooks. Leslie Nielsen, Peter MacNicol, Steven Weber, Amy Yasbeck, Lysette Anthony, Harvey Korman, Mel Brooks, Mark Blankfield, Megan Cavanagh, Clive Revill, Chuck McCann, Avery Schreiber, Charlie Callas, Anne Bancroft. Dracula gets the Mel Brooks treatment in this parody which spends so much time retelling the familiar Transylvanian's story it forgets to be funny. There are choice moments for Brooks fans . . . just not enough. The cast mugs its best, including MacNicol as Renfield, Brooks as Dr. Van Helsing, Korman in an amusing impression of Nigel Bruce, and Nielsen as the suavely sinister Count. Bancroft has a delightful cameo as "Madame Ouspenskaya." [PG-13]▼●

Dracula, Father and Son SEE: **Dracula and Son**

Dracula Has Risen From The Grave (1968-British) **C-92m.** **½ D: Freddie Francis. Christopher Lee, Rupert Davies, Veronica Carlson, Barbara Ewing, Barry Andrews, Michael Ripper. Dracula runs afoul of small-town monsignor when he pursues the churchman's beautiful blonde niece. Pretty good Hammer horror, third in the series. Sequel: TASTE THE BLOOD OF DRACULA. [G]▼●

Dracula—Prince of Darkness (1966-British) **C-90m.** ** D: Terence Fisher. Christopher Lee, Barbara Shelley, Andrew Keir, Suzan Farmer. Sequel to HORROR OF DRACULA doesn't measure up. The vampiric Count (Lee) is revived by a servant and wreaks terror on a group of tourists in a secluded castle. Techniscope.▼●◗

Dracula's Daughter (1936) **70m.** *** D: Lambert Hillyer. Gloria Holden, Otto Kruger, Marguerite Churchill, Irving Pichel, Edward Van Sloan, Nan Grey, Hedda Hopper. Sequel to the Lugosi classic depicts vampirish activities of Holden, who has a decided taste for *female* victims; Pichel adds imposing support as her sinister manservant. Hillyer, normally a B-Western director, manages to imbue this chiller with a moody, subtly sensual quality. ▼●

Dracula's Dog (1978) **C-90m.** ** D: Albert Band. Jose Ferrer, Michael Pataki, Reggie Nalder, Jan Shutan, Libbie Chase, John Levin. Transylvanian vampire and bloodthirsty dog, endowed with vampirish traits by the original Count, go to L.A. to find Dracula's last living descendant. Horror cheapie with admittedly novel twist. Retitled ZOLTAN, HOUND OF DRACULA. [R]▼

Dracula's Last Rites SEE: **Last Rites** (1980)

Dracula's Widow (1989) **C-86m.** *½ D: Christopher Coppola. Josef Sommer, Sylvia Kristel, Lenny Von Dohlen, Stefan Schnabel, Marc Coppola, Rachel Jones. Kristel plays the title character, who comes to L.A. and takes up residence at a wax museum. Dull, minor fare. Twenty-five-year-old director Coppola is the nephew of Francis. Filmed in 1987. [R]▼

Dracula Today SEE: **Dracula A.D. 1972**

Dracula vs. Frankenstein (1970) SEE: **Assignment Terror**

Dracula vs. Frankenstein (1971) **C-90m.** BOMB D: Al Adamson. J. Carrol Naish, Lon Chaney, Jr., Zandor Vorkov, Russ Tamblyn, Jim Davis, Anthony Eisley. Self-conscious comedy masquerading as horror film wasting talents of old-timers Naish and Chaney; Dracula makes deal with aging Dr. Frankenstein so as to have steady supply of blood. Regrettably, both Naish and Chaney's final film. Aka THE REVENGE OF DRACULA. [PG]▼●

Dragnet (1954) **C-89m.** *** D: Jack Webb. Jack Webb, Ben Alexander, Richard Boone, Ann Robinson, Stacy Harris, Virginia Gregg, Dennis Weaver. "This is the city . . ." While investigating brutal murder, Sgt. Friday and Officer Frank Smith ignore 57 varieties of civil liberties; feature film version of classic TV show evokes its era better than almost anything. Highly recommended on a nonesthetic level.▼

Dragnet (1987) **C-106m.** **½ D: Tom Mankiewicz. Dan Aykroyd, Tom Hanks, Christopher Plummer, Harry Morgan, Alexandra Paul, Jack O'Halloran, Elizabeth Ashley, Dabney Coleman. Aykroyd is a comic reincarnation of Jack Webb, playing Sgt. Joe Friday's dense but dedicated nephew in this parody. Hanks is fun as his freewheeling new partner, with Morgan, Webb's onetime sidekick, now promoted to captain of the L.A.P.D. Starts out quite funny, then goes flat . . . but the punchline is a howl. Aykroyd coscripted with Mankiewicz and Alan Zweibel. [PG-13]▼●◗

Dragon and the Cobra SEE: **Fist of Fear, Touch of Death**

Dragon Flies, The SEE: **Man from Hong Kong, The**

Dragonfly SEE: **One Summer Love**

Dragonfly Squadron (1954) **82m.** ** D: Lesley Selander. John Hodiak, Barbara Britton, Bruce Bennett, Jess Barker. Usual Korean War story, alternating between pilots in the air and their romantic problems on ground.▼

Dragonheart (1996) **C-103m.** *** D: Rob Cohen. Dennis Quaid, Sean Connery (voice only), David Thewlis, Dina Meyer, Julie Christie, Pete Postlethwaite, Jason Isaacs, Brian Thompson, Lee Oakes, Wolf Christian, Terry O'Neill. Highly unusual fable about a knight "of the old school" (in the 1st century A.D.) whose youthful king turns evil after having his life saved by a dragon who gives him half of his heart. Years later, the knight befriends that same dragon and joins with him to vanquish the cruel king. Unlikely premise is made plausible by Quaid's persuasive performance and the commanding presence of Connery as Drago (matched by the creature's superior, state-of-the-art digital animation). Fine score by Randy Edelman. Followed by a direct-to-video sequel. Panavision. [PG-13] ▼●◗

Dragon Murder Case, The (1934) **68m.** ** D: H. Bruce Humberstone. Warren William, Margaret Lindsay, Lyle Talbot, Eugene Pallette, Dorothy Tree. An eerie, so-called "dragon pool" is the setting for murder in this *Philo Vance* whodunit, but the suspects are so unpleasant you'll wish someone bumped them all off. William, debuting as Vance, is colorless; Pallette (as Inspector Heath) has all the good lines.

Dragon Seed (1944) **145m.** **½ D: Jack Conway, Harold S. Bucquet. Katharine Hepburn, Walter Huston, Aline MacMahon, Turhan Bey, Hurd Hatfield, Agnes Moorehead, Frances Rafferty, J. Carrol Naish, Akim Tamiroff, Henry Travers. Well-meant but overlong film of Pearl Buck's tale of Chinese town torn asunder by Japanese occupation; fascinating attempts at Oriental characterization.▼

Dragons Forever (1987-Hong Kong) **C-94m.** ***½ D: Samo Hung. Jackie Chan, Samo Hung, Yuen Biao, Yuen Wah, Benny Urquidez, Deannie Yip, Pauline Yeung. Simply delightful film has Chan playing a lawyer who enlists crook Hung and cracked friend Biao to help him spy on a woman involved with a case. Everything changes when love blossoms. Action, comedy, and romance blend together seamlessly under Hung's direction. All three stars shine in moments of incredible acrobatics and hilarious slapstick. Aka CYCLONE Z. ●◗

Dragonslayer (1981) **C-108m.** *** D: Matthew Robbins. Peter MacNicol, Caitlin Clarke, Ralph Richardson, John Hallam, Peter Eyre, Albert Salmi. Enjoyable fantasy-adventure about a sorcerer's apprentice who takes on the challenge of slaying a dragon—and finds he is in over his head. A bit scary and graphic for some kids. Filmed in England, Scotland, and Wales with a mostly British cast but American MacNicol in the lead—somewhat incongruously. Fine Alex North score. Panavision. [PG]▼●

Dragon: The Bruce Lee Story (1993) **C-119m.** *** D: Rob Cohen. Jason Scott Lee, Lauren Holly, Robert Wagner, Michael Learned, Nancy Kwan, Kay Tong Lim, Sterling Macer, Ric Young, Sven-Ole Thorson. Corny but very likable biopic about legendary action movie star who died at age 33 in 1973. Plenty of martial-arts mayhem, but also the story of a man who must overcome a variety of obstacles to find his place in the world. Adapted from a book by Lee's widow, Linda. The film's star is no relation to Bruce. Panavision. [PG-13]▼●◗

Dragonworld (1994) **C-84m.** *** D: Ted Nicolaou. Sam Mackenzie, Brittney Powell, John Calvin, Lila Kaye, John Woodvine, Courtland Mead, Andrew Keir, Jim Dunk. Pleasant children's film about a young Scottish laird forced by taxes to put his big pet dragon on display in an amusement park. Entertaining, good-looking movie (one of the best from producer Charles Band), but did the plot have to be so similar to MIGHTY JOE YOUNG? Good effects by Mark Rappaport and David Allen. [PG]▼●

Dragonwyck (1946) **103m.** **½ D: Joseph L. Mankiewicz. Gene Tierney, Walter Huston, Vincent Price, Glenn Langan, Anne Revere, Spring Byington, Henry (Harry) Morgan, Jessica Tandy. Period chiller set at a gloomy mansion on the Hudson, with good cast but episodic presentation. Mankiewicz's directorial debut; he also scripted from the Anya Seton story.

Dragoon Wells Massacre (1957) **C-88m.** ** D: Harold Schuster. Barry Sullivan, Dennis O'Keefe, Mona Freeman, Katy Jurado, Sebastian Cabot. Marauding Apaches force lawmen and renegades to join forces for self-protection; some action-packed scenes. CinemaScope.

Dragstrip Girl (1994) **C-83m. TVM** D: Mary Lambert. Mark Dacascos, Natasha

Gregson, Augusto Cesar Sandino, Christopher Crabb, Maria Celedonio, Richard Portnow, Raymond Cruz, Tracy Wells, Traci Lords. The 1950s: Social-climbing Chicano parking valet spots cars for a "chop shop" and has eyes on a rich Anglo girl in a T-bird. Hardly any dragstrip action in this dull, self-consciously "significant" remake of the 1957 cheapie. One of Showtime's "Rebel Highway" series, this uses only the title of the old American-International film. Below average.

Dr. Akagi (1998-Japanese) **C-128m.** *** D: Shohei Imamura. Akira Emoto, Kumiko Aso, Juro Kara, Masanori Sera, Jacques Gamblin, Keiko Matsuzaka. Pointed satiric drama set in the waning days of WW2 about a small-town doctor who fears that a hepatitis epidemic is about to sweep his country. Savagely lampoons Japanese military bureaucracy, but works best as a loving portrait of a dedicated man and those in his inner circle.▼

Dr. Alien (1988) **C-87m.** ** D: David DeCoteau. Judy Landers, Billy Jacoby, Olivia Barash, Stuart Fratkin, Raymond O'Connor, Arlene Golonka, Linnea Quigley, Troy Donahue, Ginger Lynn Allen, Edy Williams. Landers is an alien who disguises herself as a college professor and transforms freshman Jacoby from wimp to dreamboat. Silly stuff (with an all-star schlock movie supporting cast). [R]▼●

Drama of Jealousy, A SEE: **Pizza Triangle, The**

Dramatic School (1938) **80m.** **½ D: Robert B. Sinclair. Luise Rainer, Paulette Goddard, Alan Marshal, Lana Turner, Anthony Allen (John Hubbard), Henry Stephenson, Genevieve Tobin. Carbon-copy STAGE DOOR with Rainer the center of attraction as fanciful girl who makes good in both marriage and career; look for Ann Rutherford, Dick Haymes, Hans Conried in early bit roles.

Drango (1957) **92m.** ** D: Hall Bartlett, Jules Bricken. Jeff Chandler, Joanne Dru, Julie London, Donald Crisp. Chandler is Yankee Civil War veteran assigned to restore order to Southern town his command plundered. OK Western.

Draughtsman's Contract, The (1982-British) **C-103m.** ** D: Peter Greenaway. Anthony Higgins, Janet Suzman, Anne Louise Lambert, Hugh Fraser. Arrogant young artist takes commissions from the mistress of an estate in return for sexual favors; sumptuous-looking 17th-century tale, but cold and aloof. Will be of greater interest to fans of writer-director Greenaway. [R]▼

Draw! (1984) **C-98m. TVM** D: Steven Hilliard Stern. Kirk Douglas, James Coburn, Alexandra Bastedo, Graham Jarvis, Derek McGrath, Len Birman. Two old pros give this lighthearted Western (filmed on the range in Alberta, Canada) the traditional college try. Kirk's an over-the-hill outlaw in this misfire, and Jimbo is his old nemesis, now a boozing lawman who challenges him to one last showdown. Made for cable. Average.▼

Dr. Bethune (1990-Canadian-Chinese-French) **C-115m.** **½ D: Phillip Borsos. Donald Sutherland, Helen Mirren, Helen Shaver, Colm Feore, James Pax, Ronald Pickup, Guo Da, Anouk Aimée. Handsomely mounted but episodic account of controversial Canadian doctor Norman Bethune (well played by Sutherland), ardent anti-fascist and proponent of socialized medicine. Much terrain is covered, from his love life to his involvement in the Spanish Civil War and with Mao Tse-tung fighting the Japanese; unfortunately, you never really know what makes him tick. Original title: BETHUNE: THE MAKING OF A HERO. Released in the U.S. in 1993; Sutherland also starred in BETHUNE, a 1977 Canadian TV movie. ▼

Dr. Black and Mr. White SEE: **Dr. Black, Mr. Hyde**

Dr. Black, Mr. Hyde (1976) **C-87m.** **½ D: William Crain. Bernie Casey, Rosalind Cash, Marie O'Henry, Ji-Tu Cumbuka, Milt Kogan, Stu Gilliam. Black lab scientist Casey tests experimental serum on himself and turns into a white monster. No surprises, but not bad, either, with Casey doing first-rate job. Aka THE WATTS MONSTER and DR. BLACK AND MR. WHITE. [PG]▼

Dr. Broadway (1942) **68m.** **½ D: Anthony Mann. MacDonald Carey, Jean Phillips, J. Carrol Naish, Richard Lane, Eduardo Ciannelli, Warren Hymer. Anthony Mann's first film is a decent little B mystery centering on Carey as Times Square doc and the assorted crooks and loonies he becomes involved with. Nicely done on a low-budget and featuring a rare performance by Phillips, Ginger Rogers's stand-in.

Dr. Bull (1933) **75m.** *** D: John Ford. Will Rogers, Marian Nixon, Ralph Morgan, Rochelle Hudson, Berton Churchill, Louise Dresser, Andy Devine. Rogers in fine form as country doctor battling small-town pettiness as much as fighting illness. Stereotyped characters are perfect foils for Rogers' common-sense pronouncements; director Ford provides ideal atmosphere.

Dr. Cadman's Secret SEE: **Black Sleep, The**

Dr. Christian Responding to the phenomenal worldwide interest in the birth of the Dionne Quintuplets in Canada in 1935, 20th Century-Fox made a movie about the doctor who delivered the babies. Jean Hersholt was cast as Dr. Allan Dafoe in THE COUNTRY DOCTOR (1936) and repeated the role in two successful sequels, REUNION (1936) and FIVE OF A KIND (1938). The role fit the Danish actor like a glove, but attempts to extend the series were dashed when Dafoe refused to sell further rights to his story. Instead, Hersholt helped create a similar character called Dr. Christian, who became the focus of a successful radio series that began in 1937. (It lasted until 1953!) In 1939, RKO released the first of six independently made, low-budget films about the Good Doctor and his neighbors in River's End, Minnesota. Dorothy Lovett appears as Christian's attractive nurse, Judy Price, whose romantic entanglements provide sturdy subplot material. All six films are bucolic, low-key in nature, and heavily sentimental; they don't wear particularly well, although the doctor's efforts to help the homeless in COURAGEOUS DR. CHRISTIAN (cowritten, incidentally, by Ring Lardner, Jr.) give that particular entry a surprisingly contemporary slant.

DR. CHRISTIAN

Meet Dr. Christian (1939)
Courageous Dr. Christian (1940)
Dr. Christian Meets the Women (1940)
Remedy for Riches (1940)
Melody for Three (1941)
They Meet Again (1941)

Dr. Christian Meets the Women (1940) **68m.** ** D: William McGann. Jean Hersholt, Dorothy Lovett, Edgar Kennedy, Rod La Rocque, Frank Albertson, Marilyn (Lynn) Merrick, Maude Eburne, Veda Ann Borg. Predictable but harmless series entry, with the good doctor exposing "Professor" La Rocque's diet and physical-culture scam.▼

Dr. Cyclops (1940) **C-75m.** **½ D: Ernest Schoedsack. Albert Dekker, Thomas Coley, Janice Logan, Victor Kilian, Charles Halton. Title character (Dekker) shrinks humans to doll-size; the story is just OK, but the elaborate special effects (in color) are worth seeing.▼●

Dr. Dolittle (1998) **C-85m.** ** D: Betty Thomas. Eddie Murphy, Ossie Davis, Oliver Platt, Peter Boyle, Richard Schiff, Kristen Wilson, Kyla Pratt, Raven-Symoné, Jeffrey Tambor; voices of Ellen DeGeneres, Norm Macdonald, Garry Shandling, Julie Kavner, Jenna Elfman, Albert Brooks, Chris Rock, Reni Santoni, John Leguizamo, Gilbert Gottfried, Jonathan Lipnicki, Paul Reubens, Brian Doyle-Murray. 1990s rethink of the Hugh Lofting character has Murphy as a busy, self-absorbed doctor who reacquires the gift he had as a child to understand animals' speech. Comic chaos ensues. Murphy is likable and energetic, but the film is awfully flat; bound to appeal to kids who don't mind that seemingly every other word in the script is "butt." [PG-13]▼●◗

Dream a Little Dream (1989) **C-99m.** *½ D: Marc Rocco. Corey Feldman, Meredith Salenger, Jason Robards, Piper Laurie, Harry Dean Stanton, William McNamara, Corey Haim, Susan Blakely, Victoria Jackson, Alex Rocco, Josh Evans. Yet another personality-exchange comedy—this one with Robards and Feldman switching bodies after a bike mishap. Perfectly dreadful. Director is son of costar Alex Rocco. Direct-to-video sequel: DREAM A LITTLE DREAM 2. [PG-13]▼

Dreamboat (1952) **83m.** *** D: Claude Binyon. Ginger Rogers, Clifton Webb, Jeffrey Hunter, Anne Francis, Elsa Lanchester. Clever romp: silent-star Rogers cashes in on TV showings of her old movies, to chagrin of co-star Webb, now a distinguished professor. Scenes showing their old silent films are most enjoyable.

DreamChild (1985-British) **C-94m.** **½ D: Gavin Millar. Coral Browne, Ian Holm, Peter Gallagher, Caris Corfman, Nicola Cowper, Jane Asher, Amelia Shankley, Shane Rimmer. Woman for whom Rev. Charles Dodgson (Lewis Carroll) invented his *Alice in Wonderland* stories comes to America at age 80 for the author's centenary, unable to understand the fuss, and fearful of her own repressed memories. Fascinating material seriously flawed by romantic subplot and ludicrous recreation of N.Y.C. setting and characters of the 1930s. Browne's superb performance makes it all worthwhile. Jim Henson's Creature Shop provided Wonderland characters. Written by Dennis Potter. [PG]▼

Dream Demon (1988-British-U.S.) **C-89m.** ** D: Harley Cokliss. Kathleen Wilhoite, Jemma Redgrave, Timothy Spall, Jimmy Nail, Susan Fleetwood, Mark Greenstreet, Annabelle Lanyon, Nickolas Grace. Soon-to-be-married Redgrave has horrifying dreams, unwillingly pulling into them Wilhoite, an American in London seeking secrets of her own past. Good special effects and performances undercut by who-cares story and many repetitive sequences. Released in the U.S. in 1993. [R]▼

Dreamer (1979) **C-86m.** ** D: Noel Nosseck. Tim Matheson, Susan Blakely, Jack Warden, Richard B. Shull, Barbara Stuart, Pedro Gonzalez-Gonzalez. Bowling, a sport only slightly more cinematic than isometric exercises, gets the ROCKY treatment in this bland rags-to-riches story. Having Matheson's bowling ball made of Flubber might have helped pick up the pace. [PG]▼

Dreamer of Oz: The L. Frank Baum Story, The (1990) **C-100m. TVM** D: Jack Bender. John Ritter, Annette O'Toole, Rue McClanahan, Courtney Barilla, Charles Haid, David Schram, Nancy Lenehan. Good-hearted if superficial bio of the entrepreneur and author of *The Wonderful Wizard of Oz,* sparked by several fantasy sequences featuring Dorothy and her friends

on the Yellow Brick Road. Sci-fi writer Richard Matheson did the script. Average.
Dream for an Insomniac (1998) **C/B&W-88m.** ** D: Tiffani DeBartolo. Ione Skye, Jennifer Aniston, Mackenzie Astin, Michael Landes, Seymour Cassel. Waitress/aspiring actress (Skye) falls for the new counter-boy/poet (Astin) just 48 hours before she's about to move to L.A. Cute but sitcom-ish romantic comedy set in a Sinatra-themed, family-owned coffeehouse in San Francisco. Charismatic casting helps, particularly Aniston as Skye's flaky best friend, but you wish they'd all stop their yapping. Written by the director. Filmed in 1995. [R]▼●
Dream Girl (1948) **85m.** ** D: Mitchell Leisen. Betty Hutton, Macdonald Carey, Virginia Field, Patric Knowles, Walter Abel, Peggy Wood. Hutton stars as female Walter Mitty with constant daydreams; lowbrow version of Elmer Rice play.
Dreaming Lips (1937-British) **93m.** **½ D: Paul Czinner, Lee Garmes. Elisabeth Bergner, Raymond Massey, Romney Brent, Joyce Bland, Charles Carson, Felix Aylmer. Glamorous, pampered Bergner, wife of orchestra conductor Brent, commences a romance with world-famous (but desperately lonely) violinist Massey. A bit overdone, and the ending is a disappointment, but it's entertaining most of the way. Good star vehicle for Bergner. ▼
Dreaming Out Loud (1940) **81m.** ** D: Harold Young. Lum 'n' Abner (Chester Lauck, Norris Goff), Frances Langford, Frank Craven, Bobs Watson, Phil Harris. Radio comedians Lum 'n' Abner's screen debut is a very slight rural comedy-melodrama with music. The fabled proprietors of the Jot-Em-Down general store in Pine Ridge, Arkansas, get involved in the lives of various local residents.▼
Dreamlife of Angels, The (1998-French) **C-113m.** ***½ D: Erick Zonca. Elodie Bouchez, Natacha Régnier, Grégoire Colin, Jo Prestia, Patrick Mercado. Evocative study of two young women—one generous and impulsive, the other sullen and despairing—who meet at a clothing factory in Lille, France, and become close friends, then drift apart as one becomes involved with a club owner. An elusive story, directed with quiet precision by coscreenwriter Zonca (his feature debut), which slowly, penetratingly reveals a wealth of detail about the bonds of friendship and the vagaries of destiny. Bouchez and Régnier are outstanding. [R]▼◗
Dream Lover (1986) **C-104m.** *½ D: Alan J. Pakula. Kristy McNichol, Ben Masters, Paul Shenar, Justin Deas, John McMartin, Gayle Hunnicutt, Matthew Penn. Abysmal thriller about young woman's attempts to expunge recurring nightmare from her mind through "dream therapy." Intensely unsettling film with an interesting idea torpedoed by snail-like pacing and sterile atmosphere. What Hitchcock could have done with this! [R]▼
Dream Lover (1994) **C-103m.** **½ D: Nicholas Kazan. James Spader, Mädchen Amick, Bess Armstrong, Fredric Lehne, Larry Miller, Kathleen York, Blair Tefkin, Scott Coffey, Clyde Kusatsu, William Shockley. Handsome, wealthy architect Spader meets gorgeous, enigmatic Amick and the two become a passionate, perfect couple—until her cloudy past (eventually) raises his suspicions. Fluid camerawork (by Jean-Yves Escoffier) and some smart dialogue go out the window as plausibility level declines alarmingly. Stars register well but can't overcome a noirish mystery that just misses. Feature directing debut for screenwriter Kazan. Also available in unrated version. [R]▼●
Dream Machine, The (1990) **C-86m.** ** D: Lyman Dayton. Corey Haim, Evan Richards, Jeremy Slate, Randall England, Tracy Fraim, Brittney Lewis, Susan Seaforth Hayes. Super-wealthy Slate is murdered by an embezzler after cheating on his wife. She's just learned of his infidelity and, on an impulse, gives his new turbocharged Porsche to immature college student Haim (who doesn't know the deceased's body is stuffed in the trunk). By-the-numbers action-thriller with an intriguing (if unlikely) premise. [PG]▼●
Dream of Kings, A (1969) **C-107m.** *** D: Daniel Mann. Anthony Quinn, Irene Papas, Inger Stevens, Sam Levene, Radames Pera, Val Avery. Emotional study of robust Quinn trying to find money to take ailing son to Greece. Vivid look at Greek community in Chicago; heart-rending story by Harry Alan Petrakis. Stevens exceptional as young widow attracted to Quinn. [R]▼
Dream of Passion, A (1978-Greek) **C-106m.** *½ D: Jules Dassin. Melina Mercouri, Ellen Burstyn, Andreas Voutsinas, Despo Diamantidou, Dimitris Papa-michael. Aside from Burstyn's powerhouse performance as an American jailed in Greece for killing her three children, this attempt to parallel her story with Medea's is the kind of idea that should never have left the story conference. Mercouri is typically hammy as the actress who takes up her cause. [R]▼
Dreams (1955-Swedish) **86m.** ** D: Ingmar Bergman. Eva Dahlbeck, Harriet Andersson, Gunnar Bjornstrand, Ulf Palme, Inga Landgre. Sometimes fascinating but mostly vague—and, ultimately lesser—Bergman drama, about photo agency head Dahlbeck and model Andersson, and their dreams, torments, crises, oppression, relations with men. Aka JOURNEY INTO AUTUMN. ▼
Dreams (1990) SEE: **Akira Kurosawa's Dreams**
Dreamscape (1984) **C-99m.** *** D: Joseph Ruben. Dennis Quaid, Max von Sydow,

Christopher Plummer, Eddie Albert, Kate Capshaw, George Wendt, David Patrick Kelly. Quaid finds he can physically enter other people's dreams in this entertaining yarn; science-fantasy elements more successful than political intrigue subplot. [PG-13]▼●

Dream Street (1921) **138m.** ** D: D. W. Griffith. Carol Dempster, Ralph Graves, Charles Emmett Mack, Edward Peil, Tyrone Power (Sr.), Morgan Wallace. Disappointing silent melodrama about Gypsy Fair (Dempster), a music hall dancer, who is admired by two Irish brothers and an evil Chinese gambling den proprietor. Based on stories from *Limehouse Nights* by Thomas Burke, the book that also spawned Griffith's poetic BROKEN BLOSSOMS. Due to Dempster's limited abilities, this film never flowers. After its N.Y. premiere, it was shown with experimental sound-on-disc sequences by Orlando Kellum.▼

Dream Team, The (1989) **C-113m.** **½ D: Howard Zieff. Michael Keaton, Christopher Lloyd, Peter Boyle, Stephen Furst, Dennis Boutsikaris, Lorraine Bracco, Milo O'Shea, Philip Bosco, James Remar. Four mental-hospital patients become separated from their doctor while on a field trip to Yankee Stadium, and find themselves stranded in an even-larger looney bin: The Big Apple. Uneven farce seems inspired by ONE FLEW OVER THE CUCKOO'S NEST, and gets its mileage from the performances of its leading actors. [PG-13]▼●

Dream Wife (1953) **101m.** *½ D: Sidney Sheldon. Cary Grant, Deborah Kerr, Walter Pidgeon, Buddy Baer, Movita, Steve Forrest. Silly bedroom comedy about Grant "marrying" an Eastern princess for goodwill reasons. Cast is wasted. Also shown in computer-colored version.▼

Dream With the Fishes (1997) **C-96m.** ** D: Finn Taylor. David Arquette, Brad Hunt, Cathy Moriarty, Kathryn Erbe, Patrick McGaw, J. E. Freeman, Timi Prulhiere, Allyce Beasley, Peter Gregory. Mismatched buddy tale about a suicidal voyeur and a terminally ill drug addict who decide to "go for it" when they take off on a memorable trip that involves, among other things, nude bowling and bank holdups. Small film has its charms but seems to be trying too hard to be quirky. [R]▼

Dr. Ehrlich's Magic Bullet (1940) **103m.** ***½ D: William Dieterle. Edward G. Robinson, Ruth Gordon, Otto Kruger, Donald Crisp, Maria Ouspenskaya, Montagu Love, Sig Ruman, Donald Meek. Outstanding chronicle of 19th-century German scientist who developed cure for venereal disease. Robinson earnest in superior script by John Huston, Heinz Herald, and Norman Burnside; surprisingly compelling.▼

Dressed for Death SEE: **Straight On Till Morning**

Dressed to Kill (1941) **71m.** **½ D: Eugene Forde. Lloyd Nolan, Mary Beth Hughes, Sheila Ryan, William Demarest, Ben Carter, Virginia Brissac, Henry Daniell. Hard-boiled P.I. Michael Shayne (Nolan) probes a string of strange murders linked to a play in which the victims are all wearing theatrical costumes. Reasonably absorbing series entry.

Dressed to Kill (1946) **72m.** **½ D: Roy William Neill. Basil Rathbone, Nigel Bruce, Patricia Morison, Edmond Breon, Carl Harbord, Patricia Cameron, Tom Dillon. Music boxes made in prison hold the key to the whereabouts of stolen bank plates in this lively final entry in the Rathbone *Sherlock Holmes* series. Also shown in computer-colored version.▼●

Dressed to Kill (1980) **C-105m.** ***½ D: Brian De Palma. Michael Caine, Angie Dickinson, Nancy Allen, Keith Gordon, Dennis Franz, David Margulies, Brandon Maggart. High-tension melodrama about a psycho-killer who stalks two women—one a frustrated suburban housewife, the other a street-smart hooker who teams up with the first woman's son to trap the murderer. Writer-director De Palma works on viewer's emotions, not logic, and maintains a fever pitch from start to finish. Chilling Pino Donaggio score. Unrated version also available. Panavision. [R]▼●

Dresser, The (1983-British) **C-118m.** ***½ D: Peter Yates. Albert Finney, Tom Courtenay, Edward Fox, Zena Walker, Eileen Atkins, Michael Gough, Cathryn Harrison. Excellent film adaptation of Ronald Harwood's play about an aging actor-manager (based on real-life Donald Wolfit) whose very survival depends on the constant pampering and prodding of his dresser—who lives vicariously through the old man's performances. Finney, as Sir, and Courtenay, as Norman the dresser, are simply superb. Yates captures the look and feel of wartime England, and backstage atmosphere of a small touring company, with uncanny ability. A must for anyone who loves acting and the theater. [PG]▼●

Dressmaker, The (1988-British) **C-89m.** **½ D: Jim O'Brien. Joan Plowright, Billie Whitelaw, Peter Postlethwaite, Jane Horrocks, Tim Ransom. Medium account of two Liverpool sisters, one repressed (Plowright) and the other spirited (Whitelaw), and what happens when their naive, fragile niece falls for an American GI during WW2. Well acted, and starts off promisingly, but bogs down.▼●

Dr. Fischer of Geneva (1983-British) **C-110m. TVM** D: Michael Lindsay-Hogg. Alan Bates, James Mason, Greta Scacchi, Clarissa Kaye, Hugh Burden, Cyril Cusack, Barry Humphries. Mason is magnificent in one of his last roles, as a rich man who cynically delights in manipulating people to demonstrate man's venality. At a "bomb party," where guests risk literally being blown up in opening their million-dollar party favors, future son-in-law Bates gives Mason his comeuppance. Features an excellent supporting performance by Kaye, Mason's real-life widow, as a greedy dowager. Based on a Graham Greene story. Above average.

Dr. Giggles (1992) **C-95m.** *½ D: Manny Cotto. Larry Drake, Holly Marie Combs, Cliff De Young, Glenn Quinn, Keith Diamond, Richard Bradford, Michelle Johnson. Gory, one-note horror drama in which crazed doctor, who giggles whenever nervous, goes on a murderous rampage after escaping from a looney-bin. Drake's fine performance is wasted. Super 35. [R]▼●◗

Dr. Gillespie's Criminal Case (1943) **89m.** **½ D: Willis Goldbeck. Lionel Barrymore, Van Johnson, Donna Reed, Keye Luke, John Craven, William Lundigan, Walter Kingsford, Nat Pendleton, Marilyn Maxwell, Alma Kruger, Marie Blake, Henry O'Neill, Nell Craig. Gillespie tries to help a convicted murderer prove his innocence in this unusually serious entry which helped to establish Johnson and Reed, as well as providing an early role for young Margaret O'Brien.

Dr. Gillespie's New Assistant (1942) **87m.** **½ D: Willis Goldbeck. Lionel Barrymore, Van Johnson, Susan Peters, Richard Quine, Keye Luke, Alma Kruger, Stephen McNally, Nat Pendleton, Walter Kingsford, Nell Craig, Marie Blake, Frank Orth, Rose Hobart, Ann Richards. Three young surgeons (Johnson, Luke, and Quine) are put on "trial" by Gillespie to see who gets to replace Dr. Kildare in this satisfying entry stocked with burgeoning MGM talent. Quine and Peters were married in real life the following year.

Dr. Goldfoot and the Bikini Machine (1965) **C-90m.** ** D: Norman Taurog. Vincent Price, Frankie Avalon, Dwayne Hickman, Susan Hart, Fred Clark. Mad scientist tries to make a fortune manufacturing lifelike lady robots to marry wealthy men. Good chase scene, but otherwise just silly. Panavision. ▼

Dr. Goldfoot and the Girl Bombs (1966-Italian) **C-85m.** *½ D: Mario Bava. Vincent Price, Fabian, Franco Franchi, Moana Tahi, Laura Antonelli. Dumb sequel to DR. GOLDFOOT AND THE BIKINI MACHINE finds Price now backed by Red China, dropping actual girl bombs into the laps of unsuspecting generals.▼

Dr. Heckyl and Mr. Hype (1980) **C-99m.** **½ D: Charles B. Griffith. Oliver Reed, Sunny Johnson, Maia Danziger, Mel Welles, Virgil Frye, Jackie Coogan, Corinne Calvet. Reed is a grotesquely ugly podiatrist who drinks a potion to commit suicide, instead turns into a handsome murderer. Moderately funny comedy, also written by Roger Corman veteran Griffith. [R]▼

Drifter, The (1988) **C-90m.** **½ D: Larry Brand. Kim Delaney, Timothy Bottoms, Al Shannon, Miles O'Keeffe, Loren Haines, Thomas Wagner, Larry Brand. Interesting low-budget variation on the PLAY MISTY FOR ME/FATAL ATTRACTION formula as pretty costume designer Delaney picks up virile O'Keeffe hitchhiking, has a one-night affair, and is then hounded by him. Director Brand (who also plays the cop on the case) shows promise but film suffers from lack of a coherent scenario. [R]▼

Drifting Weeds SEE: **Floating Weeds**

Driftwood (1947) **90m.** **½ D: Allan Dwan. Ruth Warrick, Walter Brennan, Natalie Wood, Dean Jagger, Charlotte Greenwood, Jerome Cowan, H. B. Warner, Margaret Hamilton. Small-town doctor adopts a young girl who's never experienced "civilization" before. Entertaining family film with standout performance by young Natalie.▼

Drive a Crooked Road (1954) **82m.** ** D: Richard Quine. Mickey Rooney, Dianne Foster, Kevin McCarthy, Jack Kelly, Harry Landers. Quietly paced film of auto mechanic Rooney dreaming of being racing-car champ; instead becomes chump for gangsters, due to girlfriend.

Drive, He Said (1972) **C-90m.** **½ D: Jack Nicholson. William Tepper, Karen Black, Michael Margotta, Bruce Dern, Robert Towne, Henry Jaglom, Michael Warren, Charles Robinson, David (Ogden) Stiers, Cindy Williams. Confusing tale of youth alienation contains fine performances but loses itself in its attempt to cover all the bases; Dern is fabulous as gung-ho college basketball coach. Nicholson's directorial debut; he also cowrote the screenplay with Jeremy Larner. [R]

Drive-In (1976) **C-96m.** ** D: Rod Amateau. Lisa Lemole, Glen Morshower, Gary Cavagnaro, Billy Milliken, Lee Newsom, Regan Kee. Amiable low-budget trash about a night in the life of teenaged yahoos at a Texas drive-in during the unreeling of a campy disaster film (which takes up much of the screen time). Better after 20 beers. [PG]▼

Drive Me Crazy (1999) **C-91m.** ** D: John Schultz. Melissa Joan Hart, Adrian Grenier, Stephen Collins, Ali Larter, Mark Metcalf, William Converse-Roberts, Faye Grant. In order to win their dream prom dates, the most popular girl in school and a rebel outcast team up and pretend they're going steady. Predictable teen comedy could easily be called HE'S ALL THAT but is kept afloat by likable lead performances. Tries to have it both ways by featuring an onscreen number from punk girl band The Donnas and a title track by Britney Spears. [PG-13]▼◗

Driver, The (1978) **C-90m.** *** D: Walter Hill. Ryan O'Neal, Bruce Dern, Isabelle Adjani, Ronee Blakley, Matt Clark, Felice Orlandi. Tense throwback to the Hollywood film noir era pits getaway driver O'Neal against creepy cop Dern. Oddball melodrama doesn't seem like much at the time, but has a way of staying with you afterwards. Great car chase sequences. [PG—edited from original R rating]▼

Driver's Seat, The (1973-Italian) **C-101m.** BOMB D: Giuseppe Patroni Griffi. Elizabeth Taylor, Ian Bannen, Mona Washbourne, Andy Warhol, Guido Mannari. Liz is a disturbed woman who comes to Rome in search of someone to do her in. You may wish to do the same after sitting through this turkey, maybe Taylor's all-time worst. Adapted from a Muriel Spark novel. Aka PSYCHOTIC. [R]▼

Driving Miss Daisy (1989) **C-99m.** *** D: Bruce Beresford. Morgan Freeman, Jessica Tandy, Dan Aykroyd, Patti LuPone, Esther Rolle. Genteel, entertaining adaptation of Alfred Uhry's stage play about a simple black man who's hired as chauffeur for a cantankerous old Southern woman, and winds up being her most faithful companion. A smooth and enjoyable ride, with fine performances by the two leads. Aykroyd is likable in an unusual "straight" role as Tandy's son, though you can never quite forget who's playing the part (especially with such obvious makeup). Oscar winner for Best Picture, Actress, Screenplay (by Uhry), and Makeup. [PG] ▼●◗

Dr. Jekyll and Mr. Hyde (1920) **96m.** *** D: John S. Robertson. John Barrymore, Martha Mansfield, Brandon Hurst, Nita Naldi, Charles Lane, Louis Wolheim. One of several silent versions of famous tale, this one can hold its own next to the later March and Tracy filmings; Barrymore is superb as curious doctor who ventures into the unknown, emerging as evil Mr. Hyde. Bravura performance sparks well-made production.▼●◗

Dr. Jekyll and Mr. Hyde (1932) **97m.** *** D: Rouben Mamoulian. Fredric March, Miriam Hopkins, Rose Hobart, Holmes Herbert, Halliwell Hobbes. Exciting, floridly cinematic version of famous story with March in Oscar-winning portrayal of tormented doctor, Hopkins superb as tantalizing Ivy. Beware of 82m. re-issue version.▼●

Dr. Jekyll and Mr. Hyde (1941) **114m.** *** D: Victor Fleming. Spencer Tracy, Ingrid Bergman, Lana Turner, Donald Crisp, Ian Hunter, Barton MacLane, C. Aubrey Smith, Sara Allgood. Tracy and Bergman are excellent in thoughtful, lush remake of Robert Louis Stevenson's classic, which stresses Hyde's emotions rather than physical horror. Also shown in computer-colored version.▼●

Dr. Jekyll and Ms. Hyde (1995) **C-90m.** *½ D: David Price. Sean Young, Tim Daly, Lysette Anthony, Stephen Tobolowsky, Harvey Fierstein, Thea Vidale, Jeremy Piven, Polly Bergen, Stephen Shellen, Jane Connell, Julie Cobb, Robert Wuhl. Did we really need a comic retread of the classic Robert Louis Stevenson tale, with Jekyll's great-grandson (Daly) morphing into seductress Helen Hyde (Young)? If so, it should have been a lot better. [PG-13]▼●

Dr. Jekyll and Sister Hyde (1972-British) **C-94m.** **½ D: Roy Ward Baker. Ralph Bates, Martine Beswick, Gerald Sim, Lewis Fiander, Susan Broderick. Interesting twist to classic tale finds the good doctor discovering that his evil life is brought out in the form of a beautiful but dangerous woman. No thrills but fun; resemblance between Bates and Beswick is remarkable. Released in Britain at 97m. [PG]▼

Dr. Kildare From 1938 to 1947, this MGM series, set in Blair General Hospital, was one of the most successful and entertaining of all. INTERNES CAN'T TAKE MONEY (1937, Paramount) was the first film based on Max Brand's characters, with Joel McCrea as Kildare, but it was not part of the series and did not use any of the later familiar roles. The first official entry, YOUNG DR. KILDARE, starred Lew Ayres as Kildare, Lionel Barrymore as Dr. Gillespie, Laraine Day (Mary Lamont), Alma Kruger (Nurse Molly Byrd), Walter Kingsford (Dr. Carewe, head of the hospital), Nat Pendleton (Joe Wayman, ambulance driver), Emma Dunn and Samuel S. Hinds (Dr. Kildare's benevolent parents), Nell Craig (Nurse Parker), Marie Blake (Sally, switchboard operator), Frank Orth (Mike), and George Reed (Conover). Indeed, the Kildare series has more running characters than most others. Laraine Day left the series after DR. KILDARE'S WEDDING DAY, and the parents left along with Lew Ayres after DR. KILDARE'S VICTORY. Van Johnson and Keye Luke spent several films trying to become Dr. Gillespie's assistant, with Marilyn Maxwell as love interest for Van. Philip Dorn tried out in CALLING DR. GILLESPIE, and James Craig finished the series with DARK DELUSION. Lionel Barrymore appeared in all of them as the crusty Dr. Gillespie, and supported those entries with lesser plots and casts, often by himself.

DR. KILDARE

Internes Can't Take Money (1937)
Young Dr. Kildare (1938)
Calling Dr. Kildare (1939)
The Secret of Dr. Kildare (1939)
Dr. Kildare's Strange Case (1940)
Dr. Kildare Goes Home (1940)
Dr. Kildare's Crisis (1940)
The People vs. Dr. Kildare (1941)
Dr. Kildare's Wedding Day (1941)
Dr. Kildare's Victory (1942)
Calling Dr. Gillespie (1942)
Dr. Gillespie's New Assistant (1942)
Dr. Gillespie's Criminal Case (1943)
Three Men in White (1944)

Between Two Women (1944)
Dark Delusion (1947)

Dr. Kildare Goes Home (1940) **78m.** ** D: Harold S. Bucquet. Lew Ayres, Lionel Barrymore, Laraine Day, Samuel S. Hinds, Gene Lockhart, Emma Dunn, Nat Pendleton, Walter Kingsford, Alma Kruger, Nell Craig, Marie Blake. Selfless Kildare gives up chance to become Dr. Gillespie's assistant to help his overworked, smalltown physician dad set up a clinic. One of the internes is a young Arthur O'Connell.

Dr. Kildare's Crisis (1940) **75m.** **½ D: Harold S. Bucquet. Lew Ayres, Lionel Barrymore, Laraine Day, Robert Young, Emma Dunn, Nat Pendleton, Bobs Watson, Walter Kingsford, Alma Kruger, Nell Craig, Frank Orth, Marie Blake, Horace MacMahon. Kildare's impending nuptials are jeopardized by a diagnosis of possible epilepsy in his fiancée's brother (Young). Sleek entry with good production.

Dr. Kildare's Strange Case (1940) **76m.** **½ D: Harold S. Bucquet. Lew Ayres, Lionel Barrymore, Laraine Day, Shepperd Strudwick, Samuel S. Hinds, Emma Dunn, Nat Pendleton, Walter Kingsford, Alma Kruger, Nell Craig, Horace MacMahon, Marie Blake, Frank Orth. Kildare utilizes shock therapy and other "modern" techniques to help cure a mental patient. Arresting entry with numerous subplots.▼

Dr. Kildare's Victory (1942) **92m.** **½ D: W.S. Van Dyke II. Lew Ayres, Lionel Barrymore, Ann Ayars, Robert Sterling, Jean Rogers, Alma Kruger, Walter Kingsford, Nell Craig, Marie Blake, Frank Orth, Barry Nelson. Kildare, still heartsick over "Mary Lamont," falls for a socialite patient while fighting a hospital zoning problem in this busy episode. Ayres' last appearance in the series.

Dr. Kildare's Wedding Day (1941) **82m.** **½ D: Harold S. Bucquet. Lew Ayres, Lionel Barrymore, Laraine Day, Red Skelton, Fay Holden, Walter Kingsford, Alma Kruger, Samuel S. Hinds, Emma Dunn, Nils Asther, Miles Mander, Nell Craig, Frank Orth. Tragedy strikes Kildare's fiancée (Day, whom MGM was grooming for bigger roles) in this surprisingly somber episode leavened with comic relief by Skelton. Erstwhile "Dick Tracy" Ralph Byrd plays a cop.

Dr. M SEE: **Club Extinction**

Dr. Mabuse: Der Spieler (The Gambler) (1922-German) **120m.** ***½ D: Fritz Lang. Rudolf Klein-Rogge, Aud Egede Nissen, Gertrude Welcker, Alfred Abel, Lil Dagover, Paul Richter. Baroque tale about master criminal Mabuse (Klein-Rogge), who gambles with lives and fates, is an allegory of postwar German decadence. Brilliantly directed, designed, photographed; originally half of a two-part film, now shown separately.▼

Dr. Mabuse, King of Crime (1922-German) **93m.** *** D: Fritz Lang. Rudolf Klein-Rogge, Aud Egede Nissen, Gertrude Welcker, Alfred Abel. Part Two of Lang's epic work DR. MABUSE, DER SPIELER, which follows various story threads and details Mabuse's descent into madness. Not as flamboyant as Part One, but still quite good. Director Lang later made THE TESTAMENT OF DR. MABUSE (1933) and THE THOUSAND EYES OF DR. MABUSE (1960).▼

Dr. Minx (1975) **C-94m.** BOMB D: Hikmet Avedis. Edy Williams, Randy Boone, Harvey Jason, Marlene Schmidt, Alvy Moore, William Smith. Pitiful exploitation drama about Dr. Williams and her relationships with various men. Eternal starlet Edy's acting is abominable. [R]▼

Dr. No (1962-British) **C-111m.** ***½ D: Terence Young. Sean Connery, Ursula Andress, Joseph Wiseman, Jack Lord, Bernard Lee, Lois Maxwell. First James Bond film is least pretentious, with meatier story, better all-round production of Ian Fleming caper. Bond investigates strange occurrences in Jamaica, encounters master-fiend Dr. No (Wiseman).▼●◗

Drop Dead Fred (1991) **C-98m.** BOMB D: Ate De Jong. Phoebe Cates, Rik Mayall, Marsha Mason, Tim Matheson, Carrie Fisher, Keith Charles, Ron Eldard. Putrid fantasy-comedy about a repressed young woman who—as her life is crumbling around her—is revisited by her childhood make-believe "friend" Drop Dead Fred, a repulsive mischief-maker. Cates' appealing performance can't salvage this mess. Recommended only for people who think nose-picking is funny. [PG-13]▼●

Drop Dead Gorgeous (1999) **C-98m.** *½ D: Michael Patrick Jann. Kirsten Dunst, Denise Richards, Kirstie Alley, Ellen Barkin, Allison Janney, Brittany Murphy, Sam McMurray, Amy Adams, Mindy Sterling, Mo Gaffney, Nora Dunn. Annoying pseudo-documentary satire about small-town Midwestern teen beauty pageants. Full of frantic mugging and outrageous gags about eating disorders, but most of them aren't funny. Only prize-winner here is Janney as good-hearted trailer trash. To see how it's done right, watch SMILE. [PG-13]▼◗

Drop Squad (1994) **C-86m.** ** D: D. Clark Johnson. Eriq LaSalle, Vondie Curtis Hall, Ving Rhames, Kasi Lemmons, Leonard Thomas, Billy Williams, Eric A. Payne, Vanessa Williams, Nicole Powell, Paula Kelly. Unsatisfying tale of a black ad-agency employee (LaSalle) who conjures up idiotic advertising campaigns, thus forsaking his roots; he becomes the target of some vigilante deprogrammers who seek to make him aware of his ethnic and family loyalties. Well-intentioned satire of corporate racism, but neither as humorous nor as daring as it sets out to be. Executive producer is Spike Lee, who appears briefly in one of the commercials. [R]▼●◗

Drop Zone (1994) **C-102m.** **½ D: John Badham. Wesley Snipes, Gary Busey, Yancy Butler, Michael Jeter, Corin Nemec, Kyle Secor, Luca Bercovici, Malcolm-Jamal Warner, Rex Linn, Grace Zabriskie, Claire Stansfield, Andy Romano. Solid if predictable actioner with U.S. marshal Snipes going up against some sky-diving baddies out to pilfer data on undercover drug agents to sell to international narcotics dealers. The scenario is preposterous, but there are enough dazzling airborne stunts to keep you entertained. Panavision. [R]▼●◗

Dr. Otto and the Riddle of the Gloom Beam (1986) **C-97m.** ** D: John R. Cherry III. Jim Varney, Glenn Petech, Myke Mueller, Jackie Welch, Daniel Butler, Esther Huston. Varney, of ERNEST . . . fame, stars as a loony scientist who takes on various disguises to confuse those who would destroy him. Strictly for fans of the elastic-faced comic though there are a couple of genuine guffaws. [PG]▼

Drowning by Numbers (1987-British) **C-118m.** ***½ D: Peter Greenaway. Joan Plowright, Bernard Hill, Juliet Stephenson, Joely Richardson. Another bizarre, fascinating celluloid put-on from Greenaway, about an obsessive coroner and his involvement with three generations of women from the same family. Stunningly filmed and very entertaining (but recommended most enthusiastically to Greenaway fans). Not released in U.S. until 1991.▼●

Drowning Mona (2000) **C-95m.** **½ D: Nick Gomez. Danny DeVito, Bette Midler, Jamie Lee Curtis, Neve Campbell, Casey Affleck, William Fichtner, Marcus Thomas, Peter Dobson, Kathleen Wilhoite, Tracey Walter. Fairly amusing black comedy about a small town shaken by the drowning of its most reviled citizen (Midler), and the repercussions felt by her idiot son and husband, the town sheriff (DeVito), and others who knew and loathed her. [PG-13] ▼◗

Drowning Pool, The (1976) **C-108m.** **½ D: Stuart Rosenberg. Paul Newman, Joanne Woodward, Anthony Franciosa, Murray Hamilton, Melanie Griffith, Richard Jaeckel, Gail Strickland, Linda Haynes. Newman returns as private eye Harper, (based on Ross Macdonald's Archer character) in slickly made but slow whodunit; here he is called to help former lover Woodward out of a jam. Screenplay by Tracy Keenan Wynn, Lorenzo Semple, and Walter Hill. Panavision. [PG]▼

Dr. Phibes Rises Again! (1972-British) **C-89m.** **½ D: Robert Fuest. Vincent Price, Robert Quarry, Valli Kemp, Fiona Lewis, Peter Jeffrey, Peter Cushing, Beryl Reid, Terry-Thomas, Hugh Griffith. Campy sequel to THE ABOMINABLE DR. PHIBES finds Price looking for elixir to revive his dead wife, with Quarry hot on his trail throughout Egypt. [PG]▼●

Dr. Popaul SEE: **High Heels**

Dr. Socrates (1935) **70m.** *** D: William Dieterle. Paul Muni, Ann Dvorak, Barton MacLane, Raymond Brown, Mayo Methot. Enjoyable film about small-town doctor Muni who unwillingly becomes official doctor for wounded mobsters. Offbeat role for Muni, unusually good one for MacLane as loudmouthed gangster. Remade as KING OF THE UNDERWORLD with Kay Francis in the Muni role!

Dr. Strange (1978) **C-100m. TVM** D: Philip DeGuere. Peter Hooten, Clyde Kusatsu, Jessica Walter, John Mills, Philip Sterling. Marvel Comics Group hero gets a shot at a series in this pilot dealing in the occult, with tongue firmly in cheek. Plot has him joining forces with a world-weary sorcerer (played *con brio* by Sir John Mills) to stop a beautiful witch from adding to her collection of men's souls. Above average.▼

Dr. Strangelove or: How I Learned to Stop Worrying and Love the Bomb (1964-British) **93m.** **** D: Stanley Kubrick. Peter Sellers, George C. Scott, Sterling Hayden, Slim Pickens, Keenan Wynn, Peter Bull, James Earl Jones. U.S. President must contend with the Russians and his own political and military leaders when a fanatical general launches A-bomb attack on U.S.S.R. Sellers plays the President, British captain, and mad inventor of the Bomb in this brilliant black comedy, which seems better with each passing year. Sellers' phone conversation with Soviet premier is classic. Outstanding cast, incredible sets by Ken Adam. Jones' film debut. ▼●◗

Dr. Syn, Alias the Scarecrow (1962) **C-98m.** **½ D: James Neilson. Patrick McGoohan, George Cole, Tony Britton, Geoffrey Keen, Kay Walsh, Patrick Wymark. Agreeable Disney production made in England (and originally shown in three parts on the Disney TV show as *The Scarecrow of Romney Marsh*) about country vicar who in reality is a smuggler and pirate. McGoohan is well cast as the mysterious bandit-hero who conducts his nightly raids disguised as a scarecrow. Filmed before in 1937 with George Arliss; another 1962 version, NIGHT CREATURES, stars Peter Cushing. [G]▼

Dr. Terror's Gallery of Horrors SEE: **Return from the Past**

Dr. Terror's House of Horrors (1965-British) **C-98m.** **½ D: Freddie Francis. Peter Cushing, Christopher Lee, Roy Castle, Max Adrian, Michael Gough, Donald Sutherland, Neil McCallum, Edward Underdown, Ursula Howells, Jeremy Kemp, Bernard Lee. Don't let title steer you from this intelligent episodic thriller about a strange doctor (Cushing) who tells five men's fortunes on a train. Enjoyable horror-fantasy. Techniscope.▼

Drugstore Cowboy (1989) **C-100m.** ***½ D: Gus Van Sant, Jr. Matt Dillon, Kelly Lynch, James Remar, James Le Gros, Heather Graham, Beah Richards, Grace Zabriskie, Max Perlich, William S. Burroughs. Fascinating, completely credible look at the world of a junkie and his "family," who rob drugstores to support their habit. No preaching or moralizing here, which is precisely what gives the film its impact. Standout performances, particularly from Dillon and Lynch. Based on prison inmate James Fogle's unpublished autobiographical novel of the 1970s. Screenplay by Van Sant and Daniel Yost. [R]▼●◗

Drum, The (1938) SEE: **Drums**

Drum (1976) **C-110m.** BOMB D: Steve Carver. Warren Oates, Ken Norton, Isela Vega, Pam Grier, Yaphet Kotto, John Colicos, Brenda Sykes, Paula Kelly. Continuation of MANDINGO—a new and dreadful low in lurid characters and incidents. Norton in title role generates neither interest nor sympathy. [R]▼

Drum Beat (1954) **C-111m.** **½ D: Delmer Daves. Alan Ladd, Audrey Dalton, Marisa Pavan, Robert Keith, Rodolfo Acosta, Charles Bronson, Warner Anderson, Elisha Cook, Jr., Anthony Caruso, Strother Martin. In southern Oregon, former Indian fighter Ladd tries to talk Modoc chief Captain Jack (Bronson) into peace. Director Daves based his script on historical events. Bronson is especially good in an unusual role. CinemaScope.▼

Drums (1938-British) **C-99m.** *** D: Zoltan Korda. Sabu, Raymond Massey, Valerie Hobson, Roger Livesey, David Tree. Fine, colorful adventure with precocious Sabu rescuing British cavalry in early 20th-century India; atmospheric and actionful. Originally titled THE DRUM. Original British running time: 104m.▼●

Drums Across the River (1954) **C-78m.** ** D: Nathan Juran. Audie Murphy, Lisa Gaye, Walter Brennan, Lyle Bettger, Hugh O'Brian, Mara Corday, Jay Silverheels, Regis Toomey, Bob Steele. Murphy ties in with gold-jumpers overrunning Indian land, redeems himself by joining forces against these men to achieve peace.

Drums Along the Mohawk (1939) **C-103m.** ***½ D: John Ford. Claudette Colbert, Henry Fonda, Edna May Oliver, John Carradine, Jessie Ralph, Arthur Shields, Robert Lowery, Ward Bond. John Ford richly captures flavor of Colonial life in this vigorous, courageous story of settlers in upstate N.Y. during Revolutionary War. Action, drama, sentiment, humor deftly interwoven in beautiful Technicolor production. From Walter Edmonds' novel. ▼●

Drums in the Deep South (1951) **C-87m.** ** D: William Cameron Menzies. James Craig, Barbara Payton, Guy Madison, Barton MacLane, Craig Stevens. Stagnant Civil War yarn of West Pointers who find themselves fighting for opposite causes. ▼

Drums of Tahiti (1954) **C-73m.** *½ D: William Castle. Dennis O'Keefe, Patricia Medina, Francis L. Sullivan, George Keymas. Footloose American aids a Tahitian Queen who opposes annexation by the French in the late 1800s. Silly Sam Katzman production whose only novelty (in theaters) was the use of 3-D—as you can tell by flaming torches hurled at the camera!

Drunken Master (1978-Hong Kong) **C-106m.** **½ D: Yuen Woo Ping. Jackie Chan, Yuen Sui Tin, Wang Jang Lee, Hsu Hsia, Ling Yang, Dean Shek, Yuen Shun-Yee. Jackie plays Chinese folk hero Wong Fei Hung in this kung fu comedy, his first big hit. Almost plotless film has Wong studying under hard-drinking master played by Yuen Sui Tin, the director's father. Enjoyably silly, with some good stunt work and comic moments. Of note mostly for its importance to Chan's career. Aka DRUNKEN MONKEY IN THE TIGER'S EYE(!) Followed by a sequel in 1994. Widescreen.▼

Drunken Master II (1994-Hong Kong) **C-113m.** **½ D: Lau Kar Leung. Jackie Chan, Anita Mui, Ti Lung, Andy Lau, Gabriel Wong, Ken Lo, Chin Kar-Lok. Chan returns to the role that made him a star 16 years earlier. Lavishly mounted but meandering sequel has Wong Fei Hung confronting art smugglers and family strife. Chan plays the character at the same age he did in the first film, even though now he's as old as the man playing his father! Some truly amazing fight sequences, especially the complex final battle in a steel mill. The final scene is surprisingly tasteless, however. The fellow Jackie fights under the train is the film's director. Technovision.▼

Drunks (1996) **C-90m.** **½ D: Peter Cohn. Richard Lewis, Faye Dunaway, Amanda Plummer, Spalding Gray, Parker Posey, Calista Flockhart, Howard Rollins, Lisa Gay Hamilton, Dianne Wiest. Potent, if stagy, character study about alcoholics (of varied backgrounds) who tell all at an Alcoholics Anonymous meeting. Comedian Lewis is effective as a particularly pained group leader. A fine actors' showcase with some strong moments. Debuted on cable TV before theatrical release. [R]▼

Dr. Who and the Daleks (1965-British) **C-85m.** **½ D: Gordon Flemyng. Peter Cushing, Roy Castle, Jennie Linden, Roberta Tovey, Barrie Ingham. Pleasing feature inspired by the long-running British TV serial, with the Doctor and his young friends transported to another world where humans are threatened by robotlike Daleks. Followed by DALEKS—INVASION EARTH 2150 A.D. Techniscope. ▼

Dry White Season, A (1989) **C-107m.** **½ D: Euzhan Palcy. Donald Sutherland, Janet Suzman, Zakes Mokae, Jürgen Prochnow, Susan Sarandon, Marlon Brando, Winston Ntshona, Thoko Ntshinga, Susannah Harker, Rowan Elmes. Disappointing film about South African apartheid, set in 1976, with Sutherland as a schoolteacher who slowly awakens to the appalling reality of how blacks are treated in his country. Crucially important subject matter is unfortunately presented in the context of a story that's contrived and dramatically hollow. Brando is magnetic (if somewhat askew) in a showy supporting role as an outspoken barrister. [R]▼●

D2: The Mighty Ducks (1994) **C-107m.** ** D: Sam Weisman. Emilio Estevez, Kathryn Erbe, Michael Tucker, Jan Rubes, Carsten Norgaard, Maria Ellingsen, Joshua Jackson, Elden Ryan Ratliff (Hansen), Shaun Weiss, Matt Doherty. Having led his rag-tag hockey team to surprise victory in THE MIGHTY DUCKS, Estevez now gets a chance to coach Team USA (incorporating his former Ducks) in the Junior Goodwill Games—and make a bundle of money as a potential celebrity. The kind of film that gives the word "contrivance" a bad name: a Disney movie with mixed messages about competition, commercialism, puberty, and sportsmanship. Kids may like it anyway. Sports stars ranging from Wayne Gretzky to Kareem Abdul Jabbar make cameo appearances. [PG]▼●

D3: The Mighty Ducks (1996) **C-104m.** ** D: Robert Lieberman. Emilio Estevez, Jeffrey Nordling, Joshua Jackson, David Selby, Heidi Kling, Joss Ackland, Elden Ryan Ratliff (Hansen), Shaun Weiss, Vincent A. Larusso, Matt Doherty, Colombe Jacobsen, Aaron Lohr. Those adolescent hockey players have won scholarships to a fancy private school, where they have a new, no-nonsense coach (Nordling) and find themselves outsiders in a snooty varsity league. Oh yes—and Charlie (Jackson) has a girlfriend. The Ducks franchise seems to be running out of steam, but the formula still may work for undemanding kids. [PG]▼●

DuBarry Was a Lady (1943) **C-101m.** *** D: Roy Del Ruth. Red Skelton, Lucille Ball, Gene Kelly, Virginia O'Brien, Rags Ragland, Zero Mostel, Donald Meek, George Givot, Louise Beavers, Tommy Dorsey and His Orchestra. Nightclub worker Skelton pines for beautiful singing star Ball; when he swallows a Mickey Finn, he dreams he's Louis XVI, and has to contend with the prickly Madame DuBarry (Ball). Colorful nonsense, missing most of the songs from Cole Porter's Broadway score, though "Friendship" is used as the finale. Opens like a vaudeville show, with beautiful chorines and specialty acts, including young Mostel, and Dorsey's band—with Buddy Rich on drums—doing a sensational "Well, Git It." They turn up later in powdered wigs, as do The Pied Pipers, with Dick Haymes and Jo Stafford. Lana Turner has a bit part.▼●

Du Barry, Woman of Passion (1930) **90m.** ** D: Sam Taylor. Norma Talmadge, William Farnum, Conrad Nagel, Hobart Bosworth, Alison Skipworth. Early sound version of oft-told tale about the life and loves of the famous 18th-century courtesan. Stiff and primitive but with fine art direction by William Cameron Menzies.▼

Du-beat-e-o (1984) **C/B&W-87m.** *½ D: Alan Sacks. Ray Sharkey, Joan Jett, Derf Scratch, Len Lesser, Nora Gaye. Outrageous, obnoxious, gimmicky punk collage about hip filmmaker Sharkey, who has been ordered by his mob financiers to complete his rock 'n' roll movie in 31 hours. Lots of energy, but it's all sorely misplaced.▼

Dubious Patriots, The SEE: **You Can't Win 'Em All**

Duchess and the Dirtwater Fox, The (1976) **C-103m.** *½ D: Melvin Frank. George Segal, Goldie Hawn, Conrad Janis, Thayer David, Roy Jenson, Bob Hoy, Richard Farnsworth. Dumb comedy about cardsharp Segal and dance-hall cutie Hawn teaming up in the Old West. Occasional laughs, inappropriate song interludes. Panavision. [PG]▼●

Duchess of Idaho (1950) **C-98m.** **½ D: Robert Z. Leonard. Esther Williams, Van Johnson, John Lund, Paula Raymond, Amanda Blake, Eleanor Powell, Lena Horne. Williams' vehicle takes her to Sun Valley, where she's trying to help patch up roommate's romance but falls in love herself. MGM guest stars pep up the formula production.▼

Duck Soup (1933) **70m.** **** D: Leo McCarey. Groucho, Harpo, Chico, Zeppo Marx, Margaret Dumont, Louis Calhern, Raquel Torres, Edgar Kennedy, Leonid Kinskey, Charles Middleton. The Marx Brothers' most sustained bit of insanity, a flop when first released, but now considered a satiric masterpiece. In postage-stamp-sized Freedonia, Prime Minister Rufus T. Firefly (Groucho) declares war on neighboring Sylvania just for the hell of it. Enough gags for five movies, but our favorite is still the mirror sequence. Zeppo's swan song with his brothers.▼●◗

DuckTales: The Movie—Treasure of the Lost Lamp (1990) **C-73m.** **½ D: Bob Hathcock. Voices of Alan Young, Christopher Lloyd, Rip Taylor, June Foray, Chuck McCann, Richard Libertini, Russi Taylor, Joan Gerber, Terence McGovern. Disney's premier "Movietoon" feature falls somewhere between traditional studio standards and Saturday morning gruel. Story centers on an archeological trek for a genie's lamp that can, among other things, make ice cream fall from the sky, pitting

Uncle Scrooge McDuck against the evil Merlock. Mild vehicle for Huey, Dewey, Louie, and company. [G]▼●

Duck, You Sucker (1972-Italian) **C-138m.** *** D: Sergio Leone. Rod Steiger, James Coburn, Romolo Valli, Maria Monti. Big, sprawling story of Mexican revolution, and how peasant thief Steiger gets talked into taking sides by Irish explosives expert Coburn. Tremendous action sequences; Leone's wry touches and ultra-weird Ennio Morricone score make it worthwhile diversion. Aka A FISTFUL OF DYNAMITE, some prints of which run 121m. Released in Italy at 158m. Techniscope. [PG]▼●

Dude Goes West, The (1948) **87m.** ** D: Kurt Neumann. Eddie Albert, Gale Storm, James Gleason, Binnie Barnes, Gilbert Roland, Barton MacLane. Innocuous little comedy of Easterner Albert becoming a Western hero.

Dudes (1987) **C-90m.** BOMB D: Penelope Spheeris. Jon Cryer, Daniel Roebuck, Flea, Lee Ving, Catherine Mary Stewart. Incomprehensible, idiotic account of a trio of N.Y.C. punk rockers, and their fate when harassed by a gang of redneck killers in the Southwest. Thoroughly repugnant. [R]▼●

Dudes Are Pretty People (1942) **95m.** ** D: Hal Roach, Jr. Jimmy Rogers, Noah Beery, Jr., Marjorie Woodworth, Paul Hurst, Marjorie Gateson, Russell Gleason, Grady Sutton. A couple of itinerant cowboys move to a dude ranch when one of them falls for a flashy blonde. Pretty dull. Originally one of producer Hal Roach's 46m. "Streamliner" featurettes; for TV it's been spliced to its equally dull sequel, CALABOOSE.

Dudley Do-Right (1999) **C-77m.** *½ D: Hugh Wilson. Brendan Fraser, Sarah Jessica Parker, Alfred Molina, Eric Idle, Robert Prosky, Alex Rocco, Jack Kehler, Louis Mustillo; narrated by Corey Burton. Poorly conceived live-action version of the delightful Jay Ward-produced TV cartoons of the 1960s about a stalwart (if thick-headed) Mountie, his sweetheart, Nell Fenwick, and the dastardly villain, Snidely Whiplash (played with gusto by Molina). A couple of laughs here and there can't make up for a desperate, everything-but-the-kitchen-sink script. Super 35. [PG]▼●◗

Duel (1971) **C-90m. TVM** D: Steven Spielberg. Dennis Weaver, Tim Herbert, Charles Seel, Eddie Firestone. Businessman driving rented car on lonely stretch of road begins to realize that the driver of a diesel truck (whom he cannot see) is out to get him. This TV movie put Spielberg on the map, and rightly so; superb suspense film, from Richard Matheson's script. Telecast at 73m.: released theatrically in 1983 at 88m. Above average. ▼●

Duel at Apache Wells (1957) **70m.** *½ D: Joe Kane. Anna Maria Alberghetti, Ben Cooper, Jim Davis, Bob Steele, Frank Puglia. Title tells more than all in standard oater. Filmed in widescreen Naturama.

Duel at Diablo (1966) **C-103m.** *** D: Ralph Nelson. James Garner, Sidney Poitier, Bibi Andersson, Dennis Weaver, Bill Travers, William Redfield, John Crawford, John Hubbard, John Hoyt. Aging Indians vs. Cavalry formula comes alive in this exciting Western; offbeat casting with tight direction. Some may find it too violent, but a must for action and Western fans. Look for Richard Farnsworth as a wagon driver. ▼●

Duel at Silver Creek, The (1952) **C-77m.** *½ D: Don Siegel. Audie Murphy, Stephen McNally, Faith Domergue, Susan Cabot, Gerald Mohr, Lee Marvin. Ponderous oater has Murphy as the "Silver Kid" helping marshal fight town criminals.▼

Duel at the Rio Grande (1962-Italian) **C-93m.** ** D: Mario Caiano. Sean Flynn, Danielle de Metz, Folco Lulli, Armando Calvo. Bland reworking of THE MARK OF ZORRO, with Flynn (Errol's son) uneasy in lead role. Dyaliscope.

Duel in Durango SEE: **Gun Duel in Durango**

Duel in the Jungle (1954-British) **C-102m.** **½ D: George Marshall. Dana Andrews, Jeanne Crain, David Farrar, George Coulouris, Wilfrid Hyde-White. Action-packed adventure of insurance investigator tracking allegedly dead man to Africa. Strong cast.

Duel in the Sun (1946) **C-130m.** *** D: King Vidor. Jennifer Jones, Joseph Cotten, Gregory Peck, Lionel Barrymore, Lillian Gish, Herbert Marshall, Walter Huston, Butterfly McQueen, Charles Bickford, Tilly Losch, Harry Carey. Producer-writer David O. Selznick's ambitious attempt to duplicate success of GONE WITH THE WIND: big, brawling, engrossing, often stupid sex-Western, with half-breed Jones caught between brothers Peck and Cotten. Great in Technicolor, with some memorable scenes and an unexpectedly bizarre finale. From the novel by Niven Busch. Superb score by Dimitri Tiomkin.▼●◗

Duellists, The (1977-British) **C-101m.** *** D: Ridley Scott. Keith Carradine, Harvey Keitel, Edward Fox, Cristina Raines, Robert Stephens, Diana Quick, Tom Conti, Albert Finney, Peter Postlethwaite. Competent screen version of Joseph Conrad's *The Duel* concerns long-running feud between French officers Carradine and Keitel during the Napoleonic wars. Supporting players are more convincing than two leads; film is among most staggeringly beautiful of its time. Scott's first feature. [PG]▼●

Duel of Champions (1961-Italian) **C-105m.** ** D: Ferdinando Baldi. Alan

Ladd, Franca Bettoja, Franco Fabrizi, Robert Keith, Luciano Marin. Stodgy epic set in ancient Rome with bored-looking Ladd the Roman leader who challenges forces of Alba. Totalscope.▼

Duel of the Titans (1961-Italian) **C-88m.** ** D: Sergio Corbucci. Steve Reeves, Gordon Scott, Virna Lisi, Massimo Girotti. Reeves is Romulus and Scott is Remus in this fictional account of justice overcoming tyranny in ancient Rome. CinemaScope.▼

Duet for Four (1982-Australian) **C-97m.** *½ D: Tim Burstall. Mike Preston, Wendy Hughes, Michael Pate, Diane Cilento, Gary Day, Arthur Dignam, Rod Mullinar. Middle-aged Preston's life is in turmoil: his wife has a lover, his mistress wants marriage, his daughter might be a drug addict, his business may be taken over. Weak drama does not delve beneath the surface of its characters. Panavision.

Duet for One (1986) **C-107m.** **½ D: Andrei Konchalovsky. Julie Andrews, Alan Bates, Max von Sydow, Rupert Everett, Margaret Courtenay, Cathryn Harrison, Macha Meril, Liam Neeson. World-class violinist Andrews is stricken with multiple sclerosis, and her comfortable, rewarding life is shattered. Tom Kempinski based his two-character play (virtuoso and psychiatrist) on a real-life cellist, but for film it was opened up and, in the process, diluted. Husband Bates, therapist von Sydow, and rebellious protégé Everett are fine, but it's Andrews' gutsy performance that breathes life into the film. Made in England. [R]▼

Duffy (1968-U.S.-British) **C-101m.** *½ D: Robert Parrish. James Coburn, James Mason, James Fox, Susannah York, John Alderton. Scummy crime comedy about two half-brothers who decide to rob their father of bank notes he is transporting by ship. A waste of everyone's talents and lovely location photography. [M/PG]

Duffy of San Quentin (1954) **78m.** **½ D: Walter Doniger. Louis Hayward, Joanne Dru, Paul Kelly, Maureen O'Sullivan, George Macready. Low-keyed account of Warden Duffy's reforms within famed prison. Followed by THE STEEL CAGE.

Duffy's Tavern (1945) **97m.** BOMB D: Hal Walker. Barry Sullivan, Marjorie Reynolds, Bing Crosby, Dorothy Lamour, Alan Ladd, Betty Hutton, Eddie Bracken, Veronica Lake, Robert Benchley, Paulette Goddard, Brian Donlevy. Disastrous "comedy" of radio character Ed Gardner trying to save Duffy's Tavern, Victor Moore trying to save his record company. No redeeming values despite guest appearances by several dozen Paramount stars.

Duke of West Point, The (1938) **109m.** **½ D: Alfred E. Green. Louis Hayward, Joan Fontaine, Tom Brown, Richard Carlson, Alan Curtis, Donald Barry. Predictable West Point saga of honor and love at the Academy is trite but entertaining, with Fontaine winning as the ingenue.▼

Dulcima (1971-British) **C-93m.** **½ D: Frank Nesbitt. Carol White, John Mills, Stuart Wilson, Bernard Lee, Sheila Raynor. Poor White moves in with and exploits wealthy old farmer Mills. OK melodrama benefits from solid work by the stars. Original running time: 98m. [PG]

Dulcimer Street (1948-British) **112m.** **½ D: Sidney Gilliat. Richard Attenborough, Alastair Sim, Fay Compton, Stephen Murray, Wylie Watson, Susan Shaw, Joyce Carey, Ivy St. Helier, Hugh Griffith, Maurice Denham. Atmospheric account of a slum area of London and its inhabitants who champion one of their own accused of murder. Original British title: LONDON BELONGS TO ME.

Dulcy (1940) **73m.** *½ D: S. Sylvan Simon. Ann Sothern, Ian Hunter, Roland Young, Reginald Gardiner, Billie Burke, Lynne Carver, Dan Dailey, Jr. Pretty bad comedy of Chinese orphan mending new family's problems. Good cast with inferior material.

Dumb & Dumber (1994) **C-106m.** ** D: Peter Farrelly. Jim Carrey, Jeff Daniels, Lauren Holly, Teri Garr, Karen Duffy, Mike Starr, Charles Rocket, Victoria Rowell, Cam Neely, Felton Perry. No, dumb*est*: a self-proclaimed no-brainer about two idiot pals who drive cross-country to Aspen to return a briefcase which (unbeknownst to them) contains a fortune in ransom money. Cheesy, gross-out comedy has its moments here and there, and enthusiastic performances by the two stars, who deserve a better script than this. Followed by an animated TV series. [PG-13]▼●◗

Dumbo (1941) **C-64m.** **** D: Ben Sharpsteen. Voices of Sterling Holloway, Edward Brophy, Verna Felton, Herman Bing, Cliff Edwards. One of Walt Disney's most charming animated films, about pint-sized elephant with giant-sized ears, and how his friend Timothy the Mouse helps build his confidence. Never a dull moment, but pink-elephants dream sequence is special treat. Frank Churchill and Oliver Wallace's scoring earned them Oscars.▼●

Dummy (1979) **C-100m. TVM** D: Frank Perry. Paul Sorvino, LeVar Burton, Brian Dennehy, Rose Gregorio, Gregg Henry. Real-life account of the relationship between a deaf and dumb black youth accused of murder and the deaf court-appointed attorney who defended him in the precedent-setting Chicago trial. Tour-de-force roles for Sorvino, exceptionally good as the lawyer, and Burton. Ernest Tidyman's tidy script another plus. Above average.

Dune (1984) **C-140m.** *½ D: David Lynch. Kyle MacLachlan, Francesca Annis, Brad Dourif, Jose Ferrer, Linda Hunt, Freddie Jones, Richard Jordan, Virginia Madsen,

Silvana Mangano, Kenneth McMillan, Jack Nance, Sian Phillips, Jürgen Prochnow, Paul Smith, Sting, Dean Stockwell, Max von Sydow, Patrick Stewart, Sean Young, Alicia (Roanne) Witt. Elephantine adaptation of Frank Herbert's popular sci-fi novel set in the year 10,991. You know you're in trouble when film's opening narration (setting up the story) is completely incomprehensible! Visually imaginative, well cast, but joyless and oppressive—not to mention *long*. For devotees of Herbert's novel only. (A special 190-minute edition was prepared for TV, under protest from director Lynch with new narration and footage that wasn't used in the theatrical version. TV print credits the pseudonymous Allen Smithee as director.) Todd-AO 35. [PG-13]▼●◗

Dunera Boys, The (1985-Australian) **C-150m.** ★★½ D: Sam Lewin. Joseph Spano, Bob Hoskins, Joseph Furst, John Meillon, Warren Mitchell, Mary-Anne Fahey, Simon Chilvers, Steven Vidler, Moshe Kedem. Low-key, fact-based drama of Jewish refugees in England at the outset of WW2 who, because of their nationalities, are suspected of being Nazi spies and exiled to a POW camp in Australia. Hoskins plays a loutish fishmonger who's as English as Winston Churchill, but somehow is deported with the others. Fascinating subject matter is occasionally pointed, but film is overlong and uneven. Made for Australian television.▼●

Dungeonmaster, The (1985) **C-73m.** ★½ D: Rosemarie Turko, John Buechler, Charles Band, David Allen, Steve Ford, Peter Manoogian, Ted Nicolaou. Jeffrey Byron, Richard Moll, Leslie Wing. It took seven—count 'em, seven—directors to make this short, sour chronicle of a girl held hostage by a villain. Her savior (atrociously played by Byron) must overcome seven challenges. You have only one: to sit through this. [PG-13]▼●

Dungeons and Dragons SEE: **Mazes and Monsters**

Dunkirk (1958-British) **113m.** ★★★ D: Leslie Norman. John Mills, Richard Attenborough, Bernard Lee, Robert Urquhart, Ray Jackson, Lionel Jeffries. Near-epic dramatization of the rescue by the Royal Navy and small civilian craft of 300,000 British soldiers trapped on the French beach of the title in 1940. One of the last films of the famed Ealing studios. Very realistic, with a fine cast and good direction. Original British length: 135m. Metroscope.

Dunston Checks In (1996) **C-88m.** ★★½ D: Ken Kwapis. Jason Alexander, Faye Dunaway, Eric Lloyd, Rupert Everett, Graham Sack, Paul Reubens, Glenn Shadix, Nathan Davis, Jennifer Bassey. Easy-to-take kids' comedy about the sons of a hard-working hotel manager who discover that an orangutan has been sneaked into the establishment by a crafty thief. Alexander is excellent, the kids are appealing, the orangutan is just right, Everett does a Terry-Thomas homage, Dunaway goes slapstick, and everyone has a good time, including the audience. [PG]▼●

Dunwich Horror, The (1970) **C-90m.** ★★½ D: Daniel Haller. Sandra Dee, Dean Stockwell, Ed Begley, Sam Jaffe, Lloyd Bochner, Joanna Moore, Talia Coppola (Shire). Adaptation of H. P. Lovecraft's story about warlock Stockwell's sinister plans for girlfriend Dee. Often effective, but ending ruins the whole film. [M]▼●

Durant Affair, The (1962-British) **73m.** ★½ D: Godfrey Grayson. Jane Griffiths, Conrad Phillips, Nigel Green, Simon Lack. Flabby courtroom melodrama.

Dust (1985-French-Belgian) **C-88m.** ★★★½ D: Marion Hansel. Jane Birkin, Trevor Howard, John Matshikiza, Nadine Uwampa, Lourdes Christina Sayo, Rene Diaz. Birkin gives a fine performance as an unmarried woman, in need of love and affection, who murders her arrogant father (Howard) after he seduces the wife of his farm's black foreman. An intense, rewarding portrayal of isolation, oppression, and degradation.▼

Dust Be My Destiny (1939) **88m.** ★★½ D: Lewis Seiler. John Garfield, Priscilla Lane, Alan Hale, Frank McHugh, John Litel, Billy Halop, Henry Armetta, Stanley Ridges, Bobby Jordan, Charley Grapewin. Garfield is ideally cast as an alienated drifter who finds himself in jail, where he falls for vicious prison foreman's stepdaughter (Lane). The stars rise above their less-than-original material.

Dust Devil (1993-British-French) **C-87m.** ★★ D: Richard Stanley. Robert Burke, Chelsea Field, Zakes Mokae, John Matshikiza, Rufus Swart, William Hootkins, Marianne Sägebrecht. In Africa's Namibia Desert, evil spirit Burke, trapped in human form, must kill to enter a spiritual realm; he meets Field, fleeing an unhappy marriage, and is pursued by policeman Mokae. Interesting premise, good acting partly offset lethargic pace, pretentious approach. [R]▼●

Dusty (1982-Australian) **C-88m.** ★★★ D: John Richardson. Bill Kerr, Noel Trevarthen, Carol Burns, Nicholas Holland, John Stanton, Kate Edwards. Subtle, touching little film about a dingo (wild dog of the bush), captured while a puppy and eventually raised by an old man (Kerr). Adults will enjoy it as much as kids.▼

Dusty and Sweets McGee (1971) **C-95m.** ★★★½ D: Floyd Mutrux. Unconventional, no-holds-barred docudrama detailing day-to-day life of various heroin addicts in Los Angeles area. [R]

Dutch (1991) **C-105m.** ★★½ D: Peter Faiman. Ed O'Neill, Ethan Randall (Embry),

JoBeth Williams, Christopher McDonald, Ari Meyers, E. G. Daily, Kathleen Freeman. Yet another warm-hearted concoction from the John Hughes assembly line, in which a stuck-up rich kid learns all about life when he travels home for Thanksgiving with his mother's blue-collar boyfriend, Dutch. Some choice, almost Chaplinesque moments (particularly one terrific scene in a homeless shelter) and appealing performances by O'Neill and Randall can't make us forget that we've seen this formula many times before. [PG-13]▼●

Dutchman (1966-British) **55m.** **½ D: Anthony Harvey. Shirley Knight, Al Freeman, Jr. Two-character allegory, based on LeRoi Jones's play, of confrontation between sadistic white trollop Knight and naive black Freeman in a subway car. Tense and well acted, but contrived.

Dybbuk, The (1938-Polish) **125m.** *** D: Michael Waszynsky. Leon Liebgold, Lili Liliana, Max Bozyk, Abraham Morevsky, Dina Halpern. Fascinating, beautifully detailed (and restored) Yiddish-language version of Sholom Anski's famous folktale of a restless, disembodied spirit who enters the body of the woman he was pledged to wed. Of special interest as a look at a culture made extinct by Hitler. One of a dozen or so Yiddish features made in Poland prior to the Holocaust.▼

Dying Room Only (1973) **C-74m. TVM.** D: Phillip Leacock. Cloris Leachman, Ross Martin, Ned Beatty, Louise Latham, Dana Elcar, Dabney Coleman. Couple traveling back to L.A. via desert by car stop off at roadside diner; husband mysteriously disappears. Excellent mood thanks to Richard Matheson's surprise-ending script, thoughtful direction, and small ensemble cast. Above average.▼

Dying Young (1991) **C-105m.** **½ D: Joel Schumacher. Julia Roberts, Campbell Scott, Vincent D'Onofrio, Colleen Dewhurst, David Selby, Ellen Burstyn. Aimless young woman answers a classified ad and becomes nurse/companion to a 28-year-old poor-little-rich-boy who's suffering from leukemia; needless to say, they fall in love. As vehicle for Roberts' charms, it works; as love story it has its moments; but as a tearjerker it never really delivers, wandering toward an inconclusive (and unsatisfying) finale. Scott shares a few scenes with his real-life mother Dewhurst. [R]▼●

Dynamite (1929) **129m.** *** D: Cecil B. DeMille. Conrad Nagel, Kay Johnson, Charles Bickford, Julia Faye, Joel McCrea. Enough plot for seven films in this silly but fascinating early talkie; aristocratic Johnson marries miner Bickford, who's about to be executed, to gain inheritance . . . then Bickford is cleared. Typical DeMille entertainment.

Dynamite (1949) **69m.** *½ D: William H. Pine. William Gargan, Virginia Welles, Richard Crane, Irving Bacon, Frank Ferguson, Mary Newton. Young commercial dynamiter Crane clashes with older colleague Gargan over affections of Welles in standard B-opus.▼

Dynamite Chicken (1971) **C/B&W-76m.** ** D: Ernie Pintoff. Richard Pryor, John Lennon, Yoko Ono, Sha Na Na, Ace Trucking Company, Joan Baez, Ron Carey, Andy Warhol, Paul Krassner, Leonard Cohen, Malcolm X, many others. Odd, dated pastiche of songs, skits, television commercial parodies and old movie clips, filmed when nudity and profanity on celluloid were still shocking. Worth a look alone for Pryor. [R]▼

Each Dawn I Die (1939) **92m.** *** D: William Keighley. James Cagney, George Raft, George Bancroft, Jane Bryan, Maxie Rosenbloom, Stanley Ridges, Louis Jean Heydt, Abner Biberman, John Wray, Victor Jory, Thurston Hall. Reporter Cagney is framed, sent to prison, where he meets tough-guy Raft. Good performances all around—Cagney hits a white-hot peak as the embittered, stir-crazy fall guy—but last half of film becomes outrageously improbable. Music score by Max Steiner. ▼●

Eager Beavers SEE: **Swinging Barmaids**

Eagle, The (1925) **77m.** *** D: Clarence Brown. Rudolph Valentino, Vilma Banky, Louise Dresser, Albert Conti, James Marcus, George Nichols. Valentino plays a sort of Russian Robin Hood in this entertaining costume picture, winning the hand of Vilma Banky while trying to outwit Czarina Dresser, angry because he snubbed her advances.▼●

Eagle and the Hawk, The (1933) **68m.** ***½ D: Stuart Walker. Fredric March, Cary Grant, Jack Oakie, Carole Lombard, Guy Standing, Douglas Scott. Well-produced antiwar film with reluctant hero March, bullying gunner-observer Grant, everyone's friend Oakie, sympathetic society girl Lombard. Sobering John Monk Saunders story is still timely. Mitchell Leisen, credited as "associate director," reportedly directed most of the film. Originally 72m. ▼

Eagle and the Hawk, The (1950) **C-104m.** **½ D: Lewis R. Foster. John Payne, Rhonda Fleming, Dennis O'Keefe, Thomas Gomez, Fred Clark. Contrived actioner set in 1860s Mexico-Texas with O'Keefe and Payne U.S. law enforcers stifling coup to make Maximilian ruler of Mexico; Fleming is fetching love interest.

Eagle Has Landed, The (1977) **C-123m.** *** D: John Sturges. Michael Caine, Donald Sutherland, Robert Duvall, Jenny Agutter, Donald Pleasence, Anthony Quayle, Jean Marsh, Sven-Bertil Taube, John Standing, Judy Geeson, Treat Williams, Larry Hagman, Jeff Conaway. Action-packed wartime adventure taken from fanciful Jack

Higgins best-seller about Nazi plot to kidnap Winston Churchill. Hardly a dull moment, thanks to solid cast and lively, twist-laden story. Original running time in England was 134m. Panavision. [PG]▼

Eagle in a Cage (1971-British) **C-98m.** *** D: Fielder Cook. John Gielgud, Ralph Richardson, Billie Whitelaw, Kenneth Haigh, Moses Gunn, Ferdy Mayne. Fine drama of Napoleon in exile on St. Helena. Haigh is quite impressive in the title role, and is surrounded by a top cast. Screenplay by Millard Lampell. [PG]

Eagles Over London (1970-Italian) **C-97m.** **½ D: Enzo Castellari. Frederick Stafford, Van Johnson, Francisco Rabal, Evelyn Stewart, Christian Hay. German intelligence group infiltrates British High Command on the eve of Battle of Britain. Shopworn war drama. Techniscope.

Eagle Squadron (1942) **109m.** **½ D: Arthur Lubin. Robert Stack, Eddie Albert, Diana Barrymore, Nigel Bruce, Jon Hall, Evelyn Ankers, Gladys Cooper, Mary Carr. Usual WW2 action and romance as young American fliers fought the war in the RAF. Good action scenes help average script.

Eagle's Wing (1979-British) **C-111m.** *½ D: Anthony Harvey. Martin Sheen, Sam Waterston, Caroline Langrishe, Harvey Keitel, Stephane Audran, John Castle, Jorge Luke. God never intended penguins to fly or the British to make Westerns. Dreary, artsy glop entangling half a dozen plots cribbed from other, better oaters; principal one involves seesawing between renegade Indian Waterston and trapper Sheen for possession of magnificent white stallion. Billy Williams's lush cinematography doesn't help. Most U.S. prints run 98m. Panavision. [PG]▼

Eagle With Two Heads, The (1948-French) **93m.** **½ D: Jean Cocteau. Edwige Feuillere, Jean Marais, Sylvia Monfort, Jacques Varennes, Jean Debucourt, Yvonne de Bray. Stuffy, slightly crazed Queen Feuillere's husband was assassinated a decade earlier, on their wedding day. Amid much court intrigue, a poet-anarchist (Marais) who bears a striking resemblance to the deceased monarch stumbles into her quarters. While anything by Cocteau is worth a look, this romantic drama is too often static, and is his least successful film. He scripted, based on his play (which also starred Feuillere and Marais).▼

Earl Carroll Vanities (1945) **91m.** **½ D: Joseph Santley. Dennis O'Keefe, Constance Moore, Eve Arden, Otto Kruger. Republic Pictures tried hard to give this musical class, but zest and production values are lacking; Arden adds her usual quips.

Earl of Chicago, The (1940) **85m.** **½ D: Richard Thorpe. Robert Montgomery, Edward Arnold, Reginald Owen, Edmund Gwenn. Montgomery can't put over far-fetched tale of Chicago mobster inheriting English title. His awkward performance strains film's credibility.

Early Frost, An (1985) **C-100m. TVM** D: John Erman. Gena Rowlands, Ben Gazzara, Sylvia Sidney, Aidan Quinn, D.W. Moffett, John Glover, Sydney Walsh. Emotion-packed drama about the effect on a family when their son breaks the news that he not only is gay but also has contracted AIDS. Terrific work by entire cast, bringing out the best of Ron Cowen and Daniel Lipman's solid, never maudlin, Emmy-winning script (based on Sherman Yellen's story). Above average.▼●

Early Summer (1951-Japanese) **135m.** *** D: Yasujiro Ozu. Setsuko Hara, Chishu Ryu, Kuniko Miyake, Chikage Awashima, Chiyeko Higashiyama. Stirring tale of a woman (Hara) who, at 28, is aging by her society's standards. She resides with her elderly parents, and must deal with their pressure to marry the man of their choice. A sensitively rendered film about basic human emotions, made by a master filmmaker.▼●

Early to Bed (1936) **75m.** **½ D: Norman Z. McLeod. Mary Boland, Charlie Ruggles, George Barbier, Gail Patrick, Robert McWade, Lucien Littlefield. Ruggles' sleepwalking involves him in shady adventure with gangsters. Boland and Ruggles are a perfect match.

Earrings of Madame de . . . , The (1953-French-Italian) **105m.** **** D: Max Ophuls. Charles Boyer, Danielle Darrieux, Vittorio De Sica, Jean Debucourt, Lia de Léa. Captivating classic detailing the events that unravel after fickle Darrieux pawns the earrings presented her by husband Boyer. A knowing look at the effect of living a shallow, meaningless life. Masterfully acted and directed, with dazzling tracking shots. Screenplay by Marcel Achard, Ophuls, and Annette Wademant, from the novel by Louise de Vilmorin. Aka DIAMOND EARRINGS; originally released at 192m.▼●

Earth (1930-Russian) **90m.** **** D: Alexander Dovzhenko. Semyon Svashenko, Stepan Shkurat, Mikola Nademsky, Yelena Maximova. Lyrical, deservedly famous classic about collective farming in the Ukraine, with peasants opposing a landowner and the arrival of a tractor symbolizing the transformation of Soviet society. This ode to the wonders of nature is loaded with beautiful imagery. Long a staple on all-time-best film lists.▼

Earthbound (1981) **C-94m.** *½ D: James L. Conway. Burl Ives, Christopher Connelly, Meredith MacRae, Joseph Campanella, Todd Porter, Marc Gilpin, Elissa Leeds, John Schuck, Stuart Pankin. Average family from outer space lands in Middle America due to a faulty flying saucer. Will dastardly government official Campanella shoot them? Trite, dumb, idiotic. [PG]

Earth Dies Screaming, The (1964-British) **62m.** ★★½ D: Terence Fisher. Willard Parker, Virginia Field, Dennis Price, Vanda Godsell. Grim thriller with invaders taking over remote village; packs great initial suspense but labors.

Earth Girls Are Easy (1989) **C-100m.** ★★½ D: Julien Temple. Geena Davis, Jeff Goldblum, Jim Carrey, Damon Wayans, Julie Brown, Michael McKean, Charles Rocket, Larry Linville, Rick Overton, Angelyne. Infectiously goofy musical comedy about aliens landing in the San Fernando Valley and being ushered into materialistic Southern California life by a ditsy manicurist. Not enough substance to sustain a feature film, but there are some good laughs, and an endearing performance by Davis. Costar Brown (who sings airhead anthem " 'Cause I'm a Blonde") also cowrote the movie. Panavision. [PG]▼●◗

Earthling, The (1980-Australian) **C-102m.** ★★½ D: Peter Collinson. William Holden, Ricky Schroder, Jack Thompson, Olivia Hamnett, Alwyn Kurts. Holden, terminally ill, teaches Schroder, orphaned and lost, how to survive in the bush country. OK drama features much nature footage and will appeal mainly to kids. Originally released at 97m., later reedited and lengthened to 102m. Panavision. [PG]▼

Earthquake (1974) **C-129m.** BOMB D: Mark Robson. Charlton Heston, Ava Gardner, George Kennedy, Genevieve Bujold, Richard Roundtree, Lorne Greene, Barry Sullivan, Marjoe Gortner, Lloyd Nolan, Victoria Principal, Walter Matuschanskwyasky (Walter Matthau), Gabriel Dell, Pedro Armendariz, Jr., Lloyd Gough, John Randolph, Donald Moffat. Title tells the story in hackneyed disaster epic originally released in Sensurround. Marjoe as a sex deviate and Gardner as Lorne Greene's *daughter* tie for film's top casting honors. Additional footage was shot for inclusion in network showings. Won Oscar for Sound, plus special achievement for Visual Effects and citations for the development of Sensurround. Panavision. [PG]▼●◗

Earth's Final Fury SEE: **When Time Ran Out . . .**

Earth vs. the Flying Saucers (1956) **82m.** ★★★ D: Fred F. Sears. Hugh Marlowe, Joan Taylor, Donald Curtis, Morris Ankrum, Tom Browne Henry, voice of Paul Frees. Matter-of-fact presentation gives tremendous boost to familiar storyline (alien invaders order us to surrender peaceably—or else). Literate dialogue, subdued performmances, and solid Ray Harryhausen effects make this a winner that belies its B origins nearly every step of the way.▼●

Earth vs. the Spider (1958) **73m.** ★★ D: Bert I. Gordon. Ed Kemmer, June Kenny, Geene Persson, Gene Roth, Hal Torrey, Sally Fraser, June Jocelyn, Troy Patterson, Hank Patterson. A spider bigger than a bus is found in a cave; when it's apparently killed, it's put on display in a high school gym—where it is revived by the sounds of rock 'n roll! Teenager-oriented Bert I. Gordon movie is more watchable than most of his giant-thing-on-the-loose films. Aka THE SPIDER.▼

Earthworm Tractors (1936) **69m.** ★★½ D: Ray Enright. Joe E. Brown, June Travis, Guy Kibbee, Dick Foran, Carol Hughes, Gene Lockhart, Olin Howland. Broad comedy with Joe as *Saturday Evening Post* character Alexander Botts, braggart and tractor salesman extraordinaire.▼

Easiest Way, The (1931) **74m.** ★★½ D: Jack Conway. Constance Bennett, Adolphe Menjou, Robert Montgomery, Marjorie Rambeau, Anita Page, Clark Gable, Hedda Hopper. Bennett rises from dire poverty to a life of luxury after becoming the mistress of advertising mogul Menjou, but finds heartbreak when she falls for reporter Montgomery. Watered-down adaptation of notorious play about high-priced call girls starts out great, then turns into a standard romantic triangle melodrama to satisfy the Hays Office. Gable has a small, but strong role in his first film as an MGM contract player.

East End Chant SEE: **Limehouse Blues**

Easter Parade (1948) **C-103m.** ★★★½ D: Charles Walters. Judy Garland, Fred Astaire, Peter Lawford, Ann Miller, Jules Munshin. Delightful Irving Berlin musical about Astaire trying to forget ex-dance partner Miller while rising to stardom with Garland. Too good to watch just at Eastertime. Musical highlights include Astaire's solo "Stepping Out With My Baby," Miller's "Shaking the Blues Away," Fred and Judy's "A Couple of Swells," and the Fifth Avenue finale with Berlin's title song. Oscar winner for musical scoring (Johnny Green and Roger Edens). Story by Frances Goodrich and Albert Hackett; they also scripted with Sidney Sheldon.▼●

Easter Sunday SEE: **Being, The**

East is East (1999-British) **C-96m.** ★★★ D: Damien O'Donnell. Om Puri, Linda Bassett, Jordan Routledge, Archie Panjabi, Emil Marwa, Chris Bisson, Lesley Nicol, Gary Damer, Emma Rydal, Ruth Jones, John Bardon. Piquant look at a cross-cultural family in 1970s London. Pakistani immigrant George (Puri) has lived there for twenty-five years; his wife is English, and their seven children have been raised as Brits, but he clings to his old-world ways and (rather hypocritically) expects them to conform to Pakistani customs. Keenly observed social comedy-drama never betrays its stage origins; Ayub Khan-Din scripted from his play. [R]▼

East of Borneo (1931) **76m.** ★½ D: George Melford. Rose Hobart, Charles Bickford, Georges Renavent, Lupita Tovar, Noble Johnson. Headache-inducing melodrama about desperate Hobart, who treks into the jungle to find physician husband Bickford; he thinks she's cheated on him, and has become a cynical alcoholic. Dull and deadening.▼

East of Eden (1955) **C-115m.** **** D: Elia Kazan. James Dean, Julie Harris, Raymond Massey, Jo Van Fleet, Burl Ives, Richard Davalos, Albert Dekker. Emotionally overwhelming adaptation of the John Steinbeck novel about two brothers' rivalry for the love of their father; affects today's generation as much as those who witnessed Dean's starring debut. Van Fleet (in film debut) won Oscar as boys' mother. Screenplay by Paul Osborn. Remade as TV miniseries. CinemaScope.▼●

East of Elephant Rock (1977-British) **C-92m.** BOMB D: Don Boyd. Judi Bowker, John Hurt, Jeremy Kemp, Christopher Cazenove, Anton Rodgers. Inept period drama set in 1948 Malaya; final reel ripped off from W. Somerset Maugham's THE LETTER. Further sabotaged by campy songs on soundtrack as well as opening disclaimer, which invites viewers to "laugh and smile" at the film. Bowker is beautiful, as are Sri Lanka locations.▼

East of Kilimanjaro (1957-U.S.-British-Italian) **C-75m.** *½ D: Arnold Belgard, Edoardo Capolino. Marshall Thompson, Gaby Andre, Fausto Tozzi, Kris Aschan, Rolf Aschan. Dull story of cameraman Thompson and efforts to halt virus affecting cattle in title region. Filmed in Africa. Originally ran 85m.; some prints 72m. Aka THE BIG SEARCH. Vistarama.

East of Shanghai SEE: **Rich and Strange**

East of Sudan (1966-British) **C-84m.** ** D: Nathan Juran. Anthony Quayle, Sylvia Sims, Derek Fowlds, Jenny Agutter, Johnny Sekka. British trooper falls for English governess when he leads her and several others to safety from Arabs in 1880s; OK juvenile adventure. Techniscope.

East of Sumatra (1953) **C-82m.** **½ D: Budd Boetticher. Jeff Chandler, Marilyn Maxwell, Anthony Quinn, Suzan Ball, Peter Graves. Satisfactory actioner set on Pacific island. Chandler is mining engineer trying to prevent native uprising while romancing Maxwell; Quinn effective as villain. Based on a Louis L'Amour novel.

East of the River (1940) **73m.** **½ D: Alfred E. Green. John Garfield, Brenda Marshall, Marjorie Rambeau, William Lundigan, George Tobias, Jack LaRue, Douglas Fowley. Another variation of MANHATTAN MELODRAMA, with childhood pals Garfield and Lundigan growing up on opposite sides of the law. Rambeau is fine as Garfield's mother.

East Side Kids (1940) **62m.** *½ D: Robert F. Hill. Harris Berger, Hally Chester, Frankie Burke, Donald Haines, Dave O'Brien, Dennis Moore, Vince Barnett, Leon Ames. Slum kids take on counterfeiters in this cheapie Sam Katzman-Monogram production. Despite title, this has nothing to do with the subsequent Leo Gorcey-Bobby Jordan-Huntz Hall series.▼

East Side Kids Meet Bela Lugosi, The SEE: **Ghosts on the Loose**

East Side of Heaven (1939) **90m.** **½ D: David Butler. Bing Crosby, Joan Blondell, Mischa Auer, Irene Hervey, C. Aubrey Smith, Baby Sandy. Cute Crosby comedy with songs; Bing becomes guardian of abandoned baby, croons title tune, "Sing A Song of Sunbeams."

East Side Story (1997-German-French) **C/B&W-87m.** ***½ D: Dana Ranga. "Soviet musicals" sounds like an oxymoron, but more than 40 were made behind the Iron Curtain from the early '30s until the late '60s. This documentary doesn't limit itself to clips from the films, but includes interviews with filmmakers, critics, and ordinary moviegoers. Some of the musicals are propaganda featuring deliriously happy workers, but others, especially those directed by Grigori Alexandrov, look so delightful you long to see titles like THE JOLLY FELLOWS and VOLGA VOLGA, Stalin's favorite movie. An absolute must for film buffs.▼

East Side, West Side (1949) **108m.** **½ D: Mervyn LeRoy. Barbara Stanwyck, James Mason, Ava Gardner, Van Heflin, Cyd Charisse, Gale Sondergaard, William Frawley, Nancy Davis (Reagan). Stanwyck and Mason have pivotal roles as chic N.Y.C. society couple with abundant marital woes, stirred up by alluring Gardner and understanding Heflin. Static MGM version of Marcia Davenport's superficial novel.▼

East-West (1999-French-Russian-Spanish-Bulgarian) **C-121m.** ** D: Régis Wargnier. Sandrine Bonnaire, Oleg Menchikov, Catherine Deneuve, Sergei Bodrov, Jr. A doctor and his French wife join other Russian émigrés who are invited back to their homeland following WW2, but once there, their lives become a nightmare. Fascinating historical subject matter is turned into a turgid soap opera. Deneuve has a small, thankless role as a politically active stage star, but Bonnaire is luminous. [PG-13]

Easy Come, Easy Go (1947) **77m.** **½ D: John Farrow. Barry Fitzgerald, Diana Lynn, Sonny Tufts, Dick Foran, Frank McHugh, Allen Jenkins. Fitzgerald is his usual self as a horseplayer who refuses to let daughter Lynn get married.

Easy Come, Easy Go (1967) **C-95m.** *½ D: John Rich. Elvis Presley, Dodie Marshall, Pat Priest, Elsa Lanchester, Frank McHugh, Pat Harrington. Presley's a frogman diving for buried treasure in this hack-

neyed comedy. Fortunately, he doesn't sing underwater. Yet he does get to perform such classics as "The Love Machine" and "Yoga Is As Yoga Does."▼
Easy Go SEE: **Free and Easy**
Easy Life, The (1963-Italian) **105m.** *** D: Dino Risi. Vittorio Gassman, Catherine Spaak, Jean-Louis Trintignant, Luciana Angiolillo. Gassman has proper joie de vivre for playing middle-aged playboy who introduces student Trintignant to life of frolic with tragic results; well played and haunting.▼
Easy Living (1937) **86m.** *** D: Mitchell Leisen. Jean Arthur, Edward Arnold, Ray Milland, Franklin Pangborn, William Demarest, Mary Nash, Luis Alberni. Millionaire Arnold throws spoiled-wife's mink out the window; it drops on unsuspecting working girl Arthur. Arnold's son Milland, off making his career, falls in love. The girl: Arthur. Delightful comedy written by Preston Sturges.▼
Easy Living (1949) **77m.** *** D: Jacques Tourneur. Victor Mature, Lizabeth Scott, Lucille Ball, Sonny Tufts, Lloyd Nolan, Paul Stewart, Jeff Donnell, Jack Paar, Art Baker. Mature is aging football star who can't adjust to impending retirement—especially under constant pressure from grasping wife Scott. Intelligent film from Irwin Shaw story, with good performance from Lucy as team secretary in love with Mature.▼●
Easy Money (1983) **C-95m.** **½ D: James Signorelli. Rodney Dangerfield, Joe Pesci, Geraldine Fitzgerald, Candy Azzara, Taylor Negron, Jennifer Jason Leigh, Tom Ewell. Working-class slob has one year to give up all his bad habits—drinking, overeating, smoking, gambling—in order to collect big inheritance. Dangerfield's first starring comedy vehicle is pleasant enough—with a refreshing amount of restraint for an 80s comedy. Final gag is right out of W. C. Fields. [R]▼●
Easy Rider (1969) **C-94m.** ***½ D: Dennis Hopper. Peter Fonda, Dennis Hopper, Jack Nicholson, Karen Black, Luke Askew, Luana Anders, Robert Walker, Phil Spector, Toni Basil. Low-budget film of alienated youth nearly ruined Hollywood when every studio tried to duplicate its success. Tale of two cyclists chucking it all and searching for "the real America," while inevitably dated, remains quite worthwhile, highlighted by fine Laszlo Kovacs photography, great rock soundtrack, and Nicholson's star-making performance as boozy lawyer who tags along. Written by Fonda, Hopper, and Terry Southern. [R]▼●◗
Easy to Love (1953) **C-96m.** **½ D: Charles Walters. Esther Williams, Van Johnson, Tony Martin, John Bromfield, Carroll Baker. Pleasant Williams aquatic vehicle set at Florida's Cypress Gardens, with Johnson and Martin vying for her love. Spectacular production numbers by Busby Berkeley. Baker's first film.▼●
Easy to Wed (1946) **C-110m.** **½ D: Edward Buzzell. Van Johnson, Esther Williams, Lucille Ball, Keenan Wynn, Cecil Kellaway, June Lockhart. Remake of LIBELED LADY can't hold a candle to original, but remains passable comedy, with Lucy in one of her first major comedy showcases.▼
Easy Virtue (1927-British) **79m.** **½ D: Alfred Hitchcock. Isabel Jeans, Franklin Dyall, Eric Bransby Williams, Ian Hunter, Robin Irvine, Violet Farebrother. Jeans suffers nobly as the wife of an alcoholic and the lover of a suicide in this melodramatic silent Hitchcock. Laughable dramatics but imaginatively shot, based on a Noel Coward play.▼◗
Easy Way, The SEE: **Room for One More**
Easy Wheels (1989) **C-94m.** ** D: David O'Malley. Paul Le Mat, Eileen Davidson, Marjorie Bransfield, Jon Menick, Barry Livingston, Mark Holton, Theresa Randle, Danny Hicks, George Plimpton, Ted Raimi, Ben Stein. A gang of good male bikers combats a baby-stealing gang of women bikers in the Midwest. Satirical action comedy is awkwardly directed, but has some good ideas. Writer "Celia Abrams" in the credits is really Sam Raimi. [R]▼
Eat a Bowl of Tea (1989) **C-104m.** *** D: Wayne Wang. Cora Miao, Russell Wong, Victor Wong, Lau Siu Ming, Eric Tsang Chi Wai. From 1924 until the end of WW2, most Chinese women were not allowed to accompany their menfolk who emigrated to the U.S. This charming but pointed ethnic comedy chronicles what happened when the ban was lifted, as American-born Russell Wong brings Chinese-born bride Miao to N.Y.C. A film that no one else but Wang could have made. A PBS *American Playhouse* theatrical production. [PG-13]▼●
Eat Drink Man Woman (1994-Taiwan) **C-124m.** *** D: Ang Lee. Sihung Lung, Kuei-Mei Yang, Chien-Lien Wu, Yu-Wen Wang, Winston Chao, Ah-Leh Gua, Sylvia Chang. Director Lee's follow-up to THE WEDDING BANQUET is another charming study of love, family, and tradition, which follows a Taipei master chef (Lung) who has lost his taste buds and has grown apart from his three daughters. The multiple stories and their resolutions are a bit too predictable, but Lee's handling of the action is dexterous and the entire cast is winning. The presentation of food onscreen is, in all senses of the word, delectable, ranking with the dishes of TAMPOPO, BABETTE'S FEAST, and LIKE WATER FOR CHOCOLATE. Lee coscripted as well.▼●
Eaten Alive (1976) **C-96m.** **½ D: Tobe Hooper. Neville Brand, Mel Ferrer, Carolyn

Jones, Marilyn Burns, William Finley, Stuart Whitman, Robert Englund. Ill-fated Hollywood debut feature by TEXAS CHAINSAW director Hooper is a garishly stylized, unrelentingly bizarre film about a psychopath (Brand) who has a crocodile living in the front yard of his hotel. Periodically guests who upset the management are fed to this pet. Originally titled DEATH TRAP; aka STARLIGHT SLAUGHTER, LEGEND OF THE BAYOU, and HORROR HOTEL.▼●◗

Eating (1990) **C-110m.** *** D: Henry Jaglom. Frances Bergen, Lisa Richards, Nelly Alard, Gwen Welles, Mary Crosby, Marlene Giovi, Marina Gregory, Daphna Kastner, Elizabeth Kemp, Toni Basil. A group of women, attending a birthday party, sit around talking about food and life—in that order. Typically idiosyncratic, low-budget Jaglom outing, but this one really works: the conversation is fascinating and often hilarious. Frances Bergen (Edgar's widow, Candice's mom) is a revelation.▼

Eating Raoul (1982) **C-83m.** ***½ D: Paul Bartel. Paul Bartel, Mary Woronov, Robert Beltran, Susan Saiger, Buck Henry, Dick Blackburn, Edie McClurg, Ed Begley, Jr., John Paragon, Hamilton Camp. Delicious black comedy about the Blands, a super-square couple who lure wealthy swingers to their apartment and kill them, which both reduces the number of "perverts" and helps finance their dream restaurant. Sags a little here and there, but overall a bright, original, and hilarious satire; Paragon has a super bit as a sexshop owner. Directors Joe Dante and John Landis also appear. [R] ▼

Eat My Dust! (1976) **C-90m.** *½ D: Charles Griffith. Ron Howard, Christopher Norris, Warren Kemmerling, Dave Madden, Rance Howard, Clint Howard, Corbin Bernsen. Nervewracking yarn about two young drivers unable to satisfy passion for speed. Hang on! [PG]▼

Eat the Peach (1986-Irish) **C-95m.** **½ D: Peter Ormrod. Stephen Brennan, Eamon Morrissey, Catherine Byrne, Niall Toibin, Joe Lynch, Tony Doyle. Two hard-luck friends in rural Ireland, suddenly unemployed, are inspired by a scene in Elvis Presley's movie ROUSTABOUT and decide to build a "wall of death" (a huge wooden cylinder in which they ride their motorcycles in a circuslike stunt). Can fame and fortune be far behind? Uniquely dour Irish sensibility permeates this uneven but engaging little film about hopes and dreams—even cockeyed ones like these. Director Ormrod and producer John Kelleher based their script on a true story.▼

Eat the Rich (1987-British) **C-88m.** BOMB D: Peter Richardson. Nosher Powell, Lanah Pellay, Fiona Richmond, Ronald Allen, Sandra Dorne. Ironically tasteless black comedy about Pellay getting fired from his job in a restaurant, where he later returns leading a band of revolutionaries and begins serving human flesh on the menu. Weird point of view and noisy heavy metal music score by Motorhead. Many pointless cameos by the likes of Paul and Linda McCartney, Bill Wyman, Miranda Richardson and Koo Stark. [R]▼

Ebb Tide (1937) **C-94m.** **½ D: James Hogan. Frances Farmer, Ray Milland, Oscar Homolka, Lloyd Nolan, Barry Fitzgerald. Hokey but entertaining outdoors picture with Nolan a madman on strange island. Remade as ADVENTURE ISLAND.

Eboli (1979-Italian) **C-120m.** ***½ D: Francesco Rosi. Gian Maria Volonté, Irene Papas, Paolo Bonicelli, Alain Cuny, Lea Massari. Slow-moving but rewarding chronicle of anti-Facist writer/artist Carlo Levi's exile in a small, primitive southern Italian mountain village during the mid-1930s. Stunningly directed, with Volonte perfect as Levi. Video title: CHRIST STOPPED AT EBOLI; most prints with this title run 210m.▼

Echoes (1983) **C-89m.** **½ D: Arthur Allan Seidelman. Richard Alfieri, Nathalie Nell, Mercedes McCambridge, Ruth Roman, Gale Sondergaard, Mike Kellin, John Spencer. Art student Alfieri becomes obsessed by a dream in which his twin brother, who died before birth, is out to kill him. Intriguing premise, just adequate result. [R]▼

Echoes of a Summer (1976) **C-99m.** ** D: Don Taylor. Richard Harris, Lois Nettleton, Jodie Foster, Geraldine Fitzgerald, William Windom, Brad Savage. Another film in the "disease" genre, as 12-year-old Foster's stolid reaction to impending death inspires those around her. Overwritten tearjerker, but Jodie is always worth a look. [PG]

Echoes of Paradise (1987-Australian) **C-92m.** *½ D: Phillip Noyce. Wendy Hughes, John Lone, Steven Jacobs, Peta Toppano, Rod Mullinar, Gillian Jones. Frustrated Hughes' husband cheats on her, so while in Thailand she liberates herself by commencing an affair with Balinese dancer Lone. Boring (though attractive) soaper is an unfortunate misfire for talented stars and director. Australian title: SHADOWS OF THE PEACOCK. [R]▼●

Echo Park (1986-Austrian-U.S.) **C-93m.** **½ D: Robert Dornhelm. Susan Dey, Thomas Hulce, Michael Bowen, Christopher Walker, Richard (Cheech) Marin, Cassandra Peterson, Timothy Carey. Small film set in older L.A. neighborhood, which follows the fortunes of three offbeat characters: a single mother/actress, a pizza delivery man/poet, and an Austrian weight-lifter/TV hopeful. Bowen (as the latter) scores best in this mildly diverting film; first half is best. [R]▼●

Eclipse (1962-French-Italian) **123m.** ***

D: Michelangelo Antonioni. Alain Delon, Monica Vitti, Francesco Rabal, Lilla Brignone, Louis Seigner, Rosanna Rory. Obvious but fascinating drama of alienation, Antonioni-style, about a translator (Vitti) who breaks up with her boyfriend and commences an affair with stockbroker Delon. Antonioni strikingly captures Vitti's isolation, and the world (and city of Rome) as filtered through her sensibilities. Third in a trilogy, following L'AVVENTURA and LA NOTTE. Original title: L'ECLISSE. ▼

Ecstasy (1933-Czech) **88m.** ★★½ D: Gustav Machaty. Hedy Kiesler (Lamarr), Aribert Mog, Jaromir Rogoz, Leopold Kramer. A young bride discovers her husband is impotent, and has an affair. Undistinguished romantic drama was once notorious for scenes of pre-Hollywood Hedy in the buff—and showing her in the throes of sexual passion.▼

Ed (1996) **C-94m.** ★½ D: Bill Couturié. Matt LeBlanc, Jayne Brook, Bill Cobbs, Jack Warden, Charlie Schlatter, Carl Anthony Payne II, Zacharias Ward, Tommy Lasorda. Nervous pitcher getting his big break on a minor-league baseball team becomes roommate with the club's new third baseman: a full-grown chimpanzee. Uninspired vehicle for *Friends* star LeBlanc (and Hollywood debut for award-winning documentary director Couturié). Strikes out as a warm family comedy, though younger viewers may be amused. [PG]▼●

Eddie (1996) **C-100m.** ★★½ D: Steve Rash. Whoopi Goldberg, Frank Langella, Dennis Farina, Richard Jenkins, Lisa Ann Walter, John Benjamin Hickey, Troy Beyer. Gimmicky star vehicle for Whoopi finds her going overnight from rabid N.Y. Knicks fan to being coach of the team—when the cynical new owner finds there's great publicity value in it. Despite the far-fetched premise, Whoopi mines laughs—especially early on, before the film begins to take itself too seriously. Look for cameos by various N.Y. celebs and basketball stars. [PG-13]▼●◗

Eddie and the Cruisers (1983) **C-92m.** ★★ D: Martin Davidson. Tom Berenger, Michael Paré, Joe Pantoliano, Matthew Laurance, Helen Schneider, Ellen Barkin. Ideal premise—whatever happened to the members of a legendary, innovative rock 'n' roll band of the 60s—buried by terrible script. Paré plays band's iconoclastic leader, who ran his car off a pier; Barkin is TV reporter who tries to piece together story, a la CITIZEN KANE ... but there's no Rosebud here. Good song score by John Cafferty. Followed by a sequel. [PG]▼●

Eddie and the Cruisers II: Eddie Lives! (1989) **C-103m.** BOMB D: Jean-Claude Lord. Michael Paré, Marina Orsini, Bernie Coulson, Matthew Laurance, Michael Rhoades, Anthony Sherwood, Bo Diddley. Now get this: Eddie Wilson did *not* die in a 1964 New Jersey car accident; he's living incognito in Montreal (where movies can be financed more cheaply) and is only surfacing now because the producers wanted a sequel. Eddie's life signs did not extend to the box office. [PG-13]▼●

Eddie Cantor Story, The (1953) **C-116m.** ★½ D: Alfred E. Green. Keefe Brasselle, Marilyn Erskine, Aline MacMahon, Marie Windsor. If Brasselle doesn't turn you off as Cantor, MacMahon's Grandma Esther or a putty-nosed young actor (Jackie Barnett) playing Jimmy Durante certainly will.▼

Eddie Macon's Run (1983) **C-95m.** ★★½ D: Jeff Kanew. Kirk Douglas, John Schneider, Lee Purcell, Leah Ayres, Lisa Dunsheath, Tom Noonan, John Goodman. Bumpy chase-and-car-crash picture that has wrongly convicted prison escapee Schneider (in his first starring role after attaining *Dukes of Hazzard* fame) trying to elude his relentless pursuer (Douglas) and make it to Mexico. Based on the novel by James McLendon. Goodman's film debut. [PG]▼●

Eddie Murphy Raw (1987) **C-93m.** ★★ D: Robert Townsend. Occasionally uproarious but ultimately dispiriting Murphy concert film, shot at N.Y.C.'s Felt Forum. Best moments: the comic's imitations of Bill Cosby and Richard Pryor giving their opposing views on the crude tone of so much Murphy material. Worst: sexist slurs that too often predominate. Fades in the stretch; there's an amusing fictional prologue, "set" in the Murphys' home two decades ago. [R]▼

Eddy Duchin Story, The (1956) **C-123m.** ★★ D: George Sidney. Tyrone Power, Kim Novak, Victoria Shaw, James Whitmore. Glossy Hollywood bio of pianist-bandleader of 1930s and '40s; Power tries hard (Carmen Cavallaro dubs at keyboard). Tearjerker ending and theme song memorable. CinemaScope.▼●

Eden (1998) **C-106m.** ★★★ D: Howard Goldberg. Joanna Going, Dylan Walsh, Sean Patrick Flanery, Sean Christensen, Edward O. Blenis, Jr. Original, provocative film set in 1965 about a young mother with MS, married to a prep school professor, who has an out-of-body experience that leads her away from her mundane life toward an exploration of her cosmic self. No mumbo jumbo here, but instead a gripping drama in which the main character forces the people closest to her to examine their own lives. Written by the director. Made in 1996. [R]▼◗

Edge, The (1997) **C-117m.** ★★½ D: Lee Tamahori. Anthony Hopkins, Alec Baldwin, Elle Macpherson, Harold Perrineau, L. Q. Jones, Bart the Bear. Quiet billionaire Hopkins accompanies his supermodel wife on a location shoot in Alaska, then finds himself stranded in the wilderness with photographer (Baldwin) and his assistant (Perrineau) when their plane crashes. The bookish rich guy turns out to be a pretty fair survivalist, but meets his match in killer Kodiak bear. Good acting, exciting action sequences, but a stretch of credibility (more in the relationships than in the survival mode) makes this an uneven outing. Written by David Mamet. Panavision. [R]▼●◗

Edge of Darkness (1943) **120m.** ***½ D: Lewis Milestone. Errol Flynn, Ann Sheridan, Walter Huston, Nancy Coleman, Helmut Dantine, Judith Anderson, Ruth Gordon, John Beal, Roman Bohnen. Intense, compelling drama of underground movement in Norway during Nazi takeover in WW2. Eye-popping camera work complements fine performances. Scripted by Robert Rossen, from William Woods' story. Also shown in computer-colored version.▼

Edge of Doom (1950) **99m.** ** D: Mark Robson. Dana Andrews, Farley Granger, Joan Evans, Mala Powers, Adele Jergens. Granger reaches peak of histrionic despair in moody piece about young man baffled by poverty, religion, murder, and assorted other problems.

Edge of Eternity (1959) **C-80m.** ** D: Don Siegel. Cornel Wilde, Victoria Shaw, Mickey Shaughnessy, Edgar Buchanan, Rian Garrick, Jack Elam. Deputy sheriff Wilde tracks killers to Grand Canyon, leading to shoot-out on mining buckets suspended on cables way above canyon. CinemaScope.

Edge of Hell (1956) **76m.** *½ D: Hugo Haas. Hugo Haas, Francesca de Scaffa, Ken Carlton, June Hammerstein. Offbeat, minor film of pauper Haas, his beloved dog, and small boy who enters on the scene.

Edge of Sanity (1989-British) **C-90m.** *½ D: Gérard Kikoine. Anthony Perkins, Glynis Barber, Sarah Maur-Thorp, David Lodge, Ben Cole. Grotesque, overwrought travesty on *Dr. Jekyll and Mr. Hyde* (Robert Louis Stevenson is not even credited). Jekyll (Perkins) *accidentally* discovers the Hyde formula, transforms only very slightly, and becomes Jack the Ripper. Tasteless, pointless, and unpleasant. [R] ▼●

Edge of the City (1957) **85m.** **** D: Martin Ritt. John Cassavetes, Sidney Poitier, Jack Warden, Ruby Dee, Kathleen Maguire, Ruth White. Somber, realistic account of N.Y.C. waterfront life and corruption. Friendship of army deserter Cassavetes and dock worker Poitier, both conflicting with union racketeer Warden, provides focus for reflections on integration and integrity in lower-class society. Masterfully acted by all. Ritt's first film as director. Robert Alan Aurthur adapted his own 1955 TV play, *A Man Is Ten Feet Tall* (which was also film's British title), in which Poitier originated his role. Also shown in computer-colored version.

Edge of the World, The (1937-British) **74m.** *** D: Michael Powell. Niall MacGinnis, Belle Chrystall, John Laurie, Finlay Currie, Eric Berry. The life and death of an isolated Shetland island as it is evacuated of its citizens. Engrossing drama, filmed on the North Sea isle of Foula. Powell and those cast and crew still alive revisited the location 40 years later to film the documentary RETURN TO THE EDGE OF THE WORLD.▼

Edie in Ciao! Manhattan SEE: **Ciao! Manhattan**

Edison, the Man (1940) **107m.** *** D: Clarence Brown. Spencer Tracy, Rita Johnson, Lynne Overman, Charles Coburn, Gene Lockhart, Henry Travers, Felix Bressart. Sequel to YOUNG TOM EDISON perfectly casts Tracy as earnest inventor with passion for mechanical ingenuity. Facts and MGM fantasy combine well in sentimental treatment. Also shown in computer-colored version.▼●

Edith and Marcel (1983-French) **C-104m.** *½ D: Claude Lelouch. Evelyne Bouix, Marcel Cerdan, Jr., Jacques Villeret, Jean-Claude Brialy, Francis Huster, Jean Bouise, Charles Aznavour. Passionless retelling of the love affair between singer Edith Piaf and middleweight boxer Marcel Cerdan, who died in a 1949 plane crash. Bouix and Cerdan, Jr., are bland in the title roles. Originally 162m.▼

Ed's Next Move (1996) **C-88m.** *** D: John Walsh. Matt Ross, Callie Thorne, Kevin Carroll, Ramsey Faragallah, Nina Sheveleva. Sweetly engaging romantic comedy; a sincere, knowing story of the difficulties of finding love in the Big City. The title character (Ross), a Wisconsin native who comes to N.Y.C. to make his fortune, is immediately attracted to a struggling musician (Thorne), who is already involved with someone. [R]▼●

Ed TV (1999) **C-122m.** *** D: Ron Howard. Matthew McConaughey, Jenna Elfman, Woody Harrelson, Sally Kirkland, Martin Landau, Ellen DeGeneres, Rob Reiner, Dennis Hopper, Elizabeth Hurley, Adam Goldberg, Viveka Davis, Clint Howard. Entertaining yarn about a desperate cable TV network that decides to broadcast an ordinary guy's life for every waking moment of the day—turning the poor sap into an overnight celebrity. Interesting twists in Lowell Ganz and Babaloo Mandel's script keep this from being a one-joke comedy. Well cast right down the line. Remake of a Canadian film, LOUIS XIX: ROI DES ONDES. [PG-13]▼●◗

Educating Rita (1983-British) **C-110m.** *** D: Lewis Gilbert. Michael Caine, Julie Walters, Michael Williams, Maureen Lipman, Jeanne Crowley, Malcolm Douglas. Entertaining adaptation of Willy Russell's stage play about a young working-class wife who wants to better herself, and selects boozy professor Caine as her tutor. Walters is excellent in her film debut (re-creating her stage role) and Caine has one of his best roles as her mentor. [PG-13]▼●

Education of Little Tree, The (1997) **C-114m.** **½ D: Richard Friedenberg. James Cromwell, Tantoo Cardinal, Joseph Ashton, Graham Greene, Mika Boorem, Christopher Heyerdahl. An 8-year-old boy, half-white/half-Cherokee, goes to live with his grandparents in the backwoods of Tennessee in 1935 and is taught the way of life and the land. Beautifully photographed family film never fully takes hold, but fine performances and solid values make it pleasant viewing. [G]▼●

Education of Sonny Carson, The (1974) **C-105m.** **½ D: Michael Campus. Rony Clanton, Don Gordon, Joyce Walker, Paul Benjamin, Ram John Holder. Interesting if overemotional drama of rebellious black youth in Brooklyn of the 50s and 60s. Based on Carson's autobiography; the film takes on additional meaning with regard to his latter day notoriety on the N.Y.C. political scene. [R]▼

Edward, My Son (1949-British) **112m.** *** D: George Cukor. Spencer Tracy, Deborah Kerr, Ian Hunter, James Donald, Mervyn Johns, Felix Aylmer, Leueen McGrath. Film recounts rocky marriage of Tracy and Kerr who discover they drove their son to suicide. Gimmicks of Tracy talking to viewer, title character never being shown, come off as forced.

Edward Scissorhands (1990) **C-100m.** *** D: Tim Burton. Johnny Depp, Winona Ryder, Dianne Wiest, Vincent Price, Alan Arkin, Anthony Michael Hall, Kathy Baker, Conchata Ferrell, Caroline Aaron, Dick Anthony Williams. Strikingly original fable (expanded from an idea Burton hatched as a child) about a man-made boy whose creator dies before attaching human hands to his body. Now he's adopted by a relentlessly cheery Avon Lady, and taken to live in American suburbia. Mixture of fairy tale elements and social satire loses its story momentum toward the end, but that can't erase its charm or good-natured humor. Depp is perfect as the fragile scissor-handed boy, and it's great fun to watch Price as his master. [PG-13]▼●

Edward II (1991-British) **C-91m.** *** D: Derek Jarman. Steven Waddington, Kevin Collins, Andrew Tiernan, John Lynch, Dudley Sutton, Tilda Swinton, Jerome Flynn, Jody Graber, Nigel Terry, Annie Lennox. Trenchant (if unnecessarily violent) adaptation of the Christopher Marlowe play, written in 1592, about the downfall of the openly gay British monarch who rejects his queen for a male lover. Despite 14th-century setting, some characters wear contemporary clothing, and film works quite well as a condemnation of 20th-century gay-bashing. Not for all tastes—but never dull. Lennox, formerly of Eurythmics, appears in one scene singing Cole Porter's "Ev'ry Time We Say Goodbye."▼●

Ed Wood (1994) **124m.** *** D: Tim Burton. Johnny Depp, Martin Landau, Sarah Jessica Parker, Patricia Arquette, Jeffrey Jones, G. D. Spradlin, Vincent D'Onofrio, Lisa Marie, Bill Murray, Mike Starr, Max Casella, Brent Hinkley, Juliet Landau, George "The Animal" Steele. A loving look at Edward D. Wood, Jr., a man of boundless enthusiasm and no talent who made some of the worst movies of all time (including GLEN OR GLENDA and PLAN 9 FROM OUTER SPACE). Cast to perfection, with Depp ideal in the title role. Landau—in Rick Baker makeup (both men won Oscars)—is positively astonishing as the aged and impoverished Bela Lugosi, whom Wood befriended. There isn't much story thrust here, but the vivid re-creation of time and place makes this a must for any old-movie buff. [R]▼●

Eegah (1963) **C-92m.** BOMB D: Nicholas Merriwether (Arch Hall, Sr.). Arch Hall, Jr., Marilyn Manning, Richard Kiel, William Watters (Arch Hall, Sr.). Kiel, pre-James Bond, is a prehistoric giant who falls in love with teenager Manning. A staple at "All-Time Worst Film" festivals. Arch Hall, Jr., sings the memorable "I Love You, Valerie."▼●

Eel, The (1997-Japanese) **C-117m.** *** D: Shohei Imamura. Koji Yakusho, Misa Shimizu, Fujio Tsuneta, Mitsuko Baisho, Akira Emoto, Sho Aikawa, Ken Kobayashi. A businessman brutally murders his wife upon discovering that she has been cheating on him. Eight years later, he is paroled from prison, and can only relate to his pet eel, because it will not disappoint or betray him. Then he saves a woman who has attempted suicide after a bad love affair. Pensive, poignant allegorical drama.▼

Effect of Gamma Rays on Man-in-the-Moon Marigolds, The (1972) **C-100m.** *** D: Paul Newman. Joanne Woodward, Nell Potts, Roberta Wallach, Judith Lowry. Woodward gives superb performance in tale of secluded boor of a mother and her two strange daughters. Screenplay by Paul Zindel from his Pulitzer Prize-winning play. [PG]

Effi Briest (1974-German) **135m.** ***½ D: Rainer Werner Fassbinder. Hanna Schygulla, Wolfgang Schenck, Karl-Heinz Bohm, Ulli Lommel, Ursula Stratz, Irm Hermann. Sharply observed drama, set in 19th-century Germany, is one of Fassbinder's best. It's the story of the social and sexual victimization of the title character (Schygulla), an innocent teenager stifled by the conventions of society and lacking the resolve to challenge them.

Fassbinder also scripted; based on a novel by Theodor Fontane, which was filmed three times before.▼

Efficiency Expert, The (1992-Australian) **C-85m.** *** D: Mark Joffe. Anthony Hopkins, Alwyn Kurts, Rebecca Rigg, Russell Crowe, Angela Punch McGregor, Ben Mendelsohn, Bruno Lawrence, Toni Collette. Pleasant farce that follows the plight of Hopkins, an uncompromising management consultant whose attitude is ever-so-slightly altered by the various, humorously inefficient workers at a small factory. Hopkins offers a solid comic performance. Original title: SPOTTSWOOD. [PG]▼●

Egg and I, The (1947) **108m.** *** D: Chester Erskine. Claudette Colbert, Fred MacMurray, Marjorie Main, Louise Allbritton, Percy Kilbride, Richard Long, Donald MacBride, Samuel S. Hinds. Colbert is delightful as city girl who marries chicken farmer MacMurray and struggles to survive on his farm; first appearance of Ma and Pa Kettle. From Betty MacDonald's best-seller. Later a TV series.▼●

Egyptian, The (1954) **C-140m.** ** D: Michael Curtiz. Jean Simmons, Victor Mature, Gene Tierney, Michael Wilding, Bella Darvi, Peter Ustinov, Edmund Purdom, Judith Evelyn, Henry Daniell, John Carradine, Tommy Rettig. Ponderous, often unintentionally funny biblical-era soaper with Purdom cast as the sensitive, truth-seeking title character, a physician in ancient Egypt. Darvi's performance as a femme fatale is hilariously awful; see how much of her dialogue you can understand. Loosely based on Mika Waltari's novel. CinemaScope.▼●

Eiger Sanction, The (1975) **C-128m.** *½ D: Clint Eastwood. Clint Eastwood, George Kennedy, Vonetta McGee, Jack Cassidy, Thayer David, Heidi Bruhl, Reiner Schoene, Brenda Venus. Pseudo-James Bond misfire, often unintentionally funny. Thrilling mountain-climbing climax does not make up for film's many faults and ungodly length. Jack Cassidy as gay, treacherous spy contributes the only creative acting. Based on novel by Trevanian. Panavision. [R]▼●◗

8½ (1963-Italian) **135m.** **** D: Federico Fellini. Marcello Mastroianni, Claudia Cardinale, Anouk Aimée, Sandra Milo, Barbara Steele, Rossella Falk, Madeleine LeBeau, Caterina Boratto, Edra Gale, Mark Herron. Fellini's unique self-analytical movie casts Mastroianni as a filmmaker trying to develop a new project, amid frequent visions and countless subplots. A long, difficult, but fascinating film, overflowing with creative and technical wizardry. Certainly one of the most intensely personal statements ever made on celluloid. Screenplay by Fellini, Tullio Pinelli, Ennio Flaiano, and Brunello Rondi. Oscar winner for Costume Design and as Best Foreign Language Film.▼●

8½ Women (1999-British) **C-121m.** *½ D: Peter Greenaway. John Standing, Matthew Delamere, Vivian Wu, Shizuka Inoh, Barbara Sarafian, Kirina Mano, Toni Collette, Amanda Plummer, Natcha Amal, Manna Fujiwara, Polly Walker. When a successful businessman is widowed, his son tries to help him through his grief by taking him on a sexual odyssey. The women range from a former nun (Collette) to a horsewoman/pig fancier (Plummer) who wears a bizarre see-through harness. Copious male and female nudity can't keep this from being a colossal bore. A supposed homage to Fellini, this isn't in his league. [R]

18 Again! (1988) **C-100m.** **½ D: Paul Flaherty. George Burns, Charlie Schlatter, Tony Roberts, Anita Morris, Red Buttons, Miriam Flynn, Jennifer Runyon. 81-year-old Jack Watson (92-year-old Burns) becomes 18 again via his grandson's body and a bump on the head. Sound familiar? What it lacks in originality is made up in part by Schlatter's utterly charming performance as the young George, and that fountain of youth Burns (who, alas, we see precious little of). [PG]▼●

Eighteen and Anxious (1957) **93m.** ** D: Joe Parker. Martha Scott, Jim Backus, Mary Webster, William Campbell, Jackie Coogan. Oddball cast atones for amateurish muck about pregnant teen-ager forced to face life's realities.

Eighth Day, The (1996-French-Belgian) **C-118m.** **½ D: Jaco van Dormael. Daniel Auteuil, Pascal Duquenne, Miou-Miou, Isabelle Sadoyan, Henry Garcin, Michele Maes. Well-intentioned but overly familiar feel-good story of uptight, phony-baloney Belgian businessman Auteuil, who (predictably) undergoes a personality transformation after finding himself in the company of a Down's Syndrome victim (Duquenne, who actually suffers from the malady). If you've seen RAIN MAN . . . Auteuil and Duquenne both won Cannes Film Festival acting prizes. Super 35.▼●

8 Heads in a Duffel Bag (1997-U.S.-British) **C-95m.** **½ D: Tom Schulman. Joe Pesci, Andy Comeau, Kristy Swanson, Todd Louiso, George Hamilton, Dyan Cannon, David Spade, Frank Roman, Ernestine Mercer. Mob hit man Pesci's bag of the title is accidentally swapped with that of a medical student on the way to a Mexican vacation. Many black-comedy complications ensue. Occasionally very funny, but not often enough, and debuting director Schulman's timing is limp; Spade and Louiso have the best moments. [R]▼●

Eight Hundred Leagues Down the Amazon (1993) **C-75m.** *½ D: Luis Llosa. Daphne Zuniga, Barry Bostwick, Adam Baldwin, Tom Verica, E. E. Bell, Ramsay Ross. In the 19th century, planter Bostwick, his daughter Zuniga, and others drift down the Amazon on a huge raft; scheming Baldwin causes complications. Underbudgeted but overplotted, this curio is as ponderous as its little-used raft. From a novel by Jules Verne. Roger Corman executive-produced. [PG-13]▼

Eight Iron Men (1952) **80m.** **½ D: Edward Dmytryk. Bonar Colleano, Lee Marvin, Richard Kiley, Nick Dennis, Arthur Franz, Mary Castle. WW2 actioner focusing on a group of soldiers, strain they undergo during continued enemy attack.

Eight Men Out (1988) **C-119m.** *** D: John Sayles. John Cusack, Clifton James, Michael Lerner, Christopher Lloyd, John Mahoney, Charlie Sheen, David Strathairn, D. B. Sweeney, Michael Rooker, Perry Lang, James Read, Bill Irwin, Kevin Tighe, Studs Terkel, John Anderson, Maggie Renzi. Exquisitely detailed period piece about the infamous 1919 "Black Sox" World Series, in which members of the Chicago White Sox agreed to throw the games in return for cash. Writer-director Sayles (who also appears as sportswriter Ring Lardner) touches all the bases, except perhaps in terms of emotion; the story doesn't have the impact it might have, though the actual baseball scenes are superb and the key performances (by Strathairn, Sweeney, and Cusack) are top-notch. Based on a book by Eliot Asinof. [PG]▼●

8 Million Ways to Die (1986) **C-115m.** BOMB D: Hal Ashby. Jeff Bridges, Rosanna Arquette, Alexandra Paul, Randy Brooks, Andy Garcia. Dreary tale of alcoholic ex-cop who gets involved with high-priced call girl and her "friends" (a powerful pimp and a sleazy drug dealer). Slow, arid film populated by unpleasant and uninteresting characters. Remarkably poor script (cowritten by Oliver Stone) has only faint resemblance to Lawrence Block's fine novel. [R]▼●

8MM (1999) **C-123m.** ** D: Joel Schumacher. Nicolas Cage, Joaquin Phoenix, James Gandolfini, Peter Stormare, Anthony Heald, Catherine Keener, Chris Bauer, Myra Carter, Amy Morton. Private detective accepts an unusual assignment: to learn whether or not a "snuff" film in which a girl apparently dies is genuine. Despite himself, he becomes obsessed with the case and mired in a netherworld he cannot stand. An intensely grim, often unpleasant film, somewhat reminiscent of HARDCORE, is weakened by serious issues of credibility in Cage's character and motivation. Super 35. [R]▼●◗

Eight O'Clock Walk (1952-British) **87m.** **½ D: Lance Comfort. Richard Attenborough, Cathy O'Donnell, Derek Farr, Ian Hunter. Courtroom drama manages to create pace and tension, involving murder trial; nicely played by Attenborough.

Eight on the Lam (1967) **C-106m.** BOMB D: George Marshall. Bob Hope, Phyllis Diller, Jonathan Winters, Jill St. John, Shirley Eaton. Another of Hope's horrible 60s comedies casts him as a widower with seven children who finds $10,000; even Winters can't help this dud.▼●

8 Seconds (1994) **C-104m.** **½ D: John G. Avildsen. Luke Perry, Stephen Baldwin, Cynthia Geary, James Rebhorn, Carrie Snodgress, Red Mitchell, Ronnie Claire Edwards, Linden Ashby, Renee Zellweger. OK bio of rodeo legend Lane Frost gets standard Avildsen ROCKY rah-rah treatment. Perry and Geary (as his wife) put the film over, up to a point, with natural, winning performances, but day-to-day rodeo life was captured with far more flavor in THE LUSTY MEN and JUNIOR BONNER. [PG-13]▼●

84 Charing Cross Road (1987) **C-97m.** ***½ D: David Jones. Anne Bancroft, Anthony Hopkins, Judi Dench, Jean De Baer, Maurice Denham, Eleanor David, Mercedes Ruehl, Daniel Gerroll. Loving, literate, and totally disarming film about the longtime correspondence, and growing friendship, between a feisty N.Y.C. woman and the British bookseller who provides her with the rare volumes she cherishes more than anything else in life. Affectionately detailed evocation of N.Y.C. and London over twenty years' time is capped by ideal performances. Based on the memoirs of Helene Hanff and the play adapted from her book. Screenplay by Hugh Whitemore. [PG]▼●

84 Charlie Mopic (1989) **C-95m.** *** D: Patrick Duncan. Jonathan Emerson, Nicholas Cascone, Jason Tomlins, Christopher Burgard, Glenn Morshower, Richard Brooks, Byron Thomas. Imaginative low-budget film provides fresh approach to life on the front line in Vietnam. Writer-director Duncan tells his story completely from the point of view of a combat cameraman who's assigned to follow a special seven-man reconnaissance unit on a dangerous mission. Lulls in pace made up for by film's overall vitality, commanding performances by cast of unknowns. [R]▼●

80 Steps to Jonah (1969) **C-107m.** ** D: Gerd Oswald. Wayne Newton, Mickey Rooney, Jo Van Fleet, Keenan Wynn, Diana Ewing, Slim Pickens, Sal Mineo. A loner, running from the police, stumbles upon camp for blind children; new world changes his outlook on life. Major liability: casting of Newton in leading role. Music score by George Shearing. [G]

80,000 Suspects (1963-British) **113m.** ** D: Val Guest. Claire Bloom, Richard Johnson, Yolande Donlan, Cyril Cusack. Capable cast saddled with yarn of doctor (Johnson) and wife (Bloom) finding new love together while combating local small-pox outbreak. CinemaScope.

Eijanaika (1981-Japanese) **C-151m.** ***½ D: Shohei Imamura. Shigeru Izumiya, Kaori Momoi, Masao Kusakari, Ken Ogata, Shigeru Tsuyuguchi, Mitsuko Baisho. Fascinating, compelling saga of corruption, politics, greed, power, deceit, focusing on experiences of peasant who has just returned to Japan after being shipwrecked and sent to America during the 1860s. Fine performances, with a memorable finale. Cut to 127m.; video release retains original running time.▼●

El Alamein (1953) **67m.** ** D: Fred F. Sears. Scott Brady, Edward Ashley, Rita Moreno, Michael Pate. No surprises in WW2 desert actioner with Brady heading group being attacked by Nazis.

El Bruto (1952-Mexican) **83m.** ** D: Luis Buñuel. Pedro Armendariz, Katy Jurado, Andres Soler, Rosita Arenas. Armendariz is conned by scheming boss into harassing tenants he unfairly wants to evict; seduced by the boss's lusty mistress (Jurado), he then falls in love with a girl whose father he accidentally murdered. Simplistic, quite unsubtle melodrama, a disappointment from a master filmmaker. Aka THE BRUTE. ▼

El Cid (1961) **C-184m.** *** D: Anthony Mann. Charlton Heston, Sophia Loren, Raf Vallone, Genevieve Page, John Fraser, Gary Raymond, Hurd Hatfield, Massimo Serato, Herbert Lom, Michael Hordern. Mammoth spectacle with above-average script and acting in film of legendary 11th-century warrior-hero (Heston) who drove Moors from Spain. Music by Miklos Rozsa. Super Technirama 70.▼●

El Condor (1970) **C-102m.** ** D: John Guillermin. Jim Brown, Lee Van Cleef, Patrick O'Neal, Mariana Hill, Iron Eyes Cody, Elisha Cook, Jr. Slow Western about two drifters in search of some gold supposedly buried in Mexican fortress; Hill looks good even with her clothes on. [R]▼

El Diablo (1990) **C-115m. TVM** D: Peter Markle. Anthony Edwards, Louis Gossett, Jr., John Glover, M. C. Gainey, Miguel Sandoval, Sarah Trigger, Robert Beltran, Joe Pantoliano. Small-town Texas schoolteacher—who's all thumbs with a gun—teams up with black gunslinger and motley crew to go after legendary outlaw who has kidnapped a student. Lighthearted, gag-laden Western ambles into violence at the climax. Cowritten by John Carpenter and Tommy Lee Wallace along with Bill Phillips. Made for cable. Above average.▼

El Dorado (1967) **C-126m.** *** D: Howard Hawks. John Wayne, Robert Mitchum, James Caan, Arthur Hunnicutt, Edward Asner, Michele Carey, Christopher George, Charlene Holt, Paul Fix, R. G. Armstrong, Johnny Crawford, Robert Donner. Follow-up to RIO BRAVO finds aging gunfighter Wayne helping drunken sheriff pal Mitchum quell a range war. Typically smooth Hawks mix of comedy and action, with zesty Leigh Brackett script and exemplary performances, especially by Mitchum, Caan as young gambler who can't shoot, and George as ultra-cool hired gun.▼●

Eleanor and Franklin (1976) **C-208m. TVM** D: Daniel Petrie. Jane Alexander, Edward Herrmann, Rosemary Murphy, Pamela Franklin, David Huffman, MacKenzie Phillips, Lilia Skala, Ed Flanders, Anna Lee, Linda Purl, Linda Kelsey, Lindsay Crouse. Outstanding performances by the two leads and all the supporting players (Rosemary Murphy won an Emmy for her Sara Delano Roosevelt) in this multi-award-winning production adapted by James Costigan from Joseph P. Lash's Pulitzer Prize best-seller about the Roosevelts from FDR's youth to his death in 1945. Director Petrie won an Emmy, and the film itself was named Outstanding Special of the Year. Above average.▼

Eleanor and Franklin: The White House Years (1977) **C-152m. TVM** D: Daniel Petrie. Jane Alexander, Edward Herrmann, Rosemary Murphy, Walter McGinn, Blair Brown, David Healy, Anna Lee, Mark Harmon, Linda Kelsey, Peggy McKay, Donald Moffat. Follow-up to award-winning TV portrait of the Roosevelts practically duplicated the Emmy honors, with statuettes going to director Petrie and the program itself as Outstanding Special. This sequel concentrates on FDR and Eleanor during their 12-year residence at 1600 Pennsylvania Avenue. Written by James Costigan. Above average.▼

Eleanor Roosevelt Story, The (1965) **91m.** ***½ D: Richard Kaplan. Narrated by Archibald Macleish, Eric Sevareid, Francis Cole. Oscar-winning documentary account of the former First Lady, a great American citizen who overcame personal obstacles and became a beacon of human kindness. A most effective music score by Ezra Laderman.▼

Election (1999) **C-103m.** ***½ D: Alexander Payne. Matthew Broderick, Reese Witherspoon, Chris Klein, Jessica Campbell, Mark Harelik, Phil Reeves, Molly Hagan, Delaney Driscoll, Colleen Camp, Matt Malloy. Audacious, wickedly funny satire about an earnest Nebraska schoolteacher's attempt to put a roadblock in the path of an overachiever who's running unopposed for class president. Highly original story also involves adultery, lust, and lesbianism; somehow manages to avoid mean-spiritedness while taking dead aim at its subjects. Written by Payne and Jim Taylor from the novel by Tom Perrotta. Broderick and Witherspoon are exceptionally good. Super 35. [R]▼●◗

Electra Glide in Blue (1973) **C-113m.** *** D: James William Guercio. Robert Blake, Billy Green Bush, Mitchell Ryan,

Jeannine Riley, Elisha Cook, Jr., Royal Dano. Violent film about highway cop Blake making up in brains what he lacks in height. Striking action sequences and good characterizations. Panavision. [PG]▼●

Electric Dreams (1984) **C-95m.** **½ D: Steve Barron. Lenny Von Dohlen, Virginia Madsen, Maxwell Caulfield, voice of Bud Cort. Old-fashioned boy meets girl story told in rock-video terms, with a third corner to the love triangle: a jealous computer. Good idea gets sillier as it goes along. [PG]▼●

Electric Horseman, The (1979) **C-120m.** **½ D: Sydney Pollack. Robert Redford, Jane Fonda, Valerie Perrine, Willie Nelson, John Saxon, Nicolas Coster, Wilford Brimley, James B. Sikking. Innocuous rip-off of LONELY ARE THE BRAVE tries to palm off Redford as a near-derelict who steals a $12 million thoroughbred from a Vegas hotel and heads for some grazing land. Pleasant, to be sure, but considering the people involved, a disappointment. Panavision. [PG]▼●

Electronic Monster, The (1957-British) **72m.** *½ D: Montgomery Tully. Rod Cameron, Mary Murphy, Meredith Edwards, Peter Illing. Cameron investigates an actor's mysterious death, revealing strange experiments in electronic hypnosis at a clinic. Blah sci-fi programmer. Aka ESCAPEMENT. ▼

Element of Crime, The (1984-Danish) **C-104m.** *** D: Lars von Trier. Michael Elphick, Esmond Knight, Me Me Lei, Gerald Wells, Ahmed El-Shenawi, Astrid Henning Jensen, Lars von Trier. It's the post-holocaust future, and the world is suffering from an ecological imbalance; ragged cop Elphick undergoes hypnosis in order to properly investigate a series of horrible sex crimes perpetrated against young girls. Surreal, thought-provoking thriller is crammed with references to earlier films, from Hitchcock to film noir to BLADE RUNNER. Von Trier also scripted, in an impressive feature debut.▼

Elena and Her Men SEE: **Paris Does Strange Things**

Eleni (1985) **C-117m.** **½ D: Peter Yates. Kate Nelligan, John Malkovich, Linda Hunt, Oliver Cotton, Ronald Pickup, Rosalie Crutchley, Dimitra Arliss, Glenne Headly. *N.Y. Times* reporter gets himself assigned to Athens bureau so he can resolve life-long obsession with finding truth about his mother's execution by communists in Greece following WW2. Steve Tesich's script is based on Nicholas Gage's book—and life—but coldness of the lead character is just one reason this film remains aloof and uninteresting instead of being an emotional powerhouse. Nelligan plays Gage's mother in convincing flashback sequences. [PG]▼●

Elephant Boy (1937-British) **80m.** *** D: Robert Flaherty, Zoltan Korda. Sabu, W. E. Holloway, Walter Hudd, Allan Jeayes, Bruce Gordon, D. J. Williams. Interesting early-day docudrama about native boy (Sabu, in film debut) who claims he knows location of mythic elephant herd.▼●

Elephant Gun (1959-British) **C-84m.** ** D: Ken Annakin. Belinda Lee, Michael Craig, Patrick McGoohan, Anna Gaylor, Eric Pohlmann, Pamela Stirling. Jungle love triangle has virtue of on-location shooting in Africa.

Elephant Man, The (1980) **125m.** ***½ D: David Lynch. Anthony Hopkins, John Hurt, Anne Bancroft, John Gielgud, Wendy Hiller, Freddie Jones, Michael Elphick, John Standing, Phoebe Nicholls, Kathleen Byron, Kenny Baker, Patricia Hodge. Moving dramatization of the story of John Merrick, a grotesquely deformed man shown compassion for the first time in his life by an eminent doctor in turn-of-the-century London. No relation to the Broadway play (in which one had to imagine how Merrick looked). Fine performances by all; rich Victorian atmosphere created by Lynch and veteran cameraman Freddie Francis—in beautiful black and white. Screenplay by Christopher DeVore, Eric Bergren, and the director. Panavision. [PG]▼●

Elephant Stampede SEE: **Bomba and the Elephant Stampede**

Elephant Walk (1954) **C-103m.** ** D: William Dieterle. Elizabeth Taylor, Dana Andrews, Peter Finch, Abraham Sofaer. Overblown melodrama set on Ceylon tea plantation, with Taylor as Finch's new bride who must cope with environment and his father complex. Pachyderm stampede climax comes none too soon. Vivien Leigh, replaced by Taylor, can be seen in long shots.▼

Elevator to the Gallows SEE: **Frantic (1957)**

11 Harrowhouse (1974-British) **C-98m.** *** D: Aram Avakian. Charles Grodin, Candice Bergen, James Mason, Trevor Howard, John Gielgud, Helen Cherry. Funny action spoof of heist films, as diamond merchant Grodin robs the world clearinghouse for gems. Grodin also adapted Gerald A. Browne's best-selling novel. Aka ANYTHING FOR LOVE and FAST FORTUNE. Panavision. [PG]▼

El Greco (1966-Italian-French) **C-95m.** ** D: Luciano Salce. Mel Ferrer, Rosanna Schiaffino, Franco Giacobini, Renzo Giovampietro, Adolfo Celi. Despite lavish trappings, story of painter reduced to soap-opera terms falls flat. Beautiful color, but no plot of any distinction. CinemaScope.

Eliminators (1986) **C-96m.** *½ D: Peter Manoogian. Andrew Prine, Denise Crosby, Patrick Reynolds, Conan Lee, Roy Dotrice. Woman scientist, white male guide, a ninja, and a cyborg team up to battle a mad-genius industrialist who wants to take over the world. Good to see an equal-opportunity adventure, but this RAIDERS clone has little to offer but low humor. Crosby is Bing's granddaughter. [PG]▼

Elizabeth (1998-British) **C-123m.** *** D: Shekhar Kapur. Cate Blanchett, Geoffrey Rush, Joseph Fiennes, Richard Attenborough, Christopher Eccleston, Vincent Cassel, Fanny Ardant, Kathy Burke, Eric Cantona, John Gielgud, Edward Hardwicke. Queen Mary I dreads the prospect of her half-sister, a heathen Protestant, ascending to the throne, but upon Mary's death that's exactly what happens, leading to intrigues and divisiveness within the court. Elizabeth (Blanchett) tries to rule with common sense and sees no reason to abandon her lover simply to satisfy protocol. Interesting historical drama anchored by Blanchett's charismatic performance as a woman who was far ahead of her time. Oscar winner for Best Makeup. [R]▼●◗

Elizabeth of Ladymead (1948-British) **C-97m.** *** D: Herbert Wilcox. Anna Neagle, Hugh Williams, Michael Laurence, Bernard Lee, Nicholas Phipps, Isabel Jeans. Engaging comedy-drama in four episodes from husband-wife team of Wilcox-Neagle. Latter charming as English lady-of-the-manor with mind of her own welcoming home four husbands from four different British wars. Star vehicle, unsuccessful when released, quite intriguing today for its depiction of woman's role in English society. Some prints run 90m.▼

Elizabeth the Queen SEE: **Private Lives of Elizabeth and Essex, The**

Ella Cinders (1926) **60m.** *** D: Alfred E. Green. Colleen Moore, Lloyd Hughes, Vera Lewis, Doris Baker, Emily Gerdes, Jed Prouty. Moore is in top form as the much-abused stepdaughter of crotchety old Lewis, who wins a contest and treks off to Hollywood to seek fame in the movies. Bright and peppy, with Harry Langdon on hand in a most amusing cameo. Based on a popular comic strip. ▼

Ellery Queen Perhaps the most successful series of detective stories ever written, the Ellery Queen mysteries rank as one of the least successful film series. A few scattered attempts to film Queen stories in the 1930s with Donald Cook and Eddie Quillan never aroused much interest. Then in 1940, Columbia began a series starring Ralph Bellamy as Ellery Queen, Charley Grapewin as his Inspector father, Margaret Lindsay as his Girl Friday Nikki, and James Burke as Inspector Queen's dim-witted aide. The very first entry, ELLERY QUEEN, MASTER DETECTIVE, belied its title by making Bellamy an incredible "comic" bumbler, an inexplicable characterization that lasted through all of Bellamy's films in the series. Heavy doses of comedy relief in entries like ELLERY QUEEN AND THE MURDER RING were not offset by solid mystery angles, and the films, though only one hour long, moved like molasses. A switch in casting making William Gargan the lead character in 1942 did not help matters, with the actual suspects becoming more obvious than ever. Gargan's three efforts as Queen were undistinguished, and his last episode, ENEMY AGENTS MEET ELLERY QUEEN, was also the last in the short-lived series.

ELLERY QUEEN

The Spanish Cape Mystery (1935)
The Mandarin Mystery (1937)
Ellery Queen, Master Detective (1940)
Ellery Queen's Penthouse Mystery (1941)
Ellery Queen and the Perfect Crime (1941)
Ellery Queen and the Murder Ring (1941)
Close Call for Ellery Queen (1942)
Desperate Chance for Ellery Queen (1942)
Enemy Agents Meet Ellery Queen (1942)

Ellery Queen and the Murder Ring (1941) **65m.** *½ D: James Hogan. Ralph Bellamy, Margaret Lindsay, Charley Grapewin, Mona Barrie, Paul Hurst, James Burke, Blanche Yurka, George Zucco, Tom Dugan, Leon Ames. Queen (stupider than ever!) helps Pop when murder strikes, this time in a private hospital. Bellamy's final appearance in this disappointing series. Loosely adapted from *The Dutch Shoe Mystery.*

Ellery Queen and the Perfect Crime (1941) **68m.** *½ D: James Hogan. Ralph Bellamy, Margaret Lindsay, Charley Grapewin, Spring Byington, H.B. Warner, James Burke, Douglass Dumbrille, John Beal, Linda Hayes, Sidney Blackmer, Walter Kingsford, Charles Lane. Nothing perfect at all in this entry about the murder of a shady stockbroker.

Ellery Queen, Master Detective (1940) **66m.** ** D: Kurt Neumann. Ralph Bellamy, Margaret Lindsay, Charley Grapewin, James Burke, Michael Whalen, Marsha Hunt, Fred Niblo, Charles Lane, Douglas Fowley, Katherine DeMille. The "master" sleuth is turned into a buffoon in this initial series entry, centering on the murder of a millionaire at a health spa. Lindsay has some good moments as Nikki Porter. Too much talk and too little intrigue.

Ellery Queen's Penthouse Mystery (1941) **69m.** ** D: James Hogan. Ralph Bellamy, Margaret Lindsay, Charley Grapewin, Anna May Wong, James Burke, Eduardo Ciannelli, Frank Albertson, Ann Doran, Charles Lane, Russell Hicks, Tom Dugan, Mantan Moreland. Detective Queen helps out his police inspector father (Grapewin) in the case of a murdered Chinese entertainer who was smuggling jewels. Wong is good as always, but wasted here. Slow going.

El Mariachi (1992) **C-81m.** *** D: Robert Rodriguez. Carlos Gallardo, Consuelo Gomez, Peter Marquardt, Jaime de Hoyos, Reinol Martinez, Ramiro Gomez. Energetic little film about a young singing guitarist (mariachi) who comes to a small town, where he's mistaken for a ferocious prison escapee. Arresting, original (and violent) film was shot in two weeks for just $7,000, but offers more entertainment than most of today's megabuck Hollywood movies. Director Rodriguez also photographed, edited, coproduced, and wrote the picture; Gallardo also served as coproducer. In Spanish. Rodriguez later reworked this as DESPERADO. [R]▼●◗

Elmer Gantry (1960) **C-145m.** ***½ D: Richard Brooks. Burt Lancaster, Jean Simmons, Dean Jagger, Arthur Kennedy, Shirley Jones, Patti Page, Edward Andrews, Hugh Marlowe, John McIntire, Rex Ingram. Lancaster gives a vibrant Oscar-winning performance as the salesman with the gift of gab who joins evangelist Simmons's barnstorming troupe in the 1920s Midwest. Jones won Academy Award as his jilted girlfriend turned prostitute; Brooks also won an Oscar for his sprawling screenplay from Sinclair Lewis's trenchant novel.▼●

Elmer the Great (1933) **74m.** *** D: Mervyn LeRoy. Joe E. Brown, Patricia Ellis, Frank McHugh, Claire Dodd, Preston S. Foster, Russell Hopton, Sterling Holloway, Emma Dunn, J. Carrol Naish. Brown is at his best as the home-run-hitting title character, a loud-mouthed rube who arrives in the major leagues with the Chicago Cubs. Based on a play by Ring Lardner and George M. Cohan. The second in Brown's baseball trilogy, followed by ALIBI IKE. Originally made as FAST COMPANY; reworked as THE COWBOY QUARTERBACK.

Elmore Leonard's Gold Coast (1997) **C-105m. TVM** D: Peter Weller. David Caruso, Marg Helgenberger, Jeff Kober, Barry Primus, Wanda De Jesus, Richard Bradford. In this wry, sometimes violent tale of low-lifes and pretty women living in novelist Leonard's South Florida world, drifter Caruso comes to collect some money owed him by a mobster, only to find the guy dead; instead, he has a torrid romance with the mobster's sex-starved widow. Made for cable. Average.▼

El Norte (1983) **C-139m.** **** D: Gregory Nava. Zaide Silvia Gutierrez, David Villalpando, Ernesto Gomez Cruz, Alicia del Lago, Heraclio Zepeda, Stella Quan, Lupe Ontiveros. Sweeping, emotional saga of a brother and sister who leave their violence-torn village in Guatemala to find a better life in The North—El Norte. Getting to America is half the story; making a life there is the other half. Writer-director Nava presents a heightened sense of reality that removes this from the realm of documentary; a compassionate, heart-rending, unforgettable film. Cowritten and produced by Anna Thomas, for *American Playhouse.* [R]▼

E Lollipop SEE: **Forever Young, Forever Free**

Elopement (1951) **82m.** ** D: Henry Koster. Clifton Webb, Anne Francis, Charles Bickford, William Lundigan, Reginald Gardiner. Tame proceedings despite Webb's arch performance as Francis' father, who disapproves of her marriage to Lundigan.

El Paso (1949) **C-103m.** ** D: Lewis R. Foster. John Payne, Gail Russell, Sterling Hayden, Gabby Hayes. Routine Western of post-Civil War Texas, with Payne an attorney who discovers gunplay more than words will rid town of crooks.

El Super (1979) **C-90m.** *** D: Leon Ichaso, Orlando Jiminez-Leal. Raymundo Hidalgo-Gato, Zully Montero, Raynaldo Medina, Juan Granda, Hilda Lee, Elizabeth Pena. The trials of homesick exiled Cuban who labors as an apartment-house super in Manhattan. Hidalgo-Gato is excellent as a comically sad outsider, still in transit after a decade away from his homeland.▼

Elusive Corporal, The (1962-French) **108m.** **½ D: Jean Renoir. Jean-Pierre Cassel, Claude Brasseur, Claude Rich, O. E. Hasse, Jean Carmet. Pointed if predictable chronicle of French corporal who attempts to escape with his pals from a German prison camp during WW2. Sobering look at friendship and freedom, which Renoir explored more successfully in other, earlier films. The wry comic touches are an asset.▼●

Elusive Pimpernel, The (1950-British) **C-109m.** *** D: Michael Powell, Emeric Pressburger. David Niven, Margaret Leighton, Cyril Cusack, Jack Hawkins, Arlette Marchal, Robert Coote, Patrick Macnee. Colorful remake of THE SCARLET PIMPERNEL. Niven is British fop who secretly aids victims of Reign of Terror; lively fun. This was filmed as a musical—you can tell where the numbers were cut!▼

Elvira Madigan (1967-Swedish) **C-89m.** *** D: Bo Widerberg. Pia Degermark, Thommy Berggren, Lennart Malmer, Nina Widerberg, Cleo Jensen. Lovers on the run, in soft-focus photography: tightrope walker Degermark and married army officer Berggren run off together. Though based on a true story (and filmed before in 1943), stylistically this too often resembles a shampoo commercial. Still, it was a big hit, with attractive stars, lush photography, and canny use of Mozart music. [PG]▼●◗

Elvira, Mistress of the Dark (1988) **C-96m.** BOMB D: James Signorelli. Elvira (Cassandra Peterson), W. Morgan Sheppard, Daniel Greene, Susan Kellermann, Jeff Conaway, Edie McClurg, William Duell. Peterson takes her TV horror host character to the screen in this flimsy story of a TV host shaking up a small New England town which she's visiting to pick up an inheritance. Unfunny, one-joke script (cowritten by Peterson) keeps its attention firmly riveted to the star's ample bosom. More yawns than yocks. [PG-13]▼●

Elvis (1979) **C-150m. TVM** D: John Carpenter. Kurt Russell, Shelley Winters, Pat Hingle, Season Hubley, Bing Russell, Ed Begley, Jr., Joe Mantegna. The Presley saga affectionately and believably retold, from his youth to his career as a club entertainer in 1969. Russell surprisingly effective as Elvis, whose songs were dubbed by country singer Ronnie McDowell. One of the highest rated TV movies ever—even outdrawing a rerun of GONE WITH THE WIND, shown opposite it at its premiere. Written by Anthony Lawrence. Some prints run 119m. Above average.▼

Elvis and Me (1988) **C-200m. TVM** D: Larry Peerce. Dale Midkiff, Susan Walters, Billy Green Bush, Jon Cypher, Linda Miller, Anne Haney. The Presley saga, this time based on wife Priscilla's book. Midkiff gets the King's moves pretty much down, though toward the end he looks more like Johnny Cash. Elvis' songs are performed by Ronnie McDowell (as they were in the other two Presley TV movies). Originally shown in two parts. Average.▼

Elvis on Tour (1972) **C-93m.** ** D: Pierre Adidge, Robert Abel. Static study of rock 'n' roll's biggest super-star going through his paces at a series of U.S. concerts. Even the music is not up to standard. Multiple Screen. [G]▼●

Elvis: That's the Way It Is (1970) **C-97m.** *** D: Denis Sanders. Engaging look at Elvis Presley offstage, preparing major nightclub act, culminating in opening-night performance in Las Vegas. Well-filmed if one-sided documentary paints vivid picture of Elvis as master showman. Panavision.▼●◗

Embassy (1972-British) **C-90m.** **½ D: Gordon Hessler. Richard Roundtree, Chuck Connors, Max von Sydow, Ray Milland, Broderick Crawford, Marie-Jose Nat. Spotty spy thriller about Russian defector von Sydow seeking asylum and the State Department's efforts to have agent Roundtree smuggle him out of the mideast under KGB man Connors' nose. Good cast works valiantly with contrived plot, talky script. Aka TARGET: EMBASSY. [PG]▼

Embraceable You (1948) **80m.** ** D: Felix Jacoves. Dane Clark, Geraldine Brooks, S. Z. Sakall, Wallace Ford. Tough-guy Clark injures young girl, then falls in love with her, in this sentimental romance.

Embryo (1976) **C-104m.** ** D: Ralph Nelson. Rock Hudson, Diane Ladd, Barbara Carrera, Roddy McDowall, Anne Schedeen. Sometimes interesting, sometimes repulsive horror sci-fi about woman and dog grown from fetuses outside the womb—with terrifying results. Retitled CREATED TO KILL. [PG]▼

Emerald Forest, The (1985) **C-113m.** *** D: John Boorman. Powers Boothe, Meg Foster, Charley Boorman, Dira Pass. American engineer spends ten years searching for his kidnapped son, who's been raised by primitive Amazon tribe. Fascinating look at a unique civilization, but lack of emotional empathy for the father and contrived storyline weaken overall impact. Still worthwhile. Script by Rospo Pallenberg; rich music score by Junior Homrich. And a completely convincing performance by young Boorman, son of the film's director. Panavision. [R]▼●

Emergency (1962-British) **63m.** ** D: Francis Searle. Glyn Houston, Zena Walker, Dermot Walsh, Colin Tapley. Adequate programmer dealing with Walker-Walsh reaffirming their marriage while waiting for blood donor to save their daughter's life.

Emergency Call (1933) **61m.** ** D: Edward L. Cahn. William Boyd, Wynne Gibson, William Gargan, Betty Furness, Reginald Mason, George E. Stone. Boyd (pre-Hopalong Cassidy) is a naïve young surgeon who teams with sassy ambulance driver Gargan to battle racketeers trying to muscle in on hospital business. Minor programmer cowritten by Joseph L. Mankiewicz does have a certain cheesy appeal.

Emergency Hospital (1956) **62m.** ** D: Lee Sholem. Walter Reed, Margaret Lindsay, John Archer, Byron Palmer, Rita Johnson, Jim Stapleton. The title tells all in this routine melodrama detailing the problems of patients and staff in a L.A. hospital during one 12-hour shift.

Emergency Wedding (1950) **78m.** ** D: Edward Buzzell. Barbara Hale, Larry Parks, Una Merkel, Jim Backus, Queenie Smith. Sterile remake of YOU BELONG TO ME detailing jealous Parks who thinks new wife, doctor Hale, spends too much time with her male patients.

Emerson, Lake & Palmer in Concert (1981) **C-91m.** **½ D: Ron Kantor. Keith Emerson, Greg Lake, Carl Palmer. Adequate record of the veteran rock group in performance at Olympic Stadium in Montreal.

Emigrants, The (1971-Swedish) **C-148m.** *** D: Jan Troell. Max von Sydow, Liv Ullmann, Eddie Axberg, Allan Edwall. Solid if rambling tale of peasant farmer von Sydow, wife Ullmann, and fellow Swedes who emigrate to America in the 19th century. Sequel, THE NEW LAND, is even better; both have been edited together for TV, dubbed in English, and presented as THE EMIGRANT SAGA. See also THE OX. [PG]▼●

Emigrant Saga, The SEE: **Emigrants, The** and **New Land, The**

Emil and the Detectives (1964) **C-99m.**

*½ D: Peter Tewksbury. Walter Slezak, Bryan Russell, Roger Mobley, Heinz Schubert, Peter Erlich, Cindy Cassell. Turgid Disney version of Erich Kastner's children's book about a young boy who is robbed and determines to nail the thief with the help of young detective friends. Filmed in Germany, where it was made before in 1931.▼

Emily Brontë's Wuthering Heights SEE: **Wuthering Heights** (1992)

Eminent Domain (1991) **C-102m.** **½ D: John Irvin. Donald Sutherland, Anne Archer, Jodhi May, Paul Freeman, Bernard Hepton. Intriguing story of high political official (Sutherland) in pre-Solidarity Poland who wakes up one morning to discover his privileged Politburo position no longer exists and no one will give him a satisfactory reason for (or even acknowledge) the eerie snafu. Reminiscent of Kafka's *The Trial*; often disturbing, but confusing in spots. [PG-13]▼

Emma (1932) **73m.** *** D: Clarence Brown. Marie Dressler, Richard Cromwell, Jean Hersholt, Myrna Loy, John Miljan, Leila Bennett. Dressler is at her best, as down-to-earth woman who works as housemaid-nanny for family and eventually marries widowed father (Hersholt). Sentimental movie never cloys, thanks to wonderful Marie. Frances Marion's story was scripted by Leonard Praskins and Zelda Sears.

Emma (1996) **C-111m.** *** D: Douglas McGrath. Gwyneth Paltrow, Jeremy Northam, Toni Collette, Greta Scacchi, Juliet Stevenson, Alan Cumming, Polly Walker, Ewan McGregor, James Cosmo, Sophie Thompson, Phyllida Law. Charming, witty adaptation of Jane Austen's comedy of manners about a headstrong young woman who makes a habit of playing matchmaker for others, but can't recognize her own true feelings—or those of the men who surround her. Paltrow is delightful, and surrounded by an ideal (and highly attractive) cast. Thompson (sister of actress Emma T.) is wonderful as the talkative Miss Bates; that's her real-life mother, Law, playing Mrs. Bates. Script by McGrath, making his directorial debut. Oscar-winning score by Rachel Portman. [PG]▼●◗

Emperor and the Assassin, The (1999-Chinese) **C-161m.** *** D: Chen Kaige. Gong Li, Zhang Fengyi, Li Xuejian, Wang Zhiwen, Chen Kaige, Lu Xiaohe. Sweeping, fact-based account of the ruler of a Chinese kingdom (Xuejian) in 320 B.C. who is determined to annex the country's other kingdoms and become its first emperor. For this purpose, he enlists the help of his concubine (Li, ravishing as ever); she, in turn, falls for an assassin (Fengyi). The story's predictability is outweighed by the beautifully staged spectacle; this is reportedly the most expensive Chinese film ever made. [R]▼◗

Emperor Jones, The (1933) **72m.** **½ D: Dudley Murphy. Paul Robeson, Dudley Digges, Frank Wilson, Fredi Washington, Ruby Elzy. Robeson plays Pullman porter who escapes from chain gang and improbably becomes King of a Caribbean island. Pretentious adaptation of Eugene O'Neill play derives its chief interest and value from Robeson himself. Look for Moms Mabley in bit part.▼●

Emperor of Peru, The SEE: **Odyssey of the Pacific**

Emperor of the North (1973) **C-118m.** ***½ D: Robert Aldrich. Lee Marvin, Ernest Borgnine, Keith Carradine, Charles Tyner, Harry Caesar, Malcolm Atterbury, Simon Oakland, Matt Clark, Elisha Cook. Unusual, exciting (and heavily symbolic) action film set during the Depression. Sadistic conductor Borgnine will kill any tramp who tries to cop a ride on his train; legendary hobo Marvin announces he will be the first to succeed. Beautifully filmed in Oregon by Joseph Biroc; taut script by Christopher Knopf and typically muscular Aldrich direction make this a unique entertainment. Initially released as EMPEROR OF THE NORTH POLE. [PG]

Emperor's Candlesticks, The (1937) **89m.** **½ D: George Fitzmaurice. William Powell, Luise Rainer, Robert Young, Maureen O'Sullivan, Frank Morgan, Emma Dunn, Douglass Dumbrille. Powell and Rainer play cat-and-mouse as spies on opposite sides of the fence who (naturally) fall in love, in this enjoyable but wildly far-fetched story set in Czarist Russia and Vienna. Based on a novel by Baroness Orczy (who also wrote *The Scarlet Pimpernel*).

Emperor Waltz, The (1948) **C-106m.** **½ D: Billy Wilder. Bing Crosby, Joan Fontaine, Roland Culver, Lucile Watson, Richard Haydn, Sig Ruman. Lavish but lackluster musical set in Franz Joseph Austria with Bing selling record players to royalty. Awfully schmaltzy material for writer-director Wilder. Filmed in 1946. Jasper National Park in Alberta, Canada, fills in for Tyrolean Alps.▼

Empire of Passion (1978-Japanese) **C-110m.** ** D: Nagisa Oshima. Kazuko Yoshiyuki, Tatsuya Fuji, Takahiro Tamura, Takuzo Kawatani. Peasant woman Yoshiyuki has affair with village good-for-nothing Fuji; they murder her husband, whose ghost returns to haunt them. Boring, despite interesting subject matter. A follow-up to IN THE REALM OF THE SENSES. Aka IN THE REALM OF PASSION. [R]▼◗

Empire of the Ants (1977) **C-90m.** *½ D: Bert I. Gordon. Joan Collins, Robert Lansing, Albert Salmi, John David Carson, Robert Pine, Jacqueline Scott. Laughable man-vs.-giant insects chiller from H. G.

Wells' story. Vacationers on an isolated island find themselves at the mercy of voracious ants that have become monsters after feasting on a leaking barrel of radioactive waste. [PG]▼

Empire of the Sun (1987) **C-152m.** ** D: Steven Spielberg. Christian Bale, John Malkovich, Miranda Richardson, Nigel Havers, Joe Pantoliano, Leslie Phillips, Masato Ibu, Emily Richard, Rupert Frazer, Ben Stiller, Robert Stephens, Burt Kwouk. British boy, living a well-sheltered life in Shanghai, is separated from his parents and forced to fend for himself when Japan invades China at the outset of WW2. Sprawling, ambitious, but emotionally distant and loaded with cinematic crescendos (replete with crane camera shots and overbearing music by John Williams) that simply don't have the emotional content to warrant all that fuss. Tom Stoppard adapted J.G. Ballard's autobiographical novel (Ballard appears briefly in Beefeater costume in an early party scene). [PG]▼●

Empire Records (1995) **C-91m.** *½ D: Allan Moyle. Anthony LaPaglia, Debi Mazar, Liv Tyler, Maxwell Caulfield, Rory Cochrane, Johnny Whitworth, Robin Tunney, Renee Zellweger, Ethan Randall (Embry). A day in the life of a record store, which the manager is desperately trying to save from a corporate takeover. A series of noisy vignettes which add up to nothing, despite attractive young cast. Disappointing outing from Moyle, who directed the more potent PUMP UP THE VOLUME. Super 35. [PG-13]▼●

Empire Strikes Back, The (1980) **C-124m.** **** D: Irvin Kershner. Mark Hamill, Harrison Ford, Carrie Fisher, Billy Dee Williams, Anthony Daniels, David Prowse, Peter Mayhew, Kenny Baker, Frank Oz, Alec Guinness, Clive Revill, Julian Glover, John Ratzenberger, voice of James Earl Jones. Smashing sequel to STAR WARS manages to top the original in its embellishment of leading characters' personalities, truly dazzling special effects (which earned a special Oscar) and nonstop spirit of adventure and excitement. Story threads include a blossoming romance between Han Solo and Princess Leia, the cosmic education of Luke Skywalker (by the mystical Yoda), an uneasy alliance with opportunistic Lando Calrissian, and a startling revelation from Darth Vader. 1997 reissue included 3 minutes of additional footage. Full title onscreen is STAR WARS EPISODE V: THE EMPIRE STRIKES BACK. Sequel: RETURN OF THE JEDI. Panavision. [PG] ▼●

Employees Entrance (1933) **75m.** *** D: Roy Del Ruth. Warren William, Loretta Young, Wallace Ford, Alice White, Allen Jenkins. Zesty pre-Code look at life in a department store and its ruthless, amoral manager. Gripping, funny, outrageous, racy. Based on a stage play.▼●

Empty Canvas, The (1963-French-Italian) **118m.** *½ D: Damiano Damiani. Bette Davis, Horst Buchholz, Catherine Spaak, Isa Miranda, Lea Padovani, Daniela Rocca, Georges Wilson. Artist Buchholz is obsessed with model Spaak, eventually decorates her naked body with bank notes. Davis is his wealthy mother; hopefully, she was well paid for her time. Based on an Alberto Moravia novel.▼

Empty Mirror, The (1999) **C-119m.** *½ D: Barry J. Hershey. Norman Rodway, Joel Grey, Peter Michael Goetz, Glenn Shadix, Camilla Soeberg, Doug McKeon. Ignorant of time and place, we're thrust into a strange environment where Adolf Hitler encounters key people from his past as he dictates his memoirs. Surreal, ambitious film, intercut with footage from TRIUMPH OF THE WILL and Eva Braun's home movies, pretty well lives up to its title: there's not much to reflect on. Grey's appearance as Joseph Goebbels is an interesting career counterpart to his m.c. from CABARET. [PG-13]▼

Enchanted April (1935) **66m.** **½ D: Harry Beaumont. Ann Harding, Frank Morgan, Katharine Alexander, Reginald Owen, Jane Baxter, Ralph Forbes, Jessie Ralph, Charles Judels, Rafaela Ottiano. Nicely realized adaptation of Elizabeth von Arnim's novel about two repressed Englishwomen who leave their husbands to rent an Italian villa for a month—and blossom in the rarefied atmosphere. Harding is ideal in the lead, but Owen is way over the top as a British blowhard. Improved upon in the 1991 remake.

Enchanted April (1991-British) **C-101m.** ***½ D: Mike Newell. Josie Lawrence, Miranda Richardson, Joan Plowright, Polly Walker, Alfred Molina, Jim Broadbent, Michael Kitchen, Adriana Fachetti. Utterly charming film about two repressed, married women who seize an impulse and rent an Italian villa for a month, taking on two very different women as housemates for this daring adventure. Ideally cast, nicely realized, and very romantic. Screenplay by Peter Barnes. Elizabeth von Arnim's 1921 novel was filmed before in 1935. Made for British television, released theatrically in the U.S. [PG]▼●

Enchanted Cottage, The (1945) **92m.** **½ D: John Cromwell. Dorothy McGuire, Robert Young, Herbert Marshall, Mildred Natwick, Spring Byington, Hillary Brooke. Adaptation of Arthur Pinero play about two misfits, a homely woman and a disfigured man, who find each other beautiful in the enchanted cottage. Never quite as good as you'd like it to be. Previously filmed in 1924. Some prints run 78m.▼●

Enchanted Forest (1945) **C-78m.** **½ D: Lew Landers. Edmund Lowe, Brenda Joyce, Billy Severn, Harry Davenport, John

Litel. Nicely done story of young boy who learns about life from old man who lives amid nature in the forest.▼

Enchanted Island (1958) **C-94m.** *½ D: Allan Dwan. Dana Andrews, Jane Powell, Don Dubbins, Arthur Shields. Miscast, low-budget version of Herman Melville's *Typee*. Andrews is deserter from American whaling ship who finds love with native girl Powell on South Sea island; some minor uprisings by local cannibals for good measure.▼

Enchantment (1948) **102m.** *** D: Irving Reis. David Niven, Teresa Wright, Evelyn Keyes, Farley Granger, Jayne Meadows, Leo G. Carroll. Weepy romancer with elderly Niven recalling his tragic love as he watches great-niece Keyes' romance with Granger.▼●

Encino Man (1992) **C-89m.** *½ D: Les Mayfield. Sean Astin, Brendan Fraser, Pauly Shore, Megan Ward, Robin Tunney, Rick Ducommun, Mariette Hartley, Richard Masur, Rose McGowan. Nerdy teenager Astin and his weirdo pal Shore dig up a frozen caveman in Astin's suburban L.A. backyard. The scant laughs come from plunging the affable Cro-Magnon into teenage life, circa 1992. Formulaic teen comedy; Shore's bogus slang irritates, but limber, good-natured Fraser (as the cave-dude) has his moments. Followed by 1996 TV sequel ENCINO WOMAN. [PG]▼●◗

Encore (1952-British) **85m.** *** D: Pat Jackson, Anthony Pelissier, Harold French. Nigel Patrick, Roland Culver, Kay Walsh, Glynis Johns, Terence Morgan. Entertaining trilogy of Somerset Maugham stories: brothers try to outdo one another over money; busybody matron almost ruins ship cruise; apprehensive circus performer faces a crisis.▼

Encore (1978-British) SEE: **Comeback, The**

End, The (1978) **C-100m.** *** D: Burt Reynolds. Burt Reynolds, Sally Field, Dom DeLuise, Joanne Woodward, Kristy McNichol, Robby Benson, David Steinberg, Norman Fell, Carl Reiner, Pat O'Brien, Myrna Loy. Uneven but original black comedy by Jerry Belson about man who learns he's dying, and decides to commit suicide. DeLuise is achingly funny as Burt's schizophrenic sanitarium pal, and Reynolds's final soliloquy is great (in uncensored version). [R]▼●

Endangered Species (1982) **C-97m.** *½ D: Alan Rudolph. Robert Urich, JoBeth Williams, Paul Dooley, Hoyt Axton, Peter Coyote, Marin Kanter, Dan Hedaya, Harry Carey, Jr., John Considine. Self-important, preachy story—based on a serious real-life situation—about a N.Y. cop's investigation of cattle mutilations in the Western U.S. Tries to be a thriller, but telegraphs all its punches. [R]▼

Endless Descent (1991-Spanish) **C-79m.** BOMB D: Juan Piquer Simon. Jack Scalia, R. Lee Ermey, Ray Wise, Deborah Adair, John Toles Bey, Ely Pouget. With its designer and captain stereotypically clashing, a sub goes in search of another vessel, mysteriously sunk in the depths. Colorful monsters are eventually found, but you might not wait that long. ▼●

Endless Game, The (1990-British) **C-105m. TVM** D: Bryan Forbes. Albert Finney, George Segal, Derek de Lint, Monica Guerritore, Ian Holm, John Standing, Kristin Scott Thomas, Anthony Quayle, Nanette Newman. British agent, seeking the truth behind the murder of a woman who'd been a colleague and lover, finds himself knee-deep in international intrigue and political corruption. Convoluted spy thriller written by director Forbes. Quayle's last film. Made for cable. Average.▼

Endless Love (1981) **C-115m.** BOMB D: Franco Zeffirelli. Brooke Shields, Martin Hewitt, Shirley Knight, Don Murray, Richard Kiley, Beatrice Straight, James Spader, Robert Moore, Penelope Milford, Jan Miner, Tom Cruise, Jami Gertz. Scott Spencer's deservedly praised novel about an obsessive romance between two teenagers is thoroughly trashed in textbook example of how to do everything wrong in a literary adaptation. Rightfully regarded as one of the worst films of its time. Cruise's and Spader's film debuts. [R]▼●

Endless Night (1972-British) **C-99m.** *** D: Sidney Gilliat. Hayley Mills, Hywel Bennett, Britt Ekland, George Sanders, Per Oscarsson, Peter Bowles, Lois Maxwell. Gripping Agatha Christie thriller about chauffeur (Bennett) who marries rich American girl (Mills) and moves into "dream house" which turns out to be more a nightmare. Aka AGATHA CHRISTIE'S ENDLESS NIGHT.▼●

Endless Summer, The (1966) **C-95m.** *** D: Bruce Brown. Mike Hynson, Robert August. Enjoyable documentary on surfing, filmed on location around the world, with a most diverting tongue-in-cheek narrative. Followed by a sequel—28 years later. Followed in 2000 by ENDLESS SUMMER REVISITED. ▼●

Endless Summer II, The (1994) **C-107m.** *** D: Bruce Brown. Patrick O'Connell, Robert "Wingnut" Weaver. Superior sequel to Brown's 1966 surfing documentary, enhanced this time by a bigger budget and sophisticated camera work. Exotic locales and eye-popping surfing footage will make this a must-see for hot-doggers; others will still enjoy the unspoiled beauty of big-wave beaches from Alaska to Java. Several of the veteran surfers from the original documentary turn up here as does some brief topless beachbunny nudity. [PG]▼●

End of Days (1999) **C-122m.** *½ D: Peter Hyams. Arnold Schwarzenegger, Gabriel Byrne, Kevin Pollak, Robin Tunney, CCH Pounder, Rod Steiger, Derrick O'Connor, Miriam Margolyes, Udo Kier. The Devil takes the form of a wealthy New Yorker (Byrne) and sets out to find his pre-ordained bride; if he can impregnate her before midnight on New Year's Eve, 1999, he will bring about Hell on Earth, or Armageddon, or something. However, Satan never reckoned with Arnold, who's actually quite good as the burned-out cop/defender of humanity. This laughable movie is overproduced junk, a straight-to-video clunker writ large. [R]▼●◗
End of Desire (1958-French-Italian) **C-86m.** ** D: Alexandre Astruc. Maria Schell, Christian Marquand, Pascale Petit, Ivan Desny. Marquand weds Schell for her money, and she chooses to remain blind to his indiscretions. Schell is sole bright spot in this dreary tale, based on a de Maupassant short story. U.S. released in 1962.▼
End of Innocence, The (1991) **C-102m.** *½ D: Dyan Cannon. Dyan Cannon, John Heard, George Coe, Lola Mason, Rebecca Schaeffer, Steve Meadows, Billie Bird, Michael Madsen, Madge Sinclair, Renee Taylor. One woman's road to a breakdown, thanks to quarreling parents and a rich assortment of rotten men. Passionately acted by Cannon, who as a writer-director may have been in over her head. [R]▼
End of the Affair, The (1955-British) **106m.** **½ D: Edward Dmytryk. Deborah Kerr, Van Johnson, John Mills, Peter Cushing, Michael Goodliffe. Graham Greene's mystic-religious novel about a wartime love affair in London loses much in screen version, especially from mismatched stars. Remade in 1999.▼◗
End of the Affair, The (1999-British-U.S.) **C-109m.** *** D: Neil Jordan. Ralph Fiennes, Julianne Moore, Stephen Rea, Ian Hart, Samuel Bould, Jason Isaacs. Finely wrought rendition of Graham Greene's (reportedly autobiographical) novel about a WW2 love affair that takes a surprising turn when the married woman (a radiant Moore) has an unexplained change of heart. Director-screenwriter Jordan captures the understatement and nuance of a vintage British drama with his keen eye and gifted stars. [R]▼◗
End of the Game (1976-German-Italian) **C-103m.** *** D: Maximilian Schell. Jon Voight, Jacqueline Bisset, Martin Ritt, Robert Shaw, Gabriele Ferzetti, Donald Sutherland. Complex thriller about dying police commissioner Ritt, who for three decades has been trying to nail omnipotent criminal Shaw. Director Ritt, in a rare acting role, is excellent; Voight plays his assistant, and Sutherland appears as a dead man! Based on Friedrich Duerrenmatt's novel; retitled GETTING AWAY WITH MURDER for TV. [PG]
End of the Line (1987) **C-105m.** ** D: Jay Russell. Wilford Brimley, Levon Helm, Mary Steenburgen, Barbara Barrie, Kevin Bacon, Holly Hunter, Bob Balaban, Clint Howard, Rita Jenrette, Howard Morris, Bruce McGill, Trey Wilson. Two lifelong Southern railroad workers, suddenly unemployed when their parent company abandons the rails for air freight, take off for the Chicago corporate headquarters in a stolen engine. Labor of love for executive producer Steenburgen begins promisingly, quickly degenerates into silly Capra-esque fantasy. Cast makes it a curio. [PG]▼●
End of the River, The (1947-British) **80m.** ** D: Derek Twist. Sabu, Bibi Ferreira, Esmond Knight, Torin Thatcher, Robert Douglas. Native boy Sabu fights for acceptance in white world; ambitious drama suffers from mediocre casting.
End of the Road (1970) **C-110m.** ***½ D: Aram Avakian. Stacy Keach, Harris Yulin, Dorothy Tristan, James Earl Jones, Grayson Hall, Ray Brock, James Coco. Keach and Jones give stinging performances in solid filmization of bizarre John Barth novel about unstable college instructor who becomes involved with the wife of a professor. Tristan is superb in crucial and difficult role. Screenplay by Dennis McGuire, Terry Southern, and the director. [X]▼
End of the World (1977) **C-87m.** ** D: John Hayes. Christopher Lee, Sue Lyon, Kirk Scott, Lew Ayres, Macdonald Carey, Dean Jagger, Liz Ross. Lee plays a priest and his sinister "double" in this strange sci-fi tale about imminent world destruction by alien invaders. Opens strong but drifts into dullness. [PG]▼
End of the World in Our Usual Bed in a Night Full of Rain, The SEE: **Night Full of Rain, A**
End of Violence, The (1997) **C-122m.** ** D: Wim Wenders. Bill Pullman, Andie MacDowell, Gabriel Byrne, Traci Lind, Loren Dean, Daniel Benzali, Pruitt Taylor Vince, John Diehl, Peter Horton, Rosalind Chao, Frederic Forrest, Sam Fuller. Wenders' first American film since PARIS, TEXAS is gorgeous to look at but fuzzy and half-baked. Movie producer Pullman hides out with a Mexican family after surviving a professional "hit" that may have something to do with a high-tech security project being run out of L.A.'s Griffith Park Observatory. Lind is appealing as a stuntwoman, MacDowell less so packing a rod while decked out in bikini nightwear. Ry Cooder's score sells the movie to a point, just as it did for UNTIL THE END OF THE WORLD. Super 35. [R]▼●◗
Endurance (1999) **C-82m.** **½ D: Leslie Woodhead. Interesting, well-made docu-drama about Ethiopian long-distance runner

Haile Gebrselassie, who won a Gold Medal at the 1996 Atlanta Olympic Games. Dramatically recreates his difficult childhood and the decisions leading up to his extraordinary running career. (Haile is portrayed by his nephew in flashback; his sister plays his mother.) Matter-of-fact, even sleepy at times, and missing the conclusive emotional punch you're waiting for. Olympic footage directed by Bud Greenspan. Coproduced by Terrence Malick, and based on his idea. Super 35. [G]▼

Enemies, A Love Story (1989) **C-119m.** ***½ D: Paul Mazursky. Anjelica Huston, Ron Silver, Lena Olin, Margaret Sophie Stein, Alan King, Judith Malina, Rita Karlin, Phil Leeds, Elya Baskin, Paul Mazursky. Quietly haunting film about an aloof Jewish intellectual (Silver) who managed to hide from the Nazis during WW2 and now, in 1949, leads a double life in Coney Island, N.Y., married to his wartime protector (Stein) and fooling around with a sexy married woman (Olin). Things get even more complicated when his first wife (Huston), who was thought dead, turns up. Typically quixotic Isaac Bashevis Singer material—full of irony, wit, and heartbreak—is beautifully realized by Mazursky (who cowrote the screenplay with Roger L. Simon) and a perfect cast. Kudos also to Pato Guzman for his incredibly evocative production design. [R]▼●

Enemy Agents Meet Ellery Queen (1942) **64m.** *½ D: James Hogan. William Gargan, Margaret Lindsay, Charley Grapewin, Gale Sondergaard, Gilbert Roland, Sig Rumann, James Burke. Queen takes on Nazi spies in this final entry to an undistinguished series.

Enemy Below, The (1957) **C-98m.** *** D: Dick Powell. Robert Mitchum, Curt Jurgens, Theodore Bikel, Doug McClure, Russell Collins, David Hedison. Fine submarine chase tale, which manages to garner interest from usual crew interaction of U.S. vs. Germany in underwater action; the special effects for this earned Walter Rossi an Academy Award. Previously filmed in 1931 as THE SEAS BENEATH. CinemaScope.▼●

Enemy From Space (1957-British) **84m.** *** D: Val Guest. Brian Donlevy, Michael Ripper, Sidney James, Bryan Forbes, John Longden, Vera Day, William Franklyn. Even better than the original, THE CREEPING UNKNOWN, this tense, scary science-fiction thriller concerns a secret alien invasion and BODY SNATCHERS-like takeovers of human beings. Donlevy is stern as Dr. Quatermass. Video title: QUATERMASS II. Followed by FIVE MILLION YEARS TO EARTH.▼●

Enemy General, The (1960) **74m.** **½ D: George Sherman. Van Johnson, Jean-Pierre Aumont, Dany Carrel, John Van Dreelen. OSS officer Johnson and French resistance leader Aumont join forces to rescue Nazi general Van Dreelen who wants to defect to Allies; satisfactory handling of middling material.

Enemy Mine (1985) **C-108m.** **½ D: Wolfgang Petersen. Dennis Quaid, Louis Gossett, Jr., Brion James, Richard Marcus. Mortal space enemies are stranded together on a barren planet, forced to become friends in order to survive. Warmhearted science-fiction tale gets a bit too cuddly at times, but it's entertaining. Gossett's lizardlike makeup (by Chris Walas) is incredible; so is Rolf Zehetbauer's production design. Super 35. [PG-13]▼●

Enemy of the People, An (1979) **C-103m.** **½ D: George Schaefer. Steve McQueen, Charles Durning, Bibi Andersson, Richard Bradford, Robin Pearson Rose, Richard A. Dysart. Bearded scientist McQueen defies community by taking stand against polluted water system in Arthur Miller's adaptation of the Ibsen play. Sincere, plodding effort was a labor of love for McQueen, but understandably sat on the shelf for years and received limited distribution. Still superior to other films from McQueen's final period. Filmed in 1977. [G]

Enemy of the People, An (1989-Indian) **C-100m.** **½ D: Satyajit Ray. Soumitra Chatterjee, Dhritiman Chatterjee, Ruma Guhathakurta, Mamata Shankar, Dipankar Dey. Adaptation of the Ibsen play, updated and set in Bengal. Its message, about the perils of greed, religious fanaticism, and environmental pollution may be topical, but the film is too static. Still, there are enough flashes of Ray's brilliance to make it worthwhile. The director also scripted.

Enemy of the State (1998) **C-127m.** *** D: Tony Scott. Will Smith, Gene Hackman, Jon Voight, Lisa Bonet, Regina King, Stuart Wilson, Tom Sizemore, Loren Dean, Barry Pepper, Ian Hart, Jake Busey, Scott Caan, Jason Lee, Gabriel Byrne, James LeGros, Dan Butler, Jamie Kennedy, Bodhi Pine Elfman. Crackerjack thriller about a successful D.C. lawyer who happens to get in the way of a ruthless executive at the National Security Agency (Voight). The NSA official finds it necessary to ruin the attorney's reputation and throw his life into disarray . . . but the lawyer finds help from an unlikely source. Never takes a breath! Jason Robards appears unbilled. Panavision. [R]▼●◗

Enforcer, The (1951) **87m.** *** D: Bretaigne Windust. Humphrey Bogart, Zero Mostel, Ted de Corsia, Everett Sloane, Roy Roberts. When informer de Corsia dies, D.A. Bogart has to find another way to prove that Sloane is the head of a murder-for-hire ring. Loosely based on the true story of Murder, Inc., this is a generally effective, moody thriller. Mostel is particularly good as a frightened crook.▼●

Enforcer, The (1975) SEE: **Death Collector**
Enforcer, The (1976) **C-96m.** *** D: James Fargo. Clint Eastwood, Tyne Daly, Harry Guardino, Bradford Dillman, John Mitchum, DeVeren Bookwalter, John Crawford, Albert Popwell. Rule-breaking detective Dirty Harry Callahan (Eastwood) has to contend with a female partner (Daly) as he goes after an underground terrorist group in San Francisco. Violent, bubble-gum-mentality script, but it's a formula that just seems to work. Followed by SUDDEN IMPACT. Panavision. [R]▼●
England Made Me (1973-British) **C-100m.** *** D: Peter Duffell. Peter Finch, Michael York, Hildegard Neil, Michael Hordern, Joss Ackland. Unappreciated in its initial release, drama of a powerful financier in Nazi Germany of 1935 is absorbing, thoughtful fare. Made in Yugoslavia. [PG]
Englishman Who Went Up a Hill, but Came Down a Mountain, The (1995-British) **C-99m.** **½ D: Christopher Monger. Hugh Grant, Tara Fitzgerald, Colm Meaney, Ian McNeice, Ian Hart, Kenneth Griffith, Tudor Vaughn, Hugh Vaughn. Two British mapmakers raise the ire of a Welsh community during WW1 when they designate the village's prized landmark a hill and not a you-know-what. Woe be the one-joke movie when the joke isn't much of a grabber, despite being based on real Welsh legend. Agreeable cast and attractive physical trappings definitely help, though Grant's hem-haw acting style probably adds ten minutes to the running time. Panavision. [PG]▼●◗
English Patient, The (1996) **C-162m.** ***½ D: Anthony Minghella. Ralph Fiennes, Juliette Binoche, Willem Dafoe, Kristin Scott Thomas, Naveen Andrews, Colin Firth, Julian Wadham, Jürgen Prochnow, Kevin Whately. Mesmerizing adaptation (by Minghella) of Michael Ondaatje's novel about a man badly burned in a WW2 plane crash in the African desert; a Canadian nurse (Binoche) tends to him in an abandoned monastery in Italy, and slowly, bit by bit, his story emerges. Fiennes and Scott Thomas are perfectly matched in this intelligent, passionate romance about two people thrown together by chance during a tumultuous period. The story unfolds novelistically, layer by layer, drawing the viewer in with its sinuous, sensuous images and jarring depictions of wartime brutality. Strikingly photographed by John Seale. An exceptional achievement all around. Winner of nine Oscars: Best Picture, Director, Cinematography, Supporting Actress (Binoche), Art Direction, Sound, Score (Gabriel Yared), Costumes, and Editing. [R]▼●◗
Enid Is Sleeping (1990) **C-100m.** *** D: Maurice Phillips. Elizabeth Perkins, Judge Reinhold, Jeffrey Jones, Maureen Mueller, Rhea Perlman, Michael J. Pollard. Very black comedy about a woman who accidentally kills her much-hated sister—after being caught sleeping with her husband (who happens to be a police officer). Macabre humor may not be to everyone's taste, but slapstick antics with the "dead" body and genuine character development put this leagues ahead of the similar WEEKEND AT BERNIE'S. Severely cut by its studio, then reclaimed (and restored) by its star and director; a triumph for Perkins, who's never been better. Video title: OVER HER DEAD BODY. [R]▼
Enigma (1982-British-French) **C-101m.** **½ D: Jeannot Szwarc. Martin Sheen, Brigitte Fossey, Sam Neill, Derek Jacobi, Michel Lonsdale, Frank Finlay. The KGB sends out five crack assassins to eliminate five Soviet dissidents; CIA agent Sheen (who's apparently seen NOTORIOUS once too often) tries to stop them by having ex-lover Fossey cozy up to top Russian agent Neill. Fine cast does its best with so-so material; script by John Briley. [PG]▼●
Enjo (1958-Japanese) **96m.** ***½ D: Kon Ichikawa. Raizo Ichikawa, Tatsuya Nakadai, Ganjiro Nakamura, Yoko Uraji, Tanie Kitabayashi. Troubled young novice priest Ichikawa cannot handle corruption around him and burns down a temple. Perceptive psychological study of a human being's destruction; based on a Yukio Mishima novel, fashioned around a true story. Aka CONFLAGRATION. Daieiscope.▼
Enormous Changes at the Last Minute (1983) **C-115m.** **½ D: Mirra Bank, Ellen Hovde. Maria Tucci, Lynn Milgrim, David Strathairn, Ellen Barkin, Ron McLarty, Zvee Scooler, Kevin Bacon, Jeffrey DeMunn, Sudie Bond. Three separate dramas about contemporary women living in N.Y.C., and their relationships with husbands, ex-husbands, lovers, parents, children. Ambitious but uneven, with some good performances and touching moments. Screenplay by John Sayles with Susan Rice, based on the stories of Grace Paley. "Faith's Story" was filmed in 1978; "Virginia's Story" and "Alexandra's Story" in 1982. Aka TRUMPS. ▼●
Ensign Pulver (1964) **C-104m.** ** D: Joshua Logan. Robert Walker, Jr., Burl Ives, Walter Matthau, Tommy Sands, Millie Perkins, Kay Medford. Flat sequel to MISTER ROBERTS has Walker sinking in Jack Lemmon role amid synthetic seaboard and coral-isle shenanigans. Disappointing film is worth noting for its large cast of future stars: Larry Hagman, Gerald O'Loughlin, Al Freeman, Jr., James Farentino, James Coco, Diana Sands, and Jack Nicholson. Panavision.▼
Enter Arsene Lupin (1944) **72m.** ** D: Ford Beebe. Charles Korvin, Ella Raines, J. Carrol Naish, George Dolenz, Gale Sondergaard. Good supporting cast of vil-

lains gives zest to tame tale of naive heroine possessing a wealth of jewels.
Enter Laughing (1967) **C-112m.** ** D: Carl Reiner. Reni Santoni, Jose Ferrer, Shelley Winters, Elaine May, Jack Gilford, Janet Margolin, David Opatoshu, Michael J. Pollard, Don Rickles, Nancy Kovack, Rob Reiner. Reiner's funny semi-autobiographical Broadway play becomes bland screen comedy as youngster struggles to make it as an actor, despite all manner of problems in his way.▼
Enter Madame (1935) **83m.** **½ D: Elliott Nugent. Elissa Landi, Cary Grant, Lynne Overman, Sharon Lynne, Frank Albertson. Grant marries opera star Landi and winds up taking back seat to her career; pleasant romantic comedy.
Entertainer, The (1960-British) **97m.** ***½ D: Tony Richardson. Laurence Olivier, Brenda de Banzie, Roger Livesey, Joan Plowright, Daniel Massey, Alan Bates, Shirley Anne Field, Albert Finney, Thora Hird. Seedy vaudevillian (Olivier, recreating his stage role) ruins everyone's life and won't catch on. Film captures flavor of chintzy seaside resort, complementing Olivier's brilliance as egotistical song-and-dance man. Coscripted by John Osborne, from his play. Film debuts of Bates and Finney. Olivier and Plowright married the following year. Remade as a 1975 TVM starring Jack Lemmon. ▼●
Entertaining Angels: The Dorothy Day Story (1996) **C-110m.** ** D: Michael Ray Rhodes. Moira Kelly, Martin Sheen, Boyd Kestner, Lenny Von Dohlen, James Lancaster, Heather Graham, Paul Lieber, Heather Camille. By-the-numbers biography, set in the 1920s and '30s, of Dorothy Day (Kelly), the fabled Roman Catholic activist. Scenario spotlights her spiritual evolution from journalist and suffragette in Greenwich Village to her conversion to Roman Catholicism and her devotion to helping the poor. Disappointingly superficial. [PG-13]▼
Entertaining Mr. Sloane (1970-British) **C-94m.** **½ D: Douglas Hickox. Beryl Reid, Harry Andrews, Peter McEnery, Alan Webb. Acting by McEnery, Reid, and Andrews is extraordinary in story of young man who becomes involved with both brother and sister. Uneven adaptation of Joe Orton play.▼
Enter the Dragon (1973) **C-97m.** ***½ D: Robert Clouse. Bruce Lee, John Saxon, Jim Kelly, Ahna Capri, Yang Tse, Angela Mao. Almost perfect Kung Fu film that forgets about plot and concentrates on mind-boggling action. Martial arts expert Lee (in last complete film role) infiltrates strange tournament on island fortress. This was filmed after (but released before) Lee's RETURN OF THE DRAGON. 3m. added on video in 1998. Aka THE DEADLY THREE. Panavision. [R]▼●◗
Enter the Ninja (1981) **C-94m.** *½ D: Menahem Golan. Franco Nero, Susan George, Sho Kosugi, Alex Courtney, Will Hare, Zachi Noy, Dale Ishimoto, Christopher George. Ninjitsu master Nero takes on greedy Christopher George and old rival Kosugi. Third-rate chop-socky actioner and certainly no ENTER THE DRAGON. Original running time: 99m. Followed by REVENGE OF THE NINJA. [R]▼
Entity, The (1983) **C-115m.** ** D: Sidney J. Furie. Barbara Hershey, Ron Silver, Jacqueline Brooks, David Lablosa, George Coe, Margaret Blye, Alex Rocco. Woman is raped repeatedly by giant invisible mass. Her psychiatrist thinks it's all in the mind, until parapsychologists set a trap for the critter. Effectively sensational but atrociously exploitive; supposedly based on actual incident. Panavision. [R]▼
Entrapment (1999) **C-112m.** **½ D: Jon Amiel. Sean Connery, Catherine Zeta-Jones, Will Patton, Ving Rhames, Maury Chaykin. American insurance investigator Zeta-Jones convinces her boss to let her set the bait to capture world-class art thief Connery, leading to a gigantic cat-and-mouse game played out in London and Kuala Lumpur. The two stars are easy to watch, and there are lots of gimmicky action scenes, but it's all rather flat. Connery coexecutive-produced. Panavision. [PG-13] ▼●◗
Entre Nous (1983-French) **C-110m.** ***½ D: Diane Kurys. Miou Miou, Isabelle Huppert, Guy Marchand, Jean-Pierre Bacri, Robin Renucci, Patrick Bauchau. Moving, multi-layered story of two women who form a bond of friendship that lasts many years, takes many turns, and threatens their ineffectual husbands. Compassionate telling by Kurys of her own mother's story, with extraordinary performances all around. Original French title: COUP DE FOUDRE. Followed by C'EST LA VIE. Panavision. [PG]▼◗
Equinox (1971) **C-80m.** ** D: Jack Woods. Edward Connell, Barbara Hewitt, Frank Boers, Jr. (Frank Bonner), Robin Christopher, Jack Woods, Fritz Leiber. Archaeology students confront Satanism—and mutant-like monsters—while searching for vanished professor. Late-1960s amateur film (directed by later special-effects Oscar winner Dennis Muren) was reworked for theatrical release, mixing movie clichés with good special effects. This film took several years to complete, and the young cast obviously ages in it. Aka THE BEAST. [M/PG]▼
Equinox (1993) **C-110m.** ** D: Alan Rudolph. Matthew Modine, Lara Flynn Boyle, Fred Ward, Tyra Ferrell, Marisa Tomei, Kevin J. O'Connor, Tate Donovan, Lori Singer, M. Emmet Walsh, Gailard Sartain, Mark Modine. Slow-moving mystery with Modine playing two men—a weakling auto mechanic and an underworld tough-guy—

who live in the same city and lead parallel lives. Typically quirky Rudolph drama, but weaker than most; rife with commentary on contemporary mores and morals. [R]▼●

Equus (1977) **C-138m.** **½ D: Sidney Lumet. Richard Burton, Peter Firth, Colin Blakely, Joan Plowright, Harry Andrews, Eileen Atkins, Jenny Agutter. Peter Shaffer's shattering play makes bumpy screen adaptation, its vivid theatricality lost on film; Burton, however, is superb as troubled psychiatrist trying to unlock deep-rooted problems of stable boy Firth. [R] ▼●

Eraser (1996) **C-115m.** *** D: Charles Russell. Arnold Schwarzenegger, James Caan, Vanessa Williams, James Coburn, Robert Pastorelli, James Cromwell, Danny Nucci, Roma Maffia, Camryn Manheim. High-octane, high-tech, violent and cartoonish action-thriller about a specialist in the Federal Witness Protection Program who vows to keep a female witness safe and sticks to his word even after he becomes as much a target as she. Explosive, cutting-edge action and special effects give fans their money's worth, and then some. Indefensible on any artistic level, but lots of fun. Panavision. [R] ▼●◗

Eraserhead (1978) **90m.** *** D: David Lynch. John (Jack) Nance, Charlotte Stewart, Allen Joseph, Jeanne Bates, Judith Anna Roberts, Laurel Near, V. Phipps-Wilson. Brooding experimental film full of repulsive imagery tells story of zombie-like misfit, his spastic girlfriend, and their half-human offspring. Bona fide cult film is full of surreal, nightmarish tangents. Feature film debut of director Lynch.▼●

Erendira (1983-Mexican-French-German) **C-103m.** **½ D: Ruy Guerra. Irene Papas, Claudia Ohana, Michael Lonsdale, Oliver Wehe, Rufus. Strange does not begin to describe this fable of queenly Papas forcing beautiful, obedient granddaughter Ohana into prostitution in a vast, surreal desert. Ambitious and fluidly directed, but unmemorable; from a screenplay by Gabriel Garcia Marquez.▼

Eric Clapton and His Rolling Hotel (1981-British) **C-62m.** *½ D: Rex Pyke. Eric Clapton, Muddy Waters, George Harrison, Elton John. Below-average rock documentary of Clapton's '79 European tour.

Erik the Conqueror (1961-Italian) **C-81m.** ** D: Mario Bava. Cameron Mitchell, Alice Kessler, Ellen Kessler, Françoise Christophe. Unexceptional account of 10th-century Viking life, with Mitchell fighting for virtue and love. Released on video as THE INVADERS at 88m. Dyaliscope. ▼

Erik the Viking (1989) **C-104m.** BOMB D: Terry Jones. Tim Robbins, Mickey Rooney, Eartha Kitt, Terry Jones, Imogen Stubbs, John Cleese, Antony Sher, Gordon John Sinclair, Freddie Jones. Robbins is a revisionist Erik, but quick—what's the Norse expression for "unwatchable satire"? [PG-13]▼●

Erin Brockovich (2000) **C-131m.** *** D: Steven Soderbergh. Julia Roberts, Albert Finney, Aaron Eckhart, Marg Helgenberger, Cherry Jones, Conchata Ferrell, Tracey Walter, Mimi Kennedy, Peter Coyote. Brassy, divorced mother of three, at the end of her rope, talks her way into a job in Finney's law office, then becomes obsessed with a pro bono case involving residents of a California desert town who have been exposed to poisonously polluted water. Energetic, engaging David vs. Goliath story never states—or overstates—the obvious, and travels far on Roberts's charisma and Finney's expertise. That's the real Erin Brockovich playing a waitress. [R]▼◗

Ernest Goes to Camp (1987) **C-93m.** *½ D: John R. Cherry 3rd. Jim Varney, Victoria Racimo, John Vernon, Iron Eyes Cody, Lyle Alzado, Gailard Sartain. Ernest, an obnoxious dimwit popularized in a spate of TV commercials, is the star of this clumsy and unfunny comedy about a dumb cluck who wants to be a summer camp counselor in the worst way—and gets his wish. Aimed at children who aren't very bright. Followed by ERNEST SAVES CHRISTMAS. [PG]▼●

Ernest Goes to Jail (1990) **C-82m.** ** D: John Cherry. Jim Varney, Gailard Sartain, Bill Byrge, Barbara Bush, Randall (Tex) Cobb, Barry Scott, Charles Napier. Third in the surprisingly successful series about Ernest P. Worrell finds our hero in prison as the result of a switch set up by an evil inmate lookalike (also played by Varney). Harmless, predictable, and hokey, the importance of seeing Ernest may depend on your age and I.Q.—if either is 12 or below this may be the movie for you. Followed by ERNEST SCARED STUPID. [PG]▼●

Ernest Goes to School (1994) **C-90m.** BOMB D: Coke Sams. Jim Varney, Linda Kash, Bill Byrge, Corrine Koslo, Kevin McNulty, Jason Michas. Sub-atomic brain accelerator is used to make Chippewa Falls High's school custodian, Ernest, a temporary genius in an attempt to undermine a plot to close the school. Completely predictable and unfunny; fifth entry in the series is only for die-hard Ernest fans. Followed by SLAM DUNK ERNEST. [PG]▼●

Ernest Saves Christmas (1988) **C-89m.** *½ D: John Cherry. Jim Varney, Douglas Seale, Oliver Clark, Noelle Parker, Robert Lesser, Gailard Sartain, Billie Bird. The title character, who makes Gomer Pyle seem like Albert Einstein, attempts to help Santa Claus on Christmas Eve. This is one Christmas present to be opened with extreme caution . . . unless you're a fan of Ernest P. Worrell. Followed by ERNEST GOES TO JAIL. [PG]▼●

Ernest Scared Stupid (1991) **C-91m.** *½ D: John Cherry. Jim Varney, Eartha Kitt,

Austin Nagler, Jonas Moscartolo, Shay Astar. The fourth Ernest P. Worrell feature has a patently redundant title. Originally released at Halloween time, the story has dimwitted Ernest inadvertently releasing a villainous troll from its tomb. Pretty lame; Kitt is wasted as a witch. Followed by ERNEST GOES TO SCHOOL. [PG]▼●

Erotique (1993-U.S.-German) **C-93m.** ** D: Lizzie Borden, Monika Treut, Clara Law. Kamela Lopez-Dawson, Bryan Cranston, Liane Curtis, Priscilla Barnes, Camilla Soeberg, Michael Carr, Peter Kern, Marianne Sägebrecht, Tim Lounibos, Hayley Man, Choi Hark-kin. Uneven feature in three parts, each a story with a female slant. Borden's piece, about a phone sex worker exacting revenge against one of her callers, is obvious and annoying; Treut tells the trite tale of a pair of lesbians who set out to seduce a man. By far the best of the lot is Law's perceptive study of the cultural differences between a Hong Kong woman and her Australian-Chinese boyfriend. A fourth episode, the muddled account of a teacher's erotic encounter while on a trip, was excluded from the final print but added to the video release. It is directed by Ana Maria Magalhaes and stars Claudia Ohana and Guilherme Leme. Video running time is 117m.▼●◗

Errand Boy, The (1961) **92m.** **½ D: Jerry Lewis. Jerry Lewis, Brian Donlevy, Howard McNear, Sig Ruman, Fritz Feld, Iris Adrian, Kathleen Freeman, Doodles Weaver, Renee Taylor. Jerry on the loose in a movie studio has its moments. Long string of gags provide the laughter; veteran character actors produce the sparkle.▼●

Escapade (1935) **89m.** ** D: Robert Z. Leonard. William Powell, Luise Rainer, Frank Morgan, Virginia Bruce, Reginald Owen, Mady Christians, Laura Hope Crews, Henry Travers. Married woman is persuaded to pose for a roguish Viennese artist, but when the semi-nude illustration is printed, it causes a potential scandal. Sophisticated comedy/drama was Rainer's Hollywood debut film; she and Powell are charming, but the film's initial sparkle eventually goes flat—as the picture goes on. Remake of the much superior (and sexier) Austrian film MASKERADE (1934).

Escapade (1955-British) **87m.** *** D: Philip Leacock. John Mills, Yvonne Mitchell, Alastair Sim, Jeremy Spenser, Andrew Ray, Marie Lohr, Peter Asher. Mills is a professional pacifist whose life is anything but tranquil; his three sons, fearing that their parents are about to be divorced, react in a most unusual manner. Ambitious, insightful, solidly acted drama about the cynicism and hypocrisy of adults and the idealism of youth. Stick with this.▼

Escapade in Japan (1957) **C-93m.** ** D: Arthur Lubin. Cameron Mitchell, Teresa Wright, Jon Provost, Roger Nakagawa, Philip Ober, Clint Eastwood. Location filming in Japan is the prime asset of this otherwise forgettable adventure of two young boys, one American and the other Japanese, and their search for the former's parents. Eastwood is cast as a serviceman named Dumbo! Technirama.▼

Escape (1940) **104m.** *** D: Mervyn LeRoy. Norma Shearer, Robert Taylor, Conrad Veidt, Nazimova, Felix Bressart, Albert Basserman, Philip Dorn, Bonita Granville, Blanche Yurka. Countess Shearer, mistress of Nazi general Veidt, helps Taylor get his mother (Nazimova) out of German concentration camp before WW2; polished, with sterling cast. Based on Ethel Vance's 1939 best-seller.

Escape (1948) **78m.** *** D: Joseph L. Mankiewicz. Rex Harrison, Peggy Cummins, William Hartnell, Norman Wooland, Jill Esmond, Frederick Piper, Marjorie Rhodes, Betty Ann Davies, Cyril Cusack. Intelligent, well-paced story of law-abiding man for whom a chance encounter leads to a prison sentence; morally outraged, he determines to escape. Harrison is excellent as the cerebral hero of this John Galsworthy story (which was filmed before in 1930). Shot on natural locations around England. Screenplay by Philip Dunne.

Escape (1970) SEE: **McKenzie Break, The**

Escape (1987) SEE: **Escape From Sobibor**

Escape Artist, The (1982) **C-96m.** ** D: Caleb Deschanel. Griffin O'Neal, Raul Julia, Teri Garr, Joan Hackett, Gabriel Dell, Elizabeth Daily, Desiderio (Desi) Arnaz, Huntz Hall, Jackie Coogan, M. Emmet Walsh, David Clennon, Harry Anderson, Carlin Glynn, Margaret Ladd. Maddeningly muddled tale of teen-ager O'Neal, an amateur magician, and the adults who attempt to exploit him. Griffin, son of Ryan and brother of Tatum, has a pleasing screen presence. Directorial debut for cinematographer Deschanel. [PG]▼

Escape From Alcatraz (1979) **C-112m.** *** D: Donald Siegel. Clint Eastwood, Patrick McGoohan, Roberts Blossom, Jack Thibeau, Fred Ward, Paul Benjamin. Straightforward, methodical telling of true story about 1962 breakout from supposedly impregnable prison. Vivid and credible throughout. Watch for Danny Glover in his film debut. [PG]▼●◗

Escape From East Berlin (1962) **94m.** ** D: Robert Siodmak. Don Murray, Christine Kaufmann, Werner Klemperer, Ingrid van Bergen, Karl Schell. East German chauffeur becomes determined to tunnel to West Berlin, to allow his family and new girlfriend to escape Communist domination. Dated and propagandistic but based on true events.

Escape From Fort Bravo (1953) **C-98m.** *** D: John Sturges. William Holden, Eleanor Parker, John Forsythe, Polly

Bergen, William Demarest. Well-executed Western set in 1860s Arizona, balancing North-South conflict with whites vs. Indians, climaxed by tense ambush.▼

Escape From L.A. (1996) **C-101m.** ** D: John Carpenter. Kurt Russell, Stacy Keach, Steve Buscemi, Cliff Robertson, Valeria Golino, Peter Fonda, Michelle Forbes, A. J. Langer, George Corraface, Pam Grier, Robert Carradine, Bruce Campbell, Paul Bartel. In the year 2013, the Island of L.A. is a penal colony for America's undesirables. Snake Plissken (Russell) is sent there to bring back a valuable destruction device that was smuggled away by the daughter of the U.S. President. Lackluster follow-up to ESCAPE FROM NEW YORK is tongue-in-cheek, but devoid of wit, and not likely to satisfy action fans, either. Russell coproduced and cowrote the script. Onscreen title: JOHN CARPENTER'S ESCAPE FROM L.A. Panavision. [R]▼●◗

Escape From New York (1981) **C-99m.** ** D: John Carpenter. Kurt Russell, Lee Van Cleef, Ernest Borgnine, Donald Pleasence, Isaac Hayes, Adrienne Barbeau, Harry Dean Stanton, Season Hubley. For a "fun" film this is pretty bleak. The year is 1997, Manhattan is a maximum-security prison, and a character named Snake Plissken (Russell) must effect a daring rescue from within its borders. Reminiscent in some ways of Carpenter's ASSAULT ON PRECINCT 13, which was smaller—and better. Followed by ESCAPE FROM L.A. Panavision. [R]▼●

Escape From Planet Earth SEE: **Doomsday Machine, The**

Escape From Red Rock (1958) **75m.** *½ D: Edward Bernds. Brian Donlevy, Jay C. Flippen, Eilene Janssen, Gary Murray. Modest oater of rancher and girl involved in theft, being chased into Indian country by pursuing posse. Regalscope.

Escape From San Quentin (1957) **81m.** BOMB D: Fred F. Sears. Johnny Desmond, Merry Anders, Richard Devon, Roy Engel. Drab film has Desmond as runaway convict who decides to give himself and buddy up to police.

Escape From Sobibor (1987) **C-150m. TVM** D: Jack Gold. Alan Arkin, Joanna Pacula, Rutger Hauer, Hartmut Becker, Jack Shepherd. Searing drama detailing the largest prisoner escape from a WW2 Nazi death camp, with a memorable Arkin performance as the leader, and a terrific script by Reginald Rose, based on Richard Rashke's book. Top-notch production. Video title: ESCAPE. Above average.▼●◗

Escape From the Dark SEE: **Littlest Horse Thieves, The**

Escape From the Planet of the Apes (1971) **C-98m.** *** D: Don Taylor. Roddy McDowall, Kim Hunter, Bradford Dillman, Natalie Trundy, Eric Braeden, William Windom, Sal Mineo, Ricardo Montalban. Third in series is best of the sequels, with the Apes in modern-day L.A.; ingeniously paves the way for 4th and 5th entries in series. Followed by CONQUEST OF THE PLANET OF THE APES. Panavision. [G]▼●

Escape From Zahrain (1962) **C-93m.** *½ D: Ronald Neame. Yul Brynner, Sal Mineo, Madlyn Rhue, Jack Warden, James Mason, Jay Novello. Plodding film of five prisoners escaping from jail in Mideastern country, being chased across desert. Nice photography at least. Panavision.

Escape in the Desert (1945) **81m.** ** D: Edward A. Blatt. Philip Dorn, Helmut Dantine, Jean Sullivan, Alan Hale. Tame remake of THE PETRIFIED FOREST involving American flyer encountering Nazi at desert hotel.

Escape in the Fog (1945) **65m.** ** D: Oscar (Budd) Boetticher. Nina Foch, William Wright, Otto Kruger, Konstantin Shayne. Capable but unexceptional programmer of girl who has strange dream of murder being committed and encounters the dream victim in real life.

Escape Me Never (1947) **104m.** *½ D: Peter Godfrey. Errol Flynn, Ida Lupino, Eleanor Parker, Gig Young, Reginald Denny, Isobel Elsom. Sappy remake of 1935 Elisabeth Bergner vehicle, with Lupino as an itinerant waif (!) and Flynn as struggling composer who marries her but takes up with his brother's aristocratic fiancée (Parker). Forget it. ▼

Escapement SEE: **Electronic Monster, The**

Escapes (1985) **C-71m.** *½ D: David Steensland. Vincent Price, John Mitchum, Michael Patton-Hall, Todd Fulton, Ken Thorley, Jeff Boudov. Price introduces this mostly boring five-episode horror anthology. Only the second segment, detailing young Patton-Hall's plight as he loses his way in the mountains, is of the slightest interest.▼

Escape to Athena (1979-British) **C-101m.** **½ D: George Pan Cosmatos. Roger Moore, Telly Savalas, David Niven, Claudia Cardinale, Richard Roundtree, Stefanie Powers, Sonny Bono, Elliott Gould, William Holden. Agreeable time-filler, with all-star cast in outlandish adventure yarn about WW2 POWs planning escape and art heist at the same time. Released in England at 125m. Panavision. [PG]▼

Escape to Burma (1955) **C-87m.** ** D: Allan Dwan. Barbara Stanwyck, Robert Ryan, David Farrar, Murvyn Vye, Lisa Montell, Reginald Denny. Stanwyck rides herd over a tea plantation—and a pack of wild animals—but doesn't quite know how to deal with a wanted man who seeks refuge. Cast does what it can with pulp material. SuperScope.▼

Escape to Glory (1940) **74m.** *** D: John

Brahm. Constance Bennett, Pat O'Brien, John Halliday, Alan Baxter, Melville Cooper. British ship is attacked by German sub at outbreak of WW2, giving pause to various passengers on-board—including a German doctor. Thoughtful, atmospheric B-picture with minimal amount of clichés.

Escape to the Sun (1972-British-Israeli) **105m.** *½ D: Menahem Golan. Laurence Harvey, Josephine Chaplin, John Ireland, Lila Kedrova, Jack Hawkins, Clive Revill. Suspense tale about aftermath of unsuccessful attempt by Soviet Jews to hijack a plane wastes a capable cast. [PG]▼

Escape to Witch Mountain (1975) **C-97m.** *** D: John Hough. Eddie Albert, Ray Milland, Kim Richards, Ike Eisenmann, Donald Pleasence. Excellent Disney mystery-fantasy: two children with mysterious powers try to discover their origins, while being pursued by evil Milland, who wants to use their powers for his own purposes. Remade for TV. Followed by sequel RETURN FROM WITCH MOUNTAIN. [G]▼●

Escape 2000 (1981-Australian) **C-92m.** BOMB D: Brian Trenchard-Smith. Steve Railsback, Olivia Hussey, Michael Craig, Carmen Duncan, Roger Ward. Repellently violent, unpleasant ripoff of THE MOST DANGEROUS GAME, set in future society where criminals are hunted in a controlled environment. Original title: TURKEY SHOOT. Video running time: 80m. Panavision. [R]▼

Escort for Hire (1960-British) **C-66m.** ** D: Godfrey Grayson. June Thorburn, Noel Trevarthan, Peter Murray, Jill Melford, Guy Middleton. Clichéd murder yarn, enhanced by Technicolor, with Trevarthan an out-of-work actor joining escort service, becoming involved in murder.

Escort West (1959) **75m.** **½ D: Francis D. Lyon. Victor Mature, Elaine Stewart, Faith Domergue, Reba Waters, Noah Beery, Leo Gordon, Rex Ingram. Fairly good Western with Confederate soldier and 10-year-old daughter heading West, encountering two women who survived renegade attack and saved Army payroll. CinemaScope.

Especially on Sunday (1991-Italian-French-Belgian) **C-90m.** **½ D: Giuseppe Tornatore, Giuseppe Bertolucci, Marco Tullio Giordana. Philippe Noiret, Ornella Muti, Bruno Ganz, Maria Maddelena Fellini, Chiara Caselli, Andrea Prodan, Bruno Berdini, Nicoletta Braschi, Jean-Hugues Anglade. Trio of short films, each set in the Italian countryside, is a mixed bag. The first, by Tornatore (featuring Noiret as a barber who is comically harassed by a dog), is slight; the second, by Bertolucci (middle-aged Ganz picks up a pretty young woman and her mentally ill brother), is trite; the third, by Giordana (widow Fellini develops a most unusual unspoken bond with her new daughter-in-law), is the best of the lot, a thoughtful meditation on loneliness. Fellini is Federico's sister; this is her screen debut. European release version includes a fourth film, by Francesco Barilli. [R]

Espionage (1937) **67m.** **½ D: Kurt Neumann. Edmund Lowe, Madge Evans, Paul Lukas, Ketti Gallion, Skeets Gallagher, Leonid Kinskey, Billy Gilbert. Slick, fast-paced MGM B pic. Lowe and Evans are rival reporters on the trail of arms tycoon Lukas aboard the Orient Express.

Espionage Agent (1939) **83m.** ** D: Lloyd Bacon. Joel McCrea, Brenda Marshall, George Bancroft, Jeffrey Lynn, James Stephenson, Martin Kosleck. Formula spy caper with McCrea and Marshall tracking down the head of notorious spy ring.

Esther and the King (1960-U.S.-Italian) **C-109m.** ** D: Raoul Walsh. Joan Collins, Richard Egan, Denis O'Dea, Sergio Fantoni. Cardboard biblical costumer pretends to recreate 4th-century B.C. Persia, with stony performances by Collins and Egan as the king and the Jewish maiden he wants to replace murdered queen. Filmed in Italy. CinemaScope.▼

Esther Waters (1948-British) **108m.** **½ D: Ian Dalrymple. Kathleen Ryan, Dirk Bogarde, Cyril Cusack, Ivor Barnard, Fay Compton, Mary Clare. Well-appointed account of rogue Bogarde (in starring debut) involved with lovely damsels frequenting the racetracks; set in 19th-century England. Film bogs down into soaper of gloomy married life, marring initial zest.

Eternally Yours (1939) **95m.** **½ D: Tay Garnett. Loretta Young, David Niven, Hugh Herbert, C. Aubrey Smith, Billie Burke, Broderick Crawford, ZaSu Pitts, Eve Arden. Wayout idea comes off fairly well; Young is married to magician Niven, thinks his tricks are taking precedence to their married life. Also shown in computer-colored version.▼

Eternal Sea, The (1955) **103m.** **½ D: John H. Auer. Sterling Hayden, Alexis Smith, Dean Jagger, Virginia Grey. Well-played biography of Admiral John Hoskins' efforts to retain active command despite WW2 injury. Hayden is restrained in lead role; modest production values.

Eternal Song, The SEE: **A Brivele der Mamen**

Ethan Frome (1993) **C-107m.** **½ D: John Madden. Liam Neeson, Patricia Arquette, Joan Allen, Tate Donovan, Katharine Houghton, Stephen Mendillo. Stately, just-adequate adaptation of Edith Wharton's famed 1911 novella of tragedy, irony, and repression, set in rural New England: the tale of a farmer who weds a domineering woman (Allen), then falls in love with her poor but pretty cousin (Arquette). Beautifully photographed (by Bobby Bukowski) and intelligently scripted (by Richard Nelson), but not as powerful and moving as it should be. An *American Playhouse* theatrical feature. [PG]▼●

E.T. The Extra-Terrestrial (1982) **C-115m.** **** D: Steven Spielberg. Dee Wallace, Henry Thomas, Peter Coyote, Robert MacNaughton, Drew Barrymore, K.C. Martel, Sean Frye, Tom (C. Thomas) Howell. A 10-year-old boy (Thomas) befriends a creature from another planet that's been stranded on Earth. A warm, insightful story of childhood innocence, frustration, courage, and love . . . with a remarkable "performance" by E.T. An exhilarating experience for young and old alike. Screenplay by Melissa Mathison. John Williams won an Oscar for his soaring score, as did the sound and visual effects teams. Trivia note: Debra Winger contributed to E.T.'s voice. [PG]▼●

Eureka (1983) **C-130m.** ** D: Nicolas Roeg. Gene Hackman, Theresa Russell, Rutger Hauer, Jane Lapotaire, Ed Lauter, Mickey Rourke, Joe Pesci, Corin Redgrave. Klondike prospector becomes fabulously wealthy, watches his kingdom crumble 30 years later when his daughter's problems and Miami thugs converge on him at the same time. Odd drama, even for Roeg, that somehow climaxes with long, windy courtroom histrionics. Shelved by its studio, sporadically released in 1985. Aka RIVER OF DARKNESS. [R]▼

Eureka Stockade (1949-British-Australian) **103m.** *** D: Harry Watt. Chips Rafferty, Jane Barrett, Gordon Jackson, Jack Lambert, Peter Illing, Ralph Truman, Peter Finch. Stirring period drama, set in the 1850s upon the discovery of gold in Australia, chronicling the conflict between workingmen intent on panning for gold and their former employers (and government) intent on restricting their freedom. One of the former (Rafferty, in a forceful performance) attempts to mediate between the opposing groups. Aka MASSACRE HILL. ▼

Europa Europa (1991-French-German) **C-115m.** ***½ D: Agnieszka Holland. Marco Hofschneider, Rene Hofschneider, Julie Delpy, Ashley Wanninger, Piotr Kozlowski, Halina Labornarska, Hanns Zischler. German-Jewish teenage boy flees the Nazis and conceals his identity—only to find himself drafted into Hitler's army! Eye-opening, fact-based WW2 Holocaust drama, from Solomon Perel's autobiography, is both harrowing and humorous; deftly blends horrific images with black comedy to depict the growing pains of a boy becoming a man in the midst of a world in chaos. Polish writer-director Holland has made a riveting and moving film. [R]▼●

Europa '51 SEE: **Greatest Love, The**

Europeans, The (1979) **C-90m.** *** D: James Ivory. Lee Remick, Robin Ellis, Wesley Addy, Tim Choate, Lisa Eichhorn, Tim Woodward, Kristin Griffith. Meticulous film of Henry James novel vividly recreates 19th-century life in New England, as the arrival of two foreign cousins disrupts the stern-faced calm of a plain American family. Deliberately paced, but richly rewarding.▼●

Eva (1962-British) **100m.** *** D: Joseph Losey. Jeanne Moreau, Stanley Baker, Virna Lisi, Nona Medici, Francesco Rissone, James Villiers. Brooding account of writer Baker whose continued attraction for Eva (Moreau) causes wife (Lisi) to have tragic death. Premise isn't always workable, but Moreau is well cast as personification of evil. Based on a novel by James Hadley Chase. Director's cut (titled EVE) runs 120m.

Eve (1968-British-Spanish) **C-94m.** BOMB D: Jeremy Summers. Robert Walker, Jr., Celeste Yarnall, Herbert Lom, Christopher Lee, Fred Clark, Maria Rohm. Pilot is saved from Amazon savages by white jungle goddess who wields strange power over her subjects. Save yourself and don't watch.

Eve Knew Her Apples (1945) **64m.** **½ D: Will Jason. Ann Miller, William Wright, Robert Williams, Ray Walker. Sprightly musical variation of IT HAPPENED ONE NIGHT, with Miller on the lam from her marriage-minded fiancé.

Evel Knievel (1972) **C-90m.** **½ D: Marvin Chomsky. George Hamilton, Sue Lyon, Bert Freed, Rod Cameron. Biography of daredevil motorcyclist contains some great action footage; modest but effective film. Shouldn't be confused with VIVA KNIEVEL! (in which Evel played himself). [PG]▼

Evelyn Prentice (1934) **80m.** **½ D: William K. Howard. William Powell, Myrna Loy, Una Merkel, Rosalind Russell, Isabel Jewell, Harvey Stephens. Story of successful attorney who doesn't know his own wife is in trouble is too drawn-out, ultimately too implausible. Cast rises above material, but Cora Sue Collins is an obnoxious brat. Russell's first film. Remade as STRONGER THAN DESIRE.▼

Even Cowgirls Get the Blues (1994) **C-97m.** BOMB D: Gus Van Sant. Uma Thurman, Lorraine Bracco, Angie Dickinson, Rain Phoenix, John Hurt, Roseanne Arnold, Keanu Reeves, Noriyuki "Pat" Morita, Sean Young, Crispin Glover, Ed Begley, Jr., Faye Dunaway, Steve Buscemi, Heather Graham, Victoria Williams, Carol Kane, Grace Zabriskie. Tom Robbins' hopelessly dated novel about a hitchhiker with oversized thumbs is a candidate for the decade's worst movie: there is not enough peyote in the entire American Southwest to render scenes set in the feminist-collective ranch comprehensible or possible to endure. Recut by the director after its stormy reception at the Toronto Film Festival knocked it off the '93 release schedule. The k.d. lang score is the movie's sole worthy component. William S. Burroughs is briefly seen at film's beginning on a N.Y.C. street. [R]▼●

Even Dwarfs Started Small (1968-German) **96m.** *** D: Werner Herzog. Helmut Doring, Gerd Gickel, Paul Glauer, Erna Gschwnedtner, Gisela Hartwig. Unusual, disturbing, truly unsettling parable about dwarfs and midgets confined to a barren correctional institution who literally take over the asylum. Reminiscent of Tod Browning's FREAKS.▼◗

Evening Star, The (1996) **C-129m.** ** D: Robert Harling. Shirley MacLaine, Bill Paxton, Juliette Lewis, Miranda Richardson, Ben Johnson, Scott Wolf, George Newbern, Marion Ross, Mackenzie Astin, Donald Moffat, China Kantner, Jack Nicholson, Jennifer Grant. The further adventures of feisty, eccentric Aurora Greenway, who's now raised three grandchildren (born to Debra Winger in TERMS OF ENDEARMENT). Trades on the memory of a much better movie; even Nicholson's brief appearance only reminds us of the earlier film. There's barely an honest moment in the picture. Ross stands out as MacLaine's loyal longtime housekeeper and friend. Based on Larry McMurtry's novel. Johnson's final film. [PG-13]▼●

Event Horizon (1997-U.S.-British) **C-95m.** ** D: Paul Anderson. Laurence Fishburne, Sam Neill, Kathleen Quinlan, Joely Richardson, Richard T. Jones, Jack Noseworthy, Jason Isaacs, Sean Pertwee. In 2047, a rescue mission is launched to Neptune when the exploration ship *Event Horizon* reappears as mysteriously as it had vanished seven years before. The returned ship's crew is gone, but there's a disturbing presence aboard, perhaps connected to the black hole designed to warp space. Well-acted movie begins promisingly but becomes increasingly unlikely; offers no explanation for the strange events. Some intense horror scenes. Panavision. [R]▼●◗

Eve of Destruction (1991) **C-98m.** ** D: Duncan Gibbins. Gregory Hines, Renee Soutendijk, Michael Greene, Kurt Fuller, John M. Jackson, Kevin McCarthy. This muddled FRANKENSTEIN variation might have worked with a better script, and without a point of view that manages to at the same time be reverse-sexist and anti-feminist. Soutendijk gives her all in a dual role: Dr. Eve Simmons, a scientist, and Eve VIII, the android/robot bomb she's created in her own likeness—and which is running amok. Hines is the good guy who sets out to immobilize it. Dutch actress Soutendijk's U.S. film debut. [R]▼●

Eve of St. Mark, The (1944) **96m.** *** D: John M. Stahl. Anne Baxter, William Eythe, Michael O'Shea, Vincent Price, Dickie Moore. Human focus on WW2 in tale of soldier Eythe and girl friend Baxter at outset of war; not always successful Maxwell Anderson story.

Ever After (1998) **C-122m.** *** D: Andy Tennant. Drew Barrymore, Anjelica Huston, Dougray Scott, Patrick Godfrey, Megan Dodds, Melanie Lynskey, Timothy West, Judy Parfitt, Jeroen Krabbé, Richard O'Brien, Jeanne Moreau. The Queen of France (Moreau) summons the Brothers Grimm to her castle so she may tell them the true story of Cinderella: what unfolds is a charming rethinking of the classic fairy tale, with Barrymore as a feisty orphan (named Danielle) who puts her potential Prince Charming to shame with her bravery and regard for humankind. Long, but exquisitely filmed on location in France. Barrymore is a delight as a Cinderella for feminists. VHS version is rated PG. Super 35. [PG-13] ▼●◗

Evergreen (1934-British) **90m.** *** D: Victor Saville. Jessie Matthews, Sonnie Hale, Betty Balfour, Barry Mackay, Ivor MacLaren. British musical-comedy star's best known film is enjoyable fluff about young girl who becomes a stage sensation masquerading as her long-retired mother. Score includes Rodgers and Hart's "Dancing on the Ceiling."▼●

Ever in My Heart (1933) **68m.** **½ D: Archie Mayo. Barbara Stanwyck, Otto Kruger, Ralph Bellamy, Ruth Donnelly, Frank Albertson. New Englander Stanwyck, a Daughter of the American Revolution, weds German-born college professor Kruger. He becomes an American citizen—and then WW1 comes. Well-meaning soaper reflects the mood of the period, but is too hurried and simplistic to really score.

Ever Since Eve (1937) **79m.** *½ D: Lloyd Bacon. Marion Davies, Robert Montgomery, Frank McHugh, Patsy Kelly, Allen Jenkins, Louise Fazenda, Barton MacLane. Davies makes herself homely in order to avoid being harassed on the job; dreary comedy tests the mettle of Warner Bros. stock cast. This was Marion's last film.

Eversmile New Jersey (1989) **C-88m.** *½ D: Carlos Sorin. Daniel Day-Lewis, Mirjana Jokovic, Gabriela Archer, Julio De Grazia, Ignacio Quiros, Miguel Ligero, Ana Maria Glunta. If you've waited all your life to see a film about a traveling missionary dentist, wait no more: Day-Lewis plays a fanatic who works for a "dental consciousness" foundation and travels the hinterlands to spread his noble message. Offbeat, to say the least, but grows wearisome after a while. Filmed in Argentina. [PG]▼●

Every Bastard a King (1970-Israeli) **C-93m.** BOMB D: Uri Zohar. Pier Angeli, William Berger, Oded Kotler, Yehoram Gaon, Ori Levy. Story of journalist and his mistress, set against the 6-day Israeli-Egyptian War, is a slapdash effort with nothing to recommend it. Retitled EVERY MAN A KING for TV. [PG]

Everybody Does It (1949) **98m.** ***½ D: Edmund Goulding. Paul Douglas, Linda Darnell, Celeste Holm, Charles Coburn, Millard Mitchell, Lucile Watson, John Hoyt, George Tobias. Exceptionally amusing yarn of aspiring singer Holm, harried husband Douglas, and prima donna Darnell. Celeste wants vocal career, Douglas gets one instead. Remake of WIFE, HUSBAND, AND FRIEND; Nunnally Johnson adapted his earlier screenplay (based on a James M. Cain story).

Everybody Gets It in the End SEE: **Tag: The Assassination Game**

Everybody's All-American (1988) **C-127m.** *** D: Taylor Hackford. Jessica Lange, Dennis Quaid, Timothy Hutton, John Goodman, Carl Lumbly, Ray Baker, Savannah Smith Boucher, Patricia Clarkson. The twenty-five-year saga of a college football hero and his homecoming queen, who find a rocky road living happily ever after. Quaid seems too aware of the caricature he is about to become, but Lange's bittersweet performance rings true throughout and makes this film worth seeing. Based on Frank Deford's novel. [R]▼●

Everybody's Fine (1990-Italian) **C-112m.** **½ D: Giuseppe Tornatore. Marcello Mastroianni, Michele Morgan, Marino Cenna, Roberto Nobile, Valeria Cavali, Norma Martelli, Fabio Iellini, Salvatore Cascio. Mastroianni is elderly, slightly befuddled Sicilian patriarch who embarks on extended tour of Italy to visit his five grown children. Provocative idea of showing a parent's hopes and dreams dashed by reality; unfortunately, it becomes a lumbering Felliniesque travelogue. Creator of CINEMA PARADISO looks at flip side of nostalgia here with so-so success (and a typically vital Mastroianni performance). Michele Morgan is lovely in small role of woman in tour group.▼●

Everybody Sing (1938) **91m.** ** D: Edwin L. Marin. Allan Jones, Judy Garland, Fanny Brice, Reginald Owen, Billie Burke, Reginald Gardiner. Shrill musical with stupid plot, unmemorable songs; good cast fighting weak material about nutty family involved in putting on a show. After loud finale you'll be waiting for a sequel called EVERYBODY SHUT UP.▼●

Everybody Wins (1990) **C-98m.** BOMB D: Karel Reisz. Debra Winger, Nick Nolte, Will Patton, Jack Warden, Judith Ivey, Kathleen Wilhoite, Frank Converse, Frank Military. Private detective with an ax to grind ties his professional reputation to a schizoid small-town hooker who outbugs Bugs and Daffy. Arthur Miller's first screenplay since THE MISFITS (based on his one-act play "Some Kind of Love Story") gave fruit to this ironically titled fiasco; Winger flounders in a difficult—perhaps even unplayable—role. [R]▼●

Every Day's A Holiday (1937) **80m.** *** D: A. Edward Sutherland. Mae West, Edmund Lowe, Charles Butterworth, Charles Winninger, Walter Catlett, Lloyd Nolan, Louis Armstrong. Mae sells Herman Bing the Brooklyn Bridge, so police detective Lowe orders her to leave N.Y.C. She returns to help expose crooked police chief Nolan. Gay 90s setting for fast-moving West vehicle. ▼

Every Girl Should Be Married (1948) **85m.** **½ D: Don Hartman. Cary Grant, Franchot Tone, Diana Lynn, Betsy Drake, Alan Mowbray. Airy comedy of girl (Drake) setting out to trap bachelor (Grant) into marriage; Tone has thankless "other man" role. Drake also "captured" Grant in real life; they were married soon after this film came out. Also shown in computer-colored version.▼●

Every Home Should Have One SEE: **Think Dirty**

Every Little Crook and Nanny (1972) **C-91m.** ** D: Cy Howard. Lynn Redgrave, Victor Mature, Paul Sand, Austin Pendleton, John Astin, Dom DeLuise, Pat Harrington, Severn Darden. Good idea—the kidnapping of a mobster's son by nanny Redgrave—gets away in this comic crime-and-caper film. One bright spot: Mature's gangster portrayal. [PG]

Every Man a King SEE: **Every Bastard a King**

Every Man for Himself (1980-French-Swiss) **C-87m.** **½ D: Jean-Luc Godard. Isabelle Huppert, Jacques Dutronc, Nathalie Baye, Roland Amstutz, Anna Baldaccini. Self-conscious account of three characters whose lives are intertwined: Dutronc, who has left his wife for Baye; Baye, who is leaving Dutronc for life in the boondocks; and Huppert, country girl turned prostitute. Godard's "comeback" film was widely overrated, and certainly can't compare with his best work of the past.

Every Man for Himself and God Against All (1975-German) **C-110m.** **** D: Werner Herzog. Bruno S., Walter Ladengast, Brigitte Mira, Hans Musaus, Willy Semmelrogge, Michael Kroecher. Man kept in confinement from birth mysteriously appears in 1820s Nuremberg. Poignant tale based on real incident explores his alternate vision of the world and his attempts to adjust to society. Herzog's best film (from his own screenplay) features stunning performance by Bruno S. as Kaspar Hauser. The story also is recounted in KASPAR HAUSER. Aka THE MYSTERY OF KASPAR HAUSER. ▼

Every Man Is My Enemy (1967-Italian) **C-93m.** *½ D: Francesco Prosperi. Robert Webber, Elsa Martinelli, Jean Servais, Martina Berti, Pierre Zimmer. Mafia hitman Webber tries to pull off major diamond heist in Marseilles, with predictable complications. ▼

Every Night at Eight (1935) **81m.** **½ D: Raoul Walsh. George Raft, Alice Faye,

Frances Langford, Patsy Kelly, Herman Bing, Walter Catlett. Forgettable trifle about Faye, Langford, and Kelly singing their way to fame with bandleader Raft. Dorothy Fields-Jimmy McHugh score includes "I Feel a Song Comin' On" and "I'm in the Mood for Love."

Everyone Says I Love You (1996) **C-101m.** *** D: Woody Allen. Woody Allen, Goldie Hawn, Alan Alda, Julia Roberts, Drew Barrymore, Edward Norton, Tim Roth, Natalie Portman, Gaby Hoffmann, Natasha Lyonne, Lukas Haas, Billy Crudup, David Ogden Stiers. The misadventures of an upper-class Manhattan family, at home, in Venice, and in Paris. A cheerful mess that's simply an excuse for Allen to make a musical. The sheer joy of watching the cast sing wonderful old songs (only Barrymore is dubbed) makes up for all the film's shortcomings (including a lack of story, and a curious habit of the camera's wandering away from whoever is singing, for no apparent reason). Everyone seems to be having a good time, and Woody enthusiastically reprises his nebbish persona of yore. The score is brilliantly arranged by Dick Hyman. [R] ▼●◗

Everything But the Truth (1956) **C-83m.** ** D: Jerry Hopper. Maureen O'Hara, John Forsythe, Tim Hovey, Frank Faylen. When youngster Hovey joins truth pledge crusade at school, repercussions to his family and townfolk grow; cutesy.

Everything for Sale (1968-Polish) **C-105m.** *** D: Andrzej Wajda. Beata Tyszkiewicz, Elzbieta Czyzewska, Daniel Olbrychski, Andrzej Lapicki. Not top-drawer Wajda, but still an ambitious, fluidly directed examination of life on a movie set, the relationship between a director and his actors, and what happens when the leading man is accidentally killed. A very personal homage to Zbigniew Cybulski, Wajda's star of the '50s, who died in a freak mishap in 1967.

Everything Happens at Night (1939) **77m.** **½ D: Irving Cummings. Sonja Henie, Ray Milland, Robert Cummings, Maurice Moscovich, Alan Dinehart, Fritz Feld, Jody Gilbert, Victor Varconi. Rival journalists Cummings and Milland come to Swiss village in search of supposedly assassinated "peace leader," but find themselves sidetracked by pert Henie (who gets to do plenty of skiing and ice-skating). Uneven comedy/drama/romance/thriller.▼

Everything I Have Is Yours (1952) **C-92m.** ** D: Robert Z. Leonard. Marge and Gower Champion, Dennis O'Keefe, Eduard Franz. Champions play dance team who finally get Broadway break, only to discover she's pregnant. Mild musical helped by stars' multitalents.▼●

Everything's Ducky (1961) **81m.** ** D: Don Taylor. Mickey Rooney, Buddy Hackett, Jackie Cooper, Roland Winters. Nonsense of Rooney-Hackett teaming up with talking duck, with trio ending up on navy missile orbiting earth; strictly for kids.

Everything You Always Wanted to Know About Sex (But Were Afraid to Ask) (1972) **C-87m.** *** D: Woody Allen. Woody Allen, John Carradine, Lou Jacobi, Louise Lasser, Anthony Quayle, Tony Randall, Lynn Redgrave, Burt Reynolds, Gene Wilder, Jack Barry, Erin Fleming, Robert Q. Lewis, Heather MacRae, Pamela Mason, Sidney Miller, Regis Philbin, Geoffrey Holder, Jay Robinson, Robert Walden. One of Woody's most cinematic comedies, also most uneven, most tasteless. In multi-episode feature based very loosely on Dr. David Reuben's book, only a few segments stand out: final sequence inside male body during intercourse is a gem. [R]▼●

Every Time We Say Goodbye (1986-Israeli) **C-95m.** **½ D: Moshe Mizrahi. Tom Hanks, Cristina Marsillach, Benedict Taylor, Anat Atzmon, Gila Almagor. Hanks' presence adds to this otherwise average soaper-romance, about an American flyer who falls for a Sephardic Jew (Marsillach) in WW2 Jerusalem. [PG-13] ▼●

Every Which Way but Loose (1978) **C-114m.** BOMB D: James Fargo. Clint Eastwood, Sondra Locke, Geoffrey Lewis, Beverly D'Angelo, Ruth Gordon. Clint takes the first pickup truck to Stupidsville, with an orangutan as his best friend, in this bizarre change of pace for the action star. The clumsiest comedy of its year. Sequel: ANY WHICH WAY YOU CAN. [PG]▼●

Eve's Bayou (1997) **C-109m.** *** D: Kasi Lemmons. Jurnee Smollett, Meagan Good, Samuel L. Jackson, Lynn Whitfield, Debbi Morgan, Jake Smollett, Ethel Ayler, Diahann Carroll, Vondie Curtis Hall, Lisa Nicole Carson, Branford Marsalis, Victoria Rowell; narrated by Tamara Tunie. Absorbing tale of a privileged Creole family of the early 1960s, as seen through the eyes of a 10-year-old girl, who learns that her parents have very human frailties . . . and are still susceptible to age-old superstitions and even voodoo. Exceptional cast, led by young Smollett, give credence to the often fanciful story, which is drenched in Southern gothic atmosphere. Impressive writing and directing debut for Lemmons. Costar Jackson was one of the film's producers. [R]▼●◗

Evictors, The (1979) **C-92m.** *½ D: Charles B. Pierce. Michael Parks, Jessica Harper, Vic Morrow, Sue Ane Langdon, Dennis Fimple, Bill Thurman. Couple moves into eerie house, unaware of its violent history. Tired rehash of an all too familiar formula. Panavision. [PG]▼

Evil, The (1978) **C-90m.** **½ D: Gus Trikonis. Richard Crenna, Joanna Pettet,

Andrew Prine, Cassie Yates, Lynne Moody, Victor Buono, George O'Hanlon, Jr. Doctor Crenna rents "haunted" house to use as clinic, but he and associates are violently victimized by powers within. Slow-moving film covers familiar ground; some chills. Laser title: HOUSE OF EVIL. [R]▼●

Evil Dead, The (1983) **C-85m.** **½ D: Sam Raimi. Bruce Campbell, Ellen Sandweiss, Betsy Baker, Hal Delrich, Sarah York. Five kids at mountain cabin chop each other to pieces when demons possess everything. Wildly stylish, ultra-low-budget movie made by precocious college students is one of the grossest horror films ever. Borrowing inspiration from NIGHT OF THE LIVING DEAD, SUSPIRIA, THE EXORCIST and THE HOUSE ON HAUNTED HILL (just to name a few), it provides a deliriously imaginative roller coaster ride for those with strong stomachs. Video version rated R. Followed by two sequels.▼●◗

Evil Dead II (1987) **C-85m.** ** D: Sam Raimi. Bruce Campbell, Sarah Berry, Dan Hicks, Kassie Wesley, Theodore Raimi, Denise Bixler, Richard Domeier. Sequel provides "more of the same" with a similar plot about a cabin in the woods that turns out to be inhabited by evil spirits. Lots of gore and special effects, but at least there's some sense of style and humor. Almost on a par with the original. Followed by ARMY OF DARKNESS. [R]▼●◗

Evil Eye, The (1962-Italian) **92m.** **½ D: Mario Bava. Leticia Roman, John Saxon, Valentina Cortese, Dante Di Paolo. Incredible but enjoyable chiller set in Rome, with Roman involved in a series of unsolved brutal murders.

Evil in the Deep SEE: **Treasure of Jamaica Reef, The**

Evil Mind, The SEE: **Clairvoyant, The**

Evil of Frankenstein (1964-British) **C-84m.** ** D: Freddie Francis. Peter Cushing, Duncan Lamont, Peter Woodthorpe, James Maxwell, Sandor Eles. Dr. F. thaws out his monster, with all-too-predictable consequences in this Hammer Films potboiler, a sequel to REVENGE OF FRANKENSTEIN. 97m. TV print makes matters worse; some scenes have been eliminated; terrible new footage showing frightened villagers has been added; new cast includes Steven Geray, Maria Palmer, William Phipps. Followed by FRANKENSTEIN CREATED WOMAN.▼●

Evil's Bed SEE: **Scandal Sheet** (1985) ▼

Evilspeak (1982) **C-89m.** BOMB D: Eric Weston. Clint Howard, R. G. Armstrong, Joseph Cortese, Claude Earl Jones, Haywood Nelson, Charles Tyner. Orphan Howard, hassled by fellow students at military academy, seeks revenge via black magic. Haven't we seen all this before? [R]▼

Evil That Men Do, The (1984) **C-89m.** *½ D: J. Lee Thompson. Charles Bronson, Theresa Saldana, Joseph Maher, Jose Ferrer, Rene Enriquez, John Glover, Raymond St. Jacques, Antoinette Bower. Typical, violent Bronson entry, with Charlie a professional killer on the trail of a sadistic British doctor (Maher). For Bronson addicts only. [R]▼●

Evil Under the Sun (1982-British) **C-102m.** ** D: Guy Hamilton. Peter Ustinov, Jane Birkin, Colin Blakely, Nicholas Clay, Roddy McDowall, James Mason, Sylvia Miles, Denis Quilley, Diana Rigg, Maggie Smith, Emily Hone. Murder at a resort hotel, with Hercule Poirot (Ustinov) to the rescue. An all-star cast and top production values, but still blah. Based on the Agatha Christie novel, with a script by Anthony Shaffer; exteriors filmed in Majorca. [PG]▼●

Evita (1996) **C-134m.** **½ D: Alan Parker. Madonna, Antonio Banderas, Jonathan Pryce, Jimmy Nail. The world's longest music video: a lavish adaptation of Andrew Lloyd Webber and Tim Rice's 1978 stage musical about the rise of Eva Peron, from her illegitimate childhood to near-deification as First Lady in 1940s Argentina. As pageant, it works, but there is no emotional center, leaving the viewer aloof from its leading character from start to finish. Madonna parades (and sings) well enough, but Pryce's strong presence as Juan Peron and Banderas's fiery singing commentary bring it to life. Newly added song, "You Must Love Me," won an Oscar. 2.35 Research PLC. [PG]▼●◗

Evita Peron (1981) **C-200m. TVM** D: Marvin Chomsky. Faye Dunaway, James Farentino, Rita Moreno, Jose Ferrer, Pedro Armendariz, Jr., Michael Constantine, Signe Hasso, Katy Jurado, Robert Viharo, Jeremy Kemp, John Van Dreelen, Marvin Miller, Virginia Gregg. Dunaway gives a flamboyant portrayal of Argentina's charismatic First Lady, and Farentino (who replaced Robert Mitchum) is interesting as dictator Juan Peron, in this lengthy teleplay by Ronald Harwood. No relation to the Broadway musical, though the film was clearly inspired by its success. Average.

Ewok Adventure, The (1984) **C-100m. TVM** D: John Korty. Eric Walker, Warwick Davis, Fionnula Flanagan, Guy Boyd, Dan Fishman, Debbie Carrington, Burl Ives (narrator). Those furry characters from George Lucas's RETURN OF THE JEDI get their own movie and aid a couple of young space castaways who are searching for their parents. Lucas's maiden TV movie is jam-packed with cinematic wizardry, although it tends to overshadow the story that he wrote. Sequel: EWOKS: THE BATTLE FOR ENDOR. Above average. ▼●

Ewoks: The Battle for Endor (1985) **C-100m. TVM** D: Jim and Ken Wheat.

Wilford Brimley, Warwick Davis, Aubree Miller, Sian Phillips, Carel Struycken, Niki Bothelo, Eric Walker. An old hermit joins a little girl and her cuddly Ewok pal in a search for a nasty witch. Arresting (and expensive) George Lucas sequel to his earlier TV charmer THE EWOK ADVENTURE. Above average.▼●

Excalibur (1981-British) **C-140m.** ***½ D: John Boorman. Nicol Williamson, Nigel Terry, Helen Mirren, Nicholas Clay, Cherie Lunghi, Corin Redgrave, Paul Geoffrey, Patrick Stewart, Gabriel Byrne, Liam Neeson. Eccentric but spellbinding, sexually aware rendition of the King Arthur legend by a stylish filmmaker working at the peak of his powers. Written by Rospo Pallenberg and Boorman. That's the director's son, Charley Boorman, as young Mordred. Magnificent production will lose much on small TV screen. Edited for TV to 119m. [PG]▼●

Excess Baggage (1997) **C-101m.** *½ D: Marco Brambilla. Alicia Silverstone, Benicio Del Toro, Christopher Walken, Nicholas Turturro, Harry Connick, Jr., Sally Kirkland. Predictable story of rich, hostile brat Silverstone trying to get her neglectful father's attention by faking her own kidnapping. She smokes, drinks, and whines her way through this tedious "comedy" in which everybody involved in the convoluted plot is "clueless." [PG-13]▼●◗

Excessive Force (1993) **C-90m.** *½ D: Jon Hess. Thomas Ian Griffith, James Earl Jones, Charlotte Lewis, Lance Henriksen, Burt Young, Tony Todd, W. Earl Brown. Martial arts whiz Griffith wrote this violent tale, and stars as a Chicago cop who's accused of stealing millions and setting up his partners for murder. Very familiar stuff for genre fans, with nothing much to set it apart from dozens of other films languishing on the video shelf. Followed by EXCESSIVE FORCE II: FORCE ON FORCE. [R]▼

Ex-Champ (1939) **64m.** ** D: Phil Rosen. Victor McLaglen, Tom Brown, Nan Grey, Constance Moore. Routine programmer: boxer McLaglen trying to do good deed for son, in dutch with gambling syndicate.

Exclusive (1937) **85m.** **½ D: Alexander Hall. Fred MacMurray, Frances Farmer, Charlie Ruggles, Lloyd Nolan, Fay Holden, Ralph Morgan, Horace McMahon. Lively newspaper story has Farmer joining tabloid in direct competition with her father (Ruggles) and boyfriend (MacMurray), who are also reporters. Uneasy mix of comedy, romance, and melodrama.

Exclusive Story (1936) **75m.** **½ D: George B. Seitz. Franchot Tone, Madge Evans, Stuart Erwin, Joseph Calleia, Robert Barrat, J. Farrell MacDonald, Louise Henry. Fast-paced B-picture with Tone as newspaper attorney trying to get the goods on Calleia and falling in love with Evans.

Excuse My Dust (1951) **C-82m.** **½ D: Roy Rowland. Red Skelton, Sally Forrest, Macdonald Carey, Monica Lewis, William Demarest. Amiable Skelton musicomedy. Red invents automobile which almost costs him his sweetheart; her father owns town livery stable.

Executioner, The (1970-British) **C-107m.** ** D: Sam Wanamaker. Joan Collins, George Peppard, Judy Geeson, Oscar Homolka, Charles Gray, Nigel Patrick, Keith Michell. Pedestrian thriller with British spy Peppard suspecting that colleague Michell is a double agent. Panavision. [PG]▼

Executioner, Part II, The (1984) **C-85m.** BOMB D: James Bryant. Christopher Mitchum, Aldo Ray, Antoine John Mottet, Renee Harmon. Amateurish actioner, atrociously directed and acted, with homicide cop Mitchum hunting down a vigilante murderer. Has no connection to any other EXECUTIONER title. [R]▼

Executioner's Song, The (1982) **C-200m. TVM** D: Lawrence Schiller. Tommy Lee Jones, Rosanna Arquette, Christine Lahti, Eli Wallach, Jordan Clark, Steven Keats, Richard Venture, Michael LeClair, Walter Olkewicz. Jones' electrifying, Emmy-winning portrayal of convicted killer Gary Gilmore and his efforts to get the state of Utah to carry out his death sentence in 1977 keeps this lengthy film sizzling. Equally as torrid: Arquette's erotic portrait of Gilmore's jailbait girlfriend, Nicole Baker. Norman Mailer adapted his own best seller. A 97m. version, originally released to theaters in Europe, contains some nudity. Originally shown in two parts. Above average.▼

Execution of Private Slovik, The (1974) **C-120m. TVM** D: Lamont Johnson. Martin Sheen, Mariclare Costello, Ned Beatty, Gary Busey, Matt Clark, Ben Hammer, Charles Haid. Solid drama enhanced by Sheen's beautiful performance as Eddie Slovik, the only American soldier since the Civil War to be executed for desertion (in 1945). Thoughtful, literate adaptation by Richard Levinson and William Link of William Bradford Huie's controversial book. Above average.▼

Executive Action (1973) **C-91m.** BOMB D: David Miller. Burt Lancaster, Robert Ryan, Will Geer, Gilbert Green, John Anderson, Ed Lauter, Sidney Clute, Lloyd Gough, Dick Miller. Excruciatingly dull thriller promised to clear the air about JFK's assassination but was more successful at clearing theaters. Scripted by Dalton Trumbo. Ryan's last film. [PG]▼●

Executive Decision (1996) **C-132m.** *** D: Stuart Baird. Kurt Russell, Steven Seagal, Halle Berry, John Leguizamo, Oliver Platt, Joe Morton, David Suchet, Len Cariou, Mary Ellen Trainor, Marla Maples Trump, J. T. Walsh, Nicholas Pryor, B. D. Wong. The situation: Arab terrorists are in control of a 747.

The solution: *Sneak* an elite team aboard the plane, already in flight. The problems: The team has to depend on inexperienced Russell, and there's a nerve gas bomb aboard that will wipe out Washington, D.C. Tense, inventive thriller that—until a misfired final reel—delivers the goods in high style. Directing debut for top editor Baird, who might have tightened the story a bit. Panavision. [R]▼●◗

Executive Suite (1954) **104m.** *** D: Robert Wise. William Holden, June Allyson, Barbara Stanwyck, Fredric March, Walter Pidgeon, Louis Calhern, Shelley Winters, Paul Douglas, Nina Foch, Dean Jagger. Slick, multifaceted story of company power struggle with top cast, from Cameron Hawley novel . . . though similar film PATTERNS is much better. Later a TV series.▼●

Exile, The (1947) **95m.** **½ D: Max Ophuls. Douglas Fairbanks, Jr., Maria Montez, Paule Croset (Rita Corday), Henry Daniell, Nigel Bruce, Robert Coote. OK swashbuckler with exiled king Fairbanks falling in love with common girl; guest appearance by Montez.

eXistenZ (1999-Canadian-British) **C-97m.** ** D: David Cronenberg. Jennifer Jason Leigh, Jude Law, Willem Dafoe, Ian Holm, Don McKellar, Callum Keith Rennie, Sarah Polley, Christopher Eccleston. Preposterous film set in the near future about a virtual-reality game designer who gets trapped in one of her own games with a man who's supposed to be protecting her. At one point they wonder how to get out of the game; it's much easier to get out of the movie. Cronenberg also scripted this silly concoction. ▼●◗

Exit to Eden (1994) **C-113m.** *½ D: Garry Marshall. Dana Delany, Paul Mercurio, Rosie O'Donnell, Dan Aykroyd, Hector Elizondo, Stuart Wilson, Iman, Sean O'Bryan, Stephanie Niznik, Rosemary Forsyth, Donna Dixon, John Schneider. Strange cinematic catastrophe, pried from an Anne Rice novel, attempts to jerry-build a standard cop sitcom (Aykroyd and O'Donnell investigate a murder) onto the sexual shenanigans at S&M island fantasy camp. O'Donnell's bright performance is the one justification for its existence. If anything, resembles a raunchier version of Marshall's old TV show *Love, American Style.* [R]▼●

Ex-Lady (1933) **65m.** **½ D: Robert Florey. Bette Davis, Gene Raymond, Frank McHugh, Claire Dodd, Ferdinand Gottschalk. Davis, looking sensational, plays an independent-minded woman who loves Raymond but doesn't believe in marriage. Provocative and sexy, stylishly filmed, but begins to drag and become conventional by the second half. A remake of ILLICIT, filmed just two years earlier!▼

Ex-Mrs. Bradford, The (1936) **80m.** *** D: Stephen Roberts. William Powell, Jean Arthur, James Gleason, Eric Blore, Robert Armstrong. Chic à la THIN MAN comedy-mystery, with Powell teaming with ex-wife Arthur to crack a case.▼●

Exodus (1960) **C-213m.** *** D: Otto Preminger. Paul Newman, Eva Marie Saint, Ralph Richardson, Peter Lawford, Lee J. Cobb, Sal Mineo, John Derek, Hugh Griffith, Gregory Ratoff, Felix Aylmer, Jill Haworth, David Opatoshu, Marius Goring, George Maharis. Leon Uris' sprawling history of Palestinian war for liberation becomes sporadic action epic. Newman as Israeli resistance leader, Saint as non-Jewish army nurse aren't a convincing duo; supporting roles offer stereotypes. Best scene shows refugees escaping Cyprus detention center, running British blockade into homeland. Ernest Gold won an Oscar for his score. Super Panavision 70.▼●

Exorcist, The (1973) **C-121m.** ***½ D: William Friedkin. Ellen Burstyn, Max von Sydow, Linda Blair, Jason Miller, Lee J. Cobb, Kitty Winn, Jack MacGowran. Intense, well-mounted adaptation of William Peter Blatty's best-seller, calculated to keep your stomach in knots from start to finish. Blair is "normal" 12-year-old whose body is possessed by the Devil, Miller a troubled priest who attempts to confront the demon in her—and in himself. Oscar winner for Blatty's screenplay; vocal effects by Mercedes McCambridge. Followed by two sequels and countless imitations. Reissued in 2000 with 11m. of additional footage. [R]▼●◗

Exorcist II: The Heretic (1977) **C-110m.** *½ D: John Boorman. Richard Burton, Linda Blair, Louise Fletcher, Kitty Winn, James Earl Jones, Ned Beatty, Max von Sydow. Preposterous sequel to 1973 hit. Special effects are only virtue in this turkey about priest (Burton) trying to unravel mystery of demon still living inside Blair. Boorman recut the film (from 117m.) the day after its premiere, and made numerous changes—to no avail. Restored to 117m. for homevideo. [R]▼

Exorcist III, The (1990) **C-110m.** ** D: William Peter Blatty. George C. Scott, Ed Flanders, Brad Dourif, Jason Miller, Nicol Williamson, Scott Wilson, Nancy Fish, George DiCenzo, Viveca Lindfors. Police inspector Scott is confronted by a series of gruesome murders, unmistakably the work of a serial killer who was executed the same night as the exorcism of the original movie. Film begins well but grows more absurd and confusing until it self-destructs. Shows strong evidence of post-production tinkering. [R]▼●

Exotica (1994-Canadian) **C-104m.** **½ D: Atom Egoyan. Bruce Greenwood, Mia Kirshner, Don McKellar, Arsinee Khanjian, Elias Koteas, Sarah Polley, Victor Garber, David Hemblen. Five disparate characters become linked to each other's destinies, with a strip club called Exotica as the focal point. Only at the end of the film do we fully learn the "back story" that brought two key characters into each other's lives. Intriguing, like all of Egoyan's work, but not entirely satisfying. Winner of the Genie Award as Canada's Best Picture of 1994. [R]▼●

Experience Preferred . . . but Not Essential (1983-British) **C-80m.** *** D: Peter Duffell. Elizabeth Edmonds, Sue Wallace, Geraldine Griffith, Karen Meagher, Ron Bain, Alun Lewis, Robert Blythe. Simple, charming little film about a girl's experiences working as waitress for the summer at seaside resort hotel. June Roberts' script focuses on the blossoming of one young woman, while making humorous observations about the offbeat group of people around her. Short and sweet; made for British TV. [PG]▼

Experiment in Terror (1962) **123m.** *** D: Blake Edwards. Glenn Ford, Lee Remick, Stefanie Powers, Ross Martin, Roy Poole, Ned Glass. Taut suspense with bank clerk Remick terrorized by murderous extortionist Martin . . . but FBI agent Ford is on the case. Realistic, unsentimental, with convincing performances by Remick and Martin. Great Henry Mancini score, good use of San Francisco locations.▼●

Experiment Perilous (1944) **91m.** ** D: Jacques Tourneur. Hedy Lamarr, George Brent, Paul Lukas, Albert Dekker, Margaret Wycherly, Julia Dean. Static melodrama in the GASLIGHT tradition, with doctor Brent coming to the aid of—and falling in love with—fearful Lamarr, who's being terrorized by crazed husband Lukas.▼

Experts, The (1989) **C-83m.** ** D: Dave Thomas. John Travolta, Arye Gross, Charles Martin Smith, Kelly Preston, Deborah Foreman, James Keach, Jan Rubes, Brian Doyle-Murray, Rick Ducommun. Fatally bland comedy about two Manhattan hipsters who are hired to open a nightclub in a small Nebraska town—which is really an exact replica of the hamlet built in the U.S.S.R. and used to train Russian spies. Weak in all respects, and peculiarly sentimental about the 1950s. Barely released to theaters. Costars Travolta and Preston later married. [PG-13]▼●

Explorers (1985) **C-109m.** ** D: Joe Dante. Ethan Hawke, River Phoenix, Jason Presson, Amanda Peterson, Dick Miller, Robert Picardo, Dana Ivey, Meshach Taylor, Mary Kay Place. Youngster hooked on science-fiction yearns to travel into space and gets his wish, with the help of a whiz-kid friend. Opens beautifully, takes its time developing story—then makes disastrous wrong turn in space that transforms film into a shaggy-dog joke! Director Dante has restructured film somewhat for cable TV and homevideo release. That version is 107m. [PG]▼●

Explosion (1969-Canadian) **C-96m.** *½ D: Jules Bricken. Don Stroud, Richard Conte, Gordon Thomson, Michele Chicoine, Cecil Linder, Robin Ward. Teenager haunted by his brother's death in Vietnam goes to Canada to avoid the draft, but drifts into crime instead. Heavy-handed melodrama. [PG—edited from original R rating]▼

Explosive Generation, The (1961) **89m.** ** D: Buzz Kulik. William Shatner, Patty McCormack, Billy Gray, Steve Dunne, Lee Kinsolving, Virginia Field, Phillip Terry, Edward Platt, Beau Bridges. High school teacher Shatner causes an uproar when he has his students write essays on their attitudes about sex. Based-on-fact account is an intriguing relic of its era (both for its subject and cast).

Exposed (1983) **C-100m.** *½ D: James Toback. Nastassia Kinski, Rudolf Nureyev, Harvey Keitel, Ian McShane, Bibi Andersson, Ron Randell, Pierre Clementi, James Russo. Girl from the Midwest quits school, comes to N.Y.C., hits it big as a fashion model, then gets involved with enigmatic Nureyev and his plan to kill terrorist Keitel in Paris. Seems like three different movies—all of them strange. Nureyev's performance might best be described as overripe. That's writer-director Toback in the role of Kinski's professor/lover. [R]▼

Exposure (1991-Brazilian) **C-100m.** ** D: Walter Salles, Jr. Peter Coyote, Tcheky Karyo, Amanda Pays, Raul Cortez, Giulia Gam, Cassia Kiss. Slick but corny, overbaked thriller about pompously poetic American photographer (Coyote), living in Rio de Janeiro, who becomes immersed in a seamy, violent underworld (and undergoes quite a personality change), searching for killer of young prostitute. [R]▼●

Expresso Bongo (1959-British) **108m.** **½ D: Val Guest. Laurence Harvey, Sylvia Syms, Yolande Donlan, Cliff Richard, Ambrosine Phillpotts, Eric Pohlmann, Hermione Baddeley, Wilfrid Lawson, Kenneth Griffith, Susan Hampshire. Atmospheric but dated drama with Harvey shining as a high-energy, jive-spouting London hustler who thinks he's found his version of Elvis in poor young bongo-playing rocker Richard. Written by Wolf Mankowitz. DyaliScope.▼

Exterminating Angel, The (1962-Mexican) **95m.** ***½ D: Luis Buñuel. Silvia Pinal, Enrique Rambal, Jacqueline Andere, Jose Baviera, Augusto Benedico. Guests at elegant dinner party cannot bring themselves to leave, begin to starve and die after several days. Wry assault on bourgeois manners by master surrealist Buñuel.▼

Exterminator, The (1980) **C-101m.** BOMB D: James Glickenhaus. Christopher George, Samantha Eggar, Robert Ginty, Steve James, Tony Di Benedetto.

Gore galore with Vietnam veteran Ginty aping Charles Bronson in DEATH WISH as he rubs out a gang who mugged and paralyzed a friend. If you love this film, good news—there's a sequel! Unrated director's cut runs 104m. [R]▼●◗

Exterminator II (1984) **C-88m.** BOMB D: Mark Buntzman. Robert Ginty, Mario Van Peebles, Deborah Geffner, Frankie Faison, Scott Randolph, Arye Gross, John Turturro. Ginty and his blowtorch are back, hot after a gang whose most sadistic member is named X. Obnoxious, grade Z garbage. [R]▼

Extra Girl, The (1923) **69m.** **½ D: F. Richard Jones. Mabel Normand, Ralph Graves, George Nichols, Anna Hernandez, Vernon Dent. Mack Sennett silent feature is far from prime, but still has its moments, thanks to classic comedienne Normand and an obliging lion. Dramatic interludes in Hollywood rags-to-riches saga don't really work.▼●

Extraordinary Seaman, The (1969) **C-80m.** BOMB D: John Frankenheimer. David Niven, Faye Dunaway, Alan Alda, Mickey Rooney, Juano Hernandez, Jack Carter, Manu Tupou, Barry Kelley. Extraordinarily muddled "comedy" of eccentric Niven piloting long-lost abandoned ship during WW2; shows signs of tampering from original conception of film. Barely received theatrical release. Only highpoints: clips from 1940s newsreels and Faye's eye makeup. Panavision. [G]

Extreme Adventures of Super Dave, The (2000) **C-91m.** ** D: Peter MacDonald. Super Dave Osborne (Bob Einstein), Dan Hedaya, Gia Carides, Steve Van Wormer, Art Irizawa, Don Lake, Carl Michael Lindner, Ray Charles. Daredevil ace Super Dave (a kind of live-action Wile E. Coyote) faces his ultimate challenge; heavy-handed feature-length extension of the cable TV series. Einstein also coscripted. Mike Connors appears unbilled as Super Dave's grandfather. Made for theaters in 1998, released on video instead. [PG]▼◗

Extreme Close-Up (1973) **C-80m.** *½ D: Jeannot Szwarc. James McMullan, James A. Watson, Jr., Kate Woodville, Bara Byrnes, Al Checco, Antony Carbone. Ludicrous drama about snoopers and snooping equipment has topicality working for it, but that's all. Michael Crichton scripted; retitled SEX THROUGH A WINDOW. [R]▼

Extreme Justice (1993) **C-105m.** ** D: Mark L. Lester. Lou Diamond Phillips, Scott Glenn, Chelsea Field, Yaphet Kotto, Ed Lauter, Andrew Divoff, William Lucking. Renegade cop finds himself caught in the crossfire after being recruited into a secret police unit that dispenses its own justice on the mean streets of L.A. Violence for violence's sake seems to be the theme of this theatrical film that premiered on cable. [R]▼●

Extreme Measures (1996) **C-118m.** ** D: Michael Apted. Hugh Grant, Gene Hackman, Sarah Jessica Parker, David Morse, Bill Nunn, John Toles-Bey, Paul Guilfoyle, Debra Monk, J. K. Simmons. Emergency room doctor senses something fishy going on after a man who dies mysteriously vanishes from the hospital's records. Medical conspiracy thriller starts out well enough but quickly becomes obvious and hollow. Grant has one of his best parts as a dedicated doctor; his girlfriend Elizabeth Hurley produced the film. Director David Cronenberg plays the head of a medical review board. Panavision. [R]▼●◗

Extreme Prejudice (1987) **C-104m.** ** D: Walter Hill. Nick Nolte, Powers Boothe, Michael Ironside, Maria Conchita Alonso, Rip Torn, Clancy Brown, William Forsythe, Larry B. Scott. Boyhood friends Nolte and Boothe are now on opposite sides of the law, as Texas Ranger and drug kingpin on the Texas/Mexico border. Though its excesses (in characterization, music, and especially violence) are apparently deliberate, that doesn't make them any more entertaining . . . though it helps if you accept it as tongue-in-cheek. [R]▼●

Extremities (1986) **C-89m.** *½ D: Robert M. Young. Farrah Fawcett, James Russo, Diana Scarwid, Alfre Woodard. A woman is victimized by a taunting rapist in her own home but manages to turn the tables and trap him. William Mastrosimone adapted his own play, but what worked in a theater doesn't translate to film; Fawcett's adequate but one-note performance is another liability. [R]▼●

Eye Creatures, The (1965) **80m.** *½ D: Larry Buchanan. John Ashley, Cynthia Hull, Warren Hammack, Chet Davis, Bill Peck. Gory horror film about title creatures and the intrepid band that tries to fight them off. Remake of INVASION OF THE SAUCER MEN. Retitled on some cheapo TV prints as ATTACK OF THE THE EYE CREATURES (sic).▼

Eye for an Eye, An (1966) **C-92m.** ** D: Michael Moore. Robert Lansing, Pat Wayne, Slim Pickens, Gloria Talbott. Oater with twist: two physically disabled men, who can function via teamwork as one sharpshooter, hunt down killers of older man's family. Video title: TALION.▼

Eye for an Eye, An (1981) **C-106m.** ** D: Steve Carver. Chuck Norris, Christopher Lee, Richard Roundtree, Matt Clark, Mako, Maggie Cooper, Terry Kiser. Cop Norris's partner is killed by drug traffickers; he has nightmares, becomes a one-man army seeking vengeance against villain Lee and his cronies. Silly and predictable, but delivers for formula fans. [R]▼

Eye for an Eye (1996) **C-101m.** ** D: John

Schlesinger. Sally Field, Ed Harris, Kiefer Sutherland, Joe Mantegna, Beverly D'Angelo, Olivia Burnette, Alexandra Kyle, Darrell Larsen, Charlayne Woodard, Philip Baker Hall, Keith David, Natalija Nogulich, Armin Shimerman. When Field's teenage daughter is brutally raped and murdered, she seeks revenge on the creep who did it. Field is ideally cast as the mother driven to take the law into her own hands, but this is little more than DEATH WISH in drag, a manipulative movie that becomes awfully far-fetched. What's more, those attack scenes are very tough to take. [R] ▼●

Eye of the Beholder (1999-British-Canadian) **C-109m.** *½ D: Stephan Elliott. Ewan McGregor, Ashley Judd, Jason Priestley, k.d. lang, Patrick Bergin, Genevieve Bujold. Terrible but oddly watchable mess with high-tech private eye McGregor tailing sexy serial killer Judd around the U.S.—and falling in love with her in the process. Plays like a voyeuristic music video. U.S. release runs 101m. Super 35. [R]▼◗

Eye of the Cat (1969) **C-102m.** **½ D: David Lowell Rich. Michael Sarrazin, Gayle Hunnicutt, Eleanor Parker, Tim Henry, Laurence Naismith. Glossy but intriguing suspenser with seductive Hunnicutt teaming with Sarrazin to murder his aunt (Parker), who keeps a houseful of felines. Most terrifying scene has wheelchaired Parker tottering atop a San Francisco hill. Important note: new scenes were added for network TV showing to make it "less intense." Rating based on original. [M/PG]

Eye of the Devil (1967-British) **92m.** **½ D: J. Lee Thompson. Deborah Kerr, David Niven, Donald Pleasence, Edward Mulhare, Flora Robson, Emlyn Williams, Sharon Tate, David Hemmings, John Le Mesurier. Excellent cast in odd, low-key thriller set in France. The Marquis de Bellac (Niven) abruptly leaves wife in Paris to "do what he must" at ancestral estate near Bordeaux. Strange continuity due to cuts before initial release. Also titled: 13.

Eye of the Needle (1981) **C-112m.** *** D: Richard Marquand. Donald Sutherland, Kate Nelligan, Ian Bannen, Christopher Cazenove, Philip Martin Brown. Solid WW2 spy saga from Ken Follett's best-seller. Sutherland plays a super-cool German agent temporarily stranded on an island off the British coast, where he meets a lonely, sexually frustrated woman. [R] ▼●◗

Eye of the Storm (1991-German-U.S.) **C-94m.** *½ D: Yuri Zeltser. Craig Sheffer, Bradley Gregg, Lara Flynn Boyle, Leon Rippy, Dennis Hopper. After their parents are brutally murdered, and one of the boys is blinded, two brothers take over operation of the family's motel in a desolate location. When Boyle and Hopper rent a room, unsettling truths begin to emerge. Would-be thriller is tedious until the last ten minutes. Super 35. [R] ▼●

Eye of the Tiger (1986) **C-90m.** *½ D: Richard Sarafian. Gary Busey, Yaphet Kotto, Seymour Cassel, Bert Remsen, William Smith, Kimberlin Ann Brown, Denise Galik, Judith Barsi. Ex-con Busey's town is invaded by Hells Angels types, who sadistically murder his wife . . . so he goes on a one-man crusade for revenge. Sound familiar? [R]▼●

Eye on the Sparrow (1987) **C-100m. TVM** D: John Korty. Mare Winningham, Keith Carradine, Conchata Ferrell, Sandy McPeak, Kaaren Lee, Bianca Rose. Determined blind couple take on the establishment in a battle to adopt a child. Based-on-fact drama, well played by the two leads, written by Barbara Turner. Above average.▼

Eyes in the Night (1942) **80m.** **½ D: Fred Zinnemann. Ann Harding, Edward Arnold, Donna Reed, Stephen McNally, Reginald Denny, Rosemary DeCamp, Mantan Moreland, Barry Nelson. Above-par mystery with Arnold as blind detective Duncan McClain helping Reed and Harding. The dog steals the picture. Director Zinnemann's feature film debut.

Eyes of an Angel (1994) **C-91m.** *½ D: Robert Harmon. John Travolta, Ellie Raab, Tito Larriva, Jeffrey DeMunn. When single parent Travolta and his daughter flee from the mobsters who threaten him, the fight dog she secretly nursed back to health makes a preposterous cross country trip to find her. Much too violent for kids, too boring and absurd for adults. It sat on a shelf for four years; only released after Travolta's PULP FICTION success. Original title: THE TENDER. Panavision. [PG-13]▼●

Eyes of a Stranger (1981) **C-85m.** BOMB. D: Ken Wiederhorn. Lauren Tewes, Jennifer Jason Leigh, John DiSanti, Peter DuPre, Gwen Lewis. Overweight creep DiSanti rapes and kills women, and the blood flows like wine; Tewes tracks him down, while her deaf, dumb, and blind sister (Leigh) is established as a potential victim. Utter trash. Leigh's film debut. [R]▼

Eyes of Hell (1961-Canadian) **83m.** *½ D: Julian Roffman. Paul Stevens, Claudette Nevins, Bill Walker, Anne Collings, Martin Lavut, Jim Moran. Low-budget shocker—with 3-D sequences—about an ancient Aztec mask that causes wearer to hallucinate and murder. 3-D scenes were put together by famed montage expert Slavko Vorkapich. Originally released as THE MASK.▼●

Eyes of Laura Mars (1978) **C-103m.** **½ D: Irvin Kershner. Faye Dunaway,

Tommy Lee Jones, Brad Dourif, Rene Auberjonois, Raul Julia, Frank Adonis, Darlanne Fluegel, Rose Gregorio, Michael Tucker. A high-fashion photographer has frightening premonitions of grisly murders; some genuine suspense, lots of red herrings, and a silly resolution add up to an OK thriller but Dunaway's kinky colleagues and their lifestyles are a real turnoff. John Carpenter cowrote. [R]▼●◗

Eyes of the Amaryllis, The (1982) **C-84m.** ** D: Frederick King Keller. Ruth Ford, Martha Byrne, Jonathan Bolt, Guy Boyd, Katharine Houghton. Young Byrne visits beachhouse of "mad" grandmother Ford, who awaits sign from her husband who was lost at sea 30 years before. Well-intentioned but slow-paced, uninvolving adaptation of Natalie Babbitt's story. Filmed on Nantucket Island.▼

Eyes of the Underworld (1943) **61m.** **½ D: Roy William Neill. Richard Dix, Wendy Barrie, Lon Chaney (Jr.), Lloyd Corrigan, Don Porter, Billy Lee, Marc Lawrence. Police chief Dix is on the spot when mobster uncovers his old prison record; good crime story.

Eyes, the Mouth, The (1982-Italian-French) **C-100m.** ** D: Marco Bellocchio. Lou Castel, Angela Molina, Emmanuele Riva, Michel Piccoli, Antonio Piovanelli. Dreary, pretentious pap about the effect of a man's suicide on his actor-brother (Castel), mother (Riva) and pregnant lover (Molina). At one point Castel and Molina see FIST IN HIS POCKET, also directed by Bellocchio and starring Castel. We suggest the viewer do the same. [R]▼

Eyes Wide Shut (1999) **C-154m.** *** D: Stanley Kubrick. Tom Cruise, Nicole Kidman, Sydney Pollack, Marie Richardson, Todd Field, Lisa Leone, Thomas Gibson, Vinessa Shaw, Rade Sherbedgia, Leelee Sobieski, Alan Cumming, Fay Masterson. Affluent, happily married N.Y.C. doctor starts to come apart after his wife admits to having had a potent sexual fantasy about a man she never met. This leads the husband to foray into a world of sexual adventure for the first time in his life. Provocative film takes place in a distinctive Kubrick environment—contained, almost claustrophobic at times. Overlong, and flawed, but still compelling, with two megawatt star performances. Nudity is plentiful, but the European version is even more graphic. Screenplay by Kubrick and Frederic Raphael from a 1926 Arthur Schnitzler novel. Kubrick's final film. [R] ▼●◗

Eyes Without a Face SEE: **Horror Chamber of Dr. Faustus, The**

Eye Witness (1950-British) **104m.** **½ D: Robert Montgomery. Robert Montgomery, Felix Aylmer, Leslie Banks, Michael Ripper, Patricia Wayne (Cutts). Unpretentious yarn of American attorney Montgomery in London to defend friend accused of homicide, coping with contrasting British legal system while hunting title figure. Originally titled YOUR WITNESS.▼

Eyewitness (1970) SEE: **Sudden Terror**

Eyewitness (1981) **C-102m.** ** D: Peter Yates. William Hurt, Sigourney Weaver, Christopher Plummer, James Woods, Irene Worth, Kenneth McMillan, Pamela Reed, Steven Hill, Morgan Freeman. Slick but unsatisfying thriller about a building janitor who uses his second-hand knowledge of an unsolved murder to get close to a female TV news reporter with whom he's been infatuated. Steve Tesich's script is needlessly cluttered with minor characters and story twists. [R]▼●

Fabiola (1948-Italian-French) **96m.** *** D: Alessandro Blasetti. Michele Morgan, Michel Simon, Henri Vidal, Massimo Girotti, Louis Salou, Gino Cervi. Confusing but impressive epic of persecution against Christians in 4th-century Rome. Simon is the powerful, forward-thinking Fabius Severus; Morgan is Fabiola, his cavalier offspring; Vidal is Rhual, steadfast Christian gladiator. Originally released in Europe at 150m.; English-dubbed version, adapted by Marc Connelly and Fred Pressburger and featuring an altogether different storyline, opened in the U.S. in 1951.▼

Fabulous Baker Boys, The (1989) **C-113m.** **½ D: Steve Kloves. Jeff Bridges, Michelle Pfeiffer, Beau Bridges, Ellie Raab, Jennifer Tilly. Two brothers' fifteen-year partnership as a twin-piano nightclub lounge act is shaken by the addition of a feisty (and sexy) singer, who sparks changes in their act—and their relationship. Writer Kloves' directing debut is stylish and self-assured, with some great scenes and set-pieces, but it skimps on story—and never really fleshes out Jeff Bridges' sullen character. The real-life Bridges brothers are perfectly cast, Pfeiffer is ideal. Her steamy rendition of "Makin' Whoopee" atop piano considered a minor classic. [R]▼●◗

Fabulous Baron Munchausen, The (1961-Czech) **C-84m.** **½ D: Karel Zeman. Milos Kopecky, Jana Brejchova, Rudolph Jelinek, Jan Werich. Filmmaker Zeman (FABULOUS WORLD OF JULES VERNE) provides another visual delight here, but his episodic fantasy—which takes his hero from the inside of a whale to the surface of the moon—is stilted and uninvolving. Aka THE ORIGINAL FABULOUS ADVENTURES OF BARON MUNCHAUSEN.▼●

Fabulous Dorseys, The (1947) **88m.** ** D: Alfred E. Green. Tommy Dorsey, Jimmy Dorsey, Janet Blair, Paul Whiteman, William Lundigan. Limp "biography" of bandleading brothers, constantly arguing in between "Marie," "Green Eyes," and other hit songs. Musical highlight: a jam session with Art Tatum, Charlie Barnet, Ziggy Elman and Ray Bauduc.▼●

Fabulous Joe, The (1947) **C-60m.** ** D: Bernard Carr, Harve Foster. Marie Wilson, Walter Abel, Margot Grahame, Donald Meek. Abel is typecast in this segment from THE HAL ROACH COMEDY CARNIVAL. He's harassed husband who gains moral support from talking dog.▼

Fabulous Suzanne, The (1946) **71m.** ** D: Steve Sekely. Barbara Britton, Rudy Vallee, Otto Kruger, Richard Denning, Veda Ann Borg. Fair potential of romantic story of woman who has more luck at horses than with men doesn't come across, due to script and indifferent acting.

Fabulous World of Jules Verne, The (1958-Czech) **83m.** **½ D: Karel Zeman. Lubor Tolos, Arnost Navratil, Miroslav Holub, Zatloukalova. Zeman's ingenious visual effects, reproducing the look of 19th century engravings, outshine leaden enactment of fanciful sci-fi story by Verne. Released here in 1961 with Americanized names in credits and pointless introduction by Hugh Downs.▼

Face at the Window, The (1939-British) **65m.** **½ D: George King. Tod Slaughter, Marjorie Taylor, John Warwick, Robert Adair, Harry Terry. A fiendish killer known as "The Wolf" strikes terror in 1880s Paris. Who can it be? Surely not the Chevalier del Gardo (Slaughter), respected nobleman! And who is the hideous, drooling face at the window? Charming, well-produced blood-and-thunder melodrama, based on the frequently filmed play by F. Brooke Warren. The blessedly hammy Slaughter is in great form here.▼

Face Behind the Mask, The (1941) **69m.** *** D: Robert Florey. Peter Lorre, Evelyn Keyes, Don Beddoe, George E. Stone, John Tyrell. Model B film of immigrant Lorre having face disfigured in fire, donning mask, bitterly turning to life of crime. Extremely well done on slim budget.

Face in the Crowd, A (1957) **125m.** ***½ D: Elia Kazan. Andy Griffith, Patricia Neal, Anthony Franciosa, Walter Matthau, Lee Remick, Kay Medford. Perceptive script by Budd Schulberg about homespun hobo (Griffith) discovered by Neal and promoted into successful TV star. Cast gives life to fascinating story. Film debuts of Griffith and Remick. Look for young Rip Torn and Lois Nettleton. Many celebrities also appear as themselves, including Burl Ives, Mike Wallace, Betty Furness, Bennett Cerf, Faye Emerson, and Walter Winchell.▼

Face in the Rain, A (1963) **91m.** **½ D: Irvin Kershner. Rory Calhoun, Marina Berti, Niall MacGinnis, Massimo Giuliani. At times tense melodrama of Calhoun, U.S. spy, being hidden in Italy by partisan whose wife has been associating with Axis.▼

Face of a Fugitive (1959) **C-81m.** ** D: Paul Wendkos. Fred MacMurray, Lin McCarthy, Dorothy Green, James Coburn, Alan Baxter, Myrna Fahey. OK Western about MacMurray forced to start over again in a new town when he's falsely accused of murder; his past still haunts him.

Face of a Stranger (1991) **C-100m. TVM** D: Claudia Weill. Tyne Daly, Gena Rowlands, Harris Yulin, Cynthia Nixon, Kevin Tighe, Seymour Cassel. Shining performances by Rowlands as an upscale socialite suddenly left penniless when her husband drops dead and Daly as a homeless woman living across the street in a cardboard box. The common thread between them is beautifully woven by playwright Marsha Norman in her adaptation of Mary Stuart's *New York* magazine article. Above average.

Face/Off (1997) **C-138m.** *** D: John Woo. John Travolta, Nicolas Cage, Joan Allen, Alessandro Nivola, Gina Gershon, Dominique Swain, Nick Cassavetes, Colm Feore, John Carroll Lynch, CCH Pounder, Margaret Cho, Jamie Denton. Two thirds of a terrific movie: Federal agent Travolta agrees to have a heinous criminal's face grafted onto his own, in order to fool the no-good's brother into spilling vital information. But the daring plan goes awry in more ways than one. Travolta and Cage are charismatically over the top, and Woo's staging of action scenes is powerfully good . . . but the film doesn't know when to stop. Silly plotting and dialogue might have been overlooked in a tighter film. Panavision. [R] ▼●◗

Face of Fire (1959) **83m.** *** D: Albert Band. Cameron Mitchell, James Whitmore, Bettye Ackerman, Royal Dano, Robert Simon, Richard Erdman. Unique adaptation of Stephen Crane short story *The Monster* about man disfigured while saving child from fire. Uneven cast, good direction.

Face of Fu Manchu, The (1965-British) **C-96m.** *** D: Don Sharp. Christopher Lee, Nigel Green, James Robertson Justice, Howard Marion-Crawford, Tsai Chin, Walter Rilla. First of new series with Emperor Fu bent on conquering West. Great 1920s atmosphere, good international cast. Followed by THE BRIDES OF FU MANCHU. Techniscope.▼

Face of Marble (1946) **70m.** ** D: William Beaudine. John Carradine, Claudia Drake, Robert Shayne, Maris Wrixon. Another mad doctor with new technique for bringing dead back to life. Carradine is good, others less impressive.

Face of the Frog (1959-German) **92m.** **

D: Harold Reinl. Joachim Fuchsberger, Fritz Rasp, Siegfied Lowitz, Joachen Brochmann. Lowitz is Inspector Elk tracking down the "Frog" in this routine Edgar Wallace actioner; serial-like techniques utilized. Retitled: FELLOWSHIP OF THE FROG.▼

Faces (1968) **130m.** ***½ D: John Cassavetes. John Marley, Gena Rowlands, Lynn Carlin, Seymour Cassel, Fred Draper, Val Avery. Highly personal drama about assorted infidelities is one of the few Cassavetes films to make it with general public. Powerful film with great acting, especially by Carlin and Cassel. [R]▼●◗

Face That Launched a Thousand Ships, The SEE: **Loves of Three Queens**

Face to Face (1952) **92m.** **½ D: John Brahm, Bretaigne Windust. James Mason, Michael Pate, Robert Preston, Marjorie Steele. Quiet two-part film: Joseph Conrad's "Secret Sharer" faithfully filmed with Mason as captain, Pate as fugitive; Stephen Crane's "Bride Comes to Yellow Sky" bland with Preston bringing bride Steele out West.▼

Face to Face (1976-Swedish) **C-136m.** *** D: Ingmar Bergman. Liv Ullmann, Erland Josephson, Gunnar Bjornstrand, Aino Taube-Henrikson, Kari Sylwan, Sif Ruud. Brilliant Ullmann performance and Sven Nykvist photography compensate somewhat for déjà vu feeling one gets from drama about woman psychiatrist who suffers severe nervous breakdown. As harrowing as they come; not for every taste or mood. Originally a four-part Swedish TV miniseries. [R]

Face to the Wind SEE: **Cry for Me, Billy**

Facts of Life, The (1960) **103m.** *** D: Melvin Frank. Bob Hope, Lucille Ball, Ruth Hussey, Don DeFore. Sophisticated comedy with Bob and Lucy leaving their spouses for an interlude together. The two stars make a good team worth watching. ▼●

Faculty, The (1998) **C-104m.** **½ D: Robert Rodriguez. Josh Hartnett, Jordana Brewster, Elijah Wood, Salma Hayek, Piper Laurie, Famke Janssen, Chris McDonald, Robert Patrick, Bebe Neuwirth, Clea DuVall, Laura Harris, Shawn Hatosy, Usher Raymond, Jon Stewart, Daniel von Bargen. Ohio high school students who normally clash with one another band together when they discover that their teachers are being taken over by aliens. Self-referential horror film, with a healthy nod to INVASION OF THE BODY SNATCHERS, is a cut above usual teen gore fests and has a first-rate cast. Overlong but sharply written (by Kevin Williamson, from a story by David Wechter and Bruce Kimmel). [R] ▼●◗

Fade-In (1968) **C-93m.** ** D: Allen Smithee (Jud Taylor). Burt Reynolds, Barbara Loden, Noam Pitlik, Patricia Casey, James Hampton, Joseph Perry. Odd little film made concurrently with BLUE, about love affair between film editor Loden and man she meets while working on location. Not very good, but a definite curio; never released theatrically. BLUE actors Terence Stamp, Joanna Pettet, Ricardo Montalban, and Sally Kirkland can be glimpsed here. Video title: IRON COWBOY.▼

Fade to Black (1980) **C-100m.** *½ D: Vernon Zimmerman. Dennis Christopher, Linda Kerridge, Tim Thomerson, Morgan Paull, Marya Small, Mickey Rourke. Weirdo film buff Christopher does in his enemies while dressed up as his favorite cinema villains. Interesting idea ruined by excessive violence, poor performance by Christopher. Marilyn Monroe lookalike Kerridge, as Christopher's girlfriend, is like a rose in a cesspool. [R]▼◗

Fahrenheit 451 (1966) **C-111m.** *** D: François Truffaut. Julie Christie, Oskar Werner, Cyril Cusack, Anton Diffring, Jeremy Spenser, Bee Duffell, Alex Scott, Mark Lester. Odd and generally slow-going adaptation of Ray Bradbury sci-fi novel depicting future Earth civilization where all printed reading material is banned. Though viewer interest is held throughout, film has curiously reserved, unemotional feel to it. Truffaut's only film in English.▼●◗

Fail-Safe (1964) **111m.** ***½ D: Sidney Lumet. Henry Fonda, Walter Matthau, Fritz Weaver, Dan O'Herlihy, Sorrell Booke, Larry Hagman, Frank Overton, Dom DeLuise. U.S. bomber is accidentally ordered to nuke Moscow, plunging heads of American and Russian governments into crisis of decision making as time runs out. High-tension drama done with taste and intelligence. Walter Bernstein adapted the Eugene Burdick–Harvey Wheeler best-seller. Remade in 2000 for TV. ▼●

Fair Game (1995) **C-91m.** BOMB D: Andrew Sipes. William Baldwin, Cindy Crawford, Steven Berkoff, Christopher McDonald, Miguel Sandoval, Johann Carlo, Salma Hayek, John Bedford Lloyd. Totally pre-fab action thriller that almost looks as if producer Joel Silver is trying to satirize himself. Miami lawyer Crawford survives the requisite amount of firepower and fireballs during her pursuit by former KGB operatives. Baldwin is the cop trying to keep them both alive. Arguably the worst movie of 1995. In her acting debut, supermodel Crawford makes a good jogger. [R]▼●◗

Fair Wind to Java (1953) **C-92m.** **½ D: Joseph Kane. Fred MacMurray, Vera Ralston, Victor McLaglen, Robert Douglas, Philip Ahn. Hard-boiled skipper goes after treasure in the South Seas. Pretty good adventure yarn with Ralston surprisingly good as native love interest. Great climactic volcano explosion—though accompanying process-screen work is awful.

Fairy Tale: A True Story (1997-U.S.-

British) **C-99m.** *** D: Charles Sturridge. Florence Hoath, Elizabeth Earl, Paul McGann, Phoebe Nicholls, Peter O'Toole, Harvey Keitel, Tim McInnerny. Charming film, rich in period flavor, spun around a real-life incident in 1917, when two girls photographed fairies in their garden—and no less a figure than Sir Arthur Conan Doyle declared them genuine. As it deals with death (one of the girls has lost her brother to pneumonia), the horrors of WW1, and real-life characters like Doyle and Houdini (Keitel), this may actually have greater appeal to grownups than to children. Mel Gibson, whose company produced the film, has a cameo role. [PG]▼●

Faithful (1996) **C-88m.** ** D: Paul Mazursky. Cher, Chazz Palminteri, Ryan O'Neal, Paul Mazursky, Amber Smith, Elisa Leonetti. On her 20th anniversary, the unhappy, neglected wife of a wealthy businessman is seized by a hit man who ties her up and awaits a signal from her husband to murder her. Meanwhile, they engage in a lively and surprisingly revealing conversation. All too obviously derived from a stage play (by Palminteri, who also wrote the script), this interesting piece simply doesn't work on film, despite good performances. Coproduced by Robert De Niro; filmed in 1994. [R]▼●

Faithful in My Fashion (1946) **81m.** ** D: Sidney Salkow. Donna Reed, Tom Drake, Edward Everett Horton, Spring Byington, Sig Ruman. Stale comedy-romance as soldier on leave discovers his girl engaged to someone else. Good cast in familiar settings.

Faithless (1932) **76m.** **½ D: Harry Beaumont. Tallulah Bankhead, Robert Montgomery, Hugh Herbert, Louise Closser Hale, Henry Kolker. Impoverished Bankhead tries to start life fresh after dismal past; polished soaper.

Fake, The (1953-British) **80m.** ** D: Godfrey Grayson. Dennis O'Keefe, Coleen Gray, Guy Middleton, John Laurie. Famous painting is stolen, starting a police hunt; OK crime drama.

Fake-Out (1982) **C-96m.** *½ D: Matt Cimber. Pia Zadora, Telly Savalas, Desi Arnaz, Jr. Trifling combination crime drama/comedy/romance with Las Vegas performer Zadora pressured to rat on her gangster boyfriend. Pia is raped. Pia falls in love. There are car chases . . . Aka NEVADA HEAT.▼

Fakers, The SEE: **Hell's Bloody Devils**

The Falcon Michael Arlen's debonair trouble-shooter, the Falcon, served as the basis for sixteen above-average mysteries in the 1940s, and while the series cannot be called unusual, one of its entries presented a perhaps-unique situation. George Sanders had played the character in three films when, in 1942, he decided to leave the series. In THE FALCON'S BROTHER it was arranged to put him out of the way so his brother could take over for him. Sanders' real-life brother, Tom Conway, was the replacement; he carried on for nine subsequent films. John Calvert played the character in three final low-budget films which aren't really part of the main series. Various character actors came in and out of the series playing cronies of the Falcon, such as Allen Jenkins, Ed Brophy, Eddie Dunn, and Ed Gargan. James Gleason played a thick-witted inspector in the first few films, and Cliff Clark took over for the rest. In fact, some of the films had so much comedy relief, one yearned for some mystery relief from the comedy! One interesting gimmick in several films had a beautiful girl enter near the end of the picture to alert the Falcon to danger in a new location; this would lead into the next film in which the Falcon and the girl would embark upon the new mystery. One entry, THE FALCON TAKES OVER, was from a Raymond Chandler novel, FAREWELL, MY LOVELY, which was remade as MURDER, MY SWEET with Dick Powell as Philip Marlowe.

THE FALCON

The Gay Falcon (1941)
A Date With the Falcon (1941)
The Falcon Takes Over (1942)
The Falcon's Brother (1942)
The Falcon Strikes Back (1943)
The Falcon and the Co-eds (1943)
The Falcon in Danger (1943)
The Falcon in Hollywood (1944)
The Falcon in Mexico (1944)
The Falcon Out West (1944)
The Falcon in San Francisco (1945)
The Falcon's Alibi (1946)
The Falcon's Adventure (1946)
The Devil's Cargo (1948)
Appointment With Murder (1948)
Search for Danger (1949)

Falcon and the Co-eds, The (1943) **68m.** **½ D: William Clemens. Tom Conway, Jean Brooks, Rita Corday, Amelita Ward, Isabel Jewell, George Givot, Cliff Clark, Ed Gargan. There's a slew of sinister suspects when murder strikes at a girls' school, with playboy Falcon called in to investigate. Amusing entry features Dorothy Malone(y) in a bit part as a student.

Falcon and the Snowman, The (1985) **C-131m.** **½ D: John Schlesinger. Timothy Hutton, Sean Penn, David Suchet, Lori Singer, Pat Hingle, Dorian Harewood, Mady Kaplan, Richard Dysart, Chris Makepeace, Michael Ironside. True story, based on Robert Lindsay's book about two young men from affluent families who decide to sell government secrets to the Russians. Much food for thought, but we never get to share Hutton's feelings, and that keeps this well-made film somewhat aloof. Standout: Penn's performance as a desperate, amoral, drugged-out kid. [R]▼●

Falcon in Danger, The (1943) **70m.** ** D: William Clemens. Tom Conway, Jean Brooks, Elaine Shepard, Amelita Ward, Cliff Clark, Ed Gargan, Clarence Kolb, Richard Martin. Minor entry about disappearance of passengers and $100,000 from a downed airplane.

Falcon in Hollywood, The (1944) **67m.** **½ D: Gordon Douglas. Tom Conway, Barbara Hale, Veda Ann Borg, John Abbott, Sheldon Leonard, Konstantin Shayne, Emory Parnell, Frank Jenks, Rita Corday, Jean Brooks. While on vacation in Tinseltown, the Falcon probes the murder of an actor, allowing for an entertaining tour of RKO studio's back lot. Borg shines as a brassy cab driver.

Falcon in Mexico, The (1944) **70m.** **½ D: William Berke. Tom Conway, Mona Maris, Martha MacVicar (Vickers), Nestor Paiva, Mary Currier, Emory Parnell, Pedro de Cordoba. Suspenseful entry takes the Falcon from Manhattan to Mexico City to solve the murder of an art gallery owner over a new painting by a supposedly dead artist. Scenic exteriors of Mexico are rumored to be from Orson Welles' unfinished film IT'S ALL TRUE.▼

Falcon in San Francisco, The (1945) **66m.** **½ D: Joseph H. Lewis. Tom Conway, Rita Corday, Edward Brophy, Sharyn Moffett, Fay Helm, Robert Armstrong, Myrna Dell. The Falcon, sidekick Brophy, and moppet Moffett take on a gang of silk smugglers in this leisurely but well-directed entry.

Falcon Out West, The (1944) **64m.** **½ D: William Clemens. Tom Conway, Barbara Hale, Don Douglas, Carole Gallagher, Joan Barclay, Cliff Clark, Ed Gargan, Minor Watson, Lyle Talbot. The Falcon heads to Texas to catch the killer of a millionaire rancher who died in a N.Y.C. nightclub. Future leading man Lawrence Tierney plays an orchestra leader.

Falcon's Adventure, The (1946) **61m.** ** D: William Berke. Tom Conway, Madge Meredith, Edward S. Brophy, Robert Warwick, Myrna Dell, Steve Brodie, Carol Forman, Ian Wolfe. Stale rehash of A DATE WITH THE FALCON, about imperiled inventor of synthetic diamonds. Last *Falcon* entry featuring Conway.▼

Falcon's Alibi, The (1946) **62m.** ** D: Ray McCarey. Tom Conway, Rita Corday, Vince Barnett, Jane Greer, Elisha Cook, Jr., Emory Parnell, Al Bridge, Jason Robards, Sr., Jean Brooks, Myrna Dell. Basically a retread of initial entry, THE GAY FALCON, about society matron's stolen jewels. Tepid, despite a good supporting cast.

Falcon's Brother, The (1942) **63m.** **½ D: Stanley Logan. George Sanders, Tom Conway, Jane Randolph, Don Barclay, Amanda Varela, George Lewis, Cliff Clark, Edward Gargan. Enemy agents plan to assassinate a South American diplomat to sabotage U.S.-Latin American relations and the Falcon calls in his brother Tom (real-life brother Conway) to help out. Sanders' last film in the series.

Falcon Strikes Back, The (1943) **66m.** **½ D: Edward Dmytryk. Tom Conway, Harriet Hilliard (Nelson), Jane Randolph, Edgar Kennedy, Cliff Edwards, Rita Corday, Wynne Gibson, Cliff Clark, Ed Gargan. The Falcon is framed for murdering a banker as part of a war-bond racket and tracks down the real culprits in this breezy entry. A plum role for Kennedy.

Falcon Takes Over, The (1942) **62m.** *** D: Irving Reis. George Sanders, Lynn Bari, James Gleason, Allen Jenkins, Helen Gilbert, Ward Bond, Edward Gargan, Anne Revere, George Cleveland, Hans Conried, Turhan Bey. Substantial, well-meshed mystery based on Chandler's *Farewell, My Lovely,* with Sanders up to his neck in corpses and double-crossing clients, aided by reporter Bari. Bond is a memorable Moose Malloy. Remade just two years later as MURDER, MY SWEET.▼

Fallen (1998) **C-124m.** ** D: Gregory Hoblit. Denzel Washington, John Goodman, Donald Sutherland, Embeth Davidtz, James Gandolfini, Elias Koteas, Gabriel Casseus, Robert Joy. Philadelphia homicide cop investigates brutal copycat murders—but is slow to realize that there may be an explanation beyond the normal for how and why these deaths are being executed. Hybrid of supernatural and cop-thriller genres doesn't pay off, despite creepy atmosphere and solid performances. It takes much too long to get where it's going, and the finale subverts the film's own "ground rules." Panavision. [R] ▼●

Fallen Angel (1945) **97m.** **½ D: Otto Preminger. Alice Faye, Dana Andrews, Linda Darnell, Charles Bickford, Anne Revere, Bruce Cabot, John Carradine. Andrews, hard up and bitter, stops in a small California town and falls for sultry waitress Darnell. To get money to marry her, he plans to first wed mousy heiress Faye and fleece her. Slow-paced (if good-looking) film noir was an ill-fated change of pace for musical star Faye, in her last starring movie.

Fallen Angel (1981) **C-100m. TVM** D: Robert Lewis. Dana Hill, Melinda Dillon, Richard Masur, Ronny Cox, David Hayward, Virginia Kiser, Shelby Leverington. Calculating drama about a child pornographer (Masur) who entices kids to pose for him. This not unexpectedly got a huge rating on its premiere, but less predictably won an Emmy nomination as Outstanding Drama Special. Average.▼

Fallen Angels (1995-Hong Kong) **C-95m.** ** D: Wong Kar-Wai. Leon Lai, Michelle Reis, Takeshi Kaneshiro, Charlie Yeung, Karen Mok. Slickly made but emotionally uninvolving (and practically narrative-free) portrait of cultural alienation, which like its predecessor, CHUNGKING EXPRESS, focuses on two sets of characters: an assassin and the beautiful colleague who desires him; and a mute ex-con and the woman he covets. Dazzling cinematography, camera angles, and editing aside, this is mostly meandering and confusing—and as emotionally distant as the characters it portrays.▼●◗

Fallen Idol, The (1948-British) **94m.** ***½ D: Carol Reed. Ralph Richardson, Michele Morgan, Bobby Henrey, Sonia Dresdel, Jack Hawkins, Bernard Lee. Young boy idolizes a household servant who is suspected of murdering his wife. Exceptional realization of Graham Greene story "The Basement Room," told in large part from the child's point of view. Scripted by Greene, Lesley Storm, and William Templeton. Also shown in computer colored version.▼●

Fallen Sparrow, The (1943) **94m.** **½ D: Richard Wallace. John Garfield, Maureen O'Hara, Walter Slezak, Patricia Morison, Martha O'Driscoll, Bruce Edwards, John Miljan, John Banner, Hugh Beaumont. Entertaining if somewhat vague WW2 thriller with Garfield returning to N.Y.C. after fighting in the Spanish Civil War, only to find himself hunted by undercover Nazis. Promising material never really pans out.▼●

Falling Down (1993) **C-115m.** **½ D: Joel Schumacher. Michael Douglas, Robert Duvall, Barbara Hershey, Frederic Forrest, Tuesday Weld, Rachel Ticotin, Lois Smith, Michael Paul Chan, Raymond J. Barry, D. W. Moffett, Brent Hinkley, Dedee Pfeiffer, Vondie Curtis Hall, Jack Kehoe, John Diehl. Nerdy Douglas blows his cool one morning, abandons his car in freeway traffic, and starts wandering L.A. on an increasingly violent odyssey—while Duvall, his last day before retiring from the police force, sniffs him out. Dead-on portrait of a disenfranchised, modern-day American who goes off the deep end. It's vivid, it's credible, it's extremely well acted . . . but what exactly is the point? Panavision. [R]▼●◗

Falling From Grace (1992) **C-100m.** BOMB D: John Mellencamp. John Mellencamp, Mariel Hemingway, Kay Lenz, Claude Akins, Dub Taylor, Larry Crane. Warmed-over Larry McMurtry tripe about a country music star who returns to his hometown, opening old family wounds and reigniting a relationship with his one-time girlfriend, who's now married to his brother. Lenz's sexy character is the only one that avoids cliché; Mellencamp's performance is simply boring. This marked the singing star's directing debut. [PG-13]▼●

Falling in Love (1984) **C-107m.** **½ D: Ulu Grosbard. Robert De Niro, Meryl Streep, Harvey Keitel, Jane Kaczmarek, George Martin, David Clennon, Dianne Wiest. Straightforward film about two married people who—against their better judgment—have an affair. BRIEF ENCOUNTER it's not, but De Niro and especially Streep lift it out of the ordinary. [PG-13]▼●

Falling in Love Again (1980) **C-103m.** *½ D: Steven Paul. Elliott Gould, Susannah York, Stuart Paul, Michelle Pfeiffer, Kaye Ballard, Robert Hackman, Steven Paul. Amateurish slop wherein a frustrated Gould flashes back to his halcyon youth in the Bronx and his courtship of a WASP princess. Artificial, to say the least. Twenty-year-old producer-director-writer-actor Paul scores points for chutzpah, not talent, with this feature debut; also Pfeiffer's film debut. Aka IN LOVE. [PG]▼●◗

Fall of the House of Usher (1960) SEE: **House of Usher**

Fall of the Roman Empire, The (1964) **C-153m.** ***½ D: Anthony Mann. Sophia Loren, Stephen Boyd, Alec Guinness, James Mason, Christopher Plummer, Anthony Quayle, John Ireland, Omar Sharif, Mel Ferrer, Eric Porter. Intelligent scripting, good direction, and fine acting place this far above the usual empty-headed spectacle. Mason and Guinness are superb; several action sequences are outstanding. A winner all the way. Screenplay by Philip Yordan, Ben Barzman, and Basilio Franchina. Originally 172m. Ultra Panavision 70.▼●

False Face SEE: **Scalpel**

Falstaff SEE: **Chimes at Midnight**

Fame (1980) **C-134m.** **½ D: Alan Parker. Irene Cara, Lee Curreri, Eddie Barth, Laura Dean, Paul McCrane, Barry Miller, Gene Anthony Ray, Maureen Teefy, Antonia Franceschi, Anne Meara, Albert Hague. The dreams, aspirations, struggles, and failures of students at N.Y.C.'s High School for Performing Arts should have made a great film, but this one just misses the mark, despite good ingredients and Oscar-winning music (by Michael Gore) and song (by Gore and Dean Pitchford). Moments of insight, excitement, and creativity eventually get lost in abrupt, disjointed continuity, which leaves a bushel of loose ends and unresolved ideas. Later a TV series. [R]▼●

Fame Is the Spur (1946-British) **116m.** **½ D: John and Roy Boulting. Michael Redgrave, Rosamund John, Anthony Wager, Brian Weske. Thoughtful if slow-moving chronicle of a noted politician-diplomat who rises from poverty to fame.▼

Family, The (1970-Italian) **C-100m.** **½ D: Sergio Sollima. Charles Bronson, Jill Ireland, Telly Savalas, Michel Constantin, Umberto Orsini, George Savalas. Fast pacing fails to hide clichés in this action drama about an ex-con (Bronson) in single-minded hunt for the man who framed him and stole his girl. Lots of chefs involved in writing this brew, among them Lina Wertmuller. Also called VIOLENT CITY. Techniscope. [R]▼

Family, The (1987-Italian) **C-127m.** *** D: Ettore Scola. Vittorio Gassman, Fanny Ardant, Stefania Sandrelli, Andrea Occhipinti, Jo Ciampa, Philippe Noiret. Episodic, revealing chronicle of eighty years in the life of an upper-middle-class Italian clan (with some characters portrayed through the decades by several different actors). An affectionate depiction, leisurely paced but well worth catching. Don't look for any sumptuous Roman exteriors: Scola never once strays from the family's apartment! [PG]▼●

Family Affair, A (1937) **69m.** *** D: George B. Seitz. Lionel Barrymore, Mickey Rooney, Spring Byington, Cecilia Parker, Eric Linden, Julie Haydon, Charley Grapewin, Sara Haden. Amiable first entry in the *Andy Hardy* series centers on Judge Hardy (Barrymore) solving various family problems while trying to be reelected. A good intro to the sentimental charm of life in Louis B. Mayer's idealized vision of smalltown America. Byington and Barrymore's roles were taken over by Fay Holden and Lewis Stone for the rest of the series. Based on the play *Skidding* by Aurania Rouverol.

Family Business (1986-French) **C-98m.** **½ D: Costa-Gavras. Johnny Hallyday, Fanny Ardant, Guy Marchand, Laurent Romor, Remi Martin, Juliette Rennes, Caroline Pochon. Well-made but inconsequential comedy of professional safecracker Hallyday, whose wife, daughter, and (most tellingly) son are involved in various ways with his "career." The motivations of his spouse (Ardant), particularly in relation to their son, are utterly confounding. Aka CONSEIL DE FAMILLE. ▼

Family Business (1989) **C-115m.** **½ D: Sidney Lumet. Sean Connery, Dustin Hoffman, Matthew Broderick, Rosana DeSoto, Janet Carroll, Victoria Jackson, Bill McCutcheon, Deborah Rush. Brainy Broderick, estranged from father Hoffman, enlists the aid of his grandfather Connery, a career criminal, to pull off a can't-miss heist. Worth seeing for three terrific performances by the charismatic leads, even though they're never quite believable as family—and the story lets them down. Further undermined by one of the most appalling music scores of recent memory, composed by Cy Coleman. Based on a novel by Vincent Patrick. [R]▼●

Family Enforcer SEE: **Death Collector**

Family Game, The (1984-Japanese) **C-107m.** *** D: Yoshimitsu Morita. Yusaku Matsuda, Juzo Itami, Saori Yuki, Junichi Tsujita, Ichirota Miyagawa. Arrogant tutor is engaged to propel an indolent younger son into a classy school but ends up taking over entire household. Overlong, but original, satire of Japan's burgeoning middle class offers plenty of chuckles, insights into modern-day Japan.▼

Family Honeymoon (1948) **90m.** **½ D: Claude Binyon. Claudette Colbert, Fred MacMurray, Rita Johnson, Gigi Perreau. What could have been fine comedy turns out to be uneven farce as widow takes children on second honeymoon. Very good cast does its best. Also shown in computer-colored version.

Family Jewels, The (1965) **C-100m.** **½ D: Jerry Lewis. Jerry Lewis, Donna Butterworth, Sebastian Cabot, Robert Strauss, Milton Frome. Depending on your taste for Lewis, you'll either be in ecstasy or writhing on the floor in pain because he plays seven parts—all of them as potential guardians of little girl who is inheriting several million dollars.▼

Family Life (1971-British) **C-108m.** *** D: Kenneth Loach. Sandy Ratcliffe, Bill Dean, Grace Cave, Malcolm Tierney, Hilary Martyn, Alan MacNaughton. Forceful drama about a weak-willed and deeply troubled young woman (Ratcliffe) and her deepening psychological turmoil as her parents compel her to have an abortion. While Loach's left-of-center worldview makes this a politically loaded (and occasionally preachy) allegory, he and screenwriter David Mercer nonetheless paint a harrowing portrait of an uncaring medical bureaucracy. Originally titled WEDNESDAY'S CHILD.▼

Family Pictures (1993) **C-200m. TVM** D: Philip Saville. Anjelica Huston, Sam Neill, Kyra Sedgwick, Dermot Mulroney, Janet-Laine Green, Jamie Harrold. Incisive (if a tad overlong) look through the scrapbook of an American family from the 1950s through the 1990s, with a glowing performance by Huston as the coming-apart matriarch, who must contend with raising an autistic child. Adapted with feeling by Jennifer Miller from the novel by Sue Miller (no relation). Originally shown in two parts. Above average.

Family Plot (1976) **C-120m.** **½ D: Alfred Hitchcock. Karen Black, Bruce Dern, Barbara Harris, William Devane, Ed Lauter, Cathleen Nesbitt, Katherine Helmond. Hitchcock coasts along in this tongue-in-cheek thriller. Harris is phony psychic who gets involved in a murder plot hatched by sinister Devane. Mildly entertaining but never credible. Ernest Lehman scripted Hitch's 54th and final film. [PG]▼●

Family Prayers (1993) **C-108m.** ** D: Scott Rosenfelt. Joe Mantegna, Anne Archer, Patti LuPone, Julianne Michelle, Paul Reiser, Allen Garfield, Conchata Ferrell, David Margulies, Tzvi Ratner-Stauber. Overlong drama of an adolescent Jewish boy struggling to prepare for his bar mitzvah, while suffering the ups and downs of life with a gambling-addicted father. Competent editing would have made this an excellent after-school special. This sat on the shelf after completion in 1991. [PG]▼●

Family Secret, The (1951) **85m.** **½ D: Henry Levin. John Derek, Lee J. Cobb, Erin O'Brien-Moore, Jody Lawrance. Good drama involving Cobb who defends man accused for crime which son committed.▼

Family Thing, A (1996) **C-109m.** **½ D: Richard Pearce. Robert Duvall, James Earl Jones, Michael Beach, Irma P. Hall, David Keith. When tractor salesman Duvall discovers his real mother was a black woman, he travels to Chicago to meet his half-brother, policeman Jones. Issues of race and family conflict are resolved a bit too easily in this rather contrived story, made sweet and believable by the efforts of a superior cast. Hall steals every scene as their blind aunt. Duvall also coproduced. Coscripted by Billy Bob Thornton. Super 35. [PG-13]▼●

Family Viewing (1987-Canadian) **C-92m.** *** D: Atom Egoyan. David Hemblen, Aidan Tierney, Arsinée Khanjian, Gabrielle Rose, Selma Keklikian, Jeanne Sabourin, Rose Sarkisyan. Early Egoyan feature is a provocative, daring drama-cum-black comedy about a dysfunctional family and its members' fixation on television, video, and impersonal means of communication. On-target commentary on the way hollow imagery and technology have affected contemporary life. Written by the director.▼

Family Way, The (1966-British) **C-115m.** *** D: Roy Boulting. Hayley Mills, Hywel Bennett, John Mills, Marjorie Rhodes, Avril Angers, Murray Head. Winning comedy about young newlyweds' problems, including impotence, and difficulty of living in same house as his parents. This warm, gentle film was actually considered controversial in 1967 when released in U.S.! Music score by Paul McCartney.

Fan, The (1949) **89m.** ** D: Otto Preminger. Jeanne Crain, Madeleine Carroll, George Sanders, Richard Greene. Oscar Wilde's comedy of manners *Lady Windermere's Fan*, involving marital indiscretion and social-climbing in Victorian England, loses much of its wit in this version. Madeleine Carroll's last film. Remake of the classic 1925 silent.

Fan, The (1981) **C-95m.** *½ D: Edward Bianchi. Lauren Bacall, Michael Biehn, Maureen Stapleton, James Garner, Hector Elizondo, Anna Maria Horsford, Kurt Johnson, Dwight Schultz, Dana Delany, Griffin Dunne. Broadway actress Bacall is stalked by a psychotic admirer in this bloody, distasteful adaptation of the Bob Randall novel. Bacall's star appeal helps disguise the fact that this is just an exploitation cheapie in dress clothes. [R]▼●

Fan, The (1996) **C-117m.** *½ D: Tony Scott. Robert De Niro, Wesley Snipes, Ellen Barkin, John Leguizamo, Benicio Del Toro, Patti D'Arbanville-Quinn, Chris Mulkey, Dan Butler. Ridiculous retread of all-too-familiar material, with De Niro cast as a '90s Travis Bickle, a loser on the edge, whose unhealthy passion is the S.F. Giants and their newest $40 million star, Snipes. This hollow melodrama is so overheated and overhyped by souped-up visuals and sound that the viewer feels he's been assaulted as much as the victimized baseball star. Worst of all, the film puts not one but two children in jeopardy and subjects them to psychological and verbal abuse. Ugh. Panavision. [R]▼●◗

Fanatic SEE: **Die! Die! My Darling!**

Fanatics, The (1957-French) **85m.** ** D: Alex Joffe. Pierre Fresnay, Michel Auclair, Gregoire Aslan, Betty Schneider. Occasionally taut tale of assassination plot on South American dictator, efforts of one rebel member to stop bomb explosion.

Fancy Pants (1950) **C-92m.** *** D: George Marshall. Mr. Robert Hope (formerly Bob), Lucille Ball, Bruce Cabot, Jack Kirkwood, Lea Penman, Eric Blore. Amusing musical remake of RUGGLES OF RED GAP with English valet Hope accompanying nouveau riche wildcat Lucy to her Western home.▼●

Fandango (1985) **C-91m.** **½ D: Kevin Reynolds. Kevin Costner, Judd Nelson, Sam Robards, Chuck Bush, Brian Cesak, Marvin J. McIntyre, Suzy Amis, Glenne Headly. Five college pals have one last fling before moving on to face Real Life. Based on Reynolds's student film called PROOF, expanded to feature length under sponsorship of Steven Spielberg. Fresh and likable, if uneven. [PG]▼●

Fan-Fan the Tulip (1951-French) **104m.** *** D: Christian-Jaque. Gérard Philipe, Gina Lollobrigida, Noel Roquevert, Olivier Hussenot, Marcel Herrand, Sylvie Pelayo. Delightful satire of swashbuckling epics, with Philipe ideal as the sword-wielding, love-hungry 18th-century Frenchman joining Louis XV's army. Beware shorter versions. Retitled: SOLDIER IN LOVE.

Fanny (1932-French)**120m.** ***½ D: Marc Allegret. Raimu, Pierre Fresnay, Charpin, Orane Demazis, Alida Rouffe. Marius (Fresnay) abandons Fanny (Demazis) with his child; with Cesar (Raimu) playing Cupid, she marries Panisse (Charpin). Second of Marcel Pagnol's charming trilogy, preceded by MARIUS and followed by CESAR. All three were the basis of the play and movie FANNY (1961).▼●

Fanny (1961) **C-133m.** *** D: Joshua Logan. Leslie Caron, Maurice Chevalier, Charles Boyer, Horst Buchholz, Baccaloni, Lionel Jeffries. Gorgeously photographed and beautifully scored dramatic version of Marcel Pagnol's trilogy involving young girl left with child by adventure-seeking sailor. Chevalier and Boyer give flavorful performances.▼●

Fanny and Alexander (1983-Swedish) **C-197m.** **** D: Ingmar Bergman. Pernilla Allwin, Bertil Guve, Gunn Wallgren, Allan Edwall, Ewa Froling, Jan Malmsjo, Erland Josephson, Harriet Andersson. Haunting, engrossing autobiographical family saga set in turn-of-the-century Sweden; a summing up of Bergman's career (announced as his final film). Scenes of joy, exuberance, pain, torment, exquisitely expressed, and largely seen through the eyes of a young boy. This earned Oscars as Best Foreign Film, and for its costumes, art direction-set decoration, and Sven Nykvist's lovely cinematography. Edited from an even longer television mini-series. Look for Lena Olin as a maid. Bergman's family history is further explored in THE BEST INTENTIONS, SUNDAY'S CHILDREN, and PRIVATE CONFESSIONS. [R]▼●

Fanny By Gaslight SEE: **Man of Evil**

Fan's Notes, A (1972-Canadian) **C-100m.** ** D: Eric Till. Jerry Orbach, Burgess Meredith, Patricia Collins, Julia Ann Robinson, Rosemary Murphy. Confused, football-obsessed writer becomes disillusioned with the Great American Dream of success and conformity, and ends up in mental hospital. Unfortunate misfire of Frederick Exley's highly regarded novel. [R]

Fantasia (1940) **C-120m.** ***½ D: Ben Sharpsteen (production supervisor). Leopold Stokowski and the Philadelphia Orchestra; narrated by Deems Taylor. Walt Disney's eight-part marriage of music and animated images remains an amazing achievement; Taylor's narration dates it more than the content. "The Sorcerer's Apprentice" (with Mickey Mouse), "The Dance of the Hours" (with dancing hippos and alligators), "Rite of Spring" (dinosaurs stalking the earth), and "A Night on Bald Mountain" (with Chernobog, the personification of evil) are so stunning that they make up for the less compelling sequences. Also notable for groundbreaking use of multichannel stereophonic sound. Followed by FANTASIA 2000. ▼●

Fantasia 2000 (2000) **C-75m.** *** D: James Algar, Gaetan Brizzi, Paul Brizzi, Hendel Butoy, Francis Glebas, Eric Goldberg, Pixote Hunt, Don Hahn, Steve Martin, Bette Midler, James Earl Jones, Penn and Teller, Quincy Jones, Itzhak Perlman, Angela Lansbury, James Levine, Chicago Symphony Orchestra. Update of the 1940 Disney milestone suffers from the fact that marrying music and images is no longer a novel idea; TV-style host intros don't help. But there are a number of entertaining segments, including "The Pines of Rome," with its wondrous whales, "Rhapsody in Blue," a UPA-type cartoon set in N.Y.C., "Pomp and Circumstance," with Donald Duck as Noah's assistant, and the "Firebird Suite" finale. [G]

Fantasies (1981) **C-81m.** BOMB D: John Derek. Kathleen Collins (Bo Derek), Peter Hooten, Anna Alexiadis, Phaedon Gheorghitis, Therese Bohlin. Amateurish nonsense about Derek's and Hooten's efforts to renovate a Greek island into a tourist trap. Shot in 1973, when Bo was 16, as AND ONCE UPON A LOVE. [R]▼

Fantasist, The (1986-Irish) **C-98m.** **½ D: Robin Hardy. Christopher Cazenove, Timothy Bottoms, Moira Harris, John Kavanagh, Mick Lally. Eerie tale of sexual repression among the Irish: country lass Harris moves to Dublin, where she's in danger of falling prey to Bottoms, who may be the notorious "phone call killer." Well done of its type, with Hardy effectively juxtaposing calm, quiet sequences with those of terror; however, some will find repugnant the graphic violence. [R]▼

Fantastica (1980-Canadian-French) **C-104m.** ** D: Gilles Carle. Carole Laure, Lewis Furey, Serge Reggiani, Claudine Auger, John Vernon. Laure, the star of a touring musical revue, loves impresario Furey, has an affair with ecologist Reggiani, and finds a political cause. Well intentioned, but far from fantastic.

Fantastic Invasion of Planet Earth (1966) **C-91m.** *½ D: Arch Oboler. Michael Cole, Deborah Walley, Johnny Desmond. Released theatrically in 3-D, this plays like a padded *Twilight Zone* episode; young couple find themselves trapped in seemingly deserted town enclosed in a giant Baggie. The original title, THE BUBBLE, was far less misleading: there are no aliens and no "invasion" in evidence, and not much excitement, either. Originally 112m. Filmed in widescreen Space-Vision.◗

Fantastic Planet, The (1973-French) **C-72m.** **½ D: Rene Laloux. Interesting animated feature about futuristic planet where men are dominated by superdeveloped mechanized race. Worthwhile, but static and aloof. [PG]▼◗

Fantastic Voyage (1966) **C-100m.** ***½ D: Richard Fleischer. Stephen Boyd, Raquel Welch, Edmond O'Brien, Donald Pleasence, Arthur O'Connell, William Redfield, Arthur Kennedy, James Brolin. Tremendously entertaining science fiction story of medical team reduced to microscopic size, injected inside human body. Film's great widescreen effects will be lost on TV screen, but story and action will keep you glued to your seat nevertheless. Screenplay by Harry Kleiner, based on a story by Otto Klement and Jay Lewis Bixby. Won Oscars for art direction-set decoration and special visual effects. CinemaScope.▼●

Fantomas Against Scotland Yard (1966-French-Italian) **C-104m.** **½ D: Andre Hunebelle. Jean Marais, Louis De Funes, Mylene Demongeot, Henri Serre. Satirical cliffhanger-type adventure yarn, with Marais as super-criminal engaged in athletic escapades. Retitled: FANTOMAS. Franscope.

Far and Away (1992) **C-140m.** **½ D: Ron Howard. Tom Cruise, Nicole Kidman, Thomas Gibson, Robert Prosky, Barbara Babcock, Colm Meaney, Eileen Pollock, Michelle Johnson, Cyril Cusack, Clint Howard, Rance Howard. Scrappy, dirt-poor Irish tenant farmer hooks up, in unlikely fashion, with the equally feisty daughter of a wealthy landowner, and together they sail for America to seek their ultimate destiny in the 1893 Oklahoma land rush. Ideal vehicle for Tom and Nicole, who are both beautiful and engaging; problem is a dire lack of story to fill the lulls between fight scenes. Expanded for network TV showing. Filmed in Ireland and Montana. Climactic land rush really gallops in Panavision Super 70. [PG-13] ▼●◗

Faraway, So Close! (1993-German) **C/B&W-140m.** **½ D: Wim Wenders. Otto Sander, Bruno Ganz, Solveig Dommartin, Peter Falk, Willem Dafoe, Nastassja Kinski, Horst Buchholz, Lou Reed, Mikhail Gorbachev. The perfect Wenders cast (if not the perfect Wenders movie) takes up where the more successful WINGS OF DESIRE left off; this time it is angel Sander who becomes mortal, joining old celestial pal Ganz—who's now married to circus performer Dommartin, with whom he's raising a daughter and running a pizza shop in unified Germany. Lighter going than its predecessor, but also more lightweight; it's still a borderline ordeal in the beginning and final segments, despite having been trimmed from 164m.▼●

Far Country, The (1955) **C-97m.** *** D: Anthony Mann. James Stewart, Ruth Roman, Corinne Calvet, Walter Brennan, Jay C. Flippen, John McIntire, Harry Morgan. Cattleman Stewart, a confirmed loner, brings his herd to Alaska and finds nothing but trouble; solid Western set against colorful backdrop of mining camp towns.▼●

Farewell Again (1937-British) **81m.** **½ D: Tim Whelan. Leslie Banks, Flora Robson, Sebastian Shaw, Patricia Hilliard. Neatly handled minor film detailing events in the lives of British soldiers on short leave before embarking for the front again.

Farewell, Friend (1968-French-Italian) **C-115m.** ** D: Jean Herman. Alain Delon, Charles Bronson, Olga Georges-Picot, Brigitte Fossey, Bernard Fresson. Mercenaries return to Marseilles following service in Algeria, team up for robbery, and inevitably clash. Ordinary and overlong. Aka HONOR AMONG THIEVES and THE CODE. [M/PG]▼

Farewell, My Concubine (1993-Chinese) **C-155m.** ***½ D: Chen Kaige. Leslie Cheung, Zhang Fengyi, Gong Li, Lu Qi, Ying Da. Elaborate aria, no favorite at home but cowinner of Cannes' top prize, about the contentious 52-year relationship of two male childhood apprentices in the Peking Opera, one a specialist in female roles with a lifelong atttraction to his heterosexual partner, who in turn marries a beauty from a brothel. A long but consistently absorbing drama spanning China's warlord era, the Cultural Revolution, and beyond. At its best in the first half; originally 170m. [R]▼●◗

Farewell, My Lovely (1975-British) **C-97m.** *** D: Dick Richards. Robert Mitchum, Charlotte Rampling, John Ireland, Sylvia Miles, Jack O'Halloran, Anthony Zerbe, Harry Dean Stanton, Sylvester Stallone, Walter McGinn. Third film version of Raymond Chandler novel tries too hard to evoke its period, but Mitchum is appealing as a tired Philip Marlowe. Author Jim Thompson appears briefly. Filmed before as MURDER, MY SWEET and THE FALCON TAKES OVER; followed by THE BIG SLEEP (1978). [R]▼◗

Farewell to Arms, A (1932) **78m.** *** D: Frank Borzage. Helen Hayes, Gary Cooper, Adolphe Menjou, Mary Philips, Jack LaRue, Blanche Frederici. Lushly romantic adaptation of Hemingway novel about ill-fated WW1 romance between American soldier and British nurse; dated but well done. Charles Lang's exquisite cinematography won an Oscar. Remade in 1957. Also shown in computer-colored version. ▼●◗

Farewell to Arms, A (1957) **C-152m.** **½ D: Charles Vidor. Rock Hudson, Jennifer Jones, Vittorio De Sica, Alberto Sordi, Mercedes McCambridge, Elaine Stritch, Oscar Homolka. Overblown, padded remake has unconvincing leads, static treatment of WW1 story so romantically told in Hemingway novel. Hudson is American ambulance driver wounded in WW1 Italy who falls in love with nurse Jones. Last film produced by David O. Selznick. CinemaScope.▼

Farewell to Manzanar (1976) **C-105m. TVM** D: John Korty. Yuki Shimoda, Nobu McCarthy, Clyde Kusatsu, Mako, Akemi Kikiumura, Pat Morita, James Saito. Factual story of one Japanese American family's internment in WW2 detention camp. Sad, often hidden slice of American history, beautifully directed by Korty and captured in the screenplay by Jeanne Wakatuski Houston (who lived it) and her husband James D. Houston, taken from their stirring book. Not to be missed. Above average.

Farewell to the King (1989) **C-117m.** ** D: John Milius. Nick Nolte, Nigel Havers, James Fox, Marilyn Tokuda, Frank McRae, Aki Aleong, William Wise. Disappointing actioner with Nolte an army deserter who becomes the leader of a Borneo tribe during WW2. Goal: to protect his people from the atrocities of the Japanese and the lies of the British. Intriguing premise, but result sinks into cliché. Milius scripted, from Pierre Schoendoerffer's novel. [PG-13] ▼●

Far From Home (1989) **C-86m.** *½ D:

Meiert Avis. Matt Frewer, Drew Barrymore, Richard Masur, Karen Austin, Susan Tyrrell, Anthony Rapp, Jennifer Tilly, Andras Jones, Dick Miller. Dumb killer-on-the-loose programmer with sexy teen Barrymore being stalked while vacationing with her father. Of interest only for Drew's casting in her first adolescent movie role. [R]▼●

Far From Home: The Adventures of Yellow Dog (1995) **C-80m.** **½ D: Philip Borsos. Mimi Rogers, Bruce Davison, Jesse Bradford, Tom Bower, Joel Palmer, Josh Wannamaker, Margot Finley. Nicely done (if predictable) boy-and-his-dog tale, centering on young Bradford and his super-bright Golden Labrador as they survive the capsizing of their boat; the pair must struggle to outlast the elements and other assorted dangers in a forest. [PG]▼●

Far From the Madding Crowd (1967-British) **C-169m.** ***½ D: John Schlesinger. Julie Christie, Peter Finch, Terence Stamp, Alan Bates, Prunella Ransome. Shamefully underrated adaptation of Thomas Hardy novel about beautiful woman and her profound effect on three men. Superb production, with brilliant photography by Nicolas Roeg, score by Richard Rodney Bennett, script by Frederic Raphael, and performances by Finch and Bates. Panavision.▼●

Fargo (1996) **C-97m.** ***½ D: Joel Coen. Frances McDormand, William H. Macy, Steve Buscemi, Harve Presnell, Peter Stormare, Kirstin Rudrud, John Carroll Lynch, Larry Brandenburg, Steven Reevis, Jose Feliciano. The Coen Brothers put a unique spin on a murder case, layering their story with droll observations about Minnesotans and winding up with a totally disarming comedy! McDormand is terrific as an efficient (and pregnant) police chief with multiple murders on her hands; Macy is equally good as a two-bit schemer who tries to stay cool when he finds himself way over his head in a quicksand of crime. Love that Muzak in the background! Oscar winner for Best Screenplay (Joel and Ethan Coen) and Actress (McDormand). [R]▼●◗

Far Horizons, The (1955) **C-108m.** **½ D: Rudolph Maté. Fred MacMurray, Charlton Heston, Donna Reed, Barbara Hale, William Demarest. Movie fiction about Lewis and Clark expedition, beautifully photographed; sporadic action; implausible love interest. VistaVision.

Farinelli (1994-Belgian) **C-110m.** **½ D: Gérard Corbiau. Stefano Dionisi, Enrico Lo Verso, Jeroen Krabbé, Elsa Zylberstein, Caroline Cellier, Marianne Basler. Sumptuously filmed saga of two brothers in 18th-century Europe, one a composer and the other a castrato opera singer (who, despite childhood castration, still woos women energetically, with the help of his brother). Rambling script has too many flashbacks and too little insight into the brothers' motivations; still, it's provocative and good-looking. Farinelli's castrato vocals were recreated by a digitally morphed mixture of a male and female opera singer. Original title: FARINELLI IL CASTRATO. [R]▼●

Farm, The SEE: **Curse, The**

Farmer, The (1977) **C-98m.** BOMB D: David Berlatsky. Gary Conway, Angel Tompkins, Michael Dante, George Memmoli, Ken Renard. Sadistic, amateurish actioner set just after WW2. Vet Conway tries to keep Georgia farm going, gets mixed up with the syndicate. Lots of anachronisms, including the whole movie. Panavision. [R]

Farmer's Daughter, The (1940) **60m.** ** D: James Hogan. Martha Raye, Charlie Ruggles, Richard Denning, Gertrude Michael, William Frawley. Not to be confused with later film, this one is about show business on the farm circuit, worthwhile only for Raye.

Farmer's Daughter, The (1947) **97m.** ***½ D: H. C. Potter. Loretta Young, Joseph Cotten, Ethel Barrymore, Charles Bickford, Rose Hobart, Harry Davenport, Lex Barker, James Aurness (Arness), Keith Andes. Young won Oscar for her performance as headstrong Swedish girl who fights for congressional seat against the man she loves. Delightful comedy with excellent cast. Allen Rivkin and Laura Kerr adapted Juhni Tervataa's play *Hulda, Daughter of Parliament.* Later a TV series.▼

Farmer's Wife, The (1928-British) **97m.** **½ D: Alfred Hitchcock. Jameson Thomas, Lillian Hall-Davies, Gordon Harker. A Hitchcock silent comedy. Farmer Thomas, unsuccessful at finding a bride, is secretly loved by devoted housekeeper Davies. Enjoyable rustic comedy; written by the director. Based on a play by Eden Philpotts.▼◗

Farmer Takes a Wife, The (1935) **91m.** **½ D: Victor Fleming. Janet Gaynor, Henry Fonda, Charles Bickford, Slim Summerville, Jane Withers. Vintage romance of farmers living by the Erie Canal in 1800s; Fonda's first film, and he's still enjoyable as Gaynor's suitor. Remade in 1953.▼

Farmer Takes a Wife, The (1953) **C-81m.** ** D: Henry Levin. Betty Grable, Dale Robertson, Thelma Ritter, John Carroll, Eddie Foy, Jr. Musical remake of 1935 film is slow-paced account of life in 1800s along the Erie Canal.▼●

Far North (1988) **C-90m.** *½ D: Sam Shepard. Jessica Lange, Charles Durning, Tess Harper, Donald Moffat, Ann Wedgeworth, Patricia Arquette, Nina Draxton. Shepard's directing debut, which he also scripted, is a pointless, artificial drama about the various members of a Minnesota family and what happens when patriarch Durning is almost killed by a wild horse. Good cast is wasted. [PG-13]▼●

Far Off Place, A (1993) **C-105m.** *** D: Mikael Salomon. Reese Witherspoon, Ethan

Randall (Embry), Maximilian Schell, Jack Thompson, Sarel Bok, Robert Burke, Patricia Kalember, Daniel Gerroll. Borderline-slow, but head-on-straight, Disney kids' adventure about a young Bushman guide, a game warden's daughter, and a visiting city boy who flee across the desert from murderous poachers. Frank treatment of death makes this iffy for young kids, but older children should find it rewarding. Based on the books *A Story Like the Wind* and *A Far Off Place* by Laurens van der Post. Juan Ruiz-Anchia's magnificent photography is a standout. Panavision. [PG]▼●

Far Out Man (1990) **C-91m.** BOMB D: Tommy Chong. Tommy Chong, Shelby Chong, Paris Chong, C. Thomas Howell, Martin Mull, Rae Dawn Chong, Judd Nelson. Labeled "A Tommy Chong Attempt," this vanity production is high on nepotism but short on laughs—or coherence. Chong plays a burned-out, leftover 1960s druggie who's trying to find his ex-lady and their child (played by their real-life counterparts). Longtime partner Cheech Marin contributes a cameo, but is sorely missed throughout the rest of the grungy film. [R]▼●

Fashions (1934) **78m.** *** D: William Dieterle. William Powell, Bette Davis, Verree Teasdale, Reginald Owen, Frank McHugh, Phillip Reed, Hugh Herbert. Trivial but enjoyable romp of con-man Powell and designer Davis conquering the Paris fashion world. Fine cast glides along with dapper Powell; Busby Berkeley's "Spin a Little Web of Dreams" number is great fun. Original title: FASHIONS OF 1934.▼

Fast and Furious (1939) **73m.** **½ D: Busby Berkeley. Franchot Tone, Ann Sothern, Ruth Hussey, John Miljan, Allyn Joslyn, Bernard Nedell, Mary Beth Hughes. Tone and Sothern are well matched as Joel and Garda Sloane, rare-book dealers who get involved in a murder at a seaside beauty pageant. Last of three MGM B-movies about these characters written by Harry Kurnitz.

Fast and Loose (1930) **75m.** *½ D: Fred Newmeyer. Miriam Hopkins, Carol(e) Lombard, Frank Morgan, Ilka Chase, Charles Starrett. Stiff adaptation of a Broadway comedy about a society girl falling in love with an ordinary guy. Preston Sturges is credited with the dialogue. Hopkins' film debut; Lombard has a smallish role.

Fast and Loose (1939) **80m.** **½ D: Edwin L. Marin. Robert Montgomery, Rosalind Russell, Reginald Owen, Ralph Morgan, Etienne Girardot, Alan Dinehart, Jo Ann Sayers, Joan Marsh, Sidney Blackmer. Montgomery and Russell are engaging as Joel and Garda Sloane, Nick & Nora-ish rare-book dealers who become involved in solving the murder of a wealthy bibliophile. Goes on a bit too long, but still fun. Second of three MGM films about this duo, written by Harry Kurnitz. Followed by FAST AND FURIOUS.

Fast and Sexy (1958-Italian) **C-98m.** **½ D: Reginald Denham. Gina Lollobrigida, Dale Robertson, Vittorio De Sica, Carla Macelloni. Lollobrigida is fun-loving widow who returns to her village seeking new husband. Technirama.

Fast and the Furious, The (1954) **73m.** ** D: Edwards Sampson, John Ireland. John Ireland, Dorothy Malone, Iris Adrian, Bruce Carlisle, Jean Howell, Larry Thor. Ireland is fugitive on the lam from murder frameup who jockeys Malone's sports car, with uninspired romantic interludes and cops-on-the-chase sequences. Produced and written by Roger Corman, this was the first film for American Releasing Corporation—soon to be the fabled AIP (American-International Pictures).▼

Fast Break (1979) **C-107m.** *** D: Jack Smight. Gabriel Kaplan, Harold Sylvester, Mike Warren, Bernard King, Reb Brown, Mavis Washington, Bert Remsen, Richard Brestoff, Rhonda Bates, K. Callan. Basketball coach Kaplan accepts post at midwestern college, but brings his N.Y.C. street players along with him. Perfect, innocuous TV fare, with some good laughs and exciting game climax. [PG]▼

Fast Charlie, The Moonbeam Rider (1979) **C-99m.** **½ D: Steve Carver. David Carradine, Brenda Vaccaro, L. Q. Jones, R. G. Armstrong, Jesse Vint. Period action comedy-drama about a WW1 deserter who enters the first long-distance motorcycle race. Appealing performance by Vaccaro as an early-day bike groupie and picturesque recreations of post-WW1 America are definite pluses. Also known as FAST CHARLIE AND THE MOONBEAM. [PG]

Fast, Cheap & Out of Control (1997) **C/B&W-82m.** *** D: Errol Morris. Documentary filmmaker Morris (of THE THIN BLUE LINE fame) delves into the lives of four disparate men: a topiary gardener, a lion tamer, a robot scientist, and a naked-mole-rat expert. Utilizing different film formats, Morris creates a fascinating examination of lifelong passions and occupations that touches on the nature of existence itself. A completely original film, enhanced by Caleb Sampson's music. [PG]▼●

Fast Company (1938) **73m.** ** D: Edward Buzzell. Melvyn Douglas, Florence Rice, Claire Dodd, Louis Calhern, George Zucco, Shepperd Strudwick, Dwight Frye, Nat Pendleton. Lighthearted mystery about snappily married couple who find their rare-book business a springboard for sleuthing—especially when a fellow dealer is murdered and a friend of theirs is the key suspect. Based on a novel by Marco Page (a pseudonym for Harry Kurnitz, who also coscripted the film). Followed by FAST

AND LOOSE (1939). TV title: THE RARE-BOOK MURDER.

Fast Company (1953) **67m.** ** D: John Sturges. Polly Bergen, Howard Keel, Marjorie Main, Nina Foch, Iron Eyes Cody. Not very exciting musical comedy about horse who prances to music, owned by racing enthusiast Bergen.

Fastest Guitar Alive, The (1968) **C-87m.** ** D: Michael Moore. Roy Orbison, Sammy Jackson, Maggie Pierce, Joan Freeman. Doomed effort to turn recording star Orbison into a movie star—with the dumbest title imaginable for a Civil War espionage story!▼

Fastest Gun Alive, The (1956) **92m.** *** D: Russell Rouse. Glenn Ford, Jeanne Crain, Broderick Crawford, Russ Tamblyn. Sincere Western with a moral. Ford is a peace-loving storekeeper trying to live down renown as gunslinger, but there's always someone waiting to challenge him. Tamblyn has an impressive solo dance feature. Also shown in computer-colored version.▼

Fast Food (1989) **C-92m.** **½ D: Michael A. Simpson. Clark Brandon, Randal Patrick, Tracy Griffith, Jim Varney, Michael J. Pollard, Traci Lords, Pamela Springsteen, Kevin McCarthy. Two perennial college students (and hucksters) start a fast-food operation with a twist: they lace their hamburgers with aphrodisiac sauce. A notch above the usual crude teen comedies, with Varney (aka Ernest P. Worrell) as the bad guy. [PG-13]▼●

Fast Fortune SEE: **11 Harrowhouse.**

Fast Forward (1985) **C-110m.** *½ D: Sidney Poitier. John Scott Clough, Don Franklin, Tamara Mark, Tracy Silver, Cindy McGee, Gretchen F. Palmer, Irene Worth, Constance Towers. Eight squeaky-clean teens from Sandusky, Ohio, crash N.Y.C. in search of their Big Break in Show Biz. Despite the title, this film is stuck in the 1950s; break-dancing can't disguise such cornball stuff. [PG]▼●

Fast Lady, The (1963-British) **C-95m.** **½ D: Ken Annakin. James Robertson Justice, Leslie Phillips, Stanley Baxter, Kathleen Harrison, Julie Christie, Eric Barker. Enjoyable, modest farce of naive Baxter, a Scotsman living in England, learning to drive an antique car—and to woo Christie in the process. Julie, in second film role, is thoroughly charming.

Fast Times at Ridgemont High (1982) **C-92m.** *** D: Amy Heckerling. Sean Penn, Jennifer Jason Leigh, Judge Reinhold, Robert Romanus, Brian Backer, Phoebe Cates, Ray Walston, Vincent Schiavelli, Forest Whitaker, James Russo, Pamela Springsteen, Martin Brest. Brashly entertaining look at Southern California high school kids, who hang out at the Mall and think mostly about sex. Funny, surprisingly honest, with a very appealing cast and a memorable performance by Penn as a doped-out goofball named Spicoli. High-energy feature debut for director Heckerling, based on Cameron Crowe's factual book. Film debuts of Forest Whitaker, Eric Stoltz, Anthony Edwards, and Nicolas Cage (billed under his real name, Nicholas Coppola). Some footage of Sean Penn was added for pay TV—but songs on soundtrack changed, altering running time to 90m. Later a TV series. [R]▼●◗

Fast-Walking (1982) **C-115m.** **½ D: James B. Harris. James Woods, Tim McIntire, Kay Lenz, Robert Hooks, M. Emmet Walsh, Timothy Carey, Susan Tyrrell. Oddball prison picture, laced with black humor, stars Woods as Fast-Walking Miniver, mercenary prison guard who's hired to assassinate politico Hooks. McIntire gives a standout performance as a very cagey inmate in a film whose interesting but disparate elements never quite gel. [R]▼

Fast Workers (1933) **68m.** *½ D: Tod Browning. John Gilbert, Robert Armstrong, Mae Clarke, Muriel Kirkland, Vince Barnett, Virginia Cherrill, Sterling Holloway. Abysmal film based on a play called *Rivets*, about construction workers who are friendly romantic rivals. Starts out snappy, then turns to turgid dramatics. Odd material for horror director Browning, too.

Fatal Assassin SEE: **Target of an Assassin**

Fatal Attraction (1980) SEE: **Head On**

Fatal Attraction (1987) **C-119m.** **½ D: Adrian Lyne. Michael Douglas, Glenn Close, Anne Archer, Ellen Hamilton Latzen, Stuart Pankin, Ellen Foley, Fred Gwynne, Meg Mundy. Happily married man has a weekend fling with a sexy woman who turns out to be psychotic and proceeds to turn his (and his family's) life into a living hell. Audience-pleasing thriller telegraphs most of its suspense payoffs and features a finale that seems more appropriate to RAMBO. Still, it's extremely well acted and certainly holds your attention. The film's original ending, which was more subtle and intriguing (but dumped after an unsuccessful preview), is now available on video. James Dearden based his screenplay on his own British short subject, "Diversion." [R]▼●

Fatal Beauty (1987) **C-104m.** BOMB D: Tom Holland. Whoopi Goldberg, Sam Elliott, Ruben Blades, Harris Yulin, John P. Ryan, Jennifer Warren, Brad Dourif, Neill Barry, Richard (Cheech) Marin. An inexcusably awful concoction with Goldberg as a narcotics cop. There's no shortage of gratuitous violence . . . and an antidrug message to rationalize its excesses. Some of the dialogue is mind-bogglingly awful. [R]▼●

Fatal Chase SEE: **Nowhere to Hide** (1977)

Fatal Desire (1954-Italian) **80m.** ** D: Carmine Gallone. Anthony Quinn, Kerima, May Britt, Ettore Manni, Umberto Spadaro, voice of Tito Gobbi. Nonmusical version of Mascagni's opera *Cavalleria Rusticana,* about love, adultery, and revenge in small Sicilian town. Originally filmed in color and 3-D, not released in U.S. until 1963 in b&w.

Fatal Hour, The (1940) **67m.** *½ D: William Nigh. Boris Karloff, Marjorie Reynolds, Grant Withers, Charles Trowbridge, John Hamilton, Frank Puglia, Jason Robards, Sr. Slight mystery, fourth in the Mr. Wong series, with the detective becoming involved in the investigation of a cop's death.▼◗

Fatal Instinct (1993) **C-88m.** *½ D: Carl Reiner. Armand Assante, Sherilyn Fenn, Kate Nelligan, Sean Young, Christopher McDonald, James Remar, Tony Randall, Clarence Clemons, Michael Cumpsty, Blake Clark, Eartha Kitt, Bernard Hiller. Woeful, decades-belated spoof of vintage film noir, with contemporary references to BASIC INSTINCT, BODY HEAT, and FATAL ATTRACTION thrown in so that no one will feel left out of the kitchen sink. Assante shows an unexpected flair for farce as a cop/lawyer targeted for murder by wife Nelligan and her lover (McDonald); Young fares best as a blonde sexpot named Lola. [PG-13]▼●

Fatal Vision (1984) **C-200m.TVM** D: David Greene. Karl Malden, Eva Marie Saint, Gary Cole, Barry Newman, Andy Griffith, Gary Grubbs, Mitchell Ryan, Albert Salmi. Top-of-the-line filming of Joe McGinniss's book dealing with the murder case in which ex-Green Beret captain Jeffrey MacDonald was accused and then convicted of the murders of his wife and young daughters. Malden stands out in his Emmy-winning performance as MacDonald's father-in-law who, convinced of his guilt, relentlessly seeks justice. Pungent script by the prolific John Gay. Originally shown in two parts. Above average.▼●

Fatal Witness, The (1945) **59m.** *½ D: Lesley Selander. Evelyn Ankers, Richard Fraser, George Leigh, Barbara Everest, Frederick Worlock. Quickie mystery yarn with obvious plot about wealthy matron's murder, capture of culprit.

Fat City (1972) **C-100m.** *** D: John Huston. Stacy Keach, Jeff Bridges, Susan Tyrrell, Candy Clark, Nicholas Colasanto. Taut adaptation of Leonard Gardner's novel about tanktown boxer and his young protégé was Huston's best film in 20 years; Keach, Bridges, and Tyrrell are all fine. [PG]▼

Fate Is the Hunter (1964) **106m.** **½ D: Ralph Nelson. Glenn Ford, Nancy Kwan, Rod Taylor, Suzanne Pleshette, Jane Russell, Wally Cox, Nehemiah Persoff, Mark Stevens, Max Showalter, Mary Wickes. One-note drama of investigation into cause of controversial plane crash. Good cast works with routine script. Dorothy Malone appears unbilled in one key scene. CinemaScope.

Fate Takes a Hand (1961-British) **72m.** **½ D: Max Varnel. Ronald Howard, Christina Gregg, Basil Dignam, Sheila Whittingham. Agreeable format about bag of mail recovered fifteen years after a robbery; effect of letters on recipients allows for five trim little tales.

Fat Guy Goes Nutzoid (1986) **C-78m.** BOMB D: John Golden. Tibor Feldman, Peter Linari, John MacKay, Douglas Stone. Tasteless comedy about two nerds who befriend a big, fat, retarded fellow, and his antics while on the loose in N.Y.C. Linari generates some sympathy as the big guy, but vulgar script makes fun of "retards." Shot in 1983; originally titled ZEISTERS.▼

Father Brown SEE: **Detective, The** (1954-British)

Father Goose (1964) **C-115m.** *** D: Ralph Nelson. Cary Grant, Leslie Caron, Trevor Howard, Jack Good, Nicole Felsette. Grant goes native as shiftless bum on a South Seas island during WW2, who's persuaded to become a lookout for the Australian navy—and finds himself sheltering Caron and a gaggle of schoolgirls fleeing the Japanese. Lightweight and enjoyable. Oscar-winning script by Peter Stone and Frank Tarloff.▼◗

Father Hood (1993) **C-94m.** *½ D: Darrell James Roodt. Patrick Swayze, Halle Berry, Sabrina Lloyd, Brian Bonsall, Michael Ironside, Diane Ladd, Bob Gunton, Adrienne Barbeau, Georgann Johnson. Embarrassingly bad action comedy about self-centered, two-bit hood Swayze, who inexplicably hooks up with his two kids (who've been ill treated while in foster care) and takes them on a less-than-enthralling odyssey. In desperate need of a coherent script, and characters who are even slightly likable. [PG-13]▼●

Father Is a Bachelor (1950) **84m.** ** D: Norman Foster, Abby Berlin. William Holden, Coleen Gray, Mary Jane Saunders, Stuart Erwin, Sig Ruman. Vagabond Holden with five "adopted" kids meets Gray who wants to marry him; "cute" comedy.

Fatherland (1995) **C-110m. TVM** D: Christopher Menaul. Rutger Hauer, Miranda Richardson, Peter Vaughan, Michael Kitchen, Jean Marsh. Intriguing but disappointing thriller asks what would have happened if Hitler had won WW2. On the eve of a detente pact between the Fuehrer and President Kennedy, American reporter and German cop team up to solve murder that's the missing link to uncovering a Holocaust conspiracy. Terrifying premise is hampered by an unconvincing script and indifferent pacing. A rare sympathetic role for Hauer, effective cameo from Marsh as an embalmed Nazi actress. Based on the best-seller by Robert Harris. Made for cable. Average.▼

Father Makes Good (1950) **61m.** *½ D: Jean Yarbrough. Raymond Walburn, Walter Catlett, Barbara Brown, Gertrude Astor. Mild little film in Walburn series about smalltown man who purchases a cow to show his contempt for new milk tax.

Father of the Bride (1950) **93m.** **** D: Vincente Minnelli. Spencer Tracy, Elizabeth Taylor, Joan Bennett, Billie Burke, Leo G. Carroll, Don Taylor, Rusty (Russ) Tamblyn. Liz is marrying Don Taylor, but Dad (Tracy) has all the aggravation. Perceptive view of American life, witty script by Frances Goodrich and Albert Hackett (based on Edward Streeter's book), and peerless Tracy performance. Sequel: FATHER'S LITTLE DIVIDEND. Later a TV series. Remade in 1991. Also shown in computer-colored version.▼●

Father of the Bride (1991) **C-105m.** **½ D: Charles Shyer. Steve Martin, Diane Keaton, Martin Short, Kimberly Williams, Kieran Culkin, George Newbern, B. D. Wong, Peter Michael Goetz, Kate McGregor Stewart, Martha Gehman. Pleasant update of the 1950 comedy gem about a father unwilling to let go of his little girl. It's refreshing to find such ''normal'' characters in a 90s movie, but there are too many lulls (and a few too many sidesteps into silliness) for it to hit the bull's-eye as the original did. P.S.: Can we now arrange a moratorium on the song ''My Girl''? Funny cameo by SCTV's Eugene Levy. Followed by a sequel. [PG]▼●◗

Father of the Bride Part II (1995) **C-106m.** *** D: Charles Shyer. Steve Martin, Diane Keaton, Martin Short, Kimberly Williams, George Newbern, Kieran Culkin, B. D. Wong, Peter Michael Goetz, Kate McGregor Stewart, Eugene Levy. Agreeable sequel has married daughter Williams announcing that she's pregnant, which impels Dad (Martin) to confront middle age. His midlife crisis includes a rash decision to sell their house and a renewed romanticism. Longish but fun. [PG]▼●

Fathers and Sons (1992) **C-100m.** ** D: Paul Mones. Jeff Goldblum, Rory Cochrane, Mitchell Marchand, Famke Janssen, Natasha Gregson Wagner, Paul Hipp, Ellen Greene, Samuel L. Jackson, Joie Lee, Rosanna Arquette. Odd, slow-paced drama about a movie director (Goldblum) now almost a recluse, who lives on the Jersey shore with his teenage son (Cochrane). Crowded plot involves drugs, a serial killer, a prophetic book, telepathy, mutated dolphins and alcoholism. Tackles too much, but is occasionally effective; Goldblum is excellent, as usual. John C. McGinley appears unbilled. Written by the director. [R]▼

Fathers' Day (1997) **C-98m.** ** D: Ivan Reitman. Robin Williams, Billy Crystal, Julia Louis-Dreyfus, Natassja Kinski, Charlie Hofheimer, Bruce Greenwood, Jared Harris, Louis Lombardi, Patti D'Arbanville, Charles Rocket, Meagen Fay. When her 16-year-old son runs away, a desperate Kinski tells each of two ex-lovers that he's the real father, hoping that this will spur one of them to find the boy. The two men—a genuine odd couple—wind up working together on this daunting task. Lackluster remake of Francis Veber's LES COMPÈRES gets whatever mileage it has from the two comic stars' personalities . . . but the boy is extremely dislikable, and a subplot with his stepfather (Greenwood) is a complete misfire. Panavision. [PG-13]▼●◗

Father's Little Dividend (1951) **82m.** *** D: Vincente Minnelli. Spencer Tracy, Joan Bennett, Elizabeth Taylor, Don Taylor, Billie Burke, Rusty (Russ) Tamblyn. Delightful sequel to FATHER OF THE BRIDE with same cast. Now Tracy is going to be a grandfather and he doesn't look forward to it. Also shown in computer-colored version.▼●◗

Father's Love, A SEE: **Bloodbrothers**

Father, Son and the Mistress SEE: **For Richer, For Poorer**

Father's Wild Game (1950) **61m.** *½ D: Herbert I. Leeds. Raymond Walburn, Walter Catlett, Jane Darwell, Roscoe Ates, Ann Tyrrell. In this entry, Walburn is protesting inflation at the meat market and decides to hunt wild game himself.

Father Takes a Wife (1941) **79m.** **½ D: Jack Hively. Adolphe Menjou, Gloria Swanson, John Howard, Desi Arnaz, Helen Broderick, Florence Rice, Neil Hamilton. Pleasant little comedy about glamorous stage star (Swanson) who ''settles down'' and marries Menjou, but takes on opera singer Arnaz as her protege.

Father Takes the Air (1951) **61m.** *½ D: Frank McDonald. Raymond Walburn, Walter Catlett, Florence Bates, Gary Gray. Walburn is involved with local flying school, and accidentally captures a crook.

Father Was a Fullback (1949) **84m.** **½ D: John M. Stahl. Fred MacMurray, Maureen O'Hara, Betty Lynn, Rudy Vallee, Thelma Ritter, Natalie Wood. Wholesome comedy with most engaging cast. MacMurray is football coach with as many household problems as on the gridiron.▼

Fathom (1967) **C-99m.** *** D: Leslie H. Martinson. Tony Franciosa, Raquel Welch, Clive Revill, Greta Chi, Richard Briers, Ronald Fraser, Tony Adams. Fast-paced, tongue-in-cheek spy caper with sky-diver Welch getting mixed up with dubious good-guy Franciosa. Great fun, with Revill's performance as eccentric millionaire stealing the show. Music score by John Dankworth. CinemaScope.

Fat Man, The (1951) **77m.** **½ D: William Castle. J. Scott Smart, Rock Hudson, Julie London, Clinton Sundberg, Jayne Meadows, Emmett Kelly. The star of radio's popular series of the same name appeared in this one-shot film adaptation as the corpulent gourmet/detective (created by Dashiell Hammett) whose investigation of a murder leads him to a circus for whodunit showdown.

Fat Man and Little Boy (1989) **C-126m.** *** D: Roland Joffé. Paul Newman, Dwight Schultz, Bonnie Bedelia, John Cusack, Laura Dern, Ron Frazier, John C. McGinley, Natasha Richardson. Flawed but still arresting film about the development of the atomic bomb, personalizing the story by focusing on General Groves (Newman), the bullheaded Army officer who was handed the job, and the brilliant J. Robert Oppenheimer (Schultz), who organized the brain trust creating the bomb. One complaint: some decidedly non-1940s slang amid the dialogue. J-D-C Scope. [PG-13]▼●

Fatso (1980) **C-94m.** ** D: Anne Bancroft. Dom DeLuise, Anne Bancroft, Candice Azzara, Ron Carey, Michael Lombard, Sal Viscuso. Bancroft's first feature as writer-director is disappointing. Fat man DeLuise half-heartedly tries to reduce after the death of his obese cousin. Film veers unevenly between comedy and pathos, with a few too many excrement jokes, perhaps the uncredited contribution of Mel Brooks. [PG]▼

Fat Spy, The (1965) **C-75m.** *½ D: Joseph Cates. Phyllis Diller, Jack E. Leonard, Brian Donlevy, Jayne Mansfield, Jordan Christopher, The Wild Ones, Johnny Tillotson. Once-in-a-lifetime cast makes this a must for camp followers—and a sure thing to avoid for most others. Fat Jack plays dual roles, in a story of a search for the Fountain of Youth. Filmed in Florida.▼

Faust (1926-German) **116m.** *** D: F. W. Murnau. Emil Jannings, Gosta Ekman, Camilla Horn, Wilhelm (William) Dieterle, Yvette Guilbert, Eric Barcley. Oft-told story of the eternal, earthly conflict between good and evil, in which the title character bargains away his soul to Mephistopheles (Jannings). Not a classic like Murnau's THE LAST LAUGH or SUNRISE, but still a compelling, inventively directed, visually sumptuous film, highlighted by clever special effects and impressive use of light and shadow. Based on the play by Goethe. Dieterle, then an actor, later directed THE DEVIL AND DANIEL WEBSTER.▼●

Favor, The (1994) **C-97m.** ** D: Donald Petrie. Harley Jane Kozak, Elizabeth McGovern, Bill Pullman, Brad Pitt, Ken Wahl, Larry Miller, Holland Taylor. "Happily" married Kozak asks best friend McGovern to look up—and sleep with—her high school hunk boyfriend, so she can vicariously experience the affair. Pleasant cast undone by comedy material that doesn't ring true for one minute. Sat on the shelf after completion in 1991; its latter-day release did no one any favors. [R]▼●

Favor, The Watch, and the Very Big Fish, The (1991-French-British) **C-89m.** ** D: Ben Lewin. Bob Hoskins, Jeff Goldblum, Natasha Richardson, Michel Blanc, Jacques Villeret, Angela Pleasence, Jean-Pierre Cassel, Samuel Chaimovitch. Pianist Goldblum agrees to pose as Christ on the cross for a photographer specializing in Biblical pictures—and then starts taking his role too seriously. Weak attempt at farce never quite connects, despite some amusing moments scattered about. This cast deserves better. [R]▼●

Fazil (1928) **88m.** ** D: Howard Hawks. Charles Farrell, Greta Nissen, Mae Busch, Vadim Uraneff, Tyler Brooke, John Boles. Strange casting of Farrell as desert sheik is just one oddity in this opulent romance. Visually stunning but dramatically farfetched. Silent film with original score.

FBI Girl (1951) **74m.** ** D: William Berke. Cesar Romero, George Brent, Audrey Totter, Tom Drake, Raymond Burr. Title tells all in standard fare about federal agency tracking down extortion gang.

FBI Story, The (1959) **C-149m.** *** D: Mervyn LeRoy. James Stewart, Vera Miles, Murray Hamilton, Larry Pennell, Nick Adams, Diane Jergens, Joyce Taylor. Well-mounted fabrication of history of F.B.I. as seen through career of agent Stewart, allowing for episodic sidelights into action-packed capers and view of his personal life.▼●

Fear (1946) **68m.** *½ D: Alfred Zeisler. Peter Cookson, Warren William, Anne Gwynne, James Cardwell, Nestor Paiva. Rather tepid remake of Dostoyevsky's CRIME AND PUNISHMENT, suffering from low-budget production values.▼

Fear (1988) **C-96m.** *½ D: Robert A. Ferretti. Cliff DeYoung, Kay Lenz, Robert Factor, Scott Schwartz, Frank Stallone, Geri Betzler. Family on a camping trip is terrorized by escaped cons, headed by one more psychotic Vietnam veteran. Skip it. [R]▼●

Fear (1996) **C-95m.** ** D: James Foley. Mark Wahlberg, Reese Witherspoon, William Petersen, Amy Brenneman, Alyssa Milano. Squeaky-clean teen falls for sexy psycho who locks horns with protective papa in a deadly battle. Passable slasher pic is somewhat redeemed by Foley's taut, stylish direction (the roller coaster scene is pretty steamy) and decent performances. Still, it's awfully derivative, especially the final showdown at the family nest. Former rapper/Calvin Klein pinup Wahlberg is menacing as the lovestruck hood, but he could benefit from diction lessons. Executive producer Brian Grazer called this "FATAL ATTRACTION for teens." Panavision. [R] ▼●◗

Fear and Desire (1953) **68m.** ** D: Stanley Kubrick. Frank Silvera, Kenneth Harp, Paul Mazursky, Steve Coit, Virginia Leith; narrated by David Allen. Kubrick's elusive, shoestring-budget feature-film debut is an existential anti-war allegory centering on four G.I.s (including a very green Mazursky, in his film debut) stranded behind the lines of an unknown enemy and fighting a fictitious war in an unidentified country. Long suppressed by Kubrick himself—who also photographed, edited and cowrote with poet/playwright Howard Sackler—the movie contains some striking imagery and shows the germs of budding talent, but generally comes off as an arty and pretentious student film.

Fear and Loathing in Las Vegas (1998) **C-119m.** BOMB D: Terry Gilliam. Johnny Depp, Benicio Del Toro, Tobey Maguire, Craig Bierko, Katherine Helmond, Mark Harmon, Tim Thomerson, Penn Jillette, Cameron Diaz, Lyle Lovett, Flea, Gary Busey, Christina Ricci, Michael Jeter, Harry Dean Stanton, Ellen Barkin. Excruciating adaptation of Hunter S. Thompson's 1971 book, which defined the counterculture of its day. The film, however, is simply one monotonous, painfully long drug trip—replete with close-ups of vomit and swooping camera movements at any and every opportunity. Perhaps Thompson diehards will find some value here; others beware. Super 35. [R]▼●◗

Fear Chamber, The (1971-Mexican-U.S) **C-80m.** *½ D: Juan Ibanez, Jack Hill. Boris Karloff, Julissa, Carlos East, Isela Vega, Yerye Beirute. Strange film about a semi-living stone from volcano caves that requires fluid from a terrified person in order to communicate with humans; dedicated scientist Karloff and his assistants are all too eager to help. Though faintly better than the other three Mexican-American productions Karloff worked on in 1968 (just before his death), this is still awful. Aka TORTURE ZONE.▼

Fear City (1984) **C-96m.** *½ D: Abel Ferrara. Tom Berenger, Billy Dee Williams, Jack Scalia, Melanie Griffith, Rossano Brazzi, Rae Dawn Chong, Joe Santos, Michael V. Gazzo, Jan Murray, Ola Ray, Maria Conchita Alonso. Incredibly sleazy look at Manhattan lowlife—violent and repellent in the extreme. Remarkably good cast for this kind of exploitation fodder. [R]▼●

Fear Inside, The (1992) **C-115m.** *** D: Leon Ichaso. Christine Lahti, Dylan McDermott, Jennifer Rubin, David Ackroyd, Thomas Ian Nicholas, Paul Linke. Lahti shines as an agoraphobic book artist held hostage at home by a pair of killers. David Birke's well-turned screenplay owes something, it seems, to LADY IN A CAGE. Theatrical film that premiered on cable television. [R]▼●

Fear in the Night (1947) **72m.** *** D: Maxwell Shane. Paul Kelly, DeForest Kelley, Kay Scott, Ann Doran, Robert Emmett Keane. Nifty chiller in which bank teller Kelley dreams he has killed a man in a mirrored room—and wakes up to be confronted by evidence that his fantasy was in fact reality. Based on the story "Nightmare" by William Irish (Cornell Woolrich); remade under that title in 1956.▼

Fear in the Night (1972-British) **C-94m.** ** D: Jimmy Sangster. Judy Geeson, Joan Collins, Ralph Bates, Peter Cushing. A terrorized faculty wife. Nothing you haven't seen before. [PG]▼

Fear Is the Key (1972-British) **C-103m.** *½ D: Michael Tuchner. Barry Newman, Suzy Kendall, John Vernon, Dolph Sweet, Ben Kingsley. Confused, unsatisfying Alistair MacLean thriller about a man driven to extremes in pursuit of stolen booty—and revenge for the murder of his wife and child. Kingsley's debut and only film work before GANDHI. Panavision. [PG]

Fearless (1993) **C-122m.** ***½ D: Peter Weir. Jeff Bridges, Isabella Rossellini, Rosie Perez, Tom Hulce, John Turturro, Benicio Del Toro, Deirdre O'Connell, John De Lancie, Spencer Vrooman, Daniel Cerny, Eve Roberts. A man feels his life, his outlook, his entire raison d'être changed after he survives a terrible plane crash; he can no longer deal with his own family, but is drawn to another survivor (Perez), who's unable to cope with the loss of her baby in the crash. Superior writing and acting, with Bridges (good as always) matched by Rossellini (in her best performance to date, as his wife) and Perez. Screenplay by Rafael Yglesias, based on his novel. [R]▼●◗

Fearless Fagan (1952) **79m.** ** D: Stanley Donen. Carleton Carpenter, Janet Leigh, Keenan Wynn, Richard Anderson, Ellen Corby, Barbara Ruick. Title character is circus lion who accompanies his dimwitted master (Carpenter) into the Army, with predictable results. Inconsequential comedy.

Fearless Frank (1967) **C-83m.** BOMB D: Philip Kaufman. Jon Voight, Monique Van Vooren, Joan Darling, Severn Darden, Anthony Holland, Lou Gilbert, David Steinberg, Nelson Algren. Naive country boy Voight treks off to the Big City, is murdered by gangsters, and is reincarnated as a superhero and his monsterlike clone. Pretentious satire is of interest only as a curio—and as Voight's film debut. Filmed in Chicago in 1965. Aka FRANK'S GREATEST ADVENTURE and subsequently cut to 78m. Techniscope.

Fearless Vampire Killers or: Pardon Me, But Your Teeth Are in My Neck, The (1967-British) **C-98m.** ***½ D: Roman Polanski. Jack MacGowran, Roman Polanski, Sharon Tate, Alfie Bass, Ferdy Mayne, Terry Downes, Ronald Lacey. Near-brilliant mixture of humor and horror: Professor Abronsius and assistant Alfred (great bumbling idiot team) attempt to destroy family of Slovonic vampires. Full 107m. version also available. Aka DANCE OF THE VAMPIRES. Panavision.▼●

Fearmakers, The (1958) **83m.** **½ D: Jacques Tourneur. Dana Andrews, Dick Foran, Mel Tormé, Marilee Earle. Well-done Communist witch-hunt theme as returning vet Andrews discovers subversives in his Washington, D.C., ad agency.▼

Fear No Evil (1981) **C-96m.** ** D: Frank Laloggia. Stefan Arngrim, Elizabeth Hoffman, Kathleen Rowe McAllen, Frank Birney. Classic conflict between good and evil in this horror-gore film about a shy high school student who turns out to be an incarnation of Lucifer. He viciously takes on fellow students and his parents but is combated by two archangels. [R]▼

Fear of a Black Hat (1993) **C-86m.** *** D: Rusty Cundieff. Larry B. Scott, Mark Christopher Lawrence, Rusty Cundieff, Kasi Lemmons, Howie Gold, Eric Laneuville, Barry Heins. THIS IS SPINAL TAP goes rap in this nifty burlesque about those rude, crude gangsta rappers N.W.H. (Niggaz With Hats). Group members are Tasty Taste, Tone Def, and Ice Cold (the latter played by director Cundieff, who also scripted). Quite funny at times, with Cundieff cleverly chiding the self-serving "street politics" of Public Enemy and 2 Live Crew. [R]▼●

Fear on Trial (1975) **C-100m. TVM** D: Lamont Johnson. George C. Scott, William Devane, Dorothy Tristan, John Houseman, Judd Hirsch, Lois Nettleton, Milt Kogan, Ben Piazza. Superb drama about blacklisting and subsequent libel trial of 1950s broadcaster John Henry Faulk. Scott etches another memorable portrait as attorney Louis Nizer; Devane is equally as fine as Faulk. David Rintels won an Emmy for his teleplay. Above average.

Fear Strikes Out (1957) **100m.** *** D: Robert Mulligan. Anthony Perkins, Karl Malden, Norma Moore, Adam Williams, Perry Wilson. Stark account of baseball star Jimmy Piersall and his bout with mental illness; Perkins is properly intense, with Malden superb as his domineering father. VistaVision.▼●

Feast of July (1995-U.S.-British) **C-113m.** **½ D: Christopher Menaul. Embeth Davidtz, Tom Bell, Gemma Jones, James Purejoy, Greg Wise, Kenneth Anderson, Ben Chaplin. A wandering, abandoned unwed mother finds shelter with three brothers and their parents, setting off sexual sparks in the formerly placid Victorian household. Poky prestige film, produced by Merchant-Ivory and based on the H. E. Bates novel, begins and ends satisfactorily, but the middle 90 minutes is slow going. Davidtz is almost *too* ambiguous in the lead. Super 35. [R] ▼●

Feathered Serpent, The (1948) **68m.** *½ D: William Beaudine. Roland Winters, Keye Luke, Victor Sen Yung, Mantan Moreland, Carol Forman, Robert Livingston, Martin Garralaga, Nils Asther, Jay Silverheels. Even the return of Number One Son Luke can't revive this moribund *Charlie Chan* entry about the search for a priceless Mexican statue. Scripter Oliver Drake pilfered this from his own RIDERS OF THE WHISTLING SKULL (1937). ▼

Federal Hill (1994) **100m.** *** D: Michael Corrente. Nicholas Turturro, Anthony DeSando, Libby Langdon, Michael Raynor, Jason Andrews, Robert Turano, Frank Vincent. Story of male camaraderie among young Italian-Americans "from the neighborhood" (Providence, R.I.) has an awfully familiar MEAN STREETS ring to it, but it's quite well done—extremely well acted and filled with unexpected twists. Turturro gives a star-making performance as the firecracker-tempered Ralphie, though the film concentrates on Nicky (DeSando), the local hunk infatuated with a pretty archeology student who's way out of his league. Director Corrente (who also scripted) plays Fredo. Available on video in original and computer-colored versions. [R]▼●

Fedora (1978-German) **C-114m.** **½ D: Billy Wilder. William Holden, Marthe Keller, Hildegarde Knef, Jose Ferrer, Frances Sternhagen, Henry Fonda, Michael York, Mario Adorf, Stephen Collins. Stylish but ponderous filmization of Thomas Tryon's short story about a producer's disastrous attempt to lure a Garbo-esque actress out of seclusion. Wilder's potshots at today's films and filmmakers might carry more weight if this film was better. [PG]▼●

Feds (1988) **C-82m.** *½ D: Dan Goldberg. Rebecca De Mornay, Mary Gross, Fred Dalton Thompson, Ken Marshall, Larry Cedar. Pert female cop and her bookish roommate conquer male-chauvinistic colleagues during their struggle to make "the cut" at the FBI Academy. Unlike the POLICE ACADEMY farces, this is played fairly straight, perhaps in deference to Bureau cooperation; result is laughless—and thus, pointless—comedy. [PG-13]▼●

Feed (1992) **C-76m.** ** D: Kevin Rafferty, James Ridgeway. Annoying, exploitive documentary collage featuring candid shots of 1992 presidential aspirants waiting to go on the air, as they practice their familiar public postures; the material was captured off satellite video feeds. After a few cheap laughs it becomes redundant and voyeuristic . . . not to mention unfair.▼

Feeling Minnesota (1996) **C-95m.** ** D: Steven Baigelman. Keanu Reeves, Vincent D'Onofrio, Cameron Diaz, Delroy Lindo, Courtney Love, Tuesday Weld, Dan Aykroyd, Levon Helm. Baigelman's highly touted writing and directing debut explores the explosive and unpredictable relationship between two brothers and the cagey young woman who comes between them. Watchable at times, but utterly disappointing; interesting cast is left high and dry, including the always welcome Weld as the boys' mother. Movie's title was suggested by a line in a song by Soundgarden. Coproduced by Danny DeVito. Super 35. [R]▼●◗

Feet First (1930) **83m.** **½ D: Clyde Bruckman. Harold Lloyd, Barbara Kent, Robert McWade, Lillian Leighton, Henry Hall. Lloyd talkie tries to rekindle spirit of his silent comedies with middling results. Episodic film has some very funny moments, but Harold's building-ledge routine doesn't quite come off. Edited for TV.▼

Felicia's Journey (1999-Canadian-British) **C-113m.** ** D: Atom Egoyan. Bob Hoskins, Arsinée Khanjian, Elaine Cassidy, Sheila Reid, Peter McDonald, Gerard McSorley, Brid Brennan. Mild-mannered catering manager at a British factory takes a kindly interest in a young pregnant woman who's come over from Ireland looking for the boyfriend who abandoned her . . . but the man's intentions are far from pure. A disappointment from Egoyan, from whom we expect more than just another story about a psycho—however layered it may be. Egoyan scripted from William Trevor's novel. Panavision. [PG-13]▼◗

Fellini Satyricon (1970-Italian) **C-129m.** *** D: Federico Fellini. Martin Potter, Hiram Keller, Max Born, Capucine, Salvo Randone. Opinions vary on merits of this visually stunning but overindulgent spectacle on ancient Rome, but if you love Fellini, you'll be more receptive than most viewers to his unique panorama of colorful and bizarre characters. Panavision. [R]▼●

Fellini's Casanova (1976-Italian) **C-158m.** **½ D: Federico Fellini. Donald Sutherland, Tina Aumont, Cicely Browne, John Karlsen, Daniel Emilfork Berenstein. Uninvolving if opulent version of 18th-century lover's life, made entirely at Rome's Cinecitta Studios. Sutherland is enigmatic, the film stylized to a sometimes absurd degree. Nino Rota's music helps. Danilo Donati won an Oscar for his costumes. [R]▼

Fellini's Roma (1972-Italian) **C-128m.** *** D: Federico Fellini. Peter Gonzales, Britta Barnes, Pia de Doses, Fiona Florence, Marne Maitland, Renato Giovannoli, Federico Fellini. Famed director's impressionistic ode to Eternal City of his youth, his adolescence, and the present—complete with fantasy sequence and usual carnival-of-life point of view. [R]▼●

Fellowship of the Frog SEE: **Face of the Frog**

Fellow Traveler (1989-British) **C-97m.** *** D: Philip Saville. Ron Silver, Hart Bochner, Imogen Stubbs, Daniel J. Travanti, Katherine Borowitz. Excellent political thriller detailing the plight and fate of a pair of childhood pals, one (Bochner) a movie star and the other (Silver) a scriptwriter, who are both blacklisted during the McCarthy era. Especially on target as a reflection of the temper of the 1950s, with a perceptive script by Michael Eaton. Produced by HBO, the BBC, and the British Film Institute.▼

Female (1933) **60m.** *** D: Michael Curtiz. Ruth Chatterton, George Brent, Ferdinand Gottschalk, Philip Faversham, Ruth Donnelly, Johnny Mack Brown, Lois Wilson, Gavin Gordon. Chatterton runs a major auto company with an iron hand—and tries to conduct her love life the same way—until independent-minded Brent comes along. (The two stars were then married in real life.) Funny, fascinating role-reversal yarn with incredibly lavish set design—watch for the organist perched in Ruth's entrance foyer!▼●

Female (1956) SEE: **Violent Years, The**

Female and the Flesh SEE: **Light Across the Street, The**

Female Animal, The (1958) **84m.** **½ D: Harry Keller. Hedy Lamarr, Jane Powell, Jan Sterling, George Nader. Sad waste of Lamarr as mature Hollywood star who grapples with adopted daughter Powell over Nader. CinemaScope.

Female Jungle (1956) **56m.** ** D: Bruno VeSota. Jayne Mansfield, Lawrence Tierney, John Carradine, Kathleen Crowley, Rex Thorsen, Burt Carlisle, Bruno VeSota. Lukewarm melodrama of cop Tierney seeking the killer of an actress. Mansfield costars as a nymphomaniac; also known as THE HANGOVER.▼

Female on the Beach (1955) **97m.** ** D: Joseph Pevney. Joan Crawford, Jeff Chandler, Jan Sterling, Cecil Kellaway, Judith Evelyn, Natalie Schafer, Charles Drake. Hot, heavy—and very tacky—melodrama, in which fisherman-stud Chandler attempts to put the make on wealthy widow Crawford. Outrageously trashy script is crammed with sexual double entendres. A must for Crawford fans—but don't expect anything resembling a good movie.

Female Perversions (1997) **C-119m.** ** D: Susan Streitfeld. Tilda Swinton, Amy Madigan, Karen Sillas, Frances Fisher, Laila Robins, Clancy Brown, Paulina Porizkova, John Diehl, Lisa Jane Persky, Marcia Cross. Story of highly successful lawyer (Swinton), in line for a judgeship, who is consumed by self-doubt. She swings both ways sexually, and repeatedly puts her reputation at risk. That her Ph.D. candidate sister is a shoplifter is testimony to their highly dysfunctional upbringing. Disjointed, pretentious film with a title more titillating than the film itself. [R]▼

Female Space Invaders SEE: **Starcrash**

Female Trap, The SEE: **Name of the Game Is Kill, The**

Feminine Touch, The (1941) **97m.** **½ D: W. S. Van Dyke, II. Rosalind Russell, Don Ameche, Kay Francis, Van Heflin, Donald Meek, Gordon Jones, Robert Ryan.

Brittle comedy of author Ameche writing book on jealousy, finding himself a victim when he brings wife Russell to N.Y.C.; she suspects he's carrying on with glamorous Francis.

Feminine Touch, The (1956-British) **C-91m.** ** D: Pat Jackson. George Baker, Belinda Lee, Delphi Lawrence, Adrienne Corri, Diana Wynyard. Undistinguished look at student nurses' experiences as they graduate to full-time hospital jobs. Also known as THE GENTLE TOUCH.

Femme Fatale (1991) **C-90m.** BOMB D: André Guttfreund. Colin Firth, Lisa Zane, Billy Zane, Scott Wilson, Lisa Blount, Carmine Caridi. Firth is squeaky-clean newlywed whose mysterious bride vanishes on eve of their honeymoon; he then uncovers lurid underground lifestyle she came from and to which she may have returned. Lisa Zane isn't terribly enigmatic, just tedious. Psychological drama begs for a sensible screenplay. Lisa and Billy Zane are sister and brother. [Available in both R and PG versions]▼●

Fernandel the Dressmaker (1957-French) **84m.** **½ D: Jean Boyer. Fernandel, Suzy Delair, Françoise Fabian, Georges Chamarat. Undemanding plot has Fernandel wanting to be high-fashion designer rather than drab man's tailor.▼

FernGully . . . The Last Rainforest (1992) **C-76m.** *** D: Bill Kroyer. Voices of Tim Curry, Samantha Mathis, Christian Slater, Robin Williams, Grace Zabriskie, Cheech Marin, Thomas Chong, Tone Loc. Entertaining animated feature for kids, with an ecological message. Mystical miniature forest creatures are threatened when human invasion of their rainforest (with bulldozers) threatens to unleash an evil spirit who's been locked up in a tree for years. Lively and enjoyable, if not memorable, with plenty of laughs for grownups in the free-flowing dialogue of Batty Koda, a whacked-out bat voiced by Robin Williams. Followed by a video sequel, FERNGULLY 2: THE MAGICAL RESCUE. [G]▼●

Ferris Bueller's Day Off (1986) **C-103m.** **½ D: John Hughes. Matthew Broderick, Alan Ruck, Mia Sara, Jeffrey Jones, Jennifer Grey, Cindy Pickett, Lyman Ward, Edie McClurg, Charlie Sheen, Ben Stein, Del Close, Virginia Capers, Louis Anderson, Max Perlich, T. Scott Coffey, Kristy Swanson. Saga of a cocky teenager's day of adventure while cutting classes. Starts off extremely funny, with on-target jabs at high school life, then wanders through heavy-handed slapstick and moody self-serious ruminations before regaining momentum for a bright finish. Typically uneven John Hughes script. Later a TV series. Super 35. [PG-13]▼●

Ferry Cross the Mersey (1965-British) **88m.** ** D: Jeremy Summers. Gerry and The Pacemakers, Cilla Black, The Fourmost, Jimmy Saville. Gerry Marsden and The Pacemakers perform eight songs in this musical made to cash in on their popularity; most appropriately, they appear as a Liverpool band attempting to compete in a music contest.

Ferry to Hong Kong (1959-British) **C-103m.** **½ D: Lewis Gilbert. Orson Welles, Curt Jurgens, Sylvia Syms, Jeremy Spenser. Welles and Jurgens have field day as straight-faced ferry boat skipper and drunken Austrian on trip to Macao. Otherwise just routine. CinemaScope.▼

Feud, The (1989) **C-96m.** *** D: Bill D'Elia. Rene Auberjonois, Ron McLarty, Joe Grifasi, Scott Allegrucci, Gale Mayron, David Strathairn, Stanley Tucci, Lynne Killmeyer, Kathleen Doyle, Libby George. David Lynch meets Norman Rockwell in this oddly likable satire of 1950s small-town America, centering on a feud that erupts between two families in neighboring hamlets. Broadly played; has cult-status possibilities. Based on Thomas Berger's novel; coscripted by first-time director D'Elia. [R]▼

Feudin' Fools (1952) **63m.** ** D: William Beaudine. Leo Gorcey, Huntz Hall, Bennie Bartlett, David Gorcey, Bernard Gorcey, Dorothy Ford, Lyle Talbot, Benny Baker, Russell Simpson, Bob Easton. Sach inherits a farm in Kentucky and gets caught in the crossfire of a family feud. Formula *Bowery Boys* slapstick for the sticks.

Feudin', Fussin' and A-Fightin' (1948) **78m.** ** D: George Sherman. Donald O'Connor, Marjorie Main, Percy Kilbride, Penny Edwards. Title and cast names tell all; loud and brassy.

Fever (1989-Australian) **C-83m.** *** D: Craig Lahiff. Bill Hunter, Mary Regan, Gary Sweet. Virtually silent film noir in the James M. Cain/Hitchcock vein. The ingredients are a tough cop, his younger wife, her shallow lover, and a suitcase full of money. Surprising throughout. [R]▼

Fever in the Blood, A (1961) **117m.** **½ D: Vincent Sherman. Efrem Zimbalist, Jr., Angie Dickinson, Herbert Marshall, Don Ameche, Jack Kelly, Carroll O'Connor. Turgid dramatics focusing on murder trial which various candidates for governor use to further political ambitions.

Fever Pitch (1985) **C-96m.** BOMB D: Richard Brooks. Ryan O'Neal, Catherine Hicks, Giancarlo Giannini, Bridgette Andersen, Chad Everett, John Saxon, William Smith. Anachronistic look at gambling fever with newspaper columnist (and "fever" victim) O'Neal. Embarrassingly bad; overwritten by veteran Brooks with declamatory dialogue from the *Dragnet* school of scripts. [R]▼

Few Days in the Life of I. I. Oblomov, A SEE: **Oblomov**

Few Days With Me, A (1988-French)

C-131m. *** D: Claude Sautet. Daniel Auteuil, Sandrine Bonnaire, Jean-Pierre Marielle, Dominique Lavanant, Danielle Darrieux, Tanya Lopert. Intriguing chronicle of chameleonlike Auteuil, whose family owns a department-store chain, and the series of events that ensue upon his checking up on one outlet, located in a provincial town. Veers too much between comedy (some of which is hilarious) and drama.

Few Good Men, A (1992) **C-138m.** *** D: Rob Reiner. Tom Cruise, Jack Nicholson, Demi Moore, Kevin Bacon, Kiefer Sutherland, Kevin Pollak, James Marshall, J. T. Walsh, Christopher Guest, J. A. Preston, Matt Craven, Wolfgang Bodison, Cuba Gooding, Jr., Noah Wyle. Aaron Sorkin's powerful one-set play is effectively expanded for movie retelling, as a slick young Navy lawyer (Cruise) is driven to investigate the case of two Marines who killed a compatriot. Nicholson bristles as the commanding officer of the base who doesn't want the whole story told. Smashing courtroom climax, top-grade performances all around, but a handful of contrivances keep this from scoring a direct hit. Panavision. [R]▼●◗

ffolkes (1980) **C-99m.** *** D: Andrew V. McLaglen. Roger Moore, James Mason, Anthony Perkins, Michael Parks, David Hedison, Jack Watson, Lea Brodie. Moore has fun playing an eccentric counterterrorist hired by the British government when a team of terrorists threaten to blow up two North Sea oil rigs. Surprisingly little action *per se,* but an entertaining yarn. Retitled ASSAULT FORCE for TV. Aka NORTH SEA HIJACK. [PG]▼

F for Fake (1974) **C-85m.** **½ D: Orson Welles. Wellesian tomfoolery, which started out as a portrait of notorious art forger Elmyr de Hory. When one of the interviewees turned out to be Clifford Irving—who fooled the world with a bogus Howard Hughes autobiography—Welles was forced to alter his film. Now it's a free-form treatise on hoaxes, with Welles' on-camera charm compensating for some of the movie's rough edges. Joseph Cotten, Paul Stewart, and Laurence Harvey appear briefly as themselves, along with Welles' longtime companion, Oja Kodar.▼●

Fickle Finger of Fate, The (1967-U.S.-Spanish) **C-91m.** *½ D: Richard Rush. Tab Hunter, Luis Prendes, Patty Shepard, Gustavo Rojo, Fernando Hilbeck. Idiotic comedy with Hunter an American engineer falsely accused of smuggling a candlestick, known as The Finger of Fate, out of Spain. He goes undercover in an attempt to unmask the real culprit.▼

Fiddler on the Roof (1971) **C-181m.** *** D: Norman Jewison. (Chaim) Topol, Norma Crane, Leonard Frey, Molly Picon, Paul Mann, Rosalind Harris, Michele Marsh, Neva Small, Candice Bonstein, Paul (Michael) Glaser. Rousing, colorful location-filmed adaptation of Joseph Stein's hit play based on Sholem Aleichem stories of humble village of Anatevka. Topol is hearty as Tevye, trying to preserve Jewish heritage against growing odds. Sheldon Harnick–Jerry Bock score melodically performed; Isaac Stern's violin featured on soundtrack. Earned Oscars for Cinematography (Oswald Morris) and Scoring (John Williams). Reissued at 150m. For an interesting comparison, see the original Yiddish-language TEVYE. Panavision. [G]▼●◗

Field, The (1990-British) **C-107m.** ** D: Jim Sheridan. Richard Harris, John Hurt, Tom Berenger, Sean Bean, Brenda Fricker, Frances Tomelty, John Cowley, Sean McGinley, Jenny Conroy. Ireland, the 1930s: a bull of a man who's nurtured a rented field into a prime piece of land nearly goes crazy when the widow who owns it decides to sell it at auction. Grim tale of deep-rooted stubbornness (and provincial clannishness) plays out like a Greek tragedy, and despite Harris' towering performance, becomes aloof and largely unmoving. Based on a play by John B. Keane. Made by the filmmakers of MY LEFT FOOT. [PG-13]▼●◗

Field of Dreams (1989) **C-106m.** ***½ D: Phil Alden Robinson. Kevin Costner, Amy Madigan, Gaby Hoffmann, Ray Liotta, Timothy Busfield, James Earl Jones, Burt Lancaster, Frank Whaley, Dwier Brown. Costner plays a novice farmer in Iowa who hears "a voice" that inspires him to build a baseball diamond on his property, in the hope of bringing the legendary baseball star Shoeless Joe Jackson (whose career was cut short by the Black Sox scandal) back to life. A story of redemption and faith, in the tradition of the best Hollywood fantasies, with moments that are pure magic. Kudos to writer-director Robinson, who adapted W.P. Kinsella's book *Shoeless Joe*, for hitting (and maintaining) just the right note from start to finish. Lovely score by James Horner. [PG] ▼●◗

Fiendish Ghouls, The SEE: **Mania**

Fiendish Plot of Dr. Fu Manchu, The (1980-British) **C-108m.** BOMB D: Piers Haggard. Peter Sellers, Helen Mirren, Sid Caesar, David Tomlinson, Simon Williams, Steve Franken. Disastrous comedy features Sellers in a dual role, as the title character and as his archenemy, Scotland Yard detective Nayland Smith. Painfully unfunny and, sad to say, Sellers' last film. [PG]▼●

Fiend Who Walked the West, The (1958) **101m.** **½ D: Gordon Douglas. Hugh O'Brian, Robert Evans, Dolores Michaels, Linda Cristal, Stephen McNally. Interesting if not altogether successful transposition of KISS OF DEATH to Western setting, with Evans ludicrous in the Widmark psycho role. CinemaScope.▼

Fiend Without a Face (1958-British) **74m.** *½ D: Arthur Crabtree. Marshall Thompson, Kim Parker, Terence Kilburn, Michael Balfour, Gil Winfield. Scientist materializes thoughts in form of invisible brain-shaped creatures which kill people for food. Horrific climax; good special effects.▼●
Fiend With the Atomic Brain, The SEE: **Blood of Ghastly Horror**
Fiend with the Electronic Brain, The SEE: **Blood of Ghastly Horror**
Fierce SEE: **Fighting Mad** (1981)
Fierce Creatures (1997) **C-93m.** **½ D: Robert Young, Fred Schepisi. John Cleese, Jamie Lee Curtis, Kevin Kline, Michael Palin, Ronnie Corbett, Carey Lowell, Robert Lindsay. Heartless corporate mogul takes over a failing British zoo and insists it pay its own way, leaving the new zoo director (Cleese) to deal with a resentful staff and other complications. Pleasant enough farce cowritten by Cleese to reunite the cast of A FISH CALLED WANDA never quite pays off, but has its moments. Kline is fun in a dual role. Filmed in 1995, then largely rewritten and refilmed in 1996 with a new director (Schepisi); note how Lowell disappears from whole sections of the picture. Cynthia Cleese, one of the zookeepers, is John's daughter. Panavision. [PG-13] ▼●◗
Fiercest Heart, The (1961) **C-91m.** ** D: George Sherman. Stuart Whitman, Juliet Prowse, Ken Scott, Raymond Massey, Geraldine Fitzgerald. Good cast and action-packed skirmishes with Zulus can't raise this programmer to any heights. Set in Africa. CinemaScope.
Fiesta (1947) **C-104m.** ** D: Richard Thorpe. Esther Williams, Akim Tamiroff, Ricardo Montalban, John Carroll, Mary Astor, Cyd Charisse. Williams trades in her bathing suit for a toreador outfit in this weak musical opus.
15 Malden Lane (1936) **65m.** ** D: Allan Dwan. Claire Trevor, Cesar Romero, Douglas Fowley, Lloyd Nolan, Lester Matthews. Trevor lures Romero in order to crack his underworld gang in this satisfactory programmer.
5th Ave. Girl (1939) **83m.** ** D: Gregory LaCava. Ginger Rogers, Walter Connolly, Verree Teasdale, James Ellison, Tim Holt, Kathryn Adams, Franklin Pangborn, Louis Calhern, Jack Carson. Tiresome social comedy with Rogers as homeless girl taken in by unhappy millionaire Connolly; even Ginger is lifeless in this film that purports to show that poor is better than rich if you've got a head on your shoulders.▼●
Fifth Day of Peace, The (1972-Italian) **C-100m.** ** D: Guilliano Montaldo. Richard Johnson, Franco Nero, Bud Spencer, Michael Goodliffe, Helmut Schneider. Episodic story of several disillusioned WW1 German soldiers aimlessly wandering war-ravaged Italian countryside following the armistice. [PG]▼●◗
Fifth Element, The (1997-French) **C-127m.** *** D: Luc Besson. Bruce Willis, Gary Oldman, Ian Holm, Milla Jovovich, Chris Tucker, Luke Perry, Brion James, Tommy "Tiny" Lister, Jr., Lee Evans, John Neville. Wildly imaginative tale set in the 23rd century, where a world-weary Brooklyn, N.Y., cab driver finds himself involved with a strange woman who may be responsible for saving the world from destruction. A visual candy store of futuristic images, but the film's strongest suit is its sense of humor. Unfortunately, it gets a bit tedious and formulaic toward the end, with Tucker's over-the-top radio host hogging the spotlight. Conceived by Besson when he was a teenager. Super 35. [PG-13]▼●◗
Fifth Floor, The (1980) **C-90m.** BOMB D: Howard Avedis. Bo Hopkins, Dianne Hull, Patti D'Arbanville, Sharon Farrell, Mel Ferrer, Julie Adams, John David Carson. A few laughs don't compensate for derivative story of college disco dancer who is wrongly committed to an insane asylum. Collectors of screen dementia should study Hopkins's performance. [R]▼
Fifth Monkey, The (1990) **C-93m.** *** D: Eric Rochat. Ben Kingsley, Mika Lins, Vera Fischer, Silvia De Carvalho. Straightforward, extremely enjoyable tale of snake and rare animal hunter Kingsley, and his escapades while attempting to sell chimps and earn enough money to wed the woman of his dreams. Rochat, who also scripted, movingly illustrates the necessity for mankind to respect the animal world. Beautifully filmed in Brazil. [PG-13]▼●
5th Musketeer, The (1979-Austrian) **C-103m.** **½ D: Ken Annakin. Beau Bridges, Sylvia Kristel, Ursula Andress, Cornel Wilde, Ian McShane, Lloyd Bridges, Alan Hale, Jr., Jose Ferrer, Helmut Dantine, Rex Harrison, Olivia de Havilland. Lavish, well-cast remake of THE MAN IN THE IRON MASK offers nothing new, but retells Dumas' story in capable fashion. Major points of interest: Austrian location, veteran cast. Filmed in 1977. [PG]▼
Fifty/Fifty (1992) **C-101m.** *½ D: Charles Martin Smith. Peter Weller, Robert Hays, Charles Martin Smith, Ramona Rahman, Kay Tong Lim, Dom Magwili. CIA mercenaries Weller and Hays bicker and bumble through the jungle in this silly action/adventure, in which revolvers outshoot machine guns; takes a serious turn when the "heroes" finally take a stand. [R]▼
55 Days at Peking (1963) **C-150m.** *** D: Nicholas Ray. Charlton Heston, Ava Gardner, David Niven, Flora Robson, John Ireland, Paul Lukas, Jacques Sernas. Stars provide most of the interest in confusing historical account of Boxer Rebellion in 1900s China. Super Technirama 70. ▼●

54 (1998) **C-93m.** ** D: Mark Christopher. Ryan Phillippe, Salma Hayek, Neve Campbell, Mike Myers, Sela Ward, Breckin Meyer, Sherry Stringfield, Ellen Albertini Dow, Heather Matarazzo, Lauren Hutton, Michael York, Daniel Lapaine, Ron Jeremy. Dreary drama attempts to capture the spirit of hedonistic nightclub Studio 54, which flourished in the 1970s and attracted naive young people like Phillippe, who thought entry meant a stepping-stone to success and self-esteem. Clichéd story takes focus off the most interesting person onscreen—Myers, in a canny performance as Steve Rubell, the ringmaster of this nightly drug-and-sex party. Various celebrities appear as themselves. [R]▼●◗

Fifty Roads to Town (1937) **81m.** **½ D: Norman Taurog. Don Ameche, Ann Sothern, Slim Summerville, Jane Darwell, John Qualen, Stepin Fetchit, Oscar Apfel. Above-par comedy of Ameche and Sothern, both on the lam for different reasons, snowbound together in small inn.

52nd Street (1937) **80m.** ** D: Harold Young. Ian Hunter, Leo Carrillo, Pat Paterson, Kenny Baker, Ella Logan, ZaSu Pitts. Fictionalized story of how 52nd St. became nightclub row in the 1930s; soggy drama punctuated by appearances of some 52nd St. entertainers like Jerry Colonna, Georgie Tapps, Pat Harrington, Sr.

52 Miles to Midnight SEE: **Hot Rods to Hell**

52 Pick-Up (1986) **C-110m.** ** D: John Frankenheimer. Roy Scheider, Ann-Margret, Vanity, John Glover, Robert Trebor, Lonny Chapman, Kelly Preston, Clarence Williams III, Doug McClure. Self-made businessman is caught in web of blackmail and murder—and determines to break free by himself. Elmore Leonard's story is good, but the lead characters are cold, and film wallows too long in the sleazy, voyeuristic world of the bad guys. It also would have been better shorter. Same novel was adapted just two years earlier as THE AMBASSADOR. [R]▼●

Fight Club (1999) **C-139m.** ** D: David Fincher. Brad Pitt, Edward Norton, Helena Bonham Carter, Meat Loaf (Aday), Jared Leto. A disaffected office worker (Norton) whose life has turned gray finds unexpected release through violent fistfights, organized by a new "friend" (Pitt), who lives life on the edge. The impromptu battles evolve into an underground network of fight clubs where guys pummel each other . . . but the friend has an even more ambitious agenda. Draws you in with its intriguing story, black comedy, and flamboyant visuals, then shifts tone, turns heavy-handed and heads toward an alarmingly senseless resolution. Super 35. [R]▼◗

Fighter, The (1952) **78m.** **½ D: Herbert Kline. Richard Conte, Vanessa Brown, Lee J. Cobb, Roberta Haynes. Absorbing tale set in Mexico with Conte a boxer who uses winnings to buy arms to seek revenge for family's murder.▼

Fighter Attack (1953) **C-80m.** ** D: Lesley Selander. Sterling Hayden, J. Carrol Naish, Joy Page, Paul Fierro. Modest film uses flashback to recount Hayden's last important mission in WW2 Italy.▼

Fighter Squadron (1948) **C-96m.** ** D: Raoul Walsh. Edmond O'Brien, Robert Stack, John Rodney, Tom D'Andrea, Henry Hull. OK WW2 drama of dedicated flier O'Brien, has abundance of clichés weighing against good action sequences. Rock Hudson's first film.

Fight For Your Lady (1937) **67m.** **½ D: Ben Stoloff. John Boles, Jack Oakie, Ida Lupino, Margot Grahame, Gordon Jones, Erik Rhodes, Billy Gilbert. Wrestling trainer Oakie takes over singer Boles' love life when he's jilted by tony Grahame in this fluffy but funny musical comedy. Rhodes is hilarious, as usual, as Spadissimo.

Fighting Back (1982) **C-98m.** **½ D: Lewis Teague. Tom Skerritt, Patti LuPone, Michael Sarrazin, Yaphet Kotto, David Rasche, Ted Ross, Pat Cooper. A return visit to DEATH WISH territory; fed up with lackadaisical police, hotheaded South Philly deli owner (Skerritt, who's excellent) organizes Guardian Angels-like patrol to clean up criminal scum, but is unprepared for the complications which ensue. Unpleasant, but fast, slick, and convincing; these people know which buttons to push. [R]▼

Fighting Back (1982-Australian) **C-100m.** **½ D: Michael Caulfield. Lewis Fitz-Gerald, Paul Smith, Kris McQuade, Robyn Nevin, Caroline Gillmer. Ambitious if not entirely successful drama of teacher Fitz-Gerald trying to tame unruly, illiterate 13-year-old (Smith, excellent in acting debut).

Fighting Chance, The (1955) **70m.** ** D: William Witney. Rod Cameron, Julie London, Ben Cooper, Taylor Holmes, Bob Steele. Standard fare. Horse trainer and jockey friend both fall in love with London and come to odds with each other.

Fighting Coast Guard (1951) **86m.** **½ D: Joseph Kane. Brian Donlevy, Forrest Tucker, Ella Raines, John Russell, Richard Jaeckel, William Murphy, Martin Milner, Steve Brodie, Hugh O'Brian. Better than usual entry in training-for-war film, mixing romance with WW2 military action.

Fighting Father Dunne (1948) **93m.** **½ D: Ted Tetzlaff. Pat O'Brien, Darryl Hickman, Charles Kemper, Una O'Connor, Arthur Shields, Anna Q. Nilsson, Billy Gray. Road company BOYS TOWN with determined priest O'Brien devoting his life to easing the plight of poor, homeless newsboys in St. Louis. ▼

Fighting Fools (1949) **69m.** ** D: Reginald LeBorg. Leo Gorcey, Huntz Hall, Gabriel Dell, Frankie Darro, Billy Benedict, David Gorcey, Benny Bartlett, Lyle

Talbot, Evelynne Eaton, Bernard Gorcey. Familiar fisticuffs as the Bowery Boys team with boxer Darro to break up a fight fixing racket.

Fighting Guardsman (1945) **84m.** ** D: Henry Levin. Willard Parker, Anita Louise, Janis Carter, John Loder, Edgar Buchanan, George Macready. OK costumer of oppressed Frenchmen rising against tyranny in days before French Revolution.

Fighting Kentuckian, The (1949) **100m.** **½ D: George Waggner. John Wayne, Vera Ralston, Philip Dorn, Oliver Hardy, Marie Windsor. Frontierland around 1810 is setting for two-fisted saga of Kentuckian (Wayne) combating land-grabbing criminals and courting Ralston, French general's daughter. Hardy makes rare solo appearance in character role. Also shown in computer-colored version.▼

Fighting Lawman, The (1953) **71m.** *½ D: Thomas Carr. Wayne Morris, Virginia Grey, Harry Lauter, John Kellogg, Myron Healey, Dick Rich. Grey tries to work with flimsy script as gal out to grab loot from robbers, pursued by sheriff.

Fighting Mad (1976) **C-90m.** **½ D: Jonathan Demme. Peter Fonda, Lynn Lowry, John Doucette, Philip Carey, Scott Glenn, Kathleen Miller, Harry Northup. Typical revenge picture, with peaceable Fonda driven to violence by ruthless landowner who wants to take over his farm. On-target for this kind of entertainment. [R]▼

Fighting Mad (1981-U.S.-Filipino) **C-96m.** *½ D: Cirio H. Santiago. James M. Iglehart, Jayne Kennedy, Leon Isaac (Kennedy), Joonie Gamboa, Leo Martinez. Routine actioner has Iglehart, left to die by his buddies during Vietnam War, captured by Japanese soldiers still fighting WW2. Filmed in 1977. Aka FIERCE. [R]▼

Fighting Man of the Plains (1949) **C-94m.** **½ D: Edwin L. Marin. Randolph Scott, Bill Williams, Jane Nigh, Victor Jory. Scott seeks to avenge brother's murder, but kills the wrong man. OK Western, with Dale Robertson in first prominent role as Jesse James.

Fighting O'Flynn, The (1949) **94m.** **½ D: Arthur Pierson. Douglas Fairbanks, Jr., Richard Greene, Helena Carter, Patricia Medina. Enjoyable swashbuckler set in 1800s Ireland with Fairbanks and Greene vying in love and intrigue. Cowritten by Fairbanks and Robert Thoeren.

Fighting Prince of Donegal, The (1966) **C-112m.** *** D: Michael O'Herlihy. Peter McEnery, Susan Hampshire, Tom Adams, Gordon Jackson, Andrew Keir, Donal McCann. Fine Disney swashbuckler made in England, with McEnery as new head of Irish clan who tries to unite his country but runs afoul of villainous Jackson. Vivid, colorful fun.▼

Fighting Seabees, The (1944) **100m.** *** D: Edward Ludwig. John Wayne, Susan Hayward, Dennis O'Keefe, William Frawley, Leonid Kinskey, J. M. Kerrigan, Ben Welden, Paul Fix, Grant Withers, Duncan Renaldo. Spirited WW2 saga of construction company boss Wayne and naval officer O'Keefe tangling professionally and personally, with journalist Hayward the love interest. The scenario charts the manner in which the "Seabees" (or battalion of construction worker–soldiers) came to be established. Screenplay by Borden Chase and Aeneas MacKenzie. Action-packed second unit direction by Howard Lydecker.▼

Fighting 69th, The (1940) **90m.** **½ D: William Keighley. James Cagney, Pat O'Brien, George Brent, Jeffrey Lynn, Alan Hale, Frank McHugh, Dennis Morgan, Dick Foran, John Litel, George Reeves, Frank Coghlan, Jr. Overripe (but tough to dislike) WW1 tale mixes roughneck comedy, exciting battle action, sloppy sentiment, incredible characterizations (especially Cagney's) detailing exploits of famed Irish regiment. Also shown in computer-colored version.▼

Fighting Sullivans, The SEE: **Sullivans, The**

Fighting Trouble (1956) **61m.** *½ D: George Blair. Huntz Hall, Stanley Clements, Adele Jergens, Joseph Downing, Queenie Smith, David Gorcey. With Leo Gorcey gone (replaced by Clements, as "Duke"), Hall became top banana in the *Bowery Boys* series, starting with this underdeveloped crime photographers tale.

Fighting Wildcats, The (1957-British) **74m.** ** D: Arthur Crabtree. Keefe Brasselle, Kay Callard, Karel Stepanek, Ursula Howells. Innocuous intrigue set in London and Middle East involving gangsters. Original title: WEST OF SUEZ.

Fighting Youth (1935) **85m.** **½ D: Hamilton MacFadden. Charles Farrell, June Martel, Andy Devine, J. Farrell MacDonald, Ann Sheridan, Edward Nugent. Commies vs. College Football! A genuinely bizarre bit of kitsch with subversive student Sheridan squaring off against anti-radical quarterback Farrell. Definitely one for the time capsule.

Figures in a Landscape (1970-British) **C-95m.** ** D: Joseph Losey. Robert Shaw, Malcolm McDowell, Henry Woolf, Christopher Malcolm, Pamela Brown. Capable leads and some amazing helicopter stunt work offer scant compensation for muddled allegory about two fugitives in an unnamed country pursued by an unnamed enemy. Barely released. Losey fans will want to give a look. Panavision. [PG]

File of the Golden Goose, The (1969-British) **C-105m.** ** D: Sam Wanamaker. Yul Brynner, Charles Gray, Edward Woodward, John Barrie, Adrienne Corri. Strictly formula effort with American agent and Scotland Yard man going undercover in

London to get the goods on murderous counterfeiting gang. [M/PG]

File on Thelma Jordon, The (1949) **100m.** **½ D: Robert Siodmak. Barbara Stanwyck, Wendell Corey, Joan Tetzel, Stanley Ridges, Richard Rober. Paul Kelly. Tough little film noir focusing largely on romance between unhappily married assistant D.A. Corey and femme fatale Stanwyck. Handsomely photographed by George Barnes. Aka THELMA JORDON.

Fillmore (1972) **C-105m.** *** D: Richard T. Heffron. Bill Graham, The Grateful Dead, It's a Beautiful Day, Santana, Jefferson Airplane, Quicksilver Messenger Service. Good rock documentary about Fillmore West's final days is made even better by extensive footage of its magnetic owner, Bill Graham, on the phone and on stage; one of the better rock films. Multiscreen. [R]▼

Final Analysis (1992) **C-125m.** **½ D: Phil Joanou. Richard Gere, Kim Basinger, Uma Thurman, Eric Roberts, Paul Guilfoyle, Keith David, Robert Harper, Agustin Rodriguez. Stylish, sexy thriller about a San Francisco psychiatrist who becomes involved with a patient's unhappily married sister—only to find himself enmeshed in an elaborate Hitchcockian web of murder and duplicity. Basinger is surprisingly good, Gere distressingly low-key; but the film's plodding mid-section almost undermines a bravura finale. Written by Wesley Strick. Harris Yulin appears unbilled as the prosecuting attorney. [R]▼●◗

Final Approach (1991) **C-100m.** *½ D: Eric Steven Stahl. James B. Sikking, Hector Elizondo, Madolyn Smith, Kevin McCarthy, Cameo Kneuer. Pilot Sikking, testing a stealth-type jet, apparently ejects—then awakens in the office of psychiatrist Elizondo, who wants to investigate the pilot's past. Weary, hackneyed plot treated as if it sparkles with originality. This was the first film recorded with digital technology; the sound is great, but the movie isn't. Panavision. [R]▼●

Final Assignment (1980-Canadian) **C-92m.** BOMB D: Paul Almond. Genevieve Bujold, Michael York, Burgess Meredith, Colleen Dewhurst, Alexandra Stewart. Television reporter Bujold takes on the KGB when she discovers the Russians are conducting scientific experiments on children. Schlock production, with Montreal an unsatisfactory substitute for Moscow; poor script, embarrassing performances. [PG]▼

Final Chapter—Walking Tall (1977) **C-112m.** BOMB D: Jack Starrett. Bo Svenson, Margaret Blye, Forrest Tucker, Lurene Tuttle, Morgan Woodward, Libby Boone. Yet another saga about true-life Tennessee sheriff Buford Pusser, and inferior to its predecessors. Despite title, this is not the final chapter; a TV movie (A REAL AMERICAN HERO) and series followed. [R]▼●

Final Conflict, The (1981) **C-108m.** *½ D: Graham Baker. Sam Neill, Rossano Brazzi, Don Gordon, Lisa Harrow, Mason Adams. The third OMEN movie has the anti-Christ Damien Thorn (Neill) thirtyish and the U.S. Ambassador to England. For genre addicts only. Followed by a TVM OMEN IV: THE AWAKENING. Panavision. [R]▼●

Final Countdown, The (1980) **C-104m.** *** D: Don Taylor. Kirk Douglas, Martin Sheen, Katharine Ross, James Farentino, Ron O'Neal, Charles Durning. An aircraft carrier (the real-life *U.S.S. Nimitz*) enters a time-warp and finds itself in the Pacific just before the attack on Pearl Harbor. Familiar but satisfying fantasy yarn; perfect TV fare although better viewed in Panavision. [PG]▼●

Final Crash, The SEE: **Steelyard Blues**

Final Days, The (1989) **C-150m. TVM** D: Richard Pearce. Lane Smith, Richard Kiley, David Ogden Stiers, Ed Flanders, Theodore Bikel, Graham Beckel, James B. Sikking, Gregg Henry. Well-acted drama about Richard Nixon, from Watergate to his resignation, with veteran character actor Smith doing the president to a superb turn, matched by Kiley's J. Fred Buzhardt, the Special White House Counsel. Everyone else is reduced to a walk-on (although Bikel as Kissinger is really interesting casting). Craftily adapted by playwright Hugh Whitemore from the Bob Woodward–Carl Bernstein book. Above average.▼

Final Destination (2000) **C-97m.** **½ D: James Wong. Devon Sawa, Ali Larter, Kerr Smith, Kristen Cloke, Daniel Roebuck, Roger Guenveur Smith, Chad E. Donella. Before the plane carrying him and his classmates to Paris takes off, teenager Sawa has a vision of it crashing. He and others leave the plane, which (of course) does explode—but the survivors soon start dying in mysterious accidents. Horror movie has an unusual and interesting premise, but paints itself into a corner; the ending is annoyingly unsatisfactory. Feature debut for *X-Files* vet Wong. [R]▼◗

Final Exam (1981) **C-90m.** *½ D: Jimmy Huston. Cecile Bagdadi, Joel S. Rice, Ralph Brown, Deanna Robbins, Sherry Willis-Burch. Killer stalks college kids. Not as bloody as most other entries in the genre, but still not very good. [R]▼

Final Option, The (1982-British) **C-125m.** BOMB D: Ian Sharp. Lewis Collins, Judy Davis, Richard Widmark, Robert Webber, Edward Woodward, Tony Doyle, John Duttine, Kenneth Griffith, Ingrid Pitt. Laughably ridiculous account of Britain's Special Air Services team and how one officer (Collins) goes underground—more or less—to infiltrate a terrorist gang with plans to take over the American Embassy. Lots of violence, but no brains in sight. Third-billed Widmark has precious little screen time, as the U.S. Secretary of State. Original British title: WHO DARES WINS. [R]▼

Final Programme, The SEE: **Last Days of Man on Earth, The**

Final Terror, The (1981) **C-82m.** *½ D: Andrew Davis. John Friedrich, Adrian Zmed, Daryl Hannah, Rachel Ward, Mark Metcalf. Pretty bad dead-teenagers film set in the backwoods, of marginal interest for presence of latter-day stars in cast (though they don't get much of a showcase here). [R]▼

Final Test, The (1953-British) **84m.** **½ D: Anthony Asquith. Jack Warner, Robert Morley, George Relph, Adrianne Allen. Droll, minor comedy of father-son rivalry over charming Allen.

Finders Keepers (1951) **74m.** **½ D: Frederick de Cordova. Tom Ewell, Julia (Julie) Adams, Evelyn Varden, Dusty Henley. Scatterbrained comedy that chugs down at end. Ewell and Varden enliven proceedings about a little boy who comes home with a cartful of money.

Finders Keepers (1984) **C-96m.** ** D: Richard Lester. Michael O'Keefe, Beverly D'Angelo, Louis Gossett, Jr., Ed Lauter, David Wayne, Pamela Stephenson, Brian Dennehy, John Schuck, Timothy Blake, Jim Carrey, Jack Riley. Wholehearted attempt at farce, involving stolen money, con artists in disguise, a bungling hit-man, and other promising ingredients, remains disappointingly flat. Lester manages a few neat sight gags, and Wayne is genuinely funny as the world's oldest train conductor. [R]▼

Find the Lady (1976-Canadian-British) **C-79m.** *½ D: John Trent. Lawrence Dane, John Candy, Michel Rooney, Peter Cook, Alexandra Bastedo, Dick Emery. Pre-POLICE ACADEMY comedy about inept cops Dane and Candy, on the trail of a kidnapped socialite. A couple of genuine laughs, but mostly silly—and occasionally offensive. Candy and Dane played same characters a year earlier in IT SEEMED LIKE A GOOD IDEA AT THE TIME. Aka CALL THE COPS!, KOPEK AND BROOM, and GOOD IDEA! ▼

Fine Madness, A (1966) **C-104m.** *** D: Irvin Kershner. Sean Connery, Joanne Woodward, Jean Seberg, Patrick O'Neal, Colleen Dewhurst, Renee Taylor. It's stubborn, nonconformist poet Connery versus the rest of society in uneven but sometimes outrageously funny satire. Screenplay by Elliot Baker, from his novel.▼

Fine Mess, A (1986) **C-88m.** *½ D: Blake Edwards. Ted Danson, Howie Mandel, Richard Mulligan, Stuart Margolin, Maria Conchita Alonso, Jennifer Edwards, Paul Sorvino. A slapstick saga of two bumblers, with laughs few and far between. Familiar Blake Edwards trademarks, and the supposed inspiration of Laurel and Hardy's Oscar-winning short, THE MUSIC BOX, don't carry this very far. Panavision. [PG]▼●

Fine Pair, A (1968) **C-89m.** BOMB D: Francesco Maselli. Rock Hudson, Claudia Cardinale, Thomas Milian, Leon Askin, Ellen Corby, Walter Giller. N.Y.C. policeman Hudson falls for Cardinale, daughter of an old pal, and helps her rob some jewels in terrible comedy-thriller minus laughs or suspense. Panavision. [M/PG]

Fine Romance, A (1992-U.S.-Italian) **C-83m.** ** D: Gene Saks. Julie Andrews, Marcello Mastroianni, Ian Fitzgibbon, Jean-Pierre Castaldi, Jean-Jacques Dulon, Maria Machado, Catherine Jarret. Andrews and Mastroianni try (but fail) to enliven this obvious, barely funny farce, cast as a pair whose mates have run off together, and who predictably become romantically involved themselves. Scripted by Ronald Harwood. [PG-13]▼

Finger Man (1955) **82m.** ** D: Harold Schuster. Frank Lovejoy, Forrest Tucker, Peggie Castle, Timothy Carey, Glenn Gordon, Evelynne Eaton. Convincing performances uplift account of federal agents capturing liquor gang.▼

Finger of Guilt (1956-British) **85m.** **½ D: Joseph Losey. Richard Basehart, Mary Murphy, Constance Cummings, Roger Livesey, Mervyn Johns, Faith Brook. Film director Basehart is blackmailed by woman claiming to be his mistress, which threatens his career and marriage. Intriguing film with disappointing resolution; good look inside British film studio, however. Directed by blacklistee Losey under pseudonyms Alec Snowden/Joseph Walton. Originally released in England as THE INTIMATE STRANGER at 95m.

Finger on the Trigger (1965) **C-87m.** BOMB D: Sidney Pink. Rory Calhoun, James Philbrook, Todd Martin, Silvia Solar, Brad Talbot. Reb and Yankee vets join forces to secure buried treasure while holding off hostile Indians. Made in Spain. Techniscope.▼

Finger Points, The (1931) **88m.** **½ D: John Francis Dillon. Richard Barthelmess, Fay Wray, Regis Toomey, Robert Elliott, Clark Gable. Vivid though meandering melodrama about crime reporter Barthelmess on the payroll of the mob. Wray is a newspaperwoman who urges him to go straight; Gable scores as a gang boss. One of the writers was W. R. Burnett.

Fingers (1978) **C-91m.** ***½ D: James Toback. Harvey Keitel, Jim Brown, Tisa Farrow, Michael V. Gazzo, Tanya Roberts, Marian Seldes, Danny Aiello, Ed Marinaro, Zack Norman. Crude but fascinating melodrama about an aspiring concert pianist who reluctantly "collects" on debts owed to his domineering father. Powerful, disturbing film is compellingly sensual and brilliantly acted, especially by Brown in a rare subdued role. Screenplay by the director. [R]▼

Fingers at the Window (1942) **80m.** **½ D: Charles Lederer. Lew Ayres, Laraine Day, Basil Rathbone, Walter Kingsford, Miles Mander, James Flavin. Entertaining mystery of Ayres and Day tracking down maniac killer masterminding repeated axe murders.

Finian's Rainbow (1968) **C-145m.** ***½ D: Francis Ford Coppola. Fred Astaire, Petula Clark, Tommy Steele, Keenan Wynn, Al Freeman, Jr., Don Francks, Barbara Hancock. Whimsical Burton Lane-E. Y. Harburg musical fantasy about racial injustice was ahead of its time in the late '40s on Broadway, embarrassingly dated 20 years later, but Coppola and an attractive cast work wonders with it in this imaginatively filmed, widescreen winner—perhaps the best movie musical of its era. Harburg's lyrics remain elegant and witty, and Astaire is fun as the transplanted Irishman whose leprechaun comes to life in the American South. Try to see it in a theater. Panavision. [G]▼●

Finishing School (1934) **73m.** **½ D: Wanda Tuchock, George Nicholls, Jr. Frances Dee, Bruce Cabot, Ginger Rogers, Beulah Bondi, Billie Burke, John Halliday. Interesting look at exclusive girls' school where hypocrisy reigns; wealthy Dee falls in love with struggling hospital intern Cabot.▼

Finnegan Begin Again (1985) **C-105m. TVM** D: Joan Micklin Silver. Mary Tyler Moore, Robert Preston, Sylvia Sidney, Sam Waterston, David Huddleston, Bob Gunton. Delightful comedy-drama about the unlikely relationship that blossoms between a widowed schoolteacher caught in a dead-end love affair with a married mortician and an aging newspaperman with a wife at home who's drifting into senility. Preston especially is an absolute joy. Made for cable. Above average.▼

Finnegans Wake (1965) **97m.** ***½ D: Mary Ellen Bute. Page Johnson, Martin J. Kelly, Jane Reilly, Peter Haskell. James Joyce's classic story of Irish tavern-keeper who dreams of attending his own wake is brought to the screen with great energy and control.

Fiorile (1993-Italian-French-German) **C-118m.** *** D: Paolo and Vittorio Taviani. Claudio Bigagli, Galatea Ranzi, Michael Vartan, Lino Capolicchio, Constanze Engelbrecht, Athina Cenci, Giovanni Guidelli, Chiara Caselli. While driving to visit his ailing, reclusive father, a man reveals to his two children the legend of their family's history, beginning with how their ancestors came into wealth dishonestly during the Napoleonic era. Complex, ironic tale of tarnished innocence, outside forces cruelly separating lovers, and how ill-gotten wealth will in one way or another taint the spirit. [PG-13]▼●

Fire (1997-Canadian-Indian) **C-104m.** ** D: Deepa Mehta. Shabana Azmi, Nandita Das, Kulbushan Kharbanda, Jaaved Jaaferi, Ranjit Chowdhury, Kushal Rekhi. Ho-hum lesbian-feminist drama set in New Delhi, which charts the growing spiritual/sexual attraction between a long-married woman (Azmi) and her young, newlywed sister-in-law (Das). Without exception, every male character in the story is a simplistic chauvinist pig, and the result is a superficial drama that substitutes female outrage for thoughtful filmmaking.▼

Fire and Ice (1983) **C-81m.** **½ D: Ralph Bakshi. Voices of Susan Tyrrell, Maggie Roswell, William Ostrander, Stephen Mendel. Muscular hero and buxom heroine become involved in power struggle between two warring world powers. Animated sword-and-sorcery saga is no worse (and arguably no better) than an average live-action entry, and benefits from graphic design by fabled illustrator Frank Frazetta, though the animation itself has been traced from live footage. Scripted by well-known comic book writers Roy Thomas and Gerry Conway. [PG]▼●

Fire and Ice (1987-German) **C-83m.** BOMB D: Willy Bogner. Suzy Chaffee, John Eaves, narrated by John Denver. Loud, boring, interminable (even at 83m.) tale of skier "John" (Eaves), who romances skier "Suzy" (Chaffee) on the slopes. Bogner also produced, scripted, photographed, and designed the costumes. A real snooze, despite some good ski footage. [PG]▼●

Fireball, The (1950) **84m.** *** D: Tay Garnett. Mickey Rooney, Pat O'Brien, Beverly Tyler, Marilyn Monroe, Milburn Stone, Glenn Corbett. Rooney's energetic performance carries this film. Orphan boy devotes himself to becoming big-time roller-skating champ.▼

Fireball 500 (1966) **C-92m.** BOMB D: William Asher. Frankie Avalon, Annette Funicello, Fabian, Chill Wills, Harvey Lembeck, Julie Parrish. Frankie is a stock-car racer who unknowingly transports moonshine whiskey. Desperately in need of a beach ball. Panavision.

Fire Birds (1990) **C-85m.** BOMB D: David Green. Nicolas Cage, Tommy Lee Jones, Sean Young, Bryan Kestner, Dale Dye, Mary Ellen Trainor, J. A. Preston, Peter Onorati. High-tech Apache helicopters (with an assist from their pilots) take on South American drug cartels from the air. Standard military issue with a ruptured-duck script and no romantic chemistry between professional rivals Cage and Young.

Jones doesn't evoke memories of Gregory Peck in TWELVE O'CLOCK HIGH when he pep-talks Cage into a "full-tilt boogie for freedom and justice." [PG-13]▼●

Firechasers, The (1970-British) **C-101m.** ** D: Sidney Hayers. Chad Everett, Anjanette Comer, Keith Barron, Joanne Dainton, Rupert Davies, John Loder. Strong production values in familiar story of insurance investigator hunting for arsonist.

Firecreek (1968) **C-104m.** **½ D: Vincent McEveety. James Stewart, Henry Fonda, Inger Stevens, Gary Lockwood, Dean Jagger, Ed Begley, Jay C. Flippen, Jack Elam, Barbara Luna. Somber Western has makings of a classic at outset, but goes astray, and goes on too long. Stewart is mild-mannered part-time sheriff in small town terrorized by Fonda and fellow plunderers. Beautifully photographed (by William H. Clothier), but unrelentingly downbeat. Panavision.▼

Fire Down Below (1957-British) **C-116m.** **½ D: Robert Parrish. Rita Hayworth, Robert Mitchum, Jack Lemmon, Herbert Lom, Bernard Lee, Anthony Newley. Contrived but entertaining melodrama of Mitchum and Lemmon, owners of tramp boat, falling in love with shady Hayworth on voyage between islands. CinemaScope.▼

Fire Down Below (1997) **C-105m.** ** D: Felix Enriquez Alcalá. Steven Seagal, Marg Helgenberger, Kris Kristofferson, Stephen Lang, Harry Dean Stanton, Levon Helm, Richard Masur, John Diehl, Robert Ridgely, Randy Travis. You're looking for an E.P.A. agent to go work incognito avenging a murder in Appalachia—so who you gonna call? Well, how about Steve, with his standard haircut and man-in-black garb? Laughably bad, junky action outing with a reasonable pace to match its outrageousness. Marty Stuart and Travis Tritt appear as themselves. [R] ▼●◗

Firefly, The (1937) **131m.** **½ D: Robert Z. Leonard. Jeanette MacDonald, Allan Jones, Warren William, Billy Gilbert, Henry Daniell, Douglass Dumbrille, George Zucco. Tried-and-true operetta moves slowly and goes on too long, but Jones' "Donkey Serenade" and Jeanette's vivacity remain enjoyable.▼

Firefox (1982) **C-124m.** *½ D: Clint Eastwood. Clint Eastwood, Freddie Jones, David Huffman, Warren Clarke, Ronald Lacey, Stefan Schnabel, Nigel Hawthorne, John Ratzenberger. Lamentably dull, slow-moving espionage yarn, with Eastwood as burned-out U.S. pilot who goes behind Russian lines to steal the Soviets' latest aeronautic marvel: a supersonic fighting plane. Jones wins the Charles Laughton Award for Eccentric Performances. Originally released at 137m. Panavision. [PG]▼●

Fire, Ice and Dynamite (1990-German) **C-102m.** BOMB D: Willy Bogner. Roger Moore, Shari Belafonte, Simon Shepherd, Uwe Ochsenknecht, Geoffrey Moore, Connie de Groot, Marjoe Gortner, Isaac Hayes. Obscenely wealthy Moore, whose empire is crumbling, fakes suicide to test the mettle of his children and creditors in an athletic competition. Loud, lame, occasionally offensive timewaster, redeemed (just barely) by the stuntwork. As inept as Bogner's earlier FIRE AND ICE. [PG]▼

Fire in the Sky (1993) **C-107m.** ** D: Robert Lieberman. D. B. Sweeney, Robert Patrick, Craig Sheffer, Peter Berg, James Garner, Henry Thomas, Bradley Gregg, Noble Willingham, Kathleen Wilhoite. Failed sci-fi outing, allegedly based on fact, with Sweeney cast as Travis Wilson, a man who mysteriously disappeared for five days, during which time he supposedly was taken prisoner by extraterrestrials. Written by Tracy (son of Mel) Tormé, and based on Wilson's book *The Walton Experience*. Super 35. [PG-13]▼●

Firelight (1998-U.S.-British) **C-103m.** *** D: William Nicholson. Sophie Marceau, Stephen Dillane, Dominique Belcourt, Kevin Anderson, Lia Williams, Joss Ackland, Sally Dexter. A beautiful Swiss governess (Marceau) is hired to bear a child for a 19th-century British aristocrat (Dillane) whose wife is an invalid, but naturally the two of them fall helplessly in love with each other. Well-made, old-fashioned Gothic soap opera in the MADAME X/JANE EYRE vein. Written by the director. Panavision. [R]▼●

Fire Maidens of Outer Space (1955-British) **80m.** BOMB D: Cy Roth. Anthony Dexter, Susan Shaw, Paul Carpenter, Harry Fowler, Sydney Tafler. Ultracheap space opera about astronauts who land on Jupiter's 13th moon and discover a society of young lovelies in need of male companionship. Another in the So Bad It's Good Sweepstakes; you haven't lived until you've seen the Fire Maidens perform their ritual dance to "Stranger in Paradise."▼

Fireman, Save My Child (1932) **67m.** **½ D: Lloyd Bacon. Joe E. Brown, Evalyn Knapp, Lillian Bond, Guy Kibbee, Virginia Sale. Amusing Brown romp with Joe dividing his time between fire-fighting and baseball. The first in his baseball trilogy, followed by ELMER THE GREAT and ALIBI IKE.

Fireman Save My Child (1954) **80m.** *½ D: Leslie Goodwins. Spike Jones, The City Slickers, Buddy Hackett, Hugh O' Brian, Adele Jergens. Sloppy slapstick with Spike Jones et al. manning fire station in 1900s San Francisco, running amuck when they receive a new fire engine. Originally intended for Abbott and Costello, who are still visible in some long shots.

Firemen's Ball, The (1967-Czech) **C-73m.** ** D: Milos Forman. Jan Vostrcil, Josef Sebanek, Josef Valnoha, Josef Kolb, Vaclav

Stockel. Acclaimed comedy of small-town firemen's ball which turns into sprawling disaster apparently has elusive charm that completely escaped us.▼●

Fire on the Amazon (1996) **C-81m.** ** D: Luis Llosa. Craig Sheffer, Sandra Bullock, Juan Fernandez, Judith Chapman, Ramsey Ross, David Elkin, Jorge Garcia Bustamante. Well-intentioned "save the rainforest" story, marred by appallingly reckless and hostile behavior of photojournalist Sheffer, whose stupidity should have had him blown away very early in the film. Contrived romance with activist Bullock is no more believable. Filmed in 1990. Executive-produced by Roger Corman. Unrated version also available. [R]▼◗

Fire Over Africa (1954) **C-84m.** ** D: Richard Sale. Maureen O'Hara, Macdonald Carey, Binnie Barnes, Guy Middleton. O'Hara makes a pretty law enforcer traveling to Africa to track down dope-smuggling syndicate. Filmed on location.

Fire Over England (1937-British) **89m.** *** D: William K. Howard. Laurence Olivier, Flora Robson, Leslie Banks, Raymond Massey, Vivien Leigh, Tamara Desni, Morton Selten, Robert Newton, Donald Calthrop. Satisfying historical drama of British-Spanish conflict in 1500s with flawless performance by Robson (Queen Elizabeth), fine villainy by Massey, romantic support by Olivier and Leigh. Watch for James Mason in a small (unbilled) role.▼●◗

Firepower (1979-British) **C-104m.** **½ D: Michael Winner. Sophia Loren, James Coburn, O. J. Simpson, Eli Wallach, Anthony Franciosa, George Grizzard, Vincent Gardenia, Victor Mature. Another international all-star action thriller, with beautiful people in beautiful locations (this time, the Caribbean). Inane, complicated story has Loren seeking revenge for murder of her chemist husband. Passable time-filler, especially on TV. [R]▼

Fire Sale (1977) **C-88m.** BOMB D: Alan Arkin. Alan Arkin, Rob Reiner, Vincent Gardenia, Anjanette Comer, Kay Medford, Sid Caesar, Barbara Dana, Alex Rocco, Richard Libertini, Augusta Dabney. Wretched black comedy about a department store owner and his two sons gives bad taste a bad name. Truly unbearable. [PG]

Fires on the Plain (1959-Japanese) **105m.** ***½ D: Kon Ichikawa. Eiji Funakoshi, Mantaro Ushio, Yoshihiro Hamaguchi, Osamu Takizawa. Japanese soldiers struggle to survive at the finale of the Philippine campaign during WW2; focus is on travails of tubercular Funakoshi, separated from his unit. Graphically realistic, disturbing, and depressing vision of damnation on earth, with a sobering antiwar message. Daieiscope.▼●

Firestarter (1984) **C-115m.** ** D: Mark L. Lester. David Keith, Drew Barrymore, George C. Scott, Martin Sheen, Heather Locklear, Art Carney, Louise Fletcher, Moses Gunn, Freddie Jones. Silly, sometimes laughable yarn about little girl whose parents acquired unusual mental powers as a result of a government experiment and who herself can set anything on fire at will. Lumbering story wastes a lot of acting talent, though it certainly gave employment to a number of stunt people and special effects technicians. From Stephen King's best-seller. J-D-C Scope. [R]▼●◗

Firestorm (1998) **C-89m.** *½ D: Dean Semler. Howie Long, William Forsythe, Scott Glenn, Suzy Amis, Christianne Hirt, Garwin Sanford. Wily con Forsythe and cohorts have pulled off a prison escape, incinerating a Canadian forest as their "cover." This makes the job of smoke jumpers (who parachute into difficult fires) all the more risky. By-the-numbers script is fashioned as an action vehicle for athlete Long, who suggests what Ed Harris might look like if he couldn't move his facial muscles. [R] ▼●◗

Fires Within (1991) **C-86m.** ** D: Gillian Armstrong. Jimmy Smits, Greta Scacchi, Vincent D'Onofrio, Luis Avalos, Bertila Damas, Raul Davila, Bri Hathaway, Daniel Fern. Well-intentioned but underdeveloped story of anguish suffered by a Cuban political prisoner and his family when they're reunited in Miami after an eight-year separation. Smits and Scacchi certainly make a great-looking couple. [R]▼

Firewalker (1986) **C-104m.** BOMB D: J. Lee Thompson. Chuck Norris, Lou Gossett, Melody Anderson, Will Sampson, Sonny Landham, John Rhys-Davies, Ian Abercrombie. Anderson, hair perfectly intact throughout, hires Gossett and fellow mercenary Norris to find a hidden cache of loot she's imagined exists. Press releases described Norris' character as a "soldier-of-wacky-misfortune"; his light comedy skills recall a sportswriter's description of Yogi Berra playing third base—"like a man trying to put up a pup tent in a windstorm." Arguably Chuck's worst—but who wants to argue? [PG]▼●

Fire With Fire (1986) **C-103m.** **½ D: Duncan Gibbins. Craig Sheffer, Virginia Madsen, Jon Polito, Jeffrey Jay Cohen, Kate Reid, Jean Smart, D. B. Sweeney. Story of a forbidden love affair between a boy imprisoned at a juvenile detention facility and girl who *feels* imprisoned at Catholic girl's school nearby. Seems to move slowly, since there are no real surprises, but the leads are appealing and it's pleasant enough to watch . . . until ludicrous finale. Film buffs should note Ann Savage in the small role of Sister Harriet. [PG-13]▼

Fire Within, The (1963-French) **108m.** ***½ D: Louis Malle. Maurice Ronet, Lena Skerla, Yvonne Clech, Hubert Deschamps, Jeanne Moreau, Alexandra Stewart. Shattering study of alcoholism, as wealthy Ronet, released from a sanitarium after a breakdown, visits his old friends in Paris one last time. Probably Malle's best early film—photographed, scored (with the music of Erik Satie), and acted to maximum effect—and with a minimum of self-pity.▼

Fireworks (1998-Japanese) **C-103m.** *** D: Takeshi Kitano. "Beat" Takeshi, Kayoko Kishimoto, Ren Osugi, Susumu Terajima, Tetsu Watanabe, Taro Itsumi. Tough cop's world crumbles around him: his wife is dying, his partner becomes confined to a wheelchair, and a young detective dies in a shootout because of his blunder, forcing him into a deal with the yakuza. Strongly directed film begins with clear but fragmentary flashbacks; melancholy, violent, sardonic, and romantic, it's an outstanding movie of its genre. The director, who also wrote and coedited, uses "Beat" Takeshi as an acting name. Original title: HANA-BI.▼

Firm, The (1993) **C-154m.** *** D: Sydney Pollack. Tom Cruise, Gene Hackman, Jeanne Tripplehorn, Holly Hunter, Ed Harris, Hal Holbrook, Terry Kinney, Wilford Brimley, David Strathairn, Gary Busey, Steven Hill, Tobin Bell, Barbara Garrick, Jerry Hardin, Paul Colderon, Jerry Weintraub, Karina Lombard, John Beal. Slick adaptation of John Grisham's best-seller about a Harvard law school grad who's wooed by a Memphis law firm and happily signs on, never suspecting the sinister truth behind its gracious facade. Good storytelling and good performances, but it goes on too long . . . and makes some unfortunate changes from Grisham's original. Still, it's attractive and entertaining. Paul Sorvino appears unbilled as a Mafioso. [R]▼●◗

First Blood (1982) **C-97m.** *½ D: Ted Kotcheff. Sylvester Stallone, Richard Crenna, Brian Dennehy, David Caruso, Jack Starrett. Ex-Green Beret is falsely arrested by smalltown cops, escapes and leads his pursuers into all kinds of booby traps in the "jungles" of U.S. Northwest. Throws all credibility to the winds about the time he gets off with only a bad cut after jumping from a mountain into some jagged rocks. A kewpie doll to anyone who can understand more than three words of Sly's final monologue. Followed by RAMBO: FIRST BLOOD PART II. Panavision. [R]▼●◗

Firstborn (1984) **C-103m.** ** D: Michael Apted. Teri Garr, Peter Weller, Christopher Collet, Corey Haim, Sarah Jessica Parker, Robert Downey, Jr. Divorced mom is doing her best to raise two sons—until she lets her latest boyfriend (a real lout) move into the house and take over. Credible, if unappealing, drama leads to repellent conclusion, à la DEATH WISH, putting to waste the film's good qualities and performances. [PG-13]▼●

First Comes Courage (1943) **88m.** **½ D: Dorothy Arzner. Merle Oberon, Brian Aherne, Carl Esmond, Fritz Leiber, Erik Rolf. Fairly good wartime film of Norwegian Oberon using her feminine wiles to extract secrets from Nazi officer.

First Deadly Sin, The (1980) **C-112m.** *** D: Brian G. Hutton. Frank Sinatra, Faye Dunaway, David Dukes, Brenda Vaccaro, Martin Gabel, James Whitmore. Sinatra's first starring feature after 10-year absence finds him in good form in adaptation of Lawrence Sanders' best-seller about an N.Y.C. cop who stalks a psycho during his wife's illness. Dunaway's near-comatose role couldn't be more thankless, but good supporting cast and moody Gordon Jenkins score make this one of Frank's better serious vehicles. Look fast for Bruce Willis half-hidden under a cap in a bar scene. [R]▼●◗

. . . First Do No Harm (1997) **C-100m. TVM** D: Jim Abrahams. Meryl Streep, Fred Ward, Seth Adkins, Margo Martindale, Allison Janney. Streep works her special magic as a determined mom with an epileptic young son; his suffering causes her to sidestep conventional medicine and experiment with a controversial diet treatment. Inspired by actual events in the life of producer/director Abrahams, whose son's experiences led him to champion the Ketogenic Diet. Above average.▼

First Family (1980) **C-104m.** ** D: Buck Henry. Bob Newhart, Gilda Radner, Madeline Kahn, Richard Benjamin, Bob Dishy, Harvey Korman, Rip Torn, Austin Pendleton, Fred Willard, Julius Harris, Buck Henry. Almost laughless political satire, written by Henry, with Newhart a bumbling U.S. President, Kahn his inebriated First Lady, Radner their horny First Daughter. However, Newhart's conversation with African Ambassador Harris is a gem. [R]▼

First Great Train Robbery, The SEE: **Great Train Robbery, The**

First Kid (1996) **C-101m.** *** D: David Mickey Evans. Sinbad, Brock Pierce, Blake Boyd, Timothy Busfield, Art La Fleur, Robert Guillaume, Lisa Eichhorn, James Naughton, Fawn Reed, Zachery Ty Bryan, Bill Cobbs. Very entertaining Disney comedy about a hang-loose Secret Service agent on the White House detail who gets the worst assignment in town: guarding the President's bratty son. Soon enough, however, he and the boy form a bond. Subplot about a disgruntled ex-agent gets a little intense for a family film, but otherwise this is bull's-eye stuff and a great comic vehicle for Sinbad. [PG]▼●

First Knight (1995) **C-132m.** *** D: Jerry Zucker. Sean Connery, Richard Gere, Julia Ormond, Ben Cross, Liam Cunningham, Christopher Villiers, Valentine Pelka, Colin McCormack, Ralph Ineson, John Gielgud. Handsome, sweeping, romantic adventure saga that focuses on a love triangle involving King Arthur (Connery), Lady Guinevere (Ormond), and a restless, roving spirit, who lives by his wits, named Lancelot (Gere). Awkward narrative moments (and the casting of a contemporary-sounding American as Lancelot) outweighed by the overall intelligence of William Nicholson's script, John Box's breathtaking production design, Jerry Goldsmith's majestic score, and the splendid performances by Ormond and Connery. Camelot has never looked so magical. [PG-13] ▼●◗

First Lady (1937) **82m.** *** D: Stanley Logan. Kay Francis, Anita Louise, Verree Teasdale, Preston Foster, Walter Connolly, Victor Jory, Louise Fazenda. Witty adaptation of the acerbic George S. Kaufman-Katherine Dayton play, with Francis as the ambitious wife of the Secretary of State (Foster), whom she's pushing into presidential campaign against corrupt judge Connolly. Not very cinematic, but brightly acted by fine ensemble.

First Legion, The (1951) **86m.** *** D: Douglas Sirk. Charles Boyer, William Demarest, Lyle Bettger, Barbara Rush. Engrossing low-key account of Jesuit priest who is dubious about an alleged miracle occurring in his town. Boyer gives one of his best performances. ▼

First Love (1939) **84m.** *** D: Henry Koster. Deanna Durbin, Robert Stack, Helen Parrish, Eugene Pallette, Leatrice Joy, Marcia Mae Jones, Frank Jenks. Charming Cinderella story of orphaned girl (Durbin) going to live with uncle and finding romance with Stack (in his film debut). Durbin sings "Amapola" and other songs; her first screen kiss (courtesy Stack) made headlines around the world. ▼

First Love (1958-Italian) **103m.** ** D: Mario Camerini. Carla Gravina, Raf Mattioli, Lorella De Luca, Luciano Marin. Simple, unengrossing account of the pangs of adolescent love.

First Love (1970-British-French-Swiss) **C-90m.** *** D: Maximilian Schell. John Moulder-Brown, Dominique Sanda, Maximilian Schell, John Osborne. Original, often moving story of young lovers is total concept of Schell. While his direction often wanders, his script is extremely good. [R] ▼

First Love (1977) **C-92m.** ** D: Joan Darling. William Katt, Susan Dey, John Heard, Beverly D'Angelo, Robert Loggia, Swoosie Kurtz. Youthful romance between right-thinking college boy and girl who's involved with older man; muddled film with unsatisfying conclusion. [R] ▼

First Love, Last Rites (1998) **C-93m.** ** D: Jesse Peretz. Giovanni Ribisi, Natasha Gregson Wagner, Robert John Burke, Jeannetta Arnette, Donal Logue. Deadeningly slow story of two young lovers who shack up in a modest apartment on the Louisiana bayou. Feature directorial debut for music-video helmer Peretz has a sensual mood and attractive leads but is devoid of dramatic incident. Only plus: art-rockers Shudder to Think's score, which is meant to evoke old 45 singles. Based on a short story by Ian McEwan. [R] ▼●

First Man Into Space (1959-British) **77m.** ** D: Robert Day. Marshall Thompson, Marla Landi, Robert Ayres, Bill Nagy, Carl Jaffe, Bill Edwards. Daring pilot, brother of hero, disobeys orders and becomes the title character, returning to Earth a dust-encrusted, blood-drinking monster. Better than it sounds. ▼◗

First Men in the Moon (1964-British) **C-103m.** *** D: Nathan Juran. Edward Judd, Martha Hyer, Lionel Jeffries, Erik Chitty. Lavish adaptation of H. G. Wells novel is heavy-handed at times, overloaded with comic relief, but still worthwhile; good Ray Harryhausen special effects. Cameo appearance by Peter Finch. Panavision. ▼●

First Monday in October (1981) **C-98m.** **½ D: Ronald Neame. Walter Matthau, Jill Clayburgh, Barnard Hughes, James Stephens, Jan Sterling, Joshua Bryant. Talky but OK adaptation of Jerome Lawrence–Robert E. Lee stage hit about Tracy-and-Hepburn-like clash of wills between first female member of the Supreme Court (a staunch conservative) and the most liberal of her brethren. Lost some of its novelty when it happened for real just before film was released, but still amusing; *Paper Chase* alum Stephens plays . . . a law clerk. Panavision. [R] ▼●

First Name: Carmen (1983-French-Swiss) **C-85m.** *** D: Jean-Luc Godard. Maruschka Detmers, Jacques Bonnaffe, Myriem Roussel, Christophe Odent, Jean-Luc Godard. Title character is a femme fatale, terrorist, and aspiring filmmaker, and Godard plays her uncle, a famous but "sick" and "washed-up" director named Jean-Luc Godard. Funny and compelling, if you like Godard's later work; otherwise, it will seem like a waste of time and celluloid. ▼●◗

First Nudie Musical, The (1976) **C-100m.** ** D: Mark Haggard, Bruce Kimmel. Stephen Nathan, Cindy Williams, Bruce Kimmel, Diana Canova, Alexandra Morgan, Leslie Ackerman. Basically a one-joke idea that wears thin despite an air of amiability: a desperate young filmmaker (Nathan) tries to rescue his studio by making a porno musical, complete with production numbers such as "Dancing Dildos." Best contributions come from those who keep their clothes on. Kimmel also scripted and wrote most of the songs. [R] ▼

First Power, The (1990) **C-99m.** *½ D: Robert Resnikoff. Lou Diamond Phillips, Tracy Griffith, Jeff Kober, Mykel T. Williamson, Elizabeth Arlen, Dennis Lipscomb. Cat-and-mouse battle between an L.A. cop and the spirit of an executed Devil's disciple who has the ability to pop in and out of other people's bodies. Very weak supernatural horror that fails to frighten, or offer anything fresh. Griffith is Melanie Griffith's half-sister. [R]▼●

First Spaceship on Venus (1960-German) **C-78m.** ** D: Kurt Maetzig. Yoko Tani, Oldrich Lukes, Ignacy Machowski, Julius Ongewe. Expedition goes to Venus following clues left by alien ship that exploded on Earth years before. They discover war-blasted landscape and still operating machines. Well produced but stilted. International coproduction was cut by an hour in the U.S., explaining the incoherent story line. From novel by Europe's most significant sci-fi writer, Stanislaw Lem, who repudiated the film. Totalvision.▼

First Texan, The (1956) **82m.** **½ D: Byron Haskin. Joel McCrea, Felicia Farr, Jeff Morrow, Wallace Ford. McCrea is forceful as Sam Houston, leading Texans in fight against Mexico for independence; good action sequences. CinemaScope.

First Time, The (1952) **89m.** ** D: Frank Tashlin. Robert Cummings, Barbara Hale, Jeff Donnell, Mona Barrie, Cora Witherspoon. Predictable comedy pegged on young couple's many problems with raising a baby.

First Time, The (1969) **C-90m.** *½ D: James Neilson. Jacqueline Bisset, Wes Stern, Rick Kelman, Wink Roberts, Gerald Parkes. Combination of *Ozzie and Harriet* and WALK ON THE WILD SIDE concerns a teenager's sexual initiation. Artificial look at adolescence. [M]▼

First Time, The (1983) **C-95m.** *** D: Charlie Loventhal. Tim Choate, Krista Errickson, Marshall Efron, Wendy Fulton, Raymond Patterson, Wallace Shawn, Wendie Jo Sperber, Cathryn Damon. Surprisingly intelligent, funny portrait of virginal, movie-loving college freshman Choate. A cut above other films of its type, and a promising debut for young Loventhal, a protégé of Brian De Palma. Aka DOIN' IT. [R]▼

First Time Felon (1997) **C-95m. TVM** D: Charles S. Dutton. Omar Epps, Delroy Lindo, Rachel Ticotin, Charles S. Dutton, William Forsythe, Justin Pierce, Anthony "Treach" Criss, Clifton Powell. Gritty true story of Greg Yance (Epps), a drug-dealing street tough whose life is turned around as a boot-camp inmate and who finds redemption and purpose when pressed into service helping save an Illinois town in the 1993 Mississippi River floods. Dutton, who once served time in the state pen for manslaughter, has a small (unbilled) role as a con who tries to put the first-time felon straight. Written by Daniel Therriault. Made for cable. Above average.▼

First to Fight (1967) **C-97m.** **½ D: Christian Nyby. Chad Everett, Marilyn Devin, Dean Jagger, Bobby Troup, Claude Akins, Gene Hackman. Conventional WW2 yarn with Everett the one-time hero who almost loses his courage on the battlefield. Panavision.▼

First Traveling Saleslady, The (1956) **C-92m.** ** D: Arthur Lubin. Ginger Rogers, Barry Nelson, Carol Channing, David Brian, James Arness, Clint Eastwood. Rogers and Channing try to elevate this plodding comedy of girdle-sellers in the old West, but barely succeed. Carol and Clint make one of the oddest couples in screen history.

First Wives Club, The (1996) **C-102m.** **½ D: Hugh Wilson. Goldie Hawn, Bette Midler, Diane Keaton, Maggie Smith, Dan Hedaya, Stockard Channing, Sarah Jessica Parker, Victor Garber, Stephen Collins, Elizabeth Berkley, Marcia Gay Harden, Bronson Pinchot, Jennifer Dundas, Eileen Heckart, Philip Bosco, Rob Reiner, James Naughton, Debra Monk, Kate Burton. Three college pals meet up years later at a mutual friend's funeral and discover they have something in common: husbands who've dumped (or dumped on) them. Predictable, but still pretty entertaining, thanks to three lively stars and an impressive supporting cast. Diluted from Olivia Goldsmith's novel. Heather Locklear appears unbilled. [PG]▼●◗

First Yank Into Tokyo (1945) **82m.** ** D: Gordon Douglas. Tom Neal, Barbara Hale, Marc Cramer, Richard Loo, Keye Luke, Leonard Strong, Benson Fong. Low-budget quickie made to be topical isn't so anymore, and it's not too good either; Neal undergoes plastic surgery, poses as Japanese soldier to help captured American atomic scientist escape. Of note as the first Hollywood film to acknowledge the existence of nuclear firepower.▼

Fish Called Wanda, A (1988) **C-108m.** *** D: Charles Crichton. John Cleese, Jamie Lee Curtis, Kevin Kline, Michael Palin, Maria Aitken, Tom Georgeson, Patricia Hayes, Geoffrey Palmer. Funny farce about an uptight British barrister who becomes involved with a sexy con artist (Curtis), her mindlessly macho boyfriend (Kline), and their ambitious bank robbery and getaway scheme. Cleese's script includes enough bad-taste gags to either repel or delight his audience, depending on one's personal point of view. Kline won an Oscar for his flamboyant comic performance. The cast later reunited for FIERCE CREATURES. [R] ▼●◗

Fisher King, The (1991) **C-137m.** *** D: Terry Gilliam. Robin Williams, Jeff Bridges, Amanda Plummer, Mercedes Ruehl, Michael Jeter, Harry Shearer, John de Lancie, David (Hyde) Pierce. Expansive, emotional fable of a smart-aleck, self-absorbed radio personality driven into a deep funk by an unexpected tragedy—and his unlikely rescue by a strange street vigilante who's in desperate need of rescue himself. Unusual and absorbing, both comic and tender, this takes the viewer on quite a journey. Ruehl won Best Supporting Actress Oscar as Bridges' girlfriend. Look fast for Kathy Najimy. Written by Richard LaGravenese. Super 35. [R]▼●◗

Fish Hawk (1980-Canadian) **C-95m.** ** D: Donald Shebib. Will Sampson, Charlie Fields, Geoffrey Bowes, Mary Pirle, Don Francks, Chris Wiggins. Bland family film about an alcoholic Indian who tries to mend his ways—and becomes a companion to an impressionable young farm boy. This is the kind of unchallenging, inoffensive fare that gives G-rated movies a bad reputation. [G]▼

Fish That Saved Pittsburgh, The (1979) **C-102m.** *½ D: Gilbert Moses. Julius Erving, James Bond III, Stockard Channing, Jonathan Winters, Margaret Avery, Jack Kehoe, Meadowlark Lemon, Nicholas Pryor, Flip Wilson, Kareem Abdul-Jabbar. Losing basketball team tries astrology to put them in winners' circle; low-grade comedy with disco soundtrack. Game hijinks are only saving grace. [PG]▼

F.I.S.T. (1978) **C-145m.** **½ D: Norman Jewison. Sylvester Stallone, Rod Steiger, Peter Boyle, Melinda Dillon, David Huffman, Tony Lo Bianco, Kevin Conway, Cassie Yates, Henry Wilcoxon, Brian Dennehy. Stallone's one-dimensional performance prevents this well-produced epic about a Hoffa-like labor kingpin from sustaining a strong first half. Peter Boyle does well with a role inspired by former Teamster boss Dave Beck. Screenplay by Stallone and Joe Eszterhas. [PG]▼●

Fistful of Chopsticks, A SEE: **They Call Me Bruce?**

Fistful of Dollars (1964-Italian) **C-96m.** *** D: Sergio Leone. Clint Eastwood, Gian Maria Volonté, Marianne Koch, Wolfgang Lukschy, Mario Brega, Carol Brown. Sagebrush remake of YOJIMBO single-handedly invented the "spaghetti Western," made an international superstar of Eastwood, and boosted the careers of Leone and composer Ennio Morricone as well. Clint plays the laconic Man With No Name, a tough gunslinger manipulating (and manipulated by!) two rival families warring over small frontier town. Amusing, violent, and very stylish. Released in the U.S. in 1967. Sequel: FOR A FEW DOLLARS MORE. Techniscope. ▼●◗

Fistful of Dynamite, A SEE: **Duck, You Sucker**

Fist in His Pocket (1966-Italian) **105m.** **** D: Marco Bellochio. Lou Castel, Paola Pitagora, Marino Mase, Liliana Gerace, Pier Luigi Troglio. Brilliant one-of-a-kind about a mad family of epileptics whose protagonist kills his mother and drowns his younger brother, while his sis merely settles for repressed incest. One of the great, if largely unheralded, foreign films of the 60s, with Castel more than up to the demands of the difficult role.

Fist of Fear, Touch of Death (1980) **C-90m.** *½ D: Matthew Mallinson. Fred Williamson, Ron Van Clief, Adolph Caesar, Aaron Banks, Bill Louis. Boring chopsocky film chronicling the happenings at a Madison Square Garden martial arts tournament. Highlighted are short clips of legendary Bruce Lee. Aka DRAGON AND THE COBRA. [R]▼

Fist of Fury SEE: **Chinese Connection, The**

Fist Right of Freedom SEE: **Fox and His Friends**

Fists of Fury (1971-Hong Kong) **C-103m.** ** D: Lo Wei. Bruce Lee, Maria Yi, Han Ying Chieh, Tony Liu, Miao Ker Hsiu. Lee, in his initial Kung Fu actioner, plays a young fellow who takes a job in an ice house, and discovers his boss is a drug smuggler. Feeble. Original title: THE BIG BOSS. Dyaliscope. [R]▼●◗

Fitzcarraldo (1982) **C-157m.** **** D: Werner Herzog. Klaus Kinski, Claudia Cardinale, Jose Lewgoy, Miguel Angel Fuentes, Paul Hittscher. Vivid, fascinating portrait of a man obsessed (made by a man obsessed—see BURDEN OF DREAMS) who's determined to capture a shipping route on the Amazon, even though it means hauling a boat over a mountaintop, through hostile tribal territory. Then he's going to bring in grand opera! Astonishing and captivating movie, in spite of its length; admittedly not to everyone's taste. [PG]▼

Fitzwilly (1967) **C-102m.** **½ D: Delbert Mann. Dick Van Dyke, Barbara Feldon, Edith Evans, John McGiver, Harry Townes, John Fiedler, Norman Fell, Cecil Kellaway, Sam Waterston. Ordinary fluff about butler who has to rob Gimbel's on Christmas Eve to save his employer. Van Dyke's screen career was hurt by too many films like this one. Film debuts of Feldon and Waterston. Panavision.▼

Five (1951) **93m.** *** D: Arch Oboler. William Phipps, Susan Douglas, James Anderson, Charles Lampkin, Earl Lee. Intriguing, offbeat film by famed radio writer-director Oboler about the survivors of a nuclear holocaust. Talky (and sometimes given to purple prose) but interesting. Filmed in and around Oboler's Frank Lloyd Wright home.

5 Against the House (1955) **84m.** *** D: Phil Karlson. Guy Madison, Kim Novak, Brian Keith, Kerwin Mathews, William Conrad, Alvy Moore. "Perfect crime" caper has five friends set out to rob Reno, Nevada casino. Execution of robbery, along with gorgeous Novak, keep this film rolling along. Based on a novel by Jack Finney.

Five Angles on Murder SEE: **Woman in Question, The**

Five Ashore in Singapore SEE: **Singapore, Singapore**

Five Bloody Graves SEE: **Gun Riders**

5 Branded Women (1960) **106m.** ** D: Martin Ritt. Van Heflin, Silvana Mangano, Jeanne Moreau, Vera Miles, Barbara Bel Geddes, Richard Basehart, Harry Guardino, Carla Gravina, Alex Nicol, Steve Forrest. Overambitious production, badly miscast, set in WW2 Middle Europe. Five girls scorned by partisans for consorting with Nazis prove their patriotism.

Five Came Back (1939) **75m.** *** D: John Farrow. Chester Morris, Lucille Ball, Wendy Barrie, John Carradine, Allen Jenkins, Joseph Calleia, C. Aubrey Smith, Patric Knowles. This sleeper shows its age a bit, but remains interesting for colorful character studies among passengers on plane downed in headhunter-infested Amazon jungle. Remade by Farrow as BACK FROM ETERNITY.▼●

5 Card Stud (1968) **C-103m.** *½ D: Henry Hathaway. Dean Martin, Robert Mitchum, Inger Stevens, Roddy McDowall, Katherine Justice. Dino is a gambler and Mitchum virtually repeats his NIGHT OF THE HUNTER role in surprisingly disappointing Western; Maurice Jarre's Dr. Zhivago-on-the-range musical score doesn't help. Probably Hathaway's worst Western. [M/PG]▼

Five Corners (1988) **C-92m.** *** D: Tony Bill. Jodie Foster, Tim Robbins, Todd Graff, John Turturro, Elizabeth Berridge, Rose Gregorio, Gregory Rozakis, John Seitz. Moody piece about young people whose lives converge in a Bronx neighborhood in 1964. One of them, just released from prison, stirs trouble for the others. Unexpectedly melodramatic but potent and believable . . . and seemingly the only 1960s period film not to use oldies to evoke the era. James Newton Howard's moody score is much more effective, anyway. Written by John Patrick Shanley. [R]▼●◗

Five Day Lover (1961-French-Italian) **86m.** *** D: Philippe De Broca. Jean Seberg, Micheline Presle, Jean-Pierre Cassel, François Perier. Perceptive, flavorful bedroom comedy featuring Seberg as a bored housewife-mother who has an affair with Cassel, who's being kept by her friend (Presle).

Five Days from Home (1978) **C-109m.** ** D: George Peppard. George Peppard, Neville Brand, Savannah Smith, Sherry Boucher, Victor Campos, Robert Donner. Peppard breaks out of Louisiana prison, determined to reach L.A. and see his hospitalized son. Well-intentioned but improbable film. [PG]

Five Days One Summer (1982) **C-108m.** ** D: Fred Zinnemann. Sean Connery, Betsy Brantley, Lambert Wilson, Jennifer Hilary, Isabel Dean, Gerald Buhr, Anna Massey. Middle-aged man brings a young woman—ostensibly his wife—on Swiss vacation in the early 1930s where their hesitant relationship is explored against the natural drama of mountain climbing. Adaptation of a Kay Boyle story doesn't come off, despite impeccable production. Slow, ethereal, ultimately unsatisfying. Edited to 93m. for TV by Zinnemann (his final film). [PG]▼

Five Easy Pieces (1970) **C-98m.** **** D: Bob Rafelson. Jack Nicholson, Karen Black, Billy Green Bush, Fannie Flagg, Susan Anspach, Sally Struthers, Ralph Waite, Lois Smith. Brilliant character study of musician with great promise who gave up a career to work on an oil rig. Nicholson's performance is superb, but Black, Anspach, Smith, and Bush all contribute heavily. Helena Kallianiotes is hilarious as a malcontent hitchhiker; this is the film with Jack's famous "chicken salad sandwich" speech. Beautifully written by Adrien Joyce (Carole Eastman). [R]▼●◗

Five Finger Exercise (1962) **109m.** **½ D: Daniel Mann. Rosalind Russell, Jack Hawkins, Maximilian Schell, Richard Beymer, Lana Wood, Annette Gorman. Peter Shaffer's play suffers from change of locale and alteration of original ideas; now it becomes embarrassing soap opera of possessive mother in love with daughter's tutor. Stars are miscast but try their best.

5 Fingers (1952) **108m.** *** D: Joseph L. Mankiewicz. James Mason, Danielle Darrieux, Michael Rennie, Walter Hampden, Oscar Karlweis, Herbert Berghof, John Wengraf, Michael Pate. Exceptionally intelligent spy thriller with Mason as a cool customer selling high-priced secrets right under the noses of his British government employers during WW2. Based on a novel that was purportedly true! Followed by a short-lived TV series.▼●

Five Fingers of Death (1973-Chinese) **C-102m.** *½ D: Cheng Chang Ho. Lo Lieh, Wang Ping, Wang Ching-Feng. Only interesting in that it is the Kung Fu film that began the craze in America. Family honor defended with every part of the body except the mouth, which is horrendously dubbed. Shawscope.[R]

Five Gates to Hell (1959) **98m.** *½ D: James Clavell. Neville Brand, Benson Fong, Shirley Knight, Ken Scott, John Morley, Dolores Michaels, Nancy Kulp, Irish McCalla. Overly melodramatic plot of American nurses captured by Chinese mercenaries and the various ordeals they undergo. CinemaScope.

Five Golden Dragons (1967-British) **C-93m.** ** D: Jeremy Summers. Bob Cummings, Margaret Lee, Maria Perschy, Brian Donlevy, Christopher Lee, George Raft,

Dan Duryea. Cummings is naive American caught up in international crime in Hong Kong; conventional actioner. Techniscope. ▼

Five Golden Hours (1961-British-Italian) **90m.** ** D: Mario Zampi. Ernie Kovacs, Cyd Charisse, George Sanders, Kay Hammond, Dennis Price, Finlay Currie, Ron Moody. Con man Kovacs fleeces wealthy widows, but his luck is sure to change after falling for Charisse, whose husband has just died. Limp comedy wastes the talents of its cast. ▼

Five Graves To Cairo (1943) **96m.** ***½ D: Billy Wilder. Franchot Tone, Anne Baxter, Akim Tamiroff, Erich von Stroheim, Peter Van Eyck, Fortunio Bonanova. WW2 intrigue situated in Sahara oasis hotel run by Tamiroff and Baxter; Tone attempts to obtain secrets from visiting Field Marshal Rommel (von Stroheim). Billy Wilder-Charles Brackett script manages to incorporate wit and humor into genuinely exciting wartime yarn. A remake of HOTEL IMPERIAL. ▼

Five Guns West (1955) **C-78m.** ** D: Roger Corman. John Lund, Dorothy Malone, Touch (Mike) Connors, Jack Ingram. Fair Corman Western, which he coscripted, about a group of Rebel soldiers who hold up a Yankee stagecoach. This was Corman's first film as director. ▼

Five Heartbeats, The (1991) **C-120m.** *** D: Robert Townsend. Robert Townsend, Michael Wright, Leon, Harry J. Lennix, Tico Wells, Diahann Carroll, Harold Nicholas, John Canada Terrell, Chuck Patterson, Hawthorne James, Paul Benjamin. Corny but entertaining saga of a 1960s singing group's rise to fame; loosely based on R&B group The Dells. Awfully predictable, but star/director/cowriter Townsend and his cast are so likable they make up for it. The scene in which a youthful belter named Tressa Thomas helps Townsend piece together a song on the spot is worth the price of admission. Coscripted by Keenen Ivory Wayans. [R] ▼●

Five Miles to Midnight (1962) **110m.** **½ D: Anatole Litvak. Tony Perkins, Sophia Loren, Gig Young, Jean-Pierre Aumont, Pascale Roberts. Jumbled murder mystery with Perkins convincing wife Loren to collect insurance money when it's thought he's been killed, with ironic results. ▼

Five Million Years to Earth (1968-British) **C-98m.** *** D: Roy Ward Baker. James Donald, Barbara Shelley, Andrew Keir, Julian Glover, Maurice Good, Duncan Lamont. Workers unearth spaceship and remains of alien crew in modern-day London. Good cast, great script complications, and suspense in fine example of what can be done on meager budget. Only subject matter will turn some viewers off. Originally released as QUATERMASS AND THE PIT, and superior to the earlier QUATERMASS films, known in the U.S. as THE CREEPING UNKNOWN and ENEMY FROM SPACE. Followed by QUATERMASS CONCLUSION. ▼●

Five Minutes to Live SEE: **Door-to-Door Maniac**

Five of Me, The (1981) **C-100m. TVM** D: Paul Wendkos. David Birney, Dee Wallace, Mitchell Ryan, John McLiam, James Whitmore, Jr., Ben Piazza, Judith Chapman. Birney goes two up on Joanne Woodward in this male version of THE THREE FACES OF EVE, based on Henry Hawksworth's autobiographical book about how he battled four alter egos living in his body. Average. ▼

Five on the Black Hand Side (1973) **C-96m.** **½ D: Oscar Williams. Clarice Taylor, Leonard Jackson, Virginia Capers, D'Urville Martin, Glynn Turman, Godfrey Cambridge. Black family comedy about patriarchal barber was once refreshing amidst many black exploitation films, now seems foolish. [PG]

Five Pennies, The (1959) **C-117m.** **½ D: Melville Shavelson. Danny Kaye, Barbara Bel Geddes, Tuesday Weld, Louis Armstrong, Bob Crosby, Harry Guardino, Ray Anthony, Shelley Manne, Bobby Troup. Danny plays jazz trumpeter Red Nichols in this sentimental biography. Only bright spots are musical numbers, especially duets with Kaye and Armstrong. VistaVision. ▼●

Five Star Final (1931) **89m.** *** D: Mervyn LeRoy. Edward G. Robinson. H. B. Warner, Marian Marsh, George E. Stone, Ona Munson, Boris Karloff, Aline MacMahon. Powerful drama of sensationalist newspaper sometimes falls apart with bad acting by second leads, but editor Robinson and unscrupulous reporter Karloff make it a must. Remade as TWO AGAINST THE WORLD.

Five Steps to Danger (1957) **80m.** ** D: Henry S. Kesler. Ruth Roman, Sterling Hayden, Werner Klemperer, Richard Gaines. By-now clichéd spy drama, enhanced by Roman and Hayden.

5,000 Fingers of Dr. T., The (1953) **C-88m.** *** D: Roy Rowland. Peter Lind Hayes, Mary Healy, Tommy Rettig, Hans Conried. Largely ignored, one of Hollywood's best fantasies, devised by Dr. Seuss. Boy has nightmare about cruel piano teacher (Conried) ruling over land where kidnapped youngsters are forced to practice the piano. Song numbers slow the action. ▼●

Five Weeks in a Balloon (1962) **C-101m.** **½ D: Irwin Allen. Red Buttons, Barbara Eden, Fabian, Cedric Hardwicke, Peter Lorre, Richard Haydn, Barbara Luna. Innocuous entertainment with formula script from Jules Verne tale of balloon expedition to Africa. Buoyed by fine cast, including veterans Billy Gilbert, Herbert Marshall, Reginald Owen, Henry Daniell. CinemaScope.▼●

Fixed Bayonets (1951) **92m.** **½ D: Samuel Fuller. Richard Basehart, Gene Evans, Michael O'Shea, Richard Hylton, Craig Hill. Taut Korean War drama of platoon cut off from the rest of its outfit; typical tough Fuller production. James Dean is one of the soldiers.

Fixer, The (1968) **C-132m.** **½ D: John Frankenheimer. Alan Bates, Dirk Bogarde, Georgia Brown, Hugh Griffith, Ian Holm, Jack Gilford, Elizabeth Hartman, David Warner, Carol White. Good acting helps, but Bernard Malamud's acclaimed novel fails on the screen; story of unjustly imprisoned Jewish handyman in turn-of-the-century Russia concerns itself too much with the thoughts of its main character to be effective as film. [M/PG]▼

Fixer, The (1998) **C-95m. TVM** D: Charles Robert Carner. Jon Voight, Brenda Bakke, J. J. Johnston, Miguel Sandoval, Jack Wallace, Barbara Gordon, Sara Botsford. Voight plays Chicago ward heeler, a political mover and shaker who can get things done for a price and "fix any situation," but comes to reassess his life following a near fatal accident. Voight executive-produced; actor-director Tony Bill was one of the producers and has a small role as a big-ticket lawyer. Made for cable. Average.▼●

Flame, The (1947) **97m.** ** D: John H. Auer. Vera Ralston, John Carroll, Robert Paige, Broderick Crawford, Henry Travers, Constance Dowling. Routine story of woman falling in love with intended victim of blackmail plot.

Flame and the Arrow, The (1950) **C-88m.** *** D: Jacques Tourneur. Burt Lancaster, Virginia Mayo, Robert Douglas, Aline MacMahon, Nick Cravat. Bouncy, colorful action with Lancaster romping through his gymnastics as rebel leader in medieval Italy leading his people on to victory. Mayo is gorgeous heroine.▼●

Flame and the Flesh, The (1954) **C-104m.** ** D: Richard Brooks. Lana Turner, Pier Angeli, Carlos Thompson, Bonar Colleano, Charles Goldner, Peter Illing. Pointless Turner vehicle filmed in Europe involving brunette Lana being romanced by continental Thompson, which causes a lot of misery.

Flamenco (1995-Spanish) **C-100m.** ***½ D: Carlos Saura. Saura's love of flamenco saturates this ecstatic, beautifully made performance film featuring flamenco singers, dancers, and guitarists of all ages, the best of whom are nothing short of dazzling. There are neither subtitles nor dialogue—and none are needed!▼

Flame of Araby (1951) **C-77m.** **½ D: Charles Lamont. Maureen O'Hara, Jeff Chandler, Maxwell Reed, Susan Cabot. O'Hara, looking fetching as ever, rides through this costumer of the Far East, involving battle over a prize horse.▼

Flame of New Orleans, The (1941) **78m.** *** D: René Clair. Marlene Dietrich, Bruce Cabot, Roland Young, Laura Hope Crews, Mischa Auer, Andy Devine. Dietrich can have her pick of any man in New Orleans, can't decide between wealthy Young or hard-working Cabot. Picturesque, entertaining. Clair's first American film.▼

Flame of Stamboul (1951) **68m.** *½ D: Ray Nazarro. Richard Denning, Lisa Ferraday, Norman Lloyd, Nestor Paiva. Programmer about espionage in ancient title city.

Flame of the Barbary Coast (1945) **91m.** **½ D: Joseph Kane. John Wayne, Ann Dvorak, Joseph Schildkraut, William Frawley, Virginia Grey. Hick rancher Wayne competes with slick Schildkraut for savvy saloon singer Dvorak; undemanding fluff, with Republic Pictures' version of the San Francisco earthquake. Also shown in computer-colored version. ▼

Flame of the Islands (1955) **C-90m.** ** D: Edward Ludwig. Yvonne De Carlo, Howard Duff, Zachary Scott, Kurt Kasznar, Barbara O'Neil. Caribbean scenery and sultry De Carlo provide most of the spice in this tale of a cafe singer and the men who fall in love with her.▼

Flame Over India (1959-British) **C-130m.** *** D: J. Lee Thompson. Lauren Bacall, Kenneth More, Herbert Lom, Wilfrid Hyde-White. Fast-paced actioner set on northern frontier of India as British soldiers and governess Bacall seek to speed an Indian prince to safety aboard a run-down train. Originally titled NORTHWEST FRONTIER. CinemaScope.▼

Flame Within, The (1935) **71m.** ** D: Edmund Goulding. Ann Harding, Herbert Marshall, Maureen O'Sullivan, Louis Hayward. Tired story of unrequited love. Young woman psychiatrist falls in love with patient, despite fact that she knows that it could never succeed.

Flaming Feather (1951) **C-77m.** *** D: Ray Enright. Sterling Hayden, Forrest Tucker, Barbara Rush, Arleen Whelan. Rousing Western as vigilantes rescue white woman from renegade Indians.

Flaming Frontier (1958-Canadian) **70m.** *½ D: Sam Newfeld. Bruce Bennett, Jim Davis, Paisley Maxwell, Cecil Linder, Peter Humphreys. Indian war is averted by half-breed army officer; very cheap Western. Regalscope.

Flamingo Kid, The (1984) **C-100m.** *** D: Garry Marshall. Matt Dillon, Richard Crenna, Hector Elizondo, Jessica Walter, Fisher Stevens, Janet Jones, Bronson Pinchot, Martha Gehman, Brian McNamara, Steven Weber, Eric Douglas, Marisa Tomei, Tracy Reiner, John Turturro. Very likable film set in 1963, about a Brooklyn boy from a working-class family whose head is turned by a slick sharpie who holds court at the beach club where he works. Crenna scores a bull's-eye as the fat cat (and catches a glimpse of himself in *The Real McCoys* while testing his remote control TV in one scene). Nice coming-of-age story written by Neal Marshall (no relation to director). Tomei's film debut. [PG-13]▼●◗

Flamingo Road (1949) **94m.** *** D: Michael Curtiz. Joan Crawford, Zachary Scott, Sydney Greenstreet, David Brian, Gertrude Michael, Gladys George. Crawford is excellent as tough carnival dancer ditched in small town where she soon is loving Scott and Brian and matching wits with corrupt politician Greenstreet. Remade as TVM in 1980, which later spun off a TV series. ▼●

Flaming Star (1960) **C-91m.** *** D: Don Siegel. Elvis Presley, Barbara Eden, Steve Forrest, Dolores Del Rio, John McIntire. Elvis is excellent as a half-breed Indian who must choose sides when his mother's people go on the warpath. No songs after the first ten minutes but lots of action; along with JAILHOUSE ROCK, Presley's best film. CinemaScope.▼

Flap (1970) **C-106m.** ** D: Carol Reed. Anthony Quinn, Claude Akins, Tony Bill, Victor Jory, Shelley Winters. Uneven story of Indian outcast Quinn. You're supposed to pity Flapping Eagle, but script is so weak that the chances are you won't. At times funny, but supposedly tragic. Panavision. [PG]

Flareup (1969) **C-100m.** **½ D: James Neilson. Raquel Welch, James Stacy, Luke Askew, Don Chastain, Ron Rifkin, Jean Byron. Go-go dancer Raquel gets stalked from Las Vegas to L.A. by psychopathic ex-husband of friend who blames her for breakup of the marriage. Fast melodrama is helped by good location footage. [M/PG] ▼

Flash and the Firecat (1975) **C-84m.** *½ D: Ferd and Beverly Sebastian. Roger Davis, Tricia Sembera, Dub Taylor, Richard Kiel, Joan Shawlee, Philip Bruns. Road-company Bonnie and Clyde try for one big heist; film's only novelty is the characters' use of dune buggies for transportation. [PG]▼

Flashback (1990) **C-108m.** *½ D: Franco Amurri. Dennis Hopper, Kiefer Sutherland, Carol Kane, Cliff De Young, Paul Dooley, Michael McKean, Richard Masur. Young straight-arrow FBI agent (Sutherland) is ordered to transport a recently captured "underground" political fugitive to the scene of his '60s crime—disruption of a Spiro Agnew rally. Enervatingly predictable until its (surprisingly) bloody climax. Masur and McKean, who seem to be winging it, amuse as onetime political activists now trapped in a middle-class environment. [R]▼●

Flashdance (1983) **C-96m.** **½ D: Adrian Lyne. Jennifer Beals, Michael Nouri, Lilia Skala, Sunny Johnson, Kyle T. Heffner, Lee Ving, Ron Karabatsos, Belinda Bauer, Cynthia Rhodes, Liz Sagal, Robert Wuhl. How to turn a rock video into a feature film—with glitzy images, high energy, an arresting music score (principally by Giorgio Moroder), and the stupidest story this side of Busby Berkeley. Still, this concoction about a girl with the perfect fantasy life (macho welder by day, sexy dancer by night, courted by the rich and handsome boss, watched over by a patron-saint ballerina) was a smash. Title song won an Oscar. [R]▼●

Flash Fire SEE: **Dangerous Summer, A**

Flash Gordon (1936) SEE: **Spaceship to the Unknown**

Flash Gordon (1980) **C-110m.** *** D: Mike Hodges. Sam J. Jones, Melody Anderson, Topol, Max von Sydow, Ornella Muti, Brian Blessed, Timothy Dalton, Mariangela Melato. Updated version of comic strip is better than expected, thanks to eye-filling production/costume design by Danilo Donati, amusing rock score by Queen. Jones and Anderson are liabilities as Flash and Dale Arden, but Muti's evil Princess Aura (who would make any male stray from Right) leads a strong supporting cast. Todd-AO 35. [PG]▼●◗

Flash Gordon Conquers the Universe SEE: **Purple Death from Outer Space**

Flash Gordon: Mars Attacks the World SEE: **Deadly Ray from Mars, The**

Flash Gordon's Trip to Mars SEE: **Deadly Ray From Mars, The**

Flash of Green, A (1984) **C-131m.** ** D: Victor Nunez. Ed Harris, Blair Brown, Richard Jordan, George Coe, Helen Stenborg, John Glover. Reporter in a small Florida coastal town gets in over his head when he plays footsie with a scheming county commissioner who's behind a shady land-fill development racket. Capable performances and refreshingly offbeat subject matter are eventually negated by overlength and plot redundancies. Made for *American Playhouse* and produced by costar Jordan. Based on John D. MacDonald's book.▼

Flashpoint (1984) **C-94m.** ** D: William Tannen. Kris Kristofferson, Treat Williams, Rip Torn, Kevin Conway, Miguel Ferrer, Jean Smart, Roberts Blossom, Tess Harper. Two maverick Texas Border Patrol officers stumble into volatile territory when they discover a cache of money that figures in a long-dormant mystery. Intriguing overall premise (and good cast) defeated by uninteresting presentation. Bonus: the worst title song of 1984 (sung over closing credits). [R]▼●

Flatfoot SEE: **Knock Out Cop, The**

Flatliners (1990) **C-105m.** **½ D: Joel Schumacher. Kiefer Sutherland, Julia Roberts, Kevin Bacon, William Baldwin, Oliver Platt, Kimberly Scott. Offbeat but sophomoric supernatural drama (with touches of horror and humor) about medical students experimenting with life after death. Slick camerawork and effects can't camouflage the superficiality of the script, which undermines an intriguing idea. Panavision.[R]▼●◗

Flat Top (1952) **C-83m.** **½ D: Lesley Selander. Sterling Hayden, Richard Carlson, Bill Phipps, Keith Larsen. Well-paced WW2 film of training of aircraft-carrier fighter pilots. Film integrates news footage successfully.▼

Flawless (1999) **C-110m.** ** D: Joel Schumacher. Robert De Niro, Philip Seymour Hoffman, Barry Miller, Chris Bauer, Skipp Sudduth, Daphne Rubin-Vega. N.Y.C. cop suffers a stroke, and gets speech therapy lessons from the unlikeliest source imaginable, a drag queen he can't stand who happens to live in the same apartment house. Meanwhile, a local crimelord is searching for stolen money that's stashed somewhere in the building. Overlong, overplotted film (written by Schumacher) is kept afloat by the talent of its stars, De Niro and Hoffman. Panavision. [R]▼●◗

Flaxy Martin (1949) **86m.** **½ D: Richard Bare. Virginia Mayo, Zachary Scott, Dorothy Malone, Tom D'Andrea, Helen Westcott, Elisha Cook, Jr. Smooth melodrama of lawyer framed by client on a murder charge.

Flea in Her Ear, A (1968-U.S.-French) **C-94m.** ** D: Jacques Charon. Rex Harrison, Rosemary Harris, Louis Jourdan, Rachel Roberts. Unfunny farce about philandering barrister. Some of the slapstick gags go on interminably. Panavision. [M/PG]

Fled (1996) **C-98m.** *½ D: Kevin Hooks. Laurence Fishburne, Stephen Baldwin, Will Patton, Robert John Burke, Salma Hayek, Michael Nader, David Dukes, Brittney Powell, RuPaul, Taurean Blacque. Fishburne and Baldwin escape prison chained together in DEFIANT ONES style, leading to an extended chase that involves trains, trucks, cycles, cable cars, and the clichéd like. Self-conscious movie references abound in a story dealing with a secret computer disk that has the goods on a Cuban mobster. Final gag isn't that great, but it's the best thing in the movie. [R]▼●◗

Fleet's In, The (1942) **93m.** *** D: Victor Schertzinger. Dorothy Lamour, William Holden, Eddie Bracken, Betty Hutton, Betty Jane Rhodes, Leif Erickson, Cass Daley, Gil Lamb, Barbara Britton, Rod Cameron, Lorraine and Rognan, Jimmy Dorsey Orchestra with Bob Eberly and Helen O'Connell. Bouncy wartime musical with reputed romeo Holden trying to melt iceberg Lamour. Sensational score (composed by director Schertzinger and Johnny Mercer) includes "Tangerine," "I Remember You," and "Arthur Murray Taught Me Dancing in a Hurry." Feature debuts of Hutton (in a hilarious performance that made her an instant star) and Daley. Previously filmed as TRUE TO THE NAVY and LADY BE CAREFUL; remade as SAILOR BEWARE.

Flesh (1932) **95m.** *** D: John Ford. Wallace Beery, Karen Morley, Ricardo Cortez, Jean Hersholt, Herman Bing, John Miljan. Unusual, melancholy drama with Beery as simple-minded German wrestler in love with Morley—who tries to hide her shady relationship with no-good Cortez.

Flesh & Blood (1951-British) **102m.** ** D: Anthony Kimmins. Richard Todd, Glynis Johns, Joan Greenwood, Andre Morell, Freda Jackson, James Hayter, George Cole, Michael Hordern. Turbulent study of generations of family life, focusing on clashes and romances of parents and children. Set in Scotland.

Flesh + Blood (1985) **C-126m.** ** D: Paul Verhoeven. Rutger Hauer, Jennifer Jason Leigh, Tom Burlinson, Jack Thompson, Susan Tyrrell, Ronald Lacey, Brion James, Bruno Kirby. Rowdy adventure set in 16th century: Leigh is betrothed to young Prince Burlinson but falls into clutches of Hauer and his motley band of warriors. Plenty of flesh *and* blood, but it's all rather foul and nasty; Verhoeven (in his first American English-language effort) *does* score points for sheer audaciousness. Aka THE ROSE AND THE SWORD. Technovision. [R]▼

Flesh and Bone (1993) **C-127m.** **½ D: Steve Kloves. Dennis Quaid, Meg Ryan, James Caan, Gwyneth Paltrow, Scott Wilson, Christopher Rydell, Betsy Brantley, Julia Mueller. Moody but murky "sins of the father" drama, with Quaid well cast as a vending machine supplier who discovers that the tough-luck case he's been driving around Texas figured in the childhood tragedy that has dominated his life. Absolutely no dramatic payoff, but simply oozing in portent. Undeniable standouts are Philippe Rousselot's photography and the performance of newcomer Paltrow as a sexy con woman. [R]▼●

Flesh and Desire (1955-French) **94m.** ** D: Jean Josipovici. Rossano Brazzi, Viviane Romance, Peter Van Eyck, Jean-Paul Roussillon. Turgid farm romance tale of virile Brazzi's appearance setting into motion jealousy and murder.

Flesh and Fantasy (1943) **93m.** *** D: Julien Duvivier. Charles Boyer, Edward G. Robinson, Barbara Stanwyck, Robert

Benchley, Betty Field, Robert Cummings, Thomas Mitchell, Charles Winninger. Three-part film of supernatural linked by Benchley; Field is ugly girl turned beauty by Cummings' love; Robinson's life is changed by fortune-teller Mitchell; Boyer is psychic circus star haunted by Stanwyck. Robinson sequence, based on Oscar Wilde's *Lord Arthur Saville's Crime,* is the most interesting. Coproduced by Duvivier and Boyer. Look for Peter Lawford as a Mardi Gras reveler in the first sequence. Fourth episode, dropped before release, subsequently expanded into feature titled DESTINY.

Flesh and Flame SEE: **Night of the Quarter Moon**

Flesh and Fury (1952) **82m.** **½ D: Joseph Pevney. Tony Curtis, Jan Sterling, Mona Freeman, Wallace Ford, Harry Guardino. Curtis gives presentable performance as deaf prizefighter who seeks to regain hearing and love of decent girl.

Flesh and the Devil (1927) **112m.** *** D: Clarence Brown. John Gilbert, Greta Garbo, Lars Hanson, Barbara Kent, William Orlamond, George Fawcett, Eugenie Besserer. Garbo at her most seductive as temptress who comes between old friends Gilbert and Hanson. Pulsatingly romantic, beautifully filmed, probably the best Garbo-Gilbert love match. But talk about surprise endings!▼

Flesh and the Fiends, The SEE: **Mania**

Flesh and the Woman (1953-French-Italian) **C-102m.** ** D: Robert Siodmak. Gina Lollobrigida, Jean-Claude Pascal, Arletty, Raymond Pellegrin, Peter Van Eyck. Whole film is Lollobrigida, who plays dual roles: a Parisienne whose corrupt ways cause her husband to join the Foreign Legion, and a lookalike prostitute in Algiers. Remake of Jacques Feyder's 1934 French film LE GRAND JEU.

Flesh Eaters, The (1964) **87m.** *½ D: Jack Curtis. Rita Morley, Martin Kosleck, Byron Sanders, Barbara Walken. Group trapped on island with deranged scientist is attacked by tiny but plentiful creatures that eventually make a giant monster. Occasionally tense, but gruesome and generally boring. Longer version on video.▼

Flesh Feast (1970) **C-72m.** BOMB D: B. F. Grinter. Veronica Lake, Phil Philbin, Heather Hughes, Chris Martell, Martha Mischon. Lake's final film (which she coproduced) is embarrassing, amateurish gorefest. As a mad scientist working on rejuvenation, she tortures Hitler to death at film's climax (maggots eat at his face in close-up), then addresses us directly, shouting a patriotic, anti-Nazi diatribe! [R]▼

Flesh for Frankenstein SEE: **Andy Warhol's Frankenstein**

Fletch (1985) **C-96m.** **½ D: Michael Ritchie. Chevy Chase, Dana Wheeler-Nicholson, Tim Matheson, Joe Don Baker, Richard Libertini, Geena Davis, M. Emmet Walsh, George Wendt, Kenneth Mars. Chase plays a smart-ass undercover reporter (with a penchant for disguises) who goes after major drug ring. Good mystery absolutely smothered in wisecracks, some funny, some tiresome; if you're not a fan of Chevy, stay clear! Watchable but never credible. Screenplay by Andrew Bergman from Gregory McDonald's novel. Followed by a sequel. [PG]▼●◗

Fletch Lives (1989) **C-95m.** ** D: Michael Ritchie. Chevy Chase, Hal Holbrook, Julianne Phillips, Cleavon Little, R. Lee Ermey, Richard Libertini, Randall (Tex) Cobb, George Wyner, Patricia Kalember, Geoffrey Lewis, Richard Belzer. Chase returns as Fletch, the multi-personality L.A. reporter, in silly sequel. He finds himself in Louisiana, dealing with a parade of stereotypical Southern morons. For diehard Chase fans only. [PG]▼●

Flicks (1987) **C-76m.** BOMB D: Peter Winograd. Pamela Sue Martin, Joan Hackett, Martin Mull, Betty Kennedy, Paula Victor, Richard Belzer, Lincoln Kilpatrick. Lame homage to old films is structured as a night out at the movies, complete with coming attractions, cartoon, serial segments, and main feature. Unfunny writing sinks it all, with only mild diversions offered by a "Tom & Jerry" cartoon parody and a HOWARD THE DUCK forerunner about an alien moth pursuing a Bogart-type detective case on Earth. Filmed in 1981 but never released theatrically.▼

Flight (1929) **116m.** **½ D: Frank Capra. Jack Holt, Ralph Graves, Lila Lee, Alan Roscoe, Harold Goodwin, Jimmy de la Cruze. Dated story of battling buddies in the Marine flying corps, with some still-impressive aerial sequences. Costar Graves wrote the original story.

Flight Command (1940) **116m.** ** D: Frank Borzage. Robert Taylor, Ruth Hussey, Walter Pidgeon, Paul Kelly, Nat Pendleton, Shepperd Strudwick, Red Skelton, Dick Purcell. Hackneyed story with good cast as upstart Taylor tries to make the grade in naval flight squadron. Look fast for John Raitt as a cadet.

Flight Commander SEE: **Dawn Patrol, The** (1930)

Flight for Freedom (1943) **99m.** ** D: Lothar Mendes. Rosalind Russell, Fred MacMurray, Herbert Marshall, Eduardo Ciannelli, Walter Kingsford. Stilted tale of dedicated aviatrix Russell (loosely based on Amelia Earhart), who gains worldwide fame, and is romanced by self-centered flier MacMurray.

Flight From Ashiya (1964) **C-100m.** ** D: Michael Anderson. Yul Brynner, Richard Widmark, George Chakiris, Suzy Parker, Shirley Knight. Slow movie dealing with three aviators in rescue attempt over

Pacific. Big name cast will attract; stiff script. Panavision.

Flight From Destiny (1941) **73m.** *** D: Vincent Sherman. Geraldine Fitzgerald, Thomas Mitchell, Jeffrey Lynn, James Stephenson, Mona Maris, Jonathan Hale. Well-acted tale of Mitchell, with short time to live, helping young couple by clearing young Lynn of charges brought against him; Fitzgerald a joy as Lynn's wife.

Flight From Glory (1937) **67m.** *** D: Lew Landers. Chester Morris, Van Heflin, Whitney Bourne, Onslow Stevens, Richard Lane, Paul Guilfoyle. Hard-boiled, virile tale of outcast pilots stuck flying dangerous missions over the Andes. Excellent programmer that prefigures ONLY ANGELS HAVE WINGS (1939) in many respects.▼

Flight Lieutenant (1942) **80m.** *½ D: Sidney Salkow. Pat O'Brien, Glenn Ford, Evelyn Keyes, Minor Watson, Larry Parks, Lloyd Bridges, Hugh Beaumont. Commander Watson has sore memories of Ford's father (O'Brien), making life difficult, tired programmer.

Flight Nurse (1954) **90m.** *½ D: Allan Dwan. Joan Leslie, Forrest Tucker, Jeff Donnell, Arthur Franz, Ben Cooper. Trite romantic triangle, Korean War backdrop.

Flight of Rainbirds, A (1981-Dutch) **C-94m.** *** D: Ate de Jong. Jeroen Krabbé, Marijke Merckens, Henriette Tol, Huib Rooymans, Claire Wauthion. Thoughtful, whimsical tale of sex, death, and religion, with Krabbé in a dual role as an inept, 34-year-old biologist who's never had a date, let alone slept with a woman, and his Alter Ego, who informs him that he has seven days to seduce a woman; otherwise he'll die and end up in hell.▼

Flight of the Doves (1971-British) **C-105m.** ** D: Ralph Nelson. Ron Moody, Jack Wild, Dorothy McGuire, Stanley Holloway, Helen Raye, William Rushton. Calculated cuteness mars tale of two Liverpool children who flee to Ireland to visit their grandmother; good cast isn't seen to best advantage. [G]

Flight of the Eagle, The (1982-Swedish) **C-139m.** *** D: Jan Troell. Max von Sydow, Goran Stangertz, S. A. Ousdal, Eva von Hanno. Beautifully shot true story about a foolhardy but heroic balloon mission to the North Pole in 1897 strives to become its country's national film epic, but falls short of greatness. Stays in the memory, however, despite the fact that the second half of a lengthy running time deals only with three men freezing to death in the snow. Simultaneously filmed as a miniseries for Swedish TV. An Oscar nominee for Best Foreign Film.▼●

Flight of the Innocent (1992-Italian-French) **C-105m.** *** D: Carlo Carlei. Manuel Colao, Federico Pacifici, Sal Borgese, Giusi Cataldo, Lucio Zagaria, Massimo Lodolo, Francesa Neri, Jacques Perrin. Exciting, fast-paced thriller about a little Sicilian boy (well played by Colao) who finds himself immersed in Mafia warfare and is forced to flee for his life. Immensely entertaining, this film also observes the stranglehold that organized crime can have over a society. Excellent debut feature for director/coscripter Carlei. [R]▼●

Flight of the Intruder (1991) **C-113m.** *½ D: John Milius. Danny Glover, Willem Dafoe, Brad Johnson, Rosanna Arquette, Tom Sizemore, J. Kenneth Campbell, Dann Florek, Madison Mason, Ving Rhames, David Schwimmer. Dull adaptation of Stephen Coonts' novel, chronicling the exploits and frustrations of bombardiers in the Vietnam war. It plays like one of those 1950s service dramas that was "filmed in cooperation with the U.S. military," and this is incongruous given the story's setting. Super 35. [PG-13] ▼●

Flight of the Lost Balloon (1961) **C-91m.** *½ D: Nathan Juran. Marshall Thompson, Mala Powers, James Lanphier, Douglas Kennedy. Potentially interesting adventure drowns in low-budget telling of Thompson using balloon transport to travel across African wasteland to find missing explorer. Spectrascope.

Flight of the Navigator (1986) **C-90m.** **½ D: Randal Kleiser. Joey Cramer, Veronica Cartwright, Cliff De Young, Sarah Jessica Parker, Matt Adler, Howard Hesseman. 12-year-old boy is whisked away by an alien spaceship and returns home eight years later—still a 12-year-old boy. That's when the adventure really begins. Yet another film featuring a youthful hero and a cute robot; adequate entertainment for kids. The voice of the robot, billed as Paul Mall, is actually Paul Reubens, a.k.a. Pee-wee Herman. [PG]▼●

Flight of the Phoenix (1965) **C-147m.** ***½ D: Robert Aldrich. James Stewart, Richard Attenborough, Peter Finch, Hardy Kruger, Ernest Borgnine, Ian Bannen, Ronald Fraser, Christian Marquand, Dan Duryea, George Kennedy. A plane crash leaves a group of men stranded in the Sahara desert; film avoids clichés as tension mounts among the men. Stewart as the captain, Attenborough as the navigator stand out in uniformly fine cast.▼●

Flight to Fury (1966) **76m.** ** D: Monte Hellman. Dewey Martin, Fay Spain, Jack Nicholson, Jacqueline Hellman, Vic Diaz. Odd group of adventurers headed for Philippines location and hidden diamonds when plane crashes. Low-budgeter has its points, but never really comes across. Initially released at 62 minutes, later reedited.▼

Flight to Hong Kong (1956) **88m.** ** D: Joseph M. Newman. Rory Calhoun, Barbara Rush, Dolores Donlon, Soo Yong.

Standard fare of gangster in Far East preferring Rush to his smuggler friends; it almost costs him his life.

Flight to Mars (1951) **C-72m.** ** D: Lesley Selander. Marguerite Chapman, Cameron Mitchell, Virginia Huston, Arthur Franz. Adequate sci-fi about scientists and newspapermen who land on Mars and discover a lost civilization. Special effects hampered by modest budget.▼

Flight to Nowhere (1946) **75m.** BOMB D: William Rowland. Evelyn Ankers, Alan Curtis, Jack Holt, Jerome Cowan, Micheline Cheirel, John Craven, Inez Cooper, Hoot Gibson. Ultracheap, ultraboring account of former federal agent Curtis, who against his will becomes involved in an effort to recover a map of uranium deposits.▼

Flight to Tangier (1953) **C-90m.** **½ D: Charles Marquis Warren. Joan Fontaine, Jack Palance, Corinne Calvet, Robert Douglas. Fast-paced drama involving a cache of money aboard plane that has crashed, and the assorted people chasing after the loot.

Flim-Flam Man, The (1967) **C-104m.** *** D: Irvin Kershner. George C. Scott, Sue Lyon, Michael Sarrazin, Harry Morgan, Jack Albertson, Alice Ghostley, Albert Salmi, Slim Pickens. Scott is engaging as a veteran Southern con-man who takes on Sarrazin as apprentice in his travels, but finds the novice a bit too honest. Entertaining comedy. Panavision. ▼

Flintstones, The (1994) **C-92m.** **½ D: Brian Levant. John Goodman, Elizabeth Perkins, Rick Moranis, Rosie O'Donnell, Kyle MacLachlan, Halle Berry, Elizabeth Taylor, Dann Florek, Richard Moll, Jonathan Winters, voice of Harvey Korman, Sheryl Lee Ralph, Laraine Newman, Jay Leno. If you're going to make a live-action feature from a one-note, two-dimensional TV cartoon series, this is about as good as you could hope for: a bouncy concoction with an enthusiastic cast, including a surprisingly funny Taylor as Fred Flintstone's nagging mother-in-law. Mainly for kids, who should understandably lap it up. Series creators Bill Hanna and Joe Barbera, and Wilma's original voice, Jean Vander Pyl, have cameos. Followed by a prequel. [PG]▼●◗

Flintstones in Viva Rock Vegas, The (2000) **C-90m.** ** D: Brian Levant. Mark Addy, Stephen Baldwin, Kristen Johnston, Jane Krakowski, Thomas Gibson, Joan Collins, Alan Cumming, Harvey Korman, Alex Meneses, John Taylor, voice of Rosie O'Donnell. Silly FLINTSTONES prequel featuring Fred and Barney as unmarried employees of the Bedrock Quarry; they court Wilma and Betty, while Wilma is pressured to wed snooty, slimy rich boy Chip Rockefeller. The cast is game, but the result is one big cliché that only will appeal to undiscriminating youngsters. [PG]

Flipper (1963) **C-90m.** **½ D: James Clark. Chuck Connors, Luke Halpin, Kathleen Maguire, Connie Scott. Typical wholesome family fare about a boy who befriends a dolphin. Spun off into a TV series in 1964 (with Halpin) and another in 1995. Remade in 1996. ▼

Flipper (1996) **C-96m.** **½ D: Alan Shapiro. Paul Hogan, Elijah Wood, Chelsea Field, Isaac Hayes, Jonathan Banks, Jason Fuchs, Jessica Wesson. Low-key but agreeable time-filler about a teenage boy who spends the summer with his unruly uncle in Coral Key, Florida, and is befriended by a supersmart dolphin. Simplistic storytelling aimed at a juvenile crowd. Luke Halpin, star of the earlier film and TV series, appears briefly. Super 35. [PG]▼●

Flipper's New Adventure (1964) **C-103m.** ** D: Leon Benson. Luke Halpin, Pamela Franklin, Helen Cherry, Tom Helmore, Brian Kelly. Further exploits of everybody's favorite dolphin: Flipper and Halpin thwart escaped convicts' efforts to blackmail millionaire Helmore. Pleasant, inoffensive fare for kids, filmed in the Bahamas and Key Biscayne.▼

Flirt (1995-U.S.-German-Japanese) **C-85m.** **½ D: Hal Hartley. Bill Sage, Parker Posey, Martin Donovan, Dwight Ewell, Geno Lechner, Peter Fitz, Miho Nikaidoh, Toshizo Fujisawa, Chikako Hara. Quirky three-part film in which the same mini-drama is told three different ways: Flirt leaves lover to head off on a job, but the lover demands a commitment before the departure. The stories are set in N.Y.C., Berlin (with the characters gay), and Tokyo (with the male-female roles reversed). The point: male, female, gay, straight, and across the globe, people experience the same feelings and romantic crises. More interesting as an exercise than as entertainment.▼

Flirtation Walk (1934) **97m.** **½ D: Frank Borzage. Dick Powell, Ruby Keeler, Pat O'Brien, Ross Alexander, Guinn Williams, Henry O'Neill, Tyrone Power. West Point plot is clichéd and trivial as cadet Powell falls in love with officer's daughter Keeler; some fairly good numbers highlighted by "Mr. and Mrs. Is The Name."▼

Flirting (1990-Australian) **C-100m.** *** D: John Duigan. Noah Taylor, Thandie Newton, Nicole Kidman, Bartholomew Rose, Felix Nobis, Josh Picker, Liri Paramore, Marc Gray, Greg Palmer, Joshua Marshall, David Wieland, Craig Black, Leslie Hill. Charming sequel to Duigan's THE YEAR MY VOICE BROKE, which finds shy Taylor at boarding school where he falls in love with a Ugandan girl (Newton) who goes to a nearby girls' school. Nothing particularly new but still a warm, perceptive look at the pains of adolescence, with winning performances from everyone in the cast. Director Duigan also wrote the screenplay.▼●

Flirting With Disaster (1996) **C-92m.** **½ D: David O. Russell. Ben Stiller, Patricia Arquette, Téa Leoni, Alan Alda, Mary Tyler Moore, George Segal, Lily Tomlin, Josh Brolin, Richard Jenkins, Celia Weston, Glenn Fitzgerald, David Patrick Kelly, John Ford Noonan. Married and now a father, adopted Stiller decides to seek out his birth parents, with the help of a psychology grad student; taking his wife in tow, they embark on a cross-country trek that leads to calamity at every turn. Determinedly offbeat and full of comic twists, not all of which pay off; still, a cut above the norm for contemporary comedy. Moore and Segal make a great neurotic Jewish couple, matched by Tomlin and Alda as middle-aged flower children. [R] ▼●◗

Flirting With Fate (1938) **69m.** ** D: Frank McDonald. Joe E. Brown, Leo Carrillo, Beverly Roberts, Wynne Gibson, Steffi Duna, Stanley Fields, Charles Judels. Juvenile slapstick with Joe heading a vaudeville troupe stranded in South America. Carrillo fun as influential bandit, Duna's off-key singing good for a few laughs, but basically a weak comedy.

Floating Weeds (1959-Japanese) **C-119m.** ***½ D: Yasujiro Ozu. Ganjiro Nakamura, Machiko Kyo, Haruko Sugimura, Ayako Wakao. Struggling acting troupe visits remote island, where its leader (Nakamura) visits his illegitimate son and the boy's mother, with whom he had an affair years before. Powerful drama is meticulously directed, solidly acted. Ozu directed the same story, as a silent film, in 1934. Aka DRIFTING WEEDS.▼●

Floods of Fear (1959-British) **82m.** ** D: Charles Crichton. Howard Keel, Anne Heywood, Cyril Cusack, Harry H. Corbett, John Crawford. Adequate drama about prisoner Keel on the lam, who performs heroic deeds during flood, later proving innocence and winning girl's love.

Flood Tide (1958) **82m.** **½ D: Abner Biberman. George Nader, Cornell Borchers, Michel Ray, Judson Pratt. Nicely done drama in which an innocent man is convicted of murder on the say-so of a crippled, emotionally scarred ten-year-old boy. Nice-guy Nader falls for the boy's widowed mother, and attempts to elicit the truth. CinemaScope.

Florentine, The (2000) **C-104m.** **½ D: Nick Stagliano. Michael Madsen, Chris Penn, Hal Holbrook, Mary Stuart Masterson, Virginia Madsen, Jeremy Davies, Tom Sizemore, Luke Perry, James Belushi, Burt Young, Maeve Quinlan, Lillo Brancato. Agreeable if unremarkable slice of working-class life involving love, money, crime, and morality. Set and shot in Pennsylvania; the Florentine is a neighborhood bar and meeting place. Based on a stage play. Penn coproduced; Francis Ford Coppola is executive producer. Released direct to video. [R]▼

Florian (1940) **91m.** ** D: Edwin L. Marin. Robert Young, Helen Gilbert, Charles Coburn, Lee Bowman, Reginald Owen, Lucile Watson. Young and Gilbert, poor man and rich girl, marry, united by their love of horses.

Florida Special (1936) **70m.** ** D: Ralph Murphy. Jack Oakie, Sally Eilers, Kent Taylor, Frances Drake, J. Farrell MacDonald, Sam (Schlepperman) Hearn, Claude Gillingwater, Sidney Blackmer. Romance, mystery, and murder aboard southbound train. Song: "It's You I'm Talking About."

Florida Straits (1986) **C-97m. TVM** D: Mike Hodges. Raul Julia, Fred Ward, Daniel Jenkins, Jamie Sanchez, Victor Argo, Ilka Tanya Payan, Antonio Fargas. Julia leads a treasure hunt for gold buried in the Cuban jungle twenty years earlier during the Bay of Pigs invasion. Filmed on location in and around Myrtle Beach, S.C. Made for cable. Average. [PG-13]▼●

Florodora Girl, The (1930) **80m.** *** D: Harry Beaumont. Marion Davies, Lawrence Gray, Walter Catlett, Louis John Bartels, Ilka Chase, Vivien Oakland, Jed Prouty, Sam Hardy. Charming piece of nostalgia with Marion only one of famed Florodora Sextette of Gay 90s to spurn wealthy admirers and seek true love. Some scenes originally in color.

Floundering (1994) **C-97m.** *** D: Peter McCarthy. James LeGros, John Cusack, Ethan Hawke, Maritza Rivera, Kim Wayans, Ebbe Roe Smith, Steve Buscemi, Billy Bob Thornton, Alex Cox, Lisa Zane, Nelson Lyon, Olivia Barash, Sy Richardson, Jeremy Piven, Nina Siemaszko, Viggo Mortensen. Eye-opening sleeper with LeGros in a bravura performance as John Boyz, a sensitive and compassionate Southern Californian whose spirit is slowly being killed by the everyday injustices of modern urban life; through a series of bureaucratic blunders, he finds his own life in crisis. McCarthy's script is thoughtful and perceptive, and written with an acid pen. One of the most radical American films of the early 1990s.▼●◗

Flower Drum Song (1961) **C-133m.** ** D: Henry Koster. Nancy Kwan, James Shigeta, Miyoshi Umeki, Juanita Hall, Benson Fong. Pleasant enough Rodgers and Hammerstein musical. No great songs, but listenable score and good choreography stringing together story of San Francisco's Chinatown. Major problem: it goes on too long. Panavision.▼●

Flower in His Mouth, The (1975-Italian) **C-113m.** *½ D: Luigi Zampa. Jennifer O'Neill, James Mason, Franco Nero, Orazio Orlando. O'Neill moves to small Italian town, finds its people paralyzed by fear but unwilling to tell why. Murky thriller isn't worth time it takes to figure out.

Flower of My Secret, The (1995-Spanish-French) **C-100m.** **½ D: Pedro Almodóvar. Marisa Paredes, Juan Echanove, Imanol Arias, Carmen Elias, Rossy de Palma, Chus Lampreave, Joaquin Cortes, Manuela Vargas. A middle-aged woman (Paredes), who has been happy and a successful writer, seems to be suffering a breakdown. Her work and marriage (to an often absent military-strategist husband) are meaningless, and she must relearn the joys of living. A more focused, somber portrait than usual for Almodóvar—although not without farcical flare-ups—which seems strangely reminiscent of the Douglas Sirk–Jane Wyman collaborations of 1950s Hollywood. [R]▼●

Flowers in the Attic (1987) **C-95m.** ** D: Jeffrey Bloom. Louise Fletcher, Victoria Tennant, Kristy Swanson, Jeb Stuart Adams, Ben Granger, Lindsay Parker, Marshall Colt. Disappointing adaptation of the V.C. Andrews best-seller tones down the incest and sadomasochism of the story about four youngsters kept locked up by evil granny (Fletcher) in the family mansion. Material is strangely compelling nonetheless; benefits from effective casting. [PG-13]▼●

Flowing Gold (1940) **82m.** **½ D: Alfred E. Green. John Garfield, Frances Farmer, Pat O'Brien, Raymond Walburn, Cliff Edwards, Tom Kennedy. Dynamic Garfield in story that doesn't flow; standard fare in which he and O'Brien drill for oil and fight over Farmer.

Flubber (1997) **C-93m.** ** D: Les Mayfield. Robin Williams, Marcia Gay Harden, Christopher McDonald, Raymond J. Barry, Clancy Brown, Ted Levine, Wil Wheaton, Edie McClurg, voice of Jodi Benson. Surprisingly dull remake of Disney's THE ABSENT MINDED PROFESSOR, with Williams as the fragile genius who accidentally invents flubber—flying rubber—but forgets to attend his own wedding. Needlessly complicated by John Hughes' heavily rewritten script, which manages to leave out most of the funny stuff from the original, except for the springy basketball game. Nancy Olson (the female lead in 1961) has a cameo as a secretary. [PG]▼●◗

Fluffy (1965) **C-92m.** ** D: Earl Bellamy. Tony Randall, Shirley Jones, Edward Andrews, Ernest Truex, Howard Morris, Dick Sargent. Silly film dealing with professor Randall experimenting with a lion; he can't shake the beast, causing all sorts of repercussions, even winning Jones' affection.

Fluke (1995) **C-96m.** *** D: Carlo Carlei. Matthew Modine, Nancy Travis, Eric Stoltz, Max Pomeranc, Ron Perlman, Jon Polito, Bill Cobbs, Collin Wilcox Paxton, voice of Samuel L. Jackson. Touching, beautifully filmed story of a young family man killed in a mysterious car accident and reincarnated as a dog named Fluke—while on his way to rejoin his wife and son. More appropriate for older audiences than for young kids, who might be disturbed by certain scenes and themes within the picture. Fluke is played by Comet from the popular *Full House* TV series, while Samuel L. Jackson provides the voice of his dog friend, Rumbo. Based on James Herbert's best-selling novel. [PG]▼●

Fly, The (1958) **C-94m.** *** D: Kurt Neumann. Al (David) Hedison, Patricia Owens, Vincent Price, Herbert Marshall, Kathleen Freeman. Improbable but diverting sci-fi (screenplay by James Clavell!) about scientist who experiments with disintegration machine and has his atomic pattern mingled with that of a fly. "Help me! Help me!" Two sequels—RETURN OF THE FLY and CURSE OF THE FLY. Remade in 1986. CinemaScope. ▼●

Fly, The (1986) **C-100m.** **½ D: David Cronenberg. Jeff Goldblum, Geena Davis, John Getz, Joy Boushel. Goldblum is just right as slightly crazed scientist who tests himself in a genetic transporter machine—and starts to evolve into a human fly. Extremely intense, sharply written remake of the 1958 movie that (unfortunately) goes over the line to be gross and disgusting. Written by Charles Edward Pogue and director Cronenberg. An Oscar winner for makeup (Chris Walas, Stephan Dupuis). Followed by a sequel. [R]▼●

Fly II, The (1989) **C-104m.** BOMB D: Chris Walas. Eric Stoltz, Daphne Zuniga, Lee Richardson, John Getz, Frank Turner, Ann Marie Lee, Gary Chalk, Saffron Henderson, Harley Cross, Matthew Moore. A case of "like father, like son"; too bad director Walas isn't like David Cronenberg. Stoltz, son of deceased Jeff Goldblum, has attained puberty at five with the intellect to match; now he's being unknowingly exploited by—here's a novel twist—the scientists in whose care he's entrusted. Alternately dull and messy but mostly dull; can Stoltz still move his neck muscles after having shlepped all that cranial makeup here and in MASK? [R]▼●

Fly-Away Baby (1937) **60m.** ** D: Frank McDonald. Glenda Farrell, Barton MacLane, Gordon Oliver, Hugh O'Connell, Marcia Ralston, Tom Kennedy, Harry Davenport. Episode two in the *Torchy Blane* reporter series, serving mainly as a showcase for the wisecracking charms of Farrell as she takes to the air in pursuit of killers.

Fly Away Home (1996) **C-107m.** *** D: Carroll Ballard. Jeff Daniels, Anna Paquin, Dana Delany, Terry Kinney, Holter Graham, Jeremy Ratchford. First-rate family film about a girl who goes to live with her estranged father in Canada after the death of her mom and only finds happiness when she adopts a flock of baby geese. Then father and daughter embark on the adventure of teaching the birds how to migrate! Credible, involving story (inspired by a real-life incident), sparked by Paquin's and Daniels' strong performances. Photographed by Caleb Deschanel, who previously collaborated with director Ballard on THE BLACK STALLION. [PG]▼●◗

Fly by Night (1942) **74m.** **½ D: Robert Siodmak. Richard Carlson, Nancy Kelly, Albert Basserman, Walter Kingsford, Martin Kosleck, Miles Mander. Carlson is young doctor accused of murdering scientist who tracks down a Nazi spy ring in effort to clear himself. Fairly entertaining WW2 B propaganda, which aims for the Hitchcock style.

Flying (1986-Canadian) **C-94m.** ** D: Paul Lynch. Olivia d'Abo, Rita Tushingham, Keanu Reeves, Jessica Steen, Renee Murphy. Minor imitation of FLASHDANCE has statuesque d'Abo overcoming a leg injury to become a medal-winning gymnast; Tushingham (with shocking carrot-colored hair) is her tough coach. This formula has whiskers, but d'Abo is easy to watch, even though her full figure is unconvincing for a gymnast. Video title: TEENAGE DREAM. ▼

Flying Aces SEE: **Flying Deuces, The**

Flying Deuces, The (1939) **65m.** *** D: A. Edward Sutherland. Stan Laurel, Oliver Hardy, Jean Parker, Reginald Gardiner, Charles Middleton, James Finlayson. Stan and Ollie join the Foreign Legion so Ollie can forget unhappy romance; usual complications result. Good fun, faster paced than most L&H films, includes charming song and dance to "Shine On, Harvest Moon."▼●◗

Flying Down to Rio (1933) **89m.** *** D: Thornton Freeland. Dolores Del Rio, Gene Raymond, Raul Roulien, Ginger Rogers, Fred Astaire, Blanche Frederici, Eric Blore, Franklin Pangborn. Slim Del Rio vehicle memorable for its scene of dancing girls cavorting on plane wings, plus Astaire and Rogers doing "The Carioca" in their first screen teaming. Also shown in computer-colored version.▼●

Flying Fontaines, The (1959) **C-84m.** **½ D: George Sherman. Michael Callan, Evy Norlund, Joan Evans, Joe De Santis, Roger Perry, Rian Garrick. Circus yarn involving egocentric high-wire artist Callan who covets one of the showgirls, and the repercussions involved.

Flying High (1931) **80m.** **½ D: Charles F. Riesner. Bert Lahr, Charlotte Greenwood, Pat O'Brien, Kathryn Crawford, Charles Winninger, Hedda Hopper, Guy Kibbee. Dated, oddball comedy about harebrained inventor Lahr concocting an "aerocopter" machine; Lahr (in Hollywood debut) and Greenwood are fun together. Some De Sylva-Brown-Henderson songs carried over from Broadway production.

Flying Irishman, The (1939) **72m.** ** D: Leigh Jason. Douglas Corrigan, Paul Kelly, Robert Armstrong, Gene Reynolds. Routine biog, largely fictional, dealing with life of Douglas "Wrong Way" Corrigan.

Flying Leathernecks (1951) **C-102m.** *** D: Nicholas Ray. John Wayne, Robert Ryan, Jay C. Flippen, Janis Carter, Don Taylor, William Harrigan. Major Wayne is exceedingly tough on his Marines; executive officer Ryan thinks he should be a little nicer. Guess who wins this argument. Solid, if not especially original, WW2 actioner, with good aerial scenes and nice turn by Flippen as crafty sergeant.▼●

Flying Missile, The (1950) **93m.** ** D: Henry Levin. Glenn Ford, Viveca Lindfors, Henry O'Neill, Jerry Paris, Richard Quine. Clichéd WW2 story of commander Ford's attempt to modernize his fighting ship, with predictable results.

Flying Saucer, The (1950) **69m.** *½ D: Mikel Conrad. Mikel Conrad, Pat Garrison, Russell Hicks, Denver Pyle. Pedestrian espionage tale set in Alaska; the lone flying saucer, disappointingly, is from Earth.▼

Flying Scot, The SEE: **Mailbag Robbery**

Flying Serpent, The (1946) **59m.** ** D: Sherman Scott (Sam Newfield). George Zucco, Ralph Lewis, Hope Kramer, Eddie Acuff, Milton Kibbee. Zucco sole interest in serial-like B movie. Doctor protects Aztec treasure with prehistoric bird. Basically a remake of THE DEVIL BAT.◗

Flying Tigers (1942) **102m.** **½ D: David Miller. John Wayne, John Carroll, Anna Lee, Paul Kelly, Mae Clarke, Gordon Jones, James "Jimmie" Dodd. Good war film in which Wayne commands the volunteer Flying Tigers in China prior to Pearl Harbor while contending with egotistical ace pilot Carroll. Exciting dog-fight scenes. Also shown in computer-colored version.▼●

Flying Wild (1941) **62m.** ** D: William West. Leo Gorcey, Bobby Jordan, Donald Haines, Joan Barclay, David O'Brien, David Gorcey, Bobby Stone, Sunshine Sammy Morrison, Dennis Moore. The East Side Kids tackle airborne spies in this lightweight entry.▼

FM (1978) **C-104m.** **½ D: John A. Alonzo. Michael Brandon, Martin Mull, Eileen Brennan, Cleavon Little, Cassie Yates, Alex Karras, Norman Lloyd, James Keach. Hip comedy (which could well have inspired TV's *WKRP*) about various conflicts at maverick radio station, chiefly against its profit-hungry parent company. More a series of sketches than a movie, but nicely captures feel of 70s L.A. and Mull is marvelous as the station's craziest dj. Good rock soundtrack, plus concert appearances by Linda Ronstadt, Jimmy Buffett, Tom Petty, and REO Speedwagon. Panavision. [PG]▼●◗

Fog, The (1980) **C-91m.** **½ D: John Carpenter. Adrienne Barbeau, Jamie Lee Curtis, Hal Holbrook, Janet Leigh, John Houseman, Tommy Atkins, Nancy Loomis, Charles Cyphers. Carpenter's follow-up to HALLOWEEN is a well-directed but obvious ghost story about a California coastal town cursed by a hundred-year-old shipwreck. Panavision. [R]▼●

Fog Island (1945) **72m** *½ D: Terry Morse. George Zucco, Lionel Atwill, Veda Ann Borg, Jerome Cowan, Sharon Douglas. Grade-B chiller situated at eerie mansion with usual gathering of people suspecting one another of murder and intrigue; Zucco and Atwill are potentially terrific team.▼

Fog Over Frisco (1934) **68m.** **½ D: William Dieterle. Bette Davis, Lyle Talbot, Margaret Lindsay, Donald Woods, Henry O'Neill, Arthur Byron, Hugh Herbert, Alan Hale, William Demarest. Snappy melodrama of deceitful, thrill-a-minute party-girl Davis involved in stolen-securities scheme; stepsister Lindsay tries to help.

Folies Bergère (1935) **84m.** *** D: Roy Del Ruth. Maurice Chevalier, Ann Sothern, Merle Oberon, Eric Blore, Ferdinand Munier. Entertainer Chevalier is asked to pose as aristocratic businessman, forcing him to temporarily desert fiery Sothern for elegant Oberon. Delightful musical is highlighted by Busby Berkeleyish "Straw Hat" finale which won Dave Gould an Oscar for dance direction. Remade as THAT NIGHT IN RIO and ON THE RIVIERA.

Folies Bergère (1958-French) **C-90m** ** D: Henri Decoin. Jeanmaire, Eddie Constantine, Nadia Gray, Yves Robert. Slim plot boasts expansive cafe production numbers in tale of American crooner in Paris who almost loses wife when she becomes more successful in show biz than he.

Folks! (1992) **C-107m.** BOMB D: Ted Kotcheff. Tom Selleck, Don Ameche, Anne Jackson, Christine Ebersole, Wendy Crewson, Robert Pastorelli, Michael Murphy. Excruciating comedic misfire about stockbroker Selleck trying to deal with aging dad Ameche's senility and death wish. An outrageous number of mishaps to Selleck give slapstick a bad name. Mom Jackson's repeated line, "It's all my fault," is not true—blame this one on the writer and director. [PG-13]▼●

Folks at Red Wolf Inn, The SEE: **Terror House** (1972)

Follow a Star (1959-British) **93m.** *½ D: Robert Asher. Norman Wisdom, June Laverick, Jerry Desmonde, Hattie Jacques, John Le Mesurier, Richard Wattis, Ron Moody. Flabby slapstick musical involving zany Wisdom as a cleaning store worker who is stagestruck.

Follow Me, Boys! (1966) **C-131m.** **½ D: Norman Tokar. Fred MacMurray, Vera Miles, Lillian Gish, Charlie Ruggles, Elliott Reid, Kurt Russell. Mile-high Disney corn about simple fellow who settles in small town during 1930s and starts Boy Scout troop, devoting his life to this inspiring pursuit. A little less syrup would have helped, but at least it's done with great conviction.▼

Follow Me Quietly (1949) **59m.** *** D: Richard Fleischer. William Lundigan, Dorothy Patrick, Jeff Corey, Nestor Paiva, Charles D. Brown, Paul Guilfoyle. Solid little film noir about police manhunt for self-righteous psychopathic killer called The Judge. Packs style and substance into just 59 minutes.▼

Follow That Bird SEE: **Sesame Street Presents Follow That Bird**

Follow That Camel (1967-British) **C-95m.** **½ D: Gerald Thomas. Phil Silvers, Jim Dale, Peter Butterworth, Charles Hawtrey, Kenneth Williams, Anita Harris, Joan Sims. Silvers as conniving sergeant livens up otherwise standard CARRY ON outing with Foreign Legion setting.▼

Follow That Dream (1962) **C-110m.** **½ D: Gordon Douglas. Elvis Presley, Arthur O'Connell, Anne Helm, Joanna Moore, Jack Kruschen, Simon Oakland. Presley and family move to southern Florida where they intend to homestead, despite all opposition. Easygoing comedy from Richard Powell's book *Pioneer Go Home.* Elvis sings "Home Is Where the Heart Is" and "On Top of Old Smokey"! Panavision. ▼●

Follow That Woman (1945) **69m.** ** D: Lew Landers. Nancy Kelly, William Gargan, Regis Toomey, Ed Gargan, Byron Barr, Pierre Watkin. Predictable murder yarn, heightened by Kelly's sincerity as woman implicated in murder, Gargan her husband trying to solve case.

Follow the Boys (1944) **110m.** *** D: A. Edward Sutherland. Marlene Dietrich, George Raft, Orson Welles, Vera Zorina, Dinah Shore, W. C. Fields, Jeanette MacDonald, Maria Montez, Andrews Sisters, Sophie Tucker, Nigel Bruce, Gale Sondergaard. Universal Pictures' entry in all-star WW2 series has Raft organizing USO shows, Welles sawing Dietrich in half, MacDonald singing "Beyond The Blue Horizon," Fields doing classic pool-table routine, etc. Lots of fun.▼

Follow the Boys (1963) **C-95m.** ** D: Richard Thorpe. Connie Francis, Paula Prentiss, Ron Randell, Janis Paige, Russ Tamblyn, Dany Robin. Dumb comedy unspiked by Francis' singing or antics as quartet of girls chase around the French Riviera seeking husbands. Panavision.▼●

Follow the Fleet (1936) **110m.** **** D: Mark Sandrich. Fred Astaire, Ginger Rogers, Randolph Scott, Harriet Hilliard (Nelson), Astrid Allwyn, Betty Grable. Delightful musical with sailors Astaire and Scott romancing sisters Rogers and Hilliard. Irving Berlin songs include "Let's Face the Music and Dance," "Let Yourself Go," "We Saw the Sea." A reworking of SHORE LEAVE, a 1925 Richard Barthelmess silent, and the 1930 musical HIT THE DECK. That's Lucille Ball as Kitty. ▼●

Follow the Leader (1944) **64m.** ** D: William Beaudine. Leo Gorcey, Huntz Hall, Dave Durand, Bud Gorman, Bobby Stone, Gabriel Dell, Jimmy Strand, Jack LaRue, Billy Benedict, Bernard Gorcey, Joan Marsh. WW2 vets Muggs (Gorcey) and Glimpy (Hall) try to weed out a rotten apple from their ranks to clear a pal in this repetitive *East Side Kids* entry.

Follow the Sun (1951) **93m.** **½ D: Sidney Lanfield. Glenn Ford, Anne Baxter, Dennis O'Keefe, June Havoc. Fictionalized biopic of golfer Ben Hogan with hokey dramatics to fill in lean spots.

Follow Your Dreams SEE: **Independence Day**

Folly to Be Wise (1952-British) **91m.** *** D: Frank Launder. Alastair Sim, Elizabeth Allan, Roland Culver, Martita Hunt. Generally amusing nonsense with Sim an Army chaplain trying to enliven service life with various unique entertainment programs.

Food of the Gods (1976) **C-88m.** BOMB D: Bert I. Gordon. Marjoe Gortner, Pamela Franklin, Ida Lupino, Jon Cypher, Ralph Meeker, Belinda Belaski. Dreadful adaptation of H. G. Wells novel. Strange substance causes giant growth in wasps, worms, chickens and rats. Not for the squeamish. Similar to VILLAGE OF THE GIANTS, filmed by Gordon 11 years earlier. [PG]▼

Food of the Gods II (1989-Canadian) **C-91m.** BOMB D: Damian Lee. Paul Coufos, Lisa Schrage, Jackie Burroughs, Colin Fox, Frank Moore. This time, gigantic laboratory rats terrorize a college campus. No connection to the first film, or (goodness knows) H. G. Wells' novel. Ugh!▼●

Fool and His Money, A (1988) **C-84m.** BOMB D: Daniel Adams. Jonathan Penner, Sandra Bullock, Gerald Orange, George Plimpton, Jerzy Kosinski, Tama Janowitz, Jose Torres. Plimpton as "God" tells ex-musician/ex-ad man Penner to start his own business, so he founds the "Preferent Church," a religion whose main tenet is selfishness. Embarrassing attempt at satire features Bullock on the video box, but she only has about eight minutes on screen as a public defender who can't believe her boyfriend has turned into such a jerk. [R]▼

Fool for Love (1985) **C-106m.** ** D: Robert Altman. Sam Shepard, Kim Basinger, Harry Dean Stanton, Randy Quaid. Altman's inventive direction tries to breathe life into what is ultimately a photographed play, Shepard's examination of two ex-lovers who find themselves inextricably bound together. Biggest problem is generating some interest in these characters. Very much of a piece with Shepard's other work; if you're a fan, you might adjust our rating upward. [R]▼●

Foolin' Around (1980) **C-111m.** ** D: Richard T. Heffron. Gary Busey, Annette O'Toole, Cloris Leachman, Eddie Albert, John Calvin, Tony Randall. Dumb 1950s-style comedy about a good-hearted klutz who pursues a wealthy girl, although she's already engaged. Cardboard characters and clumsy slapstick. [PG]▼

Foolish (1999) **C-96m.** BOMB D: Dave Meyers, Eddie Griffin, Master P, Amy Petersen, Frank Sivero, Daphnee Lynn Duplaix, Jonathan Banks, Andrew Dice Clay, Marla Gibbs, Bill Nunn, Bill Duke, Traci Bingham. Part drama, part comedy, part concert film, total disaster. Story centers around a comic who feels he is not using his talents wisely and throwing away his potential. Yeah, that's right; he coulda been a contender. Also, nothing he says is even remotely funny. Film is also meant to capitalize on the success of hip hop star Master P, who also executive-produced. The title says it all. [R]▼●◗

Foolish Wives (1922) **107m.** *** D: Erich von Stroheim. Erich von Stroheim, Maud George, Mae Busch, Cesare Gravina, Malvine Polo. Von Stroheim's third film as director is a typically sophisticated, fascinating tale of seduction, fake counts, blackmail, suicide, lechery, and murder. Great photography by William Daniels and Ben Reynolds, and an incredible set depicting the Monte Carlo casino designed by von Stroheim and Richard Day.▼●

Fool Killer, The (1965) **100m.** *** D: Servando Gonzalez. Anthony Perkins, Edward Albert, Dana Elcar, Henry Hull, Salome Jens, Arnold Moss. Set in post-Civil War South, film relates unusual adventures of runaway orphan (Albert) and his meeting with strange young man (Perkins). Interesting and offbeat.▼

Fools (1970) **C-97m.** BOMB D: Tom Gries. Jason Robards, Katharine Ross, Scott Hylands, Roy C. Jenson, Mark Bramhall. Wretchedly acted, written, and directed drama about love affair in San Francisco between horror movie star and beautiful, neglected wife of a lawyer. Story line is vaguely similar to PETULIA but the execution certainly isn't. [PG]▼

Fools for Scandal (1938) **81m.** **½ D: Mervyn LeRoy. Carole Lombard, Fernand Gravet, Ralph Bellamy, Allen Jenkins, Isabel Jeans, Marie Wilson. Generally a misfire, despite lovely Lombard as movie star who meets impoverished Paris nobleman Gravet; Bellamy plays the sap again.

Fools of Fortune (1990-British) **C-109m.** *½ D: Pat O'Connor. Mary Elizabeth

Mastrantonio, Iain Glen, Julie Christie, Michael Kitchen, Sean McClory, Frankie McCafferty. Muddled, haphazardly organized family chronicle set against decades of fighting between the British army and the IRA, from 1920 on. Very difficult to sort out who's doing what to whom; director O'Connor may have been too close to his subject. Mastrantonio, who shows up quite late (despite her billing), is awkward as Glen's love interest. Based on William Trevor's novel. [PG-13]▼●

Fools' Parade (1971) **C-98m.** ** D: Andrew V. McLaglen. James Stewart, George Kennedy, Anne Baxter, Strother Martin, Kurt Russell, William Windom, Kathy Cannon. Another great Stewart performance can't save melodramatic treatment of Davis Grubb novel. Story of three ex-cons stalked by their former prison guard is unintentionally funny too many times to be taken seriously. [PG]

Fools Rush In (1997) **C-107m.** **½ D: Andy Tennant. Matthew Perry, Salma Hayek, Jon Tenney, Carlos Gomez, Tomas Milian, Siobhan Fallon, John Bennett Perry, Stanley DeSantis, Suzanne Snyder, Jill Clayburgh. Hard-working New Yorker Perry chances to meet self-reliant Mexican-American photographer Hayek in Las Vegas, and it's lust at first sight . . . but when she becomes pregnant, it's hard for either of them to know what course to take. Pleasant if unexceptional romantic comedy-drama with appealing and credible performances by the two stars. [PG-13]▼●◗

Footlight Glamour (1943) **75m.** **½ D: Frank Strayer. Penny Singleton, Arthur Lake, Larry Simms, Ann Savage, Jonathan Hale, Danny Mummert, Thurston Hall, Marjorie Ann Mutchie. Amusing *Blondie* entry finds the Bumsteads mixed up with the stage-struck daughter of one of Dagwood's clients.▼

Footlight Parade (1933) **104m.** ***½ D: Lloyd Bacon. James Cagney, Joan Blondell, Ruby Keeler, Dick Powell, Guy Kibbee, Ruth Donnelly, Hugh Herbert, Frank McHugh. Cagney plays a stage director who tries to outdo himself with spectacular musical numbers. Fast-paced Warner Bros. opus winds up with three incredible Busby Berkeley numbers back-to-back: "Honeymoon Hotel," "By a Waterfall," and "Shanghai Lil." Film scholars still argue over whether it's John Garfield who gets one brief shot in the latter dance number.▼●

Footlight Serenade (1942) **80m.** *** D: Gregory Ratoff. Betty Grable, Victor Mature, John Payne, Jane Wyman, Phil Silvers, James Gleason, Mantan Moreland, Cobina Wright, Jr. Cute backstage musical with cocky boxer Mature turning to Broadway and trying to woo Grable, who's secretly engaged to Payne. Good fun.▼

Footloose (1984) **C-107m.** **½ D: Herbert Ross. Kevin Bacon, Lori Singer, John Lithgow, Dianne Wiest, Christopher Penn, Sarah Jessica Parker, John Laughlin, Elizabeth Gorcey, Frances Lee McCain, Jim Young, Brian Wimmer. City kid moves to small town where dancing has been outlawed—and confronts hellfire minister (Lithgow) in effort to bring it back. Too much emphasis on hackneyed story in so-called musical (though the soundtrack did spawn a number of Top 10 hits). Bacon's charisma sparks innocuous film. [PG]▼●

Footsteps in the Dark (1941) **96m.** **½ D: Lloyd Bacon. Errol Flynn, Brenda Marshall, Ralph Bellamy, Alan Hale, Lee Patrick, Allen Jenkins. Flynn leads double life as happily married businessman and mystery writer. Silly but genial.▼

Footsteps in the Fog (1955-British) **C-90m.** *** D: Arthur Lubin. Stewart Granger, Jean Simmons, Finlay Currie, Bill Travers, Ronald Squire. Cat-and-mouse battle involving servant girl who blackmails her employer for having murdered his wife. Fine acting, rich Victorian atmosphere.

Footsteps in the Night (1957) **62m.** *½ D: Jean Yarbrough. Bill Elliott, Don Haggerty, Eleanore Tanin, Zena Marshall. Programmer detective tale with Elliott solving the motel murder of a friend.

For a Few Bullets More SEE: **Any Gun Can Play**

For a Few Dollars More (1966-Italian) **C-130m.** *** D: Sergio Leone. Clint Eastwood, Lee Van Cleef, Gian Maria Volonté, Jose Egger, Mara Krup, Rosemarie Dexter, Klaus Kinski, Mario Brega. Sequel to FISTFUL OF DOLLARS finds two gunslingers forming an uneasy alliance in their quest for outlaw Indio (Volonté) —although their reasons for chasing him are markedly different. Slightly draggy but still fun; don't miss the scene where Van Cleef strikes a match on the back of Kinski's neck! Trademark atmospheric score by Ennio Morricone. Released in the U.S. in 1967. Followed by THE GOOD, THE BAD, AND THE UGLY. Techniscope. [R—originally rated M]▼●◗

For All Mankind (1989) **C-80m.** *** D: Al Reinert. Excellent documentary on the Apollo moon flights, culled from a zillion hours of NASA footage seamlessly edited into one representative journey. Impressive, if a bit on the cold side; end credits inform us film was shot "on location." Let us hope.▼●◗

For Better, For Worse (1954-British) **C-83m.** **½ D: J. Lee Thompson. Dirk Bogarde, Susan Stephen, Cecil Parker, Dennis Price, Eileen Herlie, Athene Seyler, Thora Hird, Sidney James. Intelligently handled account of young married couple harassed by bills, in-laws, and marital adjustment.

For Better, For Worse (1974) SEE: **Zandy's Bride**

Forbidden (1932) **81m.** ** D: Frank Capra. Barbara Stanwyck, Adolphe Menjou, Ralph Bellamy, Dorothy Peterson, Henry Armetta. A spinster schoolteacher takes a cruise and falls in love with a man who can never marry her. Fine performances and stunning Joseph Walker photography buoy this BACK STREET soap opera until its ridiculous conclusion.

Forbidden (1953) **85m.** **½ D: Rudolph Maté. Tony Curtis, Joanne Dru, Lyle Bettger, Marvin Miller, Victor Sen Yung. OK suspenser in which two-fisted Curtis arrives in Macao, hired by a gangland chief to uncover the whereabouts of Dru (who just so happens to be Curtis' ex-girlfriend).

Forbidden Alliance SEE: **Barretts of Wimpole Street, The** (1934)▼

Forbidden Cargo (1954-British) **83m.** **½ D: Harold French. Nigel Patrick, Elizabeth Sellars, Terence Morgan, Jack Warner, Greta Gynt, Joyce Grenfell, Theodore Bikel. Modest drama about customs agent Patrick clashing with dope-smuggling syndicate, enlivened by a solid cast.

Forbidden Choices SEE: **Beans of Egypt, Maine, The**

Forbidden Dance, The (1990) **C-97m.** BOMB D: Greydon Clark. Laura Herring, Jeff James, Sid Haig, Richard Lynch, Barbara Brighton, Kid Creole. Brazilian jungle princess treks to America on behalf of her endangered rain forests, ends up on a TV special as . . . a lambada dancer?!? Marginally lesser of two " 'L'-word" quickies that opened the same week. Inability of ex-Miss USA Herring to dance is good for a few chuckles. [PG-13]▼●

Forbidden Fruit (1959-French) **97m.** **½ D: Henri Verneuil. Fernandel, Francoise Arnoul, Claude Nollier, Sylvie, Jacques Castelot. Unpretentious little film of Fernandel's touching love affair with a young maiden.

Forbidden Games (1951-French) **87m.** ***½ D: René Clement. Brigitte Fossey, Georges Poujouly, Louis Herbert. During WW2, young Parisian girl is orphaned and taken in by simple peasant family; she develops friendship with their youngest son, and shares with him a private world which the grownups cannot understand. Sad, intensely moving drama earned a Best Foreign Film Oscar.▼●

Forbidden Island (1959) **C-66m.** *½ D: Charles B. Griffith. Jon Hall, Nan Adams, John Farrow, Jonathan Haze, Greigh Phillips. Sleazy film with Hall a skindiver seeking to find sunken treasure before a gang of crooks uncovers the loot.

Forbidden Paradise SEE: **Hurricane** (1979)

Forbidden Planet (1956) **C-98m.** ***½ D: Fred McLeod Wilcox. Walter Pidgeon, Anne Francis, Leslie Nielsen, Warren Stevens, Jack Kelly, Richard Anderson, Earl Holliman, George Wallace, James Drury. Sci-fi version of Shakespeare's *The Tempest* remains one of the most ambitious and intelligent films of its genre; only slow, deliberate pacing works against it, as Nielsen and fellow space travelers visit planet where expatriate Pidgeon has built a one-man empire with daughter Francis and obedient Robby the Robot. Great effects, eerie electronic score. Beware 95m. reissue prints. Lavish use of wide-screen CinemaScope is severely diminished on television.▼●◗

Forbidden Street, The (1949-British) **91m.** ** D: Jean Negulesco. Dana Andrews, Maureen O'Hara, Sybil Thorndike, Wilfrid Hyde-White, Fay Compton. Fanciful melodrama, set in Victorian England, of wealthy O'Hara defying her family by marrying beneath her class; Andrews has a dual role, as a down-and-out artist (with his voice dubbed) and an ex-barrister. Scripted by Ring Lardner, Jr. Originally titled BRITANNIA MEWS.

Forbidden World (1982) **C-86m.** *½ D: Allan Holzman. Jesse Vint, June Chadwick, Dawn Dunlap, Linden Chiles, Fox Harris. Roger Corman-produced ALIEN rip-off is followup to (and uses sets from) his GALAXY OF TERROR as well as battle scenes lifted from his BATTLE BEYOND THE STARS. Lots of gore, weak special effects. Aka MUTANT. [R]▼●

Forbidden Zone (1980) **76m.** *½ D: Richard Elfman. Herve Villechaize, Susan Tyrrell, Marie-Pascale Elfman, Viva. Pastiche film set in the Sixth Dimension, an underground kingdom ruled by Villechaize and Tyrrell. Mostly a collection of bizarre, campy musical numbers, done in the style of 1930s Max Fleischer cartoons. If only everything about the film weren't so *ugly!* Has an inevitable cult following. [R]▼

Forbin Project, The SEE: **Colossus: The Forbin Project**

Forced Entry (1984) **C-83m.** *½ D: Jim Sotos. Tanya Roberts, Ron Max, Nancy Allen, Robin Leslie. Trifling junk about a rapist-killer, and his attempt to victimize housewife Roberts. Shot in 1975 as THE LAST VICTIM; supposedly re-edited five years later. [R]▼

Forced March (1989-U.S.-Hungarian) **C-104m.** **½ D: Rick King. Chris Sarandon, Renee Soutendijk, Josef Sommer, John Seitz. American actor Sarandon faces challenge after traveling to Budapest to star in a film about Miklos Radnoti, Hungarian-Jewish poet who fell victim to the Holocaust. Ambitious, potentially potent drama mostly falls flat; scenes of the actor are pointlessly interspersed with those of the film in which he is starring.▼●

Forced Vengeance (1982) **C-90m.** *½ D: James Fargo. Chuck Norris, Mary Louise

Weller, Camilla Griggs, Michael Cavanaugh, David Opatoshu, Seiji Sakaguchi. Clichéd karate nonsense with Norris, badly in need of an acting lesson, taking on Hong Kong mobster Cavanaugh. [R]▼

Force: Five (1981) **C-95m.** ** D: Robert Clouse. Joe Lewis, Pam Huntington, Master Bong Soo Han, Richard Norton, Benny "The Jet" Urquidez. Lewis and company attempt to rescue girl from the clutches of religious-cult-head Han. Retread of Clouse's much-used martial arts formula, with gimmick of disparate five-person "team" as the collective hero. Remake of HOT POTATO. [R]▼

Force of Arms (1951) **100m.** **½ D: Michael Curtiz. William Holden, Nancy Olson, Frank Lovejoy, Gene Evans, Dick Wesson. Updating of Hemingway's A FAREWELL TO ARMS to WW2 Italy, with unmemorable results. Reissued as A GIRL FOR JOE.▼

Force of Evil (1948) **78m.** *** D: Abraham Polonsky. John Garfield, Beatrice Pearson, Thomas Gomez, Roy Roberts, Marie Windsor, Howland Chamberlin, Beau Bridges. Rock-solid film noir about a racketeer's lawyer (Garfield, in a stunning performance), whose ideals have been obscured by his greed. Beautifully photographed (by George Barnes) and lit; this has become something of a cult item. Polonsky, who coscripted with Ira Wolfert, was blacklisted and didn't make another film until 1969's TELL THEM WILLIE BOY IS HERE.▼●

Force of One, A (1979) **C-90m.** **½ D: Paul Aaron. Chuck Norris, Jennifer O'Neill, Clu Gulager, Ron O'Neal, James Whitmore Jr., Clint Ritchie, Pepe Serna. Followup to GOOD GUYS WEAR BLACK has karate champ Norris using his expertise to help California town combat drug trafficking. OK action fare. [PG]▼

Forces of Nature (1999) **C-104m.** ** D: Bronwen Hughes. Sandra Bullock, Ben Affleck, Maura Tierney, Steve Zahn, Blythe Danner, Ronny Cox, Michael Fairman, Janet Carroll, David Strickland, Anne Haney, Bert Remsen. About-to-be-wed Affleck is stranded in N.Y. with fellow passenger Bullock when their plane crashes. The two strangers decide to travel together, by land, to their intended destination: Savannah, GA. What promises to be a standard road picture with two likable stars veers off-course early on thanks to Bullock's erratic character and a threadbare story; a disappointment. [PG-13]▼●◗

Force 10 From Navarone (1978-British) **C-118m.** BOMB D: Guy Hamilton. Robert Shaw, Harrison Ford, Edward Fox, Franco Nero, Barbara Bach, Carl Weathers, Richard Kiel. Awful sequel to classic GUNS OF NAVARONE, poor in all departments, although Shaw, Ford, and Nero try to give it a lift. Mixed group (naturally), hindered by traitor Nero, attempt to blow a bridge vital to Nazis. They blew the film instead. Based on the Alistair MacLean novel. Restored to 128m. on laserdisc. Panavision. [PG]▼●◗

Foreign Affair, A (1948) **116m.** ***½ D: Billy Wilder. Jean Arthur, Marlene Dietrich, John Lund, Millard Mitchell, Peter Von Zerneck, Stanley Prager. Staid Arthur is sent to Berlin to investigate post-WW2 conditions, finds romance instead, with hot competition from Dietrich. Marlene sings "Black Market," "Ruins of Berlin," but Jean Arthur's Iowa State Song equally memorable in great Wilder comedy. Written by Charles Brackett, Billy Wilder, and Richard Breen.▼

Foreign Body (1986-British) **C-108m.** **½ D: Ronald Neame. Victor Banerjee, Warren Mitchell, Trevor Howard, Geraldine McEwan, Amanda Donohoe, Denis Quilley, Eve Ferret, Anna Massey. In a real casting switch, A PASSAGE TO INDIA star Banerjee has a field day as an itinerant Indian in London who poses as a doctor and soon finds all the women dying to get him into bed. Throwback to the style of 1950s British sex comedies. [PG-13]▼

Foreign Correspondent (1940) **119m.** **** D: Alfred Hitchcock. Joel McCrea, Laraine Day, Herbert Marshall, George Sanders, Albert Basserman, Robert Benchley, Edmund Gwenn, Eduardo Ciannelli, Harry Davenport, Martin Kosleck. McCrea in title role caught in middle of spy ring with reporters Sanders and Benchley, innocent Day, suspicious father Marshall. Tremendously entertaining film with several vintage Hitchcock showpieces. Scripted by Charles Bennett and Joan Harrison; dialogue by James Hilton and Benchley.▼●

Foreign Intrigue (1956) **C-100m.** **½ D: Sheldon Reynolds. Robert Mitchum, Genevieve Page, Ingrid Thulin, Frederick O'Brady. Based on TV series, film has virtue of on-location shooting in Europe as unemotional Mitchum checks out the cause of his employer's death.

Foreign Student (1994) **C-96m.** **½ D: Eva Sereny. Robin Givens, Marco Hofschneider, Rick Johnson, Charlotte Ross, Edward Herrmann, Jack Coleman, Charles S. Dutton, Hinton Battle, Anthony Herrera. Mild, but fairly individualized, low-budget nostalgia piece about an 18-year-old Parisian's taboo romance with a beautiful black schoolteacher/domestic while attending a small college in Virginia's Shenandoah Valley in r&b 1956. Spotty little film mixes it up with subplots involving football, William Faulkner, and blues greats Howlin' Wolf and Sonny Boy Williamson; from wistful memoirs of filmmaker Philippe Labro, a huge best-seller in France. [R]▼●

Foreman Went to France, The (1941-

British) **88m.** **½ D: Charles Frend. Tommy Trinder, Clifford Evans, Constance Cummings, Robert Morley, Mervyn Johns, Gordon Jackson, Ernest Milton. Documentary-style tale of industrial engineer who journeys to France during WW2 to help save secret machinery from being confiscated by the Axis. Adapted from a J.B. Priestley story based on a true incident.▼

Forest Rangers, The (1942) **C-87m.** **½ D: George Marshall. Fred MacMurray, Paulette Goddard, Susan Hayward, Albert Dekker, Rod Cameron, Lynne Overman, Eugene Pallette. Hayward tries to show ranger MacMurray that he's made a mistake marrying wealthy Goddard in this OK romance with good action scenes. Introduced the hit song "I've Got Spurs That Jingle, Jangle, Jingle."

Forever Amber (1947) **C-140m.** *** D: Otto Preminger. Linda Darnell, Cornel Wilde, Richard Greene, George Sanders, Jessica Tandy, Anne Revere, Leo G. Carroll. "Musical beds" costumer, taken from Kathleen Winsor's once-scandalous novel, about blonde Darnell's ascension to the court of Charles II. Lengthy but colorful and entertaining, with David Raksin's outstanding score.▼●

Forever and a Day (1943) **104m.** *** D: René Clair, Edmund Goulding, Cedric Hardwicke, Frank Lloyd, Victor Saville, Robert Stevenson, Herbert Wilcox. Brian Aherne, Robert Cummings, Ida Lupino, Charles Laughton, Herbert Marshall, Ray Milland, Anna Neagle, Merle Oberon, Claude Rains, Victor McLaglen, Buster Keaton, Jessie Matthews, Roland Young, C. Aubrey Smith, Edward Everett Horton, Elsa Lanchester, Edmund Gwenn. Eighty-odd British (and American) stars contributed their services to this episodic film, about a house and its inhabitants over the years, to raise funds for British War Relief. Uneven result, but has many fine moments and star-gazing galore; once-in-a-lifetime cast.▼◗

Forever Darling (1956) **C-96m.** **½ D: Alexander Hall. Lucille Ball, Desi Arnaz, James Mason, Louis Calhern. Ball's madcap antics nearly drive husband Arnaz to divorce, but guardian angel Mason saves the day. Contrived but enjoyable.▼●

Forever Female (1953) **93m.** ***½ D: Irving Rapper. Ginger Rogers, William Holden, Paul Douglas, Pat Crowley, James Gleason, Jesse White, Marjorie Rambeau, George Reeves, King Donovan, Marion Ross. Top-notch show business comedy, with Rogers the star who finally realizes she is too old for the ingenue role, allowing writer Holden to cast Crowley in the part. Film captures flavor of the Broadway, summer stock milieux. Scripted by Philip and Julius Epstein; suggested by James M. Barrie's play *Rosalind*.▼●

Forever, Lulu (1987) **C-85m.** BOMB D: Amos Kollek. Hanna Schygulla, Deborah Harry, Alec Baldwin, Annie Golden, Paul Gleason, Dr. Ruth Westheimer. Embarrassing, amateurish imitation of DESPERATELY SEEKING SUSAN has budding novelist Schygulla becoming embroiled in a real-life mystery in N.Y.C. involving drugs and killers. Despite having the title role, singing star Harry makes only a brief cameo appearance. Israeli director Kollek also turns in a poor acting job as Schygulla's agent. Baldwin's first film. Aka CRAZY STREETS. [R]▼●

For Ever Mozart (1996-French-Swiss) **C-84m.** *** D: Jean-Luc Godard. Madeleine Assas, Frederic Pierrot, Ghalia Lacroix, Vicky Messica, Harry Cleven. One of Godard's better latter-career films is the complex, poetic account, set in four sections, of a director attempting to mount a movie. Here, Godard insightfully deals with one of his more prominent themes: how art (and, specifically, the art of cinema) relates to politics (in this case, the political implications of the war in Bosnia).▼

Forever My Love (1962-German) **C-147m.** **½ D: Ernest Marischka. Romy Schneider, Karl Boehm, Magda Schneider, Vilma Degischer. Typical German confection dealing with 19th-century Austrian Emperor Franz Josef and Empress Elizabeth.

Forever Young (1992) **C-102m.** *** D: Steve Miner. Mel Gibson, Jamie Lee Curtis, Elijah Wood, Isabel Glasser, George Wendt, Joe Morton, Nicolas Surovy, David Marshall Grant, Art LaFleur. The year is 1939, and test-pilot Gibson (whose girlfriend is comatose after being hit by a car) volunteers to be frozen as part of a cryogenics experiment. He's accidentally thawed out in 1992, and becomes involved in the lives of a young boy (Wood) and his mom (Curtis). This romantic comedy-fantasy may play out by the numbers as it tugs at your heartstrings, but it's hard to resist, thanks to a charismatic cast. [PG] ▼●◗

Forever Young, Forever Free (1976-South African) **C-85m.** **½ D: Ashley Lazarus. Jose Ferrer, Karen Valentine, Muntu Ndebele, Norman Knox, Bess Finney, Simon Sabela. The adventures of a white orphan (Knox) and his black friend (Ndebele) who leave their South African village for N.Y.C when young Knox becomes ill. Entertaining, if a bit too sugar-coated. Aka E LOLLIPOP and LOLLIPOP. [G]

Forger of London (1961-German) **91m.** ** D: Harald Reinl. Eddi Arent, Viktor de Kowa, Karin Dor, Hellmut Lange, Robert Graf. Scotland Yard investigates counterfeit gang tied in with prime suspect, an amnesiac playboy; from Edgar Wallace tale.▼

Forget Paris (1995) **C-101m.** *** D: Billy Crystal. Billy Crystal, Debra Winger, Joe Mantegna, Cynthia Stevenson, Richard Masur, Julie Kavner, William Hickey, Robert Costanzo, John Spencer, Cathy Moriarty, Tom Wright. Crystal plays a basketball referee who falls head over heels for Winger, while burying his father in Paris. Sharply written comedy (by Crystal and Lowell Ganz and Babaloo Mandel) about the trials and tribulations of making a marriage work—after falling in love. Many top basketball stars appear as themselves; Dan Castellaneta appears unbilled. [PG-13]▼●◗

Forgiven Sinner, The (1961-French) **101m.** **½ D: Jean-Pierre Melville. Jean-Paul Belmondo, Emmanuele Riva, Patricia Gozzi, Irene Tunc. Belmondo gives subdued, offbeat performance as clergyman trying to set shady woman onto the path of righteousness. Aka LEON MORIN, PRIEST. Originally ran 123m.▼

Forgotten Woman (1939) **63m.** **½ D: Harold Young. Sigrid Gurie, William Lundigan, Eve Arden, Elizabeth Risdon, Virginia Brissac. Overnight star (and overnight fade-out) Gurie is helpless woman, framed by influential gangsters, suffering on trial.

For Heaven's Sake (1926) **86m.** **** D: Sam Taylor. Harold Lloyd, Jobyna Ralston, Noah Young, James Mason, Paul Weigel. Screamingly funny silent comedy has Lloyd a blase young millionaire whose crush on Ralston inspires him to help attract "customers" for her father's Bowery Mission. Even THE FRENCH CONNECTION hasn't dimmed the luster of Lloyd's chase climax on L.A. streets.

For Heaven's Sake (1950) **92m.** **½ D: George Seaton. Clifton Webb, Joan Bennett, Robert Cummings, Edmund Gwenn, Joan Blondell. Droll fantasy with Webb and Gwenn two angels sent to earth to speed along the arrival of Bennett and Cummings' heavenly baby.

For Keeps (1988) **C-98m.** *½ D: John G. Avildsen. Molly Ringwald, Randall Batinkoff, Kenneth Mars, Miriam Flynn, Conchata Ferrell, Sharon Brown, Renee Estevez, Larry Drake. Studious teen Ringwald becomes pregnant, and must quickly face adult responsibilities. Subject matter is most worthwhile, but the result is predictable and phony. Tim Kazurinsky coauthored the screenplay. [PG-13]▼●

For Love Alone (1986-Australian) **C-102m.** *** D: Stephen Wallace. Helen Buday, Sam Neill, Hugo Weaving, Hugh Keays-Byrne. Nicely filmed romantic drama, set in the 1930s, with Australian university student Buday falling in love with her professor (Weaving); even though he treats her poorly, she decides to follow him to England. Neill does well as an altogether different man who enters her life. Based on the novel by Christina Stead.▼

For Love of Ivy (1968) **C-102m.** ** D: Daniel Mann. Sidney Poitier, Abbey Lincoln, Beau Bridges, Leon Bibb, Nan Martin, Lauri Peters, Carroll O'Connor. Family wants to keep maid, so they find her a beau; ho-hum black romance. [G]▼◗

For Love of the Game (1999) **C-137m.** **½ D: Sam Raimi. Kevin Costner, Kelly Preston, John C. Reilly, Jena Malone, Brian Cox, J. K. Simmons, Vin Scully. Likable vehicle for Costner as a 20-year baseball veteran who looks back on the last five years of his life during an eventful end-of-season game. Effectively played for star value and sentiment, but goes into extra innings for no apparent reason, stretching out a conclusion that comes as no surprise. Panavision. [PG-13]▼●◗

For Love or Money (1933) SEE: **Cash**

For Love or Money (1963) **C-108m.** **½ D: Michael Gordon. Kirk Douglas, Mitzi Gaynor, Gig Young, Thelma Ritter, William Bendix, Julie Newmar. Comedy strains to be funnier than it is. Widow Ritter hires lawyer Douglas to find spouses for her three daughters.

For Love or Money (1993) **C-95m.** ** D: Barry Sonnenfeld. Michael J. Fox, Gabrielle Anwar, Anthony Higgins, Michael Tucker, Bob Balaban, Isaac Mizrahi, Udo Kier, Simon Jones, Dianne Brill, Dan Hedaya, Fyvush Finkel, Bobby Short. Tepid APARTMENT variation about aggressive, ambitious Fox, concierge at an upscale N.Y.C. hotel, who'll do anything to please his guests. Trouble brews when he finds himself attracted to beautiful Anwar, the mistress of married Higgins (a Donald Trump clone). Fox and a fine cast try their best, but this comedy runs out of steam long before its predictable finale. [PG]▼●

For Me and My Gal (1942) **104m.** **½ D: Busby Berkeley. Judy Garland, George Murphy, Gene Kelly, Marta Eggerth, Ben Blue, Horace (Stephen) McNally, Keenan Wynn, Richard Quine. Music sustains old-hat plot of vaudeville couple determined to play Palace, circa WW1. Kelly's film debut enhanced by he and Garland singing title tune, "When You Wore a Tulip," etc. Also shown in computer-colored version.▼●

For Men Only (1952) **93m.** ** D: Paul Henreid. Paul Henreid, Kathleen Hughes, Russell Johnson, James Dobson, Margaret Field, Vera Miles, Douglas Kennedy, O. Z. Whitehead. Sincere if obvious study of fraternity hazing that gets out of hand on a college campus. Retitled: THE TALL LIE.

Formula, The (1980) **C-117m.** ** D: John G. Avildsen. George C. Scott, Marlon Brando, Marthe Keller, John Gielgud, G. D. Spradlin, Beatrice Straight, Richard Lynch, John Van Dreelen, Craig T. Nelson. Amazingly matter-of-fact thriller about a cop who investigates a friend's murder and finds him linked to a mysterious plot involving a formula for synthetic fuel. Scott and Brando are always worth watching, but writer-producer Steve Shagan telegraphs all his punches. [R]▼●

For Pete's Sake (1974) **C-90m.** ★★½ D: Peter Yates. Barbra Streisand, Michael Sarrazin, Estelle Parsons, William Redfield, Molly Picon, Louis Zorich, Vincent Schiavelli, Anne Ramsey. Amiable, featherweight comedy about devoted wife who tries to raise money for her ambitious cab-driver husband, and gets involved with assorted nuts and underworld types. Streisand is fine in forgettable film. [PG]▼

For Queen and Country (1988-British) **C-105m.** ★★★ D: Martin Stellman. Denzel Washington, Dorian Healey, Amanda Redman, Sea Chapman, Bruce Payne. Striking, laced-in-acid contemporary thriller of life in Thatcherite England. Washington is well cast as a former paratrooper who struggles for survival in an atmosphere of racism, poverty, and corruption—and then loses his British citizenship because of an immigration-law technicality. The director also cowrote the screenplay. [R]

Forrest Gump (1994) **C-142m.** ★★½ D: Robert Zemeckis. Tom Hanks, Robin Wright, Gary Sinise, Sally Field, Mykelti Williamson, Michael Humphreys, Hanna Hall, Haley Joel Osment. A slow-witted boy grows to adulthood, floating through life—like a feather—with only a vague understanding of the tumultuous times he's living through. (He manages to be on hand for virtually every socio-pop-political phenomenon of the formative Baby Boomer decades, from the rise of Elvis to the fall of Nixon.) Either you accept Hanks in this part and go with the movie's seriocomic sense of whimsy, or you don't (we didn't)—but either way it's a long journey, filled with digitized imagery that puts Forrest Gump into a wide variety of backdrops and real-life events. Based on the (more satiric) novel by Winston Groom. Oscar winner for Best Film, Best Actor (Hanks), Director, Film Editing, Visual Effects, and Adapted Screenplay. Panavision. [PG-13]▼●

For Richer, for Poorer (1992) **C-90m. TVM** D: Jay Sandrich. Jack Lemmon, Talia Shire, Joanna Gleason, Jonathan Silverman, Madeline Kahn, George Wyner. Good cast wasted in this cynical comedy about a millionaire who bankrupts himself for the excitement of starting all over again (and to teach his pampered wife and shiftless college grad son a lesson). Kahn's homeless woman/Greek chorus seems like so much padding. Made for cable. Aka FATHER, SON AND THE MISTRESS. Average. ▼●

For Richer or Poorer (1997) **C-115m.** ★★½ D: Bryan Spicer. Tim Allen, Kirstie Alley, Jay O. Sanders, Michael Lerner, Wayne Knight, Larry Miller, Miguel A. Nunez, Jr., Megan Cavanagh, Carrie Preston, Katie Moore. Crass, filthy-rich New Yorkers Allen and Alley, whose marriage is on the rocks, are forced to take it on the lam when they're accused of tax fraud—and hide out on an Amish farm, where they pretend to be cousins of farmer Sanders. Spoiled and lazy, they're forced to do hard, honest work, and actually come to like it. Predictable in every way, but pleasant enough. Super 35. [PG-13]▼●◗

For Roseanna (1997-British) **C-95m.** ★★½ D: Paul Weiland. Jean Reno, Mercedes Ruehl, Polly Walker, Mark Frankel, Giuseppe Cederna, Renato Scarpa. Sweet, well-intentioned film about a man who has promised his wife, who's terminally ill, that she will be buried in their village churchyard cemetery . . . but with only a few vacant plots left, he takes it upon himself to keep the other townspeople healthy! Winning performances and vivid Italian atmosphere help compensate for a script (by veteran TV comedy writer Saul Turteltaub) that strains credibility to the bursting point. Panavision. [PG-13] ▼●

Forsaking All Others (1934) **84m.** ★★½ D: W. S. Van Dyke II. Clark Gable, Joan Crawford, Robert Montgomery, Charles Butterworth, Billie Burke, Frances Drake, Rosalind Russell, Arthur Treacher. Gable, just back from Spain, is about to propose to Crawford but learns she's set to wed flaky Montgomery. Star trio sparkles in this so-so romantic comedy, scripted by Joseph L. Mankiewicz. Butterworth is a treat, as always.▼●

For Singles Only (1968) **C-91m.** BOMB D: Arthur Dreifuss. John Saxon, Mary Ann Mobley, Milton Berle, Lana Wood, Mark Richman, Chris Noel, The Nitty Gritty Dirt Band. Certainly not for those who like good movies. Two girls move into singles apartment where Berle is social director; result is a rape, an attempted suicide, and several songs.

Fort Algiers (1953) **78m.** ★★ D: Lesley Selander. Yvonne De Carlo, Carlos Thompson, Raymond Burr, Leif Erickson. De Carlo romps through this adventure set in Algiers, dealing with villainous Arab leader inciting the natives to rebel.

Fort Apache (1948) **127m.** ★★★ D: John Ford. John Wayne, Henry Fonda, Shirley Temple, Pedro Armendariz, John Agar, Ward Bond, George O'Brien, Victor McLaglen, Anna Lee, Irene Rich, Dick Foran, Guy Kibbee, Mae Marsh, Hank Worden. Fonda is effectively cast against type as stubborn martinet who rubs his own men—as well as neighboring Indians—the wrong way. First of Ford's cavalry trilogy tells its story slowly, deliberately, with time for comedy and telling characterizations. Followed by SHE WORE A YELLOW RIBBON. Also shown in computer-colored version.▼●

Fort Apache, The Bronx (1981) **C-125m.** ★★★ D: Daniel Petrie. Paul Newman, Edward Asner, Ken Wahl, Danny Aiello, Rachel Ticotin, Pam Grier, Kathleen Beller.

Taut urban drama about a policeman's life in a ravaged N.Y.C. neighborhood; credible and exciting, with a fine star performance from Newman. [R]▼●

Fort Defiance (1951) **C-81m.** **½ D: John Rawlins. Dane Clark, Ben Johnson, Peter Graves, Tracey Roberts. Film focuses on human relations in between preparations for threatened Indian attacks.

Fort Dobbs (1958) **90m.** ** D: Gordon Douglas. Clint Walker, Virginia Mayo, Brian Keith, Richard Eyer. Rugged Walker is believable as hero who fights all obstacles in the old West to make decent life for himself and Mayo.

For the Boys (1991) **C-145m.** **½ D: Mark Rydell. Bette Midler, James Caan, George Segal, Patrick O'Neal, Christopher Rydell, Arye Gross, Norman Fell, Rosemary Murphy, Dori Brenner, Bud Yorkin, Jack Sheldon, Melissa Manchester, Brandon Call, Billy Bob Thornton, Xander Berkeley, Vince Vaughn. Midler is in top form as U.S.O. singer who becomes a star while performing during WW2 with Caan, a sexist, self-involved king of comedy; scenario follows their tumultuous relationship over the decades. Occasionally hokey but mostly entertaining. Arliss Howard appears unbilled as Bette's G.I. husband. [R]▼●

For the First Time (1959) **C-97m.** **½ D: Rudolph Maté. Mario Lanza, Johanna Von Koszian, Kurt Kasznar, Zsa Zsa Gabor, Hans Sohnker. Lanza is typecast as fiery opera singer who falls in love with beautiful deaf girl in Capri. Not bad, with plenty of music to satisfy Lanza fans; this was his last film. Technirama. ▼●

For the Love of Benji (1977) **C-84m.** *** D: Joe Camp. Benji, Patsy Garrett. Cynthia Smith, Allen Fiuzat, Ed Nelson, Peter Bowles, Bridget Armstrong. Moviedom's smartest pooch since Lassie in his second delightful screen adventure, this time scampering through the streets of Athens with secret agents in pursuit, trying to get the formula tattoed on his paw. Fine family entertainment. Followed by OH, HEAVENLY DOG! [G]▼◗

For the Love of Mary (1948) **90m.** **½ D: Frederick de Cordova. Deanna Durbin, Edmond O'Brien, Don Taylor, Jeffrey Lynn. Airy fluff with Durbin a White House switchboard operator getting political figures and her own romance tangled up. Deanna's final film.▼

For the Love of Mike (1960) **C-84m.** **½ D: George Sherman. Richard Basehart, Stuart Erwin, Arthur Shields, Armando Silvestre. Mild happenings as Indian boy trains a horse, hoping to use prize money for a village shrine. Another intelligent Robert B. Radnitz production. CinemaScope.

For Those Who Think Young (1964) **C-96m.** ** D: Leslie Martinson. James Darren, Pamela Tiffin, Tina Louise, Paul Lynde, Woody Woodbury, Ellen McRae (Burstyn). Witless plug for Pepsi is about low-jinks at college, undistinguished by Nancy Sinatra and Claudia Martin's (daughter of Dino) presence, or cameos by George Raft, Robert Armstrong, Allen Jenkins et al. Techniscope.

Fort Massacre (1958) **C-80m.** ** D: Joseph M. Newman. Joel McCrea, Forrest Tucker, Susan Cabot, John Russell. McCrea is leader of troop which constantly is entangled with Indian skirmishes. CinemaScope.

Fort Osage (1952) **C-72m.** BOMB D: Lesley Selander. Rod Cameron, Jane Nigh, Douglas Kennedy, Iron Eyes Cody. Inept Grade-D Western involving perennial Indian uprisings.

Fortress (1993) **C-91m.** *½ D: Stuart Gordon. Christopher Lambert, Loryn Locklyn, Kurtwood Smith, Lincoln Kilpatrick, Clifton Gonzalez Gonzalez, Jeffrey Combs. Husband and wife flee futuristic society (which forbids them from having a second child) because she is pregnant again. They're captured and sent to a high-tech maximum security prison run by a sadistic warden. (Is there any other kind?) Intriguing premise is sabotaged by weak acting and a weaker script. Incredible international success resulted in a sequel. [R]▼●◗

Fort Saganne (1984-French) **C-190m.** **½ D: Alain Corneau. Gérard Depardieu, Philippe Noiret, Catherine Deneuve, Michel Duchaussoy, Roger Dumas, Sophie Marceau, Jean-Louis Richard. Handsomely mounted but clichéd and overlong epic detailing the exploits of Charles Saganne, a French officer of modest background who is posted to the Sahara in the years before WW1. Depardieu is quietly impressive, many of the desert sequences are well done, and Philippe Sarde's score adds to the atmosphere. Depiction of Depardieu's affair with journalist Deneuve is especially trite. Technovision. ▼

Fort Ti (1953) **C-73m.** ** D: William Castle. George Montgomery, Joan Vohs, Irving Bacon, James Seay. Best facet of this oater set during French-Indian war of 1760s is its 3-D gimmickry; otherwise, standard stuff.

Fortunate Pilgrim, The SEE: **Mario Puzo's "The Fortunate Pilgrim"**

Fortune, The (1975) **C-88m.** **½ D: Mike Nichols. Jack Nicholson, Warren Beatty, Stockard Channing, Scatman Crothers, Florence Stanley, Richard B. Shull. Nicholson and Beatty make like Laurel and Hardy in this uneven 1920s comedy about two bumblers who plan to murder a dizzy heiress to get her money. Worth seeing if only for Nicholson's wonderful comic performance. David Shire's period music is nice, too. Panavision. [PG]▼

Fortune and Men's Eyes (1971-Canadian) **C-102m.** **½ D: Harvey Hart. Wendell

Burton, Michael Greer, Zooey (David) Hall, Danny Freedman. Homosexuality in prison is the theme; sincere but exploitative, unpleasant. [R]▼

Fortune Cookie, The (1966) **125m.** *** D: Billy Wilder. Jack Lemmon, Walter Matthau, Ron Rich, Cliff Osmond, Judi West, Lurene Tuttle. Biting Wilder comedy about TV cameraman (Lemmon) injured during football game and shyster lawyer (Matthau) who exaggerates damages for insurance purposes. Matthau's Oscar-winning performance hits home. Scripted by Wilder and partner I.A.L. Diamond. Panavision.▼●

Fortune in Diamonds (1952-British) **74m.** ** D: David MacDonald. Dennis Price, Jack Hawkins, Siobhan McKenna. Good cast of disparate types all thirsting for cache of gems hidden in the heart of African jungle. Retitled: THE ADVENTURERS.▼

Fortunes of Captain Blood (1950) **91m.** ** D: Gordon Douglas. Louis Hayward, Patricia Medina, George Macready, Terry Kilburn. This filming of Sabatini novel lacks flair and scope of the Flynn version. Costumer recounts tale of Irish doctor (Hayward) who becomes notorious pirate to revenge wrongdoings.

Fort Utah (1968) **C-83m.** *½ D: Lesley Selander. John Ireland, Virginia Mayo, Scott Brady, John Russell, Robert Strauss, James Craig, Richard Arlen, Jim Davis, Don "Red" Barry. Former gunfighter Ireland fights Brady, who is stirring up Indians around Fort Utah. See it only if you like the cast. Techniscope.

Fort Vengeance (1953) **75m.** *½ D: Lesley Selander. James Craig, Rita Moreno, Keith Larsen, Reginald Denny, Emory Parnell. Film lacks action in its account of Pacific Northwest and mounties chasing fur thieves, quelling Indian uprisings.

Fort Worth (1951) **C-80m.** ** D: Edwin L. Marin. Randolph Scott, David Brian, Phyllis Thaxter, Helena Carter. Scott learns that pen is not mightier than the sword; he's a gunslinger who becomes newspaper editor but can only rid town of outlaws via six-shooter.

40 Carats (1973) **C-110m.** **½ D: Milton Katselas. Liv Ullmann, Gene Kelly, Edward Albert, Binnie Barnes, Deborah Raffin, Billy Green Bush, Nancy Walker, Don Porter, Rosemary Murphy, Natalie Schafer, Claudia Jennings, Brooke Palance. Bright Broadway comedy adapted from French farce suffers in transference to screen, mainly from miscasting of Ullmann as 40-ish New York divorcee, pursued by 20-ish Albert. Glossy, mildly amusing; pepped up by Barnes and Kelly. [PG]▼

Forty Deuce (1982) **C-89m.** *½ D: Paul Morrissey. Orson Bean, Kevin Bacon, Mark Keyloun, Harris Laskaway, Tommy Citera. Heavyhanded, poorly directed drama of teenage hustler Bacon attempting to sell runaway to wealthy Bean; complications arise when the boy overdoses on heroin. From an off-Broadway play by Alan Bowne. Second half of film is in widescreen.

48HRS. (1982) **C-97m.** ***½ D: Walter Hill. Nick Nolte, Eddie Murphy, Annette O'Toole, James Remar, Frank McRae, David Patrick Kelly, Sonny Landham, Brion James, James Keane, Jonathan Banks, Denise Crosby, Olivia Brown, Jim Haynie, The Busboys. Slam-bang mix of action and comedy; weary cop Nolte springs Murphy out of the jug for two days to help him catch Murphy's escaped (and *really* disturbed) partner. Naturally, they hate each other's guts at first, but. . . . Murphy, in his screen debut, is nothing short of sensational, but so is Nolte in his low-key, raspy way; scene where Murphy terrorizes a redneck bar is the standout. Written by Roger Spottiswoode, Larry Gross, Steven E. de Souza, and Hill. Sequel: ANOTHER 48HRS. [R]▼●◗

Forty Guns (1957) **80m.** **½ D: Samuel Fuller. Barbara Stanwyck, Barry Sullivan, Dean Jagger, John Ericson, Gene Barry. Florid, wildly dramatic Sam Fuller Western with Stanwyck as self-appointed land baroness of Tombstone Territory—until marshal Sullivan shows up. CinemaScope.

40 Guns to Apache Pass (1966) **C-95m.** ** D: William Witney. Audie Murphy, Michael Burns, Kenneth Tobey, Laraine Stephens, Michael Blodgett, Michael Keep. Standard Murphy Western with every horse-opera cliché intact: plot centers around missing shipment of rifles.

Forty Little Mothers (1940) **90m.** **½ D: Busby Berkeley. Eddie Cantor, Judith Anderson, Ralph Morgan, Rita Johnson, Martha O'Driscoll, Bonita Granville, Diana Lewis. Second-rate Cantor vehicle with Eddie as unemployed college professor who becomes reluctant protector of an abandoned baby, as well as a teacher in a girls' school. Veronica Lake (then known as Constance Keane) is one of his charges.

Forty Naughty Girls (1937) **63m.** BOMB D: Edward Cline. James Gleason, ZaSu Pitts, Marjorie Lord, George Shelley, Joan Woodbury, Frank M. Thomas, Tom Kennedy. Final Hildegarde Withers mystery-comedy is just plain awful, with Pitts and Gleason getting involved in a backstage murder.

49th Man, The (1953) **73m.** **½ D: Fred F. Sears. John Ireland, Richard Denning, Suzanne Dalbert, Touch (Michael) Connors, Peter Marshall. Suspenseful account of federal agents tracking down foreign spies smuggling parts of atomic bomb into U.S. for later detonation.

49th Parallel (1941-British) **107m.** ***½ D: Michael Powell. Anton Walbrook, Eric Portman, Leslie Howard, Raymond Massey, Laurence Olivier, Glynis Johns, Niall MacGinnis, Finlay Currie. Taut, exciting WW2 yarn of Nazi servicemen whose U-boat is sunk off the Canadian coast.

Top-notch cast, rich suspense and characterizations. Oscar winner for Best Story (Emeric Pressburger); screenplay by Pressburger and Rodney Ackland. U.S. title: THE INVADERS. Original British running time: 123m.▼●

40 Pounds of Trouble (1963) **C-106m.** **½ D: Norman Jewison. Tony Curtis, Phil Silvers, Suzanne Pleshette, Larry Storch, Howard Morris, Stubby Kaye, Claire Wilcox, Jack La Rue. "Cute" Curtis comedy of casino manager who "adopts" little girl with endless complications occurring. Disneyland locations and fine character actors pep it up. Carbon copy of LITTLE MISS MARKER. Panavision. ▼

42nd Street (1933) **89m.** **** D: Lloyd Bacon. Warner Baxter, Ruby Keeler, George Brent, Bebe Daniels, Dick Powell, Guy Kibbee, Una Merkel, Ginger Rogers, Ned Sparks, George E. Stone. The definitive backstage musical still has plenty of sass—along with its clichés. Ailing director Baxter puts everything into what may be his final show, then leading lady Daniels twists her ankle! Good thing Ruby Keeler's on hand. Harry Warren-Al Dubin songs include title tune, "Young and Healthy," "You're Getting to Be a Habit With Me," "Shuffle Off to Buffalo." Busby Berkeley's ground-breaking production numbers are still sensational. Scripted by Rian James and James Seymour, from Bradford Ropes' story. Adapted for the Broadway stage fifty years later. Also shown in computer-colored version.▼●

47 Ronin, Part I, The (1941-Japanese) **112m.** ***½ D: Kenji Mizoguchi. Chojuro Kawarazaki, Yoshizaburo Arashi, Utaemon Ichikawa, Mieko Takamine. Legendary samurai warriors scheme to gain revenge for the death of their leader, who was tricked and forced to commit suicide. Based on a famous Japanese story, and fascinating as both cinema and as propaganda (remember, this was made during WW2). First of Mizoguchi's two-part epic, also known as THE LOYAL 47 RONIN. Several dozen versions of this same story have been filmed in Japan.▼◗

47 Ronin, Part II, The (1942-Japanese) **113m.** ***½ D: Kenji Mizoguchi. Chojuro Kawarazaki, Yoshizaburo Arashi, Utaemon Ichikawa, Mieko Takamine. The 47 Ronin gain vengeance for their master's death. Together with its predecessor, this was the most impressive Japanese film produced during WW2; the finale is especially stirring and revealing.▼◗

43: The Petty Story SEE: **Smash-Up Alley**

42 Up (1999-British) **C/B&W-130m.** *** D: Michael Apted. Picking up where 35 UP left off, Apted revisits all but three of his lifelong subjects as they settle into middle age. As compelling as ever.

Fort Yuma (1955) **C-78m.** ** D: Lesley Selander. Peter Graves, Joan Taylor, Addison Richards, Joan Vohs. Indians go on warpath when their chief is killed. Occasionally good combat sequences.▼

For Us, the Living (1983) **C-90m. TVM** D: Michael Schultz. Howard Rollins, Jr., Irene Cara, Margaret Avery, Roscoe Lee Browne, Larry Fishburne, Janet MacLachlan, Dick Anthony Williams, Paul Winfield. Moving drama detailing the life and work of slain civil rights activist Medgar Evers (Rollins), adapted from a biography written by his widow, Myrtle (played here by Cara). A PBS *American Playhouse* presentation. Above average.▼

For Whom the Bell Tolls (1943) **C-130m.** ***½ D: Sam Wood. Gary Cooper, Ingrid Bergman, Akim Tamiroff, Arturo de Cordova, Joseph Calleia, Katina Paxinou, Vladimir Sokoloff, Mikhail Rasumny, Fortunio Bonanova. Hemingway story of U.S. mercenary Cooper fighting for Spain with motley crew of peasants, including Bergman; tense action, beautiful color, great love scenes, marvelous Victor Young score. Paxinou won Best Supporting Actress Oscar. Originally released at 170m.; archivally restored version runs 156m.▼●◗

For Your Eyes Only (1981-British) **C-127m.** *** D: John Glen. Roger Moore, Carole Bouquet, (Chaim) Topol, Lynn-Holly Johnson, Julian Glover, Jill Bennett, Cassandra Harris, Desmond Llewelyn, Lois Maxwell, Walter Gotell. After years of space-age gadgetry, cartoon villains, female mannequins, and giants with steel teeth came this one-shot return to the old days of Ian Fleming minimalism. No other James Bond film has provoked so much debate among 007 fans (even us); judge for yourself. The chases and stuntwork *are* spectacular; debuting helmer Glen directed 2nd-unit on some earlier Bonds. Look for Charles Dance as gunman. Panavision. [PG]▼●

For Your Love Only (1976-German) **C-97m.** ** D: Wolfgang Petersen. Nastassia Kinski, Christian Quadflieg, Judy Winter, Klaus Schwarzkopf. Young student Kinski has an affair with a teacher, then kills the man who tries to blackmail and seduce her. Turgid soap opera. Made for German TV; theatrical release in 1982. ▼

Foul Play (1978) **C-116m.** **½ D: Colin Higgins. Goldie Hawn, Chevy Chase, Burgess Meredith, Dudley Moore, Rachel Roberts, Eugene Roche, Marilyn Sokol, Billy Barty, Marc Lawrence, Brian Dennehy. Innocent woman (Hawn) gets caught in strange murder plot in San Francisco; no one believes her except detective Chase, who's falling in love with her. Likable stars, good fun, but protracted story, tasteless comedy, and Hitchcock plagiarism detract. Followed by a short-lived TV series. [PG] ▼●

Fountain, The (1934) **83m.** **½ D: John

Cromwell. Ann Harding, Brian Aherne, Paul Lukas, Jean Hersholt, Ian Wolfe. WW1 romance with Harding torn between former sweetheart Aherne and husband Lukas. Handsome but tedious.

Fountainhead, The (1949) **114m.** **½ D: King Vidor. Gary Cooper, Patricia Neal, Raymond Massey, Kent Smith, Robert Douglas, Henry Hull, Ray Collins, Jerome Cowan. Ambitious but confused version of Ayn Rand philosophic novel, spotlighting an idealistic architect's clash with compromises of society; cast does what it can with the script.▼●

Four Adventures of Reinette and Mirabelle (1986-French) **C-99m.** *** D: Eric Rohmer. Joelle Miquel, Jessica Forde, Philippe Laudenbach, Yasmine Haury, Marie Riviere, Beatrice Romand. Typically charming, perceptive Rohmeresque slice of life, chronicling the friendship between country girl Reinette (Miquel) and city girl Mirabelle (Forde), who become roommates in Paris. At its best when focusing on their contrasting viewpoints, and the manner in which their friendship evolves.▼

Four Against Fate SEE: **Derby Day**

Four Bags Full (1956-French) **84m.** **½ D: Claude Autant-Lara. Jean Gabin, Bourvil, Jeanette Batti, Louis de Funes. Slender comedy vehicle for two top stars, involving duo who smuggle meat across French border during WW2.▼

4 Clowns (1970) **97m.** **** D: Robert Youngson. Laurel and Hardy, Buster Keaton, Charley Chase. A must for viewers of all ages: some of the best silent comedy ever. Interesting solo footage of Laurel and Hardy; Keaton's classic SEVEN CHANCES; hilarious sequences with underrated Chase including his best short, LIMOUSINE LOVE. One of compiler Youngson's very best efforts. [G]

Four Dark Hours SEE: **Green Cockatoo, The**

Four Daughters (1938) **90m.** ***½ D: Michael Curtiz. Claude Rains, Rosemary Lane, Lola Lane, Priscilla Lane, Gale Page, John Garfield, Jeffrey Lynn, Frank McHugh, May Robson, Dick Foran. Believable, beautifully acted soaper of small-town life; four young women with musical father Rains have lives altered by four young men. Garfield is superb in first film, matched by fine cast. Max Steiner's score includes his *Symphonie Moderne*. Followed immediately by DAUGHTERS COURAGEOUS and sequels FOUR WIVES and FOUR MOTHERS. Remade as YOUNG AT HEART.▼

Four Days in September (1997-Brazilian) **C-106m.** *** D: Bruno Barreto. Alan Arkin, Pedro Cardoso, Fernanda Torres, Luiz Fernando Guimaraes, Selton Mello, Claudia Abreu, Nelson Dantas, Fisher Stevens. Emotion-charged, based-on-fact account of the events surrounding 1969 kidnapping of American ambassador (Arkin) by an idealistic yet diverse group of young Brazilian revolutionaries. All sides are given a voice in this empathetic and well-detailed political drama. [R]▼

Four Days Leave (1950) **98m.** ** D: Leopold Lindtberg. Cornel Wilde, Josette Day, Simone Signoret, Alan Hale, Jr. Rather tame account of GI Wilde finding romance while on leave in Switzerland.

Four Desperate Men (1960-Australian) **104m.** **½ D: Harry Watt. Aldo Ray, Heather Sears. Stark study of human nature as quartet of hardened thugs decide whether or not to set off huge bomb that would destroy Sydney harbor. Original title: THE SIEGE OF PINCHGUT.

Four Deuces, The (1975) **C-87m.** **½ D: William H. Bushnell, Jr. Jack Palance, Carol Lynley, Warren Berlinger, Adam Roarke, E. J. Peaker, Gianni Russo. Action comedy/drama involving Prohibition Era bootleggers. Palance is a gang lord whose mob and casino bear the film's title; Lynley is the moll he loves and fights for. [R]▼

4D Man (1959) **C-85m.** **½ D: Irvin S. Yeaworth, Jr. Robert Lansing, Lee Meriwether, James Congdon, Guy Raymond, Robert Strauss, Patty Duke. Well-handled sci-fi of scientist who learns art of transposing matter, thus giving him power to pass through any substance.▼

Four Faces West (1948) **90m.** **½ D: Alfred E. Green. Joel McCrea, Frances Dee, Charles Bickford, Joseph Calleia. Quiet Western of fugitive pursued by determined sheriff, with cast giving intelligent interpretation to standard formula. Original, and more appropriate, title: THEY PASSED THIS WAY.▼

Four Fast Guns (1959) **72m.** *½ D: William J. Hole, Jr. James Craig, Martha Vickers, Edgar Buchanan, Brett Halsey, Paul Richards. Shoot-out of good vs. bad pits brother against brother. CinemaScope.

Four Feathers, The (1939-British) **C-115m.** **** D: Zoltan Korda. John Clements, Ralph Richardson, C. Aubrey Smith, June Duprez, Allan Jeayes, Jack Allen, Donald Gray, Clive Baxter. Grand adventure from A. E. W. Mason story of tradition-bound Britisher who must prove he's not a coward by helping army comrades combat Sudan uprising. Smith is just wonderful as tale-spinning army veteran. Screenplay by R. C. Sherriff, Lajos Biro, and Arthur Wimperis. Score by Miklos Rozsa. Original release ran 130m. Previously filmed in 1921 and 1928; remade as STORM OVER THE NILE and as a TVM in 1978 with Beau Bridges. ▼●

Four Flies on Grey Velvet (1972-Italian) **C-101m.** ** D: Dario Argento. Michael Brandon, Mimsy Farmer, Bud Spencer, Francine Racette. Unabsorbing psychological murder-mystery with performers who walk through their roles in a very disinterested fashion. Techniscope.[PG]

4 for Texas (1963) **C-114m.** *** D: Robert Aldrich. Frank Sinatra, Dean Martin, Anita Ekberg, Ursula Andress, Charles Bronson, Victor Buono, Richard Jaeckel, Mike Mazurki, Jack Elam, The Three Stooges, Yaphet Kotto. Nonsensical Sinatra-Martin romp set in the old West, with their antics only outdone by Buono as villainous banker. Ekberg and Andress both outstanding scenery attractions.▼●

Four Friends (1981) **C-115m.** *** D: Arthur Penn. Craig Wasson, Jodi Thelen, Jim Metzler, Michael Huddleston, Reed Birney, James Leo Herlihy, Glenne Headly, Mercedes Ruehl. A journey of self-discovery for an idealistic young Yugoslavian immigrant (Wasson), who lives through the turbulent American 1960s. Charming, coy, powerful, sentimental, and sometimes astonishingly old-fashioned—a real mixed bag, with many rewards and not a few flaws. Largely autobiographical script by Steve Tesich. [R]▼

Four Frightened People (1934) **78m.** **½ D: Cecil B. DeMille. Claudette Colbert, Herbert Marshall, William Gargan, Mary Boland, Leo Carrillo. Four shipwrecked souls try to survive in the jungle, while the two men become increasingly interested in the plain-Jane schoolteacher who's the most frightened of the lot. DeMille's quietest movie (and a somewhat notorious flop in its day) is entertaining malarkey, with Colbert getting more glamorous in each successive scene. Filmed on the island of Hawaii.

Four Girls in Town (1956) **C-85m.** *** D: Jack Sher. George Nader, Julie Adams, Gia Scala, Marianne Cook (Koch), Elsa Martinelli, Sydney Chaplin, Grant Williams, John Gavin. Clichéd but absorbing account of four contrasting would-be stars coming to Hollywood seeking fame and romance; excellent musical score by Alex North. CinemaScope.

Four Guns to the Border (1954) **C-82m.** **½ D: Richard Carlson. Rory Calhoun, Colleen Miller, George Nader, Walter Brennan, Nina Foch. Better than usual handling of outlaws vs. Indians, with slight morality lesson for finale. From a Louis L'Amour novel.

Four Horsemen of the Apocalypse, The (1921) **131m.** *** D: Rex Ingram. Rudolph Valentino, Alice Terry, Alan Hale, Jean Hersholt, Nigel de Brulier, Wallace Beery. Famous silent spectacle cemented Valentino's popularity via legendary tango scene, but aside from that it's a relentlessly grim anti-war story of cousins who end up fighting on opposite sides during WW1. Extremely well made, with imagery that still staggers and message that cannot be overlooked. Based on the Blasco Ibanez novel. Remade in 1962.▼●

Four Horsemen of the Apocalypse (1962) **C-153m.** **½ D: Vincente Minnelli. Glenn Ford, Ingrid Thulin, Charles Boyer, Lee J. Cobb, Paul Henreid, Paul Lukas, Yvette Mimieux, Karl Boehm. Glossy, padded trash, losing all sense of reality in its telling of a family whose members fight on opposite sides during WW2. Allegedly Angela Lansbury dubbed in Thulin's lines. CinemaScope.▼●

Four Hours to Kill! (1935) **71m.** *** D: Mitchell Leisen. Richard Barthelmess, Joe Morrison, Helen Mack, Gertrude Michael, Dorothy Tree, Ray Milland, Roscoe Karns, John Howard, Noel Madison, Charles Wilson. Ingenious structure has film taking place entirely in a vaudeville theater (and lobby) where a killer (Barthelmess) escapes from the detective escorting him to execution, hoping to kill the stoolie who ratted on him. Norman Krasna's snappy script juggles numerous subplots à la GRAND HOTEL. Watch for director Leisen in a cameo as the orchestra leader.

Four Hundred Blows, The (1959-French) **99m.** **** D: François Truffaut. Jean-Pierre Léaud, Patrick Auffay, Claire Maurier, Albert Remy, Jeanne Moreau, Jean-Claude Brialy, Jacques Demy, François Truffaut. Captivating study of Parisian youth who turns to life of small-time crime as a reaction to derelict parents. First of Truffaut's autobiographical Antoine Doinel series; followed by the "Antoine et Colette" episode in LOVE AT TWENTY. Dyaliscope.▼●◗

Four in a Jeep (1951-Swiss) **97m.** **½ D: Leopold Lindtberg. Viveca Lindfors, Ralph Meeker, Joseph Yadin, Michael Medwin, Dinan, Paulette Dubost. Revealing drama, set in a post-war Vienna occupied by American, Russian, French, and British forces. American M.P. Meeker takes an interest in troubled Lindfors, whose husband has just escaped from a Russian prison camp. On-location filming helps.▼

Four Jacks and a Jill (1942) **68m.** ** D: Jack Hively. Ray Bolger, Desi Arnaz, Anne Shirley, June Havoc, Eddie Foy, Jr., Jack Durant, Henry Daniell, Fritz Feld. Struggling hoofer/pianist Bolger and his musician pals take in singing waif Shirley in this lackluster musical. Bolger's dancing is always a pleasure to watch, but Arnaz is wasted as an exiled king turned taxi driver. Remake of STREET GIRL and THAT GIRL FROM PARIS.▼

Four Jills in a Jeep (1944) **89m.** **½ D: William A. Seiter. Kay Francis, Carole Landis, Martha Raye, Mitzi Mayfair, Phil Silvers, Dick Haymes, Jimmy Dorsey and His Orchestra; guest stars Betty Grable, Alice Faye, Carmen Miranda, George Jessel. Contrived wartime entertainment with four leading ladies reenacting their actual experiences entertaining soldiers overseas (which Landis turned into a popular book of the same name). Some good musical moments but nothing to shout about.▼

Four Kinds of Love SEE: **Bambole!**

4 Little Girls (1997) **C-102m.** **** D: Spike Lee. Shattering documentary about the fatal bombing of a black Birmingham, Alabama church on September 15, 1963, which not only killed four innocent children but galvanized the entire nation and accelerated the civil rights movement. Remembering its young (ages 11 to 14) victims are families, now-grown-up friends, ministers, reporters, political activists, and the lawyer who, years later, helped convict the key perpetrator. One of filmmaker Lee's finest hours. Produced for HBO but also given theatrical release.▼

Four Men and A Prayer (1938) **85m.** *** D: John Ford. Loretta Young, Richard Greene, George Sanders, David Niven, C. Aubrey Smith, William Henry, J. Edward Bromberg, Alan Hale, Reginald Denny, John Carradine. Compelling story of four brothers determined to unravel mystery behind their father's murder; handsome, well-paced production.

Four Mothers (1941) **86m.** **½ D: William Keighley. Priscilla Lane, Rosemary Lane, Lola Lane, Gale Page, Claude Rains, Jeffrey Lynn, May Robson, Eddie Albert, Frank McHugh, Dick Foran. FOUR DAUGHTERS formula wearing thin in soapy tale of McHugh going bankrupt.

Four Musketeers, The (1975) **C-108m.** *** D: Richard Lester. Oliver Reed, Raquel Welch, Richard Chamberlain, Frank Finlay, Michael York, Christopher Lee, Jean-Pierre Cassel, Geraldine Chaplin, Simon Ward, Faye Dunaway, Charlton Heston. Second half of Lester's irreverent but amusing approach to Dumas with less emphasis on slapstick this time around. Rich cast in top form. Filmed in 1973, at the same time as THE THREE MUSKETEERS. Followed by THE RETURN OF THE MUSKETEERS. [R]▼●◗

Four Poster, The (1952) **103m.** ***½ D: Irving Reis. Rex Harrison, Lilli Palmer. Jan de Hartog play is tour de force for stars who enact various phases of married couple's life; warm, witty script; superb performances enhanced by ingenious animated interludes by UPA studio. Later became the stage musical *I DO! I DO!*

Four Rode Out (1969) **C-99m.** *½ D: John Peyser. Pernell Roberts, Sue Lyon, Leslie Nielsen, Julian Mateos. Sheriff treks across New Mexican desert when accused of robbery and murder. Inferior Western. [R]▼

Four Rooms (1995) **C-98m.** BOMB D: Allison Anders, Alexandre Rockwell, Robert Rodriguez, Quentin Tarantino. Tim Roth, Antonio Banderas, Jennifer Beals, Paul Calderon, Sammi Davis, Amanda de Cadenet, Valeria Golino, Kathy Griffin, Marc Lawrence, Madonna, David Proval, Ione Skye, Quentin Tarantino, Lili Taylor, Marisa Tomei, Tamlyn Tomita, Alicia Witt, Lana McKissack, Danny Verduzco, Salma Hayek. What a cast . . . what a waste! Embarrassingly awful compilation consisting of four short films, with the sole point of interest being which one is the worst. Set in an L.A. hotel on New Year's Eve, and linked by the participation of Ted the Bellhop (Roth). Bruce Willis appears unbilled in the final episode, by Tarantino. [R]▼●◗

Four's a Crowd (1938) **91m.** **½ D: Michael Curtiz. Errol Flynn, Olivia de Havilland, Rosalind Russell, Patric Knowles, Hugh Herbert, Lana Turner. Lightheaded romance in which everyone loves another; straight comedy's a switch for Flynn. Pleasant.

Four Seasons, The (1981) **C-107m.** *** D: Alan Alda. Alan Alda, Carol Burnett, Len Cariou, Sandy Dennis, Rita Moreno, Jack Weston, Bess Armstrong. Four stages of friendship among three middle aged couples who vacation together. As comedy it scores, with warmly winning cast, but like its main character, it professes to discuss serious issues while pulling back after just touching the surface. Alda scripted, made feature directing debut; later a TV series. [PG]▼●

Four Sided Triangle (1953-British) **81m.** BOMB D: Terence Fisher. James Hayter, Barbara Payton, Stephen Murray, John Van Eyssen, Percy Marmont. Scientist invents a duplicating machine; hoping to solve romantic triangle, he duplicates the woman he and his best friend both love. Silly programmer.▼●

Four Skulls of Jonathan Drake, The (1959) **70m.** ** D: Edward L. Cahn. Eduard Franz, Valerie French, Henry Daniell, Grant Richards, Paul Cavanagh, Howard Wendell. Acceptable horror fare involving centuries-old voodoo curse upon family and contemporary scientist who puts an end to the weird goings-on.●

Four Sons (1928) **100m.** *** D: John Ford. James Hall, Margaret Mann, Earle Foxe, Charles Morton, Francis X. Bushman Jr., George Meeker. Famous tearjerker about a Bavarian widow whose four beloved sons fight in WW1—one of them on the American side. Simple and obvious but still effective. Remade in 1940. ▼

Four Sons (1940) **89m.** **½ D: Archie Mayo. Don Ameche, Eugenie Leontovich, Mary Beth Hughes, Alan Curtis, George Ernest, Robert Lowery. Czech family affected by Nazi rise to power; not unlike MORTAL STORM, with sons choosing different allegiances. Remake of 1928 silent. ▼

Fourteen Hours (1951) **92m.** *** D: Henry Hathaway. Paul Douglas, Richard Basehart, Barbara Bel Geddes, Debra Paget, Agnes

Moorehead, Robert Keith, Howard da Silva, Jeffrey Hunter, Martin Gabel, Grace Kelly, Jeff Corey. Well-made suspense drama about a man threatening to jump off the ledge of a building, told in semidocumentary fashion. Look for Harvey Lembeck and Ossie Davis as cabbies, Joyce Van Patten as Paget's girlfriend. Grace Kelly's film debut.

1492: Conquest of Paradise (1992-U.S.-British-French-Spanish) **C-145m.** ** D: Ridley Scott. Gérard Depardieu, Sigourney Weaver, Armand Assante, Frank Langella, Loren Dean, Angela Molina, Fernando Rey, Michael Wincott, Tcheky Karyo. The second of 1992's Christopher Columbus epics, this effort is beautifully mounted, but a long haul in steerage. The burden falls on Depardieu as the famed explorer, a French actor cast as an Italian working for Spain in an English-language movie—and an actor who speaks English like Bela Lugosi reading from cue cards. Might have been better had the action aped director Scott's finale to THELMA & LOUISE, by having Columbus and crew sail off the edge of the world. Panavision. [PG-13]▼●

Fourth Man, The (1983-Dutch) **C-104m.** ***½ D: Paul Verhoeven. Jeroen Krabbé, Renee Soutendijk, Thom Hoffman, Dolf De Vries, Geert De Jong. Sexy blonde hairdresser Soutendijk may or may not have murdered three husbands but definitely *does* screw up the mind of gay writer Krabbé when he tries to find out. Stylish dream-vs.-reality black comedy deserved its art-house success; flashy direction, eroticism to spare. ▼●

Fourth Protocol, The (1987-British) **C-119m.** **½ D: John Mackenzie. Michael Caine, Pierce Brosnan, Joanna Cassidy, Ned Beatty, Betsy Brantley, Peter Cartwright, David Conville, Matt Frewer, Ray McAnally, Ian Richardson. Pretty good spy thriller adapted by Frederick Forsyth from his best-selling novel. Caine plays a British spy who's assigned to foil a Russian plot that would destroy relations between the U.S. and England by setting off a nuclear bomb near an American air base in the U.K. Brosnan does well as a Russian agent. J-D-C Scope. [R]▼●

Fourth Story (1991) **C-91m. TVM** D: Ivan Passer. Mark Harmon, Mimi Rogers, Cliff DeYoung, Paul Gleason, M. Emmet Walsh. Intriguingly twisty tale of an average Joe P.I. hired to find a beautiful woman's missing hubby who might or might not have simply split. Psychological thriller with extra trimmings supplied by writer Andrew Guerdat. Made for cable. Above average.▼

Fourth War, The (1990) **C-91m.** **½ D: John Frankenheimer. Roy Scheider, Jürgen Prochnow, Tim Reid, Harry Dean Stanton, Lara Harris, Dale Dye. Well-done but ever-so-familiar Cold War thriller in which an American colonel (Scheider) and his Soviet counterpart (Prochnow) engage in a private, potentially disastrous war. Best for fans of the genre. Stanton looks very out of place as Scheider's commanding general. [R]▼●

Four Ways Out (1951-Italian) **77m.** **½ D: Pietro Germi. Gina Lollobrigida, Renato Baldini, Cosetta Greco, Paul Muller, Enzo Maggio. Engrossing if unoriginal drama of a robbery at a soccer stadium, and the motives and fates of the various thieves. Federico Fellini worked on the original story; he and Germi were among the scriptwriters. Released in the U.S. in 1955.▼

Four Weddings and a Funeral (1994-British) **C-117m.** *** D: Mike Newell. Hugh Grant, Andie MacDowell, Kristin Scott Thomas, Simon Callow, Rowan Atkinson, James Fleet, John Hannah, Charlotte Coleman, David Bower, Corin Redgrave, Kenneth Griffiths, Jeremy Kemp, Rosalie Crutchley. Delightful contemporary comedy about a young man who can't sustain a relationship, while all his friends seem to be getting married. Then he hits it off with another wedding guest, and the plot thickens. Fine ensemble, headed by the engaging Grant, keep this buoyant under Newell's sure-handed direction. Richard Curtis' screenplay may not bear close scrutiny (that final conversation really seems out of place), but it's certainly fun. [R]▼●◗

Four Wives (1939) **110m.** **½ D: Michael Curtiz. Claude Rains, Eddie Albert, Priscilla Lane, Rosemary Lane, Lola Lane, Gale Page, John Garfield, May Robson, Frank McHugh, Jeffrey Lynn. Sentimental but well-acted sequel to FOUR DAUGHTERS, further chronicling the lives and loves of the title quartet. Garfield appears briefly in flashback.

Fox, The (1968) **C-110m.** *** D: Mark Rydell. Sandy Dennis, Keir Dullea, Anne Heywood, Glyn Morris. Nicely crafted tale of lesbians Dennis and Heywood, and what happens when intruder Dullea happens among them. Scripted by Lewis John Carlino and Howard Koch; based on a D.H. Lawrence novella. Filmed in Canada.

Fox and His Friends (1975-German) **C-123m.** **** D: Rainer Werner Fassbinder. Rainer Werner Fassbinder, Peter Chatel, Karlheinz Bohm, Adrian Hoven, Ulla Jacobsson. Compassionate, politically astute melodrama by German wunderkind Fassbinder about gay lower-class carnival performer winning lottery fortune only to have his upper-class lover exploit him. Fassbinder is brilliant in title role. Also shown as FIST RIGHT OF FREEDOM.▼

Fox and the Hound, The (1981) **C-83m.** *** D: Art Stevens, Ted Berman, Richard Rich. Voices of Mickey Rooney, Kurt Russell, Pearl Bailey, Jack Albertson, Sandy Duncan, Jeanette Nolan, Pat Buttram, John Fiedler, John McIntire, Paul Winchell, Corey Feldman. Charming Disney animated feature about the childhood friendship between two natural enemies, a fox cub and a hound pup; as they grow older their relationship is put to the test by their emerging instincts. Warm and brimming with personable characters, this one approaches the old Disney magic at times. [G]▼◗

Foxes (1980) **C-106m.** **½ D: Adrian Lyne. Jodie Foster, Cherie Currie, Marilyn Kagan, Kandice Stroh, Scott Baio, Sally Kellerman, Randy Quaid, Lois Smith, Laura Dern. Four teenaged girls try coping with the standard non-*Our Town* problems brought by growing up in San Fernando Valley. Capable cast; apparently sincere intentions undermined by choppy storyline that just isn't compelling enough. [R]▼●

Foxes of Harrow, The (1947) **117m.** **½ D: John M. Stahl. Rex Harrison, Maureen O'Hara, Richard Haydn, Victor McLaglen, Vanessa Brown, Patricia Medina, Gene Lockhart. Lavish but lumbering tale of philanderer breaking up his marriage to seek affluence and fame in New Orleans in 1820. Pretty stale despite the trimmings.

Foxfire (1955) **C-92m.** **½ D: Joseph Pevney. Jane Russell, Jeff Chandler, Dan Duryea, Mara Corday, Barton MacLane. Russell battles cultural barriers when she impulsively marries Indian mining engineer Chandler while vacationing in Arizona. Not bad; the stars are well matched. Incidentally, that's Chandler singing the title song; he also wrote the lyrics.

Foxfire (1987) **C-100m. TVM** D: Jud Taylor. Jessica Tandy, Hume Cronyn, John Denver, Gary Grubbs, Harriet Hall. Nicely realized filming of the Tandy-Cronyn Broadway production about an Appalachian farm family and the land of their roots. Tandy won an Emmy (to go with her Tony Award for the same part) as the elderly woman who refuses to leave her home in the hills where she communes with the ghost of her dead husband. Susan Cooper adapted the play she created with Cronyn. Above average.▼●

Foxfire (1996) **C-102m.** *½ D: Annette Haywood-Carter. Hedy Burress, Angelina Jolie, Jenny Lewis, Jenny Shimizu, Sarah Rosenberg, Peter Facinelli, Dash Mihok, Cathy Moriarty, Richard Beymer, John Diehl. Knee-deep adaptation of Joyce Carol Oates' novel about four high school girls who form a gang when an enigmatic female drifter comes to town. The cast tries hard but they're done in by a heavy-handed script that's more interested in giving cursory treatment to important subjects (lesbianism, drug addiction) than plausible character or plot development. Plays like an R-rated After School Special. Super 35. [R]▼●◗

Foxhole in Cairo (1960-British) **79m.** **½ D: John Moxey. James Robertson Justice, Adrian Hoven, Peter Van Eyck, Neil McCallum, Michael Caine. Sensibly told account of counterintelligence at work in Egypt during WW2.

Foxiest Girl in Paris (1956-French) **100m.** **½ D: Roger De Broin. Martine Carol, Michel Piccoli, Mischa Auer. Sultry Carol, a fashion model, becomes amateur sleuth to solve a robbery and a murder.

Foxtrap (1986-U.S.-Italian) **C-88m.** *½ D: Fred Williamson. Fred Williamson, Chris Connelly, Arlene Golonka, Donna Owen, Beatrice Palme, Cleo Sebastian, Lela Rochon. Low-budget actioner of Williamson hired to bring runaway Owen back home from Europe to her family. Little more than a fashion show by director Williamson spotlighting his favorite actor: Williamson. [R]▼

Foxtrot (1976-Mexican-Swiss) **C-91m.** ** D: Arturo Ripstein. Peter O'Toole, Charlotte Rampling, Max von Sydow, Jorge Luke, Helen Rojo, Claudio Brook. O'Toole and his wife flee Rumania in the late 1930s and retreat to an island paradise to isolate themselves from a world about to erupt into war. Shallow, predictable drama, filmed in Mexico. Alternate version with additional sex footage titled THE OTHER SIDE OF PARADISE. [R]▼

Foxy Brown (1974) **C-94m.** *½ D: Jack Hill. Pam Grier, Peter Brown, Terry Carter, Kathryn Loder. Violence and little else in tale of nurse Grier and her vendetta against drug ring that killed her lover. [R]▼●

Fra Diavolo SEE: **Devil's Brother, The**

Fragment of Fear (1971-British) **C-96m.** ** D: Richard C. Sarafian. David Hemmings, Gayle Hunnicutt, Flora Robson, Wilfrid Hyde-White, Daniel Massey, Roland Culver, Adolfo Celi, Mona Washbourne. Hemmings is good in disappointing murder mystery that begins well, then falls apart. Photographed by the great Oswald Morris. [PG]

Framed (1947) **82m.** ** D: Richard Wallace. Glenn Ford, Janis Carter, Barry Sullivan, Edgar Buchanan, Karen Morley. Title almost self-explanatory. Innocent man mistaken for robber is brought in, enabling real thief to escape.

Framed (1975) **C-106m.** **½ D: Phil Karlson. Joe Don Baker, Conny Van Dyke, Gabriel Dell, John Marley, Brock Peters, Roy Jenson. Railroaded to jail, Baker vows revenge on the corrupt cops who put him there. The writer, director, and star of WALKING TALL, old hands at this kind of action melodrama, make the most of the situation. [R]▼

Frances (1982) **C-140m.** **½ D: Graeme Clifford. Jessica Lange, Kim Stanley, Sam Shepard, Bart Burns, Jeffrey DeMunn, Jordan Charney, Lane Smith, Anjelica Huston. Biography of 1930s movie star Frances Farmer—who wound up in a barbaric insane asylum—chronicles her tragic life in some detail, but doesn't help us understand the reasons for her self-destructive tendencies. Well crafted but cold and depressing, despite impressive performances by Lange and Stanley, as Frances' crazed mother. Her story is also told in the TVM, WILL THERE REALLY BE A MORNING? and in the independent feature COMMITTED. Look for Kevin Costner, who has one line in an alley. [R]▼●◗

Francesco (1989-Italian-German) **C-105m.** BOMB D: Liliana Cavani. Mickey Rourke, Helena Bonham Carter, Andrea Ferreol, Hans Zischler, Mario Adorf, Paolo Bonacelli. Laughably inept historical drama with a miscast Rourke muttering his way through his role as Francis of Assisi(!), son of a rich Italian merchant, who undergoes a spiritual rebirth. The narrative is often confusing, the direction is slipshod, and the result is a real snooze. [PG-13]▼●◗

Francis (The Talking Mule) Never hailed as an artistic triumph, the Francis series made up for that in box-office receipts from 1949 to 1956. Based on a book by David Stern, each of the seven films dealt with a sincere but stupid young man (at West Point he is 687th in a class of 687) led into and out of trouble by a canny talking mule. The off-screen voice was Chill Wills, the on-screen bumbler was Donald O'Connor in all but the last film, which starred Mickey Rooney. O'Connor once explained, "When you've made six pictures and the mule still gets more fan mail than you do . . ." Universal worked their contract starlets (Piper Laurie, Martha Hyer, Julia Adams, etc.) into the series as love interests, but the center of attraction was always the mule. The films, except the last one, were all about on a par: silly but amusing. The first six films were directed by Arthur Lubin, who went on to create a similar TV series called *Mr. Ed*, about a talking horse.

FRANCIS (THE TALKING MULE)

Francis (1949)
Francis Goes to the Races (1951)
Francis Goes to West Point (1952)
Francis Covers the Big Town (1953)
Francis Joins the Wacs (1954)
Francis in the Navy (1955)
Francis in the Haunted House (1956)

Francis (1949) **91m.** **½ D: Arthur Lubin. Donald O'Connor, Patricia Medina, ZaSu Pitts, Ray Collins, John McIntire, Eduard Franz, Anthony (Tony) Curtis. G.I. O'Connor becomes a war hero with the help of his talking mule, but is thought to be crazy when he tries to convince his superiors of the animal's ability. Initial entry sets the tone for the rest. Video title: FRANCIS THE TALKING MULE. ▼●

Francis Covers the Big Town (1953) **86m.** **½ D: Arthur Lubin. Donald O'Connor, Nancy Guild, Yvette Dugay, Gene Lockhart, William Harrigan, Gale Gordon. O'Connor and his talking mule join a big city newspaper and get mixed up in a murder trial.▼

Francis Goes to the Races (1951) **88m.** **½ D: Arthur Lubin. Donald O'Connor, Piper Laurie, Cecil Kellaway, Jesse White, Barry Kelley, Hayden Rorke, Larry Keating. O'Connor falls for horsebreeder Kellaway's niece (Laurie) and foils some crooks when Francis coaches a sorry nag to win the big race.▼●

Francis Goes to West Point (1952) **81m.** **½ D: Arthur Lubin. Donald O'Connor, Lori Nelson, Alice Kelley, William Reynolds, Palmer Lee (Gregg Palmer), James Best, Les Tremayne, David Janssen. Francis helps O'Connor get in and out of trouble during basic training at the military school. Look for Leonard Nimoy and Paul Burke as cadets.▼

Francis in the Haunted House (1956) **80m.** ** D: Charles Lamont. Mickey Rooney, Virginia Welles, James Flavin, Paul Cavanagh, Mary Ellen Kaye, David Janssen, Richard Deacon, Timothy Carey. Rooney took over the reins from O'Connor for this final entry, a simplistic "spooky" comedy. Paul Frees also replaced Chill Wills as the voice of Francis.▼

Francis in the Navy (1955) **80m.** **½ D: Arthur Lubin. Donald O'Connor, Martha Hyer, Richard Erdman, Jim Backus, David Janssen, Clint Eastwood, Martin Milner, Paul Burke. For his last outing in the series, O'Connor plays a dual role. Typical service farce, notable for appearance of Eastwood, in his second film. Director Lubin also quit after this one and went on to produce TV's *Mr. Ed.*▼

Francis Joins the Wacs (1954) **94m.** **½ D: Arthur Lubin. Donald O'Connor, Julia (Julie) Adams, Mamie Van Doren, Chill Wills, Lynn Bari, ZaSu Pitts, Mara Corday, Allison Hayes, Joan Shawlee. An Army snafu sends Francis and O'Connor to a WAC base, causing all sorts of problems. More amiable nonsense, but then, you know you're not dealing with reality when Van Doren is cast as "Corporal Bunky Hilstrom." Wills, the voice of Francis, also appears on screen.▼

Francis of Assisi (1961) **C-111m.** **½ D: Michael Curtiz. Bradford Dillman, Dolores Hart, Stuart Whitman, Cecil Kellaway, Finlay Currie, Pedro Armendariz. Lavish religious epic dealing with story of founder of school of monks with sympathetic performance by Dillman. Good cast and atmosphere. Script tends to sag at wrong moments. CinemaScope.

Frank and Ollie (1995) **C-89m.** *** D: Theodore Thomas. Charming documentary about Frank Thomas and Ollie Johnston, friends since the early 1930s, next-door neighbors, and longtime animators at the Walt Disney studio, where they created some of the most memorable and expressive characters ever brought to life . . . from Thumper in BAMBI to Baloo and Mowgli in THE JUNGLE BOOK. Affectionate (and informative) portrait by Thomas's son and daughter-in-law, Kuniko Okubo. [PG]▼

Frankenhooker (1990) **C-90m.** *½ D: Frank Henenlotter. James Lorinz, Patty Mullen, Charlotte Helmkamp, Shirley Stoler, Louise Lasser. Grim, gory, and seldom funny horror comedy about a novice mad scientist (Lorinz) who needs body parts to sew onto the severed head he has on ice back at the lab. When he sells N.Y.C. 42nd Street hookers a deadly "supercrack," they explode—giving him all the spare limbs and organs he desires. Offensive, cheap, and ugly—even by splatter genre standards.▼●◗

Frankenstein (1931) **70m.** ***½ D: James Whale. Colin Clive, Mae Clarke, Boris Karloff, John Boles, Edward Van Sloan, Dwight Frye, Frederick Kerr, Lionel Belmore. Definitive monster movie, with Clive as the ultimate mad scientist, creating a man-made being (Karloff) but inadvertently giving him a criminal brain. It's creaky at times, and cries for a music score, but it's still impressive . . . as is Karloff's performance in the role that made him a star. Long-censored footage, restored in 1987, enhances the impact of several key scenes, including the drowning of a little girl. Based on Mary Shelley's novel. Followed by BRIDE OF FRANKENSTEIN.▼●◗

Frankenstein (1993) **C-100m. TVM** D: David Wickes. Patrick Bergin, John Mills, Randy Quaid, Lambert Wilson, Fiona Gillies, Timothy Stark. Florid version of Mary Shelley's novel, with producer-writer-director Wickes giving it a Jekyll and Hyde twist (having previously remade that Robert Louis Stevenson tale). Quaid plays the creature with sensitivity, but Mills steals the movie as the blind hermit who befriends him. Made for cable. Average.▼

Frankenstein (1994) SEE: **Mary Shelley's Frankenstein**

Frankenstein and the Monster From Hell (1974-British) **C-93m.** ** D: Terence Fisher. Peter Cushing, Shane Briant, Madeline Smith, Dave Prowse, John Stratton. Guess who runs a hospital for the criminally insane? Hammer's final entry in their Frankenstein cycle is amusing if you catch it in the right frame of mind. [R] ▼

Frankenstein Conquers the World (1965-Japanese) **C-87m.** ** D: Ishiro Honda. Nick Adams, Tadao Takashima, Kumi Mizuno. Grade-C horror film, with Adams a scientist in Tokyo trying to combat giant, newly grown Frankenstein monster terrorizing the countryside; poor special effects. Tohoscope. ▼

Frankenstein Created Woman (1967-British) **C-92m.** ** D: Terence Fisher. Peter Cushing, Susan Denberg, Robert Morris, Barry Warren, Thorley Walters, Duncan Lamont. Sequel to EVIL OF FRANKSTEIN finds Dr. Frankenstein (Cushing) tring to put the soul of recently (and wrongly) executed man into body of scarred lover (Denberg). Everything goes wrong, including script. Followed by FRANKENSTEIN MUST BE DESTROYED!▼●

Frankenstein '88 SEE **Vindicator, The**

Frankenstein General Hospital (1988) **C/B&W-92m.** BOMB D: Deborah Roberts. Mark Blankfield, Irwin Keyes, Kathy Shower, Katie Caple, Lou Cutell, Bobby "Boris" Pickett. Ghastly comedy stars Blankfield as Dr. Bob Frankenstein, who's assembling a new Monster in the basement of the hospital where he's an intern. Crude, vulgar, and completely unfunny, this is the worst Frankenstein film ever made in English. At least that's a distinction. [R]▼●

Frankenstein Island (1981) **C-89m.** BOMB D: Jerry Warren. John Carradine, Andrew Duggan, Cameron Mitchell, Steve Brodie, Robert Clarke, Katherine Victor. Low-budget filmmaker Warren's first feature in fifteen years reunites some of his old hands (like Clarke and Victor) for a sort of remake of TEENAGE ZOMBIES, with a monster who only shows up at the end, and who may or may not be Frankenstein! [PG]▼

Frankenstein Meets the Space Monster (1965) **78m.** BOMB D: Robert Gaffney. James Karen, David Kerman, Nancy Marshall, Marilyn Hanold. Low-grade horror entry dealing with interplanetary robot that goes berserk. Bizarre, Flash Gordon–esque aliens also involved. Has gained a peculiar cult reputation. Aka MARS INVADES PUERTO RICO.▼

Frankenstein Meets the Wolf Man (1943) **72m.** *** D: Roy William Neill. Lon Chaney, Jr., Patric Knowles, Ilona Massey, Bela Lugosi, Maria Ouspenskaya, Lionel Atwill, Dennis Hoey, Rex Evans, Dwight Frye. Sequel to both GHOST OF FRANKENSTEIN and THE WOLF MAN finds werewolf Chaney seeking Dr. Frankenstein, hoping to be put out of his misery. He finds the scientist is dead—but the Monster isn't. Slick, atmospheric, fast-paced fun; Lugosi's only stint as the Monster. Followed by HOUSE OF FRANKENSTEIN.▼●

Frankenstein Must Be Destroyed! (1969-British) **C-101m.** **½ D: Terence Fisher. Peter Cushing, Simon Ward, Veronica Carlson, Freddie Jones. Cushing is more cold-blooded here than usual, as he forces young couple to help his brain transplant experiments. One of the best in Hammer series. Followed by THE HORROR OF FRANKENSTEIN. [M/PG]▼●

Frankenstein—1970 (1958) **83m.** BOMB D: Howard W. Koch. Boris Karloff, Tom

Duggan, Jana Lund, Donald Barry. As last of the Frankenstein scientists, Karloff uses money from TV production shooting in his castle to revive original monster with atomic energy. Film is slow, monster unexciting, and Karloff hammy. CinemaScope.▼

Frankenstein's Daughter (1959) **85m.** BOMB D: Richard Cunha. John Ashley, Sandra Knight, Donald Murphy, Sally Todd, Harold Lloyd, Jr. Low-grade descendant of famed monster series with a new female horror-robot being created with typical results; tinsel sets.▼

Frankenstein: The True Story (1973) **C-200m. TVM** D: Jack Smight. James Mason, Leonard Whiting, Michael Sarrazin, David McCallum, Jane Seymour, Michael Wilding, Margaret Leighton, Ralph Richardson, Agnes Moorehead, John Gielgud, Tom Baker. Epic retelling of Mary Shelley's frightmare with brilliant Christopher Isherwood screenplay; not quite the letter of the novel, but competes favorably with the immortal Karloff movies on the theme by sheer spectacle. Creature, played stunningly by Sarrazin, is not the traditional stitched-together ogre, but a dashing Victorian rogue who proceeds to physically degenerate while various psychological avenues are explored. Marvelous cast in this thinking-man's horror movie. Above average.▼

Frankenstein Unbound (1990) **C-85m.** *½ D: Roger Corman. John Hurt, Raul Julia, Bridget Fonda, Nick Brimble, Catherine Rabett, Jason Patric, Michael Hutchence, Catherine Corman, Mickey Knox, voice of Terri Treas. Thoroughly expendable horror outing casts Hurt as a 21st-century scientist, not really mad, whose implosion experiments zap him back to the days of Doc Frankenstein (Julia) and Mary Shelley (Fonda). Capable cast goes slumming in schlockmeister Corman's first directorial effort in nearly twenty years. Hutchence, here Percy Shelley, was lead singer of Australian rock band INXS.▼●

Frankie and Johnny (1936) **66m.** BOMB D: Chester Erskine. Helen Morgan, Chester Morris, Lilyan Tashman, Florence Reed, Walter Kingsford. Dismally bad, cheaply made costume musical drama based on the old love-triangle song; even the great Morgan is undone. Made in 1934.▼

Frankie and Johnny (1966) **C-87m.** **½ D: Frederick de Cordova. Elvis Presley, Donna Douglas, Harry Morgan, Sue Ane Langdon, Nancy Kovack. Saloon song expanded into feature film story for Elvis. Riverboat setting, cohort Morgan, several pretty starlets, and tuneful songs make this a satisfactory time-filler.▼●

Frankie and Johnny (1991) **C-118m.** *** D: Garry Marshall. Al Pacino, Michelle Pfeiffer, Hector Elizondo, Nathan Lane, Kate Nelligan, Jane Morris, Greg Lewis, Al Fann, K Callan, Phil Leeds. Winning (if overlong) Hollywoodization of Terrence McNally's Off-Broadway play *Frankie and Johnny in the Clair de Lune*. Pacino (never more appealing) plays a man recently released from prison who gets a job as a short-order cook and falls in love with a waitress who tries to keep all social contact at arm's length. Pfeiffer manages to overcome her miscasting with an equally affecting performance. A moving ode to loneliness. Screenplay by the playwright. [R]▼●

Frankie Starlight (1995-U.S.-Irish) **C-101m.** *** D: Michael Lindsay-Hogg. Matt Dillon, Anne Parillaud, Gabriel Byrne, Rudi Davies, Corban Walker, Alan Pentony, Georgina Cates. Engagingly offbeat drama, the tale of an Irish dwarf (a man imprisoned in a child's body) who writes a revealing, autobiographical novel in which he describes his youth; his mother (Parillaud), a WW2 refugee from France; and the two men (Byrne and Dillon) who love her and become his role models. A gentle, flavorful film that moves seamlessly from the past to the present. [R]▼●

Frank's Greatest Adventure SEE: **Fearless Frank**

Frantic (1957-French) **92m.** **½ D: Louis Malle. Jeanne Moreau, Maurice Ronet, Georges Poujouly, Yori Bertin, Jean Wall. A man and woman plan to murder her husband, but fall short of committing a "perfect crime." Intriguing, but doesn't hold up. This was Malle's first non-documentary feature as director. Music score improvised by Miles Davis. Aka LIFT TO THE SCAFFOLD and ELEVATOR TO THE GALLOWS.▼

Frantic (1988) **C-120m.** **½ D: Roman Polanski. Harrison Ford, Emmanuelle Seigner, Betty Buckley, John Mahoney, Jimmie Ray Weeks, Yorgo Voyagis, David Huddleston, Gerard Klein. American doctor is drawn into espionage, and the underworld, when his wife disappears on the first day of their trip to Paris. Carefully controlled suspense thriller never really cuts loose but keeps its grip thanks to Ford's believable performance. [R]▼●◗

Fraternity Row (1977) **C-101m.** *** D: Thomas J. Tobin. Peter Fox, Gregory Harrison, Scott Newman, Nancy Morgan, Robert Emhardt, Wendy Phillips. Well-done drama of campus life at exclusive Eastern college, 1954. Writer-producer Charles Gary Allison used USC students and crew, got professional Hollywood advice for polished look at tragic, fact-based, fraternity hazing. Cliff Robertson narrates, Don McLean did original score. Costar Newman is the late son of Paul Newman. [PG]

Fraternity Vacation (1985) **C-89m.** *½ D: James Frawley. Stephen Geoffreys, Sheree J. Wilson, Cameron Dye, Leigh McCloskey, Tim Robbins, John Vernon, Britt Ekland, Nita Talbot, Max Wright, Amanda Bearse. Two frat animals, saddled with a nerdy "brother" on a pleasure trip to Palm Springs, bet a rival they can be the first to score with an aloof, beautiful blond. Less strident, and thus less offensive, than many of its ilk, but still nothing to enrich our moviegoing heritage. [R]▼

Fraulein (1958) **C-98m.** ** D: Henry Koster. Dana Wynter, Mel Ferrer, Dolores Michaels, Maggie Hayes. Bizarre post-WW2 Berlin tale of German girl helping U.S. soldier, then being held by the Communists. Wynter miscast. CinemaScope.

Fraulein Doktor (1969-Italian-Yugoslavian) **C-102m.** *** D: Alberto Lattuada. Suzy Kendall, Kenneth More, Capucine, James Booth, Alexander Knox, Nigel Green, Giancarlo Giannini. Big cast and budget in rarely seen European antiwar film centering on career of real-life double-agent during WW1. Some of the battle sequences impressive. Same story has been filmed many times before, in Hollywood as STAMBOUL QUEST and in France as MADEMOISELLE DOCTEUR. [M]

Freaked (1993) **C-79m.** ** D: Alex Winter, Tom Stern. Alex Winter, Megan Ward, Michael Stoyanov, Randy Quaid, Mr. T, Brooke Shields. Bratty movie star and entourage fall into the hands of mad circus owner who mutates them and adds them to his collection of freaks. Wildly inventive makeup and, well, freakish ideas are undercut by an in-your-face directorial style that hammers home every joke. It would make a terrific short. Winter's BILL & TED compatriot Keanu Reeves appears unbilled as Dog Boy. [R]▼●

Freakmaker SEE: **Mutations, The**

Freaks (1932) **64m.** ***½ D: Tod Browning. Wallace Ford, Olga Baclanova, Leila Hyams, Roscoe Ates, Harry Earles, Johnny Eck, Daisy and Violet Hilton, Prince Randian, Zip and Pip, Schlitze. A unique movie about a traveling sideshow and the camaraderie of its unusual performers, goaded to vengeance by cruel trapeze star Baclanova. Horror-film master Tod Browning gathered an incredible cast of real-life sideshow freaks for this bizarre and fascinating film. Severely cut in U.S. during release and banned in the U.K. for 30 years, some reissue prints are missing brief epilogue; aka NATURE'S MISTAKES. ▼●

Freaky Friday (1977) **C-97m.** *** D: Gary Nelson. Barbara Harris, Jodie Foster, John Astin, Patsy Kelly, Dick Van Patten, Sorrell Booke, Marie Windsor, Charlene Tilton. Harris and Foster shine as mother and daughter who magically switch personalities for a day; their performances make this exceptional Disney fare, even though Mary Rodgers' script winds up with formula slapstick chase. The same premise was the basis of the 1948 movie VICE VERSA and several later Hollywood comedies (including LIKE FATHER, LIKE SON and the 1988 VICE VERSA). Remade for TV in 1995. [G] ▼●

Freddie as F.R.O.7 (1992-British) **C-90m.** ** D: Jon Acevski. Voices of Ben Kingsley, Jenny Agutter, Brian Blessed, Nigel Hawthorne, Michael Hordern, Edmund Kingsley, Phyllis Logan, Victor Maddern, Jonathan Pryce, Prunella Scales, Billie Whitelaw. If James Bond was green, and animated, he might have turned out like Freddie. This toon saga of a secret agent frog is lively, but often difficult to follow. Reedited with James Earl Jones narration and retitled FREDDIE THE FROG. [PG]▼

Freddie the Frog SEE: **Freddie as F.R.O.7**

Freddy's Dead: The Final Nightmare (1991) **C-90m.** *½ D: Rachel Talalay. Robert Englund, Lisa Zane, Shon Greenblatt, Lezlie Deane, Ricky Dean Logan, Breckin Meyer, Yaphet Kotto, Elinor Donahue. Final NIGHTMARE ON ELM STREET entry has Freddy Krueger trying to break out of the town where he's been slaughtering teens in their dreams. Now the stage is set for the end-all Freddy showdown—a 10-minute 3-D finale that didn't even look good in theaters. A total yawner—but at the end, Freddy *is* dead. Cameos by Alice Cooper, Roseanne and Tom Arnold, and Johnny Depp, whose film debut was the first NIGHTMARE. [R]▼●

Free and Easy (1930) **92m.** **½ D: Edward Sedgwick. Buster Keaton, Anita Page, Robert Montgomery, Edgar Dearing, Lionel Barrymore, Dorothy Sebastian, Trixie Friganza. Interesting early-talkie musicomedy about Keaton becoming movie star; many guest appearances by Cecil B. DeMille, William Haines, *et al.* to boost uneven film. Retitled: EASY GO.▼●

Freebie and the Bean (1974) **C-113m.** *½ D: Richard Rush. James Caan, Alan Arkin, Loretta Swit, Jack Kruschen, Mike Kellin, Alex Rocco. Some good action, but mostly repellent humor as San Francisco cops Arkin and Caan nearly wreck the city trying to get the goods on a numbers racketeer. Valerie Harper has a nice cameo as Arkin's Latin wife. Later a short-lived TV series. Panavision. [R] ▼●

Free, Blonde and Twenty One (1940) **67m.** *½ D: Ricardo Cortez. Lynn Bari, Mary Beth Hughes, Joan Davis, Henry Wilcoxon. Low-grade hokum about gold-digging gals on the make for wealthy men.

Freedom Song (2000) **C-105m. TVM** D: Phil Alden Robinson. Danny Glover, Vondie Curtis-Hall, Vicellous Reon Shannon, Glynn Turman, Stan Shaw, Michael Jai White, David Strathairn. Surprisingly well turned fictional account of the civil rights movement in 1961 rural Mississippi, as viewed through the eyes of an awakening black teen, Shannon, who falls under the spell of soft-spoken SNCC advance man Curtis-Hall, who's come to town to organize sit-ins and preach nonviolence. Cowritten by Robinson. Especially memorable for the innovative score by the gospel group Sweet Honey in the Rock and James Horner. Made for cable. Above average. ▼

Free Enterprise (1999) **C-116m.** *** D: Robert Meyer Burnett. William Shatner, Rafer Weigel, Eric McCormack, Audie England, Patrick Van Horn, Jennifer Sommerfield, Phil LaMarr, Deborah Van Valkenburgh. Long-time friends and major sci-fi movie and TV buffs McCormack and Weigel are stunned to be befriended by William Shatner. But he has problems of his own, like his desire to stage *Julius Caesar* with himself in all the roles. Uneven but entertaining comedy gives Shatner a great, self-spoofing role. Written by director Burnett and Mark Altman, who based the lead characters on themselves. [R]▼●◗

Free for All (1949) **83m.** ** D: Charles Barton. Robert Cummings, Ann Blyth, Percy Kilbride, Ray Collins. Mild froth about Cummings inventing instant gasoline.

Freejack (1992) **C-108m.** *½ D: Geoff Murphy. Emilio Estevez, Mick Jagger, Rene Russo, Anthony Hopkins, Jonathan Banks, David Johansen, Amanda Plummer, Grand L. Bush, Frankie Faison, Esai Morales, John Shea. Good cast is wasted in this mindless actioner, in which race car driver Estevez dies in 1991 and finds his body snatched into the year 2009 so that it may house the soul of ruthless tycoon Hopkins. Tiresome, superficial fare. Based on the novel *Immortality, Inc.* by Robert Sheckley. Jagger plays a bounty hunter; it's his first screen acting role since PERFORMANCE in 1970. Panavision. [R]▼●◗

Free Money (1999-Canadian) **C-94m.** *½ D: Yves Simoneau. Marlon Brando, Charlie Sheen, Thomas Haden Church, Donald Sutherland, Mira Sorvino, Martin Sheen, David Arquette, J. P. Bergeron, Christin Watson, Holly Watson. How does a movie with a cast like this get rejected for theatrical release and go straight to cable? By being a frantically unfunny "comedy" that's shrill and desperate from the word go. A gargantuan, bald-headed, bushy-mustached Brando has his biggest role in years as a psychotic, small-town prison warden whose two idiot sons-in-law try to rob a train. Often embarrassing to watch. ▼◗

Free of Eden (1999) **C-92m. TVM** D: Leon Ichaso. Sidney Poitier, Sydney Poitier, Phylicia Rashad, Robert Hooks, Khalil Khan, Saundra McClain. Gutsy high-school dropout, dreaming to get out of the inner-city projects, turns up on the doorstep of a schoolteacher-turned-hard-nosed-investment-banker, and browbeats him into mentoring her toward a better life, the same kind he fought for as a young man. An obvious labor of love for proud papa Poitier (doing a TO SIR, WITH LOVE turn) and his tyro actress-daughter. Written by Delle Chatman and Yule Caise. Made for cable. Above average. ▼

Free Soul, A (1931) **91m.** **½ D: Clarence Brown. Norma Shearer, Lionel Barrymore, Clark Gable, Leslie Howard, James Gleason. A hard-drinking, free-swinging attorney successfully defends gangster Gable on a murder rap—then finds to his dismay that his equally free-spirited daughter has fallen in love with him. Dated morality play-melodrama retains interest because of its cast and Barrymore's famous courtroom finale, which clinched him an Oscar. Based on Adela Rogers St. Johns' book about her father. Remade as THE GIRL WHO HAD EVERYTHING. ▼

Freeway (1988) **C-91m.** ** D: Francis Delia. Darlanne Fluegel, James Russo, Billy Drago, Richard Belzer, Michael Callan, Joey Palese, Steve Franken, Kenneth Tobey, Clint Howard. A nurse whose husband was the victim of a freeway shooting becomes obsessed with finding the Bible-quoting murderer, who habitually phones a radio psychiatrist from his car while cruising L.A. looking for new victims. Based on a novel but prompted by similar real-life crimes in L.A., this film is surprisingly nonexploitive, but slow and unconvincing. [R]▼●

Freeway (1996) **C-102m.** *** D: Matthew Bright. Reese Witherspoon, Kiefer Sutherland, Brooke Shields, Wolfgang Bodison, Dan Hedaya, Amanda Plummer, Michael T. Weiss, Bokeem Woodbine, Brittany Murphy, Conchata Ferrell. Corrosive modern version of *Little Red Riding Hood* in which a teenage girl, on her way to grandma's, hitchhikes a ride with a psychotic child psychiatrist (Sutherland). Extremely violent satire is bolstered by Witherspoon's one-of-a-kind lethal Lolita performance and a smart screenplay by debut director Bright. Not for the faint at heart. Deliciously oddball score by Danny Elfman. Executive-produced by Oliver Stone. Followed by a direct-to-video sequel. [R]▼●◗

Free, White and 21 (1963) **104m.** BOMB D: Larry Buchanan. Frederick O'Neal, Annalena Lund, George Edgley, Johnny Hicks, George Russell. Did black businessman O'Neal rape Lund? Who cares?▼

Free Willy (1993) **C-112m.** **½ D: Simon Wincer. Jason James Richter, Lori Petty, Michael Madsen, Jayne Atkinson, Michael Ironside, Richard Riehle, August Schellenberg, Mykelti Williamson. Wayward 12-year-old, ordered to remove paint from aquarium walls, befriends and helps train an orca whale, eventually exploited by his seedy owner. Aggressively marketed sleeper hit is perfectly OK children's fare, with an appealing performance by young Richter. Michael Jackson sings "You Are Not Alone" over closing credits. Followed by two sequels and an animated TV series. Panavision. [PG]▼●◗

Free Willy 2: The Adventure Home (1995) **C-98m.** **½ D: Dwight Little. Jason James Richter, August Schellenberg, Jayne Atkinson, Jon Tenney, Elizabeth Pena,

Michael Madsen, Francis Capra, Mary Kate Schellhardt, Mykelti Williamson, M. Emmet Walsh. Richter has younger half-brother Capra forced upon him, finds young love with Schellhardt, and helps his orca friend Willy (and Willy's relatives) when an oil spill endangers the cetaceans. Overplotted children's film lacks the spark of the first, but is still good entertainment of its kind. The killer whales are almost all miniatures or computer graphics. Panavision. [PG] ▼●◗

Free Willy 3: The Rescue (1997) **C-85m.** ** D: Sam Pillsbury. Jason James Richter, August Schellenberg, Annie Corley, Vincent Berry, Patrick Kilpatrick, Tasha Simms, Peter Lacroix, Stephen E. Miller. Richter, now a teenager, gets a summer job on a marine biology research boat and clashes with a group of poachers who want to make whale sushi out of Willy and his pregnant girlfriend Nikki (or at least their animatronic/computer-graphic likenesses). Shortest entry in the series is well intentioned and easy to take, but utterly predictable and formulaic. [PG]▼●◗

Free Woman, A (1972-German) **C-100m.** **½ D: Volker Schlöndorff. Margarethe von Trotta, Friedhelm Ptok, Martin Luttge, Walter Sedlmayer. Von Trotta divorces Ptok, has trouble adjusting to life apart from husband and son as she tries to liberate herself from her traditional functions. Truthful but boring drama.

French Cancan SEE: **Only the French Can**

French Connection, The (1971) **C-104m.** **** D: William Friedkin. Gene Hackman, Fernando Rey, Roy Scheider, Tony LoBianco, Marcel Bozzuffi. Fine action film detailing attempted international heroin smuggle into N.Y.C., and maverick detective who stops it. Five Oscars include Best Picture, Actor, Director, Screenplay (Ernest Tidyman) and Editing (Jerry Greenberg), the latter particularly for one of the most exciting car chases ever filmed. Followed by a sequel and, in 1986, a TV movie, POPEYE DOYLE. [R]▼●

French Connection II (1975) **C-119m.** **½ D: John Frankenheimer. Gene Hackman, Fernando Rey, Bernard Fresson, Jean-Pierre Castaldi, Charles Milot, Cathleen Nesbitt. Gruff N.Y. cop Popeye Doyle goes to Marseilles, determined to nail narcotics king (Rey) who eluded him in America. Enjoyable opening and riveting chase finale are separated by long, agonizing drug addiction segment that weighs whole film down. [R]▼●

French Conspiracy, The (1973-French-Italian-German) **C-124m.** ** D: Yves Boisset. Jean-Louis Trintignant, Jean Seberg, Gian Maria Volonté, Roy Scheider, Michel Piccoli. Realistic but unexciting political drama centering around left-wing reporter Trintignant, pawn in a plot to assassinate Third World leader Volonté. [PG]

French Detective, The (1975-French) **C-93m.** *** D: Pierre Granier-Deferre. Lino Ventura, Patrick Dewaere, Victor Lanoux. Neat, entertaining police story with Ventura a tough, independent, middle-aged cop who, with exuberant young partner Dewaere, determinedly pursues a hood working for politician Lanoux. ▼

Frenchie (1950) **C-81m.** ** D: Louis King. Joel McCrea, Shelley Winters, John Russell, John Emery, George Cleveland, Elsa Lanchester, Marie Windsor. When her father is murdered, Winters returns home and opens a saloon, planning revenge. Bland Western based on DESTRY RIDES AGAIN.

French Key, The (1946) **64m.** **½ D: Walter Colmes. Albert Dekker, Mike Mazurki, Evelyn Ankers, John Eldredge, Frank Fenton, Richard Arlen, Byron Foulger. Dekker gives mystery drama some class in this murder yarn.

French Kiss (1995) **C-111m.** ** D: Lawrence Kasdan. Meg Ryan, Kevin Kline, Timothy Hutton, Jean Reno, Francois Cluzet, Victor Garrivier, Susan Anbeh. Charmless contrivance about a jilted woman who follows her fiancé to Paris and hooks up with a French rogue. Will these opposites ultimately attract one another? Duh! The stars' comic savvy can only carry this so far . . . though they're good, and the French scenery is nice. Soundtrack harmonica by the great Toots Thielemans. Ryan also coproduced. Panavision. [PG-13]▼●◗

French Lieutenant's Woman, The (1981-British) **C-123m.** ***½ D: Karel Reisz. Meryl Streep, Jeremy Irons, Leo McKern, Hilton McRae, Emily Morgan, Charlotte Mitchell, Lynsey Baxter. A scandalous romance between a gentleman and a tainted woman in Victorian England is contrasted with a contemporary affair between the actor and actress who are playing those roles in a movie. The juxtaposition is jarring at first, but becomes more engaging as the film progresses. Beautifully visualized, with rich period detail, superb performances; script by Harold Pinter, from John Fowles' novel. [R]▼●

French Line, The (1954) **C-102m.** ** D: Lloyd Bacon. Jane Russell, Gilbert Roland, Arthur Hunnicutt, Mary McCarty, Craig Stevens, Steven Geray, Joyce McKenzie, Paula Corday, Scott Elliot. Russell's bust in 3-D was the gimmick to sell this dull musical. All that's left is flat tale of wealthy Texas girl in Paris being romanced by Parisian. McCarty's wisecracking is a blessing. If you blink, you'll miss Kim Novak modeling a gown.▼

Frenchman's Creek (1944) **C-113m.** *** D: Mitchell Leisen. Joan Fontaine, Arturo de Cordova, Basil Rathbone, Nigel Bruce, Cecil Kellaway, Ralph Forbes, George Kirby. Colorful female fantasy escapism of Fontaine romanced by dashing pirate de

Cordova; good supporting cast. Based on a Daphne Du Maurier novel.▼

French Postcards (1979) **C-92m.** ** D: Willard Huyck. Blanche Baker, Miles Chapin, Debra Winger, Mandy Patinkin, Valerie Quennessen, David Marshall Grant, Marie-France Pisier, Jean Rochefort. Kind of follow-up to AMERICAN GRAFFITI from that film's authors (Huyck and Gloria Katz), detailing romantic misadventures of group of college students spending junior year abroad. Pleasant but forgettable comedy. [PG]▼

French Provincial (1974-French) **C-91m.** ** D: André Téchiné. Jeanne Moreau, Michel Auclair, Marie-France Pisier, Claude Mann, Orane Demazis. Moreau, as a laundry woman who marries into a bourgeois family, shines in this otherwise flaky, superficially symbolic saga of economic change in France from the 1930s through 1970s.

French Quarter (1978) **C-101m.** *** D: Dennis Kane. Bruce Davison, Lindsay Bloom, Virginia Mayo, Alisha Fontaine, Lance LeGault, Laura Misch Owens, Ann Michelle, Becky Allen, Barry Sullivan, William Sims. Neglected drive-in treat is a genuine curiosity; tongue-in-cheek melodrama mixes PRETTY BABY plot with FRENCH LIEUTENANT'S WOMAN structure (but predates both!). Tale of young Fontaine, growing up in New Orleans as Storyville prostitute at the turn of the century, is paralleled by present-day story with same cast, linked by voodoo plot device. Ends bizarrely with narrator reminding us to "hang up your speakers and drive home safely." And Dick Hyman did the music! [R]▼

French, They Are a Funny Race, The (1956-French) **83m.** ** D: Preston Sturges. Jack Buchanan, Noel-Noel, Martine Carol, Genevieve Brunet. Director-writer Sturges' last film is a misfire, with Buchanan as veddy-British major whose marriage to Frenchwoman sparks continuing nationalistic arguments. Original title: LES CARNETS DU MAJOR THOMPSON at 105m.

French Twist (1995-French) **C-100m.** **½ D: Josiane Balasko. Victoria Abril, Josiane Balasko, Alain Chabat, Ticky Holgado, Miguel Bosé, Catherine Hiegel, Catherine Samie, Catherine Lachens, Tolache Boorman. Bouncy comedy written and directed by French star Balasko (TOO BEAUTIFUL FOR YOU), who plays a gay van driver/drifter who accidentally meets a jolly housewife (Abril) and her philandering husband (Chabat). What follows is a *very* French twist on the old love triangle theme. Enjoyable farce is liberal to a fault but loses credibility as it unfolds. Still, Abril shines, as usual, in a terrific role. Original title: GAZON MAUDIT. ▼●

French Way Is, The SEE: **Love at the Top**

Frenzy (1944) SEE: **Torment**

Frenzy (1972-British) **C-116m.** ***½ D: Alfred Hitchcock. Jon Finch, Barry Foster, Barbara Leigh-Hunt, Anna Massey, Alec McCowen, Vivien Merchant, Billie Whitelaw, Jean Marsh. Hitchcock in full gear, telling story of suave London strangler (Foster) and innocent man (Finch) suspected of murder spree. All classic Hitchcock elements are here, including delicious black humor, several astounding camera shots. Script by Anthony Shaffer. [R]▼●

Frequency (2000) **C-117m.** ** D: Gregory Hoblit. Dennis Quaid, Jim Caviezel, Andre Braugher, Elizabeth Mitchell, Noah Emmerich, Shawn Doyle, Jordan Bridges. N.Y.C. cop whose fireman father died when he was six digs out his dad's old ham radio set, and by freakish fluke, finds he can communicate with his old man! Soon the father realizes he can help his son prevent crimes that are about to happen—and the son begins to wonder if he can keep his father from perishing in a flaming building. Entertaining at first but never quite convincing (like Quaid's unfortunate New York accent), this convoluted *Twilight Zone*–ish story misses the mark. Super 35. [PG-13]▼

Fresh (1994-U.S.-French) **C-112m.** *** D: Boaz Yakin. Sean Nelson, Giancarlo Esposito, Samuel L. Jackson, N'Bushe Wright, Ron Brice, Jean LaMarre, Luis Lantigua. Disturbing, controversial chronicle of 12-year-old black youth who divides his time between school and his duties as a busy heroin courier. When he witnesses a playground killing, young Fresh (unforgettably played by Sean Nelson) must use his street smarts to fight for survival. An unflinching look at the urban narcotics nightmare; some may be disturbed by the ambivalent view of the bright young protagonist as drug dealer, victim, survivor, and hero. Impressive debut for writer-director Yakin. Music by Stewart Copeland. [R] ▼●

Fresh From Paris (1955) **C-70m.** *½ D: Leslie Goodwins. Forrest Tucker, Margaret Whiting, Martha Hyer. Grade-C musical filmed at Moulin Rouge cafe in Hollywood, with tiresome musical interludes. Original title: PARIS FOLLIES OF 1956.

Fresh Horses (1988) **C-105m.** **½ D: David Anspaugh. Molly Ringwald, Andrew McCarthy, Patti D'Arbanville, Molly Hagan, Doug Hutchison, Ben Stiller, Leon Russom. Collegian McCarthy, engaged to a wealthy dullard, falls for Ringwald's underage no-no, a semi-shantytramp who lives across the river from his Cincinnati campus. Slightly better than expected, thanks to fine Midwest location work from the director of HOOSIERS. Ringwald isn't totally convincing in the kind of role Gloria Grahame invented. [PG-13]▼●

Freshman, The (1925) **70m.** **** D: Sam Taylor and Fred Newmeyer. Harold Lloyd, Jobyna Ralston, Brooks Benedict, James Anderson, Hazel Keener. One of Lloyd's best remembered films casts him as collegiate patsy who'll do anything to be popular on campus, unaware that everyone is making fun of him. Football game finale is one of several comic highlights. A real audience-rouser.▼

Freshman, The (1990) **C-102m.** ★★★ D: Andrew Bergman. Marlon Brando, Matthew Broderick, Maximilian Schell, Bruno Kirby, Penelope Ann Miller, Frank Whaley, Paul Benedict, B. D. Wong, Bert Parks. New York University film student Broderick falls in with loony mob family headed by Brando in this infectious, off-center comedy. Not an outstanding film per se, but strong cast and New York flavor, plus Bergman's original and amusing screenplay, put it over. Best of all: Marlon's knockout performance (remind you of anyone?), and his rapport with Matthew. [PG]▼●◗

Freud (1962) **120m.** ★★★½ D: John Huston. Montgomery Clift, Susannah York, Larry Parks, David McCallum, Susan Kohner, Eileen Herlie. Intelligent, unglamorous account of Sigmund Freud as young doctor, focusing on his early psychiatric theories and treatments and his struggle for their acceptance among Viennese medical colleagues. Fascinating dream sequence. Originally released at 139m. Also known as FREUD: THE SECRET PASSION.

Frida (1984-Mexican) **C-108m.** ★★★ D: Paul Leduc. Ofelia Medina, Juan Jose Gurrola, Max Kerlow, Salvador Sanchez, Claudio Brook. Solid biography effectively captures the spirit of an extraordinary woman: Frida Kahlo (Medina), Mexican artist and radical who dealt with various physical crises (resulting from polio and a paralyzing accident). Also central to her story are her relationships with Diego Rivera and Leon Trotsky. Visually captivating, with superior cinematography by Angel Goded and an unstructured narrative that not so much traces the incidents in its subject's life but paints a portrait of her.▼

Friday (1995) **C-89m.** ★½ D: F. Gary Gray. Ice Cube, Chris Tucker, Nia Long, Tiny "Zeus" Lister, Jr., John Witherspoon, Anna Maria Horsford, Regina King, Paul Jai Parker, Bernie Mac, Angela Means, Faizon Love, LaWanda Page. Rap star/actor Ice Cube coproduced, cowrote, and stars in this comedy, revealing the fun side he never showed in films like BOYZ N THE HOOD and TRESPASS. Talented cast can't rescue this practically plotless film about youth trying to survive life in L.A.'s South Central 'hood. Followed by NEXT FRIDAY. [R] ▼●◗

Friday Foster (1975) **C-90m.** ★★ D: Arthur Marks. Pam Grier, Yaphet Kotto, Godfrey Cambridge, Thalmus Rasulala, Eartha Kitt, Jim Backus, Scatman Crothers, Ted Lange, Carl Weathers. Black bubblegum nonsense based on comic strip about fashion photographer who gets involved in mystery and intrigue; here she tries to foil assassination/conspiracy plot against black politicians. [R]▼

Friday the 13th (1980) **C-95m.** ★½ D: Sean S. Cunningham. Betsy Palmer, Adrienne King, Harry Crosby, Laurie Bartram, Mark Nelson, Jeannine Taylor, Kevin Bacon. Palmer, who figures in an admittedly bravura finale, slaughters teens holed up in woodsy summer camp. Young folks unexpectedly made this gory, cardboard thriller a box-office smash—one more clue to why SAT scores continue to decline. Rates higher than BOMB simply because it's slightly better than part 2. Followed by a seemingly never-ending series of sequels and a TV series. [R]▼●

Friday the 13th, Part 2 (1981) **C-87m.** BOMB D: Steve Miner. Betsy Palmer, Amy Steel, John Furey, Adrienne King, Kirsten Baker, Stu Charno, Warrington Gillette. More nubile campers, more bloody executions. If you loved Part 1 . . . [R]▼●

Friday the 13th Part 3 (1982) **C-96m.** ★★ D: Steve Miner. Dana Kimmell, Paul Kratka, Tracie Savage, Jeffrey Rogers, Catherine Parks, Larry Zerner. Strictly amateur night in terms of acting and writing, but this entry deemphasizes explicit gore in favor of shocks, and delivers a few—especially in 3-D and widescreen. [R]▼●

Friday the 13th—The Final Chapter (1984) **C-91m.** BOMB D: Joseph Zito. Crispin Glover, Kimberly Beck, Barbara Howard, E. Erich Anderson, Corey Feldman, Ted White, Bruce Mahler, Lawrence Monoson. Why bother with a new script? Jason finally gets his—except that (title notwithstanding) the door is left open for yet another sequel! [R]▼●

Friday the 13th Part V: A New Beginning (1985) **C-102m.** BOMB D: Danny Steinmann. John Shepard, Melanie Kinnaman, Shavar Ross, Richard Young, Carol Lacatell, Corey Parker, Corey Feldman. A clever title (after . . . THE FINAL CHAPTER) for more gore galore, as gruesome and disgusting as ever. [R]▼●

Friday the 13th, Part VI: Jason Lives (1986) **C-87m.** BOMB D: Tom McLoughlin. Thom Mathews, Jennifer Cooke, David Kagan, Renee Jones, Kerry Noonan, C.J. Graham, Tony Goldwyn, Ron Palillo. Jason's summer camp has enjoyed years of tranquility after changing its name, but watch out! If you really think there's something to gain from watching Jason rise from the grave again, good luck! The pits. [R]▼●

Friday the 13th Part VII—The New Blood (1988) **C-88m.** ★½ D: John Carl Buechler. Lar Park Lincoln, Terry Kiser, Susan Blu, Kevin Blair, Susan Jennifer Sullivan, Elizabeth Kaitan. Makeup expert Buechler fails to inject much life into this endless series. Pretty, blonde Lincoln foolishly travels to Crystal Lake (with her mom and her shrink) where her talent for telekinesis brings the monstrous Jason back up from his watery grave. [R]▼●

Friday the 13th Part VIII: Jason Takes Manhattan (1989) **C-100m.** ** D: Rob Hedden. Jensen Daggett, Kane Hodder, Peter Mark Richman, Scott Reeves, Barbara Bingham, V. C. Dupree, Sharlene Martin. The best film in the "Friday" series, imaginatively directed and written by Hedden, is still just a slasher film, though less gruesome than most. Despite the title, most of the film takes place on a cruise ship. Too long and not really for fans of the series. Followed by JASON GOES TO HELL: THE FINAL FRIDAY. [R]▼●

Frieda (1947-British) **97m.** *** D: Basil Dearden. David Farrar, Glynis Johns, Mai Zetterling, Flora Robson, Albert Lieven. Interesting study of Farrar bringing German wife Zetterling back home to England, and bigotry they encounter.▼

Fried Green Tomatoes (1991) **C-130m.** *** D: Jon Avnet. Kathy Bates, Jessica Tandy, Mary Stuart Masterson, Mary-Louise Parker, Cicely Tyson, Chris O'Donnell, Stan Shaw, Gailard Sartain, Tim Scott, Gary Basaraba, Lois Smith, Grace Zabriskie. Enjoyable story-within-a-story film, in which repressed Southern wife Bates meets elderly Tandy at a nursing home and becomes captivated by her tale-spinning about two feisty female friends and their escapades in the 1920s and 30s. First-rate adaptation of Fannie Flagg's novel *Fried Green Tomatoes at the Whistle Stop Cafe* with just one problem: a couple of endings too many. Impressive feature directorial debut for producer Avnet. Flagg has an amusing cameo. Special unrated video edition runs 137m. [PG-13]▼●◗

Friendly Enemies (1942) **95m.** **½ D: Allan Dwan. Charles Winninger, Charlie Ruggles, James Craig, Nancy Kelly. Hoary WW1 play about a conflict between German immigrant friends, one of whom has assimilated and one who has not. Simplistic in the extreme, and torpedoed by its stars' burlesque accents.▼

Friendly Fire (1979) **C-145m. TVM** D: David Greene. Carol Burnett, Ned Beatty, Sam Waterston, Dennis Erdman, Timothy Hutton. Gripping if overlong Emmy-winning drama about a rural American couple who try to cope with governmental indifference to learn the truth behind their son's death in Vietnam. Burnett seems somewhat sullen in her one-note portrayal of real-life war activist Peg Mullen, but Beatty is outstanding as her husband. Script by Fay Kanin. Above average.▼

Friendly Persuasion (1956) **C-140m.** **** D: William Wyler. Gary Cooper, Dorothy McGuire, Marjorie Main, Anthony Perkins, Richard Eyer, Robert Middleton, (Peter) Mark Richman, Walter Catlett, William Schallert. Charming account (from Jessamyn West novel) of Quaker family struggling to maintain its identity amid confusion and heartbreak of Civil War. Warm, winning performances in this beautifully made film. Music by Dimitri Tiomkin. Though no screenplay credit appears, film was written by blacklisted Michael Wilson; he received posthumous credit in 1996. Remade for TV in 1975 with Richard Kiley and Shirley Knight.▼●

Friends (1971-British) **C-102m.** BOMB D: Lewis Gilbert. Sean Bury, Anicee Alvina, Pascale Roberts, Sady Rebbot, Ronald Lewis. Yucky early-teen romance about French boy and girl who run off to the seashore, set up housekeeping, and have a baby . . . then Mommy and Daddy show up to take them home. Popular in its day, primarily due to Elton John song score. Buy the album instead. Sequel (!): PAUL AND MICHELLE. [R]▼

Friends and Lovers (1931) **68m.** **½ D: Victor Schertzinger. Adolphe Menjou, Laurence Olivier, Lili Damita, Erich von Stroheim, Hugh Herbert. Unexceptional film interesting only for its cast. Menjou and Olivier are British officers stationed in India, both in love with Damita. Von Stroheim is fun to watch as Damita's sly, conniving husband.●

Friends and Lovers (1999) **C-104m.** *½ D: George Haas. Stephen Baldwin, Danny Nucci, George Newbern, Claudia Schiffer, Alison Eastwood, Suzanne Cryer, David Rasche, Neill Barry, Leon, Robert Downey, Jr., Ann Magnuson. This lame cross between the TV sitcom *Friends* and THE BIG CHILL deals with a group of friends who gather together for a Christmas ski holiday that quickly finds them coupled in unlikely romantic pairings. Embarrassing on every level, a good group of actors is wasted in this would-be farce that sets its sights low and misses the mark anyway. In her first major film role, Schiffer proves that as an actress she's a mighty fine model.▼

Friends, Lovers & Lunatics (1989-Canadian) **C-87m.** BOMB D: Stephen Withrow. Daniel Stern, Sheila McCarthy, Deborah Foreman, Page Fletcher, Elias Koteas, Damir Andrei. Perfectly dreadful romantic comedy about commercial artist Stern, desperate to win back his ex (McCarthy), who follows her and her new boyfriend on a mountain holiday. Silly, poorly scripted time-waster. Original title: CRAZY HORSE. Aka SHE DRIVES ME CRAZY. [R]▼●

Friends of Eddie Coyle, The (1973) **C-102m.** ***½ D: Peter Yates. Robert Mitchum, Peter Boyle, Richard Jordan, Steven Keats, Alex Rocco, Mitchell Ryan. Ultrarealistic depiction of criminals and police, as hardened con labors to supply guns and make deal with cops. Bleak nightmare picture of underworld enhanced by numerous Boston locations, flawless performances. Only liabilities: film's offbeat low-key narrative approach and finale. Adapted by Paul Monash from George V. Higgins's novel. [R]

Fright (1971-British) **C-87m.** ** D: Peter Collinson. Susan George, Honor Blackman, Ian Bannen, John Gregson, George Cole, Dennis Waterman. Young babysitter (George) spends terror-filled evening at country house, menaced by mental hospital escapee. Contrived, mechanical direction and so-so script. [PG]▼

Frightened Bride, The (1953-British) **75m.** ** D: Terence Young. Andre Morell, Flora Robson, Mai Zetterling, Michael Denison, Mervyn Johns. Murder haunts a family when the youngest son becomes involved in homicide.

Frightened City, The (1961-British) **97m.** **½ D: John Lemont. Herbert Lom, John Gregson, Sean Connery, Alfred Marks, Yvonne Romain. Interesting inside look at a London racketeer amalgamating various city gangs for master plan syndicate. ▼

Frighteners, The (1996-New Zealand-U.S.) **C-109m.** **½ D: Peter Jackson. Michael J. Fox, Trini Alvarado, Peter Dobson, John Astin, Jeffrey Combs, Dee Wallace Stone, Jake Busey, Chi McBride, Jim Fyfe, Troy Evans, Julianna McCarthy, R. Lee Ermey. Overlong, but original blend of paranormal, horror, and black-comedy ingredients. Fox plays a psychic investigator/exterminator on the trail of an otherworldly serial killer. Zigzags from grisly humor to slasher-movie horror. Combs (of RE-ANIMATOR fame) has a scenery-chewing role as a wacked-out FBI agent on the case. Definitely not for all tastes. Filmed in New Zealand, home of director/cowriter Jackson. Executive-produced by Robert Zemeckis. Super 35. [R]▼●◗

Fright Night (1985) **C-105m.** *** D: Tom Holland. Chris Sarandon, William Ragsdale, Amanda Bearse, Roddy McDowall, Stephen Geoffreys, Jonathan Stark. Teenage boy enlists the aid of TV horror-movie host (and erstwhile actor) to kill suave, cunning vampire who's moved in next door. Entertaining, old-fashioned horror outing energized by Richard Edlund's spectacular special effects and highlighted by two wonderful performances, by McDowall and Sarandon. Written by Holland. Followed by a sequel. Panavision. [R]▼●◗

Fright Night Part 2 (1989) **C-104m.** ** D: Tommy Lee Wallace. Roddy McDowall, William Ragsdale, Traci Lin, Julie Carmen, Jonathan Gries, Russell Clark, Brian Thompson, Merritt Butrick, Ernie Sabella. Sister of the vampire who met a grisly end in FRIGHT NIGHT seeks revenge on the duo who destroyed him. More-of-the-same sequel is definitely a comedown from the earlier film, though well produced. Panavision. [R]▼●

Fringe Dwellers, The (1986-Australian) **C-98m.** **½ D: Bruce Beresford. Kristina Nehm, Justine Saunders, Bob Maza, Kylie Belling, Denis Walker, Ernie Dingo. Ambitious young aborigine woman convinces her family to move out of their shantytown and into a prosperous, mostly white middle-class neighborhood in present-day Australia; the expected readjustment woes follow. Sincere, very well-acted drama (especially by Nehm) is undercut by sentimental, dramatically dishonest conclusion. Overall, worth a look. [PG]▼●

Frisco Jenny (1933) **70m.** **½ D: William Wellman. Ruth Chatterton, Louis Calhern, Helen Jerome Eddy, Donald Cook, James Murray, Hallam Cooley, Pat O'Malley, Harold Huber, J. Carrol Naish. Chatterton's father and lover are killed in the San Francisco earthquake, but her problems have only begun. Loose retelling of MADAME X is a tailor-made Chatterton vehicle. Good atmosphere and smart dialogue overcome film's tendency to meander.

Frisco Kid (1935) **77m.** ** D: Lloyd Bacon. James Cagney, Margaret Lindsay, Ricardo Cortez, Lili Damita, Fred Kohler, George E. Stone, Donald Woods. Routine drama of Barbary Coast with Cagney fighting his way to the top, almost dethroned by local gangs but saved by blueblood Lindsay.

Frisco Kid, The (1979) **C-122m.** **½ D: Robert Aldrich. Gene Wilder, Harrison Ford, Ramon Bieri, Val Bisoglio, George Ralph DiCenzo, Leo Fuchs, Penny Peyser. Offbeat story of Polish rabbi crossing U.S. in 1850 and developing friendship with young bank robber. Wilder's performance, and some charming vignettes, make up for many other shortcomings. [PG]▼

Frisco Sal (1945) **94m.** ** D: George Waggner. Susanna Foster, Turhan Bey, Alan Curtis, Andy Devine, Thomas Gomez, Samuel S. Hinds. Tepid costume drama of Foster out West in California, determined to find her brother's killer.

Frisky (1955-Italian) **98m.** **½ D: Luigi Comencini. Gina Lollobrigida, Vittorio De Sica, Roberto Risso, Marisa Merlini. Lollobrigida provides sufficient sex appeal to carry simple tale of flirtatious village girl who beats out competition in winning heart of police official De Sica.

Friz Freleng's Looney Looney Looney Bugs Bunny Movie SEE: **Looney Looney Looney Bugs Bunny Movie**

Fritz The Cat (1972) **C-78m.** *** D: Ralph Bakshi. X-rated animated feature somewhat based on Robert Crumb's underground comics character. Flawed but engaging, irreverent look at radical-hip lifestyles of the 1960s, geared for people who experienced that era. Imaginatively conceived cartoon. Sequel: THE NINE LIVES OF FRITZ THE CAT. [X]▼

Frogmen, The (1951) **96m.** *** D: Lloyd Bacon. Richard Widmark, Dana Andrews, Gary Merrill, Jeffrey Hunter, Robert Wagner, Jack Warden. Intriguing look at underwater demolition squads in action in the Pacific during WW2.

Frogs (1972) **C-91m.** **½ D: George McCowan. Ray Milland, Sam Elliott, Joan Van Ark, Adam Roarke, Judy Pace. Patriarchal Milland has been destroying bayou wildlife and now all the swamp critters are out to destroy his whole family. Dumb but enjoyable thriller. [PG]▼

Frogs for Snakes (1999) **C-98m.** ** D: Amos Poe. Barbara Hershey, Robbie Coltrane, Harry Hamlin, Ian Hart, John Leguizamo, Lisa Marie, Debi Mazar, Ron Perlman, Clarence Williams III. Another Tarantino wannabe, this black comedy has a clever conceit: Struggling N.Y. actors who'll do anything for a good part make money on the side as hit men for a Russian racketeer (Coltrane). Story goes nowhere, despite a good cast. Director Poe also scripted. [R]▼

From a Whisper to a Scream SEE: **Offspring, The**

From Beyond (1986) **C-85m.** **½ D: Stuart Gordon. Jeffrey Combs, Barbara Crampton, Ted Sorel, Ken Foree, Carolyn Purdy-Gordon, Bunny Summers, Bruce McGuire. The RE-ANIMATOR team returns to H. P. Lovecraft territory for this similarly demented film based on a scientist's search for a sixth sense . . . which, in time, causes his associates to go berserk. Takes its time getting revved up, but then cuts loose in outrageous fashion. As before, this is not for the squeamish, but if you liked RE-ANIMATOR . . . [R]▼●

From Beyond the Grave (1973-British) **C-97m.** *** D: Kevin Connor. Peter Cushing, Margaret Leighton, Ian Bannen, Donald Pleasence, David Warner, Diana Dors, Angela Pleasence, Nyree Dawn Porter, Lesley-Anne Down. Neat multistoried horror pic. Visitors to Cushing's antique shop, Temptations Ltd., meet terrible fates. Leighton excels as wacky clairvoyant. Retitled: CREATURES. [PG]▼●

From Dusk Till Dawn (1996) **C-108m.** ** D: Robert Rodriguez. Harvey Keitel, George Clooney, Quentin Tarantino, Juliette Lewis, Salma Hayek, Cheech Marin, Tom Savini, Fred Williamson, John Saxon, Kelly Preston, Marc Lawrence, Michael Parks, Ernest Lui, Danny Trejo, Tito Larriva. Two out-of-control criminal brothers mow their way through Texas, heading for a rendezvous in Mexico, and take a family (and their RV) hostage. But the rendezvous location turns out to be a hellish biker bar inhabited by vampires! Indefensible trash certainly works on a visceral level; how much you can take will depend on your G.Q. (grossout quotient). Rodriguez and screenwriter/actor Tarantino seem to be having fun, especially in their casting choices, but this is just a celebration of excess. In fact, it might be retitled NATURAL BORN VAMPIRES. Followed by two direct-to-video sequels. [R] ▼●◗

From Hell It Came (1957) **71m.** *½ D: Dan Milner. Tod Andrews, Tina Carver, Linda Watkins, John McNamara, Gregg Palmer, Robert Swan. Monstrous tree rises from grave of native chief's son, causing terror in South Seas village. As walking-tree movies go, this is at the top of the list.

From Hell to Borneo (1964) **C-96m.** ** D: George Montgomery. George Montgomery, Julie Gregg, Torin Thatcher, Lisa Moreno. Filmed in the Philippines, tale recounts Montgomery's efforts to maintain sanctity of his private island against aggressive crooks and smugglers.▼

From Hell to Texas (1958) **C-100m.** **½ D: Henry Hathaway. Don Murray, Diane Varsi, Chill Wills, Dennis Hopper. Sincere Western with Murray on the run with posse on his trail for accidentally killing a man. CinemaScope.

From Hell to Victory (1979-French-Italian-Spanish) **C-100m.** ** D: Hank Milestone (Umberto Lenzi). George Peppard, George Hamilton, Horst Buchholz, Capucine, Sam Wanamaker, Jean-Pierre Cassel, Anny Duperey. Friends of various nationalities are torn apart by the coming of WW2. Undistinguished, superficial actioner. Technovision.[PG]▼

From Here to Eternity (1953) **118m.** **** D: Fred Zinnemann. Burt Lancaster, Montgomery Clift, Deborah Kerr, Donna Reed, Frank Sinatra, Philip Ober, Ernest Borgnine, Mickey Shaughnessy, Jack Warden, Claude Akins, George Reeves. Toned-down but still powerful adaptation of James Jones' novel of Army life in Hawaii just before Pearl Harbor. Depiction of Japanese sneak attack combines unforgettable action scenes with actual combat footage. Brilliantly acted by entire cast, including Sinatra in his "comeback" role as the ill-fated soldier Maggio. Eight Oscars include Best Picture, Director, Screenplay (Daniel Taradash), Cinematography (Burnett Guffey), and Supporting Actors Sinatra and Reed. Remade in 1979 as a TV miniseries, which in turn spun off a brief series.▼●

From Mao to Mozart: Isaac Stern in China (1980) **C-84m.** ***½ D: Murray Lerner. Isaac Stern, David Golub, Tan Shuzhen. Moving documentary about violinist Stern's '79 tour of China. Most memorably, he tutors talented Chinese students, encouraging them to *feel* their playing. Shuzhen, deputy director of the Shanghai Conservatory of Music, describes his incarceration during the Cultural Revolution. Deservedly won Best Documentary Academy Award. [G]▼

From Nashville With Music (1969) **C-87m.** *½ D: Eddie Crandall. Marilyn Maxwell, Leo G. Carroll, (Pedro) Gonzalez-Gonzalez,

Marty Robbins, Merle Haggard, Buck Owens. Some good C&W music, but one is better off buying the performers' albums instead of suffering through this story of N.Y.C. couple who go to the Grand Ole Opry by mistake.

From Noon Till Three (1976) **C-99m.** **½ D: Frank D. Gilroy. Charles Bronson, Jill Ireland, Douglas Fowley, Stan Haze, Damon Douglas, Anne Ramsey. Likably offbeat story (adapted by Gilroy from his own novel) about a two-bit robber who enjoys a brief tryst with a woman who—after he is thought dead—fictionalizes their romance and turns him into a legendary hero. A kind of shaggy dog joke, which while pleasant, doesn't quite work. A nice change of pace for Bronson, though. [PG]▼

From Russia With Love (1963-British) **C-118m.** ***½ D: Terence Young. Sean Connery, Daniela Bianchi, Lotte Lenya, Pedro Armendariz, Robert Shaw, Bernard Lee, Lois Maxwell. Second James Bond film is one of the best; plenty of suspense and action, and one of the longest, most exciting fight scenes ever staged. Lenya makes a very sinister spy.▼●◗

From the Earth to the Moon (1958) **C-100m.** **½ D: Byron Haskin. Joseph Cotten, George Sanders, Debra Paget, Don Dubbins, Patric Knowles, Melville Cooper, Carl Esmond, Henry Daniell. Jules Verne's fiction doesn't float well in contrived sci-fi of early rocket flight to the moon. Veteran cast looks most uncomfortable.▼●◗

From the Hip (1987) **C-112m.** BOMB D: Bob Clark. Judd Nelson, Elizabeth Perkins, John Hurt, Darren McGavin, Ray Walston, Dan Monahan, David Alan Grier, Nancy Marchand, Allan Arbus, Edward Winter. Once again, Nelson plays a character only a mother could love: a lawyer who's made a name for himself by winning a hopeless case through outrageous courtroom tactics. Now he's given another challenge: defending Hurt, who's accused of murder. Hurt's flamboyant performance can't save this mongrel of a movie. J-D-C Scope.[PG] ▼●

From the Life of the Marionettes (1980-German) **C/B&W-104m.** ***½ D: Ingmar Bergman. Robert Atzorn, Christine Buchegger, Martin Benrath, Rita Russek, Lola Muethel, Walter Schmidinger, Heinz Bennent. Powerful, provocative drama about a respectable, successful businessman (Atzorn), who ravishes and strangles a prostitute. He has also been obsessed with killing his wife (Buchegger), with whom he constantly quarrels. Not coincidentally, both were minor characters in SCENES FROM A MARRIAGE. [R]▼●

From the Mixed-Up Files of Mrs. Basil E. Frankweiler (1973) **C-105m.** **½ D: Fielder Cook. Ingrid Bergman, Sally Prager, Johnny Doran, George Rose, Georgann Johnson, Richard Mulligan, Madeline Kahn. Fanciful tale of New Jersey kids Prager and Doran who hide out in N.Y.C.'s Metropolitan Museum, creating a dream world and befriending recluse Bergman, seen too briefly. Best for children. Blanche Hanalis adapted E.L. Konigsburg's novel. Reissued as THE HIDEAWAYS. Remade in 1995 for TV with Lauren Bacall. [G]▼

From the Terrace (1960) **C-144m.** *** D: Mark Robson. Paul Newman, Joanne Woodward, Myrna Loy, Ina Balin, Leon Ames, Elizabeth Allen, Barbara Eden, George Grizzard, Patrick O'Neal, Felix Aylmer, Mae Marsh. John O'Hara's ironic chronicle of young war veteran's rise to financial and social success is superficial film. Woodward is chic and Newman wooden; Loy is superb as drunken mother, Ames fine as bitter dad. CinemaScope.▼●

From This Day Forward (1946) **95m.** *** D: John Berry. Joan Fontaine, Mark Stevens, Rosemary DeCamp, Henry (Harry) Morgan, Arline Judge, Bobby Driscoll, Mary Treen. Agreeable soaper of Fontaine and Stevens readjusting their lives when he returns from war, and their struggle to get on in the world.

Front, The (1976) **C-94m.** **** D: Martin Ritt. Woody Allen, Zero Mostel, Herschel Bernardi, Michael Murphy, Andrea Marcovicci, Remak Ramsay, Joshua Shelley, Lloyd Gough, Danny Aiello, Charles Kimbrough, Josef Sommer. Bull's-eye comedy with serious theme. Allen is a schnook enlisted by blacklisted writers to put his name on their scripts during 1950s witch-hunt era, leading to various complications. Allen's casting is perfect, and Mostel is standout as "tainted" comic fighting for survival. Original script by blacklisted Walter Bernstein; Ritt, Mostel, Bernardi, Shelley, and Gough were also blacklisted in real life. [PG]▼●

Frontier Gal (1945) **C-84m.** **½ D: Charles Lamont. Yvonne De Carlo, Rod Cameron, Andy Devine, Fuzzy Knight, Andrew Tombes, Sheldon Leonard, Clara Blandick. Sex in the West as saloon queen De Carlo falls in love with outlaw Cameron; no sympathy from villain Leonard in OK Western-comedy.

Frontier Gun (1958) **70m.** ** D: Paul Landres. John Agar, Robert Strauss, Barton MacLane, Morris Ankrum. Agar is honest sheriff who discovers that gunplay is only solution to town's crooks. Regalscope.

Frontier Hellcat (1966-German) **C-98m.** **½ D: Alfred Vohrer. Stewart Granger, Elke Sommer, Pierre Brice, Gotz George. Another Karl May *Winnetou* story, which captures flavor of Old West in adventure of pioneers passing through Rockies. Ultrascope.

Frontier Marshal (1939) **71m.** *** D: Allan Dwan. Randolph Scott, Nancy Kelly, Cesar Romero, Binnie Barnes, John Carradine, Lon Chaney, Jr., Chris-Pin Martin, Eddie Foy, Jr. Colorful retelling of events leading to legendary gunfight at the O.K. Corral. Scott is fine as Tombstone's new marshal, Wyatt Earp; Romero is more moody than cold-blooded as Doc *Halliday,* and Kelly is the girl from his past who reminds Doc of his earlier, saner days as—an obstetrician! Many scenes and bits of dialogue were used in the 1946 remake, MY DARLING CLEMENTINE. Ward Bond, who plays Earp's brother in the later film, appears briefly as a cowardly town marshal.

Frontier Uprising (1961) **68m.** *½ D: Edward L. Cahn. James Davis, Nancy Hadley, Ken Mayer, Nestor Paiva. Scout leading pioneers to West Coast in 1840s discovers that Mexico and U.S. are at war.

Front Page, The (1931) **103m.** ***½ D: Lewis Milestone. Adolphe Menjou, Pat O'Brien, Mary Brian, Edward Everett Horton, Walter Catlett, Mae Clarke, George E. Stone. First filming of Hecht-MacArthur play is forceful, funny, and flamboyantly directed, with Menjou and O'Brien a good pair as battling editor and reporter in Chicago. Stands up quite well alongside remake HIS GIRL FRIDAY.▼

Front Page, The (1974) **C-105m.** *** D: Billy Wilder. Jack Lemmon, Walter Matthau, Carol Burnett, Susan Sarandon, Vincent Gardenia, David Wayne, Allen Garfield, Austin Pendleton, Charles Durning, Harold Gould, Herb Edelman, Dick O'Neill, Jon Korkes, Martin Gabel. Third filming of the Hecht-MacArthur play about wild and woolly Chicago newspapermen in the 1920s has hardly anything new to offer (except four-letter words) but remains an enjoyable vehicle for this fine cast. Only Burnett misses the boat as pathetic hooker Molly Malloy. Remade again (!) in 1988 as SWITCHING CHANNELS. Panavision. [PG]▼●◗

Front Page Story (1954-British) **99m.** **½ D: Gordon Parry. Jack Hawkins, Elizabeth Allan, Eva Bartok, Martin Miller, Derek Farr. Solid performances enhance story of many problems confronting newspaper editor: pending divorce, murder, lost children, and a rebellious staff.

Front Page Woman (1935) **82m.** **½ D: Michael Curtiz. Bette Davis, George Brent, Winifred Shaw, Roscoe Karns, Joseph Crehan. Breezy yarn of rival reporters Davis and Brent trying to outdo each other covering unusual murder and trial. Prime ingenue Davis fare.

Frozen Assets (1992) **C-96m.** *½ D: George Miller. Shelley Long, Corbin Bernsen, Larry Miller, Dody Goodman, Matt Clark, Paul Sand, Teri Copley, Gloria Camden, Gerrit Graham. Low-octane comic trifle, in which Bernsen is transferred to a new bank—only to discover it's a sperm bank (get it?). He meets repressed biologist Long and after a lot of potency jokes they find themselves drawn to each other. Misguided movie vehicle for two proven TV stars. Corbin's mother, *The Young and the Restless'* Jeanne Cooper, has a small role. [PG-13]▼

Frozen Dead, The (1966-British) **C-95m.** ** D: Herbert J. Leder. Dana Andrews, Anna Palk, Philip Gilbert, Kathleen Breck, Karel Stepanek, Edward Fox. Bizarre account of scientist Andrews who froze group of top Nazis, now trying to revive them and the Third Reich; sloppy production values mar tale. Released theatrically in b&w.

Frozen Ghost, The (1945) **61m.** **½ D: Harold Young. Lon Chaney (Jr.), Evelyn Ankers, Milburn Stone, Douglass Dumbrille, Martin Kosleck, Elena Verdugo, Tala Birell. Entertaining *Inner Sanctum* yarn with Chaney as a stage mentalist who blames himself for a man's death, and seeks refuge (!) in a creepy wax museum run by Birell.▼

Fruit Machine, The (1988-British) **C-103m.** *** D: Philip Saville. Emile Charles, Tony Forsyth, Robert Stephens, Claire Higgins, Bruce Payne, Robbie Coltrane. Diverting contemporary thriller about two gay but very different Liverpool teens (Charles and Forsyth, in spirited performances) who witness a gangland murder and must flee for their lives. Scripted by Frank (LETTER TO BREZHNEV) Clarke. Video title: WONDERLAND.▼●

F.T.A. (1972) **C-94m.** ** D: Francine Parker. Jane Fonda, Donald Sutherland, Len Chandler, Holly Near, Pamela Donegan, Michael Alaimo. Unusual, rarely-seen documentary of Fonda and Sutherland's *Free (or F***) the Army* revue, presented near Army bases and featuring antiwar skits and songs. Interesting only as a curio.

Fugitive, The (1947) **104m.** ***½ D: John Ford. Henry Fonda, Dolores Del Rio, Pedro Armendariz, J. Carrol Naish, Leo Carrillo, Ward Bond. Brooding drama set in Mexico with revolutionist priest turned in by man who once sheltered him. Superbly shot by Gabriel Figueroa. Also shown in computer-colored version.▼●

Fugitive, The (1993) **C-127m.** ***½ D: Andrew Davis. Harrison Ford, Tommy Lee Jones, Sela Ward, Julianne Moore, Joe Pantoliano, Jeroen Krabbé, Andreas Katsulas, Daniel Roebuck, L. Scott Caldwell. Slick, solid update of the 1960s TV series about a doctor wrongly convicted of murdering his wife; he takes it on the lam, with a dogged federal marshal (Jones, in an Oscar-winning performance) and his team on his trail. Great action and stunts, including an eye-popping bus crash/train wreck, but it's the cat-and-mouse game between two strong personalities—Ford and Jones—that makes this work. Scripted by Jeb Stuart and David Twohy from Twohy's story; based on coexecutive producer Roy Huggins' original TV premise. Followed by U.S. MARSHALS. [PG-13] ▼●◗

Fugitive Kind, The (1959) **135m.** **½ D: Sidney Lumet. Marlon Brando, Anna Magnani, Joanne Woodward, Maureen Stapleton, Victor Jory, R. G. Armstrong. Uneven filming of Tennessee Williams' *Orpheus Descending*, with strange casting. Wandering bum (Brando) arrives in Southern town, sparking romances with middle-aged married woman (Magnani) and spunky Woodward. Movie goes nowhere. Remade for cable TV in 1990 as ORPHEUS DESCENDING.▼

Fugitive Lovers (1934) **84m.** ** D: Richard Boleslawski. Robert Montgomery, Madge Evans, Nat Pendleton, Ted Healy, C. Henry Gordon, The Three Stooges. Genially preposterous tale of runaway chorus girl and prison escapee who are drawn together during cross-country bus trip (all of it shot with "arty" camera angles). Moves like lightning to even *more* preposterous climax in snowbound Colorado.▼

Full Body Massage (1995) **C-105m. TVM** D: Nicolas Roeg. Mimi Rogers, Bryan Brown, Elizabeth Barondes, Christopher Burgard, Heather Gunn, Patrick Neil Quinn. Offbeat, gabby, and quite sensual memory piece involving rich bitch Rogers and her substitute masseur Brown, who may once have met as children. Much of full-bodied Rogers' footage requires her to be nude, but the eroticism of the piece flags as the talk drones on. Direct-to-video production that premiered on cable. Average. ▼

Full Circle SEE: **Haunting of Julia, The**

Full Confession (1939) **73m.** ** D: John Farrow. Victor McLaglen, Sally Eilers, Joseph Calleia, Barry Fitzgerald, Elizabeth Risdon. Well-meaning but unbearably preachy melodrama in which Fitzgerald is falsely accused of murder. McLaglen confesses the crime to priest Calleia, but what can the father do?

Fuller Brush Girl, The (1950) **85m.** ** D: Lloyd Bacon. Lucille Ball, Eddie Albert, Jeff Donnell, Jerome Cowan, Lee Patrick. Low-grade slapstick with energetic Lucy as door-to-door salesgirl, mixed up with thieves.▼●

Fuller Brush Man, The (1948) **93m.** **½ D: S.Sylvan Simon. Red Skelton, Janet Blair, Don McGuire, Adele Jergens, Ross Ford, Hillary Brooke. Usual Skelton slapstick, with Red involved in murder while valiantly trying to succeed as a door-to-door salesman.▼●

Full Fathom Five (1990) **C-82m.** BOMB D: Carl Franklin. Michael Moriarty, Maria Rangel, Michael Cavanaugh, John LaFayette, Todd Field, Daniel Faraldo, Orlando Sacha. Roger Corman's "Red October" is a waterlogged mess: a group of renegades seize a Russian sub and threaten the nuclear annihilation of Houston, while the U.S. is preparing to invade Panama. Far too cheap for its ambitions. [PG]▼

Full Metal Jacket (1987) **C-116m.** *** D: Stanley Kubrick. Matthew Modine, Adam Baldwin, Vincent D'Onofrio, Lee Ermey, Dorian Harewood, Arliss Howard, Kevyn Major Howard, Ed O'Ross. Adaptation of Gustav Hasford's *The Short Timers* is divided into two sections: a harrowing look at Marine basic training on Parris Island; and combat experiences in Vietnam. The first half is so strong (thanks in part to real-life former D.I. Ermey) that the second half suffers in comparison, as it covers more familiar ground, while keeping emotions in check. Still, it's compelling, well acted, and supremely well crafted, certainly in keeping with Kubrick's recurring theme of dehumanization. Original music by Abigail Mead, aka Vivian Kubrick, the director's daughter. Filmed in England. [R]▼●◗

Full Monty, The (1997-British-U.S.) **C-95m.** ***½ D: Peter Cattaneo. Robert Carlyle, Tom Wilkinson, Mark Addy, Lesley Sharp, Emily Woof, Steve Huison, Paul Barber, Hugo Speer, Deirdre Costello. Bull's-eye comedy about unemployed Sheffield steel-mill workers who, out of desperation, the need for money, and an equal need to have something to do, decide to become male strippers. Funny, well cast, and never mean spirited, this film earns its laughs honestly. Clever screenplay by Simon Beaufoy. Oscar-winning score by Anne Dudley. [R]▼●◗

Full Moon High (1981) **C-94m.** *** D: Larry Cohen. Adam Arkin, Ed McMahon, Elizabeth Hartman, Roz Kelly, Bill Kirchenbauer, Kenneth Mars, Joanne Nail, Alan Arkin. Infectiously silly teenage werewolf comedy, with Arkin as a high-school football star whose strange, right-wing father (McMahon) takes him to Transylvania and inadvertently changes his life. Lots of off-the-wall laughs and cameos by various comedy performers. [PG]▼

Full Moon in Blue Water (1988) **C-93m.** ** D: Peter Masterson. Gene Hackman, Teri Garr, Burgess Meredith, Elias Koteas, Kevin Cooney, David Doty. Hackman is wallowing in self-pity over his drowned wife, as creditors duplicitously plot foreclosure on his coastal Texas bar. Also involved in the talky interchange are feisty bus driver Garr, Hackman's elderly father-in-law Meredith, and mentally shaky employee Koteas. This screen original by playwright Bill Bozzone feels like bad theater. [R]▼●

Full Moon in Paris (1984-French) **C-102m.** *** D: Eric Rohmer. Pascale Ogier, Fabrice Luchini, Tcheky Karyo, Christian Vadim, Virginie Thevenet. Neat little comedy from Rohmer about a headstrong young woman (Ogier), and her relationships with three men. Wonderful dialogue and characterizations, with a charming Ogier performance. [R]▼◗

Full of Life (1956) **91m.** *** D: Richard Quine. Judy Holliday, Richard Conte, Salvatore Baccaloni, Esther Minciotti. Holliday's pregnant wife antics almost matched by Baccaloni's as excitable father-in-law with his own way of running things. ▼

Full Treatment, The SEE: **Stop Me Before I Kill!**

Fun (1993) **C-105m.** *** D: Rafal Zielinski. Alicia Witt, Renee Humphrey, William R. Moses, Leslie Hope, Ania Suli. Jarring account of seemingly average young suburban teens who have just murdered a trusting elderly woman, for the "fun" of it! A thoughtful, disquieting film, every bit as impressive as HEAVENLY CREATURES, featuring riveting performances by its talented young leads. A biting commentary on "celebrity" in America. ▼

Funeral, The (1984-Japanese) **C-124m.** *** D: Juzo Itami. Nobuko Miyamoto, Tsutomu Yamazaki, Kin Sugai, Ichiro Zaitsu, Nekohachi Edoya. Itami's debut feature is an on-target black comedy that chides solemn, traditional Japanese funeral rites. The scenario details what ensues when a modern family is compelled to hold a Buddhist funeral for its patriarch—who happened to own a brothel.▼◗

Funeral, The (1996) **C-99m.** **½ D: Abel Ferrara. Christopher Walken, Chris Penn, Annabella Sciorra, Isabella Rossellini, Vincent Gallo, Benicio Del Toro, Gretchen Mol, John Ventimiglia, Paul Hipp, Victor Argo. Moody 1930s gangster film which follows what happens as thug siblings Walken and Penn respond to the murder of their Communist kid brother (Gallo). Occasionally meanders, and the flashbacks are confusing, but there's atmosphere to spare, and Ferrara vividly depicts a macho world in which one must be unfeeling and conquer his fears in order to attain "manhood." He also deals with his familiar themes of God and religion in a world of brutality. [R] ▼●

Funeral Home (1982-Canadian) **C-93m.** ** D: William Fruet. Lesleh Donaldson, Kay Hawtrey, Barry Morse, Dean Garbett, Stephen Miller, Harvey Atkin. Teenager Donaldson investigates when guests begin disappearing from grandmother Hawtrey's summer motel. OK of its type; aka CRIES IN THE NIGHT. [R]▼

Funeral in Berlin (1966) **C-102m.** ** D: Guy Hamilton. Michael Caine, Eva Renzi, Paul Hubschmid, Oscar Homolka, Guy Doleman. Second of three Harry Palmer films (based on Len Deighton's novels) featuring Caine as the British spy arranging for defection of Russian officer in charge of Berlin war security. Caine and Homolka are good, Renzi attractive, but slow-moving tale just doesn't click. Followed by BILLION DOLLAR BRAIN. Panavision.▼●

Funhouse, The (1981) **C-96m.** **½ D: Tobe Hooper. Elizabeth Berridge, Cooper Huckabee, Miles Chapin, Largo Woodruff, Sylvia Miles, William Finley, Kevin Conway. Intense drama about four teenagers who decide to spend night in funhouse of a sleazy traveling carnival. Once inside, there is sex, violence, suspense and an increasing tension as they encounter the unknown. Stylish visuals help create an eerie atmosphere in this not entirely successful chiller. Panavision. [R]▼●

Fun in Acapulco (1963) **C-97m.** **½ D: Richard Thorpe. Elvis Presley, Ursula Andress, Paul Lukas, Alejandro Rey. Scenery outshines story of Presley working as lifeguard and entertainer in Mexican resort city and performing the likes of "No Room to Rhumba in a Sports Car," "Bossa Nova Baby," and "You Can't Say No in Acapulco." Lukas is amusing as temperamental chef.▼

Funland (1986) **C-105m.** BOMB D: William Vanderkloot. David Lander, William Windom, Bruce Mahler, Robert Sacchi, Lane Davies, Mike McManus, Jan Hooks, Susan Ursitti. Limp mishmash about the various goings-on in an amusement park. Borrows elements of POLICE ACADEMY, MASH, PLAY IT AGAIN, SAM, and MAGIC—to no avail. [PG-13]▼●

Fun Loving SEE: **Quackser Fortune Has a Cousin in the Bronx**

Funny About Love (1990) **C-101m.** *½ D: Leonard Nimoy. Gene Wilder, Christine Lahti, Mary Stuart Masterson, Robert Prosky, Stephen Tobolowsky, Anne Jackson, Susan Ruttan, Jean De Baer, David Margulies. Cartoonist Wilder and caterer Lahti can't conceive, despite the latest techniques of their laugh-a-minute fertility doctor; ensuing problems force Gene to take up with college sorority sister Masterson, obviously many years younger. Terminally mild comedy with odd, ham-handed flickers of black humor. [PG-13]▼●

Funny Bones (1995-British-U.S.) **C-126m.** **½ D: Peter Chelsom. Oliver Platt, Lee Evans, Richard Griffiths, Leslie Caron, Jerry Lewis, Oliver Reed, Ian McNeice, George Carl, Freddie Davies, Ruta Lee, Harold Nicholas. Son of a famous and beloved comedian tries to make it on his own; when he fails, he goes back to Blackpool, England, to search for material—and his roots. Extraordinarily strange movie has many endearing moments (especially when it resurrects nuggets of show business past) but so many oddities that it never adds up—or figures out what it wants to be. Jerry is great, as Platt's father, and Caron is a delight as well. [R]▼●

Funny Face (1957) **C-103m.** ***½ D:

Stanley Donen. Audrey Hepburn, Fred Astaire, Kay Thompson, Michel Auclair, Suzy Parker, Ruta Lee. Stylish and highly stylized musical with Astaire as fashion photographer who turns Hepburn into chic Paris model. Top Gershwin score ("How Long Has This Been Going On," "He Loves and She Loves," "S'Wonderful," title tune), striking use of color, entertaining performance by Thompson as magazine editor. Cinematography by Ray June and John P. Fulton. Leonard Gershe based his screenplay on an unproduced stage musical—and Astaire's role was based on Richard Avedon, who's credited as visual consultant. VistaVision.▼●

Funny Farm, The (1982-Canadian) **C-95m.** ** D: Ron Clark. Miles Chapin, Eileen Brennan, Jack Carter, Tracy Bregman, Howie Mandel, Marjorie Gross, Lou Dinos, Peter Aykroyd. Young man from Ohio comes to L.A. to make it as a stand-up comic. Slow-moving film introduces many unknown comics who do short bits at a "comedy store" owned by Brennan. Some funny moments, but film as a whole is nothing much. [R]▼

Funny Farm (1988) **C-101m.** **½ D: George Roy Hill. Chevy Chase, Madolyn Smith, Joseph Maher, Jack Gilpin, Brad Sullivan, MacIntyre Dixon, Glenn Plummer, Mike Starr, Sarah Michelle Gellar. Oddly easygoing—and thus mildly endearing—Chase comedy about a N.Y. sportswriter who discovers, MR. BLANDINGS style, that country living isn't quite what it's cracked up to be. Has the look of quality (it was photographed by Miroslav Ondricek, designed by Henry Bumstead) but too many gags fizzle. Final episode is the best. [PG]▼●◗

Funny Girl (1968) **C-155m.** *** D: William Wyler. Barbra Streisand, Omar Sharif, Kay Medford, Anne Francis, Walter Pidgeon, Lee Allen, Gerald Mohr. Streisand's Oscar-winning film debut as Fanny Brice, singer-comedienne whose unhappy private life contrasted comic antics onstage. Bad as biography, but first-rate as musical, including fine Bob Merrill–Jule Styne score ("People," title tune), memorable tugboat finale to "Don't Rain on My Parade," plus Brice standards "My Man" and "Second Hand Rose." Sequel: FUNNY LADY. Panavision. [G]▼●

Funny Lady (1975) **C-137m.** **½ D: Herbert Ross. Barbra Streisand, James Caan, Omar Sharif, Roddy McDowall, Ben Vereen, Carole Wells, Colleen Camp. FUNNY GIRL sequel shows Fanny Brice at height of career, meeting and marrying ambitious showman Billy Rose (Caan). Disjointed film has fine moments of music and comedy, but a cliché-ridden script to contend with. Panavision. [PG] ▼●

Funnyman (1967) **C-98m.** *** D: John Korty. Peter Bonerz, Sandra Archer, Carol Androsky, Larry Hankin, Barbara Hiken, Gerald Hiken. Winning little film about improvisational comic (Bonerz) who's nagged by the idea that he should be doing something more "important." Features great skits by The Committee and funny animated spoofs by director Korty.

Funny Thing Happened on the Way to the Forum, A (1966) **C-99m.** **½ D: Richard Lester. Zero Mostel, Phil Silvers, Buster Keaton, Jack Gilford, Michael Crawford, Annette Andre, Michael Hordern. Frenzied adaptation of Broadway musical about conniving slave (Mostel) in ancient Rome; tries too hard, comes off forced. Still, with great comic cast, there's plenty worth seeing. Self-spoof on song "Lovely" is a highlight; score by Stephen Sondheim.▼●◗

Fun on a Weekend (1947) **93m.** ** D: Andrew L. Stone. Eddie Bracken, Priscilla Lane, Tom Conway, Allen Jenkins, Arthur Treacher, Alma Kruger. Scatterbrain fluff as Bracken and Lane maneuver their way from penniless fortune to love and riches, all in the course of a day.

Fun With Dick and Jane (1977) **C-95m.** **½ D: Ted Kotcheff. Jane Fonda, George Segal, Ed McMahon, Dick Gautier, Allan Miller, John Dehner. Lightly amusing comedy about Segal losing his job, he and wife Fonda trying to cope with no income and finally turning to crime. Falls apart after promising start, becoming fragmented and pointless. Watch for Jay Leno in a bit. [PG]▼

Furies, The (1950) **109m.** **½ D: Anthony Mann. Barbara Stanwyck, Walter Huston, Wendell Corey, Gilbert Roland, Judith Anderson, Beulah Bondi, Thomas Gomez, Albert Dekker, Blanche Yurka, Wallace Ford. Well-directed but talky psychological Western, detailing Stanwyck's complex love-hate relationship with tyrannical cattle rancher father Huston (in his final role). Heavy going at times.

Further Adventures of Tennessee Buck, The (1988) **C-88m.** **½ D: David Keith. David Keith, Kathy Shower, Brant van Hoffman, Sydney Lassick, Tiziana Stella, Patrizia Zanetti. Fun imitation of the INDIANA JONES films; big white hunter Keith goes on safari in Borneo with former *Playboy* Playmate of the Year Shower and her rich nerd husband van Hoffman. They meet up with a cannibal tribe whose women give Shower a vivid oil rubdown (the film's highlight). Actor-director Keith maintains a breezy tone. [R]▼●

Further Adventures of the Wilderness Family, The (1978) **C-105m.** *** D: Frank Zuniga. Robert Logan, Susan D. Shaw, Heather Rattray, Ham Larsen, George (Buck) Flower, Brian Cutler. This clone of 1975's family hit ADVENTURES OF . . . has same cast, same elements, same magnificent Colorado scenery. So who's to argue with success? Also known as WILDERNESS FAMILY, THE, PART 2; followed by MOUNTAIN FAMILY ROBINSON.▼

Further Perils of Laurel and Hardy, The (1968) **99m.** **½ D: Robert Youngson. Laurel and Hardy, Charley Chase, Max Davidson, James Finlayson. Repetitious format of "episodes" dulls edge of great material, but still fun, with rare L&H silent footage, pleasing interludes by Chase and Davidson.▼

Fury (1936) **94m.** ***½ D: Fritz Lang. Sylvia Sidney, Spencer Tracy, Walter Abel, Bruce Cabot, Edward Ellis, Walter Brennan, Frank Albertson. Still timely drama of lynch mobs and mob rule in small town, making hardened criminal of innocent Tracy, spoiling his love for sweetheart Sidney. Lang's first American film; he also scripted with Bartlett Cormack, from a Norman Krasna story. Also shown in computer-colored version.▼

Fury, The (1978) **C-118m.** *** D: Brian De Palma. Kirk Douglas, John Cassavetes, Carrie Snodgress, Amy Irving, Fiona Lewis, Andrew Stevens, Charles Durning, Gordon Jump, Dennis Franz. Stylish trash about young woman (Irving) with psychokinetic powers, and Douglas' desperate attempt to save his similarly gifted son from being used—or destroyed. Bloody and violent—the ultimate litmus test for those who prefer form over content. Film debut of Daryl Hannah; look fast for James Belushi as an extra. [R] ▼●

Fury at Furnace Creek (1948) **88m.** ** D: H. Bruce Humberstone. Victor Mature, Coleen Gray, Glenn Langan, Reginald Gardiner, Albert Dekker. Ordinary Western tale of Mature erasing mar on father's career against formidable opposition.

Fury at Gunsight Pass (1956) **68m.** ** D: Fred F. Sears. David Brian, Neville Brand, Richard Long, Lisa Davis. Occasionally actionful Western, in which outlaw gang takes over a town.

Fury at Showdown (1957) **75m.** *½ D: Gerd Oswald. John Derek, John Smith, Carolyn Craig, Nick Adams. Peace-loving man branded a coward, must shoot it out to rescue his girl.

Fury at Smuggler's Bay (1961-British) **92m.** ** D: John Gilling. Peter Cushing, Michele Mercier, Bernard Lee, George Coulouris, Liz Fraser. Sea yarn of pirates scavenging passing ships and reaping rewards off the English coastline. Panascope.

Fury of the Congo (1951) **69m.** *½ D: William Berke. Johnny Weissmuller, Sherry Moreland, William Henry, Lyle Talbot. Jungle Jim nonsense about a gang of smugglers who are out to capture strange animals called Okongos whose secretions form a potent narcotic.▼

Future Cop SEE: **Trancers**

Future Shock (1994) **C-93m.** ** D: Eric Parkinson, Francis "Oley" Sassone, Matt Reeves. Vivian Schilling, Scott Thompson, Martin Kove, Sam Clay, Bill Paxton, Brion James, Sidney Lassick, James Karen, Amanda Foreman, Tim Doyle. This three-story film's setup: Evil experimenters test virtual-reality scenarios on unsuspecting psychiatric patients. A frightened woman can't get her husband to understand her fears of urban violence and wolves in Malibu; a mild nerd is victimized by his punkish new roommate; a photographer becomes obsessed with guarding against accidental death. Only the final segment shows real imagination. Unrated version runs 97m. [PG-13]▼●

Futureworld (1976) **C-104m.** *** D: Richard T. Heffron. Peter Fonda, Blythe Danner, Arthur Hill, Yul Brynner, Stuart Margolin, John Ryan. Suspenseful sequel to WESTWORLD has overtones of INVASION OF THE BODY SNATCHERS as robot duplicates try to take over. Short on action but intelligently done. [PG]▼

Futz (1969) **C-92m.** *½ D: Tom O'Horgan. Seth Allen, John Bakos, Mari-Claire Charba, Peter Craig, Sally Kirkland. Director O'Horgan, whose youthful touch made this a mild off-Broadway hit, brings bizarre tale to screen with disastrous results. No plot worth describing, except that there's a man in love with a pig.▼

Fuzz (1972) **C-92m.** ** D: Richard A. Colla. Burt Reynolds, Raquel Welch, Yul Brynner, Jack Weston, Tom Skerritt, Peter Bonerz, Steve Ihnat, James McEachin, Bert Remsen. Oddball film tries to mix laughs and excitement, to be the MASH of police dramas, but doesn't have the style to pull it off; another disappointment for Reynolds fans. Script by Evan Hunter from one of his *87th Precinct* stories, written as "Ed McBain." [PG]▼

Fuzzy Pink Nightgown, The (1957) **87m.** ** D: Norman Taurog. Jane Russell, Ralph Meeker, Adolphe Menjou, Keenan Wynn, Fred Clark, Una Merkel. Mediocre comedy. When movie star is kidnapped, everyone thinks it's a publicity gag.

F/X (1986) **C-106m.** *** D: Robert Mandel. Bryan Brown, Brian Dennehy, Diane Venora, Cliff De Young, Mason Adams, Jerry Orbach, Joe Grifasi, Josie DeGuzman, Martha Gehman. Movie special-effects man is hired to stage a phony "hit" with a Mafia man the target—but quickly learns that he's been double-crossed. Fast-moving, entertaining yarn that's a lot of fun, as long as you don't think about it for a moment afterward. Dennehy and Grifasi make a hilarious pair of Mutt and Jeff cops. Angela Bassett's film debut. Followed by a sequel and a TV series. [R]▼●

F/X2 (1991) **C-109m.** **½ D: Richard Franklin. Bryan Brown, Brian Dennehy, Rachel Ticotin, Joanna Gleason, Philip

Bosco, Kevin J. O'Connor, Tom Mason, Dominic Zamprogna, Josie DeGuzman, John Walsh, James Stacy. Special-effects whiz Brown agrees to use his skills in a police case, but when things go wrong he finds himself embroiled in a deadly cover-up—and calls on his ex-cop pal Dennehy to help. Amiable sequel has some engaging gimmickry, but the story gets too lumpy. [PG-13]▼●

Gabbeh (1996-Iranian-French) **C-75m.** ***½ D: Mohsen Makhmalbaf. Shaghayegh Djodat, Hossein Moharami, Roghieh Moharami, Abbas Sayahi. Simple, sweet allegory in which an elderly woman washes a *gabbeh* (carpet) by the side of a river. From the *gabbeh* emerges a young woman, a member of a nomadic tribe who recounts a series of related stories. This elegantly lyrical, stunningly visual fable allows a peek into a non Western culture and the way it records its history.▼

Gable and Lombard (1976) **C-131m.** BOMB D: Sidney J. Furie. James Brolin, Jill Clayburgh, Allen Garfield, Red Buttons, Joanne Linville, Melanie Mayron. Pure tripe about offscreen romance of two great stars. Brolin and Clayburgh are game but one-dimensional; script and direction are hopeless. [R]

Gabriela (1983-Brazilian-Italian) **C-102m.** ** D: Bruno Barreto. Marcello Mastroianni, Sonia Braga, Antonio Cantafora, Ricardo Petraglia. Obvious tale of barkeeper Mastroianni taking on luscious, free-spirited Braga as a cook and lover. Braga's body and smile are the main interests here. Based on Jorge Amado's novel, which was developed into a top soap opera on Brazilian television. [R]▼

Gabriel Over the White House (1933) **87m.** *** D: Gregory La Cava. Walter Huston, Karen Morley, Franchot Tone, C. Henry Gordon, Samuel S. Hinds, Jean Parker, Dickie Moore. Dizzying Depression fantasy of crooked Huston elected President, experiencing mysterious change that turns him into Superpresident, determined to eliminate racketeers, find world peace. Bizarre, fascinating.▼●

Gaby (1956) **C-97m.** **½ D: Curtis Bernhardt. Leslie Caron, John Kerr, Sir Cedric Hardwicke, Taina Elg. Remake of WATERLOO BRIDGE, telling of ballerina Caron and her romance with soldier Kerr in WW2 England; not up to original. CinemaScope.

Gaby—A True Story (1987) **C-110m.** *** D: Luis Mandoki. Liv Ullmann, Norma Aleandro, Robert Loggia, Rachel Levin (Chagall), Lawrence Monoson, Robert Beltran, Tony Goldwyn. Incredible true story of Gaby Brimmer, born with cerebral palsy to wealthy European refugee parents in Mexico, leaving her body almost completely paralyzed—but not affecting her mind. Levin, who is not disabled in real life, gives a stunning performance in the lead (matched by Monoson as her boyfriend), with Aleandro a tower of strength as the woman who devotes her life to Gaby. An often painful but worthwhile film. Brimmer executive-produced. [R]▼●

Gadjo Dilo (1998-French-Romanian) **C-97m.** ** D: Tony Gatlif. Romain Duris, Rona Hartner, Izidor Serban, Ovidiu Balan, Angela Serban. During a bleak Romanian winter, a young Frenchman hoping to track down a legendary folk singer gets involved with a group of Gypsy villagers, becomes "adopted" by a loud old drunk, and falls in love with a peasant woman. Things get complicated when the drunk's real son, a Gypsy mafioso, arrives fresh from jail. Overdone and melodramatic, this story too often plays on one note. Aka CRAZY STRANGER.▼

Gaily, Gaily (1969) **C-107m.** ** D: Norman Jewison. Beau Bridges, Melina Mercouri, Brian Keith, George Kennedy, Hume Cronyn, Margot Kidder, Wilfrid Hyde-White, Melodie Johnson. Ben Hecht's colorful memories of apprenticeship on Chicago newspaper are destroyed by silly, hollow script that even changes "Hecht" to "Harvey." Expensive sets, period flavor are only bright spots in contrived comedy. Kidder's film debut. [M]

Galaxina (1980) **C-95m.** *½ D: William Sachs. Stephen Macht, Dorothy R. Stratten, James David Hinton, Avery Schreiber. Cheap STAR WARS/STAR TREK spoof reeks of low production values, boring scenario, and non-acting. Definitely not a vehicle for the late Ms. Stratten, though the film is of interest for her appearance as a robot. Panavision. [R]▼●◗

Galaxy of Terror (1981) **C-80m.** *½ D: B. D. Clark. Edward Albert, Erin Moran, Ray Walston, Bernard Behrens, Zalman King, Sid Haig. Astronauts are killed off by monsters while on mission to aid spaceship marooned on another planet. A Grade D ALIEN clone. Aka MINDWARP: AN INFINITY OF TERROR and PLANET OF HORRORS. Followed by FORBIDDEN WORLD. [R]▼●

Galaxy Quest (1999) **C-104m.** *** D: Dean Parisot. Tim Allen, Sigourney Weaver, Alan Rickman, Tony Shalhoub, Sam Rockwell, Daryl Mitchell, Enrico Colantoni, Robin Sachs, Patrick Breen, Missi Pyle. Engaging comedy about the washed-up cast of a *Star Trek*-like TV show now reduced to making personal appearances at fan conventions; suddenly they're whisked off to a starship where an alien civilization (believing their television adventures to be real) seeks their help to save the aliens from oblivion. By Grabthar's hammer, it's clever, funny, and sweet. Panavision. [PG]▼◗

Galileo (1973-British) **C-145m.** *** D:

Joseph Losey. Topol, Edward Fox, Colin Blakely, Georgia Brown, Clive Revill, Margaret Leighton, John Gielgud, Michael Gough, Judy Parfitt, Patrick Magee, Tom Conti. Bertolt Brecht's play, whose 1947 U.S. premiere was staged by director Losey, turned into unremarkable but generally satisfactory film. Topol is a little much as the scientist whose theories of the universe confound the church, but supporting actors are excellent. An American Film Theatre Production. [PG]▼

Gallant Bess (1946) **C-101m.** ** D: Andrew Marton. Marshall Thompson, George Tobias, Jim Davis, Clem Bevans, Donald Curtis, Chill Wills. Blah MGM B-movie is a grown-up version of concurrent THE YEARLING—soldier takes army horse home with him; it eventually saves his life. The first MGM film produced in CineColor, if that's your idea of a milestone.

Gallant Blade, The (1948) **C-81m.** ** D: Henry Levin. Larry Parks, Marguerite Chapman, Victor Jory, George Macready. Colorful, standard swashbuckler with dashing Parks protecting French general from villainous plot.

Gallant Hours, The (1960) **111m.** *** D: Robert Montgomery. James Cagney, Dennis Weaver, Ward Costello, Richard Jaeckel. Sincere, low-key biog of WW2 Admiral "Bull" Halsey played documentary-style. Cagney is reserved and effective, but production needs livening.▼

Gallant Journey (1946) **85m.** **½ D: William Wellman. Glenn Ford, Janet Blair, Charles Ruggles, Henry Travers, Arthur Shields, Selena Royle. Ford pioneers glider plane development in 19th century. OK, but not as stirring as it's meant to be.

Gallant Lady (1934) **86m.** ** D: Gregory LaCava. Ann Harding, Clive Brook, Otto Kruger, Tulio Carminati, Dickie Moore, Janet Beecher. Handsome but standard soaper about unwed Harding giving up baby for adoption, later hoping for second chance when adopted mother dies. Remade as ALWAYS GOODBYE.

Gallery of Horror SEE: **Return From the Past**

Gallipoli (1981-Australian) **C-110m.** ***½ D: Peter Weir. Mark Lee, Mel Gibson, Bill Kerr, Robert Grubb, David Argue, Tim McKenzie. Youthful idealists Lee and Gibson enlist in the military, meet their fate in title WW1 battle. Engrossing human drama with meticulous direction, striking feel for period detail. Final freeze-frame shot is reminiscent of Robert Capa's classic Spanish Civil War photo of soldier at the moment of death. Panavision. [PG]▼●◗

Galloping Major (1950-British) **82m.** ** D: Henry Cornelius. Basil Radford, Jimmy Hanley, Janette Scott, A. E. Matthews, Rene Ray, Joyce Grenfell, Hugh Griffith, Sidney James. Crackerjack cast enlivens this so-so comedy about a retired major (Radford) who raises the funds to purchase a racehorse, with assorted comical complications.▼

Gal Who Took the West, The (1949) **C-84m.** ** D: Frederick de Cordova. Yvonne De Carlo, Charles Coburn, Scott Brady, John Russell. De Carlo is attractive as singer in 1890s Arizona who allows Brady and Russell to court her.

Gal Young 'Un (1979) **C-105m.** ***½ D: Victor Nunez. Dana Preu, David Peck, J. Smith, Gene Densmore, Jenny Stringfellow, Tim McCormick. Low-budget gem about Prohibition-era widow Preu charmed and then exploited by foppish hustler Peck. Effective performances, use of locales (near Gainesville, Florida), depiction of the era. From Marjorie Kinnan Rawlings story.▼

Gambit (1966) **C-109m.** *** D: Ronald Neame. Michael Caine, Shirley MacLaine, Herbert Lom, Roger C. Carmel, John Abbott. Gimmicky robbery yarn with scoundrel Caine hiring Eurasian MacLaine to carry out perfect heist of invaluable piece of sculpture; great fun. Techniscope.▼

Gamble, The (1988-Italian) **C-105m.** **½ D: Carlo Vanzina. Matthew Modine, Faye Dunaway, Jennifer Beals, Corinne Clery, Federica Moro, Ana Obregon, Vernon Wells, Feodor Chaliapin, Ian Bannen. So-so adventure in the TOM JONES mold, in which roguish Modine gambles with sinister countess Dunaway. The stakes: his life, for the family fortune she won from his father. Hokey and irrational, and the ending doesn't work, but it's still amusing (because the actors don't seem to be taking it seriously). [R]▼

Gambler, The (1974) **C-111m.** ** D: Karel Reisz. James Caan, Paul Sorvino, Lauren Hutton, Morris Carnovsky, Jacqueline Brookes, Burt Young, Carmine Caridi, Vic Tayback, Steven Keats, London Lee, M. Emmet Walsh, James Woods, Stuart Margolin. Misfire about college prof Caan's compulsion to gamble; much inferior to Altman's CALIFORNIA SPLIT. Written by James Toback. [R]▼●

Gambler, The (1997-Hungarian-French) **C-97m.** ** D: Károly Makk. Michael Gambon, Jodhi May, Polly Walker, Dominic West, Luise Rainer, William Houston. An adaptation of Dostoevsky's 1866 novel, this is as much about the writing of that book as the story the author was trying to tell. Fiction and reality merge as Dostoevsky, with huge debts from his gambling habit, signs away rights to his life's work unless he can deliver a new novel in just 27 days. Lacks emotional power, despite fine performances by Gambon and Rainer (who's making her first big-screen appearance since 1943's HOSTAGES). [R]

Gambler and the Lady, The (1952-British) **71m.** *½ D: Patrick Jenkins, Sam Newfield. Dane Clark, Kathleen Byron,

Naomi Chance, Meredith Edwards, Anthony Forwood, Eric Pohlmann. Tepid little drama of gambler Clark who falls in love, altering his unorthodox way of life.

Gambler From Natchez, The (1954) **C-88m.** ** D: Henry Levin. Dale Robertson, Debra Paget, Thomas Gomez, Lisa Daniels, Kevin McCarthy, Douglas Dick, Woody Strode. Set in 1840s, film focuses on Robertson's plot to eliminate trio of men who shot his father, a gambler caught cheating.

Gamblers, The (1969) **C-93m.** **½ D: Ron Winston. Suzy Kendall, Don Gordon, Pierre Olaf, Kenneth Griffith, Stuart Margolin, Faith Domergue. A team of card sharps work a cruise ship for high stakes; interesting international cast, nice views of Dubrovnik, resort town in Yugoslavia. [G]

Gambler's Choice (1944) **66m.** ** D: Frank McDonald. Chester Morris, Nancy Kelly, Russell Hayden, Lee Patrick, Lyle Talbot, Sheldon Leonard. Another variation of MANHATTAN MELODRAMA—three kids grow up: one becomes a lawman, the other a shady gambler, the third the nice girl they both love.▼

Gambling House (1950) **80m.** ** D: Ted Tetzlaff. Victor Mature, Terry Moore, William Bendix, Cleo Moore, Ann Doran. At times overly melodramatic account of man acquitted for murder, facing deportation as undesirable alien.

Gambling Lady (1934) **66m.** **½ D: Archie Mayo. Barbara Stanwyck, Pat O'Brien, Claire Dodd, Joel McCrea, C. Aubrey Smith. Honest professional gambler Stanwyck weds society boy McCrea; her motives are suspect because, after all, she's from "the other side of the tracks." So-so drama picks up in its second half. And isn't that Tyrone Power in a bit in the Park Avenue gambling scene?

Gamblin' Man SEE: **Cockfighter**

Game, The (1997) **C-128m.** ** D: David Fincher. Michael Douglas, Sean Penn, Carroll Baker, Deborah Kara Unger, Armin Mueller-Stahl, Peter Donat, James Rebhorn. Coldhearted financial whiz (Douglas) gets an unusual birthday present from his brother (Penn)—a gift certificate for a sophisticated recreational company that stages a "game," the nature of which is never revealed. Before long, Douglas' entire existence is stripped away, on a roller-coaster ride heading straight down. Unusually mean-spirited film offers no letup—and has no sense of humor, either. Filmed in San Francisco. Super 35. [R]▼●◗

Game for Vultures (1979-British) **C-106m.** BOMB D: James Fargo. Joan Collins, Richard Harris, Richard Roundtree, Ray Milland, Jana Cilliers, Sven-Bertil Taube, Denholm Elliott, John Parsonson, Ken Gampu. Tired cast in a dreadful drama about racial strife in Rhodesia. The subject matter may be worthy, but the result couldn't be more ponderous. [R]▼

Game Is Over, The (1966-French) **C-96m.** **½ D: Roger Vadim. Jane Fonda, Peter McEnery, Michel Piccoli, Tina Marquand, Jacques Monod. Fonda marries wealthy Piccoli, falls in love with and seduces his son (McEnery). Handsome, updated version of Zola's *La Curée* is not bad; at the time, best performance of Jane's career. Panavision. [R]▼

Gamekeeper, The (1980-British) **C-84m.** *** D: Kenneth Loach. Phil Askham, Rita May, Andrew Grubb, Peter Steels, Michael Hinchcliffe. Simple, effectively subtle tale of conservative young gamekeeper Askham, who sublimates his anger at being unable to crack the British class system.

Game of Danger (1954-British) **88m.** **½ D: Lance Comfort. Jack Warner, Veronica Hurst, Derek Farr. Offbeat study of two youngsters involved in homicide, with strange effects on their lives. Original title: BANG YOU'RE DEAD.

Game of Death, A (1946) **72m.** *½ D: Robert Wise. John Loder, Audrey Long, Edgar Barrier, Russell Wade, Russell Hicks, Jason Robards (Sr.), Noble Johnson. Second official version of THE MOST DANGEROUS GAME—madman Barrier hunts humans shipwrecked on his island. Moves well, but indifferently acted; nowhere nearly as exciting as the 1932 original. Next remake: RUN FOR THE SUN.

Game of Death (1978) **C-102m.** **½ D: Robert Clouse. Bruce Lee, Gig Young, Hugh O'Brian, Colleen Camp, Dean Jagger, Kareem Abdul-Jabbar, Chuck Norris. Lee died midway through production of this karate thriller. Six years later, Clouse reassembled the surviving actors and, with the use of doubles, completed the film. Standard fare until final, incredible half hour, when Lee goes one-on-one with each of the villains in some of the most explosive fight scenes ever filmed. Aka BRUCE LEE'S GAME OF DEATH. Panavision. [R]▼●◗

Games (1967) **C-100m.** **½ D: Curtis Harrington. Simone Signoret, James Caan, Katharine Ross, Don Stroud, Estelle Winwood. After arrival of mysterious Signoret at kinky newlywed N.Y.C. apartment, borderline pranks become deadly conspiracy. The trick: guess who's double-crossing whom. Attempts at deeper meanings unfulfilling, despite good cast. Techniscope.

Games, The (1970-British) **C-97m.** *½ D: Michael Winner. Michael Crawford, Stanley Baker, Ryan O'Neal, Charles Aznavour, Jeremy Kemp, Elaine Taylor, Kent Smith, Sam Elliott, Mona Washbourne. Dull film on potentially interesting subject: preparation of four runners for grueling 26-mile marathon in the Olympics.

Rafer Johnson plays one of the commentators. Panavision. [G]

Games Girls Play SEE: **Bunny Caper, The**

Game Show Models (1977) **C-89m.** ** D: David Neil Gottlieb. John Vickery, Diane Summerfield, Thelma Houston, Gilbert De Rush, Sid Melton, Dick Miller, Willie Bobo, Rae Sperling, Charles Champlin. Odd, sometimes effective mixture of satire and sexploitation, set in the lurid, behind-the-scenes world of TV game shows. A mishmash, but any drive-in movie with a supporting cast like that is at least worth the attempt. [R]

Games of Desire (1968) **90m.** ** D: Hans Albin. Ingrid Thulin, Claudine Auger, Paul Hubschmid. Thulin is married to Sweden's ambassador to Greece, forced to make love with various men because her husband digs his male secretary. Tepid tale of depravity doesn't have many explicit scenes, which will make the film longer than anyone wants.▼

Gamma People, The (1956-British) **79m.** ** D: John Gilling. Paul Douglas, Eva Bartok, Leslie Phillips, Walter Rilla. Douglas and Phillips happen upon comic-opera country ruled by scientists trying to create geniuses; they do, but sometimes brainless "goons" also. Worse, the geniuses have no emotions. Peculiar Ruritanian sci-fi adventure.▼

Gammera, The Invincible (1966-Japanese-U.S.) **88m.** *½ D: Noriaki Yuasi. Brian Donlevy, Albert Dekker, John Baragrey. A giant, jet-propelled fire-breathing space turtle terrorizes the earth following atomic explosion. First in a series of juvenile sci-fi films. Original Japanese version—without American actors and titled GAMERA—runs 82m. Daieiscope.▼●

Gandhi (1982-British-Indian) **C-188m.** ***½ D: Richard Attenborough. Ben Kingsley, Candice Bergen, Edward Fox, John Gielgud, Trevor Howard, John Mills, Martin Sheen, Rohini Hattangandy, Ian Charleson, Athol Fugard, Roshan Seth, Saeed Jaffrey, John Ratzenberger, Geraldine James, Michael Hordern, Marius Weyers. Sweeping account of the life and times of Mohandas K. Gandhi, who rose from a position of simple lawyer to become a nation's leader and a worldwide symbol of peace and understanding. Storytelling at its best, in the tradition of great Hollywood epics, though film's second half is less riveting than the first. Kingsley gives an unforgettable performance in the lead. Eight Oscars include Best Picture, Actor, Director, Screenplay (John Briley). Look for Daniel Day-Lewis as one of three youths who accost Gandhi in the street. Panavision. [PG]▼●

Gang Busters (1955) **78m.** ** D: Bill Karan. Myron Healey, Don C. Harvey, Sam Edwards, Frank Gerstle. Standard prison-life drama, focusing on breakout plan.▼

Gang Related (1997) **C-111m.** ** D: Jim Kouf. James Belushi, Tupac Shakur, Dennis Quaid, Lela Rochon, James Earl Jones, David Paymer, Wendy Crewson, Gary Cole, T. C. Carson, Brad Greenquist. Corrupt cops Belushi and Shakur sell coke to dealers, then kill them and recycle the drugs, but their scam starts to unravel when one of their victims turns out to be an undercover DEA agent. Sleazy crime thriller maintains some interest for a while, but falls apart due to its laughably contrived script and a schizophrenic tone that alternates faux-nihilism with shameless sentimentality. The late Shakur shows some talent in his last role, but Belushi gives an embarrassingly hammy performance. Super 35. [R]▼●

Gang's All Here, The (1943) **C-103m.** **½ D: Busby Berkeley. Alice Faye, Carmen Miranda, Phil Baker, Benny Goodman and Orchestra, Eugene Pallette, Charlotte Greenwood, Edward Everett Horton, Tony DeMarco, James Ellison, Sheila Ryan. Corny but visually dazzling wartime musical, with soldier Ellison going off to battle while both Faye and Ryan believe they're engaged to him. Two socko musical numbers courtesy of Berkeley: "The Lady with the Tutti-Frutti Hat" (featuring Miranda at her best) and the finale, "The Polka Dot Polka." Faye does "No Love, No Nothin'." And, as an added kitsch treat, Benny Goodman sings! Watch for June Haver as a hat-check girl, Jeanne Crain by the swimming pool.●

Gangs, Inc. (1941) **72m.** **½ D: Phil Rosen. Joan Woodbury, Jack LaRue, Linda Ware, John Archer, Vince Barnett, Allan (Alan) Ladd, Gavin Gordon. Fast-paced programmer with innocent Woodbury seeking revenge after shielding her boyfriend, and finding herself incarcerated on a hit-and-run rap. Of note for Ladd's supporting role as a reporter. Originally titled PAPER BULLETS, then CRIME, INC.▼

Gangster, The (1947) **84m.** *** D: Gordon Wiles. Barry Sullivan, Belita, Joan Lorring, Akim Tamiroff, Harry Morgan, John Ireland, Fifi D'Orsay, Shelley Winters. Sullivan gives strong performance as man who falls victim to his slum environment and ends up a vengeful crook.▼

Gangster Story (1959) **65m.** **½ D: Walter Matthau. Walter Matthau, Carol Grace, Bruce McFarlan, Garrett Wallberg. Straightforward, tight little gangster chronicle of a criminal mastermind and a local kingpin hooking up for a bank raid. ▼

Gang That Couldn't Shoot Straight, The (1971) **C-96m.** ** D: James Goldstone. Jerry Orbach, Leigh Taylor-Young, Jo Van Fleet, Lionel Stander, Robert De Niro, Herve Villechaize. Film version of Jimmy

Breslin's best-seller about comical, twelfth-rate N.Y.C. crooks is well cast, but adapted in slapdash fashion and directed without much feeling for the material. [PG] ▼

Gang War (1958) **75m.** **½ D: Gene Fowler, Jr. Charles Bronson, Kent Taylor, Jennifer Holden, John Doucette. Grade-B film tracing the savage events resulting from a teacher testifying against gang brutality. Regalscope.

Gang War (1962-British) **65m.** ** D: Frank Marshall. Sean Kelly, Eira Heath, David Davies, Sean Sullivan. Tame account of life among London gangsters.

Gangway for Tomorrow (1943) **69m.** ** D: John H. Auer. Margo, John Carradine, Robert Ryan, Amelita Ward, William Terry, Harry Davenport, James Bell, Charles Arnt, Wally Brown, Alan Carney. Lives of five workers in wartime munitions plant told in flashbacks; dated wartime fare with occasional bright moments. Written by Arch Oboler.

Garbage Pail Kids Movie, The (1987) **C-100m.** BOMB D: Rod Amateau. Anthony Newley, MacKenzie Astin, Katie Barberi. Crude live-action kiddie film "inspired" by the popular and controversial bubble-gum cards which feature creatures with names like Greaser Greg and Valerie Vomit. They all live in a garbage pail, where they are destined to be joined by the negative of this movie. [PG]▼

Garbo Talks (1984) **C-103m.** **½ D: Sidney Lumet. Anne Bancroft, Ron Silver, Carrie Fisher, Catherine Hicks, Steven Hill, Howard da Silva, Dorothy Loudon, Harvey Fierstein, Hermione Gingold, Mary McDonnell. Silver sets out to fulfill his dying mother's last request: to meet Greta Garbo. Bancroft is a treat as the feisty mom, but film is just a series of vignettes, occasionally poignant but overall self-conscious and contrived, further undermined by Cy Coleman's saccharine score. That's writer-performer Betty Comden as Garbo in the last scene. [PG-13]▼●

Garde à Vue (1981-French) **C-87m.** *** D: Claude Miller. Lino Ventura, Michel Serrault, Romy Schneider, Guy Marchand. Prominent lawyer Serrault, suspected of raping and murdering two girls, is interrogated by police inspectors Ventura and Marchand. Tense, involving drama, with fine performances by all.

Garden, The (1990-British) **C/B&W-92m.** **½ D: Derek Jarman. Tilda Swinton, Johnny Mills, Philip MacDonald, Roger Cook, Kevin Collins, Pete Lee-Wilson, Spencer Lee, Jody Graber, Michael Gough. Surreal, deeply personal union of images and sound, which tells (in very abstract terms) the story of the Passion of Christ; however, the Christ figure is replaced by a pair of homosexual lovers, who are destined to experience suffering and humiliation. As with most of Jarman's work, some will find it thought-provoking while others will be bored (if not offended). ▼

Garden Murder Case, The (1936) **62m.** **½ D: Edwin L. Marin. Edmund Lowe, Virginia Bruce, Benita Hume, Douglas Walton, Nat Pendleton, Gene Lockhart, H. B. Warner. Philo Vance (Lowe) tracks a cunning killer who uses hypnosis to induce his victims to do themselves in. Fast-moving programmer.

Garden of Allah, The (1936) **C-80m.** ** D: Richard Boleslawski. Marlene Dietrich, Charles Boyer, Tilly Losch, Basil Rathbone, Joseph Schildkraut, Henry Kleinbach (Henry Brandon), John Carradine. Flagrantly silly romance set in the Algerian desert; full of ripe dialogue, troubled glances, beauty shots of Marlene in a variety of gorgeous sheaths and flowing gowns, and some wonderful Technicolor scenery (which helped win its cameramen, W. Howard Greene and Harold Rosson, a special Oscar). It just isn't very good. ▼

Garden of Evil (1954) **C-100m.** **½ D: Henry Hathaway. Gary Cooper, Susan Hayward, Richard Widmark, Hugh Marlowe, Cameron Mitchell, Rita Moreno. Meandering adventure set in 1850s Mexico, with trio escorting Hayward through bandit territory to save her husband. CinemaScope.

Garden of the Finzi-Continis, The (1971-Italian) **C-95m.** **** D: Vittorio De Sica. Dominique Sanda, Lino Capolicchio, Helmut Berger, Fabio Testi, Romolo Valli. Exquisitely photographed drama about aristocratic Jewish family in WW2 Italy which conveniently ignores the spectre of the concentration camp until it's too late. Sad, haunting film boosted Sanda to stardom and won an Oscar as Best Foreign Film. Screenplay by Cesare Zavattini, Vittorio Bonicelli, and Ugo Pirro; from novel by Giorgio Bassani. [R]▼●

Garden of the Moon (1938) **94m.** **½ D: Busby Berkeley. Pat O'Brien, Margaret Lindsay, John Payne, Johnnie Davis, Melville Cooper, Isabel Jeans, Penny Singleton. Nightclub owner O'Brien and bandleader Payne have running feud; plot is pleasant excuse to work in many Berkeley numbers: "Girlfriend Of The Whirling Dervish," "Love Is Where You Find It," title tune.

Gardens of Stone (1987) **C-111m.** **½ D: Francis Coppola. James Caan, Anjelica Huston, James Earl Jones, D. B. Sweeney, Dean Stockwell, Mary Stuart Masterson, Dick Anthony Williams, Lonette McKee, Sam Bottoms, Larry Fishburne. Well-acted story about life in Arlington National Cemetery's home guard during the thick of the Vietnam war—and one young soldier's determination to go into battle. Strong performances keep it going most of the way, but toward the end the dialogue sounds hollow, like the sentiment itself. Carmine

Coppola's funereal music doesn't help. Jones steals the show in a warm-hearted role; young leading lady Masterson's real-life parents, Peter Masterson and Carlin Glynn, play her folks on screen. [R]▼●

Gargoyles (1972) **C-74m. TVM** D: B. W. L. Norton. Cornel Wilde, Jennifer Salt, Bernie Casey, Grayson Hall, Woodrow Chambliss, Scott Glenn. Anthropologist Wilde and daughter on trip to Mexico, stop off at wilderness curio station, come upon unusual skeleton. A very good beginning but deteriorates halfway through story. Flawless use of locations. Outstanding—and plentiful—monster suits by Stan Winston. Average.▼●◗

Garment Jungle, The (1957) **88m.** **½ D: Vincent Sherman. Lee J. Cobb, Kerwin Mathews, Gia Scala, Richard Boone, Valerie French, Robert Loggia, Joseph Wiseman, Harold J. Stone. Well-handled account of union-gangster corruption in dressmaking industry, with romantic interludes slowing down violent pace.

Gas (1981-Canadian) **C-94m.** BOMB D: Les Rose. Donald Sutherland, Susan Anspach, Howie Mandel, Sterling Hayden, Sandee Currie, Peter Aykroyd, Helen Shaver. Noisy, moronic garbage about the effect of a phony gas shortage on an "average" American town. Car crashes *ad nauseam*, with Sutherland wasted as Nick the Noz, a hip disc jockey. [R]▼

Gas, Food Lodging (1992) **C-101m.** **½ D: Allison Anders. Brooke Adams, Ione Skye, Fairuza Balk, James Brolin, Robert Knepper, David Lansbury, Jacob Vargas, Donovan Leitch, Chris Mulkey, Tiffany Anders. Truck-stop waitress struggles to raise two daughters in a Laramie, N.M., trailer park, with the older one already jaded by men and the younger idealistic to the end. Overrated by some, but still fairly passionate despite a slender budget and minimalist cinematics. Good performances extend to Brolin's, as a wandering dad. Skye (Trudi) and Leitch (Darius) are real-life sister and brother. [R]▼●

Gaslight (1940-British) **84m.** ***½ D: Thorold Dickinson. Anton Walbrook, Diana Wynyard, Frank Pettingell, Cathleen Cordell, Robert Newton, Jimmy Hanley. First version of Patrick Hamilton's play about an insane criminal who drives his wife crazy in order to discover hidden jewels. Electrifying atmosphere, delicious performances, and a succinctly conveyed sense of madness and evil lurking beneath the surface of the ordinary. MGM supposedly tried to destroy the negative of this original when they filmed the remake. Screenplay by A. R. Rawlinson and Bridget Boland. U.S. title: ANGEL STREET.▼

Gaslight (1944) **114m.** *** D: George Cukor. Ingrid Bergman, Charles Boyer, Joseph Cotten, Dame May Whitty, Angela Lansbury, Terry Moore. The bloom has worn off this classic chiller about a man trying to drive his wife insane, but lush production, Victorian flavor, and fine performances remain intact. Bergman won Oscar; Lansbury's film debut. Filmed before in 1940. Also shown in computer-colored version.▼●

Gaslight Follies (1945) **77m.** *½ D: Joseph E. Levine. Charlie Chaplin, Harold Lloyd, Mary Pickford, Douglas Fairbanks, Marie Dressler, William S. Hart, Lillian Gish, Rudolph Valentino, many others. This pointless hodgepodge consists mostly of fleeting clips of scores of silent-era stars. Also included are newsreel excerpts, and silent versions of THE DRUNKARD and EAST LYNNE.▼

Gas-s-s-s (1970) **C-79m.** *** D: Roger Corman. Bud Cort, Cindy Williams, Robert Corff, Ben Vereen, Tally Coppola (Talia Shire), Elaine Giftos. Insane, often uproarious story focusing on reactions of youngsters in crisis: a gas kills everyone on Earth over 25. Reedited against Corman's wishes, causing much disjointedness, but stay with it. Aka GAS! OR IT BECAME NECESSARY TO DESTROY THE WORLD IN ORDER TO SAVE IT. [PG]▼

Gate, The (1987) **C-92m.** ** D: Tibor Takacs. Stephen Dorff, Christa Denton, Louis Tripp, Kelly Rowan, Jennifer Irwin, Deborah Grove, Scot Denton. It's a boring weekend: Dorff is grounded, his sister is babysitting while the parents are away—then he and a pal discover the gate to hell in their suburban backyard. Worthless first half is somewhat redeemed by amusing/scary special effects in the second; this low-budget horror film opened big the same week as ISHTAR and came close to beating it out as the No. 1 box-office attraction! Followed by a sequel. [PG-13]▼●

Gate II (1992) **C-95m.** *½ D: Tibor Takacs. Louis Tripp, Simon Reynolds, Pamela Segall, James Villemaire, Neil Munro, James Kidnie. The demons of the underworld are resummoned by now-teenaged Tripp to grant his wishes. Though his intentions are on the naive side, it's safe to say that all hell breaks loose. None of THE GATE's goofy fright made its way into this unnecessary sequel, although the special effects provide passing interest. This spent three years on the shelf. [R]▼●

Gate of Hell (1953-Japanese) **C-86m.** ***½ D: Teinosuke Kinugasa. Machiko Kyo, Kazuo Hasegawa, Isao Yamagata, Koreya Senda. Stark, stunning historical drama, set in 12th-century Japan, about a Samurai who falls in love with—and then tragically shames—a married woman. This beautiful production earned Oscars for Costume Design and Best Foreign Film.▼

Gates of Heaven (1978) **C-85m.** ***½ D: Errol Morris. Delightfully offbeat yet piercing documentary about a pet cemetery in—where else?—Southern California. At once hilarious and an allegory about the absurdity of American priorities. Not to be confused with Michael Cimino's HEAVEN'S GATE, or Stephen King's PET SEMATARY, for that matter.▼

Gates of Paris (1957-French-Italian) **96m.** *** D: René Clair. Pierre Brasseur, Georges Brassens, Henri Vidal, Dany Carrel. Sweet, human story of a souse (Brasseur), and what happens when he begins looking after a gangster (Vidal) who has taken refuge in the house of his friend (Brassens).

Gateway (1938) **73m.** ** D: Alfred L. Werker. Don Ameche, Arleen Whelan, Gregory Ratoff, Binnie Barnes, Gilbert Roland, Raymond Walburn, John Carradine, Harry Carey. Silly story of naive Irish immigrant Whelan pursued by reporter Ameche and various other men during ocean crossing; redeemed only by interesting Ellis Island background.

Gathering, The (1977) **C-92m. TVM** D: Randal Kleiser. Edward Asner, Maureen Stapleton, Lawrence Pressman, Stephanie Zimbalist, Bruce Davison, John Randolph, Gregory Harrison, Veronica Hamel, Gail Strickland. Sentimental Emmy-winning Christmas drama of a man who seeks to reunite his shattered family for one final celebration before he dies. Asner is solid as usual, but Stapleton is simply luminous as the wife who had lost him in his drive for success. Written by James Poe. Followed by a sequel. Above average.▼●

Gathering, Part II, The (1979) **C-98m. TVM** D: Charles S. Dubin. Maureen Stapleton, Efrem Zimbalist, Jr., Jameson Parker, Bruce Davison, Lawrence Pressman, Gail Strickland, Veronica Hamel. Soapy sequel: a widow's Christmas reunion with her grown children is marred by the arrival of a new man in her life. Ed Asner's photograph throughout reminds all how glowing the original was. Average.▼

Gathering of Eagles, A (1963) **C-115m.** *** D: Delbert Mann. Rock Hudson, Rod Taylor, Mary Peach, Barry Sullivan, Kevin McCarthy, Henry Silva, Leif Erickson. Crisp Strategic Air Command drama with novelty of peacetime setting; Hudson gives one of his best performances as less than likable colonel whose wife struggles to adjust to being a military spouse. Good script by Robert Pirosh. Look for Louise Fletcher as a patient's wife.▼

Gathering of Old Men, A (1987) **C-100m. TVM** D: Volker Schlöndorff. Louis Gossett, Jr., Richard Widmark, Holly Hunter, Joe Seneca, Woody Strode, Papa John Creach, Julius Harris, Will Patton. Ensemble acting at its best in this wonderful drama about a group of old black men from rural Louisiana who take the first courageous step of their long lives by coming forward en masse to take responsibility for the killing of a white racist whom one of their members has shot. Scripted by Charles Fuller, from the novel by Ernest J. Gaines—the authors, respectively, of A SOLDIER'S STORY and THE AUTOBIOGRAPHY OF MISS JANE PITTMAN. Video title: MURDER ON THE BAYOU. Above average.▼

Gatling Gun, The (1972) **C-93m.** *½ D: Robert Gordon. Guy Stockwell, Woody Strode, Patrick Wayne, Robert Fuller, Barbara Luna, John Carradine, Pat Buttram, Phil Harris. Cavalry, renegade soldiers, Apaches, fight over Gatling gun. Standard, forgettable Western. Aka KING GUN. Techniscope. [PG]▼

Gator (1976) **C-116m.** ** D: Burt Reynolds. Burt Reynolds, Jack Weston, Lauren Hutton, Jerry Reed, Alice Ghostley, Mike Douglas, Dub Taylor. Not-so-hot sequel to WHITE LIGHTNING, about Justice Dept. agent Weston and moonshiner ex-con Reynolds out to get the goods on corrupt Southern politicians. Some good action, but overlong and poorly constructed. Reynolds' directing debut. Todd-AO 35. [PG]▼●

Gator Bait (1976) **C-93m.** *½ D: Ferd and Beverly C. Sebastian. Claudia Jennings, Sam Gilman, Doug Dirkson, Clyde Ventura, Bill Thurman. All the menfolk are after sexy swamp-girl Desiree (*Playboy* Playmate of the Year Jennings) but she has a surprise or two in store for them. A tedious tease of a film, with moments of truly repellent violence. Followed by a sequel. [R]▼

Gator Bait II: Cajun Justice (1988) **C-95m.** *½ D: Ferd and Beverly C. Sebastian. Jan MacKenzie, Tray Loren, Jerry Armstrong, Paul Muzzcat, Ben Sebastian. Just what you've been waiting for: a sequel, with Loren as the brother of the character played in the original by the late Claudia Jennings. City girl MacKenzie is his new wife; after being harassed by some stereotypically slobbering backwoods boors, she goes into action. [R]▼●

Gattaca (1997) **C-112m.** *** D: Andrew Niccol. Ethan Hawke, Uma Thurman, Jude Law, Gore Vidal, Loren Dean, Alan Arkin, Xander Berkeley, Blair Underwood, Ernest Borgnine, Tony Shalhoub, Jayne Brook, Elias Koteas. In the near future, parents can choose to have all genetic imperfections eliminated from their children prior to birth. This has given rise to a new form of discrimination: the genetically perfected "Valids" vs. the naturally born "In-Valids." In-Valid Hawke pays disabled Valid Law for the rights to his identity. Bracingly intelligent, wittily ironic, and very well acted. Given the premise, however, the dull, conformist society depicted seems unconvincing. Notable directing debut for Niccol, who also scripted. Super 35. [PG-13]▼●◗

Gaucho, The (1927) **96m.** ** D: F. Richard Jones. Douglas Fairbanks, Lupe Velez, Eve Southern, Gustav von Seyffertitz, Nigel de Brulier, Geraine Greear (Joan Barclay). Corny melodramatics and moralizing and not enough action hamper this lesser Fairbanks vehicle, in which he plays a famed, egocentric South American cowboy. Mary Pickford, Fairbanks' wife, appears as "Our Lady of the Shrine."▼●

Gauntlet, The (1977) **C-109m.** **½ D: Clint Eastwood. Clint Eastwood, Sondra Locke, Pat Hingle, William Prince, Bill McKinney, Mara Corday. Eastwood stars as a none-too-clever cop escorting hooker Locke to trial; corrupt officials are determined to stop them, whatever the cost. Exciting at times, though its credibility factor is low. Panavision. [R]▼●◗

Gay Adventure, The (1953-British) **87m.** *** D: Gordon Parry. Burgess Meredith, Jean-Pierre Aumont, Paul Valenska, Kathleen Harrison. Interestingly done yarn of trio of men on a train theorizing about pretty girl sitting across from them.

Gay Bride, The (1934) **80m.** ** D: Jack Conway. Carole Lombard, Chester Morris, ZaSu Pitts, Leo Carrillo, Nat Pendleton. Unsatisfying blend of comedy and melodrama with gold-digging Lombard hitching herself to succession of gangsters.

Gay Deception, The (1935) **77m.** **½ D: William Wyler. Francis Lederer, Frances Dee, Benita Hume, Alan Mowbray, Lennox Pawle, Akim Tamiroff, Luis Alberni, Lionel Stander. Romantic trifle of working girl (Dee) on spree in N.Y.C., pursued by proletarian-posing prince (Lederer). A slight comedy engagingly handled by Wyler. The song "Paris in the Evening" was written by Preston Sturges!

Gay Desperado, The (1936) **85m.** **½ D: Rouben Mamoulian. Nino Martini, Ida Lupino, Leo Carrillo, Harold Huber, James Blakely, Stanley Fields, Mischa Auer. Jovial Mexican bandido Carrillo and his gang (who've learned how to be tough from Grade B gangster movies) recruit reluctant singer Martini and kidnap Lupino and her rich, wimpy boyfriend. Outlandishly silly, and pretty hard to take. ●

Gay Divorcee, The (1934) **107m.** ***½ D: Mark Sandrich. Fred Astaire, Ginger Rogers, Alice Brady, Edward Everett Horton, Erik Rhodes, Eric Blore, Betty Grable. Top Astaire-Rogers froth with usual needless plot and unusual musical numbers, including Oscar-winning "Continental" and Cole Porter's "Night and Day." Rhodes is memorable as would-be corespondent in divorce case. Incidentally, the Broadway hit on which this was based was called *The Gay Divorce,* but the Hollywood Production Code disapproved. ▼●

Gay Falcon, The (1941) **67m.** **½ D: Irving Reis. George Sanders, Wendy Barrie, Allen Jenkins, Anne Hunter, Gladys Cooper, Edward S. Brophy, Arthur Shields, Turhan Bey. In the first *Falcon* entry, the blithe amateur-sleuth and ladies' man is called on to break up a phony jewelry insurance scam. Very similar to Sanders' *The Saint* series, but still enjoyable. Incidentally, the title refers to the Falcon's first name, not his inclination.

Gay Lady, The (1949-British) **C-95m.** **½ D: Brian Desmond Hurst. Jean Kent, James Donald, Hugh Sinclair, Lana Morris, Bill Owen, Michael Medwin. Lightweight costume picture about saucy entertainer who marries nobility; most notable aspect of film is its stunning use of Technicolor. Look fast for Christopher Lee as a dapper stage-door Johnnie. Original British title: TROTTIE TRUE.▼

Gay Purr-ee (1962) **C-86m.** **½ D: Abe Levitow. Voices of Judy Garland, Robert Goulet, Red Buttons, Hermione Gingold, Paul Frees, Morey Amsterdam. A naive cat's misadventures in Paris. Stylish cartoon from UPA studio, written by Chuck and Dorothy Jones, lacks storytelling oomph. Chief assets are Garland and Goulet performing original songs by Harold Arlen and E. Y. Harburg, who wrote THE WIZARD OF OZ score for Judy years earlier.▼●

Gay Sisters, The (1942) **108m.** ** D: Irving Rapper. Barbara Stanwyck, George Brent, Geraldine Fitzgerald, Gig Young, Nancy Coleman, Donald Crisp, Gene Lockhart, Anne Revere. Stanwyck secretly marries Brent to gain inheritance money in thin soaper, immensely aided by Fitzgerald and Coleman as her sisters. Young took his name from the character he plays in this.

Gazebo, The (1959) **100m.** *** D: George Marshall. Glenn Ford, Debbie Reynolds, Carl Reiner, Doro Merande, John McGiver, Mabel Albertson. Offbeat comedy involving murder and a backyard gazebo that covers up crime. Character actors McGiver and Merande wrap this up, but stars are competent. Also shown in computer-colored version. CinemaScope.▼

Gazon Maudit SEE: **French Twist**

Geisha Boy, The (1958) **C-98m.** **½ D: Frank Tashlin. Jerry Lewis, Marie McDonald, Sessue Hayakawa, Nobu McCarthy, Suzanne Pleshette, Barton MacLane, Robert Hirano. Jerry, an inept magician, travels to Japan with disastrous consequences. Imaginative visual gags; there's a cute sequence featuring the Los Angeles Dodgers (and, in particular, Gil Hodges). Pleshette's film debut. VistaVision.▼

Gene Krupa Story, The (1959) **101m.** **½ D: Don Weis, Sal Mineo, Susan Kohner, James Darren, Susan Oliver, Yvonne Craig, Lawrence Dobkin, Red Nichols, Buddy Lester. Hackneyed version of great jazz drummer's life, his ups and downs, his siege of dope addiction.▼●

Genealogies of a Crime (1997-French) **C-114m.** **½ D: Raul Ruiz. Catherine Deneuve, Michel Piccoli, Melvil Poupaud, Andrzej Seweryn, Bernadette LaFont. Deneuve is dazzling in a dual role as the lawyer for and victim of a strange young man who's accused of murdering his psychiatrist aunt after she allegedly subjected him to radical mind-control treatments. Well-acted but pretentious, intentionally confusing mixture of mystery, satire, and surrealism; tricked up with meaningless flashbacks within flashbacks and other narrative and visual gimmicks.
General, The (1927) **74m.** **** D: Buster Keaton, Clyde Bruckman. Buster Keaton, Marion Mack, Glen Cavender, Jim Farley, Joseph Keaton. One of Keaton's best silent features, setting comedy against true Civil War story of stolen train, Union spies. Not as fanciful as other Keaton films, but beautifully done; Disney did same story in 1956 as THE GREAT LOCOMOTIVE CHASE. ▼●◗
General, The (1998-Irish) **124m.** **½ D: John Boorman. Brendan Gleeson, Jon Voight, Adrian Dunbar, Sean McGinley, Maria Doyle Kennedy, Angeline Ball, Eamonn Owens. Boorman scripted this character study of a true-life Dublin working-class criminal known as the General, who evaded police capture for years. Following his own skewed code of ethics, he masterminds robberies both large and small, extracts loyalty from his soldiers, loves two women simultaneously, and matches wits with a hard-nosed cop (Voight) who is determined to nail him. Interesting, well made, but overlong. Filmmaker Jim Sheridan has a bit part. Super 35. [R]▼●◗
General Della Rovere (1959-Italian) **129m.** ***½ D: Roberto Rossellini. Vittorio De Sica, Hannes Messemer, Sandra Milo, Giovanna Ralli, Anne Vernon. De Sica is brilliant as a con-man forced by the Nazis to impersonate a just-deceased Italian general and find out the identity of a Resistance leader. Will this charade somehow transform a coward into a hero?▼
General Died at Dawn, The (1936) **97m.** ***½ D: Lewis Milestone. Gary Cooper, Madeleine Carroll, Akim Tamiroff, Dudley Digges, Porter Hall, William Frawley. Fine, atmospheric drama of Oriental intrigue, with mercenary Cooper falling in love with spy Carroll while battling evil warlord Tamiroff. Author John O'Hara has cameo as reporter on train. Another celebrated writer, Clifford Odets, scripted from Charles Booth's novel.▼
General's Daughter, The (1999) **C-125m.** **½ D: Simon West. John Travolta, Madeleine Stowe, James Cromwell, Timothy Hutton, Leslie Stefanson, Daniel von Bargen, Clarence Williams III, James Woods, John Frankenheimer. Army investigator Travolta uncovers more than he ever imagined when he looks into the murder of a popular general's daughter, herself a captain. As evidence of a major scandal grows, it becomes clear that the Army's only concern is keeping a lid on the matter. Slickly done, but this twisty tale (from Nelson DeMille's best-seller) has a heavy air of contrivance about it. Panavision. [R]▼●◗
General Spanky (1936) **71m.** ** D: Fred Newmeyer, Gordon Douglas. George "Spanky" McFarland, Billie "Buckwheat" Thomas, Carl "Alfalfa" Switzer, Phillips Holmes, Ralph Morgan, Irving Pichel, Rosina Lawrence, Louise Beavers. Sluggish Civil War story, balancing kiddie antics against an adult romance, was intended to showcase three Our Gang stars in a feature-film format; it's easy to see why there wasn't an encore. Buckwheat's role as a slave in search of a master may displease contemporary audiences.▼●
Generation, A (1954-Polish) **88m.** *** D: Andrzej Wajda. Ursula Modrzinska, Tadeusz Lomnicki, Zbigniew Cybulski. Strong, necessarily downbeat drama about the Polish Resistance during World War 2 and what happens when a young man falls in love with the woman who leads the Resistance group. Wajda's first film and the first of a trilogy that includes the even better KANAL and ASHES AND DIAMONDS. Young Roman Polanski is featured in the cast.▼
Generation (1969) **C-104m.** ** D: George Schaefer. David Janssen, Kim Darby, Carl Reiner, Peter Duel, Andrew Prine, James Coco, Sam Waterston. Darby helps otherwise dreary comedy based on Broadway play about just-married couple who infuriate the girl's father when husband plans to deliver their soon-to-arrive baby himself; plays like a TV sitcom. [M/PG]▼
Genevieve (1953-British) **C-86m.** ***½ D: Henry Cornelius. Dinah Sheridan, John Gregson, Kay Kendall, Kenneth More, Geoffrey Keen, Joyce Grenfell, Michael Medwin. Lively, colorful comedy (by William Rose) pits two couples and their vintage roadsters against one another in a cross-country race. Uniquely British, brimming with charm and humor; a huge success in its day. Music score by harmonica virtuoso Larry Adler.▼
Genghis Khan (1965) **C-124m.** *½ D: Henry Levin. Omar Sharif, Stephen Boyd, James Mason, Eli Wallach, Francoise Dorleac, Telly Savalas, Robert Morley, Yvonne Mitchell, Woody Strode. Laughable epic with gross miscasting and juvenile script, loosely based on legend of Mongol leader. No sweep or spectacle, but radiant Dorleac and earnest Sharif. Panavision.
Genius at Work (1946) **61m.** *½ D: Leslie Goodwins. Wally Brown, Alan Carney, Lionel Atwill, Anne Jeffreys, Bela Lugosi, Marc Cramer. Radio detectives get involved

in real-life murder schemes of Atwill. Brown & Carney's last film as Abbott & Costello-like team is pretty weak; Lugosi is wasted. Remake of SUPER SLEUTH.

Gentle Annie (1944) **80m.** ** D: Andrew Marton. Donna Reed, Marjorie Main, Harry Morgan, James Craig, Barton MacLane. Main vehicle about female outlaw with heart of gold.

Gentle Art of Murder SEE: **Crime Does Not Pay**

Gentle Giant (1967) **C-93m.** *** D: James Neilson. Dennis Weaver, Vera Miles, Clint Howard, Ralph Meeker, Huntz Hall. Feature film which hatched TV series *Gentle Ben* is appealing children's story of boy and his pet bear.▼

Gentle Gunman, The (1952-British) **86m.** *** D: Basil Dearden. Dirk Bogarde, John Mills, Elizabeth Sellars, Robert Beatty. Unpretentious actioner of Irish revolution and enthusiast whose attempt to prove his patriotism backfires.

Gentleman After Dark (1942) **77m.** ** D: Edwin L. Marin. Brian Donlevy, Miriam Hopkins, Preston Foster, Harold Huber. Hodgepodge yarn of man escaping prison to redeem honor of his daughter by killing his shady wife; good cast stifled by sloppy script. Remake of FORGOTTEN FACES.

Gentleman at Heart, A (1942) **66m.** **½ D: Ray McCarey. Cesar Romero, Carole Landis, Milton Berle, J. Carrol Naish, Richard Derr. Modest little comedy about bookie Romero discovering there's money in art forgery.

Gentleman Jim (1942) **104m.** ***½ D: Raoul Walsh. Errol Flynn, Alexis Smith, Jack Carson, Alan Hale, John Loder, William Frawley, Minor Watson, Ward Bond, Arthur Shields. Sassy biography of polished boxer Jim Corbett in fight game's early days. Flynn is dynamic in title role (reportedly his favorite), supported by colorful cast—especially Bond in larger-than-life role as legendary champ John L. Sullivan. Scripted by Vincent Lawrence and Horace McCoy. Also shown in computer-colored version.▼●

Gentleman's Agreement (1947) **118m.** *** D: Elia Kazan. Gregory Peck, Dorothy McGuire, John Garfield, Celeste Holm, Anne Revere, June Havoc, Albert Dekker, Jane Wyatt, Dean Stockwell, Sam Jaffe. Sincere Oscar-winning adaptation of Laura Z. Hobson's novel of writer (Peck) pretending to be Jewish, discovering rampant anti-Semitism. Holm won Supporting Actress Oscar as chic but lonely fashion editor, as did Kazan for his direction. Then-daring approach to subject matter is tame now. Screenplay by Moss Hart. ▼●◗

Gentlemen Don't Eat Poets (1995-British) **C-97m.** ** D: John-Paul Davidson. Alan Bates, Sting, Theresa Russell, Lena Headey, Steven Mackintosh, Anna Massey, Trudie Styler, Maria Aitken. An English butler, in cooperation with the mistress of the house, frames his master for murder in this blackest of black British comedies. Other than its clever (and somewhat prophetic) title, this lacks the necessary wit to succeed. Sting is understated as the butler; you get the feeling he's doing it only because his wife, Trudie Styler, produced the film. Original title: THE GROTESQUE. Video title: GRAVE INDISCRETIONS. [R]▼●

Gentlemen Marry Brunettes (1955) **C-97m.** ** D: Richard Sale. Jane Russell, Jeanne Crain, Alan Young, Rudy Vallee, Scott Brady. Anita Loos' follow-up to GENTLEMEN PREFER BLONDES has Russell and Crain, two sisters in show biz in Paris, trying to avoid romances. Not up to original. CinemaScope.

Gentlemen Prefer Blondes (1953) **C-91m.** *** D: Howard Hawks. Jane Russell, Marilyn Monroe, Charles Coburn, Elliott Reid, Tommy Noonan, George "Foghorn" Winslow. Slick, colorful bauble of entertainment with two sassy leading ladies tantalizing the men of two continents; Marilyn is at her best as fortune-hunter Lorelei Lee, and Russell gives a sly, knowing comic performance as her pal. Based on the Broadway adaptation of Anita Loos' venerable story, with sprightly Leo Robin–Jule Styne songs including "Diamonds Are a Girl's Best Friend." Sequel: GENTLEMEN MARRY BRUNETTES.▼●

Gentle Rain, The (1966) **C-110m.** **½ D: Burt Balaban. Christopher George, Lynda Day, Fay Spain, Maria Helena Diaz, Lon Clark. Frigid N.Y.C. woman goes to Rio de Janeiro, falls for draughtsman who has been mute ever since he failed to save life of his former girlfriend in car crash. Fair.

Gentle Touch, The SEE: **Feminine Touch, The** (1956)

George Balanchine's The Nutcracker SEE: **Nutcracker, The** (1993)

George of the Jungle (1997) **C-91m.** **½ D: Sam Weisman. Brendan Fraser, Leslie Mann, Thomas Haden Church, Holland Taylor, John Bennett Perry, Abraham Benrubi, Greg Cruttwell, Richard Roundtree, voice of John Cleese; narrated by Keith Scott. Live-action Disney comedy feature based on Jay Ward's 1960s cartoon show about a clumsy king of the jungle. Aimed at kids, who should enjoy it thoroughly; for adults its one-note silliness wears thin, with a preponderance of story climaxes, but Fraser and Mann are immensely likable. Why couldn't they come up with at least a few funny lines for the Ape named Ape? [PG]▼●◗

George Raft Story, The (1961) **106m.** **½ D: Joseph M. Newman. Ray Danton, Jayne Mansfield, Barrie Chase, Julie London, Neville Brand, Frank Gorshin. Danton is good in title role of fast-moving account of Raft's rise from Broadway dancer to top Hollywood star. How much is true, who can say?

George's Island (1991-Canadian) **C-90m.** **½ D: Paul Donovan. Nathaniel Moreau, Ian Bannen, Sheila McCarthy, Maury Chaykin, Vicki Ridler, Brian Downcy. Young Nova Scotia boy is taken from his crusty grandpop—who has regaled him with tales of pirate ghosts and local buried treasure from Captain Kidd's raids—and must escape from a grim foster home to complete his treasure quest. Modest tale dwells too long on adult caricatures and too little on boyhood adventures.▼●

George Stevens: A Filmmaker's Journey (1984) **C/B&W-110m.** *** D: George Stevens, Jr. Katharine Hepburn, Cary Grant, Joel McCrea, Elizabeth Taylor, Fred Astaire, Ginger Rogers, and Warren Beatty are among those who help create vivid documentary portrait of director Stevens. Great clips from ALICE ADAMS, SWING TIME, GUNGA DIN, THE MORE THE MERRIER, A PLACE IN THE SUN, SHANE, GIANT, etc. Stevens, Jr., supplies personal insights, plus fascinating home movies taken by his father on film sets—and color footage shot during WW2 in Europe.▼●

George Wallace (1997) **C-180m. TVM** D: John Frankenheimer. Gary Sinise, Mare Winningham, Angelina Jolie, Clarence Williams III, Joe Don Baker, Terry Kinney, Cliff De Young. Sinise, who already gave us a definitive portrait of Truman, here portrays one of the most controversial political figures of the '50s and '60s: Alabama governor and arch-segregationist George Wallace, whose redemption comes years after being confined to a wheelchair following an assassination attempt. Multi-award-winning drama written by Paul Monash and Marshall Fraidy, from the latter's best-selling biography. Made for cable. Originally shown in two parts. Above average.▼

George Washington Slept Here (1942) **93m.** **½ D: William Keighley. Jack Benny, Ann Sheridan, Charles Coburn, Percy Kilbride, Hattie McDaniel, William Tracy, Joyce Reynolds, Lee Patrick, Charles Dingle, John Emery. Sheridan (never more beautiful) surprises her city-dweller husband Benny by buying a dilapidated country house, and pouring all their money—and patience—into the process of fixing it up. Pleasant but predictable adaptation of the Kaufman-Hart play, with Benny in good form, and Kilbride re-creating his Broadway role as the hayseed contractor.▼●

George White's Scandals (1934) **80m.** **½ D: George White, Thornton Freeland, Harry Lachman. Rudy Vallee, Jimmy Durante, Alice Faye, Adrienne Ames, Gregory Ratoff, Cliff Edwards, Dixie Dunbar, Gertrude Michael, George White. Idiotic backstage romance plot propels entertaining, expensive musical; Faye, in film debut, sings "Oh, You Nasty Man," one of several big production numbers.

George White's Scandals (1935) **83m.** ** D: George White. Alice Faye, James Dunn, Ned Sparks, Lyda Roberti, Cliff Edwards, Arline Judge, Eleanor Powell, George White, Benny Rubin. Tired show biz story of producer White seeing talented Alice in small-town show, bringing her (and her pals) to N.Y.C. where success poses problems. Story, songs all routine, but good cast gives it some life; Powell's dancing film debut. Retitled GEORGE WHITE'S 1935 SCANDALS.

George White's Scandals (1945) **95m.** ** D: Felix E. Feist. Joan Davis, Jack Haley, Phillip Terry, Martha Holliday, Bettejane (Jane) Greer, Margaret Hamilton, Glenn Tryon. Mild musical centering around the mounting of a "Scandals" stageshow, and chronicling the romances of Davis-Haley and Holliday-Terry. Tryon plays George White; the real impresario produced.▼

Georgia (1995) **C-117m.** ** D: Ulu Grosbard. Jennifer Jason Leigh, Mare Winningham, Ted Levine, Max Perlich, John Doe, John C. Reilly, Jimmy Witherspoon, Jason Carter, Tom Bower, Smokey Hormel. A strung-out, self-destructive young woman lives in the shadow of her older sister, a popular singer, and wants to *be* her—though the younger sister has no talent. Leigh is as brilliant as ever getting inside an intense and difficult character (she does her own vocals, too), but that doesn't mean we care about her much. She also coproduced the film with her mother, Barbara Turner (who wrote the screenplay). Winningham is excellent as the serene older sister and also does her own very appealing vocals. [R]▼●◗

Georgia, Georgia (1972) **C-91m.** **½ D: Stig Bjorkman. Diana Sands, Dirk Benedict, Minnie Gentry. Black singer's involvement with white photographer and American defectors. Interesting but uneven. [R]▼

Georgy Girl (1966-British) **100m.** ***½ D: Silvio Narizzano. James Mason, Alan Bates, Lynn Redgrave, Charlotte Rampling, Bill Owen, Claire Kelly, Rachel Kempson. Delightful, adult British comedy of modern-day morals, with Redgrave as ugly-duckling Georgy, Mason as the wealthy, aging married man who wants her for his mistress. Entire cast is excellent, with Rampling scoring as Georgy's bitchy roommate. Faithful adaptation of Margaret Forster novel; scripted by Forster and Peter Nichols. ▼●

Germinal (1993-French) **C-158m.** *** D: Claude Berri. Renaud, Gérard Depardieu, Miou-Miou, Jean Carmet, Judith Henry, Jean-Roger Milo, Laurent Terzieff, Jean-Pierre Bisson, Bernard Fresson, Jacques Dacqmine, Anny Duperey. Sprawling adaptation of classic 1884 Emile Zola novel, this manages to tell both the epic tale of a bleak rural community and the personal story of coal miner Depardieu's impoverished family. The action begins when a young job-seeker (played by French singer Renaud, in his feature acting debut) stirs up the work-force in the mining village and begins to politicize the populace. Impressively recreates the period, though the characters sometimes seem a bit hollow. Still, it's hard to come away unaffected. Previously filmed in France in 1963. Panavision.▼●

Geronimo (1939) **89m.** ** D: Paul H. Sloane. Preston Foster, Ellen Drew, Andy Devine, Gene Lockhart, William Henry, Ralph Morgan, Marjorie Gateson, Chief Thundercloud. Run-of-the-mill Western marred by overuse of stock footage and bad process shots to simulate outdoor scenes. Lockhart getting just deserts is best item in trivial Indian vs. cavalry contest. Remake of LIVES OF A BENGAL LANCER.

Geronimo (1962) **C-101m.** **½ D: Arnold Laven. Chuck Connors, Kamala Devi, Ross Martin, Adam West, Pat Conway, Larry Dobkin. Exciting Indians-on-the-warpath tale, with Connors satisfactory in title role. Panavision.▼●

Geronimo (1993) **C-100m. TVM** D: Roger Young. Joseph Running Fox, Nick Ramus, Michelle St. John, Michael Grey Eyes, Tailinh Forest Flower, Kimberley Norris, Jimmy Herman, Ryan Black, Geno Silva, August Schellenberg. Not to be confused with the theatrical GERONIMO: AN AMERICAN LEGEND which premiered the same week, this was first in a series of Native American film projects from TNT. An alternately elegiac and violent look at the turbulent life of the Chiricahua Apaches and their fierce warrior-leader Geronimo. Even-handed approach toward historical accuracy and exploration of an often ignored American culture. Made for cable. 10m. added for video release. Average.▼●

Geronimo: An American Legend (1993) **C-115m.** **½ D: Walter Hill. Jason Patric, Robert Duvall, Gene Hackman, Wes Studi, Matt Damon, Rodney A. Grant, Kevin Tighe, Steve Reevis, Carlos Palomino, Victor Aaron, Stuart Proud Eagle Grant, Stephen McHattie, Richard Martin, Jr., Roger Callard, Scott Wilson. Stately, intelligent—but dramatically slack—chronicle of the U.S. Army's attempts to subjugate the great Apache warrior. Strong performance by Studi in the lead, and rich characterizations by Hackman (as General Crook) and Duvall (as a veteran Indian scout), sustain interest for quite a while—along with magnificent Moab, Utah, scenery. Eventually, the film's point is made, and there's nothing left to maintain audience involvement. Screenplay by John Milius. Panavision. [R]▼●◗

Gervaise (1956-French) **116m.** *** D: René Clement. Maria Schell, Francois Perier, Suzy Delair, Armand Mestral. Splendidly acted version of Emile Zola tale of Schell struggling to keep her family going but finally succumbing to tawdry life of her drunken husband.▼

Getaway, The (1972) **C-122m.** *** D: Sam Peckinpah. Steve McQueen, Ali MacGraw, Ben Johnson, Sally Struthers, Al Lettieri, Slim Pickens, Dub Taylor, Bo Hopkins. Exciting, enjoyable film built around a chase. Bank robber McQueen and wife MacGraw take it on the lam when robbery goes haywire. Many fine vignettes, including hair-raising episode on garbage truck. Written by Walter Hill from a Jim Thompson novel. Music by Quincy Jones. Remade in 1994. Todd-AO 35. [PG] ▼●◗

Getaway, The (1994) **C-115m.** ** D: Roger Donaldson. Alec Baldwin, Kim Basinger, Michael Madsen, James Woods, David Morse, Jennifer Tilly, James Stephens, Richard Farnsworth, Philip Seymour Hoffman, Burton Gilliam, Royce D. Applegate. He's nailed for robbery and thrown in prison; she frees him by playing up to a crime kingpin; he spends the rest of the movie resenting her. Or something like that. Action, violence, and sex by the numbers in this halfhearted remake of the 1972 hit; even the usually dynamic Woods seems to be just going through the motions. Watching real-life couple Baldwin and Basinger make love is uncomfortably voyeuristic. It takes Farnsworth, in the film's closing moments, to bring it to life. One sexy scene added for video. Panavision. [R]▼●◗

Get Back (1991) **C-89m.** ** D: Richard Lester. Adequate rockumentary of Paul McCartney's 1989–90 Get Back world tour. Recommended only for fans of McCartney's music, though there is also some vintage footage of The Beatles. Director Lester made more imaginative use of McCartney when he directed him and his compadres in A HARD DAY'S NIGHT and HELP! [PG]▼

Get Bruce (1999) **C-82m.** **½ D: Andrew J. Kuehn. Slight but very amusing look at Hollywood comedy writer and self-styled character Bruce Vilanch, whose credits range from the Academy Awards to *Hollywood Squares*. Not what you'd call a probing character profile (especially since it was done with its subject's complete cooperation), but the interviews with Robin Williams, Billy Crystal, Whoopi Goldberg, and others are often hysterically funny. [R]▼◗

Get Carter (1970-British) **C-112m.** *** D: Mike Hodges. Michael Caine, Ian Hendry, Britt Ekland, John Osborne, Tony Beckley, George Sewell. Lean, tough action melodrama with Caine as small-time gangster investigating his brother's death; good work by Caine, vivid seediness captured by writer-director Hodges. Remade one year later with black cast as HIT MAN. [R]▼

Get Charlie Tully (1976-British) **C-97m.** *½ D: Cliff Owen. Dick Emery, Derren Nesbitt, Ronald Fraser, Pat Coombs, William Franklyn. Energetic, tasteless nonsense in which con man Emery frantically searches for four young women who have the location of negotiable bonds tattooed on their rear. The usually impeccable Frank Launder and Sidney Gilliat were executive producers. [PG]

Get Crazy (1983) **C-92m.** *** D: Allan Arkush. Daniel Stern, Malcolm McDowell, Gail Edwards, Allen Goorwitz (Garfield), Ed Begley, Jr., Miles Chapin, Lou Reed, Stacey Nelkin, Bill Henderson, Franklyn Ajaye, Bobby Sherman, Fabian Forte, Lori Eastside, Lee Ving. Arkush's years working at Fillmore East rock palace form the basis for wonderful cartoonlike comedy set at a trouble-plagued New Year's Eve concert. Gags fly at machine-gun pace, interspersed with delightful musical numbers; superb take-offs on Mick Jagger (McDowell), Bob Dylan (Reed), and Muddy Waters (Henderson), plus many familiar rock stars and character actors in bits. [R]▼

Get Hep to Love (1944) **71m.** *½ D: Charles Lamont. Gloria Jean, Donald O'Connor, Jane Frazee, Robert Paige. Weak musical with precocious musical personality Jean running away to find happier home and singing career.

Get on the Bus (1996) **C-120m.** *** D: Spike Lee. Ossie Davis, Charles S. Dutton, Andre Braugher, DeAundre Bonds, Albert Hall, Isaiah Washington, Thomas Jefferson Byrd, Richard Belzer, Gabriel Casseus. Vibrant, highly energized film about a busload of black men heading from L.A. to the Million Man March in Washington, D.C., in October 1995. Not a polemic, but a series of character studies and vignettes; occasional speechifying and contrivances are forgivable because, overall, the film deals so well with issues facing all Americans. Screenplay by Reggie Rock Bythewood. Kudos to Dutton as the bus company rep and Davis as the senior member of the brigade. This low-budget film was financed by fifteen African-American men, including Danny Glover, Will Smith, and Wesley Snipes. Randy Quaid appears unbilled. [R]▼●

Get On With It (1961-British) **88m.** ** D: C. M. Pennington-Richards. Bob Monkhouse, Kenneth Connor, Shirley Eaton, Eric Barker, Ronnie Stevens, Richard Wattis, Reginald Beckwith. Dental-school graduates Monkhouse and Stevens promote a new toothpaste. Intermittently funny. Aka DENTIST ON THE JOB.

Get Out Your Handkerchiefs (1978-French-Belgian) **C-109m.** ***½ D: Bertrand Blier. Gérard Depardieu, Patrick Dewaere, Carole Laure, Riton, Michel Serrault, Eleonore Hirt. Disarming black comedy about a man who will do almost anything to keep his sexually frustrated wife happy; highly unconventional. Oscar winner for Best Foreign Film. [R]▼

Get Real (1999-British) **C-109m.** **½ D: Simon Shore. Ben Silverstone, Charlotte Brittain, Brad Gorton, Louise J. Taylor, Tim Harris, Stacy Hart. Teenage schoolboy in England realizes he's gay but can't admit it to his parents, teachers, or schoolmates. Then he falls in love with the class jock. Sincere and well acted, but tends to plod at times. Scripted by Patrick Wilde from his play *What's Wrong With Angry?* Panavision. [R]▼◗

Get Shorty (1995) **C-105m.** *** D: Barry Sonnenfeld. John Travolta, Gene Hackman, Rene Russo, Danny DeVito, Dennis Farina, Delroy Lindo, James Gandolfini, David Paymer, Martin Ferrero, Miguel Sandoval. Clever black comedy about a small-time, cool-as-ice Miami enforcer coming to L.A. on business, hooking up with a slick, grade-Z producer who can fulfill his dream of being connected with the movies. Ingenious plotting, tip-top performances, and some delicious digs at Hollywood are offset by a certain aloofness. Scott Frank scripted from Elmore Leonard's novel. Bette Midler appears unbilled; other famous faces turn up in amusing cameos. [R]▼●◗

Getting Away With Murder (1976) SEE: **End of the Game**

Getting Away With Murder (1996) **C-92m.** BOMB D: Harvey Miller. Jack Lemmon, Dan Aykroyd, Lily Tomlin, Bonnie Hunt, Brian Kerwin, Jerry Adler, Andy Romano. Ethics professor Aykroyd discovers that his next-door neighbor (Lemmon) is a notorious Nazi war criminal who is plotting to leave the country. Strictly for those who found JUDGMENT AT NUREMBERG a laugh riot; a career nadir for the comic talents on both sides of the camera. Coproduced by Penny Marshall. [R]▼●

Getting Even (1986) **C-90m.** **½ D: Dwight H. Little. Edward Albert, Audrey Landers, Joe Don Baker, Blue Deckert, Caroline Williams. Farfetched suspense film has industrialist Baker holding the city of Dallas hostage for $50 million ransom or he'll unleash a lethal poison gas. Albert and Landers are the government agents out to stop him. Rousing helicopter stunts give film a lift in the final reel. Originally titled: HOSTAGE: DALLAS. [R]▼

Getting Even With Dad (1994) **C-108m.** *½ D: Howard Deutsch. Macaulay Culkin, Ted Danson, Glenne Headly, Saul Rubinek, Gailard Sartain, Hector Elizondo, Ron Canada. Ex-con cake decorator steals a rare coin collection with his two doofus pals, *just* as his 11-year-old son shows up for an extended visit. Touchy-feely comedy didn't touch many paying customers, despite Culkin's modified HOME ALONE-ing of comical villains Rubinek and Sartain; Danson's unlikely romance with policewoman Headly is as drab as the rest.▼●

Getting Gertie's Garter (1945) **72m.** **½ D: Allan Dwan. Dennis O'Keefe, Marie McDonald, Barry Sullivan, Binnie Barnes, Sheila Ryan, J. Carrol Naish, Jerome Cowan. Similar to UP IN MABEL'S ROOM, a funny little comedy of O'Keefe trying to retrieve embarrassing memento without wife's knowledge.▼

Getting It Right (1989) **C-102m.** *** D: Randal Kleiser. Jesse Birdsall, Helena Bonham Carter, Peter Cook, Lynn Redgrave, Jane Horrocks, Richard Huw, John Gielgud, Shirley Anne Field, Pat Heywood, Judy Parfitt, Bryan Pringle. Sweetly comic story of a 31-year-old virgin and his attempts to cope with people—women in particular—seems mundane and meandering at first, and just gets better as it goes along. Some wonderful characterizations, especially Redgrave as a wealthy woman with a world-weary facade who just wants to be loved. Screenplay by Elizabeth Jane Howard, from her novel. Made in England by an American director and producer. [R]▼●

Getting of Wisdom, The (1977-Australian) **C-100m.** **½ D: Bruce Beresford. Susannah Fowle, Hilary Ryan, Alix Longman, Sheila Helpmann, Patricia Kennedy, Barry Humphries, John Waters. A spirited, sensitive 13-year-old girl (Fowle) from the outback matures on her own terms at a snobbish Victorian ladies college. Fowle is miscast; however, the era is carefully recreated. Based on autobiographical novel by one Henry Handel Richardson.▼

Getting Straight (1970) **C-124m.** **½ D: Richard Rush. Elliott Gould, Candice Bergen, Jeff Corey, Max Julien, Cecil Kellaway, Robert F. Lyons, Jeannie Berlin, John Rubinstein, Brenda Sykes, Harrison Ford. A period piece, but central issue of graduate student Gould choosing between academic double-talk and his beliefs remains relevant. Gould's personality propels glossy film. Bob Kaufman adapted Ken Kolb's novel. [R]▼

Get to Know Your Rabbit (1972) **C-91m.** **½ D: Brian De Palma. Tom Smothers, John Astin, Suzanne Zenor, Samantha Jones, Allen Garfield, Katharine Ross, Orson Welles. Offbeat comedy was barely released, and heavily tampered with at that; starts with great premise of Smothers dropping out of establishment life to become tap-dancing magician, then loses itself. Still has some inventive moments, funny ideas. Filmed in 1970. [R]▼

Gettysburg (1993) **C-248m.** ***½ D: Ronald Maxwell. Tom Berenger, Jeff Daniels, Martin Sheen, Sam Elliott, Maxwell Caulfield, Kevin Conway, C. Thomas Howell, Richard Jordan, Royce D. Applegate, John Diehl, Patrick Gorman, Cooper Huckabee, James Lancaster, Brian Mallon, Andrew Prine, Stephen Lang, Richard Anderson, Bo Brinkman, Kieran Mulroney, George Lazenby, Dwier Brown, Buck Taylor. Ted Turner's answer to GONE WITH THE WIND, a magnificent re-creation of the Civil War's most famous battle. Based on Michael Shaara's Pulitzer Prize–winning novel, *The Killer Angels,* this long but engrossing slice of history was filmed on the battlefields of the Gettysburg National Military Park using over 5,000 Civil War "reenactors" in the battle scenes. Look fast for filmmaker Ken Burns as General Hancock's aide and Turner as a Reb foot soldier during Pickett's Charge. Elliott, and especially Daniels, stand out in a cast full of great performances. Final film for Richard Jordan, who has the most poignant role in the picture as General Armistead. Superb score by Randy Edelman. Also released on video in 271m. director's cut. [PG]▼●

Get Yourself A College Girl (1964) **C-88m.** *½ D: Sidney Miller. Chad Everett, Nancy Sinatra, Mary Ann Mobley, Dave Clark Five, The Animals. Songwriter who is undergraduate at a staid girls' school falls in love with a music publisher at resort hotel. Strictly for dropouts.

Ghidrah, the Three-Headed Monster (1964-Japanese) **C-85m.** **½ D: Ishiro Honda. Yosuke Natsuki, Yuriko Hoshi, Hiroshi Koizumi, Emi Ito. Clever story, works three favorites into plot (Mothra, Rodan, Godzilla), protecting people of Tokyo against rampaging title fiend. Tohoscope.▼

Ghost, The (1963-Italian) **C-96m.** **½ D: Robert Hampton (Riccardo Freda). Barbara Steele, Peter Baldwin, Leonard Elliott (Elio Jotta), Harriet White. In 1910 Scotland, adulterous wife Steele and doctor-lover are seemingly haunted by the vengeful ghost of her crippled husband, whom they murdered. Measured, moody horror, let down by routine plot; still atmospheric and watchable. Follow-up to THE HORRIBLE DR. HICHCOCK.▼

Ghost (1990) **C-122m.** *** D: Jerry Zucker. Patrick Swayze, Demi Moore, Whoopi Goldberg, Tony Goldwyn, Rick Aviles, Vincent Schiavelli, Gail Boggs, Armelia McQueen, Phil Leeds. Overlong but enjoyable mix of fantasy, thriller, and romance. Swayze is killed, and when he learns (in his ghostly state) that he was the victim of a botched hit, he tries to warn his grieving girlfriend (Moore) that she's in danger too. Storefront medium Whoopi (in an Oscar-winning role) turns out to be the only one who can convey his messages to her. Swayze runs the gamut of expressions from A to B, but the relationships are credible and as a result the fantasy works. [PG-13]▼●

Ghost and Mr. Chicken, The (1966) **C-90m.** **½ D: Alan Rafkin. Don Knotts,

Joan Staley, Skip Homeier, Dick Sargent, Reta Shaw, James Milhollin, Phil Ober, Liam Redmond, Lurene Tuttle, Charles Lane. Featherweight comedy with Knotts a would-be reporter who seizes his big chance for a scoop by spending a night in a supposedly haunted house. Full of familiar character faces. Techniscope.▼●

Ghost and Mrs. Muir, The (1947) **104m.** ***½ D: Joseph L. Mankiewicz. Gene Tierney, Rex Harrison, George Sanders, Edna Best, Vanessa Brown, Anna Lee, Robert Coote, Natalie Wood. A lonely widow is romanced by the ghost of a sea captain in her "haunted" English cottage. Charming, beautifully made fantasy, a distant cousin to later TV sitcom; lovely score by Bernard Herrmann. Philip Dunne scripted, from the R.A. Dick novel.▼●

Ghost and the Darkness, The (1996) **C-109m.** **½ D: Stephen Hopkins. Michael Douglas, Val Kilmer, Tom Wilkinson, John Kani, Bernard Hill, Brian McCardie, Henry Cele, Om Puri. In 1896, an Irish bridge builder heads to Africa for his latest project, but the campsite is soon cursed by violent and unexplainable attacks by a pair of man-eating lions. Eventually, renowned big-game hunter Douglas is called in. What begins as a rousing, old-fashioned adventure somehow loses its way—and its impact. Screenplay by William Goldman. Based on the same true story that inspired BWANA DEVIL. Panavision. [R]▼●◗

Ghost Breakers, The (1940) **85m.** *** D: George Marshall. Bob Hope, Paulette Goddard, Richard Carlson, Paul Lukas, Anthony Quinn, Willie Best, Noble Johnson, Tom Dugan, Lloyd Corrigan. More plot than usual for a Hope film as Bob and Paulette investigate eerie Cuban mansion which she's inherited. Some real chills as well as laughs in this first-rate film. Remade as SCARED STIFF (1953).▼●

Ghost Brigade (1994) **C-80m.** **½ D: George Hickenlooper. Corbin Bernsen, Adrian Pasdar, Ray Wise, Martin Sheen, Cynda Williams. Yankees and Rebs team up to confront supernatural brigade of evil soldiers that's been wreaking gruesome slaughter on both sides. Odd mix of Civil War and horror genres aspires to a Peckinpah-type brutality but generally opts for mere shock value. Putting APOCALYPSE NOW star Sheen and HEARTS OF DARKNESS documentary director Hickenlooper together gives viewer an unmistakable feeling of déjà vu, as if you're back up the delta in Cambodia looking for Col. Kurtz. [R]▼

Ghostbusters (1984) **C-107m.** *** D: Ivan Reitman. Bill Murray, Dan Aykroyd, Harold Ramis, Sigourney Weaver, Rick Moranis, Annie Potts, Ernie Hudson, William Atherton, Reginald VelJohnson. The first multimillion-dollar scare comedy, about a trio of flaky "paranormal investigators" who go into business flushing out ghosts and spirits in N.Y.C.—and find their business booming! Engagingly offbeat, even subdued at times, with Murray's flippant personality nicely contrasting Richard Edlund's eye-popping special effects. Great fun all the way; written by Aykroyd and Ramis. Followed by a sequel and an animated TV series. Panavision. [PG]▼●◗

Ghostbusters II (1989) **C-102m.** *** D: Ivan Reitman. Bill Murray, Dan Aykroyd, Sigourney Weaver, Harold Ramis, Rick Moranis, Ernie Hudson, Peter MacNicol, David Margulies, Annie Potts, Ben Stein, Janet Margolin, Harris Yulin, Philip Baker Hall. Amiable, entertaining sequel has the ghostbusting boys reteaming five years after their last adventure to save N.Y.C. from a slime attack of gargantuan proportions, generated by all the "negative energy" in the air of the Big Apple. Longish but good-natured, with some solid laughs along the way. Chloe Webb has a funny unbilled cameo as a guest on Murray's cable TV show. Panavision. [PG]▼●◗

Ghost Catchers (1944) **67m.** *** D: Edward F. Cline. Ole Olsen, Chic Johnson, Gloria Jean, Martha O'Driscoll, Leo Carrillo, Andy Devine, Walter Catlett, Lon Chaney, Jr. One of Olsen and Johnson's wackiest comedies, with duo as nightclub owners who help Southern colonel Catlett and his daughters, who have just moved into haunted house.

Ghost Chasers (1951) **69m.** **½ D: William Beaudine. Leo Gorcey, Huntz Hall, William (Billy) Benedict, David Gorcey, Buddy Gorman, Jan Kayne, Bernard Gorcey, Lloyd Corrigan. Spirited supernatural spoof, as the Bowery Boys try to expose a fake medium.▼

Ghost Comes Home, The (1940) **79m.** ** D: William Thiele. Frank Morgan, Billie Burke, Ann Rutherford, John Shelton, Reginald Owen, Donald Meek. Morgan, thought dead, returns to family which has been doing fine without him; cast does its best with fair material.

Ghost Dad (1990) **C-84m.** ** D: Sidney Poitier. Bill Cosby, Kimberly Russell, Denise Nicholas, Ian Bannen, Christine Ebersole, Barry Corbin, Salim Grant, Brooke Fontaine, Dakin Matthews, Dana Ashbrook, Arnold Stang. Overworked businessman (and widower) Cosby dies in a taxi accident, and learns he has only a few days to try to straighten out his finances so his three kids will be secure. Positive family message aside, this effects-laden fantasy plays like an extended sitcom. Younger kids may like it—others beware. [PG]▼●◗

Ghost Dog: The Way of the Samurai (1999-U.S.-French) **C-116m.** *** D: Jim Jarmusch. Forest Whitaker, John Tormey, Cliff Gorman, Henry Silva, Isaach de Bankolé, Tricia Vessey, Victor Argo. Ghost

Dog (Whitaker), a solitary hitman who lives by the code of the Samurai, finds himself a target after a job gone wrong. Typically original (though sometimes pretentious) Jarmusch mix of mysticism, action, and even comedy, anchored by Whitaker's quiet, intense performance. Very bloody at times, and not for all tastes. Written by the director. [R]▼◗

Ghost Fever (1987) **C-86m.** ** D: Alan Smithee (Lee Madden). Sherman Hemsley, Luis Avalos, Jennifer Rhodes, Deborah Benson, Diana Brookes, Myron Healey, Pepper Martin, Joe Frazier. Hemsley and Avalos make a comfortable comedy team as cops caught up with ghosts, notably one of a former slave owner (Martin). Slapstick occasionally triumphs over some tasteless material. Filmed mostly in 1984. [PG]▼●

Ghost Goes West, The (1936) **82m.** **½ D: René Clair. Robert Donat, Eugene Pallette, Jean Parker, Everly Gregg, Elsa Lanchester, Hay Petrie, Morton Selten. Bombastic American purchases a Scottish castle, unaware that it's haunted by the ghost of the current owner's fast-living ancestor. Genial but bland comedy written by Robert E. Sherwood and filmed by Clair in an oddly aloof fashion—with barely any close-ups of its leading actors!▼

Ghost in the Invisible Bikini, The (1966) **C-82m.** *½ D: Don Weis. Tommy Kirk, Deborah Walley, Aron Kincaid, Quinn O'Hara, Nancy Sinatra, Claudia Martin, Harvey Lembeck, Jesse White, Susan Hart, Basil Rathbone, Boris Karloff, Patsy Kelly, Francis X. Bushman, Benny Rubin. Seventh (and final) BEACH PARTY movie failed to provide a shot in the arm with entirely new set of characters (save Lembeck's Eric Von Zipper); larger-than-usual roster of veteran movie greats might attract masochistic film buffs. Panavision.

Ghost in the Machine (1993) **C-95m.** *½ D: Rachel Talalay. Karen Allen, Chris Mulkey, Ted Marcoux, Wil Horneff, Jessica Walter, Brandon Quintin Adams, Phil Ducommun. The spirit of a dying serial killer is sucked into a computer mainframe in Cleveland, from which he continues to pursue his latest target, single mother Allen, by killing her friends and ruining her credit. Both obvious and ludicrous. [R]▼●

Ghost in the Noonday Sun (1973-British) **C-89m.** BOMB D: Peter Medak. Peter Sellers, Anthony Franciosa, Spike Milligan, Clive Revill, Peter Boyle, Richard Willis. Absolutely atrocious pirate comedy which understandably never got full-fledged theatrical release. Milligan, who's credited with "additional dialogue," appears in one sequence with his onetime *Goon Show* colleague Sellers, but even their chemistry can't save this turkey.▼

Ghost of Dragstrip Hollow (1959) **65m.** BOMB D: William Hole, Jr. Jody Fair, Martin Braddock, Russ Bender, Leon Tyler, Elaine DuPont. Trite mixture of hot rod gangs and haunted house formulas, with most uneven results.

Ghost of Frankenstein, The (1942) **68m.** **½ D: Erle C. Kenton. Cedric Hardwicke, Lon Chaney, Jr., Lionel Atwill, Ralph Bellamy, Bela Lugosi, Evelyn Ankers, Dwight Frye. Sequel to SON OF FRANKENSTEIN. Ygor (Lugosi) returns to foul Hardwicke's plan to replace the Monster's brain with that of educated man. Good cast manages to save stale plot. Followed by FRANKENSTEIN MEETS THE WOLF MAN.▼●

Ghost of Zorro (1949) **69m.** ** D: Fred C. Brannon. Clayton Moore, Pamela Blake, Roy Barcroft, George J. Lewis, Eugene Roth. Feature version of 1949 serial is a confusing account of descendant of Zorro adopting same guise to combat outlaws destroying telegraph lines. Moore's role as the masked hero was casting inspiration for subsequent LONE RANGER TV series.▼

Ghosts Can't Do It (1990) **C-95m.** BOMB D: John Derek. Bo Derek, Anthony Quinn, Leo Damian, Don Murray, Julie Newmar, Dee Krainz. And neither (at least on film) can John and Bo. Standard Derek atrocity involves Bo's international search for the perfect male body to house the spirit of her beloved but deceased husband (Quinn). Tony looks as if he's been photographed through the Lucille Ball MAME filter for the supernatural scenes. Just when you think it can't get any worse, Donald Trump shows up in a cameo. [R]▼●

Ghost Ship, The (1943) **69m.** *** D: Mark Robson. Richard Dix, Russell Wade, Edith Barrett, Ben Bard, Lawrence Tierney. Offbeat Val Lewton melodrama about young man who signs on merchant ship run by power-crazy captain (Dix) who's obsessed with "authority." Absorbing mood-piece with unfortunately abrupt conclusion.▼●

Ghost Ship (1952-British) **69m.** ** D: Vernon Sewell. Dermot Walsh, Hazel Court, Hugh Burden, John Robinson, Joss Ambler. Small-budget yarn about young couple purchasing a haunted yacht.▼

Ghosts—Italian Style (1967-Italian) **C-92m.** ** D: Renato Castellani. Sophia Loren, Vittorio Gassman, Mario Adorf, Margaret Lee, Aldo Guiffre, Francisco Tensi. Newlyweds Loren and Gassman move into haunted house. Weak vehicle for engaging stars. [G]

Ghosts of Mississippi (1996) **C-130m.** *** D: Rob Reiner. Alec Baldwin, Whoopi Goldberg, James Woods, Craig T. Nelson, Susanna Thompson, Lucas Black, William H. Macy, Terry O'Quinn, Virginia Madsen, Bonnie Bartlett, Wayne Rogers, Diane Ladd. Straightforward drama about Mississippi assistant D.A. Bobby DeLaughter

(Baldwin), who reopens the case against the murderer of civil rights leader Medgar Evers thirty years after the fact. Reminiscent of 1960s movies in its earnestness and sobriety, it still works, but lacks the edge and energy to make it soar. Goldberg is surprisingly good as Evers' widow, and Woods has a showy part (in heavy makeup) as the aged murderer, Byron De La Beckwith. [PG-13]▼●◗

Ghosts of Rome (1961-Italian) **C-105m.** **½ D: Antonio Pietrangeli. Marcello Mastroianni, Belinda Lee, Sandra Milo, Vittorio Gassman, Franca Marzi. Scatterbrain antics of oddball characters inhabiting rundown house soon to be demolished, with prospects of finding new quarters frightening them all.

Ghosts on the Loose (1943) **65m.** ** D: William Beaudine. Leo Gorcey, Huntz Hall, Bobby Jordan, Bela Lugosi, Sunshine Sammy Morrison, Billy Benedict, Stanley Clements, Bobby Stone, Ava Gardner, Rick Vallin. Gorcey and his gang take on Nazi spies (led by Lugosi) in this misleadingly titled entry. Notable only for early appearance of ingenue Gardner. Retitled THE EAST SIDE KIDS MEET BELA LUGOSI.▼●

Ghost Story (1974) SEE: **Madhouse Mansion**

Ghost Story (1981) **C-110m.** **½ D: John Irvin. Fred Astaire, Melvyn Douglas, Douglas Fairbanks, Jr., John Houseman, Craig Wasson, Alice Krige, Patricia Neal, Ken Olin. Four elderly New Englanders are tormented by a 50-year-old secret, which now visits evil on one of their sons as well. Absorbing if not altogether satisfying simplification of Peter Straub's best-seller, which loses steam as it nears its resolution. Astaire's last film. [R]▼●◗

Ghost Town (1988) **C-85m.** **½ D: Richard Governor. Franc Luz, Catherine Hickland, Jimmie F. Skaggs, Penelope Windust, Bruce Glover, Blake Conway, Laura Schaefer. Imaginative fantasy thriller has modern-day Western sheriff Luz chosen to rid a century-old town of its curse by avenging its dead sheriff in HIGH NOON fashion. Fine special effects distinguish this modest sleeper. [R]▼●

Ghoul, The (1933-British) **73m.** **½ D: T. Hayes Hunter. Boris Karloff, Cedric Hardwicke, Ernest Thesiger, Dorothy Hyson, Anthony Bushell, Ralph Richardson, Kathleen Harrison. England's answer to Hollywood's horror films: Egyptologist Karloff wishes to be buried with a jewel he believes will allow him eternal life. It's stolen, and he rises from the dead in search of the culprit. Slow going until Karloff's resurrection; then it really hums. Richardson's film debut. Remade as 1962 comedy NO PLACE LIKE HOMICIDE! Original 79m. version is available on video.▼

Ghoul, The (1975-British) **C-88m.** **½ D: Freddie Francis. Peter Cushing, John Hurt, Alexandra Bastedo, Gwen Watford, Veronica Carlson, Steward Bevan. Innocent people fall victim to a mysterious flesh-eating "monster" in Cushing's secluded home. Fairly interesting, non-gory thriller, with Hurt as Cushing's crazed gardener.▼

Ghoulies (1985) **C-84m.** *½ D: Luca Bercovici. Peter Liapis, Lisa Pelikan, Michael Des Barres, Jack Nance, Peter Risch, Tamara de Treaux. Boring, ridiculous film about young man who invokes Satanic spirits in the form of gremlin-like creatures (who look like muppets dipped in shellac) at a creepy old mansion. Followed by three sequels. [PG-13]▼

Giant (1956) **C-201m.** **** D: George Stevens. Elizabeth Taylor, Rock Hudson, James Dean, Carroll Baker, Jane Withers, Chill Wills, Mercedes McCambridge, Dennis Hopper, Sal Mineo, Rodney (Rod) Taylor, Earl Holliman. Near-legendary epic based on Edna Ferber's novel about two generations of Texans holds up beautifully when not broken up into two nights on TV. Hudson's best performance, close to Taylor's best, and Dean's last film. Stevens won Oscar for direction. Screenplay by Fred Guiol and Ivan Moffat. ▼●

Giant Behemoth, The (1959-British) **80m.** ** D: Eugene Lourie. Gene Evans, Andre Morell, John Turner, Leigh Madison, Jack MacGowran. Enormous radioactive dinosaur menaces England, finally invades London. Animation effects directed by Willis O'Brien are fine, but film is turgid.▼●

Giant Claw, The (1957) **76m.** *½ D: Fred F. Sears. Jeff Morrow, Mara Corday, Morris Ankrum, Edgar Barrier. Lack of decent special effects ruins the running battle between colossal bird and fighter jets. Big bird is laughable.▼

Giant From the Unknown (1958) **77m.** *½ D: Richard E. Cunha. Edward Kemmer, Sally Fraser, Bob Steele, Morris Ankrum, Buddy Baer, Joline Brand, Billy Dix. Giant, depraved conquistador Baer, in suspended animation for centuries, is revived in California mountains, wreaking minor havoc. Cheap and silly.▼

Giant Gila Monster, The (1959) **74m.** *½ D: Ray Kellogg. Don Sullivan, Lisa Simone, Shug Fisher, Jerry Cortwright, Beverly Thurman, Don Flourney, Pat Simmons. Big, beaded lizard menaces small Texas town. Not as good as it sounds. Has a couple of wildly inappropriate songs.▼●

Giant Leeches, The SEE: **Attack Of The Giant Leeches**

Giant of Metropolis, The (1961-Italian) **C-82m.** ** D: Umberto Scarpelli. Gordon Mitchell, Roldano Lupi, Bella Cortez, Liana Orfei. Blah sci-fi throwaway, set in 20,000 B.C., with he-man Mitchell taking on evildoers on the lost continent of Atlantis.▼

Giants of Thessaly, The (1960-Italian) **C-86m.** ** D: Riccardo Freda. Roland Carey, Ziva Rodann, Massimo Girotti, Alberto Farnese. Episodic sword-and-sandal account of Jason (Carey) and Orpheus (Girotti) seeking golden fleece, with expected clashes with monsters, evil women, etc. Totalscope.▼

Giant Spider Invasion, The (1975) **C-82m.** BOMB D: Bill Rebane. Steve Brodie, Barbara Hale, Leslie Parrish, Alan Hale, Robert Easton, Bill Williams. Veteran cast can't do much for this tacky horror opus filmed in Wisconsin. [PG]▼

Giant Steps (1992-Canadian) **C-94m.** **½ D: Richard Rose. Billy Dee Williams, Michael Mahonen, Robyn Stevan, Ted Dykstra, Ranee Lee. Idealistic teen trumpeter Mahonen befriends his idol, Slate Thompson (Williams), a legendary, self-destructive jazz pianist attempting to remain true to his art. Well meaning but obvious and preachy.▼

G.I. Blues (1960) **C-104m.** **½ D: Norman Taurog. Elvis Presley, Juliet Prowse, Robert Ivers, Leticia Roman, Ludwig Stossel. Prowse's versatile performance as a cabaret dancer uplifts this standard Presley fare about a guitar-playing G.I. in West Germany. Elvis sings "Tonight Is So Right for Love," "Wooden Heart," "Blue Suede Shoes," and title song.▼●◗

G.I. Bro SEE: **Beyond the Living**

Gideon of Scotland Yard (1958-British) **C-91m.** *½ D: John Ford. Jack Hawkins, Dianne Foster, Cyril Cusack, Andrew Ray, James Hayter, Ronald Howard, Anna Massey, Anna Lee. A typical day in the life of a Scotland Yard inspector; Hawkins is likable but the film is unbelievably dull. A surprising dud from director Ford. British version, titled GIDEON'S DAY, runs 118m. Originally released theatrically in the U.S. in black and white.

Gideon's Day SEE: **Gideon of Scotland Yard**

Gideon's Trumpet (1980) **C-104m. TVM** D: Robert Collins. Henry Fonda, Jose Ferrer, John Houseman, Fay Wray, Sam Jaffe, Dean Jagger, Nicholas Pryor, William Prince, Dolph Sweet, Ford Rainey. Fonda is superb in the true story of a semiliterate Florida convict who changed the course of American legal history; Ferrer is equally fine as his powerful attorney, Abe Fortas. Script by David Rintels, from Anthony Lewis's book; produced by Houseman. Above average.▼

Gidget (1959) **C-95m.** **½ D: Paul Wendkos. Sandra Dee, James Darren, Cliff Robertson, Arthur O'Connell, Joby Baker, Yvonne Craig, Doug McClure, Tom Laughlin. California teenage girl hits the beach one summer and falls in love with two surfer boys. Dee is spirited in the title role of this hit movie (based on Frederick Kohner's novel about his daughter), which led to a number of sequels and two different TV series! CinemaScope.▼●

Gidget Goes Hawaiian (1961) **C-102m.** ** D: Paul Wendkos. James Darren, Michael Callan, Deborah Walley, Carl Reiner, Peggy Cass, Eddie Foy, Jr. Inane follow-up has teenager off to the Islands, with embarrassing results for all.▼

Gidget Goes to Rome (1963) **C-101m.** ** D: Paul Wendkos. Cindy Carol, James Darren, Jessie Royce Landis, Cesare Danova, Jeff Donnell. Mild follow-up has fetching teen-ager off to Italy involved in predictable romancing.▼

Gift, The (1982-French-Italian) **C-105m.** ** D: Michel Lang. Pierre Mondy, Claudia Cardinale, Clio Goldsmith, Jacques Francois, Cecile Magnet, Remi Laurent. Bank employees chip in to buy their colleague a surprise retirement gift: a beautiful prostitute. A "good clean sex farce," strained and silly, with no sex, very little nudity, and the improbable casting of beautiful Cardinale as Mondy's wife. [R]▼

Gift for Heidi, A (1958) **C-71m.** ** D: George Templeton. Douglas Fowley, Sandy Descher, Van Dyke Parks. Heidi learns the meaning of faith, hope, and charity. OK entertainment for youngsters. Inspired by Johanna Spyri's story.

Gift From Heaven, A (1994) **C-102m.** *** D: Jack Lucarelli. Sharon Farrell, Gigi Rice, David Steen, Sarah Trigger, Gene Lythgow, Mark Ruffalo, Nicholas Worth, Molly McClure. Solid characterizations add immeasurably to this complex, impassioned drama about an emotionally scarred backwoods North Carolina mother (Farrell). She gave birth to the eldest of her two grown children (Steen) when she was twelve, after being seduced by her preacher uncle: the emotional sparks begin to fly upon the arrival of an orphaned cousin (Trigger). Actor Steen also scripted the film.

Gift Horse, The (1952-British) **100m.** *** D: Compton Bennett. Trevor Howard, Richard Attenborough, Sonny Tufts, James Donald, Joan Rice, Bernard Lee, Dora Bryan, Hugh Williams, Sidney James. Solid WW2 drama with Howard as a troublesome ship's captain, disliked by his crew, who comes into his own while battling a German U-boat. Also known as GLORY AT SEA.▼

Gift of Love, The (1958) **C-105m.** ** D: Jean Negulesco. Lauren Bacall, Robert Stack, Evelyn Rudie, Lorne Greene, Anne Seymour. If you could put up with SENTIMENTAL JOURNEY you might bear this remake, which isn't even as good. Bacall dies but returns to earth as guiding spirit for her husband and daughter. Remade again for TV as SENTIMENTAL JOURNEY. CinemaScope.

Gig, The (1985) **C-92m.** *** D: Frank D. Gilroy. Wayne Rogers, Cleavon Little,

Andrew Duncan, Jerry Matz, Daniel Nalbach, Warren Vache, Joe Silver, Jay Thomas. Perceptive, touching comedy-drama about dreams, compromises, disappointments—what it means to be alive. A group of middle-class, middle-aged men play jazz both to amuse themselves and to escape from the pressures of their lives; they are hired for their first professional engagement at a small resort, and the experience proves to be unexpectedly unsettling. Gilroy also wrote the script.▼

Gigantis, the Fire Monster (1959-Japanese) **78m.** ** D: Motoyoshi, Hugo Grimaldi. Hiroshi Koizumi, Setsuko Makayama. A new Godzilla, here called Gigantis, battles spiny Angorous, trashing another Japanese city. First sequel to GODZILLA, retitled: GODZILLA RAIDS AGAIN.▼

Gigi (1948-French) **83m.** **½ D: Jacqueline Audry. Daniele Delorme, Frank Villard, Yvonne de Bray, Gaby Morlay, Jean Tissier, Madeleine Rousset. Original version of Colette's novel is not a musical but a drolly amusing (if talky and uncinematic) comedy of manners. Delorme, who starred in two more films based on Colette stories, is delightful as Gigi, the girl trained to be a courtesan by her aunt and grandmother in fin de siècle Paris. Originally 109m.

Gigi (1958) **C-116m.** **** D: Vincente Minnelli. Leslie Caron, Maurice Chevalier, Louis Jourdan, Hermione Gingold, Jacques Bergerac, Eva Gabor. Charming turn-of-the-century musical based on Colette's story of a French girl who's groomed to be a courtesan. Exquisitely filmed, perfectly cast, with memorable Lerner & Loewe score: title tune, "Thank Heaven for Little Girls," "I Remember it Well." Winner of nine Academy Awards including Best Picture, Director, Writing (Alan Jay Lerner), Cinematography (Joseph Ruttenberg), Costumes (Cecil Beaton), Song ("Gigi"), and Scoring (Andre Previn). Chevalier received an honorary Oscar. CinemaScope.▼●◗

Gigot (1962) **C-104m.** *** D: Gene Kelly. Jackie Gleason, Katherine Kath, Gabrielle Dorziat, Albert Remy, Yvonne Constant. Sentimental, well-acted tale of a deaf mute (Gleason) and a young girl in Paris. Simple film, well done; Gleason is excellent.

G.I. Jane (1997) **C-124m.** ** D: Ridley Scott. Demi Moore, Viggo Mortensen, Anne Bancroft, Scott Wilson, Jason Beghe, Daniel Von Bargen. Contrived movie about a woman selected as a test case for admitting females into naval combat. She undergoes the unbelievable rigors of Navy SEALs training, determined not to be shown favored treatment. Pumped-up Moore is perfect for the part, though it's a toss-up as to which scenes are more off-putting—her body-building workouts or her physical abuse at the hands of her Master Chief (Mortensen). Typically dense Scott soundtrack renders much of the dialogue unintelligible—but it's no loss. Too bad they didn't lose the anticlimactic final action sequence. Panavision. [R]▼●◗

Gilda (1946) **110m.** *** D: Charles Vidor. Rita Hayworth, Glenn Ford, George Macready, Joseph Calleia, Steven Geray. Highly charged story of emotional triangle—mysterious South American casino owner Macready, his new man-Friday Ford, and Macready's alluring wife (Hayworth)—unfortunately cops out with silly resolutions. Rita has never been sexier, especially when singing "Put the Blame on Mame."▼●

Gilda Live (1980) **C-90m.** **½ D: Mike Nichols. Gilda Radner, Father Guido Sarducci (Don Novello). Filmization of Radner's Broadway show, with the comedienne doing uncensored versions of her familiar *Saturday Night Live* TV characters. Best song: "Let's Talk Dirty to the Animals." [R]▼

Gilded Lily, The (1935) **80m.** *** D: Wesley Ruggles. Claudette Colbert, Fred MacMurray, Ray Milland, C. Aubrey Smith, Edward Craven, Luis Alberni, Grace Bradley. Colbert has to choose between aristocratic Milland and down-to-earth MacMurray. Fine romantic fluff. MacMurray's breezy performance here made a strong impression and boosted him to stardom.

Gildersleeve's Ghost (1944) **64m.** ** D: Gordon Douglas. Harold Peary, Marion Martin, Richard LeGrand, Amelita Ward. Programmer entry in the *Great Gildersleeve* series, involving mixture of spooks and gangsters, with predictable results.

Gimme an 'F' (1984) **C-103m.** ** D: Paul Justman. Stephen Shellen, Mark Keyloun, John Karlen, Jennifer C. Cooke, Beth Miller, Daphne Ashbrook. Harmless but highly improbable account of the trials and tribulations of a spastic cheerleading squad and its overage instructor. [R]▼

Gimme Shelter (1970) **C-91m.** **** D: David Maysles, Albert Maysles, Charlotte Zwerin. Rolling Stones, Jefferson Airplane, Melvin Belli. Outstanding documentary of the Rolling Stones and the famous Altamont Speedway free concert that resulted in chaos and murder. Chilling, beautifully handled, with the Stones performing their best songs of the period ("Satisfaction," "Sympathy for the Devil," "Brown Sugar," "Under My Thumb," etc.). [PG—edited from original R rating]▼

Ginger and Fred (1986-Italian) **C-126m.** *** D: Federico Fellini. Giulietta Masina, Marcello Mastroianni, Franco Fabrizi, Frederick Von Ledenberg, Martin Blau, Toto Mignone. Fellini satirizes TV, and the cult of instant celebrity, in this relaxed and amusing film. Ginger and Fred are, in fact, two small-time entertainers who used to *imitate* Rogers and Astaire and who are being reunited by an unctuous TV show.

The targets are a bit obvious and the pace a bit leisurely, but the climactic sequence is fun, and the two stars are wonderful to watch, as always. [PG-13]▼

Gingerbread Man, The (1998) **C-115m.** ** D: Robert Altman. Kenneth Branagh, Embeth Davidtz, Robert Downey, Jr., Daryl Hannah, Tom Berenger, Famke Janssen, Mae Whitman, Jesse James, Robert Duvall. Cocky Savannah lawyer (Branagh, with a terrific accent) sleeps with a woman he's just met (Davidtz, in a strong performance), then gets into hot water when he tries to protect her from her lunatic father. If he's so smart, how could he leave himself so vulnerable? Ask John Grisham, who wrote this thriller, which grows more implausible with each new story twist. Final showdown is especially weak. Screenplay credited to a pseudonymous Al Hayes. [R]▼●◗

Ginger in the Morning (1973) **C-89m.** **½ D: Gordon Wiles. Sissy Spacek, Monte Markham, Mark Miller, Susan Oliver, Slim Pickens. So-so romantic comedy about a lonely salesman who picks up a comely hitchhiker. He's attracted to her young, fresh independence; she's drawn to his old-fashioned romanticism. [PG]▼

Girl, a Guy, and a Gob, A (1941) **91m.** **½ D: Richard Wallace. George Murphy, Lucille Ball, Edmond O'Brien, Henry Travers, Franklin Pangborn, George Cleveland. The girl is zany stenographer Ball; the guy is shy lawyer O'Brien; the gob is happy-go-lucky Murphy. Wacky, silly three-cornered romance; plenty of slapstick and pantomime, not surprising, since film was produced by Harold Lloyd.▼

Girl Can't Help It, The (1956) **C-99m.** **½ D: Frank Tashlin. Tom Ewell, Jayne Mansfield, Edmond O'Brien, Julie London. One-joke film about press agent Ewell trying to hype gangster's girlfriend (Mansfield) to stardom. Some good Tashlin sight gags; classic performances by Fats Domino ("Blue Monday"), The Platters ("You'll Never Know"), Gene Vincent and His Blue Caps ("BeBop A Lula"), Little Richard ("She's Got It," "Ready Teddy," and "The Girl Can't Help It"). CinemaScope.▼

Girl Crazy (1932) **74m.** **½ D: William A. Seiter. Bert Wheeler, Robert Woolsey, Dorothy Lee, Eddie Quillan, Mitzi Green, Brooks Benedict, Kitty Kelly, Arline Judge, Stanley Fields, Chris Pin Martin. First screen version of the Gershwin musical comedy is a strange hybrid—neither a faithful rendition of the show nor a really good Wheeler & Woolsey vehicle. But it's not *bad,* with W&W as city slickers out West, clashing with Arizona heavy Fields. Best song, "You've Got What Gets Me," was written for the film. Perennial Marx Brothers foil Margaret Dumont has a funny uncredited cameo. Remade in 1943.

Girl Crazy (1943) **99m.** ***½ D: Norman Taurog. Mickey Rooney, Judy Garland, Gil Stratton, Robert E. Strickland, "Rags" Ragland, June Allyson, Nancy Walker, Guy Kibbee, Tommy Dorsey and his Orchestra. Rooney sent to small Southwestern school to forget girls, but meets Garland and that's that. Great Gershwin score includes "I Got Rhythm," "Embraceable You," "But Not For Me." Busby Berkeley (the original director) staged the finale. Filmed before in 1932; remade as WHEN THE BOYS MEET THE GIRLS. ▼●

Girl for Joe, A SEE: **Force of Arms**

Girlfriends (1978) **C-88m.** *** D: Claudia Weill. Melanie Mayron, Anita Skinner, Eli Wallach, Christopher Guest, Bob Balaban, Amy Wright, Viveca Lindfors, Mike Kellin, Ken McMillan, Kathryn Walker, Kristoffer Tabori. A young woman tries to cope with love, a career, and personal independence after roommate/girlfriend leaves to get married. Mayron's warm, winning performance helps likable but uneven film over rough spots. [PG]▼

Girl From Jones Beach, The (1949) **78m.** **½ D: Peter Godfrey. Ronald Reagan, Virginia Mayo, Eddie Bracken, Dona Drake, Henry Travers, Lois Wilson, Florence Bates. Breezy comedy about an artist trying to find living embodiment of the perfectly proportioned female in his illustrations. Capable romantic-comedy performance by Reagan.

Girl From Lorraine, The (1980-French-Swiss) **C-107m.** **½ D: Claude Goretta. Nathalie Baye, Bruno Ganz, Angela Winkler, Patrick Chesnais. Unemployed draughtswoman Baye, from the provinces, maintains her dignity in lonely, unfriendly Paris. Quietly rewarding drama with an extremely likable heroine; however, sometimes as dreary as some of the characters she meets. Originally titled LA PROVINCIALE.

Girl From Manhattan, The (1948) **81m.** ** D: Alfred E. Green. Dorothy Lamour, George Montgomery, Charles Laughton, Ernest Truex, Hugh Herbert, Constance Collier. Forgettable comedy-drama with model Lamour helping her uncle run his boarding house. Passable time-killer.

Girl From Mexico, The (1939) **71m.** **½ D: Leslie Goodwins. Lupe Velez, Donald Woods, Leon Errol, Linda Hayes, Donald MacBride, Ward Bond. Advertising man Woods goes to Mexico to find a star for his radio show and bumps (literally!) into Velez. Lupe's sex appeal is unleashed in this hectic comedy which led to the *Mexican Spitfire* series. Errol is very funny as her comic cohort.

Girl From Missouri, The (1934) **75m.** *** D: Jack Conway. Jean Harlow, Lionel Barrymore, Franchot Tone, Lewis Stone, Patsy Kelly, Alan Mowbray. Delightful fluff about good-girl Harlow trying to win a millionaire without sacrificing her integrity. Wise-cracking Kelly as her girlfriend is a treat.▼

Girl From Petrovka, The (1974) **C-104m.** ** D: Robert Ellis Miller. Goldie Hawn, Hal Holbrook, Anthony Hopkins, Gregoire Aslan, Anton Dolin. Old-fashioned comedy-drama about a bittersweet affair between American correspondent Holbrook and Russian Hawn. Filmed in Vienna and Hollywood. Panavision. [PG]▼

Girl From Scotland Yard, The (1937) **62m.** *½ D: Robert Vignola. Karen Morley, Robert Baldwin, Katherine Alexander, Eduardo Ciannelli. Escapist story of girl trying to track down mysterious madman with destruction ray is poorly handled; not nearly as much fun as it might have been.

Girl From 10th Avenue, The (1935) **69m.** *** D: Alfred E. Green. Bette Davis, Ian Hunter, Colin Clive, Alison Skipworth, John Eldredge, Philip Reed, Katherine Alexander. Honest working girl Davis gets alcoholic, recently jilted society lawyer Hunter back on his feet; then his ex-girlfriend decides she wants him back. Davis shines in this engrossing soaper.

Girl-Getters, The (1966-British) **79m.** *** D: Michael Winner. Oliver Reed, Jane Merrow, Barbara Ferris, Julia Foster, David Hemmings. Realistic study of hoodlum youths at British seaside resort, their prankish games and romances; intelligently portrayed. Retitled: THE SYSTEM.▼

Girl Happy (1965) **C-96m.** **½ D: Boris Sagal. Elvis Presley, Shelley Fabares, Harold J. Stone, Gary Crosby, Joby Baker, Nita Talbot, Mary Ann Mobley, Chris Noel, Jackie Coogan. Formula Presley musical with tiresome plot of Elvis in Fort Lauderdale chaperoning Fabares, daughter of Chicago mobster. Panavision.▼

Girl He Left Behind, The (1956) **103m.** **½ D: David Butler. Tab Hunter, Natalie Wood, Jessie Royce Landis, Jim Backus, Henry Jones, Murray Hamilton, Alan King, James Garner, David Janssen. Reminiscent of SEE HERE PRIVATE HARGROVE, without any of the warmth or humor. Hunter is new recruit in Army.

Girl Hunters, The (1963-British) **103m.** **½ D: Roy Rowland. Mickey Spillane, Lloyd Nolan, Shirley Eaton, Hy Gardner. Spillane plays his own fictional detective Mike Hammer in this rugged murder mystery. Since the disappearance of his devoted secretary, Hammer has been wallowing in alcohol; he sobers up, and goes into action, upon learning she might be alive. Panavision. ▼

Girl in a Million, A (1946-British) **81m.** ** D: Francis Searle. Joan Greenwood, Hugh Williams, Yvonne Owen, Edward Lexy, Jane Hylton, Michael Hordern. Sometimes wacky comedy focusing on deaf mute who uses her charm to reform several cantankerous gentlemen.

Girl in a Swing, The (1989-U.S.-British) **C-112m.** BOMB D: Gordon Hessler. Meg Tilly, Rupert Frazer, Nicholas Le Prevost, Elspet Gray, Lorna Heilbron, Helen Cherry. Antique dealer marries a mysterious German woman after a whirlwind courtship and pays the consequences, surviving her hallucinations and related erratic behavior. Despite lots of simulated (and unrated) screen sex, this is absolutely unwatchable—though Frazer looks just enough like Regis Philbin to give this stinker some unexpected subtext. [R]▼●

Girl in Black Stockings, The (1957) **73m.** ** D: Howard W. Koch. Lex Barker, Anne Bancroft, Mamie Van Doren, Ron Randell, Marie Windsor. Minor murder mystery with some nice touches and good performances; set at chic Utah resort.

Girl in Distress SEE: **Jeannie**

Girl in Every Port, A (1928) **62m.** **½ D: Howard Hawks. Victor McLaglen, Robert Armstrong, Louise Brooks, Marcia Cassajuana, Myrna Loy, William Demarest, Natalie Joyce, Sally Rand. Lusty silent comedy about two swaggering sailor pals who travel the world brawling over anything—especially women. Pretty dated, but enthusiasm still puts it over; of special interest to Hawks buffs as the earliest example of his "buddy-buddy" films. Remade as GOLDIE.

Girl in Every Port, A (1952) **86m.** ** D: Chester Erskine. Groucho Marx, William Bendix, Marie Wilson, Don DeFore, Gene Lockhart. Nonsense of two gobs who hide a racehorse aboard ship. Good cast is wasted.▼●

Girl in His Pocket (1957-French) **82m.** **½ D: Pierre Kast. Jean Marais, Agnes Laurent, Genevieve Page. Strange tale of scientist who invents shrinking formula, changing his romantic life with unforetold complications.▼

Girl, Interrupted (1999) **C-127m.** *** D: James Mangold. Winona Ryder, Angelina Jolie, Clea DuVall, Brittany Murphy, Whoopi Goldberg, Vanessa Redgrave, Jared Leto, Jeffrey Tambor, Mary Kay Place, Joanna Kerns, Kurtwood Smith, Ray Baker. Vivid adaptation of Susanna Kaysen's autobiographical book (set in the late 1960s) about a girl who enters a mental institution at the age of 18, thinking she's normal compared to most of the others—though she did try to kill herself. Jolie is incandescent in an Oscar-winning performance as the firebrand of the ward, who, like most of the others, hides her true emotions. Ryder also executive-produced. [R]▼◗

Girl in the Kremlin, The (1957) **81m.** ** D: Russell Birdwell. Lex Barker, Zsa Zsa Gabor, Jeffrey Stone, William Schallert. Espionage hokum involving Gabor in dual role as twins, one of whom is Stalin's mistress.

Girl in the Painting (1948-British) **89m.**

*** D: Terence Fisher. Mai Zetterling, Robert Beatty, Guy Rolfe, Herbert Lom, Patrick Holt. Intriguing drama of serviceman involved in strange case of amnesiac girl seeking her lost past in Germany. Retitled: PORTRAIT FROM LIFE.

Girl in the Park, The SEE: **Sanctuary of Fear**

Girl in the Red Velvet Swing, The (1955) **C-109m.** **½ D: Richard Fleischer. Ray Milland, Joan Collins, Farley Granger, Cornelia Otis Skinner, Glenda Farrell, Luther Adler. Glossy, fictionalized account of Evelyn Nesbit-Stanford White-Harry Thaw escapade of early 20th-century N.Y.C. Showgirl falls in love with prominent architect, which upsets mentally disturbed millionaire. CinemaScope.

Girl in the Woods (1958) **71m.** *½ D: Tom Gries. Forrest Tucker, Maggie Hayes, Barton MacLane, Diana Francis. Lumbering tale of lumbermen's lives.

Girl in White, The (1952) **93m.** ** D: John Sturges. June Allyson, Arthur Kennedy, Gary Merrill, Mildred Dunnock, James Arness. Humdrum biography of Emily Dunning, the first woman to work as a doctor in a N.Y.C. public hospital.

Girl Most Likely, The (1957) **C-98m.** *** D: Mitchell Leisen. Jane Powell, Cliff Robertson, Keith Andes, Tommy Noonan, Kaye Ballard, Una Merkel. Musical remake of TOM, DICK AND HARRY comes off as bright, cheerful entertainment. A girl must decide which one of the trio she'll wed; Kaye Ballard does very well in supporting role. Choreography by Gower Champion.▼●

Girl Named Tamiko, A (1962) **C-110m.** **½ D: John Sturges. Laurence Harvey, France Nuyen, Martha Hyer, Gary Merrill, Michael Wilding. Miyoshi Umeki, Lee Patrick. Overblown soaper set in Tokyo. Harvey charms Hyer into proposing marriage so he can get U.S. citizenship. Nuyen is sweet Oriental whom Harvey really loves. Panavision.

Girl Next Door, The (1953) **C-92m.** **½ D: Richard Sale. Dan Dailey, June Haver, Dennis Day, Cara Williams, Natalie Schafer. Pleasing musical of singing star Haver moving to new home and falling in love with neighbor Dailey, a cartoonist.

Girl of the Golden West, The (1938) **120m.** **½ D: Robert Z. Leonard. Jeanette MacDonald, Nelson Eddy, Walter Pidgeon, Leo Carrillo, Buddy Ebsen, Leonard Penn. Oft-produced tale of love affair of good-girl MacDonald and bandit Eddy, with tuneful Gus Kahn-Sigmund Romberg score that didn't produce any hits.▼

Girl of the Night (1960) **93m.** **½ D: Joseph Cates. Anne Francis, Lloyd Nolan, Kay Medford, John Kerr. Francis gives a vivid performance as prostitute undergoing psychoanalysis.

Girl on a Motorcycle (1968-British-French) **C-91m.** *½ D: Jack Cardiff. Marianne Faithfull, Alain Delon, Roger Mutton, Marius Goring, Catherine Jourdan. Slick cinematography (by Cardiff) only asset to sleazy tale of Faithfull abandoning her husband, riding on her motorcycle to visit exlover Delon. From Andre Pieyre de Mandiargue's novel. Trimmed from original X-rated version titled NAKED UNDER LEATHER. [R]▼●◗

Girl on the Bridge (1951) **77m.** BOMB D: Hugo Haas. Hugo Haas, Beverly Michaels, Robert Dane, Johnny Close, Anthony Jochim. Typical Haasian look at Michaels as a so-called femme fatale and her effect on the men in her life.

Girl Rush (1944) **65m.** *½ D: Gordon Douglas. Alan Carney, Wally Brown, Frances Langford, Paul Hurst, Vera Vague, Robert Mitchum. Dim-witted comedy with Carney and Brown starring as vaudeville troupers stranded in San Francisco during the gold rush. Langford is always good, but the film isn't.▼

Girl Rush, The (1955) **C-85m.** **½ D: Robert Pirosh. Rosalind Russell, Fernando Lamas, Eddie Albert, Gloria DeHaven, Marion Lorne. Russell inherits a Las Vegas casino and determines to make it go, romanced by Lamas. Minor musical numbers and forced gaiety are all too evident. VistaVision.

Girls, The (1968) **90m.** *** D: Mai Zetterling. Bibi Andersson, Harriet Andersson, Gunnel Lindblom, Gunnar Bjornstrand, Erland Josephson, Ulf Palme. Trenchant study of modern marriages and female roles, loaded with fantasy sequences. Fabulous cast drawn by actress-turned-director Zetterling from Ingmar Bergman's repertory company.

Girls About Town (1931) **82m.** *** D: George Cukor. Kay Francis, Joel McCrea, Lilyan Tashman, Eugene Pallette, Alan Dinehart, Louise Beavers. Title tells all in this Pre-Code comedy that stops just short of calling Francis and Tashman tarts. The latter (who died three years later) is likable in her best screen role, and gorgeous Travis Banton costumes add to the film. One of the best of the early Cukor films.

Girls' Dormitory (1936) **66m.** **½ D: Irving Cummings. Herbert Marshall, Ruth Chatterton, Simone Simon, Constance Collier, J. Edward Bromberg, Dixie Dunbar, Tyrone Power. Fairly standard tale of girl's infatuation for school head Marshall spotlights newcomer Simon, who does quite well, and young leading man Power in featured role.

Girls for Rent (1974) **C-92m.** BOMB D: Al Adamson. Georgina Spelvin, Susan McIver, Rosalind Miles, Preston Pierce, Robert Livingston, Kent Taylor. Low-budget quickie capitalizing on Spelvin's success in porno classic THE DEVIL IN MISS JONES; she's an evil hit lady in dreary film which deteriorates into chase filler. [R]

Girls! Girls! Girls! (1962) **C-106m.** **½ D: Norman Taurog. Elvis Presley, Stella Stevens, Laurel Goodwin, Jeremy Slate, Benson Fong, Robert Strauss, Ginny Tiu. Presley is chased by a mass of girls and can't decide which one he prefers. Along the way, he sings "Return to Sender" and some other less memorable numbers (like "Song of the Shrimp").▼

Girl Shy (1924) **88m.** *** D: Fred Newmeyer, Sam Taylor. Harold Lloyd, Jobyna Ralston, Richard Daniels, Carlton Griffin. Enjoyable Lloyd vehicle mixes comedy and sentiment with a spectacular chase finale. Harold is a small-town boy who's petrified of women but writes book on lovemaking secrets! Fantasy scenes of his love life mark highlight.▼

Girls in Prison (1956) **87m.** *½ D: Edward L. Cahn. Richard Denning, Joan Taylor, Adele Jergens, Helen Gilbert, Lance Fuller, Jane Darwell, Raymond Hatton, Mae Marsh. Tawdry study of prison life with usual female stereotype prisoners.▼

Girls in Prison (1994) **C-83m. TVM** D: John McNaughton. Missy Crider, Bahni Turpin, Ione Skye, Anne Heche, Nicolette Scorsese, Miguel Sandoval, Tom Towles, Angie Ray McKinney. 1954: Standard tale of three women in prison, with one the target of a murderer. Good performances and direction keep this watchable, despite poor attention to period detail. One of Showtime's "Rebel Highway" entries, based on old American-International pictures, this uses only the title of the 1956 film. Script by Sam Fuller and his wife, Christa Lang. Average.▼

Girls in the Night (1953) **83m.** ** D: Jack Arnold. Joyce Holden, Glenda Farrell, Harvey Lembeck, Patricia Hardy, Jaclynne Greene. Compact account of young people seeking to better their lives, blighted by N.Y.C. tenement existence.

Girl 6 (1996) **C-105m.** ** D: Spike Lee. Theresa Randle, Isaiah Washington, Spike Lee, Jenifer Lewis, Debi Mazar, Peter Berg, Michael Imperioli, Dina Pearlman, Maggie Rush, Kristen Wilson, Naomi Campbell, Desi Moreno, John Turturro, Madonna, Quentin Tarantino, Halle Berry, Richard Belzer, Ron Silver, Susan Batson, Gretchen Mol. A frustrated young actress takes (and becomes addicted to) a job as a phone-sex worker. Done in by its predictability and lack of insight into the character of Girl 6. Worth a look for Randle's appealing performance and Lee's vivid depiction of the phone-sex world. [R]▼●

Girls Just Want to Have Fun (1985) **C-87m.** **½ D: Alan Metter. Sarah Jessica Parker, Lee Montgomery, Morgan Woodward, Jonathan Silverman, Helen Hunt, Holly Gagnier, Ed Lauter, Shannen Doherty. Likable, upbeat teen comedy about girl with reactionary father who wants to enter dance contest. Clichés and contrivances are counterbalanced by believable portrayal of teenage girls, appealingly played by Parker and Hunt. [PG]▼

Girls of Pleasure Island, The (1953) **C-95m.** ** D: F. Hugh Herbert, Alvin Ganzer. Leo Genn, Don Taylor, Gene Barry, Elsa Lanchester, Audrey Dalton. Unfunny comedy involving Genn and brood of daughters combating swarm of G.I.s who establish a base on their island.

Girls of Summer SEE: **Satisfaction**

Girls of the Night (1959-French) **114m.** **½ D: Maurice Cloche. Georges Marchal, Nicole Berger, Claus Holm, Kay Fischer, Gil Vidal. Sensible telling of plight of group of prostitutes, and clergyman who tries to help them.

Girls of the Road (1940) **61m.** ** D: Nick Grinde. Ann Dvorak, Helen Mack, Lola Lane, Ann Doran, Bruce Bennett, Don Beddoe. Interesting B movie about daughter of a governor who goes incognito to learn first hand about the way young women who've taken to the hobo life are being treated. Conventional, barely believable, but starts out with some real punch.

Girls on Probation (1938) **63m.** *½ D: William McGann. Jane Bryan, Ronald Reagan, Anthony Averill, Sheila Bromley, Henry O'Neill, Elisabeth Risdon, Sig Rumann, Susan Hayward. Uninspired B picture about a young woman (Bryan) who can't seem to stay out of trouble with the law; Reagan is a lawyer who defends her and falls in love with her.

Girls on the Beach, The (1965) **C-80m.** *½ D: William N. Witney. Martin West, Noreen Corcoran, Peter Brooks, Lana Wood, The Beach Boys, Lesley Gore, Dick Miller. Three coeds promise they'll get the Beatles to make a personal appearance and then have a mite of trouble delivering. The Beach Boys sing two tunes in this predictable comedy. Reissued as SUMMER OF '64.

Girls on the Loose (1958) **78m.** ** D: Paul Henreid. Mara Corday, Lita Milan, Barbara Bostock, Mark Richman. Drama unfolds account of Corday heading robbery gang, and eventual downfall.

Girls Town (1959) **92m.** *½ D: Charles Haas. Mamie Van Doren, Mel Torme, Paul Anka, Ray Anthony, Maggie Hayes, Cathy Crosby, Gigi Perreau, Gloria Talbott, Jim Mitchum, Elinor Donahue, Sheilah Graham, The Platters, Harold Lloyd, Jr. Wisecracking bad girl Van Doren is sent to title correctional institution, where she learns that she doesn't have all the answers. Absurd in the extreme, but has definite camp value just for the cast alone . . . plus, Anka sings "Ave Maria"! As Mamie says, it's "cool, crazy, fantabulous." Retitled INNOCENT AND THE DAMNED.▼

Girls Town (1996) **C-90m.** **½ D: Jim McKay. Lili Taylor, Bruklin Harris, Anna Grace, Aunjanue Ellis, Guillermo Diaz, Ernestine Jackson, Tara Carnes, Michael Imperioli. Disparate clique of teenage girlfriends discover the depths of their individual secrets when one of their group inexplicably commits suicide. A largely improvised script results in realistic dialogue that considers the issues of teenage boredom, friendship, victimization of women, solidarity, and empowerment. A painfully unsentimental, sometimes humorous, coming-of-age in the '90s story. [R]▼●

Girl Trouble (1942) **82m.** ** D: Harold Schuster. Don Ameche, Joan Bennett, Billie Burke, Frank Craven, Vivian Blaine. Pleasant frou-frou with Ameche and Bennett involved in business and romancing, with fine support from the adept scatterbrain Burke.

Girl Who Couldn't Say No, The (1968-Italian) **C-83m.** ** D: Franco Brusati. Virna Lisi, George Segal, Lila Kedrova, Akim Tamiroff, Paola Pitagora, Felicity Mason. Square Segal and childhood friend Lisi fall for each other, but just can't maintain a permanent relationship; mild comedy. Techniscope. [M/PG]

Girl Who Had Everything, The (1953) **69m.** **½ D: Richard Thorpe. Elizabeth Taylor, Fernando Lamas, William Powell, Gig Young, James Whitmore. Murky melodrama with top cast. Girl falls in love with criminal client of her attorney father. Remake of A FREE SOUL.▼

Girl Who Knew Too Much (1969) **C-96m.** ** D: Francis D. Lyon. Adam West, Nancy Kwan, Nehemiah Persoff, Robert Alda. Adventurer who is hired to find the killer of a syndicate boss discovers Communist plot to infiltrate organized crime. [R]

Girl Who Spelled Freedom, The (1986) **C-100m. TVM** D: Simon Wincer. Wayne Rogers, Mary Kay Place, Kieu Chinh, Kathleen Sisk. A Disney delight about a real-life teenage Cambodian refugee who arrived in the States in 1979 speaking little English and became a national spelling bee champion in just four years. Australian director Wincer and writers Christopher Knopf and David A. Simons do themselves proud. Above average.▼

Girl With a Suitcase (1960-Italian) **96m.** ***½ D: Valerio Zurlini. Claudia Cardinale, Jacques Perrin, Luciana Angelillo, Corrado Pani. Impressive film of devoted but shady girl Cardinale following her ex-lover to Parma, only to fall in love with his adolescent brother. Confusing at times, but extremely well acted.▼

Girl With Green Eyes (1964-British) **91m.** *** D: Desmond Davis. Rita Tushingham, Peter Finch, Lynn Redgrave, T. P. McKenna, Marie Kean, Julian Glover. Moving drama of young farm-girl falling in love with writer Finch, highlighted by winning Tushingham performance. Redgrave scores as her roommate. Filmed in Dublin.▼

Girl With the Red Hair, The (1981-Dutch) **C-116m.** **½ D: Ben Verbong. Renee Soutendijk, Peter Tuinman, Loes Luca, Johan Leysen, Robert Delhez, Ada Bouwman. Determined student becomes a killer of Nazi informers during WW2. Tense, chilling, sober, but overlong and too often slow; good score by Nicola Piovani helps. Special color effect will be lost on TV. Based on a true story. [PG]

Girly SEE: **Mumsy, Nanny, Sonny and Girly**

Giro City SEE: **And Nothing But the Truth**

Git (1965) **C-90m.** *½ D: Ellis Kadison. Jack Chaplain, Heather North, Leslie Bradley, Richard Webb. Young boy and daughter of dog-breeder widower set out to train a renegade setter. Woof woof.▼

Give a Girl a Break (1953) **C-82m.** **½ D: Stanley Donen. Marge and Gower Champion, Debbie Reynolds, Helen Wood, Bob Fosse, Kurt Kasznar, Richard Anderson, William Ching, Larry Keating. Innocuous musical fluff about three young women competing for the starring role in a Broadway musical. Watching Marge and Gower dance is always a treat, but the real highlight is seeing two of the greatest choreographers of all time (Champion and Fosse) dancing together. Undistinguished score by Ira Gershwin and Burton Lane.▼●

Give 'Em Hell (1954-French) **90m.** **½ D: John Berry. Eddie Constantine, Mai Britt, Jean Danet, Jean Carmet. If not taken seriously, amusing gangster yarn of Johnny Jordan (Constantine), with usual amount of fisticuffs and gunplay.

Give 'Em Hell, Harry! (1975) **C-102m.** *** D: Steve Binder. James Whitmore. Straight reproduction of Whitmore's one-man stage triumph as Harry Truman, covering high points in both the political and personal life of our 33rd President. Video-taped and transferred to film for theatrical release, but original tape version used for TV. [PG]▼

Give Me a Sailor (1938) **80m.** **½ D: Elliott Nugent. Martha Raye, Bob Hope, Betty Grable, Jack Whiting, Clarence Kolb, J. C. Nugent. Fast-moving comedy with Raye an ugly duckling constantly upstaged by her prettier, self-centered sibling (Grable); Hope and Whiting are navy brothers who play out a comic/romantic scenario involving the sisters.▼

Give Me Your Heart (1936) **87m.** **½ D: Archie Mayo. Kay Francis, George Brent, Roland Young, Patric Knowles, Henry Stephenson, Frieda Inescort. Francis has a child by a married man, weds Brent yet still pines for her baby. Well made but all-too-familiar drama, highlighted by Kay's glamorous wardrobe.

Give My Regards to Broad Street (1984-British) **C-108m.** ** D: Peter Webb. Paul McCartney, Bryan Brown, Ringo Starr, Barbara Bach, Linda McCartney, Tracey Ullman, Ralph Richardson. Vanity film with silly "plot" about a missing album tape connecting a number of music video–type numbers ("Ballroom Dancing," "No More Lonely Nights"). Some of the music is good (and McCartney reprises a couple of Beatles songs) but mostly it's a big snooze. [PG] ▼●

Give My Regards to Broadway (1948) **C-89m.** ** D: Lloyd Bacon. Dan Dailey, Charles Winninger, Nancy Guild, Charles Ruggles, Fay Bainter. Blah musical of old-time vaudevillian Winninger refusing to admit that the family act should break up.

Give Us Wings (1940) **62m.** ** D: Charles Lamont. Billy Halop, Huntz Hall, Bernard Punsley, Gabriel Dell, Bobby Jordan, Victor Jory, Wallace Ford, Anne Gwynne, Shemp Howard, Milburn Stone, William (Billy) Benedict. The Little Tough Guys become pilots for a shady crop-dusting firm in this routine meller.

Gizmo (1977) **C/B&W-77m.** **½ D: Howard Smith. Entertaining compilation of film clips on 20th-century "inventors" and their often outlandish contraptions. Good fun, though it can't quite sustain feature length. [G]▼

Gladiator, The (1938) **70m.** **½ D: Edward Sedgwick. Joe E. Brown, Man Mountain Dean, June Travis, Dickie Moore, Lucien Littlefield. Timid boy (Brown) takes serum, becomes all-star hero at college. Simple, sincere, enjoyable.▼

Gladiator (1992) **C-98m.** *½ D: Rowdy Herrington. Cuba Gooding, Jr., James Marshall, Robert Loggia, Ossie Davis, Brian Dennehy, Cara Buono, John Heard, Jon Seda, Lance Slaughter. Pubescent ROCKY wannabe about a tough Chicago teenager becoming involved in the tawdry underground boxing scene. Builds to ludicrous climax with crooked fight promoter Dennehy actually getting in the ring! [R]▼●

Gladiator (2000) **C-154m.** *** D: Ridley Scott. Russell Crowe, Joaquin Phoenix, Connie Nielsen, Oliver Reed, Derek Jacobi, Djimon Hounsou, Richard Harris, David Hemmings. Impressive tale from the days of the Roman Empire, with Crowe as a dedicated soldier who refuses to transfer his loyalty to the new emperor Commodus (Phoenix) and suffers the consequences, winding up a gladiator in the Roman Colosseum. Crowe is so good—and his character so compelling—that one is willing to forgive story lulls; the spectacle is grand, but the opening battle scene stresses chaos over coherence. Reed's last film; he died during production. Super 35. [R]

Glass Alibi, The (1946) **70m.** ** D: W. Lee Wilder. Paul Kelly, Douglas Fowley, Anne Gwynne, Maris Wrixon, Jack Conrad. Satisfactory drama involving con-man who thinks marrying a dying heiress is a sure bet, till he discovers she's recovering.

Glass Bottom Boat, The (1966) **C-110m.** *** D: Frank Tashlin. Doris Day, Rod Taylor, Arthur Godfrey, Paul Lynde, Eric Fleming, Alice Pearce, Ellen Corby, John McGiver, Edward Andrews, Dom De Luise, Dick Martin. Above-average Day nonsense, with widow Doris hired by research scientist Taylor as his biographer. He tries to seduce her; she's mistaken for a Russian spy. Lots of Tashlin's trademark slapstick. Panavision.▼●

Glass Cage, The (1964) **78m.** *½ D: Antonio Santean. John Hoyt, Elisha Cook, Arline Sax, Robert Kelljan. Programmer of burglar shot in self-defense and romance developing between police investigator and suspect. Retitled: DEN OF DOOM.▼

Glass Houses (1972) **C-90m.** ** D: Alexander Singer. Jennifer O'Neill, Bernard Barrow, Deirdre Lenihan, Ann Summers, Phillip Pine, Lloyd Kino. Low-grade drama about infidelity and incestuous desire is mildly interesting in a lurid kind of way; O'Neill's first film, but released after RIO LOBO and SUMMER OF '42. [R]◗

Glass Key, The (1935) **80m.** *** D: Frank Tuttle. George Raft, Claire Dodd, Edward Arnold, Rosalind Keith, Ray Milland, Guinn Williams. Solid Dashiell Hammett story about politician Arnold getting involved in mysterious murder, Raft trying to dig out the facts. Drags during second half, but still quite good. Remade in 1942.

Glass Key, The (1942) **85m.** ***½ D: Stuart Heisler. Brian Donlevy, Veronica Lake, Alan Ladd, Joseph Calleia, William Bendix, Bonita Granville, Richard Denning. Fast-moving remake of 1935 film, with wardheeler Donlevy accused of murder, henchman Ladd bailing him out. Lake fine as mysterious love interest, Bendix effective as brutal bodyguard. Akira Kurosawa claims this was his inspiration for YOJIMBO. Dashiell Hammett novel neatly adapted by Jonathan Latimer.▼●

Glass Menagerie, The (1950) **107m.** **½ D: Irving Rapper. Jane Wyman, Kirk Douglas, Gertrude Lawrence, Arthur Kennedy. More notable for its cast and intention than results. Slow-moving version of Tennessee Williams' drama of lame girl, her faded Southern belle mother, and idealistic brother, all living in their own fragile dream worlds. Remade twice.

Glass Menagerie, The (1973) **C-100m. TVM** D: Anthony Harvey. Katharine Hepburn, Sam Waterston, Joanna Miles, Michael Moriarty. Producer David Susskind and the entire cast (Hepburn in her TV acting debut) deserve kudos for this superior version of Tennessee Williams' play (adapted by the playwright). Above average.

Glass Menagerie, The (1987) **C-134m.**

★★★ D: Paul Newman. Joanne Woodward, John Malkovich, Karen Allen, James Naughton. Respectable, well-made version of Tennessee Williams' now legendary play, with Woodward fine as Amanda Wingfield and Malkovich superb as son Tom. Woodward, Allen, and Naughton had appeared in two regional stage productions of Williams' play prior to making this film. [PG]▼●

Glass Mountain, The (1950-British) **94m.** ★★★ D: Henry Cass. Valentina Cortese, Michael Denison, Dulcie Gray, Sebastian Shaw. Beautifully made film of a British composer who writes an opera, inspired by majestic Italian Alps. A treat for music-lovers, with many singers from La Scala appearing in opera sequence.

Glass Shield, The (1995) **C-108m.** ★★ D: Charles Burnett. Michael Boatman, Lori Petty, Richard Anderson, Ice Cube, Bernie Casey, Elliott Gould, Michael Ironside, Don Harvey, Michael Gregory, M. Emmett Walsh, Sy Richardson, Natalija Nogulich, Wanda de Jesus, Victoria Dillard. Young, wide-eyed Boatman is the first black man assigned to a tight-knit office of the L.A. Sheriff's Department; he soon discovers just how dirty this precinct really is. A polemic masquerading as a movie, with heavy-handed "villains" and a story that eventually loses its focus and its momentum. [PG-13]▼●

Glass Slipper, The (1955) **C-94m.** ★★½ D: Charles Walters. Leslie Caron, Michael Wilding, Keenan Wynn, Estelle Winwood, Elsa Lanchester, Amanda Blake. Silky musical of Cinderella story with talky plot bogging down lilting fantasy dance and song sequences.▼

Glass Sphinx, The (1967-Italian-Spanish) **C-91m.** ★½ D: Luigi Scattini. Robert Taylor, Anita Ekberg, Gianna Serra, Jack Stuart, Angel Del Pozo, Jose Truchado. World-famous archeologist Taylor on trail of tomb of glass sphinx containing magic elixir; foreign agents have similar idea. Confusing and forgettable. Techniscope.▼

Glass Tomb, The (1955-British) **59m.** ★★ D: Montgomery Tully. John Ireland, Honor Blackman, Geoffrey Keen, Eric Pohlmann, Sydney Tafler, Liam Redmond, Sam Kydd. Bizarre carnival backgrounds give this typical murder tale some spice.

Glass Tower, The (1957-German) **92m.** ★★½ D: Harold Braun. Lilli Palmer, O. E. Hasse, Peter Van Eyck, Brigitte Horney, Hannes Messemer. Interesting study of overly jealous husband keeping beautiful wife Palmer a prisoner so she won't be tempted by other men; well acted.

Glass Wall, The (1953) **80m.** ★★ D: Maxwell Shane. Vittorio Gassman, Gloria Grahame, Ann Robinson, Jerry Paris, Kathleen Freeman. Drama of refugee Gassman who illegally came to N.Y.C. and, rather than accept deportation, goes on the lam.

Glass Web, The (1953) **81m.** ★★★ D: Jack Arnold. Edward G. Robinson, John Forsythe, Kathleen Hughes, Marcia Henderson, Richard Denning, Hugh Sanders. Robinson is fine as criminal research authority for TV mystery show, who's caught up in murder utilized as basis for one of the programs. Kathleen Freeman and Beverly Garland have bits. Originally shot in 3-D.

Gleaming the Cube (1989) **C-104m.** ★★ D: Graeme Clifford. Christian Slater, Steven Bauer, Ed Lauter, Micole Mercurio, Richard Herd, Charles Cyphers, Le Tuan. Rebellious young skateboarder sets out to find his brother's murderers with the help of a street-smart detective. Skateboard stunts are sensational, but the story is by-the-numbers TV stuff. The title is skateboarding jargon for reaching the ultimate—which this movie never does. Retitled A BROTHER'S JUSTICE for TV. [PG-13]▼●◗

Glen and Randa (1971) **C-94m.** ★★½ D: Jim McBride. Steven Curry, Shelley Plimpton, Woodrow Chambliss, Garry Goodrow. Years after nuclear destruction of world, teenage lovers follow comic-book "clues" and look for Metropolis. [R—originally rated X]▼●

Glengarry Glen Ross (1992) **C-100m.** ★★★ D: James Foley. Al Pacino, Jack Lemmon, Alec Baldwin, Ed Harris, Alan Arkin, Kevin Spacey, Jonathan Pryce, Bruce Altman, Jude Ciccolella. David Mamet's scorching, profane, Pulitzer Prize-winning play about an office full of desperate real-estate salesmen-cum-con-artists is faithfully reproduced (Mamet did the adaptation himself) with a gallery of stunning performances. Pacino is dynamic as the office hotshot, Lemmon totally credible as the loser, and Baldwin is dynamite (in a part created especially for the film) as an insulting "motivator." Never succeeds in being anything but a photographed play, but when the play and the actors are this good it's hard to complain. Super 35. [R] ▼●

Glenn Miller Story, The (1954) **C-116m.** ★★★ D: Anthony Mann. James Stewart, June Allyson, Charles Drake, George Tobias, Harry Morgan, Frances Langford, Louis Armstrong, Gene Krupa. Stewart is convincingly cast as the popular bandleader in this extremely sentimental (and largely fictitious) account of his life. Music's the real star here, with most of Miller's hit records recreated.▼●

Glen or Glenda (1953) **61m.** BOMB D: Edward D. Wood, Jr. Bela Lugosi, Dolores Fuller, Daniel Davis, Lyle Talbot, Timothy Farrell, "Tommy" Haynes, Charles Crafts, Conrad Brooks. Sensational but sincere "docu-fantasy" about transvestism could well be the worst movie ever made. Legendarily awful director Wood stars (under the name Daniel Davis) as Glen, who can't decide how to tell his fiancée he wants to wear her clothes. Dizzying hodgepodge of stock footage, demented dream sequences, and heartfelt plea for tolerance linked by campy Lugosi narrating from haunted house. "Bevare!" Even more inept and hilarious than Wood's infamous PLAN 9 FROM OUTER SPACE. Also released as I CHANGED MY SEX, I LED 2 LIVES, and HE OR SHE. Reissued at 67m.▼●◗

Glimmer Man, The (1996) **C-92m.** *½ D: John Gray. Steven Seagal, Keenen Ivory Wayans, Michelle Johnson, Brian Cox, Bob Gunton, John Jackson, Stephen Tobolowsky. Seagal and Wayans team up to track down a serial killer who is terrorizing the L.A. area. Tired buddy/cop picture, even by Seagal's fairly low standards; he also coproduced. [R]▼●◗

Global Affair, A (1964) **84m.** **½ D: Jack Arnold. Bob Hope, Yvonne De Carlo, Robert Sterling, John McGiver, Lilo Pulver. Unwitty Hope vehicle has Bob in charge of a baby found at U.N., with female representative from each nation demanding the child. Also shown in computer-colored version. Metroscope.▼

Gloria (1980) **C-121m.** ** D: John Cassavetes. Gena Rowlands, Buck Henry, John Adames, Julie Carmen, Lupe Guarnica. Ex-mob mistress goes on the lam with a young neighbor-boy after gangland hit-men wipe out his parents. Good-looking but way overlong melodrama, which Cassavetes may or may not be playing for laughs. Remade in 1999. [PG]▼●

Gloria (1999) **C-108m.** ** D: Sidney Lumet. Sharon Stone, Jean-Luke Figueroa, Jeremy Northam, George C. Scott, Cathy Moriarty, Bonnie Bedelia, Mike Starr. Unnecessary, sentimental remake of 1980 John Cassavetes melodrama with Stone stepping into Gena Rowlands' pumps as a tough ex–gun moll on the lam with an adorable Puerto Rican tyke (Figueroa) in tow. Still watchable, thanks to Stone's funny, full-bodied performance (once you get over her barely credible Noo Yawk accent) and her cuddly costar. [R]▼●◗

Glorifying the American Girl (1929) **87m.** **½ D: Millard Webb, John Harkrider. Mary Eaton, Edward Crandall; and as themselves: Eddie Cantor, Helen Morgan, Rudy Vallee, Florenz Ziegfeld, Adolph Zukor, Otto Kahn, Texas Guinan, Mayor & Mrs. James Walker, Ring Lardner, Noah Beery, Johnny Weissmuller. Early talkie musical revue produced by Ziegfeld himself is a routine chorus-girl-trying-to-break-into-show-biz plot, overshadowed by the novelty of seeing a dazzling and sometimes bizarre array of talent appearing as themselves (best of all: Helen Morgan). Originally released with some two-color Technicolor sequences. Archivally restored to 96m.▼

Glory (1956) **C-100m.** ** D: David Butler. Margaret O'Brien, Walter Brennan, Charlotte Greenwood, John Lupton. Bland horseracing story, with grown-up O'Brien as woman who owns champion horse. SuperScope.▼

Glory (1989) **C-122m.** **** D: Edward Zwick. Matthew Broderick, Denzel Washington, Cary Elwes, Morgan Freeman, Jihmi Kennedy, Andre Braugher, John Finn, Donovan Leitch, John David Cullum, Bob Gunton, Cliff DeYoung. Exceptional story of America's first unit of black soldiers during the Civil War and the young, inexperienced Northerner (Broderick) who's given the job of training and leading them. Based in part on the letters of that young officer and brought to life with astonishing skill and believability. Grand, moving, breathtakingly filmed (by veteran cinematographer Freddie Francis) and faultlessly performed. One of the finest historical dramas ever made. Oscar winner for Cinematography, Sound, and Supporting Actor (Washington). Screenplay by Kevin Jarre. Jane Alexander (as Broderick's mother) and Raymond St. Jacques (as Frederick Douglass) appear unbilled. [R]▼●◗

Glory Alley (1952) **79m.** **½ D: Raoul Walsh. Ralph Meeker, Leslie Caron, Gilbert Roland, Louis Armstrong, John McIntire. Just before the championship bout, boxer Meeker quits the fight game. Series of flashbacks tells his intriguing story. New Orleans backgrounds allow for some good musical interludes.

Glory at Sea SEE: **Gift Horse, The**

Glory Boy SEE: **My Old Man's Place**

Glory Brigade, The (1953) **81m.** ** D: Robert D. Webb. Victor Mature, Alexander Scourby, Lee Marvin, Richard Egan, Nick Dennis, Roy Roberts, Alvy Moore, Henry Kulky. Passable Korean War drama with Mature leading a platoon of American GIs assigned to escort some Greek soldiers into enemy territory.

Glory! Glory! (1989) **C-210m. TVM** D: Lindsay Anderson. Richard Thomas, Ellen Greene, James Whitmore, Barry Morse, Winston Reckert. Broad, often slashing satire about TV evangelism with a dynamic but foul-mouthed female rock 'n' roller being brought in to save a money-machine mega-ministry from sinking under the leadership of the charismatic founder's straight-arrow son. Lots of truths, sight gags, rock music, sex, and Mike Fash's flashy camerawork. Written with a vengeance by Stan Daniels (of *The Mary Tyler Moore Show*), and directed to a turn by sharp-eyed Anderson. Made for cable; originally shown in two parts. Above average. [R]▼●

Glory Guys, The (1965) **C-112m.** ** D: Arnold Laven. Tom Tryon, Harve Presnell, Michael Anderson, Jr., Senta Berger, James Caan, Slim Pickens, Wayne Rogers. Lumbering Cavalry Western with a love triangle thrown in. Screenplay by Sam Peckinpah. Panavision.▼

Glory Stompers, The (1967) **C-85m.** BOMB D: Anthony M. Lanza. Dennis Hopper, Jody McCrea, Chris Noel, Jock Mahoney, Lindsay Crosby. Hopper, pre-EASY RIDER, stars as motorcycle-gang leader who wears a swastika patch and mouths lines like, "Hey, like, ya know, I wanna dance with you, baby." And, from Noel: "I just want something better than being a Stompers girl." Hilariously bad; see if you can count how many times Hopper says "man." Colorscope.▼

Glove, The (1978) **C-91m.** ** D: Ross Hagen. John Saxon, Rosey Grier, Joanna Cassidy, Joan Blondell, Jack Carter, Aldo Ray, Keenan Wynn. Violent action flick (with episodic comic diversions by various "guest" veterans), pitting a world-weary bounty hunter against a vengeful ex-con who commits mayhem with a leather-laced steel riot glove. Also shown as THE GLOVE: LETHAL TERMINATOR and LETHAL TERMINATOR. [R] ▼

Glove: Lethal Terminator, The SEE: **Glove, The**

"G" Men (1935) **85m.** ***½ D: William Keighley. James Cagney, Ann Dvorak, Margaret Lindsay, Robert Armstrong, Barton MacLane, Lloyd Nolan, William Harrigan. Although raised by an underworld figure, Cagney joins F.B.I. when a pal is killed by gangsters, puts his first-hand knowledge to use. Exciting film, beautifully shot by Sol Polito; prologue with David Brian added for 1949 reissue. Also shown in computer-colored version.▼

Gnome-Mobile, The (1967) **C-90m.** *** D: Robert Stevenson. Walter Brennan, Matthew Garber, Karen Dotrice, Richard Deacon, Tom Lowell, Sean McClory, Ed Wynn. Crusty businessman Brennan, his niece and nephew discover gnomes in redwood forest, try to protect them from freak-show entrepreneur, and land-destroyers. Lively Disney fantasy outing with top special effects, broad comedy highlights. Based on Upton Sinclair novel.▼

Gnome Named Gnorm, A (1994) **C-84m.** ** D: Stan Winston. Anthony Michael Hall, Jerry Orbach, Claudia Christian, Eli Danker, Mark Harelik, Robert Z'Dar, Joseph R. Sicari, Greg Kean. An especially strange cop-and-partner action comedy teams eccentric young detective Hall with a gnome who's just burrowed up from his underground world. Short on action, whimsy, and wackiness. Special effects maestro Winston returned to what he does best after this sat on the shelf for five years. [PG]▼

GO (1999) **C-103m.** ** D: Doug Liman. Sarah Polley, Katie Holmes, Desmond Askew, Taye Diggs, William Fichtner, J. E. Freeman, Jane Krakowski, Breckin Meyer, Jay Mohr, Timothy Olyphant, Scott Wolf, James Duval. A frenetic twenty-four hours in the lives of some hedonistic L.A. teens, as seen from several points of view. Energized, well cast, and cleverly contrived, this paean to a what-the-hell lifestyle is geared to appeal to like-minded young people . . . but others may find it too much like a junior PULP FICTION. Super 35. [R]▼●◗

Goalie's Anxiety at the Penalty Kick, The (1971-German) **C-101m.** ***½ D: Wim Wenders. Arthur Brauss, Erika Pluhar, Kai Fischer, Libgart Schwarz, Marie Bardischewski. Exceptionally knowing, haunting portrait of alienation, following a professional soccer goalie (Brauss), who abandons his team and sets out on an odyssey. Stunningly directed; a film you will not soon forget. Scripted by Peter Handke, based on his novel.▼

Goat, The SEE: **La Chevre**

Go-Between, The (1970-British) **C-116m.** ***½ D: Joseph Losey. Julie Christie, Alan Bates, Dominic Guard, Margaret Leighton, Michael Gough, Michael Redgrave, Edward Fox. Beguiling film from L. P. Hartley story of boy who becomes messenger for love notes between aristocratic Christie and farmer Bates. Lushly filmed, full of nuances, fine performances. Script by Harold Pinter. A mood piece, not for all tastes. [PG]▼

GoBots: Battle of the Rock Lords (1986) **C-75m.** *½ D: Ray Patterson. Voices of Margot Kidder, Roddy McDowall, Michael Nouri, Telly Savalas. Hanna-Barbera and Tonka Toys present a 75-minute animated commercial about the war between good GoBots versus evil Renegades, and the struggle of innocent Rock people against wicked Rock Lords. Electronically altered soundtrack makes it difficult to hear big-name voice cast. [G]▼

Goddess, The (1958) **105m.** *** D: John Cromwell. Kim Stanley, Lloyd Bridges, Steven Hill, Betty Lou Holland, Patty Duke. Absorbing biography of an ambitious girl seeking Hollywood fame. Author Paddy Chayefsky based his story on Marilyn Monroe; the film captures tragedy of the real-life Monroe with fine acting by Stanley and Bridges, among others. Film debuts of Stanley and Duke.▼●

Goddess of Love (1960-Italian) **C-68m.** *½ D: W. Tourjansky. Belinda Lee, Jacques Sernas, Massimo Girotti, Maria Frau. Drivel concerning country girl who becomes prostitute when her lover is killed. Set in ancient times. Totalscope.

Godfather, The (1972) **C-175m.** ***½ D: Francis Ford Coppola. Marlon Brando, Al Pacino, James Caan, Richard Castellano, John Cazale, Diane Keaton, Talia Shire, Robert Duvall, Sterling Hayden, John Marley, Richard Conte, Al Lettieri, Abe Vigoda, Al Martino, Morgana King, Alex

Rocco. The 1970s' answer to GONE WITH THE WIND, from Mario Puzo's novel on the violent life and times of Mafia patriarch Don Corleone (Brando). Pulp fiction raised to the highest level; a film of epic proportions, masterfully done, and set to Nino Rota's memorable music. Absolutely irresistible. Academy Award winner for Best Picture, Actor (Brando), and Screenplay (Coppola and Puzo). Baby in baptism scene is actually Coppola's infant daughter Sofia—who later costarred in THE GODFATHER, PART III. Followed by two sequels. [R]▼●

Godfather Part II, The (1974) **C-200m.** **** D: Francis Ford Coppola. Al Pacino, Robert Duvall, Diane Keaton, Robert De Niro, John Cazale, Talia Shire, Lee Strasberg, Michael V. Gazzo, G.D. Spradlin, B. Kirby, Jr. (Bruno Kirby), John Aprea, Morgana King, Mariana Hill, Troy Donahue, Joe Spinell, Abe Vigoda, Fay Spain, Harry Dean Stanton, Danny Aiello, Roger Corman, James Caan. They said it couldn't be done, but cowriter-director Coppola made a sequel that's just as compelling. This one contrasts the life of melancholy ''don'' (Pacino) with early days of his father (De Niro) as an immigrant in N.Y.C. Winner of six Oscars including Best Picture, Director, Screenplay (Coppola, Mario Puzo), Supporting Actor (De Niro), Score (Nino Rota, Carmine Coppola), Art Direction/Set Decoration (Dean Tavoularis, Angelo Graham, George R. Nelson). [R]▼●

Godfather Part III, The (1990) **C-161m.** *** D: Francis Ford Coppola. Al Pacino, Diane Keaton, Talia Shire, Andy Garcia, Eli Wallach, Joe Mantegna, George Hamilton, Bridget Fonda, Sofia Coppola, Raf Vallone, Franc D'Ambrosio, Donal Donnelly, Richard Bright, Helmut Berger, Don Novello, John Savage, Mario Donatone, Al Martino. Only a filmmaker like Coppola (teamed with writer Mario Puzo) could extend his history-making Mafioso saga and make it work so well. Absorbing story of Pacino's attempt to remove himself from the world of crime, and how fate and circumstance draw him back in, with his trigger-happy nephew (Garcia) and the rest of his family in tow. Longish, but masterfully told, with one almost-fatal flaw: the casting of Coppola's daughter Sofia (an amateur) in the pivotal role of Pacino's daughter. Video release is so-called ''final director's cut,'' 9m. longer than theatrical version. Super 35. [R]▼●

Godfather: The Complete Epic, 1902–1958, The (1981) **C-386m.** ***½ D: Francis Ford Coppola. Special marathon version of THE GODFATHER and THE GODFATHER, PART II originally prepared for television (where it aired as THE GODFATHER SAGA), combining the stories of both films in chronological order, and adding 15 minutes of footage never shown in theaters. TV version had some scenes censored; it plays complete on home video.▼

God Forgives, I Don't (1969-Italian-Spanish) **C-101m.** *½ D: Giuseppe Colizzi. Terence Hill, Bud Spencer, Frank Wolff, Gina Rovere, Jose Manuel Martin. In spite of colorful title, this spaghetti Western about an attempt to find some buried loot is like a thousand others. Hill's and Spencer's first film together. Techniscope. [M]

God Is My Co-Pilot (1945) **90m.** **½ D: Robert Florey. Dennis Morgan, Raymond Massey, Andrea King, Alan Hale, Dane Clark, John Ridgely, Stanley Ridges, Donald Woods. Well-intentioned drama of WW2 pilots bogs down in clichés, still has many good scenes.

God Is My Partner (1957) **80m.** ** D: William F. Claxton. Walter Brennan, John Hoyt, Marion Ross, Jesse White, Nancy Kulp. Sincere, hokey film of old-timer who feels he owes a spiritual obligation which he can redeem by giving away his money. Regalscope.

God Said, "HA!" (1999) **C-83m.** **½ D: Julia Sweeney. Julia Sweeney. Faithful film record of Sweeney's one-woman show in which she describes, with disarming good humor, her experience caring for her brother as he died of cancer—then discovering that she had a rare form of cervical cancer herself. Quentin Tarantino coexecutive-produced. [PG-13]▼

Gods and Monsters (1998) **C-105m.** ***½ D: Bill Condon. Ian McKellen, Brendan Fraser, Lynn Redgrave, Lolita Davidovich, David Dukes, Kevin J. O'Connor. Exceptional (if entirely fictional) character study of film director James Whale (best remembered for FRANKENSTEIN and BRIDE OF FRANKENSTEIN), alone at the end of his life in the 1950s, and fearful of losing his mind. An exquisite rendering of time and place, with a superb performance by McKellen, matched by Fraser as a gardener who catches his fancy, and Redgrave as his hilariously severe but loving housekeeper. A quiet, deliberately paced film; beautifully rendered, with a unique blend of flashback and hallucination. Director Condon won an Oscar for adapting Christopher Bram's novel *Father of Frankenstein.* Super 35. ▼●◗

God's Country (1946) **C-62m.** ** D: Robert E. Tansey. Buster Keaton, Robert Lowery, Helen Gilbert, William Farnum. Chief virtue of this flabby Western is Keaton trying to recreate some of his better pantomime skits.

God's Country (1985) **C-88m.** ***½ D: Louis Malle. Poignant, insightful, occasionally hilarious documentary look at life in Glencoe, Minnesota, a small, conservative farming community. There's priceless footage from the first frame to the last. Mostly shot in 1979; Malle returned six years later to update the lives of his subjects.

God's Country and the Woman (1936) **C-80m.** ** D: William Keighley. George Brent, Beverly Roberts, Barton MacLane, Robert Barrat, Alan Hale, Joseph King. Routine tale of Brent and Roberts running rival lumber companies; color is only asset.

Godsend, The (1979-British) **C-93m.** ** D: Gabrielle Beaumont. Cyd Hayman, Malcolm Stoddard, Angela Pleasence, Patrick Barr. OMEN/EXORCIST-type horror film about an angelic little blonde girl who is left at a family farm on a rainy night by a strange woman. In the years that follow, death, disaster, and hostility are visited upon the family in this medium thriller. [R]▼

God's Little Acre (1958) **110m.** *** D: Anthony Mann. Robert Ryan, Tina Louise, Aldo Ray, Buddy Hackett, Jack Lord, Fay Spain, Michael Landon. Effective Americana of Georgia farmers as seen by Erskine Caldwell, focusing on amusing as well as lusty, violent aspects of their existence.▼

Gods Must Be Crazy, The (1981-Botswana) **C-108m.** *** D: Jamie Uys. Marius Weyers, Sandra Prinsloo, N!xau, Louw Verwey, Michael Thys. Highly original, offbeat comedy about cultural clashes in Africa, involving a bushman who encounters civilization for the first time, a pretty schoolteacher whose new assignment is a remote village, and a bumbling scientist whose attempts to make her welcome result in slapstick catastrophes. Film itself is clumsy at times, but completely disarming. It didn't receive major U.S. release until 1984, but then became the biggest foreign box-office hit in history! Uys, who also wrote and produced, plays the reverend. Followed by a sequel. Techniscope. [PG]▼●

Gods Must Be Crazy II, The (1989-U.S.-Botswana) **C-97m.** *** D: Jamie Uys. N!xau, Lena Farugia, Hans Strydom, Eiros, Nadies, Erick Bowen. Follow-up to the surprise smash-hit farce is just as funny and endearing. N!xau returns as the bushman; here, his two young children are accidentally transported to "civilization" by a pair of poachers, and he follows them with the expected, comic result. This started shooting in 1985 and sat on the shelf for several years. [PG]▼●

Gods of the Plague (1969-German) **91m.** *** D: Rainer Werner Fassbinder. Hanna Schygulla, Margarethe von Trotta, Harry Baer, Gunther Kaufmann, Ingrid Caven. A pair of pals plot a robbery, only to have their scheme disrupted by two women (both of whom love one of the men). Low-key, *noir*ish gangster film is an ode to the Hollywood films of the genre, with a French New Wave sensibility. At the same time, it's a knowing portrait of an aimless, alienated post-war German generation.▼

Godspell (1973) **C-103m.** **½ D: David Greene. Victor Garber, David Haskell, Jerry Sroka, Lynne Thigpen, Katie Hanley, Robin Lamont. Sophomoric updating of Jesus' life with young bouncy disciples following their leader around modern-day N.Y.C. Energetic adaptation of popular stage musical; brilliant use of N.Y.C. locations, good score by Stephen Schwartz including "Day by Day," but hollow and unmoving. [G]▼◗

God Told Me To SEE: **Demon**

Godzilla (1954-Japanese) SEE: **Godzilla, King of the Monsters**

Godzilla (1998) **C-139m.** **½ D: Roland Emmerich. Matthew Broderick, Hank Azaria, Jean Reno, Maria Pitillo, Harry Shearer, Kevin Dunn, Michael Lerner, Vicki Lewis, Doug Savant, Arabella Field, Bodhi Elfman. Giant lizard monster moves swiftly from the Pacific to N.Y. harbor, and terrorizes the Big Apple. Biologist Broderick hooks up with mystery man Reno and his team to stop it. Giant-scale, fx-driven no-brainer doesn't make much sense, has shallow characters, and goes on too long—but still offers a surprising amount of fun. Super 35. [PG-13]▼●◗

Godzilla, King of the Monsters (1954-Japanese) **80m.** **½ D: Terry Morse, Ishiro Honda. Raymond Burr, Takashi Shimura, Momoko Kochi, Akira Takarada. A fire-breathing lizard threatens civilization: the special effects are the star in this, the original GODZILLA movie. Originally released in Japan in 1954 as GOJIRA, at 98m; over 20m. were eliminated, and inserts with Burr were added. Updated in 1985 and reworked in 1998. ▼●◗

Godzilla 1985 (1985-Japanese) **C-91m.** BOMB D: Kohji Hashimoto, R. J. Kizer. Raymond Burr, Keiju Kobayashi, Ken Tanaka, Yasuko Sawaguchi, Shin Takuma. Supposed update of original GODZILLA yarn is just a retread, with the atomic-fueled monster threatening Tokyo all over again, and Burr back on hand in cheaply filmed insert sequences making like Greek chorus. Too straight to be funny; instead, the Big Fella is just a Big Bore. [PG]▼●

Godzilla on Monster Island (1972-Japanese) **C-89m.** ** D: Jun Fukuda. Hiroshi Ishikawa, Tomoko Umeda, Yuriko Hishimi, Minoru Takashima. Garbo talks? Ha! In this harmless, toylike movie, *Godzilla* talks, as he and spiny Angillus battle alien-summoned Ghidrah and new playmate Gigan, who has a buzz saw in his belly. Standard colorful Toho monster hijinks. Aka GODZILLA VS. GIGAN. Tohoscope. [G]▼●

Godzilla Raids Again SEE: **Gigantis the Fire Monster**

Godzilla's Revenge (1969-Japanese) **C-**

69m. **½ D: Ishiro Honda. Kenji Sahara, Tomonori Yazaki, Machiko Naka, Sachio Sakai, Chotaro Togin, Yoshibumi Tujima. Fantasy of child daydreaming of adventures with Godzilla's son and other monsters. Battle scenes are mostly stock footage from GODZILLA VS. THE SEA MONSTER and SON OF GODZILLA. Good juvenile sci-fi. Tohoscope. [G]▼●◗
Godzilla vs. Gigan SEE: **Godzilla on Monster Island**
Godzilla vs. Mechagodzilla SEE: **Godzilla vs. the Cosmic Monster**
Godzilla vs. Megalon (1976-Japanese) **C-80m.** *½ D: Jun Fukuda. Katsuhiko Sasaki, Hiroyuki Kawase, Yutaka Hayashi, Robert Dunham. Series sinks to new low as Godzilla teams up with robot superhero against Megalon and his pal Gigan. Incredibly cheap, with lots of unintended laughs. A hoho from Toho in Tohoscope. [G]▼
Godzilla vs. Monster Zero SEE: **Monster Zero**
Godzilla vs. Mothra SEE: **Godzilla vs. the Thing**
Godzilla vs. the Bionic Monster SEE: **Godzilla vs. the Cosmic Monster**
Godzilla vs. the Cosmic Monster (1974-Japanese) **C-80m.** ** D: Jun Fukuda. Masaaki Daimon, Kazuya Aoyama, Reiko Tajima, Barbara Lynn, Akihiko Hirata. Godzilla battles robot duplicate of himself, built by alien apes intent on conquering the world. He's helped this time by ancient Okinawan monster Kingseesar. Pokey until zappity-pow climax. Aka GODZILLA VS. THE BIONIC MONSTER, GODZILLA VS. MECHAGODZILLA. Tohoscope. [G]▼●
Godzilla vs. the Sea Monster (1966-Japanese) **C-85m.** **½ D: Jun Fukuda. Akira Takarada, Toru Watanabe, Jun Tazaki, Kumi Mizuno, Hideo Sunazuka. Particularly colorful and lively entry in the series, with a yachtload of castaways helping captives of paramilitary villains. Meanwhile, Godzilla battles a stupendous shrimp. P.S.: Mothra also turns up. Tohoscope.▼
Godzilla vs. the Smog Monster (1972-Japanese) **C-87m.** **½ D: Yoshimitu Banno. Akira Yamauchi, Hiroyuki Kawase, Toshio Shibaki. Godzilla freelances as do-gooder in ridding Japan of monster born of waste, fed on factory fumes and smog. Dubbed and daffy. Tohoscope. [G—edited from original PG rating]▼●
Godzilla vs. the Thing (1964-Japanese) **C-90m.** **½ D: Ishiro Honda. Okira Takarada, Yuriko Hoshi, Hiroshi Koizumi, Yu Fujiki. Vivid special effects highlight battle between reptile Godzilla and Mothra, giant moth. TV title: GODZILLA VS. MOTHRA. Tohoscope.▼●◗
Go Fish (1994) **87m.** *** D: Rose Troche. V. S. Brodie, Guinevere Turner, T. Wendy McMillan, Anastasia Sharp, Migdalia Melendez. A romantic tale about finding a soulmate; the difference here is that both partners are women. Funny, intelligent comedy about brash Turner forging a relationship with shy Brodie. Only quibble: the heavy-handed political correctness of the secondary characters. Made on a practically nonexistent budget; Troche (who coscripted with Turner) is a talent to watch. [R] ▼●
Go for Broke! (1951) **92m.** *** D: Robert Pirosh. Van Johnson, Lane Nakano, Henry Nakamura, George Miki, Henry Oyasato, Warner Anderson. Fine WW2 drama with Johnson, a bigoted Texan, assigned to train and lead the 442nd Regimental Combat Team, composed mostly of Japanese-Americans (Nisei). Crammed with ironic touches, and uncompromising in its point of view (reflecting the Nisei's collective heroic war record). Pirosh also scripted. ▼
Gog (1954) **C-85m.** ** D: Herbert L. Strock. Richard Egan, Constance Dowling, Herbert Marshall, John Wengraf. Is a series of deaths at scientific installation the result of equipment malfunction or sabotage? Title refers to one of a pair of nonhumanoid robots. OK sci-fi, originally in 3-D.
Goin' Cocoanuts (1978) **C-96m.** ** D: Howard Morris. Donny and Marie Osmond, Herbert Edelman, Kenneth Mars, Chrystin Sinclaire, Ted Cassidy, Marc Lawrence, Khigh Dhiegh, Harold Sakata. Bad guys go after Marie's necklace in Hawaii, but the villainy, like the story, is strictly kindergarten level. Kids may go for it . . . and of course, Donny and Marie get to sing. [PG]
Goin' Down the Road (1970-Canadian) **C-90m.** ***½ D: Donald Shebib. Doug McGrath, Paul Bradley, Jayne Eastwood, Cayle Chernin, Nicole Morin. Award-winning film made for less than $100,000 puts most Hollywood blockbusters to shame; modest tale of two unlucky Nova Scotians and their near-tragic finish packs a memorable punch. McGrath and Bradley are remarkably good. [PG—edited from original R rating]
Going All the Way (1997) **C-110m.** ** D: Mark Pellington. Jeremy Davies, Ben Affleck, Amy Locane, Jill Clayburgh, Lesley Ann Warren, Rose McGowan, Rachel Weisz. Listless screen version of Dan Wakefield's popular memory novel about two young army vets who become friends in 1950s Indianapolis despite having existed on wholly different social planes during their high school years. A good book but an indifferent (and familiar-seeming) coming-of-age movie, despite a Wakefield script. Set in 1954, film opens with a *huge* 1957 pop hit—never a good sign. [R]▼●
Going Ape! (1981) **C-87m.** BOMB D: Jeremy Joe Kronsberg. Tony Danza, Jessica Walter, Stacey Nelkin, Danny De Vito, Art Metrano, Joseph Maher. Inept comedy, with Danza set to inherit $5 million if he cares for a trio of orangutans. Directorial debut for screenwriter Kronsberg,

who also penned Clint Eastwood's EVERY WHICH WAY BUT LOOSE—with an orangutan prominently featured. [PG]▼

Going Berserk (1983-Canadian) **C-85m.** BOMB D: David Steinberg. John Candy, Joe Flaherty, Eugene Levy, Alley Mills, Pat Hingle, Richard Libertini, Paul Dooley, Murphy Dunne, Dixie Carter, Ernie Hudson. Awesomely inept comedy about the misadventures of a young dolt (Candy) who's set to marry the daughter of a pompous congressman. Only a performer as likable as Candy could survive such a debacle; his *SCTV* colleagues Flaherty and Levy have little to do. [R]▼●

Going Hollywood (1933) **80m.** *** D: Raoul Walsh. Marion Davies, Bing Crosby, Fifi D'Orsay, Stuart Erwin, Ned Sparks, Patsy Kelly. Enjoyable fluff with Davies following crooner Crosby to Hollywood determined to win him away from tempestuous screen star D'Orsay. Kelly all but steals film from stars. Songs include "Temptation," "We'll Make Hay While the Sun Shines," and the title tune.▼●

Going Home (1971) **C-97m.** *** D: Herbert B. Leonard. Robert Mitchum, Jan-Michael Vincent, Brenda Vaccaro, Jason Bernard, Sally Kirkland, Josh Mostel. Powerful, if downbeat, study of young man's troubled relationship with his father, who's just been released from prison after serving time for killing his wife. [PG]▼●

Going in Style (1979) **C-96m.** ***½ D: Martin Brest. George Burns, Art Carney, Lee Strasberg, Charles Hallahan, Pamela Payton-Wright. Three retirees in Queens get more than they bargain for when they rob a bank in Manhattan to relieve their boredom. Unexpected gem from a 28-year-old writer-director is predictably funny but unpredictably moving, with Burns standing out in a terrific cast. [PG]▼

Going My Way (1944) **126m.** **** D: Leo McCarey. Bing Crosby, Barry Fitzgerald, Rise Stevens, Frank McHugh, James Brown, Gene Lockhart, Jean Heather, Porter Hall, Fortunio Bonanova, Stanley Clements, Carl (Alfalfa) Switzer. Sentimental story of down-to-earth priest Father O'Malley (Crosby) winning over aging superior (Fitzgerald) and sidewalk gang of kids is hard to resist—thanks to the skills of writer-director McCarey, who won two Oscars. Academy Awards also went to Crosby, Fitzgerald, Best Picture, and Best Song: "Swinging on a Star." Sequel: THE BELLS OF ST. MARY'S. ▼●◗

Going Places (1938) **84m.** ** D: Ray Enright. Dick Powell, Anita Louise, Allen Jenkins, Ronald Reagan. Nonsensical musical with a variety of songs, steeplechase riding, and obligatory romantic interludes. Louis Armstrong and Maxine Sullivan introduce hit song "Jeepers Creepers."

Going Places (1974-French) **C-117m.** *** D: Bertrand Blier. Gérard Depardieu, Patrick Dewaere, Miou-Miou, Jeanne Moreau, Brigitte Fossey, Isabelle Huppert. Crude, overgrown juvenile delinquents Depardieu and Dewaere commit petty crimes, terrorize and share women. Funny, earthy, sometimes even lyrical examination of alienation; Moreau appears briefly as an ex-con who trysts with the boys. [R]▼

Going Steady (1958) **79m.** *½ D: Fred F. Sears. Molly Bee, Bill Goodwin, Alan Reed, Jr., Irene Hervey. Uninspired happenings involving secretly married teenagers and repercussions when in-laws discover fact. ▼

Going Undercover (1988) **C-88m.** *½ D: James Kenelm Clarke. Chris Lemmon, Jean Simmons, Lea Thompson, Mills Watson, Viveca Lindfors, Nancy Cartwright, Joe Michael Terry. Third-rate private-eye Lemmon is hired to keep an eye on rich brat Thompson during a trip to Europe—during which she's kidnapped. Obnoxious comedy was made in 1984, and (understandably) shelved. [PG-13]▼●

Goin' South (1978) **C-109m.** *** D: Jack Nicholson. Jack Nicholson, Mary Steenburgen, Christopher Lloyd, John Belushi, Veronica Cartwright, Richard Bradford, Danny DeVito, Luana Anders, Ed Begley, Jr., Anne Ramsey. Amusing Western comedy, not for all tastes, with Nicholson saving himself from lynch mob by marrying a spinster. Steenburgen is refreshingly offbeat and Belushi's disappointingly small role is a real hoot. Film debuts of both. [PG] ▼●

Goin' to Town (1935) **74m.** *** D: Alexander Hall. Mae West, Paul Cavanagh, Ivan Lebedeff, Marjorie Gateson, Tito Coral. Good West vehicle of dance-hall girl trying to crash society, highlight: Mae doing "Samson and Delilah" scenes.▼

Go Into Your Dance (1935) **89m.** **½ D: Archie L. Mayo. Al Jolson, Ruby Keeler, Glenda Farrell, Helen Morgan, Patsy Kelly, Benny Rubin, Phil Regan, Barton MacLane. Flimsy backstage plot allows real-life husband and wife Jolson and Keeler (in their only film together) to sing and dance through seven listenable Harry Warren-Al Dubin tunes, including "About a Quarter to Nine" and "A Latin from Manhattan."●

Go, Johnny, Go! (1958) **75m.** ** D: Paul Landres. Jimmy Clanton, Alan Freed, Sandy Stewart, Chuck Berry, Jo-Ann Campbell, The Cadillacs, Ritchie Valens, Eddie Cochran, Harvey (Fuqua), The Flamingos, Jackie Wilson. Orphan Clanton, booted out of church choir for playing rock 'n' roll, is transformed by Freed into "Johnny Melody," teen idol. ("He's dreamy. Oh wow, he's the living end.") Not very good, but an artifact of its era. Berry, who acts as well as sings, performs "Memphis, Tennessee," "Little Queenie" and "Johnny Be Good," Cochran performs

"Teenage Heaven," and Wilson does "You'd Better Know It."▼●

Gold (1974-British) **C-120m.** *** D: Peter Hunt. Roger Moore, Susannah York, Ray Milland, Bradford Dillman, John Gielgud. Grand-scale adventure action yarn about plot to control price of gold on world market by destroying South African mine. Moore is stalwart hero. Long but entertaining. Panavision. [PG]▼

Goldbergs, The (1950) **83m.** **½ D: Walter Hart. Gertrude Berg, Philip Loeb, Eli Mintz, Betty Walker, David Opatoshu, Barbara Rush. Warm, human story of famous radio-TV Bronx family and their everyday problems. Retitled: MOLLY.

Gold Coast SEE: **Elmore Leonard's Gold Coast**

Gold Diggers of 1933 (1933) **96m.** ***½ D: Mervyn LeRoy. Joan Blondell, Ruby Keeler, Aline MacMahon, Dick Powell, Guy Kibbee, Warren William, Ned Sparks, Ginger Rogers, Sterling Holloway. Another spectacular Busby Berkeley dance outing with familiar let's-produce-a-Broadway-show plot. Highlights: Blondell's "Forgotten Man," Rogers' "We're In The Money" (with pig-Latin chorus), chorus girls' "Shadow Waltz."▼●

Gold Diggers of 1935 (1935) **95m.** *** D: Busby Berkeley. Dick Powell, Adolphe Menjou, Gloria Stuart, Alice Brady, Glenda Farrell, Frank McHugh, Winifred Shaw. Big-scale Berkeley musical with stereotypes providing plot line and laughs between fantastic precision production numbers, including "The Words Are In My Heart," and classic, Oscar-winning "Lullaby of Broadway," sung by Wini Shaw.▼●

Gold Diggers of 1937 (1936) **100m.** **½ D: Lloyd Bacon. Dick Powell, Joan Blondell, Glenda Farrell, Victor Moore, Lee Dixon, Osgood Perkins. Those gold-diggers won't give up; this time it's a group of insurance salesmen backing a show. Top song: "With Plenty of Money and You."

Gold Diggers: The Secret of Bear Mountain (1995) **C-94m.** ** D: Kevin James Dobson. Christina Ricci, Anna Chlumsky, Polly Draper, Brian Kerwin, Diana Scarwid, David Keith. New girl in town (Ricci) makes an unlikely friend—an aggressive, unpopular kid (Chlumsky) who's prone to telling lies. However, her tallest tale may not be bogus, and leads them on a search for long-buried treasure in a watery cave. Unsatisfying conclusion shortchanges this story; its strongest asset (sure to appeal to preteen girls) is the depiction of the girls' friendship. [PG]▼●

Gold Dust Gertie (1931) **66m.** **½ D: Lloyd Bacon. Ole Olsen, Chic Johnson, Winnie Lightner, Dorothy Christy, Claude Gillingwater, Arthur Hoyt, Charley Grapewin. Olsen & Johnson are bathing-suit salesmen trying to elude their mutual ex-wife. Lightner is energetic as always in this absurd knockabout comedy with plenty of sexual innuendo.

Golden Age of Comedy, The (1957) **78m.** **** D: Compiled by Robert Youngson. Laurel and Hardy, Carole Lombard, Ben Turpin, Will Rogers, Harry Langdon. Peerless grouping of some of silent comedy's greatest moments, including Rogers' classic spoofs of silent stars, and ending with Laurel and Hardy's legendary pie fight from "Battle of the Century."▼●

Golden Arrow, The (1936) **68m.** **½ D: Alfred E. Green. Bette Davis, George Brent, Eugene Pallette, Dick Foran, Carol Hughes, Catherine Doucet. Pleasant but featherweight comedy of "heiress" Davis and down-to-earth reporter Brent establishing marriage of convenience.

Golden Blade, The (1953) **C-81m.** **½ D: Nathan Juran. Rock Hudson, Piper Laurie, Gene Evans, George Macready, Kathleen Hughes, Steven Geray. Hudson, with the help of the magical Sword of Damascus, helps Baghdad princess Laurie battle her caliph father's grand vizier (Macready) and his strong-arm son (Evans). Typical but sprightly, entertaining Arabian Nights adventure; amusing and imaginative.

Golden Boy (1939) **99m.** **½ D: Rouben Mamoulian. Barbara Stanwyck, Adolphe Menjou, William Holden, Lee J. Cobb, Joseph Calleia, Sam Levene, Don Beddoe. Clifford Odets' narrative of music-minded boy who becomes prizefighter dates badly; Holden, in starring debut, still good, but Cobb blows the works with his Henry Armetta imitation.▼●

Golden Braid (1990-Australian) **C-88m.** *** D: Paul Cox. Chris Haywood, Gosia Dobrowolska, Paul Chubb, Norman Kaye, Robert Menzies, Jo Kennedy. Thoughtful, gentle film about a clockmaker (Haywood), obsessed with all things past, and what happens when he finds a braid of blonde hair in an 18th-century cabinet. A film with a refreshing point of view: clocks may stop ticking, and human hearts may stop beating, but time still goes on—and human beings must celebrate life.

Golden Child, The (1986) **C-96m.** BOMB D: Michael Ritchie. Eddie Murphy, Charlotte Lewis, Charles Dance, Victor Wong, Randall "Tex" Cobb, James Hong, J.L. Reate. Top candidate for the worst megahit of all time. A "perfect" child (Reate) is kidnapped despite his magical powers; as foretold by an ancient oracle, only Murphy can rescue him. Lewis is more wooden than most ex-models; entire reels go by with nary a chuckle. A box-office smash—but have you ever met anyone who liked it? [PG-13] ▼●◗

Golden Coach, The (1952-Italian) **C-101m.** ***½ D: Jean Renoir. Anna Magnani, Odoardo Spadaro, Nada Fiorelli, Dante Rino, Duncan Lamont, Jean Debucourt. Delightful film about an acting troupe touring South America in the 18th century and the amorous adventures of its leading lady. Theatrical and stylized, this is one of the great films about acting—and a stunning achievement in the use of color. Ironically, it was a flop when first released, then critically rediscovered. Photographed by Claude Renoir; music by Vivaldi.▼●

Golden Earrings (1947) **95m.** **½ D: Mitchell Leisen. Ray Milland, Marlene Dietrich, Murvyn Vye, Dennis Hoey, Quentin Reynolds. Incredible yet enjoyable escapism set in WW2 Europe has Milland joining gypsy Dietrich for espionage work; Dietrich most convincing. Gypsy Vye sings the title song.▼

Golden Eye, The (1948) **69m.** *½ D: William Beaudine. Roland Winters, Victor Sen Yung, Tim Ryan, Wanda McKay, Bruce Kellogg, Evelyn Brent. Charlie Chan investigates the mystery of a supposedly barren mine that miraculously begins to yield gold in this poor entry. Aka THE MYSTERY OF THE GOLDEN EYE and CHARLIE CHAN AND THE GOLDEN EYE.

GoldenEye (1995) **C-130m.** *** D: Martin Campbell. Pierce Brosnan, Sean Bean, Izabella Scorupco, Famke Janssen, Joe Don Baker, Judi Dench, Robbie Coltrane, Tcheky Karyo, Gottfried John, Alan Cumming, Desmond Llewelyn, Samantha Bond. Brosnan's debut as 007 is a slam-bang action adventure in the best Bond tradition, with eye-popping stunts, sexy women, and international intrigue. (There are also P.C. remarks about Bond being sexist and/or an anachronism.) The crux of the story is internal sabotage within Russia, and Bond's attempt to figure out who's behind it—and how to stop them before they use their stolen weapons to harm the free world. That's Minnie Driver as the Russian nightclub singer. Panavision. [PG-13]▼●◗

Golden Gate (1993) **C-90m.** *½ D: John Madden. Matt Dillon, Joan Chen, Bruno Kirby, Teri Polo, Tzi Ma, Stan Egi, Jack Shearer. Young FBI agent Dillon pursues subversives in San Francisco during the McCarthy witchhunts, when guiltless Chinese were harassed simply for mailing money to their families back home. Potentially compelling film is poorly executed; hampered by listless direction and David Henry Hwang's meandering and melodramatic screenplay. An *American Playhouse* coproduction. [R]▼●

Golden Girl (1951) **C-108m.** **½ D: Lloyd Bacon. Mitzi Gaynor, Dale Robertson, Dennis Day, Una Merkel. Undistinguished musical set in California during Civil War, with Gaynor portraying entertainer Lotta Crabtree who's intrigued by Rebel officer Robertson.

Goldengirl (1979) **C-104m.** ** D: Joseph Sargent. Susan Anton, Curt Jurgens, Robert Culp, Leslie Caron, Harry Guardino, Jessica Walter. Statuesque Anton is more or less turned into a robot so she can become a star in the Olympics. So-so. TV version runs 117m. (though it was originally planned for miniseries length—until the U.S. decided to boycott the Moscow Olympics). [PG]▼

Golden Gloves Story, The (1950) **76m.** *½ D: Felix E. Feist. James Dunn, Dewey Martin, Kay Westfall, Kevin O'Morrison. OK fare of two boxers and effects of pending championship bout on their lives.

Golden Hawk, The (1952) **C-83m.** ** D: Sidney Salkow. Rhonda Fleming, Sterling Hayden, John Sutton, Raymond Hatton. Frank Yerby's novel of Spanish-English fight against France in 17th century, set in Caribbean seas.

Golden Heist, The SEE: **Inside Out** (1975)

Golden Horde, The (1951) **C-77m.** ** D: George Sherman. Ann Blyth, David Farrar, George Macready, Henry Brandon, Richard Egan. Typical Arabian adventure set in 13th century, with Blyth using her brains to outwit invaders of her people's city.

Golden Idol, The (1954) **71m.** *½ D: Ford Beebe. Johnny Sheffield, Anne Kimbell, Paul Guilfoyle, Leonard Mudie, Smoki Whitfield, Rick Vallin. Bomba the Jungle Boy (with the help of some "talking" drums) recovers a priceless Watusi statue stolen by evil Arabs.

Golden Madonna, The (1949-British) **88m.** **½ D: Ladislas Vajda. Phyllis Calvert, Michael Rennie, Tullio Carminati. Lively romantic yarn of Yankee lass inheriting an Italian villa and, aided by Rennie, seeking to retrieve a holy painting.

Golden Mask, The (1954-British) **C-88m.** **½ D: Jack Lee. Van Heflin, Wanda Hendrix, Eric Portman, Charles Goldner. Intelligent adventure yarn of people seeking fabulous treasure mask in Egyptian desert.

Golden Mistress, The (1954) **C-82m.** ** D: Joel Judge (Abner Biberman). John Agar, Rosemarie Bowe, Abner Biberman, Andre Narcisse. Agar comes to Bowe's rescue in hunting out alleged voodoo killers of her father.▼

Golden Needles (1974) **C-92m.** ** D: Robert Clouse. Joe Don Baker, Elizabeth Ashley, Jim Kelly, Burgess Meredith, Ann Sothern. Everyone seems out of place in this Hong Kong-L.A. filmed action pic about a scramble for golden statue containing youth-restoring acupuncture needles. Silly. Retitled THE CHASE FOR THE GOLDEN NEEDLES. Panavision. [PG]

Golden Rendezvous (1977) **C-103m.** ** D: Ashley Lazarus. Richard Harris, Ann Turkel, David Janssen, Burgess Meredith, John Vernon, Gordon Jackson, Keith Baxter, Dorothy Malone, John Carradine. Attractive cast in pointless adaptation of Alistair MacLean's novel about gambling ship held hostage by terrorists. Retitled NUCLEAR TERROR for television.▼

Golden Salamander (1950-British) **96m.** *** D: Ronald Neame. Trevor Howard, Anouk Aimée, Walter Rilla, Herbert Lom, Wilfrid Hyde-White. Courting a Tunisian girl, Howard becomes involved in gun smuggling; taut actioner.▼

Golden Seal, The (1983) **C-95m.** *** D: Frank Zuniga. Steve Railsback, Michael Beck, Penelope Milford, Torquil Campbell, Seth Sakai, Richard Narita, Sandra Seacat. Straightforward family film about a young couple and their son, living in the Aleutian islands, cut off from the world. Like the Aleut natives, the father (Railsback) has long pursued the golden seal, a near-mythical creature with an enormous bounty on its head, but it's the boy (Campbell) who finds him, and tries to protect him. Dialogue is stiff, but when the action picks up it's absorbing and enjoyable. [PG]▼

Golden Voyage of Sinbad, The (1974-British) **C-104m.** *** D: Gordon Hessler. John Phillip Law, Caroline Munro, Tom Baker, Douglas Wilmer, Gregoire Aslan, John Garfield, Jr. Delightful rehash of earlier Sinbad adventures that evokes Saturday matinee fare of the 1950s, with Ray Harryhausen's finest "Dynamation" effects: a ship's figurehead comes to life, and a six-armed statue does sword-battle with Sinbad in action highlights. Grand entertainment. [G]▼●◗

Golden West, The (1932) **74m.** **½ D: David Howard. George O'Brien, Janet Chandler, Marion Burns, Arthur Pierson, Onslow Stevens. Solid Zane Grey story of O'Brien leaving town after feud killing, encountering Indians; son, raised as an Indian after father killed in massacre. Good "B+" Western.

Goldfinger (1964-British) **C-111m.** ***½ D: Guy Hamilton. Sean Connery, Gert Frobe, Honor Blackman, Shirley Eaton, Bernard Lee, Lois Maxwell, Harold Sakata, Tania Mallett. Entertaining, exciting James Bond adventure, third in the series. Full of ingenious gadgets and nefarious villains, with hair-raising climax inside Fort Knox. Frobe (Goldfinger) and Sakata (Oddjob) are villains in the classic tradition.▼●◗

Gold for the Caesars (1964-French-Italian) **C-86m.** *½ D: Andre de Toth. Jeffrey Hunter, Mylene Demongeot, Ron Randell, Massimo Giulio Bosetti, Ettore Manni. Still another Roman slave epic starring an American actor who'd look more at home in David and Ricky Nelson's fraternity. Nothing special. Original French running time: 95m. CinemaScope.

Gold Is Where You Find It (1938) **C-90m.** **½ D: Michael Curtiz. George Brent, Olivia de Havilland, Claude Rains, Margaret Lindsay, John Litel, Barton MacLane. And gold-rush miners find it on California farmland, starting bitter feud in brisk film, perked by good cast.

Gold of Naples, The (1954-Italian) **107m.** *** D: Vittorio De Sica. Sophia Loren, Vittorio De Sica, Toto, Silvana Mangano, Paolo Stoppa. Four vignettes—poignant, perceptive, hilarious in turn: Loren as philandering wife of pizza baker; De Sica as avid cardplayer upstaged by 8-year-old; Toto as Milquetoast family man; Mangano as prostitute involved in unusual marriage. ▼

Gold of the Seven Saints (1961) **88m.** **½ D: Gordon Douglas. Clint Walker, Roger Moore, Leticia Roman, Robert Middleton, Chill Wills, Gene Evans, Roberto Contreras. Fur-trappers Walker and Moore (the latter sporting blond hair and an Irish brogue) find 125 lbs. of gold nuggets and are pursued across the desert by several parties who want to pry it loose from them. Enjoyable Western knockoff of THE TREASURE OF THE SIERRA MADRE, featuring some striking Utah scenery and a tangy script cowritten by Leigh Brackett. WarnerScope.

Gold Raiders (1951) **56m.** *½ D: Edward Bernds. George O'Brien, The Three Stooges, Sheila Ryan, Clem Bevans, Lyle Talbot. Stooges add the only life to this flabby Western, with their usual shenanigans foiling the crooks and saving the day.▼

Gold Rush, The (1925) **82m.** **** D: Charlie Chaplin. Charlie Chaplin, Georgia Hale, Mack Swain, Tom Murray. Immortal Chaplin classic, pitting Little Tramp against Yukon, affections of dance-hall girl, whims of a burly prospector. Dance of the rolls, eating leather shoe, cabin tottering over cliff—all highlights of wonderful, timeless comedy. Chaplin reedited film in 1942; that version, with his narration and music, runs 72m.▼●◗

Gold Rush Maisie (1940) **82m.** ** D: Edwin L. Marin. Ann Sothern, Lee Bowman, Virginia Weidler, John F. Hamilton, Mary Nash, Slim Summerville, Scotty Beckett. Innocuous *Maisie* entry involving a poor family's attempt to find gold.

Goldsmith's Shop, The SEE: **Jeweller's Shop, The**

Goldstein (1965) **85m.** **½ D: Benjamin Manaster, Philip Kaufman. Lou Gilbert, Ellen Madison, Thomas Erhart, Benito Carruthers, Severn Darden, Nelson Algren. The prophet Elijah (Gilbert) emerges from Lake Michigan, is pursued by sculptor Erhart. Odd, unsatisfying satire filmed in Chicago. Based on a story by Martin Buber. Original running time: 115m.

Goldwyn Follies, The (1938) **C-120m.** *½ D: George Marshall. Adolphe Menjou, Andrea Leeds, Kenny Baker, The Ritz Brothers, Zorina, Helen Jepson, Bobby Clark, Edgar Bergen & Charlie McCarthy.

Dreadful hodgepodge as producer Menjou hires Leeds as "Miss Humanity," to judge his movies from average person's point of view. She probably would have skipped this one. Ritz Bros. come off best, while Baker sings "Love Walked In" about thirty times. George Balanchine's ballet is a matter of taste. Look for Alan Ladd as an auditioning singer.▼●◗

Golem, The (1920-German) **75m.** ***½ D: Paul Wegener, Carl Boese. Paul Wegener, Albert Steinruck, Ernst Deutsch, Lyda Salmonova. Chilling, visually dazzling story of the supernatural, based on a famous Jewish folktale of the 16th century. Rudolph of Hapsburg has exiled the Jews, blaming them for a plague; a rabbi conjures up a golem (a clay monster, played by Wegener) in order to convince the king to repeal the edict. This classic of German Expressionist cinema is also a forerunner of FRANKENSTEIN, from the way the golem is brought to life to his attraction to a child. The sets were designed by famed architect Hans Poelzig. The story has been filmed many times; Wegener also codirected versions in 1914 and 1917, and Julien Duvivier filmed it in 1938, with Harry Baur.

Goliath Against the Giants (1961-Italian) **C-90m.** *½ D: Guido Malatesta. Brad Harris, Gloria Milland, Fernando Rey, Barbara Carrol. Juvenile cartoon characterizations in this sword-and-sandal, with Harris overcoming sea creatures, Amazons, and his people's enemies. SuperTotalscope.▼

Goliath and the Barbarians (1960-Italian) **C-86m.** ** D: Carlo Campogalliani. Steve Reeves, Bruce Cabot, Giulia Rubini, Chelo Alonso, Arturo Dominici, Gino Scotti. Muscleman Reeves comes to the rescue of Italy by holding off rampaging hordes pressing down from the Alps. Totalscope.

Goliath and the Dragon (1960-Italian) **C-87m.** BOMB D: Vittorio Cottafavi. Mark Forest, Broderick Crawford, Gaby Andre, Leonora Ruffo. Fantasy costumer with embarrassing performances by all; poor special effects, with Forest challenging villainous Crawford. Totalscope.▼

Goliath and the Vampires (1961-Italian) **C-91m.** *½ D: Giacomo Gentilomo. Gordon Scott, Jacques Sernas, Gianna Maria Canale. Cloak-and-sandal nonsense; spotty special effects add only color to film. U.S. release 1964. Totalscope.▼

Go, Man, Go! (1954) **82m.** **½ D: James Wong Howe. Dane Clark, Pat Breslin, Sidney Poitier, Edmon Ryan. Imaginative telling of the formation of Harlem Globetrotters and their rise as famed basketball team. A rare directorial effort by celebrated cinematographer Howe.

Go Masters, The (1982-Chinese-Japanese) **C-123m.** *** D: Junya Sato, Duan Jishun. Rentaro Mikuni, Sun Dao-Lin, Shen Guan-Chu, Misako Honno, Tsu Kasa Itoh. Sprawling, involving romance-mystery-suspenser, set between the 1920s and '50s and focusing on the relationships between two families, one Japanese and the other Chinese. Most fascinating is various characters' obsession with Go, a chesslike strategy game. The first Sino-Japanese co-production, and a smash hit in both countries.▼

Go Naked in the World (1961) **C-103m.** ** D: Ranald MacDougall. Gina Lollobrigida, Anthony Franciosa, Ernest Borgnine, Luana Patten. Turgid melodrama badly cast. Easy-loving Lollobrigida hooks Franciosa, much to his father's (Borgnine's) dismay. CinemaScope.

Gone Are the Days (1963) **97m.** *** D: Nicholas Webster. Ossie Davis, Ruby Dee, Sorrell Booke, Godfrey Cambridge, Alan Alda, Beah Richards. Davis' satiric fable *Purlie Victorious* survives cheap adaptation, thanks to buoyant performances and basic story: self-appointed preacher schemes to undo a despotic plantation owner, as a symbolic freeing of his people from ways of the Old South. Alda's film debut.▼

Gone Fishin' (1997) **C-94m.** BOMB D: Christopher Cain. Joe Pesci, Danny Glover, Rosanna Arquette, Lynn Whitfield, Nick Brimble, Carol Kane, Willie Nelson. Annoyingly unfunny gambit of two bungling buddies off to the Florida Everglades where their dream fishing vacation is a catastrophe from beginning to end. An embarrassing waste of talent. This film really smells. [PG]▼●

Gone in 60 Seconds (1974) **C-103m.** ** D: H. B. Halicki. H. B. Halicki, Marion Busia, Jerry Daugirda, James McIntire, George Cole, Parnelli Jones. Muddled drama about a car-theft ring is highlighted by a 40-minute-long chase sequence, which is well made—but so what? [PG]▼

Gone To Earth SEE: **Wild Heart, The**

Gone With the Wind (1939) **C-222m.** **** D: Victor Fleming. Clark Gable, Vivien Leigh, Leslie Howard, Olivia de Havilland, Thomas Mitchell, Barbara O'Neil, Victor Jory, Laura Hope Crews, Hattie McDaniel, Ona Munson, Harry Davenport, Ann Rutherford, Evelyn Keyes, Carroll Nye, Paul Hurst, Isabel Jewell, Cliff Edwards, Ward Bond, Butterfly McQueen, Rand Brooks, Eddie Anderson, Oscar Polk, Jane Darwell, William Bakewell, Violet Kemble-Cooper, Eric Linden, George Reeves. If not the greatest movie ever made, certainly one of the greatest examples of storytelling on film, maintaining interest for nearly four hours. Margaret Mitchell's story is, in effect, a Civil War soap opera, focusing on vixenish Southern belle Scarlett O'Hara, brilliantly played by Leigh; she won Oscar, as did the picture, McDaniel, director Fleming, screenwriter Sidney Howard (posthumously), many others. Memorable music by Max Steiner in this one-of-a-kind film meticulously produced by David O. Selznick. Followed over five decades later by a TV mini-series, *Scarlett.*▼●◗

Gong Show Movie, The (1980) **C-89m.** BOMB D: Chuck Barris. Chuck Barris, Robin Altman, Mabel King, Murray Langston, Jaye P. Morgan, Jamie Farr, Rip Taylor. Barris created a bizarre TV show that belongs in a time capsule, but this movie (which dwells on Chuck's pressures and problems as host and producer of the show) belongs in the trash bin. [R]

Good Burger (1997) **C-95m.** ** D: Brian Robbins. Kel Mitchell, Kenan Thompson, Sinbad, Abe Vigoda, Shar Jackson, Dan Schneider, Jan Schwieterman, Ron Lester, Carmen Electra, Shaquille O'Neal, Robert Wuhl. Broad, juvenile comedy aimed at fans of Kenan and Kel from their Nickelodeon TV series. The existence of a scruffy fast-food establishment (''Welcome to Good Burger, home of the good burger, may I take your order?'') is threatened by the arrival of all-powerful Mondo Burger across the street. Like fast food itself, this film offers no real nourishment, but will appeal to kids just the same. [PG]▼●

Goodbye Again (1961) **120m.** *** D: Anatole Litvak. Ingrid Bergman, Tony Perkins, Yves Montand, Jessie Royce Landis, Diahann Carroll. Francoise Sagan's chic soaper becomes teary Bergman vehicle of middle-aged woman having affair with Perkins, still craving playboy Montand. Set in Paris.▼

Goodbye Charlie (1964) **C-117m.** *½ D: Vincente Minnelli. Tony Curtis, Debbie Reynolds, Pat Boone, Walter Matthau, Martin Gabel, Ellen McRae (Burstyn). Tasteless, flat version of George Axelrod's play; crude gangster dies and comes back to earth as Reynolds. Even Matthau struggles for laughs. James Brolin is an extra in big party scene. CinemaScope.▼

Goodbye, Children SEE: **Au Revoir, les Enfants**

Goodbye, Columbus (1969) **C-101m.** *** D: Larry Peerce. Richard Benjamin, Ali MacGraw, Jack Klugman, Nan Martin, Michael Meyers. Phillip Roth's stinging portrait of successful suburban Jewish family as seen through eyes of young man (Benjamin, in his film debut) who falls in love with daughter (MacGraw, in her first starring role). Meyers steals the show as Ali's brother. Director's father Jan Peerce has a cameo role at a wedding; look for Jaclyn Smith as a model. Music composed and performed by The Association. [PG—originally rated R]▼●

Goodbye, Franklin High (1978) **C-94m.** **½ D: Mike MacFarland. Lane Caudell, Ann Dusenberry, Darby Hinton, Julie Adams, William Windom. A high-school senior faces various challenges and decisions involving a possible baseball career, a college education, his girlfriend, and his parents in this modest, likable film. [PG]

Goodbye Girl, The (1977) **C-110m.** ***½ D: Herbert Ross. Richard Dreyfuss, Marsha Mason, Quinn Cummings, Paul Benedict, Barbara Rhoades. Neil Simon's warmest comedy to date puts young actor Dreyfuss and dumped-on divorcée Mason together as unwilling tenants of the same N.Y.C. apartment, explores their growing relationship. High-caliber script and performances to match; Dreyfuss won Oscar. Nicol Williamson appears unbilled. Later a Broadway musical. [PG]▼●◗

Goodbye Lover (1999) **C-104m.** *½ D: Roland Joffé. Patricia Arquette, Dermot Mulroney, Don Johnson, Ellen DeGeneres, Mary-Louise Parker, Ray McKinnon, Andre Gregory, John Neville, Lisa Eichhorn, Barry Newman. It's double-cross upon double-cross in this comic noir exercise of battling brothers Mulroney and Johnson—and the wacko femme fatale/realtor in their lives (Arquette), who takes her marriage vows loosely, to say the least. So bad it's almost fun, from a seriously slumming director. DeGeneres' sardonic detective seems to have wandered in from another movie altogether. Telltale trouble sign: Alex Rocco and Max Perlich are billed, but hard to spot. Super 35. [R]▼●◗

Goodbye, Mr. Chips (1939-U.S.-British) **114m.** ***½ D: Sam Wood. Robert Donat, Greer Garson, Paul von Hernreid (Henreid), Terry Kilburn, John Mills. Donat won well-deserved Oscar for memorable portrayal of shy schoolmaster who devotes his life to ''his boys,'' only coming out of his shell when he meets Garson. Extreme length works against film's honest sentiment, but Donat makes it all worthwhile. Garson's film debut made her a star overnight. Based on James Hilton's novel; scripted by R. C. Sherriff, Claudine West, and Eric Maschwitz. Remade as a musical in 1969. Also shown in computer-colored version. ▼●

Goodbye, Mr. Chips (1969) **C-151m.** ** D: Herbert Ross. Peter O'Toole, Petula Clark, Michael Redgrave, George Baker, Sian Phillips, Michael Bryant. Lumbering musical remake of 1939 classic. O'Toole is good as prim schoolteacher, but Clark's role as showgirl is shallow, ludicrous. Mediocre songs don't help; what emotion there is gets lost when film plods on to modern-day anticlimax. Ross' directorial debut. Some prints are 133m. Panavision. [G]▼●

Goodbye, My Fancy (1951) **107m.** *** D: Vincent Sherman. Joan Crawford, Robert Young, Frank Lovejoy, Eve Arden. Congresswoman Crawford returns to her old college, more to see former boyfriend Young than to receive honorary degree. Lovejoy is callous newsman. Film debut of Janice Rule.

Good-bye, My Lady (1956) **95m.** **½

D: William Wellman. Walter Brennan, Phil Harris, Brandon de Wilde, Sidney Poitier. James Street novel of small boy (de Wilde), an elderly man (Brennan), and the basenji dog that brings joy into their lives is basis for easy-going, poignant film, set in the South.▼●
Goodbye, New York (1985-U.S.-Israeli) **C-90m.** **½ D: Amos Kollek. Julie Hagerty, Amos Kollek, David Topaz, Aviva Ger, Shmuel Shiloh, Jennifer Babtist. Cute but slight, sometimes flat chronicle of New Yorker Hagerty, a Jewish American Princess of Irish extraction who finds herself penniless and stranded in Israel. She eventually adjusts to life on a kibbutz, getting to know part-time soldier Kollek. [R]▼●
Goodbye, Norma Jean (1976) **C-95m.** BOMB D: Larry Buchanan. Misty Rowe, Terence Locke, Patch Mackenzie, Preston Hanson. Sleazy look at adolescent Marilyn Monroe and her rocky road to stardom; what will have to be cut for TV will leave behind even less reason to watch this piece of tripe. Techniscope. [R]▼
Goodbye People, The (1984) **C-104m.** *½ D: Herb Gardner. Judd Hirsch, Martin Balsam, Pamela Reed, Ron Silver, Michael Tucker, Gene Saks. Absolute torture (adapted by Gardner from his play) about Balsam's begging-for-bankruptcy scheme to open a tropical drink stand on some ill-located beach property. Gardner's A THOUSAND CLOWNS may strike some as sentimental and dated, but this one doesn't even have comedy to carry it. A mawkish disaster, long on the shelf. [PG]▼●
Goodbye Pork Pie (1981-New Zealand) **C-105m.** *** D: Geoff Murphy. Kelly Johnson, Tony Barry, Claire Oberman, Bruno Lawrence, John Beach, Frances Edmond. Amiable comedy/road movie about pair of alienated men, one (Johnson) in his teens and the other (Barry) about twice his age, who trek across New Zealand in a stolen car, the police on their trail. [R]▼
Good Companions, The (1933-British) **113m.** *** D: Victor Saville. Jessie Matthews, Edmund Gwenn, John Gielgud, George Zucco, Dennis Hoey, Mary Glynne, Finlay Currie, Jack Hawkins, Max Miller. J. B. Priestley's novel about a group of strangers who form traveling theatrical company turns into a delightful film. Matthews is given full rein to display her considerable musical and comedic charms; Gielgud is equally humorous and surprising. He even sings! Remade in 1956.
Good Companions, The (1956-British) **C-104m.** *** D: J. Lee Thompson. Eric Portman, Celia Johnson, Hugh Griffith, Janette Scott, John Fraser, Joyce Grenfell, Bobby Howes, Rachel Roberts, Thora Hird, Mona Washbourne, Alec McCowen, John Le Mesurier, Anthony Newley, Shirley Anne Field. Fabulous cast adds luster to this entertaining chronicle of a group of individuals who combine their resources to save a failing "concert party" (musical troupe). Based on a novel by J. B. Priestley; first filmed in 1933. CinemaScope.
Good Dame (1934) **74m.** *½ D: Marion Gering. Fredric March, Sylvia Sidney, Jack LaRue, Helene Chadwick, Noel Francis, Russell Hopton. March and Sidney deserve better than this: tired story of carnival huckster redeemed by the love of a good woman.
Good Day for a Hanging (1958) **C-85m.** **½ D: Nathan Juran. Fred MacMurray, Maggie Hayes, Robert Vaughn, Joan Blackman, James Drury, Denver Pyle. Straightforward account of MacMurray taking over for slain sheriff and bringing in killer, only to find townspeople don't care if murderer is sentenced.▼
Good Die First, The SEE: **Beyond the Law**
Good Die Young, The (1954-British) **100m.** ** D: Lewis Gilbert. Laurence Harvey, Gloria Grahame, Richard Basehart, Stanley Baker, Margaret Leighton, John Ireland, Joan Collins. Solid cast fails to enhance standard robbery tale, with a quartet of strangers coming together to commit a holdup.
Good Earth, The (1937) **138m.** **** D: Sidney Franklin. Paul Muni, Luise Rainer, Walter Connolly, Charley Grapewin, Jessie Ralph, Tilly Losch, Keye Luke, Harold Huber. Mammoth Pearl Buck novel recreated in detail, telling story of greed ruining lives of simple Chinese farming couple. Rainer won Oscar as the ever-patient wife of Muni, as did Karl Freund for his cinematography. Screenplay by Talbot Jennings, Tess Slesinger, and Claudine West. The special effects are outstanding.▼●
Good Fairy, The (1935) **97m.** ***½ D: William Wyler. Margaret Sullavan, Herbert Marshall, Frank Morgan, Reginald Owen, Alan Hale, Beulah Bondi, Cesar Romero. Sparkling romantic comedy, adapted from Molnar play by Preston Sturges; wide-eyed Sullavan tries to act as "good fairy" to struggling lawyer Marshall, while hotly pursued by wealthy Morgan. Hilarious, charming; movie spoof near beginning is priceless. Remade as I'LL BE YOURS.
Good Father, The (1987-British) **C-90m.** **½ D: Mike Newell. Anthony Hopkins, Jim Broadbent, Harriet Walter, Fanny Viner, Simon Callow, Joanne Whalley, Michael Byrne. Hopkins is excellent in the role of a father who loses custody of his child and takes out his incredible anger by befriending Broadbent and funding latter's court case to regain *his* kid's custody. Callow is terrific as an unscrupulous lawyer. Dramatically uneven, but worth a look. Made for British TV. [R]▼●
GoodFellas (1990) **C-146m.** ***½ D: Martin Scorsese. Robert De Niro, Ray Liotta, Joe Pesci, Lorraine Bracco, Paul

Sorvino, Frank Sivero, Tony Darrow, Mike Starr, Frank Vincent, Chuck Low, Frank DiLeo, Christopher Serrone, Samuel L. Jackson, Henny Youngman, Jerry Vale, Debi Mazar, Kevin Corrigan, Michael Imperioli, Illeana Douglas. A boy grows up in an Italian-American neighborhood of Brooklyn and dreams of becoming part of the Mob. Fascinating look at the allure—and the reality—of day-to-day life in a Mafia family, based on experiences of Henry Hill (Liotta), who wound up in the Federal witness protection program. The violence is (necessarily) harsh and off-putting, like the film itself at times, but it's brilliantly realized by Scorsese and cinematographer Michael Ballhaus. Major criticism: It goes on too long. Bracco and Oscar winner Pesci stand out in an exceptional cast; that's Scorsese's mother as Pesci's mom. Screenplay by the director and Nicholas Pileggi, based on the latter's book *Wiseguy*. [R]▼●◗

Good Fight, The (1983) **C/B&W-98m.** ***½ D: Mary Dore, Sam Sills, Noel Buckner. Incisive, often moving documentary of the 3,200 American men and women who were among 40,000 volunteers battling Fascism in the Spanish Civil War. Franco may have won and they may have been harassed by their own government, but they are ultimately both authentic American patriots and survivors. Cut to 85m. for PBS showings.▼●

Good Girls Go to Paris (1939) **75m.** **½ D: Alexander Hall. Melvyn Douglas, Joan Blondell, Walter Connolly, Alan Curtis, Isabel Jeans, Clarence Kolb. Spunky waitress will do anything to visit France; she sees a meal ticket in wealthy Curtis, but really loves professor Douglas. OK comedy.

Good Guys and the Bad Guys, The (1969) **C-91m.** **½ D: Burt Kennedy. Robert Mitchum, George Kennedy, David Carradine, Tina Louise, Douglas Fowley, Lois Nettleton, Martin Balsam, John Carradine. Mild Western comedy-drama has aging marshal Mitchum going after lifelong foe Kennedy, who has been abandoned by his outlaw gang for being over the hill. Panavision. [M/PG]▼

Good Guys Wear Black (1979) **C-96m.** ** D: Ted Post. Chuck Norris, Anne Archer, James Franciscus, Lloyd Haynes, Dana Andrews, Jim Backus. Norris jumps feet first through a windshield and threatens to rearrange the face of bellman Backus—all in the name of national security. Silly political paranoia thriller kills time easily enough. Follow-up: A FORCE OF ONE. [PG]▼●

Good Humor Man, The (1950) **79m.** **½ D: Lloyd Bacon. Jack Carson, Lola Albright, Jean Wallace, George Reeves, Richard Egan. Rambunctious antics with Carson in title role, getting involved in murder plot, aided by gang of "Captain Marvel Kids."▼

Good Idea! SEE: **It Seemed Like a Good Idea at the Time**

Good Luck (1997) **C-98m.** **½ D: Richard LaBrie. Gregory Hines, Vincent D'Onofrio, James Earl Jones, Max Gail, Joe Theismann, Roy Firestone, Maria O'Brien, Sara Trigger. ROCKY-like story of a blind man and a paraplegic who decide to enter a white-water rafting race in order to prove their own self-worth. The theme of triumph over adversity is familiar, but the film's heart is in the right place. Some genuinely raucous and entertaining scenes. [R]▼●◗

Good Luck, Miss Wyckoff (1979) **C-105m.** BOMB D: Marvin J. Chomsky. Anne Heywood, Donald Pleasence, Robert Vaughn, Carolyn Jones, Dorothy Malone, Ronee Blakley, John Lafayette, Earl Holliman. Repressed schoolteacher's first taste of sex comes via rape, in awkward adaptation of William Inge novel. Good cast generally wasted. Video titles: THE SIN, THE SHAMING, and SECRET YEARNINGS. [R]▼

Good Man in Africa, A (1994) **C-93m.** *½ D: Bruce Beresford. Colin Friels, Joanne Whalley-Kilmer, Sean Connery, John Lithgow, Louis Gossett, Jr., Diana Rigg, Sarah-Jane Fenton, Maynard Eziashi, Jackie Mofokeng. Crass, slapdash filming of William Boyd's novel about a weak-willed (and all-too-often insufferable) British diplomat (Friels) in a new African nation, the scenario accomplishes little more than to depict blacks as silly, unbelievable stereotypes. Connery is sorely wasted in the role of a sympathetic doctor. Boyd scripted, and also coproduced with Beresford. [R]▼●

Good Morning Babylon (1987-Italian-French-U.S.) **C-117m.** *** D: Paolo and Vittorio Taviani. Vincent Spano, Joaquim De Almeida, Greta Scacchi, Desiree Becker, Charles Dance, Omero Antonutti, David Brandon. Two Italian brothers, whose artisan family has shaped and restored cathedrals for generations, come to America in 1915 and wind up working for D.W. Griffith on his epic film INTOLERANCE. A valentine to the early days of moviemaking, and a statement about the immortality of art, be it sculpture or film. Beguilingly naive, like the period (and the people) it depicts, with a surprising turn of events for its denouement. Dance is a standout as D.W. Griffith. [PG-13]▼●

Good Morning, Miss Dove (1955) **C-107m.** *** D: Henry Koster. Jennifer Jones, Robert Stack, Kipp Hamilton, Robert Douglas, Peggy Knudsen, Marshall Thompson, Chuck Connors, Biff Elliot, Jerry Paris, Mary Wickes, Richard Deacon. For several generations, small town spinster schoolteacher has touched and helped shape lives of her students. Now hospitalized, her past is revealed through flashbacks. Sentimental, warm, and wonderful. CinemaScope.

Good Morning, Vietnam (1987) **C-120m.**

*** D: Barry Levinson. Robin Williams, Forest Whitaker, Tung Thanh Tran, Chintara Sukapatana, Bruno Kirby, Robert Wuhl, J.T. Walsh, Noble Willingham, Floyd Vivino. Williams is the whole show here, playing an Army disc jockey who turns Armed Forces radio inside out when he's brought to Saigon in 1965. His manic monologues are so uproarious that they carry the rest of the film, which has a weakly developed "story" and often irrelevant musical interludes. Apparently the real-life Adrian Cronauer, on whom story was based, wasn't nearly as funny or outrageous as Williams. [R]▼●◗

Good Mother, The (1988) **C-103m.** ** D: Leonard Nimoy. Diane Keaton, Liam Neeson, Jason Robards, Ralph Bellamy, Teresa Wright, James Naughton, Asia Vieira, Joe Morton, Katey Sagal, Tracy Griffith, Charles Kimbrough. Keaton is excellent as usual in the role of a divorced woman who finds sexual fulfillment for the first time in her life . . . but unwittingly jeopardizes her ability to raise her daughter in the process. Tedious adaptation of the Sue Miller novel. Film debut of Matt Damon (as an extra). [R]▼●

Good Neighbor Sam (1964) **C-130m.** *** D: David Swift. Jack Lemmon, Romy Schneider, Edward G. Robinson, Michael Connors, Dorothy Provine, Neil Hamilton, Joyce Jameson, Robert Q. Lewis. Good comedy of Lemmon's adventures pretending he's not married to his real wife but to luscious neighbor Schneider. Plenty of sight gags and chase scenes make this a lot of fun. Based on a novel by Jack Finney. ▼

Good News (1947) **C-95m.** *** D: Charles Walters. June Allyson, Peter Lawford, Patricia Marshall, Joan McCracken, Ray McDonald, Mel Torme, Donald MacBride, Tom Dugan, Clinton Sundberg. Spirited remake of the 1920s collegiate musical (by DeSylva, Brown, and Henderson), given a new coat of varnish by screenwriters Betty Comden and Adolph Green. Lawford is Tait College's cocky football hero, and Allyson is the brainy girl who catches him on the rebound. Vintage songs include "The Best Things in Life are Free," "Just Imagine," "Varsity Drag"; new numbers include "The French Lesson" and "Pass That Peace Pipe." Filmed previously in 1930.▼●

Good Old Boys, The (1995) **C-130m. TVM** D: Tommy Lee Jones. Tommy Lee Jones, Sissy Spacek, Frances McDormand, Sam Shepard, Terry Kinney, Wilford Brimley, Walter Olkewicz, Park Overall, Matt Damon. Jones (who not only directed but also cowrote the teleplay) ambles his grizzled way through this turn-of-the-century comedy-drama about a saddletramp torn between the footloose life he loves in the shrinking American West and settling down with the local schoolmarm. The Texas twangs make some dialogue sometimes difficult to decipher (at least for Eastern ears). From Elmer Kelton's 1978 novel. Made for cable. Above average. ▼●

Good Sam (1948) **113m.** ** D: Leo McCarey. Gary Cooper, Ann Sheridan, Ray Collins, Edmund Lowe, Joan Lorring, Ruth Roman. Almost complete misfire, despite cast and director. Cooper is an incurable good Samaritan in this lifeless comedy. Some prints run 128m.▼

Good Son, The (1993) **C-87m.** ** D: Joseph Ruben. Macaulay Culkin, Elijah Wood, Wendy Crewson, David Morse, Daniel Hugh Kelly, Jacqueline Brookes, Quinn Culkin. Superficial BAD SEED–type thriller, which exploitively casts HOME ALONE star Culkin as an unremorseful, pre-teen sociopath who terrorizes his cousin (Wood), among many others. What's next: bringing back Shirley Temple and having her place high-tech explosives on the Good Ship Lollipop? Macaulay's sister Quinn plays his sibling, and his brother Rory can be glimpsed in a key photograph. [R]▼●

Good, the Bad, and the Ugly, The (1966-Italian-Spanish) **C-161m.** ***½ D: Sergio Leone. Clint Eastwood, Lee Van Cleef, Eli Wallach, Rada Rassimov, Mario Brega, Chelo Alonso. Third and best of Leone's "Dollars" trilogy, set during Civil War; three disparate low-lifes search for Confederate government treasure chest, each possessing only partial whereabouts. Long, funny, and flamboyant, with memorable Ennio Morricone score; the quintessential spaghetti Western. Followed by ONCE UPON A TIME IN THE WEST. Techniscope. [R—originally rated M]▼●◗

Good Time Girl (1950-British) **81m.** *½ D: David MacDonald. Jean Kent, Dennis Price, Herbert Lom, Flora Robson. Inoffensive trivia about young girl prevented from wayward life by a judge's telling of tragic fate of another teen-ager.

Good Times (1967) **C-91m.** **½ D: William Friedkin. Sonny and Cher, George Sanders, Norman Alden, Larry Duran. Back when the singing duo was considered kooky, they made this enjoyable little film, with Sonny fantasizing their potential movie roles and he and Cher singing "I Got You Babe." Friedkin's first film.▼◗

Good to Go (1986) **C-87m.** ** D: Blaine Novak. Art Garfunkel, Robert Doqui, Harris Yulin, Reginald Daughtry, Richard Brooks, Hattie Winston, Anjelica Huston. Forgettable fare about journalist Garfunkel, who's framed on a rape-murder charge. Of interest mainly for its go-go music, which came out of the Washington D.C. ghetto . . . and did *not* become the national music fad of its time. Highlighted are the performances of such go-go groups as Redds & the Boys, Trouble Funk, Chuck Brown & the Soul Searchers, among others. Video title: SHORT FUSE. [R]▼

Good Wife, The (1986-Australian) **C-92m.** **½ D: Ken Cameron. Rachel Ward, Bryan Brown, Sam Neill, Steven Vidler, Jennifer Claire, Bruce Barry. Isolated, bored wife Ward becomes obsessed with the new man in town (Neill). Predictable and a bit slow but also well made and well acted. Overall, a very mixed bag. Original Australian title: THE UMBRELLA WOMAN. [R]▼

Good Will Hunting (1997) **C-126m.** *** D: Gus Van Sant. Matt Damon, Robin Williams, Ben Affleck, Minnie Driver, Stellan Skarsgård, Casey Affleck, Cole Hauser. Four working-class friends hang out together in South Boston, but one of them, pugnacious Will Hunting (Damon), has an unusual gift: he's a genius. When M.I.T. math professor Skarsgård gets wind of this, he insists that the young man stop wasting his talents, and sends him to psychologist/teacher Williams to try to crack his brittle shell. Well-acted fiction written by costars Damon and Ben Affleck doesn't bear close scrutiny but certainly entertains, with an array of good performances. Oscar nods for Best Original Screenplay and Best Supporting Actor (Williams). [R]▼●◗

Good Woman of Bangkok, The (1991-Australian) **C-82m.** **½ D: Dennis O'Rourke. Yaowaiak Chonchanakun. This "documentary fiction" alleges to follow the life of Aoi, a prostitute in Bangkok who attracted the attention of an Australian filmmaker "trying to find why love is at once so banal and so profound." Real-life scenes of the seamy side of Bangkok are interspersed with what look like authentic interviews with an old lady, and dramatized interviews with Aoi. Alternately involving and tedious, the film is compromised by the viewer's being unable to tell fiction from reality.▼

Goofy Movie, A (1995) **C-78m.** **½ D: Kevin Lima. Voices of Bill Farmer, Jason Marsden, Jim Cummings, Kellie Martin, Rob Paulsen, Wallace Shawn, Jenna Von Oy, Frank Welker, Jo Anne Worley, Julie Brown, Joey Lawrence, Pat Buttram. Ever-lovable Goofy takes his son, Max, on a road-trip vacation, but it's a culture clash between the '90s boy and his old-fashioned father. Simple, straightforward Disney cartoon feature for kids with a handful of serviceable songs and a nice "message" about father-son relationships. No Disney classic, but pleasant enough. Followed by a direct-to-video sequel. [G]▼●

Goonies, The (1985) **C-114m.** **½ D: Richard Donner. Sean Astin, Josh Brolin, Jeff Cohen, Corey Feldman, Kerri Green, Martha Plimpton, Ke Huy Quan (Jonathan Ke Quan), John Matuszak, Anne Ramsey, Joe Pantoliano. A bunch of kids go in search of hidden treasure in this old-fashioned adventure yarn (from a story by Steven Spielberg, who may have recalled Our Gang's MAMA'S LITTLE PIRATE). Big, lively, and exceptionally noisy, aimed squarely at kids, with a likable bunch of kids onscreen. Also makes appropriate use of Max Steiner's swashbuckling theme from ADVENTURES OF DON JUAN. Panavision. [PG]▼●

Goose and the Gander, The (1935) **65m.** ** D: Alfred E. Green. Kay Francis, George Brent, Genevieve Tobin, John Eldredge, Claire Dodd. Woman's story of high-living Francis keeping an eye on ex-husband Brent.

Gor (1988) **C-95m.** *½ D: Fritz Kiersch. Urbano Barbarini, Oliver Reed, Rebecca Ferratti, Larry Taylor, Graham Clarke, Arnold Vosloo, Chris Du Plessis, Paul L. Smith, Jack Palance. Ordinary sword-and-sorcery adventure in which meek American professor is magically whisked off to "counter-Earth" Gor, where he becomes a hero and battles chuckling, tyrannical Reed. Based on the first in "John Norman's" series of Edgar Rice Burroughs-inspired adventure fantasies. Palance's role is just a cameo setting up the sequel, OUTLAW OF GOR. [PG]▼

Gordon's War (1973) **C-90m.** *** D: Ossie Davis. Paul Winfield, Carl Lee, David Downing, Tony King. When a Vietnam vet comes home to find his wife hooked on drugs, he trains four-man army to destroy the pushers. Good action, but gets lost toward the end. [R]▼

Gordy (1995) **C-90m.** ** D: Mark Lewis. Doug Stone, Kristy Young, Michael Roescher, Tom Lester, Deborah Hobart, Ted Manson. Gordy is a talking pig who somehow becomes involved in big business—and a quest to save his family from the slaughterhouse. *Very* undemanding kids' film has its moments. Based on a story by *Green Acres* veterans Jay Sommers and Dick Chevillat. Besides top-billed Stone the film features such other country music stars as Roy Clark, Mickey Gilley, Jim Stafford, Box Car Willie, and Moe Bandy. [G] ▼●

Gore Vidal's Billy the Kid (1989) **C-100m. TVM** D: William A. Graham. Val Kilmer, Duncan Regehr, Wilford Brimley, Julie Carmen, Michael Parks, Rene Auberjonois, Albert Salmi. William Bonney was a likable but misunderstood teenager who got caught up in a range war, became embittered and went bad . . . according to Vidal, who depicted Billy the Kid in a 1950s teleplay that became a Paul Newman movie, THE LEFT-HANDED GUN. This one is similarly interesting if unremarkable. The author has a cameo as a minister at graveside. Made for cable. Average.▼

Gore Vidal's Lincoln (1988) **C-200m. TVM** D: Lamont Johnson. Sam Waterston, Mary Tyler Moore, John Houseman, Richard Mulligan, John McMartin, Ruby Dee, Cleavon Little, Jeffrey DeMunn, James Gammon, Deborah Adair, Robin Gammell. Thoughtful performances by Waterston (as a pensive Abe) and Moore (as an unsteady Mary Todd) firmly ground this slow-moving personal portrait of the two, from the day they came to Washington to the day they left for the President's burial in Springfield. Earnestly adapted by Ernest Kinoy from Vidal's best-seller, with a fine music score by Ernest Gold, and Emmy-winning direction by Johnson. Originally shown in two parts. Above average.▼

Gorgeous Hussy, The (1936) **102m.** **½ D: Clarence Brown. Lionel Barrymore, Joan Crawford, Robert Taylor, Franchot Tone, Melvyn Douglas, James Stewart. Star-studded cast in strained historical drama of Andrew Jackson's belle, who disgraces herself and those connected with her. Crawford et al are beautifully costumed in well-appointed settings.▼

Gorgo (1961-British) **C-78m.** *** D: Eugene Lourie. Bill Travers, William Sylvester, Vincent Winter, Bruce Seton, Joseph O'Conor. Good sci-fi story of captured baby sea monster put into London circus and gigantic parent coming to rescue it. Exciting special effects.▼●

Gorgon, The (1964-British) **C-83m.** **½ D: Terence Fisher. Peter Cushing, Christopher Lee, Richard Pasco, Barbara Shelley, Michael Goodliffe. In 19th-century Balkan village, one of the snake-headed Gorgons still survives, turning her victims to stone—but who is she by day? Good Hammer production.▼●

Gorilla, The (1939) **66m.** ** D: Allan Dwan. The Ritz Brothers, Anita Louise, Patsy Kelly, Lionel Atwill, Bela Lugosi, Joseph Calleia. Disappointing comedy-whodunit with the Ritz Brothers as fumbling detectives prowling around old-dark-house in search of murderer. Lugosi is wasted. Filmed before in 1930.▼●◗

Gorilla (1944) SEE: **Nabonga**

Gorilla at Large (1954) **C-84m.** *** D: Harmon Jones. Cameron Mitchell, Anne Bancroft, Lee J. Cobb, Raymond Burr, Peter Whitney, Lee Marvin, Warren Stevens. Offbeat murder mystery at amusement park, with exceptionally able cast. Filmed in 3-D.

Gorilla Man, The (1942) **64m.** ** D: D. Ross Lederman. John Loder, Ruth Ford, Marian Hall, Richard Fraser, Creighton Hale. Title is misleading. Pro-Nazis try to discredit RAF pilot by linking him with series of brutal murders. Grade-B material with adequate acting.

Gorillas in the Mist (1988) **C-129m.** *** D: Michael Apted. Sigourney Weaver, Bryan Brown, Julie Harris, John Omirah Miluwi, Iain Cuthbertson, Constantin Alexandrov, Waigwa Wachira. Absorbing drama based on the life of Dian Fossey, who journeyed to Africa in 1967 and, with no prior experience, set out to document the vanishing breed of mountain gorillas for *National Geographic*. Her transformation from diligent researcher to obsessive madwoman is a bit more abrupt than it ought to be, but it's still a good film, and Weaver is compelling in the lead. [PG-13]▼●◗

Gorky Park (1983) **C-128m.** *** D: Michael Apted. William Hurt, Lee Marvin, Brian Dennehy, Ian Bannen, Joanna Pacula, Alexander Knox. Absorbing murder mystery set in Russia, where police investigator Hurt doggedly pursues the case of three bodies buried in Gorky Park. Lots of twists and turns, vivid atmosphere (with Helsinki doubling for Moscow) . . . marred somewhat by unconvincing romance and protracted finale. Dennis Potter adapted Martin Cruz Smith's novel. [R]▼●

G.O.R.P. (1980) **C-90m.** BOMB D: Joseph Ruben. Michael Lembeck, Dennis Quaid, Philip Casnoff, Fran Drescher, David Huddleston, Robert Trebor, Julius Harris, Rosanna Arquette. Sophomoric, depressingly unfunny drug-oriented comedy set in a summer camp. Makes MEATBALLS seem like *Hamlet*; for people who think the word "Quaalude" is automatically funny. [R]▼

Gospel (1982) **C-92m.** ***½ D: David Leivick, Frederick A. Ritzenberg. James Cleveland and the Southern California Community Choir, Walter Hawkins and the Hawkins Family, Mighty Clouds of Joy, Shirley Caesar, Twinkie Clark and the Clark Sisters. Inspiring, tremendously entertaining concert film spotlighting top gospel performers. Each number is more rousing than the last.▼

Gospel According to St. Matthew, The (1966-Italian-French) **135m.** **** D: Pier Paolo Pasolini. Enrique Irazoqui, Margherita Caruso, Susanna Pasolini, Marcello Morante, Mario Socrate. Unconventional, austere film on life and teachings of Christ, based solely on writings of the Apostle, Matthew. Amateur cast (including director's mother) is expressive and moves with quiet dignity. Ironically, director of this masterpiece was a Marxist.▼●◗

Gospel According to Vic, The (1985-British) **C-92m.** ** D: Charles Gormley. Tom Conti, Helen Mirren, David Hayman, Brian Pettifer, Jennifer Black. Very minor comedy of Catholic schoolteacher Conti and the series of miracles that befall him. Mirren is wasted as a music teacher/love interest. Aka HEAVENLY PURSUITS. [PG-13]▼

Gospel Road, The (1973) **C-83m.** **½ D: Robert Elfstrom. Johnny Cash, June Carter, Robert Elfstrom. Musical journey through Holy Land follows story of Jesus from his birth to his death and resurrection. Sincere but not especially good. [G]▼

Gossip (2000) **C-91m.** BOMB D: Davis Guggenheim. James Marsden, Lena Headey, Norman Reedus, Joshua Jackson, Kate

Hudson, Marisa Coughlan, Eric Bogosian, Edward James Olmos, Sharon Lawrence. Inane tale of three college roomies who hatch a rumor as a class project that (naturally) gets way out of hand. Any dropout could guess these plot twists; viewer has an easier choice. Super 35. [R]▼◗

Gosta Berling's Saga SEE: **Atonement of Gosta Berling, The**

Gotcha! (1985) **C-101m.** ★★½ D: Jeff Kanew. Anthony Edwards, Linda Fiorentino, Nick Corri, Alex Rocco, Marla Adams, Klaus Loewitsch, Christopher Rydell. Nerdy college kid goes to Paris on vacation, meets seductive older woman who involves him in espionage in East Berlin. Very nearly a good movie, with some sharp dialogue to start, but loses its appeal as it loses its credibility. [PG-13] ▼●

Go Tell It on the Mountain (1984) **C-97m. TVM** D: Stan Lathan. Paul Winfield, James Bond III, Olivia Cole, Rosalind Cash, Ruby Dee, Linda Hopkins, Alfre Woodard, Ving Rhames, Giancarlo Esposito. This drama about a young black boy's efforts to gain the approval of—and, later, understand—his stern, unrelenting stepfather is poignant, intelligent, and well acted. Adapted from James Baldwin's semiautobiographical novel; a PBS *American Playhouse* presentation. Above average.▼

Go Tell the Spartans (1978) **C-114m.** ★★★½ D: Ted Post. Burt Lancaster, Craig Wasson, Jonathan Goldsmith, Marc Singer, Joe Unger, David Clennon, Dolph Sweet, James Hong. Perceptive, moving Vietnam War picture, set in early '64; Burt shines as "advisory group" commander who is already starting to have his doubts about the conflict. More realistic in dialogue and situation than other, more publicized, popular films on the subject. Wendell Mayes's cynically funny script is right on target. Based on Daniel Ford's novel *Incident at Muc Wa*. [R]▼●

Gothic (1986-British) **C-90m.** ★★ D: Ken Russell. Gabriel Byrne, Julian Sands, Natasha Richardson, Miriam Cyr, Timothy Spall. That night in 1816 when Mary Shelley (author of *Frankenstein*) and Dr. Polidori (*The Vampyre*) were inspired to write their gothic classics—previously depicted in THE BRIDE OF FRANKENSTEIN—is given the wild Ken Russell treatment here. Too weird for some, too highbrow for many horror fans, but full of Russell's hallucinatory visuals. Same story was told two years later in HAUNTED SUMMER. [R]▼●

Gotti (1996) **C-115m. TVM** D: Robert Harmon. Armand Assante, Anthony Quinn, William Forsythe, Richard S. Sarafian, Marc Lawrence, Vincent Pastore, Alberta Watson, Al Waxman. Assante scowls his slick way through this surface biodrama of cocky wiseguy John Gotti, the dapper don among N.Y. mobsters of the 1980s, whom the feds finally put away for life. Quinn plays his fictional mentor and Lawrence is aged crime kingpin Carlo Gambino. Made for cable. Average.▼●

Governess, The (1998-British) **C-112m.** ★★½ D: Sandra Goldbacher. Minnie Driver, Tom Wilkinson, Florence Hoath, Jonathan Rhys-Meyers, Harriet Walter, Arlene Cockburn, Emma Bird. Intriguing but somewhat unfocused film, set in the 1800s, about a spirited young Jewish woman who leaves her newly impoverished London family to take a job as governess on a remote Scottish island. There she develops an unusual relationship—both cerebral and passionate—with the master of the house. Slow-moving film has interesting passages but never gels. Written by the director, who bites off more than she can chew. Super 35. [R]▼◗

Government Girl (1943) **94m.** ★★½ D: Dudley Nichols. Olivia de Havilland, Sonny Tufts, Anne Shirley, Jess Barker, James Dunn, Paul Stewart, Agnes Moorehead. Production expert Tufts comes to Washington to build airplanes for the war effort; he spars with (and, of course, falls for) secretary de Havilland. Frantic comedy with serious (and still timely) overtones about government bureaucracy. Scripted by Nichols; adapted by Budd Schulberg from a story by Adela Rogers St. Johns.

Go West (1925) **69m.** ★★½ D: Buster Keaton. Buster Keaton, Howard Truesdale, Kathleen Myers, Brown Eyes. Buster plays a greenhorn named Friendless who winds up working on a cattle ranch out West, and finding his soulmate in a cow named Brown Eyes. Not one of Buster's best silents, this still has plenty of good scenes, especially the climactic stampede, executed with typically Keatonesque comic skill. ▼●◗

Go West (1940) **81m.** ★★ D: Edward Buzzell. Groucho, Chico, and Harpo Marx, John Carroll, Diana Lewis, Walter Woolf King, Robert Barrat. Big letdown from Marxes, until hilarious train-ride climax. Occasional bits sparkle through humdrum script.▼●

Go West, Young Man (1936) **82m.** ★★★ D: Henry Hathaway. Mae West, Randolph Scott, Warren William, Alice Brady, Elizabeth Patterson, Lyle Talbot, Isabel Jewell. Movie queen Mae is stuck in the sticks, but passes time nicely with handsome farm-boy. Not top-notch West, but still fun.▼

Grace of My Heart (1996) **C-115m.** ★★½ D: Allison Anders. Illeana Douglas, John Turturro, Eric Stoltz, Matt Dillon, Patsy Kensit, Bruce Davison, David Clennon, Christina Pickles, Amanda De Cadenet, Chris Isaak, Bridget Fonda, voice of Peter Fonda. Disappointing film about a great subject: the pop music world centered around N.Y.C.'s Brill Building in the 1950s and 60s. Aspiring singer-songwriter Douglas finds doors closed to her as a performer but becomes a successful pop tunesmith instead; her destiny is then linked to a succession of men in the music business. Nice moments here and there but superficial at every turn—a real shame. Full of pleasant sound-alike songs from the period, plus one showstopper, "God Give Me Strength," written by Elvis Costello and pop veteran Burt Bacharach. Executive-produced by Martin Scorsese. [R]▼●◗

Grace Quigley (1985) **C-87m.** *½ D: Anthony Harvey. Katharine Hepburn, Nick Nolte, Elizabeth Wilson, Chip Zien, Kit Le Fever, William Duell, Walter Abel, Denny Dillon. Abysmal misfire that manages to be both bland and tasteless, about lonely, elderly Hepburn, who hires hit man Nolte to kill her—and then others of her set who would all rather be dead. Filmed in 1983, first shown at 1984 Cannes Film Festival at 102m. However, another version of this exists, titled THE ULTIMATE SOLUTION OF GRACE QUIGLEY and put together by its scriptwriter, A. Martin Zweiback. Despite an uneven second half, it is a touching, funny, surreal black comedy about the problems of the elderly and the right of choice. This cut runs 94m. and is rated **½. [PG]▼

Gracie Allen Murder Case, The (1939) **74m.** **½ D: Alfred E. Green. Gracie Allen, Warren William, Ellen Drew, Kent Taylor, Jerome Cowan, Judith Barrett, Donald MacBride, William Demarest, H. B. Warner. Fitfully amusing screwball mystery with the scatterbrained Allen as herself, constantly annoying Philo Vance in his investigation of a murdered convict. This was written for the screen first, *then* as a novel by S. S. Van Dine.

Graduate, The (1967) **C-105m.** **** D: Mike Nichols. Anne Bancroft, Dustin Hoffman, Katharine Ross, Murray Hamilton, William Daniels, Elizabeth Wilson, Brian Avery, Norman Fell, Marion Lorne, Alice Ghostley. Landmark film of the late 60s that's still just as pungent—and funny—as ever. Hoffman, in his first major film role, plays ultra-naive college grad who's seduced by a middle-aged woman, then falls in love with her daughter. Perfect song score by Simon and Garfunkel. Script by Buck Henry (who plays the desk clerk) and Calder Willingham from Charles Webb's novel. Nichols won Best Director Oscar. Look fast for Mike Farrell in hotel lobby, and Richard Dreyfuss in Berkeley rooming house. Panavision. [R]▼●◗

Graduation Day (1981) **C-96m.** BOMB D: Herb Freed. Christopher George, Patch Mackenzie, E. Danny Murphy, Michael Pataki, E. J. Peaker, Vanna White. A bloody FRIDAY THE 13TH clone, done with no talent or imagination. [R]▼

Graffiti Bridge (1990) **C-91m.** *½ D: Prince. Prince, Morris Day, Jerome Benton & The Time, Jill Jones, Mavis Staples, George Clinton, Ingrid Chavez, Robin Power, T.C. Ellis, Tevin Campbell. Further auteur antics from the rocker-filmmaker (and nonactor), a sequel of sorts to PURPLE RAIN, but with murky religious overtones. Even the musical numbers, source of the film's socko CD soundtrack, are botched here. If you don't even like Prince's music, you'd better convert our rating to BOMB. Purple piffle. [PG-13]▼●

Grand Canyon (1991) **C-134m.** ** D: Lawrence Kasdan. Danny Glover, Kevin Kline, Steve Martin, Mary McDonnell, Mary-Louise Parker, Alfre Woodard, Jeremy Sisto, Tina Lifford, Patrick Malone. Ruminations on why and how Life is Lousy, especially in L.A., as a handful of disparate lives intersect: a lawyer who feels distant from his wife, a wife who's discovered an abandoned baby, a tow-truck driver who's worried about his sister's survival in a violent neighborhood, etc. Give Kasdan (and cowriter Meg Kasdan) credit for attempting to make a serious film that deals with matters of importance . . . but the results are mushy, superficial, and unconvincing. Panavision. [R]▼●◗

Grand Central Murder (1942) **73m.** **½ D: S. Sylvan Simon. Van Heflin, Patricia Dane, Cecilia Parker, Virginia Grey, Samuel S. Hinds, Sam Levene, Horace (Stephen) McNally, Tom Conway. Slick, fast-moving B whodunit, with Heflin investigating actress' murder on private train car at Grand Central Station.

Grand Duel, The (1972-Italian) **C-92m.** *½ D: Giancarlo Santi. Lee Van Cleef, Peter O'Brien, Marc Mazza, Jess Hahn, Horst Frank. Typically spare spaghetti Western with mysterious gunman Van Cleef becoming guardian angel to a man wrongly accused of murder. Aka STORM RIDER. [R]▼

Grande Bouffe, The (1973-French-Italian) **C-125m.** **½ D: Marco Ferreri. Marcello Mastroianni, Ugo Tognazzi, Michel Piccoli, Philippe Noiret, Andrea Ferreol. Four bored middle-aged men decide to commit group suicide by eating themselves to death. Outrageous idea, but overbaked—no pun intended—and excessively, graphically gross. [X]▼◗

Grand Highway, The (1987-French) **C-104m.** *** D: Jean-Loup Hubert. Anemone, Richard Bohringer, Antoine Hubert, Vanessa Guedj, Christine Pascal. Fine, subtle, slice-of-life tale of a fragile nine-year-old boy (Hubert, son of the director) and his experiences while spending three weeks in a rural village while his mother is off giving birth. Guedj is a delight as the tomboy who becomes his friend. Original title: LE GRAND CHEMIN. Remade in U.S. as PARADISE. [R] ▼

Grand Hotel (1932) **113m.** **** D: Edmund Goulding. Greta Garbo, John Barrymore, Joan Crawford, Wallace Beery, Lionel Barrymore, Lewis Stone, Jean Hersholt, Ferdinand Gottschalk, Tully Marshall, Mary Carlisle. Vicki Baum's novel and play of plush Berlin hotel where "nothing ever happens." Stars prove the contrary: Garbo as lonely ballerina, John B. her jewel-thief lover, Lionel B. a dying man, Crawford an ambitious stenographer, Beery a hardened businessman, Stone the observer. Scripted by William A. Drake. Best Picture Oscar winner; a must. Plot reworked many times (in HOTEL BERLIN, WEEKEND AT THE WALDORF, etc.). Later a Broadway musical. ▼●

Grand Illusion (1937-French) **117m.** **** D: Jean Renoir. Jean Gabin, Pierre Fresnay, Erich von Stroheim, (Marcel) Dalio, Dita Parlo, (Julien) Carette, Gaston Modot, Jean Dasté. Renoir's classic treatise on war, focusing on French prisoners during WW1 and their cultured German commandant. Beautiful performances enhance an eloquent script (by Renoir and Charles Spaak). Edited to 94m. for U.S. release in 1938. Beware of other versions with variant running times. ▼●◗

Grand Jury (1977) **C-100m.** *½ D: Christopher Cain. Bruce Davison, Meredith MacRae, Leslie Nielsen, Barry Sullivan, Sharon Thomas. Dull drama about Davison and MacRae becoming unintentionally entangled in insurance hijinks.

Grandma's Boy (1922) **81m.** *** D: Fred Newmeyer. Harold Lloyd, Mildred Davis, Anna Townsend, Charles Stevenson, Noah Young, Dick Sutherland. Lloyd's first great success casts him as a mousy small-town type inspired to fight for his girl—and his honor—by his grandma's tales of family heritage. Still entertaining.

Grand National Night (1953-British) **81m.** ** D: Bob McNaught. Nigel Patrick, Moira Lister, Beatrice Campbell, Betty Ann Davies, Michael Hordern, Noel Purcell. Melodramatic murder yarn involving the horsey set in northern England. Hordern, as a police inspector, gives the most interesting performance. Pay close attention to the surname of leading man Patrick's character.

Grand Prix (1966) **C-175m.** ** D: John Frankenheimer. James Garner, Eva Marie Saint, Yves Montand, Toshiro Mifune, Brian Bedford, Jessica Walter, Francoise Hardy. Big cast is saddled with rambling script about personal lives of auto racers and their loves; use of split screen and spectacular sequences won't mean much on TV. Deservedly won Oscars for the editing and sound effects people. Super Panavision 70. ▼●

Grand Slam (1933) **67m.** **½ D: William Dieterle. Loretta Young, Paul Lukas, Frank McHugh, Glenda Farrell, Helen Vinson, Roscoe Karns, Walter Byron. Breezy, semisatirical look at early '30s bridge-tournament stars Young and Lukas as a couple who find love and luck. Interesting use of slow motion and freeze frame for finale.

Grand Slam (1967-Italian-U.S.) **C-120m.** *** D: Giuliano Montaldo. Edward G. Robinson, Janet Leigh, Adolfo Celi, Klaus Kinski, Georges Rigaud, Robert Hoffman. International jewel-heist film, with all the trappings. Nothing new, but smoothly done, most enjoyable. Techniscope.

Grand Theft Auto (1977) **C-85m.** ** D: Ron Howard. Ron Howard, Nancy Morgan, Marion Ross, Pete Isacksen, Barry Cahill. Howard's directorial debut (he also coscripted with his actor-father Rance) is typical unsophisticated car-crash action fare, no better or worse than most. [PG] ▼●◗

Grand Tour, The (1992) **C-99m.** **½ D: David N. Twohy. Jeff Daniels, Ariana Richards, Emilia Crow, Jim Haynie, David Wells, Nicholas Guest, Robert Colbert, Marilyn Lightstone. The proprietor of a small-town hotel fears that his unexpected guests are tourists from the future, visiting for a frightening reason. Intelligent, low-key sci-fi, well acted and consistently surprising, but too drawn-out. From the novella "Vintage Season" by Lawrence O'Donnell and C. L. Moore. Filmed for theatrical release but debuted on cable TV instead. Aka DISASTER IN TIME. [PG-13] ▼

Grandview, U.S.A. (1984) **C-97m.** **½ D: Randal Kleiser. Jamie Lee Curtis, C. Thomas Howell, Patrick Swayze, Jennifer Jason Leigh, Ramon Bieri, Carole Cook, Troy Donahue, William Windom, Elizabeth Gorcey, M. Emmet Walsh, John Cusack, Joan Cusack, Michael Winslow. So-so slice of Americana, focusing on several characters in archetypal Midwestern town: a young boy coming of age, an independent young woman trying to make it on her own running her father's demolition-derby business, and a lovesick sap who's her ace driver. Passable time-filler but nothing more. [R] ▼

Grapes of Wrath, The (1940) **129m.** **** D: John Ford. Henry Fonda, Jane Darwell, John Carradine, Charley Grapewin, Dorris Bowden, Russell Simpson, John Qualen, O. Z. Whitehead, Eddie Quillan, Zeffie Tilbury, Darryl Hickman, Ward Bond, Charles Middleton, Tom Tyler, Mae Marsh, Jack Pennick. Classic Americana of Okies moving from dust bowl to California during Depression, lovingly brought to screen. Fonda, as ex-con, is unforgettable in role of his life. Darwell, as determined family matriarch, and Ford won well-deserved Oscars. Written for the screen (from John Steinbeck's classic) and produced by Nunnally Johnson. Don't miss this one.▼●

Grass (1925) **70m.** ***½ D: Merian C. Cooper, Ernest B. Schoedsack, Marguerite Harrison. Landmark ethnographic documentary, right up with NANOOK OF THE NORTH and MOANA in its impact. The highlight: Cooper, Schoedsack, and Harrison accompany the Bakhityari, a tribe of 50,000 Persian (Iranian) nomads, on their annual journey across hazardous terrain to bring their herds to pasture. Cooper and Schoedsack went on to make CHANG and then KING KONG. ▼●◗

Grass Harp, The (1996) **C-107m.** *** D: Charles Matthau. Piper Laurie, Sissy Spacek, Walter Matthau, Edward Furlong, Nell Carter, Jack Lemmon, Mary Steenburgen, Sean Patrick Flanery, Joe Don Baker, Charles Durning, Roddy McDowall, Doris Roberts, Scott Wilson; narrated by Boyd Gaines. Thoughtful drama based on Truman Capote's evocative memoir of his boyhood in the South, where he was raised by his wealthy aunt and her lightheaded sister. Exquisite performance by Laurie as the boy's free-spirited soulmate, matched by Spacek as a woman who's been hardened by life. Director Matthau appears as a customer in McDowall's barbershop. [PG] ▼●

Grasshopper, The (1970) **C-95m.** *** D: Jerry Paris. Jacqueline Bisset, Jim Brown, Joseph Cotten, Corbett Monica, Ramon Bieri. Episodic but fairly compelling chronicle of how a beautiful 19-year-old from British Columbia ends up as a burned-out Vegas call girl at age 22. Better than expected melodrama actually features Brown in a sympathetic role. Look fast for Penny Marshall. Aka THE PASSION OF EVIL and PASSIONS. [R] ▼

Grass Is Greener, The (1961) **C-105m.** *** D: Stanley Donen. Cary Grant, Deborah Kerr, Robert Mitchum, Jean Simmons. Chic drawing-room fare that suffers from staginess. Grant-Kerr marriage is threatened by Simmons and Mitchum romancing the two, respectively. Technirama. ▼●

Grass Is Singing, The (1981-British-Swedish) **C-108m.** *** D: Michael Raeburn. Karen Black, John Thaw, John Kani, John Moulder Brown, Patrick Mynhardt. Black is excellent as a lonely woman who marries farmer Thaw and cannot adjust to life in the African woodland. Filmed in Zambia; based on a novel by Doris Lessing. Released in U.S. in 1984 as KILLING HEAT.▼

Grave Indiscretions SEE: **Gentlemen Don't Eat Poets**

Grave Robbers From Outer Space SEE: **Plan 9 From Outer Space**

Graveyard, The SEE: **Persecution**

Graveyard Shift (1989) **C-89m.** **½ D: Gerard Ciccoritti. Silvio Oliviero, Helen Papas, Cliff Stoker, Dorin Ferber, Dan Rose, Don Jones. Oliviero has the perfect occupation for a modern vampire: an all-night cabdriver. His only victims are those in "their cycle of death," but things get out of hand anyway. Intelligent, well-acted low-budgeter harmed only by not knowing when to quit. Filmed in 1985. Followed by a sequel: THE UNDERSTUDY. [R] ▼

Graveyard Shift (1990) **C-87m.** BOMB D: Ralph S. Singleton. David Andrews, Kelly Wolf, Stephen Macht, Brad Dourif, Andrew Divoff, Vic Polizos. Bottom-of-the-barrel, cliché-ridden shocker chronicling the goings-on in a mysterious mill, whose workers are disappearing within its rat-infested bowels. Poorly directed, with even worse special effects. Based on a short story by Stephen King. [R]▼●

Gravy Train, The (1974) **C-96m.** **½ D: Jack Starrett. Stacy Keach, Frederic Forrest, Margot Kidder, Barry Primus, Richard Romanus, Denny Miller. OK blend of fast-moving action and comedy as West Virginia brothers Keach and Forrest develop a liking for crime. Aka THE DION BROTHERS. [R]

Grayeagle (1978) **C-104m.** **½ D: Charles B. Pierce. Ben Johnson, Iron Eyes Cody, Lana Wood, Jack Elam, Paul Fix, Alex Cord. Interesting if flawed rehash of THE SEARCHERS with Johnson tracking the Indian (Cord) who kidnapped his daughter. Good classic Western style an asset, sluggish pacing a drawback. Produced, directed, written by Pierce, who also appears. Panavision. [PG]▼

Gray Lady Down (1978) **C-111m.** ** D: David Greene. Charlton Heston, David Carradine, Stacy Keach, Ned Beatty, Ronny Cox, Rosemary Forsyth. Tired drama about rescue of nuclear submarine, captained by Heston. Good special effects, and colorful performance by Carradine as designer of experimental diving craft. Look for Christopher Reeve as one of the officers. Panavision. [PG]▼◗

Gray's Anatomy (1996) **C/B&W-80m.** *** D: Steven Soderbergh. Spalding Gray. Gray's brilliance as a raconteur shines through in this witty, inventively directed monologue charting his experience of passing his 50th birthday and finding himself afflicted with a rare eye disease. His encounters with traditional and alternative medicine are both funny and frightening.▼◗

Grazie Zia SEE: **Thank You, Aunt**

Grease (1978) **C-110m.** *** D: Randal Kleiser. John Travolta, Olivia Newton-John, Stockard Channing, Jeff Conaway, Didi Conn, Eve Arden, Sid Caesar, Joan Blondell, Edd Byrnes, Alice Ghostley, Dody Goodman, Lorenzo Lamas, Michael Tucci, Dinah Manoff, Christopher McDonald. Energetic, imaginative filming of long-running

Broadway show fantasizes 1950s life; spirited cast, clever ideas, and Patricia Birch's choreography make it fun. Hit songs (written for movie) include "You're the One That I Want," "Hopelessly Devoted To You," and title number, sung by Frankie Valli. Followed by a sequel. Panavision. [PG]▼●

Grease 2 (1982) **C-114m.** BOMB D: Patricia Birch. Maxwell Caulfield, Michelle Pfeiffer, Adrian Zmed, Lorna Luft, Didi Conn, Eve Arden, Sid Caesar, Dody Goodman, Tab Hunter, Connie Stevens. Mindless sequel to the musical hit; opens with a great back-to-school number, then goes downhill. Pedestrian music, clumsy comedy, uncharismatic leads; only the supporting players (like newcomer Luft and veteran Arden) shine through. Inauspicious directing debut for choreographer Birch. Panavision. [PG]▼●

Greased Lightning (1977) **C-94m.** ** D: Michael Schultz. Richard Pryor, Beau Bridges, Pam Grier, Cleavon Little, Vincent Gardenia, Richie Havens, Julian Bond. Spirited cast does little to enliven plodding, episodic bio of Wendell Scott, the first black racing car driver. A waste of Pryor, both dramatically and comically. [PG]▼

Greaser's Palace (1972) **C-91m.** *** D: Robert Downey. Allan Arbus, Albert Henderson, Luana Anders, George Morgan, Larry Moyer, Michael Sullivan, James Antonio, Ron Nealy. Super-offbeat Jesus Christ parody with Western setting. Drifter (Arbus) discovers "true identity" and heals "sick" cowboys in crazy, tiny town. Seven-year-old Robert Downey, Jr., appears as a mutilated child!▼

Great Adventure, The (1953-Swedish) **73m.** ***½ D: Arne Sucksdorff. Anders Norberg, Kjell Sucksdorff, Arne Sucksdorff. Outstanding story told in semidocumentary style covering four seasons of a boy's life on a farm. Written, directed, edited, and photographed by an Oscar-winning filmmaker with a special gift for capturing animal life.▼

Great Adventure, The (1975-Italian-Spanish) **C-87m.** ** D: Paul Elliotts (Gianfranco Baldanello). Jack Palance, Joan Collins, Fred Romer (Fernando Romero), Elisabetta Virgili, Manuel de Blas, Remo de Angelis. Middling Jack London tale of a boy and his dog trying to make it in the wilds of gold-rush Alaska—fighting the odds, marauding wolves, sinister town boss Palance, dancehall queen Collins.▼

Great American Broadcast, The (1941) **92m.** **½ D: Archie Mayo. Alice Faye, John Payne, Jack Oakie, Cesar Romero, The Four Ink Spots, James Newill, Mary Beth Hughes. Fictional fun of development of radio industry, with such musical guests as zany Wiere Brothers. Entertaining; bright cast.

Great American Cowboy, The (1974) **C-90m.** *** D: Kieth Merrill. Narrated by Joel McCrea. Exciting documentary on rodeo life focuses on rodeo superstar Larry Mahan and his competition with newcomer Phil Lyne. Oscar-winner as Best Documentary Feature. [G]▼

Great American Pastime, The (1956) **89m.** ** D: Herman Hoffman. Tom Ewell, Anne Francis, Ann Miller, Dean Jones, Rudy Lee. Suburbanite Ewell doesn't know what he's getting into when he begins managing his son's Little League team. Slight, forgettable programmer.

Great Balloon Adventure, The SEE: **Olly, Olly, Oxen Free**

Great Balls of Fire! (1989) **C-102m.** **½ D: Jim McBride. Dennis Quaid, Winona Ryder, Alec Baldwin, Lisa Blount, Trey Wilson, John Doe, Steve Allen, Stephen Tobolowsky, Lisa Jane Persky, Michael St. Gerard, Peter Cook. Slick, highly stylized cartoon about the rise (and temporary fall) of '50s rocker Jerry Lee Lewis, a twice-married hellraiser whose doom was sealed when he took his 13-year-old second cousin as wife No. 3. Quaid's amusing but verrrry broad lead performance is balanced by Ryder's more even-keeled portrayal of cousin Myra. Reasonably entertaining but falls far short of its potential. That's Lewis' real voice, though Quaid *is* playing the piano. [PG-13] ▼●

Great Bank Hoax, The (1977) **C-89m.** **½ D: Joseph Jacoby. Richard Basehart, Burgess Meredith, Paul Sand, Ned Beatty, Michael Murphy, Charlene Dallas, Arthur Godfrey. Unremarkable but diverting comedy, a Watergate allegory about bank officials who try to cover up embezzlement by arranging an even bigger theft. Aka THE GREAT GEORGIA BANK HOAX; originally titled SHENANIGANS. [PG]▼

Great Bank Robbery, The (1969) **C-98m.** *½ D: Hy Averback. Zero Mostel, Kim Novak, Clint Walker, Claude Akins, Akim Tamiroff, Larry Storch. Bogus preacher and company, Mexican gang led by Tamiroff, and local outlaws all compete for control of the town of Friendly. Spoof of Westerns is a total dud. Be warned. Panavision. [M/PG]

Great Battle, The (1978-German-Yugoslavian) **C-97m.** BOMB D: Humphrey Longan (Umberto Lenzi). Helmut Berger, Samantha Eggar, Giuliano Gemma, John Huston, Stacy Keach, Henry Fonda, Edwige Fenech. Amateurish muddle about WW2 combines tired vignettes with well-known stars, dubbed sequences with others, and newsreel footage narrated by Orson Welles. A waste of everybody's time. Video title: BATTLE FORCE. [PG]▼

Great British Train Robbery, The (1967-German) **104m.** *** D: John Olden, Claus Peter Witt. Horst Tappert, Hans Cossy, Gunther Neutze, Isa Miranda. Absorbing true study of mammoth robbery of British mails by an ingenious band of outlaws.
Great Caruso, The (1951) **C-109m.** *** D: Richard Thorpe. Mario Lanza, Ann Blyth, Jarmila Novotna, Dorothy Kirsten. Biographical fiction about the legendary singer, entertainingly done. Fine music makes clichés endurable.▼●
Great Catherine (1968-British) **C-98m.** *½ D: Gordon Flemyng. Peter O'Toole, Jeanne Moreau, Zero Mostel, Jack Hawkins, Akim Tamiroff. Terrible adaptation of George Bernard Shaw's comedy about Catherine the Great wastes capable cast; wait for Dietrich's THE SCARLET EMPRESS.
Great Chase, The (1963) **81m.** ***½ Narrated by Frank Gallop. Buster Keaton, Douglas Fairbanks, Sr., Pearl White, Richard Barthelmess, Lillian Gish. Entertaining silent-film compilation of great chase scenes from THE MARK OF ZORRO, WAY DOWN EAST, etc., with most of film devoted to Keaton's classic, THE GENERAL. Score composed by harmonica virtuoso Larry Adler.▼◗
Great Dan Patch, The (1949) **94m.** **½ D: Joe (Joseph M.) Newman. Dennis O'Keefe, Gail Russell, Ruth Warrick, Charlotte Greenwood. Henry Hull, John Hoyt, Arthur Hunnicutt, Clarence Muse. Acceptable yarn about the legendary trotting horse Dan Patch and his phenomenal harness-racing career. O'Keefe is Dan's owner, Warrick and Russell (in a nicely modulated performance) the two very different women in his life.▼
Great Day (1945-British) **94m.** **½ D: Lance Comfort. Eric Portman, Flora Robson, Sheila Sim, Isabel Jeans, Walter Fitzgerald, Philip Friend. English village readies itself for visit by Eleanor Roosevelt. Despite soap-opera plot, film works as a wartime curio, capturing a particular place and time.▼
Great Day in Harlem, A (1994) **C-60m.** ***½ D: Jean Bach. Dizzy Gillespie, Milt Hinton, Marian McPartland, Art Blakey, Gerry Mulligan, Sonny Rollins, Horace Silver, Bud Freeman, Art Farmer, narration by Quincy Jones. Joyous celebration of a famous photo taken for *Esquire* magazine in 1958, which gathered dozens of jazz greats on a Harlem sidewalk. What could have been a prosaic "talking head" documentary becomes instead a lively collage of sights, sounds, and memories, with charming interviews, fascinating home movies of the event, and vintage performance footage of these musicians at work. Film director Robert Benton—then *Esquire*'s art director—is one of the interviewees.▼●◗
Great Day in the Morning (1956) **C-92m.** **½ D: Jacques Tourneur. Virginia Mayo, Robert Stack, Ruth Roman, Alex Nicol, Raymond Burr. Good cast, beautiful color scenery help so-so story of pre-Civil War Colorado, when gold rush fever and separationist sentiments clashed. SuperScope.▼
Great Diamond Robbery, The (1953) **69m.** ** D: Robert Z. Leonard. Red Skelton, Cara Williams, James Whitmore, Dorothy Stickney, Steven Geray. Limp vehicle buoyed by Skelton. Red is hoodwinked by jewel thief who wants him to recut huge diamond.
Great Dictator, The (1940) **128m.** ***½ D: Charles Chaplin. Charles Chaplin, Paulette Goddard, Jack Oakie, Reginald Gardiner, Maurice Moscovich, Billy Gilbert, Henry Daniell. Chaplin's first full talkie; unusual comedy combines slapstick, satire, and social commentary, as he plays dual role of Jewish ghetto barber and dictator Adenoid Hynkel of Tomania. Unique, surprisingly effective film also features Oakie in unforgettable portrayal of "Benzino Napaloni" of rival country Bacteria.▼●◗
Great Escape, The (1963) **C-168m.** **** D: John Sturges. Steve McQueen, James Garner, Richard Attenborough, Charles Bronson, James Coburn, David McCallum, Donald Pleasence, James Donald, Gordon Jackson, John Leyton, Angus Lennie, Nigel Stock. Allied P.O.W.s plot massive escape from Nazi prison camp. Based on true story, this blockbuster was beautifully photographed by Daniel Fapp on location in Germany. Rip-roaring excitement with marvelous international cast; script by James Clavell and W. R. Burnett, from Paul Brickhill's book. Rousing score by Elmer Bernstein. Followed by a TV sequel twenty-five years later. Panavision.▼●◗
Greatest, The (1977) **C-101m.** *½ D: Tom Gries. Muhammad Ali, Ernest Borgnine, John Marley, Robert Duvall, James Earl Jones, Roger E. Mosley, Ben Johnson, Paul Winfield, Lloyd Haynes, Dina Merrill, David Clennon. Potentially exciting screen bio of the great heavyweight champ becomes an episodic mess suffering from a script devoid of dramatic focus and ham-handed direction. Ironically, Mosley's performance as Sonny Liston has the charisma Ali's lacks. Soundtrack features George Benson's "The Greatest Love of All." [PG]▼
Greatest Battle, The SEE: **Great Battle, The**
Greatest Love, The (1951-Italian) **110m.** *½ D: Roberto Rossellini. Ingrid Bergman, Alexander Knox, Giulietta Masina, Teresa Pellati, Ettore Giannini. Bergman plays a wealthy American living in Rome, who feels compelled to help people in order to restore meaning to her own life after her

son's suicide. Obvious, slow-moving story. Originally titled EUROPA '51.▼

Greatest Show on Earth, The (1952) **C-153m.** ***½ D: Cecil B. DeMille. Betty Hutton, Charlton Heston, Cornel Wilde, Dorothy Lamour, Gloria Grahame, James Stewart, Henry Wilcoxon, Lawrence Tierney, Lyle Bettger. Big package of fun from DeMille, complete with hokey performances, clichés, big-top excitement, and a swell train wreck. Stewart well cast as circus clown with mysterious past. Some funny surprise guests appear. Oscar winner for Best Picture and Story.▼●

Greatest Story Ever Told, The (1965) **C-141m.** **½ D: George Stevens. Max von Sydow, Charlton Heston, Carroll Baker, Angela Lansbury, Sidney Poitier, Shelley Winters, John Wayne, Ed Wynn, Jose Ferrer, Van Heflin, Claude Rains, Telly Savalas, many others. Some of the most spectacular scenes ever filmed lose all validity because of incessant cameos that run throughout film. Would *you* believe John Wayne as a Roman centurion supervising Christ's crucifixion? Carl Sandburg is listed in credits as a Creative Associate. Originally shown at 260m., then at 195m. Ultra Panavision 70.▼●

Great Expectations (1934) **102m.** **½ D: Stuart Walker. Jane Wyatt, Phillips Holmes, George Breakston, Henry Hull, Florence Reed, Alan Hale, Francis L. Sullivan. Acceptable version of Dickens' story about a young boy and unknown benefactor is dwarfed by '46 classic. Sullivan plays Jaggers in both films. ▼

Great Expectations (1946-British) **118m.** **** D: David Lean. John Mills, Valerie Hobson, Bernard Miles, Francis L. Sullivan, Finlay Currie, Martita Hunt, Anthony Wager, Jean Simmons, Alec Guinness, Ivor Barnard, Freda Jackson, Torin Thatcher, Eileen Erskine, Hay Petrie. One of the greatest films ever made, a vivid adaptation of Dickens's tale of a mysterious benefactor making poor young orphan a gentleman of means. Opening graveyard sequence is a gem. Oscars went to cinematographer Guy Green and art director John Bryan. Lean, Kay Walsh, Cecil McGivern, and producers Anthony Havelock-Allan and Ronald Neame all contributed to script. Filmed in 1934, 1974, and updated in 1998. Jean Simmons played Miss Havisham in a 1989 miniseries. ▼●◗

Great Expectations (1974-U.S.-British) **C-103m. TVM** D: Joseph Hardy. Michael York, Sarah Miles, James Mason, Margaret Leighton, Robert Morley, Anthony Quayle, Joss Ackland, Rachel Roberts, Heather Sears, Peter Bull. OK remake of the Dickens classic; originally produced as a musical, but songs have been deleted. Anyway, OLIVER! it ain't. Average.▼

Great Expectations (1998) **C-111m.** **½ D: Alfonso Cuarón. Ethan Hawke, Gwyneth Paltrow, Anne Bancroft, Chris Cooper, Hank Azaria, Robert De Niro, Josh Mostel, Kim Dickens, Nell Campbell, Stephen Spinella. Modern story based on the Dickens classic has Finn (né Pip) helping a convict on the Florida marshes, then being summoned to the decrepit mansion of equally decrepit Ms. Dinsmoor (née Havisham), where he meets the love of his life, the beautiful but heartless Estella. Eventually, he's whisked off to N.Y.C. to find fame and fortune as an artist. So stylishly crafted that it's a shame it doesn't add up to much of anything. The skeleton of Dickens is there, but no resonance. Panavision. [R]▼●◗

Great Flamarion, The (1945) **78m.** **½ D: Anthony Mann. Erich von Stroheim, Mary Beth Hughes, Dan Duryea, Stephen Barclay, Lester Allen, Esther Howard. Better than most von Stroheim cheapies, this one casts him as a vaudeville star who becomes romantically entangled with his scheming married assistant. ▼

Great Gabbo, The (1929) **95m.** ** D: James Cruze. Erich von Stroheim, Don Douglas, Betty Compson, Margie Kane. The idea of von Stroheim as an egomaniacal ventriloquist is irresistible, but the story is slim, predictable, and stiffly done—padded out by lots of big and unintentionally hilarious musical numbers. A curio for film buffs. Based on Ben Hecht story; some sequences originally in color.▼

Great Gambini, The (1937) **70m.** **½ D: Charles Vidor. Akim Tamiroff, Marian Marsh, Genevieve Tobin, William Demarest, Reginald Denny. Nightclub mind-reader Tamiroff predicts a murder, then becomes involved in the investigation. Interesting B-movie fluff, with added novelty of a "mystery minute" to give you a chance to guess the killer.

Great Garrick, The (1937) **91m.** *** D: James Whale. Brian Aherne, Olivia de Havilland, Edward Everett Horton, Melville Cooper, Lionel Atwill, Lana Turner, Marie Wilson. Members of the Comédie Française perpetrate a hoax to deflate the ego of pompous David Garrick (Aherne) in this entertaining, fictionalized yarn about real-life British actor.

Great Gatsby, The (1949) **92m.** **½ D: Elliott Nugent. Alan Ladd, Betty Field, Macdonald Carey, Barry Sullivan, Ruth Hussey, Shelley Winters, Howard da Silva. Misguided adaptation of F. Scott Fitzgerald's book about a mysterious young millionaire who crashes Long Island society in the 1920s. Too talky and much too literal-minded. Ladd is pretty good, but Field (as Daisy Buchanan) gives a strangely petulant performance. Filmed before in 1926 and again in 1974.

Great Gatsby, The (1974) **C-144m.** **½ D: Jack Clayton. Robert Redford, Mia

Farrow, Bruce Dern, Karen Black, Scott Wilson, Sam Waterston, Lois Chiles, Howard da Silva, Edward Herrmann, Patsy Kensit, Roberts Blossom. Bland adaptation of F. Scott Fitzgerald's jazz-age novel about a golden boy in Long Island society; faithful to the book, and visually opulent, but lacks substance and power. Script by Francis Ford Coppola; Theoni V. Aldredge's costumes and Nelson Riddle's score earned Oscars. [PG]▼●

Great Georgia Bank Hoax, The SEE: **Great Bank Hoax, The**

Great Gilbert and Sullivan, The (1953-British) **C-105m.** *** D: Sidney Gilliat. Robert Morley, Maurice Evans, Eileen Herlie, Peter Finch, Martyn Green. Agreeable production is only a superficial biography of the legendary operetta composers, but does offer many highlights from their wonderful works. Their lives are probed more incisively in TOPSY-TURVY. Original British title: THE STORY OF GILBERT AND SULLIVAN.

Great Gildersleeve, The (1943) **62m.** ** D: Gordon Douglas. Harold Peary, Nancy Gates, Freddie Mercer, Mary Field, Jane Darwell, Thurston Hall. First of series based on famous radio character Throckmorton P. Gildersleeve is moderately amusing nonsense, as Gildy enters local politics and avoids spinster Field.▼

Great Guns (1941) **74m.** ** D: Monty Banks. Stan Laurel, Oliver Hardy, Sheila Ryan, Dick Nelson, Edmund MacDonald. Later L&H Army comedy is weak, not as bad as some but far below their classic films. Look quickly for Alan Ladd.▼

Great Guy (1936) **75m.** ** D: John G. Blystone. James Cagney, Mae Clarke, James Burke, Edward Brophy, Henry Kolker, Bernadene Hayes, Edward McNamara. Second-rate Cagney in low-budget production about inspector crusading against corruption in meat business.▼

Great Impostor, The (1961) **112m.** **½ D: Robert Mulligan. Tony Curtis, Karl Malden, Raymond Massey, Edmond O'Brien, Arthur O'Connell, Gary Merrill, Frank Gorshin. Incredible story of Ferdinand Demara, who succeeded in a variety of professional guises. Film is episodic and pat.▼

Great Jesse James Raid, The (1953) **C-74m.** **½ D: Reginald Le Borg. Willard Parker, Barbara Payton, Tom Neal, Wallace Ford. Generally action-packed tale blending fact and legend about the notorious outlaw and his last big robbery caper.▼

Great John L., The (1945) **96m.** **½ D: Frank Tuttle. Greg McClure, Linda Darnell, Barbara Britton, Lee Sullivan, Otto Kruger, Wallace Ford, George Matthews, Rory Calhoun. Not bad little biography of famous boxer John L. Sullivan's rise and fall, his two loves and unhappy end.

Great K&A Train Robbery, The (1926) **53m.** ***½ D: Lewis Seiler. Tom Mix, Dorothy Dwan, William Walling, Harry Grippe, Tony. Silent screen's most popular cowboy star in one of his greatest films: rollicking fun, filmed on magnificent locations in Colorado.▼

Great Lie, The (1941) **107m.** *** D: Edmund Goulding. Mary Astor, Bette Davis, George Brent, Lucile Watson, Hattie McDaniel, Grant Mitchell, Jerome Cowan. Brent marries Davis when alliance with Astor is annulled. He is lost in plane crash, leaving Davis and pregnant Astor to battle each other and the elements. Well-mounted soaper won Astor an Oscar as fiery concert pianist.▼●

Great Locomotive Chase, The (1956) **C-85m.** *** D: Francis D. Lyon. Fess Parker, Jeffrey Hunter, Jeff York, John Lupton, Eddie Firestone, Kenneth Tobey. True story of Andrews' Raiders (filmed before by Buster Keaton as THE GENERAL) comes to life in colorful Disney film; Parker is famous Union spy who leads a rowdy band in capturing and "kidnapping" a Confederate railroad train during Civil War. Retitled ANDREWS' RAIDERS. CinemaScope.▼◗

Great Lover, The (1949) **80m.** *** D: Alexander Hall. Bob Hope, Rhonda Fleming, Roland Young, Roland Culver, George Reeves, Jim Backus. Vintage Hope; Bob's a boy scout leader on ship filled with his troop, luscious Fleming, and murderer Young.▼

Great Man, The (1956) **92m.** ***½ D: Jose Ferrer. Jose Ferrer, Dean Jagger, Keenan Wynn, Julie London, Jim Backus, Ed Wynn. Well-loved TV star dies and Ferrer prepares memorial show, only to discover star was a despicable phony. Hard-bitten look at TV industry; top performances by senior and junior Wynns. Ferrer and Al Morgan adapted Morgan's novel.

Great Man's Lady, The (1942) **90m.** **½ D: William Wellman. Barbara Stanwyck, Joel McCrea, Brian Donlevy, Thurston Hall, K. T. Stevens, Lucien Littlefield. Saga of the West is no great shakes as McCrea dreams of oil wells, Donlevy takes his girl. Stanwyck ages to 100 years to frame story.▼

Great Man Votes, The (1939) **72m.** ***½ D: Garson Kanin. John Barrymore, Peter Holden, Virginia Weidler, Donald MacBride, William Demarest. Simple, sincere, delightful film of Barrymore, once a professor, now a souse, fighting for custody of his children, suddenly elevated to new stature when election-time rolls around. MacBride fun as small-time politico, Demarest an energetic campaign promoter. ▼

Great McGinty, The (1940) **81m.** *** D: Preston Sturges. Brian Donlevy, Muriel Angelus, Akim Tamiroff, Allyn Joslyn, William Demarest, Louis Jean Heydt, Arthur Hoyt. Sturges' directorial debut (and

Oscar-winning screenplay) isn't up to his later comedy classics, but Donlevy is excellent as bum who is manipulated into governor's chair by crooked political machine—then blows it all when he tries to be honest. Typically sharp dialogue, plus fine work by Sturges' stock company of character actors. Donlevy and Tamiroff reprised their roles as a gag in Sturges' THE MIRACLE OF MORGAN'S CREEK. ▼●

Great Meadow, The (1931) **78m.** **½ D: Charles Brabin. John Mack Brown, Eleanor Boardman, Lucille LaVerne, Anita Louise, Gavin Gordon, Guinn Williams, Russell Simpson, John Miljan. Naive and primitive but still compelling story of Virginians who undertake mountainous trek to settle new land in Kentucky, circa 1777. Fairly authentic drama gives a real sense of the hardship these pioneers endured. Filmed in Realife 70mm.

Great Mike, The (1944) **70m.** ** D: Wallace W. Fox. Stuart Erwin, Robert (Buzzy) Henry, Marion Martin, Carl (Alfalfa) Switzer, Pierre Watkin, Gwen Kenyon. Slight tale of young Henry and his love for a horse who, predictably and after various complications, is destined to become a racing champ.▼

Great Missouri Raid, The (1950) **C-83m.** ** D: Gordon Douglas. Wendell Corey, Macdonald Carey, Ellen Drew, Ward Bond, Anne Revere, Bruce Bennett, Bill Williams, Edgar Buchanan. By-the-numbers account of Frank and Jesse James (played by Corey and Carey, respectively) and the Younger brothers, who are forced to become outlaws after the Civil War by a conniving army major (Bond).▼

Great Moment, The (1944) **83m.** ** D: Preston Sturges. Joel McCrea, Betty Field, Harry Carey, William Demarest, Franklin Pangborn, Grady Sutton, Louis Jean Heydt. Confused biography of anesthesia inventor wavers from comedy to drama; ineffectual, filled with frustrating flashbacks. Very offbeat for writer-director Sturges, although film was taken out of his hands and reedited. Filmed in 1942.▼●

Great Moments in Aviation SEE: **Shades of Fear**

Great Mouse Detective, The (1986) **C-80m.** *** D: John Musker, Ron Clements, Dave Michener, Burny Mattinson. Voices of Vincent Price, Barrie Ingham, Val Bettin, Susanne Pollatschek, Candy Candido, Eve Brenner, Alan Young, Melissa Manchester. Brisk animated adaptation of Eve Titus' book *Basil of Baker Street,* about a Sherlockian mouse who matches wits with the nefarious Prof. Ratigan (whose role is performed with gusto by Price). Not much depth to this Disney cartoon feature, but it *is* a lot of fun. Reissued in 1992 as THE ADVENTURES OF THE GREAT MOUSE DETECTIVE. [G]▼●

Great Muppet Caper, The (1981-British) **C-95m.** *** D: Jim Henson. The Muppet Performers (Jim Henson, Frank Oz, Dave Goelz, Jerry Nelson, Richard Hunt), Charles Grodin, Diana Rigg, John Cleese, Robert Morley, Peter Ustinov, Jack Warden. The Muppets try to solve a London jewel robbery in their second feature-film. Clever gags and ideas plus hilarious musical numbers with Miss Piggy make up for meandering script with more than its share of slow spots. [G]▼●

Great Northfield, Minnesota Raid, The (1972) **C-91m.** **½ D: Philip Kaufman. Cliff Robertson, Robert Duvall, Luke Askew, R. G. Armstrong, Dana Elcar, Donald Moffat, John Pearce, Matt Clark, Wayne Sutherlin, Elisha Cook. New-style Western showing famous robbery scheme from seamy side. Vivid portraits of Younger brothers, James brothers, but muddled point of view. [PG]▼

Great O'Malley, The (1937) **71m.** *½ D: William Dieterle. Pat O'Brien, Humphrey Bogart, Ann Sheridan, Donald Crisp, Mary Gordon, Frieda Inescort, Sybil Jason. Syrupy film of ruthless cop O'Brien and poor man Bogart who has lame daughter and turns to crime to support her. Pretty sticky.

Great Outdoors, The (1988) **C-90m.** *½ D: Howard Deutch. Dan Aykroyd, John Candy, Stephanie Faracy, Annette Bening, Chris Young, Ian Giatti, Hilary Gordon, Rebecca Gordon, Robert Prosky. Joyless scattershot comedy about disintegration of Candy clan's summer vacation by the uninvited appearance of boorish in-law Aykroyd and family. Written by John Hughes, apparently with something else on his mind. Bening's first film. [PG]▼●◗

Great Profile, The (1940) **82m.** **½ D: Walter Lang. John Barrymore, Mary Beth Hughes, Gregory Ratoff, John Payne, Anne Baxter, Lionel Atwill, Edward Brophy. Barrymore on downslide provides some laughs in self-parodying tale of aging, conceited actor.

Great Race, The (1965) **C-150m.** **½ D: Blake Edwards. Tony Curtis, Natalie Wood, Jack Lemmon, Peter Falk, Keenan Wynn, Larry Storch, Dorothy Provine, Arthur O'Connell, Vivian Vance, Ross Martin, George Macready. Long, sometimes funny, often labored comedy, not the greatest ever made, as advertised. Duel sequence and barroom brawl are highlights, but pie fight falls flat, other gimmicks don't work. Definitely a mixed bag (although Natalie never looked better); one good song, "The Sweetheart Tree." Panavision.▼●

Great Rock 'n Roll Swindle, The (1980-British) **C-103m.** *** D: Julien Temple. Malcolm McLaren, Johnny Rotten

(John Lydon), Sid Vicious, Steve Jones, Paul Cook, Ronnie Biggs, Liz Fraser. Controversial, outrageously cynical free-form documentary about the infamous, groundbreaking punk-rock band Johnny Rotten and The Sex Pistols. Film also shows how Pistols' manager Malcolm McLaren cleverly marketed the group. One of the many highlights: the late Sid Vicious' version of "My Way."▼●

Great Rupert, The (1950) **86m.** **½ D: Irving Pichel. Jimmy Durante, Terry Moore, Tom Drake, Queenie Smith, Frank Orth, Jimmy Conlin, Chick Chandler. Agreeable comedy-fantasy about a trained squirrel who finds a cache of money and gives it to impoverished vaudevillian Durante and his family. Durante is at his best, but story runs out of steam before it's through. Produced by George Pal; director Pichel appears in a brief bit.▼◗

Great Santini, The (1979) **C-116m.** **½ D: Lewis John Carlino. Robert Duvall, Blythe Danner, Michael O'Keefe, Lisa Jane Persky, Stan Shaw, Theresa Merritt, David Keith. Character study of a career Marine who, in 1962, is "a warrior without a war," except for the one he wages with his adolescent son. Compelling performances give film its meat, but dramatic structure and resolutions are not nearly as strong. Adapted by Carlino from Pat Conroy's novel. Aka THE ACE. [PG]▼●◗

Great Scout and Cathouse Thursday (1976) **C-102m.** **½ D: Don Taylor. Lee Marvin, Oliver Reed, Robert Culp, Elizabeth Ashley, Howard Platt, Strother Martin, Sylvia Miles, Kay Lenz. Broad comedy set in Colorado of 1908 involves swindles, defanged snake, kidnapped prostitutes, and robbery of proceeds from big boxing match. Could have been funnier, but Reed is a delight as an Indian(!). [PG]▼

Great Sinner, The (1949) **110m.** **½ D: Robert Siodmak. Gregory Peck, Ava Gardner, Melvyn Douglas, Walter Huston, Ethel Barrymore. Murky romance lavishly produced, meandering along with tale of Peck saving Gardner from drowning in gambling fever—then catching it himself.

Great Sioux Massacre, The (1965) **C-91m.** **½ D: Sidney Salkow. Joseph Cotten, Darren McGavin, Philip Carey, Julie Sommars, Nancy Kovack, Frank Ferguson. Good acting enhances this version of Custer's last stand. CinemaScope.

Great Sioux Uprising, The (1953) **C-80m.** **½ D: Lloyd Bacon. Jeff Chandler, Faith Domergue, Lyle Bettger, Glenn Strange. Chandler as ex-Yankee officer is adequate in formula Western about threatened Indian war.

Great Smokey Roadblock, The (1976) **C-84m.** **½ D: John Leone. Henry Fonda, Eileen Brennan, John Byner, Dub Taylor, Susan Sarandon, Melanie Mayron, Austin Pendleton. Innocuous story of aging trucker (Fonda) attempting one perfect cross-country run before his truck is repossessed; his haul is a houseful of evicted prostitutes. Some nice vignettes. Originally titled THE LAST OF THE COWBOYS, running 106m. Coproduced by Sarandon. [PG]▼

Great Spy Mission, The SEE: **Operation Crossbow**

Great St. Louis Bank Robbery, The (1959) **86m.** *½ D: Charles Guggenheim, John Stix. Steve McQueen, David Clarke, Crahan Denton, Molly McCarthy, James Dukas. Modest robbery caper with virtue of McQueen in cast.▼●

Great St. Trinian's Train Robbery, The (1966-British) **C-94m.** ** D: Frank Launder, Sidney Gilliat. Frankie Howerd, Reg Varney, Richard Wattis, Dora Bryan. Overly droll entry in popular series begins with the real Great Train Robbery, then injects political satire with usual hijinks as crooks' hiding place for loot becomes new site for infamous girls' school. Alastair Sim's presence is sorely missed.▼

Great Texas Dynamite Chase, The (1977) **C-90m.** *½ D: Michael Pressman. Claudia Jennings, Jocelyn Jones, Johnny Crawford, Chris Pennock, Tara Strohmeier. A pair of sexy female bank robbers take to the roads in this all-too-typical low-budget outing. [R]▼

Great Train Robbery, The (1979-British) **C-111m.** *** D: Michael Crichton. Sean Connery, Donald Sutherland, Lesley-Anne Down, Alan Webb, Malcolm Terris, Wayne Sleep, Robert Lang. Stylish fun as an elegant trio conspire to pull off the greatest heist of all time, in the mid-1800s: stealing shipment of gold from a moving train! Crichton based his script on true incident, filmed it against beautiful Irish countryside. British title: THE FIRST GREAT TRAIN ROBBERY. [PG]▼●◗

Great Victor Herbert, The (1939) **91m.** **½ D: Andrew L. Stone. Allan Jones, Mary Martin, Walter Connolly, Lee Bowman, Susanna Foster, Jerome Cowan. Music overshadows plot in lightweight romance about two young singers and the famed composer. Many of Herbert's most popular songs ("Ah, Sweet Mystery of Life," "March of the Toys," etc.) included.

Great Waldo Pepper, The (1975) **C-107m.** *** D: George Roy Hill. Robert Redford, Bo Svenson, Bo Brundin, Susan Sarandon, Geoffrey Lewis, Edward Herrmann, Margot Kidder, Scott Newman. Boxoffice disappointment from director of BUTCH CASSIDY and THE STING is a much more personal film, even though brilliantly photographed story of aviation pioneers wavers uncomfortably between slapstick and drama. Worth a look. Todd-AO 35. [PG]
▼●◗

Great Wall, A (1986) **C-100m.** **½ D:

Peter Wang. Peter Wang, Sharon Iwai, Kelvin Han Yee, Li Qinqin, Hy Xiaoguang. Good-natured story of culture clash that results when Chinese-American family makes its first trip to mainland China. Amiable but hardly inspired. First U.S.-Chinese coproduction is also Wang's first feature as cowriter, director, and star (he played the chef in CHAN IS MISSING by Wayne Wang—no relation). [PG]▼●

Great Waltz, The (1938) **102m.** **½ D: Julien Duvivier. Luise Rainer, Fernand Gravet, Miliza Korjus, Hugh Herbert, Lionel Atwill, Curt Bois. Music outdoes drama in this elaborately produced biography of composer Johann Strauss, with plenty of waltzes covering up a standard triangle tale. Joseph Ruttenberg's lovely cinematography earned an Oscar.▼●

Great Waltz, The (1972) **C-135m.** BOMB D: Andrew L. Stone. Horst Buchholz, Mary Costa, Rossano Brazzi, Nigel Patrick, Yvonne Mitchell, James Faulkner. Bio of Johann Strauss is unintentionally funny in the way director Stone's SONG OF NORWAY was, but after 135 minutes, even the laughs begin to subside. Filmed on location in Austria. Panavision. [G]

Great War, The (1959-Italian-French) **118m.** ** D: Mario Monicelli. Vittorio Gassman, Alberto Sordi, Silvana Mangano, Folco Lulli. Uneven, episodic comedy-drama of two gold-bricking pals during WW1, somewhat reminiscent of WHAT PRICE GLORY? but not nearly as good. Released here in 1961. CinemaScope.▼

Great White Hope, The (1970) **C-101m.** *** D: Martin Ritt. James Earl Jones, Jane Alexander, Lou Gilbert, Joel Fluellen, Chester Morris, Robert Webber, R. G. Armstrong, Hal Holbrook, Beah Richards, Moses Gunn. Supercharged adaptation of Broadway success with Jones and Alexander (in her film debut) repeating stage roles as Jack Jefferson, famed heavyweight champion, and white mistress. Not a boxing film or social doctrine, but emotional character study. Holds up until final scene, which doesn't ring true. Howard Sackler adapted his own play. Panavision. [PG]▼

Great White Hype, The (1996) **C-90m.** **½ D: Reginald Hudlin. Samuel L. Jackson, Jeff Goldblum, Damon Wayans, Peter Berg, Jon Lovitz, Corbin Bernsen, Cheech Marin, Jamie Foxx, Salli Richardson, John Rhys-Davies, Rocky Carroll. Flamboyant boxing promoter Jackson needs a new gimmick: his champ (Wayans) isn't drawing the big money anymore, so he realizes a *white* contender is required. Berg is amusing as the dumb-but-earnest rival. Occasionally very funny, often snidely cynical, but the satire is not as pointed as intended. Written by Ron Shelton and Tony Hendra. [R]▼●

Great Ziegfeld, The (1936) **176m.** ***½ D: Robert Z. Leonard. William Powell, Myrna Loy, Luise Rainer, Frank Morgan, Fanny Brice, Virginia Bruce, Reginald Owen, Ray Bolger, Stanley Morner (Dennis Morgan). Spectacular, immensely entertaining biography of flamboyant impresario Florenz Ziegfeld, with Powell quite dashing in the title role. However, Rainer (as Anna Held) is stunning, and won an Academy Award; her telephone scene is a classic. Also won Oscars for Best Picture and Dance Direction (the "A Pretty Girl Is Like A Melody" number, supervised by Seymour Felix).▼●

Greed (1925) **140m.** **** D: Erich von Stroheim. Gibson Gowland, ZaSu Pitts, Jean Hersholt, Chester Conklin, Dale Fuller. Powerful adaptation of Frank Norris' novel *McTeague,* about a simple man whose wife's obsession with money eventually drives him to madness. Even though von Stroheim's film was taken from him and severely cut by the studio (it originally ran eight hours), this remains a stunning work, one of the greatest of all silent films. The final sequences in Death Valley are unforgettable. Reconstructed in 1999, using stills to cover long-lost footage; this version runs 242m.▼●

Greedy (1994) **C-113m.** ** D: Jonathan Lynn. Michael J. Fox, Kirk Douglas, Nancy Travis, Olivia d'Abo, Phil Hartman, Ed Begley, Jr., Jere Burns, Colleen Camp, Bob Balaban, Joyce Hyser, Mary Ellen Trainor, Siobhan Fallon, Kevin McCarthy, Tom Mason, Austin Pendleton, Kirsten Dunst. Venal family can't wait for a crotchety uncle to die, so they can get their hands on his money, but when he threatens to give it all to a sexy young companion, they dig up long-estranged nephew Fox. Naming the family McTeague (after von Stroheim's GREED) is the cleverest thing in Lowell Ganz and Babaloo Mandel's wearisome script—which isn't helped by Lynn's slack-paced direction. (The director also appears as Kirk's put-upon butler.) Based, believe it or not, on Charles Dickens' *Martin Chuzzlewit*. [PG-13]▼●◗

Greeks Had a Word for Them, The (1932) **79m.** *** D: Lowell Sherman. Joan Blondell, Ina Claire, Madge Evans, David Manners, Lowell Sherman. Vintage comedy of three gold-digging girls looking for husbands; still entertaining although redone several times, including HOW TO MARRY A MILLIONAIRE. Video title: THREE BROADWAY GIRLS.▼

Greek Tycoon, The (1978) **C-106m.** *½ D: J. Lee Thompson. Anthony Quinn, Jacqueline Bisset, Raf Vallone, Edward Albert, Charles Durning, Camilla Sparv, James Franciscus, Luciana Paluzzi, Kathryn Leigh Scott, Roland Culver, Linda Thorson, Lucy Gutteridge, Henderson Forsythe. Pointless fabrication about romance and marriage of Aristotle Onassis and a certain president's widow. Beautiful settings add only luster to tepid script that doesn't even rate as good trash. Videocassette version runs 112m. Technovision.[R]▼

Green Berets, The (1968) **C-141m.** BOMB D: John Wayne, Ray Kellogg. John Wayne, David Janssen, Jim Hutton, Aldo Ray, Raymond St. Jacques, Bruce Cabot, George Takei, Jack Soo, Patrick Wayne, Mike Henry. Politics aside, this overlong, incredibly clichéd salute to the Special Forces has enough absurd situations and unfunny comedy relief to offend anyone; don't miss now-famous final scene, where the sun sets in the East. Panavision. [G]▼●◗

Green Card (1990-Australian-French) **C-108m.** ★★½ D: Peter Weir. Gérard Depardieu, Andie MacDowell, Bebe Neuwirth, Gregg Edelman, Robert Prosky, Jessie Keosian, Ann Wedgeworth, Ethan Phillips, Mary Louise Wilson, Lois Smith, Simon Jones. Young woman agrees to marry Frenchman—in name only—so he may legally remain in this country . . . but when Immigration authorities begin to investigate, she's forced to spend time with the man. Thin, scarcely credible romantic comedy, written by the director; worth watching for Depardieu, who's charming in English-language debut. [PG-13]▼●

Green Cockatoo, The (1937-British) **65m.** ★★ D: William Cameron Menzies. John Mills, Rene Ray, Robert Newton, Charles Oliver, Bruce Seton. Considering credentials of this film (story by Graham Greene, director Menzies, etc.) the results are particularly disappointing: song-and-dance man Mills tries to unravel mystery surrounding murder of his brother (Newton). Originally titled FOUR DARK HOURS.

Green Dolphin Street (1947) **141m.** ★★½ D: Victor Saville. Lana Turner, Van Heflin, Donna Reed, Richard Hart, Frank Morgan, Edmund Gwenn, Dame May Whitty, Reginald Owen, Gladys Cooper, Moyna MacGill, Linda Christian, Gigi Perreau. If only for its glossy production and Oscar-winning special effects (earthquake and resultant tidal wave), this plodding costumer has merit. Story of two sisters (Turner, Reed) after the same man in 19th-century New Zealand is tedious. ▼●

Greene Murder Case, The (1929) **69m.** ★★½ D: Frank Tuttle. William Powell, Florence Eldridge, Ulrich Haupt, Jean Arthur, Eugene Pallette. Despite creaky early-talkie technique, this is a generally satisfying *Philo Vance* mystery about the murder of a penurious Manhattan matron. Unfortunately, the killer's identity becomes painfully obvious around the halfway mark.

Green-Eyed Blonde, The (1957) **76m.** ★★ D: Bernard Girard. Susan Oliver, Tommie Moore, Juanita Moore, Evelyn Scott, Roy Glenn. Oliver in title role is properly rebellious as teenager involved in homicide and her own tragic end.

Green Fields (1937) **95m.** ★★★ D: Edgar G. Ulmer, Jacob Ben-Ami. Michael Goldstein (Gorrin), Helen Beverly, Isidore Cashier, Anna Appel, Dena Drute, Herschel Bernardi. Lovely, lyrical adaptation of Peretz Hirshbein's Yiddish stage classic about an orphaned, wandering scholar (Goldstein) who's searching for a meaningful life, and what happens when he's taken in by a peasant family. Filmed in upstate New York; codirector Ben-Ami, respected actor-director in both the Yiddish and American theater, starred in this on the stage.▼

Green Fire (1954) **C-100m.** ★★½ D: Andrew Marton. Grace Kelly, Stewart Granger, Paul Douglas, John Ericson, Murvyn Vye. Hokum about love and conflict between emerald prospector (Granger) and coffee-plantation owner (Kelly), set in Colombia, South America. Attractive stars, hot love scenes, slimy villain (Vye). CinemaScope.▼

Green for Danger (1946-British) **93m.** ★★★★ D: Sidney Gilliat. Alastair Sim, Sally Gray, Trevor Howard, Rosamund John, Leo Genn, Judy Campbell, Megs Jenkins. Exciting whodunit set in a rural English emergency hospital during WW2. Tension neatly counterbalanced by droll wit of Sim as implacable Scotland Yard inspector; a must-see classic. Written by Gilliat and Claude Guerney.▼●

Greengage Summer, The SEE: **Loss of Innocence**

Green Glove, The (1952) **88m.** ★★½ D: Rudolph Maté. Glenn Ford, Geraldine Brooks, Cedric Hardwicke, George Macready, Jany Holt, Juliette Greco. Occasionally interesting tale of ex-paratrooper Ford returning to France after WW2 to find medieval, gem-laden religious artifact, becoming involved in murder and mayhem.▼

Green Goddess, The (1930) **80m.** ★★ D: Alfred E. Green. George Arliss, Alice Joyce, H. B. Warner, Ralph Forbes, Reginald Sheffield, Nigel de Brulier, Ivan Simpson. Campy early talkie, with Arliss a self-righteous potentate who holds innocent Britishers prisoner. The closing line is a gem. A remake of Arliss' 1923 silent film.

Green Grass of Wyoming (1948) **C-89m.** ★★½ D: Louis King. Peggy Cummins, Robert Arthur, Charles Coburn, Lloyd Nolan. Atmospheric tale of rival horse-breeding families; the usual, but nicely done. Sequel to THUNDERHEAD—SON OF FLICKA, based on a novel by Mary O'Hara.

Green Grow the Rushes (1951-British) **80m.** ★★ D: Derek Twist. Richard Burton, Honor Blackman, Roger Livesey, Geoffrey Keen, Archie Duncan. Talky, fitfully funny comedy of a Kent community involved in brandy smuggling. Of interest solely for the presence of Burton, in his last British film before going Hollywood.▼

Green Hell (1940) **87m.** **½ D: James Whale. Douglas Fairbanks, Jr., Joan Bennett, John Howard, George Sanders, Alan Hale, George Bancroft, Vincent Price. Diverse group of men, led by stalwart Fairbanks, head into unexplored jungle in search of a temple of gold. Hokey but entertaining.

Green Horizon, The SEE: **Afurika Monogatari**

Green Ice (1981-British) **C-115m.** ** D: Ernest Day. Ryan O'Neal, Anne Archer, Omar Sharif, Domingo Ambriz, John Larroquette. Emerald smuggling, with good guy O'Neal, bad guy Sharif, Archer the woman in between. Painless time-killer. [PG]▼●

Green Light, The (1937) **85m.** **½ D: Frank Borzage. Errol Flynn, Anita Louise, Margaret Lindsay, Cedric Hardwicke, Henry O'Neill, Spring Byington, Erin O'Brien-Moore. Genuinely odd blend of melodrama, religion, purple prose, and medical drama with Flynn as an idealistic doctor who makes a career sacrifice and then tries to understand the larger meaning of his life. Adaptation of a Lloyd C. Douglas novel is entertaining enough but awfully hard to swallow seriously.

Green Man, The (1957-British) **80m.** *** D: Robert Day. Alastair Sim, George Cole, Terry-Thomas, Jill Adams, Avril Angers. Droll comedy of a seemingly timid clockmaker who prefers his part-time job as paid assassin.

Green Mansions (1959) **C-104m.** **½ D: Mel Ferrer. Audrey Hepburn, Anthony Perkins, Lee J. Cobb, Sessue Hayakawa, Henry Silva, Nehemiah Persoff. W. H. Hudson's romance set in South America suffers from miscast Hepburn as Rima the Bird Girl, whom fate decrees shall not leave her sanctuary. Perkins properly puzzled as male lead. CinemaScope.▼●

Green Mile, The (1999) **C-187m.** **½ D: Frank Darabont. Tom Hanks, David Morse, Bonnie Hunt, Michael Clarke Duncan, James Cromwell, Michael Jeter, Graham Greene, Doug Hutchison, Sam Rockwell, Barry Pepper, Jeffrey DeMunn, Patricia Clarkson, Harry Dean Stanton, Dabbs Greer, Eve Brent, Gary Sinise. An elderly man recalls the incident that changed his life, in 1935, when he supervised Death Row at a Louisiana state prison, and encountered a gentle black behemoth (movingly played by Duncan) with an unusual gift. Well-made film has powerful moments, but they're needlessly stretched over three hours . . . and the central conceit isn't easy to buy. Repeated scenes of executions are tough to take. Based on Stephen King's best-seller. [R]▼●◗

Green Pastures, The (1936) **92m.** ***½ D: William Keighley, Marc Connelly. Rex Ingram, Oscar Polk, Eddie Anderson, Frank Wilson, George Reed, Abraham Gleaves, Myrtle Anderson. All-black cast in Marc Connelly fable of life in heaven, and biblical stories which give more meaning to Adam, Noah, and Moses than many so-called biblical films. Ingram is fine as "de Lawd."▼

Green Promise, The (1949) **93m.** **½ D: William D. Russell. Marguerite Chapman, Walter Brennan, Robert Paige, Natalie Wood, Ted Donaldson, Connie Marshall, Milburn Stone. Thoughtful drama of stubborn, manipulative Brennan, who lords it over his children while attempting to eke out a living on a farm. Watch this and you'll learn all you'll ever need to know about 4-H Clubs!▼

Green Room, The (1978-French) **C-95m.** ** D: François Truffaut. François Truffaut, Nathalie Baye, Jean Daste, Jean-Paul Moulin, Jeanne Lobre. Truffaut stars as a death-obsessed journalist who converts a run-down chapel into a memorial for his deceased WW1 comrades. Dreary, lifeless, disappointing, with Truffaut's character engulfed in his own rhetoric. Based on writings of Henry James; coscripted by Truffaut and Jean Gruault. [PG]▼

Green Scarf, The (1955-British) **96m.** *** D: George More O'Ferrall. Michael Redgrave, Ann Todd, Kieron Moore, Leo Genn. Imaginative handling of blind man accused of homicide, defended by aging attorney; set in Paris.

Green Slime, The (1969-Japanese-U.S.) **C-99m.** *½ D: Kinji Fukasaku. Robert Horton, Richard Jaeckel, Luciana Paluzzi, Bud Widom. On space station, title substance—exposed to blood—grows into red-eyed, tentacled monsters that quickly multiply and threaten to spread to Earth. Not as much fun as it sounds. Toeiscope. [G]▼

Greenwich Village (1944) **C-82m.** **½ D: Walter Lang. Carmen Miranda, Don Ameche, William Bendix, Vivian Blaine, Felix Bressart, Tony and Sally DeMarco, The Four Step Brothers. Silly but amiable musical about a "serious" composer (Ameche) persuaded to adapt his songs for a Broadway revue starring Blaine. When it's supposed to be 1922 N.Y.C. and Carmen Miranda turns up, you know not to expect stark realism. Look fast in both party scenes to spot The Revuers (Betty Comden, Adolph Green, Judy Holliday, Alvin Hammer).

Green Years, The (1946) **127m.** **½ D: Victor Saville. Charles Coburn, Tom Drake, Hume Cronyn, Gladys Cooper, Dean Stockwell, Jessica Tandy, Norman Lloyd, Wallace Ford. Sentimental A. J. Cronin weeper of orphaned Irish lad and his experiences growing up with his mother's family in Scotland. Coburn is wonderful as his great-grandfather, an irascible teller of tall tales. Tandy plays Cronyn's *daughter* here.

Greetings (1968) **C-88m.** *** D: Brian De Palma. Jonathan Warden, Robert De Niro, Gerrit Graham, Richard Hamilton, Megan McCormick, Allen Garfield. Loose, informal, improvisational satire about the draft, sex, the counterculture. Exudes a late '60s N.Y.C.-Greenwich Village ambience not to be found in any Hollywood feature. Sequel: HI, MOM! [R—edited from original X rating]▼●

Gregory's Girl (1981-Scottish) **C-91m.** *** D: Bill Forsyth. Gordon John Sinclair, Dee Hepburn, Chic Murray, Jake D'Arcy, Alex Norton, John Bett, Clare Grogan. Bright, winning comedy of wimpy teenager Sinclair's love for Hepburn, who takes his place on the school soccer team. Enjoyable, if perhaps a bit overrated. Followed in 1999 by GREGORY'S TWO GIRLS. [PG] ▼

Gremlins (1984) **C-106m.** ** D: Joe Dante. Zach Galligan, Phoebe Cates, Hoyt Axton, Frances Lee McCain, Polly Holliday, Glynn Turman, Dick Miller, Keye Luke, Scott Brady, Judge Reinhold, Jackie Joseph, Harry Carey, Jr., Corey Feldman. A teenager's unusual new pet spawns a legion of vicious, violent monsters who turn picture-postcard town into living hell. Comic nightmare is a cross between Capra's IT'S A WONDERFUL LIFE and THE BLOB; full of film-buff in-jokes but negated by too-vivid violence and mayhem. Cameos range from animator Chuck Jones to Robby the Robot—but you have to look fast for executive producer Steven Spielberg. Howie Mandel is the voice of Gizmo. Followed by a sequel. [PG]▼●◗

Gremlins 2 The New Batch (1990) **C-106m.** *** D: Joe Dante. Zach Galligan, Phoebe Cates, John Glover, Robert Prosky, Robert Picardo, Christopher Lee, Haviland Morris, Dick Miller, Jackie Joseph, Gedde Watanabe, Keye Luke, Kathleen Freeman, voice of Tony Randall. Not so much a horror film as a goofy sendup of itself, this sequel turns the slimy creatures loose in N.Y.C. Filled with gags, movie in-jokes, satiric barbs, and gratuitous cameo appearances. Glover is especially funny as a Donald Trump/Ted Turner type, and Lee is a delight as a genetic scientist. Be sure to stay with this through the closing credits. [PG-13]▼●◗

Grendel, Grendel, Grendel (1980-Australian) **C-90m.** **½ D: Alexander Stitt. Voices of Peter Ustinov, Keith Michell, Arthur Dignam, Ed Rosser, Bobby Bright, Ric Stone. Crude but appealing animation highlights this fable about Grendel, a medieval monster only a mother could love, and his observations about the creatures he calls "man"—who murder and pillage. Based on a novel by John Gardner. Score by harmonica great Toots Thielemans.▼

Grey Fox, The (1982-Canadian) **C-92m.** *** D: Phillip Borsos. Richard Farnsworth, Jackie Burroughs, Wayne Robson, Ken Pogue, Timothy Webber. Low-key account of real-life robber Bill Miner, who switched from stagecoaches to trains after spending thirty-three years in jail. Director Borsos may be just a bit too laid back, but Farnsworth's charming and commanding performance makes up for that. The scene in which he watches THE GREAT TRAIN ROBBERY is a gem. [PG]▼●

Greyfriars Bobby (1961) **C-91m.** **½ D: Don Chaffey. Donald Crisp, Laurence Naismith, Alex Mackenzie, Kay Walsh, Duncan Macrae, Gordon Jackson. British Disney film based on true story of a Skye terrier who became "neighborhood pet" in Edinburgh during 19th century through unusual circumstances. Great charm, fine performances offset by slow pacing. A remake of CHALLENGE TO LASSIE, which also features Crisp (who played the dog's master in the earlier film). ▼

Grey Gardens (1976) **C-95m.** *** D: David and Albert Maysles. Tasteless, suspect, but riveting documentary about Edith Bouvier Beale (79) and daughter Edie (57)—aunt and cousin of Jacqueline Onassis—filmed in their rotting, filthy 28-room mansion in East Hampton, N.Y., which was officially declared a health hazard. Fascinating for voyeurs, but film would have had more depth had we been given a better picture of mother and daughter in their youth. [PG]▼

Grey Owl (1999-British-Canadian) **C-117m.** ** D: Richard Attenborough. Pierce Brosnan, Annie Galipeau, Nathaniel Arcand, Vlasta Vrana, David Fox, Charles Powell, Renee Asherson, Graham Greene. It's difficult to accept Brosnan as the title character, a celebrated North American Indian and conservationist whose true identity is discovered by a reporter in 1936; the rest of the story unfolds in flashback. Sincere but ineffectual telling of this interesting tale went straight to video in the U.S. Panavision. [PG-13]▼◗

Greystoke: The Legend of Tarzan, Lord of the Apes (1984) **C-129m.** *** D: Hugh Hudson. Christopher Lambert, Andie MacDowell, Ian Holm, Ralph Richardson, James Fox, Cheryl Campbell, Ian Charleson, Nigel Davenport. Retelling of Tarzan tale, liberally adapted from Edgar Rice Burroughs' original. Infant son of shipwrecked couple is raised by apes, discovered at manhood by a Belgian explorer, and returned to civilization—and his doting grandfather (Richardson, who's just wonderful in his final film performance). At its best in the jungle, with Rick Baker's incredible makeup effects; more sluggish back in Britain, and hampered by obvious signs of prerelease cutting. Leading lady MacDowell's voice was dubbed by Glenn Close. Expanded 135m. version available on home video. Super Techniscope. [PG]▼●

Gridlock (1980) **C-100m. TVM** D: James Frawley. Desi Arnaz, Jr., John Beck, Noah Beery, Rene Enriquez, Shelley Fabares, Phil Foster, James Gregory, Lisa Hartman, Michael Lerner, Rue McClanahan, Ed McMahon, Christopher Norris, Al Molinaro, Allen Sues, Vic Tayback, Abe Vigoda, Lyle Waggoner, Marcia Wallace, Howard Hesseman. Comic chaos involving a highway full of TV stars as the L.A. freeway system grinds to a halt following a series of freak accidents. Retitled THE GREAT AMERICAN TRAFFIC JAM. Average.▼

Gridlock'd (1997) **C-91m.** **½ D: Vondie Curtis-Hall. Tupac Shakur, Tim Roth, Thandie Newton, Charles Fleischer, Howard Hesseman, James Pickens, Jr., John Sayles, Eric Payne, Tom Towles, Vondie Curtis-Hall, Kasi Lemmons, Lucy Alexis Liu. Occasionally spunky comedy (a poor cousin to TRAINSPOTTING) about drug-addicted musicians Shakur and Roth, who struggle (mostly against an uncaring bureaucracy) as they try to kick their habits after their singer friend (Newton) overdoses. The two leads offer solid performances. Feature directorial debut for actor Curtis-Hall (who also scripted). Elizabeth Peña appears unbilled. [R]▼●◗

Grifters, The (1990) **C-114m.** *** D: Stephen Frears. Anjelica Huston, John Cusack, Annette Bening, Pat Hingle, Henry Jones, Michael Laskin, Eddie Jones, J. T. Walsh, Charles Napier, Stephen Tobolowsky, Sandy Baron, Gailard Sartain. Icy cold adaptation of Jim Thompson's novel about con artists, with steely "working-woman" Huston coming back into the life of her grown son after many years of estrangement . . . and finding that he's taken up with a woman much like herself. Bleak and fascinating, with three first-rate performances. Screenplay by Donald E. Westlake. Coproduced and narrated by Martin Scorsese. [R]▼●◗

Grim Prairie Tales (1990) **C-94m.** ** D: Wayne Coe. James Earl Jones, Brad Dourif, Will Hare, Marc McClure, Michelle Joyner, William Atherton, Lisa Eichhorn, Wendy Cooke. Horror/Western anthology framed by Jones and Dourif spinning scary tales around a campfire. The four stories vary widely in content and execution: a cowboy is buried alive by Indians; a traveling man is seduced by a pregnant, supernatural wanderer; a homesteader pursues a nocturnal hobby of lynching black men; and a gunslinger is haunted by one of his victims. This low, low-budget effort fails, for the most part, to achieve its intriguing potential. [R]▼●

Grim Reaper, The (1981-Italian) **C-81m.** *½ D: Joe D'Amato. Tisa Farrow, Saverio Vallone, Vanessa Steiger, George Eastman. Tourist Farrow and companions are stalked by killer on a Greek island. Trifling shocker. [R]▼●

Grind (1997) **C-96m.** **½ D: Chris Kentis. Billy Crudup, Adrienne Shelly, Paul Schulze, Frank Vincent, Saul Stein, Amanda Peet. Flawed but arresting drama about an ex-con/race car driver wannabe who moves in with his blue-collar brother and sister-in-law and becomes involved in an insurance scam. While the story is predictable, the film does offer a thoughtful, observant look at working-class lives, dreams and frustrations. Shot in 1994.▼

Grip of the Strangler SEE: **Haunted Strangler, The**

Grisbi (1953-French) **94m.** **½ D: Jacques Becker. Jean Gabin, Jeanne Moreau, Rene Dary, Lino Ventura, Dora Doll. Gabin is tough in unorthodox tale of Parisian underground, involving gold heist and its mysterious disappearance. Retitled: DON'T TOUCH THE LOOT.▼

Grissly's Millions (1944) **54m.** **½ D: John English. Paul Kelly, Virginia Grey, Don Douglas, Elisabeth Risdon. Programmer involving murder of wealthy man and the typical manhunt for the killer; smoothly done.

Grissom Gang, The (1971) **C-127m.** *** D: Robert Aldrich. Kim Darby, Scott Wilson, Irene Dailey, Tony Musante, Ralph Waite, Connie Stevens, Robert Lansing, Wesley Addy, Gary Grimes. Outlandish, extremely violent comic-book thriller set in the 1920s. Heiress Darby is kidnapped by family of drooling grotesques, whose leader (Wilson) starts to fall in love with her. Very funny if you appreciate the Aldrich sense of humor; otherwise, solid action fare. Remake of 1948 British film NO ORCHIDS FOR MISS BLANDISH. [R]▼

Grizzly (1976) **C-92m.** ** D: William Girdler. Christopher George, Andrew Prine, Richard Jaeckel, Joan McCall, Joe Dorsey. OK rip-off of JAWS about an 18-foot, 2000-pound grizzly bear who launches series of attacks on campers in national park. Might be subtitled "Claws." Aka KILLER GRIZZLY. Todd-AO 35. [PG] ▼◗

Grizzly Mountain (1997) **C-96m.** *½ D: Jeremy Haft. Dan Haggerty, Dylan Haggerty, Nicole Lund, Kim Morgan Greene, Perry Stephens, Martin Kove, Megan Haggerty. While camping in the Oregon mountains, two city kids go into a cave and are transported back to 1870, where they help a friendly mountain man (guess who) battle some greedy developers who want to destroy sacred Indian land. Ultra-innocuous family film features some pleasant scenery, but worthy message is lost amidst the amateurish acting, cheesy production values, and lamebrained comedy relief. [G]▼●

Groom Wore Spurs, The (1951) **80m.** ** D: Richard Whorf. Ginger Rogers, Jack Carson, Joan Davis, Stanley Ridges. Occasionally zesty comedy of attorney Rogers marrying cowboy actor Carson, divorcing him, but coming to his defense in criminal case.▼

Groove Tube, The (1974) **C-75m.** ★★½ D: Ken Shapiro. Ken Shapiro, Lane Sarasohn, Chevy Chase, Richard Belzer, Mary Mendham, Bill Kemmill. Sometimes funny, sometimes stupid collection of satirical episodes about television. Definitely has its heart in the right place, but a mixed bag. Originally X-rated, later trimmed; Chase's feature debut. [R]▼

Gross Anatomy (1989) **C-109m.** ★★½ D: Thom Eberhardt. Matthew Modine, Daphne Zuniga, Christine Lahti, Todd Field, John Scott Clough, Alice Carter, Robert Desiderio, Zakes Mokae. So-so tale of doctor-in-training Modine, who doesn't take his studies as seriously as he should. Not bad, but not particularly distinguished; Lahti is wasted as the aspiring doctors' demanding instructor. Viewers who've attended medical school may appreciate this more. [PG-13]▼●

Grosse Fatigue (1994-French) **C-87m.** ★★½ D: Michel Blanc. Michel Blanc, Carole Bouquet, Philippe Noiret, Josiane Balasko, Christian Clavier, Charlotte Gainsbourg. French variation of STARDUST MEMORIES, with Blanc finding his celebrityhood turning into a bad dream after he is accused of defiling Balasko. Intriguing, self-involved, crammed with guest appearances by familiar faces from French cinema. Blanc, Balasko, and Bouquet all play "themselves." Video title: DEAD TIRED. [R]▼

Grosse Pointe Blank (1997) **C-107m.** ★★½ D: George Armitage. John Cusack, Minnie Driver, Alan Arkin, Dan Aykroyd, Joan Cusack, Hank Azaria, K. Todd Freeman, Mitchell Ryan, Jeremy Piven, Barbara Harris, Jenna Elfman. Professional hit man combines business with pleasure when he attends his ten-year high school reunion while on assignment . . . but the girl he dumped (and all his friends) want to know why and how he disappeared. Cusack cowrote and coproduced this sharp black comedy, brimming with hip dialogue and loaded with attitude. But the climactic violence leaves a bad taste and undermines the comedy. [R]▼●◗

Gross Misconduct (1992-Canadian) **C-95m. TVM** D: Atom Egoyan. Daniel Kash, Peter MacNeill, Linda Goranson, Doug Hughes, Lenore Zann, Shaun Ashmore, Aaron Ashmore, Kirsten Kieferle, Shannon Lawson. Director Egoyan puts his spin on the dramatic and downbeat story of Canadian hockey star Brian "Spinner" Spencer, who spun out of control after achieving fame and fortune in the NHL. Fascinating portrait of a troubled young man. Written by Paul Gross. Above average.

Groundhog Day (1993) **C-103m.** ★★★ D: Harold Ramis. Bill Murray, Andie MacDowell, Chris Elliott, Stephen Tobolowsky, Brian Doyle-Murray, Marita Geraghty, Angela Paton, Rick Ducommun, Rick Overton, Robin Duke. Smug TV weatherman goes to Punxsutawney, Pa., to cover the Groundhog Day ceremony, and finds himself trapped in a daily replay of the same 24 hours. Clever comedy-fantasy keeps coming up with new twists and turns, even when you're sure there's nowhere else it can go. An ideal vehicle for Murray with many funny moments. Director-cowriter Ramis has a brief scene as a local neurologist. [PG]▼●◗

Grounds for Marriage (1950) **91m.** ★★½ D: Robert Z. Leonard. Van Johnson, Kathryn Grayson, Paula Raymond, Barry Sullivan, Lewis Stone. Cutesy musicomedy of opera star Grayson and her ex-husband, physician Johnson.

Groundstar Conspiracy, The (1972-Canadian) **C-96m.** ★★½ D: Lamont Johnson. George Peppard, Michael Sarrazin, Christine Belford. When explosion smashes secret space project, espionage work first begins. Tightly made, but poor dialogue. Panavision. [PG]▼

Ground Zero (1987-Australian) **C-109m.** ★★★ D: Michael Pattinson, Bruce Myles. Colin Friels, Jack Thompson, Donald Pleasence, Natalie Bate, Simon Chilvers, Neil Fitzpatrick, Bob Maza, Peter Cummins. Cameraman learns that his father may have died because he saw—and photographed—too much during British A-bomb testing in Australia in the 1950s. Exciting political paranoia thriller, though sluggish in spots. Pleasence is excellent in supporting role as hermitlike survivor of those tests. A fictional story based on factual events. Panavision. [PG]▼●

Group, The (1966) **C-150m.** ★★★ D: Sidney Lumet. Candice Bergen, Joan Hackett, Elizabeth Hartman, Shirley Knight, Joanna Pettet, Mary-Robin Redd, Jessica Walter, Kathleen Widdoes, James Broderick, Larry Hagman, Richard Mulligan, Hal Holbrook, Carrie Nye, Leora Dana, George Gaynes. Uneven, but generally good adaptation of Mary McCarthy's high-class soap opera about eight graduates of Vassar-type college. Knight and Hackett stand out in excellent cast. Film debuts of Bergen, Hackett, Pettet, Widdoes, and Holbrook.▼

Group Marriage (1972) **C-85m.** ★★½ D: Stephanie Rothman. Victoria Vetri, Claudia Jennings, Aimee Eccles, Zack Taylor, Jeff Pomerantz, Jayne Kennedy, Milt Kamen. Engaging drive-in comedy with something to say. Group of young Californians sets up a communal housekeeping situation, gradually adding new members. Needless to say, the neighbors are less than thrilled. Nicely done, attractive cast. [R]▼

Grumpier Old Men (1995) **C-100m.** ★★½ D: Howard Deutch. Jack Lemmon, Walter

Matthau, Ann-Margret, Sophia Loren, Daryl Hannah, Kevin Pollak, Burgess Meredith, Ann Guilbert, Max Wright, James Andelin. Now reconciled, the longtime neighbors/nemeses argue over their offsprings' impending wedding, while a new arrival in town (Loren) turns their bait shop into a restaurant. Agreeable sequel, though it's discouraging to see two great comic actors reduced to getting cheap laughs by spouting epithets at one another. Loren is a breath of fresh air as Matthau's unlikely love interest. Meredith is back in form as Lemmon's horny dad. [PG-13]▼●◗

Grumpy Old Men (1993) **C-104m.** ★★½ D: Donald Petrie. Jack Lemmon, Walter Matthau, Ann-Margret, Burgess Meredith, Daryl Hannah, Kevin Pollak, Ossie Davis, Buck Henry, Christopher McDonald. Engagingly performed but malnourished comedy about two mateless Minnesota retirees, rabid ice-fishermen, whose lifelong feud escalates when an attractive widow moves in across the street. Walter and Jack are fun as usual, but a few too many plot threads get wrapped up in the final 15 minutes. Compensations are a funny end-credit sequence and the singular chance to hear Meredith (as Lemmon's father) make endless salacious wordplays on the male organ of love. Followed by a sequel. [PG-13]▼●◗

Grunt! The Wrestling Movie (1985) **C-90m.** BOMB D: Allan Holzman. Jeff Dial, Robert Glaudini, Marilyn Dodds Farr, Greg Magic Schwartz, John Tolos, Dick Murdoch. Would-be documentary spoof about a fabled wrestler named Mad Dog Joe De Curso; lands with a thud. [R]▼

Guadalcanal Diary (1943) **93m.** ★★★½ D: Lewis Seiler. Preston Foster, Lloyd Nolan, William Bendix, Richard Conte, Anthony Quinn, Richard Jaeckel, Lionel Stander. Richard Tregaskis' hot-off-the-wire account of Marines fighting for vital Pacific base becomes one of best WW2 actioners; large, competent cast. Screenplay by Lamar Trotti. Jaeckel's film debut.▼

Guardian, The (1990) **C-93m.** ★★ D: William Friedkin. Jenny Seagrove, Dwier Brown, Carey Lowell, Brad Hall, Miguel Ferrer, Natalia Nogulich. Yuppie couple hires a nanny for their newborn child, but we know there's something odd about her: she feeds babies to a tree in a nearby gully. Friedkin's first return to horror after THE EXORCIST has a few good scenes, but a ludicrous story and a humorless approach. Seagrove is very good in an almost unplayable role. Cowritten by the director from novel *The Nanny* by Dan Greenburg. [R] ▼●◗

Guarding Tess (1994) **C-98m.** ★★★ D: Hugh Wilson. Shirley MacLaine, Nicolas Cage, Austin Pendleton, Edward Albert, James Rebhorn, Richard Griffiths, John Roselius, David Graf, Dale Dye. Secret Service agent tries to get out of his demanding and frustrating assignment, protecting a former First Lady—but she won't let him go. Extremely satisfying comedy-drama buoyed by two perfect performances, by MacLaine and Cage. Incidentally, that's director/co-writer Wilson as the voice of the President on the phone. [PG-13]▼●◗

Guardsman, The (1931) **89m.** ★★★ D: Sidney Franklin. Alfred Lunt, Lynn Fontanne, Roland Young, ZaSu Pitts, Maude Eburne, Herman Bing. The Lunts' only starring film is charming tour de force from Molnar's comedy of jealous husband testing his wife's fidelity. Remade as THE CHOCOLATE SOLDIER and LILY IN LOVE. ▼

Guerrillas in Pink Lace (1964) **C-96m.** ★½ D: George Montgomery. George Montgomery, Valerie Varda, Roby Grace, Joan Shawlee. Poorly produced yarn filmed in Philippines about Montgomery and group of showgirls on the lam from Manila and the Japanese.▼

Guess Who's Coming to Dinner (1967) **C-108m.** ★★★ D: Stanley Kramer. Spencer Tracy, Katharine Hepburn, Sidney Poitier, Katharine Houghton, Cecil Kellaway, Beah Richards, Roy E. Glenn, Sr., Virginia Christine, Isabel Sanford. Glossy tale of mixed marriage as Houghton (Hepburn's real-life niece) brings home fiancé Poitier to meet her perplexed parents. Fluff is given strength by Oscar-winning Hepburn and Tracy in his last film appearance. William Rose also took home an Oscar for his story and screenplay.▼●◗

Guest, The (1964-British) **105m.** ★★★ D: Clive Donner. Alan Bates, Donald Pleasence, Robert Shaw. Derelict Pleasence invades the world of mentally ill Shaw and his sadistic brother Bates. Superior cast and superb performances, but claustrophobically directed by Donner. Screenplay by Harold Pinter, based on his play *The Caretaker,* which was also this film's title in Britain.

Guest in the House (1944) **121m.** ★★★ D: John Brahm. Anne Baxter, Ralph Bellamy, Aline MacMahon, Ruth Warrick, Scott McKay, Marie McDonald, Jerome Cowan, Margaret Hamilton, Percy Kilbride. Atmospheric, occasionally gripping melodrama about neurotic young Baxter and her effect on the family of her betrothed. Bellamy is extremely attractive in a rare romantic lead, and Anne goes all out in this Eve Harrington–like characterization.▼

Guest Wife (1945) **90m.** ★★½ D: Sam Wood. Claudette Colbert, Don Ameche, Dick Foran, Charles Dingle, Grant Mitchell, Wilma Francis. Breezy comedy depends on stars for flair; they do just fine, with Claudette posing as Ameche's wife to husband Foran's chagrin.▼●

Guide for the Married Man, A (1967) **C-89m.** ★★★½ D: Gene Kelly. Walter

Matthau, Inger Stevens, Robert Morse, Sue Ane Langdon, Claire Kelly, Elaine Devry; guest stars Lucille Ball, Jack Benny, Polly Bergen, Joey Bishop, Sid Caesar, Art Carney, Wally Cox, Jayne Mansfield, Hal March, Louis Nye, Carl Reiner, Phil Silvers, Terry-Thomas, Ben Blue, Ann Morgan Guilbert, Jeffrey Hunter, Marty Ingels, Sam Jaffe. Consistently funny, imaginative adult comedy of Morse trying to teach faithful husband Matthau the ABC's of adultery, with the aid of many guest stars who demonstrate Morse's theories. Joke of it all is that Matthau is married to gorgeous Inger Stevens! Panavision.▼

Guilt of Janet Ames, The (1947) **83m.** *** D: Henry Levin. Rosalind Russell, Melvyn Douglas, Sid Caesar, Betsy Blair, Nina Foch, Charles Cane, Harry Von Zell. Good casting highlights well-done film of Russell at the end of her rope when husband dies and she seeks the cause.

Guilty, The (1947) **70m.** **½ D: John Reinhardt. Bonita Granville, Don Castle, Wally Cassell, Regis Toomey. At times engaging murder yarn; twin sisters clash over their love for Castle.

Guilty as Charged (1992) **C-95m.** **½ D: Sam Irvin. Rod Steiger, Lauren Hutton, Heather Graham, Lyman Ward, Isaac Hayes, Zelda Rubinstein, Irwin Keyes, Michael Beach. Religious zealot turns out to be a self-made executioner who does away with criminals in his own homemade electric chair. Very black comedy seems a likely candidate for a cult following. Steiger's performance calls to mind his work in NO WAY TO TREAT A LADY; it's also fun to watch Isaac Hayes as one of his henchmen. Stylishly directed by first-timer Irvin, a former production associate of Brian De Palma. [R]▼

Guilty Assignment SEE: **Big Town**

Guilty as Sin (1993) **C-107m.** ** D: Sidney Lumet. Rebecca De Mornay, Don Johnson, Stephen Lang, Jack Warden, Dana Ivey, Ron White, Norma Dell'Agnese, Sean McCann, Luis Guzman, Robert Kennedy. Clever lawyer De Mornay, obsessed with winning (whether or not her clients are guilty), takes the case of sleek womanizer Johnson, who's accused of murdering his wife. Then she learns she may have made a bargain with a killer—who now has designs on *her*. The idea of intelligent opponents going head to head is intriguing, but Larry Cohen's script is underplotted and ordinary. [R]▼●

Guilty Bystander (1950) **92m.** **½ D: Joseph Lerner. Zachary Scott, Faye Emerson, Mary Boland, Sam Levene, Kay Medford. Down-and-out ex-house detective finds new zest for life when estranged wife reports their child kidnapped.

Guilty by Suspicion (1991) **C-105m.** ** D: Irwin Winkler. Robert De Niro, Annette Bening, George Wendt, Patricia Wettig, Sam Wanamaker, Luke Edwards, Chris Cooper, Ben Piazza, Martin Scorsese, Barry Primus, Gailard Sartain, Stuart Margolin, Barry Tubb, Tom Sizemore, Illeana Douglas, Jon Tenney. Hollywood Blacklist drama, set in 1951, is earnest, superficial, and numbingly bland. De Niro is hotshot director who can't comprehend severity of Communist witch hunt; Bening is his sympathetic ex-wife, and Wettig (way over the top), an actress friend. Viewers unfamiliar with this dark chapter of history may find film as fascinating as intended. Wanamaker, who spent this era in exile in England, plays a villainous attorney. Veteran producer Winkler's (mediocre) writing and directing debut. [PG-13]▼●◗

Guilty Hands (1931) **71m.** *** D: W. S. Van Dyke. Lionel Barrymore, Kay Francis, Madge Evans, William Bakewell, C. Aubrey Smith, Polly Moran, Alan Mowbray. Former D.A. Barrymore tells unscrupulous lothario Mowbray that he'll kill him—and get away with it—if he dares to go through with his plan to marry Lionel's daughter. First-rate whodunit-style drama with imaginative camerawork, a solid script, some real plot twists, and an unusually lively performance from Barrymore.

Guilty of Treason (1949) **86m.** ** D: Felix E. Feist. Charles Bickford, Paul Kelly, Bonita Granville, Richard Derr, Roland Winters, John Banner. Grim, preachy red-scare time capsule about a foreign correspondent (Kelly) in Hungary, where the commies are painting liberty-loving Josef Cardinal Mindszenty (Bickford) as an anti-Semite and traitor. Granville is fatally miscast as a Hungarian schoolteacher.▼

Guinevere (1999-Canadian-U.S.) **C-104m.** **½ D: Audrey Wells. Stephen Rea, Sarah Polley, Jean Smart, Gina Gershon, Paul Dooley, Francis Guinan, Sandra Oh, Jasmine Guy, Gedde Watanabe. Well-played tale of a charming but iconoclastic photographer who acquires younger, female protégées, schooling them in the world of art as well as sex. His latest is a 20-year-old girl whose highly strung family doesn't understand her. Story sags at times, but is buoyed by Rea and Polley's enormously ingratiating performances. Written by the director. [R]▼

Gulliver's Travels (1939) **C-74m.** **½ D: Dave Fleischer. Singing voices of Lanny Ross, Jessica Dragonette. Max Fleischer's feature-length cartoon version of Jonathan Swift tale suffers from weak scripting, never getting audience involved in story. Towncrier Gabby is obnoxious, but he's got film's most memorable song, "All's Well."▼●

Gulliver's Travels (1977-British-Belgian) **C-80m.** *½ D: Peter R. Hunt. Richard Harris, Catherine Schell, Norman Shelley, Meredith Edwards, voices of Julian Glover, Murray Melvin, Bessie Love, others. Unimaginative retelling of the Jonathan Swift classic. Part live-action, part animation; the songs are the most forgettable since the 1973 LOST HORIZON. [G]▼

Gulliver's Travels (1996) **C-200m. TVM** D: Charles Sturridge. Ted Danson, Mary Steenburgen, James Fox, Edward Fox, John Gielgud, Peter O'Toole, Omar Sharif, Geraldine Chaplin, John Standing, Alfre Woodard, Edward Woodward, Ned Beatty, Kristin Scott Thomas. Elaborate production, stunning special effects, and stellar cast (some in nearly invisible roles, others like O'Toole in outré performances) give Swift justice to the 1726 political and social satire. Odd bit: Isabelle Huppert plays the voice of a horse who helps Gulliver in one of his adventures. Written by Simon Moore, this exhilarating world is quite removed from earlier film versions. Effects by Jim Henson's Creature Shop. Originally shown in two parts. Above average.▼●

Gulliver's Travels Beyond the Moon (1966-Japanese) **C-78m.** ** D: Yoshio Kuroda. OK animated feature has Gulliver and companions going into outer space; acceptable kiddie fare.

Gumball Rally, The (1976) **C-107m.** *** D: Chuck Bail. Michael Sarrazin, Tim McIntire, Raul Julia, Normann Burton, Gary Busey, Nicholas Pryor, Susan Flannery, Steven Keats, J. Pat O'Malley, Tricia O'Neil, Med Flory. First of the cross-country road-race comedies is still the only good one, with genuinely funny characters, great cars, and loads of cartoon-like action. Julia steals the film as lecherous Italian who throws out his rear-view mirror because "what's behind me is not important." Definitely superior to CANNONBALL and the later CANNONBALL RUN movies, which were all inspired by the same real-life event. Panavision. [PG]▼●

Gumby the Movie (1995) **C-90m.** ** D: Art Clokey. Voices of Charles Farrington, Art Clokey, Gloria Clokey, Manny LaCarruba. Episodic clay-animated feature starring the popular character is slow going for all but the green guy's biggest fans. Convoluted story concerns Gumby's rock group, the Clayboys, and their benefit concert to help farmers thwarted by the Blockheads. Parodies of STAR WARS, TERMINATOR 2, and various swashbuckling epics do not help. Aka GUMBY 1.▼

Gummo (1997) **C-95m.** BOMB D: Harmony Korine. Jacob Reynolds, Nick Sutton, Jacob Sewell, Darby Dougherty, Chloe Sevigny, Carisa Bara, Linda Manz, Max Perlich. Plotless, clueless, mind-numbingly awful directorial debut for Korine (the 23-year-old scriptwriter of KIDS) about a circle of pathetic poor white trash in a small Ohio town. Tries to be shocking and outrageous—two of the characters kill cats and sell their corpses to a supermarket—but succeeds only in being trite, with scenes pointlessly dragging on . . . and on. [R]▼●

Gumshoe (1971-British) **C-88m.** **½ D: Stephen Frears. Albert Finney, Billie Whitelaw, Frank Finlay, Janice Rule, Carolyn Seymour. Whimsical crime-comedy of small-time British vaudevillian who has seen too many Bogart films and decides to play private eye. Music score by Andrew Lloyd Webber. Finney also produced. [PG]▼

Gun Battle at Monterey (1957) **67m.** *½ D: Carl G. Hittleman, Sidney A. Franklin, Jr. Sterling Hayden, Pamela Duncan, Mary Beth Hughes, Lee Van Cleef, Byron Foulger, Ted de Corsia. Unremarkable oater with stern Hayden the gunslinger out for revenge against former friend.

Gun Belt (1953) **C-77m.** **½ D: Ray Nazarro. George Montgomery, Tab Hunter, Helen Westcott, Jack Elam. Notorious outlaw trying to go straight is implicated in crime by his old gang.

Gun Brothers (1956) **79m.** ** D: Sidney Salkow. Buster Crabbe, Ann Robinson, Neville Brand, Michael Ansara. Innocuous Western of two brothers, one who becomes a rancher, the other an outlaw who wants to go straight.

Gun Crazy (1949) **86m.** ***½ D: Joseph H. Lewis. Peggy Cummins, John Dall, Berry Kroeger, Morris Carnovsky, Anabel Shaw, Harry Lewis, Nedrick Young, Rusty (Russ) Tamblyn. Knockout of a sleeper in the BONNIE AND CLYDE tradition, stylishly (and sometimes startlingly) directed. Cummins is femme fatale who leads gun-crazy Dall into life of crime. Screenplay credited to MacKinlay Kantor and Millard Kaufman (who was "fronting" for then-blacklisted writer Dalton Trumbo), from Kantor's *Saturday Evening Post* story. Aka DEADLY IS THE FEMALE. Loosely remade in 1992.▼

Gun Crazy (1969) SEE: **Talent for Loving, A**

Guncrazy (1992) **C-96m.** *** D: Tamra Davis. Drew Barrymore, James LeGros, Billy Drago, Rodney Harvey, Joe Dallesandro, Michael Ironside, Ione Skye. Noirish tale of an abused teenager from the wrong side of the tracks who falls for a born-again-Christian ex-con trying to go straight, ending up on a crime spree with him. Written by Matthew Bright but bearing a more than slight resemblance to a pair of 1949 favorites, the similarly titled GUN CRAZY and THEY LIVE BY NIGHT. Made for theaters, but debuted on cable. [R]▼●◗

Gun Duel in Durango (1957) **73m.** ** D: Sidney Salkow. George Montgomery, Steve Brodie, Bobby Clark, Mary Treen. Montgomery must wipe out his outlaw gang before he can reform. Retitled: DUEL IN DURANGO.

Gunfight, A (1971) **C-90m.** **½ D: Lamont

Johnson. Kirk Douglas, Johnny Cash, Jane Alexander, Raf Vallone, Karen Black, Keith Carradine. Off-beat Western about two aging gunfighters who meet and decide to sell tickets for a winner-take-all final shootout. Cash is good in his acting debut; also Carradine's first film. [PG]▼

Gunfight at Comanche Creek (1964) **C-90m.** *½ D: Frank McDonald. Audie Murphy, Colleen Miller, Ben Cooper, DeForest Kelley, Jan Merlin, John Hubbard. Undistinguished Western. Detective Murphy infiltrates gang of outlaws forcing wanted men to participate in robberies, then killing them to collect reward money. Panavision.

Gunfight at Dodge City, The (1959) **C-81m.** ** D: Joseph M. Newman. Joel McCrea, Julie Adams, John McIntire, Nancy Gates, Richard Anderson, James Westerfield. McCrea plays Bat Masterson, who cleans up gangster-ridden town with ironic results. CinemaScope.

Gunfight at the O.K. Corral (1957) **C-122m.** *** D: John Sturges. Burt Lancaster, Kirk Douglas, Rhonda Fleming, Jo Van Fleet, John Ireland, Lee Van Cleef, Frank Faylen, Kenneth Tobey, DeForest Kelley, Earl Holliman, Dennis Hopper, Martin Milner, Olive Carey. Stimulating Western filled with tense action sequences in recreation of Doc Holliday-Wyatt Earp battle in streets of Tombstone with Clanton gang. Written by Leon Uris. Frankie Laine sings title song. VistaVision.▼●

Gunfighter, The (1950) **84m.** ***½ D: Henry King. Gregory Peck, Helen Westcott, Millard Mitchell, Jean Parker, Karl Malden, Skip Homeier, Verna Felton, Ellen Corby, Richard Jaeckel, Alan Hale, Jr. Peck is most impressive as gunslinger trying to overcome his bloody past. A classic psychological Western scripted by William Bowers and William Sellers, from a story by Bowers and Andre de Toth. Exteriors shot in Lone Pine, California. Catch this one!▼●

Gunfighters (1947) **C-87m.** **½ D: George Waggner. Randolph Scott, Barbara Britton, Dorothy Hart, Bruce Cabot, Charles Grapewin, Forrest Tucker. Strictly average story of gunfighter who vows never again to spill blood. Good cast, but there must be fifty like this one.

Gunfight in Abilene (1967) **C-86m.** **½ D: William Hale. Bobby Darin, Emily Banks, Leslie Nielsen, Michael Sarrazin. Undistinguished post-Civil War account of gun-shy Darin, town sheriff, taking up arms against outlaws. Techniscope.▼

Gunfire (1978) SEE: **China 9, Liberty 37**

Gunfire at Indian Gap (1957) **70m.** *½ D: Joseph Kane. Vera Ralston, Anthony George, George Macready, John Doucette, Barry Kelley, Glenn Strange. Exactly what the title implies, with lovely Ralston to boot. Filmed in Naturama.

Gun for a Coward (1957) **C-73m.** **½ D: Abner Biberman. Fred MacMurray, Jeffrey Hunter, Janice Rule, Chill Wills, Dean Stockwell, Josephine Hutchinson. MacMurray is rancher whose two younger brothers have contrasting personalities; predictable results. CinemaScope.

Gun Fury (1953) **C-83m.** **½ D: Raoul Walsh. Rock Hudson, Donna Reed, Phil Carey, Lee Marvin, Neville Brand, Leo Gordon. Hudson goes after men who have kidnapped his fiancée (Reed); formidable villainy, beautiful Arizona locations. Originally shown in 3-D.▼●

Gunga Din (1939) **117m.** **** D: George Stevens. Cary Grant, Victor McLaglen, Douglas Fairbanks, Jr., Joan Fontaine, Sam Jaffe, Eduardo Ciannelli, Montagu Love, Abner Biberman, Robert Coote, Lumsden Hare, Cecil Kellaway. *The* Hollywood action-adventure yarn, vaguely based on Rudyard Kipling's famous poem, about three soldier-comrades in 19th-century India battling the savage thuggee cult when they aren't busy carousing and getting into trouble. Water boy Jaffe saves the day in rousing climax. Splendid comic adventure whose story is credited to Ben Hecht and Charles MacArthur (who based the relationships of the central characters on the same marriage/rivalry device used in *The Front Page*); scripted by Joel Sayre and Fred Guiol. For years most prints ran 96m., until film was archivally restored. Shot on location in Lone Pine, California. Also shown in computer-colored version.▼●

Gung Ho! (1943) **88m.** **½ D: Ray Enright. Randolph Scott, Grace McDonald, Alan Curtis, Noah Beery Jr., J. Carrol Naish, David Bruce, Robert Mitchum, Sam Levene. Typical WW2 action film is marked by outrageous jingoism, celebrating the bloodthirsty misfits of the "gung ho" squadron as great American patriots. A jaw-dropping experience. Also shown in computer-colored version.▼

Gung Ho (1986) **C-111m.** *** D: Ron Howard. Michael Keaton, Gedde Watanabe, George Wendt, Mimi Rogers, John Turturro, Soh Yamamura, Sab Shimono, Clint Howard, Michelle Johnson. Cocky Keaton convinces Japanese company to reopen shuttered auto factory in his economically depressed hometown—but doesn't count on culture clash that follows. Extremely lightweight but entertaining comedy. Later a TV series. Panavision. [PG-13]▼●

Gun Glory (1957) **C-89m.** ** D: Roy Rowland. Stewart Granger, Rhonda Fleming, Chill Wills, James Gregory. Granger is reformed gunslinger rejected by his community until outlaw rampage allows him to redeem himself. CinemaScope.▼

Gun Hawk, The (1963) **C-92m.** **½ D: Edward Ludwig. Rory Calhoun, Rod Cameron, Ruta Lee, John Litel, Rod Lauren, Lane

Bradford. Outlaw Cameron attempts to reform Lauren, who's heading for criminal life.

Gun in Betty Lou's Handbag, The (1992) **C-89m.** *½ D: Allan Moyle. Penelope Ann Miller, Eric Thal, Alfre Woodard, William Forsythe, Cathy Moriarty, Julianne Moore, Andy Romano, Ray McKinnon, Xander Berkeley, Michael O'Neill, Billie Neal, Gale Mayron, Faye Grant, Marian Seldes, Meat Loaf, Cordell Jackson. Now *there's* a box-office title. Meek mouse Miller stumbles onto the title murder weapon, accidentally fires it in a public restroom, then capitalizes on her newfound attention by falsely confessing to the crime. Miller's considerable charm is tested and found wanting in this blandly trying comedy from the Disney assembly line. [PG-13]▼●

Gunman's Walk (1958) **C-97m.** *** D: Phil Karlson. Van Heflin, Tab Hunter, Kathryn Grant (Crosby), James Darren. Rancher Heflin tries to train sons Hunter and Darren to be respectable citizens, but clashing personalities cause outburst of violence. Tight-knit Western. CinemaScope.▼

Gunmen (1994) **C-90m.** *½ D: Deran Sarafian. Christopher Lambert, Mario Van Peebles, Denis Leary, Patrick Stewart, Kadeem Hardison, Sally Kirkland, Richard Sarafian, Robert Harper, Brenda Bakke, Deran Sarafian. U.S. agent Van Peebles and smuggler Lambert set out to recover the loot of drug lord Stewart (who's also responsible for the murder of Van Peebles' father). Strictly by-the-numbers actioner is often pointlessly violent; the in-your-face direction is no help. Real-life rappers (including Big Daddy Kane, Dr. Dre, and Ed Lover) appear as themselves. Panavision. [R]▼●

Gunmen of the Rio Grande (1965-Italian) **C-86m.** ** D: Tulio Demicheli. Guy Madison, Madeleine LeBeau, Carolyn Davys, Massimo Serato. Madison portrays Wyatt Earp, who helps heroine ward off schemes of grasping mine owner. Totalscope.▼

Gun Moll SEE: **Jigsaw** (1949)

Gunn (1967) **C-94m.** *½ D: Blake Edwards. Craig Stevens, Laura Devon, Edward Asner, Sherry Jackson, Helen Traubel, Albert Paulsen. Unsuccessful attempt to recapture flavor of *Peter Gunn* TV series; Herschel Bernardi, Lola Albright sorely missed, along with quiet understatement and wit that made it memorable. New story is tasteless, violent whodunit involving curious madam. Screenplay by Edwards and William Peter Blatty. Revived again for TV in 1989 as PETER GUNN.

Gunpoint (1966) **C-86m.** ** D: Earl Bellamy. Audie Murphy, Joan Staley, Warren Stevens, Edgar Buchanan. Murphy as sheriff gathers a posse to catch outlaw gang who have kidnapped saloon girl.

Gun Riders (1970) **C-98m.** BOMB D: Al Adamson. Jim Davis, Scott Brady, Robert Dix, John Carradine. Ruthless gunman terrorizes settlers one more time, but his heroic counterpart is there to stop him. Cast is full of Western veterans, but they're not much help. Also known as FIVE BLOODY GRAVES and LONELY MAN. Techniscope. [PG—edited from original R rating]▼

Gun Runner, The (1984-Canadian) **C-92m.** *½ D: Nardo Castillo. Kevin Costner, Sara Botsford, Paul Soles, Gerard Parkes, Ron Lea, Mitch Martin, Larry Lewis, Aline Van Dine, Ruth Dahan. Murky gangster melodrama about idealistic Costner, seeking guns for Chinese rebellion during the 1920s, returning to native Canada and becoming involved with liquor smugglers. Tedious, to say the least, this film was (understandably) shelved until Costner's stardom prompted a 1989 video release . . . but he isn't very good in this one. [R] ▼●

Gun Runners, The (1958) **83m.** ** D: Don Siegel. Audie Murphy, Eddie Albert, Patricia Owens, Everett Sloane, Jack Elam. Murphy is involved with gun-smuggling to Cuba in this bland remake of TO HAVE AND HAVE NOT.

Guns at Batasi (1964-British) **103m.** **½ D: John Guillermin. Richard Attenborough, Jack Hawkins, Mia Farrow, Flora Robson, John Leyton. Acting is all in this intelligent if predictable account of British military life in present day Africa. CinemaScope.▼

Guns for San Sebastian (1968) **C-111m.** ** D: Henri Verneuil. Anthony Quinn, Anjanette Comer, Charles Bronson, Sam Jaffe, Silvia Pinal. Quinn plays a popular bandit who helps Mexican village defeat some Yaqui Indians after he is mistaken for a priest, but he can't conquer ridiculous script. Franscope.

Guns, Girls and Gangsters (1959) **70m.** ** D: Edward L. Cahn. Mamie Van Doren, Gerald Mohr, Lee Van Cleef, Grant Richards, Elaine Edwards, John Baer, Carlo Fiore, Paul Fix. Classic 1950s trash, with the pneumatic Mamie in her prime as a Vegas nightclub singer drawn into scheme to rip off an armored truck carrying casino winnings. Vigorous direction and diverting cast.

Gun Shy (2000) **C-102m.** **½ D: Eric Blakeney. Liam Neeson, Oliver Platt, Sandra Bullock, Jose Zuniga, Richard Schiff, Andy Lauer, Mitch Pileggi, Paul Ben-Victor, Mary McCormack, Frank Vincent, Taylor Negron. Neeson gives a wonderful comic performance as an undercover DEA agent who's suffering from stress and goes to group therapy while working on a major sting operation. Platt is equally good as a not-too-bright hood, and Bullock (who produced the film) has a relatively minor role as Neeson's open-minded love interest. Plot-heavy but underdeveloped; written by the director. [R]▼◗

Gunsight Ridge (1957) **85m.** ** D: Francis D. Lyon. Joel McCrea, Mark Stevens, Joan Weldon, Addison Richards, Slim Pickens. Townsfolk finally band together to rid themselves of outlaws; OK Western.

Gunslinger (1956) **C-83m.** *½ D: Roger Corman. John Ireland, Beverly Garland, Allison Hayes, Martin Kingsley. Strange little Western of female marshal trying to maintain law and order in outlaw-ridden town.▼

Gunsmoke (1953) **C-79m.** **½ D: Nathan Juran. Audie Murphy, Susan Cabot, Paul Kelly, Charles Drake, Jack Kelly. Compact Western with Murphy reforming to run a ranch and marry his employer's daughter.▼

Guns of a Stranger (1973) **C-91m.** BOMB D: Robert Hinkle. Marty Robbins, Chill Wills, Dovie Beams, Steve Tackett, Shug Fisher. Robbins is The Drifter, a singing cowboy, in super-boring family film. Paging Gene Autry. [G]

Guns of August, The (1964) **99m.** *** D: Nathan Kroll. Straightforward documentary about World War I spans the period from Edward VII's funeral (1910) through the final Armistice eight years later. Highly competent, if not exceptional, adaptation of Barbara Tuchman's best-seller utilizes lots of rare combat footage from the time. Well worth a look.▼●

Guns of Darkness (1962) **95m.** **½ D: Anthony Asquith. David Niven, Leslie Caron, David Opatoshu, James Robertson Justice, Eleanor Summerfield, Ian Hunter. Civilized drama of Niven searching for life's meaning, set in South America.

Guns of Fort Petticoat, The (1957) **C-82m.** *** D: George Marshall. Audie Murphy, Kathryn Grant (Crosby), Hope Emerson, Jeff Donnell, Isobel Elsom. Most enjoyable Western, with Army deserter Murphy supervising a group of Texas women in the art of warfare against pending Indian attack.

Guns of Navarone, The (1961) **C-157m.** ***½ D: J. Lee Thompson. Gregory Peck, David Niven, Anthony Quinn, Stanley Baker, Anthony Quayle, James Darren, Irene Papas, Gia Scala, James Robertson Justice, Richard Harris, Albert Lieven, Bryan Forbes, Walter Gotell. Explosive action film about Allied commandos during WW2 plotting to destroy German guns; high-powered adventure throughout this first-rate production, highlighted by Oscar-winning special effects. Script by Carl Foreman from the Alistair MacLean novel. Sequel: FORCE 10 FROM NAVARONE. CinemaScope.▼●◗

Guns of the Magnificent Seven (1969) **C-106m.** **½ D: Paul Wendkos. George Kennedy, Monte Markham, James Whitmore, Reni Santoni, Bernie Casey, Joe Don Baker, Scott Thomas, Michael Ansara, Fernando Rey. Third time out, the "Seven" plot to free Mexican revolutionary leader from a well-guarded fortress. Nothing new, but well done, with plenty of action. Panavision. [G]▼

Guns of the Timberland (1960) **C-91m.** **½ D: Robert D. Webb. Alan Ladd, Jeanne Crain, Gilbert Roland, Frankie Avalon. Pat telling of loggers vs. townpeople.

Guns, Sin and Bathtub Gin SEE: **Lady in Red, The**

Gun That Won the West, The (1955) **C-71m.** ** D: William Castle. Dennis Morgan, Paula Raymond, Richard Denning, Robert Bice. Harmless Grade-B Western of cavalry's use of Springfield rifles to put down Indian uprising.◗

Gun the Man Down (1956) **78m.** ** D: Andrew V. McLaglen. James Arness, Angie Dickinson, Robert Wilke, Emile Meyer. Wounded outlaw swears vengeance on cohorts who left him during holdup. Retitled: ARIZONA MISSION.

Guru, The (1969) **C-112m.** ** D: James Ivory. Michael York, Rita Tushingham, Utpal Dutt, Saeed Jaffrey, Madhur Jaffrey. Sincere but uninvolving story of rock star York who goes to India to learn sitar, meditation from guru Dutt. Director Ivory dwells on Indian lifestyle, settings; Tushingham provides welcome lighter moments in slow-moving film. [G]

Gus (1976) **C-96m.** *** D: Vincent McEveety. Edward Asner, Don Knotts, Gary Grimes, Tim Conway, Liberty Williams, Dick Van Patten, Dick Butkus. Football-kicking mule catapults a last-place team to victory; crooks try to kidnap Gus with usual results (like slapstick chase in a supermarket). Entertaining Disney comedy. [G]▼●

Guyana: Cult of the Damned (1980-Mexican-Spanish-Panamanian) **C-90m.** *½ D: Rene Cardona, Jr. Stuart Whitman, Gene Barry, John Ireland, Joseph Cotten, Bradford Dillman, Jennifer Ashley, Yvonne De Carlo. Not easy to turn the awesomeness of the Jonestown tragedy—where cult followers committed mass suicide—into lackluster drama, but that's what they've done here. [R]

Guyana Tragedy: The Story of Jim Jones (1980) **C-192m. TVM** D: William A. Graham. Powers Boothe, Ned Beatty, Irene Cara, Veronica Cartwright, Rosalind Cash, Brad Dourif, Meg Foster, Diane Ladd, Randy Quaid, Ron O'Neal, Diana Scarwid, Madge Sinclair, LeVar Burton, James Earl Jones, Colleen Dewhurst. Gripping recreation of the late '70s tragedy in which more than 900 cult followers of Rev. Jim Jones (played with magnetism by Boothe) committed mass suicide in a jungle clearing. Kudos to Beatty, as Congressman Leo J. Ryan, to Jones, in a riveting cameo as Father Divine, and to the huge cast. Boothe won an Emmy for his performance. Script by Ernest Tidyman. Above average.▼

Guy Named Joe, A (1943) **120m.** **½ D: Victor Fleming. Spencer Tracy, Irene

Dunne, Van Johnson, Ward Bond, James Gleason, Lionel Barrymore, Barry Nelson, Esther Williams, Don DeFore. Good cast flounders in meandering fantasy about WW2 pilot Tracy coming back to Earth to give young serviceman Johnson a hand in his romance with Tracy's girlfriend Dunne. Remade in 1989 as ALWAYS.▼●

Guys and Dolls (1955) **C-150m.** *** D: Joseph L. Mankiewicz. Marlon Brando, Jean Simmons, Frank Sinatra, Vivian Blaine, Stubby Kaye, B. S. Pully, Veda Ann Borg, Sheldon Leonard, Regis Toomey. Lavish Hollywoodization of classic Broadway musical based on Damon Runyon's colorful characters with Blaine, Kaye, Pully, and Johnny Silver reprising their stage performances and Brando making a not-bad musical debut as gambler Sky Masterson. Tuneful Frank Loesser score includes "Fugue for Tinhorns," "If I Were a Bell," "Luck Be a Lady," Blaine's memorable "Adelaide's Lament," and Stubby's showstopping "Sit Down, You're Rockin' the Boat." CinemaScope.▼●◗

Guyver, The (1992-U.S.-Japanese) **C-92m.** *½ D: Screaming Mad George, Steve Wang. Mark Hamill, Vivian Wu, Jack Armstrong, David Gale, Jimmie Walker, Michael Berryman, Peter Spellos, Spice Williams, Willard Pugh, Jeffrey Combs, David Wells, Linnea Quigley. All-American Armstrong, infected by an alien gadget, becomes an armored superhero; good thing, since almost everyone else in the movie can turn into a nightmarish monster. (CIA agent Hamill turns into a big cockroach.) Clumsy clumps of humor only make the contrived plot seem even more foolish. From a Japanese comic book. Followed by GUYVER: DARK HERO. [PG-13] ▼●

Guy Who Came Back, The (1951) **91m.** ** D: Joseph M. Newman. Paul Douglas, Linda Darnell, Joan Bennett, Don DeFore, Zero Mostel. Cast is above such material but does well by it: ex-football star tries to "find himself."

Guy With a Grin SEE: **No Time for Comedy**

Gymkata (1985) **C-90m.** BOMB D: Robert Clouse. Kurt Thomas, Tetchie Agbayani, Richard Norton, Edward Bell. Champion gymnast Thomas stars in this silly martial-arts potboiler, shot in Yugoslavia by the folks who brought you ENTER THE DRAGON. Amateurish stuff, based on Dan Tyler Moore's novel, *The Terrible Game*. [R]▼

Gypsy (1962) **C-149m.** *** D: Mervyn LeRoy. Rosalind Russell, Natalie Wood, Karl Malden, Paul Wallace, Betty Bruce, Parley Baer, Harvey Korman. Entertaining screen version of bittersweet Broadway musical about the ultimate stage mother, Mama Rose, and her daughters Baby June (Havoc) and Gypsy Rose Lee. Can't lose with that Stephen Sondheim–Jule Styne score. Suzanne Cupito (Morgan Brittany) and Ann Jilliann (Jillian) both play young June. Deleted songs appear on special video edition. Remade as a TVM in 1993 with Bette Midler. Technirama. ▼●◗

Gypsy and the Gentleman, The (1958-British) **C-107m.** **½ D: Joseph Losey. Melina Mercouri, Keith Michell, Patrick McGoohan, Flora Robson. Mercouri as fiery gypsy makes a spicy drama of her love affair with a member of the nobility.

Gypsy Colt (1954) **C-72m.** **½ D: Andrew Marton. Donna Corcoran, Ward Bond, Frances Dee, Larry Keating. Tender film of faithful horse who returns to mistress after parents sell it to racing stable. Remake of LASSIE COME HOME.▼

Gypsy Fury (1951-Swedish-French) **63m.** ** D: Christian-Jaque. Viveca Lindfors, Christopher Kent (Alf Kjellin), Romney Brent, Johnny Chabot, Lauritz Falk. Fable about gypsy and the aristocratic lover who gives up all to marry her.

Gypsy Girl (1966-British) **C-102m.** **½ D: John Mills. Hayley Mills, Ian McShane, Laurence Naismith, Geoffrey Bayldon. Brooding account of backward Hayley Mills finding her first romance with McShane; atmospheric but meandering. Originally titled SKY WEST AND CROOKED.

Gypsy Moths, The (1969) **C-110m.** *** D: John Frankenheimer. Burt Lancaster, Deborah Kerr, Gene Hackman, Scott Wilson, Bonnie Bedelia, William Windom, Sheree North. Story of three skydivers in Kansas captures the Midwest well; Kerr, Wilson and Bedelia help raise potential soap opera to a higher plane. [R]

Gypsy Wildcat (1944) **C-75m.** ** D: Roy William Neill. Maria Montez, Jon Hall, Nigel Bruce, Leo Carrillo, Gale Sondergaard, Douglass Dumbrille. Lowbrow saga of princess raised by gypsies; colorful, splashy, but routine. James M. Cain was one of the writers!

Habitation of Dragons, The (1992) **C-100m. TVM** D: Michael Lindsay-Hogg. Brad Davis, Hallie Foote, Horton Foote, Jr., Frederic Forrest, Pat Hingle, Elias Koteas, Joanna Miles, Maureen O'Sullivan, Jean Stapleton, Roberts Blossom. Horton Foote's adaptation of his play about small-town life in Depression-era Texas is admirable but dreary going despite the beautiful ensemble acting. The second in Steven Spielberg/Michael Brandman/Ted Turner's "Screenworks" series of Golden Age–like TV dramas. Made for cable. Average.▼

Hackers (1995-U.S.-British) **C-105m.** **½ D: Iain Softley. Jonny Lee Miller, Angelina Jolie, Fisher Stevens, Matthew Lillard, Laurence Mason, Jesse Bradford, Renoly Santiago, Alberta Watson, Lorraine Bracco, Wendell Pierce, Penn Jillette. A group of young computer fanatics is framed for crimes committed by computer whiz and would-be master criminal Stevens, and have to use their own hacking skills to prove themselves innocent. No great shakes, but fast pace and vivid direction make it fun. Panavision. [PG-13] ▼●◗

Hadley's Rebellion (1984) **C-96m.** ** D: Fred Walton. Griffin O'Neal, William Devane, Charles Durning, Adam Baldwin, Lisa Lucas. Another teenage-problem picture, this one centering on wrestling-obsessed O'Neal. While it doesn't exploit its characters, it's still bland and superficial. [PG]▼

Hail SEE: **Hail to the Chief**

Hail Caesar (1993) **C-97m.** BOMB D: Anthony Michael Hall. Anthony Michael Hall, Robert Downey, Jr., Frank Gorshin, Samuel L. Jackson, Judd Nelson, Nicholas Pryor. Repulsive rock-star wannabe (Hall) is in love with an obnoxious debutante, whose father is involved in a plot to sabotage a peace conference. Astonishingly bad movie without a single likeable character; an inauspicious directing debut for Hall, who also stars. Downey and Nelson, who get costar billing, have a total of six minutes' screen time—and even that isn't any good. [PG]▼

Hail! Hail! Rock 'n' Roll SEE: **Chuck Berry Hail! Hail! Rock 'n' Roll**

Hail, Hero! (1969) **C-97m.** *½ D: David Miller. Michael Douglas, Arthur Kennedy, Teresa Wright, John Larch, Louise Latham, Charles Drake, Peter Strauss, Deborah Winters, Virginia Christine, John Qualen, Carmen Zapata. Talky, overblown drama about a well-scrubbed hippie (Douglas) who confronts his family as he sorts out his feelings about Vietnam war. Notable only as screen debuts for Douglas and Strauss, and a rare film contribution by musician Gordon Lightfoot, who composed and sings two songs. Originally 100m. [M/PG]▼

Hail, Mafia (1965) **89m.** **½ D: Raoul Levy. Henry Silva, Jack Klugman, Eddie Constantine, Elsa Martinelli, Micheline Presle. Fairly interesting melodrama about hired killers going after a witness to gangland mayhem; has some good European players and nice photography by Raoul Coutard. ▼

Hail Mary (1985-French-Swiss) **C-107m.** *½ D: Jean-Luc Godard. Myriem Roussel, Thierry Rode, Philippe Lacoste, Manon Anderson, Juliette Binoche. Boring, overblown updating of the story of Christ's birth, with Mary a student/basketball player/gas station attendant and Joseph her cabdriver boyfriend; although still a virgin, she finds herself pregnant. This film sparked much controversy and was even condemned by the Pope; however, all the fuss was much ado about very little. A variety of running times have been credited to this film, so beware; has been screened with THE BOOK OF MARY, an infinitely superior featurette about a girl and her bickering parents, directed by Godard associate Anne-Marie Mieville.▼●

Hail the Conquering Hero (1944) **101m.** **** D: Preston Sturges. Eddie Bracken, Ella Raines, Raymond Walburn, William Demarest, Bill Edwards, Elizabeth Patterson, Jimmy Conlin, Franklin Pangborn, Jack Norton, Paul Porcasi, Al Bridge. Frail Bracken, rejected by Marine Corps, is mistaken for war hero by home town. Satirical Sturges at his best, with Demarest and Pangborn stealing much of the crazed proceedings.▼●

Hail to the Chief (1973) **C-85m.** **½ D: Fred Levinson. Dan Resin, Richard B. Shull, Dick O'Neill, Joseph Sirola, Patricia Ripley, Gary Sandy, Willard Waterman. Paranoid President Resin gleefully becomes dictator of the land. Good cast and some hilarious bits—but the result is not as funny as it could be. Filmed in 1970. Aka HAIL and WASHINGTON, B.C. [PG]▼

Hair (1979) **C-121m.** **½ D: Milos Forman. John Savage, Treat Williams, Beverly D'Angelo, Annie Golden, Dorsey Wright, Don Dacus, Cheryl Barnes, Nicholas Ray, Charlotte Rae, Miles Chapin, Michael Jeter. James Rado-Gerome Ragni-Galt MacDermot's hit musical play celebrated the 60s as the Age of Aquarius; unfortunately, it's now a period piece and its impact considerably muffled. Story of straitlaced midwesterner who falls in with N.Y. hippies has exciting musical moments, but doesn't hang together. Choreography by Twyla Tharp. Among the singers: Nell Carter, Melba Moore, Ellen Foley, Ronnie Dyson, Charlaine Woodard. [PG]▼●◗

Hairdresser's Husband, The (1992-French) **C-84m.** *** D: Patrice Leconte. Jean Rochefort, Anna Galiena, Roland Bertin, Maurice Chevit, Philippe Clevenot. Young boy with a fixation on a bosomy haircutter grows up to marry a woman who's practically a reincarnation of his childhood dream. Skillfully assembled comedy-drama makes great use of Rochefort's basset-hound face; slight but charming. Definite U.S. remake possibilities. Panavision. [R]▼●

Hairspray (1988) **C-96m.** *** D: John Waters. Sonny Bono, Ruth Brown, Divine, Colleen Fitzpatrick, Michael St. Gerard, Debbie Harry, Ricki Lake, Leslie Ann Powers, Jerry Stiller, Shawn Thompson, Pia Zadora, Ric Ocasek, John Waters. Shock/schlock merchant Waters goes PG, with irresistible nostalgia satire about the integration of a TV teen dance program in 1962 Baltimore. "Name" performances include Harry as the shellac-haired mother of a deposed local celebrity, Zadora as a pot-smoking Bohemian, Brown as the owner of an r & b record store, and director Waters as the deranged psychiatrist. Loses steam toward the end, but still fun.

Rich soundtrack mixes chestnuts and deservedly unearthed oldies. [PG]▼●
Hairy Ape, The (1944) **90m.** ** D: Alfred Santell. William Bendix, Susan Hayward, John Loder, Alan Napier, Dorothy Comingore, Eddie Kane. One-note drama of bestial ship stoker Bendix's obsession with wealthy, bitchy passenger Hayward. Disappointing version of Eugene O'Neill play.▼
Half a Hero (1953) **71m.** ** D: Don Weis. Red Skelton, Jean Hagen, Charles Dingle, Willard Waterman, Mary Wickes, Polly Bergen. Subdued Skelton vehicle written by Max Shulman casts him in situation-comedy mold, as N.Y. magazine writer who tries suburban life for background on story. Pretty bland.
Half Angel (1951) **C-77m.** **½ D: Richard Sale. Loretta Young, Joseph Cotten, Cecil Kellaway, Basil Ruysdael, Jim Backus, Irene Ryan, John Ridgely. Pleasant comedy of Young blessed with sleepwalking troubles, leading to romantic complications.
Half A Sixpence (1967) **C-148m.** *½ D: George Sidney. Tommy Steele, Julia Foster, Penelope Horner, Cyril Ritchard, Grover Dale. Boisterous but cardboard musical based on show adapted from H. G. Wells' *Kipps,* about draper's assistant who inherits fortune, tries to crash society. Colorfully filmed in England, but totally without charm. Story first filmed in Britain (sans music) as KIPPS in 1941. Panavision.▼
Half Baked (1998) **C-85m.** *½ D: Tamra Davis. Dave Chappelle, Jim Breuer, Harland Williams, Guillermo Diaz, Clarence Williams III, Rachel True. Three potheads try to raise money for their buddy's release from jail by selling marijuana, without Chappelle's girlfriend finding out. Some surprisingly clever touches and attempts to moralize against drugs, completely overshadowed by Breuer's irritating character and general plot stupidity. Cameos include Steven Wright, Willie Nelson, Snoop Doggy Dogg, Tommy Chong and Janeane Garofalo. [R]▼●◗
Half-Breed, The (1952) **C-81m.** ** D: Stuart Gilmore. Robert Young, Janis Carter, Jack Buetel, Barton MacLane, Reed Hadley, Porter Hall. Unscrupulous profiteer incites Apaches to attack white settlers in this predictable Western.▼
Half-Human (1955-Japanese) **70m.** *½ D: Ishiro Honda, Kenneth Crane. John Carradine, Morris Ankrum, Russ Thorson, Robert Karns. Americans Carradine and Ankrum are spliced into Japanese film about an abominable snowmanlike monster and his son(!). There are indications that the original Japanese film might be OK. This version isn't. Almost no dubbing, just Carradine's narration.▼
Half Moon Street (1986) **C-90m.** BOMB D: Bob Swaim. Michael Caine, Sigourney Weaver, Keith Buckley, Patrick Kavanagh, Nadim Sawalha, Angus MacInnes. Intriguing premise has Weaver playing a Ph.D researcher by day and glorified call girl by night, Caine a British diplomat who becomes an extra special client. Sounds as if it can't miss, but is worthless on every level; perennially fresh Weaver gives the first stilted performance of her career. Adapted from *Doctor Slaughter,* the first half of Paul Theroux's two-part novella *Half Moon Street.* Look for Janet McTeer as a secretary. [R] ▼●
Half-Naked Truth, The (1932) **77m.** *** D: Gregory LaCava. Lupe Velez, Lee Tracy, Eugene Pallette, Frank Morgan. Delightful comedy about wiseguy carnival pitchman (Tracy) scheming to make Velez an instant celebrity; plenty of laughs, and wonderful performance by Morgan as neurotic Ziegfeld-ish producer.
Half Shot at Sunrise (1930) **78m.** **½ D: Paul Sloane. Bert Wheeler, Robert Woolsey, Edna May Oliver, Dorothy Lee, George MacFarlane. Pretty funny Wheeler and Woolsey comedy (their first starring vehicle) has them as WW1 soldiers AWOL in Paris and featured in a variety of misogynistic episodes as the military police close in. Best of all: the mock ballet. ▼
Half Slave, Half Free SEE: **Solomon Northrup's Odyssey**
Halfway House, The (1943-British) **95m.** **½ D: Basil Dearden. Mervyn Johns, Glynis Johns, Françoise Rosay, Tom Walls, Alfred Drayton, Sally Ann Howes. Pleasant but low-key fantasy of disparate people brought together at mysterious country inn run by quiet but all-seeing Johns and his daughter.▼
Hallelujah (1929) **106m.** ***½ D: King Vidor. Daniel L. Haynes, Nina Mae McKinney, William Fountaine, Everett McGarrity, Victoria Spivey. King Vidor's early talkie triumph, a stylized view of black life focusing on a Southern cotton-picker who becomes a preacher but retains all-too-human weaknesses. Dated in some aspects and unabashedly melodramatic, but still quite moving. Beautifully filmed on location, with outstanding musical sequences.▼●
Hallelujah, I'm a Bum (1933) **82m.** ***½ D: Lewis Milestone. Al Jolson, Madge Evans, Frank Morgan, Harry Langdon, Chester Conklin, Tyler Brooke, Edgar Connor. Fascinating Depression curio about a hobo who tries to "reform" for the sake of a beautiful woman. Provocative, politically savvy script by Ben Hecht and S. N. Behrman, rhyming dialogue and lovely songs by Rodgers and Hart (who also make cameo appearances as photographers, following the cornerstone-laying scene), and winning performances all around. Beware edited prints (reissue title: THE HEART OF NEW YORK) and the frequently screened British version, cut and redubbed as HALLELUJAH I'M A TRAMP.▼●

Hallelujah Trail, The (1965) **C-165m.** ★★½ D: John Sturges. Burt Lancaster, Lee Remick, Jim Hutton, Brian Keith, Martin Landau, Donald Pleasence, Pamela Tiffin. Narrated by John Dehner. Remick is rambunctious temperance leader out to stop cavalry-guarded shipment of whiskey en route to thirsting Denver miners; amiable but lumbering western satire goes on and on. Ultra Panavision 70.▼●

Halliday Brand, The (1957) **77m.** ★★½ D: Joseph H. Lewis. Joseph Cotten, Viveca Lindfors, Betsy Blair, Ward Bond. Brooding Western about rancher whose domination of family and workers leads to gunplay and revenge. Weak script; strong performances.

Halloween (1978) **C-93m.** ★★★ D: John Carpenter. Donald Pleasence, Jamie Lee Curtis, Nancy Loomis, P. J. Soles, Charles Cyphers, Kyle Richards. Low-budget chiller about psychotic murderer who struck on Halloween as a child, and threatens to do so again 15 years later. Well made, with lots of scares, plus in-joke references for film buffs. Followed by several sequels and myriad clones. Curtis' feature film debut. Panavision. [R]▼●◗

Halloween II (1981) **C-92m.** ★½ D: Rick Rosenthal. Jamie Lee Curtis, Donald Pleasence, Charles Cyphers, Jeffrey Kramer, Lance Guest, Pamela Susan Shoop, Dana Carvey. Explicitly bloody sequel is as bad as any of HALLOWEEN's countless clones, with maniac continuing to stalk Curtis on the same night on which the original ends. Scripted by John Carpenter and Debra Hill. Panavision. [R]▼●◗

Halloween III: Season of the Witch (1983) **C-96m.** BOMB D: Tommy Lee Wallace. Tom Atkins, Stacey Nelkin, Dan O'Herlihy, Ralph Strait, Michael Currie. Genuinely repellent 80s-style horror film, with gore galore (after a slow start), about a maniacal plot to murder millions of children on Halloween. Nice, huh? No relation to either of the earlier HALLOWEEN films, but owes more than a bit to INVASION OF THE BODY SNATCHERS. Panavision. [R]▼●◗

Halloween 4: The Return of Michael Myers (1988) **C-88m.** ★★ D: Dwight H. Little. Donald Pleasence, Ellie Cornell, Danielle Harris, George P. Wilbur, Michael Pataki, Beau Starr, Kathleen Kinmont. Unkillable monster is back, this time mindlessly headed for his hometown to murder his niece (young Harris). Standard horror thriller is technically well made but offers little novelty. [R]▼●◗

Halloween 5 (1989) **C-96m.** ★½ D: Dominique Othenin-Girard. Donald Pleasence, Danielle Harris, Donald L. Shanks, Wendy Kaplan, Ellie Cornell, Jeffrey Landman. Slightly more plot than before but still just a sequential slaughter of teenagers as Michael Myers (Shanks) again sets out to kill his young niece (Harris). Routine and plodding, with too many endings and unnecessary setup for sequel. [R]▼●

Halloween: The Curse of Michael Myers (1995) **C-88m.** ★½ D: Joe Chappelle. Donald Pleasence, Paul Stephen Rudd, Marianne Hagan, Mitchell Ryan, Kim Darby, Bradford English, Keith Bogart, Mariah O'Brien. Pursued by the masked killer, Michael's niece escapes from mysterious catacombs with her newborn baby. Then he starts killing a family which has the misfortune merely to live in his former home. Routine slash-fest, of interest only to the dedicated, even though this time it links Michael to the Druids! [R]▼●

Halloween H20: 20 Years Later (1998) **C-85m.** ★★★ D: Steve Miner. Jamie Lee Curtis, Adam Arkin, Josh Hartnett, Michelle Williams, Adam Hann-Byrd, Jodi Lyn O'Keefe, Janet Leigh, LL Cool J, Chris Durand, Joseph Gordon-Levitt. Twenty years after the killings in HALLOWEEN, Laurie Strode (Curtis) has built a new life for herself and her son, but her psychotic brother Michael Myers is after her again with a big sharp knife. Surprisingly good belated sequel is plenty scary, and has a nice sense of humor (note Leigh's car), but the plot could have used more complications. Curtis, who suggested this project, gives a terrific performance. Coexecutive-produced by Kevin Williamson. Super 35. [R]▼●◗

Halloween Party SEE: **Night of the Demons**

Halls of Anger (1970) **C-96m.** ★★½ D: Paul Bogart. Calvin Lockhart, Janet MacLachlan, James A. Watson, Jr., Rob Reiner, Jeff Bridges, Edward Asner. Standard violence-in-school story, but with a racial angle. No better or worse than a dozen other similar films. [M/PG]

Halls of Montezuma (1950) **C-113m.** ★★½ D: Lewis Milestone. Richard Widmark, Walter (Jack) Palance, Robert Wagner, Jack Webb, Reginald Gardiner, Karl Malden, Philip Ahn. Grim WW2 actioner dealing with marine action in the Pacific. Good cast makes stereotypes acceptable.▼

Hallucination SEE: **Hallucination Generation**

Hallucination Generation (1966) **90m.** BOMB D: Edward Mann. George Montgomery, Danny Stone, Renate Kasche, Tom Baker, Marianne Kanter, Steve Rowland. Silly melodrama about American hippies in Spain, and their introduction to crime. Don't miss the LSD sequence, shot in color. Video title: HALLUCINATION.▼

Hal Roach Comedy Carnival SEE: **Curley** and **Fabulous Joe, The**

Hambone and Hillie (1984) **C-89m.** ★★½ D: Roy Watts. Lillian Gish, Timothy Bottoms, Candy Clark, O. J. Simpson, Robert Walker, Jack Carter, Alan Hale, Anne Lockhart. Elderly Gish loses her devoted mutt at an airport and he races cross-country to find her. Sugar-coated soaper is no dog, but is also no BENJI. [PG]▼

Hamburger Hill (1987) **C-110m.** ** D: John Irvin. Anthony Barrile, Michael Patrick Boatman, Don Cheadle, Michael Dolan, Don James, Dylan McDermott, M. A. Nickles, Tim Quill, Courtney B. Vance, Steven Weber. Cold, clinical, yet occasionally preachy recreation of some true-life 1969 Vietnam carnage, with troops of the 101st Airborne Division encountering the enemy in mutual slaughter for the title reward. Authentic, with expertly staged battle scenes—but limited in its emotional power. Scripted by Jim Carabatsos. [R] ▼●◗

Hamburger . . . The Motion Picture (1986) **C-90m.** BOMB D: Mike Marvin. Leigh McCloskey, Dick Butkus, Randi Brooks, Chuck McCann, Jack Blessing, Charles Tyner. Anyone who watches a movie with this title deserves whatever he gets. [R]▼●

Hamlet (1948-British) **153m.** **** D: Laurence Olivier. Laurence Olivier, Eileen Herlie, Basil Sydney, Felix Aylmer, Jean Simmons, Stanley Holloway, Peter Cushing. Brilliant adaptation of Shakespeare's play about Danish prince "who just couldn't make up his mind." Hauntingly photographed in Elsinore, Denmark. Won Oscars for Best Picture, Best Actor (Olivier), Art Direction-Set Decoration and Costumes.▼●

Hamlet (1969-British) **C-114m.** **½ D: Tony Richardson. Nicol Williamson, Gordon Jackson, Anthony Hopkins, Judy Parfitt, Mark Dignam, Marianne Faithfull. Richardson and Williamson moved their boisterous interpretation of the Shakespeare play from stage to screen with only fair results; perhaps the irritating overuse of close-ups will play better on TV. Interesting casting of Faithfull as Ophelia. [G]▼

Hamlet (1990) **C-135m.** *** D: Franco Zeffirelli. Mel Gibson, Glenn Close, Alan Bates, Paul Scofield, Ian Holm, Helena Bonham Carter, Stephen Dillane, Nathaniel Parker, John McEnery. Agreeable re-do of the Shakespeare staple with Gibson giving an energetic interpretation of the Melancholy Dane. In fact, Mel comes off better than costar Close (Gertrude); Bates, as Claudius, is the standout in the stellar cast. Never as enthralling or perceptive as Kenneth Branagh's HENRY V, but still worthwhile. [PG]▼●

Hamlet (1996-U.S.-British) **C-242m.** *** D: Kenneth Branagh. Kenneth Branagh, Julie Christie, Derek Jacobi, Kate Winslet, Rufus Sewell, Richard Briers, Brian Blessed, Gérard Depardieu, Charlton Heston, Rosemary Harris, Jack Lemmon, Billy Crystal, Robin Williams, Richard Attenborough, Nicholas Farrell, John Gielgud, John Mills, Rowena King. Branagh's unexpurgated Bard workout is a movie of moments and mixed blessings, with the story's updating—to the second half of the 19th century—doing a lot to defuse any criticism of its stunt casting. Jacobi (Claudius), Christie (Gertrude), and Winslet (Ophelia) come off extremely well, though Branagh essentially gives a stage performance that's nearly as cinematically over the top as some of his directorial touches. Guest star turns are extremely variable. Gorgeously shot in 70mm by Alex Thomson. Panavision Super 70. [PG-13] ▼●

Hamlet (2000) **C-112m.** ** D: Michael Almereyda. Ethan Hawke, Kyle MacLachlan, Sam Shepard, Diane Venora, Bill Murray, Liev Schreiber, Julia Stiles, Karl Geary, Steve Zahn, Dechen Thurman, Jeffrey Wright, Paul Bartel, Casey Affleck. Transplant of Shakespeare's timeless play to modern-day N.Y.C., where the head of the Denmark Corporation has died, adds nothing to our understanding or appreciation of the story. Some clever gags and stunt casting score occasional points. Hawke, sporting a ski cap through much of the action, is easily outshone by Schreiber (as Laertes), MacLachlan (as Claudius), and Stiles (an impressive Ophelia). [R]▼◗

Hammer (1972) **C-92m.** *½ D: Bruce Clark. Fred Williamson, Bernie Hamilton, Vonetta McGee, William Smith, Charles Lampkin. Black boxer takes on the syndicate in fast, but mindless melodrama. Some violence may be cut. [R]

Hammerhead (1968-British) **C-99m.** *½ D: David Miller. Vince Edwards, Judy Geeson, Diana Dors, Peter Vaughan, Beverly Adams. Weak James Bond carbon copy, tale of supercriminal pursued by soldier of fortune. [R]

Hammersmith Is Out (1972) **C-108m.** ** D: Peter Ustinov. Elizabeth Taylor, Richard Burton, Peter Ustinov, Beau Bridges, Leon Askin, Leon Ames, John Schuck, George Raft. Grotesque comedy about mental patient, his male nurse, and a hash slinger proves once again that Liz and Dick would do anything for money; cast has more fun than viewers in this variation on the Faust legend. [R]▼

Hammett (1983) **C-97m.** *** D: Wim Wenders. Frederic Forrest, Peter Boyle, Marilu Henner, Elisha Cook, R. G. Armstrong, Richard Bradford, Roy Kinnear, Lydia Lei, Sylvia Sidney, Samuel Fuller, Royal Dano. Wenders' first American film is a real treat for detective buffs: an adaptation of Joe Gores' fiction about famed author Dashiell Hammett's involvement in a real-life mystery (elements of which would find their way into his later stories). You couldn't ask for a more faithful re-creation of 1930s studio look; a magnificent-looking (and sounding) film. Several years in production, with much of it reportedly reshot by executive producer Francis Coppola, but final result is seamless. [PG]▼

Hamster of Happiness, The SEE: **Second-Hand Hearts**

Hamsun (1996-Norwegian-Swedish-German) **C-157m.** ***½ D: Jan Troell. Max von Sydow, Ghita Norby, Anette Hoff, Asa Soderling, Gard B. Eidsvold, Eindride Eidsvold. Famed Norwegian author Knut Hamsun (von Sydow), winner of the 1920 Nobel Prize, supported the Nazi takeover of his own country. This thoughtful film illuminates the combination of naïveté, arrogance and nationalism that led to his sorry choice. Entire cast is excellent, but von Sydow and Norby (as his ego-starved wife) are brilliant, and the movie deserves to be better known. Based on a book by Thorkild Hansen.▼

Hana-Bi SEE: **Fireworks** (1998)

Hand, The (1960-British) **60m.** *½ D: Henry Cass. Derek Farr, Ronald Leigh Hunt, Reed De Rouen, Ray Cooney. Odd, infuriatingly muddled mystery in which a Scotland Yard inspector investigates the amputation of an old drunk's hand, and in so doing uncovers a fiendish plot.▼

Hand, The (1981) **C-104m.** *½ D: Oliver Stone. Michael Caine, Andrea Marcovicci, Annie McEnroe, Bruce McGill, Viveca Lindfors, Rosemary Murphy, Mara Hobel, Pat Corley, Charles Fleischer. Cartoonist Caine's drawing hand is severed in auto accident, which destroys his career and places additional strain on his shaky marriage. Life becomes even more nightmarish when the hand returns on a murderous spree; unfortunately it didn't get Caine or writer-director Stone. Stone plays a bum who gets killed. [R] ▼●

Handful of Dust, A (1988-British) **C-118m.** ***½ D: Charles Sturridge. James Wilby, Kristin Scott Thomas, Rupert Graves, Judi Dench, Anjelica Huston, Alec Guinness, Pip Torrens, Cathryn Harrison. Rich adaptation of Evelyn Waugh's ironic story about a doomed marriage among England's smart set in the early 1930s, and the unexpected results for both the stiflingly tradition-bound husband (brilliantly and movingly played by Wilby) and the nonchalantly selfish wife (perfectly essayed by Thomas). Superior script by Tim Sullivan, Derek Granger, and Sturridge is matched by an unerring eye for period detail. [PG]▼

Handgun SEE: **Deep in the Heart**

Hand in Hand (1960-British) **75m.** **½ D: Philip Leacock. Loretta Parry, Philip Needs, John Gregson, Sybil Thorndike. Good film with a moral for children, about a Jewish girl and a Catholic boy who become friends and learn about each other. Adults may find it hard to take at times.

Handle With Care (1958) **82m.** **½ D: David Friedkin. Dean Jones, Joan O'Brien, Thomas Mitchell, John Smith, Walter Abel. Earnest minor film about law student Jones investigating crime within the town where classmates are assigned mock grand-jury work.

Handle With Care (1977) **C-98m.** *** D: Jonathan Demme. Paul LeMat, Candy Clark, Ann Wedgeworth, Marcia Rodd, Charles Napier, Alix Elias, Roberts Blossom, Ed Begley, Jr. Fine character studies and vignettes make up for shortcomings in bright, original film. Loosely revolves around LeMat and his obsession with C.B. radio; subplot with bigamist truckdriver is hilarious. Written by Paul Brickman. Originally released as CITIZENS BAND. [PG]▼

Handmaid's Tale, The (1990) **C-109m.** **½ D: Volker Schlöndorff. Natasha Richardson, Robert Duvall, Faye Dunaway, Aidan Quinn, Elizabeth McGovern, Victoria Tennant, Blanche Baker, Traci Lind. Intriguing story set in a near-future world in which young, healthy white women are brainwashed to become bearers of babies for a new, "pure" generation. Richardson must overcome the jealousy of an infertile wife (Dunaway) while fending off the advances of her high-powered husband (Duvall). Interesting but best described as sterile. Scripted by Harold Pinter from the novel by Margaret Atwood. David Dukes appears unbilled as a doctor. [R]▼●

Hand of the Gallows SEE: **Terrible People, The**

Hands Across the Table (1935) **80m.** *** D: Mitchell Leisen. Carole Lombard, Fred MacMurray, Ralph Bellamy, Astrid Allwyn, Marie Prevost. Lombard sparkles as fortune-hunting manicurist who has to choose between MacMurray and Bellamy.▼

Hands of a Stranger (1962) **86m.** **½ D: Newton Arnold. Paul Lukather, Joan Harvey, James Stapleton, Irish McCalla, Barry Gordon, Sally Kellerman. Entertaining and well-directed little chiller is an unacknowledged fourth version of THE HANDS OF ORLAC. Brilliant young pianist's hands are injured in a car accident; idealistic surgeon replaces them with those of a just-deceased criminal.▼

Hands of Death SEE: **Beyond the Living**

Hands of Orlac, The (1961-British-French) **95m.** ** D: Edmond T. Greville. Mel Ferrer, Lucile Saint-Simon, Christopher Lee, Dany Carrel, Felix Aylmer, Basil Sydney, Donald Wolfit, Donald Pleasence. Pianist gets hand transplant from a strange doctor—and finds he has the impulse to kill. Flat remake of Maurice Renard's famous story, filmed before in 1924 and (as MAD LOVE) in 1935. French-language version runs 105m. Also known as HANDS OF THE STRANGLER.▼

Hands of the Ripper (1971-British) **C-85m.** **½ D: Peter Sasdy. Eric Porter, Angharad Rees, Jane Merrow, Keith Bell, Derek Godfrey. Early believer in Freud tries to help young daughter of Jack the Ripper. Great atmosphere, solid performances, but after good start, dissolves into series of bloody murders. Not bad—but hampered by addition of psychiatrist "explaining" main character for TV prints. [R]▼

Hands of the Strangler SEE: **Hands of Orlac, The**

Hands Over the City (1963-Italian) **105m.** ***½ D: Francesco Rosi. Rod Steiger, Salvo Randone, Guido Alberti, Angelo D'Alessandro, Carlo Fermariello, Dany Paris, Guglielmo Metafora, Marallo Cannavale. Steiger is at his best in this blunt, potent drama of political corruption and hypocrisy. He plays a crooked, manipulative government official intent on profiting from a lucrative land deal while ignoring the collapse of a building in a Naples ghetto. Aka HANDS ON THE CITY.

Hand That Rocks the Cradle, The (1992) **C-110m.** ** D: Curtis Hanson. Annabella Sciorra, Rebecca De Mornay, Matt McCoy, Ernie Hudson, Julianne Moore, Madeline Zima, John de Lancie, Mitchell Laurance. Demented, revenge-seeking nanny De Mornay takes a job with unsuspecting married couple Sciorra and McCoy—guess what happens next. Some good performances (especially by De Mornay) boost this otherwise derivative shocker. Tension builds, but gruesome finale is fairly predictable. McCoy may be the most sensitive husband in recent screen history. [R]▼●◗

Handyman, The (1980-Canadian) **C-99m.** ***½ D: Micheline Lanctot. Jocelyn Berube, Andree Pelletier, Jannette Bertrand, Paul Dion, Marcel Sabourin. Shy, boyish, romantic Berube—he's not exactly short, but other men seem to tower over him—has a love affair with a married woman. A sad, beautifully made little film about people who can never get what they want because they are unable to take stands.

Hangar 18 (1980) **C-93m.** *½ D: James L. Conway. Darren McGavin, Robert Vaughn, Gary Collins, James Hampton, Philip Abbott, Joseph Campanella, Pamela Bellwood, Steven Keats, Tom Hallick, William Schallert. This Sunn Classic Picture alleges that the U.S. government is concealing a captured UFO. Slickly made, but about as credible as THE THREE STOOGES IN ORBIT; shown on TV as INVASION FORCE with new ending that undermines entire film! [PG]▼

Hang 'em High (1968) **C-114m.** **½ D: Ted Post. Clint Eastwood, Inger Stevens, Ed Begley, Pat Hingle, Arlene Golonka, James MacArthur, Ruth White, Ben Johnson, Charles McGraw, Bruce Dern, Alan Hale Jr., Dennis Hopper. Slick American attempt at spaghetti Western comes off fairly well. Eastwood survives his own hanging, swears vengeance on nine men who lynched him. Fine supporting cast; nice cameo by cowboy veteran Bob Steele as dungeon prisoner. [M]▼●◗

Hanging Garden, The (1997-Canadian) **C-91m.** *** D: Thom Fitzgerald. Chris Leavins, Kerry Fox, Seana McKenna, Peter McNeill, Christine Dunsworth, Troy Veinotte, Sarah Polley, Joel S. Keller, Joan Orenstein. Strikingly original, multi-layered psychological drama about Sweet William, the product of a dysfunctional family, who returns home after a ten-year absence to attend his sister's wedding. The film moves in and out of reality, and between present and past; a telling exploration of the complexities and emotional truths of family relationships. [R]▼

Hanging Tree, The (1959) **C-106m.** *** D: Delmer Daves. Gary Cooper, Maria Schell, Karl Malden, George C. Scott, Karl Swenson, Ben Piazza, Virginia Gregg. Literate, low-key Western with outstanding performance by Schell as a blind girl nursed by Cooper, a frontier doctor with a past. Not for all tastes. Scott's first film.▼

Hanging Up (2000) **C-93m.** BOMB D: Diane Keaton. Meg Ryan, Diane Keaton, Lisa Kudrow, Walter Matthau, Adam Arkin, Duke Moosekian, Ann Bortolotti, Cloris Leachman. Three sisters live most of their lives via cell phone, but Ryan finds herself the only one willing to bear responsibility for their father, who's hospitalized and senile. It's hard to think of a movie with more strident, obnoxious characters, or a script that makes so little sense from scene to scene. Three appealing stars are hung out to dry in this seriocomedy, written by Nora and Delia Ephron, from Delia's book. [PG-13]▼◗

Hangin' With the Homeboys (1991) **C-88m.** *** D: Joseph P. Vasquez. Doug E. Doug, Mario Joyner, John Leguizamo, Nestor Serrano, Kimberly Russell, Mary B. Ward. Jarringly honest, energetically directed and acted account of a day in the lives of several young African-Americans and Puerto Ricans who've grown up on the mean streets of the South Bronx. Each is different, but all are linked in that they're traveling down a road to nowhere. [R] ▼●

Hangman, The (1959) **86m.** ** D: Michael Curtiz. Robert Taylor, Tina Louise, Fess Parker, Jack Lord, Mickey Shaughnessy, Shirley Harmer. Rugged Taylor is the lawman who must buck the entire Western town defending a man wanted for murder.

Hangman's House (1928) **72m.** *** D: John Ford. June Collyer, Larry Kent, Earle Foxe, Victor McLaglen, Hobart Bosworth. Florid melodrama of frustrated romance and family honor, with Collyer acceding to her father's wishes and marrying blackguard Foxe despite her love for Kent. Elevated by sumptuous production and Ford's sure direction, with McLaglen playing a character who is the polar opposite of his role in THE INFORMER. Steeplechase scene predates the one in THE QUIET MAN and you can spot young John Wayne as one of the animated spectators along the racetrack railing!▼

Hangman's Knot (1952) **C-81m.** **½ D: Roy Huggins. Randolph Scott, Donna Reed, Claude Jarman, Jr., Richard Denning, Lee Marvin. Above-par Scott Western involving Rebs robbing gold shipment and officer Scott deciding they should return it. ▼

Hangmen Also Die! (1943) **131m.** **½ D: Fritz Lang. Brian Donlevy, Walter Brennan, Anna Lee, Gene Lockhart, Dennis O'Keefe. OK WW2 drama written by Bertolt Brecht; lethargic Donlevy performance as assassin of notorious Nazi leader; exciting climax including frame-up of Lockhart.▼

Hangover, The SEE: **Female Jungle**

Hangover Square (1945) **77m.** *** D: John Brahm. Laird Cregar, Linda Darnell, George Sanders, Glenn Langan, Faye Marlowe, Alan Napier, Frederic Worlock. Cregar (in his final film) is delicious as unhinged composer who goes off his top and kills women whenever he hears loud noises. Barre Lyndon's script bears little relation to the Patrick Hamilton novel, but result is still entertaining, with superb Victorian London sets and evocative Bernard Herrmann score.

Hangup (1974) **C-94m.** ** D: Henry Hathaway. William Elliott, Marki Bey, Cliff Potts, Michael Lerner, Timothy Blake. Disappointing black-oriented actioner about a drug racket; Hathaway has done many fine films, but this, his last, isn't one. Bey is good as a doomed prostitute. Aka SUPER DUDE. [R]

Hanky Panky (1982) **C-110m.** *½ D: Sidney Poitier. Gene Wilder, Gilda Radner, Kathleen Quinlan, Richard Widmark, Robert Prosky, Josef Sommer, Johnny Sekka. Innocent architect Wilder is chased by spies, cops, etc. Predictable, barely funny comedy-thriller, with Radner miscast as the love interest. (The film was intended to be a followup to STIR CRAZY, but Richard Pryor's part was rewritten for Gilda.) You've seen it all before, and better. [PG]▼●

Hannah and Her Sisters (1986) **C-106m.** ***½ D: Woody Allen. Woody Allen, Michael Caine, Mia Farrow, Carrie Fisher, Barbara Hershey, Lloyd Nolan, Maureen O'Sullivan, Daniel Stern, Max von Sydow, Dianne Wiest, J.T. Walsh, Richard Jenkins, Julie Kavner, Julia Louis-Dreyfus, John Turturro, Joanna Gleason, Bobby Short. Allen strikes gold as he examines some typically interesting and neurotic New Yorkers whose lives intertwine. Superbly cast with Woody in peak form as Farrow's hypochondriac ex-husband; Wiest in a powerhouse performance as Mia's self-consumed, self-destructive sister. There's also an atypical Allen touch of warmth, even sentiment, as frosting on the cake—all of it set to some wonderful old songs. Academy Award winner for Best Supporting Actor (Caine), Best Supporting Actress (Wiest), and Woody's Original Screenplay. Tony Roberts and Sam Waterston appear unbilled. One of the children at the Thanksgiving celebrations is Soon-Yi Previn. [PG-13]▼●

Hannah Lee SEE: **Outlaw Territory**

Hanna K. (1983-French) **C-108m.** ** D: Constantine Costa-Gavras. Jill Clayburgh, Jean Yanne, Gabriel Byrne, Mohammed Bakri, David Clennon. Intriguing but unsatisfying melodrama about flaky lawyer Clayburgh and her conflicting relationships with ex-husband Yanne, Israeli district attorney Byrne and Palestinian Bakri, who's attempting to reclaim his ancestral home. Controversial because of its pro-Palestinian stand, but on artistic terms a major disappointment from Costa-Gavras. [R]▼

Hanna's War (1988) **C-148m.** *½ D: Menahem Golan. Ellen Burstyn, Maruschka Detmers, Anthony Andrews, Donald Pleasence, David Warner, Denholm Elliott, Vincenzo Ricotta, Ingrid Pitt. The true story of Hungarian freedom fighter Hanna Senesh (Detmers), based in part on her diaries, is a misguided mess. The young, Jewish WW2 martyr deserved a far better production than this overlong, uninspiring melodrama. Hanna's prison-issue designer blouses don't help matters. Panavision. [PG-13]▼●

Hannibal (1960-U.S.-Italian) **C-103m.** ** D: Edgar G. Ulmer. Victor Mature, Rita Gam, Gabriele Ferzetti, Milly Vitale. Cardboard costume saga follows Hannibal and his elephants across the Alps and into Rome . . . but *you* may not last that long. SuperCinescope.

Hannibal Brooks (1969-British) **C-101m.** **½ D: Michael Winner. Oliver Reed, Michael J. Pollard, Wolfgang Preiss, Helmut Lohner, Karin Baal, Peter Karsten. Pleasant, forgettable film of British P.O.W. Reed assigned to evacuate valuable elephant from Munich zoo during WW2; forced to go on foot, he turns trip into escape plan. Wavers from comedy to melodrama, with Pollard major comic character; good action climax. [M/PG]

Hannie Caulder (1971-British) **C-85m.** **½ D: Burt Kennedy. Raquel Welch, Robert Culp, Ernest Borgnine, Jack Elam, Strother Martin, Christopher Lee, Diana Dors. Bizarre, mystical Western about raped/widowed/homeless woman who begs bounty hunter Culp to teach her to shoot so she can seek vengeance. Neat idea to have bad guys Borgnine, Elam, and Martin play it a la The Three Stooges, but laughter is vitiated by their gory killings. Nice turn by Lee as sympathetic gunsmith. Panavision. [R]▼●

Hanoi Hilton, The (1987) **C-130m.** *½ D: Lionel Chetwynd. Michael Moriarty, Paul LeMat, Jeffrey Jones, Lawrence Pressman, Stephen Davies, David Soul, Rick

Fitts. What may have been a sincere effort to dramatize the plight of American POWs in Vietnam becomes an unbearably dull, impossibly overlong, and embarrassingly clichéd drama, which does a real disservice to its subject . . . and throws in right-wing polemics and potshots at Jane Fonda to boot. [R]▼●

Hanover Street (1979) **C-109m.** ** D: Peter Hyams. Harrison Ford, Lesley-Anne Down, Christopher Plummer, Alec McCowen, Richard Masur, Michael Sacks. WW2 romance between married Englishwoman and American soldier who's sent on daring mission behind enemy lines is slick but contrived and unconvincing. Script by director Hyams. Panavision.[PG]▼●

Hans Christian Andersen (1952) **C-120m.** **½ D: Charles Vidor. Danny Kaye, Farley Granger, Jeanmaire, Roland Petit, John Qualen. Melodic Frank Loesser score ("Inchworm," "Ugly Duckling," "Thumbelina," etc.) can't save musical biography of vagabond tale-teller. Glossy and completely fabricated—has no relation to real Andersen's life story. Some TV prints run 104m.▼●◗

Hanussen (1988-German-Hungarian) **C-115m.** ***½ D: Istvan Szabo. Klaus Maria Brandauer, Erland Josephson, Ildiko Bansagi, Walter Schmidinger, Karoly Eperjes. Brandauer offers a compelling performance as the title character, a WW1 Austrian soldier who is shot in the head—and develops the ability to read minds and foretell the future. An intriguing, insightful, based-on-fact tale; third in a trilogy, following MEPHISTO and COLONEL REDL. [R]▼●

Happening, The (1967) **101m.** ** D: Elliot Silverstein. Anthony Quinn, George Maharis, Michael Parks, Robert Walker, Faye Dunaway, Milton Berle, Oscar Homolka, Jack Kruschen, Clifton James, Eugene Roche. Lighthearted and lightheaded caper story centering around kidnapping of a now respectable former gangster (Quinn). Turns unpleasantly serious towards end. Dunaway's film debut. The title song became a No. 1 hit for The Supremes.

Happiest Days of Your Life, The (1950-British) **84m.** *** D: Frank Launder. Alastair Sim, Margaret Rutherford, Guy Middleton, Joyce Grenfell, Edward Rigby, Muriel Aked, John Bentley, Bernadette O'Farrell, Richard Wattis, Pat (Patricia) Owens. Funny comedy involving a boys' school sharing quarters with a displaced girls' academy, with frantic situations resulting. Launder and John Dighton scripted, from the latter's play.▼

Happiest Millionaire, The (1967) **C-118m.** **½ D: Norman Tokar. Fred MacMurray, Tommy Steele, Greer Garson, Geraldine Page, Gladys Cooper, Hermione Baddeley, Lesley Ann Warren, John Davidson. Lively but overlong and uninvolving Disney musical (the last film he personally oversaw) about Philadelphia household of eccentric millionaire Anthony J. Drexel Biddle (MacMurray). Lightly entertaining. Originally tradescreened at 164m., then released at 141m.; reissued in 1984 at 159m.▼◗

Happily Ever After (1990) **C-74m.** ** D: John Howley. Voices of Irene Cara, Edward Asner, Carol Channing, Dom DeLuise, Phyllis Diller, Zsa Zsa Gabor, Linda Gary, Jonathan Harris, Michael Horton, Sally Kellerman, Malcolm McDowell, Tracey Ullman, Frank Welker. All-star voice cast gives major boost to this otherwise undistinguished sequel to the story of Snow White, who's surrounded here by dwarfelles. (Don't ask.) Produced by Filmation Studios with noticeably better animation than their Saturday morning product can boast. Aka SNOW WHITE IN THE LAND OF DOOM. [G]▼●

Happiness (1965) SEE: **Le Bonheur**

Happiness (1998) **C-139m.** ***½ D: Todd Solondz. Jane Adams, Jon Lovitz, Philip Seymour Hoffman, Dylan Baker, Lara Flynn Boyle, Cynthia Stevenson, Molly Shannon, Louise Lasser, Ben Gazzara, Camryn Manheim, Jared Harris, Elizabeth Ashley, Marla Maples. Portrait of an unhappy family—three sisters, their mother and father—and others who come into their orbit, each dealing with personal demons. They range from a telephone stalker who can't confront women in person to an eternally hopeful young woman named Joy whose life is a perpetual mess. Any film that tackles such topics as masturbation and pederasts isn't going to appeal to everyone, but writer-director Solondz makes them real people and tempers everything with humor. A truly remarkable film.▼●◗

Happiness Ahead (1934) **86m.** **½ D: Mervyn LeRoy. Dick Powell, Josephine Hutchinson, Frank McHugh, John Halliday, Allen Jenkins, Ruth Donnelly. Pleasant little film about wealthy heiress pretending to be poor when she meets likable working-stiff Powell. No production numbers, really, but several nice songs, including "Pop Goes Your Heart."

Happiness Cage, The (1972) **C-94m.** **½ D: Bernard Girard. Christopher Walken, Joss Ackland, Ralph Meeker, Ronny Cox, Marco St. John, Tom Aldredge. Uneven but thought-provoking drama about doctor in Germany who utilizes shock treatment on soldiers to stabilize aggressive behavior. Video titles: THE MIND SNATCHERS and THE DEMON WITHIN. [PG]▼

Happy Anniversary (1959) **81m.** **½ D: David Miller. David Niven, Mitzi Gaynor, Carl Reiner, Loring Smith, Monique Van Vooren, Patty Duke, Elizabeth Wilson. Funny but strained comedy of married couple Niven and Gaynor being embarrassed by daughter Duke telling nation on TV that father was indiscreet in his younger days.

Happy Birthday, Gemini (1980) **C-107m.** ** D: Richard Benner. Madeline Kahn, Rita Moreno, Robert Viharo, Alan Rosenberg, Sarah Holcomb, David Marshall Grant, Timothy Jenkins. Disappointing adaptation of Albert Innaurato's long-running Broadway play *Gemini,* centering on young man's sexual identity crisis. Colorful stage characters are lost on film. [R]▼

Happy Birthday to Me (1981-Canadian) **C-108m.** BOMB D: J. Lee Thompson. Melissa Sue Anderson, Glenn Ford, Tracy Bregman, Jack Blum, Matt Craven, Lawrence Dane. Is or is not Anderson killing off her classmates at Crawford Academy because they inadvertently caused her mother's death four years earlier? More killings, more blood, more exploitation; Ford, as Anderson's psychiatrist, hit rock bottom with this appearance. [R]▼●

Happy Birthday, Wanda June (1971) **C-105m.** *** D: Mark Robson. Rod Steiger, Susannah York, George Grizzard, Don Murray, William Hickey, Pamelyn Ferdin, Steven Paul. Stagy but enjoyable film of Kurt Vonnegut, Jr., play. Male chauvinist explorer, returning home after eight years, finds his wife matured (and engaged), and his values now obsolete. Fine performances of Vonnegut's funny black-humor situations and dialogue; Hickey hilarious as Steiger's Jerry Lewis-esque buddy. [R]

Happy Ending, The (1969) **C-112m.** **½ D: Richard Brooks. Jean Simmons, John Forsythe, Lloyd Bridges, Shirley Jones, Teresa Wright, Dick Shawn, Nanette Fabray, Robert (Bobby) Darin, Tina Louise. Initially intriguing view of modern marriage drones on interminably, as Simmons walks out on husband and family trying to find herself. Michel Legrand score highlighted by "What Are You Doing the Rest of Your Life?" Panavision. [M/PG]▼

Happy Gilmore (1996) **C-92m.** ** D: Dennis Dugan. Adam Sandler, Christopher McDonald, Carl Weathers, Julie Bowen, Alan Covert, Bob Barker, Frances Bay, Joe Flaherty, Kevin Nealon, Richard Kiel, Dennis Dugan. Sporadically funny vehicle for Sandler, as a would-be hockey player whose inability to skate leads him to the pro golf tour, where he turns game on its ear with his unsportsmanlike antics. Highpoint: a brawl between Sandler and *The Price Is Right*'s Barker. Sandler cowrote the script. Ben Stiller appears unbilled. [PG-13] ▼●◗

Happy Go Lovely (1951-British) **C-87m.** ** D: Bruce Humberstone. David Niven, Vera-Ellen, Cesar Romero, Bobby Howes, Diane Hart, Gordon Jackson. The charm of its three stars uplifts this otherwise minor musical-romance, set in Edinburgh, with chorus girl Vera-Ellen getting the lead in a show when the director (Romero) thinks she's about to wed a millionaire (Niven) she's never met.▼

Happy Go Lucky (1943) **C-81m.** **½ D: Curtis Bernhardt. Mary Martin, Dick Powell, Eddie Bracken, Betty Hutton, Rudy Vallee, Mabel Paige, Eric Blore. Happy little musical has Martin chasing millionaire Vallee on Caribbean cruise. Songs include "Murder He Says."◗

Happy Hooker, The (1975) **C-96m.** ** D: Nicholas Sgarro. Lynn Redgrave, Jean-Pierre Aumont, Lovelady Powell, Nicholas Pryor, Elizabeth Wilson, Tom Poston, Conrad Janis, George Dzundza, Vincent Schiavelli, Mason Adams, Anita Morris. Xaviera Hollander's best-seller about her rise as N.Y.C.'s most prominent madam is so heavily sanitized that one wonders just what audience scripter William Richert had in mind; moderately amusing, and cast seems to be having a good time. Followed by two fictitious sequels. [R]▼●

Happy Hooker Goes Hollywood, The (1980) **C-85m.** *½ D: Alan Roberts. Martine Beswicke, Chris Lemmon, Adam West, Phil Silvers, Richard Deacon, Lindsay Bloom, Army Archerd, Edie Adams. Now Xaviera is a brunette; she and her girls rush to the aid of a corruption-riddled movie studio in this limp rehash of SILENT MOVIE. Fine comic cast is wasted, although film buffs might enjoy seeing cult actors Beswicke and Dick Miller in bed together. [R]▼●

Happy Hooker Goes to Washington, The (1977) **C-89m.** *½ D: William A. Levey. Joey Heatherton, George Hamilton, Ray Walston, Jack Carter, Phil Foster, Billy Barty, David White. Xaviera (a *blonde* this time) is called before Congress to answer charges that sex is ruining the country and subsequently gets involved in a CIA escapade. A few chuckles here and there, but overall, more silly than sexy; Hamilton and writer Bob Kaufman did considerably better with their next film, LOVE AT FIRST BITE. [R]▼

Happy Is the Bride (1957-British) **84m.** ** D: Roy Boulting. Ian Carmichael, Janette Scott, Cecil Parker, Terry-Thomas, Joyce Grenfell, John Le Mesurier, Eric Barker, Athene Seyler. Remake of 1940's QUIET WEDDING, a mild farce about a young couple's headaches as their families prepare for their nuptials. Seyler repeats her role from the original as a helpful aunt.

Happy Land (1943) **73m.** **½ D: Irving Pichel. Don Ameche, Frances Dee, Harry Carey, Ann Rutherford, Cara Williams, Richard Crane, Henry (Harry) Morgan, Dickie Moore. Sincere but not always successful Americana of grieving father learning meaning of war as he questions his son's death in WW2. Five-year-old Natalie Wood's first feature.

Happy Landing (1938) **102m.** **½ D:

Roy Del Ruth. Sonja Henie, Don Ameche, Cesar Romero, Ethel Merman, Jean Hersholt, Billy Gilbert. Predictable Henie vehicle is not up to her other musicals. Pilot Ameche lands near her home; romance blossoms instantly.▼

Happy Mother's Day, Love George (1973) **C-90m.** ** D: Darren McGavin. Patricia Neal, Cloris Leachman, Bobby Darin, Ron Howard, Simon Oakland. Unconvincing horror tale, despite some clever attempts by director McGavin to spice it up. Strange doings in seaside house include two great gory murders, but everything else is weak. Retitled: RUN, STRANGER, RUN. [PG]▼

Happy New Year (1973-French) **C-112m.** *** D: Claude Lelouch. Lino Ventura, Françoise Fabian, Charles Gerard, Andre Falcon. Two thieves plot a robbery, but one falls hard for the liberated charmer who runs the antique shop next to the target. Bright romantic caper film is easy to take. Remade in Hollywood in 1987. Retitled: THE HAPPY NEW YEAR CAPER.▼

Happy New Year (1987) **C-85m.** **½ D: John G. Avildsen. Peter Falk, Wendy Hughes, Charles Durning, Tom Courtenay, Joan Copeland. Falk is a treat to watch in this pleasant Americanization of Claude Lelouch's French comedy caper about a pair of sophisticated crooks and their plans to hit a jewelry store in West Palm Beach, Florida. Hughes is charming in her first American film; Lelouch has a cameo in the opening scene. [PG]▼

Happy New Year Caper, The SEE: **Happy New Year** (1973)

Happy Road, The (1957) **80m.** **½ D: Gene Kelly. Gene Kelly, Barbara Laage, Michael Redgrave, Bobby Clark, Brigitte Fossey. Two single parents—American Kelly and Frenchwoman Laage—are drawn together when their children run away from school together. Pleasant but minor family fare, enhanced by location filming in French countryside.

Happy, Texas (1999) **C-99m.** *** D: Mark Illsley. Jeremy Northam, Steve Zahn, William H. Macy, Ally Walker, Illeana Douglas, M.C. Gainey, Ron Perlman, Paul Dooley, Mo Gaffney. Engaging comedy about two prison escapees who steal a van and assume the identities of its owners, gay partners who stage kiddie talent contests. Holed up in a small Texas town, they're forced to assume those lives while getting more involved with the locals than they ever intended. Shot on a shoestring, but it doesn't show; Zahn is a comic standout in the first-rate cast. [PG-13]▼◗

Happy Thieves, The (1962) **88m.** **½ D: George Marshall. Rex Harrison, Rita Hayworth, Joseph Wiseman, Gregoire Aslan, Alida Valli. Sad pairing of star duo, out of place in museum theft caper, set in Spain.

Happy Time, The (1952) **94m.** **½ D: Richard Fleischer. Charles Boyer, Louis Jourdan, Bobby Driscoll, Marsha Hunt, Kurt Kasznar, Linda Christian, Marcel Dalio, Jeanette Nolan. Pleasant nostalgia dealing with everyday events in life of a typical family, set in 1920s Canada.

Happy Together (1989) **C-102m.** ** D: Mel Damski. Patrick Dempsey, Helen Slater, Dan Schneider, Marius Weyers, Barbara Babcock, Brad Pitt. Slight, predictable romantic comedy in which college students Dempsey and Slater are accidentally paired as roommates. You can just guess how this one turns out. [PG-13]▼●

Happy Together (1997-Hong Kong) **C/B&W-97m.** **½ D: Wong Kar-Wai. Leslie Cheung, Tony Leung Chiu-wai, Chang Chen. Polished production overshadows a predictable, paper-thin chronicle of a deeply troubled relationship between a constantly bickering Hong Kong gay couple in Buenos Aires. The filmmaker won a Best Director prize at Cannes for this, but pointedly the script did not.▼●◗

Happy Years, The (1950) **C-110m.** *** D: William Wellman. Dean Stockwell, Scotty Beckett, Darryl Hickman, Leo G. Carroll, Margalo Gillmore, Leon Ames. High-spirited boy in turn-of-the-century prep school finds he has trouble fitting in. Familiar comedy-drama, adapted from Owen Johnson's *Lawrenceville Stories*, is hardly typical Wellman fare, but well enough done. Robert Wagner makes his film debut.

Harbor Lights (1963) **68m.** BOMB D: Maury Dexter. Kent Taylor, Jeff Morrow, Miriam Colon, Allan Sague. Cheap film of intrigue, with B picture perennial Taylor. Congratulations to anyone who can find some relation between title and what goes on in film. CinemaScope.

Harbor of Missing Men (1950) **60m.** *½ D: R. G. Springsteen. Richard Denning, Barbra Fuller, Steven Geray, George Zucco, Ray Teal, Percy Helton. Unsparkling Republic Pictures programmer with Denning innocently involved with jewel smuggling.

Hardbodies (1984) **C-87m.** BOMB D: Mark Griffiths. Grant Cramer, Gary Wood, Michael Rapport, Sorrells Pickard, Teal Roberts, Roberta Collins, Courtney Gaines, Joyce Jameson. Three middle-aged clods rent a beach house and hire young stud Cramer to teach them how to score. An amateurish mess; even the girl-watching palls after ten minutes or so. Made for cable TV, but released to theaters first. Followed by a sequel. [R]▼●

Hardbodies 2 (1986) **C-95m.** BOMB D: Mark Griffiths. Brad Zutaut, Fabiana Udenio, James Karen, Alba Francesca, Roberta Collins. Topless tease about the daily misfortunes of an American film crew shooting an inane romance in Greece; has there ever been another time in film history when the idea of a sequel to something called HARDBODIES would have been discussed? Still, if you're partial to airplane commode jokes . . . [R]▼●

Hard-Boiled (1992-Hong Kong) **C-126m.** *** D: John Woo. Chow Yun-Fat, Tony Leung, Teresa Mo, Philip Chan, Anthony Wong, Kwan Hoi-Shan, A-Lung. Stylish, ultra-violent story of police inspector (Yun-Fat) who teams up with a mysterious hit man (Leung) to stop a gang of arms dealers. Standard plot of revenge and male bonding is springboard for unbelievable action sequences that are bloody, comic, and hypnotic. Yun-Fat is a perfectly assured hero, and director Woo (who wrote the original story) appears as a bartender.▼●◗

Hard Boiled Mahoney (1947) **63m.** **½ D: William Beaudine. Leo Gorcey, Huntz Hall, Bobby Jordan, Gabriel Dell, Billy Benedict, David Gorcey, Teala Loring, Dan Seymour, Bernard Gorcey, Betty Compson. The Bowery Boys do the sleuth bit, probing a phony fortune-teller racket in this mix of farce and mystery.▼

Hard Bounty (1995) **C-89m.** ** D: Jim Wynorski. Matt McCoy, Kelly LeBrock, John Terlesky, Felicity Waterman, Jay Richardson, Ross Hagen, Kimberly Kelley. Languid, corpse-laden Western, in which whore LeBrock and her entourage saddle up and seek revenge after tragedy strikes. McCoy is an Eastwoodesque bounty hunter known as The Holy Ghost. Western addicts might go for it; others beware. [R]▼◗

Hard Choices (1986) **C-90m.** **½ D: Rick King. Margaret Klenck, Gary McCleery, John Seitz, John Sayles, John Snyder, Martin Donovan, Spalding Gray. Teenager jailed for innocent involvement in a robbery and shooting is befriended by a young female social worker, who has more problems of her own than she cares to admit. Interesting independently produced feature loses its footing as story progresses; strongest asset is Sayles' off-handed performance as the bad guy. Made in 1984. ▼

Hard Contract (1969) **C-107m.** **½ D: S. Lee Pogostin. James Coburn, Lee Remick, Lilli Palmer, Burgess Meredith, Patrick Magee, Sterling Hayden, Karen Black. Hired killer Coburn starts to have self-doubts when a woman (Remick) humanizes him. Film is too concerned with making an "important statement" to become particularly entertaining or involving. Panavision. [PG]

Hardcore (1979) **C-108m.** **½ D: Paul Schrader. George C. Scott, Peter Boyle, Season Hubley, Dick Sargent, Leonard Gaines, David Nichols. Calvinistic Midwesterner Scott (in powerful performance) searches for teenage daughter who's inexplicably dropped out. He's heartsick after viewing porno film starring her, and his journey into netherworld of prostitution and porn is at times fascinating, sad, and repellent. Marred by unbelievable conclusion. [R]▼●

Hard Country (1981) **C-104m.** **½ D: David Greene. Jan-Michael Vincent, Kim Basinger, Michael Parks, Gailard Sartain, Tanya Tucker, Ted Neeley, Daryl Hannah, Richard Moll. Good ole boy Vincent works all day, parties all night; his girlfriend (Basinger) wants to marry him, but also wants out of Texas. Overshadowed by URBAN COWBOY, but not bad and done with conviction. Music by Michael Martin Murphey. Film debuts of Basinger and Nashville star Tucker. [PG]▼●

Hard Day's Night, A (1964-British) **85m.** **** D: Richard Lester. John Lennon, Paul McCartney, George Harrison, Ringo Starr, Wilfrid Brambell, Norman Rossington, John Junkin, Victor Spinetti, Anna Quayle. First Beatles film is director Lester's idea of a typical day in the group's life. He lets his imagination run wild; result is a visual delight, with many Beatles songs on the soundtrack (including "Can't Buy Me Love," "And I Love Her," "I Should Have Known Better," and the title tune). Original screenplay by Alun Owen. Reissued in 1982 with a short prologue. ▼●◗

Hard Driver SEE: **Last American Hero, The**

Hard Drivin' SEE: **Thunder in Carolina**

Hard Eight (1997) **C-101m.** *** D: Paul Thomas Anderson. Philip Baker Hall, John C. Reilly, Gwyneth Paltrow, Samuel L. Jackson, Phillip Seymour Hoffman. Spare but accomplished Nevada mood piece about a minor gambling pro who, for reasons that remain tantalizingly obscure for three-fourths of the movie's length, elects to tutor a much younger man in eking out a minimal living "working" casinos. Punctuated by sporadic and deftly timed spurts of violence; Paltrow is successfully cast against type as a cocktail waitress and sometime hooker with no brains at her disposal. Super 35. [R]▼●◗

Harder They Come, The (1973-Jamaican) **C-103m.** *** D: Perry Henzell. Jimmy Cliff, Janet Barkley, Carl Bradshaw, Ras Daniel Hartman, Bobby Charlton. Country-boy Cliff comes to Kingston to make it as a singer; ironically, it isn't until he turns to a life of crime that his record starts to climb the charts. Crude but powerful film almost single-handedly launched reggae music's popularity in America; still a major cult favorite. Terrific song score includes "You Can Get It If You Really Want," "Many Rivers to Cross," title tune. [R]▼●

Harder They Fall, The (1956) **109m.** ***½ D: Mark Robson. Humphrey Bogart, Rod Steiger, Jan Sterling, Mike Lane, Max Baer, Edward Andrews. Bogart's last feature casts him as cynical sportswriter-turned-press agent who realizes for the first time how badly prizefighters are manipulated by their unfeeling managers. Powerful drama by Budd Schulberg.▼

Hard, Fast and Beautiful (1951) **79m.** ** D: Ida Lupino. Claire Trevor, Sally Forrest, Carleton Young, Robert Clarke, Kenneth Patterson. Domineering mother pushes daughter into world of competitive tennis. Straightforward story, awkwardly filmed (and acted) at times. Director Lupino and Robert Ryan make cameo appearances.

Hard Feelings (1981-Canadian) **C-110m.** *** D: Daryl Duke. Carl Marotte, Charlaine Woodard, Grand Bush, Vincent Buffano, Allan Katz, Lisa Langlois. Intelligent, entertaining, moving tale of young, confused Marotte, his problems at home and school and friendship with a straightforward black girl (appealingly played by Woodard). Set in 1963, with good juxtaposition of white suburban and black urban cultures.

Hard Knocks (1980-Australian) **C-85m.** *** D: Don McLennan. Tracey Mann, John Arnold, Bill Hunter, Max Cullen, Tony Barry. Gritty, powerful drama centering on the efforts of ex-con Mann to straighten out her life, highlighted by a brilliant, multifaceted lead performance.▼

Hardly Working (1981) **C-91m.** ** D: Jerry Lewis. Jerry Lewis, Susan Oliver, Roger C. Carmel, Deanna Lund, Harold J. Stone, Steve Franken, Buddy Lester. Jerry's "comeback" (filmed in Florida in 1979) is typical lamebrain comedy (about an unemployed circus clown who bumbles from one job to another), but an older Jerry wavers between playing the oafish kid of yore and a more "mature" character. Not a very good movie; the opening montage from earlier films is much funnier than anything that follows. Trimmed from European release length. [PG]▼

Hard Man, The (1957) **C-80m.** ** D: George Sherman. Guy Madison, Lorne Greene, Valerie French, Trevor Bardette. Madison is earnest sheriff who falls in love with murdered rancher's widow.

Hard Promises (1992) **C-95m.** *½ D: Martin Davidson. Sissy Spacek, William Petersen, Brian Kerwin, Mare Winningham, Jeff Perry, Olivia Burnette, Peter MacNicol, Ann Wedgeworth, Amy Wright, Lois Smith. Petersen gets the invitation to ex-wife Spacek's new marriage one day before the ceremony, and rushes home to small Texas town to disrupt the proceedings. Surprisingly unpleasant comedy, with Petersen's loutish behavior in the establishing scenes mitigating against any potential fun. Petersen also produced. Rip Torn (Spacek's cousin) appears unbilled. [PG] ▼●

Hard Rain (1998) **C-96m.** **½ D: Mikael Salomon. Morgan Freeman, Christian Slater, Randy Quaid, Minnie Driver, Ed Asner, Michael Goorjian, Mark Rolston, Richard Dysart, Betty White. As a small Midwest town disappears under rising flood waters, a criminal gang headed by Freeman tries to catch armored car guard Slater, who's hidden the money they're after. The cast is above average, the effects are impressive, and the setting is certainly unusual, but a routine script barely keeps this afloat. Super 35. [R] ▼●◗

Hard Ride, The (1971) **C-93m.** **½ D: Burt Topper. Robert Fuller, Sherry Bain, Tony Russel, Marshall Reed, Biff Elliot, William Bonner. Ex-sergeant Fuller accompanies the body of a black buddy home from Vietnam and tries to persuade the vet's white sweetheart and the Indian leader of his motorcycle gang to attend his funeral. Not just another cycle flick, and not bad. [PG]▼

Hard Target (1993) **C-94m.** **½ D: John Woo. Jean-Claude Van Damme, Lance Henriksen, Arnold Vosloo, Yancy Butler, Kasi Lemmons, Wilford Brimley, Chuck Pfarrer. Acclaimed action-director Woo's U.S. debut is a disappointing thriller featuring Van Damme as a sailor aiding hard-luck veterans being exploited by sadistic Henriksen (who by now can play this kind of role in his sleep). Not bad of its type, but doesn't match Woo's highly touted Hong Kong–made efforts. [R]▼●◗

Hard Ticket to Hawaii (1987) **C-96m.** ** D: Andy Sidaris. Dona Speir, Hope Marie Carlton, Ronn Moss, Harold Diamond, Rodrigo Obregon, Cynthia Brimhill, Patty Duffek, Wolf Larson. Typical Andy Sidaris mix of action, beautiful scenery, and buxom bimbos baring their breasts. The story? Something about female undercover agents running a sting operation that gets them in hot water with druglords. Does anyone *care* about the story? Followed by PICASSO TRIGGER. [R]▼

Hard Times (1975) **C-97m.** *** D: Walter Hill. Charles Bronson, James Coburn, Jill Ireland, Strother Martin, Maggie Blye, Michael McGuire. Bronson is a tight-lipped streetfighter and Coburn is the sharpster who arranges his bare-knuckled bouts in 1930s New Orleans. Colorful (but violent) entertainment. Hill's directorial debut. Panavision. [PG—edited from original R rating]▼●◗

Hard to Get (1938) **80m.** *** D: Ray Enright. Dick Powell, Olivia de Havilland, Charles Winninger, Allen Jenkins, Bonita Granville, Penny Singleton. Good variation on spoiled-rich-girl-meets-poor-but-hardworking-boy idea. Winninger, as Olivia's wealthy father, and Singleton, as their maid, are hilarious. Film is full of great supporting comics (Grady Sutton, Thurston Hall, Arthur Housman, etc.), and includes "You Must Have Been a Beautiful Baby."

Hard to Handle (1933) **78m.** **½ D: Mervyn LeRoy. James Cagney, Mary Brian, Ruth Donnelly, Allen Jenkins, Emma Dunn, Claire Dodd, Robert McWade. Cagney sparkles in this otherwise so-so Depression-era comedy as a fast-talking promoter/hustler who courts pretty Brian; Donnelly is aces as her mom. The "Grapefruit Acres" and diet schemes are homages of sorts to Cagney's legendary scene with Mae Clarke in PUBLIC ENEMY.

Hard to Hold (1984) **C-93m.** *½ D: Larry Peerce. Rick Springfield, Janet Eilber, Patti Hansen, Albert Salmi, Bill Mumy. Pampered rock star collides (literally) with spirited young woman who doesn't know—or care—who he is . . . so naturally he falls in love with her. Tiresome romance designed as star vehicle for teen idol Springfield, and retitled "Hard to Watch" by some wags. [PG—edited from original R rating]▼●

Hard to Kill (1990) **C-95m.** ** D: Bruce Malmuth. Steven Seagal, Kelly LeBrock, Bill Sadler, Frederick Coffin, Bonnie Burroughs, Zachary Rosencrantz, Dean Norris. Police detective Seagal uncovers a major political corruption ring and is shot and left for dead; when he awakens from a seven-year coma, he's ripe for revenge. Full of the usual violence and chases for this genre, but Seagal is fun to watch. LeBrock, who nurses him back to health, was then the real-life Mrs. Seagal. [R] ▼●◗

Hard Traveling (1985) **C-107m.** **½ D: Dan Bessie. J. E. Freeman, Ellen Geer, Barry Corbin, James Gammon, Jim Haynie. Occasionally touching but ultimately disappointing drama about a gentle, decent, but uneducated and disadvantaged man (Freeman) who finds love and stability with widow Geer, but commits murder when unable to support her. Done in by too many flashbacks. Based on the novel *Bread and a Stone* by Alvah Bessie, father of the director. [PG]▼

Hardware (1990) **C-92m.** ** D: Richard Stanley. Dylan McDermott, Stacy Travis, John Lynch, Iggy Pop, William Hootkins, Mark Northover. Somewhere in the post-nuke future, desert scavenger McDermott presents some android remains to Travis; eventually, the stuff rekindles what is apparently its life mission—to destroy all living things (and the Travis pad, besides). Surprisingly well made, but recalls many earlier (and better) films. Heavy violence nearly earned this an X rating, before it was trimmed. [R]▼●

Hard Way, The (1942) **109m.** *** D: Vincent Sherman. Ida Lupino, Dennis Morgan, Joan Leslie, Jack Carson, Gladys George, Julie Bishop. Intriguing but artificial story of strong-willed Lupino pushing younger sister Leslie into show business career. Holds up until improbable finale, although it seems unlikely that Broadway would cheer Leslie as the greatest discovery of the age. Morgan and Carson (in first of several teamings) match Lupino's fine performance. ▼●

Hard Way, The (1991) **C-111m.** **½ D: John Badham. Michael J. Fox, James Woods, Stephen Lang, Annabella Sciorra, Penny Marshall, John Capodice, Luis Guzman, LL Cool J, Delroy Lindo, Christina Ricci, Karen Lynn Gorney. Long, loud, loose cannon of a movie about a spoiled-brat Hollywood star who attaches himself to a reckless N.Y.C. street cop to prepare for his next movie role. Some laughs, lots of action, but it all goes out of control. Panavision. [R]▼●◗

Hardys Ride High, The (1939) **80m.** **½ D: George B. Seitz. Lewis Stone, Mickey Rooney, Cecilia Parker, Fay Holden, Ann Rutherford, Sara Haden, Virginia Grey, Marsha Hunt. Financial troubles abound when the family inherits a large estate and enters the world of the nouveau riche. Haden gets some juicy scenes in this *Andy Hardy* series entry.

Harem (1985-French) **C-113m.** *½ D: Arthur Joffe. Nastassja Kinski, Ben Kingsley, Dennis Goldson, Zohra Segal, Michel Robin, Julette Simpson. Thin, boring drama about Arab prince Kingsley, who kidnaps Kinski and adds her to his harem. Solid production values can't take the place of a coherent scenario and fully fleshed-out characterizations. Panavision.▼●

Harem Girl (1952) **70m.** ** D: Edward Bernds. Joan Davis, Peggie Castle, Arthur Blake, Minerva Urecal. Wacky Davis does her best to enliven slim vehicle about her substituting for a princess.

Harlan County, U.S.A. (1977) **C-103m.** ***½ D: Barbara Kopple. Gripping, human documentary (an Academy Award winner) about the strike of Kentucky mine workers against the Eastover Mining Company, a subsidiary of Duke Power. Memorable scene of miner and Brooklyn cop having a "conversation." [PG]▼

Harlem Diary (1995) **C/B&W-96m.** **½ D: Jonathan Stack. Nine young Harlem residents, ranging in age from 12 to 26, tell their life stories, with their own video camera chronicling the ups and downs, challenges and triumphs, as they move on the rocky path toward adulthood. Interesting documentary approach showing the struggles of a group of young people trying to survive in the projects. Produced by the Discovery Channel but given a limited release in theaters before getting TV exposure. Uneven but worthwhile. ▼●

Harlem Globetrotters, The (1951) **80m.** ** D: Phil Brown. Thomas Gomez, Dorothy Dandridge, Bill Walker, Angela Clarke. Vehicle built around famed basketball team, with a few romantic interludes.

Harlem Nights (1989) **C-115m.** ** D: Eddie Murphy. Eddie Murphy, Richard Pryor, Redd Foxx, Danny Aiello, Michael Lerner, Della Reese, Berlinda Tolbert, Stan Shaw, Jasmine Guy, Lela Rochon, Arsenio

Hall, Robin Harris. Proprietor of an after-hours club in 1930s Harlem (Pryor) and his adopted son (Murphy) try standing up to a white mobster determined to cut in on their take or put them out of business. Murphy's debut as writer-director is skimpily scripted and completely devoid of energy. Even Pryor's effortless charisma can't breathe much life into this one. [R]▼●

Harlequin (1980-Australian) **C-96m.** **½ D: Simon Wincer. Robert Powell, David Hemmings, Carmen Duncan, Broderick Crawford, Gus Mercurio, Alan Cassell. Faith-healer Powell helps politician Hemmings's son, who has leukemia; however, his wife (Duncan) is also attracted to the healer. Middling drama updating story of Rasputin, Nicholas, and Alexandra. Retitled DARK FORCES. Panavision.[PG]▼

Harley Davidson & the Marlboro Man (1991) **C-99m.** *½ D: Simon Wincer. Mickey Rourke, Don Johnson, Chelsea Field, Daniel Baldwin, Giancarlo Esposito, Vanessa Williams, Tom Sizemore. Another title in search of a movie. Drifter Rourke and onetime rodeo cowboy Johnson rob a bank to help their pal, whose Rock 'n' Roll Bar and Grill is about to be closed by strong-armed creditors. Moderately futuristic comic-adventure moves fast enough, but even some unexpectedly silly encounters can't distinguish it. Touted in the studio press material as "the lighter side of Mickey Rourke." [R]▼●

Harlow (1965) **C-125m.** **½ D: Gordon Douglas. Carroll Baker, Peter Lawford, Red Buttons, Michael Connors, Raf Vallone, Angela Lansbury, Martin Balsam, Leslie Nielsen. Slick, colorful garbage will hold your interest, but doesn't ring true. Baker could never match the real Harlow, but Vallone and Lansbury are good as her stepfather and mother. Rushed through production to compete with the slipshod Carol Lynley version. Panavision.▼

Harlow (1965) **109m.** ** D: Alex Segal. Carol Lynley, Efrem Zimbalist, Jr., Barry Sullivan, Hurd Hatfield, Ginger Rogers, Hermione Baddeley, Lloyd Bochner, Audrey Totter, John Williams, Robert Strauss. Amateurish off-the-cuff tedium loosely based on screen star of the 1930s. Rogers as Mama Harlow is best. This quickie production made news in 1965 because it was produced in an unusual manner: staged as a live television show, and recorded as a kinescope.

Harmonists, The (1997-German-Austrian) **C-116m.** *** D: Joseph Vilsmaier. Ben Becker, Heino Ferch, Ulrich Noethen, Heinrich Schafmeister, Max Tidof, Kai Wiesinger, Meret Becker, Katja Riemann. Straightforward telling of a fascinating story about the formation of an innovative vocal group whose enormous popularity in late 1920s–early '30s Germany almost seems impervious to growing Nazi dictums—but inevitably runs afoul of the new government, as three of the singers are Jewish. The same story was chronicled in a German documentary, THE COMEDIAN HARMONISTS, which was this film's title in Europe. Super 35. [R]▼

Harold and Maude (1972) **C-90m.** ***½ D: Hal Ashby. Bud Cort, Ruth Gordon, Vivian Pickles, Cyril Cusack, Charles Tyner, Ellen Geer. Black comedy focuses on loving relationship between 20-year-old Cort, who's obsessed with death, and 79-year-old swinger Gordon. Dismissed at time of release, this has become a cult favorite, and the cornerstone of writer Colin Higgins' reputation. Cort's phony suicides are hilarious. Music by Cat Stevens. [PG]▼●

Harold Lloyd's World of Comedy (1962) **94m.** *** Compiled by Harold Lloyd. Harold Lloyd, Bebe Daniels, Mildred Davis. Delightful comedy scenes show why Lloyd was so popular in the 1920s. Highlights include classic building-climbing episode and other great sight gags. A real gem.

Harold Robbins' The Betsy SEE: **Betsy, The**

Harper (1966) **C-121m.** ***½ D: Jack Smight. Paul Newman, Lauren Bacall, Julie Harris, Shelley Winters, Robert Wagner, Janet Leigh, Arthur Hill, Pamela Tiffin, Robert Webber, Strother Martin, Harold Gould. High-grade action-mystery has Newman as private eye hired by Bacall to investigate disappearance of her husband; blowsy Winters, frustrated Harris are involved in fast-paced, sophisticated yarn. Screenplay by William Goldman, from Ross Macdonald's *The Moving Target.* Sequel: THE DROWNING POOL. Panavision.▼●

Harper Valley P.T.A. (1978) **C-102m.** ** D: Richard Bennett. Barbara Eden, Ronny Cox, Nanette Fabray, Susan Swift, Ron Masak, Louis Nye, Pat Paulsen, Audrey Christie, John Fiedler, Bob Hastings. Bubblegum comedy from hit Jeannie C. Riley song about small-town mother who arouses local wrath for her free-thinking ways, retaliates with series of elaborate revenges. Old pros eke some chuckles out of threadbare material. Later a TV series. [PG]▼

Harp of Burma SEE: **Burmese Harp, The**

Harrad Experiment, The (1973) **C-88m.** **½ D: Ted Post. Don Johnson, James Whitmore, Tippi Hedren, B. Kirby, Jr. (Bruno Kirby), Laurie Walters, Robert Middleton, Victoria Thompson. Fair adaptation of offbeat best-seller by Robert Rimmer in which experimental coed college pushes policy of sexual freedom. Two pairs of relationships singled out as in book, but film actually should've been longer! Improvisational group Ace Trucking Co. appears as itself. Melanie Griffith (Hedren's daughter) was an extra in this—at age 14. Look for young Gregory Harrison. Sequel: HARRAD SUMMER. [R]▼

Harrad Summer (1974) **C-103m.** **½

D: Steven H. Stern. Richard Doran, Victoria Thompson, Laurie Walters, Robert Reiser, Bill Dana, Marty Allen. Fair sequel to THE HARRAD EXPERIMENT, about sex-education school for young students, which sends them home, where they can apply what they've learned. Aka STUDENT UNION. [R]▼

Harriet Craig (1950) **94m.** *** D: Vincent Sherman. Joan Crawford, Wendell Corey, Lucile Watson, Allyn Joslyn, Ellen Corby. Remake of CRAIG'S WIFE is well cast, with Crawford in title role of perfectionist wife who'll stop at nothing to have her house and life run as she wishes.▼

Harriet the Spy (1996) **C-101m.** **½ D: Bronwen Hughes. Michelle Trachtenberg, Vanessa Lee Chester, Gregory Smith, Rosie O'Donnell, J. Smith-Cameron, Robert Joy, Eartha Kitt. Young girl is encouraged by her eccentric nanny (O'Donnell) to keep a journal of everything she sees, which eventually gets her into trouble with friends and foes alike. Gets lost somewhere in the middle, but makes an impressive recovery in the final third, when an insightful look at childhood relationships comes to the fore. Filmed mostly in Canada. Based on the popular juvenile novel by Louise Fitzhugh. [PG]▼●

Harrison Bergeron SEE: **Kurt Vonnegut's Harrison Bergeron**

Harry and Son (1984) **C-117m.** ** D: Paul Newman. Paul Newman, Robby Benson, Joanne Woodward, Ellen Barkin, Wilford Brimley, Judith Ivey, Ossie Davis, Morgan Freeman. Newman directed, coproduced and cowrote this contrived, meandering drama about the relationship between a widower father (who's just lost his job—and his self-respect) and son (who hasn't gotten his life in order yet). Newman isn't really convincing as the old man; Benson has played the younger role a bit too often. [PG]▼●

Harry and the Hendersons (1987) **C-110m.** **½ D: William Dear. John Lithgow, Melinda Dillon, Margaret Langrick, Joshua Rudoy, Kevin Peter Hall, David Suchet, Lainie Kazan, Don Ameche, M. Emmet Walsh. Family encounters a Bigfoot-type monster in the woods and takes it home, thinking it's dead. When it comes alive, the family finds itself becoming attached to the hairy fellow. Amusing but fatally overlong, this sweet-natured variation on E.T. THE EXTRA-TERRESTRIAL runs hot and cold; best recommended for kids. Lithgow is terrific as always. Rick Baker's makeup earned an Academy Award. Later a TV series. [PG]▼●

Harry and Tonto (1974) **C-115m.** *** D: Paul Mazursky. Art Carney, Ellen Burstyn, Chief Dan George, Geraldine Fitzgerald, Larry Hagman, Arthur Hunnicutt, Joshua Mostel, Melanie Mayron, Herbert Berghof, Barbara Rhoades. An old man takes a cross-country trip with his cat as companion. Art Carney won an Oscar for his performance in this bittersweet, episodic comedy. [R]▼

Harry and Walter Go to New York (1976) **C-123m.** ** D: Mark Rydell. James Caan, Elliott Gould, Diane Keaton, Michael Caine, Charles Durning, Lesley Ann Warren, Val Avery, Jack Gilford, Carol Kane. Lavish but lopsided period farce with Caan and Gould as low-grade vaudevillians in the 1890s who wind up trying their luck as safecrackers in N.Y. Spirited but strenuous comedy misses the mark. Nice art direction by Harry Horner. Panavision. [PG]▼

Harry Black and the Tiger (1958-British) **C-107m.** BOMB D: Hugo Fregonese. Stewart Granger, Barbara Rush, Anthony Steel, I. S. Johar. Moldy jungle film tangled in the underbrush, with confusing flashbacks. Filmed in India. Sorry, Harry. CinemaScope.▼

Harry in Your Pocket (1973) **C-103m.** *** D: Bruce Geller. James Coburn, Michael Sarrazin, Trish Van Devere, Walter Pidgeon. Engaging story of group of superpickpockets and how they prey upon innocent victims. Pidgeon steals the film as sleazy professional crook.

Harry's Machine SEE: **Hollywood Harry**

Harry's War (1981) **C-98m.** **½ D: Kieth Merrill. Edward Herrmann, Geraldine Page, Karen Grassle, David Ogden Stiers, Salome Jens, Elisha Cook. Easygoing postman Herrmann battles the IRS after his aunt (Page) is unfairly billed for $190,000 in back taxes. Capra-esque one-man-against-the-bureaucracy tale is sometimes touching but mostly overbaked. Herrmann performs earnestly; Merrill also wrote the screenplay. [PG]▼

Harry Tracy, Desperado (1982-Canadian) **C-100m.** **½ D: William A. Graham. Bruce Dern, Helen Shaver, Michael C. Gwynne, Gordon Lightfoot. Saga of outlaw who lives by his own moral code. Laid-back but worthwhile for Dern's fine performance and vivid recreation of Western life at the turn of the century. [PG]▼

Harum Scarum (1965) **C-86m.** **½ D: Gene Nelson. Elvis Presley, Mary Ann Mobley, Fran Jeffries, Michael Ansara, Jay Novello, Philip Reed, Theo Marcuse, Billy Barty. Visiting the Middle East gives usual Presley musical formula a change of scenery, via back-lot desert locations.▼●

Harvest (1937-French) **127m.** **** D: Marcel Pagnol. Gabriel Gabrio, Orane Demazis, Fernandel, Edouard Delmont, Henri Poupon. Simple, stark tale of peasants Gabrio and Demazis struggling against all odds to till the land and give life to the earth. Magnificent, with Fernandel memorable as Demazis' comical husband.▼

Harvey (1950) **104m.** ***½ D: Henry Koster. James Stewart, Josephine Hull, Peggy Dow, Charles Drake, Cecil Kellaway, Victoria Horne, Jesse White, Wallace Ford, Ida Moore. Stewart gives one of his best performances as tippler Elwood P. Dowd, whose companion is a six-foot invisible rabbit named Harvey (actually, he's 6 feet, 3½ inches). Hull won Oscar as distraught sister. Mary Chase and Oscar Brodney adapted Chase's Pulitzer Prize-winning play. Hull, Horne, and White recreate their Broadway roles.▼●

Harvey Girls, The (1946) **C-101m.** *** D: George Sidney. Judy Garland, Ray Bolger, John Hodiak, Angela Lansbury, Preston Foster, Virginia O'Brien, Marjorie Main, Kenny Baker, Cyd Charisse, Catherine McLeod. Westward expansion brings with it Fred Harvey's railroad station restaurants, and proper young waitresses who have civilizing influence on rowdy communities. Silly script made entertaining by good cast and a few musical highlights (like Oscar-winning "On the Atchison, Topeka, and the Santa Fe").▼●

Harvey Middleman, Fireman (1965) **C-75m.** ** D: Ernest Pintoff. Gene Troobnick, Hermione Gingold, Patricia Harty, Arlene Golonka, Will MacKenzie, Charles Durning. Low-key comedy about mildmannered fireman trying to coordinate fantasy and real life; amiable but unfocused film was animator Pintoff's first live-action feature.

Has Anybody Seen My Gal? (1952) **C-89m.** **½ D: Douglas Sirk. Charles Coburn, Piper Laurie, Rock Hudson, Gigi Perreau, Lynn Bari, William Reynolds, Larry Gates, Skip Homeier. Pleasant, lightweight 1920s nostalgia about rich old Coburn planning to leave his fortune to the family of a woman who turned down his marriage proposal years earlier. Coburn's performance is the whole show; look fast for James Dean.

Hasty Heart, The (1949-British) **99m.** ***½ D: Vincent Sherman. Ronald Reagan, Patricia Neal, Richard Todd, Anthony Nicholls, Howard Crawford. Sensitive film version of John Patrick play, focusing on proud Scottish soldier who discovers he has short time to live and friendships he finally makes among his hospital mates. Remade in 1983 for cable TV.▼

Hatari! (1962) **C-159m.** ***½ D: Howard Hawks. John Wayne, Elsa Martinelli, Red Buttons, Hardy Kruger, Gerard Blain, Bruce Cabot. Marvelous lighthearted action film of wild-animal trappers in Africa, with just-right mixture of adventure and comedy. Wayne is at his best. Notable Henry Mancini score. Filmed in Tanganyika; title is Swahili for "Danger!"▼●

Hatchet for the Honeymoon (1971-Italian-Spanish) **C-93m.** **½ D: Mario Bava. Stephen Forsyth, Dagmar Lassander, Laura Betti, Gerard Tichy, Femi Benussi. Characteristic Bava horror thriller: strong on vivid imagery, shot in fluid, cinematic style, with a screwy, hard-to-follow plot about a madman who murders brides, while haunted by the ghost of his own wife. [PG]▼

Hatchet Man, The (1932) **74m.** **½ D: William Wellman. Edward G. Robinson, Loretta Young, Dudley Digges, Blanche Frederici, Leslie Fenton. Fascinating yarn about Chinatown tongs, and Robinson's attempts to Americanize himself. Potent melodrama, once you get past obvious barrier of Caucasian cast.

Hatchet Murders, The SEE: **Deep Red**

Hate (1995-French) **95m.** *** D: Mathieu Kassovitz. Vincent Cassel, Hubert Kounde, Said Taghaoui, Karim Belkadra, Edouard Montoute. Two-fisted tale of three young hoods (an Arab, a Jew, and a black), living in the projects outside of Paris, who seek retribution when their best friend is beaten into a coma by the cops. Basically an anti-police polemic, this is short on subtlety but still powerfully effective. Bravura camerawork is reminiscent of Spike Lee, but Kassovitz's mise-en-scène is his own and aptly reflects the alienated world of lower-class kids without keys to their own city. Winner of Best Director award at Cannes. Original title: LA HAINE. [R]▼

Hatful of Rain, A (1957) **109m.** *** D: Fred Zinnemann. Eva Marie Saint, Don Murray, Anthony Franciosa, Lloyd Nolan, Henry Silva, Gerald S. O'Loughlin, William Hickey. Realistic melodrama of the living hell dope addict Murray undergoes, and the effects on those around him; fine performances. Scripted by Michael V. Gazzo, Alfred Hayes and Carl Foreman from Gazzo's play. CinemaScope.

Hats Off (1936) **70m.** ** D: Boris Petroff. Mae Clarke, John Payne, Helen Lynd, Luis Alberni, Skeets Gallagher, Franklin Pangborn. Minor musical about the travails of rival press agents. The supporting actors, particularly Alberni and Gallagher, fare best here. Payne's first starring film.▼

Hatter's Castle (1941-British) **90m.** **½ D: Lance Comfort. Deborah Kerr, James Mason, Robert Newton, Emlyn Williams. Fine cast must support fair material in tale of poor man who relentlessly pursues his dream of social acceptance; from A. J. Cronin's novel.

Hatter's Ghost, The (1982-French) **C-120m.** *½ D: Claude Chabrol. Michel Serrault, Charles Aznavour, Monique Chaumette, Aurore Clement. Disappointing murder mystery from Chabrol, based on a Georges Simenon novel. Tailor Aznavour learns that nephew Serrault is a mass killer, but is too scared to inform the police. Potentially exciting thriller is badly handled.

Haunted, The (1991) **C-100m. TVM** D: Robert Mandel. Sally Kirkland, Jeffrey DeMunn, Louise Latham, Joyce Van Patten, Stephen Markle, Diane Baker, George D. Wallace. Suburban Pennsylvania family battles demonic possession after moving into a new home. Surprisingly effective thriller based on the 1988 best-seller written by the family (and Robert Curran). Above average.

Haunted Honeymoon (1940-British) **83m.** **½ D: Arthur B. Woods. Robert Montgomery, Constance Cummings, Leslie Banks, Seymour Hicks, Robert Newton, Googie Withers. Famed amateur criminologist Lord Peter Wimsey (Montgomery) marries mystery writer (Cummings) and settles down to quiet honeymoon—until murder enters the picture and demands their involvement. Montgomery miscast as Dorothy L. Sayers' witty sleuth. Originally titled BUSMAN'S HONEYMOON.

Haunted Honeymoon (1986) **C-82m.** BOMB D: Gene Wilder. Gene Wilder, Gilda Radner, Dom DeLuise, Jonathan Pryce, Paul L. Smith, Peter Vaughan, Bryan Pringle. Tediously unfunny "scare movie" farce inspired by old Bob Hope/Red Skelton comedies; set in an old dark house full of creepy people (with one great gag lifted from Fred MacMurray's MURDER, HE SAYS). When you put Dom DeLuise in drag and still can't get laughs, you know something's wrong. [PG]▼●

Haunted House of Horror, The SEE: **Horror House**

Haunted Palace, The (1963) **C-85m.** **½ D: Roger Corman. Vincent Price, Debra Paget, Lon Chaney, Jr., Frank Maxwell, Leo Gordon, Elisha Cook, Jr., John Dierkes. When a man arrives in New England town to claim family castle, he discovers the town populated by mutants and the castle under an ancestor's evil spell, which soon possesses him. Good-looking but minor film from Corman's Edgar Allan Poe cycle, although based mainly on H. P. Lovecraft's *The Strange Case of Charles Dexter Ward.* Script by Charles Beaumont. Panavision.▼●

Haunted Strangler, The (1958-British) **81m.** **½ D: Robert Day. Boris Karloff, Anthony Dawson, Elizabeth Allan, Derek Birch, Jean Kent. Offbeat yarn of mystery writer investigating case of murderer hung twenty years ago, with dismaying results. Originally titled GRIP OF THE STRANGLER.▼●◗

Haunted Summer (1988) **C-106m.** **½ D: Ivan Passer. Phillip Anglim, Laura Dern, Alice Krige, Eric Stoltz, Alex Winter. Flawed film version of Anne Edwards' novel about the fabled and emotional meeting between poets Lord Byron and Percy Shelley, novelist Mary Godwin and Dr. John Polidori in Italy in 1816. The psychedelic '60s had nothing on *this* "summer of love" and experimentation. Beautifully filmed, and better than Ken Russell's similar GOTHIC, but it's still forced and unconvincing. [R]▼●

Haunting, The (1963) **112m.** ***½ D: Robert Wise. Julie Harris, Claire Bloom, Richard Johnson, Russ Tamblyn, Lois Maxwell, Fay Compton. 90-year-old New England haunted house is setting for chosen group being introduced to the supernatural, with hair-raising results. Don't see this one alone! Filmed in England; Nelson Gidding adapted Shirley Jackson's *The Haunting of Hill House.* Remade in 1999. Panavision. ▼●

Haunting, The (1999) **C-114m.** *½ D: Jan De Bont. Liam Neeson, Catherine Zeta-Jones, Owen Wilson, Lili Taylor, Bruce Dern, Marian Seldes, Virginia Madsen. Three people are lured to a creepy mansion under false pretenses by a psychological researcher (Neeson). Incredibly dull chiller has all the special effects money can buy but no sense, no logic, and virtually no scares. Taylor's performance as a lonely woman who feels a kinship with the house is the only redeeming feature of this clunker, which has little in common with the 1963 movie or Shirley Jackson's novel, on which it's supposedly based. Panavision. [PG-13] ▼●◗

Haunting Fear (1991) **C-88m.** *½ D: Fred Olen Ray. Brinke Stevens, Jay Richardson, Jan-Michael Vincent, Karen Black, Della Sheppard, Robert Clarke, Robert Quarry, Michael Berryman. Stevens fears being buried alive, her husband has a sexy mistress, and Vincent is lurking around in the street. Odd plot tries to bring it all together, but motivation is absent. Hasty, empty film allegedly based on Poe's "Premature Burial."▼

Haunting of Julia, The (1976-British-Canadian) **C-96m.** ** D: Richard Loncraine. Mia Farrow, Keir Dullea, Tom Conti, Jill Bennett, Robin Gammell, Cathleen Nesbitt. Occult thriller about a young woman who tries to start a new life after the death of her daughter and moves into a house inhabited by a troubled spirit. A good (if familiar) start, but soon lapses into unsatisfying contrivance. From a Peter Straub story. Originally titled FULL CIRCLE. Panavision. [R]▼

Haunts (1977) **C-98m.** *** D: Herb Freed. May Britt, Cameron Mitchell, Aldo Ray, William Gray Espy, Susan Nohr. You have to stay with it to appreciate this offbeat horror pic fully, but it's well worth the effort. Writers Anne Marisse and Herb Freed and a good cast have vividly captured small-town atmosphere when a series of murders grips the countryside. As a farm woman with demons of her own, Britt gives the best performance of her erratic career. [PG]▼

Havana (1990) **C-140m.** **½ D: Sydney Pollack. Robert Redford, Lena Olin, Alan Arkin, Tomas Milian, Daniel Davis, Tony Plana, Betsy Brantley, Lise Cutter, Richard Farnsworth, Mark Rydell. No masterpiece, overly reminiscent of CASABLANCA, and a huge box-office disaster, but still unjustly maligned as a stinker. Redford (aging, but marvelous) plays a professional gambler hoping to score in the waning hours of Batista's Cuba; Olin (surprisingly stiff) is the married Swede who takes his mind off the game. Production designer's dream is very entertaining for about 90 minutes, then tails off. Similar to the underrated Richard Lester film CUBA. Raul Julia appears unbilled. [R]▼●◗

Have Rocket, Will Travel (1959) **76m.** **½ D: David Lowell Rich. The Three Stooges, Jerome Cowan, Anna Lisa, Bob Colbert. Good slapstick with the Stooges accidentally launched into space, where they meet a unicorn and become national heroes. This was the trio's first starring feature after being rediscovered on TV, though Joe DeRita had, by this time, filled the Curly/Shemp slot.▼

Having a Wild Weekend (1965-British) **91m.** **½ D: John Boorman. Dave Clark Five, Barbara Ferris, Lenny Davidson, Rick Huxley, Mike Smith, Denis Payton, David Lodge. Just as The Dave Clark Five tried to steal some of the Beatles' thunder, this fast-paced trifle tried to capture success of A HARD DAY'S NIGHT. The Five star as stuntmen who, along with a model (Ferris), search for a dream island. Songs include "Having a Wild Weekend," "Catch Us If You Can," "I Can't Stand It." Director Boorman's first film. Originally titled CATCH US IF YOU CAN.▼

Having Wonderful Crime (1945) **70m.** **½ D: A. Edward Sutherland. Pat O'Brien, George Murphy, Carole Landis, Lenore Aubert, George Zucco. Lively mystery-comedy in which a trio of friends—brash lawyer O'Brien and wise-cracking newlyweds Murphy and Landis—become involved with a magician who disappears and his mysterious assistant. Based on characters created by Craig Rice, though the film bears no relation to Rice's novel of the same name.▼

Having Wonderful Time (1938) **71m.** **½ D: Alfred Santell. Ginger Rogers, Douglas Fairbanks, Jr., Peggy Conklin, Lucille Ball, Lee Bowman, Eve Arden, Dorothea Kent, Richard (Red) Skelton, Donald Meek, Jack Carson, Allan Lane, Grady Sutton. OK film about Catskills resort hotel; Ginger wants culture on summer vacation but gets Doug instead. Arthur Kober adapted his own Broadway comedy, but the original's satiric depiction of Jewish New Yorkers is completely homogenized. Skelton sparkles in his feature debut; Dean Jagger plays Ginger's brother and Ann Miller is visible among the campers.▼●

Hav Plenty (1998) **C-92m.** *½ D: Christopher Scott Cherot. Christopher Scott Cherot, Chenoa Maxwell, Hill Harper, Tammi Katherine Jones, Betty Vaughn. Smug, self-satisfied romantic comedy about down-and-out writer who finds unexpected sparks with his best friend when he spends New Year's weekend with her crazy friends and family. Maxwell gives a truly irritating performance as the inexplicable girl of Cherot's dreams, but the writer-director-editor-star has charisma; it's his filmmaking skills that need polishing. Dopey movie-within-a-movie ending features Shemar Moore, Nia Long, TLC's Chili, The Fugees' Lauryn Hill, and Mekhi Phifer. [R]▼

Hawaii (1966) **C-171m.** *** D: George Roy Hill. Julie Andrews, Max von Sydow, Richard Harris, Torin Thatcher, Gene Hackman, Carroll O'Connor, Jocelyne LaGarde, John Cullum, George Rose, Michael Constantine. Sprawling filmization of James Michener's novel plays well on TV, where cutting actually helps. Story (adapted by Dalton Trumbo and Daniel Taradash) follows growth of Hawaii in 1800s as fierce but well-intentioned missionary tries to bring religion to the undeveloped islands. Uneven but generally entertaining epic. Originally released at 189m.; some prints 151m. Look for Bette Midler as a passenger on the Hawaii-bound ship. Sequel: THE HAWAIIANS. Panavision.▼●

Hawaiians, The (1970) **C-134m.** *** D: Tom Gries. Charlton Heston, Geraldine Chaplin, John Phillip Law, Tina Chen, Alec McCowen, Keye Luke, Mako. Sequel to HAWAII is epic narrative of seafaring Heston returning home to a restless, changing Hawaii. Film follows several decades of relationships, conflict, hardship, progress, sex, leprosy—you name it. Compelling, colorful storytelling, with outstanding performance by Chen. Panavision.[PG]

Hawks (1988-British) **C-107m.** ** D: Robert Ellis Miller. Timothy Dalton, Anthony Edwards, Janet McTeer, Camille Coduri, Jill Bennett, Sheila Hancock, Connie Booth. Heavy-handed black comedy about British lawyer Dalton and American jock Edwards, both terminally ill with cancer but still equally red-blooded; they rip off an ambulance and head for the brothels of Amsterdam for one final fling. Uneasy mixture of humor and touchy-feely emotion does not work. Barry Gibb (of the Bee Gees, who did the music) is coauthor of the story upon which this is based. [R]▼

Hawk the Slayer (1980-British) **C-93m.** *½ D: Terry Marcel. Jack Palance, John Terry, Bernard Bresslaw, Ray Charleson, Peter O'Farrell, Harry Andrews, Roy Kinnear, Ferdy Mayne. Brothers Palance and Terry vie for a magical family sword in this period costumer. Labored, with gimmicky direction.▼●

Hawmps! (1976) **C-113m.** ** D: Joe Camp. James Hampton, Christopher Connelly, Slim

Pickens, Jack Elam, Denver Pyle. Amusing idea based on real life incident: camels trained as Army mounts in Texas desert. Some comedy results, but how far can you stretch one idea? Originally released at 126m. [G]▼

Hazard (1948) **95m.** ** D: George Marshall. Paulette Goddard, Macdonald Carey, Fred Clark, Stanley Clements. Routine comedy of private-eye Carey following Goddard, falling in love in the process.

Head, The (1959-German) **92m.** ** D: Victor Trivas. Horst Frank, Karin Kernke, Michel Simon, Helmut Schmid, Dieter Eppler. Old-fashioned chiller involving head-transplants, with obligatory murders and blood-drenched revenge; extremely eerie but not very convincing.▼

Head (1968) **C-86m.** *** D: Bob Rafelson. The Monkees, Terry (Teri) Garr, Vito Scotti, Timothy Carey, Logan Ramsey, Frank Zappa, Jack Nicholson. Far-out film debut for TV rock group was written (or concocted) by Rafelson and Nicholson before they made big splash with FIVE EASY PIECES; this overlooked item is a delightful explosion of crazy ideas with no coherent plot, many old film clips, some good songs, and such unlikely guest stars as Sonny Liston and Victor Mature. Well worth seeing. [G]▼●◗

Head Above Water (1996-U.S.-British) **C-92m.** ** D: Jim Wilson. Harvey Keitel, Cameron Diaz, Craig Sheffer, Billy Zane, Shay Duffin. Black comedy–thriller about lovely substance abuser Diaz; she's married to judge Keitel, but her male friends still carry a torch for her, with disastrous consequences. Convoluted plot twists abound, but you don't really care what happens to any of these characters. Remake of a 1987 Norwegian film, PATHFINDER, itself remade as HEAD ABOVE WATER in 1994. U.S. debut on cable TV. Super 35. [PG-13]▼●

Headin' for Broadway (1980) **C-89m.** *½ D: Joseph Brooks. Rex Smith, Terri Treas, Vivian Reed, Paul Carafotes, Gene Foote. Astonishingly amateurish film by writer-director-producer-composer Brooks about four young hopefuls auditioning for a Broadway musical. Looks like a film they tried to save in the editing room; it didn't work. [PG]

Heading for Heaven (1947) **71m.** *½ D: Lewis D. Collins. Stuart Erwin, Glenda Farrell, Irene Ryan, Milburn Stone, Selmer Jackson, Janis Wilson. Soggy account of well-meaning Erwin trying to build model middle-income-bracket community, but being fleeced by racketeers.

Heading Home (1990-British) **C-88m. TVM** D: David Hare. Gary Oldman, Joely Richardson, Stephen Dillane, Stella Gonet, Michael Bryant. Absorbing reminiscence by Richardson, about the conflict she faced as a naive young woman in love with two different men. This lovely loss-of-innocence story is quirky and unpredictable, with excellent performances by the entire cast. Above average.

Headless Body in Topless Bar (1996) **C-101m.** *½ D: James Bruce. Raymond Barry, Jennifer MacDonald, Rustam Branaman, April Grace, Taylor Nichols, David Selby, Paul Williams, Biff Yeager. This "psychological dark comedy" based on the infamous 1983 *New York Post* headline is a talky character piece about an ex-con who takes the inhabitants of a topless bar hostage after killing the bartender. Might have worked better as a one-act play—or, better yet, left on the newsstand.

Headless Ghost, The (1958-British) **61m.** BOMB D: Peter Graham Scott. Richard Lyon, Liliane Sottane, David Rose, Clive Revill, Carl Bernard, Trevor Barnett. Brainless horror-comedy with students investigating a haunted castle. Dyaliscope.▼●

Headline Hunters (1955) **70m.** ** D: William Witney. Rod Cameron, Julie Bishop, Ben Cooper, Raymond Greenleaf. Uninspired tale of fledgling reporter tracking down big-city racketeers. Remake of 1940 BEHIND THE NEWS.

Headlines of Destruction (1955-French) **85m.** ** D: John Berry. Eddie Constantine, Bella Darvi, Paul Frankeur, Walter Chiari. Interesting concept poorly executed; Darvi is defense attorney involved with Constantine in trial of man accused of murder.

Head Office (1986) **C-86m.** ** D: Ken Finkleman. Judge Reinhold, Eddie Albert, Jane Seymour, Danny DeVito, Rick Moranis, Don Novello, Michael O'Donoghue, Wallace Shawn, Lori-Nan Engler. Naive Reinhold is hired by world's most powerful multinational conglomerate after his father pulls strings, falls for board chairman's renegade daughter. Episodic, wildly uneven comedy wastes good cast, though Novello, Albert, and O'Donoghue have their funny moments, Seymour some sexy ones. Panavision. [PG-13]▼

Head On (1980-Canadian) **C-98m.** ** D: Michael Grant. Sally Kellerman, Stephen Lack, John Huston, Lawrence Dane, John Peter Linton. Strange comedy-drama with Kellerman and Lack meeting after a car accident, fulfilling each other's sex fantasies acting out bizarre games. Ambitious but unsuccessful. Retitled FATAL ATTRACTION for 1985 U.S. release. [R]▼

Head Over Heels (1979) **C-97m.** **½ D: Joan Micklin Silver. John Heard, Mary Beth Hurt, Peter Riegert, Kenneth McMillan, Gloria Grahame, Nora Heflin, Griffin Dunne. Low-key story of Heard's obsession with winning back former girlfriend Hurt; the kind of film that engenders strictly personal reactions—it will either charm or annoy you. Based on Ann Beattie's novel CHILLY SCENES OF WINTER, and reissued under that name at 93m. Jazz harmonica great Toots Thielemans is prominently featured on the soundtrack. [PG]▼

Health (1979) **C-100m.** ** D: Robert Altman. Carol Burnett, Glenda Jackson, James Garner, Lauren Bacall, Diane Stilwell, Henry Gibson, Donald Moffat, Paul Dooley, Dick Cavett, Alfre Woodard. Offbeat political satire using health-food convention in Florida hotel as basis for various backroom shenanigans. Non-Altman buffs may like this more than devotees; Woodard steals the film—no easy feat considering that incredible cast—as hotel's ultra-patient manager. Shelved for two years. Title is acronym for Happiness, Energy, And Longevity Through Health. Panavision. [PG]

Hear Me Good (1957) **80m.** *½ D: Don McGuire. Hal March, Joe E. Ross, Merry Anders, Jean Willes. Trivia concerning a fixed beauty contest. VistaVision.

Hear My Song (1991-U.S.-British) **C-104m.** *** D: Peter Chelsom. Ned Beatty, Adrian Dunbar, Shirley Anne Field, Tara Fitzgerald, David McCallum, William Hootkins, Harold Berens, James Nesbitt. Wheeler-dealer nightclub owner must redeem himself with his girlfriend—and his community—by finding expatriate Irish tenor Josef Locke and bringing him back to England for an engagement. Charmingly offbeat, old-fashioned film written by its first-time feature director and leading man Dunbar, very loosely based on real-life story. If Beatty (as Locke) didn't pull off the climactic scene, it wouldn't work—but he does. [R]▼●

Hear No Evil (1993) **C-97m.** *½ D: Robert Greenwald. Marlee Matlin, D. B. Sweeney, Martin Sheen, John C. McGinley, Christina Carlisi, Greg Elam, Charley Lang, Marge Redmond. Plotline reminiscent of WAIT UNTIL DARK, except the terrorized young woman here is deaf, not blind. You can fill in the blanks. Grade-Z thriller, only partly redeemed by the presence of Matlin. [R]▼●

Hearse, The (1980) **C-100m.** ** D: George Bowers. Trish Van Devere, Joseph Cotten, David Gautreaux, Donald Hotton, Med Flory, Donald Petrie. Passably engrossing yarn right off the woman-in-distress/house-inhabited-by-spirits assembly line, with an unsatisfying conclusion. [PG]▼

Heart (1987) **C-90m.** *½ D: James Lemmo. Brad Davis, Frances Fisher, Steve Buscemi, Robinson Frank Adu. Dreary, stereotypical boxing tale about has-been fighter Davis—complete with dishonest manager—who's pitted against a rival ten years his junior. [R]▼

Heartaches (1981-Canadian) **C-93m.** **½ D: Donald Shebib. Margot Kidder, Annie Potts, Robert Carradine, Winston Rekert, George Touliatos, Guy Sanvido. Pregnant Potts abandons husband Carradine—who is not the baby's father—and becomes the unwilling buddy of man-hunting screwball Kidder. Fine lead performances spark this minor comedy. [R]▼●

Heart and Souls (1993) **C-104m.** *** D: Ron Underwood. Robert Downey, Jr., Charles Grodin, Alfre Woodard, Kyra Sedgwick, Tom Sizemore, David Paymer, Elisabeth Shue, Eric Lloyd, Bill Calvert, Lisa Lucas, Richard Portnow, B. B. King. Four disparate San Franciscans die in a bus accident in 1959, and find themselves inexorably linked with a baby who's been born at that same exact moment; what's more, only he can see and hear them. A great showcase for Downey—whose body is inhabited, at various times, by his heavenly friends—though Woodard is equally good, as usual. Fans of mushy, sentimental, old-fashioned Hollywood fantasies (like us) should enjoy this fable; others beware. Based on a 9-minute short subject by the coauthors of this script. Look fast to see Bob Newhart's son, Robert William Newhart, impersonating his dad. Panavision. [PG-13]▼●◗

Heartbeat (1946) **102m.** ** D: Sam Wood. Ginger Rogers, Jean Pierre Aumont, Adolphe Menjou, Basil Rathbone, Melville Cooper, Mikhail Rasumny, Eduardo Ciannelli, Mona Maris, Henry Stephenson. Boring remake of the French film BATTEMENT DE COEUR (1939), with Rogers sorely miscast as an 18-year-old reform school escapee who becomes a pickpocket and ends up falling for one of her victims, a handsome young diplomat (Aumont).▼

Heart Beat (1980) **C-105m.** *½ D: John Byrum. Nick Nolte, Sissy Spacek, John Heard, Ray Sharkey, Anne Dusenberry, Kent Williams, Tony Bill, Steve Allen. Hapless chronicle of the relationship between Jack Kerouac (Heard) and Carolyn (Spacek) and Neal (Nolte) Cassady. Byrum's flaky script (based more on fiction than on fact) has no continuity whatsoever. Sharkey stands out as the Allen Ginsbergesque Ira; good period score by Jack Nitzsche. Watch for John Larroquette. [R]▼

Heartbeeps (1981) **C-79m.** *½ D: Allan Arkush. Andy Kaufman, Bernadette Peters, Randy Quaid, Kenneth McMillan, Melanie Mayron, Christopher Guest, voice of Jack Carter. Two robots fall for each other in this misfired futuristic comedy. Students of makeup might want to take a peek at Stan Winston's work. Panavision. [PG]▼●

Heartbreaker (1983) **C-90m.** ** D: Frank Zuniga. Fernando Allende, Dawn Dunlap, Peter Gonzales Falcon, Michael D. Roberts, Miguel Ferrer, Pepe Serna, Rafael Campos. Chicano Allende falls for WASP Dunlap amid an ambience of custom-fitted automobiles. Lackluster independent production is annoyingly devoid of insight into the culture it depicts. Look fast for Patty "Apollonia" Kotero. [R]▼

Heartbreakers (1984) **C-98m.** **½ D:

Bobby Roth. Peter Coyote, Nick Mancuso, Carole Laure, Max Gail, James Laurenson, Carol Wayne, Kathryn Harrold, Jamie Rose. Moody, provocative film about two male friends (avant-garde artist Coyote, second-generation businessman Mancuso) seeking creative and sexual fulfillment and trying to define their relationships with others. Highly personal, occasionally insightful film invites highly personal reactions. Bull's-eye performances, great use of L.A. locations. [R]▼

Heartbreak Hotel (1988) **C-93m.** **½ D: Chris Columbus. David Keith, Tuesday Weld, Charlie Schlatter, Jacque Lynn Colton, Angela Goethals, Chris Mulkey, Karen Landry. A reliable test of your whimsy quotient, as an Ohio teen (Schlatter) kidnaps Elvis in 1972, then transports him home to the divorced mom (Weld) who's carried a torch for the King since the mid-1950s. Keith's Presley, like the entire film, is fun, though the premise is so hard to swallow that you're likely to go with this—or reject it—all the way. Pair this with WILD IN THE COUNTRY or ROCK, ROCK, ROCK for a compatible VCR double bill. [PG-13]▼●

Heartbreak Kid, The (1972) **C-104m.** *** D: Elaine May. Charles Grodin, Cybill Shepherd, Jeannie Berlin, Eddie Albert, Audra Lindley. Neil Simon's supreme comedy of embarrassment, adapted from Bruce Jay Friedman's short story "A Change of Plan." Jewish boy (Grodin) gets married (to Berlin) but meets beautiful WASP blonde (Shepherd) on honeymoon, and determines to juggle plans. Either hilarious or horrifying, depending on your point of view; directed for maximum impact by May, whose daughter plays Grodin's bride. [PG]▼●◗

Heartbreak Ridge (1986) **C-130m.** **½ D: Clint Eastwood. Clint Eastwood, Marsha Mason, Everett McGill, Moses Gunn, Eileen Heckart, Bo Svenson, Boyd Gaines, Mario Van Peebles, Arlen Dean Snyder. Eastwood is so enjoyable to watch, as a hell-raising career marine sergeant who whips a squadron of young recruits into shape, that he makes this predictable and protracted film worthwhile. But it's still pretty thin stuff and takes longer to play out than the real-life invasion of Grenada it depicts. [R]▼●

Heartburn (1986) **C-108m.** *** D: Mike Nichols. Meryl Streep, Jack Nicholson, Jeff Daniels, Maureen Stapleton, Stockard Channing, Richard Masur, Catherine O'Hara, Steven Hill, Milos Forman, Karen Akers, Anna Maria Horsford, Mercedes Ruehl, Joanna Gleason, Yakov Smirnoff, Kevin Spacey, Natasha Lyonne. Nora Ephron adapted her own best-selling (and autobiographical) book about a sophisticated couple whose marriage seems just fine until she learns he's been having an affair—while she's pregnant! Lightweight, superficial story is supercharged by two charismatic stars, who make it a must-see. Director Forman's acting debut. [R]▼●

Heart Condition (1990) **C-95m.** **½ D: James D. Perriott. Bob Hoskins, Denzel Washington, Chloe Webb, Roger E. Mosley, Ja'net Dubois, Alan Rachins, Ray Baker, Jeffrey Meek. Superficial but entertaining yarn about a crass, bigoted L.A. cop who gets a heart transplant and learns, to his dismay, that the donor was the slick black lawyer he'd been stalking. What's more, the deceased appears as a ghost/companion who wants the cop to help avenge his murder. Outlandish premise made palatable by its two dynamic leads. [R]▼●

Heart Is a Lonely Hunter, The (1968) **C-125m.** *** D: Robert Ellis Miller. Alan Arkin, Sondra Locke, Laurinda Barrett, Stacy Keach, Jr., Chuck McCann, Biff McGuire, Percy Rodriguez, Cicely Tyson, Jackie Marlowe. Heart-rending drama of a deaf mute's lonely world, and how he helps an adolescent girl struggling to find herself. Sincere adaptation of Carson McCullers' novel, set in the Deep South, benefits from moving performances—including Arkin, Locke (whose debut film this was), and comic actor McCann, in a revelatory change-of-pace part as Arkin's simple-minded mute friend. Also marked film debut for Keach. [G]▼

Heartland (1979) **C-96m.** ***½ D: Richard Pearce. Rip Torn, Conchata Ferrell, Barry Primus, Lilia Skala, Megan Folson, Amy Wright. Simple, well-told story of hearty Americans surviving the rigors of frontier life, circa 1910. Ferrell plays a young widow who accepts a job as housekeeper for dour rancher Torn in the wilds of Wyoming. Well-acted, well-filmed, and beautifully understated; based on the actual diaries of a pioneer woman. [PG]▼

Heartland Reggae (1980-Canadian) **C-87m.** BOMB D: J. P. Lewis. Bob Marley and the Wailers, Peter Tosh, Jacob Miller and the Inner Circle Band, Althea and Donna. Shoddy documentary of '78 concert commemorating a visit to Jamaica by Haile Selassie. Even the music can't save it.▼

Heart Like a Wheel (1983) **C-113m.** **½ D: Jonathan Kaplan. Bonnie Bedelia, Beau Bridges, Leo Rossi, Hoyt Axton, Bill McKinney, Anthony Edwards, Dean Paul Martin, Paul Bartel, Dick Miller, Terence Knox. Well-made but curiously uninspiring bio of race-car driver Shirley Muldowney, who had to fight sexism—and the conflict of career vs. marriage—to become a champion on the track. Bedelia's performance is outstanding, but disjointed narrative—particularly where her relationship with racer Connie Kalitta (Bridges) is concerned—is a handicap. [PG]▼●

Heart of Darkness (1994) **C-100m. TVM** D: Nicolas Roeg. Tim Roth, John Malkovich, James Fox, Patrick Ryecart, Peter Vaughan, Iman, Isaach DeBankole, Morten Faldaas. Dark and brooding adaptation (by Benedict Fitzgerald) of Joseph Conrad's novella about the hunt in the African jungles by an ivory consortium for a maverick local manager (Malkovich) who's taken to the wilds and gone mad. Story, of course, was the basis for Coppola's APOCALYPSE NOW. Made for cable. Average. ▼●

Heart of Dixie (1989) **C-95m.** *½ D: Martin Davidson. Ally Sheedy, Virginia Madsen, Phoebe Cates, Treat Williams, Don Michael Paul, Kyle Secor, Francesca Roberts, Kurtwood Smith, Richard Bradford, Barbara Babcock. Forgettable story of Alabama college sorority in the late 1950s and one girl's awakening to larger realities of life—including the mistreatment of blacks in the South. Superficial and uninvolving, to say the least. [PG]▼●

Heart of Glass (1976-German) **C-93m.** *** D: Werner Herzog. Josef Bierbichler, Stefan Autter, Clemens Scheitz, Volker Prechtel, Sonia Skiba. A glassblower has died without revealing the secret formula of his craft, and this has a profound, disturbing effect on his fellow townspeople. Thematically muddled but visually stunning; crammed with stark, graphic, beautiful images. Based on a Bavarian legend; Herzog each day put his cast into a hypnotic trance, to attempt to achieve an effect of collective hysteria.▼

Heart of Justice, The (1993) **C-100m. TVM** D: Bruno Barreto. Jennifer Connelly, Bradford Dillman, Dennis Hopper, William H. Macy, Joanna Miles, Dermot Mulroney, Keith Reddin, Eric Stoltz, Harris Yulin. Intrepid reporter Stoltz tries to find out why a rich young man shot wealthy hack writer Hopper, and then took his own life. Vincent Price relishes his gourmet role in the opening scene. Written by costar Reddin for the "Screenworks" series, and beautifully shot by Declan Quinn. Price's final role. Made for cable. Above average.

Heart of Midnight (1988) **C-93m.** *½ D: Matthew Chapman. Jennifer Jason Leigh, Peter Coyote, Gale Mayron, Sam Schacht, Denise Dummont, Frank Stallone, Brenda Vaccaro, Steve Buscemi. Psychological thriller about a young woman teetering on the edge of sanity, who inherits a seedy sex club which attracts a sick clientele. Good performance by Leigh and artsy approach to subject are minor diversions in this muddled and unpleasant film. Written by the director. [R]▼●

Heart of the Matter, The (1953-British) **105m.** *** D: George More O'Ferrall. Trevor Howard, Elizabeth Allan, Maria Schell, Denholm Elliott. Graham Greene's novel of inner and outward conflict set in Sierra Leone, with Howard as police officer on verge of mental collapse.

Heart of the Stag (1984-New Zealand) **C-91m.** ** D: Michael Firth. Bruno Lawrence, Mary Regan, Terence Cooper, Anne Flannery. Lawrence is mysterious stranger who signs on as a farmhand and disrupts incestuous relationship of Cooper and his redheaded daughter Regan. Pretentious drama benefits from good acting, tense musical score by Leonard Rosenman. [R]▼

Hearts and Armour (1982-Italian) **C-101m.** ** D: Giacomo Battiato. Tanya Roberts, Barbara De Rossi, Zeudi Araya, Rick Edwards, Leigh McCloskey, Ron Moss. Well-mounted but confusing fantasy based on the 1516 classic *Orlando Furioso* by Ludovico Ariosto. De Rossi is a sexy female warrior in knight's armor fighting in the war between Christians and Moors. American stars such as Roberts and McCloskey add little to a film (also shot in TV miniseries form) aimed at an international audience. Technovision. ▼

Hearts and Minds (1974) **C-110m.** ***½ D: Peter Davis. Oscar-winning documentary about our misguided involvement in Vietnam was political hot potato for awhile, but may rate more frequent showings now that the country has caught up with it. Packs a wallop, regardless of one's political persuasion. [R]▼●

Hearts Divided (1936) **87m.** ** D: Frank Borzage. Marion Davies, Dick Powell, Charlie Ruggles, Claude Rains, Edward Everett Horton, Arthur Treacher. Napoleon's younger brother (Powell) woos and weds an American (Davies). This lackluster musical is based on a true story, though you'd never know it. A remake of the silent GLORIOUS BETSY.

Hearts of Darkness: A Filmmaker's Apocalypse (1991) **C-96m.** ***½ D: Fax Bahr, George Hickenlooper. Top-notch documentary detailing the disaster-laden production of Francis Coppola's 1979 Vietnam epic, APOCALYPSE NOW. Expertly mixes footage shot by Eleanor Coppola (the director's wife) during the film's shooting in the Philippines and decade-later interviews with crew and cast (excluding Marlon Brando, who declined to participate). Revealing peek into the filmmaking process and a record of events during this particular film's chaotic shoot. [R]▼●

Hearts of Fire (1987) **C-95m.** BOMB D: Richard Marquand. Fiona (Flanagan), Rupert Everett, Bob Dylan, Julian Glover, Suzanne Bertish, Ian Dury, Richie Havens, Larry Lamb, Maury Chaykin. Perfectly dreadful account of the rise of a rock singer (Fiona), and her relationships with her mentors: a British pop star (Everett) and a cynical, retired rock legend (who else but Dylan). Dylan's first screen appearance since 1977's RENALDO AND CLARA; Marquand's final credit as director. This turkey played briefly in England in 1987, and was released to video in 1990. There are 19 songs on the soundtrack (but none memorable enough to raise its rating). J-D-C Scope. [R]▼●

Hearts of the West (1975) **C-102m.** *** D: Howard Zieff. Jeff Bridges, Andy Griffith, Donald Pleasence, Blythe Danner, Alan Arkin, Richard B. Shull, Herb Edelman, Alex Rocco, Marie Windsor, Dub Taylor, William Christopher. Offbeat comedy. Starry-eyed Bridges comes to 1930s Hollywood hoping to be a Western writer, winds up starring in cheap cowboy films instead. Enjoyable but low-key. [PG]▼

Hearts of the World (1918) **122m.** **½ D: D. W. Griffith. Lillian Gish, Dorothy Gish, Robert Harron, Kate Bruce, Ben Alexander, George Fawcett, George Siegmann. Griffith's epic of WW1, shot in England and France; melodramatic story of a young man gone to war, the sufferings of his family and homeland, was made as propaganda to convince America to enter WW1. Dorothy Gish has fine comedy role, young Noel Coward a small part as villager with wheelbarrow, Erich von Stroheim a lusty German. For these highlights, other good moments, worth seeing.▼●

Heartsounds (1984) **C-127m. TVM** D: Glenn Jordan. Mary Tyler Moore, James Garner, Sam Wanamaker, Wendy Crewson, David Gardner, Carl Marotte. Justifiably acclaimed weeper, a wonderfully acted version of Martha Weinman Lear's best-seller dealing with her life when her doctor-husband suffers a series of debilitating heart attacks. Fay Kanin wrote the script and Norman Lear, the author's cousin, produced. The leads give two of the best performances of their careers. Above average.

Heart To Heart (1978-French) **C-110m.** *** D: Pascal Thomas. Daniel Ceccaldi, Laurence Ligneres, Anne Caudry, Michel Galabru, Elisa Servier. Fifteen years in the life of a family, recalled by daughter-sister Caudry. Sometimes episodic, but mostly a light, cheerful, well-acted comedy.

Heat (1972) **C-100m.** *** D: Paul Morrissey. Sylvia Miles, Joe Dallesandro, Andrea Feldman, Pat Ast, Ray Vestal. Andy Warhol meets SUNSET BOULEVARD in this hot and heavy tale of unemployed actor Dallesandro taking up with faded star Miles. Even non-fans of the Warhol group might like this. [R]▼◗

Heat (1987) **C-101m.** BOMB D: R. M. Richards. Burt Reynolds, Karen Young, Peter MacNicol, Howard Hesseman, Neill Barry, Diana Scarwid, Joe Mascolo, Alfie Wise. Dim, dingy, scattershot film (written by William Goldman, of all people) about a Las Vegas tough, whose exact livelihood is never defined, but who knows how to handle the low-lifes—and teaches "protégé" MacNicol all he knows. So what? [R]▼●

Heat (1995) **C-172m.** ***½ D: Michael Mann. Al Pacino, Robert De Niro, Val Kilmer, Jon Voight, Tom Sizemore, Diane Venora, Amy Brenneman, Ashley Judd, Mykelti Williamson, Wes Studi, Ted Levine, Dennis Haysbert, William Fichtner, Natalie Portman, Tom Noonan, Kevin Gage, Hank Azaria, Henry Rollins, Tone Loc, Jeremy Piven. Dynamite cops-and-robbers saga, with Pacino an obsessive, supersmart L.A. detective on the trail of high-tech, high-precision robber De Niro and his tight-knit gang. It turns out that the two have more in common than either one might think. A fascinating, multilayered character study studded with gripping (and often violent) action scenes, plus a chance to see two of the world's greatest actors working together—even though they share precious little screen time. Overlength is the only criticism of this crackerjack contemporary drama. Mann scripted, reworking his 1989 TV movie L.A. TAKEDOWN. Bud Cort appears unbilled. Panavision. [R] ▼●◗

Heat and Dust (1983-British) **C-130m.** *** D: James Ivory. Julie Christie, Greta Scacchi, Christopher Cazenove, Julian Glover, Susan Fleetwood, Shashi Kapoor, Madhur Jaffrey, Barry Foster, Zakir Hussain, Patrick Godfrey. Englishwomen Scacchi and great-niece Christie, sixty years apart, fall in love with India and become pregnant by natives—yet still remain outsiders in a land they can never fully comprehend. Intelligent drama, lovely performances. Screenplay by Ruth Prawer Jhabvala, from her novel. [R]▼

Heat and Sunlight (1988) **C-98m.** **½ D: Rob Nilsson. Rob Nilsson, Consuelo Faust, Don Bajema, Ernie Fosselius, Bill Bailey, Bill Ackridge. Photographer Nilsson must deal with his feelings and obsessions as his love affair with dancer Faust ends. Lively in its best moments, but also meanders and lacks structure. Characters are the most interesting element here. ▼●

Heathers (1989) **C-102m.** **½ D: Michael Lehmann. Winona Ryder, Christian Slater, Shannen Doherty, Lisanne Falk, Kim Walker, Penelope Milford, Glenn Shadix, Lance Fenton. Sharp, somewhat smug satire of high school social strata, with Ryder in a terrific performance as a girl who hangs out with the school's bitch-queens but doesn't feel quite comfortable about their reign of terror. Outrageous black humor works at first, but isn't sustained; uneven script goes far astray. Slater is commanding in his Jack Nicholsonesque performance. Feature debut for director Lehmann and writer Daniel Waters, with many virtues as well as flaws. [R]▼●◗

Heat Lightning (1934) **64m.** *** D: Mervyn LeRoy. Aline MacMahon, Ann Dvorak, Preston Foster, Lyle Talbot, Glenda Farrell, Frank McHugh, Ruth Donnelly, Jane Darwell, Edgar Kennedy. Archetypal Warner Bros. melodrama—spiced with the usual racy wisecracks—centering on jaded mechanic MacMahon and her naive younger sister (Dvorak), who run a gas-station/cafe/motel in the middle of the desert and tangle with crooks and other assorted quirky characters. Atmospheric and very well acted, with MacMahon a standout as a tough-as-nails dame who's repressed her femininity. Based on a play by George Abbott and Leon Abrams. Remade as HIGHWAY WEST (1941).

Heat of Desire (1980-French) **C-90m.** ** D: Luc Beraud. Patrick Dewaere, Clio Goldsmith, Jeanne Moreau, Guy Marchand, Pierre Dux, Jose-Luis Lopez Vasquez. Happily married university professor is whisked away for spontaneous sex by mysterious, loose living free spirit, who soon destroys his marriage and scuttles his career. Silly but sometimes sexy heavy-breather; several screen-filling shots of Goldsmith's ample frame. U.S. release: 1984. [R]▼●

Heat's On, The (1943) **80m.** ** D: Gregory Ratoff. Mae West, Victor Moore, William Gaxton, Lester Allen, Mary Roche, Hazel Scott, Xavier Cugat, Lloyd Bridges. Mae is a musical-comedy star involved with conniving producers in this flat, low-budget nightclub musical. The heat's certainly off; West's last film until MYRA BRECKINRIDGE in 1970.▼

Heat Wave (1954-British) **68m.** *½ D: Ken Hughes. Alex Nicol, Hillary Brooke, Paul Carpenter, Sidney James. Tame murder yarn, with Brooke the sultry dame involved in homicide.▼

Heatwave (1983-Australian) **C-99m.** *** D: Phillip Noyce. Judy Davis, Richard Moir, Chris Haywood, Bill Hunter, John Gregg, Anna Jemison. Radical Davis protests destruction of neighborhood for $100 million redevelopment project by firm which might have mob connections. Situation further complicated by attraction between her and project architect Moir in this Aussie counterpart to CHINATOWN. From a real-life incident, which also inspired THE KILLING OF ANGEL STREET. [R]▼

Heat Wave (1990) **C-100m. TVM** D: Kevin Hooks. Cicely Tyson, Blair Underwood, James Earl Jones, Sally Kirkland, David Strathairn, Robert Hooks, Adam Arkin, Margaret Avery, Paris Vaughan, Charlie Korsmo. Solid drama constructed around the 1965 Watts riot in Los Angeles, with strong performances by Tyson and Jones, and Underwood portraying real-life *L.A. Times* reporter Robert Richardson. Made for cable. Average. ▼●

Heaven (1987) **C-80m.** ** D: Diane Keaton. Nothing if not bizarre, this personal project of Keaton's intersperses oddly shot interviews with non sequitur clips from old movies on the subject of Heaven: how to get there, what it will be like, if it exists, etc. Clips range from METROPOLIS to THE HORN BLOWS AT MIDNIGHT—what's the point? [PG-13] ▼●

Heaven (1998) **C-103m.** ** D: Scott Reynolds. Martin Donovan, Danny Edwards, Richard Schiff, Joanna Going, Patrick Malahide, Karl Urban. An intriguing premise goes unrealized in this muddled psychological thriller about a deeply troubled architect (Donovan) with a severe gambling problem who's been rejected by his wife. Endless, confusing plot twists are set into motion when he mixes with Heaven (Edwards), a transvestite stripper who is also clairvoyant. Super 35. [R]▼

Heaven and Earth (1990-Japanese) **C-106m.** **½ D: Haruki Kadokawa. Takaai Enoki, Masahiko Tsugawa, Atsuko Asano, Tsunehiko Watase, Naomi Zaizen, Binpachi Ito, narrated by Stuart Whitman. Physically impressive, large-scale Samurai epic, notable for budget (reportedly over $40 million) and because much of it was shot in Canada! Lacks the mastery of a Kurosawa at the helm, but fans of big battle scenes may enjoy it anyway. Released in Japan at 119m.▼●

Heaven & Earth (1993) **C-140m.** **½ D: Oliver Stone. Tommy Lee Jones, Hiep Thi Le, Joan Chen, Haing S. Ngor, Debbie Reynolds, Dustin Nguyen, Conchata Ferrell, Vivian Wu, Dale Dye, Liem Whatley. Vietnamese woman's painful odyssey from a peaceful childhood in a peasant village to a lifetime of upheaval both in Vietnam and the U.S. This true story (based on two published memoirs by Le Ly Hayslip) tells of a woman forever caught between forces of North and South in her native country; between the spiritual and the practical; between Vietnamese and American ways. A jumbled narrative, difficult to watch at times, but writer-director Stone lets us share the character's emotional catharsis at the conclusion. Hayslip can be seen briefly as a jewelry broker; Jeffrey Jones appears unbilled as a priest. Panavision. [R]▼●

Heaven Can Wait (1943) **C-112m.** ***½ D: Ernst Lubitsch. Gene Tierney, Don Ameche, Charles Coburn, Marjorie Main, Laird Cregar, Spring Byington, Allyn Joslyn, Eugene Pallette, Signe Hasso, Louis Calhern. Excellent comedy-fantasy told in flashback. Ameche, who believes he's lived a life of sin, recalls his past as he requests admission to Hades. Witty Samson Raphaelson script helps make this a delight. Based on the play *Birthdays* by Laszlo Bus-Fekete.▼●

Heaven Can Wait (1978) **C-100m.** *** D: Warren Beatty and Buck Henry. Warren Beatty, Julie Christie, Jack Warden,

Dyan Cannon, Charles Grodin, James Mason, Buck Henry, Vincent Gardenia. Gentle, pleasing remake of HERE COMES MR. JORDAN with Beatty as good-natured football player who is taken to heaven ahead of schedule, and has to return to "life" in another man's body. Amiable but never moving, with Christie miscast as the woman who inspires Beatty. Scripted by Beatty and Elaine May. [PG] ▼●◗

Heaven Help Us (1985) **C-104m.** *** D: Michael Dinner. Donald Sutherland, John Heard, Andrew McCarthy, Mary Stuart Masterson, Kevin Dillon, Malcolm Danare, Jennie Dundas, Kate Reid, Wallace Shawn, Philip Bosco, Patrick Dempsey, Christopher Durang. Very funny evocation of Catholic high school life in Brooklyn, circa 1965, with solid ring of truth throughout. Shawn has hilarious cameo as priest who kicks off school dance with denunciation of lust. Impressive feature debuts for writer Charles Purpura and director Dinner. [R]▼●

Heaven Knows, Mr. Allison (1957) **C-107m.** *** D: John Huston. Deborah Kerr, Robert Mitchum. Marvelous, touching tale of nun Kerr and Marine Mitchum stranded together on a Japanese-infested Pacific island during WW2. Solid performances by the stars. CinemaScope.▼

Heavenly Bodies (1985-Canadian) **C-89m.** BOMB D: Lawrence Dane. Cynthia Dale, Richard Rebiere, Walter George Alton, Laura Henry, Stuart Stone. The world's first Aerobics Musical, and with any luck, the last. [R]▼

Heavenly Body, The (1943) **95m.** ** D: Alexander Hall. Hedy Lamarr, William Powell, James Craig, Fay Bainter, Henry O'Neill, Spring Byington. Hedy is heavenly, but script is silly; astronomer Powell suspects neglected wife Lamarr of being unfaithful with air-raid warden Craig.

Heavenly Creatures (1994-New Zealand) **C-99m.** ***½ D: Peter Jackson. Melanie Lynskey, Kate Winslet, Sarah Peirse, Diana Kent, Clive Merrison, Simon O'Connor. Dark, exhilarating story based on the true-life case of New Zealand teenagers Pauline Parker and Juliet Hulme, whose obsessive relationship drove them to murder. Very well acted, particularly by Lynskey and Winslet, and stunningly directed by Jackson, who plunges us into the bizarre fantasy world that the girls create for themselves. The real-life Hulme, it was later discovered, has written best-selling murder mysteries for years under the pseudonym Anne Perry. Jackson also cowrote the screenplay with Frances Walsh. Original New Zealand running time: 108m. Super 35.▼●

Heavenly Days (1944) **71m.** ** D: Howard Estabrook. Fibber McGee and Molly (Jim and Marion Jordan), Barbara Hale, Eugene Pallette, Gordon Oliver. Mild entry in famed radio comedians' series, with the lovable married couple off to Washington to help run the Senate.

Heavenly Kid, The (1985) **C-89m.** *½ D: Cary Medoway. Lewis Smith, Jason Gedrick, Jane Kaczmarek, Richard Mulligan, Mark Metcalf. Embarrassingly amateurish fantasy-comedy about a greasy teen of the early '60s who dies in a chicken race and can't get into heaven—until he helps out a young nerd in the 1980s. Film's better moments come toward the end, but by then you may have bailed out. [PG-13]▼

Heavenly Pursuits SEE: **Gospel According to Vic, The**

Heaven Only Knows (1947) **95m.** **½ D: Albert S. Rogell. Robert Cummings, Brian Donlevy, Jorja Curtwright, Marjorie Reynolds, Bill Goodwin, John Litel, Stuart Erwin. Oddball Western with fantasy touches as angel Cummings descends to earth to help soulless gambler. Retitled: MONTANA MIKE.

Heavens Above! (1963-British) **105m.** *** D: John Boulting. Peter Sellers, Cecil Parker, Isabel Jeans, Eric Sykes, Bernard Miles, Ian Carmichael, Irene Handl, Brock Peters, William Hartnell, Roy Kinnear, Joan Hickson. Wry satire on British clergy life; Sellers top-notch as the reverend who becomes bishop in outer space. Originally ran 118m. Produced by Roy Boulting.▼

Heaven's Gate (1980) **C-149m.** ** D: Michael Cimino. Kris Kristofferson, Christopher Walken, Isabelle Huppert, Jeff Bridges, John Hurt, Sam Waterston, Brad Dourif, Joseph Cotten, Geoffrey Lewis, Richard Masur, Terry O'Quinn, Mickey Rourke, Willem Dafoe. Writer-director Cimino's now-notorious spectacle is missing just one thing: a story. It deals, more or less, with the conflict between immigrant settlers of 19th-century Wyoming and the ruthless American empire-builders who want them eliminated. Stunningly photographed (by Vilmos Zsigmond) on magnificent locations, with incredible period detail—all to little effect, since the narrative, character motivations, and soundtrack are so hopelessly muddled. Originally shown at 219m. Panavision. [R]▼●◗

Heaven's Prisoners (1996) **C-126m.** **½ D: Phil Joanou. Alec Baldwin, Mary Stuart Masterson, Kelly Lynch, Eric Roberts, Teri Hatcher, Vondie Curtis Hall. Alcoholic former New Orleans cop Baldwin and his wife Lynch rescue a little girl from a wrecked aircraft, but this leads to involvement with drug runners and murder. Adaptation of James Lee Burke's popular novel about a Cajun detective is too long and slow, and captures little of the regional atmosphere; except for the miscast Baldwin, the cast is excellent, especially Masterson as a stripper and Roberts as a drug lord. Baldwin coexecutive-produced. [R]▼●

Heaven With a Barbed Wire Fence (1939) **62m.** **½ D: Ricardo Cortez. Jean Rogers, Raymond Walburn, Marjorie Rambeau, Glenn Ford, Nicholas (Richard) Conte, Ward Bond. Spunky little road movie with Rogers, Ford, and Conte linking up and riding the rails to California. Ford's feature debut, as well as Conte's. Coscripted by Dalton Trumbo, and based on his story.

Heaven With a Gun (1969) **C-101m.** **½ D: Lee H. Katzin. Glenn Ford, Carolyn Jones, Barbara Hershey, John Anderson, David Carradine. Peace-loving man is forced to return to world of violence in the Old West. Uneven. Panavision. [M]

Heavy (1996) **C-105m.** **½ D: James Mangold. Pruitt Taylor Vince, Liv Tyler, Shelley Winters, Deborah Harry, Joe Grifasi, Evan Dando. Somber character study about Victor (Vince), a chubby, balding, hopelessly shy pizza chef who toils in a rural eatery run by his widowed mother (Winters). Enter a pretty teen (Tyler), the new waitress; Victor fantasizes about becoming her boyfriend and savior. There is a sense of sadness and eloquence to Victor, but not quite enough. ▼●

Heavy Metal (1981-Canadian) **C-90m.** *** D: Gerald Potterton. Voices of Richard Romanus, John Candy, Joe Flaherty, Don Francks, Eugene Levy, Harold Ramis, John Vernon. Episodic animated feature is uneven, but great fun on a mindless, adolescent level. Sexy sci-fi stories and vignettes in a variety of graphic styles, many set to rock music. Our favorites: "Harry Canyon," about a N.Y.C. cabbie of the future, and "Den," a boy's macho fantasy. Film is actually the work of many animation studios, directors, and writers around the world. [R] ▼●◗

Heavy Petting (1988) **C-80m.** **½ D: Obie Benz. David Byrne, Sandra Bernhard, Allen Ginsberg, Ann Magnuson, Spalding Gray, Josh Mostel, Laurie Anderson, John Oates, Abbie Hoffman, Jacki Ochs. ATOMIC CAFE–style look at sexual mores in the 1950s, punctuated by celebrity interviews and highlighted by hysterical period film clips. Scattershot quasi-documentary lacks strong point of view, but it's tough to knock a film in which such "witnesses" as David Byrne, William S. Burroughs, and Zoe Tamerlis (of MS. 45 cultdom) offer their views on teen dating. [R]▼●

Heavy Traffic (1973) **C-76m.** ***½ D: Ralph Bakshi. Animated feature is somewhat pretentious and largely gross in telling of young New Yorker depressed by sights and sounds around him, finding refuge at drawing-board. Dazzling cinematic treatment, with often revolutionary combination of live-action and animation. Some brilliant set-pieces within loose story framework. [R—edited from original X rating]▼

Heavyweights (1994) **C-97m.** ** D: Steven Brill. Tom McGowan, Aaron Schwartz, Ben Stiller, Shaun Weiss, Tom Hodges, Leah Lail, Paul Feig, Max Goldblatt, Jeffrey Tambor, Jerry Stiller, Anne Meara. Yet another summer camp movie, this one about a haven for overweight kids where, as the press release said, "big is beautiful and thin isn't in." That is, until campers meet up with the fitness counselor of their nightmares. This heavy-handed comedy's intended "message" about self-esteem is undermined by a barrage of fat jokes! [PG] ▼●

Hedda (1975-British) **C-104m.** **½ D: Trevor Nunn. Glenda Jackson, Peter Eyre, Timothy West, Jennie Linden, Patrick Stewart. Royal Shakespeare Company production of Ibsen's *Hedda Gabler* attains a modicum of vitality from Jackson's showy performance in the title role. So-so. [PG]▼

He Got Game (1998) **C-136m.** **½ D: Spike Lee. Denzel Washington, Ray Allen, Milla Jovovich, Rosario Dawson, Hill Harper, Zelda Harris, Ned Beatty, Jim Brown, Joseph Lyle Taylor, Bill Nunn, John Turturro, Lonette McKee. A prisoner is freed for one week to convince his son—the country's hottest high school basketball player—to sign with the state governor's favorite college. Farfetched premise is played out with conviction, but its points are obvious and hammered home redundantly. Redeemed by strong characterizations and powerful moments. Many basketball stars and coaches appear as themselves; young Allen is himself an NBA player. [R]▼●◗

Heidi (1937) **88m.** **½ D: Allan Dwan. Shirley Temple, Jean Hersholt, Arthur Treacher, Helen Westley, Mady Christians, Sidney Blackmer, Sig Ruman, Marcia Mae Jones, Mary Nash. Classic children's story set in 19th-century Switzerland is good vehicle for Shirley, playing girl taken from grandfather (Hersholt) to live with cruel Nash. Nice tear-jerker for children. Also shown in computer-colored version.▼●

Heidi (1952-Swiss) **98m.** *** D: Luigi Comencini. Elsbeth Sigmund, Heinrich Gretler, Thomas Klameth, Elsie Attenhofer. Faithful, flavorful retelling of Johanna Spyri's children's classic, filmed in the story's actual locales. Sigmund is well cast in the title role. Followed by HEIDI AND PETER.▼

Heidi (1965-Austrian-German) **C-95m.** *** D: Werner Jacobs. Eva Marie Singhammer, Gertraud Mittermayr, Gustav Knuth, Lotte Ledi. Fine retelling of classic children's story about young girl who leaves her cozy home in Swiss Alps for adventures in the world below.▼

Heidi (1968) **C-110m. TVM** D: Delbert Mann. Maximilian Schell, Jean Simmons, Michael Redgrave, Walter Slezak, Jennifer Edwards, Peter Van Eyck. Well-made version of the classic story, with Edwards (daughter of Blake Edwards) leading a good cast. Script by Earl Hamner Jr. of *The Waltons* fame. Above average.▼

Heidi (1993-U.S.-Austrian-Swiss) **C-200m. TVM** D: Michael Rhodes. Jason Robards, Jane Seymour, Jane Hazlegrove, Lexi Randall, Sian Phillips, Patricia Neal, Noely Thornton, Andrew Bicknell, Basil Hoskins. Pleasant Disney retelling of the classic children's story with Thornton doing nicely in the title role. Seymour gets a stab at scenery chewing as the unpleasant governess. Denis Lewiston's Alpine photography is the real star. Originally shown in two parts. Made for cable. Average.▼

Heidi and Peter (1955-Swiss) **C-89m.** **½ D: Franz Schnyder. Heinrich Gretler, Elsbeth Sigmund, Thomas Klameth, Anita Mey. So-so follow-up to HEIDI (1952), involving her adventures with Peter and a flood that threatens their village.

Heidi Chronicles, The (1995) **C-100m. TVM** D: Paul Bogart. Jamie Lee Curtis, Tom Hulce, Peter Friedman, Kim Cattrall, Sharon Lawrence, Eve Gordon, Roma Maffia, Shari Belafonte. Wendy Wasserstein's late '80s Broadway seriocomedy (Tony Award, Pulitzer Prize) about one woman's feminist march through 30 years of America. Some of Curtis' best work is here as the smart, overachieving, but basically unhappy Heidi Holland, floundering in midlife along with her married and divorced and remarried friends. Wonderful for most of the journey, and though a bit wearying in the home stretch, it's still worth the trip. Above average. ▼

Heidi Fleiss, Hollywood Madam (1995-British) **C-107m. TVM** D: Nick Broomfield. Snoopy, loopy documentary, which profiles the madam to the stars in a superior example of ambush journalism. Features an array of characters not to be gathered in the same room: Fleiss buddy Victoria Sellers (Peter's daughter), ex–L.A. police chief Daryl Gates, and Fleiss lover/mentor Ivan Nagy, who's referred to as a pimp and a woman-beater by so many interviewees that it's easy to accept him as evil incarnate. First shown in the U.S. on cable TV, then released to theaters (to great acclaim). Above average.▼●◗

Heidi's Song (1982) **C-94m.** *½ D: Robert Taylor. Voices of Lorne Greene, Sammy Davis, Jr., Margery Gray, Michael Bell, Peter Cullen. Animated feature from Hanna-Barbera studio reprises all-too familiar Heidi tale. Despite songs by Sammy Cahn and Burton Lane, awkward continuity, lifeless animation and an excess of cute animals leave this little better than most Saturday morning fare. [G]▼

Heimat (1984-German) **C/B&W-940m.** *** D: Edgar Reitz. Marita Breuer, Dieter Schaad, Rudiger Weigang, Karin Rasenack, Willi Burger, Gertrud Bredel, Mathias Kniesbeck. No, that running time is not a typo! This is an ambitious epic, almost 16 hours in length, about life in a provincial German village between 1919 and 1982. First few hours are generally more compelling than the last. Has its boring stretches, and after a while it does seem like a glorified soap opera, but at its best, perceptive, comic, even poetic. Gernot Roll's cinematography is exquisite. Followed by a sequel: HEIMAT 2. ▼

Heiress, The (1949) **115m.** **** D: William Wyler. Olivia de Havilland, Ralph Richardson, Montgomery Clift, Miriam Hopkins, Vanessa Brown, Mona Freeman, Ray Collins, Selena Royle. Henry James' novel *Washington Square* receives superlative screen treatment with Oscar-winning de Havilland as spinster wooed by fortune-hunter Clift in 19th-century N.Y.C., despite warnings from her cruel father, Richardson. Aaron Copland's music score also won an Oscar. Adapted by Ruth and Augustus Goetz from their stage play. Remade in 1997 as WASHINGTON SQUARE. ▼●

Heir to Genghis Khan, The SEE: **Storm Over Asia**

Heist, The (1979-Italian) **C-85m.** **½ D: Sergio Gobbi. Charles Aznavour, Virna Lisi, Robert Hossein. Typical cop-chasing-gangster mishmash wastes its cast but is distinguished by some great stunt driving. Video version runs 92m.▼

Heist, The (1989) **C-97m. TVM** D: Stuart Orme. Pierce Brosnan, Tom Skerritt, Wendy Hughes, Robert Prosky, Noble Willingham. Ex-con devises intricate racetrack robbery to exact revenge on his former partner, who had framed him in an emerald-smuggling deal. Entertaining yarn with a first-rate cast, including transplanted Australian leading lady Hughes. Made for cable. Average.▼

He Knows You're Alone (1981) **C-94m.** *½ D: Armand Mastroianni. Don Scardino, Caitlin O'Heaney, Elizabeth Kemp, Tom Rolfing, Patsy Pease, Tom Hanks, Dana Barron, Paul Gleason. Yet another entry in slice-and-dice genre, this one with minor novelty of brides-to-be as victims. A bit less bloody than others of its ilk; otherwise, business as usual. Hanks' film debut. Aka BLOOD WEDDING. [R]▼

Helas Pour Moi (1993-French-Swiss) **C-84m.** **½ D: Jean-Luc Godard. Gerard Depardieu, Laurence Masliah, Bernard Verley, Jean-Louis Loca. Pensive account of an average married couple (Depardieu and Masliah) who reside in a Swiss village, and what happens when the husband's body supposedly is borrowed by a "god." Of interest as an examination of the meaning of faith, but the narrative is much too fragmented and the film too cluttered with declarations and episode headings. Godard based his screenplay in part on Greek legend. Video title: OH, WOE IS ME.▼

He Laughed Last (1956) **C-77m.** **½ D: Blake Edwards. Frankie Laine, Lucy Marlow, Anthony Dexter, Richard Long, Alan Reed, Jesse White, Florenz Ames, Henry Slate. Marlow is a 1920s flapper who inherits a gangster's nightclub in this colorful spoof of Prohibition era crime stories. Laine even gets to croon a couple of songs.

Held Up (2000) **C-91m.** *½ D: Steve Rash. Jamie Foxx, Nia Long, Barry Corbin, John Cullum, Jake Busey, Michael Shamus Wiles, Eduardo Yanez, Sarah Paulson, Julie Hagerty. While vacationing in the Grand Canyon, Long dumps her fiancé (Foxx) upon learning that he's spent their nest egg on a vintage Studebaker. Then the car is stolen . . . and finally, Foxx is taken hostage. The real crime is that time-wasters like this make it to the screen. [PG-13]▼

Helen Morgan Story, The (1957) **118m.** **½ D: Michael Curtiz. Ann Blyth, Paul Newman, Richard Carlson, Gene Evans, Alan King, Cara Williams. Fiction about dynamic 1920s and '30s torch singer, dwelling on her romances and alcoholism; Blyth never captures the star's pathos or greatness. She's dubbed by Gogi Grant. CinemaScope.▼

Helen of Troy (1955) **C-118m.** ** D: Robert Wise. Stanley Baker, Rossana Podesta, Brigitte Bardot, Jacques Sernas, Cedric Hardwicke, Harry Andrews. Sweeping pageantry, but empty script spoils this version of story about the woman who caused the Trojan War. Filmed in Italy. CinemaScope.▼●

Hell and High Water (1954) **C-103m.** **½ D: Samuel Fuller. Richard Widmark, Bella Darvi, Victor Francen, Cameron Mitchell, Gene Evans, David Wayne, Stephen Bekassy, Richard Loo. Uneven mixture of romance, espionage, and a demolition caper, stemming from U.S. sub's mission to Arctic. Tame film got a boost from being shot in CinemaScope.

Hell Below (1933) **105m.** **½ D: Jack Conway. Robert Montgomery, Walter Huston, Madge Evans, Jimmy Durante, Robert Young, Sterling Holloway, Eugene Pallette. Vintage submarine drama surpasses many more elaborate efforts; Huston is captain, Montgomery his seaman nemesis.

Hell Below Zero (1954) **C-91m.** ** D: Mark Robson. Alan Ladd, Joan Tetzel, Basil Sydney, Stanley Baker. Tepid adventure yarn casting Ladd as helper of Tetzel, who commands a whaling vessel while searching for her dad's killer. Made in England.

Hellbenders, The (1967-Italian-Spanish) **C-92m.** *½ D: Sergio Corbucci. Joseph Cotten, Norma Bengell, Julian Mateos, Gino Pernice, Angel Aranda, Maria Martin. Dreary spaghetti Western in which crazed ex-Confederate officer Cotten schemes to rekindle the rebel cause, facing a variety of complications and crises.▼

Hell Bent for Leather (1960) **C-82m.** **½ D: George Sherman. Audie Murphy, Felicia Farr, Stephen McNally, Robert Middleton, Rad Fulton, Jan Merlin, Herbert Rudley, Allan Lane, John Qualen, Bob Steele. Adequate Western with Murphy a horsetrader falsely accused of murder; greedy sheriff McNally knows he's innocent, but still heads the posse on his trail. CinemaScope.

Hellbound (1993-U.S.-Canadian-Israeli) **C-95m.** *½ D: Aaron Norris. Chuck Norris, Calvin Levels, Christopher Neame, Sheree J. Wilson, David Robb, Cherie Franklin, Jack Adalist, Erez Atar. After being imprisoned by Richard the Lion-Hearted in 1186, Satan's emissary (Neame) is freed in modern times to face a more formidable foe: Chuck Norris. Too much acting from Neame, not enough from Norris, and a silly story with little action. This sat on the shelf for two years before going direct to video. Some attractive Israeli settings. [R] ▼●▶

Hellbound: Hellraiser II (1988-British) **C-97m.** *½ D: Tony Randel. Ashley Laurence, Clare Higgins, Kenneth Cranham, Imogen Boorman, Sean Chapman, Doug Bradley, William Hope. Confusing, tedious sequel begins immediately after first film ends. Teenage heroine literally goes to Hell in effort to rescue ill-fated father, but encounters opposition from her revived stepmother and an occult-obsessed psychiatrist. But Hell is a boring, dusty labyrinth. Almost as gruesome as HELLRAISER (it's *not* a sequel to HELLBOUND), but nowhere near as entertaining. Followed by HELLRAISER III: HELL ON EARTH. [R]▼●▶

Hellcamp SEE: **Opposing Force**

Hell Canyon Outlaws (1957) **72m.** ** D: Paul Landres. Dale Robertson, Brian Keith, Rossana Rory, Dick Kallman, Buddy Baer. Triumph against outlaw forces in the Old West; that's it.

Hellcats of the Navy (1957) **82m.** **½ D: Nathan Juran. Ronald Reagan, Nancy Davis (Reagan), Arthur Franz, Harry Lauter, Selmer Jackson. Satisfactory actioner of WW2 exploits of U.S. submarine and its crew. Ronald and Nancy Reagan's only screen appearance together.▼

Hell Comes to Frogtown (1987) **C-88m.** *½ D: R. J. Kizer, Donald G. Jackson. Roddy Piper, Sandahl Bergman, Rory Calhoun, Cec Verrill, William Smith, Nicholas Worth, Kristi Sommers. Goofy post-holocaust tale with wrestler ''Rowdy'' Roddy as the only fertile male left on earth, who sets out to rescue women being held captive by frog-like mutants. At least the frog masks are good. 1992 sequel: RETURN TO FROGTOWN. [R]▼●

Hell Divers (1932) **113m.** ** D: George

Hill. Wallace Beery, Clark Gable, Conrad Nagel, Dorothy Jordan, Marjorie Rambeau, Marie Prevost, Cliff Edwards. Beery and Gable are boisterous rivals in the Naval Air Force in this often lively but overlong MGM effort, with some still-exciting aerial action. Watch for young Robert Young as a sailor.

Hell Drivers (1957-British) **91m.** **½ D: Cy Endfield. Stanley Baker, Herbert Lom, Peggy Cummins, Patrick McGoohan, Jill Ireland, Gordon Jackson, David McCallum, Sean Connery. Taut account of ex-con trucker carrying heavy cargoes over rugged roads and trying to expose boss's racket. British running time: 108m. VistaVision.

Heller in Pink Tights (1960) **C-100m.** **½ D: George Cukor. Sophia Loren, Anthony Quinn, Margaret O'Brien, Steve Forrest, Edmund Lowe. Colorful tale of theatrical troupe that travels throughout the Old West—with the law often in pursuit. Based on a Louis L'Amour novel.▼

Hellfighters (1968) **C-121m.** ** D: Andrew V. McLaglen. John Wayne, Katharine Ross, Jim Hutton, Vera Miles, Bruce Cabot, Jay C. Flippen. Broadly acted adventure about men who fight oil fires is made endurable by good cast. Wayne's character is based on real-life oil well firefighter Red Adair. Panavision. [R]▼◗

Hellfire Club, The (1961-British) **C-93m.** *** D: Robert S. Baker, Monty Berman. Keith Michell, Adrienne Corri, Peter Cushing, Peter Arne, Kai Fischer, David Lodge, Martin Stephens, Miles Malleson, Francis Matthews. Lively, entertaining 18th-century swashbuckler with familiar rightful- vs. wrongful-heir plot; acrobatic Michell makes an ideal dashing hero. The depraved, powerful, real-life club of the title serves as backdrop. Also shown in 86m. b&w print. DyaliScope.▼

Hellgate (1952) **87m.** **½ D: Charles Marquis Warren. Sterling Hayden, Joan Leslie, James Arness, Ward Bond. Offbeat account of Hayden falsely sent to prison, strange manner in which he redeems himself during prison breakout. Reworking of THE PRISONER OF SHARK ISLAND. Same topic covered later in TVM THE ORDEAL OF DR. MUDD.

Hellhole (1985) **C-95m.** *½ D: Pierre de Moro. Ray Sharkey, Judy Landers, Mary Woronov, Marjoe Gortner, Edy Williams, Terry Moore, Rick Cox, Lynn Borden. Innocent Landers is caught inside women's sanitarium where strange experiments are being conducted. They should have tried to conjure up a better script. Pretty bad, even for the genre. [R]▼●

Hell in Korea (1956-British) **81m.** **½ D: Julian Amyes. Ronald Lewis, Stephen Boyd, Victor Maddern, George Baker, Robert Shaw, Stanley Baker, Harry Andrews, Michael Medwin, Michael Caine, Percy Herbert. Standard drama about small U.N. patrol tangling with Chinese; interesting to see Caine in his first film, Shaw in his second. Aka A HILL IN KOREA.▼

Hell in the Pacific (1968) **C-103m.** *** D: John Boorman. Lee Marvin, Toshiro Mifune. Two men, one American, one Japanese, confront each other on deserted WW2 Pacific island. Gripping idea well executed, with two dynamic actors; only the finale disappoints. Panavision. ▼●◗

Hellions, The (1962-British) **C-87m.** **½ D: Ken Annakin. Richard Todd, Anne Aubrey, Lionel Jeffries, Zena Walker, Jamie Uys, Marty Wilde. Western revenge plot transferred to 19th-century South Africa; inevitable shoot-out intact. Technirama.

Hell Is for Heroes (1962) **90m.** *** D: Donald Siegel. Steve McQueen, Bobby Darin, Fess Parker, Harry Guardino, James Coburn, Mike Kellin, Nick Adams, Bob Newhart. Tough, taut WW2 film about a small squadron forced to hold off a German attack by pretending they're larger—and more powerful—than they really are. Takes its time getting started but builds in intensity to a riveting climax. Only incongruous note: presence of young Newhart, who even interpolates a variation on one of his telephone monologues into the story! Cowritten by WW2 specialist Robert Pirosh.▼●

Hell Night (1981) **C-101m.** *½ D: Tom DeSimone. Linda Blair, Vincent Van Patten, Peter Barton, Jenny Neumann, Kevin Brophy, Suki Goodwin. How's this for originality? Four college fraternity/sorority pledges must spend a night in Garth Mansion, which is haunted by ghost of retarded killer. Unfortunately, reports of his death were greatly exaggerated. What appears to be the usual teenage hack-'em-up has no nudity or explicit violence, making one wonder just what audience they had in mind. Extremely dull. [R]▼◗

Hello Again (1987) **C-96m.** ** D: Frank Perry. Shelley Long, Judith Ivey, Gabriel Byrne, Corbin Bernsen, Sela Ward, Austin Pendleton, Carrie Nye, Robert Lewis, Madeleine Potter, Illeana Douglas. Long Island housewife chokes to death but is brought back to life by her witchlike sister one year later . . . and soon discovers that she can't simply pick up her life where she left off. Contemporary comedy written by Susan Isaacs doesn't develop its premise with any logic or momentum, and quickly sags. Long tries her best. [PG]▼●

Hello, Dolly! (1969) **C-146m.** **½ D: Gene Kelly. Barbra Streisand, Walter Matthau, Michael Crawford, E. J. Peaker, Marianne McAndrew, Tommy Tune, Louis Armstrong, Danny Lockin. Splashy treatment of smash Broadway play with Jerry Herman's popular score. Dolly Levi insists on playing matchmaker, even when she herself gets matched. Overblown and unmemorable, but colorful diversion. Based on Thornton

Wilder's *The Matchmaker* (filmed in 1958). Oscar winner for Sound, Art Direction, and Score (Lennie Hayton and Lionel Newman). Some prints run 118m. Todd-AO. [G]▼●

Hello Down There (1969) **C-98m.** *½ D: Jack Arnold. Tony Randall, Janet Leigh, Jim Backus, Roddy McDowall, Ken Berry, Merv Griffin, Richard Dreyfuss. So-called comedy about family living in experimental underwater home might entertain children if you pay them to watch it. Reissued as SUB-A-DUB-DUB. [G]

Hello Elephant (1952-Italian) **78m.** *½ D: Gianni Franciolini. Vittorio De Sica, Sabu, Maria Mercader, Nando Bruno. Misfire of comedy-satire involving royalty who bestows an elephant on one of his subjects as a fitting reward. Retitled: PARDON MY TRUNK.▼

Hello Frisco, Hello (1943) **C-98m.** ** D: H. Bruce Humberstone. Alice Faye, John Payne, Jack Oakie, Lynn Bari, Laird Cregar, June Havoc, Ward Bond. Hackneyed musicomedy of Payne getting too big for his britches as Barbary Coast entrepreneur; Oscar-winning song, "You'll Never Know." Big comedown from earlier musicals with star trio.▼

Hello-Goodbye (1970-British) **C-107m.** BOMB D: Jean Negulesco. Michael Crawford, Curt Jurgens, Genevieve Gilles, Ira Furstenberg, Lon Satton. Abysmal love triangle goes nowhere, makes no sense. Awful, loose, and annoying. [PG]

Hello Mary Lou: Prom Night II (1987-Canadian) **C-96m.** **½ D: Bruce Pittman. Lisa Schrage, Michael Ironside, Wendy Lyon, Justin Louis. No relation to PROM NIGHT. Lyon, who looks great in or out of costume, is possessed by the spirit of a murdered prom queen and becomes her instrument of revenge. [R] ▼●

Hell on Devil's Island (1957) **74m.** *½ D: Christian Nyby. Helmut Dantine, William Talman, Donna Martell, Rex Ingram, Alan Lee. Low-grade exposé of unsavory working conditions in prison mining operations. Regalscope.

Hell on Frisco Bay (1955) **C-98m.** **½ D: Frank Tuttle. Alan Ladd, Edward G. Robinson, Joanne Dru, William Demarest, Paul Stewart, Fay Wray, Rodney (Rod) Taylor, Jayne Mansfield. Thirties-style gangster film recounting the exposure of crime syndicate and its head; actionful, with good cast. CinemaScope.▼

Hello, Sister! (1933) **62m.** **½ D: Erich von Stroheim, Alfred Werker. James Dunn, Boots Mallory, ZaSu Pitts, Minna Gombell. Innocuous boy-meets-girl story of special interest to film buffs. Originally filmed by von Stroheim as WALKING DOWN BROADWAY; later reedited, partially refilmed; enough bizarre touches remain to reveal von Stroheim's touch, however.

Hello Sucker (1941) **60m.** *½ D: Edward Cline. Peggy Moran, Tom Brown, Walter Catlett, Hugh Herbert. Dingy little film of Moran and Brown acquiring vaudeville booking agency, making it a success and finding love with one another.

Hellraiser (1987-British) **C-94m.** **½ D: Clive Barker. Andrew Robinson, Clare Higgins, Ashley Laurence, Sean Chapman, Oliver Smith, Robert Hines. Robinson and Higgins move into a roomy British dwelling, unaware that his half brother—and her former lover—is hiding upstairs in a kind of gelatinous/skeletal state; soon the beast is forcing her to lure stray men back to the house so he can replenish himself with their blood. Grisly but stylish directorial debut by famed horror novelist Barker; ugly fun all the way. Followed by HELLBOUND: HELLRAISER II. [R]▼●◗

Hellraiser III: Hell on Earth (1992) **C-93m.** *½ D: Anthony Hickox. Terry Farrell, Doug Bradley, Paula Marshall, Kevin Bernhardt, Ken Carpenter, Ashley Laurence. Further adventures of the grossout Pinhead goes for the jokes, not the jugular. This time Pinhead crosses paths with an ambitious TV newswoman who winds up with the grisliest (if not the biggest) story of her career. Freddy and Jason are starting to look good by comparison. [R]▼●◗

Hellraiser: Bloodline (1996) **C-85m.** BOMB D: Alan Smithee. Bruce Ramsay, Valentina Vargas, Doug Bradley, Adam Scott, Charlotte Chatton. For the fourth and apparently final chapter, Pinhead matches wits with a demon lover/cohort, ironically named Angelique (Vargas). Dull and plot-heavy, even if you're a Clive Barker devotee. Re-caulk your bathtub instead. But then, what did you expect of another film from the Smithee oeuvre? [R]▼●◗

Hell's Angels (1930) **127m.** ***½ D: Howard Hughes. Ben Lyon, James Hall, Jean Harlow, John Darrow, Lucien Prival, Roy Wilson. Hughes' expensive, indulgent WW1 aviation film is in a class by itself; slow-moving and sometimes corny storywise, but unmatched for aerial spectacle. Also the film that launched Harlow ("Would you be shocked if I put on something more comfortable?") to stardom. Two-color Technicolor party scene and tinted night sequences were restored in 1989. James Whale, credited as dialogue director, actually wrote and directed much of the film. Beware shorter prints.▼

Hell's Angels Forever (1983) **C-92m.** ** D: Richard Chase, Kevin Keating, Leon Gast. Superficial quasi-documentary portrait of the Hell's Angels, with no real information on, or insight into, the notorious cycle gang. [R]▼

Hell's Angels on Wheels (1967) **C-95m.** **½ D: Richard Rush. Adam Roarke, Jack Nicholson, Sabrina Scharf, Jana Taylor,

John Garwood. Excellent photography by then-unknown Laszlo Kovacs, and Nicholson's characterization as gas station attendant named Poet, make this one tough to resist on a trash level. Famed Angel Sonny Barger was technical advisor.▼

Hell's Bloody Devils (1970) **C-92m.** ** D: Al Adamson. Broderick Crawford, Scott Brady, John Gabriel, Kent Taylor, John Carradine, Robert Dix, Keith Andes, Jack Starrett, Anne Randall, Vicki Volante. Traveling the low road to action with, believe it or not, a gang of sadistic bikers, a band of neo-Nazis, the Vegas mob, a sinister dude named Count von Delberg—all beating one another to a pulp. Add a cast of veteran actors and, incredibly, a score by Nelson Riddle! Retitled THE FAKERS, then SMASHING THE CRIME SYNDICATE. [PG]

Hell's Crossroads (1957) **73m.** ** D: Franklin Adreon. Stephen McNally, Peggie Castle, Robert Vaughn, Barton MacLane. Oater involving members of the James Brothers outlaw gang. Naturama.

Hell's Five Hours (1958) **73m.** ** D: Jack L. Copeland. Stephen McNally, Coleen Gray, Vic Morrow, Maurice Manson. Several people are held prisoners at missile depot by Morrow, bent on blowing the place sky-high.

Hell's Half Acre (1954) **91m.** **½ D: John H. Auer. Wendell Corey, Evelyn Keyes, Elsa Lanchester, Nancy Gates, Philip Ahn, Keye Luke, Marie Windsor. A woman seeks her long-missing husband in Honolulu, where he's established a new identity. Some interesting vignettes in this OK melodrama.

Hell's Heroes (1929) **68m.** ***½ D: William Wyler. Charles Bickford, Raymond Hatton, Fred Kohler, Fritzi Ridgeway. After robbing a bank in New Jerusalem ("A Bad Town . . . for Bad Men"), three outlaws try to flee across the sweltering, windswept desert but unexpectedly wind up caring for a baby when its mother dies. First sound version of Peter B. Kyne's *Three Godfathers* is probably the most satisfying, and certainly the least sentimental; beautifully directed, tersely acted, and vividly atmospheric.

Hell's Highway (1932) **62m.** **½ D: Rowland Brown. Richard Dix, Tom Brown, C. Henry Gordon, Charles Middleton, Rochelle Hudson, Oscar Apfel, Stanley Fields, Fuzzy Knight, Clarence Muse. Dix, serving time on a blatantly misrun chain gang, has to change his escape plans when his kid brother is brought in as prisoner. Though it pales alongside I AM A FUGITIVE FROM A CHAIN GANG (released just a few months later), this highly melodramatic tale is tough, raw (touching on everything from racial prejudice to homosexuality), and pictorially striking. Biggest disappointment: the finale.

Hell Ship Mutiny (1957) **66m.** *½ D: Lee Sholem, Elmo Williams. Jon Hall, John Carradine, Peter Lorre, Roberta Haynes, Mike Mazurki, Stanley Adams. Hall looks bored in rehash of South Sea tale of ship captain overcoming sinister forces exploiting the natives.▼

Hell's Horizon (1955) **80m.** ** D: Tom Gries. John Ireland, Marla English, Bill Williams, Hugh Beaumont, Jerry Paris, Kenneth Duncan. Interaction among men of bombing squad in the Korean War.

Hell's House (1932) **72m.** ** D: Howard Higgin. Junior Durkin, Pat O'Brien, Bette Davis, Junior Coghlan, Charley Grapewin, Emma Dunn. Low-budget quickie about naive kid who takes rap for bootlegger and goes to poorly run boys' reformatory. Interesting mainly for early appearances of O'Brien and Davis.▼

Hell's Island (1955) **C-84m.** **½ D: Phil Karlson. John Payne, Mary Murphy, Francis L. Sullivan, Eduardo Noriega, Paul Picerni. Tough-talking melodrama about Payne's pursuit of stolen gem, and relationship with deceitful former girlfriend; script has echoes of THE MALTESE FALCON, and even a Sydney Greenstreet figure in the person of Sullivan. VistaVision.

Hell's Kitchen (1939) **81m.** **½ D: Lewis Seiler, E. A. Dupont. Ronald Reagan, Stanley Fields, Grant Mitchell, Margaret Lindsay, Dead End Kids. Ex-con Fields goes straight, tries to bail Dead End Kids out of trouble, sets them on the right road. Remake of THE MAYOR OF HELL.

Hell's Long Road (1963-Italian) **C-89m.** **½ D: Charles Roberti. Elena Brazzi, Kay Nolandi, Berto Frankis, Bela Kaivi, Marcello Charli. Offbeat costume sudser set in ancient Rome during rule of Nero (Frankis), focusing on personal life of arch senator (Charli) and romance with splendiferous Brazzi; vivid settings.

Hell's Outpost (1954) **90m.** ** D: Joseph Kane. Rod Cameron, Joan Leslie, Chill Wills, John Russell. Cameron is ambitious miner in this sturdy little film; Leslie is the fetching love interest.

Hellstrom Chronicle, The (1971) **C-90m.** **½ D: Walon Green. Lawrence Pressman. Documentary about man's impending struggle against insects somehow beat THE SORROW AND THE PITY for the Oscar, but sappy narration and repetitive structure lessen its effect. Still, microphotography is incredible; enjoyed brief vogue as a "head" movie. [G]▼

Hell to Eternity (1960) **132m.** **½ D: Phil Karlson. Jeffrey Hunter, David Janssen, Vic Damone, Patricia Owens, Sessue Hayakawa. Straightforward drama based on true story of WW2 hero Guy Gabaldon, who was raised by Japanese foster parents; battle scenes galore.▼

Hell Up in Harlem (1973) **C-96m.** BOMB

D: Larry Cohen. Fred Williamson, Julius W. Harris, Gloria Hendry, Margaret Avery, D'Urville Martin. Excessively violent, poorly filmed sequel to BLACK CAESAR as Fred makes N.Y.C. a decent place to live by annihilating all who stand in his way. [R]▼

Hell With Heroes, The (1968) **C-95m.** **½ D: Joseph Sargent. Rod Taylor, Claudia Cardinale, Harry Guardino, Kevin McCarthy, Peter Duel, William Marshall. OK pulp fiction about WW2 flyers Taylor and Duel who run air-cargo service, become involved with notorious smuggler Guardino and his mistress (Cardinale). Unprofound, but slickly done. Techniscope.

Hellzapoppin' (1941) **84m.** *** D: H. C. Potter. Ole Olsen, Chic Johnson, Martha Raye, Mischa Auer, Jane Frazee, Hugh Herbert, Robert Paige, Shemp Howard, Elisha Cook Jr. Famous madcap Broadway show is conventionalized by Hollywood, with romantic subplot and too many songs, but still has many inspired moments of lunacy, from a throwaway CITIZEN KANE gag to the mutterings of Hugh Herbert.

Help! (1965-British) **C-90m.** ***½ D: Richard Lester. John Lennon, Paul McCartney, George Harrison, Ringo Starr, Leo McKern, Eleanor Bron, Victor Spinetti, Roy Kinnear, Patrick Cargill. Crazy, funny film, the Beatles' second. Lots of wild gags, many songs (including "Ticket to Ride," "Another Girl," "You've Got to Hide Your Love Away," title tune). The story: a religious sect attempts to recover a sacrificial ring from Ringo. Written by Charles Wood and Marc Behm.▼●◗

Help Me Dream (1981-Italian) **C-112m.** *** D: Pupi Avati. Mariangela Melato, Anthony Franciosa, Paola Pitagora, Jean-Pierre Léaud, Alexandra Stewart. Intriguing, original, winningly nostalgic musical romance centering on affable American flyer Franciosa hiding out with Italian Melato and children in a farmhouse during WW2. An ode to an idealized America, with period songs and choreography by Hermes Pan.

Helter Skelter (1976) **C-194m. TVM** D: Tom Gries. George DiCenzo, Steve Railsback, Nancy Wolfe, Marilyn Burns, Christina Hart, Cathey Paine, Alan Oppenheimer, Skip Homeier, David Clennon, Paul Mantee, Sidney Clute. Electrifying film of prosecutor Vincent Bugliosi's best-seller, adapted by JP Miller, about the track-down and trial of Charles Manson and his spaced-out "family" in California. Serious, intense, and frightening; a vivid performance by Railsback as Manson. Originally shown in two parts. Above average.▼

He Married His Wife (1940) **83m.** ** D: Roy Del Ruth. Joel McCrea, Nancy Kelly, Roland Young, Mary Boland, Cesar Romero, Lyle Talbot, Mary Healy, Elisha Cook, Jr. Obvious, talky comedy in which McCrea, tired of paying alimony to ex-wife Kelly, schemes to get her remarried. John O'Hara was one of the writers.

Hemingway's Adventures of a Young Man (1962) **C-145m.** ** D: Martin Ritt. Richard Beymer, Diane Baker, Paul Newman, Corinne Calvet, Fred Clark, Dan Dailey, James Dunn, Juano Hernandez, Arthur Kennedy, Ricardo Montalban, Susan Strasberg, Jessica Tandy, Eli Wallach, Simon Oakland, Michael (J.) Pollard. Loosely based on autobiographical data from his stories, this pretentious, drawn-out memory of the famed author is overblown, cornball, and embarrassing. Fine cast mostly wasted. Aka ADVENTURES OF A YOUNG MAN. CinemaScope.

Hennessy (1975-British) **C-103m.** **½ D: Don Sharp. Rod Steiger, Lee Remick, Richard Johnson, Trevor Howard, Peter Egan, Eric Porter. Interesting but unbelievable thriller about Irish man whose wife and child are killed in Belfast violence, stirring him to plan bombing of Parliament on opening day when the Royal Family attends. [PG]▼

Henry Aldrich Teen-aged Henry Aldrich was Paramount's answer to MGM's Andy Hardy series, and while the Aldrich films were less popular, less prestigious, and shorter-lived, they were then, and remain today, well-crafted, entertaining little films, without any of the pretentiousness and calculated coyness that marred the Hardy series. Henry and group were the invention of Clifford Goldsmith, whose play *What a Life* opened in 1938 on Broadway, spawning a radio series with Ezra Stone repeating his stage role of Henry. In 1939, Paramount turned the hit play into a pleasant film, retaining Betty Field (as Henry's plain-jane girlfriend) and Vaughan Glaser (as dour principal Mr. Bradley) from the original cast, but bypassing Ezra Stone in favor of Jackie Cooper. Best of all, Paramount assigned their writing team of Billy Wilder and Charles Brackett to provide the script—an unlikely pair for such Middle American doings, but welcome nonetheless. In 1941, Jackie Cooper repeated his role in a second outing, LIFE WITH HENRY, a typically silly but likable effort. Then Paramount cast a newcomer, Jimmy Lydon, in the key role of Henry and surrounded him with a new supporting cast for a string of actual series films: Charles Smith as his laconic but shifty pal Dizzy, John Litel as his stern father, Olive Blakeney as his forgiving mother, and welcome Vaughan Glaser as the forever-pouting principal. A new director, ex-film editor Hugh Bennett, was added to comprise the working unit that turned out nine films over the next four years. The Aldrich films, timed around 70 minutes, fell into a pattern that proved generally successful: putting hopelessly blundering Henry into an increasingly complicated series of mishaps which would alienate him from his parents, sometimes his friends, and often the entire town, before culminating in a major action and/or slapstick climax in which Henry would be vindicated. The films are consistently well paced and slickly filmed, never belying their modest budgets, and filled with engaging players: Mary Anderson as Henry's girlfriend in several entries (later replaced by Diana Lynn, and other less notable starlets); Frances Gifford as a movie star who accepts Henry's prom invitation as a publicity stunt in HENRY ALDRICH GETS GLAMOUR, Fritz Feld as a famous musician whose Stradivarius is accidentally "borrowed" by Henry in HENRY ALDRICH SWINGS IT; Lucien Littlefield as an antagonistic teacher in two of the episodes; June Preisser as a vamp in HENRY ALDRICH FOR PRESIDENT; and Vera Vague as a potential wife for Mr. Bradley in HENRY ALDRICH PLAYS CUPID. Best of all is Francis Pierlot as a character called Nero Smith, a pyromaniac who announces his intentions to Henry, leading to suspicions and troubles galore in perhaps the best series entry, HENRY ALDRICH, EDITOR. HENRY ALDRICH'S LITTLE SECRET is the last and easily the weakest film of the nine Lydon pictures, but the other eight maintain a surprisingly good standard of filmmaking quality and good, lightweight entertainment.

HENRY ALDRICH

What a Life (1939)
Life With Henry (1941)
Henry Aldrich for President (1941)
Henry and Dizzy (1942)
Henry Aldrich, Editor (1942)
Henry Aldrich Gets Glamour (1943)
Henry Aldrich Swings It (1943)
Henry Aldrich Haunts a House (1943)
Henry Aldrich, Boy Scout (1944)
Henry Aldrich Plays Cupid (1944)
Henry Aldrich's Little Secret (1944)

Henry Aldrich, Boy Scout (1944) **66m.** **½ D: Hugh Bennett. Jimmy Lydon, Charles Smith, John Litel, Olive Blakeney, Joan Mortimer, Darryl Hickman, Minor Watson, Richard Haydn. Henry as a Scout Leader? Just a jumping-off point for him to get into more jams than usual—including a literal cliffhanger.

Henry Aldrich, Editor (1942) **71m.** *** D: Hugh Bennett. Jimmy Lydon, Charles Smith, John Litel, Olive Blakeney, Rita Quigley, Vaughan Glaser, Francis Pierlot. When a pyromaniac tells Henry where he plans to strike next—and Henry prints the news—he becomes the prime suspect! Solid series entry with a truly exciting climax, and memorable performance by Pierlot as Nero Smith.

Henry Aldrich for President (1941) **73m.** **½ D: Hugh Bennett. Jimmy Lydon, Charles Smith, June Preisser, Mary Anderson, Martha O'Driscoll, Dorothy Peterson, John Litel, Rod Cameron, Lucien Littlefield, Kenneth Howell. Henry's race for the presidency of the Centerville High School student council gets him into the usual hot water. Particularly attractive cast of young Hollywood hopefuls supports Lydon in his series debut.

Henry Aldrich Gets Glamour (1943) **75m.** **½ D: Hugh Bennett. Jimmy Lydon, Charles Smith, John Litel, Olive Blakeney, Diana Lynn, Frances Gifford, Gail Russell, Bill Goodwin, Vaughan Glaser. Henry wins first prize in a *Movieplay* magazine contest: a date with glamorous Hilary Dane (Gifford). Entertaining (if typically farfetched) entry with appealing distaff cast.

Henry Aldrich Haunts a House (1943) **73m.** **½ D: Hugh Bennett. Jimmy Lydon, Charles Smith, John Litel, Olive Blakeney, Joan Mortimer, Vaughan Glaser, Jackie Moran, Lucien Littlefield, Mike Mazurki. Henry gets into more trouble than usual when he swallows a test tube full of experimental strength serum, and stumbles into a "haunted" house. Contrived, to say the least, but fun.

Henry Aldrich Plays Cupid (1944) **65m.** **½ D: Hugh Bennett. Jimmy Lydon, Charles Smith, John Litel, Olive Blakeney, Diana Lynn, Vaughan Glaser, Vera Vague (Barbara Jo Allen), Paul Harvey, Barbara Pepper. Henry tries to marry off the school principal Mr. Bradley in this enjoyable outing which features Vera Vague as the other half of the match.

Henry Aldrich's Little Secret (1944) **75m.** ** D: Hugh Bennett. Jimmy Lydon, Charles Smith, Joan Mortimer, John Litel, Olive Blakeney, Ann Doran, John David Robb, Tina Thayer, Noel Neill. Henry tries to help out a troubled young mother by taking care of her infant in this so-so entry that brought the series to a close.

Henry Aldrich Swings It (1943) **64m.** **½ D: Hugh Bennett. Jimmy Lydon, Charles Smith, John Litel, Olive Blakeney, Mimi Chandler, Vaughan Glaser, Marion Hall, Fritz Feld, Bernard Nedell. Henry is smitten with his pretty music teacher (Hall); his Dad likes her too, but Mrs. Aldrich misunderstands, thinks her husband is unfaithful. Meanwhile, Henry forms his own band and gets into trouble with gamblers and crooks. Amusing comedy of errors.

Henry and Dizzy (1942) **71m.** **½ D: Hugh Bennett. Jimmy Lydon, Charles Smith, Mary Anderson, John Litel, Olive Blakeney, Maude Eburne, Vaughan Glaser, Shirley Coates. Typical comic misadventures of Henry and his pal Basil A. "Dizzy" Stevens, with a great climax at Lake Wopacotapotalong. Look for future

''Lois Lane'' Noel Neill as Dizzy's girlfriend, and former Little Rascal Carl ''Alfalfa'' Switzer as a bratty kid.
Henry & June (1990) **C-134m.** ***½ D: Philip Kaufman. Fred Ward, Uma Thurman, Maria de Medeiros, Richard E. Grant, Kevin Spacey, Jean-Philippe Ecoffey, Bruce Myers, Jean-Louis Bunuel. Stylish, atmospheric, and surprisingly unerotic adaptation of the Anais Nin diaries dealing specifically—and in sexually explicit fashion—with her lover (author Henry Miller) and Henry's wife June. Performed with gusto (in Ward's case, broad gusto) and distinguished by brilliant production design of randy Paris, circa 1931. Screenplay by Philip and Rose Kaufman. Controversy over the adult material in this film finally caused the MPAA to create a new NC-17 rating. [NC-17]▼●◗
Henry Fool (1998) **C-137m.** **½ D: Hal Hartley. Thomas Jay Ryan, James Urbaniak, Parker Posey, Maria Porter, James Saito, Kevin Corrigan, Liam Aiken, Miho Nikaido, Gene Ruffini. Hartley just misses the mark with this characteristically offbeat tale of Simon Grim (Urbaniak), a bashful garbageman, and the title character (Ryan), a free spirit who encourages him to begin writing poetry. An allegory that, in its best moments, serves as an ode to nonconformity and risk-taking; but it's uneven, overlong, and has too many boring stretches. Scripted by Hartley. [R]▼
Henry VIII and His Six Wives (1973-British) **C-125m.** ***½ D: Waris Hussein. Keith Michell, Donald Pleasence, Charlotte Rampling, Jane Asher, Lynne Frederick. Adapted from BBC-TV series, historical pageant divides time evenly among the wives, Rampling and Frederick coming off best. Michell is exceptional as the King. [PG]
Henry V (1945-British) **C-137m.** **** D: Laurence Olivier. Laurence Olivier, Robert Newton, Leslie Banks, Renee Asherson, Esmond Knight, Leo Genn, Ralph Truman, Harcourt Williams, Ivy St. Helier, Ernest Thesiger, Max Adrian, George Cole, Felix Aylmer, Robert Helpmann, Freda Jackson, Jimmy Hanley, John Laurie. Olivier's masterful rendition of Shakespeare play is a cinematic treat, filmed in rich color and framed by ingenious presentation of a typical performance at the Globe theater during 1500s. This earned Olivier a special Academy Award ''for his outstanding achievement as actor, producer, and director in bringing HENRY V to the screen.''▼●◗
Henry V (1989-British) **C-137m.** ***½ D: Kenneth Branagh. Kenneth Branagh, Derek Jacobi, Brian Blessed, Alec McCowen, Ian Holm, Richard Briers, Robert Stephens, Robbie Coltrane, Christian Bale, Judi Dench, Paul Scofield, Michael Maloney, Emma Thompson, Geraldine McEwan. Stunning revitalization of Shakespeare's play about the warrior-king, with Branagh (in an incredible directorial debut) breathing fire and meaning into the worthy text. A different reading from Olivier's but no less impressive; when he finishes his speech before leading his men into battle at Agincourt, you're ready to enlist! Superb music by Patrick Doyle. Supporting cast is peppered with familiar faces from the elite of British theater and film. Won Costume Design Oscar.▼●
Henry IV (1984-Italian) **C-95m.** ** D: Marco Bellochio. Marcello Mastroianni, Claudia Cardinale, Luciano Bartoli, Latou Chardons, Leopoldo Trieste. Disappointing update of Pirandello's brilliant satirical play on the nature of madness and illusion. When a nobleman falls off his horse, he comes to believe he's Emperor Henry IV . . . or does he? The two stars do what they can to extract a few moments of lucidity from the confusion, but the result is generally unrewarding. [PG-13]▼
Henry: Portrait of a Serial Killer (1990) **C-90m.** ***½ D: John McNaughton. Michael Rooker, Tracy Arnold, Tom Towles. Unpleasant, unexploitive, and brilliantly directed portrayal of diseased minds (not just Henry's), loosely based on the life of self-confessed Texas mass murderer Henry Lee Lucas. As disturbing as Michael Powell's PEEPING TOM, which it in many ways resembles. Definitely not for everyone, with some very graphic scenes; a powerful (if minimalist) movie experience. Screenplay by director McNaughton and Richard Fire. Filmed in 1986. Followed by a 1997 sequel. [X]▼●◗
Henry, the Rainmaker (1949) **64m.** *½ D: Jean Yarbrough. Raymond Walburn, Walter Catlett, William Tracy, Mary Stuart. Mild comedy of homey Walburn who develops a ''scientific'' way to make rain. First in short-lived ''Father'' series; followed by LEAVE IT TO HENRY.
Her Adventurous Night (1946) **76m.** **½ D: John Rawlins. Dennis O'Keefe, Helen Walker, Tom Powers, Fuzzy Knight. Youngster with wild imagination fabricates tale of murder and crime, causing parents to go to jail and the youth's life put in peril.
Her Alibi (1989) **C-94m.** **½ D: Bruce Beresford. Tom Selleck, Paulina Porizkova, William Daniels, James Farentino, Hurd Hatfield, Patrick Wayne, Tess Harper, Joan Copeland. Successful mystery writer hopes to cure his career slump by providing a fake alibi for accused murderer Porizkova (by putting her up in his dreamy country home and observing her behavior). Amiable but awkwardly directed comedy benefits from attractive leads and amusing supporting cast; would you believe Wayne in a ponytail and loud golf pants? [PG]▼●◗
He Ran All the Way (1951) **77m.** **½ D:

John Berry. John Garfield, Shelley Winters, Wallace Ford, Selena Royle, Gladys George, Norman Lloyd. Taut but predictable thriller with on-the-lam cop killer Garfield hiding out in Winters' home. Garfield's final film.

Herbie Goes Bananas (1980) **C-100m.** *½ D: Vincent McEveety. Charlie Martin Smith, Steven W. Burns, Cloris Leachman, John Vernon, Elyssa Davalos, Harvey Korman, Richard Jaeckel, Alex Rocco, Fritz Feld. Fourth Disney LOVE BUG epic finds Smith and Burns driving ol' '53 toward a race in Brazil, but encountering all sorts of "hilarious" obstacles along the way. One amusing scene where the VW turns matador; otherwise, strictly scrap metal. A TV series followed. [G]▼●

Herbie Goes to Monte Carlo (1977) **C-91m.** ** D: Vincent McEveety. Dean Jones, Don Knotts, Julie Sommars, Roy Kinnear, Jacques Marin. Spy ring hides diamond in Herbie the Volkswagen's gas tank while Jones is racing in Europe. Disney's LOVE BUG formula is starting to run out of gas. [G]▼●

Herbie Rides Again (1974) **C-88m.** **½ D: Robert Stevenson. Helen Hayes, Ken Berry, Stefanie Powers, Keenan Wynn, John McIntire, Huntz Hall. OK sequel to THE LOVE BUG with similar special effects, as Herbie the Volkswagen tries to help Hayes and Berry steer clear of evil Alonzo Hawk (Wynn). Typical Disney slapstick. [G]▼●

Her Bridal Night SEE: **Bride Is Much Too Beautiful, The**

Her Brother (1960-Japanese) **C-98m.** **½ D: Kon Ichikawa. Keiko Kishi, Hiroshi Kawaguchi, Kinuyo Tanaka, Masayuki Mori. Troublesome family is brought together when immature brother-son Kawaguchi contracts tuberculosis; central to the scenario is his warm relationship with his older sister (Kishi). Sentimental drama. Daieiscope.

Her Cardboard Lover (1942) **93m.** *½ D: George Cukor. Norma Shearer, Robert Taylor, George Sanders, Frank McHugh, Elizabeth Patterson. Tired comedy that chic Shearer, in her final screen appearance, is unable to salvage.

Hercules (1959-Italian) **C-107m.** **½ D: Pietro Francisci. Steve Reeves, Sylva Koscina, Gianna Maria Canale, Fabrizio Mioni, Ivo Garrani, Gina Rovere, Luciana Paoluzzi (Paluzzi). This Italian import became a surprise U.S. hit, and served as the prototype of all cloak-and-sandal pictures to come: Reeves is musclebound mythical hero in essentially a retelling of the story of Jason and the Golden Fleece. Sequel: HERCULES UNCHAINED. Dyaliscope. ▼●

Hercules (1983-Italian) **C-98m.** *½ D: Lewis Coates (Luigi Cozzi). Lou Ferrigno, Mirella D'Angelo, Sybil Danning, Ingrid Anderson, William Berger, Brad Harris, Rossana Podesta. Silly, special-effects-laden epic with Hercules (Ferrigno) attempting to rescue kidnapped Princess Anderson. However, the ex-Incredible Hulk is undeniably well cast. Followed by a sequel. [PG]▼●

Hercules (1997) **C-93m.** *** D: John Musker, Ron Clements. Voices of Tate Donovan, Susan Egan, James Woods, Danny DeVito, Rip Torn, Samantha Eggar, Bobcat Goldthwait, Matt Frewer, Hal Holbrook, Barbara Barrie; opening narration by Charlton Heston. Entertaining Disney cartoon feature based on Greek mythology. Baby Hercules is stolen from Mount Olympus by the bungling henchmen of Hades; raised as a mortal with extraordinary strength, he must prove himself a real hero to regain entry to the home of the gods. Funny, well-paced story is peppered with gags and songs (by Alan Menken and David Zippel), and a standout characterization by Woods as the garrulous and glib villain. Followed by an animated TV series and a video sequel. [G] ▼●

Hercules II (1985-Italian) **C-90m.** *½ D: Lewis Coates (Luigi Cozzi). Lou Ferrigno, Milly Carlucci, Sonia Viviani, William Berger, Carlotta Green, Claudio Cassinelli. Sequel to HERCULES (1983). Recommended for nondiscriminating viewers too young to read this. Video title: THE ADVENTURES OF HERCULES. [PG]▼

Hercules Against Rome (1960-Italian) **C-87m.** ** D: Piero Pierott. Alan Steel, Wandisa Guida, Livio Lorenzon, Daniele Vargas. Steel fights a series of unconvincing villains to protect the late emperor's daughter. Totalscope.

Hercules Against the Moon Men (1964-Italian) **C-88m.** ** D: Giacomo Gentilomo. Alan Steel, Jany Clair, Anna-Maria Polani, Nando Tamberlani. Steel is muscular hero who frees people of Samar from control of magical lunar people; potential action never occurs. Cromoscope.▼

Hercules Against the Sons of the Sun (1963-Italian) **C-91m.** ** D: Osvaldo Civirani. Mark Forest, Anna Pace, Giuliano Gemma, Andrea Rhu. Setting is pre-Columbian America, but the adventure is the same as usual. Techniscope.▼

Hercules and the Captive Women (1963-Italian) **C-87m.** ** D: Vittorio Cottafavi. Reg Park, Fay Spain, Ettore Manni, Marlo Petri. Cardboard costumer with Park vs. Spain, the despotic ruler of Atlantis. Super Technirama 70.▼

Hercules in New York (1970) **C-91m.** *½ D: Arthur Allan Seidelman. Arnold Stang, Arnold Strong (Schwarzenegger), Taina Elg, James Karen, Deborah Loomis, Ernest Graves, Tanny McDonald. Hercules journeys to Earth from Mt. Olympus and gets mixed up with wrestling promoters—and mobsters—in this lumbering comedy. Inept, but irresistible for the opportunity to watch a young, badly dubbed Schwarzenegger in his movie debut. Reissued as HERCULES—THE MOVIE at 82m, and HERCULES GOES BANANAS at 75m. For TV release a three-minute prologue has been added. Aren't you glad you asked? [G]▼●

Hercules in the Haunted World (1961-Italian) **C-83m.** ** D: Mario Bava. Reg Park, Christopher Lee, Leonora Ruffo, Giorgio Ardisson, Ida Galli. Occasionally sparked by atmospheric settings, this sword-and-sandal epic narrates adventures of Park in the devil's kingdom. Totalscope Super/100.▼

Hercules, Samson & Ulysses (1965-Italian) **C-85m.** ** D: Pietro Francisci. Kirk Morris, Richard Lloyd, Liana Orfei, Enzo Cerusico. Title alerts one for gymnastics of trio of legendary musclemen.

Hercules Unchained (1960-Italian) **C-101m.** ** D: Pietro Francisci. Steve Reeves, Sylva Koscina, Primo Carnera, Sylvia Lopez. Par-for-the-course entry featuring the muscleman hero and his princess bride setting off for the city of Thebes; along the way he will bid to prevent a war and tangle with a sinister queen. Dyaliscope.▼●

Here Comes Mr. Jordan (1941) **93m.** **** D: Alexander Hall. Robert Montgomery, Evelyn Keyes, Claude Rains, Rita Johnson, Edward Everett Horton, James Gleason, John Emery. Excellent fantasy-comedy of prizefighter Montgomery accidentally sent to heaven before his time, forced to occupy a new body on earth. Hollywood moviemaking at its best, with first-rate cast and performances; Harry Segall won an Oscar for his original story, as did Sidney Buchman and Seton I. Miller for their screenplay. Characters used again in DOWN TO EARTH; film remade as HEAVEN CAN WAIT in 1978. Look fast for a young Lloyd Bridges.▼●

Here Comes the Groom (1951) **113m.** *** D: Frank Capra. Bing Crosby, Jane Wyman, Franchot Tone, Alexis Smith, James Barton, Anna Maria Alberghetti. Crosby contrives to keep former fiancée Wyman from marrying millionaire Tone in this lightweight musical outing. Guest appearances by Louis Armstrong, Dorothy Lamour, Phil Harris, and Cass Daley, plus Oscar-winning song, "In the Cool, Cool, Cool of the Evening."▼●

Here Comes the Navy (1934) **86m.** **½ D: Lloyd Bacon. James Cagney, Pat O'Brien, Gloria Stuart, Dorothy Tree, Frank McHugh. Enjoyable but standard tale of cocky Cagney who becomes navy hero; nothing new, but well done.

Here Come the Co-Eds (1945) **87m.** **½ D: Jean Yarbrough. Bud Abbott, Lou Costello, Peggy Ryan, Martha O'Driscoll, June Vincent, Lon Chaney (Jr.), Donald Cook. Pretty zany Abbott and Costello comedy of two wacky caretakers turning formerly staid girls' school on its ear.▼

Here Come the Girls (1953) **C-78m.** **½ D: Claude Binyon. Bob Hope, Arlene Dahl, Rosemary Clooney, Tony Martin, Fred Clark, Robert Strauss, the Four Step Brothers. At times amusing romp with Hope a naive show biz-ite who becomes involved with killer on the loose.▼●

Here Come the Littles (1985-Luxembourg) **C-72m.** *½ D: Bernard Deyries. Voices of Jimmy E. Keegan, Bettina Bush, Donovan Freberg, Hal Smith. Silly, boring animated effort about tiny people with tails who live in the walls of big peoples' houses and their adventures with a 12-year-old boy. Spawned from the popular books and TV series. [G]▼

Here Come the Marines (1952) **66m.** *½ D: William Beaudine. Leo Gorcey, Huntz Hall, David Gorcey, Bennie Bartlett, Bernard Gorcey, Gil Stratton, Jr., Murray Alper, Hanley Stafford, Myrna Dell, Arthur Space, Tim Ryan. The Bowery Boys are drafted and probe a murder in this tired rehash.

Here Come the Nelsons (1952) **76m.** ** D: Frederick de Cordova. Ozzie, Harriet, David and Ricky Nelson, Rock Hudson, Ann Doran, Jim Backus, Barbara Lawrence, Sheldon Leonard, Gale Gordon. Expanded version of radio's *Adventures of Ozzie & Harriet,* spotlighting a series of typical, comical situations. Light, predictable fare that paved the way for the long-running TV series.▼

Here Come the Waves (1944) **99m.** *** D: Mark Sandrich. Bing Crosby, Betty Hutton, Sonny Tufts, Ann Doran, Gwen Crawford, Noel Neill, Catherine Craig, Mae Clarke. Zippy wartime music-comedy with Crosby cleverly cast as a Sinatra-like crooner, the idol of bobby-soxers, who joins the navy, and becomes involved with twin sisters (played by Hutton—and one's even demure!). Harold Arlen-Johnny Mercer score includes "Let's Take the Long Way Home," "(That Old) Black Magic" (reprised from STAR SPANGLED RHYTHM), and "Ac-cent-u-ate the Positive," which is performed in blackface! Yvonne De Carlo and Mona Freeman have bit parts.▼

Here Is My Heart (1934) **77m.** **½ D: Frank Tuttle. Bing Crosby, Kitty Carlisle, Roland Young, Alison Skipworth, Reginald Owen. Bing's a radio star in love with princess Carlisle in this flimsy little musical. Songs include "Love Is Just Around the Corner."

Her Enlisted Man SEE: **Red Salute**

Here on Earth (2000) **C-96m.** ** D: Mark Piznarski. Chris Klein, Leelee Sobieski, Josh Hartnett, Michael Rooker, Bruce Greenwood, Annette O'Toole, Annie Corley, Elaine Hendrix, Stuart Wilson. Spoiled preppie Klein falls for small-town girl Sobieski while rooming with her boyfriend's family for the summer. Fateful teen romantic triangle is strictly by-the-numbers. Sobieski gets points for radiantly dangling two hunky guys along; if she were any more angelic she'd explode. [PG-13]▼◗

Here We Go Again (1942) **76m.** ** D: Allan Dwan. Edgar Bergen and Charlie McCarthy, Jim and Marian Jordan (Fibber McGee and Molly), Harold Peary (The Great Gildersleeve), Ginny Simms, Bill Thompson, Isabel Randolph, Gale Gordon, Mortimer Snerd. Follow up to LOOK WHO'S LAUGHING finds Fibber and Molly on a cross-country trip for their 20th anniversary, getting involved in mild antics at resort hotel with rest of radio gang. Easy-to-take comedy, but nothing special.

Here We Go Round the Mulberry Bush (1968-British) **C-96m.** **½ D: Clive Donner. Barry Evans, Judy Geeson, Angela Scoular, Sheila White, Vanessa Howard, Denholm Elliott. British teen-ager Evans is hung up on girls, but finds his pursuits a constant dead-end. Amusing, often clever adolescent romp; music by Stevie Winwood & Traffic, Spencer Davis Group.

Her Favorite Patient SEE: **Bedside Manner**

Her First Romance (1951) **73m.** *½ D: Seymour Friedman. Margaret O'Brien, Allen Martin, Jr., Jimmy Hunt, Sharyn Moffett. O'Brien's first grown-up role and her first screen kiss are only assets of this plodding summer camp story.

Her Highness and the Bellboy (1945) **112m.** **½ D: Richard Thorpe. Hedy Lamarr, Robert Walker, June Allyson, Carl Esmond, Agnes Moorehead, Rags Ragland. Sentimental fluff of N.Y.C. bellboy Walker, crippled girlfriend Allyson, captivating Princess (Lamarr) he escorts; a bit creaky.

Her Husband's Affairs (1947) **83m.** *½ D: S. Sylvan Simon. Lucille Ball, Franchot Tone, Edward Everett Horton, Mikhail Rasumny, Gene Lockhart, Nana Bryant. Pretty sterile comedy: Ball learns not to poke into husband's business affairs.▼

Her Jungle Love (1938) **C-81m.** **½ D: George Archainbaud. Dorothy Lamour, Ray Milland, Lynne Overman, J. Carrol Naish, Dorothy Howe (Virginia Vale). Flyers Milland and Overman stranded on tropical isle with Lamour; Ray teaches her how to kiss, Naish tries to destroy everyone in this escapist fare.

Her Kind of Man (1946) **78m.** ** D: Frederick de Cordova. Dane Clark, Janis Paige, Zachary Scott, Faye Emerson, George Tobias. Lukewarm drama of young singer with gangster background making good in Big City and falling in love with gossip columnist. Fair cast.

Her Lucky Night (1945) **63m.** ** D: Edward Lilley. Andrews Sisters, Martha O'Driscoll, Noah Beery, Jr., George Barbier, Grady Sutton, Ida Moore. Minor comedy with singing trio seeking romance at any cost.

Her Majesty, Love (1931) **75m.** *½ D: William Dieterle. Marilyn Miller, W. C. Fields, Leon Errol, Ford Sterling, Chester Conklin, Ben Lyon, Virginia Sale. Unbearable musical with sweet Miller in love with Lyon in old Berlin. Errol as persistent suitor, Fields as juggling father, provide only uplifting moments.

Her Majesty Mrs. Brown SEE: **Mrs. Brown**

Her Man Gilbey (1948-British) **89m.** **½ D: Harold French. Albert Lieven, Margaret Rutherford, Peggy Cummins, Martin Miller. Capable cast nicely handles contrived yarn of quartet of people whose lives intertwine in Geneva.

Hero, The (1970) **C-97m.** **½ D: Richard Harris. Richard Harris, Romy Schneider, Kim Burfield, Maurice Kaufman, Yossi Yadin. Old-fashioned film about a soccer star and the young boy who idolizes him; partly filmed in Israel. [PG]▼

Hero (1992) **C-112m.** **½ D: Stephen Frears. Dustin Hoffman, Geena Davis, Andy Garcia, Joan Cusack, Kevin J. O'Connor, Maury Chaykin, Stephen Tobolowsky, Christian Clemenson, Tom Arnold, Warren Berlinger, Susie Cusack, James Madio, Darrell Larson. Seriocomic yarn about a ne'er-do-well (Hoffman) who saves lives after a plane crash, barely giving it a thought, until an imposter (Garcia) takes credit for the good deed, and becomes lionized by the public—and the media. Flawed but entertaining, with some glib, funny potshots at television. How many times did they watch MEET JOHN DOE before filming this? Chevy Chase, Edward Herrmann, Barney Martin, and Fisher Stevens appear unbilled. [PG-13]▼●◗

Hero Ain't Nothin' But a Sandwich, A (1978) **C-105m.** **½ D: Ralph Nelson. Cicely Tyson, Paul Winfield, Larry B. Scott, Helen Martin, Glynn Turman, David Groh. Well-meaning drama (from Alice Childress' book) about intelligent but alienated black ghetto youth who takes up drugs. Moralistic film may get PTA recommendations, but doesn't really deliver: young Scott's performance is major asset. [PG]▼●

Hero and the Terror (1988) **C-96m.** *½ D: William Tannen. Chuck Norris, Brynn Thayer, Steve W. James, Jack O'Halloran, Ron O'Neal, Billy Drago. Flat melodrama proves to be an unwise change of pace for action star Norris, here playing a "sensitive" police detective who must exorcise his personal demons by doing battle one last time with his larger-than-life maniac nemesis O'Halloran. Film's cowriter, former actor Michael Blodgett, has an endless cameo in a restaurant scene. [R]▼●

Hero At Large (1980) **C-98m.** **½ D: Martin Davidson. John Ritter, Anne Archer, Bert Convy, Kevin McCarthy, Harry Bellaver, Anita Dangler. Unemployed actor Ritter is mistaken for do-gooding "Captain Avenger"; political hucksters Convy and McCarthy attempt to co-opt him. Winning if naive satire. Look fast for Kevin Bacon. [PG]▼

Herod the Great (1960-Italian) **C-93m.** *½ D: Arnaldo Genoino. Edmund Purdom, Sylvia Lopez, Sandra Milo, Alberto Lupo. Juvenile account of ruler of ancient Judea, his warring and his jealousy of wife's admirers. Totalscope.▼

Heroes, The (1972-Italian) **C-99m.** ** D: Duccio Tessari. Rod Steiger, Rod Taylor, Rosanna Schiaffino, Claude Brasseur, Terry-Thomas. A middling script sinks this forgettable actioner about a motley crew that bands together to pull off a heist of "loot" military money. Techniscope. [PG]

Heroes (1977) **C-113m.** **½ D: Jeremy Paul Kagan. Henry Winkler, Sally Field, Harrison Ford, Val Avery, Olivia Cole, Hector Elias. Innocuous film marked Winkler's first starring role, as crazy Vietnam vet who chases a dream of wealth and success cross-country; Field is appealing as the girl he meets and wins along the way. [PG]▼

Heroes Die Hard SEE: **Mr. Kingstreet's War**

Heroes for Sale (1933) **73m.** *** D: William A. Wellman. Richard Barthelmess, Loretta Young, Aline MacMahon, Robert Barrat, Grant Mitchell, Douglass Dumbrille, Charles Grapewin, Ward Bond. Potent melodrama with Barthelmess as an American Everyman who manages to survive one calamity after another—from morphine addiction (as a result of a WW1 injury) to job-hunting during the Depression—and continues to endure, like the country itself. Ambitious script by Wilson Mizner and Robert Lord tackles everything from the hypocrisy of hero worship to Communism! A fascinating social document of the early 1930s.▼

Heroes of Telemark, The (1965-British) **C-131m.** **½ D: Anthony Mann. Kirk Douglas, Richard Harris, Michael Redgrave, Mervyn Johns, Eric Porter. Douglas and Harris spend more time battling each other than the Nazis overrunning Norway in this pictorially striking (filmed on location), predictable blow-up-the-German-factory yarn. Panavision.▼

Hero's Island (1962) **C-94m.** **½ D: Leslie Stevens. James Mason, Kate Manx, Neville Brand, Rip Torn, Warren Oates, Brendan Dillon, (Harry) Dean Stanton. Peculiar mixture of adventure and soap opera set in 18th-century on island near North Carolina, involving pirates and homesteaders. Mason coproduced. Panavision.

Her Panelled Door (1950-British) **84m.** *** D: Ladislas Vajda. Phyllis Calvert, Edward Underdown, Helen Cherry, Richard Burton. During an air raid Calvert is shellshocked, forgetting her past, leading to dramatic results.

Her Primitive Man (1944) **79m.** *½ D: Charles Lamont. Robert Paige, Louise Allbritton, Robert Benchley, Edward Everett Horton. Grade C flick with Paige pretending to be a savage to win love of anthropologist Allbritton.

Her Sister's Secret (1946) **86m.** **½ D: Edgar G. Ulmer. Nancy Coleman, Margaret Lindsay, Felix Bressart, Regis Toomey, Philip Reed, Henry Stephenson. Young woman discovers she's pregnant after brief affair. Fair weeper with competent cast.

Hers to Hold (1943) **94m.** ** D: Frank Ryan. Deanna Durbin, Joseph Cotten, Charles Winninger, Nella Walker, Gus Schilling, Ludwig Stossel, Irving Bacon. Grown-up Durbin is in love with serviceman Cotten in undistinguished romance, brightened by Deanna's singing. Songs: "Begin The Beguine," etc.

Her 12 Men (1954) **C-91m.** ** D: Robert Z. Leonard. Greer Garson, Robert Ryan, Barry Sullivan, Richard Haydn, James Arness, Tim Considine, David Stollery, Frances Bergen. Maudlin script has Greer as dedicated teacher in boys' school. A failed attempt to repeat the success of GOODBYE, MR. CHIPS.

He's a Cockeyed Wonder (1950) **77m.** *½ D: Peter Godfrey. Mickey Rooney, Terry Moore, William Demarest, Ross Ford, Mike Mazurki. Bland Rooney film has him as energetic young man who captures a gang of robbers and gets to marry his boss' daughter.

He Said, She Said (1991) **C-115m.** ** D: Ken Kwapis, Marisa Silver. Kevin Bacon, Elizabeth Perkins, Sharon Stone, Nathan Lane, Anthony LaPaglia, Stanley Anderson, Charlaine Woodard, Danton Stone. We say, piffle. Gimmick comedy charts the dissolution of a romance between two Baltimore journalists who parlay their rival point/counterpoint columns into a popular local TV spot. Kwapis' half (marginally funnier) is shown from Bacon's point of view; Silver's (marginally better, thanks to Perkins) takes overlong story from the opposite perspective. About as contemporary as a '60s TV sitcom, with clumsy fantasy sequences. Panavision. [PG-13]▼●

He's My Girl (1987) **C-104m.** ** D: Gabrielle Beaumont. T.K. Carter, David Hallyday, Misha McK, Jennifer Tilly, David Clennon. A few amusing moments cannot save this silly comedy about Carter dressing in drag to accompany pal Hallyday on a free trip to Hollywood. Lots of energy, but it's mostly for naught. [PG-13]▼

He Stayed for Breakfast (1940) **89m.** **

D: Alexander Hall. Loretta Young, Melvyn Douglas, Una O'Connor, Eugene Pallette, Alan Marshal. NINOTCHKA and COMRADE X in reverse, as Russian Douglas is Americanized by Young; trivial.

Hester Street (1975) **92m.** ***½ D: Joan Micklin Silver. Steven Keats, Carol Kane, Mel Howard, Dorrie Kavanaugh, Doris Roberts, Stephen Strimpell. Young Jewish immigrant (Kane) joins her husband in N.Y.C. at turn of the century, only to find that he has forsaken his Old World ways and expects her to do the same. Disarmingly simple story, outstanding period flavor. [PG]▼

He Walked by Night (1948) **79m.** *** D: Alfred L. Werker. Richard Basehart, Scott Brady, Roy Roberts, Whit Bissell, Jack Webb. Grade-A drama of killer hunted by police; told in semi-documentary style (and, as film buffs know, partially directed by Anthony Mann). Effective performances by all.▼●

He Was Her Man (1934) **70m.** ** D: Lloyd Bacon. James Cagney, Joan Blondell, Victor Jory, Frank Craven, Sarah Padden. Disappointing drama of safecracker Cagney on the lam, meeting Blondell, who's engaged to fisherman Jory. One of Cagney's weakest Warner Bros. vehicles.

He Who Gets Slapped (1924) **85m.** *** D: Victor Seastrom. Lon Chaney, Norma Shearer, John Gilbert, Tully Marshall, Marc McDermott, Ford Sterling. Brilliant scientist tries to bury personal tragedy under mask of circus clown, who falls in love with beautiful bareback rider (Shearer). Famous story becomes Pagliacci-type vehicle for Chaney.▼●

He Who Rides a Tiger (1966-British) **103m.** ** D: Charles Crichton. Tom Bell, Judi Dench, Paul Rogers, Kay Walsh, Ray McAnally. Cat burglar is nice to children and is further softened by love, but he still has professional problems; OK programmer.

Hex (1973) **C-92m.** *½ D: Leo Garen. Keith Carradine, Tina Herazo (Cristina Raines), Hilarie Thompson, Gary Busey, Robert Walker, Dan Haggerty, John Carradine, Scott Glenn. Off-the-wall bike movie that involves a motorcycle gang with occultism in post-WW1 Nebraska. You've been warned. Video title: THE SHRIEKING. [PG]▼●

Hexed (1993) **C-90m.** ** D: Alan Spencer. Arye Gross, Claudia Christian, Adrienne Shelly, Ray Baker, R. Lee Ermey, Michael Knight, Robin Curtis, Brandis Kemp, Norman Fell, Teresa Ganzel. Hotel clerk with delusions of grandeur gets involved with a once overweight fashion model whose long-ago act of arson killed 32 people. Very hit-and-miss—and at worst, terrible—but at least it isn't bland. Christian, as the model, is a stitch. [R]▼●

Hey Babu Riba (1986-Yugoslavian) **C-109m.** *** D: Jovan Acin. Gala Videnovic, Relja Basic, Nebojsa Bakocevic, Marko Todorovic, Dragan Bjelogrlic, Milos Zutic. Perceptive film combines nostalgia and political commentary in flashback story of four men recalling their pranks in the early 1950s when all were in love with dream girl Videnovic. Film buffs will appreciate picture being built around kids' fascination with Esther Williams in BATHING BEAUTY; also features vintage footage from the sexy Swedish classic SHE ONLY DANCED ONE SUMMER. [R]▼●

Hey Boy! Hey Girl! (1959) **81m.** *½ D: David Lowell Rich. Louis Prima, Keely Smith, James Gregory, Henry Slate, Asa Maynor, Sam Butera and The Witnesses. Minor low-budget musical about a singer (Smith) who will join Prima and the Witnesses only if they appear at a church bazaar. Louis sings the unforgettable "A Banana Split for My Baby (And a Glass of Water for Me)."

Hey Good Lookin' (1982) **C-86m.** *½ D: Ralph Bakshi. Voices of Richard Romanus, David Proval, Jesse Welles, Tina Bowman. Animated feature dips into "nostalgia" for street gangs in 1950s Brooklyn, and a sense of deja vu hangs over the proceedings. More interesting visually than Bakshi's other later films, because this one wasn't completely traced from live-action footage, but as entertainment it's vulgar and pointless. Originally made in 1975, then largely redone for 1982 release. [R]▼

Hey, Let's Twist! (1961) **80m.** BOMB D: Greg Garrison. Joey Dee, The Starliters, Peppermint Loungers, Jo Ann Campbell, Zohra Lampert, Teddy Randazzo, Allan Arbus. Let's not. This minor film about the rise, decline, and rise of the Peppermint Lounge nightclub came out at the height of the Twist dance rage and wasn't very good then . . . now it's just a bad way to kill 80 minutes. Try spotting a young Joe Pesci (then a Starliters guitarist, making his film debut) as an extra.

Hey, Rookie (1944) **77m.** **½ D: Charles Barton. Larry Parks, Ann Miller, Condos Brothers, Joe Sawyer, Jack Gilford, Selmer Jackson. Typical let's put-on-a-show-for-the-servicemen, with Miller's dancing and several specialty acts.

Hey There It's Yogi Bear (1964) **C-89m.** ** D: William Hanna, Joseph Barbera. Voices of: Mel Blanc, J. Pat O'Malley, Julie Bennett, Daws Butler, Don Messick. First full-length cartoon from Hanna-Barbera studio stars Yogi Bear in amusing musical tale for younger folk.▼●

H. G. Wells' New Invisible Man SEE: **New Invisible Man, The**

Hiawatha (1952) **C-80m.** *½ D: Kurt Neumann. Vincent Edwards, Keith Larsen, Michael Tolan, Yvette Dugay. Juvenile low-budget version of the Longfellow classic.

Hickey & Boggs (1972) **C-111m.** ★★½ D: Robert Culp. Robert Culp, Bill Cosby, Rosalind Cash, Sheila Sullivan, Isabel Sanford, Ta-Ronce Allen, Lou Frizzell. Tough melodrama by Walter Hill about two weary, hard-luck private eyes whose search for a missing girl brings death to almost everyone around them. Well made but extremely violent and downbeat; will come as a surprise to fans of the stars' tongue-in-cheek antics on their *I Spy* TV series. Many now-familiar faces appear in bits: Robert Mandan, Michael Moriarty, Vincent Gardenia, James Woods, and Ed Lauter. [PG]

Hidden, The (1987) **C-96m.** ★★★ D: Jack Sholder. Michael Nouri, Kyle MacLachlan, Ed O'Ross, Clu Gulager, Claudia Christian, Clarence Felder, William Boyett, Richard Brooks. L.A. cop Nouri pursues an alien criminal that loves violence, fast cars, and rock music—and can pass from one human body to another. FBI agent MacLachlan, helping out, is really an alien cop. Smart, fast-paced thriller effectively blends horror, sci-fi, and action with humor; good acting and savvy direction. Followed by a sequel. [R]▼●◗

Hidden II, The (1994) **C-95m.** BOMB D: Seth Pinsker. Raphael Sbarge, Kate Hodge, Jovin Montanaro, Christopher Murphy, Michael Weldon, Michael A. Nickles, Tony Di Benedetto, Tom Tayback. Fifteen years after the events in the original, the daughter of the L.A. cop who chased down the body-switching alien teams up with another alien cop, here to save us from more of the evil visitors. Cheap, slow-paced sequel distorts the premise of the original; result is stilted and routine, utterly devoid of the wit and energy that sparked the first. [R]▼●

Hidden Agenda (1990-British) **C-108m.** ★★★ D: Ken Loach. Frances McDormand, Brian Cox, Brad Dourif, Mai Zetterling, Jim Norton, Maurice Roeves. American human rights activist McDormand and British police inspector Cox (both excellent) try to unravel mystery surrounding police ambush and cover-up in strife-ridden Belfast during the early 1980s. Effective political thriller set amidst the battleground of Northern Ireland. If not exactly unbiased (director Loach is known for films which are critical of the U.K.), it *is* believable. Many small roles played by Belfast non-actors. [R]▼●

Hidden City, The (1950) **71m.** ★½ D: Ford Beebe. Johnny Sheffield, Sue England, Paul Guilfoyle, Damian O'Flynn, Leon Belasco, Smoki Whitfield. Bomba the Jungle Boy comes to the aid of a jungle orphan (England) who's actually a princess. Aka BOMBA AND THE HIDDEN CITY.

Hidden Eye, The (1945) **69m.** ★★½ D: Richard Whorf. Edward Arnold, Frances Rafferty, Ray Collins, Paul Langton, Raymond Largay, William Phillips. Follow-up to EYES IN THE NIGHT, with blind detective Arnold making good use of other senses to solve murder mystery; fast-moving, entertaining mystery.

Hidden Fear (1957) **83m.** ★½ D: Andre de Toth. John Payne, Alexander Knox, Conrad Nagel, Natalie Norwick. On-location filming in Copenhagen is chief virtue of mild hunt-down-the-murderer plot.

Hidden Fortress, The (1958-Japanese) **126m.** ★★★½ D: Akira Kurosawa. Toshiro Mifune, Misa Uehara, Minoru Chiaki, Kamatari Fujiwara, Susumu Fujita, Takashi Shimura. Autocratic young Princess Uehara and loyal general Mifune must make dangerous journey to their homeland with royal fortune, with only bare minimum of help from two bumbling misfits hoping to make off with a share of the gold. Solid comedy-adventure with great deadpan performance by Mifune; one of Kurosawa's personal favorites. Acknowledged by George Lucas as a primary inspiration for STAR WARS. Some U.S. prints cut to 90m.; released in Japan at 139m., and reissued in the U.S. in 1984 at that length. Tohoscope.▼●

Hidden Homicide (1959-British) **70m.** ★½ D: Tony Young. Griffith Jones, James Kenney, Patricia Laffan, Bruce Seton, Charles Farrell. Circumstantial evidence makes writer think he's a murderer.

Hidden in America (1996) **C-96m. TVM** D: Martin Bell. Beau Bridges, Bruce Davison, Shelton Dane, Jena Malone, Alice Krige, Josef Sommer, Frances McDormand, Jeff Bridges. Strong drama about hunger in America, with Beau Bridges as a laid-off factory worker, trying to feed his children, too proud to take handouts from wealthy, well-meaning Davison. Jeff Bridges has a small role and produced the film in conjunction with the nonprofit End Hunger Network. Hard-hitting script by Peter Silverman and Michael de Guzman. Made for cable. Above average.▼

Hidden Room, The (1949-British) **98m.** ★★★ D: Edward Dmytryk. Robert Newton, Sally Gray, Naunton Wayne, Phil Brown, Michael Balfour, Olga Lindo. Very effective suspenser involving Newton's plan to eliminate a man threatening his marriage; nifty climax. Retitled: OBSESSION.▼

Hideaway (1995) **C-112m.** BOMB D: Brett Leonard. Jeff Goldblum, Christine Lahti, Alfred Molina, Jeremy Sisto, Rae Dawn Chong, Kenneth Welsh, Alicia Silverstone. Horror film from best-selling novel by Dean R. Koontz about a man resuscitated after "dying," who returns psychically linked to a psychotic killer who's also back from the beyond—and intent on making the man's family his next victims. This goes nowhere for nearly two interminable hours; Koontz had the good sense to try and have his name taken off the picture. Super 35. [R]▼●

Hideaways, The SEE: **From the Mixed-Up Files of Mrs. Basil E. Frankweiler**
Hide in Plain Sight (1980) **C-98m.** *** D: James Caan. James Caan, Jill Eikenberry, Robert Viharo, Joe Grifasi, Barbra Rae, Kenneth McMillan, Josef Sommer, Danny Aiello. Caan made a creditable directing debut with this true story about a divorced man whose children are swept away by the U.S. government when their new father is moved underground by the Justice Department's witness relocation program. Straightforward and well done. Panavision. [PG]▼
Hideous Kinky (1999-British-French) **C-97m.** *** D: Gillies MacKinnon. Kate Winslet, Saïd Taghmaoui, Bella Riza, Carrie Mullan, Pierre Clémenti, Sira Stampe. Interesting story about an immature young woman who's left her lover, and her life, in England to seek spiritual satisfaction in Morocco—with her two young daughters in tow. Well-observed study of selfishness, spontaneity, and social mores set in the early 1970s, anchored by Winslet's fine performance. Based on an autobiographical novel by Esther Freud. Super 35. [R]▼◗
Hideous Sun Demon, The (1959) **74m.** *½ D: Robert Clarke. Robert Clarke, Patricia Manning, Nan Peterson, Patrick Whyte, Fred La Porta, Bill Hampton. Doctor exposed to radiation discovers that sunlight turns him into ghastly lizard creature. Hideously low-budget production stars the director himself as demon of title.▼
Hide-Out (1934) **83m.** **½ D: W. S. Van Dyke. Robert Montgomery, Maureen O'Sullivan, Edward Arnold, Elizabeth Patterson, Whitford Kane, Mickey Rooney, C. Henry Gordon, Edward Brophy. Big-city racketeer recovers from gunshot wound on idyllic farm where he falls in love (of course) with fetching O'Sullivan. Opens and closes great, with some humdrum stuffing in between; wonderful supporting cast (including Henry Armetta and Herman Bing as nightclub co-owners!). Remade in 1941 as I'LL WAIT FOR YOU.▼
Hideout, The (1961-French) **80m.** **½ D: Raoul Andre. Marcel Mouloudji, Yves Vincent, Francis Blanche, Louise Garletti. Diverting account of Mouloudji seeking refuge in an insane asylum during WW2, kept there as a patient.
Hider in the House (1991) **C-109m.** *½ D: Matthew Patrick. Gary Busey, Mimi Rogers, Michael McKean, Kurt Christopher Kinder, Candy Hutson, Elizabeth Ruscio, Bruce Glover. Disturbed Busey creates a secret living space in the home of a family he admires, but his efforts to try to ingratiate himself with them lead to violence. Routine thriller with a ludicrous premise; Busey is fine as the psycho. [R]▼
Hi Diddle Diddle (1943) **72m.** ** D: Andrew L. Stone. Adolphe Menjou, Martha Scott, Pola Negri, Dennis O'Keefe, Billie Burke, June Havoc. Trifling screwball comedy of newlyweds Scott and O'Keefe; her nutty mom (Burke) loses all her money and his con-man dad (Menjou) comes to her rescue, disrupting the honeymoon. Notable for appearance of silent screen vamp Pola Negri as an egotistical opera star.▼
Hiding Out (1987) **C-98m.** ** D: Bob Giraldi. Jon Cryer, Keith Coogan, Annabeth Gish, Gretchen Cryer, Oliver Cotton, Tim Quill, Anne Pitoniak, John Spencer. Silly, thoroughly unbelievable teen comedy-thriller about stockbroker Cryer, who's on the lam from thugs. He hides out by dyeing his hair and becoming an instant high-school senior. Jon's real-life mother, actress/writer Gretchen Cryer, plays Aunt Lucy. [PG-13]▼
Hiding Place, The (1975) **C-145m.** **½ D: James F. Collier. Julie Harris, Eileen Heckart, Arthur O'Connell, Jeanette Clift, Robert Rietty, Pamela Sholto. Well-meaning, sometimes effective, but draggy, predictable story of Dutch Christians aiding Jews in WW2. Produced by Billy Graham's Evangelistic Association. [PG]▼
High and Dry (1954-British) **93m.** **½ D: Alexander Mackendrick. Paul Douglas, Alex Mackenzie, James Copeland, Abe Barker. Satisfactory, minor yarn about U.S. financier Douglas in conflict with the captain of broken-down ship carrying valuable cargo; static at times. Originally titled THE MAGGIE.
High and Low (1963-Japanese) **142m.** *** D: Akira Kurosawa. Toshiro Mifune, Tatsuya Mihashi, Yutaka Sada, Tatsuya Nakadai, Kyoko Kagawa. Carefully paced study of business executive Mifune, who is financially ruined when he nobly pays ransom money to kidnappers who mistakenly stole his chauffeur's son. Based on an Ed McBain story; one color sequence. Tohoscope.▼●◗
High and the Mighty, The (1954) **C-147m.** ***½ D: William A. Wellman. John Wayne, Claire Trevor, Laraine Day, Robert Stack, Jan Sterling, Phil Harris, Robert Newton, David Brian, Paul Kelly. Granddaddy of all the airborne disaster films, and more fun than most of them put together: a GRAND HOTEL cast of characters boards a flight from Hawaii to the mainland, little dreaming of the trouble in store. Corny and predictable but great fun, bolstered by Dimitri Tiomkin's Oscar-winning music. Written by Ernest K. Gann. CinemaScope.
High Anxiety (1977) **C-94m.** **½ D: Mel Brooks. Mel Brooks, Madeline Kahn, Cloris Leachman, Harvey Korman, Dick Van Patten, Ron Carey, Howard Morris, Murphy Dunne, Jack Riley, Charlie Callas. Affectionate, well-made but uneven spoof of Hitchcock films with Brooks as psychiatrist who walks into trouble as new head of sanitarium. Isolated moments of great comedy

bolster so-so film. Future RAIN MAN director Barry Levinson, who coscripted this film, appears as a hostile hotel bellman. Kahn's father is played by special effects maestro (and real-life Hitchcock collaborator) Albert J. Whitlock. [PG]▼●

High Art (1998-Canadian) **C-101m.** *** D: Lisa Cholodenko. Ally Sheedy, Radha Mitchell, Patricia Clarkson, Tammy Grimes, Gabriel Mann, Bill Sage, David Thornton. Off-putting at first, but a clear-eyed character study of a naive young woman whose stock rises at a pretentious art magazine because of her budding relationship with a once brilliant photographer who had a breakdown years ago. The question is how deeply Mitchell is willing to immerse herself in Sheedy's hedonistic, heroin-infused, lesbian lifestyle. Sheedy is solid and understated; Clarkson is a hoot in a wonderfully showy performance as her companion, an eccentric, egomaniacal German actress. Sarita Choudhury appears unbilled. [R]▼

High Ballin' (1978-U.S.-Canadian) **C-100m.** **½ D: Peter Carter. Peter Fonda, Jerry Reed, Helen Shaver, Chris Wiggins, David Ferry, Chris Longevin. Good-buddy truckdrivers Fonda and Reed battle a rival kingpin's goons who want to force them off the road for good. Predictable action fare, with added spice from female trucker Shaver. [PG]▼

High Barbaree (1947) **91m.** ** D: Jack Conway. Van Johnson, June Allyson, Thomas Mitchell, Marilyn Maxwell, Cameron Mitchell. Navy flier's life story told in flashback as he awaits rescue in plane in ocean. Good cast in inferior story.

High Bright Sun, The SEE: **McGuire, Go Home!**

High Command, The (1937-British) **90m.** **½ D: Thorold Dickinson. Lionel Atwill, Lucie Mannheim, Steven Geray, James Mason, Allan Jeayes, Wally Patch. Crime melodrama set at an African military outpost. Atwill is a general caught up in a blackmailing scheme that leads to murder. An early role for Mason.▼

High Commissioner, The (1968-British) **C-93m.** *½ D: Ralph Thomas. Christopher Plummer, Rod Taylor, Lilli Palmer, Camilla Sparv, Daliah Lavi, Clive Revill, Franchot Tone. Wonderful cast is wasted in tired spy thriller about diplomat involved in murder at height of Cold War negotiations. British title: NOBODY RUNS FOREVER.

High Cost of Loving, The (1958) **87m.** **½ D: Jose Ferrer. Jose Ferrer, Gena Rowlands, Joanne Gilbert, Jim Backus, Bobby Troup, Edward Platt, Werner Klemperer, Nancy Kulp. Lots of familiar faces in this very mild romantic comedy about tensions that threaten marriage of Ferrer and Rowlands. Enjoyable but innocuous semi-satire. Rowlands' film debut. CinemaScope.

High Country, The (1981-Canadian) **C-101m.** BOMB D: Harvey Hart. Timothy Bottoms, Linda Purl, George Sims, Jim Lawrence, Bill Berry, Walter Mills. Feeble drama about obnoxious escaped con Bottoms and illiterate Purl eluding pursuers in the mountains. Panavision. [PG]▼

High Crime (1973-Italian) **C-100m.** ** D: Enzo G. Castellari. Franco Nero, James Whitmore, Fernando Rey, Delia Boccardo. Energetic but superficial action drama. Narc Nero going up against Mafioso Rey. You've seen it all before. Techniscope. ▼

Higher and Higher (1943) **90m.** **½ D: Tim Whelan. Michele Morgan, Jack Haley, Frank Sinatra, Leon Errol, Marcy McGuire, Victor Borge, Mary Wickes, Mel Torme. Bright, breezy, generally witless musical, with good cheer compensating for lack of material, as once-wealthy Errol schemes with his own servants to raise money. Sinatra's songs are fine: "The Music Stopped," "I Couldn't Sleep a Wink Last Night." This was his starring debut. ▼●

Higher Learning (1995) **C-127m.** **½ D: John Singleton. Omar Epps, Kristy Swanson, Laurence Fishburne, Michael Rapaport, Jennifer Connelly, Ice Cube, Jason Wiles, Tyra Banks, Cole Hauser, Bradford English, Regina King, Busta Rhymes, Jay Ferguson. Provocative drama of life at a big university where problems tend to break down along racial and sexual lines. Epps plays a young black athlete searching for direction and, sometimes blindly, raging at injustice. Fishburne is a political science professor who tries to help him see the world as it is. Credible, well-acted film goes awry when writer-director Singleton steers it toward melodrama, and foregoes student relations to focus on a group of extremist skinheads. [R]▼●

High Fidelity (2000) **C-113m.** **½ D: Stephen Frears. John Cusack, Iben Hjejle, Todd Louiso, Jack Black, Lisa Bonet, Catherine Zeta-Jones, Joan Cusack, Tim Robbins, Lili Taylor, Joelle Carter, Natasha Gregson Wagner, Sara Gilbert, Bruce Springsteen. After his girlfriend leaves, a music-obsessed Chicago record store owner (Cusack) reflects on his failed relationships. Adaptation of Nick Hornby's novel (originally set in London) is alternately insightful and annoying, embodied by Cusack's direct-to-camera chats and the fanatically detailed depiction of the music scene and its inhabitants. Cusack coproduced and cowrote the screenplay. [R]▼◗

High Flight (1957-British) **C-89m.** *½ D: John Gilling. Ray Milland, Bernard Lee, Kenneth Haigh, Anthony Newley. Stale British drama of recruits in training for the RAF—not as good as Milland's I WANTED WINGS. Last reel, in the air, only exciting part. CinemaScope.

High Frequency (1988-Italian) **C-105m.** ** D: Faliero Rosati. Vincent Spano, Oliver Benny, Anne Canovas, Isabelle Pasco, David Brandon. Satellite relay station attendant Spano and young ham operator Benny see a murder on a satellite monitor and try to warn a woman they believe will be the killer's next victim. Ersatz REAR WINDOW lifts ideas—but not substance—from the Hitchcock classic. Italian production released with English-language soundtrack. [PG]▼●

High Fury (1947-British) **71m.** ** D: Harold French. Madeleine Carroll, Ian Hunter, Michael Rennie, Michael McKeag, Anne Marie Blanc. Nice location filming in Switzerland uplifts this otherwise standard drama about the plight of war orphans. Carroll wants to adopt young McKeag against the wishes of philandering husband Rennie. Original British title: WHITE CRADLE INN.▼

High Heels (1972-French) **C-100m.** **½ D: Claude Chabrol. Jean-Paul Belmondo, Mia Farrow, Laura Antonelli, Daniel Ivernel. Well-acted but disappointing Chabrol comedy-mystery about a playboy doctor (Belmondo) attracted to women other men find unappealing. Originally titled DR. POPAUL. Aka SCOUNDREL IN WHITE. ▼

High Heels (1991-Spanish) **C-115m.** **½ D: Pedro Almodóvar. Victoria Abril, Marisa Paredes, Miguel Bosé, Feodor Atkine, Bibi Andersen, Rocio Munoz. So-so Almodóvar concoction about the conflicts and intricacies in the relationship between a famous, egocentric actress (Paredes) and her TV newscaster daughter (Abril). First half is vintage Almodóvar, but film becomes a bit more serious (than necessary) as it unfolds. Still, there are plenty of the director's outlandish touches—check out that women's prison—and also some interesting views on celebrity. Leading man Bosé (son of Italian actress Lucia Bosé and Spanish bullfighter Luis Miguel Dominguin) is a pop music star in Spain. [R]▼

High Hell (1958-British) **87m.** **½ D: Burt Balaban. John Derek, Elaine Stewart, Rodney Burke, Patrick Allen. Mine owner's wife has an affair with husband's partner; trio snowbound for winter fight about it.

High Hopes (1988-British) **C-112m.** ***½ D: Mike Leigh. Philip Davis, Ruth Sheen, Edna Dore, Philip Jackson, Heather Tobias, Lesley Manville, David Bamber. Extraordinary slice-of-life comedy-drama about love, alienation, and responsibility, centered on a young, laid-back working-class couple, his aged mother and manic sister. Writer-director Leigh offers a provocative, highly original view of life's misfits in modern-day England, and offers food for thought along with some very hearty laughs.▼

Highlander (1986) **C-111m.** *½ D: Russell Mulcahy. Christopher Lambert, Roxanne Hart, Clancy Brown, Sean Connery, Beatie Edney, Alan North. Immortal being is tracked from 16th-century Scotland to modern-day America by his eternal archenemy. Interesting notion made silly and boring. Connery, at least, shows some style in smallish role as Lambert's survival tutor. Former rock video director Mulcahy's relentlessly showy camera moves may cause you to reach for the Dramamine. Ran 17m. longer outside U.S. (and reportedly made more sense). Director's Cut edition is 5m. longer. Followed by two sequels, a TV series and an animated TV series. [R]▼●◗

Highlander II: The Quickening (1991) **C-88m.** *½ D: Russell Mulcahy. Christopher Lambert, Virginia Madsen, Michael Ironside, Sean Connery, John C. McGinley, Allan Rich, Phil Brock, Rusty Schwimmer. Lambert has saved the world by a globe-encircling shield, but years later, the shield's the problem. At least, that seems to be the setup; hard to tell in a film so awesomely dull. Connery is dull, too, and in it very briefly. We learn new stuff about the immortals that contradicts the first film without adding anything interesting. Even those who liked the first one hated this. Some video versions run 108m. J-D-C Scope. [R]▼●◗

Highlander—The Final Dimension (1994-U.S.-Canadian) **C-99m.** BOMB D: Andy Morahan. Christopher Lambert, Mario Van Peebles, Deborah Unger, Mako, Raoul Trujillo, Martin Neufeld, Michael Jayston. Conor McCloud, the wanderer from medieval Scotland, does battle in today's N.Y. with evil fellow immortal from the past, the Mongol magician Cane (Van Peebles). Foolish, badly written piffle is a sequel only to the first film, ignoring the 2nd and the TV series. Lambert is glum, Van Peebles shamelessly hammy. Dozens of unexplained elements, starting with Cane's perfect English. Video version rated R. Super 35. [PG-13] ▼●◗

High Lonesome (1950) **C-81m.** ** D: Alan LeMay. John Barrymore, Jr., Chill Wills, Lois Butler, Jack Elam. Moody little drama set in the West with Barrymore a brooding youth involved with killers.▼

Highly Dangerous (1951-British) **88m.** **½ D: Roy Baker. Dane Clark, Marius Goring, Margaret Lockwood, Wilfrid Hyde-White, Olaf Pooley, Eric Pohlmann. American reporter (Clark) accompanies scientist (Lockwood) on secret mission; well paced.

High Noon (1952) **84m.** **** D: Fred Zinnemann. Gary Cooper, Thomas Mitchell, Lloyd Bridges, Katy Jurado, Grace Kelly, Otto Kruger, Lon Chaney (Jr.), Henry (Harry) Morgan, Lee Van Cleef, Robert Wilke, Sheb Wooley. On his wedding—and retirement—day, marshal Cooper learns that a gunman is coming seeking revenge. Though he has good excuses for leaving, he feels a responsibility to stay and face the gunman—but no one in town is willing to help. The story appears to unfold in "real time," as the many on-screen clocks will verify. Legendary Western drama about a crisis of conscience, written by Carl Foreman, underscored by Tex Ritter's performance of Oscar-winning Dimitri Tiomkin–Ned Washington song, "Do Not Forsake Me, Oh My Darlin'." Oscars also went to Cooper, Tiomkin's score, and Elmo Williams' and Harry Gerstad's editing. Followed by 1980 TV sequel with Lee Majors. Also shown in computer-colored version. ▼●◗

High Plains Drifter (1973) **C-105m.** *** D: Clint Eastwood. Clint Eastwood, Verna Bloom, Marianna Hill, Mitchell Ryan, Jack Ging, Stefan Gierasch. Moody, self-conscious but compelling story of drifter hired by townspeople to protect them from vengeful outlaws who have just been released from prison. Half-serious, half tongue-in-cheek, with great role for midget Billy Curtis. Panavision. [R]▼●◗

Highpoint (1980-Canadian) **C-88m.** BOMB D: Peter Carter. Richard Harris, Christopher Plummer, Beverly D'Angelo, Kate Reid, Peter Donat, Saul Rubinek. Confused and sloppy comedy thriller (reedited by a film doctor) has Harris as an accountant mixed up in a CIA plot and international intrigue. An excuse for frequent chases culminating in a poorly photographed stunt fall off Toronto's CN tower. ▼●

High Pressure (1932) **74m.** *** D: Mervyn LeRoy. William Powell, Evelyn Brent, Frank McHugh, George Sidney, Guy Kibbee, Evalyn Knapp, Ben Alexander. Slam-bang con-man caper stars Powell as hilarious scheming promotor trying to sell artificial rubber. Typical nonstop Warner Bros. early talkie farce.

High Risk (1981) **C-94m.** **½ D: Stewart Raffill. James Brolin, Cleavon Little, Bruce Davison, Chick Vennera, Anthony Quinn, Lindsay Wagner, James Coburn, Ernest Borgnine. Preposterous movie about group of normal Americans becoming mercenaries, flying to South America, parachuting into jungle to rip off dope dealers . . . and that's just the beginning, because they soon run into bandidos. Ridiculous story, but good fun. [R]▼●◗

High Road to China (1983) **C-120m.** ** D: Brian G. Hutton. Tom Selleck, Bess Armstrong, Jack Weston, Wilford Brimley, Robert Morley, Brian Blessed. Low road to escapism, with Selleck (in his first starring feature) as a boozy ex-WW1 aerial ace hired by heiress Armstrong to find her father. Strictly mediocre, with substandard action scenes, and the flattest dialogue this side of the Great Wall. [PG]▼●

High School Caesar (1960) **72m.** ** D: O'Dale Ireland. John Ashley, Gary Vinson, Lowell Brown, Steve Stevens, Judy Nugent, Daria Massey. Rich kid Ashley, whose parents are too busy for him, gets a chip on his shoulder the size of the Rock of Gibraltar . . . and sets up his own little crime empire in school. Actually, not bad of its type.▼

High School Confidential! (1958) **85m.** *½ D: Jack Arnold. Russ Tamblyn, Jan Sterling, John Drew Barrymore, Mamie Van Doren, Diane Jergens, Ray Anthony, Jerry Lee Lewis, Jackie Coogan, Charles Chaplin, Jr., Lyle Talbot, William Wellman, Jr., Michael Landon. Amateurish, hilariously awful marijuana exposé, with young undercover agent Tamblyn obtaining evidence against dope pushers. A most fascinating cast. Retitled YOUNG HELLIONS; followed by COLLEGE CONFIDENTIAL! CinemaScope.▼●

High School High (1996) **C-86m.** ** D: Hart Bochner. Jon Lovitz, Tia Carrere, Louise Fletcher, Mekhi Phifer, Malinda Williams, John Neville. Lovitz plays an idealistic teacher who finds himself in an urban high school so mean it even has its own cemetery! Farcical at times, uncomfortably realistic at other moments, this film suffers from a severe identity crisis. AIRPLANE/NAKED GUN veterans David Zucker and Pat Proft were among the writers. [PG-13]▼●◗

High Season (1987-British) **C-92m.** ** D: Clare Peploe. Jacqueline Bisset, James Fox, Irene Papas, Sebastian Shaw, Kenneth Branagh, Lesley Manville, Robert Stephens. Romantic misfire has Bisset (stunningly lovely as always) as a photographer residing in Rhodes who becomes involved with obnoxious tourists, a spy, and her egotistical ex-hubbie Fox. Fluff offers little more than luscious views of Bisset and the Greek island setting. [R]▼●

High Sierra (1941) **100m.** *** D: Raoul Walsh. Ida Lupino, Humphrey Bogart, Alan Curtis, Arthur Kennedy, Joan Leslie, Henry Hull, Henry Travers, Barton MacLane, Jerome Cowan, Cornel Wilde, Donald MacBride, John Eldredge, Isabel Jewell, Willie Best. Bogey is Mad Dog Earle, killer with a soft heart on the lam from police, in rousing (if not exactly credible) gangster caper. Lupino as the moll and Leslie as the lame innocent Bogart befriends offer interesting contrast. Screenplay by John Huston and W. R. Burnett based on Burnett's novel. Remade as I DIED A THOUSAND TIMES, and in Western garb as COLORADO TERRITORY. Also shown in computer-colored version. ▼●

High Society (1955) **61m.** ** D: William Beaudine. Leo Gorcey, Huntz Hall, Bernard Gorcey, Amanda Blake, David (Gorcey) Condon, Addison Richards, Gavin Gordon, Paul Harvey, Bennie Bartlett. The Bowery Boys go from a greasy garage to an aristocrat's mansion when Sach is mistakenly believed to be heir to a fortune. OK, but nothing new.

High Society (1956) **C-107m.** *** D: Charles Walters. Bing Crosby, Grace Kelly, Frank Sinatra, Celeste Holm, John Lund, Louis Calhern, Louis Armstrong, Sidney Blackmer. Fluffy remake of PHILADELPHIA STORY is enjoyable, but has lost all the bite of the original. Kelly is about to marry Lund when ex-hubby Crosby arrives, along with reporters Sinatra and Holm. Cole Porter songs include "True Love," "Did You Evah?" "You're Sensational," plus Bing and Satchmo's "Now You Has Jazz." Grace Kelly's last acting role. VistaVision.▼●

High Spirits (1988) **C-97m.** BOMB D: Neil Jordan. Peter O'Toole, Daryl Hannah, Steve Guttenberg, Beverly D'Angelo, Liam Neeson, Peter Gallagher, Jennifer Tilly, Ray McAnally, Donal McCann, Connie Booth, Liz Smith. Two yuppie stereotypes and a pair of 200-year-old ghosts romp around in an Irish castle threatened with foreclosure, with O'Toole—looking a bit ghostly here himself—playing ring master. Head-splitting farce full of collapsing sets and lots of wind-machine action; cast members complained that film's producers crudely altered the original whimsical intentions of writer-director Jordan. Unbearable. [PG-13]▼●

High Stakes (1989) **C-102m.** ** D: Amos Kollek. Sally Kirkland, Robert LuPone, Richard Lynch, Sarah (Michelle) Gellar, Kathy Bates, W. T. Martin. A stripper/prostitute tries to retrieve her daughter from the Mob, while falling in love with a Wall Street speculator. A B-movie script with an A performance by Kirkland. Filmed as MELANIE ROSE and sent almost directly to video under this nondescript title. [R]▼●

High Strung (1991) **C-93m.** *½ D: Roger Nygard. Steve Oedekerk, Denise Crosby, Fred Willard, Thomas F. Wilson, Ed Williams, Jani Lane, Kirsten Dunst, Tony Sawyer. A day in the life of chronic whiner Oedekerk (who cowrote film with Robert Kuhn). Grating comedy was rereleased in 1994 to capitalize on the success of Jim Carrey, who has a very small (about 5 minutes), unbilled role. [PG]▼●

High Terrace (1956-British) **77m.** ** D: Henry Cass. Dale Robertson, Lois Maxwell, Derek Bond, Eric Pohlmann. Fledgling actress is implicated in murder in minor drama.

High Tide (1947) **72m.** **½ D: John Reinhardt. Lee Tracy, Don Castle, Julie Bishop, Regis Toomey, Anabel Shaw, Francis Ford. Low-budget gets good mileage from players convincingly relating story of newspaper's attempts to prevent racketeers taking over city.

High Tide (1987-Australian) **C-101m.** **½ D: Gillian Armstrong. Judy Davis, Jan Adele, Claudia Karvan, Colin Friels, John Clayton, Frankie J. Holden, Monica Trapaga, Mark Hembrow. Quietly emotional story of a woman who inadvertently encounters the teenage daughter she abandoned years ago. Truthfully told, well acted, and set against bleakness of an Australian coastal town, but hampered by a leading character we don't necessarily care about. It's fun to see Davis in the opening scenes playing a backup singer for a crummy Elvis impersonator! [PG-13]▼●

High Time (1960) **C-103m.** **½ D: Blake Edwards. Bing Crosby, Fabian, Tuesday Weld, Nicole Maurey. Middling Crosby vehicle has Bing a widower resuming college career and trying to be one of the boys; forced comedy. CinemaScope.

High Treason (1952-British) **93m.** **½ D: Roy Boulting. Andre Morell, Liam Redmond, Mary Morris. Well-handled drama involving complex caper to instigate chaos in English industrial life via high-explosive bomb.

High Velocity (1977) **C-105m.** ** D: Remi Kramer. Ben Gazzara, Paul Winfield, Britt Ekland, Keenan Wynn, Alejandro Rey, Victoria Racimo. Hard-nosed Vietnam vets are hired to spring an international executive who's been kidnapped. Standard action fare, unworthy of good cast. Panavision. [PG]▼

High Voltage (1929) **57m.** *½ D: Howard Higgin. William Boyd, Owen Moore, Carol(e) Lombard, Diane Ellis, Phillips Smalley, Billy Bevan. Main attraction in this deadening, laughably predictable antique is a very young Lombard (who was then billed as "Carol," without the final "e"), as one of a diverse group stranded in the wilderness after a snowstorm; she's a prisoner, in the custody of sheriff (Moore), who falls for tough guy (Boyd).▼

High Wall (1947) **99m.** *** D: Curtis Bernhardt. Robert Taylor, Audrey Totter, Herbert Marshall, Dorothy Patrick, H. B. Warner, Warner Anderson. Well-paced mystery of former air force bomber pilot who attempts to establish innocence in murder case by working with psychiatrist.

Highway Dragnet (1954) **71m.** ** D: Nathan Juran. Richard Conte, Joan Bennett, Wanda Hendrix, Reed Hadley, Mary Beth Hughes. Tawdry caper of Conte trying to prove his innocence of a murder rap. This was Roger Corman's first film, as cowriter and coproducer.

Highwayman, The (1951) **C-82m.** **½ D: Lesley Selander. Charles Coburn, Wanda Hendrix, Philip Friend, Cecil Kellaway, Victor Jory. Filmization of famous poem, involving innkeeper's daughter in love with nobleman who masquerades as bandit to help the oppressed; set in 1760s England.

Highwayman Rides, The SEE: **Billy the Kid** (1930)

Highway Patrolman (1993-U.S.-Mexican)

C-105m. **½ D: Alex Cox. Roberto Sosa, Bruno Bichir, Vanessa Bauche, Zaide Silvia Gutierrez, Pedro Armendariz, Jr., Malena Doria. Portrait of an idealistic young highway patrolman (Sosa), who is committed to upholding the law but gradually allows himself to be corrupted. Mildly entertaining and more straightforward than one might expect from filmmaker Cox; if anything, the problem is the story's lack of dramatic tension.▼

Highway 61 (1991-Canadian-British) **C-102m.** **½ D: Bruce McDonald. Don McKellar, Valerie Buhagiar, Earl Pastko, Peter Breck, Jello Biafra. An odd couple—introverted, inexperienced small-town barber McKellar and eccentric, on-the-lam roadie Buhagiar—find themselves traveling from Ontario to New Orleans, along the highway immortalized by Bob Dylan, with a coffin strapped to the roof of their car. Quirky rock 'n roll road movie is strangely likable, depending on your taste and tolerance for the material. McKellar also wrote the script. [R]▼●

Highway 301 (1950) **83m.** ** D: Andrew L. Stone. Steve Cochran, Virginia Grey, Robert Webber, Richard Egan. Good little gangster film relating robbery capers in straightforward manner.

Highway to Battle (1960-British) **71m.** ** D: Ernest Morris. Gerard Heinz, Margaret Tyzack, Peter Reynolds, Richard Shaw. Trim little film set in 1935 England involving Nazi diplomats who try to defect, chased by Gestapo agents.

Highway to Hell (1992) **C-93m.** *½ D: Ate de Jong. Patrick Bergin, Chad Lowe, Kristy Swanson, Richard Farnsworth, C. J. Graham, Lita Ford, Kevin Peter Hall. Newlyweds Lowe and Swanson have their honeymoon ruined when she's abducted by a cop from hell . . . literally! Lowe then learns that local legend gives him 24 hours to rescue his bride. Oddball yarn is unexciting and unfunny; even comic Gilbert Gottfried in a cameo as Hitler can't salvage this one. Filmed in 1989. [R] ▼●

High, Wide, and Handsome (1937) **112m.** **½ D: Rouben Mamoulian. Irene Dunne, Randolph Scott, Dorothy Lamour, Elizabeth Patterson, Charles Bickford, Raymond Walburn, Alan Hale, Akim Tamiroff, William Frawley. Jerome Kern–Oscar Hammerstein old-time musical of determined Scott drilling for oil in 19th-century Pennsylvania, fighting corrupt Hale. Corny plot put over by energetic cast; result is entertaining. Songs include "The Folks Who Live On The Hill."

High Wind in Jamaica, A (1965-British) **C-104m.** *** D: Alexander Mackendrick. Anthony Quinn, James Coburn, Dennis Price, Gert Frobe, Lila Kedrova, Nigel Davenport, Kenneth J. Warren, Deborah Baxter. Excellent cast and intelligent script about group of children who reveal their basic natures when left adrift aboard a pirate vessel. Score composed by harmonica virtuoso Larry Adler. CinemaScope.

Hi, Good Lookin' (1944) **62m.** ** D: Edward Lilley. Harriet Hilliard, Eddie Quillan, Kirby Grant, Betty Kean, Roscoe Karns, Ozzie Nelson and His Orchestra, Jack Teagarden and His Orchestra, Delta Rhythm Boys, Tip, Tap and Toe. Lightweight musical programmer serves as a showcase for Hilliard as she attempts to become a radio star with help of Grant.

Hilary and Jackie (1998-British) **C-120m.** *** D: Anand Tucker. Emily Watson, Rachel Griffiths, James Frain, David Morrissey, Charles Dance, Celia Imrie, Rupert Penry-Jones, Bill Paterson. Highly charged portrait of British cellist Jacqueline du Pré (Watson) and her complex relationship with her sister, Hilary (Griffiths), which grows more troubled as Jackie becomes a star in the classical music world. Told in nonlinear fashion, with arresting performances by both women; Watson's cello work is extraordinarily convincing. The facts (disputed by some relatives and colleagues) come from Hilary's memoir. Super 35. [R] ▼●◗

Hilda Crane (1956) **C-87m.** ** D: Philip Dunne. Jean Simmons, Guy Madison, Jean-Pierre Aumont, Judith Evelyn, Evelyn Varden. Twice-divorced Simmons returns to the college town that used to be her home, starts the local gossips to fluttering with her behavior. Not much overall, but title character is surprisingly liberated for her time, making her one of the 50s' more interesting screen heroines. CinemaScope.

Hildegarde Withers In 1932, RKO Radio Pictures purchased the rights to a story by Stuart Palmer about Hildegarde Withers, a schoolteacher with a yen for sleuthing who becomes involved with Inspector Oscar Piper of the Police Department. The role of the stubborn and occasionally thick-witted New York cop went to James Gleason, while Hildegarde found her perfect personification in character actress Edna May Oliver. When Piper gruffly asks who she is, she replies archly, "I'm a schoolteacher, and I might have done wonders with you if I'd caught you early enough." PENGUIN POOL MURDER is a first-rate mystery in every respect, but it's the relationship between Hildegarde and Oscar, which builds to a level of grudging respect and even affection, that makes it special. It took RKO more than a year to produce a sequel, which ignored the fact that the two lead characters had gotten married at the end of the first picture (clearly, it made for better material to maintain them as friendly adversaries). MURDER ON THE BLACKBOARD reunited Gleason and Oliver with the same writer (Willis Goldbeck) and director (George Archainbaud) who fashioned the original film, and yielded similarly pleasing results. Returning too were Edgar Kennedy, as one of Gleason's cops, and Gustav von Seyffertitz, as a lab technician. Another year passed before Hildegarde would call on Oscar to help solve a mystery on picturesque Catalina Island in MURDER ON A HONEYMOON, which was cowritten by Seton I. Miller and famed humorist Robert Benchley. Unfortunately, Miss Oliver left RKO just when the studio (finally) committed itself to making a more regular series with these characters. Oliver was replaced by Helen Broderick for MURDER ON A BRIDLE PATH, a terribly slow-moving mystery which gave the usually jaunty actress no material to work with, and Gleason's character the stupidest lines of the series. Then RKO cast ZaSu Pitts as Hildegarde for THE PLOT THICKENS, and things took a turn for the better. Pitts and Gleason are well teamed, and the mystery is engaging. Unfortunately, the stars' followup did not maintain that standard. FORTY NAUGHTY GIRLS is more comic than mysterious, and more heavy-handed than hilarious. With that obvious failure, RKO gave up. One of Stuart Palmer's Withers stories was later adapted as a feature called MR. O'MALLEY AND MRS. MALONE, with Marjorie Main and James Whitmore; later still, Eve Arden starred as Hildegarde in a rather freely rewritten TV movie, A VERY MISSING PERSON, with James Gregory as Oscar Piper in 1972. With only a handful of films on its roster, and only half of them worthwhile, this may not be the most significant series in Hollywood history, but at its best it remains one of the most enjoyable.

HILDEGARDE WITHERS

Penguin Pool Murder (1932)
Murder on the Blackboard (1934)
Murder on a Honeymoon (1935)
Murder on a Bridle Path (1936)
The Plot Thickens (1936)
Forty Naughty Girls (1937)

Hi-Life (1998) **C-82m.** ** D: Roger Hedden. Katrin Cartlidge, Charles Durning, Daryl Hannah, Moira Kelly, Peter Riegert, Campbell Scott, Eric Stoltz, Anne De Salvo, Saundra Santiago, Bruce McVittie, Carlos Alban. Characters and complications abound in this contrived Christmastime tale about a N.Y.C. bartender (Scott) and his attempt to raise sufficient funds to pay for what he has been led to believe is his sister's abortion. MIRACLE ON 34TH STREET it ain't, but the talented cast makes it watchable. [R]▼◗

Hill, The (1965) **122m.** ***½ D: Sidney Lumet. Sean Connery, Harry Andrews, Ian Hendry, Michael Redgrave, Ian Bannen, Alfred Lynch, Ossie Davis, Roy Kinnear, Jack Watson. Powerful drama of military prison camp, with superb performances by all. One problem: British actors bark at each other and much dialogue is unintelligible to American ears (though if you can make it through the first reel, hang on). Written by Ray Rigby. Also shown in computer-colored version.▼●

Hillbillys in a Haunted House (1967) **C-88m.** *½ D: Jean Yarbrough. Ferlin Husky, Joi Lansing, Don Bowman, John Carradine, Lon Chaney, Jr., Basil Rathbone, Molly Bee, Merle Haggard, Sonny James. Country singers Husky and Lansing spend a night in an old mansion, become involved with an espionage ring. Moronic comedy with an elderly, tired cast; a follow-up to LAS VEGAS HILLBILLYS. Sorry to say, Rathbone's last film.▼

Hill in Korea, A SEE: **Hell in Korea**

Hills Have Eyes, The (1977) **C-89m.** **½ D: Wes Craven. Susan Lanier, Robert Houston, Virginia Vincent, Russ Grieve, Dee Wallace, Martin Speer, Michael Berryman. Typical American family on camping trip is harassed by savage, cannibalistic mutants. Above average of its type, with compact direction and plenty of amusing plot twists. Extremely gory film has acquired a cult following. Followed by a sequel. [R]▼●

Hills Have Eyes Part II, The (1985-U.S.-British) **C-88m.** BOMB D: Wes Craven. Michael Berryman, John Laughin, Tamara Stafford, Kevin Blair, John Bloom. Lame sequel has a group of young motocross enthusiasts stranded in the desert, preyed upon by primitive family. Loaded with flashback footage from 1977 film, including one sequence ludicrously purporting to be a recollection by a dog! Filmed in 1983. [R]▼●

Hills of Home (1948) **C-97m.** *** D: Fred M. Wilcox. Edmund Gwenn, Donald Crisp, Tom Drake, Rhys Williams, Janet Leigh. Fine Lassie movie about doctor convincing Scottish father to urge son to study medicine.▼

Hills Run Red, The (1966-Italian) **C-89m.** ** D: Carlo Lizzani. Thomas Hunter, Henry Silva, Dan Duryea, Nando Gazzola. Civil War Western of stolen payrolls; poorly dubbed and loosely acted. Techniscope.

Hill 24 Doesn't Answer (1955-Israeli) **102m.** *** D: Thorold Dickinson. Edward Mulhare, Haya Harareet, Michael Wager, Michael Shillo, Arieh Lavi. Evocative if occasionally schmaltzy drama, played in flashbacks, of the fight for modern Israel, centering on the stories of four soldiers defending a hill outside Jerusalem during the 1948 war.▼

Hi-Lo Country, The (1998) **C-114m.** **½

D: Stephen Frears. Woody Harrelson, Billy Crudup, Patricia Arquette, Sam Elliott, Cole Hauser, Penelope Cruz, Darren Burrows, Jacob Vargas, James Gammon, Lane Smith, Katy Jurado. Story of two cowboy friends in post-WW2 New Mexico who happen to fall in love with the same woman—though she's already married. A paean to the cowboy way of life and the joys of true friendship, this film has so much going for it (including Harrelson's terrific performance as a hell-raiser and Oliver Stapleton's cinematography) that it's a shame it doesn't hit the bull's-eye . . . and Arquette is so dull. Screenplay by Walon Green from the novel by Max Evans. Executive-produced by Martin Scorsese. 2.35 Research PLC. [R]▼●◗

Hi, Mom! (1970) **C/B&W-87m.** ***½ D: Brian De Palma. Robert De Niro, Allen Garfield, Lara Parker, Jennifer Salt, Gerrit Graham, Charles Durning. Sequel to GREETINGS! is funny satire of the late '60s, with Vietnam veteran De Niro making dirty movies and bombing apartment houses. Aka CONFESSIONS OF A PEEPING JOHN and BLUE MANHATTAN. [R]▼

Hindenburg, The (1975) **C-125m.** ** D: Robert Wise. George C. Scott, Anne Bancroft, William Atherton, Roy Thinnes, Gig Young, Burgess Meredith, Charles Durning, Richard A. Dysart, Robert Clary, Rene Auberjonois, Katherine Helmond. Intriguing premise, that 1937 airship disaster was an act of sabotage, undermined by silly Grand Hotel-type characters and unexciting denouement combining original newsreel footage and newly shot material. This earned special Oscars for its visual and sound effects. 5 min. were added to film for network showing. Panavision. [PG] ▼●◗

Hindu, The SEE: **Sabaka**

Hi, Nellie! (1934) **75m.** **½ D: Mervyn LeRoy. Paul Muni, Glenda Farrell, Ned Sparks, Robert Barrat, Kathryn Sergava, Hobart Cavanaugh, Berton Churchill, Douglass Dumbrille. Minor but enjoyable newspaper yarn with Muni as hard-hitting editor who's punished by being assigned to advice-to-the-lovelorn column. Loses initial momentum with gangland subplot, but it's still entertaining. Remade as LOVE IS ON THE AIR, YOU CAN'T ESCAPE FOREVER, and THE HOUSE ACROSS THE STREET.

Hips, Hips, Hooray (1934) **68m.** *** D: Mark Sandrich. Bert Wheeler, Robert Woolsey, Dorothy Lee, Thelma Todd, Ruth Etting, George Meeker. One of Wheeler & Woolsey's best vehicles is a lavish, risqué musical comedy about their attempts to save Todd's ailing beauty business. Wild production numbers, plus a nice song from Etting, "Keep Romance Alive."▼●

Hired Gun, The (1957) **63m.** **½ D: Ray Nazarro. Rory Calhoun, Anne Francis, Vince Edwards, John Litel, Chuck Connors. Francis is fetching as condemned killer Calhoun determines to prove innocent. CinemaScope.

Hired Hand, The (1971) **C-93m.** *** D: Peter Fonda. Peter Fonda, Warren Oates, Verna Bloom, Robert Pratt, Severn Darden. First-rate photography by Vilmos Zsigmond and good performances by Oates and Bloom aid this offbeat, sometimes pretentious Western about cowboy who goes to work for the wife he deserted seven years before. TV prints run 98m., and include a scene with Larry Hagman. [PG]▼

Hired to Kill (1990) **C-91m.** *½ D: Nico Mastorakis, Peter Rader. Brian Thompson, Oliver Reed, George Kennedy, Jose Ferrer, Michelle Moffett, Barbara Lee Alexander, Jordana Capra, Kendall Conrad, Kim Lonsdale, Jude Mussetter, Penelope Reed. Mercenary Thompson poses as a gay fashion designer to spring rebel leader Ferrer from Latin American prison. His commando squad: six gorgeous women posing as fashion models! Well produced, but awesomely silly. [R]▼

Hired Wife (1940) **96m.** *** D: William A. Seiter. Rosalind Russell, Brian Aherne, Virginia Bruce, Robert Benchley, John Carroll. Secretary Russell marries boss Aherne for business reasons; then the fun begins. Hilarious trifle with cast of comedy experts.

Hireling, The (1973-British) **C-108m.** ***½ D: Alan Bridges. Robert Shaw, Sarah Miles, Peter Egan, Elizabeth Sellars, Caroline Mortimer, Patricia Lawrence. Artistic adaptation of L. P. Hartley novel of stifling class system of England. Chauffeur (Shaw) helps upper-class woman (Miles) out of mental depression, mistakenly assumes she's interested in him. Ensemble British cast, good direction. Screenplay by Wolf Mankowitz. [PG]

Hiroshima (1995-Canadian-Japanese) **C/B&W-195m. TVM** D: Roger Spottiswoode, Koreyoshi Kurahara. Kenneth Welsh, Wesley Addy, Richard Masur, David Gow, Hisashi Igawa, Sheena Larkin, Tatsuo Matsumura, Jeffrey DeMunn, Ken Jenkins, Saul Rubinek, Timothy West, Kei Sato, Kohji Takahashi. Mesmerizing account of the events leading up to the dropping of the atomic bomb, as told from both sides in two separate, interwoven films—one Canadian (with Kenneth Welsh as Truman), the other Japanese, with subtitles. Recently uncovered footage, newsreels, armed forces clips, and dramatized encounters with the leading figures of the time provide stunning results for this ambitious TV effort. Interestingly, other than a few U.S. actors, no American hands were involved, despite its dealing mainly with Harry Truman, his closest advisors, and the Manhattan Project. Made for cable. Above average. ▼●

Hiroshima, Mon Amour (1959-French-Japanese) **91m.** ***½ D: Alain Resnais. Emmanuele Riva, Eiji Okada, Stella Dassas, Pierre Barbaud, Bernard Fresson. Resnais' first feature is a thoughtful, complex study of a French film actress (Riva) and Japanese architect (Okada), each with a troubled past, who have a brief affair in postwar Hiroshima. Scripted by Marguerite Duras.▼

Hiroshima: Out of the Ashes (1990) **C-100m. TVM** D: Peter Werner. Max von Sydow, Judd Nelson, Mako, Tamlyn Tomita, Stan Egi, Sab Shimono, Pat Morita, Kim Miyori. Well-made, if naturally depressing, drama about the A-bomb as seen by the survivors at ground zero. Nelson plays an American POW being held there. John McGreevey's earnest script is based partly on Michihiko Hachiya's *Hiroshima Diary*. Above average.▼

His Brother's Wife (1936) **90m.** ** D: W. S. Van Dyke, II. Barbara Stanwyck, Robert Taylor, Jean Hersholt, Joseph Calleia, John Eldredge, Samuel S. Hinds. Glossy soaper of dedicated scientist Taylor scorning Stanwyck, who marries his brother Eldredge for spite. Stanwyck and Taylor married in real life three years later.

His Butler's Sister (1943) **94m.** ** D: Frank Borzage. Deanna Durbin, Franchot Tone, Pat O'Brien, Evelyn Ankers, Elsa Janssen, Akim Tamiroff, Walter Catlett, Alan Mowbray. Great opening (Iris Adrian and Robin Raymond as the Sunshine Twins) and moving finale (Deanna's stunning rendition of "Nessun Dorma" from *Turandot*), but in between, a tired Durbin vehicle with Tone as an aloof Broadway composer.▼

His Double Life (1933) **67m.** **½ D: Arthur Hopkins. Roland Young, Lillian Gish, Montague Love, Lucy Beaumont, Lumsden Hare. Slight, moderately entertaining tale about a shy but famous artist (Young), who is more than pleased to settle down with middle-class spinster Gish when he is thought dead. Based on Arnold Bennett's play *Buried Alive,* filmed three times in the silent era. Remade far more successfully as HOLY MATRIMONY.▼

His First Command (1929) **61m.** ** D: Gregory La Cava. William Boyd, Dorothy Sebastian, Gavin Gordon, Helen Parrish, Alphonse Ethier. Slow-moving romantic drama with Boyd offering an awkward performance as a playboy who enlists in the army to win the affection of colonel's daughter Sebastian. Forgettable.▼

His Girl Friday (1940) **92m.** **** D: Howard Hawks. Cary Grant, Rosalind Russell, Ralph Bellamy, Gene Lockhart, Helen Mack, Ernest Truex, Clarence Kolb, Porter Hall, Roscoe Karns, Abner Biberman, Cliff Edwards, John Qualen, Frank Jenks, Billy Gilbert. Splendid comedy remake of THE FRONT PAGE with Grant as conniving editor, Russell as star reporter (and his ex-wife), Bellamy as mama's boy she's trying to marry amid hot murder story. Terrific character actors add sparkle to must-see film, scripted by Ben Hecht and Charles Lederer. Remade (with the same gender twist) in 1988 as SWITCHING CHANNELS.▼●◗

His Kind of Woman (1951) **120m.** *** D: John Farrow. Robert Mitchum, Jane Russell, Vincent Price, Tim Holt, Raymond Burr, Charles McGraw, Marjorie Reynolds, Jim Backus. Mitchum blindly goes to Mexico for a payoff of 50 grand, discovers he's the soon-to-be-dead chump whose identity will help deported gangster Burr re-enter the country. Cult film is overlong, but its spoofing of he-man heroics predates the more celebrated BEAT THE DEVIL by three years; Price is hilarious as a ham actor.▼

His Majesty O'Keefe (1953) **C-92m.** **½ D: Byron Haskin. Burt Lancaster, Joan Rice, Benson Fong, Philip Ahn, Grant Taylor. Another athletic Lancaster buccaneer romp, set in the South Seas.▼

History Is Made at Night (1937) **97m.** ***½ D: Frank Borzage. Charles Boyer, Jean Arthur, Leo Carrillo, Colin Clive, Ivan Lebedeff, George Meeker, Lucien Prival, George Davis. Arthur, fleeing from a jealous husband she doesn't love, falls in love with Parisian headwaiter Boyer. Elegant, adult romantic drama, seamlessly directed by Borzage, with incredible shipboard climax and flawless performances by the two leads.▼●

History of Mr. Polly, The (1949-British) **96m.** *** D: Anthony Pelissier. John Mills, Sally Ann Howes, Finlay Currie, Betty Ann Davies, Edward Chapman, Megs Jenkins, Juliet Mills. Worthy adaptation of H. G. Wells novel about timid draper's clerk (Mills) and his relationships with women—notably a shrewish cousin and a jolly innkeeper. Amusing and enjoyable Victorian comedy.

History of the World—Part 1 (1981) **C-92m.** *½ D: Mel Brooks. Mel Brooks, Gregory Hines, Dom DeLuise, Madeline Kahn, Harvey Korman, Cloris Leachman, Ron Carey, Sid Caesar, Pamela Stephenson, Mary-Margaret Humes, Howard Morris, Spike Milligan, Barry Levinson, many guest stars. Narrated by Orson Welles. Scattershot comedy wanders from the Stone Age to Roman Empire to French Revolution, dispensing gags ranging from hilarious to hideous. After a while momentum's gone, and it all just lies there, despite efforts of a large comic cast. Caesar scores highest as a caveman in opening scenes. Hines' film debut. Panavision. [R]▼●◗

His Woman (1931) **80m.** ** D: Edward Sloman. Gary Cooper, Claudette Colbert,

Douglass Dumbrille, Harry Davenport. Stiff, early-talkie romance between skipper Cooper and passenger, nurse Colbert.
Hit! (1973) **C-134m.** *** D: Sidney J. Furie. Billy Dee Williams, Paul Hampton, Richard Pryor, Gwen Welles. Detailed and overlong, but exciting story of black U.S. agent who seeks revenge on top drug importers in Marseilles who are indirectly responsible for his daughter's death. Panavision. [R]▼
Hit, The (1984-British) **C-98m.** *** D: Stephen Frears. Terence Stamp, John Hurt, Tim Roth, Laura Del Sol, Bill Hunter, Fernando Rey. Sly, offbeat film about a criminal stool pigeon (Stamp) who's been in hiding for ten years but whose time has just run out: two hit men have tracked him down. Sharp, often very funny, and doggedly unpredictable. Written by Peter Prince; memorable theme music by Eric Clapton, assisted by Roger Waters. Film debut of Tim Roth. [R]▼●
Hit and Run (1957) **84m.** BOMB D: Hugo Haas. Hugo Haas, Cleo Moore, Vince Edwards. Trash involving Haas' efforts to rid himself of wife's young boyfriend.
Hit and Run (1982) **C-93m.** ** D: Charles Braverman. Paul Perri, Claudia Cron, Will Lee, Bart Braverman, E. Brian Dean, Donald Symington. All gloss, no substance in this implausible drama of cabdriver Perri's entanglement with mysterious, beautiful passenger Cron and murder. Also known as REVENGE SQUAD. [PG]▼
Hitcher, The (1986) **C-97m.** **½ D: Robert Harmon. Rutger Hauer, C. Thomas Howell, Jennifer Jason Leigh, Jeffrey DeMunn, John Jackson. Hitchhiker Hauer keeps reappearing in Howell's life—is he real, or an hallucination? Reminiscent of other movies, except all those other movies (DUEL, NIGHT OF THE HUNTER) are better. Not without interest, but some of the violence is genuinely grisly and unappealing. Panavision. [R]▼●◗
Hitch-Hiker, The (1953) **71m.** **½ D: Ida Lupino. Edmond O'Brien, Frank Lovejoy, William Talman, Jose Torvay. Well-made suspense yarn about two men on a hunting trip whose car is commandeered by a murderous fugitive. Good performances, especially by a venal Talman in the title role, but the film's once-powerful impact has been muted by decades of more graphic and imaginative films.▼◗
Hitler (1962) **107m.** **½ D: Stuart Heisler. Richard Basehart, Cordula Trantow, Maria Emo, Martin Kosleck, John Banner, Carl Esmond. Basehart gives a cerebral interpretation to the career of the leader of the Third Reich.▼
Hitler—Dead or Alive (1943) **70m.** ** D: Nick Grinde. Ward Bond, Dorothy Tree, Warren Hymer, Paul Fix, Russell Hicks, Felix Basch, Bobby Watson. Low-budget nonsense, with con-men shooting for high stakes by attempting to kill Hitler.▼
Hitler Gang, The (1944) **101m.** **½ D: John Farrow. Robert Watson, Martin Kosleck, Victor Varconi, Luis Van Rooten, Sig Ruman, Tonio Selwart, Ludwig Donath. Historical drama of Hitler's rise to power had greatest impact on WW2 audiences but is still fairly interesting, though dwarfed by recent documentaries.
Hitler's Children (1943) **83m.** *** D: Edward Dmytryk, Irving Reis. Tim Holt, Bonita Granville, Kent Smith, Otto Kruger, H. B. Warner, Lloyd Corrigan. Engrossing exploitation film of young people forced to live life of horror in Nazi Germany. Quite sensational in its day.▼
Hitler's Gold SEE: **Inside Out** (1975)
Hitler's Madman (1943) **84m.** **½ D: Douglas Sirk. Patricia Morison, John Carradine, Alan Curtis, Ralph Morgan, Howard Freeman, Ludwig Stossel, Edgar Kennedy. Sensationalistic saga based on true story of small Czech village destroyed by Nazis, and commander Heydrich, assassinated by determined Czechs. Look for Ava Gardner in a small part.
Hitler: The Last Ten Days (1973-British-Italian) **C-108m.** ** D: Ennio de Concini. Alec Guinness, Simon Ward, Adolfo Celi, Diane Cilento, Gabriele Ferzetti, Eric Porter, Doris Kunstmann. Strange treatment of Hitler's final tyrannies is grimly amusing at times; muddled film doesn't really work. Panavision. [PG]▼
Hit List (1989) **C-87m.** ** D: William Lustig. Jan-Michael Vincent, Lance Henriksen, Rip Torn, Leo Rossi, Jere Burns, Ken Lerner. Familiar urban thriller of ordinary guy whose child is mistakenly kidnapped by cold-eyed hit man working for flamboyant mobster Torn. Hero teams up with the real target, an informer. Lots of violent action. Torn and Henriksen are good, but you've seen it all before. [R]▼●
Hit Man (1972) **C-90m.** ** D: George Armitage. Bernie Casey, Pamela Grier, Lisa Moore, Don Diamond, Roger E. Mosley. Reworking of GET CARTER in black mold. Big rubout is key to crime story, and it loses steam before long. [R]
Hitman (1985) SEE: **American Commandos**
Hitman, The (1991) **C-95m.** *½ D: Aaron Norris. Chuck Norris, Michael Parks, Al Waxman, Alberta Watson, Salim Grant, Ken Pogue, Marcel Sabourin. Fairly awful Chuck Norris vehicle in which the star goes undercover to infiltrate an organized crime ring. Norris gets to play a heavy —even though we know all along it's a ruse. This acting "stretch" still isn't enough to distinguish the film. Stuntwork remains the only redeeming quality. [R]▼●
Hit Parade of 1943 SEE: **Change of Heart**
Hit Team, The SEE: **Company of Killers**

Hit the Deck (1955) **C-112m.** **½ D: Roy Rowland. Jane Powell, Tony Martin, Debbie Reynolds, Ann Miller, Vic Damone, Russ Tamblyn, Walter Pidgeon, Kay Armen, Gene Raymond. Second-string MGM musical of sailors on shore leave is pleasant time-filler, no more, with nice Vincent Youmans songs like "Hallelujah," "Sometimes I'm Happy," "More Than You Know." Filmed before in 1930. CinemaScope. ▼●

Hit the Ice (1943) **82m.** **½ D: Charles Lamont. Bud Abbott, Lou Costello, Ginny Simms, Patric Knowles, Elyse Knox, Sheldon Leonard, Marc Lawrence, Joseph Sawyer. Bud and Lou are newspaper photographers involved with gang of thugs in zany comedy with good gags on skating rink. ▼●

Hit the Road (1941) **61m.** ** D: Joe May. Billy Halop, Huntz Hall, Gabriel Dell, Bernard Punsley, Gladys George, Barton MacLane, Bobs Watson, Evelyn Ankers, Charles Lang, Shemp Howard. Halop, Hall and the other boys are turned into vengeful orphans when their dads are all rubbed out in a mob war. Uninteresting *Little Tough Guys* entry.▼

Hitting a New High (1937) **85m.** **½ D: Raoul Walsh. Lily Pons, Jack Oakie, Edward Everett Horton, Lucille Ball, Eric Blore, Eduardo Ciannelli. Title refers to Pons' voice, not the film per se; fluffy musical romance relies on supporting cast for entertainment.

Hi'ya, Chum (1943) **61m.** *½ D: Harold Young. Ritz Brothers, Jane Frazee, Robert Paige, June Clyde, Edmund MacDonald. Entertainers find themselves in small boomtown, and open a restaurant there. Weak musical comedy, if that's what you want to call it.

H-Man, The (1958-Japanese) **C-79m.** ** D: Ishiro Honda. Kenji Sahara, Yumi Shirakawa, Akihiko Hirata, Koreya Senda. Good special effects marred by dumb script involving radioactive liquid causing havoc in Tokyo, subplot of cops vs. underworld. Tohoscope.▼

H. M. Pulham, Esq. (1941) **120m.** ***½ D: King Vidor. Hedy Lamarr, Robert Young, Ruth Hussey, Charles Coburn, Van Heflin, Fay Holden, Bonita Granville, Leif Erickson, Sara Haden. Intelligent, mature, and witty film (based on John P. Marquand story) about a man who's lived his life as he was supposed to—not as he chose to. Lamarr is excellent as the spirited career woman who coaxes proper Bostonian Young out of his shell, ever so briefly. Scripted by Elizabeth Hill and director Vidor. Anne Revere has unbilled bit as a secretary in flashback scenes.

Hobson's Choice (1954-British) **107m.** *** D: David Lean. Charles Laughton, John Mills, Brenda de Banzie, Daphne Anderson, Prunella Scales, Richard Wattis, Helen Haye. Laughton is selfish, overbearing owner of bootshop in 1890s who's used to being tended to by his three subservient daughters; then his eldest (De Banzie) decides to take matters into her own hands. Beautifully staged and photographed (by Jack Hildyard), with Laughton having a field day in the lead. Loses momentum along the way, but still entertaining. Filmed before in 1931; remade as a TVM in 1983. ▼●

Hockey Night (1984-Canadian) **C-77m.** **½ D: Paul Shapiro. Megan Follows, Rick Moranis, Gail Youngs, Yannick Bisson, Henry Ramer, Sean McCann. A girl goalie makes the boys' hockey team in a small Canadian town. Unexceptional but still likable, and ideal nonexploitation fare for pre- and early teens.▼

Hocus Pocus (1993) **C-95m.** *½ D: Kenny Ortega. Bette Midler, Sarah Jessica Parker, Kathy Najimy, Omri Katz, Thora Birch, Vinessa Shaw, Amanda Shepherd, Larry Bagby III, Tobias Jelinek, Stephanie Faracy, Charlie Rocket, Kathleen Freeman, Don Yesso. Lonely male teen in Salem, Mass., conjures up three long-deceased witches who can only sustain themselves by sucking the life out of children. Someone certainly sucked the humor out of this ghoulish, effects-laden concoction. Hammy to the extreme, and a discredit to Disney "family entertainment." [PG]▼●◗

Hoffa (1992) **C-140m.** **½ D: Danny DeVito. Jack Nicholson, Danny DeVito, Armand Assante, J. T. Walsh, John C. Reilly, Frank Whaley, Kevin Anderson, John P. Ryan, Robert Prosky, Natalija Nogulich, Nicholas Pryor, Karen Young, Cliff Gorman. Scattershot (and sanitized) biography of legendary Teamster boss Jimmy Hoffa, transformed into a must-see by the galvanizing performance of Nicholson. DeVito indulges in visual flourishes but seldom engages our emotions; nor does David Mamet's script, which never gives us much insight into the man or his motivations. Nicholson's daughter, Jennifer Nicholson, has a bit as a nursing nun in white. Bruno Kirby appears unbilled as a nightclub comic. Panavision. [R]▼●

Hoffman (1970-British) **C-116m.** *** D: Alvin Rakoff. Peter Sellers, Sinead Cusack, Jeremy Bulloch, Ruth Dunning. Very odd, low-key dual character study with Sellers blackmailing attractive young bride-to-be to spend weekend with him. Slightly overlong; great performances. [PG]

Hog Wild (1980-Canadian) **C-97m.** *½ D: Les Rose. Michael Biehn, Patti D'Arbanville, Tony Rosato, Angelo Rizacos, Martin Doyle, Matt Craven. Dumb comedy about humorously nasty bikers who harass teenagers. Predictable, low-grade production benefits from spirited performances, especially Rosato as incoherently mumbling gang leader The Bull. [PG]▼

Holcroft Covenant, The (1985-British) **C-112m.** ** D: John Frankenheimer. Michael Caine, Anthony Andrews, Victoria Tennant, Lilli Palmer, Mario Adorf, Michael Lonsdale. Muddy, twisty, unbelievable tale from Robert Ludlum novel. Caine's late father (a comrade-in-arms of Adolf Hitler) has left a fortune behind, supposedly to make amends for his wrongdoing—and leading Caine on a globe-trotting series of adventures. Just old-fashioned enough to be watchable—but not very good. [R]▼●◗

Hold Back the Dawn (1941) **115m.** ***½ D: Mitchell Leisen. Charles Boyer, Olivia de Havilland, Paulette Goddard, Victor Francen, Walter Abel, Rosemary DeCamp. First-rate soaper with Billy Wilder-Charles Brackett script of gigolo Boyer marrying spinsterish Olivia to get into U.S. That's director Leisen in the Hollywood soundstage sequence, directing Veronica Lake and Brian Donlevy in I WANTED WINGS. Catch this one.

Hold Back the Night (1956) **80m.** **½ D: Allan Dwan. John Payne, Mona Freeman, Peter Graves, Chuck Connors. Korean War officer Payne recounts facts about bottle of liquor he always has with him.

Hold Back Tomorrow (1955) **75m.** *½ D: Hugo Haas. Cleo Moore, John Agar, Frank de Kova, Harry Guardino, Jan Englund. Strange B-film concerning condemned murderer who marries a girl on the night before his execution.

Hold 'Em Jail (1932) **74m.** **½ D: Norman Taurog. Bert Wheeler, Robert Woolsey, Betty Grable, Edgar Kennedy, Edna May Oliver, Roscoe Ates, Robert Armstrong, Paul Hurst, Warren Hymer. Silly comedy in which Wheeler and Woolsey are framed, sent to jail, and play on Warden Kennedy's football team. The climactic big game is the highlight. ▼

Hold 'Em Navy (1937) **64m.** ** D: Kurt Neumann. Lew Ayres, Mary Carlisle, John Howard, Benny Baker, Elizabeth Patterson. Ayres and Howard on the gridiron, with Carlisle the love interest. Boolah, boolah! Look for Alan Ladd in a bit part.

Hold Me Thrill Me Kiss Me (1992) **C-92m.** *** D: Joel Hershman. Max Parrish, Adrienne Shelly, Sean Young, Diane Ladd, Timothy Leary, Andrea Naschak, Bela Lehoczky. Parrish goes on the lam after shooting his fiancée (Young), a wealthy weirdo, and becomes involved with an oversexed, abusive stripper and her virginal kid sister, who live in a trailer park inhabited by assorted oddballs. Funky, extremely entertaining comedy. Fans of Pedro Almodóvar, John Waters, and early David Lynch will really go for this. Also available in unrated version. [R]▼●

Hold On! (1966) **C-85m.** *½ D: Arthur Lubin. Peter Noone, Herman's Hermits, Sue Ane Langdon, Karl Green, Shelley Fabares. Will NASA name a spaceship after Herman's Hermits? That's the burning question in this awful musical, set while the group is on a U.S. tour. One of their songs is titled "A Must to Avoid," which sums up this loser. Panavision.

Hold That Baby! (1949) **64m.** ** D: Reginald LeBorg. Leo Gorcey, Huntz Hall, Billy Benedict, David Gorcey, Bennie Bartlett, Gabriel Dell, Frankie Darro, John Kellogg, Anabel Shaw, Bernard Gorcey. The Bowery Boys find a bouncing bundle of joy in a laundromat and get mixed up in an inheritance swindle; standard series shenanigans.

Hold That Blonde (1945) **76m.** ** D: George Marshall. Eddie Bracken, Veronica Lake, Albert Dekker, Frank Fenton, George Zucco, Donald MacBride. OK comedy, sometimes strained, of kleptomaniac Bracken tangling with sultry thief Lake.

Hold That Co-Ed (1938) **80m.** *** D: George Marshall. John Barrymore, George Murphy, Marjorie Weaver, Joan Davis, Jack Haley, George Barbier. Good musicomedy supercharged by Barrymore as windy politician; he makes the whole film.

Hold That Ghost (1941) **86m.** *** D: Arthur Lubin. Bud Abbott, Lou Costello, Richard Carlson, Joan Davis, Mischa Auer, Evelyn Ankers, Marc Lawrence, Shemp Howard, Ted Lewis, The Andrews Sisters. Prime A&C, with the boys inheriting a haunted house. Fine cast includes hilarious Davis as professional radio screamer. Highlight: the moving candle.▼

Hold That Hypnotist (1957) **61m.** ** D: Austen Jewell. Huntz Hall, Stanley Clements, Jane Nigh, David (Gorcey) Condon, Robert Foulk, James Flavin, Queenie Smith, Jimmy Murphy. Hypnotized Sach regresses to a past life in the 17th century, where he gets mixed up with Blackbeard the pirate. Adequate *Bowery Boys* time passer.

Hold That Line (1952) **64m.** ** D: William Beaudine. Leo Gorcey, Huntz Hall, Gil Stratton, Jr., David Gorcey, Bennie Bartlett, Bernard Gorcey, John Bromfield, Veda Ann Borg, Taylor Holmes, Pierre Watkin. The Bowery Boys go to college and bring along some old vaudeville gags as Sach becomes a gridiron hero.

Hold Your Man (1933) **86m.** *** D: Sam Wood. Jean Harlow, Clark Gable, Stuart Erwin, Elizabeth Patterson, Blanche Friderici. Delightful film that effectively makes the transition from comedy to drama with Harlow falling for jailbound Gable. The stars are at their best here.▼

Hole in the Head, A (1959) **C-120m.** ** D: Frank Capra. Frank Sinatra, Edward G. Robinson, Eleanor Parker, Carolyn Jones, Thelma Ritter, Eddie Hodges, Keenan Wynn, Joi Lansing. Sticky story of a ne'er-do-well (Sinatra) and his son (Hodges) doesn't seem sincere. Only distinction is Oscar-winning song, "High Hopes." CinemaScope.▼●

Holiday (1930) **96m.** *** D: Edward H. Griffith. Ann Harding, Robert Ames, Mary Astor, Edward Everett Horton, Hedda Hopper, Monroe Owsley. This rediscovered version of Philip Barry's play about nonconformity is a pleasant surprise; an unstodgy early talkie with casting that in some cases (Astor, Owsley) even tops the more famous 1938 version (Horton plays the same role in both movies!).

Holiday (1938) **93m.** ***½ D: George Cukor. Katharine Hepburn, Cary Grant, Doris Nolan, Lew Ayres, Edward Everett Horton, Henry Kolker, Binnie Barnes, Jean Dixon, Henry Daniell. Fine, literate adaptation of Philip Barry's play (filmed before in 1930) about nonconformist Grant confronting stuffy N.Y.C. society family, finding his match in Hepburn (who had understudied the role in the original Broadway company a decade earlier). Screenplay by Donald Ogden Stewart and Sidney Buchman. Delightful film.▼●

Holiday Affair (1949) **87m.** *** D: Don Hartman. Robert Mitchum, Janet Leigh, Wendell Corey, Gordon Gebert, Henry (Harry) Morgan. Well-done Christmas season story about widow Leigh, her small son, two contrasting men courting her. Remade in 1997.▼

Holiday Camp (1948-British) **97m.** **½ D: Ken Annakin. Dennis Price, Flora Robson, Jack Warner. Pleasant account of life and love at British summer resort; atmospheric, with good characterizations.

Holiday for Lovers (1959) **C-103m.** **½ D: Henry Levin. Clifton Webb, Jane Wyman, Jill St. John, Carol Lynley, Paul Henreid, Gary Crosby, Jose Greco. Arch Dr. Webb and Wyman escort attractive daughters on South American vacation, with predictable mating. CinemaScope.

Holiday for Sinners (1952) **72m.** **½ D: Gerald Mayer. Gig Young, Janice Rule, Keenan Wynn, William Campbell. Strange goings-on at Mardi Gras as several people try to forget their troublesome lives and have a good time.

Holiday in Havana (1949) **73m.** ** D: Jean Yarbrough. Desi Arnaz, Mary Hatcher, Ann Doran, Steven Geray, Minerva Urecal, Sig Arno. Bargain-basement musical, with Arnaz and Hatcher playing pair of Cuban love birds. Of interest solely for Desi's presence.▼

Holiday in Mexico (1946) **C-127m.** *** D: George Sidney. Walter Pidgeon, Ilona Massey, Roddy McDowall, Jose Iturbi, Xavier Cugat, Jane Powell. Engaging, well-cast musical comedy of daughter of ambassador falling for noted musician.▼

Holiday Inn (1942) **101m.** ***½ D: Mark Sandrich. Bing Crosby, Fred Astaire, Marjorie Reynolds, Virginia Dale, Walter Abel, Louise Beavers. Entertaining musical built on paper-thin plot about a romantic triangle, and the establishment of a country inn that's open only on holidays. That's the cue for a raft of Irving Berlin holiday songs (there's even one for George Washington's birthday!) including the timeless Oscar-winner "White Christmas." Good fun, and snappier than partial remake WHITE CHRISTMAS. Bing's original Rhythm Boys partner, Harry Barris, plays the orchestra leader.▼●

Hollow Point SEE: **Wild Pair, The**

Hollow Reed (1996-British-German) **C-104m.** *** D: Angela Pope. Martin Donovan, Joely Richardson, Jason Flemyng, Ian Hart, Sam Bould. Doctor Donovan, who is divorced, senses that his young son is being abused by his ex-wife's live-in boyfriend. He decides to petition for custody, but knows his concern for his son's safety will be obscured by the fact that he is gay. Intensely dramatic, extremely well-acted psychological drama works on two levels: as a top-notch suspense thriller and a no-holds-barred indictment of homophobia. [R]▼

Hollow Triumph (1948) **83m.** *** D: Steve Sekely. Paul Henreid, Joan Bennett, Eduard Franz, Leslie Brooks. Tense melodrama of killer assuming identity of lookalike doctor. Retitled: THE SCAR.▼

Holly and the Ivy, The (1952-British) **80m.** *** D: George More O'Ferrall. Ralph Richardson, Celia Johnson, Margaret Leighton, Denholm Elliott, Hugh Williams, Roland Culver. Straightforward adaptation of Wynyard Browne play revolving around Christmas holiday with Richardson, the small-town cleric, learning about his three grown-up children; nicely acted.

Hollywood Boulevard (1936) **70m.** **½ D: Robert Florey. John Halliday, Marsha Hunt, Robert Cummings, Mae Marsh, C. Henry Gordon, Esther Ralston, Frieda Inescort, Esther Dale, Albert Conti, Charles Ray, Francis X. Bushman, Maurice Costello, Betty Compson. Halliday is vain former star who writes his memoirs for *Confidential*-type magazine, affecting lives of daughter Hunt, ex-girlfriend Ralston. Slow-moving drama is saved by sometimes crisp, perceptive dialogue, presence of silent stars Marsh, Bushman, Ray, etc. Gary Cooper appears briefly as himself.

Hollywood Boulevard (1976) **C-83m.** **½ D: Joe Dante, Allan Arkush. Candice Rialson, Mary Woronov, Rita George, Jeffrey Kramer, Dick Miller, Paul Bartel. Shameless low-budgeter splices shots from various Roger Corman films into the "story" of a would-be actress who goes to work for some schlock moviemakers. Engaging nonsense and some funny gags (especially for film buffs and Corman devotees)—though not enough to completely hide the fact that this *is* a schlock movie. Miller and Bartel are great fun as an agent and a motivation-minded director. Don't miss gag after closing credits. [R]▼

Hollywood Canteen (1944) **124m.** **½ D: Delmer Daves. Bette Davis, John Garfield, Joan Leslie, Robert Hutton, Dane Clark, Janis Paige; many guest stars including Joan Crawford, Ida Lupino, Barbara Stanwyck, Eddie Cantor, Jack Carson, Eleanor Parker, Alexis Smith, S. Z. Sakall. Amiable all-star silliness set in Hollywood's real-life haven for WW2 servicemen, featuring cofounders Davis and Garfield. Hutton plays G.I. with a crush on lovely Leslie. Best bits: Peter Lorre and Sydney Greenstreet; Jack Benny and violinist Joseph Szigeti. Roy Rogers introduces "Don't Fence Me In," later reprised by the Andrews Sisters.▼●

Hollywood Cavalcade (1939) **C-96m.** **½ D: Irving Cummings. Alice Faye, Don Ameche, J. Edward Bromberg, Al Jolson, Mack Sennett, Stuart Erwin, Buster Keaton, Rin-Tin-Tin, Jr. Colorful saga of pioneering days in Hollywood (based, very loosely, on Mack Sennett and Mabel Normand) starts out fun, with some lively re-creations of silent slapstick comedies, but gets bogged down in clichéd dramatics later on.

Hollywood Harry (1985) **C-99m.** ** D: Robert Forster. Robert Forster, Joe Spinell, Shannon Wilcox, Marji Martin, Kathrine Forster, Mallie Jackson. Down-the-tubes private eye Forster hires on to find a young girl who's turned up in an X-rated movie. Strictly standard fare. Forster also produced and scripted; his 14-year-old daughter Kathrine plays Harry's niece. Aka HARRY'S MACHINE. [PG-13]▼

Hollywood Hotel (1937) **109m.** **½ D: Busby Berkeley. Dick Powell, Rosemary Lane, Lola Lane, Ted Healy, Johnnie "Scat" Davis, Alan Mowbray, Frances Langford, Louella Parsons, Hugh Herbert, Glenda Farrell, Edgar Kennedy. Silly, paper-thin plot about Powell winning Hollywood talent contest but finding stardom elusive, buoyed by bright Johnny Mercer-Richard Whiting score, including "Hooray for Hollywood" and historic numbers by the Benny Goodman band ("Sing Sing Sing") and quartet (with Gene Krupa, Lionel Hampton, Teddy Wilson). Ronald Reagan has brief bit as radio announcer.

Hollywood Knights, The (1980) **C-95m.** *½ D: Floyd Mutrux. Tony Danza, Michelle Pfeiffer, Fran Drescher, Leigh French, Randy Gornel, Robert Wuhl, Stuart Pankin, P. R. Paul, Richard Schaal, Debra Feuer. A punk answer to AMERICAN GRAFFITI, which follows a band of high-school hell-raisers on Halloween Night, 1965, when their favorite drive-in hangout is about to close. Sophomoric humor to spare, only a small part of it funny. Danza's feature debut. [R]▼

Hollywood or Bust (1956) **C-95m.** **½ D: Frank Tashlin. Dean Martin, Jerry Lewis, Anita Ekberg, Pat Crowley. Star-struck Lewis teams up with gambler Martin on trek to crash the movie capital; typical comedy by the frantic team. Dean and Jerry's last film together opens with Jerry's "tribute" to movie fans around the world. VistaVision.▼

Hollywood Party (1934) **68m.** **½ No director credited. Jimmy Durante, Laurel and Hardy, Lupe Velez, Polly Moran, Charles Butterworth, Eddie Quillan, June Clyde, George Givot, Jack Pearl, Ted Healy and The Three Stooges, many others. Musical comedy hodgepodge built around screen star Durante throwing a gala party. Romantic subplot is for the birds, but Stan and Ollie battling fiery Velez, Durante as Schnarzan, befuddled Butterworth and opening title tune make it worthwhile. Richard Boleslawski, Allan Dwan, Roy Rowland directed various scenes without credit; TV print runs 63m., and is missing appearance by Mickey Mouse and color Disney cartoon HOT CHOCOLATE SOLDIERS.▼

Hollywood Revue of 1929, The (1929) **130m.** ** D: Charles Riesner. Conrad Nagel, Jack Benny, John Gilbert, Norma Shearer, Joan Crawford, Laurel and Hardy, Bessie Love, Lionel Barrymore, Marion Davies, Buster Keaton, Marie Dressler, Polly Moran, many others. MGM's all-star revue introducing its silent-film stars as talkie personalities, cohosted by Benny and Nagel. Definitely a curio for film buffs, rough sledding for others. TV print at 116m. is missing some material; several scenes originally filmed in color.●

Hollywood Shuffle (1987) **C-82m.** **½ D: Robert Townsend. Robert Townsend, Anne-Marie Johnson, Starletta Dupois, Helen Martin, Craigus R. Johnson. Uneven but enjoyable comedy about young black actor trying to get a foothold in Hollywood, but running into problems of stereotyping at every turn. Townsend (who also directed and cowrote, with Keenen Ivory Wayans) is so appealing, and his message is so dead on-target, that it's hard to dislike this film, even though it's strictly hit-or-miss. [R]▼●

Hollywood Story (1951) **77m.** **½ D: William Castle. Richard Conte, Julia (Julie) Adams, Richard Egan, Henry Hull. Trying to solve an old murder, producer makes a picture on the subject, hoping to uncover culprit.

Hollywood Vice Squad (1986) **C-100m.** BOMB D: Penelope Spheeris. Trish Van Devere, Ronny Cox, Frank Gorshin, Leon Isaac Kennedy, Carrie Fisher, Ben Frank, Robin Wright, Joey Travolta. Stupid comic variation on VICE SQUAD with Van Devere asking help of the cops to find her runaway daughter, who's now a hooker and heroin addict. Wright's film debut. [R]▼●

Holocaust Survivors: Remembrance of Love SEE: **Remembrance of Love**

Holocaust 2000 SEE: **Chosen, The** (1978)

Holy Man (1998) **C-114m.** ** D: Stephen Herek. Eddie Murphy, Jeff Goldblum, Kelly Preston, Robert Loggia, Jon Cryer, Eric McCormack, Sam Kitchin. Slick producer for a home shopping TV network stumbles onto a spiritual man named G who says he's on a pilgrimage. Before long, G has affected every part of the man's life and become a sensation on the air. Promising movie wanders all over the place and squanders Murphy's likable performance. It's still watchable, thanks to him, Goldblum, and Preston. Various celebrities appear in cameos, including, most curiously, designer Nino Cerutti. Panavision. [PG]▼●◗

Holy Matrimony (1943) **87m.** *** D: John M. Stahl. Monty Woolley, Gracie Fields, Laird Cregar, Una O'Connor, Alan Mowbray, Melville Cooper, Franklin Pangborn. Delightful tale of artist Woolley assuming late butler's identity to avoid publicity, finding many complications. Remake of 1933 film HIS DOUBLE LIFE.

Holy Matrimony (1994) **C-92m.** *½ D: Leonard Nimoy. Patricia Arquette, Joseph Gordon-Levitt, Armin Mueller-Stahl, Tate Donovan, John Schuck, Lois Smith, Courtney B. Vance, Jeffrey Nordling. Arquette, on the lam for robbery, hides out in a Hutterite community and (through contrived circumstances) ends up married to 12-year-old Gordon-Levitt. Bland, juvenile, comedic variation on WITNESS, but Gordon-Levitt is charming. [PG-13] ▼●

Holy Smoke (1999-U.S.-Australian) **C-114m.** ** D: Jane Campion. Kate Winslet, Harvey Keitel, Julie Hamilton, Tim Robertson, Daniel Wyllie, Sophie Lee, Kerry Walker, Pam Grier. When a young Australian woman falls under the spell of an Indian guru, her family hires an expert American cult deprogrammer to bring her back to her senses. She turns the tables and finds him surprisingly susceptible to her mind games and sexual teasing. Naked performances—in every sense of the word—by the two leads and a layered script rife with quirky humor and sexual politics can't bring credibility to Keitel's character. This is supposed to be his 190th case; what were the other 189 like? [R]▼◗

Holy Terror (1977) **C-96m.** ** D: Alfred Sole. Brooke Shields, Tom Signorelli, Louisa Horton, Paula Sheppard, Mildred Clinton, Linda Miller, Lillian Roth. Does 12-year-old Alice (Sheppard) kill her sister, parents, aunt, etc.? OK murder mystery is noteworthy mainly as Shields' feature debut—and she's bumped off in the first reel. Filmed in Paterson, N.J.; cameo appearance by Roth as a pathologist. Originally 108m. Aka ALICE, SWEET ALICE and COMMUNION. [R] ▼●◗

Hombre (1967) **C-111m.** *** D: Martin Ritt. Paul Newman, Fredric March, Richard Boone, Diane Cilento, Cameron Mitchell, Barbara Rush, Martin Balsam. Interesting Western (from an Elmore Leonard story) of Indian-raised Newman trying to survive in white man's world in Arizona circa 1880. Encounters with various characters on a stagecoach provide basis for film's action and drama; well acted, entertaining. Panavision.▼●

Home Alone (1990) **C-102m.** **½ D: Chris Columbus. Macaulay Culkin, Joe Pesci, Daniel Stern, John Heard, Roberts Blossom, Catherine O'Hara, John Candy, Billie Bird, Angela Goethals, Devin Ratray. Wildly successful comedy about an eight-year-old boy whose family inadvertently leaves him behind when they go to Paris for Christmas vacation. The plucky kid then proceeds to fend off two bumbling burglars with a variety of elaborate booby-traps. Culkin is terrific, but the film has its ups and downs; the violence, even for a cartoonish farce, is a bit extreme. Climactic scene with forbidding neighbor Blossom is certainly the film's high point. Macaulay's brother Kieran plays his cousin Fuller. Followed by two sequels. [PG]▼●◗

Home Alone 2: Lost in New York (1992) **C-120m.** ** D: Chris Columbus. Macaulay Culkin, Joe Pesci, Daniel Stern, Catherine O'Hara, John Heard, Tim Curry, Brenda Fricker, Devin Ratray, Hillary Wolf, Eddie Bracken, Dana Ivey, Rob Schneider, Kieran Culkin, Gerry Bamman. Culkin boards the wrong plane at Christmastime, is separated from his family, and ends up in N.Y.C., where he befriends pigeon-lady Fricker and contends with nitwits Pesci and Stern, more than ever a pair of cartoon characters come to life. Essentially a reworking of its smash-hit predecessor, but it manages to be even more violent. There are also shameless plugs for the Plaza Hotel, replete with a walk-on by owner Donald Trump. Written and produced by John Hughes. [PG]▼●◗

Home Alone 3 (1997) **C-102m.** **½ D: Raja Gosnell. Alex D. Linz, Olek Krupa, Rya Kihlstedt, Lenny von Dohlen, David Thornton, Haviland Morris, Kevin Kilner, Marian Seldes. Another little boy left home alone battles another gang of crooks, but this time they're high-tech industrial thieves after an important computer chip. Unexpectedly funny follow-up (rather than sequel), helped by an appealing little boy (Linz), smarter crooks, and a less sappily sentimental subplot. Written by John Hughes. [PG]▼●◗

Home and the World, The (1984-Indian) **C-130m.** ***½ D: Satyajit Ray. Soumitra Chatterjee, Victor Banerjee, Swatilekha

Chatterjee, Gopa Aich, Jennifer Kapoor. Wealthy, liberated estate owner allows his wife to break with the tradition of female seclusion—and she falls in love with his best friend, a nationalist leader. Set in early 20th-century Bengal, and based on a novel by Rabindranath Tagore; a masterful and poignant film, made by a world-class filmmaker.▼

Home at Seven (1952-British) **85m.** *** D: Ralph Richardson. Ralph Richardson, Margaret Leighton, Jack Hawkins, Campbell Singer. Taut thriller of club treasurer who can't account for a day in his life when a murder and a robbery occurred. Aka MURDER ON MONDAY.▼

Home Before Dark (1958) **136m.** *** D: Mervyn LeRoy. Jean Simmons, Dan O'-Herlihy, Rhonda Fleming, Efrem Zimbalist, Jr. Shiny but poignant telling of Simmons' readjustment to life after nervous breakdown; on-location shooting in Massachusetts.

Homebodies (1974) **C-96m.** **½ D: Larry Yust. Frances Fuller, Ian Wolfe, Ruth McDevitt, Paula Trueman, Peter Brocco, William Hansen. Bizarre horror-comedy will depend on one's taste for scenario. Elderly tenants of condemned building resort to murder to keep their home. Good cast, including Douglas Fowley as the builder. Made in Cincinnati.▼

Homeboy (1976) SEE: **Black Fist**

Homeboy (1988) **C-118m.** **½ D: Michael Seresin. Mickey Rourke, Christopher Walken, Debra Feuer, Thomas Quinn, Kevin Conway, Antony Alda, Ruben Blades. Downbeat, rainy tale of aging, alcoholic boxer Rourke, his relationship with flashy, philosophical crook Walken, and his romance with a carousel owner. Very well made, with fine, quirky performances by the leads, but so unrelentingly grim it can scarcely be called entertainment. [R]▼●

Homecoming (1948) **113m.** ** D: Mervyn LeRoy. Clark Gable, Lana Turner, Anne Baxter, John Hodiak, Ray Collins, Cameron Mitchell. Gable and Turner have exciting WW2 romance in the trenches, but that can't support 113 minutes of dreary drama; one of Gable's lesser efforts.▼

Homecoming, The (1973) **C-111m.** ***½ D: Peter Hall. Cyril Cusack, Ian Holm, Michael Jayston, Vivien Merchant, Terence Rigby, Paul Rogers. Jayston, long separated from his London family, brings wife Merchant home to meet his father and two brothers. Film version of the Harold Pinter play is among the most satisfactory of all stage-to-screen adaptations. An American Film Theater Production. [PG]▼

Homecoming—A Christmas Story, The (1971) **C-120m. TVM** D: Fielder Cook. Patricia Neal, Edgar Bergen, Ellen Corby, Andrew Duggan, Josephine Hutchinson, Cleavon Little, Dorothy Stickney, Richard Thomas, William Windom, David Huddleston. Neal is Olivia Walton in this forerunner to the long-running series *The Waltons.* Teleplay by Earl Hamner, Jr., was adapted from his own novel, previously filmed as SPENCER'S MOUNTAIN. Corby, Thomas, and a number of the other young players continued in *The Waltons* for years. Above average.▼

Home for the Holidays (1995) **C-103m.** ** D: Jodie Foster. Holly Hunter, Robert Downey, Jr., Anne Bancroft, Charles Durning, Dylan McDermott, Geraldine Chaplin, Cynthia Stevenson, Steve Guttenberg, Claire Danes, Austin Pendleton, David Strathairn, Amy Yasbeck, Shawn Hatosy. Dreary "comedy" about a woman at loose ends who flies home to spend Thanksgiving with her wildly dysfunctional family. Filled with unpleasant (and in some cases unfathomable) characters who are neither funny nor interesting. Why would *anybody* want to spend time with these people? [PG-13]▼●

Home Free All (1983) **92m.** **½ D: Stewart Bird. Allan Nicholls, Roland Caccavo, Lorry Goldman, Maura Ellyn, Shelley Wyant. Nicholls is appealing in this comedy-drama about an ex-hippie radical, a child of the 50s and 60s desperately lost in the 80s. Some hilarious moments but not as incisive as intended.▼

Home Fries (1998) **C-93m.** *½ D: Dean Parisot. Drew Barrymore, Luke Wilson, Catherine O'Hara, Jake Busey, Shelley Duvall, Kim Robillard, Daryl "Chill" Mitchell. Black-comedy misfire has two brothers giving their stepfather a unique scare at the behest of Mom. As a result, his pregnant mistress (Barrymore) is left without a father for her child; matters grow complicated when one of the brothers shows interest. She's a Podunk fast-food waitress, which explains the title, but not why this farce is so poky—and laughless. [PG-13] ▼●◗

Home From the Hill (1960) **C-150m.** *** D: Vincente Minnelli. Robert Mitchum, Eleanor Parker, George Peppard, George Hamilton, Luana Patten, Everett Sloane, Constance Ford. Overlong but generally satisfying drama about Southern landowner's conflicts with his wife and two sons—one of them illegitimate. Typical MGM gloss seems at odds with gritty subject matter; noteworthy for giving the two Georges their first big break. CinemaScope.▼●

Homegrown (1998) **C-103m.** **½ D: Stephen Gyllenhaal. Billy Bob Thornton, Hank Azaria, Kelly Lynch, Jon Bon Jovi, Ryan Phillippe, Judge Reinhold, Jon Tenney, Jamie Lee Curtis, John Lithgow, Ted Danson. When a big-time drug dealer is assassinated, three of his worker bees try to cover up the death so they can cash in on his latest marijuana crop. Needless to say, they find themselves in way over their heads. Alternately funny and serious, this unfocused film has a strong cast and interesting, often amusing vignettes, but never quite comes together. [R]▼●◗

Home in Indiana (1944) **C-103m.** *** D: Henry Hathaway. Walter Brennan, Jeanne Crain, June Haver, Charlotte Greenwood, Lon McCallister, Ward Bond, Willie Best, George Cleveland. Typical horse-racing saga gets a good rehashing here with colorful production and sincere performances; climactic race is well-handled. Remade as APRIL LOVE.

Home Is the Hero (1959-Irish) **83m.** **½ D: Fielder Cook. Walter Macken, Eileen Crowe, Arthur Kennedy, Joan O'Hara. Modest yarn with Abbey Theatre group, telling story of ex-con (Macken) trying to pick up pieces of home-life.

Home Is Where the Hart Is (1987-Canadian) **C-94m.** *½ D: Rex Bromfield. Valri Bromfield, Stephen E. Miller, Deanne Henry, Martin Mull, Eric Christmas, Leslie Nielsen, Ted Stidder. A 100-plus-year-old billionaire is kidnapped by a roller derby queen/ nurse, and his identical twin sons (who are in their 70s) set out to find him. Bizarre—and very, very bad—farce. [PG-13]▼●

Home Is Where the Heart Is SEE: **Square Dance**

Home Movies (1979) **C-90m.** *½ D: Brian De Palma. Keith Gordon, Nancy Allen, Kirk Douglas, Gerrit Graham, Vincent Gardenia, Mary Davenport. Flaky farce reminiscent of De Palma's early work. Nebbish Gordon, an "extra in his own life," is given Star Therapy treatment by egomaniacal director Douglas (who has his own life filmed constantly), and sets out to woo Allen away from his nutsy older brother (Graham). Original in concept but tiresome in execution, although nobody eats a hamburger like Allen. Most of the production crew was made up of De Palma's filmmaking students from Sarah Lawrence College. Aka THE MAESTRO. [PG]▼●

Home of Angels (1993) **C-90m.** **½ D: Nick Stagliano. Abe Vigoda, Sherman Hemsley, Lance Robinson, Smokin' Joe Frazier, Craig Sechler, Karen Wolfe. Well-meaning but artificial drama of a young boy (Robinson) whose beloved grandfather (Vigoda) suffers from Alzheimer's disease. Against his parents' wishes, he sets out to kidnap grandpa from a nursing home and bring the old man home for Christmas. Frazier appears as the boy's guardian angel. ▼

Home of Our Own, A (1993) **C-104m.** **½ D: Tony Bill. Kathy Bates, Edward Furlong, Soon-Teck Oh, Tony Campisi, Clarissa Lassig, Sarah Schaub, Miles Feulner, Amy Sakasitz, T. J. Lowther. Bates is a determined single mother in 1962 L.A. who uproots her six children and settles in a desolate Idaho town; she has almost no money but a lot of energy and a fierce fighting spirit. Young Furlong is the reluctant "man of the family." Avoids becoming overly sentimental, but film is still basically Disney fare with an edge. Campisi—Bates' persistent boyfriend—is the actress's real-life husband. Director Bill has an unbilled cameo as a doctor. [PG]▼●

Home of the Brave (1949) **85m.** *** D: Mark Robson. James Edwards, Douglas Dick, Steve Brodie, Jeff Corey, Lloyd Bridges, Frank Lovejoy. More daring when made than now, but still hard-hitting account of black soldier Edwards suffering more abuse from fellow G.I.'s than the enemy while on a mission during WW2. From an Arthur Laurents play.▼●

Home of the Brave (1986) **C-90m.** *** D: Laurie Anderson. Laurie Anderson, Adrian Belew, Richard Landry, Joy Askew, Dolette McDonald, Janice Pendarvis, William S. Burroughs. Concert film pretty well duplicates what fans of performance artist Anderson have been seeing for years; mix of music and provocative visuals doesn't quite add up to another STOP MAKING SENSE, but it's a generally rewarding introduction for the uninitiated. Mostly accessible, but the middle section will test your openness to unconventional music. ▼

Homer (1970) **C-91m.** *½ D: John Trent. Don Scardino, Alex Nicol, Tisa Farrow, Lenka Peterson, Ralph Endersby, Trudy Young. Well-meaning but cliché-ridden drama about small-town teen-ager, generation gap, Vietnam War protests, rock music, sex. You've seen it all before. [PG]

Homer and Eddie (1990) **C-99m.** BOMB D: Andrei Konchalovsky. James Belushi, Whoopi Goldberg, Karen Black, Ernestine McClendon, Nancy Parsons, Anne Ramsey, Beah Richards. He's been mentally impaired since getting smacked in childhood by a flying baseball; she's dying of brain cancer; theirs is an odyssey-by-auto punctuated by service-station knock-offs and a musical interlude where they dance with paper bags on their heads. Not to be confused with Homer & Jethro or Flo & Eddie, though you may be praying for any and all to show up. [R] ▼●

Homestretch, The (1947) **C-96m.** ** D: H. Bruce Humberstone. Cornel Wilde, Maureen O'Hara, Glenn Langan, Helen Walker, James Gleason. Harmless film of romance between young girl and horse-owner suffers from uneven acting and script.

Home, Sweet Homicide (1946) **90m.** ** D: Lloyd Bacon. Peggy Ann Garner, Randolph Scott, Lynn Bari, Dean Stockwell. Nothing-special comedy-mystery, as children of mystery writer solve local murder and find husband for their mother.

Hometown Story (1951) **61m.** ** D: Arthur Pierson. Jeffrey Lynn, Donald Crisp, Marjorie Reynolds, Alan Hale, Jr., Mari-

lyn Monroe, Barbara Brown, Glenn Tryon. Obvious programmer of recently defeated pol Lynn, who blames big business for his loss and tries to defame manufacturer Crisp. Of interest mostly for Monroe's supporting role as one of Lynn's employees.▼◗
Hometown USA (1979) **C-93m.** BOMB D: Max Baer. Gary Springer, David Wilson, Brian Kerwin, Pat Delaney, Julie Parsons, Sally Kirkland. Yet another nostalgic look at teenagers in the late 1950s is just a sloppy, sleazy, unfunny AMERICAN GRAFFITI rip-off.▼◗
Homeward Bound: The Incredible Journey (1993) **C-84m.** *** D: DuWayne Dunham. Robert Hays, Kim Greist, Jean Smart, Benj Thall, Veronica Lauren, Kevin Chevalia; voices of Michael J. Fox, Sally Field, Don Ameche. Three beloved household pets, separated from their youthful masters, embark on an almost impossible trek over mountainous terrain to rejoin them. Remake of 1963's THE INCREDIBLE JOURNEY enables us to hear the animals talking, and in true '90s fashion, their dialogue is overstuffed with lowbrow wisecracks. Still, the story is compelling, and the vocal performances excellent, especially Ameche, as the older, more faithful canine. Sure-fire Disney family entertainment. Followed by a sequel. [G]▼●◗
Homeward Bound II: Lost in San Francisco (1996) **C-88m.** **½ D: David R. Ellis. Robert Hays, Kim Greist, Veronica Lauren, Kevin Chevalia, Benj Thall, Michael Rispoli, Max Perlich; voices of Michael J. Fox, Sally Field, Ralph Waite, Sinbad, Jon Polito. Congenial sequel has the three household pets forced to fend for themselves in the City by the Bay, where Chance, Sassy, and Shadow find themselves dodging both canine and human adversaries on the city streets. Enough snappy dialogue to amuse parents as well as their kids. [G]▼●◗
Homework (1982) **C-90m.** *½ D: James Beshears. Joan Collins, Michael Morgan, Shell Kepler, Lanny Horn, Lee Purcell, Carrie Snodgress, Wings Hauser, Mel Welles, Beverly Todd, Betty Thomas. Atrocious, wildly inconsistent "comedy" about a teenage boy's sexual awakening—and embarrassment. Filmed mostly in 1979, it underwent major surgery, including attempt to simulate nude scenes with Joan Collins (using an alleged double) so it could be promoted as a young boy–older woman sex comedy à la PRIVATE LESSONS and MY TUTOR. [R] ▼●
Homicidal (1961) **87m.** **½ D: William Castle. Jean Arliss (Joan Marshall), Patricia Breslin, Glenn Corbett, Eugenie Leontovitch, Alan Bunce, Richard Rust. One of Castle's less gimmicky shockers, about pretty but rather strange young nurse who presides over creepy household consisting of mute stroke victim and decidedly unmacho young man. Shamelessly steals a great deal from PSYCHO, and much of the dialogue is ludicrous, but still manages to deliver some shudders.
Homicide (1991) **C-102m.** **½ D: David Mamet. Joe Mantegna, William H. Macy, Natalija Nogulich, Ving Rhames, Rebecca Pidgeon, Vincent Guastaferro, Lionel Mark Smith, Jack Wallace, J. J. Johnston. Urban homicide detective is pulled off a major case to take care of a seemingly routine murder of an elderly shopkeeper, but soon finds himself embroiled in a strange, conspiracy-like situation that causes him to question his own motives and his identity as a Jew. Provocative material is underdeveloped by writer-director Mamet, and laid on with too heavy a hand . . . but the "Mametspeak" and lead performance are still quite commanding. [R]▼●
Homicide Bureau (1939) **58m.** *½ D: C. C. Coleman, Jr. Bruce Cabot, Rita Hayworth, Robert Paige, Marc Lawrence, Richard Fiske, Moroni Olsen. Cabot plays a brash detective who's in perennial hot water with his superiors in this humdrum B picture. Rita's role as a lab technician is small—and dull.
Hondo (1953) **C-84m.** *** D: John Farrow. John Wayne, Geraldine Page, Ward Bond, Michael Pate, James Arness, Rodolfo Acosta, Leo Gordon, Lee Aaker, Lassie. Rousing, well-done Western with Wayne the tough, wily cavalry scout who comes upon Page and her young son living in the wilderness, unalarmed about a pending Apache uprising. Good script by James Edward Grant, from a story by Louis L'Amour. Originally shown in 3-D. Later a short-lived TV series. ▼
Honey (1981-Italian-Spanish) **C-84m.** *½ D: Gianfranco Angelucci. Clio Goldsmith, Catherine Spaak, Fernando Rey, Donatella Damiani, Susan Scott, Luc Merenda. Utterly confusing chronicle of writer Spaak forcing editor Rey to read her manuscript about the sexual awakening of young Goldsmith—or so it seems. [R]▼
Honeychile (1951) **C-90m.** *½ D: R. G. Springsteen. Judy Canova, Eddie Foy, Jr., Alan Hale, Jr., Walter Catlett. Cornball stuff involving Canova in the music-publishing business.
Honey I Blew Up the Kid (1992) **C-89m.** *** D: Randal Kleiser. Rick Moranis, Marcia Strassman, Robert Oliveri, Daniel and Joshua Shalikar, Lloyd Bridges, John Shea, Keri Russell, Ron Canada, Gregory Sierra, Julia Sweeney, Ken Tobey. Bull's-eye sequel to the surprise Disney hit HONEY, I SHRUNK THE KIDS. This time, absentminded scientist Moranis accidentally enlarges his two-year-old son, who grows to gargantuan proportions and stalks the streets of Las Vegas! Good, clean fun with terrific special effects and a lot of gen-

uine laughs; wears a bit thin after a while, but its upbeat spirit makes up for that. Video sequel: HONEY, WE SHRUNK OURSELVES. [PG]▼●

Honey, I Shrunk the Kids (1989) **C-93m.** *** D: Joe Johnston. Rick Moranis, Matt Frewer, Marcia Strassman, Kristine Sutherland, Thomas Brown, Jared Rushton, Amy O'Neill, Robert Oliveri. Cute comedy-fantasy about a quartet of kids who accidentally trigger Moranis's experimental ray gun and find themselves reduced to microscopic size—and stranded across the yard from their home. Enjoyable family fare, with engaging special effects (by such whizzes as Phil Tippett and David Allen). Followed by HONEY, I BLEW UP THE KID and later, a TV series. [PG]▼●

Honeymoon (1947) **74m.** ** D: William Keighley. Shirley Temple, Franchot Tone, Guy Madison, Lina Romay, Gene Lockhart, Grant Mitchell. Unmemorable mixture of romance and comedy in story of G.I. who longs for fiancée in Mexico during three-day pass. Good cast fails to make film click.

Honeymoon (1959-Spanish) **C-90m.** ** D: Michael Powell. Anthony Steel, Ludmilla Tcherina, Antonio, Rosita Segovia. Muddled romancer intertwined with ballet sequences, from the director of THE RED SHOES. Steel, on wedding trip with Tcherina, encounters Antonio who tries to court the ex-ballerina. Excerpts from ballets *Los Amantes de Teruel* and *El Amor Brujo.* Technirama.

Honeymoon Academy (1990) **C-94m.** *½ D: Gene Quintano. Kim Cattrall, Robert Hays, Leigh Taylor-Young, Charles Rocket, Lance Kinney, Christopher Lee. Time waster about a secret agent (Cattrall) who tries to take time off for a honeymoon in Madrid, but finds herself involved in espionage business all the same. Attempt at lighthearted chase comedy/romance doesn't come off . . . and incidentally, the film's title has nothing to do with the story. [PG-13]▼●

Honeymoon Ahead (1945) **60m.** ** D: Reginald Le Borg. Allan Jones, Raymond Walburn, Grace McDonald, Vivian Austin. Nonsensical trivia involving kindly prisoner (head of convicts' choir) and his involvement with the world outside the big walls.

Honeymoon for Three (1941) **77m.** **½ D: Lloyd Bacon. Ann Sheridan, George Brent, Charlie Ruggles, Osa Massen, Walter Catlett, Jane Wyman. Breezy comedy of novelist Brent warding off female admirers by pretending to be married; Sheridan is his witty, amorous secretary.

Honeymoon Hotel (1964) **C-89m.** *½ D: Henry Levin. Robert Goulet, Jill St. John, Nancy Kwan, Robert Morse, Elsa Lanchester, Keenan Wynn. Asinine shenanigans with bachelors Goulet and Morse arriving at resort for newlyweds. Lanchester is fun despite all. Panavision.

Honeymoon in Bali (1939) **95m.** *** D: Edward H. Griffith. Fred MacMurray, Madeleine Carroll, Allan Jones, Osa Massen, Helen Broderick, Akim Tamiroff, Astrid Allwyn, Carolyn Lee, Monty Woolley. Pleasant romantic comedy about a career woman (Carroll) who is determined never to marry—until she meets easy-to-take MacMurray. Video title: MY LOVE FOR YOURS. ▼

Honeymoon in Vegas (1992) **C-95m.** *** D: Andrew Bergman. James Caan, Nicolas Cage, Sarah Jessica Parker, Pat Morita, Johnny Williams, John Capodice, Robert Costanzo, Anne Bancroft, Peter Boyle, Burton Gilliam, Seymour Cassel, Jerry Tarkanian, Tony Shalhoub, Natasha Lyonne, Ben Stein. Cage and Parker finally decide to tie the knot—in Las Vegas—but he loses her in a rigged poker game to mobster Caan! Engaging farce from writer-director Bergman has enough twists, turns, and cockeyed humor to keep things lively from start to finish . . . including a corps of "flying Elvises." Presley music (performed by everyone from Billy Joel to Bono) fills the soundtrack. [PG-13]▼●◗

Honeymoon Killers, The (1970) **108m.** *** D: Leonard Kastle. Shirley Stoler, Tony LoBianco, Mary Jane Higby, Doris Roberts. Taut, based-on-fact account of the Lonely Hearts Killers: Martha Beck (Stoler), a rotund nurse, and Ray Fernandez (LoBianco), a gigolo. Together, they scheme to swindle and murder wealthy, lonely women. Low-budget item has deservedly developed a cult reputation over the years. Martin Scorsese was the original director; he was replaced by Donald Volkman, who in turn was replaced by Kastle (who also scripted). Same story retold in Arturo Ripstein's DEEP CRIMSON. [R]▼●

Honeymoon Lodge (1943) **63m.** ** D: Edward Lilley. David Bruce, Harriet Hilliard (Nelson), June Vincent, Rod Cameron, Franklin Pangborn, Andrew Tombes, Ozzie Nelson and His Orchestra, Veloz and Yolanda, Tip, Tap and Toe. Innocuous musical centers on Bruce and Vincent's romantic complications at a country resort. Slim pretext for some amusing songs and dances by Ozzie & Harriet and others.

Honeymoon Machine, The (1961) **C-87m.** **½ D: Richard Thorpe. Steve McQueen, Jim Hutton, Paula Prentiss, Brigid Bazlen, Dean Jagger, Jack Weston. Pleasant comedy with a spirited cast about two sailors who find a way to beat the roulette table in Venice. Easy to take, easy to forget. CinemaScope.▼

Honey Pot, The (1967) **C-131m.** **½ D: Joseph L. Mankiewicz. Rex Harrison, Susan Hayward, Cliff Robertson, Capucine,

Edie Adams, Maggie Smith, Adolfo Celi. Director/writer Mankiewicz updates *Volpone* in sly blend of high comedy and whodunit. Harrison pretends to be dying, sends for former mistresses to see their reactions; hoax evolves into elaborate murder scheme. Never as amusing as one would like it to be. Aka IT COMES UP MURDER.▼

Honeysuckle Rose (1980) **C-119m.** *** D: Jerry Schatzberg. Willie Nelson, Dyan Cannon, Amy Irving, Slim Pickens, Joey Floyd, Charles Levin, Priscilla Pointer, Mickey Rooney, Jr., Diana Scarwid. Appealing, low-key film about a country music star and his lifestyle at home in Texas and on the road, which begins to come apart when he starts fooling around with the young daughter of his longtime musical sidekick. Lots of good music by Willie, fiddler Johnny Gimble, and guest star Emmylou Harris. Officially based on INTERMEZZO, believe it or not! Retitled ON THE ROAD AGAIN. Panavision. [PG]▼●

Honey, We Shrunk Ourselves (1997) **C-75m.** **½ D: Dean Cundey. Rick Moranis, Eve Gordon, Robin Bartlett, Allison Mack, Jake Richardson, Stuart Pankin, Bug Hall. Amusing direct-to-video followup to the effects-driven comedy series. This time, crackpot inventor Moranis's machine manages to shrink him and his wife along with their best friends, leaving their collective kids on their own. Key sequences include a wild ride in a Hot Wheels car. Modestly made, yielding modest results. [PG] ▼●

Hong Kong (1951) **C-92m.** ** D: Lewis R. Foster. Ronald Reagan, Rhonda Fleming, Nigel Bruce, Marvin Miller, Lee Marvin. Mediocre account of Reagan trying to heist a valuable antique from orphaned boy but going straight before finale. Strictly backlot Hong Kong.

Hong Kong Affair (1958) **79m.** *½ D: Paul F. Heard. Jack Kelly, May Wynn, Richard Loo, Lo Lita Shek. Kelly is the Yank who comes to the Orient to investigate his property holdings, getting more than he bargained for.

Hong Kong Confidential (1958) **67m.** **½ D: Edward L. Cahn. Gene Barry, Beverly Tyler, Allison Hayes, Noel Drayton. Harmless B film about Anglo-American agents rescuing a kidnapped Arabian prince.

Honkers, The (1972) **C-102m.** **½ D: Steve Ihnat. James Coburn, Lois Nettleton, Slim Pickens, Anne Archer, Richard Anderson, Joan Huntington, Jim Davis. Theme about aging rodeo performer was handled better in J. W. COOP and JUNIOR BONNER (all made same year!); actor Ihnat died shortly after directing this film. [PG]

Honky (1971) **C-89m.** **½ D: William A. Graham. Brenda Sykes, John Nielson, William Marshall, Maia Danziger, Marion Ross, Lincoln Kilpatrick. Not-bad drama of budding romance between black Sykes and white Nielson, and the problems they encounter. Score by Quincy Jones. Panavision. [R]▼

Honky Tonk (1941) **105m.** **½ D: Jack Conway. Clark Gable, Lana Turner, Frank Morgan, Claire Trevor, Marjorie Main, Albert Dekker, Chill Wills, Veda Ann Borg. Good-gal Lana loves gambler Gable in romantic Western that's fun for a spell, then drags into talky marathon. Morgan and Wills offer fine character performances. Remade for TV in 1974. Also shown in computer-colored version.▼●

Honky Tonk Freeway (1981) **C-107m.** ** D: John Schlesinger. William Devane, Beverly D'Angelo, Beau Bridges, Jessica Tandy, Hume Cronyn, Geraldine Page, George Dzundza, Teri Garr, Joe Grifasi, Howard Hesseman, Paul Jabara, Frances Lee McCain, John Astin, David Rasche, Daniel Stern. An absurdist view of contemporary America, in fragmented vignettes of various oddballs whose lives converge in Ticlaw, Florida, a tiny town determined to attract tourists despite the lack of an exit ramp from the new freeway. As a statement on life, it's a failure; as a silly comedy, it sometimes succeeds. Reminiscent (in its narrative style) of NASHVILLE. [PG]▼

Honkytonk Man (1982) **C-122m.** *½ D: Clint Eastwood. Clint Eastwood, Kyle Eastwood, John McIntire, Alexa Kenin, Verna Bloom, Matt Clark, Barry Corbin. The kind of film that gives "change-of-pace" a bad name. Clint is Depression-era country singer hoping to make it to the Grand Old Opry before he dies of tuberculosis; son Kyle plays his nephew, who tags along. Artificial and overlong; many music greats appear in bits, including Marty Robbins, who provides film's sole touching moment and, ironically, died himself only days before the picture opened. [PG]▼●

Honolulu (1939) **83m.** **½ D: Edward Buzzell. Eleanor Powell, Robert Young, George Burns, Gracie Allen, Rita Johnson, Willie Fung, Sig Rumann, Ruth Hussey, Eddie Anderson, The Kings Men. Pleasant musical fluff with Young in a dual role, as a movie star who, seeking peace and quiet, trades places with his lookalike, a Hawaiian plantation owner. Powell has several dance features (including a tap hula!), but many of the best moments belong to Gracie. Oddly enough, this was Burns and Allen's final film together.▼

Honor Among Thieves SEE: **Farewell, Friend**

Honor Guard, The SEE: **Wolf Lake**

Hoodlum, The (1951) **61m.** ** D: Max Nosseck. Lawrence Tierney, Allene Roberts, Marjorie Riordan, Lisa Golm. Once a crook, always a crook is plot of this caper about ex-con planning bank robbery.▼

Hoodlum (1997) **C-130m.** **½ D: Bill Duke. Laurence Fishburne, Tim Roth, Vanessa L. Williams, Andy Garcia, Cicely Tyson, Chi McBride, Clarence Williams III, Richard Bradford, William Atherton, Loretta Devine, Queen Latifah. GODFATHER wannabe about 1930s Harlem racketeer Ellsworth "Bumpy" Johnson, who locks horns with Dutch Schultz (Roth) and Lucky Luciano (Garcia), and tries to carve his own niche in the numbers game. Well-crafted, multi-character gangster saga has its moments, but takes a long time to tell its story and never builds the emotional punch it seeks. One welcome novelty: a '30s-style montage illustrating Bumpy's rise to power. Fishburne also coexecutive-produced. [R] ▼●◗

Hoodlum Empire (1952) **98m.** **½ D: Joseph Kane. Brian Donlevy, Claire Trevor, Forrest Tucker, Vera Ralston, Luther Adler. Cast is sufficiently versed in format to make this exposé of a crime syndicate better than average.▼

Hoodlum Priest, The (1961) **101m.** *** D: Irvin Kershner. Don Murray, Larry Gates, Keir Dullea, Logan Ramsey, Cindi Wood. Based on real-life clergyman who devoted himself to trying to help would-be criminals, focusing on Murray's efforts to rehabilitate delinquent Dullea (in film debut); splendidly acted. Murray coproduced and cowrote (latter under pseudonym Don Deer).▼

Hoodlum Saint, The (1946) **91m.** ** D: Norman Taurog. William Powell, Esther Williams, Angela Lansbury, James Gleason, Lewis Stone, "Rags" Ragland, Frank McHugh, Slim Summerville. Confusing mishmash with Powell a cynical, money-obsessed WW1 vet who, between schemes, falls for pretty Williams. This one squeaks by solely on Powell's charm.

Hoods (1999) **C-92m.** **½ D: Mark Malone. Joe Mantegna, Kevin Pollak, Joe Pantoliano, Vincent Berry, Jennifer Tilly, Robert Costanzo, Richard Foronjy, John Capodice, Joseph Maher. Wry look at N.Y.C. mobsters and a hapless functionary who's stuck carrying out orders for his mentally incompetent father. Some genuinely funny scenes and ingratiating performances by an A-1 ensemble make this worth a look, even though the payoff is weak. Seymour Cassel and Charles Martin Smith appear unbilled. Made for theaters, debuted on cable. [R]▼◗

Hook, The (1963) **98m.** *** D: George Seaton. Kirk Douglas, Robert Walker, Jr., Nick Adams, Nehemiah Persoff. Film examines men at war (Korean) and the taking of one life, face-to-face, as opposed to killing many in battle. Earnest, thought-provoking. Music by harmonica virtuoso Larry Adler. Panavision.

Hook (1991) **C-144m.** ** D: Steven Spielberg. Dustin Hoffman, Robin Williams, Julia Roberts, Bob Hoskins, Maggie Smith, Caroline Goodall, Charlie Korsmo, Amber Scott, Phil Collins, Arthur Malet, Dante Basco, Gwyneth Paltrow. Unfortunate cheapening of the beloved James Barrie tale of Peter Pan, with Williams as a heartless corporate takeover honcho who must rediscover his true identity—as Pan—in order to save his children, who've been kidnapped by Captain Hook. Great casting in key roles is dissipated by a script that offers no joy, and very little magic—with a troupe of TV-generation Lost Boys who'd be more at home in a McDonald's commercial. (Musician David Crosby and an unrecognizable Glenn Close have bit parts as pirates.) If this is Peter Pan for the 90s, give us the 50s instead. Panavision. [PG]▼●

Hooked Generation (1969) **C-92m.** BOMB D: William Grefe. Jeremy Slate, Willie Pastrano, Steve Alaimo, John Davis Chandler, Socrates Ballis. Narcotics peddlers slaughter Cuban contacts, kidnap innocent victims; poor excuse for a film. [R]▼

Hook, Line & Sinker (1969) **C-91m.** BOMB D: George Marshall. Jerry Lewis, Peter Lawford, Anne Francis, Pedro Gonzalez-Gonzalez, Jimmy Miller, Kathleen Freeman. Potentially funny premise about supposedly dying man who runs up $100,000 in credit card debts, only to discover he's healthy, is totally botched; even Lewis fans will be bored. [G]

Hooker Cult Murders, The SEE: **Pyx, The**

Hoop Dreams (1994) **C-169m.** ***½ D: Steve James. Exceptional documentary follows two Chicago inner-city kids (Arthur Agee and William Gates), who have dreams of basketball stardom, over four years' time. This intimate and engrossing film plays like drama, not documentary, except that it takes unexpected twists and turns no writer could invent. A searing commentary on our social system, the indomitable strength of the family unit, and the unpredictability of life. Overlong, perhaps, but fascinating most of the way. Produced by Steve James, Frederick Marx, and Peter Gilbert. [PG-13]▼●

Hooper (1978) **C-100m.** *** D: Hal Needham. Burt Reynolds, Jan-Michael Vincent, Sally Field, Brian Keith, John Marley, James Best, Adam West, Robert Klein. Lighthearted look at aging ace Hollywood stunt man Reynolds, his freewheeling life-style, and the young tyro who gets him to try the biggest stunt of all. [PG] ▼●◗

Hooray for Love (1935) **72m.** *** D: Walter Lang. Ann Sothern, Gene Raymond, Bill Robinson, Maria Gambarelli, Pert Kelton, Fats Waller, Jeni Le Gon, Thurston Hall, Lionel Stander. Modest but very entertaining musical with aspiring show-biz hot-shot Raymond romancing reluctant singer Sothern. Robinson shines in "I'm Living in a Great Big Way" specialty number, ably assisted by Waller and Le Gon; Kelton adds laughs as an inept soprano.

Hoosiers (1986) **C-114m.** *** D: David Anspaugh. Gene Hackman, Barbara Hershey, Dennis Hopper, Sheb Wooley, Fern Parsons, Brad Boyle, Steve Hollar, Brad Long, David Neidorf. Hackman gets a last-chance job coaching a small-town Indiana high school basketball team in the 1950s, and faces the dual challenge of bringing the team to the state championship—and redeeming himself. Thoroughly ingratiating (and just as thoroughly calculated), this well-made slice of Americana is hard to resist. Hackman is terrific as usual; Hopper is fine in a showy role as an alcoholic basketball nut. Written by Angelo Pizzo. [PG]▼●◗

Hoosier Schoolboy (1937) **62m.** **½ D: William Nigh. Mickey Rooney, Anne Nagel, Frank Shields, Edward Pawley, William Gould. Perceptive little Depression-era melodrama detailing the myriad problems of the title character (Rooney). Scenario depicts everything from the plight of forgotten WW1 veterans to greedy capitalists who cause strikes and strife.▼

Hootenanny Hoot (1963) **91m.** ** D: Gene Nelson. Peter Breck, Joby Baker, Ruta Lee, Pam Austin, Johnny Cash, Sheb Wooley, The Brothers Four, Judy Henske. Predictable comedy about college hootenanny show brought to TV is made bearable only by presence of Cash and other country/folk performers. One of producer Sam Katzman's "topical" low-budgeters.

Hope (1997) **C-100m. TVM** D: Goldie Hawn. Jena Malone, Christine Lahti, Catherine O'Hara, Jeffrey D. Sams, J. T. Walsh, Mary Ellen Trainor. Hawn makes her directing debut with this compelling coming-of-age tale dealing with a young tomboy (wonderful, sad-faced Malone) growing up in the segregation-era South. The story, an original by Kerry Kennedy, unfolds during a single week coinciding with the 1962 Cuban Missile Crisis and has the preteen girl challenging her small town to confront the truth after a black playmate dies in a fire at the local movie house run by her bigoted uncle. Made for cable. Above average.▼●

Hope and Glory (1987-British) **C-113m.** ***½ D: John Boorman. Sarah Miles, David Hayman, Derrick O'Connor, Susan Wooldridge, Sammi Davis, Ian Bannen, Sebastian Rice-Edwards, Jean-Marc Barr, Annie Leon. A loving look back at British family life during the first years of WW2, as seen through the eyes of a young boy to whom the whole thing is a great adventure. Boorman's autobiographical tale (he scripted and produced, as well) is funny, moving and richly detailed; no one has captured the experience of living through the London air raids and bombings so well. Charley Boorman (the director's son, who starred in THE EMERALD FOREST) appears briefly as a German pilot who's been shot down. [PG-13]▼●

Hope Floats (1998) **C-114m.** *** D: Forest Whitaker. Sandra Bullock, Harry Connick, Jr., Gena Rowlands, Mae Whitman, Michael Paré, Cameron Finley, Kathy Najimy, Bill Cobbs, Connie Ray. Learning her husband has been unfaithful, Bullock moves back to her Texas hometown, taking along her lonely daughter, Whitman. Her mother immediately tries to set her up with Connick, but Bullock is having a hard time just learning about herself. Well acted, particularly by Whitman, with inventive direction, the movie is entertaining throughout, but as shapeless as soup. Excellent song score. Rosanna Arquette appears unbilled. Coexecutive-produced by Bullock. [PG-13]▼●◗

Hoppity Goes to Town (1941) **C-77m.** **½ D: Dave Fleischer. Pleasant animated feature about residents of bug-ville and their various problems—living in a human world, and threatened by villainous C. Bagley Beetle. Good-looking but uncompelling story-wise, with unmemorable Frank Loesser–Hoagy Carmichael score. Originally titled MR. BUG GOES TO TOWN.▼●

Hopscotch (1980) **C-104m.** *** D: Ronald Neame. Walter Matthau, Glenda Jackson, Sam Waterston, Ned Beatty, Herbert Lom. Entertaining contrivance about a maverick CIA operative who's fed up with his idiotic boss (Beatty) and decides to teach him a lesson by publishing his volatile memoirs. Barely believable, but fun to watch, thanks largely to Matthau. From the novel by Brian Garfield, who coproduced and coscripted the film. Panavision. [R]▼●

Horizons West (1952) **C-81m.** **½ D: Budd Boetticher. Robert Ryan, Julia (Julie) Adams, Rock Hudson, Raymond Burr, James Arness, John McIntire, Dennis Weaver. Standard Western of brothers Ryan and Hudson on opposite sides of the law; the latter attempts to block the former's efforts to ruthlessly acquire power in post–Civil War Texas.▼

Horizontal Lieutenant, The (1962) **C-90m.** ** D: Richard Thorpe. Jim Hutton, Paula Prentiss, Miyoshi Umeki, Jim Backus, Jack Carter, Marty Ingels, Charles McGraw. Artificial service comedy about inept army intelligence officer Hutton and his misadventures in the Pacific during WW2. CinemaScope.▼

Horn Blows at Midnight, The (1945) **78m.** *** D: Raoul Walsh. Jack Benny, Alexis Smith, Dolores Moran, Allyn Joslyn, Reginald Gardiner, Guy Kibbee, John Alexander, Margaret Dumont, Franklin Pangborn, Bobby (Robert) Blake. Enjoyable, original comedy-fantasy about an angel (Benny) sent to destroy earth with a blast from Gabriel's horn. Broad, funny, no classic, but not the turkey Benny so often joked about either. Franklin Pangborn is especially funny as a flustered hotel detective.▼●

Hornets' Nest (1970) **C-110m.** **½ D: Phil Karlson. Rock Hudson, Sylva Koscina, Sergio Fantoni, Jacques Sernas, Giacomo Rossi Stuart, Tom Felleghi. Hudson and group of Italian children plot to blow up Nazi-controlled dam. Reasonably well done and exciting. [M]▼

Horrible Dr. Hichcock, The (1962-Italian) **C-76m.** **½ D: Robert Hampton (Riccardo Freda). Robert Flemyng, Barbara Steele, Teresa Fitzgerald, Maria Teresa Vianello. Unaware her doctor husband is a (gulp!) necrophiliac, woman accompanies him to the mansion where his first wife apparently died twelve years earlier during sexual games. Eerie, handsome horror, with undertones of Poe. British version, TERROR OF DR. HICHCOCK, runs 88m. and is also available on tape. Followed by THE GHOST. Panoramic.▼

Horrible House on the Hill, The SEE: **Devil Times Five**

Horror Castle (1964-Italian) **C-83m.** *½ D: Anthony Dawson (Antonio Margheriti). Christopher Lee, Rossana Podesta, George Riviere, Jim Nolan, Anny Belli Uberti. Chiller about a demented WW2 victim running rampant in a Rhine castle, using assorted torture chamber devices on unsuspecting people. Effect is numbing. Aka THE VIRGIN OF NUREMBERG and TERROR CASTLE. British title: THE CASTLE OF TERROR. Totalscope.▼

Horror Chamber of Dr. Faustus, The (1959-French-Italian) **88m.** *** D: Georges Franju. Pierre Brasseur, Alida Valli, Edith Scob. Moody horror film, a classic in some circles, about a brilliant but crazed scientist/surgeon/researcher (Brasseur) and his fate after disfiguring his daughter. Originally titled LES YEUX SANS VISAGE (EYES WITHOUT A FACE).▼●

Horror Creatures of the Prehistoric Planet SEE: **Vampire Men of the Lost Planet**

Horror Express (1972-Spanish-British) **C-88m.** *** D: Eugenio Martin. Christopher Lee, Peter Cushing, Telly Savalas, Silvia Tortosa, Jorge Rigaud. Crackerjack horror movie, ingeniously staged and well acted by the genre's superstars. Turn-of-the-century chiller has a long-frozen monster coming to life while being transported from Asia to the West. Lee and Cushing are rival anthropologists aboard the train and Savalas is a power-crazed Cossack officer. Aka PANIC ON THE TRANS-SIBERIAN EXPRESS. Widescreen. [R]▼◗

Horror High SEE: **Twisted Brain**

Horror Hotel (1960-British) **76m.** **½ D: John Moxey. Dennis Lotis, Christopher Lee, Betta St. John, Patricia Jessel, Venetia Stevenson. Seventeenth-century witch burned at the stake maintains an inn to lure victims for blood sacrifice to the devil. Not bad of its type. Original British title: THE CITY OF THE DEAD.▼●◗

Horror Hotel (1976) SEE: **Eaten Alive!**

Horror House (1969-British) **C-79m.** *½ D: Michael Armstrong. Frankie Avalon, Jill Haworth, Dennis Price, George Sewell, Gina Warwick, Richard O'Sullivan. Below-standard thriller using dog-eared "let's-spend-a-night-in-a-haunted-house" script. Frankie should have stayed on the beach with Annette. Original British title: THE HAUNTED HOUSE OF HORROR. [M/PG]

Horror Island (1941) **60m.** **½ D: George Waggner. Dick Foran, Leo Carrillo, Peggy Moran, Fuzzy Knight, John Eldredge, Lewis Howard, Iris Adrian. Fast-paced, diverting B-thriller film has various colorful types converging at isolated manor; one by one, they're stalked and murdered.

Horror of Dracula (1958-British) **C-82m.** *** D: Terence Fisher. Peter Cushing, Christopher Lee, Melissa Stribling, Michael Gough, Carol Marsh, John Van Eyssen, Valerie Gaunt, Miles Malleson. Probably Hammer Films' best shocker, a handsomely mounted retelling of the Stoker tale, with fantasy elements deemphasized. Lee is smooth as the Count, and Cushing perfect as tireless Professor Van Helsing. Script by Jimmy Sangster; full-blooded score by James Bernard. Released in Britain as DRACULA; followed by six sequels, the first of which was DRACULA—PRINCE OF DARKNESS.▼●

Horror of Frankenstein, The (1970-British) **C-95m.** ** D: Jimmy Sangster. Ralph Bates, Kate O'Mara, Graham Jones, Veronica Carlson, Bernard Archard, Dennis Price, Joan Rice. New kind of Dr. Frankenstein: he arranges murder of father, cheats on his lover, kills his best friend, while creating new, laughable monster. Semi-spoof remake of CURSE OF FRANKENSTEIN. For aficionados only. Followed by FRANKENSTEIN AND THE MONSTER FROM HELL. [R]▼●

Horror of Party Beach, The (1964) **72m.** BOMB D: Del Tenney. John Scott, Alice Lyon, Allen Laurel, Marilyn Clark, Eulabelle Moore. Radioactive waste is dumped off-shore, resulting in scaly monsters who disrupt the fun of a bunch of Connecticut beach bunnies. One of the earliest anti-nuclear warning films, although for some strange reason the message fails to come across. Billed as "The First Horror Musical" by its producers, who evidently never saw Liberace in SINCERELY YOURS.▼

Horror of the Blood Monsters SEE: **Vampire Men of the Lost Planet**

Horror on Snape Island (1972-British) **C-85m.** BOMB D: Jim O'Connolly. Bryant Halliday, Jill Haworth, Anna Palk, Jack Watson, Mark Edwards, Derek Fowlds.

One of the horrors is a series of brutal murders masterminded by lunatic; another one is the film itself. Retitled TOWER OF EVIL and BEYOND THE FOG. [R]▼◗

Horror Planet (1982-British) **C-86m.** BOMB D: Norman J. Warren. Robin Clark, Jennifer Ashley, Stephanie Beacham, Steven Grives, Barry Houghton, Victoria Tennant, Judy Geeson. Obnoxious, gory garbage about male and female space travelers and their discovery of a crawling terror. Interesting cast wasted in this awful ALIEN clone. Cut for U.S. release. Original title: INSEMINOID. J-D-C Scope. [R]▼●◗

Horror Show, The (1989) **C-95m.** BOMB D: James Isaac. Lance Henriksen, Brion James, Rita Taggart, Thom Bray, Matt Clark, Dedee Pfeiffer, Lewis Arquette, Lawrence Tierney, Alvy Moore. Henriksen gives typically strong performance as cop pursued by murderous—and already executed—maniac James, who's intent on wiping out the cop's family by turning nightmares into reality. Confused, silly and boring. Known outside U.S. as HOUSE III. [R]▼

Horrors of the Black Museum (1959-British) **C-95m.** **½ D: Arthur Crabtree. Michael Gough, June Cunningham, Graham Curnow, Shirley Ann Field, Geoffrey Keen. Gruesome sequences highlight chiller about writer who uses his hypnotized helper to commit murders. CinemaScope.▼●

Horse Feathers (1932) **68m.** ***½ D: Norman Z. McLeod. Groucho, Harpo, Chico, and Zeppo Marx, Thelma Todd, David Landau, Robert Greig, Nat Pendleton. Groucho is head of Huxley College, building up football team to play rival Darwin U. in crazy Marx nonsense. The password is "swordfish." Originally released at 70m.▼●◗

Horse in the Gray Flannel Suit, The (1968) **C-113m.** *** D: Norman Tokar. Dean Jones, Diane Baker, Lloyd Bochner, Fred Clark, Ellen Janov, Kurt Russell. Cheerful Disney comedy about advertising man (Jones) who finds a way to link his daughter's devotion to horses with an ad campaign. [G]▼

Horseman on the Roof, The (1995-French) **C-122m.** **½ D: Jean-Paul Rappennau. Juliette Binoche, Olivier Martinez, Pierre Arditi, François Cluzet, Jean Yanne, Gérard Depardieu. Gorgeous but rather leisurely spectacle, set in 1832, of Italian cavalry officer (Martinez), part of an underground network spread throughout southern France, who is trying to force Austrian overlords out of Italy. On top of everything else, a cholera epidemic is ravaging the French countryside. Binoche is noblewoman who becomes the horseman's traveling companion. Exquisite Provence locations help boost this adventure saga, based on Jean Giono's 1951 novel—a literary classic in France. Depardieu has a humorous cameo as an unorthodox police superintendent. Technovision. [R]▼●

Horsemasters, The (1961) **C-87m.** ** D: William Fairchild. Annette Funicello, Janet Munro, Tommy Kirk, Donald Pleasence, Tony Britton, Jean Marsh, John Fraser, Millicent Martin. Minor family fare (originally shown on Disney TV show) about Annette learning horsemanship—and to overcome her fear of jumping—at exclusive British riding school. Filmed in England; released as a feature in Europe.▼

Horsemen, The (1971) **C-109m.** **½ D: John Frankenheimer. Omar Sharif, Leigh Taylor-Young, Jack Palance, David De, Peter Jeffrey. Sharif enters grueling buzkashi tournament to please his demanding father (Palance) and prove his machismo. Old-fashioned action-adventure mixes uncomfortably with soul-searching in Dalton Trumbo's script. Filmed in Afghanistan and Spain. Beautiful photography by Claude Renoir in Panavision. [PG]▼

Horse Named Comanche, A SEE: **Tonka**

Horseplayer, The (1990) **C-89m.** *½ D: Kurt Voss. Brad Dourif, Sammi Davis, M. K. Harris, Vic Tayback. Extremely odd story of an artist and his seductive sister who interrupt the life of a recluse when they move into his apartment building. No one is quite what they seem—but who cares? [R]▼●

Horse's Mouth, The (1958-British) **C-93m.** ***½ D: Ronald Neame. Alec Guinness, Kay Walsh, Renee Houston, Mike Morgan, Michael Gough, Ernest Thesiger. Guinness adapted Joyce Cary's story into this droll screenplay about a brilliant, eccentric, egocentric—and perpetually starving—artist whom some consider a genius. Many others, who know him more intimately, think of him as a major irritant. Score makes ideal use of Prokofiev's "Lieutenant Kije" suite.▼●

Horse Soldiers, The (1959) **C-119m.** **½ D: John Ford. John Wayne, William Holden, Constance Towers, Althea Gibson, Hoot Gibson, Anna Lee, Russell Simpson, Ken Curtis, Denver Pyle, Strother Martin, Hank Worden. Ford's only feature set during the Civil War, based on actual incidents. Union Colonel Wayne leads sabotage party deep into Rebel territory, accompanied by somewhat pacifistic doctor Holden. Large-scale actioner rates only a "medium" by Ford buffs; others may like it better.▼●

Horse Whisperer, The (1998) **C-169m.** ***½ D: Robert Redford. Robert Redford, Kristin Scott Thomas, Sam Neill, Dianne Wiest, Scarlett Johansson, Chris Cooper, Cherry Jones, Ty Hillman, Jeanette Nolan, Don Edwards. Exquisite rendering of Nicholas Evans' novel about a teenaged girl, traumatized in a horse-riding accident, whose domineering mother drives them both (and the horse) to Montana, where a renowned horse trainer tries to rehabilitate the animal—and simultaneously, the girl. Story offers a tailor-made part for Redford and an opportunity for mature romance, but like his character, Redford the filmmaker takes his time telling the story. It's risky, but it works. Screenplay by Eric Roth and Richard LaGravenese. Panavision. [PG-13]▼●◗

Horse Without a Head, The (1963) **C-89m.** *** D: Don Chaffey. Leo McKern, Jean-Pierre Aumont, Herbert Lom, Pamela Franklin, Vincent Winter. Excellent cast in entertaining British-made Disney film (first shown on the Disney TV show) about kids mixed up with bad guys on the trail of stolen loot. First-rate family fare. ▼

Hospital, The (1971) **C-103m.** ***½ D: Arthur Hiller. George C. Scott, Diana Rigg, Barnard Hughes, Nancy Marchand, Richard A. Dysart, Stephen Elliott, Jordan Charney, Roberts Blossom, Robert Walden, Lenny Baker, Frances Sternhagen, Stockard Channing, Katherine Helmond. Sardonically funny view of modern city hospital where bitterly discouraged doctor (Scott) is drawn into chaos by crazy girl (Rigg) and her scheming father. Paddy Chayefsky's Oscar-winning script makes fun of serious situation by turning it into Marx Brothers-ish lunacy; ultimate truth in what's being said leaves viewer somewhat sad. [PG]▼●

Hospital of Terror SEE: **Beyond the Living**

Hostage, The (1967) **C-84m.** **½ D: Russell S. Doughton, Jr. Don O'Kelly, (Harry) Dean Stanton, John Carradine, Ron Hagerthy, Ann Doran. Well-done low-budget film about a six-year-old who stows away on moving van driven by two killers. Shot on location in Iowa.▼

Hostage (1983-Australian-German) **C-90m.** *½ D: Frank Shields. Kerry Mack, Ralph Schicha, Judy Nunn, Clare Binney. Young, carefree Mack is blackmailed into marriage by Nazi Schicha, and her life becomes hell on earth. Intriguing scenario, based on a true story and set in the 70s, but the result is disjointed, repetitive, boring. Original title: HOSTAGE: THE CHRISTINE MARESCH STORY. Video title: SAVAGE ATTRACTION.▼

Hostage (1987) **C-95m.** ** D: Hanro Mohr. Wings Hauser, Karen Black, Kevin McCarthy, Nancy Locke (Hauser), Robert Whitehead. When a planeload of innocents is kidnapped by Arab terrorists, Hauser and McCarthy enlist ex-soldiers for a rescue mission. Black is very funny in role of a movie star tired of being a sex symbol. Filmed in South Africa. [R]▼

Hostage (1992-British) **C-101m.** ** D: Robert Young. Sam Neill, Talisa Soto, James Fox, Michael Kitchen, Art Malik, Cristina Higueras, Jean Pierre Reguerraz. British secret agent Neill wants out of the Service, but his slimy superiors won't let him go. Mildly interesting morality tale of kidnapping and ethical considerations in the world of international politics. [R]▼

Hostages (1943) **88m.** ** D: Frank Tuttle. Luise Rainer, William Bendix, Roland Varno, Oscar Homolka, Katina Paxinou, Paul Lukas. Routine tale of underground movement in WW2; Bendix outshines Rainer acting-wise.

Hostages (1993-British) **C-100m. TVM** D: David Wheatley. Kathy Bates, Colin Firth, Ciaran Hinds, Natasha Richardson, Jay O. Sanders, Josef Sommer, Harry Dean Stanton. Gritty dramatization of Western hostages held in Lebanon during the 80s, with a stark script by Bernard MacLaverty. Made for cable. Above average.▼

Hostage: The Christine Maresch Story SEE: **Hostage** (1983)

Hostile Guns (1967) **C-91m.** **½ D: R. G. Springsteen. George Montgomery, Yvonne De Carlo, Tab Hunter, Brian Donlevy, John Russell. U.S. marshal, transporting prisoners to penitentiary, discovers that female prisoner is a woman he once loved. Typical. Techniscope. ▼●

Hot Blood (1956) **C-85m.** *½ D: Nicholas Ray. Jane Russell, Cornel Wilde, Luther Adler, Joseph Calleia. Jane Russell shakes her tambourines and drives Cornel Wilde, in this supremely silly (not to mention unbelievable) gypsy yarn. CinemaScope.

Hot Box, The (1972) **C-85m.** ** D: Joe Viola. Margaret Markov, Andrea Cagan, Ricky Richardson, Laurie Rose, Charles Dierkop. Filipino-shot women's prison film adequately runs through the standard changes, as heroines break out and foment a local revolution. Cowritten and produced by Jonathan Demme. [R]▼

Hot Car Girl SEE: **Hot Rod Girl**

Hot Dog . . . The Movie (1984) **C-96m.** *½ D: Peter Markle. David Naughton, Patrick Houser, Tracy N. Smith, John Patrick Reger, Frank Koppola, Shannon Tweed. Hijinks at a ski resort: an updating of '60s Beach Party-type movies, just as dumb, but now much raunchier. Good ski sequences, but that's about it. Film is so titled to avoid confusion with HOT DOG . . . THE OPERA. [R]▼

Hotel (1967) **C-124m.** ** D: Richard Quine. Rod Taylor, Catherine Spaak, Karl Malden, Melvyn Douglas, Richard Conte, Michael Rennie, Merle Oberon, Kevin McCarthy. Adaptation of still another Arthur Hailey multicharactered novel is not all that inferior to AIRPORT, but that's faint praise; Douglas has some good scenes. Later a TV series.▼

Hotel Berlin (1945) **98m.** **½ D: Peter Godfrey. Helmut Dantine, Andrea King, Raymond Massey, Faye Emerson, Peter Lorre, Alan Hale. GRAND HOTEL author Vicki Baum tries again with sundry characters based in hotel during decline of

Nazi Germany; good cast makes it generally interesting.

Hotel Colonial (1983-Italian-U.S.) **C-104m.** BOMB D: Cinzia Torrini. John Savage, Rachel Ward, Robert Duvall, Massimo Troisi. International mishmash wastes a good cast in downbeat tale of Savage going to Colombia to investigate the death of his brother, aided by embassy attaché Ward and thwarted by evil Duvall. Pretty Mexican scenery is film's only merit. [R]▼●

Hotel for Women (1939) **83m.** ** D: Gregory Ratoff. Linda Darnell, Ann Sothern, Elsa Maxwell, Lynn Bari, Sidney Blackmer, Alan Dinehart. Weak film about group of manhunting girls, noteworthy only as Darnell's film debut. Originally titled ELSA MAXWELL'S HOTEL FOR WOMEN.

Hotel Imperial (1939) **67m.** ** D: Robert Florey. Isa Miranda, Ray Milland, Reginald Owen, Gene Lockhart, Albert Dekker. Miranda encounters intrigue while searching for man responsible for her sister's death; fairly entertaining drama. Troubled film was years in production, with numerous cast, director and title changes. A remake of 1927 silent, this was in turn remade as FIVE GRAVES TO CAIRO.

Hotel New Hampshire, The (1984) **C-110m.** *** D: Tony Richardson. Rob Lowe, Jodie Foster, Beau Bridges, Nastassja Kinski, Paul McCrane, Jennie Dundas, Dorsey Wright, Matthew Modine, Wilford Brimley, Amanda Plummer, Wallace Shawn, Anita Morris, Joely Richardson. Faithful adaptation of John Irving's sprawling seriocomic novel about an unconventional family and its bizarre adventures—social, sexual, and political—on both sides of the Atlantic. Some fine vignettes and good performances make this worth watching, though characters eventually wear out their welcome. [R]▼●

Hotel Paradiso (1966-British) **C-96m.** **½ D: Peter Glenville. Alec Guinness, Gina Lollobrigida, Robert Morley, Akim Tamiroff. Pretentious farce of manners is only fitfully amusing; meek Guinness tries to carry on his rendezvous with gorgeous neighbor Gina, but everything interferes. Panavision.▼

Hotel Reserve (1944-British) **79m.** *** D: Lance Comfort, Max Greene, Victor Hanbury. James Mason, Lucie Mannheim, Herbert Lom, Patricia Medina, Anthony Shaw, David Ward. Suspenseful, moody film about innocent Austrian medical student (Mason) who's accused of espionage while on holiday in France before WW2. Based on an Eric Ambler novel.▼

Hotel Sahara (1951-British) **96m.** **½ D: Ken Annakin. Yvonne De Carlo, Peter Ustinov, David Tomlinson, Roland Culver. Pleasant fluff about North African hotel owner and beautiful fiancée who must shift "loyalties" every time new army marches into town during WW2.

Hotel Sorrento (1995-Australian) **C-112m.** *** D: Richard Franklin. Caroline Goodall, Caroline Gillmer, Tara Morice, Joan Plowright, John Hargreaves, Ben Thomas, Ray Barrett. Atmospheric, well-acted drama, set in a small seaside Australian town, focusing on the reunion of a trio of very different sisters, one of whom has just published a highly successful autobiographical novel. What follows may be predictable, but the result is compelling nonetheless. Also known as SORRENTO BEACH. [R] ▼

Hotel Terminus: The Life and Times of Klaus Barbie (1987) **C-267m.** ***½ D: Marcel Ophuls. Sobering, Oscar-winning documentary about the infamous Nazi war criminal who, decades after WW2, was expelled from Bolivia and returned to France for trial. Filled with incisive interviews with key individuals in his life. A fine companion piece to Ophuls' THE SORROW AND THE PITY.▼●

Hot Enough for June SEE: **Agent 8¾**

Hot Lead SEE: **Run of the Arrow**

Hot Lead and Cold Feet (1978) **C-90m.** *** D: Robert Butler. Jim Dale, Darren McGavin, Karen Valentine, Jack Elam, Don Knotts, John Williams. Amiable Disney Western spoof with lots of slapstick features British comic Dale in three roles: tough patriarch, tougher gunfighter son, and meek twin, a Salvation Army lad. The brothers participate in a wild obstacle race to gain possession of the town, then to defeat villainous Mayor McGavin. Good Oregon location filming. [G]▼

Hot Line (1969) SEE: **Day the Hot Line Got Hot, The**

Hot Millions (1968-British) **C-105m.** *** D: Eric Till. Peter Ustinov, Maggie Smith, Karl Malden, Bob Newhart, Robert Morley, Cesar Romero. Wry piece of fluff about Ustinov using a computer to siphon off big bucks from huge American conglomerate. Good performers aid pleasant romp, which became one of the biggest sleepers of its year. [G]▼

Hot News (1953) **68m.** *½ D: Edward Bernds. Stanley Clements, Gloria Henry, Ted de Corsia, Veda Ann Borg. Programmer tale of dedicated newspaperman cleaning up crime syndicate involved in sporting events.

Hot Pepper (1933) **76m.** **½ D: John G. Blystone. Victor McLaglen, Edmund Lowe, Lupe Velez, El Brendel. Another reprise of feud between Flagg (McLaglen) and Quirt (Lowe) from WHAT PRICE GLORY?, now civilians involved in nightclub, with spitfire Velez the woman they fight over. Constant wisecracks are a bit forced, but stars milk script for all it's worth.

Hot Potato (1976) **C-87m.** *½ D: Oscar Williams. Jim Kelly, George Memmoli,

Geoffrey Binney, Irene Tsu, Judith Brown. Idiotic action film in which karate expert Kelly and two cohorts try to rescue kidnapped Senator's daughter from Oriental villain. Comic-book stuff. Filmed in Thailand. Remade as FORCE: FIVE. [PG]▼

Hot Pursuit (1987) **C-93m.** *½ D: Steven Lisberger. John Cusack, Robert Loggia, Wendy Gazelle, Jerry Stiller, Monte Markham, Shelley Fabares, Ben Stiller. Student Cusack, grounded by bad grades, has been prevented from taking a dream vacation with the family of his wealthy girlfriend. Then he gets last-minute reprieve from a kindly prof, and tries to catch up with them on the road. Silly comedy will probably remind you of Cusack's earlier THE SURE THING—and the comparison isn't favorable. [PG-13]▼●

Hot Resort (1985) **C-92m.** BOMB D: John Robins. Tom Parsekian, Michael Berz, Bronson Pinchot, Daniel Schneider, Frank Gorshin, Marcy Walker, Debra Kelly, Samm-Art Williams, Mae Questel. Vulgar comedy about young guys on the make, spending the summer working at a resort hotel on the Caribbean island of St. Kitts. There's pretty scenery and prettier girls but few laughs. [R]▼

Hot Rock, The (1972) **C-105m.** *** D: Peter Yates. Robert Redford, George Segal, Ron Leibman, Paul Sand, Zero Mostel, Moses Gunn, William Redfield, Charlotte Rae, Topo Swope. Light, funny caper comedy where inept robbers blunder every step of carefully planned jewel heist. Best bit: the raid on the police station. Screenplay by William Goldman from Donald Westlake's novel; followed by BANK SHOT. Panavision. [PG]▼●

Hot Rod Gang (1958) **72m.** *½ D: Lew Landers. John Ashley, Gene Vincent, Jody Fair, Steve Drexel. Low-budget relic of its era, about hot-rod-happy Ashley joining Vincent's band to earn money to enter big race.

Hot Rod Girl (1956) **75m.** BOMB D: Leslie H. Martinson. Lori Nelson, Chuck Connors, John Smith, Frank Gorshin, Roxanne Arlen, Dabbs Greer. Blah juvenile delinquency potboiler, with sympathetic cop Connors establishing drag strip to keep hot-rodding teens off the streets. Aka HOT CAR GIRL.▼

Hot Rod Rumble (1957) **79m.** *½ D: Leslie Martinson. Brett Halsey, Richard Hartunian, Joey Forman, Leigh Snowden. Title tells all in this formula programmer of juvenile delinquents.

Hot Rods to Hell (1967) **C-92m.** **½ D: John Brahm. Dana Andrews, Jeanne Crain, Mimsy Farmer, Laurie Mock. Fast-paced actioner has Andrews and family tormented by hot-rod-happy juvenile delinquents. Original title: 52 MILES TO MIDNIGHT.

H.O.T.S. (1979) **C-95m.** *½ D: Gerald Seth Sindell. Susan Kiger, Lisa London, Pamela Jean Bryant, Kimberly Cameron, Lindsay Bloom, Mary Steelsmith, Angela Aames, Danny Bonaduce, Ken Olfson. Lame-brained knock-off of ANIMAL HOUSE with two sororities at each other's throats until they settle their differences with a strip football game. Leering sexploitation fare at least has gorgeous girls (including several *Playboy* playmates) and decent production, making this best watched with the sound off. Written by two women, believe it or not, one of them actress Cheri Caffaro (whose husband produced the film). Aka T&A ACADEMY. [R]▼

Hot Shots (1956) **61m.** *½ D: Jean Yarbrough. Huntz Hall, Stanley Clements, Joi Lansing, Jimmy Murphy, David Gorcey, Queenie Smith, Robert Shayne. The Bowery Boys become caretakers to a mischievous child TV star in this threadbare entry from the tail end of the series.

Hot Shots! (1991) **C-85m.** *** D: Jim Abrahams. Charlie Sheen, Cary Elwes, Valeria Golino, Lloyd Bridges, Kevin Dunn, Jon Cryer, William O'Leary, Kristy Swanson, Efrem Zimbalist, Jr., Bill Irwin, Judith Kahan, Pat Proft, Heidi Swedberg. Sheen plays a pilot trying to overcome his father's disastrous reputation in the cockpit in this zany, often hilarious takeoff on "flyboy" movies from ONLY ANGELS HAVE WINGS to TOP GUN. Surprisingly high quotient of successful gags, including sendups of movies ranging from DANCES WITH WOLVES to ROCKY, help this comedy soar at times. Bridges is a riot as an admiral with a loose propeller. Followed by a sequel. [PG-13] ▼●

Hot Shots! Part Deux (1993) **C-89m.** **½ D: Jim Abrahams. Charlie Sheen, Lloyd Bridges, Valeria Golino, Richard Crenna, Brenda Bakke, Miguel Ferrer, Rowan Atkinson, Jerry Haleva, Mitchell Ryan, Gregory Sierra. Obligatory sequel with Rambo-like Sheen called into action to rescue U.S. soldiers who tried to rescue soldiers (and so on . . .) held captive after Desert Storm. Plenty of gags and countless movie parodies, but just as many misses as hits this time around, especially in the second half. The cast acquits itself nicely, particularly Sheen, Bridges, and Crenna (who kids his own RAMBO series role). [PG-13]▼●

Hot Spell (1958) **86m.** ** D: Daniel Mann. Shirley Booth, Anthony Quinn, Shirley MacLaine, Earl Holliman, Eileen Heckart, Warren Stevens. Quinn—not just a pig but a blue-ribbon hog—cheats on wife Booth, who spouts irritating platitudes like Hazel on speed. Well-acted but dated drama about the breakup's effect on their children; MacLaine shines as their daughter. Set in New Orleans. VistaVision ▼

Hot Spot SEE: **I Wake Up Screaming**

Hot Spot, The (1990) **C-130m.** **½ D:

Dennis Hopper. Don Johnson, Virginia Madsen, Jennifer Connelly, Charles Martin Smith, William Sadler, Jerry Hardin, Barry Corbin, Leon Rippy, Jack Nance. Sounds as if it can't miss, but does: drifter Johnson, selling used cars in a nowhere Texas burg, gets involved with boss' wife Madsen, an R-rated descendant of Barbara Stanwyck from DOUBLE INDEMNITY. Overlong by 30 minutes and never once hits the bull's-eye, but there's so much ornery sex that you may be compelled to keep watching. Connelly plays the mysterious "nice girl" (with a sensuous body) who handles the car lot's financing. Based on Charles Williams' 1952 novel *Hell Hath No Fury*. [R]▼●

Hot Stuff (1979) **C-87m.** **½ D: Dom DeLuise. Dom DeLuise, Suzanne Pleshette, Jerry Reed, Luis Avalos, Ossie Davis, Marc Lawrence. Four Miami cops set up a "Sting"-like operation to fence stolen goods. Unexceptional but pleasant trifle that surprises by treating its characters as real human beings instead of cartoon stereotypes. Cowritten by Donald Westlake. [PG]▼●

Hot Summer Night (1957) **86m.** **½ D: David Friedkin. Leslie Nielsen, Colleen Miller, Edward Andrews, Claude Akins, Paul Richards. Offbeat story about reporter seeking an interview with leader of robbery gang.

Hot Sweat SEE: **Keetje Tippel**

Hot to Trot (1988) **C-83m.** BOMB D: Michael Dinner. Bob Goldthwait, Virginia Madsen, Dabney Coleman, Cindy Pickett, Jim Metzler, Tim Kazurinsky, Gilbert Gottfried, Jack Whitaker; voices of John Candy, Burgess Meredith. Here's a fresh concept for the 1980s: a comedy about a talking horse. Goldthwait plays a semi-imbecile who gets stock tips from a whinnying pal with the voice of John Candy. As comedies go, this is the equivalent of Black Monday. Coleman, courtesy of the makeup department, wears a pair of horse teeth here; they *are* funny. [PG]▼●

Hot Water (1924) **60m.** *** D: Sam Taylor, Fred Newmeyer. Harold Lloyd, Jobyna Ralston, Josephine Crowell, Charles Stevenson, Mickey McBan, Pat Harmon. Typically entertaining silent comedy feature with Lloyd, atypically, as a put-upon husband. Not as strong as Lloyd's best comedies; built instead on three lengthy set pieces, but they're very funny indeed—especially the ride on the trolley and a trouble-prone automobile outing with the family.▼

Houdini (1953) **C-106m.** **½ D: George Marshall. Tony Curtis, Janet Leigh, Torin Thatcher, Ian Wolfe, Sig Ruman. Fanciful biography of famed escape artist; more fiction than fact, but entertaining.▼●

Hound-Dog Man (1959) **C-87m.** *** D: Don Siegel. Fabian, Carol Lynley, Stuart Whitman, Arthur O'Connell, Dodie Stevens, Betty Field, Royal Dano, Margo Moore, Claude Akins, Edgar Buchanan, Jane Darwell, L.Q. Jones. Pleasant tale of Southern country boys Fabian (in film debut) and Whitman courting Stevens and Lynley. Fabian is surprisingly good; of course, he also sings. CinemaScope.

Hound of the Baskervilles, The (1939) **80m.** *** D: Sidney Lanfield. Basil Rathbone, Nigel Bruce, Richard Greene, Wendy Barrie, Lionel Atwill, John Carradine, Beryl Mercer, Mary Gordon, E. E. Clive. Rathbone made his first appearance as Sherlock Holmes in this grade-A production based on Conan Doyle's story about mysterious murders taking place at a creepy mansion on the moors (though he's off screen for a good part of the story). Fairly faithful to the source material with the now classic closing line from cocaine-user Holmes: "Quick Watson, the needle!" (Fourth screen version of the oft-filmed novel.)▼●

Hound of the Baskervilles, The (1959-British) **C-84m.** *** D: Terence Fisher. Peter Cushing, Christopher Lee, Andre Morell, Marla Landi, Miles Malleson, John LeMesurier. Cushing is well cast as Sherlock Holmes and Lee is fine as Sir Henry Baskerville in this atmospheric Hammer Films adaptation of the Conan Doyle classic.▼●

Hound of the Baskervilles, The (1972) **C-73m. TVM** D: Barry Crane. Stewart Granger, William Shatner, Bernard Fox, John Williams, Anthony Zerbe, Jane Merrow. Ludicrous remake of Conan Doyle spellbinder with casting the least of its problems. Nuance, tension, situation all made trivial by script, pacing, production values. For masochists only. Below average.

Hound of the Baskervilles, The (1978-British) **C-84m.** BOMB D: Paul Morrissey. Dudley Moore, Peter Cook, Denholm Elliott, Joan Greenwood, Spike Milligan, Jessie Matthews, Roy Kinnear. Dreadful spoof of Conan Doyle story scripted by Cook (who plays Sherlock Holmes), Moore (as both Watson and Holmes's mother), and director Morrissey. After a few laughs it descends into dreariness and never recovers. What a waste of talent! U.S. version runs 78m., with sequences out of order. Technovision.▼

Hound of the Baskervilles, The (1983-British) **C-101m. TVM** D: Douglas Hickox. Ian Richardson, Donald Churchill, Martin Shaw, Denholm Elliott, Brian Blessed, Ronald Lacey, Eleanor Bron, Edward Judd, Glynis Barber, Nicholas Clay. Best version of the Doyle classic to date with excellent use of locations. Richardson is an energetic, witty Holmes, though story requires him to be offstage much of the time. Well paced, stylish, and atmospheric, this deserved theatrical release but didn't get it. Above average.▼◗

Hour Before the Dawn, The (1944) **75m.** ** D: Frank Tuttle. Franchot Tone, Veronica Lake, John Sutton, Binnie Barnes, Henry Stephenson, Mary Gordon, Nils Asther. Polished, empty WW2 romance-espionage, with Tone falling for Nazi spy Lake; unlikely casting doesn't help.

Hour of Decision (1957-British) **81m.** ** D: C.M. Pennington Richards. Jeff Morrow, Hazel Court, Anthony Dawson, Lionel Jeffries, Carl Bernard, Mary Laura Wood. Morrow is newspaperman who tracks down murderer of fellow columnist, discovering his wife was involved with the man.▼

Hour of Glory SEE: **Small Back Room, The**

Hour of the Assassin (1987) **C-93m.** ** D: Luis Llosa. Erik Estrada, Robert Vaughn, Alfredo Alvarez Calderon, Lourdes Berninzon. OK political thriller has Estrada called back from L.A. to South American nation of San Pedro to assassinate the newly elected democratic president. Vaughn is the CIA agent assigned to stop him. Filmed in Peru. [R]▼

Hour of the Gun (1967) **C-100m.** ** D: John Sturges. James Garner, Jason Robards, Robert Ryan, Albert Salmi, Charles Aidman, Steve Ihnat, Michael Tolan, William Windom, William Schallert, Monte Markham, Frank Converse, Jon Voight. Western about Ike Clanton and the Earp Brothers after O.K. Corral shoot-up begins well, becomes increasingly tedious. Robards has a good time as Doc Holliday; flavorful score by Jerry Goldsmith. Panavision.▼●

Hour of the Star, The (1986-Brazilian) **C-96m.** *** D: Suzana Amaral. Marcelia Cartaxo, Jose Dumont, Tamara Taxman, Fernanda Montenegro. Amaral's debut feature (made when she was 52 years old) is a subtle, touching neorealist drama about a plain, awkward, virginal country orphan (Cartaxo) and her experiences in São Paolo. Slow in spots, but still worthwhile.▼

Hour of the Wolf (1968-Swedish) **88m.** *** D: Ingmar Bergman. Liv Ullmann, Max von Sydow, Erland Josephson, Gertrud Fridh, Gudrun Brost. Lesser Bergman about painter von Sydow, wife Ullmann, and apparitions he sees when they retreat to deserted island. The acting, as usual, is first-rate.▼●

Hour of 13, The (1952) **79m.** **½ D: Harold French. Peter Lawford, Dawn Addams, Roland Culver, Colin Gordon. Mystery yarn set in 1890s London, with Lawford a ritzy thief who develops a heart of gold in order to do a good deed for society. Remake of 1934 film THE MYSTERY OF MR. X.

Hours of Love, The (1965-Italian) **89m.** **½ D: Luciano Salce. Ugo Tognazzi, Emmanuele Riva, Barbara Steele, Umberto D'Orsi, Mara Berni. Pleasant little sex farce proving the adage that illicit love is sweeter than blessed marriage. CinemaScope.

House (1986) **C-93m.** ** D: Steve Miner. William Katt, George Wendt, Richard Moll, Kay Lenz, Michael Ensign, Susan French, Mary Stavin. Horror novelist Katt, simultaneously suffering from the split-up of his marriage, son's disappearance, and Vietnam memories, is plagued by demonic fantasies when he moves to the Victorian home where his aunt hanged herself. Lots of horror effects that don't hang together, but a quirky attitude, and a sense of humor, buoy things enough to make this moderately entertaining. Followed by several sequels. [R]▼●

House II: The Second Story (1987) **C-88m.** *½ D: Ethan Wiley. Arye Gross, Jonathan Stark, Royal Dano, Lar Park Lincoln, Bill Maher, John Ratzenberger. A followup rather than a sequel to HOUSE, this incoherent mess is, if anything, a step down. Another young hero moves into another weird house, and finds himself involved with living-dead gunslingers, crystal skulls, Aztec sacrifices, pterodactyls, and a sword-wielding electrician. Busy, but chaotic and boring. [PG-13]▼●

House III SEE: **Horror Show, The**

House IV (1992) **C-100m.** BOMB D: Lewis Abernathy. Terri Treas, Scott Burkholder, Denny Dillon, Melissa Clayton, William Katt, Ned Romero, Ned Bellamy, Dabbs Greer, John Santucci. When her husband is killed and her daughter confined to a wheelchair in a car wreck, a young wife holds onto the old house he inherited, despite spooky goings-on and efforts by her brother-in-law to get her out. Slow, overlong, thrill-less, this lurches from comedy to horror, and can't even match the shoddy effects of the first two. Although Katt has the same character name as in HOUSE, he doesn't seem to be playing the same person. [R]▼●

House Across the Bay, The (1940) **86m.** **½ D: Archie Mayo. George Raft, Joan Bennett, Lloyd Nolan, Gladys George, Walter Pidgeon, June Knight. Raft's out to get Pidgeon, who has taken wife Bennett from him while he's been in jail. Familiar but exciting film.▼

House Across the Street, The (1949) **69m.** ** D: Richard Bare. Wayne Morris, Janis Paige, James Mitchell, Alan Hale, Bruce Bennett. Routine remake of Paul Muni's HI, NELLIE, with Morris as newspaperman on the scent of a murder. Paige is peppery as love interest.

House Arrest (1996) **C-108m.** **½ D: Harry Winer. Jamie Lee Curtis, Kevin Pollak, Jennifer Tilly, Kyle Howard, Christopher McDonald, Sheila McCarthy, Wallace Shawn, Ray Walston, Caroline Aaron, Mooky Arizona, Colleen Camp, Russel Harper, Jennifer Love Hewitt, Amy Sakasitz, Ben Stein. Sensitive, put-upon teenage boy is so shocked that his parents are separating that he locks them in the basement, hoping to force them to talk out their problems; soon his scheme escalates as other kids bring their parents to join them. Not as bad as it sounds, a sometimes thoughtful comedy that should have been a one-hour TV show. [PG] ▼●

Houseboat (1958) **C-110m.** ***½ D: Melville Shavelson. Cary Grant, Sophia Loren, Martha Hyer, Harry Guardino, Eduardo Ciannelli, Murray Hamilton. Loren becomes Grant's housekeeper and takes his three motherless kids in hand. Predictable romance ensues, in this delightful comedy. Guardino hilarious as houseboat handyman. VistaVision.▼●

House by the Lake (1977-Canadian) **C-89m.** *½ D: William Fruet. Brenda Vaccaro, Don Stroud, Chuck Shamata, Richard Ayres, Kyle Edwards. Violent, ugly thriller. Four morons led by Stroud invade weekend retreat of lovers Vaccaro and Shamata. Stroud and Vaccaro good, though. Original title: DEATH WEEKEND. [R]▼

House by the River, The (1950) **88m.** *** D: Fritz Lang. Louis Hayward, Jane Wyatt, Lee Bowman, Ann Shoemaker, Kathleen Freeman. Strange, moody tale of larcenous husband (Hayward) who spins web of evil that involves his wife (Wyatt) and brother (Bowman). Overwrought at times—particularly near the end—but full of fascinating touches, striking atmosphere.

House Calls (1978) **C-98m.** ***½ D: Howard Zieff. Walter Matthau, Glenda Jackson, Art Carney, Richard Benjamin, Candice Azzara, Dick O'Neill, Thayer David. Matthau plays recently widowed doctor who tries to woo feisty Jackson without sacrificing his independence, in this laughing-out-loud contemporary comedy. Cowritten by Max Shulman and Julius J. Epstein. Carney hilarious as addle-brained head of surgery at Matthau's hospital. Later a TV series. [PG]▼●

Houseguest (1995) **C-109m.** ** D: Randall Miller. Sinbad, Phil Hartman, Jeffrey Jones, Kim Greist, Stan Shaw, Tony Longo, Paul Ben-Victor, Mason Adams, Kim Murphy, Chauncey Leopardi, Talia Seider, Ron Glass. Deep-in-debt dreamer pursued by thuggish money collectors poses as a world-renowned oral surgeon and childhood friend of a suburban advertising exec. Sinbad is likable, but no funnier than the desperate rest. Woefully overextended comedy is mired in uninvolving subplots and burdened by two of the unfunniest break-ya-fingas comical thugs in screen history. The kind of movie that opens in January. [PG]▼●

Householder, The (1963-U.S.-Indian) **100m.** **½ D: James Ivory. Shashi Kapoor, Leela Naidu, Durga Khote, Hariendernath Chattopadaya. Fair comedy about perplexed schoolteacher Kapoor, coping with his arranged marriage and new obligations. Ivory's first fiction feature, and initial collaboration with longtime producer Ismail Merchant and scriptwriter Ruth Prawer Jhabvala; from her novel.▼●

Household Saints (1993) **C-124m.** *** D: Nancy Savoca. Tracey Ullman, Vincent D'Onofrio, Lili Taylor, Judith Malina, Michael Rispoli, Victor Argo, Michael Imperioli, Illeana Douglas, Joe Grifasi. Rich, almost folkloric portrait of three generations of Italian working-class N.Y.C. women: elderly immigrant Malina, whose life is ruled by old wives' tales; her daughter-in-law (Ullman), an old-maid-in-training won by Malina's son (D'Onofrio) in a pinochle game; and their religion-obsessed daughter (Taylor). As in her first feature, TRUE LOVE, director Savoca (who scripted with her husband, Richard Guay, from Francine Prose's novel) depicts Italian New Yorkers with uncanny accuracy. Jonathan Demme executive produced. [R]▼

House in Nightmare Park SEE: **Crazy House** (1975)

Housekeeper's Daughter, The (1939) **79m.** ** D: Hal Roach. Joan Bennett, Victor Mature, Adolphe Menjou, William Gargan. Pleasant murder mystery enhanced by chic Bennett, who helps crack a homicide case. Mature's film debut.

Housekeeping (1987) **C-116m.** **½ D: Bill Forsyth. Christine Lahti, Sara Walker, Andrea Burchill. Two orphaned girls meet their aunt for the first time when she comes to live with them; she turns out to be a free spirit who shuns responsibility and has a profound effect on the sisters' own relationship. Forsyth's first American film, set in the 1950s, is a quiet, offbeat, and melancholy story that unfolds like a novel but lacks a certain momentum. Still, there are many touching moments. Lahti is wonderful as always, and the girls (both movie newcomers) are excellent. Based on Marilynne Robinson's book. [PG]▼

House of Angels (1992-Swedish) **C-126m.** **½ D: Colin Nutley. Helena Bergstrom, Rikard Wolff, Per Oscarsson, Sven Wolter, Viveka Seldahl, Reine Brynolfsson, Jacob Eklund. Contemporary tale of sexy and liberal Bergstrom who, with her avant-garde pal, descends on a rural Swedish village to claim an inheritance and throws the strait-laced townfolk for a loop. Easygoing, offbeat (if longish) film is really not all that different from those classic Ealing comedies coming from 1950s Britain. U.S. theatrical version ran 119m. Aka COLIN NUTLEY'S HOUSE OF ANGELS. [R] ▼

House of Bamboo (1955) **C-102m.** **½ D: Samuel Fuller. Robert Ryan, Robert Stack, Shirley Yamaguchi, Cameron Mitchell, Sessue Hayakawa. Picturesque if not credible story of army officers and Japanese police tracking down a gang of former soldiers working for a well-organized syndicate. CinemaScope.

House of Cards (1969) **C-105m.** ** D: John

Guillermin. George Peppard, Inger Stevens, Orson Welles, Keith Michell, Ralph Michael, Maxine Audley. Down-and-out boxer/adventurer (Peppard) hired by rich widow (Stevens) to tutor her young son becomes pawn of Fascist millionaires and generals intent on retaking Europe. Sound familiar? One good chase, though. Techniscope. [G]

House of Cards (1993) **C-109m.** ** D: Michael Lessac. Kathleen Turner, Tommy Lee Jones, Park Overall, Shiloh Strong, Asha Menina, Esther Rolle, Michael Horse, Anne Pitoniak. Architect Turner and her two children return to the U.S. after several years of living among Mayan ruins (and the eerie spirituality of the Mayan Indians) of Central America. When her young daughter becomes increasingly withdrawn and shows signs of autism, Turner battles child psychologist Jones over therapy. Pokey story is less a treatise on the girl's trauma than it is on the benefits of having a well-to-do parent with lots of free time and a big backyard. [PG-13]▼●◗

House of Crazies SEE: **Asylum**

House of Dark Shadows (1970) **C-96m.** *** D: Dan Curtis. Jonathan Frid, Grayson Hall, Kathryn Leigh Scott, Roger Davis, Joan Bennett, John Karlen, Thayer David, Louis Edmonds, Nancy Barrett. Feature version of popular TV serial, recounting vampire Barnabas Collins' (Frid) quest for a cure so he can wed lovely Scott. Nothing new scriptwise, but beautiful locations, flashy direction and camerawork, and some nice jolts make it an enjoyable chiller. Followed by NIGHT OF DARK SHADOWS. [PG]▼●

House of Dracula (1945) **67m.** **½ D: Erle C. Kenton. Onslow Stevens, Lon Chaney, Jr., John Carradine, Martha O' Driscoll, Jane Adams, Lionel Atwill, Glenn Strange, Skelton Knaggs. Sequel to HOUSE OF FRANKENSTEIN takes different tack: Stevens tries "real" science to cure various Universal monsters, but finds that some of their bad habits begin to rub off. Acting, direction, eerie set design compensate for over-ambitious script, hasty resolution. ▼●

House of Evil (1971-Mexican-U.S.) **C-80m.** BOMB D: Juan Ibanez, Jack Hill. Boris Karloff, Julissa, Andres Garcia, Angel Espinosa, Beatriz Baz. The old heirs-being-killed-one-by-one story, involving crazy composer Karloff, his old house, killer toys, and an organ melody that heralds death. One of four films Karloff made back to back in 1968, constituting his last film work; this is the worst of the lot. Aka DANCE OF DEATH and SERANATA MACABRA. [PG]▼

House of Exorcism, The SEE: **Lisa and the Devil**

House of Fear (1939) **67m.** **½ D: Joe May. William Gargan, Irene Hervey, Alan Dinehart, Walter Woolf King, Dorothy Arnold, El Brendel, Harvey Stephens, Robert Coote. Murderer stalks N.Y.C. theater; offbeat show business characters in pretty good whodunit. Remake of 1929 film THE LAST WARNING.

House of Fear, The (1945) **69m.** *** D: Roy William Neill. Basil Rathbone, Nigel Bruce, Dennis Hoey, Aubrey Mather, Paul Cavanagh, Holmes Herbert, Gavin Muir. Sherlock Holmes is called in to investigate when members of an eccentric Scottish gentleman's club are knocked off one by one. Liberal, but ingenious, adaptation of Conan Doyle's "The Five Orange Pips."▼●

House of Frankenstein (1944) **71m.** **½ D: Erle C. Kenton. Boris Karloff, J. Carrol Naish, Lon Chaney, Jr., John Carradine, Elena Verdugo, Anne Gwynne, Lionel Atwill, Peter Coe, George Zucco, Glenn Strange, Sig Rumann. Episodic all-star monster opus linked by evil scientist Karloff and hunchback Naish posing as traveling horror show operators. First half has them dealing with Dracula (wonderfully played by Carradine), second picks up where FRANKENSTEIN MEETS THE WOLF MAN left off. Contrived, to say the least, but tough to dislike. Strange's first appearance as the Frankenstein Monster. Sequel: HOUSE OF DRACULA.▼●

House of Frankenstein 1997 (1997) **C-200m. TVM** D: Peter Werner. Adrian Pasdar, Greg Wise, Teri Polo, CCH Pounder, Miguel Sandoval, Jorja Fox, Peter Crombie, Karen Austin, Richard Libertini, William Converse Roberts, Gary Frank. Shamelessly overhyped two-part horror film has nothing to do with the 1944 Universal picture but deals instead with a contemporary real estate tycoon who'll stop at nothing to locate Frankenstein's monster for a theme club he's planning to build. There are werewolves, witch hunters, bloodsuckers, but precious little of the title monster—played with some humanity by Crombie (who at one point is so terrified he carries a gun!). Not much fun. Average.

House of Fright SEE: **Two Faces of Dr. Jekyll, The**

House of Games (1987) **C-102m.** *** D: David Mamet. Lindsay Crouse, Joe Mantegna, Mike Nussbaum, Lilia Skala, J.T. Walsh, Willo Hausman, Ricky Jay, Meshach Taylor, W. H. Macy. Uptight female psychiatrist (and best-selling author) becomes involved with a slick confidence man and his "team," and quickly gets in over her head. Fascinating Hitchcockian tale by David Mamet, which also marks his film directing debut. Many of his stage cronies are on hand, notably Mantegna, in a dynamic performance, and Crouse, then Mamet's wife. [R]▼●

House of God, The (1979) **C-108m.** *½ D: Donald Wrye. Tim Matheson, Charles Haid, Bess Armstrong, Michael Sacks, Lisa Pelikan, George Coe, Ossie Davis,

Howard Rollins, Jr., James Cromwell, Sandra Bernhard. Misfire black comedy about bunch of young interns coming to grips with reality of hospital pressures. A few scattered laughs, but mostly a waste of terrific (and then-unknown) talent. Adapted by Wrye from Samuel Shem's novel; never released theatrically. [R]

House of Horrors (1946) **65m.** ** D: Jean Yarbrough. Bill Goodwin, Robert Lowery, Virginia Grey, Rondo Hatton, Martin Kosleck. Slightly below average horror meller. Frustrated artist (Kosleck) uses fiend The Creeper to knock off critics. Laughable script, OK acting.▼●

House of Intrigue, The (1959-Italian) **C-94m.** **½ D: Duilio Coletti. Curt Jurgens, Dawn Addams, Folco Lulli, Dario Michaelis, Philippe Hersent. WW2 espionage caper with pleasing on-location European backgrounds. CinemaScope.

House of Mortal Sin SEE: **Confessional, The**

House of Mystery (1961-British) **56m.** **½ D: Vernon Sewell. Jane Hylton, Peter Dyneley, Nanette Newman, Maurice Kaufman, John Merivale. Nifty little story of haunted house, with its new owners learning the mysterious history of the premises; supernatural played up well.▼

House of Numbers (1957) **92m.** **½ D: Russell Rouse. Jack Palance, Barbara Lang, Harold J. Stone, Edward Platt. Palance plays dual role as man seeking to spring gangster brother from prison and take his place. CinemaScope.

House of a Thousand Dolls (1967-British-Spanish) **C-83m.** *½ D: Jeremy Summers. Vincent Price, Martha Hyer, George Nader, Anne Smyrner, Wolfgang Kieling, Sancho Garcia. Vacationing couple in Tangiers befriended by young man convinced that his fiancée has been abducted into white slavery ring. Incredible dialogue, with Price walking through film in a daze. Techniscope. ▼

House of Ricordi (1954-Italian) **C-117m.** ** D: Carmine Gallone. Paolo Stoppa, Roland Alexandre, Marta Toren, Roldano Lupi, Marcello Mastroianni. Passable biography of well-known music-publishing house, set in the 18th century, with many musical interludes. Retitled: CASA RICORDI.

House of Rothschild (1934) **88m.** *** D: Alfred L. Werker. George Arliss, Boris Karloff, Loretta Young, Robert Young, Florence Arliss, C. Aubrey Smith. Elaborate, entertaining chronicle of famed banking family, with Arliss as Nathan Rothschild at time of Napoleonic Wars, Loretta his daughter, R. Young her suitor, Karloff as civilized villain. Finale originally shot in color.

House of Seven Corpses, The (1973) **C-90m.** ** D: Paul Harrison. John Ireland, Faith Domergue, John Carradine, Carol Wells, Charles McCauley, Jerry Stricklen. A film crew uses a supposedly haunted house for location work on a horror film, and learns to regret it; low-budget, but not bad. [PG]▼

House of Strangers (1949) **101m.** *** D: Joseph L. Mankiewicz. Edward G. Robinson, Susan Hayward, Richard Conte, Luther Adler, Efrem Zimbalist, Jr., Debra Paget, Hope Emerson, Esther Minciotti. Dynamic drama of ruthless financier Robinson who uses his four sons to suit his own schemes. Unique plot line has been utilized in various disguises for many subsequent films—most memorably, five years later in the Western BROKEN LANCE. ▼

House of the Black Death (1965) **80m.** *½ D: Harold Daniels. Lon Chaney, Jr., John Carradine, Andrea King, Tom Drake, Dolores Faith, Sabrina. Warlock holds people captive in a creepy old house; terribly dragged out, grade-Z stuff.▼

House of the Long Shadows (1983-British) **C-96m.** *½ D: Pete Walker. Vincent Price, Christopher Lee, Peter Cushing, Desi Arnaz, Jr., John Carradine, Sheila Keith, Julie Peasgood, Richard Todd. Arnaz, Jr. single-handedly sinks this sixth screen version of George M. Cohan's spoof, SEVEN KEYS TO BALDPATE, miscast as a mystery writer staying the night in a spooky mansion on a bet with Todd. Notable only for its historic teaming of four all-time horror masters, all wasted in small roles. [PG]▼

House of the Seven Gables, The (1940) **89m.** *** D: Joe May. George Sanders, Margaret Lindsay, Vincent Price, Nan Grey, Alan Napier, Cecil Kellaway, Dick Foran. Good adaptation of Hawthorne's classic novel. Set in 19th-century New England; conniving Sanders frames his brother, Price, for murder of their father in effort to cheat him out of inheritance. Fine performances from all. Price also appeared in TWICE-TOLD TALES, which includes abbreviated version of *Seven Gables* novel.▼

House of the Seven Hawks, The (1959) **92m.** **½ D: Richard Thorpe. Robert Taylor, Nicole Maurey, Linda Christian, Donald Wolfit, David Kossoff, Eric Pohlmann. Diverting account of skipper Taylor involved in shipboard murder and hunt for long-lost Nazi loot. Made in England.

House of the Spirits, The (1993-German-Danish-Portuguese-U.S.) **C-138m.** ** D: Bille August. Jeremy Irons, Meryl Streep, Glenn Close, Winona Ryder, Vanessa Redgrave, Armin Mueller-Stahl, Antonio Banderas, Maria Conchita Alonso, Miriam Colon, Vincent Gallo, Jan Niklas, Teri Polo. Epic South American saga that follows a prominent family's turbulent life from the 1920s through the early 70s. Heavy with portent—and clearly written by someone for whom English is not a first language—this sprawling story tries to incorporate the mysticism of Isabel Allende's bestselling novel with sputtering results. Streep is badly miscast, and Irons struggles with his Hispanic role. Streep's 10-year-old daughter plays her character as a child. Opened in Europe at 145m. Panavision. [R]▼●

House of Unclaimed Women SEE: **School for Unclaimed Girls**

House of Usher (1960) **C-85m.** ***½ D: Roger Corman. Vincent Price, Mark Damon, Myrna Fahey, Harry Ellerbe. First-rate horror film based on classic tale by Edgar Allan Poe. When beautiful young girl's suitor arrives to ask her hand in marriage, the doors of the house of Usher fling open, and terror begins. Filmed several times before and since, but never this effectively; a great tour de force for Price. First of Corman's eight Poe adaptations. Aka FALL OF THE HOUSE OF USHER. CinemaScope. ▼●

House of Usher, The (1988) **C-90m.** *½ D: Alan Birkinshaw. Oliver Reed, Donald Pleasence, Romy Windsor, Rufus Swart, Norman Coombes, Anne Stradi. Yet another telling of the Edgar Allan Poe saga is one big yawn, with Reed as Roderick Usher, and Windsor as his prey—the woman who can bear him a son and continue the family name. Filmed in South Africa. [R]▼●

House of Wax (1953) **C-88m.** *** D: Andre de Toth. Vincent Price, Frank Lovejoy, Phyllis Kirk, Carolyn Jones, Paul Cavanagh, Charles Buchinsky (Bronson). Remake of MYSTERY OF THE WAX MUSEUM stars Price as vengeful sculptor who rebuilds his fire-destroyed showplace by using human victims as wax figures. Jones excellent as an early victim. Most popular of the era's 3-D films, a status it retains today. This is the film that launched Price on his horror film cycle after 15 years of "straight" roles. Love that paddleball man!▼●

House of Women (1962) **85m.** **½ D: Walter Doniger. Shirley Knight, Andrew Duggan, Constance Ford, Barbara Nichols, Margaret Hayes, Virginia Gregg. Trite rendition of conditions in a women's prison elevated by good cast and fast pacing. Remake of CAGED.

House of Yes, The (1997) **C-90m.** **½ D: Mark Waters. Parker Posey, Josh Hamilton, Tori Spelling, Freddie Prinze, Jr., Genevieve Bujold. On a stormy night in 1983, a young man brings his fiancée home to meet his cracked Washington, D.C., family, including his demented twin sister, Jackie-O, whose fantasies about Jacqueline Kennedy have extended to reenacting the JFK assassination—with real bullets. Well-wrought black comedy, based on the stage play by Wendy MacLeod, never quite escapes being a "play on film." Strong performances, led by Posey's, make this worth a look. [R] ▼●◗

House on Carroll Street, The (1988) **C-100m.** ** D: Peter Yates. Kelly McGillis, Jeff Daniels, Mandy Patinkin, Christopher Rhode, Jessica Tandy, Jonathan Hogan, Trey Wilson. McGillis, who's just lost her job after being branded a subversive during the McCarthy era, stumbles onto a strange espionage plot that's being covered up, and gradually persuades FBI agent Daniels that she's on to something big. Finely detailed period piece set in 1950s N.Y.C. starts off well, then chucks its relevance (and believability) for a melodramatic finale filmed à la Hitchcock at Grand Central Station . . . leaving a passel of plot holes and unanswered questions. A real disappointment from onetime black-listed writer Walter Bernstein. Patinkin is excellent as Roy Cohn-type attorney. [PG]▼●

House on Haunted Hill (1958) **75m.** *** D: William Castle. Vincent Price, Carol Ohmart, Richard Long, Alan Marshal, Elisha Cook, Jr., Carolyn Craig, Leona Anderson. Zillionaire Price offers group of people $10,000 each if they'll spend a night in spooky old mansion with murder-laden history; he even provides loaded guns as party favors. Campy fun; probably the Castle film which holds up best on TV. Originally presented theatrically with flying skeleton gimmick "Emergo." Remade in 1999. ▼●◗

House on Haunted Hill (1999) **C-93m.** *½ D: William Malone. Geoffrey Rush, Famke Janssen, Taye Diggs, Bridgette Wilson, Peter Gallagher, Chris Kattan, Ali Larter, Max Perlich, Jeffrey Combs, Lisa Loeb. Dreary remake of the 1958 movie, with two obnoxious "hosts"—a venomous married couple (Rush, Janssen)—having a party whose guest list is comprised of five strangers. Each one can win a million dollars for surviving the night in a former sanitarium with a bloodstained past. Heavy-handed, and no fun at all. [R]▼●◗

House on Marsh Road, The SEE: **Invisible Creature, The**

House on 92nd St., The (1945) **88m.** ***½ D: Henry Hathaway. William Eythe, Lloyd Nolan, Signe Hasso, Gene Lockhart, Leo G. Carroll, Lydia St. Clair. Exciting, trend-setting documentary-style drama—based on fact and staged on actual locations—about FBI counterespionage activities during WW2: Nazi agents, operating in N.Y.C., attempt to pilfer part of the atom bomb formula. Charles G. Booth earned an Oscar for his original story. Screenplay by Booth, Barre Lyndon, and John Monks, Jr. Look for E. G. Marshall, in film debut. ▼

House on Skull Mountain, The (1974) **C-89m.** *½ D: Ron Honthaner. Victor French, Janee Michelle, Jean Durand, Mike Evans, Xernona Clayton. Voodoo man Durand is on the loose in the title abode. Black horror entry (but with a white hero!)

is not particularly bloody, but also not particularly good. [PG]▼

House on Telegraph Hill, The (1951) **93m.** **½ D: Robert Wise. Richard Basehart, Valentina Cortese, William Lundigan, Fay Baker. Good cast in intriguing tale of WW2 refugee assuming dead woman's identity so that she can come to San Francisco where wealthy relatives reside.

House Party (1990) **C-100m.** *** D: Reginald Hudlin. Christopher Reid, Robin Harris, Christopher Martin, Martin Lawrence, Tisha Campbell, A. J. Johnson, Paul Anthony. Infectiously good-natured comedy about urban black teenagers and the events leading up to (and following) a house party one night. Upbeat and imaginative, cast with real-life music rappers (including Reid, who plays the leading role of Kid). A solid feature debut for young writer-director Hudlin. Followed by animated TV series *Kid 'n Play* and two sequels. [R]▼●

House Party 2 (1991) **C-94m.** ** D: Doug McHenry, George Jackson. Christopher Reid, Christopher Martin, Eugene Allen, George Anthony Bell, Georg Stanford Brown, Tony Burton, Tisha Campbell, Iman, Kamron, Queen Latifah, Martin Lawrence, Helen Martin, William Schallert. Uninspired sequel has Kid (Reid) heading off to college—if he can just hold onto the money his church congregation has raised to send him there. Reid is still appealing, but this fragmented film has little to offer, in spite of its social-consciousness rhetoric and get-an-education "message." [R]▼●

House Party 3 (1994) **C-94m.** *½ D: Eric Meza. Christopher Reid, Christopher Martin, David Edwards, Angela Means, Tisha Campbell, Bernie Mac, Gilbert Gottfried, Ketty Lester. Kid, amid jitters over his impending marriage, is trying to make it in music management by signing a feisty female rap group and dodging a vindictive tour promoter. Scattershot chuckles, but coarse, crude, and misogynistic, unlike the original. More hangover than beer blast. [R]▼●

HouseSitter (1992) **C-102m.** ** D: Frank Oz. Steve Martin, Goldie Hawn, Dana Delany, Julie Harris, Donald Moffat, Peter MacNicol, Richard B. Shull, Laurel Cronin, Christopher Durang, Cherry Jones. Unusual hybrid of comedy, farce, and screwball romance that doesn't know what it's trying to be. Martin plays a New England architect who meets kooky nonconformist Hawn; in no time she's moved into the vacant dream home he'd intended for Delany and begun spinning lies about being his Mrs. Laughs throughout, and the stars do their best, but the film is painfully Hollywood-cookie-cutter in form. [PG]▼●◗

House That Cried Murder, The (1974) **C-85m.** **½ D: Jean-Marie Pelissie. Robin Strasser, John Beal, Arthur Roberts, Iva Jean Saraceni. Strasser has some surprises in store for Roberts when he is unfaithful on their wedding day. Pretty scary thriller; also known as THE BRIDE. [PG]

House That Dripped Blood, The (1970-British) **C-101m.** **½ D: Peter Duffell. John Bennett, John Bryans, Denholm Elliott, Joanna Dunham, Tom Adams, Peter Cushing, Christopher Lee, Nyree Dawn Porter, Jon Pertwee, Ingrid Pitt. Entertaining four-part horror film written by Robert Bloch with a bit too much tongue in cheek, revolving around suitably creepy-looking mansion purchased by new, hesitant owner. Best segments: first and last. [PG]▼

House That Screamed, The (1970-Spanish) **C-94m.** *½ D: Narciso Ibanez Serrador. Lilli Palmer, Chistina Galbo, John Moulder-Brown, Mary Maude, Candida Losada. Grisly horror at a home for troubled girls, where disciplinarian Palmer and her sex-starved son (Brown) make life difficult—to say the least—for the young ladies. Franscope. [PG]

House Where Evil Dwells, The (1982) **C-88m.** ** D: Kevin Connor. Edward Albert, Susan George, Doug McClure, Amy Barrett, Mako Hattori, Toshiyuki Sasaki, Toshiya Maruyama. American family moves into stylish old house in Kyoto, Japan, ignoring warnings that it's haunted by ghosts of doomed 19th-century love triangle. A few new twists can't relieve familiar formula, and general air of silliness. Quite violent at times. [R]▼

Housewife (1934) **69m.** ** D: Alfred E. Green. Bette Davis, George Brent, Ann Dvorak, John Halliday, Ruth Donnelly. Little punch in story of struggling copywriter Brent deserting wife Dvorak for old-flame Davis (playing unsubtle vamp).

Houston Story, The (1956) **79m.** **½ D: William Castle. Gene Barry, Barbara Hale, Edward Arnold, Paul Richards, Jeanne Cooper. Barry portrays greedy oil worker who plans to take over crime syndicate involved in stealing oil.

Howards End (1992-British) **C-140m.** **** D: James Ivory. Anthony Hopkins, Vanessa Redgrave, Helena Bonham Carter, Emma Thompson, James Wilby, Sam West, Jemma Redgrave, Nicola Duffett, Prunella Scales. Sumptuous, stimulating adaptation of E. M. Forster's novel of class distinction—and what happens when members of different social strata collide in 1910 England. Thompson won an Oscar for her terrific performance as an audacious and independent young woman of no means who is ever-so-subtly seduced by Hopkins, a successful man whose social veneer masks an insidious (and even cruel) nature. Extraordinarily good on every level. Also won Oscars for Best Screenplay (by Ruth Prawer Jhabvala) and Art Direction–Set Decoration. Simon Callow appears unbilled as a lecturer. Super 35. [PG] ▼●◗

Howards of Virginia, The (1940) **122m.** **½ D: Frank Lloyd. Cary Grant, Martha Scott, Cedric Hardwicke, Alan Marshal, Richard Carlson, Paul Kelly, Irving Bacon. Historical account of Revolutionary War is OK, but too long for such standard retelling.▼

Howard Stern's Private Parts SEE: **Private Parts**

Howard the Duck (1986) **C-111m.** BOMB D: Willard Huyck. Lea Thompson, Jeffrey Jones, Tim Robbins, Paul Guilfoyle, Holly Robinson, Miles Chapin, Virginia Capers, David Paymer, Thomas Dolby, and voice of Richard Kiley. Steve Gerber's sarcastic comic-book creation is (unwisely) turned into a live-action character for this hopeless mess of a movie set in Cleveland. Gargantuan production produces gargantuan headache. Executive produced, but disowned, by George Lucas. [PG]▼●

How Do I Love Thee? (1970) **C-110m.** *½ D: Michael Gordon. Jackie Gleason, Maureen O'Hara, Shelley Winters, Rosemary Forsyth, Rick Lenz, Clinton Robinson. Pleasant cast can't do much for sloppily sentimental film about Gleason's inability to relate to his son, a philosophy professor. Plays like a TV show, a bad one at that. [PG]▼

How Funny Can Sex Be? (1976-Italian) **C-97m.** **½ D: Dino Risi. Giancarlo Giannini, Laura Antonelli, Alberto Lionello, Duilio Del Prete, Paola Barbone, Carla Mancini. Eight bawdy episodes on love, sex, and marriage. More misses than hits, but buoyed by Giannini's comic prowess and Antonelli's tantalizing beauty. Released here after Giannini's success in Wertmuller films. [R]▼

How Green Was My Valley (1941) **118m.** **** D: John Ford. Walter Pidgeon, Maureen O'Hara, Donald Crisp, Anna Lee, Master Roddy McDowall, John Loder, Sara Allgood, Barry Fitzgerald, Patric Knowles, Rhys Williams, Arthur Shields, Ann Todd, Mae Marsh. Narrated by Irving Pichel; United Kingdom version narrated by Rhys Williams. Moving drama from Richard Llewellyn's story of Welsh coal miners, centering on Crisp's large, close-knit family. Beautifully filmed, lovingly directed, winner of five Academy Awards: Best Picture, Director, Supporting Actor (Crisp), Cinematography (Arthur Miller), Art Direction. Screenplay by Philip Dunne. ▼●◗

How I Got Into College (1989) **C-89m.** ** D: Savage Steve Holland. Anthony Edwards, Corey Parker, Lara Flynn Boyle, Finn Carter, Charles Rocket, Christopher Rydell, Brian Doyle-Murray. Aimless senior applies to a small college because his high-achiever dream girl is doing the same, and gets caught up in the cutthroat recruitment machine. Mild execution of ripe satirical premise, buoyed by fantasy set pieces associated with director Holland's previous work. Has its moments, but not enough of them. [PG-13]▼●

How I Won the War (1967-British) **C-109m.** *** D: Richard Lester. Michael Crawford, John Lennon, Roy Kinnear, Jack MacGowran, Michael Hordern, Lee Montague, Alexander Knox. Pungent, if occasionally overbaked, account of a middle-aged veteran whose pompous reminiscenses of his wartime heroics cannot obscure his ineptitude in battle. A deliciously cynical parody of the lunacy of war. Interesting to see Lennon in one of his very few acting roles, as the Cockney Gripweed.▼●

Howling, The (1981) **C-91m.** *** D: Joe Dante. Dee Wallace, Patrick Macnee, Dennis Dugan, Christopher Stone, Belinda Balaski, Kevin McCarthy, John Carradine, Slim Pickens, Elisabeth Brooks, Robert Picardo, Noble Willingham, Kenneth Tobey, Dick Miller, Meshach Taylor. A female TV news reporter is sent to a strange California encounter-group community to recover from a sexual trauma, unaware that virtually everyone there is a werewolf. A hip, well-made horror film, brimming with film-buff jokes (almost every character is named after a werewolf movie director) and Rob Bottin's amazing wolf transformations. Only complaint: Why set the horror against such a patently bizarre backdrop? Coscripter John Sayles has a funny cameo as a morgue attendant. Followed by several so-called sequels. [R]▼●

Howling II: Your Sister Is a Werewolf (1985) **C-90m.** BOMB D: Philippe Mora. Christopher Lee, Annie McEnroe, Reb Brown, Sybil Danning, Marsha A. Hunt, Ferdy Mayne. Ridiculous sequel is set in Transylvania where unlikely siblings Danning and Lee head up a family of werewolves. Attempt at sending up the genre falls flat. [R]▼●

Howling III (1987-Australian) **C-94m.** ** D: Philippe Mora. Barry Otto, Imogen Annesley, Dasha Blahova, Max Fairchild, Frank Thring, Michael Pate, Barry Humphries. OK horror spoof stars Annesley, a Kim Basinger-like beauty, as an Australian marsupial werewolf, who gives birth to a cute little creature that lives in a pouch on her belly. Unusual addition to werewolf genre features some funny cameos, including Thring as an Alfred Hitchcock-style director. [PG-13]▼●

Howling IV: The Original Nightmare (1988-British) **C-92m.** BOMB D: John Hough. Romy Windsor, Michael T. Weiss, Anthony Hamilton, Susanne Severeid. Being based somewhat more closely on Gary Brandner's original novel doesn't save this film from being a turkey in wolf's clothing. Isolated in a distant cabin, a young woman battles werewolves, including her boyfriend, a newly minted howler. Shot in South Africa, unsuccessfully passing itself off as California. Poor makeup effects. [R]▼●

Howling V: The Rebirth (1989) **C-99m.**

** D: Neal Sundstrom. Victoria Catlin, Elizabeth Silverstein, Mark Faulkner, Stephanie Shockley, William Stavin. Much better than II or IV, this still suffers from a very low budget—so low there are no werewolves to be seen! All the hairy monster stuff takes place off-screen in this variation on *Ten Little Indians,* as a group in a picturesque old castle is knocked off one by one by the secret werewolf among them. Some suspense, OK performances, and a genuine surprise at the end. [R]▼●

Howling VI—The Freaks (1991) **C-102m.** *½ D: Hope Perello. Brendan Hughes, Michelle Matheson, Bruce Martyn Payne, Jered Barclay, Sean Gregory Sullivan, Antonio Fargas, Carlos Cervantes. This time the werewolf is the hero, a drifter who turns up in a Southwestern desert town just ahead of a circus full of monsters. Intelligently written, especially for this series, but pretentious, with vague Ray Bradburyesque overtones. Awkward and confusing, of appeal to buffs only. [R]▼●

How Stella Got Her Groove Back (1998) **C-124m.** ** D: Kevin Rodney Sullivan. Angela Bassett, Taye Diggs, Regina King, Whoopi Goldberg, Suzzanne Douglas, Michael J. Pagan, Sicily, Richard Lawson, Glynn Turman, Carl Lumbly. Tight-midriffed San Francisco stockbroker, age 40, romances the 20-year-old med-school hopeful she meets while vacationing in Jamaica, setting off a wave of *tsk-tsk*-ing among her friends and his parents. Overlong and dull, this occasionally lush version of Terry McMillan's novel might be more convincing if Bassett didn't look more like a 25-year-old knockout. Subplot about Goldberg's illness and subsequent hospitalization helps keep the film from getting *into* a groove. [R]▼●◗

How Sweet It Is! (1968) **C-99m.** *½ D: Jerry Paris. James Garner, Debbie Reynolds, Maurice Ronet, Paul Lynde, Marcel Dalio, Terry-Thomas. Married couple with teen-age son goes to Europe to revitalize themselves, but Mom starts to dally with sexy Frenchman. Bland comedy looks like a TV show and is about as memorable. Watch for Penny Marshall as one of the Tour Girls. Panavision.▼

How the West Was Won (1962) **C-155m.** ***½ D: John Ford ("The Civil War"), Henry Hathaway ("The Rivers, The Plains, The Outlaws"), George Marshall ("The Railroad"). Carroll Baker, Henry Fonda, Gregory Peck, George Peppard, Carolyn Jones, Eli Wallach, Robert Preston, Debbie Reynolds, James Stewart, John Wayne, Richard Widmark, All-Star Cast; narrated by Spencer Tracy. Blockbuster epic about three generations of Western pioneers isn't same experience on TV it was on Cinerama screen, but great cast, first-rate photography and lovely Alfred Newman score still make it top entertainment. Peppard stands out with excellent portrayal. This won Oscars for Story and Screenplay (James R. Webb) and Editing (Harold F. Kress). Cinerama. ▼●◗

How to Beat the High Co$t of Living (1980) **C-110m.** *½ D: Robert Scheerer. Susan Saint James, Jane Curtin, Jessica Lange, Richard Benjamin, Cathryn Damon, Fred Willard, Dabney Coleman, Eddie Albert, Art Metrano, Garrett Morris. Thoroughly blah caper comedy by Bob Kaufman about three housewives who plot a heist at the local shopping center. Worth a glance to see Coleman in rare romantic lead . . . and Saint James and Curtin years before they clicked together as *Kate and Allie*. [PG]▼

How to Be Very, Very Popular (1955) **C-89m.** **½ D: Nunnally Johnson. Betty Grable, Robert Cummings, Charles Coburn, Sheree North, Fred Clark, Alice Pearce, Orson Bean. Grable and North on the lam hide in a college fraternity in this semi-remake of SHE LOVES ME NOT. Sheree does wild "Shake, Rattle and Roll" number, stealing Grable's spotlight. This was Betty's last movie. CinemaScope.

How to Commit Marriage (1969) **C-95m.** ** D: Norman Panama. Bob Hope, Jackie Gleason, Jane Wyman, Maureen Arthur, Tim Matheson, Leslie Nielsen, Tina Louise, Irwin Corey. Above average for later Hope movies, but still a far cry from great comedy. Hope and Wyman are about to divorce when their daughter announces plans to marry Gleason's son. "Mod" elements of script were already dated when film came out. [M/PG]▼

How to Frame a Figg (1971) **C-103m.** ** D: Alan Rafkin. Don Knotts, Joe Flynn, Elaine Joyce, Edward Andrews, Yvonne Craig. Simplistic chap (Knotts) finds trouble behind every doorway as he is made patsy for crooked politicians. Usual unsubtle Knotts comedy. [G]▼

How to Get Ahead in Advertising (1989-British) **C-95m.** **½ D: Bruce Robinson. Richard E. Grant, Rachel Ward, Richard Wilson, Jacqueline Tong, John Shrapnel, Susan Wooldridge, Mick Ford. Advertising hotshot Grant is under so much pressure—and has become so negative about his manipulative profession—that his anxiety brings forth a talking boil on his shoulder with a mind of its own! Certifiably weird comedy by writer-director Robinson (reunited with the star of his first film, WITHNAIL AND I) has its share of funny and bizarre moments, but its attack on advertising is so heavy-handed that as satire it fizzles. [R]▼●

How to Make a Monster (1958) **74m.** BOMB D: Herbert L. Strock. Robert Harris, Walter Reed, Gary Clarke, Paul Brinegar. Dismal chiller involving studio makeup artist who goes berserk and turns his creations into zombie-like killers. Final 11m. of film is in color. Superama. ▼

How to Make an American Quilt (1995) **C-116m.** ** D: Jocelyn Moorhouse. Winona Ryder, Ellen Burstyn, Anne Bancroft, Maya Angelou, Kate Nelligan, Jean Simmons, Samantha Mathis, Alfre Woodard, Lois Smith, Kate Capshaw, Johnathon Schaech, Holland Taylor, Maria Celedonio, Claire Danes, Loren Dean, Melinda Dillon, Dermot Mulroney, Derrick O'Connor, Esther Rolle, Rip Torn, Mykelti Williamson, Alicia (Lecy) Goranson, Adam Baldwin. Aimless young woman leaves her fiancé behind to spend the summer with her grandmother and great-aunt. Soon she's delving into their lives and the experiences of their female friends who work together in a non-stop quilting bee. Episodic "woman's film" (based on Whitney Otto's novel) offers at least one flashback too many in its quilt-like pattern. It's genteel, good looking, and well acted, but has no narrative momentum. [PG-13]▼●◗

How to Make It SEE: **Target: Harry**

How to Make Love to a Negro Without Getting Tired (1989-Canadian) **C-97m.** *½ D: Jacques W. Benoit. Isaach de Bankolé, Maka Kotto, Antoine Durand, Jacques Legras, Roberta Bizeau, Miriam Cyr. Pretentious satire about a charming, elusive black Haitian writer (de Bankolé) living in Montreal, and how he exploits various racial stereotypes to get wealthy white girls into bed. At worst repugnant, reverse-racist, sexist, and homophobic; at best just plain silly. Coscripted by Dany Laferrière, from his autobiographical novel.

How to Marry a Millionaire (1953) **C-95m.** *** D: Jean Negulesco. Marilyn Monroe, Betty Grable, Lauren Bacall, William Powell, Rory Calhoun, David Wayne, Alex D'Arcy, Fred Clark, Cameron Mitchell. Terrific ensemble work in dandy comedy of three man-hunting females pooling resources to trap eligible bachelors. Nunnally Johnson scripted and produced this remake of THE GREEKS HAD A WORD FOR THEM, which is preceded by Alfred Newman conducting his famed "Street Scene" theme (a prologue designed to show off stereophonic sound). CinemaScope.▼●

How to Murder a Rich Uncle (1957-British) **80m.** **½ D: Nigel Patrick. Charles Coburn, Nigel Patrick, Wendy Hiller, Anthony Newley, Katie Johnson, Athene Seyler. Amusing cash-in on THE LADYKILLERS, with nouveau poor British family deciding to knock off visiting American relative Coburn for his money, succeeding only in doing themselves in. No classic, but entertaining. Script by John Paxton; Michael Caine has a tiny bit. CinemaScope.

How to Murder Your Wife (1965) **C-118m.** *** D: Richard Quine. Jack Lemmon, Virna Lisi, Terry-Thomas, Eddie Mayehoff, Claire Trevor, Sidney Blackmer, Max Showalter, Jack Albertson, Mary Wickes. Engaging comedy that almost holds up to finale. Cartoonist Lemmon marries Lisi while drunk and spends rest of film devising ways to get rid of her. Mayehoff is standout as Lemmon's lawyer friend.▼●

How to Save a Marriage (And Ruin Your Life) (1968) **C-108m.** *½ D: Fielder Cook. Dean Martin, Stella Stevens, Eli Wallach, Anne Jackson, Betty Field, Jack Albertson. Typical 1960s sex farce has swinging bachelor Dino mistaking Stella for his best friend's mistress, with predictable complications. Stevens wasted again. Panavision.

How to Steal a Million (1966) **C-127m.** *** D: William Wyler. Audrey Hepburn, Peter O'Toole, Charles Boyer, Eli Wallach, Hugh Griffith. Hepburn and O'Toole are a delightful match in this sophisticated comedy about a million-dollar theft in a Paris art museum. Boyer, O'Toole's boss, and Griffith, Hepburn's father, are equally good. Panavision.▼●

How to Stuff a Wild Bikini (1965) **C-93m.** ** D: William Asher. Annette Funicello, Dwayne Hickman, Brian Donlevy, Buster Keaton, Mickey Rooney, Harvey Lembeck, Beverly Adams, Jody McCrea, John Ashley, Bobbi Shaw. The fatigue is palpable in this sixth BEACH PARTY movie, which tries out another new leading man (with Frankie Avalon again shunted to a cameo role). As usual, the veterans—especially Rooney—liven things a little, but overall, pretty mediocre. Followed by GHOST IN THE INVISIBLE BIKINI. Panavision.▼◗

How to Succeed in Business Without Really Trying (1967) **C-121m.** ***½ D: David Swift. Robert Morse, Michele Lee, Rudy Vallee, Anthony Teague, Maureen Arthur, Sammy Smith, Robert Q. Lewis. Delightful, original musical from Broadway hit about ambitious window-washer (Morse) who uses wiles, and a handbook, to rise to prominence in Vallee's Worldwide Wicket Co. Superb farce, good Frank Loesser songs (including "Brotherhood of Man" and "I Believe in You"), imaginative staging of musical numbers by Bob Fosse. Panavision.▼●◗

How U Like Me Now (1992) **C-109m.** *** D: Darryl Roberts. Darnell Williams, Salli Richardson, Raymond Whitfield, Daniel Gardner, Byron Stewart, Darryl Roberts, Charnele Brown. Likable comedy of middle and working-class African-American twenty-somethings in Chicago, with the focus on live-in lovers Williams and Richardson, whose relationship is at a crossroads. Refreshingly, none of the characters are stereotypical ghetto cartoons. This may be favorably compared with Spike Lee's breakthrough feature, SHE'S GOTTA HAVE IT. [R]▼

Huckleberry Finn (1931) **80m.** **½ D: Norman Taurog. Jackie Coogan, Mitzi

Green, Junior Durkin, Eugene Pallette, Jackie Searl, Clarence Muse, Jane Darwell. Life on the Mississippi with Huck, Tom Sawyer, and Becky Thatcher. Charming but very, very dated; a follow-up to previous year's TOM SAWYER, with same cast.

Huckleberry Finn (1939) **90m.** *** D: Richard Thorpe. Mickey Rooney, Walter Connolly, William Frawley, Rex Ingram, Lynne Carver. Subdued Rooney fine, Ingram excellent as Huck and Jim in classic Mark Twain tale of early 19th-century America; Connolly and Frawley are amusing as riverboat con-artists. Also shown in computer-colored version.▼

Huckleberry Finn (1974) **C-118m.** ** D: J. Lee Thompson. Jeff East, Paul Winfield, Harvey Korman, David Wayne, Arthur O'Connell, Gary Merrill. Little of Mark Twain is left in this handsome but empty-headed musical version of his classic story. Score by Richard and Robert Sherman is as forgettable as their script. Panavision. [G] ▼●

Huckleberry Finn (1975) **C-78m. TVM** D: Robert Totten. Ron Howard, Donny Most, Antonio Fargas, Jack Elam, Merle Haggard, Royal Dano, Rance Howard, Clint Howard. Folksy treatment of the classic by Twain (played by Dano), minus the social criticism and sinister aspects of the literary adventure favorite. Above average.▼

Hucksters, The (1947) **115m.** *** D: Jack Conway. Clark Gable, Deborah Kerr, Sydney Greenstreet, Adolphe Menjou, Ava Gardner, Keenan Wynn, Edward Arnold. Glossy dig at advertising and radio industries, with Gable battling for integrity among yes-men. Greenstreet memorable as despotic head of soap company; Kerr's first American movie. Also shown in computer-colored version.▼●

Hud (1963) **112m.** **** D: Martin Ritt. Paul Newman, Patricia Neal, Melvyn Douglas, Brandon de Wilde, John Ashley. Excellent story of moral degradation set in modern West, with impeccable performances by all. Neal won Best Actress Oscar as family housekeeper who doesn't want to get involved with no-account Newman. Douglas received Best Supporting Oscar as Newman's ethical, uncompromising father, and James Wong Howe's cinematography also earned a statuette. Irving Ravetch and Harriet Frank, Jr. scripted from Larry McMurtry's novel *Horseman, Pass By*. Panavision.▼●

Hudson Hawk (1991) **C-95m.** ** D: Michael Lehmann. Bruce Willis, Danny Aiello, Andie MacDowell, James Coburn, Richard E. Grant, Sandra Bernhard, Donald Burton, Don Harvey, David Caruso, Andrew Bryniarski, Lorraine Toussaint, Frank Stallone, Leonardo Cimino. Wildly overblown vanity film (Willis cowrote the story *and* the title song) about a cat burglar, just sprung from prison, who's blackmailed into performing several daring art heists, including one from the Vatican! Blissfully incoherent, with some good action scenes, but nothing to hang them on except a steady stream of Willis wisecracks, only some of which are funny. [R] ▼●◗

Hudson's Bay (1940) **95m.** **½ D: Irving Pichel. Paul Muni, Gene Tierney, Laird Cregar, John Sutton, Virginia Field, Vincent Price, Nigel Bruce. Muni's good, but life of founder of Hudson Bay fur-trading company lacks punch. Expansive production.

Hudsucker Proxy, The (1994) **C-111m.** *** D: Joel Coen. Tim Robbins, Jennifer Jason Leigh, Paul Newman, Charles Durning, John Mahoney, Jim True, William Cobbs, Bruce Campbell, Joe Grifasi, Peter Gallagher, Noble Willingham, Steve Buscemi, Anna Nicole Smith, Jon Polito. A country bumpkin arrives in the Big City and becomes the unwitting pawn in a scheme to ruin a thriving corporation. The Coen brothers' most extravagant creation to date, an eye-popping 50s fantasy of big business gone berserk, with Robbins absolutely perfect as the wide-eyed patsy who miraculously rises to the top. Newman is a crafty villain, and Leigh is fun (if a bit one-note) as a fast-talking, Kate Hepburn–ish reporter. Written by Ethan and Joel Coen with Sam Raimi; the Coens rival Fellini in the selection of unusual faces to populate their films. [PG]▼●◗

Hue and Cry (1946-British) **82m.** *** D: Charles Crichton. Alastair Sim, Jack Warner, Valerie White, Harry Fowler, Jack Lambert, Frederick Piper, Joan Dowling. Snappy romp as young Fowler suspects that details in the stories published in his favorite weekly pulp magazine are being used as a code by a gang of crooks. Nicely filmed on location on the streets of post-WW2 London. The first of many good Ealing comedies; written by T.E.B. Clarke. Released in the U.S. in 1950.▼

Huey Long (1985) **C/B&W-88m.** ***½ D: Ken Burns. Entertaining, thoroughly fascinating documentary portrait of Huey Long, controversial Depression-era Louisiana governor and one of the most intriguing personalities in American history. Crammed with priceless footage; a must.▼

Huggers SEE: **Crazy Moon**

Hugo Pool (1997) **C-94m.** ** D: Robert Downey. Alyssa Milano, Patrick Dempsey, Cathy Moriarty, Malcolm McDowell, Robert Downey, Jr., Richard Lewis, Sean Penn, Bert Remsen, Chuck Barris, Ann Magnuson. Strained whimsy about an L.A. pool cleaner (Milano) and her dealings with her dysfunctional parents and assorted oddball clients, one of whom—a man suffering from Lou Gehrig's disease—she falls in love with. Self-indulgent shaggy-dog farce comes off like an actors' improv exercise and varies wildly from deadpan absurdist comedy to mawkish sentimentality. Laura

Downey (the director's wife) coscripted. [R]▼●◗
Hugo the Hippo (1976) **C-90m.** **½ D: William Feigenbaum. Voices of Burl Ives, Marie and Jimmy Osmond, Robert Morley, Paul Lynde. OK children's cartoon musical about a youngster's attempt to save a hippo from extinction in ancient Zanzibar. [G]▼
Huk (1956) **C-84m.** *½ D: John Barnwell. George Montgomery, Mona Freeman, John Baer, James Bell. Philippine-made hokum about Montgomery returning to the Islands to revenge his dad's murder.
Hullabaloo Over Georgie and Bonnie's Pictures (1978-British) **C-89m.** *** D: James Ivory. Peggy Ashcroft, Victor Banerjee, Larry Pine, Saeed Jaffrey, Aparna Sen, Jane Booker. Wry comedy about the purpose and significance of art, set in an Indian palace where various people (including a British aristocrat, wonderfully played by Ashcroft) are attempting to acquire several miniature paintings. Deftly scripted by Ruth Prawer Jhabvala. Originally produced for British television.▼
Human Beast, The SEE: **La Bête Humaine**
Human Comedy, The (1943) **118m.** ***½ D: Clarence Brown. Mickey Rooney, Frank Morgan, Jackie "Butch" Jenkins, James Craig, Marsha Hunt, Fay Bainter, Ray Collins, Darryl Hickman, Donna Reed, Van Johnson. Memorable Americana, faithfully adapted from William Saroyan's sentimental Oscar-winning story of life in a small town during WW2. Unfolds like a novel, with many lovely vignettes, and one of Rooney's best performances as a teenager with growing responsibilities. Screenplay by Howard Estabrook. P.S.: Keep an eye out for those three soldiers on leave: Barry Nelson, Don DeFore, and Robert Mitchum! Also shown in computer-colored version.▼●
Human Desire (1954) **90m.** **½ D: Fritz Lang. Glenn Ford, Gloria Grahame, Broderick Crawford, Edgar Buchanan, Kathleen Case, Diana DeLaire. Lang's follow-up to THE BIG HEAT is a well-directed but muddled account of railroad engineer Ford, just back from Korea, who becomes mixed up with married Grahame and murder. Based on Zola's *La Bête Humaine,* filmed in 1938 in France by Jean Renoir.▼
Human Duplicators, The (1965) **C-82m.** ** D: Hugo Grimaldi. George Nader, Barbara Nichols, Richard Kiel, George Macready, Dolores Faith, Hugh Beaumont, Richard Arlen. An alien giant paves the way for a major invasion by duplicating people—but then falls in love. Some imagination here, but low-budget production sinks it.▼
Human Experiments (1980) **C-82m.** *½ D: Gregory Goodell. Linda Haynes, Geoffrey Lewis, Ellen Travolta, Aldo Ray, Jackie Coogan, Darlene Carviotto. As the title says . . . [R]▼
Human Factor, The (1975-British-Italian) **C-96m.** *½ D: Edward Dmytryk. George Kennedy, John Mills, Raf Vallone, Rita Tushingham, Barry Sullivan, Arthur Franz. Violent, bloody chronicle of Kennedy tracking down the killers of his family. Decent cast wasted. [R]▼
Human Factor, The (1979) **C-115m.** ** D: Otto Preminger. Nicol Williamson, Iman, Derek Jacobi, Richard Attenborough, Robert Morley, Ann Todd, John Gielgud. Dry, unexciting filmization of Graham Greene's spy novel about a British double agent (Williamson) who's forced to defect to Russia. Top cast, script by Tom Stoppard, but results are mediocre. Preminger's final film. [R]
Human Gorilla, The SEE: **Behind Locked Doors**
Human Highway (1982) **C-88m.** *½ D: Bernard Shakey (Neil Young), Dean Stockwell. Neil Young, Russ Tamblyn, Dennis Hopper, Sally Kirkland, Dean Stockwell, Charlotte Stewart, Devo. Young and Tamblyn run a gas station in the middle of nowhere in this wacked-out, anti-nuke comedy. Notable for footage of Young in concert plus rock group Devo performing with a red, radioactive glow about them (caused by the nuclear power plant in the vicinity). ▼●
Human Jungle, The (1954) **82m.** **½ D: Joseph M. Newman. Gary Merrill, Jan Sterling, Paula Raymond, Emile Meyer, Regis Toomey, Chuck Connors, Lamont Johnson, Claude Akins. Documentary-style account of a typical day at a busy police precinct house; nicely done.
Human Monster, The (1939-British) **73m.** ** D: Walter Summers. Bela Lugosi, Hugh Williams, Greta Gynt, Edmon Ryan, Wilfred Walter. Absurd, sometimes engaging Edgar Wallace tale of evil Lugosi using blind men as pawns in elaborate murder scheme. Original title: DARK EYES OF LONDON. Remade in West Germany as DEAD EYES OF LONDON. ▼●◗
Humanoids from the Deep (1980) **C-80m.** *** D: Barbara Peeters. Doug McClure, Ann Turkel, Vic Morrow, Cindy Weintraub, Anthony Penya, Denise Galik. Mutated salmon monsters with penchant for bikinied beachgoers commit rape and other (graphic) mayhem in small oceanside town. Fast, occasionally hilarious gutter trash from the Roger Corman stable. The finale is not for squeamish viewers. Remade in 1996 for TV. [R]▼●◗
Humongous (1981-Canadian) **C-93m.** *½ D: Paul Lynch. Janet Julian, David Wallace, Janit Baldwin, John Wildman, Joy Boushel, Layne Coleman. Slow-moving horror film opens with brutal rape and follows with every cliché in the book. A group of youths who wreck their boat on a small island are picked off one at a time by a raving man-beast. Most of the action occurs in com-

plete darkness and you never even get a good look at the monster. [R]▼

Humoresque (1946) **125m.** ***½ D: Jean Negulesco. Joan Crawford, John Garfield, Oscar Levant, J. Carrol Naish, Craig Stevens, Tom D'Andrea, Peggy Knudsen, Paul Cavanagh. Ambitious violinist Garfield gets involved with wealthy, unstable patroness Crawford. No cardboard soap opera this; superb performances, handsome production, hilarious support from Levant, and a knockout finale. Perhaps Crawford's finest hour. Young Robert Blake plays Garfield as a child, and that's Isaac Stern's violin on the soundtrack. Filmed before in 1920.▼●

Hunchback SEE: **Hunchback of Notre Dame, The** (1982)

Hunchback of Notre Dame, The (1923) **93m.** *** D: Wallace Worsley. Lon Chaney, Patsy Ruth Miller, Ernest Torrence, Tully Marshall, Norman Kerry. Lavish filming of Hugo classic, capturing flair of medieval Paris and strange attraction of outcast Chaney for dancing girl (Miller). Silent classic holds up well, with Chaney's makeup still incredible.▼●◗

Hunchback of Notre Dame, The (1939) **115m.** ***½ D: William Dieterle. Charles Laughton, Sir Cedric Hardwicke, Thomas Mitchell, Maureen O'Hara, Edmond O'Brien, Alan Marshal, Walter Hampden, Harry Davenport, George Zucco, Curt Bois, George Tobias, Rod La Roque. Superb remake of Lon Chaney silent is even better than the original. Laughton, as Victor Hugo's misshapen bell-ringer Quasimodo, is haunting and unforgettable. Magnificently atmospheric studio recreation of medieval Paris also a big plus. Film debut of O'Brien, and U.S. debut of O'Hara. Also shown in computer-colored version. ▼●◗

Hunchback of Notre Dame, The (1957-French) **C-104m.** **½ D: Jean Delannoy. Gina Lollobrigida, Anthony Quinn, Jean Danet, Alain Cuny. Quinn makes a valiant try in lead, but film misses scope and flavor of Hugo novel. CinemaScope.▼●

Hunchback of Notre Dame, The (1982) **C-150m. TVM** D: Michael Tuchner. Anthony Hopkins, Derek Jacobi, Lesley-Anne Down, Robert Powell, John Gielgud, David Suchet, Gerry Sundquist, Tim Pigott-Smith, Alan Webb, Roland Culver. Rousing new production of the Victor Hugo classic, adapted by John Gay. Highlighted by Hopkins's carefully shaded portrait of Quasimodo and production designer John Stoll's detailed replica of Paris's Notre Dame Cathedral, built on the backlot of Pinewood Studios outside London. Aka HUNCHBACK. Remade again for TV in 1997 with Mandy Patinkin. Above average.▼

Hunchback of Notre Dame, The (1996) **C-85m.** *** D: Gary Trousdale, Kirk Wise. Voices of Tom Hulce, Demi Moore, Kevin Kline, Tony Jay, Jason Alexander, Heidi Mollenhauer, Paul Kandel, Charles Kimbrough, Mary Wickes, Jane Withers, David Ogden Stiers. Intensely dramatic, involving story about the pathetic, put-upon Quasimodo, his evil guardian Frollo, and the one person who shows him kindness, the gypsy Esmeralda. Disney's all-time strangest choice for an animated feature turns out surprisingly well: handsomely designed, dynamically staged, with songs that (if unmemorable) work within the fabric of the story; comic relief, however, involving Quasi's three gargoyle friends, seems contrived and out of place. [G] ▼●

Hunger, The (1983) **C-97m.** *½ D: Tony Scott. Catherine Deneuve, David Bowie, Susan Sarandon, Cliff DeYoung, Beth Ehlers, Dan Hedaya. Kinky trash masquerading as a horror film, with Deneuve as a vampire who needs fresh blood to survive. Bowie's quite good as Deneuve's companion—with an aging scene that's the film's highlight. As for the rest, beware, unless seeing Deneuve and Sarandon in bed together is your idea of a good time. Look for Ann Magnuson and Willem Dafoe in small roles. Panavision. [R]▼●

Hungry Hill (1947-British) **92m.** ** D: Brian Desmond Hurst. Margaret Lockwood, Dennis Price, Cecil Parker, Jean Simmons, Eileen Herlie, Siobhan McKenna. Based on Daphne Du Maurier's book focusing on 19th-century Irish family with their vices and virtues highlighted; capable cast, with Herlie and McKenna making their film debuts.

Hunk (1987) **C-102m.** ** D: Lawrence Bassoff. John Allen Nelson, Steve Levitt, Deborah Shelton, Rebeccah Bush, James Coco, Robert Morse, Avery Schreiber. Youthful nerd sells his soul to become a California hunk—but still has to deal with the Devil (Coco) and his beautiful emissary (Shelton). Silly stuff benefits from an attractive and colorful cast. [PG] ▼●

Hunted, The (1948) **67m.** **½ D: Jack Bernhard. Preston Foster, Belita, Pierre Watkin, Edna Holland. Trim minor film with Foster a cop out to reform girlfriend Belita; efficiently produced.

Hunted (1952) SEE: **Stranger in Between**

Hunted, The (1974) SEE: **Touch Me Not**

Hunted, The (1995) **C-118m.** *½ D: J. F. Lawton. Christopher Lambert, John Lone, Joan Chen, Yoshio Harada, Yoko Shimada. N.Y. businessman is chased by masked ninja assassins who actively conceal their identities, which at least puts them one-up on some of their fellow cast members. Slicing and dicing via DTS sound technology suggests an episode of *The Montel Williams Show* gone terribly wrong: titles of bona fide Japanese classics indicate what it's like sitting through this: GATE OF HELL,

STREET OF SHAME and—in Lambert's case—AN ACTOR'S REVENGE. [R] ▼●◗

Hunter, The (1980) **C-97m.** BOMB D: Buzz Kulik. Steve McQueen, Eli Wallach, Kathryn Harrold, LeVar Burton, Ben Johnson. Incomprehensible bio of real-life contemporary bounty hunter Ralph (Pappy) Thorson has plot holes that Hannibal could have led elephants through. McQueen's last film and probably his worst. [PG]▼●

Hunters, The (1958) **C-108m.** **½ D: Dick Powell. Robert Mitchum, Robert Wagner, Richard Egan, Mai Britt, Lee Phillips. Veteran pilot falls for wife of younger flyer—who crashes behind enemy lines. Fair of its type. CinemaScope.▼

Hunt for Red October, The (1990) **C-135m.** ***½ D: John McTiernan. Sean Connery, Alec Baldwin, Scott Glenn, Sam Neill, James Earl Jones, Joss Ackland, Richard Jordan, Peter Firth, Tim Curry, Courtney B. Vance, Jeffrey Jones, Fred Dalton Thompson, Timothy Carhart. Exciting, complex thriller from the best-seller by Tom Clancy. Connery stars as a Soviet submarine captain who may (or may not) be planning to defect to the U.S. during the maiden voyage of a supersecret nuclear sub; Baldwin is the American intelligence ace who tries to anticipate his every move. Long, potentially confusing at times, but always manages to make a course correction in the nick of time . . . and deliver another direct hit. Oscar winner for sound-effects editing. Followed by PATRIOT GAMES. Panavision. [PG]▼●◗

Hunting (1990-Australian) **C-97m.** ** D: Frank Howson. John Savage, Kerry Armstrong, Guy Pearce, Jeffrey Thomas, Rebecca Rigg, Rhys McConnochie. Ambitious but overwrought exercise in style, about beautiful but deeply troubled secretary Armstrong, who forsakes her self-pitying husband, and becomes involved with all-powerful (and predictably evil, hypocritical) empire-builder Savage. Panavision. [R]▼

Hunting Party, The (1971) **C-108m.** BOMB D: Don Medford. Oliver Reed, Candice Bergen, Gene Hackman, Simon Oakland, L. Q. Jones, Ronald Howard, G. D. Spradlin. When his wife is kidnapped and raped by Reed and his gang, Hackman sets out to kill them one by one. Fine cast wasted in repellently violent Western that adds nothing new to tired plot, unless you count the bordello-equipped train. [R]

Hunt the Man Down (1950) **68m.** ** D: George Archainbaud. Gig Young, Lynne Roberts, Willard Parker, Gerald Mohr, Paul Frees. Ordinary whodunit: public defender Young trying to solve a murder.▼

Hunt to Kill SEE: **White Buffalo, The**

hurlyburly (1998) **C-122m.** ** D: Anthony Drazan. Sean Penn, Kevin Spacey, Robin Wright Penn, Chazz Palminteri, Garry Shandling, Anna Paquin, Meg Ryan. A seamy slice of life about a circle of L.A. friends—self-absorbed, smart-assy, driven, drug-infused people desperately looking for happiness in all the wrong places. David Rabe adapted his much-admired 1984 play, but it loses something in the transition to film, becoming more realistic and less funny despite a powerhouse cast. [R]▼●◗

Hurricane, The (1937) **102m.** ***½ D: John Ford. Dorothy Lamour, Jon Hall, Mary Astor, C. Aubrey Smith, Raymond Massey, Thomas Mitchell, John Carradine, Jerome Cowan. First-rate escapism on isle of Manikoora, where idyllic native life of Hall and Lamour is disrupted by vindictive governor Massey. Climactic hurricane effects have never been equaled. Lovely score by Alfred Newman. Screenplay by Dudley Nichols and Oliver H. P. Garrett, from the novel by Charles Nordhoff and James Norman Hall. Remade in 1979. ▼●◗

Hurricane (1979) **C-119m.** BOMB D: Jan Troell. Jason Robards, Mia Farrow, Max von Sydow, Trevor Howard, Dayton Ka'ne, Timothy Bottoms, James Keach. Look what just blew in: a $22 million remake of the 1937 classic that may well put you to sleep! Retitled FORBIDDEN PARADISE for TV. Todd-AO 35. [PG]▼

Hurricane, The (1999) **C-125m.** **½ D: Norman Jewison. Denzel Washington, Vicellous Reon Shannon, Deborah Kara Unger, Liev Schreiber, John Hannah, Debbi Morgan, Dan Hedaya, Clancy Brown, Harris Yulin, David Paymer, Rod Steiger. Washington's powerful performance as wrongly imprisoned prizefighter Rubin "Hurricane" Carter makes this otherwise conventional drama worth seeing. Shannon plays a ghetto teenager who reads Carter's autobiography and determines to find a way to set him free. The boy's Canadian guardians are ill-defined characters and weaken the story, along with heavy-handed portrayals of Carter's victimizers. [R]▼●◗

Hurricane Island (1951) **C-70m.** *½ D: Lew Landers. Jon Hall, Marie Windsor, Marc Lawrence, Edgar Barrier. Low-budget nonsense involving the fountain of youth and female buccaneer.

Hurricane Smith (1952) **C-90m.** ** D: Jerry Hopper. Yvonne De Carlo, John Ireland, James Craig, Forrest Tucker. Romance and a search for gold as a ship is beached on a South Sea island.

Hurricane Streets (1998) **C-88m.** *** D: Morgan J. Freeman. Brendan Sexton III, Shawn Elliott, Isidra Vega, David Roland Frank, L. M. "Kit" Carson, Heather Matarazzo, Edie Falco. Moving drama of adolescents whose underlying decency is put to the test in a world of petty thievery in N.Y.C.'s East Village. Realistic, unsentimental acting of relative unknowns highlights this excellent first feature from writer-director Freeman (not to be confused with the actor), who puts both angst and hope into his story. [R]▼●

Hurry Sundown (1967) **C-142m.** ** D: Otto Preminger. Michael Caine, Jane Fonda, John Phillip Law, Diahann Carroll, Robert Hooks, Faye Dunaway, Burgess Meredith, Robert Reed, George Kennedy, Frank Converse, Loring Smith, Beah Richards, Madeleine Sherwood, Rex Ingram, Jim Backus. Often ludicrous, overripe melodrama with ruthless Southerner Caine determined to buy up cousin's land, stopping at nothing to achieve goal. A curio for Fonda and Caine's offbeat casting, not to mention Horton Foote as one of the scripters. Jane's saxophone "solo," though, is worth checking out. Panavision.

Hurry Up, or I'll Be 30 (1973) **C-88m.** ** D: Joseph Jacoby. John Lefkowitz, Linda De Coff, Ronald Anton, Maureen Byrnes, Danny DeVito. Mild low-budget comedy about efforts of schnook (Lefkowitz) to get his life in order before he hits 30.▼

Husbands (1970) **C-138m.** **½ D: John Cassavetes. Ben Gazzara, Peter Falk, John Cassavetes, Jenny Runacre, Jenny Lee Wright, Noelle Kao. Cassavetes' follow-up to FACES is not nearly as good; story deals with trio of middle-aged buddies who take off for Europe when their best friend dies. Some good scenes, but plagued by Cassavetes' habitual self-indulgence. Originally released at 154m. [PG]▼

Husbands and Wives (1992) **C-107m.** ***½ D: Woody Allen. Woody Allen, Blythe Danner, Judy Davis, Mia Farrow, Juliette Lewis, Liam Neeson, Sydney Pollack, Lysette Anthony, Cristi Conaway, Timothy Jerome, Ron Rifkin, Jerry Zaks, Bruce Jay Friedman, Benno Schmidt, Caroline Aaron, Nora Ephron. Long-married couple startles their best friends by announcing they're going to split up; meanwhile, the friends start to stray themselves. Perceptive, witty, knowing script by Allen is brilliantly performed (especially by Davis and Pollack), though Woody and Mia's headline-making scandal at the time of the film's release made it difficult not to grimace at some pointed dialogue. Only negative note: amateurish hand-held camera and jump-cuts are jarring and distracting. [R]▼●

Hush (1998) **C-97m.** *½ D: Jonathan Darby. Jessica Lange, Gwyneth Paltrow, Johnathon Schaech, Nina Foch, Debi Mazar, David Thornton, Hal Holbrook. Paltrow and wealthy boyfriend Schaech are manipulated by his neurotic horse-rancher mother (Lange). Viewers could read a novel while watching this "thriller" and still not miss anything. Lange appears to believe she's doing Blanche Dubois all over again. [PG-13]▼●◗

Hush . . . Hush, Sweet Charlotte (1964) **133m.** *** D: Robert Aldrich. Bette Davis, Olivia de Havilland, Joseph Cotten, Agnes Moorehead, Cecil Kellaway, Victor Buono, Mary Astor, Bruce Dern. Macabre story of a family with a skeleton in its closet, confusing at times but worth watching for its cast. Bette is Olivia's victimized cousin; Cotten is Olivia's boyfriend.▼●

Hussy (1980-British) **C-95m.** *½ D: Matthew Chapman. Helen Mirren, John Shea, Murray Salem, Paul Angelis, Jenny Runacre. Muddled, poorly directed melodrama centering on hooker Mirren, boyfriend Shea, and illicit drugs. [R]▼

Hustle (1975) **C-120m.** BOMB D: Robert Aldrich. Burt Reynolds, Catherine Deneuve, Ben Johnson, Paul Winfield, Eileen Brennan, Eddie Albert, Ernest Borgnine, Jack Carter, Catherine Bach. Pretentious, foul-mouthed, foul-minded story about an L.A. cop and a high-class call-girl who dream of escaping from their gritty life but never make it. This one's the pits. [R]▼

Hustler, The (1961) **135m.** **** D: Robert Rossen. Paul Newman, Jackie Gleason, Piper Laurie, George C. Scott, Myron McCormick, Murray Hamilton, Michael Constantine, Jake LaMotta, Vincent Gardenia. Newman is outstanding as disenchanted drifter and pool hustler who challenges legendary Minnesota Fats (Gleason). Dingy pool-hall atmosphere vividly realized in this incisive film. Cinematographer Eugen Shuftan won an Oscar. Walter Tevis novel adapted by Sidney Carroll and director Rossen. Followed years later by THE COLOR OF MONEY. CinemaScope. ▼●

Hustler Squad SEE: **Doll Squad, The**

Hustling (1975) **C-100m. TVM** D: Joseph Sargent. Lee Remick, Jill Clayburgh, Monte Markham, Alex Rocco, Dick O'-Neill, Burt Young, Melanie Mayron. Searing drama by Fay Kanin about prostitution racket, well-acted by Remick as an investigative reporter (à la Gail Sheehy, on whose book this was based) and Clayburgh, giving a gritty portrait of a hooker. Played for the sensational. Above average.▼●

Hypnotic Eye, The (1960) **79m.** ** D: George Blair. Jacques Bergerac, Merry Anders, Marcia Henderson, Allison Hayes. Partially successful chiller of theatrical mesmerizer with penchant for having female victims disfigure themselves.

Hysteria (1965-British) **85m.** **½ D: Freddie Francis. Robert Webber, Anthony Newlands, Jennifer Jayne, Maurice Denham, Lelia Goldoni, Peter Woodthorpe, Sandra Boize. After a car accident, an amnesiac Yank in London finds himself entangled in a complex murder plot that may or may not be a figment of his imagination. Twisty, reasonably intriguing Hammer Studios thriller starts out promisingly, but gets bogged down in sluggish exposition. Never totally satisfying.

Hysterical (1983) **C-87m.** BOMB D: Chris

Bearde. William, Mark and Brett Hudson, Cindy Pickett, Richard Kiel, Julie Newmar, Bud Cort, Robert Donner, Murray Hamilton, Clint Walker, Franklin Ajaye, Charlie Callas, Keenan Wynn, Gary Owens. Lame parody of AMITYVILLE/EXORCIST type pictures; the start and finish of the Hudsons' screen career. [PG]▼●

I Accuse! (1958-British) **99m.** **½ D: Jose Ferrer. Jose Ferrer, Anton Walbrook, Emlyn Williams, Viveca Lindfors, David Farrar, Leo Genn, Herbert Lom, Harry Andrews, Felix Aylmer, George Coulouris, Donald Wolfit. Sincere but pretentious treatment of the treason trial of Alfred Dreyfus (Ferrer), with Williams as his defender, Emile Zola. Screenplay by Gore Vidal. CinemaScope.

I Aim at the Stars (1960) **107m.** *** D: J. Lee Thompson. Curt Jurgens, Victoria Shaw, Herbert Lom, Gia Scala. Low-key fictional history of Nazi missile scientist Werner Von Braun and his problems adjusting to life in America.

I Am a Camera (1955-British) **98m.** ***½ D: Henry Cornelius. Julie Harris, Laurence Harvey, Shelley Winters, Ron Randell, Anton Diffring, Patrick McGoohan, Peter Prowse. Intelligent adaptation of John van Druten's play (based on Christopher Isherwood stories) about pre-war Berlin, with Harris a delight as a fun-loving young woman who'll accept anything from anyone. Screenplay by John Collier. Basis of Broadway musical and film CABARET.▼

I Am a Dancer (1973) **C-93m.** *** D: Pierre Jourdan, Bryan Forbes. Documentary on Rudolf Nureyev is handled a little better than many dance films; includes shots of rehearsals and lots of footage with Margot Fonteyn.▼

I Am a Fugitive from a Chain Gang (1932) **93m.** **** D: Mervyn LeRoy. Paul Muni, Glenda Farrell, Helen Vinson, Preston Foster, Edward Ellis, Allen Jenkins. Still packs a wallop after all these years, with Muni as innocent man brutally victimized by criminal justice system. Haunting finale is justly famous. Scripted by Sheridan Gibney and Brown Holmes, from Robert E. Burns' autobiographical story. Burns' plight is also dramatized in the made for cable TVM THE MAN WHO BROKE 1,000 CHAINS.▼●

I Am a Thief (1935) **64m.** ** D: Robert Florey. Mary Astor, Ricardo Cortez, Dudley Digges, Robert Barrat, Irving Pichel. Stilted adventure of jewel thieves and insurance fraud set on Orient Express. Good cast can't save indifferent script.

I Am Cuba (1964-Russian-Cuban) **141m.** ***½ D: Mikhail Kalatozov. Sergio Corrieri, Salvador Vud, Jose Gallardo, Raul Garcia. Luz Maria Collazo, Jean Bouise. Sweeping, eye-popping ode to Cuba and the Castro revolution. Vignettes idealize hardworking but exploited peasants and Castro's staunch, freedom-loving revolutionaries, depicting Americans as decadent, sexist swine. And the images are consistently dazzling; the film demands to be seen and savored by any lover of pure cinema. Scripted by Yevgeny Yevtushenko and Enrique Pineda Barnet; released in the U.S. in 1995. ▼●◗

I Am the Cheese (1983) **C-95m.** **½ D: Robert Jiras. Robert MacNaughton, Hope Lange, Don Murray, Robert Wagner, Cynthia Nixon, Lee Richardson, John Fiedler, Sudie Bond. Paper-thin but occasionally appealing tale of alienated teenager who has witnessed his parents' death, and his fantasies while under psychiatric care. From Robert Cormier's novel. Remade as LAPSE OF MEMORY. [PG]▼

I Am the Law (1938) **83m.** **½ D: Alexander Hall. Edward G. Robinson, Otto Kruger, Wendy Barrie, John Beal, Louis Jean Heydt, Fay Helm, Barbara O'Neil. No surprises in this story of D.A. Robinson fighting corrupt city government, but it's done so smoothly you forget you've seen it before. Don't miss E.G. dancing the Big Apple at the beginning.▼●

I Believe In You (1952-British) **93m.** **½ D: Michael Relph, Basil Dearden. Cecil Parker, Celia Johnson, Harry Fowler, Godfrey Tearle, Laurence Harvey, Joan Collins. Intelligent study of methods used by probation officers to reform their charges.

I Bury the Living (1958) **76m.** *** D: Albert Band. Richard Boone, Theodore Bikel, Peggy Maurer, Herbert Anderson. Crisp little chiller about cemetery manager who finds he may have power of life and death by sticking white (or black) pins into a map of the graveyard.▼●

I Can Get It for You Wholesale (1951) **90m.** *** D: Michael Gordon. Susan Hayward, Dan Dailey, Sam Jaffe, George Sanders, Randy Stuart, Marvin Kaplan, Harry Von Zell. Hayward is aces as a model-turned dress designer determined to make it in N.Y.C.'s garment industry. Jerome Weidman's flavorful novel was adapted by Vera Caspary and scripted by Abraham Polonsky. Aka: ONLY THE BEST.

Ice Castles (1979) **C-109m.** *** D: Donald Wrye. Lynn-Holly Johnson, Robby Benson, Colleen Dewhurst, Tom Skerritt, Jennifer Warren, David Huffman. Successful ice skating career of Iowa farm girl is interrupted after she is blinded in freak accident. Tops for the disease/affliction genre, with well-photographed skating sequences and good performances by all. [PG]▼

Ice Cold in Alex SEE: **Desert Attack**

Ice Follies of 1939, The (1939) **93m.** ** D: Reinhold Schunzel. Joan Crawford, James Stewart, Lew Ayres, Lewis Stone, Bess Ehrhardt, Lionel Stander, Roy Shipstad,

Eddie Shipstad, Oscar Johnson. Stewart and Ayres are skating partners who split after Jimmy marries Joan; rather than risk hurting their act and getting in the way of Jimmy's dream to start a musical ice revue, she goes off on her own and becomes a movie star overnight! Strange pastiche obviously concocted by MGM to showcase Shipstad and Johnson's Ice Follies show—complete with a (boring) Technicolor finale. ●

Iceland (1942) **79m.** ** D: H. Bruce Humberstone. Sonja Henie, John Payne, Jack Oakie, Felix Bressart, Osa Massen, Joan Merrill. Labored love story defeats this Henie musical, although skating and singing interludes are pleasant; song hit, "There Will Never Be Another You."▼

Iceman (1984) **C-99m.** ***½ D: Fred Schepisi. Timothy Hutton, Lindsay Crouse, John Lone, Josef Sommer, David Strathairn, Danny Glover, James Tolkan. A Neanderthal man is found frozen in ice. Scientists manage to bring him back to life, but only Hutton is interested in him as a human being and not a lab specimen. Fascinating, credible science fiction made all the more involving by Schepisi's fine direction. Haunting score by Bruce Smeaton; remarkable performance as the caveman by Lone. Story by John Drimmer; scripted by Chip Proser and Drimmer. Panavision. [PG]▼●

Iceman Cometh, The (1973) **C-178m.** ***½ D: John Frankenheimer. Lee Marvin, Fredric March, Robert Ryan, Jeff Bridges, Martyn Green, Moses Gunn, Bradford Dillman, Evans Evans. Remarkably successful film of Eugene O'Neill's play about assorted barflies in a 1912 saloon; Marvin's Hickey is only adequate, but Ryan dominates an outstanding supporting cast. An American Film Theatre production. First shown at 239m. This was March's last film. [PG]▼●◗

Ice Palace (1960) **C-143m.** **½ D: Vincent Sherman. Richard Burton, Robert Ryan, Carolyn Jones, Martha Hyer, Jim Backus, Ray Danton, Shirley Knight, Diane McBain, Karl Swenson, George Takei. Typically sprawling (and silly) Edna Ferber saga of two men whose friendship turns to bitter rivalry, and whose lives parallel the development of Alaska. Watchable, to be sure, but hokey from start to finish.▼

Ice Pirates, The (1984) **C-91m.** ** D: Stewart Raffill. Robert Urich, Mary Crosby, Michael D. Roberts, John Matuszak, Anjelica Huston, Ron Perlman, John Carradine, Robert Symonds. Spoofy blend of space opera and swashbuckler, set in an arid future where water has become the most precious of commodities. Script vacillates between clever and half-baked; claustrophobic direction (which won't help on TV) keeps this from being more than a passable rainy-afternoon flick. [PG]▼●

Ice Station Zebra (1968) **C-148m.** **½ D: John Sturges. Rock Hudson, Ernest Borgnine, Patrick McGoohan, Jim Brown, Tony Bill, Lloyd Nolan. Standard Cold War nail-biter with all-male cast has Hudson a sub commander sailing for North Pole to await orders, not knowing that Cold War incident will ensue; McGoohan a British agent out to trap a Russian spy. Based on the Alistair MacLean novel; originally in Cinerama. Infamous as Howard Hughes' favorite movie! Super Panavision 70. [G]▼●

Ice Storm, The (1997) **C-113m.** **½ D: Ang Lee. Kevin Kline, Joan Allen, Sigourney Weaver, Christina Ricci, Elijah Wood, Henry Czerny, Adam Hann-Byrd, Tobey Maguire, Jamey Sheridan, Kate Burton, Larry Pine, Katie Holmes. Icy adaptation of Rick Moody's much-praised novel about a real-life ice storm in 1973 and how it parallels activities in upscale New Canaan, Connecticut. A sober and absorbing chronicle of sexuality—repressed and unleashed—in 70s suburbia (love those clothes!), but also somewhat clinical and off-putting, until the heartrending finale. A film one can admire without actually enjoying. [PG-13] ▼●◗

Icicle Thief, The (1989-Italian) **C-85m.** **½ D: Maurizio Nichetti. Maurizio Nichetti, Caterina Sylos Labini, Heidi Komarek, Renato Scarpa. Ingenious satire of contemporary commercialism—and disrespect for the art of film on television—has Nichetti's BICYCLE THIEF–type drama being presented on TV with so many commercials that soon no one can separate the program from the ads . . . including the actors in the film! Nichetti plays with his audience, often amusingly, but pulls the rug out from under a bit too often.▼

I Come in Peace (1990) **C-92m.** ** D: Craig R. Baxley. Dolph Lundgren, Brian Benben, Betsy Brantley, Matthias Hues, David Ackroyd, Jay Bilas, Sherman Howard, Mark Lowenthal, Michael J. Pollard, Jesse Vint. Black-clad alien, who looks like a giant surfer, arrives to harvest people for their endorphins; his race is addicted to them. Basically just another cop (Lundgren) and new partner (FBI agent Benben) movie, with lots of explosions. Routine and unimaginative. [R]▼●

I Confess (1953) **95m.** **½ D: Alfred Hitchcock. Montgomery Clift, Anne Baxter, Karl Malden, Brian Aherne, Dolly Haas, O. E. Hasse. A priest hears a murderer's confession and is himself accused of the crime. Lesser Hitchcock film, made in Quebec, is nevertheless intriguing for its stark photography and symbolism. See also LE CONFESSIONALE. ▼●

I Could Go on Singing (1963-British) **C-99m.** **½ D: Ronald Neame. Judy Garland, Dirk Bogarde, Jack Klugman, Aline MacMahon, Gregory Phillips. Garland is famed singer returning to England to claim illegitimate son living with real father (Bogarde). Garland is exceptional in singing sequences revealing the true Judy; sadly, this was her last film. Panavision.▼●

I Could Never Have Sex With Any Man Who Has So Little Respect For My Husband (1973) **C-86m.** ** D: Robert McCarty. Carmine Caridi, Lynne Lipton, Cynthia Harris, Andrew Duncan, Dan Greenburg. Talky but amusingly offbeat comedy written by humorist Greenburg. A study of guilt as two couples are stuck together on vacation on Martha's Vineyard. [R]

I Cover Big Town (1947) **63m.** ** D: William C. Thomas. Philip Reed, Hillary Brooke, Robert Lowery, Robert Shayne, Louis Jean Heydt. Uninspired mystery has female reporter solving complicated murder case. Uneven cast. Retitled: I COVER THE UNDERWORLD.

I Cover the Underworld (1947) SEE: **I Cover Big Town**

I Cover the Underworld (1955) **70m.** *½ D: R. G. Springsteen. Sean McClory, Ray Middleton, Lee Van Cleef, Joanne Jordan. Republic pictures programmer of clergyman whose twin brother is an about-to-be-released gangster.

I Cover the War (1937) **68m.** ** D: Arthur Lubin. John Wayne, Gwen Gaze, Major Sam Harris, James Bush, Don Barclay. Second-rate pulp fiction about correspondent Wayne tangling with Arab rebel leader.

I Cover the Waterfront (1933) **70m.** **½ D: James Cruze. Ben Lyon, Claudette Colbert, Ernest Torrence, Hobart Cavanaugh, Maurice Black, Purnell Pratt, Wilfred Lucas. Dated but still entertaining yarn about tired but persistent waterfront reporter Lyon, who romances free-spirited Colbert to trap her father (Torrence), who has been smuggling Chinese immigrants. How long will it take for him to actually fall in love? Considered pretty raw in its day. ▼

I'd Climb the Highest Mountain (1951) **C-88m.** *** D: Henry King. Susan Hayward, William Lundigan, Rory Calhoun, Gene Lockhart, Ruth Donnelly, Barbara Bates, Lynn Bari, Alexander Knox. Simple good-hearted slice of Americana filmed on location in Georgia, with Lundigan as a preacher whose bride (Hayward) must learn a new way of life in Southern hill country. ▼

Ideal Husband, An (1948-British) **C-96m.** **½ D: Alexander Korda. Paulette Goddard, Michael Wilding, Diana Wynyard, C. Aubrey Smith, Glynis Johns, Michael Medwin. Oscar Wilde's drawing room comedy receives classy presentation but is slow-moving. Remade in 1999.▼

Ideal Husband, An (1999-British-U.S.) **C-96m.** *** D: Oliver Parker. Cate Blanchett, Rupert Everett, Jeremy Northam, Julianne Moore, Minnie Driver, John Wood, Jeroen Krabbé, Peter Vaughan, Lindsay Duncan. Delightful revision of Oscar Wilde's classic 1895 comedy about a stalwart Member of Parliament who becomes a blackmail target—and can't stand the idea that his devoted wife will find him less than perfect. One couldn't ask for a more attractive or appealing cast, though Everett practically steals the film with his effortless insouciance. [PG-13]▼◗

I Deal in Danger (1966) **C-89m.** **½ D: Walter Grauman. Robert Goulet, Christine Carere, Donald Harron, Werner Peters. Feature version of TV series *Blue Light* involves adventures of Goulet pretending to be Nazi convert in order to help Allies.

Identification of a Woman (1982-Italian-French) **C-128m.** **½ D: Michelangelo Antonioni. Tomas Milian, Daniela Silverio, Christine Boisson, Sandra Monteleoni, Giampaolo Saccarola. A familiar Antonioni theme—alienation and the difficulty of initiating relationships in contemporary society—is explored in this low-key tale of a movie director (Milian) and his involvement with two women. Atmospheric, allegorical film of interest mostly to Antonioni diehards. Released in the U.S. in 1996.▼

Identity Crisis (1990) **C-98m.** BOMB D: Melvin Van Peebles. Mario Van Peebles, Ilan Mitchell-Smith, Nicholas Kepros, Shelley Burch, Rick Aviles, Stephen J. Cannell, Olivia Brown, Larry "Bud" Melman, Bobby Rivers. Crude, messy pseudo-farce, in which the spirit of a white, stereotypically effeminate fashion designer is mysteriously transferred into the body of black, stereotypically superhip rapper (Mario Van Peebles, who overacts outrageously). Excruciating and, ultimately, boring. Scripted by Mario; produced by Melvin (who appears as a police inspector). [R]▼

Identity Unknown (1945) **71m.** **½ D: Walter Colmes. Richard Arlen, Cheryl Walker, Roger Pryor, Bobby Driscoll, Lola Lane, Ian Keith, John Forrest, Sara Padden. Occasionally moving but uneven psychological drama about a soldier with amnesia, who treks around the country attempting to discover his identity. The scenes with young Driscoll, who thinks Arlen's his dad, are a highlight.▼

I Died a Thousand Times (1955) **C-109m.** ** D: Stuart Heisler. Jack Palance, Shelley Winters, Lori Nelson, Lee Marvin, Earl Holliman, Lon Chaney (Jr.), Dennis Hopper. Overblown remake of Bogart's HIGH SIERRA with Palance as mad killer with soft spot for crippled girl (Nelson). Winters is his moll in this gangster run-through. CinemaScope. ▼●

Idiot, The (1951-Japanese) **166m.** *** D: Akira Kurosawa. Toshiro Mifune, Masayuki

Mori, Setsuko Hara, Takashi Shimura. Kurosawa coscripted this updated version of the Dostoyevsky novel, about a prince and his friend who both love the same woman. Dramatically uneven (because the release version was edited down from Kurosawa's original cut), but there are enough flashes of brilliance to make it worthwhile.▼

Idiot, The (1960-Russian) **C-122m.** **½ D: Ivan Pyrlev. Julia Borisova, Yuri Yakovlev, N. Podgorny, L. Parkhomenko, R. Maximova, N. Pazhitnov. Faithful if not inspired adaptation of Dostoyevsky novel of tormented soul and his peculiar interactions with others.

Idiot's Delight (1939) **105m.** *** D: Clarence Brown. Norma Shearer, Clark Gable, Edward Arnold, Charles Coburn, Joseph Schildkraut, Burgess Meredith, Virginia Grey. Disparate characters—including a tacky vaudevillian and his one-time flame, who's come up in the world—are forced to share each other's company in a hotel near the Italian border as WW2 is about to erupt. Robert E. Sherwood's Pulitzer Prize-winning play is badly dated, an interesting period piece, notable for its pacifist ideals . . . but frankly more interesting for Gable's famous song-and-dance routine to "Puttin' on the Ritz."▼●

Idle Hands (1999) **C-90m.** *½ D: Rodman Flender. Devon Sawa, Seth Green, Elden Henson, Jessica Alba, Fred Willard, Jack Noseworthy, Vivica A. Fox. Lazy, dope-smoking teenager Sawa discovers that his right hand is possessed, and a killer. He, or it, murders his parents and his two best friends, then he tries to remedy matters. Horror comedy (with ideas reminiscent of many other films, notably EVIL DEAD II) is doomed by too many crude and genuinely tasteless jokes. [R] ▼●◗

Idol, The (1966) **107m.** ** D: Daniel Petrie. Jennifer Jones, Michael Parks, John Leyton, Jennifer Hilary, Guy Doleman. Trash about worthless type who makes it with both mother and girl of his best friend; interesting only as chance to see latter-day Jones and watch Parks try to ape James Dean. Filmed in England.▼

Idolmaker, The (1980) **C-119m.** **½ D: Taylor Hackford. Ray Sharkey, Tovah Feldshuh, Peter Gallagher, Paul Land, Joe Pantoliano, Maureen McCormick, Olympia Dukakis. Fictionalized bio of rock producer Bob Marcucci, who guided (pushed?) Frankie Avalon and Fabian to stardom in the late '50s. A great idea overcome by a script that builds momentum and then drops the ball. Good performances, sharp direction, though little period flavor (even in rock vet Jeff Barry's slick music score). [PG]▼●◗

I Don't Buy Kisses Anymore (1992) **C-112m.** ** D: Mitchell Marcarelli. Jason Alexander, Nia Peeples, Lainie Kazan, Lou Jacobi, Eileen Brennan, Larry Storch. Chubby shoestore owner Alexander is befriended by psychology student Peeples; he wants romance, but she wants to study his compulsive eating disorder. Romantic comedy boasts a likable cast but a disappointing script that slides too easily into caricature and stereotype. [PG]▼●

I Don't Care Girl, The (1953) **C-78m.** **½ D: Lloyd Bacon. Mitzi Gaynor, David Wayne, Oscar Levant, Warren Stevens. Premise of George Jessel preparing film bio of Eva Tanguay is vehicle to recreate facets in life of the vaudeville star.

I Don't Want to Be Born SEE: **Devil Within Her, The**

I Don't Want to Talk About It (1994-Argentine) **C-102m.** **½ D: Maria Luisa Bemberg. Marcello Mastroianni, Luisina Brando, Alejandra Podesta. Memorable but not altogether compelling fable about a polished Casanova who finds himself attracted to a small town's most cultured woman—a dwarf whose physically attractive but repellently possessive mother has her own eyes set on this eligible bachelor. At 70, Mastroianni remains dashing. [PG-13]▼●

I Dood It (1943) **102m.** ** D: Vincente Minnelli. Red Skelton, Eleanor Powell, Richard Ainley, Patricia Dane, Lena Horne, Hazel Scott, Jimmy Dorsey and Orchestra. Strained, overlong musicomedy about a tailor and his movie-star sweetheart; good songs include "Star Eyes" and "Taking a Chance on Love," but patchwork film lifts its big finale from Powell's earlier BORN TO DANCE! A remake (more or less) of Buster Keaton's SPITE MARRIAGE.▼

I'd Rather Be Rich (1964) **C-96m.** **½ D: Jack Smight. Sandra Dee, Maurice Chevalier, Andy Williams, Robert Goulet, Gene Raymond, Charles Ruggles, Hermione Gingold, Allen Jenkins, Rip Taylor. Airy remake of IT STARTED WITH EVE. Dee finds substitute fiancé to please dying grandfather who wants to see her happy. Only Chevalier-Gingold scenes have spice.

I Dreamed of Africa (2000) **C-112m.** ** D: Hugh Hudson. Kim Basinger, Vincent Perez, Eva Marie Saint, Liam Aiken, Garrett Strommen. Story of Kuki Gallmann, an Italian who moves with her young son and new husband to remote African ranch. She is determined to triumph over adverse conditions, and becomes passionate about animal rights. Basinger (an animal activist herself) is effective, but biopic of privileged, determined Gallmann is never quite as compelling as intended. Super 35. [PG-13]

I Dream of Jeanie (1952) **C-90m.** ** D: Allan Dwan. Ray Middleton, Bill Shirley, Muriel Lawrence, Eileen Christy, Lynn Bari, Richard Simmons, Rex Allen, Louise Beavers, James Kirkwood, Carl "Alfalfa" Switzer. Blah biography of famed 19th-century American composer Stephen Foster (Shirley), who pines over Lawrence (even though Christy, the "Jeanie" of the title, really is the girl for him). Foster's "story" also is told in HARMONY LANE and SWANEE RIVER.▼

I Dream Too Much (1935) **95m.** **½ D: John Cromwell. Lily Pons, Henry Fonda, Eric Blore, Osgood Perkins. Opera star Pons' Hollywood debut casts her and Fonda as a married couple with career problems. Look for Lucille Ball as an American tourist in Paris.▼

I Drink Your Blood (1970) **C-72m.** ** D: David Durston. Bhaskar, Jadine Wong, Ronda Fultz, George Patterson. To get revenge on sadistic band of hippies, young boy gives them meat pies infected with rabies and they go homicidally crazy. Nuff said. [R]▼

I Eat Your Skin (1970) **82m.** BOMB D: Del Tenney. William Joyce, Heather Hewitt, Betty Hyatt Linton, Dan Stapleton, Walter Coy, Robert Stanton. Scientifically created zombies menace two-fisted hero on Caribbean island. Worthless. Filmed in 1964. Aka VOODOO BLOODBATH. [PG]▼

I Escaped from Devil's Island (1973) **C-89m.** BOMB D: William Witney. Jim Brown, Christopher George, Paul Richards, Rick Ely, Richard Rust, Jan Merlin. Produced by the Corman boys (Roger and Gene) in Mexico and the Caribbean, this actioner is an insult to vet director Witney's standing with buffs who know his earlier work. Violent, vulgar. [R]

I Escaped from the Gestapo (1943) **75m.** ** D: Harold Young. Dean Jagger, John Carradine, Mary Brian, William Henry, Sidney Blackmer, Ian Keith. Low-budget WW2 thriller; title tells the story. Retitled: NO ESCAPE.

if. . . . (1968-British) **C/B&W-111m.** **** D: Lindsay Anderson. Malcolm McDowell, David Wood, Richard Warwick, Robert Swann, Christine Noonan, Arthur Lowe, Mona Washbourne, Graham Crowden, Simon Ward. Magnificent, surrealistic study of students at boarding school who plot revolution—or do they? Originally X-rated, later trimmed for wider acceptance. Written by David Sherwin. [R]▼●

If a Man Answers (1962) **C-102m.** **½ D: Henry Levin. Sandra Dee, Bobby Darin, Micheline Presle, John Lund, Cesar Romero, Stefanie Powers, Christopher Knight, Charlene Holt. Trite pap of Dee and Darin (then married in real life) trying to outdo each other with jealousy-baiting antics.

If Ever I See You Again (1978) **C-105m.** *½ D: Joe Brooks. Joe Brooks, Shelley Hack, Jimmy Breslin, Jerry Keller, George Plimpton, Danielle Brisebois. Producer-director-writer-composer-arranger-conductor Brooks' followup to his mediocre YOU LIGHT UP MY LIFE is even worse; this time he stars, as a songwriter trying to rekindle old flame with Hack (in her starring movie debut). Breslin should stick to his typewriter. [PG]▼

If He Hollers, Let Him Go (1968) **C-106m.** *½ D: Charles Martin. Raymond St. Jacques, Kevin McCarthy, Barbara McNair, Dana Wynter, Arthur O'Connell, John Russell, Ann Prentiss, Royal Dano. Prison escapee St. Jacques tries to clear himself of false rape-murder charge. Lots of clichés, plus McNair's celebrated nude scenes. Aka DEAD RIGHT. [R]▼

If I Had a Million (1932) **83m.** ***½ D: James Cruze, H. Bruce Humberstone, Stephen Roberts, William A. Seiter, Ernst Lubitsch, Norman Taurog, Norman Z. McLeod. Gary Cooper, George Raft, Mary Boland, Charles Laughton, W. C. Fields, Wynne Gibson, Gene Raymond, Charlie Ruggles, Alison Skipworth, Jack Oakie, Frances Dee, Richard Bennett. Wealthy Bennett gives that sum to various people to see their reactions; all the episodes are good, but the most famous are Laughton's worm-turning and Fields' revenge on road hogs.●

If I Had My Way (1940) **94m.** **½ D: David Butler. Bing Crosby, Gloria Jean, Charles Winninger, El Brendel, Allyn Joslyn, Claire Dodd. Title tune is chief asset of pleasant but standard Crosby vehicle in which he helps little Gloria find her guardian, vaudevillian Winninger.

If I'm Lucky (1946) **79m.** ** D: Lewis Seiler. Vivian Blaine, Perry Como, Harry James, Carmen Miranda, Phil Silvers, Edgar Buchanan, Reed Hadley. James' band is broke and unemployed, and becomes involved with politician Buchanan's "common man" campaign. Paper-thin remake of THANKS A MILLION, occasionally uplifted by Silvers' and Miranda's spunk.

If It's Tuesday, This Must Be Belgium (1969) **C-99m.** *** D: Mel Stuart. Suzanne Pleshette, Ian McShane, Mildred Natwick, Murray Hamilton, Sandy Baron, Michael Constantine, Norman Fell, Peggy Cass, Joan Collins. Funny study of Americans abroad on quickie tour; filmed throughout Europe. Host of cameos sprinkled throughout. Rehashed as a TV movie in 1987. [G]▼●

If I Were Free (1933) **66m.** **½ D: Elliott Nugent. Irene Dunne, Clive Brook, Nils Asther, Henry Stephenson, Vivian Tobin, Tempe Pigott, Lorraine MacLean, Laura

Hope Crews, Halliwell Hobbes. Dunne and Brook shine as lovers trying to break away from their respective failing marriages. First-rate cast and production do wonders with tearjerker material.

If I Were King (1938) **101m.** *** D: Frank Lloyd. Ronald Colman, Frances Dee, Basil Rathbone, Ellen Drew, C. V. France, Henry Wilcoxon, Heather Thatcher, Sidney Toler. Colman (with that inimitable voice) is ideally cast as the French poet-rogue François Villon, who matches wits with the crafty King Louis XI (Rathbone) and falls hopelessly in love with a lady-in-waiting (Dee). Forget historical accuracy; this is just good entertainment. Scripted by Preston Sturges. Filmed before in 1920 and, as the operetta THE VAGABOND KING, in 1930 and again in 1956. Villon was also played by John Barrymore in THE BELOVED ROGUE (1927).▼

If I Were Rich SEE: **Cash**

If Looks Could Kill (1991) **C-88m.** ** D: William Dear. Richard Grieco, Linda Hunt, Roger Rees, Robin Bartlett, Gabrielle Anwar, Geraldine James, Carole Davis, Roger Daltrey. Class clown is mistaken for a top undercover agent while touring Paris with his high school class; standard flunk-out slapstick ensues. Negligible, though Hunt adds a touch of class as a whip-wielding villainess. [PG-13]▼●

If Lucy Fell (1996) **C-94m.** *½ D: Eric Schaeffer. Sarah Jessica Parker, Eric Schaeffer, Ben Stiller, Elle Macpherson, James Rebhorn, Robert John Burke, David Thornton, Dominic Chianese, Mujibur Rahman, Sirajul Islam. Puerile "romantic comedy," with writer-director Schaeffer playing an artist of arrested emotional development who shares an apartment with Parker, a therapist (!) with whom he also shares a "death pact," if neither one has found the perfect mate by the age of 30. Any resemblance between these characters and actual human beings is strictly coincidental. Schaeffer isn't dumb, however; he wrote himself a makeout scene with supermodel Macpherson. [R]▼●

I Found Stella Parish (1935) **84m.** ** D: Mervyn LeRoy. Kay Francis, Ian Hunter, Paul Lukas, Sybil Jason, Jessie Ralph, Barton MacLane. Shady actress with a past (Francis) comes to U.S. with her daughter (Jason) hoping for a quiet future; mild soaper.

I. F. Stone's Weekly (1973) **62m.** ***½ D: Jerry Bruck, Jr. Loving, concise documentary of the maverick Washington journalist is often funny and always moving. Narrated by Tom Wicker.

If These Walls Could Talk (1996) **C-100m. TVM** D: Nancy Savoca, Cher. Demi Moore, Shirley Knight, Kevin Cooney, CCH Pounder, Sissy Spacek, Xander Berkeley, Joanna Gleason, Hedy Burress, Diana Scarwid, Lindsay Crouse, Anne Heche, Eileen Brennan, Jada Pinkett, Craig T. Nelson, Cher. Strong abortion-themed trilogy about three women (coexecutive producer Moore in the '50s, Spacek in the '70s, Heche in the '90s) and the ways they deal with unplanned pregnancies in different social and political climates. Cher made her directing debut with the third tale and turns up in a red wig as an abortion clinic doctor. Nancy Savoca, director of the first two stories, wrote or cowrote all three. Above average.▼

If This Be Sin (1949-British) **98m.** ** D: Gregory Ratoff. Roger Livesey, Myrna Loy, Peggy Cummins, Richard Greene, Elizabeth Allan. Maudlin multi-love-affair story set on isle of Capri. Original British title: THAT DANGEROUS AGE.

If Winter Comes (1947) **97m.** ** D: Victor Saville. Walter Pidgeon, Deborah Kerr, Angela Lansbury, Binnie Barnes, Janet Leigh, Dame May Whitty, Reginald Owen. Good cast fails to enliven wooden drama of young man who finds happiness following code of honor; set in England.

If You Could Only Cook (1935) **70m.** *** D: William A. Seiter. Herbert Marshall, Jean Arthur, Leo Carrillo, Lionel Stander, Alan Edwards. Arthur and Marshall are superb team in this delightful comedy of wealthy automobile tycoon/inventor and penniless woman, who, for complex reasons, become mobster Carrillo's maid and butler. This film wrongly carried Frank Capra's name as director in many European prints as a fraudulent studio effort to exploit his massive popularity.

If You Could See What I Hear (1982-Canadian) **C-103m.** ** D: Eric Till. Marc Singer, R. H. Thompson, Sarah Torgov, Shari Belafonte Harper, Douglas Campbell, Helen Burns. Well-intentioned but overly cute, ultimately unreal biography of Tom Sullivan (Singer), the writer, composer, athlete, TV personality and Renaissance man who happens to be blind. [PG]▼●

If You Knew Susie (1948) **90m.** **½ D: Gordon Douglas. Eddie Cantor, Joan Davis, Allyn Joslyn, Charles Dingle. Weak film of show biz couple is a delight for Cantor-Davis fans but pointless for others.▼

I Got the Hook Up (1998) **C-93m.** BOMB D: Michael Martin. Master P, A.J. Johnson, Gretchen Palmer, Tommy "Tiny" Lister, Helen Martin, John Witherspoon, Ice Cube, Mia X, Snoop Doggy Dogg. Witless, seemingly interminable blaxploitation comedy about a couple of South Central L.A. con artists who hoodwink the whole hood when they get their hands on a truckload of "hot" beepers and cell phones. Dopey vehicle for rapper/producer Master P, and an unremarkable feature debut for R&B video director Martin. Makes FRIDAY look like RASHOMON. [R]▼●

I Hate Actors (1986-French) **C/B&W-90m.** **½ D: Gerard Krawrzyk. Jean Poiret, Michel Blanc, Bernard Blier, Michel Galabru, Guy Marchand, Dominique Lavanant. Cute, slight little satire on Hollywood, with a series of murders comically disrupting the filming of a costume epic; agent Poiret is the prime suspect. Based on a novel by Ben Hecht and filmed mostly in beautiful black-and-white; set in Tinseltown, yet all of the dialogue's in French. Look very carefully for Gérard Depardieu. [PG]

I Hate Blondes (1981-Italian) **C-89m.** *** D: Giorgio Capitani. Enrico Montesano, Jean Rochefort, Corinne Clery, Marina Langner, Paola Tedesco, Ivan Desny. Funny comedy about ghostwriter Montesano, whose work inspires a series of real-life heists. Crammed with sight gags; highlighted by a sequence in which Montesano searches for stolen jewels at a party. ▼

I Hate Your Guts! SEE: **Intruder, The** (1961)

I Have Seven Daughters SEE: **My Seven Little Sins**

I, Jane Doe (1948) **85m.** *½ D: John H. Auer. Ruth Hussey, John Carroll, Vera Ralston, Gene Lockhart, John Howard, John Litel. Ludicrous courtroom "drama" of murderess Ralston, with the victim's wife (Hussey) defending her.

Ikarie XB1 SEE: **Voyage to the End of the Universe**

I Killed Rasputin (1967-French-Italian) **C-95m.** *½ D: Robert Hossein. Gert Frobe, Peter McEnery, Geraldine Chaplin, Robert Hossein, Ira Furstenberg, Ivan Desny. Well-mounted but ponderous story of the man who befriended and then murdered Rasputin; Frobe is simply awful. Franscope. ▼

Ikiru (1952-Japanese) **143m.** **** D: Akira Kurosawa. Takashi Shimura, Nobuo Kaneko, Kyoko Seki, Miki Odagiri, Yunosuke Ito. Minor bureaucrat Shimura, dying of cancer, searches for meaning in his life. Thoughtful, poignant examination of loneliness, with a brilliant performance by Shimura. ▼●

I Know What You Did Last Summer (1997) **C-100m.** ** D: Jim Gillespie. Jennifer Love Hewitt, Sarah Michelle Gellar, Ryan Phillippe, Freddie Prinze, Jr., Johnny Galecki, Bridgette Wilson, Anne Heche, Muse Watson. In coastal North Carolina, four friends, just graduating from high school, accidentally run down a pedestrian on a lonely road. They dump the body into the sea and vow never to mention it again. But a year later, they each begin receiving the title message in the mail, and then the murders begin. . . . Tame horror film has a few effective scares, and Hewitt is good, but scripter Kevin Williamson's attempt at a SCREAM follow-up is too routine to succeed overall. Followed by I STILL KNOW WHAT YOU DID LAST SUMMER. Panavision. [R] ▼●◗

I Know Where I'm Going! (1945-British) **91m.** **** D: Michael Powell, Emeric Pressburger. Wendy Hiller, Roger Livesey, Finlay Currie, Pamela Brown, Valentine Dyall, Petula Clark. Simple film of headstrong girl (Hiller) who plans to marry for money, stranded in Scottish seacoast town for a week, where she meets and slowly falls in love with Livesey. Very little plot, but an abundance of charm and wit. A quiet gem. Beautifully scripted by the filmmakers. ▼●

I Know Why the Caged Bird Sings (1979) **C-100m. TVM** D: Fielder Cook. Diahann Carroll, Ruby Dee, Paul Benjamin, Roger E. Mosley, Esther Rolle, Madge Sinclair, Constance Good, Art Evans. Black writer Maya Angelou's remembrances of her childhood in the Depression-era South. Good is more than good as young Maya and Rolle is a tower of strength as the grandmother who raises her. Scripted by Leonora Thuna, Ralph B. Woolsey, and Angelou, from her book. Above average. ▼

Il Bell' Antonio SEE: **Bell' Antonio**

Il Bidone SEE: **Swindle, The**

Il Grido (1957-Italian) **115m.** **½ D: Michelangelo Antonioni. Steve Cochran, Alida Valli, Dorian Gray, Betsy Blair, Lyn Shaw. Leisurely paced yet compelling study of Cochran's mental disintegration due to lack of communication with those he loves; Cochran is quite good. Aka THE OUTCRY. ▼

I Like It Like That (1994) **C-105m.** *** D: Darnell Martin. Lauren Velez, Jon Seda, Tomas Melly, Desiree Casado, Isaiah Garcia, Jesse Borrego, Lisa Vidal, Griffin Dunne, Rita Moreno. Fresh, vibrant little film about a Latino woman from the Bronx whose tumultuous, love/hate relationship with her husband and three kids is rocked when she stumbles into a job—an exciting one, no less—in the record business. Writer-director Darnell Martin examines real, everyday issues with zest, humor, and the ring of truth. [R] ▼●

I Like Money (1960-British) **C-97m.** **½ D: Peter Sellers. Peter Sellers, Nadia Gray, Herbert Lom, Leo McKern, Martita Hunt, John Neville, Michael Gough, Billie Whitelaw. Subdued satirical remake of TOPAZE, with Sellers the timid schoolteacher who becomes an unscrupulous businessman. British title: TOPAZE. CinemaScope.

I Like Your Nerve (1931) **69m.** *½ D: William McGann. Douglas Fairbanks, Jr., Loretta Young, Henry Kolker, Edmund Breon, Boris Karloff. Devil-may-care Fairbanks breezes into Latin country and sets his sights on Loretta—even though she's engaged. Tiresome comic romance. Karloff has tiny role as a butler named Luigi!

I Live for Love (1935) **64m.** **½ D: Busby Berkeley. Dolores Del Rio, Everett

Marshall, Guy Kibbee, Allen Jenkins, Berton Churchill. Lesser Berkeley musical concerns backstage romance between Del Rio and Marshall. A couple of OK songs, but unfortunately no dancing.

I Live My Life (1935) **92m.** ** D: W. S. Van Dyke II. Joan Crawford, Brian Aherne, Frank Morgan, Aline MacMahon, Eric Blore, Fred Keating, Jessie Ralph, Arthur Treacher, Frank Conroy, Sterling Holloway, Vince Barnett, Hedda Hopper, Lionel Stander. Crawford and Aherne are in love, but she's flighty and he's an archeologist. Glossy and empty. Scripted by Joseph L. Mankiewicz.▼

Il Ladro di Bambini SEE: **Stolen Children**

I'll Be Home for Christmas (1998) **C-86m.** **½ D: Arlene Sanford. Jonathan Taylor Thomas, Jessica Biel, Adam LaVorgna, Sean O'Bryan, Gary Cole, Kathleen Freeman, Amzie Strickland. Conniving college kid tries to make his way cross-country to be home for Christmas dinner, only because his dad has promised him a Porsche if he does. Fairly predictable boy-gets-girl, boy-loses-girl, boy-gets-girl-again-and-learns-a-lesson comedy aimed at young fans of the teenage star. [PG]▼●◗

I'll Be Seeing You (1944) **85m.** **½ D: William Dieterle. Ginger Rogers, Joseph Cotten, Shirley Temple, Spring Byington, Tom Tully, John Derek. Overblown David Selznick schmaltz. Rogers, convict home on parole, meets disturbed soldier Cotten; they fall in love.

I'll Be Yours (1947) **93m.** **½ D: William A. Seiter. Deanna Durbin, Tom Drake, Adolphe Menjou, William Bendix, Franklin Pangborn. Pleasant but undistinguished remake of THE GOOD FAIRY with Deanna in hot water after telling white lie to wealthy and amorous Menjou.▼

I'll Cry Tomorrow (1955) **117m.** ***½ D: Daniel Mann. Susan Hayward, Richard Conte, Jo Van Fleet, Ray Danton, Eddie Albert, Margo. Superlative portrayal by Hayward of star Lillian Roth, her assorted marriages and alcoholic problems. Everything a movie biography should be. Helen Rose won an Oscar for her costumes. Also shown in computer-colored version. ▼●

I'll Do Anything (1994) **C-115m.** ** D: James L. Brooks. Nick Nolte, Albert Brooks, Julie Kavner, Joely Richardson, Tracey Ullman, Whittni Wright, Jeb Brown, Joely Fisher, Ian McKellen, Suzzanne Douglas, Robert Joy, Harry Shearer, Rosie O'Donnell, Ken Page, Woody Harrelson, Patrick Cassidy, Anne Heche. Self-absorbed actor whose career is on the ropes is suddenly forced to care for his six-year-old daughter. Writer-director Brooks tries to weave a tale of fatherhood into a cutting look behind the scenes of Hollywood, with discouragingly spotty results. Some great "in" material shares screen time with an array of truly dislikeable characters. Kavner and Albert Brooks come off best, as a neurotic match made in heaven. This is the notorious movie that was shot as a musical, before test screenings indicated all the musical numbers should come out! [PG-13]▼●

Illegal (1955) **88m.** **½ D: Lewis Allen. Edward G. Robinson, Nina Foch, Hugh Marlowe, Jayne Mansfield, Albert Dekker, Ellen Corby, DeForest Kelley, Howard St. John. Former D.A. Robinson becomes criminal attorney with gangster client, but lays reputation—and life—on the line to defend former assistant Foch for homicide. Valiant attempt to recapture spark of earlier Robinson vehicles; remake of THE MOUTHPIECE.▼

Illegal Entry (1949) **84m.** **½ D: Frederick de Cordova. Howard Duff, Marta Toren, George Brent, Gar Moore. Harsh narrative of federal agent assigned to uncover smuggling racket.

Illegal in Blue (1994) **C-94m.** **½ D: Stu Segall. Stacey Dash, Dan Gauthier, Louis Giambalvo, Trevor Goddard, Michael Durrell, Sandra Reinhardt, David Groh, Raye Birk. Cop Gauthier, on leave without pay after turning in some crooked coworkers, becomes involved with a sultry nightclub singer (Dash) who may or may not have murdered her husband. Atmospheric 1990s film noir is occasionally illogical but fun nonetheless, and quite sexy. Available on video in R and unrated versions. [R]▼

Illegally Yours (1988) **C-102m.** BOMB D: Peter Bogdanovich. Rob Lowe, Colleen Camp, Harry Carey, Jr., Kenneth Mars, Kim Myers. Juror Lowe is shocked to see that defendant Camp was once the girl he lusted for in elementary school, and snoops around on his own to clear her of the charge. Barely released, painfully unfunny farce, with Bogdanovich still trying to emulate Howard Hawks; how bizarre to see pratfalling Lowe (in glasses) aping Ryan O'Neal in WHAT'S UP DOC?—who, in turn, was aping Cary Grant in BRINGING UP BABY. [PG]▼

I'll Get By (1950) **C-83m.** **½ D: Richard Sale. June Haver, William Lundigan, Gloria DeHaven, Dennis Day, Thelma Ritter. Remake of TIN PAN ALLEY, involving songwriter and his girlfriend; Jeanne Crain, Victor Mature and Dan Dailey make guest appearances.

I'll Get You (1953-British) **79m.** ** D: Seymour Friedman, Peter Graham Scott. George Raft, Sally Gray, Clifford Evans, Reginald Tate, Patricia Laffan. OK gangster yarn of Raft (FBI man) and Gray (British Intelligence) cracking a kidnapping syndicate. Originally titled ESCAPE ROUTE.

I'll Give a Million (1938) **72m.** ** D: Walter Lang. Warner Baxter, Lynn Bari, Jean Hersholt, John Carradine, Peter Lorre. Amusing little idyll of rumor that an eccentric millionaire is posing as a hobo, causing droll results.

Illicit (1931) **81m.** *½ D: Archie Mayo. Barbara Stanwyck, James Rennie, Ricardo Cortez, Joan Blondell, Charles Butterworth, Natalie Moorhead. Independent-minded Stanwyck loves Rennie, but doesn't want marriage to taint her happiness. Boring, badly directed, overly talky "talkie." Remade two years later as EX-LADY.▼

Illicit Interlude (1951-Swedish) **94m.** **½ D: Ingmar Bergman. Maj-Britt Nilsson, Alf Kjellin, Birger Malmsten, Georg Funkquist. Moody film using flashback retells Britt-Nilsson's romance with now-dead lover, and its relationship to her present frame of mind. Original title: SUMMERPLAY; video title: SUMMER INTERLUDE.▼

Ill Met By Moonlight SEE: **Night Ambush**

I'll Never Forget What's 'is Name (1967-British) **C-99m.** ***½ D: Michael Winner. Orson Welles, Oliver Reed, Carol White, Harry Andrews, Michael Hordern, Wendy Craig, Marianne Faithfull, Peter Graves, Frank Finlay, Edward Fox. Excellent comedy-drama in which one man rebels against his good life and tries vainly to go back to simpler days. Script by Peter Draper.▼◗

I'll Never Forget You (1951) **C-90m.** **½ D: Roy (Ward) Baker. Tyrone Power, Ann Blyth, Michael Rennie, Dennis Price, Beatrice Campbell. American (Power) working in London is transported back to 18th century, where he falls in love with Blyth. Remake of BERKELEY SQUARE. Opens in b&w, switches to color.

I'll Remember April (1945) **63m.** *½ D: Harold Young. Gloria Jean, Kirby Grant, Samuel S. Hinds, Milburn Stone, Addison Richards, Mary Forbes. Jean lacks verve as goodie-goodie vocalist out to solve crime for which Dad was blamed.

I'll See You in My Dreams (1951) **110m.** **½ D: Michael Curtiz. Doris Day, Danny Thomas, Frank Lovejoy, Patrice Wymore, James Gleason. Warner Bros. formula musical biography at its hokiest: trite telling of Gus Kahn's life and times; songs include "Ain't We Got Fun," "It Had to Be You."▼●

I'll Take Romance (1937) **85m.** **½ D: Edward H. Griffith. Grace Moore, Melvyn Douglas, Stuart Erwin, Helen Westley, Margaret Hamilton. Silly story of opera star Moore kidnapped by agent Douglas has lovely title tune, operatic arias to keep it moving along.

I'll Take Sweden (1965) **C-96m.** ** D: Frederick de Cordova. Bob Hope, Dina Merrill, Tuesday Weld, Frankie Avalon, Jeremy Slate. Pseudo-sexy Hope vehicle, with everyone frantic over life and love; witless proceedings.▼

I'll Tell the World (1945) **61m.** ** D: Leslie Goodwins. Lee Tracy, Brenda Joyce, Raymond Walburn, June Preisser, Thomas Gomez, Howard Freeman, Lorin Raker. Minor comedy with idea-man Tracy saving Walburn's failing radio station.

illtown (1998) **C-97m.** *½ D: Nick Gomez. Michael Rapaport, Lili Taylor, Adam Trese, Kevin Corrigan, Paul Schulze, Angela Featherstone, Saul Stein, Tony Danza, Isaac Hayes. Good cast flounders in this downer of a drama about drug dealers Rapaport, Taylor, and Corrigan—they're the good guys—and a vengeance-seeking ex-partner (Trese) who's just been released from jail. Pretentious, boring, and crammed with fuzzy moralizing. Of note for Danza's offbeat casting as a gay crimelord. Filmed in 1995. [R]▼●

Illuminata (1999) **C-111m.** ** D: John Turturro. John Turturro, Katherine Borowitz, Susan Sarandon, Christopher Walken, Rufus Sewell, Beverly D'Angelo, Donal McCann, Georgina Cates, Ben Gazzara, Aida Turturro. Life, love, lust, and ambition in a theatrical troupe in turn-of-the-20th-century N.Y.C. (although the flavor is distinctly European). Playwright Turturro is in love with the company's star/manager, and longs to have her perform his latest play. Lively, even campy, roles for a fine cast spark this good-looking but often lumbering production, which plays like a French farce in slow motion. Turturro coscripted with Brandon Cole, based on the latter's play. [R]▼◗

Illusion Travels by Streetcar (1953-Mexican) **90m.** **½ D: Luis Buñuel. Lilia Prado, Carlos Navarro, Domingo Soler, Fernando Soto, Agustin Isunza. Two transit workers steal a streetcar destined for the scrap heap, take it on one last run, picking up odd assortment of passengers. Agreeable (if lesser) Buñuel fable.▼

Illustrated Man, The (1969) **C-103m.** ** D: Jack Smight. Rod Steiger, Claire Bloom, Robert Drivas, Don Dubbins, Jason Evers, Tim Weldon, Christie Matchett. Young wanderer Drivas meets tattooed man Steiger, searching for the strange woman (Bloom), who "illustrated" his entire body. The wanderer sees futuristic stories in three of the illustrations, all of which also star Steiger and/or Bloom and Drivas. Disappointing, slow-paced adaptation of stories from Ray Bradbury's well-regarded collection. A few good moments but weak overall. Panavision. [M/PG]▼●

I Love a Bandleader (1945) **70m.** ** D: Del Lord. Phil Harris, Leslie Brooks, Walter Catlett, Eddie Anderson, Frank Sully, Pierre Watkin. Formula claptrap about meek Harris who becomes a swinging bandleader; actors' natural abilities rise above material.

I Love a Mystery (1945) **70m.** **½ D: Henry Levin. Jim Bannon, Nina Foch, George Macready, Barton Yarborough, Carole Mathews, Lester Matthews. Bizarre, entertaining whodunit based on popular radio show, with Bannon as Jack Packard, Yarborough as Doc Young. This one involves strange Oriental cult, and a prophecy of doom for bewildered Macready. First in a short-lived series.

I Love a Soldier (1944) **106m.** ** D: Mark Sandrich. Paulette Goddard, Sonny Tufts, Beulah Bondi, Mary Treen, Barry Fitzgerald. Reteaming of Goddard and Tufts after their hit in SO PROUDLY WE HAIL! doesn't match original; story examines problems of wartime marriages.

I Loved a Woman (1933) **91m.** BOMB D: Alfred E. Green. Edward G. Robinson, Kay Francis, Genevieve Tobin, J. Farrell MacDonald, Robert Barrat. Robinson plays meat-packing plant owner whose life is destroyed by enticing, ambitious opera singer Francis. Absurd story moves like molasses; dialogue is good only for (unintended) laughs.

I Love Melvin (1953) **C-76m.** **½ D: Don Weis. Donald O'Connor, Debbie Reynolds, Una Merkel, Allyn Joslyn, Jim Backus, Richard Anderson, Noreen Corcoran. Cute musical comedy. O'Connor tries to get to first base with Reynolds by pretending he can get her picture on the cover of *Look* magazine.▼●

I Love My . . . Wife (1970) **C-95m.** ** D: Mel Stuart. Elliott Gould, Brenda Vaccaro, Angel Tompkins, Dabney Coleman, Joan Tompkins. The kind of comedy for which the word "vehicle" was invented. Rarely funny chronicle of Gould's lifelong sexual hangups suffers from witless script, bland direction. [R]▼

I Love Trouble (1948) **94m.** *** D: S. Sylvan Simon. Franchot Tone, Janet Blair, Janis Carter, Adele Jergens, Glenda Farrell. Flippant mystery with private-eye Tone romancing Blair while searching for her missing sister-in-law.

I Love Trouble (1994) **C-123m.** **½ D: Charles Shyer. Julia Roberts, Nick Nolte, Saul Rubinek, James Rebhorn, Robert Loggia, Kelly Rutherford, Olympia Dukakis, Marsha Mason, Eugene Levy, Charles Martin Smith, Dan Butler, Paul Gleason, Nora Dunn, Keith Gordon, Dorothy Lyman, Stuart Pankin, Megan Cavanagh, Jessica Lundy, Robin Duke. Rival Chicago newspaper reporters reluctantly join forces to investigate a mysterious train wreck—and, naturally, fall in love. A likable homage to vintage Hollywood bickering/bantering romantic comedies with a touch of adventure and suspense thrown in; there are even old-fashioned "wipes" between shots. Unfortunately, the film's overlength hampers its cuteness, and reveals the degree of contrivance at work. [PG]▼●◗

I Love You (1981-Brazilian) **C-104m.** *½ D: Arnaldo Jabor. Sonia Braga, Paulo Cesar Pereio, Vera Fischer, Tarcisio Meira, Maria Lucia Dahl, Regina Case. Silly, pretentiously arty chronicle of relationship between Braga and Pereio, each of whom tries to manipulate the other. Sonia, however, is lovely to look at. [R]▼

I Love You Again (1940) **99m.** ***½ D: W. S. Van Dyke II. William Powell, Myrna Loy, Frank McHugh, Edmund Lowe, Donald Douglas, Nella Walker. Hilarious story of amnesiac Powell—solid citizen in a small town—reverting to former life as con-man, but trying to forestall divorce proceedings by "his" wife (Loy). Ingenious script by Charles Lederer, George Oppenheimer and Harry Kurnitz.▼●

I Love You, Alice B. Toklas (1968) **C-93m.** ***½ D: Hy Averback. Peter Sellers, Jo Van Fleet, Leigh Taylor-Young, Joyce Van Patten. Excellent comedy about the freaking out of mild-mannered L.A. lawyer. Sellers has never been better. Written by Larry Tucker and Paul Mazursky. [R]▼●

I Love You, I Love You Not (1979) SEE: **Together?**

I Love You, I Love You Not (1996-French-German-British-U.S.) **C-92m.** ** D: Billy Hopkins. Jeanne Moreau, Claire Danes, Jude Law, James Van Der Beek, Kris Park, Lauren Fox, Emily Burkes-Nossiter, Robert Sean Leonard, Julia Stiles. Disappointingly overwrought drama about a shy teen (Danes) who attends a Manhattan prep school; she has a crush on the school hunk (Law), and encounters anti-Semitism when her classmates learn that her beloved grandmother (the ever-resplendent Moreau) is a Holocaust survivor. Scripted by Wendy Kesselman, based on her play; Danes also plays the grandmother (as a young woman) in the Holocaust sequences.▼●◗

I Love, You Love (1961-Italian) **C-84m.** **½ D: Alessandro Blasetti. Marny Trio, Fattini and Cairoli, Don Yada's Japanese Dance Troupe, The Benitez Sisters. Documentary-style survey of love in various capitals of the world, occasionally spiced by imaginative use of footage. Ultrascope.

I Love You to Death (1990) **C-96m.** **½ D: Lawrence Kasdan. Kevin Kline, Tracey Ullman, Joan Plowright, River Phoenix, William Hurt, Keanu Reeves, James Gammon, Victoria Jackson, Miriam Margolyes, Heather Graham. Lumpy black comedy about a gregarious Italian-American pizzeria owner whose constant womanizing remains a secret to his wife—until one day when she learns the truth, and then attempts to murder him, with spectacular lack of success. Kline is fun, Plowright is hilarious as his mordant, Slavic mother-in-law, but unfortunately, the film goes flat. Director Kasdan plays a lawyer in the closing scenes; Kline's real-life wife, Phoebe Cates, has an unbilled part as one of his one-night stands. Amazingly, based on a real-life couple! [R]▼●

Il Postino SEE: **Postman, The** ▼●

I, Madman (1989) **C-89m.** **½ D: Tibor Takacs. Jenny Wright, Clayton Rohner, Randall William Cook, Steven Memel, Stephanie Hodge. A young woman's reading of a novel brings its murderous, supernatural author back to life. A nice, small surprise: the story is imaginative, scary and funny, the effects are clever, and the cast above average; there's also a wow of an ending. If it had only made *sense* . . . [R]▼●

Image, The (1990) **C-110m. TVM** D: Peter Werner. Albert Finney, John Mahoney, Kathy Baker, Swoosie Kurtz, Marsha Mason, Spalding Gray. In this first cousin to NETWORK, a top TV news anchorman (Finney) chases the ratings at all costs, until a falling out with his longtime pal and a Savings & Loan scandal bring him disillusionment. Provocative, well-acted, but ultimately empty. Made for cable. Average. [R]▼

Imagemaker, The (1986) **C-93m.** ** D: Hal Wiener. Michael Nouri, Jerry Orbach, Jessica Harper, Anne Twomey, Farley Granger, Maury Povich, Marcia Gay Harden. The President's ex-media adviser, still reeling from his wife's death, has an audio tape that could incriminate his former boss; genuine or bogus, people are literally dying to get their hands on it. A muddled mess, though a sometimes entertaining one; high point is a hilariously melodramatic scene on a Washington talk show. Twomey good as an ambitious TV news reporter. [R]▼

Images (1972-U.S.-British) **C-101m.** ***½ D: Robert Altman. Susannah York, Rene Auberjonois, Marcel Bozzuffi, Hugh Millais, Cathryn Harrison. Difficult but fascinating film about a troubled woman who tries to sort out her life; images of reality and fantasy clash in a kind of continuous hallucination. Off-putting at first, but worth the effort to hang on. Filmed in Ireland. Panavision. [R]

Imaginary Crimes (1994) **C-105m.** **½ D: Anthony Drazan. Harvey Keitel, Fairuza Balk, Kelly Lynch, Vincent D'Onofrio, Elisabeth Moss, Diane Baker, Chris Penn, Amber Benson, Seymour Cassel, Annette O'Toole. Thoughtful, moving (if ultimately overly familiar) coming-of-age story with Keitel doing well as a hustler-dreamer who tries to be the best father he can to his two motherless daughters: drab 17-year-old Balk and younger sister Moss. Lynch shines in her few flashback scenes as the family's deceased wife-mother. [PG]▼●

Imagine: John Lennon (1988) **C-103m.** **½ D: Andrew Solt. Narrated by John Lennon. Unusual documentary, produced by Solt and David L. Wolper, assembled from 240 hours of footage from Yoko Ono's personal archives. Not exactly a puff job, but a bit discomforting given the obvious calculation that went into the project. Not to be missed are Lennon's confrontations with Al Capp and journalist Gloria Emerson. [R]▼●

I'm All Right Jack (1959-British) **104m.** ***½ D: John Boulting. Ian Carmichael, Terry-Thomas, Peter Sellers, Richard Attenborough, Margaret Rutherford, Dennis Price, Irene Handl, Miles Malleson. Carmichael works for his uncle and unwittingly upsets an elaborate and crooked business scheme in this memorable comedy. Sellers wonderful as labor leader. Scripted by Frank Harvey, John Boulting, and Alan Hackney, from Hackney's novel *Private Life*. Sequel to PRIVATE'S PROGRESS. Produced by Roy Boulting.▼

I Married a Communist (1950) **73m.** ** D: Robert Stevenson. Laraine Day, Robert Ryan, John Agar, Thomas Gomez, Janis Carter, Richard Rober, William Talman. Cornball acting and a "better-dead-than-Red" scenario sink this noirish melodrama, which has become a relic of its era. Ryan is a shipping executive and former political radical whose past comes back to haunt him. The "commies" (headed by Gomez) are depicted as two-bit gangsters, but Talman is especially good as a killer-for-hire. Retitled WOMAN ON PIER 13.

I Married a Monster from Outer Space (1958) **78m.** **½ D: Gene Fowler, Jr. Tom Tryon, Gloria Talbott, Ken Lynch, John Eldredge, Jean Carson, Maxie Rosenbloom. One of the silliest titles in film history obscures pretty good little rehash of INVASION OF THE BODY SNATCHERS: Talbott notices that husband Tryon (as well as some of his friends) has been behaving very peculiarly of late. Some nice, creepy moments in chiller which has slowly developed a cult following. Remade for TV in 1998.▼●

I Married an Angel (1942) **84m.** ** D: W. S. Van Dyke II. Jeanette MacDonald, Nelson Eddy, Edward Everett Horton, Binnie Barnes, Reginald Owen, Douglass Dumbrille. Playboy Eddy dreams he marries angel MacDonald in this bizarre adaptation of Rodgers and Hart musical. MacDonald and Eddy's last film together. Songs include "Spring Is Here," title tune.▼

I Married a Shadow (1982-French) **C-110m.** *** D: Robin Davis. Nathalie Baye, Francis Huster, Richard Bohringer, Madeleine Robinson, Guy Trejan. Engrossing if sometimes overwrought drama of abandoned, pregnant Baye taking on the identity of another after a train wreck. Baye is radiant, particularly in the scenes with her newborn baby. Based on a Cornell Woolrich story previously filmed as NO MAN OF HER OWN (1950). Remade in 1996 as MRS. WINTERBOURNE. Aka I MARRIED A DEAD MAN. [PG]▼

I Married a Strange Person! (1998) **C-**

74m. **½ D: Bill Plympton. Voices of Charis Michelson, Tom Larson, Richard Spore, Toni Rossi, J. B. Adams, John Russo. Animator-director-cowriter Plympton invokes Picasso's famous quote disdaining "good taste," and follows through with this wild, freeform story of a man who acquires strange powers—and an overactive imagination—just as he embarks on married life. Brash, bizarre, full of deliberately "gross" sight gags involving body parts, and often howlingly funny . . . but not for prudish viewers. Plympton fans should revel in it.▼

I Married a Witch (1942) **76m.** *** D: René Clair. Fredric March, Veronica Lake, Robert Benchley, Susan Hayward, Cecil Kellaway, Elizabeth Patterson. Witch burned in Salem centuries ago (Lake) comes back to haunt descendants of Puritan (March) who sent her to her death. Saucy comedy-fantasy based on a story by Thorne (*Topper*) Smith. Good special effects, too.▼●

I Married a Woman (1958) **84m.** ** D: Hal Kanter. George Gobel, Diana Dors, Adolphe Menjou, Jessie Royce Landis. Lackluster events concerning harassed ad man Gobel who'd rather spend time with his gorgeous wife than overtime at the office. Look fast for young Angie Dickinson and an amusing movie-star cameo.▼●

I'm Dancing as Fast as I Can (1982) **C-107m.** **½ D: Jack Hofsiss. Jill Clayburgh, Nicol Williamson, Dianne Wiest, Daniel Stern, Joe Pesci, Geraldine Page, James Sutorius, Cordis Heard, Richard Masur, Ellen Greene, John Lithgow. Successful Valium-addicted TV documentary filmmaker Clayburgh undergoes harrowing ordeal when she quits pills cold-turkey. Searing because of subject matter, but not particularly well made; still, Clayburgh and costars are first-rate. Screenplay by David Rabe (Clayburgh's husband), based on Barbara Gordon's memoir. [R]▼●

I'm Dangerous Tonight (1990) **C-100m. TVM** D: Tobe Hooper. Anthony Perkins, Mädchen Amick, Daisy Hall, R. Lee Ermey, Natalie Schafer, Mary Frann, Dee Wallace Stone. Hooper takes a Cornel Woolrich short story about a demonic Aztec cloak passing on evil powers to whomever touches it, and (with Perkins doing another of his spooky turns) very nearly pulls this one off—but not quite. Made for cable. Average.▼

I Met Him in Paris (1937) **86m.** **½ D: Wesley Ruggles. Claudette Colbert, Melvyn Douglas, Robert Young, Lee Bowman, Mona Barrie, Fritz Feld. Prolonged romantic comedy dependent entirely on charm of its stars. Vacationing Colbert, in Paris, then Switzerland, has to choose from Bowman, Young, and Douglas (you guess who wins out).

I Met My Love Again (1938) **77m.** **½ D: Arthur Ripley, Joshua Logan. Joan Bennett, Henry Fonda, Dame May Whitty, Alan Marshal, Louise Platt, Alan Baxter, Tim Holt. Familiar soaper of young girl Bennett running off with amorous author, with tragic consequences; acting surpasses script.▼

I'm From Missouri (1939) **80m.** ** D: Theodore Reed. Bob Burns, Gladys George, Gene Lockhart, William Henry, George P. Huntley, Judith Barrett, Patricia Morison. Homespun Burns sails to England with a load of Army mules and encounters London society. Episodic, occasionally funny comedy.

I'm Gonna Git You Sucka (1988) **C-87m.** *** D: Keenen Ivory Wayans. Keenen Ivory Wayans, Bernie Casey, Antonio Fargas, Steve James, Isaac Hayes, Jim Brown, Ja'net DuBois, Dawnn Lewis, John Vernon, Clu Gulager, Kadeem Hardison, Damon Wayans, Jester Hairston, Anne Marie Johnson, Gary Owens, Eve Plumb, Clarence Williams III, David Alan Grier, Kim Wayans, Robin Harris, Chris Rock. Hip spoof of '70s blaxploitation films with Wayans (who also wrote and directed) as Jack Spade, vowing to avenge the death of his brother, who died of an o.g. (overdose of gold chains). Loose and good-natured, with some laugh out-loud gags. Jim Brown and Isaac Hayes, who made so many straight-faced films of this kind, contribute some of the funniest moments. Look for Robert Townsend in a cameo. [R]▼●

Imitation General (1958) **88m.** ** D: George Marshall. Glenn Ford, Red Buttons, Taina Elg, Dean Jones, Kent Smith, Tige Andrews. Tepid, occasionally tasteless WW2 comedy defeats its game cast. Ford is a sergeant who impersonates superior officer. CinemaScope.

Imitation of Life (1934) **109m.** **½ D: John M. Stahl. Claudette Colbert, Warren William, Rochelle Hudson, Louise Beavers, Fredi Washington, Ned Sparks, Alan Hale, Henry Armetta. Believable but dated first version of Fannie Hurst's soaper of working-girl Colbert who makes good with Beavers' pancake recipe; Washington is fine as latter's daughter who passes for white. Ultrasentimental. Adapted for the screen by Preston Sturges.▼

Imitation of Life (1959) **C-124m.** ***½ D: Douglas Sirk. Lana Turner, John Gavin, Sandra Dee, Dan O'Herlihy, Susan Kohner, Robert Alda, Juanita Moore, Mahalia Jackson, Troy Donahue, Jack Weston. Plush remake of Fannie Hurst story, with Turner as career-driven actress; Moore is the good-hearted black woman who shares her life, and whose troubled daughter (Kohner) passes for white. Fine performances and direction overcome possible soapiness to make this quite credible and moving.▼

I'm Losing You (1999) **C-100m.** **½ D:

Bruce Wagner. Frank Langella, Rosanna Arquette, Salome Jens, Andrew McCarthy, Elizabeth Perkins, Amanda Donohoe, Buck Henry, Laraine Newman, Daniel von Bargen. Interesting, adult film about a Hollywood producer who learns he's dying just as his grown children (Arquette, McCarthy) are going through crises of their own. Full of incisive vignettes, though one is left wanting to know more about some of the characters. A creditable directing debut for Wagner, who adapted his own novel. Gina Gershon appears unbilled. Executive produced by David Cronenberg. [R]▼

Immediate Family (1989) **C-95m.** ★★½ D: Jonathan Kaplan. Glenn Close, James Woods, Mary Stuart Masterson, Kevin Dillon, Linda Darlow, Jane Greer, Jessica James, Mimi Kennedy. Well-off professional marrieds yearn for a child and hook up with a pregnant, underprivileged teenager via an adoption agency. Watchable change of pace from a pair of often angst-ridden leads but more slick and rose-colored than need be. Masterson stands out in a solid acting quartet. [PG-13]▼●

Immortal Bachelor, The (1979-Italian) **C-95m.** ★★½ D: Marcello Fondato. Monica Vitti, Giancarlo Giannini, Vittorio Gassman, Claudia Cardinale, Renato Pozzetto. Cleaning woman Vitti is on trial for killing philandering husband Giannini; jury member Cardinale decides she'd prefer him to her boring husband (Gassman). Slight Neapolitan comedy, with a fine cast wasted.▼

Immortal Battalion, The SEE: **Way Ahead, The**

Immortal Beloved (1994) **C-121m.** ★★★ D: Bernard Rose. Gary Oldman, Jeroen Krabbé, Isabella Rossellini, Johanna Ter Steege, Marco Hofschneider, Miriam Margolyes, Barry Humphries, Valeria Golino, Gerard Horan, Christopher Fulford, Alexandra Pigg. Handsome, absorbing biography is told in picture-puzzle style, as Beethoven's most ardent admirer and confidant (Krabbé) tries to learn the identity of the composer's "immortal beloved," addressed in a passionate letter found after his death. Filmed in and around Prague, it's a sumptuous-looking and sumptuous-*sounding* tale (with Beethoven's music performed by Sir Georg Solti and the London Symphony) but apparently takes as many liberties with the facts as those corny Hollywood composer biopics of yore. Oldman is an ideal choice for the leading role. The director also scripted. Panavision. [R]▼●◗

Immortal Monster, The SEE: **Caltiki, The Immortal Monster**

Immortal Sergeant, The (1943) **91m.** ★★½ D: John M. Stahl. Henry Fonda, Maureen O'Hara, Thomas Mitchell, Allyn Joslyn, Reginald Gardiner, Melville Cooper. OK wartime drama of inexperienced corporal (Fonda) who is forced to take command of patrol in Africa after sergeant dies.▼

Immortal Story, The (1968-French) **C-63m.** ★★★ D: Orson Welles. Orson Welles, Jeanne Moreau, Roger Coggio, Norman Eshley, Fernando Rey. Intriguing tale (from an Isak Dinesen story) about a morally bankrupt merchant (Welles) who contrives to make a myth about a sailor seducing a wealthy man's wife come true. Generally well done and, at times, dazzling; originally made for French television. ▼

I'm No Angel (1933) **87m.** ★★★½ D: Wesley Ruggles. Mae West, Cary Grant, Edward Arnold, Gertrude Michael, Kent Taylor. West in rare form as star of Arnold's sideshow who chases after playboy Grant; Mae's courtroom plea caps it.▼●◗

I'm Not Rappaport (1996) **C-136m.** ★★½ D: Herb Gardner. Walter Matthau, Ossie Davis, Amy Irving, Martha Plimpton, Craig T. Nelson, Guillermo Diaz, Boyd Gaines, Ron Rifkin, Irwin Corey. Too long—and too literal—adaptation of Gardner's 1986 Tony Award–winning Broadway play about a pair of old codgers who develop an adversarial friendship in Central Park. Strong performances by Matthau, as an aged radical and congenital tale-spinner, and Davis, as a nearly blind building superintendent just trying to hang on. The characters are so good and so likable that they almost overcome the silliness of the climactic sequence (standing up to drug pusher Nelson) . . . but not quite. [PG-13]▼●

I, Mobster (1958) **80m.** ★★½ D: Roger Corman. Steve Cochran, Lita Milan, Robert Strauss, Celia Lovsky. Rugged account of gangster Cochran and events in his crime-filled life. CinemaScope.▼

I, Monster (1971-British) **C-74m.** ★★ D: Stephen Weeks. Christopher Lee, Peter Cushing, Mike Raven, Richard Hurndall, George Merritt, Kenneth J. Warren. Good, atmospheric production and ensemble performances cannot completely redeem boring adaptation of Stevenson's *Dr. Jekyll and Mr. Hyde*. This time, early student of Freud develops serum to relieve human inhibitions. Film was intended to be shown in 3-D, which explains some of the unusual camera shots. [PG]

Impact (1949) **111m.** ★★★ D: Arthur Lubin. Brian Donlevy, Ella Raines, Helen Walker, Charles Coburn, Anna May Wong, Robert Warwick, Mae Marsh. Nice-guy Donlevy's wife is cheating on him. She and her lover plot to do him in . . . but there are complications. Entertaining, thoughtful drama will keep you guessing at every turn.▼◗

Impasse (1969) **C-100m.** ★★½ D: Richard Benedict. Burt Reynolds, Anne Francis, Vic Diaz, Jeff Corey, Lyle Bettger, Rodolfo Acosta. OK actioner with Reynolds and pals seeking out a cache of gold bullion on Corregidor. [M]

Impatient Years, The (1944) **91m.** **½ D: Irving Cummings. Jean Arthur, Lee Bowman, Charles Coburn, Edgar Buchanan, Harry Davenport, Grant Mitchell, Jane Darwell. Thin comedy of soldier Bowman returning to civilian life with wife Arthur, finding trouble readjusting.

Imperative (1982-German) **C/B&W-96m.** *** D: Krzysztof Zanussi. Robert Powell, Brigitte Fossey, Leslie Caron, Sigfrit Steiner, Matthias Habich. Unusual, intense chronicle of math professor Powell's attempt to find spiritual understanding. Occasionally overdone but still provocative and worthwhile.

Imperfect Lady, The (1947) **97m.** ** D: Lewis Allen. Teresa Wright, Ray Milland, Cedric Hardwicke, Virginia Field, Anthony Quinn, Reginald Owen. Undistinguished drama of Parliament member falling in love with ballerina in London during 1890s.

Imperial Venus (1962-French-Italian) **C-120m.** ** D: Jean Delannoy. Gina Lollobrigida, Stephen Boyd, Raymond Pellegrin, Micheline Presle, Gabriele Ferzetti, Massimo Girotti. Lumpy spectacle about how Paolina Bonaparte, Napoleon's hot-blooded sister, spread her charms around practically his entire army in her lust for power. Super Technirama 70.▼

Impersonator, The (1961-British) **64m.** ** D: Alfred Shaughnessy. John Crawford, Jane Griffiths, Patricia Burke, John Salew, Yvonne Ball. Satisfactory chiller programmer of murder in a small village, with Crawford trying to clear himself; offbeat climax.

Importance of Being Earnest, The (1952-British) **C-95m.** *** D: Anthony Asquith. Michael Redgrave, Michael Denison, Richard Wattis, Edith Evans, Margaret Rutherford, Joan Greenwood, Dorothy Tutin. Oscar Wilde's peerless comedy of manners set in Victorian England is given admirable treatment by most able cast.▼●

Impossible Object SEE: **Story of a Love Story**

Impossible Spy, The (1987-U.S.-British) **C-96m. TVM** D: Jim Goddard. John Shea, Eli Wallach, Michal Bat-Adam, Rami Danon, Sasson Gabay, Chaim Girafi. Absorbing spy thriller about Elie Cohen, an Egyptian-born Israeli who is persuaded to become a government agent and winds up leading a double life—as a mild-mannered (mostly absentee) husband and father in Israel, and as a wealthy businessman who infiltrates the highest levels of the Syrian government. Fascinating story based on the exploits of a real-life Israeli hero. Made for cable, and originally shown at 89m. Above average.▼

Impossible Years, The (1968) **C-92m.** BOMB D: Michael Gordon. David Niven, Lola Albright, Chad Everett, Ozzie Nelson, Cristina Ferrare. Stupid, leering sex farce from hit Broadway play about psychiatrist who has problems of his own with nubile young daughter; the most obscene G-rated film of all. Panavision. [G]▼

Impostor, The (1944) **95m.** **½ D: Julien Duvivier. Jean Gabin, Richard Whorf, Allyn Joslyn, Ellen Drew, Peter Van Eyck, Ralph Morgan. Well-acted but ordinary story of patriotic Frenchman who escapes prison, assumes new identity to join WW2 fight again. Retitled: STRANGE CONFESSION.

Impostors, The (1998) **C-100m.** *** D: Stanley Tucci. Stanley Tucci, Oliver Platt, Alfred Molina, Lili Taylor, Tony Shalhoub, Steve Buscemi, Allison Janney, Richard Jenkins, Isabella Rossellini, Campbell Scott, Billy Connolly, Dana Ivey, Hope Davis, Lewis J. Stadlen. A rare bird for our time: an old-fashioned farce, written and directed by and starring Tucci, who's teamed (providentially) with Platt, as unemployed actors whose audacious behavior toward popular ham actor Molina sends them scurrying and hiding out on a luxury liner. Doors slam, people trip over each other and fall in love at the drop of a hat. A treat to watch . . . especially with this cast of supremely gifted actors (including one surprise). [R]▼●◗

Impromptu (1991) **C-109m.** ***½ D: James Lapine. Judy Davis, Hugh Grant, Mandy Patinkin, Bernadette Peters, Julian Sands, Ralph Brown, Georges Corraface, Anton Rodgers, Emma Thompson, Anna Massey. Intellectual romp, in the SMILES OF A SUMMER NIGHT mold, about 19th-century superstars—Chopin, Liszt, Delacroix, George Sand, and the like—on a country holiday. Spirited performances and some timeless satire of culture vultures on the make; compared to A SONG TO REMEMBER, they *do* make them better than they used to. Film debut of stage director Lapine; screenplay by Sarah Kernochan, his wife. [PG-13]▼●

Improper Channels (1981-Canadian) **C-92m.** **½ D: Eric Till. Alan Arkin, Mariette Hartley, Sarah Stevens, Monica Parker, Harry Ditson. OK comedy with oddball architect Arkin erroneously accused of child abuse. Stevens, as his 5-year-old daughter, is cute; Hartley, as his estranged wife, is wasted. [PG]▼●

Impulse (1974) **C-91m.** BOMB D: William Grefe. Ruth Roman, William Shatner, Harold Sakata, Kim Nicholas, Jennifer Bishop, James Dobson. Distasteful Florida-made cheapie with Shatner overacting as a child-molester. Truly awful. Originally titled WANT A RIDE, LITTLE GIRL? [PG]▼

Impulse (1984) **C-91m.** *½ D: Graham Baker. Tim Matheson, Meg Tilly, Hume Cronyn, John Karlen, Bill Paxton, Amy Stryker. Matheson visits girlfriend Tilly in a small farming community, finds the citizens are robbing banks, shooting children, urinating on cars. Plodding reverse variation on INVASION OF THE BODY SNATCHERS—here, everyone exhibits *too much* emotion. [R]▼●◗

Impulse (1990) **C-108m.** *** D: Sondra Locke. Theresa Russell, Jeff Fahey, George Dzundza, Alan Rosenburg, Nicholas Mele, Eli Danker, Charles McCaughan, Lynne Thigpen, Shawn Elliott. Half-standard, half-fresh, and always tough: honest narc Russell, moonlighting as an L.A. streetwalker for the vice squad, briefly but fatefully yields to corruption after lousy hours and failed relationships combine to wear her down. Underrated sleeper doesn't exactly expand parameters of the cop genre, but benefits from a memorable central character; arguably Russell's best performance to date. [R]▼●

Impulsion SEE: **Stepmother, The**

Impure Thoughts (1985) **C-87m.** **½ D: Michael A. Simpson. Brad Dourif, Lane Davies, Terry Beaver, John Putch, Joe Conley, Mary McDonough, Mary Nell Santacroce, narration by Dame Judith Anderson. A quartet of men have died; they meet in Purgatory and recall their lives together as Catholic school students when JFK was president and no one had ever heard of Vietnam. Occasionally funny and insightful, with some truly wonderful moments, but it just doesn't hold together. [PG]▼

Inadmissible Evidence (1968-British) **96m.** **½ D: Anthony Page. Nicol Williamson, Eleanor Fazan, Jill Bennett, Peter Sallis, David Valla, Eileen Atkins. John Osborne's play about barrister who has reached saturation point with everyone and everything preserves Williamson's fine stage performance, but still a photographed play, not a film. Music by Dudley Moore. [R]

In a Lonely Place (1950) **91m.** ***½ D: Nicholas Ray. Humphrey Bogart, Gloria Grahame, Frank Lovejoy, Robert Warwick, Jeff Donnell, Martha Stewart. Mature, powerful drama about a feisty, self-destructive screenwriter (Bogart) who has an affair with starlet Grahame while trying to clear himself of a murder rap. Excellent performances in this study of two turbulent characters set against realistic and cynical Hollywood backdrop. Written by Andrew Solt.▼

In & Out (1997) **C-90m.** *** D: Frank Oz. Kevin Kline, Joan Cusack, Tom Selleck, Matt Dillon, Debbie Reynolds, Wilford Brimley, Bob Newhart, Gregory Jbara, Shalom Harlow, Lewis J. Stadlen, Ernie Sabella, Dan Hedaya, Joseph Maher, Shawn Hatosy. When a young actor (Dillon) wins an Oscar, he thanks his small-town high school teacher—who, he says, is gay. The popular teacher, days away from his wedding, denies this emphatically but still has to deal with the tumult and media frenzy that erupt. Very funny script by Paul Rudnick, played to a fare-thee-well by an expert cast. Enjoyable cameos by Whoopi Goldberg and Glenn Close at the mock Oscar ceremony. [PG-13]▼●◗

In a Shallow Grave (1988) **C-92m.** BOMB D: Kenneth Bowser. Michael Biehn, Maureen Mueller, Michael Beach, Patrick Dempsey, Thomas Boyd Mason. Gloomy, slow-moving tale of WW2 veteran Biehn, disfigured at Guadalcanal, who has retreated to his family's desolate Virginia homestead to brood about his condition (and wallow in self-pity). Biehn tries hard but is overpowered by film's snail-like pacing and bizarre, romantic story line (involving drifter Dempsey, whose character is weird in the extreme). One of the oddest and most maudlin dramas ever made. An *American Playhouse* presentation. [R]▼

In a Year of Thirteen Moons (1978-German) **C-129m.** ***½ D: Rainer Werner Fassbinder. Volker Spengler, Ingrid Caven, Gottfried John, Elisabeth Trissenaar, Eva Mattes. Extraordinary performance by Spengler in the difficult role of a pathetic transsexual conceived and abandoned by his mother while her husband was in a prison camp. Powerful, disturbing tale of loneliness, alienation, rejection, winningly written and directed by Fassbinder.▼

In Caliente (1935) **84m.** ** D: Lloyd Bacon. Dolores Del Rio, Pat O'Brien, Edward Everett Horton, Leo Carrillo, Glenda Farrell. Pedestrian romantic comedy filmed in Agua Caliente, with fast-talking magazine editor O'Brien wooing dancer Del Rio. Horton's comic relief is the saving grace, along with Busby Berkeley's production numbers for "Muchacha" and "The Lady in Red" (sung by Wini Shaw, with a novelty chorus by Judy Canova).

In Celebration (1975-British) **C-110m.** *** D: Lindsay Anderson. Alan Bates, James Bolam, Brian Cox, Constance Chapman, Gabrielle Day, Bill Owen. Overly theatrical but still taut, vivid drama depicting the pain, anger, and intense relationship of three brothers who return to the coal mining town of their youth for their parents' 40th anniversary. Based on a play by David Storey, which Anderson had directed on the stage; an American Film Theatre production. [PG]▼

Incendiary Blonde (1945) **C-113m.** *** D: George Marshall. Betty Hutton, Arturo de Cordova, Charlie Ruggles, Albert Dekker, Barry Fitzgerald, Mary Phillips, Bill Goodwin. Hollywoodized biography of 1920s nightclub queen Texas Guinan is Hutton all over. Plenty of old-time songs.

Incense for the Damned SEE: **Bloodsuckers** (1970-British)

Inchon! (1982-Korean-U.S.) **C-105m.** BOMB D: Terence Young. Laurence Olivier, Jacqueline Bisset, Ben Gazzara, Toshiro Mifune, Richard Roundtree. Empty-headed

Korean war epic produced by Rev. Sung Myung Moon's Unification Church. Olivier looks like a wax museum figure in his makeup as Gen. Douglas MacArthur. Laughable script punctuated by epic-scale battle scenes. Cut from 140m. length. [PG]

Incident, The (1967) **107m.** *** D: Larry Peerce. Tony Musante, Martin Sheen, Beau Bridges, Jack Gilford, Thelma Ritter, Brock Peters, Ruby Dee, Ed McMahon, Diana Van Der Vlis, Mike Kellin, Jan Sterling, Gary Merrill, Donna Mills. Tough, brutal story of two drunken hoods who terrorize passengers in N.Y.C. subway. Well made but unpleasant—and still topical. Film debuts of Sheen and Mills.▼●

Incident, The (1990) **C-100m. TVM** D: Joseph Sargent. Walter Matthau, Susan Blakely, Robert Carradine, Peter Firth, Barnard Hughes, Harry Morgan, William Schallert. Matthau is first-rate as a small-town lawyer during WW2 who becomes a pariah when he's forced to defend a German POW in a murder trial. Written by Michael and James Norell. Matthau's TV movie debut. Followed by AGAINST HER WILL: AN INCIDENT IN BALTIMORE in 1992. Above average.▼●

Incident at Midnight (1963-British) **58m.** ** D: Norman Harrison. Anton Diffring, William Sylvester, Tony Garnett, Martin Miller. Based on Edgar Wallace short story, film deals with drugstore hangout of dope addicts and gangsters who ply their trade there; trim yarn.

Incident at Oglala (1992) **C-89m.** *** D: Michael Apted. Narrated by Robert Redford. Incisive documentary detailing the alleged framing of Leonard Peltier, Native American who was jailed in the wake of a 1975 "incident" at South Dakota's Pine Ridge Reservation that resulted in the deaths of two FBI agents. Must viewing in tandem with the thematically related THUNDERHEART, also directed by Apted. Redford also is executive producer. [PG]▼●◗

Incident at Phantom Hill (1966) **C-88m.** **½ D: Earl Bellamy. Robert Fuller, Dan Duryea, Jocelyn Lane, Claude Akins. Solid little Western about greedy trio chasing after horde of gold, combating Indians, the elements and each other. Techniscope.

Incident at Victoria Falls (1991-Belgian-British-Italian-Luxembourg) **C-120m.** **½ D: Bill Corcoran. Christopher Lee, Patrick Macnee, Claude Akins, Richard Todd, Joss Ackland, John Indi, Stephen Gurney. Just before retiring to Sussex to raise bees, Sherlock Holmes (Lee) is persuaded by King Edward (Ackland) to bring a valuable diamond back from South Africa. This leads to an encounter with Teddy Roosevelt (Akins), lots of chugging about in steam trains, and a great deal of intrigue. Lee is fine as an aging Holmes, but Macnee's a bit too comic as Watson. Cut down from a four-hour miniseries, accounting for some story abruptness—and Jenny Seagrove's name in the credits, though she does not appear on screen. Aka SHERLOCK HOLMES AND THE INCIDENT AT VICTORIA FALLS. Followed SHERLOCK HOLMES AND THE LEADING LADY.▼

Incognito (1997-U.S.-British) **C-107m.** **½ D: John Badham. Jason Patric, Irène Jacob, Rod Steiger, Thomas Lockyer, Ian Richardson, Simon Chandler, Michael Cochrane. An art forger (Patric) who's hired to create a fake Rembrandt goes to Europe and falls for an art expert (Jacob) who happens to be the world's foremost Rembrandt authority, and forces her to go on the run with him after he's framed for murder. Barely released, would-be Hitchcockian thriller. Ian Holm appears unbilled. Panavision. [R] ▼●◗

In Cold Blood (1967) **134m.** **** D: Richard Brooks. Robert Blake, Scott Wilson, John Forsythe, Paul Stewart, Gerald S. O'Loughlin, Jeff Corey, Will Geer. Excellent semidocumentary adaptation of Truman Capote's book, tracing stories of two young killers (Blake, Wilson), their motives and eventual arrest after slaughtering innocent family. Incisive, engrossing, unsensational; masterful script, direction by Brooks, fine black-and-white photography by Conrad Hall. Remade as a TV miniseries in 1996. Panavision.▼●

Inconvenient Woman, An (1991) **C-200m. TVM** D: Larry Elikann. Jason Robards, Jill Eikenberry, Rebecca De Mornay, Peter Gallagher, Elaine Stritch, Chad Lowe, Joseph Bologna, Roddy McDowall, Roy Thinnes, Chelsea Field, Paxton Whitehead. Philandering financier tries to make the murder of his frosty wife's high-society friend look like suicide. His mistress, however, makes things difficult in this adaptation of Dominick Dunne's darkly witty tale of L.A. society. De Mornay's a delight doing a Judy Holliday type. Good if overlong script by John Pielmeier. Originally shown in two parts. Above average.▼

In Country (1989) **C-120m.** *½ D: Norman Jewison. Bruce Willis, Emily Lloyd, Joan Allen, Kevin Anderson, John Terry, Peggy Rea, Judith Ivey, Richard Hamilton, Patricia Richardson, Jim Beaver. Disappointing, poorly executed film of Vietnam vet Willis and niece Lloyd, two Kentuckians trying to come to terms with the war. Willis is good as a cynical, shell-shocked recluse, but script, from Bobbie Ann Mason's acclaimed novel, is flawed: character relationships are uneven, and too many questions are left unanswered (like Willis' medical condition). Beautifully handled concluding scenes, leading up to Washington, D.C., Veterans Memorial visit, can't redeem film. [R]▼●◗

Incredible Invasion SEE: **Sinister Invasion**

Incredible Journey, The (1963) **C-80m.** *** D: Fletcher Markle. Emile Genest, John Drainie, Tommy Tweed, Sandra Scott. Entertaining, well-made Disney story of three pets—two dogs and a cat—who make 250-mile journey across Canada on their own to be with their family of humans. Remade by Disney in 1993 as HOMEWARD BOUND: THE INCREDIBLE JOURNEY. ▼●

Incredible Melting Man, The (1978) **C-86m.** *½ D: William Sachs. Alex Rebar, Burr DeBenning, Myron Healey, Michael Aldredge, Ann Sweeney, Lisle Wilson. Rebar is only survivor of outer space mission which has turned his body into a melting muck. Cheap, old-fashioned B horror film whose only saving grace is Rick Baker's excellent makeup effects. [R]▼

Incredible Mr. Limpet, The (1964) **C-102m.** ** D: Arthur Lubin. Don Knotts, Jack Weston, Carole Cook, Andrew Duggan, Larry Keating. Knotts plays a milquetoast who dreams of becoming a fish—and miraculously gets his wish (turning into an animated cartoon figure). What's more, he helps the Navy spot Nazi submarines during WW2. Innocuous family fare goes on too long.▼●

Incredible Petrified World, The (1958) **78m.** BOMB D: Jerry Warren. John Carradine, Robert Clarke, Allen Windsor, Phyllis Coates, Lloyd Nelson, George Skaff. Four people explore the ocean depths in Dr. Carradine's diving bell and are plunged into land of catacombed tunnels. Not uninteresting sci-fi entry, but ultimately defeated by poor acting, leaden pacing.▼

Incredible Sarah, The (1976) **C-106m.** ** D: Richard Fleischer. Glenda Jackson, Daniel Massey, Yvonne Mitchell, Douglas Wilmer, David Langton, Simon Williams. Broadly sketched portrait of legendary French actress Sarah Bernhardt; Jackson chews the scenery in a flamboyant performance, but someone should have chewed up the script instead. Filmed in England. [PG]▼●

Incredible Shrinking Man, The (1957) **81m.** *** D: Jack Arnold. Grant Williams, Randy Stuart, April Kent, Paul Langton, William Schallert, Billy Curtis. Outstanding special effects highlight intelligent story. Williams' mysterious shrinkage forces him to view the world—and himself—in a different light than ever before. Existential script by Richard Matheson, from his novel.▼●

Incredible Shrinking Woman, The (1981) **C-88m.** ** D: Joel Schumacher. Lily Tomlin, Charles Grodin, Ned Beatty, Henry Gibson, Elizabeth Wilson, Mark Blankfield, Pamela Bellwood, John Glover, Mike Douglas. Semi-spoof of SHRINKING MAN with Tomlin in three roles, principally as a suburban housewife whose constant exposure to household products causes her to dwindle; she becomes a media darling, then the target of an evil corporation. Never as funny or pointed as it would like to be, but worth catching for really peculiar color schemes and an amazing performance by Rick Baker as a gorilla named Sidney. Schumacher's directorial debut. [PG]▼●

Incredible Two-Headed Transplant, The (1971) **C-88m.** *½ D: Anthony M. Lanza. Bruce Dern, Pat Priest, Casey Kasem, Albert Cole, John Bloom, Berry Kroeger. The head of an insane murderer is attached to the head of a mental retardate. Which head made this film? [PG]▼

Incredibly Strange Creatures Who Stopped Living and Became Mixed-Up Zombies, The (1963) **C-82m.** **½ D: Ray Dennis Steckler. Cash Flagg (Ray Dennis Steckler), Brett O'Hara, Atlas King, Sharon Walsh, Madison Clarke, Son Hooker. Legendary (thanks to that title) low-budget horror film about hideous goings-on at a carny sideshow, with lots of rock numbers thrown in. Truly bizarre film features gorgeously saturated color, awful acting, hideous dialogue, haunting atmosphere and little plot. Cinematography by Joe Micelli (author of *American Cinematographers' Manual*) with very young Laszlo Kovacs and Vilmos Zsigmond helping. Aka THE TEENAGE PSYCHO MEETS BLOODY MARY.▼

Incredibly True Adventures of Two Girls in Love, The (1995) **C-94m.** ** D: Maria Maggenti. Laurel Holloman, Nicole Parker, Maggie Moore, Kate Stafford, Sabrina Artel, Toby Poser, Dale Dickey. A grungily dressed, white tomboy from a lesbian household falls for a financially secure black beauty—a reciprocated romance that has the latter's snooty high school pals reeling. Given the physical characteristics of the two leads and the script's lack of mean streak, the tolerant may overlook this meagerly budgeted comedy's total lack of cinematic interest. Otherwise, it's more interminable than incredible. [R] ▼

"In" Crowd, The (1988) **C-96m.** **½ D: Mark Rosenthal. Donovan Leitch, Jennifer Runyon, Scott Plank, Joe Pantoliano, Bruce Kirby, Wendy Gazelle, Page Hannah. Surprisingly likable look at the lives and loves of those guys and gals who danced their hearts out on daily TV dance shows in the 1960s. Not as hip as John Waters' similarly themed HAIRSPRAY but fun anyway. Leitch is the son of '60s recording star Donovan. [PG]▼●

Incubus (1966) **74m.** *** D: Leslie Stevens. William Shatner, Allyson Ames, Eloise Hardt, Robert Fortier, Ann Atmar, Milos Milos. First—and so far *only*—movie ever made in the language of Esperanto concerns a beautiful succubus who tries to corrupt a pure soul, only to fall in love instead. Long-lost, genuinely creepy curio written and directed by the creator of *The Outer Limits* plays like a feature-length episode of that series—as made by Ingmar Bergman. Conrad Hall's expressionistic b&w photography of the striking Big Sur locations is a major asset.▼

Incubus, The (1982-Canadian) **C-90m.** BOMB D: John Hough. John Cassavetes, Kerrie Keane, Helen Hughes, Erin Flannery, Duncan McIntosh, John Ireland. Repulsive, poorly made horror thriller about sex murders in small Wisconsin town. [R]▼●

In Custody (1993-British-Indian) **C-123m.** ** D: Ismail Merchant. Shashi Kapoor, Shabana Azmi, Om Puri, Sushma Seth, Neena Gupta, Tinnu Anand. Silly tale of a doltish college lecturer and intellectual (Puri) who writes poetry no one will publish; he sets out to interview India's ''greatest living Urdu poet'' (Kapoor), which quickly proves to be a disheartening experience. Means to be an allegory about the lack of respect for history, intellectualism, and scholarship in modern India, but the result is only nonsensical. Disappointing effort from Merchant (better known as James Ivory's longtime producer). [PG]▼

Indecent Proposal (1993) **C-118m.** ** D: Adrian Lyne. Robert Redford, Demi Moore, Woody Harrelson, Oliver Platt, Seymour Cassel, Billy Bob Thornton, Rip Taylor, Joel Brooks, Billy Connolly, Sheena Easton, Herbie Hancock. A cocky high roller offers destitute couple Harrelson and Moore a million dollars to sleep with her for one night. They accept, but are immediately plunged into a whirlpool of remorse, jealousy, and bitterness. Intriguing premise bogged down by sheer silliness (not to mention overlength), though it remains watchable. [R]▼●

Independence Day (1983) **C-110m.** ** D: Robert Mandel. Kathleen Quinlan, David Keith, Frances Sternhagen, Cliff DeYoung, Dianne Wiest, Josef Sommer, Bert Remsen, Richard Farnsworth, Brooke Alderson, Noble Willingham, Susan Ruttan. Interesting but unfocused little picture about a young woman who's aching to leave her claustrophobic hometown but held back (in part) by romance with car mechanic Keith. Subplot about battered wife (superbly played by Wiest) seems to be a separate film altogether. Shown on TV as FOLLOW YOUR DREAMS. [R]▼

Independence Day (1996) **C-145m.** **½ D: Roland Emmerich. Will Smith, Bill Pullman, Jeff Goldblum, Mary McDonnell, Judd Hirsch, Margaret Colin, Randy Quaid, Robert Loggia, James Rebhorn, Harvey Fierstein, Adam Baldwin, Brent Spiner, James Duval, Vivica A. Fox, Lisa Jakub, Ross Bagley, Bill Smitrovich, Harry Connick, Jr. Spectacular—and spectacularly stupid—sci-fi saga of alien ships hovering over the earth and apparently planning to attack. U.S. President Pullman tries to determine how best to fight, as the stakes keep changing on an hour-to-hour basis. Big, Oscar-winning special effects are impressive, but the human stories are so dumb, the writing so lame, and some of the performances so broad they make some silly 50s sci-fi movies look brilliant by comparison. 15m. added for special edition. Super 35. [PG-13] ▼●◗

Indestructible Man (1956) **70m.** ** D: Jack Pollexfen. Lon Chaney, Jr., Casey Adams, Marion Carr, Ross Elliot, Stuart Randall, Robert Shayne. Scientist is able to return from the dead a fabled, just-executed criminal, ''Butcher Benton'' (Chaney), who goes on to seek revenge against his shyster lawyer and others. Not-bad sci-fi/horror entry will entertain fans of the genre.▼◗

Indiana Jones and the Last Crusade (1989) **C-127m.** **½ D: Steven Spielberg. Harrison Ford, Sean Connery, Denholm Elliott, Alison Doody, John Rhys-Davies, Julian Glover, River Phoenix, Michael Byrne, Alex Hyde-White. Follow-the-numbers adventure spectacle has Ford in fine form and Connery adding panache as Indy's archeologist father, whose mysterious disappearance (while searching for the Holy Grail) sets the story in motion. This deliberately old-fashioned Saturday matinée yarn has everything money can buy, but never really generates a sense of wonder and excitement. A definite improvement over the second Indiana Jones outing, but it still bears the mark of one too many trips to the well. Oscar winner for sound effects editing. Panavision. [PG-13]▼●

Indiana Jones and the Temple of Doom (1984) **C-118m.** ** D: Steven Spielberg. Harrison Ford, Kate Capshaw, Ke Huy Quan (Jonathan Ke Quan), Amrish Puri, Roshan Seth, Philip Stone, Dan Aykroyd. Headache-inducing prequel to RAIDERS OF THE LOST ARK, but this time the 1930s archaeologist/adventurer has a weaker story and wimpier heroine. Re-creates (and outdoes) a bunch of great cliffhanger stunts, but never gives us a chance to breathe . . . and tries to top the snake scene in RAIDERS by coming up with a variety of new ''gross-out'' gags. Oscar winner for Visual Effects. Followed by INDIANA JONES AND THE LAST CRUSADE. Panavision. [PG] ▼●

Indianapolis Speedway (1939) **82m.** ** D: Lloyd Bacon. Pat O'Brien, Ann Sheridan, John Payne, Gale Page, Frank McHugh, John Ridgely, Regis Toomey. Routine but watchable remake of Howard Hawks's THE CROWD ROARS, about the rivalry between brothers O'Brien and

Payne on the racetrack. James Cagney's patented cockiness, the best thing about the original, is what's missing here.

Indian Fighter, The (1955) **C-88m.** *** D: Andre de Toth. Kirk Douglas, Walter Matthau, Elsa Martinelli, Walter Abel, Lon Chaney. Exciting account of Douglas leading wagon train through rampaging Indian country. CinemaScope.▼

Indian in the Cupboard, The (1995) **C-96m.** *** D: Frank Oz. Hal Scardino, Litefoot, Lindsay Crouse, Richard Jenkins, Rishi Bhat, Steve Coogan, David Keith, Sakina Jaffrey, Vincent Kartheiser, Nestor Serrano. A boy (Scardino) receives an old cupboard as a birthday present, and finds that when he puts a plastic Indian inside and turns the key, the Indian comes to life. *Then* he learns that the Indian is not a toy, but a real person, and complications ensue—especially when his best friend conjures up a real-life cowboy. First-rate adaptation of Lynne Reid Banks' popular children's book, scripted by Melissa Mathison (of E.T. fame); full of wonder and simple wisdom . . . if a few too many giant closeups of the boy's face. [PG] ▼●

Indian Love Call SEE: **Rose Marie** (1936)

Indian Paint (1964) **C-91m.** ** D: Norman Foster. Johnny Crawford, Jay Silverheels, Pat Hogan, Robert Crawford, Jr., George J. Lewis. Fifteen-year-old Arikara (Crawford), his foal, and his coming-to-manhood. Harmless, forgettable.▼

Indian Runner, The (1991) **C-125m.** *** D: Sean Penn. David Morse, Viggo Mortensen, Valeria Golino, Patricia Arquette, Charles Bronson, Sandy Dennis, Dennis Hopper, Kenny Stabler. Mood piece about a young man's desperate attempts to understand—and get closer to—his troubled kid brother, who's just returned from Vietnam. Lethargic at times, but filled with emotion and truth, and ultimately quite moving. Strong performances all around, with offbeat but effective casting of Bronson as the boy's melancholy father. Impressive achievement for first-time writer/director Penn. Penn's real-life mother, actress Eileen Ryan, plays Mrs. Baker. Inspired by Bruce Springsteen's song "Highway Patrolman." [R]▼●

Indian Scarf, The (1963-German) **85m.** ** D: Alfred Vohrer. Heinz Drache, Gisela Uhlen, Corny Collins, Klaus Kinski. Edgar Wallace suspenser, with heirs to an estate being strangled one by one during sojourn at benefactor's country home. Ultrascope. ▼

Indian Scout SEE: **Davy Crockett, Indian Scout**

Indian Summer (1993) **C-97m.** *** D: Mike Binder. Alan Arkin, Matt Craven, Diane Lane, Bill Paxton, Elizabeth Perkins, Kevin Pollak, Vincent Spano, Julie Warner, Kimberly Williams. Good-natured yuppie nostalgia about thirtysomethings who return to the beloved summer camp of their youth for a reunion weekend. Arkin is wonderful as the camp director, and the cast couldn't be more appealing. Writer-director Binder based this on his own memories, and filmed at the actual Camp Tamakwa he attended in Canada. That's horror-film director Sam Raimi playing Arkin's flunky. Panavision. [PG-13] ▼●

Indian Summer (1995) SEE: **Alive and Kicking**

Indian Tomb, The (1959-German) **C-97m.** **½ D: Fritz Lang. Debra Paget, Paul Hubschmid, Walther Reyer, Claus Holm, Sabine Bettmann, Rene Deltman. The pace picks up a bit in this second of Lang's Indian diptych, chronicling the events leading up to lovers Paget and Hubschmid's escape from the clutches of maharajah Reyer. Paget's exotic dance is a highlight. This and Part One (THE TIGER OF ESCHNAPUR) were originally dubbed, edited down to 95m., and released as JOURNEY TO THE LOST CITY.

Indian Uprising (1952) **C-75m.** ** D: Ray Nazarro. George Montgomery, Audrey Long, Carl Benton Reid, Robert Shayne. Geronimo on the warpath again.▼

Indiscreet (1931) **81m.** *½ D: Leo McCarey. Gloria Swanson, Ben Lyon, Barbara Kent, Arthur Lake, Monroe Owsley. Tiresome romantic comedy-drama with Swanson trying to keep her scarlet past from Lyon. Art deco sets, and Gloria's rendition of two DeSylva-Brown-Henderson songs, aren't compensation enough for sitting through this one. Original running time 92m.▼

Indiscreet (1958) **C-100m.** *** D: Stanley Donen. Cary Grant, Ingrid Bergman, Cecil Parker, Phyllis Calvert, David Kossoff, Megs Jenkins. Bergman is renowned actress whom American playboy Grant romances and can't forget. Delightful comedy from Norman Krasna play *Kind Sir.* Made in England. Remade as a 1988 TVM with Robert Wagner and Lesley-Anne Down.▼

Indiscretion of an American Wife (1953-U.S.-Italian) **63m.** **½ D: Vittorio De Sica. Jennifer Jones, Montgomery Clift, Gino Cervi, Richard Beymer. Turgid melodrama set in Rome's railway station, with Jones the adulterous wife meeting lover Clift for one more clinch. De Sica's original 87m. version, titled TERMINAL STATION, was restored in 1983. Remade in 1998 for TV.▼◗

Indochine (1992-French) **C-155m.** ** D: Régis Wargnier. Catherine Deneuve, Vincent Perez, Linh Dan Pham, Jean Yanne, Dominique Blanc, Henri Marteau, Carlo Brandt, Gerard Lartigau. Soap opera set against political upheaval in French Indochina during the 1930s. Deneuve plays a wealthy French landowner who's raised an orphaned Indochinese girl, and now must contend with the fact that she's grown—and has a mind of her own. Interesting historical elements, set against a fascinating landscape, but story is mostly tripe. Even so, nabbed the Foreign Film Oscar. [PG-13] ▼●

Indomitable Teddy Roosevelt, The (1983) **C-94m.** *** D: Harrison Engle. Narrated by George C. Scott. Excellent and innovative documentary about the remarkable, larger-than-life figure who became our 26th president. Artfully mixes newsreel footage with meticulous recreations featuring Bob Boyd in the role of T.R. Set to the stirring music of John Philip Sousa.▼◗

In Dreams (1999) **C-99m.** ** D: Neil Jordan. Annette Bening, Robert Downey, Jr., Aidan Quinn, Stephen Rea, Paul Guilfoyle, Dennis Boutsikaris, Katie Sagona, Krystal Benn. Massachusetts woman is haunted by disturbing dreams which turn out to be the thoughts of a sick man who's abducting and murdering children. Is she insane, or somehow psychically connected to the killer? Extremely unpleasant adult horror film is well made but hard to watch. It's also hard to top the opening sequence, based on the real-life incident of a town being flooded to create a reservoir. Jordan coscripted with Bruce Robinson. [R]▼●◗

In Enemy Country (1968) **C-107m.** ** D: Harry Keller. Tony Franciosa, Anjanette Comer, Guy Stockwell, Paul Hubschmid, Tom Bell, Emile Genest. So-so programmer of WW2 intrigue, set in France and England, filmed on Universal's backlot. Not very convincing. Techniscope.

I Never Promised You a Rose Garden (1977) **C-96m.** *** D: Anthony Page. Bibi Andersson, Kathleen Quinlan, Ben Piazza, Lorraine Gary, Reni Santoni, Susan Tyrrell, Signe Hasso, Jeff Conaway, Diane Varsi, Barbara Steele, Sylvia Sidney, Dennis Quaid. Intelligent adaptation of Hannah Green's book about her treatment for schizophrenia as a teenager, focusing on relationship between her (Quinlan) and dedicated psychiatrist (Andersson). Graphic, clinical approach is often disturbing. [R] ▼

I Never Sang for My Father (1970) **C-93m.** ***½ D: Gilbert Cates. Melvyn Douglas, Gene Hackman, Dorothy Stickney, Estelle Parsons, Elizabeth Hubbard, Lovelady Powell. Sensitive adaptation of Robert Anderson play about grown man (Hackman) faced with problem of caring for elderly father (Douglas). Fine job all around, but extremely depressing. Scripted by the playwright. [PG]▼●

Inevitable Grace (1994) **C-103m.** BOMB D: Alex Canawati. Maxwell Caulfield, Stephanie Knights, Jennifer Nicholson, Tippi Hedren, Samantha Eggar, Sandra Knight, Rob Sheiffele, Taylor Negron. Lame psychological thriller about a psychiatrist at a mental institution who gets involved in a nasty (and ludicrous) triangle with her patient and the woman's husband. Seemingly endless movie does offer a chance to check out the acting ability of Jack Nicholson and Sandra Knight's daughter Jennifer, but that's not much of a recommendation.▼

Infamous Crimes SEE: **Philo Vance Returns**

In Fast Company (1946) **61m.** *½ D: Del Lord. Leo Gorcey, Huntz Hall, Bobby Jordan, Billy Benedict, Jane Randolph, Judy Clark, David Gorcey, Douglas Fowley. The Bowery Boys get mixed up in a full-scale taxicab war in this substandard entry.

Infernal Idol, The SEE: **Craze**

Inferno (1953) **C-107m.** **½ D: Roy (Ward) Baker. Robert Ryan, Rhonda Fleming, William Lundigan, Henry Hull, Carl Betz, Larry Keating. Fleming plots rich husband Ryan's demise, with surprising results. Good desert sequences. Originally in 3-D. Remade as a TV movie, ORDEAL.

Inferno (1980-Italian) **C-107m.** **½ D: Dario Argento. Leigh McCloskey, Irene Miracle, Sacha Pitoeff, Daria Nicolodi, Eleonora Giorgi, Veronica Lazar, Alida Valli. American returns to N.Y. from studies in Rome to investigate the gruesome murder of his sister, and discovers "evil mothers" wreaking supernatural havoc on both sides of Atlantic. Surreal, hypnotic shocker by Italian horror maestro Argento is short on sense, but long on style. Technovision. [R]▼◗

Infinity (1996) **C-117m.** **½ D: Matthew Broderick. Matthew Broderick, Patricia Arquette, Peter Riegert, Dori Brenner, Peter Michael Goetz, Željko Ivanek, Matt Mulhern, Joyce Van Patten, James LeGros. Sweet but uneven movie based on the life of Richard Feynman, whose relationship with Arline Greenbaum (Arquette) in pre-WW2 N.Y.C. takes a fateful turn when he is recruited to work on the Manhattan Project. (The theoretical physicist won the Nobel Prize in 1965.) Effective when dealing with the love story, but meanders when Feynman moves to Los Alamos. Broderick's directorial debut; scripted by his mother, Patricia Broderick. [PG]▼●◗

Information Received (1962-British) **77m.** ** D: Robert Lynn. Sabina Sesselman, William Sylvester, Hermione Baddeley, Edward Underdown. Potentially effective seesaw cat-and-mouse account of criminals Sesselman and Sylvester each trying to kill the other.

Informer, The (1929-British) **82m.** **½ D: Arthur Robison. Lya de Putti, Lars Hanson, Warwick Ward, Carl Harbord, Dennis Wyndham. Intriguing curio, part-silent and part-talkie, about Gypo Nolan (Hanson), Irish Republican Army member who, in a fit of jealousy, betrays his best friend to the police. Pales beside the more famous 1935 version of the Liam O'Flaherty novel, but not without its own merits. Silent sequences are far more effective than the talking ones. ▼

Informer, The (1935) **91m.** ***½ D: John Ford. Victor McLaglen, Heather Angel, Preston Foster, Margot Grahame, Wallace Ford, Una O'Connor, J. M. Kerrigan, Joseph Sauers (Sawyer), Donald Meek. Dated but still potent study of human nature tells of hard-drinking McLaglen, who informs on buddy to collect reward during Irish Rebellion of 1922. Powerful drama, based on Liam O'Flaherty's novel, with a memorable Max Steiner score. McLaglen's performance won the Oscar, as did Ford, Steiner, and Dudley Nichols (for Best Screenplay). Filmed before in England in 1929. Remade as UP TIGHT.▼●

Informers, The SEE: **Underworld Informers**

In for Treatment (1979-Netherlands) **C-99m.** ***½ D: Eric van Zuylen, Marja Kok. Helmert Woudenberg, Frank Groothof, Hans Man In't Veld, Marja Kok, Joop Admiraal. Simple, pointed, powerful story of a middle-aged man who checks into a hospital for tests but is really dying of cancer; he must deal with a distant, maddeningly impersonal hospital system. Hard to watch because of the subject, but still poignant and never maudlin; a production of the Werkteater, a Dutch theater collective.▼

Infra-Man (1976-Hong Kong) **C-92m.** *** D: Hua-Shan. Li Hsiu-hsien, Wang Hsieh, Yuan Man-tzu, Terry Liu, Tsen Shu-yi, Huang Chien-lung, Lu Sheng. Princess Dragon Mom (Liu) and her odd assortment of monster underlings attempt to take over the earth—and it's Infra-Man (Hsiu-hsien) to the rescue. Action-packed, with gloriously corny dialogue (dubbed), outlandish costumes and sets, adequate special effects. Great fun. Panavision. [PG]▼

Inglorious Bastards (1978-Italian) **C-100m.** ** D: Enzo G. Castellari. Ian Bannen, Bo Svenson, Fred Williamson, Peter Hooten, Michael Pergolani. Five soldiers about to be court-martialled during WW2 take off through France, hoping to make the Swiss border. Far-fetched story with a few good action scenes. Retitled COUNTERFEIT COMMANDOS. [R]▼

In God's Hands (1998) **C-96m.** ** D: Zalman King. Matt George, Matty Liu, Patrick Shane Dorian, Shaun Tomson, Maylin Pultar, Bret Michaels. Three world-class surfers (played by three actual world-class surfers) embark on the ultimate global tour of duty. Fictional film suffers from amateurishness of its cast of nonperformers, but is marginally worth seeing for gorgeous cinematography and, of course, some breathtaking wave riding. A change of pace for softcore auteur King. Super 35. [PG-13]▼◗

In God We Tru$t (1980) **C-97m.** BOMB D: Marty Feldman. Marty Feldman, Peter Boyle, Louise Lasser, Richard Pryor, Andy Kaufman, Wilfrid Hyde-White, Severn Darden. Naive monk Feldman treks to L.A. to raise money for his monastery. A comedy that is tragically unfunny—including Pryor, who plays God. Feldman also cowrote the script. [PG]▼

In Harm's Way (1965) **165m.** **½ D: Otto Preminger. John Wayne, Kirk Douglas, Patricia Neal, Tom Tryon, Paula Prentiss, Henry Fonda, Brandon de Wilde, Jill Haworth, Dana Andrews, Stanley Holloway, Burgess Meredith, Franchot Tone, Patrick O'Neal, Carroll O'Connor, Slim Pickens, Barbara Bouchet, Hugh O'Brian, George Kennedy, Bruce Cabot, Larry Hagman. Overlong, melodramatic account of warfare in the South Pacific at the outset of WW2, focusing on the exploits of larger-than-life naval officer Wayne (whose character is nicknamed "Rock"). Most interesting for its cast of old-timers and up-and-coming stars. Panavision.▼

Inheritance, The (1947-British) **98m.** *** D: Charles Frank. Jean Simmons, Derrick DeMarney, Derek Bond, Katina Paxinou, Esmond Knight. Well-appointed chiller, with Simmons as innocent preyed upon by corrupt uncle; situated in Victorian London and Paris. Based on a novel by Sheridan Le Fanu. Original British title: UNCLE SILAS.▼●◗

Inheritance, The (1976-Italian) **C-105m.** **½ D: Mauro Bolognini. Anthony Quinn, Dominique Sanda, Fabio Testi, Adriana Asti, Luigi Proietti. Moody melodrama about dying patriarch (Quinn) who wants to disown everyone but his calculating daughter-in-law (Sanda), who offers him sexual comforts. Well-acted, handsome production with emphasis on eroticism. Originally 121m. Techniscope. [R]▼◗

Inheritors, The (1998-Austrian) **C-95m.** *** D: Stefan Ruzowitzky. Simon Schwarz, Sophie Rois, Lars Rudolph, Julia Gschnitzer, Ulrich Wildgruber, Elizabeth Orth, Tilo Pruckner, Susanne Silverio. A landowner dies and bequeaths his assets to the seven lowly peasants who worked his farm. Spirited, pointed (if predictable) political allegory, set in an Austrian village in the 1930s. Vivid characterizations add punch to the proceedings. [R]▼

Inherit the Wind (1960) **127m.** ***½ D: Stanley Kramer. Spencer Tracy, Fredric March, Gene Kelly, Florence Eldridge, Dick York, Harry Morgan, Donna Anderson, Elliott Reid, Claude Akins, Noah Beery, Jr., Norman Fell. Vocals by Leslie Uggams. Absorbing adaptation of Jerome Lawrence–Robert E. Lee play based on notorious Scopes Monkey Trial of 1925, when Clarence Darrow defended and William Jennings Bryan prosecuted a schoolteacher arrested for teaching Darwin's Theory of Evolution. Names are changed (Kelly's character is based on acid-tongued H.L. Mencken), but the issue is real and still relevant. An acting tour de force, with solid support from Morgan as the judge, Reid as a lawyer, Eldridge as March's devoted wife. Only offbeat casting of Kelly doesn't quite come off. Screenplay by Nathan E. Douglas (Nedrick Young) and Harold Jacob Smith. Remade as 1988 TVM with Kirk Douglas and Jason Robards. Also remade as a TVM in 1999 with Jack Lemmon and George C. Scott.▼●

Inkwell, The (1994) **C-110m.** *½ D: Matty Rich. Larenz Tate, Joe Morton, Suzzanne Douglas, Glynn Turman, Vanessa Bell Calloway, Adrienne-Joi Johnson, Morris Chestnut, Jada Pinkett, Duane Martin, Mary Alice, Phyllis Yvonne Stickney. A 16-year-old, whose toy doll confidante naturally worries his parents, learns about love, SUMMER OF '42–style, in this Summer of '76 nostalgia piece set in a black section of Martha's Vineyard. Clumsily written and directed and (doll aside) irritatingly derivative. Filmmakers groused that the result would have been better without studio interference. [R] ▼●

In-Laws, The (1979) **C-103m.** *** D: Arthur Hiller. Peter Falk, Alan Arkin, Richard Libertini, Nancy Dussault, Penny Peyser, Arlene Golonka, Michael Lembeck, Ed Begley, Jr., Rosana (de) Soto, Art Evans, David Paymer. Wacky comedy about a dentist (Arkin) who becomes involved in the bizarre intrigues of his daughter's father-in-law-to-be (Falk), who claims to be a CIA agent. Andrew Bergman's script commendably unpredictable start to finish; Libertini hilarious as Latin dictator with a Señor Wences fetish. Enjoyable score by John Morris. [PG]▼●

In Like Flint (1967) **C-114m.** **½ D: Gordon Douglas. James Coburn, Lee J. Cobb, Jean Hale, Andrew Duggan, Anna Lee. Weak sequel to OUR MAN FLINT finds our hero going against secret society of women plotting to take over the world. CinemaScope.▼●

In Love SEE: **Falling in Love Again**

In Love and War (1958) **C-111m.** **½ D: Philip Dunne. Robert Wagner, Dana Wynter, Jeffrey Hunter, Hope Lange, Bradford Dillman, Sheree North, France Nuyen, Mort Sahl. 1940s-style WW2 film traces effects of war on three soldiers; handsome cast uplifts soaper. CinemaScope.

In Love and War (1987) **C-100m. TVM** D: Paul Aaron. Jane Alexander, James Woods, Dr. Haing S. Ngor, Richard McKenzie, Concetta Tomei. Graphic but strangely uninvolving dramatization of the book by U.S. Navy Commander James B. Stockdale and his wife Sybil about their lives when he, for eight years, was being tortured as a POW during the Vietnam War and she was waging a fight back home as an organizer of POW wives. Average.▼●

In Love and War (1996-U.S.-British) **C-115m.** BOMB D: Richard Attenborough. Sandra Bullock, Chris O'Donnell, Mackenzie Astin, Emilio Bonucci, Ingrid Lacey, Margot Steinberg. Lumbering catastrophe chronicles Ernest Hemingway's WW1 love affair with Red Cross nurse Agnes von Kurowsky, eight years his senior and the inspiration for the character Catherine Barkley in *A Farewell to Arms*. Miscast O'Donnell might actually be more credible playing Ernest Borgnine, and the leads have no chemistry. The film leans on what used to be called "scenic values" like a bookie who's been stiffed. Panavision. [PG-13]▼●◗

In Name Only (1939) **94m.** *** D: John Cromwell. Carole Lombard, Cary Grant, Kay Francis, Charles Coburn, Helen Vinson, Peggy Ann Garner. Solid soaper with wealthy, married Grant falling for widowed Lombard, trying desperately to obtain a divorce from bitchy, manipulative social climber Francis. Beautifully acted.▼●

Inner Circle, The (1991) **C-134m.** **½ D: Andrei Konchalovsky. Tom Hulce, Lolita Davidovich, Bob Hoskins, Alexandre Zbruev, Feodor Chaliapin, Jr., Bess Meyer, Maria Baranova. Intriguing if ultimately obvious, disappointing saga of life in the Soviet Union under the iron rule of Stalin. Story follows naive, humble projectionist (Hulce) who gets to screen a film for the dictator. Much more subtlety is in order here, as Hulce's performance soon becomes grating and one-dimensional. Based on a true story; some sequences were shot inside the Kremlin, and even KGB headquarters. [PG-13]▼●

Inner Sanctum (1948) **62m.** ** D: Lew Landers. Charles Russell, Mary Beth Hughes, Lee Patrick, Nana Bryant, Billy House, Roscoe Ates. Not-bad little film noir. A man kills his wife in the dark of night at a train station. A boy witnesses the crime, finds his life in jeopardy. "Inspired by" the radio series of the same name.▼

Innerspace (1987) **C-120m.** **½ D: Joe Dante. Dennis Quaid, Martin Short, Meg Ryan, Kevin McCarthy, Fiona Lewis, Vernon Wells, Robert Picardo, Wendy Schaal, Harold Sylvester, William Schallert, Henry Gibson, Orson Bean, Kevin Hooks, Kathleen Freeman, Dick Miller, Ken Tobey. Diverting tale of rambunctious Navy test pilot (Quaid) who undergoes miniaturization experiment and is accidentally injected into the body of hypochondriac Short. Heady combination of science fiction and comedy, with an off-the-wall sensibility that keeps things unpredictable . . . though tightening would have helped. Short is a delight as the comic hero. Oscar winner for Best Visual Effects. [PG]▼●

Innocent, The (1976-Italian) **C-115m.** **** D: Luchino Visconti. Giancarlo Giannini, Laura Antonelli, Jennifer O'Neill.

Director Visconti's final film is among his greatest, a lavishly mounted tragedy about a Sicilian aristocrat who has the tables turned on him by the luscious wife he has chosen to ignore. Technovision. [R]▼

Innocent, The (1985-British) **C-101m.** **½ D: John Mackenzie. Andrew Hawley, Kika Markham, Kate Foster, Liam Neeson, Patrick Daley, Tom Bell, Clive Wood, Miranda Richardson. Medium drama about a young boy (Hawley) on the edge of puberty, growing up in a Yorkshire town during the Depression. Occasionally striking but too often slow.

Innocent, The (1993-British-German) **C-107m.** ** D: John Schlesinger. Isabella Rossellini, Anthony Hopkins, Campbell Scott, Ronald Nitschke, Hart Bochner, James Grant, Jeremy Sinden. Blah Cold War/paranoia thriller, set in the 1950s, about an ingenuous British circuitry expert (Scott) sent to Berlin to help set up a complicated phone-tapping apparatus to be used against the East Germans; along the way, he becomes involved in a passionate romance. Hopkins is fine as usual (although he does seem miscast as a blustery American CIA official). The characters are strictly one-dimensional; a minor credit for all concerned. Unreleased in U.S. till 1996. [R]▼●

Innocent Affair, An (1948) **90m.** ** D: Lloyd Bacon. Fred MacMurray, Madeleine Carroll, Buddy Rogers, Rita Johnson, Alan Mowbray, Louise Allbritton, Anne Nagel. Outmoded marital sex comedy of love and jealousy, bolstered by teaming of MacMurray and Carroll—their fifth and final pairing. Retitled: DON'T TRUST YOUR HUSBAND.

Innocent and the Damned SEE: **Girls Town**

Innocent Blood (1992) **C-112m.** *** D: John Landis. Anne Parillaud, Robert Loggia, Anthony LaPaglia, David Proval, Don Rickles, Chazz Palminteri, Rocco Siusto, Tony Sirico, Tony Lip, Kim Coates, Angela Bassett, Luis Guzman, Leo Burmester, Linnea Quigley, Frank Oz. Guilty-pleasure time: a sexy French vampire (Parillaud) sinks her teeth into mob boss Loggia and unwittingly unleashes a brood of bloodsucking gangsters! Meanwhile, good cop LaPaglia tries to figure out just what's going on. Wild and woolly crossbreed of urban action thriller and vampire movie, with a wicked sense of humor; doesn't always make sense, but fun to watch (if you can take the blood). Rickles is terrific as Loggia's loyal lawyer. Landis casts other film directors, as usual, in cameo roles, including Dario Argento, Michael Ritchie, and Sam Raimi. [R]▼●◗

Innocent Bystanders (1973-British) **C-111m.** **½ D: Peter Collinson. Stanley Baker, Geraldine Chaplin, Donald Pleasence, Dana Andrews, Sue Lloyd, Derren Nesbitt. Baker plays James Bond-like character involved in international manhunt for Russian scientist who has escaped from Siberia. Well-made but standard fare, with heavy doses of sadism and violence. [PG]

Innocent Man, An (1989) **C-113m.** ** D: Peter Yates. Tom Selleck, F. Murray Abraham, Laila Robins, David Rasche, Richard Young, Badja Djola. Happily married airline mechanic is mistaken for a drug contact by a pair of on-the-take cops who've burst into his home; victim gets a hearty course of "Slammer 101" after both slugs frame him. Slick and soft at the center, despite some potentially compelling script elements; not too strong on credibility, either. [R]▼●

Innocents, The (1961-British) **100m.** ***½ D: Jack Clayton. Deborah Kerr, Michael Redgrave, Peter Wyngarde, Megs Jenkins, Pamela Franklin, Martin Stephens. First-rate thriller based on Henry James' "The Turn of the Screw," with Kerr as governess haunted by specters that may or may not be real. Script by William Archibald and Truman Capote, brilliantly realized on film. Photographed by Freddie Francis. Remade in 1992 as THE TURN OF THE SCREW. CinemaScope.▼●

Innocents in Paris (1953-British) **93m.** *** D: Gordon Parry. Alastair Sim, Ronald Shiner, Claire Bloom, Margaret Rutherford, Claude Dauphin, Laurence Harvey, Jimmy Edwards, Richard Wattis, Louis de Funes, Christopher Lee. Engaging comedy about seven diverse types crossing the Channel to France, each having wacky adventures. Original British running time 102m.

Innocent Sleep, The (1996-British) **C-95m.** ** D: Scott Michell. Rupert Graves, Annabella Sciorra, Michael Gambon, Franco Nero, John Hannah, Graham Crowden. A drunken derelict in London finds himself being pursued by a corrupt cop after witnessing a murder and stumbling onto a high-level international conspiracy. Old-fashioned, would-be Hitchcockian "innocent-man-on-the-run" thriller is extremely slow moving and murkily plotted, with a cop-out finale that fails to wrap up the myriad loose ends. Super 35. [R]▼

Innocents with Dirty Hands SEE: **Dirty Hands**

Innocent Victim (1989-British) **C-89m.** **½ D: Giles Foster. Helen Shaver, Lauren Bacall, Malcolm Stoddard, Peter Firth, Paul McGann, Katie Hardie, Tony Haygarth, Phyllida Law. When the young son of unmarried writer Shaver unexpectedly dies, her disturbed mother (Bacall) kidnaps another boy, the abused son of a would-be singer (Hardie). Deliberately paced thriller with too many plot twists; well acted, but wears out its welcome. Based on a novel by Ruth Rendell. Original British title: TREE OF HANDS.▼

Inn of the Damned (1974-Australian)

C-118m. **½ D: Terry Bourke. Judith Anderson, Alex Cord, Michael Craig, Joseph Furst, Tony Bonner, John Meillon. Bounty hunter Cord investigates the disappearances of travelers at an inn operated by sickies Anderson and Furst. Fair of its type, uplifted immeasurably by Anderson's entertaining performance.▼

Inn of the Frightened People (1971-British) **89m.** ** D: Sidney Hayers. Joan Collins, James Booth, Ray Barrett, Sinead Cusack, Tom Marshall, Kenneth Griffith. Parents of young girl who was raped and murdered take revenge on man they believe guilty. Sordid, low-budget thriller with some interesting moments. British title: REVENGE. Aka TERROR FROM UNDER THE HOUSE. ▼

Inn of the Sixth Happiness, The (1958) **C-158m.** *** D: Mark Robson. Ingrid Bergman, Curt Jurgens, Robert Donat, Ronald Squire, Athene Seyler, Richard Wattis. True story of English servant (Bergman) who, despite her lack of credentials, realizes her dream of becoming a missionary in China. Bergman is wonderful and Donat memorable in final screen performance. Simple, effective score by Malcolm Arnold. CinemaScope. ▼●

In Nome del Papa Re SEE: **In the Name of the Pope King**

Inn on the River, The (1962-German) **95m.** **½ D: Alfred Vohrer. Joachim Fuchsberger, Klaus Kinski, Brigitte Grothum, Richard Much. Remake of THE RETURN OF THE FROG, this Edgar Wallace yarn involves series of brutal murders on the waterfront by the "Shark's" gang. ▼

In Old California (1942) **88m.** ** D: William McGann. John Wayne, Binnie Barnes, Albert Dekker, Helen Parrish, Patsy Kelly, Edgar Kennedy, Dick Purcell, Harry Shannon. Wayne moves into Western town controlled by shifty Dekker, with inevitable confrontation. Also shown in computer-colored version. ▼

In Old Chicago (1938) **95m.** ***½ D: Henry King. Tyrone Power, Alice Faye, Don Ameche, Alice Brady, Andy Devine, Brian Donlevy, Phyllis Brooks, Tom Brown, Berton Churchill, Sidney Blackmer, Gene Reynolds, Bobs Watson. Lavish period-piece building up to Chicago fire of 1871; Oscar-winning Brady is Mrs. O'Leary, whose sons Power, Ameche, and Brown find their own adventures in the Windy City. Scripted by Lamar Trotti and Sonya Levien, based on a story by Niven Busch. Originally released at 115m.▼

In Old Kentucky (1935) **86m.** **½ D: George Marshall. Will Rogers, Dorothy Wilson, Bill "Bojangles" Robinson, Russell Hardie, Louise Henry, Charles Sellon. Story is as old as the hills—a family feud—but Rogers' natural charm and Bojangles' fantastic footwork make it most enjoyable.

In Old Oklahoma (1943) **102m.** **½ D: Albert S. Rogell. John Wayne, Martha Scott, Albert Dekker, Gabby Hayes, Marjorie Rambeau, Sidney Blackmer, Dale Evans. Slugger Wayne brooks no nonsense in this oil-drilling yarn; good action, obligatory romance. Aka WAR OF THE WILDCATS. ▼

In Our Hands (1984) **C-90m.** *** No director credited. Impressive record of June 1982 anti-nuclear rally in N.Y.C. Speeches and musical performances by Helen Caldicott and Benjamin Spock, Pete Seeger, Carly Simon, Peter, Paul & Mary, Holly Near, Roy Scheider, Ellen Burstyn, Jill Clayburgh, Orson Welles, Meryl Streep, and dozens of others.▼

In Our Time (1944) **110m.** **½ D: Vincent Sherman. Ida Lupino, Paul Henreid, Nazimova, Nancy Coleman, Mary Boland, Victor Francen, Michael Chekhov. Lupino and Henreid try to save Poland from Nazi takeover in plush soaper that seeks to be meaningful propaganda; Nazimova is touching as Henreid's aristocratic mother. Never quite hits the mark.

In Person (1935) **85m.** **½ D: William Seiter. Ginger Rogers, George Brent, Alan Mowbray, Grant Mitchell, Samuel S. Hinds, Joan Breslau. In between TOP HAT and FOLLOW THE FLEET, Rogers made this formula comedy about a movie star who's had a nervous breakdown; while recuperating, she spars romantically with Brent. Trivial, but pleasant.▼●

In Praise of Older Women (1978-Canadian) **C-108m.** BOMB D: George Kaczender. Tom Berenger, Karen Black, Susan Strasberg, Helen Shaver, Alexandra Stewart, Marilyn Lightstone. Hungarian stud recalls nearly two decades' worth of conquests, all of whom are paraded across the screen in various stages of undress. Strasberg and Stewart are particularly praiseworthy, but nothing else is in this tease of a movie. Remade in 1997. [R]▼

In Pursuit of Honor (1995) **C-110m. TVM** D: Ken Olin. Don Johnson, Craig Sheffer, Gabrielle Anwar, Bob Gunton, Rod Steiger, John Dennis Johnston, Robert Coleby. Invigorating retelling of a little-known episode in American history: a 1935 military mutiny involving five cavalry soldiers who chose to defy Gen. Douglas MacArthur's order to destroy hundreds of horses as part of the army's modernization program. The standard disclaimer about no animals being harmed during the filming makes the viewer wonder about how the onscreen machine-gunning of dozens of horses was accomplished. This all-American "black mark" was filmed in Australia. Written by Dennis Lynton Clark. Made for cable. Above average.▼●

Inquiry, The (1987-Italian) **C-107m.** **½ D: Damiano Damiani. Keith Carradine, Harvey Keitel, Phyllis Logan, Lina Sastri.

Intriguing story treats the resurrection of Christ as a mystery thriller. Carradine is a hardnosed investigator sent from Rome to find out what happened to the missing body of Jesus Christ; an official cover-up is presumed. Offbeat point of view holds interest. Excellent dubbing of the Italian supporting characters, but it's still distracting to hear Keitel's Bronx accent as Pontius Pilate. ▼

In Search of Gregory (1970-British) **C-90m.** ** D: Peter Wood. Julie Christie, Michael Sarrazin, John Hurt, Adolfo Celi, Paola Pitagora. Muddled film set in Geneva, about two potential lovers who fantasize about, but never meet, each other. [M/PG]

In Search of Historic Jesus (1980) **C-91m.** BOMB D: Henning G. Schellerup. John Rubinstein, John Anderson, Nehemiah Persoff, Andrew Bloch, Morgan Brittany, Walter Brooke, Royal Dano, Lawrence Dobkin. Sunn Classic drivel about Jesus and the Shroud of Turin. Film should be retitled "In Search of Morons Who Will Believe Anything." Narrated ominously by Brad Crandall. [G]▼●

In Search of Noah's Ark (1976) **C-95m.** *½ D: James L. Conway. Narrated by Brad Crandall. Cheaply made documentary reveals "new evidence" that Noah's ark really existed. Premise may hold your attention. [G]▼

In Search of the Castaways (1962) **C-100m.** **½ D: Robert Stevenson. Hayley Mills, Maurice Chevalier, George Sanders, Wilfrid Hyde-White, Michael Anderson, Jr., Keith Hamshire. Expedition tries to locate missing sea captain, in journey that encounters fire, flood, earthquake and other disasters. Disney adaptation of Jules Verne suffers from muddled continuity; good cast does its best.▼●

Insect SEE: **Blue Monkey**

Inseminoid SEE: **Horror Planet**

Inserts (1975-British) **C-99m.** BOMB D: John Byrum. Richard Dreyfuss, Jessica Harper, Veronica Cartwright, Bob Hoskins, Stephen Davies. Pretentious, unending nonsense played out by five characters on one set: decaying Hollywood mansion in early thirties where once-famous director now makes porno films. Dreadful. The British version runs 117m. [X]▼

Inside (1996) **C-94m.** ** D: Arthur Penn. Eric Stoltz, Nigel Hawthorne, Louis Gossett, Jr., Ian Roberts, Jerry Mofokeng. South African university professor Stoltz is accused of conspiring against the apartheid government and is subjected to ruthless interrogation by a sadistic colonel (Hawthorne). Years later, the colonel is subject to questioning by Gossett. The cast is first rate and the subject matter is interesting, but film lacks dramatic spark. First shown on cable TV. [R]▼●

Inside Daisy Clover (1965) **C-128m.** **½ D: Robert Mulligan. Natalie Wood, Robert Redford, Christopher Plummer, Roddy McDowall, Ruth Gordon, Katherine Bard. Potentially biting account of Wood's rise as Hollywood star in 1930s misfires; pat situations with caricatures instead of people. Panavision.▼●

Inside Detroit (1955) **82m.** ** D: Fred F. Sears. Dennis O'Keefe, Pat O'Brien, Margaret Field, Mark Damon. Ordinary exposé-style narrative of corruption in automobile industry.

Inside Job (1946) **65m.** ** D: Jean Yarbrough. Preston Foster, Ann Rutherford, Alan Curtis, Jimmy Moss. Sensible minor film of struggling young marrieds tempted to enter life of crime to solve their financial problems.

Inside Monkey Zetterland (1992) **C-93m.** **½ D: Jefery Levy. Steven Antin, Katherine Helmond, Patricia Arquette, Tate Donovan, Sandra Bernhard, Sofia Coppola, Rupert Everett, Bo Hopkins, Martha Plimpton, Debi Mazar, Ricki Lake, Lance Loud, Francis Bay. Hit-and-miss L.A. comedy about the title character (Antin), a young screenwriter, and his complex connections with family (most tellingly, soap opera star mom Helmond) and friends. Filled with moments of humor and insight, and tolerance for its various offbeat characters, but at other times affected and formulaic. Loosely autobiographical; star Antin scripted and coproduced. [R]▼●

Inside Moves (1980) **C-113m.** **½ D: Richard Donner. John Savage, David Morse, Diana Scarwid, Amy Wright, Tony Burton, Bill Henderson, Bert Remsen, Harold Russell. Offbeat drama about a young suicide survivor (Savage) who falls in with a group of upbeat misfits and learns about self-esteem. A well-meaning film with some excellent performances and emotional highpoints but a few too many story flaws—including the final scene. Russell's first film since THE BEST YEARS OF OUR LIVES. Panavision. [PG]▼●

Inside Out (1975-British) **C-97m.** **½ D: Peter Duffell. Telly Savalas, James Mason, Robert Culp, Aldo Ray, Charles Korvin. Savalas engineers break-in at maximum security prison in East Germany to free notorious war criminal who knows whereabouts of a secret cache of gold. Not bad international caper. Retitled HITLER'S GOLD and THE GOLDEN HEIST. [PG] ▼

Inside Out (1986) **C-87m.** **½ D: Robert Taicher. Elliott Gould, Howard Hesseman, Jennifer Tilly, Beah Richards, Dana Elcar, Nicole Norman. Sad little film about a man whose problems only begin with his agoraphobia—his irrational fear of being in public places. An interesting story that after a while, like its main character, has nowhere to go. Still, the vignette about the homeless man in the hallway is quite touching. [R]▼

Insider, The (1999) **C-157m.** ***½ D: Michael Mann. Al Pacino, Russell Crowe, Christopher Plummer, Diane Venora, Philip Baker Hall, Lindsay Crouse, Debi Mazar, Stephen Tobolowsky, Colm Feore, Bruce McGill, Gina Gershon, Michael Gambon, Rip Torn, Lynne Thigpen, Hallie Kate Eisenberg, Wings Hauser, Pete Hamill. Dynamic fact-based story of a gutsy segment producer for TV's *60 Minutes* (Pacino) who sniffs out a story in disaffected scientist Crowe, who's just been fired by a major tobacco company. Compelling, adult entertainment that finds great drama in the real-life machinations of TV journalism (and big business). Great performances all around. Screenplay by Mann and Eric Roth, based on a magazine story by Marie Brenner. Super 35. [R]▼◗

Insiders, The SEE: **Policewomen**

Inside Story, The (1948) **87m.** ** D: Allan Dwan. Marsha Hunt, William Lundigan, Charles Winninger, Gail Patrick. Warm, minor film set in Depression days in Vermont, involving sudden circulation of large amount of money.

Inside Straight (1951) **89m.** **½ D: Gerald Mayer. David Brian, Arlene Dahl, Barry Sullivan, Mercedes McCambridge. Study of greed and corruption as ambitious man rises to fortune in 1870s San Francisco only to find life empty.

Inside the Mafia (1959) **72m.** **½ D: Edward L. Cahn. Cameron Mitchell, Elaine Edwards, Robert Strauss, Jim L. Brown, Ted de Corsia, Grant Richards. Gunblasting account of the Black Hand organization, with cast having field-day.

Inside the Walls of Folsom Prison (1951) **87m.** ** D: Crane Wilbur. Steve Cochran, David Brian, Philip Carey, Ted de Corsia. Moderately successful account of crusade to improve harsh penitentiary conditions.

Insignificance (1985-British) **C-110m.** ***½ D: Nicolas Roeg. Gary Busey, Tony Curtis, Theresa Russell, Michael Emil, Will Sampson. Striking, gloriously cinematic examination of the meaning of fame in America and the perils of atomic warfare. The stars are cast as unnamed celebrities—a ballplayer, senator, actress, and professor—who resemble Joe DiMaggio, Joseph McCarthy, Marilyn Monroe, and Albert Einstein, and meet in a N.Y.C. hotel room in 1954. Funny, ironic, thought provoking. Wonderfully acted by all. Screenplay by Terry Johnson. [R] ▼●

In Society (1944) **75m.** ** D: Jean Yarbrough. Bud Abbott, Lou Costello, Marion Hutton, Arthur Treacher, Thomas Gomez, Thurston Hall, Kirby Grant. Minor A&C, with the boys as plumbers mistaken for members of society; hectic slapstick finale. Includes chase footage lifted from NEVER GIVE A SUCKER AN EVEN BREAK.▼

Insomnia (1997-Norwegian) **C-97m.** *** D: Erik Skjoldbjaerg. Stellan Skarsgård, Sverre Anker Ousdal, Gisken Armand, Bjorn Floberg, Maria Bonnevie, Kristian Figenschow. Moody police thriller with two criminal investigators traveling to remote, arctic Norway on a murder case; soon the relentless midnight sun and tactical missteps cause one of the men to unravel. Skarsgård is good, as always, in this psychological maelstrom.▼◗

Inspecteur Lavardin (1986-French) **C-99m.** **½ D: Claude Chabrol. Jean Poiret, Jean-Claude Brialy, Bernadette Lafont, Jacques Dacqmine, Jean-Luc Bideau, Hermine Claire, Pierre-Francois Dumeniaud, Florent Gibassier, Guy Louret, Jean Depusse. Crime and comedy make for an unusual mix in this tale of quirky police detective Poiret's murder investigation in a French seaside village. Lafont—newly widowed, wealthy, and an old flame of the inspector's—and her wacky brother (Brialy) head the list of suspects. A sequel to Chabrol's COP AU VIN/POULET AU VINAIGRE (1984) which introduced Poiret's Lavardin character in a supporting role.

Inspector Calls, An (1954-British) **80m.** *** D: Guy Hamilton. Alastair Sim, Arthur Young, Olga Lindo, Eileen Moore. J. B. Priestley play detailing British police detective Sim's investigation of girl's suicide. Via flashbacks he learns a family's responsibility for her fate. Clever plot finale.

Inspector Clouseau (1968) **C-94m.** ** D: Bud Yorkin. Alan Arkin, Delia Boccardo, Frank Finlay, Patrick Cargill, Beryl Reid, Barry Foster. Scotland Yard calls on inept French detective to crack potential robbery; in spite of Arkin's talents, Peter Sellers is too well identified with the role (from other Pink Panther movies) for one to fully accept this characterization. Besides, film isn't particularly funny. Made in England. Panavision. [G]

Inspector Gadget (1999) **C-80m.** ** D: David Kellogg. Matthew Broderick, Rupert Everett, Joely Fisher, Michelle Trachtenberg, Andy Dick, Cheri Oteri, Michael G. Hagerty, Dabney Coleman, Rene Auberjonois, Frances Bay; voices of D. L. Hughley, Don Adams. Desperate gimmick comedy for kids based on the 1980s animated TV series. After a severe accident, Broderick's body is pieced back together with cutting-edge technology, just right for chasing bad guys like Everett (aka Claw). Gizmos and slapstick galore, but precious few laughs in this Disney concoction. [PG]▼●◗

Inspector General, The (1949) **C-102m.** *** D: Henry Koster. Danny Kaye, Walter Slezak, Barbara Bates, Elsa Lanchester, Gene Lockhart, Alan Hale, Walter Catlett.

Kaye plays a buffoon who pretends to be a visiting bureaucrat in an Eastern European village. Entertaining musical adaptation of the Gogol story.▼

Inspector Maigret (1958-French) **110m.** **½ D: Jean Delannoy. Jean Gabin, Annie Girardot, Oliver Hussenot, Jeanne Boitel. Famed French detective must track down notorious woman-killer. Retitled: WOMAN-BAIT.

Inspiration (1931) **74m.** **½ D: Clarence Brown. Greta Garbo, Robert Montgomery, Lewis Stone, Marjorie Rambeau, Beryl Mercer, Oscar Apfel. Lesser Garbo vehicle about beautiful Parisian woman whose past makes her decide to leave Montgomery, even though she still loves him. A modern version of Alphonse Daudet's *Sappho.* ▼●

Instant Justice (1987-Gibraltar) **C-101m.** **½ D: Christopher Bentley (Denis Amar). Michael Paré, Tawny Kitaen, Peter Crook, Charles Napier. Solid action scenes spark routine drama of young marine Paré resigning his commission to go after the killers of his sister. Kitaen is the beautiful call girl who reluctantly helps him. Originally titled: MARINE ISSUE. [R]▼

Instinct (1999) **C-124m.** **½ D: Jon Turteltaub. Anthony Hopkins, Cuba Gooding, Jr., Donald Sutherland, Maura Tierney, George Dzundza, John Ashton, John Aylward, Thomas Q. Morris, Doug Spinuzza. Ambitious psychiatric resident (Gooding) evaluates brilliant and/or insane primatologist (Hopkins), who's been living among the Rwandan gorillas he studied and who may have murdered some park rangers. Talky drama sets off a few sparks whenever the two leads square off, and has some CUCKOO'S NEST flourishes throughout. Panavision. [R]▼●◗

Insurance Man, The (1985-British) **C-77m.** *** D: Richard Eyre. Robert Hines, Daniel Day-Lewis, Jim Broadbent, Hugh Fraser, Tony Haygarth. Dramatically uneven yet still ambitious, impressive account of a young dyeworker named Franz (Hines), whose body develops a rash, and his dealings with both the bureaucracy and a man named Mr. Kafka (Day-Lewis), a claims assessor who also writes. A tribute to Kafka and his work, with a screenplay by Alan Bennett.

Intent to Kill (1958-British) **89m.** **½ D: Jack Cardiff. Richard Todd, Betsy Drake, Herbert Lom, Warren Stevens, Carlo Justini, Alexander Knox, Lisa Gastoni, Jackie Collins. OK thriller about South American president Lom, who's been shot, and who arrives in Montreal incognito for brain surgery—where assassins plot to do him in. Scripted by Jimmy Sangster. CinemaScope.▼●

Interiors (1978) **C-93m.** ***½ D: Woody Allen. Diane Keaton, Geraldine Page, E. G. Marshall, Maureen Stapleton, Kristin Griffith, Mary Beth Hurt, Richard Jordan, Sam Waterston. Woody Allen's first screen drama as writer-director is an Ingmar Bergmanesque study of a family full of unhappy, frustrated men and women; this drama of anguished lives is not for all tastes, but extremely well done. [PG]▼●

Interlude (1957) **C-90m.** **½ D: Douglas Sirk. June Allyson, Rossano Brazzi, Marianne Cook (Koch), Jane Wyatt, Françoise Rosay. Adequate tearjerker of Allyson falling in love with Continental composer Brazzi, whose wife refuses to accept the situation. Remake of WHEN TOMORROW COMES, and remade in 1968 under same title. CinemaScope.

Interlude (1968-British) **C-113m.** *** D: Kevin Billington. Oskar Werner, Barbara Ferris, Virginia Maskell, Donald Sutherland, Nora Swinburne, Alan Webb, John Cleese. Charming, sentimental tale of symphony conductor and reporter who have an affair; told in flashback. Previously filmed as WHEN TOMORROW COMES and INTERLUDE (1957). [M/PG]

Intermezzo (1936-Swedish) **88m.** *** D: Gustav Molander. Gosta Ekman, Inga Tidblad, Ingrid Bergman, Bullen Berglund, Britt Hagman. Young pianist Bergman and famous—but married—violinist Ekman fall in love. Ingrid is ravishing in her sixth Swedish film; its remake, three years later, was to be her Hollywood debut. Coscripted by Molander. ▼●

Intermezzo (1939) **70m.** ***½ D: Gregory Ratoff. Leslie Howard, Ingrid Bergman, Edna Best, Cecil Kellaway, John Halliday. One of the best love stories ever filmed, as married Howard, renowned violinist, has an affair with musical protégée Bergman (in her first English-speaking film). Short and sweet, highlighted by Robert Henning–Heinz Provost love theme. Original title: INTERMEZZO, A LOVE STORY; Bergman played same role in Gustav Molander's Swedish version. Remade, after a fashion, as HONEYSUCKLE ROSE.▼●◗

Internal Affairs (1990) **C-117m.** ** D: Mike Figgis. Richard Gere, Andy Garcia, Nancy Travis, Laurie Metcalf, Richard Bradford, William Baldwin, Michael Beach, Annabella Sciorra, Elijah Wood. Smarmy, overripe, and overlong drama about a young cop who joins L.A.'s Internal Affairs Dept. and becomes obsessed with nailing a cocky, corrupt officer (Gere) who's a past master at manipulating people. Intriguing ideas get lost, and illogic takes over pretty quickly. [R]▼●◗

International House (1933) **70m.** ***½ D: A. Edward Sutherland. W. C. Fields, Peggy Hopkins Joyce, Stuart Erwin, George Burns, Gracie Allen, Bela Lugosi, Franklin Pangborn, Rudy Vallee, Sterling Holloway, Cab Calloway, Baby Rose Marie.

Offbeat, delightful film with early television experiment bringing people from all over the world to large Oriental hotel. Spotlight alternates between Fields and Burns & Allen, all in rare form, with guest spots by various radio entertainers. Short and sweet, a must-see film. Calloway sings the memorable "Reefer Man."▼●

International Lady (1941) **102m.** ★★½ D: Tim Whelan. Ilona Massey, George Brent, Basil Rathbone, Gene Lockhart, Martin Kosleck, Clayton Moore. Massey is a femme fatale spy, Brent the U.S. government agent involved in cracking espionage ring. Superficial but entertaining.▼

International Settlement (1938) **75m.** ★★ D: Eugene Forde. George Sanders, Dolores Del Rio, June Lang, Dick Baldwin, Leon Ames, John Carradine, Harold Huber. Mediocre tale of Shanghai intrigue with Sanders masquerading as notorious smuggler, pursued by various crooks and sultry Del Rio.

International Squadron (1941) **87m.** ★★½ D: Lothar Mendes. Ronald Reagan, James Stephenson, Olympe Bradna, William Lundigan, Joan Perry, Julie Bishop, Cliff Edwards. Air Force straightens out no-account Reagan and turns him into fighting ace. Standard war story, a remake of CEILING ZERO.

International Velvet (1978-British) **C-127m.** ★★★ D: Bryan Forbes. Tatum O'Neal, Christopher Plummer, Anthony Hopkins, Nanette Newman, Dinsdale Landen. Long overdue sequel to NATIONAL VELVET has Velvet (Newman) a grown woman with a live-in lover (Plummer) and a niece (O'Neal) primed to follow in her footsteps as an Olympic horsewoman. Too lengthy and shunned by the critics, but deftly played by Hopkins and Plummer; exquisitely filmed, entertaining. [PG]▼

Internecine Project, The (1974-British) **C-89m.** ★★ D: Ken Hughes. James Coburn, Lee Grant, Harry Andrews, Ian Hendry, Michael Jayston, Keenan Wynn. Lackluster espionage drama with Coburn as opportunist who tries to eliminate skeletons in his closet by having a handful of industrial spies kill each other off. [PG]▼

Internes Can't Take Money (1937) **77m.** ★★½ D: Alfred Santell. Barbara Stanwyck, Joel McCrea, Lloyd Nolan, Stanley Ridges, Lee Bowman, Irving Bacon, Pierre Watkin, Charles Lane, Fay Holden. Fairly successful hybrid of medical drama and gangster tale, with a bit of mother-love sentiment thrown in for good measure. Young intern McCrea helps ex-con Stanwyck rescue her daughter from crooks in the first film to be adapted from the *Dr. Kildare* stories by Max Brand.▼

Interns, The (1962) **120m.** ★★★ D: David Swift. Michael Callan, Cliff Robertson, James MacArthur, Nick Adams, Suzy Parker, Haya Harareet, Stefanie Powers, Buddy Ebsen, Telly Savalas. Glossy, renovated DR. KILDARE soap opera, kept afloat by an interesting young cast. Followed by sequel THE NEW INTERNS.▼●

Interrupted Journey (1949-British) **80m.** ★★½ D: Daniel Birt. Richard Todd, Valerie Hobson, Christine Norden, Tom Walls, Ralph Truman. Eerie film about Todd, who runs off with another woman, finds himself caught in a living nightmare. OK thriller is hampered by a cornball finale. ▼

Interrupted Melody (1955) **C-106m.** ★★★ D: Curtis Bernhardt. Eleanor Parker, Glenn Ford, Roger Moore, Cecil Kellaway, Ann Codee, Stephan Bekassy. Fine biography of Marjorie Lawrence, Australian opera star, who made a comeback after being crippled by polio. Eileen Farrell sings for Parker. William Ludwig and Sonya Levien won Oscars for their story and screenplay. CinemaScope.▼●

Intersection (1994) **C-98m.** ★½ D: Mark Rydell. Richard Gere, Sharon Stone, Lolita Davidovich, Martin Landau, David Selby, Jenny Morrison, Ron White. Dreary romantic triangle of wealthy architect Gere, who has drifted apart from his aloof wife (Stone), and taken up with spunky Davidovich. Meanwhile, all involved feel terribly guilty about the teenage daughter they're hurting. Title comes from an accident site, which prompts all this moping around in a series of flashbacks. Derived from a 1970 French feature, LES CHOSES DE LA VIE (THE THINGS OF LIFE), directed by Claude Sautet. [R]▼●

Interval (1973-Mexican) **C-84m.** ★★ D: Daniel Mann. Merle Oberon, Robert Wolders, Claudio Brook, Russ Conway, Charles Bateman, Barbara Ransom. A globetrotting woman, running from her past, finds true love with a much younger man (Wolders, who became Oberon's husband in real life). Drippy May-December romance, filmed in Mexico and produced by Oberon, whose last film this was. [PG] ▼

Interview With the Vampire: The Vampire Chronicles (1994) **C-122m.** ★½ D: Neil Jordan. Tom Cruise, Brad Pitt, Antonio Banderas, Stephen Rea, Christian Slater, Kirsten Dunst, Domiziana Giordano, Thandie Newton, Indra Ove. In contemporary San Francisco, a young man grants an interview about his two-hundred-year existence as a vampire—a "life" with which he has never felt completely comfortable. Likely to satisfy fans of Anne Rice's popular novel, and female fans of its star "hunks," but this descent into the netherworld is unappealing, unrelenting, and (after a while) downright boring. The actors can't be faulted, nor can the handsome production design. [R]▼●◗

Intervista (1987-Italian) **C-108m.** ★★★ D: Federico Fellini. Sergio Rubini, Antonella Ponziani, Maurizio Mein, Paola Liguori,

Lara Wendel, Antonio Cantafora, Nadia Ottaviani, Anita Ekberg, Marcello Mastroianni, Federico Fellini. Engaging, illuminating mock-documentary about the making of a film about Fellini; the master is depicted in production of an adaptation of Kafka's *Amerika*. Mastroianni and Ekberg (who costarred almost 30 years before in LA DOLCE VITA) appear as themselves. The film also serves as an homage to Cinecittà, the studio where Fellini shot all of his classics. To fully appreciate this very personal movie about the moviemaking process, you must be familiar with—and an admirer of—Fellini and his work. Released in the U.S. in 1992.▼

In the Army Now (1994) **C-91m.** *½ D: Daniel Petrie, Jr. Pauly Shore, Lori Petty, David Alan Grier, Andy Dick, Esai Morales, Lynn Whitfield, Art LeFleur, Tom Villard, Keith Coogan. Pauly is a pacifist who joins the army so he can "be all that he can be for free," only to learn that there's more to enlisting than receiving complimentary room and board. Latest in a long line of barracks comedies proves no competition for BUCK PRIVATES. Pauly's fans might disagree. Brendan Fraser appears unbilled. [PG] ▼●

In the Best of Families (1994) **C-200m. TVM** D: Jeff Bleckner. Kelly McGillis, Harry Hamlin, Keith Carradine, Holland Taylor, Jayne Brook, Ken Jenkins, Elizabeth Wilson, Louise Latham, Marian Seldes. 1970s Southern belle unravels and goes on a murderous spree against her own parents and those of her loving ex-husband with the help of her volatile survivalist cousin. Well-turned adaptation by Robert L. Freedman of Jerry Bledsoe's true-crime best-seller. Originally shown in two parts. Above average.

In the Bleak Midwinter SEE: **Midwinter's Tale, A**

In the Company of Men (1997) **C-93m.** ** D: Neil LaBute. Aaron Eckhart, Stacy Edwards, Matt Malloy, Mark Rector. Provocative but stark and discomfiting low-budget film about two yuppie office workers who—frustrated by the world around them, and women in particular—make a pact that while they're on assignment in another city, they'll both date a woman and then dump her, just for the satisfaction of it. The slicker of the two (Eckhart) turns out to have a hidden agenda, however. Alternately absorbing, humdrum, and distasteful. Eckhart's creepy character does get under your skin. Highly praised in some circles. Written by the director. [R]▼●◗

In the Cool of the Day (1963-British) **C-89m.** ** D: Robert Stevens. Peter Finch, Jane Fonda, Angela Lansbury, Arthur Hill, Constance Cummings, Alexander Knox, Nigel Davenport, Alec McCowen. Good cast flounders in turgid soaper, with Finch (who is married to bitchy Lansbury) mediating marital rift between Hill and his emotionally and physically fragile wife Fonda; soon Finch and Fonda fall in love. The on-location filming in Greece helps. Produced by John Houseman. Panavision.

In the Custody of Strangers (1982) **C-100m. TVM** D: Robert Greenwald. Martin Sheen, Jane Alexander, Emilio Estevez, Kenneth McMillan, Ed Lauter, Matt Clark, John Hancock, Virginia Kiser. Thoughtful drama about a middle-class family's ordeal when their teenage son (Sheen's real-life son, Estevez) is jailed on drunk charges with hardened criminals and the parents can't get him out. Written by Jennifer Miller. Above average.▼

In the Devil's Garden (1971-British) **C-89m.** *½ D: Sidney Hayers. Suzy Kendall, Frank Finlay, Freddie Jones, Lesley-Anne Down, James Laurenson, Tony Beckley. Undistinguished thriller of rapist-killer in girls' school; of interest mainly for the presence of Down, in an early role as one of the victims. Aka ASSAULT, THE CREEPERS, TOWER OF TERROR and SATAN'S PLAYTHINGS. Panavision. [R]▼

In the French Style (1963) **105m.** **½ D: Robert Parrish. Jean Seberg, Stanley Baker, Addison Powell, James Leo Herlihy, Philippe Forquet, Claudine Auger. Two short stories by Irwin Shaw are basis for this overlong account of American girl who discovers transient affairs are marring her life.

In the Good Old Summertime (1949) **C-102m.** *** D: Robert Z. Leonard. Judy Garland, Van Johnson, S. Z. "Cuddles" Sakall, Spring Byington, Clinton Sundberg, Buster Keaton. Musical remake of THE SHOP AROUND THE CORNER, with Garland and Johnson the pen pals who fall in love. Not up to most MGM Garland vehicles, but pleasant. That's young Liza Minnelli with Judy in the finale.▼●

In the Heat of Passion (1992) **C-102m.** **½ D: Rodman Flender. Sally Kirkland, Nick Corri, Jack Carter, Michael Greene, Gloria LeRoy, Carl Franklin. Low-budget but diverting film noir, with Corri a young garage mechanic who puts the moves on wealthy, mysterious Kirkland. When her husband gets in the way, what's a lover to do? Twisty tale encompasses a serial rapist and the reality-TV show tracking him, with Corri's assistance. Genuinely suspenseful, sexually frank film hindered by mediocre production values. [R]▼●

In the Heat of the Night (1967) **C-109m.** **** D: Norman Jewison. Sidney Poitier, Rod Steiger, Warren Oates, Lee Grant, Scott Wilson, Larry Gates, Quentin Dean, James Patterson, Anthony James, William Schallert. Redneck Southern sheriff grudgingly accepts help from big-city black detective in solving bizarre murder. Marvelous social thriller hasn't dated one bit—tough, funny, and atmospheric, with unbeatable acting and splendid Quincy Jones score. Five Oscars include Best Picture, Actor (Steiger), Screenplay (Stirling Silliphant), Editing (Hal Ashby). Poitier reprised his character in THEY CALL ME *MISTER* TIBBS! and THE ORGANIZATION. Followed by a TV series 20 years later. ▼●

In The Line of Fire (1993) **C-128m.** ***½ D: Wolfgang Petersen. Clint Eastwood, John Malkovich, Rene Russo, Dylan McDermott, Gary Cole, Fred Dalton Thompson, John Mahoney, Jim Curley, Clyde Kusatsu, Patrika Darbo, John Heard. Crackling, well-made thriller about a would-be presidential assassin who pulls Secret Service agent Eastwood—who failed to protect President Kennedy in 1963—into a cruel game of cat-and-mouse as he plans to murder the current president. Eastwood, as an older, vulnerable, piano-playing loner, has never been better, and Malkovich matches him as the superintelligent loony. Steve Railsback appears unbilled. Written by Jeff Maguire. Panavision. [R]▼●◗

In the Meantime, Darling (1944) **72m.** ** D: Otto Preminger. Jeanne Crain, Frank Latimore, Eugene Pallette, Mary Nash, Cara Williams, Reed Hadley, Stanley Prager, Gale Robbins. Predictable period piece about wealthy child-bride Crain, who learns duty and humility when forced to rough it after marrying G.I. Latimore. That's young Blake Edwards jitterbugging with Jeanne.

In the Money (1958) **61m.** ** D: William Beaudine. Huntz Hall, Stanley Clements, David Gorcey, Eddie LeRoy, Patricia Donahue, Paul Cavanagh, Leonard Penn. The final *Bowery Boys* outing, with Sach and the gang escorting a poodle on a cruise, and the ubiquitous thieves after a diamond concealed on the pooch.

In the Mood (1987) **C-99m.** **½ D: Phil Alden Robinson. Patrick Dempsey, Talia Balsam, Beverly D'Angelo, Michael Constantine, Betty Jinette, Kathleen Freeman, Peter Hobbs, Edith Fellows. Engaging if low-key comedy based on true story of 1944's "woo woo kid" Sonny Wisecarver, a 15-year-old California boy who made headlines because of his affairs with two "older" women, one of whom he actually married. Dempsey is ideal and Robinson's script is delightfully wry, but film lacks a certain punch. The real-life Wisecarver appears as a mailman in newsreel sequence (narrated by an uncredited Carl Reiner). Wonderful score by Ralph Burns, incorporating many vintage songs. [PG-13]▼●

In the Mouth of Madness (1995) **C-95m.** **½ D: John Carpenter. Sam Neill, Jürgen Prochnow, Charlton Heston, David Warner, John Glover, Julie Carmen, Bernie Casey, Peter Jason, Frances Bay, Hayden Christensen. From his padded cell, desperate Neill relates his story to Warner: Hired to locate reclusive horror writer Prochnow, Neill finds him in a small New England town. But then people, places, and even reality begin undergoing horrific transformations. The first two-thirds is among Carpenter's best work as a director, and Neill is outstanding, but the last third becomes pointlessly obscure, and the ending is a pretentious letdown. Derived, without credit, from concepts created by H. P. Lovecraft. Panavision. [R]▼●◗

In the Name of the Father (1993-U.S.-Irish) **C-127m.** ***½ D: Jim Sheridan. Daniel Day-Lewis, Pete Postlethwaite, Emma Thompson, John Lynch, Corin Redgrave, Beatie Edney, Daniel Massey. Searing, fact-based account of youthful Belfast no-good who's picked up—along with a friend and most of his family—by British police and accused of a terrorist bombing he had nothing to do with. Director Sheridan (reunited with his MY LEFT FOOT star) grabs you by the collar and never lets go; Day-Lewis is extraordinarily intense and believable, Postlethwaite every bit as good as his simple, straightforward dad. Gerry Conlon's book *Proved Innocent* adapted by Sheridan and Terry George. Gabriel Byrne executive-produced. [R]▼●◗

In the Name of the Pope King (1977-Italian) **C-105m.** *** D: Luigi Magni. Nino Manfredi, Danilo Mattei, Carmen Scarpitta, Giovannella Grifea, Carlo Bagno. Manfredi gives one of the best performances of his career in this moving tale, set in the mid-19th century, of a magistrate to the pontificial state whose son is suspected of terrorism. Not released in U.S. until 1986. Aka IN NOME DEL PAPA RE.▼

In the Navy (1941) **85m.** **½ D: Arthur Lubin. Bud Abbott, Lou Costello, Dick Powell, The Andrews Sisters, Claire Dodd, Dick Foran. Bud and Lou are somehow in the Navy; Lou has hallucinations and nearly wrecks the entire fleet. Powell and Andrews Sisters provide songs, and Costello shows Abbott how 7 × 13 = 28. ▼●◗

In the Realm of Passion SEE: **Empire of Passion**

In the Realm of the Senses (1976-Japanese-French) **C-105m.** **½ D: Nagisa Oshima. Tatsuya Fuji, Eiko Matsuda, Aio Nakajima, Meika Seri. Sexually insatiable Matsuda will do anything to possess husband Fuji. Explicit, controversial, often erotic and well-acted, but overall a pretentious film. The story was previously told in A WOMAN CALLED SADA ABE: BEYOND THE REALM OF THE SENSES.▼◗

In the Shadow of Kilimanjaro (1986-U.S.-British-Kenya) **C-97m.** BOMB D: Raju Patel. John Rhys-Davies, Timothy Bottoms, Michele Carey, Irene Miracle, Calvin Jung, Don Blakely, Patty Foley. There's a drought in the African bush, so 90,000 baboons are looking for dinner—and begin attacking humans. A ponderous, obvious, stupid movie that's also unnecessarily, disgustingly gory. Filmed on location in Kenya and based on a series of true events. [R]▼

In the Shadow of the Stars (1991) **C-93m.** *** D: Irving Saraf, Allie Light. Absorbing documentary about members of the chorus of the San Francisco Opera Company—the drive that makes them want to sing, the yearning to take center stage, the sacrifices made, the dreams fulfilled. Even non-opera lovers will be caught up in this very human story, simply but eloquently told (with a healthy selection of operatic excerpts). Oscar winner for Best Documentary Feature.▼

In the Soup (1992) **C/B&W-90m.** **½ D: Alexandre Rockwell. Steve Buscemi, Seymour Cassel, Jennifer Beals, Pat Moya, Will Patton, Sully Boyar, Jim Jarmusch, Carol Kane, Stanley Tucci, Rockets Redglare, Elizabeth Bracco. Absurdist comedy about a naive, ambitious writer (Buscemi) who's penned a 500-page screenplay, and the eccentric small-time hood (Cassel, in a canny, award-caliber performance) who promises to produce his film. At times very funny, but also downright silly; coscripted by Rockwell. Filmed in color, released in b&w. Both versions available on video.▼

In the Spirit (1990) **C-94m.** ** D: Sandra Seacat. Marlo Thomas, Elaine May, Peter Falk, Jeannie Berlin, Olympia Dukakis, Melanie Griffith, Michael Emil, Christopher Durang. Oddball throwback to black comedies of the 1970s, as mystic Thomas and house guest May get targeted by the mysterious killer who's murdered the prostitute next door. Packed with characters and performances that tend to grate on the nerves, though it is fun to see Thomas and May doing Abbott and Costello (or is it a neurotic version of Lucy and Ethel?). Griffith has just one scene. [R]▼

In the Wake of a Stranger (1958-British) **69m.** ** D: David Eady. Tony Wright, Shirley Eaton, Danny Green, Harry H. Corbett, Willoughby Goddard, Barbara Archer. Sailor implicated in murder tries to clear himself; just fair.

In the White City (1983-Swiss-Portuguese) **C-108m.** ***½ D: Alain Tanner. Bruno Ganz, Teresa Madruga, Julia Vonderlinn, Jose Carvalho. Involving, thought-provoking, Kafkaesque tale of seaman Ganz's experiences while in Lisbon, highlighted by his relationship with chambermaid Madruga. The work of a filmmaker in complete command of his art.▼

In This Our Life (1942) **97m.** *** D: John Huston. Bette Davis, Olivia de Havilland, George Brent, Dennis Morgan, Charles Coburn, Frank Craven, Billie Burke, Hattie McDaniel, Lee Patrick, Ernest Anderson. Fine drama of neurotic family with husband-stealing Davis ruining sister de Havilland's life, and eventually her own; Davis at histrionic height. Based on Ellen Glasgow novel. Walter Huston has cameo role as bartender in one scene. Also shown in computer-colored version.▼●

Intimacy (1966) **87m.** *½ D: Victor Stoloff. Jack Ging, Nancy Malone, Joan Blackman, Barry Sullivan, Jackie de Shannon. Grade-C drama may get more interesting response on TV than it deserves, since plot involves the spying on a Washington official by hidden cameras. Remade as THE WASHINGTON AFFAIR.

Intimate Lighting (1965-Czech) **72m.** *** D: Ivan Passer. Vera Kresadlova, Zdenek Brezusek, Karel Blazek, Jaroslava Stedra, Jan Vostrcil, Vlastmila Vlkova, Karel Uhlik. Unpretentious, day-in-the-life story of two old friends, professional musicians, reuniting after long absence at country home. Excellent performances.▼

Intimate Relations (1996-British-Canadian) **C-105m.** *** D: Philip Goodhew. Julie Walters, Rupert Graves, Matthew Walker, Laura Sadler, Holly Aird, Les Dennis, Elizabeth McKechnie. Black comedy/melodrama of romantic obsession in 1954 England. Housewife Walters (wickedly effective) takes in sailor Graves as a lodger, and in no time passions are aroused throughout the household. Interesting British Empire tale (fact-based, and for mature viewers) reminiscent in many ways of both A PRIVATE FUNCTION and HEAVENLY CREATURES. [R]▼●

Intimate Stranger, The SEE: **Finger of Guilt**

Intolerance (1916) **178m.** **** D: D. W. Griffith. Lillian Gish, Robert Harron, Mae Marsh, Constance Talmadge, Bessie Love, Seena Owen, Alfred Paget, Eugene Pallette, many others. Landmark American epic interweaves four stories of prejudice and inhumanity, from the Babylonian era to the modern day. Melodramatic, to be sure, but gains in momentum and power as it moves toward its stunning climax. That's Lillian Gish as the mother rocking the cradle; Constance Talmadge gives a most appealing and contemporary performance as the sprightly Mountain Girl. Shown in a variety of prints with variant running times—as long as 208m.▼●◗

In Too Deep (1999) **C-95m.** **½ D: Michael Rymer. Omar Epps, LL Cool J, Nia Long, Stanley Tucci, Hill Harper, Pam Grier, Veronica Webb. Police academy grad (Epps) goes undercover to take on a ruthless crimelord known as "God" (LL Cool J) but finds he can't get out. Gritty, realistic gangsploitation actually avoids most of the clichés of the genre and has a commanding, understated performance from Epps at its core. Hip-hoppers Jermaine Dupri, Mya and Nas appear in cameos. Super 35. [R]▼◗

Into the Blue (1950-British) **83m.** *½ D: Herbert Wilcox. Michael Wilding, Odile Versois, Jack Hulbert, Constance Cummings, Edward Rigby. Dreary comedy about stowaway Wilding and his adventures on a yacht. Retitled MAN IN THE DINGHY.▼

Into the Fire (1987-Canadian) **C-93m.** ** D: Graeme Campbell. Susan Anspach, Olivia d'Abo, Art Hindle. Old-fashioned murder/sex triangle thriller has the novelty of a wintry Canadian setting where lodge owner Anspach is an impressive seductress. Almost outdone by one too many plot twists. Precocious d'Abo is also a stunning, contrasting femme fatale. Aka LEGEND OF WOLF LODGE. [R]▼●

Into the Night (1985) **C-115m.** *** D: John Landis. Jeff Goldblum, Michelle Pfeiffer, Richard Farnsworth, Irene Papas, Kathryn Harrold, Paul Mazursky, Roger Vadim, Dan Aykroyd, David Bowie, Bruce McGill, Vera Miles, Clu Gulager. Engaging, episodic film about a middle-class nerd who helps a beautiful woman who's being chased by killers. Convoluted story filled with offbeat vignettes and colorful characters, many of them played by Hollywood directors (Don Siegel, Jonathan Demme, Jack Arnold, Lawrence Kasdan, Paul Bartel, David Cronenberg, Richard Franklin, Colin Higgins, Andrew Marton, Jonathan Kaufer, Amy Heckerling). Landis himself is very funny as one of the Iranian bad guys. Probably more appealing to film buffs than general audiences. [R]▼●

Into the Sun (1992) **C-100m.** *½ D: Fritz Kiersch. Anthony Michael Hall, Michael Paré, Deborah Maria Moore, Terry Kiser, Brian Haley. Hall plays a conceited actor who tags along with U.S. pilot Paré in order to research an upcoming film role. Virtually identical in plot to the Michael J. Fox/James Woods comedy THE HARD WAY, with a change in milieu (and budget). Aerial stunts aren't bad considering the threadbare production values, but it's only for those who'll try out anything that pops up on the video store shelves. [R]▼●

Into the West (1993-Irish) **C-97m.** *** D: Mike Newell. Gabriel Byrne, Colm Meaney, Ellen Barkin, Ciaran Fitzgerald, Ruaidhri Conroy, David Kelly, Johnny Murphy, John Kavanagh, Pauline Delaney. Dark, melancholy fable about two young brothers who flee their drab Dublin life (with a morose, widowed father) on the back of a mystical white horse. A highly original film with equal parts charm, dour Irish moods, and the theme of family and its inexorable pull on us all. Byrne was film's associate producer. Written by Jim Sheridan. [PG]▼●

Intrigue (1947) **90m.** ** D: Edwin L. Marin. George Raft, June Havoc, Helena Carter, Tom Tully, Marvin Miller, Dan Seymour, Philip Ahn, Michael Ansara. Predictable Raft vehicle of ex-military man with mar on his record turning Shanghai crime ring over to cops to clear himself.

Introducing Dorothy Dandridge (1999) **C-120m. TVM** D: Martha Coolidge. Halle Berry, Brent Spiner, Obba Babatunde, Loretta Devine, Cynda Williams, LaTanya Richardson, D.B. Sweeney, Klaus Maria Brandauer, William Atherton. Berry dazzles as equally dazzling Dandridge, whose performing career (and love life) took tragic turns in racist Hollywood of the 1950s. Based, a bit too obviously, on the book by Earl Mills, Dandridge's white friend, manager, and protector, played here by Spiner. Brandauer plays the despotic director Otto Preminger. Singing was dubbed by Wendi Williams. Made for cable. Average. ▼◗

Intruder, The (1955-British) **84m.** **½ D: Guy Hamilton. Jack Hawkins, Hugh Williams, Michael Medwin, Dennis Price, Dora Bryan. Hawkins is resolute army veteran who digs into past to discover why one of his old military group went astray.

Intruder, The (1962) **80m.** ***½ D: Roger Corman. William Shatner, Frank Maxwell, Beverly Lunsford, Robert Emhardt, Leo Gordon, Jeanne Cooper, Charles Beaumont, George Clayton Johnson, William F. Nolan. Racist Shatner drifts from one small Southern town to another inciting townspeople to riot against court-ordered school integration. Corman's only ''message'' film—and one of his few box-office flops—still packs a punch; low budget and location filming aid authenticity. Script by Charles Beaumont. Reissued as I HATE YOUR GUTS! and SHAME.▼

Intruder in the Dust (1949) **87m.** *** D: Clarence Brown. David Brian, Claude Jarman, Jr., Juano Hernandez, Porter Hall, Elizabeth Patterson. Black man (Hernandez, in a solid performance) is accused of murder in a Southern town, and a gathering mob wants to lynch him. First-rate adaptation of William Faulkner novel.▼

Invader, The (1936) SEE: **Old Spanish Custom, An**

Invader (1992) **C-95m.** ** D: Philip J. Cook. Hans Bachmann, A. Thomas Smith, Rick Foucheux, John Cooke, Robert Bidermann, Ralph Bluemke, Allison Sheehy. A tabloid reporter learns that aliens have taken over a U.S. Air Force base, and teams up with military types to defeat them. Low budget and weak humor hamper things, but the script is clever and the effects are very impressive for what they must have cost. [R]▼

Invaders, The SEE: **49th Parallel**

Invaders From Mars (1953) **C-78m.** *** D: William Cameron Menzies. Helena Carter, Arthur Franz, Jimmy Hunt, Leif Erickson, Hillary Brooke, Bert Freed. Starkly stylish sci-fi told from little boy's point of view, as he alone witnesses invasion of aliens who capture and brainwash residents of average small town. Remade in 1986.▼●◗

Invaders From Mars (1986) **C-100m.** *½ D: Tobe Hooper. Karen Black, Hunter Carson, Timothy Bottoms, Laraine Newman, James Karen, Louise Fletcher, Bud Cort, Jimmy Hunt. Remake of '50s fantasy favorite about a boy's nightmarish experiences when aliens land in his back yard and overtake everyone around him—even his parents. Starts fine, rapidly goes downhill toward utter disaster. Hunt, the youngster in the original film, plays a police chief here; the boy this time is real-life son of costar Black. J-D-C Scope. [PG] ▼●◗

Invasion (1966-British) **82m.** **½ D: Alan Bridges. Edward Judd, Yoko Tani, Lyndon Brook, Eric Young, Anthony Sharp, Stephanie Bidmead. Entertaining sci-fi film involving interplanetary travelers forced to land on earth, and their conflict with humans.▼

Invasion Earth 2150 A.D. SEE: **Daleks—Invasion Earth 2150 A.D.**

Invasion Force SEE: **Hangar 18**

Invasion of the Animal People (1962) **73m.** *½ D: Virgil Vogel, Jerry Warren. Robert Burton, Barbara Wilson, Sten Gester, Bengt Bomgren. John Carradine is narrator and American link for Swedish-made 1960 production about rampaging monster who escapes from spaceship and terrorizes Lapland. Low-grade nonsense.▼

Invasion of the Bee Girls (1973) **C-85m.** *** D: Denis Sanders. Victoria Vetri, William Smith, Anitra Ford, Cliff Osmond, Wright King, Ben Hammer. Wonderfully campy (and sexy) sci-fi outing about a strange force that's transforming women into dangerous creatures who you-know-what men to death in a small California town. Written by Nicholas Meyer pre-SEVEN-PER-CENT SOLUTION. [R]▼

Invasion of the Body Snatchers (1956) **80m.** ***½ D: Don Siegel. Kevin McCarthy, Dana Wynter, Larry Gates, King Donovan, Carolyn Jones, Virginia Christine. Classic, influential, and still very scary science-fiction (with McCarthy-era subtext) about small-town residents who are being replaced by inert duplicates hatched from alien "pods." Tense script by Daniel Mainwaring from Jack Finney's *The Body Snatchers*; Sam Peckinpah can be glimpsed as a meter reader. Appropriately frightening musical score by Carmen Dragon. Reissued in 1979 at 76m., minus unnecessary, studio-imposed prologue and epilogue with Whit Bissell and Richard Deacon. Remade in 1978 and 1994 (as BODY SNATCHERS). Also shown in computer-colored version. SuperScope.▼●◗

Invasion of the Body Snatchers (1978) **C-115m.** *** D: Philip Kaufman. Donald Sutherland, Brooke Adams, Leonard Nimoy, Jeff Goldblum, Veronica Cartwright. Chilling remake of 1956 classic with many new twists and turns; unfortunately, it runs out of steam and offers one climax too many. Kevin McCarthy and Don Siegel, star and director of original film, have significant cameo roles; look fast for Robert Duvall. Weird score by Denny Zeitlin. [PG] ▼●◗

Invasion of the Saucer Men (1957) **69m.** *½ D: Edward L. Cahn. Steve Terrell, Gloria Castillo, Frank Gorshin, Raymond Hatton, Ed Nelson. Slow paced, minor sci-fi comedy about bulbous-headed aliens trying to pin the death of one of them on a teenager. Cheap, but has some atmosphere and Paul Blaisdell's outlandish aliens. Remade as THE EYE CREATURES.▼

Invasion Siniestra SEE: **Sinister Invasion**

Invasion, U.S.A. (1952) **74m.** *½ D: Alfred E. Green. Gerald Mohr, Peggie Castle, Dan O'Herlihy, Phyllis Coates, Robert Bice, Tom Kennedy, Noel Neill. Red Scare movie depicting full-fledged invasion of America by "The Enemy" —while Mohr romances Castle. Hopelessly cheap and ineffectual, using tons of stock footage showing actual air battles and bombings. Trivia note: Both women who played Lois Lane on TV's *Superman* series appear in the cast.▼

Invasion U.S.A. (1985) **C-107m.** BOMB D: Joseph Zito. Chuck Norris, Richard Lynch, Melissa Prophet, Alex Colon. Political-paranoia action film about retired CIA agent (Norris) back on the job when Russian terrorists invade Florida, tryto overtake entire country by causing panic and turmoil. Repellent in the extreme. [R]▼●

Inventing the Abbotts (1997) **C-120m.** ** D: Pat O'Connor. Liv Tyler, Joaquin Phoenix, Jennifer Connelly, Billy Crudup, Joanna Going, Kathy Baker, Will Patton, Barbara Williams, Alessandro Nivola, Shawn Hatosy. Two working-class brothers try to woo the beautiful and wealthy Abbott sisters in 1950s Midwest America. Aspires to be a classic coming-of-ager like SPLENDOR IN THE GRASS, but despite a very attractive cast, the proceedings are pretty flaccid. Lush surroundings can't compensate for dull scripting; plays like an anemic Douglas Sirk melodrama or a return to Peyton Place. Michael Keaton narrates unbilled. [R]▼●

Investigation of a Citizen Above Suspicion (1970-Italian) **C-115m.** *** D: Elio Petri. Gian Maria Volonte, Florinda Bolkan, Salvo Randone, Gianni Santuccio, Arturo Dominici. Oscar-winning foreign film about powerful police chief who slashes the throat of his mistress, then waits entire movie to see if he'll be caught. Interesting, but not overly gripping. Superbly creepy score by Ennio Morricone. [R]

Invincible Six, The (1970) **C-96m.** **½ D: Jean Negulesco. Stuart Whitman, Elke

Sommer, Curt Jurgens, James Mitchum, Ian Ogilvy. Energetic action film about a motley crew on the lam who come to the aid of isolated villagers under the thumb of a bandit gang. It's THE MAGNIFICENT SEVEN transplanted to present-day mid-East in this Iranian-made production. Widescreen.▼

Invisible Agent (1942) **81m.** ** D: Edwin L. Marin. Ilona Massey, Jon Hall, Peter Lorre, Cedric Hardwicke, J. Edward Bromberg, John Litel. Hall plays agent fighting Nazis with invisibility. Fun for the kids; dialogue is witless.▼

Invisible Boy, The (1957) **85m.** **½ D: Herman Hoffman. Richard Eyer, Diane Brewster, Philip Abbott, Harold J. Stone. One of the earlier sci-fi films to deal with unwieldy computers gone berserk and power-happy; not bad. Also features Robby the Robot (FORBIDDEN PLANET).▼●

Invisible Creature, The (1959-British) **70m.** ** D: Montgomery Tully. Sandra Dorne, Patricia Dainton, Tony Wright. Oddball little film of ghost interfering with homicide plot in eerie English mansion. Retitled: THE HOUSE ON MARSH ROAD. ▼

Invisible Dr. Mabuse, The (1961-German) **89m.** **½ D: Harald Reinl. Lex Barker, Karin Dor, Siegfried Lowitz, Wolfgang Priess, Rudolf Fernau. Well-paced entry in the arch-villain series, with FBI agent Barker coming to Germany to investigate the murder of a colleague, becoming involved with Mabuse and the mysterious "Operation X." Aka THE INVISIBLE HORROR.▼

Invisible Ghost (1941) **64m.** *½ D: Joseph H. Lewis. Bela Lugosi, Polly Ann Young, John McGuire, Clarence Muse, Terry Walker, Betty Compson. Low-grade horror about domineering wife who hypnotizes her husband into murder plot.▼

Invisible Horror, The SEE: **Invisible Dr. Mabuse, The**

Invisible Invaders (1959) **67m.** *½ D: Edward L. Cahn. John Agar, Jean Byron, Robert Hutton, Philip Tonge, John Carradine, Hal Torey. Invisible aliens from the moon possess corpses and attack the living; holed up in a cave, scientists race against time to stop them. Cheap, silly, and boring.▼●

Invisible Kid, The (1988) **C-95m.** BOMB D: Avery Crounse. Jay Underwood, Karen Black, Wally Ward, Chynna Phillips, Brother Theodore, Mike Genovese, Jan King. High-school dolt stumbles onto invisibility formula, which enables him to poke into the girls' locker room and such. Crude in all respects. [PG]▼●

Invisible Man, The (1933) **71m.** ***½ D: James Whale. Claude Rains, Gloria Stuart, Una O'Connor, William Harrigan, E. E. Clive, Dudley Digges, Dwight Frye. H. G. Wells' fantasy brilliantly materializes on screen in tale of mad scientist who makes himself invisible, wreaking havoc on British country village. Rains' starring debut is dated but still enjoyable. Look fast for John Carradine phoning in a "sighting"; that's Walter Brennan whose bicycle is stolen. ▼●

Invisible Maniac, The (1990) **C-87m.** BOMB D: Rif Coogan. Noel Peters, Melissa Moore, Robert R. Ross, Jr., Shannon (Savannah) Wilsey, Rod Sweiter. Teen spoof of *The Invisible Man,* with large amounts of T & A thrown in. Amateurish production makes this film's cheap laughs unfunny and dull. [R]▼

Invisible Man Returns, The (1940) **81m.** *** D: Joe May. Cedric Hardwicke, Vincent Price, John Sutton, Nan Grey, Cecil Kellaway, Alan Napier. Fine follow-up, with Price going invisible to clear himself of murder charge. Considered by many to be Price's first horror film.▼

Invisible Man's Revenge, The (1944) **77m.** **½ D: Ford Beebe. Jon Hall, Alan Curtis, Evelyn Ankers, Leon Errol, John Carradine, Gale Sondergaard, Ian Wolfe, Billy Bevan. Hall made invisible by doctor to obtain estate; he then kills doctor after being refused visibility. Better-than-average cast saves rather innocuous script.▼●

Invisible Menace, The (1938) **55m.** ** D: John Farrow. Boris Karloff, Marie Wilson, Regis Toomey, Henry Kolker, Eddie Craven, Eddie Acuff, Charles Trowbridge. Not a horror/fantasy film, as the title implies, but a Grade B whodunit set at a military installation, with Karloff as the woebegone prime suspect. Wilson supplies incongruous comedy relief, while the FBI is rather poorly represented by Cy Kendall. Remade as MURDER ON THE WATERFRONT.

Invisible Ray, The (1936) **81m.** **½ D: Lambert Hillyer. Boris Karloff, Bela Lugosi, Frances Drake, Frank Lawton, Walter Kingsford, Beulah Bondi. Scientist Karloff contracts radiation that gives him touch of death, and slowly deteriorates his mind. Interesting yarn, but a notch below other Karloff-Lugosi vehicles.▼●

Invisible Stripes (1939) **82m.** *** D: Lloyd Bacon. George Raft, Jane Bryan, William Holden, Flora Robson, Humphrey Bogart, Paul Kelly, Moroni Olsen, Tully Marshall. Earnest account of parolee Raft trying to go straight, protecting brother Holden from gangster Bogart; subdued acting is effective.

Invisible Woman, The (1941) **72m.** *** D: A. Edward Sutherland. John Barrymore, Virginia Bruce, John Howard, Charlie Ruggles, Oscar Homolka, Margaret Hamilton, Donald MacBride, Edward Brophy, Shemp Howard, Charles Lane, Thurston Hall. Great cast in likable comedy about screwy professor Barrymore turning model Bruce invisible, arousing the curiosity of playboy sponsor Howard, as well as the more monetary interests of gangster Homolka. Slick and sprightly, with Ruggles terrific as Howard's long-suffering butler; Maria Montez has a bit as one of Bruce's fellow models.▼

Invitation (1952) **84m.** **½ D: Gottfried Reinhardt. Van Johnson, Dorothy McGuire, Louis Calhern, Ray Collins, Ruth Roman. Society tearjerker decked out in MGM gloss about invalid McGuire; her father (Calhern) tries to buy Johnson to romance dying daughter. Memorable theme by Bronislau Kaper (which was originally used in A LIFE OF HER OWN).

Invitation to a Gunfighter (1964) **C-92m.** **½ D: Richard Wilson. Yul Brynner, George Segal, Janice Rule, Pat Hingle, Brad Dexter. Cast surpasses turgid, talky script about town that hires gunslinger to kill an outcast, with surprising results.▼

Invitation to Happiness (1939) **95m.** **½ D: Wesley Ruggles. Irene Dunne, Fred MacMurray, Charles Ruggles, William Collier, Sr., Eddie Hogan. Ordinary story, well acted: society girl marries fighter, but marriage can't survive because of his driving ambition in boxing ring.

Invitation to the Dance (1956) **C-93m.** **½ D: Gene Kelly. Gene Kelly, Igor Youskevitch, Claire Sombert, David Paltenghi, Daphne Dale, Claude Bessy, Tommy Rall, Carol Haney, Tamara Toumanova, Belita. Kelly's ambitious film tells three stories entirely in dance. Earnest but uninspired, until final "Sinbad" segment with Kelly in Hanna-Barbera cartoon world. Music by Jacques Ibert, Andre Previn, and Rimsky-Korsakov. Filmed in 1952.▼

In Which We Serve (1942-British) **115m.** **** D: Noel Coward, David Lean. Noel Coward, John Mills, Bernard Miles, Celia Johnson, Kay Walsh, Joyce Carey, Michael Wilding, James Donald, Richard Attenborough. Unlike many WW2 films, this masterpiece doesn't date one bit; superb film about men on a British fighting ship, told through flashback. Written, codirected, and scored by costar Coward (who was given a special Oscar "for his outstanding production achievement"). Lean's first directing credit. Film debuts of Johnson, Attenborough, young Daniel Massey and infant Juliet Mills.▼●

I Only Want You to Love Me (1976-West German) **C-101m.** **½ D: Rainer Werner Fassbinder. Vitus Zeplichal, Elke Aberle, Alexander Allerson, Ernie Mangold, Johanna Hofer. Intriguing morality tale of decent, hardworking young bricklayer, whose Bavarian upbringing was noticeably lacking in parental affection. When he marries and moves to Munich, the lure of the big-city consumer society (and the ability to buy on credit) proves disastrous. Deliberately paced but offbeat examination of a shattered psyche. Made for TV; unreleased in the U.S. until 1994.▼

I Ought to Be in Pictures (1982) **C-107m.** ** D: Herbert Ross. Walter Matthau, Ann-Margret, Dinah Manoff, Lance Guest, Lewis Smith, Martin Ferrero, David Faustino, Michael Dudikoff. Poor formula Neil Simon sitcom, adapted from his play: 19-year-old Brooklynite Manoff hitches to L.A. to make it in movies—and establishes connection with her father (Matthau), screenwriter turned gambler-drinker. Matthau and Manoff do their best; Ann-Margret wasted as Walter's mistress. [PG]▼

I Passed for White (1960) **93m.** ** D: Fred M. Wilcox. Sonya Wilde, James Franciscus, Pat Michon, Elizabeth Council, Griffin Crafts, Isabelle Cooley. Exploitation film handled with slight dignity involving light-skinned black woman and her rich white boyfriend.

Ipcress File, The (1965-British) **C-108m.** ***½ D: Sidney J. Furie. Michael Caine, Nigel Green, Guy Doleman, Sue Lloyd, Gordon Jackson. First and best of Len Deighton's Harry Palmer series, with Caine as unemotional Cockney crook turned secret agent, involved in grueling mental torture caper. Eerie score by John Barry. Followed by two sequels—FUNERAL IN BERLIN and BILLION DOLLAR BRAIN—and a pair of cable TV followups in 1997, BULLET TO BEIJING and MIDNIGHT IN ST. PETERSBURG. Techniscope.▼●◗

Iphigenia (1977-Greek) **C-127m.** **½ D: Michael Cacoyannis. Irene Papas, Tatiana Papamoskou, Costa Kazakos, Costa Carras, Christos Tsangas. Ambitious but overdirected adaptation of Euripides' *Iphigenia in Aulis*, in which Agamemnon becomes convinced that, to earn military victory, he will have to sacrifice his daughter Iphigenia (impressively played by young Papamoskou). The elements of high drama are present, but Cacoyannis opts for eye-popping visuals rather than focusing on the heart of the story.▼

I Promise to Pay (1937) **65m.** **½ D: D. Ross Lederman. Chester Morris, Helen Mack, Leo Carrillo, Thomas Mitchell, John Gallaudet, Wallis Clark. Snappy little programmer about likable, scrupulously honest family man Morris who's taken in by loan sharks. Enjoyable (if not quite credible).

I.Q. (1994) **C-95m.** *** D: Fred Schepisi. Tim Robbins, Meg Ryan, Walter Matthau, Lou Jacobi, Gene Saks, Joseph Maher, Stephen Fry, Tony Shalhoub, Frank Whaley, Keene Curtis, Charles Durning, Alice Playten, Danny Zorn. Pleasant romantic comedy (perhaps too "cute" for some viewers) about a garage mechanic who falls in love with a customer at first sight, and gets some unusual matchmaking help from her uncle—Albert Einstein! Likable performances by well-matched Robbins and Ryan, with Matthau having fun as the cagey Professor. Set in 1950s Princeton, N.J. Super 35. [PG]▼●

I Remember Mama (1948) **134m.** ***½ D: George Stevens. Irene Dunne, Barbara Bel Geddes, Oscar Homolka, Philip Dorn, Cedric Hardwicke, Edgar Bergen, Rudy Vallee, Barbara O'Neil, Florence Bates, Ellen Corby. Beautifully realized, exquisitely detailed filming of John Van Druten's play, based on Kathryn Forbes' memoirs about growing up with her Norwegian immigrant family in San Francisco. A bit long, but richly rewarding, with top performances in each and every role. Screenplay by DeWitt Bodeen. Followed by the TV series *Mama*. Also shown in computer-colored version.▼●

Irene (1940) **104m.** **½ D: Herbert Wilcox. Anna Neagle, Ray Milland, Roland Young, Alan Marshal, May Robson, Billie Burke, Marsha Hunt, Arthur Treacher, Tommy Kelly. Pleasant remake of venerable musical (done as a silent film with Colleen Moore) minus most of the songs. Wealthy playboy Milland romances working-girl Neagle; some offbeat touches make it pleasing. "Alice Blue Gown" sequence originally filmed in color.▼

Irish Eyes Are Smiling (1944) **C-90m.** **½ D: Gregory Ratoff. Monty Woolley, June Haver, Dick Haymes, Anthony Quinn, Maxie Rosenbloom, Veda Ann Borg, Maeve McGrail. Colorful corn about Ernest R. Ball, composer of famous Irish songs, with pleasant cast and familiar tunes like "When Irish Eyes Are Smiling," "Mother Machree," and a lavish non-Ball number: "Bessie With a Bustle" (by Mack Gordon and James V. Monaco).

Irish in Us, The (1935) **84m.** ** D: Lloyd Bacon. James Cagney, Pat O'Brien, Olivia de Havilland, Frank McHugh, Allen Jenkins. Pretty stale comedy about rivalry between policemen and prizefighters, with good cast to hold one's interest.

Irishman, The (1978-Australian) **C-108m.** *** D: Donald Crombie. Michael Craig, Simon Burke, Robin Nevin, Lou Brown, Andrew Maguire. Effective, wonderfully acted drama of teamster Craig, his wife and sons, and his refusal to accept change and progress during the 1920s. A touching portrait of a family in turmoil.▼

Irish Whiskey Rebellion (1972) **C-93m.** ** D: J. C. Works (Chester Erskine). William Devane, Anne Meara, Richard Mulligan, David Groh, Judie Rolin, William Challee, Stephen Joyce. Pedestrian action tale of Irish rum-running during America's Prohibition era hoping to raise money for IRA struggles back home. Strong performances by all. [PG]

Irma la Douce (1963) **C-142m.** **½ D: Billy Wilder. Shirley MacLaine, Jack Lemmon, Lou Jacobi, Herschel Bernardi, Joan Shawlee, Hope Holiday, Bill Bixby. Wilder's straight comedy adaptation of Broadway musical is a Parisian fairytale for adults. Gendarme Lemmon falls for prostitute MacLaine and will do anything to keep her for himself. Red Light District is vividly recreated, but reteaming of stars and director can't equal THE APARTMENT. André Previn won an Oscar for his scoring. Look fast for young James Caan in walk-on. Panavision.▼●

Irma Vep (1996-French) **C-96m.** *** D: Olivier Assayas. Maggie Cheung, Jean-Pierre Léaud, Nathalie Richard, Alex Descas, Nathalie Boutefeu, Dominique Faysse, Bulle Ogier, Arsinée Khanjian, Lou Castel. Keen, insightful satire of movies and the disorder surrounding the moviemaking process. Hong Kong action-film star Cheung (cast as herself) comes to Paris to star in a reworking of Louis Feuillade's 1915–16 serial LES VAMPIRES. However, the inspiration for her character is not so much Feuillade as Michelle Pfeiffer's Catwoman in BATMAN RETURNS. Crammed with cinematic references and biting criticisms of contemporary moviemaking. The title, incidentally, is an anagram.▼●◗

Iron & Silk (1990) **C-92m.** *** D: Shirley Sun. Mark Salzman, Pan Qingfu, Jeannette Lin Tsui, Vivian Wu. Charming true story of Salzman, an American who worked for two years in China as an English teacher, while studying with martial arts great Pan Qingfu. The cultural differences are both amusing and at times serious in this spectacularly photographed family film. Screenplay by Salzman, based on his book. [PG]▼●

Iron Cowboy SEE: **Fade-In**

Iron Curtain, The (1948) **87m.** *** D: William Wellman. Dana Andrews, Gene Tierney, June Havoc, Berry Kroeger, Edna Best. Well-made, based-on-fact "anti-commie" saga of Igor Gouzenko (Andrews), who with wife Tierney attempts to defect to the West with top-secret documents. Filmed on location in Canada. Retitled: BEHIND THE IRON CURTAIN.

Iron Duke, The (1935-British) **88m.** *** D: Victor Saville. George Arliss, Gladys Cooper, Ellaline Terriss, A. E. Matthews, Allan Aynesworth, Lesley Wareing, Emlyn Williams, Felix Aylmer, Norma Varden. Arliss is his usual sterling self as the Duke of Wellington, seemingly the only man who can make peace between England, its allies, and France in 1815. Entertaining history lesson gets better and better as it draws us into international and political intrigues. Cooper is outstanding as the Duchess of Angouleme (vengeful daughter of Marie Antoinette); young Williams is fun as a malicious newspaperman.▼

Iron Eagle (1986) **C-119m.** *½ D: Sidney J. Furie. Louis Gossett, Jr., Jason Gedrick,

David Suchet, Tim Thomerson, Larry G. Scott, Caroline Lagerfelt, Jerry Levine, Michael Bowen. Dum-dum comic-book movie about an 18-year-old who commandeers an F-16 fighter jet and flies to the Middle East (playing rock music on his Walkman all the way) in order to save his dad, who's been taken prisoner. Full of jingoistic ideals, dubious ethics, and people who die and miraculously come back to life. Not boring, just stupid. Followed by three sequels. [PG-13]▼●◗

Iron Eagle II (1988-Canadian-Israeli) **C-105m.** *½ D: Sidney J. Furie. Louis Gossett, Jr., Mark Humphrey, Stuart Margolin, Alan Scarfe, Sharon H. Brandon, Maury Chaykin. Equally idiotic sequel, with General Gossett recruiting pilot Humphrey to team with his Soviet counterparts on a secret mission in the Mideast. Humphrey may be a Tom Cruise clone, but the film makes TOP GUN seem like FROM HERE TO ETERNITY. Sequels: ACES: IRON EAGLE III and IRON EAGLE IV. [PG]▼●

Iron Giant, The (1999) **C-86m.** *** D: Brad Bird. Voices of Jennifer Aniston, Eli Marienthal, Harry Connick, Jr., Vin Diesel, Christopher McDonald, James Gammon, Cloris Leachman, John Mahoney, M. Emmet Walsh. Striking and original animated feature gently pokes fun at 1950s paranoia (and sci-fi movies), as a boy befriends a huge robotic creature from outer space. That writer-director Bird and his animators can bring such feeling to a metallic character is just one of this film's triumphs. Based on the book *The Iron Man* by Ted Hughes. Celco-Widescreen. [PG]▼●◗

Iron Glove, The (1954) **C-77m.** **½ D: William Castle. Robert Stack, Ursula Thiess, Richard Stapley, Charles Irwin, Alan Hale, Jr. Typical swashbuckler about 18th-century England and Prince James, pretender to the throne.

Iron Hand, The SEE: **Chinese Connection, The**

Iron Horse, The (1924) **119m.** *** D: John Ford. George O'Brien, Madge Bellamy, Cyril Chadwick, Fred Kohler, Gladys Hulette, J. Farrell MacDonald. Epic-scale silent film about building of transcontinental railroad, intertwined with predictable human-interest subplots involving surveyor O'Brien, sweetheart Bellamy, traitor Kohler, etc. Storywise, film may seem hackneyed today, but it's important to note that this movie *invented* what later became clichés. ▼

Iron Major, The (1943) **85m.** **½ D: Ray Enright. Pat O'Brien, Ruth Warrick, Robert Ryan, Leon Ames, Russell Wade, Bruce Edwards, Barbara Hale. O'Brien goes through the paces as Frank Cavanaugh, famed football coach/WW1 hero, in this ultra-patriotic, by-the-numbers biography. Based on a story by Cavanaugh's wife Flo (played by Warrick).▼

Iron Man (1931) **73m.** ** D: Tod Browning. Lew Ayres, Jean Harlow, Robert Armstrong, John Miljan, Eddie Dillon. Routine early talkie of prizefighter Ayres and gold-digging wife Harlow (who hadn't clicked yet in films). Manager-pal Armstrong is only one who sees through her. Remade in 1937 (as SOME BLONDES ARE DANGEROUS) and 1951.

Iron Man (1951) **82m.** **½ D: Joseph Pevney. Jeff Chandler, Evelyn Keyes, Stephen McNally, Joyce Holden, Rock Hudson, Jim Backus, Jim Arness. Reworking of 1931 film focuses on Chandler as a poor, well-intentioned Pennsylvania coal miner who can't control his killer instinct once he steps into the boxing ring.

Iron Mask, The (1929) **87m.** *** D: Allan Dwan. Douglas Fairbanks, Belle Bennett, Marguerite De La Motte, Dorothy Revier, Vera Lewis, William Bakewell, Nigel de Brulier, Ullrich Haupt. Entertaining Dumas tale (later filmed as THE MAN IN THE IRON MASK) told from point of view of D'Artagnan (Fairbanks), who becomes Louis XIV's protector from birth to later time when scheming Rochefort (Haupt) tries to pass off twin brother as heir to throne. Lavish silent swashbuckler originally had talkie sequences. Final scenes are especially poignant as this was Doug's farewell to the swashbuckling genre. Most current prints are of the 1940 reissue with narration by Douglas Fairbanks, Jr.▼●

Iron Maze (1991-U.S.-Japanese) **C-102m.** *½ D: Hiroaki Yoshida. Jeff Fahey, Bridget Fonda, Hiroaki Murakami, J. T. Walsh, Gabriel Damon, John Randolph. Japanese industrialist Murakami, hoping to build an amusement park in a Pennsylvania steel town, is near-fatally assaulted; his American wife (Fonda) and a laid-off steelworker (Fahey) offer different perceptions of events leading to the incident. Muddled, pretentious RASHOMON variation, coexecutive-produced by Oliver Stone. [R]▼●◗

Iron Mistress, The (1952) **C-110m.** **½ D: Gordon Douglas. Alan Ladd, Virginia Mayo, Joseph Calleia, Phyllis Kirk. Spotty Western adventure of Jim Bowie (Ladd), who invented the famed frontier knife.

Iron Petticoat, The (1956) **C-87m.** **½ D: Ralph Thomas. Bob Hope, Katharine Hepburn, James Robertson Justice, Robert Helpmann, David Kossoff. Curious comedy made in England tries to update NINOTCHKA theme with Hepburn as humorless Russian and Hope as American military man who tries to win her over. Stars' surprising rapport is film's chief value; mediocre script and direction kill the rest. VistaVision.

Iron Sheriff, The (1957) **73m.** *½ D: Sidney Salkow. Sterling Hayden, Constance

Ford, John Dehner, Kent Taylor, Darryl Hickman. Marshal Hayden sets out to prove son is not guilty of murder.

Iron Triangle, The (1989) **C-91m.** ** D: Eric Weston. Beau Bridges, Haing S. Ngor, Johnny Hallyday, Liem Whatley, James Ishida. A U.S. army captain, serving in Vietnam in 1969, is captured by a 17-year-old Vietcong soldier, and the pair develop a bond. Intriguing as a look at the war from the side of the "enemy," but the result is confused and slight. [R]▼●

Ironweed (1987) **C-144m.** **½ D: Hector Babenco. Jack Nicholson, Meryl Streep, Carroll Baker, Michael O'Keefe, Diane Venora, Fred Gwynne, Margaret Whitton, Tom Waits, Jake Dengel, Nathan Lane, James Gammon, Joe Grifasi, Bethel Leslie, Ted Levine, Frank Whaley. William Kennedy adapted his Pulitzer Prize-winning novel about street people, set in Albany, N.Y., 1938. Nicholson plays a man trying to come to terms with the life he turned his back on years ago. Streep is his longtime companion who, like him, can't stay off the bottle for long. Babenco's first American film is strong on atmosphere and filled with haunting images . . . but it's long and unremittingly bleak, with a few too many dramatic peaks. The salvation is Nicholson and Streep, whose rich performances are a privilege to watch. [R]▼●

Iron Will (1994) **C-109m.** *½ D: Charles Haid. Mackenzie Astin, Kevin Spacey, August Schellenberg, David Ogden Stiers, Brian Cox, George Gerdes, John Terry. Youngster enters a Winnipeg-to-St. Paul dog-sled race in the WW1 era; result is so "by the numbers" that you almost expect the numerals to start flashing on the screen, à la John Waters' POLYESTER. Two additional writers polished the original script by veteran John Michael Hayes (REAR WINDOW), presumably to make it more like a bad Disney Channel entry. There's a faint pulse whenever Spacey (as a journalist) shows up on screen. [PG]▼●

Iroquois Trail, The (1950) **85m.** ** D: Phil Karlson. George Montgomery, Brenda Marshall, Dan O'Herlihy, Glenn Langan. Too often flabby account of French and Indian War, lacking sufficient plot motivation and action sequences.

Irreconcilable Differences (1984) **C-117m.** *** D: Charles Shyer. Ryan O'Neal, Shelley Long, Drew Barrymore, Sam Wanamaker, Allen Garfield, Sharon Stone, David Paymer. Bittersweet comedy about a bright young couple who marry and prosper, until success in Hollywood causes them to lose sight of what's really important in their lives. Result: Their ten-year-old daughter sues them for divorce! Perceptive script by Nancy Meyers and first-time director Shyer, with especially funny jabs at Hollywood. Also the only film in memory to drop the name of Sig Rumann! [PG]▼●

Isadora (1968-British) **C-131m.** ***½ D: Karel Reisz. Vanessa Redgrave, James Fox, Jason Robards, Ivan Tchenko, John Fraser, Bessie Love, Cynthia Harris. Extremely long but gripping study of Isadora Duncan, first of modern dancers and most prominent free-thinker of her time. Interesting technique and carefully studied performances combine together in this offbeat biography. Originally released at 168 minutes, later recut to 131 minutes and retitled THE LOVES OF ISADORA. A third version, supervised by the director, was released to television in 1987 under the original title. [M/PG]▼

I Sailed to Tahiti with an All Girl Crew (1968) **C-95m.** *½ D: Richard L. Bare. Gardner McKay, Fred Clark, Diane McBain, Pat Buttram, Edy Williams. One of the all-time camp classics, if only for its title. Unfortunately, film doesn't live down to its expectations.

I Saw What You Did (1965) **82m.** *** D: William Castle. Sara Lane, Andi Garrett, John Ireland, Joan Crawford, Leif Erickson, Patricia Breslin. Tense, gimmick-free Castle shocker about two teenage girls who dial phone numbers at random and whisper film's title; one of their "victims" is Ireland—who's just murdered his wife! Look out! Remade for TV in 1988.◗

I See a Dark Stranger SEE: **Adventuress, The**

I Sent a Letter to My Love (1981-French) **C-96m.** ***½ D: Moshe Mizrahi. Simone Signoret, Jean Rochefort, Delphine Seyrig. A woman (Signoret) cares for her paralyzed brother (Rochefort); through a newspaper personals column, they unknowingly begin a romantic correspondence. Perceptive character study, highlighted by brilliant Signoret performance; fine work by Rochefort and Seyrig (as their spinsterish friend). Director Mizrahi and Gerard Brach adapted Bernice Rubens' novel. [PG]▼

I Shot Andy Warhol (1996-U.S.-British) **C-106m.** *** D: Mary Harron. Lili Taylor, Jared Harris, Stephen Dorff, Martha Plimpton, Danny Morgenstern, Lothaire Bluteau, Michael Imperioli, Reg Rogers, Donovan Leitch, Tahnee Welch, Eric Mabius. In 1968, Valerie Solanas shot pop art icon Warhol, seriously wounding him. This film traces her bizarre life leading to that moment, including the writing of her "SCUM Manifesto" decreeing males biologically obsolete. Taylor is brilliant as the delusional Solanas, and the film depicts Warhol (Harris, son of actor Richard), his "Factory," and the period in convincing detail. Not for all tastes and slightly pretentious, but well made and fascinating. [R]▼●

I Shot Jesse James (1949) **81m.** ** D: Samuel Fuller. Preston Foster, Barbara

Britton, John Ireland, Reed Hadley, J. Edward Bromberg. Flamboyant directorial touches (in Fuller's first film) cannot redeem essential dullness of story about Bob Ford, the man who plugged Jesse in the back.▼

Ishtar (1987) **C-107m.** ** D: Elaine May. Warren Beatty, Dustin Hoffman, Isabelle Adjani, Charles Grodin, Jack Weston, Tess Harper, Carol Kane, Aharon Ipale. The HEAVEN'S GATE of movie comedies made headlines because of its huge expense and costly delays, but the only thing wrong with it is that it isn't very funny. Beatty and Hoffman go the Hope and Crosby route as untalented singer-songwriters who get involved with international intrigue in North Africa (shades of ROAD TO MOROCCO!). A blind camel and a flock of vultures steal the show. Paul Williams' deliberately awful songs are funny, too, but not funny enough to overcome the flatness of director May's script. Produced by Beatty. [PG-13]▼●

Island, The (1962-Japanese) **96m.** *** D: Kaneto Shindo. Nobuko Otowa, Taiji Tonoyama, Shinji Tanaka, Masanori Horimoto. Engrossing documentary-style study of peasant family living on rocky island near Japan, struggling to survive. Visually stunning film contains not a single word of dialogue.▼

Island, The (1980) **C-114m.** BOMB D: Michael Ritchie. Michael Caine, David Warner, Angela Punch McGregor, Frank Middlemass, Don Henderson, Zakes Mokae, Jeffrey Frank. Absolutely awful thriller about magazine reporter who investigates strange doings in the Caribbean and winds up a prisoner of primitive island tribe. You know you're in trouble when David Warner plays the most normal guy on the island! Peter Benchley scripted from his own novel. Panavision. [R]▼●

Island (1989-Australian) **C-93m.** **½ D: Paul Cox. Irene Papas, Eva Sitta, Anoja Weerasinghe, Chris Haywood, Francois Bernard. Three women—each struggling with a personal emotional crisis—meet on a remote Greek island. Knowing they are only to cross paths briefly, they unburden their innermost feelings to each other. Atmospheric psychological drama lacks a strong central core.

Island at the Top of the World, The (1974) **C-93m.** **½ D: Robert Stevenson. David Hartman, Donald Sinden, Jacques Marin, Mako, David Gwillim, Agneta Eckemyr. Disney's attempt to score again in Jules Verne territory misses bullseye; simplistic, derivative story of Arctic expedition which stumbles across "lost" Viking civilization. Mainly for kids. [G]▼◗

Island Claws (1980) **C-82m.** BOMB D: Hernan Cardenas. Robert Lansing, Steve Hanks, Nita Talbot, Barry Nelson, Jo McDonnell, Martina Deignan. Florida-lensed horror stinker (never released theatrically) blames a nuclear reactor spill for causing crabs to become giant-sized and start killing people. Very talky, cheap and unscary; Roger Corman's ATTACK OF THE CRAB MONSTERS is a lot more fun. Retitled: NIGHT OF THE CLAW.▼

Island in the Sky (1953) **109m.** **½ D: William Wellman. John Wayne, Lloyd Nolan, James Arness, Andy Devine, Walter Abel, Allyn Joslyn. Clichéd survival story of a downed transport plane and its crew under the staunch leadership of Wayne, set in Greenland during WW2. Unconvincing and talky most of the way. Look fast for Fess Parker. Written by Ernest K. Gann.

Island in the Sun (1957) **C-119m.** ** D: Robert Rossen. James Mason, Joan Fontaine, Dorothy Dandridge, Joan Collins, Michael Rennie, Diana Wynyard, John Williams, Stephen Boyd, Harry Belafonte. Misfire adaptation of Alec Waugh's book about idyllic West Indies island torn by racial struggle. Good cast can't do much with unconvincing script. CinemaScope.▼

Island of Desire (1952-British) **C-103m.** *½ D: Stuart Heisler. Linda Darnell, Tab Hunter, Donald Gray, John Laurie, Sheila Chong. Sun-drenched, romantic WW2 drama of nurse, Marine, and injured pilot all washed ashore on tropical desert island. Parched performances. British title: SATURDAY ISLAND.▼

Island of Doomed Men (1940) **67m.** ** D: Charles Barton. Peter Lorre, Robert Wilcox, Rochelle Hudson, George E. Stone, Don Beddoe, Kenneth MacDonald. Low-grade melodrama even Lorre can't save as man who traps unsuspecting victims on island, turns them into his slaves.

Island of Dr. Moreau, The (1977) **C-104m.** *** D: Don Taylor. Burt Lancaster, Michael York, Nigel Davenport, Barbara Carrera, Richard Basehart. Handsomely produced remake of ISLAND OF LOST SOULS with Lancaster heading a solid cast as demented doctor who has spent years creating half-man, half-beast "humanimals." Good horror-fantasy chiller, based on H. G. Wells' novel. Remade in 1996. [PG]▼

Island of Dr. Moreau, The (1996) **C-95m.** *½ D: John Frankenheimer. Marlon Brando, Val Kilmer, David Thewlis, Fairuza Balk, Ron Perlman, Marco Hofschneider, Temuera Morrison. Heavy-handed retelling of H. G. Wells' novel, as Thewlis is rescued at sea and brought to Dr. Moreau's island, where he's horrified to discover experiments turning animals into humans. Grotesque in the extreme, obvious, and ultimately pointless, but Brando devotees will want to check out his flamboyantly silly performance, and makeup buffs should admire Stan Winston's remarkable creations. Director's cut version runs 99m. Super 35. [PG-13]▼●◗

Island of Lost Men (1939) **63m.** *½ D: Kurt Neumann. Anna May Wong, J. Carrol Naish, Eric Blore, Ernest Truex, Anthony Quinn, Broderick Crawford. Generally dull mystery of Wong searching for Oriental general along the waterfront. A few atmospheric scenes, but stilted dialogue throughout.

Island of Lost Souls (1933) **70m.** ***½ D: Erle C. Kenton. Charles Laughton, Bela Lugosi, Richard Arlen, Stanley Fields, Kathleen Burke, Leila Hyams. Strong adaptation of H. G. Wells' novel of a mad scientist isolated on a remote island, where he transforms jungle beasts into half-human abominations (". . . are we not men?"). Laughton hams it up a bit, but despite more explicit horror films of late, this retains its frightening aura, particularly in the grisly finale. Remade as THE ISLAND OF DR. MOREAU in 1977 and 1996.▼●

Island of Lost Women (1959) **71m.** ** D: Frank Tuttle. Jeff Richards, Venetia Stevenson, John Smith, Diane Jergens, Alan Napier, June Blair. Plane forced down on remote island leads to complications with scientist and daughters who inhabit the jungle isle.

Island of Love (1963) **C-101m.** *½ D: Morton Da Costa. Robert Preston, Tony Randall, Giorgia Moll, Walter Matthau, Betty Bruce, Michael Constantine. Con artist Preston sets out to transform a Greek isle into a tourist trap while evading the clutches of vengeful gangster Matthau. Silly, unfunny comedy wastes the talents of all concerned. Panavision.

Island of Terror (1966-British) **C-90m.** ** D: Terence Fisher. Peter Cushing, Edward Judd, Carole Gray, Niall MacGinnis. Sci-fi tale about cancer research gone wild and mutations that result is directed and acted by veterans of the field, but result is nothing special.▼

Island of the Blue Dolphins (1964) **C-93m.** *½ D: James B. Clark. Celia Kaye, George Kennedy, Ann Daniel, Carlos Romero, Larry Domasin. True story of Indian girl (Kaye) abandoned on small island, befriended only by wild dogs. Set in early 19th century. Well meaning but not very good.▼

Island of the Burning Damned SEE: **Island of the Burning Doomed**

Island of the Burning Doomed (1967-British) **C-94m.** **½ D: Terence Fisher. Christopher Lee, Peter Cushing, Patrick Allen, Sarah Lawson, Jane Merrow, William Lucas. Aliens cause a massive heatwave during winter. Good sci-fi, with Lee and Cushing at their best. Also known as ISLAND OF THE BURNING DAMNED and NIGHT OF THE BIG HEAT.▼

Island of the Doomed SEE: **Man-Eater of Hydra**

Island of the Lost (1967) **C-91m.** *½ D: John Florea; Underwater sequences, Ricou Browning. Richard Greene, Luke Halpin, Mart Hulswit, Jose De Vega, Robin Mattson, Irene Tsu. Anthropologist Greene takes his family on an expedition to find an uncharted South Sea isle but becomes shipwrecked. Clean-cut, highly innocuous travelogue from the Ivan Tors studio, cowritten by Tors and actor Richard Carlson. Underwater expert Browning appeared with Carlson years before as the CREATURE FROM THE BLACK LAGOON.▼

Island Princess, The (1955-Italian) **C-98m.** ** D: Paolo Moffa. Marcello Mastroianni, Silvana Pampanini, Gustavo Rojo. Rather hackneyed yarn set in 1500s, with Mastroianni a Spanish captain falling in love with princess of the Canary Islands.

Island Rescue (1951-British) **87m.** ** D: Ralph Thomas. David Niven, Glynis Johns, George Coulouris, Barry Jones, Kenneth More, Noel Purcell, Bernard Lee, Jeremy Spenser, Anton Diffring. Lukewarm comedy involving rescue of cows from German-occupied island during WW2. Original British title: APPOINTMENT WITH VENUS.

Islands in the Stream (1977) **C-105m.** **½ D: Franklin J. Schaffner. George C. Scott, David Hemmings, Claire Bloom, Susan Tyrrell, Gilbert Roland, Richard Evans, Hart Bochner, Julius Harris. Film version of Hemingway novel about an island-dwelling sculptor and his three sons begins well but falls apart completely in the final third. Still one of the better adaptations of this author, with one of Scott's best performances. Panavision. [PG]▼●

Island Woman (1958) **72m.** *½ D: William Berke. Marie Windsor, Vincent Edwards, Marilee Earle, Leslie Scott, Maurine Duvalier, George Symonette. Sailboat captain Edwards falls for tourist Earle, while her aunt (Windsor) connives to win him for herself. Dull; spiced with calypso music.

Isle of Forgotten Sins (1943) **82m.** ** D: Edgar G. Ulmer. John Carradine, Gale Sondergaard, Sidney Toler, Frank Fenton, Rita Quigley, Veda Ann Borg, Rick Vallin, Betty Amann, Tala Birell. Standard programmer with deep sea divers Carradine and Fenton going up against conniving ship captain Toler over a gold treasure. As usual, Ulmer's direction is much better than the material. Based on his short story; retitled MONSOON.▼

Isle of Fury (1936) **60m.** ** D: Frank McDonald. Humphrey Bogart, Margaret Lindsay, Donald Woods, Paul Graetz, Gordon Hart, E. E. Clive. Mild remake of Somerset Maugham novel NARROW CORNER, involving love triangle on South Sea island; early Bogart.

Isle of Lost Women SEE: **99 Women**

Isle of Sin (1960-German) **63m.** *½ D: Johannes Kai. Christiane Nielsen, Erwin Strahl, Jan Hendriks, Slavo Schwaiger. Trite tale of passengers on plane which crashes on deserted island, with expected friction between types.

Isle of the Dead (1945) **72m.** *** D: Mark Robson. Boris Karloff, Ellen Drew, Marc Cramer, Katherine Emery, Helene Thimig, Jason Robards. Eerie horror tale of assorted characters stranded on Greek island during quarantine. Good Val Lewton production.▼●

Isle of the Snake People SEE: **Snake People**

Is My Face Red? (1932) **66m.** **½ D: William A. Seiter. Ricardo Cortez, Helen Twelvetrees, Jill Esmond, Robert Armstrong, Sidney Toler, ZaSu Pitts. Cortez does well as a wisecracking, Walter Winchell-like columnist. Some snappy dialogue, but film really goes nowhere—and main character is such a total heel that our sympathies aren't with him when script demands they should be. That's director Seiter as the ship's purser.

Isn't It Romantic? (1948) **87m.** ** D: Norman Z. McLeod. Veronica Lake, Mary Hatcher, Mona Freeman, Billy DeWolfe, Patric Knowles, Roland Culver, Pearl Bailey. No.

Isn't Life Wonderful (1924) **115m.** **½ D: D. W. Griffith. Carol Dempster, Neil Hamilton, Erville Alderson, Helen Lowell, Marcia Harris, Frank Puglia, Lupino Lane. Combination grim drama and tender love story about a family of Polish refugees in inflation-laden post-WW1 Germany. The spotlight is on Inge (Dempster) and her sweetheart Paul (Hamilton), a veteran who suffers from gas poisoning, and their attempt to build a life together. A perfect example of how the style and substance of Griffith had become dated by 1924. Nonetheless, a fascinating curio, with some stark and powerful sequences. Filmed on location in Germany.▼●

Isn't She Great (2000) **C-93m.** ** D: Andrew Bergman. Bette Midler, Nathan Lane, Stockard Channing, David Hyde Pierce, John Cleese, John Larroquette, Amanda Peet. Ill-conceived film about highly driven actress turned authoress Jacqueline Susann (*Valley of the Dolls*) and the one man who believes in her, her press agent husband, Irving Mansfield. Not funny enough to succeed as a comedy, not serious or solid enough to work as a biography; Lane is awfully hard to resist, however, as the irrepressibly upbeat Mansfield. Screenplay by Paul Rudnick, from Michael Korda's magazine article. [R]▼◗

Is Paris Burning? (1966-French-U.S.) **173m.** ** D: René Clement. Jean-Paul Belmondo, Charles Boyer, Leslie Caron, Jean-Pierre Cassel, Claude Dauphin, Alain Delon, Kirk Douglas, Glenn Ford, Gert Frobe, Daniel Gelin, Yves Montand, Anthony Perkins, Simone Signoret, Robert Stack, Orson Welles. Rambling pseudo-documentary-style recreation of WW2 France, showing liberation of Paris and Nazis' attempt to burn the city. Cameos by international players confuse blotchy film made in Europe. Screenplay by Gore Vidal and Francis Ford Coppola, from the Larry Collins-Dominique Lapierre book. Panavision.▼●

Istanbul (1957) **C-84m.** ** D: Joseph Pevney. Errol Flynn. Cornell Borchers, John Bentley, Torin Thatcher, Leif Erickson, Martin Benson, Nat "King" Cole, Werner Klemperer. Dull drama of flyer Flynn returning to Istanbul, discovering his ladylove (whom he believed had perished in a fire) to be alive and an amnesiac. Sole bright spot: Cole singing "When I Fall in Love." Remake of SINGAPORE. CinemaScope.▼

Istanbul (1990-Turkish-Swedish) **C-88m.** BOMB D: Mats Arehn. Timothy Bottoms, Twiggy, Emma Kilberg, Robert Morley, Lena Endre, Sverre Anker Ousdal. Journalist Bottoms arrives in Istanbul with his daughter to seek information on family of his wife's son, becomes enmeshed in confusing intrigue. Twiggy is a mystery woman. Murky, clumsy, international coproduction is about as interesting as watching camel spit dry. [PG-13] ▼●

I Stand Condemned (1935-British) **75m.** **½ D: Anthony Asquith. Harry Baur, Laurence Olivier, Penelope Dudley Ward, Robert Cochran, Morton Selten, Athene Seyler. Inconsequential story of jealous Russian framing young officer as a spy, to eliminate him from rivalry over woman. Worth seeing for young, dashing Olivier. British title: MOSCOW NIGHTS.▼

Is There Sex After Death? (1971) **C-97m.** *** D: Jeanne and Alan Abel. Buck Henry, Alan Abel, Marshall Efron, Holly Woodlawn, Earle Doud. Crude but funny satire of porn films. Famous hoaxer Abel (who, with his wife, also produced and scripted) plays a traveling sexologist; Efron hilarious as an X-rated-film director. [R—edited from original X rating]▼

I Still Know What You Did Last Summer (1998) **C-101m.** *½ D: Danny Cannon. Jennifer Love Hewitt, Freddie Prinze, Jr., Brandy, Mekhi Phifer, Muse Watson, Matthew Settle, Bill Cobbs, Jeffrey Combs, Jennifer Esposito, John Hawkes. Hewitt and friends win a vacation to a Caribbean island, where they are pursued by the killer with a hook from the first movie, I KNOW WHAT YOU DID LAST SUMMER. Another film in which the cast runs around screaming while being killed, one by one. Plotless mess lacks any suspense, and makes the original look like a classic. Panavision. [R] ▼●◗

It (1927) **72m.** **½ D: Clarence Badger. Clara Bow, Antonio Moreno, William Austin, Jacqueline Gadsdon (Jane Daly), Priscilla Bonner. Bow is dazzling in this otherwise ordinary tale of a spirited, gold-digging department-store salesgirl with designs on her handsome boss (Moreno). Based on Elinor Glyn's trendy story of the same title; Madame Glyn appears briefly as herself. Look for Gary Cooper in a walk-on as a reporter.▼●

It! (1967) **C-96m.** ** D: Herbert J. Leder. Roddy McDowall, Jill Haworth, Ernest Clark, Paul Maxwell, Aubrey Richards. McDowall brings hulking stone statue—the Golem, no less—to life and soon finds it makes a great murderer. Kill it! Filmed in England.

It Ain't Hay (1943) **80m.** **½ D: Erle C. Kenton. Bud Abbott, Lou Costello, Patsy O'Connor, Grace McDonald, Leighton Noble, Cecil Kellaway, Eugene Pallette, Eddie Quillan. Pretty good A&C from Damon Runyon story, "Princess O'Hara," of racehorse Teabiscuit; good supporting cast helps.

I Take This Woman (1940) **97m.** ** D: W. S. Van Dyke II. Spencer Tracy, Hedy Lamarr, Verree Teasdale, Kent Taylor, Laraine Day, Mona Barrie, Louis Calhern, Marjorie Main, Frances Drake, Jack Carson. Disappointing soaper with dedicated doctor Tracy sacrificing all for Lamarr, who at first isn't grateful. Long in production, with innumerable behind-the-scenes changes, this was a notorious dud in 1940.

Italian Connection, The (1973-Italian) **C-92m.** ** D: Fernando Di Leo. Henry Silva, Woody Strode, Mario Adorf, Luciana Paluzzi, Sylva Koscina, Adolfo Celi. Violent gangster meller has Milanese hood Adorf set up by gang boss Celi for the blame in a six-million-dollar heroin heist. For action fans only. Video title: MANHUNT. [R]▼

Italian Job, The (1969-British) **C-101m.** **½ D: Peter Collinson. Michael Caine, Noel Coward, Maggie Blye, Benny Hill, Tony Beckley, Raf Vallone. $4,000,000 in gold bullion's the object in average caper film about prison-based mastermind Coward's plan to divert authorities in Turin, Italy, causing "history's biggest traffic jam." Wild chases galore, plus truly bizarre ending, but characterizations are pat, forgettable. Panavision. [G]▼●

Italiano Brava Gente (1965-Italian) **156m.** *** D: Giuseppe De Santis. Arthur Kennedy, Peter Falk, Tatyana Samoilova, Rafaelle Pisu, Andrea Checchi. Expansive chronicle of Italian-Russian warfront during WW2, focusing on a variety of strata of soldiers and civilians. Much edited since European opening. Retitled: ATTACK AND RETREAT.▼

It All Came True (1940) **97m.** **½ D: Lewis Seiler. Ann Sheridan, Humphrey Bogart, Jeffrey Lynn, ZaSu Pitts, Jessie Busley, Una O'Connor, Grant Mitchell, Felix Bressart. Offbeat story combines comedy, drama, music, and sentiment as gangster Bogart hides out in quaint boarding house. Fine showcase for Sheridan, who sings "Angel in Disguise" and "The Gaucho Serenade."

It Always Rains on Sunday (1947-British) **92m.** ***½ D: Robert Hamer. Googie Withers, Jack Warner, John McCallum, Edward Chapman, Jimmy Hanley, John Carol, John Slater, Susan Shaw, Sydney Tafler, Alfie Bass, Betty Ann Davies, Jane Hylton, Hermione Baddeley. Excellent mosaic of characters whose lives intertwine in a drab London neighborhood. McCallum is escaped convict seeking refuge with his ex-lover, Withers (in real life, the two stars married the following year). Arthur La Bern's novel was scripted by Henry Cornelius, Angus MacPhail, and Hamer.

It Came From Beneath the Sea (1955) **80m.** *** D: Robert Gordon. Kenneth Tobey, Faith Domergue, Donald Curtis, Ian Keith, Harry Lauter. Breathtaking special effects highlight this sci-fi thriller. Huge octopus emerges from Pacific Ocean and wreaks havoc on San Francisco. First film made by Ray Harryhausen-Charles H. Schneer team.▼●

It Came From Hollywood (1982) **C-80m.** *½ D: Malcolm Leo, Andrew Solt. Dan Aykroyd, John Candy, Cheech and Chong, Gilda Radner. Contemporary comedy stars are spectacularly *un*funny introducing and narrating clips from some of Hollywood's worst movies—most of which are funny enough without additional wisecracks. What's more, this pointless, poorly constructed compilation includes scenes from *good* movies like WAR OF THE WORLDS and THE INCREDIBLE SHRINKING MAN! Even so, howlers like MARS NEEDS WOMEN and PLAN 9 FROM OUTER SPACE still offer some genuine laughs. [PG]▼●

It Came From Outer Space (1953) **81m.** *** D: Jack Arnold. Richard Carlson, Barbara Rush, Charles Drake, Russell Johnson, Joe Sawyer, Kathleen Hughes. Intriguing science-fiction based on a Ray Bradbury story. An alien ship crashes in the Arizona desert; its passengers assume the identities of nearby townspeople so they can effect repairs unnoticed—they think. Remarkably sober for its era, with crisp performances and real restraint, even in its use of 3-D. The 1996 TV movie IT CAME FROM OUTER SPACE II is a much inferior remake, rather than the sequel the title suggests. ▼●

It Came Without Warning SEE: **Without Warning**

It Comes Up Murder SEE: **Honey Pot, The**

It Conquered the World (1956) **68m.** **½ D: Roger Corman. Peter Graves, Beverly Garland, Lee Van Cleef, Sally Fraser. Low-budget sci-fi which intelligently attempts to create atmospheric excitement in yarn of carrot-shaped monster from Venus, Paul Blaisdell's finest creation. One of Corman's best early quickies, well acted and interesting but awkwardly plotted. Remade as ZONTAR, THE THING FROM VENUS.▼

It Could Happen to You (1994) **C-101m.** *** D: Andrew Bergman. Nicolas Cage, Bridget Fonda, Rosie Perez, Wendell Pierce, Isaac Hayes, Victor Rojas, Seymour Cassel, Stanley Tucci, J. E. Freeman, Red Buttons, Richard Jenkins. Charming romantic comedy about a Good Samaritan cop who shares a lottery ticket with a hard-luck waitress—little dreaming it will make them both millionaires. Warm, winning performances by Cage and Fonda carry this N.Y.-based fairy tale, with a plot not intended for close scrutiny. Inspired by a true-life story. [PG]▼●◗

It Grows on Trees (1952) **84m.** ** D: Arthur Lubin. Irene Dunne, Dean Jagger, Joan Evans, Richard Crenna, Les Tremayne. Dunne's last feature is slim vehicle of wife who discovers backyard foliage is blossoming crisp money.

It Had To Be You (1947) **98m.** **½ D: Don Hartman, Rudolph Maté. Ginger Rogers, Cornel Wilde, Percy Waram, Spring Byington, Ron Randell. Rogers has severe indecision before every scheduled marriage, until dream-lover Wilde appears. Airy, fanciful comedy.

It Had to Happen (1936) **79m.** ** D: Roy Del Ruth. George Raft, Leo Carrillo, Rosalind Russell, Alan Dinehart, Arline Judge. Italian immigrant Raft working his way to political power in N.Y.C., trying to romance upper-class Russell.

I Thank a Fool (1962-British) **C-100m.** ** D: Robert Stevens. Susan Hayward, Peter Finch, Diane Cilento, Cyril Cusack, Kieron Moore, Athene Seyler. Dreary, farfetched story about Hayward spending a year and a half in prison for mercy-killing, then becoming involved with lawyer Finch, who prosecuted her case, with bizarre results. CinemaScope.

It Happened at Nightmare Inn SEE: **Nightmare Inn**

It Happened at the World's Fair (1963) **C-105m.** *** D: Norman Taurog. Elvis Presley, Joan O'Brien, Gary Lockwood, Yvonne Craig. Entertaining Presley vehicle set at Seattle World's Fair, with Elvis and O'Brien brought together by little Ginny Tiu. Listenable tunes (including "One Broken Heart for Sale," "A World of Our Own" and "Happy Ending") help make this most enjoyable. Young Kurt Russell, who later played Elvis in a TV movie, makes his film debut in a small role. Panavision.▼

It Happened Here (1966-British) **95m.** *** D: Kevin Brownlow, Andrew Mollo. Pauline Murray, Sebastian Shaw, Fiona Lelard, Honor Fehrson. Imaginative fable of Britain taken over by the Nazis during WW2, made in semidocumentary style by two ingenious young filmmakers. Brits keep a stiff upper lip during fascist persecution; leading lady Murray is the odd woman out, as a nurse thought to be collaborating with the enemy.▼◗

It Happened in Athens (1962) **C-92m.** ** D: Andrew Marton. Jayne Mansfield, Trax Colton, Lili Valenty, Maria Xenia, Bob Mathias, Nico Minardos. Silly, juvenile charade made somewhat watchable by Mansfield in a variety of revealing costumes as an actress who agrees to marry the winner of the marathon at the 1896 Olympics. Previewed at 100m. CinemaScope.

It Happened in Brooklyn (1947) **105m.** ** D: Richard Whorf. Frank Sinatra, Kathryn Grayson, Jimmy Durante, Peter Lawford, Gloria Grahame. Hokey musical of group of Brooklynites trying to make it big in show biz; all coating, no substance. Some good songs, including "Time After Time" and wonderful Sinatra-Durante duet, "The Song's Gotta Have Heart."▼●

It Happened One Christmas (1977) **C-112m. TVM** D: Donald Wrye. Marlo Thomas, Wayne Rogers, Orson Welles, Cloris Leachman, Barney Martin, Karen Carlson, Doris Roberts. IT'S A WONDERFUL LIFE with change of sex only proves how wonderful the original by Frank Capra was—and is. This one goes on forever, and that's just one of the problems. Anyway, earnestly made. Average.

It Happened One Night (1934) **105m.** **** D: Frank Capra. Clark Gable, Claudette Colbert, Walter Connolly, Roscoe Karns, Alan Hale, Ward Bond. Legendary romantic comedy doesn't age a bit. Still as enchanting as ever, with reporter Gable and runaway heiress Colbert falling in love on rural bus trip. Hitch-hiking travails, the Walls of Jericho, other memorable scenes remain fresh and delightful. First film to win all five major Oscars: Picture, Actor, Actress, Director, and Screenplay (Robert Riskin). Based on Samuel Hopkins Adams' story "Night Bus," originally published in *Cosmopolitan.* Remade as musicals EVE KNEW HER APPLES and YOU CAN'T RUN AWAY FROM IT.▼●

It Happened One Summer SEE: **State Fair** (1945)

It Happened on 5th Avenue (1947) **115m.** ** D: Roy Del Ruth. Don DeFore, Ann Harding, Charlie Ruggles, Victor Moore, Gale Storm, Grant Mitchell. Overlong comedy about elegant N.Y.C. mansion taken over by thoughtful bum, who invites horde of friends and real owner in disguise to be his guests.▼

It Happened to Jane (1959) **C-98m.** **½ D: Richard Quine. Doris Day, Jack Lemmon, Ernie Kovacs, Steve Forrest, Teddy Rooney, Russ Brown, Mary Wickes, Parker Fennelly. Breezy, likable comedy: Doris runs a Maine lobstery, and Jack is her lawyer; together they tangle with ultracheap villain Kovacs (who hams mercilessly). Aka TWINKLE AND SHINE.

It Happened Tomorrow (1944) **84m.** *** D: René Clair. Dick Powell, Linda Darnell, Jack Oakie, Edgar Kennedy, John Philliber, Edward Brophy, George Cleveland, Sig Ruman, Paul Guilfoyle. Diverting if somewhat static fantasy yarn about a turn-of-the-century reporter who gets inside track on *tomorrow's* headlines, leading to unexpected complications. Low-key, often charming.▼

It Happens Every Spring (1949) **87m.** ***½ D: Lloyd Bacon. Ray Milland, Jean Peters, Paul Douglas, Ed Begley, Ted de Corsia, Ray Collins, Jessie Royce Landis, Alan Hale, Jr., Debra Paget. Clever little comedy of chemistry professor (Milland) accidentally discovering a chemical mixture which causes baseballs to avoid all wooden surfaces, namely baseball bats. He takes leave from academia and embarks on meteoric pitching career. A most enjoyable, unpretentious picture. Story by Shirley W. Smith and Valentine Davies; scripted by Davies.▼

It Happens Every Thursday (1953) **80m.** *** D: Joseph Pevney. Loretta Young, John Forsythe, Frank McHugh, Edgar Buchanan, Jane Darwell, Dennis Weaver. Warm comedy about married couple who buy small-town newspaper and try every method conceivable to make it click.

I, the Jury (1953) **87m.** ** D: Harry Essex. Biff Elliot, Preston Foster, Peggie Castle, Elisha Cook, Jr., John Qualen. Undistinguished Mickey Spillane caper with Mike Hammer seeking his friend's killer. Originally in 3-D; remade in 1982 in 2-D.

I, the Jury (1982) **C-111m.** ** D: Richard T. Heffron. Armand Assante, Barbara Carrera, Alan King, Laurene Landon, Geoffrey Lewis, Paul Sorvino, Judson Scott. Mickey Spillane's hard-boiled Mike Hammer seems out of place in this updated remake, though contemporary levels of violence and nudity suit the material. Lots of action and some truly beautiful women help camouflage the holes in Larry Cohen's script; Assante is a sulky Hammer. [R]▼

It Lives Again (1978) **C-91m.** *½ D: Larry Cohen. Frederic Forrest, Kathleen Lloyd, John Ryan, John Marley, Andrew Duggan, Eddie Constantine. Sequel to IT'S ALIVE offers not one but three murderous babies. More of a horror film than a thriller—and not a very good one. Constantine's first American film in many years. Aka IT'S ALIVE II; followed by IT'S ALIVE III: ISLAND OF THE ALIVE. [R]▼●

It Lives by Night SEE: **Bat People**

It Only Happens to Others (1971-French-Italian) **C-88m.** ** D: Nadine Trintignant. Marcello Mastroianni, Catherine Deneuve, Serge Marquand, Dominique Labourier, Catherine Allegret. Loss of young child causes happily married couple to withdraw from society. Heavy on the syrup. Panoramica. [PG]

It Runs in My Family (1994) **C-85m.** ** D: Bob Clark. Charles Grodin, Kieran Culkin, Mary Steenburgen, Christian Culkin, Al Mancini, Troy Evans, Roy Brocksmith, Glenn Shadix, Dick O'Neill, Wayne Grace. Followup to A CHRISTMAS STORY—with a new cast—is a huge disappointment, chronicling the same family's adventures in the early 40s—from the boy's efforts to win at top-spinning to the Old Man's feud with his hillbilly neighbors. Culkin and Grodin are no match for Peter Billingsley and Darren McGavin in the earlier film, and many of writer/narrator Jean Shepherd's nostalgic musings don't come off nearly as well as they do in his writings and broadcasts. Barely released theatrically; retitled MY SUMMER STORY. [PG]▼

It's a Big Country (1951) **89m.** **½ D: Charles Vidor, Richard Thorpe, John Sturges, Don Hartman, Don Weis, Clarence Brown, William Wellman. Ethel Barrymore, Keefe Brasselle, Gary Cooper, Nancy Davis (Reagan), Gene Kelly, Keenan Wynn, Fredric March, Van Johnson, James Whitmore. Narrated by Louis Calhern. Dore Schary's plug for America uses several pointless episodes about the variety of people and places in U.S. Other segments make up for it in very uneven film.

It's a Bikini World (1967) **C-86m.** *½ D: Stephanie Rothman. Deborah Walley, Tommy Kirk, Bob Pickett, Suzie Kaye, The Animals, The Gentrys. Superlover Kirk loves bikinied Debbie, but she doesn't dig him until he masquerades as an intellectual. Not among the best of its kind, if there even *is* a best of its kind. The Animals, however, do perform "We Gotta Get Out of This Place." Techniscope.

It's a Date (1940) **103m.** **½ D: William A. Seiter. Deanna Durbin, Walter Pidgeon, Kay Francis, Eugene Pallette, Lewis Howard, S. Z. Sakall, Samuel S. Hinds, Cecilia Loftus. Durbin faces unique growing pains when she's offered a Broadway role intended for her mother (Francis) and then is courted by a man her mother's age (Pidgeon). Star trio shines brightly in this enjoyable contrivance, which unfortunately goes on too long and ends (incongruously) with Deanna singing "Ave Maria"! Remade as NANCY GOES TO RIO.▼

It's a Dog's Life (1955) **C-88m.** **½ D: Herman Hoffman. Jeff Richards, Edmund Gwenn, Dean Jagger, Sally Fraser. Film uses gimmick of having the canine star tell his life story from slums to luxury. Retitled: BAR SINISTER. CinemaScope.▼

It's a Gift (1934) **73m.** **** D: Norman Z. McLeod. W. C. Fields, Baby LeRoy, Kathleen Howard, Tommy Bupp, Morgan Wallace. Fields is a grocery store owner who goes West with his family. Beautiful comedy routines in one of the Great Man's unforgettable films. Charles Sellon as a blind man, T. Roy Barnes as a salesman looking for Carl LaFong, contribute some hilarious moments. A remake of Fields' silent film IT'S THE OLD ARMY GAME.▼●

It's a Great Feeling (1949) **C-85m.** **½ D: David Butler. Dennis Morgan. Doris Day, Jack Carson, Bill Goodwin. Gentle spoof of Hollywood with Carson's ego making filming difficult for himself and partner Morgan; guest appearances by many Warner Bros. players and directors, including Joan Crawford, Gary Cooper, Michael Curtiz, Jane Wyman, Sydney Greenstreet, Danny Kaye, Edward G. Robinson, King Vidor, Eleanor Parker, Patricia Neal, Raoul Walsh, Ronald Reagan—and even Reagan and Wyman's daughter Maureen!▼●

It's a Great Life (1943) **75m.** **½ D: Frank Strayer. Penny Singleton, Arthur Lake, Larry Simms, Hugh Herbert, Jonathan Hale, Danny Mummert, Alan Dinehart, Irving Bacon, Marjorie Ann Mutchie. Dagwood is sent to buy a house and comes back with a horse, if you can believe it, eventually winding up in a fox hunt. Elementary *Blondie* farce raises a few laughs. Video title: BLONDIE AND DAGWOOD—IT'S A GREAT LIFE.▼

It's a Joke, Son (1947) **63m.** ** D: Ben Stoloff. Kenny Delmar, Una Merkel, June Lockhart, Kenneth Farrell, Douglass Dumbrille. Folksy comedy featuring further exploits of Senator Claghorn (Delmar) from the Fred Allen radio show.▼

It's Alive! (1974) **C-91m.** **½ D: Larry Cohen. John Ryan, Sharon Farrell, Andrew Duggan, Guy Stockwell, James Dixon, Michael Ansara. Schlocky thriller about a baby who goes on a murderous rampage. Has a devoted following, but not for all tastes. Effective score by Bernard Herrmann. Sequels: IT LIVES AGAIN and IT'S ALIVE III: ISLAND OF THE ALIVE. [PG]▼●

It's Alive II SEE: **It Lives Again**

It's Alive III: Island of the Alive (1987) **C-91m.** **½ D: Larry Cohen. Michael Moriarty, Karen Black, Laurene Landon, Gerrit Graham, James Dixon, Neal Israel, Macdonald Carey. Part 3 makes serious comments on issues ranging from the AIDS crisis to abortion as Moriarty, father of a monster baby, succeeds in preventing society from exterminating all the monster infants, who are quarantined on a desert island. Wild fun, loaded with dark humor.▼

It's All True (1993) **C/B&W-87m.** *** D: Richard Wilson, Myron Meisel, Bill Krohn. Fascinating assemblage of the remaining "lost" footage from Orson Welles' abandoned three-part documentary he was shooting in Brazil in 1942 as RKO brass was taking a knife to THE MAGNIFICENT AMBERSONS back in Hollywood. Only tantalizing snippets remain of the *My Friend Bonito* episode (shot in Mexico by Norman Foster under Welles' supervision) and of the seductive Carnaval footage (some in color); virtually intact is what would have been the original's centerpiece: the *Four Men on a Raft* tribute to Brazilian fishermen. A major contribution to movie history, albeit one for specialized tastes; film concludes with an audio track of Welles with Carmen Miranda. For film buffs who think they've experienced it all.▼●

It's Always Fair Weather (1955) **C-102m.** *** D: Gene Kelly, Stanley Donen. Gene Kelly, Dan Dailey, Michael Kidd, Cyd Charisse, Dolores Gray, David Burns. Three WW2 buddies meet ten years after their discharge and find they have nothing in common. Pungent Comden and Green script falls short of perfection but still has wonderful moments, and some first-rate musical numbers (like Cyd's "Baby, You Knock Me Out" and Dolores' "Thanks a Lot But No Thanks"). Best: the ash-can dance, although clever use of wide-screen is lost on TV. CinemaScope.▼●

It's a Mad Mad Mad Mad World (1963) **C-154m.** **½ D: Stanley Kramer. Spencer Tracy, Edie Adams, Milton Berle, Sid Caesar, Buddy Hackett, Ethel Merman, Mickey Rooney, Dick Shawn, Dorothy Provine, Phil Silvers, Jonathan Winters, Peter Falk, Jimmy Durante, Terry-Thomas, Eddie "Rochester" Anderson, William Demarest, many guest stars. Supercomedy cast in attempt at supercomedy, about group of people racing to find hidden bank loot under watchful eye of detective Tracy. Big, splashy, generally funny, but bigness doesn't equal greatness. Homevideo version restored to 175m. Filmed in Ultra Panavision 70. ▼●

It's a Pleasure! (1945) **C-90m.** ** D: William A. Seiter. Sonja Henie, Michael O'Shea, Bill Johnson, Marie McDonald, Gus Schilling, Iris Adrian. Skater Henie and hockey player O'Shea get married but can't seem to break the ice; pretty weak.▼

It's a Small World (1950) **68m.** ** D: William Castle. Paul Dale, Lorraine Miller, Will Geer, Steve Brodie, Todd Karns. Truly strange B-movie stars Dale (a deejay in real life) as a midget who suffers a succession of life's hard knocks until finally becoming "adjusted" and even finding romance in a circus. Director Castle (who appears in a cameo as a cop) makes it interesting but unnecessarily nasty for the little guy.

It's a Wonderful Life (1946) **129m.** **** D: Frank Capra. James Stewart, Donna Reed, Lionel Barrymore, Thomas Mitchell, Henry Travers, Beulah Bondi, Frank Faylen, Ward Bond, Gloria Grahame, H.B. Warner, Frank Albertson, Todd Karns, Samuel S. Hinds, Mary Treen, Sheldon Leonard, Ellen Corby. Sentimental tale of Stewart, who works all his life to make good in small town, thinking he's failed and trying to end his life. Guardian angel Travers comes to show him his mistake. Only Capra and this cast could pull it off so well; this film seems to improve with age. Capra, Frances Goodrich, Albert Hackett, and Jo Swerling expanded Philip Van Doren Stern's short story "The Greatest Gift" (which had originally been written by Stern as a Christmas card!). Remade for TV as IT HAPPENED ONE CHRISTMAS. Also shown in computer-colored version.▼●◗

It's a Wonderful World (1939) **86m.** *** D: W. S. Van Dyke II. Claudette Colbert, James Stewart, Guy Kibbee, Nat Pendleton, Frances Drake, Edgar Kennedy, Ernest Truex, Sidney Blackmer, Hans Conried. Screwball comedy with Colbert a runaway poetess, Stewart a fugitive chased by cops Pendleton and Kennedy. Very, very funny, with Stewart having a field-day. Scripted by Ben Hecht, from his and Herman J. Mankiewicz' story. We swear by our eyes!

It Seemed Like a Good Idea at the Time (1975-Canadian) **C-106m.** ** D: John Trent. Anthony Newley, Stefanie Powers, Isaac Hayes, Lloyd Bochner, Yvonne De Carlo, Henry Ramer, Lawrence Dane, John Candy. Tired comedy with a mostly tired cast, centering on Newley's attempts to woo back his remarried ex-wife. Dane and Candy appear as a pair of bumbling cops, characters they replayed a year later in FIND THE LADY. Aka GOOD IDEA! [PG]▼

It's Good to Be Alive (1974) **C-100m. TVM** D: Michael Landon. Paul Winfield, Lou Gossett, Ruby Dee, Ramon Bieri, Joe DeSantis, Ty Henderson, Lloyd Gough. The Roy Campanella story, beginning with the baseball star's crippling automobile accident in 1958. Especially strong performances by the three leads make this rewarding viewing. Above average.▼

It Should Happen to You (1954) **87m.** *** D: George Cukor. Judy Holliday, Peter Lawford, Jack Lemmon, Michael O'Shea, Vaughn Taylor. Holliday is Gladys Glover of Binghamton, N.Y., who has come to N.Y.C. to make a name for herself—and does so, by plastering her moniker across a Columbus Circle billboard. Judy is radiant in this charming romantic comedy/satire, scripted by Garson Kanin. Lemmon's first film.▼●

It Shouldn't Happen to a Dog (1946) **70m.** **½ D: Herbert I. Leeds. Carole Landis, Allyn Joslyn, Margo Woode, Henry (Harry) Morgan, Reed Hadley, John Alexander, Jean Wallace, John Ireland. Fluff about reporter Joslyn, who erroneously thinks policewoman Landis and a Doberman pinscher named Rodney robbed a bar.

It Shouldn't Happen to a Vet SEE: **All Things Bright and Beautiful**

It's in the Air (1935) **80m.** ** D: Charles Riesner. Jack Benny, Una Merkel, Ted Healy, Nat Pendleton, Mary Carlisle, Grant Mitchell. Uncharacteristic Benny as con-artist who goes to ex-wife Merkel for help. Fair comedy; mainly a curiosity item.

It's in the Bag! (1945) **87m.** *** D: Richard Wallace. Fred Allen, Binnie Barnes, Robert Benchley, Sidney Toler, Jack Benny, Don Ameche, Victor Moore, Rudy Vallee, William Bendix. Story similar to THE TWELVE CHAIRS with flea-circus promoter Allen entitled to inheritance; plot soon goes out the window in favor of unrelated but amusing episodes, including hilarious encounter between Allen and Benny.▼

It's Love Again (1936-British) **83m.** *** D: Victor Saville. Robert Young, Jessie Matthews, Sonnie Hale, Ernest Milton, Robb Wilton, Sara Allgood. Lighter-than-air musical-comedy vehicle for Matthews following her success with Saville on EVERGREEN. Young is wise-guy publicity man who dreams up idea of creating an imaginary socialite, until Matthews steps out of the chorus line to fill the role. Funny, charming and imaginatively done, with several pleasant songs.▼

It's Love I'm After (1937) **90m.** *** D: Archie Mayo. Bette Davis, Leslie Howard, Olivia de Havilland, Patric Knowles, Eric Blore, Bonita Granville, Spring Byington, Veda Ann Borg. Delightful, witty comedy of ego-struck actor Howard and his fiancée/costar Davis, who explodes when he becomes involved with infatuated admirer de Havilland. Reminiscent in spirit of TWENTIETH CENTURY; Blore is marvelous as Howard's ultradedicated valet.

It's My Party (1996) **C-109m.** **½ D: Randal Kleiser. Eric Roberts, Gregory Harrison, Margaret Cho, Bruce Davison, Lee Grant, Devon Gummersall, Marlee Matlin, Roddy McDowall, Olivia Newton-John, Bronson Pinchot, Paul Regina, George Segal, Dimitra Arlys (Arliss), Christopher Atkins, Ron Glass, Victor Love, Joel Polis, Nina Foch, Sally Kellerman, Greg Louganis. Roberts portrays a successful L.A. designer suffering from AIDS, who decides he'd prefer to die with dignity and throws himself a wild weekend party for a final fling. Quite moving and often very funny. Roberts is excellent in the lead. [R]▼●

It's My Turn (1980) **C-91m.** *** D: Claudia Weill. Jill Clayburgh, Michael

Douglas, Charles Grodin, Beverly Garland, Steven Hill, Teresa Baxter, Joan Copeland, John Gabriel, Charles Kimbrough, Jennifer Salt, Daniel Stern, Dianne Wiest. Enjoyable, low-key romantic comedy-drama about a young woman trying to balance her life as a career woman, mate, and daughter. A quirky and consistently surprising little film with good performances, especially from Grodin as Clayburgh's aloof lover. Film debut of Dianne Wiest. [R]▼●

It's Never Too Late (1956-British) **C-95m.** **½ D: Michael McCarthy. Phyllis Calvert, Guy Rolfe, Sarah Lawson, Peter Illing, Patrick Barr. Pleasant frou-frou about Calvert becoming famed writer, caught between choice of being good mother or living a celebrity's life.

It's Not the Size That Counts (1974-British) **C-90m.** BOMB D: Ralph Thomas. Leigh Lawson, Elke Sommer, Denholm Elliott, Vincent Price, Judy Geeson, George Coulouris, Milo O'Shea. Abominable sequel to PERCY, even worse, if that's possible; Lawson replaces Hywel Bennett as penis-transplant recipient. Original title PERCY'S PROGRESS. [R]▼

It'$ Only Money (1962) **84m.** *** D: Frank Tashlin. Jerry Lewis, Joan O'Brien, Zachary Scott, Jack Weston, Jesse White, Mae Questel. TV repairman Jerry wants to be a detective like his idol (White!), so he sets out to locate a missing heir—and guess who it turns out to be? Slick mystery-comedy is one of Lewis' best vehicles, thanks to solid script (by John Fenton Murray) and direction, fine cast, and memorable climax involving runaway army of robot lawn mowers.

It's Pat (1994) **C-77m.** BOMB D: Adam Bernstein. Julia Sweeney, David Foley, Charles Rocket, Kathy Griffin, Julie Hayden, Kathy Najimy, Larry Hankin, Tim Meadows, Camille Paglia. Sweeney's cheerfully obnoxious, androgynous character from *Saturday Night Live* skits is not a prime candidate for feature-film stardom, but that was obvious to most observers before this picture was ever made! If you can get through the first five minutes, you may get through the whole movie, as Pat finds true love with the equally androgynous Chris (Foley). Barely released theatrically. Sweeney coscripted. [PG-13]▼●

It's Showtime (1976) **C/B&W-86m.** *** No director credit. Enjoyable compilation of animal sequences from movies, reaching back to Rin Tin Tin's silent films. Maximum footage from NATIONAL VELVET and LASSIE COME HOME, but everything—from canine version of "Singin' in the Rain" to Bonzo the Chimp being bottle-fed by Ronald Reagan—is great fun.

It Started in Naples (1960) **C-100m.** **½ D: Melville Shavelson. Clark Gable, Sophia Loren, Vittorio De Sica, Marietto, Paolo Carlini, Claudio Ermelli. Gable is American lawyer, in Italy to bring nephew back to America, but sexy Aunt Sophia won't agree. Star duo never clicks as love match, but they do their best. Attractive fluff. VistaVision.▼

It Started With a Kiss (1959) **C-104m.** **½ D: George Marshall. Glenn Ford, Debbie Reynolds, Eva Gabor, Fred Clark, Edgar Buchanan, Harry Morgan. Airy comedy about wacky Reynolds and her army officer husband Ford, trying to make a go of marriage; set in Spain. CinemaScope.▼

It Started With Eve (1941) **90m.** *** D: Henry Koster. Deanna Durbin, Charles Laughton, Robert Cummings, Guy Kibbee, Margaret Tallichet, Walter Catlett. Delightful romantic comedy; Deanna poses as Cummings' fiancee to please his dying father (Laughton). Trouble starts when Laughton shows signs of recovery. Remade as I'D RATHER BE RICH.▼●

It's Tough to Be Famous (1932) **79m.** *** D: Alfred E. Green. Douglas Fairbanks, Jr., Mary Brian, Walter Catlett, Lilian Bond, Terrence Ray, David Landau. Pungent story of naval hero who becomes a much-manipulated media celebrity against his wishes. Done with usual Warner Bros. pizazz—and still surprisingly timely.

It's Trad, Dad! SEE: **Ring-a-Ding Rhythm**

It's Your Move (1968-Italian-Spanish) **C-93m.** ** D: Robert Fiz. Edward G. Robinson, Terry-Thomas, Adolfo Celi. Good cast aids limp tale of Englishman who uses lookalikes for four bank tellers to pull off robbery. Techniscope.

It Takes All Kinds (1969-U.S.-Australian) **C-98m.** ** D: Eddie Davis. Robert Lansing, Vera Miles, Barry Sullivan, Sid Melton, Penny Sugg. Fair double-cross drama about Miles' shielding of Lansing when he accidentally kills sailor in a brawl in Australia. Nothing special.

It Takes a Thief (1960-British) **90m.** ** D: John Gilling. Jayne Mansfield, Anthony Quayle, Carl Mohner, Peter Reynolds, Barbara Mullen, Edward Judd. Mansfield is gangland leader with big heist in the workings; supporting cast uplifts flick. Original title: THE CHALLENGE.▼

It Takes Two (1995) **C-101m.** **½ D: Andy Tennant. Kirstie Alley, Steve Guttenberg, Mary-Kate Olsen, Ashley Olsen, Philip Bosco, Jane Sibbett, Michelle Grison, Desmond Roberts, Ernie Grunwald, Lawrence Dane. Surprisingly well-wrought comedy for kids about lookalikes who trade places in order to help each other. The fabulously wealthy girl has a father who's about to marry a patently awful woman, while the orphan is about to lose her best friend, the social worker who supervises the orphanage. The twins give very likable performances, as do their adult costars. A cross between THE PRINCE AND THE PAUPER and THE PARENT TRAP. [PG]▼●

It! The Terror from Beyond Space (1958) **69m.** **½ D: Edward L. Cahn. Marshall Thompson, Shawn Smith, Kim Spalding, Ann Doran, Dabbs Greer. The second spaceship to Mars heads for Earth with the sole survivor of the *first* expedition, accused of murdering his crewmates—but the real killer is a Martian monster (Ray "Crash" Corrigan), which has crept aboard the returning ship. ALIEN owes a lot to this tidy, suspenseful, but underproduced movie, scripted by sci-fi writer Jerome Bixby.▼●

It Was a Wonderful Life (1993) **C-84m.** **½ D: Michele Ohayon. Narrated by Jodie Foster. Maddeningly uneven documentary about six formerly affluent women who, for varying reasons, have found themselves destitute and homeless. A chronicle of individuals who valiantly attempt to transcend their respective plights, done in by its all-too-often one-sided feminist proselytizing.

Ivanhoe (1952) **C-106m.** *** D: Richard Thorpe. Robert Taylor, Joan Fontaine, Elizabeth Taylor, Emlyn Williams, George Sanders, Robert Douglas, Finlay Currie, Felix Aylmer, Francis de Wolff, Guy Rolfe, Norman Wooland, Basil Sydney. Almost a classic spectacular, marred by draggy scripting of Walter Scott's epic of England in Middle Ages, in days of chivalrous knights; beautifully photographed on location in Great Britain. Remade as a TVM.▼●

Ivanhoe (1982) **C-150m. TVM** D: Douglas Camfield. James Mason, Anthony Andrews, Sam Neill, Michael Hordern, Olivia Hussey, Lysette Anthony, Julian Glover, John Rhys-Davies. Robust, florid adaptation (by John Gay) of the Scott classic. Stunningly photographed by John Coquillon and enthusiastically played by a standout cast, especially Mason as Isaac of York. Above average.▼

Ivan the Terrible, Part One (1943-Russian) **96m.** **** D: Sergei Eisenstein. Nikolai Cherkassov, Ludmila Tselikovskaya, Serafima Birman. Film spectacle of the highest order. Eisenstein's incredibly lavish, detailed chronicle of Czar Ivan IV's life from coronation to defeat to reinstatement, forging fascinating image of the man and his country. Enhanced by Prokofiev's original score. Heavy going, but worthwhile; the story continues in IVAN THE TERRIBLE, PART TWO.▼●◗

Ivan the Terrible, Part Two (1946-Russian) **88m.** ***½ D: Sergei Eisenstein. Nikolai Cherkassov, Serafima Birman, Mikhail Nazvanov, Pavel Kadochnikov, Andrei Abrikosov. Continuation of the saga of Czar Ivan IV, in which he takes on the boyars in a battle for power. Impressive film is just a shade below its predecessor. Banned by Stalin because of controversial depiction of Ivan's secret police, and not released until 1958. (The director had planned to shoot Part Three—which, needless to say, he never did.) Banquet-dance sequence was originally in color.▼●◗

I've Always Loved You (1946) **C-117m.** *** D: Frank Borzage. Philip Dorn, Catherine McLeod, William Carter, Maria Ouspenskaya, Felix Bressart. Lavish romancer with classical music background; Ouspenskaya stands out in cast.▼●

I've Heard the Mermaids Singing (1987-Canadian) **C-81m.** **½ D: Patricia Rozema. Sheila McCarthy, Paule Baillargeon, Ann-Marie McDonald, John Evans. Wistful, original comedy-drama about a young woman who's never been successful at anything but lands a job as assistant to a chic, intelligent art gallery owner whom she comes to idolize. McCarthy's winning and empathetic performance, in her film debut, keeps us hooked even when the movie starts to wander, which it does, more than once, before redeeming itself with the final shot. A slight but impressive first feature for writer-director Rozema.▼●

I've Lived Before (1956) **82m.** **½ D: Richard Bartlett. Jock Mahoney, Leigh Snowden, Ann Harding, John McIntire. Strange small-budget film about pilot who thinks he is an aviator who died in WW1.

I Vitelloni (1953-Italian) **104m.** **** D: Federico Fellini. Alberto Sordi, Franco Interlenghi, Franco Fabrizi, Leopoldo Trieste. Magnificent comedy-drama—arguably Fellini's masterpiece—about five shiftless male adolescents in a small Adriatic town who have to cope with emerging adulthood. Film's episodic structure brings to mind AMERICAN GRAFFITI; its love of humanity anticipates the director's own AMARCORD two decades later. In any event, a lovely film.▼●

Ivory Hunter (1951-British) **C-107m.** **½ D: Harry Watt. Anthony Steel, Dinah Sheridan, Harold Warrender, Meredith Edwards, William Simons. Documentary-ish account of establishment of Mount Kilimanjaro Game Preserve Park in Africa. Retitled: WHERE NO VULTURES FLY.

Ivory Hunters SEE: **Last Elephant, The**

Ivy (1947) **99m.** **½ D: Sam Wood. Joan Fontaine, Patric Knowles, Herbert Marshall, Richard Ney, Cedric Hardwicke, Lucile Watson. Average drama of murderess snared in her own seemingly faultless plans. Good cast gives film added boost.

I Wake Up Screaming (1941) **82m.** *** D: H. Bruce Humberstone. Betty Grable, Victor Mature, Carole Landis, Laird Cregar, William Gargan, Alan Mowbray, Allyn Joslyn, Elisha Cook, Jr. Entertaining whodunit with Grable and Mature implicated in murder of Betty's sister, pursued by determined cop Cregar. Twist finish to good mystery. Remade as VICKI; originally titled HOT SPOT.▼

I Walk Alone (1947) **98m.** ** D: Byron Haskin. Burt Lancaster, Lizabeth Scott,

Kirk Douglas, Wendell Corey, Kristine Miller, George Rigaud, Marc Lawrence. A prison term changes Lancaster's outlook on life, and return to outside world makes him bitter. Good cast, weak film.

I Walked with a Zombie (1943) **69m.** ***½ D: Jacques Tourneur. Frances Dee, Tom Conway, James Ellison, Edith Barrett, Christine Gordon, Theresa Harris, James Bell. Nurse Dee comes to Caribbean island to treat zombie-like wife of troubled Conway, finds skeletons in family closet, plus local voodoo rituals and legends that cannot be ignored. Exceptional Val Lewton chiller with rich atmosphere, mesmerizing story. Loosely adapted from *Jane Eyre*!▼●

I Walk the Line (1970) **C-95m.** **½ D: John Frankenheimer. Gregory Peck, Tuesday Weld, Estelle Parsons, Ralph Meeker, Lonny Chapman, Charles Durning. Rural sheriff Peck falls for moonshiner's daughter Weld, thereby destroying both his professional and personal life. Offbeat but aimless drama, helped by excellent Weld performance. Johnny Cash sings five songs. Panavision. [PG]▼

I Wanna Hold Your Hand (1978) **C-104m.** *** D: Robert Zemeckis. Nancy Allen, Bobby DiCicco, Marc McClure, Susan Kendall Newman, Theresa Saldana, Eddie Deezen, Wendie Jo Sperber, Will Jordan. Teenagers connive to get tickets for the Beatles' first appearance on *The Ed Sullivan Show*. If this original comedy seems occasionally silly and overbearing, that's the price it pays for being a generally accurate portrayal of a raucous event. Comedian Jordan is as hilariously Sullivan-like as ever. Steven Spielberg was executive producer. [PG]▼●

I Want a Divorce (1940) **75m.** **½ D: Ralph Murphy. Joan Blondell, Dick Powell, Gloria Dickson, Frank Fay, Dorothy Burgess, Jessie Ralph, Harry Davenport, Conrad Nagel. Powell and Blondell have just gotten married but already they're beginning to wonder in this light comedy. The two stars were married at the time in real life, too.

I Wanted Wings (1941) **131m.** ** D: Mitchell Leisen. Ray Milland, William Holden, Wayne Morris, Brian Donlevy, Constance Moore, Veronica Lake, Hedda Hopper. Stale plot of three men undergoing air force training served to introduce Lake as star material; that remains only real point of interest. However, the special effects for this did garner an Oscar.

I Want Her Dead SEE: **W**

I Want to Live! (1958) **120m.** ***½ D: Robert Wise. Susan Hayward, Simon Oakland, Virginia Vincent, Theodore Bikel, John Marley, Dabbs Greer, Gavin MacLeod. Hayward won an Oscar for her gutsy performance as prostitute-crook Barbara Graham who (according to the film) is framed for murder and goes to gas chamber. Smart presentation, fine acting, memorable jazz score by Johnny Mandel. Nelson Gidding and Don Mankiewicz based script on articles about Graham. Look fast for Jack Weston. Remade as a 1983 TVM with Lindsay Wagner. ▼●

I Want What I Want (1972-British) **C-91m.** **½ D: John Dexter. Anne Heywood, Harry Andrews, Jill Bennett, Nigel Flatley, Paul Rogers. Interesting little piece about sexual crisis in the life of man who wants a sex-change operation.▼

I Want You (1951) **102m.** *** D: Mark Robson. Dana Andrews, Dorothy McGuire, Farley Granger, Peggy Dow, Robert Keith, Mildred Dunnock, Martin Milner, Ray Collins, Jim Backus. Dated yet still touching Americana detailing effects of the Korean war on a small-town family. An artifact of its era, with fine performances all around. Screenplay by Irwin Shaw.▼

I Was a Communist for the FBI (1951) **83m.** **½ D: Gordon Douglas. Frank Lovejoy, Dorothy Hart, Philip Carey, James Millican. Documentary-style counterspy caper, low key and effective.

I Was a Male War Bride (1949) **105m.** *** D: Howard Hawks. Cary Grant, Ann Sheridan, Marion Marshall, Randy Stuart, William Neff, Ken Tobey. Delightful comedy of errors has French Army officer Grant trying to accompany WAC wife Sheridan back to U.S. with hilarious results. Grant in drag makes this one worth watching.▼

I Was an Adventuress (1940) **81m.** **½ D: Gregory Ratoff. Vera Zorina, Erich von Stroheim, Richard Greene, Peter Lorre, Sig Ruman. Jewel thief Zorina goes straight, marries Greene, but can't shake off former associates von Stroheim, Lorre, et al. With that cast, it should have been better.

I Was an American Spy (1951) **85m.** **½ D: Lesley Selander. Ann Dvorak, Gene Evans, Douglas Kennedy, Richard Loo, Philip Ahn, Lisa Ferraday. Dvorak is chanteuse in Manila who helps combat Japanese attack in WW2 spy story, elevated by veteran star. Song: "Because of You."

I Was a Shoplifter (1950) **82m.** **½ D: Charles Lamont. Scott Brady, Mona Freeman, Charles Drake, Andrea King, Anthony (Tony) Curtis. Fair programmer with cop Brady going undercover to bust open a shoplifting gang. Look for Rock Hudson as a department-store detective.

I Was a Spy (1933-British) **83m.** ** D: Victor Saville. Madeleine Carroll, Conrad Veidt, Herbert Marshall, Gerald du Maurier, Edmund Gwenn, Donald Calthrop, Nigel Bruce. Unmemorable account of espionage agent Carroll, a Belgian nurse who aids the British after her country is overrun by the Germans during WW1. Veidt is perfectly cast as a German commandant.▼

I Was a Teenage Boy SEE: **Something Special**

I Was a Teenage Frankenstein (1957) **72m.** *½ D: Herbert L. Strock. Whit Bissell, Gary Conway, Phyllis Coates, Robert Burton. Campy junk about mad scientist who pulls young Conway from an auto wreck and "repairs" him. Doesn't live up to that title; worth catching only for Bissell's immortal line, "Answer me! You have a civil tongue in your head! I know—I sewed it in there!" One sequence is in color.▼

I Was a Teen-age Werewolf (1957) **75m.** ** D: Gene Fowler, Jr. Michael Landon, Yvonne Lime, Whit Bissell, Vladimir Sokoloff, Guy Williams. The title tells all in this curious mating of horror movies and juvenile delinquency melodramas. Marred by low production values; memorable for Landon's presence.▼

I Was a Teenage Zombie (1987) **C-92m.** BOMB D: John E. Michalakias. Michael Ruben, George Seminara, Steve McCoy, Cassie Madden. Low-grade horror spoof concerns teen zombie Ruben battling McCoy, the zombie version of a drug pusher who's been preying on adolescents. Amateur night at the movies.▼●

I Was Happy Here SEE: **Time Lost and Time Remembered**

I Was Monty's Double (1958-British) **100m.** ***½ D: John Guillermin. M. E. Clifton-James, John Mills, Cecil Parker, Marius Goring, Michael Hordern, Leslie Phillips, Bryan Forbes. Exciting, true WW2 story of actor persuaded to pose as Gen. Montgomery in order to divert German intelligence in North Africa. Cast is first-rate.

I Went Down (1997-Irish-British) **C-107m.** **½ D: Paddy Breathnach. Brendan Gleeson, Peter McDonald, Tony Doyle, Peter Caffrey, Antoine Byrne. A good but down-on-his-luck guy is forced to pull off a kidnapping in order to work off a large debt he owes some gangsters. Quirky Irish action comedy has genuine affection for its unlikely heroes but never really catches fire, despite a wily performance from Gleeson as an aging petty thug who can't even steal a car properly. A big hit in Ireland. [R]▼

I Will, I Will . . . For Now (1976) **C-96m.** ** D: Norman Panama. Elliott Gould, Diane Keaton, Paul Sorvino, Victoria Principal, Robert Alda, Warren Berlinger, Madge Sinclair, Candy Clark. Fair satire on frigidity, infidelity, marriage counselling and a sex clinic. Gould and ex-wife Keaton spend film rediscovering each other. Panavision. [R]▼

I Woke Up Early the Day I Died (1999) **C/B&W-90m.** BOMB D: Aris Iliopulos. Billy Zane, Abraham Benrubi, Sandra Bernhard, Karen Black, Conrad Brooks, Tippi Hedren, Eartha Kitt, Ann Magnuson, Andrew McCarthy, Ron Perlman, Will Patton, Max Perlich, Summer Phoenix, Christina Ricci, John Ritter, Rick Schroeder, Nicolette Sheridan, Carel Struycken, Jonathan Taylor Thomas, Vampira, Steven Weber. An unproduced screenplay by Edward D. Wood, Jr., served as the "inspiration" for this tedious chronicle of a thief (Zane) who breaks out of a mental institution. The intention was to make a bad (read: unintentionally funny) movie in the style of Ed Wood, but the result is just boring. Made as a silent movie, with sound effects and music. Zane coproduced.▼

I Wonder Who's Killing Her Now? (1976) **C-87m.** **½ D: Steven H. Stern. Bob Dishy, Joanna Barnes, Bill Dana, Vito Scotti. Luckless husband hires someone to bump off his wife for insurance money, then tries to call it off; uneven but often funny farce, written by Woody Allen's one-time collaborator Mickey Rose. [PG]▼

I Wonder Who's Kissing Her Now (1947) **C-104m.** **½ D: Lloyd Bacon. June Haver, Mark Stevens, Martha Stewart, Reginald Gardiner, Lenore Aubert, William Frawley. Innocuous recreation of life and loves of 1890s songwriter, Joseph E. Howard. As usual, music is better than script. Gene Nelson makes his film debut.

Jabberwocky (1977-British) **C-100m.** **½ D: Terry Gilliam. Michael Palin, Max Wall, Deborah Fallender, John Le Mesurier, Annette Badland. Gilliam and Palin of MONTY PYTHON AND THE HOLY GRAIL fame give us another satire of medieval times, but the humor is even more spotty than its predecessor's. For fans. [R]▼●

J'Accuse (1937-French) **C-95m.** *** D: Abel Gance. Victor Francen, Jean Max, Delaitre, Renee Devillers. Very good—but not great—antiwar film, focusing on exploited war veteran Francen; in a vivid sequence, he calls on war casualties to rise from their graves. Previously filmed by Gance in 1918.▼

Jack (1996) **C-113m.** ** D: Francis Ford Coppola. Robin Williams, Diane Lane, Jennifer Lopez, Brian Kerwin, Fran Drescher, Bill Cosby, Michael McKean, Don Novello, Allan Rich, Adam Zolotin, Todd Bosley. A boy born prematurely—but fully developed—turns out to be aging at four times normal rate. At 10, with the physical characteristics of a 40-year-old man, he leaves his cloistered home to go to school and deal with other kids his age for the first time in his life. Williams is the perfect choice to play this man-child, but the script goes nowhere. Overlong, too adult for kids, too redundant for grownups; destined to please no one. [PG-13]▼●

Jackal, The (1997) **C-124m.** **½ D: Michael Caton-Jones. Bruce Willis, Richard

Gere, Sidney Poitier, Diane Venora, Tess Harper, J. K. Simmons, Mathilda May, Stephen Spinella, Richard Lineback. When the FBI and the KGB are stumped as to how to capture an international assassin called The Jackal, they turn to the one man who knows him—an Irish terrorist (Gere) who's serving time in a U.S. prison. Watchable globe-trotting thriller is weakened by lapses of credibility, but boosted by Gere's charismatic performance. Venora is also a standout as a no-nonsense Russian agent. Bears only the slightest resemblance to the superior THE DAY OF THE JACKAL, despite being "officially" based on that screenplay. Panavision. [R]▼●◗

Jackals, The (1967) **C-105m.** ** D: Robert D. Webb. Vincent Price, Diana Ivarson, Robert Gunner, Bob Courtney, Patrick Mynhardt. William Wellman's striking YELLOW SKY reset in the South African Transvaal, with six bandits terrorizing a grizzled old miner (Price) and his granddaughter into surrendering their gold cache.

Jackals (1986) **C-92m.** ** D: Gary Grillo. Jack Lucarelli, Gerald McRaney, Wilford Brimley, Jameson Parker, Jeannie Wilson. Predictable, forgettable action drama starring TV's *Simon & Simon* duo with ex-cop Lucarelli taking on evil McRaney, a white slave trader. You've seen this one a hundred times before. Aka AMERICAN JUSTICE. [PG]▼

Jack and His Friends (1992) **C-96m.** *½ D: Bruce Ornstein. Allen Garfield, Sam Rockwell, Judy Reyes, Paul Hecht, Alison Fraser. Silly, juvenile mishmash detailing the various problems of the fat, pathetic title character (Garfield), who discovers his wife's infidelity and is summarily kidnapped. A barely funny, ultra-low-budget comedy; after a while Jack's self-loathing becomes more obnoxious than amusing.▼

Jack & Sarah (1995-British-French) **C-110m.** **½ D. Tim Sullivan. Richard E. Grant, Samantha Mathis, Judi Dench, Ian McKellen, Cherie Lunghi, Eileen Atkins, Imogen Stubbs. A London lawyer is crushed when his young wife dies in childbirth, but he finds a reason to live in his infant daughter. He hires a young American as a nanny, which leads to romance—and complications. Good performances, particularly by the two leads, keep this uneven film watchable and pleasant. PG version available on video. [R]▼●

Jack and the Beanstalk (1952) **C/B&W-78m.** **½ D: Jean Yarbrough. Bud Abbott, Lou Costello, Dorothy Ford, Barbara Brown, Buddy Baer. A&C version of fairy tale OK for kids, but not as funny as their earlier films. Begins in sepiatone, then changes to color, like THE WIZARD OF OZ.▼●

Jackass Mail (1942) **80m.** ** D: Norman Z. McLeod. Wallace Beery, Marjorie Main, J. Carrol Naish, Darryl Hickman, William Haade, Dick Curtis. Easygoing Beery vehicle about fugitive who accidentally becomes a hero. Take it or leave it; no harm done either way.

Jack Be Nimble (1993-New Zealand) **C-93m.** **½ D: Garth Maxwell. Alexis Arquette, Sarah Smuts-Kennedy, Bruno Lawrence, Tony Barry, Elizabeth Hawthorne. Weird, clever little chiller in which the title character is adopted into a family of cretins and abused beyond endurance; he sets out to find his long-lost sister, and also to seek revenge. Doesn't quite work when it takes itself too seriously; otherwise, this is devilishly entertaining, and has cult possibilities. [R]▼●

Jack Frost (1998) **C-95m.** **½ D: Troy Miller. Michael Keaton, Kelly Preston, Mark Addy, Joseph Cross, Henry Rollins, Dweezil Zappa. A neglectful dad dies in a car accident and comes to life one year later as a snowman in his son's front yard! Warm, likable performances and an absence of treacle make this an OK family film, but it never overcomes its fundamental problem: a *very* strange premise. Panavision. [PG]▼●◗

Jackie Brown (1997) **C-154m.** *** D: Quentin Tarantino. Pam Grier, Samuel L. Jackson, Robert Forster, Michael Keaton, Bridget Fonda, Robert De Niro, Michael Bowen, Chris Tucker, Sid Haig. Leisurely paced but enjoyable adaptation of Elmore Leonard's crime caper *Rum Punch,* reset in Southern California. Grier (in a standout performance) plays a flight attendant who's been trafficking in hot money for lowlife Jackson; when caught, she plays all the angles she can think of to keep herself out of jail, managing to keep the cops, her chief client, and everyone else on ice. Dynamite performances all around sustain film through its periodic lulls. [R]▼●◗

Jackie Chan's First Strike (1996-Hong Kong) **C-110m.** **½ D: Stanley Tong. Jackie Chan, Chen Chun Wu, Jackson Lou, Bill Tung, Jouri Petrov. Hong Kong's most physically agile cop finds himself in a James Bond–like intrigue involving the CIA, Russian mafia, a nuclear device, and of course, a good-looking female scuba diver. The dubbing here is typically wretched, yet in a lark like this it really doesn't matter; the last two thirds is almost wall-to-wall action, including a doozy of a donnybrook in which Chan makes memorable use of a ladder. Technovision and Panavision. [PG-13]▼●◗

Jackie Chan's Police Story SEE: **Police Story** (1985)

Jackie Chan's Who Am I? (1998-Hong Kong) **C-108m.** *** D: Jackie Chan, Benny Chan. Jackie Chan, Michelle Ferre, Mirai Yamamoto, Ron Smerczak, Ed Nelson, Tom Pompert. Chan is part of a secret military team sent on a fatal mission; although he survives, he loses his memory, and can't understand why so many people are pursuing him. Lame dialogue and cardboard performances are outshone by one fantastic action scene after another, including a unique episode involving wooden shoes in Rotterdam. Chan also wrote the screenplay. Filmed in English. Originally 117m. Panavision. [PG-13]▼●◗

Jackie Robinson Story, The (1950) **76m.** *** D: Alfred E. Green. Jackie Robinson, Ruby Dee, Minor Watson, Louise Beavers, Richard Lane, Harry Shannon, Ben Lessy, Joel Fluellen. Straightforward bio of Robinson, the first black man to play major-league baseball. Fascinating as a social history; pointed in its presentation of the racial issues involved. Interestingly, Robinson's Negro League ball club is called the Black Panthers! Dee plays Robinson's wife; forty years later, she was cast as his mother in the TV movie THE COURT-MARTIAL OF JACKIE ROBINSON.▼

Jack Johnson (1971) **90m.** *** D: William Cayton. Narrated by Brock Peters. Documentary on world-famous heavyweight champion. Features excellent jazz score by Miles Davis. [PG]

Jack London (1943) **94m.** *½ D: Alfred Santell. Michael O'Shea, Susan Hayward, Osa Massen, Harry Davenport, Frank Craven, Virginia Mayo. Hokey, episodic "biography" of famed writer spends too much time maligning Japanese—which was supposed to give topical slant to this period drama in 1943. Aka THE ADVENTURES OF JACK LONDON and THE LIFE OF JACK LONDON.▼

Jack London's Call of the Wild (1997) **C-100m. TVM** D: Peter Svatek. Rutger Hauer, Bronwin Booth, Charles Powell, Burke Lawrence, Luc Morissette. Doubtless the most faithful version of the oft-filmed tale, this frequently harrowing French-Canadian production is told from the perspective of the often abused husky, Buck, who had been dognapped and pressed into service by Yukon miners as a sled dog. Seldom are the faces of the actors shown, and then through upward-tilted cameras. Narrated by Richard Dreyfuss. Made for cable. Average.▼

Jack London's Klondike Fever SEE: **Klondike Fever**

Jack McCall Desperado (1953) **C-76m.** ** D: Sidney Salkow. George Montgomery, Angela Stevens, Jay Silverheels, Douglas Kennedy. Civil War yarn of Southerner Montgomery capturing man who framed him as spy.▼

Jacknife (1989) **C-102m.** *** D: David Jones. Robert De Niro, Ed Harris, Kathy Baker, Charles Dutton, Loudon Wainwright III. Simple and involving story of a Vietnam vet (De Niro) who looks up an old Army buddy (Harris) and tries to get him to face up to his repressed memories of Nam, and their mutual best friend who died there. Meanwhile, a romance blossoms between De Niro and Harris' wallflower sister, with whom he lives. Three terrific performances make this a must. Stephen Metcalfe adapted his play *Strange Snow.* [R]▼●

Jack of Diamonds (1967-U.S.-German) **C-105m.** *½ D: Don Taylor. George Hamilton, Joseph Cotten, Marie Laforet, Maurice Evans, Carroll Baker, Zsa Zsa Gabor, Lilli Palmer. Hamilton plays a cat burglar who robs jewels from Baker, Gabor, and Palmer, who are "special guests" in this film. Skip this one and wait for TO CATCH A THIEF to be shown.

Jackpot, The (1950) **87m.** **½ D: Walter Lang. James Stewart, Barbara Hale, James Gleason, Fred Clark, Natalie Wood. Dated, minor comedy, uplifted by stars; Stewart is winner of radio contest but can't pay taxes on winnings.▼

Jack's Back (1988) **C-97m.** *½ D: Rowdy Herrington. James Spader, Cynthia Gibb, Rod Loomis, Rex Ryon, Robert Picardo, Chris Mulkey, Danitza Kingsley. Umpteenth retelling of the JACK THE RIPPER saga is updated to contemporary L.A. where young doctor Spader is the #1 suspect when prostitutes are killed in grisly fashion 100 years to the day after Bloody Jack's legendary crimes. Plot twist halfway through is preposterous; Spader is earnest but miscast. [R]▼●

Jack Slade (1953) **90m.** ** D: Harold Schuster. Mark Stevens, Dorothy Malone, Barton MacLane, John Litel. Oater programmer of Stevens turning criminal with tragic results; Malone is wasted.

Jackson County Jail (1976) **C-89m.** **½ D: Michael Miller. Yvette Mimieux, Tommy Lee Jones, Robert Carradine, Frederic Cook, Severn Darden, Howard Hesseman, Mary Woronov. Prisoner Yvette, dumped on by everyone she meets, goes on the lam with fellow inmate in yet another chase pic. Livelier than most, this one has developed a cult reputation. Miller later remade it for TV as OUTSIDE CHANCE; it was remade again in 1996 as MACON COUNTY JAIL. [R]▼●

Jack the Bear (1993) **C-98m.** **½ D: Marshall Herskovitz. Danny DeVito, Robert J. Steinmiller, Miko Hughes, Gary Sinise, Julia Louis-Dreyfus, Reese Witherspoon, Bert Remsen, Andrea Marcovicci. Sporadically affecting, but mostly muddled comedy-drama about the emotional unraveling of a widowed TV horror-movie host whose neighbor is a pro-Nazi psycho who poses a threat to children. Kept on track at least some of the time by Steinmiller's exceptional performance as DeVito's older son (age 12). Set in 1972; based on Dan McCall's novel. Super 35. [PG-13] ▼●

Jack the Giant Killer (1962) **C-94m.** *** D: Nathan Juran. Kerwin Mathews, Judi Meredith, Torin Thatcher, Walter Burke.

Marvelous Fantascope special effects make this costume adventure yarn (in the SINBAD tradition) great fun. Beware reissue, which was dubbed into an ersatz musical!▼●

Jack the Ripper (1960-British) **88m.** ** D: Robert Baker, Monty Berman. Lee Patterson, Eddie Byrne, George Rose, Betty McDowall. Middling retelling of notorious knife-wielder, with alternating scenes of Scotland Yard and fiend at work in London. Sometimes hits the mark with gory sensationalism.▼

Jack the Ripper (1988) **C-200m. TVM** D: David Wickes. Michael Caine, Armand Assante, Ray McAnally, Susan George, Jane Seymour, Lewis Collins, Ken Bones. Taut, evocative drama about the infamous 1888 East End London serial killer, with Caine as Scotland Yard Detective Inspector Frederick Abberline, who conducted the original investigation. In this fictionalized account, he unmasks the real murderer (based on director-cowriter Wickes' contemporary research). Originally broadcast in two parts. Above average.▼

Jacob's Ladder (1990) **C-115m.** **½ D: Adrian Lyne. Tim Robbins, Elizabeth Pena, Danny Aiello, Matt Craven, Pruitt Taylor Vince, Jason Alexander, Patricia Kalember, Eriq La Salle, Ving Rhames. Brooding, often effective tale of Vietnam vet who suffers from hallucinations, which may or may not be linked to his everyday life in N.Y.C. Nightmarish story leads to a climax that—like a bad shaggy-dog joke—negates the entire film! Bruce Joel Rubin's script is reminiscent of Ambrose Bierce's classic "An Occurrence at Owl Creek Bridge," only not as good. Macaulay Culkin appears unbilled in a key supporting role. Two deleted scenes were added for the film's cable TV debut. [R]▼●◗

Jacob the Liar (1974-East German) **C-95m.** *** D: Frank Beyer. Vlastimil Brodsky, Erwin Geschonneck, Manuela Simon, Henry Hubchen, Blanche Kommerell, Armin Mueller-Stahl. Touching, sometimes comic tale of Polish Jew Brodsky, whose false tales to fellow ghetto dwellers give some hope against their Nazi captors. Remade in 1999 as JAKOB THE LIAR.▼

Jacob Two Two Meets the Hooded Fang (1977-Canadian) **C-80m.** **½ D: Theodore J. Flicker. Stephen Rosenberg, Alex Karras, Guy L'Ecuyer, Joy Coghill, Earl Pennington, Claude Gail. Engaging fantasy for kids written by Mordecai Richler, about a boy who dreams he's sent to children's prison. Low-budget production values are unfortunate detriment. [G]▼

Jacqueline (1956-British) **C-92m.** *** D: Roy Baker. John Gregson, Kathleen Ryan, Jacqueline Ryan, Noel Purcell, Cyril Cusack. Captivating drama of lovable little Irish girl and how she helps her tippler father find work. Lots of warmth.

Jacqueline Susann's Once Is Not Enough (1975) **C-121m.** BOMB D: Guy Green. Kirk Douglas, Alexis Smith, David Janssen, Deborah Raffin, George Hamilton, Melina Mercouri, Brenda Vaccaro. Trashy film based on Susann's trashy novel of jet-set intrigue, and a blossoming young woman (Raffin) with a father-fixation. Incurably stupid, and surprisingly dull. Vaccaro offers brightest moments as unabashed man-chaser. Panavision. [R]▼

Jacques Brel Is Alive and Well and Living in Paris (1975) **C-98m.** ** D: Denis Heroux. Elly Stone, Mort Shuman, Joe Masiell, Jacques Brel. Musical revue featuring 26 bittersweet songs on life, love, war and death by Belgian balladeer Jacques Brel. No plot, no dialogue. Based on 1968 stage show. An American Film Theater Production. [PG]▼

Jacquot de Nantes (1991-French) **C-118m.** ***½ D: Agnés Varda. Philippe Maron, Edouard Joubeaud, Laurent Monnier, Brigitte de Villepoix. Deeply moving chronicle of the sum of a man's life, as Varda creates a portrait of her late husband, French filmmaker Jacques Demy. Varda cuts from interviews with Demy (lovingly photographed in extreme close-up), to clips from his films, to the re-created story of young "Jacquot" growing up in Nantes during the 1940s and developing a passion for cinema. A heartfelt valentine from one life partner to another. Released in U.S. in 1993 as JACQUOT. Varda has since directed several other celluloid tributes to Demy.▼

Jade (1995) **C-101m.** ** D: William Friedkin. David Caruso, Linda Fiorentino, Chazz Palminteri, Michael Biehn, Richard Crenna, Donna Murphy, Ken King, Holt McCallany, David Hunt, Angie Everhart, Kevin Tighe, Jay Jacobus. While investigating the brutal murder of a wealthy San Franciscan, assistant D.A. Caruso realizes to his dismay that his old flame (Fiorentino, married to his good friend Palminteri) may be involved. Sordid mystery/thriller from the seedy pen of Joe Eszterhas; has its moments (including an exciting S.F. car chase) but never rises above the mire. Unrated video edition has 12m. additional footage. [R] ▼●◗

Jade Mask, The (1945) **66m.** *½ D: Phil Rosen. Sidney Toler, Mantan Moreland, Edwin Luke, Janet Warren, Edith Evanson, Hardie Albright, Frank Reicher, Alan Bridge, Ralph Lewis. Another in the rapidly declining *Charlie Chan* series, focusing on the hunt for a murderous couple who use masquerades and trickery to make it look like their victims are still alive.▼●

Jagged Edge (1985) **C-108m.** **½ D: Richard Marquand. Jeff Bridges, Glenn Close, Peter Coyote, Robert Loggia, John Dehner, Leigh Taylor-Young, Karen Austin, Lance Henriksen, James Karen, Michael Dorn. Wealthy publishing magnate is accused of murdering his wife; hotshot lawyer Close will defend him only if she believes he's innocent. Not only is she convinced—she immediately falls in love with him! Credibility goes out the window in this otherwise well-made, often gripping combination of thriller and courtroom drama. How could such a "smart" movie allow so many silly loopholes? Loggia is terrific as usual as Close's street-smart leg man. [R]▼●◗

Jaguar (1956) **66m.** *½ D: George Blair. Sabu, Chiquita, Barton MacLane, Jonathan Hale, Mike Connors. Presence of former elephant-boy Sabu is only virtue of ridiculous programmer about mysterious murders on an oilfield.

Jaguar Lives! (1979) **C-90m.** *½ D: Ernest Pintoff. Joe Lewis, Christopher Lee, Donald Pleasence, Barbara Bach, Capucine, Joseph Wiseman, Woody Strode, John Huston. Karate champ Lewis is featured in this predictable action cheapie as a special agent sent to dispatch narcotics biggies in various world capitals. Top cast, but don't be fooled. [PG]▼

Jail Bait (1954) **70m.** *½ D: Edward D. Wood, Jr. Timothy Farrell, Lyle Talbot, Steve Reeves, Herbert Rawlinson, Dolores Fuller, Clancey Malone, Theodora Thurman, Mona McKinnon. Farrell leads young Malone into life of crime; when the law closes in, he forces Malone's plastic surgeon father to change his face. Misleadingly titled thriller is less inept than Wood's "classics," and thus less funny, but inspired teaming of Talbot and Reeves (in his first speaking part) as cops is good for a few giggles.▼●◗

Jail Bait (1972-German) **C-99m.** *** D: Rainer Werner Fassbinder. Eva Mattes, Harry Baer, Jorg von Liebenfels, Ruth Drexel, Kurt Raab, Hanna Schygulla. Another provocative, controversial exploration of emptiness in post-WW2 Germany from the prolific Fassbinder. Here, a seductive 14-year-old (Mattes) becomes involved with Baer, eventually coaxing him into murdering her father. Originally made for German television; not released in the U.S. until 1977.

Jailbreakers, The (1960) **64m.** *½ D: Alexander Grasshoff. Robert Hutton, Mary Castle, Michael O'Connell, Gabe Delutri, Anton Van Stralen. Escaped prisoners harass a young couple in a deserted town. Tepid programmer.

Jailbreakers (1994) **C-76m. TVM** D: William Friedkin. Shannen Doherty, Antonio Sabato, Jr., Adrienne Barbeau, Adrien Brody, Vince Edwards, George Gerdes, Dana Barron, Chris Conrad, Charles Napier. The 1950s: High school cheerleader's involvement with attractive hoodlum causes her problems, especially when he breaks out of jail to be with her. Unusual for depicting a motorcycle-riding rebel as a sociopath and the young heroine as irredeemable, but not very involving. One of Showtime's "Rebel Highway" entries, all based on old American-International pictures; this uses only the title of the 1960 original. Average.

Jail Busters (1955) **61m.** ** D: William Beaudine. Leo Gorcey, Huntz Hall, Bernard Gorcey, Barton MacLane, Anthony Caruso, Percy Helton, David Gorcey, Bennie Bartlett, Murray Alper, Fritz Feld, Lyle Talbot, Henry Kulky. The Bowery Boys go up the river to help clear a pal who's already there as an undercover reporter.

Jailhouse Rock (1957) **96m.** *** D: Richard Thorpe. Elvis Presley, Judy Tyler, Vaughn Taylor, Dean Jones, Mickey Shaughnessy. Elvis learns to pick a guitar in the Big House, later becomes a surly rock star. Presley's best film captures the legend in all his nostril-flaring, pre-Army glory. Great Leiber-Stoller score, including "Treat Me Nice," "Don't Leave Me Now," and terrific title song (with a dance number choreographed by Elvis). Also shown in computer-colored version. CinemaScope. ▼●◗

Jake Speed (1986) **C-104m.** BOMB D: Andrew Lane. Wayne Crawford, Dennis Christopher, Karen Kopins, John Hurt, Leon Ames, Roy London, Donna Pescow, Barry Primus, Monte Markham. Utter waste of time about a paperback hero who turns up in real life to help a damsel in distress. Crawford, who has all the star appeal of a can of tuna, presumably got the lead role because he also cowrote and coproduced the film. [PG]▼●

Jake's Women SEE: **Neil Simon's "Jake's Women"**

Jakob the Liar (1999) **C-114m.** **½ D: Peter Kassovitz. Robin Williams, Alan Arkin, Bob Balaban, Hannah Taylor Gordon, Armin Mueller-Stahl, Liev Schreiber, Michael Jeter, Nina Siemaszko, Mathieu Kassovitz. In a Polish ghetto in 1944, a wistful widower (Williams) raises hopes among his fellow townspeople after he accidentally hears an optimistic report about the war on a Nazi radio. Soon, he is besieged for more "radio reports," which he is forced to invent. Modest film from Jurek Becker's novel is only mildly successful, though Williams does his best. He also coexecutive-produced the film. Mueller-Stahl also appeared in the 1974 version. [PG-13]▼

Jalopy (1953) **62m.** ** D: William Beaudine. Leo Gorcey, Huntz Hall, David Gorcey, Bennie Bartlett, Bernard Gorcey, Robert Lowery, Murray Alper, Jane Easton, Richard Benedict. Sputtering laughs as the Bowery Boys enter an auto race with the help of a supercharged gas formula invented by Sach.

Jamaica Inn (1939-British) **98m.** ** D: Alfred Hitchcock. Charles Laughton, Maureen O'Hara, Leslie Banks, Robert Newton, Emlyn Williams, Mervyn Johns. Stodgy Victorian costumer of cutthroat band headed by nobleman Laughton; O'Hara is lovely, but plodding Hitchcock film is disappointing. Based on Daphne du Maurier novel; Hitch had far more success a year later with du Maurier's *Rebecca*. Remade for British TV in 1985 with Jane Seymour and Patrick McGoohan. ▼●◗

Jamaica Run (1953) **C-92m.** ** D: Lewis R. Foster. Ray Milland, Arlene Dahl, Wendell Corey, Patric Knowles. Ray goes salvage-diving in the Caribbean for Dahl's nutty family. Unexciting production.

Jamboree (1957) **71m.** ** D: Roy Lockwood. Kay Medford, Robert Pastine, Paul Carr, Freda Halloway, Slim Whitman, Jodie Sands, Frankie Avalon, Fats Domino, Jerry Lee Lewis, Carl Perkins, Lewis Lymon and The Teen Chords, Buddy Knox, Count Basie, Joe Williams, Sandy Singer. Slight plot—singers Carr and Halloway fall in love, are manipulated by ambitious manager Medford—highlighted by rock, rockabilly, and jazz vignettes. Avalon looks about 12 years old, and Lewis sings "Great Balls of Fire." Aka DISC JOCKEY JAMBOREE. ▼

James and the Giant Peach (1996) **C-80m.** ***½ D: Henry Selick. Paul Terry, Miriam Margolyes, Joanna Lumley, Pete Postlethwaite, Mike Starr; voices of Simon Callow, Richard Dreyfuss, Jane Leeves, Susan Sarandon, Miriam Margolyes, David Thewlis. Wondrous adaptation of Roald Dahl's fantasy about a beleaguered boy, tended by two harridan aunts, who discovers a magic pathway inside a giant peach. Together with a grasshopper, a spider, a centipede, a worm, a glowworm, and a ladybug, he sets sail for the city of his dreams—N.Y. Starts in live action, then segues to cutting-edge stop-motion animation to bring Dahl's (typically) bizarre but delightful story to life. Gets better and better as it goes along, with impeccable voice characterizations and charming songs by Randy Newman. A rare movie that creates a world all its own, and an even rarer children's film that has real wit and imagination. [PG]▼●

James Dean Story, The (1957) **82m.** ** D: George W. George, Robert Altman. Narrated by Martin Gabel. Uninspired use of available material makes this a slow-moving documentary on life of 1950s movie star.▼●◗

Jamón Jamón (1992-Spanish) **C-93m.** *** D: José Juan Bigas Luna. Penelope Cruz, Stefania Sandrelli, Anna Galiena, Juan Diego, Jordi Molla, Javier Bardem. Clever, erotic black comedy-melodrama about sex and food, which also serves to mirror Spanish society in transition. The scenario focuses on the various members of two families from different classes, and what follows after beautiful Cruz falls for (and becomes pregnant by) her boss' spoiled son (Molla). A delight from start to finish, and a sleeper hit in Europe.▼

Jam Session (1944) **77m.** ** D: Charles Barton. Ann Miller, Jess Barker, Charles Brown, Eddie Kane, Louis Armstrong, Duke Ellington and His Band, Glen Gray and His Band, Teddy Powell and His Band, Charlie Barnet Orchestra, Nan Wynn, Pied Pipers. Mild musical of showgirl Miller trying to crash Hollywood; notable for many musical guests doing enjoyable specialty numbers.

Jane Austen in Manhattan (1980) **C-108m.** *½ D: James Ivory. Robert Powell, Anne Baxter, Michael Wager, Tim Choate, John Guerrasio, Katrina Hodiak, Kurt Johnson, Sean Young. Dreary, confusing oddity about charismatic acting-teacher Powell and his rival Baxter, each trying to produce a newly discovered play written by Jane Austen. Overlong; a disappointment from director Ivory. Hodiak is the daughter of Baxter and John Hodiak.▼

Jane Austen's Mafia! (1998) **C-84m.** **½ D: Jim Abrahams. Jay Mohr, Billy Burke, Christina Applegate, Lloyd Bridges, Pamela Gidley, Olympia Dukakis, Jason Fuchs, Joe Viterelli, Tony Lo Bianco. Parody from the AIRPLANE/NAKED GUN school takes aim at THE GODFATHER and CASINO but throws in gags referring to everything from FORREST GUMP to JURASSIC PARK. Disorganized, to say the least, but full of funny stuff—funny enough to overlook many of its shortcomings. Bridges' last film. Aka MAFIA! [PG-13]▼●◗

Jane Eyre (1934) **67m.** ** D: Christy Cabanne. Virginia Bruce, Colin Clive, Beryl Mercer, Aileen Pringle, David Torrence, Lionel Belmore. Thin version of the oft-filmed Brontë novel, produced by Monogram, of all studios, with Bruce in the title role and Clive as Mr. Rochester. Still, it's not uninteresting as a curio.▼

Jane Eyre (1944) **96m.** *** D: Robert Stevenson. Orson Welles, Joan Fontaine, Margaret O'Brien, Henry Daniell, John Sutton, Agnes Moorehead, Elizabeth Taylor, Peggy Ann Garner, Sara Allgood, Aubrey Mather, Hillary Brooke. Artistically successful if slow-moving version of Charlotte Brontë novel about orphan girl who grows up to become a governess in mysterious household. One of Elizabeth Taylor's early films.▼●

Jane Eyre (1971-British) **C-110m. TVM** D: Delbert Mann. George C. Scott, Susannah York, Ian Bannen, Jack Hawkins, Rachel Kempson, Jean Marsh, Nyree Dawn Porter. Sumptuous Gothic settings and Scott's great performance highlight this pleasant if somewhat uninspired retelling of the Brontë classic. Average.

Jane Eyre (1996-French-Italian-U.S.-British) **C-117m.** ** D: Franco Zeffirelli. William Hurt, Charlotte Gainsbourg, Anna Paquin, Geraldine Chaplin, Fiona Shaw, Elle Macpherson, John Wood, Joan Plowright, Amanda Root, Charlotte Attenborough. Unremarkable remake of Brontë's classic romance features Gainsbourg as a very credible Jane. Unfortunately, there is a lack of chemistry between the leads, and a rushed ending that is completely out of sync with the rest of the film. The 1944 version remains the best attempt. [PG]▼●◗

Janie (1944) **106m.** **½ D: Michael Curtiz. Joyce Reynolds, Edward Arnold, Ann Harding, Robert Benchley, Robert Hutton, Alan Hale, Hattie McDaniel. Naive (now) but pleasant comedy about small-town teenage girl falling in love with serviceman despite father's objections to love-hungry soldiers. From the Broadway play by Josephine Bentham and Herschel Williams. Followed by JANIE GETS MARRIED.

Janie Gets Married (1946) **89m.** **½ D: Vincent Sherman. Joan Leslie, Robert Hutton, Edward Arnold, Ann Harding, Robert Benchley, Dorothy Malone. Pleasant follow-up to JANIE, with bright-eyed Leslie helping soldier-hubby Hutton readjust to civilian life.

Janis (1975) **C-96m.** *** D: Howard Alk, Seaton Findlay. Documentary on Janis Joplin was filmed with cooperation of her family, so it ignores the singer's dark side. OK within its limits, with a dozen or so songs performed (including "Piece of My Heart," "Me and Bobby McGee," "Kozmic Blues," "Mercedes Benz"). [R]▼

January Man, The (1989) **C-97m.** *½ D: Pat O'Connor. Kevin Kline, Mary Elizabeth Mastrantonio, Susan Sarandon, Harvey Keitel, Danny Aiello, Rod Steiger, Alan Rickman, Faye Grant, Tandy Cronyn. Appallingly wrongheaded mix of cop movie, romantic drama, and offbeat comedy written by John Patrick Shanley, with Kline as a self-styled eccentric whose brother, the police commissioner of N.Y.C., is forced to hire him to help catch a serial killer. Fine cast founders in this unfunny, illogical mess. [R]▼●

Japanese War Bride (1952) **91m.** **½ D: King Vidor. Don Taylor, Shirley Yamaguchi, Cameron Mitchell, Marie Windsor, Philip Ahn. Penetrating study of WW2 veterans who return to life in U.S.A. with Oriental brides.

Jason and the Argonauts (1963-British) **C-104m.** *** D: Don Chaffey. Todd Armstrong, Gary Raymond, Nancy Kovack, Honor Blackman, Nigel Green. Great special effects (by Ray Harryhausen) and colorful backgrounds in fable about Jason's search for golden fleece. Encounters with mythic monsters and gods highlight this sweeping adventure. Rich score by Bernard Herrmann.▼●◗

Jason Goes to Hell: The Final Friday (1993) **C-88m.** *½ D: Adam Marcus. John D. LeMay, Kari Keegan, Kane Hodder, Steven Williams, Steven Culp, Erin Gray, Rusty Schwimmer, Billy Green Bush. Ninth entry in the FRIDAY THE 13TH series, ignores the plots of the last six or so, and opens with Jason being blown to pieces in an ambush. However, his evil spirit takes over a convenient bystander, and reborn, he heads for home to confront his (hitherto unmentioned) sister. Erratic, illogical, and pointlessly cruel; some fans liked it because of its delight in including elements from other contemporary horror movie series. [R]▼●

Jason's Lyric (1994) **C-119m.** ** D: Doug McHenry. Allen Payne, Jada Pinkett, Forest Whitaker, Bokeem Woodbine, Treach, Lisa Carson, Suzzanne Douglas, Eddie Griffin, Lahmard Tate. Overly familiar (not to mention confusing) tale of good-and-evil brothers. Jason (Payne) is an honest and dependable workingman; Joshua (Woodbine) is a drug-abusing thief. Jason falls in love with an attractive waitress named Lyric (Pinkett)—more a romantic male fantasy than a real person—and you know what's coming. Several sex scenes were trimmed to avoid an NC-17 rating, but gruesome violence remains intact. [R]▼●◗

Jassy (1947-British) **C-96m.** **½ D: Bernard Knowles. Margaret Lockwood, Patricia Roc, Dennis Price, Dermot Walsh, Basil Sydney, Nora Swinburne. Brooding drama of gypsy girl accused of causing her husband's death; well-mounted 19th-century yarn.

Java Head (1934-British) **70m.** *** D: J. Walter Ruben. Anna May Wong, Elizabeth Allan, Edmund Gwenn, John Loder, Ralph Richardson, Herbert Lomas. Perceptive, literate account of sea captain Loder, whose roots are in a puritanical English port city, and his marriage to a Mandarin princess (Wong). Based on the Joseph Hergesheimer best-seller (which was set in Massachusetts).▼

Jawbreaker (1999) **C-90m.** *½ D: Darren Stein. Rose McGowan, Rebecca Gayheart, Julie Benz, Judy Evans Greer, Carol Kane, William Katt, Jeff Conaway, Tatyana Ali, Pam Grier, Brian Warner (Marilyn Manson), P.J. Soles, The Donnas. Monotonous—and unpleasant—black comedy about a tight-knit band of girls who rule their high school—until an accidental murder forces them to "adopt" a geeky student who could cause trouble for them. A short-subject idea padded to feature length. [R]▼●◗

Jaws (1975) **C-124m.** **** D: Steven Spielberg. Roy Scheider, Robert Shaw, Richard Dreyfuss, Lorraine Gary, Murray Hamilton, Jeffrey Kramer, Susan Backlinie, Carl Gottlieb. A rare case of a bubblegum story (by Peter Benchley) scoring as a terrific movie. The story: New England shore community is terrorized by shark attacks; local cop (Scheider), ichthyologist (Dreyfuss) and salty shark expert (Shaw) determine to kill the attacker. Hold on to your seats! Screenplay by Benchley and Gottlieb. Three Oscars include John Williams' now-classic score, Verna Fields' sensational editing. Benchley has cameo as reporter on beach. Followed by three sequels. Panavision. [PG]▼●◗

Jaws 2 (1978) **C-117m.** **½ D: Jeannot Szwarc. Roy Scheider, Lorraine Gary, Murray Hamilton, Joseph Mascolo, Jeffrey Kramer, Collin Wilcox. Just when you thought it was safe to turn on your TV set again, here comes another gratuitous sequel. The shark scenes deliver the goods, but Robert Shaw and Richard Dreyfuss are sorely needed when film is on land. Panavision. [PG]▼●

Jaws 3-D (1983) **C-97m.** ** D: Joe Alves. Dennis Quaid, Bess Armstrong, Simon MacCorkindale, Louis Gossett, Jr., John Putch, Lea Thompson. Road-company Irwin Allen-type disaster film, unrelated to first two JAWS except by contrivance; this time a shark's on the loose in Florida's Sea World. (Does this make it an unofficial remake of REVENGE OF THE CREATURE?) Might play on TV, but in theaters its only real assets were excellent 3-D effects. Retitled JAWS III for TV and homevideo. ArriVision. [PG]▼●

Jaws the Revenge (1987) **C-89m.** *½ D: Joseph Sargent. Lorraine Gary, Lance Guest, Mario Van Peebles, Karen Young, Michael Caine, Judith Barsi, Lynn Whitfield. Watchable but mediocre retread of JAWS, the fourth time around, with Gary as the widow of sheriff Scheider (from the original film) who's convinced the great white shark is deliberately seeking out and killing off members of her family. Marginal movie really sunk by stupid, abrupt finale; Caine wasted in frivolous supporting role. Set mostly in the Bahamas. [PG-13]▼●◗

Jaws of Death, The SEE: **Mako: The Jaws of Death**

Jaws of Satan (1981) **C-92m.** *½ D: Bob Claver. Fritz Weaver, Gretchen Corbett, Jon Korkes, Norman Lloyd, Diana Douglas. Ludicrous JAWS ripoff involving a deadly snake who is actually Satan himself! Filmed in 1979 and shelved . . . with good reason. [R]▼

Jayhawkers, The (1959) **C-100m.** **½ D: Melvin Frank. Jeff Chandler, Fess Parker, Nicole Maurey, Henry Silva, Herbert Rudley. Turgid Western set in 1850s, with Chandler and Parker battling for power, Maurey the love interest. VistaVision.▼

Jayne Mansfield: A Symbol of the '50s SEE: **Jayne Mansfield Story, The**

Jayne Mansfield Story, The (1980) **C-100m. TVM** D: Dick Lowry. Loni Anderson, Arnold Schwarzenegger, Raymond Buktenica, Kathleen Lloyd, G. D. Spradlin, Dave Shelley. Stunning Loni is merely OK as Jayne in this factually questionable biopic of the platinum blonde sex queen of the '50s, who according to this version would let nothing stand in her way of becoming the next Marilyn Monroe. With the exception of Mickey Hargitay (played by Schwarzenegger), all characters have fictitious names. Aka JAYNE MANSFIELD: A SYMBOL OF THE '50s. Average.▼

Jazz Boat (1960-British) **90m.** **½ D: Ken Hughes. Anthony Newley, Anne Aubrey, Lionel Jeffries, David Lodge, Bernie Winters, James Booth. Energetic caper of handyman Newley pretending to be a crook and then having to carry through, with dire results. CinemaScope.

Jazz on a Summer's Day (1959) **C-85m.** ***½ D: Bert Stern. Louis Armstrong, Big Maybelle, Chuck Berry, Dinah Washington, Gerry Mulligan, Thelonious Monk, Anita O'Day, Mahalia Jackson, Sonny Stitt, Jack Teagarden. Candid, enjoyable filmed record of the 1958 Newport Jazz Festival. A must for jazz aficionados.▼

Jazz Singer, The (1927) **89m.** **½ D: Alan Crosland. Al Jolson, May McAvoy, Warner Oland, Eugenie Besserer, Otto Lederer, William Demarest, Roscoe Karns. Legendary first talkie is actually silent with several sound musical and talking sequences. Story of Cantor Oland's son (Jolson) going into show business is creaky, but this movie milestone should be seen once. Songs: "My Mammy," "Toot Toot Tootsie Goodbye," "Blue Skies," etc. Look fast for Myrna Loy as a chorus girl. Remade twice (so far!).▼●

Jazz Singer, The (1953) **C-107m.** **½ D: Michael Curtiz. Danny Thomas, Peggy Lee, Mildred Dunnock, Eduard Franz, Tom Tully, Allyn Joslyn. Slick remake benefits from Curtiz' no-nonsense direction and presence of Lee and Dunnock . . . but it's still just *so* schmaltzy.▼

Jazz Singer, The (1980) **C-115m.** BOMB D: Richard Fleischer. Neil Diamond, Laurence Olivier, Lucie Arnaz, Catlin Adams, Franklyn Ajaye, Paul Nicholas, Sully Boyar, Mike Kellin. Cantor Olivier shouts, "I hef no son!"—one of the highpoints of this mothballed sudser in which Diamond becomes a rock star in about as much time as it takes to get a haircut. This remake may actually contain more clichés than the 1927 version! [PG]▼●◗

J. D.'s Revenge (1976) **C-95m.** ** D: Arthur Marks. Glynn Turman, Joan Pringle, Lou Gossett, Carl Crudup, James Louis Watkins, Alice Jubert. Black horror melodrama: possession of innocent man by vengeful spirit. Fairly well executed. [R]▼

Jealousy (1945) **71m.** ** D: Gustav Machaty. John Loder, Nils Asther, Jane Randolph, Karen Morley. Obvious plot line of renowned writer being murdered and wrong person accused; well served by capable cast.

Jean de Florette (1986-French) **C-122m.** ***½ D: Claude Berri. Yves Montand, Gérard Depardieu, Daniel Auteuil, Elisabeth Depardieu, Ernestine Mazurowna, Marcel Champel, Armand Meffre. Proud, cocky French farmer schemes with his simple-minded nephew to acquire some nearby farmland by making sure the new owners never discover an all-important natural spring on the property. Richly textured, emotionally powerful adaptation of Marcel Pagnol novel, exquisitely and meticulously filmed, with galvanizing performances—especially by Depardieu as the doggedly optimistic novice farmer. Story continues in MANON OF THE SPRING. Technovision. [PG]▼●

Jeanne and the Perfect Guy (1999-French) **C-98m.** **½ D: Olivier Ducastel. Virginie Ledoyen, Mathieu Demy, Valerie Bonneton, Jacques Bonnaffe. Musical comedy about a beautiful young woman who finally meets the love of her life, only to lose him when he disappears after learning he is HIV-positive. Unusual subject matter for a musical, to say the least, but Ducastel (seemingly inspired by Jacques Demy films) almost pulls it off. Downbeat subject matter is eclipsed by inventive use of songs and ultimately life-affirming message. Panavision.

Jeanne Eagels (1957) **109m.** **½ D: George Sidney. Kim Novak, Jeff Chandler, Agnes Moorehead, Gene Lockhart, Virginia Grey. Novak tries but can't rise to demands of portraying famed actress of 1920s. Chandler is her virile love interest.

Jeannie (1941-British) **101m.** *** D: Harold French. Michael Redgrave, Barbara Mullen, Wilfrid Lawson, Kay Hammond, Albert Lieven, Edward Chapman, Googie Withers, Rachel Kempson, Ian Fleming. Enjoyable comedy-romance with Scottish lass Mullen vacationing in Vienna and becoming involved with washing machine salesman Redgrave and gigolo Lieven. Anatole de Grunwald was one of the writers. Aka GIRL IN DISTRESS. Remade as LET'S BE HAPPY.

Jefferson in Paris (1995) **C-144m.** ** D: James Ivory. Nick Nolte, Greta Scacchi, Thandie Newton, Gwyneth Paltrow, Seth Gilliam, James Earl Jones, Simon Callow, Michael Lonsdale, Nancy Marchand, Jean-Pierre Aumont, Daniel Mesguich. While serving as U.S. Ambassador to France in the 1780s, a widowed Thomas Jefferson (Nolte) begins to fall in love with an Italian-born Englishwoman (Scacchi), but also finds himself attracted to a black, teenaged slave (Newton) on his household staff; meanwhile, his strong-willed daughter (Paltrow) seems to want to be the only woman in his life. Story is framed, in flashback, by Jones as free black man who claims to be Jefferson's son. Ambitious, well-appointed drama is also long and sluggish. [PG-13]▼●

Jeffrey (1995) **C-92m.** **½ D: Christopher Ashley. Steven Weber, Michael T. Weiss, Patrick Stewart, Bryan Batt, Sigourney Weaver, Nathan Lane, Olympia Dukakis, Christine Baranski, Robert Klein, Kathy Najimy, Irma St. Paule, Camryn Manheim. Thirtyish New Yorker Jeffrey (Weber), who is gay, has sworn off sex in this era of AIDS—only to meet hunky gym rat Weiss. They launch into a relationship and encounter just about every sort of "type" (gay or straight) imaginable, including Stewart (very good as a homosexual interior designer with a biting wit). Paul Rudnick's off-Broadway success works best when going for laughs; the intended poignancy of this very 90s romantic comedy is more forced. Rudnick also scripted and coproduced. Kevin Nealon appears unbilled. [R] ▼●

Jekyll & Hyde (1990-U.S.-British) **C-100m. TVM** D: David Wickes. Michael Caine, Cheryl Ladd, Joss Ackland, Ronald Pickup, Kim Thomson, Lionel Jeffries, Kevin McNally, Lee Montague. Caine, reunited with much of the same behind-the-scenes talent from JACK THE RIPPER (1988), has a high old scenery-chewing time playing the famous Robert Louis Stevenson character. Director Wickes wrote the script for this atmospheric but unmemorable remake. Average.▼

Jekyll & Hyde . . . Together Again (1982) **C-87m.** *½ D: Jerry Belson. Mark Blankfield, Bess Armstrong, Krista Errickson, Tim Thomerson, Michael McGuire, George Chakiris. Nothing here that Jerry Lewis's Nutty Professor didn't do better, as Blankfield exaggerates on his druggist character from *Fridays* TV show in tasteless excursion into cheap sex and drug jokes. A few scattered laughs in disappointing directorial debut by veteran comedy writer Belson. [R]▼

Jennie Gerhardt (1933) **85m.** *** D: Marion Gering. Sylvia Sidney, Donald Cook, Mary Astor, Edward Arnold, Louise Carter, Cora Sue Collins, H. B. Warner. Meticulously produced version of Theodore Dreiser saga of poor-girl Sidney finding kind benefactor Arnold, losing him, and living as Cook's back-street lover. Actors and elaborate production lend credibility to episodic soaper set at turn of the century.

Jennifer (1953) **73m.** **½ D: Joel Newton. Ida Lupino, Howard Duff, Robert Nichols, Mary Shipp. Turgid programmer of Lupino working at eerie old mansion where she discovers a murder.

Jennifer (1978) **C-90m.** ** D: Brice Mack. Lisa Pelikan, Bert Convy, Nina Foch, Amy Johnston, John Gavin, Jeff Corey, Wesley Eure. Unusually good cast in blatant rip-off of CARRIE, with Pelikan as ostracized high-school girl whose powers include ability to unleash deadly snakes on her victims. Retitled JENNIFER (THE SNAKE GODDESS) for TV. [PG]▼

Jennifer Eight (1992) **C-127m.** **½ D: Bruce Robinson. Andy Garcia, Uma Thurman, Lance Henriksen, Kathy Baker, Graham Beckel, Kevin Conway, John Malkovich, Perry Lang, Lenny von Dohlen. Taut, entertaining thriller in which burned-out L.A. cop Garcia relocates to a small Northern California town, where he promptly finds himself investigating a series of brutal murders. Will the next victim be beautiful, blind Thurman? Strong performances and eerie snowbound locations are plusses, but unfortunately, credibility dwindles as the story plays out. [R]▼●◗

Jennifer on My Mind (1971) **C-90m.** BOMB D: Noel Black. Michael Brandon, Tippy Walker, Lou Gilbert, Steve Vinovich, Peter Bonerz, Renee Taylor, Chuck McCann, Barry Bostwick, Jeff Conaway. Probably the worst of many drug films released in the early 70's; rootless American drifter and rich American girl smoke grass in Venice, advance to hard drugs back home. Awful script by Erich Segal; of interest mainly for presence of Robert De Niro, in small, prophetic role of gypsy cab driver. [R]

Jennifer (The Snake Goddess) SEE: **Jennifer** (1978)

Jenny (1970) **C-88m.** BOMB D: George Bloomfield. Marlo Thomas, Alan Alda, Marian Hailey, Elizabeth Wilson, Vincent Gardenia, Stephen Strimpell. Sappy soaper about filmmaker who marries pregnant girl in order to avoid the draft. Opening scene includes a clip from A PLACE IN THE SUN, which is best thing in film. [M/PG]▼

Jeopardy (1953) **69m.** **½ D: John Sturges. Barbara Stanwyck, Barry Sullivan, Ralph Meeker, Lee Aaker. Uneven thriller with Stanwyck, on vacation in Mexico, attempting to save husband Sullivan from drowning—and then being kidnaped herself by killer-on-the-lam Meeker. Starts off well, but then fizzles. Paging Alex Trebek!

Jeremiah Johnson (1972) **C-116m.** *** D: Sydney Pollack. Robert Redford, Will Geer, Stefan Gierasch, Allyn Ann McLerie, Charles Tyner, Josh Albee. Atmospheric chronicle of life of a mountain man, surviving wintry wilderness, Indians, rival trappers. Unfortunately, film doesn't know where to quit, rambling on to inconclusive ending. Geer is delightful as feisty mountain hermit. Script by John Milius and Edward Anhalt. Panavision. [PG]▼●◗

Jeremy (1973) **C-90m.** *** D: Arthur Barron. Robby Benson, Glynnis O'Connor, Len Bari, Leonard Cimino, Ned Wilson, Chris Bohn. Two shy teen-agers in N.Y.C. meet, fall in love, then separate. Poignant and real; situations, characters, and atmosphere are memorable. Some scenes cut for TV, others added from cutting-room floor to build running time. [PG]▼

Jericho SEE: **Dark Sands**

Jerk, The (1979) **C-94m.** **½ D: Carl Reiner. Steve Martin, Bernadette Peters, Catlin Adams, Mabel King, Richard Ward, Dick Anthony Williams, Bill Macy, Jackie Mason. Martin's first starring feature is a hit-or-miss comedy about the misadventures of a terminally stupid man. Some very funny moments, but after a while they're spread pretty thin. Martin later produced a TV version, THE JERK, TOO. [R]▼●◗

Jerky Boys, The (1995) **C-82m.** *½ D: James Melkonian. John G. Brennan, Kamal Ahmed, Alan Arkin, William Hickey, Alan North, Brad Sullivan, James Lorinz. Crank-call practitioners (who in real life had a hit record in N.Y.C.) who describe themselves as "two low-lifes from Queens" palm themselves off as Chicago hit men, thoroughly confusing N.Y. mobster Arkin (who must wonder what he's doing in this "comedy"). Result doesn't exactly expand the possibilities of cinema, though it may appeal to the type of person who enjoys vandalizing suburban mailboxes. [R]▼●

Jerrico, The Wonder Clown SEE: **Three Ring Circus**

Jerry Maguire (1996) **C-138m.** ***½ D: Cameron Crowe. Tom Cruise, Cuba Gooding, Jr., Renee Zellweger, Kelly Preston, Jerry O'Connell, Jay Mohr, Bonnie Hunt, Regina King, Jonathan Lipnicki, Glenn Frey, Eric Stoltz, Jann Wenner, Alexandra Wentworth, Lucy Alexis Liu. Cocky, super-successful sports agent has a crisis of conscience, which costs him his job and all but one of his clients—the most difficult one on the roster (Gooding, in a charismatic, Oscar-winning performance). His only ally is a young woman (with a little boy) who's devoted to him professionally and personally. Intelligent, original, layered screenplay (by Crowe) with characters who are actually interesting and three-dimensional. Cruise's earnestness is perfect for the part, and Zellweger is a real find. Various sports figures play themselves; Beau Bridges appears unbilled. Only complaint: It goes on too long. Some prints have a *faux* athletic shoe commercial at the end. [R]▼●◗

Jerusalem (1996-Swedish-Danish) **C-166m.** **½ D: Bille August. Maria Bonnevie, Ulf Friberg, Lena Endre, Pernilla August, Sven-Bertil Taube, Reine Brynolfsson, Olympia Dukakis, Max von Sydow. In late 19th-century Sweden, a poor, rural community is swept up in religious fervor; the town becomes bitterly divided, separating a pair of young sweethearts (Friberg, Bonnevie). When the converted emigrate to a Christian commune in Palestine, led by American Dukakis, they find new strife and strain. Long, fact-based epic (from Selma Lagerlof's novel) is earnest to a fault. Made for Swedish TV. [PG-13]▼

Jerusalem File, The (1972-U.S.-Israeli) **C-96m.** ** D: John Flynn. Bruce Davison, Nicol Williamson, Daria Halprin, Donald Pleasence, Ian Hendry, Koya Yair Rubin.

Uneasy mixture of political intrigue and straight action as American student Davison gets entangled in Arab-Israeli terrorism following the Six Day War. [PG]

Jesse James (1939) **C-105m.** *** D: Henry King. Tyrone Power, Henry Fonda, Nancy Kelly, Randolph Scott, Henry Hull, Brian Donlevy, John Carradine, Jane Darwell. Sprawling, glamorous Western with Power and Fonda as Jesse and Frank James; movie builds a case that the Old West's most notorious outlaw was misguided. Sequel: THE RETURN OF FRANK JAMES. ▼●

Jesse James Meets Frankenstein's Daughter (1966) **C-88m.** *½ D: William Beaudine. John Lupton, Narda Onyx, Cal Bolder, Estelita, Jim Davis, Steven Geray, William Fawcett. Low-budget nonsense mixes horror and Western genres, with Dr. Frankenstein's daughter practicing brain experiments—including turning Jesse's pal into a new monster. ▼

Jesse James vs. the Daltons (1954) **C-65m.** ** D: William Castle. Brett King, Barbara Lawrence, James Griffith, Bill Phipps, John Cliff. Bland shoot-out between alleged son of Jesse James and the other notorious outlaw gang.

Jesse James' Women (1954) **C-83m.** *½ D: Donald Barry. Don Barry, Jack Buetel, Peggie Castle, Lita Baron. Romancing a variety of women leaves James little time for outlaw activities; cute premise doesn't work out.

Jesse Owens Story, The (1984) **C-200m. TVM** D: Richard Irving. Dorian Harewood, Georg Stanford Brown, Debbi Morgan, Tom Bosley, LeVar Burton, Ronny Cox, Greg Morris, Ben Vereen, George Kennedy. Lovingly made biopic of famed black track star who won four gold medals at 1936 Berlin Olympics in the presence of Hitler's Nazi "super-race." Follows Owens from college days to his post-Olympic period when he was shamefully exploited. Harewood's tour-de-force performance, Harold Gast's incisive script, and Michel Legrand's score make this one of the better sports films. Originally shown in two parts. Above average. ▼

Jessica (1962) **C-112m.** **½ D: Jean Negulesco. Angie Dickinson, Maurice Chevalier, Noel-Noel, Gabriele Ferzetti, Sylva Koscina, Agnes Moorehead. Dickinson is an Italian midwife who has men in her village lusting for her, with Chevalier as the local priest. Malarkey. Panavision.

Jester, The SEE: **Der Purimshpiler**

Jesus (1979) **C-117m.** **½ D: Peter Sykes, John Krish. Brian Deacon, Rivka Noiman, Yossef Shiloah, Niko Nitai, Gadi Roi, David Goldberg. Narrated by Alexander Scourby. Straightforward but unmemorable retelling of Jesus' life, produced by The Genesis Project and filmed in Israel. [G]▼

Jesus Christ Superstar (1973) **C-103m.** *** D: Norman Jewison. Ted Neeley, Carl Anderson, Yvonne Elliman, Barry Dennen, Joshua Mostel, Bob Bingham. From record album to Broadway show to motion picture—film retains the Tim Rice–Andrew Lloyd Webber score, adds some interesting settings and visual trappings. It's not everyone's cup of religious experience, but certainly innovative. Watch for ubiquitous porno star Paul Thomas in the chorus. Todd-AO 35. [G]▼●◗

Jesus of Montreal (1989-Canadian-French) **C-119m.** ***½ D: Denys Arcand. Lothaire Bluteau, Catherine Wilkening, Johanne-Marie Tremblay, Remy Girard, Robert Lepage, Gilles Pelletier, Marie-Christine Barrault. A group of actors come together to stage an unconventional production of the Passion Play, and find themselves embroiled in controversy. Writer-director Arcand takes on religious hypocrisy, commercialism, and other social ills in this wise, profoundly moving and sometimes savagely funny film. A real gem. Arcand also appears in the role of the judge. [R]▼●

Jesus' Son (1998-Canadian) **C-109m.** ** D: Alison MacLean. Billy Crudup, Samantha Morton, Denis Leary, Jack Black, Will Patton, Greg Germann, Holly Hunter, Dennis Hopper. A stream-of-consciousness reminiscence by one young man who's swallowed up in the drug culture of the 1970s. Told in nonlinear flashback style, with vignettes involving a variety of characters who cross his path (played by Leary, Hopper, Hunter). Main problem: it's hard to care about the leading character. Based on Denis Johnson's acclaimed collection of short stories. Super 35. [R]▼

Jesus Trip, The (1971) **C-84m.** ** D: Russ Mayberry. Tippy Walker, Robert Porter, Billy "Green" Bush, Frank Orsati, Robert Tessier, Allan Gibbs. Motorcycle gang kidnaps attractive young nun in film that isn't as bad as it sounds; cast is good. [PG]▼

Jet Attack (1958) **68m.** BOMB D: Edward L. Cahn. John Agar, Audrey Totter, Gregory Walcott, James Dobson. Sloppy Korean War programmer about rescue of U.S. scientist caught behind North Korean lines. ▼

Jet Over the Atlantic (1960) **95m.** ** D: Byron Haskin. Guy Madison, Virginia Mayo, George Raft, Ilona Massey, Margaret Lindsay, George Macready, Anna Lee, Venetia Stevenson, Mary Anderson, Bret Halsey. Capable cast in clichéd situation of plane with bomb on board. Madison's the former air force pilot saving the day; predictable plot line. ▼

Jet Pilot (1957) **C-112m.** ** D: Josef von Sternberg. John Wayne, Janet Leigh, Jay C. Flippen, Paul Fix, Richard Rober, Roland Winters, Hans Conried. One of Howard Hughes' movie curios, updating his HELL'S ANGELS interest in aviation with

cold war theme, as American pilot Wayne falls in love with Russian jet ace Leigh. Ridiculous, to say the least, though some of its humor seems to have been intentional. Completed in 1950, unreleased for seven years! Incidentally, some of the stunt flying was done by Chuck Yeager.▼●◗
Jetsons: The Movie (1990) **C-81m.** ** D: William Hanna, Joseph Barbera. Voices of George O'Hanlon, Penny Singleton, Mel Blanc, Tiffany, Don Messick, Patric Zimmerman. Disappointing expansion of the 1960s animated TV sitcom has nothing to offer now-grownup fans of the series, but remains a palatable offering for very young children, with pro-social messages thrown in at the end. [G]▼●
Je Vous Aime (1981-French) **C-105m.** *½ D: Claude Berri. Catherine Deneuve, Jean-Louis Trintignant, Gérard Depardieu, Alain Souchon, Christian Marquand, Serge Gainsbourg. Shallow, solemn tale of liberated career-woman Deneuve, who is unable to remain monogamous. Good cast can do little with material; disappointing.
Jeweller's Shop, The (1987-Italian-Canadian) **C-97m.** ** D: Michael Anderson. Burt Lancaster, Ben Cross, Olivia Hussey, Andrea Occhipinti. Lancaster is a mysterious old Polish jeweler at the start of WW2 who brings together two pairs of lovers. Of particular interest both as one of the star's last film appearances and for the fact that it's based on a play by Karol Wojtyla, who later became Pope John Paul II. Aka THE GOLDSMITH'S SHOP.
Jewel of the Nile, The (1985) **C-104m.** ** D: Lewis Teague. Michael Douglas, Kathleen Turner, Danny DeVito, Spiros Focas, Avner Eisenberg, The Flying Karamazov Brothers. Contrived "high adventure" involving an evil potentate and a precious "jewel." Sequel to ROMANCING THE STONE can't capture charm of original, because the characters are set—and character change (particularly Turner's) is what made the first movie fun. Some good stunts and funny lines, but it all rings hollow. Widescreen. [PG]▼●◗
Jewel Robbery (1932) **70m.** ***½ D: William Dieterle. William Powell, Kay Francis, Hardie Albright, Henry Kolker, Spencer Charters, Alan Mowbray, Helen Vinson. Lubitsch-like bauble with wealthy, married Francis (who aches for excitement in her life) being captivated by debonair burglar Powell. Breathlessly paced, witty and charming. Screenplay by Erwin Gelsey, based on a play by Ladislaus Fodor.
Jewish Jester, The SEE: **Der Purimshpiler**
Jezebel (1938) **103m.** ***½ D: William Wyler. Bette Davis, Henry Fonda, George Brent, Margaret Lindsay, Donald Crisp, Fay Bainter, Spring Byington, Richard Cromwell, Henry O'Neill. Davis won her second Oscar as tempestuous Southern belle who goes too far to make fiancé Fonda jealous; Bainter also received Oscar as Davis' sympathetic aunt. Fine production, entire cast excellent. John Huston was one of the writers. Also shown in computer-colored version.▼●◗
Jezebels, The SEE: **Switchblade Sisters**
JFK (1991) **C/B&W-188m.** ***½ D: Oliver Stone. Kevin Costner, Sissy Spacek, Kevin Bacon, Tommy Lee Jones, Laurie Metcalf, Gary Oldman, Michael Rooker, Jay O. Sanders, Beata Pozniak, Joe Pesci, Donald Sutherland, John Candy, Jack Lemmon, Walter Matthau, Ed Asner, Vincent D'Onofrio, Sally Kirkland, Brian Doyle-Murray, Wayne Knight, Tony Plana, Tomas Milian, Sean Stone. Absolutely riveting film about New Orleans D.A. Jim Garrison and his gradual involvement (and eventual obsession) with finding the truth about President Kennedy's assassination. Full of startling scenes, and bravura acting; as dramatic moviemaking, it's superb. Not to be mistaken for a documentary, however, despite its sanctimonious attitude toward the truth. Oscar winner for Robert Richardson's cinematography and Joe Hutshing and Pietro Scalia's phenomenal editing. Screenplay by Oliver Stone and Zachary Sklar. The real Garrison can be glimpsed playing Earl Warren. Lolita Davidovich and Frank Whaley appear unbilled. Director's cut runs 205m. Panavision. [R]▼●◗
Jigsaw (1949) **70m.** ** D: Fletcher Markle. Franchot Tone, Jean Wallace, Myron McCormick, Marc Lawrence, Betty Harper (Doe Avedon). Pedestrian caper of assistant D.A. Tone on the trail of a journalist's killer, uncovering a racist hate group. Sparked by unbilled appearances of Marlene Dietrich, Henry Fonda, John Garfield, Burgess Meredith, Marsha Hunt. Retitled: GUN MOLL.▼
Jigsaw (1968) **C-97m.** **½ D: James Goldstone. Harry Guardino, Bradford Dillman, Hope Lange, Pat Hingle, Diana Hyland, Victor Jory, Paul Stewart, Susan Saint James, Michael J. Pollard, James Doohan, Kent McCord. Fast-paced, utterly confusing yarn about amnesiac Dillman trying to figure out his past and unravel murder caper he was involved in. Frantic editing and music don't help viewer; remake of MIRAGE. Made for TV but shown theatrically first.
Jigsaw Man, The (1984-British) **C-91m.** ** D: Terence Young. Michael Caine, Laurence Olivier, Susan George, Robert Powell, Charles Gray, Michael Medwin. Caine, an ex-British Secret Service honcho who defected to Russia, comes back to England (following rejuvenating plastic surgery) for one final mission. Will he serve one country, the other, or play both ends against the middle? Unfortunately this

Caine-Olivier pairing is no SLEUTH, so you won't care. [PG]▼●

Jim Buck SEE: **Portrait of a Hitman**

Jimi Hendrix (1973) **C-102m.** **½ D: Joe Boyd, John Head, Gary Weis. Documentary on life of noted black rock guitarist; good segments from various concerts, interviews with those who knew him well. Songs include "Purple Haze," "Wild Thing," "Johnny B. Goode." [R]▼

Jimmy and Sally (1933) **68m.** **½ D: James Tinling. James Dunn, Claire Trevor, Harvey Stephens, Lya Lys, Jed Prouty. Go-getter Dunn lets his ambition cloud his devotion to Trevor in amiable little film of no consequence whatsoever.

Jimmy Hollywood (1994) **C-109m.** ** D: Barry Levinson. Joe Pesci, Christian Slater, Victoria Abril, Jason Beghe, John Cothran, Jr., Rob Weiss, Chad McQueen. Well-meaning but one-note tale of hard-luck middle-aged dreamer Pesci, a would-be actor who earns fame by playing out the role of a lifetime: Jericho, an urban vigilante. Obvious look at life in seedy, contemporary Hollywood, which once was a "mecca of dreams." Pesci is good, but his character quickly becomes wearying. Watch for director Levinson at the finale. Levinson also scripted. [R]▼●

Jimmy the Gent (1934) **67m.** **½ D: Michael Curtiz. James Cagney, Bette Davis, Alice White, Allen Jenkins, Philip Reed, Mayo Methot. Crooked businessman Cagney pretends to refine himself to impress Davis in this bouncy comedy.

Jimmy the Kid (1983) **C-85m.** *½ D: Gary Nelson. Gary Coleman, Paul LeMat, Walter Olkewicz, Dee Wallace, Ruth Gordon, Don Adams, Cleavon Little, Avery Schreiber. Bored, brilliant son of wealthy husband-and-wife singing team is kidnapped by gang of pathetically incompetent bunglers who teach him how to enjoy being a kid. Coleman returns favor by bringing good cast down to his level of nonacting, consisting of endless mugging and exaggerated eyeball rolling, in this lame comedy. Based on a Donald Westlake novel, with LeMat as the same character played by Robert Redford in THE HOT ROCK. [PG]▼

Jim Thorpe—All American (1951) **107m.** **½ D: Michael Curtiz. Burt Lancaster, Charles Bickford, Steve Cochran, Phyllis Thaxter, Dick Wesson. The life of the famed American Indian athlete who was stripped of his Olympic medals for playing professional baseball. Lancaster lends dignified vigor to title role; Bickford is especially outstanding as Thorpe's mentor, legendary coach Pop Warner.▼●

Jingle All the Way (1996) **C-88m.** ** D: Brian Levant. Arnold Schwarzenegger, Sinbad, Phil Hartman, Rita Wilson, Robert Conrad, Martin Mull, James Belushi, Harvey Korman, Laraine Newman, Jake Lloyd. Neglectful father promises his son a Turbo Man action figure, then frantically searches to find the sold-out toy the day before Christmas. His chief rival in the search (Sinbad) turns out to be not just a competitor but a major sicko. Even at 88 minutes this feels prolonged and protracted, a dubious 90s addition to the canon of holiday movies. Arnold gives it his best, but he simply isn't funny. [PG] ▼●◗

Jinnah (1998-U.S.-Pakistani-British) **C-94m.** *** D: Jamil Dehlavi. Christopher Lee, James Fox, Maria Aitkin, Sashi Kapoor, Shireen Shah, Richard Lintern, Robert Ashby, Sam Dastor. Lee is outstanding as the dedicated, brittle and reserved Mohammed Ali Jinnah, founder of Pakistan, in this odd biography in which, on the verge of death, he's shown the events of his past in Ebenezer Scrooge style. Fox, Ashby and Dastor are also fine as Mountbatten, Nehru and Gandhi. A worthwhile, intelligent movie that deserves, like its subject, to be better known.▼

Jinxed! (1982) **C-103m.** ** D: Don Siegel. Bette Midler, Ken Wahl, Rip Torn, Val Avery, Jack Elam, Benson Fong. Messy black comedy about a Vegas lounge singer, the lout she lives with, and a young blackjack dealer the lout has managed to jinx at his own table. Though a characteristically ripped Rip provides some amusement, the much-reported lack of rapport between Midler/Wahl and Midler/Siegel comes through on the screen. Screenwriter "Bert Blessing" is really Frank D. Gilroy. [R]▼

Jinx Money (1948) **68m.** ** D: William Beaudine. Leo Gorcey, Huntz Hall, Gabriel Dell, Billy Benedict, David Gorcey, Bennie Bartlett, Sheldon Leonard, Donald MacBride, Wanda McKay, John Eldredge. The Bowery Boys stumble upon $50,000 of a dead gangster's loot and spend a slow hour being chased by his cohorts.

Jitterbugs (1943) **74m.** ** D: Mal St. Clair. Stan Laurel, Oliver Hardy, Vivian Blaine, Robert Bailey, Douglas Fowley, Noel Madison. One of the team's better later efforts, with Blaine sharing the spotlight and doing quite nicely. Ollie's scene with Southern belle Lee Patrick is a gem. Previously filmed as ARIZONA TO BROADWAY.

Jivaro (1954) **C-91m.** ** D: Edward Ludwig. Fernando Lamas, Rhonda Fleming, Brian Keith, Lon Chaney (Jr.), Richard Denning, Rita Moreno. Cornball adventure with beautiful Fleming arriving in the Amazon to search for her missing fiancé; promptly and predictably, she hooks up with Lamas.

J-Men Forever! (1979) **75m.** *** D: Richard Patterson. Philip Proctor, Peter Bergman, voice of M. G. Kelly. Clever stunt that really works—scenes from countless Republic serials are re-edited into new feature, with redubbed soundtrack and a few new scenes. Story (by Firesign Theatre's Proctor and Bergman) has The Lightning Bug ("From the Moon, Baby!") out to conquer Earth by flooding radio airwaves with rock; various heroes try to make the world safe for Lawrence Welk. Amazing job of editing by Gail Werbin; one great gag involves a young Leonard Nimoy. [PG]▼

Joanna (1968-British) **C-107m.** **½ D: Michael Sarne. Genevieve Waite, Christian Doermer, Calvin Lockhart, Donald Sutherland, Glenna Forster-Jones. Flashy story of wide-eyed girl falling in with loose-living London crowd, growing up through heartbreak, conflict. Sutherland steals film in flamboyant role as frail, wealthy young man trying to enjoy life to fullest. Panavision. [R]

Joan of Arc (1948) **C-100m.** **½ D: Victor Fleming. Ingrid Bergman, Jose Ferrer, Francis L. Sullivan, J. Carrol Naish, Ward Bond, Shepperd Strudwick, Hurd Hatfield, Gene Lockhart, John Emery, Cecil Kellaway, George Coulouris, John Ireland. Bergman is staunchly sincere in this overlong, faithful adaptation of Maxwell Anderson's play. Not enough spectacle to balance talky sequences. Originally released theatrically at 145m.▼●

Joan of Ozark (1942) **80m.** ** D: Joseph Santley. Judy Canova, Joe E. Brown, Eddie Foy, Jr., Jerome Cowan, Alexander Granach, Anne Jeffreys. Hillbilly Canova hunts down Nazi underground ring in U.S.

Joan of Paris (1942) **91m.** ***½ D: Robert Stevenson. Michele Morgan, Paul Henreid, Thomas Mitchell, Laird Cregar, May Robson, Alexander Granach, Alan Ladd. Excellent WW2 tale of dedicated Morgan giving herself up so Henreid and fellow-pilots can return to Allied lines. U.S. debuts for both Morgan and Henreid.▼

Jocks (1987) **C-91m.** *½ D: Steve Carver. Scott Strader, Perry Lang, Mariska Hargitay, Richard Roundtree, R. G. Armstrong, Christopher Lee, Stoney Jackson, Adam Mills, Katherine Kelly Lang, Trinidad Silva, Don Gibb. Silly teen comedy of college tennis team's hijinx in Las Vegas. Despite oddball roles for vets Lee and Armstrong, picture only comes to life on the tennis court. Filmed in 1984. [R]▼

Joe (1970) **C-107m.** **½ D: John G. Avildsen. Peter Boyle, Dennis Patrick, K. Callan, Audrey Caire, Susan Sarandon, Patrick McDermott. Sleeper film brought Boyle to prominence as hardhat bigot who practices genteel blackmail on executive Patrick, who's murdered his daughter's hippie boyfriend. Overrated film owes much to Boyle's characterization, not to contrived plot. Sarandon's film debut. [R]▼●

Joe and Ethel Turp Call on the President (1939) **70m.** **½ D: Robert Sinclair. Ann Sothern, Lewis Stone, Walter Brennan, William Gargan, Marsha Hunt, Tom Neal. Cute little B-film from Damon Runyon story about Brooklynites Sothern and Gargan who go all the way to the White House to see the President (Stone) when their favorite mailman (Brennan) is jailed for destroying a registered letter.

Joe Butterfly (1957) **C-90m.** **½ D: Jesse Hibbs. Audie Murphy, Burgess Meredith, George Nader, Keenan Wynn, Fred Clark. Another variation on TEAHOUSE OF THE AUGUST MOON, set in post-WW2 Japan. American soldiers at mercy of wily Japanese Meredith to get needed supplies. CinemaScope.

Joe Cocker: Mad Dogs and Englishmen (1971-British) **C-119m.** *** D: Pierre Adidge. Joe Cocker, Leon Russell, Chris Stainton, Carl Radle, John Price, Bobby Keys, Rita Coolidge, Claudia Linnear. Excellent rockumentary of Cocker's '70 American tour, highlighted by Cocker, Russell, and Linnear in performance. Songs include "Feelin' Alright," "With a Little Help from My Friends," "Darlin' Be Home Soon," many others. Aka MAD DOGS AND ENGLISHMEN. Multiple Screen. [PG]▼

Joe Dakota (1957) **C-79m.** **½ D: Richard Bartlett. Jock Mahoney, Luana Patten, Charles McGraw, Barbara Lawrence, Claude Akins, Lee Van Cleef. Folksy oater of Mahoney renewing a town's pride in itself.

Joe Gould's Secret (2000) **C-104m.** *** D: Stanley Tucci. Ian Holm, Stanley Tucci, Patricia Clarkson, Hope Davis, Steve Martin, Susan Sarandon, Patrick Tovatt, Celia Weston, Allan Corduner. *New Yorker* profile writer Joseph Mitchell (Tucci) is introduced to "the king of the Bohemians," street savant Joe Gould (Holm), and becomes fascinated (and sucked in) by this bombastic Greenwich Village habitue. Notable for its loving recreation of 1940s N.Y.C. and the world that Mitchell documented so vividly. Holm is simply superb. Screenplay by Howard A. Rodman. [R]▼◗

Joe Hill (1971-Swedish) **C-114m.** *** D: Bo Widerberg. Thommy Berggren, Ania Schmidt, Kelvin Malave, Everl Anderson, Cathy Smith. Fabricated story of legendary labor leader has usual Widerberg matter-of-taste glossiness, but also some affecting scenes and pleasant performances. Joan Baez sings title song. [PG]

Joe Kidd (1972) **C-88m.** ** D: John Sturges. Clint Eastwood, Robert Duvall, John Saxon, Don Stroud, Stella Garcia, James Wainwright. Eastwood is hired to hunt down some Mexican-Americans by land baron Duvall in ordinary Western; nice photography and a rousing scene where Eastwood drives a train through a barroom. Written by Elmore Leonard. Panavision. [PG]▼●◗

Joe Louis Story, The (1953) **88m.** ** D: Robert Gordon. Coley Wallace, Paul Stewart, Hilda Simms, James Edwards, John

Marley, Dots Johnson. Biopic of the heavyweight champ is interesting historically but dramatically hokey; Wallace looks the part of Louis, but is no actor.▼

Joe Macbeth (1955-British) **90m.** **½ D: Ken Hughes. Paul Douglas, Ruth Roman, Bonar Colleano, Gregoire Aslan, Sidney James. Occasionally amusing variation on Shakespeare's *Macbeth*, with Douglas a 1930s gangster whose wife (Roman) nags him into murdering his way to the top of his "profession."

Joe Palooka SEE: **Palooka**

Joe Panther (1976) **C-110m.** *** D: Paul Krasny. Brian Keith, Ricardo Montalban, Alan Feinstein, Cliff Osmond, A Martinez, Ray Tracey. Good family film about modern-day Seminole youth (Tracey) striving to make his way in the white man's world. [G]▼

Joe's Apartment (1996) **C-80m.** **½ D: John Payson. Jerry O'Connell, Megan Ward, Robert Vaughn, Don Ho, Shiek Mahmud-Bey, Jim Sterling, Sandra Denton, Toukie Smith, Scott "Bam Bam" Bigelow, Paul Bartel, voices of Billy West, Reginald Hudlin, Dave Chappelle, B. D. Wong. Joe (O'Connell) lives in a N.Y.C. slum apartment infested by thousands of singing, dancing, and talking cockroaches, who help him defeat the schemes of his evil landlord (Don Ho). To put it mildly, not for all tastes, but if you can handle break-dancing vermin, the effects are excellent, the musical numbers inventive, and the whole thing harmlessly silly. Written by the director. Based on a short that first aired on MTV in 1992. [PG-13]▼●◗

Joe Smith, American (1942) **63m.** ** D: Richard Thorpe. Robert Young, Marsha Hunt, Harvey Stephens, Darryl Hickman. Dated WW2 morale-booster about kidnapped munitions worker Young who refuses to divulge secrets to Nazis. Paul Gallico story remade as THE BIG OPERATOR. Watch for Ava Gardner in a bit.

Joe the King (1999) **C-83m.** ** D: Frank Whaley. Noah Fleiss, Val Kilmer, Karen Young, Ethan Hawke, John Leguizamo, Austin Pendleton, Max Ligosh, James Costa, Camryn Manheim, Amy Wright. A 14-year-old boy's life is one long, losing battle. With a drunken, irresponsible father (Kilmer) and an absentee mother (Young), he's descended into a life of theft and antisocial behavior. He's not really a bad kid, but there is no relief, and certainly no hope, in sight for him. Actor Whaley's writing-directing debut is a vivid portrait of working-class life, but is so dismal it might be retitled THE 800 BLOWS. [R]▼◗

Joe Versus the Volcano (1990) **C-102m.** **½ D: John Patrick Shanley. Tom Hanks, Meg Ryan, Lloyd Bridges, Robert Stack, Dan Hedaya, Abe Vigoda, Ossie Davis, Barry McGovern, Amanda Plummer, Carol Kane, Nathan Lane. Pleasant if pointless fable about a stressed-out nerd who learns he has six months to live, and accepts an eccentric millionaire's offer to enable him to live like a king—so long as he jumps into a volcano at the end of his "vacation." Unfortunately, the story also takes a dive. Writer Shanley's directorial debut turns out to be a shaggy-dog story that doesn't pay off. However, it *is* fun watching Ryan play three distinctively different women . . . and remember, luggage is everything. Panavision. [PG] ▼●

Joey (1985) **C-97m.** ** D: Joseph Ellison. Neill Barry, James Quinn, Elisa Heinsohn, Linda Thorson, Ellen Hammill, Dan Grimaldi, Frankie Lanz. Hokey but harmless ode to Oldies and Doo Wop, chronicling the troubled personal life of teen rock musician Barry and his relationship with his dad (Quinn), who used to turn out hit records but now toils in a gas station and drinks away his paycheck. Otherwise minor item features cameo appearances by The Limelights (who perform "Daddy's Home"), Silhouettes ("Get a Job"), Ad-Libs ("Boy From New York City"), Elegants ("Little Star"), Screamin' Jay Hawkins ("I Put a Spell on You") and, fleetingly, Jimmy Merchant and Herman Santiago, the only surviving Teenagers ("Why Do Fools Fall in Love?"). [PG]▼

Joey Breaker (1993) **C-92m.** **½ D: Steven Starr. Richard Edson, Cedella Marley, Fred Fondren, Erik King, Gina Gershon, Philip Seymour Hoffman, Michael Imperioli, Parker Posey. Astute, candid, but too often dramatically static portrait of a suave, self-absorbed N.Y. talent agent (Edson), and how his consciousness is raised. Marley (the daughter of Bob Marley) plays the romantic interest, a Jamaican nursing student. Starr, an ex-William Morris agent, also scripted and coproduced. [R]▼

John and Mary (1969) **C-92m.** **½ D: Peter Yates. Dustin Hoffman, Mia Farrow, Michael Tolan, Sunny Griffin, Stanley Beck, Tyne Daly, Alix Elias, Marian Mercer, Olympia Dukakis, Cleavon Little, Kristoffer Tabori. John and Mary meet, make love, but don't know if the relationship should end right there. Innocuous, uncompelling trifle. Hoffman seems to be sleepwalking; audience may join him. Panavision. [PG—originally rated R]

John Carpenter's Body Bags SEE: **Body Bags**

John Carpenter's Escape From L.A. SEE: **Escape From L.A.**

John Carpenter's Vampires SEE: **Vampires**

John F. Kennedy: Years of Lightning, Day of Drums (1964) **C-85m.** **** D: Bruce Herschensohn. Brilliant documentary, originally commissioned by the United

States Information Agency, on the life and times of John Kennedy.

John Goldfarb, Please Come Home (1965) **C-96m.** *½ D: J. Lee Thompson. Shirley MacLaine, Peter Ustinov, Richard Crenna, Scott Brady, Jim Backus, Charles Lane, Jerome Cowan, Wilfrid Hyde-White, Fred Clark, Harry Morgan, Telly Savalas, Richard Deacon, Jackie Coogan, Jerome (Jerry) Orbach, Barbara Bouchet. Trapped in desert kingdom, two Americans (pilot, woman reporter) conspire to help Arabian chief Ustinov's football team beat Notre Dame. Notre Dame University found this spoof so offensive it sued in court; the viewer has an easier alternative. Screenplay by William Peter Blatty. Look for Teri Garr. CinemaScope.

John Grisham's The Rainmaker SEE: **Rainmaker, The** (1997)

John Loves Mary (1949) **96m.** **½ D: David Butler. Ronald Reagan, Jack Carson, Patricia Neal, Wayne Morris, Edward Arnold, Virginia Field. Genial adaptation of Norman Krasna's Broadway hit about a soldier (Reagan) who does his pal a favor by marrying the fellow's British girlfriend, so she can come to the U.S.—intending to get divorce upon arrival. Naive fluff was Neal's film debut.▼

John Meade's Woman (1937) **87m.** ** D: Richard Wallace. Edward Arnold, Gail Patrick, Francine Larrimore, George Bancroft, Aileen Pringle, Sidney Blackmer. Arnold plays another Great American Businessman, marrying one girl to spite another. Idea backfires; so does film.

Johnny Allegro (1949) **81m.** **½ D: Ted Tetzlaff. Nina Foch, George Raft, George Macready, Will Geer. Seamy gangster melodrama of ex-racketeer Raft helping federal agents capture counterfeiting gang. Last half of story imitates THE MOST DANGEROUS GAME.

Johnny Angel (1945) **79m.** *** D: Edwin L. Marin. George Raft, Claire Trevor, Signe Hasso, Lowell Gilmore, Hoagy Carmichael, Marvin Miller, Margaret Wycherly, J. Farrell MacDonald. Tough, well-done melodrama, with Raft cleaning up notorious mob, solving mystery of father's murder. Trevor lends good support.▼●

Johnny Apollo (1940) **93m.** *** D: Henry Hathaway. Tyrone Power, Dorothy Lamour, Edward Arnold, Lloyd Nolan, Charles Grapewin, Lionel Atwill, Marc Lawrence. Good-natured Power turns crook, resentful of father Arnold, white-collar thief. Good acting, especially by Lamour as the girlfriend.▼

Johnny Be Good (1988) **C-84m.** BOMB D: Bud Smith. Anthony Michael Hall, Robert Downey, Jr., Paul Gleason, Uma Thurman, Steve James, Seymour Cassel, Howard Cosell, Jim McMahon, Robert Downey, Sr., Jennifer Tilly. Offensive, bottom-of-the-barrel comedy about star high-school jock Hall and how various colleges attempt to illegally recruit him. The seriousness of the issue completely eludes the makers of this turkey. R-rated scenes were added for homevideo version. [PG-13—later reedited to R]▼●

Johnny Belinda (1948) **103m.** ***½ D: Jean Negulesco. Jane Wyman, Lew Ayres, Charles Bickford, Jan Sterling, Agnes Moorehead, Stephen McNally, Rosalind Ivan, Alan Napier, Dan Seymour. Sensitively acted, atmospheric drama of young deaf-mute girl (Wyman) and doctor (Ayres) who works with her. Setting of provincial fishing-farming community vividly realized. Wyman won an Oscar for her fine performance. Elmer Harris play was scripted by Irmgard von Cube and Allen Vincent. Remade for TV in 1982 with Rosanna Arquette. Also shown in computer-colored version.▼

Johnny Bull (1986) **C-100m. TVM** D: Claudia Weill. Jason Robards, Colleen Dewhurst, Peter MacNicol, Kathy Bates, Suzanna Hamilton. Strong performances elevate this drama about a Cockney girl whose dreams of America are shattered when she and her G.I. husband move into his disgruntled parents' home in a Pennsylvania town where the mine has been played out. Award-winning first script by Kathleen Betsko Yale. Above average.

Johnny Come Lately (1943) **97m.** **½ D: William K. Howard. James Cagney, Grace George, Marjorie Main, Marjorie Lord, Hattie McDaniel, Ed McNamara. Tame but amusing Cagney vehicle, with Jimmy as wandering newspaperman who helps elderly editor George in small-town political battle.▼●

Johnny Concho (1956) **84m.** **½ D: Don McGuire. Frank Sinatra, Keenan Wynn, William Conrad, Phyllis Kirk, Wallace Ford, Dorothy Adams, Jean Byron, Claude Akins, John Qualen. Plodding Western with novelty of Sinatra as cowardly soul who must build courage for inevitable shootout. Adapted from a *Studio One* TV play.

Johnny Cool (1963) **101m.** *** D: William Asher. Henry Silva, Elizabeth Montgomery, Sammy Davis, Jr., Richard Anderson, Jim Backus, Wanda Hendrix, Brad Dexter, Joey Bishop, Marc Lawrence, John McGiver, Mort Sahl, Telly Savalas, Elisha Cook, Jr. Sadistic study of vicious gangster seeking revenge. Brutal account, realistically told.

Johnny Dangerously (1984) **C-90m.** *½ D: Amy Heckerling. Michael Keaton, Joe Piscopo, Marilu Henner, Maureen Stapleton, Peter Boyle, Griffin Dunne, Richard Dimitri, Glynnis O'Connor, Byron Thames, Danny DeVito, Dom DeLuise, Ray Walston, Sudie Bond. Lame comedy about Prohibition-era gangsters; looks like a TV show and plays that way, too, with scattershot jokes (only a few of them funny) instead of a script. [PG-13]▼

Johnny Dark (1954) **C-85m.** **½ D: George Sherman. Tony Curtis, Piper Laurie, Don Taylor, Paul Kelly, Ilka Chase, Sidney Blackmer. Curtis is energetic as auto designer who enters big race.

Johnny Doesn't Live Here Any More (1944) **77m.** **½ D: Joe May. Simone Simon, James Ellison, Minna Gombell, Alan Dinehart, Robert Mitchum, Grady Sutton. WW2 ancestor of THE APARTMENT, with Simon's flat becoming a madhouse. Retitled: AND SO THEY WERE MARRIED.

Johnny Eager (1941) **107m.** *** D: Mervyn LeRoy. Robert Taylor, Lana Turner, Edward Arnold, Van Heflin, Robert Sterling, Patricia Dane, Glenda Farrell, Barry Nelson. Slick MGM melodrama with convoluted plot about sociology student (and daughter of D.A. Arnold) Turner falling in love with unscrupulous racketeer Taylor. Heflin won Best Supporting Actor Oscar as Taylor's alcoholic friend.▼

Johnny Got His Gun (1971) **C-111m.** ** D: Dalton Trumbo. Timothy Bottoms, Kathy Fields, Marsha Hunt, Jason Robards, Donald Sutherland, Diane Varsi, David Soul, Tony Geary. Morbid film version of Trumbo's novel about WWI basket case has moving opening and climax, but everything in the middle is either talky, pretentious, or amateurish. [PG]▼●

Johnny Guitar (1954) **C-110m.** ***½ D: Nicholas Ray. Joan Crawford, Sterling Hayden, Scott Brady, Mercedes McCambridge, Ward Bond, Ben Cooper, Ernest Borgnine, Royal Dano, John Carradine, Paul Fix, Frank Ferguson. The screen's great kinky Western, a memorable confrontation between saloonkeeper Crawford and righteous hellion McCambridge, who wants her run out of town and/or hanged. Simply fascinating with symbolism rampant throughout. Script by Philip Yordan.▼●

Johnny Hamlet (1972-U.S.-Italian) **C-91m.** ** D: Enzo G. Castellari. Chip Corman, Gilbert Roland, Horst Frank. Texan returns home, gets involved in robbery, murder, and torture in undistinguished oater with Shakespearean plot line. Techniscope. [PG]

Johnny Handsome (1989) **C-94m.** ** D: Walter Hill. Mickey Rourke, Ellen Barkin, Elizabeth McGovern, Morgan Freeman, Forest Whitaker, Lance Henriksen, Scott Wilson, Blake Clark. Disfigured Rourke is imprisoned after his abandonment by fellow lowlifes during a heist; a doctor then proposes performing plastic surgery on his features, hoping to lower his recidivism potential. Eccentric, to say the least, and not totally without interest given the cast, but eventually wears out its welcome. Given Rourke's standard appearance, this must be the only skull surgery ever performed without benefit of a shampoo. [R]▼●

Johnny Holiday (1949) **92m.** *** D: Willis Goldbeck. William Bendix, Allen Martin, Jr., Stanley Clements, Jack Hagen. Remarkably sincere study of juvenile delinquent torn between friends from dishonest past and those trying to help him at reform farm.▼

Johnny in the Clouds SEE: **Way to the Stars, The**

Johnny Mnemonic (1995-Canadian) **C-98m.** *½ D: Robert Longo. Keanu Reeves, Dolph Lundgren, Takeshi, Ice-T, Dina Meyer, Udo Kier, Denis Akiyama, Henry Rollins, Tracy Tweed, Don Francks. In the very ugly future of 2021, a world-weary courier (who carries info in his head) takes one final run from Beijing to Newark, his storage capacity dangerously overloaded with volatile data sought by a huge, ruthless corporation. Intriguing premise, written by William Gibson and directed by artist Longo, goes absolutely nowhere, as uninteresting characters mouth laughable dialogue against a landscape of urban hell. Despite the computer graphics, this is cyberclaptrap. Runs about 15m. longer in Japan. [R] ▼●◗

Johnny Nobody (1961-British) **88m.** *** D: Nigel Patrick. Nigel Patrick, Yvonne Mitchell, Aldo Ray, William Bendix, Cyril Cusack. Irish priest suspects murder when drunken author is killed. Unusual plot twists with religious overtones. Neat, well-made little thriller. Warwickscope. ▼

Johnny O'Clock (1947) **95m.** **½ D: Robert Rossen. Dick Powell, Evelyn Keyes, Lee J. Cobb, Ellen Drew, Nina Foch, Jeff Chandler. Cast and director make script about high-class gambler in trouble with the law seem better than it is; Powell is fine in lead role.

Johnny One Eye (1950) **78m.** ** D: Robert Florey. Pat O'Brien, Wayne Morris, Dolores Moran, Gayle Reed. Schmaltzy Damon Runyon yarn of O'Brien, a gangster with a heart of gold, on the lam.

Johnny Reno (1966) **C-83m.** BOMB D: R.G. Springsteen. Dana Andrews, Jane Russell, Lon Chaney (Jr.), John Agar, Lyle Bettger, Tom Drake, Richard Arlen, Robert Lowery. Laughably clichéd Western has Marshal Andrews trying to save accused killer from lynching. Only for buffs who want to play "spot the star." Techniscope.▼

Johnny Rocco (1958) **84m.** ** D: Paul Landres. Richard Eyer, Stephen McNally, Coleen Gray, Russ Conway. Gangster's son (Eyer) is focal point of gangland hunt because he witnessed a killing; OK drama.

Johnny Shiloh (1963) **C-90m.** **½ D: James Neilson. Kevin Corcoran, Brian Keith, Darryl Hickman, Skip Homeier. Young Corcoran leaves his family and tags along with Civil War Army led by Keith. Set-bound adventure, but well acted and easy to watch. Originally shown in two parts on the Disney TV show.▼

Johnny Stecchino (1991-Italian) **C-100m.** *** D: Roberto Benigni. Roberto Benigni, Nicoletta Braschi, Paolo Bonacelli, Ignazio Pappalardo, Franco Volpi. A mild and meek school bus driver is the spitting image of a notorious gangster—Johnny Stecchino (''Toothpick''). When the latter's luscious girlfriend drags the naive lookalike down to her Sicilian villa all sorts of shenanigans ensue. Bright physical comedy was Italy's most successful film ever at the box office, and director-cowriter-star Benigni has thrown in a wide array of his trademark physical gags. Material wears a little thin after a while, but it's hard to dislike a film with a heroine whose favorite exclamation is ''Holy Cleopatra!'' [R]▼●

Johnny Stool Pigeon (1949) **76m.** **½ D: William Castle. Howard Duff, Shelley Winters, Dan Duryea, Anthony (Tony) Curtis. Standard drama of convict being sprung from prison so he can lead federal agents to former gang members.

Johnny Suede (1991) **C-95m.** *** D: Tom DiCillo. Brad Pitt, Calvin Levels, Alison Moir, Catherine Keener, Tina Louise, Nick Cave, Samuel L. Jackson. Pitt is perfectly cast as Johnny Suede, who sports a glorious pompadour and dreams of stardom as a Ricky Nelson-type pop singer. Clever, winningly hip little film; at its best contrasting Johnny's dream world with the reality that surrounds him.▼●

Johnny Tiger (1966) **C-102m.** **½ D: Paul Wendkos. Robert Taylor, Geraldine Brooks, Chad Everett, Brenda Scott. Set in Florida, tame tale of teacher Taylor, doctor Brooks, and half-breed Seminole Everett trying to come to conclusions about Indians' role in modern world.▼

Johnny Tremain (1957) **C-80m.** *** D: Robert Stevenson. Hal Stalmaster, Luana Patten, Jeff York, Sebastian Cabot, Dick Beymer, Walter Sande. Excellent Disney film, from Esther Forbes' novel about a young boy who gets involved in the Revolutionary War; sprinkles fiction with fact to bring history to life.▼●

Johnny Trouble (1957) **80m.** **½ D: John H. Auer. Ethel Barrymore, Cecil Kellaway, Carolyn Jones, Stuart Whitman, Jesse White, Jack Larson. Tender story of elderly Barrymore, convinced that her long-missing son will return and that he wasn't a bad boy. Ethel's final film. Remake of SOMEONE TO REMEMBER.

Johnny, We Hardly Knew Ye (1977) **C-100m. TVM** D: Gilbert Cates. Paul Rudd, Kevin Conway, Burgess Meredith, William Prince, Richard Venture, Tom Berenger, Kenneth McMillan, Shirley Rich, Joseph Bova, Brian Dennehy. Well-acted account of John F. Kennedy's first try for public office, based on 1972 best-seller. Rudd tries but lacks JFK's charisma; Meredith's charm makes up for it as ''Honey Fitz'' Fitzgerald. Average.▼

Johnny Yuma (1966-Spanish-Italian) **C-99m.** ** D: Romolo Guerrieri. Mark Damon, Lawrence Dobkin, Rosalba Neri, Louis Vanner. Blood-drenched story of man fighting for his inheritance.

John Paul Jones (1959) **C-126m.** **½ D: John Farrow. Robert Stack, Marisa Pavan, Charles Coburn, Erin O'Brien, Macdonald Carey, Jean-Pierre Aumont, Peter Cushing, Bruce Cabot, Bette Davis. Empty spectacle of 18th-century American naval hero, with cameo by Davis as Russian empress, Catherine the Great. Look for Mia Farrow (daughter of film's director and Maureen O'Sullivan) in film debut. Technirama.▼

johns (1996) **C-94m.** ** D: Scott Silver. Lukas Haas, David Arquette, Arliss Howard, Keith David, Christopher Gartin, Elliott Gould, Richard Kind, John C. McGinley. Depressing tale of friendship between two hustlers on the L.A. scene, set on the day before Christmas. Gritty and bleak with solid performances by Haas and Arquette, but the subject and tone will remind viewers of the far superior MIDNIGHT COWBOY. [R]▼

Johnstown Flood, The (1926) **70m.** **½ D: Irving Cummings. George O'Brien, Florence Gilbert, Janet Gaynor, Anders Randolf. Silent-era disaster film, and no worse than a lot of newer ones; compactly told, with still-dazzling special effects. Gaynor's first feature-length movie. Look fast for Carole Lombard as a bridesmaid.

Jo Jo Dancer, Your Life Is Calling (1986) **C-97m.** ** D: Richard Pryor. Richard Pryor, Debbie Allen, Art Evans, Fay Hauser, Barbara Williams, Carmen McRae, Paula Kelly, Diahnne Abbott, Scoey Mitchell, Billy Eckstine, Wings Hauser, E'lon Cox, Virginia Capers, Dennis Farina. Pryor examines his life, with the help of an alter-ego character; largely autobiographical film only sparks when chronicling the comedian's early life and first show-biz encounters. From there it's downhill: jumbled, at arm's-length, and boring. Pryor's directorial debut, if you don't count an earlier concert film (he also coscripted and produced). Super 35. [R]▼●

Joke of Destiny, A (1983-Italian) **C-105m.** *½ D: Lina Wertmuller. Ugo Tognazzi, Piera Degli Esposti, Gastone Moschin, Renzo Montagnani, Valeria Golino. A high government official is accidentally locked in his computer-controlled limousine, and his dilemma is dealt with as if it's a national crisis. Loud, overwrought satire has a couple of laughs but will either put you to sleep or give you a headache. Full title: A JOKE OF DESTINY, LYING IN WAIT AROUND THE CORNER LIKE A BANDIT. [PG]▼

Joker Is Wild, The (1957) **126m.** *** D: Charles Vidor. Frank Sinatra, Mitzi Gaynor, Jeanne Crain, Eddie Albert, Beverly Garland, Jackie Coogan, Sophie Tucker. Sinatra is fine in biography of nightclub performer Joe E. Lewis, with Crain and Gaynor diverting as his two loves. Cahn and Van Heusen song "All the Way" won an Oscar; in fact, the film was reissued as ALL THE WAY. VistaVision.
Jokers, The (1966-British) **C-94m.** *** D: Michael Winner. Michael Crawford, Oliver Reed, Gabriella Licudi, Harry Andrews, James Donald, Daniel Massey, Michael Hordern, Frank Finlay, Rachel Kempson, Edward Fox. Droll satire on the Establishment with Reed and Crawford two brothers from upper classes, putting everyone on and carrying out perfect caper; ironic results.
Jolly Bad Fellow, A (1964-British) **94m.** ** D: Don Chaffey. Leo McKern, Janet Munro, Maxine Audley, Duncan MacRae. Peculiar yarn of college professor who plays God by trying to kill those people whom he feels are evil parasites; strange blend of drama-satire. Retitled: THEY ALL DIED LAUGHING.
Jolson Sings Again (1949) **C-96m.** **½ D: Henry Levin. Larry Parks, Barbara Hale, William Demarest, Ludwig Donath, Tamara Shayne. Attempt to continue THE JOLSON STORY only partially succeeds, and is a curio at best . . . especially when Parks (playing Jolson) meets Parks (playing Parks). Jolson standards ("Baby Face," "Sonny Boy," "Back In Your Own Back Yard," and many others) are still great. ▼●
Jolson Story, The (1946) **C-128m.** ***½ D: Alfred E. Green. Larry Parks, Evelyn Keyes, William Demarest, Bill Goodwin, Ludwig Donath, Tamara Shayne. Hokey but very entertaining biography of all-time great Al Jolson, with Parks giving his all in story of brash vaudeville performer's rise in the show biz world. Songs: "April Showers," "Avalon," "You Made Me Love You," "My Mammy" plus many others, all dubbed by Jolson; that's the real Jolson in long shot on the runway during the "Swanee" sequence. Morris Stoloff earned an Oscar for his scoring. Sequel: JOLSON SINGS AGAIN.▼●
Jonah Who Will Be 25 in the Year 2000 (1976-Swiss) **C-115m.** ***½ D: Alain Tanner. Myriam Boyer, Jean-Luc Bideau, Miou-Miou, Roger Jendly, Jacques Denis. Sensitive, literate, engaging comedy about eight individuals affected by the political events of the late '60s. Miou-Miou is lovely as supermarket clerk with no qualms about liberating groceries. A companion to Tanner's later NO MAN'S LAND (1985). ▼
Jonathan Livingston Seagull (1973) **C-120m.** **½ D: Hall Bartlett. Voices of James Franciscus, Juliet Mills, Hal Holbrook, Kelly Harmon, Dorothy McGuire, Richard Crenna. Unique film based on Richard Bach's best-seller about an existential seagull. Superb photography allows us to take bird's point of view as he forsakes his flock to explore wonders of flying. Dialogue doesn't work nearly as well, nor does Neil Diamond's overbearing score. Panavision. [G]▼
Joni (1980) **C-108m.** **½ D: James F. Collier. Joni Eareckson, Bert Remsen, Katherine De Hetre, Cooper Huckabee, John Milford, Michael Mancini, Richard Lineback. Earnest account of Eareckson's actual struggle to rebuild her life and find religion after breaking her spine in a diving mishap. Based on a book by Eareckson; financed by Billy Graham. [G]▼
Jory (1972) **C-96m.** ** D: Jorge Fons. John Marley, B. J. Thomas, Robby Benson, Brad Dexter, Patricia Aspillaga, Linda Purl, Anne Lockhart, Howard Hesseman. Familiar Western about 15-year-old who becomes a man when father and close friends are senselessly murdered. Filmed in Mexico. [PG]▼
Joseph and His Brethren (1962) **C-103m.** ** D: Irving Rapper. Marietto, Geoffrey Horne, Belinda Lee, Finlay Currie, Antonio Segurini, Charles Borromel, Carlo Giustini. Juvenile biblical tale, lavishly produced but empty-headed. Totalscope.▼
Joseph Andrews (1977-British) **C-103m.** ** D: Tony Richardson. Ann-Margret, Peter Firth, Michael Hordern, Beryl Reid, Jim Dale, Natalie Ogle, Peter Bull, Karen Dotrice. Director Richardson returns to Henry Fielding but TOM JONES lightning fails to strike again; well-photographed farce based on concealed identities is dull throughout. [R]▼
Joseph Conrad's The Secret Agent SEE: **Secret Agent, The** (1996)
Josephine Baker Story, The (1991-U.S.-British) **C-130m. TVM** D: Brian Gibson. Lynn Whitfield, Ruben Blades, David Dukes, Louis Gossett, Jr., Craig T. Nelson, Kene Holliday, Vivian Bonnell. Lavish but skin-deep rags-to-riches-to-rags tale of the black girl from St. Louis who became the legendary toast of Paree in the '20s and '30s but still faced unrelenting racism in America. Baker's famed nearly nude "Banana Dance" is faithfully recreated, but will likely hinder commercial TV showings. Filmed on location entirely in Budapest(!) Made for cable. Average. ▼●
Josette (1938) **73m.** *½ D: Allan Dwan. Don Ameche, Simone Simon, Robert Young, Bert Lahr, Joan Davis, Tala Birell, Paul Hust, William Collier, Sr., Lynn Bari, William Demarest. Idiotic romance about two very different brothers (Ameche and Young); they become involved with virtuous Simon, who's been forced to imperson-

ate a famous chanteuse. Lahr and Davis are wasted. Among the forgettable songs: "May I Drop a Petal in Your Glass of Wine."
Josh and S.A.M. (1993) **C-98m.** ** D: Billy Weber. Jacob Tierney, Noah Fleiss, Martha Plimpton, Stephen Tobolowsky, Joan Allen, Chris Penn, Maury Chaykin, Udo Kier, Allan Arbus, Amy Wright. Odd, unsatisfying road movie about a pair of emotionally put-upon brothers, the offspring of otherwise occupied (as well as divorced) parents, who end up stealing a car and picking up hitchhiker Plimpton. The scenario strains credibility, if only because the boys are aged 12 and 7. There's the germ of an engaging film here, but the result is just too silly. [PG-13]▼●
Joshua (1976) **C-75m.** *½ D: Larry Spangler. Fred Williamson, Isela Vega, Brenda Venus, Stacy Newton, Kathryn Jackson. Modest Western of Williamson patiently tracking down and killing one by one the bandits who murdered his mother, maid to a frontier family. Embarrassing, cynical script by Williamson insults the audience; Mexican superstar Vega is wasted. Originally titled: THE BLACK RIDER. [PG—reedited from original R rating]▼
Joshua Then and Now (1985-Canadian) **C-118m.** *** D: Ted Kotcheff. James Woods, Gabrielle Lazure, Alan Arkin, Michael Sarrazin, Linda Sorenson, Alan Scarfe, Alexander Knox, Robert Joy. Unorthodox life and times of a Jewish writer in Canada whose father was a small-time gangster and who marries into a politically and socially prominent WASP family. Uneven but entertaining comedy-drama, based on Mordecai Richler's semiautobiographical novel; Woods is fine in one of his first leading-man roles, Arkin terrific as his colorful dad. If story seems abrupt at times, it's because this was shot as a TV miniseries and cut to feature length. [R]▼
Jour de Fete (1949-French) **70m.** ***½ D: Jacques Tati. Jacques Tati, Guy Decomble, Paul Frankeur, Santa Relli, Maine Vallee, Roger Rafal. In this exquisite feature-film directorial debut French comedian/mime Tati plays a postman whose attempts to modernize delivery link up a series of delightful gags built around a small town's Bastille Day celebration. Tati's cleverness and timing make him one of the most accomplished cinematic comedians since Buster Keaton. Originally filmed in color, but released in black & white with color tinting. Restored to its original color version in 1997. Some prints run 87m. Aka THE BIG DAY.▼●
Journey, The (1959) **C-125m.** *** D: Anatole Litvak. Deborah Kerr, Yul Brynner, Jason Robards, Jr., Robert Morley, E. G. Marshall, Anne Jackson, Ronny Howard, Kurt Kasznar, Anouk Aimée. Heady melodrama set in 1956 Budapest, with assorted types seeking to leave. Offbeat romance between Kerr and Communist officer Brynner. Film debuts of Robards and Howard.
Journey (1972-Canadian) **C-87m.** BOMB D: Paul Almond. Genevieve Bujold, John Vernon, Gale Garnett, George Sperdakos, Elton Hayes.Young woman, saved from drowning by head of wilderness commune, believes that she brings bad luck to everyone with whom she comes in contact. Including the people who made this film. Heavy going. [PG]▼
Journey (1995) **C-100m. TVM** D: Tom McLoughlin. Jason Robards, Brenda Fricker, Meg Tilly, Max Pomeranc, Eliza Dushku. Touching tale of an 11-year-old named Journey who is dumped with his slightly older sister by their uncaring single mom on their grandparents' doorstep. Journey then tries desperately to reassemble the family. Beautifully acted (especially by Robards and young Pomeranc) and adapted by Patricia MacLachlan from her novel. Glenn Close was one of the executive producers. Above average.▼●
Journey Back to Oz (1974) **C-90m.** **½ D: Hal Sutherland. Voices of Liza Minnelli, Milton Berle, Margaret Hamilton, Jack E. Leonard, Paul Lynde, Ethel Merman, Mickey Rooney, Rise Stevens, Danny Thomas, Mel Blanc. Long-delayed (made in 1964) animated sequel without the Wizard. Okay for the kids; main interest for grownups is familiar voices, including Minnelli in her late mother's role. [G]▼
Journey Beneath the Desert (1961-French-Italian) **C-105m.** **½ D: Edgar G. Ulmer. Haya Harareet, Jean-Louis Trintignant, Rad Fulton, Amedeo Nazzari, Georges Riviere, Giulia Rubini, Gabriele Tinti, Gian Maria Volonte. Enjoyable hokum in which three mining engineers find themselves trapped in the Lost City of Atlantis, located beneath the Sahara desert (as well as smack dab in the middle of a nuclear testing site). Aka L'ATLANTIDE. Previously filmed in 1921, 1932, and 1948 (as SIREN OF ATLANTIS). Technirama. ▼
Journey for Margaret (1942) **81m.** *** D: W. S. Van Dyke II. Robert Young, Laraine Day, Fay Bainter, Nigel Bruce, Margaret O'Brien, William Severn. Stirring WW2 drama of children left homeless by British bombing. O'Brien is very appealing scene-stealer, Young her adopted father.▼
Journey Into Autumn SEE: **Dreams** (1955)
Journey Into Fear (1942) **69m.** *** D: Norman Foster. Orson Welles, Joseph Cotten, Dolores Del Rio, Ruth Warrick, Agnes Moorehead, Everett Sloane, Jack Moss, Hans Conried. Often baffling WW2 spy drama started by Welles, taken out of his hands. Much of tale of smuggling munitions into Turkey still exciting. Cotten

and Welles scripted this adaptation of the Eric Ambler novel. Remade in 1975. Also shown in computer-colored version.▼●

Journey Into Fear (1975-Canadian) **C-103m.** ** D: Daniel Mann. Sam Waterston, Zero Mostel, Yvette Mimieux, Scott Marlowe, Ian McShane, Joseph Wiseman, Shelley Winters, Stanley Holloway, Donald Pleasence, Vincent Price. Muddled remake of 1942 film, shot throughout Europe, with Waterston as research geologist involved in international intrigue. [R]▼

Journey Into Light (1951) **87m.** **½ D: Stuart Heisler. Sterling Hayden, Viveca Lindfors, Thomas Mitchell, H. B. Warner, Ludwig Donath. Thought-provoking theme, poorly paced; Hayden is clergyman who finds his belief in God again with aid of blind Lindfors.

Journey of August King, The (1995) **C-95m.** *** D: John Duigan. Jason Patric, Thandie Newton, Larry Drake, Sam Waterston, Sara-Jane Wylde, Eric Mabius. Troubled, widowed farmer August King (Patric) comes to the assistance of Annalees Williamsburg (Newton), a vulnerable young slave who has run away from her master in 1815 North Carolina. Contemplative and civilized tale, beautifully filmed and richly humanistic. Waterston (cast as a landowner) also coproduced. Scripted by John Ehle, based on his novel. [PG-13]▼●

Journey of Hope (1990-Swiss) **C-110m.** ***½ D: Xavier Koller. Necmettin Cobanoglu, Nur Surer, Emin Sivas, Erdinc Akbas, Yaman Okay. Heartbreaking, based-on-fact account of what happens when a poor Turkish couple and their young son set off for Switzerland, in the hope of finding a better life. This could have wallowed in sentiment and clichés, but director-coscripter Koller consistently keeps it on the right emotional track. Deserving Best Foreign Film Academy Award-winner packs a real wallop.▼●

Journey of Natty Gann, The (1985) **C-101m.** *** D: Jeremy Kagan. Meredith Salenger, John Cusack, Ray Wise, Lainie Kazan, Barry Miller, Scatman Crothers, Verna Bloom, Bruce M. Fischer. Girl travels cross-country during the hardest days of the Depression, in order to be with her father; along the way she acquires an unlikely companion and protector—a wolf. Low-key but entertaining Disney film travels smoothly to expected conclusion. Rich 1930s atmosphere helps a lot, and the wolf (actually played by a dog!) is great. Widescreen. [PG]▼●

Journey of Robert F. Kennedy SEE: **Unfinished Journey of Robert F. Kennedy, The**

Journey Through Rosebud (1972) **C-93m.** **½ D: Tom Gries. Robert Forster, Kristoffer Tabori, Victoria Racimo, Eddie Little Sky, Roy Jenson, Wright King. Sympathetic but dully directed drama about the modern-day Indian's plight. Location footage in South Dakota helps. Panavision. [PG]▼

Journey Through the Past (1972) **C-78m.** *½ D: Bernard Shakey (Neil Young). Crosby, Stills, Nash and Young, Buffalo Springfield, Carrie Snodgress, Jack Nitzsche. Overblown, phony, pseudo-hip home movie centering on rock superstar Young. [R]

Journey to Freedom (1957) **60m.** *½ D: Robert C. Dertano. Jacques Scott, Genevieve Aumont, Morgan Lane, Fred Kohler, Don Marlowe, Tor Johnson. Lukewarm spy hunt, with Communist agents tracking down pro-American refugee now in the U.S.▼

Journey Together (1945-British) **95m.** **½ D: John Boulting. Richard Attenborough, Jack Watling, Edward G. Robinson, Bessie Love, David Tomlinson, John Justin, George Cole, Ronald Squire, Hugh Wakefield, Sebastian Shaw. Documentary-like chronicle of wannabe R.A.F. pilots Attenborough and Watling, and their training in England and the U.S. during WW2. Robinson is on hand in a supporting role as one of the flight instructors. Most of those involved with the film's production were then R.A.F. members. Boulting also scripted, based on a story by Terence Rattigan.▼

Journey to Italy SEE: **Strangers** (1953)

Journey to Shiloh (1968) **C-101m.** *½ D: William Hale. James Caan, Michael Sarrazin, Brenda Scott, Don Stroud, Paul Petersen, Harrison Ford. Limp Civil War programmer about young Texans anxious to engage in battle. Veterans Rex Ingram, John Doucette, and Noah Beery are lost in this jumble. Techniscope.

Journey to the Beginning of the World SEE: **Voyage to the Beginning of the World**

Journey to the Center of the Earth (1959) **C-132m.** *** D: Henry Levin. James Mason, Pat Boone, Arlene Dahl, Diane Baker, Thayer David, Alan Napier. Entertaining, old-fashioned fantasy-adventure, from Jules Verne's story of daring expedition headed by Mason; long in telling, with silly digressions, but generally fun. Remade for TV in 1999, and as WHERE TIME BEGAN. Best enjoyed in CinemaScope. ▼●◗

Journey to the Center of Time (1967) **C-82m.** *½ D: D. L. Hewitt. Scott Brady, Gigi Perreau, Anthony Eisley, Abraham Sofaer, Poupee Gamin, Lyle Waggoner. Very cheap sci-fi time travel adventure to future and past, using plot elements from earlier THE TIME TRAVELERS. Aka TIME WARP. ▼◗

Journey to the Far Side of the Sun (1969-British) **C-99m.** *** D: Robert Parrish. Roy Thinnes, Lynn Loring, Herbert Lom, Patrick Wymark. Entertaining exploration of planet hidden behind the sun. The ending makes the movie. Originally titled DOPPELGANGER. [G]▼●◗

Journey to the Lost City SEE: **Indian Tomb, The** and **Tiger of Eschnapur**

Journey to the Seventh Planet (1961-Danish) **C-83m.** *½ D: Sidney Pink. John Agar, Greta Thyssen, Ann Smyrner, Mimi Heinrich, Carl Ottosen. In year 2001, expedition to Uranus discovers hostile alien brain that can turn thoughts into reality. Cheap, clumsy, dull, with just a smidge of imagination. ▼●

Joy House (1964-French) **98m.** **½ D: René Clement. Jane Fonda, Alain Delon, Lola Albright, Sorrell Booke. Living on his looks, a playboy on the run seeks refuge in gloomy French mansion run by two American women. Fate and quicker wits than his control this brooding tale of irony. Aka THE LOVE CAGE. Franscope.▼

Joy in the Morning (1965) **C-103m.** ** D: Alex Segal. Richard Chamberlain, Yvette Mimieux, Arthur Kennedy, Sidney Blackmer. Betty Smith's gentle novel of struggling law student and his marital problems becomes mild vehicle for Chamberlain, who crusades for human dignity amid stereotypes of a college town.

Joyless Street, The (1925-German) **96m.** *** D: G.W. Pabst. Asta Nielsen, Greta Garbo, Werner Krauss, Valeska Gert, Jaro Furth, Agnes Esterhazy, Einar Hanson. Fascinating, expressionistic account of economic and moral decay, focusing on the inhabitants of one sorry Viennese street after WW1. Garbo, in her third feature, plays a professor's daughter who attempts to keep her family from starving. Many varied versions of this oft-edited title exist. Aka THE STREET OF SORROW. ▼●

Joy Luck Club, The (1993) **C-135m.** *** D: Wayne Wang. Kieu Chinh, Tsai Chin, France Nuyen, Lisa Lu, Ming-Na Wen, Tamlyn Tomita, Lauren Tom, Rosalind Chao, Andrew McCarthy, Diane Baker, Chao-Li Chi, Melanie Chang, Victor Wong, Lisa Connolly, Vu Mai, Ying Wu, Mei Juan Xi, Irene Ng. Rich tapestry of eight stories; the incredible saga of four women who survived—and prevailed—against all odds in China, and their assimilated American daughters, whose troubles seem almost trivial by comparison. Starts losing its grip in the penultimate sequence, but soars again for a powerhouse finale that will have you reaching for a crying towel. Screenplay by Amy Tan and Ronald Bass, from Tan's best-selling novel. [R]▼●

Joy of Living (1938) **90m.** *** D: Tay Garnett. Irene Dunne, Douglas Fairbanks, Jr., Alice Brady, Guy Kibbee, Jean Dixon, Eric Blore, Lucille Ball. Delightful screwball musicomedy with gay-blade Fairbanks wooing singing star Dunne.▼●

Joy of Loving SEE: **School for Love**

Joy of Sex (1984) **C-93m.** BOMB D: Martha Coolidge. Michelle Meyrink, Cameron Dye, Lisa Langlois, Charles Van Eman, Christopher Lloyd, Colleen Camp, Ernie Hudson. Virgin Meyrink, believing she has weeks to live, decides to "do it all" before she dies. Nothing of Alex Comfort's book—including his name—is left (and despite the title, no one seems to be having a good time) in embarrassingly bad high-school comedy. [R]▼

Joy Ride (1958) **60m.** *½ D: Edward Bernds. Rad Fulton, Ann Doran, Regis Toomey, Nicholas King, Robert Levin. Minor account of middle-aged man trying to reform hot-rod gang members; occasionally bristling.

Joyride (1977) **C-92m.** ** D: Joseph Ruben. Desi Arnaz, Jr., Robert Carradine, Melanie Griffith, Anne Lockhart, Tom Ligon, Cliff Lenz. Meandering tale of two young-and-footloose couples on the road to Alaska looking for adventure but drifting into crime. Four show-biz offspring play the leads: the sons of Desi Arnaz (and Lucy) and John Carradine, the daughters of Tippi Hedren and June Lockhart. [R]▼

Joysticks (1983) **C-88m.** BOMB D: Greydon Clark. Joe Don Baker, Leif Green, Jim Greenleaf, Scott McGinnis, Logan Ramsey. Loud, inane ode to video games, with meanie Baker (looking as if he just spent a week on skid row) attempting to shut down video arcade populated by requisite Lolitas, nerds, slobs, punks, etc. Original title: VIDEO MADNESS. [R]▼●

J. R. SEE: **Who's That Knocking at My Door**

Juarez (1939) **132m.** *** D: William Dieterle. Paul Muni, Bette Davis, Brian Aherne, Claude Rains, John Garfield, Gale Sondergaard, Donald Crisp, Gilbert Roland, Louis Calhern, Grant Mitchell. Interesting biography of Mexican leader (Muni), with unforgettable performance by Rains as Napoleon III; also notable is Garfield's offbeat casting as Mexican General Diaz. Elaborately done, but never as inspiring as it's intended to be.▼

Jubal (1956) **C-101m.** *** D: Delmer Daves. Glenn Ford, Ernest Borgnine, Rod Steiger, Valerie French, Felicia Farr, Noah Beery, Jr., Charles Bronson. It's Bard in the Saddle with this Western OTHELLO: when jealous rancher Borgnine seeks some lovemaking advice from cowhand Ford, along comes Steiger hinting that Ford's giving Borgnine's wife (French) a few "lessons" as well. Brooding, intense drama is pretty good on its own terms, more intriguing if you know the original. CinemaScope.▼●

Jubilee Trail (1954) **C-103m.** **½ D: Joseph Kane. Vera Ralston, Joan Leslie, Forrest Tucker, John Russell, Ray Middleton, Pat O'Brien. Expansive Republic Western vehicle for Ralston as heart-of-gold chanteuse sorting out rancher's life in old California.▼

Judas Kiss (1999) **C-97m.** *** D: Sebastian Gutierrez. Carla Gugino, Hal Holbrook, Emma Thompson, Alan Rickman, Roscoe Lee Browne, Lisa Eichhorn, Greg Wise, Philip Baker Hall, Gil Bellows. Young New Orleans pick-up gang kidnaps an important official of a computer company for a big ransom payoff—but there's more to this caper than first meets the eye. Sexy Gugino (who also coproduced the film) sparks a good cast, but the real treat is watching Thompson and Rickman drawling together as Southern investigators (one Federal, one local) on the case. Written by the director. Made for theaters; debuted on cable. Panavision. [R]▼

Judas Was a Woman SEE: **La Bête Humaine**

Jude (1996-British) **C-123m.** ** D: Michael Winterbottom. Christopher Eccleston, Kate Winslet, Rachel Griffiths, Liam Cunningham, June Whitfield, Ross Colvin Turnbull. Dour, generally uninvolving adaptation of Thomas Hardy's final novel, *Jude the Obscure,* about an unschooled but intellectually ambitious 19th-century stonemason who endures a lifetime of smashed dreams. The early going wobbily telescopes many of the book's events into the opening half hour; the movie then gets a desperately needed shot in the arm when Winslet (terrific) shows up as the cousin, lover, and academic rebel trying to exist in a society that systematically crushes rebels. Panavision. [R]▼●

Judge, The (1949) **69m.** ** D: Elmer Clifton. Milburn Stone, Katherine de Mille, Paul Guilfoyle, Stanley Waxman, Norman Budd, Jonathan Hale, John Hamilton. Well-intentioned but muddled low-budget melodrama chronicling the fate of Stone, a clever criminal attorney who gets his clients off on legal technicalities. Dreadful musical accompaniment is no help.▼

Judge and Jake Wyler, The (1972) **C-100m. TVM** D: David Lowell Rich. Bette Davis, Doug McClure, Eric Braeden, James McEachin, Kent Smith, Joan Van Ark. Tolerable whodunit with sense of humor. Eccentric judge (Davis) takes on parolee as detective partner in new agency investigating suspicious death of business-man. For TV, good banter, convincing situations. Produced and cowritten by Richard Levinson and William Link. Above average.

Judge and the Assassin, The (1975-French) **C-121m.** ***½ D: Bertrand Tavernier. Philippe Noiret, Michel Galabru, Isabelle Huppert, Jean-Claude Brialy, Renee Faure. In a way, the title tells all in this incisive, expertly directed and acted drama: Judge Noiret must determine whether murderer Galabru is insane or faking. Fascinating from start to finish. Panavision.▼●

Judge Dredd (1995) **C-96m.** ** D: Danny Cannon. Sylvester Stallone, Armand Assante, Diane Lane, Rob Schneider, Joan Chen, Jürgen Prochnow, Max von Sydow, Balthazar Getty, Joanna Miles, Mitchell Ryan. Loud, ugly adaptation of the comic book set in a future world of urban chaos where new-age police are empowered to "judge"—and kill, if need be—on the spot. Judge Dredd (Stallone) is caught in a conspiracy much bigger and more insidious than he realizes. Some interesting plotting is lost in a sea of hard-edged violence, video game–like special effects, and overripe acting. James Earl Jones reads opening narration; James Russo and Scott Wilson appear unbilled. Panavision. [R] ▼●◗

Judge Hardy and Son (1939) **95m.** **½ D: George B. Seitz. Lewis Stone, Mickey Rooney, Cecilia Parker, Fay Holden, Sara Haden, Ann Rutherford, Maria Ouspenskaya, June Preisser, Martha O'Driscoll. Rather somber Andy Hardy series entry, as the Judge tries to help an elderly couple threatened with eviction while dealing with the personal problems of his wife's illness.

Judge Hardy's Children (1938) **78m.** **½ D: George B. Seitz. Lewis Stone, Mickey Rooney, Cecilia Parker, Fay Holden, Ann Rutherford, Betty Ross Clark, Ruth Hussey. The good Judge has duties in Washington, D.C., where Andy falls for a French diplomat's daughter. Average Andy Hardy entry.

Judgement in Stone, A (1986-Canadian) **C-102m.** *½ D: Ousama Rawi. Rita Tushingham, Ross Petty, Tom Kneebone, Shelley Peterson, Jessica Stern, Jonathan Crombie, Jackie Burroughs. Tushingham is well cast in this otherwise tiresome, drawn-out chiller as a repressed, illiterate, and psychotic spinster who takes a job as a housemaid with tragic results. Aka THE HOUSEKEEPER. Remade in France as LA CÉRÉMONIE. [R] ▼●

Judge Priest (1934) **80m.** ***½ D: John Ford. Will Rogers, Tom Brown, Anita Louise, Henry B. Walthall, Stepin Fetchit, Hattie McDaniel. Exceptional slice of Americana with Rogers as commonsensical yet controversial judge in small town; full of warm and funny character vignettes, including Walthall's stirring courtroom scene. Ford remade it in 1953 as THE SUN SHINES BRIGHT.▼

Judge Steps Out, The (1949) **91m.** **½ D: Boris Ingster. Alexander Knox, Ann Sothern, George Tobias, Sharyn Moffett. Judge Knox runs away from his job and shrewish wife, hides out as a short-order cook, falls in love with Sothern. Cowritten by Alexander Knox and Boris Ingster.▼

Judgment (1990) **C-90m. TVM** D: Tom Topor. Keith Carradine, Blythe Danner,

Jack Warden, David Strathairn, Bob Gunton, Mitchell Ryan, Michael Faustino. Tense, based-on-fact drama by director Topor about deeply religious parents who confront the church when they suspect their young son is being molested by the popular new priest. Fine performances all around, especially Warden's Darrow-like attorney. Made for cable. Above average.▼

Judgment at Nuremberg (1961) **178m.** **** D: Stanley Kramer. Spencer Tracy, Burt Lancaster, Richard Widmark, Marlene Dietrich, Judy Garland, Maximilian Schell, Montgomery Clift, William Shatner. Superior production revolving around U.S. judge Tracy presiding over German war-criminal trials. Schell won Oscar as defense attorney, as did Abby Mann for his screenplay. Fine performances by Dietrich as widow of German officer, Garland as hausfrau, Clift as unbalanced victim of Nazi atrocities.▼●

Judgment in Berlin (1988) **C-92m.** ** D: Leo Penn. Martin Sheen, Sam Wanamaker, Sean Penn, Max Gail, Juerger Hemrich, Carl Lumbly, Max Volkert Martens. U.S. judge Sheen, thrown into one of those Spencer Tracy/Nuremberg situations, has to determine if the hijacking of an East German jet into Berlin is justified. Ragged but *just* watchable, with actor Penn (the director's son) turning in one unexpectedly heartfelt cameo during some climactic courtroom testimony. Shown on TV as ESCAPE TO FREEDOM. [PG]▼●

Judgment Night (1993) **C-109m.** **½ D: Stephen Hopkins. Emilio Estevez, Cuba Gooding, Jr., Denis Leary, Stephen Dorff, Jeremy Piven, Peter Greene. Sporadically tense, competently directed programmer about four suburban buddies who end up being chased through tenements and sewers after driving their fancy RV over a shooting victim in a very tough part of Chicago. Ultimately done in by standard genre clichés, but surprisingly absorbing in the early going. Leary is a standout as the chief heavy. Super 35. [R]▼●◗

Judith (1966) **C-109m.** BOMB D: Daniel Mann. Sophia Loren, Peter Finch, Jack Hawkins, Hans Verner, Zharira Charifai. Austrian Jewess Loren survives prison camp with makeup intact, comes to Israel in 1948 to locate Nazi husband who betrayed her. Film is both dull and unbelievable, a bad combination. Video title: CONFLICT. Panavision.▼

Ju Dou (1989-Chinese-Japanese) **C-95m.** ***½ D: Zhang Yimou. Gong Li, Li Wei, Li Bao-Tian, Zhang Yi, Zhen Ji-an. Striking, visually magnificent drama, set during the 1920s, telling the tragic story of a young peasant woman who's forced to wed an elderly, bitter factory owner, and commences an affair with his nephew. This was banned in China, supposedly because of its focus on individual values and unflattering depiction of the old man (in a nation ruled by a small elite group of old men); also the authorities supposedly feared that audiences would see it as a metaphor for the way China's leaders control society. First Chinese film ever to earn a Best Foreign Film Academy Award nomination—and those responsible for entering it in the competition were disciplined by their superiors. Controversy aside, a powerful, provocative film. ▼●◗

Judy Berlin (2000) **96m.** *** D: Eric Mendelsohn. Barbara Barrie, Bob Dishy, Edie Falco, Carlin Glynn, Aaron Harnick, Bette Henritze, Madeline Kahn, Julie Kavner, Anne Meara, Novella Nelson. Cross-section of residents of Long Island town dream of happiness while facing bleak reality—and a lingering solar eclipse. Original, often eloquent (if slow-paced) statement on contemporary life and love, depicted by top-notch cast of N.Y. actors, including Kahn in her final film. Writer-director Mendelsohn's feature directing debut. ▼

Juggernaut (1974-British) **C-109m.** *** D: Richard Lester. Richard Harris, Omar Sharif, David Hemmings, Anthony Hopkins, Shirley Knight, Ian Holm, Roy Kinnear, Freddie Jones. Surprisingly effective thriller about bomb threat on luxury ocean liner, and demolition experts' attempts to avoid disaster. Harris is first-rate and so is Lester's direction of a formula story. [PG]▼

Juggler, The (1953) **86m.** **½ D: Edward Dmytryk. Kirk Douglas, Milly Vitale, Paul Stewart, Alf Kjellin, Beverly Washburn. Sentimental account of Jewish refugee Douglas going to Israel to rebuild his life, overcoming bitterness from life in a concentration camp. Filmed in Israel.

Juice (1992) **C-92m.** ** D: Ernest R. Dickerson. Omar Epps, Jermaine Hopkins, Tupac Shakur, Khalil Kain, Cindy Herron, Vincent Laresca, Samuel L. Jackson. Impressively shot but overly contrived (and extremely violent) tale of four black teenage friends whose lives take a tragic turn when a store robbery goes out of control. Promising directorial debut for Spike Lee's talented cinematographer. Costar Herron (from the group En Vogue), Queen Latifah, and other rap stars appear, and perform on the soundtrack. [R]▼●

Juke Box Rhythm (1959) **81m.** *½ D: Arthur Dreifuss. Jo Morrow, Jack Jones, Brian Donlevy, George Jessel, Hans Conried, Karin Booth, Marjorie Reynolds, Fritz Feld, Johnny Otis, The Treniers, The Earl Grant Trio. Perfectly awful minor musical focusing on various schemes of clean-cut young singer Jones. However, Otis does sing ''Willie and the Hand Jive.''

Juke Girl (1942) **90m.** **½ D: Curtis

Bernhardt. Ann Sheridan, Ronald Reagan, Richard Whorf, Gene Lockhart, Betty Brewer, Faye Emerson, George Tobias, Alan Hale, Howard da Silva, Donald MacBride, William B. Davidson, Fuzzy Knight, Willie Best. Exploitation of farmers is the subject of this robust Warner Bros. film, which is spoiled by typecasting of the bad guys and a melodramatic script that veers way off-course. It does provide Reagan with one of his most interesting parts, however, as an itinerant worker who becomes a farmers' rights activist(!), battling for underdog Tobias against fat-cat Lockhart.

Jules and Jim (1961-French) **104m.** **** D: François Truffaut. Jeanne Moreau, Oskar Werner, Henri Serre, Marie Dubois, Vanna Urbino. Truffaut's memorable tale of three people in love, and how the years affect their interrelationships. A film of rare beauty and charm. Screenplay by Truffaut and Jean Gruault, based on novel by Henri-Pierre Roché. Americanized by Paul Mazursky in WILLIE AND PHIL. Franscope.▼●

Julia (1977) **C-118m.** **** D: Fred Zinnemann. Jane Fonda, Vanessa Redgrave, Jason Robards, Maximilian Schell, Hal Holbrook, Rosemary Murphy, Meryl Streep, Lisa Pelikan, Cathleen Nesbitt, John Glover. Fonda plays Lillian Hellman in adaptation of author's story in *Pentimento* about her exuberant, unusual friend Julia, and how she drew Hellman into involvement with European resistance movement in 1930s. Fine storytelling in beautifully crafted film; Robards (as Dashiell Hammett), screenwriter Alvin Sargent, and radiant Redgrave won Oscars. Streep's feature debut. [PG]▼●

Julia and Julia (1987-Italian) **C-97m.** **½ D: Peter Del Monte. Kathleen Turner, Gabriel Byrne, Sting, Gabriele Ferzetti, Angela Goodwin. Turner is compelling as a woman whose life splits in two, leaving her caught between a happily married existence with Byrne and a dangerous affair with photographer Sting. Intriguing, well-acted psychological thriller that unfortunately leads nowhere. Handsomely photographed by Giuseppe Rotunno, this theatrical release was made on high-definition video, then transferred to film. [R]▼●

Julia Has Two Lovers (1991) **C-86m.** **½ D: Bashar Shbib. Daphna Kastner, David Duchovny, David Charles, Tim Ray, Clare Bancroft, Martin Donovan. Children's author, who's "involved" with a man but convinced she can do better, develops a fantasy relationship with a telephone wrong number, who ends up engaging her in mutually stimulating chats. Cheaply made, unevenly acted, but solid-enough premise keeps you engrossed to the end. [R]▼

Julia Misbehaves (1948) **99m.** *** D: Jack Conway. Greer Garson, Walter Pidgeon, Peter Lawford, Elizabeth Taylor, Cesar Romero, Mary Boland, Nigel Bruce. Bouncy account of showgirl Garson returning to dignified husband Pidgeon when daughter Taylor is about to marry; Romero is fun as bragging acrobat. Stars seem right at home with slapstick situations.▼

Julie (1956) **99m.** ** D: Andrew L. Stone. Doris Day, Louis Jourdan, Barry Sullivan, Frank Lovejoy, Jack Kelly, Ann Robinson, Jack Kruschen, Mae Marsh. Overbaked soaper in which Day contends with jealous, psychopathic spouse Jourdan, who strangled her first husband and now threatens to kill her. Sometimes tense, but too often unintentionally funny. Also shown in computer-colored version.▼

Julie Darling (1982-Canadian-German) **C-100m.** *½ D: Paul Nicolas, Maurice Smith. Anthony Franciosa, Isabelle Mejias, Sybil Danning, Cindy Girling. Awful thriller, with teenager Mejias plotting to do in stepmom Danning after seeing her own mother raped and murdered. [R]

Julien Donkey-Boy (1999) **C-94m.** *½ D: Harmony Korine. Ewen Bremner, Chloë Sevigny, Werner Herzog, Evan Neumann, Joyce Korine, Chrissy Kobylak, Alvin Law. Korine (of KIDS fame and GUMMO infamy) scripted this disgustingly sordid freak show about a dysfunctional family including a schizophrenic (Bremner), his pregnant sis (Sevigny), and their sadistically cruel father (Herzog). The first American film to utilize the cinematic rules of Dogma 95. [R]▼

Juliet of the Spirits (1965-Italian) **C-148m.** *** D: Federico Fellini. Giulietta Masina, Sandra Milo, Mario Pisu, Valentina Cortese, Lou Gilbert, Sylva Koscina. Surrealistic fantasy triggered by wife's fears that her well-to-do husband is cheating on her. A film requiring viewer to delve into woman's psyche via a rash of symbolism; counterbalanced with rich visual delights.▼●

Julietta (1953-French) **96m.** **½ D: Marc Allegret. Jean Marais, Jeanne Moreau, Dany Robin, Denise Grey, Nicole Berger. Frilly comedy in which pert Robin dallies with handsome Marais—even though he's engaged to wed Moreau.

Julius Caesar (1953) **120m.** ***½ D: Joseph L. Mankiewicz. Marlon Brando, James Mason, John Gielgud, Louis Calhern, Edmond O'Brien, Greer Garson, Deborah Kerr, George Macready, Michael Pate, Alan Napier, Ian Wolfe, Douglass Dumbrille, Edmund Purdom. Superior adaptation of William Shakespeare's play of political power and honor in ancient Rome. Lavishly produced (by John Houseman), with an excellent cast and Oscar-winning art direction-set decoration. Screenplay by director Mankiewicz.▼●

Julius Caesar (1970) **C-117m.** **½ D: Stuart Burge. Charlton Heston, Jason Robards, John Gielgud, Richard Johnson,

Robert Vaughn, Richard Chamberlain, Diana Rigg, Jill Bennett, Christopher Lee, Michael Gough, Andre Morell. Technically ragged, but acceptable version of Shakespeare play, negated somewhat by Robards' zombielike portrayal of Brutus. The 1953 version (also starring Gielgud) is much better. Panavision. [G]▼●

Jumanji (1995) **C-104m.** ** D: Joe Johnston. Robin Williams, Bonnie Hunt, Kirsten Dunst, Bradley Pierce, Bebe Neuwirth, Jonathan Hyde, David Alan Grier, Patricia Clarkson, Adam Hann-Byrd. In 1969 New England, a boy finds a board game buried underground and soon discovers that by playing it a world of terror is unleashed; twenty-six years later, in the same house, two kids start playing the very same game and bring that boy—now a full-grown man—back to life. A phantasmagoria of digital special effects (a virulent vine, a stampede of wild animals, giant attacking mosquitoes, etc.) seems to be this film's raison d'être. Unfortunately, we're all too aware that they *are* special effects. The story doesn't seem to have much of a point, except perhaps that one shouldn't play with ancient board games. Followed by an animated TV series. [PG] ▼●◗

Jumbo SEE: **Billy Rose's Jumbo**

Jumpin at the Boneyard (1992) **C-107m.** *½ D: Jeff Stanzler. Tim Roth, Alexis Arquette, Danitra Vance, Samuel L. Jackson, Kathleen Chalfant, Luis Guzman, Elizabeth Bracco, Jeffrey Wright. Divorced, unemployed Bronx father's further burden: his younger brother, a crack addict he's reunited with after three years. Honorably intentioned but stillborn drama taking place over 24 hours. Thematically and aesthetically for masochists only. [R]▼●

Jumping Jacks (1952) **96m.** **½ D: Norman Taurog. Dean Martin, Jerry Lewis, Mona Freeman, Don DeFore, Robert Strauss. Daffy duo has good opportunity for plenty of sight gags when they join military paratroop squad.▼●

Jumpin' Jack Flash (1986) **C-100m.** *½ D: Penny Marshall. Whoopi Goldberg, Stephen Collins, John Wood, Carol Kane, Annie Potts, Peter Michael Goetz, Roscoe Lee Browne, Sara Botsford, Jeroen Krabbé, Jonathan Pryce, Jon Lovitz, Phil Hartman, Tracy Reiner, Jim Belushi, Paxton Whitehead, Tracey Ullman, Jamey Sheridan. Computer programmer is pulled into international intrigue when spy who wants in from the cold contacts her on her terminal. Lively but stupid star vehicle for Goldberg, who's infinitely better than the script. Feature directing debut for Marshall, who cast her producer-director brother Garry as a police detective, and former TV costar Michael McKean in an unbilled cameo as a British party guest. [R]▼●

Jump Into Hell (1955) **93m.** **½ D: David Butler. Jacques Sernas, Kurt Kasznar, Peter Van Eyck, Pat Blake. Neatly paced actioner of paratroopers involved in Indochina war.

June Bride (1948) **97m.** *** D: Bretaigne Windust. Bette Davis, Robert Montgomery, Fay Bainter, Tom Tully, Barbara Bates, Jerome Cowan, Mary Wickes. Flippant comedy of magazine writers Davis and Montgomery inspired by story they are doing on June brides. Breezy script by Ranald MacDougall. Don't blink or you'll miss Debbie Reynolds in her film debut.▼

June Night (1940-Swedish) **86m.** **½ D: Per Lindberg. Ingrid Bergman, Olof Widgren, Gunnar Sjoberg, Carl Strom, Marianne Lofgren, Lill-Tollie Zellman, Alf Kjellen. Generally fine performances compensate for melodramatic nature of this soaper, detailing the plight of small-town girl Bergman after she becomes involved with sailor Sjoberg. Bergman's final film before coming to Hollywood.▼●◗

Jungle, The (1952) **74m.** *½ D: William Berke. Rod Cameron, Cesar Romero, Marie Windsor, Sulchana. Romantic triangle burdens tale of expedition in India that encounters still living mammoths. Shot on location but still dull and pedestrian.▼

Jungle Book (1942) **C-109m.** *** D: Zoltan Korda. Sabu, Joseph Calleia, John Qualen, Frank Puglia, Rosemary DeCamp, Noble Johnson. Colorful Kipling fantasy of boy (Sabu) raised by wolves. Exciting family fare, fine Miklos Rozsa score. Remade twice (by Disney).▼●◗

Jungle Book, The (1967) **C-78m.** *** D: Wolfgang Reitherman. Voices of Phil Harris, Sebastian Cabot, Louis Prima, George Sanders, Sterling Holloway, J. Pat O'Malley, Verna Felton, Bruce Reitherman. Genial Disney animated feature freely adapted from Rudyard Kipling's stories. Mowgli, the boy raised by wolves, is befriended by a laid-back bear named Baloo (memorably voiced by Harris) who joins him in his jungle adventures. Hand-picked cast of actors help create some vivid characterizations in this easygoing film. Songs include "The Bare Necessities," "I Wanna Be Like You," "Trust in Me." Remade in 1998 as a live-action direct-to-video sequel: THE JUNGLE BOOK: MOWGLI'S STORY. ▼●◗

Jungle Book, The (1994) SEE: **Rudyard Kipling's The Jungle Book**

Jungle Captive (1945) **63m.** BOMB D: Harold Young. Otto Kruger, Amelita Ward, Phil Brown, Vicky Lane, Jerome Cowan, Rondo Hatton. Sloppy sequel to JUNGLE WOMAN deals with yet another mad scientist's attempt to transform ape woman into beautiful girl. Three strikes and you're out.▼

Jungle Cat (1960) **C-70m.** **½ D: James Algar. Narrated by Winston Hibler. One of Disney's weaker True-Life Adventures suffers from script and presentation, not raw material: wildlife footage of the title character, a jaguar, is excellent.▼

Jungle Cavalcade (1941) **76m.** **½ D: Clyde Elliot, Armand Denis, Frank Buck. A compilation film of Buck capturing and caging a zooful of wild animals, edited from his first three features (BRING 'EM BACK ALIVE, WHITE CARGO, FANG AND CLAW). Buck's narration is laughably hokey and self-serving, and his attitude will not endear him to animal rights activists . . . but there's still plenty of exciting footage. ▼

Jungle Fever (1991) **C-132m.** *** D: Spike Lee. Wesley Snipes, Annabella Sciorra, Spike Lee, Ossie Davis, Ruby Dee, Samuel L. Jackson, Lonette McKee, John Turturro, Frank Vincent, Anthony Quinn, Halle Berry, Tyra Ferrell, Veronica Webb, Tim Robbins, Brad Dourif, Debi Mazar, Nicholas Turturro. Engrossing look at a love affair that crosses over racial, ethnic, cultural, and geographic boundary lines, when upwardly-mobile, happily married Snipes has a fling with his new temp secretary Sciorra. Less than perfect, with a drug subplot that throws the film off-kilter toward the end—but still utterly compelling. Lee doesn't have all the answers, but he certainly raises interesting questions. Terrific songs by Stevie Wonder and score by Terence Blanchard, although the music practically drowns out the dialogue in some scenes. What's the point of that? [R]▼●◗

Jungle Fighters SEE: **Long and the Short and the Tall, The**

Jungle Gents (1954) **64m.** ** D: Edward Bernds, Austen Jewell. Leo Gorcey, Huntz Hall, David Gorcey, Bennie Bartlett, Patrick O'Moore, Laurette Luez, Bernard Gorcey, David (Gorcey) Condon, Joel Fluellen, Woody Strode. The Bowery Boys go to Africa in search of diamonds in this low-grade romp, shot on leftover sets from BOMBA, THE JUNGLE BOY. A young Clint Walker, billed as Jett Norman, appears as Tarzan.

Jungle Girl SEE: **Bomba and the Jungle Girl**

Jungle Goddess (1948) **65m.** *½ D: Lewis D. Collins. Ralph Byrd, George Reeves, Wanda McKay, Armida. Very low-budget swamp saga is good only for laughs.

Jungle Heat SEE: **Dance of the Dwarfs**

Jungle Jim When athletic Johnny Weissmuller left the Tarzan series after sixteen years in the role, enterprising producer Sam Katzman proposed a new series that would enable the more mature but still rugged star to cavort in familiar surroundings. It was Jungle Jim, presold to an anxious audience via a successful comic strip and radio show. One critic accurately summed it up as "Tarzan with clothes on." The series was considered sure-fire and performed well at the box office for seven years, despite its almost consistent mediocrity. Aimed primarily at juvenile audiences, most efforts had Jungle Jim helping some Columbia Pictures heroine in distress (a lady scientist seeking a rare drug, a WAC captain lost in the jungle, etc.) and getting tangled up with hostile natives, voodoo curses, and nefarious villains (often all three at once). In the last three films of the series (CANNIBAL ATTACK, JUNGLE MOON MEN, DEVIL GODDESS) the name Jungle Jim was dropped and Weissmuller played himself, but the format remained the same, with Johnny's ever-faithful chimpanzee friend Tamba at his side. Perhaps the highlight of the series was CAPTIVE GIRL, an average entry which had the distinction of Buster Crabbe, whose career paralleled Weissmuller's in many ways, as the villain.

JUNGLE JIM

Jungle Jim (1948)
The Lost Tribe (1949)
Captive Girl (1950)
Mark of the Gorilla (1950)
Pygmy Island (1950)
Fury of the Congo (1951)
Jungle Manhunt (1951)
Jungle Jim in the Forbidden Land (1952)
Voodoo Tiger (1952)
Savage Mutiny (1953)
Killer Ape (1953)
Valley of Head Hunters (1953)
Jungle Man-Eaters (1954)
Cannibal Attack (1954)
Jungle Moon Men (1955)
Devil Goddess (1955)

Jungle Jim (1948) **73m.** ** D: William Berke. Johnny Weissmuller, Virginia Grey, George Reeves, Lita Baron, Rick Vallin, Holmes Herbert. Weissmuller leads a perilous expedition to find a miracle drug, accompanied by scientist Grey and pre-*Superman* Reeves in this initial adventure. Not as bizarre as what would follow.▼

Jungle Jim in the Forbidden Land (1952) **65m.** *½ D: Lew Landers. Johnny Weissmuller, Angela Greene, Jean Willes, Lester Matthews, William Tannen. Weissmuller unwillingly leads an anthropologist to the land of the giant people (with the aid of some cheap stock footage) in this ridiculous entry.

Jungle Man-Eaters (1954) **68m.** *½ D: Lee Sholem. Johnny Weissmuller, Karin Booth, Richard Stapley, Bernard Hamilton, Gregory Gay, Lester Matthews. Jungle Jim vs. diamond smugglers. Ho-hum. Last of the official *Jungle Jim* entries, with Weissmuller using his real name in the final three adventures.

Jungle Manhunt (1951) **66m.** *½ D: Lew Landers. Johnny Weissmuller, Bob Water-

field, Sheila Ryan, Rick Vallin, Lyle Talbot. Real-life gridiron hero Waterfield plays a footballer lost in the jungle, but never fear, *Jungle Jim* Weissmuller is on the case.
Jungle Moon Men (1955) **70m.** *½ D: Charles S. Gould. Johnny Weissmuller, Jean Byron, Helene Stanton, Bill Henry, Myron Healey, Billy Curtis. Enjoyably bad grade-Z ripoff of *She,* about an eternally young high priestess (Stanton).
Jungle Princess, The (1936) **85m.** *** D: William Thiele. Dorothy Lamour, Ray Milland, Akim Tamiroff, Lynne Overman, Molly Lamont, Mala, Hugh Buckler. Lamour's first sarong film is quite unpretentious and pleasant; Milland is explorer who brings her back to civilization.
Jungle 2 Jungle (1997) **C-105m.** *** D: John Pasquin. Tim Allen, Martin Short, JoBeth Williams, Lolita Davidovich, David Ogden Stiers, Bob Dishy, Valerie Mahaffey, Leelee Sobieski. Very likable, if predictable, Disney comedy about a career-obsessed New Yorker who goes to Africa to get final divorce papers signed by his ex-wife and comes back with a son he never knew he had. The boy's jungle instincts are no match for life in Manhattan—though he does manage to score some points along the way. Good laughs throughout this family-oriented feature, a remake of the French hit LITTLE INDIAN, BIG CITY. [PG]▼●
Jungle Warriors (1984-German-Mexican) **C-93m.** *½ D: Ernst R. von Theumer. Nina Van Pallandt, Paul L. Smith, John Vernon, Alex Cord, Sybil Danning, Woody Strode, Dana Elcar, Louisa Moritz, Marjoe Gortner. How's this for a plot: fashion models are taken prisoner by South American drug kingpin and tortured by his kinky half-sister (Danning). Credible cast stuck in sub-par action yarn.▼
Jungle Woman (1944) **60m.** *½ D: Reginald LeBorg. Acquanetta, Evelyn Ankers, J. Carrol Naish, Samuel S. Hinds. Psychiatrist fails to cure killer-ape tendencies of Acquanetta in this sorry sequel to CAPTIVE WILD WOMAN. Tries to emulate the style of Val Lewton's classy horror movies, even eliminates ape-woman makeup (until final shot). Followed by JUNGLE CAPTIVE. ▼
Junior (1994) **C-110m.** **½ D: Ivan Reitman. Arnold Schwarzenegger, Danny DeVito, Emma Thompson, Frank Langella, Pamela Reed, Judy Collins, James Eckhouse, Aida Turturro, Welker White. Pleasant-enough comedy about a straitlaced scientist (Schwarzenegger) who's persuaded by an aggressive colleague (DeVito) to try injecting sperm into his body and becoming pregnant. Unexpected result: he doesn't want to give up his baby! This "politically correct farce" boasts enthusiastic performances from its three stars, and precious few laughs after the initial "joke" is presented. Instead, Arnold becomes a better man by experiencing childbearing like a woman. Sheesh. [PG-13]▼●◗
Junior Bonner (1972) **C-103m.** ***½ D: Sam Peckinpah. Steve McQueen, Robert Preston, Ida Lupino, Ben Johnson, Joe Don Baker, Barbara Leigh, Mary Murphy. Totally captivating rodeo comedy-drama as an aging McQueen returns to his home and family to take part in a local contest. Peckinpah's most gentle film is full of natural performances, particularly by Preston and Lupino as McQueen's estranged parents. Written by Jeb Rosebrook. Todd-AO 35. [PG]▼◗
Junior Miss (1945) **94m.** **½ D: George Seaton. Peggy Ann Garner, Allyn Joslyn, Michael Dunne, Faye Marlowe, Mona Freeman, Sylvia Field, Barbara Whiting, Mel Torme. Naive but entertaining comedy of teen-ager Garner and harried father Joslyn, based on Broadway play by Jerome Chodorov and Joseph Fields (from Sally Benson's stories).
Junkman (1982) **C-96m.** *½ D: H. B. Halicki. H. B. Halicki, Christopher Stone, Susan Shaw, Lang Jeffries, Hoyt Axton, Lynda Day George. Cars speed, crash, and practically bring each other to orgasm. Oh, yes, there *is* a story . . . [PG]▼
Juno and the Paycock (1930-British) **96m.** ** D: Alfred Hitchcock. Sara Allgood, Edward Chapman, Sidney Morgan, Marie O'Neill, John Laurie, Dennis Wyndham, John Longden. Faithful but dull, stagebound adaptation (by Hitchcock and Alma Reville) of Sean O'Casey's play about a poor Dublin family's travails during the civil war. The straightforward material defeats the director; however, Allgood is a standout as Juno. That's Barry Fitzgerald as "The Orator," in his screen debut.▼
Jupiter's Darling (1955) **C-96m.** **½ D: George Sidney. Esther Williams, Howard Keel, George Sanders, Marge and Gower Champion, Norma Varden. Lavish musical of Robert Sherwood's *Road to Rome*, which bogs down in tedium: Williams is temptress who dallies with Hannibal (Keel) to prevent attack on Rome. CinemaScope.▼●
Jupiter's Thigh (1979-French) **C-90m.** ** D: Philippe De Broca. Annie Girardot, Philippe Noiret, Frances Perrin, Catherine Alric. Blah sequel to DEAR DETECTIVE, with sleuth Girardot and professor Noiret becoming involved in intrigue while honeymooning in Greece. [PG]▼
Jupiter's Wife (1994) **C-78m.** ***½ D: Michel Negroponte. Compelling documentary about a middle-aged homeless woman whom filmmaker Negroponte chanced to encounter in N.Y.'s Central Park. She claims to have ESP and be the wife of the god Jupiter and daughter of the late actor Robert Ryan! Negroponte delves into her past and discovers quite a few surprises in

this extremely moving portrait of a shattered life. Shot on video. Shown on cable TV prior to its theatrical premiere. ▼

Jurassic Park (1993) **C-126m.** ***½ D: Steven Spielberg. Sam Neill, Laura Dern, Jeff Goldblum, Richard Attenborough, Bob Peck, Martin Ferrero, B. D. Wong, Joseph Mazzello, Ariana Richards, Samuel L. Jackson, Wayne Knight. Billionaire Attenborough invites paleontologists Dern and Neill and mathematician Goldblum to inspect his island amusement park, populated with living dinosaurs; he even has his grandchildren tag along, blissfully unconvinced that anything could go wrong. Slam-bang thriller delivers the goods with action, suspense, and hair-raising chills, plus the most astonishing special effects of this nature in cinema history: the dinosaurs seem *alive.* The story can't bear such close scrutiny, but while this thrill ride is going, you won't mind. Michael Crichton cowrote the screenplay from his own novel. Won three Oscars, for Visual Effects, Sound, and Sound Effects Editing. Followed by THE LOST WORLD: JURASSIC PARK. [PG-13]▼●

Juror, The (1996) **C-116m.** ** D: Brian Gibson. Demi Moore, Alec Baldwin, Joseph Gordon-Levitt, Anne Heche, James Gandolfini, Lindsay Crouse, Tony Lo Bianco, Michael Constantine, Matt Craven, Todd Susman, Michael Rispoli, Jack Gilpin. Shady (and, it turns out, psychopathic) underworld figure Baldwin victimizes an unsuspecting Moore so that she will sway fellow jurors into acquitting a Mafia boss. Comparisons to TRIAL BY JURY are apt, but this one goes on (much) longer and gets more ridiculous by the minute. The stars can't be faulted, but the script certainly can. Panavision. [R]▼●◗

Jury Duty (1995) **C-85m.** BOMB D: John Fortenberry. Pauly Shore, Tia Carrere, Stanley Tucci, Brian Doyle-Murray, Abe Vigoda, Charles Napier, Richard Edson, Richard Riehle, Alex Datcher, Shelley Winters, Dick Vitale, Andrew (Dice) Clay. "BOMB" may be too high a rating for this inane, insulting "comedy" featuring Shore as a jerk who would much rather face duty on a sequestered jury (and get a free hotel room) than find himself a job. Loaded with tasteless, gratuitous references to the O. J. Simpson trial. [PG-13]▼●

Jury Duty: The Comedy (1990) **C-100m. TVM** D: Michael Schultz. Stephen Baldwin, Mark Blankfield, Barbara Bosson, Heather Locklear, Bronson Pinchot, Lynn Redgrave, Tracy Scoggins, Alan Thicke, Reginald VelJohnson. A panel of familiar faces is called on to render a decision in a farcical, headline-making embezzlement trial of a mild-mannered accountant (versatile Pinchot, who plays three roles in all). The verdict: Average.

Jury of One (1974-French-Italian) **C-97m.** ** D: André Cayatte. Sophia Loren, Jean Gabin, Henri Garcin, Julien Bertheau, Michel Albertini. Plodding melodrama about a woman who goes to outrageous extremes to protect her son, on trial for murder and rape. Gabin plays the judge. Aka THE VERDICT. [R]

Just Across the Street (1952) **78m.** ** D: Joseph Pevney. Ann Sheridan, John Lund, Cecil Kellaway, Natalie Schafer, Harvey Lembeck. Mild shenanigans with working-woman Sheridan being mistaken for wealthy estate owner.

Just a Gigolo (1979-West German) **C-105m.** **½ D: David Hemmings. David Bowie, Sydne Rome, Kim Novak, David Hemmings, Maria Schell, Curt Jurgens, Marlene Dietrich. *Very* interesting cast is chief attraction of weird melodrama starring Bowie as Prussian war vet who drifts from job to job in Berlin before finally discovering his true calling. Dietrich, in her last film appearance, pops in long enough to croak the title song; Rome's spirited performance gives lift to uneven film that possibly made more sense in original 147m. version released in Europe. [R]▼●

Just a Little Harmless Sex (1999) **C-98m.** **½ D: Rick Rosenthal. Alison Eastwood, Lauren Hutton, Kimberly Williams, Jonathan Silverman, Jessica Lundy, Rachel Hunter, William Ragsdale. After a wife kicks her husband out of the house (when he reluctantly picks up a hooker one night) their marriage is thrust into crisis mode. She calls her girlfriends together for advice, and he does the same with the guys; they all converge at a local club. Minor but entertaining, even insightful, low-budget romantic comedy with a very attractive cast. [R]▼

Just an Old Sweet Song (1976) **C-78m. TVM** D: Robert Ellis Miller. Cicely Tyson, Robert Hooks, Kevin Hooks, Eric Hooks, Beah Richards, Lincoln Kilpatrick, Edward Binns, Minnie Gentry. Melvin Van Peebles' contemporary drama about a black family from Detroit whose two-week vacation in the South changes their lives. Lovingly acted family film. Above average.

Just Another Girl on the I.R.T. (1993) **C-92m.** *½ D: Leslie Harris. Ariyan Johnson, Kevin Thigpen, Ebony Jerido, Chequita Jackson, William Badget, Jerard Washington. A bright, sassy 17-year-old African-American (Johnson) desires to escape from her stifling Brooklyn housing project by going to college and then medical school, but her dreams are shattered when she finds herself pregnant. Cinematically, this is strictly amateur night; plus, the film's two white characters are thoughtless, mean-spirited stereotypes (proving that an African-American filmmaker can be as insensitive and racist as a white one). Sole merit: Johnson, who offers a spirited performance. [R] ▼

Just Around the Corner (1938) **70m.** **

D: Irving Cummings. Shirley Temple, Joan Davis, Charles Farrell, Amanda Duff, Bill Robinson, Bert Lahr, Claude Gillingwater. Simpleminded corn with Shirley singlehandedly ending the Depression, manipulating pessimistic tycoon Gillingwater into creating new jobs. But the musical numbers with Robinson are still a delight. Also shown in computer-colored version.▼

Just Ask for Diamond (1988-British) **C-94m.** *** D: Stephen Bayly. Susannah York, Patricia Hodge, Roy Kinnear, Michael Medwin, Peter Eyre, Nickolas Grace, Dursley McLinden, Colin Dale, Bill Paterson, Jimmy Nail, Saeed Jaffrey. Clever, if occasionally cartoonish, detective-film parody, about the kid brother of a dumbbell private eye and the mystery surrounding a box of candy. Best for older children (although they might not get all the references to 1940s Hollywood detective dramas). Screenplay by Anthony Horowitz, from his novel *The Falcon's Malteser.* Aka DIAMOND'S EDGE. [PG]▼

Just Before Dawn (1946) **66m.** **½ D: William Castle. Warner Baxter, Adelle Roberts, Martin Kosleck, Mona Barrie, Marian Miller, Charles D. Brown, Craig Reynolds. Dr. Ordway (Baxter) is tricked into giving a fatal injection to one of his patients and won't rest until he catches the real culprits in this dark and moody *Crime Doctor* entry.

Just Between Friends (1986) **C-110m.** **½ D: Allan Burns. Mary Tyler Moore, Ted Danson, Christine Lahti, Sam Waterston, Salome Jens, Jane Greer, James MacKrell. Genteel tearjerker about two women who strike up a friendship, unaware that they share the same man—one as wife, one as lover. Too pat, too neat and clean to really hit home, though the acting is first-rate, and Lahti is terrific as the single career woman. Nice role for Jane Greer, too, as Mary's mom. Directing debut for writer Burns. [PG-13]▼

Just Cause (1995) **C-102m.** *½ D: Arne Glimcher. Sean Connery, Laurence Fishburne, Kate Capshaw, Blair Underwood, Ed Harris, Christopher Murray, Ruby Dee, Scarlett Johansson, Daniel J. Travanti, Ned Beatty, Liz Torres, Lynne Thigpen, Kevin McCarthy, Hope Lange, Chris Sarandon, George Plimpton. Eminent Harvard Law School professor is persuaded to help a black man in Florida who's about to be executed for a heinous crime he swears he didn't commit. Starts out as an engrossing story, but goes so far afield—and becomes so preposterous (not to mention unpleasant) by the swampy climax that it winds up a huge waste of time. John Katzenbach's novel considerably changed. Connery also executive produced. Panavision. [R]▼●◗

Just for Fun (1963-British) **85m.** *½ D: Gordon Flemyng. Mark Wynter, Cherry Roland, Richard Vernon, Reginald Beckwith, John Wood, Bobby Vee, The Crickets, Freddie Cannon, Johnny Tillotson, Ketty Lester, The Tremeloes. A wisp of a plot—teens establish their own political party to run a pop election—surrounds this forgettable musical trifle. Among the more recognizable tunes are "The Night Has a Thousand Eyes" (Bobby Vee) and "Keep on Dancin' " (The Tremeloes).

Just for You (1952) **C-104m.** *** D: Elliott Nugent. Bing Crosby, Jane Wyman, Ethel Barrymore, Bob Arthur, Natalie Wood, Cora Witherspoon, Regis Toomey. Zesty musical of producer Crosby who can't be bothered with his growing children, till Wyman shows him the way. Pleasant Harry Warren–Leo Robin score, highlighted by "Zing a Little Zong." Based on Stephen Vincent Benet novel *Famous.* ▼●

Just Imagine (1930) **109m.** *½ D: David Butler. El Brendel, Maureen O'Sullivan, John Garrick, Marjorie White, Frank Albertson, Hobart Bosworth. Famous but utterly disappointing sci-fi musical set in 1980, with Brendel, officially dead since 1930, suddenly revived and unable to get used to phenomenal changes in living. Futuristic sets, gags, costumes made tremendous impression on everyone who saw film in 1930, but alas, it doesn't wear well at all. Songs by DeSylva-Brown-Henderson.

Justine (1969) **C-116m.** *** D: George Cukor. Anouk Aimée, Dirk Bogarde, Robert Forster, Anna Karina, Philippe Noiret, Michael York, John Vernon, Jack Albertson, Cliff Gorman, Michael Constantine, Marcel Dalio, Michael Dunn, Abraham Sofaer. Stylish film won't please fans of Lawrence Durrell's *Alexandria Quartet,* but works as exotic kitsch; Cukor's great use of widescreen won't mean much on TV. Filmed in Tunis. Panavision. [R]▼

Just Like a Woman (1994-British) **C-102m.** **½ D: Christopher Monger. Julie Walters, Adrian Pasdar, Paul Freeman, Gordon Kennedy, Susan Wooldridge. Amiable (if a bit overlong) comedy featuring Pasdar as Gerald, a heterosexual American in London who derives pleasure from becoming "Geraldine" and wearing women's clothes. The film works because it's never condescending toward Gerald; he's not a caricature, but rather a guy with an unusual predilection. ▼

Just Off Broadway (1942) **66m.** ** D: Herbert I. Leeds. Lloyd Nolan, Marjorie Weaver, Phil Silvers, Janis Carter. Acceptable Michael Shayne caper, with swanky dame on trial for murder; outcome is easy for mystery fans.

Just One of the Guys (1985) **C-100m.** *** D: Lisa Gottlieb. Joyce Hyser, Clayton Rohner, Billy Jacoby, Toni Hudson, William Zabka, Leigh McCloskey, Sherilyn Fenn, Arye Gross. Pretty high school senior, convinced that looks have kept patronizing male teachers from supporting her in citywide journalism competition, dons male disguise and tries again at another school. Engagingly eccentric characterizations take this fast-paced sleeper out of the ordinary; performed with gusto by a cast that's aiming to please. [PG-13]▼●

Just Tell Me What You Want (1980) **C-112m.** **½ D: Sidney Lumet. Ali MacGraw, Alan King, Myrna Loy, Keenan Wynn, Tony Roberts, Peter Weller, Judy Kaye, Dina Merrill, Joseph Maher, Michael Gross, Leslie Easterbrook, David Rasche, John Gabriel. Obnoxious tycoon King drives long-time mistress MacGraw into arms of younger man, then does everything he can to get her back. Bitchy upper-class comedy may be too strident for some tastes, but King's flamboyant performance is sensational, as is Loy's quiet one as his long-suffering secretary. Screenplay by Jay Presson Allen, from her novel. Loy's last theatrical feature. [R]▼

Just the Ticket (1999) **C-115m.** **½ D: Richard Wenk. Andy Garcia, Andie MacDowell, Richard Bradford, Laura Harris, Andre Blake, Elizabeth Ashley, Patrick Breen, Fred Asparagus, Ron Leibman, Chris Lemmon, Don Novello, Abe Vigoda, Bill Irwin. Mostly likable but lumpy comedy-drama about ne'er-do-well ticket scalper Garcia and his on-again, off-again relationship with MacDowell—who loves him but can't tolerate his utter irresponsibility. Nice characterizations, vivid filming on the streets of N.Y.C.; hurt by uneven narrative and overlength. Garcia produced the film and composed much of its music. Written by the director. [R]▼●◗

Just the Way You Are (1984) **C-94m.** *** D: Edouard Molinaro. Kristy McNichol, Michael Ontkean, Kaki Hunter, Andre Dussolier, Catherine Salviat, Robert Carradine, Lance Guest, Alexandra Paul, Timothy Daly, Patrick Cassidy. Episodic but likable film about crippled musician (McNichol) who goes to French ski resort with her leg in a cast—to see, for once, what it's like when people don't know she's handicapped. Elements of sharp comedy, escapist romance, and travelogue aren't seamlessly connected, but results are extremely pleasant, and McNichol has never been more appealing. Script by Allan Burns. [PG]▼

Just This Once (1952) **90m.** **½ D: Don Weis. Janet Leigh, Peter Lawford, Lewis Stone, Marilyn Erskine, Richard Anderson. Cute little comedy of stern Leigh in charge of playboy Lawford's dwindling fortunes, and their inevitable romance.

Just Tony (1922) **58m.** **½ D: Lynn Reynolds. Tom Mix, Claire Adams, J. P. Lockney, Duke Lee, Frank Campeau. Amiable Tom Mix Western sheds spotlight on his beloved horse Tony, tracing his life from mistreated mustang to benevolent protector of cowboy Mix.▼

Just You and Me, Kid (1979) **C-95m.** *½ D: Leonard Stern. George Burns, Brooke Shields, Lorraine Gary, Nicolas Coster, Burl Ives, Ray Bolger, Leon Ames, Carl Ballantine, Keye Luke. Burns struggles to keep awful comedy afloat, but it ain't easy. Shields plays a runaway who comes to stay with the ex-vaudevillian. Commercial interruptions might help this one. [PG]

J W Coop (1972) **C-112m.** ***½ D: Cliff Robertson. Cliff Robertson, Geraldine Page, Cristina Ferrare, R. G. Armstrong, John Crawford. Vivid character study of none-too-bright drifter who sets his sights on becoming No. 1 rodeo star. Tour de force: director/writer/star Robertson scores in all departments. [PG]▼

Kabloonak (1994-Canadian-French) **C-105m.** **½ D: Claude Massot. Charles Dance, Adamie Quasiak Knukpuk, David Bursztein, Patty Hannock, Philippe Freturn, Peter Hudson, Geoffrey Bateman. Dance (who played D.W. Griffith in GOOD MORNING, BABYLON) here portrays pioneer documentarian Robert Flaherty, who spends one year in Alaska befriending Inouit eskimos in order to make NANOOK OF THE NORTH (1922). Interesting throughout, if not particularly inspired. Aka THE STRANGER.▼

Kafka (1991) **C/B&W-98m.** **½ D: Steven Soderbergh. Jeremy Irons, Theresa Russell, Joel Grey, Ian Holm, Jeroen Krabbe, Armin Mueller-Stahl, Alec Guinness, Brian Glover, Robert Flemyng. Strikingly photographed and designed film about mild-mannered insurance clerk Franz Kafka (Irons), who becomes both curious and assertive for the first time when he begins investigating a friend's disappearance. Teasing, darkly comic tale takes elements from various Kafka stories about oppression and paranoia, and weaves them into an expressionistic tapestry. Set in 1919 Prague. Not a total success, and not for all tastes, but offers many delights, including some choice character vignettes. Written by Lem Dobbs; photographed on location in Prague by Walt Lloyd. [PG-13]▼●

Kagemusha (1980-Japanese) **C-159m.** **** D: Akira Kurosawa. Tatsuya Nakadai, Tsutomo Yamazaki, Kenichi Hagiwara, Jinpachi Nezu, Shuji Otaki. Sixteenth-century thief is spared execution if he will pose as secretly deceased warlord whose throne is coveted by others. Grand combination of humanism and spectacle from a great filmmaker in the twilight of his career. Released outside the U.S. at 179m. Aka KAGEMUSHA (THE SHADOW WARRIOR). [PG]▼●

Kaleidoscope (1966) **C-103m.** ** D: Jack Smight. Warren Beatty, Susannah York, Clive Revill, Eric Porter, Murray Melvin. Idea of Beatty-York teaming can't miss, but does, in bland comedy about American playboy/card-shark forced to capture narcotics smuggler or go to jail. Flashy but forgettable. Filmed in England.▼

Kalifornia (1993) **C-117m.** *** D: Dominic Sena. Brad Pitt, Juliette Lewis, David Duchovny, Michelle Forbes, Sierra Pecheur, Gregory Mars Martin. Offbeat road-movie thriller about a writer and a photographer, researching a coffee-table book on serial killers, who get a harsh dose of reality when they hook up with Pitt and Lewis. Effectively ironic, and well acted by its talented cast. Unrated version runs 118m. Super 35. [R] ▼●◗

Kama Sutra: A Tale of Love (1996-Indian) **C-114m.** *** D: Mira Nair. Indira Varma, Sarita Choudhury, Naveen Andrews, Ramon Tikaram, Rekha, Pearl Padamsee, Arundhati Rao. Frankly erotic, spirited feminist saga of sex and sexual politics in 16th-century feudal India, telling the story of Maya (Varma), an independent-minded servant who seduces a young king. He becomes obsessed with her, but weds a princess whom he does not love. A pointed portrait of a woman who is unwilling to accept a woman's "destiny" of being her father's property one day and her husband's property the next. Rated for video as NC-17, and as R (113m.).▼●◗

Kamikaze '89 (1982-German) **C-106m.** *** D: Wolf Gremm. Rainer Werner Fassbinder, Gunther Kaufmann, Boy Gobert, Arnold Marquis, Richy Mueller, Brigitte Mira, Frank Ripploh, Franco Nero. Police lieutenant Fassbinder (in his final screen role) attempts to foil an alleged bomb plot, set in a futuristic Germany. Exciting if sometimes confusing thriller, from Per Wahloo novel.▼

Kamilla (1981-Norwegian) **C-100m.** *** D: Vibeke Lokkeberg. Nina Knapskog, Vibeke Lokkeberg, Helge Jordal, Kenneth Johansen, Karin Zetlitz Haerem. Briskly paced yet quietly disturbing chronicle of 7-year-old Knapskog and the world around her: most distressingly, her constantly squabbling parents; most specially, the secret world she shares with a little boy. Knapskog is remarkable, and the film can be favorably compared to SMALL CHANGE and FORBIDDEN GAMES, the celluloid masterpieces about childhood.

Kanal (1956-Polish) **97m.** *** D: Andrzej Wajda. Teresa Izewska, Tadeusz Janczar, Wienczylaw Glinski, Wladyslaw (Vladek) Sheybal. Intense, almost unrelentingly graphic account of the final days of the September, 1944, Warsaw uprising in Nazi-occupied Poland. This is the second of Wajda's war trilogy, after A GENERATION and before ASHES AND DIAMONDS. Aka THEY LOVED LIFE. Not shown in U.S. until 1961.▼

Kandyland (1987) **C-93m.** BOMB D: Robert Schnitzer. Kim Evenson, Sandahl Bergman, Charles Laulette, Bruce Baum, Cole Stevens. Dumb exploitation film charts the misadventures of Evenson (a former *Playboy* model) becoming a stripper at the Kandyland club, under the tutelage of old pro Bergman. Unintentionally silly dialogue sinks this one. [R]▼●

Kangaroo (1952) **C-84m.** ** D: Lewis Milestone. Maureen O'Hara, Peter Lawford, Finlay Currie, Richard Boone. Uninspired blend of romance and adventure, salvaged by good on-location Australian landscapes and fetching O'Hara.▼

Kangaroo (1986-Australian) **C-105m.** ** D: Tim Burstall. Colin Friels, Judy Davis, John Walton, Julie Nihill, Hugh Keays-Byrne. Muddled account of controversial British writer (Friels) who exiles himself and wife Davis to Australia in the early 1920s, and develops an intellectual attachment to a group of Fascists. Potentially fascinating, insightful portrait of a man of letters and his difficulties in dealing with the real world, but there's little feel for the characters and their motivations. Adapted from D. H. Lawrence's autobiographical novel. Friels and Davis are real-life husband and wife. Panavision. [R]▼

Kansan, The (1943) **79m.** **½ D: George Archainbaud. Richard Dix, Jane Wyatt, Victor Jory, Albert Dekker, Eugene Pallette, Robert Armstrong. Zippy Western, with Dix becoming town hero, taming gangsters, but facing more trouble with corrupt town official.▼

Kansas (1988) **C-108m.** BOMB D: David Stevens. Matt Dillon, Andrew McCarthy, Leslie Hope, Brent Jennings, Brynn Thayer, Kyra Sedgwick. McCarthy gets stranded in the Midwest after his car and possessions blow up on the road, and takes it on the lam after boxcar acquaintance (and punk) Dillon implicates him in a bank robbery. Goes into fast free-fall around the time McCarthy rescues the governor's daughter from drowning (!)—and falls for the kind of farmer's daughter who wears makeup and pearls in the field. Second only to Toto as the Sunflower State's top movie dog. Super 35. [R]▼●

Kansas City (1996-U.S.-French) **C-115m.** ** D: Robert Altman. Jennifer Jason Leigh, Miranda Richardson, Harry Belafonte, Michael Murphy, Dermot Mulroney, Steve Buscemi, Brooke Smith, Jane Adams, A. C. Smith. Vividly atmospheric but dramatically lackluster portrait of K.C. in the 1930s, a hotbed of racketeering, political machines, and jazz, focusing on local mob kingpin Belafonte, young upstart Mulroney, and his wife, Leigh. Lots of flavor but little substance, and a redundant story line. Best part: the jazz, which is played almost continuously (often on-camera) by an all-star lineup including Nicholas Payton, Joshua Redman,

Mark Whitfield, Christian McBride, Cyrus Chestnut, and Ron Carter. [R]▼●

Kansas City Bomber (1972) **C-99m.** ** D: Jerrold Freedman. Raquel Welch, Kevin McCarthy, Helena Kallianiotes, Norman Alden, Jeanne Cooper, Dick Lane, Jodie Foster. Once you've seen five minutes, it doesn't pay to stay through the rest. Raquel stars as good-hearted roller derby star who has female colleagues jealous, male employers drooling. Dialogue, situations often unintentionally funny. [PG]

Kansas City Confidential (1952) **98m.** *** D: Phil Karlson. John Payne, Coleen Gray, Preston Foster, Neville Brand, Lee Van Cleef, Jack Elam, Dona Drake. Tough action drama with hard-luck ex-con Payne implicated in a bank heist, determined to quite literally unmask the real culprits. Quentin Tarantino must have seen this one prior to scripting RESERVOIR DOGS!▼

Kansas City Kitty (1944) **71m.** ** D: Del Lord. Joan Davis, Bob Crosby, Jane Frazee, Erik Rolf. Programmer sparked by Davis, involved in purchase of song-publishing company on the skids.

Kansas Pacific (1953) **C-73m.** ** D: Ray Nazarro. Sterling Hayden, Eve Miller, Barton MacLane, Reed Hadley, Irving Bacon. Inoffensive account of building of title railway during 1860s, with Reb soldiers trying to prevent its completion.▼●

Kansas Raiders (1950) **C-80m.** ** D: Ray Enright. Audie Murphy, Brian Donlevy, Marguerite Chapman, Scott Brady, Tony Curtis, Richard Arlen, Richard Long, James Best, Dewey Martin, Richard Egan. Fair Civil War Western with young Jesse James and company joining Quantrill's Raiders, who are portrayed as a vigilante group more concerned with killing and looting than fighting Northern soldiers. Most interesting are the depictions of Jesse (Murphy) as a good-boy-gone-bad and Quantrill (Donlevy) as a megalomaniac.

Karate Cop SEE: **Slaughter in San Francisco**

Karate Kid, The (1984) **C-126m.** ***½ D: John G. Avildsen. Ralph Macchio, Noriyuki (Pat) Morita, Elisabeth Shue, Randee Heller, Martin Kove, William Zabka, Chad McQueen, Tony O'Dell, Larry Drake. Teenager is beset by bullies until an unlikely mentor (the Japanese handyman in his apartment house) teaches him about self-confidence—and karate. Unabashedly old-fashioned, manipulative movie is a real audience-pleaser; from director of the original ROCKY. Winning performances by Macchio and Morita. If only they'd trimmed it a bit. Followed by three sequels (last is THE NEXT KARATE KID) and animated TV series. [PG]▼●◗

Karate Kid, Part II, The (1986) **C-113m.** **½ D: John G. Avildsen. Ralph Macchio, Noriyuki (Pat) Morita, Nobu McCarthy, Danny Kamekona, Yuji Okumoto, Tamlyn Tomita, Martin Kove. Purposeless sequel takes main characters from original film to Japan, where they're confronted by Morita's long-ago arch-enemy and his nasty nephew. Corny in the extreme (all that's missing from climax is hounds and ice floes), but made palatable by performances of Macchio and Morita. Aimed strictly at kids. [PG]▼●

Karate Kid III, The (1989) **C-111m.** BOMB D: John G. Avildsen. Ralph Macchio, Noriyuki (Pat) Morita, Robyn Elaine Lively, Thomas Ian Griffith, Martin Kove, Sean Kanan, Jonathan Avildsen. Utterly stupid sequel has the "kid" (27-year-old Macchio) being set up for slaughter by nemesis Kove (in an obligatory appearance). When Morita refuses to train him, Macchio turns instead to Griffith—a sadistic millionaire Vietnam vet (who also turns out to be a buddy of Kove's!). Will Morita save him? Naturally . . . but this film is hopeless. [PG]▼●

Kashmiri Run (1969-Spanish) **C-101m.** ** D: John Peyser. Pernell Roberts, Alexandra Bastedo, Julian Mateos, Gloria Gamata. Two men and a girl try to stay one step ahead of the Chinese Communists fleeing Tibet; plodding actioner. [R]▼

Katherine (1975) **C-100m. TVM** D: Jeremy Kagan. Art Carney, Sissy Spacek, Henry Winkler, Julie Kavner, Jane Wyatt, Hector Elias, Jenny Sullivan. Absorbing drama written by Kagan about one young woman's radical experience, from innocent to activist to terrorist. Spacek is remarkable in title role. Subsequently cut to 78m. Aka THE RADICAL. Above average. ▼●

Kathleen (1941) **88m.** ** D: Harold S. Bucquet. Shirley Temple, Herbert Marshall, Laraine Day, Gail Patrick, Felix Bressart. Predictable story of neglected daughter Temple bringing widower father Marshall and Day together.

Kathy O' (1958) **C-99m.** **½ D: Jack Sher. Dan Duryea, Jan Sterling, Patty McCormack, Mary Fickett, Sam Levene, Mary Jane Croft, Walter Woolf King, Joseph Sargent. Sluggish frolic of temperamental child star McCormack and her desperate public relations agent Duryea. CinemaScope.

Katie Did It (1951) **81m.** **½ D: Frederick de Cordova. Ann Blyth, Mark Stevens, Cecil Kellaway, Jesse White. Blyth is perkier than usual as square New England librarian who becomes hep when romanced by swinging New Yorker Stevens.

Katie's Passion SEE: **Keetje Tippel**

Kazaam (1996) **C-93m.** *½ D: Paul M. Glaser. Shaquille O'Neal, Francis Capra, Ally Walker, Marshall Manesh, James Acheson, Fawn Reed, John Costelloe. Threadbare urban fantasy has a troubled kid accidentally summoning a friendly genie from his home—a boom box. Vehicle for basketball star O'Neal confirms his pleasing personality but gets mired in a story full of grimy and unpleasant characters; far from ideal family entertainment. Glaser also wrote the story; O'Neal coexecutive-produced. [PG]▼●

Kazablan (1974-Israeli) **C-114m.** *** D: Menahem Golan. Yehoram Gaon, Arie Elias, Efrat Lavie, Joseph Graber. Entertaining musical made in Old Jaffa and Jerusalem, in English, based on a popular show. Gaon repeats his stage role as streetwise war hero out to save his neighborhood from being torn down. Excellent color and location work. Panavision. [PG]

Keep, The (1983) **C-96m.** *½ D: Michael Mann. Scott Glenn, Ian McKellen, Alberta Watson, Jürgen Prochnow, Robert Prosky, Gabriel Byrne. German soldiers try to defend a Rumanian mountain pass during WW2 by headquartering in an ancient fortress—ignoring villagers' warnings of a strange presence inside. Outlandish, incoherent, and mostly awful; recommended only for connoisseurs of Strange Cinema. Panavision. [R]▼●

Keep 'Em Flying (1941) **86m.** **½ D: Arthur Lubin. Bud Abbott, Lou Costello, Carol Bruce, Martha Raye, William Gargan, Dick Foran. Good A&C mixed in with clichéed plot of stunt-pilot Foran unable to accustom himself to Air Force discipline. Raye is fun playing twins.▼●

Keep 'Em Slugging (1943) **60m.** ** D: Christy Cabanne. Bobby Jordan, Huntz Hall, Gabriel Dell, Norman Abbott, Evelyn Ankers, Elyse Knox, Frank Albertson, Don Porter, Shemp Howard. Jordan takes over the Little Tough Guys from Billy Halop, as a clerk in a shipping company beset by hijackers.▼

Keeper of the City (1992) **C-95m. TVM** D: Bobby Roth. Louis Gossett, Jr., Peter Coyote, Renee Soutendijk, Anthony LaPaglia, Aeryk Egan, Tony Todd. Vigilante gangster killer (LaPaglia, in a De Niro turn) baffles Chicago cop Gossett and arrogant newspaperman Coyote, cleaning up the town his own way. Adapted by Gerald DiPego from his own novel. Made for cable. Average. ▼●

Keeper of the Flame (1943) **100m.** *** D: George Cukor. Spencer Tracy, Katharine Hepburn, Richard Whorf, Margaret Wycherly, Forrest Tucker, Frank Craven, Audrey Christie, Horace (Stephen) McNally, Darryl Hickman, Howard da Silva, Donald Meek. Reporter Tracy sets out to write the true story of a beloved, just-deceased American patriot. Dated, somewhat heavy-handed treatment of a still-timely theme: the pitfalls of blind hero worship. Scripted by Donald Ogden Stewart, with some interesting echoes of CITIZEN KANE.▼●

Keeping On (1981) **C-75m. TVM** D: Barbara Kopple. Dick Anthony Williams, Carol Kane, James Broderick, Marcia Rodd, Rosalind Cash, Carl Lee, Danny Glover, Trazana Beverly, Guy Boyd. Good drama of proud preacher-worker Williams trying to unionize mill with assistance of organizer Broderick. Unsubtle, but not unfair, in its pro-union viewpoint; a fictional counterpart of Kopple's documentaries, HARLAN COUNTY, U.S.A., and AMERICAN DREAM. Screenplay by Horton Foote. Originally made for PBS' *American Playhouse*. Above average.▼

Keeping the Faith (2000) **C-127m.** **½ D: Edward Norton. Ben Stiller, Edward Norton, Jenna Elfman, Anne Bancroft, Eli Wallach, Ron Rifkin, Milos Forman, Holland Taylor, Lisa Edelstein, Rena Sofer, Ken Leung, Brian George. N.Y.C. boyhood pals grow up to be a priest and a rabbi, both contemporary thinkers with great appeal to their congregations. Into their lives comes a savvy woman who was their best friend at age eight, before she moved away; now they become caught in a most unusual triangle. Smart (if predictable) comedy goes on much too long and wears out its welcome, though the trio of stars is likable throughout. Norton's directorial debut. [PG-13]▼◗

Keep It Cool SEE: **Let's Rock!**

Keep the Change (1992) **C-100m. TVM** D: Andy Tennant. William Petersen, Lolita Davidovich, Jack Palance, Rachel Ticotin, Buck Henry, Fred Dalton Thompson, Lois Smith, Jeff Korber. Leisurely tale of a California artist who returns to his Montana roots on a journey of rediscovery. Top-notch cast ambles nicely through John Miglis's adaptation of Thomas McGuane's novel. Made for cable. Above average.▼

Keep Your Powder Dry (1945) **93m.** ** D: Edward Buzzell. Lana Turner, Laraine Day, Susan Peters, Agnes Moorehead, Bill Johnson, Natalie Schafer, Lee Patrick. Hackneyed tale of WW2 WACs, glossy on the outside, empty on the inside.

Keetje Tippel (1975-Dutch) **C-107m.** **½ D: Paul Verhoeven. Rutger Hauer, Monique van de Ven, Eddie Brugman, Hannah De Leeuwe, Andrea Domburg. Slickly produced tale of a poor-but-determined young woman (van de Ven), and her struggles as she rises up the social ladder in 19th-century Amsterdam. Superficial social commentary on working class life. However, van de Ven is excellent as Keetje. Aka KATIE'S PASSION, CATHY TIPPEL, and HOT SWEAT. [R] ▼●

Kelly (1981-Canadian) **C-93m.** ** D: Christopher Chapman. Robert Logan, Twyla-Dawn Vokins, George Clutesi, Elaine Nalee, Doug Lennox. Young Vokins leaves the city to live with her father (Logan) in the wilderness. Static and boring; Logan wrote the screenplay.

Kelly and Me (1957) **C-86m** ** D: Robert

Z. Leonard. Van Johnson, Piper Laurie, Martha Hyer, Onslow Stevens. Johnson is unsuccessful hoofer who hits movie big-time with talented dog for partner. Mild musical. CinemaScope.

Kelly's Heroes (1970) **C-145m.** **½ D: Brian G. Hutton. Clint Eastwood, Telly Savalas, Don Rickles, Donald Sutherland, Carroll O'Connor, Gavin MacLeod, Stuart Margolin, (Harry) Dean Stanton. Large-scale WW2 film tries for Sergeant Bilko-ish atmosphere with middling results; hippie soldier Sutherland isn't credible in 1940s setting. Actionful aspects of Savalas and Eastwood's far-fetched gold heist behind enemy lines make film worth watching. Panavision. [PG]▼●

Kennel Murder Case, The (1933) **73m.** ***½ D: Michael Curtiz. William Powell, Mary Astor, Eugene Pallette, Ralph Morgan, Helen Vinson, Jack LaRue, Robert Barrat, Arthur Hohl, Paul Cavanagh. The definitive *Philo Vance* mystery, about an apparent suicide which Vance believes was really murder, tied to intrigue among rivals competing in a Long Island dog show. Stylish direction and photography and a fine cast make this top-notch by any standard.▼●◗

Kenner (1969) **C-92m.** ** D: Steve Sekely. Jim Brown, Madlyn Rhue, Robert Coote, Ricky Cordell, Charles Horvath. Small, bittersweet romance of soldier of fortune in Bombay (filmed on location), whose search for partner's murderer involves young native dancer. [G]

Kenny & Co. (1976) **C-90m.** **½ D: Don Coscarelli. Dan McCann, Mike Baldwin, Jeff Roth, Ralph Richmond, Reggie Bannister. Sweet-natured, upbeat look at adolescent life, focusing on one boy's growing pains. Virtually a one-man-show behind the camera by young Coscarelli. [PG]

Kenny Rogers as The Gambler (1980) **C-94m. TVM** D: Dick Lowry. Kenny Rogers, Bruce Boxleitner, Christine Belford, Harold Gould, Clu Gulager, Lance LeGault, Lee Purcell. In his first starring role Rogers brings his charisma and credible acting abilities to this Western, which used his hit song as a narrative springboard. Average; also known as THE GAMBLER; followed by two sequels, PART II—THE ADVENTURE CONTINUES and PART III—THE LEGEND CONTINUES.▼

Kentuckian, The (1955) **C-104m.** **½ D: Burt Lancaster. Burt Lancaster, Diana Lynn, Dianne Foster, Walter Matthau, John McIntire, Una Merkel, John Carradine. Minor but spirited frontier adventure set in 1820s with Lancaster (doing double duty as star and director) traveling to Texas with his son, hoping to start new life. Based on Felix Holt's novel *The Gabriel Horn*. Matthau's film debut. CinemaScope.▼●

Kentucky (1938) **C-95m.** *** D: David Butler. Loretta Young, Richard Greene, Walter Brennan, Douglass Dumbrille, Karen Morley, Moroni Olsen, Russell Hicks. Lushly filmed story of rival horsebreeding families in blue-grass country, with lovers Young and Greene clinching at finale. Brennan won Best Supporting Actor Oscar.▼

Kentucky Fried Movie, The (1977) **C-78m.** *** D: John Landis. Evan Kim, Master Bong Soo Han, Bill Bixby, George Lazenby, Henry Gibson, Donald Sutherland, Tony Dow, Boni Enten, Ursula Digard. Vulgar, often funny skits strung together. Best: a lengthy Bruce Lee takeoff, a black and white spoof of the old courtroom TV shows. Idea originated with Kentucky Fried Theatre, a Madison, Wisconsin, satirical group whose key members—Jim Abrahams, David Zucker, and Jerry Zucker—went on to do AIRPLANE! Followed a decade later by AMAZON WOMEN ON THE MOON. [R]▼

Kentucky Kernels (1934) **75m.** *** D: George Stevens. Bert Wheeler, Robert Woolsey, Mary Carlisle, Spanky McFarland, Noah Beery, Lucille LaVerne. Wheeler & Woolsey take little Spanky into the deep South to collect inheritance, but find themselves in the midst of a family feud. Good vehicle for the team with great slapstick finale.▼●

Kentucky Moonshine (1938) **85m.** ** D: David Butler. Tony Martin, Marjorie Weaver, Ritz Brothers, Slim Summerville, John Carradine. Radio singer Martin's ratings are slipping, so he travels Down South to find new talent; show-biz hopefuls Weaver and The Ritz Brothers pose as hillbillies in order to be discovered. Occasionally zany but mostly thin musical-comedy.

Kes (1969-British) **113m.** *** D: Kenneth Loach. David Bradley, Lynne Perrie, Freddie Fletcher, Colin Welland, Brian Glover, Bob Bowes. Refreshingly unsentimental account of a young working-class boy who finds release from the dreariness of his life by looking after and training a falcon. This is no typical boy-and-his-pet story; rather, it's a pointed commentary on the lack of opportunities for the lower classes in England—a theme that's been a constant in director Loach's work.

Kettles in the Ozarks, The (1956) **81m.** **½ D: Charles Lamont. Marjorie Main, Arthur Hunnicutt, Una Merkel, Ted de Corsia, Richard Eyer, David O'Brien, Joe Sawyer, Richard Deacon, Sid Tomack. With Pa now gone, Ma Kettle takes the clan to visit her hillbilly brother-in-law (Hunnicutt). Percy Kilbride is sorely missed, but the cast is peppered with familiar character faces, and Ma's showdown with the backwoods moonshiners is pretty funny.▼

Kettles on Old Macdonald's Farm, The (1957) **80m.** *½ D: Virgil Vogel. Marjorie Main, Parker Fennelly, Gloria Talbott, John Smith, Claude Akins, Roy Barcroft, Pat Morrow. Ma Kettle plays matchmaker for a spoiled debutante and a poor lumberman in this weak final series entry, with Fennelly taking over the role of Pa.▼

Key, The (1934) **69m.** **½ D: Michael Curtiz. William Powell, Edna Best, Colin Clive, Hobart Cavanaugh, Halliwell Hobbes, Phil Regan, Arthur Treacher. Powell is miscast as a soldier of fortune who goes to work for the British in wartorn Dublin, finds his old flame (Best) married to buddy Clive. Good cast makes this watchable.

Key, The (1958-British) **125m.** **½ D: Carol Reed. William Holden, Sophia Loren, Trevor Howard, Oscar Homolka, Kieron Moore, Bernard Lee. Jan de Hartog novel becomes pointless romance tale. Loren is disillusioned woman passing out key to her room to series of naval captains during WW2, hoping to make their dangerous lives a little happier. Michael Caine has a small role. CinemaScope.▼●

Key Exchange (1985) **C-90m.** *** D: Barnet Kellman. Ben Masters, Brooke Adams, Daniel Stern, Danny Aiello, Nancy Mette, Tony Roberts. Masters plays a neurotic New Yorker who exchanges apartment keys with Adams but can't commit himself to her alone. Amusing adaptation of Kevin Wade's off-Broadway play with fine performances and good use of N.Y.C. locations. [R]▼

Key Largo (1948) **101m.** ***½ D: John Huston. Humphrey Bogart, Edward G. Robinson, Lauren Bacall, Lionel Barrymore, Claire Trevor, Thomas Gomez, Jay Silverheels, Marc Lawrence, Dan Seymour, Harry Lewis. Dandy cast in adaptation of Maxwell Anderson's play about tough gangster (Robinson) holding people captive in Florida hotel during tropical storm. Trevor won Best Supporting Actress Oscar as Robinson's boozy moll. Script by Huston and Richard Brooks. Score by Max Steiner. Also shown in computer-colored version. ▼●◗

Key Man (1954) **78m.** **½ D: Paul Guilfoyle. Angela Lansbury, Keith Andes, Brian Keith. Competent little picture about illicit love affair leading to mysterious accidents involving Lansbury's architect husband.

Keys of the Kingdom, The (1944) **137m.** *** D: John M. Stahl. Gregory Peck, Thomas Mitchell, Vincent Price, Edmund Gwenn, Roddy McDowall, Cedric Hardwicke, Peggy Ann Garner. Peck is fine in this long but generally good film about missionary's life (played as boy by McDowall); from A. J. Cronin novel.▼●

Keys to Tulsa (1997) **C-113m.** *½ D: Leslie Greif. Eric Stoltz, James Spader, Deborah Kara Unger, Joanna Going, Michael Rooker, Randy Graff, Mary Tyler Moore, James Coburn, Peter Strauss, Cameron Diaz. Or, Time Spent with Low-lifes in Oklahoma. Tiresome crime melodrama about a perpetual screw-up (Stoltz) who gets involved with a blackmail scheme instigated by seedy Spader, who also happens to be married to Stoltz's longtime heartthrob Unger. Diaz is fun in the first scene, but then disappears—and with her, all hope for some form of entertainment. [R]▼●

Key to the City (1950) **101m.** **½ D: George Sidney. Clark Gable, Loretta Young, Frank Morgan, Marilyn Maxwell, Raymond Burr, James Gleason. Bland romance between Gable and Young, two mayors who meet at convention in San Francisco.▼

Key Witness (1960) **82m.** **½ D: Phil Karlson. Jeffrey Hunter, Pat Crowley, Dennis Hopper, Joby Baker, Susan Harrison, Johnny Nash, Corey Allen. Overlong but effective narrative of pressures from street gang on Hunter's family to prevent his wife from testifying in criminal case. CinemaScope.

Khartoum (1966-British) **C-134m.** ** D: Basil Dearden. Charlton Heston, Laurence Olivier, Richard Johnson, Ralph Richardson, Alexander Knox, Johnny Sekka, Michael Hordern, Nigel Green, Hugh Williams, Ralph Michael. Dull historical spectacle about "Chinese" Gordon and his famous defeat by Arab tribesmen in 1885. Olivier is good, Heston better than usual, but film is way too talky for a spectacle. Ultra Panavision 70.▼●

Khyber Patrol (1954) **C-71m.** ** D: Seymour Friedman. Richard Egan, Dawn Addams, Patric Knowles, Raymond Burr. Cast is above pedestrian film of British officers fighting in India, with usual love conflicts.

Kickboxer (1989) **C-105m.** *½ D: Mark DiSalle. Jean-Claude Van Damme, Denis Alexio, Dennis Chan, Tong Po, Haskell Anderson, Rochelle Ashana. Dull, dumb martial-arts time-killer. Van Damme seeks revenge against Thai fighter who crippled his brother. Strictly by the numbers. Followed by several unrelated sequels. [R]▼●◗

Kicked in the Head (1997) **C-88m.** BOMB D: Matthew Harrison. Kevin Corrigan, Linda Fiorentino, Michael Rapaport, James Woods, Lili Taylor, Burt Young. Woefully inept N.Y. comedy about a would-be author of a meaning-of-life book and the tiresome characters he meets in the passing parade—among them motormouthed uncle Woods and flight attendant Fiorentino. Scripted by the director and his star. Executive-produced by Martin Scorsese. [R]▼●

Kicking and Screaming (1995) **C-96m.** ** D: Noah Baumbach. Josh Hamilton, Eric Stoltz, Olivia d'Abo, Chris Eigeman, Parker Posey, Jason Wiles, Cara Buono, Carlos Jacott, Elliott Gould, Jessica Hecht. Guess what? It's another we-just-graduated-from-college-what-do-we-do-now film! This one centers on a group of young men and their life-and-death crises concerning relationships, jobs, parents, etc. Successful in spots, but should have been better. Funniest scene is the opening—a grad night lawn party. Eigeman virtually reprises the roles he had in Whit Stillman's METROPOLITAN and BARCELONA. Question: Are there any hip, low-budget American movies that *don't* feature Eric Stoltz? [R]▼●

Kid, The (1921) **60m.** ***½ D: Charles Chaplin. Charlie Chaplin, Jack (Jackie) Coogan, Edna Purviance, Chuck Reisner, Lita Grey. Chaplin's first real feature mixes slapstick and sentiment in a winning combination, as the Tramp raises a streetwise orphan. Wonderful film launched Coogan as major child star, and it's easy to see why.▼●◗

Kid Blue (1973) **C-100m.** *½ D: James Frawley. Dennis Hopper, Warren Oates, Ben Johnson, Peter Boyle, Janice Rule, Lee Purcell, Ralph Waite, Clifton James, Howard Hesseman, M. Emmet Walsh. Pseudo hip Western comedy about misfit Hopper's faltering attempts to exist in small Texas town in early 20th century. Laughs, excitement, and interest are at a minimum here in spite of cast; Hopper is too old for his role. Panavision. [PG]

Kid Brother, The (1927) **83m.** **** D: Ted Wilde, J. A. Howe. Harold Lloyd, Jobyna Ralston, Walter James, Leo Willis, Olin Francis. Delightfully winning, beautifully filmed silent comedy with Harold as Cinderella-type kid brother in robust all-male family, who gets to prove his mettle in exciting finale where he subdues beefy villain. One of Lloyd's all-time best.▼

Kidco (1984) **C-105m.** **½ D: Ronald F. Maxwell. Scott Schwartz, Cinnamon Idles, Tristine Skyler, Elizabeth Gorcey. Okay comedy about the problems of preteen entrepreneur Schwartz and his cohorts, yuppies-in-training all. Ideal fare for the money-obsessed '80s yet barely released theatrically. Based on a true-life story; filmed in 1982. [PG]▼

Kid Dynamite (1943) **73m.** ** D: Wallace Fox. Leo Gorcey, Huntz Hall, Bobby Jordan, Sunshine Sammy Morrison, Bobby Stone, Gabriel Dell, Pamela Blake, Bennie Bartlett, Dave Durand. Rambunctious *East Side Kids* entry, basically an extended fight between Muggs (Gorcey) and Danny (Jordan).▼

Kid for Two Farthings, A (1955-British) **C-96m.** *** D: Carol Reed. Celia Johnson, Diana Dors, David Kossoff, Jonathan Ashmore, Brenda De Banzie, Primo Carnera, Sidney Tafler, Lou Jacobi. Imaginative fable of a poor little London boy (Ashmore) with a vivid imagination; he looks for a unicorn he believes will work miracles, and finds instead a sick, one-horned goat. Script by Wolf Mankowitz, based on his novel.▼

Kid From Brooklyn, The (1946) **C-113m.** *** D: Norman Z. McLeod. Danny Kaye, Virginia Mayo, Vera-Ellen, Steve Cochran, Eve Arden, Walter Abel, Lionel Stander, Fay Bainter. Comedy of milkman accidentally turned into prizefighter is often overdone but still a funny Kaye vehicle; remake of Harold Lloyd's THE MILKY WAY.▼●

Kid From Cleveland, The (1949) **89m.** *½ D: Herbert Kline. George Brent, Lynn Bari, Rusty (Russ) Tamblyn, Tommy Cook, Ann Doran, Bill Veeck, the Cleveland Indians. Sports reporter Brent becomes involved with troubled (but baseball-crazy) youth Tamblyn. Numbingly awful; of interest solely for the presences of Satchel Paige, Bob Feller, Tris Speaker, Hank Greenberg and other baseball immortals.

Kid From Kansas, The (1941) **66m.** *½ D: William Nigh. Leo Carrillo, Andy Devine, Dick Foran, Ann Doran. When a fruit buyer offers ridiculously low prices for planters' crops, competitors take drastic measures; low budget, low quality.

Kid From Left Field, The (1953) **80m.** ** D: Harmon Jones. Dan Dailey, Anne Bancroft, Billy Chapin, Lloyd Bridges, Ray Collins, Richard Egan. Homey little film with Dailey as ex-baseball star turned ballpark vendor who uses his son as cover while trying to turn a losing team around. Remade as 1979 TV movie with Gary Coleman.

Kid From Spain, The (1932) **96m.** *** D: Leo McCarey. Eddie Cantor, Lyda Roberti, Robert Young, Ruth Hall, John Miljan, Stanley Fields. Lavish Cantor musical with Eddie mistaken for famed bullfighter; Roberti is his vivacious leading lady. Striking Busby Berkeley musical numbers; look for Paulette Goddard and Betty Grable in the chorus line.▼●

Kid From Texas, The (1950) **C-78m.** ** D: Kurt Neumann. Audie Murphy, Gale Storm, Albert Dekker, Shepperd Strudwick, Will Geer, William Talman, Paul Ford. Slapdash Western, Murphy's first, in which he plays Billy the Kid. He's hired by kindly New Mexico rancher Strudwick, and becomes a victim of circumstance—and an outlaw.

Kid Galahad (1937) **101m.** *** D: Michael Curtiz. Edward G. Robinson, Bette Davis, Humphrey Bogart, Wayne Morris, Jane Bryan, Harry Carey, Veda Ann Borg. Well-paced actioner of promoter Robinson making naive Morris boxing star, losing his girl Davis to him at same time. Remade in 1941 (as THE WAGONS ROLL AT NIGHT) and in 1962. Shown on TV as BATTLING BELLHOP.▼

Kid Galahad (1962) **C-95m.** **½ D: Phil Karlson. Elvis Presley, Gig Young, Lola Albright, Joan Blackman, Charles Bronson, Ned Glass. This remake lacks wallop of the original. Elvis stars as a boxer who wins championship—and sings six forgettable songs—but prefers quiet life as garage mechanic. ▼●

Kid Glove Killer (1942) **74m.** *** D: Fred Zinnemann. Van Heflin, Lee Bowman, Marsha Hunt, Samuel S. Hinds, Cliff Clark, Eddie Quillan. Solid B film about police chemist Heflin uncovering the killer of a mayor, with taut direction by Zinnemann. Look for Ava Gardner as a car hop.

Kid in King Arthur's Court, A (1995) **C-89m.** **½ D: Michael Gottlieb. Thomas Ian Nicholas, Joss Ackland, Art Malik, Paloma Baeza, Kate Winslet, Ron Moody. Innocuous kids' comedy about a teenaged boy who's magically transported to ancient Camelot, where he helps to redeem the doddering King Arthur and undo the arch-villain Lord Belasco. Parents may yawn, but it's a pleasant-enough outing for kids. Young Nicholas is engaging and Ackland is solid as a rock, playing the good King. [PG]▼●◗

Kid Millions (1934) **90m.** *** D: Roy Del Ruth. Eddie Cantor, Ethel Merman, Ann Sothern, George Murphy, Warren Hymer, The Nicholas Brothers. Elaborate Cantor musical about Eddie inheriting a fortune. Musical numbers (including one by The Nicholas Brothers) and comedy set-pieces boost a weak script. Color segment in ice-cream factory a delight. Songs include "When My Ship Comes In." Lucille Ball is one of the Goldwyn Girls in this one. ▼●

Kidnap of Mary Lou, The SEE: **Almost Human**

Kidnapped (1938) **90m.** **½ D: Alfred L. Werker. Warner Baxter, Freddie Bartholomew, Arleen Whelan, C. Aubrey Smith, Reginald Owen, John Carradine, Nigel Bruce. Good adventure yarn of 1750s Scotland and England but not Robert Louis Stevenson; fine cast in generally entertaining script.

Kidnapped (1948) **80m.** ** D: William Beaudine. Roddy McDowall, Sue England, Dan O'Herlihy, Roland Winters, Jeff Corey. Disappointing low-budget adaptation of Robert Louis Stevenson novel.

Kidnapped (1960) **C-97m.** **½ D: Robert Stevenson. Peter Finch, James MacArthur, Bernard Lee, Niall MacGinnis, John Laurie, Finlay Currie, Peter O'Toole. Disney feature filmed in England is faithful to Robert Louis Stevenson's classic novel, but surprisingly dull. Good cast and vivid atmosphere are its major assets.▼●

Kidnapped (1971-British) **C-100m.** ** D: Delbert Mann. Michael Caine, Trevor Howard, Jack Hawkins, Donald Pleasence, Gordon Jackson, Vivien Heilbron. Disappointing version of Stevenson tale is made endurable by Caine's pleasing performance as Alan Breck. Panavision. [G]

Kidnapped (1995) **C-195m. TVM** D: Ivan Passer. Armand Assante, Brian McCardie, Patrick Malahide, Michael Kitchen, Brian Blessed, Adam Blackwood, Brian McGrath. Assante swashbuckles through this full-bodied, spectacularly filmed version of the classic; probably as close to Robert Louis Stevenson as any that preceded it through the years. Adapted by John Goldsmith and Michael Barlow and enacted with verve by a cast of predominantly British, Irish, Scottish, and Welsh actors; newcomer McCardie is quite admirable as David Balfour. Shot entirely in Ireland and coexecutive produced by Francis Ford Coppola. Made for cable; originally shown in two parts. Above average. ▼

Kidnapping of the President, The (1980-U.S.-Canadian) **C-113m.** **½ D: George Mendeluk. William Shatner, Hal Holbrook, Van Johnson, Ava Gardner, Miguel Fernandes, Cindy Girling. The title tells all: Third World terrorists kidnap president Holbrook, with Secret Service chief Shatner intervening. OK actioner is certainly topical; based on Charles Templeton's novel. [R]▼

Kidnap Syndicate (1975-Italian) **C-83m.** ** D: Fernando Di Leo. James Mason, Valentina Cortese, Luc Merenda, Irina Maleeva, Vittorio Caprioli. Crime drama about the snatching of two youngsters—the son of a multimillionaire and an auto mechanic's boy—and how the industrialist's rash actions cause all manner of violence and a rampage of vengeance. [R]▼

Kid Rodelo (1966) **91m.** *½ D: Richard Carlson. Don Murray, Janet Leigh, Broderick Crawford, Richard Carlson. After jail term, cowboys go off to search for hidden $50,000 in gold. You've seen it all before. Filmed in Spain. Based on a Louis L'Amour novel.

Kids (1995) **C-90m.** **½ D: Larry Clark. Leo Fitzpatrick, Justin Pierce, Chloe Sevigny, Rosario Dawson, Yakira Peguero, Harold Hunter, Sarah Henderson. Photographer/skateboardist Clark's filmmaking debut is a cinema verité–style look at aimless N.Y.C. teens, focusing on Telly (Fitzpatrick), who loves to deflower virgins, and Jennie (Sevigny), who's facing the consequences of one such encounter. A telling portrait of 90s-style hedonism and the results of kids growing up without parents to guide them. Utterly matter-of-fact and nonjudgmental about its sexual frankness and violence, (which is precisely what disturbed many viewers). Is it purely exploitive, or true to life? You be the judge. ▼●◗

Kids Are Alright, The (1979) **C-108m.** *** D: Jeff Stein. Overlong and disjointed, yet frequently exhilarating documentary on The Who that manages to capture the anarchic spirit of the group—and of rock 'n' roll. Brief appearances by Steve Martin, Tom Smothers, and Ringo Starr, along with wild interviews with Townshend, Daltrey, Moon, and Entwistle. Songs include "Magic Bus," "Happy Jack," and several numbers from *Tommy*. [PG]▼

Kids in the Hall Brain Candy SEE: **Brain Candy**

Kid Vengeance (1977) **C-94m.** *½ D: Joe Manduke. Lee Van Cleef, Jim Brown, John Marley, Leif Garrett, Glynnis O'Connor, Matt Clark. Bloody, gory, obnoxious Western about young Garrett seeking revenge against outlaws who killed his parents and kidnapped his sister.▼

Kika (1993-Spanish) **C-111m.** *** D: Pedro Almodóvar. Peter Coyote, Veronica Forque, Victoria Abril, Alex Casanovas, Rossy de Palma, Santiago Lajusticia, Anabel Alonso, Bibi Andersson. Wacky, very adult story about free-spirited makeup artist Kika (Forque, whose performance is positively infectious) and the men in her life, including an American expatriate writer (Coyote) and a psychotic prison escapee. Almodóvar has given his favorite actress, Abril, the role of a lifetime: a tabloid TV hostess who cruises Madrid with a camera strapped to her head, seeking to capture criminal acts on videotape. Very funny, explicitly sexual film doesn't quite sustain its momentum to the end, but remains fresh and certainly different. Will undoubtedly shock those unfamiliar with Almodóvar. ▼●◗

Kikujiro (1999-Japanese) **C-116m.** ** D: Takeshi Kitano. Beat Takeshi, Yasuke Sekiguchi, Kayoko Kishimoto, Yuko Daike, Beat Kiyoshi. Half road movie, half variation on the unhappy child/crusty adult genre, a listless story of a young boy's journey to seek out his long-gone mother—with a low-life chaperone. Title character (played by the director under his "Beat Takeshi" monicker) is an unsympathetic bully, while young Sekiguchi is a bit of a lump. By the time this very protracted story tries turning fanciful by introducing two of the most unlikely bikers in history, a cutting-edge action filmmaker has lost control of his picture. [PG-13]

Kill A Dragon (1967) **C-91m.** *½ D: Michael Moore. Jack Palance, Fernando Lamas, Aldo Ray, Alizia Gur. Complicated, far-fetched tale of feudal baron in modern China and his American adversary.

Kill and Kill Again (1981) **C-100m.** ** D: Ivan Hall. James Ryan, Anneline Kriel, Ken Gampu, Norman Robinson, Michael Meyer. OK chop-socky actioner, with Ryan foiling scientist Meyer's plot to take over the world. Filmed in South Africa. [PG]▼◗

Kill, Baby . . . Kill! (1966-Italian) **C-83m.** *** D: Mario Bava. Erika Blanc, Giacomo Rossi Stuart, Fabienne Dali, Giana Vivaldi, Piero Lulli, Max Lawrence. One of horror maestro Bava's best films, spoiled only by his overuse of a zoom lens. Suicide victims in a small Transylvanian village are found with gold coins embedded in their hearts. Stylish, witty and colorful, with many astonishing sequences. Also shown in cut version under title CURSE OF THE LIVING DEAD. [PG]▼

Killbots SEE: **Chopping Mall**

Kill Castro SEE: **Cuba Crossing**

Killer SEE: **Bulletproof Heart**

Killer, The (1989-Hong Kong) **C-110m.** ***½ D: John Woo. Chow Yun-Fat, Sally Yeh, Danny Lee, Kenneth Tsang, Chu Kong, Lam Chung, Shing Fui-On. Spectacular thriller about a hit man (Yun-Fat) who forms an unusual relationship with a singer (Yeh) he accidentally blinds and the cop (Lee) assigned to stop him. Pulp melodrama achieves near-operatic grandeur, thanks to multi-leveled characterizations and story, creative direction, and phenomenal action scenes that make most American films look anemic by comparison. Woo also wrote the screenplay.▼●◗

Killer: A Journal of Murder (1996) **C-91m.** *½ D: Tim Metcalfe. James Woods, Robert Sean Leonard, Steve Forrest, Robert John Burke, Cara Buono, Ellen Greene, Jeffrey DeMunn, Christopher Petrosino, Richard Riehle, Harold Gould. In 1929, young Jewish prison guard Leonard befriends Leavenworth convict Carl Panzram (Woods), smuggling him forbidden writing supplies. Panzram, a habitual killer, writes his story, which we see in flashbacks. Woods is brilliant, but the point of view is hackneyed and outmoded. Badly written and directed. [R]▼●◗

Killer Ape (1953) **68m.** *½ D: Spencer Bennet. Johnny Weissmuller, Carol Thurston, Ray Corrigan, Max Palmer, Nestor Paiva, Nick Stuart. *Jungle Jim* Weissmuller takes on evil white hunters who are using animals to test their germ warfare weapons. Former cowboy star Corrigan, who frequently worked in an ape suit for jungle cheapies, appears here sans costume.

Killer Bait SEE: **Too Late for Tears**

Killer Bats SEE: **Devil Bat, The**

Killer Elite, The (1975) **C-122m.** ** D: Sam Peckinpah. James Caan, Robert Duvall, Arthur Hill, Bo Hopkins, Mako, Burt Young, Gig Young. Mercenary Duvall double-crosses partner Caan, leading to characteristic but lesser Peckinpah bloodbath involving the CIA. Trashy script slightly redeemed by director's flair for action sequences. Panavision. [PG]▼●◗

Killer Fish (1979-Italian-Brazilian) **C-101m.** ** D: Anthony M. Dawson (Antonio Margheriti). Lee Majors, Karen Black, James Franciscus, Margaux Hemingway, Marisa Berenson, Gary Collins. Pursuit of stolen jewels dumped in lake full of deadly piranha fish forms basis for this predictable outing filmed in Brazil. Same fishy predators were used in much more enjoyable film, PIRANHA. Also known as DEADLY TREASURE OF THE PIRANHA. [PG]▼

Killer Force (1975) **C-101m.** ** D: Val Guest. Peter Fonda, Telly Savalas, Hugh O'Brian, Christopher Lee, Maud Adams, O. J. Simpson, Ian Yule. Dirty doings at diamond syndicate's desert mine in South Africa. Has cast and potential but overly diffuse and complex. [R]▼

Killer Grizzly SEE: **Grizzly**

Killer Inside Me, The (1976) **C-99m.** *** D: Burt Kennedy. Stacy Keach, Susan Tyrrell, Keenan Wynn, Tisha Sterling, Don Stroud, Charles McGraw. Bizarre opus about a psychotic deputy sheriff (flashbacks accounting for his present state) about to go off the deep end; saved and made believable by strong performance from Keach. Panavision. [R]▼●◗

Killer Is Loose, The (1956) **73m.** *** D: Budd Boetticher. Joseph Cotten, Rhonda Fleming, Wendell Corey, Alan Hale, Michael Pate. Cop Cotten accidentally kills the wife of quiet bank-clerk-turned-robber Corey, who later escapes from prison with eye-for-an-eye revenge in mind. Fast-paced suspenseful sleeper, with excellent L.A. location photography and perhaps Corey's best performance: he's both scary and pathetic.

Killer Klowns From Outer Space (1988) **C-88m.** **½ D: Stephen Chiodo. Grant Cramer, Suzanne Snyder, John Vernon, John Allen Nelson, Peter Licassi, Michael Siegel, Royal Dano. One-of-a-kind alien invasion sci-fi featuring blood-drinking alien clowns harvesting a small city. Routinely plotted, but vividly designed, with cheeky humor, it plays its premise to the hilt, all circus bases touched. A cult favorite. [PG-13]▼●

Killer Leopard (1954) **70m.** *½ D: Ford Beebe, Edward Morey, Jr. Johnny Sheffield, Beverly Garland, Barry Bernard, Donald Murphy, Leonard Mudie, Smoki Whitfield. Bomba the Jungle Boy guides a Hollywood starlet through the bush to find her missing husband. Did this next-to-last series entry really require two directors?

Killer McCoy (1947) **104m.** *** D: Roy Rowland. Mickey Rooney, Brian Donlevy, Ann Blyth, James Dunn, Tom Tully, Sam Levene. Good drama of fighter Rooney accidentally involved in murder, with fine supporting cast of promoters and racketeers. Remake of THE CROWD ROARS (1938).

Killers, The (1946) **105m.** **** D: Robert Siodmak. Burt Lancaster, Ava Gardner, Edmond O'Brien, Albert Dekker, Sam Levene, Virginia Christine, William Conrad, Charles McGraw. Compelling crime drama (based on Hemingway story) of ex-fighter found murdered, subsequent investigation. Film provides fireworks, early success of Lancaster (in film debut) and Gardner. Miklos Rozsa's dynamic score features the familiar dum-da-dum-dum theme later utilized by *Dragnet*. Screenplay by Anthony Veiller (and, uncredited, John Huston). Reworked in 1964.▼●

Killers, The (1964) **C-95m.** **½ D: Don Siegel. Lee Marvin, John Cassavetes, Angie Dickinson, Ronald Reagan, Clu Gulager, Claude Akins, Norman Fell. Two inquisitive hit men piece together the story of the man they've just murdered, in this free adaptation of Hemingway's short story. Originally shot for TV, it was rejected as "too violent" and released to theaters instead. Some latter-day notoriety derives from Reagan's casting as a brutal crime kingpin; it was his last movie role. Marvin has a great closing line.▼

Killer's Carnival (1965) **C-95m.** **½ D: Albert Cardiff, Robert Lynn, Sheldon Reynolds. Stewart Granger, Lex Barker, Pierre Brice, Karin Dor, Pascal Petit. Three stories of intrigue set in Rome, Vienna, and Brazil; tired cast in OK espionage tales.

Killer's Curse SEE: **Beyond the Living**

Killers From Space (1954) **71m.** BOMB D: W. Lee Wilder. Peter Graves, James Seay, Steve Pendleton, Barbara Bestar, Frank Gerstle. Scientist Graves, killed in a plane crash, is brought back to life by aliens from the planet Astron Delta. They're planning to invade Earth and want him to pilfer atomic data. Poor in all departments—and too dull to be funny. ▼

Killer Shark (1950) **76m.** *½ D: Oscar (Budd) Boetticher. Roddy McDowall, Laurette Luez, Roland Winters, Edward Norris, Douglas Fowley, Dick Moore. Back Bayite McDowall learns new values as skipper of shark-hunting vessel; cheapie film.▼

Killer Shrews, The (1959) **70m.** **½ D: Ray Kellogg. James Best, Ingrid Goude, Ken Curtis, Baruch Lumet, Gordon McLendon. No, this isn't about an attack of nagging wives, it's an inventive but silly sci-fi tale of people isolated on a Texas island, menaced by title creatures created by well-intentioned scientist.▼

Killer's Kiss (1955) **67m.** ** D: Stanley Kubrick. Frank Silvera, Jamie Smith, Irene Kane, Jerry Jarret. Meandering account of revenge when boxer's courting of working-girl causes her boss to commit murder. Interesting early Kubrick; the inspiration for the film-within-a-film of STRANGERS KISS. Leading lady Kane is now TV and newspaper journalist Chris Chase.▼●◗

Killers of Kilimanjaro (1959-British) **C-91m.** ** D: Richard Thorpe. Robert Taylor, Anthony Newley, Anne Aubrey, Gregoire Aslan, Alan Cuthbertson, Donald Pleasence. Spotty adventure yarn of railroad-building in East Africa. CinemaScope.

Killer Spy (1958-French) **82m.** ** D: Georges Lampin. Jean Marais, Nadja Tiller, Andre Luguet, Bernadette Lafont. Capable cast tries to instill life into this spy-and-murder yarn; scenery outshines script.

Killers Three (1968) **C-88m.** BOMB D: Bruce Kessler. Robert Walker, Diane Varsi, Dick Clark, Norman Alden, Maureen Arthur, Merle Haggard. Knock-off of BONNIE AND CLYDE doesn't offer much by way of comparison, unless you find the idea of Dick Clark in wirerims a gas. [M/PG]

Killer That Stalked New York, The (1950) **79m.** **½ D: Earl McEvoy. Charles Korvin, Evelyn Keyes, William Bishop, Dorothy Malone, Lola Albright, Jim Backus, Whit Bissell, Richard Egan. Interesting B film of a diamond-smuggling couple sought by police because they contracted contagious disease while abroad.

Kill Her Gently (1957-British) **73m.** ** D: Charles Saunders. Marc Lawrence, Maureen Connell, George Mikell, Griffith Jones, John Gayford. Brutal B film of supposedly cured mental patient hiring two convicts-at-large to kill his wife.

Killing, The (1956) **83m.** ***½ D: Stanley Kubrick. Sterling Hayden, Coleen Gray, Vince Edwards, Jay C. Flippen, Ted de Corsia, Marie Windsor, Joe Sawyer, Elisha Cook, Timothy Carey. The film that really put Kubrick on the map—a case study of a racetrack heist, with a colorful cast of characters, including the ultimate nebbish (Cook, married to vixenish Windsor) and an ultra-cool killer for hire (Carey). Major flaw: the *Dragnet*-style narration. Kubrick scripted from Lionel White's novel *Clean Break.*▼●◗

Killing Affair, A (1988) **C-100m.** *½ D: David Saperstein. Peter Weller, Kathy Baker, John Glover, Bill Smitrovich. Dreary goings on in the Southern backwoods, circa 1943, where Weller kills Baker's hateful husband, and then develops a turbulent relationship with her. Based on Robert Houston's novel *Monday, Tuesday, Wednesday*, this marks writer Saperstein's directing debut. Filmed in 1985. [R]▼●

Killing 'em Softly (1985-Canadian) **C-81m.** BOMB D: Max Fischer. George Segal, Irene Cara, Clark Johnson, Nicholas Campbell, Joyce Gordon. Segal kills a rock band manager who owes him money; Cara's boyfriend is charged with the crime. Guess what—Segal and Cara fall in love. Sloppily made and embarrassingly bad. ▼

Killing Fields, The (1984-British) **C-141m.** ***½ D: Roland Joffé. Sam Waterston, Haing S. Ngor, John Malkovich, Julian Sands, Craig T. Nelson, Bill Paterson, Athol Fugard, Spalding Gray. Highly charged drama based on the memoirs of *N.Y. Times* reporter Sidney Schanberg, who remained in Cambodia after American evacuation—putting his native translator and assistant Dith Pran in great jeopardy. Frighteningly realistic depiction of a country torn apart by war and terrorism; an emotional powerhouse. Long but worthwhile. Impressive feature debut for documentary director Joffé; Ngor (who lived through Cambodian turmoil in real life) won Best Supporting Actor Oscar for his acting debut. Oscars also went to cinematographer Chris Menges, editor Jim Clark. [R]▼●

Killing Game, The (1967-French) **C-94m.** **½ D: Alain Jessua. Jean-Pierre Cassel, Claudine Auger, Michael Duchaussoy, Eleanore Hirt. Mystery comic strip writer comes up with his ultimate puzzler. Not bad.▼

Killing Heat SEE: **Grass Is Singing, The**

Killing in a Small Town, A (1990) **C-100m. TVM** D: Stephen Gyllenhaal. Barbara Hershey, Brian Dennehy, John Terry, Richard Gilliland, Lee Garlington, Hal Holbrook. Hershey gives a riveting Emmy-winning performance as a churchgoing wife and mother in a quiet Texas town who one day strikes her best friend 41 times with an ax. Her story unravels through the trial in Cynthia Cidre's artful adaptation of the real-life case (told in John Bloom and Jim Atkinson's book *Evidence of Love*). Above average.▼●

Killing of a Chinese Bookie, The (1976) **C-109m.** *½ D: John Cassavetes. Ben Gazzara, Timothy Agoglia Carey, Seymour Cassel, Azizi Johari, Meade Roberts, Alice Friedland. Strange, self-indulgent (even for Cassavetes) home movie centering around the owner of a strip joint, the mob and what used to be called "B-girls." Small cult may take to this; others beware. [R]▼●◗

Killing of Angel Street, The (1981-Australian) **C-101m.** **½ D: Donald Crombie. Liz Alexander, John Hargreaves, Alexander Archdale, Reg Lye, Gordon McDougall. Fair melodrama about corrupt real estate manipulators harassing homeowners to sell their property. Communist Hargreaves and geologist Alexander take on the villains when her activist father mysteriously dies. Supposedly based on actual events that also inspired HEATWAVE (1983).▼

Killing of Sister George, The (1968) **C-138m.** **½ D: Robert Aldrich. Beryl Reid, Susannah York, Coral Browne, Ronald Fraser, Patricia Medina. Overwrought but entertaining drama, with comedy touches, about soap opera actress Reid who fears her character (Sister George) is due to be "killed." Story follows her deteriorating lesbian relationship with dependent, childlike York, who's caught the eye of network executive Browne. Very good performances in this adaptation of Frank Marcus' play. [R—originally rated X]▼◗

Killing Time, The (1987) **C-94m.** ** D: Rick King. Beau Bridges, Kiefer Sutherland, Wayne Rogers, Joe Don Baker, Camelia Kath, Janet Carroll, Michael Madsen, Gracie Harrison. Stale noir-ish thriller about sex, sin, violence and duplicity in a small California town. Sutherland has murdered a deputy, assumed his identity, while new sheriff Bridges and mistress Kath plot to do in her evil husband (Rogers). DOUBLE INDEMNITY it ain't! [R]▼●

Killing Zoe (1994) **C-98m.** **½ D: Roger Avary. Eric Stoltz, Jean-Hugues Anglade, Julie Delpy, Tai Thai, Bruce Ramsey, Kario Salem, Salvator Xurev, Gary Kemp, Martin Raymond, Cecilia Peck. Writer-director Avary, coscripter of PULP FICTION, spreads mayhem and body tissue in his own Paris-set directorial debut—a Bastille Day bank caper in which some participants are preoccupied with drugs, and their imported Yank safecracker is preoccupied with a call girl who has surpassed all expectations. Plot twists and stylistic flourishes notwithstanding, zippy melodrama is too little, too late. *Extremely violent.* Quentin Tarantino coexecutive-produced. [R] ▼●◗

Kill! Kill! Kill! (1972-French-Spanish-German-Italian) **C-90m.** *½ D: Romain Gary. Jean Seberg, James Mason, Stephen Boyd, Curt Jurgens, Daniel Emilfork. Interpol agent Mason, on the trail of Italian drug kingpins, gets competition from fellow agent Boyd, who believes in playing dirty. Hardened violence clashes with writer-director Gary's purple prose. Original title KILL, at 102m.

Kill Me Again (1989) **C-94m.** **½ D: John Dahl. Val Kilmer, Joanne Whalley-Kilmer, Michael Madsen, Jonathan Gries, Pat Mulligan, Nick Dimitri, Bibi Besch. Femme fatale Whalley-Kilmer makes like Jane Greer in this contemporary film noir, sexily scamming her way through the Nevada desert (and a couple of big cities) trying to steal gangland booty. Fans of detective genre will enjoy this mild send-up of crime flicks. Fun, but also inherently derivative. [R]▼

Kill Me Tomorrow (1957-British) **80m.** ** D: Terence Fisher. Pat O'Brien, Lois Maxwell, George Coulouris, Robert Brown, Tommy Steele. Adequate B film about newspaperman cracking murder case leading to arrest of diamond-smuggling syndicate.

Kill or Be Killed (1950) **67m.** *½ D: Max Nosseck. Lawrence Tierney, George Coulouris, Marissa O'Brien, Rudolph Anders. Pedestrian account of man on lam hunted down in jungle by law enforcers.

Kill or Be Killed (1980) **C-90m.** ** D: Ivan Hall. James Ryan, Norman Combes, Charlotte Michelle, Danie DuPlessis. Karate champions lock limbs as ex-Nazi coach seeks revenge against Japanese counterpart who bested him in a tournament during WW2. A cut above the usual martial arts fodder. [PG]▼

Killpoint (1984) **C-89m.** *½ D: Frank Harris. Leo Fong, Richard Roundtree, Cameron Mitchell, Stack Pierce, Hope Holiday. Dreary, one-dimensional actioner with cop Fong and agent Roundtree on the trail of gunrunners. Sickeningly violent. [R]▼●

Kill the Umpire (1950) **78m.** **½ D: Lloyd Bacon. William Bendix, Una Merkel, Ray Collins, Gloria Henry, William Frawley, Tom D'Andrea. Lightweight comedy about baseball lover who becomes the sport's most hated man, the umpire. Ends with spectacular slapstick chase. Screenplay by Frank Tashlin.

Kilroy Was Here (1947) **68m.** *½ D: Phil Karlson. Jackie Cooper, Jackie Coogan, Wanda McKay, Frank Jenks. Supposedly topical comedy (then) is pretty limp now, with innocent victim of "Kilroy Was Here" joke trying to lead normal life despite his name.

Kim (1950) **C-113m.** ***½ D: Victor Saville. Errol Flynn, Dean Stockwell, Paul Lukas, Thomas Gomez, Cecil Kellaway. Rousing actioner based on Kipling classic, set in 1880s India, with British soldiers combatting rebellious natives. Flavorful production. Remade for TV.▼

Kim (1984) **C-150m. TVM** D: John Davies. Peter O'Toole, Bryan Brown, John Rhys-Davies, Ravi Sheth, Julian Glover, Lee Montague. Enthusiastic new version of the Kipling tale about Indian boy recruited by the British for some high adventure. Brown has the old Errol Flynn role, Sheth makes an impressive debut as Kim, and O'Toole has a high old time as an Indian mystic in a bald wig. James Brabazon wrote this colorful adaptation. Above average.▼

Kimberley Jim (1965-South African) **C-82m.** ** D: Emil Nofal. Jim Reeves, Madeleine Usher, Clive Parnell, Arthur Swemmer, Mike Holt. Minor musical of two carefree gamblers who win diamond mine in fixed poker game, and then have a change of heart. Rare screen appearance by late country singer Reeves. Scanoscope.

Kindergarten Cop (1990) **C-111m.** **½ D: Ivan Reitman. Arnold Schwarzenegger, Penelope Ann Miller, Pamela Reed, Linda Hunt, Richard Tyson, Carroll Baker, Cathy Moriarty, Park Overall, Richard Portnow, Angela Bassett. Macho cop is forced to masquerade as a kindergarten teacher in order to find a youngster who's living with his mother incognito. Amusing but overly contrived Schwarzenegger vehicle blends elements of comedy, cop thriller, and romance. Despite the presence of cute kids, this is definitely not for children—especially the finale. [PG-13]▼●◗

Kind Hearts and Coronets (1949-British) **104m.** ***½ D: Robert Hamer. Dennis Price, Alec Guinness, Valerie Hobson, Joan Greenwood, Miles Malleson, Hugh Griffith, Jeremy Spenser, Arthur Lowe. Peerless black comedy of castoff member of titled family setting out to eliminate them all. Guinness plays all eight victims! Hamer and John Dighton adapted Roy Horniman's novel *Israel Rank.*▼●

Kind Lady (1936) **76m.** **½ D: George B. Seitz. Aline MacMahon, Basil Rathbone, Mary Carlisle, Frank Albertson, Dudley Digges, Doris Lloyd, Donald Meek. MacMahon is being blackmailed and held prisoner in her own house by Rathbone and his cronies; fairly entertaining, but not as good as the remake. Adapted from the Edward Chodorov play, which was based on a Hugh Walpole story. Doris Lloyd, who plays the victim's sister here, took the role of her housemaid in the 1951 version.

Kind Lady (1951) **78m.** *** D: John Sturges. Ethel Barrymore, Maurice Evans, Angela Lansbury, Betsy Blair, Keenan Wynn, John Williams, Doris Lloyd. Creepy little chiller about a genteel older woman (Barrymore) who is victimized by a charmer (Evans), who takes over her home—and her life. Wynn is particularly effective as a thug/butler. Coscripted by Edward Chodorov, and based on his play; filmed previously in 1936.

Kind of Loving, A (1962-British) **112m.** *** D: John Schlesinger. Alan Bates, June Ritchie, Thora Hird, Bert Palmer, Gwen Nelson, Malcolm Patton, Leonard Rossiter, Peter Madden. Intelligent account of young couple forced to marry when girl becomes pregnant, detailing their home life; well acted.▼

Kindred, The (1987) **C-97m.** **½ D: Stephen Carpenter, Jeffrey Obrow. Rod Steiger, Kim Hunter, David Allen Brooks, Amanda Pays, Talia Balsam, Timothy Gibbs, Peter Frechette, Julia Montgomery. Enjoyable horror flick of teens in danger from a scientific experiment that resulted in a grotesque monster. OK special effects in a film marking Steiger's latter-day entry into Donald Pleasence-type horror roles. [R]▼●

King: A Filmed Record . . . Montgomery to Memphis (1970) **153m.** ***½ D: Joseph L. Mankiewicz, Sidney Lumet. Superior documentary covering life of Dr. Martin Luther King from 1955 until his death in 1968 is marred only by the pretentious and unnecessary "bridges" featuring such stars as Paul Newman, Joanne Woodward, and James Earl Jones. Otherwise, well-chosen compilation of news footage carries tremendous wallop. TV version is shortened to 90m.●

King and Country (1964-British) **90m.** ***½ D: Joseph Losey. Dirk Bogarde, Tom Courtenay, Leo McKern, Barry Foster, James Villiers, Peter Copley. Vivid antiwar treatise beautifully acted by strong supporting cast. Bogarde is detached Army captain lawyer assigned to defend deserter private Courtenay during WW1. Score composed by harmonica virtuoso Larry Adler. ▼

King and Four Queens, The (1956) **C-86m.** **½ D: Raoul Walsh. Clark Gable, Eleanor Parker, Jo Van Fleet, Jean Willes, Barbara Nichols, Sara Shane, Jay C. Flippen. Static misfire with Gable on the search for money hidden by husbands of four women he encounters. CinemaScope.▼

King and I, The (1956) **C-133m.** ***½ D: Walter Lang. Deborah Kerr, Yul Brynner, Rita Moreno, Martin Benson, Terry Saunders, Rex Thompson, Alan Mowbray. Excellent film adaptation of Rodgers and Hammerstein Broadway musical, based on book filmed in 1946 as ANNA AND THE KING OF SIAM (and remade as ANNA AND THE KING). Kerr plays widowed English schoolteacher who travels to Siam to teach the King's many children, and finds dealing with His Highness her greatest challenge. Brynner gives the performance of a lifetime, and won an Oscar recreating his Broadway role. Kerr is charming; her singing voice was dubbed by Marni Nixon. Songs include "Hello, Young Lovers," "Getting to Know You," "Shall We Dance." Also won Oscars for art direction-set decoration, Irene Sharaff's costumes, Alfred Newman and Ken Darby's scoring. Screenplay by Ernest Lehman. Cinema Scope 55. ▼●◗

King and I, The (1999) **C-87m.** **½ D: Richard Rich. Voices of Miranda Richardson, Christiane Noll, Martin Vidnovic, Ian Richardson, Darrell Hammond, Adam Wylie, Allen D. Hong. Condensed animated kiddie version of classic Rodgers and Hammerstein musical now includes romps with animal chums, black magic by the king's evil minister, and unfunny slapstick with his racially stereotyped sidekick. Artwork and settings are colorful and lavish, but animation is erratic. Eight songs (out of twenty) survive somewhat unscathed; Barbra Streisand sings medley over end credits. [G] ▼●◗

King and the Chorus Girl, The (1937) **94m.** **½ D: Mervyn LeRoy. Joan Blondell, Fernand Gravet, Edward Everett Horton, Jane Wyman. Gravet is nobleman on a lark, finding true love with beautiful chorine Blondell. Lively production. Written by Norman Krasna and Groucho Marx!

King Creole (1958) **116m.** **½ D: Michael Curtiz. Elvis Presley, Carolyn Jones, Dolores Hart, Dean Jagger, Liliane Montevecchi, Walter Matthau, Paul Stewart, Vic Morrow. Elvis is quite good as young New Orleans night-club singer who is eventually dragged into the criminal underworld. Toned-down adaptation of Harold Robbins' *A Stone For Danny Fisher* (which was set in Chicago), coscripted by Michael V. Gazzo. Songs include "Hard Headed Woman," "Trouble," title number. VistaVision.▼●◗

King David (1985) **C-114m.** **½ D: Bruce Beresford. Richard Gere, Edward Woodward, Alice Krige, Denis Quilley, Niall Buggy, Cherie Lunghi, Hurd Hatfield, Jack Klaff. Solid biblical story traces young David's life from boyhood battle with Goliath to uneasy reign as king; only goes awry in second half, where abruptness undermines narrative. Visually striking, with Donald McAlpine's photography, Carl Davis's music strong assets—along with outstanding performance by Woodward as deposed King Saul. Panavision. [PG-13]▼●

Kingdom, The (1994-Danish) **C-271m.** ***½ D: Lars von Trier. Ernst-Hugo Jaregard, Kirsten Rolffes, Ghita Norby, Soren Pilmark, Holger Juul Hansen, Annevig Schelde Ebbe, Jens Okking, Otto Brandenburg, Baard Owe, Solbjorg Hojfeldt. Four-hour film is actually four Danish TV episodes strung together, set and shot at the real National State Hospital in Copenhagen (known as "The Kingdom"). As virtually every critic has pointed out, this is *ER* meets *Twin Peaks,* with crackpot doctors, paranormal goings-on, sex, black humor, etc. A must for those who think they've seen everything. Note: The unusual look of the film (a brownish, dirty-looking print texture) was achieved by shooting on 16mm, transferring to video, editing on video, transferring back to 16mm, and finally blowing up to 35mm! Followed by THE KINGDOM, PART 2. ▼●

Kingdom of the Spiders (1977) **C-94m.** *** D: John (Bud) Cardos. William Shatner, Tiffany Bolling, Woody Strode, Lieux Dressler, Altovise Davis. Unsurprising but well-made chiller about veterinarian Shatner and entomologist Bolling discovering that tarantulas are going on the warpath in Arizona. [PG]▼

Kingfish: A Story of Huey P. Long (1995) **C-100m. TVM** D: Thomas Schlamme. John Goodman, Matt Craven, Anne Heche, Ann Dowd, Bob Gunton, Bill Cobbs, Hoyt Axton. Episodic look at the charismatic, boorish Depression-era Southern demagogue is anchored by Goodman's tour-de-force performance. Paul Monash's script is confused; Alexander Gruszynski's photography diffused; Schlamme's direction obtuse. Made for cable. Average.▼●

Kingfisher Caper, The (1975-South African) **C-90m.** **½ D: Dirk DeVilliers. Hayley Mills, David McCallum, Jon Cypher. Typical tale of intrigue, love and passion interwoven with a family feud over the running of a South African diamond empire. Aka DIAMOND LUST. [PG] ▼

King Gun SEE: **Gatling Gun, The**

King in New York, A (1957-British) **105m.** **½ D: Charles Chaplin. Charles Chaplin, Dawn Addams, Oliver Johnston, Maxine Audley, Harry Green, Michael Chaplin. Unseen in U.S. until 1973, supposedly anti-American film is rather mild satire of 1950s sensibilities, witch hunts, and technology. Chaplin over-indulges himself, and film lacks focus, but there are good moments, and interesting performance by son Michael as young malcontent.▼●

King in Shadow (1956-German) **87m.** ** D: Harald Braun. O. W. Fischer, Horst Buchholz, Odile Versois, Gunther Hadank. Buchholz is mentally disturbed young King of Sweden in 1760s; court intrigue encouraged by his domineering mother (Versois) makes for tepid costume tale.

King Kong (1933) **103m.** **** D: Merian C. Cooper, Ernest B. Schoedsack. Fay Wray, Robert Armstrong, Bruce Cabot, Frank Reicher, Sam Hardy, Noble Johnson, James Flavin. Classic version of beauty-and-beast theme is a moviegoing must, with Willis O'Brien's special effects and animation of monster ape Kong still unsurpassed. Final sequence atop Empire State Building is now cinema folklore; Max Steiner music score also memorable. Followed immediately by THE SON OF KONG. Remade in 1976. Also shown in computer-colored version.▼●

King Kong (1976) **C-134m.** *½ D: John Guillermin. Jeff Bridges, Charles Grodin, Jessica Lange, John Randolph, Rene Auberjonois, Julius Harris, Jack O'Halloran, Ed Lauter, John Lone. Addle-brained remake of 1933 classic has great potential but dispels all the mythic, larger-than-life qualities of the original with idiotic characters and campy approach. Highly touted special effects (which earned a special Oscar) run hot-and-cold; real marvel is Rick Baker in a gorilla suit. Extra footage added for network showing. Lange's film debut; Joe Piscopo has a small role; look fast for Corbin Bernsen playing a reporter. Followed a decade later by KING KONG LIVES. Panavision. [PG]▼●◗

King Kong Escapes (1967-Japanese) **C-96m.** BOMB D: Ishiro Honda. Rhodes Reason, Mie Hama, Linda Miller, Akira Takarada. Contrived new plot involving girl who wins ape's heart, battle against would-be world conqueror. Kong never had it so bad. Tohoscope. [G]

King Kong Lives (1986) **C-105m.** BOMB D: John Guillermin. Brian Kerwin, Linda Hamilton, John Ashton, Peter Michael Goetz, Frank Maraden, Alan Sader. Dino De Laurentiis sequel gives the ape a mate with everything he loves: She's tall, statuesque, with great mossy teeth. The Army tries to kill them (naturally), but not before a finale that actually rips off the final scene in SPARTACUS. Desperate. J-D-C Scope. [PG-13]▼●

King Kong vs. Godzilla (1962-Japanese-U.S.) **C-90m.** **½ D: Thomas Montgomery, Ishiro Honda. Michael Keith, James Yagi, Tadao Takashima, Mie Hama. All talk, talk, talk until the rousing finale, when the two monsters clash. Special effects are above average. Tohoscope.▼◗

King Lear (1971-British) **137m.** ***½ D: Peter Brook. Paul Scofield, Irene Worth, Jack MacGowran, Alan Webb, Cyril Cusack, Patrick Magee. This version of Shakespeare tragedy could be heavy going for the uninitiated, but often a strong and rewarding experience. Starkly photographed in Denmark. [PG]▼

King Lear (1987-U.S.-Swiss) **C-91m.** *½ D: Jean-Luc Godard. Peter Sellars, Burgess Meredith, Molly Ringwald, Jean-Luc Godard, Woody Allen, Norman Mailer, Kate Mailer. Bizarre, garish, contemporary punk-apocalyptic updating of Shakespeare classic. Little to be said about this pretentious mess except . . . avoid it. [PG]▼

King of Alcatraz (1938) **56m.** **½ D: Robert Florey. J. Carrol Naish, Gail Patrick, Lloyd Nolan, Harry Carey, Robert Preston, Anthony Quinn. Alcatraz escapee Naish takes over passenger ship, encountering rough and tumble seamen Nolan and Preston. Film moves like lightning, with outstanding cast making you forget this is just a B picture.

King of Burlesque (1935) **83m.** **½ D: Sidney Lanfield. Warner Baxter, Jack Oakie, Alice Faye, Mona Barrie, Dixie Dunbar. Dumb but enjoyable musical; cliché-ridden story of burlesque producer who risks all on ambitious Broadway show. Faye, Fats Waller (used all too briefly), hit song "I'm Shootin' High" provide highspots.

King of Chinatown (1939) **60m.** **½ D: Nick Grinde. Anna May Wong, Sidney Toler, Akim Tamiroff, J. Carrol Naish, Anthony Quinn, Roscoe Karns, Philip Ahn. Interesting little B movie with good cast, about underworld racketeers trying to gain power in Chinatown.

King of Comedy, The (1983) **C-109m.** ***½ D: Martin Scorsese. Robert De Niro, Jerry Lewis, Diahnne Abbott, Sandra Bernhard, Shelley Hack, Tony Randall, Ed Herlihy, Fred de Cordova. Pungent black comedy about a show-business hanger-on and world class loser who idolizes America's top TV comedian/talk-show host and figures out a bizarre scheme to get on the program. The denouement is a wow! Too mordant and "sick" for many viewers' taste, though it's all been done with a minimum of exaggeration . . . and a pair of knock-out performances by De Niro and Lewis. Written by Paul D. Zimmerman. Filmed in 1981. [PG]▼●

King of Hearts (1966-French-British) **C-102m.** *** D: Philippe De Broca. Alan Bates, Pierre Brasseur, Jean-Claude Brialy, Genevieve Bujold, Francoise Christophe, Adolfo Celi. Scotsman Bates walks into French town in WW1 that has been abandoned by everyone except those in the insane asylum. Stylish film isn't for all tastes, but has become a cult favorite. Offbeat. Techniscope.▼●

King of Jazz (1930) **C-93m.** *** D: John Murray Anderson. Paul Whiteman and His Orchestra, John Boles, Jeanette Loff, The Rhythm Boys (Bing Crosby, Al Rinker, Harry Barris). Million-dollar musical revue, shot in two-color Technicolor process, is filled with larger-than-life production numbers and wonderful songs. Highlights include Walter Lantz's cartoon sequence, Joe Venuti's swing violin, young Bing Crosby with the Rhythm Boys, and, of course, Gershwin's "Rhapsody in Blue" (which in early Technicolor is more a rhapsody in turquoise). Uneven, to be sure, but a lot of fun. Originally released at 105m.▼

King of Kings, The (1927) **115m.** *** D: Cecil B. DeMille. H. B. Warner, Ernest Torrence, Jacqueline Logan, Joseph Schildkraut, Victor Varconi, Robert Edeson, William Boyd. Lavish silent film holds up rather well, benefits from DeMille's superb storytelling skills and reverence for the subject. The Resurrection sequence is in two-color Technicolor. Remade in 1961.▼●

King of Kings (1961) **C-168m.** ***½ D: Nicholas Ray. Jeffrey Hunter, Siobhan McKenna, Robert Ryan, Hurd Hatfield, Viveca Lindfors, Rita Gam, Rip Torn. The life of Christ, intelligently told and beautifully filmed; full of deeply moving moments, such as the Sermon on the Mount, Christ's healing of the lame, and many others. Memorable Miklos Rozsa score. Not without flaws, but well worthwhile; grandly filmed in widescreen, bound to lose some of its visual impact on TV. Narrated by Orson Welles. SuperTechnirama 70.▼●

King of Kong Island (1978-Italian) **C-92m.** BOMB D: Robert Morris. Brad Harris, Esmeralda Barros, Marc Lawrence, Adrianna Alben, Mark Farran. Mercenary Harris on the trail of loony scientist Lawrence, who's been monkeying around with the brains of apes, making them act like robots. Couldn't be any worse; not even good for laughs. Aka KONG ISLAND.▼

King of Marvin Gardens, The (1972) **C-104m.** ***½ D: Bob Rafelson. Jack Nicholson, Bruce Dern, Ellen Burstyn, Julia Anne Robinson, Scatman Crothers. Pretentious but genuinely haunting, original drama about Nicholson's failure to discourage brother Dern's outlandish financial schemes. Burstyn's performance as an aging beauty is chilling in its perfection, and Laszlo Kovacs' photography rates with the best of the decade. [R]▼●◗

King of Masks, The (1997-Chinese) **C-101m.** ***½ D: Wu Tianming. Chu Yuk, Chao Yim Yin, Zhang Riuyang, Zhao Zhigang. Beautifully realized story, set in 1930s Sichuan, about an aged street performer who realizes he has no heir to whom he can pass on his ancient tradition (and secrets) . . . so he purchases a child on the black market. Simple, eloquent, and moving. Written by Wei Minglun.▼◗

King of New York (1990) **C-103m.** ** D: Abel Ferrara. Christopher Walken, David Caruso, Larry Fishburne, Victor Argo, Wesley Snipes, Janet Julian, Joey Chin, Steve Buscemi, Paul Calderon, Giancarlo Esposito. Fidgety Walken plays the ex-con lord to a band of black drug dealers who regularly annihilate their Colombian-Italian-Chinese rivals. Cult director Ferrara offers style and little more in this ultraviolent outing; one extended monsoon shootout makes this presumably tongue-in-cheek effort worth a glance on a very draggy night. Walken's improbable headquarters, the Plaza Hotel, begs for a scene between his low-rent minions and Ivana Trump in the service elevator. [R]▼●

King of the Coral Sea (1956-Australian) **74m.** **½ D: Lee Robinson. Chips Rafferty, Charles Tingwell, Ilma Adey, Rod Taylor, Lloyd Berrell, Reginald Lye. On-location filming in Australia aids this account of wetback smuggling into the mainland.

King of the Grizzlies (1970) **C-93m.** **½ D: Ron Kelly. John Yesno, Chris Wiggins, Hugh Webster, Jack Van Evera; narrated by Winston Hibler. Standard Disney animal-adventure about Indian who was "brother" to bear as a cub, and who now faces the full-grown grizzly in a different light. Filmed in the Canadian Rockies. [G]▼

King of the Gypsies (1978) **C-112m.** **½ D: Frank Pierson. Eric Roberts, Judd Hirsch, Susan Sarandon, Sterling Hayden, Annette O'Toole, Brooke Shields, Shelley Winters, Annie Potts, Michael V. Gazzo, Michael Higgins, Mary Louise Wilson, Matthew Laborteaux, Danielle Brisebois, Patti LuPone, Linda Manz, Tom Mason, Rachel Ticotin. Loose adaptation of Peter Maas' best seller about three generations of gypsies in N.Y.C. Dying Hayden passes tribe leadership to grandson Roberts (in his film debut), skipping over sleazy son Hirsch, who promptly sets out to kill his offspring. Initially fascinating melodrama turns into conventional chase thriller, but still intriguing, with fine acting, moody Sven Nykvist photography, and infectious score by David Grisman and Stephane Grappelli (who also appear in the film). [R]▼

King of the Hill (1993) **C-103m.** ***½ D: Steven Soderbergh. Jesse Bradford, Jeroen Krabbé, Lisa Eichhorn, Karen Allen, Spalding Gray, Elizabeth McGovern, Joseph Chrest, Adrien Brody, Cameron Boyd, Amber Benson, Kristin Griffith, Remak Ramsay, Katherine Heigl. A 12-year-old St. Louis boy, whose mother is ill and whose flaky father is often away, is forced to fend for himself in the depths of the Great Depression, using his wits to survive against extraordinary odds. One of the most vivid depictions of the Depression ever captured on film; full of rich, often harrowing detail that draws us in to vicariously experience everything young Aaron (Bradford) is going through. Director Soderbergh also scripted this adaptation of the memoir by A. E. Hotchner. Exceptional in every way. Super-35. [PG-13]▼●

King of the Jungle (1933) **72m.** **½ D: H. Bruce Humberstone, Max Marcin. Buster Crabbe, Frances Dee, Sidney Toler, Nydia Westman, Robert Barrat, Irving Pichel, Douglass Dumbrille. Imitation Tarzan yarn comes off well, with Crabbe being dragged into civilization against his will. Good fun.

King of the Khyber Rifles (1953) **C-100m.** **½ D: Henry King. Tyrone Power, Terry Moore, Michael Rennie, John Justin. Power is half-caste British officer involved in native skirmishes, Moore the general's daughter he loves. Film version of Talbot Mundy's novel lacks finesse or any sense of Kipling-style reality-fantasy. CinemaScope.

King of the Mountain (1981) **C-90m.** ** D: Noel Nosseck. Harry Hamlin, Joseph Bottoms, Deborah Van Valkenburgh, Richard Cox, Dennis Hopper, Dan Haggerty, Seymour Cassel. Garage mechanic Hamlin and friends guzzle beer and race their cars down L.A.'s treacherous Mulholland Drive. Pretentious, clichéd script and situations, with superficial and obvious finale. Hopper overacts outrageously as a burned-out former king of the Drive. Inspired by David Barry's feature in *New West* magazine. [PG]▼

King of the Roaring 20's—The Story of Arnold Rothstein (1961) **106m.** **½ D: Joseph M. Newman. David Janssen, Dianne Foster, Jack Carson, Diana Dors, Mickey Rooney. Slow-paced narrative of famous gambler's rise and fall miscasts lead role (real Rothstein was short and fat), slightly whitewashes him, and gets most of the facts wrong. Stray gangster-movie elements are inappropriately added. ▼

King of the Underworld (1939) **69m.** ** D: Lewis Seiler. Humphrey Bogart, Kay Francis, James Stephenson, John Eldredge, Jessie Busley. Farfetched story of doctor Francis becoming involved with Bogart's underworld gang; ludicrous finale. Remake of DR. SOCRATES.

King of the Wild Horses (1947) **79m.** *½ D: George Archainbaud. Preston Foster, Gail Patrick, Bill Sheffield, Guinn Williams. Youth's companionship with fierce stallion is focus of this mild Western.

King of the Wild Stallions (1959) **C-75m.** ** D: R. G. Springsteen. George Montgomery, Diane Brewster, Edgar Buchanan, Emile Meyer, Byron Foulger. Horse is the hero of this oater, protecting a widow and her son. CinemaScope.

King of the Zombies (1941) **67m.** *½ D: Jean Yarbrough. Dick Purcell, Joan Woodbury, Mantan Moreland, Henry Victor, John Archer. Scientist develops corps of zombies to use in WW2; ridiculous chiller saved by Moreland's comedy relief.▼●

Kingpin (1996) **C-113m.** *½ D: Peter Farrelly, Bobby Farrelly. Woody Harrelson, Randy Quaid, Vanessa Angel, Bill Murray, Chris Elliott, William Jordan, Richard Tyson, Rob Moran, Lin Shaye, Zen Gesner, Prudence Wright Holmes. Once-promising bowling champ whose career was ruined by a sleazy competitor sees his chance for reflected glory when he discovers a potential ace, who turns out to be Amish. Stupid and proud of it, this comedy goes the gross-out route and then, halfway through, asks us to care about these pinhead characters! Setups for laugh lines or visual punch lines are muffed time and time again. What a waste. 117m. R-rated version debuted on video in 1999. Super 35. [PG-13]▼●◗

King, Queen, Knave (1972-British) **C-92m.** BOMB D: Jerzy Skolimowski. David Niven, Gina Lollobrigida, John Moulder-Brown, Mario Adorf. Coarse, heavy-handed adaptation of Vladimir Nabokov novel about a klutzy youth who falls in love with his sexy aunt (Lollobrigida). Never released theatrically in the U.S. [R]▼

King Ralph (1991) **C-97m.** **½ D: David S. Ward. John Goodman, Peter O'Toole, John Hurt, Camille Coduri, Richard Griffiths, Leslie Phillips, James Villiers, Joely Richardson, Niall O'Brien, Julian Glover, Judy Parfitt. Mild, one-joke comedy about a Las Vegas lounge entertainer who is found to be the only living heir to the throne of England. Inoffensive but hardly inspired; Goodman's likability has to carry this a long, long way. Based on Emlyn Williams' novel *Headlong*. [PG]▼●◗

King Rat (1965) **133m.** *** D: Bryan Forbes. George Segal, Tom Courtenay, James Fox, Patrick O'Neal, Denholm Elliott, James Donald, John Mills, Alan Webb. James Clavell novel of WW2 Japanese POW camp, focusing on effect of captivity on Allied prisoners. Thoughtful presentation rises above clichés; many exciting scenes.▼

King Richard and the Crusaders (1954) **C-114m.** *½ D: David Butler. Rex Harrison, Virginia Mayo, George Sanders, Laurence Harvey, Robert Douglas. Cardboard costumer of Middle Ages, with laughable script. Indeed, Sanders as The Lion Heart and Harrison as a Saracen warrior do appear to be having a good time. CinemaScope.▼

Kings and Desperate Men (1983-Canadian) **C-118m.** *½ D: Alexis Kanner. Patrick McGoohan, Alexis Kanner, Andrea Marcovicci, Margaret Trudeau, Robin Spry, Frank Moore. Abrasive talk-show host McGoohan is held hostage in his studio by amateurish terrorists seeking public forum to debate plight of their comrade, convicted of manslaughter. Interesting premise sabotaged by poor direction, choppy editing. McGoohan overacts shamelessly. Trudeau has limited footage as his wife. [PG-13]▼

Kings Go Forth (1958) **109m.** *** D: Delmer Daves. Frank Sinatra, Tony Curtis, Natalie Wood, Leora Dana, Karl Swenson. Soapy but well done three-cornered romance, set in WW2 France. Two GI buddies both fall for same girl, unaware that she is half-black. Script by Merle Miller; several jazz greats, including Red Norvo and Pete Candoli, put in appearances.▼●

King's Mistress, The SEE: **King's Whore, The**

Kings of the Road (1976-German) **176m.** ***½ D: Wim Wenders. Rudiger Vogler, Hanns Zischler, Lisa Kreuzer, Rudolf Schundler, Marquard Bohm. Deliberately slow, introspective, disarming tale (written by the director) of itinerant cinema mechanic Vogler, traveling with Zischler along the underpopulated, forgotten border regions between East and West Germany—a dying area that serves as a metaphor for the decline of the German film industry. It's also about cars, rock 'n' roll, and the American cultural imperialism of Wenders' homeland. The last (and best) in Wenders' "road movie" trilogy, after ALICE IN THE CITIES and WRONG MOVE.▼

Kings of the Sun (1963) **C-108m.** **½ D: J. Lee Thompson. Yul Brynner, George Chakiris, Shirley Anne Field, Richard Basehart, Brad Dexter. Skin-deep spectacle, badly cast, telling of Mayan leader who comes to America with surviving tribesmen and encounters savage Indians. Filmed in Mexico. Panavision.

King Solomon's Mines (1937-British) **80m.** *** D: Robert Stevenson. Paul Robeson, Cedric Hardwicke, Roland Young, John Loder, Anna Lee. Robust adventure given full-blooded treatment by fine cast, exploring Africa in search of treasure-filled mines. One of Robeson's best screen roles even allows him to sing. H. Rider Haggard story remade in 1950 and 1985.▼

King Solomon's Mines (1950) **C-102m.** ***½ D: Compton Bennett, Andrew Marton. Deborah Kerr, Stewart Granger, Richard Carlson, Hugo Haas. Remake of H. Rider Haggard story is given polished production, with Granger-Kerr-Carlson trio leading safari in search for legendary diamond mines. Scripted by Helen Deutsch. This won Oscars for Cinematography (Robert Surtees) and Editing; excess footage used in WATUSI and other later jungle films. ▼●

King Solomon's Mines (1985) **C-100m.**

*½ D: J. Lee Thompson. Richard Chamberlain, Sharon Stone, Herbert Lom, John Rhys-Davies, Ken Gampu. H. Rider Haggard's adventure yarn is updated for the Indiana Jones generation, but the results are unsuccessful. Cartoon characters and outlandish cliffhanger situations abound—but where's the charm? Followed by sequel (shot simultaneously), ALLAN QUATERMAIN AND THE LOST CITY OF GOLD. J-D-C Scope. [PG-13]▼

King Solomon's Treasure (1977-Canadian-British) **C-89m.** *½ D: Alvin Rakoff. David McCallum, John Colicos, Patrick Macnee, Britt Ekland, Yvon Dufour, Ken Gampu, Wilfrid Hyde-White. Silly, low-budget adaptation of H. Rider Haggard's *Allan Quatermain* has miscast trio of Colicos, McCallum (with comedy-relief stutter) and Macnee hunting for African treasure, fighting off dinosaurs and meeting Phoenician queen Ekland. Despite obvious similarities, this is no RAIDERS OF THE LOST ARK.▼

King's Pirate, The (1967) **C-100m.** **½ D: Don Weis. Doug McClure, Jill St. John, Guy Stockwell, Mary Ann Mobley. Cardboard, juvenile swashbuckler set in 18th century, with McClure the nominal hero. Remake of AGAINST ALL FLAGS.

Kings Row (1942) **127m.** ***½ D: Sam Wood. Ann Sheridan, Robert Cummings, Ronald Reagan, Betty Field, Charles Coburn, Claude Rains, Judith Anderson, Maria Ouspenskaya. Forerunner of PEYTON PLACE still retains its sweep of life in pre-WW1 Midwestern town, with the fates of many townsfolk intertwined. Beautiful Erich Wolfgang Korngold music score backs up plush production, fine characterizations. Notable, too, as Reagan's finest performance. Screenplay by Casey Robinson, from Henry Bellamann's bestselling book. Also shown in computer-colored version.▼●

King's Story, A (1965-British) **C-100m.** *** D: Harry Booth. With the voices of Orson Welles, Flora Robson, Patrick Wymark, David Warner. Strong documentary focusing on early life of Duke of Windsor and his ultimate abdication from throne of England to marry the woman he loved.

King Steps Out, The (1936) **85m.** *** D: Josef von Sternberg. Grace Moore, Franchot Tone, Walter Connolly, Raymond Walburn, Elizabeth Risdon, Nana Bryant, Victor Jory. Fanciful musical romance with fine cast supporting Moore's lovely voice; direction big asset to otherwise average musical.▼

King's Thief, The (1955) **C-78m.** *** D: Robert Z. Leonard. David Niven, Ann Blyth, George Sanders, Edmund Purdom, Roger Moore, Alan Mowbray. Ornately produced costumer of 17th-century court intrigue involving England's King Charles II. CinemaScope.▼

King's Vacation, The (1933) **60m.** **½ D: John G. Adolfi. George Arliss, Dudley Digges, Dick Powell, Patricia Ellis, Marjorie Gateson, Florence Arliss. Refreshing story of monarch Arliss returning to ex-wife Gateson in search for "the simple life," only to find she's living even better than he is! Typical of Arliss' lighter vehicles.

King's Whore, The (1990-French-Austrian-British-Italian) **C-115m.** **½ D: Axel Corti. Timothy Dalton, Valeria Golino, Stephane Freiss, Feodor Chaliapin, Margaret Tyzack, Eleanor David, Robin Renucci. Lavishly filmed but dramatically uneven historical melodrama. In the royal court of Piedmont in Northern Italy, King Dalton becomes consumed by his burning desire for beautiful but unwilling Golino, the wife of his chamberlain. Scripted by Corti, Frederic Raphael, and Daniel Vigne. Aka THE KING'S MISTRESS. [R]▼●

Kinjite: Forbidden Subjects (1989) **C-97m.** ** D: J. Lee Thompson. Charles Bronson, Juan Fernandez, James Pax, Kumiko Hayakawa, Perry Lopez, Peggy Lipton, Amy Hathaway, Bill McKinney, Sy Richardson, Alex Hyde-White, Richard Egan, Jr. Glum urban thriller pitting supercop Bronson against scummy pimp Fernandez, who specializes in turning teenage girls to prostitution. Also involved is a Japanese businessman, newly come to L.A., whose daughter is kidnapped by the pimp. Some interesting ideas, but mostly formulaic. [R]▼●

Kipperbang (1982-British) **C-80m.** *½ D: Michael Apted. John Albasiny, Alison Steadman, Gary Cooper, Abigail Cruttenden, Maurice Lee. Annoyingly lightweight comedy detailing the romantic fantasies and predicaments of young teens and their elders—particularly, their English teacher—in 1948 Britain. Originally made for British television, released here theatrically in 1984. Original title: P'TANG YANG KIPPERBANG. [PG]▼

Kipps (1941-British) **82m.** *** D: Carol Reed. Michael Redgrave, Diana Wynyard, Arthur Riscoe, Phyllis Calvert, Max Adrian, Helen Haye, Michael Wilding. Meticulous adaptation of H. G. Wells's story about a shopkeeper who inherits money and tries to crash Society. Faithfully scripted by Sidney Gilliat, but a bit stodgy overall. Basis for musical HALF A SIXPENCE. Originally released in U.S. as THE REMARKABLE MR. KIPPS. Original British running time 108m.▼

Kismet (1944) **C-100m.** **½ D: William Dieterle. Ronald Colman, Marlene Dietrich, Edward Arnold, Florence Bates, James Craig, Joy Ann Page, Harry Davenport. Colman tries a change of pace playing the "king of beggars," a wily magician whose daughter is wooed by the handsome young

Caliph in this plot-heavy Arabian Nights-type tale. Passably entertaining but nothing special, despite opulent MGM production. Best of all is Dietrich, with tongue in cheek and body painted gold for one famous dance scene. Filmed before in 1920 and 1930; remade in 1955 after the Broadway musical version. Retitled ORIENTAL DREAM.▼

Kismet (1955) **C-113m.** **½ D: Vincente Minnelli. Howard Keel, Ann Blyth, Dolores Gray, Monty Woolley, Sebastian Cabot, Vic Damone. Handsome but uninspired filming of the Broadway musical of this Arabian Nights–type tale. Robert Wright–George Forrest songs (based on Borodin themes) include "Stranger in Paradise," "Baubles, Bangles, and Beads." CinemaScope.▼●

Kiss, The (1929) **89m.** *** D: Jacques Feyder. Greta Garbo, Conrad Nagel, Andres Randolf, Holmes Herbert, Lew Ayres, George Davis. Married Garbo gives young Ayres, who is smitten with her, an innocent goodnight kiss, which leads to misunderstanding and tragedy. Sleek, fluidly filmed Garbo vehicle was her last silent, and Ayres' first starring role. Farfetched but very enjoyable.▼●

Kiss, The (1988) **C-101m.** ** D: Pen Densham. Joanna Pacula, Meredith Salenger, Mimi Kuzyk, Nicholas Kilbertus, Jan Rubes. Occasionally scary horror film builds up to but downplays the sexual implications of its CAT PEOPLE–style story of a family curse passed down to each generation by a woman-to-woman kiss. Salenger is the unlucky target of beautiful aunt Pacula's evil smooch. [R]▼●

Kiss and Kill SEE: **Blood of Fu Manchu, The**

Kiss and Tell (1945) **90m.** **½ D: Richard Wallace. Shirley Temple, Jerome Courtland, Walter Abel, Katherine Alexander, Robert Benchley, Porter Hall. Film of successful Broadway play about wacky teenager Corliss Archer is a bit forced but generally funny; one of Temple's better grown-up roles. Sequel: A KISS FOR CORLISS.

Kiss Before Dying, A (1956) **C-94m.** *** D: Gerd Oswald. Robert Wagner, Virginia Leith, Jeffrey Hunter, Joanne Woodward, Mary Astor, George Macready. Effective chiller with Wagner superb as psychopathic killer and Astor his devoted mother; well paced. Based on an Ira Levin novel. Remade in 1991. CinemaScope.▼

Kiss Before Dying, A (1991) **C-95m.** *½ D: James Dearden. Matt Dillon, Sean Young, Max von Sydow, Diane Ladd, James Russo, Martha Gehman, Ben Browder, Joie Lee, Adam Horovitz. Almost completely ineffectual thriller about an ambitious young sicko who charms—and murders—his way into a powerful family. Young plays twin sisters, enabling us to watch her give *two* bad performances. Writer-director Dearden even dares to have her looking at Hitchcock's VERTIGO on TV, a reminder (as if we needed one) of the right way to make this kind of film. Ira Levin's novel was filmed before in 1956. [R]▼●

Kiss Before the Mirror, The (1933) **67m.** **½ D: James Whale. Frank Morgan, Paul Lukas, Nancy Carroll, Jean Dixon, Gloria Stuart, Walter Pidgeon, Donald Cook, Charles Grapewin. While defending Lukas for killing his adulterous wife, attorney Morgan begins to see the entire chain of events recurring in his own home! Strange romantic melodrama is made even stranger by being shot on leftover FRANKENSTEIN sets; good performances and typical Whale stylistics keep one watching. Remade by the director as WIVES UNDER SUSPICION.

Kiss Daddy Good Night (1987) **C-89m.** *½ D: Peter Ily Huemer. Uma Thurman, Paul Dillon, Paul Richards, Steve Buscemi, Annabelle Gurwitch, David Brisbin. Vague, forgettable melodrama-thriller about a young vamp (Thurman, in her screen debut), who seduces and robs men, and her strange relationship with older bohemian Richards. [R]▼

Kissed (1996-Canadian) **C-73m.** *½ D: Lynne Stopkewich. Molly Parker, Peter Outerbridge, Jay Brazeau, Natasha Morley, Jessie Winter Mudie. A woman infatuated with corpses since childhood gets her dream job working in a mortuary, then meets a man who becomes obsessed with her flirtation with death. Dull, occasionally repulsive thought provoker seeks poetry in necrophilia. Only pluses are Parker and Morley's transfixing performances. Educational value: everything you ever wanted to know about embalming.▼

Kisses for My President (1964) **113m.** **½ D: Curtis Bernhardt. Fred MacMurray, Polly Bergen, Arlene Dahl, Edward Andrews, Eli Wallach. Thirties-style comedy of Bergen becoming President of the U.S., with MacMurray her husband caught in unprecedented protocol. Sometimes funny, often witless.▼●

Kiss for Corliss, A (1949) **88m.** ** D: Richard Wallace. Shirley Temple, David Niven, Tom Tully, Virginia Welles. Puffed-up comedy of teenager Temple convincing all that she and playboy Niven are going together; naïve fluff. Limp follow-up to KISS AND TELL with Shirley as Corliss Archer; this was her final film. Retitled ALMOST A BRIDE.▼

Kiss From Eddie, A SEE: **Arousers, The**

Kissin' Cousins (1964) **C-96m.** **½ D: Gene Nelson. Elvis Presley, Arthur O'Connell, Glenda Farrell, Jack Albertson, Pamela Austin, Yvonne Craig, Donald Woods. Elvis has a dual role as military officer trying to convince yokel relative to allow missile site to be built on homestead; good supporting cast, usual amount of singing—mostly forgettable—and dancing. Panavision.▼

Kissing a Fool (1998) **C-93m.** *½ D: Doug Ellin. David Schwimmer, Jason Lee, Mili Avital, Bonnie Hunt, Vanessa Angel, Kari Wuhrer, Bitty Schram. Thoroughly charmless romantic comedy, told via flashback in an irritating narrative form, about a betrothed Chicago sportscaster who badgers a novelist buddy into testing his fiancée's fidelity as he himself is playing around. Subliminally sleazy but wrapped in a cozily sentimental veneer, which means the film doesn't even have the courage of its convictions. Avital is appealing as the pretty book editor who deserves better. Schwimmer also coexecutive-produced. [R]▼●◗

Kissing Bandit, The (1948) **C-102m.** ** D: Laslo Benedek. Frank Sinatra, Kathryn Grayson, Ann Miller, J. Carrol Naish, Ricardo Montalban, Mildred Natwick, Cyd Charisse, Billy Gilbert. Frail Sinatra vehicle about son of Western kissing bandit who picks up where Dad left off; song "Siesta" sums it up.▼

Kissinger and Nixon (1995) **C-100m. TVM** D: Daniel Petrie. Ron Silver, Beau Bridges, Ron White, George Takei, Kenneth Welsh, Tony Rosato, Matt Frewer, Brett Halsey. The intriguing love-hate (accent on the latter) relationship between K & N during the six-month period in 1972–73 when Kissinger was wheeling and dealing an end to the Vietnam War and Nixon was grandstanding politically, belittling Henry in the inner circle and having Alexander Haig (Frewer) spy on him. Silver and Bridges do yeoman work acting under all the facial putty and vocal mannerisms, and fight Lionel Chetwynd's somewhat telescoped vision (from Walter Isaacson's *Kissinger*) to a draw. This take on Nixon upstaged Oliver Stone's by premiering a week before the theatrical movie. Made for cable. Average. ▼●

Kiss in the Dark, A (1949) **87m.** ** D: Delmer Daves. David Niven, Jane Wyman, Victor Moore, Wayne Morris, Broderick Crawford. Drab comedy effort involving pianist Niven, who gets more than he bargained for when he inherits an apartment building.

Kiss Kiss-Bang Bang (1966-Spanish) **C-90m.** **½ D: Duccio Tessari. Giuliano Gemma, George Martin, Antonio Casas, Daniel Vargas. Routine spy yarn of British Secret Service efforts to prevent sale of secret formula to foreign powers. Techniscope.

Kiss Me Deadly (1955) **105m.** ***½ D: Robert Aldrich. Ralph Meeker, Albert Dekker, Paul Stewart, Cloris Leachman, Wesley Addy, Nick Dennis, Maxine Cooper, Gaby Rodgers, Jack Elam, Strother Martin, Jack Lambert. Meeker is a perfect Mike Hammer in moody, fast and violent adaptation of Mickey Spillane novel. Years ahead of its time, a major influence on French New Wave directors, and one of Aldrich's best films. Leachman's film debut. Some video versions have 82 seconds of additional footage which completely changes the finale. ▼●

Kiss Me Goodbye (1982) **C-101m.** ** D: Robert Mulligan. Sally Field, James Caan, Jeff Bridges, Paul Dooley, Claire Trevor, Mildred Natwick, Dorothy Fielding, William Prince. Strained romantic comedy-fantasy about young woman who's visited by her dead husband just as she's about to remarry. Attractive cast is pretty much wasted in this reworking of the Brazilian film DONA FLOR AND HER TWO HUSBANDS. [PG]▼

Kiss Me, Guido (1997) **C-86m.** **½ D: Tony Vitale. Nick Scotti, Anthony Barrile, Anthony DeSando, Craig Chester, Dominick Lombardozzi, Molly Price, Christopher Lawford. Earnest comedy about a heterosexual Pacino/De Niro wannabe (Scotti) from the Bronx who moves to Manhattan and unknowingly takes a gay roommate. Occasionally funny, even though the set-up is artificial and the characters are stereotypes. [R]▼●

Kiss Me Kate (1953) **C-109m.** ***½ D: George Sidney. Kathryn Grayson, Howard Keel, Ann Miller, Bobby Van, Keenan Wynn, James Whitmore, Bob Fosse, Tommy Rall, Kurt Kasznar, Ron Randell. Bright filmization of Cole Porter's Broadway musical, adapted from Shakespeare's *The Taming of the Shrew*. Grayson and Keel are erstwhile married couple whose off-stage and on-stage lives intertwine. Songs include "So in Love," "Always True to You in My Fashion," "Brush Up Your Shakespeare" (delightfully performed by Wynn and Whitmore); the "From This Moment On" number, highlighting Fosse and Carol Haney, is outstanding. Originally in 3-D.▼●

Kiss Me, Stupid (1964) **126m.** ** D: Billy Wilder. Dean Martin, Ray Walston, Kim Novak, Felicia Farr, Cliff Osmond, Barbara Pepper, Doro Merande, Henry Gibson, John Fiedler, Mel Blanc. Martin plays womanizing crooner named "Dino" whose interest in unsuccessful songwriter Walston might increase if he gets a crack at his wife. Lewd farce (by Wilder and I. A. L. Diamond) was condemned as "smut" when first released, and hasn't improved very much—although it does have its defenders. Panavision.▼●

Kiss of Death (1947) **98m.** *** D: Henry Hathaway. Victor Mature, Brian Donlevy, Coleen Gray, Richard Widmark, Karl Malden, Taylor Holmes, Mildred Dunnock. Famous gangster saga is showing its age, with both the cops and robbers a little too polite—except, of course, for Widmark, in his notorious film debut as giggling, psychopathic killer who shoves a wheelchair-bound old woman down a flight of stairs! Mature is solid as thief who turns state's evidence. Scripted by Ben Hecht and Charles Lederer; filmed on authentic N.Y.C. locations. Remade in 1995.▼

Kiss of Death (1995) **C-101m.** ★★½ D: Barbet Schroeder. David Caruso, Nicolas Cage, Samuel L. Jackson, Helen Hunt, Kathryn Erbe, Stanley Tucci, Michael Rapaport, Ving Rhames, Philip Baker Hall, Anthony Heald, Anne Meara. Mediocre 90s remake of 40s crime yarn (with Richard Price script) has Caruso as an ex-con trying to go straight who's swept back into the underworld—then forced to turn stoolie for the D.A. Caruso is OK—nothing more—in first starring film, but Cage is a parody of a mad-dog bad guy. Jackson shines, as usual, in a solid supporting role. Jay O. Sanders appears unbilled as a Federal agent. [R]▼●

Kiss of Evil SEE: Kiss of the Vampire

Kiss of Fire (1955) **C-87m.** ★★½ D: Joseph M. Newman. Barbara Rush, Jack Palance, Rex Reason, Martha Hyer. Run-of-the-mill costumer. Rush gives up Spanish throne to remain in America with true love.

Kiss of the Spider Woman (1985 U.S.-Brazilian) **C/B&W-119m.** ★★★ D: Hector Babenco. William Hurt, Raul Julia, Sonia Braga, Jose Lewgoy, Nuno Leal Maia, Denise Dumont. Adaptation of Manuel Puig's highly regarded novel actually gets better as it goes along, revealing layers in story of gay man and political activist locked together in South American prison cell. Hurt is superb in Oscar-winning performance as man whose only food for survival is his memory of tacky Hollywood movies. Script by Leonard Schrader. Later a Broadway musical. [R]▼●

Kiss of the Tarantula (1972) **C-85m.** ★½ D: Chris Munger. Suzanne Ling, Eric Mason, Herman Wallner, Patricia Landon, Beverly Eddins. Unstable teenager uses pet tarantulas against her stepmother and other "enemies." Heavy handed. [PG]▼

Kiss of the Vampire (1963-British) **C-88m.** ★★½ D: Don Sharp. Clifford Evans, Edward DeSouza, Noel Willman, Jennifer Daniel. Intelligent Hammer treatment of vampire tale, well done in color, with many chilling sequences. Unfortunately, much of film's punch is lost in reedited TV version known as KISS OF EVIL.▼●◗

Kiss or Kill (1997-Australian) **C-93m.** ★★★ D: Bill Bennett. Matt Day, Frances O'Connor, Chris Haywood, Barry Otto, Andrew S. Gilbert, Barry Langrishe, Max Cullen. Neat, noirish murder mystery with Day and O'Connor well cast as a pair of scam-artists who take it on the lam after their latest dupe unexpectedly dies. The style, impudence, and unusual characters overcome the formulaic story. [R]▼●

Kiss Shot (1989) **C-100m. TVM** D: Jerry London. Whoopi Goldberg, Dorian Harewood, Dennis Franz, Tasha Scott, David Marciano, Teddy Wilson. Whoopi's TV-movie debut has her a pool-playing minimum wage single mom looking for some fast money to pay the mortgage. THE HUSTLER it ain't, but Whoopi's impressive bank shots (her own, it appears) and her nice feel for romantic comedy compensate. Average.▼●◗

Kiss the Blood off My Hands (1948) **80m.** ★★ D: Norman Foster. Joan Fontaine, Burt Lancaster, Robert Newton. Disappointing romance-thriller follows the plight of two lost souls, lonely nurse–war widow Fontaine and deeply troubled ex-POW Lancaster, who's on the lam for murder in London. Some potent scenes and good Miklos Rozsa score cannot salvage tepid film.

Kiss the Boys Goodbye (1941) **85m.** ★★½ D: Victor Schertzinger. Mary Martin, Don Ameche, Oscar Levant, Virginia Dale, Barbara Jo Allen (Vera Vague), Raymond Walburn, Elizabeth Patterson, Connee Boswell. Enjoyable backstage musical of aspiring actress and director, with good support from Levant and bright score.

Kiss the Girls (1997) **C-120m.** ★★½ D: Gary Fleder. Morgan Freeman, Ashley Judd, Cary Elwes, Tony Goldwyn, Bill Nunn, Jeremy Piven, Roma Maffia, Jay O. Sanders, Alex McArthur, Mena Suvari. When a police forensic psychologist learns that his niece has been abducted, he uses his considerable skills to try and identify the culprit—a devious sicko who doesn't kill all his victims, but holds them captive instead. Surprisingly discreet for a '90s film—but in its final segments, increasingly conventional and formulaic. And too long. Freeman is—typically—solid as a rock; Judd is very good as a doctor who refuses to be treated as a victim. Panavision. [R]▼●◗

Kiss the Girls and Make Them Die (1966-Italian) **C-101m.** BOMB D: Henry Levin. Michael Connors, Dorothy Provine, Terry-Thomas, Raf Vallone, Beverly Adams, Oliver McGreevy. Dull spy spoof about power-crazy industrialist who has a satellite capable of sterilizing the world, which is something Bond, Flint, and Matt Helm wouldn't mind. Awful film.

Kiss Them for Me (1957) **C-105m.** ★★½ D: Stanley Donen. Cary Grant, Jayne Mansfield, Leif Erickson, Suzy Parker, Larry Blyden, Ray Walston. Forced comedy about romantic entanglements of navy officers on shore leave. CinemaScope.

Kiss the Other Sheik (1965-Italian-French) **C-85m.** BOMB D: Luciano Salce, Eduardo De Filippo. Marcello Mastroianni, Pamela Tiffin, Virna Lisi, Luciano Salce. Off-color and off-base comedy of crazy man and his sexy wife. Panavision.

Kiss Tomorrow Goodbye (1950) **102m.** **½ D: Gordon Douglas. James Cagney, Barbara Payton, Luther Adler, Ward Bond, Helena Carter, Steve Brodie, Barton MacLane, Rhys Williams, Frank Reicher, John Litel, William Frawley, Neville Brand, Kenneth Tobey. Violent thriller in the wake of WHITE HEAT, with Cagney as criminal so ruthless he even blackmails crooked cops! Despite impressive cast, Jimmy's practically the whole show; only Adler as shyster lawyer gives him any competition. Cagney's brother William produced—and also plays his brother.▼●

Kit Carson (1940) **97m.** *** D: George B. Seitz. Jon Hall, Lynn Bari, Dana Andrews, Harold Huber, Ward Bond, Renie Riano, Clayton Moore. Sturdy Western with Hall in title role, Andrews as cavalry officer, Bari the woman they fight over; plenty of action in Indian territory. Also shown in a computer-colored version.▼

Kitchen Toto, The (1987) **C-96m.** *** D: Harry Hook. Edwin Mahinda, Bob Peck, Phyllis Logan, Robert Urquhart, Kirsten Hughes, Edward Judd. Moving account of Kenya's final break from British rule in the mid-1950s. This complicated and violent struggle for freedom is told through the eyes of a young "kikuyu" boy slowly drawn into these events when he goes to work in the household of the British police chief after his father is murdered by terrorists. Demanding but ultimately rewarding; first-rate debut for director Hook, who grew up in Kenya during the period depicted here. [PG-13]▼●

Kitten With a Whip (1964) **83m.** ** D: Douglas Heyes. Ann-Margret, John Forsythe, Patricia Barry, Peter Brown, Ann Doran. Uninspired account of delinquent (Ann-Margret) and friends forcing businessman Forsythe to drive them to Mexico.

Kitty (1945) **104m.** *** D: Mitchell Leisen. Paulette Goddard, Ray Milland, Patric Knowles, Reginald Owen, Cecil Kellaway, Constance Collier. Overlong but entertaining costumer of girl's rise from guttersnipe to lady in 18th-century England with help of impoverished rake Milland; one of Goddard's best roles.

Kitty and the Bagman (1982-Australian) **C-95m.** **½ D: Donald Crombie. Liddy Clark, John Stanton, Val Lehman, Gerard McGuire, Collette Mann, Reg Evans. Flavorful period detail is the star of this inconsequential comedy-drama about crooked cop Stanton and young Clark, who becomes Underworld Queen of Sydney in the Roaring Twenties. Panavision. [R]▼

Kitty Foyle (1940) **107m.** ***½ D: Sam Wood. Ginger Rogers, Dennis Morgan, James Craig, Eduardo Ciannelli, Ernest Cossart, Gladys Cooper. Tender love story won Rogers an Oscar as Christopher Morley's working-girl heroine; Ciannelli memorable as speakeasy waiter.▼●

KKK SEE: **Klansman, The**

Klansman, The (1974) **C-112m.** BOMB D: Terence Young. Lee Marvin, Richard Burton, Cameron Mitchell, Lola Falana, Luciana Paluzzi, Linda Evans, O. J. Simpson. Thoroughly trashy racial melodrama casts Marvin as a Southern sheriff and Burton as a local landowner who get involved in a hotbed (and hot beds) of racial activity. Original director Sam Fuller (who is still credited as coscripter) wisely took an early hike. Aka THE BURNING CROSS and KKK. [R]▼

Klondike Annie (1936) **80m.** *** D: Raoul Walsh. Mae West, Victor McLaglen, Philip Reed, Helen Jerome Eddy, Harry Beresford, Harold Huber, Soo Young, Lucille Webster Gleason. West and McLaglen are rugged team, with Mae on the lam from police, going to the Yukon and masquerading as Salvation Army worker. West chants "I'm An Occidental Woman in An Oriental Mood For Love," and other hits. ▼●◗

Klondike Fever (1980) **C-106m.** *½ D: Peter Carter. Rod Steiger, Angie Dickinson, Jeff East, Lorne Greene, Barry Morse. Jack London (East) in Alaska during the Gold Rush. Poorly made adventure yarn. Aka JACK LONDON'S KLONDIKE FEVER. [PG]▼

Klondike Kate (1943) **64m.** *½ D: William Castle. Ann Savage, Tom Neal, Glenda Farrell, Constance Worth, Sheldon Leonard, Lester Allen. Low-budget humdrum of innocent Neal accused of murder in Alaska, fighting for his life and his girl.

Klute (1971) **C-114m.** ***½ D: Alan J. Pakula. Jane Fonda, Donald Sutherland, Charles Cioffi, Roy Scheider, Dorothy Tristan, Rita Gam, Jean Stapleton. Fine combination detective-thriller/character-study, with Sutherland a private-eye searching for suburban husband last seen in N.Y.C. Fonda won Oscar as call girl who once saw man in question. Beware: Commercial TV print runs 108m. and omits one crucial scene that helps Sutherland solve the mystery! Panavision. [R]▼●

Knack, and How to Get It, The (1965-British) **84m.** ***½ D: Richard Lester. Rita Tushingham, Ray Brooks, Michael Crawford, Donal Donnelly. One of the funniest comedies ever imported from Britain. One man's a whiz with the ladies, and his buddy simply wants to learn his secret. Fast-moving, constantly funny. Charles Wood and director Lester scripted, from Ann Jellicoe's play. Look sharp for Charlotte Rampling (as a water skier) and Jacqueline Bisset.▼●

Knave of Hearts SEE: **Lovers, Happy Lovers**

Knickerbocker Holiday (1944) **85m.** ** D: Harry Brown. Nelson Eddy, Charles Coburn, Constance Dowling, Shelley Winters, Percy Kilbride, Chester Conklin. Plodding film of Kurt Weill–Maxwell Anderson musical of N.Y.C.'s early days; score includes "September Song."▼

Knife in the Head (1978-German) **C-113m.** ***½ D: Reinhard Hauff. Bruno Ganz, Angela Winkler, Hans Christian Blech, Hans Honig, Hans Brenner. Ganz is excellent as a biogeneticist who is paralyzed after being shot in the head in a police raid, then used as a pawn by both police and political radicals. Fascinating, disturbing drama.▼

Knife in the Water (1962-Polish) **94m.** **** D: Roman Polanski. Leon Niemczyk, Jolanta Umecka, Zygmunt Malanowicz. Absorbing drama grows out of the tensions created when a couple off for a sailing weekend pick up a student hitchhiker. Polanski's first feature film is a brilliant piece of cinematic storytelling, and a must-see movie.▼●

Knight Moves (1992) **C-96m.** **½ D: Carl Schenkel. Christopher Lambert, Diane Lane, Tom Skerritt, Daniel Baldwin. Chess master Lambert finds himself a murder suspect during a competition on an island in Washington state. Meanwhile, the killer teases Lambert by providing the chess champion with clues he must decipher for himself. OK thriller; has its moments, but also more than its share of lulls. Super 35. [R]▼●

Knight of the Dragon, The SEE: **Star Knight**

Knightriders (1981) **C-145m.** *** D: George A. Romero. Ed Harris, Gary Lahti, Tom Savini, Amy Ingersoll, Patricia Tallman, Christine Forrest, Warner Shook, Brother Blue. Ambitious, unusual film about a traveling band that stages medieval fairs at which knights joust on motorcycles, and their self-styled King Arthur, who tries to get his followers to live under an old-fashioned code of honor. Finely crafted little change-of-pace for horror master Romero, who also wrote the screenplay; Stephen King has a funny cameo as a beer-guzzling spectator. [R]▼●

Knights and Emeralds (1986-British) **C-94m.** **½ D: Ian Emes. Christopher Wild, Beverly Hills, Warren Mitchell, Bill Leadbitter, Rachel Davies, Tracie Bennett. Fair chronicle of young, white, working-class musician Wild, and what happens when he begins associating with his black counterparts. A well-meaning examination of racism and its effects, combined with mostly forgettable musical numbers. Panavision. [PG]▼

Knights of the Round Table (1953) **C-115m.** **½ D: Richard Thorpe. Robert Taylor, Ava Gardner, Mel Ferrer, Stanley Baker, Felix Aylmer. MGM's first widescreen film (made in England) was excuse for this pretty but empty mini-spectacle of King Arthur's Court, revealing famous love triangle. CinemaScope.▼●

Knight Without Armour (1937-British) **101m.** *** D: Jacques Feyder. Marlene Dietrich, Robert Donat, Irene Vanbrugh, Herbert Lomas, Miles Malleson, David Tree. Secret agent Donat helps countess Dietrich flee Russian revolutionaries. Sumptuous production, charismatic stars.▼●

K-9 (1989) **C-102m.** BOMB D: Rod Daniel. James Belushi, Mel Harris, Kevin Tighe, Ed O'Neill, Jerry Lee, James Handy, Cotter Smith. Cop Belushi teams with a German shepherd (Jerry Lee) to crack a drug case. Dubbing this one a dog would be much too kind. Followed a decade later by a direct-to-video sequel, K-911. [PG-13]▼●◗

Knock Off (1998-U.S.-Hong Kong) **C-91m.** *½ D: Tsui Hark. Jean-Claude Van Damme, Rob Schneider, Lela Rochon, Michael Fitzgerald Wong, Paul Sorvino, Carmen Lee. Van Damme teams up with American agents to combat terrorists. Having Van Damme play a Hong Kong clothing designer/importer in an action film pinned to a plot about designer jeans is peculiar but not interesting . . . which also describes the movie. Director Hark abandons his usual vivid fight choreography for standard swift intercutting instead. Samo Hung appears unbilled. Super 35. [R]▼●◗

Knock on Any Door (1949) **100m.** **½ D: Nicholas Ray. Humphrey Bogart, John Derek, George Macready, Allene Roberts, Susan Perry. More a showcase for young Derek—as a "victim of society" who turns to crime—than a vehicle for Bogart, as conscience-stricken attorney who defends him. Serious but dated drama. Sequel: LET NO MAN WRITE MY EPITAPH.▼●

Knock on Wood (1954) **C-103m.** *** D: Norman Panama, Melvin Frank. Danny Kaye, Mai Zetterling, Torin Thatcher, David Burns, Leon Askin, Abner Biberman. Superior Kaye vehicle, with ventriloquist Danny involved with beautiful Zetterling and international spies; good Kaye routines.

Knockout (1941) **73m.** **½ D: William Clemens. Arthur Kennedy, Virginia Field, Anthony Quinn, Olympe Bradna, Cliff Edwards, Cornel Wilde. Slick little programmer of a prizefighter seesawing between fame and folly.

Knockout (2000) **C-100m.** *½ D: Lorenzo Doumani. Sophia-Adella Hernandez, Eduardo Yanez, Tony Plana, William McNamara, Maria Conchita Alonso, Paul Winfield. B-movie about an East L.A. homegirl (Hernandez) who becomes a boxer, following in the footsteps of her dad (Plana), who gave up life in the ring to become a cop. Potentially intriguing subject matter KO'd by hammy performances (especially McNamara as a yuppie sleaze promoter), flat direction and a clichéd script that would shame Syd Field. [R]▼◗

Knock Out Cop, The (1978-Italian-German) **C-113m.** ** D: Steno. Bud Spencer, Werner Pochat, Enzo Cannavale, Joe Stewardson, Bodo, Dagmar Lassander. Silly live-action comic strip with tough, beefy police inspector Spencer on the hunt for drug smugglers. For prepubescent boys only. Originally titled FLATFOOT. Video title: TRINITY: TRACKING FOR TROUBLE.▼

Knute Rockne, All American (1940) **96m.** *** D: Lloyd Bacon. Pat O'Brien, Gale Page, Donald Crisp, Ronald Reagan, Albert Bassermann, John Qualen. Corny but entertaining bio of famed Notre Dame football coach (O'Brien, in a standout performance), with Reagan as his star player, George Gipp. Several long-excised scenes, including O'Brien's famous locker-room pep talk and Reagan's "win just one for the Gipper" speech have now been restored to most TV prints. You *can* see it all on homevideo in any case. Also shown in computer-colored version.▼

Kolya (1996-Czech-British) **C-110m.** **½ D: Jan Sverak. Zdenek Sverak, Andrej Chalimon, Libuse Safrankova, Ondrez Vetchy, Stella Zazvorkova, Ladislav Smoljak, Irena Livanova. Sentimental tale of a mid-fiftyish cellist, an unattached lothario who unexpectedly is made guardian of a small Russian boy. Set in 1988 Prague, on the eve of independence from the Russians, this is a sweet-natured love story that unfortunately seems too pat and manufactured. You'll laugh and certainly cry, but same essential story has been told on film many times before. Lead actor/screenwriter is the director's father. Oscar winner as Best Foreign Film. [PG-13]▼●

Kona Coast (1968) **C-93m.** **½ D: Lamont Johnson. Richard Boone, Vera Miles, Joan Blondell, Steve Ihnat, Chips Rafferty, Kent Smith. Good cast in routine melodrama of fishing boat skipper's fight to get the guys who murdered his daughter. Fifties rock star Duane Eddy has small part. Filmed in Hawaii. From a screen story by John D. MacDonald.

Konga (1961-British) **C-90m.** *½ D: John Lemont. Michael Gough, Margo Johns, Jess Conrad, Claire Gordon. *Very* mad scientist Gough, intent on creating a plant-animal hybrid, occasionally enlarges his chimpanzee friend to gorilla size, then sends the ape out to kill his enemies. A climactic overdose makes Konga king-sized for an exceptionally dull rampage. Brassy, silly Herman Cohen–produced knockoff of KING KONG has only Gough's juicy, hammy performance to recommend it.▼

Kong Island SEE: **King of Kong Island**

Kongo (1932) **85m.** *** D: William Cowen. Walter Huston, Lupe Velez, Conrad Nagel, Virginia Bruce, C. Henry Gordon. Bizarre, fascinating melodrama of crippled madman Huston ruling African colony, seeking revenge on man who paralyzed him by torturing his daughter. Not for the squeamish. Remake of WEST OF ZANZIBAR.

Kon-Tiki (1951) **73m.** *** No director credited. Narrated by Ben Grauer, Thor Heyerdahl. This documentary won an Oscar in 1951; it traces Heyerdahl's raft trip from Peru to Tahiti, substantiating his theory that ancient sailing boats crossed the Pacific Ocean.▼

Kopek and Broom SEE: **Find the Lady**

Korczak (1990-Polish) **118m.** *** D: Andrzej Wajda. Wojtek Pszoniak, Ewa Dalkowska, Teresa Budzisz-Krzyzanowska, Piotr Kozlowski, Jan Peszek. Tremendously moving, real-life story of a truly remarkable man: Janusz Korczak (Pszoniak, in a powerful performance), a respected doctor, writer and children's rights advocate who operated a house for Jewish orphans in Warsaw during the 1930s and maintained his moral standards after the Nazis invaded his homeland. Simple, poignant script by Agnieszka Holland.▼

Kotch (1971) **C-113m.** ***½ D: Jack Lemmon. Walter Matthau, Deborah Winters, Felicia Farr, Charles Aidman, Darrell Larson, Larry Linville. Heartwarming comedy of elderly man who refuses to be put out to pasture by his children. Matthau superb in Lemmon's first directorial effort. [PG]▼

Koyaanisqatsi (1983) **C-87m.** **** D: Godfrey Reggio. Spellbinding, senses-staggering nonnarrative film soars across the United States in search of vistas both natural and man-made. Much of the photography is slow-motion or time-lapse (the title is Hopi Indian for "life out of balance"), all of it set to a mesmerizing score by Philip Glass. So rich in beauty and detail that with each viewing it becomes a new and different film. Should be seen in a theatre for maximum impact. Followed by POWAQQATSI.▼

Krakatoa, East of Java (1969) **C-101m.** **½ D: Bernard Kowalski. Maximilian Schell, Diane Baker, Brian Keith, Barbara Werle, John Leyton, Rossano Brazzi, Sal Mineo. Muddled epic-adventure of disparate group sailing for location of treasure-laden sunken ship. Attempt at Jules Verne-ish saga hampered by shallow characterizations, dialogue, but action footage is first-rate, climaxed by volcanic explosion and tidal wave. Heavily cut after premiere, leaving story more jumbled than before. P.S.: Krakatoa was *West* of Java. Retitled VOLCANO. Originally 136m. Super Panavision 70. [G]▼●◗

Kramer vs. Kramer (1979) **C-104m.** ****

D: Robert Benton. Dustin Hoffman, Meryl Streep, Jane Alexander, Justin Henry, Howard Duff, George Coe, JoBeth Williams. Wife walks out on upwardly mobile husband, leaving him to fend for himself and young son; intelligent, beautifully crafted, intensely moving film. Adapted by Benton from Avery Corman's novel and acted to perfection by entire cast. Oscar winner for Best Picture, Actor, Screenplay, Director, Supporting Actress (Streep). [PG]▼●

Krays, The (1990-British) **C-119m.** *** D: Peter Medak. Billie Whitelaw, Gary Kemp, Martin Kemp, Susan Fleetwood, Charlotte Cornwell, Jimmy Jewel, Avis Bunnage, Kate Hardie, Alfred Lynch, Tom Bell, Steven Berkoff, Victor Spinetti, Barbara Ferris, Julia Migenes, John McEnery, Sadie Frost. Brutal but stylish bio of the real-life twins (one gay, one straight) who ruled London's underworld in the 1960s, aided immeasurably by the title-role casting of two sibling members (not twins) of the Brit pop group Spandau Ballet. Picks up, after an iffy beginning, when the Kemps take over from an assortment of child actors; would have been even stronger had it gone beyond character study and dealt more with the lowlife Mod milieu. Whitelaw is good, as usual, as the boys' smothering mother. [R]▼●

Kremlin Letter, The (1970) **C-113m.** *½ D: John Huston. Bibi Andersson, Richard Boone, Max von Sydow, Orson Welles, Patrick O'Neal, Barbara Parkins, Dean Jagger, George Sanders, Raf Vallone. Dull, complicated thriller based on best-seller concerns efforts to retrieve bogus treaty supposedly signed by U.S. and Soviet Union that will pit them against Red China. Good cast is thrown away; film does provide rare opportunity to see Sanders in drag. Panavision. [M/PG]

Kriemhild's Revenge SEE: **Die Nibelungen**

Krippendorf's Tribe (1998) **C-94m.** ** D: Todd Holland. Richard Dreyfuss, Jenna Elfman, Natasha Lyonne, Gregory Smith, Carl Michael Lindner, Stephen Root, Elaine Stritch, Tom Poston, David Ogden Stiers, Lily Tomlin, Zakes Mokae. Widowed anthropology professor, who's spent all his grant money, is forced to present his findings on an unknown tribe in New Guinea. Trouble is, he never found such a tribe, so he makes one up, then shoots bogus videos with his three kids to back up his claims. Farcical comedy fizzles with wildly inconsistent characters (particularly Elfman) and desperate plot devices which never quite gel. [PG-13]▼●

Kristin Lavransdatter (1995-Norwegian) **C-144m.** ** D: Liv Ullmann. Elisabeth Matheson, Bjorn Skagestad, Sverre Anker Ousdal, Henny Moan, Rut Tellefsen, Erland Josephson, Lena Endre. Intense, plodding drama, set in the 14th century, about the title character (Matheson) and how pressures from family and society thwart her from being with her true love and steer her to marry another man instead. It's a conflict between religious obligation and "the sin of passion," and well acted, but never as profound or involving as intended. Ullmann also scripted, based on novel by Nobel Prize-winner Sigrid Undset. Originally shown at 180m.▼

Kronos (1957) **78m.** **½ D: Kurt Neumann. Jeff Morrow, Barbara Lawrence, John Emery, George O'Hanlon, Morris Ankrum. Diverting science-fiction with unique monster: an enormous metallic walking machine capable of absorbing the Earth's energy. Occasionally shaky special effects are compensated for by nice touch of mysterioso and convincing performances, especially by Emery as the alien's catspaw. Regalscope.▼●

Kronos (1974) SEE: **Captain Kronos: Vampire Hunter**

Krull (1983) **C-117m.** ** D: Peter Yates. Ken Marshall, Lysette Anthony, Freddie Jones, Francesca Annis, David Battley, Liam Neeson, Robbie Coltrane. Overly familiar story elements and plodding treatment keep this traditional fantasy quest from going anywhere, despite its elaborate trappings. Marshall is the young hero who must recover a magic ornament to save damsel and kingdom. Panavision. [PG]▼●

Krush Groove (1985) **C-97m.** ** D: Michael Schultz. Blair Underwood, Joseph Simmons, Sheila E., Fat Boys, Daryll McDaniels, Kurtis Blow. Yet another rap musical, with a silly (almost nonexistent) story but lots of music, rapping, and street culture artifacts. Aficionados of this kind of music rate the soundtrack very highly. [R]▼●

K-2 (1992-British) **C-111m.** **½ D: Franc Roddam. Michael Biehn, Matt Craven, Raymond J. Barry, Hiroshi Fujioka, Patricia Charbonneau, Luca Bercovici, Julia Nickson-Soul, Jamal Shah. A Seattle assistant D.A. (brash) and his physics-prof pal (gentle) attempt to climb the world's steepest and most remote mountain. Gritty outdoor expansion of Patrick Meyers' play, which won a Tony for its impressive mountain set; magnificent outdoor footage compensates for that, but not for the stock movie characterizations. Film never tops its first fifteen minutes, which are spellbinding. [R]▼●

Kuffs (1992) **C-100m.** *½ D: Bruce Evans. Christian Slater, Tony Goldwyn, Milla Jovovich, Bruce Boxleitner, George De La Pena, Troy Evans, Lu Leonard, Leon Rippy, Mary Ellen Trainor, Ashley Judd. Smarmy Slater desperately needs a job after abandoning his pregnant girlfriend; as luck would have it, his brother gets shot in the line of duty as a private policeman in San

Francisco. Unbearably flip, especially during frequent breaks for Slater's straight-to-camera narration. You keep waiting for Dirty Harry to show up and toss this kiddie cop one of his patented glares. [PG-13] ▼●

Kull the Conqueror (1997) **C-95m.** ** D: John Nicolella. Kevin Sorbo, Tia Carrere, Karina Lombard, Thomas Ian Griffith, Litefoot, Roy Brocksmith, Harvey Fierstein, Edward Tudor-Pole, Douglas Henshall, Sven Ole Thorsen. In ancient times, Kull, a barbarian from Atlantis, unexpectedly becomes king of a troubled country, and soon finds himself involved in swordfights, magic, and palace intrigue. Passionless, incoherent, and routine, with a few good performances, very uneven effects and makeup, and not enough sorcery. Based on a character created by Conan creator Robert E. Howard; in fact, this began life as a script for a third Conan movie. Super 35. [PG-13]▼●◗

Kundun (1997) **C-134m.** *** D: Martin Scorsese. Tenzin Thuthob Tsarong, Gyurme Tethong, Tulku Jamyang Kunga Tenzin, Tenzin Yeshi Paichang, Tencho Gyalpo, Tsewang Migyur Khangsar, Sonam Phuntsok, Robert Lin. The fascinating saga of the 14th Dalai Lama begins with the discovery that he has been reincarnated in the body of a two-year-old boy. We follow his journey through life, including education, exile, and a confrontation with the Chinese government, led by Mao Tse-tung. Search in vain for a Scorsese "edge"—this is just good, solid storytelling, from Melissa Mathison's script (written with the Dalai Lama's cooperation). A cast of nonprofessional actors is simply remarkable, and so is Philip Glass' score. Super 35. [PG-13]▼●◗

Kung Fu (1972) **C-75m. TVM** D: Jerry Thorpe. David Carradine, Barry Sullivan, Keith Carradine, Philip Ahn, Keye Luke, Wayne Maunder, Albert Salmi, Benson Fong, Richard Loo, Victor Sen Yung. Stylish tale of young Carradine, a half-American/half-Chinese Buddhist monk trained in karate, who flees mainland China after he's accused of murder and comes to the American West. Good performances and offbeat direction that counterpoints the script's moods. Above average; pilot for the series. Carradine reprised the role 14 years later in KUNG FU: THE MOVIE. ▼●

Kung Fu: The Movie (1986) **C-100m. TVM** D: Richard Lang. David Carradine, Kerri Keane, Mako, William Lucking, Luke Askew, Benson Fong, Keye Luke, Martin Landau, Brandon Lee. Carradine reprises his now cult role of Kwai Chang Caine from the original *King Fu* series of the early 1970s, here being stalked by evil warlord Mako, who's mixed up in California's opium trade in the late 1880s. Bruce Lee's son Brandon is "introduced" as a young Manchu assassin who clashes with Carradine, and Keye Luke repeats (in flashback only) his original part as Master Po, Carradine's blind teacher. Followed by a subsequent series, set in modern times, in which Carradine plays Caine's grandson. Average.▼

Kurt Vonnegut's "Harrison Bergeron" (1995-Canadian) **C-105m. TVM** D: Bruce Pittman. Sean Astin, Miranda de Pencier, Buck Henry, Eugene Levy, Howie Mandel, Andrea Martin, Christopher Plummer, Hayden Christensen. Witty, highly original look at Vonnegut's perfect Big Brother–style world of 2053 (from his 1961 short story). Teenage whiz Astin sees through the machinations of charmingly sinister Plummer, who keeps everybody contentedly mediocre through mind control, only to find his own stubborn intelligence has made him a dangerous outcast in need of brainwashing. Look for the star's dad, John Astin, in a brief appearance as a smarmy golf commentator. Adapted by Arthur Crimm. Made for cable. Above average.▼

Kwaidan (1964-Japanese) **C-164m.** ***½ D: Masaki Kobayashi. Rentaro Mikuni, Michiyo Aratama, Keiko Kishi, Tatsuya Nakadai, Takashi Shimura. Four tales of the supernatural, based on works by Lafcadio Hearn, focusing on samurais, balladeers, monks, spirits. Subtle, moody, well staged; stunning use of color and widescreen. Released in U.S. in 1965 at 125m., with the second episode (featuring Kishi and Nakadai) deleted. Tohoscope.▼●

La Balance (1982-French) **C-102m.** *** D: Bob Swaim. Nathalie Baye, Philippe Leotard, Richard Berry, Maurice Ronet, Christophe Malavoy, Jean-Paul Connart. Extremely tough, violent Parisian cop movie (directed and cowritten by an American) about effort to nail criminal kingpin by forcing one-time associate (Leotard) to turn informer. Baye is excellent as prostitute in love with victimized pimp. Winner of many Cesar Awards (France's Oscar) including Best Picture. [R]▼

La Bamba (1987) **C-108m.** *** D: Luis Valdez. Lou Diamond Phillips, Esai Morales, Rosana De Soto, Elizabeth Pena, Danielle von Zerneck, Joe Pantoliano, Rick Dees, Marshall Crenshaw, Brian Setzer. Solid musical biography of Ritchie Valens, a poor Mexican-American who became a rock 'n' roll sensation at age 17. Writer-director Valdez can't avoid some standard Hollywood bio trappings, but good-time music and Phillips' commanding, sympathetic performance more than compensate. Morales is excellent as Ritchie's troubled brother. Valens' music is performed by Los Lobos on soundtrack—they appear as the Tijuana band. Original music by Carlos Santana and Miles Goodman. [PG-13]▼●◗

La Belle Noiseuse (1991-French) **C-240m.** ***½ D: Jacques Rivette. Michel Piccoli,

Jane Birkin, Emmanuelle Béart, Marianne Denicourt, David Bursztein, Gilles Arbona, Bernard Dufour. Riveting story of the relationship between a once-famed artist and the young woman who inspires him to paint after 10 years of inactivity, and becomes his model. A stunning examination of the artistic process and its accompanying obsessions, with outstanding performances by Piccoli as the artist and gorgeous Beart as his subject. Extremely long, deliberately paced but always involving; beautifully directed by Rivette and photographed by William Lubtchansky. Screenplay by Rivette, Pascal Bonitzer, and Christine Laurent. Dufour, by the way, supplies the artist's hand. A new version, reworked and with a new perspective, was released in 1993. Its title: DIVERTIMENTO, running 125m. ▼

La Bête Humaine (1938-French) **99m.** ***½ D: Jean Renoir. Jean Gabin, Julien Carette, Simone Simon, Fernand Ledoux, Blanchette Brunoy, Gerard Landry. Locomotive engineer Gabin displays fits of uncontrollable violence against women. When he forms a liaison with the flirtatious wife of a deputy stationmaster, he becomes entangled in a plot to kill the husband. Sublimely atmospheric adaptation of Emile Zola's novel suited the fatalistic mood of Europe in 1938, as the Nazis overran Czechoslovakia. That's Renoir himself in the role of Cabuche; he also scripted. Aka THE HUMAN BEAST and JUDAS WAS A WOMAN. Fritz Lang remade it in the U.S. as HUMAN DESIRE.▼

La Bohème (1926) **94m.** ***½ D: King Vidor. Lillian Gish, John Gilbert, Renee Adoree, George Hassell, Roy D'Arcy, Edward Everett Horton, Karl Dane, Gino Corrado. Charming, floridly romantic silent vehicle for Gish and Gilbert (at their very best) as the star-crossed lovers who live among the starving artists in Paris' Latin Quarter. Gilbert and director Vidor had just made THE BIG PARADE together; this was a worthy followup. Based on an 1851 novel, by the way, and quite different from Puccini's famous opera.

La Boum (1981-French) **C-100m.** **½ D: Claude Pinoteau. Claude Brasseur, Brigitte Fossey, Sophie Marceau, Denise Grey, Bernard Giraudeau. Cliched but harmless chronicle of the life of pretty 13-year-old Marceau, whose parents (Brasseur, Fossey) are having marital difficulties. A French box-office smash. Sequel: LA BOUM 2.▼

La Boum 2 (1982-French) **C-109m.** **½ D: Claude Pinoteau. Sophie Marceau, Claude Brasseur, Brigitte Fossey, Pierre Cosso, Shiela O'Connor, Denise Grey. Here teenager Marceau is two years older and has a romance with another student. Her parents are still squabbling. A formula film, no better or worse than the original.

Labyrinth (1986) **C-101m.** *** D: Jim Henson. David Bowie, Jennifer Connelly, Toby Froud. Teenage girl's baby brother is kidnapped by the King of the Goblins (Bowie); in order to rescue him she must navigate a devilish labyrinth. Entertaining variation on *Alice in Wonderland* written by Monty Python's Terry Jones, executive produced by George Lucas, and filtered through the sensibilities of The Muppets' Jim Henson. A treat for kids and the young at heart (Muppet fans in particular); only weakness is that it does get slow at times. J-D-C Scope. [PG]▼●◗

Labyrinth of Passion (1982-Spanish) **C-100m.** *** D: Pedro Almodóvar. Celia Roth, Imanol Arias, Helga Line, Antonio Banderas. Zany, energetic sex farce, most of which is beyond the power of description. It does involve a gallery of comically outlandish characters scurrying about Madrid, including transvestites, punk rockers, nymphomaniacs—and Islamic fundamentalists. Occasionally crude, and always rude, but that's all part of the fun.▼●

La Cage aux Folles (1978-French-Italian) **C-91m.** *** D: Edouard Molinaro. Ugo Tognazzi, Michel Serrault, Michel Galabru, Claire Maurier, Remy Laurent, Benny Luke. A gay couple tries to act straight for the sake of Tognazzi's son, who's bringing home his fiancée and her parents. Entertaining adaptation of French stage farce, with some hilarious moments and a wonderful performance by Serrault as the more feminine half of the middle-aged twosome—but why this became such a raging success is a mystery. Followed by two sequels, as well as a hit Broadway musical. Remade in 1996 as THE BIRDCAGE. [R] ▼●

La Cage aux Folles II (1980-French) **C-101m.** **½ D: Edouard Molinaro. Michel Serrault, Ugo Tognazzi, Marcel Bozzuffi, Michel Galabru, Paola Borboni, Benny Luke. St. Tropez nightclub owner (Tognazzi) and his female-impersonator housemate (Serrault) become involved with a spy ring in this mild sequel. [R]▼●

La Cage aux Folles 3: The Wedding (1985-French-Italian) **C-87m.** *½ D: Georges Lautner. Michel Serrault, Ugo Tognazzi, Michel Galabru, Benny Luke, Stephane Audran, Antonella Interlenghi. Pointless sequel has drag queen Albin (Serrault) in line for big inhertance—if he marries and produces a son. This farce has been milked dry by now. [PG-13]▼●

La Cérémonie (1995-French-German) **C-111m.** *** D: Claude Chabrol. Isabelle Huppert, Sandrine Bonnaire, Jacqueline Bisset, Jean-Pierre Cassel, Virginie Ledoyen, Valentin Merlet. Slow-moving but effective Chabrol thriller, with Huppert and Bonnaire as lower-class pals in rural Brittany, who resent the wealthy household in which Bonnaire is employed as maid. Nice turn by Bisset, as sympathetic matriarch.▼

La Chèvre (1982-French) **C-91m.** *** D: Francis Veber. Pierre Richard, Gérard Depardieu, Michel Robin, Pedro Armendariz, Jr., Corynne Charbit, Andre Valardy. No-nonsense sleuth Depardieu sets out to locate an industrialist's daughter who's disappeared in Mexico, finds himself comically hampered by his employer's accountant (Richard), an amateur detective. Amiable, amusing comedy was a box-office smash in France. Veber also scripted. Aka THE GOAT. Americanized remake: PURE LUCK. ▼

La Chienne (1931-French) **95m.** **** D: Jean Renoir. Michel Simon, Janie Mareze, Georges Flamant, Madeleine Berubet. Renoir's first sound film, and first sound-film masterpiece: a terse, somber drama of mild-mannered bank cashier Simon, with an overbearing wife, who plays into the hands of prostitute Mareze and her scheming pimp. Renoir coscripted; Mareze died in a car accident a couple of weeks after filming was completed. Fritz Lang redid this as SCARLET STREET; what a video double bill they would make!▼●

La Chinoise (1967-French) **C-95m.** *** D: Jean-Luc Godard. Anne Wiazemsky, Jean-Pierre Léaud, Michel Semianko, Lex de Bruijn, Juliet Berto. Five young Maoists share an apartment and try to apply their politics to the reality of their lives. Godard aficionados will be fascinated; others may be bored.

La Ciudad SEE: **City, The**

La Collectionneuse (1971-French) **C-88m.** *** D: Eric Rohmer. Patrick Bauchau, Haydee Politoff, Daniel Pommerulle, Alain Jouffroy, Mijanou Bardot. No. 3 of Rohmer's "Six Moral Tales" is less compelling than later films, still intriguing for fans of contemplative stories in this series, focusing on young man's attraction to aloof young girl sharing summer villa on the Mediterranean. Made in 1967. ▼

Lacombe, Lucien (1974-French) **C-137m.** **** D: Louis Malle. Pierre Blaise, Aurore Clement, Holger Lowenadler, Therese Giehse. Brilliant, perceptive account of opportunist French peasant Blaise, who joins the Gestapo during the Nazi Occupation—after setting out to join the Resistance—and falls in love with a Jewish tailor's daughter. Subtle, complex tale of guilt, innocence, and the amorality of power; masterfully directed. [R]

L.A. Confidential (1997) **C-136m.** ***½ D: Curtis Hanson. Kevin Spacey, Russell Crowe, Guy Pearce, James Cromwell, David Strathairn, Kim Basinger, Danny DeVito, Graham Beckel, Brenda Bakke, Paul Guilfoyle, Ron Rifkin. Vividly atmospheric tale of L.A. in the early 1950s, run by corrupt cops—one of whom (Spacey) works hand in hand with the publisher of a sleazy tabloid (DeVito). Self-righteous Pearce, however, thinks he can rise above the muck in the department. Director Hanson and Brian Helgeland's Oscar-winning adaptation of the James Ellroy novel is overlong but compelling and richly detailed; a bleak worldview, to be sure. Basinger won a Best Supporting Actress Oscar as the Veronica Lake–ish call girl, but she's surrounded by Oscar-worthy costars. Super 35. [R] ▼●◗

Lad: A Dog (1962) **C-98m.** **½ D: Aram Avakian, Leslie H. Martinson. Peter Breck, Peggy McCay, Carroll O'Connor, Angela Cartwright, Maurice Dallimore. Genuine if schmaltzy version of Albert Payson Terhune novel of dog who brings new zest for life to lame child.▼

L'Addition (1985-French) **C-85m.** ** D: Denis Amar. Richard Berry, Richard Bohringer, Victoria Abril, Farid Chopel. Drab prison drama of criminal Berry vs. ruthless guard Bohringer. Never finds the spark to catch fire, despite presence of Spanish actress Abril (who resembles Rosanna Arquette). [R]▼

Ladies and Gentlemen, The Fabulous Stains (1982) **C-87m.** ** D: Lou Adler. Diane Lane, Ray Winstone, Peter Donat, David Clennon, John Lehne, Cynthia Sikes, Laura Dern, John (Fee) Waybill, Christine Lahti. Antisocial teenage girl decides to become a punk rock star and takes to the road. Unreleased major studio film is strident and unappealing, despite good cast. Lahti shines in her two scenes. Members of Clash and The Sex Pistols appear as a British punk band. [R]

Ladies and Gentlemen, the Rolling Stones (1975) **C-90m.** **½ D: Rollin Binzer. Disappointing documentary on rock group's 1972 U.S. tour is unworthy of subject, but fans should take a look. Loss of quadrophonic sound on some prints hurts. [PG]

Ladies Club, The (1986) **C-90m.** ** D: A. K. Allen. Karen Austin, Diana Scarwid, Christine Belford, Bruce Davison, Shera Danese, Beverly Todd. Policewoman and rape victim team up with other angry women to teach rapists a lesson they won't forget. May offer distaff viewers some vicarious pleasure, but it's still not a very good film. Made in 1984. [R]▼

Ladies Courageous (1944) **88m.** ** D: John Rawlins. Loretta Young, Geraldine Fitzgerald, Diana Barrymore, Evelyn Ankers, Frank Jenks, Ruth Roman, Anne Gwynne, Philip Terry, Lois Collier, Kane Richmond. Well-meant idea fails because of hackneyed script and situations; saga of the WAFs during WW2 who played a vital part in air warfare.

Ladies' Day (1943) **62m.** ** D: Leslie Goodwins. Lupe Velez, Eddie Albert, Patsy Kelly, Max Baer, Jerome Cowan, Iris Adrian, Joan Barclay. Slight baseball farce with Albert a top hurler with an eye for the ladies whose athletic skills disappear each time he gets a new girlfriend. The latest to catch his eye is movie star Velez.

Ladies in Love (1936) **97m.** **½ D: Edward Griffith. Janet Gaynor, Loretta Young, Constance Bennett, Simone Simon, Don Ameche, Paul Lukas, Tyrone Power. Man-hunting girls in Budapest stick together to find likely victims; large cast makes it entertaining; young Power seen to good advantage.

Ladies in Retirement (1941) **92m.** *** D: Charles Vidor. Ida Lupino, Louis Hayward, Evelyn Keyes, Elsa Lanchester, Edith Barrett, Isobel Elsom, Emma Dunn. Static but well-made gothic melodrama about housekeeper Lupino's attempt to cover up murder in eccentric British household. Not as potent—or as shocking—as it must have been in 1941, but still good. Remade as THE MAD ROOM.

Ladies' Man (1931) **70m.** *½ D: Lothar Mendes. William Powell, Kay Francis, Carole Lombard, Gilbert Emery, John Holland. Lifeless story of gigolo Powell becoming involved with society mother (Olive Tell) and daughter (Lombard), trying to find true happiness with Francis. Strange, downbeat film.

Ladies' Man (1947) **91m.** ** D: William D. Russell. Eddie Bracken, Cass Daley, Virginia Welles, Spike Jones and His City Slickers. Brassy comedy of hayseed inheriting a fortune, coming to N.Y.C. to paint the town.

Ladies' Man, The (1961) **C-106m.** *** D: Jerry Lewis. Jerry Lewis, Helen Traubel, Kathleen Freeman, Hope Holiday, Pat Stanley, Jack Kruschen, Doodles Weaver, Harry James and His Band. Pretty funny comedy with Jerry the handyman in a girls' school run by Mrs. Wellenmelon (Traubel). Enormous set is the real star; Buddy Lester and George Raft have amusing cameo appearances.▼●

Ladies of Leisure (1930) **98m.** **½ D: Frank Capra. Barbara Stanwyck, Ralph Graves, Lowell Sherman, Marie Prevost, Nance O'Neill, George Fawcett. Stanwyck falls in love with playboy-artist Graves, but cannot shake her reputation as gold-digger. Creaky story made worthwhile by Stanwyck's believable performance and Capra's fluent filmmaking technique. Remade as WOMEN OF GLAMOR.▼

Ladies of the Big House (1931) **76m.** **½ D: Marion Gering. Sylvia Sidney, Gene Raymond, Wynne Gibson, Purnell Pratt, Louise Beavers, Jane Darwell, Noel Francis. Sidney is framed and imprisoned; a tearful, well-acted prison drama.

Ladies of the Chorus (1949) **61m.** ** D: Phil Karlson. Adele Jergens, Rand Brooks, Marilyn Monroe, Eddie Garr, Nana Bryant. Cheapie musical about mother/daughter burlesque chorines, with young Monroe seemingly headed for the same romantic blunder that mom Jergens made. Worth a look for MM in her first sizable role. Garr (who plays a burlesque clown) is the father of Teri.▼

Ladies of the Jury (1932) **65m.** **½ D: Lowell Sherman. Edna May Oliver, Jill Esmond, Roscoe Ates, Ken Murray, Kitty Kelly, Cora Witherspoon, Florence Lake. Oliver shines as society matron evaluating a murder trial who makes a shambles of courtroom and jury room. Unfortunately, surrounding production is static and unimaginative. Title is odd misnomer, since jury is coed; Guinn Williams appears unbilled as juror with French wife. Remade in 1937 as WE'RE ON THE JURY.

Ladies Should Listen (1934) **62m.** ** D: Frank Tuttle. Cary Grant, Frances Drake, Edward Everett Horton, Nydia Westman, Ann Sheridan. Grant's life is manipulated by telephone operator Drake in flimsy comedy, no great shakes.

Ladies They Talk About (1933) **68m.** **½ D: Howard Bretherton, William Keighley. Barbara Stanwyck, Preston S. Foster, Lyle Talbot, Dorothy Burgess, Maude Eburne, Lillian Roth, Ruth Donnelly. Stanwyck is terrific as usual in punchy pre-Code women's prison picture. More than a bit silly at times.▼●

Ladies Who Do (1963-British) **85m.** **½ D: C. M. Pennington-Richards. Peggy Mount, Robert Morley, Harry H. Corbett, Nigel Davenport, Carol White, Miriam Karlin. When a charwoman discovers that waste paper scraps contain valuable stock market tips, a mild satire on British financial world unfolds.▼

La Discrète (1990-French) **C-94m.** *** D: Christian Vincent. Fabrice Luchini, Judith Henry, Maurice Garrel, Francois Toumarkine. Insightful allegory about a heartless writer/Don Juan (Luchini) who allows vengeful publisher Garrel to convince him to toy with the emotions of typist Henry, to extract raw material for a book. Solid performances (especially by Henry) help put this one over.▼

La Dolce Vita (1960-Italian) **175m.** ***½ D: Federico Fellini. Marcello Mastroianni, Anita Ekberg, Anouk Aimée, Yvonne Furneaux, Magali Noel, Alain Cuny, Annibale Ninchi, Walter Santesso, Lex Barker, Jacques Sernas, Nadia Gray. Lengthy trend-setting film, not as ambiguous as other Fellini works—much more entertaining, with strong cast. Mastroianni stars as tabloid reporter who sees his life in shallow Rome society as worthless but can't change. Story and screenplay by Fellini, Ennio Flaiano, and Tullio Pinelli, with Brunello Rondi. Piero Gherardi's costumes won an Oscar. Totalscope.▼●

L'Adolescente (1979-French-German) **C-90m.** **½ D: Jeanne Moreau. Laetitia

Chauveau, Simone Signoret, Edith Clever, Jacques Weber, Francis Huster. One-dimensional tale of anxious, confused Chauveau, just beginning her teen years at the outset of WW2. A heartfelt effort by Moreau that falls flat. Aka THE ADOLESCENT. [PG]

Lady and the Bandit, The (1951) **79m.** ** D: Ralph Murphy. Louis Hayward, Patricia Medina, Suzanne Dalbert, Tom Tully. Harmless costumer about career and love of highwayman Dick Turpin.

Lady and the Mob, The (1939) **66m.** **½ D: Ben Stoloff. Fay Bainter, Lee Bowman, Ida Lupino, Henry Armetta. Bainter gives dignity to mini-tale of eccentric rich lady involved with gangster mob.

Lady and the Monster, The (1944) **86m.** **½ D: George Sherman. Vera Ralston, Erich von Stroheim, Richard Arlen, Sidney Blackmer. Pretty good chiller of mysterious brain taking over man's life. Remade as DONOVAN'S BRAIN.

Lady and the Outlaw, The SEE: **Billy Two Hats**

Lady and the Tramp (1955) **C-75m.** ***½ D: Hamilton Luske, Clyde Geronimi, Wilfred Jackson. Voices of Peggy Lee, Barbara Luddy, Bill Thompson, Bill Baucon, Stan Freberg, Verna Felton, Alan Reed. One of Walt Disney's most endearing animated features, based on Ward Greene's story about a rakish dog named Tramp who helps pedigreed canine named Lady out of a jam—and into a romance. Elements of adventure and drama are masterfully blended with comedy and music in this stylish film, the Disney studio's first feature cartoon in CinemaScope. Songs by Sonny Burke and Peggy Lee (who's the voice of Peg, Darling, Si and Am, the Siamese cats). CinemaScope.▼●◗

Lady Be Good (1941) **111m.** *** D: Norman Z. McLeod. Eleanor Powell, Ann Sothern, Robert Young, Lionel Barrymore, John Carroll, Red Skelton, Virginia O'Brien, Dan Dailey, Jimmy Dorsey and His Orchestra. Spunky musical of married songwriters Sothern and Young, with Powell and Skelton along for good measure. Fine score: title tune, "Fascinating Rhythm," "You'll Never Know," Oscar-winning "Last Time I Saw Paris." ▼●

Lady Beware (1987) **C-108m.** **½ D: Karen Arthur. Diane Lane, Michael Woods, Cotter Smith, Viveca Lindfors, Peter Nevargic, Edward Penn, Tyra Ferrell. Lane's mildly kinky store-window displays arouse a married psychotic; he soon graduates from irritating phone calls and mail interception to breaking into her window-barred loft. Imperfect, but compelling, feminist exploitation film builds to a satisfying (and surprisingly nonviolent) conclusion; Lane's performance is uneven, but her rage convincing. Filmed and set in Pittsburgh. [R]▼●

Ladybird, Ladybird (1993-British) **C-102m.** *** D: Kenneth Loach. Crissy Rock, Vladimir Vega, Ray Winstone, Sandie Lavelle, Mauricio Venegas, Clare Perkins. Shattering, based-on-fact account of a durable but deeply troubled single mother of four (extremely well played by Rock), who has a history of being abused by men; she becomes involved with kindly Vega, but this relationship will not be without its share of crises. Another impassioned look at British working class life from director Loach. ▼

Ladybug Ladybug (1963) **84m.** *** D: Frank Perry. Jane Connell, William Daniels, James Frawley, Richard Hamilton, Kathryn Hays, Jane Hoffman, Elena Karam, Judith Lowry, Nancy Marchand, Estelle Parsons, Miles Chapin, Marilyn Rogers, Alice Playten, Christopher Howard. Ambitious and provocative (if a bit too obvious) account of some rural schoolchildren and their reactions when a civil defense system warns of an impending nuclear attack. Screenplay by Eleanor Perry, and a followup of sorts to DAVID AND LISA. Based on an actual incident.

Ladybugs (1992) **C-89m.** *½ D: Sidney J. Furie. Rodney Dangerfield, Jackée, Jonathan Brandis, Ilene Graff, Vinessa Shaw, Tom Parks, Jeanetta Arnette, Nancy Parsons, Blake Clark, Tommy Lasorda. To placate his boss and secure a promotion, Rodney becomes the coach of a girls' soccer team—complete with an in-drag male player (the son of his fiancée). Slapdash execution of what sounds like a sure-fire Dangerfield premise; the best zingers concern rival female coach Parsons. [PG-13]▼●

Lady by Choice (1934) **78m.** **½ D: David Burton. Carole Lombard, May Robson, Roger Pryor, Walter Connolly, Arthur Hohl. Enjoyable follow-up to LADY FOR A DAY; dancer Lombard takes in scraggly Robson, makes her proper lady.▼

Lady Caroline Lamb (1972-British) **C-118m.** BOMB D: Robert Bolt. Sarah Miles, Jon Finch, Richard Chamberlain, John Mills, Margaret Leighton, Ralph Richardson, Laurence Olivier. Wretched filmization of famous story; wife of English politician scandalizes everyone by her open affair with Lord Byron. Bolt's banal script is often unintentionally funny. Panavision. [PG]▼

Lady Chatterley's Lover (1981-French-British) **C-105m.** BOMB D: Just Jaeckin. Sylvia Kristel, Nicholas Clay, Shane Briant, Ann Mitchell, Elizabeth Spriggs, Peter Bennett. Dull, cheap version of the D. H. Lawrence classic, with Kristel as the lady and Clay as the lover. Kristel is beautiful, but still cannot act. From the

director of EMMANUELLE. Previously filmed in France in 1955. [R]▼●
Lady Consents, The (1936) **75m.** **½ D: Stephen Roberts. Ann Harding, Herbert Marshall, Margaret Lindsay, Walter Abel. Pat triangle with married Marshall discovering that he still loves his ex-wife.
Lady Dances, The SEE: **Merry Widow, The** (1934)
Lady Doctor (1956-Italian) **90m.** **½ D: Camillo Mastrocinque. Abbe Lane, Vittorio De Sica, Toto, Titina De Filippo, German Cobos, Teddy Reno. Pungent nonsense as Toto and De Sica try to con doctor Lane out of a fortune hidden in her house.
Lady Dracula (1973) **C-80m.** BOMB D: Richard Blackburn. Cheryl Smith, Lesley Gilb, William Whitton, Richard Blackburn. Perfectly awful low-budgeter about a lady vampire with lesbian tendencies. Bring back Gloria Holden! Aka LEGENDARY CURSE OF LEMORA and LEMORA, THE LADY DRACULA. [PG]
Lady Eve, The (1941) **94m.** ***½ D: Preston Sturges. Barbara Stanwyck, Henry Fonda, Charles Coburn, Eugene Pallette, William Demarest, Eric Blore, Melville Cooper. Stanwyck is a con artist who sets her eyes on wealthy Fonda—the dolt to end all dolts, who proclaims "snakes are my life." Sometimes silly and strident, this film grows funnier with each viewing—thanks to Sturges's script, breathless pace, and two incomparable stars. Remade as THE BIRDS AND THE BEES.▼●
Lady for a Day (1933) **96m.** **** D: Frank Capra. Warren William, May Robson, Guy Kibbee, Glenda Farrell, Jean Parker, Walter Connolly, Ned Sparks, Nat Pendleton. Wonderful Damon Runyon fable of seedy apple vendor Robson transformed into perfect lady by softhearted racketeer William. Robert Riskin adapted Runyon's story "Madame La Gimp." Sequel: LADY BY CHOICE. Remade by Capra as POCKETFUL OF MIRACLES. ▼●
Lady for a Night (1942) **87m.** ** D: Leigh Jason. Joan Blondell, John Wayne, Ray Middleton, Philip Merivale, Blanche Yurka, Edith Barrett, Hattie Noel. Plodding costume drama of wealthy, status-seeking gambling queen Blondell and her plight upon marrying impoverished society drunk Middleton. Good cast seems out of place.▼
Lady Frankenstein (1971-Italian) **C-84m.** BOMB D: Mel Welles. Joseph Cotten, Mickey Hargitay, Sarah Bey, Paul Muller, Paul Whiteman. Poor horror entry with Cotten a tired, ill-fated Baron; his daughter (Bey) takes up where he leaves off in the monster-making department. [R]▼
Lady From Cheyenne (1941) **87m.** **½ D: Frank Lloyd. Loretta Young, Robert Preston, Edward Arnold, Frank Craven, Gladys George. Average fare of schoolteacher Young (in 1869 Wyoming) striking a blow for women's rights about a century too early, as she fights for the opportunity to sit on a jury. Good supporting cast helps.
Lady From Louisiana (1941) **82m.** **½ D: Bernard Vorhaus. John Wayne, Ona Munson, Ray Middleton, Henry Stephenson, Helen Westley, Jack Pennick, Dorothy Dandridge. Wayne and Munson fall in love, then discover they're on opposite sides of gambling controversy; so-so period-piece.▼
Lady From Shanghai, The (1948) **87m.** *** D: Orson Welles. Rita Hayworth, Orson Welles, Everett Sloane, Glenn Anders, Ted de Corsia, Erskine Sanford, Gus Schilling. The camera's the star of this offbeat thriller, with the cast incidental in bizarre murder mystery about an Irish adventurer (Welles) who joins seductive Hayworth and her husband (Sloane) on a Pacific cruise. The famous hall of mirrors climax is riveting. Cinematography by Charles Lawton, Jr. Based on novel by Sherwood King, scripted and produced by Welles. That's Errol Flynn's yacht, *Zaca,* in the seagoing scenes.▼●
Lady From Texas, The (1951) **C-77m.** ** D: Joseph Pevney. Howard Duff, Mona Freeman, Josephine Hull, Gene Lockhart, Craig Stevens. Strange minor film of eccentric old lady Hull; Duff and Freeman come to her rescue.
Lady Gambles, The (1949) **98m.** *** D: Michael Gordon. Barbara Stanwyck, Robert Preston, Stephen McNally, Edith Barrett, John Hoyt, Leif Erickson. The LOST WEEKEND of gambling films, a well-acted drama chronicling Stanwyck's decline from respectable writer's wife to desperate, addicted gambler and all-around screwup. Look for Tony Curtis—then billed as "Anthony"—as a bellboy.
Lady Godiva (1955) **C-89m.** ** D: Arthur Lubin. Maureen O'Hara, George Nader, Victor McLaglen, Torin Thatcher, Robert Warwick. Cardboard costumer of famed lady and her horseback ride set in Middle Ages England—What a dull ride! Look for Clint Eastwood, billed as "First Saxon." ▼
Lady Godiva Rides Again (1951-British) **90m.** ** D: Frank Launder. Dennis Price, John McCallum, Stanley Holloway, Pauline Stroud, Diana Dors, George Cole, Kay Kendall, Sidney James, Dagmar (Dana) Wynter, Googie Withers, Alastair Sim. Intriguing cast keeps one watching this OK comedy about a simple lass who wins a beauty contest and is exposed to the seamy side of glamour. Joan Collins' film debut, as one of the contestants.
Lady Grey (1980) **C-100m.** BOMB D: Worth Keeter. Ginger Alden, David Allen Coe, Paul Ott, Herman Bloodsworth, Ed Grady, Paula Baldwin. Low-grade drama chronicling the trials of aspiring country

singer played by Elvis Presley's last girlfriend. Shot in North Carolina; an Earl Owensby production.▼

Lady Hamilton SEE: **That Hamilton Woman**

Lady Has Plans, The (1942) **77m.** ** D: Sidney Lanfield. Paulette Goddard, Ray Milland, Roland Young, Albert Dekker, Margaret Hayes, Cecil Kellaway. Jumbled spy comedy with innocent Goddard suspected of being agent and Milland tailing her in Lisbon.

Ladyhawke (1985) **C-124m.** *** D: Richard Donner. Matthew Broderick, Rutger Hauer, Michelle Pfeiffer, Leo McKern, John Wood, Ken Hutchison, Alfred Molina. Overlong but generally entertaining medieval fantasy adventure about star-crossed lovers caught in an evil spell—and a young thief who becomes their unlikely ally. Hauer and Pfeiffer are perfectly cast as stalwart hero and heroine, but Broderick's manner and dialogue seem better suited to a Woody Allen movie! Thunderous music by Andrew Powell. Technovision. [PG-13]▼●◗

Lady Ice (1973) **C-93m.** ** D: Tom Gries. Donald Sutherland, Jennifer O'Neill, Robert Duvall, Patrick Magee, Eric Braeden, Jon Cypher. Dull caper film pairs insurance investigator Sutherland and wealthy O'Neill, whose father is a major "fence" for stolen jewels. Good cast wasted. Panavision. [PG]▼

Lady in a Cage (1964) **93m.** *** D: Walter Grauman. Olivia de Havilland, Ann Sothern, Jeff Corey, James Caan, Jennifer Billingsley, Rafael Campos, Scatman Crothers. Bone-chilling psychological drama in which incapacitated widow de Havilland finds herself stuck in an elevator in her home, then is terrorized by thugs. Allegorical tale of alienation and mindless cruelty in an impersonal society; unpleasant to watch, but undeniably truthful and prophetic. Starkly directed and well acted.▼

Lady in a Jam (1942) **78m.** **½ D: Gregory La Cava. Irene Dunne, Patric Knowles, Ralph Bellamy, Eugene Pallette, Queenie Vassar. Thirties-type screwball comedy doesn't really hit bull's-eye, with wacky Dunne convincing psychiatrist Knowles to marry her to cure her ills.

Lady in Cement (1968) **C-93m.** ** D: Gordon Douglas. Frank Sinatra, Raquel Welch, Dan Blocker, Richard Conte, Martin Gabel, Lainie Kazan, Richard Deacon, Joe E. Lewis. Sequel to TONY ROME finds Sinatra discovering nude corpse with feet encased in cement. Typical private-eye hokum, with heavy doses of violence, leering sex. Panavision. [PG—originally rated R]▼●

Lady in Distress (1939-British) **76m.** *** D: Herbert Mason. Paul Lukas, Sally Gray, Michael Redgrave, Patricia Roc, Hartley Power. Redgrave falls for wife of jealous magician after witnessing what looked like her murder. Originally titled A WINDOW IN LONDON.▼

Lady in Question, The (1940) **81m.** **½ D: Charles Vidor. Brian Aherne, Rita Hayworth, Glenn Ford, Irene Rich, George Coulouris, Lloyd Corrigan. Aherne plays a juror interested in defendant Hayworth. He manages to save her, but later falls prey to jealousy. Varies awkwardly from comedy to drama.▼●

Lady in Red, The (1979) **C-93m.** **½ D: Lewis Teague. Pamela Sue Martin, Robert Conrad, Louise Fletcher, Robert Hogan, Laurie Heineman, Glenn Withrow, Christopher Lloyd, Dick Miller. Martin suffers a life on the lam, before and after her period of notoriety as girlfriend of John Dillinger (Conrad). Lurid, low-budget retread of familiar material is handled with surprising verve. A Roger Corman production; screenplay by John Sayles. Robert Forster appears uncredited in key supporting role. Retitled GUNS, SIN AND BATHTUB GIN. [R]▼

Lady in the Car With Glasses and a Gun, The (1970-French) **C-105m.** **½ D: Anatole Litvak. Samantha Eggar, Oliver Reed, John McEnery, Stephane Audran, Billie Dixon. Eggar is best thing about otherwise unexceptional film. Psychological thriller about attempt to drive young woman crazy is only occasionally interesting. Panavision. [R]

Lady in the Dark (1944) **C-100m.** **½ D: Mitchell Leisen. Ginger Rogers, Ray Milland, Jon Hall, Warner Baxter, Barry Sullivan, Gail Russell, Mischa Auer. Overproduced Technicolor adaptation of the groundbreaking Moss Hart Broadway show (minus most of the Kurt Weill–Ira Gershwin songs) about a career woman who undergoes psychoanalysis to find the root of her problems. Intriguing but ultimately ponderous.

Lady in the Iron Mask (1952) **C-78m.** ** D: Ralph Murphy. Louis Hayward, Patricia Medina, Alan Hale, John Sutton. Variation of Dumas tale, with Three Musketeers still about; moderate costumer.

Lady in the Lake (1946) **103m.** **½ D: Robert Montgomery. Robert Montgomery, Audrey Totter, Lloyd Nolan, Tom Tully, Leon Ames, Jayne Meadows. Raymond Chandler whodunit has novelty of camera taking first-person point of view of detective Philip Marlowe (Montgomery); unfortunately, confusing plot is presented in more prosaic (and dated) manner.▼●

Lady in White (1988) **C-112m.** *** D: Frank LaLoggia. Lukas Haas, Len Cariou, Alex Rocco, Katherine Helmond, Jason Presson, Jared Rushton, Renata Vanni, Angelo Bertolini. Sleeper film combines 1960s nostalgia with supernatural horror in original fashion. An inquisitive youngster

(Haas) becomes involved with ghosts in mystery story about an unsolved murder and the legendary Lady in White (Helmond) residing in a spooky house nearby. Villain's identity is a bit too easy to guess, but there are plenty of chills and great period atmosphere along the way. Director's cut version runs 6m. longer. [PG-13] ▼●◗

Lady Is Willing, The (1942) **92m.** *** D: Mitchell Leisen. Marlene Dietrich, Fred MacMurray, Aline MacMahon, Arline Judge, Stanley Ridges, Roger Clark. Agreeable comedy; glamorous Dietrich wants to adopt a baby, so she marries pediatrician MacMurray. Dramatic segment near the end spoils lively mood.▼

Lady Jane (1985-British) **C-142m.** *** D: Trevor Nunn. Helena Bonham Carter, Cary Elwes, John Wood, Michael Hordern, Jill Bennett, Jane Lapotaire, Sara Kestelman, Patrick Stewart, Warren Saire, Joss Ackland, Ian Hogg, Richard Johnson. Absorbing historical drama about the machinations that put a sixteen-year-old girl on the throne of England for just nine days. Exquisite looking, well-acted, just a trifle slow at times. Same story told before in a 1936 film, TUDOR ROSE. [PG-13]▼●

Lady Killer (1933) **74m.** *** D: Roy Del Ruth. James Cagney, Mae Clarke, Leslie Fenton, Margaret Lindsay, Henry O'Neill, Raymond Hatton, George Chandler. Vintage Cagney, with tangy tale of mobster becoming Hollywood actor, torn between two professions; Cagney repeats his Clarke slapfest.▼●

Ladykillers, The (1955-British) **C-90m.** ***½ D: Alexander Mackendrick. Alec Guinness, Katie Johnson, Cecil Parker, Herbert Lom, Peter Sellers, Danny Green, Frankie Howerd. Droll black comedy of not-so-bright crooks involved with seemingly harmless old lady. Guinness scores again (even his *teeth* are funny) with top-notch supporting cast in this little Ealing Studios gem, written by William Rose. Original British running time: 97m.▼

Lady L (1965-British) **C-107m.** **½ D: Peter Ustinov. Sophia Loren, Paul Newman, David Niven, Claude Dauphin, Philippe Noiret, Michel Piccoli. Stars and sets are elegant, but this wacky comedy set in early 20th-century London and Paris fizzles, despite Ustinov's writing, directing, and cameo appearance. Panavision.▼

Lady Liberty (1972-Italian) **C-95m.** *½ D: Mario Monicelli. Sophia Loren, William Devane, Luigi Proietti, Beeson Carroll, Danny DeVito, David Doyle, Richard Libertini, Edward Herrmann, Alan Feinstein, Christopher Norris, Susan Sarandon. Dull comedy of immigrant bride-to-be who tries to get an enormous sausage through U.S. customs. Watch for Warhol's Candy Darling in transvestite cameo; originally titled MORTADELLA. [PG]

Lady Luck (1946) **97m.** *** D: Edwin L. Marin. Robert Young, Barbara Hale, Frank Morgan, James Gleason. Hale marries gambler Young with hopes of reforming him but meets more problems than she bargained for.

Lady of Burlesque (1943) **91m.** *** D: William Wellman. Barbara Stanwyck, Michael O'Shea, J. Edward Bromberg, Iris Adrian, Marion Martin, Pinky Lee, Frank Conroy, Gloria Dickson. Stanwyck attempts to uncover—no pun intended—killer of strippers in this amusing adaptation of Gypsy Rose Lee's *G-String Murders.*▼

Lady of Secrets (1936) **73m.** **½ D: Marion Gering. Ruth Chatterton, Otto Kruger, Lionel Atwill, Marian Marsh, Lloyd Nolan, Robert Allen. Smooth but soapy story of woman whose one unhappy love affair has made her live a life of seclusion. Good cast makes standard film worth seeing.

Lady of the Tropics (1939) **92m.** ** D: Jack Conway. Hedy Lamarr, Robert Taylor, Joseph Schildkraut, Frederick Worlock, Natalie Moorhead. Sad love affair between playboy Taylor and halfbreed Lamarr in exotic setting; slow-moving.

Lady of Vengeance (1957-British) **73m.** ** D: Burt Balaban. Dennis O'Keefe, Ann Sears, Patrick Barr, Vernon Greeves. Tedious account of man hiring killer to avenge a girl's death, becoming embroiled in further murder.

Lady on a Train (1945) **93m.** *** D: Charles David. Deanna Durbin, Ralph Bellamy, Edward Everett Horton, George Coulouris, Allen Jenkins, David Bruce, Patricia Morison, Dan Duryea, William Frawley. Excellent comedy/murder-mystery with Deanna witnessing a murder, then getting involved with nutty family of the deceased tycoon. You'll never guess killer's identity in neatly plotted yarn which even allows Deanna to sing a few tunes. Based on a Leslie Charteris story.▼

Lady on the Bus (1978-Brazilian) **C-102m.** *½ D: Neville D'Almedia. Sonia Braga, Nuno Leal Maia, Paulo Cesar Pereio, Jorge Doria, Yara Amaral, Claudio Marzo. Braga, the least likely of all actresses to project frigidity, is unresponsive on her wedding night—but wait! Soon she begins sampling other men, and sampling, and sampling. . . . Follow-up to DONA FLOR AND HER TWO HUSBANDS has even more sex but far less wit and charm. A dull ride. [R]▼

Lady Pays Off, The (1951) **80m.** **½ D: Douglas Sirk. Linda Darnell, Stephen McNally, Gigi Perreau, Virginia Field. Fanciful drama of schoolteacher Darnell who must pay off gambling debts in Reno by tutoring casino owner's daughter.

Lady Possessed (1952-British) **87m.** ** D: William Spier, Roy Kellino. James Mason, June Havoc, Pamela Kellino (Mason), Fay Compton, Odette Myrtil. Bizarre

film of ill woman thinking she is controlled by will of Mason's dead wife.
Lady Says No, The (1951) **80m.** ** D: Frank Ross. David Niven, Joan Caulfield, Lenore Lonergan, James Robertson Justice. Lightweight comedy of fickle Caulfield, who won't decide if marriage is for her.▼
Lady Scarface (1941) **69m.** ** D: Frank Woodruff. Dennis O'Keefe, Judith Anderson, Frances Neal, Mildred Coles, Eric Blore, Marc Lawrence. Anderson tries to elevate this episodic yarn of police hunting for dangerous gunwoman and her gang.▼
Lady's From Kentucky, The (1939) **67m.** **½ D: Alexander Hall. George Raft, Ellen Drew, Hugh Herbert, ZaSu Pitts, Louise Beavers, Stanley Andrews. Regardless of title, Raft's horse takes precedence over his lady in this well-done horseracing saga.
Lady Sings the Blues (1972) **C-144m.** **½ D: Sidney J. Furie. Diana Ross, Billy Dee Williams, Richard Pryor, James Callahan, Paul Hampton, Sid Melton. Black version of Hollywood cliché-biography, sparked by superb performance by Ross (in her acting debut) as Billie Holiday, legendary jazz singer whose life was ruined by drug addiction. Valueless as biography, but OK as soap opera, with excellent support from Pryor as "Piano Man." Panavision. [R]▼●
Lady's Morals, A (1930) **75m.** ** D: Sidney Franklin. Grace Moore, Reginald Denny, Wallace Beery, Jobyna Howland. First attempt to make star of opera singer Moore doesn't click. She plays Jenny Lind, who learns value of love from devoted Denny.
Lady Surrenders, A SEE: **Love Story** (1944)
Lady Takes a Chance, A (1943) **86m.** *** D: William A. Seiter. Jean Arthur, John Wayne, Charles Winninger, Phil Silvers, Mary Field, Don Costello. Wayne and Arthur make fine comedy team as burly rodeo star and wide-eyed city girl who falls for him; Silvers adds zip as bus-tour guide.▼
Lady Takes a Flyer, The (1958) **C-94m.** **½ D: Jack Arnold. Lana Turner, Jeff Chandler, Richard Denning, Andra Martin. Different-type Turner fare. Lana is lady flier who marries pilot Chandler, each finds it hard to settle down to married life. CinemaScope.
Lady Takes a Sailor, The (1949) **99m.** ** D: Michael Curtiz. Jane Wyman, Dennis Morgan, Eve Arden, Robert Douglas, Allyn Joslyn. Featherweight comedy fully described by title tag.
Lady to Love, A (1930) **92m.** ** D: Victor Seastrom (Sjostrom). Edward G. Robinson, Vilma Banky, Robert Ames, Richard Carle, Lloyd Ingraham. Stilted early talkie version of Sidney Howard's play *They Knew What They Wanted,* previously filmed in 1928, and remade in 1940 under its original title. Robinson is miscast as an Italian vintner in San Francisco who gets a young mail-order bride (Banky) by sending her a picture of his hunky foreman (Ames). Between Robinson's heavy-handed Chico Marx–like dialect and Banky's Budapest accent, subtitles might have helped.
Lady Vanishes, The (1938-British) **97m.** **** D: Alfred Hitchcock. Margaret Lockwood, Michael Redgrave, Paul Lukas, Dame May Whitty, Googie Withers, Cecil Parker, Linden Travers, Catherine Lacey. An old woman's disappearance during a train ride leads baffled young woman into a dizzying web of intrigue. Delicious mystery-comedy; Hitchcock at his best, with a witty script by Frank Launder and Sidney Gilliat, and wonderful performances by Naunton Wayne and Basil Radford, who scored such a hit as a pair of twits that they repeated those roles in several other films! Based on Ethel Lina White's novel *The Wheel Spins*. Remade in 1979.▼●◗
Lady Vanishes, The (1979-British) **C-99m.** *½ D: Anthony Page. Elliott Gould, Cybill Shepherd, Angela Lansbury, Herbert Lom, Arthur Lowe, Ian Carmichael. Remake of Hitchcock classic retains basic story but is sabotaged by the obnoxious characterizations of its "screwball" stars, Gould and Shepherd. Screenplay by George Axelrod. Panavision. [PG]▼●
Lady Wants Mink, The (1953) **C-92m.** *** D: William A. Seiter. Eve Arden, Ruth Hussey, Dennis O'Keefe, William Demarest, Gene Lockhart. Most diverting little film of wife Hussey breeding mink to get the coat she's always wanted.
Lady With a Dog (1959-Russian) **90m.** **½ D: Josif Heifits. Iya Savvina, Alexei Batalov, Ala Chostakova, N. Alisova. Middle-aged man and young woman, both married, meet and fall in love on vacation. Intelligent tale of adulterous love, sensibly handled, with no contrived ending. Based on the short story by Anton Chekov, also partly the basis of DARK EYES (1987).▼
Lady With a Lamp, The (1951-British) **112m.** *** D: Herbert Wilcox. Anna Neagle, Michael Wilding, Felix Aylmer, Maureen Pryor, Gladys Young, Julian D'Albie. Methodical recreation of 19th century nurse-crusader Florence Nightingale, tastefully enacted by Neagle.
Lady With a Past (1932) **80m.** **½ D: Edward H. Griffith. Constance Bennett, Ben Lyon, David Manners, Astrid Allwyn, Merna Kennedy, Nella Walker, Blanche Frederici. Chic fluff about rich "good girl" Bennett who discovers that she's much more popular with the opposite sex when she acts "bad."
Lady Without Passport, A (1950) **72m.** **½ D: Joseph H. Lewis. Hedy Lamarr, John Hodiak, James Craig, George Mac-

ready. Turgid melodrama as Lamarr seeks to leave Havana, former romantic and business associations behind her.
Lady With Red Hair (1940) **81m.** **½ D: Curtis Bernhardt. Miriam Hopkins, Claude Rains, Richard Ainley, Laura Hope Crews, Helen Westley, John Litel, Victor Jory. Breathless pace, likable cast make up for silliness in story of actress Mrs. Leslie Carter and her colorful mentor David Belasco. Look fast for young Cornel Wilde at boarding house.
Lafayette (1962-French) **C-110m.** ** D: Jean Dreville. Jack Hawkins, Orson Welles, Howard St. John, Edmund Purdom, Vittorio De Sica, Michel Le Royer. Overblown, badly scripted costumer of famed 18th-century Frenchman; an episodic minor spectacle. Super Technirama 70. ▼
Lafayette Escadrille (1958) **93m.** **½ D: William Wellman. Tab Hunter, Etchika Choureau, Marcel Dalio, David Janssen, Clint Eastwood, Tom Laughlin. Attempted epic of famous French flying legion of WW1 becomes pat actioner with typical romantic interlude, featuring wholesome Hunter. ▼
La Femme Infidele (1969-French-Italian) **C-98m.** ***½ D: Claude Chabrol. Stephane Audran, Michel Bouquet, Maurice Ronet, Stephen Di Napolo, Michel Duchaussoy. Atmospheric drama about wife who acquires more respect for her husband when he murders her lover; Audran and Bouquet are fine in yet another memorable film from director Chabrol. Also known as UNFAITHFUL WIFE. [R]
La Femme Nikita (1990-French-Italian) **C-117m.** *** D: Luc Besson. Anne Parillaud, Jean-Hugues Anglade, Tcheky Karyo, Jeanne Moreau, Jean Reno, Jean Bouise. Slick, ultra-violent saga of a hedonistic young woman who runs with a punked-out gang—until she's recruited by a French intelligence officer, determined to make her an undercover agent and "hit-man." Stylish and compelling, if not always believable, with a star-making role for Parillaud. Remade in the U.S. as POINT OF NO RETURN, and in Hong Kong as BLACK CAT; later a U.S. cable TV series. Technovision. [R]▼●◗
L'Age d'Or (1930-French) **63m.** **** D: Luis Buñuel. Gaston Modot, Lya Lys, Max Ernst, Pierre Prévert. Bishops turn into skeletons and the cow wanders into the bedroom in Buñuel's first feature, a surrealistic masterpiece coscripted by Salvadore Dali. Right-wing agitators caused a riot at the film's first (and for a long time, only) public screening; its anticlericalism put it into the "banned film" category for decades. Still has the power to delight, if no longer shock. ▼●
La Grande Bouffe SEE: **Grande Bouffe, The**
La Grande Bourgeoise (1974-Italian) **C-115m.** **½ D: Mauro Bolognini. Catherine Deneuve, Giancarlo Giannini, Fernando Rey, Tina Aumont, Paolo Bonicelli. Strong cast adds some punch to true story about Giannini's murder of sister Deneuve's loutish husband and the political storm it generates. Stylish but not terribly compelling. [R]▼
La Gran Fiesta (1987-Puerto Rican) **C-101m.** **½ D: Marcos Zurinaga. Daniel Lugo, Miguelangel Suarez, Luis Prendes, Cordelia Gonzalez, Laura Delano, Raul Julia, E.G. Marshall, Julian Pastor. Sometimes low-keyed and other times melodramatic account of intrigue—both personal and political—among the various folk who attend the final grand ball in the Casino at Old San Juan on the eve of its takeover by U.S. Armed Forces in 1942. Interesting subject, but misses the mark.
La Guerre Est Finie (1966-French-Swedish) **121m.** ***½ D: Alain Resnais. Yves Montand, Ingrid Thulin, Genevieve Bujold, Jean Daste, Michel Piccoli. Aging, tired leftist Montand travels from Spain to Paris, reports to his political associates, and visits mistress Thulin. Complex, emotionally powerful drama, with striking direction, performances. Screenplay by Jorge Semprun. ▼
Lair of the White Worm, The (1988-British) **C-94m.** **½ D: Ken Russell. Amanda Donohoe, Hugh Grant, Catherine Oxenberg, Peter Capaldi, Sammi Davis, Stratford Johns, Paul Brooke, Christopher Gable. Typically outrageous Ken Russell farce, adapted from a novel by Bram Stoker (of *Dracula* fame). Strange doings begin when an archaeologist unearths a huge wormlike skull on the grounds of an estate; they get *curiouser* and *curiouser* when it turns out worms are the stuff of legend in that area. Bizarre, campy, and altogether outlandish. [R]▼●
Lake Placid (1999) **C-82m.** ** D: Steve Miner. Bill Pullman, Bridget Fonda, Oliver Platt, Brendan Gleeson, Betty White, David Lewis, Mariska Hargitay, Meredith Salenger. The creature terrorizing a Maine lake (which is *not* Lake Placid, N.Y.) turns out to be a very large crocodile. Between arguments, paleontologist Fonda, game warden Pullman, sheriff Gleeson and irritating, wealthy academic Platt try to figure out what to do about it. David E. Kelley, writing down to the material, provides lots of wisecracks, but few scares. Brief but tiresome film tries—but fails—to be a monster movie and environmentally correct at the same time. Adam Arkin appears unbilled. Panavision. [R]▼●◗
Lake Placid Serenade (1944) **85m.** ** D: Steve Sekely. Vera Hruba Ralston, Robert Livingston, Vera Vague (Barbara Jo Allen), Eugene Pallette, Stephanie Bachelor, Walter Catlett, John Litel; guest star, Roy Rogers. Flimsy musical romance about an

ice skater, played by real-life skating queen Ralston. Supporting cast does its best.

Lakota Woman: Siege at Wounded Knee (1994) **C-100m. TVM** D: Frank Pierson. Irene Bedard, Joseph Runningfox, Floyd Red Crow Westerman, Tantoo Cardinal, Michael Horse, Lawrence Hayne, Lois Red Elk, August Schellenberg. All-Native American cast brings alive Mary Crow Dog's moving autobiography. Bedard is especially fine as the woman who went from an abused childhood through intra-tribal politics to become an eyewitness at the famed 1973 siege at Wounded Knee. Above average. ▼●

La Lectrice (1988-French) **C-98m.** *** D: Michel Deville. Miou-Miou, Christian Ruché, Sylvie Laporte, Michel Raskine, Brigitte Catillion, Régis Royer, Maria Casarés, Pierre Dux. Fascinating, multi-textured account of Miou-Miou reading a book aloud to her boyfriend and imagining herself the heroine in the story: a professional reader who becomes involved in the lives of her various clients. Scripted by Deville and his wife, Rosalinde. [R]▼●

La Marseillaise (1938-French) **130m.** ***½ D: Jean Renoir. Pierre Renoir, Louis Jouvet, Julien Carette, Lisa Delamare. Renoir scripted this stirring account of the French Revolution, featuring dialogue extracted from documents of the 1790s. Begins with news of the fall of the Bastille reaching Louis XVI, ends with the Marseilles Battalion of the French Revolutionary Army storming the Tuilleries and marching to Valmy. Renoir opted for a humanist approach to history, avoiding what he considered the false solemnity of most historical epics. ▼

La Maternelle (1932-French) **86m.** *** D: Jean Benoit-Levy. Madeleine Renaud, Alice Tissot, Paulette Elambert, Sylvette Fillacier, Mady Berri, Henri Debain. Insightful, compassionate drama about the plight of slum children in Montmartre day nursery. The focus is on little Elambert's pain, confusion, and attachment to nurse Renaud. Its observations about children's perceptions have dated not one bit.▼

Lamb (1985-British) **C-110m.** **½ D: Colin Gregg. Liam Neeson, Hugh O'Conor, Ian Bannen, Rouan Wilmot, Frances Tomelty, Dudley Sutton. Neeson is good in this otherwise obvious drama spotlighting the complex relationship between an idealistic Brother who teaches at a Roman Catholic school for problem boys and a deeply troubled pupil (O'Conor) who is maltreated by the authoritarian headmaster. Not released in the U.S. until 1995.▼

Lambada (1990) **C-98m.** BOMB D: Joel Silberg. J. Eddie Peck, Melora Hardin, Shabba-Doo, Ricky Paull Goldin, Basil Hoffman, Dennis Burkley. By day, Peck teaches math to snots in a posh Beverly Hills high school; by night, he tries to "reach" barrio kids in an East L.A. lambada club. In other words, it's STAND AND DELIVER with better buns; avoid at all costs unless you never miss a Shabba-Doo movie. Super 35. [PG-13]▼●

Lamerica (1994-Italian-French) **C-116m.** ***½ D: Gianni Amelio. Enrico Lo Verso, Michele Placido, Carmelo Di Mazzarelli, Piro Milkani, Elida Janushi. Deeply touching, laced-in-acid drama, set in the wake of Albania's emancipation from communism and detailing the manner in which fate links up a young, arrogant Italian capitalist (Lo Verso) and the just-liberated political prisoner (Di Mazzarelli) he is attempting to exploit. A politically savvy account of how the downtrodden go from one kind of exploitation to another as political systems change. Amelio effectively captures the feeling of what it's like to be a poor and powerless refugee. Technovision.▼

Lancer Spy (1937) **84m.** *** D: Gregory Ratoff. Dolores Del Rio, George Sanders, Peter Lorre, Joseph Schildkraut, Virginia Field, Sig Ruman, Fritz Feld. Sanders disguises himself as German officer to get information in this taut thriller; Del Rio has to choose between love and loyalty to her country.

Land and Freedom (1995-U.S.-Spanish-German) **C-109m.** *** D: Kenneth Loach. Ian Hart, Rosana Pastor, Iciar Bollain, Tom Gilroy, Marc Martines, Frederic Pierrot, Angela Clarke. Perceptive, passionate account of the Spanish Civil War, centered on a young, working-class British Communist (Hart) who comes to Spain to join the anti-fascists in their battle against Franco. Rich human drama of political idealism and reality, if a bit too moralistic at times. Highlight: that pseudo-documentary ad hoc town meeting. ▼●

Land Before Time, The (1988) **C-69m.** **½ D: Don Bluth. Voices of Pat Hingle, Gabriel Damon, Helen Shaver, Candace Hutson, Judith Barsi, Will Ryan, Burke Barnes. A young dinosaur is orphaned and must make his way to a valley green with vegetation where he and his tribe can survive. Along the way he meets other young friends of different dinosaur species, and they make the trek together. Enjoyable if leisurely paced (and plotted) cartoon feature for younger viewers. Followed by five video sequels. [G]▼●◗

Land Before Time II: The Great Valley Adventure, The (1994) **C-74m.** *** D: Roy Allen Smith. Voices of Jeff Bennett, Heather Hogan, Kenneth Mars, John Ingle, Linda Gary, Candace Hutson, Scott McAfee. Charming direct-to-video sequel to earlier animated feature has young brontosaurus Littlefoot and his dino pals contending with omnivores and a baby T-Rex who wants to join their group! Kids will identify with the young reptiles in this delightful adventure. Songs by The Roches;

original theme music by James Horner. Followed by several more video sequels. [G]▼●

Land Girls, The (1998-British-French) **C-110m.** ** D: David Leland. Catherine McCormack, Rachel Weisz, Anna Friel, Steven Mackintosh, Tom Georgeson, Maureen O'Brien, Gerald Down. Disappointing soap opera based on the potentially fascinating story of the Women's Land Army, formed in 1941 to put women to work on English farms whose men had gone off to war. The three attractive young women who come to live with farmer Georgeson wind up dallying with his randy son (Mackintosh), and after a while it all seems rather silly. Leland coscripted from a novel by Angela Huth. Panavision. [R]▼●

Landlord, The (1970) **C-113m.** ***½ D: Hal Ashby. Beau Bridges, Pearl Bailey, Diana Sands, Louis Gossett, Lee Grant, Susan Anspach, Bob (Robert) Klein, Patricia (Trish) Van Devere. Vibrant comedy-drama with Bridges as aimless rich-kid who buys Brooklyn tenement planning to renovate it for himself, changing plans when he meets tenants. Delightful comic touches combined with perceptive sidelights on black experience. Ashby's first film as director. TV version runs 104m. [PG—originally rated R]▼

Land of Fury SEE: **Seekers, The** (1954)

Land of No Return, The (1978) **C-84m.** BOMB D: Kent Bateman. Mel Torme, William Shatner, Donald Moffat. The only novelty of this dreary wilderness-survival opus is the (mis)casting of Torme as an animal trainer whose plane crashes in Utah. Filmed in 1975. Also know as SNOWMAN and CHALLENGE TO SURVIVE. [G]

Land of the Minotaur (1976-U.S.-British) **C-88m.** *½ D: Costa Carayiannis. Donald Pleasence, Luan Peters, Peter Cushing, Nikos Verlekis, Costas Skouras. Tourists are kidnapped by Greek Minoan devil-worship cult, and a local priest tries to save them, in this draggy, uninteresting yarn. Aka MINOTAUR. Released in England at 94m. as THE DEVIL'S MEN. [PG]▼

Land of the Pharaohs (1955) **C-106m.** **½ D: Howard Hawks. Jack Hawkins, Joan Collins, James Robertson Justice, Dewey Martin, Alexis Minotis, Sydney Chaplin. Talky, fruity spectacle about building of the Great Pyramid, filmed on an epic scale. Hawks claimed neither he nor his writers (including William Faulkner and Harry Kurnitz) "knew how a pharaoh talked" . . . and it shows. Still worth catching for great revenge ending and now-campy villainy by Collins. CinemaScope. ▼●

Land Raiders (1970) **C-100m.** ** D: Nathan Juran. Telly Savalas, George Maharis, Arlene Dahl, Janet Landgard, Jocelyn Lane, George Coulouris, Guy Rolfe. Even if you can accept Savalas and Maharis as brothers, this Western about family feuds amidst Indian attacks has little to offer.▼

Landru SEE: **Bluebeard** (1962)

Landslide (1992-British) **C-95m.** *½ D: Jean-Claude Lord. Anthony Edwards, Tom Burlinson, Melody Anderson, Ronald Lacey, Ken James, William Colgate, Lloyd Bochner, Joanna Cassidy. Muddled, forced psychological drama/mystery about the sole survivor of a car crash (Edwards). He suffers from selective memory loss, and attempts to piece together his past while confronting shady dealings in a small town. [PG-13]▼

Land That Time Forgot, The (1975-British) **C-90m.** **½ D: Kevin Connor. Doug McClure, John McEnery, Susan Penhaligon, Keith Barron, Anthony Ainley. Edgar Rice Burroughs' 1918 sci-fi novel about Germans and Americans in WW1 submarine discovering unknown land in South America is not bad as adventure yarn, but special effects (dinosaurs, volcanic eruption) are not convincing. Sequel: THE PEOPLE THAT TIME FORGOT. [PG]▼

Land Unknown, The (1957) **78m.** ** D: Virgil Vogel. Jock Mahoney, Shawn Smith, Henry Brandon, Douglas Kennedy. Naval helicopter exploring Antarctica is forced down in lost valley of prehistoric animals. Monsters are clumsily done but film is OK. CinemaScope.▼●

La Notte (1961-French-Italian) **120m.** **½ D: Michelangelo Antonioni. Jeanne Moreau, Marcello Mastroianni, Monica Vitti, Bernhard Wicki. Moreau is bored and troubled by one-dimensional husband Mastroianni in this study of noncommunication. Moody, introverted, abstract—and superficial—filled with "empty, hopeless images." The second of a trilogy, preceded by L'AVVENTURA and followed by L'ECLISSE. Also known as THE NIGHT.▼

Lansky (1999) **C-120m. TVM** D: John McNaughton. Richard Dreyfuss, Eric Roberts, Illeana Douglas, Beverly D'Angelo, Anthony LaPaglia, Ryan Merriman, Max Perlich. The rise and fall (in writer David Mamet's spare view) of Meyer Lansky, a Jewish immigrant from Poland who palled around from boyhood with the likes of Benjamin "Bugsy" Siegel and Charles "Lucky" Luciano, became a shrewd accountant for the Mob in its heyday, and, unlike his famous underworld compatriots, managed to die peacefully after a long life. Surprisingly low-key Dreyfuss plays the title role. Made for cable. Average.◗

Lantern Hill (1990-Canadian) **C-110m. TVM** D: Kevin Sullivan. Sam Waterston, Marion Bennett, Sarah Polley, Zoe Caldwell, Colleen Dewhurst. Another heartwarmer in the ANNE OF GREEN GABLES/AVONLEA mold from the author of those books, Lucy Maud Montgomery, and the

Canadian production team that brought them so successfully to TV. In this one a 12-year-old Depression-era girl faces a formidable struggle to reunite her estranged parents. Made for cable. Above average.▼●

La Nuit de Varennes (1982-Italian-French) **C-133m.** *** D: Ettore Scola. Marcello Mastroianni, Jean-Louis Barrault, Hanna Schygulla, Harvey Keitel, Jean-Claude Brialy. Witty historical fable allows such famous figures as Casanova and Thomas Paine to cross paths at the time of the French Revolution. Original French running time 150m. Technovision. [R]▼

La Parisienne (1957-French-Italian) **C-85m.** ** D: Michel Boisrond. Brigitte Bardot, Charles Boyer, Henri Vidal, Andre Luguet, Nadia Gray, Noel Roquevert, Claire Maurier. Flimsy comedy with Bardot the daughter of the Premier of France. To get back at her Don Juan husband (Vidal), she has an affair with married prince Boyer. Aka UNE PARISIENNE.▼

La Passante (1982-French-German) **C-106m.** *** D: Jacques Rouffio. Romy Schneider, Michel Piccoli, Wendelin Werner, Helmut Griem, Gerard Klein, Dominique Labourier, Mathieu Carriere, Maria Schell. Why does nonviolence advocate Piccoli kill a Paraguayan ambassador, an ex-Nazi living under an assumed name? Interesting drama is ambitious in scope, but could have been better. Schneider, in her final film, plays both Piccoli's wife and the woman who sheltered him as a boy. ▼●

La Pelle (1981-Italian-French) **C-131m.** *½ D: Liliana Cavani. Marcello Mastroianni, Burt Lancaster, Claudia Cardinale, Ken Marshall, Alexandra King, Carlo Giuffre. Distastefully bitter panorama of American troops in Naples after the Liberation, based on the memoirs of Curzio Malaparte (played here by Mastroianni). Overlong; poorly directed and scripted (by Cavani and Robert Katz). A disaster.

La Permission SEE: **Story of a Three Day Pass, The**

La Prisonniere (1969-French) **104m.** ** D: Henri-Georges Clouzot. Laurent Terzieff, Bernard Fresson, Elsabeth Wiener, Dany Carrel, Dario Moreno, Daniel Riviere. From the director of DIABOLIQUE comes this obscure, confused study of woman obsessed with a photographer of sadomasochism. Strikingly photographed.

La Promesse (1996-Belgian-French-Luxembourgian-Tunisian) **C-93m.** ***½ D: Jean-Pierre Dardenne, Luc Dardenne. Jérémie Renier, Olivier Gourmet, Assita Ouedraogo, Rasmané Ouedraogo. Harrowing tale of a boy being raised by a father who mercilessly exploits illegal immigrants—as their supposed savior, landlord, and employer. Trouble begins when the boy, who's always obeyed his father unquestioningly, develops a friendship with one of the illegals. Moving in its understated, matter-of-fact look at a young man at a moral crossroads in his life. Remarkably raw . . . and real. Written by the directors.▼

La Provinciale SEE: **Girl from Lorraine, The**

Larceny (1948) **89m.** **½ D: George Sherman. John Payne, Joan Caulfield, Dan Duryea, Shelley Winters, Dorothy Hart. Slick but ordinary underworld tale, with roguish Payne deciding to help lovely Caulfield; Duryea is slimy villain.

Larceny, Inc. (1942) **95m.** ***½ D: Lloyd Bacon. Edward G. Robinson, Jane Wyman, Broderick Crawford, Jack Carson, Anthony Quinn, Edward Brophy. Hilarious little comedy of ex-cons Robinson, Crawford, and Brophy using luggage store as front for shady activities; villain Quinn tries to horn in. Look for Jackie Gleason in a small role as a soda jerk.

Larceny in Her Heart (1946) **68m.** ** D: Sam Newfield. Hugh Beaumont, Cheryl Walker, Ralph Dunn, Paul Bryar, Charles Wilson, Douglas Fowley. Sleuth Michael Shayne (Beaumont) gets mixed up with a femme fatale during a murder investigation in this passable minor entry, though seeing the Beaver's future TV dad in the lead may be the chief point of interest today.

L'Argent (1983-French-Swiss) **C-90m.** ***½ D: Robert Bresson. Christian Patey, Sylvie van den Elsen, Michel Briguet, Caroline Lang, Jeanne Aptekman. How the petty maneuverings of some upperclass boys and shopkeepers result in the ruin of workingman Patey: the rich lie, and get their workers to lie for them, but are aghast when the workers lie to them. Subtle, powerful film, simply and effectively directed by a master filmmaker; based on a Tolstoy story. ▼

Larger Than Life (1996) **C-93m.** *½ D: Howard Franklin. Bill Murray, Janeane Garofalo, Matthew McConaughey, Linda Fiorentino, Keith David, Pat Hingle, Jeremy Piven, Maureen Mueller, Harve Presnell, Lois Smith, Tai. Disappointing comedic misfire of motivational speaker Murray trying to get an elephant cross-country in a hurry. One hysterical sequence of Murray's mishandling of a truck is the only real laugh. Promising possibilities fall flat, with McConaughey way over the top and Fiorentino completely wasted. [PG] ▼●

La Ronde (1950-French) **97m.** ***½ D: Max Ophuls. Anton Walbrook, Serge Reggiani, Simone Simon, Simone Signoret, Daniel Gelin, Danielle Darrieux, Fernand Gravet, Odette Joyeux, Jean-Louis Barrault, Isa Miranda, Gérard Philipe. Wise, witty account of various people having affairs, forming a chain that eventually comes full circle, all held together by sarcastic Walbrook. A film of style and charm, based on an Arthur Schnitzler play. Screenplay by Jacques Natanson and director Ophuls. Remade as CIRCLE OF LOVE and CHAIN OF DESIRE.▼●

Larsen, Wolf of the Seven Seas SEE: **Wolf Larsen** (1975)

La Salamandre (1971-Swiss) **125m.** *** D: Alain Tanner. Bulle Ogier, Jean-Luc Bideau, Jacques Denis. Simple, funny examination of truth: journalist Bideau and writer Denis research facts behind the case of mysterious Ogier, accused by her uncle of attempted murder. Fine performances by the three leads.▼

La Separation (1994-French) **C-85m.** *** D: Christian Vincent. Isabelle Huppert, Daniel Auteuil, Jerome Deschamps, Karin Viard, Laurence Lerel. Knowingly detailed, beautifully acted chronicle of the simmering tensions between a married couple (Huppert and Auteuil) as their relationship disintegrates. In its best moments, this sobering film compares favorably with Bergman's SCENES FROM A MARRIAGE. Released in the U.S. in 1998.▼◗

Laserblast (1978) **C-90m.** **½ D: Michael Raye. Kim Milford, Cheryl Smith, Roddy McDowall, Ron Masak, Keenan Wynn, Dennis Burkley. Low-budget sci-fi with teen Milford finding alien ray gun which enables him to become a creature who can destroy his enemies. David Allen's stop-motion effects are a highlight. [PG]▼●◗

Laser Mission (1989-German-South African-U.S.) **C-83m.** ** D: Beau Davis. Brandon Lee, Debi Monahan, Ernest Borgnine, Werner Pochath, Graham Clarke, Maureen Lahoud, Pierre Knoessen. Free-lance secret agent Lee and tough Monahan travel across a South African desert to rescue laser expert Borgnine, kidnapped by the Soviets. Lee is appealing, but this low-rent 007-type adventure has nothing new to offer.▼●◗

Lassie (1994) **C-92m.** *** D: Daniel Petrie. Helen Slater, Thomas Guiry, Jon Tenney, Brittany Boyd, Frederic Forrest, Richard Farnsworth, Michelle Williams, Charlie Hofheimer, Clayton Barclay Jones. A city family with some problems decides to start over again at the old family farm; along the way, a remarkably smart dog "adopts" them. Young Guiry is a standout as the troubled boy who (quite credibly) changes under the influences of Lassie and his new country environment. Painted in broad strokes, for its intended youthful audience. [PG]▼●

Lassie Come Home (1943) **C-88m.** ***½ D: Fred M. Wilcox. Roddy McDowall, Donald Crisp, Dame May Whitty, Edmund Gwenn, Nigel Bruce, Elsa Lanchester, Elizabeth Taylor, and Pal. Winning, wonderful film from Eric Knight's book about a poor family forced to sell their beloved dog, who undertakes several tortuous journeys to return to them. A tearjerker of the first order, and one of the all-time great family films. Lassie is played—quite remarkably—by a male collie named Pal. Sequel: SON OF LASSIE. Remade as GYPSY COLT and THE MAGIC OF LASSIE.▼●

Lassiter (1984) **C-100m.** **½ D: Roger Young. Tom Selleck, Jane Seymour, Lauren Hutton, Bob Hoskins, Joe Regalbuto, Ed Lauter, Warren Clarke. A second-story man is shanghaied into doing espionage work in London on the eve of WW2. Stylish and nicely acted, but too plodding to overcome its basic problem of ordinariness. Selleck's second star vehicle is at least an improvement over his first (HIGH ROAD TO CHINA). [R]▼●

Last Action Hero (1993) **C-130m.** ** D: John McTiernan. Arnold Schwarzenegger, F. Murray Abraham, Art Carney, Charles Dance, Frank McRae, Tom Noonan, Robert Prosky, Anthony Quinn, Mercedes Ruehl, Austin O'Brien, Ian McKellen, Toru Tanaka, Joan Plowright, Tina Turner, Rick Ducommun, Michael V. Gazzo. Noisy, smug, self-conscious blockbuster-wannabe about a boy whose "magic ticket" transports him into an action movie alongside his No. 1 hero, Jack Slater (Schwarzenegger). Genuinely bad writing and an overall air of unpleasantness torpedo this film; good action scenes and occasional clever ideas can't save it. (And how exactly did an Ingmar Bergman picture work its way into the story?) A raft of cameo appearances add to the in-joke tone of the picture. Panavision. [PG-13] ▼●◗

Last Adventure, The (1967-French) **C-102m.** **½ D: Robert Enrico. Alain Delon, Lino Ventura, Joanna Shimkus, Hans Meyer. Two adventurers and a beautiful woman go on a very engaging treasure hunt. Techniscope.▼

Last American Hero, The (1973) **C-100m.** *** D: Lamont Johnson. Jeff Bridges, Valerie Perrine, Geraldine Fitzgerald, Art Lund, Gary Busey, Ed Lauter, Ned Beatty. Unusual, engrossing saga of Junior Jackson, North Carolinan moonshiner and racing fanatic, pitting his ability against the System. Three-dimensional, believable characters enhance cynical point of view. Retitled HARD DRIVER. Panavision. [PG] ▼

Last American Virgin, The (1982) **C-90m.** **½ D: Boaz Davidson. Lawrence Monoson, Diane Franklin, Steve Antin, Joe Rubbo, Louisa Moritz. Formula teen comedy-drama (derived from one of Cannon's Israeli-made LEMON POPSICLE films) works thanks to attractive and talented young cast. Monoson has the title role, with pals Antin and Rubbo trying desperately to find a willing girlfriend. Moritz is very funny as the stereotyped Latin bombshell. [R]▼

Last Angry Man, The (1959) **100m.** *** D: Daniel Mann. Paul Muni, David Wayne, Betsy Palmer, Luther Adler, Joby Baker, Joanna Moore, Godfrey Cambridge, Billy Dee Williams. Sentimental story of an old, dedicated family doctor in Brooklyn whose life is going to be portrayed on TV. Muni (in his last film) makes it worth seeing. Adapted by Gerald Green from his novel. Remade as 1974 TVM with Pat Hingle.▼

Last Blitzkrieg, The (1958) **84m.** ** D: Arthur Dreifuss. Van Johnson, Kerwin Mathews, Dick York, Larry Storch. WW2 actioner trying to focus on German point of view.

Last Blood SEE: **Murder in Coweta County**

Last Boy Scout, The (1991) **C-105m.** ** D: Tony Scott. Bruce Willis, Damon Wayans, Chelsea Field, Noble Willingham, Taylor Negron, Danielle Harris, Halle Berry, Bruce McGill. Hardcore action film with Willis as a fired Secret Service agent now supporting himself through sticky gumshoe hire-outs; Wayans is his buddy in bonding (and an ex-pro-football quarterback) who helps him investigate gridiron corruption. More of the same from LETHAL WEAPON screenwriter Shane Black. Violent, even by this genre's standards, but zippy enough to make it an OK view. Panavision. [R]▼●◗

Last Bridge, The (1954-Austrian-Yugoslavian) **95m.** ***½ D: Helmut Kautner. Maria Schell, Bernhard Wicki, Barbara Rutting, Carl Mohner. Schell gives well-modulated performance as German doctor captured by Yugoslavian partisans during WW2, first administering medical aid reluctantly, then realizing all people deserve equal attention. Released in the U.S. in 1957.▼

Last Butterfly, The (1991-Czech-British) **C-110m.** *** D: Karel Kachyna. Tom Courtenay, Brigitte Fossey, Ingrid Held, Freddie Jones, Milan Knazko, Josef Kemer, Linda Jablonska. Acidly ironic drama of famous French mime Courtenay, who is "hired" by the Nazis to give one performance for the children of Terezin, the infamous "city of the Jews," during WW2. It's meant for propaganda purposes, to show the world that Jews in concentration camps were living the Life of Riley. Occasionally heavy going because of subject matter, but always moving. [PG-13]▼●

Last Call (1990) **C/B&W-90m.** **½ D: Jag Mundhra. William Katt, Shannon Tweed, Joseph Campanella, Matt Roe, Stella Stevens, Karen Elise Baldwin, Joseph Dellger, Alvin Silver. After real-estate whiz Katt is cheated in a land deal by mob sleazes Roe and Campanella, he enlists super-sexbomb Tweed to help fleece them back. Straight-to-video exploiter doesn't hesitate to showcase Playmate of the Year Tweed or vintage Playboy model Stevens in numerous steamy scenes. Video version is unrated although R-rated version exists for broadcast use. [R]▼●

Last Challenge, The (1967) **C-105m.** ** D: Richard Thorpe. Glenn Ford, Angie Dickinson, Chad Everett, Gary Merrill, Jack Elam, Delphi Lawrence, Royal Dano. Punk Everett is out to get Marshal Ford in well-cast but routine Western; Angie plays saloon-keeper, which makes one wonder why the two men don't just settle their problems over a drink. Panavision.

Last Chance, The (1968-Italian) **C-91m.** ** D: Niny Rosati. Tab Hunter, Michael Rennie, Daniela Bianchi, Liz Barrett. American journalist Hunter is given valuable documents about an international crime syndicate and finds himself a hunted man. Listless thriller. Cromoscope.▼

Last Chase, The (1981-Canadian) **C-101m.** *½ D: Martyn Burke. Lee Majors, Burgess Meredith, Chris Makepeace, Alexandra Stewart, Ben Gordon. Oil shortage causes the demise of auto travel during the 1980s; 20 years later, ex-race-car driver Majors reassembles his Porsche and becomes a "symbol of freedom" as he races across the country. Flimsy drama that reeks of Reaganomics. [PG]▼

Last Circus Show, The (1974-Italian) **C-91m.** ** D: Mario Garriazzo. James Whitmore, Lee J. Cobb, Cyril Cusack, Renato Cestie. Family-style tearjerker about a young boy who tries to reunite his parents, then falls deathly ill and begs to see a circus performance. Aka THE BALLOON VENDOR. [PG]

Last Command, The (1928) **88m.** **** D: Josef von Sternberg. Emil Jannings, Evelyn Brent, William Powell, Nicholas Soussanin, Michael Visaroff, Jack Raymond, Fritz Feld. Stunning silent drama of refugee Russian general Jannings, who is now reduced to working as a Hollywood extra—and destined to appear in a movie depicting the Russian revolution. A fascinating story laced with keen perceptions of life and work in Hollywood. Lajos Biros' story was based on an actual person; Jannings' gripping performance won him an Oscar (shared for his work in THE WAY OF ALL FLESH).▼

Last Command, The (1955) **C-110m.** **½ D: Frank Lloyd. Sterling Hayden, Anna Maria Alberghetti, Richard Carlson, Arthur Hunnicutt, Ernest Borgnine, J. Carrol Naish, Ben Cooper, John Russell, Virginia Grey, Jim Davis, Eduard Franz, Otto Kruger, Slim Pickens. Elaborate, sweeping account of the battle of the Alamo, hampered by tedious script. Story centers on wandering adventurer Jim Bowie (Hayden), who is galvanized by Mexican threats against Texas. All the historical Alamo set-pieces are here, with Hunnicutt a refreshingly rustic Davy Crockett. Music by Max Steiner; title song "Jim Bowie" sung by Gordon MacRae.▼

Last Dance (1996) **C-103m.** **½ D: Bruce Beresford. Sharon Stone, Rob Morrow, Randy Quaid, Peter Gallagher, Jack Thompson, Jayne Brook, Pamala Tyson, Skeet Ulrich. Younger brother of governor's chief of staff arrives in state capitol and gets a make-work job in the Clemency Office. He throws himself into his first case, launching a crusade to save a woman convicted of double murder from being executed. Stone gives a creditable performance in this severely deglamorized role, though it's hard to empathize with a murderer heroine. (By film's end, you can't help but feel *something.*) Morrow is good, too, but his character's motivations are muddy. Suffers from comparison to the previous year's superior DEAD MAN WALKING. Charles S. Dutton appears unbilled. [R]▼●

Last Days, The (1999) **C-90m.** ***½ D: James Moll. Exceptional documentary about five survivors of the Holocaust who suffered through Hitler's "final solution" in the last year of the war in Hungary. Brilliantly compiled from archive footage; vivid interviews and contemporary visits to Germany and Hungary, with five well-chosen subjects whose stories gradually meld into a mosaic. Produced by Steven Spielberg's Shoah Foundation. Oscar winner as Best Documentary. [PG-13]▼

Last Days of Chez Nous, The (1993-Australian) **C-96m.** **½ D: Gillian Armstrong. Lisa Harrow, Bruno Ganz, Kerry Fox, Miranda Otto, Kiri Paramore, Bill Hunter. Aspiring novelist with a teenage daughter endures marital discord when her aimless younger sister moves in. Director Armstrong returns to her roots for this interesting, if not entirely successful, film about relationships—between spouses, siblings, children and parents. (Biggest problem: an enigmatic and unappealing lead character.) A movie for real grown-ups, though it lacks the emotional power of MY BRILLIANT CAREER. Offers a view of Sydney (the bleaker part) that other movies usually don't show. [R]▼

Last Days of Disco, The (1998) **C-113m.** *** D: Whit Stillman. Chloë Sevigny, Kate Beckinsale, Chris Eigeman, Mackenzie Astin, Matt Keeslar, Robert Sean Leonard, Jennifer Beals, Burr Steers, David Thornton, Jaid Barrymore, Carolyn Farina. Two friends, naive but smart Sevigny and critical Beckinsale, hang out at a trendy disco in the early 1980s, trying—like everyone they know—to make the transition from group activity to pairing off. Sardonic but sympathetic to its characters, the movie is amusing and well acted but not particularly insightful. Said to be the last in Stillman's romantic-yuppies trilogy with METROPOLITAN and BARCELONA; some of the characters from those films turn up here. [R]▼●◗

Last Days of Dolwyn, The (1949-British) **95m.** **½ D: Emlyn Williams. Edith Evans, Emlyn Williams, Richard Burton, Anthony James, Hugh Griffith. A dowager is called upon for help when her Welsh village is slated for extinction as part of a reservoir project; well acted but somewhat aloof. Written by actor-director Williams; Burton's first film. Aka WOMAN OF DOLWYN.▼

Last Days of Frankie the Fly, The (1997) **C-95m.** BOMB D: Peter Markle. Dennis Hopper, Daryl Hannah, Kiefer Sutherland, Michael Madsen, Dayton Callie. Hopper is a lowly runner for a neighborhood thug (Madsen, surprise!) who's looking to get out from under the creep's thumb—as a screenwriter. Unsympathetic characters in a harsh and violent world, spouting quirky dialogue amidst the L.A. porn scene; the price we pay for PULP FICTION keeps getting higher. Debuted on U.S. cable TV. [R]▼

Last Days of Man on Earth, The (1973-British) **C-78m.** *½ D: Robert Fuest. Jon Finch, Jenny Runacre, Sterling Hayden, Patrick Magee, Hugh Griffith, Harry Andrews. Muddled sci-fi comedy set in Lapland, London and Turkey as world nears its end. A few scattered laughs. Longer, original British version (called THE FINAL PROGRAMME, running 89m.) has more substance. Based on one of Michael Moorcock's "Jerry Cornelius" stories; film has gained cult reputation. [R]▼●

Last Days of Patton, The (1986) **C-150m. TVM** D: Delbert Mann. George C. Scott, Eva Marie Saint, Richard Dysart, Murray Hamilton, Ed Lauter, Kathryn Leigh Scott. Scott returns to the role of George S. Patton after a 16-year hiatus in this woefully overlong drama chronicling the general's controversial last days following end of WW2. Scott's deathbed scene ranks among the longest in movie history. William Luce's script was based on Ladislas Farago's book of the same name. Average.▼

Last Days of Planet Earth, The (1974-Japanese) **C-90m.** BOMB. D: Toshio Masuda. Tetsuro Tamba, Toshio Kurosawa, So Yamamura, Kaoru Yumi. The air and sea are polluted, children attend school in gas masks, parents hallucinate—all predictions of Nostradamus. Preachy, laughably staged, atrociously dubbed; presented, perhaps, by the *National Enquirer*. Original title PROPHECIES OF NOSTRADAMUS: CATASTROPHE 1999. Tohoscope.▼

Last Days of Pompeii, The (1935) **96m.** *** D: Ernest B. Schoedsack. Preston Foster, Basil Rathbone, Dorothy Wilson, David Holt, Alan Hale, John Wood, Louis Calhern. Blacksmith Foster aspires to wealth and power as gladiator; climactic spectacle scenes are thrilling and expertly done, by the same special effects team responsible for KING KONG. Also shown in computer-colored version.▼●

Last Days of Pompeii, The (1960-Italian) **C-105m.** **½ D: Mario Bonnard. Steve Reeves, Christine Kaufmann, Barbara Carroll, Anne Marie Baumann, Mimmo Palmara. New version of venerable tale focuses on muscleman Reeves and synthetic account of Christian martyrs. Very little spectacle. SuperTotalscope.▼

Last Detail, The (1973) **C-105m.** ***½ D: Hal Ashby. Jack Nicholson, Otis Young, Randy Quaid, Clifton James, Carol Kane, Michael Moriarty, Nancy Allen. Superior comedy-drama about two career sailors ordered to transport a kleptomaniac prisoner to the brig. Robert Towne's brilliant off-color dialogue contributes to a quintessential Nicholson performance. Based on a Darryl Ponicsan novel. Look quickly for Gilda Radner. [R]▼●◗

Last Dragon, The (1985) **C-109m.** ** D: Michael Schultz. Taimak, Vanity, Chris Murney, Julius J. Carry 3rd, Faith Prince, Ernie Reyes, Jr., Keshia Knight (Pulliam), William H. Macy. Juvenile film about would-be martial arts master who gets involved with glamorous video deejay (Vanity) and some overwrought gangsters. Campy and heavy-handed; strictly kid stuff, except for one gag: the name of the Chinatown warehouse. Released theatrically as BERRY GORDY'S THE LAST DRAGON. Look fast for Chazz Palminteri as a thug. [PG-13] ▼

Last Elephant, The (1990) **C-100m. TVM** D: Joseph Sargent. John Lithgow, Isabella Rossellini, James Earl Jones. Boozy one-time novelist and research scientist team up to beat the African bush to thwart elephant poachers trafficking in illegal ivory. Mediocre drama coproduced by the National Audubon Society, whose money would have been better spent on a documentary. Made for cable. Video title: IVORY HUNTERS. Average.▼●

Last Embrace (1979) **C-102m.** *** D: Jonathan Demme. Roy Scheider, Janet Margolin, John Glover, Sam Levene, Christopher Walken, Charles Napier. CIA agent Scheider sees wife ambushed, spends rest of the picture believing he's next. One of the better Hitchcock-influenced suspense thrillers offers good performances and a punchy climax at Niagara Falls. Fine Miklos Rozsa score; watch for Mandy Patinkin. [R]▼●

Last Emperor, The (1987-Italian-British-Chinese) **C-160m.** ***½ D: Bernardo Bertolucci. John Lone, Joan Chen, Peter O'Toole, Ying Ruocheng, Victor Wong, Dennis Dun, Ryuichui Sakamoto, Maggie Han, Ric Young. Remarkable film inspired by true story of Pu Yi, the last emperor of China, who is crowned at age three and lives a cloistered life in the Forbidden City until he is deposed (as a young man) during the revolution and forced to fend for himself in the outside world for the first time. A magnificent journey to another time and place, hampered by unanswered questions in the narrative and a main character who remains somewhat cold. Nothing can top the spectacle of life in the Forbidden City (where scenes were actually filmed)—or the twists of fate that fill Pu Yi's life. Photographed by Vittorio Storaro; music by Ryuichi Sakamoto, David Byrne, and Cong Su. Winner of nine Academy Awards including Best Picture, Director, Adapted Screenplay (Mark Peploe, Bertolucci), Cinematography, Art Direction, Editing, Costume Design, and Original Score. Hong Kong–produced version, based on Pu Yi's autobiography, predates this. Director's cut runs 218m. Technovision. [PG-13] ▼●◗

Last Escape, The (1970) **C-90m.** *½ D: Walter Grauman. Stuart Whitman, John Collin, Pinkas Braun, Martin Jarvis, Gunther Neutze, Margit Saad. O.S.S. Captain Whitman is ordered to sneak rocket expert out of Germany near the end of WW2 with predictable results. [G]

Last Exit to Brooklyn (1989-W. German) **C-102m.** **½ D: Uli Edel. Stephen Lang, Jennifer Jason Leigh, Burt Young, Peter Dobson, Jerry Orbach, Stephen Baldwin, Ricki Lake, John Costelloe, Alexis Arquette. Gritty, brutal but stylish adaptation of Hubert Selby, Jr.'s notorious slice-of-life novel set on the mean streets of 1952 Brooklyn, where violence—verbal, physical, sexual, and otherwise—rules. Crammed with local color, but all the characters are thoroughly repellent and the film is difficult to like and to take. Selby himself appears as a cab driver. [R]▼●

Last Fight, The (1983) **C-86m.** *½ D: Fred Williamson. Willie Colon, Ruben Blades, Fred Williamson, Joe Spinell, Darlanne Fluegel, Nereida Mercado, Jose "Chegui" Torres, Don King. Poor melodrama with salsa music star Blades a singer-turned-boxer vying for the world championship. Doesn't even come up to level of old boxing B movies. [R]▼

Last Flight, The (1931) **80m.** *** D: William Dieterle. Richard Barthelmess, John Mack Brown, Helen Chandler, Walter Byron, Elliott Nugent, David Manners. Piquant film about an ex-WW1 flying ace (Barthelmess) and his flippant friends in 1920s Paris. Written by John Monk Saunders (of WINGS fame), and based on his novel, this focuses on the same "lost generation" that Hemingway wrote about in *The Sun Also Rises*. Not a perfect film, but an interesting and unusual one. German director Dieterle's English-language debut.

Last Flight of Noah's Ark, The (1980) **C-97m.** **½ D: Charles Jarrott. Elliott Gould, Genevieve Bujold, Ricky Schroder, Tammy Lauren, John Fujioka, Yuki Shimoda, Vincent Gardenia. Typical Disney sentimentality, somewhat effective. Pilot Gould, missionary Bujold, stowaway children, and a planeload of animals are forced down in the Pacific, where they unite with two Japanese soldiers, who didn't know WW2 was over, to convert the plane into an ark. Filmed largely on Waikiki Beach. Story by Ernest K. (THE HIGH AND THE MIGHTY) Gann. [G] ▼◗

Last Frontier, The (1956) **C-98m.** **½ D: Anthony Mann. Victor Mature, Guy Madison, Robert Preston, James Whitmore, Anne Bancroft. Three wilderness scouts see their lives change with the coming of cavalry outpost and military martinet (Preston). Offbeat characterizations in this cavalry drama. Aka SAVAGE WILDERNESS. CinemaScope.▼

Last Gangster, The (1937) **81m.** *** D: Edward Ludwig. Edward G. Robinson, James Stewart, Rosa Stradner, Lionel Stander, Douglas Scott, John Carradine, Sidney Blackmer, Louise Beavers, Edward Brophy, Grant Mitchell. Robinson's dynamic performance, and slick MGM production, elevate this tale of an underworld chief who's sent away for ten years, obsessed by the thought of the son he's never met. Entertaining story by William Wellman and Robert Carson was originally to have been called *Another Public Enemy.*

Last Gentleman, The (1934) **80m.** *** D: Sidney Lanfield. George Arliss, Edna May Oliver, Charlotte Henry, Janet Beecher, Ralph Morgan, Edward Ellis, Donald Meek. Delightful comedy with Arliss as dying millionaire whose family descends on him in hopes of carting away a piece of his fortune. Ingenious denouement gives Arliss last laugh.

Last Good Time, The (1994) **C-91m.** *** D: Bob Balaban. Armin Mueller-Stahl, Maureen Stapleton, Lionel Stander, Olivia d'Abo, Adrian Pasdar, Zohra Lampert, Kevin Corrigan. Well-observed little chamber drama about an elderly widower who takes in a young woman hiding from her lowlife boyfriend. Well acted all around, and nicely detailed, with a fine score by Jonathan Tunick. [R]▼●

Last Grenade, The (1970-British) **C-94m.** **½ D: Gordon Flemyng. Stanley Baker, Alex Cord, Honor Blackman, Richard Attenborough, Rafer Johnson, Andrew Keir. Solid cast in grim, unevenly plotted tale of duel to death between two British mercenaries. Good location shooting can't hide lack of character development, motivation. Panavision. [M]

Last Hard Men, The (1976) **C-103m.** *½ D: Andrew V. McLaglen. Charlton Heston, James Coburn, Barbara Hershey, Michael Parks, Jorge Rivero, Larry Wilcox, Thalmus Rasulala, Morgan Paull, Robert Donner, Christopher Mitchum. Outlaw Coburn leads a gang of men on a jailbreak, then sets into motion plan of vengeance on sheriff Heston: kidnapping daughter Hershey and threatening to gang-rape her. Repellently violent and tasteless Western, loosely based on a Brian Garfield novel, saved only by Parks' interesting performance as reform-minded sheriff. Panavision. [R]

Last Holiday (1950-British) **89m.** *** D: Henry Cass. Alec Guinness, Beatrice Campbell, Kay Walsh, Bernard Lee, Wilfrid Hyde-White, Sidney James, Ernest Thesiger. Ordinary man is told he is dying and decides to live it up at a swank resort. A droll, biting script by J. B. Priestley (who also coproduced), with sterling performances by all.▼

Last Horror Film, The (1984) **C-87m.** BOMB D: David Winters. Caroline Munro, Joe Spinell, Judd Hamilton, David Winters. Laughably amateurish mishmash about cabbie Spinell obsessed with horror movie star Munro. He follows her to the Cannes Film Festival, where this was partially shot (in 1981). [R] ▼

Last Hour, The (1991) **C-85m.** **½ D: William Sachs. Michael Paré, Shannon Tweed, Bobby Di Cicco, Robert Pucci, Robert Miano, George Kyle, Danny Trejo, Raye Hollitt. A gangster kidnaps the ex-wife of cop Paré and current wife of high-living Pucci, who previously double-crossed the gangster, and holds her hostage in an old L.A. building. Pretty good low-rent imitation DIE HARD with atmospheric photography and occasionally amusing dialogue. [R]▼

Last House on the Left (1972) **C-91m.** BOMB D: Wes Craven. David Hess, Lucy Grantham, Sandra Cassel, Marc Sheffler, Jeramie Rain, Fred Lincoln, Gaylord St. James. Repugnant film in which sadistic, Manson-type group rapes and tortures two girls to death, only to meet even sterner justice from one girl's parents. Technically inept and really sick. Based on, believe it or not, Bergman's VIRGIN SPRING. Runs 83m. on video. [R]▼●

Last House on the Left, Part II SEE: **Twitch of the Death Nerve**

Last Hunt, The (1956) **C-108m.** **½ D: Richard Brooks. Robert Taylor, Stewart Granger, Lloyd Nolan, Debra Paget, Russ Tamblyn, Constance Ford. Rampaging buffalo herd is primary excitement of Taylor-Granger feuding partnership in 1880s West. CinemaScope.▼

Last Hurrah, The (1958) **121m.** ***½ D: John Ford. Spencer Tracy, Jeffrey Hunter, Dianne Foster, Basil Rathbone, Pat O'Brien, Donald Crisp, James Gleason, Ed Brophy, John Carradine, Ricardo Cortez, Frank McHugh, Jane Darwell, Anna Lee, Charles FitzSimmons, Ken Curtis, O. Z. Whitehead, Jack Pennick, Dan Borzage. Sentimental version of Edwin O'Connor novel of politics, loosely based on life of Boston's mayor James Curley who in this story is mounting his final election campaign. Top-notch veteran cast makes film sparkle. Remade for TV in 1977 by (and with) Carroll O'Connor.▼●◗

Last Laugh, The (1924-German) **87m.** ***½ D: F. W. Murnau. Emil Jannings, Maly Delschaft, Max Hiller, Hans Unterkirchen. Silent-film classic told entirely by camera, without title cards. Jannings plays proud doorman at posh hotel who is suddenly demoted; film details his utter and grievous humiliation. Brilliantly filmed by pioneer cameraman Karl Freund, with towering performance by Jannings. Remade in Germany in 1955.▼●

Last Light (1993) **C-104m. TVM** D: Kiefer Sutherland. Kiefer Sutherland, Forest Whitaker, Amanda Plummer, Kathleen Quinlan, Lynne Moody, Clancy Brown. Sutherland's directing debut has him as a death-row inmate whose unexpected friendship with prison guard Whitaker changes both of their lives. Hard-hitting drama, with an overly complex script by Robert Eisele. Made for cable. Above average.▼

Last Man on Earth, The (1964-U.S.-Italian) **86m.** ** D: Sidney Salkow. Vincent Price, Franca Bettoia, Emma Danieli, Giacomo Rossi-Stuart, Tony Cerevi. Often crude chiller with Price the sole survivor of plague, besieged by victims who arise at night thirsting for his blood; erratic production. Based on Richard Matheson's *I Am Legend*; remade as THE OMEGA MAN. CinemaScope. ▼●

Last Man Standing (1996) **C-101m.** ** D: Walter Hill. Bruce Willis, Christopher Walken, Bruce Dern, Alexandra Powers, David Patrick Kelly, William Sanderson, Karina Lombard, Ned Eisenberg, Michael Imperioli, R. D. Call, Leslie Mann. Willis chances to pass through a dreary Texas town where two Chicago gangs are at each other's throats—and tries to work both sides of the street to his own advantage. Remake of YOJIMBO (which itself became A FISTFUL OF DOLLARS), set in the 1930s, is rife with gunplay, but overcome by sheer boredom. Super 35. [R]▼●◗

Last Man to Hang, The (1956-British) **75m.** ** D: Terence Fisher. Tom Conway, Elizabeth Sellars, Eunice Gayson, Freda Jackson, Raymond Huntley, Anthony Newley. Forthright courtroom film of man on trial for alleged murder of wife.

Last Married Couple in America, The (1980) **C-103m.** *½ D: Gilbert Cates. George Segal, Natalie Wood, Richard Benjamin, Valerie Harper, Bob Dishy, Dom DeLuise. Likable cast in stupid sex comedy about happily married couple so upset by breakup of married friends that they begin to question their own relationship. Smutty and ridiculous. [R]▼

Last Metro, The (1980-French) **C-133m.** **½ D: François Truffaut. Catherine Deneuve, Gerard Depardieu, Jean Poiret, Heinz Bennent, Andrea Ferreol, Paulette Dubost. A beautiful actress struggles to keep her "exiled" husband's theater alive during the German occupation of Paris. A film with charm and style but no point—a problem underscored by its abrupt and quizzical finale. Watching the elegant Deneuve provides most of this film's appeal. [PG]▼●◗

Last Mile, The (1932) **70m.** *** D: Sam Bischoff. Howard Phillips, Preston S. Foster, George E. Stone, Noel Madison, Alan Roscoe, Paul Fix. Stark, atmospheric drama about life on death row, with Killer Mears (Foster) leading a takeover of the cellblock. Based on John Wexley's play. Remade in 1959.▼

Last Mile, The (1959) **81m.** **½ D: Howard W. Koch. Mickey Rooney, Clifford David, Harry Millard, Don "Red" Barry, Ford Rainey, Leon Janney. The "big house" oldie dusted off as a dramatic vehicle for Rooney.

Last Millionaire, The (1934-French) **90m.** *** D: René Clair. Max Dearly, Renée Saint-Cyr, Jose Noguero, Raymond Cordy, Paul Olivier. Light, mildly funny satire about the world's wealthiest man (Dearly), who is asked to govern a bankrupt, mythical kingdom; he is knocked on the head, and his idiotic rulings are interpreted as acts of genius. Not bad, but not up to Clair's best films of the period.

Last Movie, The (1971) **C-108m.** *½ D: Dennis Hopper. Dennis Hopper, Julie Adams, Peter Fonda, Kris Kristofferson, Sylvia Miles, John Phillip Law, Rod Cameron, Sam Fuller. Hopper's fatally pretentious follow-up to EASY RIDER is interesting only as curio; incomprehensible story of small Peruvian village after a movie company pulls out has lovely photography, good acting by Adams. Otherwise, you've been warned. Among the supporting cast: Dean Stockwell, Russ Tamblyn, Michelle Phillips. Kristofferson's film debut (he also wrote the music). Also known as CHINCHERO. [PG]▼

Last Night (1998-Canadian-French) **C-93m.** ** D: Don McKellar. Don McKellar, Sandra Oh, Sarah Polley, Callum Keith Rennie, David Cronenberg, Robin Gammel, Genevieve Bujold, Jackie Burroughs. Rumination on the last night of civilization, and how various people deal with their impending demise. Not exactly profound, though Oh's heartrending performance almost makes this worth watching. Written by leading actor McKellar, making his directorial debut. [R]▼◗

Last Night at the Alamo (1983) **80m.** *** D: Eagle Pennell. Sonny Davis, Lou Perry, Steve Matilla, Tina Hubbard, Doris Hargrave. The last night at the Alamo, no famous battle site but a small, obscure Houston bar. A fascinating portrayal of the modern-era "cowboy" as henpecked, alcoholic, ultimately pathetic. Independently produced, with a hilariously profane script by Kim Henkel, author of THE TEXAS CHAINSAW MASSACRE.▼

Last of His Tribe, The (1992) **C-90m. TVM** D: Harry Hook. Jon Voight, Graham Greene, David Ogden Stiers, Jack Blessing, Anne Archer, Daniel Benzali. Earnest dramatization of anthropologist Alfred Kroeber's discovery of the last member of a small Indian tribe in pre-WW1 California. Greene shines as Ishi, the lonely survivor, but the production lumbers and suffers from a ludicrous tacked-on ending. The subject was tackled before by Dalton Trumbo in 1978's ISHI: THE LAST OF HIS TRIBE. Made for cable. Average.▼

Last of Mrs. Cheyney, The (1929) **94m.** **½ D: Sidney Franklin. Norma Shearer, Basil Rathbone, George Barraud, Herbert Bunston, Hedda Hopper, George K. Arthur. Young woman who has charmed a group of British society types turns out to be involved with a ring of jewel thieves. Very much an early-talkie stage play, with some terribly arch performances, but still quite watchable. Based on the play by Frederick Lonsdale. Remade in 1937.●

Last of Mrs. Cheyney, The (1937) **98m.** *** D: Richard Boleslawski. Joan Crawford, William Powell, Robert Montgomery, Frank Morgan, Jessie Ralph, Nigel Bruce. Glossy remake of Norma Shearer's 1929 success, from Frederick Lonsdale's play about a chic American jewel thief in England. Great fun for star watchers, though it was considered a dated dud in 1937. Remade in 1951 as THE LAW AND THE LADY.▼

Last of Sheila, The (1973) **C-120m.** ***½ D: Herbert Ross. James Coburn, James Mason, Dyan Cannon, Ian McShane, Joan Hackett, Raquel Welch, Richard Benjamin. Super murder-puzzler about jet-set gamester who devises what turns into a deadly game of whodunit. Many red herrings make it all the more fun. Script by Anthony Perkins and Stephen Sondheim, real-life puzzle fans. [PG]▼

Last of the Badmen (1957) **C-79m.** ** D: Paul Landres. George Montgomery, Meg Randall, James Best, Michael Ansara, Keith Larsen. Western about Chicago detectives in 1880s chasing after killers of their fellow-worker. CinemaScope.

Last of the Buccaneers (1950) **C-79m.** *½ D: Lew Landers. Paul Henreid, Jack Oakie, Mary Anderson, John Dehner. Quickie costumer tainting the legendary name of Jean Lafitte with plodding account of his post–Battle of New Orleans exploits.

Last of the Comanches (1952) **C-85m.** **½ D: Andre de Toth. Broderick Crawford, Barbara Hale, Lloyd Bridges, Martin Milner, John War Eagle, William Andrews (Steve Forrest). Capable rehash of cavalrymen fighting off Indian attack. Western remake of SAHARA.▼

Last of the Cowboys, The SEE: **Great Smokey Roadblock, The**

Last of the Dogmen (1995) **C-120m.** ** D: Tab Murphy. Tom Berenger, Barbara Hershey, Kurtwood Smith, Steve Reevis, Andrew Miller, Gregory Scott Cummins, Molly Parker; narrated by Wilford Brimley. Annoyingly clichéd, eminently forgettable adventure with crackerjack tracker Berenger setting out to bring back a trio of prison escapees who meet a horrible fate as he nears their campsite. Could it have been the work of the mysterious, legendary Cheyenne "dog soldiers"? You may not want to stick around to find out. Panavision. [PG] ▼●◗

Last of the Fast Guns, The (1958) **C-82m.** ** D: George Sherman. Jock Mahoney, Gilbert Roland, Linda Cristal, Eduard Franz. Adequately told Western of search for missing man, and obstacles the hired gunslinger must overcome. CinemaScope.

Last of the Finest, The (1990) **C-106m.** ** D: John Mackenzie. Brian Dennehy, Joe Pantoliano, Jeff Fahey, Bill Paxton, Deborra-Lee Furness, Guy Boyd, Henry Darrow, Lisa Jane Persky. Honest, independent-minded L.A. cop Dennehy and his comrades discover sinister forces at work while attempting to bust drug traffickers. Dennehy's usual solid performance can't overcome occasionally outlandish scenario, with obvious parallels to the Iran-Contra affair. [R]▼●

Last of the High Kings (1996-Irish-Danish) **C-104m.** *** D: David Keating. Gabriel Byrne, Catherine O'Hara, Jared Leto, Christina Ricci, Colm Meaney, Stephen Rea, Lorraine Pilkington, Emily Mortimer, Jason Barry, Ciaran Fitzgerald. Solid coming-of-age tale, set in Dublin, which tells the story of idealistic 17-year-old Frankie (Leto) and the individuals who affect his life—beginning with his eccentric, egocentric actor father (Byrne) and his comically pro-Protestant mom (O'Hara, who has never been better). Loaded with charm and thoughtfully scripted by Keating and Byrne. Aka SUMMER FLING. [R]▼

Last of the Mobile Hot-Shots (1970) **C-108m.** ** D: Sidney Lumet. James Coburn, Lynn Redgrave, Robert Hooks, Perry Hayes, Reggie King. Ambitious flop from Tennessee Williams' *Seven Descents of Myrtle* about volatile interracial triangle set in Deep South. ("Mobile" refers to the Alabama town.) [R—edited from original X rating]▼

Last of the Mohicans, The (1920) **75m.** *** D: Maurice Tourneur, Clarence Brown. Wallace Beery, Barbara Bedford, Albert Roscoe, Lillian Hall, Henry Woodward, James Gordon, Harry Lorraine. Colorful retelling of the James Fenimore Cooper classic, pitting the villainous Magua (Beery, who's well cast) against Hawkeye, Uncas,

Chingachgook, and the story's other characters. First-rate silent drama. Look for Boris Karloff in a bit part as an Indian. Brown took over directing when Tourneur was injured during production.▼●

Last of the Mohicans, The (1936) **91m.** *** D: George B. Seitz. Randolph Scott, Binnie Barnes, Heather Angel, Hugh Buckler, Henry Wilcoxon, Bruce Cabot, Phillip Reed, Robert Barrat. Effective and exciting adaptation of James Fenimore Cooper novel about conflicts between British Army and Colonial settlers during the French and Indian War. Scott is a stout Hawkeye, Cabot an appropriately hissable Magua. Screenplay by Philip Dunne. Also shown in computer-colored version. ▼●

Last of the Mohicans, The (1992) **C-114m.** ***½ D: Michael Mann. Daniel Day-Lewis, Madeleine Stowe, Russell Means, Eric Schweig, Jodhi May, Steven Waddington, Wes Studi, Maurice Roëves, Patrice Chereau, Colm Meaney, Peter Postlethwaite. Rousing, kinetic update of the James Fenimore Cooper classic, replete with 1990s sensibilities, potent depiction of violence, and a charismatic central performance by Day-Lewis as Hawkeye. Wavers between sweep of historical fiction and smaller canvas of its love story, but never fails to entertain. Oscar winner for Best Sound. Screenplay by Mann and Christopher Crowe from Philip Dunne's script for the 1936 film. Evocative score by Randy Edelman. Expanded version runs 117m. Panavision. [R]▼●◗

Last of the Red Hot Lovers (1972) **C-98m.** BOMB D: Gene Saks. Alan Arkin, Sally Kellerman, Paula Prentiss, Renee Taylor. Appalling film version of typical Neil Simon play concerns Arkin's unsuccessful attempts to carry on sneaky love affair with three different women (not all at once). Actors scream at each other for more than an hour and a half in shoddy production for which the term "photographed stage play" must have been invented. [PG]▼●

Last of the Redmen (1947) **C-77m.** **½ D: George Sherman. Jon Hall, Michael O'Shea, Evelyn Ankers, Julie Bishop, Buster Crabbe. OK adaptation of THE LAST OF THE MOHICANS, with Hall cast as Hawkeye, O'Shea as Major Hayward and Crabbe as Magua. Story focuses on Hawkeye's attempt to escort a British general's children through dangerous Indian country.

Last of the Secret Agents?, The (1966) **C-90m.** *½ D: Norman Abbott. Marty Allen, Steve Rossi, John Williams, Nancy Sinatra, Lou Jacobi. Tiring spoof on spy movies ends up unintentional self-mockery. Strictly for Allen and Rossi fans. Look for Harvey Korman as a German colonel.

Last of the Ski Bums (1969) **C-86m.** *** D: Dick Barrymore. Ron Funk, Mike Zuetell, Ed Ricks. Made by same team that produced THE ENDLESS SUMMER, film details exploits of three men who win large sum of money, spend it on long ski holiday. Weak narrative conflicts with beauty of visuals. [G]

Last of the Vikings, The (1961-Italian) **C-102m.** ** D: Giacomo Gentilomo. Cameron Mitchell, Edmund Purdom, Isabelle Corey, Helene Remy. Filmed with gusto, elaborate epic deals with Mitchell out to punish the Norse for devastating his homelands; poorly acted. Dyaliscope.▼

L.A. Story (1991) **C-95m.** **½ D: Mick Jackson. Steve Martin, Victoria Tennant, Richard E. Grant, Marilu Henner, Sarah Jessica Parker, Kevin Pollak, Sam McMurray, Patrick Stewart, Iman. Martin wrote this amusing piece of fluff about a wacky TV weatherman trying to sort out his life. Slender story thread allows Martin to make comic observations about living in trend-conscious L.A., some of them mild, some of them worthy of laughing out loud. Several of Martin's comedy cronies make cameo appearances. A deleted scene with John Lithgow was added for the film's cable-TV debut. [PG-13]▼●◗

Last Outlaw, The (1936) **72m.** *** D: Christy Cabanne. Harry Carey, Hoot Gibson, Henry B. Walthall, Tom Tyler, Margaret Callahan. Delightful blend of comedy and Western ingredients with Carey as a once notorious bandit released from prison after twenty-five years, only to find the Old West gone. Carey is wonderful (along with entire cast). There's even a hilarious dig at singing cowboys! John Ford coauthored the story.▼

Last Outpost, The (1935) **70m.** *** D: Louis Gasnier, Charles Barton. Cary Grant, Claude Rains, Gertrude Michael, Kathleen Burke, Colin Tapley, Akim Tamiroff. Exciting action-adventure with British troops in Africa, along lines of LOST PATROL, LIVES OF A BENGAL LANCER, etc.

Last Outpost, The (1951) **C-88m.** **½ D: Lewis R. Foster. Ronald Reagan, Rhonda Fleming, Bruce Bennett, Bill Williams, Peter Hanson, Noah Beery, Jr. Burst of action saves wornout yarn of two brothers on opposite sides of Civil War, teaming up to fight off Indian attack. This was Reagan's first starring Western. Video title: CAVALRY CHARGE.▼

Last Party, The (1993) **C-96m.** *** D: Mark Benjamin, Marc Levin. Robert Downey, Jr., takes his video camera on an odyssey of America, focusing on 1992 Democratic and Republican national conventions, to get a sense of the country and its political attitudes. Along the way he interviews such colleagues as Sean Penn and Mary Stuart Masterson, and such varied notables as Oliver Stone, Spike Lee, G. Gordon Liddy, Jerry Falwell, and even his father, filmmaker Robert Downey, Sr. Not quite a documentary, but an entertaining journey (in the ROGER & ME vein); ultimately, we learn more about Downey, Jr., than we do about the state of the union.▼●

Last Picture Show, The (1971) **118m.** **** D: Peter Bogdanovich. Timothy Bottoms, Jeff Bridges, Ben Johnson, Cloris Leachman, Ellen Burstyn, Cybill Shepherd, Eileen Brennan, Clu Gulager, Sam Bottoms, Randy Quaid, John Hillerman, Noble Willingham. Brilliant study of life in small Texas town during 1950s, and how characters' lives intertwine, from Larry McMurtry's novel (he and Bogdanovich wrote the script). Oscars went to Johnson and Leachman for sensitive performances, but entire cast works at same level. Beautifully photographed in b&w by Robert Surtees. Shepherd's film debut. Sequel: TEXASVILLE. "Special Edition" reedited by Bogdanovich in 1990 includes 7m. of material originally cut from the film. [R] ▼●◗

Last Plane Out (1983) **C-92m.** *½ D: David Nelson. Jan-Michael Vincent, Julie Carmen, Mary Crosby, David Huffman, William Windom, Lloyd Battista. Political thriller produced by Jack Cox and based on his real-life experiences as a journalist in the final days of the Somoza regime in Nicaragua suffers from cornball treatment and obvious propaganda slant. Battista as Somoza is Mr. Nice Guy in this version. Low-budget production isn't helped by indifferent direction by Nelson. [PG]▼

Last Posse, The (1953) **73m.** ** D: Alfred L. Werker. Broderick Crawford, John Derek, Charles Bickford, Wanda Hendrix, Warner Anderson. Sheriff's men track down robbers, not without surprising results.

Last Prostitute, The (1991) **C-100m. TVM** D: Lou Antonio. Sonia Braga, Wil Wheaton, Woody Watson, Dennis Letts, Cotter Smith. Amiable coming-of-age story about two 1960s teens who seek out a legendary prostitute only to discover she's no longer in "business," and now runs a horse farm. Carmen Culver does a nice job of adapting William Borden's play. Made for cable. Above average. ▼

La Strada (1954-Italian) **115m.** **** D: Federico Fellini. Anthony Quinn, Giulietta Masina, Richard Basehart, Aldo Silvana, Marcella Rovere, Livia Venturini. Deceptively simple tale of brutish strongman Quinn taking simple-minded Masina with him as he tours countryside, where he encounters gentle acrobat Basehart. Best Foreign Film Oscar winner; stunning performances, haunting Nino Rota score. Story and screenplay by Fellini and Tullio Pinelli. ▼●

Last Rebel, The (1971) **C-89m.** BOMB D: Denys McCoy. Joe Namath, Jack Elam, Woody Strode, Ty Hardin, Victoria George. Namath plays Confederate soldier who raises havoc in small Missouri town after the Civil War. Film has obvious camp value, but it's not enough; Joe makes Ty Hardin look like John Gielgud. [PG]

Last Remake of Beau Geste, The (1977) **C-83m.** **½ D: Marty Feldman. Marty Feldman, Ann-Margret, Michael York, Peter Ustinov, James Earl Jones, Trevor Howard, Henry Gibson, Terry-Thomas, Spike Milligan, Roy Kinnear. After uproarious first half, Feldman's Foreign Legion spoof falters and gropes its way to weak conclusion. Enough belly-laughs to make it worthwhile, and sidesplitting performance by butler Milligan. Feldman also cowrote this, his directorial debut. [PG]▼

Last Resort (1986) **C-80m.** **½ D: Zane Buzby. Charles Grodin, Robin Pearson Rose, John Ashton, Ellen Blake, Megan Mullally, Christopher Ames, Jon Lovitz, Gerrit Graham, Mario Van Peebles, Phil Hartman. Newly unemployed Grodin decides, on impulse, to take his family to a Club Med-type vacation resort, with predictably comic results. Likable but iffy comedy does have some genuine laughs. First time director Buzby also appears as resort's baby sitter. [R]▼●

Last Reunion, The (1980) **C-98m.** *½ D: Jay Wertz. Cameron Mitchell, Leo Fong, Chanda Romero, Vic Silayan, Hal Bokar, Philip Baker Hall. Violent drama of WW2 platoon's reunion in the Philippines, where in 1945 they slaughtered a Japanese general and his wife. Now, thirty-three years later, the sole witness is out for revenge. Not very good.▼

Last Rites (1980) **C-88m.** BOMB D: Domonic Paris. Patricia Lee Hammond, Gerald Fielding, Victor Jorge, Michael Lally, Mimi Weddell. A vampire mortician harasses a family that bears the surname Fonda. The pits. Aka DRACULA'S LAST RITES. [R]▼

Last Rites (1988) **C-103m.** ** D: Donald P. Bellisario. Tom Berenger, Daphne Zuniga, Chick Vennera, Anne Twomey, Dane Clark, Paul Dooley, Vassili Lambrinos. Routine drama of a priest who uses the auspices of the church to protect a girl on a Mafia hit list. Of course, he falls in love with her. Of course, he also happens to be the son of a Mafia chieftain himself. And of course, the studio sent this one straight to video. [R]▼●

Last Roman, The (1968-German-Rumanian) **92m.** ** D: Robert Siodmak. Laurence Harvey, Orson Welles, Sylva Koscina, Honor Blackman, Michael Dunn, Harriet Andersson, Lang Jeffries, Robert Hoffman. Big cast in spears and togas look baffled at what has become of Felix Dann's German bestseller *Kamf um Rom* about the decline of the Roman Empire. Edited down from a two-part spectacular. Techniscope.▼

Last Run, The (1971) **C-99m.** **½ D: Richard Fleischer. George C. Scott, Tony Musante, Trish Van Devere, Colleen

Dewhurst. Mediocre tale of aging gangland driver who has to make one more run for his ego. Great photography by Sven Nykvist. Started by John Huston, who left early on. Panavision. [PG]

Last Safari, The (1967-British) **C-110m.** ** D: Henry Hathaway. Kaz Garas, Stewart Granger, Gabriella Licudi, Johnny Sekka, Liam Redmond. Uninteresting action tale with depressed professional hunter (Stewart) coming to terms with himself and rich young couple who hire him. Good cast can't handle script.▼

Last Seduction, The (1994) **C-110m.** *** D: John Dahl. Linda Fiorentino, Peter Berg, J. T. Walsh, Bill Nunn, Bill Pullman, Michael Raysses, Zach Phifer. Pathologically evil—and stunningly sexual—woman ditches her husband, grabs the cash he's made in a drug deal, and flees N.Y.C., encamping in a small upstate town where she attracts and mystifies a local man—her latest patsy. Fiorentino's fiery femme fatale makes Stanwyck in DOUBLE INDEMNITY look like Snow White! Sizzling, sexy thriller from modern film noir expert Dahl and writer Steve Barancik. Unrelenting meanness wears it down a bit toward the end. Made U.S. debut on cable. [R]▼●

Last September, The (1999-British-Irish-French) **C-103m.** ** D: Deborah Warner. Maggie Smith, Michael Gambon, Jane Birkin, Fiona Shaw, Lambert Wilson, Keeley Hawes, David Tennant, Gary Lydon. A less-than-compelling look at the last days of the Anglo-Irish, the British ruling class who live in cloistered elegance in Ireland as a storm brews all around them. The year is 1920, and a wealthy couple's young ward (Hawes) enters into a forbidden relationship with a young Irishman who's wanted for murder. Based on Elizabeth Bowen's novel. [R]▼

Last Stagecoach West (1957) **67m.** *½ D: Joseph Kane. Jim Davis, Victor Jory, Mary Castle, Lee Van Cleef. Fair cast cannot save bland Western about stagedriver who loses government contracts and goes out of business. Filmed in Naturama.

Last Stand at Saber River (1997) **C-100m. TVM** D: Dick Lowry. Tom Selleck, Suzy Amis, Keith Carradine, David Carradine, Haley Joel Osment, David Dukes, Harry Carey, Jr., Rachel Duncan, Tracey Needham. Bitter Reb soldier Selleck returns to his Arizona homestead to battle Union sympathizers laying claim to the spread in this energetic Western based on Elmore Leonard's novel. Made for cable. Average.▼

Last Starfighter, The (1984) **C-100m.** **½ D: Nick Castle. Lance Guest, Robert Preston, Dan O'Herlihy, Catherine Mary Stewart, Barbara Bosson, Norman Snow, Cameron Dye, Wil Wheaton. Sci-fi for kids, about a youngster whose video-game prowess makes him a prime recruit to help save real-life planet under attack. Likable but toothless adventure (with an arch-villain who simply disappears from the proceedings) benefits greatly from performances of old pros Preston and O'Herlihy, who's unrecognizable in lizard-like makeup. Preston's last film. Panavision. [PG] ▼●

Last Summer (1969) **C-97m.** ***½ D: Frank Perry. Richard Thomas, Barbara Hershey, Bruce Davison, Cathy Burns, Ralph Waite, Conrad Bain. Powerful story based on Evan Hunter novel of teenagers playing on the beach in a summer resort. Film follows their games, sexual awakenings, and how evil manifests itself with calculated determination. Cathy Burns a standout. [R—edited from original X rating]▼

Last Summer in the Hamptons (1995) **C-105m.** ** D: Henry Jaglom. Victoria Foyt, Viveca Lindfors, Jon Robin Baitz, Savannah Boucher, Roscoe Lee Browne, Andre Gregory, Nick Gregory, Melissa Leo, Roddy McDowall, Martha Plimpton, Holland Taylor, Ron Rifkin, Brooke Smith, Diane Salinger, Kristoffer Tabori. An insecure young movie star (Foyt) arrives in the summer community of East Hampton, Long Island, and becomes involved with the assorted theater folk who comprise a circle of friends-lovers-colleagues. Another of Jaglom's occasionally insightful talk-fest/confessionals in which the characters reveal their jealousies, neuroses, and feelings. For inveterate Jaglom fans only. Scripted by Jaglom and Foyt (who are husband and wife). [R]▼●

Last Sunset, The (1961) **C-112m.** *** D: Robert Aldrich. Rock Hudson, Kirk Douglas, Dorothy Malone, Joseph Cotten, Carol Lynley, Neville Brand, Regis Toomey, Jack Elam. Strange on the Range, courtesy Aldrich and scripter Dalton Trumbo; philosophical outlaw Douglas and pursuing sheriff Hudson play cat-and-mouse with each other during lengthy cattle drive. Throws in everything from incest to Indians!

Last Supper, The (1996) **C-94m.** ** D: Stacy Title. Cameron Diaz, Ron Eldard, Annabeth Gish, Jonathan Penner, Courtney B. Vance, Nora Dunn, Ron Perlman, Bill Paxton, Charles Durning, Mark Harmon, Jason Alexander, Bryn Erin. Five grad student friends decide to rid the world of antisocial extremists who don't happen to conform to their worldview. Intriguing premise plays itself out too soon and stretches credibility in the name of satire; ultimately unpleasant and unsatisfying, though the cast is excellent and some of the cameos (Paxton, Durning, Harmon, Perlman) are first-rate. Costar Penner also coproduced the film. Filmed in 1994. [R] ▼●

Last Tango in Paris (1973-French-Italian) **C-129m.** ***½ D: Bernardo Bertolucci. Marlon Brando, Maria Schneider, Jean-Pierre Léaud, Darling Legitimus, Catherine Sola, Mauro Marchetti, Dan Diament. Expatriate American in Paris tries purging himself of bad memories after his wife's suicide, enters into a tragic "no questions asked" sexual liaison with a chance acquaintance. The most controversial film of its era is still explicit by today's standards, though it's mellowed somewhat with age. A sterling showcase for Bertolucci's camera mastery; Brando's performance, then as now, is among the best of his career. [X—also shown in R-rated version]▼●◗

Last Temptation of Christ, The (1988) **C-164m.** *** D: Martin Scorsese. Willem Dafoe, Harvey Keitel, Barbara Hershey, Harry Dean Stanton, David Bowie, Verna Bloom, Andre Gregory, Juliette Caton, Roberts Blossom, Irvin Kershner, Nehemiah Persoff, Barry Miller. Thought-provoking and deeply felt drama adapted from Nikos Kazantzakis' book which speculates about Jesus' self-doubts when he realizes he has been chosen by God to carry His message. Moments of great power and beauty are diminished somewhat by mundane dialogue and slow stretches; still worthwhile, with a genuine feeling for time and place that helps make the story vivid and real. Music by Peter Gabriel. [R]▼●◗

Last Ten Days, The (1956-German) **113m.** *** D: G. W. Pabst. Albin Skoda, Oskar Werner, Lotte Tobisch, Willy Krause, Helga Kennedy-Dohrn. Finely etched study of downfall of leader of Third Reich. Retitled: LAST TEN DAYS OF ADOLPH HITLER.

Last Time I Committed Suicide, The (1997) **C-93m.** *½ D: Stephen Kay. Thomas Jane, Keanu Reeves, Adrien Brody, John Doe, Claire Forlani, Jim Haynie, Marg Helgenberger, Lucinda Jenney, Gretchen Mol. Mordantly stylized, cliché-laden story of beat icon Neal Cassady, ostensibly based on a letter he once wrote to Jack Kerouac. Totally unsympathetic, angst-filled characters are put to even greater disadvantage by a jittery camera and harsh lighting. [R]▼●

Last Time I Saw Archie, The (1961) **98m.** ** D: Jack Webb. Robert Mitchum, Jack Webb, Martha Hyer, France Nuyen, Louis Nye, Richard Arlen, Don Knotts, Joe Flynn, Robert Strauss. Webb's sole attempt at comedy is less funny than some of his more serious films; a pity, because William Bowers' script—based on his own Army experiences—had real potential, and Mitchum nicely underplays as the titular conman. (By the way, the real Archie Hall sued for invasion of privacy!)

Last Time I Saw Paris, The (1954) **C-116m.** *** D: Richard Brooks. Elizabeth Taylor, Van Johnson, Donna Reed, Walter Pidgeon, Eva Gabor, George Dolenz, Roger Moore. Updated version of F. Scott Fitzgerald story, set in post-WW2 Paris, of ruined marriages and disillusioned people. MGM gloss helps.▼●◗

Last Train From Gun Hill (1959) **C-94m.** *** D: John Sturges. Kirk Douglas, Anthony Quinn, Carolyn Jones, Earl Holliman, Brad Dexter, Brian Hutton, Ziva Rodann. Superior Western of staunch sheriff determined to leave Gun Hill with murder suspect, despite necessity for shoot-out. VistaVision.▼

Last Train From Madrid, The (1937) **77m.** *** D: James Hogan. Dorothy Lamour, Lew Ayres, Gilbert Roland, Anthony Quinn, Lee Bowman, Karen Morley, Helen Mack, Evelyn Brent, Robert Cummings, Lionel Atwill, Olympe Bradna. Imitation GRAND HOTEL linking vignettes of various people escaping from wartorn Spain during 1930s. Modest but well-made film, with impressive cast.

Last Tycoon, The (1976) **C-125m.** ***½ D: Elia Kazan. Robert De Niro, Tony Curtis, Robert Mitchum, Jeanne Moreau, Jack Nicholson, Donald Pleasence, Peter Strauss, Ingrid Boulting, Ray Milland, Dana Andrews, Theresa Russell, John Carradine, Anjelica Huston. Low-keyed but effective Harold Pinter adaptation of F. Scott Fitzgerald's final novel benefits immeasurably from De Niro's great, uncharacteristic performance as 1930s movie producer (inspired by Irving Thalberg) who is slowly working himself to death. Along with Joan Micklin Silver's TV film BERNICE BOBS HER HAIR, the best Fitzgerald yet put on the screen. Lew Ayres appears unbilled. [PG] ▼●

Last Unicorn, The (1982-British) **C-92m.** **½ D: Arthur Rankin, Jr., Jules Bass. Voices of Alan Arkin, Jeff Bridges, Mia Farrow, Tammy Grimes, Robert Klein, Angela Lansbury, Christopher Lee, Keenan Wynn, Paul Frees, Rene Auberjonois. Set in the time of Robin Hood, this pleasing animated fable tells of the adventures of a beautiful white unicorn who enters a forest in search of others of its kind. The weakest element: those bland, forgettable Jimmy Webb songs. Scripted by Peter S. Beagle, and based on his novel. [G]▼

Last Valley, The (1970-British) **C-128m.** ** D: James Clavell. Michael Caine, Omar Sharif, Florinda Bolkan, Nigel Davenport, Per Oscarsson, Arthur O'Connell. Thinking man's adventure epic is an unfortunate misfire; 17th-century story brings warrior Caine and his soldiers to peaceful valley which has remained untouched by the Thirty Years War. Todd-AO. [PG]▼◗

Last Victim, The SEE: **Forced Entry**

Last Voyage, The (1960) **C-91m.** *** D: Andrew L. Stone. Robert Stack, Dorothy Malone, George Sanders, Edmond O'Brien, Woody Strode. Engrossing drama of luxury ship that goes down at sea, and the ways the crew and passengers are affected. (To heighten the realism of the film, they really sank a ship.) Sanders is ill-fated

captain, Stack and Malone a married couple in jeopardy.▼●
Last Wagon, The (1956) **C-99m.** *** D: Delmer Daves. Richard Widmark, Felicia Farr, Susan Kohner, Tommy Rettig, Stephanie Griffin, Ray Stricklyn, Nick Adams, Timothy Carey. Widmark is condemned killer who saves remnants of wagon train after Indian attack, leading them to safety. Clichéd plot well handled. CinemaScope.
Last Waltz, The (1978) **C-117m.** **** D: Martin Scorsese. The Band, Bob Dylan, Neil Young, Joni Mitchell, Van Morrison, Eric Clapton, Neil Diamond, The Staples, Muddy Waters, Emmylou Harris, Paul Butterfield, Dr. John, Ronnie Hawkins, Ringo Starr, Ron Wood. Truly wonderful documentary about The Band's Thanksgiving, 1976, farewell concert, filmed by state-of-the-art Hollywood talent. A pair of studio-shot numbers involving The Staples and Harris are as exciting to watch as listen to, but the whole film is beautifully done. [PG]▼●
Last Wave, The (1977-Australian) **C-106m.** *** D: Peter Weir. Richard Chamberlain, Olivia Hamnett, (David) Gulpilil, Frederick Parslow, Vivean Gray, Nanjiwarra Amagula. Fascinating chiller about Australian lawyer (Chamberlain) defending aborigine accused of murder. Modern symbolism and ancient tribal rituals make for unusual and absorbing film. [PG]▼
Last Will of Dr. Mabuse, The SEE: **Testament of Dr. Mabuse, The**
Last Woman, The (1976-French) **C-112m.** ** D: Marco Ferreri. Gérard Depardieu, Ornella Muti, Michel Piccoli, Zouzou, Renato Salvatori, David Biffani, Nathalie Baye. Provocative subject matter is superficially handled in this pointlessly sensationalistic drama about macho, self-absorbed engineer Depardieu, insensitive to women and confused by a world of changing roles and relationships. His final act of self-mutilation is as ridiculous as it is shocking. [X]
Last Woman on Earth, The (1960) **C-71m.** BOMB D: Roger Corman. Antony Carbone, Edward Wain, Betsy Jones-Moreland. Dull three-cornered romance involving last survivors on earth after unexplained disaster. Screenplay by Robert Towne—his first. He also costars, using acting pseudonym Edward Wain. Vistascope.▼
Last Year at Marienbad (1961-French-Italian) **93m.** *** D: Alain Resnais. Delphine Seyrig, Giorgio Albertazzi, Sacha Pitoeff. Murky, difficult but oddly fascinating tale in which Albertazzi confronts bewildered Seyrig, claiming they'd had an affair "last year at Frederiksbad, or perhaps at Marienbad." An art-house hit in its day, beautifully photographed (by Sacha Vierny); scripted by Alain-Robbe Grillet. Dyaliscope.▼◗
Las Vegas Hillbillys (1966) **C-90m.** *½ D: Arthur C. Pierce. Ferlin Husky, Jayne Mansfield, Mamie Van Doren, Richard Kiel, Sonny James, Del Reeves, Bill Anderson, Connie Smith. How does country hick Husky become a big-time Las Vegas entrepreneur? You really don't want to know. A once-in-a-lifetime cast. Sequel: HILLBILLYS IN A HAUNTED HOUSE. ▼
Las Vegas Lady (1976) **C-87m.** BOMB D: Noel Nosseck. Stella Stevens, Stuart Whitman, George DiCenzo, Lynne Moody, Linda Scruggs, Joseph Della Sorte, Jesse White. Substandard heist pic about a security guard who flips for title femme. Even LAS VEGAS HILLBILLYS is better. [PG]▼
Las Vegas Shakedown (1955) **79m.** ** D: Sidney Salkow. Dennis O'Keefe, Coleen Gray, Charles Winninger, Thomas Gomez, Elizabeth Patterson, Robert Armstrong. Improbable yet diverting account of O'Keefe's effort to run an honest gambling house, with on-location filming in Las Vegas.▼
Las Vegas Story, The (1952) **88m.** ** D: Robert Stevenson. Jane Russell, Victor Mature, Vincent Price, Hoagy Carmichael, Brad Dexter. Synthetic murder yarn supposedly set in gambling capital, sparked by Russell's vitality.▼
La Symphonie Pastorale (1946-French) **105m.** ***½ D: Jean Delannoy. Pierre Blanchar, Michele Morgan, Jean Desailly, Line Noro, Andree Clement. Quietly powerful classic about pastor Blanchar's all-consuming passion for blind girl Morgan, whom he takes under his wing and educates. This sensitive study of moral and spiritual corruption was coscripted by the director, and based on an Andre Gide novel.▼
L.A. Takedown (1989) **C-100m. TVM** D: Michael Mann. Scott Plank, Alex McArthur, Vincent Guastaffero, Michael Rooker, Ely Pouget, Daniel Baldwin, Peter Dobson. Cop and thief engage in a violent cat-and-mouse game following a spectacular heist. Producer-director-writer Mann tried to bring same stylish approach to L.A. locations that he used for *Miami Vice.* Series pilot that didn't make it. Mann reworked this as the theatrical HEAT in 1995. Average.
L'Atalante (1934-French) **89m.** **** D: Jean Vigo. Michel Simon, Dita Parlo, Jean Dasté, Gilles Margaritis, Louis Lefèvre, Diligent Raya. Naturalism and surrealist fantasy blend beautifully in all-time masterpiece about a young couple who begin their life together sailing down the Seine on a barge. Ultimate in romantic cinema also anticipated neorealist movement by more than a decade; Vigo died at 29, just as film premiered. Restored in 1990 to its

full length; avoid 82m. version, which circulated for years.▼

Late August, Early September (1999-French) **C-112m.** *** D: Olivier Assayas. Mathieu Amalric, Virginie Ledoyen, François Cluzet, Jeanne Balibar, Arsinée Khanjian, Alex Descas, Nathalie Richard. Bittersweet, subtly rendered slice of life about various friends, lovers, and acquaintances who are unable to set down roots—professionally, personally, or romantically. The specter of mortality hangs over the proceedings as one of them, a novelist (Cluzet) who has just turned forty, suffers from an unnamed illness. A heartfelt and potent portrait of self-involvement and emotional stagnation.▼

Late Autumn (1960-Japanese) **C-127m.** *** D: Yasujiro Ozu. Setsuko Hara, Yoko Tsukasa, Mariko Okada, Keiji Sada, Shin Saburi. Widowed Hara seeks a husband for unmarried daughter Tsukasa. Solid Ozu drama reworking his LATE SPRING.

Late for Dinner (1991) **C-99m.** **½ D: W. D. Richter. Brian Wimmer, Peter Berg, Marcia Gay Harden, Peter Gallagher, Colleen Flynn, Kyle Secor, Michael Beach, Bo Brundin, Janeane Garofalo. Two friends, on the lam and in need of help, are frozen by a doctor who's experimenting with cryonics; when they're awakened twenty-nine years later, physically unchanged, they stumble to put their lives back together. Offbeat, to say the least, and movingly acted, but the transition from loopy comedy to deeply felt sentiment (in the film's denouement) doesn't quite come off. [PG]▼●

Late George Apley, The (1947) **98m.** *** D: Joseph L. Mankiewicz. Ronald Colman, Peggy Cummins, Vanessa Brown, Richard Haydn, Charles Russell, Richard Ney, Percy Waram, Mildred Natwick, Edna Best. John P. Marquand's gentle satire of Boston bluebloods is smoothly entertaining. Colman is perfectly cast as the stuffy patriarch who strives to uphold his family's social status.

Late Liz, The (1971) **C-119m.** BOMB D: Dick Ross. Anne Baxter, Steve Forrest, James Gregory, Coleen Gray, Joan Hotchkis, Jack Albertson. Campy drama about Baxter's rejection of alcohol due to religion is well-intentioned, but hardly convincing as presented here; viewers may need a good stiff drink by the time it's over. [PG]▼

La Terra Trema (1947-Italian) **160m.** **** D: Luchino Visconti. Narrated by Luchino Visconti, Antonio Pietrangeli. Powerful, lyrical neorealist classic about a poor family in a Sicilian fishing village, exploited by fish wholesalers and boat owners. Filmed on location, and in Sicilian dialect, with a non-professional cast. Francesco Rosi and Franco Zeffirelli were Visconti's assistant directors. Beware of severely edited versions.▼

Late Show, The (1977) **C-94m.** ***½ D: Robert Benton. Art Carney, Lily Tomlin, Bill Macy, Eugene Roche, Joanna Cassidy, John Considine, Howard Duff. Carney is an aging private eye who tries to solve murder of his ex-partner (Duff), "helped" by flaky, aimless young woman (Tomlin). Echoes of Chandler and Hammett resound in Benton's complex but likable script; chemistry between Carney and Tomlin is perfect. Later a short-lived TV series called *Eye to Eye*. [PG]▼●

Lathe of Heaven, The (1980) **C-105m. TVM** D: David Loxton, Fred Barzyk. Kevin Conway, Bruce Davison, Margaret Avery. Davison's dreams literally come true; egocentric Dr. Conway tries to manipulate him into eliminating war, racism, and illness. Interesting visual and laser effects do not compensate for lumbering, disconnected scenario. Based on Ursula K. LeGuin's futuristic novel. Made for PBS. Average.

Latin Lovers (1953) **C-104m.** **½ D: Mervyn LeRoy. Lana Turner, Ricardo Montalban, John Lund, Louis Calhern, Jean Hagen, Rita Moreno. Hokey romance yarn set in South America, with Turner seeking true love; pointless script.▼

Latino (1985) **C-105m.** *** D: Haskell Wexler. Robert Beltran, Annette Cardona, Tony Plana, Ricardo Lopez, Luis Torrentes, Juan Carlos Ortiz, Julio Medina, James Karen. Gut-wrenching drama of Vietnam replayed, with Chicano Green Beret Beltran "advising" the U.S.-backed Contras in their war against the Sandanistas in Nicaragua. Unabashedly left-wing; to some it will be propaganda, while to others it will be truth. Striking direction with a fine sense of irony; however, Beltran's relationship with Cardona just doesn't ring true. Filmed in Nicaragua; Wexler's first "fiction" film since MEDIUM COOL in 1969.▼●

Latitude Zero (1969-Japanese) **C-99m.** ** D: Ishiro Honda. Joseph Cotten, Cesar Romero, Richard Jaeckel, Patricia Medina, Linda Haynes, Akira Takarada. Better than average imported cast helps usual wide-eyed sci-fi adventure of underwater civilization of benevolent geniuses fighting legions of Malic (Romero), out to control world. Some good sets, but action and suspense poorly handled. Based on the old (American) radio series. Tohoscope. [G]

L'Atlantide SEE: **Journey Beneath the Desert**

La Traviata (1982-Italian) **C-112m.** **** D: Franco Zeffirelli. Teresa Stratas, Placido Domingo, Cornell MacNeil, Alan Monk, Axelle Gail. Verdi's opera, adapted from the Alexandre Dumas *Camille* saga, makes a magnificent film. If Domingo looks too old for Alfredo, he still sings beautifully, while Stratas's performance as the tragic Violetta matches her brilliant voice. The cinematography and production design are the equal of anything from the Golden Age of moviemaking in a film that even those who dislike opera will enjoy. [G]▼●

La Truite SEE: **Trout, The**

Laughing Policeman, The (1974) **C-111m.** **½ D: Stuart Rosenberg. Walter Matthau, Bruce Dern, Lou Gossett, Albert Paulsen, Anthony Zerbe, Anthony Costello, Cathy Lee Crosby, Joanna Cassidy. Reasonably engrossing San Francisco cop drama about search for mass slayer of bus passengers. Matthau and Dern are good as cops with contrasting styles. Based on the Martin Beck novel by Maj Sjowall and Per Wahloo. [R]▼

Laughing Sinners (1931) **72m.** ** D: Harry Beaumont. Joan Crawford, Clark Gable, Neil Hamilton, John Mack Brown, Marjorie Rambeau, Guy Kibbee, Roscoe Karns. Crawford attempts suicide after Hamilton dumps her; Salvation Army preacher Gable (!) stops her. The rest is predictable.▼

Laughter (1930) **81m.** **½ D: Harry D'Arrast. Nancy Carroll, Fredric March, Frank Morgan, Leonard Carey. Lumpy film with a few bright sequences about Follies girl Carroll marrying millionaire but finding life empty, unhappy.

Laughter in Paradise (1951-British) **95m.** **½ D: Mario Zampi. Alastair Sim, Joyce Grenfell, Hugh Griffith, Fay Compton, John Laurie. Notorious practical joker dies, and leaves hefty sum to four relatives if they will carry out his devilish instructions. Pleasant little comedy. Audrey Hepburn appears fleetingly as cigarette girl. Remade in 1969 as SOME WILL, SOME WON'T.

Laughter in the Dark (1969-British) **C-101m.** *½ D: Tony Richardson. Nicol Williamson, Anna Karina, Jean-Claude Drouot, Peter Bowles, Sian Phillips. Excruciating film from Nabokov novel about wealthy married man (Williamson) whose fascination with young girl (Karina) backfires at every turn, eventually ruining his life. Exceedingly unpleasant, and seemingly interminable. [X]

Laura (1944) **85m.** **** D: Otto Preminger. Gene Tierney, Dana Andrews, Clifton Webb, Vincent Price, Judith Anderson, Grant Mitchell, Lane Chandler, Dorothy Adams. Classic mystery with gorgeous Tierney subject of murder plot; detective Andrews trying to assemble crime puzzle. Fascinating, witty, classic, with Webb a standout as cynical columnist Waldo Lydecker and Price in his finest non-horror performance as suave Southern gigolo. Based on the Vera Caspary novel; also features David Raksin's theme. Rouben Mamoulian started directing film, Preminger took over. Screenplay by Jay Dratler, Samuel Hoffenstein, and Betty Reinhardt. Joseph LaShelle's cinematography earned an Oscar. Several minutes of dialogue were cut from all prints after initial release; this footage has been restored on home video.▼●

Laurel and Hardy's Laughing 20's (1965) **90m.** ***½ Compiled by Robert Youngson. Stan Laurel, Oliver Hardy, Charley Chase, Edgar Kennedy, James Finlayson, Anita Garvin. Some of L&H's best moments on film are included, with everything from pie-throwing to pants-ripping. Also some excellent sequences of Charley Chase, adding to the fun.▼●

Lavender Hill Mob, The (1951-British) **82m.** ***½ D: Charles Crichton. Alec Guinness, Stanley Holloway, Sidney James, Alfie Bass, Marjorie Fielding, John Gregson, Edie Martin. Excellent comedy with droll Guinness a timid bank clerk who has perfect scheme for robbing a gold bullion truck, with a madcap chase climax. Won an Oscar for Best Story and Screenplay (T. E. B. Clarke); look for Audrey Hepburn in opening scene.▼●

La Venexiana SEE: **Venetian Woman, The**

La Viaccia (1962-Italian) **103m.** **½ D: Mauro Bolognini. Jean-Paul Belmondo, Claudia Cardinale, Pietro Germi, Romolo Valli, Gabriella Pallotta, Gina Sammarco. Zesty yarn of country youth finding romance in the city with prostitute. Retitled: THE LOVEMAKERS.

La Vie Continue (1982-French) **C-93m.** *½ D: Moshe Mizrahi. Annie Girardot, Jean-Pierre Cassel, Pierre Dux, Giulia Salvatori, Emmanuel Gayet, Rivera Andres. Dreary sudser wastes Girardot as middle-aged woman whose husband suddenly drops dead of a heart attack; she struggles with her new-found widowhood. Loosely remade in U.S. as MEN DON'T LEAVE. [PG]▼

La Vie de Bohème (1992-Finnish-French-Swedish-German) **100m.** *** D: Aki Kaurismaki. Matti Pellonpaa, Andre Wilms, Kari Vaananen, Christine Murillo, Evelyne Didi, Samuel Fuller, Louis Malle, Jean-Pierre Léaud. Pleasantly offbeat comic/absurdist slice-of-life about three poor, struggling artists: a painter, composer and writer. While at best mediocre talent-wise, each is dedicated to the artistic life and values his books, piano, or paint over all else. A loose updating of a novel by Henri Murger, which was the inspiration for Puccini's *La Bohème*. ▼

La Vie de Chateau SEE: **Matter of Resistance, A**

La Vie Privée SEE: **Very Private Affair, A**

L'Avventura (1960-French-Italian) **145m.** ***½ D: Michelangelo Antonioni. Monica Vitti, Gabriele Ferzetti, Lea Massari, Dominique Blanchar, James Addams. Massari mysteriously disappears on an uninhabited island after arguing with boyfriend Ferzetti, impelling him and her friend Vitti to look for her. Subtle, incisive allegory of spiritual and moral decay makes for demanding viewing. Antonioni's first international suc-

cess was also the first of a trilogy (followed by LA NOTTE and L'ECLISSE).▼●
Law and Disorder (1958-British) **76m.** **½ D: Charles Crichton. Michael Redgrave, Robert Morley, Ronald Squire, Elizabeth Sellars. Brisk comedy of con-man who gives up crime to avoid embarrassment of making up stories to tell prim son.
Law and Disorder (1974) **C-103m.** *** D: Ivan Passer. Carroll O'Connor, Ernest Borgnine, Ann Wedgeworth, Anita Dangler, Leslie Ackerman, Karen Black, Jack Kehoe. Intelligent, original comedy-drama of two middle-aged New Yorkers incensed at rising crime who become auxiliary cops. At first they treat it as a lark, but soon it becomes deadly serious. Full of fine perceptions, interesting vignettes. [R]▼
Law and Jake Wade, The (1958) **C-86m.** *** D: John Sturges. Robert Taylor, Richard Widmark, Patricia Owens, Robert Middleton. Robust Western of outlaw forcing his cohort-turned-good to lead him to buried loot. Taylor and Widmark make good adversaries. CinemaScope.▼
Law and Order (1932) **70m.** ***½ D: Edward L. Cahn. Walter Huston, Harry Carey, Raymond Hatton, Russell Hopton, Ralph Ince, Andy Devine, Walter Brennan. Exceptional Western that takes a familiar story (Wyatt Earp and Doc Holliday vs. the Clantons) and reworks it with style but no flourishes. Huston plays Saint Johnson, gunslinger and lawman. Stark, realistic, with a knockout finale. Coscripted by John Huston. Remade in 1953.
Law and Order (1953) **C-80m.** ** D: Nathan Juran. Ronald Reagan, Dorothy Malone, Alex Nicol, Preston Foster, Ruth Hampton, Russell Johnson, Dennis Weaver, Jack Kelly. Lawman Reagan wants to retire to marry Malone, but first must tame bad guy Foster. Standard Western was filmed far more successfully in 1932.▼
Law and the Lady, The (1951) **104m.** **½ D: Edwin H. Knopf. Greer Garson, Michael Wilding, Fernando Lamas, Marjorie Main, Hayden Rorke, Margalo Gillmore. Stylish if standard remake of THE LAST OF MRS. CHEYNEY with Garson (gowned by Cecil Beaton) teaming up with Wilding for slick society jewel robberies.
Law Is the Law, The (1959-French) **103m.** **½ D: Christian-Jaque. Fernandel, Toto, Mario Besozzi, René Genin. Two top Continental comedians work well together in yarn of French customs official and his pal who smuggle items over the border.
Lawless, The (1950) **83m.** ** D: Joseph Losey. Gail Russell, Macdonald Carey, Lalo Rios, Lee Patrick, John Sands, Martha Hyer. Vaguely interesting study of Mexican-American fruit-pickers in Southern California, with facets of racial discrimination pointed out.
Lawless Breed, The (1952) **C-83m.** *** D: Raoul Walsh. Rock Hudson, Julia Adams, John McIntire, Mary Castle, Hugh O'Brian, Lee Van Cleef, Dennis Weaver, Michael Ansara. Solid Western drama that recounts the life and times of legendary (and misunderstood) outlaw John Wesley Hardin (well played by Hudson, in his starring debut).▼
Lawless Eighties, The (1957) **70m.** ** D: Joseph Kane. Buster Crabbe, John Smith, Ted de Corsia, Marilyn Saris. Average oater about a gunfighter who protects a circuit rider harassed by hoodlums. Filmed in Naturama.
Lawless Street, A (1955) **C-78m.** **½ D: Joseph H. Lewis. Randolph Scott, Angela Lansbury, Warner Anderson, Jean Parker, Wallace Ford, Ruth Donnelly, Michael Pate. Hard-bitten marshal Scott tries to eliminate evil forces from western town, then confronts his bittersweet past when musical star Lansbury comes to town. Entertaining Western with disappointing resolution.▼
Lawman (1971) **C-98m.** *** D: Michael Winner. Burt Lancaster, Robert Ryan, Lee J. Cobb, Robert Duvall, Sheree North, Albert Salmi, Joseph Wiseman, J.D. Cannon, Richard Jordan, John McGiver, Ralph Waite, John Beck, John Hillerman. Intriguing thought-Western about stoic marshal (Lancaster) who comes into unfamiliar town to bring back wanted men, refusing to sway from duty even though entire town turns against him. Unsatisfactory resolution mars otherwise compelling story; Ryan gives one of his finest performances as timid sheriff. [PG]▼
Lawn Dogs (1998-U.S.-British) **C-100m.** **½ D: John Duigan. Kathleen Quinlan, Sam Rockwell, Christopher McDonald, Bruce McGill, Tom Aldredge, Mischa Barton. Odd but intriguing story of the unlikely relationship that develops between a misfit kid who lives in an antiseptic, gate-guarded community, and a drop-out gardener who grew up in the area but has long been an outcast in the community. Sometimes uneasy mix of black comedy and social satire, but marked by good performances and a piquant sense of humor. [R]▼●◗
Lawnmower Man, The (1992) **C-105m.** *½ D: Brett Leonard. Jeff Fahey, Pierce Brosnan, Jenny Wright, Mark Bringleson, Geoffrey Lewis, Jeremy Slate, Dean Norris, Austin O'Brien. Scientist Brosnan needs a guinea pig for hitherto failed experiments in drug therapy and computer instruction; who better than the grinning mental defective who mows his lawn? At least the pyrotechnics at the end (simulating "virtual reality") are full of visual buzz. Fahey in a blond wig is really tough to take. Has nothing to do with the Stephen King short story it's ostensibly based on. Director's cut, available on video, has more than 30m. of additional footage. Followed by a sequel. [R]▼●◗
Lawnmower Man 2: Beyond Cyberspace

(1996-U.S.-British-Japanese) **C-93m.** ** D: Farhad Mann. Patrick Bergin, Matt Frewer, Austin O'Brien, Ely Pouget, Camille Cooper, Patrick La Brecque, Crystal Celeste Grant, Kevin Conway. Moron-turned-genius Jobe is back, still intent on ruling the world from cyberspace. This involves ruthless billionaire Conway, reclusive computer expert Bergin, doctor Pouget, and young O'Brien, returning from the original film. The plot is both complicated and simpleminded, and aimed primarily at teenage computer fans—but the standardized BLADE RUNNER future, routine action, and only intermittent computer graphics will likely leave them as disinterested as everyone else. Aka: LAWNMOWER MAN 2: JOBE'S WAR. Panavision. [PG-13]▼●◗

Law of Desire (1987-Spanish) **C-100m.** *** D: Pedro Almodóvar. Eusebio Poncela, Carmen Maura, Antonio Banderas, Miguel Molina, Bibi Andersson, Manuela Velasco, Nacho Martinez. Surreal, hedonistic, and hilarious comedy focusing on a gay love triangle, with equal doses of passion, sex, fantasy, and tragedy. Maura is a standout as a free-spirited transsexual; Almodóvar is one of the brightest talents to emerge on the international filmmaking scene during the 1980s.▼●

Law of the Lawless (1964) **C-88m.** **½ D: William F. Claxton. Dale Robertson, Yvonne De Carlo, William Bendix, Bruce Cabot, Richard Arlen, John Agar, Lon Chaney (Jr.), Kent Taylor. Veteran cast is chief interest here, with Robertson an ex-gunman turned judge. Techniscope.

Law of the Tropics (1941) **76m.** ** D: Ray Enright. Constance Bennett, Jeffrey Lynn, Regis Toomey, Mona Maris, Hobart Bosworth. Fair cast in routine drama of man discovering his wife is accused murderess. Remake of OIL FOR THE LAMPS OF CHINA.

Lawrence of Arabia (1962-British) **C-216m.** **** D: David Lean. Peter O'-Toole, Alec Guinness, Anthony Quinn, Jack Hawkins, Claude Rains, Anthony Quayle, Arthur Kennedy, Omar Sharif, Jose Ferrer. Blockbuster biography of enigmatic adventurer T. E. Lawrence is that rarity, an epic film that is also literate. Loses some momentum in the second half, but still a knockout—especially in 1989 reissue version, which restored many cuts made over the years (and made a few judicious trims in the process). Still, the only way to really appreciate this film is on a big screen. Screenplay by Robert Bolt and Michael Wilson, based on Lawrence's book *The Seven Pillars of Wisdom.* Seven Oscars include Best Picture, Director, Cinematography (Freddie Young), Score (Maurice Jarre), Editing, and Art Direction. O'Toole's first leading role made him an instant star. Beware of shorter prints. Originally 222m. Super Panavision 70. ▼●

Laws of Gravity (1991) **C-100m.** *** D: Nick Gomez. Peter Greene, Adam Trese, Edie Falco, Arabella Field, Paul Schulzie. Intense, vivid chronicle of three momentous days in the lives of a pair of young blue-collar Brooklyn thieves and their girlfriends. Shot on a minuscule budget, and distinguished by gritty, Scorsese-like realism. The performances are collectively terrific, and Jean de Segonzac's hand-held camera is a major plus. [R]▼

Law vs. Billy the Kid, The (1954) **C-73m.** ** D: William Castle. Scott Brady, Betta St. John, James Griffith, Alan Hale, Jr., Paul Cavanagh. Title gives away plot line of unmemorable Western.

Lawyer, The (1970) **C-117m.** **½ D: Sidney J. Furie. Barry Newman, Harold Gould, Diana Muldaur, Robert Colbert, Kathleen Crowley. Lively story loosely based on famous Dr. Sam Sheppard murder case; Newman is stubborn young lawyer defending doctor accused of murdering his wife, battling legal protocol and uncooperative client. Unexceptional but diverting; Newman later revived role in TV series *Petrocelli.* [R]

Lawyer Man (1932) **72m.** *** D: William Dieterle. William Powell, Joan Blondell, Claire Dodd, Sheila Terry, Alan Dinehart, David Landau, Helen Vinson, Allen Jenkins, Roscoe Karns, Sterling Holloway. Powell is aces in this amusing pre-Code drama as an ambitious lawyer—with a near-fatal eye for the ladies—who tangles with crooked politicians. Blondell is his loyal, lovesick secretary. Powell even speaks Yiddish in this one.

Lay That Rifle Down (1955) **71m.** *½ D: Charles Lamont. Judy Canova, Robert Lowery, Jacqueline de Wit, Jil Jarmyn, Richard Deacon, Tweeny Canova. Mild Cinderella story featuring Canova as an overworked drudge who finds herself contending with a nasty aunt, a greedy banker, and a pair of swindlers.▼

Lazybones (1925) **79m.** *** D: Frank Borzage. Charles "Buck" Jones, Madge Bellamy, Virginia Marshall, Edythe Chapman, Leslie Fenton, ZaSu Pitts. Story of endearing but aimless character, his romances, and the path life takes him down as years go by. Poignant evocation of small-town life from turn of the century into the 1920s. Unusual role for Jones, better known as cowboy hero.

Leadbelly (1976) **C-126m.** ***½ D: Gordon Parks. Roger E. Mosley, Paul Benjamin, Madge Sinclair, Alan Manson, Albert P. Hall, Art Evans, Loretta Greene. Poignant biography of the legendary folksinger Huddie Ledbetter, master of the 12-string guitar and long-time convict on Texas and Louisiana chain gangs. Stunning musical performances (including "Rock Island

Line," "Goodnight Irene" and many more classics), with Mosley effectively restrained in the title role. Superior entertainment. [PG]
Leader of the Band (1987) **C-90m.** ** D: Nessa Hyams. Steve Landesberg, Mercedes Ruehl, Gailard Sartain, James Martinez, Calvert DeForest (Larry "Bud" Melman). Clichés abound in this innocuous tale of unemployed musician Landesberg whipping an inept high school marching band into shape. [PG]▼●
Leading Man, The (1997-British) **C-100m.** *** D: John Duigan. Jon Bon Jovi, Anna Galiena, Lambert Wilson, Thandie Newton, Barry Humphries, David Warner. British backstage theater romance about an American movie star who seduces a playwright's lonely wife and his leading-lady mistress. While it can't quite make up its mind whether it's a comic drama or a light thriller, it's still very entertaining stuff. Bon Jovi is surprisingly good as the brash, amoral Yankee, and Galiena and Newton are fetching as the women caught in his web. [R]▼●
League of Frightened Men, The (1937) **65m.** ** D: Alfred E. Green. Walter Connolly, Lionel Stander, Eduardo Ciannelli, Irene Hervey, Victor Kilian, Walter Kingsford. Second Nero Wolfe film casts relatively amiable Connolly in the role of Rex Stout's sleuth for a none-too-inscrutable mystery about a band of former college chums who are being killed off one by one.
League of Gentlemen, The (1960-British) **114m.** ***½ D: Basil Dearden. Jack Hawkins, Nigel Patrick, Roger Livesey, Richard Attenborough, Bryan Forbes, Kieron Moore, Robert Coote, Nanette Newman. Ex-army colonel enlists the aid of former officers (through blackmail) to pull off big bank heist. High-class British humor makes this tale of crime a delight. Forbes also wrote the script. Look for Oliver Reed as a ballet dancer!▼●
League of Their Own, A (1992) **C-128m.** *** D: Penny Marshall. Tom Hanks, Geena Davis, Madonna, Lori Petty, Jon Lovitz, David Strathairn, Garry Marshall, Megan Cavanagh, Rosie O'Donnell, Renee Coleman, Ann Cusack, Tracy Reiner, Janet Jones, Tea Leoni, Bill Pullman. Thoroughly entertaining comedy about the women's baseball league that sprang up when male ballplayers were off fighting in WW2. Davis and Madonna stand out in a first-rate cast, with Hanks giving a terrific comedy performance as the drunken ex-baseball star who manages their team. Good-natured fiction that sheds light on a neglected chapter of real-life sports history. Later, briefly a TV series. Panavision. [PG]▼●◗
Lean on Me (1989) **C-109m.** **½ D: John G. Avildsen. Morgan Freeman, Beverly Todd, Robert Guillaume, Alan North, Lynne Thigpen, Robin Bartlett, Michael Beach, Ethan Phillips, Regina Taylor. The story of "Crazy Joe" Clark, the real-life baseball bat, bullhorn toting high school principal from New Jersey who whips his students into shape by alternately bolstering and bullying them. Freeman is riveting in the central role, making up for script's shortcomings and Avildsen's all-too-familiar approach. [PG-13]▼●◗
Leap Into the Void (1979-Italian) **C-120m.** *** D: Marco Bellocchio. Michel Piccoli, Anouk Aimée, Michele Placido, Gisella Burinato, Antonio Piovanelli. A compassionate comedy about a very unusual topic: suicide. Magistrate Piccoli uses Placido to try to induce his mentally ill sister (Aimee) to do herself in. Of course, things do not go as planned.
Leap of Faith (1992) **C-108m.** **½ D: Richard Pearce. Steve Martin, Debra Winger, Lolita Davidovich, Liam Neeson, Lukas Haas, Meat Loaf, Philip Seymour Hoffman, M. C. Gainey, La Chanze, Delores Hall, John Toles-Bey, Albertina Walker, Ricky Dillard. Nicely textured look at an evangelist's traveling tent show—though Martin is never credible as a religious pitchman who connects with his gullible audiences. Director Pearce has a keen eye for detail and atmosphere, but the film's story flaws are hard to overlook. The real treat: watching Winger as Martin's savvy partner in-crime. [PG-13]▼●
Learning Tree, The (1969) **C-107m.** **½ D: Gordon Parks. Kyle Johnson, Alex Clarke, Estelle Evans, Dana Elcar, Mita Waters. Parks called virtually every shot in brilliantly photographed but surprisingly mild film version of his autobiographical novel about young black growing up in Kansas. Film's appeal lies more in its intentions than in what it actually accomplishes. Panavision. [M/PG]▼
Lease of Life (1954-British) **C-94m.** **½ D: Charles Frend. Robert Donat, Kay Walsh, Denholm Elliott, Adrienne Corri, Cyril Raymond. Donat makes anything worth watching, even this mild tale of poor-but-honest country vicar with one year to live, struggling to make ends meet and maintain his integrity.
Leather Boys, The (1963-British) **105m.** *** D: Sidney J. Furie. Rita Tushingham, Colin Campbell, Dudley Sutton, Gladys Henson. Uncompromising study of impulsive Tushingham's incompatible marriage to motorcycle-loving mechanic, focusing on their opposing viewpoints and sleazy environment. Released in U.S. in 1966. CinemaScope.▼
Leatherface: Texas Chainsaw Massacre III (1990) **C-81m.** *½ D: Jeff Burr. Kate Hodge, Ken Foree, R. A. Mihailoff, Viggo Mortensen, William Butler, Joe Unger. Mostly a remake of the first film: cannibal clan battles three would-be dinners. Severely damaged by prerelease cuts designed

to reduce gore but which only make the film incoherent. Followed by TEXAS CHAINSAW MASSACRE: THE NEXT GENERATION. [R]▼●

Leather Gloves (1948) **75m.** ** D: Richard Quine, William Asher. Cameron Mitchell, Virginia Grey, Sam Levene, Jane Nigh, Henry O'Neill, Blake Edwards. Fight flick about on-the-skids boxer Mitchell lacks sufficient punch to push over clichés.

Leather Jackets (1991) **C-90m.** BOMB D: Lee Drysdale. D. B. Sweeney, Bridget Fonda, Cary Elwes, Craig Ng, Marshall Bell, Christopher Penn, Jon Polito, James LeGros, Neil Giuntoli. Leather-jacketed Elwes and friends rip off and murder a Vietnamese mob bagman, whose associates vow vengeance—and plenty of it. Newly engaged Sweeney and Fonda try to help, and get caught in the crossfire, which they deserve for being in such a turkey. What a bloody mess! [R]▼●

Leathernecks Have Landed, The (1936) **68m.** **½ D: Howard Bretherton. Lew Ayres, Isabel Jewell, Jimmy Ellison, James Burke, J. Carrol Naish, Ward Bond, Henry Mowbray. Enjoyable B-picture fare about Marine (Ayres) who, with help of beauty Jewell, starts running guns to rebel forces in Shanghai. Written by Seton I. Miller.

Leather Saint, The (1956) **86m.** **½ D: Alvin Ganzer. Paul Douglas, John Derek, Jody Lawrance, Cesar Romero, Ernest Truex. Forthright account of clergyman who becomes a boxer to earn money to help congregation. VistaVision.

Leave All Fair (1985-New Zealand) **C-88m.** *** D: John Reid. John Gielgud, Jane Birkin, Feodor Atkine, Simon Ward. Intelligent, rewarding account of the elderly John Middleton Murry (Gielgud), husband and editor of Katherine Mansfield, and his manipulative relationship with her. She's portrayed in flashback by Birkin, who also appears as a young woman who reminds Murry of her. Stick with this one.

Leave Her to Heaven (1945) **C-110m.** *** D: John M. Stahl. Gene Tierney, Cornel Wilde, Jeanne Crain, Vincent Price, Mary Philips, Ray Collins, Darryl Hickman, Gene Lockhart. Tierney's mother says, "There's nothing wrong with Ellen. It's just that she loves too much." In fact, she loves some people to death! Slick trash, expertly handled all around with Tierney breathtakingly photographed in Technicolor by Oscar-winner Leon Shamroy. And how about those incredible homes in New Mexico and Maine! Remade for TV as TOO GOOD TO BE TRUE in 1988.▼●

Leave It to Beaver (1997) **C-89m.** *** D: Andy Cadiff. Christopher McDonald, Janine Turner, Cameron Finley, Erik von Detten, Adam Zolotin, Barbara Billingsley, Ken Osmond, Frank Bank, Erika Christensen, Alan Rachins. Cute family comedy based on the vintage TV series, with Finley an appealing Theodore Cleaver, for whom things never seem to go quite right . . . especially when he volunteers to play football in order to please his dad. Brother Wally (who experiences his first taste of puppy love) and unctuous Eddie Haskell are here, too. Billingsley, Osmond, and Bank (June, Eddie, and Lumpy from the original show) make token appearances. [PG]▼●◗

Leave It to Blondie (1945) **75m.** ** D: Abby Berlin. Penny Singleton, Arthur Lake, Larry Simms, Marjorie Kent, Jonathan Hale, Chick Chandler, Marjorie Ann Mutchie, Danny Mummert, Eddie Acuff, Jack Rice. The Bumsteads enter a songwriting contest in this trivial *Blondie* entry.▼

Leave It to Henry (1949) **57m.** *½ D: Jean Yarbrough. Raymond Walburn, Walter Catlett, Gary Gray, Mary Stuart. Quickie film has Walburn destroying the town bridge when son is fired as toll-booth collector. Second in a B-picture series, followed by FATHER MAKES GOOD.

Leaving Las Vegas (1995) **C-111m.** ***½ D: Mike Figgis. Nicolas Cage, Elisabeth Shue, Julian Sands, Richard Lewis, Steven Weber, Valeria Golino, Graham Beckel, Carey Lowell, R. Lee Ermey, Mariska Hargitay, Laurie Metcalf, Julian Lennon, Lou Rawls, Ed Lauter, Xander Berkeley, Susan Barnes. Cage is a hopeless alcoholic who moves to Las Vegas, determined to drink himself to death, while Shue is a prostitute who demeans herself on a nightly basis. Their attachment to one another (and their willingness to accept each other as they are) makes this an unusually powerful and moving love story, in spite of the seamy trappings. Cage and Shue give brave, honest performances (Cage won the Best Actor Oscar). Figgis scripted from John O'Brien's novel, and also composed the score, with vocals by Sting. Ironically, O'Brien committed suicide after selling the movie rights to his book. [R] ▼●◗

Leaving Normal (1992) **C-110m.** **½ D: Edward Zwick. Christine Lahti, Meg Tilly, Lenny Von Dohlen, Maury Chaykin, James Gammon, Patrika Darbo, Eve Gordon, James Eckhouse, Brett Cullen, Rutanya Alda. An aggressively cynical cocktail waitress and her quieter, twice-wed friend take off for Alaska after failing to find fulfillment in Normal, Wyoming. Smug collection of on-the-road episodes fails to build a solid foundation, though the film does improve marginally once the characters settle down at their destination. Tilly is well cast, and Lahti is atypically insufferable. Cinematographer Ralf Bode's color vistas help. [R]▼●

Le Bal (1982-Italian-French) **C-112m.** *** D: Ettore Scola. Christophe Allwright, Marc Berman, Regis Bouquet, Chantal Capron, Nani Noel, Jean-Francois Perrier, Danielle Rochard. Original, stylish panorama of life, love, loneliness, war and peace, from the mid-30s to 80s. Set in a ballroom, with no major characters; the actors play different roles, in different time periods. No dialogue, just music and sound effects. Quite different, to state the obvious, but most definitely worthwhile.▼

Le Beau Mariage (1982-French) **C-97m.** ***½ D: Eric Rohmer. Beatrice Romand, Andre Dussollier, Feodor Atkine, Hugette Faget, Arielle Dombasle. Headstrong young woman rather arbitrarily decides she will be married (to no one in particular), initiates an embarrassing pursuit of male with other ideas. If you can accept this hard-to-swallow premise, film is a beautifully acted comedy of humiliation. Romand, incidentally, is the now-grown-up adolescent from Rohmer's CLAIRE'S KNEE, made 11 years earlier. [PG]▼

Le Beau Serge (1958-French) **97m.** *** D: Claude Chabrol. Jean-Claude Brialy, Gérard Blain, Michele Meritz, Bernadette Lafont, Edmond Beauchamp. Considered to be the first New Wave film, this rural tale also marked the feature directing debut of *Cahiers du Cinéma* film critic Claude Chabrol. When Brialy returns to his tiny home town, he is stunned to find how drastically his old school chum (Blain) has changed. Perceptive examination of the trials of life in a poor farming community and the moral questions raised by how one treats a friend. Brialy, Blain, and young Lafont (a teenaged nymphet) continued to collaborate with Chabrol (who also wrote and produced) for three decades.▼

Le Bonheur (1965-French) **C-87m.** **½ D: Agnés Varda. Jean-Claude Drouot, Claire Drouot, Sandrine Drouot, Oliver Drouot, Marie-France Boyer. Happily married carpenter Drouot falls for postal clerk Boyer, feels he can love both her and wife and they will share him. Intriguing, but emotionally uninvolving and unbelievable. Drouot's real wife and children portray his cinematic spouse and offspring. Aka HAPPINESS.▼

Le Boucher (1969-French-Italian) **C-93m.** *** D: Claude Chabrol. Stephane Audran, Jean Yanne, Antonio Passallia, Mario Beccaria, Pasquale Ferone. Another good psychological thriller from Chabrol, focusing on sympathetic murderer and his relationship with beautiful schoolteacher in small French village. Aka THE BUTCHER. [PG] ▼●

Le Caviar Rouge (1985-French-Swiss) **C-91m.** ** D: Robert Hossein. Robert Hossein, Candice Patou, Ivan Desny. Well-photographed but cold and lifeless three-character drama of spies Hossein and Patou (his real-life wife) spending a long night together in Geneva under Russian spy boss Desny's supervision to determine who is a turncoat. A very glum ending doesn't help. Though not a remake, film closely resembles the format of Hossein's 1959 drama NIGHT ENCOUNTER. [PG]

L'Eclisse SEE: **Eclipse**

Le Confessionale (1995-Canadian-British-French) **C-100m.** **½ D: Robert Lepage. Lothaire Bluteau, Patrick Goyette, Jean-Louis Millette, Kristin Scott Thomas, Richard Frechette; Marie Gignac. Elaborate, challenging, but only intermittently successful tale which intercuts two scenarios set years apart, involving a pregnant adolescent in 1952 Quebec (as Alfred Hitchcock is in town shooting I CONFESS) who is determined not to reveal her lover's identity, and the adopted brother (Bluteau) of her natural father. Fluidly directed, with clever visual references to Hitch, but the result somehow seems disconnected and unnecessarily complex. Worth a look, especially for Hitchcock aficionados. Stage director Lepage's debut feature; he also scripted.▼

Le Corbeau (1943-French) **92m.** ***½ D: Henri-Georges Clouzot. Pierre Fresnay, Ginette Leclerc, Helena Manson, Noel Roquevert, Sylvie, Louis Seigner. Ingenious suspenser detailing what happens when a series of mysterious poison pen letters begins circulating in a small French town. Quite controversial in its day, because it was financed by a German movie company and considered to be anti-French propaganda. Remade in Hollywood as THE 13TH LETTER. Aka THE RAVEN.▼

Le Crabe Tambour (1977-French) **C-120m.** ***½ D: Pierre Schoendoerffer. Jean Rochefort, Claude Rich, Jacques Dufilho, Jacques Perrin, Odile Versois, Aurore Clement. Expertly directed, detailed chronicle, mostly told in flashback, of the complex relationship between dying naval captain Rochefort and legendary officer Perrin, a character out of *Soldier of Fortune* magazine. Both, along with Rich as the doctor and Dufilho as the chief engineer, offer top-notch performances, and Raoul Coutard's cinematography is breathtaking.▼●

Leda SEE: **Web of Passion**

Le Dernier Combat (1984-French) **90m.** ** D: Luc Besson. Pierre Jolivet, Jean Bouise, Fritz Wepper, Christiane Kruger, Jean Reno. Wildly overpraised science-fiction film is basically another post-apocalypse epic. Jolivet is curious survivor wandering around a devastated landscape having odd, pointless encounters with strange people. Novelty item is without dialogue, in black and white, with stereo sound, but CinemaScope widescreen visuals are lost on TV. [R]▼

Leech Woman, The (1960) **77m.** *½ D: Edward Dein. Coleen Gray, Grant Williams, Philip Terry, Gloria Talbott, John Van Dreelen. In Africa, an aging woman obtains power that restores her youth, but requires her to murder—including her rotten husband. Back in L.A. it's more of the same. Gray is very good; the movie isn't.▼●

Left-Handed Gun, The (1958) **102m.** **½ D: Arthur Penn. Paul Newman, Lita Milan, John Dehner, Hurd Hatfield. Faltering psychological Western dealing with Billy the Kid's career, method-acted by Newman. Penn's first feature, based on a 1955 *Philco Playhouse* TV play by Gore Vidal in which Newman starred. See also GORE VIDAL'S BILLY THE KID. ▼

Left-Handed Woman, The (1978-German) **C-119m.** ** D: Peter Handke. Edith Clever, Bruno Ganz, Michel Lonsdale, Markus Muhleisen, Angela Winkler, Ines de Longchamps, Bernhard Wicki, Gérard Depardieu. Clever, as The Woman, demands that husband Ganz leave her. He complies. Time passes . . . and the audience falls asleep.

Left Hand of God, The (1955) **C-87m.** *** D: Edward Dmytryk. Humphrey Bogart, Gene Tierney, Lee J. Cobb, Agnes Moorehead, E. G. Marshall, Benson Fong. Bogart manages to be convincing as American caught in post-WW2 China, posing as clergyman with diverting results. CinemaScope.▼

Left Right and Center (1959-British) **95m.** **½ D: Sidney Gilliat. Ian Carmichael, Patricia Bredin, Alastair Sim, Eric Barker. Simple, entertaining comedy about opponents in political campaign falling in love. Sim is hilarious, as always, as Carmichael's conniving uncle.

Legacy (1975) **90m.** **½ D: Karen Arthur. Joan Hotchkis, George McDaniel, Sean Allen, Dixie Lee. Original but flawed character study of pampered, pathetic upper-class woman (Hotchkis) going through the motions of her life. She role-plays, complains, masturbates in her bath, and eventually goes batty. Hotchkis, who wrote the screenplay and play on which it's based, is extraordinary; however, direction is sometimes static and finale is anti-climactic. [R]

Legacy, The (1979) **C-100m.** **½ D: Richard Marquand. Katharine Ross, Sam Elliott, John Standing, Ian Hogg, Margaret Tyzack, Charles Gray, Lee Montague, Roger Daltrey. Two Americans find themselves among group of people shanghaied to British mansion where strange deaths and an occult ceremony await. Acceptable fare for fans of this genre. Filmed in England; aka THE LEGACY OF MAGGIE WALSH. [R]▼

Legacy of Blood SEE: **Blood Legacy**

Legacy of Maggie Walsh, The SEE: **Legacy, The**

Legacy of Rage (1986-Hong Kong) **C-87m.** **½ D: Ronny Yu. Brandon Lee, Michael Wong, Regina Kent, Onno Boelee (Bolo Yeung), Tanya George, Wai-Man Chan, Randy Mang. Lee's debut film has him framed for the murder of a cop by a mobster "friend" who then tries to steal his fiancée; eight years later he's released from prison and is out for blood. Martial arts mayhem is surprisingly kept to a bare minimum in this imitation John Woo crime drama filled with gory shootouts, bone-crushing violence and hyperkinetic car chases and explosions.▼●◗

Legal Eagles (1986) **C-114m.** **½ D: Ivan Reitman. Robert Redford, Debra Winger, Daryl Hannah, Brian Dennehy, Terence Stamp, Steven Hill, David Clennon, John McMartin, Jennie Dundas, Roscoe Lee Browne, Christine Baranski, Jay Thomas. Underwritten, overproduced romantic comedy about assistant D.A. who becomes involved with flaky lawyer (Winger) and her even flakier client (Hannah). Redford's charisma is at its brightest, which helps make up for lack of spark between him and Winger, and film's other weaknesses. Commercial TV version of this film offers a completely different ending from the original theatrical movie! Panavision. [PG]▼●◗

Legalese (1998) **C-92m. TVM** D: Glenn Jordan. James Garner, Gina Gershon, Mary-Louise Parker, Edward Kerr, Kathleen Turner, Brian Doyle-Murray. Unscrupulous attorney Garner (at his latter-day best) uses a front—a green lawyer who becomes his protégé—to defend a wiggy actress in a high-profile murder case, calling the shots and manipulating the media. Sharp contemporary comedy. Turner plays an aggressive TV tabloid reporter. Billy Ray wrote the witty, rapid-fire script. Made for cable. Above average.▼

Legend (1985-British) **C-89m.** ** D: Ridley Scott. Tom Cruise, Mia Sara, Tim Curry, David Bennent, Alice Playten, Billy Barty. Lavishly mounted fantasy, in the Grimm's Fairy Tale mold, about the demon Darkness trying to gain control over young girl who represents absolute innocence. Incredibly handsome but story lacks momentum and characters are not well defined. Kids might enjoy it. Released in U.S. in 1986 with Tangerine Dream score; in Europe it runs 20 minutes longer with Jerry Goldsmith music. Panavision. [PG]▼●

Legendary Champions, The (1968) **77m.** *** D: Harry Chapin. Narrated by Norman Rose. Excellent documentary on boxing's heavyweight champions from 1882 to 1929.

Legendary Curse of Lemora SEE: **Lady Dracula**

Legend in Leotards SEE: **Return of Captain Invincible, The**

Legend of Billie Jean, The (1985) **C-96m.** ** D: Matthew Robbins. Helen Slater, Keith Gordon, Christian Slater, Richard Bradford, Peter Coyote, Martha Gehman, Dean Stockwell. Texas girl and her brother are implicated in a shooting; unjustly accused of other crimes, they run from police and soon become rebel heroes. Slater is very good, and film is watchable, but its adult characters come out as caricatures and the "message" gets muddy. Christian Slater's first feature film. [PG-13]▼

Legend of Boggy Creek, The (1972) **C-90m.** ** D: Charles B. Pierce. Willie E. Smith, John P. Nixon, John W. Gates, Jeff Crabtree, Buddy Crabtree. Docudrama about sightings of a horrifying swamp monster in an Arkansas community. This modest but well-touted endeavor became a huge success, inspiring many similar films—including RETURN TO BOGGY CREEK and THE BARBARIC BEAST OF BOGGY CREEK PART II (which is actually the third in the series). Techniscope. [G]▼

Legend of Frenchie King, The (1971-French-Spanish-Italian-British) **C-97m.** *½ D: Christian-Jaque, Guy Casaril. Brigitte Bardot, Claudia Cardinale, Michael J. Pollard, Patty Shepard, Micheline Presle. Clumsy attempt at bawdy Western in the style of VIVA MARIA, with Bardot and her sisters as female outlaws at a French settlement in New Mexico, circa 1880. Badly dubbed. Aka PETROLEUM GIRLS. [R]▼

Legend of Gosta Berling, The SEE: **Atonement of Gosta Berling, The**

Legend of Hell House, The (1973-British) **C-95m.** *** D: John Hough. Roddy McDowall, Pamela Franklin, Clive Revill, Gayle Hunnicutt, Roland Culver, Peter Bowles. Harrowing story of occult phenomena as four researchers agree to spend one week in house known to be inhabited by malignant spirits. Not the usual ghost story, and certain to curl a few hairs. Michael Gough turns up as a corpse at conclusion. Written by Richard Matheson from his novel *Hell House*. [PG]▼●

Legend of Hillbilly John, The (1973) **C-86m.** *** D: John Newland. Susan Strasberg, Percy Rodrigues, R. G. Armstrong, Alfred Ryder, Severn Darden, Denver Pyle, Sharon Henesy, Sidney Clute, Harris Yulin, Hedges Capers. Odd, intriguing surprise, independently produced, in which two Johns—one (Pyle) an old man and the other (Capers) his grandson—set out to do battle with the devil. Based on several North and South Carolina legends and most deserving of its cult-film status. Aka WHO FEARS THE DEVIL (the title of the book upon which it's based) and MY NAME IS JOHN. [G]▼

Legend of Lobo, The (1962) **C-67m.** **½ No director credited. Narrated by Rex Allen, with songs by Sons of the Pioneers. Disney film follows a wolf named Lobo from birth to adulthood, as he learns the ways of life in the West. Well-done, if unmemorable, with bright soundtrack.▼◗

Legend of Lylah Clare, The (1968) **C-130m.** ** D: Robert Aldrich. Kim Novak, Peter Finch, Ernest Borgnine, Milton Selzer, Valentina Cortese, Michael Murphy, Lee Meriwether, Coral Browne, Ellen Corby. Has-been Hollywood director fashions young woman into the image of his late wife for screen biography; flamboyantly awful, but some think it's so bad it's good. Judge for yourself. Based on a 1963 *Dupont Show of the Week* TV play by Robert Thom. [R]

Legend of Machine Gun Kelly, The SEE: **Melvin Purvis—G-Man**

Legend of Nigger Charley, The (1972) **C-98m.** **½ D: Martin Goldman. Fred Williamson, D'Urville Martin, Don Pedro Colley, Gertrude Jeanette, Marcia McBroom, Alan Gifford. Violent, routine black Western about Virginia slave who becomes a fugitive after killing treacherous overseer; Lloyd Price sings title tune. Sequel: THE SOUL OF NIGGER CHARLEY. [PG]

Legend of 1900, The (1998-Italian) **C-116m.** ** D: Giuseppe Tornatore. Tim Roth, Pruitt Taylor Vince, Bill Nunn, Clarence Williams III, Melanie Thierry, Harry Ditson. Expansive fable about an infant named 1900, born (and abandoned) on a huge ocean liner at the turn of the 20th century; he spends his entire life on that ship, and turns out to be a uniquely gifted pianist. Ambitious tale has some wonderful moments—including a piano duel with Jelly Roll Morton (Williams)—but rambles inconclusively. Italian title: THE LEGEND OF THE PIANIST ON THE OCEAN, which runs 170m. Technovision. [R]▼

Legend of Sea Wolf SEE: **Wolf Larsen** (1975)

Legend of the Bayou SEE: **Eaten Alive!**

Legend of the Holy Drinker, The (1988-Italian) **C-125m.** ***½ D: Ermanno Olmi. Rutger Hauer, Anthony Quayle, Sandrine Dumas, Dominique Pinon, Sophie Segalen. Subtle, poetic tale of a down-and-out man (Hauer, in a very uncharacteristic performance), who drinks too much, sleeps under a bridge, and is haunted by his past. The scenario chronicles what happens when he's presented 200 francs by a stranger. As in Olmi's best films, there are often long silences—but those silences are golden.

Legend of the Lone Ranger, The (1981) **C-98m.** ** D: William A. Fraker. Klinton Spilsbury, Michael Horse, Christopher Lloyd, Jason Robards, Matt Clark, Juanin Clay, Richard Farnsworth, John Bennett Perry, John Hart. A middling effort to tell the origin of the Masked Man, which wavers between seriousness and tongue-in-cheek. Some fine action, great scenery, and a promising storyline, but sabotaged by awkward handling, uncharismatic leads (Spilsbury was dubbed to no great effect), and an awful "ballad" narration by Merle Haggard. Bring back Clayton Moore and Jay Silverheels! Panavision. [PG]▼

Legend of the Lost (1957) **C-109m.** **

D: Henry Hathaway. John Wayne, Sophia Loren, Rossano Brazzi, Kurt Kasznar, Sonia Moser. Incredibly insipid hodgepodge interesting as curio: Wayne and Brazzi on treasure hunt in Sahara battle over rights to Loren. Technirama.▼

Legend of the 7 Golden Vampires, The SEE: **Seven Brothers Meet Dracula, The**

Legend of the Werewolf (1975-British) **C-87m.** ** D: Freddie Francis. Peter Cushing, Ron Moody, Hugh Griffith, Roy Castle, David Rintoul, Lynn Dalby. Trite version has handsome Rintoul as the hairy guy, working in French zoo, tracked down by coroner-investigator Cushing. Man-to-Wolf transformation scenes are subpar.▼

Legend of the White Horse (1985-U.S.-Polish) **C-91m.** BOMB D: Jerzy Domaradzki, Janusz Morgenstern. Christopher Lloyd, Dee Wallace Stone, Allison Balson, Soon-Teck Oh, Luke Askew. Geologist Lloyd and son visit the mythical country of Karistan where his environmental impact study is impeded by a "witch," a white horse that turns into a horrible dragon, and some violent American bad guys. This supposed family film is confusing, sometimes scary, and at all times preposterous.▼

Legend of Tom Dooley, The (1959) **79m.** ** D: Ted Post. Michael Landon, Jo Morrow, Jack Hogan, Richard Rust, Dee Pollock. Landon is pleasing in title role of Rebel soldier who robs a stage for the cause, only to discover war is over and he's now an outlaw. Based on the hit song.▼

Legend of Wolf Lodge SEE: **Into the Fire**

Legends of the Fall (1994) **C-134m.** ** D: Edward Zwick. Brad Pitt, Anthony Hopkins, Aidan Quinn, Julia Ormond, Henry Thomas, Karina Lombard, Gordon Tootosis, Tantoo Cardinal, Paul Desmond. Sprawling family saga about three brothers raised in Montana by their iconoclastic father—a former cavalry officer who turned his back on bloodshed and the exploitation of Indians. Lumbering, Edna Ferber-esque plot is rife with sibling rivalry, pregnant looks, and heated exchanges. Many moviegoers—especially fans of red-hot Pitt—embraced this film, but its earnest, straight-faced story gets sillier as it goes along. Performances are fairly one-note, as well, except for Thomas as the youngest brother. Based on a novella by Jim Harrison. Oscar winner for John Toll's cinematography. [R]▼●◗

Legionnaire (1998) **C-99m.** *½ D: Peter MacDonald. Jean-Claude Van Damme, Adewale Akinnuoye-Agbaje, Steven Berkoff, Nicholas Farrell, Jim Carter, Ana Sofrenovic. Boxer Van Damme joins the French Foreign Legion in 1925 and flees to Morocco after defying a mobster who orders him to take a dive. The script is so dated and unintentionally hilarious that you keep expecting to see Ramon Novarro show up in a turban, or at least Marty Feldman; but alas, it's all played with numbing seriousness and a lack of style and imagination. Released straight to video in the U.S. Super 35. [R]▼●◗

Legion of the Damned SEE: **Battle of the Commandos**

Le Grand Chemin SEE: **Grand Highway, The**

Le Haine SEE: **Hate**

Le Jouet (1976-French) **C-92m.** **½ D: Francis Veber. Pierre Richard, Michel Bouquet, Fabrice Greco, Suzy Dyson, Jacques Francois. To show up his cutthroat father, a rich boy buys a human toy. Sometimes funny, sometimes not . . . but it's miles ahead of the American remake, THE TOY. Veber also scripted. [PG]

Le Jour Se Lève (1939-French) **93m.** ***½ D: Marcel Carné. Jean Gabin, Jacqueline Laurent, Jules Berry, Arletty, Mady Berry. A staple of French cinema, from the writer-director team that later created CHILDREN OF PARADISE; factory worker Gabin, trapped in a building, flashes back on events that drove him to murder. Generally holds up, while going a long way toward defining Gabin's screen persona. Written by Jacques Prévert, from Jacques Viot's story. U.S. title: DAYBREAK. Later remade here as THE LONG NIGHT.▼

Le Mans (1971) **C-106m.** *** D: Lee H. Katzin. Steve McQueen, Siegfried Rauch, Elga Andersen, Ronald Leigh-Hunt. Exciting study of Grand Prix auto racing with exceptionally fine camera work on the track. Panavision. [G]▼●

Le Million (1931-French) **85m.** ***½ D: René Clair. Annabella, René Lefevre, Vanda Greville, Paul Olivier, Louis Allibert. A chase after a lost lottery ticket propels this charming, whimsical, innovative gem from Clair. The actors sing some of their dialogue; as much fun today as when first released.▼●◗

Lemonade Joe (1967-Czech) **84m.** *** D: Oldrich Lipsky. Carl Fiala, Olga Schoberova, Veta Fialova, Miles Kopeck, Rudy Dale, Joseph Nomaz. Sometimes repetitious but often quite funny spoof of the American Western; title refers to hero, who drinks Kola Loca lemonade instead of booze. CinemaScope.

Lemon Drop Kid, The (1934) **71m.** ** D: Marshall Neilan. Lee Tracy, Helen Mack, William Frawley, Minna Gombell, Baby LeRoy, Robert McWade, Henry B. Walthall, Kitty Kelly, Eddie Peabody. Racetrack con-man flees to quiet burg, falls in love, and settles down. Drifts from comedy to sentiment to melodrama, killing off best Damon Runyon elements. Frawley is fun as silver-tongued tout called The Professor. Look for Ann Sheridan in bit part at the track. Remade with Bob Hope.

Lemon Drop Kid, The (1951) **91m.** *** D: Sidney Lanfield. Bob Hope, Marilyn Maxwell, Lloyd Nolan, Jane Darwell, William Frawley. Hope is hilarious as racetrack tout who owes big money to gangster and must pay or else. Adapted from Damon Runyon story, filmed before in 1934. Film introduced Livingston/Evans Christmas hit "Silver Bells." ▼●

Lemon Sisters, The (1990) **C-93m.** *½ D: Joyce Chopra. Diane Keaton, Carol Kane, Kathryn Grody, Elliott Gould, Ruben Blades, Aidan Quinn, Estelle Parsons, Richard Libertini, Nathan Lane. Dopey female buddy comedy revolving around the relationships of three women; doesn't take off despite an impressive cast. Although the laughs are few, the scene in which Kane sings "Rawhide" is almost worth a look. This film sat on the shelf awhile before its desultory release to theaters. [PG-13]▼●

Lemon Sky (1987) **C-90m. TVM** D: Jan Egleson. Kevin Bacon, Tom Atkins, Lindsay Crouse, Kyra Sedgwick, Laura White. Well acted but much too theatrical account of young Bacon, and what he finds when he visits his father (Atkins) and new stepmother (Crouse). Scripted by Lanford Wilson. Bacon and costar Sedgwick later married in real life. A PBS *American Playhouse* presentation. Average.

Lemora, The Lady Dracula SEE: **Lady Dracula**

L'Enfer (1994-French) **C-105m.** ** D: Claude Chabrol. Emmanuelle Béart, Francois Cluzet, Marc Lavoine, Nathalie Cardone, Andre Wilms, Christiane Minazzoli, Dora Doll, Jean-Pierre Cassel. Cluzet and sexy Béart marry, become settled in domesticity and seem very happy—until the husband becomes convinced that the wife is cheating on him. Chabrol ponders some interesting questions—how well can two people know each other? how far can they trust each other?—but result is one-note, with Cluzet becoming a laughable caricature of an insanely jealous man. Scripted by Chabrol, from original screenplay by Henri-Georges Clouzot (which the latter had started filming in 1964 but never completed). [R]▼◗

Leningrad Cowboys Go America (1989-Finnish) **C-80m.** *** D: Aki Kaurismaki. Matti Pellonpaa, Kari Vaananen, Jim Jarmusch, Nicky Tesco. Straight-faced comedy from the prolific Kaurismaki, about a group of dreadful musicians from Finland's tundra; they're so bad that they decide to head for the U.S.—where people will listen to "anything"—and they set out on tour through the modern wasteland of small-town America. Filmed in the U.S. and Finland, and scripted by Kaurismaki; while his films have become known and admired at festivals, this was the first to have a major theatrical release in the U.S. [PG-13]▼●

Lenny (1974) **112m.** **** D: Bob Fosse. Dustin Hoffman, Valerie Perrine, Jan Miner, Stanley Beck, Gary Morton. Powerful biography of troubled nightclub comic Lenny Bruce, whose hip humor and scatological dialogue made him a controversial figure in the 1950s. Fine direction, evocative b&w camerawork (by Bruce Surtees) showcase excellent performances by Hoffman and Perrine (as Lenny's wife, stripper Honey Harlowe). Script by Julian Barry, expanded from his Broadway play. [R]▼●

Lensman (1984-Japanese) **C-107m.** **½ D: Yoshiaki Kawajiri, Kazuyuki Hirokawa. Voices of Kerrigan Mahan, Tom Wyner, Greg Snegoff, Michael McConnohie. Japanese animated feature based on classic sci-fi novels of American E. E. "Doc" Smith, which also inspired STAR WARS. Unfortunately, this film plays like a mediocre ripoff of the George Lucas film; computer-generated animation sequences are interesting to watch but don't move the story along. For comic book buffs only.▼

Leo and Loree (1980) **C-97m.** ** D: Jerry Paris. Donny Most, Linda Purl, David Huffman, Jerry Paris, Shannon Farnon, Allan Rich. Uneven romantic comedy about Most moving to Hollywood and suffering typical difficulties of novice actors. He falls in love with Purl, daughter of an Oscar-winning actress, who is trying to make it on her own. Nothing unusual, ambitious, or offensive about it. [PG]

Léolo (1992-Canadian-French) **C-107m.** *** D: Jean-Claude Lauzon. Maxime Collin, Ginette Reno, Roland Blouin, Julien Guiomar, Pierre Bourgault, Giuditta Del Vecchio, Denys Arcand, narrated by Gilbert Sicotte. Bizarrely funny black comedy about a boy, on the verge of adolescence, surviving in the slums of Montreal. He's stifled by a family he aptly describes as a "black hole," and is convinced he's the offspring of a contaminated, sperm-laden tomato! Lauzon penned the semiautobiographical script.▼●

Leonard Part 6 (1987) **C-85m.** BOMB D: Paul Weiland. Bill Cosby, Tom Courtenay, Joe Don Baker, Moses Gunn, Pat Colbert, Gloria Foster, Victoria Rowell. With a band of mad animals knocking off the government's top-secret agents, restaurateur Cos comes out of retirement to avenge his one-time colleagues by foiling the villainess responsible. Even Cosby warned audiences to stay away from this megabomb (for which he receives story and producer credit). [PG]▼●

Leon Morin, Priest SEE: **Forgiven Sinner, The**

Leonor (1975-French-Spanish-Italian) **C-90m.** BOMB D: Juan Buñuel. Michel Piccoli, Liv Ullmann, Ornella Muti, Antonio Ferrandis, Jorge Rigaud. Medieval mishmash with Lady Liv rising from the dead a decade after husband Piccoli seals her in a tomb. Deadening and idiotic. Directed by the son of Luis Buñuel. [PG]▼

Leopard, The (1963-French-Italian) **C-205m.** **** D: Luchino Visconti. Burt Lancaster, Alain Delon, Claudia Cardinale, Rina Morelli, Paolo Stoppa. Magnificent spectacle, set in 1860 Sicily, about an aristocrat who tries coming to terms with the unification of Italy. Originally released here in a badly dubbed 165m. version, film was restored in 1983 to proper form (though Lancaster's voice is still dubbed, as it was in original *foreign* version). Delon and Cardinale are close to the final word in romantic pairings; concluding hour-long banquet scene is among the great set pieces in movie history. Technirama.

Leopard in the Snow (1978-Canadian-British) **C-90m.** **½ D: Gerry O'Hara. Keir Dullea, Susan Penhaligon, Kenneth More, Billie Whitelaw, Jeremy Kemp, Yvonne Manners. First movie produced by publishers of Harlequin Romance paperbacks is predictably tearful love story about English girl who falls for a testy, reclusive American who's afraid to admit his feelings. [PG]▼

Leopard Man, The (1943) **66m.** **½ D: Jacques Tourneur. Dennis O'Keefe, Margo, Jean Brooks, Isabel Jewell, James Bell, Margaret Landry, Abner Biberman. Intriguing but flawed Val Lewton thriller about series of murders in small New Mexico town blamed on escaped leopard. Based on novel *Black Alibi* by Cornell Woolrich. ▼●

Leopard Son, The (1996) **C-84m.** ***½ D: Hugo Van Lawick. Narrated by John Gielgud. Sweeping, beautifully filmed documentary following the birth, growing pains, and coming-of-age of a leopard cub. Shot over a two-year period in Africa's Serengeti Plain, this eye-opening film shows just how much luck plays a part in any animal's survival. This deeply moving film is best experienced on the big screen. Parents should know that there are disturbing scenes of animal death, though handled with discretion. Music by Stewart Copeland. This was Discovery Channel's first theatrical release. [G]▼●

Leo the Last (1970-British) **C-103m.** ** D: John Boorman. Marcello Mastroianni, Billie Whitelaw, Calvin Lockhart, Glenna Forster-Jones, Graham Crowden. Oddball film about reticent Mastroianni, last in a line of princes, who gradually emerges from decaying London mansion to become involved with people living on his black ghetto block. Enigmatic, unsatisfying film, with occasional bright touches. Boorman explored some of the same ideas twenty years later in WHERE THE HEART IS. [R]

Leo Tolstoy's Anna Karenina (1997) **C-108m.** ** D: Bernard Rose. Sophie Marceau, Sean Bean, Alfred Molina, Mia Kirshner, James Fox, Fiona Shaw, Danny Huston, Phyllida Law, David Schofield, Saskia Wickham, Jennifer Hall, Hamish Falconer. Practically passionless recounting of the oft-filmed tale of the title character (Marceau), a wife and mother who commences an illicit affair with dashing Count Vronsky (Bean) in 19th-century Russia. Handsomely mounted, but dramatically flat. Notable only as the first Western-produced ANNA to be filmed in Russia—notably St. Petersburg. Panavision. [R]▼●

Le Petit Théâtre de Jean Renoir SEE: **Little Theatre of Jean Renoir, The**

Lepke (1975) **C-110m.** **½ D: Menahem Golan. Tony Curtis, Anjanette Comer, Michael Callan, Warren Berlinger, Milton Berle, Vic Tayback. Cut above usual gangster film, with Curtis surprisingly convincing as title character, head of '30s Murder, Inc. Berle has serious cameo as Comer's father. Recut to 98m. by Golan for cable TV release. Panavision. [R]▼

Le Plaisir (1951-French) **97m.** ***½ D: Max Ophuls. Jean Gabin, Danielle Darrieux, Simone Simon, Claude Dauphin, Gaby Morlay, Pierre Brasseur, Pauline Dubost, Madeleine Renaud, Daniel Gelin. Three short stories by Guy de Maupassant relate the joy and irony of romance. In "Le Masque," an elderly man recovers his youth with the aid of a magic mask; in "Le Maison Tellier," a bevy of prostitutes embarks on their annual holiday in the countryside; in "Le Modele," a free-living artist weds a model after she cripples herself in a failed suicide attempt. Lush production with fluid camera and baroque set decoration, Ophuls' trademarks. Coscripted by Ophuls and Jacques Natanson. Narrated by Peter Ustinov, as the voice of de Maupassant, in the English version (Jean Servais narrates the original).▼

Leprechaun (1993) **C-92m.** BOMB D: Mark Jones. Warwick Davis, Jennifer Aniston, Ken Olandt, Mark Holton, Robert Gorman, John Sanderford, Shay Duffin, Pamela Mant. Inept horror drama in which a pint-sized Irish fairy (Davis) goes on a rampage after being ripped off of a hundred gold-pieces. Gratuitous gore and cheap shocks take the place of moviemaking skill; unfortunately, the ending leaves room for an inevitable spate of sequels. [R]▼●◗

Leprechaun 2 (1994) **C-85m.** *½ D: Rodman Flender. Warwick Davis, Charlie Heath, Shevonne Durkin, Sandy Baron, Adam Biesk, James Lancaster, Clint Howard, Kimmy Robertson. A spurned, vengeful leprechaun arrives in L.A. from ancient Ireland to claim his bride—the descendant of a lass he was tricked out of 1,000 years ago. Just another excuse for high-body-count gratuitous gore, begorrah! [R]▼●▶

Le Rouge et le Noir (1954-French-Italian) **C-145m.** ★★★ D: Claude Autant-Lara. Gérard Philipe, Danielle Darrieux, Antonella Lualdi, Jean Martinelli. Solidly acted, handsomely produced historical drama based on the Stendahl novel about a man of the lower classes (Philipe) and his obsession with making it in society in 1830 France; Darrieux and Lualdi are the women in his life. Released in the U.S. in 1958; European running time 170m. Aka THE RED AND THE BLACK, which is its video title.▼

Le Samourai (1967-French) **C-101m.** ★★★½ D: Jean-Pierre Melville. Alain Delon, Nathalie Delon, François Perier, Cathy Rosier, Jacques Leroy, Jean-Pierre Posier, Catherine Jourdan. Delon is the ultimate existential hit man in this tale of an assassin who's hired to kill a nightclub owner, but is double-crossed by his mysterious employers. Alain Delon was never better than in this quintessential Melville *policier,* a marvelously stylish meditation on crime and solitude that was a direct influence on John Woo's THE KILLER. ▼

Les Biches (1968-French-Italian) **C-104m.** ★★★½ D: Claude Chabrol. Jean-Louis Trintignant, Jacqueline Sassard, Stephane Audran, Nane Germon. Excellent film of rich, aging lesbian who picks up unformed waif who earns her living drawing on the sidewalks of Paris. [R]▼●

Les Bons Debarras (1978-Canadian) **C-115m.** ★★½ D: Francis Mankiewicz. Charlotte Laurier, Marie Tifo, Germain Houde, Louise Marleau, Roger Lebel. Fatherless 13-year-old girl (Laurier) idolizes and romanticizes her mother (Tifo), with tragic results. Cogent but overlong and repetitious drama about growing up, aided by a strong performance from Tifo.

Les Compères (1984-French) **C-92m.** ★★★ D: Francis Veber. Pierre Richard, Gérard Depardieu, Anny Duperey, Michel Aumont, Stephane Bierry. Endearing comedy in which beautiful, desperate Duperey manipulates former boyfriends Richard and Depardieu into searching for runaway son Bierry by making each think that the boy is his. This one works primarily because of the stars' knowing performances. Veber also scripted. Remade in the U.S. as FATHERS' DAY. [PG]▼

Les Diaboliques SEE: **Diabolique** (1955)

Le Sex Shop (1973-French) **C-92m.** ★★★ D: Claude Berri. Claude Berri, Juliet Berto, Nathalie Delon, Jean-Pierre Marielle, Beatrice Romand, Catherine Allegret. Amiable spoof of our preoccupation with sex; failing bookstore owner starts selling porno material, becomes increasingly fascinated by it. Clever idea well done; originally rated X because of its candid (yet unsensational) scenes. [R—edited from original X rating]▼

Les Girls (1957) **C-114m.** ★★★½ D: George Cukor. Gene Kelly, Mitzi Gaynor, Kay Kendall, Taina Elg, Jacques Bergerac, Leslie Phillips, Henry Daniell, Patrick Macnee. Charming, sprightly musical involving three show girls who (via flashback) reveal their relationship to hoofer Kelly; chicly handled in all departments, with Cole Porter tunes and Oscar-winning Orry-Kelly costumes. John Patrick adapted Vera Caspary's novel. CinemaScope.▼●

Les Miserables (1935) **108m.** ★★★½ D: Richard Boleslawski. Fredric March, Charles Laughton, Cedric Hardwicke, Rochelle Hudson, Frances Drake, John Beal, Florence Eldridge, Jessie Ralph, Leonid Kinskey. Meticulous production of Victor Hugo's classic tale. Minor thief March tries to bury past and become respectable town mayor, but police inspector Javert (Laughton) won't let him. John Carradine has bit part as student radical. Screenplay by W.P. Lipscomb.▼●

Les Miserables (1952) **104m.** ★★★ D: Lewis Milestone. Michael Rennie, Debra Paget, Robert Newton, Sylvia Sidney, Edmund Gwenn, Cameron Mitchell, Elsa Lanchester, Florence Bates. Glossy but thoughtful remake of the venerable Victor Hugo classic.

Les Miserables (1952-Italian) **118m.** ★★★ D: Riccardo Freda. Gino Cervi, Valentina Cortesa, John Hinrich, Aldo Nicodemi, Duccia Giraldi. Intelligent, handsomely mounted version of the oft-filmed Victor Hugo story, with Cervi making a fine Jean Valjean. Mario Monicelli was one of the scripters. Originally 140m. ▼

Les Miserables (1957-French-German) **C-210m.** ★★½ D: Jean-Paul Le Chanois. Jean Gabin, Daniele Delorme, Bernard Blier, Bourvil, Gianni Esposito, Serge Reggiani. Victor Hugo tale, with Gabin as Jean Valjean, Blier as Javert. Respectful but uninspiring. Often shown in two parts. Technirama.▼

Les Miserables (1978) **C-150m. TVM** D: Glenn Jordan. Richard Jordan, Anthony Perkins, Cyril Cusack, Claude Dauphin, John Gielgud, Flora Robson, Celia Johnson, Joyce Redman. Lavish remake of the perennial with a cerebral interpretation of Valjean by Jordan and a determined one of Javert by Perkins. Sparkling cameos by Dauphin (in his last role) and some British stalwarts. Above average.▼

Les Misérables (1995-French) **C-178m.** ★★★½ D: Claude Lelouch. Jean-Paul Belmondo, Michel Boujenah, Alessandra Martines, Annie Girardot, Clementine Celarie, Philippe Leotard, Rufus, Jean Marais, Micheline Presle, Darry Cowl, Salome, Ticky Holgado, Philippe Kohrsand, Nicc Croisille, Paul Belmondo. Extraordinary cycling of Victor Hugo's sprawling n into a 20th-century landscape, culmi in a story of WW2 France. Belmondo plays a simple man who takes on the qualities of Jean Valjean as he helps a Jewish family fleeing from the Nazis. Lelouch's modern parable/adaptation emphasizes the impact that one good man can have on the lives of people around him; the result is absolutely riveting. Great, humanistic storytelling. Marais (from the Cocteau classics of the 1940s) plays the Monseigneur; Presle plays the Mère Supérieure. The ballerina and her daughter are played by Lelouch's real-life wife and daughter. Super 35. [R] ▼●

Les Misérables (1998) **C-131m.** **½ D: Bille August. Liam Neeson, Geoffrey Rush, Uma Thurman, Claire Danes, Hans Matheson, Reine Brynolfsson, Mimi Newman. Respectful, well-made adaptation of the Hugo classic, with strong performances from Neeson (as Jean Valjean), Thurman (as Fantine), Danes (as Cosette), and of course Rush (as the villainous Javert). Location filming in Paris (and Prague) is another asset. Yet there is a certain fire missing, especially at the finale, which keeps this from soaring. Panavision. [PG-13]▼●◗

Les Parents Terribles (1948-French) **98m.** *** D: Jean Cocteau. Jean Marais, Josette Day, Yvonne de Bray, Marcel Andre, Gabrielle Dorziat. Absorbing drama of a dysfunctional middle-class family, with inexperienced young Marais falling in love with Day, unaware that she's been his father's mistress. De Bray is outstanding as Marais's neurotic mother, who subtly expresses incestuous feelings toward her son. Cocteau scripted based on his play (which featured these same actors). Remade in England as INTIMATE RELATIONS.▼●

Lesson Before Dying, A (1999) **C-105m. TVM** D: Joseph Sargent. Don Cheadle, Cicely Tyson, Mekhi Phifer, Irma P. Hall, Brent Jennings, Dana Ivey. Moving drama set in late '40s rural Louisiana dealing with a well-spoken black teacher persuaded to work with an illiterate plantation worker who's been railroaded onto death row. Peabody Award-winning film lovingly adapted by Ann Peacock from the longtime bestseller by Ernest J. Gaines. Above average. ▼

Lesson in Love, A (1954-Swedish) **95m.** *** D: Ingmar Bergman. Gunnar Bjornstrand, Eva Dahlbeck, Yvonne Lombard, Harriet Andersson, Ake Gronberg. Obstetrician Bjornstrand, happily married for 15 years to Dahlbeck, has an affair with a patient; Dahlbeck then returns to *her* former lover—the husband's best friend. Medium Bergman.▼

ess Than Zero (1987) **C-96m.** ** D: arek Kanievska. Andrew McCarthy, Jami tz, Robert Downey, Jr., James Spader, Bill, Nicholas Pryor, Brad Pitt. Bret Ellis' nihilistic novel about young, disengaged L.A. have-it-alls is sanitized into pointlessness, though a faithful adaptation would have turned off everyone; try to imagine it with Eddie Bracken, Veronica Lake, and Sonny Tufts. The two leads are awful, but Spader is creepy as a drug-dealing slug, Downey exceptional as a wealthy addict. *Almost* good-bad. [R]▼●

Les Visiteurs SEE: **Visitors, The** (1993-French)

Les Voleurs (1996-French) **C-117m.** ** D: André Téchiné. Catherine Deneuve, Daniel Auteuil, Laurence Côte, Fabienne Babe, Julien Rivière, Benoît Magimel, Didier Bezace, Ivan Desny. Something different from Téchiné (who last teamed with these two stars on MA SAISON PRÉFÉRÉE): a crime picture, laced with his usual emotional/sexual twists. Here, as a boy pieces together his father's death, the viewer meets his outcast uncle, a cop (Auteuil), a cipher-like professor (Deneuve), and the young woman who comes between them (Côte). More an acting exercise than a cogent drama. Aka THIEVES.▼●

Let 'Em Have It (1935) **90m.** **½ D: Sam Wood. Richard Arlen, Virginia Bruce, Alice Brady, Bruce Cabot, Harvey Stephens, Eric Linden, Joyce Compton, Gordon Jones. Predictable gangster saga is interesting for depiction of newly formed FBI at work. Some strong action scenes.▼

Let Freedom Ring (1939) **100m.** **½ D: Jack Conway. Nelson Eddy, Virginia Bruce, Victor McLaglen, Lionel Barrymore, Edward Arnold, Guy Kibbee, Raymond Walburn. Hokey but enjoyable pap of crusading Eddy righting wrongs in home town, combating crooked bosses.▼

Lethal Terminator SEE: **Glove, The**

Lethal Weapon (1987) **C-110m.** *** D: Richard Donner. Mel Gibson, Danny Glover, Gary Busey, Mitchell Ryan, Tom Atkins, Darlene Love, Traci Wolfe. Undercover cop Gibson, a borderline psychopath who's always on the edge, is partnered with stable family-man Glover, and they prove a good team as they go after a particularly scummy drug ring. Loud, violent, trashy cop movie done to a turn; fast paced and entertaining so long as you don't think about it too much. Director's cut runs 117m. Followed by three sequels. [R]▼●◗

Lethal Weapon 2 (1989) **C-113m.** *** D: Richard Donner. Mel Gibson, Danny Glover, Joe Pesci, Joss Ackland, Derrick O'Connor, Patsy Kensit, Darlene Love, Traci Wolfe, Steve Kahan. Ultraviolent, superslick sequel is just as cartoonish as the first—and possibly even more entertaining. This time around, our heroes tangle with a nefarious smuggling kingpin hiding behind diplomatic immunity, but doesn't reckon with Gibson's reckless ways. A must for action fans. Director's cut runs 118m. Panavision. [R]▼●◗

Lethal Weapon 3 (1992) **C-115m.** ★★½ D: Richard Donner. Mel Gibson, Danny Glover, Joe Pesci, Rene Russo, Stuart Wilson, Steve Kahan, Darlene Love, Traci Wolfe, Gregory Millar, Jason Meshover-Iorg, Delores Hall. Glover is about to retire when he and partner Gibson find themselves in the midst of an escalating war with a former cop turned criminal mastermind. Despite lazy writing and pointless plot turns, manages to crank out enough thrills, laughs, and violent action to rate as acceptable escapism. Director's cut runs 117m. Panavision. [R] ▼●◗

Lethal Weapon 4 (1998) **C-127m.** ★★★ D: Richard Donner. Mel Gibson, Danny Glover, Joe Pesci, Rene Russo, Chris Rock, Jet Li, Steve Kahan, Kim Chan, Darlene Love, Traci Wolfe. Those wacky cops are at it again, this time battling a Chinese ganglord—and facing domestic crises involving pregnancy and marriage. Added this time: Rock, as an overzealous cop, and Li, as a formidable bad guy. The cast is so likable and their energy so infectious that the filmmakers get away with murder, presenting an overlong, incoherent story and peppering it with supercharged action sequences. Fans of the series won't be disappointed; others needn't bother. Richard Libertini appears unbilled. Panavision. [R]▼●◗

Let Him Have It (1991-British) **C-115m.** ★★★ D: Peter Medak. Chris Eccleston, Paul Reynolds, Tom Courtenay, Tom Bell, Eileen Atkins, Clare Holman, Mark McGann, Michael Gough, Ronald Fraser, James Villiers, Murray Melvin, Norman Rossington, Clive Revill. Absorbing drama based on the true story of Derek Bentley, a slow-witted youth who was pulled into a life of crime in post-war England and sentenced to death for a murder actually committed by his youthful cohort. Medak's sympathetic point of view is abetted by vivid performances, including young Eccleston in the lead, and a gallery of top British actors in supporting roles. [R]▼●

Let It Be (1970-British) **C-80m.** ★★★ D: Michael Lindsay-Hogg. John Lennon, Paul McCartney, Ringo Starr, George Harrison. Uneven, draggy documentary is rescued and abetted by brilliant, Oscar-winning score by The Beatles. When they perform it becomes magical; when others are thrown in it becomes a bore. [G]▼●

Let It Ride (1989) **C-86m.** ★★ D: Joe Pytka. Richard Dreyfuss, Teri Garr, David Johansen (Buster Poindexter), Jennifer Tilly, Allen Garfield, Ed Walsh, Michelle Phillips, Mary Woronov, Robbie Coltrane, Richard Edson, Cynthia Nixon. Disjointed, only sporadically funny tale of a compulsive gambler who finally hits a winning streak at a Florida racetrack. First-time director Pytka tries for a Damon Runyon flavor and a fast pace, but it doesn't come off; screenwriter Nancy Dowd had her name removed from credits. [PG-13]▼●

Let No Man Write My Epitaph (1960) **106m.** ★★★ D: Philip Leacock. Burl Ives, Shelley Winters, James Darren, Jean Seberg, Ricardo Montalban, Ella Fitzgerald. Bizarre account of slum life, focusing on Darren and his dope-addicted mother involved with a variety of corrupt individuals. Sequel to KNOCK ON ANY DOOR.▼

L'Etoile du Nord (1982-French) **C-101m.** ★½ D: Pierre Granier-Deferre. Simone Signoret, Philippe Noiret, Fanny Cottencon, Julie Jezequel, Gamil Ratib. Boring tale of down-and-out Noiret murdering wealthy businessman Ratib, and his relationships with golddigger Cottencon and her mother (Signoret). Just talk, flashbacks, and more talk, with insufficient action or character development. Signoret can't save this one. Based on a Georges Simenon novel. [PG]▼

Let's Be Happy (1957-British) **C-93m.** ★★½ D: Henry Levin. Tony Martin, Vera-Ellen, Zena Marshall, Guy Middleton. Featherweight musical of girl going to Scotland to claim a castle she's inherited. CinemaScope.

Let's Dance (1950) **C-112m.** ★★½ D: Norman Z. McLeod. Betty Hutton, Fred Astaire, Roland Young, Ruth Warrick, Shepperd Strudwick, Lucile Watson, Barton MacLane, Melville Cooper. Lesser-known Astaire vehicle is still fun, with war widow Hutton attempting to shield her young son from the clutches of his wealthy, stuffy great-grandmother. Astaire is the man who loves her, and his dancing (particularly in the "Piano Dance" number) is wonderful. Songs by Frank Loesser.▼●

Let's Do It Again (1953) **C-95m.** ★★★ D: Alexander Hall. Jane Wyman, Ray Milland, Aldo Ray, Leon Ames, Tom Helmore. Musical remake of THE AWFUL TRUTH with Milland in Cary Grant's role, Wyman in Irene Dunne's, and Ray in Ralph Bellamy's. Songs add to spicy plot, but no classic like original '37 film.

Let's Do It Again (1975) **C-112m.** ★★★ D: Sidney Poitier. Sidney Poitier, Bill Cosby, Jimmie Walker, Calvin Lockhart, Joh Amos, Denise Nicholas, Lee Chamberl Hilarious follow-up to UPTOWN SA DAY NIGHT; lodge brothers Poit Cosby hypnotize Walker into great boxer, figuring they can c bets. Yes, it's an old "Bo plot, but still well done. A PIECE OF THE ACTIO

Let's Face It (1943) 7 Lanfield. Bob Hope, Pitts, Phyllis Povah Arden. Brassy co competing with wartime comedy of soldiers hired as male companions.

Let's Get Harry (1986) **C-107m.** *½ D: Alan Smithee. Michael Schoeffling, Tom Wilson, Glen Frey, Gary Busey, Robert Duvall, Rick Rossovich, Ben Johnson, Matt Clark, Gregory Sierra, Elpidia Carrillo, Mark Harmon, Jere Burns. Inherently stupid, unbelievable action yarn about a soldier of fortune's attempt to rescue pipeline worker Harmon, who's been kidnapped (along with an ambassador) by an underground group of drug dealers in South America. Busey and Duvall give lively performances, but that's all one can recommend about this turkey. Director Stuart Rosenberg had his name removed from the credits. Barely received theatrical release. Video title: THE RESCUE. [R]▼●

Let's Get Lost (1989) **119m.** *** D: Bruce Weber. Chet Baker, jazz trumpeter and singer from the "cool" school of the 1950s, is the subject of photographer Weber's high-style, black & white documentary. It's a fascinating (and sometimes disquietingly personal) look at the charismatic musician once referred to as the James Dean of jazz, whose long involvement with drugs never seemed to deter him from making beautiful music. Overlong, but worthwhile.▼

Let's Get Tough! (1942) **62m.** ** D: Wallace Fox. Leo Gorcey, Bobby Jordan, Huntz Hall, Sunshine Sammy Morrison, Bobby Stone, David Gorcey, Tom Brown, Florence Rice, Robert Armstrong, Gabriel Dell. The East Side Kids take on Japanese spies in this rampantly jingoistic entry. The kids ad lib shamelessly, with frequently amusing results.▼

Let's Go Navy! (1951) **68m.** **½ D: William Beaudine. Leo Gorcey, Huntz Hall, William Benedict, David Gorcey, Bernard Gorcey, Allen Jenkins, Buddy Gorman, Charlita, Dorothy Ford, Tom Neal, Frank Jenks. The Bowery Boys sign up and ship out to catch some crooks who are posing as gobs. One of their funniest outings.

Let's Hope It's a Girl (1985-Italian) **C-114m.** *** D: Mario Monicelli. Liv Ullmann, Philippe Noiret, Catherine Deneuve, Bernard Blier, Giuliana De Sio, ...hina Cenci, Stefania Sandrelli. Complex, ...y, seriocomic account of what happens ... Count Noiret returns to his former ...llmann) and family and attempts to ...f their estate. The men all have a ...aults, and the women can very ...ithout them. Blier is great ...ilariously senile uncle.

...e (1966-British) **C-92m.** ...astle. Nigel Green, Mary ...obert Pickering, Linda ...ez, Nestor Paiva. ...ht for this outra- ... who tries to kill his uncle because his uncle is trying to kill him over a $5 million inheritance. Lots of hokey thrills involving sharks, tarantulas and the like. Loosely based on Rohan O'Grady novel.

Let's Live a Little (1948) **85m.** **½ D: Richard Wallace. Hedy Lamarr, Robert Cummings, Anna Sten, Robert Shayne, Mary Treen. Amusing but unspectacular romantic comedy, with Lamarr and Cummings falling in love.

Let's Make It Legal (1951) **77m.** ** D: Richard Sale. Claudette Colbert, Macdonald Carey, Zachary Scott, Robert Wagner, Barbara Bates, Marilyn Monroe. Trifling comedy in which Colbert divorces Carey and is tempted to wed ex-beau Scott. Monroe is wasted as a bathing beauty.▼

Let's Make Love (1960) **C-118m.** *** D: George Cukor. Marilyn Monroe, Yves Montand, Tony Randall, Frankie Vaughan, Wilfrid Hyde-White, David Burns. Billionaire Montand hears of show spoofing him, wants to stop it, then meets the show's star, Monroe. To charm her, he hires Bing Crosby to teach him to sing, Milton Berle to coach on comedy, Gene Kelly to make him dance. Bubbly cast, snappy musical numbers. CinemaScope.▼●

Let's Make Music (1940) **85m.** **½ D: Leslie Goodwins. Bob Crosby, Jean Rogers, Elisabeth Risdon, Joseph Buloff. Nathanael West wrote this entertaining B musical about bandleader Crosby turning prim schoolteacher's football victory song into a hit. Good fun; other songs include "Big Noise from Winnetka."

Let's Make Up (1954-British) **C-94m.** ** D: Herbert Wilcox. Errol Flynn, Anna Neagle, David Farrar, Kathleen Harrison, Peter Graves. Froth about overimaginative Neagle trying to decide between suitors Flynn and Farrar. Sean Connery has a bit in his film debut. Original title: LILACS IN THE SPRING.▼

Let's Rock! (1958) **79m.** ** D: Harry Foster. Julius La Rosa, Phyllis Newman, Conrad Janis, Della Reese, Joy Harmon, Royal Teens, Paul Anka, Danny and the Juniors, Roy Hamilton, Wink Martindale. Balladeer La Rosa resists changing his singing style with the popularity of rock 'n' roll. KING LEAR it isn't. Danny and the Juniors sing "At the Hop"; the Royal Teens do "Short Shorts." Aka KEEP IT COOL.

Let's Scare Jessica to Death (1971) **C-89m.** **½ D: John Hancock. Zohra Lampert, Barton Heyman, Kevin O'Connor, Mari-Claire Costello, Gretchen Corbett. Creepy little tale of murder and deception as unstable girl gets full fright-treatment at country home. [PG]▼

Let's Spend the Night Together (1982) **C-94m.** ** D: Hal Ashby. Tired concert film, edited from three separate performances from the Rolling Stones' 1981 tour. Flirts with excitement only when lookers in appropriate garb help Mick Jagger perform "Honky Tonk Woman." This is at least the *third* Stones concert film, and the republic will stand if it's the last.[PG]▼

Let's Talk About Men (1965-Italian) **93m.** *** D: Lina Wertmuller. Nino Manfredi, Luciana Paluzzi, Margaret Lee, Milena Vukotic, Patrizia DeClara, Alfredo Baranchini. Amusing episodic film (four stories tied to a fifth): Manfredi competently and comically plays five different men involved with different women and situations. Made right after Ettore Scola's LET'S TALK ABOUT WOMEN, this took 11 years to cross the ocean but was worth the wait.

Let's Talk About Sex (1998) **C-82m.** *½ D: Troy Beyer. Troy Beyer, Paget Brewster, Randi Ingerman, Joseph C. Phillips, Michaline Babich, Tina Nguyen. Let's not and say we did. Miami advice columnist enlists her two roomies to help make a documentary about what women really think about men and sex. Intriguing concept is poorly handled with lame attempts at shock humor and mawkish dramatic material. This film would lead you to believe that the peak of sexual freedom derives from all-night, frozen-yogurt binging, teary-eyed confessionals. Directorial debut for actress Beyer, who also wrote the infantile B*A*P*S. [R]▼●

Let's Talk About Women (1964-Italian-French) **108m.** **½ D: Ettore Scola. Vittorio Gassman, Maria Fiore, Donatella Mauro, Giovanna Ralli, Antonella Lualdi, Slyva Koscina, Heidi Stroh, Rosanna Ghevardi, Walter Chiari, Eleonora Rossi-Drago, Jean Valerie. Nine-episode comedy with Gassman starring in each, and encountering a variety of women. Some segments better than others; one of the best has Gassman discovering that the prostitute he's hired is married to an old friend of his! Lina Wertmuller's LET'S TALK ABOUT MEN came a year later.

Letter, The (1940) **95m.** ***½ D: William Wyler. Bette Davis, Herbert Marshall, James Stephenson, Frieda Inescort, Gale Sondergaard. Lushly photographed Somerset Maugham drama set in Malaya, tells of murderess (Davis) who tries to cover up her deed by pleading self-defense. Davis quite appealing in her unsympathetic role. Previously filmed in 1929 (also with Herbert Marshall in cast); remade as THE UNFAITHFUL, then again for TV in 1982 with Lee Remick.▼●

Letter for Evie, A (1945) **89m.** ** D: Jules Dassin. Marsha Hunt, John Carroll, Spring Byington, Hume Cronyn, Pamela Britton, Norman Lloyd. Inconsequential romancer; Hunt is torn between pen-pal Cronyn and his buddy Carroll.

Letter From an Unknown Woman (1948) **90m.** *** D: Max Ophuls. Joan Fontaine, Louis Jourdan, Mady Christians, Marcel Journet, Art Smith. Lush romantic flavor of direction and performances obscures clichés and improbabilities in story of Fontaine's lifelong infatuation with musician Jourdan.▼●

Letter of Introduction, A (1938) **104m.** **½ D: John M. Stahl. Adolphe Menjou, Andrea Leeds, Edgar Bergen (and Charlie McCarthy), George Murphy, Rita Johnson, Eve Arden, Ann Sheridan. Smoothly done account of aspiring actress Leeds trying to make it without famous father Menjou's help; personality-plus cast.▼

Letters From My Windmill (1954-French) **140m.** ***½ D: Marcel Pagnol. Henri Velbert, Daxely, Yvonne Gamy, Rellys, Robert Vattier, Roger Crouzet. A trio of delights from Pagnol: "The Three Low Masses," "The Elixir of Father Gaucher," "The Secret of Master Cornille." The second is best, with monk Rellys leading his monastery into liquor business. Pagnol scripted, and the English subtitles were penned by Preston Sturges!▼

Letters to an Unknown Lover (1985-British-French) **C-101m.** **½ D: Peter Duffell. Cherie Lunghi, Mathilda May, Yves Beneyton, Ralph Bates, Andrea Ferreol. Unconvincing but not uninteresting tale of escaped POW Beneyton and his relationship with sisters Lunghi and May. Neat direction and an intriguing portrait of life in France during the Occupation, but the characterizations just don't hold up. Filmed in both English and French versions; the latter is titled LES LOUVES.▼

Letter to Brezhnev (1985-British) **C-94m.** *** D: Chris Bernard. Peter Firth, Alfred Molina, Alexandra Pigg, Margi Clarke, Neil Cunningham, Ken Campbell, Angela Clarke, Tracy Lea. Bored, unemployed Pigg and zany girlfriend Margi Clarke meet Russian sailors Firth and Molina, who are on leave in dreary Liverpool. There's the potential for love, yet in a few hours they'll be far apart, perhaps forever. Charming, disarming fable about taking risks and dreaming dreams, whose many assets far outweigh its few defects. Very much a product of Liverpool. [R]▼●

Letter to Mother, A SEE: **A Brivele der Mamen**

Letter to Three Wives, A (1949) **103m.** **** D: Joseph L. Mankiewicz. Jeanne Crain, Linda Darnell, Ann Sothern, Kirk Douglas, Paul Douglas, Jeffrey Lynn, Barbara Lawrence, Connie Gilchrist, Florence Bates, Thelma Ritter. Delicious Americana showing reactions of three women who receive a letter from town flirt who has run off with one of their husbands. Celeste Holm provides the voice of the letter's authoress. Mankiewicz won Oscars for his terrific script and direction. Based on a novel by John Klempner, adapted by Vera Caspary. Remade as a TVM in 1985.▼●

Let the Good Times Roll (1973) **C/B&W-98m.** *** D: Sid Levin, Bob Abel. Chuck Berry, Chubby Checker, Bo Diddley, Little Richard, Five Satins, Shirelles, Coasters, Bill Haley and The Comets. Rockumentary with flavor and wit. Study of 1950s told through incredible compilation of film footage, and some fine performances by leading rock 'n' rollers of the period in revival concerts, highlighted by terrific finale with Berry and Diddley dueting on "Johnny B. Goode." Imaginative multi-image widescreen effects are letterboxed on most TV prints. [PG]

Let Us Live (1939) **68m.** **½ D: John Brahm. Maureen O'Sullivan, Henry Fonda, Ralph Bellamy, Alan Baxter, Stanley Ridges. Weepy melodrama about innocent man Fonda convicted of murder and his girl O'Sullivan trying to clear him.

Leviathan (1989) **C-98m.** *½ D: George Pan Cosmatos. Peter Weller, Richard Crenna, Amanda Pays, Daniel Stern, Ernie Hudson, Michael Carmine, Lisa Eilbacher, Hector Elizondo, Meg Foster. Yet one more dreadful ALIEN clone, this one set underwater (like several other 1989 releases), with a team of men and women imperiled as they toil in the depths of the Atlantic. Skip it. J-D-C Scope. [R]▼●◗

Le Voyage en Douce (1980-French) **C-98m.** **½ D: Michel Deville. Dominique Sanda, Geraldine Chaplin. What do women talk about when men aren't around? Friends Sanda and Chaplin travel to the South of France; they gab, flirt, tell each other lies. Sometimes witty, but ultimately disappointing; director Deville asked 15 French writers of both sexes to provide him with sexual anecdotes, which he worked into screenplay.

Levy and Goliath (1987-French) **C-97m.** **½ D: Gerard Oury. Richard Anconina, Michel Boujenah, Jean-Claude Brialy, Saouad Amidou, Sophie Barjac, Maxime Leroux, Robert Hossein. Director Oury returns to the ethnic humor of his hit THE MAD ADVENTURE OF "RABBI" JACOB with this wacky tale of an Hassidic Jew from Antwerp (Anconina) who gets mixed up with drug smugglers in Paris while becoming romantically involved with Arab beauty Amidou. Young cast is excellent and Brialy is a hoot as a narc working undercover in drag.

Lianna (1983) **C-110m.** *** D: John Sayles. Linda Griffiths, Jane Hallaren, Jon DeVries, Jo Henderson, Jessica Wight MacDonald, Jesse Solomon, Maggie Renzi. Young woman, trapped in an unhappy marriage, finds herself attracted to another woman, and tries to come to grips with being lesbian. Writer-director Sayles hasn't a false note or an unsure line of dialogue, though the film goes on a bit too long. As usual, he's written himself a good role, as a film professor; look for Chris Elliott as a lighting technician. [R]▼

Liar Liar (1997) **C-87m.** **½. D: Tom Shadyac. Jim Carrey, Maura Tierney, Jennifer Tilly, Swoosie Kurtz, Amanda Donohoe, Jason Bernard, Mitchell Ryan, Anne Haney, Justin Cooper, Cary Elwes, Randall "Tex" Cobb, Cheri Oteri. Unscrupulous lawyer with a penchant for lying gets his just deserts when his neglected son makes a birthday wish that his Dad has to tell the truth for 24 hours—and it comes true. Carrey vehicle delivers the laughs for his fans, but once the premise unfolds it's pretty formulaic. Bob Hope lived through a similar 24 hours in NOTHING BUT THE TRUTH (1941). [PG-13]▼●◗

Liar's Moon (1981) **C-105m.** **½ D: David Fisher. Matt Dillon, Cindy Fisher, Christopher Connelly, Hoyt Axton, Maggie Blye, Susan Tyrrell, Yvonne DeCarlo, Broderick Crawford, Mark Atkins, Molly McCarthy. Hokey and obvious but still engaging soaper of poor Dillon and wealthy Fisher falling in love, with a "terrible secret" between them. Director Fisher also wrote the screenplay. Filmed with two different endings; both were released. [PG]▼

Libel (1959) **100m.** **½ D: Anthony Asquith. Dirk Bogarde, Olivia de Havilland, Robert Morley, Paul Massie, Wilfrid Hyde-White, Anthony Dawson, Richard Wattis, Millicent Martin. Engrossing if uninspired filming of Edward Wooll's vintage play about a baronet (and former prisoner of war) who is challenged in court to prove his identity—which turns out to be unusually difficult. Metroscope.

Libeled Lady (1936) **98m.** **** D: Jack Conway. Jean Harlow, William Powell, Myrna Loy, Spencer Tracy, Walter Connolly, Charley Grapewin, Cora Witherspoon. Wonderful comedy with the four stars working at full steam: conniving newspaper editor Tracy uses his fiancee (Harlow) and ex-employee (Powell) to get the goods on hot-headed heiress Loy—but everything goes wrong. Sit back and enjoy. Screenplay by Maurine Watkins, Howard Emmett Rogers, and George Oppenheimer. Remade as EASY TO WED.▼●

Liberation of L. B. Jones, The (1970) **C-102m.** **½ D: William Wyler. Lee J. Cobb, Anthony Zerbe, Roscoe Lee Browne, Lola Falana, Lee Majors, Barbara Hershey, Yaphet Kotto, Chill Wills. Wyler's final film is militant tale of racism in the South. Some good performances, especially Falana's, but slow pace and many subplots hurt. [R]▼

Liberty Heights (1999) **C-127m.** **½ D: Barry Levinson. Adrien Brody, Ben Foster, Orlando Jones, Bebe Neuwirth, Joe Mantegna, Rebekah Johnson, David Krumholtz,

Richard Kline, Vincent Guastaferro, Justin Chambers, Carolyn Murphy, James Pickens, Jr., Shane West. A family living in a Jewish suburb in 1954 Baltimore must deal with changing times and values represented by "the other kind," i.e., gentiles and African Americans. Director-writer Levinson's fourth Baltimore tale (following DINER, TIN MEN and AVALON) is well mounted and has many insightful and humorous moments, but is also surprisingly bland, with rather pedestrian plot turns and revelations of character and theme. [R]▼●◗

Licence to Kill (1989-British) **C-133m.** *** D: John Glen. Timothy Dalton, Carey Lowell, Robert Davi, Talisa Soto, Anthony Zerbe, Frank McRae, Everett McGill, Wayne Newton, Benicio Del Toro, Desmond Llewlyn, David Hedison, Priscilla Barnes. Tough, mean James Bond adventure, with Dalton pursuing a drug kingpin to avenge an attack on his best friend. Dazzling stunts, high adventure, and a sexy companion for Bond (Lowell) make this one of the best of the series since Sean Connery's departure (yet it still lacks that old-time panache). Panavision. [PG-13]▼●

Licensed to Kill SEE: **Second Best Secret Agent in the Whole Wide World**

License to Drive (1988) **C-88m.** ** D: Greg Beeman. Corey Haim, Corey Feldman, Carol Kane, Richard Masur, Heather Graham, Michael Manasseri, Harvey Miller, Nina Siemaszko, Grant Goodeve, Parley Baer. Noisy teen comedy about a 16-year-old who's just flunked his driver's test, and sneaks his grandfather's prized car out for a "dream" date that turns into a nightmare. Appealing performance by Haim, and a terrific one by the underrated Masur. Uneven comedy; low point: a long, tasteless sequence involving a drunk driver. [PG-13]▼●

License to Kill (1964-French) **95m.** ** D: Henri Decoin. Eddie Constantine, Yvonne Monlaur, Daphne Dayle, Paul Frankeur, Vladimir Inkijinoff, Charles Belmont. Constantine is modern-day Nick Carter involved with Oriental spies and superduper guided missile weapon wanted by Allies; elaborate nonsense.▼

Liebestraum (1991) **C-109m.** **½ D: Mike Figgis. Kevin Anderson, Pamela Gidley, Bill Pullman, Kim Novak, Graham Beckel, Zach Grenier, Thomas Kopache, Max Perlich, Catherine Hicks, Taina Elg. An architectural writer visits his dying mother in a small town, only to get involved in a forty-year-old sex scandal, his own adultery, and the demolition of the town's most distinctive building by his lover's husband. So-so material with a truly insane title; directed (overdirected?) with some style by the maker of STORMY MONDAY. Novak, who's wasted, spends most of the film bedridden in a gloomy hospital. Available on video in R and unrated versions. [R]▼●

Lies (1983) **C-100m.** **½ D: Ken and Jim Wheat. Ann Dusenberry, Bruce Davison, Gail Strickland, Clu Gulager, Terence Knox, Bert Remsen, Dick Miller. Not bad little thriller about an actress who's used as a pawn in elaborate inheritance scam. Well-cast low budgeter piles up too many contrivances toward the climax. [R]▼

Lies My Father Told Me (1975-Canadian) **C-102m.** ***½ D: Jan Kadar. Yossi Yadin, Len Birman, Marilyn Lightstone, Jeffrey Lynas. Tender film about young boy in Canadian-Jewish ghetto of the 1920s who idolizes his grandfather, a simple, old-fashioned junk collector. Author Ted Allan plays Mr. Baumgarten. Simple and moving drama. [PG]▼

Lieutenant Wore Skirts, The (1956) **C-99m.** **½ D: Frank Tashlin. Tom Ewell, Sheree North, Rita Moreno, Rick Jason, Les Tremayne, Jean Willes. Ewell makes nonsense acceptable as he chases after wife who reenlisted in service thinking he'd been drafted again. CinemaScope.

Life (1999) **C-108m.** **½ D: Ted Demme. Eddie Murphy, Martin Lawrence, Obba Babatundé, Ned Beatty, Bernie Mac, Miguel A. Nuñez, Jr., Clarence Williams III, Bokeem Woodbine, Nick Cassavetes, Poppy Montgomery, Noah Emmerich, Rick James, R. Lee Ermey, Lisa Nicole Carson. A slick Harlem pickpocket and a none-too-bright patsy meet up in the early 1930s and are railroaded into a Mississippi prison, where they spend the next 55 years. Broad comedy is juxtaposed against unexpectedly poignant and serious moments in this episodic film; not always on target, but entertaining just the same. Murphy and Lawrence are very funny, and age believably in Rick Baker's makeup. [R]▼●◗

Life and Adventures of Nicholas Nickleby, The SEE: **Nicholas Nickleby**

Life and Death of Colonel Blimp, The (1943-British) **C-163m.** **** D: Michael Powell, Emeric Pressburger. Roger Livesey, Deborah Kerr, Anton Walbrook, John Laurie, James McKechnie, Neville Mapp. Superb, sentimental story of a staunch British soldier, and incidents that dovetail in his long, eventful life. Opens in WW2 and flashes back as far as the Boer War. Kerr charming as three different women in the Colonel's life. (Title character bears no relation to famous David Low caricature buffoon on whom he's supposedly based.) Heavily cut for various reissues; often shown in b&w.▼●

Life and Nothing But (1990-French) **C-135m.** *** D: Bertrand Tavernier. Philippe Noiret, Sabine Azema, Pascale Vignal, Maurice Barrier, Francois Perrot. Two years after the WW1 armistice, French Army officer Noiret is still tabulating French casualties and identifying bodies, a job which brings him into contact with a wealthy and repressed young woman who's been searching obsessively for her husband. Subject matter is more compelling than the script, which loses its edge; still worthwhile. Panavision. [PG]▼●

Life and Times of Grizzly Adams, The (1976) **C-93m.** *½ D: Richard Friedenberg. Dan Haggerty, Don Shanks, Lisa Jones, Marjorie Harper, Bozo. Poorly made, clumsily scripted family/wilderness saga, about fur trapper innocently pursued for crime, who finds peace in the mountains where he befriends a massive bear. Followed by THE MARK OF THE BEAR in 1991, GRIZZLY MOUNTAIN in 1998, the 1982 made-for-TV movie THE CAPTURE OF GRIZZLY ADAMS and a TV series. [G]▼

Life and Times of Judge Roy Bean, The (1972) **C-120m.** *** D: John Huston. Paul Newman, Ava Gardner, Victoria Principal, Jacqueline Bisset, Anthony Perkins, Tab Hunter, John Huston, Stacy Keach, Roddy McDowall, Ned Beatty, Dick (Richard) Farnsworth. Tongue-in-cheek Western saga with surrealistic touches. Newman plays self-appointed "Judge" who rules over barren territory, encountering various colorful characters as town grows and matures. Engaging cameos by Keach, Huston, McDowall, and Gardner as Lillie Langtry. Written by John Milius. [PG]▼●

Life and Times of Rosie the Riveter, The (1980) **C/B&W-60m.** *** D: Connie Field. Wanita Allen, Gladys Belcher, Lyn Childs, Lola Weixel, Margaret Wright. Thoughtful, enlightening documentary about women factory workers during WW2 effectively combines period newsreel footage and interviews with five "Rosies." Aka ROSIE THE RIVETER. ▼

Life at the Top (1965-British) **117m.** **½ D: Ted Kotcheff. Laurence Harvey, Jean Simmons, Honor Blackman, Michael Craig, Donald Wolfit, Robert Morley, Margaret Johnston, Nigel Davenport. Follow-up to ROOM AT THE TOP picks up the account a decade later; film lacks flavor or life—best moments are flashbacks to Signoret-Harvey romance.

Life Begins (1932) **71m.** *** D: James Flood, Elliott Nugent. Loretta Young, Aline MacMahon, Glenda Farrell, Vivienne Osborne, Eric Linden, Preston Foster, Elizabeth Patterson, Dorothy Tree. Offbeat film of maternity ward, with fine Warner Bros. cast depicting nurses, mothers, and others involved in life-giving process. Remade as A CHILD IS BORN.

Life Begins at College SEE: **Life Begins in College**

Life Begins at Eight-Thirty (1942) **85m.** *** D: Irving Pichel. Monty Woolley, Ida Lupino, Cornel Wilde, Sara Allgood, Melville Cooper, J. Edward Bromberg. Drunken washed-up actor Woolley disrupts daughter Lupino's life. Highlight is scene of Woolley as intoxicated Santa Claus. Produced and adapted by Nunnally Johnson from Emlyn Williams's play.

Life Begins at Forty (1935) **85m.** *** D: George Marshall. Will Rogers, Rochelle Hudson, Richard Cromwell, Jane Darwell, Slim Summerville, George Barbier, Thomas Beck, Sterling Holloway. Delightful Americana, with newspaper editor Rogers trying to clear name of Cromwell, who was framed for bank robbery years ago. Rogers' comments on American life remain surprisingly contemporary.

Life Begins at 17 (1958) **75m.** *½ D: Arthur Dreifuss. Mark Damon, Dorothy Johnson, Edd Byrnes, Luana Anders, Ann Doran, Hugh Sanders. Rich punk Damon is dating plain Anders, but is only using her to get to her beauty-queen sister. Demented specimen of producer Sam Katzman's low-budget (albeit successful) 1950s teenpics.

Life Begins for Andy Hardy (1941) **100m.** *** D: George B. Seitz. Mickey Rooney, Lewis Stone, Judy Garland, Fay Holden, Ann Rutherford, Sara Haden, Patricia Dane, Ray McDonald. Andy decides to get a job in the Big Apple before starting college and is confronted with the harsh realities of life and love. Unusually adult and cynical addition to the series. Garland's third and final appearance; her songs were cut(!) from the finished film.▼●

Life Begins in College (1937) **94m.** **½ D: William A. Seiter. Joan Davis, Tony Martin, Ritz Brothers, Gloria Stuart, Nat Pendleton, Fred Stone. Sis-boom-bah college nonsense with zany Ritz trio helping the school team win the big game. Pendleton is fun as an Indian who comes to college.

Lifeboat (1944) **96m.** ***½ D: Alfred Hitchcock. Tallulah Bankhead, William Bendix, Walter Slezak, Mary Anderson, John Hodiak, Henry Hull, Heather Angel, Hume Cronyn, Canada Lee. Penetrating revelations about shipwreck survivors adrift in lonely lifeboat during WW2. Bankhead remarkable as spoiled journalist, Slezak fine as Nazi taken aboard. Only Hitchcock would take on the challenge of such a film—and succeed. Jo Swerling adapted John Steinbeck's original story. Remade as a 1993 TVM, LIFEPOD. ▼●

Lifeforce (1985) **C-101m.** ** D: Tobe Hooper. Steve Railsback, Peter Firth, Frank Finlay, Mathilda May, Patrick Stewart, Michael Gothard. Completely crazy science-fiction yarn starts as outer space saga, then becomes a vampire movie, then turns into an end-of-the-world story! Ridiculous, to say the least, but so bizarre, it's fascinating: people disintegrate, London is overrun by zombies, and controlling it all is a beautiful nude space vampiress! Don't say we didn't warn you. Based on Colin Wil-

son's novel *Space Vampires*. Foreign release version running 116m. available on video. J-D-C Scope. [R]▼●◗
Lifeguard (1976) **C-96m.** **½ D: Daniel Petrie. Sam Elliott, Anne Archer, Kathleen Quinlan, Stephen Young, Parker Stevenson, Steve Burns, Sharon Weber. After his 15-year high school reunion, Elliott can't decide whether to chuck the title job to become a salesman. Slight drama resembles made-for-TV movie, but attractive cast and locations make it pleasant enough. [PG]▼
Life in the Balance, A (1955) **74m.** ** D: Harry Horner. Ricardo Montalban, Anne Bancroft, Lee Marvin, Jose Perez. Lukewarm narrative set in a Latin American city, about a series of woman-killings; the police hunt for guilty person.
Life in the Pink SEE: **Operation Petticoat** (1977)
Life in the Theater, A (1993) **C-78m. TVM** D: Gregory Mosher. Jack Lemmon, Matthew Broderick. David Mamet adapted (and expanded) his 1977 two-character play for television: a witty, original dialogue between a veteran actor on his way down and a young, up-and-coming colleague. If you're a fan of Lemmon, Broderick, Mamet or the theater, you'll love it, though it worked better on stage than it does on film. Made for cable. Above average.▼●
Life Is a Bed of Roses (1983-French) **C-111m.** ***½ D: Alain Resnais. Vittorio Gassman, Ruggero Raimondi, Geraldine Chaplin, Fanny Ardant, Pierre Arditi, Sabine Azema. Enchanting, magical, original fable paralleling the stories of wealthy Raimondi building a "temple of happiness" circa WW1, and a conference on alternative education at that site in the present day. Resnais and screenwriter Jean Gruault beautifully illustrate that there are no simple solutions to problems, that those who impose their ideas of perfection on the world are just as dangerous as those who cause disorder. [PG]
Life Is a Long Quiet River (1987-French) **C-95m.** *** D: Etienne Chatiliez. Benoit Magimel, Valerie Lalande, Tara Romer, Jerome Floch, Sylvie Cubertafon, Emmanuel Cendrier. A mixup of babies is revealed twelve years after the fact, and two very different families must learn to deal with the life-changing events it causes. Delightful French comedy that examines the differences between the lower class and the bourgeois. Wry, winning directorial debut for Chatiliez.▼
Life Is Beautiful (1997-Italian) **C-116m.** ***½ D: Roberto Benigni. Roberto Benigni, Nicoletta Braschi, Giorgio Cantarini, Giustino Durano, Sergio Bustric, Marisa Paredes, Horst Buchholz. Extraordinary film by comedy star Benigni about an irrepressible spirit who refuses to ever give in to adversity, even when he is taken to a concentration camp with his wife (Benigni's real-life wife, Braschi) and young son. He determines that the boy will be shielded from the horrors around them—and somehow finds a way to do it. A unique and beguiling fable that celebrates the human spirit. Benigni cowrote with Vincenzo Cerami. Oscar winner for Best Foreign Language Film, Best Actor, Best Score (Nicola Piovani). Original title: LA VITA E BELLA. [PG-13]▼●◗
Life Is Cheap . . . but Toilet Paper Is Expensive (1990) **C-89m.** ** D: Wayne Wang. Spenser Nakasako, Lo Wai, Cora Miao, Victor Wong, Cheng Kwan Min. Courier is sent to Hong Kong with metal briefcase handcuffed to his wrist; upon arrival, he's unable to deliver his mysterious attaché, so he decides to take in the colorful sights of the city instead. Extremely bizarre, graphic, and dense little film, of interest mainly to fans of filmmaker Wang. Some bloody scenes threatened to earn this an X rating, so the film was released unrated and visually intact.
Life Is Sweet (1991-British) **C-102m.** *** D: Mike Leigh. Alison Steadman, Jim Broadbent, Claire Skinner, Jane Horrocks, Stephen Rea, Timothy Spall, David Thewlis. Another slice of working-class life from Leigh, focusing on an endearing couple and their iconoclastic twin daughters—one of whom (Horrocks) is waist-deep in self-loathing. More a series of vignettes than a conventional story, and filled with deliciously offbeat humor; not for every taste, but a bittersweet treat for fans of Leigh's work. Leading lady Steadman was then the director's wife.▼●
Life Less Ordinary, A (1997-British) **C-103m.** **½ D: Danny Boyle. Ewan McGregor, Cameron Diaz, Holly Hunter, Delroy Lindo, Ian Holm, Ian McNeice, Stanley Tucci, Dan Hedaya, Tony Shalhoub, Maury Chaykin, Judith Ivey. Black comedy about a janitor who kidnaps his ex-boss's daughter, a spoiled heiress who finds life a bore. Meanwhile, two emissaries from Heaven (Hunter and Lindo) have to find a way to make these two fated souls fall in love. Fans of the two likable stars will perhaps be more forgiving than others of this oddball, sporadically funny outing from the SHALLOW GRAVE/TRAINSPOTTING team. Super 35. [R]▼●◗
Life of Brian (1979-British) **C-93m.** *** D: Terry Jones. Graham Chapman, John Cleese, Terry Gilliam, Eric Idle, Terry Jones, Michael Palin. This Monty Python religious parable will probably offend every denomination equally, but it shouldn't. Story of a man whose life parallels Christ is the funniest and most sustained feature from Britain's bad boys. [R]▼●
Life of Emile Zola, The (1937) **116m.**

**** D: William Dieterle. Paul Muni, Gale Sondergaard, Joseph Schildkraut, Gloria Holden, Donald Crisp, Erin O'Brien-Moore, Morris Carnovsky, Louis Calhern, Harry Davenport, Marcia Mae Jones, Dickie Moore, Ralph Morgan. Sincere biography of famed 19th-century French writer who rose to cause of wrongly exiled Captain Dreyfus (Schildkraut); detailed production filled with fine vignettes. Won Oscars for Best Picture, Screenplay (Norman Reilly Raine, Geza Herczeg, and Heinz Herald), Supporting Actor (Schildkraut).▼●

Life of Her Own, A (1950) **108m.** **½ D: George Cukor. Lana Turner, Ray Milland, Tom Ewell, Louis Calhern, Ann Dvorak, Margaret Phillips, Jean Hagen, Barry Sullivan, Phyllis Kirk. Turner is at the center of three-cornered romance leading to heartbreak for all. MGM fluff; Dvorak wraps it up with her expert portrayal of an aging model. Bronislau Kaper's musical theme was later reused for his classic INVITATION.▼

Life of Jack London, The SEE: **Jack London**

Life of Jimmy Dolan, The (1933) **89m.** *** D: Archie Mayo. Douglas Fairbanks, Jr., Loretta Young, Guy Kibbee, Fifi D'Orsay, Aline MacMahon, Lyle Talbot. Fast-moving account of boxer Fairbanks, on the run after he thinks he killed a reporter, winding up at a home for crippled children. Look for Mickey Rooney as one of the kids, John Wayne in boxing trunks. Remade as THEY MADE ME A CRIMINAL.

Life of Oharu, The (1952-Japanese) **146m.** **½ D: Kenji Mizoguchi. Kinuyo Tanaka, Toshiro Mifune, Hisako Yamane, Yuriko Hamada, Ichiro Sugai. Clichéd account of beautiful Tanaka, banished for loving a samurai (Mifune, in a small role) below her station, ending up an aged prostitute. Also shown at 118m. and known as DIARY OF OHARU.▼●

Life of Riley, The (1948) **87m.** **½ D: Irving Brecher. William Bendix, James Gleason, Rosemary DeCamp, Bill Goodwin, Beulah Bondi, Meg Randall, Richard Long, John Brown. Adaptation of the popular radio comedy series about hard-luck working stiff Chester A. Riley. More bittersweet than the subsequent TV series but enjoyable, with the black comedy of Brown's Digger O'Dell a real novelty.

Life of the Party, The (1937) **77m.** ** D: William Seiter. Gene Raymond, Harriet Hilliard (Nelson), Ann Miller, Joe Penner, Parkyakarkas, Victor Moore, Billy Gilbert, Helen Broderick, Franklin Pangborn, Margaret Dumont. Young Raymond will forfeit $3 million if he weds Hilliard before he turns 30. Second-rate musical comedy.

Life of Vergie Winters, The (1934) **82m.** **½ D: Alfred Santell. Ann Harding, John Boles, Helen Vinson, Betty Furness, Lon Chaney, Jr., Bonita Granville. Successful adaptation of Louis Bromfield weeper chronicling life of Harding, who defies small-town gossip, following her own instincts.

Life on a String (1991-Chinese-British-German) **C-110m.** *** D: Chen Kaige. Liu Zhong Yuan, Huang Lei, Xu Qing, Ma Ling, Zhang Zhengguan. Lyrical, beautifully filmed tale of a blind boy who's told by his master that his sight will be restored if he devotes his life to music; he becomes a saintly old man (still without sight) who travels from village to village with his young disciple singing songs, which he finds spiritually nurturing. Thoughtful film crammed with poetic imagery, soundtrack of wonderful folk songs. ▼

Lifepod (1993) **C-100m. TVM** D: Ron Silver. Ron Silver, Robert Loggia, Jessica Tuck, Kelli Williams, Adam Storke, CCH Pounder, Stan Shaw. Hitchcock's LIFEBOAT reset in the future with a group of survivors stranded in deep space and a saboteur on their rescue ship. Silver made his directing debut with this crafty (and credited) reworking of Hitchcock by M. Jay Roach and Pen Densham. Above average. ▼●

Life Stinks (1991) **C-95m.** ** D: Mel Brooks. Mel Brooks, Lesley Ann Warren, Jeffrey Tambor, Stuart Pankin, Howard Morris, Rudy De Luca, Teddy Wilson, Michael Ensign, Matthew Faison, Billy Barty, Carmine Caridi. Money-hungry developer Brooks takes a bet that he won't survive on the streets of L.A. for one month without a cent. Usual Brooks smorgasbord of gags, but the success rate is pretty low. Attempts to make meaningful statement about homelessness are thin at best, tasteless at worst. Brooks also cowrote the screenplay. [PG-13]▼●

Life With Blondie (1946) **64m.** **½ D: Abby Berlin. Penny Singleton, Arthur Lake, Larry Simms, Marjorie Kent, Jonathan Hale, Ernest Truex, Marc Lawrence, Veda Ann Borg, Jack Rice, Bobby Larson, Eddie Acuff. Genial nonsense about the Bumsteads' dog, Daisy, winning a Navy pinup contest and being kidnaped by gangsters.▼

Life With Father (1947) **C-118m.** **** D: Michael Curtiz. William Powell, Irene Dunne, Elizabeth Taylor, Edmund Gwenn, ZaSu Pitts, Jimmy Lydon, Martin Milner. Rich adaptation of long-running Broadway play (by Howard Lindsay and Russel Crouse) based on Clarence Day's story of growing up in turn-of-the-century N.Y.C. with his loving but eccentric father. Utterly delightful, and a handsome production as well. Screenplay by Donald Ogden Stewart.▼●◗

Life With Henry (1941) **80m.** **½ D: Ted Reed. Jackie Cooper, Leila Ernst, Eddie Bracken, Fred Niblo, Hedda Hopper, Kay Stewart, Moroni Olsen, Rod Cam-

eron, Pierre Watkin, Lucien Littlefield, Frank M. Thomas. Followup to WHAT A LIFE brings Cooper back to role of Henry Aldrich, the perpetual foulup who this time wants to win a trip to Alaska. Bracken is fun as his comic pal.
Life With Mikey (1993) **C-91m.** *** D: James Lapine. Michael J. Fox, Christina Vidal, Nathan Lane, Cyndi Lauper, David Krumholtz, David Huddleston, Victor Garber, Tony Hendra. Former child TV star Fox lackadaisically runs a Manhattan talent agency for kids with his more dedicated brother. Then he tries to turn 10-year-old pickpocket Vidal into a star of cookie commercials and finds himself fired up in the process. Funny film, with serious overtones, is a perfect vehicle for Fox and appealing newcomer Vidal. Audition scenes are particularly good. Ruben Blades appears unbilled as Vidal's father. [PG]▼●
Lift, The (1983-Dutch) **C-98m.** **½ D: Dick Maas. Huub Stapel, Willeke Van Ammelrooy, Josine Van Dalsum, Pret Romer, Gerard Thoolen, Hans Veerman. Sleek horror thriller set in a new highrise, where the elevators are involved in a suspicious number of accidents. Maas is a better director than writer; smoothly made, suspenseful, and witty, but talky, with no satisfactory explanation for the bizarre events. [R]▼●
Lift to the Scaffold SEE: **Frantic** (1957)
Light Across the Street, The (1956-French) **76m.** **½ D: Georges Lacombe. Brigitte Bardot, Raymond Pellegrin, Roger Pigaut, Claude Romain. Above-par Bardot fare: she's wed to jealous Pellegrin, who begins to suspect she's fooling around with the new next-door neighbor. Original running time: 99m. Retitled: FEMALE AND THE FLESH.
Light Ahead, The (1939) **94m.** *** D: Edgar G. Ulmer. Isidore Cashier, Helen Beverly, David Opatoshu, Rosetta Bialis, Tillie Rabinowitz. Heartfelt, pleasingly sentimental saga, based on the writings of Mendele Mocher Sforim (Mendele the bookseller), detailing the plight of poor, luckless lovers Beverly and Opatoshu, and how they are helped by wise old bookseller Cashier in a provincial Russian town during the 1880s. Long-lost Yiddish-language gem was shot in Newton, New Jersey!▼
Light at the Edge of the World, The (1971-Spanish-Liechtensteinian) **C-119m.** *½ D: Kevin Billington. Kirk Douglas, Yul Brynner, Samantha Eggar, Jean-Claude Druout, Fernando Rey. Amidst their fight for possession of an island, lighthouse keeper Douglas and sea pirate Brynner battle it out for affections of shipwreck victim Eggar. Jules Verne tale has some excitement, but is more often unintentionally funny. Panavision. [PG]▼
Light Fingers (1957-British) **90m.** ** D: Terry Bishop. Guy Rolfe, Eunice Gayson, Roland Culver, Lonnie Donegan, Hy Hazell, Ronald Howard. Miserly husband (Culver) thinks wife is kleptomaniac; hires bodyguard butler who is really a thief. Adequate production.
Lighthorsemen, The (1987-Australian) **C-111m.** **½ D: Simon Wincer. Jon Blake, Peter Phelps, Nick Wateres, Tony Bonner, Bill Kerr, John Walton, Tim McKenzie, Sigrid Thornton, Anthony Andrews. Saga of the Australian Light Horse Brigade, and their involvement in a daunting desert campaign during WW1. Sweeping widescreen adventure, stunningly filmed, but marred by simplistic characterizations, and overlength (though trimmed for U.S. release). Climactic charge on Beersheba is genuinely exciting. Original Australian running time: 128m. Panavision. [PG]▼●
Light in the Forest, The (1958) **C-93m.** *** D: Herschel Daugherty. James MacArthur, Carol Lynley, Fess Parker, Wendell Corey, Joanne Dru, Jessica Tandy, Joseph Calleia, John McIntire. Absorbing Disney for young people, from Conrad Richter's story of a white boy, raised by Indians, who has difficulty readjusting to life with his real parents. Lynley's film debut.▼●
Light in the Jungle (1990) **C-89m.** ** D: Gray Hofmeyer. Malcolm McDowell, Susan Strasberg, Andrew Davis, John Carson, Helen Jessop, Henry Cele, Patrick Shai. Languid story of Nobel prize winner Albert Schweitzer's years as a doctor in Africa, where he battles both the superstitions of the natives and the interference of his European benefactors. Inspired visuals, but choppy storytelling hampers this potentially interesting bio. [PG]▼
Light in the Piazza (1962) **C-101m.** ***½ D: Guy Green. Olivia de Havilland, Rossano Brazzi, Yvette Mimieux, George Hamilton, Barry Sullivan. Splendid soaper about mother who's anxious to marry off retarded daughter but isn't sure she's being fair to suitor. Beautifully filmed on location in Italy. Screenplay by Julius Epstein, from Elizabeth Spencer's novel. CinemaScope.
Light It Up (1999) **C-99m.** **½ D: Craig Bolotin. Usher Raymond, Forest Whitaker, Marcello Robinson, Rosario Dawson, Robert Ri'chard, Judd Nelson, Fredro Starr, Sara Gilbert, Glynn Turman, Vanessa L. Williams. Well-intentioned but preachy drama about a group of N.Y.C. students who occupy their high school after their favorite teacher is unfairly suspended and a police officer is accidentally shot. Attempts to deal with a number of serious issues, but results are forced and melodramatic. Written by the director. [R]▼◗
Lightning Jack (1994-Australian) **C-93m.** ** D: Simon Wincer. Paul Hogan, Cuba Gooding, Jr., Beverly D'Angelo, Kamala Dawson, Pat Hingle, Richard Riehle, Frank

McRae, Roger Daltrey, L. Q. Jones, Max Cullen. Hogan attempts to repeat his "CROCODILE" DUNDEE success with this amiable but obvious, undistinguished Western/comedy. He's the whole show in his role as two-bit desperado Lightning Jack Kane, but all his charm can't save it. Gooding is his mute sidekick. Hogan also scripted and coproduced. Panavision. [PG-13]▼●

Lightning Strikes Twice (1951) **91m.** **½ D: King Vidor. Richard Todd, Ruth Roman, Mercedes McCambridge, Zachary Scott. Muddled yet engaging yarn of ex-con returning home to start new life, finding actual killer of his wife.

Lightning Swords of Death (1974-Japanese) **C-83m.** *** D: Kenji Misumi. Tomisaburo Wakayama, Masahiro Tomikawa, Goh Kato. Discredited samurai roams medieval Japan pushing his young son ahead of him in baby cart in this edited entry from *Sword of Vengeance* series. Unending action and beautifully staged fights, with climactic battle rivaling finale of THE WILD BUNCH. Very bloody, though; followed by SHOGUN ASSASSIN. Shawscope. [R]

Lightning, the White Stallion (1986) **C-95m.** *½ D: William A. Levey. Mickey Rooney, Isabel Lorca, Susan George, Billy Wesley. Extremely weak family fare with Rooney a wealthy man whose racehorse is stolen. The Mick can't save it. [PG]▼

Light of Day (1987) **C-107m.** ** D: Paul Schrader. Michael J. Fox, Gena Rowlands, Joan Jett, Michael McKean, Thomas G. Waites, Cherry Jones, Michael Dolan, Jason Miller, Michael Rooker. Family angst movie masquerading as a rock 'n' roll tale. Jett and Fox are sister and brother who perform together in a local Cleveland band that starts to gain some recognition, just as personal problems threaten to tear the family apart. Rowlands, in a gratuitous subplot, plays their dying mother. Real-life rock star Jett steals the movie with her compelling performance, but the film degenerates as it goes along. Occasional sparks can't save Schrader's muddled script. [PG-13] ▼●

Lightship, The (1985) **C-89m.** ** D: Jerzy Skolimowski. Robert Duvall, Klaus Maria Brandauer, Tom Bower, Robert Costanzo, Badja Djola, William Forsythe, Arliss Howard, Michael Lyndon. Duvall, practically unrecognizable, gives an outrageously inventive performance as a slimy homosexual thug in this otherwise muddled, pretentiously symbolic saga of a trio of criminals who besiege Brandauer's lightship. Narration, spoken by Brandauer's son (Lyndon—real-life son of Skolimowski), is laughably hokey. [PG-13]▼

Light Sleeper (1992) **C-103m.** *** D: Paul Schrader. Willem Dafoe, Susan Sarandon, Dana Delany, David Clennon, Mary Beth Hurt, Victor Garber, Jane Adams, Paul Jabara, David Spade. Quintessential Schrader Lonely Guy film, with Dafoe an aging sadsack who wants more out of life than his dead-end job taxi-ing cocaine to upscale users in N.Y. Well performed by all, and with surprising dashes of loopy humor—though leading to an inevitable bloodbath given the standard blueprint for most Schrader movies. Quite the image-altering showcase for Delany. [R]▼●◗

Light That Failed, The (1939) **97m.** *** D: William Wellman. Ronald Colman, Walter Huston, Ida Lupino, Dudley Digges, Muriel Angelus, Fay Helm, Francis McDonald. Fine cast in Kipling melodrama of London artist Colman going blind, determined to finish portrait of Lupino, whose florid cockney performance steals film.

Light Touch, The (1951) **110m.** **½ D: Richard Brooks. Stewart Granger, Pier Angeli, George Sanders, Kurt Kasznar. On-location shooting in Europe perks up lukewarm drama of art thief Granger and his innocent girlfriend Angeli.

Light Years (1988-French) **C-71m.** ** D: Rene Laloux. Voices of Glenn Close, Christopher Plummer, Jennifer Grey, John Shea, David Johansen, Terrence Mann, Penn and Teller. Pretentious animated sci-fi fantasy, about a prince who time-travels into the future; he's surrounded by characters named Ambisextra, Metamorphosis, Chief of the Deformed, and The Collective Voice (so you know this wasn't made with young children in mind). The animation is nothing special, and the talky script is by none other than Isaac Asimov. [PG]▼●

Light Years Away (1981-French-Swiss) **C-105m.** *** D: Alain Tanner. Trevor Howard, Mick Ford, Bernice Stegers, Henri Vorlogeux. Irritable old Howard, who resides in a deserted, dilapidated gas station, becomes the mentor of drifter Ford. Thoughtful yarn is well acted by its two leads. Filmed in Ireland.

Like a Crow on a June Bug SEE: **Sixteen**

Like a Turtle on Its Back (1978-French) **C-110m.** **½ D: Luc Beraud. Jean-Francois Stevenin, Bernadette Lafont, Virginie Thevenet, Veronique Silver, Claude Miller. Uneven yet absorbing tale of blocked writer Stevenin's efforts to create, offering a hint of the real struggle a writer must make to pound out meaningful sentences on his typewriter.

Like Father, Like Son (1987) **C-98m.** BOMB D: Rod Daniel. Dudley Moore, Kirk Cameron, Margaret Colin, Catherine Hicks, Patrick O'Neal, Sean Astin. Heart surgeon accidentally sprinkles an ancient Indian potion into his Bloody Mary and presto!—he and his teenage son have somehow switched identities. Moore's mugging talents get a major workout in this Hall of Fame embarrassment, first of four 1987/1988 comedies to utilize an adult-teen switcheroo theme. Later variations worked somewhat better. [PG-13]▼●

Likely Story, A (1947) **88m.** *½ D: H. C. Potter. Bill Williams, Barbara Hale, Sam Levene, Lanny Rees, Dan Tobin, Nestor Paiva. Williams and Hale, then real-life newlyweds, star in this inane comedy about a deluded, shellshocked ex-GI who thinks he's dying and the determined young artist who rescues him. Levene adds the only spark as a Runyonesque crook.

Like Water for Chocolate (1992-Mexican) **C-113m.** *** D: Alfonso Arau. Lumi Cavazos, Marco Leonardi, Regina Torne, Mario Ivan Martinez, Ada Carrasco. Striking and sensuous film (from a novel by Laura Esquivel, the director's then-wife), set in the early part of the 20th century: a young woman's life is shaped first by her stern and unyielding mother, and more important, by the overwhelming power of cooking. Sumptuous fable—not without humor—with a good cast and a top-notch performance from lead actress Cavazos. Piquant, sometimes mystical, and enjoyably unpredictable. Original running time was 144m. ▼●

Li'l Abner (1940) **78m.** *½ D: Albert S. Rogell. Granville Owen, Martha O'Driscoll, Mona Ray, Johnnie Morris, Buster Keaton, Kay Sutton. Actors in grotesque makeup bring Al Capp's Dogpatch comic strip characters to life, but despite the presence of many silent comedy veterans (Keaton, Edgar Kennedy, Chester Conklin, Billy Bevan, Al St. John, to name a few) there's nary a laugh in sight. Later musical is much better.▼

Li'l Abner (1959) **C-113m.** **½ D: Melvin Frank. Peter Palmer, Leslie Parrish, Stubby Kaye, Howard St. John, Julie Newmar, Stella Stevens, Billie Hayes, Robert Strauss. Lively Gene DePaul-Johnny Mercer musical based on Broadway version of Al Capp's comic strip; loud and brassy, with corny comedy, some good songs. Stubby Kaye is fine as Marryin' Sam; other Dogpatch characters vividly enacted. Look sharp for young Valerie Harper and Beth Howland among the chorus girls. VistaVision.▼

Lilacs in the Spring SEE: **Let's Make Up**

Lili (1953) **C-81m.** **** D: Charles Walters. Leslie Caron, Mel Ferrer, Zsa Zsa Gabor, Jean-Pierre Aumont, Amanda Blake, Kurt Kasznar. Enchanting musical with Leslie as French orphan who attaches herself to carnival and self-pitying puppeteer Ferrer. Bronislau Kaper's Oscar-winning score includes "Hi Lili, Hi Lo." Helen Deutsch scripted, from Paul Gallico's story.▼●

Lilies of the Field (1963) **93m.** *** D: Ralph Nelson. Sidney Poitier, Lilia Skala, Lisa Mann, Isa Crino, Stanley Adams. A "little" film that made good, winning Poitier an Oscar as handyman who helps build chapel for Skala and her German-speaking nuns. Quiet, well acted, enjoyable. Director Nelson followed this with a TV movie, CHRISTMAS LILIES OF THE FIELD.▼●

Lili Marleen (1981-German) **C-120m.** **½ D: Rainer Werner Fassbinder. Hanna Schygulla, Giancarlo Giannini, Mel Ferrer, Karl Heinz von Hassel, Christine Kaufmann, Hark Bohm, Karin Baal, Udo Kier. Second-rate Fassbinder about third-rate cabaret singer Schygulla, whose recording of the title song becomes a hit in Nazi Germany. Intriguing subject matter is pretentiously handled. [R]

Lilith (1964) **114m.** **½ D: Robert Rossen. Warren Beatty, Jean Seberg, Peter Fonda, Kim Hunter, Jessica Walter, Anne Meacham, Gene Hackman, Rene Auberjonois. Fairly faithful version of controversial J. R. Salamanca novel about a novice therapist who falls in love with a troubled patient. A probing if not altogether satisfying look at the many facets of madness—and love. Director-writer Rossen's last film.▼

Lillian Russell (1940) **127m.** ** D: Irving Cummings. Alice Faye, Don Ameche, Henry Fonda, Edward Arnold, Warren William, Leo Carrillo, Nigel Bruce. Strained biog of early 20th-century star; lavish backgrounds and weak plot line diminish Faye's vehicle; Arnold repeats his Diamond Jim Brady role with gusto.

Lilli Marlene (1950-British) **75m.** ** D: Arthur Crabtree. Lisa Daniely, Hugh McDermott, Richard Murdoch, Leslie Dwyer, John Blythe, Stanley Baker. Potentially exciting film is middling fare, with Daniely the girl used by the Nazis to broadcast pessimistic news to British army. Followed by THE WEDDING OF LILLI MARLENE.

Lily Dale (1996) **C-98m. TVM** D: Peter Masterson. Mary Stuart Masterson, Sam Shepard, Stockard Channing, Tim Guinee, John Slattery, Jean Stapleton. Leisurely adaptation by Horton Foote of his 1968 Off-Broadway memory play dealing with a young man whose tentative return home to 1910 Houston is fraught with anxiety and unwelcomed by his shallow sister. A family affair, with Foote as off-screen narrator (the young man in old age), actress daughter Hallie as executive producer, cousin Peter Masterson as director, and the latter's daughter Mary Stuart rather miscast in the title role (the thirtyish actress playing in her late teens). An elegantly mounted enterprise. Made for cable. Average.▼

Lily in Love (1985-U.S.-Hungarian) **C-103m.** *½ D: Karoly Makk. Christopher Plummer, Maggie Smith, Elke Sommer, Adolph Green, Szabo Sandor. Flat, unfunny (and uncredited) reworking of Molnar's THE GUARDSMAN and THE CHOCOLATE SOLDIER. Egotistical actor Plummer disguises himself as an Italian, and courts wife Smith. Tries to be charming and sophisticated, but fails dismally despite Plummer and Smith's efforts. [PG-13]▼●

Limbo (1972) **C-112m.** ** D: Mark Robson. Kathleen Nolan, Kate Jackson,

Katherine Justice, Stuart Margolin, Hazel Medina, Russell Wiggins. Emotional melodrama about three women, whose husbands are either missing or captured in Vietnam, who become friends. One of the first major Hollywood productions to examine homefront repercussions of the war, but its intentions are better than its results. Screenplay by Joan (Micklin) Silver and James Bridges. Aka WOMEN IN LIMBO. [PG]

Limbo (1999) **C-126m.** ***½ D: John Sayles. Mary Elizabeth Mastrantonio, David Strathairn, Vanessa Martinez, Kris Kristofferson, Casey Siemaszko, Leo Burmester, Kathryn Grody, Rita Taggart. Novelistic film by writer-director Sayles set in modern-day Alaska about characters who find themselves at emotional crossroads: a quiet man with a skeleton in his closet (Strathairn), an itinerant nightclub singer (Mastrantonio) with a habit of picking rotten male companions, and her teenage daughter (Martinez), who's filled with self-loathing and tired of her mother's mercurial relationships. Surprising, intelligent, and richly textured. [R]▼◗

Limehouse Blues (1934) **65m.** ** D: Alexander Hall. George Raft, Jean Parker, Anna May Wong, Kent Taylor, Billy Bevan, Robert Loraine, Eric Blore. Atmospheric but predictable melodrama of race and class differences, set in London's Limehouse district, where brutalized "white girl" Parker is taken in by half-American/half-Chinese saloonkeeper Raft. Watch for Ann Sheridan in a bit. Retitled: EAST END CHANT.

Limelight (1952) **145m.** *** D: Charles Chaplin. Charles Chaplin, Claire Bloom, Nigel Bruce, Buster Keaton, Sydney Chaplin, Norman Lloyd. Sentimental story of aging, washed-up music hall clown (Chaplin) who saves ballerina Bloom from suicide and regains his own confidence while building her up. Overlong, indulgent Chaplin effort still has many moving scenes, historic teaming of Chaplin and Keaton in comedy skit. Young Geraldine Chaplin (the director's daughter) makes her film debut as a street urchin. This won an Oscar for its score in 1972, the year in which it was first eligible for the competition—because it had not been shown in an L.A. theater until then!▼●◗

Limey, The (1999) **C-90m.** **½ D: Steven Soderbergh. Terence Stamp, Peter Fonda, Lesley Ann Warren, Luis Guzman, Barry Newman, Joe Dallesandro, Nicky Katt, Amelia Heinle. A taciturn Britisher, just out of prison, comes to L.A. to avenge the suspicious death of his daughter, who fell under the spell of a sleazy music magnate (Fonda). Stylish and understated, with great use of L.A. locations, but the story at the core isn't all that interesting. Stamp appears in flashbacks lifted from his 1967 film POOR COW. [R]▼●◗

Limping Man, The (1953-British) **76m.** ** D: Charles De Latour. Lloyd Bridges, Moira Lister, Leslie Phillips, Helene Cordet, Alan Wheatley, Rachel Roberts, Jean Marsh. Passable mystery with ex-G.I. Bridges returning to London to rekindle romance with actress Lister, and finding himself embroiled in murder and mayhem.▼

Line, The (1980) **C-94m.** *½ D: Robert Siegel. Russ Thacker, Brad Sullivan, Lewis J. Stadlen, Jacqueline Brooks, David Doyle, Erik Estrada. Poorly made anti-military drama, based on an incident in which 27 prisoners staged a sit-down strike at the Presidio, California military stockade. One-third of the film is made up of footage from Siegel's '71 film, PARADES.▼

Line King: The Al Hirschfeld Story, The (1996) **C-87m.** ***½ D: Susan Warms Dryfoos. Outstanding documentary about Al Hirschfeld, the most famous—and durable—caricaturist of the 20th century. The articulate artist is seen throughout and some of his admiring, amused subjects appear, including Lauren Bacall, Carol Channing, Joan Collins and Robert Goulet. Jules Feiffer offers commentary as well. The highest praise possible: the film is truly worthy of its subject. Beware the hour-long broadcast TV version.▼

Line of Fire SEE: **Sam's Song**

Lineup, The (1958) **86m.** **½ D: Don Siegel. Warner Anderson, Emile Meyer, Eli Wallach, Richard Jaeckel, Robert Keith. Expanded version of TV series set in San Francisco, focusing on gun-happy hoodlum after a cache of dope. Cult favorite with fans of director Siegel. Pretty ordinary except for final car-chase stunt.

Linguini Incident, The (1992) **C-98m.** *½ D: Richard Shepard. Rosanna Arquette, David Bowie, Eszter Balint, Andre Gregory, Buck Henry, Viveca Lindfors, Marlee Matlin, Lewis Arquette. Even pasta lovers should probably steer clear of this dismal trendy-cutesy-quirky caper comedy. Arquette (quite appealing) is a Houdini-obsessed waitress at a N.Y.C. restaurant who wants to rob the place, Bowie is an illegal alien bartender, and Matlin is a cashier. Story concerns magic acts, wagers, and an antique wedding ring. Julian Lennon and Iman have cameos. [R]▼●

Link (1986-British) **C-103m.** BOMB D: Richard Franklin. Terence Stamp, Elisabeth Shue, Steven Pinner, Richard Garnett. Primatologist Stamp is experimenting on chimps . . . and his activities get predictably out of hand. A horror film that's not horrifying, or suspenseful, or even mildly entertaining. [R]▼

Lion, The (1962) **C-96m.** ** D: Jack Cardiff. William Holden, Trevor Howard, Capucine, Pamela Franklin, Samuel Romboh, Christopher Agunda. Beautiful scenery of Kenya is far better than melodrama about young girl attached to pet lion, with family concerned it is turning her into a savage. CinemaScope.

Lion and the Horse, The (1952) **C-83m.** ** D: Louis King. Steve Cochran, Bob Steele, Sherry Jackson, Ray Teal. Warm B film of valiant horse who combats a fierce African lion; geared for children.

Lion Has Wings, The (1939-British) **76m.** **½ D: Michael Powell, Brian Desmond-Hurst, Adrian Brunel. Merle Oberon, Ralph Richardson, June Duprez, Robert Douglas, Anthony Bushell, Derrick de Marney, Brian Worth, Austin Trevor, Ivan Brandt. Dated British WW2 morale-builder, produced by Alexander Korda in a (then) unique "docudrama" style. Top-notch cast and technical credits boost the propagandist elements dramatizing England's entry into the war and the strength of the RAF.

Lionheart (1987) **C-104m.** *** D: Franklin J. Schaffner. Eric Stoltz, Gabriel Byrne, Nicola Cowper, Dexter Fletcher, Deborah Barrymore, Nicholas Clay. Seeking Richard the Lionhearted, who's passing through France headed for the Crusades, runaway young knight Stoltz gradually forms his own children's crusade as more and more homeless children follow him. Richly produced, well acted, with a superb Jerry Goldsmith score, it's a shame this sincere, if slight, film received almost no theatrical release. [PG]▼●

Lionheart (1991) **C-105m.** ** D: Sheldon Lettich. Jean-Claude Van Damme, Deborah Rennard, Harrison Page, Lisa Pelikan, Ashley Johnson. By-the-numbers programmer with Van Damme deserting the foreign legion, becoming a professional street-fighter, and battling a variety of villains. Only for those who like films in which fights are staged ad nauseam. Aka A.W.O.L. and WRONG BET. [R]▼●◗

Lion Hunters, The (1951) **75m.** *½ D: Ford Beebe. Johnny Sheffield, Morris Ankrum, Ann B. Todd, Douglas Kennedy, Smoki Whitfield, Robert Davis, Woodrow (Woody) Strode. It's Bomba the Jungle Boy to the rescue when a hunting expedition is slaughtering lions on sacred Masai grounds. Typical juvenile adventure with even lower production values than usual for this cut-rate series.▼

Lion in Winter, The (1968-British) **C-135m.** **** D: Anthony Harvey. Peter O'Toole, Katharine Hepburn, Jane Merrow, Anthony Hopkins, Nigel Terry, Timothy Dalton, Nigel Stock, John Castle. Brilliant, fierce, and personal drama (adapted by James Goldman from his play) of Henry II deliberating over a successor on fateful Christmas Eve. Hepburn co-won Best Actress Oscar for her strong performance as Eleanor of Aquitaine. Oscars also went to Goldman and composer John Barry. Film debuts of Hopkins and Dalton. O'Toole also played Henry II in BECKET. Panavision. ▼●

Lion Is in the Streets, A (1953) **C-88m.** **½ D: Raoul Walsh. James Cagney, Barbara Hale, Anne Francis, Warner Anderson, John McIntire, Jeanne Cagney, Lon Chaney, Jr., Frank McHugh. Cagney, in a Huey Long take-off, is lively as a swamp peddler turned politician, but rambling screenplay prevents film from having much impact. Well photographed by Harry Stradling. ▼●

Lion King, The (1994) **C-88m.** *** D: Roger Allers, Rob Minkoff. Voices of Jonathan Taylor Thomas, Matthew Broderick, James Earl Jones, Jeremy Irons, Moira Kelly, Niketa Calame, Ernie Sabella, Nathan Lane, Robert Guillaume, Rowan Atkinson, Madge Sinclair, Whoopi Goldberg, Cheech Marin, Jim Cummings. A lion cub raised to take his father's place someday as king of the jungle is sabotaged by his evil uncle—and lives in exile until he realizes his rightful place in the circle of life. With distant echoes of BAMBI, this entertaining Disney cartoon feature (highlighted by Oscar-winning Elton John–Tim Rice songs and Oscar-winning music score by Hans Zimmer) has dazzling scenics, some show-stopping animation, and outstanding voice work—but drama so intense (and comedy so hip) it's not really for very young viewers. Followed by animated TV series, a direct-to-video sequel, THE LION KING II: SIMBA'S PRIDE, and a Broadway musical. [G]▼●

Lion of the Desert (1981-Libyan-British) **C-162m.** *** D: Moustapha Akkad. Anthony Quinn, Oliver Reed, Rod Steiger, John Gielgud, Irene Papas, Raf Vallone, Gastone Moschin. Sweeping "David vs. Goliath" spectacle, with Quinn as Omar Mukhtar, guerrilla leader who stymied Italian forays into Libya between 1911 and 1931. Steiger is Benito Mussolini. Filmed in 1979. Panavision. [PG]▼◗

Lipstick (1976) **C-89m.** BOMB D: Lamont Johnson. Margaux Hemingway, Chris Sarandon, Perry King, Anne Bancroft, Robin Gammell, Mariel Hemingway. Gorgeous model is brutally raped, must ultimately take justice into her own hands. Totally wretched film gives new dimension to term, "exploitation picture." Mariel's film debut. [R]▼●

Liquidator, The (1966-British) **C-105m.** **½ D: Jack Cardiff. Rod Taylor, Trevor Howard, Jill St. John, Wilfrid Hyde-White. Nice location photography and adequate acting add up to a rather limp Bondian imitation. Even Taylor can't save this one. Panavision.

Liquid Dreams (1991) **C-92m.** **½ D: Mark Manos. Richard Steinmetz, Candice Daly, Barry Dennen, Juan Fernandez, Tracey Walter, Frankie Thorn, Paul Bartel, Mink Stole, John Doe. Beautiful Daly, determined to uncover her sister's killer, becomes immersed in a world of decadent, nightmarish dance halls and clubs, and various hidden evils. Provocative if overly slick thriller with sci-fi elements. Released on video in R and unrated versions. [R]▼

Liquid Sky (1983) **C-112m.** *** D: Slava Tsukerman. Anne Carlisle, Paula E. Sheppard, Susan Doukas, Otto Von Wernherr, Bob Brady. Gleefully nasty original about a lesbian punker whose Manhattan penthouse patio is trespassed by a UFO. A one-joke movie, but a pretty good joke; Carlisle, who also plays a gay male model, is remarkable, and there's some potent imagery despite the minuscule budget. Not for every taste, but you knew that when you read the plot synopsis. [R]▼●◗

Lisa (1962) **C-112m.** **½ D: Philip Dunne. Stephen Boyd, Dolores Hart, Leo McKern, Hugh Griffith, Donald Pleasence, Harry Andrews, Robert Stephens, Marius Goring, Finlay Currie. Jan de Hartog's suspenseful novel of Dutch-Jewish girl in post-WW2 Europe trying to get to Palestine. Exciting film despite gaps in story logic. Stylishly photographed on location by Arthur Ibbetson. CinemaScope.

Lisa and the Devil (1972-Italian-Spanish-West German) **C-95m.** **½ D: Mario Bava. Elke Sommer, Telly Savalas, Sylva Koscina, Alida Valli, Alessio Orano, Gabriele Tinti, Kathy Leone, Eduardo Fajardo. A tourist (Sommer) gets lost in an unidentified European town and winds up at an eerie mansion replete with rotting corpses, wax dummies, a blind woman, and a man who thinks she's the reincarnation of his dead wife. Oh yes, there's also an evil lollipop-sucking butler (Savalas), who just happens to be Satan. Truly strange, surreal psychological horror tale filled with hallucinatory imagery. Re-edited in 1975 as THE HOUSE OF EXORCISM, with gory new footage and unrelated scenes with Robert Alda as a priest. ▼●◗

Lisbon (1956) **C-90m.** **½ D: Ray Milland. Ray Milland, Maureen O'Hara, Claude Rains, Yvonne Furneaux, Francis Lederer, Percy Marmont, Jay Novello. On-location tale of international thief Rains hiring skipper Milland to rescue Maureen's husband from Communist imprisonment. Nice scenery, nothing special. Naturama. ▼

Listen, Darling (1938) **70m.** **½ D: Edwin L. Marin. Judy Garland, Freddie Bartholomew, Mary Astor, Walter Pidgeon, Alan Hale, Scotty Beckett. Judy and Freddie try to land mother (Astor) a husband; Garland sings "Zing Went The Strings Of My Heart."▼●

Listen to Me (1989) **C-107m.** *½ D: Douglas Day Stewart. Kirk Cameron, Jami Gertz, Roy Scheider, Amanda Peterson, Tim Quill, George Wyner, Anthony Zerbe, Christopher Atkins. Slick travesty about a renowned small-college debating squad, set on the kind of party-school campus where Dick Dale and The Del-Tones wouldn't be out of place. Climactic abortion debate—before the Supreme Court, no less—is cheap and hokey in roughly equal measure. Beware of Cameron's shifting Oklahoma accent. [PG-13] ▼●

Listen Up: The Lives of Quincy Jones (1990) **C-114m.** **½ D: Ellen Weissbrod. Ultraslick look at the life and times of Quincy Jones, the famed musician-composer-arranger-producer. Not so much a documentary as a visual and musical collage; sometimes effective, but too often plays like a music video—and is much too self-congratulatory. Dozens of Jones' friends, associates, and admirers appear, including Dizzy Gillespie, Lionel Hampton, Jesse Jackson, Frank Sinatra, Barbra Streisand, Miles Davis, Steven Spielberg, Sidney Lumet, Ella Fitzgerald, Oprah Winfrey, Ray Charles, Ice T, Melle Mel, Big Daddy Kane. [PG-13]▼●

List of Adrian Messenger, The (1963) **98m.** *** D: John Huston. George C. Scott, Clive Brook, Dana Wynter, Herbert Marshall, Tony Curtis, Kirk Douglas, Burt Lancaster, Robert Mitchum, Frank Sinatra, John Huston, Bernard Fox. Good murder mystery has a gimmick: Curtis, Douglas, Lancaster, Mitchum, and Sinatra are all heavily disguised in character roles. All that trouble wasn't necessary; the mystery is good on its own. The director's son Tony (billed as Anthony Walter Huston) plays Wynter's son. Filmed in Ireland.▼●

Lisztomania (1975-British) **C-105m.** *½ D: Ken Russell. Roger Daltrey, Sara Kestelman, Paul Nicholas, Fiona Lewis, Ringo Starr. So-called biography of Franz Liszt is, in truth, one of Ken Russell's most outlandish extravaganzas; director's devotees may enjoy this visual, aural (and sexual) assault. Others beware! Panavision. [R]▼●

Little Annie Rooney (1925) **97m.** ** D: William Beaudine. Mary Pickford, William Haines, Walter James, Gordon Griffith, Carlo Schippa. One of Mary's weaker starring vehicles mixes comedy, sentiment, melodrama, and blarney in uneven doses, as ragamuffin girl and her brother set out to avenge their father's murder.▼●

Little Ark, The (1972) **C-100m.** *** D: James B. Clark. Theodore Bikel, Philip Frame, Genevieve Ambas, Max Croiset, Johan De Slaa. Another good children's film from producer Robert Radnitz; this one concerns two Dutch youngsters who try to find their father after being separated from him during a flood. Panavision. [G]

Little Big Horn (1951) **86m.** **½ D: Charles Marquis Warren. Lloyd Bridges, John Ireland, Marie Windsor, Reed Hadley, Hugh O'Brian. Small-budget film manages to generate excitement in its account of Custer's Last Stand.▼

Little Big League (1994) **C-119m.** ** D: Andrew Scheinman. Luke Edwards, Timothy Busfield, John Ashton, Ashley Crow, Kevin Dunn, Jonathan Silverman, Dennis Farina, Jason Robards, Wolfgang Bodison, Duane Davis. A 12-year-old boy inherits the Minnesota Twins from his grandfather, and decides to manage the baseball team himself. Could have and should have been a cute family movie, but it has no energy—and goes on forever. Special appearances by real-life major leaguers Ken Griffey, Jr., Lou Piniella, Sandy Alomar, Jr., Tim Raines, Wally Joyner, and others. Directing debut for producer Scheinman. [PG] ▼●

Little Big Man (1970) **C-139m.** **** D: Arthur Penn. Dustin Hoffman, Faye Dunaway, Martin Balsam, Richard Mulligan, Chief Dan George, Jeff Corey, Alan Oppenheimer, Aimee Eccles, William Hickey. Sprawling, superb filmization of Thomas Berger's novel about Jack Crabb, 121-year-old man who reminisces about his life as young pioneer, adopted Indian, drinking pal of Wild Bill Hickok, medicine-show hustler, and survivor of Custer's Last Stand. Rich humor, colorful characterizations, moving tragedy are among ingredients, and they all click. Screenplay by Calder Willingham. Originally released at 150 minutes. Panavision. [PG]▼●

Little Bit of Heaven, A (1940) **87m.** ** D: Andrew Marton. Gloria Jean, Robert Stack, Hugh Herbert, C. Aubrey Smith, Stuart Erwin, Nan Grey. Jean has vocal outing as 12-year-old singer supporting family; OK vehicle.

Little Bit of Soul, A (1998-Australian) **C-85m.** ** D: Peter Duncan. Geoffrey Rush, David Wenham, Frances O'Connor, Heather Mitchell, John Gaden. Wacko Aussie black comedy about two scientists (and ex-lovers) working on an immortality serum who make a pact with their married benefactors—who just happen to be your average, everyday Satanists! Attempted satire of science and religion is ultimately too shrill and strained to generate many laughs despite a capable cast. Soundtrack of Louis Jordan oldies helps liven things up. [R]▼

Little Boy Lost (1953) **95m.** *** D: George Seaton. Bing Crosby, Claude Dauphin, Nicole Maurey, Gabrielle Dorziat. Synthetic tear-jerker set in post-WW2 France, where newspaperman Crosby is trying to locate his son, not knowing which boy at orphanage is his.▼

Little Buddha (1993) **C-123m.** ** D: Bernardo Bertolucci. Keanu Reeves, Chris Isaak, Bridget Fonda, Alex Wiesendanger, Ying Ruocheng, Raju Lal, Rudraprsad, Jo Champa. Disappointing, dramatically muddled Bertolucci epic with obvious similarities to THE LAST EMPEROR, telling the parallel stories of an aged Tibetan monk (Ruocheng) who believes that a young Seattle boy (Wiesendanger) is the reincarnation of his respected mentor, and the young Prince Siddhartha (Reeves), who lived 2,500 years ago. Pretty to look at, but otherwise pretty much of a bore. Technovision (35mm), Arriflex (70mm). [PG]▼●◗

Little Caesar (1930) **80m.** ***½ D: Mervyn LeRoy. Edward G. Robinson, Douglas Fairbanks, Jr., Glenda Farrell, Stanley Fields, Sidney Blackmer, Ralph Ince, George E. Stone. Small-time hood becomes underworld big-shot; Robinson as Caesar Enrico Bandello gives star-making performance in classic gangster film, still exciting. Francis Faragoh and Robert E. Lee adapted W.R. Burnett's novel.▼●

Little Cigars (1973) **C-92m.** *** D: Chris Christenberry. Angel Tompkins, Billy Curtis, Jerry Maren, Frank Delfino, Emory Souza, Felix Silla, Joe De Santis. Crime-caper comedy with a midget gang committing the mayhem. Fast and funny, with Tompkins especially good as a former mistress to gangster De Santis, and Curtis, the leader of the tiny troupe. Look for a funny bit by dwarf Angelo Rossitto during a police lineup. [PG]

Little City (1999) **C-89m.** ** D: Roberto Benabib. Jon Bon Jovi, Penelope Ann Miller, Josh Charles, Annabella Sciorra, JoBeth Williams, Joanna Going. Life and loves—gay and straight, platonic and passionate—among a group of young people in San Francisco. Pleasant-enough time-filler, with an attractive cast and postcard views of the city, but nothing special. Released direct to video. [R]▼

Little Colonel, The (1935) **80m.** *** D: David Butler. Shirley Temple, Lionel Barrymore, Evelyn Venable, John Lodge, Sidney Blackmer, Bill Robinson. Even non-fans should like this, one of Shirley's best films, as she mends broken ties between Grandpa Barrymore and Mama Venable in the Reconstruction South . . . and does that famous step dance with Robinson. Final scene was filmed in Technicolor. Also shown in computer-colored version. ▼●

Little Darlings (1980) **C-95m.** ** D: Ronald F. Maxwell. Tatum O'Neal, Kristy McNichol, Armand Assante, Matt Dillon, Maggie Blye, Nicolas Coster, Krista Erickson, Alexa Kenin, Cynthia Nixon. Tatum and Kristy wager which one will be the first to lose her virginity at summer camp. Not quite as sleazy as it sounds, but not very inspiring, either. McNichol easily outacts her costar with a solid performance. Panavision. [R]▼●

Little Dorrit (1988-British) ** D: Christine Edzard. Derek Jacobi, Alec Guinness, Roshan Seth, Sarah Pickering, Miriam Margolyes, Cyril Cusack, Max Wall, Eleanor Bron, Michael Elphick, Joan Greenwood, Patricia Hayes, Robert Morley, Sophie Ward, Bill Fraser. PART ONE: NOBODY'S FAULT **(C-177m.)** Ambitious adaptation of Charles Dickens' satiric novel concerns upstanding but ineffectual Jacobi, and the young seamstress Little Dorrit (Pickering) who lives with her father (Guinness) in debtors' prison. Low-budget production is painstakingly slow-moving: viewers will either adore this or despise it. PART TWO: LITTLE DORRIT'S STORY **(C-183m.)** Second half of saga unfortunately insists on recreating almost the entire first half *scene for scene* before moving forward. As in first part, there are several good performances (notably Guinness's) but screenplay is inadequate. [G]▼●

Little Dorrit's Story SEE: **Little Dorrit**

Little Dragons, The (1980) **C-90m.** *½ D: Curtis Hanson. Charles Lane, Ann Sothern, Chris Petersen, Pat Petersen, Sally Boyden, Rick Lenz, Sharon Weber, Joe Spinell, Tony Bill. Junior Kung Fu aficionados solve a kidnapping mystery. May appeal to the less discriminating 9-year-old. Lane and particularly Sothern are wasted. [PG]▼

Little Drummer Girl, The (1984) **C-130m.** *** D: George Roy Hill. Diane Keaton, Yorgo Voyagis, Klaus Kinski, Sami Frey, Michael Cristofer, Thorley Walters, Anna Massey. Adaptation of John Le Carré's best-selling spy thriller is long, slow, confusing, not always believable—but still worthwhile, if only for Keaton's strong performance as a mercurial pro-Palestinian actress recruited to perform as Israeli agent. Globe-trotting story about a novice caught in the world of terrorists holds interest throughout, even with its flaws. Kinski is first-rate as Israeli counterintelligence officer. [R]▼●

Little Egypt (1951) **C-82m.** **½ D: Frederick de Cordova. Mark Stevens, Rhonda Fleming, Nancy Guild, Charles Drake, Tom D'Andrea, Verna Felton, John Litel, Fritz Feld. Chicago Fair in the 1890s is setting for tale of entrepreneurs who popularized the later-famous belly dancer.

Little Fauss and Big Halsy (1970) **C-97m.** **½ D: Sidney J. Furie. Robert Redford, Michael J. Pollard, Lauren Hutton, Noah Beery, Lucille Benson. So-so character study of two motorcycle racers, one timid and gullible (Pollard), the other a self-centered braggart (Redford) who takes advantage of cohort. Beery and Benson outstanding as Pollard's folks; flavorful song score by Johnny Cash. Panavision. [R]

Little Foxes, The (1941) **116m.** ***½ D: William Wyler. Bette Davis, Herbert Marshall, Teresa Wright, Richard Carlson, Patricia Collinge, Dan Duryea, Charles Dingle. Outstanding filmization of Lillian Hellman's play of greed and corruption within a crumbling Southern family on the financial outs, headed by majestic Davis as ruthless Regina. Collinge, Duryea, Dingle, Carl Benton Reid, and John Marriott all recreate their Broadway roles, with Collinge, Duryea, Reid, and Teresa Wright making their film debuts. Scripted by Hellman. Prequel: ANOTHER PART OF THE FOREST.▼●◗

Little Fugitive (1953) **75m.** *** D: Ray Ashley, Morris Engel, Ruth Orkin. Richie Andrusco, Rickie Brewster, Winifred Cushing, Will Lee. A young boy who thinks he has killed his brother wanders lost through Coney Island. A lyrical little comedy-drama, produced independently and on a threadbare budget. A minor classic.▼●◗

Little Giant, The (1933) **74m.** *** D: Roy Del Ruth. Edward G. Robinson, Mary Astor, Helen Vinson, Kenneth Thomson, Russell Hopton. Just three years after LITTLE CAESAR, Robinson spoofed his own gangster image in this bright comedy about a bootlegger who decides to better himself and crash high society. ●

Little Giant (1946) **91m.** ** D: William A. Seiter. Bud Abbott, Lou Costello, Brenda Joyce, Jacqueline de Wit, George Cleveland, Elena Verdugo, Mary Gordon, Margaret Dumont. Fair A&C with Lou becoming a vacuum cleaner salesman in series of familiar but amusing routines. Bud and Lou work separately in this one.▼

Little Giants (1994) **C-105m.** **½ D: Duwayne Dunham. Rick Moranis, Ed O'Neill, Shawna Waldron, Mary Ellen Trainor, Matthew McCurley, Susanna Thompson, Brian Haley, Devon Sawa, Michael Zwiener, Troy Simmons, Sam Horrigan, John Madden, Harry Shearer, Dabbs Greer. Moranis has always lived in the shadow of big brother O'Neill, a swaggering football star; when Moranis' daughter—a first-rate player—doesn't get picked for O'Neill's Pop Warner football team, she persuades her dad to launch a rival team, as a haven for all the town's misfit kids. Amiable juvenile comedy is formula to the max, but knows how to please its youthful audience. Several real-life football players appear as themselves. [PG]▼●

Little Girl Who Lives Down the Lane, The (1976-Canadian) **C-94m.** *** D: Nicolas Gessner. Jodie Foster, Martin Sheen, Scott Jacoby, Mort Shuman, Alexis Smith. Complex, unique mystery with Foster as young girl whose father never seems to be home—and she gets very nervous when anyone goes near the basement. Think you've figured it out? Forget it, Charlie; you haven't even scratched the surface. Engrossing, one-of-a-kind film written by Laird Koenig. Panavision. [PG]▼●

Little Gloria . . . Happy At Last (1982) **C-200m. TVM** D: Waris Hussein. Bette Davis, Angela Lansbury, Christopher

Plummer, Maureen Stapleton, Martin Balsam, Glynis Johns, Barnard Hughes, Michael Gross, John Hillerman, Lucy Gutteridge, Jennifer Dundas. Glittering, star-laden adaptation (by William Hanley) of Barbara Goldsmith's best seller about the notorious custody trial of 10-year-old Gloria Vanderbilt in 1934. Lansbury, in her TVM debut as Gertrude Vanderbilt Whitney, Gloria's powerful aunt, is especially fine. Originally shown in two parts. Above average.▼

Little Hut, The (1957-British) **C-90m.** ** D: Mark Robson. Ava Gardner, Stewart Granger, David Niven, Finlay Currie, Walter Chiari. Busy husband Granger takes sexy wife Gardner for granted. Will her friendship with Niven stay platonic when all three are stranded on an island? Static, flat, talky sex farce, from the Andre Roussin play.

Little Indian, Big City (1994-French) **C-90m.** *½ D: Hervé Palud. Thierry Lhermitte, Ludwig Briand, Patrick Timsit, Arielle Dombasle. Dopey French kiddie comedy about a stockbroker who goes to the Amazon to divorce his estranged wife and discovers he has a 13-year-old son, whom he brings back to Paris. A big hit in France, Disney released it in the U.S., with terrible American dubbing. Jokes are mainly of the scatological variety: the little kid's name Mimi-Siku means "cat pee" in his native tongue. Americanized in 1997 as JUNGLE 2 JUNGLE. [PG]▼

Little Kidnappers, The (1953-British) **95m.** ***½ D: Philip Leacock. Jon Whiteley, Vincent Winter, Adrienne Corri, Duncan Macrae, Jean Anderson, Theodore Bikel. Splendid children's story set in Nova Scotia, 1900. Two orphan youngsters "adopt" abandoned baby when strict grandfather forbids them having a dog. Whiteley and Winter won special Oscars for outstanding juvenile performances. British title: THE KIDNAPPERS. Remade for cable.

Little Kidnappers, The (1990-Canadian) **C-100m. TVM** D: Donald Shebib. Charlton Heston, Bruce Greenwood, Leo Wheatley, Charles Miller, Patricia Gage, Leah Pinsent. Heston's the embittered grandpa to two Scottish orphans, sent to live with him in Nova Scotia, who discover an abandoned baby and are accused of being kidnappers. Agreeable remake of 1953 British film. Made for cable. Average.▼

Little Laura & Big John (1973) **C-82m.** **½ D: Luke Moberly, Bob Woodburn. Fabian Forte, Karen Black, Ivy Thayer, Ken Miller, Paul Gleason, Cliff Frates, Evie Karafotias. Surprisingly engaging road company BONNIE AND CLYDE set in Everglades country. One-time teen rock 'n' roll idol Fabian made his acting comeback in this one, although Warren Beatty needn't be too concerned about the competition. [R]▼

Little Lord Fauntleroy (1936) **98m.** *** D: John Cromwell. Freddie Bartholomew, C. Aubrey Smith, Guy Kibbee, Dolores Costello, Mickey Rooney, Jessie Ralph. Young New Yorker Bartholomew suddenly finds himself a British lord in this charming film from classic story. Handsome, well-cast production. Filmed before in 1921; remade for TV in 1980. Also shown in computer-colored version.▼

Little Lord Fauntleroy (1980) **C-100m. TVM** D: Jack Gold. Ricky Schroder, Alec Guinness, Eric Porter, Colin Blakely, Connie Booth, Rachel Kempson. Lavish TV adaptation of the classic Frances Hodgson Burnett novel about an impoverished New York youngster who becomes heir to his titled grandfather's British estate. Blanche Hanalis wrote this version, for which Arthur Ibbetson's magnificent photography won an Emmy Award. Above average.▼

Little Malcolm (1974-British) **C-112m.** ** D: Stuart Cooper. John Hurt, John McEnery, David Warner, Rosalind Ayres, Raymond Platt. Hurt is prototypical angry young man (booted out of art school) who forms neofascist cult and rails out against society in this well-acted adaptation of David Halliwell's play criticizing 1960s protest movements. Warner takes acting honors as Hurt's obsessive verbal adversary. Ex-Beatle George Harrison's first venture into film production. Original British title: LITTLE MALCOLM AND HIS STRUGGLE AGAINST THE EUNUCHS.

Little Man Tate (1991) **C-99m.** *** D: Jodie Foster. Jodie Foster, Dianne Wiest, Adam Hann-Byrd, Harry Connick, Jr., David Pierce, P.J. Ochlan, Debi Mazar, Celia Weston, Danitra Vance, Josh Mostel, George Plimpton. Moving, extraordinarily empathic look at a child genius; his single, working-class mom (Foster) can't give him the support and stimulation he needs—but neither can the director (Wiest) of a school for exceptional children who takes him under her wing. Beautifully realized by Foster in her directing debut; her performance is equally strong. Bittersweet screenplay by Scott Frank; solid jazz score by Mark Isham. Bob Balaban appears unbilled as a quizmaster. [PG]▼●

Little Man, What Now? (1934) **91m.** ***½ D: Frank Borzage. Margaret Sullavan, Douglass Montgomery, Alan Hale, Catherine Doucet, Mae Marsh, Alan Mowbray, Hedda Hopper. Impoverished German newlyweds are further strapped when wife becomes pregnant. Splendid romance was also the first Hollywood film to deal even peripherally with conditions that resulted in Hitler's rise to power. Sullavan is luminous. William Anthony McGuire scripted, from the novel by Hans Fallada.

Little Men (1940) **84m.** ** D: Norman Z. McLeod. Kay Francis, Jack Oakie, George Bancroft, Jimmy Lydon, Ann Gillis, Charles Esmond, William Demarest. Occasionally cute but slight, predictable adaptation of the Louisa May Alcott novel, focusing on rough adolescent Lydon "learning the ways" at Francis' school. Oakie easily steals the film as an irrepressible con man. Remade in 1998.▼

Little Men (1998-Canadian) **C-98m.** **½ D: Rodney Gibbons. Mariel Hemingway, Chris Sarandon, Michael Caloz, Ben Cook, Ricky Mabe, Gabrielle Boni; narrated by Kathleen Fee. Pleasant TV-style period piece based on Louisa May Alcott's followup to *Little Women*. Jo and Mr. Bhaer are now married and running a home for wayward boys; they turn their kind attention to a newly orphaned street urchin and his rowdy friend. Official title is: LOUISA MAY ALCOTT'S LITTLE MEN. [PG]▼

Little Mermaid, The (1989) **C-82m.** *** D: John Musker, Ron Clements. Voices of Jodi Benson, Pat Carroll, Samuel E. Wright, Kenneth Mars, Buddy Hackett, Christopher Daniel Barnes, Rene Auberjonois, Ben Wright. Delightful Disney animated feature loosely based on Hans Christian Andersen story about a young mermaid named Ariel who longs to be human. One could squabble about certain story points, but the film is so enjoyable it's foolish to try. Buoyant musical numbers include "Kiss The Girl," "Part of Your World," and "Under the Sea," sung by a Jamaican crab named Sebastian (Wright). Won Oscars for Best Original Score (Alan Menken) and Song ("Under the Sea," by Menken and Howard Ashman). Followed by an animated TV series and a direct-to-video sequel. [G]▼●◗

Little Minister, The (1934) **110m.** ***½ D: Richard Wallace. Katharine Hepburn, John Beal, Donald Crisp, Andy Clyde, Beryl Mercer. Charming film of James M. Barrie story about Scottish pastor falling in love, with Hepburn radiant in period romance. ▼●

Little Miss Broadway (1938) **70m.** ** D: Irving Cummings. Shirley Temple, George Murphy, Jimmy Durante, Phyllis Brooks, Edna May Oliver, George Barbier. Not bad Temple, with Shirley bringing Oliver's theatrical boarding house to life; Shirley and Durante are good together. Songs: "Be Optimistic," "If All the World Were Paper," "Hop Skip and Jump." Also shown in computer-colored version.▼

Little Miss Marker (1934) **80m.** *** D: Alexander Hall. Adolphe Menjou, Shirley Temple, Dorothy Dell, Charles Bickford, Lynne Overman, Warren Hymer. Winning Damon Runyon tale of bookie Menjou and N.Y.C. gambling colony reformed by adorable little Shirley, left as IOU for a debt. Remade as SORROWFUL JONES and 40 POUNDS OF TROUBLE, and again in 1980. Also shown in computer-colored version. ▼

Little Miss Marker (1980) **C-103m.** ** D: Walter Bernstein. Walter Matthau, Julie Andrews, Tony Curtis, Bob Newhart, Sara Stimson, Lee Grant, Brian Dennehy, Kenneth McMillan. Boring remake of the Damon Runyon story, with Matthau as the bookie, Stimson the little girl, Andrews the love interest, Curtis the heavy. Veteran screenwriter Bernstein's first directing credit. [PG]▼

Little Monsters (1989) **C-100m.** *½ D: Richard Alan Greenberg. Fred Savage, Howie Mandel, Ben Savage, Daniel Stern, Margaret Whitton, Rick Ducommun, Amber Barretto, Frank Whaley. BEETLEJUICE-inspired fantasy comedy suffers from clumsy script and obvious postproduction cuts. Boy finds prankish monster (Mandel) under his bed; their friendship leads to various crises, in our world and in the dimly lit land of the monsters. Premise was promising but results are dismal. Cast tries hard. [PG]▼●

Little Mother SEE: **Mamele**

Little Murders (1971) **C-110m.** *** D: Alan Arkin. Elliott Gould, Marcia Rodd, Vincent Gardenia, Elizabeth Wilson, Jon Korkes, Donald Sutherland, Lou Jacobi, Alan Arkin. Jules Feiffer's ultrablack comedy about life in nightmarish N.Y.C. focuses on aggressive urbanite (Rodd) who lassoes passive photographer Gould into marriage. Superb performance by Gardenia as Rodd's father, hilarious cameo by Arkin as mind-blown detective, but even funniest moments are overshadowed by frighteningly depressing atmosphere. [PG—edited from original R rating]▼

Little Nellie Kelly (1940) **100m.** **½ D: Norman Taurog. Judy Garland, George Murphy, Charles Winninger, Douglas McPhail. Lightweight musical based on George M. Cohan play about Judy patching up differences between father Murphy and grandfather Winninger. Garland sings "It's A Great Day For The Irish."▼●

Little Nemo: Adventures in Slumberland (1990-Japanese) **C-85m.** **½ D: Masami Hata, William T. Hurtz. Voices of Gabriel Damon, Mickey Rooney, Rene Auberjonois, Danny Mann, Laura Mooney, Bernard Erhard. Beautifully rendered animation about a young boy's odyssey into the world of dreams—and the perils of Nightmare Land. Starts with a knockout opening sequence, and has much to entertain youngsters (and animation buffs), but its story loses momentum. Inspired by Winsor McCay's comic strip classic. Songs by Richard M. and Robert B. Sherman. Concept for the screen by Ray Bradbury. Not released in the U.S. until 1992. [G]▼●

Little Night Music, A (1978) **C-124m.** *½ D: Harold Prince. Elizabeth Taylor, Diana Rigg, Len Cariou, Lesley-Anne Down, Hermione Gingold, Lawrence Guittard, Christopher Guard, Chloe Franks. Laughably stilted film version of the Stephen Sondheim/Hugh Wheeler stage musical which in turn was based on Ingmar Bergman's sex-at-a-country-estate comedy, SMILES OF A SUMMER NIGHT. Liz's rendition of "Send in the Clowns" is no chart buster. Filmed in Austria. [PG]▼●

Little Nikita (1988) **C-98m.** ** D: Richard Benjamin. Sidney Poitier, River Phoenix, Richard Jenkins, Caroline Kava, Richard Bradford, Richard Lynch, Loretta Devine, Lucy Deakins. Intriguing premise—young, all-American Phoenix learning that his parents are Soviet agents—fails to catch fire in this sometimes entertaining but ultimately incoherent thriller. Poitier adds a bit of spark as an FBI agent. [PG]▼●

Little Noises (1991) **C-110m.** **½ D: Jane Spencer. Crispin Glover, Tatum O'Neal, Rik Mayall, Tate Donovan, John C. McGinley, Nina Siemaszko, Carole Shelley, Steven Schub. Ambitious but muddled account of Glover, a failure who calls himself a writer (even though he's never penned anything); he finds status and monetary reward after passing off the poetry of a deaf mute orphan as his own.▼●

Little Odessa (1994) **C-98m.** *** D: James Gray. Tim Roth, Edward Furlong, Moira Kelly, Vanessa Redgrave, Maximilian Schell, Paul Guilfoyle, Natasha Andreichenko, David Vadim, Mina Bern. Melancholy drama set during a bleak Brooklyn winter, about Joshua (Roth), a hitman whose Russian-Jewish family resides in Brighton Beach. He has been disowned by his adulterous father (Schell), and his mother (Redgrave) is dying; his kid brother (Furlong) is caught between Russian and American cultures, and between his love for Joshua and the knowledge that his brother is evil. Grim, disturbing, brilliantly directed with a distinctive visual style by 24-year-old Gray (who also scripted). Super 35. [R]▼●◗

Little Old New York (1940) **100m.** **½ D: Henry King. Alice Faye, Brenda Joyce, Fred MacMurray, Richard Greene, Henry Stephenson. Claims to be story of Robert Fulton and his steamboat; merely serves as framework for standard romance.

Little Prince, The (1974-British) **C-88m.** **½ D: Stanley Donen. Richard Kiley, Steven Warner, Bob Fosse, Gene Wilder, Joss Ackland, Clive Revill, Donna McKechnie, Victor Spinetti. Antoine de St. Exupery's children's book is considered a classic, but this musical fantasy doesn't do it justice. Kiley plays aviator who counsels and guides a young boy who wants to learn about life. Unmemorable score by Lerner and Loewe is just one of this fable's major letdowns. [G]▼●

Little Princess, The (1939) **C-91m.** *** D: Walter Lang. Shirley Temple, Richard Greene, Anita Louise, Ian Hunter, Cesar Romero, Arthur Treacher, Marcia Mae Jones, Sybil Jason. Shirley stars as a Victorian waif who makes good in this lavishly mounted, colorful production. Filmed again in 1995. ▼●◗

Little Princess, A (1995) **C-97m.** *** D: Alfonso Cuaron. Eleanor Bron, Liam Cunningham, Liesel Matthews, Rusty Schwimmer, Arthur Malet, Vanessa Lee Chester, Errol Sitahal, Vincent Schiavelli. A little jewel of a movie about a fanciful young girl (Matthews) whose father deposits her at a boarding school while he goes off to fight in WW1—unaware that the headmistress is a spiteful woman. Devotees of Frances Hodgson Burnett's classic novel (filmed before with Shirley Temple) may be dismayed at liberties taken with the original—moving it to N.Y.C. in the teens, for instance—but its spirit is intact. Hard to believe this handsome production was filmed almost entirely on a Burbank studio backlot! [G] ▼●◗

Little Rascals, The (1994) **C-72m.** ** D: Penelope Spheeris. Travis Tedford, Bug Hall, Brittany Ashton Holmes, Kevin Jamal Woods, Zachary Mabry, Ross Elliot Bagley, Sam Saletta, Blake Jeremy Collins, Blake McIver Ewing, Jordan Warkol. Spanky and the members of the He-Man Woman Haters Club try to sabotage Alfalfa's budding romance with Darla. Aimed squarely at young children, who will probably enjoy it, though it's no match for the original 1930's Hal Roach comedy shorts. The kids are cute, but Alfalfa (played by Hall) is the only standout—along with Pete the Pup. Gag cameos by a few stars and celebrities seem extraneous. [PG]▼●◗

Little Riders, The (1996) **C-95m. TVM** D: Kevin Connor. Paul Scofield, Rosemary Harris, Malcolm McDowell, Noely Thornton, Renee Soutendijk, Benedick Blythe, Derek De Lint, Luke Edwards. Disney family drama about an American youngster trapped in her grandparents' village in WW2 Holland and her efforts to keep the town's treasured clock (with its little horsemen) out of Nazi hands. Pleasant production based on Margaretha Shemin's best-selling children's book. Made for cable. Average.

Little Romance, A (1979) **C-108m.** *** D: George Roy Hill. Laurence Olivier, Diane Lane, Thelonious Bernard, Arthur Hill, Sally Kellerman, David Dukes, Broderick Crawford. Engaging film about relationship of young American girl (Lane, in her film debut) living in Paris and running off with a charming French boy (Bernard), chaperoned by wily old con man (Olivier, wonderfully hammy). A throwback to director Hill's WORLD OF HENRY ORIENT in its winning treatment of adolescence, but not quite as good. Crawford has funny cameo as himself. Georges Delerue's music score won a well-deserved Oscar. Panavision. [PG]▼●

Little Sex, A (1982) **C-95m.** ** D: Bruce Paltrow. Tim Matheson, Kate Capshaw, Edward Herrmann, John Glover, Joan Copeland, Susanna Dalton, Wendie Malick,

Wallace Shawn, Melinda Culea, Bill Smitrovich. MTM Enterprises' first theatrical feature is basically an R-rated TV-movie, with Matheson marrying long-time girlfriend Capshaw hoping it will cure him of his womanizing. It doesn't. Tired but watchable comedy-drama has pretty N.Y.C. locations and pleasing performances, particularly by Herrmann as Matheson's wiser older brother. Capshaw's film debut. [R]▼

Little Shepherd of Kingdom Come, The (1961) **C-108m.** **½ D: Andrew V. McLaglen. Jimmie Rodgers, Luana Patten, Chill Wills, George Kennedy, Neil Hamilton. Bland family-type film of boy who fought for the North during Civil War and his return to rural life. Based on the 1903 novel by John William Fox. Kennedy's film debut. CinemaScope.

Little Shop of Horrors, The (1960) **70m.** ***½ D: Roger Corman. Jonathan Haze, Jackie Joseph, Mel Welles, Dick Miller, Myrtle Vail, Jack Nicholson, Marie Windsor. Classic black comedy about young schnook who develops bloodthirsty plant and is forced to kill in order to feed it. Initially infamous as The Film Shot In Two Days, but now considered one of Corman's best pictures. Nicholson has hilarious bit as masochist who thrives on dental pain; delightful screenplay by Charles Griffith (who also plays the hold-up man and is the voice of "Audrey, Jr."). Later a stage musical, which was filmed in 1986. Also shown in computer-colored version.▼●◗

Little Shop of Horrors (1986) **C-88m.** **½ D: Frank Oz. Rick Moranis, Ellen Greene, Vincent Gardenia, Steve Martin, James Belushi, John Candy, Christopher Guest, Bill Murray, voice of Levi Stubbs. Very entertaining black comedy/musical about a nebbish (played to perfection by Moranis) whose "unusual" new plant brings him good fortune—but turns into a Frankenstein. Greene (repeating her stage role) is a delight as his squeaky-voiced heartthrob, Martin hilarious as her macho boyfriend. But when Audrey II, the plant, turns *really* mean and monstrous, with super-duper special effects, the fun drains away. Based on the off-Broadway musical by Howard Ashman and Alan Menken, which in turn was based on Roger Corman's 1960 low-budget black comedy (written by Charles B. Griffith). [PG-13]▼●◗

Littlest Horse Thieves, The (1977) **C-104m.** *** D: Charles Jarrott. Alastair Sim, Peter Barkworth, Maurice Colbourne, Susan Tebbs, Andrew Harrison, Chloe Franks. Well-made Disney period piece, filmed in England, about three children's efforts to save pit-ponies who work the mines from abuse and death. Set at the turn of the century. Good location photography. Originally titled ESCAPE FROM THE DARK. [G]▼◗

Littlest Outlaw, The (1955) **C-75m.** *** D: Roberto Gavaldon. Pedro Armendariz, Joseph Calleia, Rodolfo Acosta, Andres Velasquez, Pepe Ortiz. Unpretentious little Disney film about Mexican boy (Velasquez) who runs away with a horse rather than see it killed for its misdeeds; filmed on location.▼

Littlest Rebel, The (1935) **70m.** *** D: David Butler. Shirley Temple, John Boles, Jack Holt, Karen Morley, Bill Robinson, Stepin Fetchit, Guinn "Big Boy" Williams. One of Shirley's best films, a Civil War saga set in the Old South, with our little heroine managing to wrap Union officer Holt around her little finger and protect her Confederate officer father (Boles). Temple and Robinson do some delightful dancing as well. Also shown in computer-colored version.▼

Little Theatre of Jean Renoir, The (1971-French) **C-100m.** *** D: Jean Renoir. Jeanne Moreau, Fernand Sardou, Francoise Arnoul, Jean Carmet, Marguerite Cassan, Dominique Labourier. Quartet of short sketches about human dignity and goodness of country life (as opposed to surviving in a dehumanized urban wilderness). Renoir's celluloid swan song may not be among his best, but still has much to offer. Made for television in 1969.▼●

Little Thief, The (1989-French) **C-104m.** **½ D: Claude Miller. Charlotte Gainsbourg, Didier Bezace, Simon de la Brosse, Nathalie Cardone, Raoul Billerey. So-so character portrait of the title lass, an alienated, amoral teen drifting through life in postwar France. If she comes off as a female Antoine Doinel, it's because the original story was cowritten by François Truffaut, who was supposedly planning to film this at the time of his death; resulting film lacks the director's inimitable touch. Miller was for ten years Truffaut's assistant; Gainsbourg is the daughter of Jane Birkin. [R]▼●

Little Tough Guy (1938) **80m.** ** D: Harold Young. Billy Halop, Huntz Hall, Gabriel Dell, Bernard Punsly, David Gorcey, Hally Chester, Helen Parrish, Robert Wilcox, Jackie Searl, Marjorie Main, Peggy Stewart. When his dad is railroaded into jail, young Halop rounds up his refined pals (you know—Pig, Ape, Dopey, et al.) and tears up the town. First entry of a minor series spun off from the *Dead End Kids* (see *Bowery Boys* entry for further details).▼

Little Tough Guys in Society (1938) **76m.** *½ D: Erle Kenton. Mischa Auer, Mary Boland, Edward Everett Horton, Helen Parrish, Jackie Searl, Peggy Stewart, Harold Huber, David Oliver, Frankie Thomas. Paper-thin tale of title delinquents—junior Dead End Kids—and their escapades. Auer, Boland and Horton can't save it.

Little Treasure (1985) **C-95m.** *½ D: Alan Sharp. Margot Kidder, Ted Danson, Burt Lancaster, Joseph Hacker, Malena

Doria, John Pearce. A stripper ventures to Mexico to meet her long-lost father but spends most of her time searching for treasure with a dropout American. Unsatisfying story marked directing debut for writer Sharp. Danson comes off best. [R]▼●

Little Vegas (1990) **C-91m.** ** D: Perry Lang. Anthony John Denison, Catherine O'Hara, Jerry Stiller, Michael Nouri, Perry Lang, Bruce McGill, John Sayles, Jay Thomas, Bob Goldthwait. Subtle comedy revolving around offbeat characters in trailer park located in desolate area that Mafia developers want to turn into a ''little'' Las Vegas. Intriguing possibilities, but it doesn't quite gel. [R]▼●

Little Vera (1988-Russian) **C-133m.** *** D: Vassili Pitchul. Natalia Negoda, Andrei Sokolov, Yuri Nazarov, Ludmila Zaisova, Alexander Niegreva. Groundbreaking, post-*glasnost* look at life in modern Russia. Negoda offers a fresh performance as an alienated, working-class, rock music-loving young woman; the depiction of her sexual relationship with Sokolov, plus the manner in which Western culture has affected her life, make this unlike any other Soviet film you've ever seen. Not surprisingly, it was a smash hit in its homeland.▼●

Little Voice (1998-British-U.S.) **C-96m.** *** D: Mark Herman. Jane Horrocks, Michael Caine, Brenda Blethyn, Jim Broadbent, Ewan McGregor, Annette Badland, Philip Jackson. When a sleazy talent agent (Caine) and an equally greasy nightclub owner (Broadbent) discover that the reclusive daughter of a middle-aged shrew has the uncanny ability to sing like Judy Garland and other show-business greats, they smell money. But the mousy girl, known as Little Voice, sings for other reasons entirely. Vivid adaptation of Jim Cartwright's London play *The Rise and Fall of Little Voice*, with Horrocks re-creating her sensational performance, joined by a superb cast that (to put it mildly) doesn't hold back. [R]▼●◗

Little Women (1933) **115m.** **** D: George Cukor. Katharine Hepburn, Joan Bennett, Paul Lukas, Frances Dee, Jean Parker, Edna May Oliver, Douglass Montgomery, Spring Byington. Film offers endless pleasure no matter how many times you've seen it; a faithful, beautiful adaptation of Alcott's book by Victor Heerman and Sarah Y. Mason, who deservedly received Oscars. The cast is uniformly superb. Remade in 1949, 1978 (for TV), and 1994.▼●

Little Women (1949) **C-121m.** **½ D: Mervyn LeRoy. June Allyson, Peter Lawford, Margaret O'Brien, Elizabeth Taylor, Janet Leigh, Mary Astor. Glossy remake of Louisa May Alcott's gentle account of teenage girls finding maturity and romance—patly cast.▼●

Little Women (1978) **C-200m. TVM** D: David Lowell Rich. Meredith Baxter Birney, Susan Dey, Ann Dusenberry, Eve Plumb, Dorothy McGuire, Robert Young, Greer Garson, Cliff Potts, William Shatner. Sugarplum refilming of the classic, sparked by McGuire's Marmee and Garson's Aunt March (her TV movie debut). The pallid short-lived series spun off from this adaptation by Suzanne Clauser. Above average.

Little Women (1994) **C-118m.** **** D: Gillian Armstrong. Winona Ryder, Susan Sarandon, Gabriel Byrne, Trini Alvarado, Samantha Mathis, Kirsten Dunst, Claire Danes, Christian Bale, Eric Stoltz, John Neville, Mary Wickes. Exquisite rendering of Louisa May Alcott's Civil War–era classic about four devoted sisters who eventually have to leave their New England nest. A perfect cast is led by Ryder as the headstrong Jo, with Sarandon as that tower of strength, Marmee. Not a false moment or false move in the entire film, though purists may object to Marmee mouthing 1990s-style feminist doctrine. Veteran character actress Wickes threatens to steal every scene she's in, as crotchety Aunt March. Screenplay by Robin Swicord. [PG]▼●◗

Little World of Don Camillo, The (1951-French-Italian) **96m.** **½ D: Julien Duvivier. Fernandel, Sylvie, Gino Cervi, Vera Talqui, Franco Interlenghi, Saro Urzi. Fernandel is the whole show in this comic tale of a small-town priest who's outraged when the Communists are elected to local office. Moderately funny satire of religion and politics, coscripted by Duvivier and based on the novel by Giovanni Guareschi. English language version is narrated by Orson Welles. Followed by several sequels.▼

Live a Little, Love a Little (1968) **C-90m.** ** D: Norman Taurog. Elvis Presley, Michele Carey, Don Porter, Rudy Vallee, Dick Sargent, Sterling Holloway, Eddie Hodges. Elvis manages to land two well-paying photographer's jobs and work them both by hopping back and forth from office to office. Pleasant, if standard, Presley fare. Panavision.▼

Live a Little, Steal a Lot (1975) **C-101m.** **½ D: Marvin Chomsky. Robert Conrad, Don Stroud, Donna Mills, Robyn Millan, Luther Adler, Burt Young, Paul Stewart. Unremarkable but engrossing tale based on real-life story of two Florida beach bums who engineered ''impossible'' heist of 564-carat Star of India. Fine TOPKAPI-like caper scenes, plus good speedboat chase. Originally titled MURPH THE SURF and retitled YOU CAN'T STEAL LOVE. [PG]▼

Live and Let Die (1973-British) **C-121m.** **½ D: Guy Hamilton. Roger Moore, Yaphet Kotto, Jane Seymour, Clifton James, Geoffrey Holder, Bernard Lee, Lois

Maxwell. Barely memorable, overlong James Bond movie seems merely an excuse to film wild chase sequences; superagent goes after master criminal subverting U.S. economy via drugs. Works on level of old-time serial. This was Moore's first appearance as 007; title song by Paul McCartney. [PG]▼●

Live Fast, Die Young (1958) **82m.** ** D: Paul Henreid. Mary Murphy, Norma Eberhardt, Michael Connors. Turgid B film of runaway girl and her sister who prevents her from starting a life of crime.

Live Flesh (1997-Spanish-French) **C-100m.** ***½ D: Pedro Almodóvar. Liberto Rabal, Francesca Neri, Javier Bardem, Angela Molina, Jose Sancho, Penelope Cruz. Smitten son of a prostitute is jailed for accidentally shooting and paralyzing a cop during an altercation with a dishy drug user. Upon his release, he discovers that the woman is married to his victim! What might have been a melodramatic howler is instead Almodóvar's best feature since WOMEN ON THE VERGE OF A NERVOUS BREAKDOWN. After a bumpy start, film becomes a model of how to change moods. The director scripted from the novel by Ruth Rendell. Panavision. [R]▼●

Live for Life (1967-French-Italian) **C-130m.** **½ D: Claude Lelouch. Yves Montand, Annie Girardot, Candice Bergen, Irene Tunc, Anouck Ferjac. TV documentary producer Montand leaves wife Girardot for fashion model Bergen in glossy film helped by some good acting; picture was follow-up to Lelouch's A MAN AND A WOMAN.

Live It Up SEE: **Sing and Swing**

Live, Love and Learn (1937) **78m.** **½ D: George Fitzmaurice. Robert Montgomery, Rosalind Russell, Robert Benchley, Mickey Rooney, Helen Vinson, Monty Woolley, Al Shean, Billy Gilbert. Stars glide through this formula MGM fluff, with ritzy Russell marrying nonconformist artist Montgomery.

Lively Set, The (1964) **C-95m.** **½ D: Jack Arnold. James Darren, Pamela Tiffin, Doug McClure, Marilyn Maxwell, Charles Drake, Greg Morris. Empty-headed account of cocky Darren, quitting college to become a champion sports car racer. Several forgettable songs—including The Surfaris' ''Boss Barracuda.''

Live Nude Girls (1995) **C-92m.** ** D: Julianna Lavin. Dana Delany, Kim Cattrall, Cynthia Stevenson, Laila Robins, Lora Zane, Olivia d'Abo, Glenn Quinn, Tim Choate. A bunch of galpals come together for a bachelorette party and pass the time talking, at which point assorted jealousies, fantasies, and feelings come to the surface. Well intentioned, to be sure, but oh, so predictable. [R]▼●

Lives of a Bengal Lancer, The (1935) **109m.** **** D: Henry Hathaway. Gary Cooper, Franchot Tone, Richard Cromwell, Sir Guy Standing, C. Aubrey Smith, Monte Blue, Kathleen Burke, Noble Johnson, Lumsden Hare, Akim Tamiroff, J. Carrol Naish, Douglass Dumbrille. Delightful Hollywood foray into British empire building in Northwest India. Cooper and Tone are pals in famed British regiment, Cromwell the callow son of commander Standing whom they take under their wing. Top story, action, repartee—and wonderful snake-charming scene. Grover Jones, William Slavens McNutt, Achmed Abdullah, Waldemar Young, and John Balderston coscripted; from the novel by Major Francis Yeats-Brown. Remade, with obvious changes, as GERONIMO (1939).▼●

Live Wire (1992) **C-85m.** **½ D: Christian Duguay. Pierce Brosnan, Ron Silver, Ben Cross, Lisa Eilbacher, Brent Jennings, Tony Plana, Al Waxman, Philip Baker Hall, Michael St. Gerard. FBI bomb expert Brosnan is puzzled when several people in Washington literally explode; his opponent is terrorist Cross, using a water-like explosive. Silver is a crooked senator, one of Cross' targets. OK thriller with good performances and an unusual, if absurd, premise. Theatrical film debuted on cable TV instead. Available on video in R-rated and unrated (87m.) versions.▼●

Live Wires (1946) **64m.** **½ D: Phil Karlson. Leo Gorcey, Huntz Hall, Bobby Jordan, Billy Benedict, William Frambes, Claudia Drake, Pamela Blake, Mike Mazurki. Gorcey tangles with gangsters in this first official *Bowery Boys* entry, a smooth mix of crime and slapstick. Remake of HE COULDN'T TAKE IT (1933).

Living Daylights, The (1987-British) **C-130m.** **½ D: John Glen. Timothy Dalton, Maryam d'Abo, Jeroen Krabbe, Joe Don Baker, John Rhys-Davies, Art Malik, Andreas Wisniewski, Desmond Llewelyn, Robert Brown, Geoffrey Keen, Walter Gotell. Dalton makes an impressive debut as James Bond in this entertaining, globe-trotting spy story about a double-dealing Russian general; it's brimming with great stunts and gimmicks, and eschews the smirking comic attitude of other recent Bond outings. But like some other Bonds, this one goes on far too long. Caroline Bliss debuts as Miss Moneypenny. Panavision. [PG]▼●

Living Desert, The (1953) **C-73m.** *** D: James Algar. Narrated by Winston Hibler. Disney's first True-Life Adventure feature has dazzling footage of the American desert and its inhabitants, but attracted justifiable criticism for its gimmicky treatment of some material like the famous ''scorpion dance.'' Still worthwhile. Academy Award winner.▼

Living End, The (1992) **C-92m.** *** D: Gregg Araki. Mike Dytri, Craig Gilmore, Mark Finch, Mary Woronov, Johanna Went,

Darcy Marta, Nicole Dillenberg, Paul Bartel. Frank, impertinent black comedy–road movie about Dytri and Gilmore. Each is twentyish, gay, and HIV-positive, and they set out on a nihilistic journey. Despite the characters' situation, the film is spirited and devilishly funny, but there's still no shortage of rage over their circumstances. Araki also scripted, photographed, and edited this ultra-low-budget gem.▼

Living Free (1972-British) **C-91m.** **½ D: Jack Couffer. Susan Hampshire, Nigel Davenport, Geoffrey Keen. Sequel to BORN FREE details further adventures of lioness Elsa and her three cubs. Nice photography but far too leisurely. [G]▼

Living Ghost, The (1942) **61m.** BOMB D: William Beaudine. James Dunn, Joan Woodbury, Paul McVey, Norman Willis, J. Farrell MacDonald, Jan Wiley. Dunn hams outrageously as a detective trying to find a murderer in a houseful of suspects. Grade Z comedy-mystery-thriller. Video title: A WALKING NIGHTMARE.▼

Living in a Big Way (1947) **103m.** ** D: Gregory La Cava. Gene Kelly, Marie McDonald, Charles Winninger, Phyllis Thaxter, Spring Byington. Kelly returns from WW2 to get to know his war bride for the first time and clashes with her *nouveau riche* family. A notorious flop in its day, but not all that bad; Kelly does a couple of first-rate dance numbers.▼

Living in Oblivion (1995) **C/B&W-91m.** *** D: Tom DiCillo. Steve Buscemi, Catherine Keener, Dermot Mulroney, Danielle Von Zerneck, James Le Gros, Rica Martens, Peter Dinklage, Hilary Gilford, Michael Griffiths, Matthew Grace, Robert Wightman. Clever, amusing look at a low-budget movie in progress, from several points of view. Writer-director DiCillo has several tricks up his sleeve to go along with his pointed perceptions about how egos collide—and how things go wrong on every movie set. Most of the cast also worked behind the scenes. Mulroney and Keener are married in real life. [R]▼●

Living It Up (1954) **C-95m.** *** D: Norman Taurog. Dean Martin, Jerry Lewis, Janet Leigh, Edward Arnold, Fred Clark, Sheree North, Sig Ruman. Bright remake of NOTHING SACRED. Jerry has Carole Lombard's role as supposed radiation victim brought to N.Y.C. as publicity stunt by reporter Leigh; Martin is Jerry's doctor. Scene at Yankee Stadium is a classic. That's sexy Sheree North, in her film debut, doing what was billed as "the first rock 'n' roll dance on the screen."

Living Legend (1980) **C-92m.** BOMB D: Worth Keeter. Earl Owensby, Ginger Alden, William T. Hicks, Jerry Rushing, Greg Carswell, Toby Wallace. Owensby is an Elvis Presley-like entertainer; his girlfriend is played by Alden, the real Elvis's final ladyfriend. Crude and phony; your 12-year-old cousin could make a more professional-looking film. [PG]

Living on Tokyo Time (1987) **C-83m.** **½ D: Steven Okazaki. Minako Ohashi, Ken Nakagawa, Mitzie Abe, Bill Bonham, Brenda Aoki. Occasionally amusing but mostly minor account of an Odd Couple: Ohashi, a Japanese who speaks little English; and Nakagawa, a Japanese-American who speaks no Japanese. They're set up in a marriage so that she may remain in the U.S. Filmed in San Francisco. [R]▼

Living on Velvet (1935) **80m.** ** D: Frank Borzage. Kay Francis, George Brent, Warren William, Russell Hicks, Maude Turner Gordon, Samuel S. Hinds. Romance between Brent, in state of shock, and upper-class Francis, who vanishes when he gains senses. Chic fluff.

Living Out Loud (1998) **C-100m.** **½ D: Richard LaGravenese. Holly Hunter, Danny DeVito, Queen Latifah, Martin Donovan, Richard Schiff, Elias Koteas, Suzanne Shepherd. Deeply felt comedy-drama about loneliness, focusing on a woman who can't get over the breakup of her marriage and an elevator operator in her Manhattan building who falls in love with her. Because there's no strong story line it bobs and weaves a bit, but there are many fine vignettes and moments of truth . . . and a dynamite opening, with Latifah singing a beautiful rendition of "Lush Life." Inspired in part by two Chekhov short stories. Directing debut for top screenwriter LaGravenese. Panavision. [R]▼●◗

Livin' Large (1991) **C-96m.** ** D: Michael Schultz. Terrence "T.C." Carson, Lisa Arrindell, Blanche Baker, Nathaniel "Afrika" Hall, Julia Campbell, Bernie McInerney, Loretta Devine. Young streetwise black desperately wants to be a TV newsman—and gets his chance by sheer fluke; then he learns that staying on top in the TV game means selling his soul. Farcical comedy has moments, but grows increasingly shallow, predictable; only energetic, likable cast keeps it alive. [R]▼●

Lizzie (1957) **81m.** **½ D: Hugo Haas. Eleanor Parker, Richard Boone, Joan Blondell, Hugo Haas, Ric Roman, Marion Ross, Johnny Mathis. Interesting, if ultimately pedantic, adaptation of Shirley Jackson's *The Bird's Nest*, with Parker as a mousy woman who turns out to have three distinct personalities. Boone is a psychiatrist trying to help her. A project of rare distinction for cultish director Haas, though he injects his familiar personality by playing a kibitzing neighbor. Parker is excellent. Eclipsed by release of similar (and superior) THE THREE FACES OF EVE soon after.

Lloyd's of London (1936) **115m.** ***½ D: Henry King. Freddie Bartholomew, Madeleine Carroll, Sir Guy Standing, Tyrone

Power, C. Aubrey Smith, Virginia Field, George Sanders. Handsomely mounted fiction of rise of British insurance company; young messenger boy Bartholomew grows up to be Power, who competes with Sanders for affection of Carroll.▼

Loaded (1994-British-New Zealand) **C-105m.** **½ D: Anna Campion. Oliver Milburn, Nick Patrick, Catherine McCormack, Thandie Newton, Mathew Eggleton, Danny Cunningham, Biddy Hodson, Dearbhla Molloy. Seven young-adult friends spend a weekend in the British countryside to make an amateur horror movie. They are by turns aimless, repressed, rebellious, scared (etc.); before the weekend ends, recklessness and tragedy permanently alter their relationships. Slow-moving but worthwhile film; if these were American youths, they would be far more immature and obnoxious. Feature directing debut for Anna Campion, sister of director Jane. [R]▼●

Loan Shark (1952) **74m.** ** D: Seymour Friedman. George Raft, Dorothy Hart, Paul Stewart, John Hoyt. Raft tries hard to instill life into flabby yarn about ex-convict smashing a loan-shark racket.▼

Local Boy Makes Good (1931) **67m.** **½ D: Mervyn LeRoy. Joe E. Brown, Dorothy Lee, Ruth Hall, Robert Bennett, Edward Woods. Entertaining Brown vehicle, with mousy Joe turning into a track-and-field star.

Local Hero (1983-British) **C-111m.** ***½ D: Bill Forsyth. Peter Riegert, Burt Lancaster, Fulton MacKay, Denis Lawson, Norman Chancer, Peter Capaldi, Jenny Seagrove. Enchantingly off-kilter comedy about an oil company rep (Riegert) who's assigned to buy up a Scottish coastal village which is badly needed for a refinery site. Nothing normal or predictable happens from that point on; writer-director Forsyth is more interested in quirkiness than belly-laugh gags, and his film is overflowing with ingenious characters and incidents. A little gem. [PG]▼●

Loch Ness (1996-British) **C-101m.** **½ D: John Henderson. Ted Danson, Joely Richardson, Ian Holm, Harris Yulin, James Frain, Kirsty Graham, Keith Allen, Nick Brimble. Lighthearted adventure-fantasy with jaded scientist Danson going to Scotland to prove Loch Ness monster is a hoax, only to discover some real magic and fall in love with single-mom Richardson. Innocuous, but amiable, family fare. U.S. debut on network TV. Filmed in 1994. Panavision. [PG]▼●

Locket, The (1946) **86m.** ** D: John Brahm. Laraine Day, Brian Aherne, Robert Mitchum, Gene Raymond, Sharyn Moffet, Ricardo Cortez. Another of those post-WW2 psychological dramas, with Day as a woman who makes men fall in love with her—blinding them to her true personality (and problems). Famed for its flashback within a flashback within a flashback . . . but not very good. Look for young brunette Martha Hyer as a party guest, and Ellen Corby as a household servant.●

Lock, Stock and Two Smoking Barrels (1998-U.S.-British) **C-106m.** **½ D: Guy Ritchie. Jason Flemyng, Dexter Fletcher, Nick Moran, Jason Statham, Steven Mackintosh, Vinnie Jones, Sting, Lenny McLean, P. H. Moriarty. PULP FICTION, British style: a young smart aleck tries to beat a professional gambling ring and sinks in over his head, while others peripheral to this action are drawn into a vortex of coincidence, misunderstanding, and violence. Outlandish, audacious, and funny, though it wears thin after a while, and its ultimate resolution is apparent a bit too soon. [R]▼●◗

Lock Up (1989) **C-106m.** *½ D: John Flynn. Sylvester Stallone, Donald Sutherland, Darlanne Fleugel, John Amos, Sonny Landham, Tom Sizemore, Frank McRae. With six months to go on his sentence, convict Stallone gets abducted from his country-club cell and transported to a hellhole run by old Hun-like adversary Sutherland. Missing are Linda Blair, John Vernon, a lesbian guard, and 15 gratuitous showers; you *do* get a body-shop montage backed by Ides of March's "Vehicle." Bottom of the world, ma. [R]▼●◗

Lock Up Your Daughters! (1969-British) **C-102m.** BOMB D: Peter Coe. Christopher Plummer, Susannah York, Glynis Johns, Ian Bannen, Tom Bell, Elaine Taylor. Film version of Henry Fielding play tries to be another TOM JONES, but tale of mistaken identities in 18th-century England couldn't be more forced. [R]

Locusts, The (1997) **C-124m.** *½ D: John Patrick Kelley. Ashley Judd, Kate Capshaw, Paul Rudd, Jeremy Davies, Vince Vaughn, Jessica Capshaw. A hunk of a drifter comes to town and is hired by oversexed ranch queen Kate Capshaw to work for her, both day *and* night; along the way, he develops a friendship with her highly disturbed son. Brooding drama of cruel family secrets gives viewers a reprieve whenever local-girl-with-a-heart-of-gold Judd is on screen. Set in 1950s Kansas. Super 35. [R]▼●

Lodger, The (1926-British) **75m.** *** D: Alfred Hitchcock. Ivor Novello, Malcolm Keen, June, Marie Ault, Arthur Chesney. The director's first suspense thriller, with a classic Hitchcockian theme: lodger Novello is accused by jealous detective Keen of being a killer. Memorable finale: Novello chased by bloodthirsty mob. Aka THE CASE OF JONATHAN DREW. Remade in 1932 (again with Novello), 1944, and in 1954 as MAN IN THE ATTIC. Look for Hitchcock's first cameo.▼

Lodger, The (1944) **84m.** *** D: John Brahm. Merle Oberon, George Sanders,

Laird Cregar, Sir Cedric Hardwicke, Sara Allgood, Aubrey Mather, Queenie Leonard, Doris Lloyd, Billy Bevan. That new lodger at a turn-of-the-century London boarding house may be Jack the Ripper. Good, atmospheric chiller with fine performances. Remade as MAN IN THE ATTIC.

Logan's Run (1976) **C-120m.** ** D: Michael Anderson. Michael York, Jenny Agutter, Richard Jordan, Peter Ustinov, Farrah Fawcett-Majors, Roscoe Lee Browne. Dazzling first half, showing life of unending pleasure and extinction at age 30 in the year 2274, canceled out by dreary second half. Earned a special Oscar for visual effects. From novel by William F. Nolan and George Clayton Johnson. Later a brief TV series. Todd-AO 35. [PG]▼●◗

Lola (1961-French) **90m.** *** D: Jacques Demy. Anouk Aimée, Marc Michel, Jacques Harden, Alan Scott, Elina Labourdette. Contemporary fable of love, with several disparate people's lives intertwining in port city of Nantes. Aimée is enchanting as cabaret dancer and carefree single mother; Michel is young man looking for life's meaning—and romance. Demy's first feature successfully links coincidence and Hollywood-movie fantasy with '60s realism and sexual frankness. References to Lola pop up in Demy's later films. Music score by Michel Legrand; film is dedicated to Max Ophuls. Franscope.▼

Lola (1969-British-Italian) **C-88m.** ** D: Richard Donner. Charles Bronson, Susan George, Trevor Howard, Michael Craig, Honor Blackman, Lionel Jeffries, Robert Morley, Jack Hawkins, Orson Bean, Kay Medford, Paul Ford. Sixteen-year-old nymphet initiates relationship with 38-year-old porno book writer; hyperkinetic film misses target, despite good cast and likable performance by Bronson. Released in England as TWINKY, at 98m. Aka THE STATUTORY AFFAIR. [PG]▼

Lola (1982-German) **C-114m.** ***½ D: Rainer Werner Fassbinder. Barbara Sukowa, Armin Mueller-Stahl, Mario Adorf, Mathias Fuchs, Helga Feddersen, Karin Baal, Ivan Desny. Brilliantly directed and edited chronicle of repercussions when cynical, calculating singer-whore Sukowa sets sights on respectable Mueller-Stahl, the new Building Commissioner and only honest politician in town. Striking, unusual use of lighting and color. One-third of Fassbinder's trilogy of life in postwar Germany (with THE MARRIAGE OF MARIA BRAUN and VERONIKA VOSS.) [R]

Lola Montes (1955-French) **C-110m.** *** D: Max Ophuls. Martine Carol, Peter Ustinov, Anton Walbrook, Oskar Werner, Ivan Desny. Legendary film about beautiful circus performer and her effect on various men nonetheless suffers from Carol's lack of magnetism in title role. Ophuls' superb use of widescreen won't mean much on TV; the celebrated director's last film. CinemaScope.▼●◗

Lolita (1962-British) **152m.** *** D: Stanley Kubrick. James Mason, Shelley Winters, Peter Sellers, Sue Lyon, Marianne Stone, Diana Decker. Sexually precocious Lyon becomes involved with stolid professor Mason, and bizarre Sellers provides peculiar romance leading to murder and lust. Screenplay for this genuinely strange film is credited to Vladimir Nabokov, who wrote the novel of the same name, but bears little relation to his actual script, later published. Winters is outstanding as Lyon's sex-starved mother. Reissued in U.S. with 1m. of additional dialogue from British version. Remade in 1997.▼●◗

Lolita (1997-British-French) **C-137m.** ***½ D: Adrian Lyne. Jeremy Irons, Melanie Griffith, Dominique Swain, Frank Langella, Suzanne Shepherd. Exceptional remake of Vladimir Nabokov's notorious novel about a man's overwhelming (and ultimately, self-destructive) infatuation with a nymphet. In this version we're told the source of his obsession, which is just one reason it stands up against Kubrick's 1962 version and in some ways surpasses it . . . though Peter Sellers is sorely missed. Irons is a perfect Humbert and Swain is ideal as his object of desire. Screenplay by Stephen Schiff. [R] ▼◗

Lollipop SEE: **Forever Young, Forever Free**

Lolly Madonna XXX (1973) **C-103m.** ** D: Richard C. Sarafian. Rod Steiger, Robert Ryan, Jeff Bridges, Scott Wilson, Season Hubley, Katherine Squire, Ed Lauter, Gary Busey, Randy Quaid. Modern-day Hatfield-McCoy feud erupts between two backwoods families, prompted by mistaken identity situation involving innocent girl (Hubley). Histrionics galore, but no point to it at all. Aka THE LOLLY-MADONNA WAR. Panavision. [PG]

Lolly-Madonna War, The SEE: **Lolly Madonna XXX**

London Belongs to Me SEE: **Dulcimer Street**

London Kills Me (1991-British) **C-107m.** BOMB D: Hanif Kureishi. Justin Chadwick, Steven Mackintosh, Fiona Shaw, Emer McCourt, Brad Dourif, Roshan Seth, Tony Haygarth, Stevan Rimkus, Eleanor David, Alun Armstrong. Glossy, phony tale of a homeless, rootless young man who steals and deals drugs, and decides he wants to go straight; his companions are a small-time druggie who aspires to greatness as a big-time dealer and a pretty junkie. This shallow cop-out of a movie does little more than serve as a recruiting poster for thieving and shooting heroin. Directorial debut of playwright-screenwriter Kureishi (MY

BEAUTIFUL LAUNDRETTE, SAMMY AND ROSIE GET LAID). [R]▼

London Melody (1937-British) **75m.** ** D: Herbert Wilcox. Anna Neagle, Tullio Carminati, Robert Douglas, Horace Hodges, Grizelda Hervey. Static account of Cockney street entertainer Neagle—who's made up to look like a movie queen despite her character's station in life—who is taken under the wing of diplomat Carminati. Released in the U.S. a year later as GIRL IN THE STREET.▼

Lone Gun, The (1954) **C-78m.** ** D: Ray Nazarro. George Montgomery, Dorothy Malone, Frank Faylen, Neville Brand. Standard Western of valiant hero shooting it out with outlaws, winning hand of rancher's daughter, nicely played by Malone.

Lone Hand (1953) **C-80m.** **½ D: George Sherman. Joel McCrea, Barbara Hale, James Arness, Charles Drake. Sturdy McCrea is undercover agent posing as outlaw to get the goods on a gang.

Loneliness of the Long Distance Runner, The (1962-British) **103m.** **** D: Tony Richardson. Michael Redgrave, Tom Courtenay, Avis Bunnage, Peter Madden, Alec McCowen, James Fox, Julia Foster, John Thaw. Engrossing story of rebellious young man chosen to represent reform school in track race. Superbly acted film confronts society, its mores and institutions. Screenplay by Alan Sillitoe, from his own story. Key British film of 1960s.▼●

Lonely Are the Brave (1962) **107m.** *** D: David Miller. Kirk Douglas, Gena Rowlands, Walter Matthau, Michael Kane, Carroll O'Connor, William Schallert, George Kennedy, Bill Bixby. Penetrating study of rebellious cowboy Douglas escaping from jail, pursued by posse utilizing modern means of communications and transportation. Script by Dalton Trumbo, from Edward Abbey's novel, *Brave Cowboy*. Panavision.▼●

Lonely Guy, The (1984) **C-90m.** **½ D: Arthur Hiller. Steve Martin, Charles Grodin, Judith Ivey, Robyn Douglass, Steve Lawrence, Merv Griffin, Dr. Joyce Brothers. Unusually subdued and offbeat vehicle for Martin, who's quite likable as a nerd-ish type who's just been thrown out by his girlfriend . . . only to find he's not alone. Grodin is a delight as a melancholy soulmate who inducts him into the society of Lonely Guys in N.Y.C. Too prolonged and uneven. Based on Bruce Jay Friedman's book *The Lonely Guy's Book of Life*. Adapted by Neil Simon, scripted by Ed Weinberger and Stan Daniels. [R] ▼●◗

Lonelyhearts (1958) **101m.** **½ D: Vincent J. Donehue. Montgomery Clift, Robert Ryan, Myrna Loy, Dolores Hart, Maureen Stapleton, Frank Maxwell, Jackie Coogan, Mike Kellin. Superior cast in interesting adaptation of Nathanael West's book and Howard Teichmann's play, both titled *Miss Lonelyhearts*. Clift is would-be reporter assigned to title column and becomes too deeply involved in the problems of his readers. A bit dated by today's standards, but watchable; scripted and produced by Dore Schary. West's book had previously been filmed as ADVICE TO THE LOVELORN. Film debuts of Stapleton and director Donehue.▼

Lonely Hearts (1981-Australian) **C-95m.** *** D: Paul Cox. Wendy Hughes, Norman Kaye, Jon Finlayson, Julia Blake, Jonathan Hardy. Delightfully quirky romantic comedy about an unlikely match—a middle-aged piano tuner with a flair for theatrics, and a painfully shy office worker. Lovely performances match director Cox's offbeat screenplay. [R]▼●

Lonely Lady, The (1983) **C-92m.** BOMB D: Peter Sasdy. Pia Zadora, Lloyd Bochner, Bibi Besch, Joseph Cali, Anthony Holland, Jared Martin, Ray Liotta, Kenneth Nelson. Terrible movie about an aspiring screenwriter who's used and abused while on her way to the Top in Hollywood; adapted from the Harold Robbins novel. Pia does her best, but this is rock-bottom stuff, not even fun on a trash level (although there's campy dialogue to spare). Filmed mostly in Italy. [R]▼●

Lonely Man, The (1957) **87m.** *** D: Henry Levin. Anthony Perkins, Jack Palance, Elaine Aiken, Neville Brand, Claude Akins. Solid acting and taut direction remove sting of hackneyed gunslinger-trying-to-reform plot. VistaVision.▼

Lonely Passion of Judith Hearne, The (1987-British) **C-116m.** **½ D: Jack Clayton. Maggie Smith, Bob Hoskins, Wendy Hiller, Marie Kean, Ian McNeice, Alan Devlin, Rudi Davies, Prunella Scales. Smith gives a knockout performance as a lonely, driven Irish woman whose life takes another turn for the worse after moving into a boardinghouse run by snippy Kean. Hoskins is equally fine as a garrulous gentleman with whom she sparks a relationship based on mutual misunderstanding. In fact, all the performances are superb in this long-awaited adaptation of Brian Moore's 1955 novel about a woman's blind faith in the church—and total lack of faith in herself . . . but dramatically the story has a few too many peaks and valleys. [R]▼

Lonely Woman, The SEE: **Strangers** (1953)

Lone Ranger, The (1956) **C-86m.** **½ D: Stuart Heisler. Clayton Moore, Jay Silverheels, Lyle Bettger, Bonita Granville, Perry Lopez, Robert J. Wilke. Action-packed feature version of the popular TV series, focusing on the Masked Man and Tonto as they tangle with scheming rancher Bettger, who has been stirring up trouble with the Indians.▼

Lone Ranger and the Lost City of Gold, The (1958) **C-80m.** ** D: Lesley Selander. Clayton Moore, Jay Silverheels, Douglas Kennedy, Charles Watts. Typical Lone Ranger Western is fine for younger audiences, involving hooded killers and mysterious clues to a hidden treasure city.▼

Loners, The (1972) **C-79m.** ** D: Sutton Roley. Dean Stockwell, Todd Susman, Scott Brady, Gloria Grahame, Pat Stich, Alex Dreier, Tim Rooney. Standard bike movie with several screen veterans and a plot involving three drop-out cyclists who turn their backs on society and take it on the lam across the Southwest. [R]▼

Lonesome Gun SEE: **Stranger on the Run**

Lone Star (1952) **94m.** **½ D: Vincent Sherman. Clark Gable, Ava Gardner, Lionel Barrymore, Beulah Bondi, Broderick Crawford, Ed Begley. Texas fights for independence, with good guy Gable vs. badman Crawford, Ava the woman in between. OK oater. Also shown in computer-colored version.▼

Lone Star (1996) **C-134m.** *** D: John Sayles. Kris Kristofferson, Chris Cooper, Elizabeth Peña, Joe Morton, Ron Canada, Miriam Colon, Clifton James, Matthew McConaughey, Stephen J. Lang, Tony Plana, Frances McDormand. Absorbing multicharacter story set in small Texas border town, where the memory of a former sheriff looms large—especially to his son, who's the current lawman. Keenly observed character studies are woven together by writer-director Sayles with his usual eye for detail and ear for good dialogue. Super 35. [R]▼●◗

The Lone Wolf Michael Lanyard, better known as the Lone Wolf, was a jewel thief who would always sacrifice his own ambitions to help a lady in distress. Created by Louis Joseph Vance in 1914, his impact was such that Lanyard's nickname became a part of our language. The character was featured in a number of silent films, portrayed by such formidable actors as Henry B. Walthall and Jack Holt. Columbia Pictures starred Bert Lytell in a series of Lone Wolf outings that spanned the early talkie era. When the studio made THE LONE WOLF RETURNS, in 1935, it was a chance for moviegoers to reacquaint themselves with an already familiar character (and for Columbia a chance to dust off the script of its same-named 1926 production). Melvyn Douglas played the dapper character in this stylish and delightful film; three years later the studio cast Francis Lederer in THE LONE WOLF IN PARIS, with Frances Drake as a rival thief. Then in 1939, Warren William took over the role and played a reformed Lanyard in a series of nine low-budget, fast-moving, enjoyable films which lacked the class of the first two entries but had a certain charm of their own. There was a heavy accent on comedy, and Eric Blore was added to the cast as Lanyard's light-fingered valet Jamison, who not only served as comic relief but usually got tangled up in the plot as well. William's best effort by far was his first, THE LONE WOLF SPY HUNT, a reworking of 1929's THE LONE WOLF'S DAUGHTER by mystery writer Jonathan Latimer, in which the leading man was aided by a delightfully screwball Ida Lupino as his girlfriend, an alluring Rita Hayworth as a slinky spy, Ralph Morgan as the spy leader, and Virginia Weidler as his curious daughter. Subsequent films in the series couldn't match that cast—or that script—but they were generally entertaining grade-B fare. After a respite of a few years, Gerald Mohr took up the role for several fair-to-middling efforts like 1947's THE LONE WOLF IN LONDON, which brought back valet Eric Blore. Ron Randell played Lanyard in the final entry, THE LONE WOLF AND HIS LADY (1949).

THE LONE WOLF

The Lone Wolf Returns (1935)
The Lone Wolf in Paris (1938)
The Lone Wolf Spy Hunt (1939)
The Lone Wolf Strikes (1940)
The Lone Wolf Meets a Lady (1940)
The Lone Wolf Takes a Chance (1941)
The Lone Wolf Keeps a Date (1941)
Secrets of the Lone Wolf (1941)
Counter-Espionage (1942)
One Dangerous Night (1943)
Passport to Suez (1943)
The Notorious Lone Wolf (1946)
The Lone Wolf in London (1947)
The Lone Wolf in Mexico (1947)
The Lone Wolf and His Lady (1949)

Lone Wolf & Cub: Sword of Vengeance (1972-Japanese) **C-83m.** *** D: Kenji Misumi. Tomisaburo Wakayama, Yunosuke Itoo, Fumio Watanabe, Shigeru Tsuyuguchi, Tomoko Mayama, Tomoo Uchida. In 17th-century Japan, Itto Ogami (Wakayama), the Shogun's executioner, is framed by the Yagyu clan, who also murder his wife. Embittered, he becomes a traveling assassin for hire, wheeling his young son Daigoro around Japan in a baby cart loaded with more gadgets than James Bond's Aston-Martin. First in the outstanding series is largely a setup for the sequels, but it's still beautifully stylized, gorily violent, and intelligent. Based on a long-running *manga* (comic book) series written by Kazuo Koike, illustrated by Goseki Kojima. LIGHTNING SWORDS OF DEATH and SHOGUN ASSASSIN were composed of segments from this and/or the sequels. Tohoscope.▼●

Lone Wolf and Cub 2: Baby Cart at the River Styx (1972-Japanese) **C-81m.** ***½ D: Kenji Misumi. Tomisaburo Wakayama, Kayo Matsuo, Minoru Ooki, Shooji Kobayashi, Shin Kishida, Akihiro Tomikawa.

Ogami is hired to kill a defecting worker who knows the secret of a dye process, the basis of the prosperity of a province. Best in the series, with amazing fights (Ogami is attacked with a *radish* at one point), superlative photography, great period atmosphere, and a sense of humor about itself. As with all in the series, very violent and bloody, with some nudity. Tohoscope.▼●

Lone Wolf & Cub 3: Baby Cart to Hades (1972-Japanese) **C-89m.** *** D: Kenji Misumi. Tomisaburo Wakayama, Goo Katoo, Yuuko Hama, Isao Yamagata, Michitaro Mizushima, Ichiroo Takatani. A man whose insane lord was betrayed hires Ogami to kill the betrayer, now an important official. First in the series to climax with Wakayama defeating a virtual army singlehanded. More conventional than those on either side of it, it's still an accomplished, stylish film. As always, the rating depends on one's tolerance—or fondness—for violent movies. Tohoscope.▼●

Lone Wolf & Cub 4: Baby Cart in Peril (1972-Japanese) **C-81m.** **½ D: Buiichi Saito. Tomisaburo Wakayama, Yooichi Hayashi, Michie Azuma, Akihiro Tomikawa, So Yamamura. This time, Ogami is hired to kill a tattooed woman, an expert with a short sword, who's carving up those connected to the man who raped her. Meanwhile, more Yagyu assassins try to kill our stone-faced hero. Stylistically overblown, with flashbacks, narration, and voice-overs galore; slowly paced, but has a great climactic fight. Tohoscope.▼●

Lone Wolf & Cub 5: Baby Cart in the Land of Demons (1973-Japanese) **C-89m.** *** D: Kenji Misumi. Tomisaburo Wakayama, Michiyo Yasuda, Akihiro Tomikawa, Shingo Yamashiro, Tomomi Satoo, Akira Yamauchi, Eijii Okada, Minoru Ooki. One by one, five samurai face Ogami to test his skills before hiring him. As each one dies, he gives Ogami another part of his instructions: to kill their lord, his concubine, and their five-year-old daughter. Grimmest of the lot, but also graced with the finest photography in the series and a powerful incident centering on Daigoro, Ogami's young son. Tohoscope. ▼●

Lone Wolf & Cub 6: White Heaven in Hell (1974-Japanese) **C-83m** *** D: Yoshiyuki Kuroda. Tomisaburo Wakayama, Akihiro Tomikawa, Junko Hitomi, Goroo Mutsumi, Minoru Ooki, Isao Kimura. Ogami is confronted by the last remaining son of his arch-enemy, Retsudo Yagyu; this time, the supernatural plays a part, and for the first time the Lone Wolf is afraid—but not for long. The photography particularly resembles the comic books. Robust battle on a snowy mountain climaxes the series, one of the best, not just in Japanese cinema history, but *world* cinema. Tohoscope.▼●

Lone Wolf and His Lady, The (1949) **60m.** *½ D: John Hoffman. Ron Randell, June Vincent, Alan Mowbray, William Frawley, Colette Lyons, Douglass Dumbrille. The Wolf turns newshound to cover the exhibition of a famous gem, and of course it's stolen, and of course he's suspected. Randell previously helped kill the *Bulldog Drummond* series, and does the same here in this final entry. Mowbray inherits Eric Blore's role as Jamison the valet.

Lone Wolf in London, The (1947) **68m.** ** D: Leslie Goodwins. Gerald Mohr, Nancy Saunders, Eric Blore, Evelyn Ankers, Richard Fraser, Queenie Leonard, Alan Napier. Some valuable jewels are stolen and Scotland Yard naturally suspects the Wolf. Glib entry not helped by Mohr's lack of charm.

Lone Wolf in Mexico, The (1947) **69m.** ** D: D. Ross Lederman. Gerald Mohr, Sheila Ryan, Jacqueline de Wit, Eric Blore, Nestor Paiva, John Gallaudet. Mohr's third and final appearance as the Wolf, as the series was becoming increasingly prosaic. This time he's accused of both robbery and murder down Mexico way.

Lone Wolf in Paris, The (1938) **66m.** ** D: Albert S. Rogell. Francis Lederer, Frances Drake, Walter Kingsford, Leona Maricle, Olaf Hytten, Albert Van Dekker. Lederer takes over for this one entry, becomes mixed up in political intrigue when he's hired by a princess to steal back her mother's crown jewels from a greedy duke.

Lone Wolf Keeps a Date, The (1941) **65m.** ** D: Sidney Salkow. Warren William, Frances Robinson, Bruce Bennett, Eric Blore, Thurston Hall, Jed Prouty, Don Beddoe. Listless episode has the Lone Wolf mixed up with a kidnapped millionaire and stolen ransom money in Miami.

Lone Wolf McQuade (1983) **C-107m.** **½ D: Steve Carver. Chuck Norris, David Carradine, Barbara Carrera, Leon Isaac Kennedy, Robert Beltran, L.Q. Jones, R.G. Armstrong, Sharon Farrell. Maverick Texas Ranger Norris takes on gun-running operation headed by Carradine. Played as a spaghetti Western, providing perfect milieu for Norris' fighting skills. A little long, with a sappy emotional sub-plot, but mostly good action fare. [PG]▼●

Lone Wolf Meets a Lady, The (1940) **71m.** ** D: Sidney Salkow. Warren William, Eric Blore, Jean Muir, Victor Jory, Roger Pryor, Warren Hull, Thurston Hall, Fred A. Kelsey, Bruce Bennett. The nonchalant reformed crook comes to the aid of a socialite (Muir) whose $100,000 necklace is lifted on the eve of her wedding. Standard entry with a plethora of complications.

Lone Wolf Returns, The (1935) **69m.** *** D: Roy William Neill. Melvyn Douglas, Gail Patrick, Tala Birell, Arthur Hohl, Thurston Hall, Raymond Walburn, Douglass Dumbrille. Urbane jewel thief Douglas wants to retire but is blackmailed by gangsters into helping them pull a heist. Stylish and delightfully lighthearted caper; filmed before in 1926.

Lone Wolf Spy Hunt, The (1939) **67m.** *** D: Peter Godfrey. Warren William, Ida Lupino, Rita Hayworth, Virginia Weidler, Ralph Morgan, Tom Dugan, Don Beddoe, Marc Lawrence, James Craig. Highly satisfactory blend of screwball comedy and genuine suspense as spies in Washington, D.C., kidnap Lanyard in an attempt to steal military secrets. William's first effort as the Lone Wolf, and certainly his best, with a top-notch cast worthy of a bigger budget. Script by ace mystery writer Jonathan Latimer (his first), based on 1929's THE LONE WOLF'S DAUGHTER. Hayworth, not yet a star, makes a sultry femme fatale.

Lone Wolf Strikes, The (1940) **57m.** **½ D: Sidney Salkow. Warren William, Joan Perry, Eric Blore, Alan Baxter, Astrid Allwyn, Montagu Love, Robert Wilcox, Don Beddoe, Fred A. Kelsey. Nimble entry focusing on an heiress's stolen string of pearls which the Lone Wolf is trying to return to its owner.

Lone Wolf Takes a Chance, The (1941) **76m.** **½ D: Sidney Salkow. Warren William, June Storey, Henry Wilcoxon, Eric Blore, Thurston Hall, Don Beddoe, Evalyn Knapp, Fred Kelsey, Regis Toomey. The Lone Wolf is framed for murder and uncovers a counterfeiting racket in an attempt to prove his innocence. Well-paced entry; early appearance by Lloyd Bridges.

Long Ago Tomorrow (1970-British) **C-100m.** ** D: Bryan Forbes. Malcolm McDowell, Nanette Newman, Georgia Brown, Bernard Lee, Gerald Sim, Michael Flanders. Rather wrong-headed drama of love between paraplegics. Could have been sensitive if script and direction weren't so porous and obvious. Original British title: THE RAGING MOON. [PG]▼

Long and the Short and the Tall, The (1961-British) **105m.** *** D: Leslie Norman. Richard Todd, Laurence Harvey, Richard Harris, David McCallum, Ronald Fraser. Well-delineated account of British patrol unit during WW2, focusing on their conflicting personalities and raids on Japanese. Retitled: JUNGLE FIGHTERS.

Long Arm, The SEE: **Third Key, The**

Long Dark Hall, The (1951-British) **86m.** **½ D: Anthony Bushell, Reginald Beck. Rex Harrison, Lilli Palmer, Tania Held, Henrietta Barry. Sturdy melodrama of man accused of killing girlfriend, with wife remaining loyal to him.▼

Long, Dark Night, The SEE: **Pack, The**

Long Day Closes, The (1992-British) **C-83m.** *** D: Terence Davies. Leigh McCormack, Marjorie Yates, Anthony Watson, Aysee Owens, Nicholas Lamont, Tina Malone. Poignant, painterly slice of life, an autobiographical remembrance by writer-director Davies of working-class England in the 1950s. The depiction of family life is far rosier than in Davies' earlier DISTANT VOICES, STILL LIVES, picturing a dreary postwar England yearning for an idealized beauty found in Hollywood movies and romantic pop songs. [PG]▼

Long Day's Dying, The (1968-British) **C-93m.** *½ D: Peter Collinson. David Hemmings, Tom Bell, Tony Beckley, Alan Dobie. Dull story of three British soldiers and their German captive during weary trek through European countryside. Techniscope. [R]

Long Day's Journey Into Night (1962) **136m.** **** D: Sidney Lumet. Katharine Hepburn, Ralph Richardson, Jason Robards, Jr., Dean Stockwell, Jeanne Barr. Faithful, stagy adaptation of Eugene O'Neill's detailed study of family in the 1910s. Hepburn is dope-addicted wife, Richardson her pompous actor husband, Stockwell the son dying of TB, and Robards the alcoholic son. Originally 174m.▼●

Long Days of Summer, The (1980) **C-105m. TVM** D: Dan Curtis. Dean Jones, Joan Hackett, Ronnie Scribner, Louanne, Donald Moffat, Andrew Duggan, Michael McGuire, Leigh French. Sequel to WHEN EVERY DAY WAS THE FOURTH OF JULY recreates pre–WW2 America as seen through the eyes of a young Jewish boy and shows his lawyer dad's battle against the prejudices of his staid New England town. Average. ▼

Long Duel, The (1967-British) **C-115m.** **½ D: Ken Annakin. Yul Brynner, Trevor Howard, Harry Andrews, Andrew Keir, Charlotte Rampling. Brynner leads peasant revolt against British raj in 1920s India; routine adventure saga. Look for Edward Fox. Panavision.

Longest Day, The (1962) **180m.** **** D: Ken Annakin, Andrew Marton, Bernhard Wicki. John Wayne, Rod Steiger, Robert Ryan, Peter Lawford, Henry Fonda, Robert Mitchum, Richard Burton, Richard Beymer, Jeffrey Hunter, Sal Mineo, Roddy McDowall, Eddie Albert, Curt Jurgens, Gert Frobe, Sean Connery, Robert Wagner, Red Buttons, Mel Ferrer, many others. One of the last great epic WW2 films. Brilliant retelling of the Allied invasion of Normandy, complete with all-star international cast, re-creation of historical events on a grand scale; Oscar-winning special effects and cinematography. Also shown in computer-colored version. CinemaScope. ▼●◗

Longest Yard, The (1974) **C-123m.** ***½ D: Robert Aldrich. Burt Reynolds, Eddie Albert, Ed Lauter, Michael Conrad, Jim Hampton, Bernadette Peters, Charles Tyner, Mike Henry, Harry Caesar, Richard Kiel, Robert Tessier, Malcolm Atterbury. Convict Reynolds, a former football pro, quarterbacks a squad of dirty players against warden Albert's hand-picked team. An audience picture if there ever was one; hilarious bone-crunching comedy written by Tracy Keenan Wynn. [R]▼●

Long Gone (1987) **C-110m. TVM** D: Martin Davidson. William L. Petersen, Virginia Madsen, Dermot Mulroney, Larry Riley, Katy Boyer, Henry Gibson, Teller. Engaging baseball comedy about a third-rate minor league team's battle for the championship. Sassy script by Michael Norell, and performances (Petersen as the team's brash player/manager, and Madsen as a small-town beauty queen). Made for cable. Above average.▼●

Long Goodbye, The (1973) **C-112m.** **½ D: Robert Altman. Elliott Gould, Nina Van Pallandt, Sterling Hayden, Henry Gibson, Mark Rydell, Jim Bouton, David Arkin, Warren Berlinger. Strange, almost spoofy updating of Raymond Chandler's novel, with Gould as a shabby Philip Marlowe involved with mysterious Van Pallandt, alcoholic Hayden, evil Gibson, missing pal Bouton, and Jewish gangster Rydell. Some nice touches, especially John Williams' jokey score, but Altman's attitude toward the genre borders on contempt. Screenplay by Leigh Brackett, who had earlier coscripted THE BIG SLEEP. Look for Arnold Schwarzenegger as a muscleman, David Carradine as a prisoner. Beware TV prints minus the original ending! Panavision. [R]▼●

Long Good Friday, The (1980-British) **C-114m.** ***½ D: John Mackenzie. Bob Hoskins, Helen Mirren, Eddie Constantine, Dave King, Bryan Marshall, Derek Thompson, George Coulouris, Stephen Davies, Pierce Brosnan. Occasionally confusing but otherwise terrific portrait of hoodlum rivalry in contemporary London; takes its rightful place with the best gangster movies of all time. Hoskins, brilliant as underworld entrepreneur, is matched by Mirren as subtly sexy mistress. Original screenplay by Barrie Keeffe. [R]▼●◗

Long Gray Line, The (1955) **C-138m.** *** D: John Ford. Tyrone Power, Maureen O'Hara, Robert Francis, Ward Bond, Donald Crisp, Betsy Palmer, Phil Carey, Harry Carey, Jr. Lengthy sentimental melodrama of West Point athletic trainer Power and his many years at the Academy. O'Hara is radiant as his wife. CinemaScope.▼

Long Haul, The (1957-British) **88m.** ** D: Ken Hughes. Victor Mature, Diana Dors, Patrick Allen, Gene Anderson. Mature is truck driver whose turbulent marriage paves way for his becoming involved with crooks. Minor fare.▼

Long Hot Summer, The (1958) **C-117m.** *** D: Martin Ritt. Paul Newman, Joanne Woodward, Anthony Franciosa, Orson Welles, Lee Remick, Angela Lansbury. Well-blended William Faulkner short stories make a flavorful, brooding drama of domineering Southerner (Welles) and a wandering handyman (Newman), who decides to stick around and marry daughter Woodward. Excellent Alex North score, weak finish to strong film; the Newmans' first film together. Remade for TV. CinemaScope.▼●

Long Hot Summer, The (1985) **C-200m. TVM** D: Stuart Cooper. Ava Gardner, Judith Ivey, Don Johnson, Jason Robards, William Russ, Cybill Shepherd, Wings Hauser, William Forsythe, Albert Hall. Surprisingly good remake of the Faulkner tale of sex and sin in a small Southern town. Johnson and Ivey stand out in the roles taken in 1958 film by Paul Newman and Joanne Woodward. Rita Mae Brown and Dennis Turner based their screenplay on the earlier one by Irving Ravetch and Harriet Frank, Jr., as much as on Faulkner's story, *The Hamlet.* Originally shown in two parts. Above average.▼

Long John Silver (1954-Australian) **C-109m.** **½ D: Byron Haskin. Robert Newton, Connie Gilchrist, Kit Taylor, Grant Taylor. Newton reprises title role from TREASURE ISLAND (with same director as the Disney film) and chews the scenery in this loose adaptation of Robert Louis Stevenson. Look for Rod Taylor in a small role. Aka RETURN TO TREASURE ISLAND. CinemaScope.▼

Long Kiss Goodnight, The (1996) **C-120m.** **½ D: Renny Harlin. Geena Davis, Samuel L. Jackson, Craig Bierko, Yvonne Zima, Tom Amandes, Brian Cox, Patrick Malahide, David Morse, Joseph McKenna, G. D. Spradlin, Alan North. If you find a kitchen sink, it's the one screenwriter Shane Black forgot to throw into this over-the-top action yarn, which starts out seriously, then changes tone. Davis plays an amnesiac with a young daughter, whose happy life is disrupted when she's forced to confront her past—as a professional undercover assassin! Jackson is a low-rent private eye who goes along for this roller-coaster ride, full of large-scale stunts and humor with Davis as a combination Pauline (as in PERILS OF . . .) and Rambo. No one seems to mind or care that a child is also part of the mayhem. Super 35. [R]▼●◗

Long Live Your Death SEE: **Don't Turn the Other Cheek**

Long, Long Trailer, The (1954) **C-96m.** **½ D: Vincente Minnelli. Lucille Ball, Desi Arnaz, Marjorie Main, Keenan Wynn, Gladys Hurlbut. Pleasant vehicle for Lucy and Desi, on honeymoon with cumbersome trailer that creates havoc for the duo. Plenty of slapstick.▼●

Long Lost Father (1934) **63m.** **½ D: Ernest B. Schoedsack. John Barrymore, Helen Chandler, Donald Cook, Alan Mowbray, Claude King. Minor Barrymore vehicle casts him as man who deserted daughter Chandler years ago, tries to make up for it when she gets in a jam.

Long Memory, The (1952-British) **91m.** *** D: Robert Hamer. John Mills, John McCallum, Elizabeth Sellars, Geoffrey Keen, John Chandos, Vida Hope. Mills is framed for murder by girlfriend Sellars. When released from prison twelve years later, he sets out to prove his innocence. Well-done drama.

Long Night, The (1947) **101m.** ** D: Anatole Litvak. Henry Fonda, Barbara Bel Geddes, Vincent Price, Ann Dvorak, Queenie Smith. Plodding drama of killer hiding out overnight with girl who tries to get him to confess; pretty tired drama. Remake of Jean Gabin film LE JOUR SE LÈVE.

Long Pants (1927) **61m.** ** D: Frank Capra. Harry Langdon, Gladys Brockwell, Al Roscoe, Alma Bennett, Frankie Darro, Priscilla Bonner. Langdon's followup to THE STRONG MAN is one of the most curious silent comedies ever made: a dark, mostly unfunny story of a boy in knickers who fantasizes about being a great lover (based on books he's read), and gets his chance when a sexy femme fatale passes through town. However, this does require that he murder his hometown bride first! For what it's worth, Capra didn't complete the film, and didn't like what was done with it. ▼●

Long Ride from Hell, A (1970-Italian) **C-94m.** *½ D: Alex Burks (Camillo Bazzoni). Steve Reeves, Wayde Preston, Dick Palmer, Silvana Venturelli, Lee Burton, Ted Carter. Title is another instance of truth-in-advertising; dreary Western coauthored by Reeves has to do with rancher who tries to clear himself of phony train-robbery charge. [R]

Long Ride Home, The SEE: **Time for Killing, A**

Long Riders, The (1980) **C-100m.** *** D: Walter Hill. David, Keith and Robert Carradine, Stacy and James Keach, Randy and Dennis Quaid, Nicholas and Christopher Guest, Pamela Reed, Savannah Smith, James Whitmore, Jr., Harry Carey, Jr. *All in the Family* out West. The Carradines, Keaches, Quaids, and Guests portray, respectively, the Younger, James, Miller, and Ford brothers in this stylish but extremely bloody film. Typically meticulous direction by Hill, with David Carradine and Reed igniting sparks as Cole Younger and Belle Starr. Excellent score by Ry Cooder. [R]▼●

Long Shadow, The (1961-British) **64m.** *½ D: Peter Maxwell. John Crawford, Susan Hampshire, Bill Nagy, Humphrey Lestocq. Flabby espionage caper set in 1950s Vienna, with Crawford an American foreign correspondent caught up in it all.

Long Ships, The (1964-British-Yugoslavian) **C-125m.** ** D: Jack Cardiff. Richard Widmark, Sidney Poitier, Rosanna Schiaffino, Russ Tamblyn, Oscar Homolka, Colin Blakely. Fairly elaborate but comic-book-level costume adventure of Vikings battling Moors for fabled treasure. Good cast deserves better. Super Technirama 70.▼

Long Shot, The (1976) SEE: **Target of an Assassin**

Longshot, The (1986) **C-89m.** BOMB D: Paul Bartel. Tim Conway, Jack Weston, Harvey Korman, Ted Wass, Jonathan Winters, Stella Stevens, Anne Meara, George DiCenzo. Four lower-middle-class losers borrow $5,000 from the local break-ya-fingas financier to finance a sure thing at the track. Pathetic comedy is full of toilet gags and can't even coast on the good will established by the cast in better days. Mike Nichols *(Mike Nichols!!!)* executive produced. [PG-13]▼

Long Summer of George Adams, The (1982) **C-100m. TVM** D: Stuart Margolin. James Garner, Joan Hackett, Anjanette Comer, Alex Harvey, Juanin Clay, David Graf. Lighthearted homespun period piece, adapted by John Gay from Weldon Hill's book, with Garner as a small-town railroad man who's done out of a job by diesel power. Garner and his *Rockford Files/ Maverick* production gang give this one the charm it exudes, along with some lovely bits of Americana. Above average.

Longtime Companion (1990) **C-96m.** *** D: Norman René. Stephen Caffrey, Patrick Cassidy, Brian Cousins, Bruce Davison, John Dossett, Mark Lamos, Dermot Mulroney, Mary-Louise Parker, Michael Schoeffling, Campbell Scott, Robert Joy. Emotional pre-PHILADELPHIA examination of AIDS in the '80s, focusing on a closely knit group of gay men in N.Y.C. Film spans the entire decade, from first reports of a mystery illness to a time when the disease became a tragic part of everyday life. Craig Lucas's script is insightful, heart-wrenching, and funny. Entire cast is excellent, especially Davison. A PBS *American Playhouse* presentation. [R]▼●

Long Tomorrow, The SEE: **Cry For Me, Billy**

Long Voyage Home, The (1940) **105m.** ***½ D: John Ford. John Wayne, Thomas Mitchell, Ian Hunter, Ward Bond, Barry Fitzgerald, Wilfrid Lawson, Mildred Natwick, John Qualen, Arthur Shields, Joe Sawyer, J. Warren Kerrigan. Evocative look at men who spend their lives at sea, adapted (by Dudley Nichols) from four short O'Neill plays. Richly textured drama with many beautiful vignettes; exquisitely photographed by Gregg Toland. ▼●

Long Wait, The (1954) **93m.** ** D: Victor Saville. Anthony Quinn, Charles Coburn, Gene Evans, Peggie Castle, Dolores Donlan, Mary Ellen Kay. Meandering, actionless account of man with loss of memory discovering he's been framed for several crimes.

Long Walk Home, The (1990) **C-97m.** *** D: Richard Pearce. Sissy Spacek, Whoopi Goldberg, Dwight Schultz, Ving Rhames, Dylan Baker. Narrated by Mary Steenburgen. Perceptive, extremely well-acted account of the life and changing times in the segregated American South of the mid-1950s. The focus is on the consciousness-raising of Spacek, a privileged pillar of Southern womanhood; Goldberg is her hard-working housekeeper, who's struggling to help support her own family. Fine sense of period detail; most intriguing of all, John Cork's script mirrors the connection between feminism and the civil rights movement. [PG]▼●

Long Way Home, The (1997) **C-119m.** ***½ D: Mark Jonathan Harris. Narrated by Morgan Freeman. Exceptional, Oscar-winning documentary about the incredible story of Jews who—once freed from Nazi concentration camps—were forced to endure yet another ordeal. Unwelcome in their homelands, bereft of families, they were held in squalid detention camps or arrested for illegal immigration until the formation of the state of Israel in 1948. Well told through the use of archival footage, on-camera interviews, and the words of survivors and participants. ▼●

Look Back in Anger (1959-British) **99m.** ***½ D: Tony Richardson. Richard Burton, Claire Bloom, Edith Evans, Mary Ure, Gary Raymond, Glen Byam Shaw, Donald Pleasence. John Osborne's trend-setting angry-young-man play, with Burton rebelling against life and wife, realistically filmed and acted; dialogue bristles.▼●

Look Down and Die SEE: **Steel**

Looker (1981) **C-94m.** BOMB D: Michael Crichton. Albert Finney, James Coburn, Susan Dey, Leigh Taylor-Young, Dorian Harewood, Tim Rossovich, Darryl Hickman. Conglomerate-head Coburn produces the computerized images of gorgeous models to hawk products and political candidates on TV—and also murders his subjects. As he is losing all his clients, Beverly Hills plastic surgeon Finney investigates. Intriguing premise is illogically and boringly handled; even Finney cannot save this turkey. Watch for Vanna White. Panavision. [PG]▼●

Look for the Silver Lining (1949) **C-100m.** **½ D: David Butler. June Haver, Ray Bolger, Gordon MacRae, Charles Ruggles, Rosemary DeCamp. Superficial biography of Marilyn Miller's career in show business, with vintage vaudeville numbers bolstering trivial plot line.▼

Look in Any Window (1961) **87m.** ** D: William Alland. Paul Anka, Ruth Roman, Alex Nicol, Gigi Perreau, Jack Cassidy. Unhappy home life sets Anka on path of crime. Ho-hum.

Looking for Danger (1957) **62m.** ** D: Austen Jewell. Huntz Hall, Stanley Clements, Eddie LeRoy, David (Gorcey) Condon, Jimmy Murphy, Otto Reichow, Lili Kardell, Percy Helton. Genial *Bowery Boys* caper, relating a flashback adventure in North Africa to trap some Nazis during WW2.

Looking for Love (1964) **C-83m.** BOMB D: Don Weis. Connie Francis, Susan Oliver, Jim Hutton, Barbara Nichols, Danny Thomas, Johnny Carson, George Hamilton, Paula Prentiss. They should have looked for a script instead. Plastic show-biz romance with little help from various guest stars, including Carson (who wound up making HORN BLOWS AT MIDNIGHT-type jokes about this—his only film appearance).

Looking for Mr. Goodbar (1977) **C-135m.** *½ D: Richard Brooks. Diane Keaton, Richard Gere, William Atherton, Tuesday Weld, Richard Kiley, LeVar Burton, Tom Berenger, Brian Dennehy. Sordid rewrite (by director Brooks) of Judith Rossner's novel begins as intelligent study of repressed young girl, then wallows endlessly in her new ''liberated'' lifestyle. Keaton's performance outclasses this pointless movie. Story recycled in the TVM TRACKDOWN: FINDING THE GOODBAR KILLER. [R]▼●

Looking for Richard (1996) **C-109m.** ***½ D: Al Pacino. Al Pacino, Frederic Kimball, Harris Yulin, Penelope Allen, Alec Baldwin, Kevin Spacey, Estelle Parsons, Winona Ryder, Aidan Quinn. Fascinating documentary-style film about Pacino's staging of *Richard III* and his simultaneous exploration of the relevance of Shakespeare to people in every walk of life. Every scene is dissected—by actors and scholars—before we see it performed, bringing this play to vivid life, especially for those of us who aren't already Shakespeare buffs. A treat from start to finish. Among the interviewees: Kenneth Branagh, Kevin Kline, James Earl Jones, Rosemary Harris, Peter Brook, Derek Jacobi, Vanessa Redgrave, and John Gielgud. [PG-13]▼●

Looking Forward (1933) **82m.** **½ D: Clarence Brown. Lionel Barrymore, Lewis Stone, Benita Hume, Elizabeth Allan, Phillips Holmes, Colin Clive, Doris Lloyd. Stone gives one of his best performances as a man trying to keep his London department store (founded by his family 200 years ago) afloat during the depths of the Depression; Barrymore is a mousy clerk who's been with the store for forty years. Superficial but pleasant drama boasts that its title came from a speech by F.D.R.

Looking Glass War, The (1970-British) **C-108m.** *½ D: Frank R. Pierson. Christopher Jones, Pia Degermark, Ralph Richardson, Anthony Hopkins, Paul Rogers,

Susan George, Anna Massey, Ray McAnally, Vivien Pickles. Dull film version of John le Carré's best-seller has Jones risking his life to photograph a rocket in East Berlin. Good opportunity to study the leads' bone structure, since they never change facial expressions. Panavision. [M/PG]▼

Lookin' to Get Out (1982) **C-104m.** BOMB D: Hal Ashby. Jon Voight, Burt Young, Ann-Margret, Bert Remsen, Jude Farese, Allen Keller, Richard Bradford, Angelina Jolie. Voight coscripted, coproduced, and tries out his Al Pacino impression in this embarrassing, implausible comedy about two losers who con their way into a suite at the MGM Grand with a plan to win big at blackjack. Remsen's performance as a wily old card shark is the only bright spot in this utter catastrophe. Shot in 1980; unfortunately, it recovered. [R]▼

Looks and Smiles (1981-British) **104m.** *** D: Kenneth Loach. Graham Green, Carolyn Nicholson, Tony Pitts, Phil Askham, Cilla Mason. Working-class teenager Green cannot find a job or place for himself in society. Solid, realistic story of alienation, frustration, anger.

Look Who's Laughing (1941) **78m.** ** D: Allan Dwan. Edgar Bergen, Jim and Marion Jordan (Fibber McGee and Molly), Lucille Ball, Harold Peary (The Great Gildersleeve), Lee Bonnell. Bergen's plane inadvertently lands in Wistful Vista, where he becomes involved in a municipal squabble with Fibber and Molly. Slim vehicle for radio favorites only comes alive when Charlie McCarthy takes the spotlight.▼●

Look Who's Talking (1989) **C-90m.** *** D: Amy Heckerling. John Travolta, Kirstie Alley, Olympia Dukakis, George Segal, Abe Vigoda; voice of Bruce Willis. Amiable comedy about an unmarried woman who has a baby (by her no-good married boyfriend) and then sets out to find a suitable "daddy" for him. Good showcase for costars Alley and Travolta. Written by director Heckerling. One quibble: though set in N.Y.C., it's all too obvious that it was shot somewhere else (Vancouver, to be precise). Followed by two sequels and the TV series *Baby Talk*. [PG-13]▼●◗

Look Who's Talking Now (1993) **C-92m.** ** D: Tom Ropelewski. John Travolta, Kirstie Alley, George Segal, Olympia Dukakis, David Gallagher, Tabitha Lupien, Lysette Anthony; voices of Danny DeVito, Diane Keaton. Third entry in the series isn't bad, thanks to some cute dogplay and the delightful voice-over work by DeVito and Keaton, as a kind of live-action LADY AND THE TRAMP, who wreak havoc on the lives of the Umbriacco family. Passable family entertainment. [PG-13]▼●

Look Who's Talking Too (1990) **C-81m.** BOMB D: Amy Heckerling. John Travolta, Kirstie Alley, Olympia Dukakis, Elias Koteas, Twink Caplan, Gilbert Gottfried, Lorne Sussman; voices of Bruce Willis, Roseanne Barr, Damon Wayans, Mel Brooks. Militantly offensive sequel adds a baby girl to the formula—with the voice of Barr. It took a million bad poo-poo jokes and a gratuitous Travolta dance number to pad the running time. Climactic apartment fire may traumatize young children. [PG-13]▼●

Looney, Looney, Looney Bugs Bunny Movie, The (1981) **C-80m.** **½ D: Friz Freleng. Voice of Mel Blanc. Feature-length compilation of classic Warner Bros. cartoons is divided into three parts. In the first, Yosemite Sam must return Bugs Bunny to the Devil in order to save his own soul. Second part has Bugs rescuing Tweety from gangsters Rocky and Muggsy. Third and best segment is a parody of Hollywood award shows featuring Freleng's wonderful 1957 cartoon THE THREE LITTLE BOPS. Also includes Bugs Bunny's Oscar-winning KNIGHTY KNIGHT BUGS (1958). Official billing is FRIZ FRELENG'S LOONEY, LOONEY, LOONEY BUGS BUNNY MOVIE. [G] ▼

Loophole (1954) **80m.** **½ D: Harold D. Schuster. Barry Sullivan, Charles McGraw, Dorothy Malone, Don Haggerty, Mary Beth Hughes, Don Beddoe. Imaginative handling of oft-told tale of bank employee accused of theft, catching actual crooks.

Loophole (1980-British) **C-105m.** **½ D: John Quested. Albert Finney, Martin Sheen, Susannah York, Colin Blakely, Jonathan Pryce, Robert Morley, Alfred Lynch, Christopher Guard. Slick but very ordinary caper film about an unemployed architect who's persuaded to participate in an ambitious break-in of "impenetrable" London bank. Aka BREAK IN.▼

Loose Cannons (1990) **C-94m.** *½ D: Bob Clark. Gene Hackman, Dan Aykroyd, Dom DeLuise, Ronny Cox, Nancy Travis, Robert Prosky, Paul Koslo, Dick O'Neill, Jan Triska, David Alan Grier. Below-rock-bottom car-chase excuse about two D.C. cops caught between ex-Nazis and Israeli adversaries scuffling over a mysterious Hitler home movie. Unfunny and offensive, film stagnated on the shelf while the studio figured out what to do with it. Career nadir for most of its participants. Panavision. [R]▼●

Loose in London (1953) **63m.** **½ D: Edward Bernds. Leo Gorcey, Huntz Hall, David Gorcey, Bernard Gorcey, John Dodsworth, Norma Varden, Angela Greene, Walter Kingsford, Joan Shawlee. When Sach is thought to be related to a dying British earl, the Bowery Boys head to England and expose some scheming heirs in this enjoyable romp.

Loose Shoes (1980) **C-74m.** **½ D: Ira

Miller. Bill Murray, Howard Hesseman, David Landsburg, Ed Lauter, Susan Tyrrell, Avery Schreiber, Misty Rowe, Jaye P. Morgan, Buddy Hackett, Murphy Dunne. Very mixed bag of spoofs of coming-attractions previews, some hilarious, some duds. Highlights: "Skateboarders From Hell," "The Yid and the Kid" (Chaplin), "The Sneaker" (Woody Allen), "Welcome to Bacon County," "Jewish Star Wars," and unbearably funny "Darktown After Dark." Dunne also composed score and songs. Filmed mostly in 1977. Originally titled COMING ATTRACTIONS. Aka QUACKERS. [R]▼

Loot (1970-British) **C-101m.** **½ D: Silvio Narizzano. Lee Remick, Richard Attenborough, Roy Holder, Hywel Bennett, Milo O'Shea, Dick Emery, Joe Lynch. Frantic black comedy from Joe Orton's stage hit. Holder and Bennett knock over a bank, hide the swag in the coffin of the former's mother, and then have a spot of trouble retrieving it. Despite Mod trappings, basically an old-fashioned, door-slamming farce; funny for those in the mood. [PG—originally rated R]▼

Looters, The (1955) **87m.** **½ D: Abner Biberman. Rory Calhoun, Julie Adams, Ray Danton, Thomas Gomez. OK drama of survivors of plane crash fighting amongst themselves for money aboard wreckage.

Lord Jeff (1938) **86m.** ** D: Sam Wood. Freddie Bartholomew, Mickey Rooney, Charles Coburn, Herbert Mundin, Terry Kilburn, Gale Sondergaard, Peter Lawford, Monty Woolley. Acceptable family film about good-boy Bartholomew led astray, sent to straighten out at naval school.

Lord Jim (1965) **C-154m.** **½ D: Richard Brooks. Peter O'Toole, James Mason, Curt Jurgens, Eli Wallach, Jack Hawkins, Paul Lukas, Daliah Lavi, Akim Tamiroff. Overlong, uneven adaptation of Joseph Conrad's story about idealistic young man in British Merchant Marine in the 19th century discredited as a coward who lives with scar for the rest of his life. Film's great moments provided by outstanding supporting cast. Super Panavision 70.▼

Lord Love a Duck (1966) **104m.** *** D: George Axelrod. Tuesday Weld, Roddy McDowall, Lola Albright, Martin West, Ruth Gordon, Harvey Korman, Martin Gabel, Sarah Marshall, Lynn Carey. Madcap black comedy about progressive Southern California high school where botany is called "plant skills." Film wavers uncomfortably between comedy and drama at times, but really delivers some belly laughs. Terrific performances in movie that was ahead of its time. Directorial debut of co-writer Axelrod.▼

Lord of Illusions (1995) **C-108m.** **½ D: Clive Barker. Scott Bakula, Kevin J. O'Connor, Famke Janssen, Vincent Schiavelli, Barry Del Sherman, Sheila Tousey, Joel Swetow, Joseph Latimore, Susan Traylor, Daniel Von Bargen. Private eye Bakula, a specialist in the supernatural, is in L.A. on a "normal" case when a stage magician is apparently killed during a performance. This is linked to the pending resurrection of an evil sorcerer, and soon Bakula is battling the forces of darkness again. Intelligent thriller, written by the director, is better than the usual genre fodder, but it's thinly plotted, and condescends slightly to its audience. Also available in 122m. unrated "director's cut." [R] ▼●◗

Lord of the Flies (1963-British) **90m.** *** D: Peter Brook. James Aubrey, Tom Chapin, Hugh Edwards, Roger Elwin, Tom Gaman. Unique story of a group of British schoolboys stranded on remote island. Their gradual degeneration into a savage horde is compelling. Adapted from William Golding's novel. Remade in 1990.▼●

Lord of the Flies (1990) **C-90m.** **½ D: Harry Hook. Balthazar Getty, Chris Furrh, Danuel Pipoly, Badgett Dale, Edward and Andrew Taft. Color update of the novel-to-film turns William Golding's savage schoolboys into TV-savvy American kids; it may make the story more immediate (though even that's arguable), but it also purges the original of its poetry. Visceral, and improves as it progresses, but inferior to Peter Brook's 1963 version whose amateur actors, by and large, were superior to this brood. [R]▼●

Lord of the Jungle (1955) **69m.** *½ D: Ford Beebe. Johnny Sheffield, Wayne Morris, Nancy Hale, Paul Picerni, William Phipps, Smoki Whitfield, Leonard Mudie, Harry Lauter, Joel Fluellen, Juanita Moore. Bomba the Jungle Boy tries to weed out a rogue elephant to save the entire herd from extinction; final entry of this shoddy series.

Lord of the Rings, The (1978) **C-133m.** **½ D: Ralph Bakshi. Voices of Christopher Guard, William Squire, John Hurt, Michael Sholes, Dominic Guard. Ambitious animated version of J. R. R. Tolkien's fantasy saga covers 1½ books of his trilogy (ending rather abruptly). Story of different races in Middle Earth competing for ownership of all-powerful Rings is inspired and exciting, but begins to drag—and confuse—during last hour. Bakshi's technique awkwardly combines animation and live-action tracings. [PG]▼

Lords of Discipline, The (1983) **C-102m.** **½ D: Franc Roddam. David Keith, Robert Prosky, G. D. Spradlin, Rick Rossovich, John Lavachielli, Mitchell Lichtenstein, Mark Breland, Michael Biehn, Barbara Babcock, Judge Reinhold, Bill Paxton, Jason Connery, Matt Frewer, Sophie Ward. Familiar but satisfactory military school drama, set in 1964 South Carolina. Keith plays senior asked to keep an eye on first black cadet (Breland) who's being systematically tortured by secret society called "The Ten." Good performances, especially by Prosky as school's number-two officer; based on the Pat Conroy novel. Unbelievable as it may appear, most of the film was shot in England! [R]▼●

Lord's of Flatbush, The (1974) **C-88m.** *** D: Stephen F. Verona, Martin Davidson. Perry King, Sylvester Stallone, Henry Winkler, Paul Mace, Susan Blakely, Paul Jabara, Dolph Sweet. Fun story of a Flatbush gang, circa 1957, with original music score. Training ground for two future stars, with Stallone writing some of the dialogue and Winkler trying out his Fonzie character. Look for Ray Sharkey as a student, Armand Assante as a wedding guest. [PG]▼●◗

Lords of the Deep (1989) **C-79m.** BOMB D: Mary Ann Fisher. Bradford Dillman, Priscilla Barnes, Daryl Haney, Melody Ryane, Eb Lottimer, Stephen Davies. In undersea base of future, menace seems to be manta-shaped aliens, but it's really loony leader Dillman. Clumsy, cheap, and amateurish, this was the fourth and last of 1989's undersea sci-fi thrillers, and the worst by far. Roger Corman appears unbilled (which is just as well). [PG-13]▼

Lords of Treason SEE: **Secret Honor**

Lorenzo's Oil (1992) **C-135m.** *** D: George Miller. Nick Nolte, Susan Sarandon, Peter Ustinov, Kathleen Wilhoite, Gerry Bamman, Margo Martindale, James Rebhorn, Ann Hearn, Zack O'Malley Greenburg. True-life story of Michaela and Augusto Odone, who learned their son had adrenoleukodystrophy, an incurable degenerative disease, and proceeded to turn the medical community upside down to keep him alive. Powerful film transcends its "disease of the week" roots, thanks to a highly cinematic visual style and an intelligent script (cowritten by director Miller, a physician by training, and Nick Enright). Nolte and Sarandon are excellent, and Ustinov offers fine support as a sympathetic doctor. The physical torture that Lorenzo goes through is often painful to watch. [PG-13] ▼●

Lorna Doone (1935-British) **89m.** *** D: Basil Dean. John Loder, Margaret Lockwood, Victoria Hopper, Roy Emerson, Edward Rigby, Mary Clare, Roger Livesey. Well-photographed tale of 17th-century love affair between farmer and outlaw's daughter (though she is hiding her true identity). Lovely locations, fine acting; remade in 1951 and for TV in 1990.

Lorna Doone (1951) **C-88m.** **½ D: Phil Karlson. Barbara Hale, Richard Greene, Carl Benton Reid, William Bishop. Middling screen version of Richard D. Blackmore's novel of 1680s England, with farmers rebelling against oppressive landlords. Done on small budget, but not bad.

Lorna Doone (1990-British) **C-90m. TVM** D: Andrew Grieve. Clive Owen, Sean Bean, Polly Walker, Billie Whitelaw, Miles Anderson, Rachel Kempson. Lushly photographed but uninspired rendition of Blackmore's novel about love, outlaws on horseback, and revenge in 17th-century England. Average. ▼

Los Amigos SEE: **Deaf Smith & Johnny Ears**

Loser Takes All (1956-British) **C-88m.** ** D: Ken Annakin. Rossano Brazzi, Glynis Johns, Robert Morley, Tony Britton, Geoffrey Keen, Peter Illing. Brazzi and Johns celebrate their honeymoon in Monte Carlo and try out their "perfect system" for winning at roulette, with unusual effect on their marriage. On-location filming helps. Remade in 1990 as STRIKE IT RICH. CinemaScope.

Losing Chase (1996) **C-92m.** *** D: Kevin Bacon. Helen Mirren, Kyra Sedgwick, Beau Bridges, Michael Yarmush, Lucas Denton, Nancy Beatty. Well-acted character-driven drama, set on Martha's Vineyard, about a psychologically troubled woman (Mirren) and her complex relationship with the new mother's helper (Sedgwick) hired to look after her children. This premiered on cable TV prior to theatrical release; Bacon's feature directing debut. Sedgwick (Bacon's wife) executive-produced. [R]▼●

Losing Ground (1982) **C-86m.** *** D: Kathleen Collins. Seret Scott, Bill Gunn, Duane Jones, Billie Allen, Gary Bolling, Norberto Kerner, Maritza Rivera. Clever script uplifts this comedy of uptight philosophy professor Scott who examines her feelings when artist husband Gunn paints beautiful Rivera. Unique in that the leading characters are middle-class blacks.

Losing Isaiah (1995) **C-108m.** *** D: Stephen Gyllenhaal. Jessica Lange, Halle Berry, David Strathairn, Cuba Gooding, Jr., Daisy Eagan, Marc John Jeffries, Samuel L. Jackson, Joie Susannah Lee, Regina Taylor, La Tanya Richardson, Jacqueline Brookes. Dedicated white Chicago social worker adopts a black infant who's been thrown in the trash (literally) by his crack-addicted mother; several years later, when the young woman straightens out her life, she goes to court to reclaim her son. Wrenching (and believable) drama scores points by making all of its characters human and flawed; first-rate performances make the most of Naomi Foner's intelligent script. Only disappointment is the final scene, which isn't very satisfying. Incidentally, Jackson and Richardson, who play opposing attorneys, are real-life husband and wife. [R]▼●

Losin' It (1983) **C-104m.** **½ D: Curtis Hanson. Tom Cruise, Jackie Earle Haley, John Stockwell, Shelley Long, John P. Navin, Jr., Henry Darrow, Hector Elias, Rick Rossovich. Pleasant enough but predictable film about three teenagers out for a wild time in Tijuana—with more bluster than experience. Appealing cast gives it extra value. [R]▼●

Los Olvidados (1950-Mexican) **88m.** ***½ D: Luis Buñuel. Alfonso Mejia, Roberto Cobo, Stella Inda, Miguel Inclan. Gripping story of juvenile delinquency among slums of Mexico, with surreal dream sequences interspersed. An offbeat winner from Buñuel, aka THE YOUNG AND THE DAMNED.▼●

Loss of Innocence (1961-British) **C-99m.** **½ D: Lewis Gilbert. Kenneth More, Danielle Darrieux, Susannah York, Maurice Denham. York gives poignant performance as teenager who, through love affair, becomes a woman; events leave her and younger sister and brother stranded on the Continent. Original title: THE GREENGAGE SUMMER.

Loss of Sexual Innocence, The (1999-British) **C-106m.** BOMB D: Mike Figgis. Julian Sands, Saffron Burrows, Stefano Dionisi, Kelly MacDonald, Gina McKee, Jonathan Rhys-Meyers, Bernard Hill, Rossy De Palma. An outlandish, pretentious and pointless film with parallel story threads from different phases of a man's life contrasting contemporary sexual relations and the first loss of innocence in the Garden of Eden. Almost plays like a parody of an ''art'' film.▼◗

Lost (1955-British) **C-89m.** **½ D: Guy Green. David Farrar, David Knight, Julia Arnall, Anthony Oliver, Marjorie Rhodes. Offbeat account of effects of a child kidnapping on parents, police, press and crooks.

Lost and Found (1979) **C-112m.** ** D: Melvin Frank. George Segal, Glenda Jackson, Maureen Stapleton, Hollis McLaren, John Cunningham, Paul Sorvino, John Candy, Martin Short. Widowed college prof and British divorcee meet in a French ski resort and quickly cool their romance by marrying. Attempt to recapture the success of the overrated A TOUCH OF CLASS is just more old fashioned nonsense posing as hip comedy. [PG]▼

Lost & Found (1999) **C-95m.** *½ D: Jeff Pollack. David Spade, Sophie Marceau, Patrick Bruel, Artie Lange, Mitchell Whitfield, Martin Sheen, Jon Lovitz, Estelle Harris, Rose Marie, Marla Gibbs, Carole Cook. Spade plots to win his beautiful new neighbor's affections while they search for her missing dog—which he has kidnapped. Crude, offensive, unoriginal, often painful to watch; only redeeming feature is an engaging Marceau. Fundamental error: her ''slimy'' ex-boyfriend is more likable than the leading man. Spade also takes credit as cowriter. [PG-13] ▼●◗

Lost Angel (1944) **91m.** **½ D: Roy Rowland. Margaret O'Brien, James Craig, Marsha Hunt, Philip Merivale, Henry O'Neill, Donald Meek, Keenan Wynn, Bobby (Robert) Blake. O'Brien is winning as precocious child—trained as a genius by scientists—who learns life's simple pleasures when she moves in with reporter Craig. Look for Ava Gardner as a hat-check girl.

Lost Angels (1989) **C-116m.** ** D: Hugh Hudson. Donald Sutherland, Adam Horovitz, Amy Locane, Don Bloomfield, Celia Weston, Graham Beckel, Kevin Tighe, John C. McGinley, Park Overall. Sincere but obvious and compromised drama of teenager Horovitz, unjustly sent to a mental clinic treating teenagers far more troubled than he. Sutherland is sole sympathetic psychiatrist. Shallow story grows increasingly incoherent and uninvolving. Horovitz, of singing group Beastie Boys, is good in acting debut. Super 35. [R]▼●

Lost Boundaries (1949) **99m.** *** D: Alfred L. Werker. Beatrice Pearson, Mel Ferrer, Richard Hylton, Susan Douglas, Canada Lee, Rev. Robert Dunn, Carleton Carpenter. Penetrating, well-meaning if slow-moving account of a dedicated, light-skinned Negro doctor (Ferrer, in his screen debut) who (with his family) passes for white in a small New Hampshire town. A clear-eyed look at segregated America.

Lost Boys, The (1987) **C-97m.** ** D: Joel Schumacher. Jason Patric, Corey Haim, Dianne Wiest, Barnard Hughes, Edward Herrmann, Kiefer Sutherland, Jami Gertz, Corey Feldman, Jamison Newlander. Family moves to California town where the local teenage gang turns out to be a pack of vampires! Slick movie aimed at juvenile audiences; both the humor and the plotting are pretty obvious. Only real fireworks come at the end during final showdown. Panavision. [R]▼●◗

Lost Command (1966) **C-130m.** *** D: Mark Robson. Anthony Quinn, Alain Delon, George Segal, Michele Morgan, Maurice Ronet, Claudia Cardinale, Gregoire Aslan, Jean Servais. Taut, well-made story of French-Algerian guerrilla warfare in North Africa, with Quinn as the peasant who has risen to a position of command. Fine international cast, good direction, and some top-notch action sequences blend very well. Panavision.▼

Lost Continent (1951) **86m.** ** D: Samuel Newfield. Cesar Romero, Hillary Brooke, John Hoyt, Whit Bissell, Sid Melton, Acquanetta. Lavish production values are obviously lacking as Romero leads expedition to prehistoric mountaintop to recover missing rocket. Video includes tinted sequences. ▼

Lost Continent, The (1968-British) **C-89m.** **½ D: Michael Carreras. Eric Porter, Hildegard Knef, Suzanna Leigh, Tony Beckley, Nigel Stock, Neil McCallum. Tramp steamer wanders into the seaweed-choked Sargasso Sea and finds isolated freak civilization derived from Spanish monarchy. Good cast handles lopsided script straightfaced; occasional good action. Based on Dennis Wheatley's novel *Uncharted Seas.* [G]▼◗

Lost Highway (1997-U.S.-French) **C-135m.** **½ D: David Lynch. Bill Pullman, Patricia Arquette, Balthazar Getty, Robert Blake, Natasha Gregson Wagner, Richard Pryor, Lisa Boyle, Michael Massee, Jack Nance, Henry Rollins, Gary Busey, Robert Loggia, Marilyn Manson, Giovanni Ribisi. Very bizarre Lynchian story that makes *Twin Peaks* seem as easy to follow as a *Sesame Street* episode. Basic plot involves Pullman as a jazz musician who, believing his wife is having an affair, suddenly finds himself the main suspect in her murder. Or is he? Or was she? Lynch fans will have fun trying to figure it out; others will find it incomprehensible. Blake is particularly enigmatic as a mystery man with a bad makeup job. Panavision. [R]▼●

Lost Honeymoon (1947) **71m.** ** D: Leigh Jason. Franchot Tone, Ann Richards, Tom Conway, Frances Rafferty, Una O'Connor, Clarence Kolb. Trivial comedy of ex-GI Tone aware that he had amnesia while stationed in London during WW2, but unaware that he had married and fathered two children.▼

Lost Honor of Katharina Blum, The (1975-German) **C-106m.** ***½ D: Volker Schlöndorff, Margarethe von Trotta. Angela Winkler, Mario Adorf, Dieter Laser, Heinz Bennent, Jürgen Prochnow. Solid drama about a woman persecuted because she is suspected of aiding terrorists that is also a stinging commentary on individual freedom, political repression, and the dangers of media manipulation. Based on the Henrich Boll novel; remade as a TVM, THE LOST HONOR OF KATHRYN BECK. [R]▼

Lost Honor of Kathryn Beck, The (1984) **C-100m. TVM** D: Simon Langton. Marlo Thomas, Kris Kristofferson, George Dzundza, Edward Winter, David Rasche, Linda Thorson. Thomas seeks to clear her reputation, smeared by the police and press after she spent the night with a man, unaware he was a long-sought terrorist. Uneven Americanization of the 1975 Volker Schlöndorff–Margarethe von Trotta film THE LOST HONOR OF KATHARINA BLUM, adapted by Loring Mandel. Noted cinematographer Gordon Willis and British TV director Langton made their American TV movie debuts here. Also known as ACT OF PASSION. Average.▼

Lost Horizon (1937) **132m.** **** D: Frank Capra. Ronald Colman, Jane Wyatt, John Howard, Edward Everett Horton, Margo, Sam Jaffe, H. B. Warner, Isabel Jewell, Thomas Mitchell. James Hilton's classic story about five people stumbling into strange Tibetan land where health, peace, and longevity reign. A rare movie experience, with haunting finale. Screenplay by Robert Riskin. After being shown in edited reissue prints for years, this classic has been restored to its original length—though several scenes are still missing, and are represented by dialogue only, illustrated with stills. Remade with music in 1973.▼●◗

Lost Horizon (1973) **C-143m.** *½ D: Charles Jarrott. Peter Finch, Liv Ullmann, Sally Kellerman, George Kennedy, Michael York, Olivia Hussey, Bobby Van, James Shigeta, Charles Boyer, John Gielgud. First half-hour copies 1937 film scene-for-scene, and everything's fine; then we get to Shangri-La and awful Burt Bacharach–Hal David songs, and it falls apart. "Lost" is right. Originally released at 150m. Panavision. [G]

Lost in a Harem (1944) **89m.** **½ D: Charles Riesner. Bud Abbott, Lou Costello, Marilyn Maxwell, John Conte, Douglass Dumbrille, Lottie Harrison, Jimmy Dorsey Orchestra. Slicker-than-usual A&C (made on infrequent trip to MGM), but strictly routine. Some good scenes here and there with sultan Dumbrille; Maxwell is perfect harem girl.▼●

Lost in Alaska (1952) **76m.** *½ D: Jean Yarbrough. Bud Abbott, Lou Costello, Mitzi Green, Tom Ewell, Bruce Cabot. Unremarkable slapstick set in 1890s, with A&C off to the wilds to help a friend but doing more hindering.▼

Lost in America (1985) **C-91m.** *** D: Albert Brooks. Albert Brooks, Julie Hagerty, Garry Marshall, Art Frankel, Michael Greene. Two yuppies drop out of the rat race and take to the road ("just like EASY RIDER") in this low-key, often hilarious satire of upwardly mobile types. Written by Brooks and Monica Johnson. And isn't that Albert's voice on the phone as the Mercedes salesman? [R]▼●

Lost in Space (1998) **C-122m.** ** D: Stephen Hopkins. Gary Oldman, William Hurt, Matt LeBlanc, Mimi Rogers, Heather Graham, Lacey Chabert, Jack Johnson, Jared Harris, Edward Fox; voice of Dick Tufeld. In 2058, with the hope of opening a gateway to a new planet for denizens of the overcrowded Earth, a family is launched into space, accompanied by a he-man pilot and the weasely doctor who tried to sabotage the journey. The 1960s TV series is recreated on a lavish scale, but hurt by crudely episodic story, grim tone, and paper-thin characters. Oldman, curiously, *underplays* the role of Dr. Smith, the inept saboteur. Angela Cartwright, Mark Goddard, Marta Kristen, and June Lockhart, stars of the original TV series, have cameo roles. Panavision. [PG-13]▼●◗

Lost in the Stars (1974) **C-114m.** *** D: Daniel Mann. Brock Peters, Melba Moore, Raymond St. Jacques, Clifton Davis, Paula Kelly. Good American Film Theatre version of the Kurt Weill-Maxwell Anderson musical, based on Alan Paton's CRY, THE BELOVED COUNTRY (filmed on its own in 1951). Owes much of its power to Peters' portrayal of the South African minister. Filmed in Jamaica, B.W.I., and Hollywood. [G]▼

Lost in Yonkers (1993) **C-112m.** **½ D: Martha Coolidge. Richard Dreyfuss, Mercedes Ruehl, Irene Worth, David Strathairn, Brad Stoll, Mike Damus, Robert Guy Miranda, Jack Laufer, Susan Merson. Struggling widower leaves his two sons with his steely German mother, and his sweet but simple-minded grown-up sister, while he goes off to make a living during WW2. Faithful adaptation of Neil Simon's Pulitzer Prize–winning comedy-drama. Simon's script, and Coolidge's direction, try to make you forget it's a photographed play, and they almost succeed. Worth seeing if only to watch Ruehl and Worth repeat their moving, Tony Award-winning stage performances. [PG]▼●

Lost Man, The (1969) **C-122m.** **½ D: Robert Alan Aurthur. Sidney Poitier, Joanna Shimkus, Al Freeman, Jr., Michael Tolan, Leon Bibb, Richard Dysart, David Steinberg, Paul Winfield. Uncomfortable updating of ODD MAN OUT from an Irish setting to present-day black underground has some tension, but doesn't really work. Three stars are good. Panavision. [M/PG]▼

Lost Missile, The (1958) **70m.** ** D: Lester Berke. Robert Loggia, Ellen Parker, Larry Kerr, Philip Pine. Super-hot alien missile circles Earth, setting fires and melting cities. Loggia races against time to destroy it before it reaches N.Y.C. Too cheap for its ideas, but Loggia is good. Ending is surprisingly downbeat.

Lost Moment, The (1947) **88m.** *** D: Martin Gabel. Robert Cummings, Susan Hayward, Agnes Moorehead, Joan Lorring, Eduardo Ciannelli. Henry James' *Aspern Papers* becomes offbeat drama. Publisher Cummings in Italy seeking lost love letters of famous writer, comes across neurotic Hayward who claims to have access to them.▼●

Lost One, The (1951-German) **97m.** ** D: Peter Lorre. Peter Lorre, Karl John, Renate Mannhardt, Johanna Hofer. Lorre's only film as director is a talky, grim, but not uninteresting drama about the downfall of a German researcher (played by Peter himself, with appropriate weariness), whose girlfriend is thought to have been passing on his discoveries to the British during WW2. Of interest mostly as a footnote to Lorre's career; based on a true story.▼

Lost Patrol, The (1934) **73m.** **** D: John Ford. Victor McLaglen, Boris Karloff, Wallace Ford, Reginald Denny, Alan Hale, J. M. Kerrigan, Billy Bevan. McLaglen's small British military group lost in Mesopotamian desert, as Arabs repeatedly attack the dwindling unit. Classic actioner filled with slice-of-life stereotypes, headed by religious fanatic Karloff. Fast-moving fun, great Max Steiner score. Scripted by Dudley Nichols, from Philip MacDonald's novel *Patrol.* Previously filmed in 1929, as a British silent starring Victor McLaglen's brother, Cyril, in the lead role; reworked many times (BAD LANDS, SAHARA, BATAAN, etc.). ▼●

Lost Squadron, The (1932) **79m.** **½ D: George Archainbaud. Richard Dix, Mary Astor, Erich von Stroheim, Joel McCrea, Dorothy Jordan, Robert Armstrong. WW1 pilots forced to find work as stunt fliers for movies; interesting idea boosted by von Stroheim's overacting as director "Arthur von Furst."▼●

Lost Tribe, The (1949) **72m.** ** D: William Berke. Johnny Weissmuller, Myrna Dell, Elena Verdugo, Joseph Vitale, Ralph Dunn, George J. Lewis. Action-packed *Jungle Jim* romp, with Weissmuller fighting lions, tigers and sharks to help save an African city from plunderers.

Lost Volcano, The (1950) **67m.** *½ D: Ford Beebe. Johnny Sheffield, Donald Woods, Marjorie Lord, John Ridgely, Robert Lewis, Elena Verdugo, Tommy Ivo. Bomba the Jungle Boy (Sheffield) fights greedy African guides who are after buried treasure. ▼

Lost Weekend, The (1945) **101m.** **** D: Billy Wilder. Ray Milland, Jane Wyman, Philip Terry, Howard da Silva, Doris Dowling, Frank Faylen, Mary Young. Unrelenting drama of alcoholism—and a landmark of adult filmmaking in Hollywood. Milland's powerful performance won him an Oscar; there's fine support from bartender da Silva, sanitarium aide Faylen. Won Academy Awards for Best Picture, Director, Actor, Screenplay (Wilder and Charles Brackett). ▼●

Lost World, The (1925) **65m.** **½ D: Harry Hoyt. Bessie Love, Wallace Beery, Lewis Stone, Lloyd Hughes. Silent film version of A. Conan Doyle adventure yarn is remarkable for special effects recreating prehistoric beasts encountered on scientific expedition to remote plateau. Interesting as precursor to KING KONG—in story structure and in Willis O'Brien's special effects. Originally 108m.; remade twice.▼●◗

Lost World, The (1960) **C-98m.** ** D: Irwin Allen. Michael Rennie, Jill St. John, David Hedison, Claude Rains, Fernando Lamas, Richard Haydn. Despite cinematic advances, this remake of the 1925 film doesn't match original's special effects. OK juvenile entry of an expedition into remote territory hopefully inhabited by prehistoric monsters. CinemaScope.▼

Lost World, The (1993-Canadian) **C-99m.** *½ D: Timothy Bond. John Rhys-Davies, David Warner, Eric McCormack, Nathania Stanford, Darren Peter Mercer, Tamara Gorski, Innocent Chosa, Kate Egan. In 1912, an expedition journeys to an African plateau where dinosaurs still live. Rhys-Davies as

Professor Challenger and Warner as his rival are good, but others in the too-large cast are amateurish, and the dinosaurs are not only badly done, but extremely scarce. A cheap, insignificant version of Conan Doyle's wonderful novel, which still deserves a lavish remake. Sequel, RETURN TO THE LOST WORLD (1994), was shot simultaneously. ▼

Lost World: Jurassic Park, The (1997) **C-134m.** **½ D: Steven Spielberg. Jeff Goldblum, Julianne Moore, Pete Postlethwaite, Arliss Howard, Richard Attenborough, Vince Vaughn, Vanessa Lee Chester, Peter Stormare, Harvey Jason, Richard Schiff, Thomas F. Duffy, Joseph Mazzello, Ariana Richards. It turns out that madman Attenborough left a menagerie of dinosaurs behind on a *second* island—and wants to sponsor an expedition there. Goldblum knows the dangers, but his girlfriend is already there and he's forced to follow, along with assorted others. Havoc ensues. Completely contrived sequel to JURASSIC PARK benefits from Goldblum's deprecating dialogue and superior special effects. Enough cliffhanger-style action scenes to make up for the lulls. [PG-13] ▼●

Lottery Bride, The (1930) **80m.** **½ D: Paul Stein. Jeanette MacDonald, John Garrick, Joe E. Brown, ZaSu Pitts, Robert Chisholm. Delightfully creaky musical with Norwegian setting; Jeanette must deny her true love when she becomes lottery bride for his older brother. Impressive sets, forgettable music, enjoyable comic relief from Brown and Pitts. ▼

Lotus Eaters, The (1993-Canadian) **C-101m.** *** D: Paul Shapiro. Sheila McCarthy, R. H. Thomson, Michele-Barbara Pelletier, Aloka McLean, Tara Frederick, Frances Hyland, Andrea Libman, Gabe Khouth, Paul Soles. Amiably amusing 1960s nostalgia set on an island in Western Canada, where a change of wind (signified by the arrival of a new schoolteacher) blows a gust of drama into the lives of a mildly eccentric school principal, his wife, and their two impressionable daughters. Winner of three Genie Awards including Best Actress for McCarthy and Best Screenplay (Peggy Thomson). [PG-13] ▼

Louisa (1950) **90m.** *** D: Alexander Hall. Ronald Reagan, Charles Coburn, Ruth Hussey, Edmund Gwenn, Spring Byington, Piper Laurie, Scotty Beckett, Martin Milner. Delightful romantic yarn of Byington seeking to become a December bride, undecided between Coburn and Gwenn; most disarming. Film debut of Piper Laurie.

Louisa May Alcott's Little Men SEE: **Little Men** (1998)

Louisiana Hayride (1944) **67m.** ** D: Charles Barton. Judy Canova, Ross Hunter, Minerva Urecal, Lloyd Bridges, Russell Hicks. Hillbilly Canova goes Hollywood in this typical cornball vehicle.

Louisiana Purchase (1941) **C-98m.** **½ D: Irving Cummings. Bob Hope, Vera Zorina, Victor Moore, Irene Bordoni, Dona Drake. Brassy Irving Berlin musicomedy, with Hope's comedy very funny, especially famous filibuster scene in Congress. Zorina, Moore and Bordoni re-create their Broadway roles. Opening scene of chorus girls (including Barbara Britton, Margaret Hayes and Jean Wallace) singing lines about characters being fictitious is probably a movie first . . . and last. Best tune: "It's a Lovely Day Tomorrow." ▼

Louisiana Story (1948) **77m.** **** D: Robert Flaherty. Classic, influential documentary set in the Louisiana bayous, with a young boy observing oil drillers at work. Beautifully made; produced by the Stanydard Oil Company. Music by Virgil Thomson. ▼

Louis L'Amour's The Shadow Riders SEE: **Shadow Riders, The**

Loulou (1980-French) **C-110m.** ***½ D: Maurice Pialat. Isabelle Huppert, Gérard Depardieu, Guy Marchand, Humbert Balsan, Bernard Tronczyk. Huppert leaves stable hubby for topsy-turvy life with loutish Depardieu. Two leads have terrific sexual rapport in dynamic star vehicle. ▼

Lovable Cheat, The (1949) **75m.** ** D: Richard Oswald. Charlie Ruggles, Peggy Ann Garner, Richard Ney, Alan Mowbray, Fritz Feld, Ludwig Donath, Buster Keaton, Curt Bois. Interesting more for cast and credits than actual achievement, this rather odd independent production (based on a Balzac play) centers on the comic antics of Ruggles battling against his creditors. ▼

Love (1927) **82m.** **½ D: Edmund Goulding. Greta Garbo, John Gilbert, George Fawcett, Emily Fitzroy, Brandon Hurst, Philippe De Lacy. Silent version of *Anna Karenina* in modern setting, as married Garbo falls in love with dashing military guard Gilbert, an affair doomed from start. Lesser entry for famed screen lovers, with Gilbert's eyebrow-raising gestures at their worst. Garbo's 1935 remake (ANNA KARENINA) is much better. MGM actually filmed two endings—one happy, one sad. ▼●

Love Affair (1932) **68m.** ** D: Thornton Freeland. Dorothy Mackaill, Humphrey Bogart, Jack Kennedy, Barbara Leonard, Astrid Allwyn. Romance between a spoiled heiress and a dedicated aircraft engineer; pretty tired stuff, even with the curiosity value of a clean-cut Bogart as leading man.

Love Affair (1939) **87m.** ***½ D: Leo McCarey. Irene Dunne, Charles Boyer, Maria Ouspenskaya, Lee Bowman, Astrid Allwyn, Maurice Moscovich, Joan Brodel (Leslie). Superior comedy-drama about shipboard romance whose continuation onshore is interrupted by unforseen circumstances. Dunne and Boyer are a marvelous match. Screenplay by Delmer Daves and Donald Ogden Stewart, from story by Mildred Cram and Leo McCarey. Remade by

McCarey as AN AFFAIR TO REMEMBER, and a second time (by Warren Beatty). Beware public-domain videocassette version, which has planted an entirely new music score on the soundtrack!▼◗

Love Affair (1994) **C-108m.** **½ D: Glenn Gordon Caron. Warren Beatty, Annette Bening, Katharine Hepburn, Garry Shandling, Chloe Webb, Pierce Brosnan, Kate Capshaw, Paul Mazursky, Brenda Vaccaro, Glenn Shadix, Barry Miller, Harold Ramis, Elya Baskin, Taylor Dayne, Carey Lowell, Dan Castellaneta, Rosalind Chao, Wendie Jo Sperber, Frank Campanella, Ray Charles. Soulless remake of the 1939 weepie (itself remade as AN AFFAIR TO REMEMBER), with Beatty as an ex-jock-turned-sportscaster and ladies man who chances to meet Bening on an eventful plane ride. Frustrating film runs hot and cold; high point is the sequence with Hepburn as Beatty's feisty aunt. Intrusive songs on the soundtrack are a debit, Conrad Hall's silky cinematography is a plus, but the biggest letdown is the ending, which stops short of a big, old-fashioned sentimental Hollywood finish—just what the movie really needs. Beatty produced and co-wrote with Robert Towne. [PG-13] ▼●

Love Among the Ruins (1975) **C-102m. TVM** D: George Cukor. Katharine Hepburn, Laurence Olivier, Colin Blakely, Joan Sims, Richard Pearson, Leigh Lawson. Grand romantic comedy teaming two acting legends for the first time. Aging actress being sued by a young gigolo for breach of promise is defended by a prominent barrister who had been her long-ago lover. Rich and lustrous with Emmy Awards for its two stars, to director Cukor (his TV movie debut) and to writer James Costigan. Bouquets all around. Above average.▼●

Love Among Thieves (1987) **C-100m. TVM** D: Roger Young. Audrey Hepburn, Robert Wagner, Jerry Orbach, Samantha Eggar, Patrick Bauchau. Romantic thriller uniting an elegant lady (Hepburn, of course, in her only TV movie) with a raffish, cigar-chomping stranger, roughing it in the wilds of Mexico after she has pulled a daring jewel heist to bargain for her abducted fiancé's life. Regrettably it's no CHARADE for Audrey. Average.

Love and a .45 (1994) **C-101m.** **½ D: C. M. Talkington. Gil Bellows, Renee Zellweger, Rory Cochrane, Jeffrey Combs, Jace Alexander, Michael Bowen, Ann Wedgeworth, Peter Fonda. Derivative (although not uninteresting) young-lovers-on-the-lam melodrama, about a white-trash couple who become criminals and outlaws. Features the same over-the-top comic-book violence that made RESERVOIR DOGS an instant cult favorite. [R]▼◗

Love and Anarchy (1973-Italian) **C-108m.** *** D: Lina Wertmuller. Giancarlo Giannini, Mariangela Melato, Lina Polito, Eros Pagni, Pina Cel, Elena Fiore. Italian bumpkin Giannini tries to assassinate Mussolini in 1932, falls for a prostitute in the brothel serving as his base of operation. Uneven but stylish drama helped establish Wertmuller's reputation in the U.S. [R]▼◗

Love and Basketball (2000) **C-124m.** *** D: Gina Prince-Bythewood. Sanaa Lathan, Omar Epps, Alfre Woodard, Dennis Haysbert, Debbi Morgan, Harry J. Lennix, Kyla Pratt, Glenndon Chatman. A most agreeable hybrid of love story and coming-of-age saga. Lathan plays a precocious, talented basketball player, Epps the cocky son of an NBA professional; their relationship goes through many phases from the time they're 11 years old to young adulthood, as the story breaks down into four "quarters." A crowd-pleaser from start to finish, if a little long; only the final resolution seems contrived. Feature debut for writer-director Prince-Bythewood. [R]▼◗

Love and Bullets (1979-British) **C-103m.** ** D: Stuart Rosenberg. Charles Bronson, Rod Steiger, Jill Ireland, Strother Martin, Bradford Dillman, Henry Silva, Michael V. Gazzo. Bronson is supposed to nab gangster's moll Ireland for the FBI, but falls in love with her during his pursuit in Switzerland. Routine action yarn . . . for Bronson fans only. Panavision. [PG]▼

Love and Death (1975) **C-82m.** *** D: Woody Allen. Woody Allen, Diane Keaton, Harold Gould, Alfred Lutter, Olga Georges-Picot, Zvee Scooler. One of Woody's most pretentious films won applause for its spoofs of Russian literature and foreign films, but this tale of a devout coward in the Napoleonic wars is more like a remake of Bob Hope's MONSIEUR BEAUCAIRE. Funny but uneven, with music by Prokofiev. [PG]▼●

Love and Death on Long Island (1997-Canadian-British) **C-93m.** ***½ D: Richard Kwietniowski. John Hurt, Jason Priestley, Fiona Loewi, Sheila Hancock, Maury Chaykin, Gawn Granger, Elizabeth Quinn. Quiet gem about an eccentric, reclusive British writer who stumbles into the wrong movie theater and, while watching HOT PANTS COLLEGE II, becomes intrigued, and then obsessed, with one of its cast members (Priestley). Before long, he flies to Long Island, N.Y., in the hope of somehow consummating his fantasy relationship with the actor. A marvel of nuance and quiet observation, with Hurt simply perfect in the lead; impressive feature directing debut for Kwietniowski, who also scripted (from Gilbert Adair's novel). [PG-13]▼◗

Love and Fear (1988-Italian-German-French) **C-114m.** *** D: Margarethe von Trotta. Fanny Ardant, Greta Scacchi, Valeria Golino, Peter Simonischek, Sergio Castellito, Agnes Sorel, Paolo Hendel. Involving if occasionally melodramatic account of the lives and loves of a trio of sisters: the oldest (Ardant) is an intellectual and all too aware of passing time and advancing age; the middle one (Scacchi) has no professional identity and lives by her emotions; the youngest (Golino) is a passionate, idealistic premed student. Crammed with ideas and observations about how life is in constant flux; loosely based on Chekhov's *Three Sisters.*

Love and Human Remains (1993-Canadian) **C-100m.** *** D: Denys Arcand. Thomas Gibson, Ruth Marshall, Cameron Bancroft, Mia Kirshner, Joanne Vannicola, Matthew Ferguson, Rick Roberts. Arcand's first English-language film is a provocative portrait of confused, restless urban singles, focusing on a pair of ex-lovers who are still roommates: Gibson, a gay, 30-ish former teen TV star who now works as a waiter, and Marshall, who's straight and desperate for tenderness. Meanwhile, there's a maniac on the loose murdering unsuspecting women! An astute look at what it means to fall in love in the era of AIDS, ambiguous sexuality, and pervasive violence. Scripted by Brad Fraser, based on his play. ▼●

Love and Kisses (1965) **C-87m.** **½ D: Ozzie Nelson. Rick Nelson, Kristin Nelson, Jack Kelly, Jerry Van Dyke, Pert Kelton, Madelyn Hines. Harmless fare. Rick gets married, disrupting his family's life.

Love and Larceny (1963-Italian) **94m.** **½ D: Dino Risi. Vittorio Gassman, Anna Maria Ferrero, Dorian Gray, Peppino De Filippo. Saucy comedy of exuberant conman Gassman making no pretense about his carefree life and pleasures. Totalscope.▼

Love and Learn (1947) **83m.** ** D: Frederick de Cordova. Jack Carson, Robert Hutton, Martha Vickers, Janis Paige, Otto Kruger. Overdone idea of songwriters Carson and Hutton waiting for their big break; young girl comes to their aid, but she doesn't save film.

Love and Marriage (1964-Italian) **106m.** **½ D: Gianni Puccini, Mino Guerrini. Sylva Koscina, Philippe Leroy, Amadeo Girard, April Hennessy. Funny film in four segments relating to male-female relationships of an amorous variety.

Love and Money (1982) **C-90m.** ** D: James Toback. Ray Sharkey, Ornella Muti, Klaus Kinski, Armand Assante, King Vidor, Susan Heldfond, William Prince. Convoluted drama about Sharkey's entanglement in international scheme plotted by billionaire businessman Kinski; has its bright spots, but disappoints nonetheless because director Toback distances himself from his material. Sex scenes with Sharkey and Muti were toned down before film's release. Of interest mainly for presence of legendary director Vidor as Sharkey's senile grandfather. Completed in 1980. [R]

Love and Other Catastrophes (1996-Australian) **C-76m.** **½ D: Emma-Kate Croghan. Frances O'Connor, Alice Garner, Radha Mitchell, Matt Day, Matthew Dyktynski. Agreeable comedy about the various crises, crushes and romances among a group of twentysomething Melbourne University students who are male and female, straight and gay. An amusing look at a point in young adulthood in which switching one's major is a pivotal life decision; also refreshing in its depiction of the easy mixing and socializing between characters with different sexual preferences. A promising debut for 23-year-old director/coscripter Croghan. [R] ▼

Love and Pain (and the Whole Damn Thing) (1972) **C-110m.** *** D: Alan J. Pakula. Maggie Smith, Timothy Bottoms. Charming story of two introverts who miraculously and humorously find each other, fall in love while touring Spain; written by Alvin Sargent. [PG]

Love and the Frenchwoman (1961-French) **143m.** *** D: Jean Delannoy, Michel Boisrond, René Clair, Christian-Jaque, Jean-Paul Lechanois. Martine Lambert, Claude Rich, Dany Robin, Jean-Paul Belmondo, Annie Girardot, Martine Carol. Savory account of the seven ages of love in a woman's life, sensitively acted.▼

Love and the Midnight Auto Supply (1978) **C-93m.** *½ D: James Polakof. Michael Parks, Linda Cristal, Scott Jacoby, Colleen Camp, John Ireland, Rory Calhoun, Rod Cameron. Yahoo action-comedy has ringleader of stolen auto-parts gang turning Robin Hood to help farm workers combat corrupt politicians. Retitled MIDNIGHT AUTO SUPPLY. [PG]

Love at First Bite (1979) **C-96m.** *** D: Stan Dragoti. George Hamilton, Susan St. James, Richard Benjamin, Dick Shawn, Arte Johnson, Sherman Hemsley, Isabel Sanford, Barry Gordon, Ronnie Schell, Eric Laneuville. Silly but likable comedy about Count Dracula's adventures in New York City, and love affair with fashion model St. James. Hamilton's comic performance is bloody good. Written by Robert Kaufman. [PG]▼●

Love at First Sight (1974-Canadian) **C-85m.** BOMB D: Rex Bromfield. Mary Ann McDonald, Dan Aykroyd, Jane Mallett, George Murray, Barry Morse, Mignon Elkins, Les Carlson. Excruciatingly dumb comedy with Aykroyd (pre-*Saturday Night Live*, and in his first starring role) cast as a young man who's blind, and in love with McDonald. Very predictable, and very unfunny. Aka LOVE IS BLIND and AT FIRST SIGHT.▼

Love at Large (1990) **C-97m.** ** D: Alan Rudolph. Tom Berenger, Anne Archer, Elizabeth Perkins, Kate Capshaw, Annette O'Toole, Ted Levine, Ann Magnuson, Kevin J. O'Connor, Ruby Dee, Barry Miller, Neil Young. A challenge to Rudolph cultists everywhere, this coy mess involves rival private detectives (male and female) who keep tripping over each other while following a case that's already plagued by problems of mistaken identity. Made watchable by the director's typically beguiling use of color and decor, plus his penchant for offbeat casting. Rocker Neil Young has a straight part (uh . . . so to speak). [R]▼●

Love at Stake (1987) **C-83m.** **½ D: John Moffitt. Patrick Cassidy, Kelly Preston, Bud Cort, Barbara Carrera, Stuart Pankin, Dave Thomas, Georgia Brown, Annie Golden. Wacky, overlooked comedy spoofs the Salem witch trials in the irreverent Mel Brooks tradition (producer Michael Gruskoff coproduced several Brooks pictures). Ingenues Cassidy and Preston (who plays baker Sarah Lee) are appealing, but the show is stolen by Carrera as a very sexy witch and Pankin and Thomas as corrupt officials. Dr. Joyce Brothers cameos as a defense witness at the witch trial and is branded a heretic! [R]▼●

Love at the Top (1974-French) **C-105m.** ** D: Michel Deville. Jean-Louis Trintignant, Jean-Pierre Cassel, Romy Schneider, Jane Birkin, Florinda Bolkan, Georges Wilson. Slick but superficial, muddled account of club-footed writer Cassel advising Trintignant on how to become rich and sleep with lots of women. Birkin, Bolkan, and Schneider are attractive, but it's all window dressing. Aka THE FRENCH WAY IS. [R]

Love at Twenty (1962-International) **113m.** **½ D: François Truffaut, Renzo Rossellini, Shintaro Ishihara, Marcel Ophuls, Andrzej Wajda. Jean-Pierre Léaud, Eleonora Rossi-Drago, Zbigniew Cybulski, Nami Tamura, Marie-France Pisier, Barbara Lass. Quintet of middling stories produced in France, Germany, Italy, Japan, Poland; variations on theme of love among younger generation. Truffaut's ANTOINE ET COLETTE is a sequel to THE 400 BLOWS (the first of his Antoine Doinel films). Original French running time: 123m. Totalscope.

Love Before Breakfast (1936) **70m.** **½ D: Walter Lang. Carole Lombard, Preston Foster, Cesar Romero, Janet Beecher, Betty Lawford, Douglas Blackley (Robert Kent). Fast-starting comedy slows down to obvious ending, but Lombard (as object of Foster's and Romero's attention) is always worth watching. Preston Sturges worked uncredited on the script.

Love Bug, The (1969) **C-107m.** ***½ D: Robert Stevenson. Dean Jones, Michele Lee, Buddy Hackett, David Tomlinson, Joe Flynn, Benson Fong, Iris Adrian. Delightful Disney comedy about a Volkswagen with a mind of its own; subtle it ain't, but the slapstick and stunts are great fun to watch. Followed by three HERBIE sequels and a 1997 made-for-TV movie. ▼●

Love Cage, The SEE: **Joy House**

Love Child (1982) **C-96m.** ** D: Larry Peerce. Amy Madigan, Beau Bridges, Mackenzie Phillips, Albert Salmi, Joanna Merlin, Rhea Perlman. Trifling melodrama of prisoner Madigan who has baby by Bridges and fights for the right to motherhood. Plays like an R-rated made-for-TV movie; based on a true story. [R]▼

Love Crazy (1941) **99m.** **½ D: Jack Conway. William Powell, Myrna Loy, Gail Patrick, Jack Carson, Florence Bates, Sidney Blackmer, Sig Ruman. One misunderstanding leads to another in this energetic marital farce that loses steam halfway through. Highlighted by Powell's attempts to prove himself insane, and Carson's hilarious characterization as Ward Willoughby.▼

Love Crimes (1992) **C-85m.** BOMB D: Lizzie Borden. Sean Young, Patrick Bergin, Arnetia Walker, James Read, Ron Orbach, Wayne Shorter. Astonishingly inept, confusing thriller with Young (in a lifeless performance) playing an assistant district attorney who becomes involved with Bergin who, posing as a fashion photographer, exploits and rips off unsuspecting women. The director's cut (which is unrated and runs 97m.) is far more coherent, particularly with regard to the motivations of Young's character and the gradations of her relationship with Bergin. However, the scenario remains obvious and superficial. That version is rated **. Both are available on video. [R]▼

Loved One, The (1965) **116m.** ***½ D: Tony Richardson. Robert Morse, Jonathan Winters, Anjanette Comer, Rod Steiger, Dana Andrews, Milton Berle, James Coburn, John Gielgud, Tab Hunter, Margaret Leighton, Liberace, Roddy McDowall, Robert Morley, Lionel Stander, Ayllene Gibbons, Bernie Kopell, Alan Napier, Jamie Farr. Correctly advertised as the picture with something to offend everyone. Britisher Morse attends to uncle's burial in California, encountering bizarre aspects of funeral business. Often howlingly funny, and equally gross. Once seen, Mrs. Joyboy can never be forgotten. Based on the Evelyn Waugh novel, adapted by Terry Southern and Christopher Isherwood.▼●

Love Field (1992) **C-104m.** **½ D: Jonathan Kaplan. Michelle Pfeiffer, Dennis Haysbert, Stephanie McFadden, Brian Kerwin, Louise Latham, Peggy Rea, Beth Grant, Johnny Ray McGhee, Cooper Huckabee, Mark Miller. Small, sensitive film of Dallas beautician (a platinum-blond Pfeiffer) who is enthralled by President and Mrs. Kennedy—and is like an excited schoolgirl at the thought of their fateful 1963 visit to her hometown. (Love Field is the name of Dallas's airport.) Really a road movie, with Pfeiffer deserting her husband and traveling halfway across the country with the unlikely duo of black father and daughter (Haysbert and McFadden). Rich performances (especially Pfeiffer's), rural flavor, and an unflinching look at race relations almost compensate for the sometimes overly contrived plot. [PG-13]▼●

Love Finds Andy Hardy (1938) **90m.** *** D: George B. Seitz. Lewis Stone, Mickey Rooney, Judy Garland, Cecilia Parker, Fay Holden, Ann Rutherford, Betsy Ross Clark, Lana Turner, Gene Reynolds. One of the best of the series finds young Andrew frantically trying to juggle two girlfriends at the same time. Classy support by ingenues Garland and Turner. Judy sings three songs, including "Meet the Beat of My Heart."▼●

Love From a Stranger (1937-British) **90m.** ** D: Rowland V. Lee. Ann Harding, Basil Rathbone, Binnie Hale, Bruce Seton, Bryan Powley, Jean Cadell. Working girl Harding wins fortune in a lottery, is swept off her feet by suave Rathbone, but after their marriage she begins to suspect he's not quite what he seemed. Stagy but interesting thriller features Rathbone's most unbridled performance, quite a sight to see. From Frank Vosper's play of a story by Agatha Christie. Joan Hickson, later TV's shrewd Miss Marple, plays a scatterbrained maid. Remade in 1947.▼

Love From a Stranger (1947) **81m.** **½ D: Richard Whorf. Sylvia Sidney, John Hodiak, John Howard, Isobel Elsom, Ernest Cossart. Capable cast goes through familiar paces in SUSPICION-like story of woman who learns her new husband may be a murderer. Filmed before in 1937; from an Agatha Christie story.▼

Love God?, The (1969) **C-101m.** ** D: Nat Hiken. Don Knotts, Anne Francis, Edmond O'Brien, James Gregory, Maureen Arthur, Maggie Peterson, Jesslyn Fax. Comedy for those who are amused by Knotts playing Hugh Hefner type; film is final work of Nat Hiken, who created Sergeant Bilko in better days. Techniscope. [M]▼

Love Goddesses, The (1965) **87m.** *** Compiled by Saul J. Turell and Graeme Ferguson. Marilyn Monroe, Mae West, Jean Harlow, Theda Bara, Rita Hayworth, Claudette Colbert, Dorothy Lamour, many others. Compilation covers a lot of ground, featuring many major female stars from silent days to the present. Not always the ideal clips, but well done, with many welcome classic scenes. Some color sequences. Revised for 1972 theatrical reissue.▼●▶

Love Happy (1949) **91m.** **½ D: David Miller. Harpo, Chico, and Groucho Marx, Ilona Massey, Vera-Ellen, Marion Hutton, Raymond Burr, Eric Blore. No NIGHT AT THE OPERA, but even diluted Marx Brothers are better than none. Putting on a musical forms background for Harpo's antics, with Chico in support, Groucho in a few unrelated scenes. Marilyn Monroe has a brief bit. Among the writers were Ben Hecht and Frank Tashlin. ▼●

Love Has Many Faces (1965) **C-105m.** **½ D: Alexander Singer. Lana Turner, Cliff Robertson, Hugh O'Brian, Ruth Roman, Stefanie Powers, Virginia Grey. Timid attempt at lurid soaper; playgirl Turner's costume changes are the highlights. O'Brian and Robertson are gigolos. Filmed in Acapulco.▼

Love Hurts (1990) **C-106m.** ** D: Bud Yorkin. Jeff Daniels, Judith Ivey, Cynthia Sikes, John Mahoney, Cloris Leachman, Amy Wright, Mary Griffin, Brady Quaid. Unhappily divorced Daniels goes home for his sister's wedding, only to find his exwife and their kids staying with his folks. Bittersweet comedy-drama has some good moments, but not enough. Mahoney and Leachman's performances as Daniels' parents border uncomfortably on caricature. [R]▼

Love in a Goldfish Bowl (1961) **C-88m.** BOMB D: Jack Sher. Tommy Sands, Fabian, Jan Sterling, Edward Andrews. Film is as bad as its title, a worthless, boring trifle about teenagers taking over a beach house. Forget it. Panavision.

Love in a Taxi (1980) **C-90m.** ***½ D: Robert Sickinger. Diane Sommerfield, James H. Jacobs, Earl Monroe, Malik Murray, Lisa Jane Persky. Wonderful little film about love blooming between Jewish cabbie Jacobs and black clerk Sommerfield. Made with care and affection, an audience-pleaser, with nice performances all around.

Love in Bloom (1935) **75m.** ** D: Elliott Nugent. George Burns, Gracie Allen, Joe Morrison, Dixie Lee, J. C. Nugent, Lee Kohlmar. Burns and Allen are forced to take back seat to sappy romantic story about struggling songwriter and his girlfriend; George and Gracie give this minor film its only value.▼

Love in Germany, A (1984-German) **C-110m.** **½ D: Andrzej Wajda. Hanna Schygulla, Marie-Christine Barrault, Armin Mueller-Stahl, Elisabeth Trissenaar, Daniel Olbrychski, Piotr Lysak, Bernhard Wicki. German shopkeeper, her husband off fighting at the front, risks life and reputation by romancing a much younger Polish POW. Wimpy Lysak doesn't look as if he could drive a girl's hopscotch team into sexual delirium, creating severe credibility problems in this subpar Wajda effort. Barrault is effectively cast against type as conniving Nazi sympathizer. [R]▼

Love-Ins, The (1967) **C-92m.** BOMB D: Arthur Dreifuss. James MacArthur, Susan Oliver, Richard Todd, Mark Goddard, Carol Booth. Professor Timothy Leary—er, Richard Todd—advocates LSD, becomes a hippie messiah. A bad trip.

Love in the Afternoon (1957) **130m.** ***½ D: Billy Wilder. Gary Cooper, Audrey Hepburn, Maurice Chevalier, John McGiver. Forget age difference between Cooper and Hepburn and enjoy sparkling romantic comedy, with Chevalier as Audrey's private-eye dad. McGiver lends good support in witty comedy set in Paris. Wilder's first film cowritten with I.A.L. Diamond, and a tribute to his idol, Ernst Lubitsch.▼●

Love in the City (1953-Italian) **90m.** ** D: Michelangelo Antonioni, Federico Fellini, Dino Risi, Carlo Lizzani, Alberto Lattuada, Francesco Maselli, Cesare Zavattini. Ugo Tognazzi, Maresa Gallo, Caterina Rigoglioso, Silvio Lillo, Angela Pierro. The title tells all in this episodic, six-part neorealist chronicle—filmed cinema verité style—of various aspects of romance in Rome. This was supposed to be the first edition of a film journal, known as "The Spectator." Originally 110m.; the Lizzani-directed sequence, about prostitution, was deleted from foreign-release prints.▼

Love Is a Ball (1963) **C-111m.** **½ D: David Swift. Glenn Ford, Hope Lange, Charles Boyer, Ricardo Montalban, Telly Savalas. Forced froth trying hard to be chic; gold-digging and romance on the Riviera. Panavision.

Love Is a Dog From Hell (1987-Belgian) **C-90m.** *** D: Dominique Deruddere. Josse De Pauw, Geert Hunaerts, Florence Beliard, Anne Van Essche, Amid Chakir, Michael Pas, Carmela Locantorc. Weird yet fascinating, well-acted three-part fantasy chronicling one person's descent from 12-year-old innocent to grungy barfly—and necrophiliac. Originally 30m. long, then expanded to feature length. Script by Marc Didden and Deruddere, loosely based on Charles Bukowski's *The Copulating Mermaid of Venice, Calif.*

Love Is All There Is (1996) **C-90m.** *½ D: Renee Taylor, Joseph Bologna. Renee Taylor, Joseph Bologna, Lainie Kazan, Paul Sorvino, Barbara Carrera, Angelina Jolie, Nathaniel Marston, William Hickey, Abe Vigoda, Connie Stevens, Dick Van Patten. Taylor and Bologna scripted this loud, sentimental, silly romantic comedy of two rival Italian catering families whose children fall in love. This modern-day *Romeo and Juliet* makeover is set in City Island, The Bronx, where the scenery upstages the largely wasted cast. Filmed in 1994. [R]▼●

Love Is a Many Splendored Thing (1955) **C-102m.** *** D: Henry King. William Holden, Jennifer Jones, Murray Matheson, Torin Thatcher, Jorja Curtright, Virginia Gregg, Isobel Elsom, Richard Loo, Soo Yong, Philip Ahn, James Hong, Keye Luke. Well-mounted soaper set in Hong Kong at time of Korean War. Eurasian doctor Jones falls in love with war correspondent Holden. Effective telling of true story, beautifully executed, with Oscar-winning costumes (Charles LeMaire), scoring (Alfred Newman) and title song (Sammy Fain and Paul Francis Webster). CinemaScope.▼●◗

Love Is a Racket (1932) **72m.** ** D: William Wellman. Douglas Fairbanks, Jr., Ann Dvorak, Frances Dee, Lee Tracy, Lyle Talbot, Andre Luguet, Warren Hymer. Attractive cast in curiously unappealing story of a Broadway columnist and his private intrigues. Tracy, who portrayed Winchell types so often, here plays the columnist's legman.

Love Is Better Than Ever (1952) **81m.** **½ D: Stanley Donen. Elizabeth Taylor, Larry Parks, Josephine Hutchinson, Tom Tully, Ann Doran, Elinor Donahue, Kathleen Freeman. Forgettable froth involving talent agent Parks and dance teacher Taylor. Mild MGM musical, but Liz looks terrific. Gene Kelly has an unbilled cameo.▼

Love Is Blind SEE: **Love at First Sight**

Love Is Forever (1983) **C-150m. TVM** D: Hall Bartlett. Michael Landon, Priscilla Presley, Moira Chen, Jurgen Prochnow, Edward Woodward. Controversial dramatization of journalist John Everingham's heralded rescue of his Laotian girlfriend following Communist takeover of her country. Behind-the-scenes details of this film's production are more interesting than the film itself, which was aimed for theatrical release as COMEBACK. Produced by Landon, who also reportedly took a hand in directing. Moira Chen is better known as softcore pornography actress Laura Gemser. Revamped and reedited for later showing at 100m. Average. Video title: PASSION AND VALOR.▼◗

Love Is Never Silent (1985) **C-100m. TVM** D: Joseph Sargent. Mare Winningham, Phyllis Frelich, Ed Waterstreet, Fredric Lehne, Cloris Leachman, Sid Caesar. Compelling period drama of a girl torn between being her deaf parents' link to the world and having a life of her own. Winningham is winning as usual, as are Frelich and Waterstreet, both stars of the National Theatre of the Deaf. Darlene Craviotto's loving script is based on Joanne Greenberg's novel *In This Sign.* Emmy winner for Best Director and Outstanding Drama/Comedy Special. Above average.

Love Is News (1937) **78m.** ** D: Tay Garnett. Tyrone Power, Loretta Young, Don Ameche, Slim Summerville, George Sanders, Jane Darwell, Stepin Fetchit, Pauline Moore, Elisha Cook, Jr., Dudley Digges, Walter Catlett. Heiress Young decides to get even with relentless reporter Power by announcing she's going to marry him—so he'll see what it's like to be in the spotlight for a change. Comedy misfire was remade more successfully as THAT WONDERFUL URGE, with Power repeating his starring role.

Love Is on the Air (1937) **61m.** ** D: Nick Grinde. Ronald Reagan, June Travis, Eddie Acuff, Ben Welden, Robert Barrat, Addison Richards. Reagan's first film casts him as a brash headline-making radio personality who goes after corrupt city officials—

but is sidetracked by his cautious boss. Passable B picture with meaningless title; one of several remakes of Paul Muni's HI, NELLIE.

love jones (1997) **C-110m.** **½ D: Theodore Witcher. Larenz Tate, Nia Long, Isaiah Washington, Bill Bellamy, Bernadette Clark, Lisa Nicole Carson, Khalil Kain. Age-old boy-meets-girl love story given '90s treatment, set in the upwardly mobile black culture of Chicago. Slightly overlong but refreshing date movie is energized by the chemistry of leads Tate and Long, and fine supporting performances. [R]▼●◗

Love Laughs at Andy Hardy (1946) **94m.** **½ D: Willis Goldbeck. Mickey Rooney, Lewis Stone, Sara Haden, Bonita Granville, Fay Holden, Lina Romay, Dorothy Ford, Addison Richards, Hal Hackett. Andy (played by a 26-year-old Rooney) returns to college after serving in WW2 to find that his sweetheart is engaged to someone else. The naive Hardy sentimentality was out of tune with the postwar mood and the series came to a close after this (although a reunion film was made twelve years later).▼

Loveless, The (1983) **C-84m.** **½ D: Kathryn Bigelow, Monty Montgomery. J. Don Ferguson, Willem Dafoe, Marin Kanter, Robert Gordon, Tina L'Hotsky, Liz Gans. A group of bikers stop in a small Southern town while on their way to the races at Daytona. Uneven homage to THE WILD ONE: pretentious and practically plotless, with about five times as much rockabilly music as dialogue; still, visually stunning, like an Edward Hopper painting of the 1950s. [R]▼

Love Letter, The (1999) **C-88m.** ** D: Peter Ho-sun Chan. Kate Capshaw, Blythe Danner, Ellen DeGeneres, Geraldine McEwan, Julianne Nicholson, Tom Everett Scott, Tom Selleck, Gloria Stuart. Low-key romantic comedy of New England seaside hamlet; bookstore owner/single mom Capshaw finds a love letter that inadvertently gets passed around town. Fun at first, but slows to a crawl at the midway point. Capshaw coproduced; her daughters Jessica Capshaw and Sasha Spielberg briefly appear. Based on the novel by Cathleen Schine. [PG-13]▼●◗

Love Letters (1945) **101m.** ** D: William Dieterle. Jennifer Jones, Joseph Cotten, Ann Richards, Anita Louise, Cecil Kellaway, Gladys Cooper, Reginald Denny. Artificial soaper of amnesiac Jones cured by Cotten's love; only real asset is Victor Young's lovely title song. Ayn Rand adapted Chris Massie's book, *Pity My Simplicity.*▼

Love Letters (1983) **C-98m.** *** D: Amy Jones. Jamie Lee Curtis, James Keach, Amy Madigan, Bud Cort, Matt Clark, Bonnie Bartlett, Sally Kirkland. Moving drama about a young single woman (nicely played by Curtis) who discovers deceased mother's correspondence with lover, then takes up with a married man of her own (Keach). Originally titled MY LOVE LETTERS. Aka PASSION PLAY. [R]▼●

Love Lottery, The (1954-British) **C-89m.** ** D: Charles Crichton. David Niven, Peggy Cummins, Anne Vernon, Herbert Lom, Hugh McDermott. Niven is movie star involved in international lottery; the winner gets him! Vernon is girl he really loves. Potential satire never comes off. Humphrey Bogart has guest bit in finale.

Lovely To Look At (1952) **C-105m.** **½ D: Mervyn LeRoy. Kathryn Grayson, Red Skelton, Howard Keel, Ann Miller, Marge & Gower Champion, Zsa Zsa Gabor. Second screen version of ROBERTA is a lesser MGM musical, but definitely has its moments as American comic Skelton inherits half-interest in a Paris dress salon run by Grayson and Marge Champion. Miller and the Champions add punch to the musical sequences; Vincente Minnelli directed the fashion show sequence. Songs include "Smoke Gets in Your Eyes," "I Won't Dance," and title tune.▼●

Lovely Way to Die, A (1968) **C-103m.** **½ D: David Lowell Rich. Kirk Douglas, Sylva Koscina, Eli Wallach, Kenneth Haigh, Sharon Farrell, Gordon Peter, Martyn Green. Odd detective suspenser. Douglas is likable cop turned private-eye assigned by D.A. (Wallach) to protect Koscina, awaiting murder trial. Pacing and script offbeat at right moments, otherwise standard. Look for Ali MacGraw in screen debut. Techniscope.

Love Machine, The (1971) **C-108m.** *½ D: Jack Haley, Jr. John Phillip Law, Dyan Cannon, Robert Ryan, Jackie Cooper, David Hemmings, Shecky Greene, Maureen Arthur. Ridiculous screen version of Jacqueline Susann's best-seller about Robin Stone (Law), ruthless TV executive who uses others for self-gain. [R]▼

Lovemakers, The SEE: **La Viaccia**

Love Maniac, The SEE: **Blood of Ghastly Horror**

Love Me Forever (1935) **90m.** **½ D: Victor Schertzinger. Grace Moore, Leo Carrillo, Robert Allen, Spring Byington, Douglass Dumbrille. Entertaining musical of down-and-out singer who miraculously rises to top and becomes star. Good cast helped make Moore become star in real life too.

Love Me or Leave Me (1955) **C-122m.** ***½ D: Charles Vidor. Doris Day, James Cagney, Cameron Mitchell, Robert Keith, Tom Tully. Engrossing musical bio (from an Oscar-winning story by Daniel Fuchs) of singer Ruth Etting, whose life and career were dominated by a gangster called the Gimp. Day and Cagney give strong performances. Score includes Doris' hit

"I'll Never Stop Loving You," plus oldies like "Ten Cents a Dance," "Shaking the Blues Away." CinemaScope.▼●

Love Me Tender (1956) **89m.** **½ D: Robert D. Webb. Richard Egan. Debra Paget, Elvis Presley, Robert Middleton, William Campbell, Neville Brand, Mildred Dunnock. Presley's film debut is Civil War yarn of conflicting politics among sons in a Southern family, and their mutual love for Paget. Elvis' singing ("Let Me," "We're Gonna Move (to a Better Home)," "Poor Boy," and the title tune) highlights so-so Western. Elvis's swivel hips *might* not be authentic period detail! CinemaScope.▼

Love Me Tonight (1932) **96m.** **** D: Rouben Mamoulian. Maurice Chevalier, Jeanette MacDonald, Charlie Ruggles, Myrna Loy, C. Aubrey Smith, Charles Butterworth, Robert Greig. One of the best musicals ever made; Chevalier plays a tailor who falls in love with a princess (MacDonald). Along the way they get to sing Rodgers and Hart's "Lover," "Mimi," "Isn't It Romantic?" among others. Mamoulian's ingenious ideas, and mobile camera, keep this fresh and alive. Screenplay by Samuel Hoffenstein, Waldemar Young, and George Marion, Jr., from a play by Leopold Marchand and Paul Armont. Originally released at 104m.

Love Nest (1951) **84m.** ** D: Joseph M. Newman. June Haver, William Lundigan, Frank Fay, Marilyn Monroe, Jack Paar, Leatrice Joy. Cheerful but bland comedy about an Army returnee whose wife has bought a broken-down brownstone apartment, and whose tenants become part of their lives. Interesting only for early looks at Monroe and future TV host Paar.▼

Love of Sunya, The (1927) **77m.** *** D: Albert Parker. Gloria Swanson, John Boles, Anders Randolph, Andres de Segurola, Hugh Miller, Pauline Garon. Lavish vehicle for silent-star Swanson has Eastern yogi enabling her to envision her life with two potential husbands—neither of whom is the man she truly loves. Soap opera deluxe, remake of earlier EYES OF YOUTH.▼

Love on a Pillow (1962-French) **C-102m.** ** D: Roger Vadim. Brigitte Bardot, Robert Hossein, James Robertson Justice, Jean-Marc Bory. Charitable Bardot bestows her pleasures on young man, hoping to divert his intended suicide; saucy little comedy. Franscope.

Love on the Dole (1941-British) **100m.** *** D: John Baxter. Deborah Kerr, Clifford Evans, Mary Merrall, George Carney, Geoffrey Hibbert, Joyce O'Neill. Serious, well-acted study of struggling London family during Depression. From Walter Greenwood novel.▼

Love on the Ground (1984-French) **C-126m.** *½ D: Jacques Rivette. Geraldine Chaplin, Jane Birkin, Andre Dussollier, Jean-Pierre Kalfon, Facundo Bo, Laszlo Szabo. Boring, confusing, pretentious story of actresses Chaplin and Birkin, hired by Kalfon to rehearse and perform his play—whose ending has not yet been written. For Rivette admirers only.

Love on the Run (1936) **80m.** ** D: W. S. Van Dyke II. Joan Crawford, Clark Gable, Franchot Tone, Reginald Owen, Mona Barrie, Ivan Lebedeff, Charles Judels, William Demarest, Donald Meek. Roving newspaper correspondent Gable takes it on the lam with frustrated heiress Crawford and becomes involved with international spies. This stale IT HAPPENED ONE NIGHT variation relies solely on its star power. ●

Love on the Run (1979-French) **C-90m.** *** D: François Truffaut. Jean-Pierre Léaud, Marie-France Pisier, Claude Jade, Dani, Dorothee, Rosy Varte, Julien Bertheau, Daniel Mesguich. Further romantic adventures of Truffaut's alter ego, Antoine Doinel (Léaud): Here, he divorces wife Jade and sets out again on his hopeless chase after love. Fine, but not top-notch Truffaut. Fifth entry in series, following BED AND BOARD; included are clips of others, which don't work here. Léaud's final appearance as Doinel. [PG]▼●◗

Love Parade, The (1929) **110m.** *** D: Ernst Lubitsch. Maurice Chevalier, Jeanette MacDonald, Lillian Roth, Lionel Belmore, Lupino Lane, Ben Turpin. Initial teaming of Chevalier and MacDonald is enjoyable operetta with chic Lubitsch touch, about love among the royalty of Sylvania. Acrobatic comedian Lane and personality performer Roth make wonderful second leads. Virginia Bruce is one of Jeanette's ladies-in-waiting. "Dream Lover" is film's best song. Score by Victor Schertzinger (later a film director himself) and Clifford Grey. MacDonald's film debut.●

Love Potion No. 9 (1992) **C-96m.** ** D: Dale Launer. Tate Donovan, Sandra Bullock, Mary Mara, Dale Midkiff, Hillary Bailey Smith, Dylan Baker, Anne Bancroft. Sluggish, often silly comedy in which two timid people, biochemist Donovan and animal psychologist Bullock, become human guinea pigs for a love potion. Launer also produced and scripted; loosely based on the classic Leiber-Stoller Golden Oldie. [PG-13]▼●

Lover, The (1992-French) **C-110m.** **½ D: Jean-Jacques Annaud. Jane March, Tony Leung, Frédérique Meininger, Arnaud Giovaninetti, Melvil Poupaud, Lisa Faulkner, Xiem Mang. Narrated by Jeanne Moreau. Exotic, soft-core adaptation of Marguerite Duras' autobiographical novel about a teenage girl who's initiated into sex by an older Chinese dandy in 1929 Indochina. Borderline tedious, yet offbeat and well-mounted enough to amuse anyone inclined to see it in the first place. Peripheral characters are more interesting than the two leads (at least when clothed). Sexier European version is available unrated. [R]▼●

Lover Boy (1954) SEE: **Lovers, Happy Lovers!**

Loverboy (1989) **C-98m.** *½ D: Joan Micklin Silver. Patrick Dempsey, Kate Jackson, Robert Ginty, Nancy Valen, Charles Hunter Walsh, Barbara Carrera, Bernie Coulson, Ray Girardin, Robert Camilletti, Vic Tayback, Kim Miyori, Kirstie Alley, Carrie Fisher. Paper-thin comedy of pizza delivery boy Dempsey turning on a bevy of frustrated older women, with resulting predictable complications. Curiously anachronistic, and not even up to sitcom level; a major disappointment from the otherwise dependable Silver. [PG-13]▼●

Lover Come Back (1946) **90m.** **½ D: William A. Seiter. Lucille Ball, George Brent, Vera Zorina, Carl Esmond, William Wright, Charles Winninger. Bright little comedy of Lucy suing Brent for divorce when she sees his companion during war, photographer Zorina. Retitled WHEN LOVERS MEET.

Lover Come Back (1961) **C-107m.** ***½ D: Delbert Mann. Rock Hudson, Doris Day, Tony Randall, Edie Adams, Jack Oakie, Jack Kruschen, Ann B. Davis, Joe Flynn, Jack Albertson, Howard St. John, Donna Douglas. Early Day-Hudson vehicle is one of the best. Funny, fast-moving comedy has ad exec Doris trying to get account away from rival Rock—unaware that the product doesn't exist! Edie Adams stands out in fine supporting cast.▼●

Lovers, The (1958-French) **88m.** *** D: Louis Malle. Jeanne Moreau, Alain Cuny, Jose Luis de Villalonga, Jean-Marc Bory, Gaston Modot. Chic, once-controversial tale of wealthy, married, spiritually-empty Moreau and her two very different extramarital involvements. Malle's first major international success, and one of Moreau's most important early credits. Dyaliscope.▼

Lovers (1991-Spanish) **C-103m.** ***½ D: Vicente Aranda. Victoria Abril, Jorge Sanz, Maribel Verdu. Handsome youth snuggles up with his sexy older landlady, while leaving his deceptively innocent fiancée in the lurch. Erotic true-crime saga, based on a murder case from 1955 Franco Madrid. Impressively acted and photographed. Screenplay by director Aranda, Alvaro Del Amo, and Carlos Perez Merinero.▼

Lovers and Liars (1979-Italian) **C-96m.** ** D: Mario Monicelli. Goldie Hawn, Giancarlo Giannini, Claudine Auger, Aurore Clement, Laura Betti, Andrea Ferreol. Forgettable black comedy centering on complications surrounding romance between American tourist Hawn and Italian bank exec Giannini. Aka TRAVELS WITH ANITA; originally ran 125m. [R]▼●◗

Lovers and Lollipops (1955) **80m.** **½ D: Morris Engel, Ruth Orkin. Lori March, Gerald O'Loughlin, Cathy Dunn, William Ward. Sweet but flawed little film about 7-year-old Dunn becoming jealous when her widowed mother begins dating a nice guy. The story rambles, and the music score is intrusive, but the N.Y.C. location footage is exceptional, as it was in Engel and Orkin's landmark film LITTLE FUGITIVE.▼

Lovers and Other Strangers (1970) **C-106m.** ***½ D: Cy Howard. Gig Young, Bea Arthur, Bonnie Bedelia, Anne Jackson, Harry Guardino, Michael Brandon, Richard Castellano, Bob Dishy, Marian Hailey, Cloris Leachman, Anne Meara. Vividly real, genuinely funny movie about side-effects, reverberations when young couple gets married. Film won fame for Castellano, with catch-line "So what's the story?" just one of many memorable vignettes. Gig Young delightful as perennially cheerful father of the bride. From the play by Renee Taylor and Joseph Bologna (they scripted with David Z. Goodman); with Oscar-winning song, "For All We Know." Diane Keaton's film debut. [PG—originally rated R]▼

Lovers, Happy Lovers (1954-British) **103m.** *** D: René Clement. Gérard Philipe, Valerie Hobson, Joan Greenwood, Margaret Johnston, Natasha Parry. Philipe is wed to Hobson but tries to seduce her friend (Parry) in this witty, deftly ironic sex comedy. Original title: KNAVE OF HEARTS. Retitled: LOVER BOY.

Lover's Knot (1996) **C-88m.** *½ D: Pete Shaner. Bill Campbell, Jennifer Grey, Tim Curry, Adam Baldwin, Dr. Joyce Brothers, Anne Francis, Zelda Rubinstein, Dawn Wells. Cutesy romantic trifle in which cupid Curry must bring together a poetry scholar and a beautiful doctor, then keep them an item for the rest of this movie's seemingly endless running time. Cupid's bow definitely misses the funny bone here; just a space-filler at the video store. [R]▼

Lovers Like Us (1975-French) **C-103m.** **½ D: Jean-Paul Rappeneau. Catherine Deneuve, Yves Montand, Luigi Vanucchi, Tony Roberts, Dana Wynter. Globetrotting screwball comedy has Deneuve and Montand running away from their respective spouses, meeting and falling in love with each other. Nothing special, but easy to take. [PG]▼

Lovers of Paris (1957-French) **115m.** **½ D: Julien Duvivier. Gérard Philipe, Danielle Darrieux, Dany Carrel. Spirited drama of Philipe coming to Paris bent on success and marriage; Darrieux is his perfect choice. Original title: POT-BOUILLE.

Lovers of the Arctic Circle (1998-Spanish) **C-112m.** ★★★ D: Julio Medem. Najwa Nimri, Fele Martinez, Nancho Novo, Maru Valdivielso, Kristel Díaz, Victor Hugo Oliveira. Beguiling romantic drama about two young people who first meet as eight-year-old schoolmates and gradually realize they are destined to be together; in fact, their entire lives are linked by a series of odd parallels. It's no coincidence that the main characters' names, Anna and Otto, are palindromes; director Medem's conceit is that love is circular and eternal. Only sour note is film's conclusion. Super 35. [R]▼

Lovers on the Bridge, The (1991-French) **C-129m.** ★★½ D: Léos Carax. Juliette Binoche, Denis Lavant, Klaus-Michael Grüber, Daniel Buain, Marion Stalens, Edith Scob. Binoche is a lustrous presence in this otherwise hot-and-cold tale as a homeless, half-blind painter who, with manipulative street-performer Lavant, camps out on Paris's crumbling Pont Neuf Bridge while it's closed down for restoration. Some dazzling imagery combined with an air of pretension make this a decidedly mixed bag. Released in the U.S. in 1999. [R]▼

Loves and Times of Scaramouche, The (1975-Italian) **C-95m.** ★½ D: Enzo G. Castellari. Michael Sarrazin, Ursula Andress, Aldo Maccione, Giancarlo Prete, Michael Forest. Scaramouche has his way with women, and runs afoul of an oafish Napoleon in this energetic but empty-headed farce. Maccione adds some laughs as Bonaparte. Poorly dubbed. Filmed in Rome and Zagreb.▼

Love Serenade (1996-Australian) **C-101m.** ★★½ D: Shirley Barrett. Miranda Otto, Rebecca Frith, George Shevtsov, John Alansu, Jessica Napier. Oddball black comedy about a desperate, clingy beautician (Frith) and her reclusive younger sister (Otto) vying for the affections of a self-centered hipster deejay (Shevtsov)—who seems to be the only eligible man in town. Often poignant and deadpan funny, but the ending is unsatisfying. Worth seeing for the performances, especially Otto, a compendium of hilariously paranoid body tics. Film takes its title from a Barry White song, one of many featured on the groovy '70s soundtrack. Written by the director. Super 35. [R]▼

Love She Sought, The (1990) **C-100m. TVM** D: Joseph Sargent. Angela Lansbury, Denholm Elliott, Robert Prosky, Cynthia Nixon, Gary Herschberger. Fine adult drama about devoted unmarried church teacher who, on retirement, decides to look up her longtime pen pal in Ireland, with whom she's fallen in love through his letters. A great Lansbury performance and a wonderful one by Elliott help put this classy adaptation of John Hassler's misty-eyed book *A Green Journey* over the top. Ron Cowen and Daniel Lipman coscripted. Above average.

Lovesick (1983) **C-95m.** ★★ D: Marshall Brickman. Dudley Moore, Elizabeth McGovern, Alec Guinness, John Huston, Wallace Shawn, Alan King, Renee Taylor, Ron Silver, Gene Saks, David Strathairn. "Sick" is right; this romantic comedy (about a psychiatrist who falls in love with his newest patient) needs a shot of adrenalin. Fine cast founders; Guinness's turn as the shade of Sigmund Freud is a waste. Only Silver gets real laughs as a Pacino-like actor. [PG]▼●◗

Love's Labour's Lost (2000-U.S.-British-French) **C-95m.** ★½ D: Kenneth Branagh. Kenneth Branagh, Natascha McElhone, Alicia Silverstone, Nathan Lane, Adrian Lester, Alessandro Nivola, Matthew Lillard, Timothy Spall, Carmen Ejogo, Emily Mortimer, Geraldine McEwan, Richard Briers, Richard Clifford. Shakespeare's comic romp becomes a 1930s musical. The King of Navarre (Nivola) and three comrades swear off women—just as the King of France's daughter (Silverstone) arrives with three attractive friends. Hollywood-inspired production numbers are downright embarrassing at times; everyone tries hard, but only Lane emerges unscathed. Uses old Fred & Ginger songs, but reminds one more of Burt & Cybill (from AT LONG LAST LOVE). Panavision. [PG]

Love Slaves of the Amazon (1957) **C-81m.** ★★ D: Curt Siodmak. Don Taylor, Eduardo Ciannelli, Gianna Segale, Harvey Chalk. Title tag removes all surprises about this programmer.

Loves of a Blonde (1965-Czech) **88m.** ★★★½ D: Milos Forman. Hana Brejchova, Josef Sebanek, Vladimir Pucholt, Jan Vostrell, Vladimir Mensik. Sweet, poignant tale of idealistic shoe-factory worker Brejchova, and what happens after she spends the night with—and falls in love with—womanizing pianist Pucholt. Gentle comedy-drama is both entertaining and revealing.▼●

Loves of Carmen, The (1948) **C-99m.** ★★½ D: Charles Vidor. Rita Hayworth, Glenn Ford, Ron Randell, Victor Jory, Luther Adler. Hayworth's beauty is all there is in this colorful but routine retelling of the story of a gypsy man-killer, minus Bizet's music.▼●◗

Loves of Edgar Allan Poe, The (1942) **67m.** ★★ D: Harry Lachman. Linda Darnell, John Shepperd (Shepperd Strudwick), Virginia Gilmore, Jane Darwell, Mary Howard, Henry (Harry) Morgan. Plodding biography of 19th-century writer and women who influenced him.

Loves of Isadora, The SEE: **Isadora**

Loves of Three Queens (1953-Italian) **C-90m.** ★★ D: Marc Allegret. Hedy Lamarr, Massimo Serato, Cathy O'Donnell, Luigi Tosi, Guido Celano, Robert Beatty. Three-part film involving lives and loves of Genevieve of Brabant, Empress Josephine, and Helen of Troy (Lamarr). Originally three-hour meandering epic, now chopped down;

still lacks continuity or interest. Retitled: THE FACE THAT LAUNCHED A THOUSAND SHIPS.▼

Love Songs (1986-Canadian-French) **C-107m.** ** D: Elie Chouraqui. Catherine Deneuve, Richard Anconina, Christopher Lambert, Jacques Perrin, Nick Mancuso, Dayle Haddon, Charlotte Gainsbourg. Lightweight, predictable soap opera about the loves and ambitions of rock singers (Anconina, Lambert), focusing mostly on the latter's relationship with an older woman (Deneuve). Attempts to be touching and bittersweet but doesn't ring true. ▼

Lovespell (1979) **C-91m.** BOMB D: Tom Donovan. Richard Burton, Kate Mulgrew, Nicholas Clay, Cyril Cusack, Geraldine Fitzgerald, Niall Toibin, Diana Van Der Vlis, Niall O'Brien. Thoroughly inept retelling of the romantic Tristan and Isolde legend. One-take-only filming on Irish locations has static direction and writing from a *Classics Illustrated* comic book. Mulgrew is too old for the Isolde role, and her American accent clashes with the rest of the cast. Aka TRISTAN AND ISOLDE.▼

Love Stinks (1999) **C-93m.** *½ D: Jeff Franklin. French Stewart, Bridgette Wilson, Bill Bellamy, Tyra Banks, Steve Hytner, Jason Bateman, Tiffani-Amber Thiessen, Colleen Camp. Love is not the only thing that stinks in this barely funny (and mean-spirited) tale of a television comedy writer (Stewart) who becomes romantically involved with a sociopathic beauty-from-hell (Wilson). Plays like a one-note, R-rated TV sitcom episode. [R]▼◗

Love Story (1944-British) **108m.** *** D: Leslie Arliss. Margaret Lockwood, Stewart Granger, Patricia Roc, Tom Walls, Reginald Purdell, Moira Lister. No relation to later hit film, this one has dying pianist Lockwood finding true love at summer resort with pilot Granger, whose eyesight is failing. Originally released here as A LADY SURRENDERS.

Love Story (1970) **C-99m.** *** D: Arthur Hiller. Ali MacGraw, Ryan O'Neal, Ray Milland, John Marley, Katherine Balfour, Russell Nype, Tom (Tommy) Lee Jones. Just what it says: simple, modern boy-meets-girl story set against New England college backdrop, tinged with tragedy of girl's sudden illness. Straightforward filming of Erich Segal's book can't hold a candle to older Hollywood schmaltz, but on its own terms, pretty good (and a box-office smash). Francis Lai won an Oscar for his score. Followed by OLIVER'S STORY. [PG]▼●

Love Streams (1984) **C-141m.** ** D: John Cassavetes. Gena Rowlands, John Cassavetes, Diahnne Abbott, Risa Martha Blewitt, Seymour Cassel, Margaret Abbott. Typical Cassavetes fodder about a brother and sister with a strong emotional bond: for her, love never ends; and for him, love is an abstract undone by the harsh realities of life. Cassavetes aficionados will probably like it; for others, only marginally bearable. Based on a play by Ted Allan, who cowrote screenplay with Cassavetes. [PG-13]▼

Love That Brute (1950) **85m.** **½ D: Alexander Hall. Paul Douglas, Jean Peters, Cesar Romero, Joan Davis, Arthur Treacher, Keenan Wynn, Peter Price, Jay C. Flippen. Douglas is well cast as a loud-talking, good-natured prohibition racketeer with a yen for innocent Peters. Romero, who's the heavy here, had the lead in TALL, DARK AND HANDSOME, of which this is a remake.

Love Thy Neighbor (1940) **82m.** ** D: Mark Sandrich. Jack Benny, Fred Allen, Mary Martin, Verree Teasdale, Eddie "Rochester" Anderson, Virginia Dale, Theresa Harris. Contrived attempt to capitalize on Benny-Allen radio feud. Martin still good, though, and Rochester has some sprightly scenes, but disappointment for fans of both Benny and Allen.

Love Under Fire (1937) **75m.** **½ D: George Marshall. Loretta Young, Don Ameche, Frances Drake, Walter Catlett, Sig Ruman, John Carradine, Holmes Herbert. Romance and adventure as detective Ameche has to arrest alleged thief Young in Madrid amid Spanish Civil War. Disjointed but enjoyable.

Love! Valour! Compassion! (1997) **C-110m.** **½ D: Joe Mantello. Jason Alexander, Randy Becker, Stephen Bogardus, John Glover, John Benjamin Hickey, Justin Kirk, Stephen Spinella. Entertaining but overlong adaptation of Terrence McNally's Tony Award–winning play about eight gay male acquaintances who spend countryside weekends at their host's dream Victorian home over three summer holidays. Too much of the text tiresomely depends on Backbiting! Pettiness! and Sniping!, though Glover (reprising his Tony Award–winning performance) is impressive in a dual role as twins of wildly differing dispositions (last name, uh, Jeckyll). [R]▼●

Love Walked In (1998-U.S.-Argentinian) **C-90m.** ** D: Juan J. Campanella. Denis Leary, Terence Stamp, Aitana Sanchez-Gijon, Danny Nucci, Moira Kelly, Michael Badalucco, Marj Dusay. Routine, low-rent film noir about a sour nightclub pianist who agrees to use his beautiful girlfriend as bait to entrap a wealthy admirer. Object: a big cash payoff. Adequate but uninspired time filler. [R]▼

Love With the Proper Stranger (1963) **100m.** *** D: Robert Mulligan. Natalie Wood, Steve McQueen, Edie Adams, Herschel Bernardi, Tom Bosley. Nifty, cynical romance tale of working girl Wood and trumpet player McQueen. Much N.Y.C. on-location filming, nice support from

Adams. Written by Arnold Schulman. Good bit: the title tune.▼●

Love Your Mama (1993) **C-92m.** ** D: Ruby Oliver. Carol E. Hall, Audrey Morgan, Andre Robinson, Earnest Rayford III, Kearo Johnson, Jacqueline Williams. Low-budget, semi-autobiographical melodrama about a mother in a Southside Chicago ghetto whose tribulations include an unfaithful, alcoholic husband, a pregnant teenage daughter, and two sons whose lives seem to be headed nowhere. Debuting writer-director Oliver must be commended for surmounting all obstacles to get her vision on the screen; in point of fact, her saga of getting the movie made is more inspiring than the film itself. [PG-13]▼

Loving (1970) **C-90m.** ***½ D: Irvin Kershner. George Segal, Eva Marie Saint, Sterling Hayden, Keenan Wynn, Nancie Phillips, Janis Young, Roy Scheider, Sherry Lansing. Extremely good drama chronicles Segal's marital and occupational problems. Director Kershner has great feeling for day-to-day detail; film's superb climax involves public lovemaking. [R]

Loving Couples (1980) **C-97m.** ** D: Jack Smight. Shirley MacLaine, James Coburn, Susan Sarandon, Stephen Collins, Sally Kellerman, Nan Martin. Couples MacLaine/Coburn and Sarandon/Collins switch partners. A titillating title for a predictable comedy. [PG]▼

Loving You (1957) **C-101m.** **½ D: Hal Kanter. Elvis Presley, Lizabeth Scott, Wendell Corey, Dolores Hart, James Gleason. Publicist Liz and country-western musician Corey discover gas station attendant Presley and promote him to stardom. Elvis's second movie is highlighted by his performance of "Teddy Bear" and the title tune. VistaVision.▼●

Lovin' Molly (1974) **C-98m.** ** D: Sidney Lumet. Anthony Perkins, Beau Bridges, Blythe Danner, Edward Binns, Susan Sarandon, Conard Fowkes. Danner is just right in otherwise indifferent filmization of Larry McMurtry's novel *Leaving Cheyenne,* about two friends in Texas and their lifelong love for the same woman. [R]

Low Down Dirty Shame, A (1994) **C-108m.** **½ D: Keenen Ivory Wayans. Keenen Ivory Wayans, Charles S. Dutton, Jada Pinkett, Salli Richardson, Andrew Divoff, Corwin Hawkins, Gary Cervantes, Gregory Sierra, Kim Wayans. Occasionally amusing comedy-actioner with Wayans as a private detective hired by the DEA to uncover some missing drug money. However, you might say that it's a low-down dirty shame that this film isn't funnier—or that Wayans (who also scripted) so often resorts to unsubtle stereotyping for cheap laughs. Pinkett really scores as Wayans' loyal assistant. [R]▼●

Lower Depths, The (1936-French) **92m.** **½ D: Jean Renoir. Jean Gabin, Louis Jouvet, Suzy Prim, Vladimir Sokoloff, Junie Astor, Robert Le Vignan. Sordid drama about assorted characters in a squalid home for derelicts. Pepel (Gabin), a professional thief, loves the younger sister of his mistress, and commits murder to save her from the clutches of a police officer to whom she has been "given" as a bribe. Loose adaptation of the 1902 Maxim Gorki play changes the setting from Czarist Russia to an imaginary land. Renoir scripted with Charles Spaak. Remade 21 years later by Akira Kurosawa, who was more faithful to the play. Original title: LES BAS-FONDS. ▼

Lower Depths, The (1957-Japanese) **125m.** *** D: Akira Kurosawa. Toshiro Mifune, Isuzu Yamada, Ganjiro Nakamura, Kyoko Kagawa. Well-directed and acted but endlessly talky drama of tortured, poverty-stricken souls, with Mifune a thief who becomes involved with Kagawa. Based on a Maxim Gorki play.▼

Low Life, The (1996) **C-98m.** ** D: George Hickenlooper. Rory Cochrane, Kyra Sedgwick, Sean Astin, Ron Livingston, Christian Meoli, Sara Melson, James Le Gros, Shawnee Smith, J. T. Walsh, Renee Zellweger. Wannabe writer Cochrane comes to L.A. and finds himself surrounded by aimless companions and a woman (Sedgwick) who cannot commit. Well acted, but depressing and unfulfilling. [R]▼●

Loyal 47 Ronin, The SEE: **47 Ronin, Part I and Part II, The**

Loyalties (1986-Canadian-British) **C-97m.** **½ D: Anne Wheeler. Kenneth Welsh, Tantoo Cardinal, Susan Wooldridge, Vera Martin, Christopher Barrington-Leigh. Nicely paced but predictable psychological drama about an ever-so-proper British couple (Welsh, Wooldridge) who've settled in a remote Canadian village, and what happens when they take on half-Indian Cardinal as a housekeeper. [R]▼

L. 627 (1992-French) **C-145m.** *** D: Bertrand Tavernier. Didier Bezace, Charlotte Kady, Philippe Torreton, Nils Tavernier, Jean-Paul Comart, Jean-Roger Milo, Lara Guirao. "Lulu" Marguet is a career cop who fights drug dealers with a keen sense of commitment—which is more than can be said for many of his colleagues. Pungent satire of contemporary French police force, and the way an "elite" drug-busting unit tries to function amid the absurdities of red tape and administrative bungling. Funny, yet frightening. Director Tavernier's son plays Vincent.▼

L-Shaped Room, The (1963-British) **125m.** *** D: Bryan Forbes. Leslie Caron, Tom Bell, Brock Peters, Avis Bunnage, Emlyn Williams, Cicely Courtneidge, Bernard Lee, Patricia Phoenix, Nanette Newman. French woman crosses the Channel to face pregnancy alone, comes to meet interesting assortment of characters in shabby London boarding house. Caron is superb in the lead.▼

Lt. Robin Crusoe, USN (1966) **C-110m.** BOMB D: Byron Paul. Dick Van Dyke, Nancy Kwan, Akim Tamiroff, Arthur Malet, Tyler McVey. Labored Disney comedy is unworthy of Van Dyke, who plays modern-day Robinson Crusoe, a navy pilot who drifts onto deserted island, becomes involved with pretty native girl. Film has virtually nothing of merit to recommend. Story by Retlaw Yensid (spell it backwards).▼

Lucas (1986) **C-100m.** *** D: David Seltzer. Corey Haim, Kerri Green, Charlie Sheen, Courtney Thorne-Smith, Winona Ryder, Thomas E. Hodges. Thoroughly winning story of a precocious 14-year-old boy who develops a serious crush on the new girl in town—and the various ramifications that follow. One of the few Hollywood films about young people in the 80s that doesn't paint its characters in black and white only. A real sleeper, marking writer Seltzer's directing debut as well as screen debut for Ryder. [PG-13]▼

Lucie Aubrac (1997-French) **C-116m.** **½ D: Claude Berri. Carole Bouquet, Daniel Auteuil, Patrice Chereau, Jean-Roger Milo, Heino Ferch, Pascal Greggory. Married couple Auteuil and Bouquet are members of the Resistance in Lyon, France. When he is captured by the Gestapo, she determines to free him. WW2 drama emphasizes real-life love story but suffers from deliberate pacing. Based on the book *Outwitting the Gestapo* by Lucie Aubrac herself. Leading French director Chereau portrays Max. Technovision. [R]▼

Lucifer Project, The SEE: **Barracuda**

Luckiest Man in the World, The (1989) **C-82m.** *** D: Frank D. Gilroy. Philip Bosco, Doris Belack, Joanne Camp, Matthew Gottlieb, Arthur French, Stan Lachow. Scrooge-like businessman Bosco is almost killed in a plane crash, and abruptly decides to change his ways. Gilroy also scripted this unpretentious, well-acted little tale; the "voice" in the bathroom is that of Moses Gunn.

Luck of Ginger Coffey, The (1964-Canadian-U.S.) **100m.** *** D: Irvin Kershner. Robert Shaw, Mary Ure, Liam Redmond, Tom Harvey, Libby McClintock. Effective kitchen-sink drama with Shaw in one of his best performances as an out-of-work Irish-born dreamer, approaching middle age, who moves to Montreal with wife Ure and their teenage daughter, hoping to find success. Scripted by Brian Moore, based on his novel.▼

Luck of the Irish, The (1948) **99m.** **½ D: Henry Koster. Tyrone Power, Anne Baxter, Cecil Kellaway, Lee J. Cobb, Jayne Meadows. Leprechaun Kellaway becomes reporter Power's conscience in this "cute" but unremarkable romance.

Lucky Devils (1932) **64m.** ** D: Ralph Ince. William Boyd, Dorothy Wilson, William Gargan, Bruce Cabot, Creighton Chaney (Lon Chaney, Jr.), Roscoe Ates, William Bakewell, Bob Rose, Julie Haydon, Betty Furness. Stuntman Gargan likes extra Wilson, but she loves stuntman Boyd. Hokey programmer, but great opening scene; Hollywood-on-film buffs will surely want to see it.

Lucky Jim (1957-British) **95m.** **½ D: John Boulting. Ian Carmichael, Terry-Thomas, Hugh Griffith, Sharon Acker, Jean Anderson. Comic misadventures of puckish history professor at provincial British university; amusing adaptation of Kingsley Amis book, though not up to Boulting Brothers standard.▼

Lucky Jordan (1942) **84m.** **½ D: Frank Tuttle. Alan Ladd, Helen Walker, Marie McDonald, Mabel Paige, Sheldon Leonard, Lloyd Corrigan. Far-fetched story of smart-mouthed hood Ladd reluctantly drafted into the army, becoming entangled with U.S.O. worker Walker (in her feature debut) and Nazi spies.

Lucky Lady (1975) **C-118m.** ** D: Stanley Donen. Gene Hackman, Liza Minnelli, Burt Reynolds, Geoffrey Lewis, John Hillerman, Robby Benson, Michael Hordern. Star trio make an engaging team, as amateur rum-runners in the 1930s who practice a menage-a-trois after business hours . . . script goes astray and drags along to a limp, hastily refilmed conclusion. Unfortunate waste of talent; written by Willard Huyck and Gloria Katz. [PG]

Lucky Losers (1950) **69m.** ** D: William Beaudine. Leo Gorcey, Huntz Hall, Hillary Brooke, Gabriel Dell, Lyle Talbot, Bernard Gorcey, Billy Benedict, Joseph Turkel, Frank Jenks, David Gorcey. Stale *Bowery Boys* comedy, with Slip and Sach trading their overalls for pinstripes when they land jobs as stockbrokers.

Lucky Luciano (1974-Italian-French-U.S.) **C-110m.** ** D: Francesco Rosi. Gian-Maria Volonte, Rod Steiger, Edmond O'Brien, Vincent Gardenia, Charles Cioffi. Fair international coproduction about the deported crime kingpin, given a good interpretation by Volonte. Former federal narcotics agent Charles Siragusa, Luciano's real-life nemesis, plays himself. [R]▼

Lucky Me (1954) **C-100m.** ** D: Jack Donohue. Doris Day, Robert Cummings, Phil Silvers, Eddie Foy, Nancy Walker, Martha Hyer, Bill Goodwin. Bright-faced but doggedly mediocre musical set in Miami, with Doris as star of Silvers' third-rate theatrical troupe who attracts the attention of Broadway songwriter Cummings. Look for young Angie Dickinson in first film appearance. CinemaScope. ▼●

Lucky Nick Cain (1951) **87m.** **½ D: Joseph M. Newman. George Raft, Coleen Gray, Charles Goldner, Walter Rilla. Acceptable gangster yarn of Raft involved with counterfeiting gang, accused of murder; filmed in Italy.

Lucky Night (1939) **82m.** *½ D: Norman Taurog. Myrna Loy, Robert Taylor, Henry O'Neill, Joseph Allen, Douglas Fowley, Charles Lane, Marjorie Main. Incoherent, interminable mess, in which magnate's daughter Loy and down-and-out gambler Taylor meet, get drunk, and get married—all in one evening. Sounds far more promising than it plays.

Lucky Partners (1940) **99m.** ** D: Lewis Milestone. Ronald Colman, Ginger Rogers, Jack Carson, Spring Byington, Cecilia Loftus, Harry Davenport. Far-fetched comedy about Colman and Rogers winning sweepstakes together, then taking "imaginary" honeymoon. Stars try to buoy mediocre script.▼

Lucky Star, The (1980-Canadian) **C-110m.** *** D: Max Fischer. Louise Fletcher, Rod Steiger, Lou Jacobi, Brett Marx, Helen Hughes. Entertaining tale of a young Jewish boy (Marx) whose parents are taken away by the Nazis. He is sheltered on a Rotterdam farm and singlehandedly goes up against German Colonel Steiger. A sleeper. [PG]

Lucky Stiff, The (1949) **99m.** ** D: Lewis R. Foster. Dorothy Lamour, Brian Donlevy, Claire Trevor, Irene Hervey, Marjorie Rambeau. Sturdy cast in slim vehicle of lawyer setting trap for actual killer after girl suspect has death sentence reprieved. Produced by, of all people, Jack Benny!

Lucky Stiff (1988) **C-82m.** ** D: Anthony Perkins. Joe Alaskey, Donna Dixon, Jeff Kober, Morgan Sheppard, Barbara Howard, Charles Frank, Fran Ryan, Leigh McCloskey, Bill Quinn. Uneven black comedy about cannibalism improves as it goes along. Fat Alaskey, full of jokes and yearning to be married, is romanced by gorgeous Dixon, but doesn't know that she's selected him as Mr. Christmas Dinner for her inbred family. Awkwardly structured script and odd rhythms of film are helped by Alaskey's ingratiating performance. [PG]▼●

Lucky 13 SEE: **Running Hot**

Lucky to Be a Woman (1956-Italian) **95m.** **½ D: Alessandro Blasetti. Charles Boyer, Sophia Loren, Marcello Mastroianni, Nino Besozzi, Titina De Filippo. Boyer is lecherous count who helps make peasant gal Loren a cultured movie star; Mastroianni is her photographer boyfriend; charmingly acted. Aka WHAT A WOMAN! Panoramica. ▼

Lucy Gallant (1955) **C-104m.** **½ D: Robert Parrish. Charlton Heston, Jane Wyman, Thelma Ritter, Claire Trevor, William Demarest, Wallace Ford. Spiritless soaper of success-bent Wyman rejecting suitors Heston et al., wanting to get ahead instead; set in Western oil town. Wyman plays dressmaker, and veteran Hollywood costume designer Edith Head makes a rare on-screen appearance near the end. VistaVision.

Ludwig (1972-Italian-French-German) **C-173m.** ** D: Luchino Visconti. Helmut Berger, Romy Schneider, Trevor Howard, Silvana Mangano, Helmut Griem, Gert Frobe. Lavish film about Mad King of Bavaria keeps main character so cold, aloof that one feels no sympathy; after nearly three hours, effect is deadening. Authentic locations are breathtaking. Schneider and Howard excellent, but slow-moving film doesn't work. Incredibly, the original version of this runs 246m.! Video runs 231m. Panavision. [PG]▼

Lullaby of Broadway (1951) **C-92m.** **½ D: David Butler. Doris Day, Gene Nelson, Gladys George, S. Z. Sakall, Billy de Wolfe, Florence Bates, Anne Triola. Musical comedy star Day returns to N.Y.C., unaware that her singer mother has hit the skids. Warner Bros. musical is decent but no big deal; good cast and lots of great old songs keep it moving.▼●

Lulu Belle (1948) **87m.** ** D: Leslie Fenton. Dorothy Lamour, George Montgomery, Albert Dekker, Otto Kruger, Glenda Farrell. Hackneyed drama of singer stepping on anyone and everyone to achieve fame.

Lumiere (1976-French) **C-95m.** **½ D: Jeanne Moreau. Jeanne Moreau, Francine Racette, Lucia Bose, Caroline Cartier, Marie Henriau, Keith Carradine, Bruno Ganz, François Simon. Elaborate but not very involving drama about four actresses of different ages and status and their relationships with careers, men, each other. Curio is worth seeing for Moreau's directorial debut. [R]▼

Luminarias (2000) **C-100m.** *** D: Jose Luis Valenzuela. Evelina Fernandez, Marta DuBois, Angela Moya, Diana Ortelli, Sal Lopez, Scott Bakula, Cheech Marin, Robert Beltran, Andrew Kim, Pepe Serna, Liz Torres. Four L.A. Latina women of a certain age cling to one another as they try to find the right men—while battling their own social prejudices. A sharply observed portrait of women with ethnic identity crises, told with vigor and humor. Written by its impressive leading lady, Fernandez. [R]

Luna (1979) **C-144m.** *** D: Bernardo Bertolucci. Jill Clayburgh, Matthew Barry, Veronica Lazar, Renato Salvatori, Fred Gwynne, Alida Valli, Roberto Benigni. Initially dazzling tale of male adolescent's identity crisis becomes ponderous when it turns into a mother-son soap opera with incestuous implications. Cinematically exciting, though, with a bravura finale. [R]

Lunatics: A Love Story (1992) **C-87m.** **½ D: Josh Becker. Theodore Raimi, Deborah Foreman, Bruce Campbell, Brian McCree, Eddie Rosmaya, Michele Stacey.

Raimi is a gentle paranoid, confined by his fears to his lonely, foil-lined L.A. apartment; Foreman is convinced she causes the death of everyone she loves. Odd low-budget comedy has real, if eccentric, charm. "Presented" by Sam Raimi. [PG-13]▼

Lunatics and Lovers (1975-Italian) **C-93m.** *½ D: Flavio Mogherini. Marcello Mastroianni, Claudia Mori, Lino Morelli, Flora Carabella, Adriano Celentano. Aristocrat Mastroianni has an imaginary wife; an organ grinder convinces prostitute Mori to "impersonate" her. When it's not silly, it's dull.▼

Lunch Wagon (1980) **C-88m.** **½ D: Ernest Pintoff. Pamela Jean Bryant, Rosanne Katon, Candy Moore, Rick Podell, Rose Marie, Chuck McCann, Vic Dunlop, Jimmy Van Patten, Dick Van Patten. Above average drive-in comedy about trio of young lovelies who set up their lunch truck at a prime construction site, unaware that their competition is really a cover for a planned bank robbery. Good cast, spirited direction; Dale Bozzio sings "Mental Hopscotch." Reissued as LUNCH WAGON GIRLS and COME 'N' GET IT. [R]▼

Lunch Wagon Girls SEE: **Lunch Wagon**

Lured (1947) **102m.** **½ D: Douglas Sirk. George Sanders, Lucille Ball, Charles Coburn, Alan Mowbray, Cedric Hardwicke, Boris Karloff, George Zucco. Ball turns detective in this melodrama, encounters strange characters and harrowing experiences while tracking murderer; pretty good, with top cast. Remake of Robert Siodmak's 1940 French film PIEGES. ▼

Lure of the Swamp (1957) **74m.** *½ D: Hubert Cornfield. Marshall Thompson, Willard Parker, Joan Vohs, Jack Elam. Tawdry B film of man's lust for wealth, leading to destruction of group hunting loot in murky swamp. Regalscope.

Lure of the Wilderness (1952) **C-92m.** **½ D: Jean Negulesco. Jeffrey Hunter, Jean Peters, Constance Smith, Walter Brennan, Jack Elam. Remake of SWAMP WATER doesn't match earlier version's atmosphere of Southern swamps where murderer holds young man hostage to keep his whereabouts secret.

Lurking Fear (1994) **C-76m.** *½ D: C. Courtney Joyner. Jon Finch, Blake Bailey, Ashley Lauren, Jeffrey Combs, Allison Mackie, Paul Mantee, Vincent Schiavelli. On a hot, sunny Christmas in Massachusetts, crooks and monster fighters confront one another in an old church, waiting for the creatures who live in tunnels below to make their annual attack. Seedy and tiresome, this seems more derived from KEY LARGO than from H. P. Lovecraft's story. Shot in Romania, and looks it. From Full Moon.▼●

Lush Life (1994) **C-96m. TVM** D: Michael Elias. Jeff Goldblum, Forest Whitaker, Kathy Baker, Lois Chiles, Tracey Needham, Zack Norman, Jack Sheldon. Nicely played character study with Goldblum and Whitaker as working musicians and buddies on the N.Y. music scene. Baker is Goldblum's long-suffering wife, who wants to get out of the City and lead a more "normal" life. Sags a bit along the way, but still satisfying, especially for jazz fans; tasty score supervised by Lennie Niehaus. Above average.▼

Lust for a Vampire (1971-British) **C-95m.** *½ D: Jimmy Sangster. Ralph Bates, Yutte Stensgaard, Barbara Jefford, Michael Johnson, Suzanna Leigh, Mike Raven, Christopher Neame. Carmilla, the seductress from THE VAMPIRE LOVERS, preys on students at a girls' school. Third-rate Hammer horror, anemically produced. Followed by TWINS OF EVIL. Original title: TO LOVE A VAMPIRE. [R]▼

Lust for Gold (1949) **90m.** **½ D: S. Sylvan Simon. Ida Lupino, Glenn Ford, Gig Young, Jay Silverheels, Eddy Waller. Lupino gets overly dramatic as grasping woman stopping at nothing to obtain riches of gold-laden mine.▼

Lust for Life (1956) **C-122m.** **** D: Vincente Minnelli. Kirk Douglas, Anthony Quinn, James Donald, Pamela Brown, Everett Sloane, Niall MacGinnis, Noel Purcell, Henry Daniell, Jill Bennett, Lionel Jeffries, Eric Pohlmann. Brilliant adaptation of Irving Stone's biography of painter Van Gogh, vividly portraying his anguished life. Quinn won well-deserved Oscar for performance as painter-friend Gauguin, in this exquisite color production. Script by Norman Corwin. Produced by John Houseman. Fine music score by Miklos Rozsa. CinemaScope.▼●

Lust in the Dust (1985) **C-85m.** BOMB D: Paul Bartel. Tab Hunter, Divine, Lainie Kazan, Geoffrey Lewis, Henry Silva, Cesar Romero, Gina Gallego, Woody Strode, Pedro Gonzales-Gonzales. Hunter and Divine descend on a New Mexico hellhole—he (like most of the cast) to locate some buried treasure, she (he?) to fulfill a dream of becoming a saloon singer. Dreadful attempt at camp despite an apparently whimsical casting director; what's to say about a movie where Divine's warbling is the comical highlight? [R]▼●

Lusty Men, The (1952) **113m.** *** D: Nicholas Ray. Susan Hayward, Robert Mitchum, Arthur Kennedy, Arthur Hunnicutt, Frank Faylen. Intelligent, atmospheric rodeo drama, with ex-champ Mitchum becoming mentor of novice Kennedy—and finding himself attracted to Kennedy's no-nonsense wife (Hayward). Solid going most of the way—until that hokey finale. Well-directed by Ray.▼●

Luther (1973-British) **C-112m.** **½ D: Guy Green. Stacy Keach, Patrick Magee, Hugh Griffith, Robert Stephens, Alan Badel, Judi

Dench. Sincere but placid American Film Theatre recreation of John Osborne's play about Martin Luther (Keach), leader of the Protestant Reformation.▼

Luv (1967) **C-95m.** *½ D: Clive Donner. Jack Lemmon, Peter Falk, Elaine May, Eddie Mayehoff, Paul Hartman, Severn Darden. Murray Schisgal's three-character hit play about pseudo-intellectuals was not a natural for the screen anyway, but this version is truly an abomination. The cast tries. Look for a young Harrison Ford. Panavision.▼●

Luxury Liner (1948) **C-98m.** ** D: Richard Whorf. George Brent, Jane Powell, Lauritz Melchior, Frances Gifford, Xavier Cugat. MGM fluff aboard a cruise ship, with Powell singing her heart out.●

Lydia (1941) **104m.** *** D: Julien Duvivier. Merle Oberon, Edna May Oliver, Alan Marshal, Joseph Cotten, Hans Yaray, George Reeves. Sentimental tale of elderly woman (Oberon) meeting her former beaux and recalling their courtship. Remake of Duvivier's own French classic, UN CARNET DE BAL.▼

Lydia Bailey (1952) **C-89m.** **½ D: Jean Negulesco. Dale Robertson, Anne Francis, Luis Van Rooten, Juanita Moore, William Marshall. Handsome but empty version of Kenneth Roberts actioner of 1800s Haiti and revolt against French rulers.

M (1931-German) **99m.** **** D: Fritz Lang. Peter Lorre, Ellen Widmann, Inge Landgut, Gustav Grundgens. Harrowing melodrama about psychotic child murderer brought to justice by Berlin underworld. Riveting and frighteningly contemporary; cinematically dazzling, especially for an early talkie. Lorre's performance is unforgettable. Original 111m. version, available on video, features a different ending: a brief courtroom coda that subtly changes film's final message. Remade in 1951.▼●◗

M (1951) **88m.** *** D: Joseph Losey. David Wayne, Howard da Silva, Luther Adler, Karen Morley, Jorja Curtright, Martin Gabel, Norman Lloyd. Interesting, intelligent re-thinking of Fritz Lang classic set in L.A., with Wayne as child-killer hunted down by community of criminals.

Ma and Pa Kettle Betty MacDonald's best-selling book *The Egg and I* told of the hardships a city girl faced moving with her husband to a rural chicken farm. Among the problems were the incredible local characters, two of whom, Ma and Pa Kettle, were given prime footage in the screen version of THE EGG AND I. Played by veterans Marjorie Main and Percy Kilbride, the "hillbilly" duo (who actually resided in Cape Flattery, Washington) created a hit and became the stars of their own series. The Kettle movies, shot on the Universal back lot for a relative pittance, and seldom praised by critics, earned millions and millions of dollars for the studio. Rambunctious Ma and hesitant Pa's adventures were not exactly out of Noel Coward, but they knew how to please their audience with gags that were tried and true. What's more, Main and Kilbride were absolutely perfect in the leads. Meg Randall and Lori Nelson took turns playing the eldest daughter in the Kettles' tremendous brood (ranging somewhere from twelve to fifteen children). Ray Collins and Barbara Brown were introduced as the snobby Bostonian in-laws the Parkers in MA AND PA KETTLE BACK ON THE FARM, and various actors took turns playing Pa's Indian farmhands, with Oliver Blake winning the best showcase as Geoduck in MA AND PA KETTLE AT HOME (also the series' funniest entry). In 1955 Percy Kilbride left the series. Arthur Hunnicutt played a backwoods brother-in-law in THE KETTLES IN THE OZARKS, and Parker Fennelly (best remembered as Titus Moody) took on the role of Pa in THE KETTLES ON OLD MACDONALD'S FARM, but neither actor caught on, and the series came to an end in 1957. Some Hollywood pundits concluded that such cornball humor had run its course, but in the 1960s a TV series called *The Beverly Hillbillies* came along to prove them wrong.

MA AND PA KETTLE

Ma and Pa Kettle (1949)
Ma and Pa Kettle Go to Town (1950)
Ma and Pa Kettle Back on the Farm (1951)
Ma and Pa Kettle at the Fair (1952)
Ma and Pa Kettle On Vacation (1953)
Ma and Pa Kettle at Home (1954)
Ma and Pa Kettle at Waikiki (1955)
The Kettles in the Ozarks (1956)
The Kettles on Old Macdonald's Farm (1957)

Ma and Pa Kettle (1949) **75m.** **½ D: Charles Lamont. Marjorie Main, Percy Kilbride, Richard Long, Meg Randall, Patricia Alphin, Esther Dale. The Kettles and their fifteen kids are threatened with eviction, but Pa wins a tobacco slogan contest and they all move into a luxurious "home of the future." First in the series of lowbrow bread-and-butter programmers that turned into a box-office bonanza. The futuristic home is a lot of fun. Video title: FURTHER ADVENTURES OF MA AND PA KETTLE.▼●

Ma and Pa Kettle at Home (1954) **81m.** *** D: Charles Lamont. Marjorie Main, Percy Kilbride, Alan Mowbray, Ross Elliot, Alice Kelley, Brett Halsey, Mary Wickes, Irving Bacon, Emory Parnell, Oliver Blake. Sixth and best entry in the series has the Kettles trying to impress an

Eastern magazine editor (Mowbray) in order to win a scholarship prize. One slapstick gag follows another, leading to a wild climactic chase; there's some homespun sentiment, too, as we spend Christmas with the Kettles (and, at last count, fifteen kids).▼

Ma and Pa Kettle at the Fair (1952) **78m.** **½ D: Charles Barton. Marjorie Main, Percy Kilbride, Lori Nelson, James Best, Esther Dale, Russell Simpson, Emory Parnell. Standard entry centering on the Kettles' efforts to win money at a country fair (with Ma's cooking) to send their daughter to college. Funny finale features Pa in a hectic horse race.▼

Ma and Pa Kettle at Waikiki (1955) **79m.** ** D: Lee Sholem. Marjorie Main, Percy Kilbride, Lori Nelson, Byron Palmer, Loring Smith, Lowell Gilmore, Mabel Albertson, Esther Dale, Ida Moore. To help out a relative, the Kettles travel to Hawaii where Pa immediately blows up the family pineapple factory and gets himself kidnaped. Pretty weak. Kilbride's last film.▼

Ma and Pa Kettle Back on the Farm (1951) **80m.** ** D: Edward Sedgwick. Marjorie Main, Percy Kilbride, Richard Long, Meg Randall, Barbara Brown, Ray Collins, Emory Parnell, Peter Leeds. The Kettles have to contend with their snobby in-laws while dealing with crooks who think there are uranium deposits on their land. Typical cornball entry.▼

Ma and Pa Kettle Go to Town (1950) **70m.** **½ D: Charles Lamont. Marjorie Main, Percy Kilbride, Richard Long, Meg Randall, Gregg Martell, Charles McGraw, Jim Backus, Elliott Lewis, Bert Freed, Hal March. The Kettles get mixed up with crooks on a trip to New York, and their country smarts naturally subdue the city slickers. One of the series' best.▼

Ma and Pa Kettle On Vacation (1953) **75m.** ** D: Charles Lamont. Percy Kilbride, Marjorie Main, Ray Collins, Bodil Miller, Sig Ruman, Barbara Brown, Oliver Blake, Teddy Hart. The formula's wearing thin, as Ma and Pa travel to Paris as the guests of the Parkers and get mixed up with spies and femmes fatales. Look fast for a young Rita Moreno.▼

Ma Barker's Killer Brood (1960) **82m.** ** D: Bill Karn. Lurene Tuttle, Tris Coffin, Paul Dubov, Nelson Leigh. Energetic performance by Tuttle in lead role and occasional bursts of gunplay hoist this programmer gangster yarn above tedium.▼

Mac (1992) **C-118m.** *** D: John Turturro. John Turturro, Michael Badalucco, Carl Capotorto, Katherine Borowitz, John Amos, Olek Krupa, Ellen Barkin, Joe Paparone. Rock-solid tale of a trio of Italian-American brothers in Queens, New York, during the mid-1950s. The eldest (Turturro), a carpenter, is fiercely determined to realize his American Dream: his boss is a stubborn, penny-pinching contractor, so he starts up his own construction company, convinced that he can build superior houses and be a better boss. Crammed with offbeat humor, but most refreshing as a sincere depiction of the lives and struggles of blue-collar Americans. Turturro's directorial debut; he coscripted with Brandon Cole. The film is dedicated to Turturro's father, a carpenter, and inspired by the senior Turturro's life. [R]▼●

Macabra SEE: **Demonoid, Messenger of Death**

Macabre (1958) **73m.** ** D: William Castle. William Prince, Jim Backus, Christine White, Jacqueline Scott. Weird goings-on in small town when doctor's wife and her sister are murdered. Film promises much, delivers little. Famous for Castle's gimmick of handing out policies insuring moviegoers for $1,000 against death by fright.

Mac and Me (1988) **C-93m.** *½ D: Stewart Raffill. Christine Ebersole, Jonathan Ward, Katrina Caspary, Lauren Stanley, Jade Calegory. Slight E.T. clone about Mac, an outer space creature, and his plight in suburban L.A. More a TV commercial than a movie: There's a production number set in a McDonald's, and the alien survives by sipping Coca-Cola. [PG]▼●

Macao (1952) **80m.** ** D: Josef von Sternberg. Robert Mitchum, Jane Russell, William Bendix, Gloria Grahame, Thomas Gomez, Philip Ahn. Flat yarn supposedly set in murky title port, with Russell a singer and Mitchum the action-seeking man she loves.▼●

Macaroni (1985-Italian) **C-104m.** **½ D: Ettore Scola. Jack Lemmon, Marcello Mastroianni, Daria Nicolodi, Isa Danieli, Maria Luisa Saniella. Uptight American businessman goes to Naples and finds some unfinished personal business left over from his last visit—when he was an amorous soldier during WW2. Two of the world's most endearing actors try to keep this souffle from falling, and almost succeed. [PG]▼●

MacArthur (1977) **C-130m.** *** D: Joseph Sargent. Gregory Peck, Dan O'Herlihy, Ed Flanders, Sandy Kenyon, Dick O'Neill, Marj Dusay, Art Fleming. Solid, absorbing saga of flamboyant military chief during WW2 and Korean War. Peck is excellent but film doesn't pack the punch of PATTON. Originally trade-screened at 144m. then cut for release. [PG]▼●

MacArthur's Children (1985-Japanese) **C-115m.** ***½ D: Masahiro Shinoda. Masako Natsume, Shima Iwashita, Hiromi Go, Takaya Yamauchi, Yoshiyuka Omori, Shiori Sakura, Juzo Itami. Extremely poignant, proud, loving remembrance of life in a small Japanese fishing village immediately following that nation's defeat in WW2. Most effectively delineated are the Japanese reaction to losing the war, as well

as the cultural effects of the American occupation—from styles of dress to baseball. [PG]▼●
Macbeth (1948) **89m.** *** D: Orson Welles. Orson Welles, Jeanette Nolan, Dan O'Herlihy, Edgar Barrier, Roddy McDowall, Robert Coote, Erskine Sanford, Alan Napier, Peggy Webber, John Dierkes. Welles brought the Bard to Republic Pictures with this moody, well-done adaptation, filmed entirely on bizarre interiors (which deliberately emphasize its theatricality). Most revival houses now show Welles' original version, which runs 105m. and has the actors speaking with authentic Scot accents. ▼●
Macbeth (1971-British) **C-140m.** ***½ D: Roman Polanski. Jon Finch, Francesca Annis, Martin Shaw, Nicholas Selby, John Stride, Stephan Chase. Gripping, atmospheric, and extremely violent recreation of Shakespeare tragedy of young Scots nobleman lusting for power, driven onward by crazed wife and prophecies. Great example of film storytelling, thanks to excellent direction. Todd-AO 35. [R]▼●
Machine, The (1994-French-German) **C-96m.** *** D: François Dupeyron. Gérard Depardieu, Nathalie Baye, Didier Bourdon, Natalia Woerner, Erwan Baynaud, Marc Andreoni, Julie Depardieu. Scientist Depardieu's experiment works better than he expected, and he switches minds with a psychotic killer of women. Suspenseful, well-plotted Gallic variation on old themes; good direction, better acting. From the novel *La Machine* by Rene Belletto.▼
Machine-Gun Kelly (1958) **80m.** **½ D: Roger Corman. Charles Bronson, Susan Cabot, Barboura Morris, Morey Amsterdam, Wally Campo, Jack Lambert, Connie Gilchrist. With typical efficiency, Corman gives this gangster chronicle pacing and more than passing interest. Bronson is fine in title role. Superama.▼
Machine Gun McCain (1968-Italian) **C-94m.** ** D: Giuliano Montaldo. John Cassavetes, Britt Ekland, Peter Falk, Gabriele Ferzetti, Salvo Randone, Gena Rowlands. Junk about just-released gangster who tries to rob Mafia-controlled casino in Las Vegas. Techniscope.[PG]
Machismo SEE: **Cry Blood Apache**
Macho Callahan (1970) **C-99m.** **½ D: Bernard Kowalski. David Janssen, Lee J. Cobb, Jean Seberg, David Carradine, Pedro Armendariz, Jr., James Booth, Richard Anderson. Janssen miscast as Civil War P.O.W.-escapee, out to kill man who got him arrested in first place; will recognize latter by his yellow shoes. Interesting view of West, but dialogue often unbelievable. Panavision. [R]▼
Maciste—The Mighty (1960-Italian) **C-87m.** ** D: Carlo Campogalliani. Mark Forest, Chelo Alonso, Angelo Zanolli, Federica Ranchi. Forest in title role tries to instill some animation in wooden tale of old Egypt and the barbaric Persians. Totalscope.
Mack, The (1973) **C-110m.** ** D: Michael Campus. Max Julien, Don Gordon, Richard Pryor, Carol Speed, Roger E. Mosley, William C. Watson. Extremely violent melodrama about a black pimp in Oakland was one of the most popular blaxploitation films; strange, because it's utterly ordinary. [R]▼●
Mackenna's Gold (1969) **C-128m.** **½ D: J. Lee Thompson. Gregory Peck, Omar Sharif, Telly Savalas, Camilla Sparv, Keenan Wynn, Julie Newmar, Lee J. Cobb, Raymond Massey, Burgess Meredith, Anthony Quayle, Edward G. Robinson, Eli Wallach, Ted Cassidy, Eduardo Ciannelli. Overblown adventure saga about search for lost canyon of gold, with doublecrosses, conflicts, mysterious clues, etc. Super cast saddled with ludicrous script, made worse by pre-release tampering that cut extremely long film, leaving abrupt denouement, several loose ends. Fine Quincy Jones score; produced by Carl Foreman (who also scripted) and Dimitri Tiomkin. Narrated by Victor Jory. Super Panavision 70. [M]▼●
Mackintosh and T.J. (1975) **C-96m.** ** D: Marvin J. Chomsky. Roy Rogers, Clay O'Brien, Billy Green Bush, Andrew Robinson, Joan Hackett. Old-fashioned modern-day Western about an aging ranch hand and a young boy. Those charmed by idea of Roy Rogers' comeback will want to see it; others beware. Music by Waylon Jennings. [PG]
Mackintosh Man, The (1973) **C-105m.** **½ D: John Huston. Paul Newman, Dominique Sanda, James Mason, Harry Andrews, Ian Bannen, Nigel Patrick, Michael Hordern. Well-made espionage thriller has only one problem: it's all been done before. Filmed in Ireland, England, and Malta; screenplay credited to Walter Hill. [PG]▼
Mack the Knife (1989) **C-120m.** BOMB D: Menahem Golan. Raul Julia, Richard Harris, Julia Migenes, Roger Daltrey, Julie Walters, Rachel Robertson, Clive Revill. Name cast over-emotes in this ill-conceived, overly stylized version of *The Threepenny Opera.* More a filmed stage revue than anything else, and not a very good one; Golan adapted the script, and completely misses the spirit of the original. This one blots the memory of Brecht and Weill (not to mention Bobby Darin). [PG-13]▼●
Macomber Affair, The (1947) **89m.** ***½ D: Zoltan Korda. Gregory Peck, Joan Bennett, Robert Preston, Reginald Denny, Carl Harbord. Penetrating, intelligent filmization of Hemingway story about conflicts that develop when hunter Peck takes married couple (Preston, Bennett) on safari. Bristling performances help make this one of the most vivid screen adaptations of a

Hemingway work. Based on "The Short Happy Life of Francis Macomber"; scripted by Casey Robinson and Seymour Bennett.
Macon County Line (1974) **C-89m.** **½ D: Richard Compton. Alan Vint, Cheryl Waters, Max Baer, Jr., Jesse Vint, Joan Blackman, Geoffrey Lewis, James Gammon, Leif Garrett. Bloody thriller based on fact, set in 1954 Georgia; three outsiders are pursued for a murder they didn't commit. Baer produced and wrote it; Bobbie Gentry sings her own theme song. Followed by RETURN TO MACON COUNTY. [R]▼◗
Macumba Love (1960) **C-86m.** *½ D: Douglas Fowley. Walter Reed, Ziva Rodann, William Wellman, Jr., June Wilkinson. Trivia of author delving into voodoo practices in South America.▼
Mad About Men (1954-British) **C-90m.** ** D: Ralph Thomas. Glynis Johns, Donald Sinden, Anne Crawford, Margaret Rutherford, Dora Bryan, Noel Purcell. Mermaid and young woman look-alike change places in this pleasant fantasy, and love takes its course. Sequel to MIRANDA.
Mad About Music (1938) **98m.** *** D: Norman Taurog. Deanna Durbin, Herbert Marshall, Gail Patrick, Arthur Treacher, Helen Parrish, Marcia Mae Jones, William Frawley. Excellent Durbin vehicle; busy mother Patrick leaves Deanna in Swiss girls' school, where she pretends Marshall is her father. Holds up better than remake TOY TIGER.▼
Madadayo (1993-Japanese) **C-134m.** *** D: Akira Kurosawa. Tatsuo Matsumura, Kyoko Kagawa, Hisashi Igawa, George Tokoro. Kurosawa's final film, made when he was 83, is a gentle and contemplative series of vignettes depicting two decades in the life of a revered professor—his retirement in 1943, the bombing of his house during an air raid, building a new home, finding and losing a stray cat, etc.—all centered around a string of birthday parties thrown for him by his ex-students at which he shouts "madadayo!" ("not yet!") to indicate he's not ready to be taken by death. A warmhearted and life-affirming finale to the career of a cinematic master.
Mad Adventures of "Rabbi" Jacob, The (1974-French) **C-96m.** *** D: Gerard Oury. Louis De Funes, Suzy Delair, Marcel Dalio, Claude Giraud, Claude Pieplu. Broad slapstick comedy about hotheaded, bigoted businessman who—for complicated reasons—is forced to disguise himself as a rabbi. Uneven but often quite funny, with echoes of silent-screen humor. [G]
Madame (1961-French) **C-104m.** **½ D: Christian-Jaque. Sophia Loren, Robert Hossein, Julien Bertheau, Marina Berti. Uninspired remake of MADAME SANS-GENE (filmed in 1925) with Loren, who uses looks and wits to rise from laundress to nobility in Napoleonic France. Super Technirama 70.
Madame Bovary (1934-French) **102m.** ** D: Jean Renoir. Valentine Tessier, Pierre Renoir, Max Dearly, Daniel Lecourtois, Fernand Fabre, Alice Tissot, Helena Manson. Uneven, unsatisfying version of the oft-filmed Flaubert story, about the romantic, ill-fated title character. Originally three hours long, Renoir (who also scripted) was forced to drastically edit it. While the first version may have been more compelling than the existing film, the fact remains that Tessier is miscast as Emma Bovary.▼
Madame Bovary (1949) **115m.** ***½ D: Vincente Minnelli. Jennifer Jones, James Mason, Van Heflin, Louis Jourdan, Christopher Kent (Alf Kjellin), Gene Lockhart, Gladys Cooper, George Zucco, Henry (Harry) Morgan. Gustave Flaubert's 19th-century heroine sacrifices her husband and their security for love, meets a horrible end. Once-controversial adaptation looks better every year, despite an odd "framing" device involving Flaubert's morals trial. Justifiably celebrated ball sequence is among the greatest set pieces of Minnelli's—or anyone else's—career. Screenplay by Robert Ardrey. Previously filmed in 1932 (as UNHOLY LOVE) and 1934 (in France, by Jean Renoir); remade in France in 1991.▼●
Madame Bovary (1991-French) **C-130m.** ** D: Claude Chabrol. Isabelle Huppert, Jean-Francois Balmer, Christopher Malavoy, Jean Yanne, Lucas Belvaux, Jean-Claude Bouilland. Huppert's persona is far too chilly to convey the passion of Emma Bovary in this faithful but exhaustingly dull rendering of Flaubert's classic. Vincente Minnelli's version may turn the novel upside-down, but it's a far more significant movie. Even viewers with unusually refined auteurist radar would have a tough time pegging this as a Chabrol. [PG-13] ▼●
Madame Butterfly (1932) **86m.** **½ D: Marion Gering. Sylvia Sidney, Cary Grant, Charlie Ruggles, Irving Pichel, Helen Jerome Eddy. Puccini opera (minus music) of Oriental woman in love with American (Grant) is sensitive, tragic romance, dated but well handled.
Madame Curie (1943) **124m.** *** D: Mervyn LeRoy. Greer Garson, Walter Pidgeon, Henry Travers, Albert Basserman, Robert Walker, C. Aubrey Smith. Despite stretches of plodding footage, bio of famed female scientist is generally excellent. Garson and Pidgeon team well, as usual.▼●
Madame Racketeer (1932) **71m.** **½ D: Alexander Hall, Henry Wagstaff Gribble. Alison Skipworth, Richard Bennett, George Raft, Evalyn Knapp, Gertrude Messinger, J. Farrell MacDonald, Robert McWade. Entertaining vehicle for Skip-

worth as con-woman supreme known as The Countess, who reveals a heart of gold when she encounters her two grown daughters for the first time.

Madame Rosa (1977-French) **C-105m.** **½ D: Moshe Mizrahi. Simone Signoret, Samy Ben Youb, Claude Dauphin, Gabriel Jabbour, Michal Bat-Adam, Costa-Gavras. Signoret's magnetic performance gives substance to interesting but aimless film about an aging madam who earns her keep sheltering prostitutes' children. Won Best Foreign Film Oscar. [PG]▼

Madame Sin (1972) **C-90m. TVM** D: David Greene. Robert Wagner, Bette Davis, Catherine Schell, Paul Maxwell, Denholm Elliott, Gordon Jackson. Evil genius (Davis) uses former C.I.A. agent as pawn for control of Polaris submarine. Elaborate production has Bad beating out Good at end; with Bette in charge, it's well worth seeing. Above average.▼

Madame Sousatzka (1988) **C-122m.** *** D: John Schlesinger. Shirley MacLaine, Navin Chowdhry, Peggy Ashcroft, Twiggy, Shabana Azmi, Leigh Lawson, Geoffrey Bayldon, Lee Montague. Eccentric, reclusive London piano teacher (MacLaine, wearing clanky jewelry and piles of makeup) implores her students to cultivate their artistic spirit and bring passion to their music. She meets her match in her star pupil, a 15-year-old boy of Indian heritage. Beautifully made film succeeds largely due to the strong emotions being played out, and to the superb supporting cast (especially young Chowdhry and mother Azmi—the latter a major star in her native India). [PG-13]▼●

Madame X (1929) **90m.** ** D: Lionel Barrymore. Ruth Chatterton, Lewis Stone, Raymond Hackett, Holmes Herbert, Eugenie Besserer, Sidney Toler, Ullrich Haupt. Leaden weeper, filmed previously in 1906, 1916, and 1920, about cold, cruel husband Stone forcing wife Chatterton onto the streets. Their son comes of age believing she's dead . . . and then gets to defend her on a murder charge. A curio at best; the remakes are better. Plays on TV as ABSINTHE. ●

Madame X (1937) **71m.** **½ D: Sam Wood. Gladys George, John Beal, Warren William, Reginald Owen, William Henry, Henry Daniell, Phillip Reed, Ruth Hussey. Alexandre Bisson's stalwart soap opera gets polished MGM treatment and a fine performance by Gladys George as the woman whose ultimate sacrifice is never detected by her son. Goes astray toward the end (with Beal a bit much), but worth a look.▼

Madame X (1966) **C-100m.** **½ D: David Lowell Rich. Lana Turner, John Forsythe, Constance Bennett, Ricardo Montalban, Burgess Meredith, Keir Dullea, Virginia Grey. Plush remake of perennial soaper of attorney defending a woman accused of murder, not knowing it's his mother. Fine cast and varied backgrounds bolster Turner's pivotal performance. Constance Bennett's last film.▼

Madame X (1981) **C-100m. TVM** D: Robert Ellis Miller. Tuesday Weld, Len Cariou, Eleanor Parker, Robert Hooks, Jerry Stiller, Jeremy Brett, Martina Deignan, Robin Strand, Tom Tully. Hard to believe this hardy soap opera would show up again, but here it is, updated somewhat by writer Edward Anhalt (who also appears in the film as a judge). Average.

Madam Satan (1930) **115m.** *** D: Cecil B. DeMille. Kay Johnson, Reginald Denny, Roland Young, Lillian Roth, Elsa Peterson, Tyler Brooke. Bizarre semimusical extravaganza with placid Johnson posing as wicked Madam Satan to win back errant husband Denny. Mad party scene on Zeppelin is certainly an eye-popper.▼

Mad at the World (1955) **72m.** *½ D: Harry Essex. Frank Lovejoy, Keefe Brasselle, Cathy O'Donnell, Karen Sharpe. Pointless study of Brasselle seeking vengeance on teenage slum gang who harmed his baby; Lovejoy is detective on case.

Mad Bomber, The (1972) **C-95m.** ** D: Bert I. Gordon. Vince Edwards, Chuck Connors, Neville Brand, Hank Brandt, Cristina Hart. Hardnosed cop Edwards relentlessly dogs paranoid villain Connors who's out to waste those he imagines have wronged him. Aka THE POLICE CONNECTION. [R]▼

Mad Checkmate SEE: **It's Your Move**

Mädchen in Uniform SEE: **Mäedchen in Uniform** (1931)

Mad City (1997) **C-114m.** ** D: Costa-Gavras. John Travolta, Dustin Hoffman, Alan Alda, Mia Kirshner, William Atherton, Raymond J. Barry, Ted Levine, Robert Prosky, Blythe Danner. Recently fired museum guard Travolta tries to get his job back at gunpoint, accidentally taking some children hostage and giving disgraced TV newsman Hoffman a chance to get back into the big time. Well-crafted movie with a knockout performance by Hoffman is unfortunately routine and obvious. Does anyone still find it outrageous that a TV newsman might exploit his subjects for self-gain? Bill Nunn appears unbilled. Super 35. [PG-13]▼●◗

Maddening, The (1996) **C-97m.** *½ D: Danny Huston. Burt Reynolds, Angie Dickinson, Mia Sara, Brian Wimmer, Josh Mostel, William Hickey, Kayla Buglewics, Candace Hutson. Addled Angie and brutal Burt hold Mia and her young daughter captive in backwoods Florida, while her estranged husband searches for her. Over-the-top Southern gothic saddled with a familiar, predictable plot and uneven acting. Filmed in 1994. [R]▼●

Mad Doctor, The (1941) **90m.** ** D: Tim Whelan. Basil Rathbone, Ellen Drew, John Howard, Barbara Jo Allen (Vera Vague), Ralph Morgan, Martin Kosleck. Not a horror film, but a polished B about suave medico who marries women and murders them for their money. Interesting for a while, but misses the mark.

Mad Doctor of Blood Island (1969) **C-85m.** BOMB D: Gerry DeLeon, Eddie Romero. John Ashley, Angelique Pettyjohn, Ronald Peary, Alicia Alonzo. Newcomers to remote tropical island quickly discover why it has a reputation for evil. It's a tossup which is worse: the dialogue, the music, or the hyperactive zoom lens. Filmed in Philippines. Retitled TOMB OF THE LIVING DEAD; followed by a sequel(!), BEAST OF BLOOD. [M/PG]▼

Mad Doctor of Market Street, The (1942) **61m.** *½ D: Joseph H. Lewis. Lionel Atwill, Una Merkel, Claire Dodd, Nat Pendleton, Anne Nagel. Mini-chiller from Universal Pictures about insane scientist on Pacific isle using natives for strange experiments.

Mad Dog SEE: **Mad Dog Morgan**

Mad Dog and Glory (1993) **C-96m.** *** D: John McNaughton. Robert De Niro, Uma Thurman, Bill Murray, Kathy Baker, David Caruso, Mike Starr, Tom Towles, J. J. Johnston, Richard Belzer. Offbeat concoction from street-smart writer Richard Price, about a nerdy cop (De Niro) who does a favor for a Chicago hood (Murray), and is repaid by having Thurman delivered to him as a "present" for one week. Though it's low-key, and doesn't quite hit the bull's-eye, it's still oddly endearing. Coproduced by Price, Martin Scorsese, and Barbara De Fina. [R]▼●◗

Mad Dog Coll (1961) **86m.** *½ D: Burt Balaban. John Davis Chandler, Brooke Hayward, Kay Doubleday, Jerry Orbach, Telly Savalas. Minor crime melodrama about the career of Vincent "Mad Dog" Coll, the most vicious killer in all gangland. Hayward is the daughter of Margaret Sullavan, and the author of *Haywire*; that's Vincent Gardenia as Dutch Schultz, Gene Hackman (in his film debut) as a cop.

Mad Dog Morgan (1976-Australian) **C-102m.** *** D: Philippe Mora. Dennis Hopper, Jack Thompson, David Gulpilil, Frank Thring, Michael Pate. Hopper gives lively performance as legendary Australian outlaw of the 1800s in this moody, well-made, but extremely violent film; TV print runs 93m. Retitled: MAD DOG. Panavision. [R]▼

Mad Dogs and Englishmen SEE: **Joe Cocker: Mad Dogs and Englishmen**

Mad Dog Time (1996) **C-93m.** ** D: Larry Bishop. Ellen Barkin, Gabriel Byrne, Richard Dreyfuss, Jeff Goldblum, Diane Lane, Gregory Hines, Kyle MacLachlan, Burt Reynolds, Christopher Jones, Henry Silva, Michael J. Pollard, Billy Idol, Billy Drago, Paul Anka, Rob Reiner, Richard Pryor, Angie Everhart. On another, but almost identical, Earth, gangsters rule supreme. Sleek Goldblum is continually challenged by upstarts, primarily MacLachlan, but his real rival is big boss Dreyfuss, fresh out of prison. Dry and intelligent, but slow and ostentatiously stylish. Goldblum is sensational, however. Written by the director, the son of Joey Bishop, who appears unbilled. Retitled TRIGGER HAPPY. [R]▼●

Made For Each Other (1939) **93m.** *** D: John Cromwell. Carole Lombard, James Stewart, Charles Coburn, Lucile Watson, Alma Kruger, Esther Dale, Ward Bond, Louise Beavers. First-rate soaper of struggling young marrieds Stewart and Lombard battling illness, lack of money, Stewart's meddling mother Watson. Fine acting makes this all work. Also shown in computer-colored version.▼◗

Made for Each Other (1971) **C-107m.** *** D: Robert B. Bean. Renee Taylor, Joseph Bologna, Paul Sorvino, Olympia Dukakis. Exceptionally funny tale of two oddball types who meet at encounter session and fall in love. Original screenplay by Taylor and Bologna. [PG]◗

Made in America (1993) **C-110m.** ** D: Richard Benjamin. Whoopi Goldberg, Ted Danson, Will Smith, Nia Long, Paul Rodriguez, Jennifer Tilly, Peggy Rea, Clyde Kusatsu, Lu Leonard. Fiercely proud, independent Goldberg is forced to reveal to her teenage daughter that she was conceived from a sperm bank. The daughter then learns that her "father" is a blowhard car salesman—who's white. Dishearteningly stupid movie based on a clever premise. The two ladies trapped in Whoopi's store, by the way, are Frances Bergen (Candice's mother) and '50s TV leading lady Phyllis Avery. [PG-13]▼●◗

Made in Heaven (1987) **C-103m.** ** D: Alan Rudolph. Timothy Hutton, Kelly McGillis, Maureen Stapleton, Don Murray, Marj Dusay, Ray Gideon, Amanda Plummer, Mare Winningham, Timothy Daly. Young man dies and goes to heaven, where he meets a yet-unborn beauty and falls in love. The Big Question: how long will it take for them to meet, in their new identities on earth, and realize that they were "made for each other"? Potentially sweet fantasy-romance is undermined by too many kinky touches and inside-joke cameos (Debra Winger, in drag, plays Hutton's guardian angel). This is apparently director Rudolph's idea of a mainstream Hollywood movie. Among the other cameos: Neil Young, Tom Petty, Ellen Barkin, Ric Ocasek, David Rasche, Tom Robbins, Gary Larson. [PG]▼●

Made in Italy (1967-Italian-French) **101m.** **½ D: Nanni Loy. Virna Lisi, Anna Magnani, Sylva Koscina, Walter Chiari,

Lea Massari, Alberto Sordi, Jean Sorel, Catherine Spaak. Enjoyable collage of short vignettes about natives, tourists, sophisticates, laborers and all others in Italy. Episodic, of course, but well done. Techniscope.

Made in Paris (1966) **C-101m.** **½ D: Boris Sagal. Ann-Margret, Louis Jourdan, Richard Crenna, Edie Adams, Chad Everett. Witless, unpolished shenanigans of Ann-Margret, fashion designer in France, falling for Jourdan. Panavision.

Madeleine (1950-British) **101m.** **½ D: David Lean. Ann Todd, Leslie Banks, Elizabeth Sellars, Ivor Barnard. Superior cast improves oft-told drama of woman accused of murdering her lover. A vehicle for Lean's then wife, Ann Todd, and one of the filmmaker's few disappointments. Retitled: STRANGE CASE OF MADELEINE.▼

Madeleine (1958-German) **86m.** *½ D: Kurt Meisel. Eva Bartok, Sabina Sesselmann, Ilse Steppat, Alexander Kerst. Unsensational study of prostitutes, with a witless plot of Bartok trying to shed her shady past.

Madeline (1998) **C-90m.** *** D: Daisy von Scherler Mayer. Frances McDormand, Hatty Jones, Nigel Hawthorne, Ben Daniels, Stéphane Audran. Genteel adaptation of Ludwig Bemelmans' beloved children's books about a mischievous orphan girl and the wise nun, Miss Clavel (McDormand), who looks after her and her classmates. Combining elements from several stories with new plot devices, the film captures the spirit of the books and benefits from location filming in Paris. Too bland for older children—and, most likely, their parents—but just right for young ones. [PG] ▼●◗

Mademoiselle (1966-British-French) **103m.** ** D: Tony Richardson. Jeanne Moreau, Ettore Manni, Keith Skinner, Umberto Orsini, Jane Berretta, Mony Rey. Ponderous, sometimes hilariously pretentious film written by Jean Genet, about a sexually repressed schoolteacher in a small French village who secretly poisons animals, sets fires and tries to destroy an Italian woodcutter whom she can't seduce. Woeful foray into arty s&m was shot in both French and English-language versions. Panavision.

Mademoiselle Fifi (1944) **69m.** **½ D: Robert Wise. Simone Simon, John Emery, Kurt Kreuger, Alan Napier, Jason Robards, Sr., Helen Freeman. A laundress reveals more integrity and patriotic spirit than her condescending fellow passengers on an eventful coach ride during the Franco-Prussian war. Uneven Val Lewton production (with allegorical implications about WW2), adapted from two Guy de Maupassant stories.▼●

Mademoiselle Striptease SEE: **Please! Mr. Balzac**

Mad Executioners, The (1963-German) **94m.** ** D: Edwin Zbonek. Wolfgang Preiss, Harry Riebauer, Rudolph Fernau, Chris Howland. Muddled Edgar Wallace-ish suspenser about Scotland Yard inspector setting up his own court of justice to execute criminals. Ultrascope.▼

Mad Genius, The (1931) **81m.** *** D: Michael Curtiz. John Barrymore, Marian Marsh, Donald Cook, Carmel Myers, Charles Butterworth, Mae Madison, Frankie Darro, Luis Alberni, Boris Karloff. Followup to SVENGALI has Barrymore a deranged entrepreneur who lives vicariously through Cook's dancing career. Bizarre, entertaining film with hilarious Butterworth as Barrymore's crony, Alberni as a dope fiend. Karloff has small role near the beginning as the sadistic father.

Mad Ghoul, The (1943) **65m.** **½ D: James Hogan. David Bruce, Evelyn Ankers, George Zucco, Turhan Bey, Charles McGraw, Robert Armstrong, Milburn Stone, Rose Hobart. Strong cast buoys grim story of scientist and his strange life-preserving methods. ▼

Madhouse (1974-British) **C-89m.** *** D: Jim Clark. Vincent Price, Peter Cushing, Robert Quarry, Adrienne Corri, Natasha Payne, Linda Hayden. Price plays horror-film actor making a TV comeback after a long mental breakdown—until he's implicated in a series of grisly homicides. Good, if somewhat unimaginative, adaptation of Angus Hall novel *Devilday*. [PG]▼

Madhouse (1990) **C-90m.** *½ D: Tom Ropelewski. John Larroquette, Kirstie Alley, Alison LaPlaca, John Diehl, Jessica Lundy, Bradley Gregg, Dennis Miller, Robert Ginty. Larroquette and Alley find themselves unable to enjoy their new home when unwanted house guests drop in and *never* leave. Gags are drawn out endlessly; though Larroquette is a talented farceur, he can't sustain the whole film. Humor here would never pass muster on the stars' later TV series. [PG-13]▼●

Madhouse Mansion (1974-British) **C-86m.** **½ D: Stephen Weeks. Marianne Faithfull, Leigh Lawson, Anthony Bate, Larry Dann, Sally Grace, Penelope Keith, Vivian Mackerell, Murray Melvin, Barbara Shelley. Bizarre, sometimes effective chiller about affable chap Dann, who with a couple of mysterious college acquaintances spends a holiday in a spooky old house that seems to be caught in a time warp. Originally titled GHOST STORY. ▼

Madigan (1968) **C-101m.** ***½ D: Donald Siegel. Richard Widmark, Henry Fonda, Harry Guardino, Inger Stevens, James Whitmore, Susan Clark, Michael Dunn, Sheree North. Excellent, unpretentious film blends day-to-day problems of detective Madigan (Widmark) with endless dilemmas facing police commissioner Fonda. Shot largely on location in N.Y.C.; fine work by Guardino, Whitmore, and supporting cast. Adapted as TV series. Techniscope.▼●◗

Madigan's Million (1968) **C-86m.** BOMB D: Stanley Prager. Dustin Hoffman, Elsa Martinelli, Cesar Romero. Pre-GRADUATE Hoffman is caught in amateurish movie released to capitalize on later success; he plays bumbling Treasury agent sent to Italy to recover money stolen by recently murdered gangster Romero. Inept. [G]▼

Madison Avenue (1962) **94m.** ★★½ D: H. Bruce Humberstone. Dana Andrews, Eleanor Parker, Jeanne Crain, Eddie Albert, Howard St. John, Henry Daniell. Tightly produced programmer centering on machinations in N.Y.C.'s advertising jungle. CinemaScope.

Mad Little Island (1957-British) **C-94m.** ★★½ D: Michael Relph. Jeannie Carson, Donald Sinden, Roland Culver, Noel Purcell, Ian Hunter, Duncan MacRae, Catherine Lacey, Jean Cadell, Gordon Jackson. Sequel to TIGHT LITTLE ISLAND finds that little Scottish isle's tranquility disturbed again, this time by imminent installation of missile base. Not up to its predecessor, but on its own terms, decent enough. Original title: ROCKETS GALORE!

Mad Love (1935) **70m.** ★★★ D: Karl Freund. Peter Lorre, Frances Drake, Colin Clive, Isabel Jewell, Ted Healy, Sara Haden, Edward Brophy, Keye Luke. Famous *Hands of Orlac* story refitted for Lorre as mad doctor in love with married Drake. He agrees to operate on her pianist husband's injured hands, with disastrous results. Stylishly directed by legendary cameraman Freund; only debit is unwelcome comedy relief by Healy.▼●

Mad Love (1995) **C-95m.** ★½ D: Antonia Bird. Chris O'Donnell, Drew Barrymore, Joan Allen, Jude Ciccolella, Kevin Dunn, Liev Schreiber, Richard Chaim, Robert Nadir, Amy Sakasitz, Matthew Lillard, T.J. Lowther, Elaine Miles. Teen-lovers-on-the-lam movie with a difference: she's mentally unstable. Attractive young stars do the best they can, but the script peters out and leaves them nothing to work with. A waste of time. By the way, this is not a remake of the 1935 movie; too bad—they could have used a dose of Peter Lorre. [PG-13] ▼●◗

Mad Magazine Presents Up the Academy SEE: **Up the Academy**

Mad Magician, The (1954) **72m.** ★★½ D: John Brahm. Vincent Price, Mary Murphy, Eva Gabor, Patrick O'Neal, John Emery. In this imitation of HOUSE OF WAX (filmed in 3-D, like its predecessor) Price plays a demented magic-act inventor who kills famous magicians and then impersonates them.

Madman (1978-Israeli) **C-92m.** ★½ D: Dan Cohen. Michael Beck, F. Murray Abraham, Alan Feinstein, Sigourney Weaver, Esther Zevko. Bitterly vengeful Soviet-Jewish mental patient joins the Israeli army, intent on killing Russians. Slow, poorly directed film lacks conviction. Casting of Weaver, in her first leading role, and future Oscar-winner Abraham, gives this film its only distinction. [R]▼

Mad Max (1979-Australian) **C-93m.** ★★★½ D: George Miller. Mel Gibson, Joanne Samuel, Hugh Keays-Byrne, Steve Bisley, Tim Burns, Roger Ward. In the desolate near-future, the police have their hands full keeping roads safe from suicidally daring drivers and roving gangs. Top cop Gibson tires and quits, but when his wife and child are murdered by vicious cyclists, he embarks on high-speed revenge. Weird atmosphere and characters combine with amazing stunt work in this remarkable action film. Thrown away by its U.S. distributor (which also redubbed it with American voices), later found its audience in the wake of successful sequel. Todd-AO 35. [R]▼●◗

Mad Max 2 SEE: **Road Warrior, The**

Mad Max Beyond Thunderdome (1985-Australian) **C-106m.** ★★½ D: George Miller, George Ogilvie. Mel Gibson, Tina Turner, Angelo Rossitto, Helen Buday, Rod Zuanic, Frank Thring, Angry Anderson. In the desolate future Mad Max comes upon Turner's cutthroat city of Bartertown, survives a battle-to-the-death in Roman-style Thunderdome arena, and is exiled to the desert, where he's rescued by tribe of wild children. Thunderous film has lots of action and stunts, and even some philosophical moments, but lacks the kinetic energy of THE ROAD WARRIOR (MAD MAX 2). Panavision. [PG-13]▼●◗

Madmen of Mandoras SEE: **They Saved Hitler's Brain**

Mad Miss Manton, The (1938) **80m.** ★★½ D: Leigh Jason. Barbara Stanwyck, Henry Fonda, Sam Levene, Frances Mercer, Stanley Ridges, Vicki Lester, Whitney Bourne, Hattie McDaniel, Penny Singleton, Grady Sutton. Socialite Stanwyck involves her friends in murder mystery; trivial but enjoyable film, with sleuthing and slapstick combined.▼●

Mad Monster, The (1942) **72m.** ★½ D: Sam Newfield. Johnny Downs, George Zucco, Anne Nagel, Sarah Padden, Glenn Strange, Gordon DeMain. Dull, low-budget mad-scientist thriller drags heavy feet for unintended laughs. Zucco effortlessly steals show as crazed doctor changing man into beast.▼

Mad Monster Party? (1967) **C-94m.** ★★ D: Jules Bass. Voices of Phyllis Diller, Boris Karloff, Gale Garnett, Ethel Ennis. Famous monsters are brought together by Frankenstein, who wants to announce his retirement, in this silly animated kiddie feature.▼

Madness of King George, The (1994-British-U.S.) **C-107m.** ★★★ D: Nicholas Hytner. Nigel Hawthorne, Helen Mirren, Ian Holm, Rupert Everett, Rupert Graves, John Wood, Amanda Donohoe, Julian Rhind-Tutt. In the late 18th century, England's benevolent King George (Hawthorne) suddenly takes ill, and shows signs of mental instability—opening the door for court intrigue and the usurping of the throne by his ne'er-do-well son, the Prince of Wales (Everett). Hawthorne vividly re-creates his stage performance (surrounded by a first-rate cast) in Alan Bennett's adaptation of his witty and intriguing play; Bennett also appears in a cameo near the end as a member of Parliament. First film for theater director Hytner. Oscar winner for Art Direction.▼●

Madonna of the Seven Moons (1946-British) **105m.** *** D: Arthur Crabtree. Phyllis Calvert, Stewart Granger, Patricia Roc, Jean Kent, John Stuart, Peter Glenville. Calvert is pushed in two directions because of strange gypsy curse; she is wife, mother, and mistress at same time. Taut melodrama, may be considered camp in some circles.

Madonna's Secret, The (1946) **79m.** ** D: William Thiele. Francis Lederer, Gail Patrick, Ann Rutherford, Linda Stirling, John Litel. OK whodunit involving hunt for killer of murdered artist's model.

Madonna Truth or Dare SEE: **Truth or Dare**

Madron (1970) **C-93m.** ** D: Jerry Hopper. Richard Boone, Leslie Caron, Paul Smith, Gabi Amrani, Chaim Banai, Avraham Telya. A nun who survived wagon-train massacre and a scowling gunslinger try to elude Apaches on the warpath in this ho-hum Western shot in Israel's Negev Desert. [PG]▼

Mad Room, The (1969) **C-92m.** ** D: Bernard Girard. Stella Stevens, Shelley Winters, James Ward, Carol Cole, Severn Darden, Beverly Garland, Michael Burns. Mild but unexceptional remake of LADIES IN RETIREMENT concerns the skeletons in Stella's closet. Grisly tale has a few shocking scenes. [M]▼

Mad Wednesday SEE: **Sin of Harold Diddlebock, The**

Madwoman of Chaillot, The (1969) **C-132m.** ** D: Bryan Forbes. Katharine Hepburn, Charles Boyer, Claude Dauphin, Edith Evans, John Gavin, Paul Henreid, Oscar Homolka, Margaret Leighton, Giulietta Masina, Nanette Newman, Richard Chamberlain, Yul Brynner, Donald Pleasence, Danny Kaye. Unfortunate misfire, with Hepburn as eccentric woman who refuses to believe the world no longer beautiful. Stellar cast wasted in heavy-handed allegory that just doesn't work; adapted from Jean Giraudoux's play. [G] ▼●

Maedchen in Uniform (1931-German) **98m.** ***½ D: Leontine Sagan. Dorothea Wieck, Hertha Thiele, Emilia Unda, Hedwig Schlichter, Ellen Schwannecke. Winning drama about sensitive student Thiele forming lesbian relationship with teacher Wieck in oppressive girls boarding school. Simply, sympathetically handled by Sagan; this highly acclaimed and once-controversial film was based on a novel written by a woman, Christa Winsloe, who also co-scripted. Beware of edited prints. Title sometimes is listed as MÄDCHEN IN UNIFORM. Remade in 1958.▼

Maedchen in Uniform (1958-German) **C-91m.** **½ D: Geza von Radvanyi. Lilli Palmer, Romy Schneider, Christine Kaufmann, Therese Giehse. Rather talky story of girls' school and one particularly sensitive youngster (Schneider) who is attracted to her teacher (Palmer). Remake of famous 1931 movie is shade above average.

Maestro, The SEE: **Home Movies**

Mafia! SEE: **Jane Austen's Mafia!**

Mafia Princess (1986) **C-100m. TVM** D: Robert Collins. Tony Curtis, Susan Lucci, Kathleen Widdoes, Chuck Shamata, Louie DiBianco. Silver-haired Curtis is terrific as Chicago mob boss Sam Giancana, while Lucci hones her well-established soap opera bitch role as his petulant, self-centered daughter in this adaptation of Antoinette Giancana's best-selling autobiography. Script doesn't quite complement performances, though. Average.▼

Mafu Cage, The (1978) **C-102m.** *½ D: Karen Arthur. Lee Grant, Carol Kane, Will Geer, James Olson. Grant and Kane are sisters in this offbeat, unfocused melodrama of incest, jealousy, and murder. Mafu is Kane's pet orangutan; each protagonist in turn assumes animal's caged, victimized role. Retitled MY SISTER, MY LOVE and THE CAGE. [R]▼

Maggie, The SEE: **High and Dry**

Magic (1978) **C-106m.** ** D: Richard Attenborough. Anthony Hopkins, Ann-Margret, Burgess Meredith, Ed Lauter, Jerry Houser, David Ogden Stiers. Ludicrous thriller about demented ventriloquist Hopkins who's tormented by his dummy—even as he tries to rekindle romance with high-school sweetie Ann-Margret. Wait for a rerun of DEAD OF NIGHT (1945) instead. Screenplay by William Goldman, from his novel. [R]▼●◗

Magic Bow, The (1947-British) **105m.** **½ D: Bernard Knowles. Stewart Granger, Phyllis Calvert, Jean Kent, Dennis Price, Cecil Parker. As usual, music overshadows weak plot in biography of violinist Paganini.▼

Magic Box, The (1951-British) **C-103m.** **** D: John Boulting. Robert Donat, Maria Schell, Margaret Johnston, Robert Beatty; guests Laurence Olivier, Michael Redgrave, Eric Portman, Glynis Johns, Emlyn Williams, Richard Attenborough, Stanley Holloway, Margaret Rutherford, Peter Ustinov, Bessie Love, Cecil Parker, etc. Practically every British star appears in this superb biography of William Friese-Greene, the forgotten inventor of movies. Beautifully done; one scene where Donat perfects the invention, pulling in a cop off the street (Olivier) to see it, is a gem.

Magic Bubble, The SEE: **Unbecoming Age**

Magic Carpet, The (1951) **C-84m.** ** D: Lew Landers. Lucille Ball, John Agar, Patricia Medina, Raymond Burr, George Tobias. Mild costumer that has virtue of Ball as heroine, and little else.

Magic Christian, The (1969-British) **C-93m.** *** D: Joseph McGrath. Peter Sellers, Ringo Starr; guest stars Richard Attenborough, Christopher Lee, Raquel Welch, Laurence Harvey, Yul Brynner, Wilfrid Hyde-White, Spike Milligan, Dennis Price, John Cleese, Graham Chapman, Roman Polanski. In series of wacky schemes, world's wealthiest man and his protégé wreak havoc on society by demonstrating how people will do *anything* for money. Fiendishly funny adaptation of Terry Southern's insane novel, scripted by Southern and McGrath, with contributions from Sellers, Cleese, and Chapman. Some prints run 88m. [M/PG]▼●

Magic Face, The (1951) **89m.** ** D: Frank Tuttle. Luther Adler, Patricia Knight, William L. Shirer, Ilka Windish. Low-key study of impersonator who murders Hitler and assumes his place; Adler rises above material.

Magic Fire (1956) **C-95m.** ** D: William Dieterle. Yvonne De Carlo, Carlos Thompson, Rita Gam, Valentina Cortese, Alan Badel. Uninspired musical biography of 19th-century German composer Richard Wagner.

Magic Flute, The (1974-Swedish) **C-134m.** ***½ D: Ingmar Bergman. Ulric Cold, Josef Kostlinger, Erik Saeden, Birgit Nordin, Irma Urrila, Hakan Hagegard. Lively, intelligent filmization of Mozart's opera of activities surrounding the kidnapping of Urrila, the Queen's daughter, by sorcerer Cold. Shot for Swedish TV, released as a feature in the U.S. [G]▼●◗

Magic Garden of Stanley Sweetheart, The (1970) **C-117m.** *½ D: Leonard Horn. Don Johnson, Linda Gillin, Michael Greer, Dianne Hull, Holly Near, Victoria Racimo. Vapid film from Robert Westbrook's novel about sexual and drug-oriented experiences of aimless college student trying to put his head together. A yawn, except for Greer, and Stanley's underground film "Headless." [R]

Magician, The (1958-Swedish) **102m.** *** D: Ingmar Bergman. Max von Sydow, Ingrid Thulin, Gunnar Bjornstrand, Naima Wifstrand, Bibi Andersson, Erland Josephson. Complex, provocative account of Albert Emanuel Vogler (von Sydow), a 19th-century hypnotist-magician who has studied with Mesmer but finds himself debt-ridden and charged with blasphemy. A thoughtful (and too-long underrated) portrait of a man who is part-faker, part-genius.▼●

Magician of Lublin, The (1979) **C-105m.** *½ D: Menahem Golan. Alan Arkin, Louise Fletcher, Valerie Perrine, Shelley Winters, Lou Jacobi, Maia Danziger, Lisa Whelchel. Turn-of-the-century Jewish magician tries for the big time in stilted, poorly acted version of Isaac Bashevis Singer's Polish-based novel. However, you do get to see Winters destroy a jailhouse even more impressively than Sam Jaffe's elephant did in GUNGA DIN. [R]▼

Magic in the Water (1995-Canadian) **C-98m.** *½ D: Rick Stevenson. Mark Harmon, Harley Jane Kozak, Joshua Jackson, Sarah Wayne, Willie Nark-Orn, Frank Sotonoma Salsedo, Morris Panych. In the laid-back community of Glenorky a number of residents believe there's a monster that lives in the lake; a vacationing family comes to learn there is some "truth" to the myth. All the magic *must* be in the water; there's certainly none on the screen. Routine family film feels like recycled Spielberg. [PG] ▼●

Magic of Lassie, The (1978) **C-100m.** **½ D: Don Chaffey. James Stewart, Lassie, Mickey Rooney, Alice Faye, Stephanie Zimbalist, Pernell Roberts, Michael Sharrett, Mike Mazurki. Stewart is worth watching in this bland remake of LASSIE COME HOME, as grandfather of Zimbalist and Sharrett, who are forced to turn over their beloved Lassie to mean owner Roberts. Songs performed by Pat and Debby Boone, plus Faye and even Stewart. [G]▼

Magic Sword, The (1962) **C-80m.** **½ D: Bert I. Gordon. Basil Rathbone, Estelle Winwood, Gary Lockwood, Anne Helm, Liam Sullivan, Jacques Gallo. Entertaining, often (unintentionally) hilarious adventure. Young knight Lockwood sets out to rescue beautiful princess Helm, who's been kidnapped by evil sorcerer Rathbone. In their better moments, Lockwood and Helm seem like refugees from a Beach Party movie; Rathbone and Winwood offer knowingly hammy performances.▼●

Magic Town (1947) **103m.** *** D: William Wellman. James Stewart, Jane Wyman, Kent Smith, Regis Toomey, Donald Meek. Intriguing satire of pollster Stewart finding perfect average American town, which ruins itself when people are told his discovery. Doesn't always hit bull's-eye but remains engrossing throughout; written by Frank Capra's frequent scripter, Robert Riskin. Also shown in computer-colored version. ▼●

Magic World of Topo Gigio, The (1965-Italian) **C-75m.** *½ D: Luca de Rico. Ermanno Roveri, Ignazio Colnaghi, Frederica Milani, Topo Gigio. Unsuccessful attempt to build a feature-film around the little puppet mouse who scored such success on TV's *Ed Sullivan Show* in the 1960s.

Magnet, The (1951-British) **78m.** *** D: Charles Frend. William Fox, Kay Walsh, Stephen Murray. Disarming study of fun-loving children at play, told intelligently from their own point of view; no phony psychology thrown in. Young William Fox is known today as James Fox.

Magnetic Monster, The (1953) **76m.** **½ D: Curt Siodmak. Richard Carlson, King Donovan, Jean Byron, Byron Foulger. Magnetic isotope is stolen, grows in size and creates havoc; stunning climax features special effects lifted from 1930s German film, GOLD.▼●

Magnificent Ambersons, The (1942) **88m.** **** D: Orson Welles. Tim Holt, Joseph Cotten, Dolores Costello, Anne Baxter, Agnes Moorehead, Ray Collins, Richard Bennett, Erskine Sanford. Brilliant drama from Booth Tarkington novel of family unwilling to change its way of life with the times; mother and son conflict over her lover. Welles' follow-up to CITIZEN KANE is equally exciting in its own way, though film was taken out of his hands, recut and reshot by others. Previously filmed in 1925 as PAMPERED YOUTH. Also shown in computer-colored version.▼●

Magnificent Brute, The (1936) **80m.** ** D: John G. Blystone. Victor McLaglen, Binnie Barnes, William Hall, Jean Dixon. Pertly acted love triangle, with McLaglen the roughneck blast furnace boss, involved in romance and stolen money.

Magnificent Cuckold, The (1966-Italian) **111m.** **½ D: Antonio Pietrangeli. Claudia Cardinale, Ugo Tognazzi, Michele Girardon, Bernard Blier. Saucy sex comedy of marital infidelity, with Tognazzi, the businessman husband of Cardinale, outwitted by his curvaceous wife.

Magnificent Doll (1946) **95m.** ** D: Frank Borzage. Ginger Rogers, Burgess Meredith, David Niven, Horace (Stephen) McNally, Peggy Wood. Rogers just isn't right as Dolley Madison, and historical drama with Meredith as President Madison and Niven as Aaron Burr falls flat.▼

Magnificent Dope, The (1942) **83m.** *** D: Walter Lang. Henry Fonda, Lynn Bari, Don Ameche, Edward Everett Horton, Hobart Cavanaugh, Pierre Watkin. Entertaining comedy of hopeless hayseed Fonda who shows up sharper Ameche in big city; Bari is the girl between them.▼

Magnificent Fraud, The (1939) **78m.** **½ D: Robert Florey. Akim Tamiroff, Lloyd Nolan, Patricia Morison, Mary Boland, George Zucco, Steffi Duna, Robert Warwick. Actor who's a master of disguise is recruited to take the place of a recently assassinated Latin American dictator. Good premise is hampered by an unconvincing romantic subplot involving gangster Nolan. Still, it's a great showcase for Tamiroff. Supposedly this was the inspiration for MOON OVER PARADOR.

Magnificent Matador, The (1955) **C-94m.** **½ D: Budd Boetticher. Anthony Quinn, Maureen O'Hara, Manuel Rojas, Thomas Gomez, Richard Denning, Lola Albright. Another of director Boetticher's bullfighting films has Quinn an aging matador who reexamines his commitment to bullfighting, while protecting his young "protege" (Rojas) and being romanced by American O'Hara. CinemaScope.▼

Magnificent Obsession (1935) **101m.** *** D: John M. Stahl. Irene Dunne, Robert Taylor, Betty Furness, Charles Butterworth, Sara Haden, Ralph Morgan, Arthur Treacher. Dated but sincere adaptation of Lloyd Douglas' story about drunken playboy who mends his ways, becomes respected surgeon in order to restore the eyesight of a woman (Dunne) he blinded in an auto accident. Soap opera gave Taylor his first important lead—and made him a star. Original running time was 112m. Remade in 1954.

Magnificent Obsession (1954) **C-108m.** *** D: Douglas Sirk. Jane Wyman, Rock Hudson, Barbara Rush, Otto Kruger, Agnes Moorehead, Gregg Palmer. Director Sirk pulls out all the stops in this baroque, melodramatic remake of 1935 film which remains faithful to original story. Like its predecessor, a smash hit which (once again) boosted its male lead to stardom.▼

Magnificent Rebel, The (1962) **C-95m.** **½ D: Georg Tressler. Karl Boehm, Ernst Nadhering, Ivan Desny, Gabriele Porks. Boehm makes an intense Beethoven in this rather serious Disney film, not really for kids at all. Great musical sequences and very good German location photography, though romantic angle of story never really compels attention. Released theatrically in Europe, shown in U.S. as two-part Disney TV show.

Magnificent Roughnecks (1956) **73m.** BOMB D: Sherman A. Rose. Jack Carson, Mickey Rooney, Nancy Gates, Jeff Donnell. Allied Artists disaster with two "comics" as partners trying to wildcat oilfields.

Magnificent Seven, The (1960) **C-126m.** ***½ D: John Sturges. Yul Brynner, Steve McQueen, Eli Wallach, Horst Buchholz, James Coburn, Charles Bronson, Robert Vaughn, Brad Dexter. Enduringly popular Western remake of THE SEVEN SAMURAI, about paid gunslingers who try to rout the bandits who are devastating a small Mexican town. Great cast of stars-to-be; memorable Elmer Bernstein score. Followed by three sequels, starting with RETURN OF THE SEVEN, and a TV series. Remade as a TVM in 1998. Panavision. ▼●

Magnificent Seven Ride!, The (1972) **C-100m.** **½ D: George McCowan. Lee Van Cleef, Stefanie Powers, Mariette Hartley, Michael Callan, Luke Askew, Pedro Armendariz, Jr. Newly married gunfighter decides to help his buddy fight bandits after they kidnap his wife. Fourth "ride" for the Seven isn't bad. [PG]

Magnificent Sinner (1959-French) **C-97m.** ** D: Robert Siodmak. Romy Schneider, Curt Jurgens, Pierre Blanchar, Monique Melinand. Lackluster proceedings of Schneider as mistress to Russian Czar, involved in court intrigue. Remake of 1938 French film KATIA with Danielle Darrieux.

Magnificent Yankee, The (1950) **80m.** *** D: John Sturges. Louis Calhern, Ann Harding, Eduard Franz, James Lydon, Philip Ober, Richard Anderson, Hayden Rorke, John Hamilton. Genteel, entertaining saga of Oliver Wendell Holmes and his devoted wife, spanning many decades from the day they arrive in Washington, D.C., in 1902 so he may join the Supreme Court. A pleasure from start to finish, with Calhern re-creating his triumphant Broadway role.▼

Magnolia (1999) **C-188m.** *** D: Paul Thomas Anderson. Tom Cruise, Julianne Moore, John C. Reilly, Jason Robards, Philip Seymour Hoffman, Melora Walters, William H. Macy, Philip Baker Hall, Jeremy Blackman, Michael Bowen, Melinda Dillon, April Grace, Luis Guzman, Ricky Jay, Alfred Molina, Michael Murphy, Henry Gibson, Felicity Huffman, Eileen Ryan. A mosaic of misery, with an array of characters ranging from a dying man and his angelic male nurse to a precocious kid pressured to perform on a TV game show—who must deal with anger, guilt, isolation, the sins of the fathers, and ultimately, forgiveness, on an almost biblical level. Fine performances in this emotionally exhausting film, including a dynamic Cruise as a self-invented Pied Piper of satyrdom. Overall impact is muted by the film's sheer length. Haunting songs by Aimee Mann. Written by the director. Panavision. [R]▼◗

Magnum Force (1973) **C-124m.** **½ D: Ted Post. Clint Eastwood, Hal Holbrook, Mitchell Ryan, David Soul, Felton Perry, Robert Urich, Kip Niven, Tim Matheson. Eastwood's second go-round as individualistic San Francisco cop Dirty Harry Callahan. This time he traces a series of mysterious slayings to the police department itself, and finds himself in extra-hot water. Some brutal scenes; not nearly as stylish as the original. Written by John Milius and Michael Cimino. Look for Suzanne Somers at gangster's pool party. Followed by THE ENFORCER. Panavision. [R]▼●

Magus, The (1968-British) **C-117m.** BOMB D: Guy Green. Anthony Quinn, Michael Caine, Candice Bergen, Anna Karina, Paul Stassino, Julian Glover. Pretentious, hopelessly confusing story from John Fowles' novel about a magus, or magician (Quinn), who tries to control destiny of Caine, new arrival on his Greek island. At first mazelike story is fun, but with no relief it grows tiresome. Panavision.

Mahler (1974-British) **C-115m.** *** D: Ken Russell. Robert Powell, Georgina Hale, Richard Morant, Lee Montague, Rosalie Crutchley. Not for every taste (could it be a Russell film if it were?) but one of the director's best films; a gorgeously shot, set, and costumed bio about the turn-of-the-century composer and his tormented life. If you think this means it's refined, check out the purposely anachronistic Nazi humor. Energetic to a fault. [PG]▼◗

Mahogany (1975) **C-109m.** *½ D: Berry Gordy. Diana Ross, Billy Dee Williams, Anthony Perkins, Jean-Pierre Aumont, Beah Richards, Nina Foch. Silly, contrived affair about fashion designer who becomes world famous, then finds happiness only in arms of unsuccessful boy friend. Wooden performances except for Perkins' extension of PSYCHO role. Panavision. [PG]▼●

Maid, The (1991-U.S.-French) **C-91m.** ** D: Ian Toynton. Martin Sheen, Jacqueline Bisset, Jean-Pierre Cassel, Victoria Shalet, James Faulkner. Wall Street ladies' man Sheen poses as a "maid" to ingratiate himself with French businessmom Bisset and her spoiled young daughter. Warm but predictable romantic comedy which gets off to a faulty start. [PG]▼

Maid in Paris (1957-French) **84m.** ** D: Pierre Gaspard-Hutt. Dany Robin, Daniel Gelin, Marie Daems, Tilda Thamar. Bland story of girl going to the big city seeking romance.

Maid of Salem (1937) **86m.** *** D: Frank Lloyd. Claudette Colbert, Fred MacMurray, Louise Dresser, Gale Sondergaard, Beulah Bondi, Bonita Granville, Virginia Weidler, Donald Meek, Harvey Stephens, Edward Ellis, Mme. Sul-te-wan. Colonial witch-burning era is backdrop for fine drama with many similarities to Arthur Miller's *The Crucible* (minus the philosophy).

Maids, The (1975-British) **C-95m.** ** D: Christopher Miles. Glenda Jackson, Susannah York, Vivien Merchant, Mark Burns. Jean Genet's windy, pointless, exasperating play about two maids who hate their mistress. Excellent acting wasted on tripe. An American Film Theater Production. [PG]▼

Maid's Night Out (1938) **64m.** ** D: Ben Holmes. Joan Fontaine, Allan Lane, Hedda Hopper, George Irving, William Brisbane, Billy Gilbert, Cecil Kellaway. On a wager, Lane (who wants to study the home life of fish) delivers milk for his father's company and mistakes debutante Fontaine for a servant. Inane screwball comedy with one clever bit: Hopper's in the cast, and one of Lane's projects involves a fish that eats its young—named Louella! Look for Jack Carson as a roller coaster operator. ▼

Maid to Order (1987) **C-96m.** **½ D: Amy Jones. Ally Sheedy, Beverly D'Angelo, Michael Ontkean, Valerie Perrine, Dick Shawn, Tom Skerritt, Merry Clayton, Begona Plaza. Cute fairytale comedy about spoiled rich girl who's robbed of her identity, and forced to work as a maid for a gaudy and self-centered Malibu couple (played to perfection by Perrine and Shawn). D'Angelo is fun as her fairy godmother, and Ontkean is a sweet Prince Charming. Clayton scores as the household cook who belts out two numbers. Film's good-heartedness makes up for its shortcomings. [PG]▼●

Mailbag Robbery (1958-British) **70m.** ** D: Compton Bennett. Lee Patterson, Kay Callard, Alan Gifford, Kerry Jordan. Title explains full contents of programmer. Video title: THE FLYING SCOT.▼

Mail Order Bride (1964) **C-83m.** **½ D: Burt Kennedy. Buddy Ebsen, Keir Dullea, Lois Nettleton, Warren Oates, Marie Windsor, Barbara Luna. Harmless—and plotless—Western with rambunctious young rancher Dullea marrying widow Nettleton to satisfy his late father's old friend (Ebsen). Climactic shoot-out is virtual duplicate of the one in RIDE THE HIGH COUNTRY. Panavision.

Main Attraction, The (1962) **C-90m.** *½ D: Daniel Petrie. Pat Boone, Mai Zetterling, Nancy Kwan, Yvonne Mitchell, Kieron Moore. Boone is fatally out of his depth as a guitar-playing drifter in Europe who causes romantic complications when he falls in with a traveling circus. Filmed in England. Metroscope.

Main Event, The (1979) **C-112m.** *½ D: Howard Zieff. Barbra Streisand, Ryan O'Neal, Paul Sand, Whitman Mayo, Patti D'Arbanville, Richard Lawson, James Gregory, Rory Calhoun, Ernie Hudson. Tortuous farce about a bankrupt executive who inherits a hapless boxer and goads him into resuming his career. O'Neal comes off slightly better than Streisand, but only because his yelling and screaming isn't as abrasive as hers; D'Arbanville tops them both as a girl with a *really* bad cough. [PG] ▼●

Main Street After Dark (1944) **57m.** **½ D: Edward L. Cahn. Edward Arnold, Audrey Totter, Dan Duryea, Hume Cronyn, Selena Royle. Offbeat drama of family pickpocket gang put out of business by civic clean-up campaign.

Main Street to Broadway (1953) **102m.** **½ D: Tay Garnett. Tom Morton, Mary Murphy, Clinton Sundberg, Rosemary DeCamp, guest stars Ethel Barrymore, Lionel Barrymore, Shirley Booth, Rex Harrison, Lilli Palmer, Helen Hayes, Henry Fonda, Tallulah Bankhead, Mary Martin, others. Very slight story of romance, struggle, and success on the Great White Way; chief interest is large cast of Broadway stars in cameo appearances. Rodgers & Hammerstein appear on camera and contribute a song, "There's Music in You."▼

Maisie Maisie was a middling series of ten MGM features made between 1939 and 1947, starring lively Ann Sothern as a brassy showgirl involved in a progression of topical if trivial situations encompassing the changing role of American women during WW2 America. The series never rose above the B category; all were filmed in black and white and ran about 85 minutes. Production values were too often static, utilizing rear projection and indoor sets to establish the varied locales of the episodes. The Maisie series relied almost exclusively on Miss Sothern's vivacious personality to carry the slight tales of the conventional tough-girl-with-a-heart-of-gold. Her costars were competent contract players such as Robert Sterling (Sothern's then-husband), Lew Ayres, John Hodiak and George Murphy. Unlike the Andy Hardy series, few fledgling starlets appeared in these features, although guests like Red Skelton helped out from time to time. In general the series lacked a basic continuity and flavor; and earlier entries such as MAISIE and CONGO MAISIE, while no classics, had more punch than later efforts such as UNDERCOVER MAISIE.

MAISIE

Maisie (1939)
Congo Maisie (1940)
Gold Rush Maisie (1940)
Maisie Was a Lady (1941)
Ringside Maisie (1941)
Maisie Gets Her Man (1942)
Swing Shift Maisie (1943)
Maisie Goes to Reno (1944)
Up Goes Maisie (1946)
Undercover Maisie (1947)

Maisie (1939) **74m.** **½ D: Edwin L. Marin. Ann Sothern, Robert Young, Ruth Hussey, Ian Hunter, Anthony Allan, Cliff Edwards, George Tobias. First entry in the series is a mild romantic comedy, centering on the sassy showgirl's adventures on a Wyoming ranch where she falls for foreman Young and clears him of a murder charge.

Maisie Gets Her Man (1942) **85m.** **½ D: Roy Del Ruth. Ann Sothern, Red Skelton, Leo Gorcey, Pamela Blake, Allen Jenkins, Donald Meek, Walter Catlett, Fritz Feld, Rags Ragland, Frank Jenks. Maisie joins a theatrical agency in Chicago and starts a stage act with hick Skelton. Amusing entry brightened by a strong supporting cast of veteran comics.

Maisie Goes to Reno (1944) **90m.** **½ D: Harry Beaumont. Ann Sothern, John Hodiak, Tom Drake, Marta Linden, Paul Cavanagh, Ava Gardner, Bernard Nedell, Donald Meek. OK series entry with Maisie taking a trip to Reno where she has her hands full intervening in the divorce of a soldier and his wife (a young Gardner).

Maisie Was a Lady (1941) **79m.** **½ D: Edwin L. Marin. Ann Sothern, Lew Ayres, Maureen O'Sullivan, C. Aubrey Smith, Edward Ashley, Joan Perry, Paul Cavanagh. Maisie gets a job as maid to a family of bluebloods and straightens out their sorry personal lives in this well-cast entry with Ayres taking a break from *Dr. Kildare.*

Maitresse (1976-French) **C-112m.** *** D: Barbet Schroeder. Gérard Depardieu, Bulle Ogier, Andre Rouyer, Nathalie Keryan, Roland Bertin, Tony Taffin. Wickedly amusing comedy about a woman (Ogier) who earns her keep as a dominatrix, and puts her profession aside in her romantic relationship with Depardieu. Decidedly not for all tastes, but delicious fun for those who are game.▼

Major and the Minor, The (1942) **100m.** ***½ D: Billy Wilder. Ginger Rogers, Ray Milland, Rita Johnson, Robert Benchley, Diana Lynn, Frankie Thomas, Jr., Charles Smith, Larry Nunn, Norma Varden. Memorable comedy of working girl Rogers disguised as 12-year-old to save train fare, becoming involved with Milland's military school. Wilder's first directorial effort (written with Charles Brackett) is still amusing. Story suggested by Edward Childs Carpenter's play *Connie Goes Home*, and *Saturday Evening Post* story "Sunny Goes Home" by Fannie Kilbourne. That's Ginger's real-life mom playing her mother near the end of the film. Remade as YOU'RE NEVER TOO YOUNG.▼

Major Barbara (1941-British) **121m.** **** D: Gabriel Pascal. Wendy Hiller, Rex Harrison, Robert Morley, Robert Newton, Emlyn Williams, Sybil Thorndike, Deborah Kerr, David Tree, Stanley Holloway. Topnotch adaptation of Shaw play about wealthy girl who joins Salvation Army; Harrison is a professor who woos her. Excellent cast in intelligent comedy (scripted by Anatole de Grunwald and Shaw). Kerr's film debut. Also shown at 115m.▼

Major Dundee (1965) **C-124m.** **½ D: Sam Peckinpah. Charlton Heston, Richard Harris, Jim Hutton, James Coburn, Michael Anderson, Jr., Senta Berger, Mario Adorf, Brock Peters, Warren Oates, Slim Pickens, Ben Johnson, R.G. Armstrong, L.Q. Jones. Very fine cast and lavish production make up for overlong, confused story of cavalry officer (Heston) who leads assorted misfits against Apaches. Peckinpah disowned the film, which was recut by others. Panavision.▼●

Majority of One, A (1962) **C-153m.** **½ D: Mervyn LeRoy. Rosalind Russell, Alec Guinness, Ray Danton, Madlyn Rhue, Mae Questel. Compared to Broadway play, this is overblown, overacted account of Jewish matron Russell falling in love with Japanese widower Guinness. Written by Leonard Spiegelgass.▼

Major League (1989) **C-107m.** **½ D: David S. Ward. Tom Berenger, Charlie Sheen, Corbin Bernsen, Margaret Whitton, James Gammon, Rene Russo, Wesley Snipes, Dennis Haysbert, Charles Cyphers, Bob Uecker. Bitchy baseball team owner Whitton seeks to get out of her Cleveland franchise by organizing a team that's guaranteed to lose games—and fans. Pleasant but completely unremarkable baseball comedy, with no surprises whatsoever. Followed by two sequels. [R]▼●◗

Major League II (1994) **C-104m.** *½ D: David S. Ward. Charlie Sheen, Tom Berenger, Corbin Bernsen, Dennis Haysbert, James Gammon, Omar Epps, Eric Bruskotter, Bob Uecker, David Keith, Alison Doody, Margaret Whitton, Takaaki Ishibashi, Michelle Burke, Randy Quaid. Excruciatingly unfunny, decidedly minor-league sequel, with most of the principals returning for a second season; the key exclusion is Wesley Snipes, replaced by Epps as Willie Mays Hayes. Crammed with cheap jokes; except for Uecker's quips, there's barely a laugh in sight. What's more, it's shamelessly loaded with plugs for commercial products. [PG] ▼●◗

Major League: Back to the Minors (1998) **C-100m.** ** D: John Warren. Scott Bakula, Corbin Bernsen, Dennis Haysbert, Takaaki Ishibashi, Jensen Daggett, Eric Bruskotter, Ted McGinley, Bob Uecker, Walt Goggins, Kenneth Johnson, Lobo Sebastian, Peter MacKenzie. Ex-ballplayer Bakula hires on as manager of a minor league team, transforming it from loser to contender. Sound familiar? Ho-hum comedy isn't as irritating as MAJOR LEAGUE II and does have Uecker around for laughs, but that's about it. [PG-13]▼●◗

Major Payne (1995) **C-97m.** *½ D: Nick Castle. Damon Wayans, Karyn Parsons, William Hickey, Michael Ironside, Albert Hall, Steven Martini, Orlando Brown, Andrew Harrison Leeds, Joda Blare-Hershman, Damien Wayans, R. Stephen Wiles. Major Benson Payne is a warrior without a war, a disciplinarian with a rigid military mentality who is oblivious to humanity and feeling. This is about to change upon his taking command of a group of underage cadets. Thoroughly inane, by-the-numbers comedy, with a miscast Wayans too often hard to take in the title role. A remake of THE PRIVATE WAR OF MAJOR BENSON (1955). Wayans coscripted and coexecutive produced. [PG-13] ▼●◗

Make a Wish (1937) **76m.** ** D: Kurt Neumann. Basil Rathbone, Bobby Breen, Marion Claire, Ralph Forbes, Henry Armetta, Leon Errol, Donald Meek, Billy Lee. Inconsequential musical about a summer camp for boys where singing prodigy Breen encounters composer Rathbone. Supporting comedians offer most of the film's best moments.▼

Make Haste to Live (1954) **90m.** **½ D: William A. Seiter. Dorothy McGuire, Stephen McNally, Mary Murphy, Edgar Buchanan, John Howard, Carolyn Jones. McGuire gives believable performance as woman faced with criminal husband who's returned to seek vengeance.▼

Make Me an Offer (1955-British) **C-88m.** **½ D: Cyril Frankel. Peter Finch, Adrienne Corri, Rosalie Crutchley, Finlay Currie. Satisfactory highbrow shenanigans in the antique-buying field, with Finch after priceless vase.▼

Make Mine Laughs (1949) **64m.** *½ D: Richard Fleischer. Frances Langford, Joan Davis, Leon Errol, Ray Bolger, Gil Lamb. RKO mini-musical, no more than uninspired footage lumped together à la vaudeville.

Make Mine Mink (1960-British) **100m.** *** D: Robert Asher. Terry-Thomas, Athene Seyler, Hattie Jacques, Billie Whitelaw, Elspeth Duxbury, Raymond Huntley, Ron Moody, Jack Hedley, Kenneth Williams, Sidney Tafler. Former military man Terry-Thomas organizes unlikely band of fur thieves in this delightful British farce. Beware of shorter version on tape.▼

Make Mine Music (1946) **C-74m.** **½ D: Joe Grant (production supervisor). Voices of Nelson Eddy, Dinah Shore, Jerry Colonna, The Andrews Sisters, Andy Russell, Sterling Holloway, and music by The Benny Goodman Quartet. Ten-part Walt Disney animated feature with such segments as "Peter and the Wolf," "Johnny Fedora and Alice Blue Bonnet," and "Casey at the Bat." At its worst when it tries to be "arty," and at its best when it offers bright, original pieces like "The Whale Who Wanted to Sing at the Met," and the dazzling Benny Goodman number "After You've Gone." A mixed bag, to be sure. ▼

Maker, The (1997) **C-98m.** ** D: Tim Hunter. Matthew Modine, Mary-Louise Parker, Jonathan Rhys-Meyers, Fairuza Balk, Jesse Borrego, Michael Madsen, Lawrence Pressman. Troubled teenager, just coming of age, falls prey to his long-lost older brother who leads him into a life of crime. Off-putting at first, interesting for a while, but overall an unsatisfying brew of ingredients. Never released theatrically. Panavision. [R]▼

Make Way for a Lady (1936) **65m.** ** D: David Burton. Herbert Marshall, Anne Shirley, Gertrude Michael, Margot Grahame, Clara Blandick, Frank Coghlan, Jr. Routine comedy of Shirley playing matchmaker for her widowed father Marshall; pleasant enough.

Make Way For Tomorrow (1937) **92m.** ***½ D: Leo McCarey. Victor Moore, Beulah Bondi, Fay Bainter, Thomas Mitchell, Porter Hall, Barbara Read, Louise Beavers. Sensitive film of elderly couple in financial difficulty, shunted aside by their children, unwanted and unloved; shatteringly true, beautifully done.

Make Your Own Bed (1944) **82m.** *½ D: Peter Godfrey. Jack Carson, Jane Wyman, Alan Hale, Irene Manning, George Tobias, Ricardo Cortez. Forced comedy of detective Carson disguised as butler, Wyman as maid, to get lowdown on racketeer.

Making It (1971) **C-97m.** ** D: John Erman. Kristoffer Tabori, Joyce Van Patten, Marlyn Mason, Bob Balaban, Lawrence Pressman, Louise Latham, Dick Van Patten. Uneven, seriocomic "youth picture" with Tabori (son of Viveca Lindfors, impressive in his first starring role) as a 17-year-old with little but sex on his mind—until he shares a traumatic experience with his mother. Filmed in Albuquerque. [R]

Making Love (1982) **C-113m.** **½ D: Arthur Hiller. Michael Ontkean, Kate Jackson, Harry Hamlin, Wendy Hiller, Arthur Hill, Nancy Olson, Terry Kiser. Repressed homosexual doctor jeopardizes 8-year marriage by coming out of the closet with sexually carefree novelist. Soaper is easy to take, but that's its problem; script, direction, nonstereotyped performances, lack edge in bland attempt to avoid offending anyone. From the director of LOVE STORY. [R]▼

Making Mr. Right (1987) **C-95m.** **½ D: Susan Seidelman. John Malkovich, Ann Magnuson, Glenne Headly, Ben Masters, Laurie Metcalf, Polly Bergen, Harsh Nayyar, Hart Bochner, Polly Draper, Susan Anton. Nerdy scientist Malkovich has created a nearly human android in his own image; public relations whiz Magnuson is hired to sell the concept of Ulysses to the public. Hit-or-miss comedy has good performances and many effective moments, but misses the bull's-eye. Filmed and set in Miami Beach. [PG-13]▼●

Making the Grade (1984) **C-105m.** *½ D: Dorian Walker. Judd Nelson, Jonna Lee, Carey Scott, Dana Olsen, Gordon Jump, Walter Olkewicz, Ronald Lacey, Scott McGinnis. Spoiled rich kid hires young hustler to take his place at prep school. Better than the average raunchy youth comedies of the 80s, but that's faint praise. Andrew Clay plays a character here named Dice. [R]▼

Makioka Sisters, The (1985-Japanese) **C/B&W-140m.** ** D: Kon Ichikawa. Keiko Kishi, Yoshiko Sakuma, Sayuri Yoshinaga, Yuko Kotegawa, Juzo Itami. Emotionally distant, occasionally confusing tale of four upper-class sisters, two married and two single, and the manner in which they contend with tradition and social change in pre-WW2 Osaka. Ichikawa coscripted, from a highly regarded novel by Junichiro Tanizaki.▼●

Mako: The Jaws of Death (1976) **C-93m.**

★★½ D: William Grefe. Richard Jaeckel, Jennifer Bishop, Harold Sakata, John Chandler, Buffy Dee. Good horror premise has Jaeckel a friend and protector of sharks who goes berserk when both he and his "friends" are exploited. Shown theatrically as THE JAWS OF DEATH. [PG]▼

Malaga (1960-British) **97m.** ★★½ D: Laslo Benedek. Trevor Howard, Dorothy Dandridge, Edmund Purdom, Michael Hordern. Bizarre casting in routine robbery tale is primary diversion. Originally titled MOMENT OF DANGER.

Malaya (1949) **98m.** ★★½ D: Richard Thorpe. Spencer Tracy, James Stewart, Valentina Cortese, Sydney Greenstreet. Routine WW2 melodrama set in the Pacific, about Allies' efforts to smuggle out rubber. Good cast let down by so-so script.▼

Malcolm (1986-Australian) **C-86m.** ★★★ D: Nadia Tass. Colin Friels, John Hargreaves, Lindy Davies, Chris Haywood, Charles "Bud" Tingwell, Beverly Phillips, Judith Stratford. Charming, disarmingly offbeat comedy about a slow-witted young man with a genius for Rube Goldberg-like mechanical devices and his unusual entry into a life of crime. Surefooted directorial debut for actress Tass, whose husband David Parker wrote the screenplay (and designed the Tinkertoys) and whose real-life brother was the inspiration for the character of Malcolm. Infectious music score performed by The Penguin Cafe Orchestra. Australian Film Institute winner for Best Picture and other awards. [PG-13]▼●

Malcolm X (1972) **92m.** ★★★ No director credited. Excellent documentary about the life and times of the black revolutionary leader, which allows him to speak for himself. (Passages from his autobiography are spoken by James Earl Jones; his eulogy is read, as it was in real life, by Ossie Davis.) A fascinating time capsule and history lesson. Particularly interesting to see alongside Spike Lee's later film, which was produced and cowritten by Marvin Worth and Arnold Perl, the same partnership responsible for this Oscar-nominated documentary. [PG]▼

Malcolm X (1992) **C-201m.** ★★★½ D: Spike Lee. Denzel Washington, Angela Bassett, Albert Hall, Al Freeman, Jr., Delroy Lindo, Spike Lee, Theresa Randle, Kate Vernon, Lonette McKee, Tommy Hollis, Giancarlo Esposito, Craig Wasson, John Ottavino, David Patrick Kelly, Shirley Stoler. Sweeping biography of the black leader, tracing his transformation from street hustler to prison inmate to religious convert—and his ascension to national leadership while preaching the words of Elijah Muhammad. Compelling every step of the way, with a superb performance by Washington, and sure-footed guidance from director/cowriter Lee. A surprisingly measured and intelligent portrait of a still-controversial figure, with Lee's expected indulgences limited to the main title sequence and epilogue. Screenplay by Lee and Arnold Perl, based on the book *The Autobiography of Malcolm X,* as told to Alex Haley. [PG-13]▼●◗

Male Animal, The (1942) **101m.** ★★★½ D: Elliott Nugent. Henry Fonda, Olivia de Havilland, Joan Leslie, Jack Carson, Herbert Anderson, Don DeFore, Hattie McDaniel, Eugene Pallette. Intelligent, entertaining Elliott Nugent-James Thurber comedy of college professor Fonda defending his rights, while losing wife de Havilland to old flame Carson. Excellent performances in this fine, contemporary film, with spoof on typical football rallies a highlight. Remade as SHE'S WORKING HER WAY THROUGH COLLEGE.▼

Male Hunt (1964-French) **92m.** ★★★ D: Edouard Molinaro. Jean-Paul Belmondo, Jean-Claude Brialy, Catherine Deneuve, Francoise Dorleac, Marie Laforet. Spicy romp about trio of Frenchmen avoiding the clutches of marriage-minded women.

Male of the Century, The (1975-French) **C-90m.** ★★½ D: Claude Berri. Juliet Berto, Claude Berri, Hubert Deschamps, Laszlo Szabo, Yves Afonso. Writer-director Berri stars in this slight, occasionally perceptive comedy as a jealous chauvinistic husband; his wife is taken hostage during a bank robbery . . . and he's positive that she's becoming sexually involved with her captor.

Malibu (1934) SEE: **Sequoia**

Malibu Beach (1978) **C-94m.** ★½ D: Robert J. Rosenthal. Kim Lankford, James Daughton, Susan Player-Jarreau, Stephen Oliver, Michael Luther. BEACH BLANKET BINGO 1970s style—without Frankie and Annette, and with pot instead of booze. If you're desperate . . . [R]▼

Malibu Express (1985) **C-101m.** ★★ D: Andy Sidaris. Darby Hinton, Sybil Danning, Art Metrano, Shelley Taylor Morgan, Lori Sutton, Barbara Edwards, Kimberly McArthur, Lynda Wiesmeier. Hinton is a private detective working on a complex espionage and blackmail case, but this film is just an excuse to showcase the charms of numerous *Playboy* centerfold models (accounting for its frequent programming on pay-cable services). A loose remake of Sidaris' 1973 STACEY. [R]▼

Malibu High (1979) **C-92m.** BOMB D: Irv Berwick. Jill Lansing, Stuart Taylor, Katie Johnson, Tammy Taylor, Garth Howard, Phyllis Benson. Sleazy, decidedly unpleasant story of a high-school girl who turns out to be something of a sociopath. Not the innocent youth opus its title might lead you to expect. [R]▼

Malice (1993) **C-107m.** ★★½ D: Harold Becker. Alec Baldwin, Nicole Kidman, Bill Pullman, Bebe Neuwirth, George C. Scott,

Anne Bancroft, Peter Gallagher, Josef Sommer, Tobin Bell, Debrah Farentino, Gwyneth Paltrow. A professor at a New England college finds himself undermined—and overshadowed—by the arrival in town of a hotshot surgeon who rents a room from him and his wife. The plot thickens, and gets progressively sillier, in this slick, engrossing, sexy thriller. Good performances help disguise story holes until the denouement, when it all goes to pieces. Overheated and fairly absurd. [R]▼●◗

Malice in Wonderland (1985) **C-100m. TVM** D: Gus Trikonis. Elizabeth Taylor, Jane Alexander, Richard Dysart, Joyce Van Patten, Jon Cypher, Leslie Ackerman, Bonnie Bartlett, Thomas Byrd, Rick Lenz, John Pleshette, Tim Robbins. Liz and Jane as Louella Parsons and Hedda Hopper give stylish oomph to this atmospheric but historically muddled account of the monumental feud between the legendary Hollywood gossip columnists. Jacqueline Feather and David Seidler based their lighthearted script on George Eels's book, *Hedda and Louella*. Aka THE RUMOR MILL. Average.▼

Malicious (1973-Italian) **C-97m.** **½ D: Salvatore Samperi. Laura Antonelli, Turi Ferro, Alessandro Momo, Angela Luce, Pino Caruso, Tina Aumont. Seriocomic slice of life about a sexy, though innocent young woman who comes to work as housekeeper for a widower and his three sons—and tantalizes both the father and one of his teenage boys. Intriguing but often unpleasant look at mores, morals, and hypocrisy, with typically titillating role for Antonelli. Originally titled MALIZIA. Techniscope. [R]▼

Malizia SEE: **Malicious**

Mallrats (1995) **C-95m.** *½ D: Kevin Smith. Shannen Doherty, Jeremy London, Jason Lee, Claire Forlani, Jason Mewes, Kevin Smith, Michael Rooker, Renee Humphrey, Ethan Suplee, Ben Affleck, Joey Lauren Adams, Priscilla Barnes. Inert, unfunny film, from the creator of CLERKS, about a band of friends, enemies, former girl- and boyfriends, and geeks who hang out at a suburban mall. Don't look for more story than that . . . or much else. Comic book legend Stan Lee plays himself in a rather contrived subplot. [R]▼●◗

Malone (1987) **C-92m.** *½ D: Harley Cokliss. Burt Reynolds, Cliff Robertson, Kenneth McMillan, Cynthia Gibb, Scott Wilson, Lauren Hutton. Robertson is a megalomaniac plotting to take over America; lucky for us the mountain-town gas station essential to his plans is the same one ex-CIA agent Reynolds stops at for a fill-up. Hybrid of SHANE and a modern-day shoot-em-up turns pretty ludicrous after a passable beginning; note how quickly Burt recovers from a golf ball-size bullet wound. [R]▼●

Malta Story (1953-British) **98m.** **½ D: Brian Desmond Hurst. Alec Guinness, Jack Hawkins, Anthony Steel, Muriel Pavlow. On-location filming of this WW2 British-air-force-in-action yarn is sparked by underplayed acting.▼

Maltese Bippy, The (1969) **C-88m.** ** D: Norman Panama. Dan Rowan, Dick Martin, Carol Lynley, Julie Newmar, Mildred Natwick, Fritz Weaver, Robert Reed. Werewolves, haunted houses, good cast, but few true laughs in tired horror-movie spoof. Film tried to cash in on the great success of Rowan and Martin's *Laugh-In* TV show—and their "bippy" catchword. Panavision. [G]

Maltese Falcon, The (1931) **80m.** *** D: Roy Del Ruth. Bebe Daniels, Ricardo Cortez, Dudley Digges, Robert Elliott, Thelma Todd, Una Merkel, Dwight Frye. First film version of Dashiell Hammett story is quite good, with Cortez more of a ladies' man than Bogart; otherwise very similar to later classic. Retitled DANGEROUS FEMALE for TV. Remade in 1936 (as SATAN MET A LADY) and 1941.▼

Maltese Falcon, The (1941) **100m.** **** D: John Huston. Humphrey Bogart, Mary Astor, Peter Lorre, Sydney Greenstreet, Ward Bond, Gladys George, Barton MacLane, Elisha Cook, Jr., Lee Patrick, Jerome Cowan. Outstanding detective drama improves with each viewing; Bogey is Dashiell Hammett's "hero" Sam Spade, Astor his client, Lorre the evasive Joel Cairo, Greenstreet (in his talkie film debut) the Fat Man, and Cook the neurotic gunsel Wilmer. Huston's first directorial effort (which he also scripted) moves at lightning pace, with cameo by his father Walter Huston as Captain Jacobi. Previously filmed in 1931 and in 1936 (as SATAN MET A LADY). Also shown in computer-colored version.▼●◗

Mama Dracula (1980-French-Belgian) **C-90m.** BOMB D: Boris Szulzinger. Louise Fletcher, Maria Schneider, Marc-Henri Wajnberg, Alexander Wajnberg, Jess Hahn. Dreadful vampire satire with Fletcher as the title character, an eternity away from the cuckoo's nest.▼

Mama, There's a Man in Your Bed (1989-French) **C-111m.** *** D: Coline Serreau. Daniel Auteuil, Firmine Richard, Pierre Vernier, Maxime Leroux, Gilles Privat, Muriel Combeau, Catherine Salviat. Unlikely romance between the harried CEO of a yogurt company and the financially strapped cleaning woman who will do anything to keep her five children (from five different marriages) from going hungry. Clever, heartwarming story from the director of THREE MEN AND A CRADLE has a lot to say about class and color differences in a world none too tolerant of either. Original French title: ROMUALD ET JULIET.▼●

Mambo (1954-U.S.-Italian) **94m.** **½ D:

Robert Rossen. Silvana Mangano, Michael Rennie, Shelley Winters, Vittorio Gassman, Eduardo Ciannelli, Mary Clare, Katherine Dunham. Offbeat romance set in Venice; young saleswoman, her love life complicated by a penniless gambler and a sickly count, becomes a famous dancer. Strong cast keeps it watchable. Original Italian running time 107m.▼

Mambo Kings, The (1992) **C-104m.** **½ D: Arne Glimcher. Armand Assante, Antonio Banderas, Cathy Moriarty, Maruschka Detmers, Desi Arnaz, Jr., Celia Cruz, Roscoe Lee Browne, Vondie Curtis-Hall, Tito Puente, Talisa Soto. Two brothers leave Cuba for the U.S. in the early 1950s and try to establish their own band. Colorful adaptation of Oscar Hijuelos' Pulitzer Prize–winning novel *Mambo Kings Play Songs of Love* is disappointingly underwritten and one-dimensional. Most intriguing sequence involves Desi Jr. playing his father and inviting the brothers to appear on an episode of *I Love Lucy*. [R]▼●

Mame (1974) **C-131m.** BOMB D: Gene Saks. Lucille Ball, Robert Preston, Beatrice Arthur, Bruce Davison, Joyce Van Patten, Don Porter, Audrey Christie, Jane Connell, Kirby Furlong, John McGiver. Hopelessly out-of-date musical taken from Jerry Herman's Broadway hit and based on AUNTIE MAME will embarrass even those who love Lucy. Calling Fred and Ethel Mertz! Bea Arthur recreates her Tony-winning stage role; Lucy's final feature film. Panavision. [PG]▼●

Mamele (1938-Polish) **100m.** **½ D: Joseph Green, Konrad Tom. Molly Picon, Edmund Zayenda, Max Bozyk, Gertrude Bullman, Simcha Fostel. Picon shines in this otherwise all-too-obvious Yiddish-language musical comedy as the youngest daughter of a widower who's forced to play Mama to the rest of her family. Based on a play which starred Picon over a decade earlier. The title's English-language translation is LITTLE MOTHER.▼

Mamma Roma (1962-Italian) **110m.** ***½ D: Pier Paolo Pasolini. Anna Magnani, Ettore Garofolo, Franco Citti, Silvana Corsini, Luisa Orioli, Paolo Volponi. Magnani dominates the screen as the title character, an earthy, larger-than-life woman attempting to abandon her career as a prostitute and enter the middle class. The scenario charts her complex relationship with (and high hopes for) her adolescent son, with whom she is reunited after many years. Pasolini scripted this fascinating, intensely involving drama which is loaded with cinematic references; Mamma Roma would be the same character Magnani played in Rossellini's OPEN CITY had that character not been killed at the finale! Watch for Lamberto Maggiorani, the star of De Sica's THE BICYCLE THIEF, in a small but pivotal role. Released theatrically in the U.S. in 1994.▼

Mammy (1930) **84m.** ** D: Michael Curtiz. Al Jolson, Lois Moran, Louise Dresser, Lowell Sherman, Hobart Bosworth. Story of backstage shooting in a minstrel troupe is only tolerable during musical numbers; Jolson sings "Let Me Sing and I'm Happy," "To My Mammy," and "The Call of the South." Some sequences originally filmed in color.●

Mam'zelle Pigalle (1956-French) **C-77m.** ** D: Michel Boisrond. Brigitte Bardot, Jean Bretonniere, Françoise Fabian, Bernard Lancret, Mischa Auer. Dull doings with Bardot as a schoolgirl who pursues crooner Bretonniere and becomes mixed up with counterfeiters. Scripted by Boisrond and Roger Vadim. Retitled: NAUGHTY GIRL and THAT NAUGHTY GIRL. CinemaScope.▼

Man, The (1972) **C-93m.** ** D: Joseph Sargent. James Earl Jones, Martin Balsam, Burgess Meredith, Lew Ayres, William Windom, Barbara Rush, Janet MacLachlan. Black Senator Jones becomes President of U.S. after freak disaster kills chief executive in Europe. Originally made for TV but released theatrically; marginally interesting Rod Serling adaptation of Irving Wallace bestseller plus acceptable performances add up to forgettable experience. Cameo appearance by Jack Benny. [G]

Man About the House, A (1947-British) **83m.** **½ D: Leslie Arliss. Kieron Moore, Margaret Johnston, Dulcie Gray, Guy Middleton, Felix Aylmer. Murky drama of repressed Victorian sisters Johnston and Gray, who travel to the Italian villa they have inherited and contend with earthy but manipulative Moore.▼

Man About Town (1939) **85m.** **½ D: Mark Sandrich. Jack Benny, Dorothy Lamour, Edward Arnold, Binnie Barnes, Phil Harris, Betty Grable, Monty Woolley, Eddie "Rochester" Anderson. Jack tries to crash London society; lively but undistinguished musical.

Man About Town (1947-French-U.S.) **89m.** ** D: René Clair. Maurice Chevalier, Francois Perier, Marcelle Derrien, Dany Robin, Raymond Cordy, Paul Olivier. Minor Clair farce with Chevalier a middle-aged film director in 1906 Paris who takes on sensitive young Derrien as his protegé. Originally titled LE SILENCE EST D'OR, running 106m. U.S. version is neither dubbed nor subtitled: Chevalier narrates the goings-on on the soundtrack—which doesn't quite work. It also includes a special prologue, filmed under the supervision of Robert Pirosh, in which Chevalier sings "Place Pigalle."

Man Afraid (1957) **84m.** **½ D: Harry Keller. George Nader, Phyllis Thaxter, Tim Hovey, Reta Shaw, Martin Milner.

Well-acted story of clergyman Nader protecting family against father of boy he killed in self-defense. CinemaScope.

Man Alive (1945) **70m.** **½ D: Ray Enright. Pat O'Brien, Adolphe Menjou, Ellen Drew, Rudy Vallee, Fortunio Bonanova, Joseph Crehan, Jonathan Hale, Minna Gombell, Jason Robards, Sr. Amusing comedy of O'Brien, supposedly dead, playing ghost to scare away wife's new love interest; moves along at brisk pace.

Man Alone, A (1955) **C-96m.** **½ D: Ray Milland. Ray Milland, Mary Murphy, Ward Bond, Raymond Burr, Lee Van Cleef. Intelligent oater of fugitive from lynch mob (Milland) hiding with sheriff's daughter (Murphy) in small town. Milland's first directorial attempt isn't bad.▼

Man and a Woman, A (1966-French) **C-102m.** ***½ D: Claude Lelouch. Anouk Aimée, Jean-Louis Trintignant, Pierre Barouh, Valerie Lagrange. Moving romantic drama about young widow and widower who fall in love; one of the 1960s' most popular love stories, thanks to intelligent script, winning performances, innovative direction and camerawork, Francis Lai's music score. Oscar winner for Best Foreign Film, Best Original Screenplay. Remade by cowriter/director Lelouch in 1977 as ANOTHER MAN, ANOTHER CHANCE, and followed by A MAN AND A WOMAN: 20 YEARS LATER.▼

Man and a Woman: 20 Years Later, A (1986) **C-108m.** *½ D: Claude Lelouch. Anouk Aimée, Jean-Louis Trintignant, Richard Berry, Evelyne Bouix, Robert Hossein, Marie-Sophie Pochat. Badly misconceived sequel to one of the '60s' essential "date" movies finds former script girl Aimee now a film producer, race driver Trintignant involved in a Paris-to-Dakar rally. Silly film-within-a-film pays homage to DIAL M FOR MURDER and—in one desert scene—the opening to HATARI! Someone should have reminded Lelouch that "hatari!" means "danger" in Swahili. [PG]▼

Man and Boy (1972) **C-98m.** **½ D: E. W. Swackhamer. Bill Cosby, Gloria Foster, Leif Erickson, George Spell, Douglas Turner Ward, John Anderson, Yaphet Kotto, Henry Silva, Dub Taylor. Civil War veteran and young son take after the thief who has stolen their horse in a kind of black BICYCLE THIEF. Decent enough family film with Cosby in rare dramatic role. [G]▼

Man at the Carlton Tower (1961-British) **57m.** ** D: Robert Tronson. Maxine Audley, Lee Montague, Allan Cuthbertson, Terence Alexander. Routine Edgar Wallace thriller churned out against backdrop of plush London hotel involving jewel robbery and murder.

Man at the Top (1975-British) **C-92m.** *** D: Mike Vardy. Kenneth Haigh, Nanette Newman, Harry Andrews, John Quentin, Mary Maude. Feature spin-off of British TV show which in turn is a spin-off of ROOM AT THE TOP, with Haigh as Joe Lampton, now caught in EXECUTIVE SUITE-type business conflicts.

Man, a Woman and a Bank, A (1979-Canadian) **C-100m.** **½ D: Noel Black. Donald Sutherland, Brooke Adams, Paul Mazursky, Allen Magicovsky, Leigh Hamilton. Needless but inoffensive caper movie about a $4 million bank heist, with pleasing performances by the three leads. Magicovsky isn't too appealing as a suicidal whipped cream freak, but how many suicidal whipped cream freaks do you know that *are*? [PG]▼

Man Bait (1952-U.S.-British) **78m.** **½ D: Terence Fisher. George Brent, Marguerite Chapman, Diana Dors, Raymond Huntley, Peter Reynolds. British-made suspense programmer has Brent a book dealer entangled in blackmail and murder. British title: THE LAST PAGE.

Man Beast (1955) **72m.** BOMB D: Jerry Warren. Rock Madison, Virginia Maynor, George Skaff, Lloyd Nelson, Tom Maruzzi. An expedition goes in search of the abominable snowman but comes up with a turkey instead.▼

Man Behind the Gun, The (1952) **C-82m.** ** D: Felix E. Feist. Randolph Scott, Patrice Wymore, Philip Carey, Dick Wesson, Lina Romay. Army man Scott goes undercover to investigate southern California secessionist movement in 1850s. Formula stuff.

Man Betrayed, A (1941) **83m.** ** D: John H. Auer. John Wayne, Frances Dee, Edward Ellis, Wallace Ford, Ward Bond, Harold Huber, Alexander Granach. Country lawyer crusades against father of girlfriend to prove that he's crooked politician. Minor melodrama with the Duke in one of his oddest roles. Retitled: WHEEL OF FORTUNE.▼

Man Between, The (1953-British) **101m.** *** D: Carol Reed. James Mason, Claire Bloom, Hildegarde Neff, Geoffrey Toone. Hardened black-market dealer falls in love and finds himself torn between East and West. Taut, moody, and well-acted drama set in post-WW2 Berlin.

Man Bites Dog (1992-Belgian) **88m.** *** D: Rémy Belvaux, André Bonzel, Benôt Poelvoorde. Benôt Poelvoorde, Jacqueline Poelvoorde Pappaert, Nelly Pappaert, Hector Pappaert, Jenny Drye. Controversial, no-holds-barred portrait of an unashamedly brutal serial killer (played by codirector Poelvoorde). The nonstop, graphic brutality can be viewed either as sensationalism, a sick joke, or as a comment on violence on screen and in society. Shot in cinéma-vérité documentary style; codirectors

Belvaux and Bonzel play a reporter and cameraman making a film about the killer (whose actions clearly are spurred on by their presence). Definitely not for all tastes. Available on video in original NC-17 version and edited, unrated version. [NC-17] ▼

Man Called Adam, A (1966) **102m.** ** D: Leo Penn. Sammy Davis, Jr., Ossie Davis, Cicely Tyson, Louis Armstrong, Frank Sinatra, Jr., Peter Lawford, Mel Torme, Lola Falana, Gerald O'Loughlin. Pretentious melodrama of trumpet-player Davis trying to find some purpose in life; amateurishly produced.▼

Man Called Dagger, A (1968) **C-86m.** BOMB D: Richard Rush. Terry Moore, Jan Murray, Sue Ane Langdon, Paul Mantee, Eileen O'Neill, Maureen Arthur. Ex-Nazi scientist journeys to L.A. followed by secret agent Richard Dagger to assist former S.S. colonel (Murray!) in world-conquering plan. Embarrassing script, acting.

Man Called Flintstone, The (1966) **C-87m.** **½ D: Joseph Barbera, William Hanna. Voices of Alan Reed, Mel Blanc, Jean Vander Pyl, June Foray. Feature-length cartoon based on TV series of Stone Age characters satirizes superspy films. Mainly for kids.▼●

Man Called Gannon, A (1969) **C-105m.** *½ D: James Goldstone. Tony Franciosa, Michael Sarrazin, Judi West, Susan Oliver, John Anderson, Gavin MacLeod. Remade version of MAN WITHOUT A STAR is poor substitute. It's ranch-war time again. . . . Techniscope. [M/PG]

Man Called Horse, A (1970) **C-114m.** **½ D: Elliot Silverstein. Richard Harris, Judith Anderson, Jean Gascon, Manu Tupou, Corinna Tsopei, Dub Taylor. English aristocrat gets captured by Sioux Indians, undergoes torture to prove his worth. Sometimes gripping, sometimes gory; fine score by Leonard Rosenman. Followed by RETURN OF A MAN CALLED HORSE and TRIUMPHS OF A MAN CALLED HORSE. Panavision. [M/PG]▼●

Man Called Peter, A (1955) **C-119m.** *** D: Henry Koster. Richard Todd, Jean Peters, Marjorie Rambeau, Doris Lloyd, Emmett Lynn. Moving account of Scotsman Peter Marshall who became clergyman and U.S. Senate chaplain; sensitively played by Todd, with fine supporting cast. CinemaScope.▼

Man Called Sledge, A (1970-Italian) **C-93m.** ** D: Vic Morrow. James Garner, Dennis Weaver, Claude Akins, John Marley, Laura Antonelli, Wade Preston. Violent Western about a gunman whose gang goes after a cache of gold stored in a prison, and then fights over the loot. Notable mainly for Garner's atypical role as brutal outlaw. Techniscope. [R]▼

Manchu Eagle Murder Caper Mystery, The (1973) **C-80m.** **½ D: Dean Hargrove. Gabriel Dell, Will Geer, Joyce Van Patten, Anjanette Comer, Jackie Coogan, Huntz Hall, Barbara Harris. Fairly successful satire of tough private eye melodramas of 1940s. Cast and director on top of their material help make up for cheapness of production. [PG]

Manchurian Candidate, The (1962) **126m.** ***½ D: John Frankenheimer. Frank Sinatra, Laurence Harvey, Janet Leigh, Angela Lansbury, Henry Silva, James Gregory, John McGiver, Leslie Parrish, Khigh Deigh. Tingling political paranoia thriller about strange aftermath of a Korean war hero's decoration and his mother's machinations to promote her Joseph McCarthy-like husband's career. Harrowing presentation of Richard Condon story (adapted by George Axelrod). Score by David Amram. Rereleased theatrically in 1987. ▼●◗

Man Could Get Killed, A (1966) **C-99m.** **½ D: Ronald Neame, Cliff Owen. James Garner, Melina Mercouri, Sandra Dee, Tony Franciosa, Robert Coote, Roland Culver. Businessman Garner is mistaken for international spy in this so-so secret agent spoof with beautiful Rome and Lisbon locations. Bert Kaempfert's score introduces the hit tune "Strangers in the Night." Panavision.

Mandalay (1934) **65m.** *½ D: Michael Curtiz. Kay Francis, Lyle Talbot, Warner Oland, Raffaela Ottiano, Ruth Donnelly. Strange, silly, largely incoherent film set in Rangoon, about a woman with a past who helps a man on the run. Francis abandons convention to become the notorious Spot White (who "should be called Spot Cash," according to one observer). Shirley Temple is supposed to be in this film, but *we* can't find her.

Mandarin Mystery, The (1937) **63m.** *½ D: Ralph Staub. Eddie Quillan, Charlotte Henry, Rita Le Roy, Wade Boteler, Franklin Pangborn, George Irving. Famous sleuth Ellery Queen solves locked-room murder puzzle and recovers stolen stamp worth $50,000. Hopelessly muddled script and fatal miscasting of diminutive Quillan as EQ sabotages this low-budget mystery. TV version cut to 54m.▼

Mandela (1987) **C-135m. TVM** D: Philip Saville. Danny Glover, Alfre Woodard, John Matshikiza, Warren Clarke, Allan Corduner, Julian Glover. Danny Glover and Woodard are perfectly cast in this literate, poignant (and partisan) social history as Nelson and Winnie Mandela, who lead a lifelong struggle against South African apartheid . . . much of the time with Nelson in hiding, and finally imprisoned. Ronald Harwood's script is simple and effective; filmed on location in Zimbabwe. Made for cable. Above average.▼

Mandela (1996) **C-120m.** *** D: Jo Me-nell, Angus Gibson. Documentary chronicling the life of one of South Africa's greatest leaders, famed political prisoner and Nobel prizewinner Nelson Mandela. From his tribal upbringing to his work with the African National Congress, viewers are given a sense of what shaped his future role under apartheid rule to then become South Africa's first black president. Insightful and inspiring. Coproduced by Jonathan Demme. ▼●

Mandela and de Klerk (1997) **C-115m. TVM** D: Joseph Sargent. Sidney Poitier, Michael Caine, Tina Lifford, Ben Kruger, Jerry Mofokeng, Ian Roberts, Gerry Maritz. Poitier offers another towering performance as Nelson Mandela, toward the end of his 27 years in prison and as the newly installed president; bald-pated Caine is equally splendid as pragmatic F. W. de Klerk, who knows that the days of Apartheid are numbered. An arresting if talky drama, filmed on location in South Africa and at Robbin Island, where Mandela long had been imprisoned. Made for cable. Above average. ▼●

Man Detained (1961-British) **59m.** **½ D: Robert Tronson. Bernard Archard, Elvi Hale, Paul Stassino, Michael Coles. Trim Edgar Wallace yarn, enhanced by Hale's performance as secretary involved with counterfeiting gang and murder.

Mandingo (1975) **C-127m.** BOMB D: Richard Fleischer. James Mason, Susan George, Perry King, Richard Ward, Brenda Sykes, Ken Norton, Lillian Hayman, Roy Poole, Ji-Tu Cumbuka, Paul Benedict, Ben Masters. Trashy potboiler will appeal only to the s & m crowd. Mason is a bigoted plantation patriarch, George his oversexed daughter, Norton—what else?—a fighter. Stinko! Based on the Kyle Onstott novel, the first of a long series, although only one more—DRUM—was filmed. [R]▼●

Mandroid (1993) **C-80m.** ** D: Jack Ersgard. Brian Cousins, Jane Caldwell, Michael Dellafemina, Curt Lowens, Patrick Ersgard, Costel Constantin, Robert Symonds. Intrigue centers on remote-controllable robot of the title, and an absurd "Supercon" drug that does whatever the plot requires. There's even an invisible man. Acceptable comic book–style thriller set in Eastern Europe, with weak script but good direction. Sequel: INVISIBLE: THE CHRONICLES OF BENJAMIN KNIGHT. From Full Moon. [R]▼●

Mandy SEE: **Crash of Silence**

Man-Eater SEE: **Shark!**

Man-Eater of Hydra (1967-West German-Spanish) **C-88m.** ** D: Mel Welles. Cameron Mitchell, Elisa Montes, George Martin, Kay Fischer, Ralph Naukoff. Remote island with meat-eating plants is setting for predictable, mildly entertaining horror pic. Interesting special effects and atmosphere obscure silly script. Alternate title: ISLAND OF THE DOOMED. Techniscope.

Man-Eater of Kumaon (1948) **79m.** **½ D: Byron Haskin. Sabu, Wendell Corey, Joanne Page, Morris Carnovsky, Argentina Brunetti. Good adventure tale of hunter determined to kill deadly tiger on the loose.

Man Facing Southeast (1986-Argentine) **C-108m.** *** D: Eliseo Subiela. Lorenzo Quinteros, Hugo Soto, Ines Vernengo. Intriguing movie about a staff psychiatrist at a large mental hospital who tries to penetrate the enigma of a new patient who claims to be an alien visitor—and who, in fact, does seem to possess unusual powers. Fascinating at first, slow going at times, this is the kind of film that deliberately leaves the viewer to draw his own conclusions . . . and that is a great part of its mystique. [R]▼●

Manfish (1956) **C-76m.** ** D: W. Lee Wilder. John Bromfield, Lon Chaney (Jr.), Victor Jory, Barbara Nichols. Variation of Edgar Allan Poe's "Gold Bug" story is timid account of treasure hunt in Jamaica. ▼

Man for All Seasons, A (1966-British) **C-120m.** **** D: Fred Zinnemann. Paul Scofield, Wendy Hiller, Leo McKern, Robert Shaw, Orson Welles, Susannah York, John Hurt, Nigel Davenport, Vanessa Redgrave. Splendid film based on Robert Bolt's play about Sir Thomas More's personal conflict when King Henry VIII asks his support in break with Pope and formation of Church of England. Scofield's rich characterization matched by superb cast, vivid atmosphere. Six Oscars: Best Actor, Director, Picture, Screenplay (Robert Bolt), Cinematography (Ted Moore), Costumes. Remade for TV in 1988. ▼●◗

Man for All Seasons, A (1988) **C-150m. TVM** D: Charlton Heston. Charlton Heston, Vanessa Redgrave, John Gielgud, Richard Johnson, Roy Kinnear, Martin Chamberlain. A fine showcase for Heston, who plays Thomas More in Robert Bolt's reworking of his outstanding stage play. Having recently performed the part on stage in London, Heston opted to direct and star in this TV adaptation, with able support from Gielgud and Redgrave (who had a small part in the 1966 movie version). Made for cable. Above average.▼

Man Friday (1976-British) **C-115m.** *½ D: Jack Gold. Peter O'Toole, Richard Roundtree, Peter Cellier, Christopher Cabot, Joel Fluellen. Defoe classic rewritten to conform to today's racial standards. Amid gore and confusing flashbacks, Friday revolts against bondage, outwits master Crusoe, and also drives him mad (as shown in Cannes, Crusoe, having failed to "educate" Friday to British standards, and himself refused admission to Friday's tribe, blows his brains out!). [PG]▼

Man From Bitter Ridge, The (1955) **C-80m.** **½ D: Jack Arnold. Lex Barker, Mara Corday, Stephen McNally, Trevor Bardette. Peppy oater of Barker tracking down outlaws by tying in with local banker.
Man From Button Willow, The (1965) **C-84m.** ** D: David Detiege. Cartoon Western featuring the voices of Dale Robertson, Edgar Buchanan, Howard Keel, Herschel Bernardi, Ross Martin and others is only for small kiddies; story deals with America's first undercover agent in 1869 who prevents crooks from forcing settlers to get rid of their land.▼
Man From Cairo (1953-Italian) **81m.** ** D: Ray Enright. George Raft, Gianna Maria Canale, Massimo Serato, Irene Papas. Disappointing mishmash of intrigue set in Africa, with everyone scurrying about for gold.
Man From Colorado, The (1948) **C-99m.** *** D: Henry Levin. Glenn Ford, William Holden, Ellen Drew, Ray Collins, Edgar Buchanan. Unusual Western of brutal Ford appointed Federal judge, taking tyrannical hold of the territory.▼
Man From Dakota, The (1940) **75m.** **½ D: Leslie Fenton. Wallace Beery, John Howard, Dolores Del Rio, Donald Meek, Robert Barrat. Above-average Beery vehicle set in Civil War times, with glamorous Del Rio helping him and Howard, Union spies, cross Confederate lines.
Man From Del Rio (1956) **82m.** ** D: Harry Horner. Anthony Quinn, Katy Jurado, Peter Whitney, Douglas Fowley, John Larch, Whit Bissell. Dank Western of Mexican gunslinger Quinn saving a town from outlaws.
Man From Down Under, The (1943) **103m.** **½ D: Robert Z. Leonard. Charles Laughton, Binnie Barnes, Richard Carlson, Donna Reed, Christopher Severn, Clyde Cook. Overblown, over-plotted vehicle for Laughton, who's delightful as a bluff, bragging Aussie who raises two French orphans from WW1 as his own. Look for young Peter Lawford as an Australian soldier toward the end of the film.
Man From Frisco, The (1944) **91m.** **½ D: Robert Florey. Michael O'Shea, Anne Shirley, Dan Duryea, Gene Lockhart, Stephanie Bachelor, Ray Walker. O'Shea is pushy shipbuilding genius who meets resistance from residents of small town where he wants to build a new plant. Fairly entertaining action hokum with a little too much romance.
Man From Galveston, The (1963) **57m.** ** D: William Conrad. Jeffrey Hunter, Preston Foster, James Coburn, Joanna Moore, Edward Andrews, Kevin Hagen, Martin West, Ed Nelson. Unsatisfying little Western with lawyer Hunter defending ex-girlfriend Moore on a murder charge in a frontier town.
Man From God's Country (1958) **C-72m.** ** D: Paul Landres. George Montgomery, Randy Stuart, Gregg Barton, Kim Charney, Susan Cummings. Quiet oater involving land-hungry ranchers trying to outfox the railroad. CinemaScope.
Man From Hong Kong, The (1975-Australian-Chinese) **C-103m.** ** D: Brian Trenchard Smith. Jimmy Wang Yu, George Lazenby, Ros Spiers, Hugh Keays-Byrne, Rebecca Gilling. Undemanding action fans should get their fill in this stunt-crazy story of Hong Kong emissary (and Kung Fu expert) called to Sydney to help nail drug kingpin. Originally titled THE DRAGON FLIES; surprisingly triggered a hit song, "Sky High." Panavision. [R]
Man From Laramie, The (1955) **C-104m.** *** D: Anthony Mann. James Stewart, Arthur Kennedy, Donald Crisp, Cathy O'Donnell, Alex Nicol, Aline MacMahon, Wallace Ford. Taut action tale of revenge, with Stewart seeking those who killed his brother. CinemaScope.▼◗
Man From O.R.G.Y. (1970) **C-92m.** *½ D: James A. Hill. Robert Walker, Steve Rossi, Slappy White, Louisa Moritz. Banal counterespionage comedy-drama. Who's got the secrets? [R]
Man From Planet X, The (1951) **70m.** **½ D: Edgar G. Ulmer. Robert Clarke, Margaret Field, Raymond Bond, William Schallert. Scottish Highlands are visited by alien from wandering planet; at first he is benign, but evil designs of Schallert turn him against human race. Extremely cheap, but atmospheric; script is stilted but story is strong and somewhat unusual.▼●
Man From Snowy River, The (1982-Australian) **C-115m.** ***½ D: George Miller. Kirk Douglas, Tom Burlinson, Sigrid Thornton, Jack Thompson, Lorraine Bayly, Tommy Dysart, Bruce Kerr. Grand, old-fashioned Western saga, based on epic Australian poem, about strong-willed young man who goes to work for an empire-building cattleman, and falls in love with his daughter. Hokey, simplistic, but great fun, with eye-filling scenery and incredible action scenes with some wild horses. Douglas has fun in a dual role; Thompson's part is virtually a cameo. Followed by RETURN TO SNOWY RIVER. Panavision. [PG]▼●
Man From the Alamo, The (1953) **C-79m.** *** D: Budd Boetticher. Glenn Ford, Julia (Julie) Adams, Victor Jory, Hugh O'Brian, Chill Wills, Jeanne Cooper, Neville Brand. Ford escapes from the Alamo to warn others, but is branded a deserter, and forced to prove himself anew in further battles against the Mexicans. Typically offbeat Boetticher Western, well acted and exciting.▼
Man From the Diner's Club, The (1963) **96m.** **½ D: Frank Tashlin. Danny Kaye, Martha Hyer, Cara Williams, Telly

Savalas, Everett Sloane, George Kennedy. Silly shenanigans of Diner's Club employee Kaye involved with Damon Runyonish gangsters. Danny has certainly had more inspired antics than these, but okay slapstick. Screenplay by William Peter Blatty. Look for Harry Dean Stanton as a beatnik.

Man From Yesterday, The (1932) **71m.** *** D: Berthold Viertel. Claudette Colbert, Clive Brook, Charles Boyer, Andy Devine, Alan Mowbray. Story of Colbert marrying Boyer thinking husband Brook has died is surprisingly well done, thanks mainly to top performances.

Manganinnie (1980-Australian) **C-90m.** **½ D: John Honey. Mawuyul Yanthalawuy, Anna Ralph, Phillip Hinton, Elaine Mangan. White child Ralph, separated from her family, is watched over by aborigine Yanthalawuy, separated from her tribe. Slow and uninvolving, though the scenery is pretty.

Mangler, The (1995) **C-106m.** *½ D: Tobe Hooper. Robert Englund, Ted Levine, Daniel Matmor, Jeremy Crutchley, Vanessa Pike. An evil, gargantuan steam iron and speed-folder at a rural industrial laundry has been eating the employees lately; a local cop tries to exorcise the demons responsible. Englund is good as the laundry's crazed owner, but ridiculous "scares" and lack of logic defeat this forgettable genre entry based on a Stephen King short story. Horror fans will be disappointed with the results of this Englund-Hooper-King convergence. Unrated version available on video. [R]▼●

Mango Tree, The (1977-Australian) **C-93m.** **½ D: Kevin Dobson. Christopher Pate, Geraldine Fitzgerald, Robert Helpmann, Diane Craig, Gerald Kennedy, Gloria Dawn. A young man's coming of age in Australia, around the time of WW1; pictorially pleasing, with a warm performance by Fitzgerald as the young man's wise, gentle grandmother, but nothing out of the ordinary. Written and produced by former actor Michael Pate, whose son plays the lead. Panavision.▼

Manhandled (1949) **97m.** ** D: Lewis R. Foster. Dorothy Lamour, Dan Duryea, Sterling Hayden, Irene Hervey, Philip Reed. Crooked private eye Duryea tries to pin robbery-murder rap on innocent Lamour. Turgid drama that reliable cast can't salvage.

Manhattan (1979) **96m.** ***½ D: Woody Allen. Woody Allen, Diane Keaton, Michael Murphy, Mariel Hemingway, Meryl Streep, Anne Byrne, Tisa Farrow. Bittersweet slice-of-life about a N.Y.C. comedy writer and his cerebral friends; blisteringly accurate and ultimately poignant, a worthy followup to Woody's ANNIE HALL. Magnificently photographed (in b&w) by Gordon Willis, with splendid use of Gershwin music on the soundtrack. Wallace Shawn's role is especially funny; that's Mark Linn-Baker as one of the Shakespearean actors, and Karen Allen (in blonde wig) and David Rasche on TV show. Panavision. [R]▼●

Manhattan by Numbers (1993) **C-88m.** **½ D: Amir Naderi. John Wojda, Branislav Tomich, Mary Chang Faulk, Matt Friedson, Frank Irwin. Evocative account of a day in the life of an out-of-work N.Y.C. journalist (Wojda), who is about to be evicted from his apartment and, perhaps, join the hordes of homeless on the city streets. It may be Christmastime, but there is little to cheer about; N.Y.C. is somberly depicted as a dreary, graffiti-littered urban landscape in which there is mostly despair amid rare acts of kindness. Gato Barbieri's fine score helps set and sustain mood; big disappointment is illogically upbeat finale.

Manhattan Melodrama (1934) **93m.** *** D: W. S. Van Dyke II. Clark Gable, William Powell, Myrna Loy, Leo Carrillo, Isabel Jewell, Mickey Rooney, Nat Pendleton. Boyhood pals remain adult friends though one is a gangster and the other a D.A. (a plot device reused many times). What might be unbearably corny is top entertainment, thanks to this star trio and a director with gusto. Arthur Caesar's original story won an Oscar. Footnoted in American history as the film John Dillinger saw just before being gunned down at the Biograph Theatre in Chicago. Also shown in computer-colored version.▼●

Manhattan Merry-Go-Round (1938) **80m.** ** D: Charles Riesner. Phil Regan, Ann Dvorak, Leo Carrillo, James Gleason. Gangster Carrillo takes over a record company. Flimsy script, with romantic subplot, is just an excuse for none-too-thrilling specialty numbers by Gene Autry, Cab Calloway, Ted Lewis, Louis Prima, The Kay Thompson Singers, and Joe DiMaggio (!), to name just a few.▼

Manhattan Murder Mystery (1993) **C-108m.** *** D: Woody Allen. Woody Allen, Diane Keaton, Alan Alda, Anjelica Huston, Jerry Adler, Lynn Cohen, Ron Rifkin, Joy Behar, Marge Redmond, Aida Turturro. Slight but enjoyable caper, with Allen and Keaton as a married couple who suspect their seemingly harmless neighbor has murdered his wife. A return (of sorts) to "earlier, funnier" filmmaking for Allen, this is no classic but it is consistently entertaining, with the usual quota of one-liners and some very funny set pieces. Best of all is the marvelous chemistry between Allen and Keaton (taking over the role originally intended for Mia Farrow), who play off each other's neuroses with intuitive ease. Allen cowrote the screenplay with his ANNIE HALL and MANHATTAN collaborator Marshall Brickman. [PG]▼●◗

Manhattan Project, The (1986) **C-117m.**

** D: Marshall Brickman. John Lithgow, Christopher Collet, Cynthia Nixon, Jill Eikenberry, John Mahoney, Sully Boyar, Gregg Edelman, Robert (Sean) Leonard. Precocious teenager breaks into top-secret plant, steals some plutonium, and builds his own nuclear reactor, ostensibly to make a point but also to show off. Slick, extremely well-acted film is blatantly irresponsible and has us cheering for the kid as he outwits the dopey grownups and nearly blows up the world! [PG-13]▼●

Man Hunt (1941) **105m.** ***½ D: Fritz Lang. Walter Pidgeon, Joan Bennett, George Sanders, John Carradine, Roddy McDowall. Farfetched yet absorbing drama of man attempting to kill Hitler, getting into more trouble than he bargained for. Tense, well-done. Screenplay by Dudley Nichols, from Geoffrey Household's novel. Remade as ROGUE MALE.

Manhunt (1973) SEE: **The Italian Connection**

Manhunt, The (1986-Italian) **C-89m.** ** D: Larry Ludman (Fabrizio De Angelis). John Ethan Wayne, Raymund Harmstorf, Henry Silva, Bo Svenson, Ernest Borgnine. Wayne (son of John Wayne) is a young, would-be horse trainer unjustly arrested as a horse thief. Cast uplifts routine plot in this made-in-U.S.A. Italian production, filmed in 1984. ▼

Manhunter (1986) **C-119m.** *** D: Michael Mann. William L. Petersen, Kim Greist, Joan Allen, Brian Cox, Dennis Farina, Stephen Lang, Tom Noonan. Forceful contemporary cops-and-robbers melodrama told with *Miami Vice* stylistics (and hard-pounding music) by that show's creator, writer-director Mann. Petersen plays a troubled former FBI agent who's called back to service to capture a serial killer, which he does by getting himself to think just like the murderer! Gripping all the way and surprisingly nonexploitive, considering subject matter. Don't examine story too carefully or the holes start to show through. Jailed killer Hannibal Lecter figures in the story; later he'd become the subject of his own story, THE SILENCE OF THE LAMBS. Based on Thomas Harris' novel *Red Dragon.* Alternate TV title: RED DRAGON. Super 35. [R]▼●

Manhunt in the Jungle (1958) **C-79m.** BOMB D: Tom McGowan. Robin Hughes, Luis Alvarez, James Wilson, Jorge Montoro, John B. Symmes. Hackneyed safari set in Brazil.

Mania (1959-British) **87m.** *** D: John Gilling. Peter Cushing, Donald Pleasence, George Rose, June Laverick, Dermot Walsh, Billie Whitelaw. Deliciously lurid shocker with Cushing going all out as an Edinburgh scientist who employs grave-robbers Pleasence and Rose to supply him with corpses for his experiments. Originally titled THE FLESH AND THE FIENDS (and released at 97m.). Aka PSYCHO KILLERS and THE FIENDISH GHOULS; the latter runs 74m. Dyaliscope. ▼

Maniac (1934) **51m.** BOMB D: Dwain Esper. Bill Woods, Horace Carpenter, Ted Edwards, Phyllis Diller (not the comedienne), Theo Ramsey, Jenny Dark. Typically delirious Esper schlockfest—filmed mostly in somebody's basement—about a lunatic who murders a mad doctor and assumes his identity. High points include a passionate soliloquy on insanity, pulling out a cat's eye and eating it, and a climactic fight between two women armed with hypodermic needles!▼

Maniac (1962-British) **86m.** **½ D: Michael Carreras. Kerwin Mathews, Nadia Gray, Donald Houston, Justine Lord. One of the better British thrillers made in wake of PSYCHO, with Mathews as vacationing artist in France arousing hatred of girlfriend's sick father. Good plot twists. Written by Jimmy Sangster. Megascope.▼

Maniac (1977) SEE: **Ransom**

Maniac (1980) **C-87m.** BOMB D: William Lustig. Joe Spinell, Caroline Munro, Gail Lawrence (Abigail Clayton), Kelly Piper, Rita Montone, Tom Savini. Unrelenting exercise in nihilistic gore about a cretin who murders women and then scalps them so that he can dress up his mannequins. Although an excellent character actor, coscriptwriter-producer-star Spinell bears most of the blame for this claustrophobic, sickening film. [R]▼◗

Maniac Cop (1988) **C-85m.** *½ D: William Lustig. Tom Atkins, Bruce Campbell, Laurene Landon, Richard Roundtree, William Smith, Robert Z'dar, Sheree North. Potentially intriguing premise, of a killer on the police force striking terror in the hearts of N.Y.C. residents, is bungled by failed black humor and ham-fisted direction into standard stalk-and-slash fare. Best work is done by North as a crippled, embittered policewoman. Followed by several sequels. [R]▼●◗

Manifesto (1988-U.S.-Yugoslavian) **C-96m.** **½ D: Dusan Makavejev. Camilla Søeberg, Alfred Molina, Simon Callow, Eric Stoltz, Lindsay Duncan, Rade Šerbedžija, Svetozar Svetković, Chris Haywood, Patrick Godfrey, Linda Marlowe, Gabrielle Anwar, Ronald Lacey. Set in the 1920s, this anarchic dark comedy depicts a small Balkan community that's a hotbed of assassination plots, sexual freedom, and repressive ideas. Loosely derived from a story by Emile Zola, the film is brightly colored and impishly written (by the director), but eventually becomes *too* anarchic for its own good. More notable for what it attempts than what it achieves. Makavejev's first film in Yugoslavia after a 17-year exile. Video title: A NIGHT OF LOVE. [R]▼

Man I Killed, The SEE: **Broken Lullaby**

Manila Calling (1942) **81m.** ** D: Herbert I. Leeds. Lloyd Nolan, Carole Landis, Cornel Wilde, James Gleason, Martin Kosleck, Ralph Byrd, Elisha Cook, Jr., Louis Jean Heydt. Pat WW2 film of one guy taking 'em all on with his small but dedicated outfit.

Man I Love, The (1946) **96m.** *** D: Raoul Walsh. Ida Lupino, Robert Alda, Bruce Bennett, Andrea King, Dolores Moran, Martha Vickers, Alan Hale. Slick, well-acted melodrama casts Ida as nightclub singer pursued by no-good mobster Alda. Forget logic and just enjoy. This film inspired Scorsese's NEW YORK, NEW YORK.▼●

Man I Married, The (1940) **77m.** *** D: Irving Pichel. Joan Bennett, Francis Lederer, Lloyd Nolan, Anna Sten, Otto Kruger. Strong story of German Lederer taken in by Nazi propaganda while American wife Bennett tries to stop him. Taut, exciting script.

Man in a Cocked Hat (1959-British) **88m.** *** D: Jeffrey Dell, Roy Boulting. Terry-Thomas, Peter Sellers, Luciana Paluzzi, Thorley Walters, Ian Bannen, John Le Mesurier, Miles Malleson. Screwball farce about Island of Gallardia, a British protectorate forgotten for 50 years; when rediscovered, bumbling Terry-Thomas of the Foreign Office is left in charge. British title: CARLTON-BROWNE OF THE F.O.▼

Man in a Uniform (1993-Canadian) **C-99m.** *** D: David Wellington. Tom McCamus, Brigitte Bako, Kevin Tighe, David Hemblen, Graham McPherson. Startlingly effective TAXI DRIVER variation about an actor (McCamus, who is excellent) who wins a role as a cop on a TV series and begins wearing his costume uniform in public, with jarring results. Film effectively examines the difference between real and reel life in an impersonal, randomly violent society. Well worth watching. Original title: I LOVE A MAN IN UNIFORM. ▼

Man in Grey, The (1943-British) **116m.** *** D: Leslie Arliss. Margaret Lockwood, James Mason, Phyllis Calvert, Stewart Granger, Helen Haye, Martita Hunt. Wealthy Calvert befriends impoverished schoolmate Lockwood; years later, Lockwood repays the kindness by trying to steal her husband. Elaborate costume drama, told in flashback, is entertaining, and notable for boosting Mason (as Calvert's hateful husband) to stardom. Originally shown in the U.S. at 93m.▼

Man in Half Moon Street, The (1944) **92m.** **½ D: Ralph Murphy. Nils Asther, Helen Walker, Brandon Hurst, Reginald Sheffield. Not-bad horror tale of scientist Asther experimenting with rejuvenation; done on better scale than many of these little epics. Remade as THE MAN WHO COULD CHEAT DEATH.

Man in Hiding (1953-British) **79m.** *½ D: Terence Fisher. Paul Henreid, Lois Maxwell, Kieron Moore, Hugh Sinclair. Tame detective-capturing-elusive-killer plot.

Man in Love, A (1987-French-Italian) **C-117m.** *** D: Diane Kurys. Peter Coyote, Greta Scacchi, Peter Riegert, Claudia Cardinale, Jamie Lee Curtis, John Berry, Vincent Lindon, Jean Pigozzi. Full-blooded romance about a married American actor who falls in love with his leading lady while making a movie in Rome. Coyote and Scacchi are believable (and extremely sexy) in this sensual and intelligent film, written by Israel Horovitz and director Kurys, whose first English language film this is. Technovision. [R]▼●

Man Inside, The (1958-British) **90m.** *½ D: John Gilling. Jack Palance, Anita Ekberg, Nigel Patrick, Anthony Newley, Sidney James, Donald Pleasence, Eric Pohlmann. Shoddy robbery caper with private investigator hunting jewel thieves throughout Europe. CinemaScope.▼

Man Inside, The (1990-U.S.-French) **C-93m.** ** D: Bobby Roth. Jürgen Prochnow, Peter Coyote, Nathalie Baye, Dieter Laser, Monique van de Ven, Phillip Anglim, Henry G. Sanders. Crusading West German investigative reporter infiltrates a scandal-sheet newspaper in order to write an indictment of their sleazy practices. A misfire, despite its intriguing premise and cast; it may just be that the film bites off more than it can chew. Story seems dated already. [PG]▼●

Man in the Attic (1954) **82m.** **½ D: Hugo Fregonese. Jack Palance, Constance Smith, Byron Palmer, Frances Bavier, Rhys Williams, Sean McClory, Isabel Jewell, Leslie Bradley. Flavorful account of notorious Jack the Ripper, with Palance going full-blast. Remake of THE LODGER.

Man in the Dark (1953) **70m.** **½ D: Lew Landers. Edmond O'Brien, Audrey Totter, Ruth Warren, Ted de Corsia, Horace McMahon. Convict O'Brien undergoes brain surgery to eliminate criminal bent, and loses memory in the process; his old cohorts only care that he remember where he stashed their stolen loot. Routine remake of THE MAN WHO LIVED TWICE was originally shown in 3-D.

Man in the Dinghy SEE: **Into the Blue**

Man in the Glass Booth, The (1975) **C-117m.** **½ D: Arthur Hiller. Maximilian Schell, Lois Nettleton, Luther Adler, Lawrence Pressman, Henry Brown, Richard Rasof. American Film Theatre version of Robert Shaw's play about a glib Jewish industrialist brought to trial for Nazi war crimes. Schell is good, but overall effect is contrived. Shaw had his name removed from credits of film. [PG]▼

Man in the Gray Flannel Suit, The (1956) **C-153m.** ***½ D: Nunnally Johnson. Gregory Peck, Jennifer Jones, Fredric March, Marisa Pavan, Lee J. Cobb, Keenan Wynn, Gene Lockhart, Gigi Perreau, Arthur O'Connell, Henry Daniell. Sloan Wilson's slick novel of Madison Avenue executive struggling to get ahead and to find meaning in his home life. Nice cameo by Ann Harding as March's wife. Scripted by the director; music by Bernard Herrmann. CinemaScope.▼●

Man in the Iron Mask, The (1939) **110m.** *** D: James Whale. Louis Hayward, Joan Bennett, Warren William, Joseph Schildkraut, Alan Hale, Walter Kingsford, Marion Martin. Rousing adventure of twin brothers: one becomes King of France, the other a carefree gay blade raised by D'Artagnan (William) and the 3 Musketeers. Fine swashbuckler. Filmed in 1929 with Douglas Fairbanks as THE IRON MASK.▼

Man in the Iron Mask, The (1977) **C-100m. TVM** D: Mike Newell. Richard Chamberlain, Patrick McGoohan, Louis Jourdan, Jenny Agutter, Vivien Merchant, Ian Holm, Ralph Richardson. Stylish romantic adventure in this William Bast adaptation of the Dumas classic acted with panache by a sterling cast. Chamberlain can swashbuckle with the best of them. Grand entertainment. Above average.▼

Man in the Iron Mask, The (1998) **C-132m.** *** D: Randall Wallace. Leonardo DiCaprio, Jeremy Irons, John Malkovich, Gérard Depardieu, Gabriel Byrne, Anne Parillaud, Judith Godreche, Edward Atterton, Peter Sarsgaard, Hugh Laurie. Handsome retelling of the durable Alexandre Dumas tale of a man unjustly imprisoned and encased in an iron mask—because his very existence threatens the reigning king of France, the young, selfish Louis XIV. The fate of both are soon in the hands of the aging but still passionate Musketeers. It would be hard to miss with that cast; the film is quite enjoyable, but it does go on too long. [PG-13]▼●◗

Man in the Middle (1964-British) **94m.** ** D: Guy Hamilton. Robert Mitchum, France Nuyen, Barry Sullivan, Keenan Wynn, Alexander Knox, Trevor Howard. Unconvincing, confusing film of Howard Fast novel *The Winston Affair*, about American military officer accused of homicide; static courtroom sequences. CinemaScope.

Man in the Moon (1961-British) **98m.** *** D: Basil Dearden. Kenneth More, Shirley Anne Field, Norman Bird, Michael Hordern, John Phillips. Top comedy satirizing space race. Government recruits man unaffected by cold, heat, speed, etc., to be perfect astronaut.

Man in the Moon, The (1991) **C-99m.** *** D: Robert Mulligan. Sam Waterston, Tess Harper, Gail Strickland, Reese Witherspoon, Jason London, Emily Warfield, Bentley Mitchum, Ernie Lively. Ingratiatingly old-fashioned weeper set in rural Louisiana in 1957, about a 14-year-old girl in love with an older boy, who in turn prefers her college-bound sis. Newcomer Witherspoon is unforgettable as the younger sister—more early adolescent lightning for director Mulligan, who guided TO KILL A MOCKINGBIRD and SUMMER OF '42. Nicely shot by Freddie Francis. Waterston has some effective scenes as the girls' father. [PG-13]▼●

Man in the Net, The (1959) **97m.** **½ D: Michael Curtiz. Alan Ladd, Carolyn Jones, Diane Brewster, Charles McGraw, John Lupton, Tom Helmore. Fair drama of Ladd trying to clear himself of murder charge for wife's death.

Man in the Raincoat, The (1957-French-Italian) **97m.** ** D: Julien Duvivier. Fernandel, John McGiver, Bernard Blier, Claude Sylvain, Jean Rigaux, Rob Murray. Middling comedy-mystery with Fernandel as a bumbling musician who accidentally becomes involved with murder. Tries hard and has its moments but simply doesn't gel. ▼

Man in the Road, The (1957-British) **83m.** *½ D: Lance Comfort. Derek Farr, Ella Raines, Donald Wolfit, Karel Stepanek. Despite sturdy cast, humdrum telling of Communists trying to get scientist to divulge secret formula.

Man in the Saddle (1951) **C-87m.** ** D: Andre de Toth. Randolph Scott, Joan Leslie, Ellen Drew, Alexander Knox. Scott is involved in romantic triangle causing death on the range; justice triumphs.▼

Man in the Santa Claus Suit, The (1979) **C-100m. TVM** D: Corey Allen. Fred Astaire, Gary Burghoff, John Byner, Bert Convy, Nanette Fabray, Harold Gould. Yuletide fantasy of how Astaire (playing seven different characters) affects the lives of various familiar TV faces. He also sings the title song—delightfully. Average.▼

Man in the Shadow (1957) **80m.** **½ D: Jack Arnold. Jeff Chandler, Orson Welles, Colleen Miller, James Gleason. Welles chomps his way through role of rancher responsible for helper's death. Chandler is the earnest sheriff. CinemaScope.▼

Man in the Shadow (1957-British) SEE: **Violent Stranger**

Man in the Vault (1956) **73m.** *½ D: Andrew V. McLaglen. William Campbell, Karen Sharpe, Anita Ekberg, Berry Kroeger, Paul Fix. Programmer of drab locksmith involved in robbery; nothing special.

Man in the White Suit, The (1951-British) **84m.** ***½ D: Alexander Mackendrick. Alec Guinness, Joan Greenwood, Cecil Parker, Michael Gough, Ernest Thesiger, Vida Hope, George Benson, Edie Martin. Guinness is inventor who discovers a fabric that can't wear out or soil; dismayed

garment manufacturers set out to bury his formula. Most engaging comedy. Screenplay by Roger Macdougall, John Dighton, and Mackendrick, from Macdougall's play.▼●
Man in the Wilderness (1971) **C-105m.** *** D: Richard C. Sarafian. Richard Harris, John Huston, John Bindon, Ben Carruthers, Prunella Ransome, Henry Wilcoxon. Trapper Harris abandoned in wasteland, must fight for survival, and revenge as well. Well-made, engrossing, but bloody film. Panavision. [PG]▼
Manitou, The (1978) **C-104m.** BOMB D: William Girdler. Tony Curtis, Susan Strasberg, Michael Ansara, Ann Sothern, Burgess Meredith, Stella Stevens. Long-dead Indian medicine man gets himself resurrected through a fetus on Strasberg's neck. Veterans Curtis, Sothern, and Meredith look properly embarrassed. Based on a novel by Graham Masterson. Panavision. [PG]▼●
Man Killer (1933) **67m.** **½ D: Michael Curtiz. William Powell, Margaret Lindsay, Ruth Donnelly, Arthur Hohl, Natalie Moorehead, Arthur Byron. Powell accepts job with shady private-detective Hohl and agrees to dupe wealthy Lindsay, but falls in love with her instead. Warner Bros. programmer picks up after a slow start. Originally released as PRIVATE DETECTIVE 62.
Man Made Monster (1941) **59m.** ** D: George Waggner. Lionel Atwill, Lon Chaney, Jr., Anne Nagel, Frank Albertson, Samuel S. Hinds, William Davidson, Ben Taggart, Connie Bergen. Sci-fi yarn of scientist Atwill making Chaney invulnerable to electricity and able to kill with his touch; fairly well done. Reissued as ATOMIC MONSTER.▼
Man Named John, A (1965-Italian-French) **C-94m.** *** D: Ermanno Olmi. Rod Steiger. Excellent documentary on Pope John XXIII, encompassing many facets of his life, work, and beliefs on mankind. Aka AND THERE CAME A MAN.
Mannequin (1937) **95m.** **½ D: Frank Borzage. Joan Crawford, Spencer Tracy, Alan Curtis, Ralph Morgan, Leo Gorcey, Elisabeth Risdon. Prototype rags-to-riches soaper, with working-girl Crawford getting ahead via wealthy Tracy. Predictable script, but nice job by stars, usual MGM gloss (even in the tenements!).▼●
Mannequin (1987) **C-89m.** BOMB D: Michael Gottlieb. Andrew McCarthy, Kim Cattrall, Estelle Getty, G. W. Bailey, James Spader, Meshach Taylor, Carole Davis. Cattrall is an ancient Egyptian spirit who embodies a department store mannequin; McCarthy is the only one who sees her come to life, and falls in love with her. Attempt to recreate the feeling of old screwball comedies is absolute rock-bottom fare. Dispiriting to anyone who remembers what movie comedy ought to be. Followed by a sequel. [PG]▼●
Mannequin Two: On the Move (1991) **C-95m.** BOMB D: Stewart Raffill. Kristy Swanson, William Ragsdale, Meshach Taylor, Terry Kiser, Stuart Pankin, Cynthia Harris. This inept sequel to MANNEQUIN makes you think the original was not so bad by comparison. Again, a window dresser (Ragsdale) in a department store frees the spirit of a medieval peasant (Swanson) who has been imprisoned inside a mannequin's form for—quite logically—1,000 years. Torpor ensues. [PG]▼●
Manny & Lo (1996) **C-97m.** *** D: Lisa Krueger. Scarlett Johansson, Aleksa Palladino, Mary Kay Place, Paul Guilfoyle, Glenn Fitzgerald, Novella Nelson. Orphaned 11-year-old Manny (Johansson) and her more naive 16-year-old sister Lo (Palladino) sleep in model homes and drive about in an old station wagon, until it's obvious Lo is pregnant, so they kidnap prissy Place to help with the delivery while hiding out in a woodsy cabin. Wise, warm comedy-drama is fresh and unexpected; a notable debut for writer-director Krueger. Place is particularly good. [R]▼●
Man of Aran (1934-British) **73m.** **** D: Robert Flaherty. Colman (Tiger) King, Maggie Dillane. Superb, classic documentary about day-to-day existence, and constant fight for survival, of fisherman in remote Irish coastal community. Scenes at sea are breathtaking.▼
Man of a Thousand Faces (1957) **122m.** ***½ D: Joseph Pevney. James Cagney, Dorothy Malone, Jane Greer, Marjorie Rambeau, Jim Backus, Jeanne Cagney, Robert J. Evans, Roger Smith, Jack Albertson, Snub Pollard. Surprisingly dedicated, well-acted biography of silent star Lon Chaney. Cagney as Chaney, Malone as disturbed first wife, Greer as wife who brings him happiness, are all fine. Chaney's life and career are recreated with taste (if not accuracy). Touching portrayal of movie extra by Rambeau. Ralph Wheelwright's story was adapted by R. Wright Campbell, Ivan Goff, and Ben Roberts. CinemaScope. ▼●◗
Man of Conflict (1953) **72m.** ** D: Hal Makelim. Edward Arnold, John Agar, Susan Morrow, Russell Hicks. Lukewarm drama of generation clash between father Arnold and son Agar over business and philosophy of life.
Man of Conquest (1939) **105m.** **½ D: George Nicholls, Jr. Richard Dix, Gail Patrick, Edward Ellis, Joan Fontaine. Republic Pictures tried to give this biography of Texas' Sam Houston good production values, but script slows down action.
Man of Evil (1944-British) **90m.** ** D: Anthony Asquith. Phyllis Calvert, James Mason, Stewart Granger, Wilfrid Lawson, Jean Kent. Elaborate but ponderous costumer

of maniac who tries to run people's lives to suit his fancy; overdone and not effective. Original title: FANNY BY GASLIGHT.▼

Man of Flowers, A (1984-Australian) **C-91m.** **½ D: Paul Cox. Norman Kaye, Alyson Best, Chris Haywood, Sarah Walker, Julia Blake, Bob Ellis, Barry Dickins. Kaye, a wealthy flower-loving bachelor with a mother fixation, pays artist's model Best $100 a week to disrobe for him on call. Original but monotonal mix of somberness and silliness; may catch your interest if you're in the right mood. Werner Herzog plays Kaye's father in flashback. ▼●

Man of Iron (1956-Italian) **116m.** *** D: Pietro Germi. Pietro Germi, Luisa Della Noce, Sylva Koscina, Carlo Giuffre. Somber account of Germi, railroad engineer, whose life takes a tragic turn, affecting his whole family; realistically presented. Original title: THE RAILROAD MAN.

Man of Iron (1980-Polish) **C-152m.** ***½ D: Andrzej Wajda. Jerzy Radziwilowicz, Krystyna Janda, Marian Opiana. Sequel to MAN OF MARBLE finds documentary filmmaker Janda married to son of the fallen hero whose life she had been researching. Rousing march for Solidarity is not quite up to its predecessor, but two films taken together are as epic in scope as our own GODFATHER sagas. Lech Walesa appears briefly as himself. [PG]▼●

Man of La Mancha (1972) **C-130m.** BOMB D: Arthur Hiller. Peter O'Toole, Sophia Loren, James Coco, Harry Andrews, John Castle. Plodding, abysmal adaptation of Dale Wasserman's popular musical based on Cervantes' *Don Quixote,* with Joe Darion-Mitch Leigh score. Beautiful source material has been raped, murdered, and buried. [PG]▼●

Man of Legend (1971-Italian-Spanish) **C-97m.** **½ D: Sergio Grieco. Peter Strauss, Tina Aumont, Luciana Paluzzi, Massimo Serato. WWI German soldier, mistaken for spy and condemned to death, flees to Africa, joins French Foreign Legion, falls in with Moroccan rebels and steals the heart of the chief's daughter. Uninspired sex-and-sand saga. [R]▼

Man of Marble (1977-Polish) **C-160m.** **** D: Andrzej Wajda. Krystyna Janda, Jerzy Radziwilowicz, Tadeusz Lomnicki, Jacek Lomnicki, Krystyna Zachwatowicz. Compelling, controversial, brilliantly directed tale of determined filmmaker Janda retracing the life of Radziwilowicz, naive bricklayer lionized in the 1950s as a worker-hero of the State. Wajda celebrates the role of filmmaker as a speaker of truth; ironically, the film's finale, an explanation of the bricklayer's fate, was excised by the Polish censors. Followed by MAN OF IRON.▼

Man of No Importance, A (1994-British) **C-98m.** **½ D: Suri Krishnamma. Albert Finney, Brenda Fricker, Michael Gambon, Tara Fitzgerald, Rufus Sewell, Patrick Malahide, David Kelly, Mick Lally. While staging Oscar Wilde's controversial *Salome* at his local Dublin church, a theater-loving bus conductor examines his repressed sexual feelings—toward both his leading actress and the bus's handsome driver. Initially lightweight comedy-drama gradually becomes more complex, possibly taking on more than it can handle; Finney, however, devours the role with his usual feeling and conviction. [R]▼●

Man of the Century (1999) **80m.** ** D: Adam Abraham. Gibson Frazier, Susan Egan, David Margulies, Frank Gorshin, Bobby Short, Anne Jackson, Gary Beach, Marisa Ryan, Lester Lanin. A snappy-talking newspaper reporter named Johnny Twennies (Frazier) lives in a 1920s world, immersed in its slang, customs, and music, unaware of the realities around him, or the very contemporary sexual longing of his girlfriend (Egan). An obvious labor of love, this somewhat amateurish film has enthusiasm to spare, and some amusing cameos, but one overriding problem: it makes no sense. Written by the director and his star. [R]▼

Man of the House (1995) **C-96m.** ** D: James Orr. Chevy Chase, Farrah Fawcett, Jonathan Taylor Thomas, George Wendt, David Shiner, Art LaFleur, Richard Portnow. Thomas is the center of attention in this tepid comedy, as the sometimes overbearing son of Fawcett, whom district attorney Chase intends to marry. Stepdad-to-be attempts to ingratiate himself with the boy, who plots to eliminate the man from his mom's life. The humor—what there is of it—is plenty predictable, but kids will probably lap it up. [PG]▼●

Man of the West (1958) **C-100m.** *** D: Anthony Mann. Gary Cooper, Julie London, Lee J. Cobb, Arthur O'Connell, Jack Lord, John Dehner, Royal Dano. Dismissed in 1958, this powerful story deserves another look. Cooper plays a reformed outlaw who is forced to rejoin his ex-boss (Cobb) to save himself and other innocent people from the gang's mistreatment. Strong, epic-scale Western, with script by Reginald Rose. CinemaScope.▼

Man of the World (1931) **71m.** ** D: Richard Wallace. William Powell, Carole Lombard, Wynne Gibson, Guy Kibbee, George Chandler. Routine tale of good-girl Lombard in love with con-man Powell. If Carole's performance seems heartfelt it may be due to the fact the two stars married the same year.

Man of the Year (1996) **C-87m.** ** D: Dirk Shafer. Odd combination of documentary and "mockumentary" (à la THIS IS SPINAL TAP) tells the story of Dirk Shafer, the *Playgirl* Centerfold Star of 1992 who hid his gay lifestyle in order to become a symbol of heterosexual male beefcake . . . and an expert on "what women want from a man." The potentially rich premise doesn't really pay off, as the "real" footage used here is far more interesting than the re-creations.▼◗

Man on a String (1960) **92m.** *** D: Andre de Toth. Ernest Borgnine, Kerwin Mathews, Colleen Dewhurst, Alexander Scourby, Glenn Corbett. Fictionalized account of counterspy Boris Morros, involved in Russian-U.S. Cold War conflict. Taut action sequences.

Man on a Swing (1974) **C-110m.** **½ D: Frank Perry. Cliff Robertson, Joel Grey, Dorothy Tristan, Elizabeth Wilson, George Voskovec. Mysterious clairvoyant (Grey) offers to help a cop (Robertson) solve sex-slaying that's been troubling him, but generates more questions than answers. Intriguing idea sadly misses the mark by building up to an unsatisfying conclusion. Based on a true story. [PG]

Man on a Tightrope (1953) **105m.** **½ D: Elia Kazan. Fredric March, Gloria Grahame, Terry Moore, Cameron Mitchell, Adolphe Menjou, Richard Boone, Robert Beatty. Passable based-on-fact account of an obscure, downtrodden little circus troupe and its escape from Communist-ruled Czechoslovakia to freedom in Austria. Has its moments, but the characters are far too broadly drawn. Scripted by Robert E. Sherwood.

Man on Fire (1957) **95m.** **½ D: Ranald MacDougall. Bing Crosby, Mary Fickett, Inger Stevens, E.G. Marshall, Malcolm Broderick, Anne Seymour, Richard Eastham. Divorced father (Crosby) refuses to grant his remarried ex-wife partial custody of their son in this modest domestic drama.

Man on Fire (1987-French-Italian) **C-93m.** BOMB D: Elie Chouraqui. Scott Glenn, Jade Malle, Paul Shenar, Brooke Adams, Jonathan Pryce, Joe Pesci, Danny Aiello. International mishmash of pacifist Glenn, hired as young Malle's bodyguard, who turns into a minor league Rambo when she is kidnapped. Good cast wasted. [R]▼●

Manon of the Spring (1986-French) **C-113m.** *** D: Claude Berri. Yves Montand, Emmanuelle Béart, Daniel Auteuil, Hippolyte Girardot, Elisabeth Depardieu, Gabriel Bacquier. Conclusion of the story begun in JEAN DE FLORETTE resumes with Manon, now a beautiful, free-spirited young shepherdess, learning the truth behind her father's death, and plotting her revenge on the pathetic Auteuil and the scheming Montand. Berri spins his story slowly, deliberately, savoring every moment leading to the unexpected conclusion. Only thing missing in this second half is the strong presence of Gérard Depardieu. Technovision. [PG]▼●

Man on the Eiffel Tower, The (1949) **C-97m.** *** D: Burgess Meredith. Charles Laughton, Franchot Tone, Burgess Meredith, Robert Hutton, Jean Wallace, Patricia Roc, Wilfrid Hyde-White, Belita. Intriguing treatment of Georges Simenon yarn with Laughton as Inspector Maigret and Tone as a madman who thinks he has all the angles on carrying out a perfect crime. This was Meredith's directing debut, shot entirely in Paris in the experimental Anscocolor process.▼

Man on the Flying Trapeze, The (1935) **65m.** ***½ D: Clyde Bruckman. W. C. Fields, Mary Brian, Kathleen Howard, Grady Sutton, Vera Lewis, Walter Brennan. Hilarious Fieldsian study in frustration, with able assistance from hardboiled wife Howard, good-for-nothing Sutton. Best sequence has W. C. receiving four traffic tickets in a row!

Man on the Moon (1999) **C-118m.** ** D: Milos Forman. Jim Carrey, Danny DeVito, Courtney Love, Paul Giamatti, Vincent Schiavelli, Peter Bonerz, Gerry Becker, Leslie Lyles. The writers of ED WOOD and THE PEOPLE VS. LARRY FLYNT, reteamed with FLYNT director Forman, strike out with this bio of the late comedy performer Andy Kaufman. Carrey perfectly embodies his subject, but it's impossible to get inside Kaufman's head and understand what made him so very, very strange, onstage and off . . . if indeed it's even worth the effort. Some of Kaufman's real-life acting colleagues appear as themselves. Panavision. [R]▼●◗

Man on the Roof (1977-Swedish) **C-110m.** ***½ D: Bo Widerberg. Gustav Lindstedt, Hakan Serner, Sven Wallter, Thomas Hellberg. A cop killer is the subject of a Stockholm manhunt in this police film with substance and style. Absorbing for its look at police methodology as well as its suspense and action. Based on the Martin Beck novel by Maj Sjowall and Per Wahloo (Walter Matthau played Beck in THE LAUGHING POLICEMAN). [R]▼

Man or Gun (1958) **79m.** ** D: Albert Gannaway. Macdonald Carey, Audrey Totter, James Craig, James Gleason. Bland Western with Carey cleaning up the town. Filmed in Naturama.

Man Outside, The (1968-British) **C-98m.** **½ D: Samuel Gallu. Van Heflin, Heidelinde Weis, Pinkas Braun, Peter Vaughan, Charles Gray, Ronnie Barker. Heflin is fired from CIA job but cannot extricate himself from international tug-of-war over Russian defector; unpretentious spy stuff. Techniscope. [G]●.

Man Outside (1986) **C-109m.** *½ D: Mark Stouffer. Robert Logan, Kathleen Quinlan, Bradford Dillman, Levon Helm, Andrew Barach, Alex Liggett. Why has Logan dropped out and chosen to isolate himself and live off the land in rural Arkansas? Anthropology professor Quinlan decides to find out and promptly falls for him . . . even as he's accused of kidnapping a young boy. Slickly made but obvious, overbaked, and a bore. In addition to Helm, other former members of The Band (Rick Danko, Garth Hudson, Richard Manuel) are in the cast. [PG-13]▼●

Manpower (1941) **102m.** *** D: Raoul Walsh. Edward G. Robinson, Marlene Dietrich, George Raft, Alan Hale, Walter Catlett, Frank McHugh, Eve Arden. Lively, typical Warner Bros. film, with nightclub "hostess" Dietrich coming between Robinson and Raft. Scene in a diner is worth the price of admission.

Man-Proof (1938) **74m.** ** D: Richard Thorpe. Myrna Loy, Franchot Tone, Rosalind Russell, Walter Pidgeon, Nana Bryant, Rita Johnson, Ruth Hussey. Flimsy plot with bright stars: Loy and Russell both love Pidgeon, but Tone is ready to step in any time.

Man's Best Friend (1993) **C-97m.** **½ D: John Lafia. Ally Sheedy, Lance Henriksen, Robert Costanzo, Fredric Lehne, John Cassini, J. D. Daniels, William Sanderson, Trula Marcus, Rick Barker. Investigative reporter Sheedy rescues big doggy, Max, from scientist Henricksen's vivesection lab . . . but Max is genetically engineered with many odd abilities—and a bad attitude. Modestly clever thriller pushes clichés associated with dogs (mailmen, junkyards, cats) to amusingly violent extremes. Derivative but fun. Written by the director. [R]▼●

Man's Castle (1933) **66m.** ***½ D: Frank Borzage. Spencer Tracy, Loretta Young, Marjorie Rambeau, Arthur Hohl, Walter Connolly, Glenda Farrell, Dickie Moore. Typically lovely Borzage romance; penniless Young moves in with shantytown tough-guy Tracy, hoping to develop a real relationship in spite of his reluctance. Tracy's ultra-macho character is a bit tough to stomach at times, but film's enormous heart conquers all, bolstered by appealing performances. Originally released at 75m.

Man's Favorite Sport? (1964) **C-120m.** **½ D: Howard Hawks. Rock Hudson, Paula Prentiss, John McGiver, Maria Perschy, Roscoe Karns, Charlene Holt. Amusing, often labored variation on Hawks' own BRINGING UP BABY. Fishing "expert" Hudson, who in reality has never fished, is forced to enter big tournament by pushy Prentiss (in her best performance). Loaded with slapstick and sexual innuendo; Norman Alden is hilarious as wisecracking Indian guide.▼

Mansfield Park (1999-British) **C-99m.** **½ D: Patricia Rozema. Frances O'Connor, Embeth Davidtz, Jonny Lee Miller, Alessandro Nivola, Harold Pinter, Lindsay Duncan, Sheila Gish. In early 19th-century England, an impoverished girl is sent to live with wealthy relatives. Working as their servant she grows to be an astute, imaginative and surprisingly independent-minded woman. Very loosely based on Jane Austen's novel and personal journals. O'Connor shines as the heroine among a top-notch cast, but story lacks the wit and satirical edge of other Austen adaptations. [PG-13]▼◗

Mansion of the Doomed (1977) **C-85m.** *½ D: Michael Pataki. Richard Basehart, Gloria Grahame, Trish Stewart, Lance Henriksen, Al Ferrara. Eye surgeon Basehart seeks eyeballs for blinded daughter from hapless victims who pile up in basement. Cheap horror opus.▼

Man They Could Not Hang, The (1939) **65m.** **½ D: Nick Grinde. Boris Karloff, Lorna Gray, Robert Wilcox, Roger Pryor, Ann Doran. First of series of four Karloff vehicles with basically same plot; hanged man brought back to life seeks revenge on his killers. Good of its type.▼

Man to Man Talk (1958-French) **89m.** ** D: Luis Saslavski. Yves Montand, Nicole Berger, Yves Noel. Trite little tale of father forced to explain facts of life to youngster when mother is having a baby. Retitled: PREMIER MAY.

Man-Trap (1961) **93m.** **½ D: Edmond O'Brien. Jeffrey Hunter, David Janssen, Stella Stevens, Hugh Sanders. Capable cast involved in adultery, robbery and disaster; unusual fling at directing by O'Brien. Panavision.

Man Trouble (1992-U.S.-Italian) **C-100m.** *½ D: Bob Rafelson. Jack Nicholson, Ellen Barkin, Beverly D'Angelo, Harry Dean Stanton, Michael McKean, Veronica Cartwright, David Clennon, Paul Mazursky, Saul Rubinek, Lauren Tom. Opera singer Barkin is troubled by a frightening break-in and other harassment so she hires guard-dog specialist Nicholson to beef up security. This mongrel of a screwball comedy consistently misses the target. Particularly disappointing in light of reteaming Nicholson with FIVE EASY PIECES director Rafelson and writer Carole Eastman. Way below par for all concerned. [PG-13]▼●

Manuela SEE: **Stowaway Girl**

Man Under Suspicion (1984-German) **C-126m.** **½ D: Norbert Kuckelmann. Maximilian Schell, Lena Stolze, Robert Aldini, Wolfgang Kieling, Kathrin Ackermann, Reinhard Hauff. Lawyer Schell investigates the motives behind a young man's act of violence at a political rally. Provocative subject matter—how the roots of fascism must be destroyed before they are given the opportunity to blossom—but low-keyed to the point of tedium, and much too long, though final twenty minutes are fairly effective.

Man Upstairs, The (1958-British) **88m.** *** D: Don Chaffey. Richard Attenborough, Bernard Lee, Donald Houston, Virginia Maskell. Compact study, excellently acted, of Attenborough, a man gone berserk much to everyone's amazement.

Man Upstairs, The (1992) **C-100m. TVM** D: George Schaefer. Katharine Hepburn, Ryan O'Neal, Henry Beckman, Helena Carroll, Brenda Forbes. Escaped petty jewel thief finds friendship and redemption while hiding out in the home of an elderly woman. Lightweight comedy-drama brought Hepburn back before the cameras, reuniting her with director Schaefer and writer James Prideaux for the third time on TV. Executive produced by Burt Reynolds, who had originally hoped to costar until scheduling intervened. Average.▼

Man Who Broke 1,000 Chains, The (1987) **C-115m. TVM** D: Daniel Mann. Val Kilmer, Charles Durning, Sonia Braga, James Keach, Elisha Cook, William Sanderson, Kyra Sedgwick, Billy Bob Thornton. The episodic adventures of Robert Elliot Burns, whose life inspired the Paul Muni classic I AM A FUGITIVE FROM A CHAIN GANG, of which this drama is *not* a remake. Made for cable. Average.▼

Man Who Broke the Bank at Monte Carlo, The (1935) **66m.** **½ D: Stephen Roberts. Ronald Colman, Joan Bennett, Colin Clive, Nigel Bruce, Montagu Love. Flimsy film carried by Colman charm, translating famous title song into story of man who calculates to clean out treasury of Riviera gambling establishment.

Man Who Came to Dinner, The (1941) **112m.** ***½ D: William Keighley. Bette Davis, Ann Sheridan, Monty Woolley, Billie Burke, Jimmy Durante, Richard Travis, Grant Mitchell, Mary Wickes, Elizabeth Fraser, Reginald Gardiner. Pompous critic Woolley (recreating his Broadway role) is forced to stay with Burke's Midwestern family for the winter, driving them crazy with assorted wacky friends passing through. Delightful adaptation of George S. Kaufman–Moss Hart play. Scripted by the Epstein brothers. Also shown in computer-colored version. ▼●

Man Who Captured Eichmann, The (1996) **C-100m. TVM** D: William A. Graham. Robert Duvall, Arliss Howard, Jeffrey Tambor, Jack Laufer, Nicolas Surovy, Joel Brooks, Sam Robards, Michael Tucci, Rita Zohar. Duvall's rather mild-mannered Adolph Eichmann is living warily in exile in postwar Argentina, when the elusive Nazi suddenly is snatched off the street by Israel's Mossad and engages in a Hannibal Lecter–like confrontation of wills with agent Peter Malkin (Howard). This engrossing film is based on Malkin's memoir *Eichmann in My Hands*. Made for cable. Above average.▼

Man Who Changed His Mind, The SEE: **Man Who Lived Again, The**

Man Who Cheated Himself, The (1950) **81m.** **½ D: Felix E. Feist. Lee J. Cobb, Jane Wyatt, John Dall, Terry Frost. Good cast uplifts typical murder film.

Man Who Could Cheat Death, The (1959-British) **C-83m.** **½ D: Terence Fisher. Anton Diffring, Hazel Court, Christopher Lee, Arnold Marle, Delphi Lawrence. OK remake of THE MAN IN HALF MOON STREET, about sculptor with somewhat messy method of retarding the aging process; typical Hammer production.

Man Who Could Work Miracles, The (1936-British) **82m.** ***½ D: Lothar Mendes. Roland Young, Ralph Richardson, Edward Chapman, Ernest Thesiger, Joan Gardner, George Zucco, Wallace Lupino, Joan Hickson, George Sanders, Torin Thatcher. H. G. Wells' fantasy of timid British department store clerk (Young) endowed with power to do anything he wants. Special effects are marvelous, supported by good cast, in charming film.▼●

Man Who Cried Wolf, The (1937) **66m.** **½ D: Lewis R. Foster. Lewis Stone, Tom Brown, Barbara Read, Robert Gleckler, Forrester Harvey. Actor Stone confesses to various murders, convinces cops he's crazy, planning perfect alibi for real killing. Cheaply filmed; Stone is mainstay of film, with Marjorie Main in good supporting role as society woman.

Man Who Dared, The (1933) **75m.** **½ D: Hamilton McFadden. Preston Foster, Zita Johann, Joan Marsh, Frank Sheridan. Modest but engrossing biography of Anton Cermak, Bohemian immigrant who became Chicago mayor and died when hit by bullet intended for FDR. Foster is excellent.

Man Who Died Twice, The (1958) **70m.** ** D: Joseph Kane. Rod Cameron, Vera Ralston, Mike Mazurki, Gerald Milton. Ralston's last film to date is mild account of chanteuse involved in murder. Filmed in Naturama.

Man Who Fell to Earth, The (1976-British) **C-140m.** ***½ D: Nicolas Roeg. David Bowie, Rip Torn, Candy Clark, Buck Henry, Bernie Casey, Jackson D. Kane. Title character ostensibly heads world conglomerate, but is actually here to find water for his planet. Highly original, fabulously photographed adaptation of Walter Tevis' classic fantasy novel is riveting for the first two-thirds, goes downhill toward the end. Still tops of its kind. Originally released in the U.S. at 118m. Remade as 1987 TVM. Panavision. [R]▼●◗

Man Who Finally Died, The (1962-British) **100m.** ** D: Quentin Lawrence. Stanley Baker, Peter Cushing, Mai Zetterling, Eric Portman, Niall MacGinnis, Nigel Green, Barbara Everest. Tepid attempt at Hitchcock-like thriller: Baker returns to German home town and tries to discover what happened to his father during WW2. CinemaScope.

Man Who Had Power Over Women, The (1970-British) **C-89m.** **½ D: John

Krish. Rod Taylor, James Booth, Carol White, Penelope Horner, Charles Korvin, Clive Francis, Magali Noel. Seriocomic satire about an executive with ethics in a London talent agency. Andrew Meredith's script (from the Gordon Williams novel) tends toward overstatement, which a good cast tries to moderate. [R]▼

Man Who Haunted Himself, The (1970-British) **C-94m.** ** D: Basil Dearden. Roger Moore, Hildegarde Neil, Alastair Mackenzie, Hugh Mackenzie, Kevork Malikyan. Strange psychological drama about Moore encountering a duplicate of himself in the aftermath of a car crash. Mildly interesting; good location footage of London. [PG]▼

Man Who Knew Too Little, The (1997) **C-94m.** ** D: Jon Amiel. Bill Murray, Peter Gallagher, Joanne Whalley, Alfred Molina, Richard Wilson, Geraldine James, John Standing, Anna Chancellor, Nicholas Woodeson. Curiously flat Murray vehicle about a dolt who visits his brother in England, is signed up for an "interactive theater" experience, but walks instead into the midst of a complex espionage scheme. Murray is game as always, in the kind of situation that used to serve Bob Hope and Danny Kaye so well, but the script lets him down. The title is the funniest part of the picture. [PG]▼●◗

Man Who Knew Too Much, The (1934-British) **75m.** *** D: Alfred Hitchcock. Leslie Banks, Edna Best, Peter Lorre, Nova Pilbeam, Frank Vosper, Pierre Fresnay. Film buffs argue which version of exciting story is better. We vote this one, with Hitchcock in fine form weaving dry British humor into a story of heart-pounding suspense; young girl is kidnapped to prevent her parents from revealing what they've learned about assassination plot.▼●◗

Man Who Knew Too Much, The (1956) **C-120m.** **½ D: Alfred Hitchcock. James Stewart, Doris Day, Brenda De Banzie, Bernard Miles, Ralph Truman, Daniel Gelin, Alan Mowbray, Carolyn Jones, Hillary Brooke. Hitchcock's remake of his 1934 film is disappointing. Even famous Albert Hall assassination sequence rings flat in tale of American couple accidentally involved in international intrigue. Doris's "Que Sera, Sera" won Jay Livingston and Ray Evans Best Song Oscar. Composer Bernard Herrmann is conducting orchestra at the climax. VistaVision. ▼●◗

Man Who Lived Again, The (1936-British) **61m.** *** D: Robert Stevenson. Boris Karloff, Anna Lee, John Loder, Frank Cellier, Lyn Harding, Cecil Parker. Mad doctor Karloff has been transferring personalities from one monkey to another. How soon will he be experimenting with human subjects? Solid, above-par chiller. Original British title: THE MAN WHO CHANGED HIS MIND.▼

Man Who Lived Twice, The (1936) **73m.** **½ D: Harry Lachman. Ralph Bellamy, Marian Marsh, Thurston Hall, Isabel Jewell, Nana Bryant, Ward Bond. Killer (Bellamy) ditches his cohorts, undergoes brain surgery which literally changes him into a new man. Interesting premise should have made for better film. Remade as MAN IN THE DARK.

Man Who Loved Cat Dancing, The (1973) **C-122m.** *** D: Richard C. Sarafian. Burt Reynolds, Sarah Miles, George Hamilton, Lee J. Cobb, Jack Warden, Bo Hopkins, Robert Donner, Jay Silverheels. Western tale of defiant woman who leaves her husband and takes up riding along with a band of outlaws. Sluggish in spots, but enjoyable; script by Eleanor Perry. Panavision. [PG]▼

Man Who Loved Redheads, The (1955-British) **C-103m.** *** D: Harold French. John Justin, Moira Shearer, Roland Culver, Denholm Elliott, Harry Andrews, Patricia Cutts. Delightful British comedy written by Terence Rattigan about a man with lifelong crush on redheads, dating back to boyhood meeting with beautiful Shearer. American print runs 89m.

Man Who Loved Women, The (1977-French) **C-119m.** *** D: François Truffaut. Charles Denner, Brigitte Fossey, Nelly Borgeaud, Leslie Caron, Genevieve Fontanel. Charming, sophisticated comedy about a bachelor who is obsessed with women and, it turns out, they with him. To make sense of the fact that he falls in love with almost every woman he meets, he writes his autobiography. Remade in 1983.▼●

Man Who Loved Women, The (1983) **C-110m.** ** D: Blake Edwards. Burt Reynolds, Julie Andrews, Kim Basinger, Marilu Henner, Barry Corbin, Cynthia Sikes, Jennifer Edwards, Tracy Vaccaro. Lackluster, snail's pace remake of the François Truffaut film—minus the climactic revelation that gave the earlier movie its point. Reynolds gives one of his most appealing performances, but spends an eternity discussing his adoration of women with stone-faced psychoanalyst Andrews. Director-writer Edwards gave coscreenplay credit to his own psychiatrist! [R]▼●

Man Who Never Was, The (1956-British) **C-103m.** *** D: Ronald Neame. Clifton Webb, Gloria Grahame, Robert Flemyng, Josephine Griffin, Stephen Boyd. Good WW2 spy yarn based on true story of Allies planting elaborate red herring to divert attention from invasion of Sicily. CinemaScope.▼

Man Who Played God, The (1932) **81m.** **½ D: John G. Adolfi. George Arliss, Bette Davis, Violet Heming, Louise Closser Hale, Donald Cook, Ray Milland. Well-acted tale of musician Arliss going deaf, infatuated student Davis sticking by him. Not as stagy as other Arliss films, with

Bette getting her first big break and young Milland in a small role. Remade as SINCERELY YOURS.

Man Who Reclaimed His Head, The (1934) **80m.** *** D: Edward Ludwig. Claude Rains, Lionel Atwill, Joan Bennett, Baby Jane, Henry O'Neill, Wallace Ford. Odd drama adapted from Jean Bart stage play, told in flashback. Struggling writer and advocate of world peace used by capitalists (led by Atwill) to their own, selfish ends. Unusual story well acted, especially by Rains, but too slowly paced.

Man Who Shot Liberty Valance, The (1962) **123m.** **** D: John Ford. James Stewart, John Wayne, Vera Miles, Lee Marvin, Edmond O'Brien, Andy Devine, Woody Strode, Jeanette Nolan, Ken Murray, John Qualen, Strother Martin, Lee Van Cleef, John Carradine, Carleton Young. Tenderfoot lawyer Stewart helps civilize the West, but needs help from he-man Wayne to do so. Panned and patronized upon original release, but now regarded as an American classic by virtually every Ford scholar; one of the great Westerns. Producer Willis Goldbeck and James Warner Bellah adapted Dorothy Johnson's story.▼●

Man Who Skied Down Everest, The (1976-Canadian) **C-86m.** **½ D: F. R. Crawley. Irresistible idea for a documentary (Japanese sports figure Yuichiro Miura's 1970 skiing expedition) sabotaged by inane narration on soundtrack of English language version. Oscar winner for Best Documentary. CinemaScope. [G]▼

Man Who Talked Too Much, The (1940) **75m.** **½ D: Vincent Sherman. George Brent, Virginia Bruce, Brenda Marshall, Richard Barthelmess, William Lundigan, George Tobias. Good courtroom drama with D.A. Brent and lawyer Lundigan, brothers fighting same case. Remake of THE MOUTHPIECE, made again as ILLEGAL.

Man Who Turned to Stone, The (1957) **80m.** BOMB D: Leslie Kardos. Victor Jory, Ann Doran, Charlotte Austin, William Hudson, Paul Cavanagh, Jean Willes, Victor Varconi. Jory and his followers stay immortal by siphoning off the life forces of others. If they don't get renewed, they petrify. So does the movie.▼

Man Who Understood Women, The (1959) **C-105m.** **½ D: Nunnally Johnson. Leslie Caron, Henry Fonda, Cesare Danova, Myron McCormick, Marcel Dalio, Conrad Nagel. Unsatisfactory narrative of movie-maker genius Fonda who hasn't slightest notion of how to treat wife Caron. CinemaScope.

Man Who Wagged His Tail, The (1957-Spanish-Italian) **91m.** **½ D: Ladislao Vajda. Peter Ustinov, Pablito Calvo, Aroldo Tieri, Silvia Marco. Scrooge-like slumlord Ustinov is transformed into a dog. OK fantasy filmed in Madrid and Brooklyn. Released in the U.S. in 1961.▼

Man Who Wasn't There, The (1983) **C-111m.** BOMB D: Bruce Malmuth. Steve Guttenberg, Jeffrey Tambor, Lisa Langlois, Art Hindle, Morgan Hart, Bill Forsythe, Vincent Baggetta. Inept—not to mention inane—invisibility comedy that touted its 3-D effects but offered little in *any* dimension. Better writing, directing, and acting can be found at a nursery school pageant. Panavision. [R]▼

Man Who Watched Trains Go By SEE: **Paris Express, The**

Man Who Would Be King, The (1975) **C-129m.** ***½ D: John Huston. Sean Connery, Michael Caine, Christopher Plummer, Saeed Jaffrey, Shakira Caine. Old-fashioned adventure and derring-do from Kipling via Huston: two British soldier-pals try to bamboozle high priests of remote Kafiristan into turning over their riches by convincing them that Connery is a god. Caine and Connery are ideal, script is superb, and film is entertaining, if not quite in the realm of GUNGA DIN. Panavision. [PG]▼●◗

Man Who Wouldn't Die, The (1942) **65m.** ** D: Herbert I. Leeds. Lloyd Nolan, Marjorie Weaver, Helene Reynolds, Henry Wilcoxon. Nolan is efficient as wisecracking detective Mike Shayne with a tougher caper than usual.

Man Who Wouldn't Talk, The (1940) **72m.** ** D: David Burton. Lloyd Nolan, Jean Rogers, Onslow Stevens, Eric Blore, Mae Marsh. Routine drama with Nolan refusing to defend himself on murder charge; silly ending. Based on one-act play *The Valiant*, filmed in 1929 with Paul Muni.

Man Who Wouldn't Talk, The (1958-British) **97m.** *½ D: Herbert Wilcox. Anna Neagle, Anthony Quayle, Zsa Zsa Gabor, Katherine Kath, Dora Bryan. Britain's foremost female lawyer (Neagle) defends Quayle on murder charge, even though he cannot speak, for fear of revealing top-secret information. Dreadful.

Man With a Cloak, The (1951) **81m.** **½ D: Fletcher Markle. Barbara Stanwyck, Joseph Cotten, Louis Calhern, Leslie Caron, Jim Backus, Margaret Wycherly, Joe DeSantis. Intriguing little mystery, set in 19th-century N.Y.C.; housekeeper Stanwyck plots to kill Calhern for his money and romances Cotten, whose identity is kept secret until the climax. Not bad, with spooky David Raksin score, but having Barbara sing was a mistake.

Man With a Million (1954-British) **C-92m.** ** D: Ronald Neame. Gregory Peck, Jane Griffiths, Ronald Squire, A. E. Matthews, Wilfrid Hyde-White, Reginald Beckwith. Often tedious telling of Mark Twain story "The Million Pound Bank Note," in which penniless American Peck is given the title sum of money on a wager, leading to various complications. Original title: THE MILLION POUND NOTE. Remade as A MILLION TO JUAN.

Man With Bogart's Face, The (1980) **C-106m.** **½ D: Robert Day. Robert Sacchi, Michelle Phillips, Olivia Hussey, Franco Nero, Misty Rowe, Victor Buono, Herbert Lom, Sybil Danning, Dick Bakalyan, George Raft, Mike Mazurki, Yvonne DeCarlo, Henry Wilcoxon, Victor Sen Yung, Jay Robinson. Offbeat mystery about present-day detective who has plastic surgery to resemble his idol and immediately becomes involved in MALTESE FALCON-esque case. Not really a comedy, although it has its lighter moments; good fun, especially for buffs. Adapted from his own novel and produced by Andrew J. Fenady; Raft's final film. Aka SAM MARLOWE, PRIVATE EYE. [PG]▼

Man With Connections, The (1970-French) **C-93m.** **½ D: Claude Berri. Guy Bedos, Yves Robert, Rosy Varte, Georges Geret, Zorica Lozic. Good-natured comedy about young Frenchman who tries to use "pull" to make Army hitch as pleasant as possible. Autobiographical film is, like Berri's others, amiable, quietly entertaining. [R]

Man With Nine Lives, The (1940) **73m.** **½ D: Nick Grinde. Boris Karloff, Roger Pryor, Jo Ann Sayers, Stanley Brown, John Dilson, Hal Taliaferro. Scientist Karloff seeks cure for cancer by freezing bodies in suspended animation. Hokey, but fun when Karloff himself thaws out. Also known as BEHIND THE DOOR.▼

Man With One Red Shoe, The (1985) **C-93m.** ** D: Stan Dragoti. Tom Hanks, Dabney Coleman, Lori Singer, Charles Durning, Carrie Fisher, Edward Herrmann, Jim Belushi, Irving Metzman, Gerrit Graham, David L. Lander, David Ogden Stiers. Flat remake of THE TALL BLOND MAN WITH ONE BLACK SHOE, about an innocent guy wrongly targeted by CIA types for elimination. Wastes the considerable comic talents of its cast—and doesn't allow leading man Hanks to be funny at all! [PG]▼

Man Without a Country, The (1973) **C-78m. TVM** D: Delbert Mann. Cliff Robertson, Beau Bridges, Peter Strauss, Robert Ryan, Walter Abel, John Cullum, Geoffrey Holder, Shepperd Strudwick, Patricia Elliott. Tour-de-force performance by Robertson as Philip Nolan makes this Sidney Carroll adaptation of the Edward Everett Hale classic shine. Not much action but a magnificent character study. Above average.

Man Without a Face, The (1993) **C-114m.** *** D: Mel Gibson. Mel Gibson, Nick Stahl, Margaret Whitton, Fay Masterson, Gaby Hoffmann, Geoffrey Lewis, Richard Masur, Michael DeLuise, Ethan Phillips, Jean De Baer, Viva. Literate, absorbing drama exploring the evolving relationship between lonely 12-year-old Stahl, who's intent on gaining entrance to a military academy, and reclusive, facially scarred ex-teacher Gibson, who becomes his mentor. Despite some dramatic lapses, Gibson's directorial debut is more than respectable; he and Stahl offer excellent performances. From Isabelle Holland's novel. [PG-13]▼●

Man Without a Star (1955) **C-89m.** *** D: King Vidor. Kirk Douglas, Jeanne Crain, Claire Trevor, Richard Boone, Jay C. Flippen, William Campbell. Boisterous Western with drifter Douglas befriending young Campbell, tangling with manipulative rancher Crain. Kirk even gets to sing and play the banjo in this one. Remade as A MAN CALLED GANNON.▼

Man Without a World, The (1991) **98m.** *** D: Eleanor Antin. Christine Berry, Anna Henriques, Pier Marton, George Leonard, Don Sommese, Marcia Goodman. Unusual, fascinating fiction written, produced, and directed by performance artist Antin and presented as a long-lost, recently discovered silent "Yiddish shtetl film" made decades ago in Cracow by one Yevgeny Antinov, the "controversial Soviet silent film director." The scenario is a folktale about daily life in a shtetl (Jewish village), centering on a young girl (Berry) who falls in love with a poet (Marton). A valentine to shtetl life and silent film technique; however, you won't find its frank sexuality and nudity in any real period Yiddish film. Antin herself appears as a gypsy dancer.

Man With the Balloons, The (1965-Italian-French) **85m.** ** D: Marco Ferreri. Marcello Mastroianni, Catherine Spaak. Mastroianni plays successful businessman who loses his girl, eventually goes mad because he becomes obsessed with finding out how much air a balloon needs before it bursts. Offbeat idea, to be sure, but result is just plain silly. Panoramica.

Man With the Golden Arm, The (1955) **119m.** *** D: Otto Preminger. Frank Sinatra, Eleanor Parker, Kim Novak, Darren McGavin, Arnold Stang, Doro Merande. Then-daring film of drug addiction is now dated, but still powerful; Sinatra is the junkie, Parker the crippled wife. Memorable Elmer Bernstein jazz score.▼●

Man With the Golden Gun, The (1974-British) **C-125m.** *** D: Guy Hamilton. Roger Moore, Christopher Lee, Britt Ekland, Maud Adams, Herve Villechaize, Clifton James, Richard Loo, Marc Lawrence, Bernard Lee, Lois Maxwell, Desmond Llewelyn. Moore's second shot as super agent James Bond is good, gimmicky fun but the actor had one more film to go (THE SPY WHO LOVED ME) before actually growing into the character; Lee is excellent as assassin Scaramanga. Great car stunts, worldwide locales. [PG]▼●◗

Man With the Gun (1955) **83m.** **½ D: Richard Wilson. Robert Mitchum, Jan Sterling, Angie Dickinson, Barbara Lawrence, Karen Sharpe, Henry Hull. Mitchum as lawman who brings peace to a Western town is the whole show.

Man With the Synthetic Brain, The SEE: **Blood of Ghastly Horror**

Man With Two Brains, The (1983) **C-93m.** *** D: Carl Reiner. Steve Martin, Kathleen Turner, David Warner, Paul Benedict, Richard Brestoff, James Cromwell, George Furth, Randi Brooks. While trapped in a loveless marriage with venal Turner, brilliant surgeon Michael Hfuhruhurr (Martin) falls in love with a brain in a jar (voiced by Sissy Spacek) and immediately starts searching for a new "home" for it. As silly as it sounds, but put your brain in neutral and the laughs are there, particularly the decor of Warner's condo and the identity of "The Elevator Killer." [R]▼●◗

Man With Two Faces, The (1934) **72m.** **½ D: Archie Mayo. Edward G. Robinson, Mary Astor, Ricardo Cortez, Mae Clarke, Louis Calhern. Minor but entertaining yarn (from a play by Alexander Woollcott and George S. Kaufman) about a ham actor who tries to protect his sister from her sinister husband.

Man, Woman and Child (1983) **C-99m.** *** D: Dick Richards. Martin Sheen, Blythe Danner, Sebastian Dungan, Arlene McIntyre, Missy Francis, Craig T. Nelson, David Hemmings, Nathalie Nell. Unabashed tearjerker (from Erich Segal's book) about a happily married man, with two children, who learns that a brief affair he had with a Frenchwoman ten years ago produced a son—and that the boy has just been orphaned. Simple, honestly sentimental movie. [PG]▼

Manxman, The (1929-British) **90m.** **½ D: Alfred Hitchcock. Carl Brisson, Malcolm Keen, Anny Ondra, Randle Ayrton. Fisherman Brisson and lawyer Keen, best friends since childhood, both love Ondra. OK melodrama was Hitchcock's last silent film.▼◗

Many Happy Returns (1934) **60m.** **½ D: Norman McLeod. George Burns, Gracie Allen, Joan Marsh, George Barbier, Franklin Pangborn, Ray Milland, William Demarest, Guy Lombardo and His Royal Canadians. Gracie wants to replace father's department store with a bird sanctuary! Typically silly Burns and Allen comedy, with Lombardo providing the music. For Larry Adler's harmonica number, Guy Lombardo's band appears on screen, but the music was performed by Duke Ellington!

Many Rivers to Cross (1955) **C-92m.** **½ D: Roy Rowland. Robert Taylor, Eleanor Parker, Victor McLaglen, James Arness, Josephine Hutchinson, Rosemary DeCamp. Parker shows more vim and vigor than Taylor in this 1800s Western, centering on her yen for him. Raucous, energetic frontier comedy. CinemaScope.

Map of the Human Heart (1993-British-Australian-French-Canadian) **C-126m.** *** D: Vincent Ward. Jason Scott Lee, Anne Parillaud, Patrick Bergin, John Cusack, Robert Joamie, Annie Galipeau, Jeanne Moreau, Ben Mendelson, Clotilde Courau. Fascinating, if not altogether successful, fable about an Inuit Eskimo boy plucked from his Canadian homeland and taken to "civilization" by a mapmaker in the 1930s. The rest of the young man's life unfolds like a strange dream. Director Ward's sometimes hallucinatory images and a mystical atmosphere make this a compelling film to watch even when it falters storywise. Filled with extraordinary performances, including a cameo by the always wonderful Moreau. Super 35. [R]▼●

Map of the World, A (1999) **C-126m.** *** D: Scott Elliott. Sigourney Weaver, Julianne Moore, David Strathairn, Ron Lea, Arliss Howard, Chloë Sevigny, Louise Fletcher. School nurse Weaver, whose family life is fragmented, observes the world with ironic detachment until she's imprisoned for abusing a student. She regards jail as almost a vacation from her responsibilities, but cannot evade her own memories. Excellent performances, especially by Weaver, enliven this intelligent adaptation of the novel by Jane Hamilton. The middle seems to mark time, but the first third is outstanding. [R]▼◗

Maracaibo (1958) **C-88m.** **½ D: Cornel Wilde. Cornel Wilde, Jean Wallace, Abbe Lane, Francis Lederer, Michael Landon. Wilde is expert firefighter who goes to Venezuela to combat oil blaze, romancing ex-girlfriend between action scenes. VistaVision.

Mara Maru (1952) **98m.** **½ D: Gordon Douglas. Errol Flynn, Ruth Roman, Raymond Burr, Richard Webb, Nestor Paiva. Turgid adventure pits Flynn against Burr as they vie for sunken treasure, with Roman the love interest.

Mara of the Wilderness (1965) **C-90m.** **½ D: Frank McDonald. Adam West, Linda Saunders, Theo Marcuse, Denver Pyle, Sean McClory. Sometimes diverting account of Saunders, who grew up in the wild north country, with West trying to rehabilitate her.▼

Marathon Man (1976) **C-125m.** **½ D: John Schlesinger. Dustin Hoffman, Laurence Olivier, Roy Scheider, William Devane, Marthe Keller, Fritz Weaver, Marc Lawrence, Richard Bright. Glossy thriller adapted by William Goldman from his book. Basic premise of graduate student Hoffman propelled into dizzying world of international intrigue spoiled by repellent violence and some gaping story holes. Hoffman and arch-villain Olivier are superb but film doesn't do them justice. [R]▼●

Marat/Sade (Persecution and Assassination of Jean-Paul Marat as Performed by the Inmates of the Asylum at Charenton Under the Direction of the Marquis de Sade, The) (1966-British) **C-115m.** **** D: Peter Brook. Patrick Magee, Clifford Rose, Glenda Jackson, Ian Richardson, Brenda Kempner, Ruth Baker, Michael Williams, Freddie Jones. Chilling adaptation of Peter Weiss play about "performance" staged by inmates of French insane asylum, under direction of Marquis de Sade. Lurid atmosphere is so vivid that it seems actors are breathing down your neck; brilliantly directed by Brook. Not for weak stomachs. Screenplay by Adrian Mitchell; Jackson's starring film debut.▼●◗

Marauders, The (1955) **C-81m.** ** D: Gerald Mayer. Dan Duryea, Jeff Richards, Keenan Wynn, Jarma Lewis. OK story of rancher fighting against greedy cattle ranchers.

Marcello Mastroianni: I Remember, Yes I Remember (1997-Italian) **C/B&W-98m.** *** D: Anna Maria Tató. Film lovers in general and fans of the late actor in particular should savor this full-bodied documentary portrait, made by Mastroianni's longtime companion, who filmed him not long before his death in 1996. Mastroianni reminisces, jokes, reflects on his career and the directors with whom he worked—and, most tellingly, exudes a love of and passion for life. Originally 199m.; made for Italian television.▼◗

March of the Wooden Soldiers SEE: **Babes in Toyland** (1934)

March or Die (1977) **C-104m.** ** D: Dick Richards. Gene Hackman, Terence Hill, Max von Sydow, Catherine Deneuve, Ian Holm. Homage to French Foreign Legion adventures of filmdom's past. Good cast wages losing battle with static script and walks downheartedly through action scenes. Disappointing epic-that-might-have-been. Additional footage tacked on for network showing. [PG]▼

Marco (1973) **C-109m.** ** D: Seymour Robbie. Desi Arnaz, Jr., Jack Weston, Zero Mostel. Lavish but lumbering musical, filmed on Oriental locations, with Arnaz as young Marco Polo and Mostel as Kublai Khan. Disappointing. [G]▼

Marco Polo (1962-Italian) **C-90m.** **½ D: Hugo Fregonese. Rory Calhoun, Yoko Tani, Robert Hundar, Camillo Pilotto, Pierre Cressoy, Michael Chow. Unspectacular epic about medieval adventurer and his journey to China. Calhoun and film lack needed vigor. CinemaScope.

Marco the Magnificent (1965) **C-100m.** **½ D: Denys De La Patelliere, Noel Howard. Horst Buchholz, Anthony Quinn, Omar Sharif, Elsa Martinelli, Akim Tamiroff, Orson Welles. Laughable mini-epic, extremely choppy, with episodic sequences pretending to recount events in life of medieval adventurer. Franscope.

Mardi Gras (1958) **C-107m.** **½ D: Edmund Goulding. Pat Boone, Christine Carere, Tommy Sands, Sheree North, Gary Crosby. Perky, unpretentious musical with energetic cast. Boone wins military school raffle date with movie star Carere. CinemaScope.

Margaret's Museum (1995-Canadian) **C-118m.** **½ D: Mort Ransen. Helena Bonham Carter, Kate Nelligan, Clive Russell, Craig Olejnik, Andrea Morris, Peter Boretski, Kenneth Welsh. Bonham Carter has one of her better roles as a maverick who lives in a Nova Scotia mining town that seems to be on the edge of civilization; she despises the mines, which have killed her father and brother and embittered her mother (Nelligan). Then she falls in love with a burly former miner (Russell). Well meaning—with some strong moments—but gloomy and predictable. [R]▼●

Margie (1946) **C-89m.** *** D: Henry King. Jeanne Crain, Glenn Langan, Lynn Bari, Alan Young, Barbara Lawrence, Conrad Janis, Esther Dale, Hobart Cavanaugh, Ann Todd, Hattie McDaniel. Sweet nostalgia about ultra-sensitive teen (Crain) in 1920s who gets more than a crush on her handsome new French teacher. The manner in which the teacher relates to Margie is innocent enough, but it surely would get him thrown in jail today! Loaded with snippets of period songs ("April Showers," "My Time Is Your Time," the title tune, etc.).

Margin for Error (1943) **74m.** ** D: Otto Preminger. Joan Bennett, Milton Berle, Otto Preminger, Carl Esmond, Howard Freeman, Ed McNamara. Dated, awkward "comedy" of Jewish cop Berle assigned to guard German consul in N.Y.C. during WW2. Director Preminger should have told actor Preminger to stop overacting.

Marianne (1929) **112m.** *** D: Robert Z. Leonard. Marion Davies, George Baxter, Lawrence Gray, Cliff Edwards, Benny Rubin. Davies' first talkie also one of her best; fine vehicle for her charm and comic talent as French girl pursued by two American soldiers during WW1.

Marianne and Juliane (1982-German) **C-106m.** ***½ D: Margarethe von Trotta. Jutta Lampe, Barbara Sukowa, Rudiger Vogler, Doris Schade, Franz Rudnick. Profound, multileveled, and memorable chronicle of the relationship between two sisters, alike in some ways yet so very different in others. Juliane (Lampe) is a feminist editor working within the system; Marianne (Sukowa) is a radical political terrorist. Superbly acted, a must-see.▼

Maria's Lovers (1984) **C-100m.** ** D: Andrei Konchalovsky. Nastassia Kinski,

John Savage, Robert Mitchum, Keith Carradine, Anita Morris, Bud Cort, Karen Young, Tracy Nelson, John Goodman, Vincent Spano, Bill Smitrovich. Young soldier returns home from WW2, after suffering nervous breakdown, and finds himself unable to consummate his love with new bride. Richly atmospheric film, set in Pennsylvania mining town, has fine performances and other attributes, but is unrelievedly ponderous. Opening sequence cleverly integrates footage from John Huston's famous documentary LET THERE BE LIGHT with newly shot material of Savage. [R]▼

Marie (1985) **C-112m.** *** D: Roger Donaldson. Sissy Spacek, Jeff Daniels, Keith Szarabajka, Morgan Freeman, Fred (Dalton) Thompson, Don Hood, John Cullum. Solid drama about divorcée and mother of three who takes a job in Tennessee state government, then blows the whistle on corruption and finds herself in very hot water. Might be hard to believe if it wasn't true (though knowing the outcome of the case will certainly remove a lot of the suspense). Based on Peter Maas' book; defense attorney Thompson plays himself. J-D-C Scope. [PG-13]▼

Marie Antoinette (1938) **149m.** **½ D: W. S. Van Dyke II. Norma Shearer, Tyrone Power, John Barrymore, Robert Morley, Gladys George, Anita Louise, Joseph Schildkraut. Opulent MGM production of life of 18th-century French queen lacks pace but has good acting, with great performance by Morley as Louis XVI. Shearer captures essence of title role as costumer retells her life from Austrian princess to doomed queen of crumbling empire.▼●

Marie Antoinette (1955-French) **C-108m.** **½ D: Jean Delannoy. Michele Morgan, Richard Todd, Jean Morel. Epic on life of famed 18th-century French queen has marvelous Morgan in title role but lacks perspective and scope.

Marie Galante (1934) **88m.** ** D: Henry King. Spencer Tracy, Ketti Gallian, Ned Sparks, Helen Morgan, Sig Rumann, Leslie Fenton, Jay C. Flippen, Stepin Fetchit. So-so adventure in which down-on-her-luck Gallian links up with good-guy Tracy to thwart a scheme to blow up the Panama Canal. French actress Gallian's first American film; she's attractive, but her career went nowhere. Morgan sings two forgettable songs.▼

"Marihuana" (1936) **58m.** BOMB D: Dwain Esper. Harley Wood, Hugh McArthur, Pat Carlyle, Paul Ellis, Dorothy Dehn, Richard Erskine. Some naive, fun-loving kids puff on the title weed, offered them by a man you know is evil incarnate because he has a mustache, and the result is nude swimming, a drowning . . . and worse! This exploitation fare is a real scream, almost mind-boggling in its dopiness. And don't forget that it was researched "with the help of federal, state and police narcotic officers." A companion piece to REEFER MADNESS. Originally titled "MARIJUANA"—THE DEVIL'S WEED.▼

Marilyn (1963) **83m.** **½ Narrated by Rock Hudson. Standard, often patronizing documentary on Marilyn Monroe built around clips from most of her movies, including the unfinished SOMETHING'S GOT TO GIVE. CinemaScope.▼

Marine Issue SEE: **Instant Justice**

Marine Raiders (1944) **91m.** ** D: Harold D. Schuster. Pat O'Brien, Robert Ryan, Ruth Hussey, Frank McHugh, Barton MacLane. Typical RKO WW2 film, this time focusing on marine training.▼

Marines, Let's Go (1961) **C-104m.** *½ D: Raoul Walsh. Tom Tryon, David Hedison, Barbara Stuart, William Tyler. Tedium about four soldiers, their comic adventures on leave in Tokyo, and their dramatic encounters on Korean battlefield. CinemaScope.

Mario Puzo's "The Fortunate Pilgrim" (1988) **C-250m. TVM** D: Stuart Cooper. Sophia Loren, Edward James Olmos, Hal Holbrook, John Turturro, Anna Strasberg, Yorgo Voyagis, Roxann Biggs, Ed Wiley, Mirjana Karanovic, Ron Marquette, Annabella Sciorra. Atmospheric adaptation of the novel Puzo wrote prior to *The Godfather* paced by Loren's strong performance as turn-of-the-century Italian immigrant who brings her family to N.Y.C. (Belgrade, Yugoslavia, stands in for the Big Apple) and spends the next three decades searching for the American dream. Writer John McGreevey kept the saga sprawling, and Reginald Morris's cinematography is impressive. The composers, unfortunately, thought they were scoring grand opera—perhaps because producers Carlo Ponti and son Alex were able to enlist Pavarotti to sing Caruso-style on the soundtrack. Originally shown in two parts. Above average.

Marius (1931-French) **125m.** *** D: Alexander Korda. Raimu, Pierre Fresnay, Charpin, Alida Rouffe, Orane Demazis. Amusing, flavorful if a bit too theatrical satire of provincial life, centering on the love of Marius (Fresnay) for Fanny (Demazis). Raimu is wonderful as Cesar, cafe owner and father of Marius. Screenplay by Marcel Pagnol; first of a trilogy, followed by FANNY and CESAR. All three were the basis of the play and movie FANNY (1961).▼●

Marjoe (1972) **C-88m.** **½ D: Howard Smith, Sarah Kernochan. Oscar-winning documentary about life of fake evangelist Marjoe Gortner is certainly interesting, but is a little too pleased with itself, a little too pat to be totally convincing. Marjoe himself is likable enough. [PG]▼

Marjorie Morningstar (1958) **C-123m.** **½ D: Irving Rapper. Gene Kelly, Natalie Wood, Claire Trevor, Ed Wynn, Everett Sloane, Carolyn Jones, Martin Milner, Martin Balsam, Ruta Lee. Wood is only adequate as Herman Wouk's heroine in tale of N.Y.C. girl aspiring to greatness but ending up a suburban housewife, with Kelly her summer romance.▼●

Mark, The (1961-British) **127m.** ***½ D: Guy Green. Stuart Whitman, Maria Schell, Rod Steiger, Brenda De Banzie, Maurice Denham, Donald Wolfit, Paul Rogers, Donald Houston. Whitman is excellent in his portrayal of emotionally broken sex criminal who has served time, now wants to make new start. Thoughtful, well-acted adult drama written by Sidney Buchman and Stanley Mann. CinemaScope.▼

Marked for Death (1990) **C-94m.** ** D: Dwight H. Little. Steven Seagal, Basil Wallace, Keith David, Tom Wright, Joanna Pacula, Elizabeth Gracen, Bette Ford, Danielle Harris, Al Israel, Arlen Dean Snyder, Jimmy Cliff. Familiar, brainless actioner with ex-drug agent Seagal taking on Jamaican dope pushers who've, as the title says, marked him and his family for extinction. Cliff and band appear briefly and perform on soundtrack. Super 35. [R]▼●◗

Marked Woman (1937) **99m.** *** D: Lloyd Bacon. Bette Davis, Humphrey Bogart, Lola Lane, Isabel Jewell, Jane Bryan, Eduardo Ciannelli, Allen Jenkins, Mayo Methot. Bristling gangster drama of D.A. Bogart convincing Bette and four girlfriends to testify against their boss, underworld king Ciannelli.▼●

Mark of the Gorilla (1950) **68m.** *½ D: William Berke. Johnny Weissmuller, Trudy Marshall, Suzanne Dalbert, Onslow Stevens, Selmer Jackson, Robert Purcell, Pierce Lyden. A ruthless gang in search of gold disguise themselves as apes in this ludicrous *Jungle Jim* entry.

Mark of the Hawk, The (1957-British) **C-83m.** *** D: Michael Audley. Eartha Kitt, Sidney Poitier, Juano Hernandez, John McIntire. Unusual tale intelligently acted, set in contemporary Africa, with peaceful vs. violent means for racial equality the main theme. Originally titled ACCUSED. Aka SHAKA LULU. SuperScope 235.▼

Mark of the Renegade (1951) **C-81m.** **½ D: Hugo Fregonese. Ricardo Montalban, Cyd Charisse, J. Carrol Naish, Gilbert Roland. Peculiar Western tale of 1820s, with Montalban an outlaw who romances Charisse.

Mark of the Vampire (1935) **61m.** *** D: Tod Browning. Lionel Barrymore, Elizabeth Allan, Bela Lugosi, Lionel Atwill, Carol Borland, Jean Hersholt, Donald Meek. Delightful, intriguing tale of vampires terrorizing rural village; inspector Atwill, vampire expert Barrymore investigate. Beautifully done, with an incredible ending. Remake of Browning's silent LONDON AFTER MIDNIGHT.▼●

Mark of the Vampire (1957) SEE: **Vampire, The**

Mark of the Whistler (1944) **61m.** *** D: William Castle. Richard Dix, Janis Carter, Porter Hall, Paul Guilfoyle, John Calvert. Dix is a tramp who pretends to be the long-lost owner of a dormant trust fund in this compelling entry of *The Whistler* series, based on a story by Cornell Woolrich.

Mark of Zorro, The (1920) **90m.** ***½ D: Fred Niblo. Douglas Fairbanks Sr., Marguerite De La Motte, Noah Beery, Robert McKim, Charles Mailes. Silent classic with Fairbanks as the masked hero of old California; perhaps Doug's best film—his first swashbuckler. Nonstop fun.▼●◗

Mark of Zorro, The (1940) **93m.** ***½ D: Rouben Mamoulian. Tyrone Power, Linda Darnell, Basil Rathbone, Gale Sondergaard, Eugene Pallette, J. Edward Bromberg, Montagu Love. Lavish swashbuckler with Power as son of California aristocrat in 1800s, alternately a foppish dandy and a dashing masked avenger of evil: climactic swordplay with Rathbone a swashbuckling gem. Great score by Alfred Newman.▼●

Mark of Zorro, The (1974) **C-78m. TVM** D: Don McDougall. Frank Langella, Ricardo Montalban, Gilbert Roland, Yvonne de Carlo, Louise Sorel, Anne Archer, Robert Middleton. Langella buckles and swashes in this tepid remake. Montalban is properly villainous, Roland surprisingly spry at wall-scaling. Best of all: unforgettable Alfred Newman musical score from the 1940 film, interpolated here. Average.

Marksman, The (1953) **62m.** *½ D: Lewis D. Collins. Wayne Morris, Elena Verdugo, Frank Ferguson, Rick Vallin. Flabby little tale of Morris, a law enforcer with a telescopic gun, chasing after outlaws.

Mark Twain and Me (1991-Canadian) **C-95m. TVM** D: Daniel Petrie. Jason Robards, Talia Shire, R. H. Thomson, Fiona Reid, Chris Wiggins, Amy Stewart. Nicely played, tender-hearted Disney film about youngster Dorothy Quick's encounter with a deceptively gruff, aging Mark Twain (an almost unrecognizable Robards) that led to Quick's autobiographical book, *Enchantment: A Little Girl's Friendship with Mark Twain.* Delightfully adapted by Cynthia Whitcomb. Made for cable. Above average.▼

Marlene (1984-German) **C/B&W-96m.** *** D: Maximilian Schell. Utterly, unexpectedly fascinating look at Marlene Dietrich, built on unusual foundation of a tape-recorded interview with Schell that she refused to allow to be filmed! How Schell turns this liability into an asset for the film—just one of its layers—and how Dietrich reveals so much about herself even in her stubborn rejection of basic interview questions, is all part of the film's mystique (and Marlene's). Includes most of her finest moments on screen.▼●

Marlowe (1969) **C-95m.** *** D: Paul Bogart. James Garner, Gayle Hunnicutt, Carroll O'Connor, Rita Moreno, Sharon Farrell, William Daniels, Jackie Coogan, Bruce Lee. Slick updating of Raymond Chandler's *The Little Sister* with Garner as Philip Marlowe, hired by girl to find missing brother. Really belongs in 1940s, but works fairly well; Moreno memorable as stripper who helps solve case in exciting finale, plus hilarious scene where Lee reduces Marlowe's office to rubble. [M/PG]▼

Marnie (1964) **C-129m.** *** D: Alfred Hitchcock. Sean Connery, Tippi Hedren, Diane Baker, Martin Gabel, Louise Latham, Alan Napier. This story of a habitual thief (Hedren) whose employer (Connery) is determined to understand her illness was considered a misfire in 1964 . . . but there's more than meets the eye, especially for Hitchcock buffs. Script by Jay Presson Allen. Look for Bruce Dern, Mariette Hartley, and Melody Scott Thomas in small roles.▼●

Maroc 7 (1967-British) **C-91m.** ** D: Gerry O'Hara. Gene Barry, Elsa Martinelli, Cyd Charisse, Leslie Phillips. Slow robbery-murder tale of secret agent out to catch split-personality thief. Panavision.▼

Marooned (1969) **C-134m.** ** D: John Sturges. Gregory Peck, Richard Crenna, James Franciscus, David Janssen, Gene Hackman, Lee Grant, Nancy Kovack, Mariette Hartley. Glossy but disappointing story of astronauts unable to return to earth, while space agency head Peck tries to keep lid from blowing off. Alternately boring and excruciating; climactic scenes in space produce agony, not excitement. Oscar-winning special effects are chief asset. Retitled SPACE TRAVELLERS. Panavision. [M/PG]▼●

Marquise of O, The (1976-French-German) **C-102m.** *** D: Eric Rohmer. Edith Clever, Bruno Ganz, Peter Luhr, Edda Seippel, Otto Sander. Delicate, disarmingly simple story set in 18th-century Italy; a young widow saved from rape by a Russian soldier during Franco-Prussian war finds herself pregnant some months later, and doesn't understand how. Beautiful period flavor, but film's charm is very low-key. [PG]▼

Marriage Circle, The (1924) **90m.** *** D: Ernst Lubitsch. Florence Vidor, Monte Blue, Marie Prevost, Creighton Hale, Adolphe Menjou, Harry Myers, Dale Fuller, Esther Ralston. Classic, influential silent comedy about the flirtations and infidelities of several well-to-do characters in Vienna, the "city of laughter and romance." Lubitsch's initial American comedy of manners, inspired by Chaplin's A WOMAN OF PARIS. Remade by Lubitsch and George Cukor as the musical ONE HOUR WITH YOU. ▼

Marriage-Go-Round, The (1960) **C-98m.** **½ D: Walter Lang. Susan Hayward, James Mason, Julie Newmar, Robert Paige, June Clayworth. Film version of Leslie Stevens' saucy play about marriage: Mason is professor attracted to free-love-oriented Newmar. Amusing, but lacks real bite. CinemaScope.

Marriage Is a Private Affair (1944) **116m.** *** D: Robert Z. Leonard. Lana Turner, James Craig, John Hodiak, Frances Gifford, Hugh Marlowe, Keenan Wynn. Somewhat dated, glossy MGM yarn of manchasing Turner, not about to be stopped just because she's married.

Marriage Italian-Style (1964-Italian) **C-102m.** *** D: Vittorio De Sica. Sophia Loren, Marcello Mastroianni, Aldo Puglisi, Pia Lindstrom, Vito Moriconi, Marilu Tolo. Spicy account of Loren's efforts to get long-time lover Mastroianni to marry her and stay her husband. Based on Eduardo De Filippo's 1946 play *Filumena*. ▼

Marriage of a Young Stockbroker, The (1971) **C-95m.** **½ D: Lawrence Turman. Richard Benjamin, Joanna Shimkus, Elizabeth Ashley, Adam West, Patricia Barry, Tiffany Bolling. Humorous and sad depiction of marital breakdown; husband indulges in voyeurism, wife has own problems. Good cast working with script that seems uncertain as to what point it wants to drive across. Director Turman, who'd produced THE GRADUATE, hoped lightning would strike twice with this adaptation of novel by same author, Charles Webb. [PG—edited from original R rating]▼

Marriage of Maria Braun, The (1978-German) **C-120m.** ***½ D: Rainer Werner Fassbinder. Hanna Schygulla, Ivan Desny, Gottfried John, Klaus Lowitsch, Gisela Uhlen. Schygulla shines in the Joan Crawfordesque role of a penniless soldier's wife who builds an industrial empire after the end of WW2. Riveting; the first of Fassbinder's three parables of postwar Germany, followed by LOLA and VERONIKA VOSS. [R]▼

Marriage on the Rocks (1965) **C-109m.** **½ D: Jack Donohue. Frank Sinatra, Deborah Kerr, Dean Martin, Cesar Romero, Hermione Baddeley, Tony Bill, Nancy Sinatra, John McGiver, Trini Lopez. Frank and Deborah have marital spat, get quickie Mexican divorce, she ends up married to his best pal, Dino. A waste of real talent. Panavision.▼

Married Man, A (1984-British) **C-200m. TVM** D: John Davies. Anthony Hopkins, Ciaran Madden, Lise Hilboldt, Yvonne Coulette, John LeMesurier, Sophie Ashton. Veddy-British domestic drama about a bored barrister, his proper wife and his paramour.

Mixed in with the suds and lather is a murder, but despite another of Hopkins' always interesting performances, this is a lethargic exercise that easily could have been halved. Originally shown in two parts. Average.▼

Married to It (1993) **C-112m.** ** D: Arthur Hiller. Beau Bridges, Stockard Channing, Robert Sean Leonard, Mary Stuart Masterson, Cybill Shepherd, Ron Silver, Don Francks, Donna Vivino, Jimmy Shea, Nathaniel Moreau, Gerry Bamman, Ed Koch. Several married couples meet in Manhattan and become the unlikeliest of friends. Each spouse manages to embrace several annoyingly bland clichés: yuppie, young newlywed, ex-hippie, bitchy step-mother—you get the picture. Cast of decent actors can't begin to save the pedestrian script. This one sat on the shelf for a couple of years. [R]▼●

Married to the Mob (1988) **C-103m.** *** D: Jonathan Demme. Michelle Pfeiffer, Matthew Modine, Dean Stockwell, Mercedes Ruehl, Alec Baldwin, Joan Cusack, Trey Wilson, Charles Napier, Tracey Walter, Al Lewis, Nancy Travis, David Johansen (Buster Poindexter), Chris Isaak, Oliver Platt, Todd Solondz. A woman tries to escape from the Mafia after the death of her hit man husband, only to find that the local boss has the hots for her. Amiable, entertaining farce with right-on performances by Pfeiffer and Stockwell (in a neat comic turn as the mafioso). Only director Demme could make a mob movie with likable characters in it! Score by David Byrne. [R]▼●

Married Woman, A (1964-French) **94m.** ** D: Jean-Luc Godard. Macha Meril, Philippe Leroy, Bernard Noel. Turgid three-cornered romance, with Meril unable to decide between husband Leroy and lover Noel; then, she finds herself pregnant. Godard narrates this pretentious allegory of middle-class alienation.▼

Marrying Kind, The (1952) **93m.** *** D: George Cukor. Judy Holliday, Aldo Ray, Madge Kennedy, Sheila Bond, John Alexander, Rex Williams, Phyllis Povah, Peggy Cass, Mickey Shaughnessy, Griff Barnett. Bittersweet drama of young couple on verge of divorce recalling their life together via flashbacks; sensitive performers outshine talky script—but story and situations haven't dated one bit.▼

Marrying Man, The (1991) **C-115m.** **½ D: Jerry Rees. Kim Basinger, Alec Baldwin, Robert Loggia, Elisabeth Shue, Armand Assante, Paul Reiser, Fisher Stevens, Peter Dobson, Gretchen Wyler. Engaged L.A. playboy joyrides with buddies to post-WW2 Las Vegas—and falls for a gorgeous chanteuse who happens to be Bugsy Siegel's mistress. Neil Simon original is already a legend for its on-set hijinks, in-fighting, and star egos, causing just about everyone down to the Key Grip to disown the thing. In truth, the picture's fairly entertaining, with sexy Baldwin and super-sultry Basinger hard to resist. [R]▼●

Marry Me Again (1953) **73m.** ** D: Frank Tashlin. Robert Cummings, Marie Wilson, Mary Costa, Jess Barker. Mild shenanigans of aviator Cummings and beauty contest winner Wilson's on-again, off-again romance.

Marry Me, Marry Me (1969-French) **C-87m.** *** D: Claude Berri. Elisabeth Wiener, Regine, Claude Berri, Luisa Colpeyn. Delightful story of love and (what else?) marriage, Berri-style. [M/PG]▼

Mars Attacks! (1996) **C-103m.** **½ D: Tim Burton. Jack Nicholson, Glenn Close, Annette Bening, Pierce Brosnan, Danny DeVito, Martin Short, Sarah Jessica Parker, Michael J. Fox, Rod Steiger, Tom Jones, Lukas Haas, Natalie Portman, Jim Brown, Pam Grier, Paul Winfield, Sylvia Sidney, Lisa Marie, Joe Don Baker, Christina Applegate, Barbet Schroeder. Overly self-satisfied spoof of 50s alien-invasion movies (and 50s attitudes) has Martians landing in flying saucers. President Nicholson urges calm and reason, but the little guys turn out to be predators . . . nasty ones at that! Great effects and animation (of the Martian characters) but awfully broad and one-note in tone, spoofing something that's already funny in the straight-faced originals of the period. One can't completely dislike a film in which Slim Whitman figures so prominently, however. Inspired by a gum card series of the same name. Panavision. [PG-13]▼●◗

Marseilles Contract, The SEE: **Destructors, The** (1974)

Marshal's Daughter, The (1953) **71m.** *½ D: William Berke. Ken Murray, Laurie Anders, Preston Foster, Hoot Gibson. Cornpone oater with Murray and Anders ridding their town of outlaws; Tex Ritter even sings a song, with veteran Gibson in supporting role.▼

Mars Invades Puerto Rico SEE: **Frankenstein Meets the Space Monster**

Mars Needs Women (1968) **C-80m.** *½ D: Larry Buchanan. Tommy Kirk, Yvonne Craig, Byron Lord, Roger Ready, Warren Hammack, Anthony Houston. Just as the title suggests, Martians Kirk and four pals, hoping to increase birthrate on their planet, arrive here to capture live women. Strangely sincere but extremely silly and distended. Texas-made film written by the director. Most important revelation: Mars abandoned neckties 50 years ago.▼●

Marsupials, The: The Howling III SEE: **Howling III**

Martha (1973-West German) **C-112m.** **½ D: Rainer Werner Fassbinder. Margit Carstensen, Karlheinz Bohm, Gisela Fackeldey, Adrian Hoven, Peter Chatel. Unsubtle account of spinsterish Carstensen, who has spent her life under the control of her father. He dies and she immediately marries, with disastrous results. A film very much of the early 1970s, a time when women were discovering feminism. Now it serves as a curio and a history lesson. Cineastes take note: Martha's last name is Heyer (as in Martha Hyer), and she lives on Douglas Sirk Street! First made available in the U.S. in 1994.

Martha + Ethel (1994) **C/B&W-80m.** *** D: Jyll Johnstone. Incisive documentary look at the title duo, one a German refugee and the other an African-American, who were the childhood nannies of director Johnstone and Barbara Ettinger, the film's producer. A valentine to two totally dissimilar women, and a keenly observed examination of U.S. cultural change during the second half of the 20th century. [G]▼●

Martians Go Home (1990) **C-89m.** *½ D: David Odell. Randy Quaid, Margaret Colin, Anita Morris, Barry Sobel, Vic Dunlop, John Philbin, Gerrit Graham, Ronny Cox, Harry Basil. TV songwriter Quaid accidentally summons a billion green wisecracking Martians to Earth; chaos (limited by the film's low budget) ensues. Fredric Brown's classic sci-fi humor novel misfires on the screen, partly because the pesky Martians are all played by mediocre standup comics. [PG-13]▼●

Martin (1978) **C-95m.** *** D: George A. Romero. John Amplas, Lincoln Maazel, Christine Forrest, Elayne Nadeau, Tom Savini, Sarah Venable, George A. Romero. Typical Romero mix of social satire and stomach-churning gore: 17-year-old Amplas thinks he's a vampire (lacking fangs, he must resort to razor blades); thanks to his frequent calls to a late-night radio show, he's also something of a local celebrity! Intriguing little shocker is worth seeing, but not right after dinner. [R]▼●

Martin Lawrence: You So Crazy SEE: **You So Crazy**

Martin's Day (1984-Canadian) **C-98m.** ** D: Alan Gibson. Richard Harris, Lindsay Wagner, James Coburn, Justin Henry, Karen Black, John Ireland. Creditable cast in utterly ordinary "family film" about escaped prisoner who kidnaps (and ultimately befriends) young boy. Bland and unconvincing. [PG]▼

Marty (1955) **91m.** ***½ D: Delbert Mann. Ernest Borgnine, Betsy Blair, Joe Mantell, Joe De Santis, Esther Minciotti, Augusta Ciolli, Karen Steele, Jerry Paris, Frank Sutton. Oscar for Borgnine as Bronx butcher who doesn't plan to find love, but does, in this moving Paddy Chayefsky script, originally a TV play; also won Oscars for Chayefsky, Mann, and Best Picture.▼●

Marvin and Tige (1983) **C-104m.** **½ D: Eric Weston. John Cassavetes, Gibran Brown, Billy Dee Williams, Denise Nicholas Hill, Fay Hauser. Tearjerker about a loser (Cassavetes) who takes in an aimless eleven-year-old (Brown) who tried to kill himself. Well acted, and well intentioned, but pretty standard stuff. [PG]▼

Marvin's Room (1996) **C-98m.** ***½ D: Jerry Zaks. Meryl Streep, Leonardo DiCaprio, Diane Keaton, Robert De Niro, Hume Cronyn, Gwen Verdon, Dan Hedaya, Hal Scardino, Victor Garber. Affecting adaptation of Scott McPherson's Off-Broadway play about a woman who's devoted her adult life to caring for her stroke-ridden father and a dithery aunt; now she must call on her long-estranged sister and nephews to help out in her own health emergency. A poignant and pointed look at family ties, old wounds, love, and responsibility, with uniformly fine performances. Cronyn adds immeasurable strength, though he says not a word. Rachel Portman's beautiful score is another asset. Broadway director Zaks' film debut. [PG-13]▼●◗

Marx Brothers at the Circus SEE: **At the Circus**

Marx Brothers Go West SEE: **Go West**

Mary & Tim (1996) **C-100m. TVM** D: Glenn Jordan. Candice Bergen, Thomas McCarthy, Richard Kiley, Louise Latham, Kelli Williams, Shirley Knight, Debra Mooney, Sean O'Bryan. Veteran Bergen and newcomer McCarthy are the lonely older widow and the mentally challenged younger man who comes into her life in this well-turned remake of TIM, the 1979 Australian film which effectively introduced Mel Gibson to American audiences. Colleen McCullough wrote the novel on which this was based before her more famous *The Thorn Birds*. Average.

Mary Burns, Fugitive (1935) **84m.** *** D: William K. Howard. Sylvia Sidney, Melvyn Douglas, Pert Kelton, Alan Baxter, Wallace Ford, Brian Donlevy. Fine gangster melodrama. Sidney is dragged into underworld, valiantly tries to escape her gangster lover (Baxter).

Maryjane (1968) **C-104m.** *½ D: Maury Dexter. Fabian, Diane McBain, Michael Margotta, Kevin Coughlin, Patty McCormack, Terri (Teri) Garr. 1960s version of REEFER MADNESS casts Fabian as high school art teacher who tries to keep his students from smoking grass; terrible, but may play better if you're stoned.

Maryland (1940) **C-92m.** **½ D: Henry King. Walter Brennan, Fay Bainter, Brenda Joyce, John Payne, Charles Ruggles, Marjorie Weaver. Predictable story given elaborate treatment. Bainter refuses to let son Payne ride horses since his father was killed that way. Beautiful color scenery.

Mary, Mary (1963) **C-126m.** **½ D: Mervyn LeRoy. Debbie Reynolds, Barry

Nelson, Michael Rennie, Diane McBain, Hiram Sherman. Unremarkable, stagy adaptation of Jean Kerr's sex comedy about divorced couple trying to screw up each other's new romances. Stick with THE AWFUL TRUTH.

Mary of Scotland (1936) **123m.** ***½ D: John Ford. Katharine Hepburn, Fredric March, Florence Eldridge, Douglas Walton, Moroni Olsen, John Carradine, Robert Barrat, Ian Keith, Ralph Forbes, Alan Mowbray, Donald Crisp. Lavish historical drama in which Mary Queen of Scots (Hepburn) returns to her homeland from France, to rule "fairly and justly." She falls in love with Lord March, and contends with various treacheries. Based on a play by Maxwell Anderson.▼●

Mary Poppins (1964) **C-140m.** **** D: Robert Stevenson. Julie Andrews, Dick Van Dyke, David Tomlinson, Glynis Johns, Ed Wynn, Hermione Baddeley, Karen Dotrice, Matthew Garber, Arthur Treacher, Reginald Owen. There's charm, wit, and movie magic to spare in Walt Disney's adaptation of P.L. Travers's book about a "practically perfect" nanny who brings profound change to the Banks family of London, circa 1910. Oscars went to Richard and Robert Sherman for their tuneful score, the song "Chim-Chim-Cheree," the formidable Visual Effects team, Cotton Warburton for his editing, and Andrews, in her film debut (though Van Dyke is equally good as Bert, the whimsical jack of all trades). That's Jane Darwell, in her last screen appearance, as the bird lady. A wonderful movie. Scripted by co-producer Bill Walsh and Donald Da Gradi.▼●◗

Mary, Queen of Scots (1971) **C-128m.** *** D: Charles Jarrott. Vanessa Redgrave, Glenda Jackson, Patrick McGoohan, Timothy Dalton, Nigel Davenport, Trevor Howard, Daniel Massey, Ian Holm. Inaccurate history lesson but good costume drama, with strong performances from Redgrave as Mary, Jackson as Queen Elizabeth, rivals for power in Tudor England. Panavision. [PG]▼

Mary Reilly (1996) **C-108m.** **½ D: Stephen Frears. Julia Roberts, John Malkovich, Glenn Close, George Cole, Michael Gambon, Kathy Staff, Michael Sheen, Bronagh Gallagher, Linda Bassett, Ciaran Hinds. Intriguing premise: the story of Dr. Jekyll and Mr. Hyde from the point of view of a housemaid in his employ. Unfortunately, this chamber drama is played out in ponderous fashion and almost sinks under its own weight, despite the interesting performances by its stars. (Admittedly, Roberts' Irish accent comes and goes at whim.) Close is fun in a flamboyant part as a madam. Screenplay by Christopher Hampton from the novel by Valerie Martin. [R]▼●

Mary Shelley's Frankenstein (1994) **C-128m.** ** D: Kenneth Branagh. Robert De Niro, Kenneth Branagh, Tom Hulce, Helena Bonham Carter, Aidan Quinn, Ian Holm, Richard Briers, John Cleese, Robert Hardy, Cherie Lunghi. Hugely disappointing, "faithful" rendition of the Frankenstein saga. Energetic to a fault, with a camera that refuses to stand still. Branagh allows us to understand what makes Dr. F. tick, but the story goes askew once his monster is unleashed. And what's with that story framework with sea captain Quinn? De Niro's monster remains doggedly De Niro-ish, and makes one yearn for Karloff. (Even Peter Boyle would do.) [R]▼●◗

Mary White (1977) **C-100m. TVM** D: Jud Taylor. Ed Flanders, Kathleen Beller, Fionnula Flanagan, Tim Matheson, Donald Moffat. Moving drama, told poetically, based on the writings of Pulitzer Prize-winning newsman William Allen White after the tragic death of his teenaged daughter in 1921. Leisurely paced, not for every taste, but class tells and so does Ed Flanders, who is superb. Script by Caryl Ledner. Above average.▼

Ma Saison Préférée (1993-French) **C-124m.** *** D: André Téchiné. Catherine Deneuve, Daniel Auteuil, Marthe Villalonga, Jean-Pierre Bouvier, Chiara Mastroianni, Carmen Chaplin, Anthony Prada. Story of intertwining relationships, and more interestingly, familial bonds and duties. Deneuve (married, with successful small business but stress at home) and eccentric brother Auteuil (a bachelor and neurosurgeon) make realistic, offbeat leads as adults trying to understand and enjoy life. Deneuve and Marcello Mastroianni's real-life daughter, Chiara, makes her film debut, playing Deneuve's daughter. Talky, but worthwhile. Panavision.▼●◗

Masculine-Feminine (1966-French-Swedish) **103m.** *** D: Jean-Luc Godard. Jean-Pierre Léaud, Chantal Goya, Marlene Jobert, Michel Debord, Catherine-Isabelle Duport, Eva-Britt Strandberg, Brigitte Bardot. Engaging, original concoction mixes politics, sex, comedy, nostalgia with standard boy-meets-girl theme. Interviewer/journalist Léaud has affair with would-be rock star singer Goya; they're Godard's "children of Marx and Coca-Cola." Adapted, oddly enough, from a Guy de Maupassant story!▼

MASH (1970) **C-116m.** **** D: Robert Altman. Donald Sutherland, Elliott Gould, Tom Skerritt, Sally Kellerman, Robert Duvall, Jo Ann Pflug, Rene Auberjonois, Roger Bowen, Gary Burghoff, Fred Williamson, John Schuck, Bud Cort, G. Wood. Altman's first major success gave new meaning to the word "irreverence," set new style for contemporary filmmaking; follows black-comedy exploits of wild and woolly medical unit during Korean War in hilarious, episodic fashion. Oscar-winning screenplay by Ring Lardner, Jr.; reissued in 1973 at 112m., with new title music by Ahmad Jamal. Later a hit TV series (*M*A*S*H*). [PG—edited from original R rating] Panavision.▼●

Mask, The (1961) SEE: **Eyes of Hell**

Mask (1985) **C-120m.** ***½ D: Peter Bogdanovich. Cher, Sam Elliott, Eric Stoltz, Estelle Getty, Richard Dysart, Laura Dern, Harry Carey, Jr., Lawrence Monoson, Marsha Warfield, Barry Tubb, Andrew Robinson. Irresistible film based on true story of Rocky Dennis, teenage boy whose face has been terribly disfigured by a rare disease, and his mother Rusty, who's instilled a sense of confidence and love in her son, though her own defenses are easily broken down. Anna Hamilton Phelan's script dodges cliché, while Cher and Stoltz make their characters warm and real. A winner. [PG-13]▼●◗

Mask, The (1988-Italian) **C-90m.** *½ D: Fiorella Infascelli. Helena Bonham Carter, Michael Maloney, Feodor Chaliapin, Roberto Herlitzka. Trivial, dull account of self-centered count's son Maloney, who becomes obsessed with pretty young actress Carter. She's put off by him, so he commences to woo her by donning various masks and changing his identity. Extremely slow-moving.

Mask, The (1994) **C-101m.** **½ D: Charles Russell. Jim Carrey, Cameron Diaz, Peter Riegert, Peter Greene, Amy Yasbeck, Richard Jeni, Orestes Matacena, Timothy Bagley, Nancy Fish, Ben Stein. A wimpy bank clerk discovers a mask that turns him into a sizzling Superdude who acts out his alter ego's fantasies. Pretty entertaining, though it's seamier (and more violent) than it needs to be, and has some real lulls during its plottier moments. The already rubber-faced Carrey is aided and abetted by stunning digital computer effects, inspired by the manic 1940s cartoons of Tex Avery. Based on the comic book. Followed by an animated TV series. [PG-13]▼●◗

Mask of Diijon, The (1946) **73m.** ** D: Lewis Landers. Erich von Stroheim, Jeanne Bates, Denise Vernac, William Wright, Edward Van Sloan. Stroheim is hypnotist who has delusions of grandeur, and schemes in murder attempts; exciting finish.▼◗

Mask of Dimitrios, The (1944) **95m.** *** D: Jean Negulesco. Peter Lorre, Sydney Greenstreet, Zachary Scott, Faye Emerson, Victor Francen, George Tobias, Steve Geray, Eduardo Ciannelli, Florence Bates. Fine, offbeat melodrama with mild-mannered mystery writer Lorre reviewing life of notorious scoundrel Scott (in film debut). Frank Gruber adapted Eric Ambler's novel, *A Coffin for Dimitrios.* As always, Lorre and Greenstreet make a marvelous team.▼

Mask of Fu Manchu, The (1932) **68m.** **½ D: Charles Brabin. Boris Karloff, Lewis Stone, Karen Morley, Myrna Loy, Charles Starrett, Jean Hersholt. Elaborate chiller of Chinese madman Karloff menacing expedition in tomb of Ghengis Khan. Adaptation of Sax Rohmer novel is ornate and hokey, but fun; Loy is terrific as Fu's deliciously evil daughter.▼●

Mask of the Avenger (1951) **C-83m.** ** D: Phil Karlson. John Derek, Anthony Quinn, Jody Lawrance, Arnold Moss. Not up to snuff; man posing as count of Monte Cristo is involved in swordplay.

Mask of Zorro, The (1998) **C-136m.** *** D: Martin Campbell. Antonio Banderas, Anthony Hopkins, Catherine Zeta-Jones, Stuart Wilson, Matt Letscher, Maury Chaykin, Tony Amendola, Pedro Armendariz, L.Q. Jones, Victor Rivers. An aging Zorro passes the mantle of public protector to a younger man, who's reluctant at first but soon relishes his secret identity with cape and sword. Exquisite, exciting, with great swordplay and horse action—but has too much of everything, as if the filmmakers want to wear you out. Banderas is an ideal Zorro, Hopkins a surprisingly engaging one, Zeta-Jones a saucy and beautiful heroine. Panavision. [PG-13]▼●◗

Masque of the Red Death, The (1964) **C-86m.** ***½ D: Roger Corman. Vincent Price, Hazel Court, Jane Asher, David Weston, Patrick Magee, Skip Martin, Nigel Green, John Westbrook. The most Bergman-like of Corman's films, an ultra-stylish adaptation of the Poe tale (with another, *Hop Frog,* worked in as a subplot), starring Price as evil Prince Prospero, living it up in eerie, timeless castle while Plague ravages the countryside. Beautifully photographed in England by Nicolas Roeg. Remade in 1989. Panavision.▼●

Masque of the Red Death (1989) **C-83m.** ** D: Larry Brand. Adrian Paul, Clare Hoak, Jeff Osterhage, Patrick Macnee, Tracy Reiner. Roger Corman produced this remake of one of his best films. Poe's Prince Prospero (Paul) is still dissipated, but this time more thoughtful and troubled. Despite an interesting approach to figure of the Red Death and literate (if talky) script, overall cheapness and very slow pace cripple this medieval melodrama. [R]▼

Masquerade (1965-British) **C-101m.** **½ D: Basil Dearden. Cliff Robertson, Jack Hawkins, Marisa Mell, Michel Piccoli, Bill Fraser, John LeMesurier. Above-average spy satire highlighted by Robertson's portrayal of recruited agent. Good support casting with good location shooting to give Arabic atmosphere.

Masquerade (1988) **C-91m.** **½ D: Bob Swaim. Rob Lowe, Meg Tilly, Kim Cattrall, Doug Savant, John Glover, Dana Delany, Erik Holland. Lowe essentially has the ambiguous Cary Grant SUSPICION role: Does he really love delicate (and in this case, filthy rich) spouse Tilly—or is he planning to murder her at the first opportunity? Romantic suspense thriller has its moments, and might have had more with a better leading man. Merely OK, with Tilly, Glover, Delany and lovely Hamptons scenery offering compensation. [R]▼●

Masquerade in Mexico (1945) **96m.** ** D: Mitchell Leisen. Dorothy Lamour, Arturo de Cordova, Patric Knowles, Ann Dvorak, George Rigaud, Natalie Schafer, Billy Daniels. Frivolous plot, forgettable songs combine in this limp musicomedy of bullfighters, romance, and Mexican intrigue. Remake of MIDNIGHT (1939) by the same director.

Masquerader, The (1933) **78m.** **½ D: Richard Wallace. Ronald Colman, Elissa Landi, Halliwell Hobbes, Helen Jerome Eddy. Dated but enjoyable film goes on theory that two Colmans are better than one; journalist pretends he is his drug-addict cousin, a member of Parliament. Hobbes is splendid as loyal and long-suffering butler.

Massacre (1934) **70m.** **½ D: Alan Crosland. Richard Barthelmess, Ann Dvorak, Dudley Digges, Claire Dodd, Henry O'Neill, Robert Barrat. Unusual story about college-educated Sioux (Barthelmess) who tries to fight injustice and discrimination against his people back on the reservation. Interesting attempt to show an enlightened view of contemporary Indians, in the context of typical Warner Bros. melodramatic fodder.

Massacre (1956) **C-76m.** ** D: Louis King. Dane Clark, James Craig, Marta Roth, Miguel Torruco, Jaime Fernandez. Uninspired account of greedy Indian gunsellers.

Massacre at Central High (1976) **C-85m.** *** D: Renee Daalder. Derrel Maury, Andrew Stevens, Kimberly Beck, Robert Carradine, Roy Underwood, Steve Bond. Newcomer to California high school doesn't like the way students are being terrorized by a gang, so he decides to eliminate them, in ultra-violent fashion . . . but that's not the end of the story. Seemingly typical blend of teen and revenge formulas given offbeat twists by writer-director Daalder. [R]▼

Massacre at Fort Holman SEE: **Reason to Live, a Reason to Die, A**

Massacre Hill SEE: **Eureka Stockade**

Massacre in Rome (1973-French-Italian) **C-103m.** *** D: George Pan Cosmatos. Richard Burton, Marcello Mastroianni, Leo McKern, John Steiner, Anthony Steel. Good drama: priest Mastroianni opposed to idealistic German Colonel Burton, who must execute 330 Roman hostages in retaliation for deaths of 33 Nazi soldiers. [PG]▼

Massacre River (1949) **75m.** *½ D: John Rawlins. Guy Madison, Rory Calhoun, Johnny Sands, Carole Mathews, Cathy Downs. Minor Western, with trio of soldiers fighting over women.

Mass Appeal (1984) **C-100m.** *** D: Glenn Jordan. Jack Lemmon. Zeljko Ivanek, Charles Durning, Louise Latham, Lois de Banzie, James Ray, Talia Balsam, Gloria Stuart. Feisty young seminarian rattles the complacency of a popular parish priest in this entertaining filmization of Bill C. Davis' glib Broadway play. Lemmon is first-rate as usual, and though film belies its stage origins it still works fine. [PG]▼●

Master Gunfighter, The (1975) **C-121m.** BOMB D: Frank Laughlin. Tom Laughlin, Ron O'Neal, Lincoln Kilpatrick, Geo Anne Sosa, Barbara Carrera, Victor Campos. BILLY JACK'S creator-star is an intense gunfighter who hates to kill but does it just the same. Lots of rhetoric. Remake of a 1969 Japanese samurai film, GOYOKIN. Panavision. [PG]

Mastermind (1976) **C-131m.** *** D: Alex March. Zero Mostel, Bradford Dillman, Keiko Kishi, Gawn Grainger, Herbert Berghof, Jules Munshin, Sorrell Booke. Enjoyable spoof of Charlie Chan films with Mostel as Inspector Hoku, who tries to protect robot-like invention sought by international interests. Some good slapstick, rousing car chase. Received limited release after sitting on shelf since 1969. [G]▼

Master Minds (1949) **64m.** ** D: Jean Yarbrough. Leo Gorcey, Huntz Hall, Billy Benedict, Bennie Bartlett, David Gorcey, Gabriel Dell, Alan Napier, Jane Adams, Bernard Gorcey. Sach's ability to predict events puts him in a carnival where he ends up the unwilling participant in a mad scientist's brain transplant experiment. Typical *Bowery Boys* nonsense.

Masterminds (1997) **C-105m.** *½ D: Roger Christian. Patrick Stewart, Vincent Kartheiser, Brenda Fricker, Brad Whitford, Matt Craven, Annabelle Gurwitch. High-tech action/adventure yarn finds evil genius Stewart taking over an exclusive private school for ransom, but former student and computer whiz kid Kartheiser stands in his way. Kids might find the attitude-driven script harmless fantasy, but adults may cringe watching Fricker and Stewart in this DIE HARD for preteens. Super 35. [PG-13]▼●

Master of Ballantrae, The (1953) **C-89m.** **½ D: William Keighley. Errol Flynn, Roger Livesey, Anthony Steel, Yvonne Furneaux. Robert Louis Stevenson's historical yarn has Flynn involved in plot to make Bonnie Prince Charles king of England; on-location filming in Scotland,

Sicily, and England adds scope to costumer. Remade for TV.▼●

Master of Ballantrae, The (1984) **C-150m. TVM** D: Douglas Hickox. Richard Thomas, Michael York, John Gielgud, Brian Blessed, Timothy Dalton, Nickolas Grace, Finola Hughes, Ian Richardson. Lavish swashbuckler with York in the old Errol Flynn part and Thomas as the brother with whom he battles for the old family homestead and the honor of joining Bonnie Prince Charlie's cause. R. L. Stevenson done to a TV T. Above average.

Master of the House (1925-Danish) **81m.** *** D: Carl Theodor Dreyer. Johannes Meyer, Astrid Holm, Karin Mellemose, Mathilde Nielson, Clara Schonfeld. Solid domestic comedy-drama about a haughty brute who criticizes and humiliates his wife and children until his elderly nanny steps in to teach him a lesson in obedience. Scenario by Dreyer and Sven Rindom, from Rindom's play. So popular at time of its release that, in Paris alone, it was shown at 57 theaters in just three weeks.▼

Master of the World (1961) **C-104m.** *** D: William Witney. Vincent Price, Charles Bronson, Mary Webster, Henry Hull, Richard Harrison. Sci-fi adventure adapted from two Jules Verne novels about a 19th-century genius (Price) seeking to stop war from his ingenious flying machine, a cross between a zeppelin and a helicopter. Bronson (oddly cast) admires his ends, deplores his methods, and sets out to stop him. Very well done. Screenplay by Richard Matheson.▼●

Master Race, The (1944) **96m.** **½ D: Herbert J. Biberman. George Coulouris, Stanley Ridges, Osa Massen, Nancy Gates, Lloyd Bridges, Carl Esmond, Morris Carnovsky, Helen Beverly. The Germans are losing WW2 and Nazi Colonel Coulouris goes incognito in a Belgian village, schemes to keep the "Master Race" alive. Thoughtful if overly melodramatic account; the character of the heroic Russian doctor/POW (Esmond) is most intriguing.▼

Masters of the Universe (1987) **C-106m.** ** D: Gary Goddard. Dolph Lundgren, Frank Langella, Courteney Cox, James Tolkan, Meg Foster, Christina Pickles, Billy Barty, Jon Cypher. He-Man (Lundgren) comes to Earth seeking a key that controls the power of the universe, stolen by cosmic crud Skeletor (unrecognizable Langella); somehow two teen puppy-lovers get involved. Elaborate comic book nonsense (which has had another life in kiddie animation) is dumb but inoffensive. [PG]▼●

Masterson of Kansas (1954) **C-73m.** ** D: William Castle. George Montgomery, Nancy Gates, James Griffith, Jean Willes, Benny Rubin. Despite presence of trio of famed gunmen—Doc Holliday, Wyatt Earp and Bat Masterson—film is just standard.

Master Spy (1964-British) **71m.** **½ D: Montgomery Tully. Stephen Murray, June Thorburn, Alan Wheatley, John Carson. OK drama of Allied counteragent escaping from Communist prison.

Master Touch, The (1973-Italian-German) **C-96m.** ** D: Michele Lupo. Kirk Douglas, Florinda Bolkan, Giuliano Gemma, Rene Koldehoff. Safecracker Douglas, just out of jail, attempts to trip up a foolproof alarm and rip off a safe for $1 million. Deadening. Techniscope. [PG]▼

Matador (1986-Spanish) **C-106m.** *** D: Pedro Almodóvar. Assumpta Serna, Antonio Banderas, Nacho Martinez, Carmen Maura, Eva Cobo, Julieta Serrano, Chus Lampreave. Dazzling black comedy chronicles plight of retired matador Martinez, passing time by compulsively watching snuff films—and his young, troubled protégé (Banderas). Opening sequence is a real stunner.▼●

Mata Hari (1932) **90m.** *** D: George Fitzmaurice. Greta Garbo, Ramon Novarro, Lionel Barrymore, Lewis Stone, C. Henry Gordon, Karen Morley. Garbo is the alluring spy of WW1, beguiling everyone from Novarro to Barrymore. Highlights: Garbo's exotic dance sequence, Morley stalked by gang executioner. That's an unbilled Mischa Auer in opening scene as condemned man who won't betray Garbo's love.▼●

Mata Hari (1985) **C-108m.** *½ D: Curtis Harrington. Sylvia Kristel, Christopher Cazenove, Oliver Tobias, Gaye Brown, Gottfried John. The famous femme fatale of WW1 *must* have been more interesting than this! Kristel's frequent nudity is only possible attraction. [R]▼

Mata Hari's Daughter (1954-Italian) **C-102m.** ** D: Renzo Meruis. Frank Latimore, Ludmilla Tcherina, Erno Crisa. Humdrum account of alleged daughter of famed WW1 spy in 1940 Java involved in espionage; sterile dubbing. Retitled: DAUGHTER OF MATA HARI.

Match Factory Girl, The (1990-Finnish) **C-70m.** *** D: Aki Kaurismaki. Kati Outinen, Elina Salo, Esko Nikkari, Vesa Vierikko. A drab, oppressed young woman allows herself to fall for the wrong man; he unceremoniously dumps her, but her reaction is anything but passive. Clever, ironic pitch-black comedy from prolific Kaurismaki. ▼

Match King, The (1932) **80m.** **½ D: Howard Bretherton, William Keighley. Warren William, Lili Damita, Glenda Farrell, Harold Huber, John Wray, Hardie Albright. Clever, ambitious young man will stop at nothing to succeed, becomes a multimillionaire buying exclusive rights to manufacture matches around the world! Interesting if uneven, story is doubly compelling because it's mostly true, based on life of Ivar Kreuger.

Matchless (1967-Italian) **C-104m.** ** D: Alberto Lattuada. Patrick O'Neal, Ira Furstenberg, Donald Pleasence, Henry Silva. Dashing, romantic 007-like journalist is pursued for his knowledge of a chemical formula and his magical ring, which makes him invisible. Usual imitation James Bond potboiler.

Matchmaker, The (1958) **101m.** ★★★ D: Joseph Anthony. Shirley Booth, Anthony Perkins, Shirley MacLaine, Paul Ford, Robert Morse, Wallace Ford. Endearing Thornton Wilder comedy about middle-aged widower deciding to rewed . . . but the matchmaker he consults has plans of her own. Solid performances, fine period detail; later musicalized as HELLO, DOLLY! VistaVision.▼●

Matchmaker, The (1997-U.S.-Irish) **C-96m.** ★★★ D: Mark Joffe. Janeane Garofalo, David O'Hara, Milo O'Shea, Denis Leary, Jay O. Sanders, Rosaleen Linehan, Paul Hickey, Maria Doyle Kennedy, Robert Mandan. Cute comedy about a campaign worker for a less than exemplary U.S. Senator from Massachusetts, who's given the job of tracing his relatives to a small village in Ireland and setting up a photo opportunity to entice the state's Irish-American vote. Garofalo arrives in the remote village during its annual matchmaking festival and, despite everything, gets caught up in a relationship. Fanciful, rather than realistic, but entertaining. Super 35. [R] ▼●◗

Matewan (1987) **C-130m.** ★★★½ D: John Sayles. Chris Cooper, Will Oldham, Mary McDonnell, Bob Gunton, James Earl Jones, Kevin Tighe, Gordon Clapp, Josh Mostel, Joe Grifasi, Maggie Renzi, David Strathairn. Compelling and compassionate drama about labor troubles in the heart of coal-mining country, Matewan, West Virginia, in the 1920s. As usual, writer-director Sayles (who appears briefly as a preacher) makes every note ring true in this meticulous period piece; he even cowrote some phony labor songs! Beautifully photographed by Haskell Wexler. [PG-13]▼●◗

Matilda (1978) **C-103m.** BOMB D: Daniel Mann. Elliott Gould, Robert Mitchum, Harry Guardino, Clive Revill, Karen Carlson, Lionel Stander, Larry Pennell, Art Metrano. Good cast wasted in awful kiddie pic about a boxing kangaroo, played by a man in a suit (Gary Morgan). Paul Gallico's novel loses everything in translation. [G]▼

Matilda (1996) **C-93m.** ★★½ D: Danny DeVito. Danny DeVito, Rhea Perlman, Embeth Davidtz, Pam Ferris, Mara Wilson, Paul Reubens, Tracey Walter, Kiami Davael. Cursed with a cretinous family and a witch of a school principal, a bright young girl learns self-reliance—and develops unusual powers. Wilson's irresistible charm anchors this very black comedy from the book by Roald Dahl. The bizarre goings-on, and the strange sensibilities, may play better on the printed page (and in a reader's imagination) than they do when acted out literally on-screen. Anne Ramsey being dead, DeVito had to find another harpy—in this case the furious Ferris. Jon Lovitz appears unbilled; DeVito narrates. Super 35. [PG] ▼●◗

Matinee (1993) **C-98m.** ★★★ D: Joe Dante. John Goodman, Cathy Moriarty, Simon Fenton, Omri Katz, Lisa Jakub, Kellie Martin, Jesse Lee, Lucinda Jenney, James Villemaire, Robert Picardo, Jesse White, Dick Miller, John Sayles, David Clennon, Luke Halpin. Goodman is delightful as a movie schlockmeister (inspired by real-life producer William Castle) previewing his latest scare-the-pants-off-'em horror movie at a Key West theater—the very weekend of the Cuban missile crisis, when everyone's nerves are on edge. Sweet-natured film, full of nostalgia and in-jokes for film buffs, but a little slow (and soft) until it gets rolling. Film-within-a-film, MANT, is a real hoot, with appearances by sci-fi stalwarts William Schallert, Kevin McCarthy, Robert Cornthwaite. [PG]▼●◗

Matinee Idol, The (1928) **56m.** ★★★ D: Frank Capra. Johnnie Walker, Bessie Love, Lionel Belmore, Ernest Hilliard, Sidney D'Albrook. Delightful farce about Broadway star Walker who, while stranded in the country, appears incognito in Love's local play, then brings her amateur theater group to N.Y. to put on a hilariously bad Civil War show. Long-lost Capra silent is an expert mixture of comedy, romance, and sentiment.▼◗

Mating Game, The (1959) **C-96m.** ★★★ D: George Marshall. Debbie Reynolds, Tony Randall, Paul Douglas, Fred Clark, Una Merkel, Philip Ober, Charles Lane. Zippy comedy romp of tax agent Randall falling in love with farm girl Reynolds, with Douglas rambunctious as Debbie's father. CinemaScope.▼

Mating of Millie, The (1948) **87m.** ★★½ D: Henry Levin. Glenn Ford, Evelyn Keyes, Ron Randell, Willard Parker, Virginia Hunter. Ford tries to help Keyes trap a husband so she can adopt a child, but falls in love with her himself. Predictable but pleasant.

Mating Season, The (1951) **101m.** ★★★½ D: Mitchell Leisen. Gene Tierney, John Lund, Miriam Hopkins, Thelma Ritter, Jan Sterling, Larry Keating, James Lorimer. Excellent, underrated comedy with cynical undertones about the American dream. Hardworking Lund marries socialite Tierney, suffers embarrassment when his plain-talking mother (Ritter) comes to town and is mistaken for servant. Ritter is simply superb. Written by Walter Reisch, Richard Breen, and producer Charles Brackett.

Matrix, The (1999) **C-136m.** ★★½ D: The Wachowski Brothers. Keanu Reeves, Laurence Fishburne, Carrie-Anne Moss, Hugo Weaving, Gloria Foster, Joe Pantoliano, Marcus Chong. A computer hacker (Reeves) discovers the world he is living in is an illusion maintained by computers that have taken over the world . . . and he is thought to be "the chosen one" to save humanity. Cutting-edge visuals and production design compete with an overlong script, written by the directors, that's got a high MJQ (Mumbo-Jumbo Quotient), and a tendency to keep changing its own complicated "rules." Martial arts scenes are highlights. Oscar winner for Film Editing, Sound, Sound Effects Editing, and Visual Effects. Super 35. [R]▼●◗

Mattei Affair, The (1973-Italian) **C-118m.** **½ D: Francesco Rosi. Gian Maria Volonte, Luigi Squarizina, Peter Baldwin. Semi-documentary study of rise of Italian industrialist and his mysterious death. [R]

Matter of Innocence, A (1967-British) **C-102m.** **½ D: Guy Green. Hayley Mills, Trevor Howard, Sashi Kapoor, Brenda De Banzie. Plain Jane (Mills) travels to Singapore with aunt, has an affair with Eurasian Kapoor and becomes a woman. Trite soaper with unusual role for suave Howard; from Noel Coward story "Pretty Polly." Techniscope.

Matter of Life and Death, A (1946) SEE: **Stairway to Heaven**

Matter of Resistance, A (1966-French) **92m.** **½ D: Jean-Paul Rappeneau. Catherine Deneuve, Philippe Noiret, Pierre Brasseur, Mary Marquet, Henri Garcin, Carlos Thompson. Pleasant French comedy of bored housewife (Deneuve) who welcomes arrival of soldiers to her village prior to Normandy invasion. Originally titled LA VIE DE CHATEAU.

Matter of Time, A (1976) **C-99m.** BOMB D: Vincente Minnelli. Liza Minnelli, Ingrid Bergman, Charles Boyer, Spiros Andros, Tina Aumont, Anna Proclemer. Depressing schmaltz about a chambermaid in pre-WW1 Europe taught to love life by a batty contessa. Director Minnelli's worst film, though, for his part, he denounced this version as edited. Final film for both Boyer and the director. Bergman's daughter, Isabella Rossellini, makes her screen debut as a nun. [PG]▼

Matter of WHO, A (1961-British) **90m.** **½ D: Don Chaffey. Terry-Thomas, Alex Nicol, Sonja Ziemann, Guy Deghy, Richard Briers, Carol White, Honor Blackman. Occasionally entertaining mystery with Thomas in a rare straight role as a World Health Organization bureaucrat who turns detective to trace a smallpox carrier.▼

Matt Helm (1975) **C-78m. TVM** D: Buzz Kulik. Tony Franciosa, Ann Turkel, Gene Evans, Patrick Macnee, Hari Rhodes, James Shigeta, Laraine Stephens, John Vernon, Catherine Bach. Private eye Helm finds himself neck deep in international black market arms operation while trying to protect a movie star whose life is threatened. When ol' Dino played Helm in four movies, he was a crack secret agent. Pilot to the short-lived series. Average.

Maurice (1987-British) **C-135m.** *** D: James Ivory. James Wilby, Hugh Grant, Rupert Graves, Denholm Elliott, Simon Callow, Billie Whitelaw, Ben Kingsley, Judy Parfitt, Phoebe Nicholls, Barry Foster. Typically meticulous Merchant-Ivory production of a literary work (by E. M. Forster) about a young Britisher's coming of age in the 1910s, and coming to terms with his homosexuality. Beautifully realized and extremely well acted all around . . . but overlong. Helena Bonham Carter (the star of Ivory's previous hit, A ROOM WITH A VIEW) makes a cameo appearance. [R]▼●

Maurie (1973) **C-113m.** ** D: Daniel Mann. Bernie Casey, Bo Svenson, Janet MacLachlan, Stephanie Edwards, Paulene Myers, Bill Walker. Well-meaning but downbeat tearjerker based on true story of basketball star Maurice Stokes (Casey). His sudden paralysis spurs teammate Jack Twyman (Svenson) to devote himself to Maurie's rehabilitation. Too similar to other sports-tragedy films to stand out. Shown on TV as BIG MO. [G]▼

Maverick (1994) **C-129m.** **½ D: Richard Donner. Mel Gibson, Jodie Foster, James Garner, Graham Greene, James Coburn, Alfred Molina, Paul Smith, Geoffrey Lewis, Max Perlich, Dub Taylor. Lackadaisical update of the fondly remembered 60s TV show relies heavily on personal charm to carry a thin storyline that moseys along much too slowly—and much too long. Gibson is fun as a wily cardsharp on his way to a big-stakes poker game, and the cast is peppered with familiar faces from the world of vintage TV Westerns and contemporary country music; look for a couple of cameos by stars of earlier movies from director Donner. Garner, who starred in the old TV series, is cast here as a marshal. Script by William Goldman. Panavision. [PG]▼●◗

Maverick Queen, The (1956) **C-92m.** **½ D: Joseph Kane. Barbara Stanwyck, Barry Sullivan, Scott Brady, Mary Murphy, Wallace Ford. Stanwyck is peppy as outlaw who's willing to go straight for lawman Sullivan. Filmed in Naturama.▼

Ma Vie en Rose (1997-Belgian-French-British) **C-88m.** *** D: Alain Berliner. Michele Laroque, Jean-Philippe Ecoffey, Helene Vincent, Georges Du Fresne, Julien Riviere. Ludovic (Du Fresne), a sweet little boy who resides with his parents in a Belgian suburb, has decided that, when he grows up, he wants to be a girl. To him this is perfectly logical; he already favors wearing dresses and makeup, and is determined to eventually wed the boy-next-door. Needless to say, mom and dad are perplexed and none too pleased. All points of view are well served in this charming and compassionate comedy-drama. [R]▼◗

Max and Helen (1990-U.S.-British) **C-100m. TVM** D: Philip Saville. Treat Williams, Alice Krige, Martin Landau, Jonathan Phillips, Adam Kotz, Jodhi May.

Plodding adaptation of Simon Wiesenthal's book about a pair of lovers, separated during the war in a German labor camp, who manage to find one another two decades later. Williams' miscasting as a blank-faced German Jew who becomes a Paris doctor is counterbalanced by Landau's thoughtful, soft-spoken turn as Wiesenthal. Made for cable. Average.▼●

Max Dugan Returns (1983) **C-98m.** ★★★ D: Herbert Ross. Marsha Mason, Jason Robards, Donald Sutherland, Matthew Broderick, Dody Goodman, Sal Viscuso, David Morse, Kiefer Sutherland, Charlie Lau. Sweet, simple Neil Simon comedy about a long-lost father who tries to make amends to his daughter (a struggling schoolteacher and single parent) by showering her with presents—using money he's obtained by slightly shady means. Acted with verve and sincerity by a perfect cast. Film debuts of Matthew Broderick and Kiefer Sutherland. [PG]▼●

Max Havelaar (1976-Dutch-Indonesian) **C-167m.** ★★ D: Fons Rademakers. Peter Faber, Sacha Bulthuis, Elang Mohanad, Adenan Soesilanigrat. Uneven chronicle of colonial exploitation in 19th century Dutch East Indies (now Indonesia), with Faber an officer struggling to change the rules. Tries hard, but predictable and unexciting most of the way.

Maxie (1985) **C-90m.** ★★ D: Paul Aaron. Glenn Close, Mandy Patinkin, Ruth Gordon, Barnard Hughes, Valerie Curtin, Googy Gress, Harry Hamlin. Roaring twenties flapper inhabits the body of hardworking eighties woman, and titillates her husband to boot! *Very* old-fashioned screwball comedy-fantasy just doesn't come off, despite good intentions. Incidentally, the actress playing Maxie in authentic silent movie footage is Carole Lombard. [PG]▼●

Maxime (1958-French) **93m.** ★★½ D: Henri Verneuil. Michele Morgan, Charles Boyer, Arletty, Felix Marten. Morgan is good match for Parisian scoundrel Boyer in this love tale set in 1910s.

Maximum Overdrive (1986) **C-97m.** BOMB D: Stephen King. Emilio Estevez, Pat Hingle, Laura Harrington, Yeardley Smith, John Short, J. C. Quinn. Customers and employees of interstate truck stop are terrorized by the trucks themselves, which have come to demonic life as part of a global rebellion of machines. Novelist King, making his directing debut, said he set out to create a junk movie, nothing more . . . but he made it stupid and boring. Remade as a 1997 cable movie, TRUCKS. J-D-C Scope. [R]▼●

Maximum Risk (1996) **C-100m.** ★★½ D: Ringo Lam. Jean-Claude Van Damme, Natasha Henstridge, Jean-Hugues Anglade, Zach Grenier, Paul Ben-Victor, Frank Senger. The FBI and the Russian mafia are both after former French soldier Van Damme, who's out to avenge the death of an identical twin brother that everyone seems to think he is. He even inherits the brother's dishy girlfriend in the deal. Marginally closer to a real movie than most Van Damme efforts, thanks to some stylish touches by Hong Kong action specialist Lam. Super 35. [R]▼●◗

Maya (1966) **C-91m.** ★★ D: John Berry. Clint Walker, Jay North, I. S. Johar, Sajid Kahn, Jairaj, Sonia Sahni. Silly juvenile jungle tale has young North temporarily losing respect for his big-game hunter father Walker, who has lost his nerve. Panavision.▼

Maya Lin: A Strong Clear Vision (1994) **C-96m.** ★★½ D: Freida Lee Mock. Respectful, Oscar-winning documentary about artist Maya Lin, best known as the designer of the Washington, D.C., Vietnam Veterans Memorial. While effective as a record of the artist's creative process, her conception for the Memorial and the controversy it created, this is not a particularly insightful or memorable film.▼

Maybe I'll Come Home in the Spring (1970) **C-74m. TVM** D: Joseph Sargent. Sally Field, Jackie Cooper, Eleanor Parker, Lane Bradbury, David Carradine, Harry Lauter. Year in the life of Miller family: Denise (Field) can't take home life, splits for commune existence, returns after disillusionment and drug experiences take toll. Experiences after she returns make film worthwhile, refusing to pull punches. Game attempt by Bruce Feldman at scripting without cliché. Linda Ronstadt performs the songs. Aka DEADLY DESIRE. Above average.▼

Maybe . . . Maybe Not (1995-German) **C-93m.** ★★ D: Sönke Wortmann. Til Schweiger, Katja Riemann, Joachim Król, Rufus Beck, Antonia Lang, Armin Rohde. Thrown out for cheating on his girlfriend, a heterosexual male finds respite at the home of a gay acquaintance. While the ensuing advances of gay suitors are somewhat humorous, the film is filled with characters about whom we care very little. The most successful German film to date, it is based on a series of German comic books, entitled "Der Bewegte Mann" and "Pretty Baby," by comic artist Ralf König. [R]▼●

Mayerling (1936-French) **92m.** ★★★ D: Anatole Litvak. Charles Boyer, Danielle Darrieux, Suzy Prim, Jean Dax, Vladimir Sokoloff. Touching, well-made romantic tragedy based on true story of Austrian Crown Prince Rudolph, who dared to fall in love with a commoner. Good performances spark international hit; miles ahead of 1969 remake.▼

Mayerling (1969-British) **C-140m.** ★★½ D: Terence Young. Omar Sharif, Catherine Deneuve, James Mason, Ava Gardner, James Robertson Justice, Genevieve Page. Remake of 1936 version casts Sharif as Austrian prince who defies convention, and his father (Mason), by falling in love with commoner Deneuve. Old-fashioned tragic romance is pleasant but uncompelling. Justice steals film as spirited Prince of Wales. Panavision. [M/PG] ▼

Mayflower Madam (1987) **C-100m. TVM** D: Lou Antonio. Candice Bergen, Chris Sarandon, Caitlin Clarke, Jim Antonio, Chita Rivera, Sydney Biddle Barrows. Drama (un)inspired by the life of Sydney Biddle Barrows, onetime debutante and Mayflower descendant who became the proprietor of a high-class N.Y.C. escort service supplying expensive "fantasy girls." Bergen tries hard to look interested as Barrows, and Barrows herself turns up as a pal. Interesting only for a rare TV appearance by Chita Rivera as Barrows' lawyer. Below average.▼

May Fools (1990-French-Italian) **C-108m.** **½ D: Louis Malle. Michel Piccoli, Miou-Miou, Michel Duchaussoy, Dominique Blanc, Bruno Carette, Harriet Walter, Francois Berleand, Martine Gautier, Paulette Dubost. Ensemble piece, set in the French countryside in 1968. A grandmother's death brings assorted relatives to their ancestral home; most of them, like Miou-Miou, are more money-grubbing than grieving. Piccoli is splendid as the head of the clan, a contented vintner who truly mourns his late mother. There are romantic entanglements, an interesting subtext of Paris student rebellion, jazzy Stephane Grappelli score—but it's all rather slight. Not top-notch Malle, but still diverting. [R]▼●

Mayor of Hell, The (1933) **90m.** *** D: Archie Mayo. James Cagney, Madge Evans, Allen Jenkins, Dudley Digges, Arthur Byron, Frankie Darro, Allen "Farina" Hoskins. Fascinating, somewhat strange melodrama with political-machine appointee Cagney taking a genuine interest in the way kids are being mistreated at reform school run by slimy Digges. Climax is both unexpected and bizarre. Remade as CRIME SCHOOL and HELL'S KITCHEN.

Maytime (1937) **132m.** *** D: Robert Z. Leonard. Jeanette MacDonald, Nelson Eddy, John Barrymore, Herman Bing, Tom Brown, Lynne Carver, Rafaela Ottiano, Paul Porcasi, Sig Ruman, Walter Kingsford, Harry Davenport. One of singing duo's best films, despite occasional heavy-handedness and piercing operatic sequence near the end (composed especially for film, based on Tchaikovsky's Fifth Symphony). Exquisite filming of simple story: opera star and penniless singer fall in love in Paris, but her husband/mentor (Barrymore) interferes. Only song retained from Sigmund Romberg's hit Broadway score is "Will You Remember (Sweetheart)."▼●

Maytime in Mayfair (1949-British) **C-96m.** **½ D: Herbert Wilcox. Anna Neagle, Michael Wilding, Peter Graves, Tom Walls, Nicholas Phipps, Thora Hird. Pleasant, light-as-a-soufflé romantic trifle in which Wilding inherits a London dress shop which he intends to sell . . . until he meets the manager (Neagle).▼

Maze, The (1953) **81m.** ** D: William Cameron Menzies. Richard Carlson, Veronica Hurst, Hillary Brooke, Michael Pate, Katherine Emery. Mysterious doings at a Scottish castle; a low-budgeter with a ludicrous (and unsatisfying) payoff. Stylishly composed as a 3-D movie by designer-director Menzies.

Mazes and Monsters (1982-Canadian) **C-100m. TVM** D: Steven H. Stern. Tom Hanks, Wendy Crewson, David Wallace, Chris Makepeace, Lloyd Bochner, Peter Donat, Anne Francis, Murray Hamilton, Vera Miles, Louise Sorel, Susan Strasberg. Four college students become involved in the medieval fantasy world of game-playing. Tom Lazarus's intriguing "Dungeons and Dragons" script from Rona Jaffe's book makes this an engrossing suspenser. Above average.▼

M. Butterfly (1993) **C-101m.** ** D: David Cronenberg. Jeremy Irons, John Lone, Barbara Sukowa, Ian Richardson, Annabel Leventon, Shizuko Hoshi, The Beijing Opera Troupe. Surprisingly tame and conventional Cronenberg rendering of David Henry Hwang's Tony–winning Broadway play—about the bizarrely extended relationship between a French diplomatic functionary and a Chinese diva/spy who managed to conceal the fact from him that she was a man. Cinematic closeups blatantly telegraph Lone's maleness; it's symptomatic of the movie's failure that office politics and even Irons' weary marriage are more compelling than the central ruse. [R]▼●

McBain (1991) **C-102m.** ** D: James Glickenhaus. Christopher Walken, Maria Conchita Alonso, Michael Ironside, Steve James, Jay Patterson, T.G. Waites, Victor Argo, Chick Vennera. To pay back a debt, ex-Vietnam P.O.W. Walken joins rebels in a battle against a corrupt Colombian dictatorship. Predictable, by-the-numbers actioner. [R]▼●

McCabe & Mrs. Miller (1971) **C-121m.** ***½ D: Robert Altman. Warren Beatty, Julie Christie, Rene Auberjonois, John Schuck, Bert Remsen, Keith Carradine, William Devane, Shelley Duvall, Michael Murphy, Hugh Millais, Jack Riley. Richly textured mood piece about an ambitious small-timer who opens bordello in turn-of-the-century boom town. Altman deglamorizes Hollywood image of period with his realistic visions. Beatty is first-rate as the two-bit braggart McCabe. Edmund Naughton's novel *McCabe* adapted by Brian McKay and Altman. Panavision. [R]▼●

McConnell Story, The (1955) **C-107m.** *** D: Gordon Douglas. Alan Ladd, June Allyson, James Whitmore, Frank Faylen. Weepy yet effective fictional biography of jet test pilot, with Allyson as his understanding wife. CinemaScope.▼●

McCullochs, The SEE: **Wild McCullochs, The**

McGuffin, The (1985-British) **C-95m.** ** D: Colin Bucksey. Charles Dance, Ritza Brown, Francis Matthews, Brian Glover, Phyllis Logan, Jerry Stiller, Anna Massey, Ann Todd, Bill Shine. Meandering, confusing thriller about film critic Dance, whose curiosity about a couple of his neighbors leads to his involvement in murder and mayhem. Starts off nicely but goes downhill all too quickly. An homage to Hitchcock in general, REAR WINDOW in particular.▼

McGuire, Go Home! (1965-British) **C-101m.** **½ D: Ralph Thomas. Dirk Bogarde, George Chakiris, Susan Strasberg, Denholm Elliott. Set in 1954 Cyprus; peppy account of terrorist campaign against British occupation, with side-plot of officer Bogarde in love with American girl Strasberg. Video titles: A DATE WITH DEATH; THE HIGH BRIGHT SUN.▼

McHale's Navy (1964) **C-93m.** **½ D: Edward J. Montagne. Ernest Borgnine, Joe Flynn, Tim Conway, George Kennedy, Claudine Longet, Bob Hastings, Carl Ballantine, Billy Sands, Gavin MacLeod, Jean Willes. Theatrical feature inspired by popular TV series finds the PT-73 crew doing everything possible to try and raise money to pay off gambling debts. Usual blend of slapstick and snappy dialogue; entertaining for fans.▼

McHale's Navy (1997) **C-109m.** ** D: Bryan Spicer. Tom Arnold, Dean Stockwell, Ernest Borgnine, Debra Messing, David Alan Grier, Tim Curry, Brian Haley, French Stewart, Bruce Campbell, Tommy Chong. Former Navy man who now wheels and deals from a remote Pacific island is called back to service to do battle with "the second-best terrorist in the world." Broad approach, simplistic script make this strictly a juvenile outing. Very loosely based on the 1960s TV series; Borgnine, who played McHale back then, appears here as a Pentagon security chief. [PG] ▼●

McHale's Navy Joins the Air Force (1965) **C-90m.** **½ D: Edward J. Montagne. Tim Conway, Joe Flynn, Bob Hastings, Ted Bessell, Susan Silo, Henry Beckman, Billy Sands, Gavin MacLeod, Tom Tully, Jacques Aubuchon. Rather unusual comedy with little relation to either the first feature or the TV series (including no Borgnine). Ensign Parker (Conway) is mistaken for an Air Force hot-shot, and the more he screws up, the higher he's promoted! John Fenton Murray's intricate script adds some mild satire to normal quota of slapstick; a genuine curio.▼

McKenzie Break, The (1970) **C-106m.** *** D: Lamont Johnson. Brian Keith, Helmut Griem, Ian Hendry, Jack Watson, Patrick O'Connell. Daring escape from a P.O.W. camp for Germans in Scotland makes for engrossing movie fare. Aka ESCAPE. [PG]▼◗

McLintock! (1963) **C-122m.** *** D: Andrew V. McLaglen. John Wayne, Maureen O'Hara, Patrick Wayne, Stefanie Powers, Yvonne De Carlo, Chill Wills, Bruce Cabot, Jack Kruschen, Jerry Van Dyke, Perry Lopez, Strother Martin. Brawling cattle baron G. W. McLintock (Wayne) locks horns with his feisty, estranged wife (O'Hara) who has returned home to get a divorce; their daughter visiting from college only complicates matters. Rowdy slapstick seldom stops—a giant mud pit free-for-all and a public spanking for O'Hara are just a few of the stops along the way in this Western version of *The Taming of the Shrew.* Not recommended for feminists. Produced by Michael Wayne. Panavision.▼●◗

McMasters, The (1970) **C-89/97m.** **½ D: Alf Kjellin. Burl Ives, Brock Peters, David Carradine, Nancy Kwan, Jack Palance, John Carradine. Pretty grim drama of bigotry and violence gone crazy as black Union soldier (Peters) returns to ranch of former master (Ives), eventually made co-owner of land. Dual running times indicate two different endings: bad guys (led by Palance) win out or good guys emerge victorious. Both versions were released to theaters. [PG]▼

McQ (1974) **C-116m.** ** D: John Sturges. John Wayne, Eddie Albert, Diana Muldaur, Colleen Dewhurst, Clu Gulager, David Huddleston, Al Lettieri, Julie Adams. An aging Duke tries to be Clint Eastwood as a Firebird-driving cop out to get the gangster who murdered his partner. Good action, but that's about all. Panavision. [PG]▼●

McVicar (1980-British) **C-111m.** *** D: Tom Clegg. Roger Daltrey, Adam Faith, Cheryl Campbell, Brian Hall, Steven Berkoff, Jeremy Blake, Ian Hendry. Impressive drama about John McVicar (Daltrey), England's Public Enemy Number 1, and his escape from prison. Screenplay by McVicar, who adapted his book; Daltrey is surprisingly good; Faith and Campbell fine as his prison buddy/fellow escapee and his common-law wife. [R]▼●

Meal, The (1975) **C-90m.** ** D: R. John Hugh. Dina Merrill, Carl Betz, Leon Ames, Susan Logan, Vicki Powers, Steve Potter. Symbolic but brutal film about a wealthy woman who invites a group of the rich and powerful to a banquet, lets them devour the feast as they expose and devour each other's lives. Aka DEADLY ENCOUNTER. [R] ▼

Me and Him (1989-U.S.-West German) **C-94m.** BOMB D: Doris Dörrie. Griffin Dunne, Ellen Greene, Kelly Bishop, Carey Lowell, Craig T. Nelson, Mark Linn-Baker. Embarrassingly unfunny story of a man and his talking sex organ. Based on an Italian novel, clever idea goes absolutely limp. Linn-Baker supplies the voice of Dunne's "special friend." [R]▼●

Me and My Gal (1932) **78m.** *** D: Raoul Walsh. Spencer Tracy, Joan Bennett, Marion Burns, George Walsh, J. Farrell MacDonald, Noel Madison. Wholly entertaining film blending comedy, romance, melodrama in one neat package; cop Tracy falls in love with waitress Bennett, whose sister and father become involved with a gangster. Stars at their most charming, with bottomless reserve of snappy dialogue.

Mean Dog Blues (1978) **C-108m.** **½ D: Mel Stuart. George Kennedy, Gregg Henry, Kay Lenz, Scatman Crothers, Tina Louise, Felton Perry, Gregory Sierra, James Wainwright, William Windom. Henry is railroaded onto prison farm run by Kennedy and a team of bloodthirsty Dobermans; unsurprising but well-made action film. [R]▼

Me and the Colonel (1958) **109m.** **½ D: Peter Glenville. Danny Kaye, Curt Jurgens, Nicole Maurey, Françoise Rosay. Franz Werfel's *Jacobowsky and the Colonel* is source for spotty satire; Jacobowsky is played by Kaye, and Jurgens is the anti-Semitic military officer, both brought together during crisis in WW2. Filmed in France.▼

Me and the Kid (1993) **C-94m.** *½ D: Dan Curtis. Danny Aiello, Alex Zuckerman, Joe Pantoliano, Cathy Moriarty, David Dukes, Anita Morris, Abe Vigoda, Demond Wilson, Rick Aiello, Ben Stein. Rich kid is kidnapped in a bungled robbery attempt and sets out on the road with a couple of cons—who get more than they bargained for. Low-budget attempt to cash in on the HOME ALONE bonanza, with a decent cast wasted; recommended only for the most undemanding young viewers. [PG]▼●

Meanest Man in the World, The (1943) **57m.** *** D: Sidney Lanfield. Jack Benny, Priscilla Lane, Eddie "Rochester" Anderson, Edmund Gwenn, Matt Briggs, Anne Revere. Snappy yarn of good-natured lawyer Benny discovering that he can only succeed in business by being nasty. Benny-Rochester repartee is hilarious; film is a must for Benny devotees. That's cult figure Tor Johnson as a wrestler.

Mean Frank and Crazy Tony (1975-Italian) **C-85m.** ** D: Michele Lupo. Lee Van Cleef, Tony Lo Bianco, Jean Rochefort, Jess Hahn. Cute Italian gangster film closely resembles the buddy-format of a Western, with Lo Bianco the young groupie who attaches himself to his hero Van Cleef. U.S. version of this 1973 Dino De Laurentiis production was prepared by film doctor Simon Nuchtern. [R]▼

Mean Johnny Barrows (1976) **C-85m.** ** D: Fred Williamson. Fred Williamson, Jenny Sherman, Aaron Banks, Anthony Caruso, Luther Adler, Stuart Whitman, Roddy McDowall, Elliott Gould. Mean but dull; Vietnam vet gets involved with the Mafia. Slow-paced, notable for unlikely cast and Gould's incongruous comedy relief. [R]▼

Mean Season, The (1985) **C-103m.** **½ D: Phillip Borsos. Kurt Russell, Mariel Hemingway, Richard Jordan, Richard Masur, Joe Pantoliano, Andy Garcia. Miami newspaper reporter (Russell, in a very credible performance) becomes sole contact for crazed killer, but as the headlines (and murders) continue, it becomes a question of who is "using" whom. Intriguing and initially believable idea goes awry in latter half of this mean movie. [R]▼●

Mean Streets (1973) **C-110m.** **** D: Martin Scorsese. Robert De Niro, Harvey Keitel, David Proval, Amy Robinson, Richard Romanus, Cesare Danova, George Memmoli, Robert Carradine, David Carradine. Masterpiece about small-time hood Keitel, irresponsible friend De Niro and their knockabout cronies in N.Y.C.'s Little Italy. Technically dazzling film put director Scorsese on the map and deservedly so. [R]▼●◗

Meantime (1983-British) **C-104m.** **½ D: Mike Leigh. Marion Bailey, Phil Daniels, Tim Roth, Pam Ferris, Jeff Robert, Alfred Molina, Gary Oldman. Downbeat kitchen-sink drama about the problems of a working-class London family; no one captures this milieu quite like director Leigh, though it can be pretty bleak. Molina and Oldman later costarred in PRICK UP YOUR EARS.▼◗

Meatballs (1979-Canadian) **C-92m.** *½ D: Ivan Reitman. Bill Murray, Harvey Atkin, Kate Lynch, Russ Banham, Kristine DeBell, Sarah Torgov. Alternately cruel and sloppily sentimental comedy about summer camp will no doubt wow fifth graders of all ages, though myopic screen characters named "Spaz" aren't really all that funny. Pretty desperate. Followed by several so-called sequels. [PG] ▼●◗

Meatballs Part II (1984) **C-87m.** ** D: Ken Wiederhorn. Richard Mulligan, John Mengatti, Hamilton Camp, Kim Richards, Tammy Taylor, John Larroquette, Archie Hahn, Misty Rowe, Paul Reubens (Pee-wee Herman), Vic Dunlop, Felix Silla, Elayne Boosler. In-name-only sequel throws in everything from Jewish aliens to FROM HERE TO ETERNITY take-off, as the fate of Camp Sasquatch rides on a boxing match against nearby Camp Patton ("Where Outdoor Living Molds Killers"). Slightly better than its predecessor (which isn't saying much). [PG]▼●

Meatballs III (1987) **C-94m.** *½ D: George Mendeluk. Sally Kellerman, Patrick Dempsey, Al Waxman, Isabelle Mejias, Shannon Tweed, Ian Taylor, George Buza. What do you say about a movie dealing with a dead porno star who coaches a teen-age nerd on how to lose his virginity at summer camp? As little as possible. [R]▼●

Mechanic, The (1972) **C-100m.** **½ D: Michael Winner. Charles Bronson, Keenan Wynn, Jan-Michael Vincent, Jill Ireland. Detailed study of James Bond-type assassin and youth he trains to take his place. Worth it for the double-twist ending; terse script by Lewis John Carlino. [PG]▼●

Medal for Benny, A (1945) **77m.** ***½ D: Irving Pichel. Dorothy Lamour, Arturo de Cordova, J. Carrol Naish, Mikhail Rasumny, Fernando Alvarado, Charles Dingle, Frank McHugh. Small town hypocritically honors one of its war dead. Excellent comedy-drama scripted by Frank Butler from a story by John Steinbeck and Jack Wagner.

Medicine Ball Caravan (1971) **C-90m.** **½ D: Francois Reichenbach. B. B. King, Alice Cooper, Delaney and Bonnie, Doug Kershaw, David Peel. The Caravan is a 150-member troupe that traveled the U.S. during the summer of '70 to spread peace, love, music—and make a movie. Superficially arty direction; Martin Scorsese was associate producer and supervising editor. Techniscope. [R]

Medicine Hat Stallion, The SEE: **Peter Lundy and the Medicine Hat Stallion**

Medicine Man, The (1930) **66m.** *½ D: Scott Pembroke. Jack Benny, Betty Bronson, Eva Novak, E. Alyn Warren, Billy Butts, Adolph Milar, George E. Stone, Tommy Dugan. Smooth-talking carny medicine man comes to the aid of Bronson and her brother, who live with maybe the most abusive father in screen history! Dull melodrama would be worthless if not for curiosity value of Benny in the lead. ▼

Medicine Man (1992) **C-106m.** **½ D: John McTiernan. Sean Connery, Lorraine Bracco, Jose Wilker. Connery plays a research scientist, sequestered in the Brazilian rain forest, who's found the cure for cancer—but can't duplicate it. Bracco is his brainy superior from the U.S. who's come to check up on him. Connery carries this movie singlehandedly, and as usual he's commanding to watch, but the film is weak, and Bracco's abrasive performance (and poorly written character) practically sink it. Panavision. [PG-13]▼●◗

Mediterraneo (1991-Italian) **C-92m.** *** D: Gabriele Salvatores. Diego Abatantuono, Claudio Bigagli, Giuseppe Cederna, Claudio Bisio, Gigio Alberti, Ugo Conti, Vanna Barba. It's 1941 and Greek-island males are off fighting in WW2, so some stranded Italian soldiers partake in la dolce vita—for years. Sweet memory movie with double-digit guffaws, though a slight choice to have won the Best Foreign Film Oscar. ▼●

Medium, The (1951) **84m.** **½ D: Gian-Carlo Menotti. Marie Powers, Anna Maria Alberghetti, Leo Coleman, Belva Kibler. Murky filmization of Gian-Carlo Menotti opera about eccentric spiritualist, the girl living in her seedy apartment, the outcast mute boy in love with girl.▼

Medium Cool (1969) **C-110m.** **** D: Haskell Wexler. Robert Forster, Verna Bloom, Peter Bonerz, Marianna Hill, Harold Blankenship, Peter Boyle. Arresting, unique film of TV cameraman who remains detached though surrounded by events demanding his involvement. Director/writer/cameraman Wexler used real footage of his actors at 1968 Democratic convention in Chicago, and subsequent riots, as basis for ultrarealistic film. Score by Mike Bloomfield; Paul Butterfield and The Mothers of Invention are among the artists on the soundtrack. [R]▼●

Medusa Touch, The (1978-British-French) **C-110m.** ** D: Jack Gold. Richard Burton, Lino Ventura, Lee Remick, Harry Andrews, Alan Badel, Marie-Christine Barrault, Jeremy Brett, Michael Hordern, Gordon Jackson, Derek Jacobi. Burton has spent his whole life willing people's deaths, and now he's completely out of control; Remick is his psychiatrist in this derivative, unappealing film. [PG]▼

Meet Boston Blackie (1941) **61m.** *** D: Robert Florey. Chester Morris, Rochelle Hudson, Richard Lane, Charles Wagenheim, Constance Worth. First in the *Boston Blackie* series is a slick and fast-paced mystery-comedy, introducing Morris as the whimsical ex-thief tracking down spies hiding out at Coney Island. Franz Planer's stylish cinematography enhances this solid programmer.

Meet Danny Wilson (1952) **86m.** **½ D: Joseph Pevney. Frank Sinatra, Shelley Winters, Alex Nicol, Raymond Burr. Minor but engaging musical about a young singer and his piano-playing pal, who make the mistake of signing a contract with nightclub owner/racketeer Burr—then moving in on his "girl." No original songs, but Sinatra does sing plenty of old favorites and even does a winning duet with Winters on "A Good Man Is Hard to Find."▼

Meet Dr. Christian (1939) **63m.** ** D: Bernard Vorhaus. Jean Hersholt, Dorothy Lovett, Robert Baldwin, Enid Bennett, Paul Harvey, Marcia Mae Jones, Jackie Moran. Typically folksy entry in film series of small-town doctor who solves everyone's difficulties.▼

Meeting at Midnight SEE: **Black Magic** (1944)

Meetings With Remarkable Men (1979-British) **C-110m.** **½ D: Peter Brook. Terence Stamp, Dragan Maksimovic, Mikica Dimitrijevic, Athol Fugard, Warren Mitchell, Gerry Sundquist, Bruce Myers, Natasha Parry, Martin Benson. Uneven account of

G. I. Gurdjieff (Maksimovic), the famed, inspirational cult leader, focusing on his quest through Asia to uncover the meaning of human existence. Has its moments of insight, but will ultimately be of interest only to those fascinated by the subject. Based on Gurdjieff's memoirs. [G]▼

Meeting Venus (1991-British) **C-117m.** *** D: Istvan Szabo. Glenn Close, Niels Arestrup, Erland Josephson, Johanna Ter Steege, Jay O. Sanders, Maria de Medeiros, Ildiko Bansagi, Dorottya Udvaros, Victor Poletti, Macha Meril. During the tumultuous preparations for a multinational production of Wagner's *Tannhauser*, a Hungarian conductor (Arestrup) and a Swedish diva (Close, who's outstanding) find themselves involved in an affair. Witty, knowing romantic farce about the politics of art, which also works as a metaphor for the aftereffects of European reunification. Veteran Hungarian director Szabo's first film in English. Close's singing voice is dubbed by Kiri Te Kanewa. [PG-13]▼●

Meet Joe Black (1998) **C-178m.** ** D: Martin Brest. Anthony Hopkins, Brad Pitt, Claire Forlani, Jake Weber, Marcia Gay Harden, Jeffrey Tambor, David S. Howard. Death comes to claim a billionaire industrialist (Hopkins), and decides to take human form (Pitt), emerging as a mysterious stranger with a childlike manner and a fondness for peanut butter. Odd rethinking of DEATH TAKES A HOLIDAY adds subplots that make it go on for days, toward a preposterous and unsatisfying conclusion. Hopkins is terrific, but Death's character simply makes no sense. Sumptuous production design. [PG-13] ▼●◗

Meet John Doe (1941) **132m.** *** D: Frank Capra. Gary Cooper, Barbara Stanwyck, Edward Arnold, Walter Brennan, Spring Byington, James Gleason, Gene Lockhart. Overlong but interesting social commentary, with naive Cooper hired to spearhead national goodwill drive benefitting corrupt politician Arnold. Wordy idealism can't bury good characterizations; usual Capra touches exulting populism. Virtually all existing prints (from reissue) run 123m. Also shown in computer-colored version.▼●◗

Meet Me After the Show (1951) **C-86m.** **½ D: Richard Sale. Betty Grable, Macdonald Carey, Rory Calhoun, Eddie Albert, Lois Andrews, Irene Ryan. Undistinguished Grable musical lacking bounce of her other vehicles, with usual show biz storyline.

Meet Me at the Fair (1953) **C-87m.** **½ D: Douglas Sirk. Dan Dailey, Diana Lynn, Hugh O'Brian, Carole Mathews, Rhys Williams, Chet Allen, Scatman Crothers. Dailey is good as a sideshow medicine man who helps a young orphan and courts Lynn; pleasant musical.

Meet Me in Las Vegas (1956) **C-112m.** **½ D: Roy Rowland. Dan Dailey, Cyd Charisse, Agnes Moorehead, Lili Darvas, Jim Backus; guest stars Jerry Colonna, Paul Henreid, Lena Horne, Frankie Laine, Mitsuko Sawamura. Charisse's dancing is highlight of mild musical involving rancher Dailey and ballet star Cyd in gambling capital. Cameos by many top stars add to the flavor. George Chakiris and Liliane Montevecchi are among the dancers. CinemaScope.▼●

Meet Me in St. Louis (1944) **C-113m.** **** D: Vincente Minnelli. Judy Garland, Margaret O'Brien, Lucille Bremer, Tom Drake, Mary Astor, Leon Ames, Marjorie Main, June Lockhart, Harry Davenport, Joan Carroll, Hugh Marlowe. Captivating musical based on Sally Benson's slice of Americana about a family's experiences during the year of the St. Louis World's Fair, 1903. Judy sings wonderful Ralph Blane–Hugh Martin songs "The Boy Next Door," "Have Yourself a Merry Little Christmas," "The Trolley Song," while Margaret O'Brien steals every scene she's in as little sister Tootie. (In fact, she won a special Oscar, as the year's best child actress.) Screenplay by Irving Brecher and Fred F. Finkelhoffe. Years later adapted for Broadway.▼●

Meet Me Tonight SEE: **Tonight at 8:30**

Meet Mr. Lucifer (1953-British) **83m.** ** D: Anthony Pelissier. Stanley Holloway, Peggy Cummins, Jack Watling, Barbara Murray, Joseph Tomelty, Gordon Jackson, Jean Cadell, Kay Kendall, Ian Carmichael. Meek little satire on the evils of television, with Holloway in dual role as Devil and his earthly helper.

Meet Nero Wolfe (1936) **73m.** **½ D: Herbert Biberman. Edward Arnold, Lionel Stander, Joan Perry, Victor Jory, Nana Bryant, Dennie Moore. Rex Stout's corpulent detective makes his screen debut, with Arnold faithfully playing him as demanding and difficult—in short, none too endearing (though he laughs a bit too much); Stander is his legman, Archie. The mystery itself (with two seemingly unrelated murders) is not bad. Bonus: a young and beautiful Rita Cansino (later Hayworth) in a minor role. Followed by THE LEAGUE OF FRIGHTENED MEN.

Meet the Applegates (1991) **C-90m.** **½ D: Michael Lehman. Ed Begley, Jr., Stockard Channing, Dabney Coleman, Bobby Jacoby, Cami Cooper, Glenn Shadix, Susan Barnes. Brazilian beetles in human form assimilate (sort of) in U.S. suburbia, but still manage to stock their quota of human prey in the basement. Spotty, but sometimes funny comedy, wittily designed but marred by a weak conclusion. Released on video, for no apparent reason, as THE APPLEGATES. [R] ▼●

Meet the Baron (1933) **68m.** **½ D:

Walter Lang. Jack Pearl, Jimmy Durante, ZaSu Pitts, Ted Healy and His Stooges, Edna May Oliver. Comic hodgepodge was an attempt to fashion a movie vehicle for radio comedian Pearl, in character as the tale-spinning, malaprop-laden Baron Munchausen. Supporting comics steal the show, especially Healy and his (Three) Stooges. There's also—out of left field—a Busby Berkeleyish musical number with nearly nude coeds singing "Clean as a Whistle" while taking a shower!
Meet the Chump (1941) **60m.** ** D: Edward Cline. Hugh Herbert, Lewis Howard, Jeanne Kelly (Brooks), Anne Nagel, Kathryn Adams, Shemp Howard, Richard Lane. Wacky Hugh plays inept trustee of estate due young Howard, desperate to find a way to cover the fact that he's dissipated $10 million. Mildly amusing, but generally routine.
Meet the Deedles (1998) **C-92m.** *½ D: Steve Boyum. Steve Van Wormer, Paul Walker, A. J. Langer, John Ashton, Dennis Hopper, Megan Cavanaugh, Eric Braeden, Richard Lineback, M. C. Gainey, Robert Englund. Idiotic BILL & TED clone about twin surfer dude brothers from Hawaii whose filthy rich father schemes to teach them responsibility by dispatching them to a summer camp. Bottom-of-the-barrel Disney wipeout; less discriminating teens might go for it for about three minutes. Hopper plays a villainous ex-park ranger, and Bart the Bear has a cameo. [PG]▼●
Meet the People (1944) **100m.** **½ D: Charles Riesner. Lucille Ball, Dick Powell, Virginia O'Brien, Bert Lahr, Rags Ragland, June Allyson, Bobby (Robert) Blake, Mata and Hari. OK musicomedy of ex-stage star Ball trying to revive career; so-so score, many guests (Spike Jones, Vaughn Monroe, etc.).
Meet the Stewarts (1942) **73m.** **½ D: Alfred E. Green. William Holden, Frances Dee, Grant Mitchell, Anne Revere, Mary Gordon, Marjorie Gateson, Margaret Hamilton, Don Beddoe. Wealthy girl marries hard-working Holden, can't adjust to new financial arrangement; not earthshaking, but enjoyable.
Meet Wally Sparks (1997) **C-104m.** *½ D: Peter Baldwin. Rodney Dangerfield, Debi Mazar, Cindy Williams, Burt Reynolds, David Ogden Stiers, Alan Rachins. Embarrassingly unfunny vehicle for Dangerfield, as a trashy TV talk show host attempting to save his program. Instead of successfully satirizing elements of the morally bankrupt TV talk genre, the screenplay (cowritten by Dangerfield) sinks to its level. Look for mercifully short cameos from Tony Danza, Tim Allen, Roseanne, Jay Leno, and Gilbert Gottfried. [R] ▼●◗
Megaforce (1982) **C-99m.** BOMB D: Hal Needham. Barry Bostwick, Persis Khambatta, Michael Beck, Edward Mulhare, George Furth, Henry Silva. Atrocious bubble-gum movie about an ultra-modern fighting force headed by one Ace Hunter (Bostwick, badly miscast). Embarrassing performances, clunky hardware, uninspired action scenes. [PG]▼
Mein Kampf (1961-Swedish) **117m.** *** D: Erwin Leiser. Narrated by Claude Stephenson. Technically smooth, impressive documentary chronicle of the horrors of Nazi Germany. Restrained narration allows the visuals to speak for themselves. ▼●
Melba (1953-British) **C-113m.** **½ D: Lewis Milestone. Patrice Munsel, Robert Morley, Sybil Thorndike, Martita Hunt, John McCallum. Occasionally interesting biography of Australian opera star Nellie Melba.
Melinda (1972) **C-109m.** *½ D: Hugh A. Robertson. Calvin Lockhart, Rosalind Cash, Vonetta McGee, Paul Stevens, Rockne Tarkington. Black disc jockey goes after his girlfriend's killers in violent melodrama; typical of the films that helped kill the blaxploitation genre. [R]
Mélo (1986-French) **C-110m.** *** D: Alain Resnais. Sabine Azéma, Pierre Arditi, Andre Dussollier, Fanny Ardant, Jacques Dacqmine, Catherine Arditi. Different sort of film experiment from innovator Resnais, rigorously adapting Henry Bernstein's 1929 play about a tragic love triangle. Top-notch acting and direction make this one a winner, but the (intentionally) stagy production makes it not for all tastes.
Melody (1971-British) **C-103m.** *** D: Waris Hussein. Jack Wild, Mark Lester, Tracy Hyde, Sheila Steafel, Kate Williams, Roy Kinnear. Adolescent view of life, disarmingly played by Lester and Wild (from OLIVER!) as friends who rebel against adult establishment, particularly when Lester and girlfriend Hyde decide they want to get married. Music by The Bee Gees. [G]▼
Melody Cruise (1933) **76m.** **½ D: Mark Sandrich. Charlie Ruggles, Phil Harris, Helen Mack, Greta Nissen, Chick Chandler, June Brewster. Sexy (pre-Production Code) musical comedy with Harris romancing Mack and Ruggles providing the laughs. Notable for its imaginative use of photography and optical effects, which virtually steal the show. Director Sandrich went on to do the Astaire-Rogers musicals. Look for Betty Grable in a bit.▼
Melody for Three (1941) **67m.** ** D: Erle C. Kenton. Jean Hersholt, Fay Wray, Walter Woolf King, Astrid Allwyn, Schuyler Standish, Irene Ryan. Wray's presence uplifts this adequate entry in Hersholt's *Dr. Christian* series; she's the music-teacher mother of violin prodigy Standish, and is divorced from orchestra conductor King. You can be sure that, by the final reel, the kindly doctor will reunite them.▼
Melvin and Howard (1980) **C-95m.** ***½ D: Jonathan Demme. Paul LeMat, Jason Robards, Mary Steenburgen, Jack Kehoe, Pamela Reed, Dabney Coleman, Michael

J. Pollard, Gloria Grahame, Elizabeth Cheshire, Martine Beswicke, Charles Napier, John Glover. Wonderful slice-of-life comedy based on the story of Melvin Dummar, who once gave a lift to a grizzled Howard Hughes and later produced a will naming himself as heir to the Hughes fortune. An endearing, bittersweet American fable, with Oscar-winner Steenburgen providing most of the comic highlights, including a memorable TV talent contest. Bo Goldman's script also won an Academy Award. (That's the real Melvin Dummar behind a bus station lunch counter.) [R]▼◗

Member of the Wedding, The (1952) **91m.** *** D: Fred Zinnemann. Ethel Waters, Julie Harris, Brandon de Wilde, Arthur Franz, Nancy Gates, James Edwards. Carson McCullers' sensitive account of child Harris prodded into growing up by her brother's forthcoming marriage. Waters, Harris and de Wilde movingly re-create their Broadway roles, the latter two making their film debuts. Slow but worthwhile. Remade for cable TV in 1997.▼

Member of the Wedding, The (1997) **C-100m. TVM** D: Fielder Cook. Alfre Woodard, Anna Paquin, Corey Dunn, Enrico Colantoni, Pat Hingle. Heartfelt version of Carson McCullers' novel and play about a young white girl's struggle with adolescence and her relationship with the family cook in mid-1940s Georgia. Woodard is splendid and Oscar-winning New Zealander Paquin makes her American TV debut as Frankie. Filmed before in 1952; a 1982 "live" TV version starred Pearl Bailey. Made for cable. Above average.▼●

Memed My Hawk (1987-British) **C-101m.** ** D: Peter Ustinov. Peter Ustinov, Herbert Lom, Denis Quilley, Michael Elphick, Simon Dutton, Leonie Mellinger, Barry Dennen, Siobhan McKenna, T.P. McKenna, Michael Gough. Disappointing drama with Ustinov cast as Abdi Aga, slimy, self-centered dictator of a Turkish village. Boring, despite the cast. Scripted by Ustinov, from the Yashar Kemal novel. [PG-13]

Memoirs of an Invisible Man (1992) **C-99m.** ** D: John Carpenter. Chevy Chase, Daryl Hannah, Sam Neill, Michael McKean, Stephen Tobolowsky, Rosalind Chao. Clever (but endless) special effects are the star of this stale, paper-thin dud. Chase plays a securities analyst who's rendered invisible after an accident, and finds himself involved in a by-the-numbers spy scenario. Panavision. [PG-13] ▼●

Memoirs of a Survivor (1981-British) **C-117m.** *½ D: David Gladwell. Julie Christie, Christopher Guard, Leonie Mellinger, Debbie Hutchings, Nigel Hawthorne, Pat Keen. Christie's presence cannot save this dismal, badly directed fantasy about a woman and a teenager (Mellinger) surviving in a decayed urban civilization. Good idea—film is based on a Doris Lessing novel—but poorly realized.

Memories of Me (1988) **C-105m.** ** D: Henry Winkler. Billy Crystal, Alan King, JoBeth Williams, Janet Carroll, David Ackroyd, Phil Fondacaro, Robert Pastorelli, Sidney Miller. A heart surgeon, who recently suffered a heart attack himself, seeks out his father, from whom he's been estranged, hoping to put his life in order. Contrived comedy-drama combines comic shtick with mawkish emotional scenes and never quite manages to be convincing. Crystal cowrote the screenplay and coproduced with King. [PG-13]▼●

Memory of Justice, The (1976-German-U.S.) **C-278m.** **** D: Marcel Ophuls. Outstanding documentary from the director of THE SORROW AND THE PITY questions how one country can pass judgment on the atrocities of others by examining the Nuremberg trials and their aftermath, the French performance in Algeria and the American intervention in Vietnam. Always riveting in spite of its mammoth length. [PG]▼

Memory of Us (1974) **C-93m.** **½ D: H. Kaye Dyal. Ellen Geer, Jon Cypher, Barbara Colby, Peter Brown, Robert Hogan, Rose Marie, Will Geer. Modest, interesting contemporary drama about a happily married woman who begins to question her role as wife and mother; script by star Ellen Geer, whose father Will makes brief appearance. [PG]▼

Memphis Belle (1990-British) **C-101m.** ** D: Michael Caton-Jones. Matthew Modine, Eric Stoltz, Tate Donovan, D.B. Sweeney, Billy Zane, Sean Astin, Harry Connick, Jr., Reed Edward Diamond, Courtney Gains, Neil Giuntoli, David Strathairn, John Lithgow, Jane Horrocks. If you can make it through the first hour (a virtual catalogue of war-movie clichés) this film ultimately provides an exciting fictional reenactment of the famous B-17's final bombing raid over Germany during WW2. Still, it's hard to believe that such a cornball script could be concocted in 1990. Coproduced by Catherine Wyler, whose father, William Wyler, made the 1944 documentary THE MEMPHIS BELLE. [PG-13]▼●◗

Me Myself and I (1992) **C-97m.** **½ D: Pablo Ferro. JoBeth Williams, George Segal, Don Calfa, Shelley Hack, Betsy Lynn George, Bill Macy, Sharon McNight, Ruth Gilbert. Novelist-TV writer Segal becomes involved with his next-door neighbor, a schizophrenic (well-played by Williams) who is intelligent and nurturing when "sane," but otherwise totally off-the-wall. Bizarre comedy is uneven, sometimes enjoyable and other times annoying.▼

Me Myself I (1999-Australian-French) **C-104m.** **½ D: Pip Karmel. Rachel Griffiths, David Roberts, Sandy Winton, Yael Stone, Shaun Loseby, Trent Sullivan. Fiercely independent career woman realizes that she may have made a mistake putting off marriage and family. She gets to see how the other half lives when she comes face-to-face with the husband and kids she would have experienced had she gone the "soccer mom" route. Comedy-drama takes its time unfolding, but Griffiths is good as always in a "dream" role. Directing debut for Karmel, the editor of SHINE. [R]▼

Men, The (1950) **85m.** ***½ D: Fred Zinnemann. Marlon Brando, Teresa Wright, Everett Sloane, Jack Webb, Richard Erdman, Dorothy Tree, Howard St. John, DeForest Kelley. Brando excels in film debut as ex-GI adjusting to life in wheelchair after wartime injury; low-key acting is most effective. Story and screenplay by Carl Foreman. Retitled: BATTLE STRIPE. ▼●

Men . . . (1985-German) **C-99m.** ***½ D: Doris Dörrie. Heiner Lauterbach, Uwe Ochsenknecht, Ulrike Kriener, Janna Marangosoff. Ingenious comedy-satire about an uptight adman who becomes haplessly jealous when he learns that his wife's having an affair. He promptly befriends her lover and becomes his roommate, with hilarious results. ▼

Men (1998) **C-93m.** ** D: Zoe Clarke-Williams. Sean Young, John Heard, Dylan Walsh, Richard Hillman, Jr., Karen Black, Beau Starr, Shawnee Smith, Glenn Shadix, Annie McEnroe. Trite, pretentious tearjerker about a young woman whose journey of self-discovery and sexual fulfillment takes her from N.Y. to California, where she gets involved with a married middle-aged man and a radical young photographer. Young is good, even if she's too old for the part, but much of her dialogue is unintentionally funny. Karen Black, who cowrote the script, livens things up with a cameo as a blind lesbian with an indecipherable accent. [R]▼●◗

Menace, The (1932) **64m.** ** D: Roy William Neill. H. B. Warner, Bette Davis, Walter Byron, Natalie Moorhead, William B. Davidson, Crauford Kent. Man seeks revenge on his stepmother and her cohorts, who framed him for his father's murder. Based on an Edgar Wallace story; handsome, but stodgy, and pretty obvious. Davis plays a demure British ingenue.

Menace in the Night (1958-British) **78m.** *½ D: Lance Comfort. Griffith Jones, Lisa Gastoni, Vincent Ball, Eddie Byrne. Tired tale of witness to murder being pressured by gang not to testify.

Menace II Society (1993) **C-97m.** *** D: Allen and Albert Hughes. Tyrin Turner, Larenz Tate, Jada Pinkett, Vonte Sweet, MC Eiht, Ryan Williams, Too $hort, Samuel L. Jackson, Charles Dutton, Glenn Plummer, Bill Duke. Powerful, unflinching story of life in the Watts district of Los Angeles and one teenager (Turner) who is too immersed in that violent world to get out. Social points are often hammered home, but the atmosphere of tension and random brutality is captured with searing authenticity. Extremely bloody (and profane) but gripping and well acted in naturalistic fashion. Strong debut by Hughes Brothers, who also cowrote story with screenwriter Tyger Williams. [R]▼●◗

Men Against the Sky (1940) **75m.** *½ D: Leslie Goodwins. Richard Dix, Wendy Barrie, Kent Taylor, Edmund Lowe, Granville Bates, Grant Withers. Veteran cast in RKO programmer about personnel at aircraft-building plant.

Menage (1986-French) **C-84m.** *** D: Bertrand Blier. Gérard Depardieu, Michel Blanc, Miou-Miou, Bruno Cremer, Jean-Pierre Marielle. Outrageous, fast-paced farce about a roguish, gay crook (Depardieu), who thoroughly disrupts the lives of an impoverished couple (Blanc and Miou-Miou)—sexually and otherwise. Peters out at the end but still worth a look. Panavision.▼

Men Are Not Gods (1936-British) **90m.** **½ D: Walter Reisch. Miriam Hopkins, Gertrude Lawrence, Sebastian Shaw, Rex Harrison, A.E. Matthews. Talky predecessor to A DOUBLE LIFE, with Harrison et al. almost making their play-acting *Othello* come true.▼

Me, Natalie (1969) **C-111m.** **½ D: Fred Coe. Patty Duke, James Farentino, Martin Balsam, Elsa Lanchester, Salome Jens, Nancy Marchand, Deborah Winters, Al Pacino. Soap opera-ish tale about unattractive N.Y.C. girl struggling to find herself gets tremendous boost by Duke's great performance; otherwise, film wavers uncomfortably between comedy and drama. Pacino's feature debut. [M/PG]

Men at Work (1990) **C-99m.** ** D: Emilio Estevez. Charlie Sheen, Emilio Estevez, Leslie Hope, Keith David, Dean Cameron, John Getz, Cameron Dye, John Putch. Estevez and real-life brother Sheen play garbage men whose freewheeling lifestyle is interrupted when they discover a dead body along their route. Estevez also wrote the screenplay. Laurel and Hardy they're not, but this sibling duo does provide some undemanding fun—if you check your brain at the door. [PG-13]▼●

Men Don't Leave (1990) **C-115m.** *** D: Paul Brickman. Jessica Lange, Arliss Howard, Joan Cusack, Chris O'Donnell, Charlie Korsmo, Kathy Bates. Widowed Lange, left broke with two sons, relocates from small-town Maryland to downtown Baltimore high rise. Erratic but well-performed comedy-drama is compromised by introduction of movie-predictable Mr. Right. Good moments abound, though, particularly between Lange and Cusack. And ultimately, film offers a good cry. Brickman's second directorial credit, following a seven-year lay-off after RISKY BUSINESS. Remake of

French film LA VIE CONTINUE. [PG-13]▼●

Men in Black (1997) **C-98m.** *** D: Barry Sonnenfeld. Tommy Lee Jones, Will Smith, Linda Fiorentino, Rip Torn, Vincent D'Onofrio, Tony Shalhoub, Siobhan Fallon. Hip, funny spin on the usual sci-fi invasion saga. Street-smart NYPD cop Smith is recruited to join Jones on the super-secret team that keeps an eye on thousands of aliens who already populate our planet, without most of us knowing it. When one especially violent visitor starts acting up, it's a race to find the prize he's looking for before Earth is destroyed. Outrageous and original at every turn, with great aliens by Rick Baker (Academy Award winner for Best Makeup, with David LeRoy Anderson), sharp pacing that never lets up, and a snappy script by Ed Solomon, based on the Malibu comic by Lowell Cunningham. [PG-13]▼●◗

Men in Her Diary (1945) **73m.** **½ D: Charles Barton. Peggy Ryan, Jon Hall, Louise Allbritton, Ernest Truex, Virginia Grey, William Terry, Alan Mowbray, Eric Blore, Maxie Rosenbloom. Zesty comedy of jealous wife, helpless husband, and knockout secretary; vivacious Allbritton, who never really got her due in films, is seen to good advantage here.

Men in Her Life, The (1941) **90m.** **½ D: Gregory Ratoff. Loretta Young, Conrad Veidt, Dean Jagger, Eugenie Leontovich, John Shepperd (Shepperd Strudwick), Otto Kruger. Ballerina Young marries her dancing teacher but recalls many suitors she's known in the past. Fairly interesting love-life saga.

Men in War (1957) **104m.** **½ D: Anthony Mann. Robert Ryan, Aldo Ray, Robert Keith, Vic Morrow, James Edwards, Scott Marlowe, Victor Sen Yung. Standard war film set in Korea in 1950s, with good action scenes distinguishing usual story. ▼●◗

Men in White (1934) **80m.** **½ D: Richard Boleslawski. Clark Gable, Myrna Loy, Jean Hersholt, Elizabeth Allan, Otto Kruger, Wallace Ford, Henry B. Walthall, Samuel S. Hinds. Sterling cast in sterile filming of Sidney Kingsley's play; Gable is doctor torn between study with Hersholt and marriage to society girl Loy.

Men of America (1932) **57m.** *** D: Ralph Ince. William Boyd, Charles "Chic" Sale, Dorothy Wilson, Ralph Ince, Henry Armetta, Alphonse Ethier, Theresa Maxwell Conover, Eugene Strong, Fatty Layman. Interesting Depression-era Western has rancher Boyd the object of suspicion when gangsters on the lam murder a local farmer. Boyd must avoid a lynching by rounding up the gang. Pre-"Hopalong Cassidy" Boyd, wearing a black shirt but a white hat here, fills the role nicely. Produced by David O. Selznick.

Men of Boys Town (1941) **106m.** **½ D: Norman Taurog. Spencer Tracy, Mickey Rooney, Bobs Watson, Larry Nunn, Darryl Hickman, Henry O'Neill, Lee J. Cobb. If you liked BOYS TOWN . . .▼

Men of Respect (1991) **C-113m.** *½ D: William Reilly. John Turturro, Katherine Borowitz, Dennis Farina, Peter Boyle, Rod Steiger, Lilia Skala, Steven Wright, Stanley Tucci. Pretentious modern-day *Macbeth*: Hood Turturro, pushed by an ambitious wife, rises to the top by helping blow away mob rivals. The classic sleepwalking scene (you keep wondering how it will be staged) takes place in a courtyard with Borowitz carrying a flashlight! Overacted and underlit. Columbia Pictures' first gangster/Shakespeare hybrid since JOE MACBETH; we're in no hurry for them to try it again. [R]▼●

Men of Sherwood Forest (1954-British) **C-77m.** ** D: Val Guest. Don Taylor, Reginald Beckwith, Eileen Moore, David King Wood. Yet another Robin Hood yarn, with Taylor properly sword-wielding and cavalier.▼

Men of Steel SEE: **Steel**

Men of the Fighting Lady (1954) **C-80m.** *** D: Andrew Marton. Van Johnson, Walter Pidgeon, Louis Calhern, Dewey Martin, Keenan Wynn, Frank Lovejoy, Robert Horton, Bert Freed. Above-par Korean War actioner, focusing on lives of men on U. S. aircraft carrier.▼●

Men of Two Worlds (1946-British) **C-107m.** ** D: Thorold Dickinson. Phyllis Calvert, Eric Portman, Robert Adams, Cathleen Nesbitt, Orlando Martins, Cyril Raymond. Unhappy conglomeration of clichés about well-meaning British officials trying to protect natives in Africa. Retitled WITCH DOCTOR.▼

Men's Club, The (1986) **C-100m.** BOMB D: Peter Medak. David Dukes, Richard Jordan, Harvey Keitel, Frank Langella, Roy Scheider, Craig Wasson, Treat Williams, Stockard Channing, Cindy Pickett, Gwen Welles, Ann Dusenberry, Jennifer Jason Leigh, Ann Wedgeworth. Jumbled, barely released expansion of Leonard Michaels' novel (scripted by the author) about seven males who try starting an encounter group in Jordan's home. Undistinguished performances despite that interesting cast; only noteworthy aspect is the elegant brothel for high-rollers, "The House of Affection." Ridiculous finale. [R]▼●

Men Who Tread on the Tiger's Tail, The (1945-Japanese) **60m.** **½ D: Akira Kurosawa. Denjiro Okochi, Susumu Fujita, Kenichi Enomoto, Suhu Nishina, Masayuki Mori, Takashi Shimura. Lyrical, humanistic (if modestly produced) fable, set in the 12th century and based on a Kabuki play about a lord who is being hunted by his brother; he and six generals dress as monks and set out on a journey across a heavily fortified barrier. Banned first by Japanese censors, who alleged it was not true to its source material, then by the country's post-WW2 military occupiers because of its depiction of feudal militarism; released in 1953. Enomoto is especially good as a porter.▼

Men With Guns (1998) **C-126m.** *** D: John Sayles. Federico Luppi, Damián Delgado, Dan Rivera González, Damián Alcázar, Mandy Patinkin, Katherine Grody, Tania Cruz. Dedicated, idealistic Central American doctor decides to track down former students from a government-sponsored program to bring good medicine to remote villages and tribes. This trek becomes an odyssey of discovery for the affluent but naive doctor, who acquires some unlikely companions along the way. Writer-director Sayles takes us on a road we've never traveled before—in Spanish, no less—and though it's long, it's a fascinating journey. [R]▼●◗

Men Without Souls (1940) **62m.** ** D: Nick Grinde. Barton MacLane, John Litel, Rochelle Hudson, Glenn Ford, Don Beddoe, Cy Kendall. Strictly standard prison film, with young Ford caught up in prison scandal. MacLane repeats role from dozens of other bighouse epics.

Men With Wings (1938) **C-105m.** **½ D: William A. Wellman. Fred MacMurray, Louise Campbell, Ray Milland, Andy Devine, Walter Abel, Virginia Weidler. Fictional tale of the epic of flight, with usual love triangle. After good start, it drags on. Donald O'Connor is one of the kids in the opening scenes.

Mephisto (1981-Hungarian) **C-135m.** *** D: Istvan Szabo. Klaus Maria Brandauer, Krystyna Janda, Ildiko Bansagi, Karin Boyd, Rolf Hoppe. Brandauer is magnetic as a vain, brilliant German actor who sells himself to gain prestige when the Nazis come to power. Engrossing drama is handsomely produced if a bit uneven. Based on a novel by Klaus Mann, son of Thomas, who committed suicide allegedly because he could not get the book published. Oscar winner for Best Foreign Film. First of a trilogy, followed by COLONEL REDL and HANUSSEN.▼

Mephisto Waltz, The (1971) **C-108m.** *** D: Paul Wendkos. Alan Alda, Jacqueline Bisset, Barbara Parkins, Curt Jurgens, Brad Dillman, William Windom, Kathleen Widdoes. Chiller about young journalist who falls prey to Satanic cult after meeting dying concert pianist Jurgens; good occult story with some truly frightening moments. Adapted by Ben Maddow from the Fred Mustard Stewart novel. [R]▼

Mercenaries, The SEE: **Cuba Crossing**

Mercenary, The (1968-Italian) **C-105m.** **½ D: Sergio Corbucci. Franco Nero, Tony Musante, Jack Palance, Giovanna Ralli. Better-than-average Italian pasta Western with loads of action and violence and a welcome serving of humor. At odds with one another: a stalwart mercenary (Nero), his sadistic rival (Palance), a patriotic revolutionary (Musante), a lusty peasant girl, a greedy mineowner. Video title: A PROFESSIONAL GUN. Techniscope. [PG]▼

Merchant of Four Seasons, The (1971-German) **C-88m.** *** D: Rainer Werner Fassbinder. Hans Hirschmuller, Irm Hermann, Hanna Schygulla, Andrea Schober. Fruit peddler trapped in unhappy marriage and frustrated with life disintegrates mentally and emotionally in this surprisingly rich and poignant meditation on mundane existence and failed dreams.▼

Mercury Rising (1998) **C-112m.** **½ D: Harold Becker. Bruce Willis, Alec Baldwin, Miko Hughes, Chi McBride, Kim Dickens, Robert Stanton, Bodhi Pine Elfman, Carrie Preston, L. L. Ginter, Camryn Manheim. An autistic nine-year-old boy innocently cracks a top-secret government code; cold-eyed bureaucrat Baldwin orders him killed, while over-the-hill FBI agent Willis tries to protect him. Except for the boy's autism, a routine suspense thriller, but well made and interesting throughout. Willis's standard action hero character shows a softer side here, while Baldwin plays an out-and-out heavy. Panavision. [R]▼●◗

Meridian (1990) **C-85m.** ** D: Charles Band. Sherilyn Fenn, Malcolm Jamieson, Charlie, Hilary Mason, Alex Daniels. Gothic tale about art student (Fenn) who becomes heiress to Italian castle—and its curse. OK variation on *Beauty and the Beast* doesn't hold up past the first hour, in spite of extensive nudity. Aka KISS OF THE BEAST. From Full Moon. [R]▼●

Merlin (1998) **C-180m. TVM** D: Steve Barron. Sam Neill, Helena Bonham Carter, John Gielgud, Rutger Hauer, Miranda Richardson, Isabella Rossellini, Martin Short, Billie Whitelaw; voice of James Earl Jones. In this exhilarating, effects-driven, multimillion-dollar fantasy based on the Arthurian legend, the true stars are those wizards toiling in London's FrameStore and the Jim Henson Creature Shop, crafting a dazzling array of form-shifting, morphing characters who people this magical tale set in Camelot. Look fast for the venerable Gielgud, who despite prominent billing is on screen for less than 10 seconds and utters a word or two before the title credits. Originally shown in two parts. Above average.▼◗

Merlin and the Sword SEE: **Arthur the King**

Mermaids (1990) **C-111m.** *** D: Richard Benjamin. Cher, Bob Hoskins, Winona Ryder, Michael Schoeffling, Christina Ricci, Caroline McWilliams, Jan Miner. Saucy, sexy single mother of two is a source of constant embarrassment to her teenage daughter, who's trying to deal with her own sexual awakening—and not having an easy time of it. Lively mix of

comedy and drama set in New England in the early 1960s. Funny and affecting, with a standout performance by Ryder; based on a novel by Patty Dann. [PG-13]▼●
Merrill's Marauders (1962) **C-98m.** **½ D: Samuel Fuller. Jeff Chandler, Ty Hardin, Peter Brown, Andrew Duggan, Will Hutchins, Claude Akins, John Hoyt. Gritty war film; a WW2 actioner with Chandler (his last screen role) cast as Brig. Gen. Frank Merrill, leader of a band of GIs battling the Japanese in the Burmese jungle. Fuller coscripted. CinemaScope.▼●
Merrily We Go to Hell (1932) **78m.** *½ D: Dorothy Arzner. Fredric March, Sylvia Sidney, Adrienne Allen, Skeets Gallagher, Kent Taylor, Cary Grant. Plodding story (despite intriguing title) of heiress Sidney marrying reporter March on whim, discovering that he's a problem drinker. Starts well but sinks fast.
Merrily We Live (1938) **90m.** *** D: Norman Z. McLeod. Constance Bennett, Brian Aherne, Alan Mowbray, Billie Burke, Bonita Granville, Tom Brown, Ann Dvorak, Patsy Kelly. It's all been done before, but fluttery Burke hires suave Aherne as butler to tame spoiled Bennett. Engaging fun.
Merry Andrew (1958) **C-103m.** **½ D: Michael Kidd. Danny Kaye, Pier Angeli, Baccaloni, Robert Coote. Danny is a British teacher-archeologist with a yen for the circus and one of its performers (Angeli) in this bright musicomedy. Not as wacky as earlier Kaye efforts, but good. CinemaScope.
Merry Christmas, Mr. Lawrence (1983-British-Japanese) **C-122m.** *** D: Nagisa Oshima. Tom Conti, David Bowie, Ryuichi Sakamoto, Takeshi, Jack Thompson. Oshima's first film in English (for the most part) is strange, haunting drama set in Japanese POW camp, centering on test of wills between martinet commander Sakamoto and British major Bowie. Quite rewarding for those willing to stick with it, but it does take some effort; splendid performances all around, especially Takeshi as tough sergeant and Conti as title character, camp's only bilingual prisoner. Japanese music superstar Sakamoto also composed the score. [R]▼
Merry Go Round of 1938 (1937) **87m.** **½ D: Irving Cummings. Bert Lahr, Jimmy Savo, Billy House, Mischa Auer, Alice Brady, Joy Hodges, Louise Fazenda. Disappointing backstage story with sentimental overtones as comedy foursome adopts little girl. Good specialty acts, great cast make tired tale endurable.
Merry Monahans, The (1944) **91m.** **½ D: Charles Lamont. Donald O'Connor, Peggy Ryan, Jack Oakie, Ann Blyth, Rosemary De Camp, John Miljan. Spirited cast does its best with bland, utterly predictable vaudeville saga, filled with period tunes like "When You Wore a Tulip."
Merry War, A (1997-British) **C-102m.** *** D: Robert Bierman. Richard E. Grant, Helena Bonham Carter, Julian Wadham, Jim Carter, Harriet Walter, Lesley Vickerage, Liz Smith, Barbara Leigh-Hunt. Sweet, enjoyable comedy-satire about an advertising man (Grant) who is captivated by the concept of offering his life to "art." He quits his day job and embraces a Bohemian lifestyle as he sets out to become a full-time poet, all the while maintaining a relationship with his ex–coworker/girlfriend (Bonham Carter). Based on *Keep the Aspidistra Flying*, a semi-autobiographical novel by George Orwell; it played the film festival circuit under that title.▼◗
Merry Widow, The (1925) **113m.** *** D: Erich von Stroheim. Mae Murray, John Gilbert, Roy D'Arcy, Tully Marshall, Josephine Crowell. A prince (Gilbert) is ordered to woo a rich American widow (Murray). Lavish, well-produced silent version of the Franz Lehar operetta is probably von Stroheim's most "normal" film, though he still manages to inject his usual bizarre touches (including a character with a foot fetish). See if you can spot young Clark Gable as an extra. Remade twice.
Merry Widow, The (1934) **99m.** *** D: Ernst Lubitsch. Maurice Chevalier, Jeanette MacDonald, Una Merkel, Edward Everett Horton, George Barbier, Herman Bing. Lavish, delightful filming of Lehar operetta, with usual Lubitsch charm and handpicked cast. Infectious score still first-rate. Retitled: THE LADY DANCES. ▼●
Merry Widow, The (1952) **C-105m.** **½ D: Curtis Bernhardt. Lana Turner, Fernando Lamas, Una Merkel, Richard Haydn. Franz Lehar's operetta seems dated and trite in plush but unenthusiastic remake.▼
Merton of the Movies (1947) **82m.** ** D: Robert Alton. Red Skelton, Virginia O' Brien, Gloria Grahame, Leon Ames, Alan Mowbray, Hugo Haas. Lifeless remake of George S. Kaufman–Marc Connelly play (filmed before in 1924 and 1932) about movie-struck simpleton's adventures in Hollywood. A real disappointment. Choreographer Alton's directing debut.▼
Mesmerized (1986-British-Australian-New Zealand) **C-97m.** *½ D: Michael Laughlin. Jodie Foster, John Lithgow, Michael Murphy, Harry Andrews, Dan Shor, Reg Evans. Weird, ultimately silly drama about innocent orphan Foster who weds older man Lithgow in late-19th-century New Zealand. Laughlin adapted from Jerzy Skolimowski story. Aka SHOCKED. Panavision. [PG]▼●◗
Message, The SEE: **Mohammad, Messenger of God**
Message from Space (1978-Japanese) **C-105m.** **½ D: Kinji Fukasaku. Vic Morrow, Sonny Chiba, Philip Casnoff, Peggy Lee Brennan, Sue Shiomi, Tetsuro Tamba. Embattled planet sends SOS, and intergalactic team comes to its rescue. Cardboard performances take back seat to special effects and

"cute" robot, both obviously patterned after STAR WARS. Toeiscope. [PG]

Message in a Bottle (1999) **C-132m.** ★★½ D: Luis Mandoki. Kevin Costner, Robin Wright Penn, Paul Newman, John Savage, Illeana Douglas, Robbie Coltrane, Jesse James, Bethel Leslie, Tom Aldredge, Viveka Davis, Raphael Sbarge, Rosemary Murphy. Sappy, old-fashioned romance based on Nicholas Sparks' novel about a Chicago newspaper researcher who finds a bottle washed ashore and in it a passionate letter from a man to his lover. She becomes obsessed with tracking down the writer, and when she finds him (widower Costner) she doesn't reveal that their meeting was not by chance. Too long, too slow, but enjoyable escapism if you buy into it, with Wright Penn nicely cast against type, and Newman in fine form as Costner's starchy father. Panavision. [PG-13]▼●◗

Message to Garcia, A (1936) **77m.** ★★★ D: George Marshall. Wallace Beery, Barbara Stanwyck, John Boles, Alan Hale, Mona Barrie, Herbert Mundin. Historical fiction about agent Boles trying to reach General Garcia during Spanish-American war, with dubious help of roguish Beery and well-bred Stanwyck. Very entertaining.

Message to Love: The Isle of Wight Festival (1996) **C-128m.** ★★★ D: Murray Lerner. The Who, The Doors, Joan Baez, Joni Mitchell, Jimi Hendrix, Jethro Tull, Emerson, Lake and Palmer, Tiny Tim, The Moody Blues, Kris Kristofferson, Miles Davis, Donovan. Top-notch documentary chronicling the on- and offstage activities at Great Britain's version of Woodstock/Altamont: the 1970 Isle of Wight Festival, a musical smorgasbord that was as ineptly organized as it was musically significant. Priceless footage of vintage rock acts, including Hendrix and The Doors' Jim Morrison just before their deaths. Because of financing problems, it took Lerner a quarter-century to complete this.▼●◗

Messenger of Death (1988) **C-91m.** ★½ D: J. Lee Thompson. Charles Bronson, Trish Van Devere, Laurence Luckinbill, Jeff Corey, Marilyn Hassett, John Ireland, Daniel Benzali. Boring Bronson vehicle casts him as a reporter determined to get to the bottom of an odd murder case involving two warring Mormon sects led by Corey and Ireland. By-the-numbers filmmaking wastes a potentially interesting look at a different culture. [R]▼●

Messenger: The Story of Joan of Arc, The (1999-French-U.S.) **C-148m.** ★★½ D: Luc Besson. Milla Jovovich, John Malkovich, Faye Dunaway, Dustin Hoffman, Pascal Greggory, Vincent Cassel, Tchéky Karyo, Richard Ridings, Desmond Harrington, Timothy West. Arresting approach to the story of Joan of Arc, with a vibrant Jovovich as the peasant girl who leads her countrymen into battle. But in this version (scripted by Besson and Andrew Birkin) she also questions herself, which causes the film to lose momentum after a rousing first half that's filled with vivid, in-your-face battle scenes. Alternate version runs 158m. Super 35. [R]▼◗

Metalstorm: The Destruction of Jared-Syn (1983) **C-84m.** BOMB D: Charles Band. Jeffrey Byron, Tim Thomerson, Kelly Preston, Mike Preston, Richard Moll. Derivative sci-fi film set in the future, with an intrepid hunter searching out megalomaniac who wants to rule the planet. Even 3D couldn't do much to help this amateurish—and seemingly interminable—outing. StereoScope. [PG]▼●

Metamorphosis (1990) **C-96m.** ★½ D: G. L. Eastman. Gene LeBrock, Catherine Baranov, Harry Cason, David Wicker, Stephen Brown, Jason Arnold. Low-budget, technically inept ripoff of THE FLY (1986), with self-obsessed professor/genius who tests his experimental immortality drug on himself. Result: he slowly devolves to a sawed-off dinosaur, then primordial slime. Movie treats its tired clichés with awed respect for their presumed originality. [R]▼

Meteor (1979) **C-103m.** ★½ D: Ronald Neame. Sean Connery, Natalie Wood, Karl Malden, Brian Keith, Henry Fonda, Martin Landau, Trevor Howard, Richard Dysart. Switzerland, Hong Kong, and Manhattan all get a big piece of the rock when a giant meteor comes crashing to Earth. Late entry in Hollywood's disaster cycle wastes fine cast with dull script, shoddy effects. Panavision. [PG]▼●◗

Meteor Man, The (1993) **C-100m.** ★½ D: Robert Townsend. Robert Townsend, Marla Gibbs, Eddie Griffin, Robert Guillaume, James Earl Jones, Roy Fegan, Cynthia Belgrave, Marilyn Coleman, Don Cheadle, Bill Cosby, Frank Gorshin, Sinbad, Luther Vandross. Townsend plays a timid inner-city schoolteacher (with a fear of heights) who's hit by an odd emerald meteor that turns him into a superhero. Townsend also wrote this "Superman N the Hood" tale, full of pro-social values—but not many laughs. As a comedy it just doesn't fly. [PG]▼●

Metro (1997) **C-117m.** ★★½ D: Thomas Carter. Eddie Murphy, Michael Rapaport, Michael Wincott, Carmen Ejogo, Denis Arndt, Art Evans, Donal Logue, Kim Miyori. Murphy is a self-assured hostage negotiator for the San Francisco police, but this action film needs his thousand-watt personality to keep it afloat. Plotting is cluttered and predictable, with a heinous villain (Wincott) who proves so indestructible that when he finally dies, there's no satisfaction because we're not sure he's really finished! Action highlight: a runaway cable car. Panavision. [R]▼●◗

Metroland (1998-British) **C-97m.** ★★½ D: Philip Saville. Christian Bale, Emily Watson, Lee Ross, Elsa Zylberstein, Rufus, Jonathan Aris, Ifan Meredith, Amanda Ryan, John Wood. 1977: Chris (Bale), a comfortably married man, is visited by his oldest friend, a vagabond poet, who forces him to reflect on his Bohemian days in late '60s Paris and question the value of middle-class existence in London suburbia. A thoughtful though basically unsurprising examination of compromised dreams, bolstered by the performances of Bale and Watson. Adrian Hodges adapted Julian Barnes' novel. ▼◗

Metropolis (1926-German) **120m.** **** D: Fritz Lang. Brigitte Helm, Alfred Abel, Gustav Froelich, Rudolf Klein-Rogge, Fritz Rasp. Classic silent-film fantasy of futuristic city and its mechanized society, with upper-class young man abandoning his life of luxury to join oppressed workers in a revolt. Heavy going at times, but startling set design and special effects command attention throughout. Many shorter prints exist; reissued in 1984 at 87m. with color-tints and score by Giorgio Moroder. ▼●◗

Metropolitan (1935) **75m.** **½ D: Richard Boleslawski. Lawrence Tibbett, Virginia Bruce, Alice Brady, Cesar Romero, Thurston Hall, Luis Alberni, Ruth Donnelly, George Marion, Sr., Jane Darwell. Enjoyable if predictable musical with Tibbett ideally cast as a talented but struggling opera singer who yearns for stardom. Tibbett's many songs include "Road to Mandalay" and "Figaro," which he performs most impressively.

Metropolitan (1990) **C-98m.** *** D: Whit Stillman. Carolyn Farina, Edward Clements, Christopher Eigeman, Taylor Nichols, Allison Rutledge-Parisi, Dylan Hundley, Isabel Gillies, Bryan Leder, Will Kempe, Elizabeth Thompson. Title might suggest teeming masses, but this thoroughly original little film looks instead at N.Y.C.'s upper crust—specifically, the inner circle of debutantes (who haven't yet "come out"), preppies, and their way of life. Social comedy, brimming with irony, is set during Christmas season, with loner Clements drawn into small clique of friends. Sharply written by first-time director Stillman, and well acted by cast of newcomers; Eigeman, as Nick, is a standout. [PG-13] ▼●

Mexican Hayride (1948) **77m.** ** D: Charles Barton. Bud Abbott, Lou Costello, Virginia Grey, Luba Malina, John Hubbard, Pedro de Cordoba, Fritz Feld. Lackluster A&C vehicle, with the boys on a wild goose chase with a mine deed in Mexico. Based on a Cole Porter Broadway musical, but without the songs! ▼

Mexican Manhunt (1953) **71m.** *½ D: Rex Bailey. George Brent, Hillary Brooke, Morris Ankrum, Karen Sharpe. Actors walk through thin script about solving of old crime.

Mexican Spitfire Fiery Mexican beauty Lupe Velez had personality to burn, but by the late 1930s Hollywood had seemingly run out of ideas to showcase her talent. Then in 1939 RKO cast her in a grade-B comedy called THE GIRL FROM MEXICO, with Donald Woods as an American who falls in love with her, and veteran comic Leon Errol as Woods' Uncle Matt, who becomes her soulmate. The combination of slapstick-style farce and the charisma of Velez clicked with audiences, and before year's end the studio had a followup film in theaters called MEXICAN SPITFIRE, which launched the official series. The second film expanded Errol's comic opportunities by introducing a second character for him to play, a tippling British visitor called Lord Epping. As Uncle Matt's wife, Elisabeth Risdon doesn't approve of his friendship with Lupe—but as a social climber, she's forced to kowtow to the aristocratic Epping. Two-reel comedy writers stitched the stories together from this foundation, and Errol was in his element. His routines are often hilarious; what's more, he and Lupe have a great screen rapport. Once the formula was set, however, it never varied, and at times it's hard to distinguish one Spitfire film from another. If ever a series was carried by the sheer force of its stars' personalities, this is it; when the surrounding material is good, the Spitfire films are very funny indeed, but too often a sense of deja vu hangs over the proceedings, and even Lupe's hundred-watt star power can't take it very far.

MEXICAN SPITFIRE

The Girl From Mexico (1939)
Mexican Spitfire (1939)
Mexican Spitfire Out West (1940)
Mexican Spitfire's Baby (1941)
Mexican Spitfire at Sea (1942)
Mexican Spitfire Sees a Ghost (1942)
Mexican Spitfire's Elephant (1942)
Mexican Spitfire's Blessed Event (1943)

Mexican Spitfire (1939) **67m.** *** D: Leslie Goodwins. Lupe Velez, Leon Errol, Donald Woods, Linda Hayes, Cecil Kellaway, Elisabeth Risdon. First official entry in the series is a retread of THE GIRL FROM MEXICO, but shifts focus from bland leading man Woods to hilarious Errol in dual role of Uncle Matt and the tipsy Lord Epping. Meanwhile, Matt's wife (Risdon) attempts to break up her nephew's marriage to the fiery Carmelita. Some solid belly laughs here. ▼

Mexican Spitfire at Sea (1942) **73m.** ** D: Leslie Goodwins. Lupe Velez, Leon Errol, Charles "Buddy" Rogers, ZaSu Pitts, Elisabeth Risdon, Florence Bates, Marion Martin, Lydia Bilbrook. Protracted shipboard antics as the Spitfire causes chaos on

an ocean liner in pursuit of a business deal. Series was simply repeating itself by now.
Mexican Spitfire Out West (1940) **76m.** **½ D: Leslie Goodwins. Lupe Velez, Leon Errol, Donald Woods, Elisabeth Risdon, Cecil Kellaway. The tempestuous Latin bombshell decides that her hubby isn't paying enough attention to her, so she goes to Reno for a divorce. Lively farce repeats many gags from first Spitfire film, but they're still funny.
Mexican Spitfire's Baby (1941) **69m.** ** D: Leslie Goodwins. Lupe Velez, Leon Errol, Charles "Buddy" Rogers, Elisabeth Risdon, Lydia Bilbrook, ZaSu Pitts, Fritz Feld. The Spitfire and her husband (Rogers, replacing Donald Woods) get more than they bargained for when their newly adopted French war orphan turns out to be a very grownup (and very sexy) blonde, nicely played by Marion Martin.
Mexican Spitfire's Blessed Event (1943) **63m.** **½ D: Leslie Goodwins. Lupe Velez, Leon Errol, Walter Reed, Elisabeth Risdon, Lydia Bilbrook, Hugh Beaumont, Alan Carney, Wally Brown. Last entry in the frantic series revolves around the Spitfire's often riotous masquerade of motherhood in an effort to help her husband clinch a big business deal.
Mexican Spitfire Sees a Ghost (1942) **70m.** ** D: Leslie Goodwins. Lupe Velez, Leon Errol, Charles "Buddy" Rogers, Elisabeth Risdon, Donald MacBride, Minna Gombell, Mantan Moreland. Errol's riotous turn in three roles fails to save this weak "haunted" house comedy.
Mexican Spitfire's Elephant (1942) **64m.** **½ D: Leslie Goodwins. Lupe Velez, Leon Errol, Walter Reed, Elisabeth Risdon, Marion Martin, Lydia Bilbrook, Lyle Talbot, Luis Alberni. Smugglers on a ship use Errol to unwittingly smuggle a gem through customs in a miniature elephant in this frenetic farce.
MGM's Big Parade of Comedy (1964) **100m.** **½ Compiled by Robert Youngson. Fifty of the greatest stars of all time appear in this compilation, but too briefly. Harlow's scenes are seconds long; you can miss others if you blink. Still worthwhile for many priceless sequences with Garbo, Laurel and Hardy, Keaton, Gable, Robert Benchley, Marion Davies, Marx Brothers, et al.▼
Miami Blues (1990) **C-99m.** ** D: George Armitage. Fred Ward, Alec Baldwin, Jennifer Jason Leigh, Nora Dunn, Charles Napier, Jose Perez, Paul Gleason, Obba Babatunde, Martine Beswicke. Psychopathic thief and murderer (Baldwin) arrives in Miami, hooks up with a naive young woman who's blind to his problems, and sets a world-weary cop on his trail by stealing the detective's badge and I.D. Three dynamic performances and some hip, high-style filmmaking command your attention—but the rampant amorality and violence leave a bad taste. Jonathan Demme and costar Ward were among the producers. From the Charles Willeford novel. [R]▼●
Miami Expose (1956) **73m.** *½ D: Fred F. Sears. Lee J. Cobb, Patricia Medina, Edward Arnold, Michael Granger. Boring round-up of criminal syndicate in Sunshine State.
Miami Rhapsody (1995) **C-95m.** ** D: David Frankel. Sarah Jessica Parker, Mia Farrow, Antonio Banderas, Gil Bellows, Paul Mazursky, Carla Gugino, Naomi Campbell, Kevin Pollak, Mark Blum, Ben Stein. Young woman is afraid of committing to marriage, given the tumult of her parents' and siblings' marital lives. Only problem is that she can't seem to stop *talking* about it. Light comedy, with serious undertones, almost sinks under the weight of talk: an incessant stream of one-line, sitcom-style jokes. Written by the director. Overbearing big band–style score by Mark Isham. [PG-13]▼●
Miami Story, The (1954) **75m.** ** D: Fred F. Sears. Barry Sullivan, Luther Adler, John Baer, Adele Jergens, Beverly Garland. Stern ex-con Sullivan redeems himself in Florida resort city.
Michael (1996) **C-105m.** *** D: Nora Ephron. John Travolta, Andie MacDowell, William Hurt, Robert Pastorelli, Bob Hoskins, Jean Stapleton, Teri Garr, Wally Ward, Joey Lauren Adams, Carla Gugino, Tom Hodges, Wallace Langham. A pair of cynical reporters and a phony "angel expert" discover that a dotty old lady's claim that the archangel Michael is living with her is true. Michael, however, turns out not to be your average angel. Genial, wry movie never goes quite where you expect and takes its sweet time getting there, but the trip is charming, and Travolta, as the seedy, randy Michael, is perfectly cast. Ideal music score by Randy Newman. [PG]▼●◗
Michael Collins (1996-U.S.-Irish) **C-132m.** *** D: Neil Jordan. Liam Neeson, Aidan Quinn, Julia Roberts, Stephen Rea, Alan Rickman, Ian Hart, Brendan Gleeson, Charles Dance. Politically charged story of Irish rebel leader Collins (Neeson), who with charm, guts, and idealistic fervor leads the fight against British rule in the teens and 20s. Dynamic and powerful first half gives way to more sober and inevitable conclusion, in which Collins is forced to become a diplomat and compromiser—sowing the seeds of his own demise. Neeson is excellent and surrounded by a first-rate cast in this persuasive, believable, and violent period piece, beautifully filmed by Chris Menges. Jordan also scripted. [R]▼●◗
Michael Shayne Having enjoyed considerable success with the Charlie Chan and Mr. Moto films, the B-picture unit of

20th Century-Fox was on the lookout for another detective to head his own series. In 1940 the studio purchased the rights to Brett Halliday's contemporary private eye character Michael Shayne, and cast reliable supporting actor Lloyd Nolan in the role. The kickoff film, MICHAEL SHAYNE, PRIVATE DETECTIVE, was based on Halliday's novel *Dividend on Death,* and (like the Chans and Motos) surrounded the starring sleuth with seasoned character actors and attractive ingenues from the contract roster. Oddly enough, none of the subsequent Shayne films utilized Halliday stories for their source material, though they *did* turn to other prominent authors of mystery and pulp fiction, including (on one occasion) no less than Raymond Chandler, whose Philip Marlowe tale *The High Window* was turned into the Shayne vehicle TIME TO KILL. Historically, the Shayne series is significant because it presented a self-assured (and down-to-earth) private investigator on the screen *before* the vogue for Sam Spade/Philip Marlowe-type hard-boiled detectives flourished in the 1940s. And if Lloyd Nolan hasn't quite the charisma of Bogart, he was certainly adequate in the role, more so than Hugh Beaumont, who portrayed Shayne in a series of forgettable low-budgeters made for PRC later in the 1940s.

MICHAEL SHAYNE

Michael Shayne, Private Detective (1940)
Sleepers West (1941)
Dressed to Kill (1941)
Blue, White and Perfect (1941)
The Man Who Wouldn't Die (1942)
Just Off Broadway (1942)
Time to Kill (1942)
Murder Is My Business (1946)
Larceny in Her Heart (1946)
Blonde for a Day (1946)
Three on a Ticket (1947)
Too Many Winners (1947)

Michael Shayne, Private Detective (1940) **77m.** **½ D: Eugene Forde. Lloyd Nolan, Marjorie Weaver, Joan Valerie, Walter Abel, Elizabeth Patterson, Donald MacBride. Nolan gives vivid portrayal of detective Shayne, keeping an eye on heavy gambler Weaver in average private-eye thriller.

Michael Strogoff SEE: **Soldier and the Lady, The**

Michigan Kid (1947) **C-69m.** ** D: Ray Taylor. Jon Hall, Victor McLaglen, Rita Johnson, Andy Devine, Byron Foulger. Colorful but routine refilming of Rex Beach story of female ranch owner Johnson falling victim to corrupt town government.▼

Mickey (1948) **C-87m.** ** D: Ralph Murphy. Lois Butler, Bill Goodwin, Irene Hervey, Hattie McDaniel, John Sutton, Rose Hobart, Skippy Homeier. Silly, predictable yarn of spirited teen Butler, a tomboy who learns how to be a young lady—and who plays matchmaker for her widowed dad (Goodwin).▼

Mickey Blue Eyes (1999-U.S.-British) **C-103m.** **½ D: Kelly Makin. Hugh Grant, James Caan, Jeanne Tripplehorn, Burt Young, James Fox, Joe Viterelli, Gerry Becker, Maddie Corman. Fitfully amusing farce about a N.Y.C. art auctioneer who asks his girlfriend to marry him—never dreaming that she's part of an Italian mob family. Soon, he's pressed into doing favors for some of "the boys." Starts out funny but sputters sooner than it should. [PG-13] ▼●◗

Mickey One (1965) **93m.** **½ D: Arthur Penn. Warren Beatty, Hurd Hatfield, Alexandra Stewart, Franchot Tone, Teddy Hart, Jeff Corey, Kamatari Fujiwara, Donna Michelle. Nightclub comic in trouble with mob takes it on the lam and assumes a new identity. Offbeat, to say the least; Penn's version of a French New Wave film; heavy with visual symbols but we're not quite sure what it's all about. Fine jazz score by Eddie Sauter with solos by Stan Getz.▼●

Micki + Maude (1984) **C-118m.** **½ D: Blake Edwards. Dudley Moore, Amy Irving, Ann Reinking, Richard Mulligan, George Gaynes, Wallace Shawn, John Pleshette, Lu Leonard, Priscilla Pointer, George Coe. Dudley has a wife and a girlfriend—and they're both pregnant! Surprisingly warmhearted comedy that turns into old-fashioned farce. Runs out of steam somewhere along the line but benefits from winning performances by all three leads. Panavision. [PG-13]▼●

Microcosmos (1996-French-Swiss-Italian) **C-77m.** ***½ D: Claude Nuridsany, Marie Perennou. Strikingly visual nature documentary using high-powered lenses to record a magical universe that hardly can be seen by the human eye: the world of insects, in which beetles, snails, caterpillars, ladybugs, and dragonflies exist amid grass and vines, dewdrops and poppies. An immensely entertaining, endlessly fascinating visual treat; stunningly photographed and edited. U.S. prints feature narration by Kristen Scott Thomas. [G]▼●

Midas Run (1969) **C-106m.** **½ D: Alf Kjellin. Fred Astaire, Richard Crenna, Anne Heywood, Ralph Richardson, Roddy McDowall, Cesar Romero. British secret serviceman plots a daring gold heist in this routine caper film, enlivened by Astaire's peerless presence in lead. Fred Astaire, Jr., appears briefly as plane's copilot. [M/PG]

Middle Age Crazy (1980-Canadian) **C-95m.** *½ D: John Trent. Bruce Dern, Ann-Margret, Graham Jarvis, Eric Christmas, Deborah Wakeham. Title tells all:

40-year-old Dern buys a Porsche, some new threads, and leaves wife Ann-Margret for pro-football cheerleader Wakeham. Nothing new; inspired by the hit song. [R]▼

Middle of the Night (1959) **118m.** **½ D: Delbert Mann. Kim Novak, Fredric March, Glenda Farrell, Jan Norris, Lee Grant, Effie Afton, Martin Balsam. Slow-moving screen version of Paddy Chayefsky play, with March a middle-aged man about to marry much younger Novak.

Middle of the World, The (1974-French-Swiss) **C-115m.** *** D: Alain Tanner. Olimpia Carlisi, Philippe Leotard, Juliet Berto, Jacques Denis, Roger Jendly. Intelligent, quietly effective tale of married engineer Leotard, running for political office, who has scandalous affair with waitress Carlisi.

Midnight (1934) **80m.** **½ D: Chester Erskine. Sidney Fox, O. P. Heggie, Henry Hull, Margaret Wycherly, Lynne Overman, Richard Whorf, Humphrey Bogart. Jury foreman is persecuted by the press—and even his family—after sending woman to the electric chair. Dated but interesting theatrical piece, reissued as CALL IT MURDER to capitalize on Bogart's later stardom.▼●◗

Midnight (1939) **94m.** ***½ D: Mitchell Leisen. Claudette Colbert, Don Ameche, John Barrymore, Francis Lederer, Mary Astor, Hedda Hopper, Monty Woolley. Penniless Colbert masquerades as Hungarian countess in chic Parisian marital mixup; near-classic comedy written by Billy Wilder and Charles Brackett. Barrymore's antics are especially memorable. Remade as MASQUERADE IN MEXICO.▼

Midnight (1981) **C-94m.** **½ D: John Russo. Lawrence Tierney, Melanie Verliin, John Amplas, John Hall, Charles Jackson, Doris Hackney. Low-budget horror, shot in Pennsylvania, isn't bad. Unfortunate teenager Verliin, driven out of her home by a lecherous policeman stepfather (Tierney), meets two young thieves and then a family of cultists who sacrifice young women. Russo adapted his own novel. Aka BACKWOODS MASSACRE. Followed by a sequel. [R]▼

Midnight (1989) **C-86m.** *½ D: Norman Thaddeus Vane. Lynn Redgrave, Tony Curtis, Steven Parrish, Frank Gorshin, Wolfman Jack, Rita Gam, Gustav Vintas, Karen Witter. Tiresome story of TV horror-movie hostess who finds people around her mysteriously dying. Always-watchable Redgrave does her best, but meager, slow-moving script does her in. A longer "director's cut" had theatrical showings following its video release. [R]▼●

Midnight Auto Supply SEE: **Love and the Midnight Auto Supply**

Midnight Clear, A (1992) **C-107m.** ***½ D: Keith Gordon. Peter Berg, Kevin Dillon, Arye Gross, Ethan Hawke, Gary Sinise, Frank Whaley, John C. McGinley, Larry Joshua, Curt Lowens. Top-notch anti-war drama, about a squad of young American GI's (led by Hawke) on a mission in the Ardennes Forest near the end of WW2. Refreshingly unhurried film is filled with insight, irony, and eloquence. Extremely well acted and directed; Gordon also scripted, from William Wharton's novel. [R]▼●

Midnight Cop (1989-West German) **C-96m.** **½ D: Peter Patzak. Armin Mueller-Stahl, Michael York, Morgan Fairchild, Frank Stallone, Julia Kent, Monica Bleibtreu, Allegra Curtis, Henry Friedman. Slow but interesting murder mystery pitting quirky Berlin cop against both a serial killer and a blackmailer. Overdone tenor sax jazz score and murky plot developments hamper things, but Mueller-Stahl is very good. [R]▼

Midnight Cowboy (1969) **C-113m.** **** D: John Schlesinger. Dustin Hoffman, Jon Voight, Sylvia Miles, John McGiver, Brenda Vaccaro, Barnard Hughes, Ruth White, Jennifer Salt, Bob Balaban. Emotionally shattering dramatization of James Leo Herlihy's novel was rated X in 1969, but it's essentially an old-fashioned story with some unusual modern twists: hayseed Voight comes to N.Y.C., becomes a free-lance stud, and develops unusual and deep friendship with seedy Ratso Rizzo (Hoffman). Seamiest side of N.Y.C. is backdrop for compelling, keen-eyed character study that if anything looks better today than it did when it came out. Won Best Picture, Director, Screenplay (Waldo Salt) Oscars. Graphic effects by Pablo Ferro. Please don't watch it on commercial TV: the most lenient prints run 104m. and are ludicrously dubbed to remove profane language. [R—edited from original X rating]▼●◗

Midnight Crossing (1988) **C-104m.** *½ D: Roger Holzberg. Faye Dunaway, Daniel J. Travanti, Kim Cattrall, Ned Beatty, John Laughlin. Hokey, boring, needlessly violent soaper-adventure, with insurance agent Travanti intent on recovering some booty he and his late pal buried years before. Dunaway is thanklessly cast as his wife, who is blind. [R]▼●

Midnight Express (1978) **C-121m.** ***½ D: Alan Parker. Brad Davis, Irene Miracle, Bo Hopkins, Randy Quaid, John Hurt, Mike Kellin, Paul Smith. Riveting, harshly violent story of young American Billy Hayes (Davis), who faces physical and emotional brutalization in Turkish prison after being caught drug-smuggling. Great moviemaking, though not as faithful to Hayes' true story as filmmakers would have us believe. Oscar winner for Oliver Stone's script and Giorgio Moroder's score. [R]▼●◗

Midnight in the Garden of Good and Evil

(1997) **C-155m.** ★★ D: Clint Eastwood. Kevin Spacey, John Cusack, Jack Thompson, The Lady Chablis, Alison Eastwood, Irma P. Hall, Paul Hipp, Jude Law, Dorothy Loudon, Anne Haney, Kim Hunter, Geoffrey Lewis, Richard Herd, James Moody. Meandering adaptation of John Berendt's best-seller about some of the more eccentric denizens of Savannah, Georgia. Cusack plays a N.Y. reporter assigned to cover Spacey's A-list Christmas party; when that gracious, noveau riche bon vivant is accused of murder later the same night, Cusack decides to stick around and see what happens. Never terribly compelling, despite several likable performances, and fatally overlong. [R]▼●◗

Midnight Lace (1960) **C-108m.** ★★★ D: David Miller. Doris Day, Rex Harrison, John Gavin, Myrna Loy, Roddy McDowall, Herbert Marshall, Natasha Parry, Anthony Dawson. Shrill murder mystery; unbelievable plot line, but star cast and decor smooth over rough spots. Set in London; redone as a TVM in 1980.▼

Midnight Madness (1980) **C-110m.** BOMB D: David Wechter, Michael Nankin. David Naughton, Debra Clinger, Eddie Deezen, Brad Wilkin, Maggie Roswell, Stephen Furst. Idiotic comedy about college students participating in an all-night scavenger hunt. Nothing to stay up for (unless you want to see Michael J. Fox in his feature film debut). [PG]▼

Midnight Man, The (1974) **C-117m.** ★★½ D: Roland Kibbee, Burt Lancaster. Burt Lancaster, Susan Clark, Cameron Mitchell, Morgan Woodward, Joan Lorring, Ed Lauter, Catherine Bach, Linda Kelsey, Harris Yulin. Involved, overlong mystery with Lancaster as college security officer looking into a coed's murder. Lancaster and Kibbee also cowrote and coproduced. [R]

Midnight Mary (1933) **74m.** ★★★ D: William A. Wellman. Loretta Young, Ricardo Cortez, Franchot Tone, Andy Devine, Una Merkel, Frank Conroy, Warren Hymer, Ivan Simpson, Harold Huber. Visually arresting story, told in flashback, of hard luck Young, orphaned at nine, seduced at sixteen, sent to prison. Loaded with Wellman flourishes, and Loretta is mesmerizingly beautiful. Story by Anita Loos.

Midnight Run (1988) **C-122m.** ★★★½ D: Martin Brest. Robert De Niro, Charles Grodin, Yaphet Kotto, John Ashton, Dennis Farina, Joe Pantoliano, Wendy Phillips, Richard Foronjy. Socko action-comedy with bounty hunter (and ex-cop) De Niro determined to bring bail-jumper Grodin, an embezzling accountant, from N.Y. to L.A. What De Niro *doesn't* know is that the Mob is also on Grodin's trail—with orders to kill. Sensational byplay between the stars is matched by first-rate action and a sharply written script by George Gallo. Director Brest handles the blend of violence and comedy as well as he did in BEVERLY HILLS COP. Dynamic music score by Danny Elfman. Followed by a TV series. [R]▼●◗

Midnight Story, The (1957) **89m.** ★★½ D: Joseph Pevney. Tony Curtis, Marisa Pavan, Gilbert Roland, Ted de Corsia, Kathleen Freeman. Atmospheric murder yarn with Curtis an ex-cop seeking the culprit who killed neighborhood priest. CinemaScope.

Midsummer Night's Dream, A (1935) **117m.** ★★★ D: Max Reinhardt, William Dieterle. James Cagney, Dick Powell, Joe E. Brown, Jean Muir, Hugh Herbert, Olivia de Havilland, Ian Hunter, Frank McHugh, Victor Jory, Ross Alexander, Verree Teasdale, Anita Louise, Mickey Rooney, Arthur Treacher, Billy Barty. Hollywood-Shakespeare has good and bad points; Cagney as Bottom and the Mendelssohn music are among good parts; Hugh Herbert and other incongruous cast members make up the latter. After a while Rooney (as Puck) gets to be a bit too much. Hal Mohr's glistening cinematography won an Oscar—the only one ever awarded on a write-in. This was the only sound film of esteemed European stage director Reinhardt. Film debut of Olivia de Havilland (who had appeared in Reinhardt's Hollywood Bowl production of the play a year earlier). Originally 132m.▼●

Midsummer Night's Dream, A (1966) **C-93m.** ★★½ D: Dan Eriksen. Suzanne Farrell, Edward Villella, Arthur Mitchell, Mimi Paul, Nicholas Magallanes. Filmed record of New York City Ballet's presentation of Shakespeare's comedy is mostly for dance buffs; makes some attempt to be cinematic, but not enough. Panavision.

Midsummer Night's Dream, A (1968-British) **C-124m.** ★★½ D: Peter Hall. Diana Rigg, David Warner, Michael Jayston, Ian Richardson, Judi Dench, Ian Holm, Bill Travers, Helen Mirren. Fine cast of England's Royal Shakespeare Co. in middling performance of the Shakespeare classic.▼

Midsummer Night's Dream, A (1999) **C-115m.** ★★½ D: Michael Hoffman. Kevin Kline, Michelle Pfeiffer, Rupert Everett, Stanley Tucci, Calista Flockhart, Anna Friel, Christian Bale, Dominic West, David Strathairn, Sophie Marceau, Roger Rees, Max Wright, Gregory Jbara, Bill Irwin, Sam Rockwell, Bernard Hill, John Sessions. Shakespeare's classic comedy transported from ancient Greece to late-19th-century Italy (complete with newly invented bicycles). Young love runs wild, with Everett and Pfeiffer as King and Queen of the Fairies, Tucci a spirited Puck and Kline (in his element) a buffoonish Bottom. Works better in parts than as a whole, but still enjoyable for lovers of the play. Full on-screen title is WILLIAM SHAKESPEARE'S A MID-

SUMMER NIGHT'S DREAM. 2.35 Research PLC. [PG-13]▼●◗

Midsummer Night's Sex Comedy, A (1982) **C-88m.** ★★★ D: Woody Allen. Woody Allen, Mia Farrow, Jose Ferrer, Mary Steenburgen, Tony Roberts, Julie Hagerty. SMILES OF A SUMMER NIGHT, Woody Allen-style; a quirky, entertaining diversion about sexual byplay among three couples on a summer weekend in the country, circa 1900. Appealing cast (including Farrow, in first film with Woody), exquisite Gordon Willis photography. [PG]▼

Midway (1976) **C-132m.** ★★ D: Jack Smight. Charlton Heston, Henry Fonda, James Coburn, Glenn Ford, Hal Holbrook, Robert Mitchum, Cliff Robertson, Toshiro Mifune, Robert Wagner, Edward Albert, Robert Webber, Ed Nelson, James Shigeta, Monte Markham, Christopher George, Glenn Corbett. Prominent cast acts to reels of stock shots from THIRTY SECONDS OVER TOKYO, antique Japanese war films, and actual wartime footage. Silly soap opera (Heston's ensign son in love with Japanese girl) doesn't help. Still, some of the drama and impact of the great naval battle comes through. *Many* familiar faces in cast: Tom Selleck, Kevin Dobson, Pat Morita, Dabney Coleman, Erik Estrada, Steve Kanaly, etc. Panavision. [PG]▼●◗

Midwinter's Tale, A (1995-British) **98m.** ★★½ D: Kenneth Branagh. Michael Maloney, Richard Briers, Mark Hadfield, Nicholas Farrell, Gerard Horan, John Sessions, Celia Imre, Hetta Charnley, Julia Sawalha, Joan Collins, Jennifer Saunders. Unemployed actor decides to mount a free-form production of *Hamlet* in a remote English town with an all-volunteer cast and crew. Uneven comedy hits its stride in the final portion of the film as the cast and production for the play come together and the parallels between their real lives and their stage lives are revealed. A little too pat, but likable. Original screenplay by Branagh, who tailored many of the parts for these specific actors. Original British title: IN THE BLEAK MIDWINTER. [R]▼●

Mifune (1999-Danish) **C-99m.** ★★½ D: Soren Kragh-Jacobsen. Anders W. Berthelsen, Iben Hjejle, Jesper Asholt, Emil Tarding, Anders Hove, Sofie Gråbol, Paprika Steen, Mette Bratlann. A newly married businessman returns home to take care of his mentally handicapped brother after their father dies. Complications follow when the housekeeper he hires turns out to be an ex-hooker with problems of her own. Filmed according to the spartan cinematic rules of Dogma 95, this has good acting and lovely isolated moments, but not enough to overcome a thin story with few surprises. Mifune, by the way, refers to actor Toshiro. [R]

Mighty, The (1998) **C-100m.** ★★★½ D: Peter Chelsom. Kieran Culkin, Elden Henson, Sharon Stone, Gena Rowlands, Harry Dean Stanton, Gillian Anderson, James Gandolfini, Meat Loaf, Jenifer Lewis. Beautifully realized story of two young misfits who bond together and become, in their hearts and imaginations, invincible as the knights of old. Poetic and heart-rending, with remarkable performances by the youthful leading actors. Screenplay by Charles Leavitt from the novel *Freak the Mighty* by Rodman Philbrick. [PG-13]▼●◗

Mighty Aphrodite (1995) **C-95m.** ★★★ D: Woody Allen. F. Murray Abraham, Woody Allen, Claire Bloom, Helena Bonham Carter, Olympia Dukakis, Michael Rapaport, Mira Sorvino, David Ogden Stiers, Jack Warden, Peter Weller, Steven Randazzo, Donald Symington, Rosemary Murphy. Highly entertaining fluff with Woody as a happily married man whose wife convinces him to adopt a baby; then, years later, he becomes obsessed with learning about (and getting to know) the boy's real mother. Sorvino is sensational in an Oscar-winning, star-making performance as the woman in question. [R] ▼●◗

Mighty Barnum, The (1934) **87m.** ★★★ D: Walter Lang. Wallace Beery, Adolphe Menjou, Virginia Bruce, Rochelle Hudson, Janet Beecher, Herman Bing. Fanciful biography of world-famous showman, with Menjou as his reluctant partner Bailey. More Beery than Barnum.

Mighty Ducks, The (1992) **C-100m.** ★★ D: Stephen Herek. Emilio Estevez, Joss Ackland, Lane Smith, Heidi Kling, Josef Sommer, Joshua Jackson, Elden Ratliff (Hansen), Shaun Weiss, Matt Doherty. Harmless, clichéd Disney yarn of self-centered yuppie lawyer Estevez who's busted for drunk-driving, ordered to do community service, and assigned to coach a ragtag inner-city peewee hockey team. Guess what happens next. (Anaheim-based pro hockey team was formed by Disney in 1993 called . . . you guessed it.) Followed by D2: THE MIGHTY DUCKS, D3: THE MIGHTY DUCKS, an animated series, and a TVM based on that series. [PG]▼●◗

Mighty Joe Young (1949) **94m.** ★★★ D: Ernest B. Schoedsack. Terry Moore, Ben Johnson, Robert Armstrong, Mr. Joseph Young, Frank McHugh. Updating of KING KONG theme has comparable (and Oscar-winning) special effects by Willis O'Brien and Ray Harryhausen, but no matching story line, and Moore is no Fay Wray. Mr. Young is good, though. Last sequence was originally shown with color tints, which have been restored for homevideo and most TV prints. Also shown in computer-colored version. Remade in 1998. ▼●

Mighty Joe Young (1998) **C-114m.** ★★★ D: Ron Underwood. Bill Paxton, Charlize Theron, David Paymer, Regina King, Rade Sherbedgia (Serbedzija), Peter Firth, Linda Purl, Robert Wisdom, Lawrence Pressman,

John Alexander. Entertaining update of the 1949 movie: Theron is raised in the jungle alongside a giant gorilla. In order to protect Joe from poachers, she agrees to bring him to an L.A. animal habitat—but no one understands the big guy as she does. What is more, a bad guy is out to get him, leading to an inevitable rampage. Good fun, earnestly done. Terry Moore (star of the 1949 film) and Ray Harryhausen (who helped animate the original Joe) have a cameo together; so does Dina Merrill, whose husband produced the film. Joe was designed by Rick Baker. [PG]▼●◗

Mighty McGurk, The (1946) **85m.** *½ D: John Waters. Wallace Beery, Dean Stockwell, Dorothy Patrick, Edward Arnold, Aline MacMahon, Cameron Mitchell. Formula Beery vehicle with the star a punchy prizefighter and Stockwell as adorable boy he adopts.

Mighty Morphin Power Rangers: The Movie (1995-U.S.-Japanese) **C-95m.** **½ D: Bryan Spicer. Karan Ashley, Johnny Yong Bosch, Steve Cardenas, Jason David Frank, Amy Jo Johnson, David Yost, Paul Schrier, Jason Narvy, Paul Freeman, Gabrielle Fitzpatrick, Nicholas Bell. The teenage Rangers temporarily lose their powers when primordial bad guy Ivan Ooze reappears after centuries of captivity and attacks their mentor, sending them on a quest for renewed power. Juvenile fantasy/adventure aimed squarely at the huge audience of the same-named TV series . . . and not bad, for what it is. Followed by TURBO: A POWER RANGERS MOVIE, then in 1999 a direct-to-video sequel. [PG] ▼●

Mighty Quinn, The (1989) **C-98m.** **½ D: Carl Schenkel. Denzel Washington, Robert Townsend, James Fox, Mimi Rogers, M. Emmet Walsh, Sheryl Lee Ralph, Art Evans, Esther Rolle, Norman Beaton, Keye Luke. Washington plays the independent-minded police chief of a Caribbean island who's determined to get to the bottom of a murder, even though it apparently involves political sensitivities—and his boyhood pal, a now-notorious character played by Townsend. Colorful locale spices this ordinary tale and makes it a pleasant time-filler. [R]▼●

Mighty Ursus, The (1962-Italian) **C-92m.** ** D: Carlo Campogalliani. Ed Fury, Christina Gajoni, Maria Orfei, Mario Scaccia, Mary Marlon, Luis Prendez. In title role Fury does expected gymnastics, rescuing his woman from marauding natives. Totalscope.

Migrants, The (1974) **C-78m. TVM** D: Tom Gries. Cloris Leachman, Ron Howard, Sissy Spacek, Cindy Williams, Ed Lauter, Lisa Lucas, Mills Watson, Claudia McNeil, Dolph Sweet. Acclaimed Tennessee Williams drama, adapted for TV by Lanford Wilson, using one fictional family's plight as a microcosm for the migratory worker's "harvest of shame" that Edward R. Morrow graphically documented years earlier. Produced on tape. Above average.▼

Mikado, The (1939) **C-90m.** *** D: Victor Schertzinger. Kenny Baker, John Barclay, Martyn Green, Jean Colin, Constance Wills. Baker may not be the ideal Nanki-Poo, but this color film of Gilbert and Sullivan's operetta is still worthwhile, with the marvelous G&S songs intact. ◗

Mike's Murder (1984) **C-109m.** *½ D: James Bridges. Debra Winger, Mark Keyloun, Darrell Larson, Paul Winfield, Brooke Alderson, William Ostrander, Dan Shor. One of the worst movies ever made by a filmmaker of Bridges' stature; after an acquaintance is butchered in a drug deal, Winger decides to investigate for herself. Filmed in 1982, followed by years at the editing table to no avail; Winfield provides only life as jaded record exec. Escapes BOMB rating only because several critics thought highly of it. [R]▼

Mikey and Nicky (1976) **C-116m.** **½ D: Elaine May. Peter Falk, John Cassavetes, Ned Beatty, Rose Arrick, Carol Grace, Joyce Van Patten. Ragged film (in the editing room for several years) improves as it goes along, examining relationship between small-time hoods who were childhood pals, one of whom may be fingering the other for hit-man Beatty. Superb performances by Falk and Cassavetes. [R]▼

Milagro Beanfield War, The (1988) **C-117m.** ***½ D: Robert Redford. Ruben Blades, Richard Bradford, Sonia Braga, Julie Carmen, James Gammon, Melanie Griffith, John Heard, Carlos Riquelme, Daniel Stern, Chick Vennera, Christopher Walken, Freddy Fender, Robert Carricart, M. Emmet Walsh, Trinidad Silva. Spirited, fanciful tale of a rugged individualist (dirt-poor, hard-luck Vennera) who decides to stand up to the big, brash developers who plan to milk his (and his neighbors') New Mexico land for all it's worth. Distilled from John Nichols' sprawling novel by Nichols and David Ward, this film takes a whimsical tone that's positively infectious . . . aided by a top ensemble cast, beautiful scenery, and Dave Grusin's lyrical, Oscar-winning score. [R]▼●

Mildred Pierce (1945) **109m.** ***½ D: Michael Curtiz. Joan Crawford, Jack Carson, Zachary Scott, Eve Arden, Ann Blyth, Bruce Bennett, Lee Patrick, Butterfly McQueen. Crawford won an Oscar as housewife-turned-waitress who finds success in business but loses control of ungrateful daughter Blyth—especially when she finds they're competing for the love of the same man. Solid adaptation (scripted by Ranald MacDougall) of James M. Cain's novel with top supporting cast. Also shown in computer-colored version.▼●

Miles From Home (1988) **C-114m.** *½ D:

Gary Sinise. Richard Gere, Kevin Anderson, Penelope Ann Miller, Laurie Metcalf, John Malkovich, Brian Dennehy, Judith Ivey, Helen Hunt, Terry Kinney. The "Farm of the Year" from 1959 goes bankrupt in 1988; heir Gere burns it down rather than see it taken over by the bank, then takes off on a Midwest spree accompanied by acquiescent brother Anderson. Gere's actions (and performance) are so off-putting that you begin to wonder if he doesn't deserve his fate, which can hardly be the point. Miller and Metcalf put spins on marginal roles. [R]▼●

Milkman, The (1950) **97m.** ** D: Charles T. Barton. Donald O'Connor, Jimmy Durante, Piper Laurie, Joyce Holden, William Conrad, Henry O'Neill, Jess Barker, Frank Nelson. War vet O'Connor's dad owns a dairy; when father refuses to hire him, he takes a job with the rival company, which employs his pal Durante. Mindless comedy, worth watching only for Durante and his irrepressible personality.

Milk Money (1994) **C-102m.** *½ D: Richard Benjamin. Melanie Griffith, Ed Harris, Michael Patrick Carter, Malcolm McDowell, Anne Heche, Casey Siemaszko, Philip Bosco. "Family-values" comedy about a 12-year-old who raises funds to ogle a sexy hooker—who later turns up in his hometown! Not as grubby as it sounds, but still an unlikely candidate to contribute to anyone's Irving G. Thalberg Award chances. McDowell overplays it, if that's possible in this kind of DOA dud, as a mobster who pursues Griffith to the climactic school dance. [PG-13]▼●

Milky Way, The (1936) **89m.** *** D: Leo McCarey. Harold Lloyd, Adolphe Menjou, Verree Teasdale, Helen Mack, William Gargan, George Barbier, Dorothy Wilson, Lionel Stander. Milquetoasty milkman is recruited by scheming fight promoter Menjou after inadvertently knocking out the middleweight champion! Bland but entertaining film is one of Lloyd's best talkies. Remade, almost scene for scene, as THE KID FROM BROOKLYN, with Danny Kaye, but they couldn't top the hilarious ducking scene with Lloyd and matron Marjorie Gateson. Some prints run 83m.▼●

Milky Way, The (1969-French) **C-102m.** ***½ D: Luis Buñuel. Paul Frankeur, Laurent Terzieff, Alain Cuny, Bernard Verley, Michel Piccoli, Pierre Clementi, Georges Marchal, Delphine Seyrig. Two men making religious pilgrimage through France form basis for string of Buñuel "jokes," parables, surrealistic visions. Heretical, funny, haunting, thoroughly enjoyable. [M/PG]▼●

Millennium (1989) **C-108m.** ** D: Michael Anderson. Kris Kristofferson, Cheryl Ladd, Robert Joy, Daniel J. Travanti, Brent Carver, Maury Chaykin, David McIlwraith, Al Waxman, Lloyd Bochner. Intriguing premise features time travelers from the future kidnapping doomed passengers from crashing airliners; suspicious crash investigator Kristofferson becomes involved with Ladd, one of the time travelers. Story slowly falls apart, decaying into sheer corn. Highly regarded sci-fi writer John Varley adapted his own short story "Air Raid," but someone didn't trust the audience's intelligence. [PG-13]▼●◗

Miller's Crossing (1990) **C-115m.** **½ D: Joel Coen. Gabriel Byrne, Albert Finney, Marcia Gay Harden, John Turturro, Jon Polito, J.E. Freeman, Mike Starr, Al Mancini, Michael Jeter, Steve Buscemi. Moody, stylish, and pretentious take on gangster films by the Coen brothers (Joel directed and cowrote with producer-brother Ethan). Byrne plays a black-hearted Irish mobster with a code of ethics known only to himself, and a vow of loyalty to crime kingpin Finney. Dense and dour, it's almost doggedly off-putting at first, but gets more involving as its serpentine story unfolds. Some bravura moments, as you'd expect from the Coens, along with Barry Sonnenfeld's compelling cinematography. Frances McDormand has unbilled bit as a secretary. [R]▼●

Millerson Case, The (1947) **72m.** **½ D: George Archainbaud. Warner Baxter, Nancy Saunders, Barbara Pepper, Clem Bevans, Griff Barnett, Paul Guilfoyle. The Crime Doctor (Baxter) probes the death of a physician and battles typhoid in the backwoods of Virginia in this entry that's par for the series.

Millionaire, The (1931) **80m.** **½ D: John Adolfi. George Arliss, Evalyn Knapp, David Manners, Noah Beery, Florence Arliss, J. Farrell MacDonald, James Cagney. One of Arliss' audience-proof formula films, about a Henry Ford-like industrialist who's forced to retire—but can't stay idle for long. Pleasant fluff, with Cagney memorable in a one-scene appearance as a go-getting insurance salesman. Based on a story by Earl Derr Biggers—with dialogue by Booth Tarkington! Remade as THAT WAY WITH WOMEN.

Millionaire for Christy, A (1951) **91m.** *** D: George Marshall. Fred MacMurray, Eleanor Parker, Richard Carlson, Una Merkel. 1930s-type screwball comedy; fast, unpretentious, very funny, with winning performances by Parker and MacMurray in tale of gold-digging girl out to snare rich husband.

Millionairess, The (1960-British) **C-90m.** **½ D: Anthony Asquith. Sophia Loren, Peter Sellers, Alastair Sim, Vittorio De Sica, Dennis Price. Loren is an heiress who thinks money can buy anything, until she meets Indian doctor Sellers, who won't sell his principles, or his love. Sophia is stunning, but this adaptation of G. B. Shaw's play is heavy-handed comedy. CinemaScope.▼◗

Million Dollar Baby (1941) **102m.** **½ D: Curtis Bernhardt. Priscilla Lane, Jeffrey Lynn, Ronald Reagan, May Robson, Lee Patrick, Helen Westley. The sudden acquisition of a million dollars causes strain between wide-eyed Lane and her boyfriend (Reagan), a poor but proud pianist. Innocuous comedy sparked by Robson's patented performance as gruff but good-hearted millionairess.

Million Dollar Duck, The (1971) **C-92m.** **½ D: Vincent McEveety. Dean Jones, Sandy Duncan, Joe Flynn, Tony Roberts, James Gregory, Lee H. Montgomery. A duck who lays golden eggs spurs predictable twists and turns in this standard Disney comedy. [G]▼

Million Dollar Kid (1944) **65m.** ** D: Wallace Fox. Leo Gorcey, Huntz Hall, Billy Benedict, Al Stone, Bobby Stone, Dave Durand, Gabriel Dell, Louise Currie, Noah Beery, Sr., Iris Adrian. Fair *East Side Kids* entry about a rich kid who's leading a life of crime and taken in by the boys in an attempt to reform him.▼

Million Dollar Legs (1932) **64m.** ***½ D: Edward Cline. W. C. Fields, Jack Oakie, Susan Fleming, Lyda Roberti, Andy Clyde, Ben Turpin, Dickie Moore, Billy Gilbert, Hugh Herbert. Wacky nonsense with Fields as President of Klopstokia, a nutty country entering the Olympics. Oakie is a young American pursuing W. C.'s daughter (Fleming). Joseph Mankiewicz was one of the writers of this little gem.▼

Million Dollar Legs (1939) **65m.** **½ D: Nick Grinde. Betty Grable, Jackie Coogan, Donald O'Connor, Larry (Buster) Crabbe, Peter Lind Hayes, Richard Denning. Title supposedly refers to winning horse, but Grable is star so draw your own conclusions. Pleasant college comedy of school trying to keep on its feet has nothing to do with W. C. Fields film of same name. Look fast for William Holden.▼

Million Dollar Manhunt (1956-British) **79m.** BOMB D: Maclean Rogers. Richard Denning, Carole Mathews, Ronald Adam, Danny Green, Brian Worth, Hugh Moxey. Drab account of American agent Denning on the tail of counterfeiters and $12 million printed in Nazi Germany. Aka ASSIGNMENT REDHEAD.

Million Dollar Mermaid (1952) **C-115m.** **½ D: Mervyn LeRoy. Esther Williams, Victor Mature, Walter Pidgeon, David Brian, Donna Corcoran, Jesse White, Maria Tallchief. Williams does OK as real-life aquatic star Annette Kellerman, alternating her swimming with romancing Mature. Some typically elaborate production numbers by Busby Berkeley.▼●

Million Dollar Mystery (1987) **C-95m.** ** D: Richard Fleischer. Eddie Deezen, Penny Baker, Tom Bosley, Rich Hall, Wendy Sherman, Rick Overton, Mona Lyden, Kevin Pollak. Bosley, in his dying breath, informs customers at a roadside diner that $4 million is hidden nearby—giving them just enough clues to send the rabid group scrambling in the same direction. Shameless rip-off of IT'S A MAD MAD MAD MAD WORLD is directed with more gusto than you'd expect from Fleischer. See how many plugs for Glad Bags (cosponsor, along with De Laurentiis Entertainment Group, of a real-life promotional million-dollar treasure hunt) you can spot. [PG]▼●

Million Dollar Weekend (1948) **72m.** ** D: Gene Raymond. Gene Raymond, Francis Lederer, Stephanie Paull (Osa Massen), Robert Warwick, James Craven. Average mystery yarn with veteran cast. Stockbroker steals firm's money and heads for Hawaii, where complications snowball.▼

Million Eyes of Su-Muru, The (1967) **C-95m.** ** D: Lindsay Shonteff. Frankie Avalon, George Nader, Shirley Eaton, Wilfrid Hyde-White, Klaus Kinski. Tongue-in-cheek tale of murder and women's organization bent on enslaving all of mankind. From a Sax Rohmer story. Techniscope.

Million Pound Note, The SEE: **Man With a Million**

Millions Like Us (1943-British) **103m.** *** D: Frank Launder, Sidney Gilliat. Eric Portman, Patricia Roc, Gordon Jackson, Anne Crawford, Megs Jenkins, Basil Radford, Naunton Wayne, Irene Handl, Brenda Bruce. Memorable depiction of ordinary people coping with war. Roc is an airplane-factory worker during WW2, rooming in nearby hostel with women from varied social classes. Boasts realistic approach sorely missing from SWING SHIFT forty years later.

Million to Juan, A (1993) **C-97m.** **½ D: Paul Rodriguez. Paul Rodriguez, Tony Plana, Bert Rosario, Polly Draper, Jonathan Hernandez, Larry Linville, Victor Rivers, David Rasche, Edward James Olmos, Pepe Serna, Paul Williams, Cheech Marin, Ruben Blades. Poor but honest, much put-upon Rodriguez, widowed with a ten-year-old son, is inexplicably given a check for $1 million. Predictable comedy-fantasy is uplifted by some sweet, touching moments. Based on a Mark Twain story, "The Million Pound Bank Note"; previously filmed as MAN WITH A MILLION. [PG]▼

Million to One, A (1937) **60m.** *½ D: Lynn Shores. Herman Brix (Bruce Bennett), Joan Fontaine, Monte Blue, Kenneth Harlan, Suzanne Kaaren, Reed Howes. Static account of athlete preparing for the Olympic decathlon; a showcase for Brix's abilities—in fact, he competed in the 1932 games as a shot-putter. Fontaine is the society girl who falls for him.▼

Mill on the Floss, The (1937-British) **94m.** ** D: Tim Whelan. Frank Lawton, Victoria Hopper, Fay Compton, Geraldine Fitzgerald, Griffith Jones, Mary Clare, James Mason. Disappointing, dramatically uneven adaptation of George Eliot novel about a feud between a mill owner and solicitor; the latter's crippled son (Lawton) falls for the former's daughter (Fitzgerald), and various complications and tragedies ensue.▼

Mimi (1935-British) **98m.** *½ D: Paul Stein. Gertrude Lawrence, Douglas Fairbanks, Jr., Diana Napier, Harold Warrender, Carol Goodner, Austin Trevor. Lawrence is badly miscast as the tragic heroine in this straight adaptation of *La Boheme,* set in Paris' Latin Quarter, though she does get to perform one song. Incredibly sluggish, even in current 62m. prints.▼

Mimic (1997) **C-105m.** *** D: Guillermo Del Toro. Mira Sorvino, Jeremy Northam, Charles S. Dutton, Alexander Goodwin, Giancarlo Giannini, Josh Brolin, F. Murray Abraham. Entomologist Sorvino creates a non-breeding insect to wipe out a plague of disease-carrying cockroaches. This works, but three years later, the *cure* is getting out of hand. The hybrids bred after all, and have become giants, capable of disguising themselves as their favorite prey: people. Lively, scary sci-fi thriller becomes too conventional in the last third, but until then it's great fun. From a short story by Donald A. Wollheim. [R]▼●◗

Min and Bill (1930) **70m.** **½ D: George Hill. Marie Dressler, Wallace Beery, Dorothy Jordan, Marjorie Rambeau, Frank McGlynn. Sentimental early talkie with unforgettable team of Beery and Dressler as waterfront characters trying to protect Jordan from her alcoholic mother (Rambeau). Dressler won an Academy Award for her performance.▼

Mina Tannenbaum (1994-French) **C-123m.** *** D: Martine Dugowson. Romane Bohringer, Elsa Zylberstein, Florence Thomassin, Jean-Philippe Ecoffey, Nils Tavernier, Stephane Slima, Hugues Quester. Entertaining melodrama about the friendship between two Jewish Parisian girls, an introspective artist and a brash reporter, and its disintegration when they fall in love with the same man. First half plays like a Nora Ephron coming-of-age comedy, while the rest is pure Max Ophuls. Despite the unevenness, the film is buoyed by two great performances from Zylberstein and Bohringer (in the title role). [R]▼

Minbo: Anti-Extortion Woman (1992-Japanese) **C-123m.** *** D: Juzo Itami. Nobuku Miyamoto, Akira Takarada, Masahiro Murata, Yasuo Daichi, Hideji Otaki, Hoboru Mitani, Shiro Ito, Akira Nakao. Wonderful wish-fulfillment comedy with the canny, super-competent (but diminutive) Miyamoto helping hapless hotel managers to confront the most intimidating Yakuza members in Hong Kong. A big hit in Japan, this film also inspired real-life Yakuza to attack writer-director Itami. Aka MINBO: THE GENTLE ART OF JAPANESE EXTORTION.▼

Mind Benders, The (1963-British) **101m.** *** D: Basil Dearden. Dirk Bogarde, Mary Ure, John Clements, Michael Bryant, Wendy Craig, Edward Fox. Top cast in slow-moving but compelling account of experiments in sensory deprivation, with espionage theme worked into plot.

Mind Field (1990-Canadian) **C-92m.** ** D: Jean-Claude Lord. Michael Ironside, Lisa Langlois, Sean McCann, Christopher Plummer, Stefan Wodoslawsky, Harvey Atkin, Eugene Clark. Montreal cop Ironside is plagued by problems on the job, mysterious killings, and strange LSD-like flashbacks connected to CIA researcher Plummer. Complicated, slow movie tries to cover too much ground (including police unions and JFK's assassination), scores few goals. [R]▼●

Mind Games SEE: **Agency**

Mind of Mr. Soames, The (1970-British) **C-95m.** ***½ D: Alan Cooke. Terence Stamp, Robert Vaughn, Nigel Davenport, Christian Roberts. Exceptionally fine sci-fi tale of man who has been in a coma since birth; finally revived, he must be taught thirty years' worth of knowledge in brief span of time. [M/PG]

Mind Snatchers, The SEE: **Happiness Cage, The**

Mindwalk (1991) **C-110m.** ** D: Bernt Capra. Liv Ullmann, Sam Waterston, John Heard, Ione Skye. Unusual ecological talkfest may be the MY DINNER WITH ANDRE of the environmental movement. Mainly a conversation on the sad state of the world among three people (a poet, a physicist, and a politician) roaming a picturesque French isle. Sometimes fascinating; mostly static, pretentious. If you met up with any of these people at a party, you'd be fumbling for the car keys. [PG]▼

Mindwarp: An Infinity of Terror SEE: **Galaxy of Terror**

Mine Own Executioner (1947-British) **108m.** *** D: Anthony Kimmins. Burgess Meredith, Dulcie Gray, Kieron Moore, Christine Norden, Barbara White, John Laurie, Michael Shepley. Engrossing drama about a brilliant, dedicated psychoanalyst (Meredith), who can't seem to sort out his own problems, and his efforts to help a schizophrenic ex-POW (Moore). Perceptive screenplay by Nigel Balchin, from his novel; solid performances all around, and some arresting visual highlights.▼

Miniskirt Mob, The (1968) **C-82m.** *½ D: Maury Dexter. Jeremy Slate, Diane

McBain, Sherry Jackson, Patty McCormack, Ross Hagen, Harry Dean Stanton, Ronnie Rondell. McBain plays leader of female motorcycle gang, even though she looks as if she'd be more comfortable on a Tournament of Roses float. Those who like the title will probably like the film.

Ministry of Fear (1944) **85m.** *** D: Fritz Lang. Ray Milland, Marjorie Reynolds, Carl Esmond, Dan Duryea, Hillary Brooke, Alan Napier, Percy Waram. Atmospheric thriller of wartime London, with Milland framed in complicated espionage plot; good cast, fine touches by director Lang. From the Graham Greene novel.▼

Miniver Story, The (1950) **104m.** **½ D: H. C. Potter. Greer Garson, Walter Pidgeon, John Hodiak, Leo Genn, Cathy O'Donnell, Henry Wilcoxon, Reginald Owen, Peter Finch. Sequel to MRS. MINIVER (filmed this time in England) doesn't work as well, but Garson and Pidgeon have some poignant scenes as family reunited in post-WW2 England. Young James Fox, billed as William, makes his film debut.▼

Minnesota Clay (1965-French-Italian-Spanish) **C-95m.** ** D: Sergio Corbucci. Cameron Mitchell, Georges Riviere, Ethel Rojo, Diana Martin, Anthony Ross. Standard European oater, with Mitchell giving a good performance as gunslinger who escapes prison to find the man who can clear him. He's going blind and faces his enemies aided by a heightened sense of hearing. Widescreen.

Minnie and Moskowitz (1971) **C-114m.** *** D: John Cassavetes. Gena Rowlands, Seymour Cassel, Val Avery, Timothy Carey, Katherine Cassavetes, Elsie Ames. One of Cassavetes' most likable films chronicles manic romance between lonely museum curator (Rowlands) and crazy parking-lot attendant (Cassel). Touching, amusing, and most enjoyable. [PG]▼◗

Minotaur, The (1961-Italian) **C-92m.** *½ D: Silvio Amadio. Bob Mathias, Rosanna Schiaffino, Alberto Lupo, Rik Battaglia. Occasional atmosphere and Schiaffino's appearance still cannot elevate story of mythological hero thwarting attempt of evil queen to subjugate city-dwellers with hideous monster. Totalscope.

Minotaur (1976) SEE: **Land of the Minotaur**

Minus Man, The (1999) **C-113m.** **½ D: Hampton Fancher. Owen Wilson, Janeane Garofalo, Brian Cox, Sheryl Crow, Mercedes Ruehl, Dennis Haysbert, Dwight Yoakam. Serial killer takes up residence in a middle-age suburban couple's spare room and hires on as a fellow postal worker with his landlord. Film's low-budget creepiness, though fairly effective, would have played better years ago before the screen's oversaturation with quiet, sensitive psychotics. Interesting for its sometimes-successful casting against type: comedic Wilson as the killer, the usually acerbic Garofalo as a lonely alcoholic and rocker Crow as a bar-hopper with asthma. [R]▼◗

Minute to Pray, a Second to Die, A (1967-Italian) **C-97m.** *** D: Franco Giraldi. Alex Cord, Arthur Kennedy, Robert Ryan, Mario Brega. Outlaw seeks refuge in Escondido from outlaws, bounty hunters, territorial lawmen, and anyone out to take advantage of his occasional paralytic seizures. Outstanding color photography adds to great atmosphere. Aka OUTLAW GUN. [R]▼

Miracle, The (1959) **C-121m.** **½ D: Irving Rapper. Carroll Baker, Roger Moore, Walter Slezak, Vittorio Gassman, Katina Paxinou, Dennis King, Isobel Elsom. Claptrap vehicle resurrected as glossy, empty spectacle of 1810s Spain, with Baker the would-be nun unsure of her decision, Moore the soldier she romances. Technirama.▼

Miracle, The (1991-British) **C-100m.** *** D: Neil Jordan. Beverly D'Angelo, Donal McCann, Niall Byrne, Lorraine Pilkington, J. G. Devlin. Evocative coming-of-age drama about Byrne and Pilkington, a pair of bright, bored Irish teens who view the world with youthful cynicism, and become intrigued by a beautiful mystery woman (D'Angelo) arriving in town. Soon Byrne is pursuing her romantically, but he has no idea how her presence will affect his life. Collectively well-acted, with intelligent, precise script by Jordan. [R]▼●

Miracle in Milan (1951-Italian) **95m.** ***½ D: Vittorio De Sica. Francesco Golisano, Paolo Stoppa, Emma Gramatica, Guglielmo Barnabo. Toto the Good (Golisano) brings cheer to a dreary village of poor people, aided by the old lady who raised him, who is now in heaven. Bitingly comic condemnation of the manner in which displaced Europeans were treated after WW2.▼●

Miracle in the Rain (1956) **107m.** **½ D: Rudolph Maté. Jane Wyman, Van Johnson, Peggie Castle, Fred Clark, Eileen Heckart, Josephine Hutchinson, Barbara Nichols, William Gargan, Alan King, Arte Johnson. Above-par soaper of two lost souls, Wyman and Johnson, falling in love in N.Y.C. during WW2.

Miracle in the Wilderness (1991) **C-110m. TVM** D: Kevin James Dobson. Kris Kristofferson, Kim Cattrall, John Dennis Johnston, Dennis Oliver, Sheldon Peters Wolfchild, Jonelle Nadine Romero. Old West holiday tale about a kidnapped frontier family which shares the traditional Christmas story with a vengeful Blackfoot chief and his tribe who are heading for Canada (with the U.S. Cavalry in pursuit). Based on Paul Gallico's novella. Made for cable. Average.▼

Miracle Mile (1989) **C-87m.** *½ D: Steve DeJarnatt. Anthony Edwards, Mare Winningham, John Agar, Lou Hancock, Mykel T. Williamson, Kelly Minter, Kurt Fuller, Denise Crosby, Robert Doqui, Danny De La Paz. Good-natured musician who's just gotten to first base with a coffee shop waitress picks up a ringing pay phone and learns that the U.S. has fired a nuclear warhead—which means that the end of the world is about an hour away. Artificial and overwrought from the word go, the film loses all hope of credibility in its final half-hour when illogic really takes over. Credible costars Edwards and Winningham can't do anything with this material. [R]▼●

Miracle of Fatima SEE: **Miracle of Our Lady of Fatima, The**

Miracle of Morgan's Creek, The (1944) **99m.** ★★★★ D: Preston Sturges. Eddie Bracken, Betty Hutton, William Demarest, Diana Lynn, Brian Donlevy, Akim Tamiroff, Porter Hall, Almira Sessions, Jimmy Conlin. Frantic, hilarious comedy of Betty attending all-night party, getting pregnant and forgetting who's the father. Bracken and Demarest have never been better than in this daring wartime farce. Filmed in 1942; sort of remade as ROCK-A-BYE BABY. ▼●

Miracle of Our Lady of Fatima, The (1952) **C-102m.** ★★★ D: John Brahm. Gilbert Roland, Angela Clarke, Frank Silvera, Jay Novello, Sherry Jackson. Thoughtful account of religious miracle witnessed by farm children in 1910s; intelligent script. Retitled: MIRACLE OF FATIMA. ▼●

Miracle of the Bells, The (1948) **120m.** ★½ D: Irving Pichel. Fred MacMurray, Valli, Frank Sinatra, Lee J. Cobb, Charles Meredith. Contrived story of miracle occurring when movie star is laid to rest in coal-mining home town; often ludicrous, despite sincere cast. Screenplay by Ben Hecht and Quentin Reynolds. Also shown in computer-colored version.▼

Miracle of the Hills (1959) **73m.** ★½ D: Paul Landres. Rex Reason, Theona Bryant, Jay North, Gilbert Smith, Tracy Stratford, Gene Roth. Timid little Western of town-running gal who bucks new clergyman. CinemaScope.

Miracle of the White Stallions (1963) **C-117m.** ★½ D: Arthur Hiller. Robert Taylor, Lilli Palmer, Curt Jurgens, Eddie Albert, James Franciscus, John Larch. Long, talky, confusing drama about evacuation of prized Lippizan show-horses from Vienna during WW2. A most un-Disneylike Disney film.▼

Miracle on Main Street (1939) **68m.** ★★ D: Steve Sekely. Margo, Walter Abel, Jane Darwell, Lyle Talbot, William Collier, Sr. Limp drama about depressed carnival dancer Margo, and what happens after she finds an abandoned baby on Christmas Eve. Artistically ambitious B movie that doesn't work.

Miracle on 34th Street (1947) **96m.** ★★★½ D: George Seaton. Maureen O'Hara, John Payne, Edmund Gwenn, Gene Lockhart, Natalie Wood, Porter Hall, William Frawley, Jerome Cowan. Classic Valentine Davies fable of Kris Kringle (Gwenn) working in Macy's, encountering an unbelieving child (Wood), and going on trial to prove he's Santa. Delightful comedy-fantasy won Oscars for Gwenn, Davies, and screenwriter Seaton. Thelma Ritter's auspicious screen debut; an amusing bit for young Jack Albertson, as a postal employee. Remade in 1973 (for TV) and 1994. Also shown in computer-colored version. ▼●◗

Miracle on 34th Street (1973) **C-100m. TVM** D: Fielder Cook. Jane Alexander, David Hartman, Roddy McDowall, Sebastian Cabot, Suzanne Davidson, Jim Backus, Tom Bosley, David Doyle, James Gregory, Roland Winters. Heartwarming humor and old-fashioned whimsy in this TV adaptation of the 1947 Christmas classic. Good cast, but the plot comes off awfully dated. Average.

Miracle on 34th Street (1994) **C-114m.** ★★½ D: Les Mayfield. Richard Attenborough, Elizabeth Perkins, Dylan McDermott, Mara Wilson, Robert Prosky, J. T. Walsh, James Remar, Jane Leeves, Simon Jones, William Windom. Pretty good remake of the 1947 charmer. Attenborough is wonderful as the man who calls himself Kris Kringle, and Wilson is irresistible as the little girl who doesn't believe in Santa. Loses its way whenever it veers from the original script—as in the relationship between Mara's mom (Perkins) and her neighbor/friend (McDermott) . . . and when it manages to keep the adorable youngster offscreen. Tellingly, this version is almost 20 minutes longer than the earlier film. Produced and written by John Hughes. Joss Ackland appears unbilled. [PG]▼●

Miracles (1986) **C-86m.** ★½ D: Jim Kouf. Tom Conti, Teri Garr, Paul Rodriguez, Christopher Lloyd, Adalberto Martinez, Jorge Russek. Conti and Garr, recently divorced, are whisked away to South American hellhole by jewel thief Rodriguez in this clone of ROMANCING THE STONE. The stars do their best, but we've seen it all before, and better. Written by first-time director Kouf. Super Techniscope. [PG]▼

Miracles Still Happen (1974-U.S.-Italian) **C-93m.** ★½ D: Giuseppe Scotese. Susan Penhaligon, Paul Muller, Graziella Galvani, Clyde Peters. Teenager Penhaligon treks through the Amazon alone after surviving a plane crash. Inferior, poorly made programmer, based on a true story. Original running time: 97m.▼

Miracle Woman, The (1931) **90m.** ★★★ D: Frank Capra. Barbara Stanwyck, David

Manners, Sam Hardy, Beryl Mercer, Russell Hopton. Stanwyck plays an evangelist (patterned after Aimee Semple McPherson) whose splashy sermons become big business. Manners is a blind man who falls in love with her. Story contrivances overcome by fine performances, direction, and camerawork (by Joseph Walker).▼

Miracle Worker, The (1962) **107m.** ***½ D: Arthur Penn. Anne Bancroft, Patty Duke, Victor Jory, Inga Swenson, Andrew Prine, Beah Richards, Kathleen Comegys. Austerely beautiful treatment of William Gibson's play about Annie Sullivan (Bancroft), the remarkable woman who accepts the challenge of getting through to blind, deaf Helen Keller (Duke). There is absolutely no sentiment, which only increases the emotional power of the piece. Bancroft and Duke had been playing these parts on Broadway for over a year, but you'd never know it from their spontaneous and totally compelling performances, which earned them both Oscars. Originally staged as a 1957 *Playhouse 90* on TV, also directed by Penn. Remade for TV in 1979 with Duke in the role of Sullivan.▼●

Miracle Worker, The (1979) **C-100m. TVM** D: Paul Aaron. Patty Duke Astin, Melissa Gilbert, Diana Muldaur, Charles Siebert, Anne Seymour, Stanley Wells. Powerful refilming of the William Gibson classic about young Helen Keller's first encounters with Anne Sullivan, who would be her teacher and life-long companion. Having Patty Duke Astin—who won an Oscar as Keller in 1962—play Sullivan was more a novelty than an inspired piece of casting, making this one just a notch below its predecessor. Above average.▼

Miraculous Journey (1948) **C-83m.** *½ D: Peter Stewart (Sam Newfield). Rory Calhoun, Andrew Long, Virginia Grey, George Cleveland. Substandard psychological study of victims of plane crash in jungle.

Mirage (1965) **109m.** *** D: Edward Dmytryk. Gregory Peck, Diane Baker, Walter Matthau, Kevin McCarthy, Jack Weston, Leif Erickson, Walter Abel, George Kennedy. Fine Hitchcock-like thriller, with Peck the victim of amnesia, and everyone else out to get him. Matthau steals film as easygoing private-eye; interesting on-location footage in N.Y.C. Remade as JIGSAW (1968).▼●

Miranda (1948-British) **80m.** **½ D: Ken Annakin. Googie Withers, Glynis Johns, Griffith Jones, John McCallum, David Tomlinson, Margaret Rutherford, Maurice Denham. Cute movie (adapted by Peter Blackmore from his play) about a happily married doctor who's abducted by a mermaid; she agrees to send him back to dry land only if she can accompany him to see what the human world is like. Charming fluff. Amusing to see Johns and Tomlinson together years before they were husband and wife in MARY POPPINS. Title song by Jean Sablon. Followed by a sequel, MAD ABOUT MEN.

Mirror, The (1976-Russian) **C-106m.** ***½ D: Andrei Tarkovsky. Margarita Terekhova, Philip Yankovsky, Ignat Daniltsev, Oleg Yankovsky. Extremely personal, moving tale of life in Russia during WW2. Superbly directed; overall, it works most effectively as an homage to childhood innocence.▼

Mirror Crack'd, The (1980-British) **C-105m.** **½ D: Guy Hamilton. Angela Lansbury, Elizabeth Taylor, Rock Hudson, Kim Novak, Tony Curtis, Edward Fox, Geraldine Chaplin, Wendy Morgan, Charles Gray, Pierce Brosnan. A mild Agatha Christie whodunit made enjoyable by its quartet of 1950s stars, particularly Taylor and Novak, fun as catty rival movie stars. Lansbury is a crisp Miss Marple. Rather flat in theaters, this ought to play better on TV. A highlight: the b&w movie-within-a-movie "Murder at Midnight." [PG]▼●

Mirror Has Two Faces, The (1958-French) **98m.** **½ D: André Cayatte. Michele Morgan, Bourvil, Gerald Oury, Ivan Desny, Elizabeth Manet, Sylvie, Sandra Milo. Morgan is quite good as woman who begins life anew after plastic surgery. Remade in U.S. in 1996.

Mirror Has Two Faces, The (1996) **C-126m.** **½ D: Barbra Streisand. Barbra Streisand, Jeff Bridges, Lauren Bacall, Mimi Rogers, George Segal, Pierce Brosnan, Brenda Vaccaro, Austin Pendleton, Elle Macpherson. A nerdy college prof, smarting from love affairs gone bad, enters into a cerebral relationship with fellow professor Streisand in which sex plays no part. Then she begins to long for something more. A Very Barbra Movie—she even co-wrote the love theme—that deals with self-image and the impact of physical beauty, then undermines its own convictions in a nonsensical climax. Still, entertaining and attractively cast, with Bacall terrific as Streisand's self-absorbed mother. Based on the 1958 French movie. [PG-13]▼●◗

Misadventures of Merlin Jones, The (1964) **C-88m.** *½ D: Robert Stevenson. Tommy Kirk, Annette Funicello, Leon Ames, Stuart Erwin, Alan Hewitt, Connie Gilchrist. Skimpy Disney comedy about college brain (Kirk) and his misadventures with mind-reading and hypnotism. Sequel: THE MONKEY'S UNCLE.▼

Misadventures of Mr. Wilt, The (1989-British) **C-92m.** **½ D: Michael Tuchner. Griff Rhys-Jones, Mel Smith, Alison Steadman, Diana Quick, Jeremy Clyde, Roger Allam. Two stars of the hit British TV series *Alas Smith and Jones* are featured in this silly farce about college lecturer Henry Wilt (Rhys-Jones), who hates his bitchy wife—and becomes the prime suspect when the police think she's been murdered. Smith is the twit of an inspector assigned to the case. Funny—if it hits you in the right mood. Based on Tom Sharpe's best-seller. Original British title: WILT.▼

Mischief (1985) **C-93m.** ** D: Mel Damski. Doug McKeon, Catherine Mary Stewart, Kelly Preston, Chris Nash, D. W. Brown, Jami Gertz, Terry O'Quinn. Amiable but leaden-paced teen movie set in 1950s. Likable cast and vivid period atmosphere are chief assets—but any film that shows a clip from REBEL WITHOUT A CAUSE and then tries to duplicate the scene is asking for trouble. [R]▼●

Misery (1990) **C-107m.** **½ D: Rob Reiner. James Caan, Kathy Bates, Richard Farnsworth, Frances Sternhagen, Lauren Bacall, Graham Jarvis. Stephen King white-knuckler about a successful romance novelist who's nursed back to health after a snowy car crash by his Number One Fan—who turns out to be a serious sicko. Extremely well acted, but the suspense ebbs and flows; there was much more nuance, and more interesting development of the relationship between fan and prisoner, in the novel. Bates won an Oscar for her unforgettable performance. Screenplay by William Goldman; striking cinematography by Barry Sonnenfeld. J. T. Walsh has unbilled cameo as a park ranger. Later adapted as a stage play in London. [R]▼●◗

Misfit Brigade, The (1987-U.S.-British) **C-99m.** ** D: Gordon Hessler. Bruce Davison, David Patrick Kelly, David Carradine, D. W. Moffett, Jay O. Sanders, Keith Szarabajka, Oliver Reed. At once clichéd and lighthearted (!) DIRTY DOZEN variation, about a group of German prisoners who find themselves recruited into the military by the Nazis (who are desperate for fighting men). Aka WHEELS OF TERROR. [R]▼

Misfits, The (1961) **124m.** *** D: John Huston. Clark Gable, Marilyn Monroe, Montgomery Clift, Thelma Ritter, Eli Wallach, James Barton, Estelle Winwood. Unsatisfying but engrossing parable authored by Arthur Miller, involving disillusioned divorcee Monroe and her brooding cowboy friends. Both Monroe's and Gable's last film.▼●

Mishima (1985) **C/B&W-120m.** *** D: Paul Schrader. Ken Ogata. Narration read by Roy Scheider. Ambitious, highly stylized drama about Japan's most controversial post-WW2 author, playwright, actor, director, and militarist, Yukio Mishima, whose passion to merge life and art led to his ritualistic suicide in 1970. Scenes of Mishima's life (shot in black & white) are contrasted with vivid dramatizations (in opulent color) of key fictional works that grappled with his emotional crises. Long, difficult, not always successful, but fascinating. Beautifully photographed by John Bailey, swept along by stunning Philip Glass score. [R]▼●

Miss Annie Rooney (1942) **84m.** ** D: Edwin L. Marin. Shirley Temple, William Gargan, Guy Kibbee, Dickie Moore, Peggy Ryan, Gloria Holden, Selmer Jackson, June Lockhart, Virginia Sale. Moore gives Shirley her first screen kiss in slight tale of girl from wrong side of tracks in love with rich boy. Also shown in computer-colored version. ▼

Miss Europe SEE: **Prix de Beauté**

Miss Evers' Boys (1997) **C-105m. TVM** D: Joseph Sargent. Alfre Woodard, Laurence Fishburne, Craig Sheffer, Joe Morton, Obba Babatunde, E. G. Marshall, Ossie Davis, Thom Gossom, Jr., Von Coulter. Dramatization of a shameful medical experiment kept secret for nearly forty years: the Tuskegee Study, in which the U.S. Public Health Service withheld treatment from a group of African-American men with syphilis. Woodard plays a caring nurse and co-conspirator, until urged by her conscience (four decades later) to tell of the sordid affair to a Senate subcommittee. Adapted by writer Walter Bernstein from the play by David Feldshuh. Made for cable. Above average.▼●

Miss Firecracker (1989) **C-102m.** *** D: Thomas Schlamme. Holly Hunter, Mary Steenburgen, Tim Robbins, Alfre Woodard, Scott Glenn, Ann Wedgeworth, Trey Wilson, Amy Wright, Bert Remsen. Beth Henley's Off-Broadway play, *The Miss Firecracker Contest,* becomes a most enjoyable movie, with a peerless Hunter recreating her stage role. In a Mississippi hamlet, lonely, pitiful (and hilarious) Hunter yearns for love and self-esteem. Cast is first-rate in this sweet-natured comedy-drama, scripted by Henley; reminiscent of 1930s screwball films. Director Schlamme's feature debut; that's his real-life wife, Christine Lahti, as a neighbor (holding their own newborn baby!). [PG]▼●

Miss Grant Takes Richmond (1949) **87m.** **½ D: Lloyd Bacon. Lucille Ball, William Holden, Janis Carter, James Gleason, Frank McHugh. Ball is wacky secretary innocently involved with crooks; she's the whole show.▼

Missiles From Hell (1958-British) **72m.** ** D: Vernon Sewell. Michael Rennie, Patricia Medina, Milly Vitale, David Knight, Christopher Lee. British work with Polish partisans during WW2 to obtain projectile weapon held by Nazis; choppy editing.

Missile to the Moon (1959) **78m.** *½ D: Richard Cunha. Richard Travis, Cathy Downs, K.T. Stevens, Tommy Cook. Preposterous low-budget sci-fi about lunar expedition finding sinister female presiding over race of moon-women. Lots of laughs, for all the wrong reasons. Remake of CAT WOMEN OF THE MOON (ROCKET TO THE MOON).▼

Missing (1982) **C-122m.** ***½ D: Constantin Costa-Gavras. Jack Lemmon, Sissy Spacek, Melanie Mayron, John Shea, Charles Cioffi, David Clennon, Joe Regalbuto, Richard Venture, Janice Rule. A carefully manipulated drama that works, because of Costa-Gavras' convincing direction, and Lemmon's emphatic performance as a stiff-backed father who comes to a politically volatile Latin American country in search of his missing son—unable and unwilling to believe that American representatives there might not be telling him the truth. Based on the true experiences of Ed Horman; Costa-Gavras and Donald Stewart earned Oscars for their screenplay adaptation. [PG]▼●

Missing Corpse, The (1945) **62m.** *½ D: Albert Herman. J. Edward Bromberg, Isabel Randolph, Frank Jenks, Eric Sinclair, Paul Guilfoyle. Slight, silly comedy-melodrama in which newspaper publisher Bromberg finds himself implicated in the murder of a slimy rival.▼

Missing Guest, The (1938) **68m.** *½ D: John Rawlins. Paul Kelly, Constance Moore, William Lundigan, Edwin Stanley, Selmer Jackson, Billy Wayne. As in many 1930s B melodramas, a newspaper reporter (named "Scoop," no less) is on hand when murders are being committed, this time in a haunted house. Routine. Filmed before as SECRET OF THE BLUE ROOM, later as MURDER IN THE BLUE ROOM.

Missing in Action (1984) **C-101m.** ** D: Joseph Zito. Chuck Norris, M. Emmet Walsh, David Tress, Lenore Kasdorf, James Hong. Colonel Norris, an ex-POW in Vietnam, returns to Asia to liberate American prisoners. A simplistic, revisionist fantasy-actioner, in the mold of UNCOMMON VALOR and RAMBO: FIRST BLOOD PART 2. Followed by a prequel. [R]▼●

Missing in Action 2—The Beginning (1985) **C-96m.** *½ D: Lance Hool. Chuck Norris, Soon-Teck Oh, Steven Williams, Bennett Ohta, Cosie Costa. In this limp prequel to you-know-what, Norris escapes from a POW camp in Vietnam. For Norris lovers only. Followed by BRADDOCK: MISSING IN ACTION III. [R] ▼●

Missing Juror, The (1944) **66m.** *** D: Oscar (Budd) Boetticher. Jim Bannon, Janis Carter, George Macready, Jean Stevens, Joseph Crehan, Carole Mathews. Brisk, engrossing drama of unknown killer taking revenge on jury that sent innocent man to his death; low budget, but quite good.

Missing Pieces (1983) **C-96m. TVM** D: Mike Hodges. Elizabeth Montgomery, Louanne, John Reilly, Ron Karabatsos, Robin Gammell, Julius Harris. Montgomery turns private eye to track down the killers of her reporter husband in this engaging thriller which director Hodges adapted from Karl Alexander's novel *A Private Investigation*. Karabatsos nearly steals the film from her as the world-weary detective for whom she goes to work. Above average.▼

Missing Pieces (1996) **C-93m.** ** D: Leonard Stern. Eric Idle, Robert Wuhl, Lauren Hutton, Richard Belzer, Bob Gunton, Bernie Kopell, James Hong. Silly slapstick farce about two pals who try to solve the riddle of a mysterious inheritance that's made them a target for some deadly criminals. Amiable enough, but the gags are hit-or-miss. Filmed in 1990, never released theatrically in the U.S. [PG]▼●

Mission, The (1986-British) **C-125m.** **½ D: Roland Joffé. Robert De Niro, Jeremy Irons, Ray McAnally, Aidan Quinn, Cherie Lunghi, Ronald Pickup, Chuck Low, Liam Neeson, Daniel Berrigan. Productive (and profitable) Jesuit mission in the jungles of Brazil is threatened by greedy merchants and political factions within the church, in the late 18th century. Magnificent-looking film (Chris Menges' cinematography won an Oscar), rich in imagery, goes on so long—to such an inevitable conclusion—that its dramatic power is drained. Literate, high-minded screenplay by Robert Bolt; fine performances by Irons and De Niro. J-D-C Scope. [PG] ▼●

Missionary, The (1982-British) **C-90m.** ** D: Richard Loncraine. Michael Palin, Maggie Smith, Phoebe Nicholls, Trevor Howard, Denholm Elliott, Michael Hordern, Graham Crowden. Fans of Monty Python's Palin may be surprised by this mild comedy, which he also wrote and coproduced. Returning from Africa, young man of the cloth is recruited to run a home for fallen women ("Women who've tripped?") and quickly finds himself the recipient of, uh, fringe benefits. Great supporting cast, gorgeous locations, beautiful cinematography (by Peter Hannan) overwhelm modest picture. Panavision. [R]▼●

Mission Batangas (1969) **C-100m.** *½ D: Keith Larsen. Dennis Weaver, Vera Miles, Keith Larsen, Vic Diaz. Callous American flyer in early WW2 eventually becomes a hero; poor excuse for a war movie.▼●

Mission Hill (1982) **C-90m.** ***½ D: Robert Jones. Brian Burke, Alice Barrett, Barbara Orson, Robert Kerman, Daniel Silver, Nan Mulleneaux, John Mahoney. Solid, uncompromising drama of working-class dreams and disappointments, centering on aspiring singer Barrett and her troublesome teenage brother (Burke). Sensitively directed; filmed in Boston.

Mission: Impossible (1996) **C-110m.** **½ D: Brian De Palma. Tom Cruise, Jon Voight, Emmanuelle Béart, Henry Czerny, Jean Reno, Ving Rhames, Kristin Scott Thomas, Vanessa Redgrave. Slick update of the vintage TV spy series about a crack undercover unit is full of high-tech hijinks, as ''team leader'' Cruise tries to learn what went wrong on a crucial mission in Prague—and discover who set them up. Energy wanes at several junctions, only to be revved up again for a train-and-helicopter chase finale. Lalo Schifrin's memorable TV theme is reused here, at a much higher decibel level. Cruise coexecutive-produced. Emilio Estevez appears unbilled. Followed by a sequel. Panavision. [PG-13] ▼●◗

Mission: Impossible 2 (2000) **C-126m.** ** D: John Woo. Tom Cruise, Thandie Newton, Dougray Scott, Ving Rhames, Richard Roxburgh, John Polson, Brendan Gleeson, Radé Sherbedgia. Cruise is called into action in Sydney when a ruthless renegade spy (Scott) captures a virus and its antidote and murders its creator. Cruise looks great, performs nifty martial-arts stunts and engages in hair-raising car and motorcycle chases, but there isn't a character to care about, or a story worth two hours' time; after a while it's simply boring, in spite of Woo's flamboyant treatment (and a script by Robert Towne). Anthony Hopkins appears unbilled. Panavision. [PG-13]

Mission Mars (1968) **C-95m.** *½ D: Nick Webster. Darren McGavin, Nick Adams, George DeVries, Heather Hewitt, Michael DeBeausset, Shirley Parker. Typical astronaut drama has three U.S. space men battling unseen forces while on a mission.▼

Mission of the Shark (1991) **C-100m. TVM** D: Robert Iscove. Stacy Keach, Richard Thomas, Don Harvey, Bob Gunton, Steve Landesburg, Carrie Snodgress, Andrew Prine, Stacy Keach, Sr. True WW2 drama about a long-hushed-up naval scandal, torpedoing of the U.S.S. *Indianapolis* (which had just delivered parts of the A-bomb to be dropped on Hiroshima) and the loss of many American sailors in shark-infested waters. Keach (Jr.) is Charles McVay, whose career was ruined; Keach (Sr.) is his admiral father. Most of the harrowing action takes place in the water. Written by Alan Sharp. Above average.▼

Mission Over Korea (1953) **85m.** *½ D: Fred F. Sears. John Hodiak, John Derek, Maureen O'Sullivan, Audrey Totter. Substandard Korean War tale.

Mission Stardust (1967-W. German-Italian-Spanish) **C-95m.** *½ D: Primo Zeglio. Essy Persson, Lang Jeffries, John Karelsen, Pinkas Braun, Luis Davila. Space expedition from Earth lands on Moon and encounters alien space ship whose beings are suffering from a mysterious disease. Based on first of internationally popular *Perry Rhodan* series of novels, but worthless nonetheless. Techniscope. [G]▼

Mission to Mars (2000) **C-112m.** ** D: Brian De Palma. Gary Sinise, Tim Robbins, Don Cheadle, Connie Nielsen, Jerry O'Connell, Kim Delaney, Elise Neal. Stupefyingly dull drama about a pioneering voyage to Mars in the year 2020, marked by mishap, tragedy, and some mind-blowing cosmic discoveries. Film takes a matter-of-fact approach to space travel that soon becomes deadening, with a spell-it-all-out climax for those who still don't get 2001: A SPACE ODYSSEY. There is, however, an ingenious bit of product placement for Dr Pepper. Armin Mueller-Stahl appears unbilled. Panavision. [R]▼●◗

Mission to Moscow (1943) **123m.** ***½ D: Michael Curtiz. Walter Huston, Ann Harding, Oscar Homolka, George Tobias, Gene Lockhart, Frieda Inescort, Eleanor Parker. Fascinating propaganda of real-life ambassador Joseph Davies (played by Huston) in then-peaceful Russia. Well-done, giving interesting insights to American concepts of USSR at the time. Davies himself introduces the film.

Mississippi (1935) **73m.** ***½ D: A. Edward Sutherland. Bing Crosby, W. C. Fields, Joan Bennett, Queenie Smith, Gail Patrick, Claude Gillingwater. Fine cast in musicomedy of riverboat captain Fields and singer Crosby, with Rodgers-Hart score including ''It's Easy To Remember But So Hard to Forget.'' Unforgettable poker game with Fields. Based on Booth Tarkington's ''Magnolia,'' filmed before as THE FIGHTING COWARD. Look quickly for Ann Sheridan.

Mississippi Blues (1983) **C-96m.** *** D: Bertrand Tavernier, Robert Parrish. Easygoing documentary from American Parrish and Frenchman Tavernier about the American South—its country folk, its landscape, its customs and, most wonderfully, its music.

Mississippi Burning (1988) **C-125m.** *** D: Alan Parker. Gene Hackman, Willem Dafoe, Frances McDormand, Brad Dourif, R. Lee Ermey, Gailard Sartain, Stephen Tobolowsky, Michael Rooker, Pruitt Taylor Vince, Park Overall. Two FBI agents—one a tight-jawed, by-the-book type, the other an experienced Southern lawman who knows how to handle people—head the government investigation into the disappearance of three civil rights workers in Mississippi during the summer of 1964. Vivid re-creation of the period and setting helps carry a less-than-perfect script (inspired by real-life events); Hackman gives a dynamic performance as the former small-town sheriff who figures out how to crack the case. Peter Biziou's cinematography won an Oscar. [R]▼●◗

Mississippi Gambler (1953) **C-98m.** **½ D. Rudolph Maté. Tyrone Power, Piper Laurie, Julia (Julie) Adams, John McIntire, Dennis Weaver. Power is title figure with ambitions of establishing a gambling business in New Orleans.

Mississippi Masala (1992) **C-118m.** **½

D: Mira Nair. Denzel Washington, Sarita Choudhury, Roshan Seth, Sharmila Tagore, Charles S. Dutton, Joe Seneca, Ranjit Chowdhry. Affecting, leisurely paced story of interracial romance between Washington and Choudhury and the problems it causes their respective communities in Greenwood, Mississippi. Starts out fine, with lively characters and interesting observations of a transplanted Indian lifestyle in the Deep South, then bogs down in standard—and extenuated—melodrama. Good performances by Washington (as always) and especially by Seth as Choudhury's proud lawyer father who wants to return home to Uganda. "Masala," by the way, is a collection of hot and colorful spices. Director Nair also appears as a gossipmonger. [R]▼●

Mississippi Mermaid (1969-French-Italian) **C-123m.** *** D: François Truffaut. Jean-Paul Belmondo, Catherine Deneuve, Michel Bouquet, Nelly Borgeaud. One of the director's few flops, but any film with Belmondo-Deneuve-Truffaut combo is of interest; story concerns tobacco planter whose mail-order bride turns out to be Deneuve. Always buy brand names. Originally shown in the U.S. at 110m. Dyaliscope. [PG]▼●

Miss Julie (1950-Swedish) **87m.** *** D: Alf Sjoberg. Anita Bjork, Ulf Palme, Marta Dorff, Anders Henrikson. Masterful adaptation of August Strindberg's tragic play about the love affair between an aristocratic young woman and a commoner. Superbly acted and photographed, with imaginative use of flashbacks. A milestone in Swedish cinema. Remade in 1999.▼

Miss Julie (1999-British-U.S.) **C-103m.** **½ D: Mike Figgis. Saffron Burrows, Peter Mullan, Maria Doyle Kennedy. Pungent adaptation of August Strindberg's fiery 19th-century play about the mistress of a household who toys with the affections of her footman—who in turn plays sexual games with her. Well acted, vigorously filmed, but awfully dismal. [R]▼

Miss Mary (1986-Argentine) **C-100m.** **½ D: Maria Luisa Bemberg. Julie Christie, Nacha Guevara, Luisina Brando, Iris Marga, Eduardo Pavlovsky, Gerardo Romano. Proper, prim British governness Christie arrives in Argentina in 1938, to look after the children in a proper, prim, upper-class family. A few nice touches but mostly forgettable tale of unreleased passion and emerging sexuality. An offbeat role for Christie.▼

Missouri Breaks, The (1976) **C-126m.** BOMB D: Arthur Penn. Marlon Brando, Jack Nicholson, Kathleen Lloyd, Randy Quaid, Frederic Forrest, Harry Dean Stanton. Dynamite star combo in hired gun vs. horse thief confrontation—all for naught. Jumbled, excessively violent pseudo-event; a great director's worst film and one of the worst "big" movies ever made. [PG]▼●

Missouri Traveler, The (1958) **C-104m.** **½ D: Jerry Hopper. Brandon de Wilde, Lee Marvin, Gary Merrill, Mary Hosford, Paul Ford. Folksy, minor account of orphaned youth (de Wilde) finding new roots in Southern country town in 1910s; earnest but predictable.▼

Miss Pinkerton (1932) **66m.** ** D: Lloyd Bacon. Joan Blondell, George Brent, John Wray, Ruth Hall, C. Henry Gordon, Elizabeth Patterson, Holmes Herbert. Nurse Blondell has sixth sense for mysteries, decides to go after one in easy-to-take story.

Miss Robin Crusoe (1954) **C-75m.** *½ D: Eugene Frenke. Amanda Blake, George Nader, Rosalind Hayes. Female version of Robinson Crusoe; nothing added, a lot to be desired.

Miss Robin Hood (1952-British) **78m.** ** D: John Guillermin. Margaret Rutherford, Richard Hearne, Edward Lexy, Frances Rowe. OK mixture of fantasy and farce, Rutherford an elderly nut seeking retrieval of family whiskey formula; Hearne is meek girl's-magazine writer aiding her.

Miss Rose White (1992) **C-100m. TVM** D: Joseph Sargent. Kyra Sedgwick, Amanda Plummer, Maximilian Schell, Maureen Stapleton, Milton Selzer, Penny Fuller. 1940s N.Y. career woman who has hidden her Jewishness comes to grips with her Polish immigrant sister, long thought to have died in the Holocaust. Well-acted but slow-moving adaptation by Anna Sandor of Barbara Lebow's 1987 Off-Broadway play, *A Shayna Maidel*. Above average.▼

Miss Sadie Thompson (1953) **C-91m.** *** D: Curtis Bernhardt. Rita Hayworth, Jose Ferrer, Aldo Ray, Russell Collins, Charles Bronson. Rita gives a provocative performance in musical of Somerset Maugham's RAIN, previously made as SADIE THOMPSON and DIRTY GERTIE FROM HARLEM, U.S.A. Originally in 3-D. ▼●

Miss Susie Slagle's (1945) **88m.** ** D: John Berry. Veronica Lake, Sonny Tufts, Joan Caulfield, Lillian Gish, Ray Collins, Billy DeWolfe, Lloyd Bridges. Mild tale of turn-of-the-century boarding house for aspiring doctors and nurses.

Miss Tatlock's Millions (1948) **101m.** **½ D: Richard Haydn. John Lund, Wanda Hendrix, Barry Fitzgerald, Monty Woolley, Robert Stack, Ilka Chase, Dorothy Stickney. Original comedy of Hollywood stuntman Lund hired to masquerade as a wealthy nitwit; offbeat, to say the least. Haydn, billed as "Richard Rancyd," appears as a lawyer; watch for cameos by Ray Milland and director Mitchell Leisen.▼

Mister Buddwing (1966) **100m.** ** D: Delbert Mann. James Garner, Jean Simmons, Suzanne Pleshette, Angela Lansbury,

Katharine Ross, Raymond St. Jacques, Nichelle Nichols. Misfire; over-familiar amnesia plot with Garner trying to fill in his past, meeting assorted women who might have been part of his prior life.

Mister Cory (1957) **C-92m.** **½ D: Blake Edwards. Tony Curtis, Charles Bickford, Martha Hyer, Kathryn Grant (Crosby). Curtis does OK as poor-boy-turned-rich-gambler who returns to home town to show off his wealth. CinemaScope.

Mister Drake's Duck (1950-British) **76m.** *** D: Val Guest. Douglas Fairbanks, Jr., Yolande Donlan, Howard Marion-Crawford, Reginald Beckwith. American newlyweds Fairbanks and Donlan buy a small English farm, then run into maddening military bureaucracy when one—but *which* one?—of their 60 ducks lays uranium eggs. Mild but diverting spoof of post-war red tape, with good performances.▼

Mister 880 (1950) **90m.** *** D: Edmund Goulding. Dorothy McGuire, Burt Lancaster, Edmund Gwenn, Millard Mitchell, Minor Watson. Easygoing comedy, with Gwenn an elderly N.Y.C. counterfeiter tracked down by federal agent Lancaster. Script by Robert Riskin, based on a true story.

Mister Frost (1990-French-British) **C-92m.** ** D: Philip Setbon. Jeff Goldblum, Alan Bates, Kathy Baker, Jean-Pierre Cassel, Daniel Gelin, Francois Negret, Maxime Leroux, Vincent Schiavelli, Catherine Allegret, Charley Boorman. Goldblum is blithe, cheerful serial killer who tells psychiatrist Baker that he's really the Devil, something ex-cop Bates already believes. It all has to do with Lucifer's annoyance over lack of belief in him. Goldblum is clearly having a great time, but you're not likely to. [R]▼●

Mister Johnson (1991) **C-101m.** **½ D: Bruce Beresford. Pierce Brosnan, Edward Woodward, Maynard Eziashi, Beatie Edney, Denis Quilley, Nick Reding. Africa, 1923: an ambitious, educated (and larcenous) black man who works for the local British magistrate continually gets into trouble by being too smart for his own good. Handsome, well-made, well-acted film still leaves one wanting to know more about Mister Johnson and what makes him tick. Based on a novel by Joyce Cary. [PG-13]▼●◗

Mister Moses (1965-British) **C-113m.** **½ D: Ronald Neame. Robert Mitchum, Carroll Baker, Ian Bannen, Alexander Knox, Raymond St. Jacques, Reginald Beckwith. Malarkey of rugged Mitchum and virtuous Baker leading African native tribe to their new homeland. Panavision.

Mister Roberts (1955) **C-123m.** **** D: John Ford, Mervyn LeRoy. Henry Fonda, James Cagney, William Powell, Jack Lemmon, Betsy Palmer, Ward Bond, Nick Adams, Philip Carey, Harry Carey, Jr., Ken Curtis, Martin Milner, Jack Pennick, Perry Lopez, Pat Wayne. Superb comedy-drama with Fonda recreating his favorite stage role as restless officer on WW2 cargo ship who yearns for combat action but has to contend with an irascible and eccentric captain (Cagney) instead. Fonda, Cagney, Powell (in his last screen appearance) as a philosophical doctor, and Lemmon (in an Oscar-winning performance) as the irrepressible Ensign Pulver, are all terrific. Thomas Heggen and Joshua Logan's Broadway hit was adapted for film by Logan and Frank Nugent. LeRoy replaced Ford as director sometime during production . . . but it certainly doesn't show. Sequel: ENSIGN PULVER. CinemaScope.▼●◗

Mister Scoutmaster (1953) **87m.** *** D: Henry Levin. Clifton Webb, Edmund Gwenn, George Winslow, Frances Dee, Veda Ann Borg. Child-hater Webb becomes scoutmaster in this airy film which will appeal mainly to kids.

Mister Superinvisible (1973-Italian-German-Spanish) **C-91m.** **½ D: Anthony M. Dawson (Antonio Margheriti). Dean Jones, Ingeborg Schoener, Gastone Moschin, Peter Carsten. Engaging comedy made in Geneva has American researcher Jones becoming invisible as he seeks a cure for the common cold. Good for kids, okay for grownups. Techniscope. [G]▼

Mister Universe (1951) **89m.** *½ D: Joseph Lerner. Jack Carson, Janis Paige, Vincent Edwards, Bert Lahr, Robert Alda. Quickie comedy with good cast wasted on bad material; young Edwards plays wrestler promoted by Carson.

Mister V SEE: **Pimpernel Smith**

Mistress (1991) **C-109m.** ** D: Barry Primus. Robert Wuhl, Martin Landau, Jace Alexander, Robert De Niro, Danny Aiello, Eli Wallach, Laurie Metcalf, Sheryl Lee Ralph, Jean Smart, Tuesday Knight, Christopher Walken, Ernest Borgnine, Stefan Gierasch, Roberta Wallach. Hollywood comedy-drama about a washed-up writer (Wuhl) who gets a chance to try to realize his dream—thanks to a has-been producer (Landau, who's marvelous). Plot concerns rounding up the money—and placating the money-men's mistresses. Paper-thin story has several choice moments, but never builds to a satisfying result. Veteran actor Primus' feature directing debut; De Niro coproduced. [R]▼●

Mistrial (1997) **C-105m. TVM** D: Heywood Gould. Bill Pullman, Robert Loggia, Blair Underwood, Roma Maffia, Josef Sommer, Leo Burmester, James Rebhorn, Jon Seda, Kate Burton. Cop Pullman goes bonkers when the perp who gunned down his two fellow officers is set free on a technicality and holds the courtroom hostage while conducting his own second trial. Taut but talky vigilante drama, written by director

Gould, executive-produced by Renny Harlin and then-wife Geena Davis. Made for cable. Average.▼

Misty (1961) **C-92m.** *** D: James B. Clark. David Ladd, Pam Smith, Arthur O'Connell, Anne Seymour. Marguerite Henry's popular children's book is nicely realized, with Ladd and Smith as children on island off Virginia coast who fall in love with a wild horse. CinemaScope.▼●

Misunderstood (1984) **C-91m.** **½ D: Jerry Schatzberg. Gene Hackman, Henry Thomas, Rip Torn, Huckleberry Fox, Maureen Kerwin, Susan Anspach. Boy cries out for the love of his father, who's too busy (and too consumed by the loss of his wife) to understand how much the boy needs his attention—and affection. Extremely well acted but emotionally uneven drama. Filmed in Tunisia in 1982. [PG]▼

Mitchell (1975) **C-96m.** **½ D: Andrew V. McLaglen. Joe Don Baker, Martin Balsam, Linda Evans, John Saxon, Merlin Olsen, Morgan Paull. Baker plays tough cop whose singleminded pursuit of drug ring leads to expected action and violence; slick handling of typical action fodder. [R]▼

Mi Vida Loca (My Crazy Life) (1994) **C-92m.** *** D: Allison Anders. Angel Aviles, Seidy Lopez, Jacob Vargas, Marlo Marron, Jessie Borrego, Magali Alvarado, Julian Reyes, Salma Hayek. Powerful look at hopes and realities of Latina gang girls in L.A.'s Echo Park area. Episodic structure takes some getting used to (as do some of the performances), but writer-director Anders ultimately succeeds in capturing the frustrations of the characters' world and the cycle of social rituals and violence affecting them daily.▼

Mixed Blood (1985-French) **C-97m.** *½ D: Paul Morrissey. Marilia Pera, Richard Ulacia, Linda Kerridge, Geraldine Smith. Wildly overrated black comedy set in the "alphabet city" district of East Greenwich Village where Brazilian crime matriarch Pera has run-in with rival gang's young punks. Leading man Ulacia's acting is embarrassing, while director Morrissey's tongue-in-cheek violence is strictly amateur night. ▼

Mixed Company (1974) **C-109m.** **½ D: Melville Shavelson. Barbara Harris, Joseph Bologna, Tom Bosley, Lisa Gerritsen, Dorothy Shay. Less than heartwarming but still entertaining comedy of losing basketball coach Bologna coping with wife Harris' adopting orphans of mixed ethnic backgrounds. [PG]

Mixed Nuts (1994) **C-97m.** *½ D: Nora Ephron. Steve Martin, Madeline Kahn, Rita Wilson, Robert Klein, Anthony LaPaglia, Juliette Lewis, Rob Reiner, Adam Sandler, Liev Schreiber, Joely Fisher, Parker Posey, Jon Stewart, Haley Joel Osment. Genuinely strange black comedy (or is it black farce?) about the genially bumbling staff of a suicide helpline in Venice, California, and their misadventures on Christmas Eve. Occasional laughs sputter through the haze, but this oddity never really finds its comic center. Written by Ephron and her sister Delia, based on a 1982 French film, LE PERE NOEL EST UNE ORDURE. Garry Shandling and Steven Wright appear unbilled. [PG-13]▼●

Mix Me a Person (1962-British) **116m.** *½ D: Leslie Norman. Anne Baxter, Donald Sinden, Adam Faith, Jack MacGowran, Topsy Jane, Walter Brown. Unexceptional drama of psychiatrist Baxter proving teenager Faith innocent of murdering a policeman.

Moana (1925) **85m.** ***½ D: Robert Flaherty. Ta'avale, Fa'amgase, Tu'ugaita, Moana, Pe'a. Flaherty's follow-up to NANOOK OF THE NORTH is at once a realistic yet poetic look at life in the South Seas, focusing on a young Polynesian (Moana) and his family. Filmed over a two-year period on the island of Savai'i, in the Somoas. A classic, influential film (although not as highly regarded as NANOOK or LOUISIANA STORY).▼●

Mob, The (1951) **87m.** ** D: Robert Parrish. Broderick Crawford, Betty Buehler, Richard Kiley, Otto Hulett, Neville Brand, Ernest Borgnine, John Marley, Charles Bronson. Study of lawman cracking waterfront gang syndicate; Crawford is good but script is second-rate. Interesting cast.

Mo' Better Blues (1990) **C-127m.** ** D: Spike Lee. Denzel Washington, Spike Lee, Wesley Snipes, Giancarlo Esposito, Robin Harris, Joie Lee, Bill Nunn, John Turturro, Dick Anthony Williams, Cynda Williams, Nicholas Turturro, Samuel L. Jackson, Ruben Blades, Abbey Lincoln, Tracy Camilla Johns, Joe Seneca. Backstage look at a self-centered jazz trumpeter who manages to keep everyone at arm's length—including the two ladies in his life. Colorful, musically alive, with some good vignettes from members of Lee's stock company, but it goes on forever—with barely enough story to keep it afloat. Branford Marsalis' Quartet with Terence Blanchard is featured on the soundtrack; music score by Bill Lee (Spike's father). [R]▼●

Mobsters (1991) **C-104m.** ** D: Michael Karbelnikoff. Christian Slater, Patrick Dempsey, Costas Mandylor, Richard Grieco, F. Murray Abraham, Michael Gambon, Lara Flynn Boyle, Anthony Quinn, Christopher Penn, Nicholas Sadler. What promised to be YOUNG TOMMY GUNS turns out to be simply boring: a fanciful rehash of the Prohibition Era, with youthful actors as Lucky Luciano, Frank Costello, Bugsy Siegel, and Meyer Lansky. Long, convoluted, and unrewarding. Only distinction: Richard Sylbert's handsome production design. [R]▼●

Mob Town (1941) **70m.** *½ D: William

Nigh. Billy Halop, Huntz Hall, Gabriel Dell, Bernard Punsly, Dick Foran, Anne Gwynne, Darryl Hickman, Samuel S. Hinds. Cop Foran tries to reform Halop after his gangster brother is sent to the death house, but Halop and his gang have other ideas. Insubstantial *Little Tough Guys* entry.

Moby Dick (1930) **75m.** **½ D: Lloyd Bacon. John Barrymore, Joan Bennett, Walter Long, Nigel de Brulier, Noble Johnson, Virginia Sale. Barrymore is a vivid Captain Ahab, though film is more Hollywood than Melville. Pointless love story added to original narrative, as in Barrymore's earlier silent-film version, THE SEA BEAST. Remade in 1956.

Moby Dick (1956) **C-116m.** *** D: John Huston. Gregory Peck, Richard Basehart, Friedrich Ledebur, Leo Genn, Orson Welles, James Robertson Justice, Harry Andrews, Bernard Miles, Royal Dano. Moody version of Herman Melville sea classic, with Peck lending a deranged dignity to the role of Captain Ahab. Fine scenes throughout, including second-unit camera work by the great Freddie Young. Screenplay by Huston and Ray Bradbury. Remade in 1998 as a TV miniseries with Patrick Stewart. ▼●

Model and the Marriage Broker, The (1951) **103m.** *** D: George Cukor. Jeanne Crain, Scott Brady, Thelma Ritter, Zero Mostel, Michael O'Shea, Frank Fontaine, Nancy Kulp. Poignant, perceptive little comedy-drama chronicling the affairs of marriage broker Ritter, who plays Cupid for model Crain and X-ray technician Brady. However, most of her clients don't have pretty faces: they're shy, lonely, desperate for companionship. A winner.

Model For Murder (1958-British) **75m.** ** D: Terry Bishop. Keith Andes, Hazel Court, Jean Aubrey, Michael Gough. Andes is American in England seeking late brother's girlfriend, becoming involved in jewel robbery. Adequate yarn.

Model Shop (1969-French) **C-95m.** *** D: Jacques Demy. Anouk Aimée, Gary Lockwood, Alexandra Hay, Carole Cole, Severn Darden, Tom Fielding. Twenty-four hours in life of disenchanted young architect (Lockwood), his affair with recently abandoned fashion model (Aimée). Director Demy's eye for L.A. is striking, but overall feel to story is ambiguous. [M/PG]

Model Wife (1941) **78m.** **½ D: Leigh Jason. Joan Blondell, Dick Powell, Lee Bowman, Charlie Ruggles, Lucile Watson, Ruth Donnelly, Billy Gilbert. Joan's boss won't let her get married, but she does, to Powell, and has to keep it a secret. Fairly amusing comedy.

Modern Affair, A (1996) **C-90m.** ** D: Vern Oakley. Lisa Eichhorn, Stanley Tucci, Caroline Aaron, Wesley Addy, Robert LuPone, Tammy Grimes, Robert Joy. Small, moderately amusing comedy about a successful corporate executive who undergoes artificial insemination, gets pregnant, and then impulsively tracks down the anonymous sperm donor. Results are predictable, but Tucci and Eichhorn lift the material up a couple of notches. This forgettable concoction may play better on the small screen. [R]▼

Modern Girls (1986) **C-84m.** BOMB D: Jerry Kramer. Daphne Zuniga, Virginia Madsen, Cynthia Gibb, Clayton Rohner, Chris Nash, Steve Shellen. Three femme free spirits club-hop raucous L.A. punk spots in the course of a single early a.m.; a spiritual odyssey it's not. Trashy, barely released bomb degrades young performers who've made much stronger impressions in other films; low point is Madsen's near gang rape on a pool table. [PG-13] ▼●

Modern Love (1990) **C-109m.** ** D: Robby Benson. Robby Benson, Karla DeVito, Rue McClanahan, Burt Reynolds, Frankie Valli, Louise Lasser, Kaye Ballard, Lou Kaplan. Paper-thin comedy which director-star Benson also produced and scripted. The film should be titled FAMILY AFFAIR: DeVito, Benson's wife, plays his on-screen mate, and their daughter Lyric is cast as the couple's offspring. The scenario—the duo meet, fall in love, wed, and deal with various "modern problems"—is run-of-the-mill. Filmed in South Carolina, while Benson was teaching a university moviemaking class. [R]▼

Modern Problems (1981) **C-91m.** *½ D: Ken Shapiro. Chevy Chase, Patti D'Arbanville, Mary Kay Place, Nell Carter, Brian Doyle-Murray, Dabney Coleman, Mitch Kreindel. Air-traffic controller Chase acquires telekinetic powers. A couple of funny bits; mostly flat, boring. [PG]▼

Modern Romance (1981) **C-93m.** **½ D: Albert Brooks. Albert Brooks, Kathryn Harrold, Bruno Kirby, Jane Hallaren, James L. Brooks, George Kennedy. Writer-director Brooks plays a world-class neurotic who's obsessively devoted to Harrold but unable to maintain a normal relationship with her. Alternately obnoxious and hilarious, with wonderful in-jokes about moviemaking (Brooks plays a film editor); Brooks' brother Bob Einstein plays a sporting-goods salesman in a nice cameo. Real-life writer-director James L. Brooks plays a director; he returned the favor by writing Albert a plum role in BROADCAST NEWS several years later. [R]▼●

Moderns, The (1988) **C-128m.** **½ D: Alan Rudolph. Keith Carradine, Linda Fiorentino, John Lone, Genevieve Bujold, Geraldine Chaplin, Wallace Shawn, Kevin J. O'Connor. Beautifully mounted but dramatically flawed period piece about a community of "artistes" in 1926 Paris. Bland Carradine is a major liability as an art forger; portraits of Hemingway and Gertrude Stein are less than half baked. Lone and Fiorentino are standouts as a menacing U.S rubber baron and wife, she a lost love of Carradine's. Worthy but iffy. [R]▼●

Modern Times (1936) **89m.** **** D: Charlie Chaplin. Charlie Chaplin, Paulette Goddard, Henry Bergman, Chester Conklin, Stanley ''Tiny'' Sandford. Charlie attacks the machine age in inimitable fashion, with sharp pokes at other social ills and the struggle of modern-day survival. Goddard is the gamin who becomes his partner in life. Chaplin's last silent film (with his own music—including ''Smile''—sound effects and gibberish song) is consistently hilarious, and unforgettable. Final shot is among Chaplin's most famous and most poignant. One of Goddard's sisters early on is young Gloria DeHaven (daughter of Chaplin's assistant director). ▼●

Modesty Blaise (1966-British) **C-119m.** ** D: Joseph Losey. Monica Vitti, Dirk Bogarde, Terence Stamp, Harry Andrews, Michael Craig, Scilla Gabel, Tina Marquand, Clive Revill, Alexander Knox. Director Losey ate watermelon, pickles, and ice cream, went to sleep, woke up, and made this adaptation of the comic strip about a sexy female spy. Filmed at the height of the pop-art craze, it tries to be a spoof at times, doesn't know what it's supposed to be at other moments.

Modigliani of Montparnasse SEE: **Montparnasse 19**

Mod Squad, The (1999) **C-94m.** *½ D: Scott Silver. Claire Danes, Giovanni Ribisi, Omar Epps, Dennis Farina, Josh Brolin, Michael Lerner, Steve Harris, Richard Jenkins, Bodhi Elfman. Brain-dead rehash of the late '60s–early '70s TV series. Here, the title trio—all young delinquents recruited to work undercover in the LAPD—go into action in a scenario involving the theft of confiscated drugs and other mayhem. Plays like an extended, R-rated episode that was spit out of a computer. [R]▼●◗

Mogambo (1953) **C-115m.** ***½ D: John Ford. Clark Gable, Ava Gardner, Grace Kelly, Donald Sinden, Philip Stainton, Eric Pohlmann, Laurence Naismith, Denis O'Dea. Lusty remake of RED DUST. Gable repeats his role, Ava replaces Harlow, Kelly has Mary Astor's part. John Lee Mahin reworked his 1932 screenplay. Romantic triangle in Africa combines love and action; beautifully filmed by Robert Surtees and Freddie Young.▼●

Mogul, The SEE: **Ratings Game, The**

Mohammad, Messenger of God (1977-Arabic) **C-180m.** *** D: Moustapha Akkad. Anthony Quinn, Irene Papas, Michael Ansara, Johnny Sekka, Michael Forest, Neville Jason. Spectacle of the beginnings of Moslem religion is sincere effort, more impressive with action than religious angles. In accordance with the religion, Mohammad is never shown. Aka THE MESSAGE. Panavision. [PG]▼◗

Mohawk (1956) **C-79m.** **½ D: Kurt Neumann. Scott Brady, Rita Gam, Neville Brand, Lori Nelson, Allison Hayes, John Hoyt, Vera Vague (Barbara Jo Allen), Mae Clarke, Ted de Corsia. Unintentionally hilarious hokum of devil-may-care painter Brady attempting to thwart Iroquois uprising while tangling with squaw Gam, among other femmes. There's plenty of heavy breathing, 1950s-style, here.▼●◗

Mokey (1942) **88m.** ** D: Wells Root. Dan Dailey, Donna Reed, Bobby (Robert) Blake, William ''Buckwheat'' Thomas, Cordell Hickman, Matt Moore, Etta McDaniel. Reed has problems with her stepson, who almost winds up in reform school. Typical of genre.

Mole People, The (1956) **78m.** ** D: Virgil Vogel. John Agar, Cynthia Patrick, Hugh Beaumont, Alan Napier. Agar and others find lost underground civilization of albino Sumerians, who have half-human creatures of the title as their slaves. Probably the worst of Universal-International's '50s sci-fi movies.▼

Moll Flanders (1996) **C-123m.** **½ D: Pen Densham. Robin Wright, Morgan Freeman, Stockard Channing, John Lynch, Brenda Fricker, Geraldine James, Aisling Corcoran, Jeremy Brett. Daniel Defoe's 18th-century heroine was the inspiration for this newly spun tale of a girl, born to poverty and abuse, who spends her whole life standing up to men (and women) who would ''use'' her. Wright is rock-solid as Moll, but the interesting story has its share of lulls. Filmmaker Jim Sheridan plays a priest. Panavision. [PG-13]▼●◗

Molly (1950) SEE: **Goldbergs, The**

Molly (1999) **C-91m.** *½ D: John Duigan. Elisabeth Shue, Aaron Eckhart, Thomas Jane, Jill Hennessy, D.W. Moffett, Elizabeth Mitchell, Lucy Liu. Female spin on CHARLY is a saccharine vehicle for Shue as a childlike autistic person who gets a major brain upgrade. Solid support from Eckhart as her reluctant older brother and Jane as her shy boyfriend can't make up for a major case of the cutes. Film preaches endlessly (and irresponsibly) about how kooky and free-spirited autistic people can be and how wretched we are for not enjoying the simple things in life as they do. [PG-13]▼◗

Molly and Lawless John (1971) **C-97m.** ** D: Gary Nelson. Vera Miles, Sam Elliott, Clu Gulager, John Anderson. Slow-moving but not-uninteresting feminist Western, with Miles doing well as a repressed sheriff's wife who chooses to assist a brash young killer (Elliott) in a prison escape. Their developing relationship forms the basis of the story. [PG]▼

Molly and Me (1945) **76m.** *** D: Lewis Seiler. Gracie Fields, Monty Woolley, Roddy McDowall, Reginald Gardiner, Natalie Schafer, Edith Barrett, Doris Lloyd. Unemployed actress-turned-housekeeper Fields goes about brightening the life (and solving the problems) of her new boss, a dour and snippy disgraced politician (Woolley). Well played by a fine cast, with Gardiner almost stealing the film as Woolley's butler.

Molly Maguires, The (1970) **C-123m.** **½ D: Martin Ritt. Sean Connery, Richard Harris, Samantha Eggar, Frank Finlay, Art Lund, Anthony Costello. Well-crafted film about secret society of Irish mineworkers in Pennsylvania, circa 1876, led by Connery; newcomer Harris is working as informer. Vivid atmosphere, good performances, but downbeat film lacks appeal, and is hurt by inconclusive ending. Panavision. [M/PG]▼●

Mom and Dad (1947) **97m.** **½ D: William Beaudine. Hardie Albright, Lois Austin, George Eldredge, June Carlson, Jimmy Clarke. The saga of pretty, innocent Joan Blake, whose repressive mother neglects to inform her about the birds and bees; she does "it," and finds herself "in trouble." Even though this notorious film opens with the National Anthem, and is a "vital educational production, appealing to all true-Americans," it was banned as obscene in some communities. Today, it's pretty tame; a fascinating curio.▼

Mom and Dad Save the World (1992) **C-88m.** *½ D: Greg Beeman. Teri Garr, Jeffrey Jones, Jon Lovitz, Thalmus Rasulala, Wallace Shawn, Eric Idle, Dwier Brown, Kathy Ireland. Perfectly dreadful comedy/fantasy about the megalomaniacal ruler of a tiny planet (Lovitz) who's about to blow up Earth. He becomes attracted to a suburban Mom (Garr) and spirits her and her husband (Jones) to his planet so she can be his bride. Some imaginative visuals can't buoy this strained and unfunny concoction. [PG]▼●

Moment by Moment (1978) **C-102m.** BOMB D: Jane Wagner. Lily Tomlin, John Travolta, Andra Akers, Bert Kramer, Shelley R. Bonus. Role-reversal romance with Travolta as sex object, Tomlin as bored Malibu resident gives new dimension to the word "dreary." Panavision. [R]

Moment of Danger SEE: **Malaga**

Moment of Truth, The (1952-French) **90m.** ** D: Jean Delannoy. Michele Morgan, Jean Gabin, Daniel Gelin, Simone Paris. Effective playing of trite yarn of married couple realizing how little they know each other.

Moment to Moment (1966) **C-108m.** **½ D: Mervyn LeRoy. Jean Seberg, Honor Blackman, Sean Garrison, Arthur Hill. Unconvincing, confused murder mystery set on the Riviera, but filmed largely on Universal's sound stage.▼

Mommie Dearest (1981) **C-129m.** **½ D: Frank Perry. Faye Dunaway, Diana Scarwid, Steve Forrest, Howard da Silva, Mara Hobel, Rutanya Alda, Harry Goz. Vivid, well-crafted filmization of Christina Crawford's book about growing up the adopted and abused daughter of movie queen Joan Crawford (brilliantly played by Dunaway). Knowing that the story is (allegedly) real makes watching this film a creepy experience, something akin to voyeurism . . . though now it's seen as a camp classic! [PG]▼●

Mommy (1995) **C-89m.** **½ D: Max Allan Collins. Patty McCormack, Jason Miller, Brinke Stevens, Majel Barrett, Mickey Spillane, Rachel Lemieux, Sarah Jane Miller. Pretty good little thriller set (and shot) in Muscatine, Iowa, with McCormack as The Bad Seed grown up: a smothering mommy who murders freely to get her way (and to protect her beloved daughter). Now the daughter starts to wonder how to deal with Mommy. McCormack is chillingly good, and the film seldom betrays its low-budget status. Scripted by the director, who also wrote (and sings) several songs on the soundtrack! Followed by MOMMY 2: MOMMY'S DAY.▼●

Mo' Money (1992) **C-91m.** ** D: Peter Macdonald. Damon Wayans, Marlon Wayans, Stacey Dash, Joe Santos, John Diehl, Harry J. Lennix, Almayvonne. Slapdash, needlessly violent comedy-actioner which barely runs on the energy of its talented stars. Damon Wayans plays a streetwise jerk who, in order to woo Dash, takes a job on the bottom rung of the credit card company where she works, and (with kid brother Marlon) becomes involved with fraud, blackmail, and mayhem. Damon Wayans also scripted and executive produced. [R]▼●

Mona Lisa (1986-British) **C-104m.** *** D: Neil Jordan. Bob Hoskins. Cathy Tyson, Michael Caine, Robbie Coltrane, Clarke Peters, Kate Hardie, Zoe Nathenson, Sammi Davis. Absorbing adult drama about a small-time hood who's given a job driving around a high-priced callgirl but remains naive about the life she leads, and about the degree of depravity his underworld chums have sunk to. Director Jordan (who cowrote screenplay with David Leland) leads us into this nether world along with Hoskins, allowing us to discover things at the same time. Hoskins and newcomer Tyson are terrific; Caine is wonderfully slimy in support. [R]▼●

Mondo Cane (1963-Italian) **C-105m.** **½ Producer: Gualtiero Jacopetti. First and best of Italian shockumentaries, with dubbed American narration; focuses on bizarre peculiarities of man in various parts of the world. Features hit song "More."▼●

Money for Nothing (1993) **C-100m.** ** D: Ramon Menendez. John Cusack, Debi Mazar, Michael Madsen, Benicio Del Toro, Michael Rapaport, Maury Chaykin, James Gandolfini, Fionnula Flanagan, Philip Seymour Hoffman. True story of unemployed longshoreman who finds over a million bucks which has fallen out of an armored car; he sees it as his ticket to the good life, but it doesn't work out that way. Earnest but drab treatment of an interesting story; promoted as a comedy, which it is not. The real-life Joey Coyle, on whom the film is based, committed suicide shortly before its release. Panavision. [R]▼●

Money From Home (1953) **C-100m.** **½ D: George Marshall. Dean Martin, Jerry Lewis, Pat Crowley, Robert Strauss, Jack Kruschen. Average hijinks of duo involved with gangsters, steeplechase racing, Arab ruler and his harem. Originally in 3-D.

Money Jungle, The (1968) **C-95m.** ** D: Francis D. Lyon. John Ericson, Lola Albright, Leslie Parrish, Nehemiah Persoff, Charles Drake, Kent Smith, Don Rickles. Geologists involved in oil-rights bidding are being knocked off, but Ericson is there to stop them; good cast wasted.

Money Money Money (1973-French) **C-113m.** *** D: Claude Lelouch. Lino Ventura, Jacques Brel, Charles Denner, Aldo Maccione, Charles Gerard. Gang of successful thieves decide that changing times demand their switch to political crimes, which pay more handsomely. Clever, funny spoof of our heated political era as seen through eyes of men whose only belief is in money. [PG]

Money Pit, The (1986) **C-91m.** ** D: Richard Benjamin. Tom Hanks, Shelley Long, Alexander Godunov, Maureen Stapleton, Joe Mantegna, Philip Bosco, Josh Mostel. A young couple's slapstick misadventures trying to repair and remodel a lemon of a house. Hanks and Long are very likable, but this yuppie update of MR. BLANDINGS BUILDS HIS DREAM HOUSE loses all contact with reality (and humor). Starts out funny but just gets worse and worse. Produced by Steven Spielberg and Co. [PG]▼●

Money Talks (1997) **C-95m.** ** D: Brett Ratner. Chris Tucker, Charlie Sheen, Heather Locklear, Paul Sorvino, Veronica Cartwright, Gerard Ismael, Paul Gleason, David Warner. TV newsman Sheen stumbles into a big story involving fugitive Tucker, and is forced to palm off the hustler as a longtime friend to fiancée Locklear and her rich parents. Surprise box-office success is familiar and lightweight, but has one genuine spark of whimsy: Tucker's phony masquerade as ''Vic Damone, Jr.,'' brought on by the movie's amusingly concocted TV ad for an album of Vic Sr.'s hit recordings. Tucker coexecutive produced. Super 35. [R]▼●◗

Money to Burn (1973) **C-73m. TVM** D: Robert Michael Lewis. E. G. Marshall, Mildred Natwick, Alejandro Ray, Cleavon Little, David Doyle, Charles McGraw, Ronald Feinberg, Lou Frizzell. Marshall's the standout in tale of fairly clever scheme to make use of counterfeit currency printed up in federal penitentiary. Average.▼

Money Train (1995) **C-103m.** ** D: Joseph Ruben. Wesley Snipes, Woody Harrelson, Jennifer Lopez, Robert Blake, Chris Cooper, Joe Grifasi. The costars of WHITE MEN CAN'T JUMP try to reignite their chemistry as randy N.Y.C. transit cops—and brothers (!)—who fight over the same woman, argue over Woody's gambling fever, and get involved in the theft of a money-laden subway car. Violent, overly contrived buddy flick with some big subterranean action scenes. The stars are funny together, but Blake is way over the top as the boys' megalomaniac supervisor. All in all, ''token'' entertainment. Super 35. [R] ▼●◗

Money Trap, The (1966) **92m.** **½ D: Burt Kennedy. Glenn Ford, Rita Hayworth, Elke Sommer, Joseph Cotten, Ricardo Montalban. Ford is detective turned crook in pedestrian murder yarn. Hayworth most convincing as middle-aged woman no longer self-sufficient. Rare non-Western from Kennedy; adapted by Walter Bernstein from Lionel White's novel. Panavision.

Money, Women and Guns (1958) **C-80m.** ** D: Richard Bartlett. Jock Mahoney, Kim Hunter, Tim Hovey, Gene Evans. Modest Western about lawman sent to track down killers and to find heirs to victim's will. CinemaScope.

Mongols, The (1961-Italian) **C-102m.** ** D: Andre de Toth, Leopoldo Savona. Jack Palance, Anita Ekberg, Antonella Lualdi, Franco Silva. Unimaginative spectacle set in 13th century, with Palance the son of Genghis Khan on the rampage in Europe, Ekberg his girl. CinemaScope.▼

Mon Homme (1996-French) **C-95m.** *** D: Bertrand Blier. Anouk Grinberg, Gérard Lanvin, Valeria Bruni Tedeschi, Olivier Martinez, Sabine Azema, Bernard Le Coq. Gleefully amoral sex fable about a sweet-natured, nymphomaniac prostitute (Grinberg) and what happens when she falls in love with a homeless man and turns him into her pimp. Full of typically perverse and surreal Blier touches, but also surprisingly affecting. Aka MY MAN. Panavision. ▼

Monika SEE: **Summer With Monika**

Monitors, The (1969) **C-92m.** ** D: Jack Shea. Guy Stockwell, Susan Oliver, Avery Schreiber, Larry Storch, Ed Begley, Keenan Wynn, Alan Arkin, Xavier Cugat, Stubby Kaye, Jackie Vernon, Everett Dirksen. Great cast wasted in this failed attempt at science fiction satire filmed in Chicago by Second City company. Alien Monitors control Earth and keep everything peaceful, but rebels plot against them. From novel by popular sci-fi writer Keith Laumer. [M/PG]▼

Monkey Business (1931) **77m.** ***½ D: Norman Z. McLeod. Groucho, Harpo, Chico, Zeppo Marx, Thelma Todd, Ruth Hall, Harry Woods. Four brothers stow away on luxury liner; Groucho goes after Thelma, all four pretend to be Maurice Chevalier to get off ship. Full quota of sight gags and puns in typically wacky comedy, co-scripted by S.J. Perelman; their first film written directly for the screen.▼●◗

Monkey Business (1952) **97m.** *** D: Howard Hawks. Ginger Rogers, Cary Grant, Charles Coburn, Marilyn Monroe, Hugh Marlowe. Grant discovers rejuvenation serum, which affects him, wife Rogers, boss Coburn, and secretary Monroe in this zany comedy. Coburn's classic line to MM: "Find someone to type this." Written by Ben Hecht, Charles Lederer, and I.A.L. Diamond; that's Hawks' voice during the opening credits.▼●

Monkey Grip (1982-Australian) **C-101m.** **½ D: Ken Cameron. Noni Hazlehurst, Colin Friels, Alice Garner, Harold Hopkins, Candy Raymond. Unmemorable drama detailing the trials of singleminded single mother Hazlehurst, particularly her relationship with obnoxious drug addict boyfriend Friels. Nice performance by Hazlehurst, but ultimately just a superficial soap opera.▼

Monkey Hustle (1977) **C-90m.** *½ D: Arthur Marks. Yaphet Kotto, Rosalind Cash, Rudy Ray Moore, Kirk Calloway, Randy Brooks. Appealing cast is only saving grace of dumb comedy actioner designed for black audiences, shot in Chicago. Kotto is a black Fagin; ghetto neighborhood's impending demise for an expressway forms a bit of plot. [PG]▼

Monkey on My Back (1957) **93m.** **½ D: Andre de Toth. Cameron Mitchell, Paul Richards, Dianne Foster, Jack Albertson, Kathy Garver. Mitchell as fighter Barney Ross, who became a dope addict, turns in sincere performance. Well-meant, engrossing little film.

Monkeys, Go Home! (1967) **C-101m.** ** D: Andrew V. McLaglen. Maurice Chevalier, Dean Jones, Yvette Mimieux, Bernard Woringer, Clement Harari, Yvonne Constant. Disney trivia about a man who inherits French olive farm and trains monkeys to pick his crop. Gossamer-thin, for kids only. Chevalier's final film appearance.▼

Monkey Shines: An Experiment in Fear (1988) **C-115m.** ** D: George Romero. Jason Beghe, John Pankow, Kate McNeil, Joyce Van Patten, Christine Forrest, Stephen Root, Stanley Tucci, Janine Turner. A cute monkey (injected with human brain cells) is enlisted to help a quadraplegic get on with his life. From that premise writer-director Romero tries to build horror and suspense, but it only works in spurts, and taxes our credibility (and our patience) far too often. [R]▼●

Monkey's Uncle, The (1965) **C-87m.** ** D: Robert Stevenson. Tommy Kirk, Annette Funicello, Leon Ames, Frank Faylen, Arthur O'Connell, Norman Grabowski. Juvenile Disney comedy has Kirk again as Merlin Jones, college whiz-kid who first tries sleep-learning method on monkey, then sets himself up in makeshift flying machine. Flight sequences provide brightest moments. Unforgettable title song warbled by Annette and The Beach Boys. Sequel to THE MISADVENTURES OF MERLIN JONES.▼

Monkey Trouble (1994) **C-95m.** *** D: Franco Amurri. Thora Birch, Harvey Keitel, Mimi Rogers, Christopher McDonald, Kevin Scannell. Nicely done family film about Eva (Birch), a clever nine-year-old who yearns for a pet; she adopts a Capuchin monkey, whom she hides from her parents. Splendid change-of-pace for Keitel, as a gypsy who'd been using the monkey to pick pockets; the monkey, whom Eva names "Dodger" (played by "Finster"), is a real scene-stealer. Kids Eva's age should love it. Amurri scripted, with Stu Krieger. Ridley Scott executive produced. [PG] ▼●

Monolith (1994) **C-95m.** BOMB D: John Eyres. Bill Paxton, Lindsay Frost, John Hurt, Louis Gossett, Jr., Paul Ganus, Musetta Vander, Andrew Lamond. Nonsensical sci-fi/action adventure of cops Paxton and Frost chasing an invincible killer alien. Attempts at repartee are embarrassing. [R]▼●

Monolith Monsters, The (1957) **77m.** ** D: John Sherwood. Lola Albright, Grant Williams, Les Tremayne, Trevor Bardette. Engrossing sci-fi mystery set in desert town. When exposed to water, fragments of shattered meteorites grow and reproduce—wreaking havoc on innocent bystanders. Story by sci-fi director Jack Arnold.▼●

Mon Oncle (1958-French) **C-126m.** **** D: Jacques Tati. Jacques Tati, Jean-Pierre Zola, Adrienne Servantie, Alain Bercourt. Tati's first color film is a masterpiece. M. Hulot's simple, uncluttered life is sharply contrasted to that of his sister and brother-in-law, who live in an ultramodern, gadget-laden home reminiscent of those in Buster Keaton's silent classics. Continuous flow of sight gags (including the funniest fountain you'll ever see) makes this easygoing, nearly dialogue-less comedy a total delight. Oscar winner as Best Foreign Film. Aka MY UNCLE and MY UNCLE, MR. HULOT. Original U.S. release ran 110m.▼●

Mon Oncle Antoine SEE: **My Uncle Antoine**

Mon Oncle d'Amerique (1980-French) **C-123m.** ***½ D: Alain Resnais. Gerard Depardieu, Nicole Garcia, Roger Pierre, Marie Dubois, Nelly Bourgeaud, Henri Laborit. Intensely directed, acted, and written (by Jean Gruault) film illustrating research scientist Laborit's theories on human conduct. The focus is on the intertwined lives of a plant manager (Depardieu), actress (Garcia), and media executive (Pierre). Intelligent, thought-provoking. [PG]▼

Monsieur Beaucaire (1946) **93m.** *** D: George Marshall. Bob Hope, Joan Caulfield, Patric Knowles, Marjorie Reynolds, Cecil Kellaway, Joseph Schildkraut, Reginald Owen, Constance Collier. Pleasing Hope vehicle with Bob in costume as barber sent on mission as dead duck sure to be murdered. Plush settings, funny gags.▼

Monsieur Hire (1989-French) **C-88m.** ***½ D: Patrice Leconte. Michel Blanc, Sandrine Bonnaire, Luc Thuillier, Eric Berenger. Bald, middle-aged Peeping Tom falls in love with the object of his obsession—a young woman, peripherally involved in a murder, who lives across the courtyard. Cold, but involving and terrifically acted version of a Georges Simenon novel; the short running time helps. Previously filmed in 1946 as PANIQUE. Panavision. [PG-13]▼●

Monsieur Verdoux (1947) **123m.** ***½ D: Charles Chaplin. Charles Chaplin, Martha Raye, Isobel Elsom, Marilyn Nash, Irving Bacon, William Frawley. Chaplin's controversial black comedy about a Parisian Bluebeard who murders wives for their money was years ahead of its time; its wry humor and pacifist sentiments make it quite contemporary when seen today. Broad comic sequence with Raye is particular highlight.▼●◗

Monsignor (1982) **C-122m.** ** D: Frank Perry. Christopher Reeve, Genevieve Bujold, Fernando Rey, Jason Miller, Joe Cortese, Adolfo Celi, Leonardo Cimino, Tomas Milian, Robert J. Prosky. Saga of ambitious priest who commits every heresy imaginable (including having an affair with a nun!) while operating as the Vatican's business manager. Grows more ridiculous as it goes along—with unintentional comedy on a grand scale—culminating in an astonishing final shot involving the Pope. Another camp classic from the producer and director of MOMMIE DEAREST. [R]▼

Monsignor Quixote (1988-British) **C-118m.** **½ D: Rodney Bennett. Alec Guinness, Leo McKern, Ian Richardson, Graham Crowden, Maurice Denham, Philip Stone, Rosalie Crutchley, Valentine Pelka, Don Fellows. To his surprise, a quiet, provincial Spanish priest (Guinness), a descendant of Don Quixote, is appointed monsignor. To celebrate, he and a local Communist politician (McKern) take a journey that mirrors the adventures of Cervantes's knight errant. Gentle film features fine acting and an interesting story but never engages the emotions. Based on a Graham Greene novel. Made for British television.▼

Monsoon (1943) SEE: **Isle of Forgotten Sins**

Monsoon (1953) **C-79m.** *½ D: Rodney Amateau. Ursula Thiess, Diana Douglas, George Nader, Ellen Corby. Trite drama of several people destroyed by their passions; set in India.

Monster, The (1925) **86m.** ** D: Roland West. Lon Chaney, Gertrude Olmstead, Hallam Cooley, Johnny Arthur, Charles Sellon. Overdose of comedy relief hampers moody Chaney mad-doctor doings; still OK, though, as whole film has tongue-in-cheek. From Crane Wilbur's play.▼

Monster, The (1994-Italian) **C-112m.** **½ D: Roberto Benigni. Roberto Benigni, Michel Blanc, Nicoletta Braschi, Jean-Claude Brialy, Massimo Girotti, Dominique Lavanant, Ivano Marescotti. Bumbling Benigni is mistaken by the police for a wanted serial killer, and he's followed by an attractive female cop hoping to get the goods on him. Moderately amusing comedy will mostly please those who already adore Benigni; others will find fewer laughs. Original title: IL MOSTRO.▼◗

Monster and the Girl, The (1941) **65m.** **½ D: Stuart Heisler. Ellen Drew, Robert Paige, Paul Lukas, Joseph Calleia, George Zucco, Rod Cameron. Unusual B-film starts off with story of gangsters dragging Drew into life of prostitution, then veers off into horror as Zucco transfers her dead brother's brain into body of a gorilla! White slavery angle more original than the mad-scientist stuff.▼

Monster Club, The (1980-British) **C-97m.** *½ D: Roy Ward Baker. Vincent Price, John Carradine, Donald Pleasence, Stuart Whitman, Warren Saire, Richard Johnson, Britt Ekland, Simon Ward, Anthony Steel, Patrick Magee. A trio of horror stories, all told by vampire Price. Disappointing and unimaginative, with only the barest of shudders; never released theatrically in the U.S. The club, by the way, is a disco patronized by Transylvanians.▼●

Monster From Green Hell (1957) **71m.** *½ D: Kenneth Crane. Jim Davis, Robert E. Griffin, Barbara Turner, Joel Fluellen, Vladimir Sokoloff, Eduardo Ciannelli. Laboratory wasps are sent into orbit, crash-land in Africa as giant mutations. Standard 1950s sci-fi formula stuff, with lots of talk, little action. Uses ample stock footage from STANLEY AND LIVINGSTONE. Climax originally filmed in color.▼

Monster From the Ocean Floor, The (1954) **64m.** BOMB D: Wyott Ordung. Anne Kimball, Stuart Wade, Wyott Ordung. Producer Roger Corman's first effort is a dreadful film about a squid-like creature pursued by a minisubmarine; 20,000 yawns under the sea.▼

Monster in a Box (1992) **C-96m.** *** D: Nick Broomfield. The second film adaptation of a Spalding Gray monologue, this one chronicling various adventures from L.A. to the Soviet Union which interrupt Gray's efforts to write a huge autobiographical novel (the monster of the title). The direction and the music are more obtrusive than in the previous SWIMMING TO CAMBODIA, but Gray's stories and observations are still funny, profound, and extremely compelling. Our favorite anecdote: Gray's semi-disastrous stint as the Stage Manager in a N.Y. revival of *Our Town.*▼

Monster in the Closet (1986) **C-87m.** *** D: Bob Dahlin. Donald Grant, Denise DuBarry, Claude Akins, Howard Duff, Henry Gibson, Donald Moffat, Paul Dooley, John Carradine, Jesse White, Stella Stevens. Perceptive and funny homage to 1950s sci-fi flicks. Clark Kent–type reporter Grant and scientist DuBarry team up to track down and destroy California monsters who pop out of closets and kill people. A must for buffs. Filmed in 1983. [PG]▼◗

Monster in the Night SEE: **Monster on the Campus**

Monster Island (1981-U.S.-Spanish) **C-100m.** *½ D: Juan Piquer Simon. Terence Stamp, Peter Cushing, Ian Serra, David Hatton, Blanca Estrada. Humdrum actioner, with Serra and Hatton shipwrecked on an island loaded with gold and strange creatures. Based on a story by Jules Verne.

Monster Maker, The (1944) **62m.** ** D: Sam Newfield. J. Carrol Naish, Ralph Morgan, Wanda McKay, Terry Frost. Peculiarly distasteful horror yarn with mad scientist Naish infecting his enemies with acromegaly "germs," causing hideous deformities.▼●◗

Monster of Piedras Blancas, The (1958) **71m.** *½ D: Irvin Berwick. Les Tremayne, Forrest Lewis, Jeanne Carmen, John Harmon, Frank Arvidson. Sluggish chiller with humanoid sea monster thirsting for blood on a deserted seacoast; obvious and amateurish. ▼

Monster on the Campus (1958) **76m.** **½ D: Jack Arnold. Arthur Franz, Joanna Moore, Judson Pratt, Nancy Walters, Troy Donahue. Mild-mannered college prof Franz, experimenting with the body of a fish long thought to be extinct, is unaware that its blood occasionally turns him into a murderous Neanderthal man. Silly script saved by Arnold's efficient direction and Franz's sensitive performance. Aka MONSTER IN THE NIGHT.▼●

Monster Squad, The (1987) **C-81m.** **½ D: Fred Dekker. Andre Gower, Robby Kiger, Stephen Macht, Duncan Regehr, Tom Noonan, Brent Chalem, Ryan Lambert, Ashley Bank. Young friends belong to a club that's devoted to monsters, but they unexpectedly encounter the horror heavies in real life when Dracula (accompanied by the Frankenstein monster, the Mummy, the Wolf Man, and the Gill Man) comes to their town in search of an amulet vital to his continued existence. Affectionate homage to classic horror films and their monster stars is ultimately too bland and unbelievable (even for a kiddie horror film). Climactic showdown boasts Richard Edlund's super-duper special effects. Panavision. [PG-13] ▼●

Monster That Challenged the World, The (1957) **83m.** **½ D: Arnold Laven. Tim Holt, Audrey Dalton, Hans Conried, Casey Adams. Above-average giant-bug-on-the-loose film is set in the Salton Sea, where colossal mollusks (like big caterpillars in snail shells) menace mankind. Intelligent, low-key, with good monsters.▼●

Monster Walks, The (1932) **63m.** **½ D: Frank Strayer. Rex Lease, Vera Reynolds, Mischa Auer, Sheldon Lewis, Sleep 'N'Eat (Willie Best). Campy old-house thriller, good for some fun. Heiress Reynolds is marked for death by paralyzed uncle Lewis, who wants moronic Auer to kill her and blame it on an ape that's kept in the cellar for scientific experiments. Willie bests Mischa for laughs, but it's a close race.▼

Monster Zero (1966-Japanese) **92m.** *½ D: Ishiro Honda. Nick Adams, Akira Takarada. Godzilla and Rodan are swiped from Earth to battle Ghidrah on an alien planet. Lesser monster movie from the Toho Studio. Aka GODZILLA VS. MONSTER ZERO. Tohoscope.▼●◗

Monstrosity (1964) **72m.** *½ D: Joseph Mascelli. Frank Gerstle, Erika Peters, Judy Bamber, Frank Fowler, Marjorie Eaton. Eaton is wealthy matron who hires doctor (Gerstle) to perform brain transplant on her; lumbering mess. Narrated by Bradford Dillman. Retitled: THE ATOMIC BRAIN.▼

Montana (1950) **C-76m.** **½ D: Ray Enright. Errol Flynn, Alexis Smith, S. Z. Sakall, Monte Blue, Douglas Kennedy. Slick yet unexciting Western with formula Warner Bros. plot line and type casting; minor Flynn vehicle. ▼

Montana (1990) **C-100m. TVM** D: William A. Graham. Gena Rowlands, Richard Crenna, Lea Thompson, Justin Deas, Elizabeth Berridge, Darren Dalton, Scott Coffey. In this contemporary Larry McMurtry Western, Rowlands and Crenna (doing a Gabby Hayes turn!) are a brawling couple caught in changing times: she wants to hold onto the family ranch, he wants to sell it to a power company for oil drilling. Colorful but talkative tale about values. Made for cable. Average.▼

Montana Belle (1952) **C-81m.** ** D: Allan Dwan. Jane Russell, George Brent, Scott Brady, Andy Devine, Forrest Tucker. Mildly interesting Western with Russell as Belle Starr, involved with fellow-outlaws, the Dalton Brothers. Filmed in 1948.▼

Montana Mike SEE: **Heaven Only Knows**

Montana Moon (1930) **89m.** ** D: Mal

St. Clair. Joan Crawford, John Mack Brown, Dorothy Sebastian, Ricardo Cortez, Benny Rubin, Cliff Edwards, Karl Dane. OUR DANCING DAUGHTERS goes west, with hot jazz baby Joan marrying down-to-earth cowboy Brown. Dated, and stiff as a board.

Montana Territory (1952) **C-64m.** ** D: Ray Nazarro. Lon McCallister, Wanda Hendrix, Preston Foster, Jack Elam, Clayton Moore. McCallister is deputized cowboy who's out to bring in the outlaws.

Monte Carlo (1930) **90m.** **½ D: Ernst Lubitsch. Jeanette MacDonald, Jack Buchanan, ZaSu Pitts, Claude Allister. Dated but enjoyable musical froth with Jeanette an impoverished countess wooed by royal Buchanan, who's incognito, of course. Lubitsch's methods of integrating songs into the film were innovations in 1930; most memorable is "Beyond the Blue Horizon." ●

Monte Carlo or Bust SEE: **Those Daring Young Men in Their Jaunty Jalopies**

Monte Carlo Story, The (1957-Italian) **C-99m.** ** D: Samuel Taylor. Marlene Dietrich, Vittorio De Sica, Arthur O'Connell, Natalie Trundy, Mischa Auer. Charming stars try to support thin story of troubled romance between two compulsive gamblers; filmed on location. Technirama.

Montenegro (1981-Swedish-British) **C-98m.** *** D: Dusan Makavejev. Susan Anspach, Erland Josephson, Per Oscarsson, John Zacharias, Svetozar Cvetkovic, Patricia Gelin. Bored middle-class housewife Anspach becomes sexually liberated when she accidentally falls in with Yugoslav workers who frequent a boisterous bar. Funny and entertaining. Aka MONTENEGRO—OR PIGS AND PEARLS. [R]▼●◗

Monterey Pop (1969) **C-88m.** ***½ D: James Desmond, Barry Feinstein, D.A. Pennebaker, Albert Maysles, Roger Murphy, Richard Leacock, Nick Proferes. Otis Redding. Mamas and Papas, Jimi Hendrix, The Who, Janis Joplin, Animals, Jefferson Airplane. First major rock concert film, shot at 1967 Monterey Pop Festival, is still one of the best ever, with Joplin's "Ball and Chain" and Hendrix's pyrotechnical "Wild Thing" among the highlights. Video version includes 9m. extra footage. ▼●

Monte Walsh (1970) **C-106m.** *** D: William Fraker. Lee Marvin, Jeanne Moreau, Jack Palance, Mitch Ryan, Jim Davis, Allyn Ann McLerie, Richard Farnsworth. Melancholy Western with Marvin a veteran cowboy who finds himself part of a dying West. Sensitive filming of novel by Jack Schaefer (who wrote SHANE). Fine performance by Palance in atypical good-guy role. Directorial debut for noted cinematographer Fraker. Panavision. [PG]▼

Month by the Lake, A (1995) **C-94m.** **½ D: John Irvin. Vanessa Redgrave, Edward Fox, Uma Thurman, Alida Valli, Alessandro Gassman. Garrulous, unmarried Brit (Redgrave) vacations at Italy's Lake Como on the eve of WW2. She's interested in a fellow hotel guest, stiff-upper-lip Fox, but her hesitancy opens the door for flirtatious American Thurman. Sweetly entertaining (and picturesque), if painted in very broad strokes. That's Vittorio Gassman's son as the young lothario. Based on the novella by H. E. Bates. [PG]▼●

Month in the Country, A (1987-British) **C-96m.** *** D: Pat O'Connor. Colin Firth, Kenneth Branagh, Natasha Richardson, Patrick Malahide, Tony Haygarth, Jim Carter. Occasionally slow but still thoughtful, rewarding drama about shellshocked WW1 vet Firth, and his experiences while uncovering a medieval painting on a church wall in a remote Yorkshire town. Screenplay by Simon Gray, from a novel by J. R. Carr. Stick with this one. [PG]▼●

Montparnasse 19 (1958-French-Italian) **120m.** **½ D: Jacques Becker. Gérard Philipe, Lilli Palmer, Anouk Aimée, Gerard Sety, Lila Kedrova, Lino Ventura. Unusual biography of Modigliani, with Philipe as the struggling early-20th-century painter; plays up the women in his life but at the same time presents a harshly realistic view of the Parisian art world and its denizens. Philipe is fine as the impoverished, boozing—and romantic—lead (the French star died in 1959, at age thirty-six). Film was prepared by (and is dedicated to) director Max Ophuls, who died prior to shooting. Aka MODIGLIANI OF MONTPARNASSE and MODIGLIANI. ▼

Monty Python and the Holy Grail (1975-British) **C-90m.** **½ D: Terry Gilliam, Terry Jones. Graham Chapman, John Cleese, Terry Gilliam, Eric Idle, Terry Jones, Michael Palin. The Python troupe's second feature is wildly uneven, starting out well and then getting lost—in the "story" of a medieval crusade. Some inspired lunacy, and a lot of dry stretches; awfully bloody, too. Recommended for fans only. [PG]▼●◗

Monty Python Live at the Hollywood Bowl (1982-British) **C-77m.** *** D: Terry Hughes, "Monty Python." Graham Chapman, John Cleese, Terry Gilliam, Eric Idle, Terry Jones, Michael Palin, Neil Innes, Carol Cleveland. Britain's bad boys invade Los Angeles with this madcap series of sketches and routines, including many old favorites. A must for Python aficionados. Videotaped, then transferred to film. [R]▼●

Monty Python's Life of Brian SEE: **Life of Brian**

Monty Python's The Meaning of Life (1983-British) **C-103m.** *** D: Terry Jones. Graham Chapman, John Cleese, Terry Gilliam, Eric Idle, Terry Jones, Michael Palin, Carol Cleveland, Simon Jones. Original, outrageous comedy exploring various facets of life and death—from procreation to the Grim Reaper himself—with typical Python irreverence. Highlights include the world's most obese man (an unforgettable scene, like it or not) and a cheerful, elaborate production number about sperm! A barrel of bellylaughs for Python fans; others beware. [R]▼●◗

Monument Ave. (1998) **C-90m.** ** D: Ted Demme. Denis Leary, Billy Crudup, Ian Hart, Jason Barry, Colm Meaney, Martin Sheen, Jeanne Tripplehorn, Famke Janssen, Noah Emmerich, John Diehl. Substitute Boston-Irish hoods for Martin Scorsese's Italian counterparts, and you get a sense of what this aspires to be. Serviceable drama deals with the tension between an older mentor and his band of younger car thieves, as well as the women who mourn at the funerals their actions have engendered. Might have been more impressive had it come out ten years earlier. [R]▼●◗

Moon and Sixpence, The (1942) **89m.** *** D: Albert Lewin. George Sanders, Herbert Marshall, Doris Dudley, Eric Blore, Albert Bassermann, Molly Lamont, Elena Verdugo, Florence Bates, Heather Thatcher. Surprisingly adult adaptation of W. Somerset Maugham's novel based on the life of Paul Gauguin, with Sanders as the restless (and selfish) spirit who turns his back on his family and society, to become a painter. A postscript, tacked on to satisfy Hollywood's moral code, weakly tries to undermine the character that Sanders and writer-director Lewin have just portrayed so well! Climactic scene of paintings originally shown in color.▼

Moonfire (1970) **C-107m.** BOMB D: Michael Parkhurst. Richard Egan, Charles Napier, Sonny Liston, Dayton Lummis, Joaquin Martinez. Trucker Napier unknowingly becomes involved in blackmail plot. Atrociously scripted and directed; though toplined, Egan has about eight lines; Boxer Liston, as "The Farmer," proved himself no actor.▼

Moonfleet (1955) **C-89m.** **½ D: Fritz Lang. Stewart Granger, Jon Whiteley, George Sanders, Viveca Lindfors, Joan Greenwood, Ian Wolfe. Tepid 18th-century story of Britisher Granger becoming a buccaneer. CinemaScope.●

Moon 44 (1990-West German) **C-102m.** *½ D: Roland Emmerich. Michael Paré, Lisa Eichhorn, Malcolm McDowell, Dean Devlin, Brian Thompson, Stephen Geoffreys, Mechmed Yilmaz, Leon Rippy, Roscoe Lee Browne. In the 21st century, a multinational company forces its prisoners to protect their claim on a "moon" from takeover attempt by rival company. Paré plays a tough undercover agent. Annoyingly derivative, drearily obvious sci-fi epic. Panavision. [R]▼●

Moon in the Gutter, The (1983-French) **C-126m.** *½ D: Jean-Jacques Beineix. Nastassia Kinski, Gerard Depardieu, Victoria Abril, Vittorio Mezzogiorno, Dominique Pinon. Overbaked, pompously surreal tale of dockworker Depardieu, seeking his sister's rapist, and his involvement with wealthy, beautiful Kinski. Both stars couldn't be worse. Panavision. [R]▼

Moon Is Blue, The (1953) **99m.** **½ D: Otto Preminger. William Holden, David Niven, Maggie McNamara, Tom Tully, Dawn Addams, Gregory Ratoff. Once-saucy sex comedy about a young woman who flaunts her virginity now seems tame, too much a filmed stage play, with most innuendoes lacking punch. Adapted by F. Hugh Herbert from his stage hit. Hardy Kruger (who has a small part here) played the lead in a German-language version that Preminger filmed simultaneously.▼●

Moon Is Down, The (1943) **90m.** *** D: Irving Pichel. Cedric Hardwicke, Henry Travers, Lee J. Cobb, Dorris Bowden, Margaret Wycherly, Peter Van Eyck, William Post, Jr. Fine drama from Steinbeck novel of Norway's invasion by Nazis, tracing local effect and reactions.

Moonlight and Cactus (1944) **60m.** *½ D: Edward Cline. Andrews Sisters, Elyse Knox, Leo Carrillo, Eddie Quillan, Shemp Howard, Minerva Urecal. Singing trio find themselves out West running a ranch and chasing romance. Lightweight production.

Moonlight and Valentino (1995) **C-104m.** *** D: David Anspaugh. Elizabeth Perkins, Whoopi Goldberg, Kathleen Turner, Gwyneth Paltrow, Jon Bon Jovi, Jeremy Sisto, Josef Sommer. A young woman cannot deal with the reality of suddenly being widowed—despite the support of her best friend, her younger sister, and her ex-stepmother, who rally around her. Unusual subject matter portrayed with skill and unpredictability, though some will find it too talky and/or too studied in its quirkiness. Perkins gives an outstanding performance. Ellen Simon (daughter of Neil) adapted her stage play, based on her own experience. Peter Coyote appears unbilled as Goldberg's husband. Panavision. [R] ▼●

Moonlighter, The (1953) **75m.** ** D: Roy Rowland. Barbara Stanwyck, Fred MacMurray, Ward Bond, William Ching, John Dierkes, Jack Elam. Dull Western loses its 3-D virtue on TV; MacMurray is a rustler and Stanwyck his ex-girlfriend.

Moonlighting (1982-British) **C-97m.** **** D: Jerzy Skolimowski. Jeremy Irons, Eugene Lipinski, Jiri Stanislav, Eugeniusz Haczkiewicz. Slow-paced but mesmerizing allegory about a Polish man sent to London with a trio of workmen to renovate a wealthy man's apartment. The supervisor (Irons) must keep their job a secret, since they have no work permits; the pressure increases when he learns that Poland has imposed martial law. Fascinating study of loneliness and desperation, full of irony and bittersweet humor; Irons is superb. Written and directed by Polish emigré Skolimowski. [PG]▼●

Moonlight Sonata (1938-British) **80m.** **½ D: Lothar Mendes. Ignace Jan Paderewski, Charles Farrell, Marie Tempest, Barbara Greene, Eric Portman. Well-made but stodgy romance, set in household of Swedish baroness, is excuse for screen appearance by famous concert pianist.▼

Moon Over Broadway (1997) **C-92m.** *** D: D. A. Pennebaker, Chris Hegedus. Revealing—and entertaining—documentary about the Broadway production of Ken Ludwig's comedy *Moon Over Buffalo,* starring Carol Burnett, in her first Broadway play in many years, and Philip Bosco. The assorted behind-the-scenes power trips, emotions, and distresses are captured in vivid detail; a fascinating look at what goes into creating a high-profile Broadway production. A must for theater buffs.

Moon Over Burma (1940) **76m.** ** D: Louis King. Dorothy Lamour, Preston Foster, Robert Preston, Doris Nolan, Albert Basserman, Frederick Worlock. Island setting tries to cover up for same old triangle with Foster and Preston fighting over Lamour.

Moon Over Harlem (1939) **70m.** **½ D: Edgar G. Ulmer. Bud Harris, Cora Green, Izinetta Wilcox, Earl Gough, Zerritta Stepteau, Petrina Moore, Christopher Columbus and His Swing Band, Sidney Bechet and His Clarinet. Fascinating all-black melodrama with music, about a wealthy widow who marries a heel, and the daughter she unjustly accuses of trying to seduce him. Oh yes, there's a subplot about gangsters preying on pushcart vendors. Possibly the cheapest of Ulmer's fabled ultra-low-budget projects; shot in just four days, but retains a real sense of time and place.▼

Moon Over Miami (1941) **C-91m.** *** D: Walter Lang. Don Ameche, Betty Grable, Robert Cummings, Carole Landis, Charlotte Greenwood, Jack Haley. Grable, sister Landis, and Greenwood go fortune-hunting in Miami, come up with more than they bargained for in smoothly entertaining musical romance, especially nice in color. Tuneful songs include title number, "You Started Something." Remake of THREE BLIND MICE, also remade as THREE LITTLE GIRLS IN BLUE.▼

Moon Over Parador (1988) **C-105m.** **½ D: Paul Mazursky. Richard Dreyfuss, Raul Julia, Sonia Braga, Jonathan Winters, Michael Greene, Polly Holliday, Charo, Marianne Sägebrecht, Sammy Davis, Jr., Dick Cavett, Ed Asner, Ike Pappas. Amiable comedy about an American actor who's shanghaied into portraying a recently deceased Latin American dictator; reluctant at first, he soon finds he enjoys the charade (and the despot's sexy companion). Entertaining enough, but never quite hits the bull's-eye. Cowriter/director Mazursky has a hilarious cameo in drag. Inspired by THE MAGNIFICENT FRAUD (1939). [PG-13]▼●

Moon Pilot (1962) **C-98m.** *** D: James Neilson. Tom Tryon, Brian Keith, Edmond O'Brien, Dany Saval, Tommy Kirk, Bob Sweeney, Kent Smith. Dated but enjoyable Disney comedy about astronaut Tryon who meets mysterious girl from another planet (Saval) just before his mission.▼

Moonraker, The (1958-British) **C-82m.** *** D: David MacDonald. George Baker, Sylvia Syms, Marius Goring, Peter Arne, Gary Raymond. Colorful action-packed adventure, set in 1650s England. The Earl of Dawlish (Baker) leads a double life as the dashing and mysterious hero known as The Moonraker, who sides with the royalists and protects Prince Charles Stuart against Oliver Cromwell.▼

Moonraker (1979) **C-126m.** ** D: Lewis Gilbert. Roger Moore, Lois Chiles, Michael Lonsdale, Richard Kiel, Corinne Clery, Bernard Lee, Desmond Llewelyn, Lois Maxwell. James Bond no longer resembles Ian Fleming's creation; now he's a tired punster pursuing an intergalactic madman. Overblown comic-strip adventure is strictly for the bubble-gum set . . . but tune in for eye-popping free-fall opening, the best part of this movie. Lee's last appearance as "M." Panavision. [R]▼●◗

Moonrise (1948) **90m.** **½ D: Frank Borzage. Dane Clark, Gail Russell, Ethel Barrymore, Allyn Joslyn, Henry (Harry) Morgan, Lloyd Bridges, Selena Royle, Rex Ingram, Harry Carey, Jr. Uneven script does in this psychological melodrama of angry, alienated Clark and his plight after accidentally killing the banker's son who's been taunting him for years. But it's beautifully directed; check out stunning opening shot, and opening sequence. ▼●

Moonrunners (1974) **C-102m.** ** D: Gy Waldron. James Mitchum, Kiel Martin, Arthur Hunnicutt, Joan Blackman, Waylon Jennings, Chris Forbes. Action-comedy about modern day bootleggers sputters because of Mitchum's lethargic acting and the script's lack of credibility. Later developed into the *Dukes of Hazzard* TV series. [PG]

Moonshine County Express (1977) **C-95m.** **½ D: Gus Trikonis. John Saxon, Susan Howard, William Conrad, Morgan Woodward, Claudia Jennings, Jeff Corey, Dub Taylor, Maureen McCormick. Murdered moonshiner's three sexy daughters decide to compete with local biggie (Conrad) whom they believe caused their father's death. Strong cast buoys good action programmer. [PG]▼

Moonshine War, The (1970) **C-100m.** ** D: Richard Quine. Richard Widmark, Alan Alda, Patrick McGoohan, Melodie Johnson, Will Geer, Joe Williams, Lee Hazlewood. Tediously plotted mixture of comedy and drama during late Prohibition era enlivened by unusual cast and honest attempt to evoke country atmosphere. Script by Elmore Leonard, from his novel. Look for Teri Garr as the tourist's wife. Panavision. [PG]

Moon's Our Home, The (1936) **83m.** ** D: William A. Seiter. Margaret Sullavan, Henry Fonda, Charles Butterworth, Beulah Bondi, Walter Brennan. Flyweight comedy about turbulent courtship and marriage of movie star and N.Y. novelist; too silly to matter, though stars do their best. (Footnote: Fonda and Sullavan had already been married and divorced when this film was made.)▼

Moon-Spinners, The (1964) **C-118m.** **½ D: James Neilson. Hayley Mills, Eli Wallach, Pola Negri, Peter McEnery, Joan Greenwood, Irene Papas. Disney's attempt at Hitchcock-like intrigue with a light touch has Hayley a vacationer in Crete who becomes involved with jewelry-smuggling ring. Too long and muddled to hit bullseye, but still entertaining, with Negri (off-screen since 1943) an enjoyable villainess.▼●

Moonstruck (1987) **C-102m.** **** D: Norman Jewison. Cher, Nicolas Cage, Vincent Gardenia, Olympia Dukakis, Danny Aiello, Julie Bovasso, John Mahoney, Louis Guss, Feodor Chaliapin, Anita Gillette. A gem of a movie that unfolds like a good play, without ever seeming static or stagy. Cher plays an independent young widow who agrees to marry an older man (Aiello) —and then finds herself inexorably drawn to his misfit younger brother (Cage). John Patrick Shanley's script is brimming with wonderful vignettes and acute observations about Italian-American families. Cher, Dukakis (terrific as the mother), and Shanley won Oscars for their work. [PG]▼●◗

Moontide (1942) **94m.** **½ D: Archie Mayo. Jean Gabin, Ida Lupino, Thomas Mitchell, Claude Rains, Jerome Cowan, Helene Reynolds, Ralph Byrd, (Victor) Sen Yung, Tully Marshall. Jean Gabin's portrayal of rough seaman who cares for potential suicide (Lupino) saves an otherwise average "realistic" movie.

Moontrap (1989) **C-92m.** **½ D: Robert Dyke. Walter Koenig, Bruce Campbell, Leigh Lombardi, Robert Kurcz. OK entertainment, as aging space shuttle pilot and younger partner are sent to the Moon to investigate alien artifacts, but inadvertently restart alien machinery designed to invade the Earth. Very low-budget production shows ingenuity in its special effects and imagination in the story, but dramatic values are highly variable. [R]▼●

Moon Zero Two (1970-British) **C-100m.** *½ D: Roy Ward Baker. James Olson, Catherina Von Schell (Catherine Schell), Warren Mitchell, Adrienne Corri, Ori Levy, Dudley Foster. Sci-fi adventure is almost like a Western, with people making mining claims on the moon and having to fight for their rights. You've seen it before without the craters.▼

More American Graffiti (1979) **C-111m.** *½ D: B. W. L. Norton. Candy Clark, Bo Hopkins, Ron Howard, Paul Le Mat, Mackenzie Phillips, Charles Martin Smith, Cindy Williams, Anna Bjorn, Scott Glenn, Mary Kay Place, Rosanna Arquette, Delroy Lindo. More is less, in this sequel to 1973 hit, placing that film's likable characters in a quartet of pointless vignettes. Look sharp for Harrison Ford as a motorcycle cop. Panavision (part). [PG]▼●

More Dead Than Alive (1969) **C-101m.** ** D: Robert Sparr. Clint Walker, Vincent Price, Anne Francis, Paul Hampton. Modest Western about a gunslinger traveling in a side show as sharpshooter. Not a horror film, despite title and presence of Price. [M/PG]

More Needful Things SEE: **Needful Things**

More Than a Miracle (1967-Italian-French) **C-105m.** ** D: Francesco Rosi. Sophia Loren, Omar Sharif, Dolores Del Rio, Georges Wilson, Leslie French, Marina Malfatti. Sophia has never looked better but this absurd fairy tale about a prince and a peasant girl is just a waste of time. Franscope.

More Than a Secretary (1936) **77m.** ** D: Alfred E. Green. Jean Arthur, George Brent, Lionel Stander, Ruth Donnelly, Reginald Denny, Dorothea Kent. Arthur's charm gives distinction to routine comedy of secretary in love with handsome boss Brent.

More Than Friends (1979) **C-100m. TVM** D: Jim Burrows. Penny Marshall, Rob Reiner, Kay Medford, Claudette Nevins, Howard Hesseman, Dabney Coleman. Occasionally hilarious romantic comedy by Reiner loosely based on his early courtship of then real-life wife Marshall. Above average.

More the Merrier, The (1943) **104m.** *** D: George Stevens. Jean Arthur, Joel McCrea, Charles Coburn, Richard Gaines, Bruce Bennett, Ann Savage, Ann Doran, Frank Sully, Grady Sutton. The wartime housing shortage forces Arthur to share a Washington, D.C., apartment with McCrea and crafty old codger Coburn (who won an Oscar for this comic performance). Highly entertaining, with Arthur at her peerless best. Remade as WALK, DON'T RUN.▼●

Morgan! (1966-British) **97m.** ***½ D: Karel Reisz. Vanessa Redgrave, David Warner, Robert Stephens, Irene Handl. Decidedly offbeat gem. Artist Warner verges on insanity, keyed off by wife Redgrave's divorcing him, and goes on eccentric escapades. Script by David Mercer, from his play. Vanessa's film debut. Complete title is MORGAN—A SUITABLE CASE FOR TREATMENT.▼●

Morgan Stewart's Coming Home (1987) **C-96m.** *½ D: Alan Smithee. Jon Cryer, Lynn Redgrave, Nicholas Pryor, Viveka Davis, Paul Gleason. Inane comedy from the notorious, and pseudonymous, director Smithee (in this case Paul Aaron) about a teenager who returns home from boarding school and tries to change the ways of his obnoxious, politically ambitious parents. Plays like an unsold sitcom pilot. Redgrave is wasted, and even Cryer's considerable charm can't make this worth coming home to see. [PG-13]▼●

Morgan the Pirate (1961-Italian) **C-95m.** ** D: Andre de Toth. Steve Reeves, Valerie Lagrange, Lydia Alfonsi, Chelo Alonso. Considering cast and Reeves' career, fairly lively and interesting swashbuckler based on life of illustrious pirate. Original Italian running time: 105m. CinemaScope.▼●

Morituri SEE: **Saboteur: Code Name Morituri**

Morning After, The (1986) **C-103m.** ** D: Sidney Lumet. Jane Fonda, Jeff Bridges, Raul Julia, Diane Salinger, Richard Foronjy, Geoffrey Scott, James (Gypsy) Haake, Kathleen Wilhoite, Frances Bergen, Rick Rossovich. So-called thriller about alcoholic actress waking in bed with a dead man and not knowing how it happened. Tiresome story and ill-defined characters send this one down the tubes, despite promising star combo. Look fast for Kathy Bates as neighbor of victim. [R]▼●

Morning Glory (1933) **74m.** *** D: Lowell Sherman. Katharine Hepburn, Adolphe Menjou, Douglas Fairbanks, Jr., C. Aubrey Smith, Mary Duncan. Dated but lovely film from Zoe Akins' play about stage-struck young girl called Eva Lovelace who tries to succeed in N.Y.C. Good cast, sharp script, but it's magically compelling Hepburn who makes this memorable; she won her first Oscar for her work. Remade in 1958 as STAGE STRUCK.▼●

Morocco (1930) **92m.** *** D: Josef von Sternberg. Gary Cooper, Marlene Dietrich, Adolphe Menjou, Francis McDonald, Eve Southern, Paul Porcasi. Dietrich is alluring and exotic in her first Hollywood film, as a cabaret singer (improbably stuck in Morocco) who must choose between wealthy Menjou and Foreign Legionnaire Cooper. A treat. Marlene sings three numbers, including ''What Am I Bid.''▼●

Morons From Outer Space (1985-British) **C-87m.** **½ D: Mike Hodges. Griff Rhys Jones, Mel Smith, James B. Sikking, Dinsdale Landen, Jimmy Nail, Joanne Pearce, Paul Brown. Chaos reigns supreme in this inventive, uneven, but sometimes hilarious comedy about some very human aliens with British accents—who also happen to be brainless twits—and what happens when their spaceship crash-lands on Earth. Sight gags galore. [PG-13]▼

Mortadella SEE: **Lady Liberty**

Mortal Kombat (1995) **C-102m.** *½ D: Paul Anderson. Christopher Lambert, Robin Shou, Linden Ashby, Cary-Hiroyuki Tagawa, Bridgette Wilson, Talisa Soto, Trevor Goddard. Shou, Ashby, and Wilson are among those kompeting in a martial arts tournament with nothing less than the fate of Earth in the balance. Elaborate special effects and impressive set design are helpless against a weak story, uneven akting, and komikally thin karakters. (Lambert plays a god of elektricity with a penchant for lame wisekracks; Tagawa is a mugging villain.) Mostly just one fight after another, but that's what you might expect from a movie based on a video game. Followed by a sequel. [PG-13]▼●◗

Mortal Kombat: Annihilation (1997) **C-95m.** BOMB D: John Leonetti. Robin Shou, Talisa Soto, James Remar, Brian Thompson, Lynn ''Red'' Williams, Irina Pantaeva. Mind-numbing sequel rehashes battle between good and evil for the fate of mankind (*yawn*). OK visual effects but endless fight scenes and dreadful acting stop film dead in its tracks. Of interest only to *American Gladiator* fanatics and vidkids with really low attention spans. Remar's morph from David Carradine–style kung fu sensei to turbo warrior is unintentionally hilarious. Supermodel Pantaeva's inauspicious acting debut. [PG-13]▼●◗

Mortal Storm, The (1940) **100m.** ***½ D: Frank Borzage. Margaret Sullavan, James Stewart, Robert Young, Frank Morgan, Robert Stack, Bonita Granville, Irene Rich, Maria Ouspenskaya, Gene Reynolds, Ward Bond. Nazi takeover in Germany splits family, ruins life of father, professor Morgan; Stewart tries to leave country with professor's daughter (Sullavan). Sincere filming of Phyllis Bottome's novel is beautifully acted, with one of Morgan's finest performances. Screenplay by Claudine West, Andersen Ellis, and George Froeschel. Film debut of Dan Dailey (billed as Dan Dailey, Jr.); look sharp in second classroom scene for Tom Drake.▼

Mortal Thoughts (1991) **C-104m.** **½ D: Alan Rudolph. Demi Moore, Glenne Headly, Bruce Willis, John Pankow, Harvey Keitel, Billie Neal. Two police detectives question a woman about the incidents surrounding the murder of her best friend's husband, an abusive lout. Interesting, flashback-framed film boasts some good performances, but a cast of characters it's hard to care much about, and a conclusion that pulls the rug out from everything else we've just seen. Meaningless ''touches'' (like use of slow-motion) don't add anything. Moore coproduced. [R]▼●◗

Moscow Does Not Believe in Tears (1980-Russian) **C-152m.** *** D: Vladimir Menshov. Vera Alentova, Irina Muravyova, Raisa Ryazonova, Natalia Vavilova, Alexei Batalov. A trio of young women come to Moscow during the late '50s to seek love and work. Enjoyable if slow-moving; closer in spirit to THE BEST OF EVERYTHING than WAR AND PEACE. Oscar winner as Best Foreign Film.▼

Moscow Nights SEE: **I Stand Condemned**

Moscow on the Hudson (1984) **C-115m.** ***½ D: Paul Mazursky. Robin Williams, Maria Conchita Alonso, Cleavant Derricks, Alejandro Rey, Savely Kramarov, Elya Baskin. Fine original comedy-drama by Mazursky and Leon Capetanos about a Russian musician who defects during a trip to N.Y.C. —in Bloomingdale's, no less—and tries to come to grips with his new life in a new land. Full of endearing performances, perceptive and bittersweet moments—but a few too many false endings. Williams is superb in the lead. [R]▼●

Moses (1975-British-Italian) **C-141m. TVM** D: Gianfranco DeBosio. Burt Lancaster, Anthony Quayle, Ingrid Thulin, Irene Papas, William Lancaster, Mariangela Melato, Laurent Terzieff. Theatrical version of the six-hour *Moses—the Lawgiver* is not very impressive, with so-so special effects and a solid cast wasted. Screenplay by Anthony Burgess and Vittorio Bonicelli, but you're better off reading the book. Below average.▼

Mosquito Coast, The (1986) **C-117m.** ***½ D: Peter Weir. Harrison Ford, Helen Mirren, River Phoenix, Jadrien Steele, Hilary Gordon, Rebecca Gordon, Conrad Roberts, Andre Gregory, Dick O'Neill, Martha Plimpton, Butterfly McQueen, Jason Alexander. Utterly compelling, novelistic saga of iconoclastic inventor and idealist (Ford, in a knockout performance) who moves his family to remote village in Central America where he creates an incredible utopia . . . and proceeds to play God. Not for all tastes, since Ford's character is unsympathetic (though he was even worse in Paul Theroux's novel!). Beautifully crafted, with fine screenplay by Paul Schrader. A serious and emotionally gripping film. [PG]▼●◗

Mosquito Squadron (1969-British) **C-90m.** **½ D: Boris Sagal. David McCallum, Suzanne Neve, David Buck, David Dundas, Dinsdale Landen, Charles Gray. Good ensemble performances in tired story of Canadian-born RAF pilot (McCallum)'s crucial behind-the-lines mission to destroy Germany's ultimate weapon project. [G]

Moss Rose (1947) **82m.** **½ D: Gregory Ratoff. Peggy Cummins, Victor Mature, Ethel Barrymore, Vincent Price, Margo Woode. OK period-piece of ambitious chorus girl who blackmails her way into high society; scheme nearly backfires on her.

Most Beautiful, The (1944-Japanese) **85m.** ** D: Akira Kurosawa. Takashi Shimura, Ichiro Sugai, Soji Kiyokawa, Takako Irie, Yoko Yaguchi. One of Kurosawa's earliest features includes considerable WW2 propaganda; young women factory workers are exhorted by foreman Shimura (star of Kurosawa's IKIRU and SEVEN SAMURAI) to become production warriors by increasing output of optical weaponry. Tearful young girl Yaguchi later married Kurosawa. Not released in America until 1987.

Most Dangerous Game, The (1932) **63m.** *** D: Ernest B. Schoedsack, Irving Pichel. Joel McCrea, Fay Wray, Leslie Banks, Robert Armstrong, Noble Johnson. Vivid telling of Richard Connell's famous, oft-filmed story about a megalomaniac named Count Zaroff who hunts human beings on his remote island. Banks is a florid, sometimes campy villain. Made at the same time as KING KONG by many of the same people. Remade as GAME OF DEATH and RUN FOR THE SUN, and ripped off many other times.▼●◗

Most Dangerous Man Alive (1961) **82m.** ** D: Allan Dwan. Ron Randell, Debra Paget, Elaine Stewart, Anthony Caruso, Gregg Palmer. Inventive premise adequately handled; escaped convict involved in chemical explosion is transformed into "iron man" and seeks revenge on enemies. Director Dwan's last picture.

Most Dangerous Sin, The SEE: **Crime and Punishment** (1958)

Most Wanted (1976) **C-78m. TVM** D: Walter Grauman. Robert Stack, Shelly Novack, Leslie Charleson, Tom Selleck, Kitty Winn, Sheree North, Stephen McNally. Stack heads special police unit in search of a nun killer and winds up with another TV series. Average.▼

Most Wanted (1997) **C-99m.** ** D: David Glenn Hogan. Keenen Ivory Wayans, Jon Voight, Jill Hennessy, Paul Sorvino, Robert Culp, Wolfgang Bodison, Simon Baker Denny, David Groh, John Diehl, Eric Roberts. Wayans coexecutive-produced and scripted this slick but boring, predictable, and instantly forgettable actioner about a G.I., trained as a government assassin, who takes it on the lam after being framed for murdering the First Lady. Voight makes the most of his role as a creepy, power-obsessed general. Super 35. [R]▼●◗

Most Wanted Man SEE: **Most Wanted Man in the World, The**

Most Wanted Man in the World, The (1953-French) **85m.** ** D: Henri Verneuil. Fernandel, Zsa Zsa Gabor, Nicole Maurey, Alfred Adam. Fernandel vehicle is heavy-handed buffoonery, with bucolic comic mistaken for arch-criminal. Retitled: THE MOST WANTED MAN.

Most Wonderful Moment, The (1957-Italian) **94m.** ** D: Luciano Emmer. Marcello Mastroianni, Giovanna Ralli, Marisa Merlini, Ernesto Calindri. By-the-numbers soaper of poor young obstetrician Mastroianni, and what happens when his girlfriend, nurse Ralli, becomes pregnant.▼

Motel Hell (1980) **C-92m.** *½ D: Kevin

Connor. Rory Calhoun, Paul Linke, Nancy Parsons, Nina Axelrod, Wolfman Jack, Elaine Joyce, Dick Curtis, John Ratzenberger. Just *what* are Calhoun and his rotund sister putting in their smoked sausage out there in the boondocks? Good to see Rory and Wolfman sharing screen credit, but scattered laughs and a lively finish fail to distinguish this gory horror comedy. [R]▼●

Mother (1996) **C-104m.** *** D: Albert Brooks. Albert Brooks, Debbie Reynolds, Rob Morrow, Lisa Kudrow, John C. McGinley, Isabel Glasser, Peter White. Typically low-key but likable Brooks movie about a twice-divorced man who decides to move back in with his mother in an attempt to understand the root of his problems with women. A benign comedy of recognition, with Brooks as endearing as ever and Reynolds in a well-modulated, non-jokey performance as Mother. Brooks scripted with frequent collaborator Monica Johnson. [PG-13]▼●

Mother and Daughter: The Loving War (1980) **C-100m. TVM.** D: Burt Brinckerhoff. Tuesday Weld, Frances Sternhagen, Kathleen Beller, Jeanne Lang, Ed Winter. A young woman turns to her mother for help when her teenage daughter begins to rebel—just as *she* did twenty years earlier. Harry Chapin appears as himself (performing songs cowritten with wife Sandy Chapin). Teleplay by Rose Leiman Goldemberg. Above average.▼

Mother Carey's Chickens (1938) **82m.** ** D: Rowland V. Lee. Fay Bainter, Anne Shirley, Ruby Keeler, James Ellison, Walter Brennan, Frank Albertson, Virginia Weidler, Ralph Morgan, Margaret Hamilton. Pleasant if predictable, sentimental soaper of the Carey family and its attempt to set down roots despite poverty and tragedy. Based on the novel by Kate Douglas Wiggin and play by Wiggin and Rachel Crothers. Remade as SUMMER MAGIC by Disney.

Mother Didn't Tell Me (1950) **88m.** **½ D: Claude Binyon. Dorothy McGuire, William Lundigan, June Havoc, Gary Merrill, Jessie Royce Landis. Naive young woman marries a doctor, not contemplating demands of being a professional man's wife. McGuire brightens this lightweight comedy.

Mother Is a Freshman (1949) **C-81m.** **½ D: Lloyd Bacon. Loretta Young, Van Johnson, Rudy Vallee, Barbara Lawrence, Robert Arthur, Betty Lynn. Refreshing, wholesome confection; Young and daughter Lynn both attend college, vying for Van's affection.

Mother, Jugs & Speed (1976) **C-95m.** *** D: Peter Yates. Bill Cosby, Raquel Welch, Harvey Keitel, Allen Garfield, Larry Hagman, Bruce Davison, Dick Butkus, L.Q. Jones, Toni Basil. Hilarious black comedy about a rundown ambulance service more interested in number of patients serviced than their welfare. Hagman especially good as oversexed driver. Panavision. [PG]▼

Mother Kusters Goes to Heaven (1975-German) **C-120m.** *** D: Rainer Werner Fassbinder. Brigitte Mira, Ingrid Caven, Karl-Heinz Bohm, Margit Carstensen, Irm Hermann, Gottfried John. Potent, controversial film about political exploitation and the impact of industrialized society on the individual. It's the story of Frau Kusters (nicely played by Mira), who's exploited by the Left, the Right and the media after her factory-worker husband murders one of his bosses and commits suicide to protest the possibility of his being laid off. While the scenario is rife with cynicism, Frau Kusters is such a sympathetic character that the film exudes empathy for all humankind.▼

Mother Lode (1982) **C-101m.** ** D: Charlton Heston. Charlton Heston, Nick Mancuso, Kim Basinger, John Marley. Heston's a meanie here—in twin brother roles—playing a Scottish miner who'll stop at nothing to get his sullied hands on a mother lode of gold in the mountains of British Columbia. Lackluster script was written by his son, Fraser Clarke Heston, who also produced the film. Reissued as SEARCH FOR THE MOTHER LODE: THE LAST GREAT TREASURE. [PG]▼

Mother Night (1996) **C/B&W-110m.** *** D: Keith Gordon. Nick Nolte, Sheryl Lee, Alan Arkin, John Goodman, Kirsten Dunst, Arye Gross, Frankie Faison, David Strathairn, Bernard Behrens, Brawley Nolte. American prisoner in an Israeli jail writes his memoirs, flashing back to his upbringing in Germany, where his career as a successful playwright was interrupted by his recruitment as a U.S. spy. His mission: to pose as a Nazi propagandist on the radio. Nolte takes on the challenging role in this adaptation of Kurt Vonnegut's provocative novel by writer-producer Robert B. Weide. Somber, fascinating, and unsettling. Vivid contributions by Arkin, Goodman, and others in supporting roles. Vonnegut himself makes a cameo appearance near the end of the film. [R]▼●

Mother Riley Meets the Vampire SEE: **Vampire Over London**

Mother's Boys (1994) **C-95m.** ** D: Yves Simoneau. Jamie Lee Curtis, Peter Gallagher, Joanne Whalley-Kilmer, Vanessa Redgrave, Luke Edwards, Colin Ward, Joey Zimmerman, Joss Ackland. Curtis makes an unwise return to the horror genre in this silly mom-who-deserted-family-wants-them-back revenge film. Gallagher, in a rare sympathetic turn, plays the husband, and Edwards is the eldest of three sons (and the one whose buttons Mother tries her best to push). Suspense is minimal, and story is too undernourished to have much bite. Despite one (odd) nude scene, Jamie Lee fans would fare better re-renting HALLOWEEN. [R]▼●◗

Mother's Day (1980) **C-98m.** *½ D: Charles Kaufman. Tiana Pierce, Nancy Hendrickson, Deborah Luce, Rose Ross, Holden McGuire, Billy Ray McQuade. Just about the final word in the horror-misogyny genre. Three college chums are victimized by, then turn the tables on, a hillbilly mother and her two sons. No MURDER, HE SAYS, but Drano/electric carving-knife finale does boast showmanship.▼

Mother's Prayer, A (1995) **C-100m. TVM** D: Larry Elikann. Linda Hamilton, Noah Fleiss, Bruce Dern, Kate Nelligan, RuPaul, Corey Parker, S. Epatha Merkerson. Single mom Hamilton discovers she's dying of AIDS and desperately tries to find a good home for her eight-year-old son. Loving performances by the two leads drive this well-crafted film that's more life-affirming than harrowing; a fact-based story written by producer Lee Rose. Made for cable. Above average.▼

Mother Teresa (1986) **C-81m.** ***½ D: Ann and Jeanette Petrie. Narrated by Richard Attenborough. Revealing, compelling documentary look at the Nobel Peace prize-winning nun who for decades has been ministering to Calcutta's poor. She's seen traveling the globe, from Africa to Guatemala, Beirut to the South Bronx. An appropriately sober but life-affirming film.▼

Mother Wore Tights (1947) **C-107m.** *** D: Walter Lang. Betty Grable, Dan Dailey, Mona Freeman, Connie Marshall, Vanessa Brown, Veda Ann Borg. One of Grable's most popular films, about a vaudeville family. Colorful production, costumes, nostalgic songs and an Oscar-winning Alfred Newman score, plus specialty act by the great Señor Wences. Narrated by Anne Baxter.▼

Mothra (1961-Japanese) **C-100m.** **½ D: Ishiro Honda, Lee Kresel. Franky Sakai, Hiroshi Koizumi, Kyoko Kagawa, Emi Itoh, Yumi Itoh, Jelly Itoh, Ken Uehara. Colorful Japanese monster movie about a giant caterpillar who invades Tokyo to rescue tiny twin girls, who are guiding it with their supernatural powers. Caterpillar then turns into a giant moth (natch), which carries on the destruction. Mothra (or its descendants) turned up in later films too. Tohoscope.▼

Motorcycle Gang (1957) **78m.** *½ D: Edward L. Cahn. Anne Neyland, John Ashley, Carl (Alfalfa) Switzer, Raymond Hatton, Edmund Cobb. Cheap production dealing with crackdown on rampaging cycle gang.▼

Motorcycle Gang (1994) **C-84m. TVM** D: John Milius. Gerald McRaney, Jake Busey, John Cassini, Richard Edson, Carla Gugino, Elan Oberon, Marshall Teague, Robert Miranda. The 1950s: Father, mother, and teenaged daughter drive across the Southwest, but run afoul of the title criminals, led by Busey in the kind of role his father Gary used to play. Lots of talk, not much action, but it has a raw, brutal climax. One of Showtime's "Rebel Highway" entries, all based on old American-International pictures; this uses only the title of the 1957 film. Average.

Moulin Rouge (1952) **C-123m.** ***½ D: John Huston. Jose Ferrer, Zsa Zsa Gabor, Suzanne Flon, Eric Pohlmann, Colette Marchand, Christopher Lee, Michael Balfour, Peter Cushing. Rich, colorful film based on life of Henri de Toulouse-Lautrec, the 19th century Parisian artist whose growth was stunted by childhood accident. Huston brilliantly captures the flavor of Montmartre, its characters, and Lautrec's sadly distorted view of life. Excellent cast; memorable theme song by Georges Auric. Oscar winner for its stunning art direction-set decoration and costumes.▼●

Mountain, The (1956) **C-105m.** **½ D: Edward Dmytryk. Spencer Tracy, Robert Wagner, Claire Trevor, William Demarest, Richard Arlen, E. G. Marshall. Turgid tale of brothers Tracy and Wagner climbing peak to reach wreckage, for different reasons. VistaVision.▼

Mountain Family Robinson (1979) **C-100m.** **½ D: John Cotter. Robert F. Logan, Susan Damante Shaw, William Bryant, Heather Rattray, Ham Larsen, George (Buck) Flower. Kids may not understand "déjà vu," but they'll feel it if they watch this clone of earlier Wilderness Family pictures. Not bad, but so similar to others it hardly seems worth the effort. [G]▼

Mountain Men, The (1980) **C-102m.** BOMB D: Richard Lang. Charlton Heston, Brian Keith, Victoria Racimo, Stephen Macht, John Glover, Seymour Cassel, David Ackroyd, Victor Jory. Heston and Keith star as fur trappers in this unnecessarily bloody, crude, tiresome good-guys-vs.-Indians epic. Screenplay by Fraser Clarke Heston, the star's son. Panavision. [R]▼●

Mountain Road, The (1960) **102m.** **½ D: Daniel Mann. James Stewart, Lisa Lu, Glenn Corbett, Henry (Harry) Morgan, Frank Silvera, James Best. Stewart is always worth watching, but this saga of American squadron working in China during waning days of WW2 is pretty flat.▼

Mountains of the Moon (1990) **C-135m.** ***½ D: Bob Rafelson. Patrick Bergin, Iain Glen, Richard E. Grant, Fiona Shaw, John Savident, James Villiers, Adrian Rawlins, Delroy Lindo, Paul Onsongo, Bernard Hill, Roshan Seth, Anna Massey, Leslie Phillips, Roger Rees. Captivating saga of explorer Sir Richard Burton and his search for the source of the Nile River in the late 1800s. Bergin is a charismatic lead, with Glen as John Hanning Speke, the dilettante who accompanies him. Vivid, stimulating, and satisfying; manages to embrace the sweep of an epic film along with a compellingly personal story. Screenplay by Rafelson and William Harrison, based on the latter's biographical novel *Burton and Speke* and on actual journals of the two explorers. [R]▼●◗

Mourning Becomes Electra (1947) **173m.** **½ D: Dudley Nichols. Rosalind Russell, Michael Redgrave, Raymond Massey, Katina Paxinou, Nancy Coleman, Leo Genn, Kirk Douglas. Eugene O'Neill's play set in New England and adapted from the Greek tragedy *Oresteia.* Civil War general is killed by wife and their children seek revenge. Heavy, talky drama, even in 105m. version shown on TV.▼●

Mouse and His Child, The (1977) **C-83m.** BOMB D: Fred Wolf, Chuck Swenson. Voices of Peter Ustinov, Alan Barzman, Marcy Swenson, Cloris Leachman, Andy Devine, Sally Kellerman. Boring animated film about a toy mouse and his child, and their adventures in the real world. Talk, talk, talk and no action. [G]▼

Mouse Hunt (1997) **C-97m.** **½ D: Gore Verbinski. Nathan Lane, Lee Evans, Vicki Lewis, Maury Chaykin, Eric Christmas, Michael Jeter, Debra Christofferson, Camilla Soeberg, William Hickey, Christopher Walken. Two hapless brothers inherit a musty old house and a string factory from their father; the house has promise but is inhabited by one small, very crafty rodent who defies extermination. Black comedy and slapstick combine for surprisingly clever results, but after a while it's simply exhausting. Lane and Evans are an ideal (and very funny) team, but Laurel & Hardy and The Three Stooges did this sort of thing in twenty minutes flat. [PG]▼●◗

Mouse on the Moon, The (1963-British) **C-82m.** ***½ D: Richard Lester. Margaret Rutherford, Bernard Cribbins, Ron Moody, Terry-Thomas, Michael Crawford. Hilarious sequel to THE MOUSE THAT ROARED, about Duchy of Grand Fenwick. Tiny country enters space race, with little help from its befuddled Grand Duchess, Margaret Rutherford.

Mouse That Roared, The (1959-British) **C-83m.** ***½ D: Jack Arnold. Peter Sellers, Jean Seberg, David Kossoff, William Hartnell, Monty Landis, Leo McKern. Hilarious satire about the Duchy of Grand Fenwick declaring war on the U. S. Sellers stars in three roles, equally amusing. Gag before opening titles is a masterpiece. Roger Macdougall and Stanley Mann adapted Leonard Wibberley's novel. Sequel: THE MOUSE ON THE MOON. ▼●

Mousey (1974) **C-78m. TVM** D: Daniel Petrie. Kirk Douglas, Jean Seberg, John Vernon, Bessie Love, Suzanne Lloyd, Sam Wanamaker, James Bradford. Thriller about a milquetoast teacher (Douglas) who stops at nothing to take vengeance on his ex-wife. Tightly made, and Kirk's wonderfully sinister. Released theatrically overseas as CAT AND MOUSE. Above average.

Mouthpiece, The (1932) **90m.** ***½ D: Elliott Nugent, James Flood. Warren William, Sidney Fox, Mae Madison, Aline MacMahon, John Wray, Guy Kibee. Solid story based on life of flamboyant attorney William Fallon; up-and-coming prosecutor in D.A.'s office turns to defending people instead, becomes slick and successful, leaving morals behind. First-rate all the way. Scripted by Joseph Jackson and Earl Baldwin. Remade as THE MAN WHO TALKED TOO MUCH and ILLEGAL.

Mouth to Mouth (1978-Australian) **C-95m.** ***½ D: John Duigan. Kim Krejus, Sonia Peat, Ian Gilmour, Sergio Frazetto, Walter Pym. A pair of unemployed, aimless teenage couples steal and hustle to survive. Fascinating, funny, sad, with lively direction by Duigan.

Mouth to Mouth (1995-Spanish) **C-105m.** **½ D: Manuel Gomez Pereira. Javier Bardem, Maria Barranco, Aitana Sanchez-Gijon, Josep Maria Flotats, Myriam Mezieres. Moderately amusing comedy about an out-of-work actor who soon finds his thespian talents in hot demand on a phone-sex line. Complications arise when he becomes romantically involved with one of his customers. Attractive cast makes this erotic romp actually funnier than it has a right to be. Original title: BOCA A BOCA. Panavision. [R]▼

Move (1970) **C-90m.** BOMB D: Stuart Rosenberg. Elliott Gould, Paula Prentiss, Genevieve Waite, John Larch, Joe Silver, Ron O'Neal. One of those comedies that helped to kill Gould's career within a year; porn-writer/dog-walker has problems when he moves from one apartment to another, but not as many as viewers will have trying to make sense out of the film. Panavision. [R]

Move Over, Darling (1963) **C-103m.** **½ D: Michael Gordon. Doris Day, James Garner, Polly Bergen, Chuck Connors, Thelma Ritter, Fred Clark, Don Knotts, Elliott Reid, John Astin, Pat Harrington, Jr. Woman long thought dead returns from desert island sojourn, to find her husband has remarried. Slick, amusing remake of MY FAVORITE WIFE, with strong cast of character actors milking every laugh. Film was intended to star Marilyn Monroe and Dean Martin, under the title SOMETHING'S GOT TO GIVE, but production was halted early on, and Marilyn died shortly thereafter. CinemaScope.▼

Movers and Shakers (1985) **C-79m.** *½ D: William Asher. Walter Matthau, Charles

Grodin, Vincent Gardenia, Tyne Daly, Bill Macy, Gilda Radner. Satiric look at movie-making in the 80s, written and coproduced by Grodin, who spent years trying to get it made. Talented cast (including cameos by Steve Martin and Penny Marshall) largely wasted in this unfunny comedy sprinkled with just an occasional insight or laugh. Too bad ... *Love in Sex* had great possibilities. [PG]▼

Movie Crazy (1932) **84m.** *** D: Clyde Bruckman. Harold Lloyd, Constance Cummings, Kenneth Thomson, Sydney Jarvis, Eddie Fetherstone. Lloyd's best talkie recaptures the spirit of his silent-comedy hits, telling story of small-town boy who goes to Hollywood with stars in his eyes, gets rude awakening but finally makes good. Includes his famous magician's coat scene. Cummings is a charming leading lady.

Movie Maker, The (1967) **C-91m. TVM** D: Josef Leytes. Rod Steiger, Robert Culp, Anna Lee, James Dunn, Sally Kellerman. Strong performances by Steiger and Culp in drama detailing rivalry for control of movie studio. Stagy enactment of Rod Serling script. Originally a two-part *Chrysler Theatre* of 1965 titled "A Slow Fade to Black." Above average.

Movie Maker, The (1986) SEE: **Smart Alec**

Movie Movie (1978) **C/B&W-107m.** *** D: Stanley Donen. George C. Scott, Trish Van Devere, Eli Wallach, Red Buttons, Barbara Harris, Barry Bostwick, Harry Hamlin, Art Carney, Rebecca York, Ann Reinking, Kathleen Beller. Affectionate parody of 1930s double feature: "Dynamite Hands" is b&w boxing saga with Hamlin in the John Garfield-ish role; "Baxter's Beauties of 1933" is Busby Berkeley-type musical, with numbers staged by Michael Kidd (who plays Hamlin's father in first story). There's even a Coming Attractions prevue! Introduced by George Burns. [PG]▼

Movie Struck SEE: **Pick a Star**

Moving (1988) **C-89m.** *½ D: Alan Metter. Richard Pryor, Beverly Todd, Randy Quaid, Dave Thomas, Dana Carvey, Stacey Dash, Gordon Jump, Morris Day, Rodney Dangerfield, King Kong Bundy. Mass transit engineer Pryor falls into a dream job following his unexpected and unceremonious firing—only hitch: he and the family must relocate from New Jersey to Boise, Idaho. Wallows in the predictable (kids rebel, the movers are psychos), with a modest chuckle every half-hour or so. Pryor seems uncomfortable as Ozzie Nelson. [R]▼●

Moving Target (1967-Italian) **C-92m.** *½ D: Sergio Corbucci. Ty Hardin, Michael Rennie, Grazielle Granata, Paola Pitagora, Vittorio Caprioli. Incredibly plotted spy/counterspy stuff set in Athens, marred even further by sadistic, explicitly violent action.▼◗

Moving the Mountain (1994-British) **C/B&W-83m.** ***½ D: Michael Apted. Life-affirming documentary about young Chinese student Li Lu and others of his generation who became demonstrators at Tiananmen Square in 1989. The film also chronicles Li Lu's life during the Cultural Revolution and his reasons for deciding to defy his government. Revealing, never less than riveting; the "mountain" of the title is communist Chinese authorities. ▼●

Moving Violation (1976) **C-91m.** ** D: Charles S. Dubin. Stephen McHattie, Kay Lenz, Eddie Albert, Lonny Chapman, Will Geer, Jack Murdock, John S. Ragin. Redneck sheriff goes after young couple, leading to usual car chases. So what else is new? [PG]▼

Moving Violations (1985) **C-90m.** *½ D: Neal Israel. John Murray, Jennifer Tilly, James Keach, Brian Backer, Sally Kellerman, Fred Willard, Lisa Hart Carroll, Wendie Jo Sperber, Clara Peller, Nedra Volz, Ned Eisenberg. Threadbare comedy of adventures in traffic violations school; more potholes than laughs. Incidentally, wiseacre star Murray is Bill M.'s brother. [PG-13]▼●

Mozambique (1965-British) **C-98m.** *½ D: Robert Lynn. Steve Cochran, Hildegarde Neff, Vivi Bach, Paul Hubschmid, Martin Benson. Tiresome programmer with world-weary pilot Cochran unknowingly becoming immersed in drug smuggling and white slavery. Techniscope.

Mr. Ace (1946) **84m.** **½ D: Edwin L. Marin. George Raft, Sylvia Sidney, Stanley Ridges, Sara Haden, Jerome Cowan. Ordinary dirty-politics drama of office-seeking Sidney using Raft to achieve her goals.▼●◗

Mr. & Mrs. Bridge (1990) **C-124m.** ** D: James Ivory. Paul Newman, Joanne Woodward, Blythe Danner, Simon Callow, Kyra Sedgwick, Robert Sean Leonard, Margaret Welsh, Saundra McClain, Diane Kagan, Austin Pendleton, Remak Ramsay. Portrait of strait-laced, well-to-do Kansas City couple, and how they are affected by the demands of their growing children, and the changes that overtake them in the 1930s and 40s. A plethora of intriguing but undeveloped, half-baked story threads make it frustrating and unsatisfying. Newman and Woodward are excellent, as usual. Based on two novels by Evan S. Connell, *Mrs. Bridge* (1959) and *Mr. Bridge* (1969). [PG-13]▼●

Mr. and Mrs. Loving (1996) **C-105m. TVM** D: Richard Friedenberg. Timothy Hutton, Lela Rochon, Ruby Dee, Corey Parker, Isaiah Washington, Lawrence Dane, Jackie Richardson, Bill Nunn. Hutton and Rochon play the real-life Lovings, an interracial couple of the 1950s, who violated local statutes against racial intermingling. Their case triggered a landmark Supreme Court decision overturning all such anti-miscegenation laws. Rochon's maturing from uneducated young wife to civil rights activist is the heart and soul of this trenchant little film, written by first-time director Friedenberg, with a fine score by Branford Marsalis. Hutton also served as coexecutive producer. Made for cable. Above average. ▼

Mr. and Mrs. North (1941) **67m.** **½ D: Robert B. Sinclair. Gracie Allen, William Post, Jr., Paul Kelly, Rose Hobart, Virginia Grey, Tom Conway. Radio characters come to screen in comedy involving dead bodies being discovered; sometimes funny, sometimes forced, though it's interesting to see Gracie without George. Later a TV series.

Mr. & Mrs. Smith (1941) **95m.** *** D: Alfred Hitchcock. Carole Lombard, Robert Montgomery, Gene Raymond, Jack Carson, Philip Merivale, Betty Compson, Lucile Watson. Madcap comedy of Lombard and Montgomery discovering their marriage wasn't legal. One of Hitchcock's least typical films, but bouncy nonetheless; written by Norman Krasna.▼●

Mr. Arkadin (1955-Spanish-French) **99m.** **½ D: Orson Welles. Orson Welles, Michael Redgrave, Patricia Medina, Akim Tamiroff, Mischa Auer, Katina Paxinou, Robert Arden. Overblown Welles curiosity (thematically similar to CITIZEN KANE) in which he stars as a famed tycoon with a shady past; the scenario follows his actions after being threatened with blackmail by his daughter's suitor. Filmed in English and Spanish-language versions. Aka CONFIDENTIAL REPORT.▼●

Mr. Baseball (1992) **C-113m.** **½ D: Fred Schepisi. Tom Selleck, Ken Takakura, Aya Takanashi, Toshi Shioya, Dennis Haysbert. Pleasant if uninspired comedy about a washed-up big leaguer who's traded to Japan, where his smart-ass attitude almost does him in with his team, his manager, and the young Japanese woman who takes a liking to him. Selleck is ingratiating as usual. Panavision. [PG-13]▼●◗

Mr. Belvedere Goes to College (1949) **83m.** ** D: Elliott Nugent. Clifton Webb, Shirley Temple, Tom Drake, Alan Young, Jessie Royce Landis, Kathleen Hughes. The sharp-tongued character from SITTING PRETTY enrolls in college, with predictable results. Nothing special. Jeff Chandler has bit as a policeman.

Mr. Belvedere Rings the Bell (1951) **87m.** **½ D: Henry Koster. Clifton Webb, Joanne Dru, Hugh Marlowe, Zero Mostel, Doro Merande, Billy Lynn. Another follow-up to SITTING PRETTY isn't as witty. Webb enters old folks' home to prove his theory that age has nothing to do with leading a full life.

Mr. Billion (1977) **C-93m.** ** D: Jonathan Kaplan. Terence Hill, Valerie Perrine, Jackie Gleason, Slim Pickens, Chill Wills, William Redfield. Uninspired comedy about a lowly Italian mechanic (Hill, in his American debut) on a mad, cross-country scramble to claim a billion dollar legacy, and the attempts of scoundrels to swindle him out of it. [PG]▼

Mr. Blandings Builds His Dream House (1948) **94m.** *** D: H. C. Potter. Cary Grant, Myrna Loy, Melvyn Douglas, Reginald Denny, Sharyn Moffett, Connie Marshall, Louise Beavers, Ian Wolfe, Lurene Tuttle, Lex Barker. Slick comedy of city couple attempting to build a house in the country; expertly handled, with Cary at his peak. And no one ever described room colors better than Loy! Norman Panama and Melvin Frank scripted, from Eric Hodgins' novel. Also shown in computer-colored version. ▼●

Mr. Bug Goes to Town SEE: **Hoppity Goes to Town**

Mr. Death: The Rise and Fall of Fred A. Leuchter, Jr. (1999) **C-92m.** *** D: Errol Morris. Documentarian Morris has found another oddball to profile: a milquetoast type who's had a lifelong fascination with instruments of death. After becoming an expert at building and repairing electric chairs and the like, he's hired by Holocaust deniers to gather "evidence" as to whether Hitler's gas chambers in Poland were really used for their stated purpose. Leuchter strikes the viewer as amusing at first, then misguided, possibly insidious, and ultimately pathetic. Music by Caleb Sampson. [PG-13]▼◗

Mr. Deeds Goes to Town (1936) **115m.** **** D: Frank Capra. Gary Cooper, Jean Arthur, George Bancroft, Lionel Stander, Douglass Dumbrille, Mayo Methot, Raymond Walburn, Walter Catlett, H. B. Warner. Cooper is Longfellow Deeds, who inherits 20 million dollars and wants to give it all away to needy people. Arthur is appealing as the hard-boiled big-city reporter who tries to figure out what makes him tick. Capra won his second Oscar for this irresistible film, written by Robert Riskin (from Clarence Budington Kelland's story "Opera Hat"). Later a short-lived TV series.▼●◗

Mr. Denning Drives North (1953-British) **93m.** **½ D: Anthony Kimmins. John Mills, Phyllis Calvert, Eileen Moore, Sam Wanamaker. Cast's sincerity makes this murder yarn palatable, the biggest hunt being for the corpus delicti.

Mr. Destiny (1990) **C-110m.** ** D: James Orr. James Belushi, Linda Hamilton, Michael Caine, Jon Lovitz, Hart Bochner, Rene Russo, Bill McCutcheon, Pat Corley, Courteney Cox, Kathy Ireland. Blah, by-the-numbers fantasy with Belushi an average, bored working stiff who gets to go back in time and replay an at-bat in a high school baseball game—which significantly alters his fate. Well-intentioned but heavy-handed; comparisons to IT'S A WONDERFUL LIFE are more hopeful than actual. [PG-13]▼●

Mr. Forbush and the Penguins SEE: **Cry of the Penguins**

Mr. Hex (1946) **63m.** **½ D: William Beaudine. Leo Gorcey, Huntz Hall, Bobby Jordan, Gabriel Dell, Billy Benedict, David Gorcey, Gale Robbins, Ian Keith, Bernard Gorcey. Satisfying *Bowery Boys* silliness, as Sach is turned into a pugilistic powerhouse with the help of a hypnotist.▼

Mr. Hobbs Takes a Vacation (1962) **C-116m.** **½ D: Henry Koster. James Stewart, Maureen O'Hara, Fabian, John Saxon, Marie Wilson, Reginald Gardiner, Lauri Peters, John McGiver. Glossy Hollywood family fare, '60s-style, about various misadventures as Stewart and O'Hara's clan rent a house by the ocean for the summer. Based on a novel by Edward Streeter, the same man who wrote *Father of the Bride*. CinemaScope.▼

Mr. Holland's Opus (1995) **C-142m.** *** D: Stephen Herek. Richard Dreyfuss, Glenne Headly, Jay Thomas, Olympia Dukakis, W. (William) H. Macy, Alicia Witt, Jean Louisa Kelly, Nicholas John Renner, Joseph Anderson, Anthony Natale, Joanna Gleason. Disney dips into GOODBYE, MR. CHIPS for this sentimental, old-fashioned story of a musician who reluctantly takes a job as a high school music teacher, then spends the next thirty years of his life dedicated to imbuing students with a love of music. It's his own family that suffers. Too much time is spent on the climactic school play, but it's still a heartwarming tearjerker and Dreyfuss is perfect in the lead. Panavision. [PG] ▼●◗

Mr. Hulot's Holiday (1953-French) **86m.** ***½ D: Jacques Tati. Jacques Tati, Nathalie Pascaud, Michelle Rolla, Valentine Camax, Louis Perrault. Tati introduced his delightful Hulot character in this amusing excursion to a French resort town; a fond throwback to the days of silent-screen comedy. French version runs 114m.▼●

Mr. Imperium (1951) **C-87m.** **½ D: Don Hartman. Lana Turner, Ezio Pinza, Marjorie Main, Barry Sullivan, Cedric Hardwicke, Debbie Reynolds. Threadbare romance between Turner and Pinza, now a monarch; colorful but paper-thin.▼

Mr. Jealousy (1998) **C-105m.** **½ D: Noah Baumbach. Eric Stoltz, Annabella Sciorra, Chris Eigeman, Carlos Jacott, Marianne Jean-Baptiste, Brian Kerwin, Peter Bogdanovich, Bridget Fonda. Stoltz meets Sciorra and they hit it off, but his suspicions and jealousy over her former boyfriend start driving them both crazy. Talky but humorous romance with real N.Y.C. flavor and some priceless group therapy sequences. Stoltz also executive-produced. [R]▼

Mr. Jones (1993) **C-114m.** *½ D: Mike Figgis. Richard Gere, Lena Olin, Anne Bancroft, Tom Irwin, Delroy Lindo, Bruce Altman, Lauren Tom, Anna Maria Horsford, Lucinda Jenney, Taylor Negron. A manic depressive and a shrink on the rebound have a professionally taboo romance. Gere's behavior—bounding on stage during a concert, tightrope-walking a high construction beam—turns this into THE JESTER OF TIDES. Gere is OK; Olin gives an awkward performance and is horribly lit. Sat on the shelf for a year. [R]▼●◗

Mr. Kingstreet's War (1973) **C-92m.** **½ D: Percival Rubens. John Saxon, Tippi Hedren, Rossano Brazzi, Brian O'Shaughnessy. Loner and his wife find idyllic life at African game preserve disrupted by WW2 and set out to do something about it. Interesting and unusual. Aka HEROES DIE HARD.▼

Mr. Klein (1977-French) **C-122m.** **½ D: Joseph Losey. Alain Delon, Jeanne Moreau, Michael Lonsdale, Juliet Berto, Suzanne Flon. French-Catholic art dealer exploits Jews desperately in need of money during WW2, has tables turned on him when he's mistaken for a Jew with same name. Intriguing premise only partially fulfilled due to overlength, occasionally self-conscious direction. A curiosity. [PG]▼

Mr. Love (1985-British) **C-98m.** *** D: Roy Battersby. Barry Jackson, Maurice Denham, Christina Collier, Helen Cotterill, Julia Deakin, Linda Marlowe, Margaret Tyzack. Gentle, winning tale of quiet, reserved gardener Jackson, in a loveless marriage for almost 30 years and whom most everybody thinks is a joke—so why do all those women appear at his funeral? The CASABLANCA scene is a gem. [PG-13]▼

Mr. Lucky (1943) **100m.** *** D: H. C. Potter. Cary Grant, Laraine Day, Charles Bickford, Gladys Cooper, Alan Carney, Henry Stephenson, Paul Stewart, Kay Johnson, Florence Bates. Gambling-ship-owner Grant intends to fleece virtuous Day, instead falls in love and goes straight. Basis for later TV series has spirited cast, engaging script. Love that rhyming slang!▼●

Mr. Magoo (1997) **C-87m.** *½ D: Stanley Tong. Leslie Nielsen, Kelly Lynch, Matt Keeslar, Nick Chinlund, Stephen Tobolowsky, Ernie Hudson, Jennifer Garner, Malcolm McDowell, Miguel Ferrer. Alarmingly unfunny feature based on the famous nearsighted cartoon character (revived in the animated credits, with Greg Burson filling in for Jim Backus as the voice of Magoo). Nielsen does his best, as always, but the pointlessly complicated plot—about the theft of a precious ruby—just goes on and on. And there are an awful lot of mean-spirited characters for a kids' movie. Inauspicious Hollywood debut for Jackie Chan's frequent director and collaborator; even the closing outtakes aren't funny! [PG]▼●◗

Mr. Majestyk (1974) **C-103m.** **½ D: Richard Fleischer. Charles Bronson, Al Lettieri, Linda Cristal, Lee Purcell, Paul Koslo, Alejandro Rey. Above average Bronson thriller, casting him as Colorado watermelon farmer (!) marked for destruction by syndicate hit man Lettieri; surprisingly tongue-in-cheek script by Elmore Leonard. [PG]▼

Mr. Mom (1983) **C-91m.** **½ D: Stan Dragoti. Michael Keaton, Teri Garr, Martin Mull, Ann Jillian, Christopher Lloyd, Frederick Koehler, Taliesin Jaffe, Graham Jarvis, Jeffrey Tambor. Pleasant enough rehash of age-old sitcom premise: Mom gets a job when dad gets fired, leaving him to learn the perils of running a household. Likable stars make it palatable, but you've seen it all before. [PG]▼●◗

Mr. Moto With the Charlie Chan films going strong, John P. Marquand's character of a seemingly timid but cunning and intelligent sleuth named Mr. Moto seemed a natural for the movies. Twentieth Century-Fox, the same studio that was making the Chans, inaugurated the series in 1937 with THINK FAST, MR. MOTO, with the offbeat casting of Peter Lorre in the lead. Lorre fell into the role of the crafty Moto quite well, and played the character in all eight Moto films, through 1939. The series was entertaining, but somehow lacked the heart of the Chan films. Fortunately, they were endowed with slick productions and fine casts of character actors, which tended to overshadow the films' shortcomings. Moto globe-trotted from country to country, solving various mysteries with and without the help of police authorities, and confronted such formidable villains as Sig Ruman, Sidney Blackmer, John Carradine, Leon Ames, Ricardo Cortez, Jean Hersholt and Lionel Atwill. Needless to say, the diminutive Lorre was victorious in every encounter, with the negligible help of such "assistants" as dim-witted Warren Hymer in MR. MOTO IN DANGER ISLAND. Many consider THANK YOU, MR. MOTO (1938) the best of the series, with our hero hunting for a valuable map leading to an ancient treasure. In 1965 Fox decided to revive the long-dormant Moto character in a very low-budget second feature called, appropriately enough, THE RETURN OF MR. MOTO. Movie villain Henry Silva starred as Moto, but the film was cheaply done and completely unfaithful to the original conception of the character. With luck, future movie historians will ignore it and realize that for everyone Peter Lorre was *the* Mr. Moto.

MR. MOTO

Think Fast, Mr. Moto (1937)
Thank You, Mr. Moto (1938)
Mr. Moto's Gamble (1938)
Mr. Moto Takes a Chance (1938)
Mysterious Mr. Moto (1938)
Mr. Moto's Last Warning (1939)
Mr. Moto in Danger Island (1939)
Mr. Moto Takes a Vacation (1939)
The Return of Mr. Moto (1965)

Mr. Moto in Danger Island (1939) **63m.** **½ D: Herbert I. Leeds. Peter Lorre, Jean Hersholt, Amanda Duff, Warren Hymer, Richard Lane, Leon Ames. Moto faces death at every turn as he tracks a diamond smuggling ring to Puerto Rico. Minor entry highlighted by Hymer as the dim-witted "Twister McGurk." Remake of MURDER IN TRINIDAD (1934) with Moto character grafted onto original plot. Aka DANGER ISLAND.

Mr. Moto's Gamble (1938) **71m.** **½ D: James Tinling. Peter Lorre, Keye Luke, Dick Baldwin, Lynn Bari, Douglas Fowley, Jayne Regan, Harold Huber. Moto probes the death of a boxer and discovers a crooked gambling racket. *Charlie Chan* fans will note a guest appearance by Number One Son (Luke) assisting Moto. Originally scripted as a Chan film but reassigned to Moto after the sudden death of Warner Oland.

Mr. Moto's Last Warning (1939) **71m.** *** D: Norman Foster. Peter Lorre, Ricardo Cortez, Virginia Field, John Carradine, George Sanders, Robert Coote, John Davidson. Moto battles a fine rogues' gallery of character villains, as murderous saboteurs converge on the Suez Canal and do their best to dispose of the pesky sleuth.▼

Mr. Moto Takes a Chance (1938) **63m.** **½ D: Norman Foster. Peter Lorre, Rochelle Hudson, Robert Kent, J. Edward Bromberg, Chick Chandler, George Regas. Moto teams up with a British spy (Hudson) to uncover a munitions site in the jungles of Indochina. Bromberg is improbably but effectively cast as potentate.

Mr. Moto Takes a Vacation (1939) **63m.** **½ D: Norman Foster. Peter Lorre, Joseph Schildkraut, Lionel Atwill, Virginia Field, Iva Stewart, Victor Varconi. A pleasure trip becomes business for Moto as he tries to thwart criminal mastermind after the Queen of Sheba's crown as it's being transported to a museum. Brisk final entry in the Lorre series.

Mr. Muggs Rides Again (1945) **63m.** *½ D: Wallace Fox. Leo Gorcey, Huntz Hall, Billy Benedict, Johnny Duncan, Bud Gorman, Nancy Brinkman, Minerva Urecal, George Meeker, Mende Koenig, Pierre Watkin, Bernard Gorcey. Jockey Gorcey is suspended after being framed by some crooked gamblers, but (surprise!) redeems himself in the end. Lame *East Side Kids* romp.

Mr. Muggs Steps Out (1943) **63m.** **½ D: William Beaudine. Leo Gorcey, Huntz Hall, Billy Benedict, Bobby Stone, Bud Gorman, Dave Durand, Jimmy Strand, Joan Marsh, Gabriel Dell, Noah Beery, Sr. Gorcey gets a job as chauffeur to a society lady and ends up catching some jewel thieves. Some good laughs as crude Gorcey and the East Side Kids crash snooty high society.

Mr. Music (1950) **113m.** **½ D: Richard Haydn. Bing Crosby, Nancy Olson, Charles Coburn, Ruth Hussey, Marge and Gower Champion, Peggy Lee, Groucho Marx. Easygoing vehicle for crooner Crosby as Broadway songwriter who wants to live the easy life. Remake of ACCENT ON YOUTH.▼●

Mr. Nanny (1993) **C-84m.** *½ D: Michael Gottlieb. Terry "Hulk" Hogan (Bollea), Sherman Hemsley, Austin Pendleton, Robert Gorman, Madeline Zima, David Johansen, Mother Love. Lamebrained comedy featuring Hogan as a struggling wrestler hired to look after a pair of spoiled, ignored rich kids (whom weirdo Johansen is plotting to kidnap). Strictly for die-hard fans of the Hulkster. Hemsley and Hogan are no threat to Clark and McCullough. [PG]▼●

Mr. Nice Guy (1997-Hong Kong) **C-113m.** *** D: Samo Hung. Jackie Chan, Richard Norton, Miki Lee, Karen McLymont, Gabrielle Fitzpatrick, Vince Poletto. Jackie, a TV chef(!), is pursued by two sets of bad guys who are after an incriminating videotape that's fallen into his hands. One of Jackie's better later films, set in Melbourne and, like almost all his best movies, an action comedy. Dazzling and exciting fights abound, the best (and funniest) staged at a construction site. Only the climax, involving a colossal truck flattening a luxury home, is below par for the astounding Mr. Chan. Director Samo, Jackie's lifelong friend, has a cameo as an irritated bicyclist. Technovision. [PG-13]▼●◗

Mr. North (1988) **C-92m.** **½ D: Danny Huston. Anthony Edwards, Robert Mitchum, Lauren Bacall, Harry Dean Stanton, Anjelica Huston, Mary Stuart Masterson, Virginia Madsen, Tammy Grimes, David Warner, Hunter Carson, Christopher Durang, Mark Metcalf, Katharine Houghton. Bright but penniless young man makes a major impact on Newport high society in the 1920s by being forthright, ingenious, and possessing an unusual amount of electricity in his body! Agreeable fable based on Thornton Wilder's *Theophilus North* has many assets (fine cast, beautiful locations) as well as some liabilities (uneven performances, shifts of tone). Coscripted by John Huston, who also executive produced just before his death; this marks his son's theatrical feature debut as director. [PG]▼●

Mr. Patman (1980-Canadian) **C-105m.** *½ D: John Guillermin. James Coburn, Kate Nelligan, Fionnula Flanagan, Les Carlson, Candy Kane, Michael Kirby. Coburn is well cast in this convoluted, poorly made tale of a charming but slightly mad psycho-ward orderly and his shenanigans. Disappointing. Aka CROSSOVER. ▼

Mr. Peabody and the Mermaid (1948) **89m.** **½ D: Irving Pichel. William Powell, Ann Blyth, Irene Hervey, Andrea King, Clinton Sundberg. Mild comedy-fantasy by Nunnally Johnson has its moments, with unsuspecting Powell coming across a lovely mermaid while fishing. Powell makes anything look good.▼

Mr. Perrin and Mr. Traill (1948-British) **90m.** ** D: Lawrence Huntington. Marius Goring, David Farrar, Greta Gynt, Raymond Huntley. Lukewarm study of progressive vs. conservative schoolteaching.

Mr. Quilp (1975-British) **C-118m.** *** D: Michael Tuchner. Anthony Newley, David Hemmings, David Warner, Michael Hordern, Jill Bennett, Sarah Jane Varley. Entertaining musical version of Dickens' *The Old Curiosity Shop* with songs by Newley and musical score by Elmer Bernstein. Lighthearted until last reel when it goes serious in the Dickens vein. Retitled THE OLD CURIOSITY SHOP. Remade for cable in 1995. Panavision. [G]

Mr. Ricco (1975) **C-98m.** ** D: Paul Bogart. Dean Martin, Eugene Roche, Thalmus Rasulala, Geraldine Brooks, Denise Nicholas, Cindy Williams, Philip Michael Thomas. Martin in offbeat casting as criminal lawyer involved with racist killings, sex and assorted violence, but looks too tired to care. Good mystery angle. Panavision. [PG]

Mr. Robinson Crusoe (1932) **76m.** *** D: Edward Sutherland. Douglas Fairbanks Sr., William Farnum, Earle Browne, Maria Alba. An aging but agile Doug is up to his old tricks, betting that he can survive on a South Sea island à la Robinson Crusoe. Great fun; lovely score by Alfred Newman. Also released in silent version.▼●

Mr. Rock and Roll (1957) **86m.** ** D: Charles Dubin. Alan Freed, Little Richard, Clyde McPhatter, Frankie Lymon and the Teenagers, Teddy Randazzo, Chuck Berry, Rocky Graziano, Lois O'Brien, Lionel Hampton, Ferlin Husky, The Moonglows, Brook Benton, LaVern Baker. The saga of how Alan Freed "discovered" rock 'n' roll. In AMERICAN HOT WAX, Berry played opposite Tim McIntire portraying Freed; here, he acts with the real McCoy. Vintage footage of McPhatter, Lymon, Little Richard; Rocky Graziano is along for comic relief. Also of note: The

1999 TVM MR. ROCK 'N' ROLL: THE ALAN FREED STORY.

Mr. Sardonicus (1961) **89m.** ** D: William Castle. Ronald Lewis, Audrey Dalton, Guy Rolfe, Oscar Homolka. Recluse count with face frozen in hideous grin lures wife's boyfriend/doctor to castle to cure him. Minor fare despite good ending; Castle gave the theatrical audiences the option of voting "thumbs up" or "thumbs down" via a "Punishment Poll" (but only one conclusion was filmed). Screenplay by Ray Russell from his novella *Sardonicus*.▼

Mrs. 'Arris Goes to Paris (1992) **C-100m. TVM.** D: Anthony Shaw. Angela Lansbury, Omar Sharif, Diana Rigg, Lothaire Bluteau, John Savident, Lila Kaye, Tamara Gorski. Lansbury soufflé based on Paul Gallico's novel (and unproduced play) about an English charwoman who decides she simply must have an original Dior gown from Paris. A lightweight charmer best received by the star's legion of fans, directed by her son (both taking a break from *Murder, She Wrote*). Average.▼

Mr. Saturday Night (1992) **C-119m.** **½ D: Billy Crystal. Billy Crystal, David Paymer, Julie Warner, Helen Hunt, Mary Mara, Jerry Orbach, Ron Silver, Sage Allen, Jackie Gayle, Carl Ballantine, Slappy White, Conrad Janis, Jerry Lewis. Saga of a comedian who turns out to be his own worst enemy. Many moments of truth and insight, but too long, with too many climaxes, and Crystal's old-age makeup is garish and unbelievable. It's also tough to make an appealing movie about an unappealing character. The real treat is watching Paymer in a terrific performance as Crystal's long-suffering brother. Crystal's directing debut; he also cowrote with Lowell Ganz and Babaloo Mandel (both of whom appear fleetingly as inept TV writers). [R]▼●◗

Mrs. Brown (1997-British-U.S.-Irish) **C-103m.** *** D: John Madden. Judi Dench, Billy Connolly, Geoffrey Palmer, Antony Sher, Gerald Butler, Richard Pasco, David Westhead. Rewarding drama, set in the 1860s. Queen Victoria (Dench) has been in mourning for years, following the death of her beloved husband Albert; living in Windsor Castle, away from London and public life, she only comes out of her shell when her husband's trusted Highland horseman, John Brown (Connolly), refuses to coddle her. An unusual relationship develops between the two—much to the consternation of everyone else on the Queen's staff. Richly detailed, with two superb performances at the forefront; Sher is also impressive as the bemused Benjamin Disraeli. Screenplay by Jeremy Brock. [PG]▼●◗

Mrs. Brown, You've Got a Lovely Daughter (1968-British) **C-110m.** ** D: Saul Swimmer. Herman's Hermits, Stanley Holloway, Mona Washbourne, Sara Caldwell, Lance Percival. A silly excuse for a movie, with Herman and his Hermits heading for London to enter their greyhound in a race. In between the suspense they sing "There's a Kind of Hush All Over the World" and the title tune. Panavision. [G]▼

Mrs. Dalloway (1998-British-Netherlands) **C-97m.** *** D: Marleen Gorris. Vanessa Redgrave, Natascha McElhone, Rupert Graves, Michael Kitchen, Alan Cox, Lena Headey, Amelia Bullmore, Sarah Badel, Oliver Ford Davies, Katie Carr, John Standing, Robert Hardy, Margaret Tyzack, Phyllis Calvert. Redgrave is radiant as the wife of a British M.P. who, on the day of a major soiree, thinks back to her youth when she chose between a safe, secure life and a more daring existence with a man who truly loved her. McElhone is an excellent match for Redgrave in the flashback scenes. Thoughtful, intelligent drama adapted by actress Eileen Atkins from the Virginia Woolf novel. [PG-13]▼●

Mrs. Delafield Wants to Marry (1986) **C-100m. TVM** D: George Schaefer. Katharine Hepburn, Harold Gould, Denholm Elliott, David Ogden Stiers, Charles Frank, Kathryn Walker, Bibi Besch, Brenda Forbes, John Pleshette. Sunny romantic comedy created especially for Kate by Broadway playwright James Prideaux; a December/December relationship between a high society WASP and her kindly Jewish doctor. Above average.

Mrs. Doubtfire (1993) **C-125m.** *** D: Chris Columbus. Robin Williams, Sally Field, Pierce Brosnan, Harvey Fierstein, Polly Holliday, Lisa Jakub, Matthew Lawrence, Mara Wilson, Robert Prosky, Anne Haney, Scott Capurro. Crowd-pleasing comedy (with serious overtones) about a free spirit whose wife divorces him after fourteen years; he can't bear being separated from his three kids, so he disguises himself as a dowdy British housekeeper (under an Oscar-winning makeup job) and gets himself hired to look after them. Williams is in peak form, and director Columbus keeps story and characters reasonably realistic in order to drive home a humanistic message. Based on the book *Alias Madame Doubtfire* by Anne Fine. Williams and his wife produced. Panavision. [PG-13]▼●◗

Mr. Sebastian SEE: **Sebastian**

Mr. Skeffington (1944) **127m.** *** D: Vincent Sherman. Bette Davis, Claude Rains, Walter Abel, Richard Waring, Jerome Cowan, Charles Drake, Gigi Perreau. Grand soap opera spanning several decades of N.Y.C. life from 1914 onward. Davis is vain society woman who marries stockbroker Rains for convenience, discovering his true love for her only after many years. Lavish settings, bravura Davis performance. Restored to original 146m. release for homevideo.▼●

Mr. Skitch (1933) **70m.** **½ D: James Cruze. Will Rogers, Rochelle Hudson, ZaSu Pitts, Eugene Pallette, Harry Green, Charles Starrett. Airy Rogers vehicle follows family's adventures driving to California. Pure fluff, highlighted by British entertainer Florence Desmond's comic impressions of costar Pitts and Greta Garbo.▼

Mrs. Mike (1949) **99m.** **½ D: Louis King. Dick Powell, Evelyn Keyes, J. M. Kerrigan, Angela Clarke. Powell and Keyes are pleasing duo, as Canadian mountie indoctrinates his urban wife to rural life.▼

Mrs. Miniver (1942) **134m.** ***½ D: William Wyler. Greer Garson, Walter Pidgeon, Dame May Whitty, Teresa Wright, Reginald Owen, Henry Travers, Richard Ney, Henry Wilcoxon, Helmut Dantine, Peter Lawford. Moving drama about middle-class English family learning to cope with war. Winner of six Academy Awards—for Garson, Wright, director Wyler, and Best Picture, among others—this film did much to rally American support for our British allies during WW2, though its depiction of English life was decidedly Hollywoodized. Screenplay by Arthur Wimperis, George Froeschel, James Hilton, and Claudine West; based on Jan Struther's novel. Sequel: THE MINIVER STORY. Also shown in computer-colored version.▼●

Mr. Smith Goes to Washington (1939) **129m.** **** D: Frank Capra. James Stewart, Jean Arthur, Claude Rains, Edward Arnold, Guy Kibbee, Thomas Mitchell, Eugene Pallette, Beulah Bondi, Harry Carey, H. B. Warner, Charles Lane, Porter Hall, Jack Carson. Stewart is young idealist who finds nothing but corruption in U.S. Senate. Fine Capra Americana, with Stewart's top performance bolstered by Arthur as hard-boiled dame won over by earnest Mr. Smith, and a stellar supporting cast; Carey is magnificent as the Vice President. Brilliant script by Sidney Buchman; however, Lewis R. Foster's Original Story received the Oscar. Later a brief TV series. Remade as BILLY JACK GOES TO WASHINGTON.▼●◗

Mrs. Munck (1996) **C-100m. TVM** D: Diane Ladd. Diane Ladd, Bruce Dern, Kelly Preston, Shelley Winters, Jim Walton, Scott Fisher, Seymour Cassel. A wronged woman takes revenge on her former husband—now old and wheelchair-bound—by taking him in and torturing him. A field day for Ladd, who wrote (from Ella Leffland's novel) and directed, with real-life ex-husband Dern as a costar. On its debut it was accompanied by a ''making of'' short by their daughter, actress Laura Dern. Made for video; debuted on cable. Average.▼

Mr. Soft Touch (1949) **93m.** ** D: Henry Levin, Gordon Douglas. Glenn Ford, Evelyn Keyes, John Ireland, Beulah Bondi, Percy Kilbride, Ted de Corsia. Ford and Keyes are mild romantic duo in unimportant story of ex-G.I. involved with social worker and gangster-run nightclub.

Mrs. O'Malley and Mr. Malone (1950) **69m.** ** D: Norman Taurog. Marjorie Main, James Whitmore, Ann Dvorak, Fred Clark, Dorothy Malone, Phyllis Kirk. Main is rambunctious but can't elevate film about small-towner winning prize contest, involved with murder on a N.Y.C-bound train. Whitmore is most enjoyable.

Mrs. Parker and the Vicious Circle (1994) **C/B&W-125m.** **½ D: Alan Rudolph. Jennifer Jason Leigh, Campbell Scott, Matthew Broderick, Andrew McCarthy, Peter Gallagher, Jennifer Beals, Gwyneth Paltrow, Sam Robards, Martha Plimpton, Tom McGowan, Stephen Baldwin, Wallace Shawn, Lili Taylor, James Le Gros, Keith Carradine, Nick Cassavetes, Jane Adams, Gary Basaraba, Rebecca Miller, Heather Graham, Jake Johannsen, Chip Zien. Closeup look at Dorothy Parker, fabled writer and charter member of the Algonquin Round Table in the 1920s; a vivid recreation of that period and those celebrated wits, but Parker's chronic unhappiness (and Leigh's often mannered performance) makes for tough going in this longish film. Scott is a standout as Robert Benchley in the well-chosen supporting cast; the famous humorist's grandson, author Peter Benchley, appears early on as editor Frank Crowninshield. Stanley Tucci appears unbilled near the end. Super 35. [R] ▼●

Mrs. Parkington (1944) **124m.** *** D: Tay Garnett. Greer Garson, Walter Pidgeon, Edward Arnold, Gladys Cooper, Agnes Moorehead, Peter Lawford, Dan Duryea, Lee Patrick. Determined Garson has lofty ambitions, marries wealthy but homespun Pidgeon, and pushes her way into society; overlong, well-mounted soaper.▼

Mrs. Pollifax—Spy (1971) **C-110m.** *½ D: Leslie Martinson. Rosalind Russell, Darren McGavin, Nehemiah Persoff, Harold Gould, John Beck, Dana Elcar. A bored widow volunteers as a CIA agent—and gets accepted—in this lame comedy spy caper. Russell's last theatrical film (for which she did the screenplay, under pseudonym) is also one of her worst. [G]

Mrs. Santa Claus (1996) **C-100m. TVM** D: Terry Hughes. Angela Lansbury, Charles Durning, Michael Jeter, Terrence Mann, David Norona, Debra Wiseman. In this tuneful star vehicle (though the score's hardly memorable), Angela finds herself stranded in 1910 Manhattan when her sleigh is downed by a wind current while she is checking out a new round-the-world night-before-Xmas route for hubby. Lansbury's often overlooked singing talents are spotlighted in this original television musical reuniting her with composer Jerry Herman, who wrote both *Mame* and *Dear World,* the shows for which she won two of her four Broadway Tonys. Average.▼●

Mrs. Soffel (1984) **C-110m.** ** D: Gillian Armstrong. Diane Keaton, Mel Gibson, Matthew Modine, Edward Herrmann, Trini Alvarado, Jennie Dundas, Danny Corkill, Terry O'Quinn. Interesting but gloomy, emotionally aloof rendering of true story, set in 1901, when wife of Pittsburgh prison warden falls in love with convicted murderer Gibson. Well made, but a pall hangs over entire film. [PG-13]▼●

Mrs. Wiggs of the Cabbage Patch (1934) **80m.** *** D: Norman Taurog. W. C. Fields, Pauline Lord, ZaSu Pitts, Evelyn Venable, Kent Taylor, Donald Meek, Virginia Weidler. Venerable melodrama about a good-hearted woman and her ever-growing brood gets a shot of comic adrenalin from Fields, who's perfectly matched with Pitts. Not a typical Fields vehicle by any means. Based on the 1901 novel by Alice Hegan Rice; filmed before in 1914 and 1919; remade in 1942.▼

Mrs. Wiggs of the Cabbage Patch (1942) **80m.** **½ D: Ralph Murphy. Fay Bainter, Hugh Herbert, Vera Vague (Barbara Jo Allen), Barbara Britton, Carolyn Lee, Billy Lee, Carl Switzer, Moroni Olsen. Abandoned wife with large family waits patiently for husband to return. A notch above average.

Mrs. Winterbourne (1996) **C-104m.** **½ D: Richard Benjamin. Shirley MacLaine, Ricki Lake, Brendan Fraser, Miguel Sandoval, Loren Dean, Peter Gerety, Susan Haskell. Wide-eyed Lake, alone in the world, is impregnated by her sleazy boyfriend, who then kicks her out; a coincidental meeting with another pregnant woman on a train leads to mistaken identity, and she's taken in by a wealthy Boston family who think she's one of their own. Likable comedy goes flat, but benefits from earnest performances. Based on Cornell Woolrich's *I Married a Dead Man,* which was filmed before, more seriously, as NO MAN OF HER OWN (1950) and I MARRIED A SHADOW (1982). Paula Prentiss (Mrs. Richard Benjamin) appears unbilled as an obnoxious nurse. [PG-13] ▼●

Mr. Sycamore (1974) **C-88m.** *½ D: Pancho Kohner. Jason Robards, Sandy Dennis, Jean Simmons, Robert Easton, Mark Miller. A milquetoasty mailman with a nagging wife (and a crush on local librarian) decides to escape rat race by turning into a tree! A definite curio, sadly defeated by heavy-handed treatment of material.▼

Mr. Toad's Wild Ride SEE: **Wind in the Willows, The**

Mr. Universe (1988-Hungarian) **C-96m.** *½ D: Gyorgy Szomjas. Mickey Hargitay, Laszlo Szabo, George Pinter, Mariska Hargitay. Tedious film mixes fact and fancy as a Hungarian dreamer comes to America to make a movie about Hungarian-born Mickey Hargitay, husband of Jayne Mansfield and a former Mr. Universe. Could have been an intriguing look at the American dream, as seen through a foreigner's eyes, but turns out pretentious and boring.

Mr. Winkle Goes to War (1944) **80m.** **½ D: Alfred E. Green. Edward G. Robinson, Ruth Warrick, Ted Donaldson, Robert Armstrong, Bob Haymes, Richard Lane. Wilbert Winkle (Robinson) is timid, henpecked, physically unfit and past forty, yet he's drafted into WW2. Clever, insightful little comedy.▼

Mr. Wise Guy (1942) **70m.** *½ D: William Nigh. Leo Gorcey, Huntz Hall, Bobby Jordan, David Gorcey, Sunshine Sammy Morrison, Guinn Williams, Bill Lawrence, Joan Barclay, Gabriel Dell, Bobby Stone, Billy Gilbert, Benny Rubin, Douglas Fowley, Ann Doran, Jack Mulhall, Warren Hymer. Trivial (but well cast) *East Side Kids* romp, about corruption at a reform school, from which they break out to catch a killer.▼

Mr. Wonderful (1993) **C-98m.** **½ D: Anthony Minghella. Matt Dillon, Annabella Sciorra, Mary-Louise Parker, William Hurt, Vincent D'Onofrio, David Barry Gray, Bruce Kirby, Dan Hedaya, Bruce Altman. Onetime childhood sweethearts Dillon and Sciorra get divorced, after she broadens her blue-collar horizons; to get out of paying her alimony, he tries to marry her off. Takes its time, but succeeds when exploring its characters' feelings. The attractive (and competent) cast helps. [PG-13]▼●◗

Mr. Wong Author Hugh Wiley created a distinguished, gentlemanly Oriental detective named Mr. Wong for a *Collier's* magazine story in 1935. Three years later, inspired no doubt by the success of the Charlie Chan and Mr. Moto films, Poverty Row studio Monogram Pictures decided to bring Mr. Wong to life on screen. In what was considered a casting coup, the studio managed to sign Boris Karloff for the part, and it is his presence that lends these films what meager distinction they have. The mysteries themselves aren't bad (particularly in the first entry, MR. WONG, DETECTIVE), but there's far too much talk, and no production niceties whatsoever. Running characters, like the gruff and skeptical Captain Street, played by Grant Withers, and an obnoxious reporter played by Marjorie Reynolds, are heavy-handed, to say the least. When Karloff left the series in 1940, Monogram experimented by hiring Charlie Chan's former Number One Son, Keye Luke, to play a younger version of Wong, in PHANTOM OF CHINATOWN. It was an interesting idea that didn't come off.

MR. WONG

Mr. Wong, Detective (1938)
Mystery of Mr. Wong (1939)
Mr. Wong in Chinatown (1939)
The Fatal Hour (1940)
Doomed to Die (1940)
Phantom of Chinatown (1941)

Mr. Wong, Detective (1938) **69m.** ** D: William Nigh. Boris Karloff, Grant Withers, Maxine Jennings, Evelyn Brent, Lucien Prival, William Gould. First and best of six films in which Karloff portrays Hugh Wiley's Chinese detective Mr. Wong. The murder is neatly carried out—and the murderer's identity is a real surprise. Monogram Pictures' attempt to emulate the success of the Charlie Chan and Mr. Moto series.▼●◗

Mr. Wong in Chinatown (1939) **70m.** *½ D: William Nigh. Boris Karloff, Grant Withers, William Royle, Marjorie Reynolds, Peter George Lynn, Lotus Long, Richard Loo. Blah Mr. Wong mystery, third in the series, with the sleuth becoming involved in the case of a Chinese princess' murder.▼

Mr. Write (1994) **C-89m.** BOMB D: Charlie Loventhal. Paul Reiser, Jessica Tuck, Martin Mull, Doug Davidson, Jane Leeves, Calvert De Forest, Gigi Rice, Tom Wilson, Wendi Jo Sperber, Darryl M. Bell, voice of Ben Stein. Astonishingly awful comedy about a would-be writer with no talent who falls head over heels for an advertising executive (Tuck) when he chances to work on a TV commercial. Clichéd at best, annoyingly amateurish at worst. This was completed in 1992 before Reiser launched his TV series *Mad About You*. [PG-13]▼●

Mr. Wrong (1985) SEE: **Dark of the Night**

Mr. Wrong (1996) **C-92m.** ** D: Nick Castle. Ellen DeGeneres, Bill Pullman, Joan Cusack, Dean Stockwell, Joan Plowright, Ellen Cleghorne, John Livingston, Robert Goulet, Polly Holliday, Louie Anderson. Single DeGeneres finds the perfect man in Pullman . . . or so she thinks. Not the light, funny romantic comedy you might expect, but a dark-humored attempt at satire on stalking. DeGeneres, in her starring debut, turns in a fine performance opposite the always reliable Pullman, but an uneven script works against the cast. [PG-13]▼●

Ms. Don Juan (1973-French) **C-87m.** *½ D: Roger Vadim. Brigitte Bardot, Maurice Ronet, Robert Hossein, Mathieu Carriere, Jane Birkin, Michele Sand. Bardot, in title role, seduces and/or humiliates everyone in her sight: a priest (who's also her cousin), a politician, a businessman. Glossy but limp; may be good for some unintended laughs.▼

Ms. 45 (1981) **C-84m.** **½ D: Abel Ferrara. Zoe Tamerlis, Steve Singer, Jack Thibeau, Peter Yellen, Darlene Stuto. Tamerlis is raped twice, gets her ''revenge'' by murdering every male in sight. Well-made, violent role-reversal formula film with echoes of PSYCHO, REPULSION, CARRIE, etc., which won some strong reviews and a cult reputation. Aka ANGEL OF VENGEANCE. [R]▼●

Much Ado About Nothing (1993-British-U.S.) **C-111m.** *** D: Kenneth Branagh. Kenneth Branagh, Michael Keaton, Robert Sean Leonard, Keanu Reeves, Emma Thompson, Denzel Washington, Richard Briers, Kate Beckinsale, Brian Blessed, Richard Clifford, Ben Elton, Gerard Horan, Phyllida Law, Imelda Staunton, Jimmy Yuill. Shakespeare's comedy of the wooing of Benedick (played by actor-director-screenwriter Branagh) and Beatrice (his then wife, Thompson) is set and shot entirely in and around an Italian villa in Tuscany and features a top-notch supporting cast. The film is rowdy, high spirited, and remarkably fast paced; this exhilaration brings vigor to the Bard's text, though the poetry sometimes gets lost in the shenanigans. Branagh does impressive job, but cannot match earlier Shakespearean effort, HENRY V (1989). [PG-13]▼●◗

Muddy River (1982-Japanese) **105m.** ***½ D. Kohei Oguri. Nobutaka Asahara, Takahiro Tamura, Yumiko Fujita, Minoru Sakurai, Makiko Shibato. Life in postwar Japan, as perceived by two young boys. Stunning, memorable Ozu-like tale, with lovely b&w photography. Independently produced.

Mudlark, The (1950) **99m.** *** D: Jean Negulesco. Irene Dunne, Alec Guinness, Finlay Currie, Anthony Steel, Andrew Ray, Beatrice Campbell, Wilfrid Hyde-White. Offbeat drama of Queen Victoria (Dunne), a recluse since her husband's death, coming back to reality after meeting waif who stole into her castle. Dunne does quite well as Queen, with Guinness a joy as Disraeli. Filmed in England.

Mug Town (1943) **60m.** ** D: Ray Taylor. Billy Halop, Huntz Hall, Bernard Punsly, Gabriel Dell, Grace McDonald, Edward Norris, Murray Alper, Tommy Kelly. The Little Tough Guys take on racketeers in this ''patriotic'' series entry.

Mulan (1998) **C-88m.** *** D: Barry Cook, Tony Bancroft. Voices of Ming-Na Wen, Lea Salonga, Eddie Murphy, B. D. Wong, Donny Osmond, Harvey Fierstein, Miguel Ferrer, Pat Morita, June Foray, Miriam Margolyes, George Takei, James Shigeta, Gedde Watanabe, James Hong. Disney's animated musical rendering of an ancient Chinese legend, about a headstrong daughter who disguises as a boy in order to take her father's place in the Imperial Army—and bring honor to her family. Strikingly staged and designed, with a strong and appealing leading character; the constant comedy "relief," while funny, seems jarring and unnecessary in such a strong dramatic tale. [G]▼●◗

Mulholland Falls (1996) **C-107m.** ★★ D: Lee Tamahori. Nick Nolte, Melanie Griffith, Chazz Palminteri, Michael Madsen, Chris Penn, Treat Williams, Jennifer Connelly, Andrew McCarthy, John Malkovich, Daniel Baldwin, Kyle Chandler, Ed Lauter, Aaron Neville. L.A. period piece (and CHINATOWN wannabe) about an elite squad of cops who make their own rules . . . until their leader (Nolte) becomes personally involved in a murder case with far-reaching consequences. Story unfolds in an obvious, heavy-handed way, and much of the cast is wasted. Tiresome, redundant score by Dave Grusin. That's production designer Richard Sylbert (who also worked on CHINATOWN) as the coroner. William L. Petersen, Rob Lowe, Louise Fletcher, and Bruce Dern appear unbilled. [R]▼●

Multiplicity (1996) **C-117m.** ★★½ D: Harold Ramis. Michael Keaton, Andie MacDowell, Harris Yulin, Richard Masur, Eugene Levy, Ann Cusack, Brian Doyle-Murray. Working stiff who feels pulled in all directions by his job and his family finds a solution: he clones himself—again and again and again. Amusing gimmick comedy, in the same vein as Ramis' GROUNDHOG DAY, but not quite as good. Keaton has a field day with his multiple characters, but the premise is stretched way beyond credibility and wears thin. Panavision. [PG-13]▼●◗

Mumford (1999) **C-112m.** ★★½ D: Lawrence Kasdan. Loren Dean, Hope Davis, Jason Lee, Alfre Woodard, Mary McDonnell, Pruitt Taylor Vince, Zooey Deschanel, Martin Short, David Paymer, Jane Adams, Ted Danson, Kevin Tighe, Dana Ivey. Quirky, novelistic film about a quiet, clean-cut psychologist who wins over a small town with his commonsense approach to their problems—while remaining an enigma himself. Original and amusing in a nice, old-fashioned way, but awfully tidy. Written by Kasdan. Super 35. [R]▼◗

Mummy, The (1932) **72m.** ★★★½ D: Karl Freund. Boris Karloff, Zita Johann, David Manners, Arthur Byron, Edward Van Sloan, Bramwell Fletcher, Noble Johnson. Horror classic stars Karloff as Egyptian mummy, revived after thousands of years, believing Johann is reincarnation of ancient mate. Remarkable makeup and atmosphere make it chills ahead of many follow-ups.▼●

Mummy, The (1959-British) **C-88m.** ★★½ D: Terence Fisher. Peter Cushing, Christopher Lee, Yvonne Furneaux, Eddie Byrne, Felix Aylmer, Raymond Huntley. Against warnings of severe consequences, archaeologists desecrate ancient tomb of Egyptian Princess Ananka. They return to England and those consequences. Stylish Hammer horror film.▼●

Mummy, The (1999) **C-124m.** ★½ D: Stephen Sommers. Brendan Fraser, Rachel Weisz, John Hannah, Arnold Vosloo, Kevin J. O'Connor, Jonathan Hyde, Oded Fehr. Hokey, jokey, Indiana Jones–ish adventure yarn has little to do with earlier Mummy movies. Librarian and Egyptologist Weisz (a clumsy character in the first scene—then, oddly, never again) hires Fraser to lead her to the "lost" city of Hamunaptra, where the tomb of Imhotep (Vosloo) is desecrated, to everyone's regret. Special effects galore, but no sense of awe or wonder; what's more, it goes on forever. Is that Dick Foran in the mummy attack scene? Panavision. [PG-13] ▼●◗

Mummy's Curse, The (1944) **62m.** ★★½ D: Leslie Goodwins. Lon Chaney, Jr., Peter Coe, Virginia Christine, Kay Harding, Dennis Moore, Martin Kosleck, Kurt Katch. Kharis and the reincarnated Ananka, last seen slipping into a New England swamp, are unaccountably dug up in a Louisiana bayou, where he's soon strangling people again. Surprisingly eerie and effective, with a good performance by Christine. Silent star William Farnum has a bit role as a caretaker. Last of the series.▼●

Mummy's Ghost, The (1944) **60m.** ★½ D: Reginald LeBorg. Lon Chaney, Jr., John Carradine, Ramsay Ames, Robert Lowery, Barton MacLane, George Zucco. Sequel to THE MUMMY'S TOMB finds seemingly unkillable Kharis and his mentor (Carradine) on the trail of a woman who is the reincarnation of Princess Ananka. Least interesting of the series, with nothing new or different to offer. Followed by THE MUMMY'S CURSE.▼●

Mummy's Hand, The (1940) **67m.** ★★★ D: Christy Cabanne. Dick Foran, Wallace Ford, Peggy Moran, Cecil Kellaway, George Zucco, Tom Tyler, Eduardo Ciannelli, Charles Trowbridge. Archeologists seeking lost tomb of Egyptian princess get more than they bargained for when they find it guarded by a living—and very deadly—mummy. First of the "Kharis" series is entertaining blend of chills and comedy, with good cast, flavorful music and atmosphere. Not a sequel to THE MUMMY (1932), although it does utilize flashback footage; itself followed by three sequels. ▼●

Mummy's Shroud, The (1967-British) **C-90m.** BOMB D: John Gilling. Andre Morell, John Phillips, David Buck, Elizabeth Sellars, Maggie Kimberley, Michael Ripper. British expedition takes mummy of child pharaoh back to Cairo; boy's guardian, also a mummy, murders those responsible. One of the least of the Hammer horrors. Narrated by Peter Cushing. ▼●

Mummy's Tomb, The (1942) **61m.** ★★ D:

Harold Young. Lon Chaney, Jr., Elyse Knox, John Hubbard, Turhan Bey, Dick Foran, Wallace Ford, George Zucco, Mary Gordon. Sequel to THE MUMMY'S HAND finds Kharis (now played by Chaney) transported to America to kill off surviving members of the expedition. Weak script and too much stock footage are the real villains. ▼●

Mumsy, Nanny, Sonny and Girly (1970-British) **C-101m.** BOMB D: Freddie Francis. Vanessa Howard, Michael Bryant, Ursula Howells, Pat Heywood, Howard Trevor. Rock-bottom murder tale of eccentric family where children's "game-playing" has lethal overtones. Stupid. Aka GIRLY. [R]▼

Munster, Go Home (1966) **C-96m.** **½ D: Earl Bellamy. Fred Gwynne, Yvonne De Carlo, Terry-Thomas, Hermione Gingold, John Carradine, Debby Watson, Butch Patrick. Monster family goes to England to claim a castle they've inherited; juvenile production based on the popular TV sitcom. TVM HERE COME THE MUNSTERS followed in 1995.

Muppet Christmas Carol, The (1992) **C-85m.** *** D: Brian Henson. Michael Caine, Kermit the Frog, Miss Piggy, Fozzie Bear, The Great Gonzo, Animal, Rizzo the Rat (Frank Oz, Dave Goelz, Steve Whitmire, Jerry Nelson). Delightful adaptation of the Dickens perennial, with a human Scrooge (Caine, in a nicely modulated performance) surrounded by mostly Muppet characters. Jerry Juhl's script neatly balances humor with the story's robust melodrama, and Paul Williams's songs add perfect punctuation. [G]▼●

Muppet Movie, The (1979) **C-94m.** *** D: James Frawley. Kermit the Frog, Miss Piggy, Fozzie Bear, and the Muppets (Jim Henson, Frank Oz, Jerry Nelson, Richard Hunt, Dave Goelz), Charles Durning, Austin Pendleton; 15 guest stars. Enjoyable showcase for Jim Henson's irresistible characters, charting Kermit's odyssey from a Georgia swamp to Hollywood. Unnecessary movie-star cameos and pedestrian music score can't dim Muppets' appeal in their first feature film. Trimmed from 97m. after initial release. [G]▼●

Muppets from Space (1999) **C-82m.** **½ D: Tim Hill. Gonzo, Kermit the Frog, Miss Piggy (Dave Goelz, Steve Whitmire, Frank Oz), Jeffrey Tambor, F. Murray Abraham, Ray Liotta, David Arquette, Andie MacDowell, Pat Hingle, Hollywood Hulk Hogan. Gonzo learns that he's really a stranded alien, and that others of his race are on the way. Conspiracy-minded Tambor is sure this means an invasion. Weak Muppet outing turns the story over to supporting characters, and loses the edge that sparked their earlier adventures. OK overall. [G]▼◗

Muppets Take Manhattan, The (1984) **C-94m.** *** D: Frank Oz. Kermit the Frog, Miss Piggy, Fozzie Bear, Gonzo, et al. (Jim Henson, Frank Oz, Jerry Nelson, Richard Hunt, Dave Goelz, Steve Whitmire), Dabney Coleman, Art Carney, James Coco, Joan Rivers, Gregory Hines, Linda Lavin, surprise guest stars. The Muppets try to crash Broadway with their college show, but Kermit soon discovers there's a broken heart for every light . . . Enjoyable outing with bouncy songs, nice use of N.Y.C. locations. [G]▼●

Muppet Treasure Island (1996) **C-99m.** **½ D: Brian Henson. Kermit the Frog, Miss Piggy, Gonzo, Fozzie Bear (Steve Whitmire, Frank Oz, Dave Goelz), Tim Curry, Kevin Bishop, Billy Connolly, Jennifer Saunders. The Muppets take on Robert Louis Stevenson's classic pirate story, with Kermit the Frog as Captain Smollett and Miss Piggy as "Benjamina" Gunn. Good fun, but seems longer than it is, and Curry is—of all things—a bit more subdued as Long John Silver than you'd expect. Of course, after Robert Newton, anyone would seem subdued! [G]▼●

Murder! (1930-British) **104m.** *** D: Alfred Hitchcock. Herbert Marshall, Norah Baring, Phyllis Konstam, Edward Chapman. Good early Hitchcock casts Marshall as actor who serves on jury at murder trial and believes accused woman innocent.▼◗

Murder Ahoy (1964-British) **93m.** **½ D: George Pollock. Margaret Rutherford, Lionel Jeffries, Charles Tingwell, William Mervyn, Joan Benham, Stringer Davis, Miles Malleson. This time out, Miss Marple investigates murder on a naval cadet training-ship. Original screenplay (by David Persall and Jack Seddon) based on wonderful Agatha Christie character.▼●

Murder at 45 R.P.M. (1959-French) **105m.** ** D: Etienne Perier. Danielle Darrieux, Michel Auclair, Jean Servais, Henri Guisol. Darrieux is a popular singer who publicly professes her love for her songwriter husband, while having an affair with her accompanist; after dying in a car "accident," the husband seemingly returns from his grave. Neat plot twists cannot uplift this slow-moving suspenser.▼

Murder at 1600 (1997) **C-107m.** ** D: Dwight Little. Wesley Snipes, Diane Lane, Alan Alda, Daniel Benzali, Ronny Cox, Dennis Miller, Tate Donovan, Diane Baker, Charles Rocket, Harris Yulin, Nicholas Pryor. Muddled, predictable mystery thriller in which Washington, D.C., homicide cop Snipes wades his way through assorted cover-ups and intrigue upon discovery of the bloody corpse of a beautiful White House staffer in an Oval Office bathroom. One Good Cop vs. Big Bad Bureaucracy scenario is done in by its endless plot holes, not to mention ludicrous finale. [R] ▼●◗

Murder at the Baskervilles SEE: **Silver Blaze**

Murder at the Gallop (1963-British) **81m.** ***½ D: George Pollock. Margaret Rutherford, Robert Morley, Flora Robson, Charles Tingwell, Duncan Lamont, Stringer Davis, James Villiers, Robert Urquhart. Amateur sleuth Miss Marple suspects foul play when wealthy old recluse dies. Based on Agatha Christie's *After the Funeral.*▼●
Murder at the Vanities (1934) **89m.** **½ D: Mitchell Leisen. Jack Oakie, Kitty Carlisle, Carl Brisson, Victor McLaglen, Donald Meek, Gail Patrick, Toby Wing, Gertrude Michael, Jessie Ralph, Dorothy Stickney, Duke Ellington. Offbeat murder mystery set backstage at Earl Carroll's Vanities, with detective McLaglen holding everyone under suspicion, including show's stars (Carlisle, Brisson). Songs include "Cocktails for Two," bizarre "Sweet Marijuana" number; look for Ann Sheridan as chorus girl.▼
Murder Between Friends (1994) **C-100m. TVM** D: Waris Hussein. Timothy Busfield, Stephen Lang, Martin Kemp, Lisa Blount, O'Neal Compton, Alex Courtney, Karen Moncrieff. Intriguing real-life whodunit about a New Orleans woman's murder: was it her husband or his best friend? Each of them insists the other is guilty. The plot takes another twist every ten minutes, so stay alert. Above average.
Murder by Contract (1958) **81m.** ** D: Irving Lerner. Vince Edwards, Philip Pine, Herschel Bernardi, Caprice Toriel. Intriguing little film about a hired killer and what makes him tick; ultimately sabotaged by pretentious dialogue and posturing.
Murder by Death (1976) **C-94m.** *** D: Robert Moore. Peter Sellers, Peter Falk, David Niven, Maggie Smith, James Coco, Alec Guinness, Elsa Lanchester, Eileen Brennan, Nancy Walker, Estelle Winwood, Truman Capote. Capote invites world's greatest detectives to his home and involves them in a baffling whodunit. Neil Simon spoofs such characters as Charlie Chan, Miss Marple, and Sam Spade in this enjoyable all-star comedy, with marvelous sets by Stephen Grimes. Simon followed this with THE CHEAP DETECTIVE. [PG]▼●
Murder by Decree (1979-Canadian-British) **C-121m.** *** D: Bob Clark. Christopher Plummer, James Mason, Donald Sutherland, Genevieve Bujold, Susan Clark, David Hemmings, Frank Finlay, John Gielgud, Anthony Quayle. Sherlock Holmes investigates slayings of prostitutes by Jack the Ripper, with surprising results. Involved, often lurid story doesn't sustain through conclusion, but flaws overshadowed by warm interpretations of Holmes and Watson by Plummer and Mason. For another version of Holmes vs. the Ripper, see A STUDY IN TERROR. [PG]▼●
Murder by Natural Causes (1979) **C-100m. TVM** D: Robert Day. Hal Holbrook, Katharine Ross, Richard Anderson, Barry Bostwick, Bill Fiore, Jeff Donnell. Outstanding thinking man's thriller that has the unfaithful wife of a famed mentalist trying to do him in by literally scaring him to death. Well acted and written—and don't blink for the last reel or you'll miss countless clever twists. One of the best from the writing/producing team of Richard Levinson and William Link. Above average.▼
Murder by Phone (1980-Canadian) **C-79m.** ** D: Michael Anderson. Richard Chamberlain, John Houseman, Sara Botsford, Robin Gammell, Gary Reineke, Barry Morse. Talented cast and director go slumming in this hoary horror exercise involving a crazed killer who literally phones in his murders, doing in his victims by ingenious long distance device. Filmed as BELLS. [R]▼
Murder by Proxy SEE: **Blackout** (1954)
Murder by Television (1935) **60m.** *½ D: Clifford Sandforth. Bela Lugosi, June Collyer, Huntley Gordon, George Meeker, Claire McDowell. A professor who perfects the technology of television is murdered; Lugosi, his assistant, is a prime suspect. Grade Z production holds some interest as a curio.▼
Murder by the Clock (1931) **76m.** **½ D: Edward Sloman. William "Stage" Boyd, Lilyan Tashman, Irving Pichel, Regis Toomey, Blanche Frederici, Sally O'Neil, Lester Vail. Creepy, creaky mystery designed and played like a horror film. Complicated plot involves elderly woman who installs a horn in her crypt in case she's buried alive, a mysterious reincarnation drug, and drooling half-wit Pichel. Plenty of atmosphere if not much sense.
Murder Clinic (1966-Italian-French) **C-87m.** *½ D: William Hamilton (Elio Scardamaglia). William Berger, Francoise Prevost, Mary Young, Barbara Wilson, Delphia Maurin. Period thriller of isolated clinic peopled with eccentric patients, terrorized by monster which roams in corridors and woods outside. Slow going. Techniscope.
Murder, Czech Style (1968-Czech) **90m.** **½ D: Jiri Weiss. Rudolf Hrusinsky, Kyeta Fialova, Vaclav Voska, Vladimir Mensik. Clever, gentle spoof of romantic triangle melodramas, with pudgy middle-aged clerk (Hrusinsky) marrying beautiful woman, realizing she's been cheating on him, planning revenge, via dream sequences.▼
Murderers Among Us: The Simon Wiesenthal Story (1989-U.S.-British-Hungarian) **C-175m. TVM** D: Brian Gibson. Ben Kingsley, Renee Soutendijk, Craig T. Nelson, Louisa Haigh, Jack Shepherd, Paul Freeman. Moving but overlong drama with a mesmerizing Kingsley as the Holocaust survivor who dedicated the rest of his life to hunting down the war's Nazi bigwigs. Abby Mann's thoughtful script, written

with Robin Vote and Ron Hutchinson, has been criticized for its historical selectivity (giving, for instance, Wiesenthal's still-controversial role in the capture of Eichmann a scant five minutes), but the exceptionally strong death camp scenes rank alongside those of TV's WAR AND REMEMBRANCE in impact. Made for cable. Above average.▼

Murderers' Row (1966) **C-108m.** BOMB D: Henry Levin. Dean Martin, Ann-Margret, Karl Malden, Camilla Sparv, James Gregory, Beverly Adams. Malden kidnaps A-M's father, threatens to melt Washington, D.C. with a "helio beam"; only Matt Helm can save both. (What if he'd had to make a choice?) Second Helm caper—after THE SILENCERS—offers one funny jibe at Frank Sinatra, absolutely nothing else. Sequel: THE AMBUSHERS.▼

Murder Game, The (1966-British) **75m.** *½ D: Sidney Salkow. Ken Scott, Marla Landi, Trader Faulkner, Conrad Phillips, Gerald Sim, Duncan Lamont. Routine murder-blackmail drama about woman who skips out on her husband, changes her name, then marries again.

Murder, He Says (1945) **93m.** *** D: George Marshall. Fred MacMurray, Helen Walker, Marjorie Main, Jean Heather, Porter Hall, Peter Whitney, Barbara Pepper, Mabel Paige. Zany slapstick of pollster MacMurray encountering Main's family of hayseed murderers. Too strident at times, but generally funny; clever script by Lou Breslow.▼

Murder, Inc. (1960) **103m.** *** D: Burt Balaban, Stuart Rosenberg. Stuart Whitman, May Britt, Henry Morgan, Peter Falk, David J. Stewart, Simon Oakland, Morey Amsterdam, Sarah Vaughan, Joseph Campanella. Solid little fact-based chronicle of the title crime organization, with Falk in particular scoring as Abe Reles, the syndicate's ill-fated number-one killer. Lots of familiar faces (Vincent Gardenia, Sylvia Miles, Seymour Cassel) in supporting roles. CinemaScope.

Murder in Coweta County (1983) **C-100m. TVM** D: Gary Nelson. Johnny Cash, Andy Griffith, Earl Hindman, June Carter Cash, Cindi Knight, Ed Van Nuys. No-nonsense county sheriff Cash stops at nothing—including his legal jurisdiction—to track down local bigwig Griffith, who thinks he's gotten away with murder. Dennis Nemac wrote the straightforward script from Margaret Anne Barnes's book about an actual 1948 Georgia murder. Aka LAST BLOOD. Average.▼

Murder in Greenwich Village (1937) **68m.** ** D: Albert S. Rogell. Richard Arlen, Fay Wray, Raymond Walburn, Wyn Cahoon, Scott Colton, Thurston Hall. Dated romantic mystery comedy with heiress Wray using photographer Arlen as alibi for whereabouts when murder took place. Mystery is secondary, solved only as an afterthought.

Murder in Mississippi (1990) **C-200m. TVM** D: Roger Young. Tom Hulce, Blair Underwood, Josh Charles, Jennifer Grey, CCH Pounder, Andre Braugher, John Dennis Johnson, Greg Kinnear. Riveting drama about Mickey Schwerner, James Chaney, and Andrew Goodman, three young civil rights workers whose killing in the summer of 1964 became one of the landmarks in the movement. Drama, written by Stanley Weiser, is the flip side of the theatrical (and partly fictional) MISSISSIPPI BURNING. Broadcast in two parts. Above average.

Murder in New Hampshire: The Pamela Smart Story (1991) **C-100m. TVM** D: Joyce Chopra. Helen Hunt, Chad Allen, Larry Drake, Howard Hesseman, Ken Howard, Michael Learned. Hunt's an eye-opener as the schoolteacher tried and convicted for plotting the murder of her husband with her lover, one of her students. This one made it to television just months after the sleazy, headline-making court case ended. Though it happened in Derry, New Hampshire, it was filmed in Charlotte, South Carolina—which isn't quite a match. Average.▼◗

Murder in Texas (1981) **C-200m. TVM** D: Billy Hale. Katharine Ross, Sam Elliott, Farrah Fawcett, Andy Griffith, Craig T. Nelson, Dimitra Arliss, Barry Corbin, Pamela Meyers, Bill Dana. Dramatization of the murder case revolving around Houston plastic surgeon Dr. John Hill, who was accused of killing his socially prominent first wife. John McGreevey based his script on the book *Prescription: Murder*, written by Hill's second wife, Ann Kurth (played by Ross). Andy Griffith won an Emmy Award nomination for his performance as Hill's father-in-law, wealthy oilman Ash Robinson. Above average.▼

Murder in the Air (1940) **55m.** ** D: Lewis Seiler. Ronald Reagan, John Litel, James Stephenson, Eddie Foy, Jr., Lya Lys. The fourth and final Ronald Reagan Brass Bancroft film, with the Secret Service agent assigned to stop enemy spies from stealing government plans.

Murder in the Blue Room (1944) **61m.** ** D: Leslie Goodwins. Anne Gwynne, Donald Cook, John Litel, Grace McDonald, Betty Kean, June Preisser, Regis Toomey, Bill Williams. Film has distinction of being an Old Dark House musical, but otherwise has nothing to recommend it. Typical brassy songs against OK whodunit background; filmed before as THE MISSING GUEST and SECRET OF THE BLUE ROOM.

Murder in the First (1995) **C-122m.** **½ D: Marc Rocco. Christian Slater, Kevin

Bacon, Gary Oldman, Embeth Davidtz, William H. Macy, Stephen Tobolowsky, Brad Dourif, R. Lee Ermey, Mia Kirshner, Stefan Gierasch. Young lawyer in the public defender's office is given his first assignment: defending an Alcatraz prisoner who murdered a fellow inmate. Only extenuating circumstance: the young prisoner was driven to madness by unspeakably brutal treatment for three straight years. Bacon's bravura performance is the centerpiece of this imperfect but commanding drama, which is a bit too self-satisfied and manipulative. Based on a true story, and set in the 1930s and 40s. Bacon's wife Kyra Sedgwick is amusingly cast in a cameo. With this film, director Rocco has used up his moving-camera allotment for at least ten years. [R]▼●◗

Murder in the Music Hall (1946) **84m.** ★★½ D: John English. Vera Hruba Ralston, William Marshall, Helen Walker, Nancy Kelly, William Gargan, Ann Rutherford, Julie Bishop, Jerome Cowan, Edward Norris, Jack LaRue. Neat little mystery in which troubled "ballet on ice" performer Ralston finds herself in the wrong place at the right time, and is accused of murder. To the rescue comes her bandleader boyfriend (Marshall).

Murder in the Ring SEE: **Ripped Off**

Murder Is My Beat (1955) **77m.** ★★ D: Edgar G. Ulmer. Paul Langton, Barbara Payton, Robert Shayne, Selena Royle. Standard B treatment of alleged killer Payton discovering actual criminal.

Murder Is My Business (1946) **64m.** ★★ D: Sam Newfield. Hugh Beaumont, Cheryl Walker, Lyle Talbot, George Meeker, Pierre Watkin. Programmer Mike Shayne caper, with Beaumont a tame shamus on prowl for killer.

Murder Man, The (1935) **70m.** ★★★ D: Tim Whelan. Spencer Tracy, Virginia Bruce, Lionel Atwill, Harvey Stephens, Robert Barrat, James Stewart. Tracy is good as usual playing a hard-drinking newspaper reporter who specializes in covering murders. Snappy little film also offers Stewart in his first feature appearance (playing a fellow reporter named Shorty).

Murder Mansion, The (1970-Spanish) **C-90m.** ★★ D: F. Lara Polop. Analia Gade, Evelyn Stewart (Ida Galli), Andres Resino. Travelers are lost in a fog, find themselves stranded in eerie old house with strange mistress and ghosts. A couple of good scares.▼

Murder Most Foul (1965-British) **90m.** ★★★ D: George Pollock. Margaret Rutherford, Ron Moody, Charles Tingwell, Andrew Cruickshank, Stringer Davis, Francesca Annis, Dennis Price, James Bolam. When Miss Marple is lone jury member who believes defendant is innocent, she sets out to prove it. Based on Agatha Christie's *Mrs. McGinty's Dead.*▼●

Murder, My Sweet (1944) **95m.** ★★★½ D: Edward Dmytryk. Dick Powell, Claire Trevor, Anne Shirley, Otto Kruger, Mike Mazurki, Miles Mander. Adaptation of Raymond Chandler's book *Farewell My Lovely* gave Powell new image as hard-boiled detective Philip Marlowe, involved in homicide and blackmail. Still packs a wallop. Scripted by John Paxton. Story previously used for THE FALCON TAKES OVER; remade again as FAREWELL, MY LOVELY in 1975. Also shown in computer-colored version.▼●

Murder of Mary Phagan, The (1988) **C-250m. TVM** D: Billy Hale. Jack Lemmon, Peter Gallagher, Richard Jordan, Robert Prosky, Paul Dooley, Rebecca Miller, Kathryn Walker, Charles Dutton, Kevin Spacey, Wendy J. Cooke. Leisurely, atmospheric retelling of the controversial 1913 Leo Frank murder case in which a Jewish factory manager in Atlanta was convicted of killing a young female employee and sentenced to hang. Lemmon excels as then-Governor John M. Slaton, who put his political career on the line by reexamining the case. Fictionalized version of the incident was filmed in 1937 as THEY WON'T FORGET. Larry McMurtry's story was adapted by George Stevens, Jr., and Jeffrey Lane, whose script easily might have been shortened. Originally shown in two parts. Above average. [PG]▼

Murder on a Bridle Path (1936) **65m.** ★½ D: Edward Killy, William Hamilton. James Gleason, Helen Broderick, Louise Latimer, Owen Davis, Jr., John Arledge, John Carroll, Leslie Fenton, Christian Rub, Gustav von Seyffertitz. Broderick takes over the role of Hildegarde Withers for this extremely unsatisfying series mystery about a socialite who's killed during an early morning horseback ride. A terrific finale can't make up for sixty minutes of deadly dullness.

Murder on a Honeymoon (1935) **74m.** ★★★ D: Lloyd Corrigan. Edna May Oliver, James Gleason, Lola Lane, Chick Chandler, George Meeker, Dorothy Libaire, Morgan Wallace, Leo (G.) Carroll. After a murder takes place on a seaplane ride to Catalina Island, Hildegarde Withers (who happened to be on the plane) gets Inspector Oscar Piper to come there and solve the crime. Entertaining entry in the Withers series, cowritten by Robert Benchley and actually filmed on the picturesque island.

Murder on Approval (1955-British) **70m.** ★★ D: Bernard Knowles. Tom Conway, Delphi Lawrence, Brian Worth, Michael Balfour, Campbell Cotts. Blah thriller with Conway playing a private eye hired to investigate the sale of a supposedly counterfeit stamp. Original British title: BARBADOS QUEST.▼

Murder on Monday SEE: **Home at Seven**

Murder on the Bayou SEE: **Gathering of Old Men, A**

Murder on the Blackboard (1934) **72m.**

*** D: George Archainbaud. Edna May Oliver, James Gleason, Bruce Cabot, Gertrude Michael, Regis Toomey, Tully Marshall, Edgar Kennedy, Jackie Searle, Fredrik Vogeding, Gustav von Seyffertitz. A young female schoolteacher is murdered, and fellow teacher Hildegarde Withers (Oliver) becomes involved in solving the case with Inspector Oscar Piper. Enjoyable entry in the brief Withers series.

Murder on the Orient Express (1974-British) **C-127m.** *** D: Sidney Lumet. Albert Finney, Lauren Bacall, Martin Balsam, Ingrid Bergman, Jacqueline Bisset, Jean-Pierre Cassel, Sean Connery, John Gielgud, Wendy Hiller, Anthony Perkins, Vanessa Redgrave, Rachel Roberts, Richard Widmark, Michael York, Colin Blakely, George Coulouris. Elegant all-star production of Agatha Christie's whodunit set in the 1930s, with unrecognizable Finney as super-sleuth Hercule Poirot, and all his suspects on the same railroad train. Colorful entertainment, but awfully sluggish; sharp viewers will be able to guess the denouement, as well. Bergman won Best Supporting Actress Oscar. First of several lavish Christie adaptations; followed by DEATH ON THE NILE. [PG]▼●

Murder Ordained (1987) **C-200m. TVM** D: Mike Robe. Keith Carradine, JoBeth Williams, Terry Kinney, Guy Boyd, Terence Knox, Darrell Larson, M. Emmet Walsh. Well-crafted drama based on events surrounding a pair of real-life murders in Kansas involving a Lutheran minister, his married lover, and their respective spouses. Writers Robe and James Sadwith based their script on newspaper accounts by a pair of women reporters who are depicted in the film. Originally shown in two parts. Above average.▼

Murder Over New York (1940) **65m.** **½ D: Harry Lachman. Sidney Toler, Marjorie Weaver, Robert Lowery, Ricardo Cortez, Donald MacBride, Melville Cooper, (Victor) Sen Yung. Charlie Chan (Toler) uncovers a gang of saboteurs while in Manhattan for a police convention. Briskly paced, well-directed entry.▼

Murder, She Said (1961-British) **87m.** *** D: George Pollock. Margaret Rutherford, Arthur Kennedy, Muriel Pavlow, James Robertson Justice, Charles Tingwell, Thorley Walters. Miss Marple takes a job as a domestic in order to solve a murder she witnessed. Based on Agatha Christie's *4:50 From Paddington*; first of four films starring Rutherford as Marple. Trivia note: Rutherford has several scenes with Joan Hickson, later to play Miss Marple herself in a fine British TV series.▼●

Murders in the Rue Morgue (1932) **75m.** **½ D: Robert Florey. Bela Lugosi, Sidney Fox, Leon Waycoff (Ames), Brandon Hurst, Arlene Francis, Bert Roach, Noble Johnson. Expressionistic horror film based on Poe story, with Lugosi as fiendish Dr. Mirakle, with eyes on lovely Fox as the bride of his pet ape. Considered strong stuff back then. John Huston was one of the writers. Remade as PHANTOM OF THE RUE MORGUE, and twice more under original title.▼●

Murders in the Rue Morgue (1971) **C-87m.** *½ D: Gordon Hessler. Jason Robards, Herbert Lom, Christine Kaufmann, Lilli Palmer, Adolfo Celi, Maria Perschy, Michael Dunn. Sensationalistic reworking of Poe story; players at Grand Guignol-type theater suddenly become victims of real-life murders, gory goings-on. Set in Paris, but filmed in Spain. [PG]▼

Murders in the Rue Morgue, The (1986) **C-100m. TVM** D: Jeannot Szwarc. George C. Scott, Rebecca De Mornay, Ian McShane, Neil Dickson, Val Kilmer. Another tour-de-force for George C. Scott, in this fifth film version of the Poe tale of a hideous double murder in 19th-century Paris. David Epstein's script and Bruno de Keyzer's atmospheric location photography add to the panache. One quibble: why are the store signs in English, the street designations in French? Above average.▼●

Murders in the Zoo (1933) **62m.** *** D: A. Edward Sutherland. Lionel Atwill, Charles Ruggles, Randolph Scott, Gail Patrick, John Lodge, Kathleen Burke. Astonishingly grisly horror film about an insanely jealous zoologist and sportsman (Atwill) who dispatches his wife's suitors (genuine and otherwise) with the help of various animals. Pretty potent stuff, right from the opening scene of Atwill sewing a victim's mouth shut!▼

Murder Will Out (1952-British) **83m.** *** D: John Gilling. Valerie Hobson, Edward Underdown, James Robertson Justice, Henry Kendall. Underplayed suspenser with creditable red herrings to engage the viewer. Retitled: THE VOICE OF MERRILL.

Murder With Mirrors (1985) **C-100m. TVM** D: Dick Lowry. Helen Hayes, Bette Davis, John Mills, Leo McKern, Liane Langland, Dorothy Tutin. Miss Marple tries to unmask the villain who'd stoop to murder to steal her dear old friend's ancestral home. Hayes and Davis act together for the first time in this amiable version of Agatha Christie's mystery, adapted by George Eckstein. Average.▼

Muriel (1963-French-Italian) **C-115m.** *** D: Alain Resnais. Delphine Seyrig, Jean-Pierre Kérien, Nita Klein, Claude Sainval, Jean-Baptiste Thierée. Poignant drama of alienation, about a widow (Seyrig) and her stepson (Thierée); she's haunted by the memory of her first love, he by his involvement in the torture and death of a woman named Muriel during the Algerian War.▼

Muriel's Wedding (1994-Australian) **C-105m.** ***½ D: P. J. Hogan. Toni Collette, Bill Hunter, Rachel Griffiths, Jeanie Drynan, Gennie Nevinson, Matt Day, Chris Haywood, Daniel Lapaine. Ugly duckling with a strikingly dysfunctional family (and a blustery, small-time politico father) yearns for a happier life, and starts on that road by leaving her home town of Porpoise Spit for Sydney, in the company of her fast-track girlfriend. Not the simple, straight-ahead "feel good" movie you might expect, but a darker, more idiosyncratic comedy-drama about friendship, dreams, reality, and the joys of ABBA music. A very satisfying film, full of wonderful performances; written by the director. [R]▼●◗

Murmur of the Heart (1971-French-German-Italian) **C-118m.** ***½ D: Louis Malle. Lea Massari, Benoit Ferreux, Daniel Gelin, Marc Winocourt, Michel Lonsdale. Fresh, intelligent, affectionately comic tale of bourgeois, sensuous Massari and her precocious 14-year-old son (Ferreux), builds to a thoroughly delightful resolution. Wonderful performances. [R]▼●

Murph the Surf SEE: **Live a Little, Steal a Lot**

Murphy's Law (1986) **C-100m.** *½ D: J. Lee Thompson. Charles Bronson, Kathleen Wilhoite, Carrie Snodgress, Robert F. Lyons, Richard Romanus, Angel Tompkins, Bill Henderson, James Luisi, Janet MacLachlan, Lawrence Tierney. All-too-typical Bronson vehicle about a cop framed for murders by psychopathic ex-con he originally sent to prison; only novelty is that the psycho is a woman (Snodgress). Strictly formula; violent and unpleasant. [R]▼●

Murphy's Romance (1985) **C-107m.** *** D: Martin Ritt. Sally Field, James Garner, Brian Kerwin, Corey Haim, Dennis Burkley, Georgann Johnson, Charles Lane. Young divorcée (with 12-year-old son) makes fresh start in small Arizona community, where she's attracted to older, laid-back, widowed pharmacist—and vice versa. Charming, easygoing comedy written by Irving Ravetch and Harriet Frank, Jr. (from Max Schott's novella), with Garner in a standout performance as Murphy, the last of the rugged individualists. In fact, this earned him his first Oscar nomination. [PG-13] ▼●◗

Murphy's War (1971-British) **C-108m.** *** D: Peter Yates. Peter O'Toole, Sian Phillips, Philippe Noiret, Horst Janson, John Hallam, Ingo Morgendorf. Well-staged, gripping action sequences combine with psychological study of Irish seaman (O'Toole) only survivor of German massacre, out to get revenge. Good idea, but nonaction sequences tend to bog film down; script by Stirling Silliphant. Panavision. [PG]▼

Murrow (1986) **C-110m. TVM** D: Jack Gold. Daniel J. Travanti, Dabney Coleman, Edward Herrmann, David Suchet, John McMartin, Robert Vaughn, Kathryn Leigh Scott. Plodding made-for-cable biopic of Edward R. Murrow, which was pilloried by his contemporaries, many of whom are portrayed (Coleman as CBS founder and board chairman William S. Paley, Herrmann as Murrow's longtime producer and associate Fred Friendly, McMartin as former CBS president Frank Stanton, Bob Sherman as *60 Minutes* producer Don Hewitt, etc.). A glum Travanti, though, does an admirable job in the lead. Written by Ernest Kinoy. Average.▼

Muscle Beach Party (1964) **C-94m.** **½ D: William Asher. Frankie Avalon, Annette Funicello, Buddy Hackett, Luciana Paluzzi, Don Rickles, John Ashley, Jody McCrea, Morey Amsterdam, Peter Lupus, Candy Johnson, Dan Haggerty. Followup to BEACH PARTY picks up the pace as the gang finds the beach has been invaded by Rickles and his stable of body-builders. Usual blend of surf, sand, and corn; Rickles' first series appearance and the screen debut of "Little" Stevie Wonder. Sequel: BIKINI BEACH. Panavision.▼●

Muse, The (1999) **C-96m.** *** D: Albert Brooks. Albert Brooks, Sharon Stone, Andie MacDowell, Jeff Bridges, Mark Feuerstein, Steven Wright, Bradley Whitford. Brooks plays a Hollywood screenwriter who's told that he's out of touch—until he hooks up with a bona fide muse (Stone), a capricious woman whose working methods are unconventional at best. As with so many of Brooks' movies, the parts are greater than the whole, but his gibes at Hollywood are priceless, and some of the cameo appearances (which we won't give away) are very funny indeed. [PG-13]▼◗

MUSE Concert: No Nukes, The SEE: **No Nukes**

Music Box (1989) **C-123m.** **½ D: Costa-Gavras. Jessica Lange, Armin Mueller-Stahl, Frederic Forrest, Donald Moffat, Lukas Haas, Cheryl Lynn Bruce, Michael Rooker. Chicago criminal attorney Lange is thrown for a loop when her Hungarian-immigrant dad is accused of heinous war crimes and threatened with deportation. She defends him in a sensational trial but has trouble—legally and emotionally—proving his innocence. What could have been a crackling political thriller becomes a high-gloss melodrama instead, plodding and far-fetched, though Lange is good in (rare) ethnic role, and Mueller-Stahl is strong as the enigmatic elder. A disappointment from the director of Z and MISSING. Panavision. [PG-13]▼●

Music for Millions (1944) **120m.** **½ D: Henry Koster. Margaret O'Brien, Jimmy Durante, June Allyson, Marsha Hunt, Hugh

Herbert, Jose Iturbi, Connie Gilchrist, Harry Davenport, Marie Wilson, Larry Adler, Ethel Griffies. Teary tale of war-bride Allyson, a cellist in Iturbi's orchestra, gallantly waiting to have a baby—and for husband's return. O'Brien is her precocious kid sister. While there's plenty of Chopin and Debussy, Durante steals film with "Umbriago." Watch for Ava Gardner in a bit.

Music in Darkness SEE: **Night Is My Future**

Music in My Heart (1940) **70m.** ** D: Joseph Santley. Tony Martin, Rita Hayworth, Edith Fellows, Alan Mowbray, Eric Blore, George Tobias. Routine musical of Continental Martin cast in show where he meets lovely Hayworth. One good song, "It's a Blue World."▼

Music in the Air (1934) **85m.** *** D: Joe May. Gloria Swanson, John Boles, Douglass Montgomery, June Lang, Reginald Owen, Al Shean. Predictable plot given chic treatment; leading-lady Swanson and lyricist Boles constantly quarreling, trying jealousy ploy when naive young couple come on the scene. Good Jerome Kern-Oscar Hammerstein score enhances bright production.

Music Is Magic (1935) **65m.** **½ D: George Marshall. Alice Faye, Ray Walker, Bebe Daniels, Frank Mitchell, Jack Durant, Rosina Lawrence, Thomas Beck, Hattie McDaniel. Limp musical with Faye as a struggling vaudevillian who heads for Hollywood. Will she find stardom? Daniels is outstanding as a vain, aging movie star; her young boyfriend (Beck) is named Tony Bennett!

Music Lovers, The (1971-British) **C-122m.** **½ D: Ken Russell. Glenda Jackson, Richard Chamberlain, Max Adrian, Christopher Gable, Kenneth Colley. Occasionally striking but self-indulgent and factually dubious account of Tchaikovsky (Chamberlain), who marries and abandons the whorish Nina (Jackson). Overacted, overdirected. Panavision. [R]▼●

Music Man, The (1962) **C-151m.** ***½ D: Morton Da Costa. Robert Preston, Shirley Jones, Buddy Hackett, Hermione Gingold, Paul Ford, Pert Kelton, Ronny Howard. Peerless Preston reprises his Broadway performance as super salesman/con man Prof. Harold Hill, who mesmerizes Iowa town with visions of uniformed marching band. Faithful filmization of Meredith Willson's affectionate slice of Americana. Score includes "76 Trombones," "Till There Was You," and showstopping "Trouble." Technirama.▼●◗

Music of Chance, The (1993) **C-98m.** **½ D: Philip Haas. James Spader, Mandy Patinkin, M. Emmet Walsh, Charles Durning, Joel Grey, Samantha Mathis, Christopher Penn. A man gives a lift to a fellow stumbling alongside a country road, learns he's a high-stakes poker player, and decides to back him in an upcoming game against two eccentric millionaires. Low-key adaptation of Paul Auster's existential novel offers as many questions as answers while it spins its interesting—but oddball—tale. Co-scripted by director Haas, a documentarian making his feature debut. Superior performances by a hand-picked cast; Spader is a particular standout as a slimeball with his own peculiar code of ethics.▼●

Music of the Heart (1999) **C-124m.** *** D: Wes Craven. Meryl Streep, Aidan Quinn, Angela Bassett, Gloria Estefan, Jane Leeves, Cloris Leachman, Kieran Culkin, Charlie Hofheimer, Jay O. Sanders. Newly single woman moves to East Harlem and starts a violin class, against all odds, giving her kids a sense of discipline, purpose, and pride. Pamela Gray's script sidesteps the obvious as often as possible, and makes many of the student characters worth caring about. Reaches its emotional peak before the climactic concert—but still a sweet, upbeat film. Inspired by the documentary SMALL WONDERS about the real-life Roberta Guaspari. Isaac Stern, Itzhak Perlman, and many other noted musicians appear as themselves. [PG]▼◗

Music Teacher, The (1988-Belgian) **C-95m.** **½ D: Gerard Corbiau. Jose Van Dam, Anne Roussel, Philippe Volter, Sylvie Fennec, Patrick Bauchau, Johan Leyson. A familiar plot and stale script sink this musical drama detailing what happens when opera star Van Dam retires at the pinnacle of his fame to train fetching young Roussel and petty thief Volter. The charisma and magnificent singing voice of Van Dam, the Belgian bass-baritone, almost (but not quite) redeem this. [PG]▼●

Musketeers of the Sea (1960-Italian) **C-116m.** ** D: Massimo Patrizi. Robert Alda, Pier Angeli, Aldo Ray. Anonymous sea yarn, standard in all departments, involving search for gold in Maracaibo.

Mussolini: The Decline and Fall of Il Duce (1985) **C-192m. TVM** D: Alberto Negrin. Susan Sarandon, Anthony Hopkins, Bob Hoskins, Annie Girardot, Barbara De Rossi, Fabio Testi, Kurt Raab. The focus, despite the title (and Hoskins's shadowy portrayal of Benito), is on Il Duce's crafty son-in-law, Count Galeazzo Ciano (Hopkins). Muddled drama as viewed through the eyes of Mussolini's daughter, Edda (Sarandon). Originally shown in two parts and made for cable. Aka MUSSOLINI AND I. Average.▼

Mustang Country (1976) **C-79m.** *** D: John Champion. Joel McCrea, Robert Fuller, Patrick Wayne, Nika Mina. Excellent Western set along Montana-Canadian border in 1925. 70-year-old McCrea most convincing as ex-rancher and rodeo star who shares adventures with runaway

Indian boy while hunting a wild stallion. [G]

Mutant SEE: **Forbidden World**

Mutations, The (1973-British) **C-92m.** ** D: Jack Cardiff. Donald Pleasence, Tom Baker, Brad Harris, Julie Ege, Michael Dunn, Jill Haworth. Scientist Pleasence crossbreeds humans with plants—and his unsuspecting university students are abducted as guinea pigs. Predictable story with truly grotesque elements and characters. Not recommended for dinnertime viewing. Video title: THE FREAKMAKER. [R]▼

Mute Witness (1995-British-German-Russian) **C-98m.** **½ D: Anthony Waller. Marina Sudina, Fay Ripley, Evan Richards, Oleg Jankowskij, Igor Volkow, Sergei Karlenkov, Alex Bureew. The mute makeup artist on an American horror movie being shot in Moscow sees a snuff film being shot after-hours, and soon finds hit men from the Russian Mafia out to kill her. Impressive directing debut for Waller, who makes superb use of locations, but his script is second-rate; the story goes on too long, and is riddled with coincidences. Alec Guinness appears unbilled as a master criminal. [R]▼●

Mutilator, The SEE: **Dark, The**

Mutineers, The (1949) **60m.** *½ D: Jean Yarbrough. Jon Hall, Adele Jergens, George Reeves, Noel Cravat. Hastily-thrown-together flick of Hall and mates combating rebellion aboard ship. Retitled: PIRATE SHIP.▼

Mutiny (1952) **C-77m.** *½ D: Edward Dmytryk. Mark Stevens. Angela Lansbury, Patric Knowles, Gene Evans, Rhys Williams. Sleep-inducing actioner set amidst the War of 1812, with rival sailors Stevens and Knowles vying for adventuress Lansbury.▼

Mutiny in Outer Space (1965) **81m.** *½ D: Hugo Grimaldi. William Leslie, Dolores Faith, Pamela Curran, Richard Garland, Harold Lloyd, Jr., James Dobson, Glenn Langan. Creeping fungus starts killing astronauts on the way back from trip to the moon in mediocre sci-fi meller.

Mutiny on the Bounty (1935) **132m.** **** D: Frank Lloyd. Charles Laughton, Clark Gable, Franchot Tone, Herbert Mundin, Eddie Quillan, Dudley Digges, Donald Crisp, Movita, Henry Stephenson, Spring Byington, Ian Wolfe, Mamo. Storytelling at its best, in this engrossing adaptation of the Nordhoff-Hall book about mutiny against tyrannical Captain Bligh (Laughton) on voyage to the South Seas. Whole cast is good, but Laughton is unforgettable. Scripted by three top writers: Talbot Jennings, Jules Furthman, and Carey Wilson. Oscar winner for Best Picture; leagues ahead of its 1962 remake and the 1984 film THE BOUNTY. Also shown in computer-colored version.▼●

Mutiny on the Bounty (1962) **C-179m.** **½ D: Lewis Milestone. Marlon Brando, Trevor Howard, Richard Harris, Hugh Griffith, Richard Haydn, Tim Seely, Percy Herbert, Tarita, Gordon Jackson. Lavish remake of 1935 classic can't come near it, although visually beautiful; Howard good as Captain Bligh, but Brando is all wrong as Fletcher Christian. Best thing about this version is spectacular score by Bronislau Kaper. Ultra Panavision 70.▼●

My American Cousin (1985-Canadian) **C-95m.** *** D: Sandy Wilson. Margaret Langrick, John Wildman, Richard Donat, Jane Mortifee. Well-acted, nostalgic coming-of-age story set in British Columbia in the summer of 1959, about a young girl's infatuation with her James Dean-like California cousin. Winner of six Genie awards (Canada's Oscar) including Best Picture. Donat, who plays the father, is Robert Donat's son. Followed by a sequel, AMERICAN BOYFRIENDS. [PG]▼●

My Antonia (1995) **C-100m. TVM** D: Joseph Sargent. Jason Robards, Eva Marie Saint, Neil Patrick Harris, Elina Lowensohn, Anne Tremko, Travis Fine, Jan Triska. Loving re-creation of Willa Cather's thinly veiled autobiography (adapted by Victoria Riskin) of life in Nebraska in late 1890s. Harris, a local farm boy raised by his grandparents, and Lowensohn, a young girl from an immigrant family, shine amid the grainfields as they grow from teenagers to adulthood while maintaining the special bond developed between them. P.S.: The "city" home into which Robards moves wife Saint and grandson is the actual childhood home of Henry Fonda. Made for cable. Above average.▼

My Beautiful Laundrette (1985-British) **C-98m.** ***½ D: Stephen Frears. Saeed Jaffrey, Roshan Seth, Daniel Day-Lewis, Gordon Warnecke, Derrick Branche, Shirley Anne Field. Extremely entertaining, perceptive examination of both race relations and the economic state in Britain, centering on a pair of young friends, Omar (Warnecke) and Johnny (Day-Lewis) and what happens when they take over a beat-up laundrette. On-target script by Hanif Kureishi, a Pakistani playwright who resides in England. Originally made for British TV. [R]▼●

My Best Fiend (1999-German-British) **C-95m.** ***½ D: Werner Herzog. Klaus Kinski starred in many of Werner Herzog's most notable films, but his intensity, ego and near-demented behavior made the productions tough going for everyone; at times the director and star actually plotted to murder each other. Hosting this unique documentary, Herzog revisits the locations of his Kinski films, musing over the actor's bizarre behavior. Funny, insightful, touching and deeply engrossing, it can't really explain Kinski, but it's a grand journey. Claudia Cardinale and Eva Mattes are among those interviewed.

My Best Friend Is a Vampire (1988) **C-90m.** *½ D: Jimmy Huston. Robert Sean Leonard, Evan Mirand, Cheryl Pollak, René Auberjonois, Cecilia Peck, Fannie Flagg, Kenneth Kimmins, David Warner, Paul Wilson. One-joke comedy, in the wake of TEEN WOLF, has a high-school kid transformed into a vampire and trying to cope with it as a fact of life. Solid supporting cast does what it can to help. [PG]▼

My Best Friend's Girl (1983-French) **C-99m.** **½ D: Bertrand Blier. Coluche, Isabelle Huppert, Thierry Lhermitte, Daniel Colas, Francois Perrot. Medium sex comedy with Lhermitte bringing home pick-up Huppert; she moves in, and his best friend (Coluche) falls for her. A familiar Blier theme (the sexual relationship between one woman and two men) is indifferently handled. Panavision.▼

My Best Friend's Wedding (1997) **C-105m.** *** D: P. J. Hogan. Julia Roberts, Dermot Mulroney, Cameron Diaz, Rupert Everett, Philip Bosco, M. Emmet Walsh, Rachel Griffiths, Carrie Preston, Susan Sullivan, Chris Masterson, Harry Shearer. Roberts and Mulroney are old friends, and former lovers, who have pacted to wed at age 28 if they're both still single. When Mulroney springs fiancée Diaz on Julia, she starts to freak out and tries to sabotage the nuptials. Smart and funny romantic comedy (written by Ronald Bass) with Roberts scoring in a tailor-made role, and Everett stealing every scene he's in as her gay pal. Panavision. [PG-13]▼●◗

My Bill (1938) **64m.** **½ D: John Farrow. Kay Francis, Bonita Granville, Anita Louise, Bobby Jordan, Dickie Moore. Francis is poverty-stricken widow with four children, involved in scandal; OK soaper.

My Blood Runs Cold (1965) **104m.** **½ D: William Conrad. Troy Donahue, Joey Heatherton, Barry Sullivan, Jeanette Nolan. Young man thinks girl is long-dead ancestor, and recalls love affair from generations before. Not all that bad, but not worth missing *I Love Lucy* for, either. Panavision.

My Bloody Valentine (1981-Canadian) **C-91m.** *½ D: George Mihalka. Paul Kelman, Lori Hallier, Neil Affleck, Keith Knight, Alf Humphreys. Another gory HALLOWEEN/FRIDAY THE 13TH clone. Coalminer axes various victims (male as well as female) in the friendly little town of Valentine Bluffs. Ecch. [R]▼●

My Blue Heaven (1950) **C-96m.** **½ D: Henry Koster. Betty Grable, Dan Dailey, David Wayne, Jane Wyatt, Mitzi Gaynor, Una Merkel. Pleasing musicomedy with Grable and Dailey as radio stars who try to adopt a child.

My Blue Heaven (1990) **C-95m.** *** D: Herbert Ross. Steve Martin, Rick Moranis, Joan Cusack, Melanie Mayron, Bill Irwin, Carol Kane, William Hickey, Deborah Rush, Daniel Stern, Ed Lauter, Julie Bovasso, Colleen Camp. Lightweight but entertaining comedy about an Italian hood from N.Y.C. who's moved to suburban California as part of the FBI's witness protection program, where he's watched over by straight-arrow G-man Moranis. No fireworks, but does have some good laughs, and enjoyable performances. Written by Nora Ephron. [PG-13]▼●◗

My Bodyguard (1980) **C-96m.** **½ D: Tony Bill. Chris Makepeace, Adam Baldwin, Martin Mull, Ruth Gordon, Matt Dillon, John Houseman, Joan Cusack, Craig Richard Nelson. Pleasant little film about high-school boy who hires a behemoth classmate to protect him from toughs at school. Totally likable but ultimately simplistic comedy-drama. Filmed in and around Chicago; look for Tim Kazurinsky, George Wendt, and Jennifer Beals as a classmate. Bill's directorial debut. [PG]▼

My Body, My Child (1982) **C-100m. TVM** D: Marvin J. Chomsky. Vanessa Redgrave, Joseph Campanella, Stephen Elliott, James Naughton, Gail Strickland, Jack Albertson. A woman's choice: having an abortion or giving birth to a deformed child. Redgrave gives it stature, and Albertson, as her invalid father, turns in an Emmy-nominated performance in his final role. Written by Louisa Burns-Bisogno. Above average.

My Boyfriend's Back (1989) **C-100m. TVM** D: Paul Schneider. Sandy Duncan, Judith Light, Jill Eikenberry, Stephen Macht, Alan Feinstein, John Sanderford. A '60s teen singing group's reluctant reunion 25 years later for a TV special triggers suppressed emotions and recriminations among the three women. Nice attitudes, much insight, in this unexpectedly delightful comedy-drama written by Lindsay Harrison. Look for vintage rockers Gary Lewis, Mary Wells, Peggy March, Gary Puckett, The Penguins. Above average.

My Boyfriend's Back (1993) **C-84m.** *½ D: Bob Balaban. Andrew Lowery, Traci Lind, Danny Zorn, Edward Herrmann, Mary Beth Hurt, Matthew Fox, Philip Seymour Hoffman, Austin Pendleton, Cloris Leachman, Jay O. Sanders, Paul Dooley, Bob Dishy, Paxton Whitehead, Renee Zellweger. Terminally moronic comedy about a teen (Lowery) who is killed and comes back to life to take pretty Lind to the prom. Easy-to-please thirteen-year-olds might like it; others, beware. Talented cast is wasted. [PG-13]▼

My Boys Are Good Boys (1978) **C-90m.** *½ D: Bethel Buckalew. Ralph Meeker, Ida Lupino, Lloyd Nolan, David F. Doyle,

Sean T. Roche. Odd little film mixes 1940s approach to juvenile delinquency with far-fetched story of teenagers robbing armored car. Produced by Meeker and his wife. [PG]▼

My Brilliant Career (1979-Australian) **C-101m.** ***½ D: Gillian Armstrong. Judy Davis, Sam Neill, Wendy Hughes, Robert Grubb, Max Cullen, Pat Kennedy. Excellent portrait of a headstrong young woman determined to live a life of independent and intelligent pursuits in turn-of-the-century Australia. Armstrong's eye for detail and Davis's performance dominate this fine import, based on a true story. Panavision. [G]▼

My Brother's Keeper (1949-British) **96m.** ** D: Alfred Roome. Jack Warner, Jane Hylton, George Cole, Bill Owen, David Tomlinson, Christopher Lee. Hunt-the-escaped convicts film has gimmick of the two escaped prisoners being handcuffed together.

My Brother's Wedding (1983) **C-115m.** *** D: Charles Burnett. Everett Silas, Jessie Holmes, Gaye Shannon-Burnett, Ronnie Bell, Dennis Kemper, Sally Easter. Impressive, knowing tragicomedy from the talented director of TO SLEEP WITH ANGER, about a 30-year-old product of the Watts ghetto who is pleased with his lot in life and despises his lawyer brother's upward mobility. Now he reluctantly agrees to be best man at his brother's nuptials. Impressively captures the urban black experience.

My Brother Talks to Horses (1946) **93m.** ** D: Fred Zinnemann. "Butch" Jenkins, Peter Lawford, Beverly Tyler, Edward Arnold, Charlie Ruggles, Spring Byington. Gimmick comedy that's fun at the start but drags to slow finish.

My Chauffeur (1986) **C-97m.** ** D: David Beaird. Deborah Foreman, Sam Jones, E.G. Marshall, Sean McClory, Howard Hesseman. Heavily male chauvinist chauffeur service has to contend not only with Foreman's hiring, but her emergence as the most popular employee on the staff. Strange mix of 30s screwball with today's cruder comedies doesn't really come off, yet is enough of a curiosity to keep you watching. [R]▼●

My Cousin Rachel (1952) **98m.** *** D: Henry Koster. Olivia de Havilland, Richard Burton, Audrey Dalton, John Sutton, Ronald Squire. Successful filmization of Daphne du Maurier mystery, with Burton (in his American debut) trying to discover if de Havilland is guilty or innocent of murder and intrigue.

My Cousin Vinny (1992) **C-119m.** **½ D: Jonathan Lynn. Joe Pesci, Ralph Macchio, Marisa Tomei, Mitchell Whitfield, Fred Gwynne, Lane Smith, Austin Pendleton, Bruce McGill. Very likable (if much too lackadaisical) comedy about Brooklyn "lawyer" Pesci's attempt to defend his innocent cousin (Macchio) and a friend on a murder charge in the Deep South. Pesci is perfect in a tailor-made part, and Tomei (in an Oscar-winning performance) is a delight to watch as his girlfriend. But there's no reason for this simple comedy to take so long to get where it's going. [R]▼●

My Crazy Life SEE: **Mi Vida Loca**

My Darling Clementine (1946) **97m.** **** D: John Ford. Henry Fonda, Linda Darnell, Victor Mature, Walter Brennan, Cathy Downs, Tim Holt, Ward Bond, Alan Mowbray, John Ireland, Jane Darwell, Grant Withers, J. Farrell McDonald. Beautifully directed, low-key Western about Wyatt Earp (Fonda) and Doc Holliday (Mature), leading to inevitable gunfight at O.K. Corral. Full of wonderful details and vignettes; exquisitely photographed by Joseph P. MacDonald. One of director Ford's finest films, and an American classic. Screenplay by Samuel G. Engel and Winston Miller, from a story by Sam Hellman. Based on a book by Stuart N. Lake. Remake of FRONTIER MARSHAL (1939). In 1994 an archival print was found of the 104m. preview version, containing a number of minor differences and a slightly different finale.▼●

My Darling Shiksa SEE: **Over the Brooklyn Bridge**

My Daughter Joy SEE: **Operation X**

My Dear Secretary (1948) **94m.** **½ D: Charles Martin. Laraine Day, Kirk Douglas, Keenan Wynn, Helen Walker, Rudy Vallee, Florence Bates, Alan Mowbray. Entertaining (if trivial) comedy of wannabe writer Day hiring on as secretary to best-selling author Douglas. Wynn steals the show as Douglas's comical pal.▼

My Demon Lover (1987) **C-86m.** ** D: Charles Loventhal. Scott Valentine, Michelle Little, Arnold Johnson, Gina Gallego, Robert Trebor. Trendy horror comedy has Valentine turning into a variety of monsters whenever he becomes sexually aroused, with Little the modern girl who tries to save him. Cast, including knockout beauty Gallego, is far better than the special effects-oriented material would indicate. [PG-13] ▼●

My Dinner With Andre (1981) **C-110m.** **½ D: Louis Malle. Andre Gregory, Wallace Shawn. Playwright-actor Shawn has dinner with his old friend, theater director Gregory, who's been having a series of strange life-experiences; they talk about them and their philosophies for nearly two hours. A daring and unique film, written by its two principals, with moments of insight, drama, and hilarity—but not enough to sustain a feature-length film. [PG]▼●◗

My Dog Skip (2000) **C-95m.** *** D: Jay Russell. Frankie Muniz, Diane Lane, Kevin Bacon, Luke Wilson, Caitlin Wachs, Bradley Coryell, Clint Howard; narrated by Harry Connick, Jr. Sweet (but not cloying) family film based on Mississippi-born author Willie Morris' memoir of growing up in the 1940s with his beloved English fox terrier, who helps see him through childhood, boyhood, adolescence and young manhood. Warm and winning for grownups as well as children . . . but have a handkerchief handy! [PG]▼●◗

My Dream Is Yours (1949) **C-101m.** **½ D: Michael Curtiz. Jack Carson, Doris Day, Lee Bowman, Adolphe Menjou, Eve Arden. Carson makes Day a radio star in standard musicomedy; highlights are Bugs Bunny dream sequence, Edgar Kennedy's performance as Day's uncle. Remake of TWENTY MILLION SWEETHEARTS, with Doris stepping into Dick Powell's role (and reprising the 1934 hit "I'll String Along With You").▼●

My Enemy, The Sea SEE: **Alone on the Pacific**

My Fair Lady (1964) **C-170m.** ***½ D: George Cukor. Rex Harrison, Audrey Hepburn, Stanley Holloway, Wilfrid Hyde-White, Gladys Cooper, Jeremy Brett, Theodore Bikel, Henry Daniell, Mona Washbourne, Isobel Elsom. Ultrasmooth filmization of Lerner and Loewe's enchanting musical from Shaw's PYGMALION, with Prof. Henry Higgins (Harrison) transforming guttersnipe Hepburn into regal lady, to win a bet. Sumptuously filmed, with "The Rain in Spain," fantasy "Just You Wait," Harrison's soliloquys among highlights. Eight Oscars include Picture, Actor, Director, Cinematography (Harry Stradling), Costumes (Cecil Beaton), Score Adaptation (Andre Previn), Art Direction (Beaton and Gene Allen). Super Panavision 70.▼●◗

My Family/Mi Familia (1995) **C-128m.** *** D: Gregory Nava. Jimmy Smits, Esai Morales, Edward James Olmos, Eduardo Lopez Rojas, Jenny Gago, Elpidia Carrillo, Lupe Ontiveros, Jacob Vargas, Jennifer Lopez, Maria Canals, Leon Singer, Michael De Lorenzo, Jonathan Hernandez, Constance Marie, Mary Steenburgen, Scott Bakula, DeDee Pfeiffer. A Mexican-American writer (Olmos) looks back at his family's colorful history since immigrating to L.A. in the 1920s. Evocative, well-cast, multigenerational saga indulges in melodrama at times, but never seems false, and redeems itself with a healthy sense of humor. Written by Nava and producer Anna Thomas, who also made EL NORTE. [R] ▼●

My Father Is Coming (1991-German) **C-82m.** *** D: Monika Treut. Alfred Edel, Shelley Kastner, Mary Lou Graulau, David Bronstein, Michael Massee, Annie Sprinkle, Fakir Musafar. Engrossing low-budget drama of German-born Kastner, who's struggling to find someone to love (whether it be male or female), and make it as an actress in N.Y.C.; her father's visit proves to be an awakening for both parent and child. In its best moments, an astute commentary on the importance of accepting who you are, as well as the differences in others. Notable for the appearances of porn star/performance artist Annie Sprinkle and "modern primitive" Fakir Musafar (who must be seen to be believed).▼

My Father's Glory (1990-French) **C-110m.** ***½ D: Yves Robert. Philippe Caubere, Nathalie Roussel, Didier Pain, Therese Liotard, Julien Caimaca. Richly rewarding reminiscence, set in rural France at the turn of the century, chronicling the life of a precocious little boy and his family and a summer trip to Provence, where the child becomes immersed in the country and village life. Based on Marcel Pagnol's childhood memoirs. This is storytelling, and moviemaking, of the first order. The story continues in MY MOTHER'S CASTLE. [G]▼

My Father, The Hero (1994) **C-90m.** *** D: Steve Miner. Gérard Depardieu, Katherine Heigl, Dalton James, Lauren Hutton, Faith Prince, Stephen Tobolowsky, Ann Hearn, Robyn Peterson, Frank Renzulli. Longtime absentee father takes his resentful 14-year-old daughter on a Caribbean vacation, where (to impress potential suitors) she spins a web of lies—starting with the "fact" that he's not her father, but her lover. Depardieu recreates his role from the 1991 French film MON PÈRE, CE HÉROS, and brings his considerable charisma and credibility to a potentially silly comedy, making it a lot of fun. [PG]▼●

My Favorite Blonde (1942) **78m.** *** D: Sidney Lanfield. Bob Hope, Madeleine Carroll, Gale Sondergaard, George Zucco, Victor Varconi. Bob and his trained penguin become sitting ducks when spy Madeleine uses them to help deliver secret orders; very funny Hope vehicle.▼

My Favorite Brunette (1947) **87m.** *** D: Elliott Nugent. Bob Hope, Dorothy Lamour, Peter Lorre, Lon Chaney, John Hoyt, Reginald Denny. Better-than-usual Hope nonsense with Bob as a photographer mixed up with mobsters; Lorre and Chaney add authenticity. Two very funny surprise cameos at beginning and end of film. Also shown in computer-colored version.▼●◗

My Favorite Martian (1999) **C-93m.** ** D: Donald Petrie. Christopher Lloyd, Jeff Daniels, Elizabeth Hurley, Daryl Hannah, Wallace Shawn, Christine Ebersole, Michael Lerner, Ray Walston. Strictly juvenile update of the 1960s TV sitcom, with Lloyd as the Martian who lands on Earth and moves in with good-natured lunkhead Daniels, a TV news producer. Broad, sometimes crass special-effects comedy for undemanding kids. The presence of Walston (from the original show) may bring a smile to those who remember the series. An unbilled Wayne Knight provides the voice of the Suit. [PG]▼●◗

My Favorite Season SEE **Ma Saison Préférée**

My Favorite Spy (1942) **86m.** ** D: Tay Garnett. Kay Kyser, Ellen Drew, Jane Wyman, Robert Armstrong, William Demarest, Una O'Connor, Helen Westley, George Cleveland, Ish Kabibble. How did we win WW2 with bandleader Kyser as spy? Nonsensical musicomedy tries to explain.●

My Favorite Spy (1951) **93m.** *** D: Norman Z. McLeod. Bob Hope, Hedy Lamarr, Francis L. Sullivan, Mike Mazurki, John Archer, Iris Adrian, Arnold Moss. Bob resembles murdered spy, finds himself thrust into international intrigue. Fast-moving fun, with glamorous Hedy aiding Bob on all counts.

My Favorite Wife (1940) **88m.** *** D: Garson Kanin. Cary Grant, Irene Dunne, Gail Patrick, Randolph Scott, Ann Shoemaker, Scotty Beckett, Donald MacBride. Dunne, supposedly dead, returns to U.S. to find hubby Grant remarried to Patrick, in familiar but witty marital mixup, remade as MOVE OVER, DARLING. Produced and co-written (with Sam and Bella Spewack) by Leo McCarey. Also shown in computer-colored version.▼●

My Favorite Year (1982) **C-92m.** *** D: Richard Benjamin. Peter O'Toole, Mark Linn-Baker, Jessica Harper, Joseph Bologna, Bill Macy, Lainie Kazan, Anne DeSalvo, Lou Jacobi, Adolph Green, George Wyner, Selma Diamond, Cameron Mitchell. Enjoyable comedy about a young writer on TV's top comedy show in 1954 who's given the job of chaperoning that week's guest star, screen swashbuckler and off-screen carouser Alan Swann (O'Toole, in a tailor-made role). Shifts gears, and focus, a bit too often, but has many good moments, and likable performances (including Bologna as Sid Caesar-ish TV star). The woman O'Toole dances with in night club is 1930s leading lady Gloria Stuart. Benjamin's directorial debut. Musicalized on Broadway a decade later (also with Kazan). [PG]▼●

My Fellow Americans (1996) **C-101m.** *** D: Peter Segal. Jack Lemmon, James Garner, Dan Aykroyd, Lauren Bacall, John Heard, Bradley Whitford, Sela Ward, Wilford Brimley, Esther Rolle. Two ex-presidents of the U.S.—longtime enemies—are forced to work together to uncover a plot to blame one of them for a dirty deal conducted by the current head of state. On the lam and left to their own devices, they have to deal with ordinary citizens for the first time in years. Breezy comedy, short on subtlety and long on punchlines and occasional bathroom humor . . . but it works, thanks to the charisma and professionalism of Lemmon and Garner. Bacall (as Lemmon's wife) has almost nothing to do. [PG-13] ▼●◗

My First Love (1988) **C-100m. TVM** D: Gilbert Cates. Beatrice Arthur, Richard Kiley, Joan Van Ark, Anne Francis, Richard Herd, Barbara Barrie. Pleasant comedy about a widow, challenged by her friends to take another chance at love, who seeks out the one-time high school sweetheart she hasn't seen in years. Average.

My First Wife (1984-Australian) **C-95m.** **½ D: Paul Cox. John Hargreaves, Wendy Hughes, Lucy Angwin, Anna Jemison, David Cameron. Painful, provocative drama about self-centered man who literally goes crazy when his wife leaves him after ten years. Achingly real, superbly acted, but slow and talky at times. Cox coscripted with Bob Ellis, based on his own experiences. ▼

My Foolish Heart (1949) **98m.** *** D: Mark Robson. Dana Andrews, Susan Hayward, Kent Smith, Lois Wheeler, Jessie Royce Landis, Robert Keith, Gigi Perreau. Deftly handled sentimental WW2 romance tale between soldier Andrews and Hayward; Victor Young's lovely theme helps. Based on J. D. Salinger's story "Uncle Wiggily in Connecticut," the only one of the author's works ever adapted to film.▼●

My Forbidden Past (1951) **81m.** **½ D: Robert Stevenson. Robert Mitchum, Ava Gardner, Melvyn Douglas, Janis Carter. Silly tripe about Gardner, who's got a skeleton in her family closet, seeking revenge on Mitchum for jilting her. Fast-moving, watchable nonsense set in antebellum New Orleans.▼

My Friend Flicka (1943) **C-89m.** *** D: Harold Schuster. Roddy McDowall, Preston Foster, Rita Johnson, Jeff Corey, James Bell. Sentimental story of boy who loves rebellious horse; nicely done, beautifully filmed in color. Followed by sequel THUNDERHEAD, SON OF FLICKA and a TV series.▼

My Friend Irma (1949) **103m.** ** D: George Marshall. Marie Wilson, John Lund, Diana Lynn, Don DeFore, Dean Martin, Jerry Lewis, Hans Conried. Based on radio series, movie concerns Wilson in title role as dumb blonde, Lynn as her level-headed pal, encountering wacky Martin and Lewis in their film debut. Followed by a sequel. Later a TV series.▼●

My Friend Irma Goes West (1950) **90m.** **½ D: Hal Walker. John Lund, Marie Wilson, Dean Martin, Jerry Lewis, Corinne Calvet, Diana Lynn, Lloyd Corrigan, Donald Porter, Kenneth Tobey. Daffy Irma (Wilson) and pals join Martin and Lewis on their trek to Hollywood.

My Gal Sal (1942) **C-103m.** *** D: Irving Cummings. Rita Hayworth, Victor Mature, John Sutton, Carole Landis, James Gleason, Phil Silvers, Mona Maris, Walter Catlett. Nostalgic Gay 90s musical about songwriter Paul Dresser (Mature) in love with beautiful singer Hayworth. Includes Dresser's songs, such as title tune and other old-time numbers. The two stars (and knockout Technicolor) really put this one across. That's co-choreographer Hermes Pan featured with Rita in the "Gay White Way" number. Based on the story *My Brother Paul* by Theodore Dreiser.

My Geisha (1962) **C-120m.** **½ D: Jack Cardiff. Shirley MacLaine, Yves Montand, Edward G. Robinson, Bob Cummings, Yoko Tani. Occasionally amusing comedy. MacLaine is movie star who tries the hard way to convince husband-director Montand that she's right for his movie. Loosely based on MacLaine's relationship with husband Steve Parker (who produced the film). Filmed in Japan. Technirama.▼●

My Giant (1998) **C-97m.** **½ D: Michael Lehmann. Billy Crystal, Gheorghe Muresan, Kathleen Quinlan, Joanna Pacula, Zane Carney, Jere Burns, Dan Castellaneta, Harold Gould, Doris Roberts, Lorna Luft, Estelle Harris, Steven Seagal. Ne'er-do-well showbiz agent chances to meet a 7'7" giant in Romania—and sees in him a way to resurrect his career and win back his estranged wife and kid. Sweet and amusing as long as Muresan's stomping around but the film turns borderline mawkish toward the end. Crystal is likeable as always, and real-life Washington Wizards center Muresan is winning in the title role. That's Crystal's daughter Lindsay as a put-upon production assistant. [PG-13]▼●◗

My Girl (1991) **C-102m.** **½ D: Howard Zieff. Dan Aykroyd, Jamie Lee Curtis, Macaulay Culkin, Anna Chlumsky, Richard Masur, Griffin Dunne, Ann Nelson, Peter Michael Goetz, Tom Villard, Ray Buktenica. Likable if soft-centered tale of an 11-year-old girl crying for attention from her widowed father, a mortician who doesn't know how to reach out to his precocious daughter. Bittersweet comedy touches on love, friendship, puberty, and most of all, death, but its telling moments are muted by an overall air of predictability. Appealing cast sparked by Chlumsky's mature performance. Followed by a Culkin-less sequel. [PG]▼●◗

My Girl 2 (1994) **C-99m.** **½ D: Howard Zieff. Dan Aykroyd, Jamie Lee Curtis, Anna Chlumsky, Austin O'Brien, Richard Masur, Christine Ebersole, John David Souther, Angeline Ball, Aubrey Morris, Gerrit Graham, Ben Stein, Keone Young, Anthony R. Jones, Jodie Markell, Richard Beymer, George D. Wallace. Budding teenager Chlumsky travels to L.A. (where her uncle lives) to try and learn something about her mother, who died giving birth to her; her companion on this odyssey is the son of her uncle's girlfriend. Bland but likeable fodder aimed squarely at young viewers. [PG]▼●

My Girlfriend's Boyfriend SEE: **Boyfriends and Girlfriends**

My Girl Tisa (1948) **95m.** **½ D: Elliott Nugent. Lilli Palmer, Sam Wanamaker, Akim Tamiroff, Alan Hale, Hugo Haas, Gale Robbins, Stella Adler. Sincere but uninspiring tale of devoted immigrant girl Palmer working to bring her father to the U. S. Palmer is fine as usual in lead.▼

My Gun Is Quick (1957) **88m.** *½ D: George White, Phil Victor. Robert Bray, Whitney Blake, Pamela Duncan, Donald Randolph. Drab Mickey Spillane yarn about detective Mike Hammer tracking down a murderer.

My Heroes Have Always Been Cowboys (1991) **C-106m.** **½ D: Stuart Rosenberg. Scott Glenn, Kate Capshaw, Ben Johnson, Balthazar Getty, Tess Harper, Gary Busey, Mickey Rooney, Clarence Williams III, Dub Taylor, Clu Gulager, Dennis Fimple. Aging collection of contusions (Glenn) comes home from the rodeo circuit to care for his father, only to battle sis and her husband, who'd just as soon the old man be put away. If you've seen Sam Peckinpah's sublime JUNIOR BONNER (which also featured Johnson) this has got to ring a bit hollow. Capable cast looks good in blue jeans, but cowpie cinema has been better served. [PG]▼●

My Left Foot (1989-Irish) **C-103m.** ***½ D: Jim Sheridan. Daniel Day-Lewis, Brenda Fricker, Ray McAnally, Hugh O'Conor, Fiona Shaw, Cyril Cusack, Adrian Dunbar, Ruth McCabe, Alison Whelan. Exhilarating film with Day-Lewis in a tour de force as Christy Brown, feisty Irish artist-writer who was born with cerebral palsy. This is no disease-of-the-week weeper; it's an intensely moving story with just the right touches of humor, warmth, and poignancy. Fricker and McAnally are ideal as Christy's parents, and O'Conor is absolutely remarkable as the young Christy. Sheridan coscripted (with Shane Connaughton) from Brown's autobiography. Lovely score by Elmer Bernstein. Both Day-Lewis and Fricker won Oscars for their performances. [R]▼●◗

My Life (1993) **C-112m.** **½ D: Bruce Joel Rubin. Michael Keaton, Nicole Kidman, Haing S. Ngor, Bradley Whitford, Queen Latifah, Michael Constantine, Rebecca Schull, Mark Lowenthal, Lee Garlington, Toni Sawyer. Successful ad executive, whose wife is pregnant, learns he's dying and doesn't know how to deal with the unfinished business in his life (particularly his feelings of anger toward his family) or the fact that he may never see his child. Many truthful and poignant moments in this unabashed tearjerker, but contrivances ultimately take over—especially toward the finale. Directing debut for screenwriter Rubin (the screenwriter of another misty-eyed Hollywood concoction, GHOST). [PG-13]▼●

My Life and Times with Antonin Artaud (1994-French) **93m.** ** D: Gérard Mordillat. Sami Frey, Marc Barbé, Julie Jézéquel,

Valerie Jeannet, Clotilde de Bayser, Charlotte Valandrey. Slow-moving fiction set in 1946, depicting the curious friendship between Jacques Prevel (Barbé), an eager, starving young poet, and Artaud (Frey), the brilliant but tortured, self-involved and drug-addicted writer/actor/intellectual who has just been released from an asylum. A real downer, of interest mainly to aficionados of Artaud. Crisply filmed in B&W; also in 1993, Mordillat codirected a companion documentary, THE TRUE STORY OF ARTAUD THE MOMO.▼

My Life as a Dog (1985-Swedish) **C-101m.** *** D: Lasse Hallström. Anton Glanzelius, Tomas von Brömssen, Anki Liden, Melinda Kinnaman, Kicki Rundgren, Ing-mari Carlsson. Warm-hearted look at the tumultuous life of an irrepressibly mischievous 12-year-old boy who's shipped off to live with relatives in a rural village in 1950s Sweden. Both comedic and poignant, this is ultimately an honest depiction of the often confusing nature of childhood. Glanzelius is excellent in the lead; based on an autobiographical novel by Reidar Jönsson. Later a cable-TV series. ▼●◗

My Life's in Turnaround (1994) **C-84m.** *½ D: Eric Schaeffer, Donal Lardner Ward. Eric Schaeffer, Donal Lardner Ward, Lisa Gerstein, Dana Wheeler Nicholson, Debra Clein, Sheila Jaffe, John Dore, John Sayles, Martha Plimpton, Phoebe Cates, Casey Siemaszko. Tired inside-Hollywood (or fringes-of-Hollywood) comedy might elicit a few approving snorts from the rarefied audience for which it's intended. Aspiring filmmakers exploit any presumed break that comes their way, be it a taxicab encounter with Phoebe Cates or a restaurant encounter with Martha Plimpton. Someone should have put *this* in turnaround.▼

My Life So Far (1999-British-Scottish) **C-93m.** *** D: Hugh Hudson. Colin Firth, Mary Elizabeth Mastrantonio, Malcolm McDowell, Rosemary Harris, Irène Jacob, Robert Norman, Tchéky Karyo, Brendan Gleeson. Delightful memoir of growing up in an eccentric family, set in the Scottish highlands during the 1920s and '30s. Firth is a dreamer/inventor, Mastrantonio his patient wife, McDowell his scheming man-about-town brother who has no patience for Firth's peccadilloes, and Jacob the alluring Frenchwoman who captures the imagination of every male in the household. Spirited, funny, and handsomely made. Based on the book *Son of Adam* by Sir Denis Forman. [PG-13]▼◗

My Life to Live (1963-French) **85m.** *** D: Jean-Luc Godard. Anna Karina, Saddy Rebbot, Andre S. Labarthe, Guylaine Schlumberger. Complex, fascinating 12-chapter portrait of a prostitute (Karina, who was then wed to Godard), told in documentary style. Probing look at the manner in which women and men view one another—and a celluloid valentine to Karina, upon whose mere presence Godard seems to be transfixed. Aka VIVRE SA VIE. ▼●◗

My Life With Caroline (1941) **81m.** **½ D: Lewis Milestone. Ronald Colman, Anna Lee, Charles Winninger, Reginald Gardiner, Gilbert Roland. Colman's charm sustains this frothy comedy of man suspecting his wife of having a lover.

My Little Chickadee (1940) **83m.** **½ D: Edward Cline. Mae West, W. C. Fields, Joseph Calleia, Dick Foran, Ruth Donnelly, Margaret Hamilton, Donald Meek. Team of West and Fields out West is good, but should have been funnier; W. C.'s saloon scenes are notable. The two stars also wrote screenplay.▼●

My Little Girl (1986) **C-113m.** *** D: Connie Kaiserman. Mary Stuart Masterson, James Earl Jones, Geraldine Page, Pamela Payton Wright, Anne Meara, Peter Gallagher, Page Hannah, Erika Alexander, Traci Lin, Jordan Charney, Jennifer Lopez. Subtle, perceptive account of affluent, romantic, naive young Masterson, who volunteers to work one summer in a children's detention center. Extremely well played by all, with a special nod to Alexander and Lin (as a pair of troubled, abused girls). [R]▼●

My Little Pony (1986) **C-89m.** ** D: Michael Joens. Voices of Danny DeVito, Madeline Kahn, Tony Randall, Cloris Leachman, Rhea Pearlman. Animated fantasy pits the good Little Ponies against an evil witch. Highlight is an encounter with the Smooze, an evergrowing mass of living lava—a good idea hampered by bad animation. Too "cute" for anyone over the age of 7. Followed by a TV series. [G]▼

My Love Came Back (1940) **81m.** **½ D: Curtis Bernhardt. Olivia de Havilland, Jeffrey Lynn, Eddie Albert, Jane Wyman, Charles Winninger, Spring Byington, Grant Mitchell. Entertaining little romance of violinist de Havilland looking for husband.

My Love for Yours SEE: **Honeymoon in Bali**

My Love Letters SEE: **Love Letters** (1983)

My Lucky Star (1938) **84m.** **½ D: Roy Del Ruth. Sonja Henie, Richard Greene, Cesar Romero, Buddy Ebsen, Joan Davis, Arthur Treacher, Billy Gilbert, Louise Hovick (Gypsy Rose Lee), George Barbier. Typical Henie vehicle with the skating star becoming the belle of a college campus—and helping department-store heir Romero score a hit with his dad. Finale is an imaginative "Alice in Wonderland" ice ballet.▼

My Main Man From Stony Island SEE: **Stony Island**

My Man SEE: **Mon Homme**

My Man Adam (1985) **C-84m.** ** D: Roger L. Simon. Raphael Sbarge, Page

Hannah, Veronica Cartwright, Larry B. Scott, Dave Thomas, Charlie Barnett, Austin Pendleton. Yet another youth wish-fulfillment comedy, done as a teen version of UP THE SANDBOX. Sbarge is a pizza delivery boy who fantasizes about dreamgirl Hannah (Daryl's redheaded sister, in her first starring role) and becomes involved in a real-life murder adventure. Barely released film is pleasant but uneventful. [R]▼

My Man and I (1952) **99m.** **½ D: William Wellman. Shelley Winters, Ricardo Montalban, Wendell Corey, Claire Trevor. Trials and tribulations of kindly Mexican worker Montalban; good cast helps OK script.

My Man Godfrey (1936) **95m.** ***½ D: Gregory La Cava. William Powell, Carole Lombard, Gail Patrick, Alice Brady, Eugene Pallette, Alan Mowbray, Mischa Auer, Franklin Pangborn. Delightful romp with Lombard and crazy household hiring Powell as butler thinking he's a tramp who needs a job; he teaches them that money isn't everything. Mischa Auer is impressive as starving artist, sheltered by patroness Brady. But Pallette—as harried head of household—has some of the best lines. Screenplay by Morrie Ryskind and Eric Hatch, from Hatch's novel. Jane Wyman is an extra in the party scene. Classic screwball comedy; remade in 1957.▼●

My Man Godfrey (1957) **C-92m.** **½ D: Henry Koster. June Allyson, David Niven, Martha Hyer, Eva Gabor, Jeff Donnell. Shallow compared to original, but on its own a harmless comedy of rich girl Allyson finding life's truths from butler Niven. CinemaScope.▼

My Mother's Castle (1990-French) **C-98m.** *** D: Yves Robert. Julien Caimaca, Philippe Caubere, Nathalie Roussel, Didier Pain, Therese Liotard. Sweet, warm continuation of the story which begins in MY FATHER'S GLORY. Here, young Marcel further enjoys weekend family outings to his beloved Provence. Based on Marcel Pagnol's childhood memoirs; a notch below the first film, but still most worthwhile (and must-viewing in tandem with its predecessor, as well as with Claude Berri's JEAN DE FLORETTE and MANON OF THE SPRING).▼

My Name Is Bill W. (1989) **C-100m. TVM** D: Daniel Petrie. James Woods, James Garner, JoBeth Williams, Fritz Weaver, Robert Harper, Gary Sinise, George Coe. Woods gives another flamboyant acting lesson as Bill Wilson, a fall-down drunk who sees the light, and joins a fellow boozer, Dr. Robert Smith (Garner), to found Alcoholics Anonymous. Strong script by William G. Borchert. Above average.▼

My Name Is Ivan (1962-Russian) **94m.** *** D: Andrei Tarkovsky. Kolya Burlaiev, Valentin Zubkov, Ye Zharikov, Nikolai Grinko. Taut, poignant account of 12-year-old Burlaiev, whose family is slaughtered during WW2, and his plight as he's sent as a spy into Nazi territory. Tarkovsky's first feature. Retitled: THE YOUNGEST SPY.▼●

My Name is Joe (1998-British-German) **C-105m.** **½ D: Ken Loach. Peter Mullan, Louise Goodall, Gary Lewis, Lorraine McIntosh, David McKay, Anne-Marie Kennedy, David Hayman, Scott Hannah. Likable loser Mullan is a recovering alcoholic eking out a life in Glasgow, Scotland. Mullan's tentative romance with health-care worker Goodall is worth a look . . . and more engaging than the melodramatic turn the story takes involving local thugs. [R]▼

My Name Is John SEE: **Legend of Hillbilly John, The**

My Name Is Julia Ross (1945) **65m.** *** D: Joseph H. Lewis. Nina Foch, Dame May Whitty, George Macready, Roland Varno, Anita Bolster, Doris Lloyd. An unsuspecting young woman answers newspaper ad for a job and winds up the prisoner of a crazy family. Often cited as a model B movie, it does go a long way on a low budget, though it's a bit more obvious now than it must have been in 1945. Foch's performance is still a standout. Later the inspiration for DEAD OF WINTER.

My Name Is Nobody (1973-Italian-French-German) **C-115m.** *** D: Tonino Valerii. Henry Fonda, Terence Hill, Jean Martin, Leo Gordon, R. G. Armstrong, Steve Kanaly, Geoffrey Lewis. Underrated, enjoyable if overlong Western spoof with Hill as an easygoing gunman who worships aging Fonda, a gunfighter who wants to retire. Filmed in the U.S. and Spain; produced by Sergio Leone. Released in Italy at 130m. Panavision. [PG]▼

My Neighbor Totoro (1988-Japanese) **C-86m.** *** D: Hayao Miyazaki. Voices of Lisa Michaelson, Cheryl Chase, Greg Snegoff, Natalie Core, Kenneth Hartman. Gentle, infectious animated tale of two young sisters in rural Japan and their magical adventures with Totoro, a giant furry forest spirit. Beautiful art direction and excellent English language dubbing raise this a couple of notches above other Japanimation imports. Ideal for small fry and parents; older kids may chafe at the story's leisurely pace. Wait til you see the 12-legged cat-bus! Story and script by Miyazaki, the "Walt Disney of Japan." Released in U.S. in 1993. [G]▼●

My New Gun (1992) **C-99m.** **½ D: Stacy Cochran. Diane Lane, James LeGros, Stephen Collins, Tess Harper, Bill Raymond, Bruce Altman, Maddie Corman, Natasha Lyonne, Philip Seymour Hoffman. Deadpan comedy about a quietly put-upon suburban housewife whose life takes unexpected turns when her loutish husband insists on buying her a .38 pistol. Some amusing moments and wry performances, but the film seems a bit undernourished. Feature debut for writer-director Cochran. [R]▼●

My New Partner (1984-French) **C-106m.** **½ D: Claude Zidi. Philippe Noiret, Thierry Lhermitte, Regine, Grace de Capitani, Claude Brosset. So-so comedy-drama about corrupt veteran cop Noiret, and how he responds when teamed with by-the-book rookie Lhermitte. Noiret is fine as always, but the film is strictly standard (despite its great popularity in France and its Best Picture/Director César awards). Followed by a sequel. [R]▼●

My New Partner 2 (1990-French) **C-107m.** **½ D: Claude Zidi. Philippe Noiret, Thierry Lhermitte, Guy Marchand, Line Renaud, Grace de Capitani, Michel Aumont, Jean-Pierre Castaldi, Jean-Claude Brialy, Jean Benguigui. Intricately plotted sequel finds the amiably corrupt French cops suspended from the force and plotting to oust their replacements, who turn out to be even more corrupt than they were! Breezy farce deals frivolously with such serious issues as police brutality, but has several amusing sequences and benefits from the comic chemistry of its stars. Not released in the U.S. until 1997. Aka MY NEW PARTNER AT THE RACES.

My Night at Maud's (1969-French) **105m.** *** D: Eric Rohmer. Jean-Louis Trintignant, Françoise Fabian, Marie-Christine Barrault, Antoine Vitez. No. 3 of Rohmer's "Six Moral Tales" is most intellectual, with Trintignant as moral Catholic man infatuated with woman completely unlike himself. Talky, fascinating, more specialized in appeal than later entries in series. Barrault's first film. [PG]▼●◗

My Old Man's Place (1972) **C-93m.** **½ D: Edwin Sherin. Mitchell Ryan, Arthur Kennedy, William Devane, Michael Moriarty, Topo Swope. Moriarty (in his first film) returns home from war with two soldier pals; inevitable tensions lead to rape and murder. Not profound, but moody and interesting. Original title: GLORY BOY. [R]▼

My Outlaw Brother (1951) **82m.** ** D: Elliott Nugent. Mickey Rooney, Wanda Hendrix, Robert Preston, Robert Stack, Jose Torvay. Texas Ranger Preston takes on villainous Stack, the brother of dude Rooney. Strictly conventional south-of-the-border oater.▼

My Own Private Idaho (1991) **C-102m.** **½ D: Gus Van Sant. River Phoenix, Keanu Reeves, James Russo, William Richert, Rodney Harvey, Flea, Grace Zabriskie, Tom Troupe, Udo Kier. Uniquely distinctive portrayal of male street-hustling in the American Northwest, with Phoenix as a narcoleptic sex-for-hiree and Reeves as the son of Portland's mayor—slumming in the trade. Film opens terrifically, promising to surpass even Van Sant's DRUGSTORE COWBOY—then gets bogged down in a long, dreadfully conceived gay variation on Shakespeare's *Henry IV, Part I,* from which it never fully recovers. Many potent scenes, though, and Phoenix is excellent; cult status is assured. [R]▼●

My Own True Love (1949) **84m.** ** D: Compton Bennett. Melvyn Douglas, Phyllis Calvert, Wanda Hendrix, Philip Friend, Binnie Barnes. Calvert is placed in the awkward position of choosing between two suitors, a father and son; drama lacks ring of truth.

My Pal Gus (1952) **83m.** **½ D: Robert Parrish. Richard Widmark, Joanne Dru, Audrey Totter, George Winslow, Regis Toomey. Wholesome film of Widmark coming to realize importance of son Winslow, finding romance with teacher Dru.

My Pleasure Is My Business (1974-Canadian) **C-85m.** BOMB D: Al Waxman. Xaviera Hollander, Henry Ramer, Colin Fox, Kenneth Lynch, Jayne Eastwood. "The Happy Hooker" makes her own attempt at acting in this witless comedy which purports to tell her true story (albeit just as cleaned-up as THE HAPPY HOOKER itself). Hollander is so expressionless she can't even play herself well. [R]▼

Myra Breckinridge (1970) **C-94m.** BOMB D: Michael Sarne. Mae West, John Huston, Raquel Welch, Rex Reed, Roger Herren, Farrah Fawcett, Jim Backus, John Carradine, Andy Devine, Grady Sutton. Gore Vidal's loosely structured comic novel about sex-change operation was probably unfilmable, but this version doesn't even give book a chance; as bad as any movie ever made, it tastelessly exploits many old Hollywood favorites through film clips. That's Tom Selleck—minus mustache—as one of Mae's "studs." Panavision. [R—edited from original X rating]▼

My Reputation (1946) **94m.** *** D: Curtis Bernhardt. Barbara Stanwyck, George Brent, Warner Anderson, Lucile Watson, John Ridgely, Eve Arden. Well-mounted Warner Bros. soaper; widow Stanwyck is center of scandal when she dates Brent soon after her husband's death.

Myrt and Marge (1934) **62m.** ** D: Al Boasberg. Myrtle Vail, Donna Damerel, Eddie Foy, Jr., Grace Hayes, Ted Healy, Howard, Fine, and Howard (The 3 Stooges), Bonnie Bonnell. Lackluster backstage musical, based on popular radio show of the same name. Mainly a curio for fans of the Stooges, who get to sing as well as clown.

My Science Project (1985) **C-94m.** BOMB D: Jonathan Beteul. John Stockwell, Danielle Von Zerneck, Fisher Stevens, Raphael Sbarge, Dennis Hopper, Barry Corbin, Ann Wedgeworth, Richard Masur. Laughless, often tasteless comedy about high school kids who unearth an other-worldly device that can create time and space warps. Lost in the quagmire is Hopper in funny role as a latter-day

hippie science teacher. Panavision. [PG]▼●◗
My Seven Little Sins (1954-French) **C-98m.** ** D: Jean Boyer. Maurice Chevalier, Collette Ripert, Paolo Stoppa, Delia Scala. Pleasant, inconsequential musicomedy, with Chevalier an old roué "adopting" group of Riviera chorines. Retitled: I HAVE SEVEN DAUGHTERS.
My Side of the Mountain (1969) **C-100m.** **½ D: James B. Clark. Ted Eccles, Theodore Bikel, Tudi Wiggins, Frank Perry, Peggi Loder. Children should enjoy this tale about 13-year-old Canadian boy who runs away from home to get closer to nature. Panavision. [G]▼
My Sister Eileen (1942) **96m.** **½ D: Alexander Hall. Rosalind Russell, Brian Aherne, Janet Blair, George Tobias, Allyn Joslyn, Elizabeth Patterson, June Havoc. Amusing tale of two Ohio girls trying to survive in Greenwich Village apartment; strained at times. Belongs mainly to Russell as older sister of knockout Blair. Ruth McKinney, Joseph Fields, and Jerome Chodorov adapted their Broadway hit (based on McKinney's autobiographical book). Remade as a musical in 1955 (and musicalized on Broadway as *Wonderful Town*). ▼●
My Sister Eileen (1955) **C-108m.** ***½ D: Richard Quine. Betty Garrett, Janet Leigh, Jack Lemmon, Kurt Kasznar, Dick York, Horace McMahon, Bob Fosse, Tommy Rall. Delightful, unpretentious musical version of 1942 movie about Ohio girls seeking success in the big city, moving into nutty Greenwich Village apartment. Especially interesting to see young Lemmon singing and equally young Fosse dancing; this was the first film he choreographed on his own. Not to be confused with the Broadway musical *Wonderful Town*, based on the same source. CinemaScope.▼●
My Sister, My Love SEE: **Mafu Cage, The**
My Six Convicts (1952) **104m.** *** D: Hugo Fregonese. Millard Mitchell, Gilbert Roland, John Beal, Marshall Thompson, Alf Kjellin, Henry (Harry) Morgan, Jay Adler, Regis Toomey, John Marley, Charles Buchinsky (Bronson). Unusual comedy of prison life centering on title group who manage to make jail routine tolerable, egged on by prison psychiatrist.
My Six Loves (1963) **C-101m.** **½ D: Gower Champion. Debbie Reynolds, Cliff Robertson, David Janssen, Eileen Heckart, Hans Conried, Alice Pearce, Jim Backus. Syrupy fluff of theater star Reynolds "adopting" six waifs. VistaVision.
My Son John (1952) **122m.** **½ D: Leo McCarey. Helen Hayes, Robert Walker, Dean Jagger, Van Heflin, Frank McHugh, Richard Jaeckel. Archetypal apple-pie parents (Hayes, Jagger) suspect their son (Walker) of being a Communist in this reactionary period piece. Dramatically overwrought, but fascinating as social history. Walker (who's superb) died before film was finished; most shots of him in final reel are cribbed from STRANGERS ON A TRAIN.
My Son, My Son (1940) **115m.** ** D: Charles Vidor. Madeleine Carroll, Brian Aherne, Louis Hayward, Laraine Day, Henry Hull, Josephine Hutchinson, Scotty Beckett. Drawn-out, unconvincing tale of rags-to-riches Aherne who spoils his son, and lives to regret it. Some good performances wasted on banal script.▼
My Son the Fanatic (1997-British) **C-89m.** *** D: Udayan Prasad. Om Puri, Rachel Griffiths, Stellan Skarsgård, Akbar Kurtha, Gopi Desai, Harish Patel, Bhasker Patel. Writer Hanif Kureishi again examines a Pakistani coming to terms with his life in England. In this case it's a taxi driver (Puri) who's alienated from his wife, and whose son is rebelling against him for reasons he can't understand—even while he fosters a relationship with prostitute Griffiths. A multilayered story, pointed and insightful.▼◗
My Son, the Hero (1962-Italian) **C-122m.** ** D: Duccio Tessari. Pedro Armendariz, Jacqueline Sassard, Antonella Lualdi, Giuliano Gemma. Costume picture about evil King Cadmus of Thebes, who defies the gods and faces the wrath of the Titans. Originally released in the U.S. at 111m., with comic dubbing à la WHAT'S UP, TIGER LILY?, which it preceded.
My Son, the Vampire SEE: **Vampire Over London**
My Stepmother Is an Alien (1988) **C-108m.** *½ D: Richard Benjamin. Dan Aykroyd, Kim Basinger, Jon Lovitz, Alyson Hannigan, Joseph Maher, Ann Prentiss (voice of purse), Seth Green, Wesley Mann, Harry Shearer (voice of Carl Sagan). Luscious Basinger, who knows nothing of romance or sex, marries widowed scientist (Aykroyd); he wants to settle into domesticity, while her mind is only on saving her planet from destruction. Somehow, Jimmy Durante imitations get worked into this new low in "high-concept" comedy. [PG-13]▼●◗
Mysterians, The (1957-Japanese) **C-85m.** **½ D: Ishiro Honda. Kenji Sahara, Yumi Shirakawa, Momoko Kochi, Akihiko Hirata. Centuries after the destruction of their planet, the title aliens land on Earth, install an impregnable dome by a lake, and demand women. The world does not take this well. Colorful special effects and fast pace make this one of the better Japanese sci-fis. Tohoscope.▼
Mysterious Doctor, The (1943) **57m.** **½ D: Ben Stoloff. John Loder, Eleanor Parker, Bruce Lester, Lester Matthews, Forrester Harvey. Standard story of a doctor who murders people to keep secret of his being Nazi. Moor locations interesting; cast adequate.

Mysterious Intruder (1946) **61m.** **½ D: William Castle. Richard Dix, Nina Vale, Regis Toomey, Pamela Blake, Charles Lane, Helen Mowery, Mike Mazurki. Dix is an unscrupulous private eye who resorts to murder in an attempt to find some rare Jenny Lind wax recordings in this atmospheric *Whistler* series entry.

Mysterious Island (1961-British) **C-101m.** *** D: Cy Endfield. Michael Craig, Joan Greenwood, Michael Callan, Gary Merrill, Herbert Lom. Deliberately paced fantasy adventure based on two-part Jules Verne novel, a sequel to his *20,000 Leagues Under the Sea*. Confederate prison escapees hijack observation balloon and are blown off course; find uncharted island with gigantic animals. Great special effects by Ray Harryhausen; rousing Bernard Herrmann score. Filmed before in 1929.▼●

Mysterious Island of Captain Nemo, The (1974-French-Italian) **C-96m.** ** D: Juan Antonio Bardem, Henri Colpi. Omar Sharif, Philippe Nicaud, Gerard Tichy, Jess Hahn, Rafael Bardem, Ambrose M'Bia. Jules Verne's Nemo (Sharif) again sees service in juvenile-level action piece, a bit less acceptable than others of genre. [PG]

Mysterious Lady (1928) **96m.** **½ D: Fred Niblo. Greta Garbo, Conrad Nagel, Gustav von Seyffertitz, Albert Pollet, Edward Connelly. Austrian military officer (Nagel) falls in love with Garbo, unaware that she's a Russian spy. Another contrived plot made worthwhile by Garbo herself.▼

Mysterious Magician, The (1965-German) **95m.** **½ D: Alfred Vohrer. Joachim Fuchsberger, Eddi Arent, Sophie Hardy, Karl John, Heinz Drache. Mysterious murderwave in London causes Scotland Yard to suspect that the "Wizard," archfiend, is still alive; enjoyable suspenser from Edgar Wallace story. Ultrascope.▼

Mysterious Mr. Moto (1938) **62m.** **½ D: Norman Foster. Peter Lorre, Henry Wilcoxon, Mary Maguire, Erik Rhodes, Harold Huber, Leon Ames, Forrester Harvey. The Oriental sleuth travels to London, where a secret assassination society has Scotland Yard baffled.

Mysterious Mr. Wong, The (1935) **63m.** ** D: William Nigh. Bela Lugosi, Wallace Ford, Arline Judge, Fred Warren, Lotus Long, Robert Emmett O'Connor. Lugosi, complete with Hungarian accent, plays the title character: a power-mad Chinaman obsessed with possessing twelve coins that were once the property of Confucius. He's also cast as Wong's shy, quiet alter-ego in this campy programmer. Not related in any way to Boris Karloff's MR. WONG series.▼

Mystery, Alaska (1999) **C-118m.** ** D: Jay Roach. Russell Crowe, Burt Reynolds, Hank Azaria, Mary McCormack, Lolita Davidovich, Colm Meaney, Maury Chaykin, Ron Eldard, Michael McKean, Mike Myers, Little Richard. Remote Alaskan town's hockey team is given the chance to play against the professional N.Y. Rangers as a publicity stunt. A hodgepodge of characters and an inevitable big-game finale, coupled with derivative storylines, prove that David E. Kelley (who coscripted and coproduced) should stick to TV. Crowe is the only one to rise above the material. Super 35. [R]▼●◗

Mystery Date (1991) **C-99m.** **½ D: Jonathan Wacks. Ethan Hawke, Teri Polo, Brian McNamara, Fisher Stevens, B. D. Wong, Tony Rosato, Don Davis, James Hong, Victor Wong. Shy Hawke dreams of dating a dishy neighbor, so older brother McNamara rings her up and arranges a date . . . but it turns out he has an agenda of his own, which includes a corpse in the trunk of the car Hawke is driving. Surprisingly black youth comedy with more than a few unexpected twists. Wong is a scream as a criminal rival in McNamara's high-stakes schemes. [PG-13]▼●

Mystery in Mexico (1948) **66m.** ** D: Robert Wise. William Lundigan, Jacqueline White, Ricardo Cortez, Tony Barrett, Jacqueline Dalya, Walter Reed. Competent but overly familiar second-feature mystery about insurance investigator Lundigan who goes to Mexico City to find out what happened to White's brother.

Mystery Liner (1934) **62m.** ** D: William Nigh. Noah Beery, Astrid Allyn (Allwyn), Cornelius Keefe, Gustav von Steyffertitz, Edwin Maxwell, Ralph Lewis, Zeffie Tilbury. A mysterious secret radio-control weapon being developed aboard a cruise ship is sought by various parties in this intriguing but slow-paced B-picture. That's a clean-shaven Gabby Hayes as the crew member named Wathman! Based on an Edgar Wallace novel. ▼◗

Mystery Men (1999) **C-111m.** **½ D: Kinka Usher. Hank Azaria, Claire Forlani, Janeane Garofalo, Greg Kinnear, William H. Macy, Kel Mitchell, Lena Olin, Paul Reubens, Geoffrey Rush, Ben Stiller, Wes Studi, Tom Waits, Jenifer Lewis, Ricky Jay, Louise Lasser, Eddie Izzard. Silly, flimsy story of wannabe superheroes with specious powers uniting to rescue a genuine hero from an evil villain. Good dialogue and a fun cast make up for the overblown special effects and cluttered array of characters. [PG-13]▼●◗

Mystery of Edwin Drood, The (1935) **87m.** **½ D: Stuart Walker. Claude Rains, Douglass Montgomery, Heather Angel, David Manners, E. E. Clive, Francis (L.) Sullivan, Valerie Hobson. Seemingly respectable Rains is actually responsible for series of horrible murders. All-British cast in pretty good Hollywood adaptation of Charles Dickens' unfinished novel, which inspired a Broadway musical in the 1980s. Remade in 1993.▼

Mystery of Edwin Drood, The (1993-British) **C-102m.** ** D: Timothy Forder. Robert Powell, Michelle Evans, Jonathan Phillips, Rupert Rainsford, Finty Williams, Peter Pacey, Nanette Newman, Freddie Jones, Gemma Craven, Rosemary Leach, Ronald Fraser. Dickens' unfinished novel of a suspicious choirmaster, whose deadly jealousy over his fiancée gets him into hot water, gets another go-round here, but the results are mediocre at best. Powell is an uncharismatic lead, but the cast is peppered with familiar British actors.▼

Mystery of Kaspar Hauser, The SEE: **Every Man for Himself and God Against All**

Mystery of Marie Roget, The (1942) **91m.** **½ D: Phil Rosen. Maria Montez, Maria Ouspenskaya, John Litel, Patric Knowles, Charles Middleton. Poe story provides basis for fairly good murder mystery. Detective tries to unravel mystery of actress' strange disappearance.▼

Mystery of Mr. Wong (1939) **67m.** *½ D: William Nigh. Boris Karloff, Grant Withers, Dorothy Tree, Lotus Long, Morgan Wallace, Holmes Herbert. Modest Mr. Wong mystery, second entry in the series, has Oriental sleuth becoming embroiled in mystery surrounding a rare gem and a suspiciously changed will.▼

Mystery of Mr. X, The (1934) **85m.** *** D: Edgar Selwyn. Robert Montgomery, Elizabeth Allan, Lewis Stone, Ralph Forbes, Henry Stephenson, Forrester Harvey, Ivan Simpson, Leonard Mudie. Stylish, highly enjoyable mixture of suspense and light comedy, with urbane London jewel thief Montgomery suspected of a string of police murders and trying to clear himself while romancing Scotland Yard chief's daughter. Montgomery and Allan were then husband and wife.

Mystery of Picasso, The (1956-French) **C-85m.** *** D: Henri-Georges Clouzot. Fascinating documentary about Pablo Picasso, who discusses his work and creates a number of paintings before the camera (all of which were destroyed after shooting ended, meaning that they exist only on film). Photographed by Claude (nephew of Jean and grandson of Auguste) Renoir. CinemaScope (part).▼●

Mystery of Rampo, The SEE: **Rampo**

Mystery of the Black Jungle (1956-German) **72m.** *½ D: Ralph Murphy. Lex Barker, Jane Maxwell, Luigi Tosi, Paul Muller. Embarrassing lowjinks set in India involving idol-worshiping natives. Retitled: THE BLACK DEVILS OF KALI.▼●

Mystery of the Golden Eye SEE: **Golden Eye, The**

Mystery of the Mary Celeste SEE: **Phantom Ship**

Mystery of the Wax Museum (1933) **C-77m.** **½ D: Michael Curtiz. Lionel Atwill, Fay Wray, Glenda Farrell, Allen Vincent, Frank McHugh, Arthur Edmund Carewe. Vintage horror film strays somewhat into excess "comic relief" and contrivances, but plot of madman Atwill encasing victims in wax, with Wray next on his list, is still exciting. Filmed in early two-color Technicolor; noteworthy as first horror film with contemporary urban setting. Remade as HOUSE OF WAX.▼●

Mystery of the White Room (1939) **58m.** *** D: Otis Garrett. Bruce Cabot, Helen Mack, Constance Worth, Joan Woodbury, Mabel Todd, Tom Dugan. Very good *Crime Club* mystery of murders in an operating room; modest, nicely done.

Mystery of Thug Island, The (1964-Italian-West German) **C-96m.** *½ D: Luigi Capuano. Guy Madison, Peter Van Eyck, Giacomo Rossi Stuart, Ivan Desny, Inge Schoener. Below-average formula drama with the daughter of a British Army captain abducted in India, becoming member of a sect. Bulk of the film takes place 15 years later. Euroscope.

Mystery Science Theater 3000: The Movie (1996) **C-73m.** *** D: Jim Mallon. Michael J. Nelson, Trace Beaulieu, Kevin Murphy, Jim Mallon, John Brady. Theatrical presentation of cable TV cult favorite has shorter running time than an average episode but just as many laughs. Nelson plays a hapless human trapped on orbiting spaceship with crew of wisecracking puppet robots, forced to watch an edited version of 1955's sci-fi outing THIS ISLAND EARTH. Silhouettes of Nelson and robots appear at lower right of screen, and their running commentary during the film is often hilarious. Brief framing setup and occasional break segments throughout are not so clever, especially compared to original series created by comedian Joel Hodgson. [PG-13]▼●◗

Mystery Street (1950) **93m.** **½ D: John Sturges. Ricardo Montalban, Sally Forrest, Bruce Bennett, Elsa Lanchester, Marshall Thompson, Jan Sterling, Eamon Ryan, Betsy Blair. To solve the crime, the skeleton of a murdered B-girl is studied by Cape Cod cop Montalban and Harvard doctor Bennett in an early movie depiction of forensic science. Intelligent, realistic mystery is well acted and engrossing, if slow paced.

Mystery Submarine (1950) **78m.** **½ D: Douglas Sirk. Macdonald Carey, Marta Toren, Carl Esmond, Ludwig Donath. Involved plot of military officer Carey being instrumental in destruction of Nazi sub in South America.

Mystery Submarine (1963-British) **90m.** *½ D: C. M. Pennington-Richards. Edward Judd, James Robertson Justice, Laurence Payne, Arthur O'Sullivan, Albert Lieven. Tame WW2 espionage tale of German sub manned by British crew—captured by English fleet. Aka DECOY.

Mystery Train (1989) **C-113m.** *** D:

Jim Jarmusch. Masatoshi Nagase, Youki Kudoh, Screamin' Jay Hawkins, Cinque Lee, Nicoletta Braschi, Elizabeth Bracco, Joe Strummer, Rick Aviles, Steve Buscemi, Tom Noonan, Rockets Redglare, Rufus Thomas, voice of Tom Waits. Typically quirky slice-of-life from Jarmusch, trio of stories depicts foreigners' stays in sleazy Memphis hotel. Jarmusch's minimalist style results in some slow stretches, but there are enough genuinely funny moments to make this worth seeing. [R]▼●◗

Mystic Pizza (1988) **C-104m.** ** D: Donald Petrie. Julia Roberts, Annabeth Gish, Lili Taylor, Vincent D'Onofrio, William R. Moses, Adam Storke, Conchata Ferrell, Joanna Merlin, Matt Damon. The amorous adventures of three young women who work at a pizzeria in Mystic, Connecticut. Superficial in the extreme but geared to appeal to a young female audience. A "nice little film" that isn't all that good. [R]▼●

Mystique SEE: **Circle of Power**

My Summer Story SEE: **It Runs in My Family**

My Sweet Charlie (1970) **C-97m. TVM** D: Lamont Johnson. Patty Duke, Al Freeman Jr., Ford Rainey, William Hardy, Chris Wilson, Noble Willingham. White unwed mother and black N.Y.C lawyer are thrown together in abandoned house in rural Texas. Good adaptation of David Westheimer novel; excellent performances; believable and moving. A television landmark by Richard Levinson and William Link; this earned theatrical showings after TV debut. Above average. [G]▼

My Teenage Daughter SEE: **Bad Girl**

Myth of Fingerprints, The (1997) **C-90m.** ** D: Bart Freundlich. Blythe Danner, Roy Scheider, Julianne Moore, Noah Wyle, Arija Bareikis, Brian Kerwin, Michael Vartan, Laurel Holloman, Hope Davis, James Le Gros. A dysfunctional New England family reunion at Thanksgiving reveals WASP angst simmering below the surface of gentility. Too many characters leave little time for any depth of understanding. Notable casting includes Wyle as Scheider's son; he was also associate producer. [R]▼◗

My Tutor (1983) **C-97m.** ** D: George Bowers. Matt Lattanzi, Caren Kaye, Kevin McCarthy, Arlene Golonka, Clark Brandon, Bruce Bauer, Crispin Glover. Rich, hunky (but still virginal) Lattanzi won't graduate high school unless he passes French, so his folks hire beautiful Kaye to spend the summer tutoring him. Earns points for sincerity, but credulity is low. [R]▼●

My 20th Century (1989-Hungarian) **92m.** *** D: Ildiko Enyedi. Dorotha Segda, Oleg Jankovskij, Paulus Manker, Peter Andorai, Gabor Maté. Compelling tale of twin sisters, born in 1880 Budapest, who are separated during childhood; one becomes a seductress, the other an anarchist. Enyedi incisively depicts an era that begins with promise, as Thomas Edison (Andorai) demonstrates the wonders of electricity, but develops into an age in which human relations do not keep pace with technological innovation. Segda is excellent as both sisters, and also appears as their mother. Enyedi also scripted.▼●

My Uncle SEE: **Mon Oncle**

My Uncle Antoine (1971-Canadian) **C-104m.** **½ D: Claude Jutra. Jean Duceppe, Olivette Thibault, Claude Jutra, Jacques Gagnon, Helene Loiselle. Fifteen-year-old Gagnon observes those around him while growing up in a small mining town during the 1940s. Not bad, but nothing special. Video title: MON ONCLE ANTOINE. ▼

My Uncle, Mr. Hulot SEE: **Mon Oncle**

My Wife's Best Friend (1952) **87m.** ** D: Richard Sale. Anne Baxter, Macdonald Carey, Cecil Kellaway, Leif Erickson, Frances Bavier. Unexceptional film of married couple confessing their past indiscretions when their plane seems about to crash.

My Wild Irish Rose (1947) **C-101m.** ** D: David Butler. Dennis Morgan, Andrea King, Arlene Dahl, Alan Hale, George Tobias. Irish songs galore support limp biography of songwriter Chauncey Olcott.

Nabonga (1944) **75m.** *½ D: Sam Newfield. Buster Crabbe, Julie London, Fifi D'Orsay, Barton MacLane, Bryant Washburn. Incredible cheapie of plane-crash survivor (London) making friends with local gorilla. Good for laughs, anyway. Retitled: GORILLA.▼◗

Nada (1974-French-Italian) **C-107m.** ***½ D: Claude Chabrol. Fabio Testi, Michel Duchaussoy, Maurice Garrel, Michel Aumont, Lou Castel, Didier Kaminka, Viviane Romance, Mariangela Melato. Riveting political thriller about a group of hapless left-wing terrorists who kidnap the American Ambassador to France, but then have to deal with a fascistic police chief who's even more violent than they are and doesn't care about getting the hostage back alive. Chabrol is at the top of his cool, calculated, and ultra-cynical form in this superbly filmed blend of razor-sharp action and absurdist humor. Written by Chabrol and Jean Patrick Manchette, from the latter's novel. Original running time: 134m. Aka THE NADA GANG.▼

Nadia (1984) **C-100m. TVM** D: Alan Cooke. Talia Balsam, Jonathan Banks, Joe Bennett, Simone Blue, Johann Carlo, Conchata Ferrell, Carrie Snodgress. Nadia Comaneci, the young Rumanian athlete whose gymnastic feats during the 1976 Olympics enthralled the world, gets a curiously flat retelling of her story, with all of the lead actors either British or American (some working with Mittle-European accents) and the rest of the cast fleshed out with

Yugoslavians. Gymnastic gyrations remain wondrous as performed by contemporary Olympic-class performers. Average.▼

Nadine (1987) **C-82m.** *** Robert Benton. Jeff Bridges, Kim Basinger, Rip Torn, Gwen Verdon, Glenne Headly, Jerry Stiller, Jay Patterson. Lightweight but pleasing comedy set in 1954 Austin, about a pregnant but nearly divorced hairdresser who accidentally witnesses a murder while trying to retrieve some nude "art studies" she posed for in a weak moment. Very well cast, with Basinger a surprising standout; catchy credit tune is performed by Sweethearts of the Rodeo. [PG]▼●

Nadja (1994) **92m.** *** D: Michael Almereyda. Elina Lowensohn, Peter Fonda, Suzy Amis, Galaxy Craze, Martin Donovan, Jared Harris, Karl Geary. Cleverly amusing vampire movie with the vampirish title character (perfectly played by Lowensohn) stalking the streets and late-night clubs of Manhattan's East Village. Fonda is a hoot as "Dr. Van Helsing," who has murdered Nadja's father and now is after her and her twin brother. Most enjoyable, but the stylish visuals sometimes swallow up the story. Filmed in black-and-white, in part using a plastic toy Pixelvision video camera! Executive produced by David Lynch, who appears as a morgue attendant. [R]▼●

Nails (1992) **C-100m.** **½ D: John Flynn. Dennis Hopper, Anne Archer, Tomas Milian, Keith David, Carlos Carrasco, Charles Hallahan, Cliff De Young. Wired Hopper slips into his profane, law-bending cop bit, battling druggies and crooked politicians. Misplaced theatrical release debuted on cable.▼●

Naked (1993-British) **C-131m.** *** D: Mike Leigh. David Thewlis, Lesley Sharp, Katrin Cartlidge, Greg Cruttwell, Claire Skinner, Peter Wight, Ewen Bremner, Susan Vidler, Deborah MacLaren. Unique, contemporary, energized examination of a drifter from Manchester (Thewlis) who arrives unannounced at an ex-girlfriend's London flat and proceeds to verbally abuse and amuse everyone in sight. Bleak, often brutal, and frequently hilarious look at people drifting in an alienated modern society, with a very impressive performance by Thewlis; its only real shortcoming is its overlength. Another challenging film from the always original writer-director Leigh.▼●

Naked Alibi (1954) **86m.** **½ D: Jerry Hopper. Sterling Hayden, Gloria Grahame, Gene Barry, Marcia Henderson, Casey Adams, Chuck Connors. Dismissed from force because of "police brutality," ex-cop Hayden continues to stalk cop-killer suspect Barry.

Naked and the Dead, The (1958) **C-131m.** *** D: Raoul Walsh. Aldo Ray, Cliff Robertson, Raymond Massey, William Campbell, Richard Jaeckel, James Best, Joey Bishop, L. Q. Jones, Robert Gist, Lili St. Cyr, Barbara Nichols. Norman Mailer's intensive novel about WW2 soldiers in the Pacific gets superficial but rugged filmization. Ray is the tough sergeant, Robertson the rich-kid lieutenant, Bishop the comic Jew, Jones the hick, Gist the loner, etc. RKO-Scope/WarnerScope.▼

Naked Ape, The (1973) **C-85m.** *½ D: Donald Driver. Johnny Crawford, Victoria Principal, Dennis Oliveri, Diana Darrin. Tongue-in-cheek *Playboy* production loosely based on the pop anthropology of Desmond Morris's nonfiction best-seller. Snickering sex jokes and mediocre animation (by Charles Swenson) add nothing to this episodic summary of 10 million years of Man's evolution. Musical score by Jimmy Webb. [PG]

Naked Brigade, The (1965) **99m.** ** D: Maury Dexter. Shirley Eaton, Ken Scott, Mary Chronopoulou, John Holland, Sonia Zoidou. Mild WW2 actioner of Eaton hiding from Nazi invasion of Crete.

Naked Cage, The (1986) **C-97m.** ** D: Paul Nicholas. Shari Shattuck, Angel Tompkins, Lucinda Crosby, Faith Minton, Christina Whitaker, John Terlesky. Standard women's prison drama as innocent Stattuck is framed for a bank robbery and ends up in the slammer. [R]▼

Naked City, The (1948) **96m.** *** D: Jules Dassin. Barry Fitzgerald, Howard Duff, Don Taylor, Dorothy Hart, Ted de Corsia, House Jameson, Frank Conroy, David Opatoshu. Time (and decades of TV cop shows) have dulled the edge of this once-trendsetting crime drama, produced by columnist Mark Hellinger on the streets of N.Y.C., following the investigation of a murder case step by step. Fitzgerald is still first-rate, cast against type as the detective in charge, and the cast is peppered with soon-to-be-familiar character actors (Arthur O'Connell, Paul Ford, James Gregory, Celia Adler, et al.). Cinematographer William Daniels and editor Paul Weatherwax won Oscars for their work. Screenplay by Albert Maltz and Malvin Wald. Later a TV series.▼●◗

Naked Dawn, The (1955) **C-82m.** **½ D: Edgar G. Ulmer. Arthur Kennedy, Betta St. John, Roy Engel, Eugene Iglesias, Charita. Modern Western about a snowballing series of crimes. Based on a story by Gorky, and much admired by Ulmer buffs.

Naked Earth (1958-British) **96m.** *½ D: Vincent Sherman. Juliette Greco, Richard Todd, John Kitzmiller, Finlay Currie. Misguided soap opera set in 1890s Africa, trying to build up aspiring star Greco. CinemaScope.

Naked Edge, The (1961) **99m.** **½ D: Michael Anderson. Gary Cooper, Deborah Kerr, Eric Portman, Diane Cilento, Hermione Gingold, Michael Wilding. Uneven suspenser of Kerr thinking husband Cooper is guilty of murder. Cooper's last film, made in London.▼

Naked Face, The (1985) **C-103m.** **½

D: Bryan Forbes. Roger Moore, Rod Steiger, Elliott Gould, Anne Archer, David Hedison, Art Carney. Change of pace for Moore, playing a psychiatrist suspected of murdering one of his patients. Low-budget adaptation of Sidney Sheldon novel crudely injects clues and red herrings. [R]▼

Naked Gun: From the Files of Police Squad!, The (1988) **C-85m.** *** D: David Zucker. Leslie Nielsen, George Kennedy, Priscilla Presley, Ricardo Montalban, O.J. Simpson, Nancy Marchand. A failed (but loyally supported) TV sitcom, *Police Squad,* is reincarnated as a hilarious feature film, with a deadpan, dead-perfect Nielsen as Lt. Frank Drebin, the stupidest law officer since Inspector Clouseau. Writers David and Jerry Zucker, Jim Abrahams, and Pat Proft can't keep their momentum from slowing a bit during the baseball game finale, but they provide solid, silly laughs from start to finish. Followed by two sequels. [PG-13]▼●

Naked Gun 2½: The Smell of Fear, The (1991) **C-85m.** **½ (what else?) D: David Zucker. Leslie Nielsen, Priscilla Presley, George Kennedy, O. J. Simpson, Robert Goulet, Richard Griffiths, Jacqueline Brookes, Lloyd Bochner, Tim O'Connor, Peter Mark Richman. Frank Drebin is back, this time to save America from a plot hatched by oil, coal, and nuclear power brokers to keep the country from adopting a new energy policy. Lots of gags, some of them funny, but film lacks the freshness of its predecessor and empties out its bag of tricks sooner than it should. [PG-13]▼●

Naked Gun 33⅓: The Final Insult (1994) **C-82m.** **⅓ (what else?) D: Peter Segal. Leslie Nielsen, Priscilla Presley, George Kennedy, O.J. Simpson, Fred Ward, Kathleen Freeman, Anna Nicole Smith, Ellen Greene, Ed Williams, Randall "Tex" Cobb. Sloppy sequel in which a now retired Frank Drebin returns to Police Squad for one more case . . . losing the love of his wife in the process. The most slapdash slapstick yet, with some real laughs here and there, and a passel of cameo appearances at the climactic Oscar ceremony. [PG-13]▼●

Naked Heart, The (1950-British) **96m.** ** D: Marc Allegret. Michele Morgan, Kieron Moore, Françoise Rosay, Jack Watling. Little of consequence happens in this sad story based on book *Maria Chapdelaine* by Louis Hémon. Filmed before in 1935 (in France) and 1983 (in Canada).

Naked Hills, The (1956) **C-73m.** *½ D: Josef Shaftel. David Wayne, Keenan Wynn, James Barton, Marcia Henderson, Jim Backus. Raggedy account of Wayne who has gold fever and spends life searching for ore, ignoring wife and family.▼

Naked in New York (1994) **C-91m.** **½ D: Dan Algrant. Eric Stoltz, Mary-Louise Parker, Ralph Macchio, Kathleen Turner, Tony Curtis, Timothy Dalton, Jill Clayburgh, Roscoe Lee Browne. Unsuccessful, but generally watchable backstage comedy about an aspiring playwright who can't decide whether to pursue his career in N.Y.C. or remain with the woman he loves in their Ivy League environment. Stoltz and Macchio aren't aggressive enough for their roles, but Turner (as a soap actress) and Curtis (a Broadway producer) give mild film a boost. Amusing literati cameos; Martin Scorsese executive-produced. [R]▼●

Naked in the Sun (1957) **C-79m.** ** D: R. John Hugh. James Craig, Lita Milan, Barton MacLane, Tony Hunter. Somewhat sluggish account of Indian tribes involved with slave traders.▼

Naked Jungle, The (1954) **C-95m.** *** D: Byron Haskin. Eleanor Parker, Charlton Heston, Abraham Sofaer, William Conrad. High-class South American jungle adventure, with Heston and wife Parker surrounded on their plantation by advancing army of red ants. Produced by George Pal.▼●

Naked Kiss, The (1964) **93m.** *** D: Samuel Fuller. Constance Towers, Anthony Eisley, Michael Dante, Virginia Grey, Patsy Kelly, Betty Bronson. In-your-face melodrama opens with a bang and never lets up, as prostitute Towers arrives in a small town hoping to start a new life and almost succeeds. By turns lurid, sentimental, romantic, surprising; a melange that could only have been concocted by writer-director Fuller. ▼●◗

Naked Lunch (1991-Canadian-British) **C-115m.** *** D: David Cronenberg. Peter Weller, Judy Davis, Ian Holm, Julian Sands, Roy Scheider, Monique Mercure, Nicholas Campbell, Michael Zelniker, Robert A. Silverman, Joseph Scorsiani. A no-holds-barred, graphic filming of William S. Burroughs' thoroughly unfilmable 1959 novel, weaving elements of the author's life in with the fictional material. Weller is an aspiring writer and N.Y.C. exterminator in 1953; when his loony drug-addict wife (Davis, who's great) dies, the real story takes off. He is immersed in an extended, drug-laced odyssey to a Casablanca-like community that's seething with oddballs and weirdos. Cronenberg was undeniably the right person to direct this, but be warned: mutating, oozing typewriter-size talking bugs fill the screen throughout. [R]▼●

Naked Maja, The (1959) **C-111m.** ** D: Henry Koster. Ava Gardner, Anthony Franciosa, Amedeo Nazzari, Gino Cervi, Massimo Serato, Lea Padovani, Carlo Rizzo. Mishmash involving 18th-century Spanish painter Goya and famed model for title painting. Technirama.▼

Naked Night, The SEE: **Sawdust and Tinsel**

Naked Paradise (1957) **C-68m.** BOMB D: Roger Corman. Richard Denning, Beverly Garland, Lisa Montell, Richard (Dick) Miller, Leslie Bradley. On-location filming in Hawaii can't salvage this balderdash about crooks using cruise boat to rob a local plantation. Retitled: THUNDER OVER HAWAII. Remade as BEAST FROM HAUNTED CAVE and CREATURE FROM THE HAUNTED SEA.

Naked Prey, The (1966) **C-94m.** *** D: Cornel Wilde. Cornel Wilde, Gert Van Den Bergh, Ken Gampu. Harrowing, well-done safari movie. African natives give prisoner Wilde headstart before they close in on him for kill, forcing Wilde to combat them with savage tactics; memorable brutal sequences. Panavision.▼●

Naked Runner, The (1967-British) **C-104m.** *½ D: Sidney J. Furie. Frank Sinatra, Peter Vaughan, Toby Robins, Edward Fox. Dull spy melodrama focusing on American who is pawn in bizarre plot to get him to assassinate enemy agent. Farfetched, too heavily plotted. Techniscope. ▼

Naked Space SEE: **Creature Wasn't Nice, The**

Naked Spur, The (1953) **C-91m.** ***½ D: Anthony Mann. James Stewart, Janet Leigh, Ralph Meeker, Robert Ryan, Millard Mitchell. One of the best Westerns ever made: a tough, hard little film about self-styled bounty hunter Stewart trying to capture Ryan, who stirs tension among Stewart's newly acquired "partners." Strikingly directed and photographed (by William Mellor) on location in the Rockies. Written by Sam Rolfe and Harold Jack Bloom.▼

Naked Street, The (1955) **84m.** ** D: Maxwell Shane. Farley Granger, Anthony Quinn, Anne Bancroft, Peter Graves, Jerry Paris, Jeanne Cooper. Capable cast wasted in bland yarn of reporter exposing crime syndicate.

Naked Tango (1991) **C-90m.** ** D: Leonard Schrader.Vincent D'Onofrio, Mathilda May, Esai Morales, Fernando Rey, Cipe Lincovski, Josh Mostel, Constance McCashin. Very dark look at the Tango underground of 1920s Buenos Aires, in which the famous dance symbolizes the obsessive and strange passions of three people caught up in this forbidden world. Uneasy mixture of sex and violence, with an unconvincing central performance by D'Onofrio, though stunning production design and cinematography compensate a little for the murky storytelling. A real letdown from the producer (David Weisman), screenwriter (Schrader), and author (Manuel Puig) of KISS OF THE SPIDER WOMAN. [R]

Naked Truth, The SEE: **Your Past Is Showing**

Naked Under Leather SEE: **Girl on a Motorcycle**

Naked Warriors SEE: **Arena, The**

Naked Weekend, The SEE: **Circle of Power**

Naked Youth (1959) **69m.** BOMB D: John F. Schreyer. Carol Ohmart, Robert Hutton, Steve Rowland, Jan Brooks, Robert Arthur, John Goddard. Awful potboiler about drug smuggling, murder and some youths who escape from the "State Boys Honor Farm." That "Switch"—short for switchblade—is a real peach. Plenty of blasting saxophones and bongo drums on the soundtrack. Aka WILD YOUTH.▼

Name of the Game Is Kill, The (1968) **C-88m.** ** D: Gunnar Hellstrom. Jack Lord, Susan Strasberg, Collin Wilcox, Tisha Sterling, T. C. Jones. Crazy melodrama concerns refugee Lord's problems in Arizona when he gets mixed up with a trio of sisters and their mother. Retitled THE FEMALE TRAP.

Name of the Rose, The (1986-Italian-German-French) **C-130m.** ** D: Jean-Jacques Annaud. Sean Connery, F. Murray Abraham, Christian Slater, Elya Baskin, Feodor Chaliapin, Jr., William Hickey, Michael Lonsdale, Ron Perlman, narrated by Dwight Weist. Unusual film (to say the least) based on Umberto Eco's best-seller, which places a Sherlock Holmesian monk (Connery) in the midst of a mysterious Italian abbey during the inquisition of the 13th century. Too provocative to dismiss, too lumbering to thoroughly enjoy, buoyed considerably by Connery's charismatic performance. [R]▼●

Namu, the Killer Whale (1966) **C-88m.** **½ D: Laslo Benedek. Robert Lansing, John Anderson, Lee Meriwether, Richard Erdman, Robin Mattson. Intriguing tale, based on true story of naturalist Lansing capturing and training a killer whale. Nicely done, good family fare. Aka NAMU, MY BEST FRIEND. ▼

Nana (1934) **89m.** **½ D: Dorothy Arzner. Anna Sten, Phillips Holmes, Lionel Atwill, Muriel Kirkland, Richard Bennett, Mae Clarke. Initially interesting adaptation of Emile Zola story of luxury-loving woman in tragic love affair runs out of steam towards the middle. Producer Samuel Goldwyn's first attempt to make a new Garbo out of exotic but wooden Sten.

Nancy Drew Carolyn Keene's series of juvenile mystery novels debuted in 1930 and immediately captured the fancy of young readers. In 1938 Warner Bros. purchased the screen rights, and found the perfect actress to bring Nancy to life: Bonita Granville. Her Nancy is brainy, feisty, resourceful, and full of energy—boundless energy. Frankie Thomas, Jr. plays her boyfriend and crime-solving cohort, and John Litel is (type)cast as her attorney father. Other characters and incidents were combined or compressed from Keene's books, but only two scripts were actually adapted from novels: NANCY DREW, DETECTIVE and NANCY DREW AND THE HIDDEN STAIRCASE, the best in the series and ironically the last. All four films were directed by William Clemens with typical Warner Bros. zip and pace; they're more densely plotted than one might expect for B pictures, and though they're aimed at a younger audience, they seldom skirt the grim realities of crime and murder. The four films are very much of a piece, and hew to a Hollywood formula; if they're not quite as good as the books, they're still fun to watch.

NANCY DREW

Nancy Drew, Detective (1938)
Nancy Drew—Reporter (1939)
Nancy Drew—Troubleshooter (1939)
Nancy Drew and the Hidden Staircase (1939)

Nancy Drew and the Hidden Staircase (1939) **60m.** **½ D: William Clemens. Bonita Granville, Frankie Thomas, John Litel, Frank Orth, Renie Riano, Vera Lewis, John Ridgely. Nancy comes to the aid of two aging sisters plagued by mysterious occurrences in their old mansion; best of the short-lived series, and only one of two actually based on a Carolyn Keene novel, *The Hidden Staircase.*
Nancy Drew, Detective (1938) **66m.** **½ D: William Clemens. Bonita Granville, John Litel, James Stephenson, Frankie Thomas, Frank Orth, Renie Riano, Dick Purcell. Nancy investigates a wealthy woman's disappearance in the series' debut film, with Granville's energetic performance scoring a bull's-eye. Based on *The Password to Larkspur Lane*.
Nancy Drew—Reporter (1939) **68m.** **½ D: William Clemens. Bonita Granville, John Litel, Frankie Thomas, Mary Lee, Dickie Jones. One of the series' best entries has school newspaper reporter Nancy determined to prove a girl innocent of murder charges.▼◗
Nancy Drew—Troubleshooter (1939) **69m.** ** D: William Clemens. Bonita Granville, Frankie Thomas, Jr., John Litel, Aldrich Bowker, Renie Riano. More emphasis on comedy than mystery in this series potboiler with Nancy helping to clear a friend of her Dad's who's been accused of murder.
Nancy Goes to Rio (1950) **C-99m.** **½ D: Robert Z. Leonard. Ann Sothern, Jane Powell, Barry Sullivan, Carmen Miranda, Louis Calhern, Fortunio Bonanova, Hans Conried. Agreeable if artificial MGM musical (remake of Deanna Durbin's IT'S A DATE), with Sothern and Powell as mother and daughter who compete for a plum acting role and, through misunderstanding, the same man.▼●
Nancy Steel Is Missing (1937) **85m.** **½ D: George Marshall. Victor McLaglen, Walter Connolly, Peter Lorre, June Lang, Jane Darwell, John Carradine. Story of ex-con McLaglen passing off Lang as long-ago kidnapped child is pat but smooth-going.
Nanny, The (1965-British) **93m.** *** D: Seth Holt. Bette Davis, Wendy Craig, Jill Bennett, James Villiers, Pamela Franklin, William Dix, Maurice Denham. Twisting, scary plot plus fine direction reap results. Suspects of child murder narrowed to governess Davis and disturbed youngster Dix. Unusual Hammer production, written by Jimmy Sangster. From the novel by Evelyn Piper.▼
Nanook of the North (1922) **65m.** ***½ D: Robert Flaherty. Pioneer documentary of Eskimos' daily life withstands the test of time quite well, remains as absorbing saga, well filmed. Set the standard for many documentaries to follow. Soundtrack added in 1939. The film's production is recreated in KABLOONAK. ▼◗
Napoleon (1927-French) **235m.** **** D: Abel Gance. Albert Dieudonné, Antonin Artaud, Pierre Batcheff, Armand Bernard, Harry Krimer, Albert Bras, Abel Gance. Hard to put into words the impact of this monumental silent epic. Dieudonné mesmerizingly plays the famed emperor; notable sequences include snowball fight, the Reign of Terror, and eye-popping three-screen Polyvision finale. Recut and shortened many times over the years (often by Gance himself), finally painstakingly pieced together by historian Kevin Brownlow and reissued in 1981 with a serviceable music score by Carmine Coppola. Not the kind of film one can best appreciate on TV. Filmed in part-widescreen triptych.▼●
Napoleon and Samantha (1972) **C-92m.** **½ D: Bernard McEveety. Michael Douglas, Jodie Foster, Johnny Whitaker, Will Geer, Arch Johnson, Henry Jones. Disney tale of two kids who run away with pet lion is OK family fare. Foster's film debut. [G]▼
Narrow Corner, The (1933) **71m.** *** D: Alfred E. Green. Douglas Fairbanks, Jr., Patricia Ellis, Ralph Bellamy, Dudley Digges, William V. Mong, Sidney Toler, Henry Kolker, Willie Fung. Fairbanks is on the lam, and winds up on an East Indies island where he finds friendship—and illicit romance. Remarkably adult adaptation of W. Somerset Maugham novel (made in the pre-Production Code era), with only minor flaws. Remade as ISLE OF FURY.
Narrow Margin, The (1952) **70m.** ***½ D: Richard Fleischer. Charles McGraw, Marie Windsor, Jacqueline White, Queenie Leonard. Hard-boiled cop, transporting a gangster's widow against his will to the trial in which she'll testify, must dodge hit-men aboard their train who are trying to silence her. One of the best B's ever made—fast-paced, well-acted, impressively shot in claustrophobic setting. Photographed by George E. Diskant; scripted by Earl

Fenton, from a story by Martin Goldsmith and Jack Leonard. Remade in 1990. Also shown in computer-colored version.▼●

Narrow Margin (1990) **C-97m.** **½ D: Peter Hyams. Gene Hackman, Anne Archer, James B. Sikking, J.T. Walsh, M. Emmet Walsh, Susan Hogan, Nigel Bennett, J.A. Preston, Harris Yulin. Hackman is superb as an assistant D.A. who accompanies murder witness Archer on an eventful train ride through the Canadian Rockies—pursued by henchmen of the gangster who set up the killing she saw. Some sharp dialogue for Hackman, and a great action climax atop the train, but dramatically it misses the bull's-eye—and cannot top the original 1952 film. Panavision. [R]▼●◗

Nashville (1975) **C-159m.** **** D: Robert Altman. Henry Gibson, Karen Black, Ronee Blakley, Keith Carradine, Geraldine Chaplin, Lily Tomlin, Michael Murphy, Barbara Harris, Allen Garfield, Ned Beatty, Barbara Baxley, Shelley Duvall, Keenan Wynn, Scott Glenn, Jeff Goldblum, Gwen Welles, Bert Remsen, Robert Doqui. Altman's brilliant mosaic of American life as seen through 24 characters involved in Nashville political rally. Full of cogent character studies, comic and poignant vignettes, done in seemingly free-form style. Carradine's song "I'm Easy" won an Oscar; Elliott Gould and Julie Christie appear as themselves. Screenplay by Joan Tewkesbury. Panavision. [R]▼●

Nashville Girl (1976) **C-93m.** ** D: Gus Trikonis. Monica Gayle, Glenn Corbett, Roger Davis, Johnny Rodriguez, Jesse White. OK low-budgeter about small-town girl who wants to make it big as a singer and falls in with typical no-good types in the music biz. Country superstar Rodriguez makes his movie debut. Reissued as COUNTRY MUSIC DAUGHTER. [R]▼

Nasty Girl, The (1990-German) **C/B&W-92m.** ***½ D: Michael Verhoeven. Lena Stolze, Monika Baumgartner, Michael Gahr, Fred Stillkrauth, Elisabeth Bertram, Robert Giggenbach. Biting serio-comic story of a young woman (Stolze) from a small Bavarian town whose attempts to enter a national essay contest on the subject of "My Hometown During the Third Reich" results in her obsessive quest for the truth. Stolze convincingly ages from adolescence to womanhood in this remarkable film, which is based on a true story (and scripted by the director). Verhoeven's visual style is equally striking, mixing real locations and theatrical backdrops for his actors. [PG-13]▼●

Nasty Habits (1977) **C-96m.** *½ D: Michael Lindsay-Hogg. Glenda Jackson, Melina Mercouri, Geraldine Page, Sandy Dennis, Anne Jackson, Anne Meara, Susan Penhaligon, Edith Evans, Rip Torn, Eli Wallach, Jerry Stiller. Labored comedy sets allegory of Nixon and Watergate scandal in Philadelphia convent, with Jackson as conniving Mother Superior, Dennis a dead ringer for John Dean. A one-joke film. [PG]▼

Nasty Rabbit, The (1964) **C-85m.** ** D: James Landis. Arch Hall, Jr., Micha Terr, Melissa Morgan, John Akana. Weak spoof with serious overtones involving Russian attempt to set loose a disease-infected rabbit in the U. S. Retitled: SPIES A GO GO. Techniscope.▼

Nate and Hayes (1983-U.S.-New Zealand) **C-100m.** ** D: Ferdinand Fairfax. Tommy Lee Jones, Michael O'Keefe, Max Phipps, Jenny Seagrove, Grant Tilly, Peter Rowley. An adventure movie for people who've never seen a *real* adventure movie: watchable enough but pretty pale. Seagoing rogue "Bully" Hayes (Jones) helps a young missionary rescue his fiancee, who's been kidnapped by a scurrilous pirate. Lots of serial-type action, but the leading characters lack charisma. Cowritten by John Hughes. [PG]▼●

National Lampoon Goes to the Movies (1981) **C-89m.** BOMB D: Henry Jaglom, Bob Giraldi. Peter Riegert, Diane Lane, Candy Clark, Teresa Ganzel, Ann Dusenberry, Robert Culp, Bobby DiCicco, Fred Willard, Joe Spinell, Mary Woronov, Dick Miller, Robby Benson, Richard Widmark, Christopher Lloyd, Elisha Cook, Julie Kavner, Henny Youngman. Incredibly idiotic parody of the movies, presented in three excruciating parts, each one worse than the next. "Personal growth" films, Harold Robbins/Sidney Sheldon soap operas and police movies are spoofed; a fourth segment, parodying disaster films and featuring Allen Goorwitz (Garfield), Marcia Strassman and Kenneth Mars, was excised. It's easy to see why this never received theatrical release. Aka NATIONAL LAMPOON'S MOVIE MADNESS. [R] ▼

National Lampoon's Animal House (1978) **C-109m.** ** D: John Landis. John Belushi, Tim Matheson, John Vernon, Verna Bloom, Thomas Hulce, Cesare Danova, Peter Riegert, Stephen Furst, Donald Sutherland, Karen Allen, Sarah Holcomb, Bruce McGill, Martha Smith, Mary Louise Weller, James Daughton, Kevin Bacon, Mark Metcalf, James Widdoes. Spoof of early 1960s college life is only sporadically funny, depends largely on Belushi's mugging as frat-house animal. Not nearly as roisterous or amusing as any issue of the *Lampoon*, but it became a tremendous hit—and spawned a number of truly terrible imitations—as well as a short-lived TV series, *Delta House*. [R]▼●◗

National Lampoon's Christmas Vacation (1989) **C-97m.** *** D: Jeremiah S. Chechik. Chevy Chase, Beverly D'Angelo, Randy Quaid, Diane Ladd, John Randolph, E. G. Marshall, Doris Roberts, Julia Louis-Dreyfus, Mae Questel, William Hickey,

Brian Doyle-Murray, Juliette Lewis, Johnny Galecki, Nicholas Guest, Miriam Flynn. Funny (if typically spotty, sometimes tasteless) saga of the Griswold family's disaster-filled holiday season, with Chase as the terminally stupid head of the household. Sprinkles some believably poignant moments into its slapstick brew with surprising deftness. Third in the VACATION series. Written by John Hughes. Followed by VEGAS VACATION. [PG-13]▼●◗

National Lampoon's Class Reunion (1982) **C-84m.** BOMB D: Michael Miller. Gerrit Graham, Michael Lerner, Fred McCarren, Miriam Flynn, Stephen Furst, Marya Small, Shelley Smith, Zane Buzby, Anne Ramsey. Spectacularly unfunny comedy about a high school reunion shaken by mad killer on the prowl. If you went to school with people like this, no jury in the world would convict you for turning homicidal, either. [R]▼◗

National Lampoon's European Vacation (1985) **C-94m.** *½ D: Amy Heckerling. Chevy Chase, Beverly D'Angelo, Jason Lively, Dana Hill, Eric Idle, Victor Lanoux, John Astin, Paul Bartel, Mel Smith, Robbie Coltrane. Pretty sorry sequel to VACATION, with idiotic Chase and his family stumbling through Europe. Misfire gags right and left, and surprising sexism in a film directed by a woman. Script by John Hughes and Robert Klane. Followed by NATIONAL LAMPOON'S CHRISTMAS VACATION. [PG-13]▼●

National Lampoon's Loaded Weapon 1 (1993) **C-83m.** ** D: Gene Quintano. Emilio Estevez, Samuel L. Jackson, Jon Lovitz, Tim Curry, Kathy Ireland, Frank McRae, William Shatner, James Doohan, Charlie Sheen, Bill Nunn, F. Murray Abraham, Richard Moll, Denis Leary, Corey Feldman, Phil Hartman, J. T. Walsh, Erik Estrada, Larry Wilcox, Paul Gleason, Allyce Beasley, Rick Ducommun, Charles Napier, Beverly Johnson, Denise (Lee) Richards. Lethal Weapon, Loaded Weapon, get it? Quality-caboose of the movie-spoof genre initiated by AIRPLANE! has at least a few laugh-out-loud gags: a takeoff on the BASIC INSTINCT interrogation scene and a skewering of the standard cop film convenience-store shootup. Estevez is no Leslie Nielsen, but you knew that. [PG-13]▼●◗

National Lampoon's Movie Madness SEE: **National Lampoon Goes to the Movies**

National Lampoon's Senior Trip (1995) **C-91m.** ** D: Kelly Makin. Matt Frewer, Valerie Mahaffey, Lawrence Dane, Tommy Chong, Jeremy Renner, Rob Moore. Conniving senator is exposed by the expected array of *Lampoon* honor-rollers: dopers, dropouts, the class tramp, a Cheetos freak, a self-described "frigid head case," etc. Lower-than-low humor, but fairly fast paced. [R] ▼●

National Lampoon's Vacation (1983) **C-98m.** *** D: Harold Ramis. Chevy Chase, Beverly D'Angelo, Anthony Michael Hall, Imogene Coca, Randy Quaid, Dana Barron, Christie Brinkley, John Candy, Eddie Bracken, Brian Doyle-Murray, Eugene Levy. Enjoyable lightweight comedy about a sappy middle-class family's cross-country trip by car. Given the obvious premise, there are a surprising number of genuine laughs—including the ultimate fate of Aunt Edna. Written by John Hughes. Followed by three sequels, starting with NATIONAL LAMPOON'S EUROPEAN VACATION. [R] ▼●◗

National Velvet (1944) **C-125m.** **** D: Clarence Brown. Mickey Rooney, Elizabeth Taylor, Donald Crisp, Anne Revere, Angela Lansbury, Reginald Owen, Norma Varden, Jackie "Butch" Jenkins, Terry Kilburn. Outstanding family film about a girl who determines to enter her horse in the famed Grand National Steeplechase. Taylor is irresistible, Rooney was never better, and they're surrounded by a perfect supporting cast. Revere won a Best Supporting Actress Oscar as Taylor's mother. Screenplay by Theodore Reeves and Helen Deutsch, from Enid Bagnold's novel. Followed years later by a sequel, INTERNATIONAL VELVET, and a TV series. ▼●◗

Native Son (1950) **91m.** **½ D: Pierre Chenal. Richard Wright, Jean Wallace, Gloria Madison, Nicholas Joy, Charles Cane, George Rigaud. Well-meaning but superficial, ultimately disappointing filming of Richard Wright's milestone novel and play, with the author himself starring as Bigger Thomas, frightened black chauffeur who unintentionally kills a white woman. Defeated by its low budget, but still a curio. Remade in 1986.▼

Native Son (1986) **C-112m.** **½ D: Jerrold Freedman. Victor Love, Matt Dillon, Elizabeth McGovern, Geraldine Page, Oprah Winfrey, Akosua Busia, Carroll Baker, John McMartin, Art Evans, John Karlen, Willard E. Pugh, David Rasche, Ving Rhames. Second, star-studded filming of Richard Wright's landmark 1940 novel. Nineteen-year-old Bigger Thomas (played by newcomer Love) is a poor black in 1930s Chicago whose life takes a tragic turn. Capable cast and serviceable script cannot overcome film's deliberate alterations and softening of some of the novel's key plot points and themes. Still, for those unfamiliar with the book, an OK melodrama. A coproduction of PBS's *American Playhouse.* [PG]▼●

Natural, The (1984) **C-134m.** **½ D: Barry Levinson. Robert Redford, Robert Duvall, Glenn Close, Kim Basinger, Wilford Brimley, Richard Farnsworth, Barbara Hershey, Robert Prosky, Joe Don Baker. Serpentine saga of a young man with a gift for baseball, whose life takes more than a few surprising turns. Freely adapted from Bernard Malamud's offbeat novel, with heavy doses of sentiment and larger-than-life imagery (courtesy of cinematographer Caleb Deschanel). Some effective moments, with a fine cast, but too long and inconsistent. Best of all: Randy Newman's score. Darren McGavin appears unbilled. [PG] ▼●

Natural Born Killers (1994) **C-119m.** *½ D: Oliver Stone. Woody Harrelson, Juliette Lewis, Robert Downey, Jr., Tommy Lee Jones, Tom Sizemore, Russell Means, Rodney Dangerfield, Edie McClurg, Steven Wright, Joe Grifasi, Pruitt Taylor Vince, Balthazar Getty, Dale Dye, James Gammon, Arliss Howard. Supposed satire of America's infatuation with outlaws and social miscreants, focusing on a hedonistic couple who murder more than fifty people on their "honeymoon." Whatever points Stone wants to make are delivered early on, with a bludgeon; the rest is all sound and fury. 60s-inspired hyperkinetic filmmaking style soon becomes boring and repetitious. Story by Quentin Tarantino; three others (including Stone) are credited with the screenplay. Director's cut (with 3m. of new footage) available on video. [R]▼●◗

Natural Enemies (1979) **C-100m.** *½ D: Jeff Kanew. Hal Holbrook, Louise Fletcher, Peter Armstrong, Beth Berridge, Steve Austin, Jose Ferrer, Viveca Lindfors. Successful publisher Holbrook wakes up one day with the urge to kill his family. Cold, uninvolving, and (needless to say) strange little film, written, directed and edited by Kanew. [R]▼

Nature's Mistakes SEE: **Freaks**

Naughty Arlette SEE: **Romantic Age, The**

Naughty But Nice (1939) **90m.** **½ D: Ray Enright. Dick Powell, Ann Sheridan, Gale Page, Helen Broderick, Ronald Reagan, Allen Jenkins, ZaSu Pitts, Jerry Colonna. Stuffy music professor Powell unwittingly writes popular song hit, leading to various complications and gradual personality change. Silly but fun; songs adapted from Wagner, Liszt, Mozart, Bach.

Naughty Girl SEE: **Mam'zelle Pigalle**

Naughty Marietta (1935) **106m.** **½ D: W. S. Van Dyke II. Jeanette MacDonald, Nelson Eddy, Frank Morgan, Elsa Lanchester, Douglass Dumbrille, Cecilia Parker. First teaming of Eddy and MacDonald has her a French princess running off to America, falling in love with Indian scout Eddy. Agreeable operetta with Victor Herbert score, including "The Italian Street Song," "Tramp, Tramp, Tramp," and the immortal "Ah, Sweet Mystery of Life." ▼●

Naughty Nineties, The (1945) **76m.** ** D: Jean Yarbrough. Bud Abbott, Lou Costello, Alan Curtis, Rita Johnson, Henry Travers, Lois Collier, Joe Sawyer, Joe Kirk. Ordinary A&C comedy of riverboat gamblers, sparked by duo's verbal exchanges (including "Who's on First?") and slapstick finale.▼●

Naughty Wives (1974-British) **C-84m.** BOMB D: Wolf Rilla. Brendan Price, Graham Stark, Chic Murray, Felicity Devonshire, Sue Longhurst. Silly sex farce about Price's misadventures as a door-to-door salesman. Quite a comedown for Rilla, who made the classic VILLAGE OF THE DAMNED. Opens with a highlights-of-the-action montage edited for U.S. release by Jonathan Demme. [R]

Navajo Joe (1966-Italian-Spanish) **C-89m.** *½ D: Sergio Corbucci. Burt Reynolds, Aldo Sanbrell, Tanya Lopert, Fernando Rey. Sole survivor of massacre swears revenge on his enemies in this tepid Western, of interest only for Reynolds' presence. Techniscope.▼

Navigator, The (1924) **69m.** **½ D: Buster Keaton, Donald Crisp. Buster Keaton, Kathryn McGuire, Frederick Vroom. Buster plays (yet again) a pampered millionaire who—by sheer circumstance, with a dash of stupidity—winds up on a huge, deserted ship with the woman he wants to marry. Many great gags and amusing sequences, but this silent doesn't have the momentum of Buster's best comedies. ▼●◗

Navigator, The: A Medieval Odyssey (1988-New Zealand) **C/B&W-92m.** *** D: Vincent Ward. Hamish McFarlane, Bruce Lyons, Chris Haywood, Marshall Napier, Noel Appleby, Paul Livingston, Sarah Pierse. Engrossing, very imaginative tale of psychic boy in tiny medieval English village who, to protect villagers from the plague, leads a tunneling expedition—which emerges in a modern city in 1988. Directed and written with great clarity, the film has much of the feel of a genuine medieval fable. Beautifully produced on a low budget. [PG]▼

Navy Blue and Gold (1937) **94m.** **½ D: Sam Wood. Robert Young, James Stewart, Florence Rice, Billie Burke, Lionel Barrymore, Tom Brown, Samuel S. Hinds, Paul Kelly. Hackneyed but entertaining saga of three pals (one rich and innocent, one a cynic, and one mysterious "with a past") going to Annapolis. Predictable football game climax is fun. That's Dennis Morgan (billed under his real name, Stanley Morner) dancing with Billie Burke.▼

Navy Blues (1941) **108m.** *** D: Lloyd Bacon. Ann Sheridan, Jack Oakie, Martha Raye, Jack Haley, Herbert Anderson, Jack Carson. Brassy musical with fine cast (including young Jackie Gleason), with Raye stealing most of the film.

Navy Comes Through, The (1942) **82m.** **½ D: A. Edward Sutherland. Pat O'Brien, George Murphy, Jane Wyatt, Jackie Cooper, Carl Esmond, Max Baer, Desi Arnaz, Ray Collins. Ultrapatriotic time-capsule with U.S. Navy (led by

O'Brien), stationed aboard a merchant marine ship, heroically battling the Nazis.▼

Navy SEALS (1990) **C-113m.** ** D: Lewis Teague. Charlie Sheen, Michael Biehn, Joanne Whalley-Kilmer, Rick Rossovich, Cyril O'Reilly, Bill Paxton, Dennis Haysbert, Paul Sanchez. Middle Eastern terrorists are mere putty in the hands of U.S. Navy's elite commando unit (SEa, Air, Land); "inspired" by the actual team formed under J.F.K.'s administration. G.I. Joe-level action is name of the game here. Sheen's character operates at the maturity level of Dennis the Menace. [R] ▼●◗

Navy vs. the Night Monsters, The (1966) **C-90m.** BOMB D: Michael Hoey. Mamie Van Doren, Anthony Eisley, Pamela Mason, Bill Gray, Bobby Van, Walter Sande, Edward Faulkner, Phillip Terry. 1) Look at the title. 2) Examine the cast. 3) Be aware that the plot involves omniverous trees. 4) Don't say you weren't warned.▼

Navy Wife (1956) **83m.** *½ D: Edward Bernds. Joan Bennett, Gary Merrill, Shirley Yamaguchi, Maurice Manson, Judy Nugent, Martin Milner, Dennis Weaver. Trivial tale of Japanese women revolting to obtain equal treatment from their men as they observe American military and their wives.

Nazarin (1958-Mexican) **92m.** *** D: Luis Buñuel. Francisco Rabal, Rita Macedo, Marga Lopez, Ignacio Lopez Tarso, Ofelia Guilmain. Powerful and pointed (if relentlessly grim) drama about saintly priest Rabal, and how hypocritical peasants deal with him as he tries to interpret the lessons of Christ. ▼●

Nazi Agent (1942) **83m.** ** D: Jules Dassin. Conrad Veidt, Anne Ayars, Dorothy Tree, Frank Reicher, Sidney Blackmer, Martin Kosleck, Marc Lawrence, William Tannen. Veidt plays twin brothers: one a peaceful American; the other a Nazi official. When the latter blackmails the former into spying, the good Veidt kills the bad Veidt and impersonates him. Slow-moving, rather arid tale that could have been much better. Dassin's first feature; good photography by Harry Stradling.

Neanderthal Man, The (1953) **78m.** *½ D: E. A. Dupont. Robert Shayne, Richard Crane, Robert Long, Doris Merrick. Shayne turns a tiger into a sabertooth and himself into a murderous caveman in this below-par 50s entry. Colorless and cheap; director Dupont was a long way from his German classic VARIETY.●

Near Dark (1987) **C-95m.** **½ D: Kathryn Bigelow. Adrian Pasdar, Jenny Wright, Lance Henriksen, Bill Paxton, Jenette Goldstein, Tim Thomerson. Better-than-average vampire yarn actually plays more like a werewolf film. Cowboy Pasdar is literally bitten by Wright and joins a band of hillbilly bloodsuckers who roam the West in a van. Stylishly directed horror film reunites three cast members from ALIENS: Henriksen, Paxton and Goldstein. [R] ▼●

Nearly a Nasty Accident (1962-British) **86m.** ** D: Don Chaffey. Jimmy Edwards, Kenneth Connor, Shirley Eaton, Richard Wattis, Ronnie Stevens, Jon Pertwee, Eric Barker. Minor comedy of mechanic who innocently puts the touch of disaster on everyone.

'Neath Brooklyn Bridge (1942) **61m.** ** D: Wallace Fox. Leo Gorcey, Huntz Hall, Bobby Jordan, Sunshine Sammy Morrison, Stanley Clements, Bobby Stone, Anne Gillis, Noah Beery, Jr., Marc Lawrence, Gabriel Dell, Dave O'Brien. The East Side Kids band together when Jordan is framed for murder in this terse entry.▼

Nebraskan, The (1953) **C-68m.** ** D: Fred F. Sears. Phil Carey, Roberta Haynes, Wallace Ford, Richard Webb, Lee Van Cleef, Jay Silverheels. Tame Western of Army scout Carey single-handedly trying to prevent Indian uprising. Originally in 3-D.

Necessary Roughness (1991) **C-108m.** *½ D: Stan Dragoti. Scott Bakula, Robert Loggia, Hector Elizondo, Harley Jane Kozak, Larry Miller, Sinbad, Fred Dalton Thompson, Rob Schneider, Jason Bateman, Andrew Bryniarski, Andrew Lauer, Louis Mandylor. A 34-year-old quarterback at a Texas college reeling from NCAA penalties discovers that his cute no-nonsense prof is closet football junkie. Formulaic enough to insult anyone's intelligence, with a cast of quirky teammates transparently contrived (swimsuit model Kathy Ireland is the squadron's placekicker). Beware of Bill Conti's feel-good score. [PG-13]▼●

Necromancy (1972) **C-83m.** *½ D: Bert I. Gordon. Orson Welles, Pamela Franklin, Michael Ontkean, Lee Purcell, Harvey Jason. High priest Welles tries to manipulate Franklin into becoming a witch. Mindless, poorly crafted thriller was originally released without its nude coven scenes, if anybody cares. Some prints run 75m. Video titles: THE WITCHING and ROSEMARY'S DISCIPLES. [PG]▼

Ned Kelly (1970-British) **C-100m.** **½ D: Tony Richardson. Mick Jagger, Clarissa Kaye, Mark McManus, Frank Thring. Ambitious telling of the life and adventures of Australia's most famous outlaw, emphasizing the Irish-British conflict at the heart of his story. Many good songs on the soundtrack, written by Shel Silverstein. Retitled NED KELLY, OUTLAW. [PG]▼

Needful Things (1993) **C-120m.** *½ D: Fraser C. Heston. Max von Sydow, Ed Harris, Bonnie Bedelia, Amanda Plummer, J. T. Walsh, Ray McKinnon, Duncan Fraser, Valri Bromfield. Bottom-of-the-barrel bore about a devilish old man (von Sydow) who opens a curiosity shop in a small Maine town, with predictably horrific results.

Scripted by W. D. Richter, based on the best-seller by (who else?) Stephen King. Also shown on TV in 186m. version called MORE NEEDFUL THINGS. [R] ▼●◗

Negatives (1968-British) **C-90m.** ** D: Peter Medak. Peter McEnery, Diane Cilento, Glenda Jackson, Maurice Denham, Steven Lewis, Norman Rossington. Strange movie about unmarried couple who dress up like notorious Dr. Crippen and his wife for kicks; he later switches his characterization to Baron von Richtofen. Jackson is good, but direction is too mannered. [R]▼

Negotiator, The (1998) **C-138m.** *** D: F. Gary Gray. Samuel L. Jackson, Kevin Spacey, David Morse, Ron Rifkin, John Spencer, J.T. Walsh, Regina Taylor, Siobhan Fallon, Paul Giamatti. One of Chicago's top police hostage negotiators (Jackson) is framed for embezzling money from his union's pension fund—and has a murder pinned on him, to boot. His only chance is to take hostages and clear himself with the help of another crack negotiator (Spacey). Highly watchable, if not 100% credible, but the two stars (and a strong supporting cast) make the most of it. Super 35. [R]▼●◗

Neighbors (1981) **C-94m.** BOMB D: John G. Avildsen. John Belushi, Dan Aykroyd, Cathy Moriarty, Kathryn Walker, Lauren-Marie Taylor, Tim Kazurinsky. Appallingly unfunny and tiresome "comedy" based on Thomas Berger's novel about a middle-class milquetoast whose suburban existence is shaken by the arrival of bizarre and destructive neighbors. Screenplay credited to Larry Gelbart. Pointless; sadly, Belushi's last film. [R]▼●

Neil Simon's "Broadway Bound" (1992) **C-100m. TVM** D: Paul Bogart. Anne Bancroft, Hume Cronyn, Corey Parker, Jonathan Silverman, Jerry Orbach, Michele Lee. Disappointing adaptation of Neil Simon's terrific Broadway play, the final part of his autobiographical trilogy, following BRIGHTON BEACH MEMOIRS and BILOXI BLUES. Silverman plays the young man who's aching to leave the family homestead in Brooklyn and make good on his own. Average.▼

Neil Simon's "Jake's Women" (1996) **C-100m. TVM** D: Glenn Jordan. Alan Alda, Anne Archer, Julie Kavner, Lolita Davidovich, Mira Sorvino, Joyce Van Patten, Kimberly Williams. Alda and Van Patten repeat their Broadway roles in Simon's flaccid adaptation of his semiautobiographical 1991 play about a writer in midlife crisis, using his separated mate, girlfriend, sister, therapist, and dead former wife as sounding boards. Average.▼

Neil Simon's Odd Couple II SEE: **Odd Couple II, The**

Nell (1994) **C-113m.** ** D: Michael Apted. Jodie Foster, Liam Neeson, Natasha Richardson, Richard Libertini, Nick Searcy, Robin Mullins, Jeremy Davies. The death of a hermit woman brings a small-town Southern doctor into the backwoods, where he discovers she had a daughter who's been raised completely apart from civilization. He becomes fascinated—and so does a research scientist at a nearby university, who wants to "capture" the woman. Intriguing premise goes flat as the story loses focus, and the characters' motivations and relationships grow fuzzy. Foster gives a bravura performance but it's hard to forget it *is* a performance. Panavision. [PG-13]▼●

Nelly et Monsieur Arnaud (1995-French-Italian-German) **C-106m.** *** D: Claude Sautet. Emmanuelle Béart, Michel Serrault, Jean-Hugues Anglade, Claire Nadeau, Françoise Brion, Michel Lonsdale. Subtle, beautifully acted story of a 25-year-old woman in debt and stuck in a nowhere marriage, who meets an elegant and instantly infatuated man some 40 years her senior who offers to pay her bills and give her a job typing his memoirs. Sautet proves that in his 70s he's still as effective as ever in painting the difficulties and heartbreak of human relationships. ▼

Nelson Affair, The (1973-British) **C-118m.** **½ D: James Cellan Jones. Glenda Jackson, Peter Finch, Michael Jayston, Anthony Quayle, Margaret Leighton, Dominic Guard, Nigel Stock, Barbara Leigh-Hunt. Handsome retelling of Lord Nelson-Lady Hamilton affair, making the "Lady" a slut; interesting but claustrophobic—even climactic sea battle was shot indoors! British title: A BEQUEST TO THE NATION. Panavision. [PG]

Nemesis (1993) **C-94m.** *½ D: Albert Pyun. Olivier Gruner, Tim Thomerson, Marjorie Monaghan, Merle Kennedy, Brion James, Deborah Shelton, Cary-Hiroyuki Tagawa, Nicholas Guest, Jackie Earle Haley. In 2027, tough cop Gruner, who's had many body parts replaced with mechanical duplicates, fights a group of androids (here called "cyborgs") intent on conquering world. Just another amalgam of ideas borrowed from better movies. Gruner has some appeal, though. Followed by two direct-to-video sequels. Super 35. [R]▼●◗

Nenette et Boni (1996-French) **C-103m.** *** D: Claire Denis. Alice Houri, Gregoire Colin, Valeria Bruni-Tedeschi, Vincent Gallo, Jacques Nolot. Arresting, emotionally involving chronicle of two children of divorced parents: Nenette (Houri), who is fifteen and very pregnant, and lonely eighteen-year-old Boni (Colin), who is erotically obsessed with a baker's wife. A potent exploration of a brother-sister bond and how a dysfunctional family damages its youngest and most vulnerable members.▼

Neon Bible, The (1995-U.S.-British) **C-92m.** ** D: Terence Davies. Gena Rowlands, Denis Leary, Diana Scarwid, Jacob

Tierney, Leo Burmester, Frances Conroy, Peter McRobbie. Slow-as-molasses Truman Capote–like reminiscence about a young boy coming of age in the American South and his eccentric, melancholy Aunt Mae (Rowlands, who is good as always). Despite its abundant atmosphere and good intentions, this cannot compare with Davies' earlier works. He scripted, based on a novel by John Kennedy Toole. J-D-C Scope.▼●◗

Neptune Disaster, The SEE: **Neptune Factor, The**

Neptune Factor, The (1973-Canadian) **C-98m.** ** D: Daniel Petrie. Ben Gazzara, Yvette Mimieux, Walter Pidgeon, Ernest Borgnine. Deep-sea-diving sub races to save three men trapped by an earthquake in ocean floor laboratory. Soggy underwater yarn lifts its plot almost in toto from MAROONED. Aka AN UNDERWATER ODYSSEY and THE NEPTUNE DISASTER. Panavision. [G]▼

Neptune's Daughter (1949) **C-93m.** *** D: Edward Buzzell. Esther Williams, Red Skelton, Keenan Wynn, Betty Garrett, Ricardo Montalban, Mel Blanc. Musical romance with Esther a bathing-suit designer, Skelton a no-account mistaken for polo star by Garrett. Bubbly fun, with Academy Award-winning song: "Baby It's Cold Outside."▼●

Nest, The (1980-Spanish) **C-109m.** *** D: Jaime De Arminan. Hector Alterio, Ana Torrent, Luis Politti, Agustin Gonzalez, Patricia Adriani. Diverting but predictable drama detailing the relationship between wealthy, aging widower Alterio and alienated 13-year-old Torrent. Helped immeasurably by Arminan's precise script and direction. [PG]▼

Nest, The (1988) **C-88m.** ** D: Terence H. Winkless. Robert Lansing, Lisa Langlois, Franc Luz, Terri Treas, Stephen Davies, Diana Bellamy, Nancy Morgan. Trifling, ever so familiar chronicle of a failed scientific experiment resulting in the creation of large, hungry cockroaches. Neither the best nor the worst of its type. [R]▼

Nesting, The (1981) **C-104m.** ** D: Armand Weston. Robin Groves, Christopher Loomis, Michael David Lally, John Carradine, Gloria Grahame, Bill Rowley. Gothic novelist moves into eerie Victorian mansion to which she's mysteriously drawn. Starts off interestingly but wanders and drags on to unsatisfying finish. [R]▼

Net, The (1995) **C-118m.** **½ D: Irwin Winkler. Sandra Bullock, Jeremy Northam, Dennis Miller, Diane Baker, Wendy Gazelle, Ken Howard, Ray McKinnon. The techno-thriller as plodding Sandra Bullock vehicle: She plays a mousy, vulnerable computer whiz. When bad guys need a disc she possesses, they stop at nothing—including deleting, then manipulating her identity on official computer records. Anyone who's ever seen a *real* thriller will be ahead of this story at every turn. Later a cable TV series. [PG-13]▼●◗

Network (1976) **C-121m.** **** D: Sidney Lumet. William Holden, Faye Dunaway, Peter Finch, Robert Duvall, Ned Beatty, Beatrice Straight, Wesley Addy, Darryl Hickman, Ken Kercheval, William Prince, Marlene Warfield. Paddy Chayefsky's outrageous satire on television looks less and less like fantasy as the years pass; uninhibited tale chronicles fourth-place network that will air anything for a big rating, including a patently insane, profanity-shouting "mad prophet of the airwaves" (Finch). Entire cast explodes, particularly Dunaway as ruthless programmer, Holden as conscientious newsman, Duvall as shark-like v.p., and Beatty as evangelistical board chairman. Well-deserved Oscars went to Finch (posthumously), Dunaway, Straight, and Chayefsky. [R]▼●◗

Nevada (1944) **62m.** ** D: Edward Killy. Robert Mitchum, Anne Jeffreys, Guinn "Big Boy" Williams, Nancy Gates, Harry Woods. Standard Zane Grey Western of good-guy Mitchum mopping up gang of outlaws. Filmed before in 1935.

Nevada Heat SEE: **Fake-Out**

Nevadan, The (1950) **C-81m.** ** D: Gordon Douglas. Randolph Scott, Dorothy Malone, Forrest Tucker, George Macready, Jock Mahoney. Stern Scott is the lawman who tracks down crooks, still finding time to court Malone. Shown on TV in b&w.▼

Nevada Smith (1966) **C-135m.** *** D: Henry Hathaway. Steve McQueen, Karl Malden, Brian Keith, Arthur Kennedy, Suzanne Pleshette, Raf Vallone, Pat Hingle, Howard da Silva, Martin Landau. Good Western story. Smith swears revenge for senseless murder of his parents at the hands of outlaw gang. Based on character from THE CARPETBAGGERS. Remade as a TVM in 1975. Panavision.▼●

Never a Dull Moment (1943) **60m.** **½ D: Edward Lilley. Ritz Brothers, Frances Langford, Stuart Crawford, Elisabeth Risdon, Mary Beth Hughes, George Zucco, Jack LaRue, Franklin Pangborn. Pretty good comedy with the Ritzes getting involved with gang of hoods; fast-paced, with LaRue enjoyable as semicomic heavy.

Never a Dull Moment (1950) **89m.** ** D: George Marshall. Irene Dunne, Fred MacMurray, William Demarest, Andy Devine, Gigi Perreau, Natalie Wood, Philip Ober, Ann Doran. Chic Park Avenue songwriter Dunne weds rancher MacMurray, and adjusts to life in rural Wyoming. Silly, predictable comedy is only of interest for its cast; you'll find this especially annoying if you're a feminist or an Indian.▼●

Never a Dull Moment (1968) **C-100m.** ** D: Jerry Paris. Dick Van Dyke, Edward G. Robinson, Dorothy Provine, Henry Silva,

Joanna Moore, Tony Bill. Tired Disney comedy belies title, as TV performer Van Dyke gets involved with gangsters; even Robinson's performance is lifeless.▼

Never Been Kissed (1999) **C-107m.** **½ D: Raja Gosnell. Drew Barrymore, David Arquette, Michael Vartan, Molly Shannon, John C. Reilly, Garry Marshall, Leelee Sobieski, Sean Whalen, Jordan Ladd, Jessica Alba. Twenty-five-year-old newspaper copy editor gets her first chance as a reporter by going undercover and pretending to be a 17-year-old high school student. All this does is bring back vivid memories of her nerdy school days, while the assignment remains vague and unfulfilled. Star vehicle, if ever there was one, is buoyed by Barrymore's charm (she also coproduced), but burdened with a muddled and barely believable story. Super 35. [PG-13] ▼●◗

Never Cry Wolf (1983) **C-105m.** *** D: Carroll Ballard. Charles Martin Smith, Brian Dennehy, Zachary Ittimangnaq, Samson Jorah. Smith plays real-life Canadian author Farley Mowat who braved the Arctic, alone, to study behavior of wolves . . . and wound up learning as much about himself. Uneven, but filled with striking moments and passages, plus a wonderful performance by Smith. There's also the irony of a Walt Disney production in which the leading character takes to eating mice! [PG]▼●◗

NeverEnding Story, The (1984-West German-British) **C-92m.** *** D: Wolfgang Petersen. Noah Hathaway, Barret Oliver, Tami Stronach, Moses Gunn, Patricia Hayes, Sydney Bromley, Gerald MacRaney, voice of Alan Oppenheimer. Magical, timeless fantasy built around young Oliver visualizing what he's reading from a mystical book: boy warrior Hathaway is the only hope of saving the empire of Fantasia from being swallowed up by The Nothing. Amazing, unique effects, characters, and visual design (and a not-so-subtle message that Reading Is Good). Followed by two live-action sequels, and an animated TV movie and series. Technovision. [PG]▼●

NeverEnding Story II: The Next Chapter, The (1990-U.S.-German) **C-89m.** *½ D: George Miller. Jonathan Brandis, Kenny Morrison, Clarissa Burt, John Wesley Shipp, Martin Umbach, Alexandra Johnes. Mom's dead, dad's busy, and the swim coach says he suffers from a "high wimp factor." So, it's back to Fantasia (a magic land) for the young boy who loses himself in a storybook, where a child empress (as childlike as Drew Barrymore) is in danger. Poky and cheesy, though kids might take to some of the animal sidekicks. Followed by a direct-to-video sequel. Panavision. [PG]▼●

Never Fear (1950) **82m.** **½ D: Ida Lupino. Sally Forrest, Keefe Brasselle, Hugh O'Brian, Eve Miller, Lawrence Dobkin. Young dancer Forrest's life comes apart when she develops polio. Sincere drama scripted by Lupino and her then-husband, Collier Young. Aka THE YOUNG LOVERS. ▼

Never Forget (1991) **C-100m. TVM** D: Joseph Sargent. Leonard Nimoy, Blythe Danner, Dabney Coleman, Paul Hampton, Jason Presson, Juliet Sorcey. Middling drama about concentration camp survivor Mel Mermelstein's real-life fight against a neo-Nazi group which challenges him to prove the Holocaust actually happened. Made for cable. Average.▼●

Never Give a Inch SEE: **Sometimes a Great Notion**

Never Give a Sucker an Even Break (1941) **71m.** ***½ D: Edward Cline. W. C. Fields, Gloria Jean, Leon Errol, Susan Miller, Franklin Pangborn, Margaret Dumont. Completely insane comedy with Fields (in his last starring film) playing himself; no coherent plot, but a lot of funny scenes. Dumont plays "Mrs. Hemoglobin." Climactic chase is a classic, reused by Abbott and Costello in IN SOCIETY. Story by "Otis Criblecoblis."▼●

Never Let Go (1960-British) **90m.** ** D: John Guillermin. Richard Todd, Peter Sellers, Elizabeth Sellars, Carol White, Mervyn Johns. Sellers gives heavy-handed performance as ruthless and sadistic racketeer in weak story about car thievery. Billed as his first dramatic role, it was a poor choice.▼

Never Let Me Go (1953) **94m.** **½ D: Delmer Daves. Clark Gable, Gene Tierney, Bernard Miles, Richard Haydn, Kenneth More, Belita, Theodore Bikel. Unconvincing yet smooth account of Gable trying to smuggle ballerina-wife Tierney out of Russia.▼

Never Love a Stranger (1958) **91m.** ** D: Robert Stevens. John Drew Barrymore, Lita Milan, Peg Murray, Robert Bray, Steve McQueen. Chronicle of a racketeer, from Harold Robbins' novel; predictable all the way.▼

Never Never Land (1980-British) **C-86m.** *** D: Paul Annett. Petula Clark, Cathleen Nesbitt, John Castle, Anne Seymour, Evelyn Laye, Roland Culver, Heather Miller. Nice little film about lonely child (Miller), her fascination with Peter Pan and connection with elderly Nesbitt. Best for the kids. [G]

Never on Sunday (1960-Greek) **91m.** ***½ D: Jules Dassin. Melina Mercouri, Jules Dassin, Georges Foundas, Titos Vandis, Mitsos Liguisos, Despo Diamantidou. Charming idyll of intellectual boob coming to Greece, trying to make earthy prostitute Mercouri cultured. Grand entertainment, with Oscar-winning title song by Manos Hadjidakis. Later a Broadway musical, *Illya Darling*.▼●

Never Put It in Writing (1964) **93m.** *½

D: Andrew Stone. Pat Boone, Milo O'Shea, Fidelma Murphy, Reginald Beckwith, Harry Brogan. Grade-B comedy, set in London, with Pat trying to retrieve a letter that will get him fired from his job if the boss sees it. Not much.

Never Say Die (1939) **80m.** ★★★ D: Elliott Nugent. Martha Raye, Bob Hope, Andy Devine, Gale Sondergaard, Sig Ruman, Alan Mowbray, Monty Woolley. Bob marries Martha at Swiss spa of Bad Gaswasser, thinking he has only two weeks to live. Good cast in lively, trivial romp. Cowritten by Preston Sturges.▼

Never Say Goodbye (1946) **97m.** ★★½ D: James V. Kern. Errol Flynn, Eleanor Parker, Lucile Watson, S. Z. Sakall, Hattie McDaniel, Forrest Tucker, Donald Woods. Flynn tries hard in routine comedy of husband rewinning his divorce-bound wife.▼

Never Say Goodbye (1956) **C-96m.** ★★½ D: Jerry Hopper. Rock Hudson, Cornell Borchers, George Sanders, Ray Collins, David Janssen, Shelley Fabares. Spotty tear-jerker of Hudson and Borchers, long separated, discovering one another again and creating fit home for their child. Remake of THIS LOVE OF OURS. Clint Eastwood is cast as Rock's lab assistant.

Never Say Never Again (1983) **C-137m.** ★★½ D: Irvin Kershner. Sean Connery, Klaus Maria Brandauer, Max von Sydow, Barbara Carrera, Kim Basinger, Bernie Casey, Alec McCowen, Edward Fox, Rowan Atkinson. Connery's stylish performance and self-deprecating humor make his return performance as James Bond (after twelve years) a real treat—but the film, a remake of THUNDERBALL, is uneven and overlong. Brandauer is a smooth villain, and Carrera a memorably sexy villainess, Fatima Blush. Panavision. [PG]▼●

Never So Few (1959) **C-124m.** ★★½ D: John Sturges. Frank Sinatra, Gina Lollobrigida, Peter Lawford, Steve McQueen, Richard Johnson, Paul Henreid, Brian Donlevy, Dean Jones, Charles Bronson. WW2 action/romance tale; salty performances which make one forget the clichés and improbabilities. CinemaScope. ▼●

Never Steal Anything Small (1959) **C-94m.** ★★½ D: Charles Lederer. James Cagney, Shirley Jones, Roger Smith, Cara Williams, Nehemiah Persoff, Royal Dano, Horace McMahon. Odd musical comedy-drama, with Cagney a waterfront union racketeer who'll do anything to win union election. From Maxwell Anderson-Rouben Mamoulian play *The Devil's Hornpipe.* CinemaScope.▼

Never Steal Anything Wet SEE: **Catalina Caper**

Never Talk to Strangers (1995-U.S.-Canadian) **C-102m.** ★½ D: Peter Hall. Rebecca De Mornay, Antonio Banderas, Dennis Miller, Len Cariou, Beau Starr, Tim Kelleher, Eugene Lipinski, Phillip Jarrett, Harry Dean Stanton. Criminal psychologist falls for a charming, mysterious stranger, while at the same time unexplained, terrifying incidents begin occurring. Standard-issue thriller would be more at home on television. De Mornay also coexecutive produced. [R]▼●◗

Never the Twain Shall Meet (1931) **79m.** ★½ D: W. S. Van Dyke. Leslie Howard, Conchita Montenegro, C. Aubrey Smith, Karen Morley, Mitchell Lewis, Clyde Cook. Rich, proper Howard loves rich, proper Morley . . . and then he becomes the guardian of beautiful, uninhibited Montenegro. Wooden soaper of clashing cultures.

Never to Love SEE: **Bill of Divorcement, A** (1940)

Never Too Late (1965) **C-105m.** ★★½ D: Bud Yorkin. Paul Ford, Connie Stevens, Maureen O'Sullivan, Jim Hutton, Jane Wyatt, Henry Jones, Lloyd Nolan. Occasionally amusing film version of hit Broadway play about impending parenthood of middle-agers Ford and O'Sullivan. Older performers are funny; Hutton, Stevens, script, and direction are not. Panavision.▼

Never Too Young To Die (1986) **C-92m.** ★½ D: Gil Bettman. John Stamos, Vanity, Gene Simmons, George Lazenby, Peter Kwong, Ed Brock, John Anderson, Robert Englund. Stamos, son of a spy, takes up with Vanity, one of his father's associates, to find out who murdered his dad. Pretty awful, though Simmons scores a few points for outrageousness in his portrayal of a power-crazed hermaphrodite. [R]▼●

Never Trust a Gambler (1951) **79m.** ★½ D: Ralph Murphy. Dane Clark, Cathy O'Donnell, Tom Drake, Jeff Corey, Myrna Dell. Hackneyed account of man on the run, seeking shelter from ex-wife who has fallen in love with detective seeking him.

Never Wave at a WAC (1952) **87m.** ★★½ D: Norman Z. McLeod. Rosalind Russell, Marie Wilson, Paul Douglas, Arleen Whelan, Hillary Brooke, Louise Beavers, Frieda Inescort. Expanded from a TV play, this farce involves socialite Russell joining the WACs, forced to buckle down to hard work; Wilson as dumb comrade-at-arms is most diverting.▼

New Adventures of Pippi Longstocking, The (1988) **C-100m.** ★★ D: Ken Annakin. Tami Erin, Eileen Brennan, Dennis Dugan, Dianne Hull, George DiCenzo, John Schuck, Dick Van Patten. Dreary Americanization of Astrid Lindgren's popular books about a plucky young girl—here, transformed into a tiresome troublemaker. May entertain undiscriminating children; adults should avoid at all costs. [G]▼●

New Adventures of Tarzan, The (1935) **75m.** ★½ D: Edward Kull, W. F. McGaugh. Herman Brix (Bruce Bennett), Ula Holt, Don Castello, Frank Baker, Lewis Sargent, Dale Walsh. Feature version of the serial about the search for priceless Mayan idol in Guatemala. Strictly for the kiddies. Shot on location by Edgar Rice Burroughs' own company, but no threat to Johnny Weissmuller and MGM. TV print of this feature is completely redubbed by voices other than the actors on-screen!▼

New Age, The (1994) **C-110m.** *½ D: Michael Tolkin. Peter Weller, Judy Davis, Patrick Bauchau, Corbin Bernsen, Jonathan Hadary, Patricia Heaton, Samuel L. Jackson, Audra Lindley, Paula Marshall, Adam West. Deadening deadpan satire, which its studio barely released, about a married couple who launch a born-to-go-bust boutique after they both lose their glitzy jobs on the same Recession-era day. Tolkin wrote THE PLAYER; perhaps this film would have benefitted from Robert Altman's wag-in-the-moon viewpoint. Jackson's sequence, in which he "motivates" some scam-artist telemarketers, is the only one with any real juice. [R]▼●

New Centurions, The (1972) **C-103m.** *** D: Richard Fleischer. George C. Scott, Stacy Keach, Jane Alexander, Rosalind Cash, Scott Wilson, Erik Estrada, Clifton James, Isabel Sanford, James B. Sikking, Ed Lauter, William Atherton, Roger E. Mosley. Fine, episodic adaptation by Stirling Silliphant of Joseph Wambaugh novel of rookie cops on modern-day L.A. police force, ultimately pessimistic in outlook. Great casting, performances; good storytelling. Panavision. [R]▼●

New Faces (1954) **C-99m.** **½ D: Harry Horner. Ronny Graham, Robert Clary, Eartha Kitt, Alice Ghostley, Paul Lynde, Carol Lawrence. Vaudeville hodgepodge of variety numbers, based on Leonard Sillman's popular Broadway revue, which was springboard for much new talent. One of the writers was Melvin (Mel) Brooks. CinemaScope.▼

New Faces of 1937 (1937) **100m.** ** D: Leigh Jason. Joe Penner, Milton Berle, Parkyakarkus, Harriet Hilliard (Nelson), Jerome Cowan. Silly movie with same initial premise as THE PRODUCERS, as Berle is patsy left as owner of unwatchable Broadway show. Comic highlight is Berle's stockbroker skit with Richard Lane; Ann Miller featured in finale as one of the New Faces.●

New Interns, The (1964) **123m.** **½ D: John Rich. Michael Callan, Dean Jones, Telly Savalas, Inger Stevens, George Segal, Greg Morris, Stefanie Powers, Lee Patrick, Barbara Eden. Follow-up to THE INTERNS contains unusual hospital soap opera with better than average cast and a nifty party sequence.

New Invisible Man, The (1957-Mexican) **89m.** ** D: Alfred B. Crevenna. Arturo de Cordova, Ana Luisa Peluffo, Augusto Benedico, Raul Meraz. OK updating of the classic story, with de Cordova falsely convicted of murder; he's rendered invisible so he can prove his innocence. A remake of THE INVISIBLE MAN RETURNS. Aka H. G. WELLS' NEW INVISIBLE MAN.▼

New Jack City (1991) **C-97m.** ** D: Mario Van Peebles. Wesley Snipes, Ice T, Allen Payne, Chris Rock, Mario Van Peebles, Judd Nelson, Michael Michele, Bill Nunn, Russell Wong, Vanessa Williams, Nick Ashford, Thalmus Rasulala. N.Y.C. police detective hires two maverick ex-cops to bring down a Napoleonic druglord who's made his fortune selling crack (and whose role model, apparently, is the Al Pacino character in SCARFACE!). Lots of emotional energy, and strong performances, but its clearly stated anti-drug message is clouded by overblown melodrama—and several climaxes too many. [R]▼●◗

New Jersey Drive (1995) **C-95m.** ** D: Nick Gomez. Sharron Corley, Gabriel Casseus, Saul Stein, Gwen McGee, Andre Moore, Donald Adeosun Faison. Two teenagers are drawn into the underground world of carjacking in Newark, N.J., and soon find the full weight of the local police force coming down around them. Spike Lee executive-produced this gritty, well-meaning drama of urban youth gone wrong; unfortunately, it never shifts into high gear. Corley makes his film debut here; at one time he lived the life he portrays on screen. [R] ▼●◗

New Kids, The (1985) **C-90m.** ** D: Sean Cunningham. Shannon Presby, Lori Loughlin, James Spader, John Philbin, Eric Stoltz. Unexciting thriller about a brother and sister (Presby, Loughlin), two nice kids who are harassed by meanie Spader and his cronies. There's no gratuitous gore, but there are also no real chills. [PG]▼●

New Kind of Love, A (1963) **C-110m.** **½ D: Melville Shavelson. Paul Newman, Joanne Woodward, Thelma Ritter, Eva Gabor, Maurice Chevalier, George Tobias, Marvin Kaplan, Robert Clary. Silly but enjoyable fluff with sportswriter Newman and fashion buyer Woodward tangling, and then falling in love, in Paris. The stars really put this one over; Chevalier plays himself, singing (among others) the title song.▼

New Land, The (1972-Swedish) **C-161m.** ***½ D: Jan Troell. Max von Sydow, Liv Ullmann, Eddie Axberg, Hans Alfredson, Monica Zetterlund, Per Oscarsson. Sequel to THE EMIGRANTS follows same characters as they settle in Minnesota, up to the ends of their lives. Superior performances, photography, many stirring scenes. A real winner; both films have been edited together for TV, dubbed in English, and presented as THE EMIGRANT SAGA. See also THE OX. [PG]▼●

New Leaf, A (1971) **C-102m.** **½ D:

Elaine May. Walter Matthau, Elaine May, Jack Weston, George Rose, William Redfield, James Coco, Graham Jarvis, Doris Roberts, Renee Taylor, David Doyle. Amusing comedy of destitute playboy Matthau planning to marry and murder klutzy May in order to inherit her fortune. Many funny moments, and May is terrific, but it's wildly uneven. Director/writer/star May disavowed finished film, which was reedited by others. [G]▼

New Life, A (1988) **C-104m.** **½ D: Alan Alda. Alan Alda, Ann-Margret, Hal Linden, Veronica Hamel, John Shea, Mary Kay Place, Beatrice Alda. Pleasant but pat comedy about a middle-aged couple's trials and tribulations after divorcing. Alda (sporting a beard and curly hair) also wrote the script. [PG-13]▼●

Newman's Law (1974) **C-98m.** *½ D: Richard Heffron. George Peppard, Roger Robinson, Eugene Roche, Gordon Pinsent, Louis Zorich, Abe Vigoda. Honest cop Peppard, bounced from the force for alleged corruption, investigates the case on his own. Dreary and predictable. [PG]▼

New Mexico (1951) **C-76m.** **½ D: Irving Reis. Lew Ayres, Marilyn Maxwell, Robert Hutton, Andy Devine, Raymond Burr. Moderately exciting Western of cavalry vs. Indians.

New Moon (1940) **105m.** **½ D: Robert Z. Leonard. Jeanette MacDonald, Nelson Eddy, Mary Boland, George Zucco, H. B. Warner, Grant Mitchell, Stanley Fields. Nelson and Jeanette in old Louisiana, falling in love, singing "One Kiss," "Softly as in a Morning Sunrise," "Lover Come Back to Me," "Stout-Hearted Men." Oscar Hammerstein-Sigmund Romberg score sung before in 1930 filming with Lawrence Tibbett and Grace Moore.▼●

New Orleans (1947) **89m.** **½ D: Arthur Lubin. Arturo de Cordova, Dorothy Patrick, Billie Holiday, Louis Armstrong, Woody Herman & Band, Meade Lux Lewis, other jazz stars. Hackneyed fictionalization of the birth of jazz, spanning 40 years, but there's plenty of good music. Holiday (cast as a maid!) does "Do You Know What It Means to Miss New Orleans" with Armstrong and all-star band, and it's sublime. Shelley Winters appears briefly as de Cordova's secretary.▼

New Orleans After Dark (1958) **69m.** *½ D: John Sledge. Stacy Harris, Louis Sirgo, Ellen Moore, Tommy Pelle. Programmer about capture of dope smugglers.▼

New Orleans Uncensored (1955) **76m.** *½ D: William Castle. Arthur Franz, Beverly Garland, Helene Stanton, Michael Ansara. Weak exposé account of racketeer-busting in Louisiana, with competent cast trying to overcome script.

New Rose Hotel (1999) **C-92m.** *½ D: Abel Ferrara. Christopher Walken, Willem Dafoe, Asia Argento, Yoshitaka Amano, Annabella Sciorra, Gretchen Mol, John Lurie, Ryuichi Sakamoto. Ludicrously steamy sleaze in which a pair of industrial spies (Walken, Dafoe) attempt to entice a brilliant geneticist (Amano) into switching firms by hiring a hooker (Argento) to seduce him. Meant to be a moody morality tale, but comes off silly and pompous. Based on a short story by sci-fi/cyberpunk writer William Gibson. Shot in 1997. [R]▼◗

Newsfront (1978-Australian) **C-110m.** *** D: Phillip Noyce. Bill Hunter, Gerard Kennedy, Angela Punch, Wendy Hughes, Chris Haywood, John Ewart, Bryan Brown. Enjoyable, well-crafted tale of newsreel filmmakers—centering on dedicated cameraman Hunter—is a valentine to the movie newsreel industry. Among highlights are actual late 1940s and 1950s newsreel footage, nicely integrated into scenario. [PG]▼●

News Hounds (1947) **68m.** ** D: William Beaudine. Leo Gorcey, Huntz Hall, Bobby Jordan, Billy Benedict, David Gorcey, Gabriel Dell, Bernard Gorcey, Tim Ryan, Bill Kennedy, Robert Emmett Keane, Christine McIntyre, Anthony Caruso. Scoop Mahoney and Shutterbug Sach vs. sports-fixing mobsters. The usual *Bowery Boys* hokum.

Newsies (1992) **C-125m.** *½ D: Kenny Ortega. Christian Bale, Bill Pullman, Robert Duvall, Ann-Margret, Michael Lerner, Kevin Tighe, Charles Cioffi, David Moscow, Luke Edwards, Max Casella. Or, *Howard the Paperboy*. Ambitious musical about the 1899 strike by urchin peddlers of Pulitzer's *New York World* and William Randolph Hearst's *Journal*. Done in by lackluster score, and cramped production numbers that seem cheap despite the film's hefty production budget. Duvall, looking like one of the Smith Brothers, plays Pulitzer; Ann-Margret needlessly pads film's bloated running time as musical performer who inexplicably befriends the lads. Score by Alan Menken and Jack Feldman. Directing debut for choreographer Ortega. Panavision. [PG]▼●

Newton Boys, The (1998) **C-113m.** ** D: Richard Linklater. Matthew McConaughey, Ethan Hawke, Skeet Ulrich, Vincent D'Onofrio, Julianna Margulies, Dwight Yoakam, Chloe Webb, Bo Hopkins. Lackadaisical true-life saga of four Texas brothers who robbed banks across the country from 1919 to 1924 and lived to tell about it. Gen-X auteur Linklater is largely unsuccessful at making a period actioner; indifferent pacing and superficial characterizations make this "The Mild Bunch." Best performance comes from Yoakam as a meek safecracking expert. Terrific honkytonk score by a group called Bad Livers (!); if you stick it out, the end credits feature interview footage of the real Newton Boys that's more

entertaining than anything that preceded it. Panavision. [PG-13]▼●◗
New Wave SEE: **Nouvelle Vague**
New Year's Day (1989) **C-89m.** ★★½ D: Henry Jaglom. Henry Jaglom, Gwen Welles, Maggie Jakobson, Melanie Winter, David Duchovny, Milos Forman, Michael Emil, Tracy Reiner. Another personal, hit-and-miss film from Jaglom, who plays a writer attempting to reclaim the N.Y.C. apartment he's sublet to Jakobson, Winter, and Welles. Typically, there is much talk about relationships and sex (among other subjects); some of it illuminating, much of it pretentious. Odd casting: filmmaker Forman as the apartment house janitor. [R] ▼
New Year's Evil (1981) **C-90m.** BOMB D: Emmett Alston. Roz Kelly, Kip Niven, Chris Wallace, Grant Cramer, Louisa Moritz. Atrocious thriller revolving around disc jockey Kelly and killer Niven. Another HALLOWEEN ripoff. [R]▼
New York Confidential (1955) **87m.** ★★½ D: Russell Rouse. Broderick Crawford, Richard Conte, Marilyn Maxwell, Anne Bancroft, J. Carrol Naish. Energetic cast perks up formula exposé of racketeer narrative.
New York New York (1977) **C-164m.** ★½ D: Martin Scorsese. Robert De Niro, Liza Minnelli, Lionel Stander, Georgie Auld, Mary Kay Place, George Memmoli, Barry Primus, Dick Miller, Diahnne Abbott. Elaborate but off-putting musical drama loosely based on THE MAN I LOVE; saxophonist De Niro and vocalist Minnelli love and fight with each other right through the Big Band era. Some people consider this film extraordinary, but we're not among them; kudos, though, to production designer Boris Leven, music arranger Ralph Burns, and the Kander-Ebb title song. Initially released at 153m., then cut to 137m., and finally reissued in 1981 at current length with splashy "Happy Endings" number (featuring Larry Kert) added. [PG]▼●
New York Stories (1989) **C-123m.** ★★½ D: Martin Scorsese, Francis Coppola, Woody Allen. Nick Nolte, Rosanna Arquette, Steve Buscemi, Peter Gabriel, Deborah Harry, Heather McComb, Talia Shire, Giancarlo Giannini, Don Novello, Chris Elliott, Carole Bouquet, Woody Allen, Mia Farrow, Mae Questel, Julie Kavner, Mayor Edward I. Koch, Adrien Brody, Illeana Douglas, Kirsten Dunst. Three-part anthology film: Scorsese's is an obvious, heavy-handed tale of a macho artist (Nolte) and his assistant/lover (Arquette) who wants to fly the coop. Coppola's is a cute but pointless variation on the old children's book *Eloise* about a little rich girl who lives in a N.Y.C. hotel while her parents globetrot. Finally, we get to the good stuff, with Allen in great form as a man literally haunted by his nagging mother (Questel, a howl). A waste of time until the concluding sequence. [PG]▼●
New York Town (1941) **76m.** ★★½ D: Charles Vidor. Fred MacMurray, Mary Martin, Robert Preston, Akim Tamiroff, Lynne Overman, Eric Blore, Fuzzy Knight. Bright little comedy of wide-eyed Martin manhunting in N.Y.C., assisted by photographer MacMurray. Songs include "Love In Bloom." Preston Sturges worked uncredited on the script.
Next Best Thing, The (2000) **C-108m.** BOMB D: John Schlesinger. Madonna, Rupert Everett, Benjamin Bratt, Michael Vartan, Josef Sommer, Lynn Redgrave, Malcolm Stumpf, Neil Patrick Harris, Illeana Douglas. Awful soap opera about yoga instructor having a child with her best friend, who's gay, which works fine until she falls in love with another man. Unconvincing, even condescending at times, despite its self-satisfied script. Everett keeps telling Madonna how beautiful she is, but it takes late '40s-style Joan Crawford lighting to try to put that over. Super 35. [PG-13]▼●◗
Next Door (1994) **C-95m. TVM** D: Tony Bill. James Woods, Randy Quaid, Kate Capshaw, Lucinda Jenney, Miles Feulner, Billy L. Sullivan, Joe Minares, Ivory Ocean. Two bickering neighbors (Woods and Quaid) wage a war of cruel pranks in this black comedy about suburbia. Stars can't save this mix of humor and terror; a failed social commentary about keeping up with the Joneses. Average.▼
Next Friday (2000) **C-92m.** ★½ D: Steve Carr. Ice Cube, Mike Epps, Justin Pierce, John Witherspoon, Don "D.C." Curry, Jacob Vargas, Lobo Sebastian, Rolando Molina, Lisa Rodriguez, Tommy "Tiny" Lister, Jr. Slacker/stoner (Cube) finds that his problems are just beginning when, to escape the wrath of bully Lister, he is dispatched from the 'hood to his uncle and cousin in the 'burbs. Shrill, stupid sequel to FRIDAY is a sloppy pastiche of crude comic skits filled with lame stereotypes. Cube scripted and coexecutive-produced. [R]▼●◗
Next Karate Kid, The (1994) **C-104m.** ★★ D: Christopher Cain. Noriyuki "Pat" Morita, Hilary Swank, Michael Ironside, Constance Towers, Chris Conrad. Harmless, formulaic KARATE KID sequel (fourth in the series) with a twist: the "kid" is now a girl (Swank), an alienated teen who is taught self-esteem and martial arts by the benevolent Mr. Miyagi (Morita). [PG]▼●
Next Man, The (1976) **C-108m.** ★★★ D: Richard C. Sarafian. Sean Connery, Cornelia Sharpe, Albert Paulsen, Adolfo Celi, Charles Cioffi. Good melodrama in which scenery (N.Y.C., Bavaria, London, Morocco, etc.) and violence are blended to tell of international hit lady Sharpe falling

in love with Saudi Arabian ambassador Connery as he tries to arrange peace with Palestine. Video titles: DOUBLE HIT and THE ARAB CONSPIRACY. [R]▼

Next of Kin (1989) **C-108m.** *½ D: John Irvin. Patrick Swayze, Liam Neeson, Adam Baldwin, Helen Hunt, Andreas Katsulas, Bill Paxton, Ben Stiller, Michael J. Pollard. Chicago cop Swayze, of Appalachian descent, takes on Mr. Mob with the help of backwoods brother Neeson. High-concept, low-rent star vehicle. Would *you* stay in a hotel managed by Pollard? [R]▼●

Next One, The (1984) **C-105m.** ** D: Nico Mastorakis. Keir Dullea, Adrienne Barbeau, Jeremy Licht, Peter Hobbs. Dullea, a Christ-like visitor from the future, washes up on a Greek island where widow Barbeau, living with her young son, falls in love with him. Mediocre sci-fi strains for significance. Filmed in 1981. ▼

Next Stop, Greenwich Village (1976) **C-109m.** *** D: Paul Mazursky. Lenny Baker, Shelley Winters, Ellen Greene, Christopher Walken, Lou Jacobi, Mike Kellin, Lois Smith, Dori Brenner, Antonio Fargas, Jeff Goldblum. Comic, poignant film about Brooklyn boy Baker who moves to Greenwich Village in 1953 hoping to become an actor. Wonderful period atmosphere and characterizations; Winters is excellent as Baker's domineering mother. Look fast for Bill Murray in a bar. Semiautobiographical script by Mazursky. [R]▼

Next Stop Wonderland (1998) **C-104m.** *** D: Brad Anderson. Hope Davis, Alan Gelfant, Holland Taylor, Jose Zuniga, Phil (Philip Seymour) Hoffman, Robert Klein, Roger Rees. Unabashedly old-fashioned romantic comedy about a recently jilted nurse (Davis) whose love life takes a new turn when her meddling mother (Taylor, fun as ever) secretly places a personals ad for her. Somewhere amidst a sea of overeager bachelors is her Mr. Right (Gelfant), but their lives seem to intersect without so much as a meeting. Indie spin on SLEEPLESS IN SEATTLE has silly subplots but is bolstered by a wintry Boston locale, charm to spare, and a wonderfully bittersweet performance from Davis. [R]▼●

Next Time We Love (1936) **87m.** *** D: Edward H. Griffith. Margaret Sullavan, James Stewart, Ray Milland, Grant Mitchell, Robert McWade, Anna Demetrio, Hattie McDaniel. Trim romantic soaper with Milland in love with actress Sullavan, who is married to struggling reporter Stewart. Preston Sturges worked uncredited on the script.

Next to No Time (1958-British) **C-93m.** *** D. Henry Cornelius. Kenneth More, Betsy Drake, Bessie Love, Harry Green, Patrick Barr, Roland Culver. Whimsical comedy from Paul Gallico story, about mild-mannered engineer (More) who loses inhibitions on ocean voyage where he's trying to put over important business deal.

Next Voice You Hear, The (1950) **83m.** **½ D: William Wellman. James Whitmore, Nancy Davis (Reagan), Lillian Bronson, Jeff Corey. The voice of God is heard on the radio and has a profound impact on Anytown, U.S.A. Ambitious if not terribly successful message film produced by Dore Schary.▼

Niagara (1953) **C-89m.** *** D: Henry Hathaway. Marilyn Monroe, Joseph Cotten, Jean Peters, Casey Adams, Don Wilson, Richard Allan. Black murder tale of couple staying at Niagara Falls, the wife planning to kill husband. Produced and cowritten by Charles Brackett; good location work.▼●

Niagara, Niagara (1998) **C-96m.** *½ D: Bob Gosse. Robin Tunney, Henry Thomas, Michael Parks, Stephen Lang, John MacKay. A teenage girl with Tourette's syndrome meets her soul mate while they're both shoplifting. Any film that launches a "romance" on that note provides ample warning for viewers who dare to continue. Tunney is unflinching in her performance as the gratingly foul-mouthed girl in this notably unpleasant film that adds a novel spin to lovers-on-the-lam cinema. [R] ▼

Nice Girl? (1941) **95m.** *** D: William A. Seiter. Deanna Durbin, Franchot Tone, Walter Brennan, Robert Stack, Robert Benchley. Little Deanna grows up in this cute comedy, with Tone and Stack developing amorous ideas about her. Songs: "Love At Last," "Thank You America." Video includes alternate ending. ▼

Nice Girl Like Me, A (1969-British) **C-91m.** ** D: Desmond Davis. Barbara Ferris, Harry Andrews, Gladys Cooper, Bill Hinnant, James Villiers. Orphaned Ferris accidentally becomes impregnated twice by different men, is looked after by caretaker Andrews, whom she really loves. Appealing, silly and predictable. [M/PG]▼

Nice Girls Don't Explode (1987) **C-92m.** ** D: Chuck Martinez. Barbara Harris, Michelle Meyrink, William O'Leary, Wallace Shawn, James Nardini. Silly comedy (with a memorable title) about a girl who causes things to explode, especially when she gets amorous. Harris and Meyrink, as mother and daughter who share this curse, give it their best, but the sparks don't ignite. [PG]▼●

Nice Little Bank That Should be Robbed, A (1958) **87m.** ** D: Henry Levin. Tom Ewell, Mickey Rooney, Mickey Shaughnessy, Dina Merrill. Cast is game, but story is pure cornball about goofy crooks using their gains to buy a racehorse. CinemaScope.

Nicholas and Alexandra (1971-British) **C-183m.** **½ D: Franklin Schaffner. Michael Jayston, Janet Suzman, Tom Baker, Harry Andrews, Jack Hawkins, Laurence

Olivier, Michael Redgrave, Alexander Knox, Curt Jurgens. Lavishly filmed (with Oscar-winning art direction-set decoration and costumes), well-acted chronicle of Russian leaders, and revolution that turned their world upside down. Sure and steady, but eventually tedious, despite cameos by Olivier et al. Panavision. [PG]▼●◗

Nicholas Nickleby (1947-British) **108m.** *** D: Alberto Cavalcanti. Derek Bond, Cedric Hardwicke, Alfred Drayton, Bernard Miles, Sally Ann Howes, Mary Merrall, Sybil Thorndike, Cathleen Nesbitt. Dickens's classic tale of young man's struggle to protect his family from scheming uncle and a cruel world is vividly brought to life. Can't compare with the Royal Shakespeare Company's 8½ hour stage version—but still quite good. Some American prints run 95m.▼

Nick Carter Detective Nick Carter was created in 1886 and became the busiest crime solver in American literature, being featured in hundreds of short stories in magazines and books. He was the hero of a number of silent films both here and in France, but for all his durability on the printed page he never enjoyed great success on screen. MGM launched a series in 1939 which cast urbane Walter Pidgeon as the detective, but only three films resulted. All of them are fast paced, flippant, and somewhat outlandish (like the original stories), with typical MGM polish distinguishing them from other studios' grade-B product, but their chief distinction is the casting of Donald Meek as Bartholomew, The Bee-Man, an off-center oddball who foists himself upon Nick. Nothing about Pidgeon, or the characterization of Carter, created any compelling reason to want to see more. Carter was later played in France by Eddie Constantine, and in a short-lived series, but his most striking screen appearance came in a 1978 Czech film called, variously, NICK CARTER IN PRAGUE and DINNER FOR ADELE, which finally attempted to reproduce the time and atmosphere of the original pulp stories.

NICK CARTER

Nick Carter—Master Detective (1939)
Phantom Raiders (1940)
Sky Murder (1940)

Nick Carter in Prague SEE: **Dinner for Adele**

Nick Carter—Master Detective (1939) **60m.** ** D: Jacques Tourneur. Walter Pidgeon, Rita Johnson, Henry Hull, Donald Meek, Milburn Stone, Addison Richards, Sterling Holloway. Pidgeon is good, tracking down industrial spy in slickly done detective film. Starts out very snappy, then slows to a crawl and loses its way. Memorable for some striking aerial shots.

Nickel Mountain (1985) **C-88m.** **½ D: Drew Denbaum. Michael Cole, Heather Langenkamp, Patrick Cassidy, Brian Kerwin, Grace Zabriskie, Don Beddoe, Ed Lauter. Warm drama of unwed teenage mother growing up in rural America, befriended by pathetic older man. Winning performance by Langenkamp. Adapted from John Gardner's novel; filmed in 1983.▼

Nickelodeon (1976) **C-121m.** *** D: Peter Bogdanovich. Ryan O'Neal, Burt Reynolds, Tatum O'Neal, Brian Keith, Stella Stevens, John Ritter, Jane Hitchcock, Harry Carey, Jr. Heartfelt valentine to early days of moviemaking, with O'Neal literally stumbling into his job as director, Reynolds an overnight screen hero. Based on reminiscences of such veterans as Raoul Walsh and Allan Dwan, film unfortunately loses steam halfway through. Entertaining on the whole, sparked by fine cast; script by Bogdanovich and W.D. Richter. [PG]

Nickel Ride, The (1975) **C-99m.** ** D: Robert Mulligan. Jason Miller, Linda Haynes, Victor French, John Hillerman, Bo Hopkins. Uneven and generally obscure little drama about a syndicate contact man (Miller) who keeps keys to L.A. warehouses used by dealers in stolen goods. Panavision. [PG]

Nick of Time (1995) **C-89m.** **½ D: John Badham. Johnny Depp, Christopher Walken, Charles S. Dutton, Courtney Chase, Marsha Mason, Roma Maffia, Peter Strauss, Gloria Reuben, Bill Smitrovich, G. D. Spradlin. Businessman arrives in L.A. with his young daughter and within moments, she's taken hostage while he's instructed to commit murder! Watchable suspense yarn draws you in, but hurls credibility roadblocks in your path at every turn. A game cast gives it 100 percent. Attempt to create heightened suspense by playing out the story in "real time" (with endless closeups of clocks) doesn't pay off at all. [R]▼●◗

Nico-Icon (1995-German) **C/B&W-75m.** *** D: Susanne Ofteringer. Fascinating documentary about a compelling, sadly tragic subject: Christa Päffgen, the beautiful but self-destructive German-born model and singer who re-created herself as Nico, one of Andy Warhol's "Superstars." Nico was no candidate for Mother-of-the-Year: she was a heroin addict who initiated her own son into using the drug! Warhol's interview, along with one of Nico filmed two years before her death in 1988, are among the highpoints. Lou Reed, Jackson Browne, and Paul Morrissey are among those seen on-camera in this trenchant documentary. ▼●◗

Night, The SEE: **La Notte**

Night After Night (1932) **70m.** ** D: Archie Mayo. George Raft, Mae West,

Constance Cummings, Wynne Gibson, Roscoe Karns, Louis Calhern, Alison Skipworth. Story of nightclub owner Raft's infatuation with "classy" Cummings is a crashing bore, but when Mae West comes on the screen lights up. It's her film debut, and she's in rare form.▼●

Night Ambush (1957-British) **93m.** *** D: Michael Powell, Emeric Pressburger. Dirk Bogarde, Marius Goring, David Oxley, Cyril Cusack, Christopher Lee. Taut WW2 actioner set in Crete, with fine British cast. Originally released in England as ILL MET BY MOONLIGHT at 104m. VistaVision.▼

Night and Day (1946) **C-128m.** ** D: Michael Curtiz. Cary Grant, Alexis Smith, Monty Woolley, Ginny Simms, Jane Wyman, Eve Arden, Mary Martin, Victor Francen, Alan Hale, Dorothy Malone. Music only worthy aspect of fabricated biography of songwriter Cole Porter, stiffly played by Grant, who even sings "You're The Top." Martin recreates "My Heart Belongs To Daddy" in film's highlight.▼●

Night and the City (1950) **101m.** **½ D: Jules Dassin. Richard Widmark, Gene Tierney, Googie Withers, Hugh Marlowe, Francis L. Sullivan, Herbert Lom, Mike Mazurki, Kay Kendall. Interesting film noir portrait of assorted losers in the netherworld of London, focusing on a young American hustler (Widmark) who's desperate to succeed. Marvelous showcase for Sullivan as an oily nightclub owner. Filmed in England. Remade in 1992.▼

Night and the City (1992) **C-98m.** **½ D: Irwin Winkler. Robert De Niro, Jessica Lange, Cliff Gorman, Alan King, Jack Warden, Eli Wallach, Barry Primus, Gene Kirkwood, Pedro Sanchez. De Niro is dynamic as always, playing a hustler who tries promoting a boxing match—setting himself up for personal and professional disaster at every turn. Colorful N.Y.C. ambience and solid cast combat the utter predictability of the story. Screenplay by Richard Price (who also plays a doctor), based on the 1950 film and its source novel by Gerald Kersh. [R]▼●

Night at the Opera, A (1935) **92m.** **** D: Sam Wood. Groucho, Chico, Harpo Marx, Kitty Carlisle, Allan Jones, Walter Woolf King, Margaret Dumont, Sigfried Rumann. The Marx Brothers invade the world of opera with devastating results. Arguably their finest film (a close race with DUCK SOUP), with tuneful music and appealing romance neatly interwoven. One priceless comedy bit follows another: the stateroom scene, the Party of the First Part contract, etc. This is as good as it gets.▼●

Night at the Roxbury, A (1998) **C-82m.** *½ D: John Fortenberry. Will Ferrell, Chris Kattan, Molly Shannon, Dan Hedaya, Loni Anderson, Elisa Donovan, Gigi Rice, Richard Grieco, Dwayne Hickman, Colin Quinn, Michael Clarke Duncan. The uncool Butabi Brothers from *Saturday Night Live* get (rather than rate) their feature film debut: a limp comedy about their attempt to wile themselves into the town's trendiest nightspot. Talk about the last days of disco; five minutes of material gets stretched into nearly an hour and a half. The two stars also scripted. Chazz Palminteri has a cameo. Grieco completists should be aware that he plays himself. [PG-13]▼●◗

Night Before, The (1988) **C-85m.** ** D: Thom Eberhardt. Keanu Reeves, Lori Loughlin, Theresa Saldana, Trinidad Silva, Suzanne Snyder, Morgan Lofting, Gwil Richards, Michael Greene. Mild (and all-too-familiar) comic misadventures, as a high-school nerd tries to remember what happened to him the previous night on the way to the prom. [PG-13]▼

Nightbreaker (1989) **C-100m. TVM** D: Peter Markle. Martin Sheen, Emilio Estevez, Lea Thompson, Melinda Dillon, Joe Pantoliano, Nicholas Pryor. A naive doctor witnesses the U.S. Government's use of the military as guinea pigs in 1950s atomic tests in Nevada. Sheen and real-life son Estevez play the same character, in the '50s and '80s respectively. T.S. Cook's emotional script is based on Howard Rosenberg's novel *Atomic Soldiers.* Made for cable. Above average.▼●

Nightbreed (1990-U.S.-Canadian) **C-99m.** **½ D: Clive Barker. Craig Sheffer, Anne Bobby, David Cronenberg, Charles Haid, Hugh Quarshie, Hugh Ross, Doug Bradley, Catherine Chevalier, Bob Sessions, Malcolm Smith, Oliver Parker, John Agar. Mistaken for a serial killer, Sheffer is killed at the gates of mysterious Midian, "where the monsters go." He returns from the dead to join the monsters there, confusing girlfriend Bobby and enticing his psychiatrist Cronenberg, the real killer. Intelligent, imaginative horror epic, but as adapted by Barker from his novel *Cabal*, the complicated film never becomes fully involving. Eye-popping apocalyptic climax. [R]▼●

Night Caller (1975-French-Italian) **C-91m.** ** D: Henri Verneuil. Jean-Paul Belmondo, Charles Denner, Adalberto-Maria Meril, Lea Massari, Rosy Varte. Detective Belmondo tackles both a bank robbery case and an obscene phone caller who murders women at the end of the line. Action but little else. [R]

Night Caller from Outer Space (1965-British) **84m.** **½ D: John Gilling. John Saxon, Maurice Denham, Patricia Haines, Alfred Burke, Jack Watson, Aubrey Morris. Well-done sci-fi thriller of alien kidnapping humans to take back to his home, a moon of Jupiter. U.S. theatrical title: BLOOD BEAST FROM OUTER SPACE. ▼●◗

Night Call Nurses (1972) **C-85m.** ** D: Jonathan Kaplan. Patti Byrne, Alana Collins, Mittie Lawrence, Dick Miller, Dennis Dugan, Stack Pierce. Kaplan's feature debut is typical drive-in sex comedy; lighthearted and fast-paced, with good comic performances by Dugan and the ubiquitous Miller. Third in Roger Corman-produced series; followed by THE YOUNG NURSES. [R]▼

Night Club Scandal (1937) **70m.** **½ D: Ralph Murphy. John Barrymore, Lynne Overman, Louise Campbell, Charles Bickford, Evelyn Brent, Elizabeth Patterson, J. Carrol Naish. Enjoyable B mystery with detectives seeking murderer who tried to frame innocent man. Remake of 1932 film GUILTY AS HELL.

Nightcomers, The (1972-British) **C-96m.** ** D: Michael Winner. Marlon Brando, Stephanie Beacham, Thora Hird, Harry Andrews, Verna Harvey, Christopher Ellis, Anna Palk. Poor direction hurts attempt to chronicle what happened to the children in Henry James' *Turn of the Screw* before original story began. [R]▼●

Night Court (1932) **90m.** ** D: W.S. Van Dyke. Phillips Holmes, Walter Huston, Anita Page, Lewis Stone, Mary Carlisle, John Miljan, Jean Hersholt. Slimy, crooked night court judge Huston will stop at nothing to avoid being pinned by city watchdog Stone; that includes framing an innocent young couple. Watchable but far from subtle, or surprising, until final twist.

Night Creature (1978) **C-83m.** BOMB D: Lee Madden. Donald Pleasence, Nancy Kwan, Ross Hagen, Lesly Fine, Jennifer Rhodes. Macho writer Pleasence lives on Xanadu-like island retreat near Thailand, but a prowling leopard is giving him the jitters. Low-grade thriller, minus the thrills. Aka OUT OF THE DARKNESS. [PG]▼

Night Creatures (1962-British) **C-81m.** **½ D: Peter Graham Scott. Peter Cushing, Yvonne Romain, Patrick Allen, Oliver Reed, Michael Ripper, Martin Benson, David Lodge. In 18th century England, country parson is also the notorious "dead" pirate leader of smugglers who pose as ghosts. Good fun with some scary moments. Remake of DR. SYN. Original British title: CAPTAIN CLEGG.

Night Crossing (1981-British) **C-106m.** **½ D: Delbert Mann. John Hurt, Jane Alexander, Glynnis O'Connor, Doug McKeon, Beau Bridges, Ian Bannen, Klaus Lowitsch, Kay Walsh. Unexceptional though well-cast and not unexciting tale of two families' escape from East Berlin via hot-air balloon. A Walt Disney production, based on a true story. [PG]▼

Night Digger, The (1971-British) **C-100m.** *** D: Alastair Reid. Patricia Neal, Pamela Brown, Nicholas Clay, Jean Anderson, Graham Crowden, Yootha Joyce. Odd, usually effective psychological thriller adapted from Joy Cowley novel by Roald Dahl. With the unexpected arrival of young handyman, sad relationship between two country women takes turn for the better, until they discover what he does on off-hours. Excellent performances, fine Bernard Herrmann score. Aka THE ROAD BUILDER. [R]

Night Editor (1946) **68m.** ** D: Henry Levin. William Gargan, Janis Carter, Jeff Donnell, Coulter Irwin. Minor yarn about Gargan, a law enforcer gone wrong, trying to redeem himself.

Night Evelyn Came Out of the Grave, The (1971-Italian) **C-90m.** *½ D: Emilio Miraglia. Anthony Steffen, Marina Malfatti, Rod Murdock, Giacomo Rossi-Stuart, Umberto Raho. Dreadful horror whodunit about British lord released from psychiatric clinic following wife's death, who begins to suspect she is still alive when her crypt is discovered empty. Techniscope. [R]▼

Nightfall (1956) **78m.** *** D: Jacques Tourneur. Aldo Ray, Brian Keith, Anne Bancroft, Jocelyn Brando, James Gregory, Frank Albertson. Fast-moving, well-made story of innocent man wanted by police for killing of friend, chased by actual killers for stolen money he found.

Nightfall (1988) **C-82m.** BOMB D: Paul Mayersberg. David Birney, Sarah Douglas, Alexis Kanner, Andra Millian, Charles Hayward, Susie Lindeman, Starr Andreeff. Hopelessly muddled adaptation of Isaac Asimov's classic short story about an alien world in a three-star solar system whose inhabitants face the coming darkness of nightfall (occurring only once every 1000 years) with abject terror. Birney is miscast in this cheesy production. [PG-13]▼

Night Falls on Manhattan (1997) **C-113m.** **½ D: Sidney Lumet. Andy Garcia, Richard Dreyfuss, Lena Olin, Ian Holm, Ron Leibman, James Gandolfini, Colm Feore, Shiek Mahmud-Bey, Paul Guilfoyle. Cop turned lawyer joins the D.A.'s staff in N.Y.C. and rises to the top by prosecuting a headline-making case in which his father, a veteran detective, was shot. Then he has to deal with the stickier issue of police corruption, which hits awfully close to home. Intense and watchable saga (adapted by Lumet from Robert Daley's novel *Tainted Evidence*) suffers from one major flaw: its central character's naïveté. He's constantly shocked by what we in the audience already know—or have guessed. Leibman is dynamite as the bombastic D.A. [R]▼●◗

Night Fighters (1960-British) **85m.** **½ D: Tay Garnett. Robert Mitchum, Anne Heywood, Dan O'Herlihy, Cyril Cusack, Richard Harris, Marianne Benet. Sporadically actionful tale of Irish Revolution, with Mitchum joining the cause against his will. Original title: A TERRIBLE BEAUTY.

Night Flier, The (1998) **C-99m.** **½ D: Mark Pavia. Miguel Ferrer, Julie Entwisle, Dan Monahan, Merton H. Moss. Black-hearted tabloid reporter meets his match when he tracks a mysterious bloodsucking serial killer who flies a black Cessna plane from crime scene to crime scene. Genuinely creepy mood is bolstered by Ferrer's enjoyably hissable heavy. Not-bad directorial debut for Pavia until the film's final third, which descends into typical gorefest shtick. Originally shown on cable, then released in theaters. Aka STEPHEN KING'S THE NIGHT FLIER. [R]▼●◗

Night Flight From Moscow (1973-French-Italian-West German) **C-113m.** **½ D: Henri Verneuil. Yul Brynner, Henry Fonda, Dirk Bogarde, Philippe Noiret, Virna Lisi, Farley Granger, Robert Alda, Marie Dubois, Elga Andersen. Espionage thriller about the defection of Russian diplomat Brynner is compromised by the middling screenplay adapted from Pierre Nord's cloak-and-dagger novel *Le 13e Suicide*. Originally titled THE SERPENT. Panavision. [PG]▼

Nightflyers (1987) **C-89m.** *½ D: T.C. Blake (Robert Collector). Catherine Mary Stewart, Michael Praed, John Standing, Lisa Blount, Glenn Withrow. Dreary, derivative sci-fi about a dangerous and harmful force wreaking havoc among scientists aboard a spaceship. Director Collector had his name removed from the credits. Based on a novella by George R. R. Martin. [R]▼●

Nightforce (1987) **C-82m.** *½ D: Lawrence D. Foldes. Linda Blair, James Van Patten, Richard Lynch, Chad McQueen, Dean R. Miller, James Marcel, Claudia Udy, Bruce Fisher, Cameron Mitchell. Cornball action film has Blair and fellow youngsters organizing a commando mission to Central America to free a kidnapped daughter of a U. S. senator. [R]▼

Night Freight (1955) **79m.** **½ D: Jean Yarbrough. Forrest Tucker, Barbara Britton, Keith Larsen, Thomas Gomez. Straightforward tale about railroad competing with trucking line for survival.

Night Full of Rain, A (1978-Italian) **C-104m.** ** D: Lina Wertmuller. Giancarlo Giannini, Candice Bergen, Allison Tucker, Jill Eikenberry, Michael Tucker, Anne Byrne. Wertmuller's first English language effort (shot in Rome and San Francisco) is unsatisfying fantasy drama about relationship between journalist Giannini and feminist wife Bergen, who's quite good. Full title: THE END OF THE WORLD IN OUR USUAL BED IN A NIGHT FULL OF RAIN. [R]▼

Night Gallery (1969) **C-98m. TVM** D: Boris Sagal, Steven Spielberg, Barry Shear. Roddy McDowall, Ossie Davis, Barry Sullivan, Tom Bosley, George Macready, Joan Crawford, Richard Kiley, Sam Jaffe. Three-story anthology, each part revolving around lessons learned (via Rod Serling) from paintings: despicable nephew (McDowall) speeds up death of wealthy old uncle who is resurrected via spooky oil painting; cruel art collector (Crawford) arranges for eye transplant from living donor; death camp Nazi (Kiley) in South American country picks the worst possible place to evade pursuers. Effective mixture of melodrama, morality, and supernatural spawned popular series; middle tale was Spielberg's maiden directorial effort. Above average.▼

Night Game (1989) **C-95m.** *½ D: Peter Masterson. Roy Scheider, Karen Young, Richard Bradford, Paul Gleason, Carlin Glynn. Texas police detective goes after a serial killer. What a shame to find good actors and a talented director wasting their time with such third-rate material. [R]▼●

Night Games (1980) **C-100m.** *½ D: Roger Vadim. Cindy Pickett, Joanna Cassidy, Barry Primus, Paul Jenkins, Gene Davis. Frigid housewife will make it only with guy who shows up at night in a bird suit. Vadim may be kidding, but it's tough to tell. [R]▼

Night Has a Thousand Eyes (1948) **80m.** **½ D: John Farrow. Edward G. Robinson, Gail Russell, John Lund, Virginia Bruce, William Demarest. Intriguing story of magician who has uncanny power to predict the future; script is corny at times. Based on a story by Cornell Woolrich.

Night Has Eyes, The (1942-British) **79m.** **½ D: Leslie Arliss. James Mason, Joyce Howard, Mary Clare, Wilfrid Lawson, Tucker McGuire. OK mystery of schoolteacher Howard discovering why a friend disappeared in the Yorkshire Moors; Mason is a shellshocked composer she loves. Aka TERROR HOUSE.▼

Nighthawks (1981) **C-99m.** *** D: Bruce Malmuth. Sylvester Stallone, Billy Dee Williams, Lindsay Wagner, Persis Khambatta, Nigel Davenport, Rutger Hauer, Joe Spinell, Catherine Mary Stewart. Exciting story of two N.Y.C. street cops reassigned to special unit that's tracking a ruthless international terrorist (Hauer). On target from the first scene to the fade-out, with plenty of hair-raising moments along the way. [R]▼●

Night Heaven Fell, The (1958-French) **C-90m.** **½ D: Roger Vadim. Brigitte Bardot, Alida Valli, Stephen Boyd, Pepe Nieto. Turgid drama of Bardot dallying with Boyd, who's planning to kill her uncle. CinemaScope.▼

Night Holds Terror, The (1955) **86m.** ** D: Andrew L. Stone. Jack Kelly, Hildy Parks, Vince Edwards, John Cassavetes, Jack Kruschen, Joel Marston, Jonathan Hale. Somber little film of family being held captive for ransom.

Night in Casablanca, A (1946) **85m.** *** D: Archie Mayo. Groucho, Harpo, Chico Marx, Lisette Verea, Charles Drake, Lois Collier, Dan Seymour, Sig Ruman. No classic, but many funny sequences in latter-day Marx outing, ferreting out Nazi spies in Casablanca hotel.▼

Nightingale Sang in Berkeley Square, A (1979) **C-102m.** **½ D: Ralph Thomas. Richard Jordan, David Niven, Oliver

Tobias, Elke Sommer, Gloria Grahame, Hugh Griffith, Richard Johnson. American ex-con Jordan, released from a British prison, is coerced into taking part in an elaborate bank heist masterminded by Niven. Grahame, seen briefly as Jordan's brassy mom, is a joy to watch in one of her last roles. Video titles: THE BIG SCAM and THE MAYFAIR BANK CAPER.▼

Night in Heaven, A (1983) **C-80m.** ** D: John G. Avildsen. Lesley Ann Warren, Christopher Atkins, Robert Logan, Carrie Snodgress, Deborah Rush, Sandra Beall, Alix Elias, Denny Terrio, Andy Garcia. Teacher Warren lets her friends drag her to a male strip joint, where the star attraction (Atkins) is a student she's flunking. Offbeat romantic drama penned by Joan Tewkesbury had real possibilities, but many of them were apparently left on the cutting room floor (note brief running time). Still worth a peek for fine performance by Warren. [R]▼

Night in New Orleans, A (1942) **75m.** *½ D: William Clemens. Preston Foster, Patricia Morison, Albert Dekker, Charles Butterworth, Dooley Wilson, Cecil Kellaway. Thin yarn of Morison trying to clear husband Foster of murder charge.

Night in Paradise (1946) **C-84m.** **½ D: Arthur Lubin. Merle Oberon, Turhan Bey, Thomas Gomez, Gale Sondergaard, Ray Collins, Ernest Truex. Tongue-in-cheek costumer of Aesop wooing lovely princess Oberon in ancient times; colorful, at least.

Night in the Life of Jimmy Reardon, A (1988) **C-90m.** **½ D: William Richert. River Phoenix, Ann Magnuson, Meredith Salenger, Ione Skye, Louanne, Matthew L. Perry. Richert's film of his own youthful novel (*Aren't You Even Gonna Kiss Me Goodbye?*) doesn't work overall . . . but it has something. Phoenix is a high school Romeo preparing for a fall from grace when his more affluent friends prepare to leave for ritzier colleges; Magnuson's cameo (as an amorous family friend) is a standout, but other performances fall short. Handsomely photographed by John Connor. [R]▼●

Night Into Morning (1951) **86m.** *** D: Fletcher Markle. Ray Milland, John Hodiak, Nancy Davis (Reagan), Lewis Stone, Jean Hagen, Rosemary DeCamp. Small-town professor loses family in fire, almost ruins own life through drink and self-pity. Realistic settings in modest production, with fine performance by Milland.

Night Is My Future (1948-Swedish) **87m.** **½ D: Ingmar Bergman. Mai Zetterling, Birger Malmsten, Olof Winnerstrand, Naima Wifstrand, Hilda Borgstrom. Somber, brooding tale of young Malmsten, blinded while in military service; he struggles for self-respect, and is befriended by housemaid Zetterling. Early, minor Bergman. Aka MUSIC IN DARKNESS.▼

Nightjohn (1996) **C-95m.** **TVM** D: Charles Burnett. Beau Bridges, Carl Lumbly, Lorraine Toussaint, Bill Cobbs, Kathleen York, Allison Jones. Well-crafted, moving Disney adaptation of novelist Gary Paulsen's fictional account of life among Southern slaves in the 1830s, with one (Lumbly), self-taught, engaging in the forbidden practice of secretly teaching others to read and write. Except for Bridges doing a Simon Legree turn as plantation owner, the performances are heartrending, the story (script by Bill Cain) sometimes harrowing. Made for cable. Above average.▼

Night Key (1937) **67m.** ** D: Lloyd Corrigan. Boris Karloff, Warren Hull, Jean Rogers, Hobart Cavanaugh. Middling yarn about crooks forcing elderly inventor to help them with their crimes.

Nightkill (1980-German) **C-97m.** **½ D: Ted Post. Jaclyn Smith, Mike Connors, James Franciscus, Robert Mitchum, Fritz Weaver, Sybil Danning. Confused suspense drama involving a love triangle that ends in murder and a cat-and-mouse game between a wealthy widow and a mysterious investigator. Filmed on location in Arizona by a German company. ▼

Nightmare (1942) **81m.** **½ D: Tim Whelan. Diana Barrymore, Brian Donlevy, Gavin Muir, Henry Daniell, Hans Conried, Arthur Shields. Occasionally flavorful mystery with gambler Donlevy breaking into Barrymore's home on the night husband Daniell is murdered, and their subsequent flight from both the police and Nazi spies.

Nightmare (1956) **89m.** **½ D: Maxwell Shane. Edward G. Robinson, Kevin McCarthy, Connie Russell, Virginia Christine. McCarthy is musician involved in bizarre murder set in New Orleans; OK mystery, with Robinson sparking proceedings. Remake of FEAR IN THE NIGHT.

Nightmare (1964) **83m.** **½ D: Freddie Francis. David Knight, Moira Redmond, Jennie Linden, Brenda Bruce, George A. Cooper, Clytie Jessop, Irene Richmond. Linden returns to her family mansion, plagued by nightmares, and fears that she may be turning into an insane killer, like her mother before her. Typical Hammer Films it's-all-a-plot plot in DIABOLIQUE vein is heightened by elegant camera work and good performances. Hammerscope. ▼●

Nightmare (1976) SEE: **Nightmare in Badham County**

Nightmare (1981) **C-97m.** BOMB D: Romano Scavolini. C. J. Cooke, Mik Cribben, Kathleen Ferguson. Psycho who had a traumatic childhood murders, murders, and murders again. Should be rated D for disgusting. [R]▼

Nightmare Alley (1947) **111m.** ***½ D: Edmund Goulding. Tyrone Power, Joan Blondell, Coleen Gray, Helen Walker, Taylor Holmes, Mike Mazurki, Ian Keith,

Julia Dean. Morbid but fascinating story of carnival heel Power entangled with mind-reading Blondell, blackmailing psychiatrist Walker, other assorted sideshow weirdos in highly original melodrama. Compelling look at carny life. Jules Furthman scripted, from William Lindsay Gresham's novel.

Nightmare Before Christmas, The (1993) **C-75m.** *** D: Henry Selick. Voices of Danny Elfman, Chris Sarandon, Catherine O'Hara, William Hickey, Glenn Shadix, Paul Reubens, Ken Page. Highly imaginative, stop-motion animation feature about Jack Skellington, the Pumpkin King, who tires of the old routine in Halloween Town and becomes enamored of Christmas instead—unaware that his brand of Grand Guignol and the wintry holiday don't really go together. Constantly surprising visuals and character delineation mesh with Danny Elfman's lively score (he also provides Jack's beautiful singing voice). Produced by Tim Burton, who concocted the story and many of the designs years earlier. [PG]▼●◗

Nightmare Castle (1966-Italian) **90m.** ** D: Allan Grunewald (Mario Caiano). Barbara Steele, Paul Mueller, Helga Line, Lawrence Clift. Typically atmospheric European horror film about doctor experimenting in regeneration of human blood through electrical impulses. Good photography.▼

Nightmare City SEE: **City of the Walking Dead**

Nightmare Honeymoon (1973) **C-115m.** ** D: Elliot Silverstein. Dack Rambo, Rebecca Dianna Smith, Pat Hingle, Bob Steele, David Huddleston, John Beck, Jeanette Nolan. Young couple suffers at the hands of rural killers and rapists; routine and unpleasant.

Nightmare in Blood (1976) **C-89m.** **½ D: John Stanley. Jerry Walter, Dan Caldwell, Barrie Youngfellow, Kathleen Quinlan, Kerwin Mathews. Horror film actor visiting fan convention turns out to be a real vampire after all; low-budget spoof made in San Francisco will appeal particularly to horror buffs for its many in-jokes. Techniscope. [R]▼

Nightmare in Chicago (1964) **C-80m. TVM** D: Robert Altman. Philip Abbott, Robert Ridgley, Ted Knight, Charles McGraw, John Alonzo, Barbara Turner. Psychotic killer, known to tri-state police via newspapers as Georgie Porgie, terrorizes Chicago area for 72 hours in mad murder spree. Totally location-shot, film does resemble nightmare. Interesting early credit for director Altman; expanded from a one-hour 1964 episode of *Kraft Suspense Theater*. Above average.

Nightmare Inn (1970-Spanish) **C-95m.** ** D: Eugenio Martin. Judy Geeson, Aurora Bautista, Esperanza Roy, Victor Alcazar, Lone Fleming. Geeson goes to small Spanish inn looking for relative who has disappeared, and confronts two mad sisters who run establishment; several murders follow. Passable thriller. Video title: IT HAPPENED AT NIGHTMARE INN.▼

Nightmare in the Sun (1964) **C-80m.** *½ D: Marc Lawrence. John Derek, Aldo Ray, Arthur O'Connell, Ursula Andress, Sammy Davis, Jr., Allyn Joslyn, Keenan Wynn. Turgid account of what happens when sexy Andress picks up hitchhiker Derek. Look for Richard Jaeckel and Robert Duvall as motorcyclists!▼

Nightmare in Wax (1969) **C-91m.** ** D: Bud Townsend. Cameron Mitchell, Anne Helm, Scott Brady, Berry Kroeger, Victoria Carroll. Paraphrase of HOUSE OF WAX has Mitchell as former movie makeup man whose wax museum is full of actors "missing" from the studio. [M]▼

Nightmare of Terror SEE: **Demons of the Mind**

Nightmare on Elm Street, A (1984) **C-92m.** **½ D: Wes Craven. John Saxon, Ronee Blakley, Heather Langenkamp, Amanda Wyss, Nick Corri, Johnny Depp, Charles Fleischer, Robert Englund. Several teenagers discover they're all having nightmares about the same character, scar-faced Fred Krueger—a kind of ghost who can enter their dreams at will, and kill them in macabre ways. It's up to surviving teen Nancy (Langenkamp) to try to stop him. Imaginative premise given routine treatment, but this box-office smash led to a handful of sequels and a TV series, *Freddy's Nightmares.* [R]▼●◗

Nightmare on Elm Street Part 2, A: Freddy's Revenge (1985) **C-84m.** ** D: Jack Sholder. Mark Patton, Kim Myers, Robert Rusler, Clu Gulager, Hope Lange, Marshall Bell, Sydney Walsh, Robert Englund. Reworking of first film's story (set five years later) has teenage boy plagued by dreams of demonic Freddy, who is intent on taking over both his mind *and* body . . . so he can kill all the neighborhood teens. Gruesome special effects dominate this slasher saga. [R]▼●

Nightmare on Elm Street 3, A: Dream Warriors (1987) **C-96m.** *** D: Chuck Russell. Heather Langenkamp, Patricia Arquette, Larry Fishburne, Priscilla Pointer, Craig Wasson, Robert Englund, Brooke Bundy, Rodney Eastman, John Saxon, Dick Cavett, Zsa Zsa Gabor. When troubled teens in a psychiatric hospital begin to be visited in their dreams by the chuckling, murderous shade of Freddy Krueger, Nancy (Langenkamp), the survivor of the first film and now a psychiatrist, helps another doctor and the frightened teens battle Freddy. Well written and imaginatively directed, this is the best of the Elm Street films, and boasts some of the most startling effects as well. [R]▼●

Nightmare on Elm Street 4, A: The Dream Master (1988) **C-92m.** ** D: Renny Harlin. Robert Englund, Rodney Eastman, Danny Hassel, Andras Jones, Tuesday Knight, Toy Newkirk, Ken Sagoes, Brooke Theiss, Lisa Wilcox, Brooke Bundy. Revived by flaming dog urine (!), Freddy Krueger finally kills all the children of those who originally burned him to death, and looks for new teens to terrorize, but he's opposed by a "dream master," his spiritual opposite. Series was showing its age by this point, with extravagant effects, a thin story, and far too many wisecracks. A 1989 sequel and TV series followed. [R]▼●

Nightmare on Elm Street, A: The Dream Child (1989) **C-89m.** *½ D: Stephen Hopkins. Robert Englund, Lisa Wilcox, Kelly Jo Minter, Erika Anderson, Whitby Hertford, Danny Hassel. Fifth and least in the NIGHTMARE series, with everyone except Englund just going through the paces. Here, scarred, dream-haunting Freddy Krueger (Englund) uses the unborn child of Wilcox to strike at her friends. As usual, special effects are a highlight but don't save the film from being a bore. [R]▼●

Nightmares (1983) **C-99m.** ** D: Joseph Sargent. Cristina Raines, Timothy James, William Sanderson, Emilio Estevez, Moon Zappa, Lance Henriksen, Robin Gammell, Richard Masur, Veronica Cartwright, Bridgette Andersen, Albert Hague. Four-part film (originally made for TV) with *Twilight Zone* aspirations but uninspired writing, and mostly predictable outcomes. Hasn't anyone read O. Henry lately? Themes range from a knife-wielding loony on the loose to a kid who becomes obsessed with beating a video arcade game. [R]▼◗

Night Monster (1942) **73m.** **½ D: Ford Beebe. Irene Hervey, Don Porter, Nils Asther, Lionel Atwill, Leif Erickson, Bela Lugosi, Ralph Morgan. Intriguing grade-B thriller about creepy figure stalking country estate, murdering doctors who are treating crippled Morgan.▼

'Night, Mother (1986) **C-96m.** ** D: Tom Moore. Sissy Spacek, Anne Bancroft. Unhappy young woman who lives with her mother decides to commit suicide; her mother spends the night trying to talk her out of it. Well acted, directed, and edited, but still just a photographed stage drama, missing the electricity of a live performance . . . and without the element of doubt about its conclusion that marked Marsha Norman's Pulitzer Prize-winning play. [PG-13]▼●

Night Moves (1975) **C-95m.** ***½ D: Arthur Penn. Gene Hackman, Jennifer Warren, Susan Clark, Edward Binns, Harris Yulin, Kenneth Mars, James Woods, Melanie Griffith, Dennis Dugan, Max Gail. L.A. detective Hackman puts aside his marital woes to track nymphet Griffith to Florida Keys. Complicated but underrated psychological suspenser by Alan Sharp leads to stunning climax. [R]▼●

Night Must Fall (1937) **117m.** *** D: Richard Thorpe. Robert Montgomery, Rosalind Russell, Dame May Whitty, Alan Marshal, Kathleen Harrison, E. E. Clive, Beryl Mercer. Famous film of Emlyn Williams' suspenseful play. Young woman (Russell) slowly learns identity of mysterious brutal killer terrorizing the countryside. Montgomery has showy role in sometimes stagy but generally effective film, with outstanding aid from Russell and Whitty. Screenplay by John Van Druten. Remade in 1964.▼

Night Must Fall (1964-British) **105m.** **½ D: Karel Reisz. Albert Finney, Susan Hampshire, Mona Washbourne, Sheila Hancock, Michael Medwin, Joe Gladwin, Martin Wyldeck. Cerebral attempt to match flair of original, this remake is too obvious and theatrical for any credibility. Reisz and Finney produced.

Night My Number Came Up, The (1955-British) **94m.** **** D: Leslie Norman. Michael Redgrave, Sheila Sim, Alexander Knox, Denholm Elliott, Ursula Jeans, Michael Hordern, George Rose, Alfie Bass. First-rate suspense film will have you holding your breath as it recounts tale of routine military flight, the fate of which may or may not depend on a prophetic dream. Screenplay by R. C. Sherriff, from an article by Victor Goddard.▼

Night Nurse (1931) **72m.** *** D: William Wellman. Barbara Stanwyck, Ben Lyon, Joan Blondell, Clark Gable, Charlotte Merriam, Charles Winninger. Excellent, hard-bitten tale of nurse (Stanwyck) who can't ignore strange goings-on in home where she works. Blondell adds zingy support; one of Gable's most impressive early appearances. Still potent today.▼●

Night of Adventure, A (1944) **65m.** **½ D: Gordon Douglas. Tom Conway, Audrey Long, Nancy Gates, Emory Parnell, Jean Brooks, Louis Borell, Edward Brophy, Addison Richards. Entertaining little drama with lawyer Conway attempting to exonerate bored wife Long's suitor on a murder rap, all the while avoiding scandal. A remake of HAT, COAT AND GLOVE.

Night of Dark Shadows (1971) **C-97m.** BOMB D: Dan Curtis. David Selby, Lara Parker, Kate Jackson, Grayson Hall, John Karlen, Nancy Barrett. Ripoff exploitation film bears little resemblance to popular TV serial in predictable yawner about ghosts and reincarnation in New England. Follow-up to HOUSE OF DARK SHADOWS lacks everything that made first one so good. [PG] ▼●

Night of January 16th, The (1941) **79m.** *½ D: William Clemens. Robert Preston,

Ellen Drew, Nils Asther, Donald Douglas, Rod Cameron, Alice White, Cecil Kellaway. Hit Broadway play receives lackluster screen treatment; a talky and uninspired whodunit.
Night of Love, A SEE: **Manifesto**
Night of Mystery (1937) **66m.** ** D: E. A. Dupont. Grant Richards, Roscoe Karns, Helen Burgess, Ruth Coleman, Elizabeth Patterson, Harvey Stephens, June Martel. Tedious remake of THE GREENE MURDER CASE (1929) with Richards no match for William Powell as detective Philo Vance.
Night of Terror (1933) **60m.** BOMB D: Ben Stoloff. Sally Blane, Wallace Ford, Tully Marshall, Bela Lugosi, George Meeker, Edwin Maxwell, Bryant Washburn. Empty, inept "B" chiller about ugly homicidal madman prowling the grounds of swanky estate. Top-billed Lugosi is wasted in nothing part as Hindu servant. Almost worth sitting through for really unbelievable ending.
Night of the Big Heat SEE: **Island of the Burning Doomed**
Night of the Blood Beast (1958) **65m.** *½ D: Bernard Kowalski. Michael Emmet, Angela Greene, John Baer, Ed Nelson, Tyler McVey. Astronaut returns from space apparently dead; when he awakens, he's found to have alien embryos within him—a pregnant man! The alien also turns up murderously. Well-directed but too low-budget to succeed.▼
Night of the Blood Monster (1970-Spanish-Italian-West German) **C-84m.** *½ D: Jess Frank (Jesus Franco). Christopher Lee, Maria Schell, Leo Genn, Maria Rohm, Margaret Lee. Lee is fine as Judge Jeffreys, a brutal magistrate presiding over "Bloody Assizes" after the Monmouth Rebellion against King James II, but movie itself is tedious and grisly. CinemaScope. [PG]
Night of the Claw SEE: **Island Claws**
Night of the Comet (1984) **C-94m.** **½ D: Thom Eberhardt. Catherine Mary Stewart, Kelli Maroney, Robert Beltran, Geoffrey Lewis, Mary Woronov, Sharon Farrell, Michael Bowen. World comes to an end, leaving only a couple of California valley girls behind! Smart satire, with clever and occasionally chilling moments, but plays all its cards too soon. [PG-13]▼
Night of the Cyclone (1990) **C-90m.** *½ D: David Irving. Kris Kristofferson, Jeff Meek, Marisa Berenson, Alla Kurot, Winston Ntshona, Dick Reineke, Marcel van Heerden, Gerrit Graham. Unimaginative, predictable thriller with some mildly unusual character relationships, about cop (Kristofferson) who goes to Caribbean island when his teenage daughter doesn't return from a modeling job. Plot takes odd turns, but they aren't *interesting* turns. Graham is billed as "Bud T. Chud." [R]▼●
Night of the Demon SEE: **Curse of the Demon**
Night of the Demons (1987) **C-89m.** *½ D: Kevin S. Tenney. Cathy Podewell, Alvin Alexis, William Gallo, Mimi Kinkade, Linnea Quigley, Lance Fenton. On Halloween night, wouldn't you know it, some Typical Teenagers pick the wrong possessed mortuary to party in. Everything about this amateurish movie is gratuitous, including the movie itself. Good makeup, though . . . especially the prosthetics on Quigley! Aka HALLOWEEN PARTY. Followed by two sequels. [R]▼●
Night of the Eagle SEE: **Burn, Witch, Burn!**
Night of the Following Day, The (1969) **C-93m.** **½ D: Hubert Cornfield. Marlon Brando, Richard Boone, Rita Moreno, Pamela Franklin, Jess Hahn, Gerard Buhr. Good cast makes this sordid tale of young girl's kidnapping somewhat more interesting than it should be; pretty rough in spots. Filmed in France. [R]▼
Night of the Fox (1990-U.S.-British-French-German) **C-200m. TVM** D: Charles Jarrott. George Peppard, Deborah Raffin, Michael York, David Birney, John Mills, John Standing, Amadeus August, Andrea Occhipinti, Andrea Ferreol. Bloated WW2 espionage tale based on Jack Higgins' novel about behind-the-German-lines attempt to rescue an American flyer who's carrying plans of the D-Day invasion. Complications arise when a Rommel-lookalike enters the picture. Look quickly for legendary chanteuse Patachou and Juliet Mills in cameos. Originally shown in two parts. Cut to 95m. for video release. Average.▼
Night of the Generals (1967-British) **C-148m.** *½ D: Anatole Litvak. Peter O'Toole, Omar Sharif, Tom Courtenay, Donald Pleasence, Joanna Pettet, Christopher Plummer, John Gregson, Philippe Noiret. A WW2 whodunit, film has potential but gets lost in murky script, lifeless performances. A dud. Panavision. ▼●
Night of the Ghouls SEE: **Revenge of the Dead**
Night of the Grizzly, The (1966) **C-102m.** **½ D: Joseph Pevney. Clint Walker, Martha Hyer, Keenan Wynn, Nancy Kulp, Ron Ely, Regis Toomey, Jack Elam. Acceptable Western of rancher Walker overcoming all obstacles, even a persistent vicious bear, to Western life. Techniscope.▼
Night of the Hunter, The (1955) **93m.** ***½ D: Charles Laughton. Robert Mitchum, Shelley Winters, Lillian Gish, Evelyn Varden, Peter Graves, James Gleason, Billy Chapin, Sally Jane Bruce. Atmospheric allegory of innocence, evil and hypocrisy, with psychotic religious fanatic Mitchum chasing homeless children for money stolen by their father. Mitchum is marvelously menacing, matched by Gish

as wise matron who takes in the kids. Starkly directed by Laughton; his only film behind the camera. Screenplay by James Agee, from the Davis Grubb novel. Remade as a TVM in 1991 with Richard Chamberlain.▼●◗

Night of the Iguana, The (1964) **118m.** *** D: John Huston. Richard Burton, Deborah Kerr, Ava Gardner, Sue Lyon, Skip Ward, Grayson Hall, Cyril Delevanti. Plodding tale based on Tennessee Williams play; alcoholic former clergyman Burton, a bus-tour guide in Mexico, is involved with Kerr, Gardner, and Lyon. Dorothy Jeakins won an Oscar for her costumes. Also shown in computer-colored version. ▼●

Night of the Juggler (1980) **C-101m.** *½ D: Robert Butler. James Brolin, Cliff Gorman, Richard Castellano, Abby Bluestone, Linda G. Miller, Julie Carmen, Barton Heyman, Mandy Patinkin. A sickie mistakenly kidnaps the daughter of an ex-cop (Brolin), who then leads a city-wide rampage to get her back. Fast-paced but wildly implausible movie paints a notably ugly portrait of N.Y.C. and its people. [R]▼

Night of the Laughing Dead SEE: **Crazy House** (1975)

Night of the Lepus (1972) **C-88m.** *½ D: William F. Claxton. Stuart Whitman, Janet Leigh, Rory Calhoun, DeForest Kelley, Paul Fix, Melanie Fullerton. Rabbits weighing 150 pounds and standing four feet high terrorize the countryside; National Guard, not Elmer Fudd, comes to the rescue. [PG]

Night of the Living Dead (1968) **96m.** ***½ D: George A. Romero. Duane Jones, Judith O'Dea, Russell Streiner, Karl Hardman, Keith Wayne. Romero's first feature is the touchstone modern horror film: seven people barricade themselves inside a farmhouse while an army of flesh-eating zombies roams the countryside. Once considered the *ne plus ultra* of gore, film is less stomach-churning by today's standards, yet its essential power to chill remains undiminished despite scores of imitations. Shoestring production values merely add to authentic feel. Don't watch this alone! Remade in 1990. Sequel: DAWN OF THE DEAD. Also shown in computer-colored version.▼●◗

Night of the Living Dead (1990) **C-96m.** ** D: Tom Savini. Tony Todd, Patricia Tallman, Tom Towles, McKee Anderson, William Butler, Katie Finnerman. Until near the end, this is a scene-for-scene remake of the disturbing original; it's in color, with a tougher heroine and more potent violence, but it has almost none of the impact of the first version. Makeup expert Savini's direction can't overcome the extreme familiarity of the material. Romero scripted, none too well. [R]▼●◗

Night of the Quarter Moon (1959) **96m.** *½ D: Hugo Haas. Julie London, John Drew Barrymore, Nat King Cole, Dean Jones, James Edwards, Anna Kashfi, Agnes Moorehead, Jackie Coogan. Trite handling of miscegenation theme; good cast wasted. Retitled: FLESH AND FLAME. CinemaScope.

Night of the Shooting Stars, The (1982-Italian) **C-106m.** ***½ D: Paolo and Vittorio Taviani. Omero Antonutti, Margarita Lozano, Claudio Bigagil, Massimo Bonetti, Norma Martel. Extraordinarily touching, involving, richly textured drama of a group of Tuscan villagers during WW2, in final days before liberation by Americans. With simple, lyrical images, the filmmakers unravel this life-affirming story of war's absurdities—and hope, survival. [R]▼

Night on Earth (1991) **C-125m.** *** D: Jim Jarmusch. Winona Ryder, Gena Rowlands, Giancarlo Esposito, Armin Mueller-Stahl, Rosie Perez, Isaach De Bankolé, Beatrice Dalle, Roberto Benigni, Paolo Bonacelli, Matti Pellonpaa. Exhilirating five-part slice-of-life, each story unraveling at the same time in L.A., N.Y.C., Paris, Rome, and Helsinki. All are set in taxis, and spotlight brief but eloquent encounters between cab driver and passenger. The best of many highlights: the scene in which black Brooklynite Esposito and East German refugee Mueller-Stahl reveal to each other their names. Jarmusch's most fully developed feature to date. [R]▼●

Night Passage (1957) **C-90m.** *** D: James Neilson. James Stewart, Audie Murphy, Dan Duryea, Brandon de Wilde, Dianne Foster. Soundly handled Western of Stewart working for railroad and brother Murphy belonging to gang planning to rob train payroll; exciting climactic shoot-out. Technirama.

Night Patrol (1985) **C-82m.** BOMB D: Jackie Kong. Linda Blair, Pat Paulsen, Jaye P. Morgan, Jack Riley, Billy Barty, Murray Langston, Pat Morita, Andrew (Dice) Clay. Threadbare rip-off of POLICE ACADEMY combines Barty's flatulence with crude one-liners you simply won't believe. See if you can figure out why the opening sequence has subtitles. [R]▼●

Night People (1954) **C-93m.** *** D: Nunnally Johnson. Gregory Peck, Broderick Crawford, Anita Bjork, Rita Gam, Walter Abel, Buddy Ebsen. Sensibly told, intertwining plots of Cold War espionage; filmed on location in Berlin. CinemaScope.

Night Plane From Chungking (1943) **69m.** **½ D: Ralph Murphy. Ellen Drew, Robert Preston, Otto Kruger, Steven Geray, (Victor) Sen Yung, Tamara Geva, Soo Yong. Adequate adventure yarn about a plane shot down in the jungle, with captain Preston falling for Drew while going up against the Japanese.

Night Porter, The (1974-Italian) **C-115m.**

** D: Liliana Cavani. Dirk Bogarde, Charlotte Rampling, Philippe Leroy, Gabriele Ferzetti, Isa Miranda. Sleazy, bizarre drama, set in 1957, about a sado-masochistic relationship between an ex-Nazi and the woman he used to abuse sexually in a concentration camp. [R]▼●◗

Night Runner, The (1957) **79m.** ** D: Abner Biberman. Ray Danton, Colleen Miller, Merry Anders, Eddy Waller. Violent B film of insane Danton on killing spree, about to gun down his girlfriend.

Night School (1981) **C-88m.** BOMB D: Ken Hughes. Leonard Mann, Rachel Ward, Drew Snyder, Joseph R. Sicari. Female students attending title place of learning are being decapitated. Not as graphically bloody as others of its genre, but still pretty bad. Ward's feature debut. [R]▼

Night Shadows (1984) **C-99m.** ** D: John (Bud) Cardos. Wings Hauser, Bo Hopkins, Lee Montgomery, Jennifer Warren, Jody Medford, Cary Guffey. Yet another tale of toxic waste creating monsters that terrorize small Southern town. Same old stuff, with inferior special effects and makeup. [R]

Night Shift (1982) **C-105m.** *** D: Ron Howard. Henry Winkler, Michael Keaton, Shelley Long, Gina Hecht, Pat Corley, Bobby DiCicco, Nita Talbot, Richard Belzer, Charles Fleischer, Shannen Doherty. A nebbish takes a night job at the city morgue, seeking peace and quiet, but his new assistant draws him into wild scheme to start a prostitution business! Delightful, good-natured comedy (despite seamy subject matter) written with verve by Lowell Ganz and Babaloo Mandel. (Soundtrack features Rod Stewart singing "That's What Friends Are For," years before it became a hit.) Winkler has never been better; Keaton's smash debut performance made him an instant star. Is this a great country or what? Look for Kevin Costner as an extra. [R]▼●◗

Nights of Cabiria (1957-Italian) **117m.** **** D: Federico Fellini. Giulietta Masina, Francois Perier, Amedeo Nazzari, Franca Marzi, Dorian Gray. Masina is a joy as waifish prostitute dreaming of rich, wonderful life but always finding sorrow. Basis for Broadway musical and film SWEET CHARITY. One of Fellini's best, and a most deserving Oscar winner as Best Foreign Film. Restored in 1998 to put back a 7m. sequence Fellini was forced to cut after the premiere.▼◗

Nights of Rasputin (1960-French-Italian) **87m.** ** D: Pierre Chenal. Edmund Purdom, Gianna Maria Canale, John Drew Barrymore, Jany Clair. Purdom is miscast as Rasputin in this plodding biography of the conniving, libidinous hypnotist who gained influence in Czarina Alexandria's court prior to WW1. European version runs 93m., and is in color. Aka THE NIGHT THEY KILLED RASPUTIN.▼

Night Song (1947) **101m.** ** D: John Cromwell. Dana Andrews, Merle Oberon, Ethel Barrymore, Hoagy Carmichael, Jacqueline White. Overlong, soapy drama of socialite Oberon falling in love with blind pianist Andrews. Barrymore is very good in the unusual role of comic relief. Artur Rubinstein and conductor Eugene Ormandy appear in the climactic concert sequence, playing the concerto composed especially for the film by Leith Stevens.

Night Stalker, The (1971) **C-73m. TVM** D: John Llewellyn Moxey. Darren McGavin, Carol Lynley, Simon Oakland, Ralph Meeker, Claude Akins, Kent Smith, Barry Atwater. Wise-guy reporter assigned to series of strange murders in Las Vegas. Near-brilliant mixture of double-edged horror, comedy; well-constructed script by Richard Matheson. Kudos to flawless cast. Sequel: THE NIGHT STRANGLER. Later a TV series. Above average.▼●◗

Night Stalker, The (1987) **C-89m.** ** D: Max Kleven. Charles Napier, Michelle Reese, Katherine Kelly Lang, Robert Viharo, Robert Zdar, Joey Gian, Leila Carlin, Gary Crosby, James Louis Watkins, Ola Ray, Tally Chanel, Joan Chen. Napier steps out impressively from supporting roles to star as a down and out L.A. cop who goes after a serial killer preying on prostitutes. Standard B-movie was made in 1985. [R]▼

Night Star Goddess of Electra SEE: **War of the Zombies**

Night Strangler, The (1972) **C-74m. TVM** D: Dan Curtis. Darren McGavin, Simon Oakland, Jo Ann Pflug, Richard Anderson, John Carradine, Margaret Hamilton, Wally Cox. Sequel to THE NIGHT STALKER finds McGavin eking out living in Seattle; he latches onto series of murders involving blood drainage by syringe, discovers secret underground city and lone "resident." Above average.▼●◗

Night Sun (1990-Italian-French-German) **C-112m.** *** D: Paolo and Vittorio Taviani. Julian Sands, Charlotte Gainsbourg, Nastassja Kinski, Massimo Bonetti, Margarita Lozano, Rudiger Vogler. Evocative film about an idealistic, sensitive young man (Sands), who wishes to find inner peace in a world of temptation. Based on the Tolstoi story "Father Sergius"; Sands' voice is dubbed into Italian by Giancarlo Giannini. Technovision.▼

Night the Lights Went Out in Georgia, The (1981) **C-120m.** **½ D: Ronald F. Maxwell. Kristy McNichol, Mark Hamill, Dennis Quaid, Sunny Johnson, Don Stroud, Arlen Dean Snyder. Kristy, the more ambitious half of brother-sister country music duo, tries in vain to keep sibling Quaid out of romantic scrapes. Poor beginning and conclusion somewhat redeemed by rather appealing middle. Inspired by title-named hit record. [PG]▼

Night the World Exploded, The (1957) **64m.** ** D: Fred F. Sears. Kathryn Grant, William Leslie, Tris Coffin, Raymond Greenleaf, Marshall Reed. Scientists discover a strange, exploding mineral that threatens to bring about title catastrophe and rush to prevent it. OK idea hampered by low budget.

Night They Killed Rasputin, The SEE: **Nights of Rasputin**

Night They Raided Minsky's, The (1968) **C-99m.** *** D: William Friedkin. Jason Robards, Britt Ekland, Norman Wisdom, Forrest Tucker, Harry Andrews, Joseph Wiseman, Denholm Elliott, Elliott Gould, Jack Burns, Bert Lahr, narrated by Rudy Vallee. Flavorful period-piece about Amish girl (Ekland) who comes to N.Y.C., gets involved with burlesque comic Robards and accidentally invents the striptease. Many nice backstage and onstage moments. Abruptness of Lahr's role is due to his death during filming. Produced and cowritten by Norman Lear. [M/PG]▼

Night Tide (1963) **84m.** **½ D: Curtis Harrington. Dennis Hopper, Linda Lawson, Gavin Muir, Luana Anders, Marjorie Eaton, Tom Dillon, H. E. West, Cameron. Lonely sailor Hopper falls for Lawson, who works as a mermaid at the Santa Monica pier, but learns she may be a killer—and a descendant of the sirens. Odd, dreamy little drama is strangely compelling, though not a horror film, as often promoted. Written by the director.▼●

Night to Remember, A (1943) **91m.** ***½ D: Richard Wallace. Loretta Young, Brian Aherne, Jeff Donnell, William Wright, Sidney Toler, Gale Sondergaard, Donald MacBride, Blanche Yurka. Sparkling comedy-mystery of whodunit author Aherne and wife Young trying to solve murder.▼●

Night to Remember, A (1958-British) **123m.** **** D: Roy (Ward) Baker. Kenneth More, David McCallum, Jill Dixon, Laurence Naismith, Frank Lawton, Honor Blackman, Alec McCowen, George Rose. Meticulously produced documentary-style account of sinking of the "unsinkable" passenger liner *Titanic*. Superb combination of disaster spectacle and emotional byplay; a notable contrast to Hollywood's *Titanic* films. Vivid adaptation by Eric Ambler of Walter Lord's book. ▼●◗

Night Train (1940) SEE: **Night Train to Munich**

Night Train (1959-Polish) **90m.** ** D: Jerzy Kawalerowicz. Lucyna Winnicka, Leon Niemczyk, Teresa Szmigielowna, Zbigniew Cybulski. Murky account of young woman on a train, forced to share compartment with a doctor; their lack of communication and presence of killer on train are film's focal points.

Night Train to Munich (1940-British) **93m.** *** D: Carol Reed. Rex Harrison, Margaret Lockwood, Paul Von Hernried (Henreid), Basil Radford, Naunton Wayne, Felix Aylmer, Roland Culver. Expert Hitchcockian thriller about British intelligence agent Harrison trying to rescue Czech scientist who escaped from the Nazis to London only to be kidnapped back to Berlin. Stylishly photographed (by Otto Kanturek), sharply scripted by Frank Launder and Sidney Gilliat, who also wrote Hitchcock's THE LADY VANISHES (which introduced the comic characters reprised here by Radford and Wayne). Based on Gordon Wellesley's novel *Report on a Fugitive*. Originally released in U.S. as NIGHT TRAIN.▼●

Night Train to Venice (1995-German) **C-98m.** BOMB D: Carlo U. Quinterio. Hugh Grant, Tahnee Welch, Malcolm McDowell, Kristina Soderbaum, Rachel Rice. Upon completing a book on neo-Nazis, writer Grant travels to Venice to meet with a publisher—and is followed (and menaced) by skinheads. If you're looking for a boyishly charming Grant, look elsewhere; he's a dull dolt in this trashy film, made in 1993 and passed over for theatrical release. [R]▼●

Night Unto Night (1949) **85m.** ** D: Don Siegel. Ronald Reagan, Viveca Lindfors, Broderick Crawford, Rosemary DeCamp, Osa Massen, Art Baker, Craig Stevens. Somber, unconvincing film about relationship of dying scientist and mentally disturbed widow. Finished in 1947 and shelved for two years. Reagan's performance isn't bad, but script is against him.

Night Visitor, The (1970) **C-106m.** **½ D: Laslo Benedek. Max von Sydow, Liv Ullmann, Trevor Howard, Per Oscarsson, Rupert Davies, Andrew Keir. An inmate plots to escape from an asylum for the criminally insane for one night, to avenge himself on people who put him away. Heavy in detail, but interesting. Filmed in Denmark and Sweden. [PG] ▼◗

Night Visitor (1990) **C-94m.** ** D: Rupert Hitzig. Derek Rydall, Allen Garfield, Teresa Vander Woude, Elliott Gould, Michael J. Pollard, Brooke Bundy, Richard Roundtree, Shannon Tweed. Teenage Rydall discovers his most hated teacher (Garfield) is a Satanist and serial killer of prostitutes; when no one believes him, he turns to retired cop Gould for help. Silly, unconvincing blend of teenage comedy and thriller, helped by good performances. [R]▼

Night Walker, The (1964) **86m.** *** D: William Castle. Barbara Stanwyck, Robert Taylor, Lloyd Bochner, Rochelle Hudson, Judi Meredith, Hayden Rorke. One of the better Castle horror films has Stanwyck as wealthy widow discovering cause of recurring dreams about lost husband. Effective psychological thriller with good cast, unusual script by Robert Bloch.▼

Night Warning (1982) **C-94m.** **½ D: William Asher. Jimmy McNichol, Susan Tyrrell, Bo Svenson, Marcia Lewis, Julia Duffy. Explosive, tour-de-force acting by Tyrrell distinguishes this formula horror film. She's a sexually repressed aunt, overly protective of her nephew McNichol, who finally turns to murder. [R]▼

Night Watch (1973-British) **C-105m.** **½ D: Brian G. Hutton. Elizabeth Taylor, Laurence Harvey, Billie Whitelaw, Robert Lang, Tony Britton. Woman (Taylor) believes she has witnessed a murder, but cannot prove it. Tired plot based on Lucille Fletcher play. [PG]▼

Nightwatch (1998) **C-101m.** **½ D: Ole Bornedal. Nick Nolte, Patricia Arquette, Ewan McGregor, Josh Brolin, Lauren Graham, Alix Koromzay, Lonny Chapman, John C. Reilly, Brad Dourif. McGregor hires on as a part-time night watchman in spooky morgue, while a serial killer is on a city-wide rampage. Arquette is his girlfriend, Brolin his daredevil buddy, and Nolte the police inspector on the case. Remake of writer-director Bornedal's own 1995 Danish hit, NATTEVAGTEN, is stylishly creepy, but weighs down in the final third. And remember: Don't let that door close. Super 35. [R]▼●◗

Night We Never Met, The (1993) **C-99m.** ** D: Warren Light. Matthew Broderick, Annabella Sciorra, Kevin Anderson, Louise Lasser, Jeanne Tripplehorn, Justine Bateman, Michael Mantell, Christine Baranski, Doris Roberts, Dominic Chianese, Garry Shandling, Ranjit Chowdhry, Katharine Houghton, Tim Guinee. Disappointing romantic comedy in which about-to-be-married yuppie Anderson time-shares his rent-controlled N.Y.C. apartment with Broderick and Sciorra; all are strangers, and use the pad on alternate days. [R]▼●

Nightwing (1979) **C-105m.** *½ D: Arthur Hiller. Nick Mancuso, David Warner, Kathryn Harrold, Stephen Macht, Strother Martin, Pat Corley. Warner is an oddball who comes to Arizona to kill vampire bats in their caves. Well . . . it's a living. From a Martin Cruz Smith novel. [PG]▼●

Night Without Sleep (1952) **77m.** ** D: Roy Baker. Linda Darnell, Gary Merrill, Hildegarde Neff, Hugh Beaumont, Mae Marsh. Pat treatment of man thinking he's committed murder.

Night Without Stars (1951-British) **86m.** **½ D: Anthony Pelissier. David Farrar, Nadia Gray, Maurice Teynac, June Clyde, Gerard Landry. Adequate mystery with partially blind lawyer Farrar becoming involved with Gray, and a murder.

Night World (1932) **56m.** *** D: Hobart Henley. Lew Ayres, Mae Clarke, Boris Karloff, Dorothy Revier, Russell Hopton, Clarence Muse, Hedda Hopper, Bert Roach, George Raft. Outrageous little pre-Code item about the various goings on in a Prohibition-era nightclub. Karloff is its corrupt owner; Ayres a troubled young man whose mother has murdered his father; Clarke a wiscracking chorus girl; Muse a philosophical doorman; Raft (in a small role) a Broadway tinhorn. Add to this some vintage Busby Berkeley choreography . . . and the result is a real curio.

Night Zoo (1987-Canadian) **C-115m.** ** D: Jean-Claude Lauzon. Roger Le Bel, Gilles Maheu, Lyne Adams, Lorne Brass, Germain Houde. French-Canadian melodrama, wildly overrated on its home turf, unconvincingly mixes a moving story of love between ex-con Maheu and his father with a brutal tale of sex and drugs. Title refers to a ludicrous climax at the local zoo. Graphic sex scenes almost reduce this one to exploitation film level.▼●

Nijinsky (1980-British) **C-125m.** **½ D: Herbert Ross. Alan Bates, George De La Pena, Leslie Browne, Ronald Pickup, Alan Badel, Colin Blakely, Ronald Lacey, Carla Fracci, Jeremy Irons, Janet Suzman, Sian Phillips. Handsome but disappointing chronicle of the homosexual relationship between the legendary dancer Nijinsky (De La Pena) and Ballet Russe impresario Sergei Diaghilev (Bates). Worthy subject matter defeated by soap-opera scenario, allegedly inauthentic characterizations. Fine performance by Bates, superb one by Badel as a wealthy patron. Irons' film debut. [R]▼

Nikki, Wild Dog of the North (1961) **C-74m.** *** D: Jack Couffer, Don Haldane. Jean Coutu, Emile Genest, Uriel Luft, Robert Rivard. Wolfdog Nikki is separated from his master, a Canadian trapper, and fends for himself in a variety of adventures. Exciting Disney film.▼◗

Nil by Mouth (1997-British) **C-128m.** *** D: Gary Oldman. Ray Winstone, Kathy Burke, Charlie Creed-Miles, Laila Morse, Edna Dore, Chrissie Coterill, Jon Morrison. First-time director Oldman also scripted this gritty, in-your-face, cinéma vérité–style portrait of a desperate, dysfunctional family in working-class South London, focusing on an unhappily married couple (Winstone, Burke). Often difficult to watch with its unrelenting rage, despair, and (domestic) violence, but it's heartfelt and well acted (particularly by Burke). [R]▼

Nina Takes a Lover (1994) **C-100m.** ** D: Alan Jacobs. Laura San Giacomo, Paul Rhys, Michael O'Keefe, Cristi Conaway, Fisher Stevens. Nina's husband is out of town for a few weeks, and on the spur of the moment she takes a lover—a Welsh artist. If this is what "woman's pictures" have come to in the 90s, heaven help the genre. Stevens steals every scene he's in—and gives the film its only injection of life—as Nina's friend's lover. [R] ▼●

Nine ½ Weeks (1986) **C-113m.** *½ D: Adrian Lyne. Mickey Rourke, Kim Basinger, Margaret Whitton, David Margulies, Christine Baranski, Dwight Weist, Roderick Cook. Saga of an obsessive sexual relationship; uninvolving and unerotic, not to mention degrading. Promises sexual fireworks, but all it delivers is a big tease (some explicit material was cut prior to release). Video version is more explicit, though not so much as European version. Followed in 1997 by a direct-to-video sequel, ANOTHER 9½ WEEKS. [R] ▼●◗

Nine Girls (1944) **78m.** **½ D: Leigh Jason. Ann Harding, Evelyn Keyes, Jinx Falkenburg, Anita Louise, Jeff Donnell, Nina Foch, Marcia Mae Jones, Leslie Brooks, Lynn Merrick, Shirley Mills, William Demarest. Wisecrack-laden comedy mystery about murder at a sorority house.

Nine Hours to Rama (1963) **C-125m.** **½ D: Mark Robson. Horst Buchholz, Jose Ferrer, Robert Morley, Diane Baker, Harry Andrews. Ambitious attempt to make meaningful story of events leading up to assassination of Mahatma Gandhi; bogs down in trite script. Filmed on location in India. CinemaScope.

Nine Lives Are Not Enough (1941) **63m.** **½ D: A. Edward Sutherland. Ronald Reagan, Joan Perry, James Gleason, Peter Whitney, Faye Emerson, Howard da Silva. Reagan is an aggressive newspaperman who solves a murder case. Enjoyable, fast-paced Warner Bros. B entry.

Nine Lives of Fritz the Cat, The (1974) **C-76m.** **½ D: Robert Taylor. Voices of Skip Hinnant, Reva Rose, Bob Holt, Robert Ridgely, Pat Harrington. Animated sequel to X-rated original finds Fritz in the 70s, now on welfare with a nagging wife. He smokes pot for escape, and imagines himself in eight other lives—including being an astronaut, as an orderly to Adolf Hitler, and an aide to President Kissinger(!). Not as bold (or as memorable) as the first film, but certainly lively, with some funny moments. [R]

Nine Months (1995) **C-103m.** ** D: Chris Columbus. Hugh Grant, Julianne Moore, Jeff Goldblum, Tom Arnold, Joan Cusack, Robin Williams, Ashley Johnson, Emily Yancy, Kristin Davis. Farcical tale of a couple whose blissful five-year relationship is blindsided by unexpected pregnancy: He simply can't deal with it. Slick Hollywood concoction tries to coast on Grant's boyish charm and Moore's radiant beauty, with Arnold adding bombastic comedy relief. But utter predictability and oafish silliness drain it dry. Williams' pair of scenes as a nervous, malaprop-spouting Russian obstetrician are definite high point. Based on popular 1994 French movie, NEUF MOIS. Panavision. [PG-13]▼●

976-Evil (1989) **C-89m.** **½ D: Robert Englund. Stephen Geoffreys, Patrick O'Bryan, Sandy Dennis, Jim Metzler, Maria Rubell, Robert Picardo, Lezlie Deane, J.J. Cohen, Darren Burrows. Snappy CARRIE-like outsider's-revenge horror flick. Introverted teenager Geoffreys calls 976 number that provides him with satanic powers. Story is confusing, and script too jokey, but as often as not, it delivers the goods. Director Englund is Freddy Krueger in the NIGHTMARE ON ELM STREET series. [R]▼●

1918 (1984) **C-94m.** **½ D: Ken Harrison. William Converse-Roberts, Hallie Foote, Matthew Broderick, Rochelle Oliver, Michael Higgins, Jeannie McCarthy, Bill McGhee, Horton Foote, Jr. Stagy, PBSy Horton Foote drama concerns the catastrophic late teens influenza epidemic that hit America—and its tragic effect on a small Texas town. Will probably be seen to best advantage on the small screen; Hallie Foote (the playwright's daughter) is excellent as a woman (based on her own real-life grandmother) whose husband and infant are both stricken. Produced for *American Playhouse*; followed by prequels ON VALENTINE'S DAY and CONVICTS. 1918 and ON VALENTINE'S DAY were telecast as STORY OF A MARRIAGE.▼

1984 (1956-British) **91m.** *** D: Michael Anderson. Edmond O'Brien, Michael Redgrave, Jan Sterling, David Kossoff, Mervyn Johns, Donald Pleasence. Thought-provoking version of George Orwell's futuristic novel. Lovers O'Brien and Sterling trapped in all-powerful state, try valiantly to rebel against "Big Brother." Remade in 1984.

Nineteen Eighty-Four (1984-British) **C-115m.** *** D: Michael Radford. John Hurt, Richard Burton, Suzanna Hamilton, Cyril Cusack, Gregor Fisher, James Walker, Phyllis Logan. Appropriately grim, well-cast version of the Orwell classic, with Hurt as the government functionary who illegally falls in love, Hamilton as his bedmate, and Burton—excellent in his final feature—as the party official who somehow seems human even when feeding his victims' faces to the rats. Superior to the 1956 version, though the oppressive gloominess of the second half does wear you down. Seedily impressive production design. [R] ▼●

1941 (1979) **C-118m.** **½ D: Steven Spielberg. Dan Aykroyd, Ned Beatty, John Belushi, Treat Williams, Nancy Allen, Robert Stack, Tim Matheson, Toshiro Mifune, Christopher Lee, Warren Oates, Bobby DiCicco, Dianne Kay, Murray Hamilton, Lorraine Gary, Slim Pickens, Eddie Deezen, John Candy, many others. Gargantuan comedy from the bigger-is-funnier school of filmmaking. Some excellent vignettes and dazzling special effects in freewheeling story of war panic in L.A. following Pearl Harbor attack, but on the whole suffers from overkill. Written by Bob Gale and Robert Zemeckis. 26m. of footage added for network TV and special laserdisc editon. Panavision. [PG]▼●◗

1900 (1977-Italian-French-German) **C-311m.** ***½ D: Bernardo Bertolucci. Robert De Niro, Gerard Depardieu, Donald Sutherland, Burt Lancaster, Dominique Sanda, Stefania Sandrelli, Sterling Hayden. Sweeping spectacle of 20th-century Italy focusing on two contrasting families. Ambitious, powerful film was a glorious mess when released here at 243 min.; 1991 restoration *still* seems choppy, but potent, beautiful images compensate for eventually oppressive length. [NC-17—edited from original R rating]▼●

Nineteen Nineteen (1985-British) **C/B&W-99m.** ** D: Hugh Brody. Paul Scofield, Maria Schell, Frank Finlay, Diana Quick, Clare Higgins, Colin Firth. Scofield and Schell are former patients of Sigmund Freud, who come together years later to reminisce and remember. Slow and boring, wasting talents of a fine cast.

1990: The Bronx Warriors (1983-Italian) **C-84m.** BOMB D: Enzo G. Castellari. Vic Morrow, Christopher Connelly, Fred Williamson, Mark Gregory, Stefania Girolami. Bronx gang leaders vs. nasty corporation agent Morrow. Gregory plays a character named Trash, which is the best way to describe this movie. Filmed in the Bronx and Rome. Sequel: ESCAPE FROM THE BRONX. Panavision. [R]▼

1969 (1988) **C-93m.** ** D: Ernest Thompson. Robert Downey, Jr., Kiefer Sutherland, Bruce Dern, Mariette Hartley, Joanna Cassidy, Winona Ryder. Sutherland is terrific as a sensitive antiwar youth, and Hartley fine as his understanding mother, in this story of troubled times and troubled lives. But playwright Thompson's earnest directorial debut is disconnected and ultimately disappointing. [R] ▼●

Nine to Five (1980) **C-110m.** **½ D: Colin Higgins. Jane Fonda, Lily Tomlin, Dolly Parton, Dabney Coleman, Sterling Hayden, Elizabeth Wilson, Henry Jones, Lawrence Pressman, Marian Mercer. Three savvy secretaries have to contend with a doltish boss—and inadvertently find their chance to take revenge. The first half of this comedy is dynamite, culminating in Tomlin's Disneyesque fantasy of murdering the slavedriver, but film takes a disastrous turn, losing its bearings and momentum. Appealing performances by the star trio help make up for the ultimate silliness. Parton's first film. Later a TV series. [PG]▼●

Ninety Degrees in the Shade (1964-Czech) **90m.** **½ D: Jiri Weiss. Anne Heywood, James Booth, Donald Wolfit, Ann Todd. Turgid account of Heywood, who works in food store, accused of theft; intertwined with passionate love episodes. Czech-made, with British stars. CinemaScope.

99 and 44/100% Dead (1974) **C-98m.** BOMB D: John Frankenheimer. Richard Harris, Chuck Connors, Edmond O'Brien, Bradford Dillman, Ann Turkel. Idiotic, poorly made gangster melodrama with satirical overtones: hit-man Harris is hired by mobster O'Brien to knock off rival Dillman. The pits. Panavision. [PG]▼

99 River Street (1953) **83m.** *** D: Phil Karlson. John Payne, Evelyn Keyes, Brad Dexter, Peggie Castle, Ian Wolfe, Frank Faylen. Rugged crime caper with Payne caught up in tawdry surroundings, trying to prove himself innocent of murder charge. Unpretentious film really packs a punch.

99 Women (1969-Spanish-German-British-Italian) **C-90m.** *½ D: Jess Franco. Maria Schell, Luciana Paluzzi, Mercedes McCambridge, Herbert Lom. Absurd drama about lesbianism in women's prison may have some scenes cut for some TV stations, unless film puts the censors to sleep. Also known as ISLE OF LOST WOMEN. SuperScope. [R]▼

92 in the Shade (1975) **C-93m.** *** D: Thomas McGuane. Peter Fonda, Warren Oates, Margot Kidder, Burgess Meredith, Harry Dean Stanton, Sylvia Miles, Elizabeth Ashley, William Hickey, Louise Latham. National Book Award-nominated novel about rival fishing boat captains in Florida Keys; directed by the author. Wildly uneven but well cast and frequently hilarious. [R]▼

Ninja III—The Domination (1984) **C-95m.** **½ D: Sam Firstenberg. Lucinda Dickey, Jordan Bennett, Sho Kosugi, David Chung. Follow-up to REVENGE OF THE NINJA about an evil Ninja, "killed" by the police, who forces his spirit on innocent Dickey. Lots of action; good of its type. [R]▼

Ninotchka (1939) **110m.** ***½ D: Ernst Lubitsch. Greta Garbo, Melvyn Douglas, Ina Claire, Bela Lugosi, Sig Ruman, Felix Bressart, Alexander Granach, Richard Carle. Amid much outdated sociological banter, a lighthearted Garbo still shines. Lubitsch's comedy pegged on tale of cold Russian agent Garbo coming to Paris, falling in love with gay-blade Douglas. Supporting cast shows fine comedy flair. Script by Billy Wilder, Charles Brackett, and Walter Reisch was basis for Broadway musical and film SILK STOCKINGS.▼●

Ninth Configuration, The (1980) **C-118m.** ***½ D: William Peter Blatty. Stacy Keach, Scott Wilson, Jason Miller, Ed Flanders, Neville Brand, Moses Gunn, George Di Cenzo, Robert Loggia, Tom Atkins, Alejandro Rey, Joe Spinell, Steve Sandor. In old castle used by U.S. government as asylum, new head shrink Keach quickly proves to be nuttier than any of the patients. Hilarious yet thought-provoking, with endlessly quotable dialogue and an amazing barroom fight scene. Blatty also produced and adapted his novel *Twinkle, Twinkle, Killer Kane* (this film's title at one point). Myriad versions run anywhere from 99m. to 140m.; above time is Blatty's cut, and rating applies to this version only. Panavision. [R]▼●

Ninth Gate, The (1999-French-Spanish-U.S.) **C-133m.** ** D: Roman Polanski. Johnny Depp, Frank Langella, Lena Olin, Emmanuelle Seigner, Barbara Jefford, Jack Taylor, José Lopez Rodero, James Russo. Mercenary N.Y.C. rare-book sleuth Depp combs Europe for an ancient demonic tome. Part mystery, part travelogue, with traces of Polanski's sardonic wit, but can't hold a satanic candle to his 1968 ROSEMARY'S BABY. One scene is strikingly similar to a sequence in Kubrick's EYES WIDE SHUT. Also shown at 127m. Super 35. [R]▼◗

Nitwits, The (1935) **81m.** *** D: George Stevens. Bert Wheeler, Robert Woolsey, Betty Grable, Fred Keating, Evelyn Brent, Erik Rhodes, Hale Hamilton, Willie Best. Enjoyable comedy-musical-mystery with Wheeler and Woolsey seeking to uncover the identity of the Black Widow, a blackmailer-killer. Grable plays Wheeler's girlfriend, a murder suspect. Based on a story by Stuart Palmer.●

Nixon (1995) **C-190m.** *** D: Oliver Stone. Anthony Hopkins, Joan Allen, Powers Boothe, Ed Harris, Bob Hoskins, E. G. Marshall, David Paymer, David Hyde Pierce, Paul Sorvino, Mary Steenburgen, J. T. Walsh, James Woods, Brian Bedford, Kevin Dunn, Fyvush Finkel, Annabeth Gish, Tony Goldwyn, Larry Hagman, Ed Herrmann, Madeline Kahn, Saul Rubinek, Tony Lo Bianco, Corey Carrier, Tony Plana, Dan Hedaya, Michael Chiklis, John C. McGinley, John Diehl, Robert Beltran, Joanna Going, George Plimpton, Donna Dixon, James Karen. Controversial, fragmented portrait of the U.S. politician and president, presented as a driven man beset by deep-rooted insecurities. Younger viewers might have a hard time keeping track of the players, and may fall prey to director-cowriter Stone's expected, and outrageous, historical inventions. Overlong, to be sure, but still compelling, with Hopkins' persuasive lead performance, and an array of fine supporting players, especially Allen as Pat Nixon. Panavision. [R]▼●◗

Noah's Ark (1929) **100m.** **½ D: Michael Curtiz. Dolores Costello, George O'Brien, Noah Beery, Louise Fazenda, Gwynne (Guinn) Williams, Paul McAllister, Myrna Loy. Hokey and derivative story (by Darryl F. Zanuck) has devil-may-care O'Brien, gallivanting through Europe, falling in love with German girl Costello on the eve of WW1, and finally realizing his duty and enlisting in the U.S. Army. Somehow all this is paralleled to the days of Noah in a lengthy flashback sequence. Biblical segment is dazzlingly elaborate and full of great special effects. Silent film with somewhat awkward talking sequences; originally 135m., restored in 1989; beware of 1957 reissue prints running 75m.

Nob Hill (1945) **C-95m.** **½ D: Henry Hathaway. George Raft, Joan Bennett, Vivian Blaine, Peggy Ann Garner, Alan Reed, B. S. Pully, Emil Coleman, Smith and Dale, Rory Calhoun. Gold Coast saloon owner Raft has his head turned when socialite Bennett shows an interest in him. Predictable formula musical given handsome Technicolor production.

No Big Deal (1983) **C-86m.** **½ D: Robert Charlton. Kevin Dillon, Christopher Gartin, Mary Joan Negro, Jane Krakowski, Tammy Grimes, Sylvia Miles. Fair drama about troubled, alienated, streetwise teen Dillon and his attempt to fit in with his peers. A decent effort at portraying adolescent problems, but the result is a bit too pat. Interestingly, Miles is cast as a strict, bureaucratic school principal.▼

No Blade of Grass (1970) **C-97m.** *½ D: Cornel Wilde. Nigel Davenport, Jean Wallace, John Hamill, Lynne Frederick, Patrick Holt, Anthony May. Sober-sided film trying to drive home ecology message is just an update of films like PANIC IN YEAR ZERO, with family fleeing virus-stricken London for Scottish countryside, facing panic and attack along the way. Based on John Christopher's popular novel. Panavision. [R]

Nobody Lives Forever (1946) **100m.** *** D: Jean Negulesco. John Garfield, Geraldine Fitzgerald, Walter Brennan, Faye Emerson, George Coulouris, George Tobias. Well-done but familiar yarn of con-man Garfield fleecing rich widow Fitzgerald, then falling in love for real.

Nobody Loves Me (1994-German) **C-104m.** **½ D: Doris Dörrie. Maria Schrader, Pierre Sanoussi-Bliss, Michael von Au, Elisabeth Trissenaar, Peggy Parnass. Quirky oddity about the trials of Fanny Fink (Schrader), a death-obsessed airport security officer who is turning thirty. She says she doesn't need a man, but is nonetheless desperate to find one. Her gay next-door neighbor (and kindred spirit) tells her she will soon be meeting the love of her life. Not without interest but too often as flaky and unglued as its main character.

Nobody Runs Forever SEE: **High Commissioner, The**

Nobody's Children (1994) **C-100m. TVM** D: David Wheatley. Ann-Margret, Dominique Sanda, Reiner Schone, Clive Owen,

Jay O. Sanders. A-M (as the real-life Carol Stevens) goes to Romania in 1990 to adopt a child and gets entangled in Red red tape and a political thriller. A notch above the usual. Made for cable. Above average.

Nobody's Fault SEE: **Little Dorrit**

Nobody's Fool (1986) **C-107m.** **½ D: Evelyn Purcell. Rosanna Arquette, Eric Roberts, Mare Winningham, Jim Youngs, Louise Fletcher, Gwen Welles, Stephen Tobolowsky, Charlie Barnett, Lewis Arquette. Innocuous romantic comedy by Beth Henley about a flaky waitress in a small Southwestern town who's become an outcast (after having a baby out of wedlock), and only begins to find herself when she meets Roberts, who's passing through town. Very modest film that benefits from a relaxed and unmannered performance by Roberts. [PG-13]▼●

Nobody's Fool (1994) **C-110m.** ***½ D: Robert Benton. Paul Newman, Jessica Tandy, Bruce Willis, Melanie Griffith, Dylan Walsh, Pruitt Taylor Vince, Gene Saks, Josef Sommer, Philip Seymour Hoffman, Philip Bosco. Picaresque look at a small-town ne'er-do-well and his extended (dysfunctional) family of cronies; after turning his back on his real family years ago, he now finds himself spending time with his grown-up son and his young grandson. An irresistibly appealing Newman is surrounded by wonderful actors in this charmingly unpredictable character study—including Willis, as his friendly nemesis. Benton scripted, from Richard Russo's novel. Elizabeth Wilson appears unbilled as Newman's ex-wife. [R]▼●

Nobody's Perfect (1968) **C-103m.** **½ D: Alan Rafkin. Doug McClure, Nancy Kwan, James Whitmore, David Hartman, Gary Vinson. Witless military service comedy involving pat shenanigans of U.S. submarine based in Japan, with every predictable gimmick thrown in. Techniscope.

Nobody's Perfect (1989-Swiss-U.S.) **C-91m.** **½ D: Robert Kaylor. Chad Lowe, Gail O'Grady, Patrick Breen, Kim Flowers, Eric Bruskotter, Robert Vaughn. Shy guy at a new college wants to make friends with an attractive girl, but is too tongue-tied, so at a friend's urging, disguises himself as a girl and ends up his target's roommate. Little comedy based on the last line of SOME LIKE IT HOT is predictable but entertaining. [PG-13]▼●

Nobody's Perfekt (1981) **C-95m.** BOMB D: Peter Bonerz. Gabe Kaplan, Alex Karras, Robert Klein, Susan Clark, Paul Stewart, Alex Rocco, Peter Bonerz. Entirely unfunny comedy, made in Miami, about three misfits who decide to fight City Hall when their car is totalled in a pothole and—because of a loophole—they can't sue. Klein does awful imitations of James Cagney and Bette Davis. An inauspicious theatrical directing debut for Bonerz. [PG]▼

Nobody Waved Goodbye (1965-Canadian) **80m.** *** D: Don Owen. Peter Kastner, Julie Biggs, Claude Rae, Toby Tarnow, Charmion King, Ron Taylor. Straightforward, perceptive account of alienated teenager Kastner. A sequel, UNFINISHED BUSINESS, is set 20 years later, and details the plight of Kastner and Biggs's own teen offspring.

Nocturna (1978) **C-83m.** BOMB D: Harry Tampa (Harry Hurwitz). Yvonne de Carlo, John Carradine, Nai Bonet, Brother Theodore. Grade-Z sleaze with a tired Carradine phoning in his performance as Dracula. The Count, in trouble with the taxman, turns his castle into a disco! [R]▼

Nocturne (1946) **88m.** **½ D: Edwin L. Marin. George Raft, Lynn Bari, Virginia Huston, Joseph Pevney, Myrna Dell. A ladykiller-songwriter is murdered, the police think it's suicide, but stubborn tough-guy cop Raft knows otherwise. Moderately entertaining mystery.▼●

No Deposit, No Return (1976) **C-112m.** **½ D: Norman Tokar. David Niven, Darren McGavin, Don Knotts, Herschel Bernardi, Barbara Feldon, Brad Savage, Kim Richards, Charlie Martin Smith, Vic Tayback, John Williams. Two neglected kids stage their own bogus kidnapping to stir up attention and enable them to join their mother in Hong Kong. OK Disney slapstick comedy. [G]▼

No Down Payment (1957) **105m.** *** D: Martin Ritt. Joanne Woodward, Jeffrey Hunter, Sheree North, Tony Randall, Cameron Mitchell, Patricia Owens, Barbara Rush, Pat Hingle. Turgid suburban soaper of intertwining problems of several young married couples. CinemaScope.

No Drums, No Bugles (1971) **C-85m.** **½ D: Clyde Ware. Martin Sheen. Nicely done drama, based on West Virginia legend about conscientious objector during Civil War who spends three years in a cave rather than fight. Good acting by Sheen, who's the only one on screen for most of film. Techniscope. [G]▼

No Escape (1943) SEE: **I Escaped From the Gestapo**

No Escape (1953) **76m.** *½ D: Charles Bennett. Lew Ayres, Marjorie Steele, Sonny Tufts, Gertrude Michael. Modest narrative about couple seeking actual killer to clear themselves of homicide charge. Retitled: CITY ON A HUNT.

No Escape (1994) **C-118m.** ** D: Martin Campbell. Ray Liotta, Lance Henriksen, Stuart Wilson, Kevin Dillon, Ian McNeice, Michael Lerner, Ernie Hudson. Odd mix of high tech and MOST DANGEROUS GAME finds Liotta in a maximum security prison (year 2022) before escaping to a jungle colony where isolated inmates are left to die. Not the worst of its grungy ilk, but too protracted. Wilson is amusing as a key nemesis. Arriscope. [R]▼●◗

No Highway in the Sky (1951) **98m.** *** D: Henry Koster. James Stewart, Marlene Dietrich, Glynis Johns, Jack Hawkins, Janette Scott, Elizabeth Allan, Ronald Squire, Niall MacGinnis, Kenneth More, Maurice Denham, Wilfrid Hyde-White. Offbeat, engrossing drama with Stewart as an engineer who desperately tries to convince others that aircraft can suffer from metal fatigue, and should be grounded after a given time. Dietrich is a glamorous passenger on the fateful flight. Based on a novel by Nevil Shute. Made in England, where it was released as NO HIGHWAY.▼

No Holds Barred (1952) **65m.** ** D: William Beaudine. Leo Gorcey, Huntz Hall, Leonard Penn, Marjorie Reynolds, Bernard Gorcey, David Gorcey, Tim Ryan, Bennie Bartlett, Henry Kulky. Freak-of-nature Sach develops some amazing physical attributes and becomes a wrestling star in this unsurprising *Bowery Boys* match.

No Holds Barred (1989) **C-91m.** ** D: Thomas J. Wright. Hulk Hogan, Joan Severance, Kurt Fuller, Tiny Lister, Mark Pellegrino, Jesse (The Body) Ventura, Bill Henderson. For those who can't get enough of Hulk Hogan, he appears here as a TV wrestling star who must defend himself after refusing a greedy businessman's offer to switch networks. Aimed squarely at the legion of Hulkster fans. [PG-13]▼●

Noises Off (1992) **C-104m.** **½ D: Peter Bogdanovich. Carol Burnett, Michael Caine, Denholm Elliott, Julie Hagerty, Marilu Henner, Mark Linn-Baker, Christopher Reeve, John Ritter, Nicollette Sheridan. Energetic filming of Michael Frayn's play, a clever variation on a traditional British sex farce—with the added dimension of behind-the-scenes tumult among the acting troupe. This kind of door-slamming comedy doesn't ever work on film—but Bogdanovich comes closer than anyone ever has before, with the help of a willing cast. [PG-13]▼●

No Leave, No Love (1946) **119m.** ** D: Charles Martin. Van Johnson, Keenan Wynn, Pat Kirkwood, Guy Lombardo, Edward Arnold, Marie Wilson. No script, no laughs; Johnson and Wynn are sailors on the town in this overlong romantic comedy.

No Looking Back (1980) SEE: **Out of the Blue**

No Looking Back (1998) **C-96m.** ** D: Edward Burns. Lauren Holly, Edward Burns, Jon Bon Jovi, Blythe Danner, Connie Britton. Working-class romantic triangle provides nice lead role for Holly as waitress with an OK but dead-end life with boyfriend Bon Jovi, thrown off balance by return of old sweetheart Burns. Attractive cast can't overcome a very slight story; the strong soundtrack (Sheryl Crow, Bruce Springsteen, etc.) overpowers the script. Executive-produced by Robert Redford. [R] ▼●

No Love for Johnnie (1961-British) **110m.** *** D: Ralph Thomas. Peter Finch, Stanley Holloway, Mary Peach, Mervyn Johns, Donald Pleasence, Dennis Price, Oliver Reed. Civilized study of politician who cares only about winning the election. CinemaScope.▼

Nomads (1986) **C-95m.** *½ D: John McTiernan. Lesley-Anne Down, Pierce Brosnan, Adam Ant, Anna-Maria Monticelli, Hector Mercado, Mary Woronov. Doctor (Down) treats an apparent madman, then undergoes a hallucinatory rerun of his recent experiences: he's a French anthropologist who's come to L.A. and has been drawn to a band of strange street people. Potentially interesting idea for a half-hour *Twilight Zone* but pretty deadly as a feature. Unpleasant, too. [R]▼

No Man Is an Island (1962) **C-114m.** **½ D: John Monks, Jr., Richard Goldstone. Jeffrey Hunter, Marshall Thompson, Barbara Perez, Ronald Remy, Paul Edwards, Jr., Rolf Bayer, Vicente Liwanag. Spotty production values mar true story of serviceman Hunter trapped on Guam during the three years Japanese controlled area. ▼

No Man of Her Own (1932) **85m.** **½ D: Wesley Ruggles. Clark Gable, Carole Lombard, Dorothy Mackaill, Grant Mitchell, Elizabeth Patterson, Lillian Harmer, George Barbier. Snappy story of heel reformed by good girl, noteworthy for only co starring of Gable and Lombard (then not married).▼●

No Man of Her Own (1950) **98m.** **½ D: Mitchell Leisen. Barbara Stanwyck, John Lund, Jane Cowl, Phyllis Thaxter, Richard Denning, Milburn Stone. Turgid drama based on Cornell Woolrich tale of Stanwyck assuming another's identity, later being blackmailed by ex-boyfriend. Remade in 1982 as I MARRIED A SHADOW and in 1996 as MRS. WINTERBOURNE.

No Man's Land (1985-French-Swiss) **C-110m.** *** D: Alain Tanner. Hugues Quester, Myriam Mezieres, Jean-Philippe Ecoffey, Betty Berr, Marie-Luce Felber. Sober, provocative account of several characters involved with smuggling contraband across the French-Swiss border, focusing on their motivations and disillusionment. May be effectively contrasted to Tanner's earlier JONAH WHO WILL BE 25 IN THE YEAR 2000.

No Man's Land (1987) **C-106m.** ** D: Peter Werner. Charlie Sheen, D.B. Sweeney, Lara Harris, Randy Quaid, Bill Duke, R.D. Call, M. Emmet Walsh. Rookie cop goes undercover to trap a wealthy young auto buff who operates a hot car ring, finds he likes his target, the target's sister, *and* stealing Porsches. Good premise largely botched. [R]▼●

No Man's Woman (1955) **70m.** ** D: Franklin Adreon. Marie Windsor, John Archer, Patric Knowles, Nancy Gates, Louis Jean Heydt. OK whodunit about finding murderer of strong-willed woman.

No Mercy (1986) **C-105m.** *½ D: Richard Pearce. Richard Gere, Kim Basinger, Jeroen Krabbé, George Dzundza, Gary Basaraba, William Atherton, Ray Sharkey. Chicago cop Gere storms into Louisiana Bayou country seeking the killer of his partner, falls for Cajun beauty Basinger—who's been "sold" to the kingpin perpetrator of the murder. Even mindless melodramas have to make sense, at least on their own terms; this one's pretty ridiculous. The two sexy stars don't really click. [R]▼●◗

No Minor Vices (1948) **96m.** ** D: Lewis Milestone. Dana Andrews, Lilli Palmer, Louis Jourdan, Jane Wyatt, Norman Lloyd, Bernard Gorcey, Beau Bridges. Pretentious comedy in which stereotypically eccentric artist Jourdan attempts to come between pediatrician Andrews and wife Palmer. Starts off well but bogs down.

No More Ladies (1935) **81m.** **½ D: Edward H. Griffith. Joan Crawford, Robert Montgomery, Charlie Ruggles, Franchot Tone, Edna May Oliver, Gail Patrick. Crawford marries playboy Montgomery, tries to settle him down by making him jealous over her attention to Tone. Airy comedy. Joan Burfield (Fontaine) made her film debut here.

No More Women (1934) **77m.** *** D: Albert Rogell. Victor McLaglen, Edmund Lowe, Sally Blane, Minna Gombell, Alphonse Ethier, Tom Dugan. Typically lusty vehicle for the two stars, as rival deep-sea divers who swear off brawling over "dames"—until the new owner of their ship turns out to be gorgeous Blane! Good action and underwater sequences.

No My Darling Daughter (1961-British) **97m.** **½ D: Ralph Thomas. Michael Redgrave, Michael Craig, Juliet Mills, Roger Livesey, Rad Fulton, Renee Houston. Generally funny film with Mills, rich industrialist's daughter, torn between two suitors, playboy and hard-working businessman.

No Name on the Bullet (1959) **C-77m.** *** D: Jack Arnold. Audie Murphy, Charles Drake, Joan Evans, Virginia Grey, Warren Stevens, Edgar Stehli, R. G. Armstrong, Willis Bouchey, Karl Swenson, Charles Watts, Jerry Paris, Whit Bissell. A quiet, cultured gunman (Murphy, in a fine performance) rides into a small town to kill someone, though no one but he knows who his target is. Guilt and paranoia create their own victims. Slow, philosophical, and intelligent, this is the best of sci-fi director Arnold's several Westerns. CinemaScope.▼

None But the Brave (1965) **C-105m.** **½ D: Frank Sinatra. Frank Sinatra, Clint Walker, Tommy Sands, Tony Bill, Brad Dexter. Taut war drama focusing on crew of cracked-up plane and Japanese army patrol who make peace on a remote island during WW2. Panavision.▼●

None But the Lonely Heart (1944) **113m.** **½ D: Clifford Odets. Cary Grant, Ethel Barrymore, Barry Fitzgerald, Jane Wyatt, Dan Duryea, George Coulouris, June Duprez. Odets' moody drama of a Cockney drifter features one of Grant's most ambitious performances, and some fine moments, but suffers from censorship restrictions of the time, and misplaced WW2 rhetoric. Barrymore won Supporting Actress Oscar as Grant's dying mother. Also shown in computer-colored version.▼●

None Shall Escape (1944) **85m.** *** D: Andre de Toth. Marsha Hunt, Alexander Knox, Henry Travers, Richard Crane, Dorothy Morris, Trevor Bardette. Trial of Nazi officer reviews his savage career, in taut drama that retains quite a punch. Released before, but set after, the end of WWII.

Non-Stop New York (1937-British) **71m.** *** D: Robert Stevenson. John Loder, Anna Lee, Francis L. Sullivan, Frank Cellier, Desmond Tester. Fast-paced, tongue-in-cheek Hitchcock-like yarn about a woman who can provide alibi for innocent man accused of murder—but no one believes her. Love that luxury airplane!▼

No Nukes (1980) **C-103m.** *** D: Julian Schlossberg, Danny Goldberg, Anthony Potenza. Jackson Browne, Crosby, Stills & Nash, The Doobie Brothers, John Hall, Gil Scott-Heron, Bonnie Raitt, Carly Simon, Bruce Springsteen, James Taylor, Jesse Colin Young, Jane Fonda. Super-Springsteen joins several appealing, if long in the tooth, fellow rock stars to protest nuclear power. Pleasant, if not very magnetic, concert film-documentary does boast chillingly hilarious clip from pro-nuke "Big Picture" episode from early '50s. Aka THE MUSE CONCERT: NO NUKES. [PG] ▼

No One Man (1932) **73m.** ** D: Lloyd Corrigan. Carole Lombard, Ricardo Cortez, Paul Lukas, George Barbier. Another tired love triangle, with spoiled rich-girl Lombard caught between suave but heartless Cortez and earnest doctor Lukas. Becomes laughable before long.

Noose Hangs High, The (1948) **77m.** **½ D: Charles Barton. Bud Abbott, Lou Costello, Joseph Calleia, Leon Errol, Cathy Downs, Mike Mazurki, Fritz Feld. Mistaken identity leads to complications with the boys robbed of a large sum of money; typical A&C, bolstered by presence of Errol. Highlight: "Mudder and Fodder."▼

No Place for Jennifer (1951-British) **89m.**

** D: Henry Cass. Leo Genn, Rosamund John, Beatrice Campbell, Guy Middleton. Low-key sob story of little girl with bleak future when parents divorce.
No Place Like Home (1989) **C-100m. TVM** D: Lee Grant. Christine Lahti, Jeff Daniels, Scott Marlowe, Kathy Bates, CCH Pounder. Hard-hitting drama about a working-class family in Pittsburgh who find themselves out on the street and in the world of the homeless. Lahti shows why there are few better actresses around. Written by Ara Watson and Sam Blackwell, based on incidents in director Grant's documentary HOMELESS. Above average.
No Place Like Homicide! (1962-British) **87m.** ** D: Pat Jackson. Kenneth Connor, Sidney James, Shirley Eaton, Donald Pleasence, Dennis Price, Michael Gough. At times strained satire about group of people gathered at haunted house for the reading of a will. Remake of THE GHOUL. British title: WHAT A CARVE UP!▼
No Place to Hide (1956) **C-71m.** **½ D: Josef Shaftel. David Brian, Marsha Hunt, Hugh Corcoran, Ike Jariega, Jr., Celia Flor. Tense account of search for two children who accidentally have disease-spreading pellets in their possession; filmed in Philippines.
No Place to Land (1958) **78m.** *½ D: Albert Gannaway. John Ireland, Mari Blanchard, Gail Russell, Jackie Coogan. Sleazy little film of three-cornered romance, leading nowhere. Naturama.
No Questions Asked (1951) **81m.** **½ D: Harold F. Kress. Barry Sullivan, Arlene Dahl, Jean Hagen, George Murphy, William Reynolds, Mari Blanchard. Snappy little film of Sullivan seeking easy road to success via crime rackets.
Nora Prentiss (1947) **111m.** **½ D: Vincent Sherman. Ann Sheridan, Kent Smith, Robert Alda, Bruce Bennett, Rosemary DeCamp. Chanteuse Sheridan ruins doctor Smith's life; contrived but glossy melodrama.
Norma Jean & Marilyn (1996) **C-129m. TVM** D: Tim Fywell. Mira Sorvino, Ashley Judd, Josh Charles, Ron Rifkin, Peter Dobson, Lindsay Crouse, David Dukes, John Rubinstein, Taylor Nichols. Offbeat psychological study of Marilyn Monroe by writer Jill Isaacs, with the two lead actresses battling as the alter egos of the screen icon, from childhood to her final days. Nudity will deter this from being broadcast (it premiered on cable). Above average. ▼●
Normal Life (1996) **C-102m.** *** D: John McNaughton. Luke Perry, Ashley Judd, Darwin Moxey, Tom Towles, Penelope Milford. Fascinating true-crime story of a straight-arrow suburban cop who becomes the classic enabler to a drug-addicted shopaholic wife, leading him to a successful run as a bank robber! Perry and (especially) Judd are terrific in this downbeat, straightforward, morbidly compelling tale of twisted love. Made for theatrical release, debuted on cable TV. [R]▼●
Norman . . . Is That You? (1976) **C-91m.** ** D: George Schlatter. Redd Foxx, Pearl Bailey, Dennis Dugan, Michael Warren, Tamara Dobson, Vernee Watson, Jayne Meadows. Leering comedy based on flop Broadway show and revamped with black stars: Foxx is distraught when he discovers his son is gay, and determines to "straighten him out." Shot on videotape. [PG]▼
Norman Loves Rose (1982-Australian) **C-98m.** **½ D: Henri Safran. Carol Kane, Tony Owen, Warren Mitchell, Myra de Groot, David Downer. OK comedy of teenager Owen enamored with sister-in-law Kane. She becomes pregnant, and who is the father? [R]▼
Norma Rae (1979) **C-113m.** *** D: Martin Ritt. Sally Field, Ron Leibman, Beau Bridges, Pat Hingle, Barbara Baxley, Gail Strickland, Lonny Chapman, Noble Willingham, Grace Zabriskie. Field is excellent in Oscar-winning performance as real-life poor Southern textile worker gradually won over toward unionization by N.Y.C. labor organizer. Entertaining, though not entirely believable; haunting theme "It Goes Like it Goes" sung by Jennifer Warnes, also won an Oscar. Panavision. [PG]▼●
No Road Back (1957-British) **83m.** ** D: Montgomery Tully. Sean Connery, Skip Homeier, Paul Carpenter, Patricia Dainton, Norman Wooland, Margaret Rawlings. Blind and deaf woman sacrifices everything for son, becomes involved with criminals—who then try to pin robbery on the innocent son. Plodding melodrama.
No Room for the Groom (1952) **82m.** **½ D: Douglas Sirk. Tony Curtis, Piper Laurie, Spring Byington, Don DeFore, Jack Kelly. Harmless shenanigans of ex-G.I. Curtis returning home to find it filled with in-laws.
Norseman, The (1978) **C-90m.** *½ D: Charles B. Pierce. Lee Majors, Cornel Wilde, Mel Ferrer, Jack Elam, Chris Connelly, Kathleen Freeman, Susie Coelho (Bono), Denny Miller. Stodgy period adventure casts Majors as 11th-century Viking prince who sails to North America in search of his father, a Norse king abducted by Indians. Panavision. [PG]▼
North (1994) **C-88m.** *½ D: Rob Reiner. Elijah Wood, Bruce Willis, Jason Alexander, Julia Louis-Dreyfus, Dan Aykroyd, Reba McEntire, Kathy Bates, Abe Vigoda, John Ritter, Faith Ford, Richard Belzer, Jon Lovitz, Alan Arkin, Alan Rachins, Matthew McCurley, Alexander Godunov, Kelly McGillis, Rosalind Chao, Ben Stein. Eleven-year-old boy who's convinced his folks don't appreciate him goes to court and wins the right to choose new parents, then

travels the world to find the ideal mom and dad. Wrong-headed movie never connects, and leads to an unemotional and predictable finale. Reiner coscripted with Alan Zweibel, on whose novel this was based. [PG]▼●

North Avenue Irregulars, The (1979) **C-99m.** **½ D: Bruce Bilson. Edward Herrmann, Barbara Harris, Susan Clark, Karen Valentine, Michael Constantine, Cloris Leachman, Patsy Kelly, Virginia Capers. Young priest (Herrmann) enlists churchgoing ladies for crime-fighting brigade; innocuous Disney comedy starts well but reverts to formula, including obligatory car pile-up finale. Fine actresses like Harris, Clark, and Leachman wasted. [G]▼◗

North by Northwest (1959) **C-136m.** **** D: Alfred Hitchcock. Cary Grant, Eva Marie Saint, James Mason, Leo G. Carroll, Martin Landau, Jessie Royce Landis, Philip Ober, Adam Williams, Josephine Hutchinson, Edward Platt. Quintessential Hitchcock comedy-thriller, with bewildered ad-man Grant chased cross country by both spies (who think he's a double agent) and the police (who think he's an assassin). One memorable scene after another, including now-legendary cropdusting and Mount Rushmore sequences; one of the all-time great entertainments. Witty script by Ernest Lehman, exciting score by Bernard Herrmann. VistaVision. ▼●

North Dallas Forty (1979) **C-119m.** ***½ D: Ted Kotcheff. Nick Nolte, Mac Davis, Charles Durning, Dayle Haddon, G. D. Spradlin, Bo Svenson, Steve Forrest, John Matuszak, Dabney Coleman. Seriocomic version of Peter Gent's best-seller about labor abuse in the National Football League is the best gridiron film ever made and one of the best on any sport. Boasts Super Bowl-level performances for the most part. Scripted by its producer (Frank Yablans), director, and author. Panavision. [R]▼●◗

Northern Lights (1979) **90m.** ***½ D: John Hanson, Rob Nilsson. Robert Behling, Susan Lynch, Joe Spano, Henry Martinson, Marianne Astrom-DeFina, Ray Ness, Helen Ness. Incisive, unforgettable Americana about the struggles of farmers in pre-WW1 North Dakota, with Behling attempting to organize populist Nonpartisan League. Fine first feature for Hanson and Nilsson.▼

Northern Lights (1997) **C-95m. TVM** D: Linda Yellen. Diane Keaton, Maury Chaykin, Joseph Cross, Kathleen York, John Hoffman. Quirky Disney comedy about a compulsive, dyed-in-the-wool Noo Yawker who ends up in a New England burg to claim an inheritance. There she encounters all manner of daffy small-towners in this quite unorthodox tale adapted by Hoffman from his one-man off-Broadway show (he wrote, directed, and played all the parts; here he has a supporting role as a local bumbler). The film was executive-produced by, among others, Keaton and Meg Ryan. Made for cable. Above average.

Northern Pursuit (1943) **94m.** **½ D: Raoul Walsh. Errol Flynn, Julie Bishop, Helmut Dantine, John Ridgely, Gene Lockhart, Tom Tully. Mountie Flynn tracks his man, a downed Nazi pilot, throughout Canada in this standard but slickly done drama.▼

North Sea Hijack SEE: **ffolkes**

North Shore (1987) **C-96m.** ** D: William Phelps. Matt Adler, Nia Peeples, John Philbin, Gerry Lopez, Cristina Raines, Gregory Harrison. The top young surfer in Arizona (think about it) pits himself against the famed title Oahu waves, as well as the family of the native Hawaiian local he loves. Exceptional surfing photography carries a generally dippy script only so far. [PG]▼

North Star, The (1943) **105m.** **½ D: Lewis Milestone. Anne Baxter, Dana Andrews, Walter Huston, Ann Harding, Erich von Stroheim, Jane Withers, Farley Granger, Walter Brennan. Dramatic battle sequences in WW2 Russia marred by uninteresting stretches until German von Stroheim matches wits with village leader Huston. Good performances all around; script by Lillian Hellman. Later edited to 82m. to deemphasize the good Russians and retitled ARMORED ATTACK. Also shown in computer-colored version.▼

North to Alaska (1960) **C-122m.** *** D: Henry Hathaway. John Wayne, Stewart Granger, Ernie Kovacs, Fabian, Capucine, Mickey Shaughnessy, Joe Sawyer, John Qualen. Fast-moving actioner with delightful tongue-in-cheek approach; prospectors Wayne and Granger have their hands full dealing with latter's kid brother Fabian, con artist Kovacs, and gold-digging (in the other sense) Capucine. CinemaScope.▼●

Northwest Frontier SEE: **Flame Over India**

North West Mounted Police (1940) **C-125m.** **½ D: Cecil B. DeMille. Gary Cooper, Madeleine Carroll, Preston Foster, Paulette Goddard, Robert Preston, George Bancroft, Akim Tamiroff, Lon Chaney, Jr., Robert Ryan. DeMille at his most ridiculous, with Cooper as Dusty Rivers, Goddard a fiery half-breed in love with Preston, Lynne Overman as Scottish philosopher in superficial tale of Texas Ranger searching for fugitive in Canada. Much of outdoor action filmed on obviously indoor sets.

Northwest Outpost (1947) **91m.** *½ D: Allan Dwan. Nelson Eddy, Ilona Massey, Hugo Haas, Elsa Lanchester, Lenore Ulric. Rudolf Friml operetta of California calvarymen lumbers along pretty lamely.▼

Northwest Passage (Book I—Rogers' Ran-

gers) (1940) **C-125m.** ***½ D: King Vidor. Spencer Tracy, Robert Young, Walter Brennan, Ruth Hussey, Nat Pendleton, Robert Barrat, Addison Richards. Gritty, evocative filming of Kenneth Roberts' book about Rogers' Rangers and their stoic leader (Tracy), enduring hardships and frustrations while opening up new territory in Colonial America. Young and Brennan are greenhorns who learn hard knocks under taskmaster Tracy. The river-fording sequence is a knockout.▼●

Northwest Stampede (1948) **C-79m.** **½ D: Albert S. Rogell. Joan Leslie, James Craig, Jack Oakie, Chill Wills, Victor Kilian, Stanley Andrews. Lightweight oater about lady rancher Leslie competing with cowboy Craig for prize horses.

Norwood (1970) **C-96m.** ** D: Jack Haley, Jr. Glen Campbell, Kim Darby, Joe Namath, Carol Lynley, Pat Hingle, Tisha Sterling, Dom DeLuise, Billy Curtis. Ex-Marine Campbell hits the road for series of unrelated adventures with service buddy Namath, a midget, a Greenwich Village girl, a shiftless brother-in-law, a dancing chicken, and a young girl with whom he falls in love. Easy to take, but pointless. Look for Cass Daley and Jack Haley (the director's father) in a brief appearance. [G]

No Sad Songs for Me (1950) **89m.** *** D: Rudolph Maté. Margaret Sullavan, Wendell Corey, Viveca Lindfors, Natalie Wood, Ann Doran. Moving account of dying mother Sullavan preparing her family to go on without her. Ironically, Sullavan's last film.

Nosferatu (1922-German) **84m.** ***½ D: F. W. Murnau. Max Schreck, Alexander Granach, Gustav von Wangenheim, Greta Schroeder. Early film version of *Dracula* is brilliantly eerie, full of imaginative touches that none of the later films quite recaptured. Schreck's vampire is also the ugliest in film history. Remade in 1979. ▼●◗

Nosferatu the Vampyre (1979-West German) **C-107m.** ***½ D: Werner Herzog. Klaus Kinski, Isabelle Adjani, Bruno Ganz, Roland Topor. Spooky, funny, reverent remake of F. W. Murnau's vampire masterpiece should please Dracula fans of all persuasions. Kinski is magnificent as the good Count, and Adjani's classic beauty is utilized to the hilt. English-language version, which runs 96m., also exists; even though the German version is dubbed, it's still preferable. [PG]▼●◗

No Small Affair (1984) **C-102m.** ** D: Jerry Schatzberg. Jon Cryer, Demi Moore, George Wendt, Peter Frechette, Elizabeth Daily, Ann Wedgeworth, Jeffrey Tambor, Tim Robbins, Jennifer Tilly, Rick Ducommun, Tate Donovan. Self-possessed, smart-assy, but virginal teenager becomes obsessed with an "older woman"—struggling rock singer Moore—and will do just about anything to make her like him. Some good moments here and there, but basically unappealing characters torpedo its chances. [R]▼●

Nostalghia (1983-Italian-Russian) **C/B&W-126m.** ***½ D: Andrei Tarkovsky. Oleg Yankovsky, Erland Josephson, Domiziana Giordano, Laura Del Marchi, Delia Boccardo, Patrizia Terreno. Deeply personal, stunningly directed tale of a Russian poet (Yankovsky) and his beautiful translator (Giordano) who are trekking across Italy, inquiring into the life of a long-dead composer. The poet is so immersed in himself that he barely can communicate with those around him; then he meets a recluse (Josephson) who is certain that the end of the world is near. A provocative, insightful epic, lovingly rendered by one of the cinema's true poets.▼●◗

Nostradamus (1994-British-German) **C-118m.** ** D: Roger Christian. Tchéky Karyo, F. Murray Abraham, Rutger Hauer, Amanda Plummer, Julia Ormond, Anthony Higgins. Cornball biographical drama about the fabled 16th-century astrologer-physician (Karyo), who is seen prophesizing everything from Hitler's rise to the Kennedy assassination—all the while retaining his allure for the females of his own time. Best watched when in a silly mood. [R]▼●

No Surrender (1985-British-Canadian) **C-103m.** **½ D: Peter K. Smith. Michael Angelis, Ray McAnally, Avis Bunnage, James Ellis, Bernard Hill, Mark Mulholland, Joanne Whalley, Michael Ripper, Elvis Costello. Interesting parable of modern British society and its problems, set in a remote nightclub where two warring sets of old folks come into conflict, paralleling the troubles in Northern Ireland. Ambitious script by Alan Bleasdale tries to cover too much ground, but McAnally's strong performance as a ruthless IRA gunman stands out. [R]▼

Not as a Stranger (1955) **135m.** *** D: Stanley Kramer. Olivia de Havilland, Frank Sinatra, Robert Mitchum, Charles Bickford, Gloria Grahame, Broderick Crawford, Lee Marvin, Lon Chaney, Henry (Harry) Morgan, Virginia Christine, Jerry Paris. Morton Thompson novel of Mitchum marrying nurse de Havilland who supports him through medical school despite oft-strained relationship. Glossy tribute to medical profession contains excellent performances by all. Producer Kramer's directorial debut.▼

Notebook on Cities and Clothes (1989-German) **C-80m.** *** D: Wim Wenders. Fascinating documentary about Yohji Yamamoto, the influential Japanese high-fashion designer. The film is as much an observation of the moviemaking process (and a collaboration between filmmaker and subject) as it is a straight-on look at Yamamoto and his world.▼

No-Tell Hotel, The SEE: **Rosebud Beach Hotel, The**

Notes From Underground (1995) **C-88m.** *** D: Gary Walkow. Henry Czerny, Sheryl Lee. Biting adaptation of the Dostoyevsky novella features a soul-baring performance by Czerny as Underground Man: a sarcastic loner-loser who is at once miserable and proud, brutal and deeply human. At the crux of the narrative is his recollection of a party at school, where his presence was unwanted, and his attempt to connect with a prostitute (Lee). Difficult to watch, at times, because of its stinging insights and emotional truths, but well worth the effort.

Not for Publication (1984-U.S.-British) **C-88m.** ** D: Paul Bartel. Nancy Allen, David Naughton, Laurence Luckinbill, Alice Ghostley, Richard Paul, Barry Dennen, Cork Hubbert, Paul Bartel. Unsuccessful attempt to replicate an old-fashioned screwball comedy. Allen leads double life as the star reporter of a sleazy N.Y.C. tabloid and a worker in the reelection campaign of oddball mayor Luckinbill. Along the way shy photographer Naughton falls for her. [R]▼

Nothing but a Man (1964) **92m.** ***½ D: Michael Roemer. Ivan Dixon, Abbey Lincoln, Julius Harris, Gloria Foster, Martin Priest, Leonard Parker, Yaphet Kotto, Stanley Greene. Quietly powerful look at blacks in the South, with Dixon as a railroad worker who tries to settle down for the first time in his life with schoolteacher Lincoln, and has to deal with a level of prejudice—and self-denial—he's never faced before. Perceptive and honest, this film manages to make its points without melodrama. A small gem. Look for Esther Rolle and Moses Gunn in small roles.▼●

Nothing but the Best (1964-British) **C-99m.** ***½ D: Clive Donner. Alan Bates, Denholm Elliott, Harry Andrews, Millicent Martin, Pauline Delany. Biting look at social-climbing playboy Bates who commits murder to get ahead in the world. Written by Frederic Raphael.

Nothing but the Night (1972-British) **C-90m.** *½ D: Peter Sasdy. Christopher Lee, Peter Cushing, Diana Dors, Georgia Brown, Keith Barron, Fulton Mackay, Gwyneth Strong. Uninvolving supernatural thriller about a cult that attempts immortality by projecting their personalities into the bodies of children. Filmed by Lee's production banner in a failed attempt to encourage more serious genre films. Aka THE DEVIL'S UNDEAD and THE RESURRECTION SYNDICATE. [PG]▼

Nothing but the Truth (1941) **90m.** *** D: Elliott Nugent. Bob Hope, Paulette Goddard, Edward Arnold, Leif Erickson, Helen Vinson, Willie Best. Entertaining comedy based on sure-fire idea: Bashful stockbroker Hope wagers that he can tell the absolute truth for 24 hours. Good fun. Filmed before in 1920 (with Taylor Holmes) and 1929 (with Richard Dix); also an ancestor of Jim Carrey's LIAR LIAR.

Nothing but Trouble (1944) **69m.** ** D: Sam Taylor. Stan Laurel, Oliver Hardy, Mary Boland, Philip Merivale, David Leland, Henry O'Neill. Lesser L&H vehicle with duo hired as servants, meeting young boy king whose life is in danger. Boland is amusing as usual.▼

Nothing but Trouble (1991) **C-93m.** BOMB D: Dan Aykroyd. Chevy Chase, Dan Aykroyd, John Candy, Demi Moore, Taylor Negron, Bertila Damas, Valri Bromfield. Chase and Moore, off on a weekend, get nabbed for speeding in a hellhole town under the complete domination of ancient judge Aykroyd (unrecognizable under mounds of makeup); rest of film deals with their attempted escape. Stupefyingly unwatchable; Aykroyd's directorial debut (he also wrote it). And yes, his nose *is* supposed to look like a penis. Watch for Tupac Shakur as a "digital underground member." [PG-13]▼●◗

Nothing in Common (1986) **C-118m.** ** D: Garry Marshall. Tom Hanks, Jackie Gleason, Eva Marie Saint, Hector Elizondo, Barry Corbin, Bess Armstrong, Sela Ward, John Kapelos, Jane Morris, Dan Castellaneta, Tracy Reiner. Interminably long, highly uneven comedy-drama about a perpetual adolescent who's forced to deal with his aging, unloving father when his mom leaves him flat. Some poignant, relevant conclusions about love and responsibility (and some funny shots at the advertising business) are undermined by overlength and meandering nature of film. Hanks is excellent; Gleason is abrasive (in his last film appearance). Later a TV series. Super 35. [PG]▼●

Nothing Lasts Forever (1984) **C/B&W-82m.** **½ D: Tom Schiller. Zach Galligan, Apollonia van Ravenstein, Lauren Tom, Dan Aykroyd, Imogene Coca, Eddie Fisher, Sam Jaffe, Paul Rogers, Mort Sahl, Bill Murray, Anita Ellis. Strange, occasionally entertaining comedy of aspiring artist Galligan's experiences in a N.Y.C. of the future—and also on a trip to the moon. A most unusual cast; much better seen than described. Written by first-time director Schiller, produced by Lorne Michaels, both of TV's *Saturday Night Live*. [PG]

Nothing Personal (1980-U.S.-Canadian) **C-97m.** *½ D: George Bloomfield. Donald Sutherland, Suzanne Somers, Lawrence Dane, Roscoe Lee Browne, Dabney Coleman, Saul Rubinek, Catherine O'Hara, John Dehner. Sutherland is a professor attempting to stop a corporation from slaughtering baby seals, Somers a lawyer who helps him. Inane romantic comedy. Look for appearances by Craig Russell, Tony Rosato, Joe Flaherty, and Eugene Levy. [PG]▼

Nothing Sacred (1937) **C-75m.** ***½ D: William Wellman. Carole Lombard, Fredric

March, Walter Connolly, Charles Winninger, Sig Rumann, Frank Fay. Classic comedy about hotshot reporter (March) who exploits Vermont girl's ''imminent'' death from radium poisoning for headline value in N.Y.C. Ben Hecht's cynical script vividly enacted by March and Lombard (at her best). Gershwinesque music score by Oscar Levant.Trivia note: Connolly's character is named Oliver Stone! Remade as LIVING IT UP. ▼●◗
Nothing to Lose (1997) **C-97m.** **½ D: Steve Oedekerk. Martin Lawrence, Tim Robbins, John C. McGinley, Giancarlo Esposito, Kelly Preston, Michael McKean, Rebecca Gayheart, Samaria Graham, Irma P. Hall, Steve Oedekerk. Stunned to find his wife in bed with his boss, Robbins drives away in a daze—only to be carjacked by out-of-work Lawrence. Having nothing to lose, Robbins roars off into the desert with his surprised passenger; this being a buddy comedy, they try to help each other out. OK comedy, with a likable cast, is undercut by predictability (and not exploiting the premise for its full comic value). [R]▼●◗
No Time for Comedy (1940) **98m.** **½ D: William Keighley. James Stewart, Rosalind Russell, Genevieve Tobin, Charles Ruggles, Allyn Joslyn, Louise Beavers. Slick but dated adaptation of S. N. Behrman play about actress who tries to keep her playwright-husband from taking himself too seriously. Smoothly done but artificial. Aka GUY WITH A GRIN.
No Time for Flowers (1952) **83m.** ** D: Don Siegel. Viveca Lindfors, Paul Christian, Ludwig Stossel, Manfred Ingor. Low-grade version of NINOTCHKA set in Prague; a pale shadow of its ancestor.
No Time for Love (1943) **83m.** **½ D: Mitchell Leisen. Claudette Colbert, Fred MacMurray, Ilka Chase, Richard Haydn, Paul McGrath, June Havoc. Cute but obvious romance between famous magazine photographer Colbert and down-to-earth MacMurray. The stars give this a lift.
No Time for Sergeants (1958) **119m.** ***½ D: Mervyn LeRoy. Andy Griffith, Myron McCormick, Nick Adams, Murray Hamilton, Don Knotts. Funny military comedy based on Ira Levin's Broadway play (which got its start as a 1955 *U.S. Steel Hour* TV play). Griffith and McCormick repeat roles as hayseed inducted into service and his harried sergeant. Griffith's best comedy, with good support from Adams, and, in a small role as a noncommissioned officer, Knotts. Script by John Lee Mahin. Followed years later by a TV series.▼●
No Time to Be Young (1957) **82m.** ** D: David Lowell Rich. Robert Vaughn, Roger Smith, Merry Anders, Kathy Nolan, Tom Pittman, Dorothy Green. Pedestrian programmer about a trio of troubled young men: arrogant Vaughn's just been booted out of college; confused Smith is hung up on older woman; and insecure Pittman lies to his girlfriend. Skip it.
Not My Kid (1985) **C-100m. TVM** D: Michael Tuchner. George Segal, Stockard Channing, Andrew Robinson, Gary Bayer, Nancy Cartwright, Tate Donovan, Viveka Davis. Drug abuse by a teenage daughter shatters a family in emotionally charged dramatization of book by producer Beth Polson and Dr. Miller Newton. Christopher Knopf's incisive script helps make this one of the best films on the subject. Above average.▼
Not of This Earth (1957) **67m.** **½ D: Roger Corman. Paul Birch, Beverly Garland, Morgan Jones, William Roerick. Above par low-budget entry from Roger Corman with blank-eyed Birch as an alien vampire here to get blood for his atom war-ravaged home world. Good supporting cast; great bit by Dick Miller. Remade in 1988, 1996 (for TV), and 1997 (as STAR PORTAL).
Not of This Earth (1988) **C-80m.** ** D: Jim Wynorski. Traci Lords, Arthur Roberts, Lenny Juliano, Ace Mask, Roger Lodge. Strictly standard remake of the Roger Corman quickie, in which Roberts comes to earth in search of blood to replenish his dying planet's population. Film's chief interest is the casting of ex-porn queen Lords as a nurse. [R]▼
Not One Less (1999-Chinese) **C-106m.** ** D: Zhang Yimou. Wei Minzhi, Zhang Huike, Tian Zhenda, Gao Enman, Sun Zhimei. A young student (Wei) is asked to act as teacher to her near-peers in a rural Chinese village after the regular schoolmaster leaves for a month to tend to his ailing mother. The stipulation: She must not permit any dropouts if she wants to earn an extra 10 yuan in pay. Based-on-fact story results in a notably slight exercise for China's top filmmaker. The actors are non-professionals, and show it, in lifeless and repetitive scenes. [G]
Notorious (1946) **101m.** ***½ D: Alfred Hitchcock. Cary Grant, Ingrid Bergman, Claude Rains, Louis Calhern, Leopoldine Konstantin, Reinhold Schunzel, Moroni Olsen. Top-notch espionage tale by Ben Hecht, set in post-WW2 South America, with Ingrid marrying spy Rains to aid U.S. and agent Grant. Frank, tense, well acted, with amazingly suspenseful climax (and one memorably passionate love scene). Remade for cable TV in 1992.▼●◗
Notorious Gentleman (1945-British) **123m.** *** D: Sidney Gilliat. Rex Harrison, Lilli Palmer, Godfrey Tearle, Griffith Jones, Margaret Johnston, Guy Middleton, Jean Kent. Philandering life of irresponsible playboy is told with wit and style in this handsome production. British title: THE RAKE'S PROGRESS.
Notorious Landlady, The (1962) **123m.** **½ D: Richard Quine. Kim Novak, Jack Lemmon, Fred Astaire, Lionel Jeffries, Estelle Winwood, Maxwell Reed. Lemmon

entranced by houseowner Novak, decides to find out if she really did kill her husband; set in London. Offbeat comedy-mystery written by Quine and Larry Gelbart.

Notorious Lone Wolf, The (1946) **64m.** ** D: D. Ross Lederman. Gerald Mohr, Janis Carter, Eric Blore, John Abbott, William B. Davidson, Don Beddoe, Adele Roberts, Peter Whitney. The Lone Wolf returns from WW2 and is embroiled in a museum jewel theft. Mohr replaced Warren William for this humdrum entry.

Notorious Mr. Monks, The (1958) **70m.** ** D: Joseph Kane. Vera Ralston, Don Kelly, Paul Fix, Leo Gordon. Tame Ralston vehicle involving a hitchhiker and murder. Naturama.

Notorious Sophie Lang (1934) **64m.** **½ D: Ralph Murphy. Gertrude Michael, Paul Cavanagh, Alison Skipworth, Leon Errol, Arthur Hoyt. Tightly knit yarn of police using title character (Michael) to lead them to international crime ring.

Not Quite Jerusalem SEE: **Not Quite Paradise**

Not Quite Paradise (1986-British) **C-105m.** **½ D: Lewis Gilbert. Joanna Pacula, Sam Robards, Todd Graff, Kevin McNally, Selina Cadell, Kate Ingram, Libby Morris. Love on a kibbutz; pleasant, low-key story of volunteers from the U.S., England, and other nations adjusting to the hard life on an Israeli farm, where Yank Robards falls in love with sabra Pacula. Not much oomph but an OK, old-fashioned romance. Originally titled: NOT QUITE JERUSALEM. [R]▼

No Trees in the Street (1958-British) **108m.** ** D: J. Lee Thompson. Sylvia Syms, Stanley Holloway, Herbert Lom, Ronald Howard, Joan Miller. Lower-class British life examined for its strengths and weaknesses; too sterile a human document.

Notting Hill (1999-British) **C-123m.** *** D: Roger Michell. Julia Roberts, Hugh Grant, Hugh Bonneville, Emma Chambers, James Dreyfus, Rhys Ifans, Tim McInnerny, Gina McKee. Bemused London bookshop owner chances to meet world-famous movie star, and sparks fly . . . but their budding relationship is bumpier than either could imagine. Enjoyable romantic comedy is a complete contrivance, but so smoothly done, and so engagingly performed, that you don't much mind. Written by Richard Curtis, whose script for FOUR WEDDINGS AND A FUNERAL made Grant a star. Alec Baldwin and Matthew Modine appear unbilled. Super 35. [PG-13]▼●◗

Not Wanted (1949) **94m.** **½ D: Elmer Clifton. Sally Forrest, Keefe Brasselle, Leo Penn, Dorothy Adams. Well-intentioned account of unwed mother seeking affection and understanding; produced and co-scripted by Ida Lupino (who also apparently directed most of the film).▼

Not With My Wife You Don't! (1966) **C-118m.** **½ D: Norman Panama. Tony Curtis, Virna Lisi, George C. Scott, Carroll O'Connor, Richard Eastham. Trivial fluff about air force officer Curtis and bored wife Lisi; pointless and aimless, but attractive to the eye.▼

Not Without My Daughter (1991) **C-114m.** *** D: Brian Gilbert. Sally Field, Alfred Molina, Sheila Rosenthal, Roshan Seth, Sarah Badel, Mony Rey, Georges Corraface. American woman accompanies her Iranian-born husband on a visit to his homeland. Once there, he decides to stay, and she learns (to her horror) that in Iran she has no rights, as a wife or as a woman, so she must find a way to flee the country with her daughter. Absorbing film based on real-life experience of Betty Mahmoody; the drama works because Field is so believable, and because her husband is not portrayed as a one-dimensional monster. Filmed in Israel. [PG-13]▼●

Nouvelle Vague (1990-French-Swiss) **C-88m.** **½ D: Jean-Luc Godard. Alain Delon, Domiziana Giordano, Roland Amstutz, Laurence Cote, Christophe Odent. Delon and Giordano are cast as a handsome, ultra-rich, powerful couple; the narrative focuses on sexual and political issues that run through all of Godard's films. This one's strictly a matter of taste—and one's tolerance for latter-day Godard. Aka NEW WAVE.▼

Novel Affair, A (1957-British) **C-83m.** *** D: Muriel Box. Ralph Richardson, Margaret Leighton, Patricia Dainton, Carlo Justini, Marjorie Rhodes, Megs Jenkins. Amusing tale of Leighton who writes a sexy novel, finding the fantasy come true. Nearly everyone plays dual roles, in real life and scenes from the novel! Original British title: THE PASSIONATE STRANGER.

Now About All These Women SEE: **All These Women**

Now and Forever (1934) **81m.** **½ D: Henry Hathaway. Gary Cooper, Carole Lombard, Shirley Temple, Sir Guy Standing, Charlotte Granville. Standard jewel-thief-going-straight yarn; Lombard overshadowed by Cooper and Temple. On tape only in a computer-colored version. ▼

Now and Forever (1983-Australian) **C-93m.** ** D: Adrian Carr. Cheryl Ladd, Robert Coleby, Carmen Duncan, Christine Amor, Aileen Britton. Chic Ladd's husband is unfaithful, then is falsely accused of rape and sent to jail. This puts quite a strain on their marriage. Based on Danielle Steel's novel. If you like Harlequin romances . . . Panavision. [R]▼●

Now and Then (1995) **C-96m.** **½ D: Lesli Linka Glatter. Christina Ricci, Thora Birch, Gaby Hoffman, Ashleigh Aston Moore, Demi Moore, Melanie Griffith, Rosie O'Donnell, Rita Wilson, Willa Glen, Bonnie Hunt, Janeane Garofalo, Lolita Davidovich, Cloris Leachman, Hank Azaria. Essentially a distaff version of STAND BY ME in which we get to know four friends during their last summer of adolescence in 1970. The film is bookended by sequences of the friends reminiscing at a baby shower twenty years later. Nicely done, but covers awfully familiar territory; strongest asset is the lovely performances of its young stars. Moore also produced. Brendan Fraser appears unbilled. [PG-13]▼●◗

No Way Out (1950) **106m.** *** D: Joseph L. Mankiewicz. Richard Widmark, Linda Darnell, Stephen McNally, Sidney Poitier, Ruby Dee, Ossie Davis, Bill Walker. Violent tale of racial hatred involving bigot Widmark, who has gangster pals avenge his brother's death by creating race riots. Once-provocative film is still engrossing but seems a bit artificial at times. Film debuts of Poitier, Dee, and Davis.▼

No Way Out (1972-Italian) **C-100m.** *½ D: Duccio Tessari. Alain Delon, Richard Conte, Carla Gravina, Roger Hanin, Nicoletta Machiavelli. Boring Mafia movie about a hitman (Delon) who turns on his bosses, four crime kingpins, when they kill his wife and child to dissuade him from calling it quits. Also called BIG GUNS. Techniscope. [R]

No Way Out (1987) **C-116m.** *** D: Roger Donaldson. Kevin Costner, Gene Hackman, Sean Young, Will Patton, Howard Duff, George Dzundza, Jason Bernard, Iman, Fred Dalton Thompson, David Paymer. Taut melodramatic thriller about a murder and cover-up within the inner circles of the federal government. Young is tantalizingly sexy as the woman involved with both CIA liaison Costner and Secretary of Defense Hackman. Hard to tell at first that this is a remake of THE BIG CLOCK, but it is—except for a ludicrous (and totally unnecessary) "twist" ending. Script by Robert Garland, who also produced. Super 35. [R]▼●◗

No Way to Treat a Lady (1968) **C-108m.** ***½ D: Jack Smight. Rod Steiger, Lee Remick, George Segal, Eileen Heckart, Murray Hamilton, Michael Dunn, Barbara Baxley, Ruth White, Doris Roberts, David Doyle. Delicious blend of romantic comedy and murder, with Steiger as flamboyant ladykiller, Segal as "Mo Brummel," cop on his trail, Remick as Segal's new lady-friend who could be next victim. Script by John Gay, from the William Goldman novel.

Nowhere (1997) **C-85m.** ** D: Gregg Araki. James Duval, Rachel True, Nathan Bexton, Christina Applegate, Chiara Mastroianni, Debi Mazar, Kathleen Robertson, Jordan Ladd, Sarah Lassez, Guillermo Diaz, Jeremy Jordan, Alan Boyce, Jaason Simmons, Ryan Phillippe, Heather Graham, Scott Caan, John Ritter, Beverly D'Angelo, Denise Richards, Rose McGowan, Mena Suvari. CALIGULA for the CLUELESS set. Araki's slickest film to date focuses on a herd of oversexed L.A. teens searching for true love in the wasteland of SoCal. Pop visual design and eclectic cast make for some twisted fun, although the director's taste for gallows humor and brutal violence isn't for everyone. Various pop culture celebrities turn up in cameos. Filmed in 1995. [R]▼●

Nowhere to Go (1958-British) **97m.** *** D: Seth Holt. George Nader, Maggie Smith, Bernard Lee, Geoffrey Keen, Bessie Love. Unsung, beautifully realized film noir stars Nader as a smooth Canadian burglar in England who hides out with Smith while on the run. Brilliant deep-focus photography by Paul Beeson and a moody score by jazz trumpeter Dizzy Reece stand out. Smith's film debut. Metroscope.

Nowhere to Hide (1987-Canadian) **C-90m.** ** D: Mario Azzopardi. Amy Madigan, Daniel Hugh Kelly, Robin MacEachern, Michael Ironside, John Colicos. Obvious thriller with Madigan cast as the wife of Marine Kelly. He's killed while investigating suspicious helicopter crashes . . . and she becomes a target. Madigan is much better than the material. [R]▼

Nowhere to Run (1993) **C-95m.** *½ D: Robert Harmon. Jean-Claude Van Damme, Rosanna Arquette, Kieran Culkin, Ted Levine, Joss Ackland, Tiffany Taubman. Embarrassingly awful Van Damme vehicle, in which he's an escaped con who comes to the aid of widow-in-distress Arquette and her two kids. Based on a story by Joe Eszterhas and Richard Marquand; Eszterhas also scripted. [R]▼●◗

Now, Voyager (1942) **117m.** ***½ D: Irving Rapper. Bette Davis, Paul Henreid, Claude Rains, Gladys Cooper, Bonita Granville, John Loder, Ilka Chase, Lee Patrick, Mary Wickes, Janis Wilson. Vintage, first-class soaper with Bette as sheltered spinster brought out of her shell by psychiatrist Rains, falling in love with suave Henreid, helping shy girl Wilson. All this set to beautiful, Oscar-winning Max Steiner music makes for top entertainment of this kind. Olive Higgins Prouty's bestseller was adapted by Casey Robinson.▼●

Now You See Him, Now You Don't (1972) **C-88m.** **½ D: Robert Butler. Kurt Russell, Cesar Romero, Joe Flynn, Jim Backus, William Windom, Michael McGreevy, Ed Begley, Jr. Follow-up to THE COMPUTER WORE TENNIS SHOES has student Russell inventing an invisible spray, which of course is coveted by a gang of crooks. Some good special effects in this so-so Disney comedy. [G]▼

Nuclear Run SEE: **Chain Reaction** (1980)

Nuclear Terror SEE: **Golden Rendezvous**

Nude Bomb, The (1980) **C-94m.** **½ D: Clive Donner. Don Adams, Andrea Howard, Vittorio Gassman, Dana Elcar, Pamela Hensley, Sylvia Kristel, Robert Karvelas, Norman Lloyd, Rhonda Fleming, Joey Forman. Secret Agent 86 from 1960s *Get*

Smart sitcom returns in feature-length spoof about a madman whose bombs will destroy the world's clothing; coscripter Bill Dana has a funny bit as fashion designer Jonathan Levinson Siegel. Agreeable time-filler. Shown on TV as THE RETURN OF MAXWELL SMART. Followed by the TV movie GET SMART, AGAIN! [PG]▼●

Nude in a White Car (1960-French) **87m.** **½ D: Robert Hossein. Marina Vlady, Robert Hossein, Odile Versois, Helena Manson, Henri Cremieux. Hossein's only clue to a crime is title person; suspenser set on French Riviera. Retitled: BLONDE IN A WHITE CAR.

Nudo di Donna (1981-Italian-French) **C-105m.** *** D: Nino Manfredi. Nino Manfredi, Eleonora Giorgi, Jean-Pierre Cassel, Georges Wilson. Suffering marital problems with wife of 16 years (Giorgi), Manfredi becomes infatuated with a nude rearview photo and takes up with its model, who looks just like his wife! Stunning location photography in Venice and a solid cast highlight this social comedy.▼●

Number One (1969) **C-105m.** *½ D: Tom Gries. Charlton Heston, Jessica Walter, Bruce Dern, John Randolph, Diana Muldaur. Heston turns in his loincloth for a jockstrap in this ludicrous drama about a New Orleans Saints quarterback who's fighting advancing age; interesting subject matter deserves better treatment. [M/PG]

Number One Fan (1994) **C-93m.** ** D: Jane Simpson. Chad McQueen, Catherine Mary Stewart, Renee Ammann, Paul Bartel, Eric Da Re, Charles Matthau, Dean Norris, Hoyt Axton. Action movie megastar McQueen allows himself to be seduced by kittenish fan, who turns out to be a psycho. Oh-so-familiar erotic thriller is entertaining nonetheless, until preposterous finale. McQueen reminds one of Bruce Willis rather than his late father Steve; Matthau is the son of Walter (and looks it); Da Re is the son of Aldo Ray. Watch for Mary Woronov and Dick Miller in cameos. [R] ▼●

Number One With a Bullet (1987) **C-101m.** **½ D: Jack Smight. Robert Carradine, Billy Dee Williams, Valerie Bertinelli, Peter Graves, Doris Roberts, Bobby Di Cicco. Carradine and Williams do well in this otherwise standard actioner, cast as a pair of "odd couple" detectives out to dethrone a drug kingpin. [R]▼

Number Seventeen (1932-British) **63m.** *** D: Alfred Hitchcock. Leon M. Lion, Anne Grey, John Stuart, Donald Calthrop, Barry Jones, Garry Marsh. Entertaining comedy-thriller has tramp Lion stumbling upon a jewel thieves' hideout. Exciting chase sequence involves a train and bus (though the "special effects" are pretty obvious). Screenplay by Hitchcock.▼●

Number Six (1962-British) **59m.** ** D: Robert Tronson. Nadja Regin, Ivan Desny, Brian Bedford, Michael Goodliffe. Regin is heiress mixed up in espionage and murder; OK Edgar Wallace suspenser.

Numero Deux (1975-French) **C-88m.** **½ D: Jean-Luc Godard. Sandrine Battistella, Pierre Dudry, Alexandre Rignault, Rachel Stefanopoli. Fascinating but self-conscious and confusing aural and visual smorgasbord detailing the effects of capitalism on a modern family. Shot on videotape. ▼

Nun and the Sergeant, The (1962) **74m.** ** D: Franklin Adreon. Robert Webber, Anna Sten, Leo Gordon. Hari Rhodes, Robert Easton, Dale Ishimoto, Linda Wong. Set in Korea during the war; title tells rest.

Nuns on the Run (1990-British) **C-90m.** **½ D: Jonathan Lynn. Eric Idle, Robbie Coltrane, Camille Coduri, Janet Suzman, Doris Hare, Lila Kaye, Robert Patterson. Genial farce about two career henchmen, fed up with their violent young boss, who try to make a score for themselves but bungle the job and hide out in a convent, disguised as nuns. Idle and Coltrane are great, and the film is genuinely funny at times—enough to forgive its periodic lulls. Written by director Lynn. [PG-13]▼●

Nun's Story, The (1959) **C-149m.** ***½ D: Fred Zinnemann. Audrey Hepburn, Peter Finch, Edith Evans, Peggy Ashcroft, Dean Jagger, Mildred Dunnock. Tasteful filming of Kathryn Hulme book, with Hepburn the nun who serves in Belgian Congo and later leaves convent. Colleen Dewhurst, as a homicidal patient, is electrifying. Screenplay by Robert Anderson.▼●

Nunzio (1978) **C-87m.** **½ D: Paul Williams. David Proval, James Andronica, Tovah Feldshuh, Morgana King, Vincent Russo, Theresa Saldana, Monica Lewis. Retarded Brooklyn grocery delivery boy Proval, imagines he's Superman, falls in love with bakery assistant Feldshuh. Mild story enhanced by Proval's fine performance; script by Andronica, who plays his tough but loving brother. [R]

Nurse Edith Cavell (1939) **108m.** *** D: Herbert Wilcox. Anna Neagle, Edna May Oliver, George Sanders, ZaSu Pitts, May Robson, H. B. Warner, Robert Coote. Neagle is fine as dedicated WW1 nurse who worked with the Brussels underground to aid wounded soldiers. Sturdy production.▼

Nurse on Wheels (1963-British) **86m.** *** D: Gerald Thomas. Juliet Mills, Ronald Lewis, Joan Sims, Noel Purcell, Raymond Huntley, Jim Dale. The trials of nurse Mills, who settles down to practice in a rural community. Entertaining, often touching.

Nurse Sherri SEE: **Beyond the Living**

Nutcracker (1982-British) **C-101m.** *½ D: Anwar Kawadri. Joan Collins, Carol White, Paul Nicholas, Finola Hughes, William Franklyn, Leslie Ash. Silly soaper about a Russian dancer who defects and joins the ballet company of a powerful, rich bitch (who else but Collins, in a role she can play in her sleep—and does). [R]

Nutcracker, The (1993) **C-92m.** ** D: Emile Ardolino. Darci Kistler, Damian Woetzel, Kyra Nichols, Bart Robinson Cook, Macaulay Culkin, Jessica Lynn Cohen; narrated by Kevin Kline. Much-too-stagy version of the famed, beloved ballet, set on Christmas Eve and telling the story of a little girl (Cohen) who finds herself in a fantasy-world of oversized toys. Culkin (the film's star attraction) is nothing special as the Nutcracker Prince. Adapted by Peter Martins, from the New York City Ballet production. Aka GEORGE BALANCHINE'S THE NUTCRACKER. [G]▼●◗

Nutcracker Prince, The (1990-Canadian) **C-75m.** *½ D: Paul Schibli. Voices of Kiefer Sutherland, Megan Follows, Peter O'Toole, Mike McDonald, Peter Boretski, Phyllis Diller. Young girl dreams of aiding toy soldiers in battle against evil Mouse King in this flat reworking of the classic story, set to Tchaikovsky music. Slow-paced low-budget animated feature based on the E. T. A. Hoffmann book *The Nutcracker and the Mouse King*; a Disney wannabe that simply isn't. [G]▼●

Nutcracker, The Motion Picture (1986) **C-89m.** **½ D: Carroll Ballard. Hugh Bigney, Vanessa Sharp, Patricia Barker, Wade Walthall, Russell Burnett, voice of Julie Harris. Much of this version of *The Nutcracker,* performed by the Pacific Northwest Ballet, is like a music video: quick cutting and close-ups of legs, faces, and elbows. Very annoying. But the Tchaikovsky music is, of course, wonderful, as are Maurice Sendak's sets and costumes. [G]▼

Nuts (1987) **C-116m.** *** D: Martin Ritt. Barbra Streisand, Richard Dreyfuss, Maureen Stapleton, Eli Wallach, Robert Webber, James Whitmore, Karl Malden, Leslie Nielsen, William Prince, Hayley Taylor Block. Compelling drama about a belligerent woman assigned a Legal Aid lawyer who must fight for her right to stand trial for manslaughter, when both the state and her own parents insist that she's not in her right mind. Peerless cast of pros, and nimble staging by Ritt, manage to make you forget that this was a stage play, until the climax, when Streisand delivers a lengthy monologue—in loving close-up (she also produced). Tom Topor adapted his play, with Darryl Ponicsan and Alvin Sargent. Streisand also composed the score. [R]▼●

Nutty, Naughty Chateau (1964-French) **C-100m.** **½ D: Roger Vadim. Monica Vitti, Curt Jurgens, Jean-Claude Brialy, Sylvie, Jean-Louis Trintignant, Françoise Hardy. Bizarre minor comedy involving the strange inhabitants of a castle romping about in 1750s styles; most diverting cast. Based on a Françoise Sagan play. Franscope.

Nutty Professor, The (1963) **C-107m.** *** D: Jerry Lewis. Jerry Lewis, Stella Stevens, Del Moore, Kathleen Freeman, Med Flory, Howard Morris, Elvia Allman, Henry Gibson. Jerry's wildest (and most narcissistic) comedy casts him as chipmunk-faced college professor who does Jekyll-and-Hyde transformation into swaggering Buddy Love (whom some have interpreted as a Dean Martin caricature). More interesting than funny, although "Alaskan Polar Bear Heater" routine with Buddy Lester is a riot; Lewis buffs regard this as his masterpiece. Remade in 1996. ▼●

Nutty Professor, The (1996) **C-95m.** *** D: Tom Shadyac. Eddie Murphy, Jada Pinkett, James Coburn, Dave Chappelle, Larry Miller, John Ales. Sherman Klump is a sweet stumblebum of a science professor who's grossly overweight; when he meets a beautiful young teaching assistant, he becomes motivated to try his lab experiments with DNA restructuring on himself and he's transformed into a thin, testosterone-overloaded superstud. Not only is Eddie appealing and convincing as the prof, and hilarious as his alter ego, but through camera magic (and the eye-popping, Oscar-winning makeup by Rick Baker and David Leroy Anderson) he also plays almost every member of his family! One ingredient Jerry Lewis never thought of: enough flatulence jokes to last ten lifetimes. [PG-13]▼●◗

Oak, The (1992-French-Romanian) **C-105m.** *** D: Lucian Pintilie. Maia Morgenstern, Razvan Vasilescu, Victor Rebenguic, Dorel Visan. Schoolteacher Morgenstern sets out on a journey of self-discovery after her father (a former secret-police honcho) dies. Fascinating allegory–road movie mirroring the downfall of Communism in Romania. A highly personal film, strikingly directed by Pintilie, who also scripted.▼

Oasis (1955-French) **C-84m.** ** D: Yves Allegret. Michele Morgan, Pierre Brasseur, Cornell Borchers, Carl Raddatz. Morgan's radiance brightens this oft-told story of gold-smuggling in Africa. CinemaScope.

Oasis, The (1984) **C-90m.** **½ D: Sparky Greene. Chris Makepeace, Scott Hylands, Richard Cox, Dori Brenner, Rick Podell, Mark Metcalf, Anne Lockhart. Unrelentingly grim, harrowing (and bloody) account of interaction among plane crash survivors in Mexican desert. Opening sequence is a stunner, but overall, too unpleasant.

Objective, Burma! (1945) **142m.** ***½ D: Raoul Walsh. Errol Flynn, William Prince, James Brown, George Tobias, Henry Hull, Warner Anderson. Zestful WW2 action film with Flynn and company as paratroopers invading Burma to wipe out important Japanese post; top excitement. Screenplay by Ranald MacDougall and Lester Cole. Reworked as DISTANT DRUMS, also directed by Walsh. Some prints cut to 127m. Also shown in computer-colored version. ▼●

Object of Beauty, The (1991) **C-97m.** **½ D: Michael Lindsay-Hogg. John Malkovich, Andie MacDowell, Lolita Davidovich, Rudi Davies, Joss Ackland, Bill Paterson, Ricci Harnett, Peter Riegert. Jet-set couple, who thrive on living beyond their means, find themselves stranded in a London hotel and decide to unload her coveted Henry Moore artifact—the one that may have been stolen by the hotel's newly hired deaf-mute maid. Definitely offbeat, but never really gets going; just enough style to keep it afloat, and the leads are well cast. [R]▼◗

Object of my Affection, The (1998) **C-112m.** *** D: Nicholas Hytner. Jennifer Aniston, Paul Rudd, Alan Alda, Nigel Hawthorne, John Pankow, Tim Daly, Allison Janney, Steve Zahn, Amo Gulinello, Bruce Altman, Joan Copeland. Young woman invites a gay schoolteacher who's just been dumped by his boyfriend to move into her spare room. They enjoy each other's company so much that she proposes a long-term, nonsexual "arrangement." Appealing actors carry this longish, serpentine, unconventional romantic comedy, written by Wendy Wasserstein, from the novel by Stephen McCauley . . . though the supporting actors (Alda, Janney, Hawthorne) threaten to steal it from the stars. [R]▼●

Obliging Young Lady (1941) **80m.** **½ D: Richard Wallace. Eve Arden, Edmond O'Brien, Ruth Warrick, Joan Carroll, Franklin Pangborn, George Cleveland. Agreeable comedy about youngster, center of custody fight, finding herself the focal point at a country resort.

Oblomov (1980-Russian) **C-146m.** ***½ D: Nikita Mikhalkov. Oleg Tabakov, Yuri Bogatryev, Elena Soloyei, Andrei Popov. Thirtyish civil servant and absentee landlord, nicely played by Tabakov, retires to a listless existence in bed. Lyrical adaptation of Ivan Goncharov's 1858 novel; flashback sequences of Oblomov as a boy in his mother's arms are wonderful. Outstanding cinematography. Aka A FEW DAYS IN THE LIFE OF I. I. OBLOMOV. ▼

Oblong Box, The (1969-British) **C-91m.** ** D: Gordon Hessler. Vincent Price, Christopher Lee, Alastair Williamson, Hilary Dwyer, Peter Arne, Maxwell Shaw, Sally Geeson. Price plays British aristocrat tormented by disfigured brother who's out for revenge after briefly being buried alive. Hammy performances, long drawn-out narrative, lackluster direction. [M]▼●

Obsessed (1951-British) **78m.** ** D: Maurice Elvey. David Farrar, Geraldine Fitzgerald, Roland Culver, Jean Cadell. A schoolteacher (Farrar) and the paid companion (Fitzgerald) of his long-ill and mean-spirited wife have fallen in love. Both become murder suspects when the wife is poisoned. Lackluster mystery, based on a hit stage play. Original British title: THE LATE EDWINA BLACK.▼

Obsessed (1989-Canadian) **C-100m.** **½ D: Robin Spry. Kerrie Keane, Daniel Pilon, Saul Rubinek, Lynne Griffin, Alan Thicke, Colleen Dewhurst. Good but slightly meandering drama pitting Keane against Rubinek, the thoughtless hit-and-run driver who killed her son. Well cast and engrossing, marred slightly by tendency toward sensationalism. [PG-13]▼●

Obsession (1949) SEE: **Hidden Room, The**

Obsession (1976) **C-98m.** **½ D: Brian De Palma. Cliff Robertson, Genevieve Bujold, John Lithgow, Sylvia Kuumba Williams, Wanda Blackman. Viewers who don't remember Hitchcock's VERTIGO might enjoy this rehash by De Palma and writer Paul Schrader. Robertson loses his wife and child to kidnappers, then miraculously finds wife "reborn" in another woman. Holds up until denouement. Superb Bernard Herrmann score. Panavision. [PG]▼●

Obsession (1980) SEE: **Circle of Two**

O.C. & Stiggs (1987) **C-109m.** ** D: Robert Altman. Daniel H. Jenkins, Neill Barry, Paul Dooley, Jane Curtin, Jon Cryer, Ray Walston, Louis Nye, Tina Louise, Martin Mull, Dennis Hopper, Melvin Van Peebles. Quirky (even by Altman standards) film recounts title teens' summer adventures, which consist mainly of making life miserable for the Schwab family and the cutthroat insurance agent father (Dooley) who cut off Stiggs' grandfather's old-age policy. Not without its moments and Altman weirdos—including Hopper as a drug- and gun-dealing vet, Louise as the sexy school nurse, and Curtin as the drunken Schwab matriarch—but ultimately incoherent. Sat on the shelf for several years. [R]▼

Ocean's Eleven (1960) **C-127m.** **½ D: Lewis Milestone. Frank Sinatra, Dean Martin, Sammy Davis, Jr., Peter Lawford, Angie Dickinson, Richard Conte, Cesar Romero, Patrice Wymore, Joey Bishop, Akim Tamiroff, Henry Silva, Ilka Chase, Norman Fell. Fanciful crime comedy about eleven-man team headed by Danny Ocean (Sinatra) attempting to rob five Vegas casinos simultaneously. Entire Rat Pack's in it, but no one does much, including some surprise guests. There is a clever twist ending, though. Panavision.▼●

Octagon, The (1980) **C-103m.** ** D: Eric Karson. Chuck Norris, Karen Carlson, Lee Van Cleef, Art Hindle, Jack Carter. OK Kung Fu drama with Norris taking on all comers when hired by Carlson for protection from Ninja assassins. Fair of its kind, with above-average production values. [R]▼●

Octaman (1971) **C-90m.** BOMB D: Harry Essex. Kerwin Mathews, Pier Angeli, Jeff

Morrow, Jerry Guardino, Norman Fields. Rick Baker's "octopus" creation almost—but not quite—makes this dreadful thriller about the title monster discovered on an expedition to Mexico tolerable. Angeli died during shooting.▼

October (1928-Russian) **103m.** *** D: Sergei Eisenstein, Grigori Alexandrov. Nikandrov, N. Popov, Boris Livanov. Brilliant reconstruction of the Russian Revolution contains some of Eisenstein's most striking use of montage, though most impressive sequences—such as the masterful massacre around the bridges of St. Petersburg—are in the film's first half. Based on John Reed's *Ten Days That Shook the World*, the film's alternate title.▼●◗

October Man, The (1947-British) **98m.** *** D: Roy (Ward) Baker. John Mills, Joan Greenwood, Edward Chapman, Joyce Carey, Kay Walsh, Felix Aylmer, Juliet Mills. Stranger with history of mental disorders is suspected of murder and must prove innocence, even to himself. Strong character study and good local atmosphere enhance suspenseful mystery written by Eric Ambler. British running time 110m.▼

October Moth (1959-British) **54m.** *½ D: John Kruse. Lee Patterson, Lana Morris, Peter Dyneley, Robert Crawdon. Turgid melodrama set on lonely farm, with Morris trying to cope with dim-witted brother who has injured a passerby.

October Sky (1999) **C-108m.** ***½ D: Joe Johnston. Jake Gyllenhaal, Chris Cooper, Laura Dern, Chris Owen, William Lee Scott, Chad Lindberg, Natalie Canerday, Scott Miles. Sincere, heartwarming drama based on the true story of Homer Hickam, Jr. (Gyllenhaal), who grew up in an insular West Virginia coal-mining town. When he sees *Sputnik* soaring across the nighttime sky in 1957, he becomes obsessed with the idea of building his own rocket and enlists his friends to share the dream . . . against the wishes of his father, a harsh man who's the mine foreman. Rich performances, well-drawn characters, and an old-fashioned sense of can-do American spirit make this something special. Written by Lewis Colick from Hickam's book *Rocket Boys*. Panavision. [PG]▼●◗

Octopussy (1983-British) **C-130m.** ***½ D: John Glen. Roger Moore, Maud Adams, Louis Jourdan, Kristina Wayborn, Kabir Bedi, Steven Berkoff, Desmond Llewelyn, Vijay Amritraj, Lois Maxwell. Grand escapist fare as Moore, growing nicely into the role of James Bond, matches wits with a handful of nemeses, including title-named character (Adams), whose motives—and modus operandi—are more than a bit vague. Film throws in everything but the kitchen sink for the sake of an entertaining show. Panavision. [PG]▼●

Odd Angry Shot, The (1979-Australian) **C-92m.** **½ D: Tom Jeffrey. John Hargreaves, Graham Kennedy, Bryan Brown, John Jarratt. Interesting film about a group of Australian professional soldiers stationed in Vietnam. Personal drama emphasized more than combat in poignant, sometimes broadly comic work about soldiers dealing with a war they don't think is really theirs.▼

Oddball Hall (1990) **C-87m.** ** D: Jackson Hunsicker. Don Ameche, Burgess Meredith, Bill Maynard, Tullio Moneta, Tiny Skefile. Four jewel thieves hole up in an African town, posing as members of a fraternal order called The Oddballs, and waiting to collect on a heist they pulled off years ago; a simpleminded native comes along seeking their help, and they mistake him for an Oddball chieftain. Simplistic farce is good-natured but heavy-handed; the only thing missing is laughs. [PG]▼●

Odd Birds (1985) **C-90m.** **½ D: Jeanne Collachia. Michael Moriarty, Donna Lai Ming Lew, Nancy Lee, Bruce Gray, Karen Maruyama, Scott Crawford. Awkward direction and uneven performances defeat this sensitive drama about a dreamy teenager with braces who yearns for a career as an actress, and her friendship with compassionate but disillusioned brother-teacher Moriarty. Nice feel for the way real teen girls acted back in 1965, and for the pain of being fifteen and shy.▼

Odd Couple, The (1968) **C-105m.** *** D: Gene Saks. Jack Lemmon, Walter Matthau, John Fiedler, Herb Edelman, Monica Evans, Carole Shelley. Film version of Neil Simon stage hit about two divorced men living together, sloppy Oscar (Matthau) and fussy Felix (Lemmon). Lemmon's realistic performance makes character melancholy instead of funny; other surefire comic sequences remain intact. Later developed into two TV series. Followed by a sequel. Panavision. ▼●

Odd Couple II, The (1998) **C-96m.** *½ D: Howard Deutch. Jack Lemmon, Walter Matthau, Christine Baranski, Barnard Hughes, Jonathan Silverman, Jean Smart, Lisa Waltz, Mary Beth Peil, Jay O. Sanders, Rex Linn, Alice Ghostley, Florence Stanley, Estelle Harris, Amy Yasbeck. Neil Simon wrote this sorry sequel reuniting Felix and Oscar after seventeen years when their children announce their impending marriage. The two cronies meet up in L.A., get lost while driving to the ceremony, and find themselves in a series of escalating mishaps. Sporadically funny one-liners can't save this tired film. A real shame. Officially titled NEIL SIMON'S THE ODD COUPLE II. Super 35. [PG-13]▼●◗

Odd Job, The (1978-British) **C-86m.** **½ D: Peter Medak. Graham Chapman, David Jason, Diana Quick, Simon Williams, Edward Hardwicke. British update of time-worn premise (used as early as 1916 by Douglas Fairbanks in FLIRTING WITH

FATE): an unhappy man, jilted by his wife, hires a hit man to murder her, then has a change of heart . . . but convincing the hired killer is a formidable challenge! Coscripted by Bernard McKenna and Chapman, of Monty Python fame.▼

Odd Jobs (1984) **C-88m.** ** D: Mark Story. Paul Reiser, Robert Townsend, Scott McGinnis, Paul Provenza, Julianne Phillips, Leon Askin, Richard Dean Anderson. Lame comedy about five college students working for a moving company over the summer. Radio personality Don Imus has a cameo. [PG-13]▼

Odd Man Out (1947-British) **115m.** **** D: Carol Reed. James Mason, Robert Newton, Kathleen Ryan, Robert Beatty, Cyril Cusack, F.J. McCormick, William Hartnell, Fay Compton, Denis O'Dea, Dan O'Herlihy. Incredibly suspenseful tale of Irish rebel leader hunted by police after daring robbery. Watch this one! Scripted by R. C. Sherriff and F. L. Green, from the latter's novel. Remade as THE LOST MAN. ▼●◗

Odd Obsession (1959-Japanese) **C-96m.** **½ D: Kon Ichikawa. Machiko Kyo, Ganjiro Nakamura, Tatsuya Nakadai, Junko Kano. Elderly, vain Nakamura tempts beautiful wife (Kyo) into an affair with his young doctor (Nakadai). Uneven soap opera; a few bright moments, but disappointing overall. Original running-time 107m. Remade in Italy in 1984 as THE KEY, which is also this film's alternative title (a literal translation of the Japanese title, KAGI). Daieiscope.▼

Odds Against Tomorrow (1959) **95m.** *** D: Robert Wise. Harry Belafonte, Robert Ryan, Shelley Winters, Ed Begley, Gloria Grahame. Brutal robbery story with entire cast pulling out all stops; taut, exciting drama. Jazz score by John Lewis. Film debut of Wayne Rogers.▼●

Odessa File, The (1974-British) **C-128m.** **½ D: Ronald Neame. Jon Voight, Maximilian Schell, Maria Schell, Mary Tamm, Derek Jacobi, Klaus Lowitsch. Voight carries this plodding adaptation of the Frederick Forsyth best-seller, set in 1963, about a German journalist who tracks down former Nazis. OK time killer, no more. Music score by Andrew Lloyd Webber. Panavision. [PG]▼●◗

Ode to Billy Joe (1976) **C-108m.** ** D: Max Baer. Robby Benson, Glynnis O'Connor, Joan Hotchkis, Sandy McPeak, James Best, Terence Goodman. Bobbie Gentry's 1967 song hit provides basis for standard rural romance that grows progressively ridiculous. Benson and O'Connor, reunited after JEREMY, still have appeal. [PG]▼

Odette (1950-British) **100m.** *** D: Herbert Wilcox. Anna Neagle, Trevor Howard, Marius Goring, Peter Ustinov, Bernard Lee. Neagle is excellent in true story of Odette Churchill, undercover British agent imprisoned by Nazis during WW2.

Odongo (1956-British) **C-85m.** BOMB D: John Gilling. Rhonda Fleming, Macdonald Carey, Juma, Eleanor Summerfield, Francis De Wolff. Juvenile jungle flick about search for missing native boy. CinemaScope.

Odyssey of the Pacific (1981-Canadian-French) **C-100m.** ** D: Fernando Arrabal. Mickey Rooney, Monique Mercure, Jean-Louis Roux, Guy Hoffman. Slight tale of Rooney, a retired train engineer living near an abandoned railway station, befriending a trio of homeless youngsters. Originally titled THE EMPEROR OF PERU.▼

Oedipus Rex (1957-Canadian) **C-87m.** **½ D: Tyrone Guthrie. Douglas Rain, Douglas Campbell, Eric House, Eleanor Stuart. Restrained, professional rendering of Sophocles' Greek tragedy.▼

Oedipus Rex (1967-Italian) **C-110m.** **½ D: Pier Paolo Pasolini. Franco Citti, Silvana Mangano, Alida Valli, Carmelo Bene, Julian Beck. Pictorially arresting but dull, disappointing adaptation of Sophocles' *Oedipus Rex* and *Oedipus at Colonus*, with Citti, as Oedipus, murdering his father and marrying his mother. Presented in both contemporary and historical settings; that's Pasolini himself as the High Priest.▼●

Oedipus the King (1968-British) **C-97m.** **½ D: Philip Saville. Christopher Plummer, Orson Welles, Lilli Palmer, Richard Johnson, Cyril Cusack, Roger Livesey, Donald Sutherland. Film version of Sophocles play is OK for students who have a test on it the next day, but others won't appreciate this version. Static, despite that cast. [G]

Off Beat (1986) **C-92m.** ** D: Michael Dinner. Judge Reinhold, Meg Tilly, Cleavant Derricks, Joe Mantegna, Jacques D'Amboise, James Tolkan, Amy Wright, John Turturro, Anthony Zerbe, Julie Bovasso, Fred Gwynne, Harvey Keitel, Austin Pendleton, Penn Jillette, Bill Sadler, Christopher Noth. Library worker Reinhold, filling in for policeman friend at rehearsal for a dance recital, falls in love with female cop. Modest comedy works hard to live up to its name but comes up short. Reinhold and Tilly are so low-key, they almost disappear! Great cast can't save it. Written by playwright Mark Medoff (who plays Sgt. Tiegher). [PG]▼●

Offence, The (1973-British) **C-112m.** *** D: Sidney Lumet. Sean Connery, Trevor Howard, Vivien Merchant, Ian Bannen, Derek Newark. Intense drama about how London detective Connery's frustrations cause him to beat a suspect to death; a fine performance by Connery. [R]▼

Officer and a Gentleman, An (1982) **C-125m.** **½ D: Taylor Hackford. Richard Gere, Debra Winger, David Keith, Louis Gossett, Jr., Robert Loggia, Lisa

Blount, Lisa Eilbacher, Victor French, Grace Zabriskie, David Caruso. Two misfitsseek direction in their dead-end lives—he by enrolling in Naval Officer Candidate School, she by trying to snag him as a husband. Four-letter words and steamy sex scenes can't camouflage a well-worn Hollywood formula script—with virtually every plot point telegraphed ahead of time! Made agreeable by an appealing cast, though even Gossett's Oscar-winning performance as a drill instructor is just a reprise of earlier work like Jack Webb's in THE D.I. Film's love song, "Up Where We Belong," also won an Oscar. [R]▼●

Office Space (1999) **C-89m.** ** D: Mike Judge. Ron Livingston, Jennifer Aniston, David Herman, Ajay Naidu, Diedrich Bader, Stephen Root, Gary Cole, Richard Riehle. Fitfully funny satire of office life in modern-day corporate America, with Livingston as a computer programmer who hates his job and eventually finds a way to express his disdain for his company—and his boss (Cole). Dry and undernourished, though there are some laughs along the way. Live-action writing and directing debut for Judge, creator of the animated TV series *Beavis and Butt-head* and *King of the Hill.* [R]▼●◗

Official Story, The (1985-Argentina) **C-113m.** **** D: Luis Puenzo. Norma Aleandro, Hector Alterio, Analia Castro, Chunchuna Villafane. Aleandro is exceptional as woman who lives the good life, sheltered from political turmoil that surrounds her in Argentina . . . until she begins to suspect that her adopted daughter may have been the offspring of a political prisoner. One of those rare films that manages to make a strong political statement in the midst of a crackling good story. Hard to believe it was director Puenzo's first feature film (he also scripted with Aida Bortnik). Oscar winner as Best Foreign Language Film. A knockout.▼●◗

Of Flesh and Blood (1962-French) **C-92m.** **½ D: Christian Marquand. Robert Hossein, Renato Salvatori, Anouk Aimée, André Bervil, Jean Lefebvre. Murky account of passerby Salvatori having an affair with Aimée, involved with card-cheat-turned-murderer Hossein. Franscope.

Off Limits (1953) **87m.** **½ D: George Marshall. Bob Hope, Mickey Rooney, Marilyn Maxwell, Eddie Mayehoff, Stanley Clements, Jack Dempsey, Marvin Miller, Tom Harmon, Carolyn Jones. Peppy but predictable comedy with fight manager Hope finding himself in the army; he attempts to romance Maxwell (whose nephew, Rooney, wants Hope to train him as a boxer).▼

Off Limits (1988) **C-102m.** *½ D: Christopher Crowe. Willem Dafoe, Gregory Hines, Fred Ward, Amanda Pays, Scott Glenn, Kay Tong Lim, David Alan Grier, Keith David. Sluggish, predictable, unusually sordid melodrama about two pros in the U.S. Army's Criminal Investigation Detachment (CID) who track down the ghoul murdering Vietnamese hookers in 1968 Saigon. Dafoe's googoo eyes at nun Pays are good for a few unintentional chuckles; if you can't guess the murderer, get a new hobby. [R]▼●

Offspring, The (1986) **C-99m.** *½ D: Jeff Burr. Vincent Price, Clu Gulager, Terry Kiser, Harry Caesar, Cameron Mitchell, Rosalind Cash, Susan Tyrrell, Martine Beswick, Angelo Rossitto, Lawrence Tierney. Small-town historian Price spins a quartet of horror tales, each of which took place in his hamlet. None is worth listening to. Helluva cast, however. Aka FROM A WHISPER TO A SCREAM. [R] ▼●

Off the Wall (1983) **C-85m.** BOMB D: Rick Friedberg. Paul Sorvino, Rosanna Arquette, Patrick Cassidy, Billy Hufsey, Ralph Wilcox, Dick Chudnow, Monte Markham, Brianne Leary, Mickey Gilley, Lewis Arquette. Phony comedy set in a Tennessee prison. Rosanna Arquette is wasted as daughter of state governor (Markham). [R]▼

Of Human Bondage (1934) **88m.** *** D: John Cromwell. Leslie Howard, Bette Davis, Frances Dee, Kay Johnson, Reginald Denny, Alan Hale, Reginald Owen. Smoothly filmed, well-acted version of W. Somerset Maugham's story of doctor Howard's strange infatuation with a vulgar waitress (Davis). Many find Davis' performance overdone, but by any standards it's powerfully impressive, and put her on the map in Hollywood. Howard, lovely Johnson, others are superb. Remade in 1946 (with Eleanor Parker) and 1964. Also shown in computer-colored version.▼●

Of Human Bondage (1964-British) **98m.** **½ D: Ken Hughes. Kim Novak, Laurence Harvey, Siobhan McKenna, Robert Morley, Roger Livesey, Nanette Newman, Brenda Fricker. Third and least successful filming of Maugham novel of doctor's passion for lowbrow waitress, marred by miscasting and general superficiality.▼

Of Human Hearts (1938) **100m.** **½ D: Clarence Brown. Walter Huston, James Stewart, Gene Reynolds, Beulah Bondi, Guy Kibbee, Charles Coburn, John Carradine, Ann Rutherford. Odd blend of potent 19th-century Americana and mile-high corn, in tale of dedicated preacher Huston who never established rapport with his son. When Abraham Lincoln (Carradine) lectures Stewart about neglecting his mother, it gets to be a bit much.▼

Of Life and Love (1957-Italian) **103m.** **½ D: Aldo Fabrizi, Luchino Visconti, Mario Soldati, Giorgio Pastina. Anna Magnani, Walter Chiari, Natale Cirino, Turi Pandolfini, Myriam Bru, Lucia Bose.

Four satisfactory episodes, three of which are based on Pirandello tales; fourth is actual event in Magnani's life (''The Lapdog''). Actually distilled from two Italian episodic features from 1953 and 1954.

Of Love and Desire (1963) **C-97m.** *½ D: Richard Rush. Merle Oberon, Steve Cochran, Curt Jurgens, John Agar, Steve Brodie. Beautiful settings (including Oberon's lavish Mexican home) offset overwrought sexual drama of neurotic woman who plays with the affection of several men—including her own stepbrother.

Of Love and Shadows (1994-Spanish-Argentinian) **C-109m.** *½ D: Betty Kaplan. Antonio Banderas, Jennifer Connelly, Stefania Sandrelli, Diego Wallraft, Camillo Gallardo. Young fashion journalist meets a mysterious photographer and—well, more than just film develops. Adapted from an Isabel Allende novel, this love story set against the backdrop of a Chilean military dictatorship in 1973 is a complete misfire. Convoluted plot makes little sense, and there's no chemistry between the attractive leads. [R]▼

Of Mice and Men (1939) **107m.** **** D: Lewis Milestone. Lon Chaney, Jr., Burgess Meredith, Betty Field, Charles Bickford, Bob Steele, Noah Beery, Jr. Chaney gives best performance of his career as feeble-brained Lennie who, with migrant-worker Meredith, tries to live peacefully on ranch. John Steinbeck's morality tale remains intact in sensitive screen version. The film's action begins *before* the main title credits—an arty innovation for 1939. Script by Eugene Solow. Music by Aaron Copland. Remade twice.▼●◗

Of Mice and Men (1981) **C-125m. TVM** D: Reza Badiyi. Robert Blake, Randy Quaid, Lew Ayres, Pat Hingle, Mitchell Ryan, Cassie Yates, Ted Neeley, Whitman Mayo. Fulfilling a long-time dream, producer-star Blake turns out a sturdy remake of the Steinbeck classic with his *Baretta* and *Joe Dancer* production buddies. Above average.▼

Of Mice and Men (1992) **C-110m.** *** D: Gary Sinise. John Malkovich, Gary Sinise, Alexis Arquette, Sherilyn Fenn, Joe Morton, Richard Riehle, Casey Siemaszko, John Terry, Ray Walston, Noble Willingham. More than respectable rendering of the Steinbeck warhorse, with Malkovich and Sinise respectively cast as Lennie and George—the sweet simpleton and his weary protector. Rescued from mothballs (and high school English) by the subtext of today's homeless; robust performances and impressive sun-baked look (photographed by Kenneth MacMillan) make it worthwhile. Screenplay by Horton Foote. [PG-13]▼●

Of Unknown Origin (1983-Canadian) **C-88m.** ** D: George Pan Cosmatos. Peter Weller, Jennifer Dale, Lawrence Dane, Kenneth Welsh, Louis Del Grande, Shannon Tweed. N.Y.C. businessman, bachelor-ing it temporarily, is driven to distraction by a giant rodent on the loose in his apartment. Slightly better than simultaneously released rat-themed DEADLY EYES. [R]▼

Ogre, The (1996-German-French-British) **C-117m.** **½ D: Volker Schlöndorff. John Malkovich, Gottfried John, Armin Mueller-Stahl, Marianne Sägebrecht, Volker Spengler, Heino Ferch, Dieter Laser. Seriocomic anti-Nazi parable is not nearly as good as Schlöndorff's classic THE TIN DRUM, but it's an interesting (if heavy-handed), horrific fairy tale about a childlike Frenchman (a miscast Malkovich) who willingly goes to work for the Nazis after being captured during the war and is used to ''recruit'' German children to join the army. Super 35.▼

Oh, Alfie SEE: **Alfie Darling**

O Happy Day SEE: **Seventeen and Anxious**

O'Hara's Wife (1982) **C-87m.** **½ D: William S. Bartman. Edward Asner, Mariette Hartley, Jodie Foster, Perry Lang, Tom Bosley, Ray Walston, Allen Williams, Mary Jo Catlett, Richard Schaal, Nehemiah Persoff. Only Asner is aware of the presence of wife Hartley, who's a ghost. Earnest but forgettable. [PG]▼

Oh Dad, Poor Dad, Mama's Hung You in the Closet and I'm Feeling So Sad (1967) **C-86m.** **½ D: Richard Quine. Rosalind Russell, Robert Morse, Barbara Harris, Hugh Griffith, Jonathan Winters, Lionel Jeffries, Cyril Delevanti. Impressive cast tries to sustain black comedy about overpossessive widow (Russell) and weirdo son (Morse) taking vacation on tropical island accompanied by coffin of her late husband. From the Arthur Kopit play.▼

O. Henry's Full House (1952) **117m.** **½ D: Henry Hathaway, Howard Hawks, Henry King, Henry Koster, Jean Negulesco. Fred Allen, Anne Baxter, Charles Laughton, Marilyn Monroe, Gregory Ratoff, Jeanne Crain, Oscar Levant, Jean Peters, Richard Widmark, Farley Granger. Five varying stories by O. Henry, introduced by John Steinbeck; cast better than script. ''The Clarion Call,'' ''Last Leaf,'' ''Ransom of Red Chief,'' ''Gift of the Magi,'' and ''Cop and the Anthem.''

Oh, God! (1977) **C-104m.** *** D: Carl Reiner. George Burns, John Denver, Teri Garr, Paul Sorvino, George Furth, Ralph Bellamy, Barnard Hughes, David Ogden Stiers. God appears in person of Burns to summon Denver as his messenger, to tell the world that he's alive and well. Film eschews cheap jokes to build a credible story with warm performances and upbeat message. Followed by a pair of sequels. [PG]▼●

Oh God! Book II (1980) **C-94m.** *½ D: Gilbert Cates. George Burns, Suzanne Pleshette, David Birney, Louanne, Howard Duff, Hans Conried, Wilfrid Hyde-White, Conrad Janis. Burns returns as title character; here, he enlists a child (Louanne) to remind the world that God is not dead. Contrived sequel with just a trickle of laughs; Pleshette, as usual, is wasted. [PG]▼

Oh, God! You Devil (1984) **C-96m.** ** D: Paul Bogart. George Burns, Ted Wass, Ron Silver, Roxanne Hart, Eugene Roche, Robert Desiderio. Third go-round for Burns gives him dual role of God *and* the Devil, with Wass as struggling songwriter and performer who sells his soul for success. Good cast and good-natured attitude can't overcome blandness and predictability of this comedy. Written by Andrew Bergman. [PG]▼●

Oh, Heavenly Dog! (1980) **C-103m.** **½ D: Joe Camp. Chevy Chase, Benji, Jane Seymour, Omar Sharif, Donnelly Rhodes, Robert Morley, Alan Sues. Private eye Chase returns to earth in the form of a dog to solve his own murder. Benji (in his third film) is as adorable as ever as Chase's alter ego. Filmed in England. Followed by BENJI THE HUNTED. [PG]▼

Oh, Men! Oh, Women! (1957) **C-90m.** **½ D: Nunnally Johnson. Ginger Rogers, David Niven, Dan Dailey, Barbara Rush, Tony Randall. Often bouncy sex farce revolving around psychiatrist and his assorted patients. Randall's feature debut. CinemaScope.

Oh . . . Rosalinda!! (1955-British) **C-101m.** **½ D: Michael Powell, Emeric Pressburger. Michael Redgrave, Ludmilla Tcherina, Anton Walbrook, Mel Ferrer, Dennis Price, Anthony Quayle, Annelise Rothenberger, singing voices of Sari Barabas, Alexander Young, Dennis Dowling, Walter Berry. Johann Strauss' opera *Die Fledermaus* is updated to contemporary Vienna but retains its elements of a masked ball, mistaken identity, flirtation, etc. Not entirely successful, but still stylish, witty, and colorful, as you'd expect from the team that brought you THE RED SHOES and TALES OF HOFFMAN. Redgrave, Quayle, and Rothenberger use their own singing voices, by the way. CinemaScope.

Oh! Susanna (1951) **C-90m.** ** D: Joseph Kane. Rod Cameron, Forrest Tucker, Adrian Booth, Chill Wills. Too much feuding between cavalry officers and too little real action mar this Western.

Oh! What a Lovely War (1969-British) **C-139m.** **½ D: Richard Attenborough. Laurence Olivier, John Gielgud, Ralph Richardson, Michael Redgrave, John Mills, Vanessa Redgrave, Dirk Bogarde, Susannah York, Maggie Smith, Jack Hawkins, Kenneth More, Corin Redgrave, Jane Seymour. Actor Attenborough's directing debut; impressive but cumbersome series of vignettes on WW1, ranging from colorful musical numbers to poignant human sidelights. Adapted from stage show. Beautifully designed, wildly cinematic, but too drawn-out to make maximum antiwar impact. Panavision. [G]

Oh, Woe Is Me SEE: **Hèlas Pour Moi**

Oh, You Beautiful Doll (1949) **C-93m.** **½ D: John M. Stahl. June Haver, Mark Stevens, S. Z. Sakall, Charlotte Greenwood, Gale Robbins, Jay C. Flippen. Chipper period musical about song plugger who turns serious composer's works into popular songs. Based on true story of Fred Fisher. Songs include title tune, "Peg o' My Heart," "Dardanella."

Oil (1977-Italian) **C-95m.** BOMB D: Mircea Dragan. Stuart Whitman, Woody Strode, Ray Milland, George Dinica, William Berger, Tony Kendall. A Sahara oilfield ablaze. After the 28th shot of the fire, you'll be ready to douse your TV set.▼

Oil for the Lamps of China (1935) **110m.** *** D: Mervyn LeRoy. Pat O'Brien, Josephine Hutchinson, Jean Muir, Lyle Talbot, Arthur Byron, John Eldredge, Henry O'Neill, Donald Crisp, Keye Luke. Dated but absorbing saga (from best-selling book by Alice Tisdale Hobart) about a man who dedicates his life to working for big oil company, which shows little regard for him in return; set mostly in China. Hutchinson's role, as his dedicated wife, is particularly interesting today in light of her comments about a woman's place in a man's life . . . while the film's foreword (and *deus ex machina* ending) indicates an uneasiness about attacking powerful oil companies too harshly!

Okinawa (1952) **67m.** ** D: Leigh Jason. Pat O'Brien, Cameron Mitchell, James Dobson, Richard Denning, Richard Benedict, Alvy Moore. Adequate programmer about men on a warship during the Pacific campaign of WW2.

Oklahoma! (1955) **C-145m.** ***½ D: Fred Zinnemann. Gordon MacRae, Shirley Jones, Charlotte Greenwood, Rod Steiger, Gloria Grahame, Eddie Albert, James Whitmore, Gene Nelson, Barbara Lawrence, Jay C. Flippen. Expansive film version of Rodgers and Hammerstein's landmark 1943 Broadway musical, filled with timeless songs (and the beautiful voices of MacRae and Jones to sing them) . . . plus a fine supporting cast led by incomparable Grahame as Ado Annie. Enough fine ingredients to make up for overlength of film. Songs include "Oh, What a Beautiful Mornin' " and showstopping title tune. This was filmed in two versions, one in Todd-AO and the other in CinemaScope—it's the latter version that's been used for TV and video. In 1994 the Todd-AO negative (made from entirely separate "takes") was used for laserdisc; many think it's markedly superior.▼●◗

Oklahoma Annie (1952) **C-90m.** *½ D: R. G. Springsteen. Judy Canova, John Russell, Grant Withers, Allen Jenkins, Almira Sessions. Rambunctious Canova is involved with mopping up corruption in her Western town. ▼

Oklahoma Crude (1973) **C-108m.** *** D: Stanley Kramer. George C. Scott, Faye Dunaway, John Mills, Jack Palance, Harvey Jason, Woodrow Parfrey. Old-fashioned, nonthink entertainment. Strong-willed, man-hating Dunaway determined to defend lone oil well from pressures of Palance, who represents big oil trust, hires drifter Scott to help her. Scott gives brilliant comic performance in mildly enjoyable film. Panavision. [PG]▼

Oklahoma Kid, The (1939) **80m.** *** D: Lloyd Bacon. James Cagney, Humphrey Bogart, Rosemary Lane, Donald Crisp, Harvey Stephens, Charles Middleton, Ward Bond. Cagney's the hero, Bogey's the villain in this sturdy Western about a cowboy seeking redress for the lynching of his father. Classic scene has Cagney singing "I Don't Want to Play in Your Yard."▼

Oklahoman, The (1957) **C-80m.** **½ D: Francis D. Lyon. Joel McCrea, Barbara Hale, Brad Dexter, Gloria Talbott, Verna Felton, Douglas Dick, Michael Pate. Town doc McCrea tries to keep Indian Pate from getting rooked out of his land. Pretty routine, though Talbott cultists may want to see her play an Indian maiden the same year she had the title role in DAUGHTER OF DR. JEKYLL. Laundry note: Hale wears the same outfit in a disturbingly high number of scenes. CinemaScope.▼

Oklahoma Territory (1960) **67m.** ** D: Edward L. Cahn. Bill Williams, Gloria Talbott, Ted de Corsia, Grant Richards, Walter Sande. Western concentrating on Williams' effort to find actual killer of local Indian agent.

Oklahoma Woman, The (1956) **72m.** BOMB D: Roger Corman. Richard Denning, Peggie Castle, Cathy Downs, Touch (Mike) Connors, Tudor Owen, Richard (Dick) Miller. Grade Z Corman quickie Western about ex-con Denning attempting to stay clean but tangling instead with the title character, who is "queen of the outlaws." SuperScope.

Old Acquaintance (1943) **110m.** *** D: Vincent Sherman. Bette Davis, Miriam Hopkins, Gig Young, John Loder, Dolores Moran, Phillip Reed, Roscoe Karns, Anne Revere. Well-matched stars of THE OLD MAID are reunited as childhood friends who evolve personal and professional rivalry that lasts 20 years. Davis is noble and Hopkins is bitchy in this entertaining film. John Van Druten and Lenore Coffee scripted, from the former's play. Remade as RICH AND FAMOUS.

Old Boyfriends (1979) **C-103m.** BOMB D: Joan Tewkesbury. Talia Shire, Richard Jordan, Keith Carradine, John Belushi, John Houseman, Buck Henry. Distressing botch of an intriguing idea about woman who seeks out her former lovers in an attempt to analyze her past. Shire is too lightweight to carry the acting load, and Belushi is totally wasted. Written by Paul and Leonard Schrader. [R]▼●

Old Curiosity Shop, The (1975) SEE: **Mr. Quilp**

Old Curiosity Shop, The (1995) **C-200m. TVM** D: Kevin Connor. Peter Ustinov, James Fox, Tom Courtenay, Julia McKenzie, Sally Walsh, Adam Blackwood. Picturesque Disney re-creation of Dickens' classic, with newcomer Walsh as Little Nell, Ustinov chewing the scenery as her skinflint grandfather, and Courtenay as moneylender Quilp. John Goldsmith's adaptation was lovingly filmed in and around Dublin. Previously filmed three times in the silent era, then in 1935, and in 1975 (as MR. QUILP). Originally shown in two parts. Made for cable. Above average.▼●

Old Dark House, The (1932) **71m.** ***½ D: James Whale. Boris Karloff, Melvyn Douglas, Charles Laughton, Gloria Stuart, Lilian Bond, Ernest Thesiger, Raymond Massey, Eva Moore. Outstanding melodrama (with tongue-in-cheek) gathers stranded travelers in mysterious household, where brutish butler Karloff is just one of many strange characters. A real gem, based on J. B. Priestley's *Benighted*; screenplay by Benn W. Levy and R. C. Sherriff. Remade in England in 1963. ▼●◗

Old Dark House, The (1963-British) **C-86m.** **½ D: William Castle. Robert Morley, Janette Scott, Joyce Grenfell, Tom Poston, Mervyn Johns, Fenella Fielding, Peter Bull. Uneven blend of comedy and chiller, with Poston at loose ends in eerie mansion. Released theatrically in b&w. Check out the 1932 version instead.

Old Dracula (1974-British) **C-89m.** *½ D: Clive Donner. David Niven, Teresa Graves, Peter Bayliss, Jennie Linden, Linda Hayden. Niven somehow maintains his dignity in this one-joke Dracula spoof that has him extracting samples from the necks of various Playboy Bunnies in search of correct blood type to resurrect his departed wife. British title: VAMPIRA. [PG]

Old Enough (1984) **C-91m.** **½ D: Marisa Silver. Sarah Boyd, Rainbow Harvest, Neill Barry, Danny Aiello, Susan Kingsley, Roxanne Hart, Fran Brill, Alyssa Milano, Anne Pitoniak. Two adolescent girls from wildly diverse socioeconomic backgrounds forge a tenuous friendship, then try to keep it going through thick and thin. Boyd (the rich one) has infinitely more screen appeal than counterpart Harvest, which further undercuts an already too-mild comedy. Funny subplot about sexy hairdresser who lives in Harvest's building. Written by first-time director Silver. [PG]▼

Oldest Profession, The (1967-French-German-Italian) **C-97m.** *½ D: Franco Indovina, Mauro Bolognini, Philippe De Broca, Michel Pfleghar, Claude Autant-Lara, Jean-Luc Godard. Elsa Martinelli, Jeanne Moreau, Raquel Welch, Anna Karina, France Anglade, Jean-Pierre Léaud. Totally unfunny six-part story of prostitution through the ages. Original French running time: 115m.▼●

Old Explorers (1990) **C-100m.** ** D: William Pohland. Jose Ferrer, James Whitmore, Jeffrey Gadbois, Caroline Kaiser, William Warfield, Christopher Pohland, Storm Richardson, Dominique Berrand. Two elderly pals—Ferrer and Whitmore—get together once a week to spin tales and embark on flights of fancy. Imagining themselves as famed adventurers (usually African explorer Henry Stanley or Troy archaeologist Henry Schliemann), they recount fictional quests for lost treasures and safaris to mythical lands. Extremely slow pace robs this interesting idea of its potential. [PG]▼●

Old-Fashioned Way, The (1934) **74m.** ***½ D: William Beaudine. W. C. Fields, Judith Allen, Joe Morrison, Baby LeRoy, Jack Mulhall, Oscar Apfel. Fields is in fine form managing troupe of old-time melodrama *The Drunkard,* encountering various troubles as they travel from town to town. Baby LeRoy has memorable scene throwing W. C.'s watch into a jar of molasses; also contains Fields' classic juggling routine.

Old Gringo (1989) **C-119m.** *** D: Luis Puenzo. Jane Fonda, Gregory Peck, Jimmy Smits, Patricio Contreras, Jenny Gago, Jim Metzler, Gabriela Roel, Anne Pitoniak, Pedro Armendariz, Jr. A youngish spinster, a fiery young Mexican general, and an aging American writer, Ambrose Bierce, cross paths amid the tumult of Pancho Villa's revolution in 1913. Intense, epic scale drama has its share of flaws, but its rich atmosphere and superlative star performances make it well worth seeing. Director Puenzo and Aida Bortnik wrote the screenplay, from Carlos Fuentes' novel. [R]▼●

Old Heidelberg SEE: **Student Prince in Old Heidelberg, The**

Old Hutch (1936) **80m.** ** D: J. Walter Ruben. Wallace Beery, Eric Linden, Cecilia Parker, Elizabeth Patterson, Robert McWade. Cute story of shiftless bum discovering $100,000, trying to use it without arousing suspicion. Filmed before in 1920 with Will Rogers as HONEST HUTCH.

Old Ironsides (1926) **111m.** *** D: James Cruze. Charles Farrell, Esther Ralston, Wallace Beery, George Bancroft, Charles Hill Mailes, Johnnie Walker. Elaborate, expansive hokum based on the American merchant marine's run-ins with Mediterranean pirates in the early 19th century. Full of rollicking, boisterous seamen—and in their midst, a prim leading lady and leading man. Subtle it ain't, but certainly entertaining, especially with Gaylord Carter's rousing organ score on the homevideo release. Boris Karloff has small role as a Saracen sailor.▼

Old Lady Who Walked in the Sea, The (1995-French) **C-95m.** *** D: Laurent Heynemann. Jeanne Moreau, Michel Serrault, Luc Thuillier, Geraldine Danon. Moreau's star presence sparks this entertaining, often outrageous comedy, in which she plays a veteran swindler-hustler-blackmailer named Lady M—an aged, wrinkled version of Barbara Stanwyck's LADY EVE—who becomes the mentor of a good-looking but unrefined young beach boy (Thuillier). Serrault is excellent as always as Moreau's longtime partner-in-crime.▼

Old Maid, The (1939) **95m.** ***½ D: Edmund Goulding. Bette Davis, Miriam Hopkins, George Brent, Jane Bryan, Donald Crisp, Louise Fazenda, Jerome Cowan, James Stephenson. Soap opera par excellence based on Zoe Akins play and Edith Wharton novel about the rivalry, romantic and otherwise, between cousins Davis and Hopkins. The two female stars create fireworks as they enact this chronicle of love and hate in the 1860s–80s.▼●

Old Man (1997) **C-100m. TVM** D: John Kent Harrison. Jeanne Tripplehorn, Arliss Howard, Leo Burmester, Daro Latiolas, Ray McKinnon, Jerry Leggio. Playwright/author Horton Foote scripted this adaptation of William Faulkner's short story (originally part of Faulkner's 1939 novel *The Wild Palms*) about two lost souls—a pregnant farm woman living in the bayous and a convict conscripted to help battle a flood along the Mississippi in 1927. This essentially two-person drama, imaginatively shot on location in the Louisiana swamps, provides its stars with meaty roles that they devour. Above average.▼●

Old Man and the Sea, The (1958) **C-86m.** *** D: John Sturges. Spencer Tracy, Felipe Pazos, Harry Bellaver. Well-intentioned but uneven parable of aging fisherman's daily battle with the elements. Tracy is the whole film, making the most of Hemingway's un-filmic story; Dimitri Tiomkin's expressive score won an Oscar. Remade as a TVM in 1990 with Anthony Quinn.▼●◗

Old Man Rhythm (1935) **75m.** **½ D: Edward Ludwig. Charles "Buddy" Rogers, George Barbier, Barbara Kent, Grace Bradley, Betty Grable, Eric Blore. Business tycoon Barbier goes back to college to keep an eye on his playboy son (Rogers) in this light, fluffy musical; songwriter Johnny Mercer appears as one of the students.

Old Spanish Custom, An (1936-British) **61m.** BOMB D: Adrian Brunel. Buster Keaton, Lupita Tovar, Esme Percy, Lyn Harding, Hilda Moreno. Depressing, bottom-of-the-barrel comedy, with Buster a wealthy yachtsman who docks in Spain and is duped by temptress Tovar. Only for terminally curious Keaton fans. Original title: THE INVADER.▼

Old Yeller (1957) **C-83m.** *** D: Robert Stevenson. Dorothy McGuire, Fess Parker, Tommy Kirk, Kevin Corcoran, Jeff York, Beverly Washburn, Chuck Connors. Disney's first film about a boy and his dog, from Fred Gipson's popular novel, is still one of the best. Atmospheric recreation of farm life in 1869 Texas, where Kirk becomes attached to a yellow hunting dog. Sequel: SAVAGE SAM.▼●

Oleanna (1994) **C-89m.** ** D: David Mamet. William H. Macy, Debra Eisenstadt. Maddeningly uneven two-character drama about a frustrated, self-involved male professor whose connection with a troubled, vulnerable female student leads to dire consequences. Potentially dynamic material suffers from too much staginess and dramatic obviousness. Scripted by Mamet, based on his play.▼●

Oliver! (1968-British) **C-153m.** ***½ D: Carol Reed. Ron Moody, Oliver Reed, Shani Wallis, Mark Lester, Jack Wild, Harry Secombe, Hugh Griffith, Sheila White. Fine film of Lionel Bart's hit stage musical of Dickens' *Oliver Twist* about young boy (Lester) swept into gang of youthful thieves led by scurrilous Fagin (Moody). Colorful atmosphere; rousing score including "Consider Yourself," "As Long as He Needs Me." Six Oscars including Best Picture, Director, Art Direction, Scoring (John Green), and a special prize to Onna White for her spirited choreography. Panavision. [G] ▼●◗

Oliver & Company (1988) **C-72m.** **½ D: George Scribner. Voices of Joey Lawrence, Billy Joel, Cheech Marin, Richard Mulligan, Roscoe Lee Browne, Sheryl Lee Ralph, Dom DeLuise, Taurean Blacque, Robert Loggia, Bette Midler, Natalie Gregory. Free adaptation of Dickens' *Oliver Twist* in the cartoon world: homeless kitten falls in with the jaunty Dodger and his canine pals, who work for Fagin, a human nebbish in debt to the heartless Sikes. Dodger (Joel) has the film's best song, "Why Should I Worry?"—but an excitable Chihuahua voiced by Marin provides the biggest laughs. Disney's grittiest (grungiest?) animated feature is no classic, but it's likeable enough. [G]▼●

Oliver's Story (1978) **C-92m.** *½ D: John Korty. Ryan O'Neal, Candice Bergen, Nicola Pagett, Edward Binns, Ray Milland, Swoosie Kurtz, Charles Haid, Kenneth McMillan, Josef Sommer. Vapid sequel to LOVE STORY pits money against money this time around, as O'Neal romances heiress to Bonwit Teller fortune. [PG]▼

Oliver Twist (1922) **77m.** *** D: Frank Lloyd. Jackie Coogan, Lon Chaney, Gladys Brockwell, George Siegmann, Esther Ralston. Entertaining silent version of the Charles Dickens classic, geared as a vehicle for Coogan, who was then at the height of his juvenile stardom. Chaney, that master of makeup, is ideally cast as Fagin. ▼●

Oliver Twist (1933) **77m.** ** D: William Cowen. Dickie Moore, Irving Pichel, William "Stage" Boyd, Doris Lloyd, Barbara Kent. Superficial, low-budget version of Dickens's story is mediocre by any standards, but pales particularly in comparison to the later British classic.▼

Oliver Twist (1948-British) **105m.** **** D: David Lean. Alec Guinness, Robert Newton, John Howard Davies, Kay Walsh, Francis L. Sullivan, Anthony Newley, Henry Stephenson. Superlative realization of Dickens tale of ill-treated London waif involved with arch-fiend Fagin (Guinness) and his youthful gang, headed by the Artful Dodger (Newley). Later musicalized as OLIVER! Original British running time: 116m.▼●◗

Oliver Twist (1982) **C-100m. TVM** D: Clive Donner. George C. Scott, Tim Curry, Michael Hordern, Timothy West, Eileen Atkins, Cherie Lunghi, Richard Charles, Lysette Anthony. Full-bodied Fagin by George C. paces this umpteenth version of the Dickens classic, from James Goldman's script. Remade again for TV in 1997 with Richard Dreyfuss. Above average.▼

Olivier Olivier (1992-French) **C-110m.** ***½ D: Agnieszka Holland. Francois Cluzet, Brigitte Rouan, Jean-Francois Stevenin, Gregoire Colin, Marina Golovine, Emmanuel Morozof, Faye Gatteau, Frederick Quiring. Exceptional, fact-based account of a country couple whose young son mysteriously disappears. Six years later he "reappears," but is no longer the special child who was a joy to his family; now he's a Parisian street hustler who claims to have forgotten his childhood. A fascinating film, with characters who prove to be far more intricate than they first appear. Holland also scripted. [R]▼●

Olly, Olly, Oxen Free (1978) **C-83m.** ** D: Richard A. Colla. Katharine Hepburn, Kevin McKenzie, Dennis Dimster, Peter Kilman. Hepburn plays a colorful junk dealer who befriends two young boys and helps them realize their dream of hot-air ballooning. Kate's always worth watching, but except for airborne scenes, this film is nothing special. Aka THE GREAT BALLOON ADVENTURE. [G]▼

O Lucky Man! (1973-British) **C-178m.** **** D: Lindsay Anderson. Malcolm McDowell, Rachel Roberts, Arthur Lowe, Ralph Richardson, Alan Price, Lindsay Anderson, Helen Mirren, Mona Washbourne. Mammoth allegory with surrealistic flavor about young coffee salesman who pushes his way to the top only to fall and rise again. Brilliant performances (several actors have multiple roles) throughout; incredible score by Alan Price. Written by David Sherwin. [R]▼●

Olympia (1936-German) **220m.** **** D: Leni Riefenstahl. Two-part record of the 1936 Berlin Olympics, highlighted by truly eyepopping cinematography, camera movement and editing. Of course, it's all supposed to be a glorification of the Nazi state. Various edited versions exist (some of which omit all footage of Hitler, who appears throughout the original print).▼

Omar Khayyam (1957) **C-101m.** **½ D: William Dieterle. Cornel Wilde, Debra Paget, John Derek, Raymond Massey, Michael Rennie, Yma Sumac, Sebastian Cabot. Childish but spirited costumer set in medieval Persia; cast defeated by juvenile script. VistaVision.▼

Omega Code, The (1999) **C-99m.** *½ D: Rob Marcarelli. Casper Van Dien, Michael York, Catherine Oxenberg, Michael Ironside, Jan Triska, Gregory Wagrowski. TV motivational guru Van Dien gets involved with wealthy businessman York, whose eventual plans to dominate the world are tied in with secret messages encoded in the Torah. Financed by televangelist Paul Crouch of the Trinity Broadcasting Network, film did grass-roots box-office business until rank-and-file filmgoers saw it for what it was: glorified direct-to-video cheese that somehow wangled theatrical bookings. [PG-13]▼◗

Omega Man, The (1971) **C-98m.** **½ D: Boris Sagal. Charlton Heston, Rosalind Cash, Anthony Zerbe, Paul Koslo, Lincoln Kilpatrick, Eric Laneuville. Visually striking but unsatisfying second filming of Richard Matheson's sci-fi thriller *I Am Legend.* Heston is under siege by a race of zombies spawned by apocalyptic germ warfare. Heston is superior to Vincent Price (who had role in THE LAST MAN ON EARTH). Panavision. [PG]▼●

Omega Syndrome (1987) **C-88m.** ** D: Joseph Manduke. Ken Wahl, George DiCenzo, Doug McClure, Nicole Eggert. Standard-issue tale of down-and-out reporter Wahl who whips into action (with Army buddy DiCenzo) when his teenage daughter (Eggert) is kidnapped by right-wing terrorists. [R]▼●

Omen, The (1976) **C-111m.** **½ D: Richard Donner. Gregory Peck, Lee Remick, Billie Whitelaw, David Warner, Harvey Stephens, Patrick Troughton, Leo McKern. Effective but sensationalistic horror piece on the coming of the "antiChrist," personified in young son of Peck and Remick, Americans living in England. Discreet use of gore and a now-famous decapitation, for those who like that kind of thing. Jerry Goldsmith's score won an Oscar. Followed by three sequels beginning with DAMIEN—OMEN II. Panavision. [R]▼●

On a Clear Day You Can See Forever (1970) **C-129m.** **½ D: Vincente Minnelli. Barbra Streisand, Yves Montand, Bob Newhart, Larry Blyden, Simon Oakland, Jack Nicholson. Colorful entertainment from Alan Jay Lerner-Burton Lane show about girl (Streisand) whose psychiatrist (Montand) discovers that she lived a former life, in 19th-century England. Sumptuous flashback scenes outclass fragmented modern-day plot, much of it apparently left on cutting-room floor. Glossy but never involving. Panavision. [G]▼●

On an Island With You (1948) **C-107m.** **½ D: Richard Thorpe. Esther Williams, Peter Lawford, Ricardo Montalban, Jimmy Durante, Cyd Charisse, Xavier Cugat, Leon Ames, Marie Windsor. Splashy, colorful Williams vehicle of movie star who finds off-screen romance on location in Hawaii.▼

On Any Sunday (1971) **C-91m.** *** D: Bruce Brown. Steve McQueen, Mert Lawwill, Malcolm Smith. Fine documentary on many aspects of motorcycling by Bruce Brown of ENDLESS SUMMER fame. Followed by a sequel. Followed in 2000 by ON ANY SUNDAY REVISITED. [G]▼◗

On Any Sunday II (1981) **C-90m.** ** D: Ed Forsyth, Don Shoemaker. Undistinguished sequel to ON ANY SUNDAY, documenting the exploits of championship motorcyclists. For cycle fans only. [PG]▼

On Approval (1943-British) **80m.** *** D: Clive Brook. Beatrice Lillie, Clive Brook, Googie Withers, Roland Culver. Minor British gem showcasing the hilarious Bea Lillie as woman who decides to give her prospective husband a trial run, with unexpected results. Drawing-room comedy par excellence. Leading-man Brook also directed, produced, and cowrote script (from Frederick Lonsdale's play)—the only time he ever worked behind the camera!▼●◗

On Borrowed Time (1939) **99m.** *** D: Harold S. Bucquet. Lionel Barrymore, Cedric Hardwicke, Beulah Bondi, Una Merkel, Ian Wolfe, Philip Terry, Eily Malyon. Engrossing fable of Death, Mr. Brink (Hardwicke), coming for grandpa Barrymore, finding himself trapped in tree by Lionel and grandson Bobs Watson. Engaging whimsy from the play by Lawrence Edward Watkin.▼●

Once Again (1986) **C-105m.** ** D: Amin Q. Chaudhri. Richard Cox, Jessica Harper, Martin Balsam, Frances Sternhagen, Harley Cross. Overage rock musician Cox and cynical stewardess Harper have long been estranged when their respective parents (Balsam, Sternhagen) announce their plans to marry. Tries to be charming, touching, and cute, but the script just isn't there.

Once Around (1991) **C-115m.** **½ D: Lasse Hallström. Richard Dreyfuss, Holly Hunter, Danny Aiello, Gena Rowlands,

Laura San Giacomo, Roxanne Hart, Danton Stone, Tim Guinee, Greg Germann, Griffin Dunne. Repressed Bostonian Hunter is swept off her feet by amorous (and obnoxious) supersalesman Dreyfuss, who immediately alienates her close-knit family, and puts her in the center of an emotional tug-of-war. Malia Scotch Marmo's script embraces both offbeat romantic comedy and intense family drama, some of it extremely moving, some of it off-base. As an acting showcase, however, it's superb. Coproduced by costar Dunne; Hallström's U.S. directorial debut. [R]▼●

Once a Thief (1950) **88m.** ** D: W. Lee Wilder. June Havoc, Cesar Romero, Marie McDonald, Lon Chaney, Jr., Iris Adrian. OK little film of shoplifter Havoc and her tawdry romance with Romero.

Once a Thief (1965-U.S.-French) **107m.** ** D: Ralph Nelson. Ann-Margret, Alain Delon, Van Heflin, Jack Palance, John Davis Chandler, Jeff Corey, Tony Musante. When young ex-con tries to go straight, he finds himself the pawn in another crime. Not at all interesting. Panavision.

Once Before I Die (1965) **C-97m.** **½ D: John Derek. Ursula Andress, John Derek, Rod Lauren, Richard Jaeckel, Ron Ely. Brutal, offbeat story of band of American soldiers in Philippines during WW2, trying to survive Japanese attack. Andress is only woman in group, and you can guess the rest.▼

Once Bitten (1985) **C-93m.** BOMB D: Howard Storm. Lauren Hutton, Jim Carrey, Karen Kopins, Cleavon Little, Thomas Ballatore, Skip Lackey. Inept comedy about vampiress (Hutton) who intrudes on amorous pursuits of some teenagers because she needs the blood of a virgin to maintain her youthful glow. Pretty anemic; Carrey is very restrained. [PG-13]▼●

Once In a Lifetime (1932) **75m.** *** D: Russell Mack. Jack Oakie, Sidney Fox, Aline MacMahon, Russell Hopton, ZaSu Pitts, Louise Fazenda, Onslow Stevens, Gregory Ratoff. Stagebound but still hilarious adaptation of Kaufman-Hart play about a trio of connivers who take advantage of Hollywood's state of panic when talkies arrive by pretending to be vocal coaches. Oakie is great as a simpleton, Ratoff in his element as a bombastic studio chief.

Once in Paris . . . (1978) **C-100m.** *** D: Frank D. Gilroy. Wayne Rogers, Gayle Hunnicutt, Jack Lenoir, Clement Harari, Tanya Lopert, Doris Roberts. Gilroy produced, directed, and wrote this charming tale of Hollywood screenwriter who goes to Paris to work on script, falls in love instead. Lovely location filming; Lenoir steals the film as Rogers' all-knowing chauffeur (which he actually was prior to this picture). [PG]▼

Once Is Not Enough SEE: **Jacqueline Susann's Once Is Not Enough**

Once More My Darling (1949) **94m.** **½ D: Robert Montgomery. Robert Montgomery, Ann Blyth, Jane Cowl, Taylor Holmes, Charles McGraw. Satisfying comedy of young girl infatuated with middle-aged movie star.

Once More, With Feeling (1960-British) **C-92m.** **½ D: Stanley Donen. Yul Brynner, Kay Kendall, Maxwell Shaw, Mervyn Johns. Despite sparkling Kendall (her last film) as musical conductor Brynner's dissatisfied wife, this marital sex comedy fizzles.

Once Upon a Crime (1992) **C-94m.** *½ D: Eugene Levy. John Candy, James Belushi, Cybill Shepherd, Sean Young, Richard Lewis, Ornella Muti, Giancarlo Giannini, George Hamilton, Joss Ackland, Elsa Martinelli. One of the loudest—and dumbest—comedies of the early 90s, about a group of strangers traveling through Europe who get mixed up with a murder and a missing dachshund. The real crime is the waste of a good cast. Directed by *SCTV* performer Levy. Based on a forgettable 1964 film, AND SUDDENLY IT'S MURDER! [PG]▼●

Once Upon a Forest (1993) **C-80m.** ** D: Charles Grosvenor. Voices of Michael Crawford, Ben Vereen, Ellen Blain, Ben Gregory, Paige Gosney, Elizabeth Moss, Janet Waldo, Susan Silo. Pro-social animated tale of young "furlings" who leave their forest home to find a cure for a friend who's become ill breathing fumes from a chemical spill. Message of environmental awareness is imparted in a steady story with typically cute characters, but there's nothing terribly compelling about the film. [G]▼●

Once Upon a Honeymoon (1942) **117m.** **½ D: Leo McCarey. Ginger Rogers, Cary Grant, Walter Slezak, Albert Dekker, Albert Basserman, Ferike Boros, Harry Shannon, Hans Conried. Strange but intriguing curio with status-seeking ex-burlesque queen Rogers marrying secret Nazi bigwig Slezak . . . and radio commentator Grant coming to her rescue. Some boring stretches do it in; however, the scenes in which the star duo are mistaken for Jews and almost sent to a concentration camp are fascinating.▼●

Once Upon a Horse (1958) **85m.** **½ D: Hal Kanter. Dan Rowan, Dick Martin, Martha Hyer, Leif Erickson, Nita Talbot, John McGiver, David Burns, James Gleason. Oddball Western spoof runs hot and cold, with some nutty gags and enough spark to make it worth watching. Old-time Western stars Bob Steele, Kermit Maynard, Tom Keene, Bob Livingston appear briefly as themselves. CinemaScope.

Once Upon A Scoundrel (1973) **C-90m.** **½ D: George Schaefer. Zero Mostel,

Katy Jurado, Tito Vandis. Priscilla Garcia. A Martinez. Minor but enjoyable comedy about selfish Mexican land baron Mostel, who schemes to frame the fiancé of the young girl he craves, and how he is hoodwinked into "dying" by Jurado. [G]▼

Once Upon a Texas Train (1988) **C-100m. TVM** D: Burt Kennedy. Willie Nelson, Richard Widmark, Angie Dickinson, Stuart Whitman, Shaun Cassidy, Chuck Connors, Kevin McCarthy, Ken Curtis, Gene Evans, Jack Elam, Royal Dano, Harry Carey, Jr., Dub Taylor. Entertainingly lighthearted Western with a stellar cast of veterans—and Shaun Cassidy as a young turk out to scotch the train robbery plans that have pitted aging ex-con Nelson and his gang of old codgers against longtime adversary lawman Widmark and his over-the-hill posse. Old Western hand Kennedy also wrote and produced. Video title: TEXAS GUNS. Average.▼●

Once Upon a Time (1944) **89m.** **½ D: Alexander Hall. Cary Grant, Janet Blair, James Gleason, Ted Donaldson, Art Baker. Amusing comedy-fantasy of entrepreneur Grant promoting a dancing caterpillar; trivial fun. Based on a Norman Corwin radio play, from Lucille Fletcher short story.

Once Upon a Time in America (1984) **C-139m.** *** D: Sergio Leone. Robert De Niro, James Woods, Elizabeth McGovern, Tuesday Weld, Larry Rapp, William Forsythe, James Hayden, Treat Williams, Darlanne Fleugel, Burt Young, Joe Pesci, Danny Aiello, Jennifer Connelly, Brian Bloom, James Russo, T. Scott Coffey. Long, engrossing homage to the gangster film, following the rise and fall of Jewish childhood pals on N.Y.C.'s Lower East Side. Shorn of 88m. for U.S. release, story ceases to make sense at several points, and characters appear and disappear with amazing suddenness. Even so, Leone's feel for this genre, compelling performances by De Niro and Woods, and stunning art direction make this well worth watching. Complete 227m. version is quite a different film—and not without flaws of its own. (Even this long version is minus several minutes of violent footage—notably from a key rape sequence—which exist in European prints.) Originally released in U.S. at 139m. Shown on network TV at 192m. [R]▼●

Once Upon a Time in the West (1968-U.S.-Italian) **C-165m.** ***½ D: Sergio Leone. Charles Bronson, Henry Fonda, Claudia Cardinale, Jason Robards, Gabriele Ferzetti, Paolo Stoppa, Frank Wolff, Jack Elam, Woody Strode, Lionel Stander, Keenan Wynn. Leone's follow-up to his "Dollars" trilogy is languid, operatic masterpiece. Plot, admittedly lifted from JOHNNY GUITAR, has landowner Cardinale waiting for the railroad to come through, unaware she's been targeted by hired killer Fonda (brilliantly cast as one of the coldest villains in screen history). Exciting, funny, and reverent, with now-classic score by Ennio Morricone; not to be missed. Story by Leone, Bernardo Bertolucci, and Dario Argento. Beware chopped-up 140m. version. Techniscope. [M/PG] ▼●

Once Upon a Time . . . When We Were Colored (1996) **C-111m.** **½ D: Tim Reid. Al Freeman, Jr., Phylicia Rashad, Paula Kelly, Leon, Richard Roundtree, Salli Richardson, Isaac Hayes, Polly Bergen. Well-meaning saga of a boy's childhood in a tight-knit black community on the Mississippi Delta, spanning the 1940s to the early '60s. Sometimes suffers from schmaltz and heavyhanded symbolism, but there are some lovely moments. Freeman and Roundtree are standouts. [PG]▼●◗

Once Were Warriors (1994-New Zealand) **C-103m.** ***½ D: Lee Tamahori. Rena Owen, Temuera Morrison, Mamaengaroa Kerr-Bell, Julian (Sonny) Arahanga, Taungaroa Emile, Clifford Curtis, Julian Arahanga. Shattering drama about a poor, urbanized Maori family, and the wife's growing realization that she can no longer endure her "macho" husband's abuse—both physical and psychological. Striking and powerful film marks Tamahori's directing debut; trenchant script by Riwia Brown, based on Alan Duff's novel, a best-seller in New Zealand. Not to be missed. [R] ▼●

Once You Kiss a Stranger (1969) **C-106m.** BOMB D: Robert Sparr. Paul Burke, Carol Lynley, Martha Hyer, Peter Lind Hayes, Philip Carey, Stephen McNally, Whit Bissell. Thinly disguised remake of STRANGERS ON A TRAIN, with Lynley as nut who pulls golfer Burke into bizarre "reciprocal murder" scheme. Slick but empty-headed, laughable. [M/PG]

On Dangerous Ground (1952) **82m.** *** D: Nicholas Ray. Ida Lupino, Robert Ryan, Ward Bond, Charles Kemper, Anthony Ross, Ed Begley, Ian Wolfe, Cleo Moore, Olive Carey. Effective mood-piece with hardened city cop Ryan softened by blind-girl Lupino, whose brother is involved in rural manhunt. Bernard Herrmann's score was reportedly his favorite work. Produced by John Houseman.▼●

On Deadly Ground (1994) **C-101m.** *½ D: Steven Seagal. Steven Seagal, Michael Caine, Joan Chen, John C. McGinley, R. Lee Ermey, Shari Shattuck, Billy Bob Thornton. After the critical/popular success of UNDER SIEGE, Seagal's clout was such that he was allowed to direct this fast-fader about the raping of Alaska's interior by an oil company run by evil Caine. Spiritual mumbo-jumbo halfway through looks like an outtake from THE DOORS, and the star's anticlimactic final speech (after the obligatory wrist-snapping has concluded) had fans bolting for the exits. Caine looks as

if he's undergone cosmetic surgery by Dwight Frye. Clairmont-Scope. [R]▼●◗
On Dress Parade (1939) **62m.** ** D: William Clemens. Billy Halop, Leo Gorcey, Bobby Jordan, Huntz Hall, Gabriel Dell, Bernard Punsly, Frankie Thomas, Selmer Jackson, John Litel. Last of the official *Dead End Kids* movies sends the young punks off to military school where they're (unconvincingly) turned into squeaky-clean, well-behaved little cadets. Simple programmer; also known as THE DEAD END KIDS ON DRESS PARADE.
One Against the Wind (1991-U.S.-Luxembourg) **C-100m. TVM** D: Larry Elikann. Judy Davis, Sam Neill, Denholm Elliott, Anthony Higgins, Christien Anholt, Kate Beckinsale, Frank Middlemass. Davis is the whole show as real-life Mary Lindell, well-to-do Britisher living with her teenage children in Paris during WW2 and smuggling Allied soldiers out from under the noses of the Nazis. Good script by Chris Bryant. Above average.▼
One and Only, The (1978) **C-98m.** **½ D: Carl Reiner. Henry Winkler, Kim Darby, Gene Saks, Herve Villechaize, Harold Gould, William Daniels, Polly Holliday, Ed Begley, Jr., Brandon Cruz, Charles Frank, Mary Woronov. Winkler is a brash college kid determined to make it in show biz, but winds up a flamboyant wrestler. Some truly funny moments build to gradual disenchantment with his basically obnoxious character. Written by Steve Gordon. [PG]▼
One and Only, Genuine, Original Family Band, The (1968) **C-117m.** **½ D: Michael O'Herlihy. Walter Brennan, Buddy Ebsen, Lesley Ann Warren, John Davidson, Janet Blair, Kurt Russell. Musical family becomes involved in 1888 Presidential campaign; innocuous Disney entertainment with forgettable songs by the Sherman Brothers. Goldie (billed as Goldie Jeanne) Hawn debuts in tiny part as giggling dancer. [G]▼●
One Big Affair (1952) **80m.** ** D: Peter Godfrey. Evelyn Keyes, Dennis O'Keefe, Mary Anderson, Connie Gilchrist. On-location filming in Mexico highlights this lightweight romance yarn.
One Body Too Many (1944) **75m.** ** D: Frank McDonald. Jack Haley, Jean Parker, Bela Lugosi, Blanche Yurka, Lyle Talbot, Douglas Fowley. Old dark house comedy about the reading of a will. Haley is carefree salesman mistaken for private eye, forced to solve caper.▼
One Crazy Summer (1986) **C-93m.** ** D: Savage Steve Holland. John Cusack, Demi Moore, Joel Murray, Curtis Armstrong, Bobcat Goldthwait, Tom Villard, William Hickey, Joe Flaherty. Holland's followup to BETTER OFF DEAD is another loosely connected comedy (styled like a cartoon) about a teenage misfit spending summer on Nantucket Island in New England. Some good sight gags and bright moments but no story or real characterizations to hang on to. [PG]▼●
One Cup of Coffee SEE: **Pastime**
One Dangerous Night (1943) **77m.** **½ D: Michael Gordon. Warren William, Marguerite Chapman, Eric Blore, Mona Barrie, Tala Birell, Margaret Hayes, Ann Savage, Thurston Hall, Fred Kelsey. Solid entry in *The Lone Wolf* series about a murdered blackmailing gigolo, with the Wolf suspected by both cops and crooks of the crime. Gerald Mohr, who later played the Lone Wolf, has a supporting role here.
One Dark Night (1983) **C-89m.** *½ D: Tom McLoughlin. Meg Tilly, Robin Evans, Leslie Speights, Elizabeth Daily, Adam West. Teenagers spend the night in a mausoleum. You've seen it all before, and you don't want to see it again. [PG]▼
One Day in the Life of Ivan Denisovich (1971-British-Norwegian) **C-100m.** **½ D: Caspar Wrede. Tom Courtenay, Espen Skjonberg, James Maxwell, Alfred Burke, Eric Thompson. Another instance where a novel was just too difficult to film; Alexander Solzhenitsyn's story of a prisoner in Siberian labor camp only occasionally works on the screen. Good photography by Sven Nykvist; script by Ronald Harwood. [G]▼●
One Deadly Summer (1983-French) **C-133m.** *** D: Jean Becker. Isabelle Adjani, Alain Souchon, Francois Cluzet, Manuel Gelin, Jenny Cleve, Suzanne Flon, Michel Galabru, Maria Machado. Overlong but engrossing drama with astonishing performance by Adjani as young sexpot whose disturbed behavior masks elaborate revenge plan. Extremely well acted, especially by Souchon as her likable beau and Flon as his deaf aunt, but Adjani's character is just too obnoxious to warrant much sympathy. Sebastien Japrisot's screenplay (from his novel) retains unusual device of having several characters take turns narrating. [R]▼
One Desire (1955) **C-94m.** **½ D: Jerry Hopper. Anne Baxter, Rock Hudson, Julie Adams, Natalie Wood, Betty Garde. Baxter's strong performance as woman in love with gambler Hudson elevates standard soaper.
One Down Two to Go (1983) **C-84m.** BOMB D: Fred Williamson. Fred Williamson, Jim Brown, Jim Kelly, Richard Roundtree, Paula Sills, Laura Loftus, Tom Signorelli, Joe Spinell. Kung fu tournament promoter Roundtree is ripped off, and Williamson, Brown, and Kelly go into action. Bottom-of-the-barrel blaxploitation actioner. [R]▼
one eight seven (1997) **C-119m.** **½ D: Kevin Reynolds. Samuel L. Jackson, John Heard, Kelly Rowan, Clifton Gonzalez

Gonzalez, Karina Arroyave, Jonah Rooney. N.Y.C. high school teacher Jackson is stabbed by a student, and relocates to L.A.'s San Fernando Valley. But conditions at the school there are equally rough, and soon some of his students turn up dead. Pretentious treatment of a genuine problem: violence in American schools. A corny, obvious script doesn't help, but the fine acting from all concerned does. Title refers to California state penal code for murder. [R]▼●◗

One-Eyed Jacks (1961) **C-141m.** *** D: Marlon Brando. Marlon Brando, Karl Malden, Pina Pellicer, Katy Jurado, Ben Johnson, Slim Pickens, Timothy Carey, Elisha Cook, Jr., Margarita Cordova. Fascinating but flawed psychological Western with outlaw Brando seeking revenge on former friend Malden, now a sheriff. Visually striking, and a rich character study, but overlong. Brando's only directing effort to date. VistaVision.▼●◗

One Eyed Soldiers (1966-U.S.-British-Yugoslavian) **C-80m.** *½ D: Jean Christophe. Dale Robertson, Luciana Paluzzi, Guy Deghy, Andrew Faulds, Mila Avramovic. Dying man leaves his daughter a clue to whereabouts of money in Swiss bank, leading to international scramble for the loot. If you're hoping for a fresh approach, forget it. Techniscope.

One False Move (1992) **C-105m.** *** D: Carl Franklin. Bill Paxton, Cynda Williams, Billy Bob Thornton, Michael Beach, Jim Metzler, Earl Billings, Natalie Canerday, Robert Ginnaven, Robert Anthony Bell, Kevin Hunter. Savvy L.A. cops end up in Dirt Road, Ark., awaiting three squabbling killers who are wanted for a grisly drug ripoff. Exceptionally trim—a nasty story (with a good romantic twist) methodically tracking its way toward an impending blood bath. Thornton scripted with Tom Epperson. [R]▼●◗

One Fatal Hour SEE: **Two Against the World**

One Fine Day (1996) **C-108m.** *** D: Michael Hoffman. Michelle Pfeiffer, George Clooney, Mae Whitman, Alex D. Linz, Charles Durning, Jon Robin Baitz, Ellen Greene, Joe Grifasi, Pete Hamill, Anna Maria Horsford, Sheila Kelley, Robert Klein, Amanda Peet, Bitty Schram, Holland Taylor, Rachel York. A rarity in the '90s: a genuinely nice movie about two harried and self-absorbed New Yorkers who meet by chance while taking care of their young children during an impossibly hectic career day. He's a hotshot newspaper columnist, she's with an architectural firm. Cute, funny romantic comedy will surely strike many chords with parents. Pfeiffer (never more likeable) also produced. [PG]▼●◗

One Flew Over the Cuckoo's Nest (1975) **C-133m.** **** D: Milos Forman. Jack Nicholson, Louise Fletcher, Brad Dourif, William Redfield, Michael Berryman, Peter Brocco, Will Sampson, Danny DeVito, Christopher Lloyd, Scatman Crothers, Vincent Schiavelli, Sydney Lassick, Louisa Moritz. Ken Kesey's story is a triumph of the human spirit; a feisty misfit (Nicholson) enters an insane asylum and inspires his fellow patients to assert themselves, to the chagrin of strong-willed head nurse (Fletcher). The first film since IT HAPPENED ONE NIGHT to win all five top Oscars: Best Picture, Actor, Actress, Director, Screenplay (Lawrence Hauben, Bo Goldman). Lloyd's film debut. [R]▼●◗

One Foot in Heaven (1941) **108m.** ***½ D: Irving Rapper. Fredric March, Martha Scott, Beulah Bondi, Gene Lockhart, Elisabeth Fraser, Harry Davenport, Laura Hope Crews, Grant Mitchell. Superior acting in honest, appealing story of minister and wife facing various problems as church life and 20th century America clash. Very entertaining, with memorable scene of minister March going to his first movie (a William S. Hart silent).

One Foot in Hell (1960) **C-90m.** **½ D: James B. Clark, Alan Ladd, Don Murray, Dan O'Herlihy, Dolores Michaels, Barry Coe, Larry Gates, Karl Swenson. Ambitious but peculiar production of sheriff seeking retribution against small town for negligent death of his wife; cowritten by Aaron Spelling. CinemaScope.

One for the Book SEE: **Voice of the Turtle, The**

One Frightened Night (1935) **65m.** **½ D: Christy Cabanne. Charley Grapewin, Mary Carlisle, Arthur Hohl, Wallace Ford, Lucien Littlefield, Regis Toomey, Hedda Hopper, Evalyn Knapp, Rafaela Ottiano. Fast-moving, intricately plotted little chiller about crusty old millionaire Grapewin, who wishes to give away his fortune so as to avoid a new inheritance tax.▼

One From the Heart (1982) **C-100m.** ** D: Francis Coppola. Frederic Forrest, Teri Garr, Raul Julia, Nastassia Kinski, Lainie Kazan, Harry Dean Stanton, Allen Goorwitz (Garfield), Luana Anders. Lavishly produced but practically plotless romantic comedy about couple (Forrest, Garr) who quarrel, then seek out other partners (Kinski, Julia). Dean Tavoularis' stylized Las Vegas set and the cinematography by Vittorio Storaro and Ronald V. Garcia are astonishing! Unfortunately, pretty images do not a film make. Tom Waits songs fill the soundtrack while the actors play out one of Coppola's most surreal entertainments. A must for the curious—others beware. Look sharp for Rebecca De Mornay as a restaurant patron. [R]▼●

Onegin (1999-British) **C-106m.** *** D: Martha Fiennes. Ralph Fiennes, Liv Tyler, Toby Stephens, Lena Headey, Martin Donovan,

Alun Armstrong, Harriet Walter, Irene Worth, Jason Watkins, Francesca Annis. Visually beautiful, sensitively directed love story, set in 1820s St. Petersburg and based on Pushkin's *Eugene Onegin*, about an aristocratic bachelor who inherits a country estate and becomes involved in a paradoxical relationship with a daughter of his new neighbor. Many nice, subtle touches, though Tyler is miscast. Director Martha is the sister of Ralph (who also executive produced); brother Magnus Fiennes composed the music and sister Sophie Fiennes has a cameo.▼◗

One Girl's Confession (1953) **74m.** ** D: Hugo Haas. Cleo Moore, Hugo Haas, Glenn Langan, Russ Conway. Cleo steals from her loutish guardian, then serves jail sentence knowing the loot is waiting for her. Typical Hugo Haas production, with intriguing premise but flimsy development. Moore is presented as (unbelievably) chaste—but our first look at her is in an alluring low-cut bathing suit. Thanks, Hugo.

One Good Cop (1991) **C-114m.** ** D: Heywood Gould. Michael Keaton, Rene Russo, Anthony LaPaglia, Kevin Conway, Rachel Ticotin, Tony Plana, Benjamin Bratt, Charlaine Woodard. Superficial look at dedicated N.Y.C. cop (and happily married man) who—faced with the prospect of fatherhood—is forced to examine his goals and his morality. Mix of urban grittiness and heart-tugging sentiment doesn't work, especially with its many convenient dramatic turns and shortcuts. Those three little girls *are* adorable, though. [R]▼●

One Good Turn (1954-British) **78m.** ** D: John Paddy Carstairs. Norman Wisdom, Joan Rice, Shirley Abicair, William Russell, Thora Hird. Minor musical vehicle for man-on-the-street comedian Wisdom, putting forth such homey tunes as "Take a Step in the Right Direction."●

One Heavenly Night (1931) **82m.** ** D: George Fitzmaurice. Evelyn Laye, John Boles, Leon Errol, Lilyan Tashman, Hugh Cameron. Lesser Goldwyn musical features Laye as a Budapest flower girl posing as a famous singer in order to trap Count Boles. OK for fanciers of old-fashioned romantic nonsense. Elegant photography by Gregg Toland and George Barnes.

One Horse Town SEE: **Small Town Girl** (1936)

One Hour With You (1932) **80m.** ***½ D: Ernst Lubitsch, George Cukor. Maurice Chevalier, Jeanette MacDonald, Genevieve Tobin, Roland Young, Charlie Ruggles. Chic romance of happily married couple upset by arrival of flirtatious Tobin. Chevalier is delightful as always, talking (and singing) directly to the camera. Remake of Lubitsch's 1924 THE MARRIAGE CIRCLE; started by Cukor, completed by Lubitsch with Cukor as his assistant. ●

One Hundred and One Dalmatians (1961) **C-79m.** *** D: Wolfgang Reitherman, Hamilton Luske, Clyde Geronimi. Voices of Rod Taylor, Lisa Davis, Cate Bauer, Ben Wright, Fred Warlock, J. Pat O'Malley, Betty Lou Gerson. Likable, low-key Disney cartoon feature set in England, about the theft and recovery of some adorable dalmatian puppies by a flamboyant villainess named Cruella De Vil. The story's told from a doggy point-of-view, which is just one ingredient of the film's great appeal. Remade in 1996.▼●

101 Dalmatians (1996) **C-103m.** **½ D: Stephen Herek. Glenn Close, Jeff Daniels, Joely Richardson, Joan Plowright, Hugh Laurie, Mark Williams, John Shrapnel. Remake of the Disney animated favorite starts out charmingly well, with Daniels and Richardson a perfect pair (along with their dogs Pongo and Perdita), and Close a flamboyantly funny Cruella De Vil. But once the dalmatian puppies are stolen and Cruella's bumbling henchmen take over, this John Hughes's script becomes yet another heavy-handed HOME ALONE retread, full of mechanical slapstick gags. Panavision. [G] ▼●◗

One Hundred Men and a Girl (1937) **84m.** ***½ D: Henry Koster. Deanna Durbin, Leopold Stokowski, Adolphe Menjou, Alice Brady, Eugene Pallette, Mischa Auer, Frank Jenks, Billy Gilbert. Superior blend of music and comedy as Deanna pesters conductor Stokowski to give work to her unemployed father and musician friends. Brimming with charm—and beautiful music, with Charles Previn's score earning an Oscar.▼●

100 Rifles (1969) **C-110m.** ** D: Tom Gries. Jim Brown, Raquel Welch, Burt Reynolds, Fernando Lamas, Dan O'Herlihy, Hans Gudegast (Eric Braeden). Overripe Western saga has deputy Brown going after Reynolds, fleeing with shipment of guns into Mexico, but meeting and falling for guerrilla leader Welch. Reynolds easily steals film. [PG]▼

One in a Million (1936) **95m.** *** D: Sidney Lanfield. Sonja Henie, Adolphe Menjou, Don Ameche, Ned Sparks, Jean Hersholt, The Ritz Brothers, Arline Judge, Borrah Minevich and His Harmonica Rascals. Debut vehicle for skating star Henie was built around then-timely Winter Olympics. Sonja plays a competitor who may get in trouble by having compromised her amateur status. Still fun; fine supporting cast.▼

One Is a Lonely Number (1972) **C-97m.** *** D: Mel Stuart. Trish Van Devere, Monte Markham, Janet Leigh, Melvyn Douglas, Jane Elliott, Jonathan Lippe. Sympathetic performance by Van Devere helps this better-than-usual soaper about life of

an attractive divorcee; good supporting work by Douglas and Leigh. [PG]
One Last Fling (1949) **74m.** ** D: Peter Godfrey. Alexis Smith, Zachary Scott, Douglas Kennedy, Ann Doran, Veda Ann Borg, Helen Westcott. Limp tale of overly suspicious wife checking up on her husband by going to work for him.
One Little Indian (1973) **C-90m.** **½ D: Bernard McEveety. James Garner, Vera Miles, Clay O'Brien, Pat Hingle, Andrew Prine, Jodie Foster. Garner is AWOL cavalry corporal escaping through desert with young Indian boy and a camel. Unusual Disney comedy-drama. [G]▼◗
One Magic Christmas (1985) **C-88m.** *** D: Phillip Borsos. Mary Steenburgen, Gary Basaraba, Harry Dean Stanton, Arthur Hill, Elizabeth Harnois, Robbie Magwood, Michelle Meyrink, Elias Kóteas, Jan Rubes, Sarah Polley, Graham Jarvis. Wife and mom enduring hard times has lost the Christmas spirit, but Santa Claus and guardian angel conspire with her daughter to show her the light. Entertaining Disney family fare, though pretty serious at times . . . and Stanton is the unlikeliest guardian angel in movie history! Made in Canada. [G]▼●
One Man Force (1989) **C-89m.** ** D: Dale Trevillion. John Matuszak, Ronny Cox, Charles Napier, Sharon Farrell, Sam Jones, Richard Lynch, Stacey Q. Formula action vehicle for former football star Matuszak, who plays an L.A. cop who goes off the deep end when drug dealers murder his partner. Matuszak died suddenly before this film's release. [R]▼●
One Man Jury (1978) **C-104m.** *½ D: Charles Martin. Jack Palance, Christopher Mitchum, Pamela Shoop, Angel Tompkins, Joe Spinell, Cara Williams. DIRTY HARRY rip-off with Palance as vigilante cop who administers his own brand of violent justice on some particularly repulsive felons. [R]▼
One Man's Hero (1999) **C-121m.** **½ D: Lance Hool. Tom Berenger, Daniela Romo, Stephen Tobolowsky, Joaquim de Almeida, Mark Moses, James Gammon, Patrick Bergin. When his men are sent to prison just before the outbreak of the Mexican-American war, Berenger attempts to free them and is attacked by the U.S. Army. The fleeing squadron is then captured by guerrilla forces, but they form a bond and decide to fight together. Obviously a labor of love for star/producer Berenger, and based on a true story, but more earnest than exciting. Super 35. [R]▼◗
One Man's Way (1964) **105m.** *** D: Denis Sanders. Don Murray, Diana Hyland, Veronica Cartwright, Ian Wolfe, Virginia Christine, Carol Ohmart, William Windom. Tasteful fictionalized biography of Norman Vincent Peale, his religious convictions and preaching; Murray is earnest in lead role.▼
One Million B.C. (1939) **80m.** **½ D: Hal Roach, Hal Roach, Jr. Victor Mature, Carole Landis, Lon Chaney, Jr., John Hubbard, Mamo Clark, Jean Porter. Bizarre caveman saga told in flashback is real curio, made on a big scale. Excellent special effects—from prehistoric monsters to an erupting volcano—which have turned up as stock footage in countless cheapies. Longtime rumors that D. W. Griffith directed parts are not true. Remade in 1966 as ONE MILLION YEARS B.C.
One Million Years B.C. (1966-British) **C-100m.** **½ D: Don Chaffey. Raquel Welch, John Richardson, Percy Herbert, Robert Brown, Martine Beswick. Hammer remake of 1939 prehistoric adventure boosted fur-bikinied Welch to stardom; watchable saga with spectacular Ray Harryhausen dinosaurs and percussive score by Mario Nascimbene.▼●
One Minute to Zero (1952) **105m.** ** D: Tay Garnett. Robert Mitchum, Ann Blyth, William Talman, Richard Egan, Charles McGraw, Margaret Sheridan, Eduard Franz. Romance and war combine uneasily in this muddled Korean War melodrama. Mitchum is a colonel attempting to do his job despite the intrusions of girlfriend Blyth, a United Nations envoy.▼
One More River (1934) **90m.** *** D: James Whale. Diana Wynyard, Colin Clive, Frank Lawton, Mrs. Patrick Campbell, Jane Wyatt, Reginald Denny, C. Aubrey Smith, Henry Stephenson, Lionel Atwill, Alan Mowbray. Heartfelt, nicely acted but dated drama chronicling a divorce: ruthless husband Clive accuses wife Wynyard of indiscretion with young Lawton. From John Galsworthy's last novel. Film debut of Jane Wyatt.
One More Saturday Night (1986) **C-95m.** BOMB D: Dennis Klein. Tom Davis, Al Franken, Moira Harris, Frank Howard, Bess Meyer, Dave Reynolds. Unfunny comedy written by and starring the nerdy duo from TV's *Saturday Night Live*. Unlike one of their TV skits, this feature, about various goings-on during a Saturday evening in Minnesota, runs an hour and a half. Forget it. [R]▼●
One More Time (1970) **C-93m.** *½ D: Jerry Lewis. Peter Lawford, Sammy Davis, Jr., Esther Anderson, Maggie Wright. Sequel to SALT AND PEPPER is even worse, with Sammy essentially imitating Jerry Lewis (who directed) as he and Lawford struggle to survive after losing their nightclub—and Lawford assumes his twin brother's identity. Excruciatingly bad; of interest as the only feature Lewis ever directed in which he didn't star. [PG]
One More Tomorrow (1946) **88m.** ** D: Peter Godfrey. Ann Sheridan, Dennis

Morgan, Jack Carson, Alexis Smith, John Loder, Jane Wyman, Reginald Gardiner. Light-comedy players flounder in reworking of Philip Barry's THE ANIMAL KINGDOM, about a wealthy playboy (Morgan) and a radical magazine editor (Sheridan) who fall in love but *don't* get married—to their eventual regret.

One More Train to Rob (1971) **C-108m.** **½ D: Andrew V. McLaglen. George Peppard, Diana Muldaur, John Vernon, France Nuyen, Steve Sandor. Peppard seeks revenge on former robbery partner who sent him to jail. Unremarkable Western has some flavor, nice supporting cast of familiar faces. [PG]

One Mysterious Night (1944) **61m.** *** D: Oscar (Budd) Boetticher. Chester Morris, Janis Carter, Richard Lane, William Wright, George E. Stone, Robert Williams, George McKay. Brisk and breezy *Boston Blackie* entry, with the capricious ex-thief jolted into action when he's accused of stealing a precious gem from a museum. 19-year-old Dorothy Malone (billed as Maloney) appears in one of her first roles as Eileen. TV title: BOSTON BLACKIE'S APPOINTMENT WITH DEATH.

One Night in Lisbon (1941) **97m.** **½ D: Edward H. Griffith. Fred MacMurray, Madeleine Carroll, Patricia Morison, Billie Burke, John Loder. Mild screwball comedy with gorgeous Carroll falling in love with flier MacMurray despite interference from his ex (Morison).

One Night in the Tropics (1940) **82m.** **½ D: A. Edward Sutherland. Allan Jones, Nancy Kelly, Bud Abbott, Lou Costello, Robert Cummings, Leo Carrillo, Mary Boland. Ambitious but unmemorable musical with songs by Jerome Kern, Oscar Hammerstein and Dorothy Fields, from Earl Derr Biggers' gimmicky story *Love Insurance* (filmed before in 1919 and 1924). Abbott and Costello, in film debut, have secondary roles to Jones-Kelly-Cummings love triangle, but get to do a portion of their "Who's on First?" routine.▼

One Night of Love (1934) **84m.** ***½ D: Victor Schertzinger. Grace Moore, Tullio Carminati, Lyle Talbot, Mona Barrie, Luis Alberni, Jessie Ralph. Classic musical, with an Oscar-winning Louis Silvers score, of aspiring opera star Moore and her demanding teacher Carminati. A delight from start to finish, and a must for music lovers; remains remarkably fresh and entertaining. Unquestionably Moore's best film.▼●

One Night Stand (1997) **C-103m.** ** D: Mike Figgis. Wesley Snipes, Nastassja Kinski, Kyle MacLachlan, Ming-Na Wen, Robert Downey, Jr., John Calley, Glenn Plummer, Amanda Donohoe, John Ratzenberger, Julian Sands, Thomas Haden Church, Donovan Leitch, Ione Skye, Xander Berkeley. Flashy but empty drama about a TV commercials director (Snipes) caught up in a plastic, unfeeling world, whose life is in for quite a jolt upon renewing a friendship with seriously ill Downey and having a chance encounter with Kinski. Figgis turns up as a hotel clerk. [R] ▼●◗

One Night With You (1948-British) **90m.** ** D: Terence Young. Nino Martini, Patricia Roc, Bonar Colleano, Guy Middleton, Stanley Holloway, Miles Malleson, Christopher Lee. Diluted musical with socialite Roc intrigued by singer Martini.

...... **One of Our Aircraft Is Missing** (1942-British) **106m.** ***½ D: Michael Powell, Emeric Pressburger. Godfrey Tearle, Eric Portman, Hugh Williams, Bernard Miles, Hugh Burden, Emrys Jones, Googie Withers, Joyce Redman, Pamela Brown, Peter Ustinov, Hay Petrie, Roland Culver, Robert Helpmann, John Longden. Thoughtful study of RAF pilots who crash-land in the Netherlands and seek to return to England. Powell and Pressburger scripted, from the latter's story. Powell makes an appearance as a dispatcher. Some U.S. prints run 82m.▼

One of Our Dinosaurs Is Missing (1976) **C-93m.** BOMB D: Robert Stevenson. Peter Ustinov, Helen Hayes, Clive Revill, Derek Nimmo, Joan Sims. The Disney studio's answer to insomnia, a boring film about spy with secret formula hidden in dinosaur bone, and a group of nannies determined to retrieve stolen skeleton. Filmed in England. [G]▼

One on One (1977) **C-98m.** *** D: Lamont Johnson. Robby Benson, Annette O'Toole, G. D. Spradlin, Gail Strickland, Melanie Griffith. Benson cowrote this sincere, upbeat film about naive basketball player who tries to buck corrupt world of college athletics, and sadistic coach Spradlin. Director Johnson plays Benson's alumni big brother. [PG]▼

One Plus One SEE: **Sympathy for the Devil**

One Potato, Two Potato (1964) **92m.** ***½ D: Larry Peerce. Barbara Barrie, Bernie Hamilton, Richard Mulligan, Robert Earl Jones, Harry Bellaver, Faith Burwell, Tom Ligon. Frank study of interracial marriage, beautifully acted by Barrie and Hamilton. Perceptive script by Raphael Hayes and Orville H. Hampton.

One Rainy Afternoon (1936) **79m.** **½ D: Rowland V. Lee. Francis Lederer, Ida Lupino, Roland Young, Hugh Herbert, Erik Rhodes, Mischa Auer. Silly but likable piece of froth about a charming, impetuous young man who causes a stir by kissing a young woman in a movie theater. The song "Sweet Rendezvous" was written by Preston Sturges!▼

One Romantic Night (1930) **71m.** *½ D:

Paul L. Stein. Lillian Gish, Rod La Rocque, Conrad Nagel, Marie Dressler, O. P. Heggie, Albert Conti. Static, wooden version of Molnar's *The Swan*, with princess Gish (in her talkie debut) half-heartedly pursued by playboy prince La Rocque while adored by commoner Nagel. Dressler comes off best, as Gish's dowager mother. Filmed previously in 1925 and again in 1956 (with Grace Kelly) as THE SWAN.

One Russian Summer (1973-Italian-British) **C-112m.** BOMB D: Antonio Calenda. Oliver Reed, John McEnery, Carol Andre, Raymond Lovelock, Zova Velcova, Claudia Cardinale. Cripple McEnery, with a score to settle, stirs up trouble for sadistic, temperamental landowner Reed, who laughs like a hyena and chews up the scenery. Fancy camerawork, one-dimensional characterizations; a mess. From M. Lermontov's novel *Vadim.* [R]▼

One Sings, the Other Doesn't (1977-French) **C-105m.** ** D: Agnés Varda. Therese Liotard, Valerie Mairesse, Ali Raffi, Robert Dadies, Francis Lemaire. Simplistic, sugar-coated feminist story paralleling the lives of two women from the early '60s to 1976. An honest attempt to examine the meaning of womanhood, but awfully superficial.▼

One Spy Too Many (1966) **C-102m.** ** D: Joseph Sargent. Robert Vaughn, David McCallum, Rip Torn, Dorothy Provine, Leo G. Carroll. Torn tries to take over the world, with Vaughn and McCallum to the rescue. Forgettable feature, edited from *The Man from U.N.C.L.E.* TV series.

One Step to Eternity (1955-French) **94m.** ** D: Henri Decoin. Danielle Darrieux, Michel Auclair, Corinne Calvet, Gil Delamare. Capable cast led astray by meandering production about unknown persons trying to kill four women.

One Step to Hell (1968) **C-90m.** ** D: Sandy Howard. Ty Hardin, Pier Angeli, George Sanders, Rossano Brazzi, Helga Line, Jorge Rigaud. Crude period melodrama in turn-of-the-century African bush. Lawman Hardin pursues gang of vicious killers.▼

One Summer Love (1976) **C-98m.** ** D: Gilbert Cates. Beau Bridges, Susan Sarandon, Mildred Dunnock, Ann Wedgeworth, Michael B. Miller, Linda Miller. Ambitious but muddled drama of Bridges, just out of a mental hospital, attempting to trace his family; Sarandon, who sells candy in a movie theater, takes a liking to him. Screenplay by N. Richard Nash; originally released as DRAGONFLY. [PG]▼

One Sunday Afternoon (1933) **69m.** *** D: Stephen Roberts. Gary Cooper, Fay Wray, Neil Hamilton, Frances Fuller, Roscoe Karns, Jane Darwell. Cooper is at boyish best in this original version of James Hagan's play about a turn-of-the-century dentist and how his infatuation with a sexy vamp (Wray) who weds his rival almost ruins his marriage and his life. Touching and lovingly made piece of Americana, exuding period charm and atmosphere, though darker in tone than the two Warner Bros. remakes by Raoul Walsh: as THE STRAWBERRY BLONDE in 1941, then under the original title as a 1948 Technicolor musical.

One Sunday Afternoon (1948) **C-90m.** **½ D: Raoul Walsh. Dennis Morgan, Janis Paige, Don DeFore, Dorothy Malone, Ben Blue. Musical remake of the 1933 Gary Cooper feature (and 1941's THE STRAWBERRY BLONDE) set in 1910, about a dentist who wonders if he married the right girl; pleasant but nothing more. Attractive cast, unmemorable songs.

One That Got Away, The (1958-British) **106m.** *** D: Roy (Ward) Baker. Hardy Kruger, Colin Gordon, Michael Goodliffe, Terence Alexander. Kruger gives sincere performance as Nazi prisoner in England who believes it is his duty to escape and get back to Germany. Many exciting moments.▼

One Third of a Nation (1939) **79m.** **½ D: Dudley Murphy. Sylvia Sidney, Leif Erickson, Myron McCormick, Hiram Sherman, Sidney Lumet, Iris Adrian, Byron Russell. Sidney is a poor girl yearning to escape from the N.Y.C. tenements; young Lumet is her troubled brother, Erickson an unknowing slumlord who falls for her. Still timely social document.▼

1001 Arabian Nights (1959) **C-75m.** **½ D: Jack Kinney. Voices of Jim Backus, Kathryn Grant (Crosby), Dwayne Hickman, Hans Conried, Herschel Bernardi, Alan Reed. Elaborate updating of Arabian Nights tales featuring nearsighted Mr. Magoo has a nice score, pleasing animation.▼

One Touch of Venus (1948) **81m.** **½ D: William A. Seiter. Ava Gardner, Robert Walker, Dick Haymes, Eve Arden, Olga San Juan, Tom Conway. Young man in love with department-store window statue of Venus doesn't know what to do when she magically comes to life. Amusing, but misses the bull's-eye, despite its having been a hit on Broadway. Lovely Kurt Weill–Ogden Nash score includes "Speak Low."▼●

One Tough Cop (1998) **C-94m.** *½ D: Bruno Barreto. Stephen Baldwin, Chris Penn, Gina Gershon, Mike McGlone, Paul Guilfoyle, Amy Irving, Victor Slezak, Luis Guzman. Baldwin is miscast as renegade 1980s N.Y.P.D. detective Bo Dietl who, in this hackneyed, highly fictionalized account of his exploits—based on his "autobiographical novel"—stands up to the nasty Feds when they pressure him to rat out his boyhood best friend, who's now a mob boss. Graphic violence and nonstop torrent of four-letter words are the only differences between this and a routine TV cop show. [R]▼●◗

One-Trick Pony (1980) **C-98m.** ** D: Robert M. Young. Paul Simon, Blair Brown, Rip Torn, Joan Hackett, Mare Winningham, Allen Goorwitz (Garfield), Lou Reed, The B-52's, Harry Shearer, The Lovin' Spoonful, Sam and Dave, Tiny Tim. Aging rock star tries to salvage marriage while trying to weather changes in audience tastes. Good premise, impressive supporting cast undermined by haphazard construction, lack of Simon's appeal as a leading man. Scripted and scored by Simon; one of those Hare Krishnas is Daniel Stern. [R]▼●

One True Thing (1998) **C-127m.** ***½ D: Carl Franklin. Meryl Streep, Renee Zellweger, William Hurt, Tom Everett Scott, Lauren Graham, Nicky Katt, James Eckhouse, Gerrit Graham, Diana Canova. Exceptional, moving family drama about a young woman forced to temporarily move back in with her parents and come to terms with both her mother (an expert homemaker to whom she's never related) and her literary lion of a father (whom she's always idolized). Superb acting and the constant ring of truth distinguish this adaptation by Karen Croner of Anna Quindlen's bestselling novel. [R]▼●◗

One, Two, Three (1961) **108m.** **** D: Billy Wilder. James Cagney, Arlene Francis, Horst Buchholz, Pamela Tiffin, Lilo Pulver, Howard St. John, Hans Lothar, Leon Askin, Red Buttons. Hilarious Wilder comedy about Coke executive in contemporary West Berlin freaking out when the boss's visiting daughter secretly weds a Communist. Cagney is a marvel to watch in this machine-gun-paced comedy, his last film appearance until 1981's RAGTIME. Andre Previn's score makes inspired use of Khachaturian's "Sabre Dance." The script, by Wilder and I.A.L. Diamond, was inspired by a Ferenc Molnar one-act play. Panavision. ▼●

One Way Passage (1932) **69m.** ***½ D: Tay Garnett. Kay Francis, William Powell, Aline MacMahon, Warren Hymer, Frank McHugh, Herbert Mundin. Tender shipboard romance of con-man Powell and fatally ill Francis, splendidly acted, with good support by MacMahon and McHugh as two other con-artists playing Cupid. Robert Lord won an Oscar for his original story. Remade as TILL WE MEET AGAIN.

One-Way Street (1950) **79m.** **½ D: Hugo Fregonese. James Mason, Marta Toren, Dan Duryea, William Conrad, Jack Elam, King Donovan. Turgid crime drama chronicling what happens after doctor Mason strips hood Duryea of $200,000—and his moll (Toren). Look for Rock Hudson as a truck driver.

One-Way Ticket to Hell SEE: **Teenage Devil Dolls**

One Way to Love (1945) **83m.** ** D: Ray Enright. Chester Morris, Janis Carter, Marguerite Chapman, Willard Parker. Pleasant programmer about two radio writers finding romance and new program ideas on cross-country train trip.

One Wild Moment (1977-French) **C-88m.** ** D: Claude Berri. Jean-Pierre Marielle, Victor Lanoux, Agnes Soral, Christine Dejoux, Martine Sarcey. Lightweight, unsatisfying sex farce about two middle-aged buddies (Marielle, Lanoux) who vacation with their sexy teen daughters (Soral, Dejoux). Not nearly as clever as other Berri comedies. Remade as BLAME IT ON RIO. Panavision. [R]▼

One Woman or Two (1985-French) **C-97m.** *½ D: Daniel Vigne. Gérard Depardieu, Sigourney Weaver, Dr. Ruth Westheimer, Michel Aumont, Zabou. Paleontologist Depardieu discovers the fossil remains of the first Frenchwoman; crass ad exec Weaver is intent on exploiting this to hype perfume. An utterly silly BRINGING UP BABY derivation, with its two stars wasted. [PG-13]▼

One Woman's Story SEE: **Passionate Friends, The**

On Golden Pond (1981) **C-109m.** *** D: Mark Rydell. Katharine Hepburn, Henry Fonda, Jane Fonda, Doug McKeon, Dabney Coleman, William Lanteau. Fonda, in his last feature, is no less than brilliant as crochety retired professor Norman Thayer, Jr., angry at being 80 years old and scared of losing his faculties. Hepburn fine as his devoted, all-knowing wife who shares his summers at Maine lakefront home; Jane is his alienated daughter. Sometimes simplistic comedy-drama, scripted by Ernest Thompson from his play, gets a heavy dose of Star Quality. Fonda, Hepburn, and writer Thompson all won Academy Awards for their work. [PG]▼●◗

On Her Majesty's Secret Service (1969-British) **C-140m.** ***½ D: Peter R. Hunt. George Lazenby, Diana Rigg, Gabriele Ferzetti, Telly Savalas, Bernard Lee, Lois Maxwell, Desmond Llewelyn, Catharina Von Schell (Catherine Schell), Bessie Love, Joanna Lumley. Usual globe-hopping Bond vs. Blofeld plot with novel twist: agent Bond ends up marrying Italian contessa (Rigg)! Lazenby, first non-Connery Bond, is OK, but incredible action sequences take first chair; some 007 fans consider this the best of the series. Panavision. [M/PG]▼●◗

Onion Field, The (1979) **C-127m.** *** D: Harold Becker. John Savage, James Woods, Franklyn Seales, Ted Danson, Ronny Cox, Dianne Hull, Christopher Lloyd, Priscilla Pointer, Pat Corley. Heart-wrenching true story about a cop who cracks up after witnessing his partner's murder and fleeing; adapted by author Joseph Wambaugh without any studio interference. Well-acted and impassioned, but never quite peaks. [R]▼●

Onionhead (1958) **110m.** **½ D: Norman Taurog. Andy Griffith, Felicia Farr, Walter Matthau, Erin O'Brien, Joe Mantell, Ray Danton, James Gregory, Joey Bishop, Roscoe Karns, Claude Akins, Peter Brown, Tige Andrews. Film tries to capture flavor of NO TIME FOR SERGEANTS, with Griffith in the Coast Guard this time.▼

Only Angels Have Wings (1939) **121m.** ***½ D: Howard Hawks. Cary Grant, Jean Arthur, Richard Barthelmess, Rita Hayworth, Thomas Mitchell, Sig Ruman, John Carroll, Allyn Joslyn, Noah Beery, Jr. Quintessential Howard Hawks movie, full of idealized men and women (and what men and women!) in this look at relationships among mail pilots stationed in South America—and how things heat up when a showgirl (Arthur) is tossed into the stew. An important star-boosting showcase for Hayworth, too. Jules Furthman scripted, from a story by Hawks.▼◗

Only Game in Town, The (1970) **C-113m.** *** D: George Stevens. Elizabeth Taylor, Warren Beatty, Charles Braswell, Hank Henry, Olga Valery. Romance of chorus girl and gambler takes place in Las Vegas, but was shot in Paris and suffers for it; restriction of action to indoor scenes slows pace of this pleasant adaptation of Frank D. Gilroy's play. Beatty is excellent. Stevens' final film. [M/PG]▼

Only the Best SEE: **I Can Get It for You Wholesale**

Only the French Can (1955-French) **C-93m.** *** D: Jean Renoir. Jean Gabin, Francoise Arnoul, Maria Felix, Edith Piaf. Not top-drawer Renoir, but still an impressive, enjoyable fiction about beginnings of the Moulin Rouge and impresario Gabin's creation of the cancan. Originally released in the U.S. in 1956; a brilliantly beautiful restored version, with approximately 10m. of additional footage, opened theatrically in 1985. Originally released in France as FRENCH CANCAN at 102m. ▼●

Only the Lonely (1991) **C-102m.** *** D: Chris Columbus. John Candy, Maureen O'Hara, Ally Sheedy, James Belushi, Anthony Quinn, Kevin Dunn, Milo O'Shea, Bert Remsen, Joe V. Greco, Macaulay Culkin. Chicago cop, who still lives with his mom, falls in love—and has to overcome both his mother's resistance and his feelings of guilt over leaving her. Sweet, sentimental update of MARTY shines with performances that are right on-target, including O'Hara's first since 1973's THE RED PONY. [PG-13]▼●◗

Only the Strong (1993) **C-96m.** ** D: Sheldon Lettich. Mark Dacascos, Stacey Travis, Geoffrey Lewis, Paco Christian Prieto, Todd Susman, Jeffrey Anderson Gunter. Ex–Green Beret, his old Miami high school now threatened by a drug lord, turns a dozen of the joint's worst malcontents into crimebusters by teaching them a rhythmic, Brazilian form of martial arts called capoeira. Real-life martial arts champ Dacascos is appealing in a can't-act kind of way. Dopey but inoffensive; at its best in potently choreographed fight scenes. [PG-13]▼●

Only the Valiant (1951) **105m.** ** D: Gordon Douglas. Gregory Peck, Barbara Payton, Ward Bond, Gig Young, Lon Chaney, Jr., Neville Brand, Jeff Corey. Unmemorable oater of army officer Peck showing his courage by holding off the rampaging Indians.▼●

Only Thrill, The (1998) **C-108m.** *½ D: Peter Masterson. Diane Keaton, Sam Shepard, Diane Lane, Robert Patrick, Tate Donovan, Sharon Lawrence, Stacey Travis. A fine cast can't save this drab tearjerker about the thwarted affair between a widowed seamstress and a small-town Texas shopkeeper that begins in 1966, spans three decades, and begins to repeat itself when their grown children fall in love. Stagy, contrived, and never plausible, with some hilariously unconvincing old-age wigs and makeup effects. [R]▼

Only Two Can Play (1962-British) **106m.** *** D: Sidney Gilliat. Peter Sellers, Mai Zetterling, Virginia Maskell, Richard Attenborough, Kenneth Griffith. Well-intentioned filming of Kingsley Amis novel, striving for quick laughs rather than satire. Sellers is librarian flirting with society woman Zetterling.▼

Only When I Larf (1968-British) **C-104m.** **½ D: Basil Dearden. Richard Attenborough, David Hemmings, Alexandra Stewart, Nicholas Pennell. Fun con-game film finds three confidence men scheming to sell militant African diplomat scrap metal in ammunition cases. [G]

Only When I Laugh (1981) **C-120m.** *** D: Glenn Jordan. Marsha Mason, Kristy McNichol, James Coco, Joan Hackett, David Dukes, John Bennett Perry, Kevin Bacon. Bittersweet Neil Simon comedy about alcoholic actress Mason struggling to stay off the bottle and her relationship with teenaged daughter McNichol. Fine performances by the leads, superior ones by Coco as a gay failed actor and Hackett as an aging Park Avenue beauty. Screenplay by Simon, loosely based on his play *The Gingerbread Lady*. [R]▼●

Only Yesterday (1933) **105m.** *** D: John M. Stahl. Margaret Sullavan, John Boles, Billie Burke, Reginald Denny, Edna May Oliver, Benita Hume. Though Boles is a drag, Sullavan's performance in her screen debut is still luminous enough to carry this familiar, flash-backed unwed mother saga spanning from the end of WW1 to the Depression. Opening scenes, depicting effect of the stock market crash on a group of partying high-rollers, are extremely evocative but tend to overshadow the rest of the film.

Only You (1992) **C-85m.** ** D: Betty Thomas. Andrew McCarthy, Kelly Preston, Helen Hunt, Daniel Roebuck, Denny Dillon, Kid Creole and The Coconuts. McCarthy, dumped by his dishy girlfriend-of-the-moment, meets sexy Preston and winds up taking her on his vacation jaunt to an idyllic beach resort . . . but are looks really everything? Pleasant-enough romantic comedy, with a capable and attractive cast, gets just too predictable to sustain itself. Reni Santoni appears unbilled. Released direct to video. Clairmont-Scope. [PG-13]▼●

Only You (1994) **C-108m.** *** D: Norman Jewison. Marisa Tomei, Robert Downey, Jr., Bonnie Hunt, Joaquim De Almeida, Fisher Stevens, Billy Zane, Adam LeFevre, John Benjamin Hickey, Siobhan Fallon, Phyllis Newman. Likable confection about a young woman who spends her whole life searching for her perfect mate—whose name was conjured up in childhood on a Ouija board; fate and happenstance bring her to Europe to meet her "other half." Tomei's earnest and appealing performance makes the far-fetched story work. Director Jewison provides a dreamy travelogue of Italy (photographed by Sven Nykvist, no less) as her backdrop. Like so many contemporary romantic comedies, this one invokes an earlier one (ROMAN HOLIDAY) to justify its existence. [PG]▼●◗

On Moonlight Bay (1951) **C-95m.** **½ D: Roy Del Ruth. Doris Day, Gordon MacRae, Billy Gray, Mary Wickes, Leon Ames, Rosemary DeCamp. Turn-of-the-century, folksy musical based on Booth Tarkington's *Penrod* stories with tomboy (Day) and next door neighbor (MacRae) the wholesome young lovers. Sequel: BY THE LIGHT OF THE SILVERY MOON. ▼●

On My Own (1992-Italian-Canadian-Australian) **C-93m.** ***½ D: Antonio Tibaldi. Judy Davis, Matthew Ferguson, David McIlwraith, Nicolas Van Burek, Michele Melega, Colin Fox, Jan Rubes. Complex, deeply felt, hauntingly powerful coming-of-age drama about 15-year-old Ferguson, who attends a boys' prep school. His parents are divorced; he's physically and emotionally distanced from his father, and learns that his mother (Davis, who is superb) is a schizophrenic. The scenario details how he is affected by her illness, her personality, and her fate.▼

On My Way to the Crusades, I Met a Girl Who . . . (1968-Italian) **C-93m.** BOMB D: Pasquale Festa Campanile. Tony Curtis, Monica Vitti, Hugh Griffith, John Richardson, Ivo Garrani, Nino Castelnuovo. Weak comedy about Vitti's chastity belt was held back from release for a long time, and no wonder. Aka THE CHASTITY BELT. [R]

On Our Merry Way (1948) **107m.** ** D: King Vidor, Leslie Fenton. Burgess Meredith, Paulette Goddard, Henry Fonda, James Stewart, Fred MacMurray, William Demarest, Dorothy Lamour, Victor Moore, Harry James, Eduardo Ciannelli, Dorothy Ford, Hugh Herbert. Silly multi-episode comedy, with a buoyant Meredith posing as an inquiring reporter and asking people what impact a baby has had on their life. Strained slapstick throughout. Protracted sequence, with Stewart and Fonda as laconic musician pals, was written by John O'Hara. Aka A MIRACLE CAN HAPPEN.◗

On Stage Everybody (1945) **65m.** ** D: Jean Yarbrough. Jack Oakie, Peggy Ryan, Otto Kruger, Julie London, Wallace Ford, King Sisters. Run-of-the-mill Universal musical, with frantic Oakie helping to put on the big radio variety program.

On the Avenue (1937) **89m.** *** D: Roy Del Ruth. Dick Powell, Madeleine Carroll, Alice Faye, Ritz Brothers, Alan Mowbray, Billy Gilbert, Cora Witherspoon, Joan Davis, Sig Rumann. Tasteful, intelligent musical of socialite Carroll getting involved with stage star Powell. One good Irving Berlin song after another: "I've Got My Love To Keep Me Warm," "This Year's Kisses," "Let's Go Slumming," "The Girl on the Police Gazette."▼

On the Beach (1959) **133m.** **** D: Stanley Kramer. Gregory Peck, Ava Gardner, Fred Astaire, Anthony Perkins, Donna Anderson, John Tate, Guy Doleman. Thoughtful version of Nevil Shute's novel about Australians awaiting effects of nuclear fallout from explosion that has destroyed the rest of the world. Good performances by all, including Astaire in his first dramatic role. Screenplay by John Paxton. Remade for cable TV in 2000. ▼●◗

On the Beat (1962-British) **105m.** **½ D: Robert Asher. Norman Wisdom, Jennifer Jayne, Raymond Huntley, David Lodge. Overly cute comedy with Wisdom a dumb-bunny helping Scotland Yard round up a criminal gang; too many pat routines and stereotyped performances.

On the Double (1961) **C-92m.** *** D: Melville Shavelson. Danny Kaye, Dana Wynter, Wilfrid Hyde-White, Margaret Rutherford, Diana Dors. Danny's resemblance to English general makes him valuable as a WW2 spy. At one point he does a Marlene Dietrich imitation! Repeats dual-identity gimmick from Kaye's earlier ON THE RIVIERA with equally entertaining results. Panavision.

On the Edge (1985) **C-92m.** ** D: Rob Nilsson. Bruce Dern, Bill Bailey, Jim

Haynie, John Marley, Pam Grier. Well-meaning but predictable, ultimately disappointing tale of middle-aged Dern, who attempts to redeem his life by competing in a grueling footrace. Available in unrated version. [PG-13]▼

On the Fiddle SEE: **Operation Snafu**

On the Isle of Samoa (1950) **65m.** *½ D: William Berke. Jon Hall, Susan Cabot, Raymond Greenleaf, Henry Marco. Sloppy little story of Hall finding love with native girl, inspiring him to clear up his shady past.

On the Loose (1951) **78m.** *½ D: Charles Lederer. Joan Evans, Melvyn Douglas, Lynn Bari, Robert Arthur, Hugh O'Brian. Lukewarm drama of overindulgent parents and their wayward daughter.

On the Nickel (1980) **C-96m.** **½ D: Ralph Waite. Donald Moffat, Ralph Waite, Penelope Allen, Hal Williams, Jack Kehoe. Odd, sentimental film about bums Moffat and Waite and their experiences on L.A.'s skid row. Directed, scripted, and produced by Waite, light years away from *The Waltons*. [R]▼

On the Right Track (1981) **C-98m.** **½ D: Lee Philips. Gary Coleman, Lisa Eilbacher, Michael Lembeck, Norman Fell, Maureen Stapleton, Bill Russell, Herb Edelman. Coleman is a lovable 10-year-old shoeshine boy who lives out of a train station locker and predicts horserace winners like the hero of THREE MEN ON A HORSE; Stapleton is on hand as a bag lady. Coleman's theatrical starring debut is hardly feature-film material. [PG]▼

On the Riviera (1951) **C-90m.** *** D: Walter Lang. Danny Kaye, Gene Tierney, Corinne Calvet, Marcel Dalio, Jean Murat. Bouncy musicomedy with Danny in dual role as entertainer and French military hero. ''Ballin' the Jack,'' other songs in lively film. Gwen Verdon is one of chorus girls. Remake of Maurice Chevalier's FOLIES BERGERE.

On the Road Again SEE: **Honeysuckle Rose**

On the Ropes (1999) **C-94m.** ***½ D: Nanette Burstein, Brett Morgen. Compelling documentary about a former boxer named Harry Keitt who works with young people at a Brooklyn gym, hoping to give them focus and purpose as well as a possible career after they're showcased at the Golden Gloves. The film follows three of his protégés—a promising young woman who's been dealt a bad hand, a cocky young man who thinks he knows the answers, and a real comer who's too easily seduced by the lure of fame and fortune. Rich, real, often heartbreaking . . . a must-see. ▼

On the Threshold of Space (1956) **C-98m.** **½ D: Robert D. Webb. Guy Madison, Virginia Leith, John Hodiak, Dean Jagger, Warren Stevens. Capable cast merely bridges the span between sequences of astronaut endurance tests and other space-flight maneuvers. CinemaScope.

On the Town (1949) **C-98m.** **** D: Gene Kelly, Stanley Donen. Gene Kelly, Frank Sinatra, Vera-Ellen, Betty Garrett, Ann Miller, Jules Munshin, Alice Pearce, Florence Bates. Three sailors have 24 hours to take in the sights and sounds of N.Y.C. Exuberant MGM musical, innovatively shot on location all over the City, isn't much in terms of plot and discards some of the best songs from the Betty Comden–Adolph Green–Leonard Bernstein show on which it's based . . . but it's still terrific entertainment. Highlight: ''New York, New York.'' Oscar winner for Roger Edens and Lennie Hayton's musical scoring. An impressive directing debut for Kelly and Donen.▼●◗

On the Waterfront (1954) **108m.** **** D: Elia Kazan. Marlon Brando, Karl Malden, Lee J. Cobb, Rod Steiger, Pat Henning, Eva Marie Saint, Leif Erickson, Tony Galento, John Hamilton, Nehemiah Persoff. Budd Schulberg's unflinching account of N.Y.C. harbor unions (suggested by articles by Malcolm Johnson), with Brando unforgettable as misfit, Steiger his crafty brother, Cobb his waterfront boss, and Saint the girl he loves. That classic scene in the back of a taxicab is just as moving as ever. Winner of eight Oscars: Best Picture, Director, Actor (Brando), Supporting Actress (Saint), Story & Screenplay, Cinematography (Boris Kaufman), Art Direction-Set Decoration (Richard Day), and Editing (Gene Milford). Leonard Bernstein's music is another major asset. Film debuts of Saint, Martin Balsam, Fred Gwynne, and Pat Hingle. Adapted as a Broadway show decades later.▼●

On the Yard (1979) **C-102m.** ** D: Raphael D. Silver. John Heard, Thomas D. Waites, Mike Kellin, Richard Bright, Joe Grifasi, Lane Smith. Convict Heard makes a fatal mistake by mixing it up with jailhouse kingpin Waites. So-so prison picture seems hardly worth the effort, though Kellin is memorable as an aging loser trying to get paroled. [R]▼

On Trial (1953-French) **70m.** ** D: Julien Duvivier. Madeleine Robinson, Daniel Gelin, Eleonora Rossi-Drago, Charles Vanel, Anton Walbrook, Jacques Chabassol. Chabassol, son of D.A. Vanel, investigates conviction of Gelin, discovering disparity between justice and truth; well-intentioned film gone astray.

On Valentine's Day (1986) **C-106m.** **½ D: Ken Harrison. William Converse-Roberts, Hallie Foote, Michael Higgins, Steven Hill, Rochelle Oliver, Richard Jenkins, Carol Goodheart, Horton Foote, Jr., Matthew Broderick. Literate but unmemorable account of the various goings-on in a small Texas town in 1917. Interesting characterizations, good performances, but doesn't add up to much. Semiautobiographical screenplay by Horton Foote. Followed by CONVICTS; both are prequels to **1918**. Produced for PBS's *American Playhouse,* where it was telecast (along with **1918**) as STORY OF A MARRIAGE. [PG]▼

On Your Toes (1939) **94m.** **½ D: Ray Enright. Vera Zorina, Eddie Albert, Frank McHugh, Alan Hale, James Gleason, Donald O'Connor. Long-winded backstage story about jealousy and attempted murder has little to do with George Abbott's Broadway hit; even the Rodgers and Hart songs are gone, relegated to background music! Fortunately, Zorina's dancing of "Slaughter on Tenth Avenue" remains, with choreography by George Balanchine.

Open City (1945-Italian) **105m.** **** D: Roberto Rossellini. Aldo Fabrizi, Anna Magnani, Marcello Pagliero, Maria Michi, Vito Annicchiarico, Nando Bruno, Harry Feist. Classic Rossellini account of Italian underground movement during Nazi occupation of Rome; powerful moviemaking gem. Cowritten by Rossellini, Federico Fellini, and Sergio Amidei. Aka ROME, OPEN CITY.▼●◗

Open Doors (1990-Italian) **C-109m.** *** D: Gianni Amelio. Gian Maria Volonte, Ennio Fantastichini, Renzo Giovampietro, Renato Carpentieri, Tuccio Musumeci. Stimulating drama about jurist Volonte, presiding over a murder trial in Fascist Italy. A thoughtful look at the personal implications of judging others, of what it means to condemn another to death even if he is obviously guilty. It also focuses on the need to probe for truth and justice in spite of political repression. [R]▼

Opening Night (1977) **C-144m.** *** D: John Cassavetes. Gena Rowlands, John Cassavetes, Ben Gazzara, Joan Blondell, Paul Stewart, Zohra Lampert. Fascinating if you appreciate Cassavetes' style (he also wrote it); interminable if you don't. Rowlands is an actress facing a midlife crisis triggered by the death of an adoring fan on the opening night of her new play. Blondell fine as the sympathetic authoress, Cassavetes himself no less interesting as Rowlands' costar.▼●◗

Open Season (1974-Spanish) **C-103m.** BOMB D: Peter Collinson. Peter Fonda, John Phillip Law, Richard Lynch, William Holden, Cornelia Sharpe. Sordid mixture of violence and sex as three Vietnam War buddies hunt humans. Video title: RECON GAME. [R]▼

Open Season (1996) **C-97m.** *** D: Robert Wuhl. Robert Wuhl, Rod Taylor, Helen Shaver, Gailard Sartain, Maggie Han, Steven C. White, Timothy Arrington, Barry Flatman, Dina Merrill, Saul Rubinek, Tom Selleck, Alan Thicke, Jimmie Walker, Joe Piscopo. Smart, funny satire of television and our competitive society. Wuhl plays a nerdy but straight-arrow worker bee at a ratings company who through personal integrity and candor has a knack for getting himself into trouble; then he stumbles into a job in public broadcasting. Fine supporting cast, including Taylor in a pungent performance as a messianic programming chief. Filmed in 1993. [R] ▼●

Open Your Eyes (1998-Spanish-French-Italian) **C-117m.** *½ D: Alejandro Amenábar. Penélope Cruz, Eduardo Noriega, Chete Lera, Fele Martínez, Najwa Nimri. A handsome young man falls in love, but his jealous former girlfriend deals him a cruel blow. Murky psychological thriller bounces from present-day reality to a nightmarish vision of the past and present. The hero becomes a tortured soul, but why do we in the audience have to suffer too? [R]▼

Operation Amsterdam (1960-British) **105m.** **½ D: Michael McCarthy. Peter Finch, Eva Bartok, Tony Britton, Alexander Knox, Malcolm Keen. Standard wartime suspense fare as British expedition tries to sneak a cache of diamonds out of Holland before Nazis can get to them.▼

Operation Bikini (1963) **83m.** ** D: Anthony Carras. Tab Hunter, Frankie Avalon, Eva Six, Scott Brady, Gary Crosby, Jim Backus. Occasionally perky cast livens tame WW2 narrative of attempt to destroy sunken treasure before enemy grabs it. Some color sequences.

Operation C.I.A. (1965) **90m.** **½ D: Christian Nyby. Burt Reynolds, Kieu Chinh, Danielle Aubry, John Hoyt, Cyril Collack. Burt attempts to thwart an assassination in Saigon. Neat little actioner, and an intriguing look at a Vietnam of politics and spies, where innocent old men and children die.▼

Operation Condor SEE: **Armour of God 2: Operation Condor**

Operation Conspiracy (1957-British) **69m.** *½ D: Joseph Sterling. Philip Friend, Mary Mackenzie, Leslie Dwyer, Allan Cuthbertson. Timid little espionage film. Retitled: CLOAK WITHOUT DAGGER.

Operation Crossbow (1965) **C-116m.** ***½ D: Michael Anderson. George Peppard, Sophia Loren, Trevor Howard, Tom Courtenay, Anthony Quayle, John Mills, Sylvia Syms, Richard Todd, Lilli Palmer. Fine "impossible mission" tale of small band of commandos out to destroy Nazi secret missile stronghold during WW2. Sensational ending, and the pyrotechnics are dazzling. Scripted by Robert Imrie (Emeric Pressburger), Derry Quinn, and Ray Rigby. Retitled THE GREAT SPY MISSION. Panavision.▼●

Operation Cross Eagles (1969) **C-90m.** *½ D: Richard Conte. Richard Conte, Rory Calhoun, Aili King, Phil Brown.

Undistinguished war film about a WW2 mission in Yugoslavia to rescue captured American officer.▼

Operation Daybreak (1976) **C-102m.** **½ D: Lewis Gilbert. Timothy Bottoms, Martin Shaw, Joss Ackland, Nicola Pagett, Anthony Andrews, Anton Diffring. Well-made but uninspiring account of Czech underground's attempt to assassinate Reinhard "Hangman" Heydrich, Hitler's right-hand man, during WW2. Retitled PRICE OF FREEDOM. [PG]▼

Operation Disaster (1951-British) **102m.** *** D: Roy (Ward) Baker. John Mills, Helen Cherry, Richard Attenborough, Lana Morris, Nigel Patrick. Vivid actioner of submarine warfare during WW2, tautly presented. Originally titled MORNING DEPARTURE.

Operation Double 007 SEE: **Operation Kid Brother**

Operation Dumbo Drop (1995) **C-107m.** **½ D: Simon Wincer. Danny Glover, Ray Liotta, Denis Leary, Doug E. Doug, Corin Nemec, Dinh Thien Le, Tcheky Karyo, Hoang Ly, James Hong. In the midst of the Vietnam War, a new, by-the-book captain (Liotta) arrives in a strategic village to take the place of Glover, but finds himself on an unlikely adventure to replace the hamlet's all-important elephant. Surprisingly flat until the climax, when things finally pick up. Also an odd choice of setting and subject for a Disney family film . . . which explains the lack of swearing and the toning-down of Leary's conniving character. Panavision. [PG]▼●

Operation Eichmann (1961) **93m.** **½ D: R. G. Springsteen. Werner Klemperer, Ruta Lee, Donald Buke, Barbara Turner, John Banner. Fairly intriguing account of the Nazi leader's postwar life and his capture by Israelis.▼

Operation Haylift (1950) **75m.** ** D: William Berke. Bill Williams, Ann Rutherford, Jane Nigh, Tom Brown. Minor account of air force assisting farmers to save stranded cattle during snowstorm.

Operation Kid Brother (1967-Italian) **C-104m.** *½ D: Alberto De Martino. Neil Connery, Daniela Bianchi, Adolfo Celi, Bernard Lee, Anthony Dawson, Lois Maxwell. Screen debut of Sean Connery's brother in James Bond spinoff is a disaster, in tale of master criminal (Celi)'s plan to blackmail Allied governments into controlling half of world's gold supply. Aka: OPERATION DOUBLE 007; video title: SECRET AGENT 00. Techniscope.▼

Operation M SEE: **Hell's Bloody Devils**

Operation Mad Ball (1957) **105m.** ** D: Richard Quine. Jack Lemmon, Kathryn Grant (Crosby), Mickey Rooney, Ernie Kovacs, Arthur O'Connell, James Darren, Roger Smith. Weak service comedy about crafty soldiers planning wild party off base. Dull stretches, few gags. O'Connell comes off better than supposed comedians in film.

Operation Mermaid SEE: **Bay of Saint Michel, The**

Operation Overthrow SEE: **Power Play**

Operation Pacific (1951) **111m.** *** D: George Waggner. John Wayne, Patricia Neal, Ward Bond, Scott Forbes. Overzealous Wayne is ultradedicated to his navy command; the few WW2 action scenes are taut, and Neal makes a believable love interest.▼●

Operation Petticoat (1959) **C-124m.** ***½ D: Blake Edwards. Cary Grant, Tony Curtis, Dina Merrill, Gene Evans, Arthur O'Connell, Richard Sargent, Virginia Gregg, Robert F. Simon, Gavin McLeod, Madlyn Rhue, Marion Ross, Nicky Blair. Hilarious comedy about submarine captain Grant who's determined to make his injured ship seaworthy again, and con-artist Curtis who wheels and deals to reach that goal. Some truly memorable gags; Grant and Curtis are a dynamite team in this happy film. Remade for TV in 1977.▼●

Operation Secret (1952) **108m.** ** D: Lewis Seiler. Cornel Wilde, Steve Cochran, Phyllis Thaxter, Karl Malden, Dan O'Herlihy Tame WW2 actioner involving a traitor in midst of Allied division.

Operation Snafu (1961-British) **97m.** **½ D: Cyril Frankel. Alfred Lynch, Sean Connery, Cecil Parker, Stanley Holloway, Alan King, Wilfrid Hyde-White, Eric Barker, Kathleen Harrison. Sluggish WW2 account of two buddies becoming heroes unintentionally; most capable cast. Retitled: OPERATION WARHEAD. Originally titled ON THE FIDDLE.▼

Operation Snafu (1970-Italian-Yugoslavian) **C-97m.** BOMB D: Nanni Loy. Peter Falk, Jason Robards, Martin Landau, Nino Manfredi, Scott Hylands, Slim Pickens, Frank Latimore, Anthony Dawson. Aggressively unfunny comedy about a group of Algeria-based soldiers led by Falk on special mission to Sicily during WW2. Actual title on film is SITUATION NORMAL ALL FOULED UP. Techniscope.

Operation Snatch (1962-British) **83m.** ** D: Robert Day. Terry-Thomas, George Sanders, Lionel Jeffries, Jackie Lane, Lee Montague. Fitfully funny satire involving British attempt to keep "their flag flying" on Gibraltar during WW2.

Operation St. Peter's (1968-Italian) **C-100m.** ** D: Lucio Fulci. Edward G. Robinson, Lando Buzzanca, Jean-Claude Brialy. Average heist film with a twist: attempt to steal Michelangelo's Pietà from Vatican—it's tough to fence. Techniscope. [G]

Operation Thunderbolt (1977) **C-125m.** *** D: Menahem Golan. Yehoram Gaon, Klaus Kinski, Assaf Dayan, Shai K. Ophir,

Sybil Danning. Stunning retelling of the famed raid by Israeli commandos on July 4, 1976 to rescue 104 hijacked passengers from a plane at Entebbe in Uganda. The stamp of official Israeli approval given this film and dedicated performances by a basically Israeli cast make this one outshine both star-laden American-made dramatizations, RAID ON ENTEBBE and VICTORY AT ENTEBBE. [PG]▼

Operation Warhead SEE: **Operation Snafu**

Operation X (1950-British) **79m.** ** D: Gregory Ratoff. Edward G. Robinson, Peggy Cummins, Richard Greene, Nora Swinburne. Heady yarn with Robinson overly ambitious businessman forgetting his scruples. Original title: MY DAUGHTER JOY.

Operator 13 (1934) **86m.** **½ D: Richard Boleslavsky. Marion Davies, Gary Cooper, Katharine Alexander, Jean Parker, Ted Healy, Russell Hardie, The Four Mills Brothers, Sidney Toler. Davies plays an actress who's recruited as a Union spy during the Civil War; she spends the first half of the film in blackface disguise, the second half falling in love with Confederate officer Cooper. Patently absurd but still somehow entertaining.

O Pioneers! (1992) **C-100m. TVM** D: Glenn Jordan. Jessica Lange, David Strathairn, Tom Aldredge, Reed Diamond, Anne Heche, Heather Graham, Leigh Lawson, Graham Beckel. Lange, in her TV movie debut, is the centerpiece as a hearty prairie woman in this admirable but lifeless adaptation of Willa Cather's 1913 classic about the hardships and rewards of Nebraska farm life. Done better several months earlier in an *American Playhouse* version with Mary McDonnell. Average.▼●

Opium Connection, The SEE: **Poppy Is Also a Flower, The**

Opportunity Knocks (1990) **C-105m.** **½ D: Donald Petrie. Dana Carvey, Robert Loggia, Todd Graff, Julia Campbell, Milo O'Shea, James Tolkan, Doris Belack, Sally Gracie, Del Close. Innocuous comedy about a con artist who assumes someone else's identity and falls into a plum job with a bathroom-fixture tycoon, who happens to have a cute daughter. First starring showcase for *Saturday Night Live* comic Carvey lets him do his dialect shticks, but never catches fire. [PG-13]▼●

Opposing Force (1986) **C-97m.** ** D: Eric Karson. Tom Skerritt, Lisa Eichhorn, Anthony Zerbe, Richard Roundtree, Robert Wightman, John Considine. Eichhorn, only female in a military experiment designed to simulate p.o.w.-torture conditions, falls victim to madman commander Zerbe—who justifies his rape of her as a training technique. Barely released action film builds modest suspense, then fizzles out. Aka HELLCAMP. [R] ▼

Opposite of Sex, The (1998) **C-105m.** *** D: Don Roos. Christina Ricci, Martin Donovan, Lisa Kudrow, Lyle Lovett, Johnny Galecki, William Scott Lee, Ivan Sergei. Bold, clever black comedy about a truculent 16-year-old girl who runs away from home to stay with her gay half-brother, willfully disrupts his relationships, and sets his life into a spin. Writer-director Roos creates a gallery of unusual and interesting characters, but it's a tie who has the smartest, funniest lines—Ricci, as the smart-alecky heroine/narrator, or Kudrow, as the brother's sour confidante. Not for all tastes. [R]▼●◗

Opposite Sex, The (1956) **C-117m.** *** D: David Miller. June Allyson, Joan Collins, Dolores Gray, Ann Sheridan, Ann Miller, Leslie Nielsen, Jeff Richards, Agnes Moorehead, Charlotte Greenwood, Joan Blondell, Sam Levene, Alice Pearce, Barbara Jo Allen, Carolyn Jones, Alan Marshal, Dick Shawn, Jim Backus, Harry James, Art Mooney, Dean Jones. Well-heeled musical remake of Clare Boothe Luce's THE WOMEN has stellar cast, but still pales next to brittle original (Shearer, Crawford, Russell, etc.). Major difference: music and men appear in this expanded version. CinemaScope.▼●

Opposite Sex (And How to Live With Them), The (1993) **C-86m.** BOMB D: Matthew Meshekoff. Arye Gross, Courteney Cox, Kevin Pollak, Julie Brown, Mitchell Ryan, Phil Bruns, Mitzi McCall, B. J. Ward, Jack Carter, Kimberlin Brown, Kimber Sissons, Andrea Evans. Painfully strained comedy about courtship rituals between a Jewish jock male and a WASP female with hoity-toity friends. Complete with annoying first-person, eyes-into-the-camera chat-ups to us by all four leads. Sat on the shelf, unreleased, roughly dating back to the Polk Administration. [R]▼●

Optimists, The (1973-British) **C-110m.** *** D: Anthony Simmons. Peter Sellers, Donna Mullane, John Chaffey, David Daker. Entertaining comedy-drama of London busker (street entertainer) Sellers and the two tough little kids he takes in hand. Songs by Lionel Bart include effective "Sometimes." Alternate TV version runs 94m. [PG]

Orca (1977) **C-92m.** ** D: Michael Anderson. Richard Harris, Charlotte Rampling, Will Sampson, Peter Hooten, Bo Derek, Keenan Wynn, Robert Carradine. Killer whale avenges himself on bounty hunter Harris and crew for killing pregnant mate. For undiscriminating action fans whose idea of entertainment is watching Bo getting her leg bitten off. Panavision. [PG]▼●

Orchestra Conductor, The (1980-Polish) **C-101m.** ** D: Andrzej Wajda. John Gielgud, Krystyna Janda, Andrzej Seweryn,

Jan Ciercierski. Uneven drama about aged Polish conductor Gielgud returning to his hometown. Excellent cast is defeated by a superficially philosophical script. Video title: THE CONDUCTOR.▼

Orchestra Rehearsal (1979-Italian) **C-72m.** **½ D: Federico Fellini. Baldwin Baas, Clara Colosimo, Elizabeth Lubi, Ronoldo Bonacchi, Ferdinando Villella. Heavy-handed allegory that examines an orchestra as microcosm of troubled world; occasional moments of wit and insight, but overall a disappointment. Made for Italian television. Music by Nino Rota. [R] ▼●◗

Orchestra Wives (1942) **98m.** **½ D: Archie Mayo. George Montgomery, Ann Rutherford, Glenn Miller and his Band, Lynn Bari, Carole Landis, Cesar Romero, Virginia Gilmore, Mary Beth Hughes, The Nicholas Brothers, Jackie Gleason, Henry (Harry) Morgan. Hokey storyline (with hotshot trumpeter Montgomery impetuously marrying moony-eyed fan Rutherford) serves as a nice showcase for Miller's band, and features such hits as "Serenade in Blue," "At Last," and "I've Got a Gal in Kalamazoo," featuring Tex Beneke, The Modernaires, and a snazzy dance routine by The Nicholas Brothers. That's young Jackie Gleason as the band's bass player . . . and look fast for Dale Evans as Rutherford's soda-fountain pal.▼●

Ordeal by Innocence (1984) **C-87m.** *½ D: Desmond Davis. Donald Sutherland, Faye Dunaway, Christopher Plummer, Sarah Miles, Ian McShane, Diana Quick, Annette Crosbie. Agatha Christie mystery has American Sutherland as amateur sleuth in 1950s English hamlet. Cast wasted, logic absent in utterly pointless film. Score by Dave Brubeck. Made in England. [PG-13]▼●

Ordered to Love (1960-German) **82m.** **½ D: Werner Klinger. Maria Perschy, Marisa Mell, Rosemarie Kirstein, Birgitt Bergen. Potentially explosive film gets tame treatment; account of Nazi "breeding" camps for new generation of master race soldiers.▼

Order of Death SEE: **Corrupt**

Orders Are Orders (1954-British) **78m.** ** D: David Paltenghi. Margot Grahame, Maureen Swanson, Peter Sellers, Tony Hancock, Sidney James. Hancock as befuddled lieutenant is best item in this slapstick yarn of movie company using an Army barracks for headquarters. Based on a 1932 play, filmed once before.▼

Orders to Kill (1958-British) **93m.** **½ D: Anthony Asquith. Eddie Albert, Paul Massie, Lillian Gish, James Robertson Justice. Low-key account of American agent sent into France to kill a traitor.

Ordet (1955-Danish) **125m.** **** D: Carl Dreyer. Henrik Malberg, Emil Hass Christensen, Preben Lerdorff Rye. Two rural families, at odds with each other over religious differences, are forced to come to grips with their children's love for each other. Arguably Dreyer's greatest film, but certainly the movies' final word on the struggle between conventional Christianity and more personalized religious faith. Truly awe-inspiring, with a never-to-be-forgotten climactic scene. Based on a play by Kaj Munk, filmed before in 1943.▼

Ordinary People (1980) **C-123m.** **** D: Robert Redford. Donald Sutherland, Mary Tyler Moore, Judd Hirsch, Timothy Hutton, M. Emmet Walsh, Elizabeth McGovern, Dinah Manoff, James B. Sikking. Superb adaptation of Judith Guest's novel about a well-to-do family's deterioration after the death of the eldest son, told mostly from the point of view of his guilt-ridden younger brother. Intelligent, meticulously crafted film, an impressive directorial debut for Redford, who won an Academy Award, and young Hutton, who took the Best Supporting Actor prize. Other Oscars for screenwriter Alvin Sargent and for Best Picture of the Year. McGovern's film debut. [R]▼●

Oregon Trail, The (1959) **C-86m.** ** D: Gene Fowler, Jr. Fred MacMurray, William Bishop, Nina Shipman, Gloria Talbott, Henry Hull, John Carradine. Uneventful Western with MacMurray a reporter investigating Indian attacks on settlers; set in 19th-century Oregon. CinemaScope.

Organization, The (1971) **C-107m.** *** D: Don Medford. Sidney Poitier, Barbara McNair, Sheree North, Gerald S. O'Loughlin, Raul Julia, Fred Beir, Allen Garfield, Ron O'Neal, Dan Travanty (Daniel J. Travanti), Max Gail. Poitier, in his third and final appearance as Virgil Tibbs (from IN THE HEAT OF THE NIGHT), tries to bust open a major dope-smuggling operation. Exciting chase sequences, realistic ending. [PG]▼

Organizer, The (1963-Italian) **126m.** *** D: Mario Monicelli. Marcello Mastroianni, Annie Girardot, Renato Salvatori, Bernard Blier. Serious look at labor union efforts in Italy, with Mastroianni giving low-keyed performance in title role.▼

Orgasmo SEE: **Paranoia** (1968)

Orgazmo (1997) **C-90m.** **½ D: Trey Parker. Trey Parker, Dian Bachar, Robyn Lynne Raab, Michael Dean Jacobs, Ron Jeremy, Andrew W. Kemler, David Dunn, Matt Stone. Surprisingly slick—and undeniably funny—low-budget farce about a young Mormon on a mission who winds up being recruited to star in a porno movie being shot in L.A. Written by Parker, and featuring his pal Stone (together, the creators of *South Park*); raunchy and offensive, but also surprisingly conventional in its storytelling. Unrated version also available. [NC-17] ▼

Oriental Dream SEE: **Kismet** (1944)

Original Fabulous Adventures of Baron

Munchausen, The SEE: **Fabulous Baron Munchausen, The**

Original Gangstas (1996) **C-98m.** ** D: Larry Cohen. Fred Williamson, Jim Brown, Pam Grier, Paul Winfield, Isabel Sanford, Oscar Brown, Jr., Richard Roundtree, Ron O'Neal, Christopher B. Duncan, Eddie Bo Smith, Jr., Dru Down, Robert Forster, Charles Napier, Wings Hauser. Fast-paced but very violent action thriller marks a return to the blaxploitation films of the 70s, reuniting many of the genre's top stars. When a gang shoots the father of a former bad boy turned good guy, he enlists the services of his ex-buddies to rid the town of this new urban terror. Serviceable but hardly inspired; it's still fun to see these actors doing what comes naturally. Williamson also produced. [R]▼●◗

Orlando (1993-British) **C-93m.** *** D: Sally Potter. Tilda Swinton, Billy Zane, Lothaire Bluteau, John Wood, Charlotte Valandrey, Heathcote Williams, Quentin Crisp, Peter Eyre, Ned Sherrin, Jimmy Somerville. Well, it's certainly unique: the story of someone who lives four hundred years (Swinton, in a stunning performance)—first as a man, and later as a woman—evolving from a young nobleman in the era of Queen Elizabeth I (Quentin Crisp portrays the monarch!) to a highly sensitized contemporary woman of the 20th century. Set in, on, and around various continents, time frames, and locales, this adaptation of Virginia Woolf's 1928 book (scripted by the director) is highly recommended for fans of the offbeat. Swinton's young daughter, Jessica, portrays Orlando's daughter at the finale. [PG-13]▼●◗

Orphans (1987) **C-120m.** **½ D: Alan J. Pakula. Albert Finney, Matthew Modine, Kevin Anderson. Young punk brings a well-heeled drunk home one night, planning to fleece him, but soon learns that his "victim" is no dummy; in fact, he quickly takes over the lives of the hot-tempered mugger and his slow-witted younger brother. Lyle Kessler's script (from his own play) fails to adapt its stage conventions to the new medium . . . but the performances are so powerful, and the material so emotional, that it's still worthwhile. Besides, Finney can do no wrong. [R]▼●

Orphans of the Storm (1922) **125m.** *** D: D. W. Griffith. Lillian Gish, Dorothy Gish, Joseph Schildkraut, Morgan Wallace, Lucille LaVerne, Sheldon Lewis, Frank Puglia, Creighton Hale, Monte Blue, Louis Wolheim. Griffith's epic film about sisters cruelly separated, one blind and raised by thieves, one innocent and plundered by lecherous aristocrats. Implausible plot segues into French Revolution, with lavish settings and race-to-the-rescue climax. For all its creaky situations, and extreme length, still a dazzling film. Based on a 19th-century French play, *The Two Orphans*, which was filmed before in 1915 and again in 1933 and 1955.▼●◗

Orpheus (1949-French) **95m.** *** D: Jean Cocteau. Jean Marais, Francois Perier, Maria Casarés, Marie Dea, Juliette Greco, Roger Blin. Compelling cinematic allegory set in modern times with poet Marais encountering Princess of Death, exploring their mutual fascination. Heavy-handed at times, but still quite special. Remade by Jacques Demy as PARKING. Original French running time: 112m.▼

Orpheus Descending (1990) **C-150m. TVM** D: Peter Hall. Vanessa Redgrave, Kevin Anderson, Anne Twomey, Miriam Margolyes, Sloane Shelton, Patti Allison. Tennessee Williams' drama about an Italian immigrant in a sweltering Southern town who finds romance with a wandering young stud, and tries recapturing her youth with him while her husband lies dying upstairs. Solid adaptation of Hall and Redgrave's acclaimed London and N.Y. stage production; much better than its previous filming as THE FUGITIVE KIND. Scripted by the director. Made for cable. Above average.▼

Oscar, The (1966) **C-119m.** **½ D: Russell Rouse. Stephen Boyd, Elke Sommer, Eleanor Parker, Milton Berle, Joseph Cotten, Jill St. John, Ernest Borgnine, Edie Adams, Tony Bennett, Jean Hale. Shiny tinsel view of Hollywood and those competing for Academy Awards; Parker as love-hungry talent agent comes off best. Loosely based on Richard Sale novel, with many guest stars thrown in. Some of the dialogue is so bad it's laughable.▼

Oscar (1991) **C-109m.** **½ D: John Landis. Sylvester Stallone, Ornella Muti, Don Ameche, Peter Riegert, Tim Curry, Vincent Spano, Marisa Tomei, Eddie Bracken, Linda Gray, Chazz Palminteri, Kurtwood Smith, Yvonne De Carlo, Ken Howard, William Atherton, Martin Ferrero, Harry Shearer, Richard Romanus, Kirk Douglas. Stallone is surprisingly enjoyable in a comic change-of-pace, playing 1930s gangster Angelo "Snaps" Provolone, who's trying to go straight, despite the domestic and financial chaos that surrounds him. Farcical comedy, complete with mistaken identities and slamming doors, offers showcases for Palminteri as Snaps' henchman, Curry as a priggish speech teacher, Bracken as a stuttering stoolie, and Shearer and Ferrero as the Finuccis but never quite takes wing. Based on a French play, filmed before in 1957 with Louis de Funes. [PG]▼●

Oscar and Lucinda (1997-Australian) **C-132m.** **½ D: Gillian Armstrong. Ralph Fiennes, Cate Blanchett, Ciaran Hinds, Tom Wilkinson, Josephine Byrnes, Richard Roxburgh, Billie Brown. Odd romance of two Australian misfits in the mid 1800s: scarred and tormented clergyman's son Fiennes and independent Victorian heiress Blanchett, both of whom are gambling fanatics. The wager of their lives becomes surreal, as an iron-and-glass church is transported by sea and overland into the wilderness. Eccentricity upstages romance and passion in this adaptation of Peter Carey's novel. Reminiscent of Herzog's FITZCARRALDO. Panavision. [R]▼●

Oscar Wilde (1960-British) **96m.** *** D: Gregory Ratoff. Robert Morley, Phyllis Calvert, John Neville, Ralph Richardson, Dennis Price, Alexander Knox. Morley is ideally cast as famed 19th-century playwright and wit, in film that focuses on his traumatic trials and eventual conviction for sodomy. Released at the same time as THE TRIALS OF OSCAR WILDE with Peter Finch.

O'Shaughnessy's Boy (1935) **88m.** **½ D: Richard Boleslawski. Wallace Beery, Jackie Cooper, Spanky McFarland, Henry Stephenson, Leona Maricle, Sara Haden. Sentimental tale of Beery searching for his son, taken from him by cruel wife.

O.S.S. (1946) **107m.** *** D: Irving Pichel. Alan Ladd, Geraldine Fitzgerald, Patric Knowles, Richard Benedict, Richard Webb, Don Beddoe, Onslow Stevens. Brisk WW2 espionage film with Ladd and company on important mission in France unaware that D-Day is rapidly approaching.▼

Ossessione (1942-Italian) **140m.** ***½ D: Luchino Visconti. Massimo Girotti, Clara Calamai, Juan deLanda, Elio Marcuzzo. Visconti's first feature triggered the great era of Italian neorealism, transplanting James Cain's *The Postman Always Rings Twice* quite successfully to Fascist Italy; however, as an unauthorized version of the book, it was not permitted to be shown in the U.S. until 1975. Heavy going at times, but fascinating nonetheless. Filmed earlier in France, twice later in the U.S.▼

O.S.S. 117 Double Agent (1967-French-Italian) **C-90m.** *½ D: Andre Hunebelle. John Gavin, Curt Jurgens, Margaret Lee, Luciana Paluzzi. Gavin is a poor man's James Bond in this plodding thriller about a spy who takes on an assassination bureau.

O.S.S. 117—Mission for a Killer (1966-French) **C-84m.** **½ D: Andre Hunebelle. Frederick Stafford, Mylene Demongeot, Raymond Pellegrin. At times interesting malarkey about super spy trying to combat a world-hungry political organization. Franscope.

Osterman Weekend, The (1983) **C-102m.** **½ D: Sam Peckinpah. Rutger Hauer, John Hurt, Craig T. Nelson, Dennis Hopper, Chris Sarandon, Meg Foster, Helen Shaver, Cassie Yates, Burt Lancaster. Intriguing, sometimes confusing adaptation of Robert Ludlum thriller about a controversial talk-show host who's recruited by the CIA to expose some friends who are supposedly Soviet agents. Consistently interesting but aloof and cold, despite a top-notch cast. Peckinpah's final film. [R]▼●

Otello (1986-Italian) **C-120m.** ***½ D: Franco Zeffirelli. Placido Domingo, Katia Ricciarelli, Justino Diaz, Petra Malakova, Urbano Barberini. Beautifully filmed version of the Verdi opera, with Domingo in fine voice in the title role; he is more than ably assisted by Ricciarelli as wife Desdemona and Diaz as the evil, manipulative Iago. Nearly flawless in all respects; a must for opera buffs. [PG]▼●

Othello (1952-Italian) **92m.** ***½ D: Orson Welles. Orson Welles, Micheal MacLiammoir, Suzanne Cloutier, Robert Coote, Michael Lawrence, Fay Compton, Doris Dowling. Riveting, strikingly directed version of the Shakespeare play with Welles in the title role, lied to by Iago (MacLiammoir) into thinking that wife Desdemona (Cloutier) has been unfaithful. Shot, incredibly, between 1949 and 1952, because of budget difficulties; one of the most fascinating (and underrated) attempts at Shakespeare ever filmed. Joseph Cotten appears as a Senator, Joan Fontaine as a Page. Reconstructed (with its music score rerecorded) for 1992 reissue.▼●◗

Othello (1965-British) **C-166m.** **** D: Stuart Burge. Laurence Olivier, Frank Finlay, Maggie Smith, Joyce Redman, Derek Jacobi, Edward Hardwicke, Mike Gambon, John McEnery. Brilliant transferral to the screen of Shakespeare's immortal story of the Moor of Venice. Burge directed the filming, Olivier staged the production. Panavision.▼

Othello (1995-U.S.-British) **C-125m.** *** D: Oliver Parker. Laurence Fishburne, Kenneth Branagh, Irène Jacob, Nathaniel Parker, Michael Maloney, Anna Patrick, Nicholas Farrell, Indra Ove, Michael Sheen, Pierre Vaneck, Gabriele Ferzetti, Andre Oumansky, Philip Locke, John Savident. Though not as brilliantly cinematic as Welles' version, Parker's film may be more accessible to modern audiences, as the dialogue is delivered in a naturalistic fashion. Fishburne is very good in the title role, bringing out the warrior Moor's essential innocence and passion, but Branagh is brilliant as the witty, scheming Iago; Jacob, as Desdemona, is less satisfactory. Overall, an intelligent, respectable adaptation. [R] ▼●◗

Other, The (1972) **C-100m.** *** D: Robert Mulligan. Uta Hagen, Diana Muldaur, Chris Udvarnoky, Martin Udvarnoky, Norma Connolly, Victor French, Portia Nelson, John Ritter. Eerie tale of supernatural, with twin brothers representing good and evil. Stark, chilling mood tale adapted by Thomas Tryon from his novel. [PG]▼

Other Love, The (1947) **95m.** **½ D: Andre de Toth. Barbara Stanwyck, David Niven, Richard Conte, Maria Palmer, Joan

Lorring, Gilbert Roland, Richard Hale, Lenore Aubert. Dying Stanwyck decides to live wild life with gambler Conte, unaware that doctor Niven loves her. Not convincing, but enjoyable.

Other Men's Women (1931) **70m.** **½ D: William A. Wellman. Grant Withers, Mary Astor, Regis Toomey, James Cagney, Joan Blondell. Love triangle set in the world of railroad men; interesting melodrama, dated in some ways, but vivid in its atmosphere, with great action finale. Cagney and Blondell have supporting roles.

Other People's Money (1991) **C-101m.** **½ D: Norman Jewison. Danny DeVito, Gregory Peck, Penelope Ann Miller, Piper Laurie, Dean Jones, Tom Aldredge, R. D. Call. Ruthless Wall Street predator known as Larry the Liquidator sets his sights on acquiring—and destroying—the New England wire and cable company run in traditional and familial style by Peck . . . but he doesn't count on having to battle a lawyer as smart (or as appealing) as Miller, who just happens to be Peck's daughter. A great vehicle for DeVito, though lacking the bite (and the ethnicity) of Jerry Sterner's off-Broadway play. Slick and engaging, but never really satisfying. [R]▼●

Other Side of Midnight, The (1977) **C-165m.** BOMB D: Charles Jarrott. Marie-France Pisier, John Beck, Susan Sarandon, Raf Vallone, Clu Gulager, Christian Marquand, Michael Lerner, Howard Hesseman. Trashy Sidney Sheldon novel gets the treatment it deserves in ponderous story, set from 1939–1947, about a woman who parlays her body into film stardom. Dull, as opposed to lively, drek. [R]▼

Other Side of Paradise, The SEE: **Foxtrot**

Other Side of the Mountain, The (1975) **C-101m.** **½ D: Larry Peerce. Marilyn Hassett, Beau Bridges, Belinda J. Montgomery, Nan Martin, William Bryant, Dabney Coleman, Dori Brenner, Griffin Dunne. Pleasantly performed but undistinguished true-life tragedy about skier Jill Kinmont, once a shoo-in for the Olympics until a sporting accident left her paralyzed from the shoulders down. Followed by 1978 sequel. [PG]▼

Other Side of the Mountain Part 2, The (1978) **C-100m.** **½ D: Larry Peerce. Marilyn Hassett, Timothy Bottoms, Nan Martin, Belinda J. Montgomery, Gretchen Corbett, William Bryant. Smooth continuation of story of crippled skier Jill Kinmont (Hassett), who finds true love with trucker Bottoms. Timothy's real-life father James plays his dad in this film. [PG]▼

Other Sister, The (1999) **C-129m.** **½ D: Garry Marshall. Juliette Lewis, Diane Keaton, Tom Skerritt, Giovanni Ribisi, Poppy Montgomery, Sarah Paulson, Linda Thorson, Juliet Mills, Hector Elizondo. Sentimental but unfocused film about a mentally challenged girl and her first attempts to free herself from a smothering mother. Appealing performances by Lewis and Ribisi (as her boyfriend) help make up for the wandering nature of the screenplay, though it would be hard not to shed a tear by the end. Super 35. [PG-13]▼●◗

Other Voices, Other Rooms (1997-U.S.-British) **C-94m.** ** D: David Rocksavage. Lothaire Bluteau, Anna Thomson, David Speck, Aubrey Dollar, Frank Taylor, April Turner. Colorless coming-of-age drama about a boy (Speck) who goes off to live with his father in a secluded, decaying mansion, and bonds with a couple of eccentric characters. Based on Truman Capote's early autobiographical novel, and much inferior to THE GRASS HARP (which is similar in theme and also based on Capote).

Other Woman, The (1954) **81m.** BOMB D: Hugo Haas. Hugo Haas, Cleo Moore, Lance Fuller, Lucille Barkley, Jack Macy, John Qualen. Typical Hugo Haas fare involving a girl's plot for revenge on her former boss.

Otley (1969-British) **C-90m.** ** D: Dick Clement. Tom Courtenay, Romy Schneider, Alan Badel, James Villiers, Leonard Rossiter, Fiona Lewis, Freddie Jones, Ronald Lacey. Static spy spoof about petty thief and beautiful secret agent is helped a bit by Courtenay and Schneider, but otherwise has little to recommend it. [M/PG]

Our Betters (1933) **83m.** **½ D: George Cukor. Constance Bennett, Gilbert Roland, Charles Starrett, Anita Louise, Alan Mowbray, Minor Watson, Violet Kemble Cooper. Dated but enjoyable film of Somerset Maugham drawing-room comedy about British lord marrying rich American girl. Costars Bennett and Roland later married in real life.

Our Blushing Brides (1930) **104m.** **½ D: Harry Beaumont. Joan Crawford, Anita Page, Dorothy Sebastian, Robert Montgomery, Raymond Hackett, John Miljan, Hedda Hopper, Edward Brophy, Albert Conti. Level-headed department-store worker Crawford and flighty roommates Page and Sebastian try to nab rich husbands. Crawford shines in this otherwise unconvincing drama.

Our Daily Bread (1934) **74m.** **½ D: King Vidor. Karen Morley, Tom Keene, John Qualen, Barbara Pepper, Addison Richards, Harry Holman. Landmark experiment by always innovative filmmaker Vidor, who stepped outside the studio system to make this bold, back-to-the-soil drama about communal living. Unfortunately, the acting—especially by leading man Keene—is so pedestrian as to sabotage the film. Climactic irrigation sequence is justly famous, however.▼●

Our Dancing Daughters (1928) **83m.** *** D: Harry Beaumont. Joan Crawford, Johnny

Mack Brown, Dorothy Sebastian, Nils Asther, Anita Page, Kathlyn Williams, Edward Nugent. One of the best Jazz Age silents, with absurdly melodramatic story: flapper Joan loses Johnny to Anita Page, who's been pushed into marriage against her will. Crystallization of the Roaring 20s. Silent film with synchronized music track (and even an occasional bit of off-screen dialogue).▼●

Our Girl Friday SEE: **Adventures of Sadie, The**

Our Hearts Were Growing Up (1946) **83m.** **½ D: William D. Russell. Gail Russell, Diana Lynn, Brian Donlevy, James Brown, Bill Edwards, William Demarest. Follow-up to enjoyable OUR HEARTS WERE YOUNG AND GAY doesn't match it, with girls on their own at Princeton.

Our Hearts Were Young and Gay (1944) **81m.** *** D: Lewis Allen. Gail Russell, Diana Lynn, Charlie Ruggles, Dorothy Gish, James Brown, Bill Edwards, Beulah Bondi. Extremely pleasant fluff from Cornelia Otis Skinner's book, detailing her travels to Europe during 1920s with her girlfriend Emily Kimbrough. Sequel: OUR HEARTS WERE GROWING UP.

Our Hitler (1980-German) **C-420m.** ** D: Hans-Jurgen Syberberg. Heinz Schubert, Peter Kern, Hellmut Lange, Rainer von Artenfels, Martin Sperr. Frightfully pretentious, stage-influenced 7-hour rationalization of Hitler's rise to power would probably play better if shown in four parts, as it was on German TV. A stimulating intellectual exercise for some, a laxative for most; distributed in the U.S. by Francis Ford Coppola.

Our Hospitality (1923) **74m.** **** D: Buster Keaton, Jack Blystone. Buster Keaton, Natalie Talmadge, Joe Keaton, Joe Roberts. Buster goes to the South to claim a family inheritance, and falls in love with the daughter of a longtime rival clan. Sublime silent comedy, one of Buster's best, with a genuinely hair-raising finale. Incidentally, Buster married his leading lady in real life.▼●◗

Our Little Girl (1935) **63m.** **½ D: John Robertson. Shirley Temple, Rosemary Ames, Joel McCrea, Lyle Talbot, Erin O'Brien-Moore. Usual Temple plot of Shirley bringing separated parents McCrea and Ames together again. Also shown in computer-colored version.▼

Our Man Flint (1966) **C-107m.** **½ D: Daniel Mann. James Coburn, Lee J. Cobb, Gila Golan, Edward Mulhare, Benson Fong, Gianna Serra. One of the countless James Bond spoofs, this saga of the man from Z.O.W.I.E. starts briskly, becomes forced after a while. Coburn makes a zesty hero, Golan an attractive decoration; look for James Brolin as a technician. Followed by a sequel (IN LIKE FLINT) and a TVM in 1976. CinemaScope. ▼●

Our Man in Havana (1960-British) **107m.** **½ D: Carol Reed. Alec Guinness, Burl Ives, Maureen O'Hara, Ernie Kovacs, Noel Coward, Ralph Richardson, Jo Morrow. Weak satirical spy spoof, adapted by Graham Greene from his novel. Guinness is vacuum cleaner salesman who becomes British agent. CinemaScope.

Our Miss Brooks (1956) **85m.** **½ D: Al Lewis. Eve Arden, Gale Gordon, Nick Adams, Robert Rockwell, Richard Crenna, Don Porter, Jane Morgan. Fairly amusing feature based on beloved TV series has Arden's Brooks trying to snag Rockwell's Mr. Boynton and interest Adams in journalism. Crenna's screeching serenade, "It's Magic," is a high point.▼

Our Modern Maidens (1929) **75m.** *** D: Jack Conway. Joan Crawford, Rod La Rocque, Douglas Fairbanks, Jr., Anita Page, Josephine Dunn, Edward Nugent, Albert Gran. Entertaining silent jazz-age saga about a young "modern" (Crawford) who disdains conventional morality and tries to help the career of her fiancé (Fairbanks) by coming on to worldly diplomat La Rocque. Special treat for film buffs: Doug Jr. does impressions of John Barrymore, John Gilbert, and his own father! This late-silent release has a synchronized music score, with crowd noises and sound effects. Crawford and Fairbanks were married in real life at this time.▼●

Our Mother's House (1967-British) **C-105m.** *** D: Jack Clayton. Dirk Bogarde, Margaret Brooks, Louis Sheldon-Williams, John Gugolka, Pamela Franklin, Mark Lester. Children's scheme to carry on normally when their mother dies works well until their worthless father shows up. Fine performances from all in offbeat film.

Our Relations (1936) **74m.** *** D: Harry Lachman. Stan Laurel, Oliver Hardy, Alan Hale, Sidney Toler, Daphne Pollard, Betty Healy, James Finlayson, Arthur Housman, Iris Adrian, Lona Andre. Stan and Ollie get into snowballing comedy of errors with their long-lost twins. Lots of fun; best scenes in Hale's beer garden.▼●

Our Sons (1991) **C-100m. TVM** D: John Erman. Julie Andrews, Ann-Margret, Hugh Grant, Zeljko Ivanek, Tony Roberts. Two middle-aged mothers whose sons are a gay couple cross paths when one of the young men is stricken with AIDS. Ann-Margret plays Arkansas barmaid whose long estrangement from her son will end if wealthy Andrews (in her TV-movie debut) can deliver her to his hospital bed. Film is overloaded with two-character conversations; what's more, the young men's heartfelt scenes are much more compelling than those of the female stars, which throws off the story's intended focus. Average.▼

Our Time (1974) **C-88m.** **½ D: Peter

Hyams. Pamela Sue Martin, Parker Stevenson, Betsy Slade, George O'Hanlon, Jr., Karen Balkin. Nice nostalgic tale of young love, set in a Massachusetts girls' school in 1955. Bad color photography mars otherwise effective comedic and dramatic elements. Shown on network TV as DEATH OF HER INNOCENCE. [PG]▼

Our Town (1940) **90m.** ***½ D: Sam Wood. William Holden, Martha Scott, Frank Craven, Fay Bainter, Beulah Bondi, Thomas Mitchell, Guy Kibbee, Stuart Erwin. Sensitive adaptation of Thornton Wilder's Pulitzer Prize-winning play about small New England town with human drama and conflict in every family. Splendid score by Aaron Copland and production design by William Cameron Menzies. Screenplay by Wilder, Harry Chandlee, and Frank Craven. Craven, Doro Merande, Arthur Allen, and Scott (in her film debut) recreate their Broadway roles.▼◗

Our Very Own (1950) **93m.** **½ D: David Miller. Ann Blyth, Farley Granger, Jane Wyatt, Donald Cook, Ann Dvorak, Natalie Wood, Martin Milner. Melodramatic account of Blyth's shock upon discovering she's an adopted child.▼

Our Vines Have Tender Grapes (1945) **105m.** ***½ D: Roy Rowland. Edward G. Robinson, Margaret O'Brien, James Craig, Frances Gifford, Agnes Moorehead, Jackie "Butch" Jenkins, Morris Carnovsky. Excellent view of American life in Wisconsin town with uncharacteristic Robinson as O'Brien's kind, understanding Norwegian father.▼

Our Wife (1941) **95m.** **½ D: John M. Stahl. Melvyn Douglas, Ruth Hussey, Ellen Drew, Charles Coburn, John Hubbard. Douglas adds dignity to this OK marital comedy involving musician seeking divorce to marry another.

Our Winning Season (1978) **C-92m.** ** D: Joseph Ruben. Scott Jacoby, Deborah Benson, Dennis Quaid, Randy Herman, Joe Penny, Jan Smithers, P. J. Soles. Yet another 1960s high school film focuses mostly on growing pains of aspiring track star Jacoby; not bad, but awfully familiar. [PG]

Out (1982) **C-83m.** **½ D: Eli Hollander. Peter Coyote, O-Lan Shepard, Jim Haynie, Danny Glover, Scott Beach. Medium road movie of existential revolutionary Coyote and his odyssey through America from the 1960s to 1980s. Sometimes imaginative, thanks to Hollander and Ronald Sukenick's clever script, but often boring as well. Aka DEADLY DRIFTER. ▼

Out All Night (1933) **68m.** ** D: Sam Taylor. ZaSu Pitts, Slim Summerville, Laura Hope Crews, Shirley Grey, Alexander Carr, Shirley Temple. OK film from long-run teaming of Pitts and Summerville; this time, Slim is dominated by his mother (Crews); she's not pleased when he falls in love with ZaSu.

Outback (1971-U.S.-Australian) **C-99m.** *** D: Ted Kotcheff. Gary Bond, Donald Pleasence, Chips Rafferty, Sylvia Kay, Jack Thompson. Intriguing film about sensitive schoolteacher whose personality disintegrates after interaction with rough, primitive men in Australian outback. Toned down for TV from original 114m. version; still unlikely to be endorsed by Australian tourist commission. Original title: WAKE IN FRIGHT. [R]

Outbreak (1995) **C-127m.** **½ D: Wolfgang Petersen. Dustin Hoffman, Rene Russo, Morgan Freeman, Kevin Spacey, Cuba Gooding, Jr., Donald Sutherland, Patrick Dempsey, Zakes Mokae, Dale Dye, Jim Antonio, Lance Kerwin. Crusading military research medico Hoffman must stop a deadly virus that's somehow made its way from Africa to the U.S.—little dreaming that his Army superiors have an agenda of their own. Dynamite suspense thriller with a surprising sense of humor goes almost completely awry in the second half, turning Hoffman into a kind of superhero and everyone else into a caricature or stick figure. What a shame! J.T. Walsh appears unbilled. [R]▼●◗

Outcast, The (1937) **77m.** **½ D: Robert Florey. Warren William, Karen Morley, Lewis Stone, Jackie Moran, John Wray, Esther Dale, Slim Pickens, Bob Steele, Harry Carey, Jr. Doctor (William) is acquitted of charges that he caused a patient's death—but his troubles are far from over. Obvious but occasionally potent melodrama, coscripted by Dore Schary, that's uplifted by William and Stone, the latter cast as a crusty lawyer who's retired to the small town in which William settles.

Outcast, The (1954) **C-90m.** **½ D: William Witney. John Derek, Joan Evans, Jim Davis, Catherine McLeod, Ben Cooper. Simply told Western of Derek battling to win his rightful inheritance.▼

Outcast, The (1962-Japanese) **118m.** ***½ D: Kon Ichikawa. Raizo Ichikawa, Shiho Fujimura, Hiroyuki Nagato, Rentaro Mikuni. Schoolteacher Ichikawa hides his identity as member of an outcast class until a writer he greatly respects is murdered. Intense drama is well made, fascinating.

Outcast of the Islands (1951-British) **102m.** *** D: Carol Reed. Ralph Richardson, Trevor Howard, Robert Morley, Wendy Hiller, Kerima, George Coulouris, Wilfrid Hyde-White. Compelling adaptation of Joseph Conrad story set on Malayan island, where a desperate, misguided man turns to crime and soon becomes the object of massive manhunt. Screenplay by William Fairchild. Good job all around. Some TV prints run 94m.

Outcasts of Poker Flat, The (1952) **81m.** **½ D: Joseph M. Newman. Anne Baxter, Miriam Hopkins, Dale Robertson, Cameron Mitchell, John Ridgely. Obvious, uninspired version of Bret Harte tale of social rejects trapped together in cabin during snowstorm. Filmed before in 1937.

Out Cold (1989) **C-89m.** ** D: Malcolm Mowbray. John Lithgow, Teri Garr, Randy Quaid, Bruce McGill, Lisa Blount, Alan Blumenfeld, Morgan Paull, Barbara Rhoades, Tom Byrd, Fran Ryan. Lithgow plays a meek butcher who wrongly believes he has killed his partner after discovering him frozen to death in the freezer. A wonderfully adept cast tries to pull off this black comedy, but the script knocks their efforts out cold. Aka STIFFS. [R]▼●

Outcry, The SEE: **Il Grido**

Outfit, The (1974) **C-103m.** **½ D: John Flynn. Robert Duvall, Karen Black, Joe Don Baker, Robert Ryan, Timothy Carey, Richard Jaeckel, Sheree North, Marie Windsor, Jane Greer, Henry Jones, Joanna Cassidy, Elisha Cook, Jr., Anita O'Day. Engagingly trashy mob melodrama, with ex-con Duvall tackling the syndicate responsible for his brother's death. Solid supporting cast helps. Based on a novel by Donald E. Westlake (writing as Richard Stark). [PG]▼

Out for Justice (1991) **C-91m.** ** D: John Flynn. Steven Seagal, William Forsythe, Jerry Orbach, Jo Champa, Shareen Mitchell, Sal Richards, Gina Gershon, Jay Acovone. As if he doesn't have enough trouble snapping wrists when he steps by his scum-infested deli, cop Seagal's main target is childhood buddy Forsythe—from the old Brooklyn neighborhood. Some may consider this one a Seagal stretch, but don't warm up the AFI Lifetime Achievement Award just yet. Super 35. [R]▼●◗

Outing, The SEE: **Scream** (1983)

Outland (1981) **C-109m.** **½ D: Peter Hyams. Sean Connery, Peter Boyle, Frances Sternhagen, James B. Sikking, Kika Markham, Clarke Peters, John Ratzenberger. HIGH NOON on Jupiter's volcanic moon Io, as 21st-century marshal Connery discovers that this outer-space mining planet is riddled with corruption—and he's the only one willing to do anything about it. Slickly made, but predictable and unpleasant in tone. Script by director Hyams. Panavision. [R]▼●◗

Outlaw, The (1943) **115m.** *** D: Howard Hughes. Jane Russell, Jack Buetel, Walter Huston, Thomas Mitchell, Mimi Aguglia, Joe Sawyer. Notorious "sex western" (and Russell's ballyhooed screen debut) is actually compelling—if offbeat—story of Billy the Kid, with principal honors going to Huston as Doc Holliday. Filmed in 1941 and directed mostly by Howard Hawks, though Hughes' interest in Russell's bosom is more than evident. Some prints run 95m. and 103m., but no one seems to have uncensored 117m. version.▼●◗

Outlaw Blues (1977) **C-100m.** *** D: Richard T. Heffron. Peter Fonda, Susan Saint James, John Crawford, James Callahan, Michael Lerner. Ex-convict Fonda is promoted into a country star by back-up singer Saint James, to the consternation of star Callahan, who had stolen Fonda's song. Saint James is good in her first major movie role; the picture is fun when it isn't too silly. [PG]▼

Outlaw Gun SEE: **Minute to Pray, a Second to Die, A**

Outlaw—Josey Wales, The (1976) **C-135m.** **½ D: Clint Eastwood. Clint Eastwood, Chief Dan George, Sondra Locke, Bill McKinney, John Vernon, Paula Trueman, Sam Bottoms. Long, violent Western set in post-Civil War era; Eastwood is a peaceful farmer who turns vigilante when Union soldiers murder his family. He in turn has a price on his head, propelling cat-and-mouse chase odyssey. Clint took over direction from Philip Kaufman, who also cowrote the screenplay. Followed by THE RETURN OF JOSEY WALES—without Eastwood. Panavision. [PG]▼●◗

Outlaw of Gor (1989) **C-89m.** *½ D: John "Bud" Cardos. Urbano Barberini, Jack Palance, Rebecca Ferrati, Donna Denton, Nigel Chipps, Russel Savadier. Worthless sequel to GOR (which wasn't any good in the first place). Earthman hero is magically transported back to the barbaric planet Gor, where he's soon branded an assassin by evil priest Palance and wicked queen Denton. Lots of swords, no sorcery. Based on the John Norman novel. Filmed in 1987. [PG-13]▼

Outlaw's Daughter, The (1954) **C-75m.** *½ D: Wesley Barry. Bill Williams, Kelly Ryan, Jim Davis, George Cleveland, Elisha Cook. Weak oater of stagecoach robbery and girl implicated because her elderly father used to be an outlaw.

Outlaws Is Coming, The (1965) **89m.** **½ D: Norman Maurer. The Three Stooges, Adam West, Nancy Kovack, Mort Mills, Don Lamond, Emil Sitka, Joe Bolton, Henry Gibson. The Stooges' last feature is one of their best, with some sharp satire and good Western atmosphere as the boys, their cowardly friend (West), and Annie Oakley (Kovack) combat an army of gunslingers and a genteel crook. Local TV kiddie-show hosts cast as outlaws, Gibson as a hip Indian.▼

Outlaw's Son (1957) **89m.** ** D: Lesley Selander. Dane Clark, Ben Cooper, Lori Nelson, Ellen Drew, Eddie Foy III. Clark is most earnest in modest Western about outlaw and the son he deserted years before.

Outlaw Stallion, The (1954) **C-64m.** *½ D: Fred F. Sears. Phil Carey, Dorothy Patrick, Billy Gray, Roy Roberts, Gordon Jones. Programmer of horse thieves conning ranch woman and her son to get their herd.

Outlaw Territory (1953) **C-79m.** **½ D: John Ireland, Lee Garmes. Macdonald Carey, Joanne Dru, John Ireland, Don Haggerty, Peter Ireland, Frank Ferguson.

Carey is hired killer who runs afoul of marshal Ireland, and arouses the interest of cafe-owner Dru, against her better judgment. Routine Western shot in 3-D; original title: HANNAH LEE.

Out of Africa (1985) **C-161m.** ***½ D: Sydney Pollack. Meryl Streep, Robert Redford, Klaus Maria Brandauer, Michael Kitchen, Malick Bowens, Joseph Thiaka, Stephen Kinyanjui, Michael Gough, Suzanna Hamilton, Rachel Kempson, Graham Crowden. Exquisite, intelligent romantic drama based on life of Karen Blixen, who married for convenience, moved from Denmark to Nairobi, and fell in love with a British adventurer and idealist (before gaining latter-day fame as author Isak Dinesen). Pollack's film brilliantly captures time and place, with superb performances by Streep and Brandauer, sumptuous photography by David Watkin, and a rich score by John Barry. Film's only fault is overlength—and biggest challenge is asking us to accept Redford as an Englishman. Oscars include Best Picture, Director, Screenplay (Kurt Luedtke, who synthesized five books into one seamless script), Cinematography, and Music Score. Footage added for network TV showing. [PG]▼●◗

Out of Bounds (1986) **C-93m.** *½ D: Richard Tuggle. Anthony Michael Hall, Jenny Wright, Jeff Kober, Glynn Turman, Raymond J. Barry, Pepe Serna, Meat Loaf. Iowa farm kid comes to L.A. and within twenty-four hours is hunted by the police (for murders he didn't commit) and a scuzzy drug dealer (whose stash he mistakenly took from the airport). Outlandishly unbelievable teen thriller might be retitled OUT OF BRAINS. [R]▼●

Out of Control (1985) **C-78m.** BOMB D: Allan Holzman. Martin Hewitt, Betsy Russell, Claudia Udy, Andrew J. Lederer, Cindi Dietrich, Richard Kantor, Sherilyn Fenn. Embarrassing teen-exploitation film has eight kids surviving a plane crash on small island where they play sex games, get drunk, and get in trouble with local drug runners. Wastes a catchy title song performed by the Brothers Johnson. [R]▼

Out of It (1969) **95m.** **½ D: Paul Williams. Barry Gordon, Jon Voight, Lada Edmund, Jr., Gretchen Corbett, Peter Grad. Generally amusing film about high school intellectual (Gordon) bucking high school athlete (Voight). A throwback to the days when life was one big Archie comic book. [M/PG]

Out of Season (1975-British) **C-90m.** ** D: Alan Bridges. Vanessa Redgrave, Cliff Robertson, Susan George, Edward Evans, Frank Jarvis. Mood-triangle affair: dark stranger returns to English seaside resort twenty years after affair with woman who now has grown daughter. Hints of incest and unresolved ending. [R]▼

Out of Sight (1966) **C-87m.** *½ D: Lennie Weinrib. Jonathan Daly, Karen Jensen, Robert Pine, Carole Shelayne, Gary Lewis and The Playboys, The Turtles, Freddie and The Dreamers, Dobie Gray. A butler and a blonde band together to halt a spy organization's conspiracy against rock groups. Idiotic combination beach party–spy movie that fails in both departments.

Out of Sight (1998) **C-122m.** **½ D: Steven Soderbergh. George Clooney, Jennifer Lopez, Ving Rhames, Steve Zahn, Dennis Farina, Albert Brooks, Don Cheadle, Catherine Keener, Nancy Allen. Career criminal Clooney busts out of Florida prison and uses federal agent Lopez as a shield; though they go separate ways, they've obviously fallen in love and have a need to reconnect, despite their conflicting views of the law. Interesting Elmore Leonard crime caper (adapted by Scott Frank), with a heavy dose of humor, has an appealing cast but needs a shot of adrenaline. Michael Keaton and Samuel L. Jackson appear unbilled. Techniscope. [R] ▼●◗

Out of the Blue (1947) **84m.** **½ D: Leigh Jason. Virginia Mayo, George Brent, Turhan Bey, Ann Dvorak, Carole Landis, Hadda Brooks. Naive Brent is in trouble when far from innocent young woman is discovered unconscious in his apartment; fluffy fun. Dvorak is a delight in an offbeat role.▼●

Out of the Blue (1980) **C-94m.** **½ D: Dennis Hopper. Linda Manz, Sharon Farrell, Dennis Hopper, Raymond Burr, Don Gordon. Manz, daughter of ex-biker Hopper and junkie Farrell, cannot cope with the problems of her elders, with tragic results. Taut, low-key drama; could be retitled "Child of Easy Rider." TV title: NO LOOKING BACK. [R]▼◗

Out of the Clouds (1957-British) **C-88m.** ** D: Michael Relph, Basil Dearden. Anthony Steel, James Robertson Justice, Gordon Harker, Bernard Lee, Megs Jenkins. Work and play among commercial pilots; nothing special.

Out of the Dark (1988) **C-89m.** **½ D: Michael Schroeder. Cameron Dye, Lynn Danielson, Tracey Walter, Silvana Gallardo, Karen Black, Bud Cort, Starr Andreeff, Geoffrey Lewis, Paul Bartel, Divine, Lainie Kazan, Tab Hunter. A clown-masked killer murders the employees of an L.A. telephone sex-talk service, one by one. Good cast and sense of humor relieve heavy-handed visual approach to the material. [R]▼●

Out of the Darkness (1978) SEE: **Night Creature**

Out of the Darkness (1985) **C-100m. TVM** D: Jud Taylor. Martin Sheen, Hector Elizondo, Matt Clark, Jennifer Salt, Eddie Egan. Sheen gives a shining performance as Eddie Zigo, the N.Y.C. cop who broke the Son of Sam case in the late '70s.

Refreshingly, this one focuses on the cop rather than the criminal. T. S. Cook's suspenseful script is a model of its type. Above average. ▼●

Out of the Fog (1941) **93m.** *** D: Anatole Litvak. Ida Lupino, John Garfield, Thomas Mitchell, Eddie Albert, George Tobias, Leo Gorcey, John Qualen, Aline MacMahon. Fine filmization of Irwin Shaw play *The Gentle People*, with racketeer Garfield terrorizing Brooklyn fishermen Qualen and Mitchell—and falling in love with the latter's daughter (Lupino). Scripted by Robert Rossen, Jerry Wald, and Richard Macauley.

Out of the Frying Pan SEE: **Young and Willing**

Out of the Past (1947) **97m.** ***½ D: Jacques Tourneur. Robert Mitchum, Jane Greer, Kirk Douglas, Rhonda Fleming, Richard Webb, Steve Brodie, Virginia Huston, Paul Valentine, Dickie Moore. Mitchum finds he can't escape former life when one-time employer (gangster Douglas) and lover (Greer) entangle him in web of murder and double-dealings. Classic example of 1940s film noir, with dialogue a particular standout. Script by Geoffrey Homes (Daniel Mainwaring), from his novel *Build My Gallows High*. Remade as AGAINST ALL ODDS. Also shown in computer colored version. ▼●

Out of this World (1945) **96m.** **½ D: Hal Walker. Eddie Bracken, Veronica Lake, Diana Lynn, Cass Daley, Parkyakarkus, Donald MacBride, Florence Bates, Gary, Philip, Dennis and Lindsay Crosby. Bracken becomes pop crooner (with a very familiar-sounding voice); a cute idea mercilessly padded with loud musical specialties by Daley, Lynn, and guest stars.

Out of Towners, The (1970) **C-97m.** *½ D: Arthur Hiller. Jack Lemmon, Sandy Dennis, Sandy Baron, Anne Meara, Ann Prentiss, Graham Jarvis, Ron Carey, Phil Bruns, Carlos Montalban, Billy Dee Williams, Paul Dooley, Dolph Sweet, Robert Walden, Richard Libertini. Excruciating Neil Simon script about stupidly stubborn Lemmon and wife Dennis having everything imaginable go wrong on trip to N.Y.C. More harrowing than funny, with curiously unsympathetic leading characters. Remade in 1999. [G] ▼●

Out-of-Towners, The (1999) **C-92m.** **½ D: Sam Weisman. Goldie Hawn, Steve Martin, Mark McKinney, John Cleese, Gregory Jbara, Ernie Sabella, Josh Mostel, Joe Grifasi, John Pizzarelli. It's one calamity after another when a middle-aged Ohio couple travels to N.Y.C. so he can go on a job interview. Less abrasive and farcical than Neil Simon's 1970 original, this has its fair share of laughs, with Cleese well cast as a haughty hotel manager . . . but it's Martin's fine performance that really stands out. That's Hawn's real-life son (Oliver Hudson) in the film's opening scenes. [PG-13] ▼●◗

Out on a Limb (1987) **C-200m. TVM** D: Robert Butler. Shirley MacLaine, Charles Dance, John Heard, Anne Jackson, Jerry Orbach. MacLaine stars as herself in this lumbering film of her best-selling book about her passionate love affair with an unnamed British politician (played by Dance) and her spiritual trek that gave her the chance to look at herself as an "outer being." Jackson plays Bella Abzug as a sounding board for Shirley, who cowrote the teleplay with Colin Higgins. Originally shown in two tiresome parts. Average. ▼

Out on a Limb (1992) **C-93m.** BOMB D: Francis Veber. Matthew Broderick, Jeffrey Jones, Heidi Kling, John C. Reilly, Marian Mercer, Larry Hankin. Obnoxious comedy with Broderick cast as a yuppie who comes to the aid of his kid sister in a small town inhabited by one too many screwballs. As illogical as it is crude, and desperately unfunny. [PG] ▼●

Out on Probation SEE: **Daddy-O**

Outpost in Malaya (1952-British) **88m.** **½ D: Ken Annakin. Claudette Colbert, Jack Hawkins, Anthony Steel, Jeremy Spencer. Mostly about marital disharmony on a rubber plantation. Original title: PLANTER'S WIFE.

Outpost in Morocco (1949) **92m.** ** D: Robert Florey. George Raft, Marie Windsor, Akim Tamiroff, John Litel, Eduard Franz. Cardboard adventure yarn with French Foreign Legionnaire Raft attempting to quell tribal revolt, becoming romantically involved with emir's daughter Windsor (who looks to be as Moroccan as Maureen O'Hara). ▼

Outrage (1950) **75m.** **½ D: Ida Lupino. Mala Powers, Tod Andrews, Robert Clarke, Raymond Bond, Lilian Hamilton, Hal March, Jerry Paris. Innocent young Powers is sexually molested, and then further victimized by her gossipy, narrow-minded neighbors. The scenario's sugary optimism—specifically relating to a sympathetic preacher—is much too pat, but Lupino (who also coscripted) deserves an A for effort in tackling a then-touchy theme.

Outrage, The (1964) **97m.** **½ D: Martin Ritt. Paul Newman, Edward G. Robinson, Claire Bloom, Laurence Harvey, William Shatner, Albert Salmi. Western remake of RASHOMON is pretentious fizzle, with Newman hamming it as Mexican bandit who allegedly rapes Bloom while husband Harvey stands by. Robinson as philosophical narrator is best thing about film. Also shown in computer-colored version. Panavision. ▼

Outrage (1993-Italian-Spanish) **C-108m.** *½ D: Carlos Saura. Francesca Neri, Antonio Banderas, Lali Ramon, Walter Vidarte, Coque Malla, Achero Manas, Rodrigo

Valverde. When reporter Banderas falls for circus performer Neri, they have a brief fling at happiness. Unfortunately, a (predictable) rape scene, which is horrifyingly graphic, and a subsequent shooting spree relegate this to the ranks of only diehard Banderas fans. Panavision. [R]▼●◗

Outrageous! (1977-Canadian) **C-100m.** *** D: Richard Benner. Craig Russell, Hollis McLaren, Richert Easley, Allan Moyle, Helen Shaver. Excellent comedy-drama about a very odd couple: gay hairdresser and a pregnant mental patient. McLaren's effective emoting is outshone by female impersonator Russell's flamboyant playing and imitations of Garland, Davis, Bankhead, etc. Followed ten years later by TOO OUTRAGEOUS! [R]▼

Outrageous Fortune (1987) **C-100m.** *** D: Arthur Hiller. Bette Midler, Shelley Long, Peter Coyote, Robert Prosky, John Schuck, George Carlin, Anthony Heald, Ji-Tu Cumbuka, Chris McDonald, Robert Pastorelli. Raucously funny tale of a female odd couple who learn they were both having a fling with the same man, after he apparently dies in a mysterious explosion . . . then things *really* get going! Bright script by Leslie Dixon is a perfect showcase for Midler and Long. [R]▼●

Outriders, The (1950) **C-93m.** ** D: Roy Rowland. Joel McCrea, Arlene Dahl, Barry Sullivan, Claude Jarman, Jr., Ramon Novarro, James Whitmore. Standard account of Reb soldiers trying to capture gold shipment for Confederate cause.

Outside Chance of Maximilian Glick, The (1988-Canadian) **C-96m.** *** D: Allan A. Goldstein. Saul Rubinek, Jan Rubes, Noam Zylberman, Susan Douglas Rubes, Fairuza Balk, Nigel Bennet. Pleasing tale of bright 12-year-old Zylberman, growing up in a small Canadian town in the early 1960s, who's caught between his own dreams and desires and his family's traditional Jewish values. Despite its cop-out ending, this intelligent little comedy-drama is perfect fare for preteens. [G]▼

Outside In (1972) **C-90m.** ** D: Allen Baron. Darrell Larson, Heather Menzies, Dennis Olivieri, Peggy Feury, Logan Ramsey, John Bill. Slow-moving, boring time-capsule detailing draft-dodger Larson's plight as he returns to L.A. from Canada for his father's funeral. Retitled RED WHITE AND BUSTED. [R]

Outside Man, The (1973) **C-104m.** *** D: Jacques Deray. Jean-Louis Trintignant, Ann-Margret, Angie Dickinson, Roy Scheider, Michel Constantin, Georgia Engel, Ted de Corsia, John Hillerman, Alex Rocco, Talia Shire. Okay French-American actioner, made in L.A., as interesting for its cast as its offbeat quality. Hired killer Trintignant kills gang boss Ted de Corsia, then must elude Scheider, who's out to eliminate him. Ann-Margret's plunging neckline and a shootout around de Corsia's bier (he's embalmed in a sitting position) are worth looking at, also Engel's dumb housewife. [PG]▼

Outside Ozona (1998) **C-100m.** ** D: J.S. Cardone. Robert Forster, Sherilyn Fenn, Kevin Pollak, Penelope Ann Miller, David Paymer, Meat Loaf, Swoosie Kurtz, Taj Mahal, Lois Red Elk. Various characters' lives intersect during an eventful day and evening as a long-dormant serial killer begins to strike again, a radio d.j. vents his frustrations on the air, and several others take to the road. Only fitfully interesting, despite a good cast. [R]▼◗

Outside Providence (1999) **C-103m.** **½ D: Michael Corrente. Shawn Hatosy, Jon Abrahams, Alec Baldwin, George Wendt, Tommy Bone, Jonathan Brandis, Jack Fever, Adam Lavorgna, Jesse Leach, Gabriel Mann, Kristen Shorten, Amy Smart. Unremarkable coming-of-age saga set in 1970s New England, with Hatosy as a rowdy blue-collar teen who winds up going away to prep school and falling in love. Notable mainly for casting of Baldwin as an Archie Bunker type, at which he's only marginally convincing. Screenplay by Corrente and Bobby and Peter Farrelly (based on the latter's novel). [R]▼◗

Outsider, The (1961) **108m.** *** D: Delbert Mann. Tony Curtis, James Franciscus, Bruce Bennett, Gregory Walcott, Vivian Nathan. Thoughtful biopic with Curtis giving one of his best performances as a reluctant American hero: Ira Hamilton Hayes, the Pima Indian who was one of the marines to raise the U.S. flag at Iwo Jima.

Outsider, The (1979) **C-128m.** *** D: Tony Luraschi. Craig Wasson, Patricia Quinn, Sterling Hayden, Niall Toibin, Elizabeth Begley, T. P. McKenna, Frank Grimes. A young American raised on his grandfather's stories of fighting "the Tans" in Ireland goes there to join the IRA—and is used for political and public-relations purposes. No-frills narrative, authentic and interesting, filmed on location. Script by director Luraschi. [R]

Outsiders, The (1983) **C-91m.** **½ D: Francis Coppola. C. Thomas Howell, Matt Dillon, Ralph Macchio, Patrick Swayze, Rob Lowe, Diane Lane, Emilio Estevez, Tom Cruise, Leif Garrett, Tom Waits, Sofia Coppola. Florid, highly stylized treatment of S. E. Hinton's best-selling book about troubled teenagers in 60s Oklahoma, as seen through the eyes of a boy (Howell) who likes poetry and *Gone With the Wind.* Ambitious film evokes GWTW and 50s melodramas (right down to overstated music score by Carmine Coppola), but never quite connects, despite some powerful moments. Hinton makes a cameo appearance as a nurse. Followed by another Coppola-

Hinton project, RUMBLE FISH. Later a TV series. Panavision. [PG]▼●◗

Outside the Law (1956) **81m.** *½ D: Jack Arnold. Ray Danton, Leigh Snowden, Grant Williams, Onslow Stevens. Half-baked yarn of Danton proving his worth by snaring counterfeiters.

Outside the Wall (1950) **80m.** **½ D: Crane Wilbur. Richard Basehart, Dorothy Hart, Marilyn Maxwell, Signe Hasso, Harry Morgan. Excellent cast carries off this tale of former convict snafuing a robbery syndicate.

Out to Sea (1997) **C-106m.** ** D: Martha Coolidge. Jack Lemmon, Walter Matthau, Dyan Cannon, Brent Spiner, Gloria De Haven, Elaine Stritch, Hal Linden, Donald O'Connor, Edward Mulhare, Rue McClanahan, Alexandra Powers, Sean O'Brien, Estelle Harris. A chronic con man fools his pal into joining him for a Caribbean cruise—neglecting to inform him that he's signed them both on as dance hosts. The two likable stars are cast adrift with a boatload of talented costars—and a stupid script that should have been deep-sixed before they ever set sail. [PG-13] ▼●

Outward Bound (1930) **84m.** *** D: Robert Milton. Leslie Howard, Douglas Fairbanks, Jr., Helen Chandler, Beryl Mercer, Alec B. Francis, Alison Skipworth, Montagu Love. Illicit lovers Fairbanks and Chandler, "half-way" persons who have attempted suicide, find themselves aboard a mysterious ocean liner. Well-acted allegory, from Sutton Vane's play. Remade as BETWEEN TWO WORLDS.

Out West With the Hardys (1938) **84m.** **½ D: George B. Seitz. Lewis Stone, Mickey Rooney, Cecilia Parker, Fay Holden, Ann Rutherford, Sara Haden, Don Castle, Virginia Weidler, Gordon Jones. Adventures on a ranch where a friend of the family is having water rights problems. OK *Andy Hardy* outing.

Overboard (1987) **C-112m.** *** D: Garry Marshall. Goldie Hawn, Kurt Russell, Edward Herrmann, Katherine Helmond, Michael Hagerty, Roddy McDowall. Cute comedy about a spoiled heiress who falls off her yacht, suffers amnesia, and is "claimed" at the hospital by her supposed husband, a rough-hewn carpenter with a pack of unruly kids. Lightweight and good-natured, with appealing performances by the star duo. McDowall also served as executive producer; director Marshall has a cameo as a drummer, and Hector Elizondo does an unbilled bit as skipper of a garbage scow. [PG] ▼●◗

Overcoat, The (1959-Russian) **73m.** **** D: Alexei Batalov. Roland Bykov, Y. Tolubeyev. Charming, fully realized rendition of Gogol's oft-filmed story about lowly clerk and the effect a new overcoat has on his life. Runs full gamut of emotions in simple, moving style; not shown here until 1965.▼

Over-Exposed (1956) **80m.** *½ D: Lewis Seiler. Cleo Moore, Richard Crenna, Isobel Elsom, Raymond Greenleaf, Shirley Thomas. Flabby study of blackmail, with Cleo Moore vacationing from Hugo Haas spectacles . . . some vacation!

Overexposed (1990) **C-80m.** ** D: Larry Brand. Catherine Oxenberg, David Naughton, Jennifer Edwards, William Bumiller, John Patrick Reger, Gretchen Eichholz, Karen Black. Soap opera star Oxenberg is apparently being stalked by an angry fan, but she also has recurring and horrifying memories of a burning child at a birthday party. Well made on a tight budget, but the clueless story develops too slowly, and the ending is weirdly protracted. [R]▼

Over Forty (1982-Canadian) **C-105m.** ***½ D: Anne Claire Poirier. Roger Blay, Monique Mercure, Pierre Theriault, Patricia Nolin, Jacques Godin, Luce Guilbeault. The Gang, a group of men and women who grew up together, reunite after 30 years to sing, then reminisce, then reveal. THE BIG CHILL for the 1940s generation but with far more depth; a magical gem of a movie about the essence of friendship, the passage of time, the capacity of innocence. Aka BEYOND FORTY.

Over Her Dead Body SEE **Enid Is Sleeping**

Overlanders, The (1946-Australian-British) **91m.** ***½ D: Harry Watt. Chips Rafferty, John Nugent Hayward, Daphne Campbell, John Fernside, Jean Blue, Peter Pagan, Helen Grieve. Riveting account of Australian cattle drovers, headed by indomitable Rafferty, bringing their herds across the continent during WW2. Based on actual events. Simple, straightforward, and enormously entertaining.▼

Overland Pacific (1954) **C-73m.** ** D: Fred F. Sears. Jock Mahoney, Peggie Castle, Adele Jergens, William Bishop. Mahoney is staunch railroad investigator trying to thwart Indian attacks on the trains.

Over My Dead Body (1942) **68m.** **½ D: Malcolm St. Clair. Milton Berle, Mary Beth Hughes, Reginald Denny, Frank Orth, William Davidson. Berle gives peppery performance in farfetched yarn about amateur sleuth who accidentally frames himself for murder.

Overnight (1986-Canadian) **C-96m.** **½ D: Jack Darcus. Gale Garnett, Victor Ertmanis, Alan Scarfe, Duncan Fraser, Ian White, Barbara Gordon. Fair film industry satire about a serious but unemployed actor (Ertmanis), who takes a job in a porn movie about a vampire nymphomaniac. A few bright lines but too much silliness.

Over the Brooklyn Bridge (1984) **C-106m.** ** D: Menahem Golan. Elliott Gould, Margaux Hemingway, Sid Caesar, Burt

Young, Shelley Winters, Carol Kane. Brooklyn Jewish restaurant owner Gould wants to borrow money from uncle Caesar to open a fancy Manhattan eatery, but the family objects to his Catholic girlfriend (Hemingway). Some good supporting players (especially Caesar) cannot save this stupid comedy. That's Sarah Michelle Gellar playing Young's daughter. [R]▼

Over the Edge (1979) **C-95m.** ***½ D: Jonathan Kaplan. Michael Kramer, Pamela Ludwig, Matt Dillon, Vincent Spano, Tom Fergus, Andy Romano, Ellen Geer, Lane Smith, Harry Northup. Powerful, disturbing chronicle of alienated youth in a suburban planned community; 14-year-old rebels without causes who play with guns, deal and abuse drugs, taunt cops, chug whiskey till they're blotto. Perceptive script by Charlie Haas and Tim Hunter; stunning music score by Sol Kaplan; taut direction. A winner. Dillon's film debut. [PG]▼

Over the Moon (1937-British) **C-78m.** *½ D: Thornton Freeland, William K. Howard. Merle Oberon, Rex Harrison, Ursula Jeans, Robert Douglas, Louis Borell, Zena Dare, David Tree, Elisabeth Welch, Wilfrid Hyde-White, Evelyn Ankers. Disappointingly bad comedy of country girl squandering inherited fortune. Interesting cast cannot save clinker. Beware black-and-white prints.

Over the Top (1987) **C-93m.** BOMB D: Menahem Golan. Sylvester Stallone, Robert Loggia, Susan Blakely, Rick Zumwalt, David Mendenhall, Chris McCarty, Terry Funk. Mawkish, heavy-handed variation on THE CHAMP, with Stallone competing with his fat-cat father-in-law for the custody (and affection) of his son. It all climaxes at an arm-wrestling championship in Las Vegas. Stallone tries to underplay (speaking so quietly that you often can't hear what he's saying), but when push comes to shove, he *will* drive his truck through a living room! Panavision. [PG] ▼●

Over 21 (1945) **102m.** *** D: Charles Vidor. Irene Dunne, Alexander Knox, Charles Coburn, Jeff Donnell, Lee Patrick, Phil Brown. Zesty comedy of middle-aged Knox trying to survive in officer's training for WW2 service, with help of wife Dunne; from Ruth Gordon's play.

Owl and the Pussycat, The (1970) **C-95m.** *** D: Herbert Ross. Barbra Streisand, George Segal, Robert Klein, Allen Garfield, Roz Kelly. Hit Broadway comedy about semi-illiterate prostitute and stuffy intellectual sometimes substitutes bombast for wit, but the laughs are there. The Streisand-Segal pairing really works; adapted by Buck Henry from Bill Manoff's play. Originally released at 98m. Panavision. [PG]▼●

Ox, The (1991-Swedish) **C-91m.** *** D: Sven Nykvist. Stellan Skarsgard, Ewa Froling, Lennart Hjulstrom, Max von Sydow, Liv Ullmann, Erland Josephson. Acclaimed cinematographer Nykvist directed and coscripted this stark, compelling chronicle of a desperately poor family's struggle for survival in famine-ravaged Sweden during the mid-1800s. Based on a true story; the plight of their countrymen who chose to leave Sweden and settle in the U.S. is depicted in Jan Troell's THE EMIGRANTS and THE NEW LAND (which also starred von Sydow and Ullmann). ▼

Ox-Bow Incident, The (1943) **75m.** **** D: William A. Wellman. Henry Fonda, Dana Andrews, Mary Beth Hughes, Anthony Quinn, William Eythe, Henry (Harry) Morgan, Jane Darwell, Frank Conroy, Harry Davenport. The irony and terror of mob rule are vividly depicted in this unforgettable drama about a lynch mob taking the law into its own hands, despite protests of some level-headed onlookers. Based on Walter Van Tilburg Clark's book; superb script by Lamar Trotti.▼●

Oxford Blues (1984) **C-97m.** **½ D: Robert Boris. Rob Lowe, Ally Sheedy, Julian Sands, Amanda Pays, Michael Gough, Aubrey Morris, Gail Strickland, Alan Howard, Cary Elwes. Lightweight remake of A YANK AT OXFORD, with rough-edged Lowe pursuing titled beauty Pays while building "character" on the rowing team. Boris' wildly inconsistent script is salvaged by engaging performances. [PG-13] ▼●

Pacific Destiny (1956-British) **C-97m.** ** D: Wolf Rilla. Denholm Elliott, Susan Stephen, Michael Hordern, Gordon Jackson, Inia Te Wiata. Boring (but true) story of Arthur Grimble, who serves in South Seas for British Colonial service circa 1912, and tries to quell native disputes. CinemaScope.

Pacific Heights (1990) **C-102m.** **½ D: John Schlesinger. Melanie Griffith, Matthew Modine, Michael Keaton, Mako, Nobu McCarthy, Laurie Metcalf, Carl Lumbly, Dorian Harewood, Luca Bercovici, Sheila McCarthy, Dan Hedaya, Miriam Margolyes, Nicholas Pryor. Young couple purchases a Victorian home in San Francisco, fixes it up and rents out two of its apartments, unaware that one of their tenants is a nut case. Likable and reasonably credible, but too often obvious—and never really bothers to explain Keaton's bizarre, destructive behavior. Cleverest touch: making Modine the weaker and Griffith the stronger of the twosome. Beverly D'Angelo appears unbilled in key supporting role . . . and Melanie's mom, Tippi Hedren, plays a Beverly Hills matron. [R]▼●

Pacific Liner (1939) **75m.** ** D: Lew

Landers. Chester Morris, Wendy Barrie, Victor McLaglen, Barry Fitzgerald. Formula programmer focusing on breakout of epidemic and mutiny aboard a ship; cast is better than the material.

Pacific Vibrations (1971) **C-92m.** **½ D. John Severson. Jock Sutherland, Rolf Aurness, Corky Carroll, Tom Stone, Mike Tabeling. Colorful surfing documentary. [G]

Pack, The (1977) **C-99m.** **½ D: Robert Clouse. Joe Don Baker, Hope Alexander-Willis, Richard B. Shull, R. G. Armstrong, Ned Wertimer, Bibi Besch. Predictable but well-made story of resort islanders terrorized by abandoned dogs who have become a bloodthirsty pack. Aka THE LONG, DARK NIGHT. [R]▼

Package, The (1989) **C-108m.** ** D: Andrew Davis. Gene Hackman, Joanna Cassidy, Tommy Lee Jones, John Heard, Dennis Franz, Pam Grier, Kevin Crowley, Reni Santoni, Ike Pappas, Thalmus Rasulala. Slack political paranoia thriller with Hackman as a career Army sergeant who learns he's been used as a pawn in a conspiracy plot engineered by Russian and American military dissidents. Hackman is always worth watching, but the story loses ground (and credibility) just when it ought to be peaking. [R]▼●◗

Pack of Lies (1987) **C-100m. TVM** D: Anthony Page. Ellen Burstyn, Teri Garr, Alan Bates, Sammi Davis, Ronald Hines, Clive Swift, Daniel Benzali. Top-notch filming of Hugh Whitemore's play about a suburban London couple whose friendship with the neighbors across the street is torn apart when they allow British Intelligence to use their house to spy on their best pals. Ralph Gallup's adaptation and Burstyn's performance earned Emmy nominations. Above average.▼

Pack Up Your Troubles (1932) **68m.** **½ D: George Marshall, Ray McCarey. Stan Laurel, Oliver Hardy, Mary Carr, James Finlayson, Charles Middleton, Grady Sutton, Billy Gilbert. Daffy duo are drafted during WW1; after some Army shenanigans they try to locate relatives of late pal's daughter. Good fun.▼

Pack Up Your Troubles (1939) **75m.** ** D: H. Bruce Humberstone. Ritz Brothers, Jane Withers, Lynn Bari, Joseph Schildkraut, Stanley Fields, Leon Ames. Watch the Ritz Brothers' opening routine, then forget the rest of this WW1 hodgepodge, especially when Jane is focus of the film.

Paco (1976) **C-97m.** *½ D: Robert Vincent O'Neil. Jose Ferrer, Panchito Gomez, Allen Garfield, Pernell Roberts. South American urchin Gomez visits uncle Ferrer in the big city, finds him to be a Fagin-like leader of a band of juvenile thieves. Obvious and slow-moving; producer-writer Andre Marquis cast himself in vanity role as a great actor. Some prints run 87m. [G]▼

Pad and How to Use It, The (1966) **C-86m.** **½ D: Brian Hutton. Brian Bedford, Julie Sommars, James Farentino, Edy Williams. Peter Shaffer play *The Private Ear* is basis for sex romp involving Bedford's attempt to become Sommars' lover.

Paddy (1970-Irish) **C-97m.** ** D: Daniel Haller. Milo O'Shea, Des Cave, Dearbhla Molloy, Judy Cornwell, Donal LeBlanc. Irish lover Cave tries to juggle varied sexual encounters with uninspired home life in ordinary comedy-drama. [PG]▼

Padre Padrone (1977-Italian) **C-114m.** ** D: Vittorio and Paolo Taviani. Omero Antonutti, Saverio Marioni, Marcella Michelangeli, Fabrizio Forte. Sad, illiterate Sardinian boy, brutalized by his peasant father, still grows up to master Greek and Latin and graduate college. Even sadder still, uninvolving and curiously forgettable. Based on an autobiographical book by Gavino Ledda.▼●◗

Pagan Love Song (1950) **C-76m.** ** D: Robert Alton. Esther Williams, Howard Keel, Minna Gombell, Rita Moreno. Stale MGM musical; Keel goes to Tahiti, romances Williams.▼

Pagans, The (1958-Italian) **80m.** *½ D: Ferrucio Cereo. Pierre Cressoy, Helen Remy, Vittorio Sanipoli, Luigi Tosi, Franco Fabrizi. Uninspired costumer set in Rome, with the Spanish invaders ramming the city walls.

Pagemaster, The (1994) **C-75m.** ** D: Maurice Hunt (animation), Joe Johnston (live action). Macaulay Culkin, Christopher Lloyd, Ed Begley, Jr., Mel Harris; voices of Patrick Stewart, Whoopi Goldberg, Frank Welker, Leonard Nimoy. Phobically nervous young boy seeks shelter from a storm in the local library, and is transported to an animated world by living books who represent Adventure, Fantasy, and Horror. Uninspired, often boring cartoon feature (with live-action framework) resembles a TV special more than a movie. Heavy-handed message about the wonder of books might better be told by a book itself. [G]▼●

Page Miss Glory (1935) **90m.** **½ D: Mervyn LeRoy. Marion Davies, Pat O'Brien, Dick Powell, Mary Astor, Frank McHugh, Lyle Talbot, Patsy Kelly, Allen Jenkins, Barton MacLane. Fine cast overshadows Davies in this amiable spoof of publicity stunts, with con-man O'Brien winning beauty contest with composite photograph of nonexistent girl.

Paid (1931) **80m.** **½ D: Sam Wood. Joan Crawford, Kent Douglass (Douglass Montgomery), Robert Armstrong, Marie Prevost, John Miljan, Polly Moran. Not-bad early Crawford. Innocent girl sent to prison; she hardens and seeks revenge. Remade as WITHIN THE LAW.

Paid in Full (1950) **105m.** **½ D: William Dieterle. Robert Cummings, Lizabeth Scott, Diana Lynn, Eve Arden, Ray Collins, Stanley Ridges, John Bromfield, Frank McHugh. Kind-hearted Scott loves nice-guy Cummings, but keeps her feelings to herself because he naively desires to wed her selfish kid sister (Lynn). Turgid soaper, with a based-on-fact scenario. Film debut of Carol Channing, playing a dress-shop patron.

Paid to Kill (1954-British) **70m.** ** D: Montgomery Tully. Dane Clark, Paul Carpenter, Thea Gregory, Anthony Forwood. Oft-told premise of man who hires hood to kill him for insurance and changes his mind.

Pain in the A——, A (1974-French-Italian) **C-90m.** *** D: Edouard Molinaro. Lino Ventura, Jacques Brel, Caroline Cellier, Nino Castelnuovo, Jean-Pierre Darras. Very funny black comedy about the chance meeting of a hit man trying to make good on a contract and a pathetic would-be suicide who's likely to mess up the job. Wonderful performances by Ventura and Brel in adaptation of Francis Veber's stage hit, later Americanized as BUDDY BUDDY. [PG]▼

Painted Desert, The (1931) **75m.** **½ D: Howard Higgin. William Boyd, Helen Twelvetrees, William Farnum, J. Farrell MacDonald, Clark Gable. Conflict and romance between the adopted son (Boyd) and daughter of two long-feuding Westerners. A bit stiff, though the scenery is beautiful; notable mainly for Gable's talkie debut. Some action shots are missing, abruptly cut out to use in 1938 remake.▼

Painted Hills, The (1951) **C-65m.** **½ D: Harold F. Kress. Lassie, Paul Kelly, Bruce Cowling, Gary Gray, Art Smith, Ann Doran. Nicely photographed adventure drama set in the West during the 1870s. Lassie stars as Shep, a collie who is ever-loyal to her prospector owner, with the story involving greed and a gold strike.▼

Painted Veil, The (1934) **83m.** **½ D: Richard Boleslawski. Greta Garbo, Herbert Marshall, George Brent, Warner Oland, Jean Hersholt, Cecilia Parker, Keye Luke. Set in mysterious Orient, film tells Somerset Maugham's story of unfaithful wife mending her ways. Mundane script uplifted by Garbo's personality, supported by Marshall as her husband, Brent as her lover. Remade as THE SEVENTH SIN.▼●

Painting the Clouds With Sunshine (1951) **C-87m.** ** D: David Butler. Dennis Morgan, Virginia Mayo, Gene Nelson, Lucille Norman, Virginia Gibson, Tom Conway. Lukewarm musical of trio of gold-diggers in Las Vegas searching for rich husbands, a mild reworking of an old musical formula.

Paint It Black (1989) **C-101m.** ** D: Tim Hunter. Rick Rossovich, Sally Kirkland, Martin Landau, Julie Carmen, Doug Savant, Peter Frechette, Jason Bernard. Meandering, disappointing thriller with Rossovich a sculptor who's ripped off by his lover, art dealer Kirkland, then victimized by weirdo Savant. Never released theatrically. [R]▼●

Paint Your Wagon (1969) **C-166m.** *** D: Joshua Logan. Lee Marvin, Clint Eastwood, Jean Seberg, Harve Presnell, Ray Walston, Tom Ligon, Alan Dexter. Splashy, expensive musical from Lerner-Loewe play about gold-rush days in No-Name City, California, where prospectors Marvin and Eastwood share one wife (Seberg) whom they bought at auction. Pure entertainment; witty, often risqué script (by Paddy Chayefsky!). Presnell outshines cast of nonsingers with "They Call the Wind Maria." Marvin, however, vocalizes his rendition of "Wand'rin' Star." Beware of shorter prints. Panavision. [M]▼●

Paisan (1946-Italian) **90m.** ***½ D: Roberto Rossellini. Carmela Sazio, Gar Moore, Bill Tubbs, Harriet White, Maria Michi, Robert van Loon, Dale Edmonds, Carla Pisacane, Dots Johnson. Early Rossellini classic, largely improvised by a mostly non-professional cast. Six vignettes depict life in Italy during WW2; best has American nurse White searching for her lover in battle-torn Florence. Written by Rossellini and Federico Fellini; Giulietta Masina has a bit part. Italian running time 115m.▼

Pajama Game, The (1957) **C-101m.** ***½ D: George Abbott, Stanley Donen. Doris Day, John Raitt, Carol Haney, Eddie Foy, Jr., Barbara Nichols, Reta Shaw. Adaptation of the Broadway musical hit—with much of its original cast intact—virtually defines the word "exuberance." Day is a joy as the head of a factory grievance committee who unexpectedly falls in love with the new foreman (Raitt, in his only starring film). Richard Adler and Jerry Ross's songs include "Hey, There." Dancer Haney stands out in her "Steam Heat" feature and in the energetic "Once a Year Day" picnic number. Choreography by Bob Fosse.▼●

Pajama Party (1964) **C-85m.** ** D: Don Weis. Tommy Kirk, Annette Funicello, Dorothy Lamour, Elsa Lanchester, Harvey Lembeck, Jody McCrea, Buster Keaton, Susan Hart, Donna Loren. Fourth BEACH PARTY movie moves indoors, changes director and star (although Frankie Avalon and Don Rickles do have cameos). Kirk plays Martian teenager who drops in and is understandably perplexed. Just fair, though it's always nice to see Keaton at work. Teri Garr is one of the dancers buried in the sand. Went back outside for BEACH BLANKET BINGO. Panavision. ▼

Paleface, The (1948) **C-91m.** *** D: Norman Z. McLeod. Bob Hope, Jane Russell, Robert Armstrong, Iris Adrian, Robert

Watson. Enjoyable comedy-Western, a spoof of THE VIRGINIAN, has timid Bob backed up by sharpshooting Russell in gunfighting encounters; Oscar-winning song "Buttons and Bows." Remade as THE SHAKIEST GUN IN THE WEST. Sequel: SON OF PALEFACE. ▼●

Pale Rider (1985) **C-113m.** ** D: Clint Eastwood. Clint Eastwood, Michael Moriarty, Carrie Snodgress, Christopher Penn, Richard Dysart, Sydney Penny, Richard Kiel, Doug McGrath, John Russell. Eastwood Western starts out just fine, the saga of a Good Stranger coming to the aid of some struggling miners, but winds up draggy, pretentious, and dull—with so much cloning of SHANE as to be preposterous. Well crafted, but attempts to be mythical come off as heavy-handed and ridiculous. Panavision. [R]▼●◗

Pal Joey (1957) **C-111m.** *** D: George Sidney. Rita Hayworth, Frank Sinatra, Kim Novak, Barbara Nichols, Elizabeth Patterson, Bobby Sherwood. Heel-hero of John O'Hara/Rodgers & Hart musical is transformed here into a flippant nice guy who seeks to build a sleek nightclub in San Francisco. Hayworth and Novak battle over Frank with diverting results. Songs: "Bewitched, Bothered, and Bewildered" (with sanitized lyrics), "My Funny Valentine," "The Lady Is a Tramp," etc. Look fast for Robert Reed. ▼●◗

Pallbearer, The (1996) **C-97m.** **½ D: Matt Reeves. David Schwimmer, Gwyneth Paltrow, Barbara Hershey, Michael Rapaport, Toni Collette, Carol Kane, Michael Vartan, Bitty Schram, Jean DeBaer. *Friends* star Schwimmer's first film vehicle: a nerd is recruited to be a pallbearer for a "friend" he can't quite remember. Soon he's involved with the dead fellow's sexy mother (Hershey), even while pursuing a girl he had a crush on in high school (Paltrow). Protracted story is alternately touching and infuriating, as it slowly covers well-worn territory, with occasional moments of poignancy. Schwimmer's character is alarmingly one-note. [PG-13]▼●◗

Palm Beach Story, The (1942) **90m.** ***½ D: Preston Sturges. Claudette Colbert, Joel McCrea, Rudy Vallee, Mary Astor, Sig Arno, Robert Dudley, William Demarest, Jack Norton, Franklin Pangborn, Jimmy Conlin. Hilarious screwball comedy with Claudette running away from hubby McCrea, landing in Palm Beach with nutty millionairess Astor and her bumbling brother Vallee; overflowing with Sturges madness—from the mystifying title sequence to the arrival of the Ale & Quail Club (not to mention the Wienie King!).▼●

Palmetto (1998-U.S.-German) **C-113m.** **½ D: Volker Schlöndorff. Woody Harrelson, Elisabeth Shue, Gina Gershon, Rolf Hoppe, Michael Rapaport, Chloe Sevigny, Tom Wright. An exercise in formula film noir with embittered Florida ex-newspaperman Harrelson—just out of jail—a none-too-bright patsy for crafty (and sexy) Shue, who hires him to help her stage a phony kidnaping. Stylish and steamy, with lots of twists and turns . . . but follows a much too familiar pattern. Based on the vintage novel *Just Another Sucker* by James Hadley Chase. Super 35. [R]▼●◗

Palm Springs Weekend (1963) **C-100m.** **½ D: Norman Taurog. Troy Donahue, Connie Stevens, Stefanie Powers, Robert Conrad, Ty Hardin, Jack Weston, Andrew Duggan, Carole Cook, Jerry Van Dyke, Billy Mumy. Cast tries to play teenagers; yarn of group on a spree in resort town is mostly predictable.▼●

Palmy Days (1931) **77m.** **½ D: A. Edward Sutherland. Eddie Cantor, Charlotte Greenwood, Charles Middleton, George Raft, Walter Catlett. Cantor is the patsy for a shady fortune-teller in this so-so musical, hampered by silly comic scenes which don't quite work. Notable mostly for Busby Berkeley overhead shots and Cantor performing "My Baby Said Yes, Yes" and "There's Nothing Too Good for My Baby." ▼●

Palombella Rossa (1989-Italian) **C-87m.** **½ D: Nanni Moretti. Nanni Moretti, Mariella Valentini, Silvio Orlando, Alfonso Santagata, Claudio Morganti, Asia Argento. Off-the-wall satire about the choices, both political and personal, one makes in life. The hero is Michele (Moretti), a comical communist politician/water polo player; most of the film is set during a competition in which Michele constantly debates the merits of his politics. A representative introduction to one of Italy's most popular comic actor–directors. ▼

Palooka (1934) **86m.** *** D: Benjamin Stoloff. Jimmy Durante, Stu Erwin, Lupe Velez, Marjorie Rambeau, Robert Armstrong, Mary Carlisle, William Cagney, Thelma Todd. Not much relation to Ham Fisher's comic strip, but delightful entertainment with Erwin as naive young man brought into fight game by flashy promoter Knobby Walsh (Durante). Fine cast includes James Cagney's lookalike brother William, and has Schnozzola in top form. Aka JOE PALOOKA.▼

Palookaville (1996) **C-92m.** *** D: Alan Taylor. William Forsythe, Vincent Gallo, Adam Trese, Frances McDormand, Robert LuPone, Lisa Gay Hamilton, Kim Dickens, Bridgit Ryan. Charming, whimsical look at a trio of lifelong friends and their amateur foray into the world of petty crime. Set in New Jersey, this comically poignant tale has everyday characters, struggling to survive, who get themselves into some genuinely suspenseful situations. A real sleeper, inspired by the Italian film BIG DEAL ON MADONNA STREET. [R]▼●

Panama Deception, The (1992) **C-91m.** *** D: Barbara Trent. Narrated by Elizabeth Montgomery. Powerful, aptly titled, Oscar-winning documentary which traces U.S. involvement in Panama through the decades, spotlighting the 1989 invasion (and condemning American foreign policy under Presidents Reagan and Bush). The mass media is portrayed as little more than an arm of the White House. Originally shot on video.▼●

Panama Hattie (1942) **79m.** **½ D: Norman Z. McLeod. Ann Sothern, Red Skelton, Rags Ragland, Ben Blue, Marsha Hunt, Virginia O'Brien, Alan Mowbray, Lena Horne, Dan Dailey, Carl Esmond. Cole Porter's Broadway musical (which starred Ethel Merman) about nightclub owner in Panama, falls flat on screen. Porter's score mostly absent, but Lena sings "Just One of Those Things," and sprightly Sothern sings "I've Still Got My Health."▼

Panama Sal (1957) **70m.** BOMB D: William Witney. Elena Verdugo, Carlos Rivas, Joe Flynn, Edward Kemmer. Lowjinks blend of poor comedy and flat songs. Naturama.

Pan Americana (1945) **84m.** ** D: John H. Auer. Philip Terry, Eve Arden, Robert Benchley, Audrey Long, Bettejane (Jane) Greer. Another 40's gesture toward Latin-American goodwill. Magazine staff visits Latin America, with writer Long becoming involved with photographer Terry. Crammed with Latin-American musical and specialty numbers.

Pancho Villa (1972-Spanish) **C-92m.** ** D: Eugenio Martin. Telly Savalas, Clint Walker, Anne Francis, Chuck Connors, Angel del Pozo, Luis Davila. Noisy but dull period piece has Savalas chewing up scenery in title role, Walker playing gunrunner on his payroll, and Connors as polo-playing military martinet. Hang on, though, for smashing climax as two trains collide head-on. [PG]▼●◗

Pandemonium (1982) **C-82m.** ** D: Alfred Sole. Tom Smothers, Carol Kane, Miles Chapin, Debralee Scott, Candy Azzara, Marc McClure, Judge Reinhold, Paul Reubens (Pee-wee Herman); guest stars, Tab Hunter, Donald O'Connor, Eve Arden, Eileen Brennan. Sporadically funny spoof of slasher films, set in a school for cheerleaders. Some clever ideas (in keeping with Canadian origin of many of those films, hero Smothers is a Mountie), but too often just forced. Panavision. [PG]▼

Pandora and the Flying Dutchman (1951-British) **C-123m.** ** D: Albert Lewin. James Mason, Ava Gardner, Nigel Patrick, Sheila Sim, Harold Warrender, Marius Goring, Pamela Kellino (Mason). Sorry to say, a big Technicolor bore, one of writer-director Lewin's misfires, about a woman who destroys the lives of all the men around her; then mystical, otherworldly Mason materializes. Intriguing but unconvincing tale, inspired by the legend of The Flying Dutchman, a man cursed to live for all eternity until he can find a woman capable of loving him. Only real attribute is Gardner's breathtaking beauty.▼●

Pandora's Box (1928-German) **109m.** **** D: G. W. Pabst. Louise Brooks, Fritz Kortner, Franz (Francis) Lederer, Carl Goetz. Hypnotic silent film stars legendary Brooks as flower girl who becomes protégée—then wife—of editor, with bizarre and unexpected consequences. Striking sexuality and drama, with Brooks an unforgettable Lulu. Scripters Pabst and Laszlo Wajda adapted two plays by Franz Wedekind. ▼

Panga SEE: **Curse III: Blood Sacrifice**

Panic Button (1964) **90m.** BOMB D: George Sherman. Maurice Chevalier, Eleanor Parker, Jayne Mansfield, Michael Connors, Akim Tamiroff. Good cast is wasted in this amateurish, pathetically unfunny production involving the making of a TV pilot in Italy that's supposed to flop so gangster producers will have legitimate tax loss. Wait for a rerun of THE PRODUCERS. Totalscope.▼

Panic in Needle Park, The (1971) **C-110m.** ***½ D: Jerry Schatzberg. Al Pacino, Kitty Winn, Alan Vint, Richard Bright, Kiel Martin, Michael McClanathan, Warren Finnerty, Marcia Jean Kurtz, Raul Julia, Joe Santos, Paul Sorvino. Easily the best of many drug-abuse films made in the early 1970s. Spunky small-time crook and decent young girl get hooked on heroin and go straight downhill. Pacino and Winn are tremendous. Screenplay by Joan Didion and John Gregory Dunne, from James Mills' book; produced by Dominick Dunne. [PG—edited from original R rating]▼●

Panic in the City (1968) **C-97m.** ** D: Eddie Davis. Howard Duff, Linda Cristal, Stephen McNally, Nehemiah Persoff, Anne Jeffreys, Oscar Beregi, Dennis Hopper. Blah thriller with federal agent Duff attempting to prevent some commie swine from setting off an atomic bomb in L.A. Watch for Mike Farrell as a hospital radiologist.▼

Panic in the Parlor (1956-British) **81m.** **½ D: Gordon Parry. Peggy Mount, Shirley Eaton, Gordon Jackson, Ronald Lewis. Broad but diverting humor about sailor Lewis coming home to get married, and the chaos it causes all concerned. Look for Michael Caine in a bit as a sailor. Originally titled: SAILOR BEWARE!

Panic in the Streets (1950) **93m.** ***½ D: Elia Kazan. Richard Widmark, Paul Douglas, Barbara Bel Geddes, (Walter) Jack Palance, Zero Mostel. Taut drama involving gangsters, one of whom is a carrier of pneumonic plague, and the manhunt to find him. Makes fine use of New Orleans locale; Edward and Edna Anhalt won an Oscar for their story. Screenplay by Richard Murphy. ▼●

Panic in Year Zero (1962) **95m.** **½ D: Ray Milland. Ray Milland, Jean Hagen, Frankie Avalon, Mary Mitchel, Joan Freeman, Richard Garland. Intriguing film about family that escapes atomic bomb explosion to find a situation of every-man-for-himself. Loud, tinny music spoils much of film's effectiveness. CinemaScope.●

Panic on the Trans-Siberian Express SEE: **Horror Express**

Pantaloons (1957-French) **C-93m.** **½ D: John Berry. Fernandel, Carmen Sevilla, Christine Carrere, Fernando Rey. Fernandel is peppy in this brisk little period-piece as a phony gay-blade intent on female conquests.▼

Panther (1995) **C-124m.** ** D: Mario Van Peebles. Kadeem Hardison, Bokeem Woodbine, Joe Don Baker, Courtney B. Vance, Tyrin Turner, Marcus Chong, Anthony Griffith, Bobby Brown, Nefertiti, James Russo, Jenifer Lewis, Chris Rock, Roger Guenveur Smith, Michael Wincott, Richard Dysart, M. Emmet Walsh, Dick Gregory, Jerry Rubin, James LeGros, Robert Culp, Mario Van Peebles. Despite its impressive cast, an annoyingly simple-minded and (no pun intended) whitewashed account of the militant Black Panthers, who had had their fill of the everyday oppression against Black America and began confronting authority during the Vietnam era, becoming pivotal countercultural figures. Fascinating, politically loaded subject matter yearns for a more complex, intelligent cinematic rendering. Scripted by the director's dad, Melvin, based on his novel; both coproduced. [R] ▼●◗

Panther Island SEE: **Bomba on Panther Island**

Papa, Mama, the Maid and I (1956-French) **94m.** **½ D: Jean-Paul Le Chanois. Fernand Ledoux, Gaby Morlay, Nicole Courcel, Robert Lamoureux. Sometimes saucy sex comedy, fully explained by title.

Papa's Delicate Condition (1963) **C-98m.** **½ D: George Marshall. Jackie Gleason, Glynis Johns, Charlie Ruggles, Laurel Goodwin, Charles Lane, Elisha Cook, Juanita Moore, Murray Hamilton. Amusing nostalgia of Corinne Griffith's childhood; Gleason dominates everything as tipsy father; set in 1900s. Oscar-winning song, "Call Me Irresponsible."▼●

Paper, The (1994) **C-112m.** **½ D: Ron Howard. Michael Keaton, Glenn Close, Robert Duvall, Marisa Tomei, Randy Quaid, Jason Robards, Jason Alexander, Spalding Gray, Catherine O'Hara, Lynne Thigpen, Jack Kehoe, Roma Maffia, Clint Howard, Geoffrey Owens, William Prince, Augusta Dabney, Bruce Altman. Twenty-four hours in the life of a N.Y. newspaper and its harried editors, who are trying to manage their troubled private lives against the unyielding demands of a deadline (and a few small questions about ethics). Over-the-top, far-fetched, downright silly at times, but so adrenalized—barely stopping to take a breath—that it's fun to watch just the same. Many N.Y. journalists appear in cameo roles. Music by Randy Newman. [R] ▼●◗

Paperback Hero (1973-Canadian) **C-94m.** **½ D: Peter Pearson. Keir Dullea, Elizabeth Ashley, John Beck, Dayle Haddon. Local hockey hero/womanizer leads fantasy life as town gunslinger. Interesting and well-acted, but ultimately a misfire. [R]▼

Paperback Romance (1994-Australian) **C-93m.** ** D: Ben Lewin. Gia Carides, Anthony LaPaglia, Rebecca Gibney, Robyn Nevin, Jacek Koman. Paper-thin black comedy about a disabled romance novelist (Carides) who breaks her leg while stalking handsome, roguish jeweler LaPaglia. Thus, he doesn't realize that she's handicapped; she tells him she was in a skiing accident. Would-be spoof of schmaltzy novels substitutes slapstick violence for actual laughs. The stars are a real-life couple, but seem mismated in this film. [R]▼

Paper Bullets SEE: **Gangs, Inc.**

Paper Chase, The (1973) **C-111m.** ***½ D: James Bridges. Timothy Bottoms, Lindsay Wagner, John Houseman, Graham Beckel, Edward Herrmann, Craig Richard Nelson, James Naughton, Bob Lydiard, David Clennon, Lenny Baker. Near-classic comedy-drama about pressures of freshman year at Harvard Law School; Bottoms' obsession with tyrannical professor Kingsfield (Houseman) becomes even more complicated when he discovers his girl friend is Kingsfield's daughter! Splendidly adapted by Bridges from the John Jay Osborn, Jr., novel, with wonderful Gordon Willis photography and peerless acting, led by Houseman's Oscar-winning performance in the role that made him a "star" (and which he continued in the subsequent TV series). Panavision. [PG] ▼●

Paperhouse (1988-British) **C-94m.** *** D: Bernard Rose. Charlotte Burke, Elliott Spiers, Glenne Headly, Ben Cross, Gemma Jones, Sarah Newbold. Insightful fantasy drama of girl on the verge of puberty who has vivid dreams that both reflect her own life and seem to be affecting the life of a boy she has never met—while awake. Tense, even frightening, psychologically valid and well acted . . . but not to every taste. Feature debut of music-video director Rose. [PG-13]▼●

Paper Lion (1968) **C-107m.** *** D: Alex March. Alan Alda, Lauren Hutton, Alex Karras, David Doyle, Ann Turkel, John Gordy, Roger Brown, Sugar Ray Robinson. Funny film, loosely based on George Plimpton's book, about that writer's experiences when he becomes honorary member of Detroit Lions football team. Even non-football fans should enjoy this one, especially scenes with Karras (then a member of the team). Look for Roy Scheider in small role. Techniscope. [G]▼

Paper Mask (1991-British) **C-105m.** *** D: Christopher Morahan. Paul McGann, Amanda Donohoe, Frederick Treves, Tom Wilkinson, Barbara Leigh-Hunt, Jimmy Yuill. Taut chiller is a darkly cynical look at the medical profession. McGann plays a lowly hospital orderly who takes on the identity of a doctor who's been killed in a car crash and gets a job the deceased had applied for in a busy emergency room. Alternately tense, horrifying, and hilarious. [R]▼

Paper Moon (1973) **102m.** **** D: Peter Bogdanovich. Ryan O'Neal, Tatum O'Neal, Madeline Kahn, John Hillerman, P. J. Johnson, Burton Gilliam, Randy Quaid. Unbeatable entertainment, harking back to Damon Runyonesque 1930s, as con man O'Neal unwillingly latches onto young girl (his real-life daughter) who's pretty sharp herself. Tatum made her film debut here, and won an Oscar for her scene-stealing work; Kahn is fun, too, as Trixie Delight. Script by Alvin Sargent from Joe David Brown's *Addie Pray*. Later a TV series. [PG]▼●

Paper Tiger (1975-British) **C-99m.** ** D: Ken Annakin. David Niven, Toshiro Mifune, Hardy Kruger, Ando, Ivan Desny, Ronald Fraser. Lackluster tale of a plucky kidnapped lad (Ando) and his English tutor (Niven). Since the boy is the son of Japanese ambassador Mifune, Niven sees the chance to act out his many tales of heroism that have impressed the youngster. Tepid action involving political terrorism and Disney-style cuteness muck up the proceedings entirely. Panavision. [PG]▼

Papillon (1973) **C-150m.** *** D: Franklin J. Schaffner. Steve McQueen, Dustin Hoffman, Victor Jory, Don Gordon, Anthony Zerbe, George Coulouris, Robert Deman, Bill Mumy, Gregory Sierra. Henri Charrière—"the butterfly"—(McQueen) is determined to escape from Devil's Island, despite the odds, in this exciting adventure yarn. Extreme length and graphic realism work against its total success. Script by Dalton Trumbo and Lorenzo Semple, Jr., from Charrière's best-selling book; that's Trumbo cast as the Commandant. Music by Jerry Goldsmith. Cut to 132m. after original release. Panavision. [PG—originally rated R]▼●◗

Parachute Battalion (1941) **75m.** ** D: Leslie Goodwins. Edmond O'Brien, Nancy Kelly, Robert Preston, Harry Carey, Buddy Ebsen, Paul Kelly. Efficient pre-WW2 programmer; gets a bit sticky with flag-waving.

Parachute Jumper (1933) **65m.** **½ D: Alfred E. Green. Douglas Fairbanks, Jr., Leo Carrillo, Bette Davis, Frank McHugh, Claire Dodd. Former flyers Fairbanks and McHugh strike up fast friendship with Davis, but all three are victimized by involvement with gangster Carrillo. Fast-moving, enjoyable Warner Bros. programmer.

Parade (1974-French-Swedish) **C-85m.** ** D: Jacques Tati. Jacques Tati, Karl Kossmayr, Pia Colombo. Disappointing final feature from the beloved French comic, combining assorted provincial circus acts with Tati himself performing mime routines. The result is a curio for sure, solely of interest for fans of Tati. Shot mostly on video, and transferred to celluloid. Originally made for television.▼●

Parade, The (1984) **C-100m. TVM** D: Peter H. Hunt. Michael Learned, Frederic Forrest, Rosanna Arquette, Maxwell Caulfield, James Olson, Geraldine Page. Three generations of women find their lives in turmoil when the husband of one comes home seeking revenge after seven years in prison, as the town prepares for its July 4th parade. N. Richard Nash's compact story and teleplay revive pleasant memories of his writings during TV's Golden Age. Above average.

Paradine Case, The (1948) **116m.** **½ D: Alfred Hitchcock. Gregory Peck, (Alida) Valli, Ann Todd, Charles Laughton, Charles Coburn, Ethel Barrymore, Louis Jourdan, Leo G. Carroll, John Williams. Talk, talk, talk in complicated, stagy courtroom drama, set in England. Below par for Hitchcock; producer David O. Selznick also wrote the script. Originally 132m., then cut to 125m. and finally 116m.▼◗

Paradise (1982) **C-100m.** *½ D: Stuart Gillard. Willie Aames, Phoebe Cates, Tuvia Tavi, Richard Curnock, Neil Vipond, Aviva Marks. Silly BLUE LAGOON rip-off, with Aames and Cates discovering sex while stranded in the desert. Both, however, do look good sans clothes. [R]▼

Paradise (1991) **C-110m.** *** D: Mary Agnes Donoghue. Melanie Griffith, Don Johnson, Elijah Wood, Thora Birch, Sheila McCarthy, Eve Gordon, Louise Latham. Poignant and appealing story of a boy (Wood) who's sent to friends of his mother's in a quiet country town for the summer; there he's befriended by a precocious girl (Birch), and tries to learn what makes the married couple he's staying with so cold to one another. Idyllic film takes perhaps too much time to reach its (inevitable) climax, but offers many lovely moments. Birch is a standout. Directorial debut for screenwriter Donoghue, who adapted her script from 1988 French film LE GRAND CHEMIN (THE GRAND HIGHWAY). [PG-13]▼●

Paradise Alley (1961) **85m.** *½ D: Hugo Haas. Marie Windsor, Hugo Haas, Billy Gilbert, Carol Morris, Chester Conklin, Margaret Hamilton, Corinne Griffith. Grade-D mishmash about elderly moviemaker involved in amateur film production. Interesting only for veteran cast. Original title: STARS IN THE BACK YARD.

Paradise Alley (1978) **C-109m.** *½ D: Sylvester Stallone. Sylvester Stallone, Lee Canalito, Armand Assante, Frank McRae, Anne Archer, Kevin Conway, Joyce Ingalls, Tom Waits, Ray Sharkey. Sly made his directorial debut with this Damon Runyonesque story of three none-too-bright brothers from the N.Y.C. tenements, one of whom hopes to make it big as a wrestler. Some nice moments lost in comic-book-level dramatics. Director Stallone clearly admires his star (he also croons the title song!). [PG]▼●

Paradise for Three (1938) **75m.** ** D: Edward Buzzell. Frank Morgan, Robert Young, Mary Astor, Edna May Oliver, Florence Rice, Reginald Owen, Henry Hull. Strange story of American businessman trying to mingle with German people to discover how they live. Good cast helps fair script.

Paradise, Hawaiian Style (1966) **C-91m.** **½ D: Michael Moore. Elvis Presley, Suzanna Leigh, James Shigeta, Donna Butterworth, Marianna Hill, Irene Tsu, Julie Parrish, Philip Ahn, Mary Treen. Rehash of Presley's earlier BLUE HAWAII, with Elvis a pilot who runs a charter service while romancing local dolls. Attractive fluff.▼

Paradise Lagoon SEE: **Admirable Crichton, The**

Paradise Lost: The Child Murders at Robin Hood Hills (1996) **C-150m.** **½ D: Joe Berlinger, Bruce Sinofsky. Documentary chronicling the trial of three teenage boys charged in the gruesome 1993 murders of three 8-year-old boys in West Memphis, Ark. Interviews with key participants, townsfolk, and families help draw viewers into the insular community, but film plays like an overlong segment of a TV news magazine, and the fascinating case is dragged out by an occasionally meandering narrative. Debuted on cable TV, then went to theaters. Followed up in 2000 with REVELATIONS: PARADISE LOST 2. ▼●

Paradise Road (1997-U.S.-Australian) **C-115m.** **½ D: Bruce Beresford. Glenn Close, Pauline Collins, Cate Blanchett, Frances McDormand, Julianna Margulies, Jennifer Ehle, Elizabeth Spriggs, Tessa Humphries, Johanna Ter Steege, Wendy Hughes, Susie Porter, Sab Shimono. Beresford scripted and researched this heartfelt (though cliché-ridden) based-on-fact account of a band of women who become united as they are held in a Japanese POW camp in Sumatra during WW2; they form a symphonic chorus and create beautiful harmony amid their misery. Not without many dramatically effective moments, but done in by repetition and predictability. Panavision. [R]▼●

Parallax View, The (1974) **C-102m.** ***½ D: Alan J. Pakula. Warren Beatty, Paula Prentiss, William Daniels, Walter McGinn, Hume Cronyn, Anthony Zerbe, Kenneth Mars. Director-photographer-production designer team later responsible for ALL THE PRESIDENT'S MEN gives this political thriller a brilliant "look" as reporter Beatty investigates a senator's assassination. Frightening story unfolds with each piece of evidence he uncovers. Gripping to the very end. Panavision. [R]▼◗

Parallel Lives (1994) **C-95m. TVM** D: Linda Yellen. James Belushi, James Brolin, LeVar Burton, Lindsay Crouse, Jill Eikenberry, Ben Gazzara, Jack Klugman, David Lansbury, Liza Minnelli, Dudley Moore, Gena Rowlands, Ally Sheedy, Helen Slater, Mira Sorvino, Paul Sorvino, Robert Wagner, Patricia Wettig, JoBeth Williams, Treat Williams, Matthew Perry. Men and women of various ages come together for a fraternity-sorority reunion, resulting in emotional conflict, sexual couplings—and murder. Much of the dialogue was improvised, resulting in narrative incoherence; some nice moments, but ultimately just a muddy acting exercise. Check out this movie's predecessor, CHANTILLY LACE, instead—featuring much of the same cast and crew. Made for cable. Average ▼

Paramount on Parade (1930) **77m.** **½ D: Dorothy Arzner, Otto Brower, Edmund Goulding, Victor Heerman, Edwin Knopf, Rowland V. Lee, Ernst Lubitsch, Lothar Mendes, Victor Schertzinger, A. Edward Sutherland, Frank Tuttle. Jean Arthur, Clara Bow, Maurice Chevalier, Gary Cooper, Nancy Carroll, Leon Errol, Stuart Erwin, Kay Francis, Fredric March, Helen Kane, Jack Oakie, William Powell, Buddy Rogers, many others. Early-talkie variety revue designed to show off Paramount's roster of stars. Some amusing songs and skits, but a lot of dry spots in between. Highlights include Nancy Carroll's "Dancing to Save Your Sole" and Chevalier's two numbers. Film originally ran 102m. with several sequences in color; current prints feature director Edmund Goulding and such stars as Gary Cooper and Jean Arthur "introducing" a sequence that never comes!

Paranoia (1968) **C-91m.** BOMB D: Umberto Lenzi. Carroll Baker, Lou Castel, Colette Descombes, Tino Carraro. Trash about sultry widow involved in various sexual encounters. Aka ORGASMO. Cromoscope. ▼

Paranoia (1969) SEE: **Quiet Place to Kill, A**

Paranoiac (1963-British) **80m.** **½ D: Freddie Francis. Janette Scott, Oliver Reed, Liliane Brousse, Alexander Davion, Sheila Burrell, Maurice Denham. Murder, impersonation, insanity all part of thriller set in large English country estate. CinemaScope. ▼●

Parasite (1982) **C-85m.** BOMB D: Charles Band. Robert Glaudini, Demi Moore, Luca Bercovici, James Davidson, Al Fann, Cherie Currie, Vivian Blaine. In repressive near-future, scientist who's developed voracious parasites flees with one inside him and (surprise, surprise) it gets loose. Set in the California desert, with several revolting sequences copied from ALIEN. Filmed in 3-D, with blood and parasites thrust at the viewer. StereoScope. [R]▼●◗

Parasite Murders, The SEE: **They Came From Within**

Paratrooper (1953-British) **C-87m.** ** D: Terence Young. Alan Ladd, Leo Genn, Susan Stephen, Harry Andrews, Donald Houston, Anthony Bushell, Stanley Baker, Anton Diffring. Minor Ladd vehicle involving special tactical forces and Ladd's guilt-ridden past. Original title: THE RED BERET.

Pardners (1956) **C-90m.** **½ D: Norman Taurog. Dean Martin, Jerry Lewis, Lori Nelson, Jackie Loughery, John Baragrey, Agnes Moorehead, Jeff Morrow, Lon Chaney, Jr. Ironically titled M&L vehicle (they were already on the road to their breakup) is pleasant remake of RHYTHM ON THE RANGE, with Jerry as Manhattan millionaire who cleans up Western town in his own inimitable fashion. Written by Sidney Sheldon. VistaVision.▼

Pardon Mon Affaire (1977-French) **C-105m.** *** D: Yves Robert. Jean Rochefort, Claude Brasseur, Guy Bedos, Victor Lanoux, Daniele Delorme, Anny Duperey. Sprightly comedy about efforts of happily married Rochefort to meet and court a dazzling model he spots in a parking garage. Another enjoyable French farce from director Robert. Sequel: WE WILL ALL MEET IN PARADISE. Later Americanized as THE WOMAN IN RED. [PG]▼●

Pardon Mon Affaire, Too SEE: **We Will All Meet in Paradise**

Pardon My French (1951-U.S.-French) **81m.** **½ D: Bernard Vorhaus. Paul Henreid, Merle Oberon, Paul Bonifas, Maximilliene, Jim Gerald. Fluff of Oberon inheriting a mansion in France occupied by charming composer Henreid.

Pardon My Past (1945) **88m.** *** D: Leslie Fenton. Fred MacMurray, Marguerite Chapman, Akim Tamiroff, William Demarest, Rita Johnson, Harry Davenport. Excellent tale of unsuspecting look-alike for famous playboy, incurring his debts and many enemies; fine comedy-drama.

Pardon My Rhythm (1944) **62m.** ** D: Felix E. Feist. Gloria Jean, Evelyn Ankers, Patric Knowles, Bob Crosby. Naive minor musical set in ultra-wholesome high school, with Gloria the singing belle of the ball.

Pardon My Sarong (1942) **84m.** *** D: Erle C. Kenton. Lou Costello, Bud Abbott, Lionel Atwill, Virginia Bruce, Robert Paige, William Demarest, Leif Erickson, Samuel S. Hinds, Nan Wynn, Four Ink Spots, Tip, Tap, Toe. A&C in good form as bus drivers who end up on tropical island, involved with notorious jewel thieves. ▼

Pardon My Trunk SEE: **Hello Elephant**▼

Pardon Us (1931) **55m.** **½ D: James Parrott. Stan Laurel, Oliver Hardy, Wilfred Lucas, Walter Long, James Finlayson, June Marlowe. L&H's first starring feature film is amusing spoof of THE BIG HOUSE and prison films in general; slow pacing is its major debit, but many funny bits make it a must for fans of Stan and Ollie.▼●

Parenthood (1989) **C-124m.** ***½ D: Ron Howard. Steve Martin, Mary Steenburgen, Dianne Wiest, Jason Robards, Rick Moranis, Tom Hulce, Martha Plimpton, Keanu Reeves, Harley Kozak, Dennis Dugan, Leaf Phoenix, Paul Linke. Insightful multi-character comedy about the trials and tribulations of parenthood, as seen from several points of view within the same large family. Warm, winning, and truthful; Martin is ideal in the lead, and surrounded by a perfect ensemble. Screenplay by Lowell Ganz and Babaloo Mandel (from a story they concocted with fellow parent Ron Howard). Followed by a TV series. [PG-13]▼●◗

Parents (1989) **C-82m.** ** D: Bob Balaban. Randy Quaid, Mary Beth Hurt, Sandy Dennis, Bryan Madorsky, Juno Mills-Cockell, Kathryn Grody, Deborah Rush, Graham Jarvis. Coal-black horror comedy set in the 1950s centers on a young boy who worries about where his highly conformist parents get all that meat they eat . . . and what goes on down in the basement. Well-acted but thinly plotted; a good sense of visual style and amusing production design can't keep it afloat. Feature directing debut for actor Balaban. [R]▼●◗

Parent Trap, The (1961) **C-124m.** *** D: David Swift. Hayley Mills, Maureen O'Hara, Brian Keith, Charlie Ruggles, Una Merkel, Leo G. Carroll, Joanna Barnes, Cathleen Nesbitt, Nancy Kulp, Frank DeVol. Hayley plays twins who've never met until their divorced parents send them to the same summer camp; after initial rivalry they join forces to reunite their mom and dad. Attempt to mix slapstick and sophistication doesn't work, but overall it's fun. Erich Kastner's story filmed before as 1954 British film TWICE UPON A TIME. Hayley starred—as mom—in 1986 and 1989 TV sequels. Remade in 1998.▼●

Parent Trap, The (1998) **C-128m.** *** D: Nancy Myers. Lindsay Lohan, Dennis Quaid, Natasha Richardson, Elaine Hendrix, Lisa Ann Walter, Simon Kunz, Polly

Holliday, Maggie Wheeler, Ronnie Stevens. Delightful remake of the 1961 Disney hit about eleven-year-old girls who've been raised separately, meet each other for the first time at summer camp, and contrive to bring their parents back together—though Mom lives in London and Dad in California's Napa Valley. Nicely updated to the 1990s without losing the appeal of the original. Joanna Barnes, who played the "other woman" in the 1961 movie, appears here as that character's mother. [PG]▼●◗

Paris After Dark (1943) **85m.** **½ D: Leonide Moguy. George Sanders, Philip Dorn, Brenda Marshall, Madeleine LeBeau, Marcel Dalio. Preachy but effective melodrama of French patriot Dorn, who returns to Paris from concentration camp where he was coerced into accepting Nazi domination. Look for Peter Lawford as a young Resistance fighter.

Paris Blues (1961) **98m.** *** D: Martin Ritt. Paul Newman, Joanne Woodward, Diahann Carroll, Sidney Poitier, Louis Armstrong, Serge Reggiani. Film improves with each viewing; offbeat account of musicians Newman and Poitier in Left Bank Paris, romancing tourists Woodward and Carroll. Great Duke Ellington score, including explosive "Battle Royal" number; a must for jazz fans.▼

Paris Calling (1941) **95m.** *** D: Edwin L. Marin. Elisabeth Bergner, Randolph Scott, Basil Rathbone, Gale Sondergaard, Eduardo Ciannelli, Lee J. Cobb. Exciting story of underground movement in Paris to destroy Nazis occupying France.

Paris Does Strange Things (1956-French) **C-98m.** ** D: Jean Renoir. Ingrid Bergman, Jean Marais, Mel Ferrer, Jean Richard, Magali Noel, Juliette Greco, Pierre Bertin. Claude Renoir's exquisite cinematography highlights this otherwise so-so account of impoverished Polish princess Bergman's romantic intrigues with Marais and Ferrer. Overrated by some; far from Renoir's (or Bergman's) best. French-language version, called ELENA AND HER MEN, is better, and runs 95m.▼

Paris Express, The (1953-British) **C-80m.** **½ D: Harold French. Claude Rains, Marta Toren, Marius Goring, Anouk (Aimée), Herbert Lom, Lucie Mannheim, Felix Aylmer, Ferdy Mayne, Eric Pohlmann. A clerk embezzles money, hoping to use it for travel, but gets into more of an adventure than he bargained for. Middling crime yarn based on a Georges Simenon novel. Original British title: THE MAN WHO WATCHED TRAINS GO BY.▼

Paris Follies of 1956 SEE: **Fresh From Paris**

Paris Holiday (1958) **C-100m.** **½ D: Gerd Oswald. Bob Hope, Fernandel, Anita Ekberg, Martha Hyer, Preston Sturges. Mixture of French and American farce humor makes for uneven entertainment, with Hope in France to buy a new screenplay. Features writer-director Sturges in a small acting role. Technirama.▼

Paris Honeymoon (1939) **92m.** **½ D: Frank Tuttle. Bing Crosby, Shirley Ross, Edward Everett Horton, Akim Tamiroff, Ben Blue, Rafaela Ottiano, Raymond Hatton. Texan Crosby visits France planning to marry Ross, but meets native Franciska Gaal and falls in love with her.

Paris Is Burning (1990) **C-78m.** ***½ D: Jennie Livingston. Funny, revealing, and compact documentary about N.Y.C. "drag balls"—in which black and Latino men don "vogue-ing" disguises as everything from flamboyant queens to businessmen or members of the military. Fresh and uncondescending, with a powerful element of tragedy near the end. ▼●

Paris Model (1953) **81m.** *½ D: Alfred E. Green. Eva Gabor, Tom Conway, Paulette Goddard, Marilyn Maxwell, Cecil Kellaway, Barbara Lawrence, Florence Bates. Lackluster vehicle for veteran actors, revolving around a dress and four women who purchase copies of same.

Paris Playboys (1954) **62m.** *½ D: William Beaudine. Leo Gorcey, Huntz Hall, Bernard Gorcey, Veola Vonn, Steven Geray, David (Gorcey) Condon, Bennie Bartlett. Sach impersonates a missing French professor and gets mixed up in a spy ring. Feeble *Bowery Boys* slapstick.

Paris, Texas (1984) **C-150m.** **½ D: Wim Wenders. Harry Dean Stanton, Nastassja Kinski, Dean Stockwell, Aurore Clement, Hunter Carson, Bernhard Wicki. Man who's been lost four years tries to put his life back together—and win back his wife and son. Oblique, self-satisfied, and slow, like all of Sam Shepard's writing, but distinguished by fine performances and rich Southwestern atmosphere by Wenders and cinematographer Robby Müller. This won raves from many critics, so it may be a matter of personal taste. [R]▼●

Paris Trout (1991) **C-100m.** ***½ D: Stephen Gyllenhaal. Dennis Hopper, Barbara Hershey, Ed Harris, Ray McKinnon, Tina Lifford, Darnita Henry, Eric Ware. Jarring drama, set in the late 1940s, about the mind and soul of an unrepentant racist, with Hopper (never better) as a Southerner who kills a 12-year-old black girl and cannot comprehend how he can be condemned for his action. Probing, bristling script by Pete Dexter, based on his National Book Award–winning novel. Though made as a theatrical film, this debuted in the U.S. on cable TV instead. [R]▼●

Paris Underground (1945) **97m.** **½ D: Gregory Ratoff. Constance Bennett, Gracie Fields, George Rigaud, Kurt Kreuger, Leslie Vincent, Charles Andre. Well-acted story of American Bennett and Brit-

isher Fields working in underground movement even while imprisoned in Nazi POW camp.
Paris Was Made for Lovers SEE: **Time for Loving, A**
Paris—When It Sizzles (1964) **C-110m.** *½ D: Richard Quine. William Holden, Audrey Hepburn, Noel Coward, Gregoire Aslan. Labored, unfunny comedy defeats a game cast, in story of screenwriter and secretary who act out movie fantasies in order to finish script. Paris locations, cameos by Marlene Dietrich and other stars don't help.▼
Park Row (1952) **83m.** *** D: Samuel Fuller. Gene Evans, Mary Welch, Herbert Heyes, Tina Rome, Forrest Taylor. Good, tough little film with newsman Evans starting his own paper, rivaling newspaper magnate Welch in 1880s N.Y.C.
Parlor, Bedroom and Bath (1931) **75m.** ** D: Edward Sedgwick. Buster Keaton, Charlotte Greenwood, Reginald Denny, Cliff Edwards, Dorothy Christy, Joan Peers, Sally Eilers, Natalie Moorhead, Edward Brophy. Buster plays a poor sap who's hired to pose as a great lover in this adaptation of a venerable stage farce filmed before in 1920. Great moments with Buster are few and far between in this contrived vehicle, but at least he's surrounded by compatible costars.▼●
Parnell (1937) **119m.** *½ D: John Stahl. Clark Gable, Myrna Loy, Edna May Oliver, Edmund Gwenn, Alan Marshal, Donald Crisp, Billie Burke, Donald Meek. Biography of popular and powerful Irish nationalist leader of the late 1800s whose career was destroyed by the exposure of adulterous affair. Plodding film fails to realize great story potential; this was (understandably) a notorious flop in 1937.
Parole, Inc. (1949) **71m.** ** D: Alfred Zeisler. Michael O'Shea, Turhan Bey, Evelyn Ankers, Virginia Lee, Lyle Talbot, Michael Whelan. By-the-numbers programmer in which federal agent O'Shea goes undercover to determine why dangerous convicts are mysteriously being granted paroles. ▼
Parrish (1961) **C-140m.** *½ D: Delmer Daves. Claudette Colbert, Troy Donahue, Karl Malden, Dean Jagger, Connie Stevens, Diane McBain, Sharon Hugueny, Sylvia Miles, Madeleine Sherwood. Slurpy soaper is so bad that at times it's funny; emotionless Donahue lives with his mother (Colbert, in her last theatrical film) on Jagger's tobacco plantation and falls in love with three girls there. Malden overplays tyrannical tobacco czar to the nth degree. Carroll O'Connor and Vincent Gardenia have small roles.▼
Parson and the Outlaw, The (1957) **C-71m.** *½ D: Oliver Drake. Anthony Dexter, Sonny Tufts, Marie Windsor, Buddy Rogers, Jean Parker, Bob Steele. Minor version of life and times of Billy the Kid.
Parson of Panamint, The (1941) **84m.** **½ D: William McGann. Charlie Ruggles, Ellen Drew, Phillip Terry, Joseph Schildkraut, Porter Hall. Minor offbeat Western with Terry as preacher in mining town, involved in murder while reforming the community.
Parting Glances (1986) **C-90m.** **½ D: Bill Sherwood. John Bolger, Richard Ganoung, Steve Buscemi, Adam Nathan, Patrick Tull, Kathy Kinney. Two longtime gay roommates spend their final 24 hours together before one leaves N.Y.C. on a job transfer. Earnest, intelligent drama is OK within its modest framework; subsidiary characters—one of them dying of AIDS (and played by Buscemi, in an eye-opening performance)—are more compelling than the two protagonists. This was Sherwood's only feature; he died of AIDS in 1990.▼
Partners (1982) **C-98m.** BOMB D: James Burrows. Ryan O'Neal, John Hurt, Kenneth McMillan, Robyn Douglass, Jay Robinson, Denise Galik, Rick Jason. Foolish, offensive parody of CRUISING, with straight cop O'Neal impersonating homosexual while investigating gay murder. Hurt is wasted as O'Neal's partner, who really is gay. Screenplay by Francis (LA CAGE AUX FOLLES) Veber. Undistinguished feature debut for TV comedy director Burrows. [R]▼
Parts: The Clonus Horror (1978) **C-90m.** ** D: Robert S. Fiveson. Tim Donnelly, Dick Sargent, Peter Graves, Paulette Breen, David Hooks, Keenan Wynn. Cleanly made programmer about an insidious government plan to start cloning the population. Watchable but uninspired. Video title: THE CLONUS HORROR. [R]▼
Part-Time Wife (1961-British) **70m.** *½ D: Max Varnel. Anton Rodgers, Nyree Dawn Porter, Kenneth J. Warren, Henry McCarthy. Lumbering account of Rodgers loaning wife Porter to scoundrel friend Warren, who wants to make an impression; wooden farce.
Part 2, Sounder (1976) **C-98m.** ***½ D: William A. Graham. Harold Sylvester, Ebony Wright, Taj Mahal, Annazette Chase, Darryl Young. Excellent follow-up to SOUNDER, retaining the dignity and human values in the continuing tale of a proud family of Depression-era Southern sharecroppers. [G]
Part 2, Walking Tall (1975) **C-109m.** ** D: Earl Bellamy. Bo Svenson, Luke Askew, Robert DoQui, Bruce Glover, Richard Jaeckel, Noah Beery, Jr. Tepid follow-up to ultraviolent movie about club-swinging Tennessee Sheriff Buford Pusser. Svenson now takes the role of the one-man crusader against organized crime, but makes him come off like a standard TV hero rather

than a real-life character. Sequel: FINAL CHAPTER—WALKING TALL. [PG]▼

Party, The (1968) **C-99m.** *** D: Blake Edwards. Peter Sellers, Claudine Longet, Marge Champion, Denny Miller, Gavin MacLeod, Steve Franken, Carol Wayne. Side-splitting gags highlight loosely structured film about chic Hollywood party attended by bumbling Indian actor (Sellers). Doesn't hold up to the very end, but has some memorable set-pieces. Panavision. ▼●

Party Crashers, The (1958) **78m.** *½ D: Bernard Girard. Mark Damon, Bobby Driscoll, Connie Stevens, Frances Farmer. Sleazy goings-on of teen-age gangs who become involved in reckless mayhem. Both Driscoll's and Farmer's last film.

Party Girl (1958) **C-99m.** *** D: Nicholas Ray. Robert Taylor, Cyd Charisse, Lee J. Cobb, John Ireland, Kent Smith. Crooked lawyer (Taylor) and showgirl (Charisse) try to break free from Chicago mob life. Charisse has a couple of torrid dance numbers; Ray's stylish treatment has won this film a cult following. CinemaScope. ▼●

Party Girl (1995) **C-98m.** **½ D: Daisy von Scherler Mayer. Parker Posey, Omar Townsend, Sasha von Scherler, Guillermo Diaz, Anthony DeSando, Donna Mitchell, Liev Schreiber, Nicole Bobbitt. Slim, low-budget film is fun, with Posey perfectly cast as a young N.Y.C. career woman without a career. Deciding she should be doing something more with her life than just throwing wild parties, she seeks job fulfillment (with admittedly no skills), and the N.Y. Public Library system will never be the same again. Posey is trendy and insouciant, likable and hilarious, and supporting cast scores as well—including the director's mother as Posey's godmother. Best bit: the Dewey Decimal Record-Spinning System! Later a TV series. [R]▼●

Party Girls For Sale SEE: **They Were So Young**

Party Line (1988) **C-91m.** BOMB D: William Webb. Richard Hatch, Shawn Weatherly, Leif Garrett, Greta Blackburn, Richard Roundtree. Sleazy, amateurish story capitalizing on the party-line fad in which young swingers call a special phone number to get a date—in this case, with murder. You'll want to hang up on this one long before the final credits. [R]▼●

Party's Over, The (1966-British) **94m.** ** D: Guy Hamilton. Oliver Reed, Ann Lynn, Clifford David, Louise Sorel, Eddie Albert. Sordid drama of wealthy American girl becoming involved with group of aimless London youths, with tragic results.

Party Wire (1935) **72m.** *** D: Erle C. Kenton. Jean Arthur, Victor Jory, Helen Lowell, Robert Allen, Charley Grapewin, Matt McHugh. Arthur is delightful as small-town girl wooed by prosperous prodigal son Jory, only to have their courtship maliciously distorted by local gossips via communal telephone party line. Insightful look at provincial mores employs a healthy dose of generic Capra-style humor.

Pascali's Island (1988-British) **C-104m.** **½ D: James Dearden. Ben Kingsley, Charles Dance, Helen Mirren, George Murcell, Sheila Allen, Nadim Sawalha. A largely ignored Turkish spy for the collapsing Ottoman Empire forms a duplicitous alliance with a mysterious Brit to rob the Greek island of Nisi of an archeological treasure. Well-acted drama isn't wholly successful, but it certainly holds your interest. Scripted by the director. [PG-13]▼●

Passage, The (1979-British) **C-99m.** *½ D: J. Lee Thompson. Anthony Quinn, James Mason, Malcolm McDowell, Patricia Neal, Kay Lenz, Christopher Lee, Paul Clemens, Michael Lonsdale, Marcel Bozzuffi. Trashy WW2 story of Basque guide Quinn helping chemist Mason and his family escape over the Pyrenees with Nazi fanatic McDowell in hot pursuit. McDowell's campy performance must be seen to be disbelieved. Technovision. [R]

Passage to India, A (1984-British) **C-163m.** *** D: David Lean. Judy Davis, Victor Banerjee, Peggy Ashcroft, James Fox, Alec Guinness, Nigel Havers, Richard Wilson, Antonia Pemberton, Michael Culver, Art Malik, Saeed Jaffrey. Meticulous adaptation of E. M. Forster novel set in the late 1920s, about an East/West culture clash, as a young, headstrong British woman goes to India for the first time, accompanied by the mother of her fiancé. Not a great movie, but so rich in flavor, nuance, and the sheer expressiveness of *film* that it offers great satisfaction, despite its shortcomings (and extreme length). Ashcroft won Best Supporting Actress Oscar for her fine performance as Mrs. Moore. Maurice Jarre also got an Oscar for his anachronistic score. Lean's last film. [PG]▼●

Passage to Marseille (1944) **110m.** **½ D: Michael Curtiz. Humphrey Bogart, Claude Rains, Michele Morgan, Philip Dorn, Sydney Greenstreet, Peter Lorre, George Tobias, Helmut Dantine, John Loder, Victor Francen, Vladimir Sokoloff, Edward (Eduardo) Ciannelli, Hans Conried. WW2 Devil's Island escape film marred by flashback-within-flashback confusion. Not a bad war film, just too talky; a disappointment considering the cast. Also shown in computer-colored version.▼●

Passage West (1951) **C-80m.** *½ D: Lewis R. Foster. John Payne, Dennis O'Keefe, Arleen Whelan, Mary Beth Hughes, Frank Faylen, Dooley Wilson. Outlaws join up with wagon train with predictable results.

Passed Away (1992) **C-96m.** **½ D: Charlie Peters. Bob Hoskins, Jack Warden, William Petersen, Helen Lloyd Breed, Maureen Stapleton, Pamela Reed, Tim Curry, Peter Riegert, Blair Brown, Patrick Breen, Nancy Travis, Teri Polo, Frances McDormand. Likable if lightweight black comedy about the death of a patriarch (Warden) and how it affects the various members of his colorful family. Pleasantly offbeat, with a very appealing cast, though Hoskins is never quite convincing as an American. Peters also scripted. [PG-13]▼

Passenger, The (1975-Italian) **C-119m.** **½ D: Michelangelo Antonioni. Jack Nicholson, Maria Schneider, Jenny Runacre, Ian Hendry, Steven Berkoff, Ambrose Bia. Enigmatic narrative about dissatisfied TV reporter on assignment in Africa who exchanges identities with an Englishman who has died suddenly in a hotel room. Some found this brilliant; judge for yourself. [PG]▼●

Passenger 57 (1992) **C-84m.** **½ D: Kevin Hooks. Wesley Snipes, Bruce Payne, Tom Sizemore, Alex Datcher, Bruce Greenwood, Robert Hooks, Elizabeth Hurley, Michael Horse, Ernie Lively. Snipes is a crack anti-terrorist expert planning early retirement when he is thrust into the middle of an airline hijacking perpetrated by vile arch-criminal (Payne). Watchable action fare has a few too many coincidences but delivers both on the ground and in the air, thanks largely to the two charismatic opponents. Costar Robert Hooks, who plays FBI agent Henderson, is the director's father. Panavision and J-D-C Scope. [R]▼●◗

Passing of Evil, The SEE: **Grasshopper, The**

Passion (1954) **C-84m.** ** D: Allan Dwan. Cornel Wilde, Yvonne De Carlo, Raymond Burr, Lon Chaney, Jr., Rodolfo Acosta, John Qualen, Anthony Caruso, Stuart Whitman. By-the-numbers Western set in Old California, with Wilde seeking vengeance against the murderers of his loved ones. Chaney and Burr lend solid support as a moronic thug and corrupt lawman.▼

Passion (1982-French-Swiss) **C-87m.** **½ D: Jean-Luc Godard. Isabelle Huppert, Hanna Schygulla, Michel Piccoli, Jerzy Radziwilowicz, Laszlo Szabo. Characters named Isabelle, Hanna, Michel, Jerzy and Laszlo are connected with the making of a film called PASSION, which seems to be more the visualization of a Rembrandt or Delacroix than an actual movie. Meanwhile, the extras are treated like cattle, and the moviemaking art is tainted by commerce. Truffaut's DAY FOR NIGHT celebrates the joy of filmmaking; this is, in its own way, an anti-movie. [R]▼

Passion and Valor SEE: **Love Is Forever**

Passionate Friends, The (1949-British) **95m.** **½ D: David Lean. Ann Todd, Trevor Howard, Claude Rains, Betty Ann Davies, Isabel Dean, Wilfrid Hyde-White. Predictable love triangle among the upper classes, enhanced by strong cast and Lean's craftsmanship. Based on H. G. Wells novel. Originally released in U.S. as ONE WOMAN'S STORY.

Passionate Plumber, The (1932) **73m.** ** D: Edward Sedgwick. Buster Keaton, Jimmy Durante, Irene Purcell, Polly Moran, Gilbert Roland, Mona Maris. Stilted adaptation of HER CARDBOARD LOVER as vehicle for Keaton, hired by Parisienne Purcell to make lover Roland jealous. Truly funny moments few and far between. ▼●

Passionate Sentry, The (1952-British) **84m.** ** D: Anthony Kimmins. Nigel Patrick, Peggy Cummins, Valerie Hobson, George Cole, A. E. Matthews, Anthony Bushell. Wispy romantic comedy about madcap gal who falls in love with a guard at Buckingham Palace. Retitled: WHO GOES THERE?

Passionate Stranger, The SEE: **Novel Affair, A**

Passionate Thief, The (1960-Italian) **105m.** **½ D: Mario Monicelli. Anna Magnani, Toto, Ben Gazzara, Fred Clark, Edy Vessel. Offbeat serio-comedy with Magnani a film extra, Gazzara a pickpocket, Toto an unemployed actor—all meshed together in a minor tale of love and larceny.▼

Passione d'Amore (1981-Italian-French) **C-118m.** **½ D: Ettore Scola. Bernard Giraudeau, Laura Antonelli, Valerie D' Obici, Jean-Louis Trintignant, Massimo Girotti, Bernard Blier. Hideous D'Obici pursues handsome cavalry officer Giraudeau, who's in love with gorgeous Antonelli. Intriguing Beauty and the Beast story is not completely convincing—and far from Scola's best work. Later musicalized for Broadway by Stephen Sondheim, as *Passion.* Aka PASSION OF LOVE.▼

Passion Fish (1992) **C-135m.** *** D: John Sayles. Mary McDonnell, Alfre Woodard, David Strathairn, Vondie Curtis-Hall, Angela Bassett, Nora Dunn, Sheila Kelley, Mary Portser, Maggie Renzi. Bitchy soap opera actress is paralyzed in an accident, and returns to her family home in Louisiana where she can be miserable to her heart's content—until her newest nurse/companion (Woodard) stands up to her. Funny, affecting, and satisfying entertainment—if a wee bit long. McDonnell's natural aloofness is put to perfect use by writer-director Sayles, who's given her the part of a lifetime. [R]▼●◗

Passion Flower (1930) **79m.** **½ D: William DeMille. Kay Francis, Kay Johnson, Charles Bickford, Winter Hall, Lewis Stone, ZaSu Pitts, Dickie Moore. Heiress Johnson defies her father by marrying the family chauffeur (Bickford), only to lose him to her glamorous cousin (Francis). Well-acted, effective triangle tale with some touching moments.

Passion Flower Hotel, The SEE: **Boarding School**

Passion in the Desert (1998-British) **C-**

93m. **½ D: Lavinia Currier. Ben Daniels, Michel Piccoli, Paul Meston, Kenneth Collard, Nadi Odeh, Auda Mohammed Badoul. Unusual drama, from Balzac novella, of French army captain (Daniels) and a painter in his charge (Piccoli) who get stranded in the Egyptian desert during 1798 Napoleonic campaign. The officer eventually comes face-to-face with a leopard, and their unorthodox relationship forms the crux of this story. Impressively crafted (cinematographer Alexei Rodionov also shot ORLANDO), though not for all tastes. Shot in 1995. [PG-13]▼

Passion of Anna, The (1969-Swedish) **C-101m.** ***½ D: Ingmar Bergman. Liv Ullmann, Bibi Andersson, Max von Sydow, Erland Josephson, Erik Hell. Stark drama, beautifully acted, about von Sydow, living alone on a barely populated island, and relationship with widow Ullmann, architect Josephson, and wife Andersson. Superior cinematography by Sven Nykvist. Original title was simply—and more accurately—A PASSION. [R]▼

Passion of Ayn Rand, The (1999) **C-115m. TVM** D: Christopher Menaul. Helen Mirren, Eric Stoltz, Julie Delpy, Peter Fonda, Sybil Temchen, Don McKellar. Passionate dramatization of the real-life 15-year love affair between novelist-philosopher Ayn Rand (author of *The Fountainhead*) and her handsome young protégé, Nathaniel Branden—in plain sight of Branden's girlfriend (later wife, who wrote the best-selling biography on which this was based) and Rand's rather ineffectual spouse, actor-turned-painter Frank O'Connor. Mirren's imperious, often arch Rand (née Alice Rosenbaum) is a true joy. Script by Howard Korder and Mary Gallagher. Made for cable. Above average. ▼

Passion of Beatrice, The SEE: **Beatrice**

Passion of Evil, The SEE: **Grasshopper, The**

Passion of Joan of Arc, The (1928-French) **117m.** **** D: Carl Theodor Dreyer. Maria Falconetti, Eugene Sylvain, Maurice Schutz. Joan of Arc's inquisition, trial, and burning at the stake; the scenario is based on transcript of historical trial. Masterfully directed, with groundbreaking use of close-ups; Falconetti glows in the title role. Photographed by Rudolph Maté.▼

Passion of Love SEE: **Passion d'Amore**

Passion of Mind (2000) **C-105m.** ** D: Alain Berliner. Demi Moore, Stellan Skarsgård, William Fichtner, Sinead Cusack, Peter Riegert. Romantic piffle about a woman who's either a Provence widow who dreams she's a glamorous New York literary agent . . . or vice versa. Matters are complicated when she falls in love with two very different men. Indie vehicle for Moore is sleek and watchable but plays like an International Foods Coffee version of THE DOUBLE LIFE OF VERONIQUE. Also similar to JULIA AND JULIA, although in this version scripter Ron Bass actually bothers to solve the mystery. Super 35. [R]

Passion Play SEE: **Love Letters** (1983)

Passions SEE: **Grasshopper, The**

Passport to Adventure SEE: **Passport to Destiny**

Passport to China (1961-British) **C-75m.** ** D: Michael Carreras. Richard Basehart, Alan Gifford, Athene Seyler, Burt Kwouk, Eric Pohlmann. Uninspired help-the-refugee-out-of-Red-China caper.

Passport to Destiny (1944) **64m.** ** D: Ray McCarey. Elsa Lanchester, Gordon Oliver, Lloyd Corrigan, Gavin Muir, Lenore Aubert, Fritz Feld. Tidy programmer with Elsa a patriotic scrubwoman determined to eliminate the Fuehrer. Retitled: PASSPORT TO ADVENTURE.

Passport to Pimlico (1949-British) **85m.** ***½ D: Henry Cornelius. Stanley Holloway, Margaret Rutherford, Betty Warren, Hermione Baddeley, Barbara Murray, Basil Radford, Naunton Wayne, Paul Dupuis, Michael Hordern. Salty farce of ancient treaty enabling small group of Brits to form their own bounded territory in the middle of London. Screenplay by Cornelius and T.E.B. Clarke.▼

Passport to Suez (1943) **71m.** **½ D: Andre De Toth. Warren William, Ann Savage, Eric Blore, Robert Stanford, Sheldon Leonard, Lloyd Bridges, Gavin Muir. Nazi spies lead sleuth William on a wild goose chase as part of a plan to blow up the Suez Canal in this well-made *Lone Wolf* entry with more comedy relief from Blore than usual.

Passport to Treason (1955-British) **70m.** *½ D: Robert S. Baker. Rod Cameron, Lois Maxwell, Clifford Evans. Minor drama, with Cameron trying to solve homicide case for sake of friend.

Pass the Ammo (1988) **C-97m.** BOMB D: David Beaird. Bill Paxton, Linda Kozlowski, Tim Curry, Annie Potts, Dennis Burkley, Glenn Withrow, Anthony Geary, Richard Paul. Shrill, heavy-handed spoof of televangelists that blunts its satiric edge by making its "heroes" (a young couple out to rob the church) so thoroughly disreputable. This subject cries for a better comedy. [R]▼●

Password Is Courage, The (1963-British) **116m.** *** D: Andrew L. Stone. Dirk Bogarde, Maria Perschy, Alfred Lynch, Nigel Stock, Reginald Beckwith, Richard Marner. Bogarde tops a fine cast in droll account of British soldier's plot to escape from WW2 prison camp. Metroscope.

Past Caring (1985-British) **C-77m.** ** D: Richard Eyre. Denholm Elliott, Emlyn Williams, Connie Booth, Joan Greenwood, Dave Atkins. Tepid, disappointing tale of roguish Elliott, approaching old age, who finds himself incarcerated in a home for senile senior citizens. Williams scores as an elderly homosexual bent on reliving his youth.

Pastime (1991) **C-94m.** **½ D: Robin B. Armstrong. William Russ, Glenn Plummer, Scott Plank, Noble Willingham, Jeffrey Tambor, Dierdre O'Connell, Ricky Paull Goldin. Quiet character study set in the world of minor-league baseball, circa 1957, focusing on a 41-year-old relief pitcher whose platitudes and gung-ho attitude alienate him from his younger, cockier teammates. Well-acted but drowsy little film does manage to catch the ambience of small-time baseball. Real-life major-league greats Ernie Banks, Bob Feller, Harmon Killebrew, Bill Mazeroski, Don Newcombe, and Duke Snider appear in minor roles. Film's climax shot at now-demolished Comiskey Park in Chicago. Aka ONE CUP OF COFFEE. [PG]▼●

Past Midnight (1992) **C-100m.** **½ D: Jan Eliasberg. Rutger Hauer, Natasha Richardson, Clancy Brown, Guy Boyd, Ernie Lively, Tom Wright. Romantic thriller of social worker becoming obsessed with her paroled killer client. Hauer (who's Dutch) and Richardson (who's British) sport pretty fair American accents playing two Oregonians. A theatrical film that premiered on cable TV instead. [R]▼●

Pat and Mike (1952) **95m.** *** D: George Cukor. Spencer Tracy, Katharine Hepburn, Aldo Ray, William Ching, Jim Backus, Carl (''Alfalfa'') Switzer, Charles Buchinski (Bronson), William Self, Chuck Connors. Hepburn is Pat, top female athlete; Tracy is Mike, her manager, in pleasing comedy, not up to duo's other films. Ray is good as thick-witted sports star. Written by Ruth Gordon and Garson Kanin; many sports notables appear briefly. Also shown in computer-colored version. ▼●

Patch Adams (1998) **C-115m.** **½ D: Tom Shadyac. Robin Williams, Daniel London, Monica Potter, Philip Seymour Hoffman, Bob Gunton, Josef Sommer, Irma P. Hall, Frances Lee McCain, Harve Presnell, Peter Coyote, Michael Jeter, Harold Gould, Ellen Albertini Dow, Richard Kiley. Pleasant movie based on the true story of a man who wants desperately to be a doctor and help people but rejects the sober protocol of medical school in favor of clowning and making a personal connection with patients. A natural role for Williams if there ever was one but the story, heroes and villains, are all set up a little too easily and obviously for us to derive real satisfaction at the end. Panavision. [PG-13]▼●◗

Patch of Blue, A (1965) **105m.** *** D: Guy Green. Sidney Poitier, Shelley Winters, Elizabeth Hartman, Wallace Ford, Ivan Dixon, John Qualen, Elisabeth Fraser. Sensitive drama of blind girl (Hartman) falling in love with black man (Poitier); well acted, not too sticky. Winters won Oscar as Hartman's harridan mother. Panavision.▼●

Paternity (1981) **C-94m.** *½ D: David Steinberg. Burt Reynolds, Beverly D' Angelo, Norman Fell, Paul Dooley, Elizabeth Ashley, Lauren Hutton, Juanita Moore, Mike Kellin. Bachelor Burt, the manager of Madison Square Garden, yearns to be a papa, so he hires waitress-music student D'Angelo as surrogate mother. Predictable comedy with lethargic performances. Actor-comic Steinberg's directorial debut. [PG]▼●

Pat Garrett & Billy the Kid (1973) **C-122m.** ** D: Sam Peckinpah. James Coburn, Kris Kristofferson, Richard Jaeckel, Katy Jurado, Chill Wills, Jason Robards, Bob Dylan, Rita Coolidge, Jack Elam, R. G. Armstrong, Slim Pickens, Harry Dean Stanton, L. Q. Jones, Barry Sullivan, Elisha Cook, Jr. Revisionist look at Sheriff Garrett (Coburn) and his pursuit of ex-crony Billy the Kid (Kristofferson) is interesting but far from grade-A Peckinpah; for one thing, there isn't enough contrast in the two low-key lead performances. Dylan's role is insignificant, but his score does include the hit ''Knockin' on Heaven's Door.'' The director's version now appears on homevideo and cable, and is a definite improvement over the badly paced 103m. that opened in 1973. Panavision. [R]▼●

Pather Panchali (1955-Indian) **112m.** ***½ D: Satyajit Ray. Kanu Banerji, Karuna Banerji, Subir Banerji, Runki Banerji, Uma Das Gupta, Chunibala Devi. Unrelenting study of a poverty-stricken Indian family in Bengal. Grippingly realistic, with Karuna and Subir Banerji outstanding as the mother and her young son Apu. Ray's feature debut, and the first of his ''Apu'' trilogy. Music by Ravi Shankar.▼

Pathfinder, The (1952) **C-78m.** *½ D: Sidney Salkow. George Montgomery, Helena Carter, Jay Silverheels, Elena Verdugo, Chief Yowlachie. Low-budget version of James Fenimore Cooper tale of 1750s Great Lakes area, with Indian and French attacks on Americans. Remade for TV in 1996.

Pathfinder (1988-Norwegian) **C-88m.** ***½ D: Nils Gaup. Mikkel Gaup, Nils Utsi, Svein Scharffenberg, Helgi Skulason, Sara Marit Gaup, Sverre Porsanger. A young boy agrees to lead a group of cutthroats to the hiding place of his fellow villagers, but takes them on a wild goose chase instead. Stunning realization of an ancient folk tale from Lapland is the first film ever made in the Lapp language—and a whale of an adventure, too. Panavision.▼

Pathfinder, The (1996-Canadian) **C-105m. TVM** D: Donald Shebib. Kevin Dillon, Graham Greene, Laurie Holden, Jaimz Woolvett, Michael Hogan, Frances Hyland, Russell Means, Stacy Keach. Atmospheric though episodic retelling of James Fenimore Cooper's French and Indian Wars saga and the friendship between Indian-raised Natty Bumppo and his adopted father Chingachgook. Keach chews the scenery in a few scenes as a pompous French general. Made for cable. Average.▼●

Paths of Glory (1957) **86m.** **** D: Stanley Kubrick. Kirk Douglas, Ralph Meeker, Adolphe Menjou, George Macready, Wayne Morris, Richard Anderson, Timothy Carey, Suzanne Christian, Bert Freed. During WW1, French general Macready orders his men on a suicidal charge; when they fail, he picks three soldiers to be tried and executed for cowardice. Shattering study of the insanity of war has grown even more profound with the years; stunningly acted and directed. Calder Willingham, Jim Thompson, and Kubrick adapted Humphrey Cobb's novel—based on fact.▼●◗

Patrick (1978-Australian) **C-96m.** *½ D: Richard Franklin. Susan Penhaligon, Robert Helpmann, Robert Thompson, Rod Mullinar, Bruce Barry, Julia Blake. Patrick's in a comatose state after violently murdering his mum, but his psychokinetic powers are still intact, as the hospital staff soon discovers in this tacky thriller. [PG]▼

Patriot, The (1986) **C-88m.** *½ D: Frank Harris. Gregg Henry, Simone Griffeth, Michael J. Pollard, Jeff Conaway, Leslie Nielsen, Stack Pierce, Glenn Withrow. Underwater action dominates this low-key action film. Dishonorably discharged Henry is recruited to retrieve a stolen nuclear warhead and redeem himself. [R]▼●

Patriot, The (1998) **C-90m.** BOMB D: Dean Semler. Steven Seagal, Gailard Sartain, L.Q. Jones, Camilla Belle, Dan Beene, Ron Andrews. A paunchy, sleepy-eyed Seagal plays a peaceful, bespectacled, ponytailed Rocky Mountain doctor who's kind to kids, animals and local Native Americans, but will snap your spine and shove the stem of a wine glass into your skull if he has to. Of course, he's the perfect man to combat a neo-Nazi militia using chemical warfare. Rock bottom, irresponsible star vehicle dumbs down and bloodies up serious subject matter for the yahoo crowd. Premiered in the U.S. on cable. Panavision. [R]▼◗

Patriot Games (1992) **C-116m.** *** D: Phillip Noyce. Harrison Ford, Anne Archer, Patrick Bergin, Thora Birch, Sean Bean, Richard Harris, James Earl Jones, James Fox, Samuel L. Jackson, Polly Walker. Edge-of-the-seat thriller has ex-CIA agent Jack Ryan (Ford) intervening in a terrorist attack—inspiring an Irish radical (Bean) to swear vengeance on him and his family. Ford's an ideal hero in this adaptation of Tom Clancy's book, with Archer and Birch rounding out the kind of family you want to root for—and do. Only the climactic chase doesn't ring true. Alec Baldwin previously played Ryan in THE HUNT FOR RED OCTOBER. Followed by CLEAR AND PRESENT DANGER. Panavision. [R]▼●◗

Patsy, The (1964) **C-101m.** ** D: Jerry Lewis. Jerry Lewis, Ina Balin, Everett Sloane, Keenan Wynn, Peter Lorre, John Carradine, Neil Hamilton, Nancy Kulp. When a top comedian is killed in a plane crash, his sycophants try to groom a bellhop (guess who?) into taking his place. Forced, unfunny combination of humor and pathos, much inferior to somewhat similar ERRAND BOY. Lorre's last film. ▼●

Pattern for Plunder SEE: **Bay of St. Michel, The**

Patterns (1956) **83m.** ***½ D: Fielder Cook. Van Heflin, Everett Sloane, Ed Begley, Beatrice Straight, Elizabeth Wilson. Trenchant, masterfully acted drama of greed and abuse of power in corporate America, about an all-powerful company head (Sloane) who makes life miserable for humanistic underling Begley. Much better than the similar EXECUTIVE SUITE. Scripted by Rod Serling from his 1956 *Kraft TV Theatre* production (which also starred Sloane and Begley).▼

Patti Rocks (1988) **C-86m.** ** D: David Burton Morris. Chris Mulkey, John Jenkins, Karen Landry, David L. Turk, Stephen Yoakum. Married male chauvinist engages an estranged male pal to accompany him on a marathon drive to visit the woman he's impregnated; she turns out to be a self-assured, no-nonsense type—the very opposite of how she's been portrayed. Low budget film has a compelling idea, but doesn't play nearly as well as it should. Same characters previously seen in Victoria Wozniak's LOOSE ENDS (1975). [R]▼●

Patton (1970) **C-169m.** **** D: Franklin Schaffner. George C. Scott, Karl Malden, Stephen Young, Michael Strong, Frank Latimore, James Edwards, Lawrence Dobkin, Michael Bates, Tim Considine. Milestone in screen biographies; Scott unforgettable as eccentric, brilliant General George Patton, whose temper often interferes with his command during WW2. Malden equally impressive as General Omar Bradley in intelligently written, finely wrought biographical war drama. Winner of seven Oscars, including Best Picture, Actor, Director, Screenplay (Francis Ford Coppola and Edmund H. North). Scott reprised the role 16 years later in the TVM, THE LAST DAYS OF PATTON. Dimension-150. [M/PG]▼●◗

Patty Hearst (1988) **C-108m.** *½ D: Paul Schrader. Natasha Richardson, William Forsythe, Ving Rhames, Dana Delany, Frances Fisher, Jodi Long, Olivia Barash. Stillborn dramatization of the newspaper heiress's kidnapping and subsequent brainwashing by the

Symbionese Liberation Army. Film never recovers from a deadly opening half hour that attempts to convey, from victim's point of view, the effects of highly orchestrated psychological torture. Richardson makes a strong impression, despite having almost nothing to work with. Screenplay by Nicholas Kazan. [R]▼●

Paula (1952) **80m.** **½ D: Rudolph Mate. Loretta Young, Kent Smith, Alexander Knox, Tommy Rettig. Young gives credibility to role of woman who repents for hit-and-run accident by helping injured child regain his speech.

Paul and Michelle (1974-British) **C-103m.** BOMB D: Lewis Gilbert. Sean Bury, Anicee Alvina, Keir Dullea, Catherine Allegret, Ronald Lewis. Why anyone would even *want* a sequel to FRIENDS requires investigation; further antics of those lovable teeny-boppers have about as much bearing on real life as anything Dullea encountered while going through the 2001 space-warp. [R]▼

Paulie (1998) **C-91m.** *** D: John Roberts. Gena Rowlands, Tony Shalhoub, Cheech Marin, Bruce Davison, Trini Alvarado, Jay Mohr, Buddy Hackett, Hallie Kate Eisenberg, Matt Craven, Bill Cobbs. Satisfying, enjoyable family film. A caged parrot in the basement of a scientific institution relates his colorful life story—passing from one owner to the next—to a friendly (and lonely) janitor. A sweet-natured film that dares not to be stupid; adults should enjoy it along with their kids. Mohr, who plays the sleazy Benny, is also the voice of Paulie. Written by Laurie Craig. [PG]▼●◗

Pauline at the Beach (1983-French) **C-94m.** *** D: Eric Rohmer. Amanda Langlet, Arielle Dombasle, Pascal Greggory, Feodor Atkine, Simon de la Brosse, Rosette. Witty, entertaining comedy of morals and manners that contrasts the hypocrisy of adult relationships and the straightforwardness of young people, as seen when a teenage girl (Langlet) spends the summer with her sexy, self-possessed older cousin (Dombasle). The third of Rohmer's "Comedies and Proverbs" series. [R]▼●

Pawnbroker, The (1965) **116m.** **** D: Sidney Lumet. Rod Steiger, Geraldine Fitzgerald, Brock Peters, Jaime Sanchez, Thelma Oliver, Juano Hernandez, Raymond St. Jacques. Important, engrossing film; Steiger is excellent as Sol Nazerman, a Jewish pawnbroker in Harlem who lives in a sheltered world with haunting memories of Nazi prison camps. Notable editing by Ralph Rosenblum and music by Quincy Jones. Edward Lewis Wallant's novel was adapted by David Friedkin and Morton Fine.▼●

Pawnee (1957) **C-80m.** ** D: George Waggner. George Montgomery, Bill Williams, Lola Albright, Francis J. McDonald, Raymond Hatton. Pat Western about Indian-raised white man with conflicting loyalties.

Payback (1999) **C-102m.** *½ D: Brian Helgeland. Mel Gibson, Gregg Henry, Maria Bello, Deborah Kara Unger, David Paymer, Bill Duke, Jack Conley, William Devane, Kris Kristofferson, John Glover, Lucy Alexis Liu. A slick robber is double-crossed and becomes so determined to exact revenge on his betrayer (Henry) and the crime syndicate to which he belongs that he takes on all comers, no matter how great the odds. Brutal story grows more ridiculous with each new plot turn. Based on *The Hunter,* the same Richard Stark (Donald E. Westlake) novel as POINT BLANK. James Coburn appears unbilled. Super 35. [R]▼●◗

Payday (1973) **C-103m.** ***½ D: Daryl Duke. Rip Torn, Ahna Capri, Elayne Heilveil, Cliff Emmich, Michael C. Gwynne. Solidly acted, sharply scripted (by Don Carpenter) tale of life on the road with country singer Torn. Engrossing and very well done: a sleeper. [R]▼

Payment Deferred (1932) **81m.** *** D: Lothar Mendes. Charles Laughton, Maureen O'Sullivan, Dorothy Peterson, Verree Teasdale, Ray Milland, Billy Bevan. Very theatrical yet engrossing little film about a milquetoast who finds himself tangled up in murder. Laughton is at his most idiosyncratic, with all manner of facial grimaces and gestures.

Payment on Demand (1951) **90m.** *** D: Curtis Bernhardt. Bette Davis, Barry Sullivan, Peggie Castle, Jane Cowl, Kent Taylor, Betty Lynn, John Sutton, Frances Dee, Otto Kruger. Well-handled chronicle of Davis-Sullivan marriage, highlighting events which lead to divorce.

Pay or Die (1960) **111m.** **½ D: Richard Wilson. Ernest Borgnine, Zohra Lampert, Al Austin, John Duke, Robert Ellenstein, Franco Corsaro, John Marley, Mario Siletti. Flavorful account of Mafia activities in 1910s N.Y.C.; sturdy performances.▼

Payroll (1961-British) **94m.** **½ D: Sidney Hayers. Michael Craig, Francoise Prevost, Billie Whitelaw, William Lucas, Kenneth Griffith, Tom Bell. Well-handled account involving widow of payroll guard tracking down culprits.

PCU (1994) **C-80m.** ** D: Hart Bochner. Jeremy Piven, Chris Young, David Spade, Megan Ward, Jon Favreau, Jessica Walter, Sarah Trigger, Jake Busey, Gale Mayron, Kevin Thigpen, George Clinton and Parliament Funkadelic. Political correctness is out of control at Port Chester University which leads to the inevitable clash between a cadre of overly militant student groups and a coed group of dormies who revel in their political *in*correctness. As campus comedies go, this one gets failing grades. [PG-13]▼●

Peace Killers, The (1971) **C-88m.** *½ D: Douglas Schwartz. Clint Ritchie, Jesse Walton, Paul Prokop, Darlene Duralia. Motorcycle hoods ravage peaceful commune like Attila the Hun. Sick, Sick, Sick. [R]▼

Peacemaker, The (1956) **82m.** ** D: Ted Post. James Mitchell, Rosemarie Bowe, Robert Armstrong, Jan Merlin, Dorothy Patrick, Jess Barker. Ex-gunslinger, now clergyman, tries to clean up the town.

Peacemaker (1990) **C-90m.** ** D: Kevin S. Tenney. Robert Forster, Lance Edwards, Hilary Shepard, Robert Davi, Bert Remsen. Yet another alien cop after alien villain movie, pitting Forster against Edwards, with novel twist: both claim to be the cop, causing Earthwoman Shepard any number of problems. Lots of stunts and action, but also lots of absolutely awful wisecracks. Written by the director. [R]▼●

Peacemaker, The (1997) **C-123m.** **½ D: Mimi Leder. George Clooney, Nicole Kidman, Armin Mueller-Stahl, Marcel Iures, Alexander Baluev, Rene Medvesek, Gary Werntz, Randall Batinkoff, Michael Boatman. A nuclear explosion in Russia—which turns out to be a terrorist act—triggers immediate response by a U.S. government troubleshooter team led by an inexperienced Kidman and a cocky, shoot-from-the-hip field agent (Clooney). Good action scenes are set in the midst of a confusing, barely believable yarn, which yields diminishing results as one climax after another piles up. Super 35. [R]▼●◗

Pearl, The (1948) **77m.** *** D: Emilio Fernandez. Pedro Armendariz, Maria Elena Marques. Mexican-filmed John Steinbeck tale of poor fisherman whose life is unhappily altered by finding valuable pearl; a bit heavy-handed. Beautifully photographed by Gabriel Figueroa.▼

Pearl of Death, The (1944) **69m.** *** D: Roy William Neill. Basil Rathbone, Nigel Bruce, Evelyn Ankers, Miles Mander, Rondo Hatton, Dennis Hoey, Richard Nugent. Deft *Sherlock Holmes* entry has the sleuth searching for six busts of Napoleon, one of which contains the Borgia pearl, before all the owners are murdered by ''The Creeper'' (Hatton). Suspenseful story inspired Universal to recast Hatton in several more ''Creeper'' films.▼

Pearl of the South Pacific (1955) **C-86m.** *½ D: Allan Dwan. Virginia Mayo, Dennis Morgan, David Farrar, Murvyn Vye. Greedy fortunehunters mix with island natives as they search for a hidden temple and untold riches. A so-bad-it's-funny relic of its era. SuperScope.▼

Pebble and the Penguin, The (1995-U.S.-Irish) **C-74m.** *½ No director credited. Voices of Martin Short, James Belushi, Tim Curry, Annie Golden, Angelyne Ball, B.J. Ward, Hamilton Camp, Will Ryan; narrated by Shani Wallis. Nice-guy penguin ends up on an aquatic globe-trotting odyssey with a gruff sidekick named Rocko, all for the love of a lady who's coveted by an evil penguin rival. Some movies have the smell of doom all over them; this animated feature for kids from the Don Bluth studio (with songs by Barry Manilow) is one of them. [G]▼●◗

Pecker (1998) **C-87m.** *** D: John Waters. Edward Furlong, Christina Ricci, Lili Taylor, Mary Kay Place, Martha Plimpton, Brendan Sexton III, Patricia Hearst, Jean Schertler, Bess Armstrong, Mink Stole. Pecker (Furlong) is a happy-go-lucky guy who loves taking pictures of life as he sees it. When a N.Y.C. art gallery owner ''discovers'' his work and he's embraced by the art scene, he loses his anonymity, and many of his most cherished friendships. Another slice of Baltimore life from Waters, perhaps his cheeriest yet, with doggedly likable characters in some of the unlikeliest settings. [R] ▼●◗

Peck's Bad Boy (1921) **51m.** *** D: Sam Wood. Jackie Coogan, Wheeler Oakman, Doris May, Raymond Hatton, Lillian Leighton. Still-fresh and enjoyable vehicle for child-star Coogan as young mischief-maker; clever card-titles written by humorist Irvin S. Cobb.▼●

Peck's Bad Boy (1934) **70m.** **½ D: Edward Cline. Jackie Cooper, Thomas Meighan, Jackie Searle, O. P. Heggie. Cooper is ideally cast as the title character, who enjoys an idyllic relationship with widowed dad Meighan. Trouble comes when his obnoxious aunt and bratty cousin arrive on the scene.▼

Peck's Bad Boy With the Circus (1938) **78m.** ** D: Edward Cline. Tommy Kelly, Ann Gillis, Edgar Kennedy, Billy Gilbert, Benita Hume, Spanky MacFarland, Grant Mitchell. Standard circus story slanted for kiddies. Kennedy and Gilbert wrap this one up.▼

Pedestrian, The (1974-German) **C-97m.** ***½ D: Maximilian Schell. Gustav Rudolf Sellner, Peter Hall, Maximilian Schell, Gila von Weitershausen. Excellent award-winner examines death and guilt, when successful industrialist Sellner is revealed to have been a Nazi officer who participated in the slaughter of a Greek village. Veteran actresses Elisabeth Bergner, Françoise Rosay, Lil Dagover and Peggy Ashcroft appear in one scene. [PG]▼

Peeper (1975) **C-87m.** *½ D: Peter Hyams. Michael Caine, Natalie Wood, Kitty Winn, Thayer David, Liam Dunn, Dorothy Adams. Tepid take-off of 40s detective dramas with Caine becoming involved with a weird family while trying to locate the long-lost daughter of his client. Best bit: the opening credits, recited by Bogart impersonator Jerry Lacy. Aka FAT CHANCE. Panavision. [PG]

Peeping Tom (1960-British) **C-101m.** ***

D: Michael Powell. Carl Boehm, Moira Shearer, Anna Massey, Maxine Audley, Brenda Bruce, Martin Miller. Sensational film—denounced in 1960—went on to develop a fervent following; personal feelings will dictate your reaction to story of psychopathic murderer who photographs his victims at the moment of death. Originally released in the U.S. at 86m. Director Powell plays the father of Boehm in the home-movie sequences. ▼●

Pee-wee's Big Adventure (1985) **C-90m.** **½ D: Tim Burton. Pee-wee Herman (Paul Reubens), Elizabeth Daily, Mark Holton, Diane Salinger, Tony Bill, Cassandra Peterson, James Brolin, Morgan Fairchild, Jan Hooks, Phil Hartman. A live-action cartoon (directed by former animator Burton) featuring the cartoonish Pee-wee, a nine-year-old boy in a grown-up's body. Some real laughs and clever ideas as Pee-wee searches for his stolen bicycle, but not enough to sustain a feature-length film. Best sequence: the tour of the Alamo. Wonderful music by Danny Elfman. [PG]▼●

Peggy (1950) **C-77m.** **½ D: Frederick de Cordova. Diana Lynn, Charles Coburn, Charlotte Greenwood, Rock Hudson, Jerome Cowan, Barbara Lawrence. Lightweight comedy of sisters Lynn and Lawrence entered in Rose Bowl Parade beauty contest.

Peggy Sue Got Married (1986) **C-104m.** **½ D: Francis Coppola. Kathleen Turner, Nicolas Cage, Barry Miller, Catherine Hicks, Joan Allen, Kevin J. O'Connor, Jim Carrey, Lisa Jane Persky, Barbara Harris, Don Murray, Maureen O'Sullivan, Leon Ames, Helen Hunt, John Carradine, Sofia Coppola, Sachi Parker. 43-year-old woman, on the verge of divorce, magically travels back in time to her senior year in high school and has to deal with (among other things) her boyfriend and future husband. Turner's radiant star-power bolsters this pleasant, often wistful film, whose script leaves far too many plot threads dangling. Cage's annoying performance as the boyfriend is another debit. [PG-13]▼●◗

Peg o' My Heart (1933) **89m.** *** D: Robert Z. Leonard. Marion Davies, Onslow Stevens, J. Farrell MacDonald, Irene Browne, Juliette Compton, Alan Mowbray. Sweet, old-fashioned vehicle for Davies as spunky Irish lass who's separated from her father and brought to ritzy English manor, to fulfill terms of inheritance. Corny but fun. Filmed in 1923 with Laurette Taylor.

Peking Blonde (1967-French) **C-80m.** *½ D: Nicolas Gessner. Mirielle Darc, Claudio Brook, Edward G. Robinson, Pascale Roberts, Francoise Brion. Obscure melodrama with Chinese, Russian and American spies searching for missile information and a pearl. Robinson looks bored in a small role as a CIA agent. Aka THE BLONDE FROM PEKING. Franscope.▼

Peking Express (1951) **95m.** **½ D: William Dieterle. Joseph Cotten, Corinne Calvet, Edmund Gwenn, Marvin Miller, Benson Fong. Remake of SHANGHAI EXPRESS lacks flavor or distinction. Cotten is the doctor and Calvet the shady lady he encounters on train.

Peking Opera Blues (1986-Hong Kong) **C-104m.** ***½ D: Tsui Hark. Lin Ching-Hsia, Sally Yeh, Cherie Chung, Mark Cheng, Po-chih Leong. Marvelously entertaining adventure yarn, set in 1913 China, which follows three women who become entangled with revolutionary guerillas. Dazzling mix of comedy, drama, action and incredible stunts, all set at a breathless pace by Hark. Proves you can make 'em like they used to, but not (perhaps) in America.◗

Pelican Brief, The (1993) **C-141m.** *** D: Alan J. Pakula. Julia Roberts, Denzel Washington, Sam Shepard, John Heard, Tony Goldwyn, James B. Sikking, William Atherton, Robert Culp, Stanley Tucci, Hume Cronyn, John Lithgow, Anthony Heald, Cynthia Nixon, Jake Weber. Entertaining thriller based on John Grisham's best-selling book about a law student whose theory (or brief) about the conspiracy behind the assassination of two Supreme Court justices places her in jeopardy. The only person who can help her: investigative reporter Washington. Well cast (with Julia a perfect pick for the lead) and well crafted, though the suspense starts to peter out toward the finish. Panavision. [PG-13]▼●◗

Pelle the Conqueror (1988-Danish-Swedish) **C-150m.** ***½ D: Bille August. Max von Sydow, Pelle Hvenegaard, Erik Paaske, Kristina Törnqvist, Morten Jorgensen. Wonderful 19th-century drama about a humble old widower (von Sydow) and his young son Pelle (Hvenegaard), Swedish immigrants in Denmark. They are simple folk with simple, modest dreams, yet they must valiantly struggle for survival in a world rife with everyday cruelties and injustices. The life-sustaining closeness between father and son is especially poignant. Martin Andersen Nexo's four-volume novel (only a fraction of which is depicted here) was adapted by the director. Oscar winner as Best Foreign Film. [PG-13]▼●

Penalty, The (1941) **81m.** ** D: Harold S. Bucquet. Edward Arnold, Lionel Barrymore, Marsha Hunt, Robert Sterling, Gene Reynolds, Veda Ann Borg. Unengrossing mystery-drama of F.B.I. agent's scheme to catch gangster by using his son for bait. Good cast in dull script.

Pendulum (1969) **C-106m.** **½ D: George Schaefer. George Peppard, Jean Seberg, Richard Kiley, Charles McGraw, Madeleine Sherwood, Robert F. Lyons, Marj Dusay, Isabel Sanford, Dana Elcar. Half-baked whodunit has intriguing aspects but leaves too many loose ends, as police captain Peppard is suddenly accused of murder. Smoothly done, with flashy role for Sherwood as mother of young criminal, good score by Walter Scharf, but no great shakes. [M]▼●

Penelope (1966) **C-97m.** *½ D: Arthur Hiller. Natalie Wood, Ian Bannen, Dick Shawn, Peter Falk, Jonathan Winters, Lila Kedrova, Lou Jacobi, Jerome Cowan. Neglected Nat robs her husband's bank of $60,000 in this quite unfunny comedy; Winters' bit lasts only three minutes. Panavision.

Penguin Pool Murder (1932) **70m.** *** D: George Archainbaud. Edna May Oliver, James Gleason, Mae Clarke, Robert Armstrong, Donald Cook, Clarence Wilson, Edgar Kennedy, Rochelle Hudson, Gustav von Seyffertitz, Sidney Miller. Schoolteacher Hildegarde Withers (Oliver) helps cigar-chomping cop Oscar Piper (Gleason) to solve a grisly murder in an aquarium. First of the short-lived but entertaining *Hildegarde Withers* series based on the stories of Stuart Palmer.●

Penitent, The (1988) **C-94m.** **½ D: Cliff Osmond. Raul Julia, Armand Assante, Rona Freed, Julie Carmen, Lucy Reina. Odd, ironic little fable bites off more than it can chew, with ex-con Assante seducing pal Julia's young wife. Set in a remote town whose villagers each year reenact Christ's crucifixion—which, of course, plays a major part in the proceedings. Actor Osmond's directing debut. Filmed in 1986. [PG-13]▼

Penitentiary (1979) **C-99m.** **½ D: Jamaa Fanaka. Leon Isaac Kennedy, Thommy Pollard, Hazel Spears, Badja Djola, Gloria Delaney, Chuck Mitchell. Predictable but impassioned prison film, produced, directed and written by Fanaka, about a young black man (Kennedy) wrongly accused and imprisoned who improves his lot by boxing. Hard-hitting look at corruption, violence and homosexuality of daily prison life. Followed by several sequels. [R]▼

Penitentiary II (1982) **C-103m.** BOMB D: Jamaa Fanaka. Leon Isaac Kennedy, Ernie Hudson, Mr. T., Glynn Turman, Peggy Blow, Malik Carter, Cephaus Jaxon, Marvin Jones. Atrocious, disappointing sequel, with Kennedy back in prison and the ring. Leon Isaac plays "Too Sweet," the villain's name is "Half Dead," the viewer is "Ripped Off." [R]▼

Penitentiary III (1987) **C-91m.** *½ D: Jamaa Fanaka. Leon Isaac Kennedy, Anthony Geary, Steve Antin, Ric Mancini, Kessler Raymond, Jim Bailey. An improvement over number II—but that's not saying very much. Here, Kennedy is back in jail, where both warden and mob kingpin want him for their boxing teams. Silly and mindless time killer. [R]▼

Penn & Teller Get Killed (1989) **C-90m.** ** D: Arthur Penn. Penn Jillette, Teller, Caitlin Clarke, David Patrick Kelly, Jon Cryer, Christopher Durang, Leonardo Cimino, Celia McGuire. The bad boys of magic, guesting on a nationally televised talk show, touch off gore galore when partner Penn speculates how much fun life might be if some viewer would attempt to kill him. Barely released effort does have the courage of some sicko comic convictions. [R]▼●

Pennies From Heaven (1936) **81m.** **½ D: Norman Z. McLeod. Bing Crosby, Edith Fellows, Madge Evans, Donald Meek, Louis Armstrong. Minor but pleasant Crosby vehicle about a self-styled troubadour and drifter who befriends orphaned girl (Fellows) and her grandfather (Meek). Bing's rendition of title tune is classic.▼

Pennies From Heaven (1981) **C-107m.** *** D: Herbert Ross. Steve Martin, Bernadette Peters, Christopher Walken, Jessica Harper, Vernel Bagneris, John McMartin, Jay Garner, Tommy Rall. A unique, remarkable film, parts of which are greater than the whole. Dennis Potter adapted his own British TV mini-series about a sheet-music salesman during the Depression whose restless, unhappy life is sharply contrasted with cheery songs of the day. Stunning 1930s-style musical numbers (set to original recordings) clash with bleak, Edward Hopper-esque vision of the period. The mixture is intellectually provocative, but troubling as entertainment. Beautifully photographed by Gordon Willis and designed by Ken Adam. [R]▼●

Penn of Pennsylvania SEE: **Courageous Mr. Penn**.

Penny Princess (1951-British) **C-91m.** *** D: Val Guest. Dirk Bogarde, Yolande Donlan, Kynaston Reeves. Charming froufrou of American Donlan going to Europe to collect inheritance of small principality, and Bogarde who courts her.

Penny Serenade (1941) **118m.** ***½ D: George Stevens. Irene Dunne, Cary Grant, Beulah Bondi, Edgar Buchanan, Ann Doran, Eva Lee Kuney. Quintessential soap opera, with Dunne and Grant as couple who adopt baby after their unborn baby dies. A wonderful tearjerker; scripted by Morrie Ryskind, from Martha Cheavens's story. Also shown in computer-colored version. ▼●◗

Penrod and His Twin Brother (1938) **63m.** ** D: William McGann. Billy Mauch, Bobby Mauch, Frank Craven, Spring Byington, Charles Halton. Penrod gets blamed for something he didn't do; answer is his lookalike who's really guilty. Vaguely captures 1900s Midwest America.

Penrod and Sam (1937) **64m.** **½ D: William McGann. Billy Mauch, Frank Craven, Spring Byington, Craig Reynolds, Bernice Pilot. Based on Booth Tarkington characters, family-style film relates tale of Mauch getting involved with bank robbers.

Penrod's Double Trouble (1938) **61m.** ** D: Lewis Seiler. Billy Mauch, Bobby Mauch, Dick Purcell, Gene Lockhart, Kathleen Lockhart, Hugh O'Connell. There's a reward up for Penrod's return, but a lookalike is turned in instead. OK for younger audiences; based on Booth Tarkington characters.

Penthouse (1933) **90m.** ***½ D: W. S. Van Dyke. Warner Baxter, Myrna Loy, Charles Butterworth, Mae Clarke, C. Henry Gordon. Terrific comedy-melodrama, with Baxter as criminal lawyer who enlists the help of sprightly call-girl Loy to nail a crime kingpin. A neglected gem. Remade as SOCIETY LAWYER. ●

Penthouse, The (1967-British) **C-96m.** *½ D: Peter Collinson. Suzy Kendall, Terence Morgan, Tony Beckley, Martine Beswick. Lurid thriller of adulterous couple whose "love nest" is invaded by two thugs who, by torture, bring out true nature of the pair.

People Against O'Hara, The (1951) **102m.** **½ D: John Sturges. Spencer Tracy, Pat O'Brien, Diana Lynn, John Hodiak, Eduardo Ciannelli, Jay C. Flippen, James Arness, Arthur Shields, William Campbell. Middling drama, with Tracy a noted criminal lawyer who repents for unethical behavior during a case. Look fast for Charles Bronson as one of Campbell's brothers.●

People Next Door, The (1970) **C-93m.** ** D: David Greene. Deborah Winters, Eli Wallach, Julie Harris, Stephen McHattie, Hal Holbrook, Cloris Leachman, Rue McClanahan, Nehemiah Persoff. JP Miller's adaptation of his TV play has dated pretty badly; Wallach and Harris' handwringing concern over their junkie teenage daughter now seems stiff, and Winters' overacting just the opposite. Good cast and intentions, but there are many other, better films on the topic. [R]▼

People's Enemy SEE: **Prison Train**

People That Time Forgot, The (1977-British) **C-90m.** **½ D: Kevin Connor. Patrick Wayne, Doug McClure, Sarah Douglas, Dana Gillespie, Thorley Walters, Shane Rimmer. OK sequel to THE LAND THAT TIME FORGOT. Wayne leads a party back to mysterious island in 1919 to find friend McClure, lost three years before. Based on Edgar Rice Burroughs' book, film has some pretty fierce monsters, though special effects are erratic. [PG]▼

People Toys SEE: **Devil Times Five**

People Under the Stairs, The (1991) **C-102m.** *½ D: Wes Craven. Brandon Adams, Everett McGill, Wendy Robie, A. J. Langer, Ving Rhames, Sean Whalen. Hoping to help his ailing mother and prevent their eviction from a ghetto slum, 13-year-old Adams finds himself trapped in the bizarre home of their insane, murderous landlords, McGill and Robie. Very strange horror movie (with occasional comedy touches) turns out to be a social parable about the exploitation of the Have-Nots by the Haves. Ambitious but extremely uneven. [R]▼●

People vs. Dr. Kildare, The (1941) **78m.** ** D: Harold S. Bucquet. Lew Ayres, Lionel Barrymore, Laraine Day, Bonita Granville, Alma Kruger, Red Skelton, Tom Conway, Walter Kingsford, Chick Chandler, Diana Lewis, Marie Blake, Nell Craig, Frank Orth. Verbose Kildare entry finds the medic being sued for malpractice after operating on ice skater Granville's leg. Skelton's comic relief is more annoying than amusing.

People Vs. Larry Flynt, The (1996) **C-127m.** ***½ D: Milos Forman. Woody Harrelson, Courtney Love, Edward Norton, Brett Harrelson, Donna Hanover, James Cromwell, Crispin Glover, Vincent Schiavelli, James Carville, Richard Paul, Oliver Reed, Miles Chapin. Engrossing saga of an unlikely American "hero": controversial, self-proclaimed smut peddler Larry Flynt, who starts *Hustler* magazine in the 1970s and quickly discovers that he must fight for freedom of speech in order to keep it on the newsstands. Harrelson is perfect as the mercurial, unpredictable publisher, Love is just right as his loyal but unconventional wife, and Norton is excellent as his long-suffering lawyer. Climactic showdown at the Supreme Court is a dramatic powerhouse. Screenplay by Scott Alexander and Larry Karaszewski. The real Flynt appears briefly as a Cincinnati judge. Panavision. [R]▼●◗

People Will Talk (1935) **67m.** **½ D: Alfred Santell. Mary Boland, Charles Ruggles, Leila Hyams, Dean Jagger, Ruthelma Stevens, Hans Steinke. Slim comedy about married couple pretending to fight to teach daughter a lesson. Boland and Ruggles could read a newspaper and make it funny.

People Will Talk (1951) **110m.** ***½ D: Joseph L. Mankiewicz. Cary Grant, Jeanne Crain, Finlay Currie, Walter Slezak, Hume Cronyn, Sidney Blackmer, Margaret Hamilton. Genuinely offbeat, absorbing comedy-drama of philosophical doctor Grant, who insists on treating his patients as human beings; a small-minded colleague (Cronyn) is intimidated by his radical approach to doctoring and sets out to defame him. Fine cast in talky but most worthwhile film, which features obvious parallels to the then-current HUAC investigation and McCarthy witchhunt.▼

Pepe (1960) **C-157m.** BOMB D: George Sidney. Cantinflas, Dan Dailey, Shirley Jones, 35 guest stars. Incredibly long, pointless film wastes talents of Cantinflas and many, many others (Edward G. Robinson, Maurice Chevalier, etc.). This one's only if you're desperate. Originally released at 195m. CinemaScope.

Pepe Le Moko (1937-French) **86m.** **** D: Julien Duvivier. Jean Gabin, Mireille Balin, Gabriel Gabrio, Lucas Gridoux. Gabin is magnetic (in role that brought him international prominence) as gangster who eludes capture in Casbah section of Algiers, until he is lured out of hiding by a beautiful woman. Exquisitely photographed and directed; faithfully remade the following year as ALGIERS, later musicalized as CASBAH.▼

Pepi, Luci, Bom (1980-Spanish) **C-80m.** *½ D: Pedro Almodóvar. Carmen Maura, Felix Rotaeta, Olvido Gara, Eva Siva. Almodóvar's initial feature is the story of Pepi (Maura), an heiress/rape victim who becomes an advertising executive; meanwhile, housewife Luci (Siva), whose husband had raped Pepi, leaves him and commences a lesbian relationship with Bom (Gara), a rock singer. Raunchy and outrageous, but poorly made and devoid of laughs. Aka PEPI, LUCI, BOM AND THE OTHER GIRLS and PEPI, LUCI, BOM AND OTHER GIRLS LIKE MOM.▼

Peppermint Soda (1977-French) **C-97m.** *** D: Diane Kurys. Eleanore Klarwein, Odile Michel, Coralie Clement, Marie-Veronique Maurin. Sensitive, keenly realized autobiographical (by Kurys, who also scripted) examination of early adolescence, complete with disciplinarian teacher, parents' divorce, menstrual cramps, first love. Followed by COCKTAIL MOLOTOV; same theme reworked by Kurys 13 years later in C'EST LA VIE. [PG]▼

Percy (1971 British) **C-100m.** *½ D: Ralph Thomas. Hywel Bennett, Denholm Elliott, Elke Sommer, Britt Ekland, Cyd Hayman, Janet Key. Bennett receives the world's first penis transplant and, curious, sets out to learn about its previous owner. Some interesting points could've been made, but Thomas apparently thought he was making a *Carry On* film; too bad. Followed by PERCY'S PROGRESS. [R]

Percy and Thunder (1992) **C-90m. TVM** D: Ivan Dixon. James Earl Jones, Courtney B. Vance, Billy Dee Williams, Robert Wuhl, Gloria Reuben, Gloria Foster, Zakes Mokae, Lloyd Battista, John Capodice, Tony Cox, Henry Darrow, Antonio Fargas. Percy (Jones) is a crafty, ornery fight trainer who "coulda been a contender." Thunder (Vance) is the up-and-coming middleweight boxer he trains. Together they maintain their integrity and resist corruption, even when dealing with a slick, all-powerful Don King–like promoter (Williams). Jones' performance is the entire show in this otherwise ordinary boxing drama. Made for cable. Average.▼

Percy's Progress SEE: **It's Not the Size That Counts**

Perez Family, The (1995) **C-112m.** **½ D: Mira Nair. Marisa Tomei, Anjelica Huston, Alfred Molina, Chazz Palminteri, Trini Alvarado, Celia Cruz, Diego Wallraff, Angela Lanza, Ranjit Chowdhry, Ellen Cleghorne, Jose Felipe Padron, Lazaro Perez, Vincent Gallo. Cuban plantation owner, imprisoned for twenty years, is finally released in 1980 and allowed to join the boat migration to Florida, where he yearns to see his wife and daughter; along the way he meets a fiery young woman who has no ties but longs for a better life in America. Meandering comedy-drama has some pleasant and poignant moments, but never quite takes off. Strongest asset: Tomei's strong, sexy (and convincing) performance. Adapted by Robin Swicord from Christine Bell's novel. [R] ▼●

Perfect (1985) **C-120m.** *½ D: James Bridges. John Travolta, Jamie Lee Curtis, Jann Wenner, Anne De Salvo, Stefan Gierasch, Laraine Newman, Marilu Henner, David Paymer. *Rolling Stone* reporter Travolta is writing an exposé of L.A. health clubs but finds himself attracted to aerobics instructor Curtis, whom he's about to trash in print. A smug, overlong, misguided, miscast movie, with hints of intelligent intentions; written by Bridges and reporter Aaron Latham. Real-life *Rolling Stone* editor Wenner plays himself. Wait till you hear John and Jamie Lee expound on Emersonian values! Panavision. [R]▼●

Perfect Couple, A (1979) **C-110m.** *** D: Robert Altman. Paul Dooley, Marta Heflin, Titos Vandis, Belita Moreno, Henry Gibson, Dimitra Arliss, Alan Nicholls, Ted Neeley. Offbeat but endearing romantic comedy about unlikely match-up (by computer dating) of straitlaced Dooley, under the thumb of his overbearing father, and singer Heflin, whose life is wrapped up with her familial rock group. Enjoyable music by Neeley's *ad hoc* group Keepin' 'em Off the Streets. [PG]

Perfect Friday (1970-British) **94m.** *** D: Peter Hall. Stanley Baker, Ursula Andress, David Warner, Patience Collier, T.P. McKenna. Staid bank employee Baker decides to break loose, and plans daring heist, with beautiful Andress and her oddball husband Warner in cahoots. Entertaining caper movie with some delicious twists. [R]

Perfect Furlough, The (1958) **C-93m.** **½ D: Blake Edwards. Tony Curtis, Janet Leigh, Keenan Wynn, Linda Cristal, Elaine Stritch, King Donovan, Troy Donahue. Diverting comedy of soldier Curtis winning trip to France, romancing military psychiatrist Leigh. CinemaScope.▼

Perfect Gentlemen (1978) **C-100m. TVM** D: Jackie Cooper. Lauren Bacall, Ruth Gordon, Sandy Dennis, Lisa Pelikan, Robert Alda, Stephen Pearlman. Engaging bank heist tale by Nora Ephron involving three prison widows and a safe-cracking old lady. Bacall's TV movie debut. Above average.

Perfect Harmony (1991) **C-95m. TVM**

D: Will Mackenzie. Peter Scolari, Darren McGavin, Catherine Mary Stewart, Moses Gunn, Cleavon Little, Justin Whalin, Eugene Boyd, David Faustino, Richie Havens. Simplistic Disney drama of racial conflict at an exclusive Southern boys school in the 50s. Aimed squarely at younger viewers. Made for cable. Average.▼
Perfectly Normal (1990-Canadian-British) **C-106m.** ** D: Yves Simoneau. Robbie Coltrane, Michael Riley, Deborah Duchene, Kenneth Welsh, Eugene Lipinski. Slight, peculiar comedy about "perfectly normal" guy (Riley) who meets obnoxious restaurateur (Coltrane) with a shady past. Using Riley's inheritance, they open an Italian bistro where the waiters sing opera. Mild farce is too sluggish and awkward. Cowritten by Lipinski. Inventive photography by Alain Dostie. Video version runs 106m. [R]▼
Perfect Marriage, The (1946) **87m.** **½ D: Lewis Allen. Loretta Young, David Niven, Eddie Albert, Charles Ruggles, Virginia Field, Rita Johnson, ZaSu Pitts. Niven's tired of wife Young; Young's tired of husband Niven. Sharply observed, if talky, marital comedy. Scripted by Leonard Spiegelgass, based on a play by Samson Raphaelson.▼
Perfect Match, The (1987) **C-92m.** **½ D: Mark Deimel. Marc McClure, Jennifer Edwards, Diane Stilwell, Rob Paulsen, Wayne Woodsen, Karen Witter, Jeane Byron. Likable leads in a modest romantic comedy about two singles who meet through the newspaper's personal ads. [PG]▼
Perfect Murder, A (1998) **C-105m.** *** D: Andrew Davis. Michael Douglas, Gwyneth Paltrow, Viggo Mortensen, David Suchet, Sarita Choudhury, Constance Towers, Novella Nelson. Entertaining suspense yarn which adds a few interesting twists to DIAL M FOR MURDER. Douglas is the cold-blooded husband who hires someone to kill his wife—but this time, the man he hires is her lover! The stars are perfectly cast, and the story unfolds in slick and skillful fashion. Paltrow is a perfect '90s stand-in for Grace Kelly. Special edition video includes an alternate ending. [R]▼●◗
Perfect Specimen, The (1937) **97m.** **½ D: Michael Curtiz. Errol Flynn, Joan Blondell, Hugh Herbert, Edward Everett Horton, Dick Foran, May Robson, Beverly Roberts, Allen Jenkins. Fairly amusing whimsy about super-rich Flynn, who's kept locked up and sheltered by grandmother Robson until vivacious Blondell comes crashing through his fence and they go off on a whirlwind courtship.
Perfect Strangers (1945) SEE: **Vacation From Marriage**
Perfect Strangers (1950) **88m.** **½ D: Bretaigne Windust. Ginger Rogers, Dennis Morgan, Thelma Ritter, Margalo Gillmore, Paul Ford, Alan Reed. Rogers and Morgan are jury members who fall in love; engaging romance story.
Perfect Strangers (1984) **C-91m.** ** D: Larry Cohen. Anne Carlisle, Brad Rijn, John Woehrle, Matthew Stockley, Stephen Lack, Ann Magnuson. Three-year-old Stockley witnesses Rijn carrying out gangland slaying . . . then Rijn strikes up a romance with Stockley's mom (Carlisle) in this listlessly acted will-he-or-won't-he suspense yarn. Carlisle was seen to much better effect as the star of LIQUID SKY. Aka BLIND ALLEY. [R]▼
Perfect Tribute, The (1991) **C-100m. TVM** D: Jack Bender. Jason Robards, Lukas Haas, Campbell Scott, Katherine Helmond, Ed Flanders, Jose Ferrer, Jeanne Tripplehorn. Southern teenager searches for his older brother, who's dying in a northern hospital during Civil War, and chances to meet Abraham Lincoln, who's ambling about Washington alone, disheartened because he feels his Gettysburg Address was misunderstood. Heartwarming historical fiction. Leisurely adaptation by Dennis Brown, from Mary Raymond Shipman Andrews' classic book. Above average.
Perfect Weapon, The (1991) **C-85m.** *½ D: Mark DiSalle. Jeff Speakman, John Dye, Mako, James Hong, Mariska Hargitay, Dante Basco, Seth Sakai. The Korean mob makes a very stupid move: they kill the Asian mentor of an American "weapon" with revenge on his mind. Indistinguishable from other martial-arts/vengeance sagas, which is certainly the least of its problems; to keep things simple, Speakman's character (a loner) is named Jeff. [R]▼●
Perfect Woman, The (1949-British) **89m.** **½ D: Bernard Knowles. Patricia Roc, Stanley Holloway, Miles Malleson, Nigel Patrick, Irene Handl, Patti Morgan. Screwy scientist tries to improve on nature by making a "perfect" robot woman, modeled on his niece. Naturally mix-ups follow in this OK British comedy.
Perfect World, A (1993) **C-137m.** ** D: Clint Eastwood. Kevin Costner, Clint Eastwood, Laura Dern, T. J. Lowther, Keith Szarabajka, Leo Burmester, Paul Hewitt, Bradley Whitford, Ray McKinnon, Jennifer Griffin, Bruce McGill. A prison escapee (Costner) in 1963 Texas takes young boy along with him as hostage, though they quickly build a relationship; meanwhile, an iconoclastic Texas Ranger (Eastwood) tries to pick up the convict's trail. Something new in screen entertainment: A manhunt movie with no urgency, and no suspense. In its place are some interesting character vignettes, and a lot of moral ambiguity. Costner, however, is commanding, in an unusually forceful performance. Panavision. [PG-13]▼●
Performance (1970-British) **C-105m.** *** D: Donald Cammell, Nicolas Roeg. James Fox, Mick Jagger, Anita Pallenberg, Michele

Breton, Ann Sidney, John Burdon. Psychological melodrama about criminal on the lam hiding out with rock performer, and how their lives intertwine. Not for all tastes, but a bizarre and unique film; Jagger's performance of "Memo from Turner" a highlight. [R—edited from original X rating]▼●

Perfumed Nightmare, The (1977-Filipino) **C-93m.** ***½ D: Kidlat Tahimik. Kidlat Tahimik, Dolores Santamaria, Georgette Baudry, Katrin Muller, Harmut Lerch. Surreal, whimsical, thoroughly original fable of an idealistic young Filipino (played by the director), fascinated by American culture and technology, and his awakening to the disadvantages of "progress" while in Paris. Crammed with striking images and a dazzling soundtrack.▼

Perilous Holiday (1946) **89m.** *** D: Edward H. Griffith. Pat O'Brien, Ruth Warrick, Alan Hale, Edgar Buchanan, Audrey Long. Another good O'Brien vehicle, with troubleshooter encountering dangerous counterfeiting gang south of the border.

Perilous Journey, A (1953) **90m.** ** D: R. G. Springsteen. Vera Ralston, David Brian, Scott Brady, Virginia Grey, Charles Winninger, Ben Cooper, Hope Emerson, Veda Ann Borg, Leif Erickson. Predictable but diverting Western of a ship manned by women who are heading to California to find husbands.

Perils From the Planet Mongo (1940) **91m.** **½ D: Ford Beebe, Ray Taylor. Buster Crabbe, Carol Hughes, Charles Middleton, Frank Shannon, Anne Gwynne. Truncated version of FLASH GORDON CONQUERS THE UNIVERSE serial. On Mongo, Flash, Dale Arden, and Dr. Zarkov contend with the planet's civilizations, eventually restore Prince Barin as rightful ruler and return to Earth. Uninspired handling of footage from this great serial.

Perils of Gwendoline in the Land of the Yik Yak, The (1984-French) **C-88m.** BOMB D: Just Jaeckin. Tawny Kitaen, Brent Huff, Zabou, Bernadette Lafont, Jean Rougerie. Idiotic adaptation of erotic French comic strip, seemingly a RAIDERS OF THE LOST ARK spoof, with virginal Kitaen searching for her long-lost dad. Lots of nudity, little else. Panavision. [R]▼●

Perils of Pauline, The (1947) **C-96m.** *** D: George Marshall. Betty Hutton, John Lund, Constance Collier, Billy de Wolfe, William Demarest. Lively, entertaining musical-comedy purports to be biography of silent-screen heroine Pearl White, but isn't; energetic Hutton, good Frank Loesser songs, colorful atmosphere, and presence of silent-film veterans make up for it . . . until sappy denouement.▼◗

Perils of Pauline, The (1967) **C-99m.** ** D: Herbert Leonard, Joshua Shelley. Pamela Austin, Pat Boone, Terry-Thomas, Edward Everett Horton, Hamilton Camp. Cutesy expanded TV pilot. Boone travels the globe seeking childhood sweetheart Austin; overlong, mainly for kids.

Period of Adjustment (1962) **112m.** *** D: George Roy Hill. Tony Franciosa, Jane Fonda, Jim Hutton, Lois Nettleton, John McGiver, Jack Albertson. Newlyweds (Fonda and Hutton) try to help troubled marriage of Nettleton and Franciosa, in this heartwarming comedy based on a Tennessee Williams play. Engaging performers make the most of both comic and tender moments.▼

Permanent Midnight (1998) **C-85m.** **½ D: David Veloz. Ben Stiller, Elizabeth Hurley, Maria Bello, Owen Wilson, Lourdes Benedicto, Peter Greene, Cheryl Ladd, Fred Willard, Charles Fleischer, Janeane Garofalo. Adequate film of TV writer Jerry Stahl's drug-abuse–packed memoirs, showing how—for a while—he was able to maintain professional productivity while making a fool of himself at parties and acting irresponsibly toward the British woman he marries (Hurley) so she can obtain a U.S. visa. Bello plays the hotel bedmate to whom he unloads his past in the subplot that frames the story, and Stahl himself appears as a doctor. Inevitably episodic. [R]▼●◗

Permanent Record (1988) **C-91m.** *** D: Marisa Silver. Alan Boyce, Keanu Reeves, Michelle Meyrink, Jennifer Rubin, Pamela Gidley, Michael Elgart, Richard Bradford, Barry Corbin, Kathy Baker. Teen drama packs a wallop in tale of model student Boyce whose unexpected suicide throws high school classmates and officials into turmoil: if he went that route, who's safe? Subtle treatment by Silver of a pressing social problem, aided by excellent cast, especially Reeves as Boyce's underachieving pal. [PG-13]▼●

Permission to Kill (1975-British) **C-96m.** *** D: Cyril Frankel. Dirk Bogarde, Ava Gardner, Bekim Fehmiu, Timothy Dalton, Frederic Forrest. Fascinating expose of spying as dirty business. Bogarde, spy chief of "Western Intelligence Liaison," tries to prevent Fehmiu, head of "National Freedom Party" from returning to his dictator-controlled country. Beautiful, exciting production. [PG]▼

Perri (1957) **C-75m.** *** D: N. Paul Kenworthy, Jr., Ralph Wright. Narrated by Winston Hibler. Unusual Disney film combines elements of BAMBI with True-Life nature photography, in a romanticized look at a squirrel through the cycle of four seasons in the forest. Based on Felix Salten's book.

Perry Mason Long before Raymond Burr made the part of Perry Mason his own on television, Erle Stanley Gardner's crusading attorney was featured in a half-dozen screen adventures. Created in 1933, Perry made his film debut just one year later in THE CASE OF THE HOWLING

DOG, based on one of Gardner's best-selling novels. (In fact, all of the Mason films were adaptations of books from the series, which was not the norm for Hollywood.) Leading man Warren William had played both detectives and lawyers before, but the screenwriters (and possibly, directors) of these films kept changing their minds about the way Perry should be portrayed. He was definitely flashier than the Mason depicted on the printed page (with plush offices that could have been created only in Hollywood), and overall spent less time in the courtroom, but in THE CASE OF THE LUCKY LEGS he's portrayed as a constant tippler (à la Nick Charles) and in THE CASE OF THE CURIOUS BRIDE he's positively giddy. Continuity was further undermined by recasting Perry's secretary Della Street from one film to the next; only Claire Dodd managed to play the role twice in succession, winning Perry's marriage proposal at the end of THE CURIOUS BRIDE and honeymooning in THE VELVET CLAWS. After just a couple of films, Warner Bros. downgraded the series from "A" status to "B," and after four pictures, William left. Ricardo Cortez succeeded him, but just for one picture; by the time Donald Woods inherited the role, it was clear that Warners had lost all interest. It remained for television to really capitalize on Erle Stanley Gardner's durable character some twenty years later.

PERRY MASON

The Case of the Howling Dog (1934)
The Case of the Curious Bride (1935)
The Case of the Lucky Legs (1935)
The Case of the Velvet Claws (1936)
The Case of the Black Cat (1936)
The Case of the Stuttering Bishop (1937)

Persecution (1974-British) **C-92m.** *½ D: Don Chaffey. Lana Turner, Trevor Howard, Ralph Bates, Olga Georges-Picot. Overwrought, disjointed thriller with Lana as monstrous cat-loving mother of Bates, whom she torments his entire life. Slow, unpleasant, and unintentionally hilarious. Aka THE TERROR OF SHEBA and THE GRAVEYARD. [PG]▼

Persona (1966-Swedish) **81m.** ***½ D: Ingmar Bergman. Bibi Andersson, Liv Ullmann, Gunnar Bjornstrand, Margaretha Krook. Actress Ullmann withdraws and becomes mute, is cared for by nurse Andersson; their minds and personalities switch. Haunting, poetic, for discerning viewers; also shown at 85m. and 90m.▼●

Personal Affair (1954-British) **82m.** ** D: Anthony Pelissier. Gene Tierney, Leo Genn, Glynis Johns, Walter Fitzgerald, Pamela Brown. Timid murder story involving suspected schoolteacher.▼

Personal Best (1982) **C-124m.** ***½ D: Robert Towne. Mariel Hemingway, Scott Glenn, Patrice Donnelly, Kenny Moore, Jim Moody, Larry Pennell. Athletes Hemingway and Donnelly have lesbian relationship while training for the 1980 Olympics. Annoying direction—too many close-ups of feet—but scores touchdowns galore when dealing with feelings, and women's relationship to manipulative coach Glenn. Perceptive, sensitive performance by Hemingway. Directing debut for top screenwriter Towne. [R]▼

Personal Foul (1987) **C-92m.** *** D: Ted Lichtenfeld. David Morse, Adam Arkin, Susan Wheeler Duff, F. William Parker. Honest, heartfelt tale of drifter/ex-con Morse and teacher Arkin, who meet, become pals, and then rivals for Duff (who lights up the screen in her every scene). Sometimes lags but still sweet and ingratiating.

Personal Property (1937) **84m.** **½ D: W. S. Van Dyke II. Jean Harlow, Robert Taylor, Una O'Connor, Reginald Owen, Cora Witherspoon. Taylor stiffly maneuvers through a series of masquerades, and finally courts Harlow in this MGM fluff. Remake of 1932 film THE MAN IN POSSESSION.▼

Personal Services (1987-British) **C-105m.** **½ D: Terry Jones. Julie Walters, Alec McCowen, Danny Schiller, Shirley Stelfox, Victoria Hardcastle, Tim Woodward, Dave Atkins. Naive working woman stumbles into a career as a madam, and becomes bolder as business prospers. Bittersweet comedy, based on the real experiences of Cynthia Payne, is unabashedly adult, but uneven in tone. Benefits from a terrific performance by Walters. Written by David Leland. Payne's earlier years are dramatized in WISH YOU WERE HERE. [R]▼●

Personals, The (1981) **C-88m.** *** D: Peter Markle. Bill Schoppert, Karen Landry, Paul Eiding, Michael Laskin, Vickie Dakil. Sweet, lovable—but also honest, realistic—little comedy about what happens when recently divorced, slightly balding Schoppert places a personal ad. Perhaps a bit too much extraneous footage, but still it works nicely, and "Shelly" is a riot. Filmed independently, in Minneapolis. [PG]▼

Persuader, The (1957) **72m.** ** D: Dick Ross. William Talman, James Craig, Kristine Miller, Darryl Hickman. Another Western involved with clergyman taking up arms to combat outlaws.

Persuasion (1995-British-U.S.-French) **C-107m.** *** D: Roger Michell. Amanda Root, Ciaran Hinds, Susan Fleetwood, Corin Redgrave, Fiona Shaw, John Woodvine, Phoebe Nicholls, Samuel West, Sophie Thompson, Judy Cornwell, Felicity Dean. A young woman has never recovered from her break with a dashing but impoverished sailor whom she was advised to turn away. Seven years later, they meet again in the midst of a tumultuous period in which her family tries to adjust to poverty. A lovingly crafted, beautifully acted adaptation of Jane Austen, this film demands patience but provides ample rewards. Impeccable yet understated period detail brings early-19th-century England to life. Made for British TV. [PG]▼●◗

Pest, The (1997) **C-82m.** *½ D: Paul Miller. John Leguizamo, Jeffrey Jones, Edoardo Ballerini, Freddy Rodriguez, Tammy Townsend, Joe Morton, Aries Spears. In a manic performance that makes Jim Carrey look like Ben Kingsley, Leguizamo plays a con artist with a unique talent for transforming himself into just about every type of persona. Soon he finds himself pursued by a variety of whacked-out bad guys. Leguizamo is definitely a talent, but this is a poor showcase; he also cowrote and coproduced. [PG-13]▼●

Pete Kelly's Blues (1955) **C-95m.** **½ D: Jack Webb. Jack Webb, Janet Leigh, Edmond O'Brien, Peggy Lee, Andy Devine, Lee Marvin, Jayne Mansfield, Ella Fitzgerald, Martin Milner. Realistic to the point of tedium. Recreates the 1920's jazz age and musicians involved. Cast perks goings-on, despite Webb. Peggy Lee, in a rare dramatic role, was nominated for an Academy Award. CinemaScope.▼●

Pete 'n' Tillie (1972) **C-100m.** **½ D: Martin Ritt. Walter Matthau, Carol Burnett, Geraldine Page, Barry Nelson, Rene Auberjonois, Lee H. Montgomery, Henry Jones, Kent Smith. Slick comedy-drama has its moments as wry bachelor Matthau laconically woos and marries Burnett. Later turn to melodrama doesn't work, however, and supporting characters Page and Auberjonois don't make sense. Enough good points for innocuous entertainment; adapted by Julius J. Epstein from Peter de Vries' *Witch's Milk.* Panavision. [PG]▼

Peter Ibbetson (1935) **88m.** *** D: Henry Hathaway. Gary Cooper, Ann Harding, John Halliday, Ida Lupino, Douglass Dumbrille, Virginia Weidler, Dickie Moore, Doris Lloyd. Most unusual fantasy-romance, based on George du Maurier novel about sweethearts who are separated in childhood but whose destinies draw them together years later, and for all eternity. Someone more ethereal than Harding might have put this over better, but it's still a moving and strikingly artistic endeavor. Beautifully photographed by Charles Lang.

Peter Lundy and the Medicine Hat Stallion (1977) **C-100m. TVM** D: Michael O'Herlihy. Leif Garrett, Milo O'Shea, Mitch Ryan, Bibi Besch, Charles Tyner, John Anderson, John Quade. Teenaged frontier lad becomes a Pony Express rider in the mid-1800s in this Disney-like adventure tale. Good family entertainment. Video titles: THE MEDICINE HAT STALLION and ROUGH RIDER. Above average.▼

Peter Pan (1924) **102m.** *** D: Herbert Brenon. Betty Bronson, Ernest Torrence, Anna May Wong, Mary Brian, Virginia Browne Faire, Esther Ralston, Cyril Chadwick, Philippe De Lacey. Delightful adaptation of the James M. Barrie classic about the boy who can fly and never wants to grow up, and his adventures as he flies off with Wendy Darling and her brothers to Never Never Land. Bronson makes the role of Peter all her own in this charming fantasy.▼◗

Peter Pan (1953) **C-77m.** *** D: Hamilton Luske, Clyde Geronimi, Wilfred Jackson. Voices of Bobby Driscoll, Kathryn Beaumont, Hans Conried, Bill Thompson, Heather Angel, Paul Collins, Candy Candido, Tom Conway. Delightful Walt Disney cartoon feature of the classic James M. Barrie story, with Peter leading Wendy, Michael, and John Darling to Neverland, where they do battle with Captain Hook and his band of pirates. Musical highlight: "You Can Fly," as the children sail over the city of London. ▼●◗

Peter Rabbit and Tales of Beatrix Potter (1971-British) **C-90m.** ***½ D: Reginald Mills. Beautiful ballet film with Royal Ballet Company tells the adventures of several creatures that live by the pond; interesting version of Beatrix Potter tales. British title: TALES OF BEATRIX POTTER. [G]▼

Peter's Friends (1992-British) **C-100m.** ***½ D: Kenneth Branagh. Kenneth Branagh, Emma Thompson, Rita Rudner, Stephen Fry, Hugh Laurie, Imelda Staunton, Alphonsia Emmanuel, Tony Slattery, Alex Lowe, Richard Briers. A collegiate musical troupe's weekend reunion, after ten years, sparks feelings of love, envy, anger, and self-doubt. Glibly described as a British BIG CHILL, it stands on its own, filled with honest humor, heartache, and finely etched performances. Thompson is a standout as the group nerd, and Rudner (who also wrote this with real-life husband Martin Bergman) is very funny as a self-absorbed Hollywood star. Thompson's mother, actress Phyllida Law, turns in a fine performance as the housekeeper.▼●

Pete's Dragon (1977) **C-134m.** ** D: Don Chaffey. Helen Reddy, Jim Dale, Mickey Rooney, Red Buttons, Shelley Winters, Sean Marshall, Jane Kean, Jim Backus, Jeff Conaway, voice of Charlie Callas. Heavy-handed Disney musical about orphaned boy and his only friend, a protective dragon. Endearing animated "monster" almost makes up for the live actors' tiresome mugging. Another try for MARY POPPINS magic that doesn't come close. Some prints run 121m.; the 1985 reissue was further cut to 104m. [G]▼●

Petrified Forest, The (1936) **83m.** ***½ D: Archie Mayo. Leslie Howard, Bette Davis, Dick Foran, Humphrey Bogart, Genevieve Tobin, Charley Grapewin, Porter Hall. Solid adaptation of Robert Sherwood play, focusing on ironic survival of the physically fit in civilized world. Bogart is Duke Mantee, escaped gangster, who holds writer Howard, dreamer Davis, and others hostage at roadside restaurant in Arizona. Stagy, but extremely well-acted and surprisingly fresh. Howard and Bogart recreate their Broadway roles. Scripted by Charles Kenyon and Delmer Daves. Remade as ESCAPE IN THE DESERT. Also shown in computer-colored version.▼●

Petroleum Girls SEE: **Legend of Frenchie King, The**

Pet Sematary (1989) **C-102m.** BOMB D: Mary Lambert. Dale Midkiff, Fred Gwynne, Denise Crosby, Brad Greenquist, Michael Lombard, Blaze Berdahl, Miko Hughes. Couple is shocked to discover that danger lurks for their kids just outside a newly purchased rural home; aside from a spooked adjacent pet cemetery, they somehow failed to notice that semis roar down their front-yard highway every 90 seconds or so. A box-office hit whose contempt for its audience was sensed even by undiscriminating moviegoers. Stephen King, who has a cameo as a minister, scripted from his own best-seller. Followed by a sequel. [R]▼●

Pet Sematary II (1992) **C-100m.** BOMB D: Mary Lambert. Edward Furlong, Anthony Edwards, Clancy Brown, Jared Rushton, Darlanne Fluegel, Sarah Trigger, Lisa Waltz, Jason McGuire. The son of an accidentally killed horror-movie actress discovers the pet cemetery that brings the dead back to life, causing the same kind of gore and horror as in the first film. Brown is a hoot as a resurrected sheriff, but the movie is mean-spirited and gruesome, much worse than the original BOMB! [R]▼●

Petticoat Fever (1936) **81m.** ** D: George Fitzmaurice. Robert Montgomery, Myrna Loy, Reginald Owen, Irving Bacon. Limp farce set in Labrador, with patronizing Montgomery romancing Loy (despite presence of stuffed-shirt fiancé Owen). The stars are defeated by their one-note material.

Petty Girl, The (1950) **C-87m.** **½ D: Henry Levin. Robert Cummings, Joan Caulfield, Elsa Lanchester, Melville Cooper, Mary Wickes, Tippi Hedren. Mild comedy of pin-up artist George Petty (Cummings) falling for prudish Caulfield; Lanchester steals every scene she's in.

Petulia (1968) **C-105m.** **** D: Richard Lester. Julie Christie, George C. Scott, Richard Chamberlain, Shirley Knight, Arthur Hill, Joseph Cotten, Pippa Scott, Kathleen Widdoes, Richard Dysart, Austin Pendleton, Rene Auberjonois, The Grateful Dead, Big Brother and the Holding Company. Brilliant film, set against mid-60s San Francisco scene, about recently divorced doctor and his relationship with unhappily married kook. Terrific acting, especially by Scott and Knight, in one of decade's top films; script by Lawrence B. Marcus. From John Haase's novel *Me and the Arch Kook Petulia.* [R]▼

Peyton Place (1957) **C-157m.** ***½ D: Mark Robson. Lana Turner, Hope Lange, Arthur Kennedy, Lloyd Nolan, Lee Philips, Terry Moore, Russ Tamblyn, Betty Field, David Nelson, Mildred Dunnock, Diane Varsi, Barry Coe, Leon Ames, Lorne Greene. Grace Metalious's once-notorious novel receives Grade A filming. Soap opera of life behind closed doors in a small New England town boasts strong cast, fine Franz Waxman score. Original running time: 162m. Sequel: RETURN TO PEYTON PLACE. Later a hit TV series. CinemaScope.▼●

Phaedra (1962-U.S.-French-Greek) **115m.** *** D: Jules Dassin. Melina Mercouri, Anthony Perkins, Raf Vallone, Elizabeth Ercy. Mercouri, wife of shipping magnate Vallone, has an affair with stepson Perkins. Well-acted and directed; inspired by Euripides' *Hippolytus.*

Phantasm (1979) **C-87m.** *½ D: Don Coscarelli. Michael Baldwin, Bill Thornbury, Reggie Bannister, Kathy Lester, Angus Scrimm. Two dull brothers take on a flying object that punctures skulls and a creepy cemetery worker whose ties are so thin he belongs playing "Louie, Louie" at a 1964 prom. Followed by three sequels. [R]▼●

Phantasm II (1988) **C-90m.** *½ D: Don Coscarelli. James Le Gros, Reggie Bannister, Angus Scrimm, Paula Irvine, Samantha Phillips, Kenneth Tigar. Bigger-budgeted sequel to the 1979 cult success is similar—psychic teenagers experiencing recurring nightmarish visions of The Tall Man (Scrimm)—only with more graphic and unrelenting gore. [R]▼●

Phantasm III (1994) **C-91m.** *½ D: Don Coscarelli. Reggie Bannister, A. Michael Baldwin, Angus Scrimm, Bill Thornbury, Gloria Lynne Henry, Kevin Connors, Cindy Ambuehl, John Chandler, Brooks Gardner. More flying silver spheres, cannibal gnomes, stolen bodies, explosions, and The Tall Man—still doesn't make much sense. The end is especially unsatisfying, with limp humor, unnecessary sex scenes, and amateurish acting. Followed by another video sequel. [R]▼●

Phantom, The (1996-U.S.-Australian) **C-101m.** ** D: Simon Wincer. Billy Zane, Kristy Swanson, Treat Williams, Catherine Zeta Jones, James Remar, Cary-Hiroyuki Tagawa, Casey Siemaszko, Samantha Eggar, Patrick McGoohan. Lead-footed emulation of Saturday matinee serials, using Lee Falk's masked comic-strip hero ("the ghost who walks"), who starred in a bona fide serial in 1943. His longtime attempt to vanquish a society of evil puts him face-to-face with megalomaniac Xander Drax (a campy Williams). Well-meaning INDIANA JONES wannabe has no energy and offers large-scale stunts without knowing how to stage them! Panavision. [PG] ▼●◗

Phantom Creeps, The (1939) **79m.** ** D: Ford Beebe, Saul A. Goodkind. Bela Lugosi, Robert Kent, Regis Toomey, Dorothy Arnold, Edward Van Sloan, Edward Norris. U.S. government and hostile spies vie to gain control of the "secret element," an invention of mad scientist Dr. Zorka (Lugosi). So bad it's actually quite entertaining; the whole kettle of fish is thrown in here, including stock footage of the Hindenburg disaster! And look for Lee J. Cobb as a road-crew foreman. Edited down from a 12-episode Universal serial of the same title.▼

Phantom Express, The (1932) **66m.** ** D: Emory Johnson. William Collier, Jr., Sally Blane, J. Farrell MacDonald, Hobart Bosworth, Axel Axelson, Lina Basquette. Melodramatic, ever-so-obvious account of some villains attempting to sabotage a railroad . . . and it's the company president's son (Collier) to the rescue. Notice those violins after engineer Smokey North is sacked from his job!▼

Phantom From Space (1953) **72m.** *½ D: W. Lee Wilder. Ted Cooper, Rudolph Anders, Noreen Nash, Harry Landers, Jim Bannon. An invisible alien crash-lands near L.A., wreaks accidental havoc as he makes his way across the city. OK idea hampered by low budget—and lack of talent.▼

Phantom Lady (1944) **87m.** ***½ D: Robert Siodmak. Ella Raines, Franchot Tone, Alan Curtis, Thomas Gomez, Elisha Cook, Jr., Fay Helm, Andrew Tombes, Regis Toomey. First-rate suspense yarn of innocent man (Curtis) framed for murder of his wife. Secretary Raines seeks real killer with help of Curtis' best friend (Tone) and detective (Gomez). Sexual innuendo in drumming scene with Cook is simply astonishing—the solo was reportedly dubbed by Buddy Rich. Based on a Cornell Woolrich novel; screenplay by Bernard C. Schoenfeld.▼

Phantom of Chinatown (1941) **61m.** BOMB D: Phil Rosen. Keye Luke, Lotus Long, Grant Withers, Paul McVey, Charles Miller. Sixth and final mystery in the Mr. Wong series is bottom-of-the-barrel fare, with Luke replacing Boris Karloff as a younger version of the Oriental sleuth. He's on the trail of a killer out to obtain an ancient scroll and locate an oil deposit.▼◗

Phantom of Crestwood, The (1932) **77m.** *** D: J. Walter Ruben. Ricardo Cortez, Karen Morley, Anita Louise, Pauline Frederick, H. B. Warner, Sam Hardy, Skeets Gallagher. First-rate whodunit with crafty Morley calling together the men in her life for mass-blackmail scheme, resulting in murder. Eye-riveting flashback technique highlights solid mystery.●

Phantom of Liberty, The (1974-French) **C-104m.** ***½ D: Luis Buñuel. Jean-Claude Brialy, Adolfo Celi, Michel Piccoli, Monica Vitti. A dreamlike comedy of irony, composed of surreal, randomly connected anecdotes. Highlighted is a dinner party, in which the openness of eating and the privacy of defecating are reversed, and a sequence in which adults fret over a young girl's disappearance—even though she remains present all along. [R]▼●

Phantom of Paris, The (1931) **73m.** ** D: John S. Robertson. John Gilbert, Leila Hyams, Lewis Stone, Jean Hersholt, C. Aubrey Smith, Natalie Moorhead, Ian Keith. Gilbert elevates this otherwise static, talky melodrama as a dapper magician-illusionist accused of murdering the father of the woman he loves—with an ironic twist. Police detective Stone is his cold-hearted nemesis. Based on a novel by Gaston (*The Phantom of the Opera*) LeRoux.

Phantom of Terror, The SEE: **Bird With the Crystal Plumage, The**

Phantom of the Opera, The (1925) **79m.** ***½ D: Rupert Julian. Lon Chaney, Mary Philbin, Norman Kerry, Snitz Edwards, Gibson Gowland. Classic melodrama with Chaney as the vengeful composer who lives in the catacombs under the Paris Opera House, and kidnaps young Philbin as his singing protegee. Famous unmasking scene still packs a jolt, and the Bal Masque is especially impressive in two-color Technicolor. One of Chaney's finest hours. Most prints are of the 1929 reissue version, but the original is available on laserdisc. Remade several times, and transformed into a Broadway musical.▼●◗

Phantom of the Opera (1943) **C-92m.** *** D: Arthur Lubin. Claude Rains, Susanna Foster, Nelson Eddy, Edgar Barrier, Jane Farrar, Miles Mander, J. Edward Bromberg, Hume Cronyn, Fritz Leiber, Leo Carrillo, Steven Geray, Fritz Feld. First talkie version of venerable melodrama often has more opera than Phantom, but Rains gives fine, sympathetic performance as disfigured composer worshipping young soprano Foster. Oscar winner for Cinematography (Hal Mohr and W. Howard Greene) and Art Direction.▼●

Phantom of the Opera, The (1962-British) **C-84m.** ** D: Terence Fisher. Herbert Lom, Heather Sears, Thorley Walters, Edward DeSouza, Michael Gough, Miles Malleson. Lom stars in this third screen version of the story. It's more elaborate than most Hammer horror films, but also more plodding, with only occasional moments of terror. Made worse by expansion to 90m. for TV, with added subplot of detectives investigating the murderer.▼●

Phantom of the Opera, The (1983) **C-100m. TVM** D: Robert Markowitz. Maximilian Schell, Jane Seymour, Michael York,

Jeremy Kemp, Diana Quick. Sumptuous 80s version of the grand guignol classic is highlighted by Schell's scenery-chewing portrait of the deranged Hungarian voice teacher who's not just another pretty face. Sherman Yellen's adaptation and Stan Winston's "Phantom" makeup aren't to be overlooked either, though this version goes far astray from the original Gaston Leroux novel—it isn't even set in Paris! Above average.

Phantom of the Opera, The (1989) **C-90m.** *½ D: Dwight H. Little. Robert Englund, Jill Schoelen, Alex Hyde-White, Billy Nighy, Stephanie Lawrence, Terence Harvey. Good-looking but gory, slow-moving remake, shot in Budapest but set in London. Closer to original novel than other versions. Its changes are no improvements; instead of a mask, the Phantom stitches dead flesh onto his scarred face and has made a deal with the devil. He's still killing people to advance the career of a chosen singer. No chandelier, either. Englund ("Freddy Krueger") ranges from effective to hammy as the Phantom. [R]▼●

Phantom of the Opera, The (1990-U.S.-British) **C-200m. TVM** D: Tony Richardson. Burt Lancaster, Charles Dance, Teri Polo, Ian Richardson, Andrea Ferreol, Adam Storke, Jean-Pierre Cassel. Handsome but almost high-camp remake of the venerable story, with Dance making a romantic Phantom; Lancaster is his resigned but protective father, while Polo plays Christine as if she's Cinderella. It's so tame we never see the Phantom's face. The operatic interludes are atrociously dubbed. Adapted by the estimable Arthur Kopit from his 1983 play. Originally shown in two parts. Average.◗

Phantom of the Opera, The (1999-Italian) **C-99m.** ** D: Dario Argento. Julian Sands, Asia Argento, Andrea Di Stefano, Nadia Rinaldi, Coralina Cataldi Tassoni, Istvan Bubik. Argento's gory and erotic take on the classic tale with Sands as the mysterious phantom, who, in this version, is abandoned in the sewer below the opera house as an infant and raised by a loving family of rats! The director's daughter plays the beautiful young singer with whom he becomes obsessed. Disappointingly routine and unimaginative, with only a few of the director's expected flamboyant flourishes. [R]▼◗

Phantom of the Paradise (1974) **C-92m.** *** D: Brian De Palma. Paul Williams, William Finley, Jessica Harper, George Memmoli, Gerrit Graham. Effective rock version of . . . OPERA, with Finley out for revenge against producer (Williams, miscast but not bad) who stole his songs. A flop in its time—it was sold as a spoof—but now finding a cult; ironically, many of the "weird" rock performers (including Graham as "Beef") seem pretty tame alongside some of today's artists. Williams also composed the score, and Sissy Spacek was the set decorator! [PG]▼●

Phantom of the Rue Morgue (1954) **C-84m.** ** D: Roy Del Ruth. Karl Malden, Claude Dauphin, Patricia Medina, Steve Forrest, Allyn Ann McLerie, Erin O'Brien-Moore. Remake of MURDERS IN THE RUE MORGUE suffers from Malden's hamminess in the equivalent of Lugosi's role, plus little real atmosphere. On the other hand, there *is* Merv Griffin as a college student! Originally in 3-D.▼

Phantom Planet, The (1961) **82m.** *½ D: William Marshall. Dean Fredericks, Coleen Gray, Tony Dexter, Dolores Faith, Francis X. Bushman. Astronaut crash-lands on an invisible asteroid, is shrunken to the tiny size of its inhabitants, and becomes involved in their war with silly-looking aliens. Bushman plays tiny folks' leader Sesom, but he's no Moses, backward or forward. Fascinatingly terrible movie.▼

Phantom President, The (1932) **80m.** ** D: Norman Taurog. George M. Cohan, Claudette Colbert, Jimmy Durante, Sidney Toler. Musical antique about presidential candidate, with lookalike entertainer (Cohan) falling in love with former's girl (Colbert). Interesting only as a curio, with forgettable Rodgers–Hart score.

Phantom Raiders (1940) **70m.** **½ D: Jacques Tourneur. Walter Pidgeon, Donald Meek, Joseph Schildkraut, Florence Rice, Nat Pendleton, John Carroll. Slick, fast-paced Nick Carter detective entry has our hero investigating sabotage in the Panama Canal after Allied ships are sunk.

Phantoms (1998) **C-95m.** **½ D: Joe Chappelle. Peter O'Toole, Joanna Going, Rose McGowan, Liev Schreiber, Ben Affleck, Clifton Powell, Nicky Katt. Sisters are frightened to find a Rocky Mountain town totally deserted, except for a few dead bodies; sheriff Affleck shows up to help, followed by scientist O'Toole. The answer is a mysterious underground monster from the beginning of time: intelligent, deadly, and amorphous. Not-bad thriller with good performances, astute use of locations, and some suspenseful scenes. Adapted from his own novel by Dean R. Koontz. Aka DEAN KOONTZ'S PHANTOMS. [R]▼●◗

Phantom Ship (1935-British) **80m.** ** D: Denison Clift. Bela Lugosi, Shirley Grey, Arthur Margetson, Edmund Willard, Dennis Hoey, Ben Welden, Gibson Gowland. Slow-paced "explanation" of one of the great unsolved maritime mysteries, the disappearance of the crew of the *Mary Celeste,* in 1872. Routine but holds interest. Lugosi is broad but entertaining as superstitious one-armed seaman. All exteriors filmed on a real ship. Original title: MYSTERY OF THE MARY CELESTE. ▼

Phantom Stagecoach, The (1957) **69m.**

*½ D: Ray Nazarro. William Bishop, Kathleen Crowley, Richard Webb, Frank Ferguson. Programmer Western about clashing stagecoach lines competing for business.
Phantom Thief, The (1946) **65m.** **½ D: D. Ross Lederman. Chester Morris, Jeff Donnell, Richard Lane, Dusty Anderson, George E. Stone, Frank Sully, Marvin Miller. Murder strikes at a seance and Boston Blackie is called in to investigate. Neat series entry with plenty of haunted-house comic relief from Stone.
Phantom Tollbooth, The (1969) **C-90m.** *** D: Chuck Jones, Abe Levitow (animation); David Monahan (live-action). Butch Patrick, and voices of Hans Conried, Mel Blanc, Candy Candido, June Foray, Les Tremayne, Daws Butler. Unusual animated feature (the first for both Jones and MGM), based on Norton Juster's book about bored little boy who enters strange world where letters and numbers are at war. A bit sophisticated for the Saturday matinee crowd, and the songs are pretty icky, but still quite worthwhile, especially for Jones fans. [G]▼●
Pharaoh's Curse (1957) **66m.** *½ D: Lee Sholem. Mark Dana, Ziva Rodann, Diane Brewster, George Niese, Kurt Katch, Terence de Marney. 1903 Egyptian expedition is menaced by a rapidly aging vampiric reincarnate and his mysterious sister. Pompous, slow-moving; more supernatural melodrama than horror.▼
Pharaoh's Woman, The (1960-Italian) **C-87m.** ** D: Giorgio Rivalta. Linda Cristal, Pierre Brice, Armando Francioli, John Drew Barrymore. Senseless epic set in Egypt with Francioli combating Barrymore, pretender to the throne; ornate settings. Techniscope.▼●
Phar Lap (1983-Australian) **C-108m.** *** D: Simon Wincer. Tom Burlinson, Martin Vaughan, Judy Morris, Ron Leibman, Celia de Burgh, Vincent Ball. Entertaining chronicle of champion New Zealand–born racehorse Phar Lap, who suddenly and mysteriously died in 1933 in America. Nicely directed and acted; Down Under, the story is now a legend. Reedited for U.S. release from original 118m. Panavision. [PG]▼
Phase IV (1974) **C-86m.** **½ D: Saul Bass. Nigel Davenport, Lynne Frederick, Michael Murphy, Alan Gifford, Helen Horton, Robert Henderson. Feature directing debut of famed title-maker Bass is visually stunning but rather incomprehensible science fiction about colony of super-intelligent ants (normal-sized, for a change) running rampant at a lonely scientific outpost. Difficult, but not without its rewards. [PG] ▼●
Phat Beach (1996) **C-99m.** ** D: Doug Ellin. Jermaine "Huggy" Hopkins, Brian Hooks, Eric Fleeks, Alma Collins, Claudia Kaleem, Jennifer Lucienne, Coolio, Gregg D. Vance, Tre Black, Tiny "Zeus" Lister, Jr. A wannabe writer (Hopkins) dreams of meeting the perfect girl at the beach, so he heads off to the surf with his best friend. Hopkins' earnest, charming performance saves this from being a typical hit-the-beach and hit-on-the-girls film. Coolio and Y?N-Vee perform on screen. [R]▼●
Phenix City Story, The (1955) **100m.** *** D: Phil Karlson. John McIntire, Richard Kiley, Kathryn Grant (Crosby), Edward Andrews. Fast-paced exposé film, compactly told, with realistic production, fine performances as lawyer returns to corrupt home town, tries to do something about it. Sometimes shown without 13-minute prologue.
Phenomena SEE: **Creepers**
Phenomenon (1996) **C-124m.** ** D: Jon Turteltaub. John Travolta, Kyra Sedgwick, Forest Whitaker, Robert Duvall, Jeffrey DeMunn, Brent Spiner, Richard Kiley, Tony Genaro, Sean O'Bryan, Ellen Geer. Intriguing, humanistic story has ordinary-guy Travolta struck by a bolt of light that transforms him into a genius . . . a "blessing" that turns out to be a curse. Unfortunately, the story heads nowhere and takes its sweet time getting there. Beautiful Northern California setting and lovely Thomas Newman score support Travolta's empathic performance . . . all for naught. Long, slow, and squishy in the center. Panavision. [PG]▼●◗
PHFFFT (1954) **91m.** *** D: Mark Robson. Judy Holliday, Jack Lemmon, Jack Carson, Kim Novak, Donald Curtis. Saucy sex romp by George Axelrod, with Holliday and Lemmon discovering that they were better off before they divorced.▼
Philadelphia (1993) **C-119m.** **½ D: Jonathan Demme. Tom Hanks, Denzel Washington, Jason Robards, Mary Steenburgen, Antonio Banderas, Ron Vawter, Robert Ridgely, Charles Napier, Lisa Summerour, Joanne Woodward, Roger Corman, John Bedford Lloyd, Anna Deavere Smith, Tracey Walter, Obba Babatunde, Kathryn Witt, Bradley Whitford. Up-and-coming lawyer Hanks is battling AIDS; when he's fired from his prosperous Main Line Philadelphia law firm (for trumped-up reasons), he decides to bring suit. The only lawyer who'll take his case: ambulance-chaser Washington, who doesn't like gays. Well-meaning, mainstream look at AIDS and American homophobia succeeds as a tract but falls short as drama. Hanks is terrific in an Oscar-winning performance, but we don't know anything about him, or his lover (Banderas); his Norman Rockwellian family is (alas) too good to be true. That's the Rev. Robert Castle (subject of Demme's documentary COUSIN BOBBY) as Hanks' father. Bruce Springsteen also won an Oscar for Best Song. [PG-13]▼●◗
Philadelphia Experiment, The (1984) **C-102m.** **½ D: Stewart Raffill. Michael Paré,

Nancy Allen, Eric Christmas, Bobby Di Cicco, Kene Holliday. Sailor on WWII ship falls through a hole in time and winds up in 1984. Just entertaining enough to cover production flaws and some gaping story holes. Followed by a sequel. [PG]▼●

Philadelphia, Here I Come (1975) **C-95m.** **½ D: John Quested. Donal McCann, Des Cave, Siobhan McKenna, Eamon Kelly, Fidelma Murphy, Liam Redmond. Brian Friel adapted his stage play about a young man and his alter ego who debate whether or not he should leave his dreary Irish home town and join an aunt in Philadelphia, U.S.A. Filmed on location; fine performances. ▼

Philadelphia Story, The (1940) **112m.** **** D: George Cukor. Cary Grant, Katharine Hepburn, James Stewart, Ruth Hussey, John Howard, Roland Young, John Halliday, Virginia Weidler, Mary Nash, Henry Daniell, Hillary Brooke. Talky but brilliant adaptation of Philip Barry's hit Broadway comedy about society girl who yearns for down-to-earth romance; Grant is her ex-husband, Stewart a fast-talking (!) reporter who falls in love with her. Entire cast is excellent, but Stewart really shines in his offbeat, Academy Award-winning role. Donald Ogden Stewart's script also earned an Oscar. Later musicalized as HIGH SOCIETY. Also shown in computer-colored version.▼●◗

Philo Vance Debonair detective Philo Vance, created by master novelist S. S. Van Dine (real name Willard Wright) enjoyed a long and varied screen career, in the guise of many different actors, in films made over a span of some twenty years by several different studios. The man most closely identified with the role was William Powell, who starred in the first three mysteries for Paramount: THE CANARY MURDER CASE, THE GREENE MURDER CASE, and BENSON MURDER CASE. While these very early talkies are somewhat stilted (particularly CANARY, which was completed as a silent film, then hastily adapted for sound), the whodunit angles are first-rate, as urbane Powell solves the bizarre N.Y.C.-based murders. Eugene Pallette was a fine foil as skeptical Sergeant Heath of the homicide squad, with E. H. Calvert as the N.Y.C. D.A. MGM interrupted this series with one of its own, BISHOP MURDER CASE, casting Basil Rathbone as Vance; though a clever whodunit, with the villain matching his crimes to Mother Goose rhymes, the film was all but done in by a snail-like pacing. Powell's last appearance as Vance was in Warner Bros.' THE KENNEL MURDER CASE, probably the best film in the series, brilliantly directed by Michael Curtiz, and also one of the most complex cases of all. None of the later Vance outings reached this peak of ingenuity and sophisticated filmmaking, and Warren William simply marked time in THE DRAGON MURDER CASE at Warners. MGM's next duo cast Paul Lukas in THE CASINO MURDER CASE, and Edmund Lowe in THE GARDEN MURDER CASE; slickly done, they suffered from formula scripting, acting, and direction. Wilfrid Hyde-White starred in a British production of THE SCARAB MURDER CASE in 1936, but this one never found its way to America. Meanwhile, Paramount remade THE GREENE MURDER CASE as NIGHT OF MYSTERY, a routine "B" with Grant Richards, and Warren William returned for THE GRACIE ALLEN MURDER CASE, with Vance taking back seat to the comedienne, whose stupidity became a bit overpowering in this story written for her by Van Dine. Warners then redid THE KENNEL MURDER CASE as CALLING PHILO VANCE, another forgettable "B" with James Stephenson in the role. Philo Vance went into retirement until 1947, when cheapie company PRC brought him back for three final outings, all surprisingly good little whodunits: William Wright starred in PHILO VANCE RETURNS, and Alan Curtis was a deadpan hero in PHILO VANCE'S GAMBLE and the best of all, PHILO VANCE'S SECRET MISSION, with perky Sheila Ryan as his sleuthing girlfriend. The character of Philo Vance, sophisticated and aloof, did not really fit the hard-boiled detective image of the 1940s and 1950s, so the character never appeared again onscreen, but his better outings, from the beginning and end of his film career, remain first-rate murder mysteries today.

PHILO VANCE

Canary Murder Case (1929)
The Greene Murder Case (1929)
Bishop Murder Case (1930)
Benson Murder Case (1930)
The Kennel Murder Case (1933)
The Dragon Murder Case (1934)
Casino Murder Case (1935)
The Garden Murder Case (1936)
Night of Mystery (1937)
The Gracie Allen Murder Case (1939)
Calling Philo Vance (1940)
Philo Vance Returns (1947)
Philo Vance's Gamble (1947)
Philo Vance's Secret Mission (1947)

Philo Vance Returns (1947) **64m.** ** D: William Beaudine. William Wright, Terry Austin, Leon Belasco, Clara Blandick, Iris Adrian, Frank Wilcox. Vance (Wright) tries to solve the murder of a philandering Casanova in this first of three not-bad entries by poverty-row studio PRC. Ignoring the Van Dine books, Vance is now a hard-boiled, wisecracking private eye.▼

Philo Vance's Gamble (1947) **62m.** ** D: Basil Wrangell. Alan Curtis, Terry Austin, Frank Jenks, Tala Birell, Gavin Gordon. Vance (Curtis) is up to his neck in corpses when he takes on a gang of jewel thieves in this acceptable mystery given a (low-budget) film noir mood.

Philo Vance's Secret Mission (1947) **58m.** **½ D: Reginald Le Borg. Alan Curtis, Sheila Ryan, Tala Birell, Frank Jenks, James Bell. Not-bad little mystery (last in the series) has Vance joining a detective magazine as technical advisor, only to see the publisher get bumped off.

Phobia (1980-Canadian) **C-90m.** BOMB D: John Huston. Paul Michael Glaser, Susan Hogan, John Colicos, David Bolt, Patricia Collins, David Eisner. Absolutely terrible film about psychiatrist whose patients, suffering from various phobias, are being murdered one by one. Relentlessly stupid, illogical, and unpleasant. [R]▼

Phoenix (1997) **C-107m.** ** D: Danny Cannon. Ray Liotta, Anjelica Huston, Anthony LaPaglia, Daniel Baldwin, Jeremy Piven, Kari Wuhrer, Xander Berkeley, Tom Noonan, Giancarlo Esposito, Giovanni Ribisi, Brittany Murphy. Gambling-addicted Arizona cop Liotta, deeply in debt to a bookie, hatches a heist with his three corrupt cop buddies to rip off a local loan shark, but naturally things unravel in typical B-movie fashion. Stylishly made neo-noir boasts a superior cast but is sunk by repellent characters and a depressingly derivative, post-modern Tarantino-esque script. Premiered on cable a year before 1998 theatrical release. Panavision. [R]▼◗

Phone Call From a Stranger (1952) **96m.** *** D: Jean Negulesco. Bette Davis, Shelley Winters, Gary Merrill, Michael Rennie, Keenan Wynn, Evelyn Varden, Warren Stevens, Beatrice Straight, Craig Stevens. Engrossing narrative of Merrill, survivor of a plane crash, visiting families of various victims.▼

Phony American, The (1962-German) **72m.** **½ D: Akos Rathony. William Bendix, Christine Kaufmann, Michael Hinz, Ron Randell. Strange casting is more interesting than tale of a German WW2 orphan, now grown up, wishing to become an American, and a U.S. air force pilot.

Photo Finish (1957-French) **110m.** ** D: Norbert Carbonnaux. Fernand Gravet, Jean Richard, Micheline, Louis de Funes. Strained comedy about con-men at work at the racetrack.

Phynx, The (1970) **C-92m.** BOMB D: Lee H. Katzin. A. Michael Miller, Ray Chippeway, Dennis Larden, Lonny Stevens, Lou Antonio, Mike Kellin, Joan Blondell, George Tobias, Richard Pryor. A way-off-base satire about a rock group (Miller, Chippeway, Larden, Stevens) recruited to spy behind Iron Curtain and the kidnapping of America's pop-culture heroes (in cameos, Leo Gorcey, Huntz Hall, Guy Lombardo, Joe Louis, Johnny Weissmuller, Col. Sanders, Ruby Keeler, Xavier Cugat, Dick Clark, George Jessel, and many others). Diehards may want to see some of these stars, but it's hardly worth it. [M/PG]

Physical Evidence (1989) **C-99m.** *½ D: Michael Crichton. Burt Reynolds, Theresa Russell, Ned Beatty, Kay Lenz, Ted McGinley, Tom O'Brien. Boring drama with Reynolds going through the paces as a tough cop who's been suspended from the force, and is now the prime suspect in a murder case. Russell is badly miscast as a public defender who takes up his cause. [R]▼●

π (1998) **85m.** **½ D: Darren Aronofsky. Sean Gullette, Mark Margolis, Ben Shenkman, Pamela Hart, Stephen Pearlman, Ajay Naidu. An obsessed math genius thinks the orderliness of numbers may be able to conquer the stock market or determine God's identity, yet his own disordered life finds him at the brink of madness. Filmed in inky 16mm black and white for around $60,000, this attention-getter is a true original. Well acted by a no-name cast and, we hope, a harbinger of things to come from filmmaker Aronofsky. Cowritten by the director, Eric Watson, and leading actor Gullette. [R] ▼●◗

Piaf—The Early Years (1974-U.S.-French) **C-104m.** **½ D: Guy Casaril. Brigitte Ariel, Pascale Christophe, Guy Trejan, Pierre Vernier, Jacques Duby, Anouk Ferjac. Maddeningly uneven depiction of the early life and career of the legendary singer. Fascinating subject matter, good Ariel performance and great music, but melodramatic and sloppily directed. Based on the best-selling book by Simone Berteaut, Piaf's half-sister (played here by Christophe). Unreleased in America until 1982. [PG]

Piano, The (1993-New Zealand-French) **C-121m.** ***½ D: Jane Campion. Holly Hunter, Harvey Keitel, Sam Neill, Anna Paquin, Kerry Walker, Geneviève Lemon, Tungia Baker, Ian Mune. Haunting, unpredictable tale of love and sex told from a woman's point of view. In the late 19th century, a Scottish woman, her illegitimate daughter (Paquin), and her beloved piano arrive in remote New Zealand for an arranged marriage to farmer Neill. Then headstrong Hunter (who has been mute since childhood) strikes a bargain with moody neighbor Keitel (a Maori convert) involving the piano that leads to eye-opening consequences for the entire community. Writer-director Campion has fashioned a highly original fable, showing the tragedy and triumph erotic passion can bring to one's daily life. Hunter and Paquin both won Oscars for their performances, Campion for her screenplay. [R] ▼●◗

Piano for Mrs. Cimino, A (1982) **C-100m.**

TVM D: George Schaefer. Bette Davis, Penny Fuller, Keenan Wynn, Alexa Kenin, George Hearn, Christopher Guest, Graham Jarvis. A widow, diagnosed as senile by her doctor and declared incompetent by the courts, fights to regain control of her estate and her life, with Bette Davis giving another postgraduate acting course (sometimes a smidge too obviously) to her army of students and fans. John Gay wrote the sensitive script. Above average.▼

Picasso Mystery, The SEE: **Mystery of Picasso, The**

Picasso Summer, The (1969) **C-90m.** *½ D: Serge Bourguignon. Albert Finney, Yvette Mimieux. Boring, rambling tale of young couple so enamored by paintings that they take European vacation to find Picasso himself. Animated sequence midway can stand on its own. Based on the Ray Bradbury story. [M/PG]

Picasso Trigger (1989) **C-99m.** ** D: Andy Sidaris. Steve Bond, Dona Speir, John Aprea, Hope Marie Carlton, Harold Diamond, Roberta Vasquez, Guich Koock, Bruce Penhall. Harmless, low-budget James Bond-like thriller with U.S. agent Bond tracking assassin Aprea, who uses fish (from a painting he admires) as his emblem. Sequel to HARD TICKET TO HAWAII and MALIBU EXPRESS has usual mix of action and T&A, and some peculiar gadgets (a killer crutch?). [R]▼

Piccadilly Incident (1946-British) **88m.** *** D: Herbert Wilcox. Anna Neagle, Michael Wilding, Michael Laurence, Reginald Owen, Frances Mercer. Familiar Enoch Arden theme of supposedly dead wife appearing after husband has remarried. Good British cast gives life to oft-filmed plot.

Piccadilly Jim (1936) **100m.** **½ D: Robert Z. Leonard. Robert Montgomery, Madge Evans, Frank Morgan, Eric Blore, Billie Burke. Fine light-comedy players in P. G. Wodehouse story of father and son's romantic pursuits; overlong.

Pick a Star (1937) **70m.** **½ D: Edward Sedgwick. Jack Haley, Rosina Lawrence, Patsy Kelly, Mischa Auer, Tom Dugan, Stan Laurel, Oliver Hardy. Mistaken as L&H vehicle, actually a Hal Roach production about small-town girl (Lawrence) hoping for stardom in Hollywood. Sappy story, bizarre musical production numbers, but guest stars Stan and Ollie have two very funny scenes. Retitled: MOVIE STRUCK.▼●

Picking up the Pieces (2000) **C-95m.** ** D: Alfonso Arau. Woody Allen, Maria Grazia Cucinotta, Cheech Marin, David Schwimmer, Kiefer Sutherland, Alfonso Arau, Sharon Stone, Andy Dick, Fran Drescher, Joseph Gordon-Levitt, Elliott Gould, Lupe Ontiveros, Lou Diamond Phillips, Pepe Serna, Kathy Kinney, Tony Plana, Richard Sarafian, Danny de la Paz, Mia Maestro. A butcher who's hacked his wife into pieces flees to a New Mexico town, where the woman's hand becomes a focal point of worship—and ballyhoo. Whimsical black comedy is an almost total misfire, but the stellar cast maintains interest. Made for theaters but U.S. debut was on cable.

Pickle, The (1993) **C/B&W-103m.** *½ D: Paul Mazursky. Danny Aiello, Dyan Cannon, Clotilde Courau, Shelley Winters, Barry Miller, Jerry Stiller, Chris Penn, Little Richard, Jodi Long, Rebecca Miller, Stephen Tobolowsky, Caroline Aaron, Ally Sheedy, Spalding Gray, Griffin Dunne, Isabella Rossellini, Dudley Moore, Donald Trump. Misfire about an aging, self-involved film director (Aiello) who's in desperate need of a hit, and whose most recent credit is a sci-fi epic about an overgrown pickle. *The Turkey* would be a more apt title for this opus, scripted by Mazursky, who also has a cameo. [R]▼●

Pick-up (1933) **80m.** **½ D: Marion Gering. Sylvia Sidney, George Raft, Lillian Bond, William Harrigan, Clarence Wilson, Brooks Benedict, Robert McWade, Louise Beavers. Occasionally entertaining little drama about ex-con Sidney, who's down on her luck; she conceals her identity, and becomes involved with cabdriver Raft.

Pickup (1951) **78m.** *½ D: Hugo Haas. Beverly Michaels, Hugo Haas, Allan Nixon, Howland Chamberlin, Jo Carroll Dennison. First of writer-producer-director-actor Haas' tawdry low-budget melodramas is a kind of poor man's THE POSTMAN ALWAYS RINGS TWICE, with gold-digger Michaels marrying aging railroad inspector thinking he's got lots of dough. Not as enjoyably bad as Hugo's later efforts.

Pickup Alley (1957-British) **92m.** *½ D: John Gilling. Victor Mature, Anita Ekberg, Trevor Howard, Eric Pohlmann. Lackluster account of federal agent's tracking down of dope-smuggling syndicate. CinemaScope.

Pick-up Artist, The (1987) **C-81m.** *½ D: James Toback. Molly Ringwald, Robert Downey (Jr.), Dennis Hopper, Danny Aiello, Mildred Dunnock, Harvey Keitel, Brian Hamill, Vanessa Williams, Victoria Jackson, Polly Draper, Robert Towne, Lorraine Bracco, Bob Gunton. Womanizing youth meets his match when he falls for the daughter of a boozy gambler in hock to the mob. Standard Toback lowlifes integrated into a conventionally romantic framework. Dismal, dour and deadeningly dull. [PG-13]▼●

Pickup on 101 (1972) **C-93m.** ** D: John Florea. Jack Albertson, Lesley Ann Warren, Martin Sheen, Michael Ontkean, Hal Baylor, George Chandler. Coed who wants to be liberated hits the road with rock musician and friendly hobo in this inoffensive melodrama. Video title: WHERE THE EAGLE FLIES. [PG]▼

Pickup on South Street (1953) **80m.** ***½ D: Samuel Fuller. Richard Widmark, Jean Peters, Thelma Ritter, Richard Kiley, Murvyn Vye, Milburn Stone. Pickpocket

Widmark inadvertently acquires top-secret microfilm, and becomes target for espionage agents. Tough, brutal, well-made film, with superb performance by Ritter as street peddler who also sells information. Story by Dwight Taylor; screenplay by the director. Remade as THE CAPE TOWN AFFAIR.▼

Pick-up Summer (1981-Canadian) **C-92m.** BOMB D: George Mihalka. Michael Zelniker, Carl Marotte, Karen Stephen, Helene Udy. Boys and girls prepare for pinball and beauty contests, with motorcycle rowdies thrown in for good measure. Less rewarding than an average *Archie* comic book. Aka PINBALL SUMMER and PINBALL PICK-UP. [R]▼

Pickwick Papers, The (1954-British) **109m.** *** D: Noel Langley. James Hayter, James Donald, Hermione Baddeley, Kathleen Harrison, Hermione Gingold, Joyce Grenfell, Alexander Gauge, Lionel Murton, Nigel Patrick. Flavorful, episodic version of Dickens' classic—especially the sly actor whose underhanded enterprises pay off.▼

Picnic (1955) **C-115m.** ***½ D: Joshua Logan. William Holden, Rosalind Russell, Kim Novak, Betty Field, Cliff Robertson, Arthur O'Connell, Verna Felton, Susan Strasberg, Nick Adams, Phyllis Newman, Elizabeth W. Wilson. Excellent film of William Inge play about drifter (Holden) who stops over in Kansas, stealing alluring Novak from his old buddy Robertson (making his film debut). Russell and O'Connell almost steal film in second leads, and supporting roles are expertly filled; script by Daniel Taradash. CinemaScope.▼●◗

Picnic at Hanging Rock (1975-Australian) **C-110m.** *** D: Peter Weir. Rachel Roberts, Dominic Guard, Helen Morse, Jacki Weaver, Vivean Gray, Margaret Nelson, Anne (Louise) Lambert. Moody, atmospheric film set in 1900 about three school-girls and their teacher who mysteriously disappear during an outing one sunny day. Eerie and richly textured by director Weir; based on a novel by Joan Lindsay. Reedited by Weir in 1998; that version is about 7m. shorter. [PG]▼●◗

Picture Bride (1994-Japanese) **C-95m.** *** D: Kayo Hatta. Youki Kudoh, Akira Takayama, Tamlyn Tomita, Cary-Hiroyuki Togawa, Toshiro Mifune. A young Japanese woman trying to leave her unhappy past behind travels to Hawaii in the early 1900s as a "picture bride," but soon finds that her new married life is a lot different than she imagined it would be. Slow-moving but engrossing study of the pioneer spirit in Hawaii. Mifune has a nice cameo as a silent-film narrator. [PG-13] ▼●

Picture Mommy Dead (1966) **C-88m.** **½ D: Bert I. Gordon. Don Ameche, Martha Hyer, Zsa Zsa Gabor, Signe Hasso, Susan Gordon. Hokey melodrama with Hyer newly married to Ameche, battling stepdaughter Gordon, possessed by late mother's spirit.▼

Picture of Dorian Gray, The (1945) **110m.** ***½ D: Albert Lewin. George Sanders, Hurd Hatfield, Donna Reed, Angela Lansbury, Peter Lawford, Lowell Gilmore; narrated by Cedric Hardwicke. Haunting Oscar Wilde story of man whose painting ages while he retains youth. Young Lansbury is poignant, singing "The Little Yellow Bird" (and her real-life mother Moyna MacGill is the Duchess). Sanders leaves indelible impression as elegant heavy. Several color inserts throughout the film. Harry Stradling's cinematography won an Oscar. Remade in 1971 as DORIAN GRAY. ▼●

Picture Perfect (1997) **C-100m.** *** D: Glenn Gordon Caron. Jennifer Aniston, Jay Mohr, Kevin Bacon, Olympia Dukakis, Illeana Douglas, Kevin Dunn, Faith Prince, Anne Twomey. Cute starring vehicle for Aniston (of TV's *Friends*), an up-and-comer in the advertising world who invents a fiancé to become more the kind of person her boss wants working for him. Then she has to hire a guy to act the part at a business dinner, and things get complicated. Barely credible romantic comedy is little more than an excuse to showcase Aniston's appeal—but quite watchable on that basis. [PG-13]▼●◗

Picture Show Man, The (1977-Australian) **C-99m.** ** D: John Power. Rod Taylor, John Meillon, John Ewart, Harold Hopkins, Patrick Cargill, Judy Morris. Meandering tale of a traveling showman in 1920s Australia who brings moving pictures to small towns throughout the country. A lovely idea (based on the memoirs of Lyle Penn) that has moments of charm and period atmosphere, but no story, and not much energy. Top-billed Taylor (an Aussie by birth) appears sporadically as Meillon's rival—from Texas! [PG]

Picture Snatcher (1933) **77m.** *** D: Lloyd Bacon. James Cagney, Ralph Bellamy, Alice White, Patricia Ellis, Ralf Harolde. Fast, funny, exciting little film based on true story of daring photographer who got taboo photo of woman in electric chair. Remade as ESCAPE FROM CRIME.

Picture This: The Times of Peter Bogdanovich in Archer City, Texas (1992) **C-57m.** *** D: George Hickenlooper. Absorbing documentary about filmmaker Bogdanovich's return to the scene of his first great success, THE LAST PICTURE SHOW, to make a sequel, TEXASVILLE. Cybill Shepherd, Jeff Bridges, Timothy and Sam Bottoms, Polly Platt, Randy Quaid and others recall how the first film affected their lives (including some surprisingly candid revelations)—and the townspeople compare Larry McMurtry's locally based fiction to their perception of the truth.▼●

Piece of the Action, A (1977) **C-135m.** **½ D: Sidney Poitier. Sidney Poitier, Bill Cosby, James Earl Jones, Denise Nicholas, Hope Clark, Tracy Reed, Titos

Vandis, Ja'net DuBois. Third Poitier-Cosby teaming casts them as con men obliged to help social worker set ghetto kids on the right track. Typical comic crime material offset by serious, preachy moments. [PG]▼

Pieces (1983-Italian-Spanish) **C-85m.** BOMB D: Juan Piquer Simon. Christopher George, Edmund Purdom, Lynda Day George, Paul Smith. Gorefest about a sickie who slices up coeds to create a life-sized jigsaw puzzle. View at your own risk.▼

Pied Piper, The (1942) **86m.** *** D: Irving Pichel. Monty Woolley, Roddy McDowall, Otto Preminger, Anne Baxter, Peggy Ann Garner. Woolley, not very fond of children, finds himself leading a swarm of them on chase from the Nazis. Entertaining wartime film scripted by Nunnally Johnson from a Nevil Shute novel. Remade for TV as CROSSING TO FREEDOM (1990, with Peter O'Toole).

Pied Piper, The (1972-British) **C-90m.** ***½ D: Jacques Demy. Donovan, Donald Pleasence, Michael Hordern, Jack Wild, Diana Dors, John Hurt. Chilling story of piper who rids evil hamlet of rats. While originally conceived as children's tale, director Demy succeeds in weaving grimy portrait of the Middle Ages. [G]

Pie in the Sky (1996) **C-95m.** ** D: Bryan Gordon. Josh Charles, Anne Heche, John Goodman, Christine Lahti, Peter Riegert, Bob Balaban, Christine Ebersole, Wil Wheaton, Dey Young. Comedy about a helicopter traffic reporter who has as many problems sorting out his love life as he does with freeway gridlock. Romantic tale boasts an attractive (and impressive) cast that it almost completely wastes, although Heche is a wonderfully affecting leading lady. Perfect video fodder for your next traffic jam. [R]▼●

Pierrot le Fou (1965-French-Italian) **C-110m.** *** D: Jean-Luc Godard. Jean-Paul Belmondo, Anna Karina, Dirk Sanders, Raymond Devus, Samuel Fuller, Jean-Pierre Léaud. Belmondo and Karina run away together to the South of France; he is leaving his rich wife, she is escaping her involvement with gangsters. Complex, confusing, but engrossing drama, which exudes an intriguing sense of spontaneity. Allegedly shot without a script; also shown at 90m. and 95m. Techniscope.▼●◗

Pier 13 (1940) **66m.** *½ D: Eugene Forde. Lynn Bari, Lloyd Nolan, Joan Valerie, Douglas Fowley, Chick Chandler. Routine programmer in which cop Nolan romances Bari, suspects her sister (Valerie) of being in cahoots with waterfront thief Fowley.

Pigeons (1971) **C-87m.** *½ D: John Dexter. Jordan Christopher, Jill O'Hara, Robert Walden, Kate Reid, William Redfield, Lois Nettleton, Elaine Stritch, Melba Moore. Smug film about 24-year-old Princeton graduate who drives a taxi in Manhattan. The character is unattractive and film looks as if it were designed for stage, not screen. Aka THE SIDELONG GLANCES OF A PIGEON KICKER. [R]

Pigeon That Took Rome, The (1962) **101m.** **½ D: Melville Shavelson. Charlton Heston, Elsa Martinelli, Harry Guardino, Baccaloni, Marietto, Gabriella Pallotta, Debbie Price, Brian Donlevy. Sometimes amusing WW2 comedy of Heston, behind enemy lines, using pigeons to send message to Allies, romancing local girl in whose home he is based. Panavision.

Pigskin Parade (1936) **93m.** *** D: David Butler. Stuart Erwin, Patsy Kelly, Jack Haley, Johnny Downs, Betty Grable, Arline Judge, Dixie Dunbar, Judy Garland, Anthony (Tony) Martin, Elisha Cook, Jr., Grady Sutton, The Yacht Club Boys. Entertaining college football musicomedy with Erwin the hayseed who becomes a gridiron hero, Kelly the coach's wife who knows more about the game than the coach (Haley). Cook appears as an anarchy-spouting campus radical! Garland plays Erwin's kid sister, in her feature debut, and she swings "It's Love I'm After." Alan Ladd appears as a student, and sings with The Yacht Club Boys.▼●

Pilgrimage (1933) **95m.** **½ D: John Ford. Henrietta Crosman, Heather Angel, Norman Foster, Marian Nixon, Lucille La Verne, Hedda Hopper, Charles Grapewin. Unusual film, beautifully directed by Ford, about old woman who breaks up son's romance by sending him off to war (WW1), living to regret it, but finding solace on visit to France. Delicately sentimental, it works up to a point, then goes overboard, but still has some memorable sequences.

Pillars of the Sky (1956) **C-95m.** **½ D: George Marshall. Jeff Chandler, Dorothy Malone, Ward Bond, Keith Andes, Lee Marvin, Sydney Chaplin. Chandler is apt as swaggering army officer fighting Indians, courting Malone. CinemaScope.

Pillow Book, The (1996-British-Dutch-French) **C-126m.** **½ D: Peter Greenaway. Vivian Wu, Ewan McGregor, Yoshi Oida, Ken Ogata, Hideko Yoshida, Judy Ongg, Ken Mitsuishi. Sensual, if dramatically exasperating, convolution about a young woman (Wu) who seeks revenge for wrongs perpetrated against her calligrapher father, who painted elaborate words and characters on her body during an unconventional childhood. Gorgeously shot by Sacha Vierny, film belatedly hits its stride with its heroine's romance with a doomed lover (McGregor), only to fade fatally during a grueling final half hour. Wu, though, is extraordinary, both as a character and a photographic subject. Super 35.▼◗

Pillow of Death (1945) **66m.** ** D: Wallace Fox. Lon Chaney, Jr., Brenda Joyce, J. Edward Bromberg, Rosalind Ivan, Clara Blandick. Another Chaney *Inner Sanctum* vehicle about lawyer turning to murder to clear the way for his true love.▼

Pillow Talk (1959) **C-105m.** ***½ D: Michael Gordon. Doris Day, Rock Hudson, Tony Randall, Thelma Ritter, Nick Adams, Julia Meade, Allen Jenkins, Lee Patrick, William Schallert, Frances Sternhagen. Rock pursues Doris, with interference from Randall and sideline witticisms from Ritter. Imaginative sex comedy has two stars sharing a party line without knowing each other's identity. Fast-moving; plush sets, gorgeous fashions. Oscar-winning story and screenplay by Stanley Shapiro, Russell Rouse, Clarence Greene, and Maurice Richlin. CinemaScope. ▼●◗

Pillow to Post (1945) **92m.** ** D: Vincent Sherman. Ida Lupino, Sydney Greenstreet, William Prince, Stuart Erwin, Ruth Donnelly, Barbara Brown. Obvious WW2 comedy of salesgirl Lupino having soldier Prince pose as her husband so she can get a room; good cast saddled with predictable script.

Pilot, The (1979) **C-99m.** ** D: Cliff Robertson. Cliff Robertson, Diane Baker, Frank Converse, Dana Andrews, Milo O'Shea, Ed Binns, Gordon MacRae. Airline pilot who flies at the end of a bottle discovers that his world is collapsing. Predictable drama given a boost by Walter Lassally's spectacular aerial photography and John Addison's soaring (and seemingly misplaced) score. Video title: DANGER IN THE SKIES. Panavision. [PG]▼

Pilot #5 (1943) **70m.** **½ D: George Sidney. Franchot Tone, Marsha Hunt, Gene Kelly, Van Johnson, Alan Baxter, Dick Simmons. GI pilot Tone volunteers to take on a suicide mission. As he flies to his death, his buddies recall his troubled past (including his involvement with a Huey Long–like governor). Good cast uplifts so-so curio; it's intriguing to see Kelly in a supporting part, as a morally bankrupt hothead. Watch for Peter Lawford at the opening, and see if you can spot Ava Gardner.

"Pimpernel" Smith (1941-British) **122m.** *** D: Leslie Howard. Leslie Howard, Mary Morris, Francis L. Sullivan, Hugh McDermott. Zesty updating of THE SCARLET PIMPERNEL to WW2, with Howard replaying the role of the savior of Nazi-hounded individuals. Retitled: MISTER V.▼

Pinball Pick-Up SEE: **Pick-Up Summer**

Pinball Summer SEE: **Pick-Up Summer**

Pink Cadillac (1989) **C-122m.** ** D: Buddy Van Horn. Clint Eastwood, Bernadette Peters, Timothy Carhart, Tiffany Gail Robinson, Angela Louise Robinson, John Dennis Johnston, Geoffrey Lewis, William Hickey, James (Jim) Carrey. Harmless but off-the-cuff throwaway comedy about a bail-bond bounty hunter who helps the wife of his latest target rescue her kidnapped baby from the neo-Nazi associates of her weakling husband. No Edsel, but at two hours, seriously in need of a tuneup. Eastwood's uncharacteristically broad performance does more for the film than the film does for him. [PG-13]▼●

Pink Floyd—The Wall (1982-British) **C-99m.** **½ D: Alan Parker. Bob Geldof, Christine Hargreaves, James Laurenson, Eleanor David, Bob Hoskins. Visualization of Pink Floyd's somber best-selling album, about a rock star's mental breakdown, is perhaps the longest rock video to date, and certainly the most depressing. Many of the images are hypnotic, but self-indulgence, and a relentlessly downbeat theme, erode one's interest after a while. Striking animated sequences by Gerald Scarfe, who also designed the film. Panavision. [R]▼●◗

Pink Jungle, The (1968) **C-104m.** **½ D: Delbert Mann. James Garner, Eva Renzi, George Kennedy, Nigel Green, Michael Ansara, George Rose. Offbeat blend of comedy and adventure with photographer Garner and model Renzi involved in diamond smuggling in South America. Film shifts gears too often, but provides lighthearted entertainment. Techniscope.▼

Pink Motel (1983) **C-88m.** BOMB D: Mike MacFarland. Phyllis Diller, Slim Pickens, Terri Berland, Brad Cowgill, Cathryn Hartt, Andrea Howard, Tony Longo. Diller and Pickens run a hot-sheets motel in this R-rated movie version of TV's *Love—American Style.* Corny dialogue, listless direction. [R]▼

Pink Nights (1985) **C-84m.** ** D: Philip Koch. Shaun Allen, Kevin Anderson, Peri Kaczmarek, Larry King, Jonathan Jancovic Michaels, Jessica Vitkus. Inconsequential teen comedy about Anderson, who does not seem to have much luck with the opposite sex, and how he comes to live with a trio of girls. [PG]▼●

Pink Panther, The (1964) **C-113m.** ***½ D: Blake Edwards. Peter Sellers, David Niven, Capucine, Robert Wagner, Claudia Cardinale, Brenda DeBanzie, John LeMesurier, Fran Jeffries. Delightful caper comedy introduced bumbling Inspector Clouseau to the world (as well as the cartoon character featured in the opening titles), so obsessed with catching notorious jewel thief "The Phantom" that he isn't even aware his quarry is also his wife's lover! Loaded with great slapstick and especially clever chase sequence; beautiful European locations, memorable score by Henry Mancini. Followed by A SHOT IN THE DARK. Technirama.▼●◗

Pink Panther Strikes Again, The (1976-British) **C-103m.** ***½ D: Blake Edwards. Peter Sellers, Herbert Lom, Colin Blakely, Leonard Rossiter, Lesley-Anne Down, Burt Kwouk, Andre Maranne. Fifth PINK PANTHER is one of the funniest. Sellers' former boss (Lom) goes crazy, threatens to destroy the world with a ray-gun he has commandeered. Sellers' hilarious Inspector Clouseau is backed up by better-than-usual gags—with the usual number of pain-and-destruction jokes thrown in for good measure. Sequel: REVENGE OF THE PINK PANTHER. Panavision. [PG]▼●◗

Pinky (1949) **102m.** *** D: Elia Kazan. Jeanne Crain, Ethel Barrymore, Ethel Waters, Nina Mae McKinney, William Lundigan. Pioneer racial drama of black girl passing for white, returning to Southern home; still has impact, with fine support from Mmes. Waters and Barrymore.▼

Pinocchio (1940) **C-88m.** **** D: Ben Sharpsteen, Hamilton Luske. Voices of Dickie Jones, Christian Rub, Cliff Edwards, Evelyn Venable, Walter Catlett, Frankie Darro. Walt Disney's brilliant, timeless animated cartoon feature, based on the Collodi story about an inquisitive, tale-spinning wooden puppet who wants more than anything else to become a real boy. Technically dazzling, emotionally rich, with unforgettable characters and some of the scariest scenes ever put on film (Lampwick's transformation into a jackass, the chase with Monstro the whale). A joy, no matter how many times you see it. Songs include Oscar-winning "When You Wish Upon a Star." ▼●◗

Pinocchio and the Emperor of the Night (1987) **C-87m.** ** D: Hal Sutherland. Voices of Edward Asner, Tom Bosley, Lana Beeson, Linda Gary, Jonathan Harris, James Earl Jones, Ricky Lee Jones, Don Knotts, William Windom. Uninspired continuation of the Pinocchio story: now a real boy, Pinocchio is guided by "Gee Whillikers," a wooden bug come to life, and they enjoy many adventures which parallel the Disney classic. Fully animated by Filmation Studios, but an embarrassment next to the 1940 gem. [G]▼●

Pinocchio in Outer Space (1964-U.S.-French) **C-90m.** ** D: Ray Goosens. Voices of Arnold Stang, Jess Cain. Watchable cartoon adventure for kids, with unmemorable songs.▼

Pin Up Girl (1944) **C-83m.** **½ D: Bruce Humberstone. Betty Grable, Martha Raye, John Harvey, Joe E. Brown, Eugene Pallette, Mantan Moreland, Charlie Spivak Orchestra. One of Grable's weaker vehicles, despite support from Raye and Brown; songs are nil, so is plot.▼●

Pioneer Builders SEE: **Conquerors, The**

Pipe Dreams (1976) **C-89m.** **½ D: Stephen Verona. Gladys Knight, Barry Hankerson, Bruce French, Sherry Bain, Wayne Tippit, Altovise Davis, Sally Kirkland. Singing star Knight makes acting debut in highly dramatic story set against Alaskan pipeline. Excellent location shooting. Soundtrack filled with songs by Knight and her group, the Pips. [PG]▼

Pippi Longstocking (1997-Swedish-Canadian) **C-77m.** **½ D: Clive Smith. Voices of Catherine O'Hara, Dave Thomas, Wayne Robson, Gordon Pinsent, Melissa Altro. Faithful animated version of Astrid Lindgren's story about the world's strongest girl, Miss Pippilotta Delicatessa Windowshade Mackrelmint Efraimsdottir Longstocking, age 9, as she encounters school, friends, the circus, and burglars, all for the first time. Nelvana studio's bright artwork and the script's cheerful characterizations will please fans, but the songs are dreary. Followed by a direct-to-video sequel. [G]▼

Piranha (1978) **C-92m.** *** D: Joe Dante. Bradford Dillman, Heather Menzies, Kevin McCarthy, Keenan Wynn, Dick Miller, Barbara Steele, Belinda Balaski, Bruce Gordon, Paul Bartel. Fast-paced, funny spoof of JAWS and countless 1950s sci-fi films; in-jokes and campy supporting cast will make it particular fun for film buffs. Written by John Sayles (who also plays a small role). Followed by a sequel. Remade for TV in 1996. [R]▼◗

Piranha Part Two: The Spawning (1981-Italian-U.S.) **C-95m.** *½ D: James Cameron. Tricia O'Neil, Steve Marachuk, Lance Henriksen, Ricky G. Paul, Ted Richert, Leslie Graves. A sequel in name only, this silly horror film is set at a Club Med-type resort where human mating rituals are interrupted by the spawning ritual of mutated flying fish crossed with grunions, which are oversize, deadly killers. You'd have to be psychic to have spotted any talent from director Cameron in this debut picture. [R]▼●

Pirate, The (1948) **C-102m.** *** D: Vincente Minnelli. Judy Garland, Gene Kelly, Walter Slezak, Gladys Cooper, Reginald Owen, George Zucco, The Nicholas Brothers. Judy thinks circus clown Kelly is really Caribbean pirate; lavish costuming, dancing and Cole Porter songs (including "Be a Clown") bolster stagy plot. Kelly's dances are exhilarating, as usual. Based on S. N. Behrman play.▼●

Pirate and the Slave Girl (1961-Italian) **C-87m.** ** D: Piero Pierotti. Lex Barker, Massimo Serato, Chelo Alonso, Michele Malaspina, Enzo Maggio. Formula costumer with Barker the hero who sees the light of the true cause, helping benevolent pirates vs. wicked governor. Colorscope.

Pirate Movie, The (1982-Australian) **C-99m.** BOMB D: Ken Annakin. Kristy McNichol, Christopher Atkins, Ted Hamilton, Bill Kerr, Maggie Kirkpatrick, Garry McDonald. Appalling "update" of Gilbert & Sillivan's *The Pirates of Penzance* not only trashes the original but fails on its own paltry terms—as a teenybopper comedy with bubblegum music. Parodies (and steals from) so many other films it should have been called THE RIP-OFF MOVIE. [PG]▼

Pirates (1986-French-Tunisian) **C-124m.** **½ D: Roman Polanski. Walter Matthau, Damien Thomas, Richard Pearson, Cris Campion, Charlotte Lewis, Olu Jacobs, Roy Kinnear, Ferdy Mayne, Tony Peck. Rich-looking, robust pirate comedy, filmed on a grand scale (in widescreen), with plenty of broad comedy, a delightful performance by Matthau, a rousing score by Philippe Sarde . . . and a certain lack of story. It's still fun. Panavision. [PG-13] ▼

Pirate Ship SEE: **Mutineers, The**

Pirates of Blood River, The (1962-British) **C-87m.** ** D: John Gilling. Kerwin Mathews, Glenn Corbett, Christopher Lee, Marla Landi, Oliver Reed, Andrew Keir, Peter Arne. Earnest but hackneyed account of Huguenots fighting off buccaneers. Hammerscope.

Pirates of Capri, The (1949) **94m.** ** D: Edgar G. Ulmer. Louis Hayward, Binnie Barnes, Alan Curtis, Rudolph (Massimo) Serato. Below-average adventure film has Neapolitan natives revolting against tyrant. Lots of action but not much else. Filmed in Italy. Retitled: CAPTAIN SIROCCO.

Pirates of Monterey (1947) **C-77m.** ** D: Alfred L. Werker. Maria Montez, Rod Cameron, Mikhail Rasumny, Philip Reed, Gilbert Roland, Gale Sondergaard. Dull film of exciting period in history, the fight against Mexican control of California in the 1800s.

Pirates of Penzance, The (1983) **C-112m.** *** D: Wilford Leach. Kevin Kline, Angela Lansbury, Linda Ronstadt, George Rose, Rex Smith, Tony Azito. Joseph Papp's hit stage revival of the Gilbert and Sullivan perennial is transferred to film with the original cast (plus Lansbury) and director—who decided to make no bones about its theatricality! Not for G&S purists, perhaps, but fun. Splendid production design by Elliot Scott. Panavision. [G]▼●

Pirates of Tortuga (1961) **C-97m.** ** D: Robert D. Webb. Ken Scott, John Richardson, Letitia Roman, Dave King, Rafer Johnson. Lumbering costumer involving buccaneer Sir Henry Morgan and a Caribbean pirate stronghold. CinemaScope.

Pirates of Tripoli (1955) **C-72m.** ** D: Felix E. Feist. Paul Henreid, Patricia Medina, Paul Newland, John Miljan, William Fawcett. Veteran cast in tired costumer, with colorful scenery the only virtue.

Pistol for Ringo, A (1966-Italian) **C-97m.** **½ D: Duccio Tessari. Montgomery Wood, Fernando Sancho, Hally Hammond, Nieves Navarro. Wood is the gun-shooting hero in Texas where he combats maurauding Mexicans hiding out at a ranch. Techniscope.

Pit and the Pendulum (1961) **C-80m.** ***½ D: Roger Corman. Vincent Price, John Kerr, Barbara Steele, Luana Anders, Antony Carbone. Slick horror tale set right after Spanish Inquisition. Price thinks he is his late father, the most vicious torturer during bloody inquisition. Beautifully staged; watch out for that incredible pendulum . . . and bear with slow first half. The second of Corman's Poe adaptations, scripted by Richard Matheson. Panavision. ▼●

Pit and the Pendulum, The (1991) **C-97m.** *** D: Stuart Gordon. Lance Henriksen, Rona De Ricci, Jonathan Fuller, Frances Bay, Mark Margolis, Jeffrey Combs, Oliver Reed. In 1492, Torquemada (Henriksen), Spain's Grand Inquisitor, is haunted by his lust for a baker's wife accused of witchcraft. Strong, well-researched script (by Dennis Paoli) owes little to Poe, but is vividly realized by Gordon; graphic scenes of torture are appropriate here, and Henriksen's intense performance is mesmerizing. The best Full Moon release to date. Shot in Spain. Available in both R and unrated versions. [R]▼●◗

Pitch Black (2000-U.S.-Australian) **C-107m.** ** D: David Twohy. Radha Mitchell, Vin Diesel, Cole Hauser, Keith David, Lewis Fitz-Gerald, Claudia Black, Rhiana Griffith. Ambitious but formulaic sci-fi/horror film set in the future, with a motley planeload of passengers crash-landing on a remote planet. Not only do they have to contend with a violent, amoral ex-con (the imposing Diesel) in their midst, but an unknown terror that's magnified by the threat of total darkness. Some exciting scenes and effects, but weighed down by a feeling of déjà vu. Super 35. [R]▼

Pitfall (1948) **84m.** *** D: Andre de Toth. Dick Powell, Lizabeth Scott, Jane Wyatt, Raymond Burr, John Litel, Byron Barr. Married man's brief extramarital fling may cost him his job and marriage. Intriguing film noir look at the American dream gone sour, typefied by Powell's character, who's got a house, a little boy, and a perfect wife—but feels bored and stifled.▼●

Pit Stop (1969) **92m.** **½ D: Jack Hill. Brian Donlevy, Richard Davalos, Ellen McRae (Burstyn), Sid Haig, Beverly Washburn, George Washburn. Surprisingly entertaining micro-budget drive-in fare about rivalry on the stock-car racing circuit, with some genuinely hair-raising footage during figure-eight races.▼

Pittsburgh (1942) **90m.** ** D: Lewis Seiler. Marlene Dietrich, John Wayne, Randolph Scott, Frank Craven, Louise Allbritton, Thomas Gomez, Shemp Howard. Big John loves the coal and steel business more than he does Marlene, which leaves field open for rival Scott. Slow-moving.▼

Pixote (1981-Brazilian) **C-127m.** **** D: Hector Babenco. Fernando Ramos da Silva, Marilia Pera, Jorge Juliano, Gilberto Moura, Jose Nilson dos Santos, Edilson Lino. Chilling drama about an abandoned 10-year-old street criminal who pimps, sniffs glue, and murders three people before the finale. Haunting performance by the baby-faced da Silva; Pera equally superb as a prostitute. Extraordinarily graphic film is not for the squeamish.▼

Pizza Triangle, The (1970-Italian) **C-99m.** **½ D: Ettore Scola. Marcello Mastroianni, Monica Vitti, Giancarlo Giannini. Scene-stealing stars compete in this flamboyant black comedy of two guys both in love with flower seller Vitti. Colorful photography by Carlo Di Palma. Aka A DRAMA OF JEALOUSY. Panavision. [R]

P.J. (1968) **C-109m.** ** D: John Guillermin. George Peppard, Raymond Burr, Gayle Hunnicutt, Brock Peters, Wilfrid Hyde-White, Coleen Gray, Susan Saint James. Private-eye takes job bodyguarding tycoon's mistress. OK for those who'll sit through any film of this genre, but no big deal; TV print runs 101m., and cuts out much violence—including memorable subway death. Techniscope.

P.K. and the Kid (1982) **C-89m.** ** D: Lou Lombardo. Paul Le Mat, Molly Ringwald, Alex Rocco, Fionnula Flanagan, Charles Hallahan, Bert Remsen, Esther Rolle, Leigh Hamilton. Stillborn tale of arm wrestling (made several years before the Sylvester Stallone classic OVER THE TOP, but released afterward) teams strong-wristed Le Mat with runaway teen Ringwald on the road to nowhere. With that cast and a mood resembling Le Mat's MELVIN AND HOWARD, this should have been more interesting. [PG-13]▼●

Place Called Glory, A (1966-German) **C-92m.** ** D: Ralph Gideon (Sheldon Reynolds). Lex Barker, Pierre Brice, Marianne Koch, Jorge Rigaud. German-made Western with Karl May's recurring characters Winnetou and Old Shatterhand. Plot killed by dubbing. Techniscope.▼

Place for Lovers, A (1968-Italian-French) **C-90m.** BOMB D: Vittorio De Sica. Faye Dunaway, Marcello Mastroianni, Caroline Mortimer, Karin Engh. One well-known critic called this "the most godawful piece of pseudo romantic slop I've ever seen!" Love story about American fashion designer and Italian engineer marks career low points for all concerned. [R]

Place in the Sun, A (1951) **122m.** *** D: George Stevens. Montgomery Clift, Elizabeth Taylor, Shelley Winters, Keefe Brasselle, Raymond Burr, Anne Revere. Ambitious remake of Theodore Dreiser's AN AMERICAN TRAGEDY derives most of its power from Clift's brilliant performance, almost matched by Winters as plain girl who loses him to alluring Taylor. Depiction of the idle rich, and American morals, seems outdated, and Burr's scenes as fiery D.A. are downright absurd. Everyone gets A for effort; six Oscars included Best Direction, Screenplay (Michael Wilson, Harry Brown), Score (Franz Waxman), Cinematography (William C. Mellor), Film Editing, and Costume Design.▼●

Place of One's Own, A (1945-British) **92m.** **½ D: Bernard Knowles. James Mason, Margaret Lockwood, Barbara Mullen, Dennis Price, Helen Haye, Ernest Thesiger. Well-made film about couple who buy "haunted" house, and young woman who becomes possessed by spirit of former owner. Well acted but low-key. Mason plays unusual role of older, retired man.

Places in the Heart (1984) **C-102m.** *** D: Robert Benton. Sally Field, Lindsay Crouse, Ed Harris, Amy Madigan, John Malkovich, Danny Glover, Terry O'Quinn, Bert Remsen, Ray Baker. Writer-director Benton's affectionate look at life in his hometown, Waxahachie, Texas, during the Depression 1930s. A bit too calculated and predictable, but Field is so good (as a young widow determined to survive as a cotton farmer), and film is so well made (beautifully shot by Nestor Almendros), it's hard not to like. Field won Best Actress Oscar for her performance as did Benton for his original screenplay. [PG]▼●

Plague (1978-Canadian) **C-88m.** BOMB D: Ed Hunt. Daniel Pilon, Kate Reid, Celine Lomez, Michael J. Reynolds, Brenda Donohue, Barbara Gordon. Deadly bacterium is on the loose. Phony and stultifyingly boring. Orginally titled M3: THE GEMINI STRAIN. [PG]

Plague, The (1991-French-British-Argentine) **C-105m.** *½ D: Luis Puenzo. William Hurt, Sandrine Bonnaire, Jean-Marc Barr, Robert Duvall, Raul Julia, Victoria Tennant. Obvious, muddled adaptation (by director Puenzo) of the Albert Camus novel, focusing on a dedicated doctor (Hurt), a French TV reporter (Bonnaire) and cameraman (Barr), and various other characters whose lives become intertwined during a deadly plague in a South American city. A major disappointment. Never released theatrically in the U.S. [R]▼

Plague Dogs, The (1982) **C-86m.** *** D: Martin Rosen. Voices of John Hurt, James Bolam, Christopher Benjamin, Judy Geeson, Barbara Leigh-Hunt, Nigel Hawthorne, Patrick Stewart. Unusual animated adventure, adapted from Richard Adams's novel about a pair of dogs who escape from animal experimentation lab and are hunted down like criminals. A bit slow-moving but beautifully animated and most worthwhile; a poignant plea for animal rights. For adults and older children only. A follow-up to WATERSHIP DOWN from same producer-director.▼

Plague of the Zombies, The (1966-British) **C-90m.** **½ D: John Gilling. Andre Morell, Diane Clare, Brook Williams, Jacqueline

Pearce, John Carson. Beautiful low-key photography and direction in fairly tense story of voodoo cult in Cornish village. Minor but effective Hammer horror.▼●

Plainsman, The (1936) **113m.** *** D: Cecil B. DeMille. Gary Cooper, Jean Arthur, James Ellison, Charles Bickford, Porter Hall, Victor Varconi, Helen Burgess, John Miljan, Gabby Hayes, Paul Harvey, Frank McGlynn, Sr. Typical DeMille hokum, a big, outlandish Western which somehow manages to involve Wild Bill Hickok, Calamity Jane, Buffalo Bill, George Custer and Abraham Lincoln in adventure of evil Bickford selling guns to the Indians. About as authentic as BLAZING SADDLES, but who cares—it's still good fun. Look for Anthony Quinn as a Cheyenne warrior. Remade in 1966. ▼●

Plainsman, The (1966) **C-92m.** *½ D: David Lowell Rich. Don Murray, Guy Stockwell, Abby Dalton, Bradford Dillman, Leslie Nielsen. Static remake of the Cooper-Arthur vehicle is dull even on its own.

Plainsman and the Lady (1946) **87m.** ** D: Joseph Kane. William Elliott, Vera Ralston, Gail Patrick, Joseph Schildkraut, Andy Clyde. Uninspiring saga of pony express pioneer battling slimy villains and winning lovely Ralston.

Plainsong (1982) **C/B&W-78m.** ***½ D: Ed Stabile. Jessica Nelson, Teresanne Joseph, Lyn Traverse, Steve Geiger, Sandon McCall, Howard Harris. Extremely moving, starkly realistic yet poetic drama of life and death in pioneer Nebraska, focusing on experiences of three young women settlers. Wonderfully directed; filmed, incredibly, in New Jersey.

Plan B (1997) **C-102m.** **½ D: Gary Leva. Jon Cryer, Lisa Darr, Lance Guest, Mark Matheisen, Sara Mornell. Amiable low-budget film about a group of friends, their romantic snafus, and the roadblocks they encounter in reaching their goals—to become a published novelist, to find the perfect guy, to get that big break as an actor, to conceive a child. Likable performances, reasonably credible situations and dialogue, but there are at least three endings. [R]▼

Planes, Trains & Automobiles (1987) **C-93m.** **½ D: John Hughes. Steve Martin, John Candy, Laila Robins, Michael McKean, Kevin Bacon, Dylan Baker, William Windom, Edie McClurg, Ben Stein. Bittersweet farce about a businessman trying to get home for Thanksgiving who encounters disaster at every turn and has to share most of it with a lout who becomes his steadfast companion. Martin mostly plays straight to the overbearing Candy, but writer-director Hughes refuses to make either one a caricature—which keeps this amiable film teetering between slapstick shenanigans and compassionate comedy. Hurt by an awful music score. [R]▼●

Planet Earth (1974) **C-78m. TVM** D: Marc Daniels. John Saxon, Janet Margolin, Ted Cassidy, Diana Muldaur, Johana DeWinter, Christopher Gary. Sci-fi fun as future race of humans finds itself in combat with a sadistic matriarchy. Reworking of Gene Roddenberry's GENESIS II, though not as elaborate. Average.▼

Planet of Blood (1966) **C-81m.** **½ D: Curtis Harrington. John Saxon, Basil Rathbone, Judi Meredith, Dennis Hopper, Florence Marly. Eerie space opera (utilizing effects footage cribbed from a big-budget Russian film) about a space vampire brought to Earth. Best thing is the bizarre climax, if you can wait that long. Originally titled QUEEN OF BLOOD.▼●

Planet of Horrors SEE: **Galaxy of Terror**

Planet of the Apes (1968) **C-112m.** ***½ D: Franklin J. Schaffner. Charlton Heston, Roddy McDowall, Kim Hunter, Maurice Evans, James Whitmore, James Daly, Linda Harrison. Intriguing, near-classic sci-fi. Heston leads a group of surviving astronauts in shocking future world where apes are masters, humans slaves. Only liabilities: somewhat familiar plot, self-conscious humor; otherwise, a must-see. Michael Wilson and Rod Serling scripted from Pierre Boulle's novel, spawning four sequels and two TV series. Won a special Oscar for make-up created by John Chambers. Panavision. [G]▼●

Planet of the Vampires (1965-Italian) **C-86m.** **½ D: Mario Bava. Barry Sullivan, Norma Bengell, Angel Aranda, Evi Marandi, Fernando Villena. Eerily photographed, atmospheric science-fantasy of spaceship looking for missing comrades on misty planet where strange power controls their minds. Shown on TV as THE DEMON PLANET. Colorscope.▼●

Planet on the Prowl SEE: **War Between the Planets**

Planets Against Us (1961-Italian-French) **85m.** *½ D: Romano Ferara. Michel Lemoine, Maria Pia Luzi, Jany Clair, Marco Guglielmi, Otello Toso. Human-like aliens come to earth and destroy everyone they touch. Pretty bad.▼

Plan 9 From Outer Space (1959) **79m.** BOMB D: Edward D. Wood, Jr. Gregory Walcott, Tom Keene, Duke Moore, Mona McKinnon, Dudley Manlove, Joanna Lee, Tor Johnson, Lyle Talbot, Bela Lugosi, Vampira, Criswell. Hailed as the worst movie ever made; certainly one of the funniest. Pompous aliens believe they can conquer Earth by resurrecting corpses from a San Fernando Valley cemetery. Lugosi died after two days' shooting in 1956; his remaining scenes were played by a taller, younger man holding a cape over his face! So mesmerizingly awful it actually improves (so to speak) with each viewing. And remember: it's all based on sworn testimony! Aka GRAVE ROBBERS FROM OUTER SPACE; followed by REVENGE OF THE DEAD.▼●◗

Planter's Wife SEE: **Outpost in Malaya**

Platinum Blonde (1931) **90m.** *** D: Frank Capra. Jean Harlow, Loretta Young, Robert Williams, Louise Closser Hale, Donald Dillaway, Walter Catlett. Snappy comedy about wisecracking reporter who marries wealthy girl (Harlow) but can't stand confinement of life among high society. Despite engaging presence of Harlow and Young, it's Williams' show all the way.▼

Platinum High School (1960) **93m.** ** D: Charles Haas. Mickey Rooney, Terry Moore, Dan Duryea, Yvette Mimieux, Conway Twitty, Jimmy Boyd. Limp attempt at sensationalism, with Rooney a father discovering that his son's death at school wasn't accidental. Retitled: TROUBLE AT 16.▼

Platoon (1986) **C-120m.** ***½ D: Oliver Stone. Tom Berenger, Willem Dafoe, Charlie Sheen, Forest Whitaker, Francesco Quinn, John C. McGinley, Richard Edson, Kevin Dillon, Reggie Johnson, Keith David, Johnny Depp. Penetrating first-person account of life on the line as a young soldier in the Vietnam War. Harrowingly realistic and completely convincing, though the motives and reactions of its main character (played by Sheen, based on writer-director Stone) are hard to relate to—leaving this otherwise excellent film with a certain degree of aloofness. Academy Award winner for Best Picture, Director, Film Editing (Claire Simpson), and Sound. [R]▼●◗

Platoon Leader (1988) **C-100m.** BOMB D: Aaron Norris. Michael Dudikoff, Robert F. Lyons, Michael De Lorenzo, Rick Fitts, Jesse Dabson. Obnoxious, bloody PLATOON rip-off, about a group of American GIs battling the commies in Southeast Asia. Director Norris is the brother of Chuck. [R]▼●

Playboy of the Western World, The (1962-Irish) **C-100m.** *** D: Brian Desmond Hurst. Gary Raymond, Siobhan McKenna, Elspeth March, Michael O'Brian, Liam Redmond, Niall MacGinnis. Simple and eloquent, if a bit stagy, version of J. M. Synge's classic satire. Boyish, boastful Christy Mahon (Raymond) charms a small Irish village with his tale of how he did in his dad.▼

Playboys, The (1992) **C-110m.** **½ D: Gillies MacKennon. Albert Finney, Aidan Quinn, Robin Wright, Milo O'Shea, Alan Devlin, Niamh Cusack, Ian McElhinney, Niall Buggy, Adrian Dunbar. A young woman scandalizes her provincial Irish village in the 1950s by having a child out of wedlock, and refusing to name the father; the arrival of a traveling dramatic troupe stirs things up even more. Flavorful but heavy-handed tale; good performances can only do so much with a script that's so predictable. [PG-13]▼●

Play Dirty (1968-British) **C-117m.** *** D: Andre de Toth. Michael Caine, Nigel Davenport, Nigel Green, Harry Andrews, Aly Ben Ayed. British army captain leads group of ex-cons into the North African campaign in WW2; film invites comparison with THE DIRTY DOZEN and holds its own quite well. Panavision. [M/PG]

Player, The (1992) **C-123m.** *** D: Robert Altman. Tim Robbins, Greta Scacchi, Fred Ward, Whoopi Goldberg, Peter Gallagher, Brion James, Cynthia Stevenson, Vincent D'Onofrio, Dean Stockwell, Richard E. Grant, Dina Merrill, Sydney Pollack, Lyle Lovett, Randall Batinkoff, Gina Gershon. Sharp black comedy about a paranoid young movie executive (Robbins) who is threatened by a disgruntled screenwriter—until he begins taking the law into his own hands. Biting examination of Hollywood greed and power, with eternal renegade Altman near the top of his form (especially during the eight-minute opening tracking shot). Hilarious performances, scores of star cameos (several by Altman alumni like Elliott Gould, Lily Tomlin, Sally Kellerman, and Cher), *many* inside jokes . . . but a bit too much plot. Adapted by Michael Tolkin from his novel; Tolkin and his lookalike brother, Stephen, also appear as a pair of writers who meet with Robbins. [R]▼●◗

Players (1979) **C-120m.** BOMB D: Anthony Harvey. Ali MacGraw, Dean-Paul Martin, Maximilian Schell, Pancho Gonzalez, Steve Guttenberg, Melissa Prophet. Aspiring tennis pro has to choose between forehand and foreplay when he falls for a "kept" woman. There's something wrong with any movie where Pancho Gonzalez gives the best performance. [PG]▼

Players (1980) SEE: **Club, The**

Players Club, The (1998) **C-104m.** ** D: Ice Cube. LisaRaye, Bernie Mac, Monica Calhoun, A. J. Johnson, Ice Cube, Alex Thomas, Faizon Love, Charles O. Murphy, Adele Givens, Chrystale Wilson, Larry McCoy, Dick Anthony Williams, Tiny Lister, Jamie Foxx, John Amos, Michael Clarke Duncan. A college journalism major looks back on the sleazy events that took place during her long employment at a black strip club, among them the lurid apartment parties that took place on the side. Not a bad hook, but the film is done in by its seen-it-all-before limitations and pedestrian script. Cube also wrote and executive-produced. [R]▼●

Play Girl (1940) **75m.** ** D: Frank Woodruff. Kay Francis, Nigel Bruce, James Ellison, Margaret Hamilton, Mildred Coles, Katharine Alexander. Contrived programmer with Francis playing an aging gold digger who takes pretty but destitute Coles under her wing, but doesn't count on her protegée falling in love.

Playgirl (1954) **85m.** **½ D: Joseph Pevney. Shelley Winters, Barry Sullivan, Gregg Palmer, Richard Long, Kent Taylor. Winters is most comfortable in drama about girl involved with gangsters.

Playgirl After Dark SEE: **Too Hot to Handle** (1959)

Playgirl Gang SEE: **Switchblade Sisters**

Playgirl Killer, The SEE: **Decoy for Terror**

Playing by Heart (1998) **C-120m.** ** D: Willard Carroll. Sean Connery, Gena Rowlands, Gillian Anderson, Angelina Jolie, Madeleine Stowe, Anthony Edwards, Ryan Phillippe, Dennis Quaid, Ellen Burstyn, Jay Mohr, Jon Stewart, Patricia Clarkson, Nastassja Kinski, Daniel von Bargen. Talky film—with its heart in the right place—about a handful of L.A. men and women and their fouled-up relationships, ranging from an older couple whose marriage is strained by an illness and a long-ago affair, to a woman who comes to terms with her son for the first time as he lies in a hospital bed dying of AIDS. Attractive, well-cast, but dreary multi-story mosaic, written by director Carroll. Panavision. [R] ▼●◗

Playing for Keeps (1986) **C-102m.** *½ D: Bob Weinstein, Harvey Weinstein. Daniel Jordano, Matthew Penn, Leon W. Grant, Mary B. Ward, Marisa Tomei, Jimmy Baio, Harold Gould. After finishing high school, a group of friends band together to save a run-down hotel from a greedy developer in an unfriendly town. A youth comedy from the 80s that's aged; worth seeing only for a young Marisa Tomei. Also notable as the only directorial effort by the founders and honchos of Miramax. Beware of the frequently used montage! [PG-13]▼

Playing for Time (1980) **C-150m. TVM** D: Daniel Mann. Vanessa Redgrave, Jane Alexander, Maud Adams, Viveca Lindfors, Shirley Knight, Melanie Mayron, Marisa Berenson, Verna Bloom, Martha Schlamme, Marta Heflin. Outstanding drama about Fania Fenelon, who survived Auschwitz by performing in a bizarre orchestra "playing for time" while other inmates are marched to their death. Redgrave, as Fenelon, and Alexander, as the orchestra's leader, won Emmy Awards for their performances (Knight also received a nomination). Arthur Miller's stunning teleplay earned him an Emmy, and the film itself won as Outstanding Drama Special. Above average.▼

Playing God (1997) **C-93m.** *½ D: Andy Wilson. David Duchovny, Timothy Hutton, Angelina Jolie, Michael Massee, Peter Stormare, Gary Dourdan, John Hawkes, Andrew Tiernan. Preposterous story of drug-addicted ex-surgeon Duchovny hired by gangster Hutton to be the personal emergency physician for his shot-up and slashed cronies. The improvised medical treatment is so completely laughable, it upstages the absurdity of the story line. Why this movie was ever made is truly a case for *The X-Files*. [R]▼●◗

Play It Again, Sam (1972) **C-87m.** ***½ D: Herbert Ross. Woody Allen, Diane Keaton, Tony Roberts, Jerry Lacy, Susan Anspach, Jennifer Salt, Joy Bang, Viva. Delightful adaptation of Woody's own play about film buff coached by the ghost of Bogart in fumbling attempts to impress a girl after his wife divorces him. More "conventional" than other early Allen films, but just as funny. [PG]▼●

Play It As It Lays (1972) **C-99m.** **½ D: Frank Perry. Tuesday Weld, Anthony Perkins, Tammy Grimes, Adam Roarke, Ruth Ford, Eddie Firestone. Film version of Joan Didion's best seller about neglected wife of self-centered film director is helped by Weld-Perkins casting. Story is believable enough, but rambles inconclusively. Look for Tyne Daly as a journalist. [R]

Play It Cool (1962-British) **82m.** *½ D: Michael Winner. Billy Fury, Michael Anderson, Jr., Dennis Price, Richard Wattis, Anna Palk, Keith Hamshere, Ray Brooks. Mild rock 'n' roll entry, with thin plot line of groovy group preventing a rich girl from going wrong.

Play It to the Bone (1999) **C-124m.** **½ D: Ron Shelton. Woody Harrelson, Antonio Banderas, Lolita Davidovich, Tom Sizemore, Lucy Liu, Robert Wagner, Richard Masur, Willie Garson, Cylk Cozart, Aida Turturro, Jack Carter. Two boxer friends are hired as last-minute substitutes on a primo Las Vegas fight card, and express their doubts and fears while driving from L.A. to Vegas with their mutual ex-girlfriend. Relaxed pace of Shelton's script challenges the viewer to stay interested through the long road trip up to the stormy and eventful fight and its aftermath. Many sports and show-business celebrities appear as themselves. Panavision. [R]▼●◗

Playmates (1941) **94m.** *½ D: David Butler. Kay Kyser, Lupe Velez, John Barrymore, May Robson, Patsy Kelly, Peter Lind Hayes. Poor musical "comedy" about a has-been Shakespearean actor who teams up with bandleader Kyser in order to pay back taxes. Crude and tasteless; this was Barrymore's last film.▼

Play Misty for Me (1971) **C-102m.** *** D: Clint Eastwood. Clint Eastwood, Jessica Walter, Donna Mills, John Larch, Irene Hervey, Jack Ging, Johnny Otis, Cannonball Adderley Quintet. Well-done shocker of late night radio D.J. stalked by homicidal ex-fan Walter. Eastwood's first film as director; *his* frequent director, Don Siegel, plays Murphy the bartender. [R]▼●

Play Time (1967-French) **C-108m.** **** D: Jacques Tati. Jacques Tati, Barbara Dennek,

Jacqueline Lecomte, Valerie Camille, Leon Doyen. M. Hulot (Tati) wanders through an unrecognizable modern Paris of steel and glass skyscrapers. Sight and sound gags abound in this superbly constructed film, the various episodes of which are linked by Hulot's trying to keep an appointment. Art Buchwald provided dialogue for English-speaking scenes. Cut from original 155m. French version.▼●

Plaza Suite (1971) **C-115m.** *** D: Arthur Hiller. Walter Matthau, Maureen Stapleton, Barbara Harris, Lee Grant, Louise Sorel. One of Neil Simon's funniest plays well-adapted to screen. Three separate stories about people staying in certain room at famed N.Y.C. hotel, with Matthau in all three vignettes. Best one is the last, with Matthau as flustered father of a reluctant bride. [PG]▼●

Pleasantville (1998) **C/B&W-123m.** **½ D: Gary Ross. Tobey Maguire, Jeff Daniels, Joan Allen, William H. Macy, J. T. Walsh, Reese Witherspoon, Don Knotts, Jane Kaczmarek. A brother and sister are magically transported into their TV set and the black-and-white world of a '50s sitcom called *Pleasantville,* where everything is swell. Soon, they infiltrate this perfect environment with their worldly sensibilities, and the façade is easily cracked. Excellent performances and a striking visual design (the black-and-white world and its people slowly acquire color) spark this satire, which bites off more than it can chew, becoming slow and somber. Anyway, hooray for Don Knotts! Directing debut for screenwriter Ross. [PG-13] ▼●◗

Please Believe Me (1950) **87m.** **½ D: Norman Taurog. Deborah Kerr, Robert Walker, James Whitmore, Peter Lawford, Mark Stevens, Spring Byington. Pleasant fluff of Britisher Kerr aboard liner headed for America, wooed by assorted bachelors aboard, who think she's an heiress.

Please Don't Eat the Daisies (1960) **C-111m.** *** D: Charles Walters. Doris Day, David Niven, Janis Paige, Spring Byington, Richard Haydn, Patsy Kelly, Jack Weston, Margaret Lindsay. Bright film based on Jean Kerr's stories about a drama critic and his family. Doris sings title song; her kids are very amusing, as are Byington (the mother-in-law), Kelly (housekeeper), and especially Paige as a temperamental star. Later a TV series. CinemaScope.▼●

Please! Mr. Balzac (1956-French) **99m.** ** D: Marc Allegret. Daniel Gelin, Brigitte Bardot, Robert Hirsch, Darry Cowl. Low-brow THEODORA GOES WILD variation, following Bardot's plight after she pens an anonymous, scandalous book. Scripted by Allegret and Roger Vadim. Aka MADEMOISELLE STRIPTEASE and PLUCKING THE DAISY. ▼

Please Murder Me (1956) **78m.** **½ D: Peter Godfrey. Angela Lansbury, Raymond Burr, Dick Foran, John Dehner, Lamont Johnson. Lansbury and Burr's energetic performances elevate this homicide yarn.

Please Turn Over (1960-British) **86m.** **½ D: Gerald Thomas. Ted Ray, Jean Kent, Leslie Phillips, Joan Sims, Julia Lockwood, Tim Seely. OK froth about teen daughter's lurid novel-writing and the repercussions it causes.

Pleasure Cruise (1933) **72m.** **½ D: Frank Tuttle. Roland Young, Genevieve Tobin, Ralph Forbes, Una O'Connor, Herbert Mundin, Minna Gombell. Husband and wife take "separate vacations," but he jealously follows her on board ocean liner. Chic Lubitsch-like comedy runs out of steam halfway through.

Pleasure Garden, The (1925-British) **75m.** ** D: Alfred Hitchcock. Virginia Valli, Carmelita Geraghty, Miles Mander, John Stuart, George Snell. Hitchcock's first feature, shot in Munich; uneven account of a pair of chorus girls, one (Valli) sweet and knowing, the other (Geraghty) a waif who becomes a glamorous bitch. Forgettable silent melodrama.

Pleasure of His Company, The (1961) **C-115m.** ***½ D: George Seaton. Fred Astaire, Lilli Palmer, Debbie Reynolds, Tab Hunter, Gary Merrill, Charlie Ruggles. Delightful fluff, from Samuel Taylor and Cornelia Otis Skinner's play about charming ex-husband who comes to visit, enchanting his daughter and hounding his wife's new husband. Entire cast in rare form. Taylor also scripted.

Pleasure Seekers, The (1964) **C-107m.** **½ D: Jean Negulesco. Ann-Margret, Pamela Tiffin, Tony Franciosa, Carol Lynley, Gene Tierney, Brian Keith, Gardner McKay, Isobel Elsom. Glossy, semi-musical remake of THREE COINS IN THE FOUNTAIN (by same director) about three girls seeking fun and romance in Spain. CinemaScope.

Plenty (1985) **C-124m.** **½ D: Fred Schepisi. Meryl Streep, Charles Dance, Tracey Ullman, John Gielgud, Sting, Ian McKellen, Sam Neill, Burt Kwouk. Filmization of David Hare's play about a British woman who (like Britain itself) experiences her finest hours during WW2, working for the underground . . . and never finds fulfillment or satisfaction the rest of her life. Superlative performances (Gielgud is a particular delight as aging career diplomat) and moments of insight and wit can't overcome the fact that central character played by Streep is so tedious. Schepisi makes excellent use of widescreen. Panavision. [R] ▼●◗

Plot Against Harry, The (1989) **80m.** *** D: Michael Roemer. Martin Priest, Ben Lang, Maxine Woods, Henry Nemo, Jacques Taylor, Jean Leslie, Ellen Herbert, Sandra Kazan. Amusing, perceptive slice of N.Y.C. life about an aging racketeer, just sprung from prison, who finds the old order changing, and his life coming apart at the seams. Sad-faced Priest is perfectly cast in this modest, location-filmed production, which was shot in 1969 but never released—until film-festival showings in 1989 won critical acclaim and a distributor.▼

Plot Thickens, The (1936) **67m.** **½ D: Ben Holmes. James Gleason, ZaSu Pitts, Oscar Apfel, Owen Davis, Jr., Arthur Aylesworth, Paul Fix, Barbara Barondess. Pitts takes on the role of sleuthing schoolteacher Hildegarde Withers for this amiable comic whodunit with a plot that (as the title indicates) grows more elaborate as it goes along.

Plough and the Stars, The (1936) **78m.** ** D: John Ford. Barbara Stanwyck, Preston Foster, Barry Fitzgerald, Una O'Connor, J. M. Kerrigan, Bonita Granville, Arthur Shields. Dreary, theatrical filmization of Sean O'Casey's play with Foster as Irish revolutionary leader and Stanwyck as long-suffering wife who fears for his life; script by Dudley Nichols.

Ploughman's Lunch, The (1983-British) **C-100m.** *** D: Richard Eyre. Jonathan Pryce, Tim Curry, Rosemary Harris, Frank Finlay, Charlie Dore. Complex, cynical condemnation of British manners, morals and politics, centering on the activities of thoroughly self-centered radio reporter Pryce and others during the Falklands war. Quite perceptive, within the confines of its viewpoint. [R]▼

Plucking the Daisy SEE: **Please! Mr. Balzac**

Plumber, The (1980-Australian) **C-76m.** *** D: Peter Weir. Judy Morris, Ivar Kants, Robert Coleby, Candy Raymond. Obnoxious plumber tears apart bathroom of unwilling tenants; film's single joke is stretched no further than it will go in slight but amusing black comedy made for Australian television.▼

Plunderers, The (1948) **C-87m.** ** D: Joseph Kane. Rod Cameron, Ilona Massey, Adrian Booth, Forrest Tucker. OK Republic Western involving outlaws and Army joining forces against rampaging redskins: clichés are there.

Plunderers, The (1960) **93m.** **½ D: Joseph Pevney. Jeff Chandler, John Saxon, Dolores Hart, Marsha Hunt, Jay C. Flippen, Ray Stricklyn, James Westerfield. Above-par study of outlaws interacting with honest townsfolk.

Plunderers of Painted Flats (1959) **77m.** *½ D: Albert C. Gannaway. Corinne Calvet, John Carroll, Skip Homeier, George Macready, Edmund Lowe, Bea Benadaret, Madge Kennedy, Joe Besser. Flabby Western of cowpoke seeking his father's killer. Filmed in widescreen Naturama.

Plunder of the Sun (1953) **81m.** **½ D: John Farrow. Glenn Ford, Diana Lynn, Patricia Medina, Francis L. Sullivan. Competent cast in above-average goings-on. Ford is involved with treasure hunt and murder in Mexico.

Plunder Road (1957) **71m.** **½ D: Hubert Cornfield. Gene Raymond, Jeanne Cooper, Wayne Morris, Elisha Cook, Jr., Stafford Repp. A little sleeper about robbery caper, with competent cast giving life to intriguing story. Regalscope.▼

Plunkett & Macleane (1999-British) **C-102m.** *** D: Jake Scott. Robert Carlyle, Jonny Lee Miller, Liv Tyler, Michael Gambon, Alan Cumming, Ken Stott, Claire Rushbrook. Rousing action-adventure about two of England's most notorious 18th-century highwaymen. Plays like BUTCH CASSIDY, with anachronistic hipster humor and a bumping techno score from Craig Armstrong. Don't think too hard about this flashy import; just sit back and enjoy the ride. As a bisexual dandy, Cumming cuts quite a swath. The debuting director is Ridley Scott's son. Super 35. [R]▼◗

Plymouth Adventure (1952) **C-105m.** **½ D: Clarence Brown. Spencer Tracy, Gene Tierney, Van Johnson, Leo Genn, Dawn Addams, Lloyd Bridges, Barry Jones. Superficial soap opera, glossily done, of the cynical captain of the *Mayflower* (Tracy) and the settlers who sailed from England to New England in the 17th century. This won an Oscar for its special effects.▼

Poacher's Daughter, The (1960-Irish) **74m.** **½ D: George Pollock. Julie Harris, Harry Brogan, Tim Seeley, Marie Keen, Brid Lynch, Noel Magee. Harris lends authenticity in title role as simple girl who straightens out her philandering boyfriend. Originally titled SALLY'S IRISH ROGUE.

Pocahontas (1995) **C-82m.** *** D: Mike Gabriel, Eric Goldberg. Voices of Irene Bedard, Judy Kuhn, Mel Gibson, David Ogden Stiers, John Kassir, Russell Means, Christian Bale, Linda Hunt, Billy Connolly, Frank Welker, Michelle St. John, James Apaumut Fall. More serious in tone than most Disney cartoon features, this one tells of the brave and free-spirited woman who defied her father—and her tribe—by falling in love with Capt. John Smith, part of a plundering party from england. entertaining if not particularly memorable, with Pocahontas a strong and appealing character, and her sidekicks, Meeko (a raccoon) and Flit (a hummingbird), providing delightful comedy relief. Songs by Alan Menken and Stephen Schwartz include one standout, "Colors of the Wind." Both that song and Menken's music score won Oscars. Direct-to-video sequel: POCAHONTAS II: JOURNEY TO A NEW WORLD. [G]▼●◗

Pocketful of Miracles (1961) **C-136m.**

**½ D: Frank Capra. Bette Davis, Glenn Ford, Hope Lange, Arthur O'Connell, Thomas Mitchell, Peter Falk, Edward Everett Horton, Ann-Margret, Mickey Shaughnessy, David Brian, Sheldon Leonard, Barton MacLane, John Litel, Jerome Cowan, Fritz Feld, Jack Elam, Ellen Corby. Capra's final film, a remake of his 1934 LADY FOR A DAY, is just as sentimental, but doesn't work as well. Bette is Apple Annie, a Damon Runyon character; Ford is Dave the Dude, the racketeer who turns her into a lady. Ann-Margret is appealing in her first film. Panavision.▼●

Pocket Money (1972) **C-102m.** **½ D: Stuart Rosenberg. Paul Newman, Lee Marvin, Strother Martin, Christine Belford, Kelly Jean Peters, Fred Graham, Wayne Rogers, Hector Elizondo, Richard Farnsworth. Debt-ridden cowboy and shifty pal get mixed up with crooked cattleman in modern-day Western. Strangely tepid comedy is helped by good Laszlo Kovacs photography, nice bit by Peters. Marvin's car is the damnedest thing you'll ever see. Screenplay by Terrence Malick. [PG]▼

Poetic Justice (1993) **C-110m.** ** D: John Singleton. Janet Jackson, Tupac Shakur, Regina King, Joe Torry, Maya Angelou, Tyra Ferrell, Roger Guenveur Smith, Q-Tip, Tone Loc, Billy Zane, Lori Petty. Ambitious but fatally pretentious saga of a melancholy South Central L.A. beautician (Jackson), who has retreated from the world after her boyfriend's murder; mailman Shakur attempts to break through to her, with predictable results. Implausibly, the poetry this otherwise ordinary woman composes actually is the work of Maya Angelou (who appears onscreen as Aunt June). Jackson is OK in her screen debut. [R]▼●◗

Point, The (1971) **C-73m. TVM** D: Fred Wolf. Engaging children's cartoon about boy banished from homeland because his head is rounded, not pointed like everybody else's. Charming score by Harry Nilsson. First network airing narrated by Dustin Hoffman; his voice was replaced by Alan Thicke's for later showings. Ringo Starr narrates the video version. Above average. ▼●

Point Blank (1967) **C-92m.** ***½ D: John Boorman. Lee Marvin, Angie Dickinson, Keenan Wynn, Carroll O'Connor, Lloyd Bochner, Michael Strong, John Vernon. Marvin, shot and left for dead by unfaithful wife and mobster boyfriend, gets revenge two years later. Taut thriller, ignored in 1967, but now regarded as a top film of the decade. Based on the novel *The Hunter* by Donald E. Westlake (writing as Richard Stark). Remade as PAYBACK in 1999. Panavision. ▼●

Point Break (1991) **C-122m.** **½ D: Kathryn Bigelow. Patrick Swayze, Keanu Reeves, Gary Busey, Lori Petty, John McGinley, James LeGros, John Philbin, Sydney Walsh, Vincent Klyn, Julian Reyes, Tom Sizemore. Maverick FBI agent Reeves is sent undercover into Southern California's surfing community to investigate a baffling series of perfect bank robberies. Incredible, mind-numbing plotline redeemed by great surfing and skydiving scenes. Assured, fast-moving direction by Bigelow keeps this movie hanging five, if not ten . . . though Swayze is in desperate need of a hair stylist here. Super 35. [R]▼●

Point of No Return (1993) **C-109m.** *½ D: John Badham. Bridget Fonda, Gabriel Byrne, Dermot Mulroney, Anne Bancroft, Harvey Keitel, Miguel Ferrer, Olivia d'Abo, Richard Romanus, Lorraine Toussaint, Geoffrey Lewis, Calvin Levels. An awful, slicked-up Hollywoodization of LA FEMME NIKITA, with punkish criminal Fonda recruited by the U.S. government to shoot up a chi-chi Washington restaurant (with the *Washington Post* nowhere in sight). Not a genuine emotion to be found until Mulroney shows up; even then, not many more. Panavision. [R]▼●◗

Point Zero SEE: **Ski Bum, The**

Poison (1991) **C-85m.** *** D: Todd Haynes. Edith Meeks, Larry Maxwell, Susan Norman, Scott Renderer, James Lyons. Jarring, disturbing film about what it means to be different, to be alienated from the mainstream, consisting of three skillfully interwoven stories: a mock documentary about a seven-year-old who's shot and killed his father, and summarily disappeared; a 1950s sci-fi movie parody, in which a brilliant scientist ingests some serum and becomes disfigured; and the chronicle of a gay thief who arrives at a prison. Scripted by Haynes, and inspired by the writings of Jean Genet. [NC-17]▼●

Poison Ivy (1953-French) **90m.** ** D: Bernard Borderie. Eddie Constantine, Dominique Wilms, Howard Vernon, Dario Moreno, Gaston Modot. Constantine is again FBI agent Lemmy Caution, involved in stolen gold shipment in North Africa: grade-B actioner.

Poison Ivy (1992) **C-89m.** ** D: Katt Shea Ruben. Drew Barrymore, Sara Gilbert, Tom Skerritt, Cheryl Ladd, Leonardo DiCaprio. Blah melodrama about a sluttish teen (Barrymore, who is well cast), and the insidious influence she has on the members of a wealthy, troubled family: shy Gilbert, her alcoholic dad (Skerritt) and dying mom (Ladd), and even the pet pooch. More subtlety and character development would have helped. Followed by two direct-to-video sequels. [R]▼●◗

Pokémon: The First Movie (1998-Japanese) **C-75m.** *½ D: Kunihiko Yuyama. Voices of Veronica Taylor, Philip Bartlett, Rachel Lillis, Eric Stuart, Addie Blaustein. Kids' video game/TV show/card game phenomenon hits the big screen with OK story about a mutated Pokémon clone, Mewtwo, who plans to take over the world. Not very exciting, with barely adequate animation, but kids probably won't mind. Subtitle onscreen is MEWTWO STRIKES BACK. Followed by a sequel. [G]▼◗

Police (1984-French) **C-113m.** **½ D: Maurice Pialat. Gérard Depardieu, Sophie Marceau, Richard Anconina, Pascale Rocard, Sandrine Bonnaire. Taut but repetitive drama about the thin line separating cop and criminal. Depardieu is a brutal, sex-obsessed, love-starved policeman attempting to break up a drug ring; he becomes involved with tough young Marceau, one of the dealers. ▼

Police Academy (1984) **C-95m.** **½ D: Hugh Wilson. Steve Guttenberg, G. W. Bailey, George Gaynes, Kim Cattrall, Bubba Smith, Michael Winslow, Andrew Rubin, David Graf, Bruce Mahler, Leslie Easterbrook, Georgina Spelvin. Generally good-natured comedy (with typical 80's doses of sexism and tastelessness) about a group of weirdos and misfits who enroll in big-city police academy. Winslow's comic sound effects are perfect antidote for slow spots in script. Followed by far too many sequels, a TV series, and an animated TV series. [R] ▼●◗

Police Academy 2: Their First Assignment (1985) **C-87m.** BOMB D: Jerry Paris. Steve Guttenberg, Bubba Smith, David Graf, Michael Winslow, Bruce Mahler, Marion Ramsey, Colleen Camp, Howard Hesseman, Art Metrano, George Gaynes, Ed Herlihy. Dreadful follow-up to 1984 hit (with different writers and director responsible). There are *Dragnet* episodes with more laughs than this movie. [PG-13] ▼●

Police Academy 3: Back in Training (1986) **C-82m.** *½ D: Jerry Paris. Steve Guttenberg, Bubba Smith, David Graf, Michael Winslow, Marion Ramsey, Leslie Easterbrook, Art Metrano, Tim Kazurinsky, Bobcat Goldthwait, George Gaynes, Shawn Weatherly. An improvement over #2, but that's not saying much: just another collection of pea-brained gags and amateurish performances. [PG]▼●

Police Academy 4: Citizens on Patrol (1987) **C-87m.** BOMB D: Jim Drake. Steve Guttenberg, Bubba Smith, Michael Winslow, David Graf, Tim Kazurinsky, Sharon Stone, Leslie Easterbrook, Marion Ramsey, Lance Kinsey, G. W. Bailey, Bobcat Goldthwait, George Gaynes, Billie Bird. More of the same, only worse. [PG]▼●

Police Academy 5: Assignment Miami Beach (1988) **C-90m.** BOMB D: Alan Myerson. Bubba Smith, George Gaynes, G.W. Bailey, David Graf, Michael Winslow, Leslie Easterbrook, Marion Ramsey, Janet Jones, Matt McCoy. Gaynes is in Miami to receive an award before his mandatory retirement; arch-rival Bailey comes along to gum up the works. Fourth attempt to improve on imperfection is no charm; what can you say about a sequel that Steve Guttenberg won't even appear in? [PG] ▼●

Police Academy 6: City Under Siege (1989) **C-83m.** BOMB D: Peter Bonerz. Bubba Smith, David Graf, Michael Winslow, Leslie Easterbrook, Marion Ramsey, Lance Kinsey, Matt McCoy, Bruce Mahler, G.W. Bailey, George Gaynes, Kenneth Mars, Gerrit Graham. Those wacky cops are back to solve a crime wave perpetrated by a trio that makes The Three Stooges look like Nobel laureates. This entry is only—repeat *only*—for those who thought POLICE ACADEMY 5 was robbed at Oscar time. [PG]▼●

Police Academy VII: Mission to Moscow (1994) **C-83m.** BOMB D: Alan Metter. G. W. Bailey, George Gaynes, Michael Winslow, David Graf, Leslie Easterbrook, Claire Forlani, Ron Perlman, Christopher Lee, Charlie Schlatter. They waited five years to make another chapter in this mindless series. It wasn't worth the wait. [PG] ▼●

Police Connection SEE: **Mad Bomber, The**

Police Force SEE: **Police Story** (1985)

Police Story (1985-Hong Kong) **C-89m.** *** D: Jackie Chan. Jackie Chan, Bridget Lin, Maggie Cheung, Cho Yuen, Bill Tung, Kenneth Tong. Lightning-paced kung fu comedy about cop Chan, a one-man police force attempting to get the goods on some thugs. Crammed with incredible stuntwork; a real popcorn movie that's perfect for fans of the genre. Aka JACKIE CHAN'S POLICE STORY and POLICE FORCE. Followed by three sequels. CinemaScope.▼●

Police Story Part 2 (1988-Hong Kong) **C-90m.** ** D: Jackie Chan. Jackie Chan, Maggie Cheung, Bill Thung, Lam Kowk-Hung, Crystal Kwok, Choh Yuen, Henny Ho. This sequel is a slight step down for Chan as his Hong Kong cop tries to stop a wave of bomb threats. Some awesome stunts and fine comic touches, but not as well constructed as its predecessor. Followed by a third installment. Technovision.▼●

Police Story III: Supercop (1992-Hong Kong) **C-96m.** **½ D: Stanley Tong. Jackie Chan, Michelle (Yeaoh) Khan, Maggie Cheung, Yuen Wah, Bill Tung Piu, Ken Tsang. Third in series benefits greatly from presence of Khan, a fine action star in her own right. The two stars play cops teaming up against drug smugglers. Highlights include Khan jumping a motorcycle onto a moving train and Chan dangling from a careening helicopter. Plot slows down at times, but climactic action sequences make up for it. 1996 U.S. release version cut to 91m. and redubbed in English with a new music score. Aka SUPERCOP. Followed by POLICE STORY IV: CRIME STORY. Technovision. [R]▼●◗

Policewomen (1974) **C-99m.** *½ D: Lee Frost. Sondra Currie, Tony Young, Phil Hoover, Jeanne Bell, William Smith, Wes Bishop. Unexceptional, violent actioner with talented Currie as karate-expert cop. Aka THE INSIDERS. [R]▼

Polish Wedding (1998) **C-101m.** *** D: Theresa Connelly. Gabriel Byrne, Lena Olin, Claire Danes, Mili Avital, Daniel Lapaine, Rade Serbedzija, Adam Trese, Ramsey Krull, Steven Petraca. Picaresque slice of life about a Polish-American family in Detroit. The mother of the household (Olin) is an incredible life force who is fiercely proud of her family; her husband (Byrne) has long since resigned himself to a passive role. But their daughter (Danes) is eager to experience life—perhaps too eager. First time writer-director Connelly perfectly captures the look and feel of this unusual family and the suburban atmosphere in which they live. [PG-13]▼●

Pollyanna (1920) **60m.** *** D: Paul Powell. Mary Pickford, Katherine Griffith, Herbert Ralston, Helen Jerome Eddy, William Courtleigh, Herbert Prior. Delightful silent-film adaptation of Eleanor Porter's book about "the glad girl," who smiles through adversity and brings cheer even to the crabby old aunt who takes her in when she's orphaned. Pickford is at her most charming; neat blend of sentiment, slapstick, and wholesome ideals. Remade by Disney in 1960. ▼●

Pollyanna (1960) **C-134m.** ***½ D: David Swift. Hayley Mills, Jane Wyman, Richard Egan, Karl Malden, Nancy Olson, Adolphe Menjou, Donald Crisp, Agnes Moorehead. Disney's treatment of Eleanor Porter story is first-rate, as "the glad girl" spreads cheer to misanthropes of a New England town, including her own Aunt Polly (Wyman). Fine direction and script by Swift, excellent performances all around. Mills was awarded a special Oscar for Outstanding Juvenile Performance. First filmed in 1920 with Mary Pickford. Remade for TV in 1989 as POLLY.▼●

Polly of the Circus (1932) **69m.** ** D: Alfred Santell. Clark Gable, Marion Davies, Raymond Hatton, C. Aubrey Smith, David Landau, Maude Eburne. Ill-conceived vehicle for Davies as sexy trapeze artist who falls in love with minister Gable. Ray Milland has bit part as church usher.

Polo Joe (1936) **62m.** ** D: William McGann. Joe E. Brown, Carol Hughes, Skeets Gallagher, Joseph King, Gordon (Bill) Elliott, George E. Stone. Typical Brown comedy in which Joe's got to learn polo fast to impress his girl.

Poltergeist (1982) **C-114m.** ***½ D: Tobe Hooper. Craig T. Nelson, JoBeth Williams, Beatrice Straight, Dominique Dunne, Oliver Robins, Heather O'Rourke, Zelda Rubinstein, Richard Lawson, James Karen. A young family finds its home invaded by unfriendly spirits, who "kidnap" their 5-year-old girl! Sensationally scary ghost story co-written and co-produced by Steven Spielberg. Paced like a roller-coaster ride, with dazzling special effects—and a refreshing sense of humor. Followed by two sequels. J-D-C Scope. [PG]▼●◗

Poltergeist II (1986) **C-91m.** **½ D: Brian Gibson. JoBeth Williams, Craig T. Nelson, Heather O'Rourke, Oliver Robins, Zelda Rubinstein, Will Sampson, Julian Beck, Geraldine Fitzgerald. The Freeling family is terrorized again by otherworld creatures. Another pointless sequel made palatable by some jolting state-of-the-art special effects and a still-very-likable family. Be warned that an actor receives billing as The Vomit Creature. Panavision. [PG-13]▼●

Poltergeist III (1988) **C-97m.** ** D: Gary Sherman. Tom Skerritt, Nancy Allen, Heather O'Rourke, Zelda Rubinstein, Lara Flynn Boyle, Kip Wentz, Richard Fire. O'Rourke moves in with uncle Skerritt and aunt Allen—and is still pursued by strange, evil forces. Undistinguished and occasionally plodding; eerily, young O'Rourke died four months before the film's release. [PG-13] ▼●

Polyester (1981) **C-86m.** **½ D: John Waters. Divine, Tab Hunter, Edith Massey, Mary Garlington, Ken King, David Samson, Mink Stole, Stiv Bators. Waters' first mainstream feature is wacky middle-class satire; housewife Francine Fishpaw (Divine), driven to the brink by nightmarish husband, children, and mother, is "rescued" by handsome drive-in owner Todd Tomorrow (Hunter). Less offensive than Waters' underground films, but still not for all tastes; Vincent Peranio's sets are hilariously hideous. Released in "Odorama" —with audience members given scratch-and-sniff cards. [R]▼●

Pom-Pom Girls, The (1976) **C-90m.** ** D: Joseph Ruben. Robert Carradine, Jennifer Ashley, Lisa Reeves, Michael Mullins, Bill Adler. Comedy about spoiled suburban teenagers who celebrate their senior year having food fights, making love in the back of vans, and stealing a fire truck. Routinely good-natured mayhem. [PG—edited from original R rating]▼

Pompatus of Love, The (1996) **C-99m.** ** D: Richard Schenkman. Jon Cryer, Adrian Pasdar, Tim Guinee, Adam Oliensis, Mia Sara, Kristin Scott Thomas, Arabella Field, Paige Turco, Dana Wheeler-Nicholson, Kristen Wilson, Michael McKean, Fisher Stevens, Jennifer Tilly, Roscoe Lee Browne, Jenny McCarthy. Yet another smug and talky ensemble comedy about self-absorbed guys struggling with life and love in the '90s. Though it's an obvious labor of love for cowriters Schenkman, Cryer, and Oliensis, it's just a passable example of a deadly subgenre. Title takes its name from a song lyric in "The Joker," which is sung here by the original artist, Steve Miller, and also by Sheryl Crow. [R]▼●◗

Ponette (1996-French) **C-97m.** **½ D: Jacques Doillon. Victoire Thivisol, Matiaz Bureau Caton, Delphine Schiltz, Xavier Beauvois, Claire Nebout, Marie Trintignant. Heart-rending, if unfulfilling, tale of a 4-year-old (Thivisol) who survives a car accident in which her mother is killed. Poignant look at the death of a parent, as the young girl tries to understand and cope with her mom's absence. Doillon, who also scripted, truly captures life through the eyes of a child, but there's more emotion than substance, and the ending is a cop-out. Thivisol's amazingly naturalistic performance is the film's greatest strength.▼●◗

Pontiac Moon (1994) **C-108m.** *½ D: Peter Medak. Ted Danson, Mary Steenburgen, Ryan Todd, Eric Schweig, Cathy Moriarty, Max Gail, Lisa Jane Persky, J. C. Quinn, John Schuck, Don Swayze. Eccentric pop (Danson) takes 11-year-old son on dusty road trip to coincide with Apollo XI moon landing in July 1969. Think agoraphobic mom (Steenburgen) will finally have the guts to leave the house and follow them? 11-year-olds may like this. Panavision. [PG-13]▼●

Pontius Pilate (1962-Italian-French) **C-100m.** ** D: Irving Rapper. Jean Marais, Jeanne Crain, Basil Rathbone, John Drew Barrymore, Massimo Serato, Leticia Roman. Adequate retelling of events before and after Christ's crucifixion from viewpoint of Roman procurator. Dubbing and confused script hamper good intentions. Barrymore plays Christ *and* Judas. CinemaScope.

Pony Express (1953) **C-101m.** *** D: Jerry Hopper. Charlton Heston, Rhonda Fleming, Jan Sterling, Forrest Tucker. Exuberant action Western (set in 1860s) of the founding of mail routes westward, involving historical figures Buffalo Bill and Wild Bill Hickok.▼

Pony Express Rider (1976) **C-100m.** *** D: Robert Totten. Stewart Peterson, Henry Wilcoxon, Buck Taylor, Maureen McCormick, Joan Caulfield, Ken Curtis, Slim Pickens, Dub Taylor, Jack Elam. Good family outing with Peterson joining Pony Express in 1861 to help find the man whom he believes has killed his father. [G]▼

Pony Soldier (1952) **C-82m.** **½ D: Joseph M. Newman. Tyrone Power, Cameron Mitchell, Robert Horton, Thomas Gomez, Penny Edwards. Power is sturdy in actioner about Canadian mounties and their efforts to stave off Indian war.▼

Poodle Springs (1998) **C-105m. TVM** D: Bob Rafelson. James Caan, Dina Meyer, David Keith, Joe Don Baker, Tom Bower, Brian Cox, Nia Peeples. Semi-retired and newly married (to a much younger, wealthy woman), Philip Marlowe finds himself out of his social league while immersed in intrigue surrounding the murder of another investigator in the small desert town of Poodle Springs. Tom Stoppard wrote the script, based on the best-seller by Robert Parker, from the final Marlowe story begun but never finished by Raymond Chandler. Caan is quite good as the world-weary dick. Made for cable. Average.

Poor Cow (1967-British) **C-104m.** **½ D: Kenneth Loach. Carol White, Terence Stamp, John Bindon, Kate Williams, Queenie Watts, Malcolm McDowell. OK drama about working-class loners, centering on promiscuous White's relationship with husband (Bindon), a thief, and his best friend (Stamp), whom she really loves. McDowell's film debut; Loach's feature directorial debut.

Poor Little Rich Girl (1936) **72m.** ***½ D: Irving Cummings. Shirley Temple, Alice Faye, Jack Haley, Gloria Stuart, Michael Whalen, Jane Darwell, Claude Gillingwater, Henry Armetta. One of Shirley's best films, a top musical on any terms, with Temple running away from home, joining vaudeville team of Haley and Faye, winning over crusty Gillingwater, eventually joining her father (Whalen) and lovely Stuart. Best of all is closing "Military Man" number. Also shown in computer-colored version.▼●

Pop Always Pays (1940) **67m.** **½ D: Leslie Goodwins. Leon Errol, Dennis O'Keefe, Walter Catlett, Adele Pearce, Marjorie Gateson, Tom Kennedy. Sometimes funny comedy with Errol, much to his regret, promising to allow daughter Pearce to wed O'Keefe if the latter can save $1,000—which he also promises to match.▼

Popcorn (1970) **C-85m.** *½ D: Peter Clifton. Mick Jagger, Jimi Hendrix, Rolling Stones, Otis Redding, Bee Gees, Joe Cocker. Don't be misled by the talent assembled; most of them seem to have been captured during their worst performances for this concert film. [G]

Popcorn (1991) **C-93m.** ** D: Mark Herrier. Jill Schoelen, Tom Villard, Dee Wallace Stone, Tony Roberts, Ray Walston, Elliott Hurst, Yvette Solar, Derek Rydall, Malcolm Danare, Bruce Glover. Film students put on a round-the-clock fundraiser of schlocky '50s horror pics—and who should be haunting the premises and projection booth but a ghoulish psychopathic killer? Amusing idea, awkwardly executed, though there are some knowing recreations of vintage black & white B's. Stone, Roberts, and Walston must have been hired for about a day's shooting apiece. [R] ▼●

Pope, The SEE: **Pope John Paul II**

Pope Joan (1972-British) **C-132m.** BOMB

D: Michael Anderson. Liv Ullmann, Keir Dullea, Robert Beatty, Jeremy Kemp, Olivia de Havilland, Patrick Magee, Maximilian Schell, Trevor Howard, Franco Nero, Nigel Havers, Lesley-Anne Down, Andre Morell. Dim story of woman who, disguised as man, works her way up to the papacy, only to be destroyed when revealed. Performers seem to be embarrassed, as well they should; screenplay by John Briley. Also shown in 112m. version. Reissued as THE DEVIL'S IMPOSTOR, with much material cut. Panavision. [PG]

Pope John Paul II (1984) **C-150m. TVM** D: Herbert Wise. Albert Finney, Michael Crompton, Jonathan Newth, Nigel Hawthorne, Brian Cox, Caroline Bliss, John McEnery, Ronald Pickup, Lee Montague. Finney adds another memorable portrait to his diverse gallery of colorful, full-bodied portrayals. His charismatic Karol Wojtyla is a reverential tour de force, covering the Pontiff's adult life from an adversary of Nazism and Communism in Poland to his installation as Pope in 1978. Script by Christopher Knopf. Aka THE POPE. Above average. ▼

Pope Must Die, The (1991-British) **C-97m.** **½ D: Peter Richardson. Robbie Coltrane, Beverly D'Angelo, Herbert Lom, Alex Rocco, Paul Bartel, Salvatore Cascio, Balthazar Getty, Peter Richardson, Robert Stephens, Annette Crosbie. So-so satire with Coltrane an honest small-town priest who, via computer error, becomes the new pontiff and finds himself in conflict with cardinal Rocco and mobster Lom. Occasionally clever but goes overboard once too often, descending into outright silliness. Controversy over the title in U.S. release caused its distributor to rename it THE POPE MUST DIET(!) [R]▼●

Pope of Greenwich Village, The (1984) **C-120m.** *** D: Stuart Rosenberg. Eric Roberts, Mickey Rourke, Daryl Hannah, Geraldine Page, Kenneth McMillan, Tony Musante, M. Emmet Walsh, Burt Young, Jack Kehoe, Philip Bosco, Val Avery, Joe Grifasi. Richly textured, sharply observant film about a young hustler in N.Y.C.'s Little Italy and his inability to separate himself from a cousin (Roberts) who's a perpetual screw-up. Not so much a story as a collection of character studies; Page stands out in great supporting cast, as harridan mother of crooked cop. Based on Vincent Patrick's novel. [R]▼●

Popeye (1980) **C-114m.** BOMB D: Robert Altman. Robin Williams, Shelley Duvall, Ray Walston, Paul Smith, Paul Dooley, Richard Libertini, Wesley Ivan Hurt, Linda Hunt. The beloved sailorman (Williams, in his starring debut) boards a sinking ship in this astonishingly boring movie. A game cast does its best with Jules Feiffer's unfunny script, Altman's cluttered staging, and some alleged songs by Harry Nilsson. Tune in an old Max Fleischer cartoon instead. Technovision. [PG]▼●

Popi (1969) **C-115m.** *** D: Arthur Hiller. Alan Arkin, Rita Moreno, Miguel Alejandro, Ruben Figueroa. Charming story of poverty in the ghetto, focusing on one man's often zany antics in securing better life for his children. Odd ending for far-fetched story. [G]▼

Poppy (1936) **75m.** **½ D: A. Edward Sutherland. W. C. Fields, Rochelle Hudson, Richard Cromwell, Catherine Doucet, Lynne Overman. Mild Fields, re-creating his stage role as Hudson's ever-conniving dad. Too much romantic subplot, not enough of W. C.'s antics. The Great Man also starred in a silent version, SALLY OF THE SAWDUST.

Poppy Is Also a Flower, The (1966) **C-100m.** BOMB D: Terence Young. Senta Berger, Stephen Boyd, E. G. Marshall, Trevor Howard, Eli Wallach, Marcello Mastroianni, Angie Dickinson, Rita Hayworth, Yul Brynner, Trini Lopez, Gilbert Roland, Bessie Love. Incredibly bad anti-drug feature from story by Ian Fleming, originally produced as United Nations project for TV. Acting is downright poor at times. Though never referred to that way, title actually appears on screen as POPPIES ARE ALSO FLOWERS. Aka THE OPIUM CONNECTION.▼

Popsy Pop SEE: **Butterfly Affair, The**

Porgy and Bess (1959) **C-138m.** **½ D: Otto Preminger. Sidney Poitier, Dorothy Dandridge, Pearl Bailey, Sammy Davis, Jr., Brock Peters, Diahann Carroll, Ivan Dixon, Clarence Muse. Classic Gershwin folk opera about love, dreams, and jealousy among poor folk of Catfish Row; a bit stiff, but full of incredible music: "Summertime," "It Ain't Necessarily So," "I Got Plenty Of Nothin." Davis shines as Sportin' Life. Music arrangers Andre Previn and Ken Darby won Oscars. Final film of producer Samuel Goldwyn. Todd-AO.

Pork Chop Hill (1959) **97m.** *** D: Lewis Milestone. Gregory Peck, Harry Guardino, Rip Torn, George Peppard, James Edwards, Bob Steele, George Shibata, Biff Elliot, Woody Strode, Robert Blake, Norman Fell, Martin Landau, Bert Remsen, (Harry) Dean Stanton, Gavin McLeod. Gritty Korean War combat film about the taking of a seemingly worthless hill, and the political (and communications) problems that interfere with lieutenant Peck's efforts to get the job done. Impressive cast of stars-to-be. Based on a true story.▼●◗

Porky's (1981-Canadian) **C-94m.** **½ D: Bob Clark. Dan Monahan, Mark Herrier, Wyatt Knight, Roger Wilson, Kim Cattrall, Scott Colomby, Kaki Hunter, Nancy Parsons, Alex Karras, Susan Clark. A lusty, fun-loving bunch of high school guys in

South Florida circa 1954 discover that sex is great, revenge is sweet, and Jews are OK after all. Some belly laughs. This raunchy, low-budget comedy made a fortune—and spawned two sequels. [R]▼●◗
Porky's II: The Next Day (1983-Canadian) **C-95m.** *½ D: Bob Clark. Dan Monahan, Wyatt Knight, Mark Herrier, Roger Wilson, Kaki Hunter, Scott Colomby, Nancy Parsons, Edward Winter. In-name-only sequel has same cast of kids in new (and tamer) set of escapades—with no coherency, and not even the raunchiness that made the first film so popular. Sequel: PORKY'S REVENGE. [R]▼●
Porky's Revenge (1985) **C-91m.** BOMB D: James Komack. Dan Monahan, Wyatt Knight, Tony Ganios, Kaki Hunter, Mark Herrier, Scott Colomby. Will the gang throw the big high school basketball game or won't they? Beware of high-school seniors with post-collegiate hairlines; these guys are starting to look older than the mid-'50s Bowery Boys. This *Revenge* is preferable to Montezuma's—but not by much. [R]▼●
Porridge SEE: **Doing Time**
Port Afrique (1956-British) **C-92m.** ** D: Rudolph Maté. Pier Angeli, Phil Carey, Eugene Deckers, James Hayter, Rachel Gurney, Anthony Newley, Christopher Lee. Bernard Dyer's picaresque actioner gets middling screen version; adulterous wife's past comes to light when husband investigates her death.
Portnoy's Complaint (1972) **C-101m.** BOMB D: Ernest Lehman. Richard Benjamin, Karen Black, Lee Grant, Jack Somack, Jeannie Berlin, Jill Clayburgh. Karen Black's excellent portrayal of "The Monkey" is buried in otherwise incredibly inept filmization of Philip Roth's novel about a not exactly warm relationship between Jewish boy and his mother. Terrible directorial debut by famed screenwriter Lehman. Panavision. [R]▼
Port of Call (1948-Swedish) **95m.** ** D: Ingmar Bergman. Nine-Christine Jonsson, Bengt Eklund, Erik Hell, Berta Hall, Mimi Nelson. Slim, minor early Bergman drama about troubled young outcast Jonsson and her relationship with seaman Eklund. Setting is a grim harbor slum, and film's ultimately hopeful, upbeat tone just doesn't ring true.▼
Port of Hell (1954) **80m.** ** D: Harold Schuster. Wayne Morris, Dane Clark, Carole Mathews, Otto Waldis, Marshall Thompson, Marjorie Lord, Tom Hubbard. Poor production values detract from tense situation of skipper et al. trying to take an A-bomb out to sea before it explodes.
Port of New York (1949) **86m.** ** D: Laslo Benedek. Scott Brady, Richard Rober, K. T. Stevens, Yul Brynner. Gloomy tale of customs agents cracking down on narcotics smuggling; Brynner's film debut . . . with hair!▼
Port of Seven Seas (1938) **81m.** ** D: James Whale. Wallace Beery, Frank Morgan, Maureen O'Sullivan, John Beal, Jessie Ralph. Marcel Pagnol's FANNY isn't quite suitable Beery material, but he and good cast try their best as O'Sullivan falls in love with adventuresome sailor in Marseilles. Script by Preston Sturges.
Portrait, The (1993) **C-100m. TVM** D: Arthur Penn. Gregory Peck, Lauren Bacall, Cecilia Peck, Paul McCrane, Mitchell Laurance, Donna Mitchell. High-powered cast and director give an amiable, loving spin to the tale of an aging couple, still very much in love, and their petulant adult daughter (well played by Peck's real-life daughter), who comes home to paint their portrait. An opened-up adaptation by Lynn Roth of Tina Howe's three-character 1983 Off-Broadway play *Painting Churches.* Peck was the film's coexecutive producer. Made for cable. Above average.▼●
Portrait in Black (1960) **C-112m.** **½ D: Michael Gordon. Lana Turner, Anthony Quinn, Sandra Dee, John Saxon, Richard Basehart, Lloyd Nolan, Ray Walston, Anna May Wong. Average murder/blackmail mystery filled with gaping holes that producer Ross Hunter tried to hide with glamorous decor and offbeat casting.▼
Portrait of a Hitman (1977) **C-86m.** BOMB D: Allan A. Buckhantz. Jack Palance, Richard Roundtree, Rod Steiger, Bo Svenson, Ann Turkel, Philip Ahn. Gangster Steiger hires "sensitive" hit man Palance to kill Svenson, but there are complications: Svenson is a pal who once saved Palance's life, and both of them are in love with Turkel. B-movie has ragged structure that makes it seem like an unfinished feature. Originally titled JIM BUCK.▼
Portrait of a Lady, The (1996-British) **C-144m.** ** D: Jane Campion. Nicole Kidman, John Malkovich, Barbara Hershey, Mary-Louise Parker, Martin Donovan, Shelley Winters, Richard E. Grant, Shelley Duvall, Christian Bale, Viggo Mortensen, John Gielgud. Long, often boring, and strikingly ineffectual adaptation of Henry James' novel about a young American woman, determined to live an independent life in Europe during the late 1800s. For reasons never made clear in the film, she decides to marry a man who turns out to be a spiteful, manipulative rotter. Good performances and handsome production can't overcome the dreariness of the material. A very odd, "Campionesque" prologue attempts to set a contemporary tone for what is to follow. Super 35. [PG-13]▼●◗
Portrait of a Mobster (1961) **108m.** **½ D: Joseph Pevney. Vic Morrow, Leslie Parrish, Peter Breck, Ray Danton, Norman Alden, Ken Lynch. Pretty good gang-

ster movie following the career of Dutch Schultz (Morrow), centering on his relationship with a woman who marries a crooked cop. Danton reprises his role as Legs Diamond from an earlier film.

Portrait of a Sinner (1959-British) **96m.** **½ D: Robert Siodmak. William Bendix, Nadja Tiller, Tony Britton, Donald Wolfit, Adrienne Corri, Joyce Carey. Tiller is effective in leading role as corrupting female who taints all in her path. Based on Robin Maugham story. Original British title: THE ROUGH AND THE SMOOTH.▼

Portrait of Clare (1951-British) **94m.** ** D: Lance Comfort. Margaret Johnston, Richard Todd, Robin Bailey, Ronald Howard. Unpretentious little film, pegged on gimmick of woman telling granddaughter about her past romances.

Portrait of Jennie (1948) **86m.** *** D: William Dieterle. Jennifer Jones, Joseph Cotten, Ethel Barrymore, Lillian Gish, Cecil Kellaway, David Wayne, Albert Sharpe, Henry Hull, Florence Bates, Felix Bressart. Strange otherworldly girl Jones inspires penniless artist Cotten. David O. Selznick craftsmanship and a fine cast work wonders with foolish story based on the Robert Nathan novella. Originally released with last reel tinted green and final shot in Technicolor; the special effects earned an Academy Award.▼

Portrait of the Artist as a Young Man, A (1979) **C-98m.** *** D: Joseph Strick. Bosco Hogan, T. P. McKenna, John Gielgud, Rosaleen Linehan, Maureen Potter, Niall Buggy, Brian Murray. Literate adaptation (by Judith Rascoe) of James Joyce's legendary first novel; it focuses on Stephen Dedalus (Hogan), who questions his faith as he reaches manhood in turn-of-the-century Dublin. McKenna, Linehan, and Potter play, respectively, Simon and May Dedalus, and Dante; in ULYSSES, which Strick made a dozen years before, they appeared as Buck Mulligan, Nurse Callan, and Josie Breen respectively. Filmed in Ireland.▼

Poseidon Adventure, The (1972) **C-117m.** *** D: Ronald Neame. Gene Hackman, Ernest Borgnine, Red Buttons, Carol Lynley, Roddy McDowall, Stella Stevens, Shelley Winters, Jack Albertson, Leslie Nielsen, Pamela Sue Martin, Arthur O'Connell, Eric Shea. Mindless but engrossing, highly charged entertainment—the vanguard of the decade's "disaster film" genre. Luxury cruise ship capsized by tidal wave, leaving small band of survivors to make way to top (bottom) of ship and hopefully escape. Introductory sequences are laughably bad, but one soon gets caught up in the story and ignores script's weaknesses. Oscar-winning song: "The Morning After"; also earned a special Oscar for special effects. Sequel: BEYOND THE POSEIDON ADVENTURE. Panavision. [PG]▼●◗

Positive I.D. (1987) **C-95m.** ** D: Andy Anderson. Stephanie Rascoe, John Davies, Steve Fromholtz, Laura Lane, Gail Cronauer, Matthew Sacks. Married woman unable to put her life back together after a violent rape, decides instead to adopt a new identity and live a secret life away from her family. Intriguing story always seems to be leading somewhere but never does, until the final sequence. Well made on a minuscule budget in Texas by writer-producer-director Anderson. [R]▼

Positively True Adventures of the Alleged Texas Cheerleader-Murdering Mom, The (1993) **C-105m. TVM** D: Michael Ritchie. Holly Hunter, Beau Bridges, Swoosie Kurtz, Gregg Henry, Matt Frewer, Frankie Ingrassia, Elizabeth Ruscio, Andy Richter, Giovanni Ribisi. Mirthful retelling of the same headline-making story (a Texas mother plots to kill her daughter's competitor for a spot on the high school cheerleader squad) told drearily straight in the earlier WILLING TO KILL: THE TEXAS CHEERLEADER STORY. Ritchie made this one in his SMILE mold from a smile-inducing script by Jane Anderson. Hunter won an Emmy for her portrayal of the obsessed Houston housewife. And don't miss those closing credits! Made for cable. Above average.▼●

Posse (1975) **C-94m.** *** D: Kirk Douglas. Kirk Douglas, Bruce Dern, Bo Hopkins, James Stacy, Luke Askew, David Canary. Offbeat but solid Western about a cynical lawman who tries to fulfill political ambitions by capturing an escaped robber, only to find the people are siding with the outlaw! Well photographed (by Fred Koenekamp) and well performed. Panavision. [PG]▼●

Posse (1993-U.S.-British) **C-109m.** ** D: Mario Van Peebles. Mario Van Peebles, Stephen Baldwin, Charles Lane, Tiny Lister, Jr., Big Daddy Kane, Billy Zane, Blair Underwood, Melvin Van Peebles, Salli Richardson, Tone Loc, Pam Grier, Vesta Williams, Isaac Hayes, Robert Hooks, Richard Jordan, Paul Bartel, Stephen J. Cannell, Nipsey Russell, Reginald VelJohnson, Woody Strode, Aaron Neville, Warrington and Reginald Hudlin. Noisy, violent, but politically correct Western about a mostly black posse who do battle with a pompous, racist colonel, and a vicious white sheriff who wants to take over a peaceful black frontier settlement. Game attempt at a new take on the Old West, but at its core it's thoroughly conventional. Follow-up: LOS LOCOS. Panavision. [R]▼●◗

Posse From Hell (1961) **C-89m.** **½ D: Herbert Coleman. Audie Murphy, John Saxon, Zohra Lampert, Vic Morrow, Lee Van Cleef. Gunslinger Murphy, a loner, agrees to pursue four deadly outlaws after they've robbed a bank and kidnapped a young woman, but he's saddled with an inexperienced posse. Murphy vehicle is surprisingly thoughtful and well written.

Possessed (1931) **76m.** *** D: Clarence Brown. Joan Crawford, Clark Gable, Wallace Ford, Skeets Gallagher, John Miljan. Factory girl Crawford becomes the mistress of Park Avenue lawyer Gable. Fascinating feminist drama, crammed with symbolism and featuring a radiant Crawford. Outrageous pre-Code script by Lenore Coffee.▼

Possessed (1947) **108m.** *** D: Curtis Bernhardt. Joan Crawford, Van Heflin, Raymond Massey, Geraldine Brooks, Stanley Ridges. Crawford gives fine performance in intelligent study of woman whose subtle mental problems ruin her life. Heflin and Massey are the men in her life; Brooks, as Massey's daughter, is radiant in her film debut. Also shown in computer-colored version.▼●

Possession (1981-French-West German) **C-127m.** *½ D: Andrzej Zulawski. Isabelle Adjani, Sam Neill, Heinz Bennent, Margit Carstensen, Michael Hogben. Adjani "creates" a monster, to the consternation of husband Neill, lover Bennent—and the viewer. Confusing drama of murder, horror, intrigue, though it's all attractively directed. Filmed in English; hacked down to 81m. for American release. [R]▼

Possession of Joel Delaney, The (1972) **C-105m.** *** D: Waris Hussein. Shirley MacLaine, Perry King, Lisa Kohane, David Elliott, Michael Hordern, Miriam Colon, Lovelady Powell. Uneven but satisfying mix of horror and social commentary with unsympathetic, affluent Manhattanite MacLaine threatened by mysterious transformations of her brother Joel (King). Offbeat throughout. [R]▼

Possessors, The (1958-French) **94m.** **½ D: Denys De La Patelliere. Jean Gabin, Jean Desailly, Pierre Brasseur, Emmanuele Riva, Bernard Blier. Diffuse yet forceful study of patriarch Gabin forcing issues to make his family self-sufficient.

Postal Inspector (1936) **58m.** ** D: Otto Brower. Ricardo Cortez, Patricia Ellis, Michael Loring, Bela Lugosi, David Oliver, Wallis Clark. A real-life postal inspector's life could never be this unusual: a novel romantic tale, a big robbery, and a major flood are all worked into this routine B picture. Lugosi plays a nightclub owner forced into crime by gambling debts. Oh, yes, there's also a song titled "Let's Have Bluebirds On All Our Wallpaper."▼

Postcards From the Edge (1990) **C-101m.** ***½ D: Mike Nichols. Meryl Streep, Shirley MacLaine, Dennis Quaid, Gene Hackman, Richard Dreyfuss, Rob Reiner, Mary Wickes, Conrad Bain, Annette Bening, Simon Callow, Gary Morton, CCH Pounder, Sidney Armus, Robin Bartlett, Anthony Heald, Dana Ivey, Oliver Platt, Michael Ontkean, J.D. Souther. Brilliantly cinematic rendering of Carrie Fisher's novel about a young woman falling prey to drugs while trying to pursue an acting career—in the shadow of a famous show-business mother. Vividly real, bitingly funny. MacLaine and Streep both have show-stopping musical numbers. Fisher wrote the screenplay. [R]▼●

Postman, The (1994-Italian-French) **C-113m.** *** D: Michael Radford. Massimo Troisi, Philippe Noiret, Maria Grazia Cucinotta, Linda Moretti, Renato Scarpa. A moving film detailing the friendship between exiled Chilean poet Pablo Neruda and the simple Italian man who delivers his mail every day. International talents combined to tell a universal story of how one person can affect another, no matter how different their life experiences may be. Noiret is masterful as always, and Troisi is understated and unforgettable in his final film role; he died of heart disease just twelve hours after the movie finished shooting. Oscar winner for Original Dramatic Score (Luis Bacalov). Original title: IL POSTINO.▼●

Postman, The (1997) **C-177m.** *½ D: Kevin Costner. Kevin Costner, Will Patton, Larenz Tate, Olivia Williams, James Russo, Daniel Von Bargen, Tom Petty, Scott Bairstow, Roberta Maxwell, Joe Santos, Peggy Lipton, Giovanni Ribisi, Shawn Hatosy. Long, boring, pretentious allegory about an itinerant performer in the post-apocalyptic future who passes himself off as a U.S. mail carrier. In that guise, he personifies hope for several isolated communities who've been beaten down by the cruel tactics of a demagogue (Patton, in a one-note performance). A well-meaning (but complete) misfire. That's Costner's son in the film's final shot; one daughter plays a mail carrier, the other sings "America the Beautiful." Mary Stuart Masterson appears unbilled. Panavision. [R] ▼●◗

Postman Always Rings Twice, The (1946) **113m.** **** D: Tay Garnett. Lana Turner, John Garfield, Cecil Kellaway, Hume Cronyn, Audrey Totter, Leon Ames, Alan Reed, Wally Cassell. Garfield and Turner ignite the screen in this bristling drama of lovers whose problems just begin when they do away with her husband (Kellaway). Despite complaints of changes in James M. Cain's original story (mostly for censorship purposes), the film packs a real punch and outshines the more explicit 1981 remake. Harry Ruskin and Niven Busch scripted (from Cain's novel). Filmed twice before, in France and Italy. Also shown in computer-colored version.▼●

Postman Always Rings Twice, The (1981) **C-123m.** *½ D: Bob Rafelson. Jack Nicholson, Jessica Lange, John Colicos, Michael Lerner, Christopher Lloyd, John P. Ryan, Anjelica Huston. Exceedingly unpleasant adaptation of James M. Cain's Depression-era novel about a drifter and a sensual young woman who conspire to free her from her loveless marriage. David Mamet's screenplay may be more faithful to Cain than the 1946 version, but who cares? Despite its much-touted sex scenes (more violent than erotic), it's dreary and forgettable. Moodily photographed by Sven Nykvist. [R]▼●◗

Postman's Knock (1962-British) **87m.** ** D: Robert Lynn. Spike Milligan, Barbara Shelley, John Wood, Miles Malleson, Ronald Adam, Wilfrid Lawson. Milligan is an overly efficient postal worker who upsets the equilibrium of the London post office—and some ambitious thieves. Scattered laughs in this heavy-handed comedy.

Postmark for Danger (1955-British) **84m.** *½ D: Guy Green. Terry Moore, Robert Beatty, William Sylvester, Geoffrey Keen, Josephine Griffin, Allan Cuthbertson. Hokey, overbaked murder mystery about what happens when an artist's journalist brother is "accidentally" killed in a car crash, and the actress who supposedly died with him mysteriously appears.▼

Potemkin (1925-Russian) **65m.** **** D: Sergei Eisenstein. Alexander Antonov, Vladimir Barsky, Grigori Alexandrov, Mikhail Goronorov. Landmark film about 1905 Revolution. Unlike many staples of film history classes, this one has the power to grip any audience. Odessa Steps sequence is possibly the most famous movie scene of all time. ▼●◗

Pot o' Gold (1941) **86m.** ** D: George Marshall. James Stewart, Paulette Goddard, Horace Heidt, Charles Winninger, Mary Gordon, Jed Prouty. Very minor item about harmonica-playing, music-mad Stewart, and his experiences with a band of struggling musicians. Stewart called this his worst movie! Look briefly for Art Carney as a radio announcer.▼●◗

Pound Puppies and the Legend of Big Paw (1988) **C-76m.** *½ D: Pierre DeCelles. Voices of George Rose, B. J. Ward, Ruth Buzzi, Brennan Howard. Yet another TV-style cartoon based on merchandising characters, with the Pound Puppies trying to retrieve a magical bone that's been stolen from a museum. Yawn. [G]▼

Pourquoi Pas! SEE: **Why Not!**

Powaqqatsi (1988) **C-97m.** **½ D: Godfrey Reggio. Follow-up to KOYAANISQATSI is a visual collage in which scenes of various cultures around the world are edited together to show how Third World societies have been exploited. Beautifully photographed, but the result is somehow shallow—much like a coffee-table picture book—and not nearly as impressive as its predecessor. Music is again by Philip Glass. [G]▼

Powder (1995) **C-111m.** ** D: Victor Salva. Mary Steenburgen, Sean Patrick Flanery, Lance Henriksen, Jeff Goldblum, Brandon Smith, Bradford Tatum, Susan Tyrrell, Missy Crider, Ray Wise. Rural teen Flanery, whose skin is ghostly white and whose nickname is Powder, is the local pariah; he's scary, shy, brilliant, and seems to have electromagnetic powers (and an odd relationship to lightning storms). Suddenly he's thrust into dealing with people and prejudices for the first time in his life. Combines a zillion 1950s and 1960s B-movie themes (including reform school) into a contemporary fable. Earnest, but doesn't add up to very much. [PG-13]▼●◗

Powder River (1953) **C-78m.** ** D: Louis King. Rory Calhoun, Corrine Calvet, Cameron Mitchell, Carl Betz. Straightforward minor Western, with Calhoun becoming town sheriff and clearing up a friend's murder.

Power, The (1968) **C-109m.** *** D: Byron Haskin. George Hamilton, Suzanne Pleshette, Richard Carlson, Yvonne De Carlo, Earl Holliman, Gary Merrill, Ken Murray, Barbara Nichols, Arthur O'Connell, Nehemiah Persoff, Aldo Ray, Michael Rennie. Research team discovers one of their number is an evil super-genius with powerful ESP abilities who starts killing the others one by one. Can Hamilton identify the man with the power before the villain kills him too? Could you ever doubt George Hamilton? Good, underrated George Pal production. Panavision. ●

Power (1986) **C-111m.** *½ D: Sidney Lumet. Richard Gere, Julie Christie, Gene Hackman, Kate Capshaw, Denzel Washington, E. G. Marshall, Beatrice Straight, Fritz Weaver, Michael Learned, J. T. Walsh, E. Katherine Kerr, Matt Salinger. Slick, sanctimonious story of ruthless political media manipulator (Gere) who, it turns out, isn't as smart as he thinks he is. Subject isn't headline news anymore, but this movie treats it that way. Downright embarrassing at times. [R]▼●◗

Power and the Glory, The (1933) **76m.** *** D: William K. Howard. Spencer Tracy, Colleen Moore, Ralph Morgan, Helen Vinson. Considered by many a precursor to CITIZEN KANE, Preston Sturges' script tells rags-to-riches story of callous industrialist (Tracy) in flashback. Silent-star Moore gives sensitive performance as Tracy's wife.

Power and the Prize, The (1956) **98m.** **½ D: Henry Koster. Robert Taylor, Elisabeth Mueller, Burl Ives, Charles Coburn, Cedric Hardwicke, Mary Astor. Sporadically effective study of big men in corporation and their private lives. CinemaScope.

Power of One, The (1992) **C-111m.** ** D: John G. Avildsen. Stephen Dorff, Armin Mueller-Stahl, Morgan Freeman, John Gielgud, Fay Masterson, Marius Weyers, Tracy Brooks Swope, John Osborne. Precisely what you'd expect when the director of ROCKY and THE KARATE KID tackles a movie about apartheid. Rah-rah mawkishness tells of a white South African lad who promotes integration by getting into the boxing ring with his oppressed black buddies. Offensive trivialization of a great subject, but at least the first half offers Freeman and Mueller-Stahl as the youth's mentors; when they're written out of the script in hour two, film becomes an ordeal to watch. [PG-13]▼●◗

Power of the Whistler (1945) **66m.** **½ D: Lew Landers. Richard Dix, Janis Carter, Jeff Donnell, Loren Tindall, Tala Birell, John Abbott. Carter tries to help amnesiac Dix recall his identity, only to discover that he's an escaped psycho killer. Third *Whistler* entry is a little padded but still genuinely eerie.

Power Play (1978-Canadian-British) **C-102m.** *½ D: Martyn Burke. Peter O'Toole, David Hemmings, Donald Pleasence, Barry Morse, Jon Granik. Story of a military coup in a country that looks vaguely European but where everybody sounds British or Canadian. Flat, unsuspenseful drama. Aka OPERATION OVERTHROW.▼

Powers Girl, The (1942) **93m.** ** D: Norman Z. McLeod. George Murphy, Anne Shirley, Dennis Day, Benny Goodman, Carole Landis. Trifling plot revolving about Shirley's attempt to become member of famed modeling school, with musical numbers tossed in.

P.O.W.: Prisoners of War SEE: **Secret of Blood Island, The**

P.O.W. The Escape (1986) **C-90m.** *½ D: Gideon Amir. David Carradine, Charles R. Floyd, Mako, Steve James, Phil Brock. Mindless, one-dimensional RAMBO variation, about some American P.O.W.s, headed by Col. Carradine, who battle their way to freedom as Saigon falls to the Commies. Formerly titled BEHIND ENEMY LINES. [R]▼●

Powwow Highway (1989) **C-90m.** *** D: Jonathan Wacks. Gary Farmer, A Martinez, Amanda Wyss, Joanelle Romero, Sam Vlahos, Wayne Waterman, Margo Kane, Graham Greene, Wes Studi. Big, amiable Cheyenne, on a "medicine" journey to New Mexico in a beat-up Buick, gives a lift to a lifelong friend, an Indian activist. Not a totally successful film, but unusual and satisfying, with a standout performance by Farmer, an immensely likable actor who makes his character both endearing and ennobling. [R]▼

Practically Yours (1944) **90m.** ** D: Mitchell Leisen. Claudette Colbert, Fred MacMurray, Gil Lamb, Robert Benchley, Rosemary DeCamp, Cecil Kellaway. Stars' expertise redeems contrived story of girl intercepting pilot's message to his dog.

Practical Magic (1998) **C-104m.** ** D: Griffin Dunne. Sandra Bullock, Nicole Kidman, Aidan Quinn, Stockard Channing, Dianne Wiest, Chloe Webb, Goran Visnjic, Evan Rachel Wood, Alexandra Artrip, Mark Feuerstein. Two sisters grow up under the curse of their ancestor (a woman hanged as a witch): any man whom they truly love is doomed. Free-spirited Kidman ignores the threat and leaves their New England home. Bullock lives with her witchly aunts, all too aware of the prophecy . . . until circumstance brings the sisters back together to work some magic of their own. Extremely likable stars make this watchable, but it's a lumpy brew. Based on a book by Alice Hoffman. Super 35. [PG-13]▼●◗

Practice Makes Perfect (1978-French) **C-104m.** *** D: Philippe de Broca. Jean Rochefort, Nicole Garcia, Annie Girardot, Danielle Darrieux, Catherine Alric, Lila Kedrova, Jean Desailly. Funny, knowing comedy about bored, self-centered concert pianist, supposedly living ideal life, eventually receiving his retribution. Rochefort is perfectly cast as engaging womanizer.▼

Prancer (1989) **C-102m.** *** D: John Hancock. Sam Elliott, Rebecca Harrell, Cloris Leachman, Rutanya Alda, Abe Vigoda, Ariana Richards, Michael Constantine, John Joseph Duda. Eight-year-old farm girl Harrell, who marches to her own beat—and whose widowed father (Elliott) is knuckling under to financial pressure—nurses a wounded reindeer she believes is one of Santa's own. While it occasionally is a bit too obvious and cute, it's a charming fantasy about a child's undying devotion to an animal. [G]▼●

Prayer for the Dying, A (1987-British) **C-107m.** *½ D: Mike Hodges. Mickey Rourke, Bob Hoskins, Alan Bates, Sammi Davis, Christopher Fulford, Liam Neeson, Alison Doody. Ponderous adaptation of Jack Higgins' novel about an IRA hit man (Rourke, with a dubious Irish accent) who can't escape his chosen calling, even when he tries to. Hoskins is badly miscast as a priest who becomes entangled with Rourke, while Bates chews it up as a flamboyant racketeer who doubles as a mortician. Heavy going all the way. [R]▼●

Prayer of the Rollerboys (1991) **C-94m.** **½ D: Rick King. Corey Haim, Patricia Arquette, Christopher Collet, Julius Harris, Devin Clark, Mark Pellegrino, Morgan Weisser, Jake Dengel, J.C. Quinn. To save his kid brother, orphan Haim goes undercover and joins the Rollerboys, a gang of high-powered, racist-fascist punks whose leader (Collet) might be the great-grandson of Hitler. Set in a future America in which anarchy and homelessness reign; provocative idea weakened by needlessly excessive violence—and a painfully predictable ending. [R]▼●

Preacher's Wife, The (1996) **C-125m.** **½ D: Penny Marshall. Denzel Washington, Whitney Houston, Courtney B. Vance, Gregory Hines, Jennifer Lewis, Lionel Richie, Justin Pierre Edmund, Shari Headley, Cissy Houston, Paul Bates, Loretta Devine,

Toukie Smith. Appropriately old-fashioned remake of 1947's THE BISHOP'S WIFE concerns a semi-addled angel sent down here to assist a personally and professionally troubled clergyman only to become smitten with the latter's lovely spouse. Much too leisurely and long, but a notable showcase for its stars, and a rare contemporary Christmas movie to recapture the spirit of vintage holiday classics. With Houston as the wife, the gospel numbers have zing. [PG]▼●

Predator (1987) **C-107m.** *** D: John McTiernan. Arnold Schwarzenegger, Carl Weathers, Elpidia Carrillo, Bill Duke, Jesse Ventura, Sonny Landham, Richard Chaves, R.G. Armstrong, Shane Black, Kevin Peter Hall. Schwarzenegger and his super-SWAT-team-for-hire are assigned by the U.S. to a delicate rescue mission in South American jungle . . . but Arnold and his men soon find themselves battling a faceless, ferocious enemy that's picking them off one by one. Solid, suspenseful action film takes time getting started, but emerges a grabber. Followed by a sequel. [R]▼●◗

Predator 2 (1990) **C-108m.** **½ D: Stephen Hopkins. Danny Glover, Gary Busey, Ruben Blades, Maria Conchita Alonso, Bill Paxton, Kevin Peter Hall, Robert Davi, Adam Baldwin, Kent McCord, Calvin Lockhart, Morton Downey, Jr. Fast-paced (if too derivative) sequel, minus Arnold Schwarzenegger. This time, cop Glover and cronies take on the title alien in 1997 L.A. Good production design and lots of hit-'em-across-the-face action, but don't look for anything resembling inventive dialogue or character development. Then again, you wouldn't expect either from a film with Morton Downey, Jr., in its cast. [R]▼●

Prefontaine (1997) **C-106m.** ** D: Steve James. Jared Leto, R. Lee Ermey, Ed O'Neill, Amy Locane, Lindsay Crouse, Laurel Holloman, Breckin Meyer, Brian McGovern, Kurtwood Smith. Peter Anthony Jacobs. Steve Prefontaine, an athlete from Coos Bay, Oregon, attends college, where he excels in running, eventually going to the Munich Olympics. Well-intentioned but TV-movie-like biopic fails to reveal why the runner is remembered today. Seems endless, but well acted. Story also told in 1998's WITHOUT LIMITS. [PG-13]▼●

Prehistoric Women (1950) **C-74m.** BOMB D: Gregg Tallas. Laurette Luez, Allan Nixon, Joan Shawlee, Judy Landon, Jo Carroll Dennison. Sexy, lonely cavewomen (who have their hair permed and faces made up!) set out to find some cave-hunks. Incredibly silly—and incredibly boring—programmer.▼

Prehistoric Women (1967-British) **C-91m.** *½ D: Michael Carreras. Michael Latimer, Martine Beswick, Edina Ronay, Carol White, John Raglan, Stephanie Randall, Steven Berkoff. Idiotic Hammer adventure in which Great White Hunter stumbles into lost Amazon civilization where blondes have been enslaved by brunettes. Honest! Nevertheless, this does have a cult following, due to Beswick's commanding, sensual performance as the tribe's leader. Released in Britain as SLAVE GIRLS, at 74m. CinemaScope.▼●◗

Prehistoric World SEE: **Teenage Caveman**

Prehysteria (1993) **C-86m.** **½ D: Albert Band, Charles Band. Brett Cullen, Colleen Morris, Samantha Mills, Austin O'Brien, Tony Longo, Stuart Fratkin, Stephen Lee. A family of raisin farmers (!) tries to protect five unusual critters their dog has hatched from eggs she stole from a greedy entrepreneur. An idea that will enchant children of all ages—pet dinosaurs the size of cats—overcomes a routine script. Followed by two sequels. From Full Moon. [PG]▼●

Prelude to a Kiss (1992) **C-106m.** **½ D: Norman René. Alec Baldwin, Meg Ryan, Kathy Bates, Ned Beatty, Patty Duke, Sydney Walker, Stanley Tucci, Richard Riehle, Rocky Carroll, Annie Golden. It's love at first sight for Baldwin and Ryan, and soon they're wed—but on their honeymoon, he gets the strange feeling she's not the person he fell in love with. Winningly acted romantic comedy turns very, very odd, with a plot twist that's hard to swallow, and even harder to find endearing. A game attempt by all, including featured character actor Walker. Craig Lucas adapted his own play, with Baldwin recreating his original N.Y. stage role and Walker repeating the part he played on tour. [PG-13]▼●

Premature Burial, The (1962) **C-81m.** ** D: Roger Corman. Ray Milland, Hazel Court, Richard Ney, Heather Angel, Alan Napier, John Dierkes. Title tells the story in another of Corman's Poe adaptations, with Milland oddly cast as medical student with phobia of accidental entombment. Lavish (for this series), but not one of director's best. Panavision.▼●

Premier May SEE: **Man to Man Talk**

Premonition, The (1976) **C-94m.** ** D: Robert Allen Schnitzer. Sharon Farrell, Richard Lynch, Jeff Corey, Ellen Barber, Edward Bell. Muddled script works against eerie atmosphere in this supernatural tale that stresses parapsychology as clue to young girl's disappearance. Mediocre results. Filmed in Mississippi. [PG]▼

Prescription: Murder (1967) **C-99m.** **TVM** D: Richard Irving. Peter Falk, Gene Barry, Katherine Justice, William Windom, Nina Foch, Anthony James, Virginia Gregg. Doc Fleming (Barry) thinks he's committed fool-proof murder of wife, so at first he humors efforts of seemingly slow-witted police lieutenant (Falk) to check alibi. Interesting debut of Falk's Columbo character with excellent cast, subplots. Adapted by Richard Levinson and William Link from their Broadway play (with Thomas Mitchell as Columbo). Followed by RANSOM FOR A DEAD MAN. Video title: COLUMBO: PRESCRIPTION MURDER. Above average.▼

Presenting Lily Mars (1943) **104m.** ** D: Norman Taurog. Judy Garland, Van Heflin, Fay Bainter, Richard Carlson, Spring Byington, Marta Eggerth, Marilyn Maxwell, Ray McDonald, Leonid Kinskey, Connie Gilchrist, Bob Crosby, Tommy Dorsey. Well, there she is, and there lies the script. Stale story of determined girl getting big chance on Broadway only comes alive when Judy sings. From a Booth Tarkington novel.▼●

President's Analyst, The (1967) **C-104m.** **** D: Theodore J. Flicker. James Coburn, Godfrey Cambridge, Severn Darden, Joan Delaney, Pat Harrington, Will Geer, William Daniels. Totally nutty, brilliantly maneuvered satire of many sacred cows, as Coburn is pursued by half the government when he quits title job. The ending is a beauty. Screenplay by the director. Edited for video release. Panavision.▼●

President's Lady, The (1953) **96m.** *** D: Henry Levin. Charlton Heston, Susan Hayward, John McIntire, Fay Bainter, Carl Betz. Heston as Andrew Jackson and Hayward the lady with a past he marries work well together in this fictional history of 1800s America, based on the Irving Stone novel. Heston would again play "Old Hickory" five years later in THE BUCCANEER. ▼

President's Mystery, The (1936) **80m.** *** D: Phil Rosen. Henry Wilcoxon, Betty Furness, Sidney Blackmer, Evelyn Brent, Barnett Parker. Utterly fascinating Depression-era curio about a prominent lawyer/lobbyist (Wilcoxon) who reluctantly helps greedy capitalists kill some pro–labor/small business legislation. Believing his life empty, he liquidates his assets and "reinvents" himself—but not without murderous complications. This would make a great double bill with King Vidor's OUR DAILY BREAD. Based on an idea by F.D.R., developed as a magazine article by six writers (including S. S. Van Dine)! Screenplay by Lester Cole and Nathanael West.▼

Presidio, The (1988) **C-97m.** **½ D: Peter Hyams. Sean Connery, Mark Harmon, Meg Ryan, Jack Warden, Mark Blum, Dana Gladstone, Jenette Goldstein, Don Calfa. San Francisco cop Harmon investigates a murder that took place on local military base, and clashes with an old nemesis, the presidio's chief provost Connery—whose daughter he's attracted to. Strictly formula stuff, though slickly done, with some good S.F. chase scenes. Panavision. [R]▼●◗

Press for Time (1966-British) **C-102m.** ** D: Robert Asher. Norman Wisdom, Angela Browne, Derek Bond, Derek Francis. Bumbling son of a commoner is sent by his government minister granddad to work as a reporter on a provincial newspaper. Wisdom has fun doing three roles; infectious musical score by Mike Vickers.

Pressure Point (1962) **91m.** *** D: Hubert Cornfield. Sidney Poitier, Bobby Darin, Peter Falk, Carl Benton Reid, Mary Munday, Barry Gordon, Howard Caine. Intelligent drama, with Poitier the prison psychiatrist trying to ferret out the problems of his Nazi patient (Darin). Based on a true case from Dr. Robert M. Lindner's *The Fifty-Minute Hour*.▼

Prestige (1932) **71m.** **½ D: Tay Garnett. Ann Harding, Melvyn Douglas, Adolphe Menjou, Clarence Muse, Ian MacLaren. Flamboyant direction and solid performances elevate hackneyed melodrama about life at French Army outpost in the Far East where White Supremacy—and Douglas' sanity—are threatened.

Presumed Innocent (1990) **C-127m.** *** D: Alan J. Pakula. Harrison Ford, Brian Dennehy, Raul Julia, Bonnie Bedelia, Paul Winfield, Greta Scacchi, John Spencer, Joe Grifasi, Tom Mardirosian, Anna Maria Horsford, Sab Shimono, Christine Estabrook, Michael Tolan. Solid, well-cast screen version of Scott Turow's crackling best-seller about a prosecutor assigned to investigate the murder of a sexy assistant prosecutor with whom he'd had an affair. Soon, he's charged with the murder himself! Slow going at times, film misses its potential for greatness but still delivers many powerful moments. Screenplay by Pakula and Frank Pierson. [R]▼●◗

Prêt-à-Porter SEE: **Ready to Wear**

Pretender, The (1947) **69m.** **½ D: W. Lee Wilder. Albert Dekker, Catherine Craig, Linda Stirling, Charles Drake, Charles Middleton, Alan Carney. Dekker gives sharply etched performance as N.Y.C. financier trying to do in a competitor, discovering he may be the victim instead.

Pretty Baby (1950) **92m.** ** D: Bretaigne Windust. Dennis Morgan, Betsy Drake, Zachary Scott, Edmund Gwenn, Barbara Billingsley. Coy minor comedy involving working-girl Drake, who snowballs a gimmick to a get a subway seat on the morning train into a good job and romance.

Pretty Baby (1978) **C-109m.** **½ D: Louis Malle. Keith Carradine, Susan Sarandon, Brooke Shields, Antonio Fargas, Frances Faye, Gerrit Graham, Mae Mercer, Diana Scarwid, Barbara Steele. Malle's first American film is beautifully mounted but distressingly low-keyed story of marriage between a 12-year-old New Orleans prostitute and an older photographer, set around time of WW1. Shields is striking in title role, but Carradine is pretty lifeless. Designed and cowritten (with Malle) by Polly Platt; photographed by Sven Nykvist. [R]▼●

Pretty Boy Floyd (1960) **96m.** ** D: Herbert J. Leder. John Ericson, Barry Newman, Joan Harvey, Herb (Jason) Evers, Carl York, Peter Falk, Roy Fant, Shirley Smith. Average chronicle of infamous 1930s gangster, played energetically by Ericson.

Pretty in Pink (1986) **C-96m.** *** D: Howard Deutch. Molly Ringwald, Jon Cryer, Andrew McCarthy, Harry Dean Stanton, Annie Potts, James Spader, Alexa Kenin, Andrew "Dice" Clay, Margaret Colin, Gina Gershon, Dweezil Zappa, Kristy Swanson. A high school have-not finds herself in a quandary when one of the "richies" asks her out; her fellow outcast and fanatical devotee (Cryer) isn't too happy, either. Credible look at growing pains by writer-producer John Hughes, nicely acted, if a bit slow and self-serious. Stanton, as Molly's dad, has never been so tender on screen! [PG-13]▼●

Prettykill (1987) **C-95m.** BOMB D: George Kaczender. David Birney, Season Hubley, Susannah York, Yaphet Kotto, Suzanne Snyder. Noxious exploitation film about down on his luck cop and his girlfriend/hooker enmeshed in a case of a slasher who preys on prostitutes. Snyder gives an overwrought performance as a sweet young thing with a dual personality (she lapses into her southern fried incestuous father's voice at times!). [R]▼●

Pretty Maids All in a Row (1971) **C-92m.** *** D: Roger Vadim. Rock Hudson, Angie Dickinson, Telly Savalas, John David Carson, Roddy McDowall, James Doohan, Keenan Wynn, Amy (Aimee) Eccles, Barbara Leigh. Silly but enjoyable black comedy; high school guidance-counselor/coach Hudson advises frustrated Carson in sexual matters, while school is plagued with murders of pretty female students. Written and produced by Gene Roddenberry. [R] ▼

Pretty Poison (1968) **C-89m.** *** D: Noel Black. Anthony Perkins, Tuesday Weld, Beverly Garland, John Randolph, Dick O'Neill. Oddball arsonist Perkins enlists aid of sexy high-schooler Weld for scheme he's hatching, but soon discovers that she's got stranger notions than he does! Bright screenplay by Lorenzo Semple, Jr. (from Stephen Geller's novel, *She Let Him Continue*), sparked by Weld's vivid performance. [R]▼

Pretty Village, Pretty Flame (1996-Yugoslavian) **C-125m.** *** D: Srdjan Dragojevic. Dragan Bjelogrlic, Nikola Pejakovic, Velimir Bata Zivojinovic, Dragan Maksimovic. Biting allegorical anti-war drama about two young men, one Muslim, the other Serbian, who came of age together as best pals (depicted in poignant flashbacks) and now find themselves on opposite sides in the Bosnian civil war—and inexorably heading toward a confrontation.▼◗

Pretty Woman (1990) **C-117m.** *** D: Garry Marshall. Richard Gere, Julia Roberts, Ralph Bellamy, Jason Alexander, Laura San Giacomo, Hector Elizondo, Alex Hyde-White, Elinor Donahue, Larry Miller, Jane Morris. Surprisingly successful variation on an old formula: wealthy, cold-blooded business tycoon Gere chances to meet Hollywood Boulevard hooker Roberts. He hires her to be his companion for a week, spruces her up, and—well, you can figure out the rest. Light, charming, and thoroughly entertaining, with Roberts a delight in a star-making role. Director's cut runs 124m. [R]▼●◗

Price Above Rubies, A (1998) **C-117m.** **½ D: Boaz Yakin. Renée Zellweger, Christopher Eccleston, Glenn Fitzgerald, Allen Payne, Julianna Margulies, Kathleen Chalfant, Edie Falco, John Randolph, Kim Hunter, Phyllis Newman. An unhappy Hasidic housewife in N.Y.C. yearns for sexual liberation and the freedom to pursue a career. This had critics divided, but offers a truly three-dimensional heroine, and Zellweger is convincing. Worth a look for those who seek mature, alternative fare. [R]▼◗

Priceless Beauty (1988-Italian) **C-97m.** ** D: Charles Finch. Christopher Lambert, Diane Lane, Francesco Quinn, J. C. Quinn, Claudia Ohana, Monica Scattini, Joaquin D'Almeida. Reclusive former rock star, consumed by guilt over his brother's death, finds a magic lamp in the ocean and inside it a beautiful genie who tries to rebuild his self-esteem and capacity to love. Mediocre romance (starring then-real-life husband and wife Lambert and Lane) struggles to be whimsical. [R]▼●

Price of Fear, The (1956) **79m.** **½ D: Abner Biberman. Merle Oberon, Lex Barker, Charles Drake, Gia Scala, Warren Stevens. Middling account of Oberon involved in hit-and-run accident which snowballs her life into disaster.

Price of Freedom, The SEE: **Operation Daybreak**

Price of Glory (2000) **C-118m.** **½ D: Carlos Avila. Jimmy Smits, Jon Seda, Clifton Collins, Jr. (Clifton Gonzales Gonzales), Maria del Mar, Sal Lopez, Louis Mandylor, John Verea, Paul Rodriguez, Ron Perlman. Boxing saga centered around a Latino family has familiar feel as Smits pushes his three sons toward a success that eluded him in his fighting days. Earnest performances, and some good action in the ring, but plays like a TV movie. [PG-13] ▼◗

Prick Up Your Ears (1987-British) **C-108m.** *** D: Stephen Frears. Gary Oldman, Alfred Molina, Vanessa Redgrave,

Wallace Shawn, Julie Walters, James Grant, Frances Barber, Lindsay Duncan, Janet Dale. Chillingly realistic and evocative look at young British playwright Joe Orton, who was murdered by his longtime lover Kenneth Halliwell in 1967. Stunning performances by Oldman (as Orton), Molina (as the tormented Halliwell) and Redgrave (as Orton's agent) make up for some lags in Alan Bennett's script. Unflinching look at homosexuality in England during the 50s and 60s (when it was a crime), but film offers no insight into Orton's great theatrical success. [R]▼●

Pride and Prejudice (1940) **118m.** **** D: Robert Z. Leonard. Greer Garson, Laurence Olivier, Edna May Oliver, Edmund Gwenn, Mary Boland, Maureen O'Sullivan, Karen Morley, Melville Cooper, E. E. Clive, Ann Rutherford, Marsha Hunt. Outstanding adaptation of Jane Austen's novel about five husband-hunting sisters in 19th-century England. Excellent cast, fine period flavor in classic comedy of manners; Aldous Huxley was one of the screenwriters. Cedric Gibbons and Paul Groesse's art direction deservedly earned an Oscar. Also shown in computer-colored version.▼●

Pride and the Passion, The (1957) **C-132m.** **½ D: Stanley Kramer. Cary Grant, Frank Sinatra, Sophia Loren, Theodore Bikel, John Wengraf. Miscast actioner involving capture of huge cannon by British naval officer (Grant) in 19th-century Spain. Spectacle scenes—filmed on location—are impressive; but most of the film is ridiculous. From the C.S. Forester novel. VistaVision.▼●

Pride of St. Louis, The (1952) **93m.** **½ D: Harmon Jones. Dan Dailey, Joanne Dru, Richard Crenna, Hugh Sanders, Richard Hylton, James Brown. Dailey does well in this otherwise formula biography of brash, colorful Hall of Fame pitcher Dizzy Dean. Watch for Chet Huntley as a baseball broadcaster.▼

Pride of the Blue Grass (1954) **C-71m.** ** D: William Beaudine. Lloyd Bridges, Vera Miles, Margaret Sheridan, Arthur Shields, Joan Shawlee. Familiar racetrack story; competent production.

Pride of the Bowery (1941) **61m.** ** D: Joseph H. Lewis. Leo Gorcey, Bobby Jordan, Sunshine Sammy Morrison, Donald Haines, Bobby Stone, Carleton Young, Kenneth Howell, David Gorcey, Mary Ainslee. The East Side Kids are sent to a Civilian Conservation Corps. camp where Muggs is in training for a big boxing match; some well-shot ring scenes.▼

Pride of the Marines (1945) **119m.** ***½ D: Delmer Daves. John Garfield, Eleanor Parker, Dane Clark, John Ridgely, Rosemary DeCamp, Ann Doran, Ann Todd, Warren Douglas. Ensemble acting by Warner Bros. stock company enhances true account of Marine blinded during Japanese attack, with Garfield as injured Al Schmid, Clark as sympathetic buddy. Screenplay by Albert Maltz.

Pride of the Yankees, The (1942) **127m.** **** D: Sam Wood. Gary Cooper, Teresa Wright, Babe Ruth, Walter Brennan, Dan Duryea, Ludwig Stossel, Addison Richards, Hardie Albright. Superb biography of baseball star Lou Gehrig, with Cooper giving excellent performance; fine support from Wright as devoted wife. Truly memorable final sequence. Script by Jo Swerling and Herman J. Mankiewicz, with Oscar-winning editing by Daniel Mandell. Also see A LOVE AFFAIR: THE ELEANOR AND LOU GEHRIG STORY. Also shown in computer-colored version.▼●◗

Priest (1994-British) **C-97m.** ***½ D: Antonia Bird. Linus Roache, Tom Wilkinson, Cathy Tyson, Robert Carlyle, James Ellis, Lesley Sharp, Robert Pugh, Christine Tremarco, Paul Barber, Rio Fanning. Provocative drama about a man of the cloth who finds himself caught between sacred vows and his own personal beliefs, in particular his closeted homosexuality. Deft blend of melodrama and tract that manages to deal with homosexuality, abuse, incest, and the politics of the Church with incisive results—and even a dark sense of humor. Flawlessly acted. Written by Jimmy McGovern. Originally shown at 105m. and trimmed for U.S. release. [R]▼●◗

Priest of Love (1981-British) **C-125m.** *** D: Christopher Miles. Ian McKellen, Janet Suzman, Ava Gardner, Penelope Keith, Jorge Rivero, John Gielgud, Sarah Miles. Literate account of the last years of D. H. Lawrence (McKellen)—"the one who writes the dirty books"—highlighted by his relationship with his wife (Suzman) and the publication of *Lady Chatterley's Lover.* Slow-moving but rewarding; 11 years earlier, Miles directed the screen version of Lawrence's THE VIRGIN AND THE GYPSY. [R]▼

Priest's Wife, The (1971-Italian-French) **C-106m.** *½ D: Dino Risi. Sophia Loren, Marcello Mastroianni, Venantino Venantini, Jacques Stany, Pippo Starnazza, Augusto Mastrantoni. Barely entertaining mixture of drama and humor with Loren as disillusioned singer who thinks she can convince priest (Mastroianni) to obtain release from his vow of celibacy and marry her. Weightier handling of subject matter can be heard on radio talk shows; film seems designed merely as vehicle for two stars. [PG]

Primal Fear (1996) **C-129m.** *** D: Gregory Hoblit. Richard Gere, Laura Linney, John Mahoney, Alfre Woodard, Frances McDormand, Edward Norton, Terry O'Quinn, Andre Braugher, Steven Bauer, Joe Spano, Tony Plana, Stanley Anderson, Maura Tierney, Jon Seda. Hotshot Chicago attorney defends an altar boy accused of brutally murdering a much-loved archbishop—even though all evidence seems to point to the young man's guilt. Gere gives a solid performance in one of his very best roles, as a cocky lawyer who—for once—doesn't have all the answers. Newcomer Norton is also very impressive. Film loses some of its impact by going on too long and by following unrelated story tangents. Still, an intelligent, absorbing drama. [R] ▼●◗

Primary Colors (1998) **C-143m.** ***½ D: Mike Nichols. John Travolta, Emma Thompson, Kathy Bates, Adrian Lester, Billy Bob Thornton, Maura Tierney, Larry Hagman, Diane Ladd, Paul Guilfoyle, Caroline Aaron, Rob Reiner, Ben Jones, Mykelti Williamson, Bonnie Bartlett, Tony Shalhoub, Allison Janney. Dynamic adaptation of political roman à clef by Anonymous (Joe Klein) about a Southern governor's Presidential race—and an idealistic staffer (Lester) who sees in him both a true believer in people power and an insatiable womanizer who'll do anything to cover his tracks. Travolta is extraordinarily good in a Bill Clinton–esque characterization, and Nichols has cast every part around him with an unerring eye. Bates is a powerhouse as Travolta's longtime political conscience and troubleshooter. Smart, funny, foul-mouthed screenplay by Elaine May. Super 35. [R] ▼●◗

Prime Cut (1972) **C-86m.** *** D: Michael Ritchie. Lee Marvin, Gene Hackman, Angel Tompkins, Gregory Walcott, Sissy Spacek, Janit Baldwin. Mob hijinks at a Kansas City slaughterhouse inspire well-cast, fast-moving, tongue-in-cheek trash that fans of sleazy crime melodramas should love. Spacek's first film. Panavision. [R]▼

Prime of Miss Jean Brodie, The (1969) **C-116m.** ***½ D: Ronald Neame. Maggie Smith, Robert Stephens, Pamela Franklin, Gordon Jackson, Celia Johnson, Jane Carr. Oscar-winning showcase for Smith as eccentric teacher in Edinburgh school who wields a spellbinding influence on her "girls." Remarkable character study, adapted by Jay Presson Allen from stage version of Muriel Spark's novel; filmed on location. Smith and Stephens were then real-life husband and wife. Later remade as a TV mini-series. [M/PG]▼

Prime Target (1991) **C-84m.** *½ D: David Heavener. David Heavener, Tony Curtis, Isaac Hayes, Robert Reed, Andrew Robinson, Jenilee Harrison, Michael Gregory, Don Stroud. Vanity production for writer-director-producer-star Heavener, who casts himself in the Eastwood/Norris mold as a tough cop accompanying mafioso Curtis to a new prison, with predictable complications along the way. For only the most undemanding fans. [R]▼

Primrose Path (1940) **93m.** **½ D: Gregory La Cava. Ginger Rogers, Joel McCrea, Marjorie Rambeau, Miles Mander, Henry Travers. Girl from wrong side of the tracks falls in love with ambitious young McCrea; starts engagingly, drifts into dreary soap opera and melodramatics. Rambeau is excellent as Ginger's prostitute mother.▼

Prince and the Pauper, The (1937) **120m.** ***½ D: William Keighley. Errol Flynn, Billy and Bobby Mauch, Claude Rains, Alan Hale, Montagu Love, Henry Stephenson, Barton MacLane. Rousing filmization of Mark Twain's story of young look-alikes, one a mistreated urchin, the other a prince, exchanging places. Top-billed Flynn, cast as the boys' rescuer, doesn't appear until second half of film. Great music score by Erich Wolfgang Korngold. Remade as CROSSED SWORDS. Also available in computer-colored version.▼●

Prince and the Pauper, The (1978) SEE: **Crossed Swords**

Prince and the Showgirl, The (1957) **C-117m.** **½ D: Laurence Olivier. Marilyn Monroe, Laurence Olivier, Sybil Thorndike. Jeremy Spenser, Richard Wattis. Thoughtful but slow-moving comedy of saucy American showgirl Monroe being romanced by Prince Regent of Carpathia (Olivier) during the 1911 coronation of George V. Filmed in England, with delightful performances by Monroe and Olivier. Script by Terence Rattigan from his play *The Sleeping Prince*.▼●

Prince Brat and the Whipping Boy SEE: **Whipping Boy, The**

Prince Jack (1984) **C-100m.** ** D: Bert Lovitt. Robert Hogan, James F. Kelly, Kenneth Mars, Lloyd Nolan, Cameron Mitchell, Robert Guillaume, Theodore Bikel, Jim Backus, Dana Andrews. Yet another chronicle of life among the Kennedys, here focusing mainly on the men and their personalities. Superficial at best.▼

Prince of Darkness (1987) **C-110m.** BOMB D: John Carpenter. Donald Pleasence, Lisa Blount, Jameson Parker, Victor Wong, Dennis Dun, Susan Blanchard, Anne Howard, Alice Cooper. The anti-God entombs wayward son Satan in a cannister of glop in an abandoned L.A. church; it's up to priest Pleasence and the grad students of prof Wong to clean up the mess. Not for nothing is the religious sect involved called "Brotherhood of Death." Panavision. [R]▼●◗

Prince of Egypt, The (1998) **C-97m.** **½ D: Brenda Chapman, Steve Hickner, Simon Wells. Voices of Val Kilmer, Ralph Fiennes, Michelle Pfeiffer, Sandra Bullock, Jeff Goldblum, Danny Glover, Patrick Stewart, Helen Mirren, Steve Martin, Martin Short. Animated retelling of the story of Moses features some of the most spectacular animation in the history of the medium, dra-

matic staging, and an ambitious song score by Stephen Schwartz . . . but the parts are greater than the whole, and the story drags at times. An impressive achievement, but liable to test the endurance of young children. Features Oscar-winning song "When You Believe." [PG]▼●◗
Prince of Foxes (1949) **107m.** **½ D: Henry King. Tyrone Power, Wanda Hendrix, Orson Welles, Marina Berti, Everett Sloane, Katina Paxinou. Lavish, incredibly handsome costume epic of Renaissance-era Italy (filmed on location), with adventurer Power defying all-powerful Cesare Borgia. Story elements—from Samuel Shellabarger novel—don't match impact of Leon Shamroy's sumptuous cinematography.
Prince of Pennsylvania, The (1988) **C-87m.** **½ D: Ron Nyswaner. Fred Ward, Keanu Reeves, Bonnie Bedelia, Amy Madigan, Jeff Hayenga, Tracey Ellis. Extremely quirky character comedy of free spirit Reeves (with a strange half-Mohawk hairdo) "finding" himself while battling with his equally wacko dad (Ward, in a marvelous performance). Madigan is excellent as the older woman whom Reeves romances; in-joke has her dressing up in a Freddy Krueger mask for a fake kidnapping. Writer Nyswaner (SMITHEREENS) turns director; many striking scenes unfortunately fail to grip as a whole. [R]▼●
Prince of Pirates (1953) **C-80m.** **½ D: Sidney Salkow. John Derek, Barbara Rush, Whitfield Connor, Edgar Barrier. Enjoyable little costumer involving French-Spanish wars.
Prince of Players (1955) **C-102m.** **½ D: Philip Dunne. Richard Burton, Maggie McNamara, Raymond Massey, Charles Bickford, John Derek, Eva Le Gallienne, Mae Marsh, Sarah Padden. Burton is 19th-century actor Edwin Booth, embroiled in more offstage drama than on. Shakespearean excerpts thrown in; well performed by earnest cast. Derek plays John Wilkes Booth. Script by Moss Hart. CinemaScope.
Prince of the City (1981) **C-167m.** *** D: Sidney Lumet. Treat Williams, Jerry Orbach, Richard Foronjy, Don Billett, Kenny Marino, Carmine Caridi, Bob Balaban, James Tolkan, Lindsay Crouse, Matthew Laurance, Lee Richardson, Lane Smith, Peter Michael Goetz, Lance Henriksen. Emotionally powerful story (which unfortunately is true) about a cop in a N.Y.C. special investigations unit who blows the whistle on department corruption but finds himself more a victim than a hero. Standout performances by Williams, fellow cop Orbach, weasely prosecutor Tolkan, but film's extreme length hurts overall impact; there are more details than really necessary to tell the story. Script by Lumet and Jay Presson Allen. [R]▼●
Prince of Thieves, The (1948) **C-72m.** ** D: Howard Bretherton. Jon Hall, Patricia Morison, Adele Jergens, Alan Mowbray, Michael Duane. Colorful swashbuckler of Robin Hood and Maid Marian, aimed at juvenile audiences.▼
Prince of Tides, The (1991) **C-132m.** *** D: Barbra Streisand. Nick Nolte, Barbra Streisand, Blythe Danner, Kate Nelligan, Jeroen Krabbé, Melinda Dillon, George Carlin, Jason Gould, Brad Sullivan. Nolte is both compelling and believable as a man who keeps a lifetime of harrowing memories bottled up inside—until he's forced to spill them to a psychiatrist in order to help save his suicidal sister. How much you like (or believe) Streisand's performance as the doctor may affect your feelings about the film, but she's certainly managed to tell a good story, rich in emotion. Gould (son of Streisand and Elliott Gould) plays Barbra's teenage son. Screenplay by Pat Conroy and Becky Johnston, from Conroy's sprawling novel. Streisand also coproduced the film. [R]▼●
Princess Academy, The (1987-U.S.-French-Yugoslavian) **C-90m.** BOMB D: Bruce Block. Eva Gabor, Lar Park Lincoln, Lu Leonard, Richard Paul, Carole Davis, Badar Howar. Allegedly titillating comedy about young women at a Swiss school who compare notes on losing virginity and snaring rich husbands. In any language, it stinks. [R]▼
Princess and the Goblin, The (1991-Hungarian-Welsh) **C-82m.** *½ D: Jozsef Gemes. Voices of Claire Bloom, Joss Ackland, Sally Ann Marsh, Peter Murray, Rik Mayall, Victor Spinetti, Roy Kinnear. Static animated version of George MacDonald's 1872 novel-length fairy tale. Princess Irene and miner's son Curdi head off a revolt of subterranean goblins through a series of unexplained events and unresolved encounters. Plot holes aside, the animation is stiff. Released in U.S. in 1994. [G]▼●
Princess and the Pirate, The (1944) **C-94m.** *** D: David Butler. Bob Hope, Virginia Mayo, Walter Slezak, Walter Brennan, Victor McLaglen, Hugo Haas, Marc Lawrence. One of Bob's wackiest; he and glamorous Virginia are on the lam from pirate McLaglen, trapped by potentate Slezak. Brennan is hilarious as a pirate; great closing gag, too. ▼●◗
Princess Bride, The (1987) **C-98m.** **½ D: Rob Reiner. Cary Elwes, Mandy Patinkin, Chris Sarandon, Christopher Guest, Wallace Shawn, Andre the Giant, Fred Savage, Robin Wright, Peter Falk, Peter Cook, Carol Kane, Billy Crystal, Mel Smith. Revisionist fairy tale/adventure about a beautiful young woman and her one true love, who must find and rescue her after a long separation. Some wonderful scenes and character vignettes are periodically undermined by a tendency toward comic

shtick (as in Crystal's cameo appearance) and occasional incoherency (as in the opening scenes with Castilian-tongued Patinkin and marble-mouthed Andre the Giant). Best of all: the swashbuckling sequences. Bonus for old-movie buffs: watching Guest, as Count Rugen, imitate Henry Daniell (from THE SEA HAWK). Screenplay by William Goldman, from his novel. [PG]▼●

Princess Caraboo (1994–U.S.-British) **C-96m.** *** D: Michael Austin. Phoebe Cates, Jim Broadbent, Wendy Hughes, Kevin Kline, John Lithgow, Stephen Rea, Peter Eyre, Jacqueline Pearce, Roger Lloyd Pack, John Wells, John Lynch. Pleasing fairy tale–like yarn about young "mystery woman" Cates who is believed to be a princess from a distant land, and is taken in by a well-meaning British lady (Hughes) in the early 1800s. Based on a true story, believe it or not; handsomely made, acted with gusto by a first-rate cast. Ideal family entertainment. Photographed by the great Freddie Francis. [PG]▼●

Princess Comes Across, The (1936) **76m.** *** D: William K. Howard. Carole Lombard, Fred MacMurray, Douglass Dumbrille, Alison Skipworth, William Frawley, Porter Hall, Sig Ruman, Mischa Auer. Lombard, posing as royalty on ocean voyage, meets romantic MacMurray; together they are involved in whodunit. And Fred sings "My Concertina." Delightful blend of comedy and mystery.▼

Princess Mononoke (1997-Japanese) **C-115m.** ***½ D: Hayao Miyazaki. Voices of Billy Crudup, Claire Danes, Minnie Driver, Billy Bob Thornton, Gillian Anderson, Jada Pinkett Smith. Extraordinary animated fable, full of astonishing sights; while the story is difficult to follow at times, it's worth the effort. Wounded by a dying boar god, a young man tries to get help from a forest spirit. He's aided by a girl who lives with wolf-gods, and opposed by a shrewd woman who is devoted to technology. Writer-director Miyazaki largely created his own mythology, and raises worthy questions about mankind's place in the natural world. Complex, thoughtful animated movie aimed at adults rather than children; this was the biggest box-office hit in Japanese history. [PG-13]▼◗

Princesse Tam Tam (1935-French) **77m.** *** D: Edmond T. Greville. Josephine Baker, Albert Prejean, Robert Arnoux, Germaine Aussey, Georges Peclet, Viviane Romance, Jean Galland. Baker lives up to her legend in this disarming reworking of *Pygmalion*: a poor, beautiful, wild African lass is polished and educated by writer Prejean, then passed off as an Indian princess—much to the consternation of his snobbish, two-timing wife. Charming story (by Pepito Abatino, then Baker's husband), lavish Busby Berkeley-ish musical numbers. Partially filmed in Tunisia.▼●

Princess of the Nile (1954) **C-71m.** **½ D: Harmon Jones. Debra Paget, Jeffrey Hunter, Michael Rennie, Dona Drake, Wally Cassell, Jack Elam, Lee Van Cleef. Hokey script diverts any potential this costumer may have had.

Princess O'Rourke (1943) **94m.** **½ D: Norman Krasna. Olivia de Havilland, Robert Cummings, Charles Coburn, Jack Carson, Jane Wyman, Harry Davenport, Gladys Cooper. Very dated comedy starts charmingly with pilot Cummings falling in love with Princess de Havilland, bogs down in no longer timely situations, unbearably coy finale involving (supposedly) F.D.R. himself. Krasna won Best Screenplay Oscar.

Princess Yang Kwei Fei (1955-Japanese) **C-91m.** **** D: Kenji Mizoguchi. Machiko Kyo, Masayuki Mori, So Yamamura, Eitaro Shindo, Sakae Ozawa. Emperor Mori takes country girl Kyo as his concubine. He is forced out of power by his greedy family: she is killed, and he worships her statue. Breathtakingly beautiful, poetic love story/fable/tragedy.▼

Prince Valiant (1954) **C-100m.** **½ D: Henry Hathaway. James Mason, Janet Leigh, Robert Wagner, Debra Paget, Sterling Hayden, Victor McLaglen, Donald Crisp, Brian Aherne. Hal Foster's famed comic-strip character is the hero of this cardboard costumer decked out in 20th Century-Fox splendor, battling and loving in Middle Ages England. Script by Dudley Nichols. CinemaScope.▼

Prince Who Was a Thief, The (1951) **C-88m.** **½ D: Rudolph Maté. Tony Curtis, Piper Laurie, Everett Sloane, Jeff Corey, Betty Garde. Juvenile costumer with Curtis fighting to regain his rightful seat on the throne; sparked by enthusiastic performances.

Principal, The (1987) **C-109m.** ** D: Christopher Cain. James Belushi, Louis Gossett, Jr., Rae Dawn Chong, Michael Wright, J.J. Cohen, Esai Morales, Troy Winbush. Following some drunken vandalism on his estranged spouse's car, schoolteacher Belushi is "promoted" to top job at the district's most crime-ridden school. Unlikely mix of comedy and drama benefits from likable performances and a reasonably tense HIGH NOON finale between Belushi and the school's leading thug. [R]▼●

Priscilla, Queen of the Desert SEE: **Adventures of Priscilla, Queen of the Desert, The**

Prison (1988) **C-102m.** ** D: Renny Harlin. Lane Smith, Viggo Mortensen, Chelsea Field, Andre De Shields, Lincoln Kilpatrick, Ivan Kane. The spirit of a prisoner who was executed twenty years ago seeks revenge on his one-time guard—

who's now the warden (Smith). OK special effects and location atmosphere are strongest assets of this clichéd horror film. [R]▼●

Prisoner, The (1955-British) **91m.** *** D: Peter Glenville. Alec Guinness, Jack Hawkins, Raymond Huntley, Wilfrid Lawson. Grim account of cardinal in iron curtain country undergoing grueling interrogation. Guinness-Hawkins interplay is superb.▼

Prisoner of Honor (1991-British) **C-115m. TVM** D: Ken Russell. Richard Dreyfuss, Oliver Reed, Peter Firth, Jeremy Kemp, Brian Blessed, Peter Vaughan, Kenneth Colley, Lindsay Anderson. Murky, Russellized look at l'affair Dreyfus in turn-of-the-century France, with actor (and coproducer) Dreyfuss playing Georges Picquart, the doubting French colonel who comes to believe Alfred Dreyfus's innocence and is court-martialed for his support. Interesting if episodic script by Ron Hutchinson. Made for cable. Above average.▼●

Prisoner of Second Avenue, The (1975) **C-105m.** ***½ D: Melvin Frank. Jack Lemmon, Anne Bancroft, Gene Saks, Elizabeth Wilson, Florence Stanley, M. Emmet Walsh. Neil Simon walks a tightrope between comedy and melancholia, and never falls, thanks to warm performances by Lemmon, as suddenly unemployed executive who has a nervous breakdown, and Bancroft, as his understanding wife. Look for Sylvester Stallone as an alleged pickpocket, F. Murray Abraham as a cabbie. Panavision. [PG]▼●

Prisoner of Shark Island, The (1936) **95m.** ***½ D: John Ford. Warner Baxter, Gloria Stuart, Claude Gillingwater, John Carradine, Harry Carey, Arthur Byron, Ernest Whitman, Francis McDonald. Excellent film based on true story of Dr. Samuel Mudd, who innocently treated John Wilkes Booth's leg after Lincoln assassination, and was sentenced to life imprisonment. Gripping story; Baxter superb, Carradine memorable as villainous sergeant, Whitman fine as Baxter's black comrade. Scripted by Nunnally Johnson. Remade as HELLGATE and the TV movie THE ORDEAL OF DR. MUDD.

Prisoner of the Iron Mask, The (1962-Italian) **C-80m.** **½ D: Francesco De Feo. Michael Lemoine, Wandisa Guida, Andrea Bosic, Jany Clair, Giovanni Materassi. Usual costume shenanigans: an evil count imprisons a man who has proof of the nobleman's treachery. Based not on the expected Dumas novel, but on his *Ten Years After*. D'Artagnan and The Three Musketeers do not appear. Techniscope.

Prisoner of the Mountains (1996-Russian) **C-98m.** ***½ D: Sergei Bodrov. Oleg Menshikov, Sergei Bodrov, Jr., Jemal Sikharulidze, Susanna Mekhralieva, Alexei Jharkov. Simple, devastating account of two Russian soldiers captured by Chechen rebels and held in an impoverished mountaintop village. Film is based on a Tolstoy story, but seems more pertinent in its present-day setting. Director's son portrays the younger of the two prisoners, an impressionable soldier barely out of school. Catch this one. ▼●

Prisoner of the Volga (1960-Yugoslavian) **C-102m.** ** D: W. Tourjansky. John Derek, Elsa Martinelli, Dawn Addams, Wolfgang Preiss, Gert Frobe. Well-mounted but ordinary costume drama of soldier who suffers when he seeks revenge on general who impregnated his wife. Totalscope.

Prisoner of War (1954) **80m.** ** D: Andrew Marton. Ronald Reagan, Steve Forrest, Dewey Martin, Oscar Homolka, Robert Horton, Paul Stewart, Harry Morgan, Stephen Bekassy. Sincere but two-dimensional drama exposing mistreatment of American P.O.W.s during Korean War.

Prisoner of Zenda, The (1937) **101m.** **** D: John Cromwell. Ronald Colman, Madeleine Carroll, Douglas Fairbanks, Jr., C. Aubrey Smith, Raymond Massey, Mary Astor, David Niven, Montagu Love, Alexander D'Arcy. Lavish costume romance/adventure with excellent casting; Colman is forced to substitute for lookalike cousin, King of Ruritanian country, but commoner Colman falls in love with regal Carroll. Fairbanks nearly steals the show as villainous Rupert of Hentzau. Screenplay by John L. Balderston, from Anthony Hope's novel. Previously filmed in 1914 and 1922, then again in 1952 and 1979. Also shown in computer-colored version.▼●

Prisoner of Zenda, The (1952) **C-101m.** **½ D: Richard Thorpe. Stewart Granger, Deborah Kerr, Jane Greer, Louis Calhern, Lewis Stone, James Mason, Robert Douglas, Robert Coote. Plush but uninspired remake of the Anthony Hope novel, chronicling the swashbuckling adventures of Granger, a dead ringer for a small European country's king. Stick with the Ronald Colman version; this one copies it scene for scene.▼●

Prisoner of Zenda, The (1979) **C-108m.** BOMB D: Richard Quine. Peter Sellers, Lynne Frederick, Lionel Jeffries, Elke Sommer, Gregory Sierra, Jeremy Kemp, Catherine Schell. Famous swashbuckler is played for laughs, but there aren't any. A return to the kind of picture that helped to destroy Sellers' career. [PG]▼

Prisoners of the Casbah (1953) **C-78m.** *½ D: Richard Bare. Gloria Grahame, Turhan Bey, Cesar Romero, Nestor Paiva. Low-budget costumer with diverting cast in stale plot of princess and her lover fleeing killers in title locale. Turhan Bey's last movie—for 40 years.

Prisoners of the Sun (1991-Australian) **C-109m.** *** D: Stephen Wallace. Bryan

Brown, George Takei, Terry O'Quinn, John Bach, Toshi Shioya, John Clarke, Deborah Unger, Russell Crowe. Gritty, gripping post-WW2 drama, set on an Indonesian island where the Japanese had established a POW camp for Australian flyers. The war has ended, and truth-seeking military lawyer Brown must deal with bureaucracy, politics, and clashing cultures as he sets out to prosecute different Japanese charged with mistreating and murdering POWS. Incisive, well-acted tale. [R]▼●

Prison Train (1938) **84m.** **½ D: Gordon Wiles. Fred Keating, Linda Winters (Dorothy Comingore), Clarence Muse, Faith Bacon, Alexander Leftwich, Nestor Paiva. Stylized, atmospheric little chronicle of racketeer Keating, who's convicted of murder and is traveling cross-country to begin doing time at Alcatraz. Hampered by its ultra-low budget but still a nice surprise. Aka PEOPLE'S ENEMY.▼

Private Affairs (1988-Italian) **C-104m.** BOMB D: Francesco Massaro. Kate Capshaw, David Naughton, Giuliana de Sio, Michele Placido, Luca Barbareschi. Various romantic complications among the boring people, mostly connected with the Roman fashion industry. Characters are as dull as the thin, diffuse plot; as near to unwatchable as a movie can be.▼

Private Affairs of Bel Ami, The (1947) **112m.** ***½ D: Albert Lewin. George Sanders, Angela Lansbury, Ann Dvorak, Frances Dee, Albert Basserman, Warren William, John Carradine. Delicious, literate adaptation (by Lewin) of Guy de Maupassant's "story of a rogue." Sanders, who gets ahead by using his charm on prominent women, denies himself the real love of Lansbury. Fine performances; beautifully photographed by Russell Metty.▼

Private Benjamin (1980) **C-100m.** *** D: Howard Zieff. Goldie Hawn, Eileen Brennan, Armand Assante, Robert Webber, Sam Wanamaker, Barbara Barrie, Mary Kay Place, Harry Dean Stanton, Albert Brooks, Hal Williams, P. J. Soles, Sally Kirkland, Richard Herd, Gretchen Wyler, Craig T. Nelson. A bubbleheaded Jewish American Princess enlists in the Army, and after a disastrous initiation finds direction and self-esteem for the first time in her life. Entertaining comedy with more substance than one might expect; Goldie is terrific in this tailor-made vehicle (which she produced). Later a TV series. [R] ▼●◗

Private Buckaroo (1942) **68m.** ** D: Edward Cline. The Andrews Sisters, Dick Foran, Joe E. Lewis, Donald O'Connor, Peggy Ryan, Jennifer Holt. Mini-musical from Universal Pictures is vehicle for 1940s favorite sister trio, accompanied by Harry James, et al in Army camp show.▼

Private Confessions (1997-Swedish) **C-127m.** *** D: Liv Ullmann. Pernilla August, Max von Sydow, Samuel Froler, Anita Bjork, Vibeke Falk, Thomas Hanzon. Intimate, compassionate autobiographical drama (an extension of THE BEST INTENTIONS) scripted by Ingmar Bergman, which further examines the stormy relationship between his parents: a strict, detached Lutheran minister (Froler) and a dynamic, restless woman caught in an unhappy marriage (August). Von Sydow brilliantly plays a fatherly priest. An exploration of religion, faith, and loneliness. Edited from a Swedish TV miniseries.▼

Private Detective 62 SEE: **Man Killer**

Private Duty Nurses (1971) **C-80m.** BOMB D: George Armitage. Kathy Cannon, Joyce Williams, Pegi Boucher, Joseph Kaufmann, Herbert Jefferson, Jr., Paul Hampton, Paul Gleason. Second of Roger Corman's five "nurse" pictures is the worst. Glum and humorless, it spends more time on then-new waterbeds than in the hospital; dull cast doesn't help. Followed by NIGHT CALL NURSES. [R]▼

Private Eyes (1953) **64m.** **½ D: Edward Bernds. Leo Gorcey, Huntz Hall, David (Gorcey) Condon, Bennie Bartlett, Rudy Lee, William Phillips, Joyce Holden, Bernard Gorcey, Chick Chandler, Myron Healey. Good *Bowery Boys* entry, as they open a detective agency when Sach develops the ability to read minds. Look for Lee Van Cleef in a bit.

Private Eyes, The (1980) **C-91m.** **½ D: Lang Elliott. Tim Conway, Don Knotts, Trisha Noble, Bernard Fox, John Fujioka, Fred Stuthman. Conway and Knotts are bumbling Scotland Yard sleuths—and Abbott and Costello incarnate—in this silly, well-mounted murder-in-an-old-dark-house mystery. One of the better Conway-Knotts comedies. [PG]▼●

Private Files of J. Edgar Hoover, The (1977) **C-112m.** **½ D: Larry Cohen. Broderick Crawford, Dan Dailey, Jose Ferrer, Rip Torn, Michael Parks, Raymond St. Jacques, Ronee Blakley, Celeste Holm, Howard da Silva, June Havoc, John Marley, Andrew Duggan, Lloyd Nolan. Sleazy bio of former FBI chief makes for great camp with its all-star lineup of real-life politicians—not to mention that cast! [PG]▼

Private Function, A (1985-British) **C-93m.** **½ D: Malcolm Mowbray. Michael Palin, Maggie Smith, Liz Smith, Denholm Elliott, Richard Griffiths, John Normington, Bill Paterson, Peter Postlethwaite. Droll, very British comedy by Alan Bennett set in post-WW2 England, where food rationing is still in force and a contraband pig becomes the center of attention. Often funny, but also cynical and cruel. Smith is hilarious as the social-climbing wife of milquetoasty podiatrist Palin. [R]▼

Private Hell 36 (1954) **81m.** **½ D: Don Siegel. Ida Lupino, Steve Cochran, Howard Duff, Dean Jagger, Dorothy Malone. Well-balanced account of guilt overcoming two cops who retrieve stolen money but keep some for themselves. Interesting low-budgeter with first-rate cast, but gets awfully talky in the second half. Lupino also wrote and produced the film with Collier Young.▼●

Private Lessons (1981) **C-87m.** *½ D: Alan Myerson. Sylvia Kristel, Howard Hesseman, Eric Brown, Pamela Bryant, Ed Begley, Jr., Crispin Glover. Male adolescent from wealthy family finds sexual delight with the maid, unaware that she has other plans for him. Surprise box-office hit is pretty mild piece of sleaze. Written by humorist Dan Greenburg (who also appears as a desk clerk). Followed by an in-name-only sequel 13 years later. [R]▼●

Private Life of Don Juan, The (1934-British) **80m.** ** D: Alexander Korda. Douglas Fairbanks, Merle Oberon, Binnie Barnes, Joan Gardner, Benita Hume, Athene Seyler, Melville Cooper. Lifeless costumer with aging Fairbanks in title role, pursuing a bevy of beauties in his final film.▼

Private Life of Henry VIII, The (1933-British) **97m.** **** D: Alexander Korda. Charles Laughton, Binnie Barnes, Robert Donat, Elsa Lanchester, Merle Oberon, Miles Mander, Wendy Barrie, John Loder. Sweeping historical chronicle of 16th-century British monarch, magnificently captured by Oscar-winning Laughton in a multifaceted performance. Lanchester fine as Anne of Cleves, with top supporting cast. Also shown in computer-colored version.▼●

Private Life of Sherlock Holmes, The (1970) **C-125m.** ***½ D: Billy Wilder. Robert Stephens, Colin Blakely, Genevieve Page, Irene Handl, Stanley Holloway, Christopher Lee, Clive Revill. Atypical but extremely personal Wilder film takes melancholy look at famed sleuth. Acting, photography and score are tops in neglected film whose reputation should soar in future years. Intended as a 3½-hour film. A 12m. sequence ("The Dreadful Business of the Naked Honeymooners") restored to laserdisc. Made in England. Panavision. [PG]▼●

Private Lives (1931) **84m.** *** D: Sidney Franklin. Norma Shearer, Robert Montgomery, Una Merkel, Reginald Denny, Jean Hersholt. Sparkling, witty adaptation of the Noël Coward comedy about a divorced couple (Shearer and Montgomery) who marry others and find themselves honeymooning at the same hotel.▼●

Private Lives of Adam and Eve, The (1960) **C/B&W-87m.** BOMB D: Albert Zugsmith, Mickey Rooney. Mickey Rooney, Mamie Van Doren, Fay Spain, Mel Torme, Martin Milner, Tuesday Weld, Cecil Kellaway, Paul Anka, Ziva Rodann. Perfectly awful fantasy about a stranded Nevada couple, Ad (Milner) and Evie (Van Doren), who dream that they are back in the Garden of Eden. Rooney chews the scenery as the Devil.

Private Lives of Elizabeth and Essex, The (1939) **C-106m.** ***½ D: Michael Curtiz. Bette Davis, Errol Flynn, Olivia de Havilland, Donald Crisp, Alan Hale, Vincent Price, Henry Stephenson, Henry Daniell, James Stephenson, Ralph Forbes, Robert Warwick, Leo G. Carroll. Colorful, elaborate costume drama with outstanding performance by Davis as queen whose love for dashing Flynn is thwarted. Not authentic history, but good drama. Norman Reilly Raine and Aeneas MacKenzie adapted Maxwell Anderson's play *Elizabeth the Queen*. Adult film debut of Nanette Fabray (billed as Fabares). Aka ELIZABETH THE QUEEN. ▼

Private Matter, A (1992) **C-89m. TVM** D: Joan Micklin Silver. Sissy Spacek, Aidan Quinn, Estelle Parsons, Sheila McCarthy, Leon Russom, William H. Macy. Spacek sparks as the real-life Sherri Finkbine, who in the early sixties came up against right-to-lifers when trying to abort her unborn baby after discovering doctors had prescribed thalidomide for her. Intelligent script by William Nicholson. Made for cable. Above average.▼●

Private Navy of Sgt. O'Farrell, The (1968) **C-92m.** BOMB D: Frank Tashlin. Bob Hope, Phyllis Diller, Jeffrey Hunter, Gina Lollobrigida, Mylene Demongeot, John Myhers, Mako. Hope tries to import some beautiful nurses to improve his men's morale, gets Diller instead. Of the many terrible Hope comedies of the 1960s, this may be the worst. Unfunny and offensive. [G]

Private Number (1936) **80m.** **½ D: Roy Del Ruth. Robert Taylor, Loretta Young, Patsy Kelly, Basil Rathbone, Marjorie Gateson, Paul Harvey, Joe (E.) Lewis. Young is charming as a maid who becomes romantically involved with her employers' son (Taylor), causing various complications. Rathbone is effective as the villain in this otherwise OK melodrama. Filmed previously in 1919 (with Fannie Ward) and 1931 (with Constance Bennett), as COMMON CLAY.

Private Parts (1972) **C-87m.** *** D: Paul Bartel. Ann Ruymen, Lucille Benson, Laurie Main, John Ventantonio. Truly perverse black-comedic suspense film about runaway teenage girl staying at her aunt's strange hotel where occupants are extremely weird. There's a series of murders but the focus is more on sexual eccentricities including voyeurism, narcissism and transvestism. If Andy Warhol's CHELSEA GIRLS had been codirected by Alfred

Hitchcock and John Waters it would come close to this directorial debut by Bartel. Clearly not for every taste. [R]▼

Private Parts (1997) **C-109m.** *** D: Betty Thomas. Howard Stern, Robin Quivers, Mary McCormack, Fred Norris, Paul Giamatti, Gary Dell'Abate, Jackie Martling, Carol Alt, "Stuttering John" Melendez, Allison Janney, Michael Murphy, Reni Santoni. Horatio Alger–like saga of radio phenomenon Howard Stern, who only achieves success on the air when he starts giving vent to his most outrageous ideas. This, of course, pits him against one station management after another. Highly entertaining, even to non-Stern listeners, and evidence that (as Stern has said all along) he's actually an ordinary guy with a loving wife; all the rest is a performance. Stern's real-life wife plays an NBC switchboard operator. [R]▼●◗

Private Resort (1985) **C-85m.** BOMB D: George Bowers. Rob Morrow, Johnny Depp, Hector Elizondo, Dody Goodman, Tony Azito, Emily Longstreth, Karyn O' Bryan, Hilary Shapiro, Michael Bowen, Andrew (Dice) Clay. Imbecilic sex comedy about a couple of young fellows on the make at a resort hotel. Notable only for its two up-and-coming stars. [R]▼●

Private's Affair, A (1959) **C-92m.** **½ D: Raoul Walsh. Sal Mineo, Christine Carere, Barry Coe, Barbara Eden, Gary Crosby, Terry Moore, Jim Backus, Jessie Royce Landis. Energetic young cast involved in putting on the "big Army show" on TV. CinemaScope.

Private School (1983) **C-97m.** BOMB D: Noel Black. Phoebe Cates, Betsy Russell, Matthew Modine, Michael Zorek, Fran Ryan, Julie Payne, Ray Walston, Sylvia Kristel. Raunchy teenage hijinks at a girls' school, with ample nudity but no brains in sight. Even voyeurs might have a hard time sloshing through this heavy-handed, amateurish "comedy." [R]▼●

Privates on Parade (1982-British) **C-100m.** **½ D: Michael Blakemore. John Cleese, Denis Quilley, Nicola Pagett, Patrick Pearson, Michael Elphick. Uneven adaptation of Peter Nichols' British play about SADUSEA (Song And Dance Unit, South East Asia), based in Singapore in the late 40s. Quilley is an aging queen who directs and stars in their camp shows, Cleese his thick-witted commander. Some funny musical numbers mix awkwardly with satire—and unexpected drama. [R] ▼●

Private's Progress (1956-British) **99m.** *** D: John Boulting. Richard Attenborough, Jill Adams, Dennis Price, Terry-Thomas, Ian Carmichael, Peter Jones, Christopher Lee. Prize collection of funny men, splendidly played by cast, involved in Army shenanigans. Sequel: I'M ALL RIGHT JACK.▼

Private War of Major Benson, The (1955) **C-105m.** **½ D: Jerry Hopper. Charlton Heston, Julie Adams, William Demarest, Tim Hovey, Sal Mineo, David Janssen, Tim Considine, Milburn Stone. Hovey is the little boy at military school who charms rugged commander-turned-schoolmaster Heston into sympathetic person. Remade as MAJOR PAYNE (1995).▼

Private Worlds (1935) **84m.** **½ D: Gregory La Cava. Claudette Colbert, Charles Boyer, Joan Bennett, Joel McCrea, Helen Vinson, Esther Dale, Jean Rouverol. Dated but engrossing tale of mental institution, with doctors Boyer and Colbert giving restrained performances; noteworthy support by Bennett.

Privilege (1967-British) **C-101m.** *** D: Peter Watkins. Paul Jones, Jean Shrimpton, Marc London, Max Bacon, Jeremy Child. Overambitious yet effective account of 1970s England where all-powerful welfare state manipulates masses through such media as pop singers. Jones is good as disillusioned teen-age idol.

Prix de Beauté (1930-French) **94m.** **½ D: Augusto Genina. Louise Brooks, Jean Bradin, Georges Charlia, Gaston Jacquet, A. Nicolle. Brooks is the whole show in this, her first sound film (and last major screen role). The story may be clichéd—a melodrama in which she's cast as a typist who becomes a beauty queen—but Brooks is as lovely and sensuous as ever. The final sequence is truly memorable. René Clair, originally scheduled to direct, had a hand in the script. Aka MISS EUROPE.▼

Prize, The (1963) **C-136m.** *** D: Mark Robson. Paul Newman, Elke Sommer, Edward G. Robinson, Diane Baker, Kevin McCarthy, Micheline Presle, Leo G. Carroll. Irving Wallace novel is mere stepping stone for glossy spy yarn set in Stockholm, involving participants in Nobel Prize ceremony. Newman and Sommer make handsome leads; Robinson has dual role. Fast-moving fun; script by Ernest Lehman. Panavision.▼

Prize Fighter, The (1979) **C-99m.** ** D: Michael Preece. Tim Conway, Don Knotts, David Wayne, Robin Clarke, Cisse Cameron, Mary Ellen O'Neill. If you like Knotts and Conway, you'll probably get through this lame, kiddie-oriented comedy about a dumb boxer and his smart-aleck manager, set in the 1930s. [PG]▼

Prizefighter and the Lady, The (1933) **102m.** *** D: W. S. Van Dyke. Myrna Loy, Max Baer, Otto Kruger, Walter Huston, Jack Dempsey, Primo Carnera, Jess Willard, James J. Jeffries. Entertaining film breathes life into potential clichés; real-life boxing champ Baer plays a prizefighter who falls for high-class gangster's moll Loy. Exciting prize-fight finale.●

Prize of Arms, A (1961-British) **105m.**

**½ D: Cliff Owen. Stanley Baker, Tom Bell, Helmut Schmid, John Phillips. Hindered by heavy British accents ruining much dialogue, tale unfolds methodical plan for big heist of Army funds.

Prize of Gold, A (1955-British) **C-98m.** *** D: Mark Robson. Richard Widmark, Mai Zetterling, Nigel Patrick, Donald Wolfit, Eric Pohlmann. Taut caper in post-WW2 Berlin involving a planned heist of gold from the air lift circuit.

Prizzi's Honor (1985) **C-129m.** ***½ D: John Huston. Jack Nicholson, Kathleen Turner, Anjelica Huston, Robert Loggia, William Hickey, John Randolph, Lee Richardson, Michael Lombard, Lawrence Tierney, Joseph Ruskin, Stanley Tucci. Delicious, very offbeat black comedy about a slow-witted hit man from a close-knit Mafia family who gets more than he bargained for when he falls in love with Turner. Nicholson is a joy to watch, matched by a superlative cast (Randolph is a treat as his father). Huston wrings every drop of irony from Richard Condon and Janet Roach's wry screenplay (based on Condon's novel). Beautifully photographed by Andrzej Bartkowiak. Anjelica Huston won Best Supporting Actress Oscar for her sly performance, directed by her father. [R]▼●◗

Problem Child (1990) **C-81m.** *½ D: Dennis Dugan. John Ritter, Michael Oliver, Jack Warden, Amy Yasbeck, Gilbert Gottfried, Michael Richards. Botched comic twist on THE BAD SEED has Ritter as an unlucky father who adopts devil-child Oliver. A promising opening leads nowhere as bad performances and crude jokes prevail. Followed by a sequel, a TV movie, and an animated TV series. [PG]▼●◗

Problem Child 2 (1991) **C-91m.** *½ D: Brian Levant. John Ritter, Michael Oliver, Jack Warden, Laraine Newman, Amy Yasbeck, Ivyann Schwan, Gilbert Gottfried, Paul Willson, Charlene Tilton, James Tolkan, Martha Quinn. The sequel no one asked for has Ritter adopting a second demon-child, this one female and hell-bent to give her stepbrother a run for his money. Any parent who lets an impressionable child watch this stuff ought to have his or her head examined! Followed by a 1995 TVM sequel. [PG-13]▼●

Prodigal, The (1955) **C-114m.** **½ D: Richard Thorpe. Lana Turner, Edmund Purdom, James Mitchell, Louis Calhern, Audrey Dalton, Neville Brand, Taina Elg, Cecil Kellaway, Henry Daniell, Walter Hampden, Joseph Wiseman. Juvenile biblical semi-spectacle, with Turner the evil goddess of love corrupting Purdom; glossy MGM vehicle. CinemaScope.▼●

Producers, The (1967) **C-88m.** ***½ D: Mel Brooks. Zero Mostel, Gene Wilder, Kenneth Mars, Dick Shawn, Lee Meredith, Christopher Hewett, Andreas Voustinas, Estelle Winwood, Renee Taylor, Bill Hickey. Classic piece of insanity stars incomparable Mostel as hard-luck Broadway producer Max Bialystock, who cons meek accountant Wilder into helping him with outrageous scheme: selling 25,000% of a play that's certain to flop, then heading to Rio with the excess cash. One of those rare films that gets funnier with each viewing, highlighted by legendary "Springtime for Hitler" production number. Brooks' first feature earned him an Oscar for his screenplay. Listen for his voice dubbed into "Springtime For Hitler."▼●

Professional, The (1994-U.S.-French) **C-109m.** ** D: Luc Besson. Jean Reno, Gary Oldman, Natalie Portman, Danny Aiello, Ellen Greene. Hit man (Reno) allies with alienated young girl (Portman, in her film debut) and together they battle thugs and cops in N.Y.C. Well-directed U.S. debut for Frenchman Besson (LA FEMME NIKITA) suffers from overly familiar, artificial situations and a bizarre, scenery-chewing performance from Oldman. This was rereleased in France in 1996 as LEON: VERSION INTEGRALE, with 26m. of additional footage. Technovision. [R]▼●◗

Professional Gun, A SEE: **Mercenary, The**

Professionals, The (1966) **C-117m.** *** D: Richard Brooks. Lee Marvin, Robert Ryan, Woody Strode, Burt Lancaster, Jack Palance, Ralph Bellamy, Claudia Cardinale. Bellamy employs four soldiers-of-fortune to rescue his wife from Mexican varmint Palance. Far-fetched story, but real action, taut excitement throughout; beautifully photographed by Conrad Hall. Panavision. ▼●◗

Professional Soldier (1936) **78m.** **½ D: Tay Garnett. Victor McLaglen, Freddie Bartholomew, Gloria Stuart, Constance Collier, Michael Whalen. McLaglen is hired to kidnap young king Bartholomew, but mutual friendship gets in the way. Good teaming supports average script, based on a Damon Runyon story.

Professional Sweetheart (1933) **68m.** ** D: William A. Seiter. Ginger Rogers, ZaSu Pitts, Norman Foster, Frank McHugh, Edgar Kennedy, Betty Furness, Gregory Ratoff, Sterling Holloway, Franklin Pangborn. Good cast can't put over weak radio spoof, with Rogers as airwaves star who becomes engaged to hick Foster in publicity stunt.

Professor Beware (1938) **87m.** **½ D: Elliott Nugent. Harold Lloyd, Phyllis Welch, William Frawley, Etienne Girardot, Raymond Walburn, Lionel Stander, Thurston Hall. One of Lloyd's last vehicles has good moments, but tale of archeologist searching for rare tablet is thin.

Profile of Terror SEE: **Sadist, The**

Profumo di Donna SEE: **Scent of a Woman** (1974)

Program, The (1993) **C-114m.** ** D: David S. Ward. James Caan, Halle Berry, Omar Epps, Craig Sheffer, Kristy Swanson, Abraham Benrubi, Duane Davis, Andrew Bryniarski, Joey Lauren Adams. Ambitious but seriously flawed attempt to examine the problems of college football players, and expose abuses in contemporary university sports programs. Few of the characters are sympathetic, so it's difficult to care about them or their plight. Of note primarily because of the notorious studio deletion, after the film's opening weeks, of a sequence involving jocks lying in the middle of a busy street to prove their manliness. This came (incredibly) after one teenager was killed, and others seriously injured, allegedly imitating the sequence. [R]▼●

Project A (1983-Hong Kong) **C-106m.** *** D: Jackie Chan. Jackie Chan, Yuen Biao, Samo Hung, Dick Wei, Isabella Wong. Turn-of-the-century adventure finds Chan in the Hong Kong coast guard battling pirates, teaming up with cop Yuen and thief Samo. Fantastic action comedy, with many moments reminiscent of Chan's hero, Buster Keaton. The bicycle chase is a highlight. Considered by some to be Chan's best film. Followed by a sequel. Technovision.▼◗

Project A, Part II (1987-Hong Kong) **C-108m.** *** D: Jackie Chan. Jackie Chan, Maggie Cheung, David Lam, Rosamund Kwan, Carina Lau, Bill Tung Pui. Terrific sequel has Jackie dodging vengeful pirates from the first film while fighting corrupt officials. Nice mix of farce and jaw-dropping action. Chan re-creates one of Buster Keaton's most famous stunts at the end of the film. Technovision.▼◗

Projected Man, The (1967-British) **C-77m.** ** D: Ian Curteis. Bryant Halliday, Mary Peach, Norman Wooland, Ronald Allen, Derek Farr. Using a teleportation machine something like that in all the FLY movies, scientist accidentally disfigures himself and gains the touch of death. Not bad but unoriginal. Techniscope.

Projectionist, The (1971) **C-85m.** **½ D: Harry Hurwitz. Chuck McCann, Ina Balin, Rodney Dangerfield, Jara Kohout, Harry Hurwitz, Robert Staats. Independently made film has ups and downs, but many pearly moments in story of daydreaming projectionist McCann who envisions himself a superhero, Captain Flash. Many film clips imaginatively used: best of all is coming-attractions trailer for the end of the world. [PG]▼

Project Moon Base (1953) **63m.** ** D: Richard Talmadge. Donna Martell, Hayden Rorke, Ross Ford, Larry Johns, Herb Jacobs. In the near future, three people make the first trip to the Moon from the American space station circling the Earth, but one of them is an enemy spy. Mediocre acting in this routine but scientifically accurate story. Famed sci-fi writer Robert A. Heinlein cowrote the movie; the low budget shows.▼

Project X (1968) **C-97m.** **½ D: William Castle. Christopher George, Greta Baldwin, Henry Jones, Monte Markham, Phillip Pine, Harold Gould. Offbeat but ultimately unconvincing mixture of time travel, biological warfare, and psychology in tale of future Earth civilization searching for secret germ formula. Their amnesiac secret agent has it; how to get it?

Project X (1987) **C-108m.** **½ D: Jonathan Kaplan. Matthew Broderick, Helen Hunt, Bill Sadler, Johnny Ray McGhee, Jonathan Stark, Robin Gammell, Stephen Lang, Jean Smart, Dick Miller. Young military foul-up is assigned to top secret lab where he works with chimps—and soon becomes enraged at the tests they're being subjected to. Watchable but patently predictable story, with a finale vaguely reminiscent of a 1960s Disney comedy. The chimps (especially Willie, in the role of Virgil) are great, however. [PG]▼●

Promise, The (1979) **C-98m.** BOMB D: Gilbert Cates. Kathleen Quinlan, Stephen Collins, Beatrice Straight, Laurence Luckinbill, William Prince. Boy loves girl. Girl loses face in car accident. Boy thinks girl dead. Girl gets new face from plastic surgeon. Boy falls for old girl's new face. Viewer runs screaming from room. Panavision. [PG]▼

Promise (1986) **C-100m. TVM** D: Glenn Jordan. James Garner, James Woods, Piper Laurie, Peter Michael Goetz, Michael Alldredge, Alan Rosenberg. Footloose bachelor Garner honors a long-ago promise made to his recently deceased mother to care for his schizophrenic brother in this beautifully written (by Richard Friedenberg) drama of love and responsibility. Garner coproduced. Emmy winner for Woods, Laurie, writing, directing, and Outstanding Special. Above average.

Promise, The (1994-German-French-Swiss) **C-119m.** *** D: Margarethe von Trotta. Corinna Harfouch, Meret Becker, August Zirner, Anian Zollner, Pierre Besson, Hans Kremer. Pointed account of star-crossed German lovers, covering a thirty-year timespan, beginning with their separation while trying to escape from East to West in 1961. Their relationship mirrors German history during this period, and serves as a metaphor for a divided, and then reunified, nation. Another provocative, politically savvy drama from von Trotta. [R]▼

Promise at Dawn (1970-U.S.-French) **C-101m.** **½ D: Jules Dassin. Melina Mercouri, Assaf Dayan, Francois Raffoul, Despo, Fernand Gravey, Perlo Vita (Jules Dassin). Seventh teaming of Mercouri and husband Dassin, who produced, directed, wrote, and also does a bit role as Russian silent-film star Ivan Mousjoukine. It's mostly Mercouri's show, an uneven but well-acted chronicle of the life of writer Romain Gary and his resourceful actress mother. Dayan is good as the young adult Gary. [PG]▼

Promised Land (1988) **C-101m.** **½ D: Michael Hoffman. Jason Gedrick, Kiefer Sutherland, Meg Ryan, Tracy Pollan, Googy Gress, Deborah Richter, Sondra Seacat. Uneven but moody little sleeper, set in the rural Northwest, about two casual high school acquaintances whose lives intersect tragically a couple of years after graduation. Ryan is a standout as a tattooed, rod-packing high school hellcat. Aka YOUNG HEARTS. [R]▼●

Promise Her Anything (1966) **C-98m.** **½ D: Arthur Hiller. Warren Beatty, Leslie Caron, Bob Cummings, Hermione Gingold, Lionel Stander, Keenan Wynn. Limp premise of blue-moviemaker (Beatty) taking care of neighbor Caron's baby. Filmed in England but supposed to be Greenwich Village; screenplay by William Peter Blatty. Look for Bessie Love as a petshop customer, Donald Sutherland as a baby's father.▼

Promises in the Dark (1979) **C-115m.** **½ D: Jerome Hellman. Marsha Mason, Ned Beatty, Susan Clark, Michael Brandon, Kathleen Beller, Paul Clemens, Donald Moffat. Unrelievedly depressing (though well-made) film about young girl (Beller) dying of cancer, and her compassionate doctor (Mason). Directorial debut of producer Hellman. [PG]▼

Promises! Promises! (1963) **75m.** BOMB D: King Donovan. Jayne Mansfield, Marie McDonald, Tommy Noonan, Mickey Hargitay, Fritz Feld, T. C. Jones, Claude Stroud, Marjorie Bennett, Eddie Quillan, Eileen Barton, Imogene Coca. Dreadful comedy about couples Mansfield-Noonan and McDonald-Hargitay, and their sexual shenanigans on a cruise. Notorious in its day for Jayne's baring her bod, a first for its time. Still, beware: it *is* a truly bad movie. Mansfield was in real life married to Hargitay; Noonan coproduced and coscripted.▼

Prom Night (1980-Canadian) **C-91m.** ** D: Paul Lynch. Leslie Nielsen, Jamie Lee Curtis, Casey Stevens, Antoinette Bower, Robert Silverman. Killer menaces teens who were responsible for the death of a little girl six years earlier. Not the worst of its type, but that's nothing to brag about. Followed by several sequels. [R]▼●◗

Prom Night II SEE: **Hello Mary Lou: Prom Night II**

Prom Night III: The Last Kiss (1989-U.S.-Canadian) **C-97m.** *½ D: Ron Oliver and Peter Simpson. Tim Conlon, Cyndy Preston, David Stratton, Courtney Taylor, Dylan Neal, Jeremy Ratchford. More high school horror, with another prom queen back from the dead, only this time it's not revenge that motivates her murder spree, but love. The comedy works slightly better than the horror, but a leaden pace torpedoes it, and a rotten ending sinks it. [R]▼

Prom Night IV: Deliver Us From Evil (1992-Canadian) **C-95m.** *½ D: Clay Borris. Nikki de Boer, Alden Kane, Joy Tanner, Alle Ghadban, Ken McGregor, Brock Simpson. Murderous, psychotic priest, just awakened from a 33-year coma, stalks randy teenagers in an isolated vacation home. Resolutely routine slasher movie with slight novelty of religious fanaticism. Only reference to earlier films: an on-screen toast to Jamie Lee Curtis. [R]▼●

Promoter, The (1952-British) **88m.** *** D: Ronald Neame. Alec Guinness, Glynis Johns, Valerie Hobson, Petula Clark, Edward Chapman. Charming comedy about a likable but penniless young man who sees how to get ahead in the world—and seizes his opportunity. Script by Eric Ambler from Arnold Bennett's story *The Card,* also its title in England.▼

Proof (1992-Australian) **C-91m.** ***½ D: Jocelyn Moorhouse. Hugo Weaving, Genevieve Picot, Russell Crowe, Heather Mitchell, Jeffrey Walker, Frank Gallacher. A blind cynic who impulsively shoots photographs of everything is perversely manipulated by the housekeeper who'd like to bed him; into their circle comes a far less complex dishwasher, who puts a fresh spin on their sicko games. Assuredly made film is effectively cold, cut to the bone and reminiscent of THE SERVANT. Moorhouse also scripted. [R]▼●

Prophecy (1979) **C-95m.** *½ D: John Frankenheimer. Talia Shire, Robert Foxworth, Armand Assante, Richard Dysart, Victoria Racimo. Classical musician and her doctor husband fight off what appears to be a giant salami in upstate Maine after mercury poisoning turns animals into huge mutants and worse. Ridiculous horror film is good for a few laughs. Panavision. [PG]▼

Prophecy, The (1995) **C-93m.** ** D: Gregory Widen. Christopher Walken, Elias Koteas, Virginia Madsen, Eric Stoltz, Viggo Mortensen, Amanda Plummer. Seminarian Koteas abandons the church during his own ordination to become . . . a homicide cop. Soon he's investigating why Stoltz has murdered an eyeless hermaphrodite with the physiological profile of an aborted fetus. There's either too much mumbo or too much jumbo in this oddball horror pic. Give it perverse points, though, for managing to work in a Korean War subplot and for casting Walken as the Angel Gabriel. Followed by two direct-to-video sequels. Super 35. [R]▼●◗

Proposition, The (1998) **C-110m.** ** D: Lesli Linka Glatter. Kenneth Branagh, William Hurt, Madeleine Stowe, Blythe Danner, Robert Loggia, Neil Patrick Harris,

Josef Sommer. Heavy-handed soap opera set in the 1930s gives Branagh a thankless role as a priest with more ties than one could ever imagine to wealthy Boston bigwig Hurt who can't give his wife the one thing he wants most: a child. A fine cast flounders with purple paperback fodder; sputteringly silly at times. [R]▼●

Proprietor, The (1996) **C-113m.** ** D: Ismail Merchant. Jeanne Moreau, Sean Young, Sam Waterston, Austin Pendleton, Josh Hamilton, Nell Carter, Christopher Cazenove, Pierre Vaneck, Jean-Pierre Aumont, Marc Tissot. Wildly uneven story set in Paris and N.Y.C. finds author Moreau exploring two distinct cultures, past and present life experiences, and relationships old and new as she examines the meaning of her life and the importance of memories. It's always nice to see Moreau in a major role, but this muddled vehicle isn't worthy of her. Rare directorial effort for producer Merchant. Super 35. [R]▼●

Prospero's Books (1991-British-Dutch) **C-129m.** **½ D: Peter Greenaway. John Gielgud, Michael Clark, Michel Blanc, Erland Josephson, Isabelle Pasco, Tom Bell. Original, daring but unsatisfactory adaptation of Shakespeare's *The Tempest*, with almost all of the dialogue spoken by 87-year-old Gielgud (in the role of Prospero); the other actors are little more than extras, and there's a mindboggling amount of nudity. Crammed with stunning, layered imagery, beautiful production design and cinematography—which tend to lessen the impact of the dialogue. Enjoyment will depend on your tolerance for Greenaway's approach to the material. [R]▼●

Protector, The (1985-U.S.-Hong Kong) **C-91m.** *½ D: James Glickenhaus. Jackie Chan, Danny Aiello, Sandy Alexander, Roy Chiao, Bill Wallace. Dismal attempt to bring Chan to the American market as a N.Y.C. cop(!). Leaden directing, cold tone, and lack of comedy smother Chan's gifts; his frustrations with this film led him to make the vastly superior POLICE STORY. ▼◗

Protocol (1984) **C-96m.** ** D: Herbert Ross. Goldie Hawn, Chris Sarandon, Richard Romanus, Andre Gregory, Gail Strickland, Cliff De Young, Keith Szarabajka, Ed Begley, Jr., James Staley, Kenneth Mars, Jean Smart, Joel Brooks, Daphne Maxwell, Amanda Bearse. Kenneth McMillan. Or, Goldie Goes to Washington: a contrived comedy vehicle for Hawn as inadvertent heroine (and overnight celebrity) who's rewarded with do-nothing government job . . . but soon becomes a pawn for dealing with Middle Eastern potentate. Some funny moments give way to obvious satire and a hard-to-swallow finish in which Goldie makes like Capra's Mr. Smith. [PG]▼●◗

Prototype (1983) **C-100m. TVM** D: David Greene. Christopher Plummer, David Morse, Frances Sternhagen, James Sutorius, Stephen Elliott, Arthur Hill. Richard Levinson and William Link's ingenious updating of the Frankenstein legend has Nobel Prize-winning scientist Plummer developing the first android, then stealing him from the Pentagon's clutches, fearing they plan on reprogramming "it" for a destructive mission. Above average.▼

Proud and Profane, The (1956) **111m.** **½ D: George Seaton. William Holden, Deborah Kerr, Thelma Ritter, Dewey Martin, William Redfield, Ross Bagdasarian, Marion Ross. Spotty WW2 romance story has many parallels to FROM HERE TO ETERNITY, but Kerr-Holden romance is never believable. VistaVision.

Proud and the Beautiful, The SEE: **Proud Ones, The** (1953)

Proud and the Damned, The (1973) **C-94m.** ** D: Ferde Grofe, Jr. Chuck Connors, Jose Greco, Cesar Romero, Aron Kincaid, Anita Quinn. Uneven performances and script in formula story of Civil War veterans and mercenaries drifting through Latin America, caught up in local revolution. [PG]▼

Proud Ones, The (1953-French-Mexican) **94m.** ***½ D: Yves Allegret. Michele Morgan, Gérard Philipe, Victor Manuel Mendoza, Michele Cordoue. Well-bred Morgan and down-and-out doctor Philipe cross paths in Vera Cruz, Mexico, in this absorbing tale of love, religion, and the effects of a deadly plague on the impoverished populace. Striking and atmospheric; based on Jean-Paul Sartre novel *L'Amour Redempteur* (set in China!). Original title: LES ORGUEILLEUX. Aka THE PROUD AND THE BEAUTIFUL.▼

Proud Ones, The (1956) **C-94m.** **½ D: Robert D. Webb. Robert Ryan, Virginia Mayo, Jeffrey Hunter, Robert Middleton, Walter Brennan. Staunch acting involving the inevitable showdown between disabled sheriff and outlaws perks up this Western. CinemaScope.

Proud Rebel, The (1958) **C-103m.** *** D: Michael Curtiz. Alan Ladd, Olivia de Havilland, Dean Jagger, David Ladd, Cecil Kellaway, Henry Hull, John Carradine, (Harry) Dean Stanton. Well-presented study of two-fisted Ladd seeking medical help for mute son (played by Ladd's real-life son); de Havilland is the woman who tames him. ▼●◗

Proud Valley (1940-British) **77m.** **½ D: Pen Tennyson. Paul Robeson, Edward Chapman, Simon Lack, Rachel Thomas, Edward Rigby. Mild drama of Welsh coal-mining village beset by mine shutdown; uplifted only by Robeson's commanding presence and fine voice.▼

Providence (1977-British) **C-104m.** ** D: Alain Resnais. Dirk Bogarde, John Gielgud, Ellen Burstyn, David Warner, Elaine Stritch. Odd fantasy marked director Resnais'

English-language debut. Writer Gielgud tries to complete his last novel, juxtaposes imagined thoughts about his family with real-life encounters. Muddled drama by David Mercer; interesting Miklos Rozsa score. [R]▼

Prowler, The (1951) **92m.** **½ D: Joseph Losey. Van Heflin, Evelyn Keyes, John Maxwell, Katharine Warren. Fairly good thriller about sector car cop Heflin, who complains he's had one too many "lousy breaks." He becomes obsessed with, and seduces, married Keyes . . . and plots to do in her husband.

Prowler, The (1981) **C-88m.** *½ D: Joseph Zito. Vicki Dawson, Christopher Goutman, Cindy Weintraub, Farley Granger, John Seitz. WW2 veteran kills ex-girlfriend and her new amour with a pitchfork, then suddenly resumes his murderous ways 35 years later. Illogically plotted, with gruesome special effects by Tom Savini. [R]▼

Prudence and the Pill (1968-British) **C-98m.** **½ D: Fielder Cook, Ronald Neame. Deborah Kerr, David Niven, Robert Coote, Irina Demick, Joyce Redman, Judy Geeson, Keith Michell. Labored comedy treatment of modern sexual mores. Niven thinks he can patch up his in-name-only marriage by substituting aspirin for his wife's birth control pills. Good cast and performances, but weak script. [R]

Psyche '59 (1964-British) **94m.** **½ D: Alexander Singer. Patricia Neal, Curt Jurgens, Samantha Eggar, Ian Bannen, Elspeth March. Turgid melodrama involving infidelity, with good cast doing their best.

Psychic, The (1978-Italian) **C-89m.** BOMB D: Lucio Fulci. Jennifer O'Neill, Gabriele Ferzetti, Marc Porel, Gianni Garko, Evelyn Stewart. O'Neill has frightening premonitions of deaths in this low-grade thriller. [R]▼

Psychic Killer (1975) **C-90m.** BOMB D: Raymond Danton. Jim Hutton, Julie Adams, Paul Burke, Aldo Ray, Neville Brand, Whit Bissell. Ugly, violent shocker of mental institute patient who acquires psychic powers to revenge himself on those who wronged him. Lots of cameos: Rod Cameron, Nehemiah Persoff, Della Reese, others. [PG]▼◗

Psycho (1960) **109m.** **** D: Alfred Hitchcock. Anthony Perkins, Janet Leigh, Vera Miles, John Gavin, Martin Balsam, John McIntire, Simon Oakland, John Anderson, Frank Albertson, Patricia Hitchcock. The Master's most notorious film is still terrifying after all these years, as larcenous Leigh picks the wrong place to spend a night: The Bates Motel (12 cabins, 12 vacancies . . . and 12 showers), run by a peculiar young man and his crotchety old "mother." Hitchcock's murder set-pieces are so potent, they can galvanize (and frighten) even a viewer who's seen them before! Bernard Herrmann's legendary (and endlessly imitated) score adds much to the excitement. Script by Joseph Stefano from the Robert Bloch novel. Followed by three sequels (the last for cable TV) and a TV movie (BATES MOTEL) decades later, and remade in 1998. ▼●◗

Psycho (1998) **C-109m.** BOMB D: Gus Van Sant. Vince Vaughn, Anne Heche, Julianne Moore, Viggo Mortensen, William H. Macy, Robert Forster, Philip Baker Hall, Anne Haney, Chad Everett, Rance Howard, Rita Wilson, James Remar, James LeGros. Slow, stilted, completely pointless scene-for-scene remake of the Hitchcock classic (with a few awkward new touches to taint its claim as an exact replica). The result is an insult, rather than a tribute, to a landmark film. [R]▼●◗

Psycho II (1983) **C-113m.** **½ D: Richard Franklin. Anthony Perkins, Vera Miles, Meg Tilly, Robert Loggia, Dennis Franz, Hugh Gillin. Surprisingly good sequel, with Perkins in a wonderfully canny reprise of his role as Norman Bates—now being released from asylum, supposedly rehabilitated, returning to his mother's creaky old mansion. Director Franklin builds some terrific suspense scenes, but finally goes for graphic violence toward the end, and tacks on a silly conclusion, undermining an otherwise first-rate shocker. [R] ▼●◗

Psycho III (1986) **C-96m.** *½ D: Anthony Perkins. Anthony Perkins, Diana Scarwid, Jeff Fahey, Roberta Maxwell, Hugh Gillin, Lee Garlington. Pointless sequel plays Norman Bates strictly for laughs, but maintains a slasher-film mentality. No suspense, just some gratuitous blood and unpleasantness. Perkins' directorial debut. Good night, Norman. [R]▼●

Psycho IV: The Beginning (1990) **C-100m. TVM** D: Mick Garris. Anthony Perkins, Henry Thomas, Olivia Hussey, CCH Pounder, Warren Frost, Donna Mitchell. Perkins returns as Norman Bates, more paranoid than ever as he recalls his childhood and his loony, overbearing mother, played as a semi-slut by Hussey. Joseph Stefano, who did the screenplay for Hitchcock's original, wrote the script for this one too—but *enough already*. Made for cable. Average.▼●

Psycho a Go-Go! SEE: **Blood of Ghastly Horror**

Psycho-Circus (1967-British-West German) **C-65m.** **½ D: John Moxey. Christopher Lee, Heinz Drache, Margaret Lee, Suzy Kendall, Leo Genn, Cecil Parker, Klaus Kinski. Confused (due to distributor cuts) Edgar Wallace-based story of murderer stalking odd assortment of characters in big top. Is it hooded Gregor the lion-tamer? Short running time gives film old-style serial-type pacing. Original title: CIRCUS OF FEAR.▼

Psycho Killers, The SEE: **Mania**

Psychomania (1963) **93m.** *½ D: Richard Hilliard. Lee Philips, Shepperd Strudwick, Jean Hale, Lorraine Rogers, Margot Hartman, Kaye Elhardt, James Farentino, Dick Van Patten, Sylvia Miles. War hero turned painter, suspected of murdering two beautiful young women, undertakes his own investigation. Exploitive independent production filmed in Connecticut. Originally titled VIOLENT MIDNIGHT.▼

Psychomania (1973-British) **C-95m.** **½ D: Don Sharp. George Sanders, Nicky Henson, Mary Larkin, Patrick Holt, Beryl Reid. Pact with Devil brings British motorcycle gang back from the grave. Lots of weird violence as undead bikers blaze a kamikaze trail of destruction across prepunk England. Screenplay by Julian Halevy. Aka THE DEATH WHEELERS. ▼

Psychopath, The (1966-British) **83m.** *** D: Freddie Francis. Patrick Wymark, Margaret Johnston, John Standing, Judy Huxtable. A demented killer leaves dolls as his calling card at the scene of the murders; well-made thriller from Robert Bloch script. Techniscope.

Psycho Sisters SEE: **So Evil, My Sister**

Psychotic SEE: **Driver's Seat, The**

Psych-Out (1968) **C-82m.** **½ D: Richard Rush. Susan Strasberg, Jack Nicholson, Adam Roarke, Dean Stockwell, Max Julien, Bruce Dern, Henry Jaglom, The Strawberry Alarm Clock, The Seeds, Garry Marshall. Deaf runaway Strasberg comes to Haight-Ashbury looking for missing brother Dern, falls in with rock band led by ponytailed Nicholson. Any serious intentions have long since vanished; gloriously goofy dialogue ("C'mon! Warren's freakin' out at the gallery!") and psychedelic Laszlo Kovacs camerawork make this—depending on your age and sensibilities—either amusing nostalgia or a campy embarrassment. Produced by Dick Clark!▼●

PT 109 (1963) **C-140m.** ** D: Leslie Martinson. Cliff Robertson, Robert Culp, Ty Hardin, James Gregory, Robert Blake, Grant Williams. Standard (but overlong) action film based on true story of PT-boat commander John F. Kennedy during WW2; for younger audiences. Panavision.▼●

PT Raiders SEE: **Ship That Died of Shame, The**

Puberty Blues (1981-Australian) C-86m. **½ D: Bruce Beresford. Neil Schofield, Jad Capelja, Geoff Rhoe, Tony Hughes, Sandy Paul. Teenage growing pains, told (refreshingly) from the girls' point of view; simple, honest, but somewhat familiar. Based on a best-selling Australian book by two former surfing groupies. Panavision. [R]▼

Public Access (1992) **C-86m.** **½ D: Bryan Singer. Ron Marquette, Dina Brooks, Burt Williams, Larry Maxwell, Charles Kavanaugh, Brandon Boyce. Eerie tale of a stranger who starts his own cable-TV call-in show, ostensibly to investigate what's wrong with "our town." Debut for THE USUAL SUSPECTS director Singer is a suspenseful, disquieting film marred by a total lack of motivation for the main character. Fine music score by John Ottman, who also edited the picture. [R]▼●◗

Public Be Damned SEE: **World Gone Mad, The**

Public Enemy, The (1931) **84m.** ***½ D: William Wellman. James Cagney, Jean Harlow, Eddie Woods, Beryl Mercer, Donald Cook, Joan Blondell, Mae Clarke. Prohibition gangster's rise and fall put Cagney on the map, and deservedly so; he makes up for film's occasional flaws and dated notions. Still pretty powerful, this is the one where Cagney smashes a grapefruit in Clarke's face. Originally released at 96m. ▼●

Public Enemy's Wife (1936) **69m.** **½ D; Nick Grinde. Pat O'Brien, Margaret Lindsay, Robert Armstrong, Cesar Romero, Dick Foran. Romero is good as mobster serving life whose insane jealousy over wife (Lindsay) makes her a perfect pawn for G-Man O'Brien. Not-bad Warner Bros. B.

Public Eye, The (1972-British) **C-95m.** **½ D: Carol Reed. Mia Farrow, Topol, Michael Jayston, Margaret Rawlings, Annette Crosbie, Dudley Foster. Stuffy husband hires private-eye to watch his wife, but the sleuth falls for her. Fair expansion of Peter Shaffer's play. Farrow is good, but Topol's grin is flashed once too often. Panavision. [G]

Public Eye, The (1992) **C-99m.** **½ D: Howard Franklin. Joe Pesci, Barbara Hershey, Stanley Tucci, Jerry Adler, Jared Harris, Dominic Chianese, Richard Foronjy, Richard Riehle, Gerry Becler, Bob Gunton, Del Close, Nick Tate. Intriguing mood-piece with a perfect Pesci role: a 1940s photographer who roams the streets of N.Y.C. at night in search of dramatic photo opportunities. An encounter with beautiful Hershey leads only to trouble, however. Great atmosphere and style are undone by an ungainly script and an unconvincing romantic subplot. Script by director Franklin, inspired by famed real-life photographer Weegee, some of whose shots are used in the film. Robert Zemeckis was film's executive producer. [R]▼●

Public Hero No. 1 (1935) **91m.** **½ D: J. Walter Ruben. Lionel Barrymore, Jean Arthur, Chester Morris, Joseph Calleia, Paul Kelly, Lewis Stone. Highly uneven hybrid of gangster yarn with light comedy and romance. Interesting ingredients don't mix, though it's always a pleasure to watch

Arthur. Remade in 1942 as THE GETAWAY.

Public Pigeon No. One (1957) **C-79m.** ** D: Norman Z. McLeod. Red Skelton, Vivian Blaine, Janet Blair, Allyn Joslyn, Jay C. Flippen. Bland Skelton vehicle with Red accidentally exposing gang of crooks; typical slapstick. Based on a *Climax* TV episode of 1956 in which Skelton starred.

Pucker Up and Bark Like a Dog (1990) **C-94m.** ** D: Paul S. Parco. Jonathan Gries, Lisa Zane, Barney Martin, Sal Lopez, Christopher Maher, Wendy O. Williams, Nicholas Worth, Robert Culp, Isabel Sanford, Paul Bartel, Phyllis Diller. Talented but insecure artist falls for an aspiring actress in this slimly plotted L.A. slice of life. Cast is appealing, punk rocker Williams has a great cameo, but the best thing about this film is its title. [R]▼

Pufnstuf (1970) **C-98m.** **½ D: Hollingsworth Morse. Jack Wild, Billie Hayes, Martha Raye, "Mama" Cass Elliott, Billy Barty, Angelo Rossitto, Johnny Silver. OK theatrical feature based on Sid and Marty Krofft's TV series *H.R. Pufnstuf*, with Wild as young boy brought by a magic flute to Oz-like kingdom ruled by bumbling witches. Fine for kids; Hayes is fun as "Witchiepoo." [G]

Pulp (1972) **C-95m.** *** D: Michael Hodges. Michael Caine, Mickey Rooney, Lionel Stander, Lizabeth Scott, Nadia Cassini, Al Lettieri, Dennis Price. Rooney, a retired expatriate Hollywood actor, hires paperback writer Caine to ghost his autobiography. Uneven, but good fun and well acted, especially by Rooney. [PG]▼

Pulp Fiction (1994) **C-154m.** ***½ D: Quentin Tarantino. John Travolta, Samuel L. Jackson, Uma Thurman, Harvey Keitel, Tim Roth, Amanda Plummer, Maria de Medeiros, Ving Rhames, Eric Stoltz, Rosanna Arquette, Christopher Walken, Bruce Willis. Audacious, outrageous look at honor among lowlifes, told in a somewhat radical style overlapping a handful of separate stories. Jackson and Travolta are magnetic as a pair of hit men who have philosophical debates on a regular basis; Willis is compelling as a crooked boxer whose plan to take it on the lam hits a few detours. (In fact, there are no slackers in this cast.) This voluble, violent, pumped-up movie isn't for every taste—certainly not for the squeamish—but it's got more vitality than almost any other film of 1994. Tarantino is featured onscreen as Jimmy of Toluca Lake. Roger Avary gets costory credit with Tarantino (they won the Original Screenplay Oscar). Danny DeVito was one of the executive producers. Panavision. [R]▼●◗

Pulse (1988) **C-91m.** **½ D: Paul Golding. Joey Lawrence, Cliff De Young, Roxanne Hart, Charles Tyner, Myron Healey. What's got into the appliances in the home of Lawrence and his family? Scary, tense film, written by the director, a cut above the usual sci-fi/horror thriller but seriously damaged by a lack of any explanation for its outrageous premise (a living, evil short circuit). Excellent special effects. [PG-13]▼●

Pumping Iron (1977) **C-85m.** *** D: George Butler, Robert Fiore. Arnold Schwarzenegger, Louis Ferrigno, Matty and Victoria Ferrigno, Mike Katz. Fascinating documentary about men's bodybuilding, centering on Schwarzenegger and his pursuit of yet another Mr. Olympia title. Schwarzenegger exudes charm and registers strong screen presence; his main rival is Ferrigno, pre-*Incredible Hulk*. Followed by a distaff sequel. [PG]▼●

Pumping Iron II: The Women (1985) **C-107 min.** *** D: George Butler. Pouty-lipped sexpot Rachel McLish, manlike Australian Bev Francis, and two dozen more female bodybuilders compete in a Vegas non-event where winners are offered a choice of "cash, check, or chips." Funny, if suspiciously stagy look at the profession buoyed by some hilariously incompetent judges and an "in it for the money" emcee job by smiling George Plimpton.▼●

Pumpkin Eater, The (1964-British) **110m.** *** D: Jack Clayton. Anne Bancroft, Peter Finch, James Mason, Cedric Hardwicke, Alan Webb, Richard Johnson, Maggie Smith, Eric Porter. Intelligent if overlong drama chronicling the plight of the mother of eight children, who discovers her third husband has been unfaithful. Fine performances all around, with Bancroft a standout. Script by Harold Pinter, from the Penelope Mortimer novel. ▼

Pumpkinhead (1988) **C-86m.** **½ D: Stan Winston. Lance Henriksen, Jeff East, John DiAquino, Kimberly Ross, Joel Hoffman, Cynthia Bain, Kerry Remsen, Florence Schauffler, Buck Flower, Tom Woodruff, Jr. Makeup expert Winston made his directorial debut with this interesting horror film set in the backwoods. When his young son is accidentally killed by "city folk," a storekeeper unleashes a powerful, fiendish demon on the interlopers. When he changes his mind, he finds he has no more control over the monstrous killer. Slides into the routine at times, but a nice try. Followed by a sequel. [R]▼●

Pump Up the Volume (1990) **C-100m.** **½ D: Allan Moyle. Christian Slater, Ellen Greene, Annie Ross, Samantha Mathis, Scott Paulin, Lala, Cheryl Pollak, Mimi Kennedy. Slater is terrific as Hard Harry, a high school kid by day who runs a pirate radio station by night, stirring up passions among his young listeners and enraging the adult population in the process. Though uneven, this does have some pertinent things to say that you don't always find in a youth-appeal film. [R]▼●◗

Punchline (1988) **C-128m.** *** D: David Seltzer. Sally Field, Tom Hanks, John Goodman, Mark Rydell, Kim Greist, Pam Matteson, Taylor Negron, Barry Neikrug, Mac Robbins, Max Alexander, Paul Kozlowski, Barry Sobel, Damon Wayans. Well-written, well-cast movie about aspiring stand-up comics, focusing on brash young Hanks, who's got real talent but also a knack for pushing people away, and Field, a housewife and mom who feels driven to become a comedienne. Seltzer's serious script is compassionate and believable and manages to avoid clichés and easy answers. Field and (especially) Hanks are first-rate; actor-turned-director Rydell is perfect as the unctuous nightclub owner/entrepreneur. Director Paul Mazursky also appears in the opening scene. [R]▼●

Punisher, The (1989-U.S.-Australian) **C-92m.** ** D: Mark Goldblatt. Dolph Lundgren, Louis Gossett, Jr., Jeroen Krabbe, Kim Miyori, Nancy Everhard, Brian Rooney, Bryan Marshall, Barry Otto, Zoshka Mizak. A cop whose family was wiped out by gangsters retaliates: *he* wipes out gangsters (125 in five years, and still counting). Cop Gossett and, especially, gangster Krabbe come close to rising above silly script, adapted from a Marvel Comics character created by Gerry Conway. Went straight to video in U.S. two years after being made. Shot in Australia but set in U.S. [R]▼●◗

Puppetmaster (1989) **C-90m.** *½ D: David Schmoller. Paul LeMat, Irene Miracle, Matt Roe, William Hickey, Kathryn O'Reilly, Robin Frates, Merrya Small. Psychics drawn to a remote hotel find a malignant associate has committed suicide. They're then stalked by five living puppets left there in 1939 by famous, mystical puppeteer Toulon (Hickey)—plus another menace. Clumsy, talky script helped by (too scant) special effects by David Allen Productions. Followed by several sequels. [R]▼●

Puppet Master II (1990) **C-90m.** ** D: David Allen. Elizabeth Maclellan, Collin Bernsen, Steve Welles, Gregory Webb, Charlie Spradling, Jeff Weston, Nita Talbot. The living puppets bring Toulon, inexplicably costumed as the Invisible Man, back from the dead; then, seeking brains for his life-giving elixir, they terrorize a group of paranormal researchers investigating the old hotel. Slow-paced thriller is an inauspicious directorial debut for effects maestro Allen. [R]▼●

Puppet Master III: Toulon's Revenge (1991) **C-86m.** ** D: David De Coteau. Guy Rolfe, Richard Lynch, Ian Abercrombie, Kristopher Logan, Aron Eisenberg, Walter Gotell, Sarah Douglas, Matthew Faison, Michelle Bauer. The mild best in this low-budget series (so far) is set in Nazi Germany, pitting the kindly old creator of living puppets (Rolfe) against Nazis who want to create an army of zombies. Minor but OK little thriller. [R]▼●

Puppet Masters, The (1994) **C-109m.** **½ D: Stuart Orme. Donald Sutherland, Eric Thal, Julie Warner, David Keith, Will Patton, Richard Belzer, Tom Mason, Yaphet Kotto. U.S. security agency, headed by shrewd, sardonic Sutherland, discovers that the Midwest has been invaded by alien parasites who control the actions of human beings. Good script and performances are hampered by unimaginative direction. Movie imitations of Robert A. Heinlein's classic 1950 sci-fi novel took the edge off this official adaptation before it reached the screen. Aka ROBERT A. HEINLEIN'S THE PUPPET MASTERS. Panavision. [R]▼●

Puppet on a Chain (1970-British) **C-98m.** *½ D: Geoffrey Reeve. Sven-Bertil Taube, Barbara Parkins, Alexander Knox, Patrick Allen, Vladek Sheybal. Half-baked version of Alistair MacLean's best-seller about international drug trafficking; only an exciting speedboat chase (directed by Don Sharp) keeps this film from total disaster. [PG]▼

Puppetoon Movie, The (1987) **C-80m.** **½ No director credited. Arnold Leibovit compiled this collage of George Pal's animated short subjects from the 1930s and '40s. Some of them (JOHN HENRY AND THE INKI POO, TUBBY THE TUBA, JASPER IN A JAM) are terrific, but they're better seen one or two at a time. Still, there's some delightful entertainment here.▼●

Purchase Price, The (1932) **68m.** ** D: William A. Wellman. Barbara Stanwyck, George Brent, Lyle Talbot, Hardie Albright, David Landau, Murray Kinnell, Leila Bennett. Pre-Code Warner Bros. film about nightclub singer Stanwyck, who's seen and done it all, taking it on the lam and becoming—of all things—a mail-order bride for a naive North Dakota farmer. Starts out snappy, winds up silly, though Stanwyck is always worth watching.▼

Pure Country (1992) **C-112m.** ** D: Christopher Cain. George Strait, Lesley Ann Warren, Isabel Glasser, Kyle Chandler, John Doe, Rory Calhoun, Molly McClure. Tuckered-out country star revisits his rural roots, falls for a redheaded rodeo aspirant who doesn't realize who he is. Strait showcase is mostly pure tedium, though film picks up some in hour two with the appearance of Glasser and (as her pop) cowboy vet Calhoun. [PG]▼●◗

Pure Formality, A (1994-Italian-French) **C-108m.** ** D: Giuseppe Tornatore. Gérard Depardieu, Roman Polanski, Sergio Rubini, Nicola DiPinto, Paolo Lombardi. Police inspector Polanski, investigating a just-committed murder, interrogates world-famous novelist Depardieu, who can't remember what he was doing that afternoon. Widescreen but mostly confined to a dark, leaky room; film is maddeningly tedious and directed to the hilt. Not quite what you expect from the maker of CINEMA PARADISO. Panavision. [PG-13]▼●

Pure Hell of St. Trinian's, The (1960-British) **94m.** ** D: Frank Launder. Cecil Parker, Joyce Grenfell, George Cole, Thorley Walters. Absence of Alastair Sim from series lessens glow; outrageous girls' school is visited by sheik seeking harem.

Pure Luck (1991) **C-96m.** ** D: Nadia Tass. Martin Short, Danny Glover, Sheila Kelley, Sam Wanamaker, Scott Wilson, Harry Shearer. A business magnate's accident-prone daughter disappears while vacationing in Mexico, and the father sends detective Glover to find her—accompanied by a man as unlucky as the woman he's out to find. Short's perpetual pratfalls are good for a few laughs, but otherwise this is pretty weak. American remake of French farce LE CHEVRE. [PG]▼●

Purgatory (1999) **C-100m. TVM** D: Uli Edel. Sam Shepard, Randy Quaid, Eric Roberts, Peter Stormare, Brad Rowe, Donnie Wahlberg, John David Souther, Amelia Heinle, Shannon Kenny, R. G. Armstrong. Enjoyable made-for-TV Western with a supernatural twist: Roberts and his vicious band of outlaws lose their way after a robbery and wind up in the town of Refuge, where there are no guns and the citizens look strangely familiar—especially to the youngest outlaw, who's addicted to dime novels. *Twilight Zone*–ish story is fairly obvious but well played. Average. ▼

Purim Player, The SEE: **Der Purimshpiler**

Purlie Victorious SEE: **Gone Are The Days**

Purple Death From Outer Space (1940) **87m.** **½ D: Ford Beebe, Ray Taylor. Buster Crabbe, Carol Hughes, Charles Middleton, Frank Shannon, Anne Gwynne. Edited version of FLASH GORDON CONQUERS THE UNIVERSE serial has Flash, Dale Arden, and Dr. Zarkov discovering Ming's new plan to control Earth. Uninspired handling of original footage.

Purple Gang, The (1960) **85m.** ** D: Frank McDonald. Barry Sullivan, Robert Blake, Elaine Edwards, Marc Cavell, Jody Lawrance, Suzy Marquette, Joseph Turkel. Capable cast, limp police-vs.-gangster yarn.

Purple Haze (1982) **C-104m.** *** D: David Burton Morris. Peter Nelson, Chuck McQuary, Bernard Baldan, Susanne Lack, Bob Breuler, Joanne Bauman, Katy Horsch. Overlong yet involving chronicle of alienated youth Nelson, just expelled from college, and his experiences during the summer of 1968. McQuary is excellent as his comical, "chemically dependent" friend. Effective use of period music. [R]

Purple Heart, The (1944) **99m.** *** D: Lewis Milestone. Dana Andrews, Farley Granger, Sam Levene, Richard Conte, Tala Birell, Nestor Paiva, Benson Fong, Marshall Thompson, Richard Loo. Absorbing tale of U.S. air force crew shot down during Tokyo raid receives strong performances by good cast. Produced and co-written by Darryl F. Zanuck.▼

Purple Hearts (1984) **C-115m.** ** D: Sidney J. Furie. Cheryl Ladd, Ken Wahl, Stephen Lee, David Harris, Lane Smith, Annie McEnroe, Paul McCrane, James Whitmore, Jr., Lee Ermey. Navy medic falls in love with feisty nurse in Vietnam. What starts out as good bread-and-butter story gets worse as it goes along toward silly conclusion. Overlong, to boot. Panavision. [R]▼

Purple Hills, The (1961) **C-60m.** *½ D: Maury Dexter. Gene Nelson, Joanna Barnes, Kent Taylor, Russ Bender. Cheapie oater, with ex-dancer Nelson unconvincing as cowpoke on the run from rampaging Indians. CinemaScope.

Purple Mask, The (1955) **C-82m.** ** D: H. Bruce Humberstone. Tony Curtis, Colleen Miller, Gene Barry, Dan O'Herlihy, Angela Lansbury, George Dolenz, Allison Hayes. Wooden historical adventure with Curtis as a Scarlet Pimpernel–like swashbuckling hero who goes up against Napoleon in 1803 France. CinemaScope.

Purple Noon (1960-French-Italian) **C-118m.** *** D: René Clement. Alain Delon, Marie Laforet, Maurice Ronet, Frank Latimore, Ave Ninchi. Marvelously photographed (in southern Italy, by Henri Decae), tautly directed suspenser about Delon, who envies playboy-friend Ronet and schemes to murder him and assume his identity. Based on Patricia Highsmith's *The Talented Mr. Ripley*. That's Romy Schneider among the friends stopping by cafe in opening scene. Remade as THE TALENTED MR. RIPLEY; also see THE AMERICAN FRIEND. ▼●

Purple People Eater (1988) **C-87m.** *½ D: Linda Shayne. Ned Beatty, Shelley Winters, Neil (Patrick) Harris, Peggy Lipton, Chubby Checker, Little Richard, James Houghton, Thora Birch, Molly Cheek. Corny, unimaginative (if harmless) children's picture based on the famous novelty song hit of 1959, with the title character (looking like a kid in a Halloween costume) coming to Earth to form a rock band with neighborhood teens. The song's original writer-performer, Sheb Wooley, appears as a trapeze teacher. [PG] ▼●

Purple Plain, The (1954-British) **C-100m.** *** D: Robert Parrish. Gregory Peck, Bernard Lee, Win Min Than, Maurice Denham, Brenda De Banzie. Eric Ambler thriller set in WW2 Burma; Peck is neurotic pilot whose plane crashes, forcing him to fight his way to freedom and new sense of values.

Purple Rain (1984) **C-111m.** **½ D:

Albert Magnoli. Prince, Apollonia Kotero, Morris Day, Olga Karlatos, Clarence Williams III, Jerome Benton, Billy Sparks, The Revolution, The Time. Prince's film debut is about a young Minneapolis black who struggles to gain acceptance for his own brand of futuristic (and sexy) rock music . . . but it's *not* autobiographical. Right. Dynamic concert sequences are undercut by soppy storyline and sexist, unappealing characters—especially Prince's. Oscar-winning song score includes title tune, "When Doves Cry." [R]▼●◗

Purple Rose of Cairo, The (1985) **C-82m.** ***½ D: Woody Allen. Mia Farrow, Jeff Daniels, Danny Aiello, Dianne Wiest, Van Johnson, Zoe Caldwell, John Wood, Milo O'Shea, Edward Herrmann, Karen Akers, Deborah Rush, Michael Tucker, Glenne Headly. Bittersweet comedy-fantasy about a Depression-era movie fan whose latest idol walks right off the screen and into her life! Farrow and Daniels' wonderful performances help offset the cold cleverness of Allen's script. The finale is a heartbreaker. [PG]▼●

Purple Taxi, The (1977-French-Italian-Irish) **C-107m.** *½ D: Yves Boisset. Charlotte Rampling, Philippe Noiret, Agostina Belli, Peter Ustinov, Fred Astaire, Edward Albert. Confusing, overblown drama about expatriates in Ireland, with Astaire miscast as eccentric doctor who drives title vehicle. Based on Michel Deon's bestselling novel. Originally 120m. [R]▼

Pursued (1947) **101m.** *** D: Raoul Walsh. Teresa Wright, Robert Mitchum, Judith Anderson, Dean Jagger, Alan Hale, Harry Carey, Jr., John Rodney. Grim Western of determined Mitchum out to find father's killers; very well acted, suspenseful.▼●

Pursuers, The (1961-British) **63m.** ** D: Godfrey Grayson. Cyril Shaps, Francis Matthews, Susan Denny, Sheldon Lawrence. Trim programmer with Matthews tracking down Nazi war criminal Shaps in England; conventionally told.

Pursuit of D. B. Cooper, The (1981) **C-100m.** ** D: Roger Spottiswoode. Robert Duvall, Treat Williams, Kathryn Harrold, Ed Flanders, Paul Gleason, R. G. Armstrong. What may have happened to the "legendary" D. B. Cooper (Williams, in a disappointing performance), who hijacked a plane in 1972 and bailed out with $200,000, never to be heard from again. Who cares? Lackluster comedy-chase story, with Duvall wasted as one of Cooper's pursuers. Film was plagued with problems, multiple directors, hastily refilmed ending—and it shows. [PG]▼●

Pursuit of Happiness, The (1971) **C-98m.** *** D: Robert Mulligan. Michael Sarrazin, Barbara Hershey, Robert Klein, Sada Thompson, Arthur Hill, E. G. Marshall, Barnard Hughes, Rue McClanahan. Director Mulligan has made lots of overrated films, but never got enough credit for this sympathetic tale of young man sent to jail more for his attitude in court than any particular offense. Good performances. Watch for William Devane, Charles Durning. [PG]▼

Pursuit of The Graf Spee (1956-British) **C-119m.** **½ D: Michael Powell, Emeric Pressburger. John Gregson, Anthony Quayle, Peter Finch, Ian Hunter, Bernard Lee, Patrick Macnee, Christopher Lee. Taut documentary-style account of WW2 chase of German warship by British forces. Original title: THE BATTLE OF THE RIVER PLATE. VistaVision.▼

Pursuit to Algiers (1945) **65m.** **½ D: Roy William Neill. Basil Rathbone, Nigel Bruce, Marjorie Riordan, Rosalind Ivan, Martin Kosleck, John Abbott. Lesser *Sherlock Holmes* entry is still diverting tale of heir to an Eastern throne on a perilous Mediterranean voyage.▼

Pushing Hands (1992-U.S.-Taiwanese) **C-100m.** *** D: Ang Lee. Sihung Lung, Lai Wang, Bo Z. Wang, Deb Snyder, Haan Lee, Emily Liu. Cultures clash and a family is strained to the breaking point when a Chinese-American brings his father, a tai chi master who speaks no English, to live with his American wife and son in a N.Y. suburb. Writer-director Lee's first feature is (like his later work) a keenly observed slice of life, with both humor and humanity. Lung, who plays the father, took similar roles in Lee's followup films THE WEDDING BANQUET and EAT DRINK MAN WOMAN.▼●◗

Pushing Tin (1999) **C-124m.** **½ D: Mike Newell. John Cusack, Billy Bob Thornton, Cate Blanchett, Angelina Jolie, Jake Weber, Vicki Lewis. Seriocomic slice of life about the high-pressure world of air-traffic controllers. Best-of-the-best Cusack gets caught in a macho competition with the new guy, Zen cowboy Thornton. MASH-like ensemble film starts off extremely well, with strong performances and snappy repartee, but crash-lands in its second half, becoming a dull domestic romantic comedy about Cusack trying to win back his estranged wife. Blanchett's quite good in an underwritten role as a Longuyland housewife. First feature script by *Cheers* creators Glen and Les Charles. Super 35. [R]▼●◗

Pushover (1954) **88m.** **½ D: Richard Quine. Fred MacMurray, Kim Novak, Phil Carey, Dorothy Malone, E. G. Marshall. MacMurray is cop who falls in love with gangster moll Novak; good cast covers familiar ground.▼

Putney Swope (1969) **C/B&W-85m.** *** D: Robert Downey. Arnold Johnson, Pepi Hermine, Ruth Hermine, Allen Garfield, Antonio Fargas. Hilarious, but dated, story of blacks taking over Madison Avenue ad agency, instituting considerable changes. Best bit: series of commercial spoofs. Fargas, as The Arab, steals the film. Actor billed as "Mel Brooks" is not the Brooks we know and love. [R]▼

Puttin' on the Ritz (1930) **88m.** ** D: Edward Sloman. Harry Richman, Joan Bennett, James Gleason, Aileen Pringle, Lilyan Tashman. Famed nightclub entertainer Richman made his film debut in this primitive early talkie about vaudevillian who can't handle success and turns to drink. You may do the same after watching Richman's performance—though he does introduce the title song by Irving Berlin. Partially redeemed by a few production numbers originally filmed in Technicolor, including a charming "Alice in Wonderland." Sets by William Cameron Menzies.

Puzzle of a Downfall Child (1970) **C-104m.** ** D: Jerry Schatzberg. Faye Dunaway, Barry Primus, Viveca Lindfors, Barry Morse, Roy Scheider, Barbara Carrera. Puzzling is the word for this confusing story of fashion model trying to put together the pieces of her unhappy life. [R]

Puzzle of the Red Orchid, The (1962-German) **94m.** ** D: Helmut Ashley. Christopher Lee, Marisa Mell, Klaus Kinski, Fritz Rasp, Adrian Hoven. Moderate Edgar Wallace entry; Scotland Yard and F.B.I. track down international crime syndicate. Retitled: THE SECRET OF THE RED ORCHID.▼

Pygmalion (1938-British) **95m.** **** D: Anthony Asquith, Leslie Howard. Leslie Howard, Wendy Hiller, Wilfrid Lawson, Marie Lohr, David Tree. Superlative filmization of the witty G. B. Shaw play which became MY FAIR LADY. Howard excels as the professor, with Hiller his Cockney pupil. Shaw's screenplay won an Oscar, as did its adaptation by Ian Dalrymple, Cecil Lewis, and W. P. Lipscomb. Edited by David Lean.▼●

Pygmy Island (1950) **69m.** *½ D: William Berke. Johnny Weissmuller, Ann Savage, David Bruce, Tristram Coffin, Steven Geray, William Tannen, Billy Curtis, Billy Barty, Pierce Lyden. *Jungle Jim* Weissmuller leads a search party to find missing Savage in this silly entry exemplified by having famous white midget Curtis as the leader of the pygmy tribe.

Pyrates (1991) **C-95m.** BOMB D: Noah Stern. Kevin Bacon, Kyra Sedgwick, Bruce Martyn Payne, Kristin Dattilo, Buckley Norris. Photography student Bacon and cellist Sedgwick meet, and the sex between them is so intense that they literally start fires. Crudely scripted, ineptly directed; see this only if you're interested in Bacon and Sedgwick's buns. (In real life they're husband and wife.) Set in Chicago, this film gives new meaning to the term "Windy City." [R]▼

Pyro (1964-Spanish) **C-99m.** **½ D: Julio Coli. Barry Sullivan, Martha Hyer, Sherry Moreland, Soledad Miranda. Strange chiller of man burned in fire seeking revenge on ex-girlfriend who started it.

Pyromaniac's Love Story, A (1995) **C-94m.** ** D: Joshua Brand. William Baldwin, John Leguizamo, Sadie Frost, Erika Eleniak, Michael Lerner, Joan Plowright, Armin Mueller-Stahl, Mike Starr, Julio Oscar Mechoso. A bakery burns to the ground, the work of an unknown arsonist, and the act evokes such unique emotions among a varied group of romantics that just about everyone claims responsibility for the deed—except the real culprit. Minor attempt at generating the same loopy romantic spirit as films like MOONSTRUCK. Feature directing debut for Brand, who co-created the TV series *St. Elsewhere* and *Northern Exposure*. [PG] ▼●

Pyx, The (1973-Canadian) **C-111m.** ***½ D: Harvey Hart. Karen Black, Christopher Plummer, Donald Pilon, Lee Broker, Yvette Brind'Amour. Excellent blend of horror, science-fiction and detective thriller with a mystical theme. Police sergeant Plummer investigates prostitute Black's death, finds a devil cult, numerous decadent suspects and a new twist on Catholic guilt. Aka THE HOOKER CULT MURDERS. Panavision. [R]▼

Q (1982) **C-93m.** *** D: Larry Cohen. David Carradine, Michael Moriarty, Richard Roundtree, Candy Clark, John Capodice, James Dixon, Malachy McCourt. Through plot tissue that discourages elaboration, a prehistoric Aztec deity finds itself flying out of its nest atop a Manhattan skyscraper to rip the heads off rooftop sunbathers and other assorted victims; somehow, all this is integrated into a standard N.Y.C. cop story. Spirited, occasionally hilarious trash sparked by Moriarty's eccentric performance as the loser who knows where the beast resides and intends to cash in on it. Aka THE WINGED SERPENT. [R] ▼●◗

Q & A (1990) **C-132m.** ** D: Sidney Lumet. Nick Nolte, Timothy Hutton, Armand Assante, Patrick O'Neal, Lee Richardson, Luis Guzman, Charles Dutton, Jenny Lumet, Paul Calderon, Leonard Cimino. Wet-behind-the-ears Assistant D.A. (Hutton) is assigned to investigate an incident in which veteran street cop Nolte killed a Puerto Rican druggie . . . and soon finds himself waist-deep in corruption. Gritty, graphic, well-acted story gets slower as it goes along, dragging toward an increasingly predictable conclusion. Lumet scripted from Edwin Torres' novel. Ruben Blades' "Don't Double-Cross The Ones You Love" bids fair to become the worst movie song of the 90s. [R] ▼●◗

Q Planes (1939-British) **78m.** *** D: Tim Whelan. Laurence Olivier, Ralph Richardson, Valerie Hobson, George Curzon, David Tree, George Merritt, Gus McNaughton. Delightful tongue-in-cheek espionage tale, with masterminds stealing British aircraft secrets. Richardson is a joy as lighthearted inspector who cracks the case. Retitled: CLOUDS OVER EUROPE.▼●

Quackers SEE: **Loose Shoes**

Quackser Fortune Has a Cousin in the Bronx (1970-Irish) **C-90m.** ***½ D: Waris Hussein. Gene Wilder, Margot Kidder, Eileen Colgen, Seamus Ford. Delightfully offbeat love story. Quackser Fortune follows the horses around Dublin selling their manure for gardening. The day the horses are replaced by cars he falls in love with an American coed. Original in every way. Screenplay by Gabriel Walsh. Reissued as FUN LOVING. [PG]▼●◗

Quadrophenia (1979-British) **C-115m.** ***½ D: Franc Roddam. Phil Daniels, Mark Wingett, Philip Davis, Leslie Ash, Garry Cooper, Sting. Superior mixture of early '60s "Angry Young Man" drama and rock movie tells of teenage gang battles between Mods and Rockers on the English seaside. A real sleeper. Inspired by The Who's record album. Sting makes an impressive acting debut. [R]▼●

Quality Street (1937) **84m.** *** D: George Stevens. Katharine Hepburn, Franchot Tone, Fay Bainter, Eric Blore, Cora Witherspoon, Estelle Winwood, Bonita Granville, Joan Fontaine, William Bakewell. Hepburn is radiant in delicate adaptation of James Barrie's whimsical play: "old maid" masquerades as her own niece in order to win back the love of a man who hasn't seen her in ten years. Filmed before in 1927, with Marion Davies. ▼●

Quantez (1957) **C-80m.** **½ D: Harry Keller. Fred MacMurray, Dorothy Malone, Sydney Chaplin, John Gavin, John Larch, Michael Ansara. Above-par Western involving robbery gang heading for Mexico border, encountering stiff opposition along the way. CinemaScope.

Quantrill's Raiders (1958) **C-68m.** ** D: Edward Bernds. Steve Cochran, Diane Brewster, Leo Gordon, Gale Robbins. Predictable Civil War account of the outlaw's planned attack on a Kansas arsenal. CinemaScope.

Quare Fellow, The (1962-Irish) **85m.** ***½ D: Arthur Dreifuss. Patrick McGoohan, Sylvia Syms, Walter Macken, Dermot Kelly, Jack Cunningham, Hilton Edwards. Irish-made adaptation of Brendan Behan play deals with new prison guard, well-played by McGoohan, who changes mind about capital punishment. Finely acted; excellent script by director Dreifuss.

Quarrel, The (1991-Canadian) **C-88m.** **½ D: Eli Cohen. R. H. Thompson, Saul Rubinek. A pair of former friends, both Jews, meet by accident and pass the day discussing the implications of the Holocaust and how it has altered their lives. Provocative subject matter, based on a story by Chaim Grade, but the result is as static as it is thoughtful.▼◗

Quartet (1948-British) **120m.** **** D: Ken Annakin, Arthur Crabtree, Harold French, Ralph Smart. Basil Radford, Naunton Wayne, Mai Zetterling, Ian Fleming, Jack Raine, Dirk Bogarde. Superb movie with Somerset Maugham introducing four of his tales, each with different casts and moods. Its success prompted a sequel, TRIO.▼

Quartet (1981-British-French) **C-101m.** *** D: James Ivory. Alan Bates, Maggie Smith, Isabelle Adjani, Anthony Higgins, Pierre Clementi, Daniel Mesguich, Virginie Thevenet, Suzanne Flon. Adjani is taken in by Bohemian Bates and victimized wife Smith when her husband (Higgins) is imprisoned; Bates seduces her into becoming his lover. Expertly acted drama of decadence and change; based on a book by Jean Rhys. [R]▼

Quatermass and the Pit SEE: **Five Million Years to Earth**

Quatermass Conclusion, The (1980-British) **C-107m.** **½ D: Piers Haggard. John Mills, Simon MacCorkindale, Barbara Kellerman, Margaret Tyzack, Brewster Mason. Mills is fine as heroic Professor Bernard Quatermass (of earlier screen and television adventures) in this entertaining though poorly produced sci-fi adventure. He comes to the rescue when a death beam from outer space evaporates the world's young. Made for British TV. Original title: QUATERMASS.▼

Quatermass II SEE: **Enemy From Space**

Quatermass Xperiment, The SEE: **Creeping Unknown, The**

Quatorze Juillet (1932-French) **98m.** *** D: René Clair. Annabella, Georges Rigaud, Pola Illery, Paul Olivier, Raymond Cordy. Delightful comedy about life in Paris on Bastille Day, centering on the adventures of flower-girl Annabella and her taxi-driver boyfriend. Filled with fresh, funny touches; Clair at his best. Aka JULY 14TH.

Quebec (1951) **C-85m.** ** D: George Templeton. John Barrymore, Jr., Corinne Calvet, Barbara Rush, Patric Knowles. Historical nonsense set in 1830s Canada during revolt against England. Filmed on location.▼

Queen Bee (1955) **95m.** *** D: Ranald MacDougall. Joan Crawford, Barry Sullivan, Betsy Palmer, John Ireland, Fay Wray, Tim Hovey. Crawford in title role has field-day maneuvering the lives of all in her Southern mansion, with husband Sullivan providing the final ironic twist.▼

Queen Christina (1933) **97m.** **** D: Rouben Mamoulian. Greta Garbo, John Gilbert, Ian Keith, Lewis Stone, C. Aubrey Smith, Gustav von Seyffertitz, Reginald Owen. Probably Garbo's best film, with a haunting performance by the radiant star as 17th-century Swedish queen who relinquishes her throne for her lover, Gilbert. Garbo and Gilbert's love scenes together are truly memorable, as is the famous final shot. Don't miss this one.▼●

Queenie (1987) **C-200m. TVM** D: Larry Peerce. Mia Sara, Kirk Douglas, Martin Balsam, Claire Bloom, Topol, Joel Grey, Sarah Miles, Joss Ackland. Lavishly produced but unenthralling adaptation of Michael Korda's best-seller tracing the rise of an exotic young girl from Calcutta's slums to the brink of Hollywood stardom. Queenie's character is based on Merle Oberon, while Douglas plays a thinly disguised Alexander Korda, the author's late movie-mogul uncle. Stellar cast is of little help to the unseasoned Sara, miscast in the title role. Originally shown in two parts. Average.▼

Queen Kelly (1928) **96m.** ***½ D: Erich von Stroheim. Gloria Swanson, Seena Owen, Walter Byron, Tully Marshall, Madame Sul Te Wan. A convent girl is swept off her feet by a roguish prince—then sent to live in East Africa where her aunt runs a brothel! Fascinating, extravagantly decadent von Stroheim melodrama that was never completed; this restored version wraps up story with stills and subtitles. A must for film buffs; exquisitely photographed, with scene-stealing performance by Owen as the mad queen. The European-release version, in which the girl meets with an entirely different fate, is also available.▼●

Queen Margot (1994-French-German-Italian) **C-143m.** ***½ D: Patrice Chéreau. Isabelle Adjani, Daniel Auteuil, Jean-Hugues Anglade, Vincent Perez, Virna Lisi, Jean-Claude Brialy, Dominique Blanc, Pascal Greggory, Claudio Amendola, Miguel Bosé, Asia Argento, Barbet Schroeder. Enormous production, based on a Dumas novel, of the events surrounding notorious St. Bartholomew's Day massacre in 16th-century France. Young Margot (Adjani) is forced to marry Henri de Navarre (Auteuil) by her scheming mother, Catherine de Medici (Lisi), with unexpected and terrible consequences. Excellent film (produced by Claude Berri) boasts strong performances in every role, sumptuous decor, and surprisingly erotic love scenes. Intricate, intelligent and often moving epic. Scripted by Daniele Thompson and director Chéreau. Previously filmed in 1954, with Jeanne Moreau. Original French version runs 166m. [R]▼●

Queen of Babylon, The (1954-Italian) **C-98m.** *½ D: Carlo Bragaglia. Rhonda Fleming, Ricardo Montalban, Roldano Lupi, Carlo Ninchi. American stars can't elevate elephantine study of ancient Babylonia.

Queen of Blood SEE: **Planet of Blood**

Queen of Burlesque (1946) **70m.** *½ D: Sam Newfield. Evelyn Ankers, Carleton G. Young, Marion Martin, Rose La Rose, Alice Fleming, Craig Reynolds. Low-budget suspenser unstrung backstage at burlesque theater.▼

Queen of Destiny SEE: **Sixty Glorious Years**

Queen of Hearts (1989-British) **C-112m.** ***½ D: Jon Amiel. Vittorio Duse, Joseph Long, Anita Zagaria, Eileen Way, Vittorio Amandola, Ian Hawkes, Tat Whalley. Extraordinary and unusual film, better seen than described, about an Italian couple who lead a pleasantly quixotic life in England running a family café. Tony Grisoni's original screenplay embraces elements of romance, humor, melodrama, mysticism, and fantasy in a heady mix. Remarkable first feature for director Amiel, who did *The Singing Detective* for British TV. [PG]▼

Queen of Outer Space (1958) **C-79m.** ** D: Edward Bernds. Zsa Zsa Gabor, Eric Fleming, Laurie Mitchell, Patrick Waltz, Paul Birch, Lisa Davis, Dave Willock. Manned rocketship from Earth is abducted to Venus, where the planet is ruled entirely by women. Silly, to say the least, but at least some of the laughs were intentional. Zsa Zsa, incidentally, does *not* play the title character! CinemaScope.▼

Queen of Spades, The (1949-British) **95m.** *** D: Thorold Dickinson. Anton Walbrook, Edith Evans, Ronald Howard, Mary Jerrold, Yvonne Mitchell, Anthony Dawson. Unusual, macabre fantasy from Alexander Pushkin story about Russian officer obsessed with learning the secret of winning at cards. Well-mounted production, set in 1806.▼

Queen of Spades (1960-Russian) **C-100m.** **½ D: Roman Tikhomirov. Oleg Strizhenov, Zurab Anzhaparidze, Olga Krasina, Tamara Milashkina. Stark version of Tchaikovsky opera *Pikovaya Dama,* performed by Bolshoi Theater company; deals with young man consumed by gambling urge, leading to his and girlfriend's destruction.▼

Queen of the Gorillas SEE: **Bride and the Beast, The**

Queen of the Jungle (1935) **87m.** BOMB D: Robert Hill. Mary Kornman, Reed Howes, Dickie Jones, Marilyn Spinner, Lafe McKee. Hilariously awful feature adapted from cheapie serial that rivals anything ever made by Edward Wood. A little girl is accidentally cast off in a balloon; she lands in the middle of the African jungle and grows up to become the title monarch. A laugh riot.▼

Queen of the Nile (1962-Italian) **C-85m.** ** D: Fernando Cerchio. Jeanne Crain, Vincent Price, Edmund Purdom, Amedeo Nazzari. Dull account of court life in 2000 B.C. Egypt. Not even campy. SuperCinescope.

Queen of the Stardust Ballroom (1975) **C-100m. TVM** D: Sam O'Steen. Maureen Stapleton, Charles Durning, Michael Brandon, Michael Strong, Charlotte Rae. Beautifully realized love story between a widowed grandmother and a married mailman who meet at a local dance hall. A filmed song of joy by Jerome Kass, with sensitive performances by the two leads. Later a Broadway musical, *Ballroom*. Above average.▼◗

Queen's Guards, The (1960-British) **C-110m.** ** D: Michael Powell. Daniel Massey, Robert Stephens, Raymond Massey, Ursula Jeans. Tedious, patriotic chronicle of young Massey distinguishing himself in service, saving family name; humdrum film. CinemaScope.

Queens Logic (1991) **C-112m.** **½ D: Steve Rash. Kevin Bacon, Linda Fiorentino, John Malkovich, Joe Mantegna, Ken Olin, Tony Spiridakis, Tom Waits, Chloe Webb, Jamie Lee Curtis, Kelly Bishop, Ed Marinaro. Title refers not to royalty, but to the N.Y.C. borough. Robust performances half-spark a BIG CHILL-type reunion pic, as old pals and their mates reunite for a wedding. Actor Spiridakis penned the so-so script. Unusually fine rock-oldie score helps. [R]▼●◗

Quemada! SEE: **Burn!**

Quentin Durward (1955) **C-101m.** **½ D: Richard Thorpe. Robert Taylor, Kay Kendall, Robert Morley, George Cole, Alec Clunes, Duncan Lamont, Marius Goring. Taylor plays Sir Walter Scott's dashing Scots hero in this handsome but static costumer about Louis XI's reign in 15th-century France. CinemaScope.

Querelle (1982-German) **C-120m.** BOMB D: Rainer Werner Fassbinder. Brad Davis, Franco Nero, Jeanne Moreau, Gunther Kaufmann, Hanno Poschl. Or, "A Guy in Every Port." Davis is the French sailor whose venture into an infamous whorehouse in Brest permits him to discover his true homosexual nature. Fassbinder's final film was rejected even by his admirers; gamy but slickly produced adaptation of Jean Genet novel induces boredom and giggles in equal measure. Technovision. [R]▼

Quest, The (1986-Australian) **C-93m.** *½ D: Brian Trenchard-Smith. Henry Thomas, Tony Barry, Rachel Friend, Tamsin West, Dennis Miller, Katya Manning. Abortive Australian attempt to capitalize on young Thomas' success as the star of E.T.; here he plays a precocious child who, along with a couple of pals, visits an aboriginal burial ground where a Loch Ness-style monster lives. Competently made but uninteresting. [PG]▼

Quest, The (1996) **C-95m.** **½ D: Jean-Claude Van Damme. Jean-Claude Van Damme, Roger Moore, James Remar, Jack McGee, Janet Gunn, Aki Aleong, Louis Mandylor. Epic martial-arts story with high-kicking Van Damme as N.Y.C. pickpocket whose efforts to elude the police lead him to the Far East and into the most exclusive and prestigious fight in the "world." Besides Jean-Claude, film features fifteen of the world's greatest martial arts champions. A passable but uninspired directing debut for the star, who also gets story credit. Super 35. [PG-13]▼●◗

Quest for Camelot (1998) **C-85m.** **½ D: Frederick Du Chau. Voices of Jessalyn Gilsig, Cary Elwes, Gary Oldman, Eric Idle, Don Rickles, Jane Seymour, Celine Dion, Bryan White, Pierce Brosnan, Gabriel Byrne, Jaleel White, Bronson Pinchot, John Gielgud. Pretty good Disney-derivative cartoon, about the plucky daughter of a slain knight who wants to follow in her father's footsteps—and does just that when King Arthur's sword, Excalibur, is stolen. Too dark and violent for very young kids, but agreeable enough as it treads a familiar story path, with romance, songs, and comic relief. [G]▼●◗

Quest for Fire (1981-French-Canadian) **C-97m.** ***½ D: Jean-Jacques Annaud. Everett McGill, Rae Dawn Chong, Ron Perlman, Nameer El Kadi. Peaceful tribe living 80,000 years ago is attacked by apes and wolves and loses its fire, essential for survival. They don't know how to make fire, so three of their own trek off to find it again. Not the epic intended, but still funny, tense, touching—and fascinating. Special languages devised by Anthony Burgess, and body languages and gestures by Desmond Morris; the makeup earned an Academy Award. Filmed in Kenya, Scotland, Iceland, and Canada. Panavision. [R]▼●

Quest for Love (1971-British) **C-90m.** *** D: Ralph Thomas. Tom Bell, Joan Collins, Denholm Elliott, Laurence Naismith, Lyn Ashley, Juliet Harmer, Neil McCallum, Simon Ward. Intriguing sci-fi story of man who accidentally passes into another dimension on Earth almost identical to ours, with some strange differences. Based on a short story by John Wyndham. ▼

Question of Adultery, A (1959-British) **86m.** **½ D: Don Chaffey. Julie London, Anthony Steel, Basil Sydney, Donald Houston, Anton Diffring, Andrew Cruickshank. Tepid drama involving pros and cons of artificial insemination. Retitled: THE CASE OF MRS. LORING.

Question of Love, A (1978) **C-100m. TVM** D: Jerry Thorpe. Gena Rowlands, Jane Alexander, Ned Beatty, Clu Gulager, Bonnie Bedelia, James Sutorius, Jocelyn Brando. Top-notch cast enriches this sensitive fact-based drama by William Blinn about two lesbians and the custody battle one has with her ex-husband over their young son. Above average.▼

Quick and the Dead, The (1987) **C-93m. TVM** D: Robert Day. Sam Elliott, Kate Capshaw, Tom Conti, Kenny Morrison, Matt Clark. Lean Louis L'Amour Western out of the SHANE school involving a homesteading couple, their young son, and a mysterious stranger who rides into their lives when they come under attack by a ruthless gang. James Lee Barrett's script recaptures the flavor of the old movie West. Made for cable. Above average.▼

Quick and the Dead, The (1995) **C-105m.** ** D: Sam Raimi. Sharon Stone, Gene Hackman, Russell Crowe, Leonardo DiCaprio, Tobin Bell, Roberts Blossom, Kevin Conway, Keith David, Lance Henriksen, Pat Hingle, Gary Sinise, Olivia Burnette, Fay Masterson, Bruce Campbell. Female stranger comes to the town of Redemption to enter its annual quick-draw competition; her real motive is to seek revenge on the town's evil boss, Herod (Hackman), for what he did to her family years ago. Sluggish Western tries to turn Stone into The Man With No Name, but even on a parody level, it doesn't work; endless close-ups of her beautiful face reveal nothing. One would expect more razzle-dazzle from director Raimi. Woody Strode appears briefly as a coffin maker in the opening scene; this was his final film. [R]▼●◗

Quick Before It Melts (1964) **C-98m.** **½ D: Delbert Mann. George Maharis, Robert Morse, Anjanette Comer, James Gregory, Yvonne Craig, Doodles Weaver, Howard St. John, Michael Constantine. Trivia involving Maharis and Morse in the Antarctic; they have bright idea of bringing in a planeload of girls, with predictable results. Panavision.

Quick Change (1990) **C-88m.** *** D: Howard Franklin, Bill Murray. Bill Murray, Geena Davis, Randy Quaid, Jason Robards, Bob Elliott, Philip Bosco, Phil Hartman, Kurtwood Smith, Jamey Sheridan, Kathryn Grody, Stanley Tucci, Tony Shalhoub. Very low-key but funny outing for Murray as a malcontent who stages a clever bank robbery—disguised as a clown—but can't seem to get out of N.Y.C. with his accomplices, Davis and Quaid. It's possible that only New Yorkers will truly appreciate the anti-City sentiments (and often hilarious vignettes) that permeate the film. Jay Cronley's novel was previously filmed in 1985 as HOLD-UP, with Jean-Paul Belmondo. [R]▼●

Quick Gun, The (1964) **C-87m.** ** D: Sidney Salkow. Audie Murphy, Merry Anders, James Best, Ted de Corsia, Frank Ferguson, Raymond Hatton. Formula Murphy Western, with Audie redeeming himself by combating town outlaws. Techniscope.

Quick, Let's Get Married (1971) **C-96m.** BOMB D: William Dieterle. Ginger Rogers, Ray Milland, Barbara Eden, Michael Ansara, Walter Abel, Elliott Gould. Bordello madam Rogers and adventurer Milland perpetrate "miracle" hoax on gullible prostitute (Eden). Gould makes inauspicious film debut as deaf mute. This embarrassment was filmed in 1964. Aka SEVEN DIFFERENT WAYS.

Quick Millions (1931) **72m.** **½ D: Rowland Brown. Spencer Tracy, Marguerite Churchill, Sally Eilers, Robert Burns, John Wray, George Raft. OK gangster film with Tracy as ambitious truck driver who climbs to top of the rackets. Nothing special, except to see dynamic early Tracy.

Quicksand (1950) **79m.** **½ D: Irving Pichel. Mickey Rooney, Jeanne Cagney, Barbara Bates, Peter Lorre, Taylor Holmes, Wally Cassell, Jimmy Dodd. Minor film noir about auto mechanic Rooney, who is hot for trampy Cagney, and what happens when he "borrows" $20 from his boss's cash register. Lorre is wonderfully menacing as a sleazy penny arcade owner.▼

Quicksilver (1986) **C-106m.** *½ D: Tom Donnelly. Kevin Bacon, Jami Gertz, Paul Rodriguez, Rudy Ramos, Andrew Smith, Gerald S. O'Loughlin, Larry Fishburne, Louis Anderson. The lives of big-city bicycle messengers (confusingly shot in three *different* cities), and one white-collar dropout in particular. Low-gear all the way. [PG]▼●

Quiet American, The (1958) **120m.** **½ D: Joseph L. Mankiewicz. Audie Murphy, Michael Redgrave, Claude Dauphin, Giorgia Moll, Bruce Cabot. Sanitized version of the Graham Greene novel, with the book's "un-American" feeling eliminated; naive American Murphy arrives in Saigon with his own plan to settle country's conflicts. More a murder mystery than the political thriller intended.

Quiet Earth, The (1985-New Zealand) **C-100m.** **½ D: Geoff Murphy. Bruno Lawrence, Alison Routledge, Peter Smith. Intriguing (and extremely good-looking) end-of-the-world saga; not entirely successful but well worth a look. [R]▼●

Quiet Man, The (1952) **C-129m.** **** D: John Ford. John Wayne, Maureen O'Hara, Barry Fitzgerald, Victor McLaglen, Mildred Natwick, Arthur Shields, Ward Bond, Ken Curtis, Mae Marsh, Jack MacGowran, Sean McClory, Francis Ford. American boxer Wayne returns to his native Ireland and falls in love with a spirited lass (O'Hara)—but has to deal with local customs (including the payment of a dowry) and the young woman's bullheaded brother (McLaglen). Boisterous blarney, with beautiful Technicolor scenery, and equally beautiful music by Victor Young. This film was clearly a labor of love for Ford and his Irish-American stars. Maurice Walsh's story was scripted by Frank Nugent. Oscar winner for Best Director and Cinematography (Winton C. Hoch and Archie Stout).▼●◗

Quiet Place to Kill, A (1969-Italian-Spanish) **C-88m.** BOMB D: Umberto Lenzi. Carroll Baker, Jean Sorel, Marina Coffa, Anna Proclemer, Alberto Dalbes. Dreary drama of Baker and ex-husband

Sorel covering up the latter's accidental murder of his new wife. Cut to 77m., and also known as PARANOIA; not to be confused with Lenzi's not dissimilar ORGASMO (1968), starring Baker, which was also shown as PARANOIA. Techniscope.▼

Quiet Please, Murder (1942) **70m.** **½ D: John Larkin. George Sanders, Gail Patrick, Richard Denning, Sidney Blackmer, Lynne Roberts, Kurt Katch, Minerva Urecal, Theodore von Eltz. Offbeat, intriguing yarn of master forger Sanders stealing priceless Shakespeare volume, passing off his copies as the original. Murder and romance expertly woven into story.

Quiet Room, The (1996-Australian) **C-91m.** ***½ D: Rolf de Heer. Celine O'Leary, Paul Blackwell, Chloe Ferguson, Phoebe Ferguson. Revealing and compelling portrait of the disintegration of a marriage as seen completely through the eyes and mind of a seven-year-old girl. Writer-director de Heer vividly captures the truth about the experience through the self-imposed silence of a wise child who clearly sees through adult evasiveness and lies. [PG]▼

Quigley Down Under (1990) **C-119m.** *** D: Simon Wincer. Tom Selleck, Laura San Giacomo, Alan Rickman, Chris Haywood, Ron Haddrick, Tony Bonner, Jerome Ehlers, Conor McDermottroe, Roger Ward, Ben Mendelsohn. Selleck is excellent as a self-assured sharpshooter who travels to Australia to work for despotic land baron Rickman—and takes an instant dislike to him, spawning a deadly game of cat-and-mouse in which only one will be left alive. Expertly filmed on exquisite locations, with its good qualities outweighing occasional dips in interest. Panavision. [PG-13]▼●

Quiller Memorandum, The (1966-British) **C-105m.** *** D: Michael Anderson. George Segal, Alec Guinness, Max von Sydow, Senta Berger, George Sanders, Robert Helpmann, Robert Flemyng. Good Harold Pinter script about American secret agent who investigates neo-Nazi movement in modern-day Berlin. A relief from most spy films of the 60s. Based on novel *The Berlin Memorandum* by Elleston Trevor (using pseudonym Adam Hall). Panavision. ▼

Quincannon, Frontier Scout (1956) **C-83m.** *½ D: Lesley Selander. Tony Martin, Peggie Castle, John Bromfield, John Smith, Ron Randell. Martin is miscast in title role of programmer.

Quintet (1979) **C-110m.** ** D: Robert Altman. Paul Newman, Bibi Andersson, Fernando Rey, Vittorio Gassman, Nina Van Pallandt, Brigitte Fossey, David Langton. Pretentious, unappealing story about cutthroat game of survival in a frozen city of the future. Not as puzzling as it is ponderous. [R]▼

Quiz Show (1994) **C-130m.** ***½ D: Robert Redford. John Turturro, Rob Morrow, Ralph Fiennes, Paul Scofield, David Paymer, Hank Azaria, Christopher McDonald, Johann Carlo, Elizabeth Wilson, Allan Rich, Mira Sorvino, George Martin, Paul Guilfoyle, Griffin Dunne, Timothy Busfield, Jack Gilpin, Bruce Altman, Carole Shelley, Illeana Douglas, Calista Flockhart. Engrossing story of the TV quiz show scandal of the late 1950s, focusing on a hotheaded sore loser (Turturro, in a sensational performance) and his successor on *Twenty-One*: instant hero Charles Van Doren (Fiennes), scion of a socially prominent, intellectual family. Overlength is its only weakness—but it never ceases to be real (if not always exactly truthful). Scofield is a joy to watch as the elder Van Doren, and director Martin Scorsese is well cast as the cold-blooded sponsor of the show. That's film director Barry Levinson as TV host Dave Garroway; look sharp for an unbilled Ethan Hawke in a Columbia University classroom. [PG-13]▼●◗

Quo Vadis? (1951) **C-171m.** *** D: Mervyn LeRoy. Robert Taylor, Deborah Kerr, Peter Ustinov, Leo Genn, Patricia Laffan, Finlay Currie, Abraham Sofaer, Buddy Baer. Gargantuan MGM adaptation of Henryk Sienkiewicz' novel set during the reign of Nero; Roman soldier Taylor has to figure out how to romance Christian Kerr without both of them ending up as lunch for the lions. Meticulous production includes fine location shooting and Miklos Rozsa score based on music of the era. Remade for Italian TV.▼●

Quo Vadis? (1985-Italian) **C-200m. TVM** D: Franco Rossi. Klaus Maria Brandauer, Frederic Forrest, Cristina Raines, Barbara DeRossi, Francesco Quinn, Marie-Theres Relin, Gabriele Ferzetti, Massimo Girotti, Leopoldo Trieste, Max von Sydow. Bloated, slow-moving adaptation of the Henryk Sienkiewicz saga, notable solely for Brandauer's extravagant Nero. That's Anthony Quinn's son Francesco (in his first important role) in the old Robert Taylor part. Made for Italian television, first shown in the U.S. on cable TV. Average. [R]▼●

Rabbit, Run (1970) **C-94m.** ** D: Jack Smight. James Caan, Carrie Snodgress, Anjanette Comer, Jack Albertson, Melodie Johnson, Henry Jones, Carmen Matthews, Nydia Westman, Josephine Hutchinson, Ken Kercheval, Arthur Hill. Brilliant cast, brilliant book (by John Updike), but dull film about former high school athlete who finds that life is tougher than being on the playing field. Panavision. [R]

Rabbit Test (1978) **C-86m.** **½ D: Joan Rivers. Billy Crystal, Alex Rocco, Joan Prather, Doris Roberts, George Gobel, Imogene Coca, Paul Lynde. Rivers' only film to date is like low-budget Mel Brooks: wacky comedy surrounding slim plot about first pregnant man. Some wild ideas, mostly in bad taste. Many guest-star cameos (including Rivers as a nurse). [PG]▼●

Rabbit Trap, The (1959) **72m.** **½ D: Philip Leacock. Ernest Borgnine, David Brian, Bethel Leslie, Kevin Corcoran, June Blair, Jeanette Nolan, Don Rickles. Intelligent if slow-moving study of motivational factors behind Borgnine's compulsive work life and ignoring of his family. Script by JP Miller, from his TV play.

Rabid (1977-Canadian) **C-90m.** **½ D: David Cronenberg. Marilyn Chambers, Frank Moore, Joe Silver, Patricia Gage, Susan Roman. Motorcyclist Chambers has plastic surgery after an accident, develops an insatiable hankering for human blood. Good of its type; well directed by cult favorite Cronenberg. Porn star Chambers removes her clothes—but nothing more. [R]▼

Race for Life (1954-British) **68m.** *½ D: Terence Fisher. Richard Conte, Mari Aldon, George Coulouris, Peter Illing, Alec Mango. Formula programmer with Conte as an American racing his way around some of Europe's fastest tracks against wishes of wife Aldon. Competent stock-car footage in this pre-horror Hammer production.

Race for Your Life, Charlie Brown (1977) **C-75m.** **½ D: Bill Melendez. Voices of Duncan Watson, Greg Felton, Stuart Brotman, Gail Davis, Liam Martin. Third animated feature based on Charles Schulz's *Peanuts* comic strip is set in summer camp, highlighted by treacherous raft race. Mildly entertaining, but lacks punch. [G]▼●

Racers, The (1955) **C-112m.** **½ D: Henry Hathaway. Kirk Douglas, Bella Darvi, Gilbert Roland, Lee J. Cobb, Cesar Romero, Katy Jurado. Hackneyed sports-car racing yarn, not salvaged by Douglas' dynamics or European location shooting. CinemaScope.▼

Race Street (1948) **79m.** ** D: Edwin L. Marin. George Raft, William Bendix, Marilyn Maxwell, Frank Faylen, Henry (Harry) Morgan, Gale Robbins. Ordinary crime story of San Francisco bookie-turned nightclub owner Raft, who "likes to do things his own way." He plays footsie with cop Bendix while going up against the protection racket responsible for his best friend's murder.●

Race the Sun (1996) **C-105m.** ** D: Charles T. Kanganis. Halle Berry, James Belushi, Kevin Tighe, Bill Hunter, Eliza Dushku, J. Moki Cho, Casey Affleck, Steve Zahn. An idealistic teacher (Berry) and gruff mechanic (Belushi) team up to mentor eight poverty-stricken kids who build a solar-powered car and take it to a racing competition across Australia. Clichés abound in this "feel-good" film, and the leads are annoying, but the kids are charming (in particular, Cho). Exotic locales help. Written by Barry Morrow (RAIN MAN). [PG]▼●

Race to the Yankee Zephyr (1981-Australian-New Zealand) **C-108m.** ** D: David Hemmings. Ken Wahl, Lesley Ann Warren, Donald Pleasence, George Peppard, Bruno Lawrence. Addle-brained drama about good guys Wahl and Pleasence and nemesis Peppard attempting to recover $50 million in gold from DC-3 wrecked during WW2. Video title: TREASURE OF THE YANKEE ZEPHYR. Panavision. [PG]▼

Race With the Devil (1975) **C-88m.** *½ D: Jack Starrett. Peter Fonda, Warren Oates, Loretta Swit, Lara Parker, R. G. Armstrong. Two vacationing couples are pursued by local satanic witches after witnessing a human sacrifice. It takes quite a human sacrifice to sit through this hybrid car-chase/horror film. [PG]▼

Rachel and the Stranger (1948) **79m.** *** D: Norman Foster. Loretta Young, William Holden, Robert Mitchum, Tom Tully, Sara Haden. Charming pioneer love story of a farmer, his indentured servant wife, and the farmer's wandering minstrel friend who visits their homestead. Three attractive stars at their prime. Originally reviewed at 93m. Also shown in computer-colored version.▼●

Rachel Papers, The (1989-British) **C-95m.** **½ D: Damian Harris. Dexter Fletcher, Ione Skye, Jonathan Pryce, James Spader, Bill Paterson, Lesley Sharp, Michael Gambon. Young Britisher relentlessly pursues an American girl, with the help of his computer. Skye shines (in a role similar to the one she had in SAY ANYTHING . . .) but this is really a showcase for Fletcher. Sporadically charming, adapted by first-time director Harris from Martin Amis' novel. [R]▼

Rachel, Rachel (1968) **C-101m.** ***½ D: Paul Newman. Joanne Woodward, James Olson, Kate Harrington, Estelle Parsons, Donald Moffat, Terry Kiser. Beautifully sensitive, mature film about spinster schoolteacher trying to come out of her shell. Woodward is superb; husband Newman's directorial debut. Screenplay by Stewart Stern, from a novel by Margaret Laurence. [R]▼

Rachel River (1987) **C-90m.** **½ D: Sandy Smolan. Zeljko Ivanek, Pamela Reed, Craig T. Nelson, James Olson, Alan North, Viveca Lindfors, Jo Henderson, Jon De Vries. Occasionally contrived but mostly intelligent chronicle of Reed, a rural Minnesota mother and radio journalist, and the various people who inhabit her town. Thoughtful performances overcome the occasional insipidness. Screenplay by Judith Guest; a PBS *American Playhouse* theatrical production. [PG-13]▼

Racing Fever (1964) **C-80m.** BOMB D: William Grefe. Joe Morrison, Charles Martin, Maxine Carroll, Barbara Biggart. Torrid trash of speedboat racing, an accidental killing, and revenge.

Racing With the Moon (1984) **C-108m.** *** D: Richard Benjamin. Sean Penn, Elizabeth McGovern, Nicolas Cage, John Karlen, Rutanya Alda, Carol Kane, Crispin Glover, Michael Madsen, Dana Carvey. Teenage romance set in small California town just as the young man is about to go off to fight in WW2. Appealing stars and loving eye for 1940s detail make up for slow pace. That bowling alley is a gem! [PG]▼●

Rack, The (1956) **100m.** *** D: Arnold Laven. Paul Newman, Wendell Corey, Walter Pidgeon, Edmond O'Brien, Anne Francis, Lee Marvin, Cloris Leachman. Newman is pensively convincing as Korean War veteran—brainwashed as a P.O.W. —now on trial for treason, with Pidgeon as his overbearing father and Francis his friend. Slick production adapted from Rod Serling teleplay. Robert Blake, Dean Jones, and Rod Taylor have small roles.

Racket, The (1951) **88m.** *** D: John Cromwell. Robert Mitchum, Robert Ryan, Lizabeth Scott, Ray Collins, William Talman, Robert Hutton, William Conrad, Don Porter. Police officer Mitchum and gangster Ryan spend almost as much time fighting their corrupt superiors as they do each other. Unusual film noir with strong performances (especially Ryan's) and bizarre ending; based on play previously filmed by producer Howard Hughes in 1928. Coscripted by W.R. Burnett; some scenes were directed by Nicholas Ray. Also shown in computer-colored version. ▼●

Racket Busters (1938) **71m.** ** D: Lloyd Bacon. George Brent, Humphrey Bogart, Gloria Dickson, Allen Jenkins, Walter Abel, Henry O'Neill, Penny Singleton. Mobster Bogie's going to take over the trucking business, but Brent doesn't want to cooperate. Standard programmer moves along well; cowritten by Robert Rossen.

Rad (1986) **C-91m.** BOMB D: Hal Needham. Bart Connor, Lori Laughlin, Talia Shire, Jack Weston, Ray Walston. Connor is supposed to take his SATs, but wouldn't you know it, there's a big BMX race on the same Saturday? ''Rad'' is short for *radical*—as in ''Radical, man''—which this trash definitely is not: Didn't we see this same plot in late '50s hot-rod and late '70s roller-disco movies? [PG]▼●

Radical, The SEE: **Katherine**

Radioactive Dreams (1986) **C-98m.** ** D: Albert Pyun. John Stockwell, Michael Dudikoff, Lisa Blount, George Kennedy, Don Murray, Michele Little. So-so post-apocalypse drama about Stockwell and Dudikoff, who've come to maturity in a bomb shelter. They've read all of Raymond Chandler's Philip Marlowe books and have taken on the private eye's personality. Nicely filmed, but it doesn't hold up. [R]▼●

Radio Days (1987) **C-85m.** *** D: Woody Allen. Mia Farrow, Seth Green, Julie Kavner, Josh Mostel, Michael Tucker, Dianne Wiest, Wallace Shawn, Tito Puente, Danny Aiello, Jeff Daniels, Tony Roberts, Diane Keaton, Kitty Carlisle Hart, Kenneth Mars. Richly nostalgic reminiscence (narrated by Woody) about growing up in 1940s Queens, mixing family vignettes with incidents about radio performers from that medium's golden age. The narrative never really gels, though it's always enjoyable to watch . . . especially with Allen's eye for detail and ear for dialogue. Beautifully photographed by Carlo Di Palma and designed by Santo Loquasto; filled with wonderful vintage music. [PG]▼●

Radio Flyer (1992) **C-120m.** ** D: Richard Donner. Lorraine Bracco, John Heard, Elijah Wood, Joseph Mazzello, Adam Baldwin, Ben Johnson. Two young, devoted brothers must find a way to survive their mother's marriage to an abusive drunk; their salvation is escape into a secret world, where they hatch a master plan for their Radio Flyer wagon. Spielberg-like view of childhood seems to suggest fantasy as a solution to child abuse! Despite moving performances from the two boys, this concept just doesn't work. Tom Hanks appears unbilled. Panavision. [PG-13]▼●

Radio Inside (1994) **C-91m.** **½ D: Jeffrey Bell. William McNamara, Elisabeth Shue, Dylan Walsh, Ilse Earl, Pee Wee Love, Ara Madzounian, Steve Zurk. A young man, trying to cope with the death of his father and his own aimlessness, goes to live with his brother and soon falls for the brother's girlfriend. Gentle tale with some good performances, especially by McNamara. ▼●

Radioland Murders (1994) **C-112m.** *½ D: Mel Smith. Brian Benben, Mary Stuart Masterson, Ned Beatty, Scott Michael Campbell, Brion James, Michael Lerner, Michael McKean, Jeffrey Tambor, Stephen Tobolowsky, Christopher Lloyd, Larry Miller, Anita Morris, Corbin Bernsen, Bobcat Goldthwait, Robert Walden, Rosemary Clooney, Dylan Baker, Billy Barty, Tracy Byrd, Candy Clark, Anne De Salvo, Jennifer Dundas, Bo Hopkins, Robert Klein, Harvey Korman, Joey Lawrence, Peter MacNicol, Jack Sheldon. Frenetic, wearisome farce about backstage murders on opening night of a Chicago radio network in 1939. Many talented performers are given nothing to do. Executive producer George Lucas apparently concocted this story years earlier. Arriscope. [PG]▼●◗

Radio On (1979-British) **101m.** **½ D: Chris Petit. David Beames, Lisa Kreuzer, Sting. Downbeat, rambling story of disc jockey who travels across Britain because of the mysterious circumstances of his brother's recent death. Written and directed by Petit, disciple of German director Wim

Wenders (film's associate producer); plot is only hinted at in this meditation on the bleakness of modern life.

Radium City (1987) **C/B&W-110m.** *** D: Carole Langer. Solid documentary about the young women of Ottawa, Ill., who in the 1920s were hired to paint radium on clock dials . . . and how they paid for their labor with their lives. A poignant, touching human drama.

Ra Expeditions, The (1971-Norwegian) **C-93m.** *** D: Lennart Ehrenborg. Narrated by Thor Heyerdahl and Roscoe Lee Browne. Exciting documentary about modern adventurer Heyerdahl's determination to cross the Atlantic in a papyrus boat, to prove theory that such a voyage was made thousands of years ago. Fine follow-up to KON-TIKI. [G]

Rafferty and the Gold Dust Twins (1975) **C-92m.** **½ D: Dick Richards. Alan Arkin, Sally Kellerman, Mackenzie Phillips, Alex Rocco, Charlie Martin Smith, Harry Dean Stanton. Appealing but aimless film about a pair of women who force nebbish Arkin to drive them to New Orleans from L.A. Retitled RAFFERTY AND THE HIGHWAY HUSTLERS for TV. Panavision. [R]▼

Raffles (1930) **72m.** *** D: Harry D'Arrast, George Fitzmaurice. Ronald Colman, Kay Francis, Bramwell Fletcher, Frances Dade, David Torrence, Alison Skipworth. Colman is his usual charming self in a breezy tale of gentleman thief who constantly eludes Scotland Yard. Good fun all the way. Screenplay by Sidney Howard, based on E. W. Hornung's novel *The Amateur Cracksman*, filmed in 1917 with John Barrymore, in 1925 with House Peters, remade in 1940 with David Niven. ▼●

Raffles (1940) **72m.** **½ D: Sam Wood. David Niven, Olivia de Havilland, Dudley Digges, Dame May Whitty, Douglas Walton, Lionel Pape. Niven is good but can't match Ronald Colman in this nearly scene-for-scene remake of the 1930 film about a gentleman thief (with a notably different finale). Medium-grade fluff.●

Rage (1966-U.S.-Mexican) **C-103m.** *½ D: Gilberto Gazcon. Glenn Ford, Stella Stevens, David Reynoso, Armando Silvestre, Ariadna Welter. Overstated drama of misanthropic doctor Ford who contracts rabies and races clock across Mexican desert to get help.

Rage (1972) **C-104m.** ** D: George C. Scott. George C. Scott, Richard Basehart, Martin Sheen, Barnard Hughes, Nicolas Beauvy, Paul Stevens. When peaceful rancher Scott's young son is killed by chemical testing, he seeks revenge on those responsible for accident. Good photography, but Scott's transition from nice-guy to killer isn't convincing. Scott's directorial debut. Panavision. [PG]▼

Rage at Dawn (1955) **C-87m.** ** D: Tim Whelan. Randolph Scott, Forrest Tucker, Mala Powers, J. Carrol Naish, Edgar Buchanan, Myron Healey. Ever-so-familiar Western about a secret agent (Scott) who goes undercover to ferret out the Reno brothers, a notorious outlaw gang, in post–Civil War Indiana.▼●

Rage: Carrie 2, The (1999) **C-104m.** ** D: Katt Shea. Emily Bergl, Jason London, Dylan Bruno, J. Smith-Cameron, Amy Irving, Zachery Ty Bryan, John Doe, Gordon Clapp, Rachel Blanchard, Mena Suvari. Years after CARRIE, another teenaged outsider in the same town is picked on by cruel fellow students, and again unleashes her telekinetic powers in climactic revenge. Well-acted but routine movie clumsily linked to the original. Irving's character, the only one from the original, is synthetically injected into the plot. [R]▼●◗

Rage in Harlem, A (1991) **C-115m.** **½ D: Bill Duke. Forest Whitaker, Gregory Hines, Robin Givens, Danny Glover, Zakes Mokae, Badja Djola, John Toles-Bey, Ron Taylor, Stack Pierce, George Wallace, T. K. Carter, Willard E. Pugh, Samm-Art Williams, Tyler Collins, Screamin' Jay Hawkins. Smooth operator from Mississippi (Givens) comes to Harlem to unload a stash of gold, and hooks up with a naive, nerdy mama's boy (Whitaker) who sees himself as her protector. Earnest attempt to recreate author Chester Himes' 1950s Harlem milieu doesn't quite come together in spite of some good performances. Can't hold a candle to COTTON COMES TO HARLEM (though the cop characters Gravedigger Jones and Coffin Ed reappear in this story). [R]▼●

Rage in Heaven (1941) **83m.** ** D: W. S. Van Dyke II. Robert Montgomery, Ingrid Bergman, George Sanders, Lucile Watson, Oscar Homolka, Philip Merivale, Matthew Boulton. Disappointing adaptation of James Hilton novel about mentally disturbed steel mill owner who plots unusual murder-revenge scheme; set in England.

Rage of Paris, The (1938) **75m.** *** D: Henry Koster. Danielle Darrieux, Douglas Fairbanks, Jr., Mischa Auer, Louis Hayward, Helen Broderick. Fast-talkers team up to use lovely Darrieux to snare rich husband; fast-paced comedy is fun, Darrieux a delight. Same team that Hollywoodized neophyte Deanna Durbin concocted this winsome image for the French actress. Look quickly for Mary Martin.▼

Rage of the Buccaneers, The (1962-Italian) **C-88m.** ** D: Mario Costa. Ricardo Montalban, Vincent Price, Giulia Rubini, Liana Orfei. Juvenile but bouncy yarn which is set more on land than at sea, with pirate Montalban vs. Price, villainous governor's secretary. Totalscope.

Rage to Live, A (1965) **101m.** ** D: Walter Grauman. Suzanne Pleshette, Bradford

Dillman, Ben Gazzara, Peter Graves, Bethel Leslie, James Gregory. Poor version of John O'Hara novel of free-swinging girl who tries marriage only to discover she still needs to have affairs with men. Panavision.

Raggedy Ann and Andy (1977) **C-85m.** *½ D: Richard Williams. Voices of Didi Conn, Mark Baker, Fred Stuthman, Joe Silver. Slow-moving, uninvolving children's cartoon with endless songs by Joe Raposo that stop action dead in its tracks. Appealing characters with nowhere to go; only highlight is Camel with Wrinkled Knees singing "Song Blue." Panavision. [G]▼

Raggedy Man (1981) **C-94m.** *** D: Jack Fisk. Sissy Spacek, Eric Roberts, William Sanderson, Tracey Walter, Sam Shepard, Henry Thomas, Carey Hollis, Jr. A young divorced woman with two children tries to forge a life for herself and her family in a small Texas town during WW2. Absorbing slice-of-life Americana with a misconceived melodramatic finale. Directorial debut for art director Fisk, who's Spacek's husband. [PG]▼●

Raging Bull (1980) **C/B&W-128m.** **** D: Martin Scorsese. Robert De Niro, Cathy Moriarty, Joe Pesci, Frank Vincent, Nicholas Colasanto, Theresa Saldana, John Turturro. Extraordinarily compelling look at prizefighter Jake La Motta, whose leading opponent outside the ring was always himself. That such an unappealing man could inspire so vivid a portrait is a tribute to the collaboration of Scorsese, De Niro, and writers Paul Schrader and Mardik Martin. There's not a false note in characterization or period detail. De Niro and editor Thelma Schoonmaker won richly deserved Academy Awards. [R]▼●◗

Raging Moon SEE: **Long Ago, Tomorrow**

Raging Tide, The (1951) **93m.** **½ D: George Sherman. Richard Conte, Shelley Winters, Stephen McNally, Alex Nicol, Charles Bickford. Stereotyped script, typecast acting make this murderer-on-the-run yarn tame. Adapted by Ernest K. Gann from his novel.

Ragman's Daughter, The (1972-British) **C-94m.** *** D: Harold Becker. Simon Rouse, Victoria Tennant, Patrick O'Connell, Leslie Sands. Stylishly filmed kitchen-sink drama written by Alan Sillitoe. Rouse is a young thief who falls in love with beautiful Tennant. Becker's first feature.

Ragtime (1981) **C-155m.** *** D: Milos Forman. James Cagney, Elizabeth McGovern, Howard E. Rollins, Jr., Mary Steenburgen, James Olson, Brad Dourif, Kenneth McMillan, Mandy Patinkin, Donald O'Connor, Pat O'Brien, Debbie Allen, Moses Gunn, Norman Mailer, Jeff Daniels, John Ratzenberger, Samuel L. Jackson, Fran Drescher, Michael Jeter. E. L. Doctorow's semi-fictional mosaic of 1906 America is glorious until Michael Weller's script narrows its focus to just one story thread: a black man's fanatical pursuit of justice. While the initial momentum is lost, there's still much to enjoy: fine performances (including Cagney's last in a theatrical film, after a 20-year hiatus), and Randy Newman's delightful score. Jeff Daniels' film debut. Todd-AO 35. [PG]▼●

Raid, The (1954) **C-83m.** *** D: Hugo Fregonese. Van Heflin, Anne Bancroft, Richard Boone, Lee Marvin, Tommy Rettig, James Best, Peter Graves, Claude Akins. Well-handled (and true) story of Confederate prisoners escaping from jail in upper New England, with Bancroft and Rettig trying to snafu their marauding.

Raiders, The (1952) **C-80m.** **½ D: Lesley Selander. Richard Conte, Viveca Lindfors, Barbara Britton, Hugh O'Brian, Richard Martin, William Reynolds. Sometimes with-it oater about judge during California gold rush days, leading a land-grabbing gang. Retitled: RIDERS OF VENGEANCE.

Raiders, The (1963) **C-75m.** **½ D: Herschel Daugherty. Robert Culp, Brian Keith, Judi Meredith, James McMullan, Alfred Ryder, Simon Oakland. Enthusiastic cast helps this story of cattle drives and the railroad expansion westward.

Raiders of Old California (1957) **72m.** BOMB D: Albert Gannaway. Jim Davis, Arleen Whelan, Lee Van Cleef, Louis Jean Heydt. Minor Western set in the 1850s.

Raiders of the Lost Ark (1981) **C-115m.** **** D: Steven Spielberg. Harrison Ford, Karen Allen, Wolf Kahler, Paul Freeman, Ronald Lacey, John Rhys-Davies, Denholm Elliott, Anthony Higgins, Alfred Molina. A roller-coaster ride of a movie, rekindling the spirit of Saturday matinee serials but outdoing them for genuine thrills and chills. Ford plays Indiana Jones, an archeologist-adventurer who goes globe-trotting in search of a unique religious artifact and runs into bloodcurdling danger every step of the way. Perhaps a bit too much at times, but why carp? Conceived by Spielberg and George Lucas, with Philip Kaufman; scripted by Lawrence Kasdan. Visual effects, editing, sound effects editing, and art direction-set decoration all earned Oscars. Followed by two INDIANA JONES films and TV series *The Young Indiana Jones Chronicles*. Panavision. [PG]▼●

Raiders of the Seven Seas (1953) **C-88m.** **½ D: Sidney Salkow. John Payne, Donna Reed, Gerald Mohr, Lon Chaney, Jr. Pirate Barbarossa saves countess from marriage to cutthroat, eventually falls in love.

Raid on Entebbe (1977) **C-150m. TVM** D: Irvin Kershner. Peter Finch, Charles Bronson, Horst Buchholz, Martin Balsam, John Saxon, Jack Warden, Sylvia Sidney, Yaphet Kotto, Robert Loggia, James

Woods, Dinah Manoff. Intelligent drama about Israeli commando rescue of hijacked hostages at Entebbe, Uganda, on July 4, 1976. Finch's last film garnered him an Emmy nomination. Covers same ground as VICTORY AT ENTEBBE and OPERATION THUNDERBOLT. Above average.▼

Raid on Rommel (1971) **C-99m.** *½ D: Henry Hathaway. Richard Burton, John Colicos, Clinton Greyn, Wolfgang Preiss. Poor excuse to utilize old desert footage (mostly from TOBRUK) and new faces in worn-out WW2 actioner. Techniscope. [PG]▼●◗

Railroaded! (1947) **72m.** *** D: Anthony Mann. John Ireland, Sheila Ryan, Hugh Beaumont, Ed Kelly, Jane Randolph, Keefe Brasselle. Another tight, well-made, low-budget film noir by Anthony Mann. Ireland is a ruthless gangster after Ryan; Beaumont is the cop trying to save her. ▼●

Railroad Man, The SEE: **Man of Iron** (1956)

Rails Into Laramie (1954) **C-81m.** ** D: Jesse Hibbs. John Payne, Mari Blanchard, Dan Duryea, Joyce MacKenzie, Barton MacLane, Lee Van Cleef. Pat movie of Payne's efforts to clean up title town and keep railroad construction moving westward.

Railway Children, The (1972-British) **C-102m.** *** D: Lionel Jeffries. Dinah Sheridan, Bernard Cribbins, William Mervyn, Iain Cuthbertson, Jenny Agutter, Gary Warren. Charming story of youthful trio whose one goal is to clear their father of false espionage prison sentence. Lovely Yorkshire locales add to overall effectiveness. From the novel by E. Nesbit. [G]▼

Railway Station Man, The (1992-British) **C-100m. TVM** D: Michael Whyte. Julie Christie, Donald Sutherland, John Lynch, Frank MacCusker, Mark Tandy, Niall Cusack. Christie mesmerizes as an Irish war widow who, pining for her son who has joined the IRA, falls for Sutherland, a reclusive hook-handed American who has taken up residence in the town railway station. Stark but stunning adaptation by playwright Shelagh Delaney of Jennifer Johnston's novel. Made for cable. Above average.▼●

Rain (1932) **93m.** **½ D: Lewis Milestone. Joan Crawford, Walter Huston, William Gargan, Guy Kibbee, Walter Catlett, Beulah Bondi. Considered a flop in 1932, this version of Maugham's story looks better today. Crawford is good as South Seas island trollop confronted by fire-and-brimstone preacher Huston. Director Milestone does gymnastics with camera during stagier scenes; an interesting antique. Previously filmed as SADIE THOMPSON, then again as DIRTY GERTIE FROM HARLEM U.S.A. and MISS SADIE THOMPSON. Some prints run 77m.▼◗

Rainbow, The (1989-British) **C-104m.** **½ D: Ken Russell. Sammi Davis, Amanda Donohoe, Paul McGann, Christopher Gable, David Hemmings, Glenda Jackson. Director Russell's most restrained film in years (a relative term) is a prequel to his hit adaptation of D.H. Lawrence's *Women in Love*, with Davis as a sheltered young schoolteacher who's taken under the wing (sexually and otherwise) of worldly Donohoe. Many beautiful and striking moments don't quite gel, but still worth watching. Jackson appears as the mother of the character she played in WOMEN IN LOVE. [R]▼●

Rainbow Island (1944) **C-97m.** **½ D: Ralph Murphy. Dorothy Lamour, Eddie Bracken, Gil Lamb, Barry Sullivan, Anne Revere, Olga San Juan, Elena Verdugo, Yvonne De Carlo, Reed Hadley, Marc Lawrence. Good cast main asset in musical comedy of merchant marines stranded on island with beautiful natives. Lamour, in her umpteenth sarong, wisely keeps her tongue in her cheek.

Rainbow Jacket, The (1954-British) **C-99m.** ** D: Basil Dearden. Kay Walsh, Bill Owen, Fella Edmonds, Robert Morley, Wilfrid Hyde-White, Honor Blackman. Colorful racetrack sequences spark this predictable study of Owen, veteran jockey gone wrong, who teaches Edmonds how to race properly.

Rainbow 'Round My Shoulder (1952) **C-78m.** ** D: Richard Quine. Frankie Laine, Billy Daniels, Charlotte Austin, Ida Moore, Arthur Franz, Barbara Whiting, Lloyd Corrigan. Young girl wants to be a movie star, her socialite grandma forbids it, and no surprises ensue. Blah musical written by Quine and Blake Edwards.

Rainbow Thief, The (1990) **C-92m.** *½ D: Alexandro Jodorowsky. Peter O'Toole, Omar Sharif, Christopher Lee, Jude Alderson, Jane Chaplan. Impenetrable parable about an eccentric prince (and heir to a fortune) who lives underground, aided and abetted by a colorful thief. There may be some point to all of this, but it would require too much time to figure out. There's a reason this film never made it to theaters, despite its cast and director.▼

Rainbow Trail, The (1925) **58m.** *** D: Lynn Reynolds. Tom Mix, Anne Cornwall, George Bancroft, Lucien Littlefield, Mark Hamilton, Vivien Oakland. Sequel to RIDERS OF THE PURPLE SAGE, another robust Zane Grey tale about man who determines to penetrate isolated Paradise Valley, where his uncle trapped himself with a young woman. Handsome production of oft-filmed story.

Rainbow Warrior (1994-U.S.-New Zealand) **C-93m.** *½ D: Michael Tuchner. Jon Voight, Sam Neill, Bruno Lawrence,

Kerry Fox, John Callen, Stacey Pickren. True story of 1985 bombing of a Greenpeace boat in New Zealand and the ensuing investigation. Complex tale of international conflict/intrigue is uninvolving. Neill gives a standout performance as a police superintendent. [PG]▼●

Raining Stones (1993-British) **C-90m.** *** D: Kenneth Loach. Bruce Jones, Julie Brown, Ricky Tomlinson, Tom Hickey, Gemma Phoenix. Riveting drama focusing on a struggling out-of-work laborer (Jones) in grimy Manchester, England, a good Catholic who does whatever he can to scrape together enough money to support his wife and daughter. When faced with purchasing his child's communion dress, he unknowingly borrows its cost from a vicious, usurious loan shark. With telling irony, Loach vividly captures the frustrations and anger of honest workingfolk. ▼◗

Rainmaker, The (1956) **C-121m.** *** D: Joseph Anthony. Burt Lancaster, Katharine Hepburn, Wendell Corey, Lloyd Bridges, Earl Holliman, Cameron Prud'homme, Wallace Ford. Lancaster is in top form as a charismatic con man who offers hope to a Southwestern town beset by drought, and a woman whose life is at a crossroads. Hepburn is wonderful. N. Richard Nash play was later musicalized on Broadway as *110 in the Shade*. VistaVision.▼●

Rainmaker, The (1997) **C-135m.** *** D: Francis Ford Coppola. Matt Damon, Danny DeVito, Claire Danes, Jon Voight, Mickey Rourke, Mary Kay Place, Danny Glover, Teresa Wright, Johnny Whitworth, Dean Stockwell, Virginia Madsen, Roy Scheider, Randy Travis, Andrew Shue. Solid, surefooted adaptation of John Grisham's bestseller about an idealistic lawyer, fresh from school, who goes to work for a shameless ambulance-chaser, but focuses on the case most important to him: exposing an insurance company's refusal to pay a claim for a young man who is dying of leukemia. In the midst of this, he finds himself falling in love with a battered woman. Cast to perfection, and filmed on location in Memphis . . . the finale, though, seems curiously subdued. Coproduced by Michael Douglas. Officially titled JOHN GRISHAM'S THE RAINMAKER. Panavision. [PG-13]▼●◗

Rain Man (1988) **C-133m.** *** D: Barry Levinson. Dustin Hoffman, Tom Cruise, Valeria Golino, Jerry Molen, Jack Murdock, Michael D. Roberts, Bonnie Hunt. Young, self-centered hotshot goes home to the Midwest for his father's funeral, and learns not only that he's been cut out of his inheritance, but that he has a grown brother who's autistic, and who's been kept in an institution for most of his life. The balance of the film details the growing relationship between the two men. Top-drawer performances from Hoffman, as the idiot savant, and Cruise, as his selfish sibling, make this a must-see, even though the story meanders and becomes predictable. Director Levinson is the psychiatrist near the end. Winner of Oscars for Best Picture, Director, Actor (Hoffman), and Screenplay (Ronald Bass and Barry Morrow). [R] ▼●◗

Rain or Shine (1930) **92m.** **½ D: Frank Capra. Joe Cook, Louise Fazenda, Joan Peers, Dave Chasen, William Collier, Jr., Tom Howard. Curious little circus film spotlights puckish Broadway clown Cook (and his stooges Chasen and Howard) in a storyline so thin it's hardly there. Personality and Capra's early talkie technique make this worth seeing for film buffs.

Rain People, The (1969) **C-102m.** *** D: Francis Ford Coppola. James Caan, Shirley Knight, Robert Duvall, Marya Zimmet, Tom Aldredge, Laurie Crewes. Pregnant Long Island housewife, unable to take married life, flees husband and picks up simple-minded football player on the road. Strong acting and direction triumph over weak script in film whose subject matter was years ahead of its time. [R]▼

Rains Came, The (1939) **104m.** **½ D: Clarence Brown. Myrna Loy, Tyrone Power, George Brent, Brenda Joyce, Nigel Bruce, Maria Ouspenskaya, Joseph Schildkraut, Mary Nash, Jane Darwell, Marjorie Rambeau, Henry Travers, H. B. Warner, Laura Hope Crews. Louis Bromfield novel reduced to Hollywood hokum, with married socialite Loy setting out to seduce dedicated Indian surgeon Power. Outstanding earthquake and flood scenes; the special effects earned an Academy Award. Remade as THE RAINS OF RANCHIPUR.▼

Rains of Ranchipur, The (1955) **C-104m.** **½ D: Jean Negulesco. Lana Turner, Richard Burton, Fred MacMurray, Joan Caulfield, Michael Rennie, Eugenie Leontovich. Superficial remake of THE RAINS CAME; story of wife of Englishman having affair with Hindu doctor. CinemaScope.

Raintree County (1957) **C-168m.** *** D: Edward Dmytryk. Elizabeth Taylor, Montgomery Clift, Eva Marie Saint, Lee Marvin, Nigel Patrick, Rod Taylor, Agnes Moorehead, Walter Abel. Humongous MGM attempt to outdo GWTW, with Taylor as spoiled Civil War-era belle who discovers marriage isn't all it's cracked up to be. Solid acting and memorable Johnny Green score help compensate for rambling, over-long script; Clift was disfigured in near-fatal car accident during production, and his performance understandably suffers for it. Reissued on video in 1999 with 15m. additional footage from ''Roadshow Version.'' MGM Camera 65.▼●

Rain Without Thunder (1992) **C-86m.** *** D: Gary Bennett. Betty Buckley, Jeff Daniels, Frederic Forrest, Graham Greene, Linda Hunt, Carolyn McCormick, Austin

Pendleton, Alyssa Rallo, Ali Thomas, Steve Zahn, Robert Earl Jones. Unique futuristic drama, told in documentary style and set in an America in which abortion is illegal. Young Thomas is incarcerated for aborting her pregnancy, and her mother (Buckley) is also put behind bars, convicted under New York State's new Unborn Child Kidnapping Act. Chilling (and politically loaded) tale. [PG-13] ▼

Raise the Red Lantern (1991-China-Taiwan-Hong Kong) **C-125m.** **** D: Zhang Yimou. Gong Li, Ma Jingwu, He Caifei, Cao Cuifeng, Jin Shuyuan, Kong Lin, Ding Weimin, Cui Zhihgang. Striking look at the life of a young concubine in 1920s China, as university-educated girl (Gong Li) is sent to feudal nobleman's palatial home to become his newest wife. The relationships between her and her predecessors—all of whom live on the premises—and the interaction among the women, the servants, and their master are brilliantly played out. An extraordinary view of sex, loyalty, intrigue, and female bonding. Deliberately paced, but worth watching for the changes in emotion that register on actress Gong Li's face alone. Screenplay by Ni Zhen, from a novel by Su Tong. ▼●

Raise the Titanic! (1980-British) **C-112m.** *½ D: Jerry Jameson. Jason Robards, Richard Jordan, David Selby, Anne Archer, Alec Guinness, J. D. Cannon. Long, dull adaptation of Clive Cussler's best-seller about intrigue leading to the biggest salvage job of all time. Silly plotting and laughable dialogue undermine excitement of climactic ship-raising. Technovision. [PG] ▼●

Raising a Riot (1954-British) **C-90m.** ** D: Wendy Toye. Kenneth More, Ronald Squire, Mandy Miller, Shelagh Fraser, Bill Shine. Predictable situation comedy of More, on vacation in countryside, trying to cope with his rambunctious children.

Raising Arizona (1987) **C-92m.** ***½ D: Joel Coen. Nicolas Cage, Holly Hunter, Trey Wilson, John Goodman, William Forsythe, Sam McMurray, Frances McDormand, Randall (Tex) Cobb, M. Emmet Walsh. Formidably flaky comedy about an odd couple (chronic convenience-store robber Cage and former law-enforcement officer Hunter) who decide to kidnap one of a set of quintuplets, since they can't have a child of their own. Aggressively wacked-out sense of humor may not be for all tastes, but it's a heady mix of irony and slapstick. Look out for those chase scenes! Written by Ethan and Joel Coen; spry cinematography by Barry Sonnenfeld and music by Carter Burwell. [PG-13] ▼●◗

Raising Cain (1992) **C-95m.** ** D: Brian De Palma. John Lithgow, Lolita Davidovich, Steven Bauer, Frances Sternhagen, Gregg Henry, Tom Bower, Mel Harris, Teri Austin, Gabrielle Carteris, Barton Heyman. Lithgow is the whole show here—literally—with more roles than you can count in this over-the-top thriller about a pair of twin brothers who'll stop at nothing to procure children for their father's scientific experiments. Tongue-in-cheek De Palma exercise (with nods to Hitchcock, Welles, and Michael Powell) is laced with satire, but the chills—and chuckles—don't add up to much. Not for the faint-hearted. [R] ▼●◗

Raising the Wind (1961-British) **C-91m.** **½ D: Gerald Thomas. James Robertson Justice, Leslie Phillips, Sidney James, Paul Massie, Kenneth Williams. Zany shenanigans of eccentric group of students at a London school of music; well paced.

Raisin in the Sun, A (1961) **128m.** **** D: Daniel Petrie. Sidney Poitier, Claudia McNeil, Ruby Dee, Diana Sands, Ivan Dixon, John Fiedler, Louis Gossett. Lorraine Hansberry play receives perceptive handling by outstanding cast in drama of black Chicago family's attempts to find sense in their constrained existence. Remade for TV in 1991. ▼●◗

Rake's Progress, The SEE: **Notorious Gentleman**

Rally 'Round the Flag, Boys! (1958) **C-106m.** **½ D: Leo McCarey. Paul Newman, Joanne Woodward, Joan Collins, Jack Carson, Dwayne Hickman, Tuesday Weld, Gale Gordon. Disappointing film of Max Shulman's book about small community in uproar over projected missile base. CinemaScope.

Rambling Rose (1991) **C-112m.** *** D: Martha Coolidge. Laura Dern, Robert Duvall, Diane Ladd, Lukas Haas, John Heard, Kevin Conway, Robert J. Burke, Lisa Jakub, Evan Lockwood. Evocative tale set in 1930s Georgia, with Dern as an oversexed, lost-soul of a girl who comes to work for a genteel family headed by Duvall and Ladd. Colorful, nicely detailed, and well-acted, with many pleasant surprises along the way. Ladd and Dern were the first real-life mother and daughter to be nominated for Oscars in the same year. Screenplay by Calder Willingham from his autobiographical novel. [R] ▼●◗

Rambo: First Blood Part II (1985) **C-95m.** ** D: George P. Cosmatos. Sylvester Stallone, Richard Crenna, Charles Napier, Julia Nickson, Steven Berkoff, Martin Kove. Comic-book action saga of one-man army who goes to Cambodia in search of American MIAs and finds he's been duped by Uncle Sam. Never boring but incredibly dumb; if one were to take it seriously, it would also be offensive, as it exploits real-life frustrations of MIA families and Vietnam vets. Followed by RAMBO III. Panavision. [R] ▼●◗

Rambo III (1988) **C-101m.** **½ D: Peter Macdonald. Sylvester Stallone, Richard

Crenna, Marc de Jonge, Kurtwood Smith, Spiros Focas, Sasson Gabai. A definite improvement over PART II, this one remains firmly footed in the genre of Idiot Action Movies, as our brawny hero goes behind Russian-dominated battle lines in Afghanistan to rescue his friend and former superior (Crenna) from a prison fortress. Lots of explosions to keep things lively—and some (unintentionally?) hilarious dialogue too. J-D-C Scope. [R]▼●◗

Ramona (1936) **C-90m.** ** D: Henry King. Loretta Young, Don Ameche, Kent Taylor, Pauline Frederick, Jane Darwell, Katherine DeMille. Oft-told tale doesn't wear well, with aristocratic Spanish girl Young and outcast Indian Ameche in love and shunned by society. Settings are picturesque.

Rampage (1963) **C-98m.** **½ D: Phil Karlson. Robert Mitchum, Elsa Martinelli, Jack Hawkins, Sabu, Cely Carillo, Emile Genest. German gamehunter (Hawkins), his mistress (Martinelli), and hunting guide (Mitchum) form love triangle, with men battling for Elsa. Elmer Bernstein's score is memorable.

Rampage (1992) **C-97m.** ** D: William Friedkin. Michael Biehn, Alex McArthur, Nicholas Campbell, Deborah van Valkenburgh, John Harkins, Art La Fleur, Billy Green Bush, Royce D. Applegate, Grace Zabriskie, Carlos Palomino, Andy Romano. A prosecutor has to prove that a serial killer's unspeakably heinous crimes were the product of a legally sane mind. Very rough, not for the squeamish, and not for too many others, either. Shot in 1987. McArthur is exceptionally creepy as the killer. [R]▼●

Rampage at Apache Wells (1966-German) **C-90m.** ** D: Harold Philipps. Stewart Granger, Pierre Brice, Macha Meril, Harold Leipnitz. Granger stars as Old Shatterhand, who fights for rights of Indians taken in by crooked white men. Adequate acting but atrocious dubbing. Ultrascope.

Ramparts of Clay (1971-French-Algerian) **C-85m.** *** D: Jean-Louis Bertucelli. Leila Schenna. Intriguing film about Tunisian woman, disillusioned with her way of life, who becomes involved with strike between a wealthy company and poor villagers. Very strong for patient, critical viewers; for others, boredom. [PG]▼

Rampo (1994-Japanese) **C-100m.** *** D: Kazuyoshi Okuyama. Naoto Takenaka, Michiko Hada, Masahiro Motoki, Mikijiro Hira. Japanese mystery writer Edogawa Rampo hears of a bizarre murder that is eerily close to the plot of one of his banned murder thrillers. When he meets the widow of the murdered man, he discovers her to be exactly like his fictional heroine. This elegant and lush film was reshot (more than 60 percent new footage) after producer Okuyama was dissatisfied with first director Rentaro Mayuzumi's efforts. Aka THE MYSTERY OF RAMPO. [R]▼

Ramrod (1947) **94m.** **½ D: Andre de Toth. Veronica Lake, Joel McCrea, Arleen Whelan, Don DeFore, Preston Foster, Charles Ruggles, Donald Crisp, Lloyd Bridges. Fairly good Western of territorial dispute between ranch-owner Lake and her father (Ruggles). Good supporting cast.▼

Ran (1985-Japanese-French) **C-161m.** ***½ D: Akira Kurosawa. Tatsuya Nakadai, Akira Terao, Jinpachi Nezu, Daisuke Ryu, Mieko Harada, Peter, Hisashi Igawa. Beautifully filmed adaptation of Shakespeare's *King Lear*, with Nakadai as a warlord who turns over his domain to his eldest son, inducing a power struggle by his two younger sons. Slowly paced and overly expository at the start, epic picks up with two superb battle scenes. Harada is excellent in supporting role as the most evil of women, getting her just desserts in violent fashion. Oscar winner for Costume Design. [R]▼●◗

Rancho Deluxe (1975) **C-93m.** ***½ D: Frank Perry. Jeff Bridges, Sam Waterston, Elizabeth Ashley, Charlene Dallas, Clifton James, Slim Pickens, Harry Dean Stanton, Richard Bright, Patti D'Arbanville. Off-beat present-day comedy centers on two casual cattle rustlers; cult favorite written by Thomas McGuane (92 IN THE SHADE), with music by Jimmy Buffett (who also appears in the film). TV version runs 95m. [R]▼●

Rancho Notorious (1952) **C-89m.** *** D: Fritz Lang. Marlene Dietrich, Arthur Kennedy, Mel Ferrer, Lloyd Gough, Gloria Henry, William Frawley, Jack Elam, George Reeves. Entertaining, unusual Western with Kennedy looking for murderer of his sweetheart, ending up at Marlene's bandit hideout. Colorful characters spice up routine story by Daniel Taradash.▼●

Random Harvest (1942) **126m.** ***½ D: Mervyn LeRoy. Ronald Colman, Greer Garson, Philip Dorn, Susan Peters, Henry Travers, Reginald Owen, Bramwell Fletcher, Margaret Wycherly, Ann Richards. Colman is left an amnesiac after WW1, and saved from life in a mental institution by vivacious music-hall entertainer Garson. Supremely entertaining James Hilton story given top MGM treatment, with Colman and Garson at their best. Screenplay by Claudine West, George Froeschel, Arthur Wimperis, and Hilton.▼●

Random Hearts (1999) **C-133m.** *½ D: Sydney Pollack. Harrison Ford, Kristin Scott Thomas, Charles S. Dutton, Bonnie Hunt, Dennis Haysbert, Sydney Pollack, Paul Guilfoyle, Peter Coyote, Bill Cobbs, Richard Jenkins, Edie Falco. Sub-par political movie, sub-par D.C. cop movie and sub-par romance get bludgeoned into one in this critical/commercial flop about a police sergeant and congresswoman who discover that their mates—recently killed in the same airliner crash—were having an affair.

Gloomy, lugubrious, heavily altered adaptation of Warren Adler's novel suffers from one of the rare constipated Ford performances. Every once in a while it wakes up long enough to remember it's an Internal Affairs movie and that a few heads have to be bashed. [R]▼◗

Rangers of Fortune (1940) **80m.** **½ D: Sam Wood. Fred MacMurray, Albert Dekker, Gilbert Roland, Patricia Morison, Dick Foran, Joseph Schildkraut. Smartly-whipped-together yarn of trio fleeing Mexicans, stopping off in Southwestern town to offer assistance.

Ransom (1956) **109m.** **½ D: Alex Segal. Glenn Ford, Donna Reed, Leslie Nielsen, Juano Hernandez, Alexander Scourby, Juanita Moore, Robert Keith. Brooding narrative of Ford's efforts to rescue his son who's been kidnapped. Remade in 1996.

Ransom (1977) **C-90m.** **½ D: Richard Compton. Oliver Reed, Deborah Raffin, Stuart Whitman, Jim Mitchum, John Ireland, Paul Koslo. Pretty good programmer about a town's efforts to catch a killer. Originally titled ASSAULT ON PARADISE, then MANIAC.▼

Ransom (1996) **C-120m.** *** D: Ron Howard. Mel Gibson, Rene Russo, Gary Sinise, Delroy Lindo, Lili Taylor, Brawley Nolte, Liev Schreiber, Evan Handler, Donnie Wahlberg, Dan Hedaya. Gripping thriller about a ragged team of kidnappers who snatch the son of a self-made millionaire; soon, what should have been a standard kidnap-and-ransom transaction becomes a dangerous game of cat and mouse between the tycoon and the cocky ringleader. Plenty of twists and turns in this remake of the 1956 film of the same name. That's Nick Nolte's son as the victim. Coscenarist Richard Price appears briefly as Sinise's partner in an early scene. [R]▼●◗

Rapa Nui (1994) **C-107m.** *½ D: Kevin Reynolds. Jason Scott Lee, Esai Morales, Sandrine Holt, Zac Wallace, George Henare, Eru Potaka-Dewes. Lumbering, highly romanticized saga of Easter Island ("Rapa Nui"), the remote southern Pacific outpost whose mammoth human-faced statues have long baffled historians. Set in 1680, prior to Dutch colonization, with hero Lee (of the Long Ear tribe) and villain Morales (of the Short Ears) as rivals since boyhood, now facing civil war. Climactic endurance test—a grueling race on land and sea—resembles one of those splashy MTV "sports" events. Coproduced by Kevin Costner. Panavision. [R]▼●

Rape of Love (1977-French) **C-117m.** ** D: Yannick Bellon. Nathalie Nell, Alain Foures, Michele Simonnet, Pierre Arditi, Daniel Auteuil, Bernard Granger. Nurse Nell is raped by four drunken jerks, but that's not the end of her ordeal. Not ineffective as a consciousness-raising tool, but still overly preachy; director Bellon has a tendency to depict all her male characters as insensitive chauvinists.▼

Rape of Malaya SEE: **Town Like Alice, A**

Rape Squad (1974) **C-90m.** **½ D: Bob Kelljan. Jo Ann Harris, Peter Brown, Jennifer Lee, Steve Kanaly, Lada Edmund, Jr. Well-told vigilante tale has raped women banding together to avenge themselves on sadistic Brown, who gets off by forcing women to sing "Jingle Bells" as he assaults them. Video title: ACT OF VENGEANCE. [R]▼

Rapid Fire (1992) **C-95m.** ** D: Dwight H. Little. Brandon Lee, Powers Boothe, Nick Mancuso, Raymond J. Barry, Kate Hodge, Tzi Ma, Tony Longo, Michael Paul Chan, Dustin Nguyen, John Vickery. Showcase for Bruce Lee's handsome son is more like *Enter the Lizard,* though its script is freewheeling enough to include stopoffs in a nude modeling class, an abandoned bowling alley, and Beijing's Tiananmen Square. A bounty of bullets, but the only love scene backs its standard gauzy navel-'n'-nipple expedition with a strident guitar and an unfortunately named tune: "I Can't Find My Way." Mancuso's amusing bad guy is a standout. [R]▼●

Rappin' (1985) **C-92m.** ** D: Joel Silberg. Mario Van Peebles, Tasia Valenza, Charles Flohe, Leo O'Brien, Eriq La Salle, Richie Abanes, Kadeem Hardison, Harry Goz. Just what the world needs, another breakdancing–rap music musical. This one chronicles the plight of breakdancer/ex-con Van Peebles and his conflicts with street gangster Flohe and contractor Goz. [PG]▼

Rapture (1965-French) **104m.** *** D: John Guillermin. Melvyn Douglas, Dean Stockwell, Patricia Gozzi, Gunnel Lindblom, Leslie Sands. Intensive, sensitive account of Gozzi's tragic romance with Stockwell, a man on the run. CinemaScope.

Rapture, The (1991) **C-102m.** *** D: Michael Tolkin. Mimi Rogers, Patrick Bauchau, David Duchovny, Kimberly Cullum, Will Patton, James Le Gros. Beautiful, hedonistic young woman with droning, dead-end job opts for super-Fundamentalist religious fanaticism. Singular drama about one woman's literal ascension to heaven features swinging group sex, one genuinely shocking maternal act, and a straight-faced cameo by at least one Horseman of the Apocalypse. Not for every taste, this much-debated film truly rushes in where virtually no others have dared to tread. Scripted by first-time director Tolkin. Rogers gives a four-barrelled performance. [R]▼●

Rare-Book Murder, The SEE: **Fast Company** (1938)

Rare Breed, The (1966) **C-108m.** *** D: Andrew V. McLaglen. James Stewart, Maureen O'Hara, Brian Keith, Juliet Mills, Jack Elam, Ben Johnson, Don Galloway. Cowhand Stewart is changed by British O'Hara's conviction that her Hereford bull, new to Texas, will produce better cattle. Keith (in red wig and beard) has a grand time as a Scottish rancher. Odd part-comedy Western on the unusual subject of improving cattle breeds. Hampered only by too much obvious studio shooting. Panavision. ▼

Rare Breed, A (1981) **C-94m.** *½ D: David Nelson. George Kennedy, Forrest Tucker, Tracy Vaccaro, Tom Hallick, Don DeFore. Old-fashioned story of a girl and her horse, with unconvincing depiction of the real-life incident of racehorse Carnauba kidnapped in Italy for ransom. Cute, squeaky-clean tomboy Vaccaro became a *Playboy* magazine Playmate two years after filming this family picture, whose director is the former actor offspring of Ozzie and Harriet. [PG]▼

Rascal (1969) **C-85m.** **½ D: Norman Tokar. Steve Forrest, Bill Mumy, Pamela Toll, Bettye Ackerman, Elsa Lanchester, Henry Jones. Disney adaptation of Sterling North's well-regarded autobiographical novel about his boyhood friendship with raccoon; reworked to Disney formula, with pleasant but predictable results. [G]

Rashomon (1950-Japanese) **88m.** **** D: Akira Kurosawa. Toshiro Mifune, Machiko Kyo, Masayuki Mori, Takashi Shimura. Kurosawa's first huge international success is superlative study of truth and human nature; four people involved in a rape-murder tell varying accounts of what happened. The film's very title has become part of our language. Oscar winner as Best Foreign Film. Remade as THE OUTRAGE.▼●

Rasputin (1985-Russian) **C-107m.** *** D: Elem Klimov. Alexei Petrenko, Anatoly Romashin, Velta Linei, Alice Freindlikh. Complex, impressive drama with Petrenko appropriately (and at times brilliantly) oily as the famed mad monk. A good film which might have been great if so many hands had not tinkered with it. It allegedly was completed in 1977, screened at the Moscow Film Festival in 1981 (at 148m.), and barred from the West until 1985. Sovscope.▼

Rasputin (1996) **C-105m. TVM** D: Uli Edel. Alan Rickman, Greta Scacchi, Ian McKellen, David Warner, John Wood, James Frain, Julian Curry. Opulent, revisionist retelling of the tale of the Mad Monk who befriended and advised Russia's last royal family, with a wicked, wild-eyed performance by Rickman as the drunken, womanizing mystic. Equally impressive: McKellen's compassionate Tsar Nicholas. This take, by writer Peter Pruce, has Stolypin, the Tsar's prime minister (John Wood), part of the conspiracy to do in Rasputin in 1916, Stolypin's own murder in 1911 notwithstanding. Made for cable. Above average.▼●

Rasputin and the Empress (1932) **123m.** *** D: Richard Boleslavsky. John, Ethel and Lionel Barrymore, Ralph Morgan, Diana Wynyard, Tad Alexander, C. Henry Gordon, Edward Arnold, Jean Parker. Good drama that should have been great, with all three Barrymores in colorful roles, unfolding story of mad monk's plotting against Russia. Contrary to expectations, it's Lionel, not John, who plays Rasputin. The three Barrymores' only film together; Ethel's talkie debut. Wynyard's first film.▼●

Rasputin—the Mad Monk (1966-British) **C-92m.** ** D: Don Sharp. Christopher Lee, Barbara Shelley, Richard Pasco, Francis Matthews. Confused historical drama of "monk" who actually controlled Russia before Revolution. Script uncommonly bad; Lee's performance manages to redeem film. CinemaScope.▼●◗

Ratboy (1986) **C-105m.** *½ D: Sondra Locke. Sondra Locke, Robert Townsend, Christopher Hewett, Larry Hankin, Gerrit Graham, Louie Anderson. Window dresser Locke stumbles across a half-man, half-rat—then tries to parlay him into show-biz success. Locke's directorial debut is technically competent, but film plays like an E.T./ELEPHANT MAN derivation that's no longer fresh. Barely released. [PG-13]▼

Ratings Game, The (1984) **C-102m. TVM** D: Danny DeVito. Danny DeVito, Rhea Pearlman, Gerrit Graham, Kevin McCarthy, Jayne Meadows, Steve Allen, George Wendt, Ronny Graham, Huntz Hall, Barry Corbin, Jerry Seinfeld, Michael Richards. Rollicking send-up of the television business and its incessant quest for ratings. Danny's a third-rate producer turned fawned-over power broker when his truly awful idea becomes the biggest hit since the invention of the wheel. Written by Jim Mulholland and Michael Barrie. Made for cable. Aka THE MOGUL. Above average.▼●

Rationing (1944) **93m.** **½ D: Willis Goldbeck. Wallace Beery, Marjorie Main, Donald Meek, Gloria Dickson, Henry O'Neill, Connie Gilchrist. Butcher in small town is main character in story of problems during WW2; typical Beery vehicle.

Raton Pass (1951) **84m.** **½ D: Edwin L. Marin. Dennis Morgan, Patricia Neal, Steve Cochran, Scott Forbes, Dorothy Hart. Middling Warner Bros. Western, with Morgan and Neal married couple fighting each other for cattle empire.

Rat Pack, The (1998) **C-118m. TVM** D: Rob Cohen. Ray Liotta, Joe Mantegna, Don Cheadle, Angus Macfadyen, William Petersen, Bobby Slayton, Željko Ivanek, Dan O'Herlihy, Veronica Cartwright. Sinatra's ring-a-ding days with his showbiz pals seem to be a never-ending bachelor party during the late '50s and early '60s, in a story of how power, celebrity and politics collided. A surprisingly watchable yarn—even for those who remember the Real Thing. Liotta's miscasting as the "Rat Pack" leader is offset by Mantegna's on-the-mark Dean Martin and Cheadle's terrific Sammy Davis. Made for cable TV. Average.▼◗

Rat Race, The (1960) **C-105m.** *** D: Robert Mulligan. Tony Curtis, Debbie Reynolds, Jack Oakie, Kay Medford, Don Rickles, Joe Bushkin. Comedy-drama of would-be musician (Curtis) and dancer (Reynolds) coming to N.Y.C., platonically sharing an apartment, and falling in love. Nice comic cameos by Oakie and Medford. Script by Garson Kanin, from his play.

Rats, The SEE: **Deadly Eyes**

Rat's Tale, A (1997-German) **C-89m.** ** D: Michael F. Huse. Lauren Hutton, Beverly D'Angelo, Jerry Stiller, Josef Ostendorf; voices of Dee Bradley Baker, Lynsey Bartilson. A colony of rats living underground in N.Y.C. is threatened by a greedy developer who wants to tear down their wharf—and in the meantime is using a toxic pesticide. Furry marionettes star in this English-language version of a German film with a handful of live actors and occasional special effects. Amusing for young children, but its pacing and European sensibility may not suit some fidgety viewers. Based on the award-winning book by Tor Seidler. [G]▼●

Rattle of a Simple Man (1964-British) **96m.** *** D: Muriel Box. Harry H. Corbett, Diane Cilento, Thora Hird, Michael Medwin. Pleasant saucy sex comedy of timid soul Corbett spending the night with Cilento to win a bet; set in London.▼

Ravagers, The (1965) **79m.** *½ D: Eddie Romero. John Saxon, Fernando Poe, Jr., Bronwyn Fitzsimmons, Mike Parsons, Kristina Scott. Uninspired account of Allied fight against Japanese in WW2 Philippines; filmed on location. Fitzsimmons, incidentally, is Maureen O'Hara's daughter.

Ravagers (1979) **C-91m.** BOMB D: Richard Compton. Richard Harris, Ann Turkel, Ernest Borgnine, Art Carney, Anthony James, Woody Strode, Alana Hamilton. This instant tax loss finds Harris searching for civilization in 1991 after most human life has been wiped out. Instead, he finds Borgnine. Panavision. [PG]

Raven, The (1935) **62m.** *** D: Louis Friedlander (Lew Landers). Boris Karloff, Bela Lugosi, Irene Ware, Lester Matthews, Samuel S. Hinds. Momentous teaming of horror greats with Lugosi as doctor with Poe-obsession, Karloff a victim of his wicked schemes. Hinds is subjected to torture from "The Pit and the Pendulum" in film's climax. Great fun throughout.▼●

Raven, The (1943-French) SEE: **Le Corbeau**

Raven, The (1963) **C-86m.** *** D: Roger Corman. Vincent Price, Boris Karloff, Peter Lorre, Hazel Court, Jack Nicholson, Olive Sturgess. Funny horror satire finds magicians Price and Lorre challenging power-hungry colleague Karloff. Climactic sorcerer's duel is a highlight. Screenplay by Richard Matheson, "inspired" by the Poe poem. Panavision.▼●

Raven Dance (1994) **C-91m.** BOMB D: Jimmy Lifton. Roddy McDowall, Sally Kellerman, Veronica Cartwright, Tracy Wells, William Sanderson, Mark Ruffalo, Carlton Beener, Sarah Douglas, Lois Nettleton. A young heiress and her disturbed brother, the only orphans in a convent, are targeted by her half-sister Kellerman and scheming doctor McDowall. Ghosts and a demonic mirror create complications. Awesomely amateurish but serenely smug, this is an unwatchable mess. Aka MIRROR MIRROR 2. [R]▼

Ravenous (1999) **C-98m.** **½ D: Antonia Bird. Guy Pearce, Robert Carlyle, Jeffrey Jones, David Arquette, Jeremy Davies, John Spencer, Stephen Spinella, Neal McDonough, Joseph Running Fox, Sheila Tousey. In 1847, cavalry officer Pearce is sent to a remote California fort, where a stranger (Carlyle) stumbles out of the wintry darkness with a horrifying tale of cannibalism, a tale that isn't over yet . . . Unique blend of comedy, Western, horror and satire is, obviously, not for every "taste." Grisly and off-putting, but ambitious and intelligent as well. Super 35. [R]▼●◗

Ravine, The (1969-Italian-Yugoslavian) **C-97m.** ** Paolo Cavara. David McCallum, Nicoletta Machiavelli, John Crawford, Lars Loch, Demeter Bietnc. Tepid story of German soldier (McCallum) who falls in love with sniper he is supposed to kill during WW2.

Ravishing Idiot (1964-French-Italian) **110m.** ** D: Edouard Molinaro. Anthony Perkins, Brigitte Bardot, Gregoire Aslan, André Luguet. Perkins, disenchanted with capitalism, is recruited by a Soviet spy to pilfer a secret NATO file. Silly, mostly unfunny Cold War comedy.▼

Raw Courage SEE: **Courage** (1984)

Raw Deal (1948) **78m.** *** D: Anthony Mann. Dennis O'Keefe, Claire Trevor, Marsha Hunt, Raymond Burr, John Ireland. Beautifully made, hard-boiled story of O'Keefe escaping from jail and taking out revenge on slimy Burr, who framed him; what's more, he gets caught between love of two women. Tough and convincing, with Burr a sadistic heavy.▼●

Raw Deal (1986) **C-97m.** *½ D: John Irvin. Arnold Schwarzenegger, Kathryn Harrold, Darren McGavin, Sam Wanamaker, Paul Shenar, Steven Hill, Joe Regalbuto, Robert Davi, Ed Lauter, Blanche Baker. Stupid action movie about brawny ex-Fed who helps an old pal clean some dirty laundry—and bust a major crime ring. Sense of humor helps . . . but not enough. J-D-C Scope. [R]▼●◗

Raw Edge (1956) **C-76m.** **½ D: John

Sherwood. Rory Calhoun, Yvonne De Carlo, Mara Corday, Rex Reason, Neville Brand. Bizarre premise routinely told; rancher's workers plan to kill him, with his widow to be the prize stake.

Rawhide (1951) **86m.** **½ D: Henry Hathaway. Tyrone Power, Susan Hayward, Hugh Marlowe, Dean Jagger, Edgar Buchanan, Jack Elam, George Tobias, Jeff Corey. Climactic shoot-out sparks this Western of outlaws holding group of people captive at stagecoach station. Script by Dudley Nichols. Remake of 1935 gangster film SHOW THEM NO MERCY. Retitled: DESPERATE SIEGE.▼

Rawhide Trail, The (1958) **67m.** *½ D: Robert Gordan. Rex Reason, Nancy Gates, Richard Erdman, Ann Doran. Humdrum tale of duo proving their innocence of helping the Indians attack settlers.

Rawhide Years, The (1956) **C-85m.** ** D: Rudolph Maté. Tony Curtis, Colleen Miller, Arthur Kennedy, William Demarest, William Gargan. Youthful Curtis perks this routine fare of gambler trying to clear himself of murder charge.

Raw Meat (1972-British) **C-87m.** **½ D: Gary Sherman. Donald Pleasence, David Ladd, Sharon Gurney, Christopher Lee, Norman Rossington, Clive Swift. Entertaining though overdone horror tale of descendants of people trapped in an abandoned underground tunnel preying as cannibals on modern-day London travelers. Good atmosphere; filmed at the Russell Square station. Originally titled DEATHLINE. [R]

Raw Wind in Eden (1958) **C-89m.** **½ D: Richard Wilson. Esther Williams, Jeff Chandler, Rossana Podesta, Carlos Thompson, Rik Battaglia. Plane carrying rich couple on way to yachting party crashes on isolated island. Entertaining adventure yarn is mixed with romance and jealousy. Filmed in Italy. CinemaScope.

Raymie (1960) **72m.** ** D: Frank McDonald. David Ladd, Julie Adams, John Agar, Charles Winninger, Richard Arlen, Frank Ferguson. Quiet little film about youngster (Ladd) whose greatest ambition is to catch the big fish that always eludes him. Jerry Lewis sings the title song.

Razorback (1984-Australian) **C-95m.** BOMB D: Russell Mulcahy. Gregory Harrison, Arkie Whiteley, Bill Kerr, Chris Haywood. Ludicrous horror film about a giant pig terrorizing the Australian countryside. Inauspicious feature debut by music video director Mulcahy. Panavision. [R]▼

Razor's Edge, The (1946) **146m.** ***½ D: Edmund Goulding. Tyrone Power, Gene Tierney, John Payne. Anne Baxter, Clifton Webb, Herbert Marshall, Lucile Watson, Frank Latimore. Slick adaptation of Maugham's philosophical novel, with Marshall as the author, Power as hero seeking true meaning of life, Baxter in Oscar-winning role as a dipsomaniac, Elsa Lanchester sparkling in bit as social secretary. Screenplay by Lamar Trotti. Long but engrossing; remade in 1984.▼●

Razor's Edge, The (1984) **C-128m.** **½ D: John Byrum. Bill Murray, Theresa Russell, Catherine Hicks, Denholm Elliott, James Keach, Peter Vaughan, Brian Doyle-Murray, Saeed Jaffrey. Ambitious, if anachronistic, remake of 1946 film with enough plot for *five* movies. Young American survives WW1 and begins to question meaning of his life—while his closest friends go through personal crises of their own. It's hard to read much spiritual thought on Murray's deadpan face, but he gives it a good try (and cowrote script with director Byrum). Russell comes off best in the showy role previously played by Anne Baxter. Warts and all, it's still an interesting film. J-D-C Scope. [PG-13]▼●

Reach for Glory (1963-British) **89m.** **½ D: Philip Leacock. Harry Andrews, Kay Walsh, Oliver Grimm, Michael Anderson, Jr., Martin Tomlinson, Alexis Kanner. Sensitive, if minor tale about WW2 England, involving youths and their special code of ethics, leading to one member's death.

Reach for the Sky (1956-British) **123m.** **½ D: Lewis Gilbert. Kenneth More, Muriel Pavlow, Alexander Knox, Sydney Tafler, Nigel Green. Sensibly told account of British pilot Douglas Bader, who overcomes the loss of his legs in a crash to continue his flying career. British running time: 135m.▼

Reaching for the Moon (1931) **62m.** **½ D: Edmund Goulding. Douglas Fairbanks, Sr., Bebe Daniels, Edward Everett Horton, Jack Mulhall, Helen Jerome Eddy, Bing Crosby. Enjoyable Depression comedy depicting effect of booze on financier Fairbanks, with Horton as his valet, Bebe the girl, and Crosby singing one Irving Berlin song. Originally 91m.▼

Reaching for the Sun (1941) **90m.** **½ D: William Wellman. Joel McCrea, Ellen Drew, Eddie Bracken, Albert Dekker, Billy Gilbert, George Chandler. OK comedy of North Woods clam-digger who journeys to Detroit to earn money for outboard motor by working on auto assembly line.

Ready to Rumble (2000) **C-107m.** *½ D: Brian Robbins. David Arquette, Oliver Platt, Scott Caan, Bill Goldberg, Rose McGowan, Joe Pantoliano, Martin Landau, Diamond Dallas Page, Caroline Rhea. Lowbrow timewaster about simpleminded wrestling addicts Arquette and Caan, who believe the "sport" is for real, and try to help salvage the career of their disgraced favorite wrestler (Platt, embarrassingly miscast). Our "heroes" are portable-toilet maintenance workers, which allows for plenty of bathroom humor. Made in conjunction with WCW (World Championship Wrestling); a number of its stars appear in cameos. [PG-13]▼◗

Ready to Wear (Prêt-à-Porter) (1994) **C-133m.** BOMB D: Robert Altman. Marcello Mastroianni, Sophia Loren, Kim Basinger, Julia Roberts, Tim Robbins, Anouk Aimée, Stephen Rea, Forest Whitaker, Lauren Bacall, Linda Hunt, Sally Kellerman, Tracey Ullman, Danny Aiello, Teri Garr, Rupert Everett, Richard E. Grant, Lili Taylor, Jean-Pierre Cassel, Jean Rochefort, Michel Blanc, Lyle Lovett, François Cluzet, Sam Robards, Ute Lemper, Chiara Mastroianni, Harry Belafonte, Cher. Mind-numbingly awful Altman collage about the fashion industry as it descends on Paris for the annual runway shows. No plot, no momentum, no point to any of this; a particularly egregious waste of Loren and Mastroianni (who reprise the striptease from YESTERDAY, TODAY AND TOMORROW). Most telling comment is made within the film itself: characters keep stepping in dog poop. Super 35. [R]▼●◗

Ready, Willing and Able (1937) **95m.** ** D: Ray Enright. Ruby Keeler, Lee Dixon, Allen Jenkins, Louise Fazenda, Carol Hughes, Ross Alexander, Winifred Shaw, Teddy Hart. Undistinguished Warner Bros. musical about college girl who impersonates British star in order to land Broadway role. Notable only for introduction of "Too Marvelous for Words," with a production number featuring a giant typewriter!

Real Blonde, The (1998) **C-105m.** **½ D: Tom DiCillo. Matthew Modine, Catherine Keener, Daryl Hannah, Maxwell Caulfield, Elizabeth Berkley, Marlo Thomas, Bridgette Wilson, Kathleen Turner, Christopher Lloyd, Dave Chappelle, Daniel Von Bargen, Denis Leary, Buck Henry, Steve Buscemi, Alexandra Wentworth. N.Y.C. slice-of-life about a wannabe actor and his girlfriend, a makeup artist to a top fashion model. Attempts to tackle such issues as illusion vs. reality, superficiality, sexual role-playing and the worlds of modeling and soap operas. A mixed bag with good individual scenes and performances. How well you respond may depend on your tolerance for Modine's character, who's a jerk. [R]▼●◗

Real Genius (1985) **C-104m.** **½ D: Martha Coolidge. Val Kilmer, Gabe Jarret, Michelle Meyrink, William Atherton, Jonathan Gries, Patti D'Arbanville. Idealistic whiz-kid is recruited by self-styled genius (Atherton) to join his college think tank—only to find that its members are being exploited, co-opted, and generally burned out. Potentially clever satire turns into just another youth/revenge comedy with caricatures instead of characters. Panavision. [PG]▼●

Real Glory, The (1939) **95m.** *** D: Henry Hathaway. Gary Cooper, David Niven, Andrea Leeds, Reginald Owen, Kay Johnson, Broderick Crawford, Vladimir Sokoloff, Henry Kolker. Cooper's fine as Army medic who solves all of Philippines' medical and military problems almost single-handedly after destructive Spanish-American War. Excellent action scenes.▼

Reality Bites (1994) **C-99m.** **½ D: Ben Stiller. Winona Ryder, Ethan Hawke, Ben Stiller, Janeane Garofalo, Steve Zahn, Swoosie Kurtz, Joe Don Baker, John Mahoney, Harry O'Reilly, Susan Norfleet, David Pirner, Keith David, Kevin Pollak, Karen Duffy, David Spade, Renee Zellweger. An incisive examination of Generation X, whose young people are confused, and repelled by the world being handed to them; on the other hand, a traditional love triangle, with Ryder trying to choose between straight-arrow Stiller and laid-back superdude Hawke (who's so cool he doesn't unwrap a candy bar before biting off a piece). Generally well done, with Ryder especially appealing, and Garofalo a standout as her best friend. Debuting director Stiller features his mom, Anne Meara, as a newspaperwoman, and his sister, Amy, as Ryder's "Psychic Phone Partner." Written by Helen Childress (who has a bit as a waitress). Jeanne Tripplehorn has unbilled cameo. Coproduced by Danny DeVito. [PG-13]▼●◗

Real Life (1979) **C-99m.** **½ D: Albert Brooks. Albert Brooks, Charles Grodin, Frances Lee McCain, J. A. Preston, Matthew Tobin. Writer-director-comedian Brooks' first feature doesn't sustain its comic premise as well as his hilarious short subjects, but still presents the world's greatest put-on artist in a compatible vehicle, as a shifty opportunist who sets out to make a filmed record of a typical American family. Written by Brooks, Monica Johnson, and Harry Shearer. [PG]▼

Real McCoy, The (1993) **C-106m.** *½ D: Russell Mulcahy. Kim Basinger, Val Kilmer, Terence Stamp, Gailard Sartain, Zach English, Raynor Scheine. Lame, completely inept caper film with Basinger cast as a cat burglar/ex-con who wants to go straight, but is forced into pulling off one last heist when her son is kidnapped. [PG-13]▼●◗

Real Men (1987) **C-96m.** *½ D: Dennis Feldman. James Belushi, John Ritter, Barbara Barrie, Bill Morey, Iva Andersen, Mark Herrier. Unfunny spy satire with CIA agent Belushi recruiting reluctant Ritter as a courier. Barely released to theaters, and with good reason. [PG-13] ▼●

Re-Animator (1985) **C-86m.** *** D: Stuart Gordon. Jeffrey Combs, Bruce Abbott, Barbara Crampton, Robert Sampson, David Gale. Knockout horror thriller and black comedy about H. P. Lovecraft's character Herbert West (Combs), an uppity young medical student who develops a serum to bring the dead back to life. Debut film director Gordon goes entertainingly over the line, especially in an off-color scene involving heroine Crampton and a lustful severed head. Major defect: Richard Band's music score, which is too reminiscent of Bernard Herrmann's classic PSYCHO sound track. *Lengthened* (and toned down) by Gordon for homevideo. Sequel: BRIDE OF RE-ANIMATOR. [R was surrendered] ▼●◗

Reap the Wild Wind (1942) **C-124m.** *** D: Cecil B. DeMille. Ray Milland, John Wayne, Paulette Goddard, Raymond Massey, Robert Preston, Susan Hayward, Charles Bickford, Hedda Hopper, Louise Beavers, Martha O'Driscoll, Lynne Overman. Brawling DeMille hokum of 19th-century salvagers in Florida, with Goddard as fiery Southern belle, Milland and Wayne fighting for her, Massey as odious villain. Exciting underwater scenes, with the special effects earning an Oscar. Milland good in off-beat characterization. ▼●◗

Rear Window (1954) **C-112m.** **** D: Alfred Hitchcock. James Stewart, Grace Kelly, Wendell Corey, Thelma Ritter, Raymond Burr, Judith Evelyn, Ross Bagdasarian. One of Hitchcock's most stylish thrillers has photographer Stewart confined to wheelchair in his apartment, using binoculars to spy on courtyard neighbors, and discovering a possible murder. Inventive Cornell Woolrich story adapted by John Michael Hayes. Stewart, society girlfriend Kelly, and no-nonsense nurse Ritter make a wonderful trio. Remade for TV in 1998 with Christopher Reeve. ▼●

Reason to Live, a Reason to Die, A (1974-Italian-French-German-Spanish) **C-92m.** ** D: Tonino Valerii. James Coburn, Telly Savalas, Bud Spencer, Robert Burton. Union Colonel Coburn and seven condemned men attempt to recapture a Missouri fort from brutal Confederate Major Savalas. So-so Western, aka MASSACRE AT FORT HOLMAN. Techniscope. [PG] ▼

Rebecca (1940) **130m.** **** D: Alfred Hitchcock. Laurence Olivier, Joan Fontaine, George Sanders, Judith Anderson, Nigel Bruce, Reginald Denny, C. Aubrey Smith, Gladys Cooper, Florence Bates, Leo G. Carroll, Melville Cooper. Hitchcock's first American film is sumptuous David O. Selznick production of Daphne du Maurier novel of girl who marries British nobleman but lives in shadow of his former wife. Stunning performances by Fontaine and Anderson; haunting score by Franz Waxman. Screenplay by Robert E. Sherwood and Joan Harrison. Academy Award winner for Best Picture and Cinematography (George Barnes). ▼●◗

Rebecca of Sunnybrook Farm (1917) **71m.** **½ D: Marshall Neilan. Mary Pickford, Eugene O'Brien, Josephine Crowell, Mayme Kelso, Marjorie Daw, Helen Jerome Eddy. Formulaic Pickford vehicle about spunky girl who's sent to live with her two harsh aunts; mixes sentiment, melodrama, and comedy, but lacks the spontaneity and spark of other Pickford films. Look for young ZaSu Pitts, in her film debut, as a spectator at Mary's circus. Kate Douglas Wiggin's 1903 story was remade in 1932 and 1938. ▼●

Rebecca of Sunnybrook Farm (1938) **80m.** **½ D: Allan Dwan. Shirley Temple, Randolph Scott, Jack Haley, Gloria Stuart, Phyllis Brooks, Helen Westley, Slim Summerville, William Demarest. Contrived but entertaining, with surefire elements from earlier Temple movies tossed into simple story of Scott trying to make Shirley a radio star. No relation to Kate Douglas Wiggin's famous story. Also shown in computer-colored version. ▼●

Rebel (1974) **C-80m.** *½ D: Robert Allen Schnitzer. Antony Page, Sylvester E. Stallone, Rebecca Grimes, Henry G. Sanders. Tiresome, justifiably obscure time-capsule featuring Stallone, pre–ROCKY stardom, as an alienated political radical (an interesting contrast to Rambo). Original title: NO PLACE TO HIDE. [PG] ▼

Rebel (1985-Australian) **C-91m.** ** D: Michael Jenkins. Matt Dillon, Debbie Byrne, Bryan Brown, Bill Hunter, Ray Barrett, Julie Nihill, Kim Deacon. Odd mixture of drama and music in this tale of traumatized AWOL American GI Dillon, who attaches himself to Sydney cabaret performer Byrne during WW2. Plenty of flash and style, little substance; and Dillon is fatally miscast. Panavision. [R] ▼●

Rebel in Town (1956) **78m.** ** D: Alfred L. Werker. John Payne, Ruth Roman, J. Carrol Naish, Ben Cooper, John Smith. Sensitive minor Western; renegade is present when his brother accidentally kills a child. Ironic events bring him into contact with boy's father.

Rebel Rousers (1970) **C-78m.** **½ D: Martin B. Cohen. Cameron Mitchell, Jack Nicholson, Bruce Dern, Diane Ladd, (Harry) Dean Stanton. Architect Mitchell isn't pleased when Dern holds drag-race to see who will "win" Mitchell's pregnant girlfriend. Nicholson, decked out in outrageous striped pants, steals the show in this amusing time-capsule. Filmed in 1967. Aka REBEL WARRIORS. [R] ▼●◗

Rebel Set, The (1959) **72m.** *½ D: Gene Fowler, Jr. Gregg Palmer, Kathleen Crowley, Edward Platt, Ned Glass, John Lupton, Don Sullivan, Robert Shayne. Perfectly dreadful crime drama is not without interest as an artifact of its time, with its message that "intellectuals" are inherently corrupt and not to be trusted. Platt *is* hilariously cast as a bearded coffee-house owner who recruits an out-of-work actor, a failed novelist, and a rich brat to participate in a robbery. ▼

Rebel Son, The (1939-British) **88m.** ** D: Alexis Granowsky, Adrian Brunel, Albert de Courville. Harry Baur, Anthony Bushell, Roger Livesey, Patricia Roc, Joan Gardner, Frederick Culley, Joseph Cunningham. Ineffectual English-language version of 1936 French film TARASS BOULBA (which also starred the legendary Baur) makes liberal use of action footage from the original, highlighting tale of 16th-century battle between Cossacks and Poles. Remade as TARAS BULBA. (Absurdly) retitled THE BARBARIAN AND THE LADY, and cut to 70m.

Rebel Warriors SEE: **Rebel Rousers**

Rebel Without a Cause (1955) **C-111m.** **** D: Nicholas Ray. James Dean, Natalie Wood, Sal Mineo, Jim Backus, Ann Doran, William Hopper, Rochelle Hudson, Corey Allen, Edward Platt, Dennis Hopper, Nick Adams. This portrait of youthful alienation spoke to a whole generation and remains wrenchingly powerful, despite some dated elements. The yearning for self-esteem, the barrier to communication with parents, the comfort found in friendships, all beautifully realized by director Ray, screenwriter Stewart Stern, and a fine cast (far too many of whom met early ends). This was Dean's seminal performance and an equally impressive showcase for young Mineo. CinemaScope.▼●

Reckless (1935) **96m.** ** D: Victor Fleming. Jean Harlow, William Powell, Franchot Tone, May Robson, Ted Healy, Nat Pendleton, Rosalind Russell, Henry Stephenson, Leon Waycoff (Ames), Allan Jones, Mickey Rooney, Farina (Allen Hoskins). Big cast, big production, musical numbers—all can't save script of chorus girl tangling up several people's lives. Tired and phony.▼●

Reckless (1984) **C-90m.** **½ D: James Foley. Aidan Quinn, Daryl Hannah, Kenneth McMillan, Cliff DeYoung, Lois Smith, Adam Baldwin, Dan Hedaya, Jennifer Grey, Pamela Springsteen. Rebellious teenager from wrong side of tracks takes up with straight-arrow coed, who finds in him a sense of danger and excitement missing from her comfortable existence. Nothing here we haven't seen in 1950s films about alienated youth—except for some very contemporary sex scenes—done with sincerity and a pulsing rock soundtrack. Quinn's film debut. [R]▼●

Reckless (1995) **C-92m.** *½ D: Norman Rene. Mia Farrow, Scott Glenn, Mary-Louise Parker, Tony Goldwyn, Stephen Dorff, Eileen Brennan, Giancarlo Esposito. It's Christmas Eve, and a ditsy, seemingly happy wife (Farrow) is informed by her suddenly remorseful husband that he has taken out a contract on her life. A potentially clever spoof of middle-class marital relations and phony holiday cheer quickly descends into a meandering, thoroughly ridiculous comedy-of-the-absurd. Farrow's character babbles on incessantly; it's no wonder she drives men—as well as the audience—crazy. [PG-13]▼

Reckless Kelly (1993-Australian-U.S.) **C-94m.** ** D: Yahoo Serious. Yahoo Serious, Melora Hardin, Alexei Sayle, Hugo Weaving, Kathleen Freeman, John Pinette, Bob Moss, Martin Ferrero. Modern descendant of Australia's legendary Robin Hood–like outlaw Ned Kelly (who travels around on a sputtering, klunky motorcycle) goes to L.A. to raise money to save his family's island hideout, and gets mixed up with moviemakers. Engagingly silly at the start, with some very funny sight gags, but increasingly tiresome as it moves stateside. Leading man Serious also directed, cowrote, and (according to the credits) performed his own stunts. Super 35. [PG]▼

Reckless Moment, The (1949) **82m.** ***½ D: Max Opuls (Ophuls). James Mason, Joan Bennett, Geraldine Brooks, Henry O'Neill, Shepperd Strudwick. Bennett becomes a murderer, pursued by blackmailer Mason. First-rate suspenser. Henry Garson and R.W. Soderborg adapted Elizabeth S. Holding's novel *The Blank Wall.*▼

Reckoning, The (1969-British) **C-111m.** **½ D: Jack Gold. Nicol Williamson, Rachel Roberts, Paul Rogers, Ann Bell. Contrived, latter day "angry young man" film, with Williamson (excellent as usual) as brooding businessman incapable of living in harmony with society, out to avenge long-ago slight to his father. [R]

Recon Game SEE: **Open Season**

Record City (1977) **C-90m.** *½ D: Dennis Steinmetz. Leonard Barr, Ed Begley, Jr., Sorrell Booke, Dennis Bowen, Jack Carter, Ruth Buzzi, Michael Callan, Alice Ghostley, Frank Gorshin, Kinky Friedman. CAR WASH-type youth comedy with music, set in a record store. Shot on tape. [PG]

Red (1994-Swiss-French-Polish) **C-99m.** *** D: Krzysztof Kieslowski. Irène Jacob, Jean-Louis Trintignant, Frederique Feder, Jean-Pierre Lorit, Juliette Binoche, Julie Delpy, Benoit Regent, Zbigniew Zamachowski. Final film in Kieslowski's "Three Colors" trilogy which, like BLUE and WHITE, can stand alone with its self-contained story. Fashion model Jacob meets embittered, retired judge Trintignant by accident, then develops relationship with him and enters his cloistered, secret world. Set in Geneva, this is a tale of several intertwining lives: a look at communication—and lack of same—in modern society. Acclaimed, but not for all tastes. This final chapter is subtitled "Fraternity."▼●

Red and the Black, The SEE: **Le Rouge et le Noir**

Red Badge of Courage, The (1951) **69m.** ***½ D: John Huston. Audie Murphy, Bill Mauldin, Douglas Dick, Royal Dano, John Dierkes, Arthur Hunnicutt, Tim Durant, Andy Devine. Narrated by James

Whitmore. Yankee soldier Murphy flees under fire and is guiltstricken over his apparent lack of courage. Stephen Crane's Civil War novel receives both epic and personal treatment by director Huston. Sweeping battle scenes and some truly frightening Rebel cavalry charges highlight this study of the fine line between cowardice and bravery. Many memorable vignettes: scene of Yankee general promising to share supper with half a dozen *different* platoons after the upcoming battle is a classic. Heavily re-edited after oddly negative previews; the film's troubled production is recounted in Lillian Ross' book *Picture*. Remade for TV in 1974.▼

Red Ball Express (1952) **83m.** **½ D: Budd Boetticher. Jeff Chandler, Alex Nicol, Charles Drake, Hugh O'Brian, Jack Kelly, Jacqueline Duval, Sidney Poitier, Jack Warden. Pretty good WW2 story about real-life truck convoy that was hurriedly created to bring supplies to Patton's Army deep inside German-held territory in France. Screenplay by John Michael Hayes.▼

Red Beard (1965-Japanese) **185m.** **½ D: Akira Kurosawa. Toshiro Mifune, Yuzo Kayama, Yoshio Tsuchiya, Reiko Dan, Kyoko Kagawa, Terumi Niki. Tough but kind doctor Mifune takes intern Kayama under his wing in charity clinic. Unoriginal drama is also way overlong. Tohoscope.▼●

Red Beret, The SEE: **Paratrooper**

Red Canyon (1949) **C-82m.** ** D: George Sherman. Ann Blyth, Howard Duff, George Brent, Edgar Buchanan, Chill Wills, Jane Darwell, Lloyd Bridges. Routine Zane Grey Western of wild horses being tamed.

Red Circle, The (1960-German) **94m.** **½ D: Jurgen Roland. Fritz Rasp, Karl Saebisch, Renate Ewert, Klaus-Jurgen Wussow. Scotland Yard investigates series of murders with each victim having telltale circle mark on his neck; slickly paced.▼

Red Corner (1997) **C-122m.** **½ D: Jon Avnet. Richard Gere, Bai Ling, Bradley Whitford, Byron Mann, Peter Donat, Robert Stanton, Tsai Chin, James Hong, Tzi Ma. American lawyer, representing cable/satellite TV interests in China, is framed for murdering a sexy model with whom he slept one night. His chances for justice are slim until the female lawyer assigned to his case (Ling) is bold enough to help him fight the system and figure out who's really behind this crime. Repetition and elements of illogic and predictability weaken an otherwise interesting yarn. [R]▼●◗

Red Dance, The (1928) **103m.** **½ D: Raoul Walsh. Charles Farrell, Dolores Del Rio, Ivan Linow, Boris Charsky, Dorothy Revier. Opulent production makes up for silly story of romance and intrigue during the Russian revolution.

Red Danube, The (1949) **119m.** **½ D: George Sidney. Walter Pidgeon, Ethel Barrymore, Peter Lawford, Angela Lansbury, Janet Leigh. Louis Calhern, Francis L. Sullivan. Meandering drama of ballerina Leigh pursued by Russian agents, aided by amorous Lawford; heavy-handed at times.

Red Dawn (1984) **C-114m.** *½ D: John Milius. Patrick Swayze, C. Thomas Howell, Lea Thompson, Charlie Sheen, Powers Boothe, Ben Johnson, Harry Dean Stanton, Jennifer Grey. Small-town teens become guerrilla fighters when Commies invade U.S. Good premise gunned down by purple prose and posturing—not to mention violence. [PG-13]▼●◗

Red Desert (1964-French-Italian) **C-118m.** ** D: Michelangelo Antonioni. Monica Vitti, Richard Harris, Rita Renoir, Carlo Chionetti. Vague, boring tale of Vitti alienated from her surroundings and on the verge of madness. Antonioni's first color film does have its followers, though. ▼●

Red Dragon, The (1945) **64m.** *½ D: Phil Rosen. Sidney Toler, Fortunio Bonanova, Benson Fong, Robert Emmett Keane, Willie Best, Carol Hughes. Assembly-line *Charlie Chan* mystery centering on the search for a secret bomb formula.

Red Dragon (1967-German) **C-88m.** **½ D: Ernst Hofbauer. Stewart Granger, Rosanna Schiaffino, Horst Frank, Suzanne Roquette. Granger is F.B.I. agent in Hong Kong chasing smuggling gang, Schiaffino another agent. Well paced, but predictable. Ultrascope.▼

Red Dragon (1986) SEE: **Manhunter**

Red Dust (1932) **83m.** ***½ D: Victor Fleming. Clark Gable, Jean Harlow, Mary Astor, Donald Crisp, Gene Raymond, Tully Marshall, Willie Fung. Robust romance of Indochina rubber worker Gable, his floozie gal Harlow, and visiting Astor, who is married to Raymond, but falls for Gable. Harlow has fine comic touch. Tart script by John Lee Mahin. Remade as MOGAMBO. Also shown in computer-colored version. ▼●

Red Earth, White Earth (1989) **C-100m. TVM** D: David Greene. Genevieve Bujold, Timothy Daly, Richard Farnsworth, Ralph Waite, Alberta Watson, Billy Merasty. Contemporary drama involving a three-generation farm family caught up in personal problems, trouble on the land, and political turmoil with local Indian factions. Trenchant script by Michael De Guzman adapted from Will Weaver's novel. Above average.

Red Firecracker, Green Firecracker (1994-Hong Kong) **C-116m.** *** D: He Ping. Hing Jing, Wu Gang, Zhao Xiaorui, Gao Yang. Evocative, romantic tale, beautifully directed and photographed and set in the early 20th century. The heroine is a young woman (Jing) who wears men's clothes and successfully operates her family's fireworks manufacturing business. Her priorities begin to change when she is attracted to a good-looking, wandering artist (Gang). [R]▼●◗

Red Garters (1954) **C-91m.** **½ D: George Marshall. Rosemary Clooney, Jack Carson, Guy Mitchell, Pat Crowley, Gene Barry, Cass Daley, Frank Faylen, Reginald Owen, Buddy Ebsen. Musical Western spoof gets A for effort—with strikingly stylized color sets, offbeat casting—but falls short of target.▼●

Redhead and the Cowboy, The (1950) **82m.** **½ D: Leslie Fenton. Glenn Ford, Rhonda Fleming, Edmond O'Brien, Morris Ankrum. Action-packed Civil War Western with dance-hall girl Fleming acting as Confederate courier; along the way, she gets apolitical cowboy Ford involved in her cause.

Red-Headed Stranger (1986) **C-105m.** *½ D: William Wittliff. Willie Nelson, Morgan Fairchild, Katharine Ross, Royal Dano, Sonny Carl Davis. Limp drama, screenwriter Wittliff's directorial debut, about a preacher (Nelson), his wayward wife (Fairchild, in an awful performance), a "good woman" (Ross), and some hooligans that have overridden his town. Adapted from Willie's 1975 album . . . and proof that hit records don't necessarily make good movies. Shot in 1984. [R]▼●

Red-Headed Woman (1932) **79m.** *** D: Jack Conway. Jean Harlow, Chester Morris, Una Merkel, Lewis Stone, May Robson, Leila Hyams, Charles Boyer. Harlow has never been sexier than in this precensorship story (by Anita Loos) of a gold-digging secretary who sets out to corral her married boss (Morris).▼●

Redhead From Wyoming, The (1952) **C-80m.** **½ D: Lee Sholem. Maureen O'Hara, Alexander Scourby, Alex Nicol, Jack Kelly, William Bishop, Dennis Weaver. Saucy Western pepped up by exuberant O'Hara as girl who falls in love with sheriff while protecting local cattle rustler.▼

Red Heat (1988) **C-106m.** *½ D: Walter Hill. Arnold Schwarzenegger, James Belushi, Peter Boyle, Ed O'Ross, Larry Fishburne, Gina Gershon, Richard Bright, Oleg Vidov, Pruitt Taylor Vince. Grim-faced Soviet cop tracks a scummy Russian drug dealer to Chicago, where he's partnered with belligerent Belushi from the Chicago P.D. Cheerless, foul-mouthed action film with two of the least appealing characters imaginable as the good guys. This was the first American production allowed to shoot scenes in Moscow's Red Square (. . . but *why*?). [R] ▼●◗

Red, Hot and Blue (1949) **84m.** ** D: John Farrow. Betty Hutton, Victor Mature, June Havoc, Jane Nigh, William Demarest, William Talman, Art Smith, Raymond Walburn. Strained Hutton musical-comedy about an ambitious girl trying to make it in showbiz, clashing with boyfriend Mature, a "serious" theater director. The gangster who frames the story is played by songwriter Frank Loesser, who also contributed the score.

Red House, The (1947) **100m.** *** D: Delmer Daves. Edward G. Robinson, Lon McCallister, Allene Roberts, Judith Anderson, Rory Calhoun, Julie London. Ona Munson. Title refers to strange old house containing many mysteries, providing constant fear for farmer Robinson. Exciting melodrama with fine cast.▼◗

Red Inn, The (1951-French) **100m.** **½ D: Claude Autant-Lara. Fernandel, Françoise Rosay, (Julien) Carette, Gregoire Aslan, Marie-Claire Olivia. Bizarre, ironic black comedy about what happens when stagecoach passengers seek refuge at an inn run by murderous thieves Rosay and Carette. Fernandel is the dissipated monk who intercedes on the travelers' behalf.

Red Kiss (1986-French) **C-112m.** *** D: Vera Belmont. Charlotte Valandrey, Lambert Wilson, Marthe Keller, Gunter Lamprecht, Laurent Terzieff. Sincere, thoughtful drama about the coming of age of teen Valandrey in early 1950s Paris. She's a committed Stalinist, as are her parents, but she also is fascinated by American culture—and falls in love with photographer Wilson. Original title: ROUGE BAISER.▼●

Red Light (1949) **83m.** ** D: Roy Del Ruth. George Raft, Virginia Mayo, Gene Lockhart, Barton MacLane, Henry (Harry) Morgan, Raymond Burr. Turgid drama of innocent Raft seeking revenge when freed from prison, hunting brother's killer.

Red Line 7000 (1965) **C-110m.** **½ D: Howard Hawks. James Caan, Laura Devon, Gail Hire, Charlene Holt, John Robert Crawford, Marianna Hill, James Ward, Norman Alden, George Takei. Attempt by director Hawks to do same kind of expert adventure pic he'd done for 40 years is sabotaged by overly complex script and indifferent acting, but is a faster and less pretentious racing-car drama than GRAND PRIX. Originally ran 127m. ▼●

Red Menace, The (1949) **87m.** *½ D: R. G. Springsteen. Robert Rockwell, Hanne Axman, Betty Lou Gerson, Barbara Fuller. War vet Rockwell is duped by the Commies! McCarthyesque propaganda is now an unintentionally funny antique. Narrated by "Lloyd G. Davies, member of the City Council, Los Angeles, California"! ▼●

Red Mountain (1951) **C-84m.** **½ D: William Dieterle. Alan Ladd, Lizabeth Scott, John Ireland, Arthur Kennedy. When Confederate raider Quantrill (Ireland) tries to establish his own empire in the West during the Civil War, it's up to Southern rebel Ladd and neutral Kennedy to stop him.

Redneck (1972-Italian-British) **C-89m.** BOMB D: Silvio Narizzano. Franco Nero, Telly Savalas, Mark Lester, Ely Galleani, Duilio Del Prete, Maria Michi. Tawdry, sadistic crime drama about two inept (and unappealing) robbers on the lam who inadvertently "kidnap" a young boy. Unpleasant and unbelievable. [R]▼

Red Planet Mars (1952) **87m.** **½ D: Harry Horner. Peter Graves, Andrea King, Marvin Miller, Herbert Berghof, House Peters, Vince Barnett. Outrageous sci-fi of scientist deciphering messages from Mars which turn out to be from God! Hilariously ludicrous anti-Communist propaganda (*Red* Planet Mars, get it?).▼●

Red Pony, The (1949) **C-89m.** *** D: Lewis Milestone. Myrna Loy, Robert Mitchum, Peter Miles, Louis Calhern, Shepperd Strudwick, Margaret Hamilton, Beau Bridges. Tasteful version of John Steinbeck book about boy attached tô horse, seeking escape from bickering family; leisurely pacing. Fine Steinbeck script and Aaron Copland score. Remade as a TVM. ▼●

Red Pony, The (1973) **C-100m. TVM** D: Robert Totten. Henry Fonda, Maureen O'Hara, Ben Johnson, Jack Elam, Clint Howard, Richard Jaeckel, Julian Rivero, Victor Sen Yung. Beautifully realized remake of the Steinbeck novella, minus the Billy Buck character played by Mitchum in the original. Fonda is especially good as the gruff father who loves his son in his own distant way. Adapted by Robert Totten and Ron Bishop. Above average.

Red River (1948) **133m.** **** D: Howard Hawks. John Wayne, Montgomery Clift, Walter Brennan, Joanne Dru, John Ireland, Noah Beery, Jr., Paul Fix, Coleen Gray, Harry Carey, Jr., Harry Carey, Sr., Chief Yowlatchie, Hank Worden. One of the greatest American adventures is really a Western MUTINY ON THE BOUNTY: Clift (in his first film) rebels against tyrannical guardian Wayne (brilliant in an unsympathetic role) during crucial cattle drive. Spellbinding photography by Russell Harlan, rousing Dimitri Tiomkin score; an absolute must. Many TV stations still show mutilated 125m. version (with Brennan's narration in place of diary pages, which Hawks preferred). Screenplay by Borden Chase and Charles Schnee, from Chase's *Saturday Evening Post* story. If you blink, you'll miss Shelley Winters dancing with Ireland around a campfire. Remade for TV in 1988 with James Arness. ▼●◗

Red Rock West (1993) **C-98m.** *** D: John Dahl. Nicolas Cage, Dennis Hopper, Lara Flynn Boyle, Timothy Carhart, J. T. Walsh, Dan Shor, Dwight Yoakam. Rock-solid little thriller, crammed with twists, turns and suspense, about honest, unemployed Cage, who's mistaken for a contract killer hired to do in seductive, adulterous Boyle. Nothing that occurs is logical or probable, but the film is so good (and so funny) that you are willing to go along for the ride. Hopper aficionados will savor his performance as "Lyle, from Dallas," the smarmiest of psychos, who is the real hit man. This debuted on cable TV. [R]▼●◗

Reds (1981) **C-200m.** *** D: Warren Beatty. Warren Beatty, Diane Keaton, Edward Herrmann, Jerzy Kosinski, Jack Nicholson, Paul Sorvino, Maureen Stapleton, Nicolas Coster, Gene Hackman, William Daniels, Max Wright, M. Emmet Walsh, Ian Wolfe, Bessie Love, George Plimpton, Dolph Sweet, Josef Sommer. Sprawling, ambitious film about American idealist/journalist John Reed's involvement with Communism, the Russian Revolution, and a willful, free-thinking woman named Louise Bryant. Provocative political saga is diffused, and overcome at times, by surprisingly conventional, often sappy approach to the love story (climaxed by Bryant's Little Eva-like journey to Russia over the ice floes). Interesting but wildly overpraised film won Oscars for Beatty as Best Director (he also produced and co-scripted), Stapleton as Best Supporting Actress, Vittorio Storaro for Best Cinematography. [PG]▼●

Red Salute (1935) **78m.** **½ D: Sidney Lanfield. Barbara Stanwyck, Robert Young, Hardie Albright, Cliff Edwards, Ruth Donnelly, Gordon Jones. Runaway screwball Stanwyck meets no-nonsense soldier Young in this imitation IT HAPPENED ONE NIGHT with wild sociopolitical wrinkle: Barbara's boyfriend (Albright) is a student radical who makes Communist speeches! A real oddity. Aka HER ENLISTED MAN and RUNAWAY DAUGHTER.▼

Red Scorpion (1989) **C-102m.** BOMB D: Joseph Zito. Dolph Lundgren, M. Emmet Walsh, Al White, T.P. McKenna, Carmen Argenziano, Brion James, Regopstann. Bottom-of-the-barrel actioner with Lundgren a Soviet officer sent to Africa to murder a rebel leader. Followed by direct-to-video sequel RED SCORPION 2. [R] ▼●◗

Red Shoes, The (1948-British) **C-133m.** **** D: Michael Powell, Emeric Pressburger. Anton Walbrook, Marius Goring, Moira Shearer, Robert Helpmann, Leonide Massine, Albert Basserman, Ludmilla Tcherina, Esmond Knight. A superb, stylized fairy tale. Young ballerina is torn between two creative, possessive men, one a struggling composer, the other an autocratic dance impresario. Landmark film for its integration of dance in storytelling, and a perennial favorite of balletomanes. Brian Easdale's score and Hein Heckroth and Arthur Lawson's art direction-set decoration won Oscars, and Jack Cardiff's cinematography *should* have. Shearer is exquisite in movie debut.▼●◗

Red Skies of Montana (1952) **C-99m.** **½ D: Joseph M. Newman. Richard Widmark, Jeffrey Hunter, Constance Smith, Richard Boone, Richard Crenna, Charles Buchinsky (Bronson). Trite account of forest-fire fighters, salvaged by spectacular fire sequences.

Red Sky at Morning (1970) **C-112m.** *** D: James Goldstone. Richard Thomas, Catherine Burns, Desi Arnaz, Jr., Richard Crenna, Claire Bloom, John Colicos, Harry Guardino, Strother Martin, Nehemiah Persoff. Unspectacular but pleasing adaptation of Richard Bradford's novel about adolescence in New Mexico during WW2. Comparable to SUMMER OF '42, and in many ways better; Thomas is superb. [PG]

Red Sonja (1985) **C-89m.** *½ D: Richard Fleischer. Brigitte Nielsen, Arnold Schwarzenegger, Sandahl Bergman, Paul Smith, Ernie Reyes, Jr., Ronald Lacey, Pat Roach. Spectacularly silly sword-and-sorcery saga with female lead, based on pulp writings of Robert E. Howard (of CONAN fame). Might amuse juvenile viewers, but only point of interest for adults is deciding who gives the worse performance, Nielsen or villainess Bergman. Schwarzenegger has a brief guest spot. Technovision. [PG-13] ▼●

Red Sorghum (1987-Chinese) **C-91m.** ***½ D: Zhang Yimou. Gong Li, Jiang Wen, Liu Ji, Teng Rijun, Qian Ming. Evocative, beautifully filmed combination drama/black comedy/fairy tale/epic which chronicles a most untraditional union between a pair of rural lovers during the 1920s. The years pass, a new decade arrives, and with it come Japanese invaders. A triumph for director Yimou. CinemaScope.▼

Red Stallion, The (1947) **C-82m.** *½ D: Lesley Selander. Robert Paige, Noreen Nash, Ted Donaldson, Jane Darwell. Weak little film of ranch boy and his pet horse.▼

Red Stallion in the Rockies (1949) **C-85m.** ** D: Ralph Murphy. Arthur Franz, Wallace Ford, Ray Collins, Jean Heather, Leatrice Joy. OK outdoor drama of two men rounding up herd of wild horses.

Red Sun (1972-Italian-French-Spanish) **C-112m.** ** D: Terence Young. Charles Bronson, Ursula Andress, Toshiro Mifune, Alain Delon, Capucine. East meets West in this odd story of samurai warrior pursuing valuable Japanese sword stolen from train crossing American West. Intriguing elements, and refreshingly tongue-in-cheek, but a misfire. [PG]▼◗

Red Sundown (1956) **C-81m.** **½ D: Jack Arnold. Rory Calhoun, Martha Hyer, Dean Jagger, Robert Middleton, James Millican. Virile cast adds zest to standard yarn of bad-guy-gone-good (Calhoun), squeezing out the criminal elements in town.

Red Tent, The (1971-Italian-Russian) **C-121m.** *** D: Mickail K. Kalatozov. Sean Connery, Claudia Cardinale, Hardy Kruger, Peter Finch, Massimo Girotti, Luigi Vannucchi, Mario Adorf. Top-notch adventure saga for kids and adults alike, based on true story of explorer General Nobile (Finch) whose 1928 Arctic expedition turns into disaster. Exciting scenes of survival against elements, dramatic rescue, marred by awkward flashback framework. [G]▼●

Red Tide, The SEE: **Blood Tide**

Red Tomahawk (1967) **C-82m.** *½ D: R. G. Springsteen. Howard Keel, Joan Caulfield, Broderick Crawford, Scott Brady, Wendell Corey, Richard Arlen, Tom Drake, Ben Cooper, Donald Barry. Captain Keel saves town from Sioux in routine Western with many likable performers in the cast.

Red Violin, The (1998-Canadian-Italian) **C-131m.** ** D: François Girard. Carlo Cecchi, Irene Grazioli, Jean-Luc Bideau, Jason Flemyng, Greta Scacchi, Sylvia Chang, Samuel L. Jackson, Colm Feore, Monique Mercure, Don McKellar, Sandra Oh. Multi-episode film follows the fate of a cursed violin from 17th-century Italy to 18th-century Vienna, 19th-century England, 20th-century China and present-day Montreal. The stories are mostly downbeat and/or frustrating, and the wrapup segment with appraiser Jackson is hard to swallow. Colorful locales and intriguing premises maintain minimal interest throughout. McKellar, who plays Jackson's cohort in the final episode, also coscripted with the director. Oscar-winning score by John Corigliano.▼◗

Red, White and Busted SEE: **Outside In**

Reefer Madness (1936) **67m.** BOMB D: Louis Gasnier. Dave O'Brien, Dorothy Short, Warren McCollum, Lillian Miles, Carleton Young, Thelma White. The granddaddy of all "Worst" movies; one of that era's many low-budget "Warning!" films depicts (in now-hilarious fashion) how one puff of pot can lead clean-cut teenagers down the road to insanity and death. Miles' frenzied piano solo is a highlight, but in this more enlightened age, overall effect is a little sad. Originally titled THE BURNING QUESTION, then TELL YOUR CHILDREN; beware shorter prints.▼●◗

Ref, The (1994) **C-93m.** **½ D: Ted Demme. Denis Leary, Judy Davis, Kevin Spacey, Robert J. Steinmiller, Jr., Glynis Johns, Raymond J. Barry, Richard Bright, Christine Baranski, Bill Raymond, Bob Ridgely, B. D. Wong. A cocky cat burglar on the lam holds a squabbling yuppie couple hostage on Christmas Eve and quickly learns he's gotten himself into a no-win situation. This caustic comedy is meatier than you might expect, with top-notch performances by Spacey and Davis, but it gets unexpectedly serious—then silly and illogical. Still worth a look. Director Demme is Jonathan's nephew. [R]▼●

Reflecting Skin, The (1990-British-Canadian) **C-95m.** **½ D: Philip Ridley. Viggo Mortensen, Lindsay Duncan, Jeremy Cooper, Sheila Moore, Duncan Fraser, David Longworth. Weird, jarring chiller, set in rural Idaho in the early '50s, about a boy (Cooper) who's convinced that the young widow who lives next door is a vampire. He's especially distraught when his older brother becomes her lover. Offbeat to say the least, and not for all tastes, but still worth a look.▼●

Reflection of Fear, A (1973) **C-89m.** **½ D: William A. Fraker. Robert Shaw, Mary Ure, Sally Kellerman, Sondra Locke, Signe Hasso. Muddled story of beautiful girl who becomes the crucial link in chain of violence and murder. [PG]▼

Reflections in a Golden Eye (1967) **C-108m.** **½ D: John Huston. Elizabeth Taylor, Marlon Brando, Brian Keith, Julie Harris, Robert Forster, Zorro David. Kinky version of Carson McCullers' novel about homosexual army officer in the South. Not really very good, but cast, subject matter, and Huston's pretentious handling make it fascinating on a minor level. Panavision.▼

Reflections of Murder (1974) **C-100m. TVM** D: John Badham. Tuesday Weld, Joan Hackett, Sam Waterston, Lucille Benson, Michael Lerner, R. G. Armstrong. Lance Kerwin. Wife and mistress conspire to kill a tyrannical schoolteacher who then returns to haunt them. First-class performances make this new version of French classic DIABOLIQUE a superior thriller. Script by Carol Sobieski. Above average.▼

Reformer and the Redhead, The (1950) **90m.** **½ D: Norman Panama, Melvin Frank. June Allyson. Dick Powell, David Wayne, Cecil Kellaway, Ray Collins. Sassy shenanigans with Allyson, a zoo-keeper's daughter, courted by lawyer Powell.

Reform School Girl (1957) **71m.** BOMB D: Edward Bernds. Gloria Castillo, Ross Ford, Edward Byrnes, Ralph Reed, Luana Anders, Jack Kruschen, Sally Kellerman. Hokey time-capsule about a pretty teen from "the other side of the tracks" (Castillo). After a fatal car mishap, she ends up in reform school. Will she or won't she squeal on the party responsible for her dilemma?▼

Reform School Girl (1994) **C-83m. TVM** D: Jonathan Kaplan. Aimee Graham, Teresa DiSpina, Carolyn Seymour, Matt LeBlanc, Nick Chinlund, Harry Northrup. The 1950s: Unable to prove her innocence, teenaged Donna lands in juvie jail, where the unethical warden coerces her into track and field events. Some directorial flair, but pacing is off and acting is stylistically uneven, but with surprisingly tender lesbian love scenes. One of Showtime's "Rebel Highway" entries, all based on old American-International pictures; partly a remake of the 1957 film of the same name. Average.▼

Reform School Girls (1986) **C-94m.** *½ D: Tom DeSimone. Linda Carol, Wendy O. Williams, Pat Ast, Sybil Danning, Charlotte McGinnis, Sherri Stoner, Denise Gordy, Tiffany Schwartz. Comic strip–styled spoof of women's prison films offers some knowing winks (director DeSimone also made THE CONCRETE JUNGLE), but the level of exaggeration is a turnoff, such as imagining veteran rock singer Williams as a teenager. Carol is the innocent young girl learning the ropes in prison, while chubby Ast, an Andy Warhol film graduate, was born to play a prison matron—yet even her campy acting becomes monotonous. [R]▼●

Regarding Henry (1991) **C-107m.** ** D: Mike Nichols. Harrison Ford, Annette Bening, Bill Nunn, Mikki Allen, Donald Moffat, Nancy Marchand, Elizabeth Wilson, Robin Bartlett, John Leguizamo. High-powered lawyer suffers brain injury and has to start his life all over again—learning to walk, talk, and ultimately, return to his family and job. Potentially interesting story is given polished presentation, but is so placid, and so unrealistic—even trivializing the recovery process—it never achieves any emotional impact. [PG-13]▼●

Regeneration (1915) **72m.** ***½ D: Raoul Walsh. Rockcliffe Fellowes, Anna Q. Nilsson, William Sheer, Carl Harbaugh, James Marcus, Maggie Weston. Still stirring and cinematically impressive early gangster film (and social tract) charting the plight and fate of Owen (Fellowes), a surly, charismatic Irish hood, and how his life is affected by Mamie Rose (Nilsson), a young woman who deserts her upper-class roots for life as "a settlement worker in the gangster's district." This vividly realistic melodrama, which portrays the effect of poverty on the human spirit, was filmed on location in N.Y.C.'s Bowery.▼●

Regeneration (1997-British-Canadian) **C-96m.** **½ D: Gillies MacKinnon. Jonathan Pryce, James Wilby, Jonny Lee Miller, Stuart Bunce, David Hayman, Tanya Allen, John Neville. Famed WW1 poet and decorated British war hero Siegfried Sassoon is declared mentally unstable and sent to a military psychiatric hospital after publishing a denouncement of the war. Strong acting and superb cinematography enhance this talky, stagy adaptation of Pat Barker's prize-winning novel. Pryce is exceptional as an army doctor who tries to heal the soldiers' wounded psyches. Aka BEHIND THE LINES. [R]▼

Reggae Sunsplash (1980-German-Jamaican) **C-107m.** **½ D: Stefan Paul. Bob Marley, Peter Tosh, Third World, Burning Spear. OK documentary, filmed at the '79 Sunsplash II Festival in Montego Bay, benefits from commanding presences of Marley and company.▼

Reg'lar Fellers (1941) **66m.** ** D: Arthur Dreifuss. Billy Lee, Carl "Alfalfa" Switzer, Buddy Boles, Janet Dempsey, Sarah Padden, Roscoe Ates, Dick Van Patten, Joyce Van Patten. Extremely dated comedy, based on Gene Byrnes' popular comic strip, chronicling the escapades of some typically all-American youngsters who help soften miserable, kid-hating Padden. "Alfalfa" fans will not be disappointed.▼

Reign of Terror (1949) **89m.** *** D: Anthony Mann. Robert Cummings, Arlene Dahl, Richard Hart, Richard Basehart, Arnold Moss, Beulah Bondi. Vivid costume drama set during French Revolution, with valuable diary eluding both sides of battle. Moss is particularly good as the elegantly, eloquently evil Foucher. Stunningly photographed by John Alton; every shot is a painting! Aka THE BLACK BOOK. ▼

Reincarnation of Peter Proud, The (1975) **C-104m.** **½ D: J. Lee Thompson. Michael Sarrazin, Jennifer O'Neill, Margot Kidder, Cornelia Sharpe, Paul Hecht, Tony Stephano. The soul of a man murdered years before roosts inside Sarrazin, in moderately gripping version of Max Ehrlich's book, adapted by the author. [R]▼●

Reindeer Games (2000) **C-104m.** *½ D: John Frankenheimer. Ben Affleck, Gary Sinise, Charlize Theron, Dennis Farina, James Frain, Donal Logue, Danny Trejo, Isaac Hayes, Gordon Tootoosis, Clarence Williams III. After five years in prison, a car thief assumes the identity of his cellmate and takes up with his comrade's gorgeous pen-pal girlfriend. Soon he finds himself in a quicksand pit of crime. Ridiculous story isn't believable for one minute, especially with the shallow performances of its usually capable cast (who all seem to be playing "grown-up" parts from an old movie script). Super 35. [R]▼◗

Reivers, The (1969) **C-107m.** ***½ D: Mark Rydell. Steve McQueen, Sharon Farrell, Will Geer, Michael Constantine, Rupert Crosse, Mitch Vogel, Lonny Chapman, Juano Hernandez, Clifton James, Bruce White, Dub Taylor, Allyn Ann McLerie, Diane Ladd; narrated by Burgess Meredith. Picaresque film from Faulkner novel about young boy (Vogel) in 1905 Mississippi who takes off for adventurous automobile trip with devil-may-care McQueen and buddy Crosse. Completely winning Americana, full of colorful episodes, equally colorful characters. Screenplay by Irving Ravetch (who also produced) and Harriet Frank, Jr. Aka THE YELLOW WINTON FLYER. Panavision. [M]▼

Relentless (1948) **C-93m.** **½ D: George Sherman. Robert Young, Marguerite Chapman, Willard Parker, Akim Tamiroff. Satisfactory Western about cowpoke and his gal trying to prove him innocent of murder charge.

Relentless (1989) **C-93m.** *½ D: William Lustig. Judd Nelson, Robert Loggia, Leo Rossi, Meg Foster, Patrick O'Bryan, Ken Lerner, Mindy Seeger, Angel Tompkins. Nelson gives his one memorable performance to date, as a serial killer. Otherwise thoroughly routine, and that goes double for the finale. Followed by three sequels, beginning with DEAD ON: RELENTLESS II. [R]▼●

Relic, The (1997) **C-110m.** **½ D: Peter Hyams. Penelope Ann Miller, Tom Sizemore, Linda Hunt, James Whitmore, Clayton Rohner, Chi Muoi Lo, Thomas Ryan, Robert Lesser, Lewis Van Bergen, Constance Towers, John Kapelos, Audra Lindley. As a big natural history museum hosts a glittering reception, a monster runs amok in the shadows. Yes, it's "ALIEN in a museum," but not bad. The monster, done both "live" and by computer graphics, is especially impressive, but the explanation for it is laughable. Panavision. [R]▼●◗

Reluctant Astronaut, The (1967) **C-101m.** ** D: Edward Montagne. Don Knotts, Leslie Nielsen, Joan Freeman, Arthur O'Connell, Jesse White. Featherweight comedy dealing with hicksville alumnus Knotts becoming title figure; predictable and often not even childishly humorous. For kids only.▼●

Reluctant Debutante, The (1958) **C-94m.** **½ D: Vincente Minnelli. Rex Harrison, Kay Kendall, John Saxon, Sandra Dee, Angela Lansbury. Bright drawing-room comedy which Harrison, Kendall, and Lansbury make worthwhile: British parents must present their Americanized daughter to society. CinemaScope.▼●

Reluctant Dragon, The (1941) **C/B&W-72m.** *** D: Alfred L. Werker (live-action). Robert Benchley gets a tour of the Walt Disney studio in this pleasant feature that incorporates a number of first-rate cartoon sequences (*Baby Weems, The Reluctant Dragon*), offers some interesting glimpses of studio at work. Clarence "Ducky" Nash and Florence Gill do cartoon voices, Ward Kimball animates Goofy, Frances Gifford shows Benchley around, and young Alan Ladd appears as one of the story men. Opens in b&w, turns to beautiful Technicolor hues.▼

Reluctant Saint, The (1962-U.S.-Italian) **105m.** **½ D: Edward Dmytryk. Maximilian Schell, Ricardo Montalban, Lea Padovani, Akim Tamiroff, Harold Goldblatt, Mark Damon. Loosely biographical account of St. Joseph of Cupertino, a 17th-century Franciscan whose modest upbringing and simple intellect would never have foretold the religious life he would lead (or the great number of miracles he would perform). Unusual fare; worth a look.

Reluctant Spy, The (1963-French) **93m.** **½ D: Jean-Charles Dudrumet. Jean Marais, Genevieve Page, Maurice Teynac, Jean Gallar. Marais properly spoofs James

Bond spy thrillers as secret agent chasing around the Continent.

Reluctant Widow, The (1951-British) **86m.** *½ D: Bernard Knowles. Jean Kent, Guy Rolfe, Kathleen Byron, Paul Dupuis. Mild drama set in late 18th century, of governess Kent marrying rogue Rolfe.

Remains of the Day, The (1993) **C-135m.** ***½ D: James Ivory. Anthony Hopkins, Emma Thompson, James Fox, Christopher Reeve, Peter Vaughan, Hugh Grant, Michael Lonsdale, Tim Pigott-Smith, Patrick Godfrey. HOWARDS END leads are reunited as servants at a baronial English country home—Hopkins a self-sacrificing butler who serves with the utmost discretion, and Thompson an efficient and bright head housekeeper. The two collide over work—and especially over overtures of romance. Looming over these personal stories is the (fascinating) larger tale of the misguided lord of the manor (Fox), who is excitedly making alliances with Nazi sympathizers. Kazuo Ishiguro's novel was adapted by Ruth Prawer Jhabvala, and though film can't quite dispel its literary origin, even almost-great Merchant–Ivory is better than most anything else around. Coproduced by Mike Nichols. Super 35. [PG]▼●

Remains to Be Seen (1953) **89m.** *** D: Don Weis. Van Johnson, June Allyson, Angela Lansbury, Louis Calhern, Dorothy Dandridge. Disarming comedy based on Howard Lindsay–Russel Crouse play, with Allyson a singer and Johnson the apartment-house manager involved in swank East Side N.Y.C. murder; script by Sidney Sheldon.

Remarkable Andrew, The (1942) **80m.** **½ D: Stuart Heisler. William Holden, Ellen Drew, Brian Donlevy, Montagu Love, George Watts, Brandon Hurst, Gilbert Emery, Rod Cameron, Richard Webb, Frances Gifford. Far-fetched but well-played fantasy in which small-town bookkeeper Holden is falsely accused of embezzlement; the ghost of Pres. Andrew Jackson (Donlevy) comes to his rescue, among other pillars of U.S. history. Script by Dalton Trumbo, based on his novel.

Remarkable Mr. Pennypacker, The (1959) **C-87m.** **½ D: Henry Levin. Clifton Webb, Dorothy McGuire, Charles Coburn, Ray Stricklyn, Jill St. John, Ron Ely, David Nelson. Prodded along by Webb's brittle manner, period tale unfolds of Pennsylvania businessman who leads dual life, with two families (seventeen kids in all). CinemaScope.

Rembrandt (1936-British) **84m.** ***½ D: Alexander Korda. Charles Laughton, Elsa Lanchester, Gertrude Lawrence, Edward Chapman, Roger Livesey, Raymond Huntley, John Clements, Marius Goring, Abraham Sofaer. Handsome bio of Dutch painter, full of visual tableaux and sparked by Laughton's excellent performance. One of Gertrude Lawrence's rare film appearances. ▼●

Remedy for Riches (1940) **60m.** ** D: Erle C. Kenton. Jean Hersholt, Dorothy Lovett, Edgar Kennedy, Jed Prouty, Walter Catlett, Maude Eburne, Robert Baldwin, Warren Hull. There's more comedy than drama in this moderately entertaining *Dr. Christian* series entry. A swindler "uncovers" oil in dear old River's End, and the townsfolk line up to invest their hard-earned savings.▼

Remember? (1939) **83m.** ** D: Norman Z. McLeod. Robert Taylor, Greer Garson, Lew Ayres, Billie Burke, Reginald Owen, Laura Hope Crews, Henry Travers, Sig Ruman. Blah comedy about bickering couple taking potion which gives them amnesia—whereupon they fall in love all over again. Nice try, but no cigar.

Remember Last Night? (1935) **81m.** **½ D: James Whale. Edward Arnold, Constance Cummings, Robert Young, Sally Eilers, Robert Armstrong, Reginald Denny, Monroe Owsley, Gustav von Seyffertitz, Arthur Treacher. Freewheeling, perpetually tipsy couple find themselves—and their society friends—involved with multiple murders; detective Arnold tries to get them to take matters seriously enough to solve the mystery. Lightheaded comedy-whodunit is more shrill than funny, though stellar cast of character actors and Whale's trademarked stylistics make it worth watching.

Remember My Name (1978) **C-96m.** *** D: Alan Rudolph. Geraldine Chaplin, Anthony Perkins, Moses Gunn, Berry Berenson, Jeff Goldblum, Timothy Thomerson, Alfre Woodard, Dennis Franz. Dream-like film presents fragmented story of woman returning from prison, determined to disrupt her ex-husband's new life. Moody, provocative film definitely not for all tastes; striking blues vocals on soundtrack by Alberta Hunter. Produced by Robert Altman. Woodard's film debut. [R]

Remember the Day (1941) **85m.** *** D: Henry King. Claudette Colbert, John Payne, John Shepperd (Shepperd Strudwick), Ann Todd, Douglas Croft, Jane Seymour, Anne Revere. Pleasant, tug-at-your-heartstrings Americana, told in flashback, about the effect teacher Colbert has on a student (Croft, who grows up to be presidential nominee Shepperd). Payne is the fellow teacher with whom Colbert falls in love.

Remember the Night (1940) **94m.** *** D: Mitchell Leisen. Barbara Stanwyck, Fred MacMurray, Beulah Bondi, Elizabeth Patterson, Sterling Holloway. Beautifully made, sentimental story of prosecutor MacMurray falling in love with shoplifter Stanwyck during Christmas court recess; builds masterfully as it creates a very special mood. Script by Preston Sturges.▼

Remembrance of Love (1982) **C-100m. TVM** D: Jack Smight. Kirk Douglas, Pam

Dawber, Chana Eden, Robert Clary, Yoram Gall, Michael Goodwin, Eric Douglas. Widower has an emotional reunion with a woman he had loved as a teenager in the Warsaw Ghetto forty years earlier. Melodramatically written by Harold Jack Bloom. Video title: HOLOCAUST SURVIVORS: REMEMBRANCE OF LOVE. Average.▼

Remo Williams: The Adventure Begins . . . (1985) **C-121m.** **½ D: Guy Hamilton. Fred Ward, Joel Grey, Wilford Brimley, J. A. Preston, George Coe, Charles Cioffi, Kate Mulgrew, Michael Pataki, William Hickey. Bubble-gum action-adventure yarn based on the popular *Destroyer* books by Richard Sapir and Warren Murphy, with Ward a N.Y.C. cop recruited by secret society out to avenge society's wrongs (motto: "Thou shalt not get away with it") . . . then he's trained for job by inscrutable Korean Sinanju master (Grey). Comes close to scoring bulls-eye but misfires too many times—and goes on too long. [PG-13]▼●

Renaissance Man (1994) **C-129m.** **½ D: Penny Marshall. Danny DeVito, Gregory Hines, James Remar, Cliff Robertson, Lillo Brancato, Jr., Stacey Dash, Kadeem Hardison, Richard T. Jones, Khalil Kain, Peter Simmons, Greg Sporleder, Mark Wahlberg, Ben Wright, Ed Begley, Jr., Isabella Hoffmann. A man whose life and career have hit a stone wall gets hired to teach some of the Army's least intelligent recruits some basics of reading. Overlong, overtly corny "feel-good" movie, bolstered by sincere and persuasive performances. Also stands as the kindest portrait of the U.S. Army in recent history. [PG-13]▼●

Renaldo and Clara (1978) **C-292m.** BOMB. D: Bob Dylan. Bob Dylan, Sara Dylan, Sam Shepard, Ronee Blakley, Ronnie Hawkins, Joni Mitchell, Harry Dean Stanton, Arlo Guthrie, Bob Neuwirth, Joan Baez, Allen Ginsberg, Mick Ronson, Roberta Flack. Self-important, poorly made fictionalized account of Dylan's *Rolling Thunder Revue.* Dylan plays Renaldo; his wife Sara is Clara. Pretentious and obnoxious. Dylan later cut it to 122m.; what's left is mostly concert footage, but it doesn't help much. Sam Shepard's first film. [R]

Rendezvous (1935) **91m.** ** D: William K. Howard. William Powell, Rosalind Russell, Binnie Barnes, Lionel Atwill, Cesar Romero. OK WW1 intrigue, with Powell assigned to office work instead of combat during war, running into notorious spy ring. Russell's "comedy" character is only obtrusive here.

Rendez-vous (1985-French) **C-82m.** *** D: André Téchiné. Juliette Binoche, Lambert Wilson, Wadeck Stanczak, Jean-Louis Trintignant, Olimpia Carlisi, Dominique Lavanant. Stylish melodrama perceptively investigates the borderline between play-acting and real life as stage actress (Binoche) becomes involved with obsessive live-sex show star Wilson and his mentor, a renowned director (Trintignant). Morbid mood and extreme sex scenes may repel some audiences; stunning widescreen photography will suffer on TV. CinemaScope.▼●

Rendezvous at Midnight (1935) **64m.** ** D: Christy Cabanne. Ralph Bellamy, Valerie Hobson, Catherine Doucet, Irene Ware, Helen Jerome Eddy. Fair whodunit of city commissioner being murdered just as his replacement (Bellamy) begins to investigate his corrupt administration.

Rendezvous in Paris (1996-French) **C-100m.** ***½ D: Eric Rohmer. Clara Bellar, Antoine Basler, Aurore Rauscher, Serge Renko, Michael Kraft, Benedicte Loyen. Three thoroughly enchanting tales of love, trust and ambivalence, set in the lush urban landscape of Paris. Whether it be a young woman deciding if her boyfriend can be trusted, an "almost" affair between an engaged female student and another man, or a joyless painter and his potentially amorous encounters, these tales are simply told, with a complexity just below the surface that completely captivates.▼

Rendezvous With Annie (1946) **89m.** **½ D: Allan Dwan. Eddie Albert, Faye Marlowe, Gail Patrick, Phillip Reed, C. Aubrey Smith, Raymond Walburn, William Frawley. Frantic comedy concerning G.I. Albert stationed in England who goes AWOL for a few days to see wife back in the States; engaging cast and some funny moments.

Renegade Girls SEE: **Caged Heat**

Renegades (1930) **84m.** ** D: Victor Fleming. Warner Baxter, Myrna Loy, Noah Beery, Gregory Gaye, George Cooper, C. Henry Gordon, Bela Lugosi. Stodgy story of renegades from Foreign Legion outpost in Morocco, one of whom (Baxter) has been betrayed by seductive spy Loy. Complex story builds to offbeat, and downbeat, ending.

Renegades (1946) **C-88m.** **½ D: George Sherman. Evelyn Keyes, Willard Parker, Larry Parks, Edgar Buchanan, Jim Bannon, Forrest Tucker, Ludwig Donath. Hokey Western has Keyes torn between a good doctor and member of an outlaw family. Soapy scenes offset by good action and Buchanan's standout portrayal of a bible-spouting bandit. Keyes' garish, Technicolor-red hair has to be seen to be believed.

Renegades (1989) **C-106m.** ** D: Jack Sholder. Kiefer Sutherland, Lou Diamond Phillips, Jami Gertz, Rob Knepper, Bill Smitrovich, Floyd Westerman. An undercover cop and a Lakota Indian put aside their differences to team up and chase down a criminal who's done them both wrong. Yet another buddy/cop movie which is just an excuse to keep stuntmen gainfully employed . . . though it does give Sutherland and Phillips a chance to use the gunslinging technique they learned in YOUNG GUNS. [R]▼●◗

Rent-a-Cop (1988) **C-96m.** BOMB D: Jerry London. Burt Reynolds, Liza Minnelli, James Remar, Richard Masur, Dionne Warwick, Bernie Casey, Robby Benson, Michael Rooker. Chicago dick Reynolds is suspended after his botched hotel drug bust leaves half a dozen dead; Minnelli's eyewitness hooker helps him track down the bullet-happy killer responsible. Burt seems fatigued but is at least easier to take than his costar's lounge-act prostie. [R]▼●

Rentadick (1972-British) **C-94m.** ** D: Jim Clark. James Booth, Julie Ege, Ronald Fraser, Donald Sinden, Michael Bentine, Richard Briers, Spike Milligan. Out of the nether-land between *The Goon Show* and *Monty Python* comes this romp written by Python pals John Cleese and Graham Chapman, spoofing formula private-eye flicks. An experimental nerve gas that paralyzes from the waist down has been stolen and Rentadick, Inc. is hired to track down the culprits.▼

Rent-a-Kid (1995-U.S.-Canadian) **C-89m.** **½ D: Frank Gerber. Leslie Nielsen, Christopher Lloyd, Matt McCoy, Sherry Miller, Amos Crawley, Cody Jones, Tabitha Lupien, Tony Rosato. When the head of an orphanage takes a vacation, dad Nielsen takes over with a scheme to raise money by renting out children. While predictable, this silly premise is surprisingly and sensitively realized when three children are rented by a hip 90s couple thinking about adopting. A decent family film. [G]▼●

Rented Lips (1987) **C-82m.** ** D: Robert Downey. Martin Mull, Dick Shawn, Jennifer Tilly, Robert Downey, Jr., Mel Welles, Shelley Berman, Edy Williams, June Lockhart, Kenneth Mars, Eileen Brennan, Pat McCormick, Michael Horse. Highly uneven comedy, written and produced by Mull, about a pair of down-on-their-luck educational filmmakers (with films like "Aluminum, Your Shiny Friend" to their credit) who become involved with a porno film crew. Cast of old pros and familiar faces helps. [R]▼

Repeat Performance (1947) **93m.** *** D: Alfred L. Werker. Louis Hayward, Joan Leslie, Tom Conway, Benay Venuta, Richard Basehart, Virginia Field. Narrated by John Ireland. On New Year's Eve, woman gets chance to relive the past year, leading up to the moment she murdered her husband. Fine premise smoothly executed in this B production; Basehart's first film. Remade for TV in 1989 as TURN BACK THE CLOCK.

Repentance (1987-Russian) **C-155m.** ** D: Tengiz Abuladze. Avtandil Makharadze, Zeinab Botsvadze, Ketevan Abuladze, Edisher Giorgobiani, Kakhi Kavsadze. A beloved city father dies, but why is his body mysteriously—and continuously—exhumed? This allegory about small town smallmindedness and political repression offers a critical look at the Stalin era, but the result bogs down into a talkfest, and is much too obvious and boring. Completed in 1984; the final part of a trilogy, following THE PLEA (1968) and THE WISHING TREE (1977). [PG]▼●

Replacement Killers, The (1998) **C-86m.** **½ D: Antoine Fuqua. Chow Yun-Fat, Mira Sorvino, Michael Rooker, Jürgen Prochnow, Kenneth Tsang, Til Schweiger. Chow's American debut is a disappointingly routine action yarn about a hired assassin who—after failing to kill a cop, as ordered—becomes a target himself. Not bad, but nothing special; hardly a star-making vehicle for this established Hong Kong favorite. John Woo executive-produced. Super 35. [R]▼●◗

Replica of a Crime SEE: **Amuck**

Repo Man (1984) **C-92m.** **½ D: Alex Cox. Emilio Estevez, Harry Dean Stanton, Vonetta McGee, Olivia Barash, Sy Richardson, Tracey Walter, Susan Barnes, Fox Harris, The Circle Jerks. Instant cult-movie about a new-wave punk who takes a job repossessing cars. Mixes social satire and science-fiction with engaging results, though a little of this film goes a long way. Stanton is perfect as a career repo man who shows Estevez the ropes. Michael Nesmith was executive producer. Cox prepared a special version for TV. [R]▼●

Report to the Commissioner (1975) **C-112m.** **½ D: Milton Katselas. Michael Moriarty, Yaphet Kotto, Susan Blakely, Hector Elizondo, Tony King, Michael McGuire, Dana Elcar, Robert Balaban, William Devane, Stephen Elliott, Richard Gere, Vic Tayback, Sonny Grosso. Rookie cop Moriarty accidentally kills undercover cop Blakely and becomes embroiled in department-wide cover-up. Brutal melodrama ranges from realistic to overblown; taut but not always convincing. Script by Abby Mann and Ernest Tidyman. Gere's film debut. [PG]▼

Repossessed (1990) **C-84m.** *½ D: Bob Logan. Linda Blair, Ned Beatty, Leslie Nielsen, Anthony Starke, Lana Schwab, Thom J. Sharp. AIRPLANE-style spoof of THE EXORCIST, with Blair herself as a housewife possessed anew by the same demon she was rid of as a child. Too few gags, too many targets, and a poor finale. Blair and Nielsen (as the exorcist) are good. Written by director Logan. [PG-13]▼●

Reprieve SEE: **Convicts Four**

Reprisal! (1956) **C-74m.** **½ D: George Sherman. Guy Madison, Felicia Farr, Kathryn Grant, Michael Pate, Edward Platt. Madison has to clear himself of murder charge when a powerful rancher is killed. Decent cast in ordinary grade-B Western drama.

Reptile, The (1966-British) **C-90m.** ***

D: John Gilling. Noel Willman, Jennifer Daniels, Ray Barrett, Jacqueline Pearce. Hammer chiller about village girl with strange power to change into snake. Excellent direction, sympathetic characterizations.▼●

Reptilicus (1962) **C-90m.** BOMB D: Sidney Pink. Carl Ottosen, Ann Smyrner, Mimi Heinrich, Asbjorn Andersen, Marla Behrens. The tail of a prehistoric monster—recently discovered—spawns the full-sized beast. Only good for laughs as script hits every conceivable monster-movie cliché, right to the final shot. Filmed in Denmark.▼

Repulsion (1965-British) **105m.** **** D: Roman Polanski. Catherine Deneuve, Ian Hendry, John Fraser, Patrick Wymark, Yvonne Furneaux, James Villiers. Polanski's first English-language film is excellent psychological shocker depicting mental deterioration of sexually repressed girl left alone in her sister's apartment for several days. Hasn't lost a bit of its impact; will leave you feeling uneasy for days afterward. Screenplay by Polanski and Gerard Brach.▼●

Requiem for a Gunfighter (1965) **C-91m.** *½ D: Spencer G. Bennet. Rod Cameron, Stephen McNally, Mike Mazurki, Olive Sturgess, Tim McCoy, John Mack Brown, Bob Steele, Lane Chandler, Raymond Hatton. Veteran cast is sole virtue of low-budget Western. Cameron impersonates a judge to ensure that justice is done at murder trial. Techniscope.

Requiem for a Heavyweight (1962) **100m.** *** D: Ralph Nelson. Anthony Quinn, Jackie Gleason, Mickey Rooney, Julie Harris, Nancy Cushman, Madame Spivy, Cassius Clay (Muhammad Ali). Grim account of fighter, Quinn, whose ring career is over, forcing him into corruption and degradation. His sleazy manager Gleason, sympathetic trainer Rooney, and Harris as unrealistic social worker are all fine. Adapted by Rod Serling from his great teleplay; original running time 87m.▼

Requiem for Dominic (1990-Austrian) **C-90m.** **½ D: Robert Dornhelm. Felix Mitterer, Viktoria Schubert, August Schmolzer, Angelica Schutz, Antonia Rados, Nikolas Vogel. True story about Romanian-born Austrian who returns to his homeland to be with his best friend, who's now accused of committing eighty murders. Set at the beginning of the anti-Communist movement in late 1989. Sometimes powerful, highly political film; director Dornhelm was a childhood friend of the accused man depicted in the story.▼●

Rescue, The (1986) SEE: **Let's Get Harry**

Rescue, The (1988) **C-98m.** BOMB D: Ferdinand Fairfax. Kevin Dillon, Christina Harnos, Marc Price, Ned Vaughan, Ian Giatti, Charles Haid, Edward Albert. Dumb, obnoxious actioner featuring the exploits of a group of teens as they attempt to liberate their POW dads—and really do Rambo proud in the process. A sick movie aimed at less discriminating 13-year-old boys. [PG]▼●

Rescuers, The (1977) **C-76m.** *** D: Wolfgang Reitherman, John Lounsbery, Art Stevens. Voices of Bob Newhart, Eva Gabor, Geraldine Page, Joe Flynn, Jeanette Nolan, Pat Buttram, Jim Jordan, John McIntire. Engaging, well-plotted Disney animated feature about Bernard and Bianca, members of the all-mouse Rescue Aid Society, and their efforts to save a little girl who's been kidnaped. Highlighted by some great supporting characters, including Orville the Albatross (voiced by radio's Fibber McGee, Jim Jordan), Evinrude the dragonfly, and the villainess Madame Medusa. Followed by a sequel. [G]▼●

Rescuers Down Under, The (1990) **C-74m.** *** D: Hendel Butoy, Mike Gabriel. Voices of Bob Newhart, Eva Gabor, George C. Scott, John Candy, Tristan Rogers, Adam Ryen, Frank Welker. Entertaining—if plotty—sequel to the 1977 Disney animated feature, with amorous mice Bernard and Bianca, the unlikely agents from the Rescue Aid Society, traveling to Australia to help a young boy in trouble. Animation buffs will notice considerable computer-assisted animation, especially the villain's demon tractor. [G]▼●

Reservoir Dogs (1992) **C-99m.** *** D: Quentin Tarantino. Harvey Keitel, Tim Roth, Michael Madsen, Chris Penn, Steve Buscemi, Lawrence Tierney, Randy Brooks, Kirk Baltz, Eddie Bunker, Quentin Tarantino, voice of Steven Wright. Precocious "shock" debut from writer director costar Tarantino echoes THE ASPHALT JUNGLE and THE KILLING: Post-mortem dissection of a fatally bungled jewel robbery boasts at least one unwatchably graphic torture scene and the 1992 movie year's No. 1 mortality rate. Flashy—maybe *too* flashy—but fundamentally a story well told; nearly every performance is better than expected, with Tierney in his best role since the '40s. Keitel coproduced; Monte Hellman was one of the executive producers. Super 35. [R]▼●◗

Resting Place (1986) **C-100m. TVM** D: John Korty. John Lithgow, Richard Bradford, Morgan Freeman, CCH Pounder, G. D. Spradlin, Frances Sternhagen, M. Emmet Walsh. Army officer encounters racial tension while trying to secure the burial of a black Vietnam War hero in an all-white Georgia cemetery in the 1970s. Beautiful script by Walter Halsey Davis, well performed by all. Above average.

Rest Is Silence, The (1960-German) **106m.** *** D: Helmut Kautner, Hardy Kruger, Peter Van Eyck, Ingrid Andree, Adelheid Seeck, Rudolf Forster, Boy Gobert. Updating of Hamlet, with young man trying to prove uncle killed his father.

Restless Breed, The (1957) **C-81m.** ** D: Allan Dwan. Scott Brady, Anne Bancroft, Jim Davis, Scott Marlowe, Evelyn Rudie. Usual Western fare of Brady out to get his father's killer.▼●

Restless Years, The (1958) **86m.** ** D: Helmut Kautner. John Saxon, Sandra Dee, Margaret Lindsay, Teresa Wright, James Whitmore, Luana Patten, Virginia Grey, Jody McCrea, Alan Baxter. Capable cast tries hard in this overblown relic of its era, an Edward Anhalt–scripted PEYTON PLACE clone, in which illegitimate Dee is overprotected by neurotic mom Wright; trouble comes when sensitive outsider Saxon—from "the wrong side of the tracks"—takes an interest in her. CinemaScope.

Restoration (1995) **C-117m.** *** D: Michael Hoffman. Robert Downey, Jr., Sam Neill, David Thewlis, Polly Walker, Meg Ryan, Ian McKellen, Hugh Grant, Hugh McDiarmid. In 1600s England, a young doctor torn between duty and debauchery opts for the latter when he becomes a court favorite of King Charles II, and a dummy bridegroom for one of the king's mistresses. Vivid period piece with contemporary parallels depends on Downey to draw us in—and he's excellent. Opulent production and an earnest cast buoy this film through its metamorphosis from costume romp to social drama, though it does sag during the second half. Oscar winner for Art Direction and Costume Design. Filmed in England and Wales. [R]▼●◗

Resurrection (1980) **C-103m.** ***½ D: Daniel Petrie. Ellen Burstyn, Sam Shepard, Richard Farnsworth, Roberts Blossom, Clifford David, Pamela Payton-Wright, Eva LeGallienne. Beautifully realized story (by Lewis John Carlino) about a woman who returns to life from the brink of death with amazing healing powers. Burstyn's moving performance is the centerpiece of a wonderful and underrated film. [PG]▼

Resurrection of Zachary Wheeler, The (1971) **C-100m.** *** D: Bob Wynn. Angie Dickinson, Bradford Dillman, James Daly, Leslie Nielsen, Jack Carter. Offbeat mixture of sci-fi and action. U.S. Senator brought to mysterious clinic in Alamogordo, New Mexico after car crash, is accidentally recognized by TV reporter. Only unconvincing aspect: fadeout explanation by clinic director. Shot on video. [G]▼

Resurrection Syndicate, The SEE: **Nothing but the Night**

Retreat, Hell! (1952) **95m.** **½ D: Joseph H. Lewis. Frank Lovejoy, Richard Carlson, Russ Tamblyn, Anita Louise. Grim drama chronicling the Marine withdrawal from Korea's Changjin Reservoir in the wake of a massive Chinese offensive.▼

Return, The (1980) **C-91m.** BOMB D: Greydon Clark. Jan-Michael Vincent, Cybill Shepherd, Martin Landau, Raymond Burr, Neville Brand, Brad Rearden, Vincent Schiavelli. Deadeningly dull story of a "close encounter" and how it affects two children and an old man in a small New Mexico town. Inept from start to finish. Retitled THE ALIEN'S RETURN.▼

Return (1985) **C-82m.** ** D: Andrew Silver. Karlene Crockett, John Walcutt, Lisa Richards, Frederic Forrest, Anne Lloyd Francis. Hokey, superficial tale of Crockett attempting to understand and unravel the mystery of her grandfather's death. Her investigation leads her to his birthplace and a series of bizarre secrets. Interesting premise, disappointing result. [R]▼●

Return From the Ashes (1965-British) **105m.** *** D: J. Lee Thompson. Maximilian Schell, Samantha Eggar, Ingrid Thulin, Herbert Lom, Talitha Pol. Engrossing melodrama of a philandering husband taking up with his stepdaughter when his wife is supposedly killed. Trio of stars lend credibility to the far-fetched proceedings. Panavision.

Return From the Past (1967) **C-84m.** BOMB D: David L. Hewitt. Lon Chaney, John Carradine, Rochelle Hudson, Roger Gentry. Veteran stars wasted in utter monstrosity; five tales of supernatural told here are five too many. Original titles: GALLERY OF HORROR, DR. TERROR'S GALLERY OF HORRORS, THE BLOOD SUCKERS. Totalvision.▼

Return From the Sea (1954) **80m.** ** D: Lesley Selander. Jan Sterling, Neville Brand, John Doucette, Paul Langton, John Pickard. Tepid story of Brand-Sterling romance, set in San Diego.

Return From Witch Mountain (1978) **C-95m.** *** D: John Hough. Bette Davis, Christopher Lee, Kim Richards, Ike Eisenmann, Denver Pyle, Jack Soo, Dick Bakalyan. Sequel to ESCAPE TO WITCH MOUNTAIN has Davis and Lee kidnapping Eisenmann, hoping to put his special powers to evil use. Good fun from Disney. [G]▼●

Return of a Man Called Horse, The (1976) **C-129m.** *** D: Irvin Kershner. Richard Harris, Gale Sondergaard, Geoffrey Lewis, Bill Lucking, Jorge Luke, Enrique Lucero. Excellent sequel has Harris returning from England to right wrongs done the Yellow Hand Sioux by whites. Sun Vow ceremony now performed by dozen braves. Magnificent score by Laurence Rosenthal; followed by TRIUMPHS OF A MAN CALLED HORSE. Panavision. [PG]▼●

Return of a Stranger (1961-British) **63m.** **½ D: Max Varnel. John Ireland, Susan Stephen, Cyril Shaps, Timothy Beaton. Taut thriller of psychopath Shaps released from prison, terrorizing former victim Stephen and husband Ireland.

Return of Bulldog Drummond, The (1934-British) **71m.** *** D: Walter Summers. Ralph Richardson, Ann Todd, Francis L. Sullivan, Claud Allister, Joyce Kennedy. Richardson gives a full-blooded

performance as Drummond in this serial-like account of the ex-Army officer on a bloody vigilante campaign to end crime in England by eliminating all foreigners! Wildly entertaining, and a revelation to those only familiar with genteel British cinema.
Return of Captain Invincible, The (1983-Australian-U.S) **C-90m.** **½ D: Philippe Mora. Alan Arkin, Christopher Lee, Kate Fitzpatrick, Michael Pate. Bizarre, campy comedy about drunken, derelict ex-superhero persuaded to come out of retirement sounds better than it works. Oddly placed musical numbers seem to aim for ROCKY HORROR ambiance. Aka LEGEND IN LEOTARDS. Panavision. [PG] ▼●
Return of Count Yorga (1971) **C-97m.** **½ D: Bob Kelljan. Robert Quarry, Mariette Hartley, Roger Perry, Yvonne Wilder. The Count goes out for more blood, wreaking havoc on nearby orphanage. [PG]▼
Return of Don Camillo, The (1965-Italian) **115m.** **½ D: Julien Duvivier. Fernandel, Gino Cervi, Charles Vissieres, Edouard Delmont. Fernandel is again the irresponsible smalltown Italian priest involved in more projects of goodwill.
Return of Dracula, The (1958) **77m.** ** D: Paul Landres. Francis Lederer, Norma Eberhardt, Ray Stricklyn, Jimmie Baird. Low-budget flick about the Count (Lederer) killing a man, taking his papers, and coming to U.S. Lederer thwarted by mediocre script. TV title: THE CURSE OF DRACULA. ▼●
Return of Dr. X, The (1939) **62m.** ** D: Vincent Sherman. Humphrey Bogart, Rosemary Lane, Dennis Morgan, John Litel, Huntz Hall, Wayne Morris. Only Bogart as a creepy lab assistant makes this low-grade sci-fi yarn worth viewing. Despite the title, not a sequel to DR. X.
Return of Frank James, The (1940) **C-92m.** *** D: Fritz Lang. Henry Fonda, Gene Tierney, Jackie Cooper, Henry Hull, John Carradine, J. Edward Bromberg, Donald Meek. Fonda reprises role from 1939 JESSE JAMES in story of attempt to avenge his brother's death; colorful production was Tierney's film debut.▼●
Return of Jack Slade, The (1955) **79m.** ** D: Harold Schuster. John Ericson, Mari Blanchard, Neville Brand, Angie Dickinson. To redeem his father's wrongdoings, Ericson joins the law to fight outlaws; adequate Western. SuperScope.
Return of Jafar, The (1994) **C-66m.** ** D: Toby Shelton, Tad Stones, Alan Zaslove. Voices of Jason Alexander, Jonathan Freeman, Gilbert Gottfried, Liz Callaway, Brad Kane, Dan Castellaneta, Frank Welker. Made-for-video sequel to Disney's animated smash ALADDIN, with the parrot Iago trying to renounce his evil master and befriend Aladdin and Jasmine. This episodic "feature" is actually four segments of the Aladdin TV series strung together. Not bad, with some listenable songs, but Robin Williams' comedy is sorely missed (the Genie is voiced here by Castellaneta)—and so is the indefinable "oomph" of a theatrical production. [G]▼●
Return of Jesse James, The (1950) **75m.** **½ D: Arthur Hilton. John Ireland, Ann Dvorak, Henry Hull, Hugh O'Brian, Reed Hadley. Compact budget Western dealing with rumors that lookalike for outlaw is notorious gunslinger.
Return of Josey Wales, The (1986) **C-90m.** BOMB D: Michael Parks. Michael Parks, Rafael Campos, Bob Magruder, Paco Vela, Everett Sifuentes, Charlie McCoy. Incomprehensible sequel to OUTLAW . . . , minus Clint Eastwood! Here, Wales takes on, and repeatedly embarrasses, a determined but ineffectual lawman.▼
Return of Martin Guerre, The (1982-French) **C-111m.** *** D: Daniel Vigne. Gérard Depardieu, Nathalie Baye, Roger Planchon, Maurice Jacquemont, Bernard Pierre Donnadieu. Blockbuster art house hit, based on fact, about a sixteenth-century peasant who returns to his wife and family a much better person than the misfit he was seven years earlier; could it be that he's really an impostor? No artistic groundbreaker, but a solid romance and history lesson, well acted by the two leads. Special video edition runs 123m. Remade in 1993 as SOMMERSBY. ▼●◗
Return of Maxwell Smart, The SEE: **Nude Bomb, The**
Return of Monte Cristo, The (1946) **91m.** ** D: Henry Levin. Louis Hayward, Barbara Britton, George Macready, Una O'Connor, Henry Stephenson. Rather ordinary swashbuckler of original count's, young descendant, thwarted in attempt to claim inheritance by dastardly villain.
Return of Mr. Moto, The (1965-British) **71m.** *½ D: Ernest Morris. Henry Silva, Terrence Longdon, Suzanne Lloyd, Marne Maitland, Martin Wyldeck. Silva is miscast as the Oriental sleuth in a drab, lifeless update involving an international crime syndicate out to control world oil production (no, it's not OPEC).
Return of October, The (1948) **C-98m.** ** D: Joseph H. Lewis. Glenn Ford, Terry Moore, Albert Sharpe, James Gleason, Steve Dunne. Moore is wholesome girl who thinks her horse (October) is a reincarnation of her favorite uncle, much to her relatives' consternation. Weird comedy written by Norman Panama and Melvin Frank.
Return of Peter Grimm, The (1935) **82m.** **½ D: George Nicholls, Jr. Lionel Barrymore, Helen Mack, Edward Ellis, Donald Meek, Allen Vincent. Patriarch of a close-knit family returns from the dead to make amends for all he did wrong in his lifetime. Hoary old

David Belasco play gets full-blooded treatment from Barrymore and a cast of pros.▼

Return of Rin Tin Tin, The (1947) **C-65m.** **½ D: Max Nosseck. Bobby (Robert) Blake, Donald Woods, Rin Tin Tin (III), Claudia Drake, Gaylord Pendleton, Earl Hodgins. Easy-to-take low-budget tale of young boy who comes out of his shell whenever he's with Rin Tin Tin, but bad man takes the dog away. Filmed in ultracheap Vitacolor process. Aka THE ADVENTURES OF RIN TIN TIN.▼

Return of Sabata, The (1972-Italian-Spanish) **C-106m.** *½ D: Frank Kramer (Gianfranco Parolini). Lee Van Cleef, Reiner Schone, Annabelle Incontrera, Jacqueline Alexandre, Pedro Sanchez (Ignazio Spalla). Last of the spaghetti Western series—and not a moment too soon—finds Van Cleef chasing down some baddies who bilked him out of $5,000. Techniscope. [PG]

Return of Sherlock Holmes, The (1987) **C-100m. TVM** D: Kevin Connor. Margaret Colin, Michael Pennington, Lila Kaye, Connie Booth, Nicholas Guest. Dr. Watson's modern-day great-granddaughter, a private eye from Boston, stumbles upon Sherlock Holmes' body in frozen suspension and restores the inimitable Victorian Era sleuth to life in the 1980s. Lighthearted fluff; this original bit of Holmesiana is not to be confused with the British series with Jeremy Brett shown on PBS. Average.

Return of Sophie Lang, The (1936) **65m.** **½ D: George Archainbaud. Gertrude Michael, Sir Guy Standing, Ray Milland, Elizabeth Patterson, Colin Tapley, Paul Harvey. Jewel-thief-gone-straight Michael seeks Milland's help in staying out of public eye. OK low-budgeter.

Return of Superfly, The (1990) **C-95m.** *½ D: Sig Shore. Nathan Purdee, Margaret Avery, Leonard Thomas, Christopher Curry, David Groh. Belated (and unnecessary) sequel with Purdee replacing Ron O'Neal as Priest; he's now an ex-drug dealer who goes up against his vicious, violent former cronies. Only interest is Curtis Mayfield's reworking of his original SUPERFLY score to incorporate rap music. [R]▼

Return of Swamp Thing, The (1989) **C-88m.** *½ D: Jim Wynorski. Dick Durock, Heather Locklear, Louis Jourdan, Sarah Douglas, Daniel Taylor, Ronreaco Lee. The vegetable man superhero learns that mad scientist Jourdan, who's been blending people with animals, has similar designs on his chirpy stepdaughter Locklear. Oafish spoof sequel to straight original can't find a style, and wastes time with two unfunny little boys. The comic books are much better. [PG-13]▼●

Return of the Ape Man (1944) **60m.** ** D: Philip Rosen. Bela Lugosi, John Carradine, Judith Gibson, Michael Ames (Tod Andrews), Frank Moran, Mary Currier. Scientist Lugosi transplants Carradine's brain into body of recently discovered Missing Link (Moran!). Typical Monogram fare; no relation to THE APE MAN.

Return of the Bad Men (1948) **90m.** **½ D: Ray Enright. Randolph Scott, Robert Ryan, Anne Jeffreys, George "Gabby" Hayes, Jacqueline White, Steve Brodie, Lex Barker. Newly settled Oklahoman Scott gets one female outlaw (Jeffreys) to go straight, but has a tougher time dealing with Billy the Kid, The Dalton Gang, The Younger Brothers, and a particularly nasty Sundance Kid (Ryan) in this routine Western. Also shown in computer-colored version.▼

Return of the Dragon (1973-Hong Kong) **C-91m.** **½ D: Bruce Lee. Bruce Lee, Chuck Norris, Nora Miao. Country hick Lee visits relatives who run Chinese restaurant in Italy and helps fight off gangsters trying to take over. Many fine comic and action sequences, including final battle with Chuck Norris in Roman Colosseum. This was made before (but released after) ENTER THE DRAGON, which was Lee's final completed film. Aka WAY OF THE DRAGON. Widescreen. [R]▼●◗

Return of the Fly, The (1959) **80m.** **½ D: Edward L. Bernds. Vincent Price, Brett Halsey, David Frankham, John Sutton, Dan Seymour, Danielle De Metz. Adequate sequel to THE FLY proves "like father, like son." Youth attempts to reconstruct his late father's teleportation machine and likewise gets scrambled with an insect. Followed six years later by CURSE OF THE FLY. CinemaScope.▼●

Return of the Frontiersman (1950) **C-74m.** ** D: Richard Bare. Gordon MacRae, Rory Calhoun, Julie London, Jack Holt, Fred Clark. Easygoing yarn of sheriff's son falsely accused of murder.

Return of the Jedi (1983) **C-131m.** ***½ D: Richard Marquand. Mark Hamill, Harrison Ford, Carrie Fisher, Billy Dee Williams, Anthony Daniels, Peter Mayhew, Sebastian Shaw, Ian McDiarmid, David Prowse, Alec Guinness, Kenny Baker, Denis Lawson, Warwick Davis, voices of James Earl Jones, Frank Oz. Third installment in the STAR WARS saga is a sheer delight, following the destiny of Luke Skywalker as his comrades reunite to combat a powerful Death Star. Some routine performances are compensated for by ingenious new characters and Oscar-winning special effects. More sentimental and episodic than its predecessors, but carried out in the best tradition of Saturday matinee serials, from which it draws its inspiration. Full title onscreen is: STAR WARS EPISODE VI: RETURN OF THE JEDI. Special edition released in 1997 features enhanced effects and 4m. of additional footage. Followed by two Ewok adventures for TV and the prequel STAR WARS EPISODE I: THE

PHANTOM MENACE. J-D-C Scope. [PG] ▼●

Return of the Killer Tomatoes! (1988) **C-99m.** *½ D: John De Bello. Anthony Starke, George Clooney, Karen Mistal, Steve Lundquist, Charlie Jones, John Astin. Sequel to ATTACK OF THE KILLER TOMATOES!, this is a mild improvement. In a tomato-fearing world, mad scientist Astin is turning tomatoes into people and vice-versa; our hero falls for an attractive one-time tomato. Too long, too silly, but has its moments. Followed by KILLER TOMATOES STRIKE BACK. [PG]▼●

Return of the Living Dead, The (1985) **C-90m.** ** D: Dan O'Bannon. Clu Gulager, James Karen, Don Calfa, Thom Mathews, Beverly Randolph, John Philbin. What starts out as a spoof of George Romero's zombie films (with wonderful comic performance by Karen as supervisor of medical warehouse) loses its footing when the tone, and the violence, turn serious. Directing debut for sci-fi screenwriter O'Bannon. Followed by two sequels. [R]▼●

Return of the Living Dead Part II (1988) **C-89m.** ** D: Ken Wiederhorn. James Karen, Thom Mathews, Michael Kenworthy, Marsha Dietlein, Dana Ashbrook, Suzanne Snyder. Awkward title identifies this as a sequel not to the George Romero zombie classics but rather the 1985 comedy offshoot. Inquisitive kids release deadly gas from a misplaced military canister, causing corpses from a nearby cemetery to rise and wreak havoc. [R]▼●

Return of the Living Dead III (1993) **C-97m.** **½ D: Brian Yuzna. Mindy Clarke, J. Trevor Edmond, Kent McCord, Sarah Douglas, James T. Callahan, Mike Moroff, Sal Lopez. A very different approach from the first two entries results in a serious thriller about a teenager who uses the zombie gas to resurrect his girlfriend, with horrendous results. An intelligent, gruesomely imaginative, and tragic love story, but it doesn't know when to quit. [R]▼●

Return of the Magnificent Seven SEE: **Return of the Seven**

Return of the Musketeers, The (1989-British-French-Spanish) **C-101m.** **½ D: Richard Lester. Michael York, Oliver Reed, Frank Finlay, C. Thomas Howell, Kim Cattrall, Richard Chamberlain, Philippe Noiret, Roy Kinnear, Geraldine Chaplin, Christopher Lee, Eusebio Lazaro, Jean-Pierre Cassel, Billy Connolly. Twenty years after the death of Milady de Winter, d'Artagnan (York) tries to reunite the remaining musketeers to save Queen Anne from the machinations of the devious Cardinal Mazarin (deliciously played by Noiret). Lester's follow-up to his two 70s classics is only partially successful, straining for a jaunty charm that just isn't there, but actually gets better as it goes along. Released directly to cable-TV in the U.S. in 1991. Sadly, Roy Kinnear, who played Planchet in all three films, died in an equestrian accident during production. Based on the Alexandre Dumas novel *Twenty Years Later.* [PG]▼●

Return of the Pink Panther, The (1975-British) **C-113m.** **½ D: Blake Edwards. Peter Sellers, Christopher Plummer, Catherine Schell, Herbert Lom, Burt Kwouk, Peter Arne, Gregoire Aslan, Andre Maranne, Victor Spinetti. Fourth PANTHER film, and first with Sellers since A SHOT IN THE DARK. Inspector Clouseau is a superb comedy character, but director-writer Edwards thinks big, violent gags are funny. Best part of this diamond-heist farce is the opening title, animated by Richard Williams and Ken Harris. Immediate sequel—THE PINK PANTHER STRIKES AGAIN—is much better. Panavision. [G] ▼●◗

Return of the Scarlet Pimpernel, The (1938-British) **88m.** ** D: Hans Schwartz. Barry K. Barnes, Sophie Stewart, Margaretta Scott, James Mason, Francis Lister, Anthony Bushell. Far below stunning original, with lower production values and less-than-stellar cast in costumer set in 1790s London and Paris. Original British running time: 94m.

Return of the Secaucus Seven (1980) **C-106m.** *** D: John Sayles. Mark Arnott, Gordon Clapp, Maggie Cousineau, Adam Lefevre, Bruce MacDonald, Jean Passanante, Maggie Renzi, David Strathairn. A simple low-budget film about a weekend reunion of good friends who shared the 60s radical college life and have since gone in different directions. Credible, winning performances (including one by director-writer Sayles, as Howie) enhance a script that seems to tell the story of an entire generation. Filmed with unknown actors for a reported budget of $60,000! An interesting precursor to THE BIG CHILL. [R]▼

Return of the Seven (1966) **C-96m.** ** D: Burt Kennedy. Yul Brynner, Robert Fuller, Warren Oates, Jordan Christopher, Claude Akins, Emilio Fernandez. The gang has reformed for more protection in this drab sequel to THE MAGNIFICENT SEVEN; it was a lot more fun when Eli Wallach was the heavy. Followed by GUNS OF THE MAGNIFICENT SEVEN. Aka RETURN OF THE MAGNIFICENT SEVEN. Panavision.▼●

Return of the Soldier, The (1981-British) **C-101m.** ** D: Alan Bridges. Alan Bates, Julie Christie, Glenda Jackson, Ann-Margret, Ian Holm, Frank Finlay. A shell-shocked soldier comes home from WW1 with no memory of the last twenty years, but feels a vague dissatisfaction with his life, as personified by wife Christie. Top cast in this adaptation of Rebecca West's first novel, but it's slow going, and ultimately not that interesting.▼

Return of the Street Fighter (1974-Japanese) **C-76m.** ** D: Shigehiro Ozawa. Shinichi "Sonny" Chiba, Yoko Ichiji, Masafumi Suzuki, Donald Nakajima, Milton Ishibashi, Zulu Yachi, Claude Gannyon. After refusing to carry out a hit for the mob, Chiba is targeted for execution himself. First sequel in the series is just a routine continuation of the original—a mélange of hilariously bad dubbing and brutal martial arts action—highlighted by a vicious fight in a steam bath. Followed by THE STREET FIGHTER'S LAST REVENGE. Actionscope. [R]▼●

Return of the Tall Blond Man With One Black Shoe, The (1974-French) **C-84m.** **½ D: Yves Robert. Pierre Richard, Mireille Darc, Michel Duchaussoy, Jean Rochefort, Jean Carmet. Sequel to the 1972 hit reunites the principals for a lesser if still entertaining sendup of the spy game. Spy chief Rochefort wants violinist Richard killed, but the tall blond avoids danger without even realizing what's happening. Nice shots of Rio and a fairly deft James Bond takeoff help offset slow buildup.▼

Return of the Texan (1952) **88m.** ** D: Delmer Daves. Dale Robertson, Joanne Dru, Walter Brennan, Richard Boone, Robert Horton. Flabby Western about Robertson et al fighting to save his ranch.

Return of the Texas Chainsaw Massacre SEE: **Texas Chainsaw Massacre: The Next Generation**

Return of the Vampire, The (1943) **69m.** ** D: Lew Landers, Kurt Neumann. Bela Lugosi, Frieda Inescort, Nina Foch, Roland Varno, Miles Mander, Matt Willis. Lugosi plays a vampire in wartorn London (with a werewolf assistant!) in limp attempt to capitalize on previous success as Dracula. Final scene is memorable, though.▼●

Return of the Whistler, The (1948) **63m.** **½ D: D. Ross Lederman. Michael Duane, Lenore Aubert, Richard Lane, James Cardwell, Ann Doran. The final *Whistler* series entry, about Duane's efforts to find his wealthy fiancée, who's been kidnapped and put in an asylum by a man who claims that she's already his wife. Intriguing Cornell Woolrich story.

Return to Boggy Creek (1977) **C-87m.** ** D: Tom Moore. Dawn Wells, Dana Plato. More sightings of monsters in this sequel to THE LEGEND OF BOGGY CREEK, but this time two children are involved. G-rated nonsense may intrigue young viewers. Followed by THE BARBARIC BEAST OF BOGGY CREEK PART II, which is actually the third Boggy Creek film. [G]▼

Return to Earth (1976) **C-78m. TVM** D: Jud Taylor. Cliff Robertson, Ralph Bellamy, Shirley Knight, Charles Cioffi, Stefanie Powers. Robertson is A-OK in real-life drama of the breakdown of astronaut Buzz Aldrin after his 1969 moonwalk. Adapted by George Malko from the book Aldrin wrote with Wayne Warga. Above average.▼

Return to Macon County (1975) **C-90m.** *½ D: Richard Compton. Don Johnson, Nick Nolte, Robin Mattson, Robert Viharo, Eugene Daniels, Matt Greene. Unworthy follow-up to MACON COUNTY LINE, as youngsters get mixed up in drag races, sex, the law, violence and murder, in about that order. Nolte's first film. [PG]▼

Return to Me (2000) **C-116m.** *** D: Bonnie Hunt. David Duchovny, Minnie Driver, Carroll O'Connor, Robert Loggia, Bonnie Hunt, David Alan Grier, Joely Richardson, James Belushi, Eddie Jones, William Bronder. Thoroughly engaging romantic comedy-drama about a man who loses his wife, then chances to meet a woman whose life has been saved by a heart transplant. Sincere performances by the leads and a joyous ensemble (including O'Connor as Driver's Irish grandfather and Loggia as her Italian uncle) make this heartwarmer a pleasure to watch. Impressive feature directing debut for Hunt, who costars and wrote the script with Don Lake (who plays the hair transplant man). [PG]▼◗

Return to Oz (1985) **C-110m.** ** D: Walter Murch. Nicol Williamson, Jean Marsh, Fairuza Balk, Piper Laurie, Matt Clark. Distressingly downbeat sequel to THE WIZARD OF OZ, with Dorothy fleeing a spooky sanitarium in Kansas to return to her beloved land—only to find evil rulers now in charge. Many colorful characters, but few engender any warmth or feeling. Best moments involve Will Vinton's Claymation effects, where rock faces come to life. Best sequence: final showdown with the Nome King. Inauspicious directing debut for celebrated sound technician Murch (who cowrote script). [PG]▼●

Return to Paradise (1953) **C-100m.** ** D: Mark Robson. Gary Cooper, Roberta Haynes, Barry Jones, Moira MacDonald. Lackluster South Sea tale of beach bum Cooper in love with native girl; loosely based on James Michener's story. Filmed in Samoa.▼

Return to Paradise (1998) **C-109m.** **½ D: Joseph Ruben. Vince Vaughn, Anne Heche, Joaquin Phoenix, David Conrad, Jada Pinkett Smith, Vera Farmiga. Two years after a wild, carefree trip to Malaysia, a woman tracks down two young men in N.Y.C. and tells them that if they don't return, the friend they made during their trip will be hanged for possession of hashish that really belonged to them. A rare contemporary film about responsibility, and a crisis of conscience, is weakened by the introduction of a love story. Still interesting, however, with strong performances all around. Remake of the 1990 French film FORCE MAJEURE. Super 35. [R]▼●◗

Return to Peyton Place (1961) **C-122m.** ** D: Jose Ferrer. Carol Lynley, Jeff Chandler, Eleanor Parker, Mary Astor, Robert Sterling, Luciana Paluzzi, Brett Halsey, Gunnar Hellstrom, Tuesday Weld, Bob Crane. Muddled follow-up to PEYTON PLACE suffers from faulty direction, and, save for stalwarts Astor and Parker, miscasting. Followed by TV movie MURDER IN PEYTON PLACE. CinemaScope. ▼

Return to Salem's Lot, A (1987) **C-96m.** ** D: Larry Cohen. Michael Moriarty, Ricky Addison Reed, Samuel Fuller, Andrew Duggan, Evelyn Keyes, Jill Gatsby, June Havoc, Ronee Blakley, James Dixon, David Holbrook. Anthropologist Moriarty, trying to befriend his estranged son, is lured to a small Maine town where the populace—almost all vampires—want him to write their history. Typically cheap, oddball Cohen film, which he cowrote, has little to do with Stephen King's novel or the TV movie based on it. [R]▼

Return to Sender (1963-British) **63m.** ** D: Gordon Hales. Nigel Davenport, Yvonne Romain, Geoffrey Keen, William Russell, John Horsley. Programmer action tale of revenge, from Edgar Wallace yarn of industrialist's plot to ruin a D.A.'s career and life.

Return to Snowy River (1988-Australian) **C-97m.** **½ D: Geoff Burrowes. Tom Burlinson, Sigrid Thornton, Brian Dennehy, Nicholas Eadie, Bryan Marshall. Follow-up to THE MAN FROM SNOWY RIVER is not nearly as good. Young Burlinson must again prove his worth as he battles villainous Eadie, who's become engaged to his beloved (Thornton). All those shots of galloping horses, however, are still eye-popping. Panavision. [PG]▼●

Return to the Blue Lagoon (1991) **C-100m.** BOMB D: William A. Graham. Brian Krause, Milla Jovovich, Lisa Pelikan, Garette Patrick Ratliff, Courtney Barilla. The two-year-old son of LAGOON 1's deceased parents is rescued by a ship carrying a widow and her year-old daughter; circumstances (read: cholera) force the trio onto another tropical island, so the kids can eventually partake in PG-13 prurience. How would *you* like to be a sequel to a movie whose only claim to fame was being the definitive Brooke Shields vehicle? [PG-13]▼●

Return to the Edge of the World (1978-British) **C/B&W-85m.** *** D: Michael Powell. Michael Powell, John Laurie, Hamish Sutherland. In the mid-1930s Powell directed a drama about the depopulation of an island, THE EDGE OF THE WORLD, shot on location on Foula in the North Sea. Forty years later he and the cast and crew still living—most poignantly, the actor John Laurie—returned for a reunion. This fascinating film includes footage of this trip, plus the original feature.

Return to the Lost World (1994-Canadian) **C-99m.** *½ D: Timothy Bond. John Rhys-Davies, David Warner, Eric McCormack, Nathania Stanford, Darren Peter Mercer, Tamara Gorski, Innocent Chosa, Kate Egan. In this sequel to THE LOST WORLD (1993), shot at the same time in 1991, bad Belgians begin to exploit The Lost World, so Challenger (Rhys-Davies) and friends come to the rescue. Long, weary sequel has even fewer dinosaurs than the first film, if that's possible. An insult to Conan Doyle. Good performances by Rhys-Davies and Warner are lost in this world. [PG]▼●

Return to Treasure Island (1954) **C-75m.** *½ D: E. A. Dupont, Tab Hunter, Dawn Addams, Porter Hall, James Seay, Harry Lauter. Poor updating of Stevenson novel, with student Hunter vying with crooks for buried treasure.

Return to Treasure Island (1954-Australian) SEE: **Long John Silver**

Reuben, Reuben (1983) **C-101m.** *** D: Robert Ellis Miller. Tom Conti, Kelly McGillis, Roberts Blossom, Cynthia Harris, E. Katherine Kerr, Joel Fabiani, Kara Wilson, Lois Smith. Boozy Scottish poet (an amalgam of Dylan Thomas and Brendan Behan) sponges off hospitable women in New England college town—then falls in love with beautiful young student McGillis (in her film debut). Deliciously witty script by Julius J. Epstein (adapted from writings of Peter DeVries) and fine performances help offset general feeling of anachronism about the film . . . and a curious finale. [R]▼

Reunion (1989-French-German-British) **C-110m.** *** D: Jerry Schatzberg. Jason Robards, Christian Anholt, Samuel West, Alexander Trauner, Françoise Fabian, Maureen Kerwin, Barbara Jefford. Elderly Jewish man (Robards) journeys back to Stuttgart, Germany, to seek out boyhood friend he hasn't seen since leaving for the U.S. in 1933. Much of the film is told in flashback, with Anholt giving a fine performance as high-school age Robards, and West equally good as his Aryan chum. Screenplay by Harold Pinter; veteran art director Trauner, who designed the film, has a small role as a porter. Panavision. [PG-13]▼

Reunion in France (1942) **104m.** ** D: Jules Dassin. Joan Crawford, John Wayne, Philip Dorn, Reginald Owen, Albert Bassermann, John Carradine, Henry Daniell. Glossy romance, with Frenchwoman Crawford believing fiancé Dorn is a Nazi collaborator; she hides (and falls for) American flyer Wayne. Propaganda elements date badly. Watch for Ava Gardner as a salesgirl.▼

Reunion in Reno (1951) **79m.** **½ D: Kurt Neumann. Mark Stevens, Peggy Dow, Gigi Perreau, Frances Dee, Leif Erickson. Diverting comedy of Perreau deciding to divorce her parents so she won't be in the way.

Reunion in Vienna (1933) **98m.** *** D: Sidney Franklin. John Barrymore, Diana Wynyard, Frank Morgan, May Robson, Eduardo Ciannelli, Una Merkel, Henry Travers. Too-literal adaptation of Robert Sherwood's dated stage play depends on its stars' considerable charm to come across. Barrymore provides most of the film's life with hilarious performance as exiled nobleman who returns to Vienna and tries to rekindle romance with Wynyard under the nose of her tolerant husband (Morgan).

Reveille With Beverly (1943) **78m.** ** D: Charles Barton. Ann Miller, William Wright, Dick Purcell, Franklin Pangborn, Larry Parks. Columbia Pictures mini-musical, with Miller a versatile disk jockey throwing "big show" for servicemen. Jazz fans will shoot that rating higher, since guest stars include Frank Sinatra, Mills Brothers, Bob Crosby, Count Basie, and Duke Ellington.

Revenge (1971) **C-78m. TVM** D: Jud Taylor. Shelley Winters, Stuart Whitman, Bradford Dillman, Carol Rossen, Roger Perry, Gary Clarke. Winters plots to avenge her daughter's rape by imprisoning the man she suspects of the deed in a cage in her basement. Shelley tears it up in Joseph Stefano's adaptation of Elizabeth Davis' novel, and John A. Alonzo's striking photography doesn't hurt one bit. Above average.

Revenge (1971-British) SEE: **Inn of the Frightened People**

Revenge (1979) SEE: **Blood Feud**

Revenge (1986) **C-100m.** BOMB D: Christopher Lewis. Patrick Wayne, John Carradine, Bennie Lee McGowan. Boring, filmed sequel to the videotaped horror opus BLOOD CULT details the further goings-on of a Tulsa, Oklahoma, devil-worship cult led this time by (who else?) Carradine, that preys on students for human sacrifices. Strictly for fans of mindless violence; never released theatrically. Director Lewis is (gulp!) Loretta Young's son. [R]▼

Revenge (1990) **C-124m.** *½ D: Tony Scott. Kevin Costner, Anthony Quinn, Madeleine Stowe, Sally Kirkland, Tomas Milian, Joaquin Martinez, James Gammon, Miguel Ferrer, Joe Santos, John Leguizamo. Navy pilot Costner (yes, Tony—we *know* you directed TOP GUN) visits power-broker pal Quinn at his posh Mexican estate; soon he and Stowe (Quinn's young Mrs.) are enjoying a closet quickie, in both senses of the term. Ponderous mix of the slick and the sordid died at the box office; the second half—source of the film's title—is especially tough to endure. Panavision. [R]▼●◗

Revenge of Dracula, The SEE: **Dracula vs. Frankenstein** (1971)

Revenge of Frankenstein (1958-British) **C-91m.** *** D: Terence Fisher. Peter Cushing, Francis Matthews, Eunice Gayson, Michael Gwynn, Lionel Jeffries, John Welsh. Sequel to THE CURSE OF FRANKENSTEIN is quite effective with the good doctor still making a new body from others, ably assisted by hunchback dwarf and young medical student. Thought-provoking script has fine atmosphere, especially in color. Followed by EVIL OF FRANKENSTEIN.▼●

Revenge of the Creature (1955) **82m.** ** D: Jack Arnold. John Agar, Lori Nelson, John Bromfield, Nestor Paiva, Robert B. Williams. OK sequel to THE CREATURE FROM THE BLACK LAGOON destroys much of that film's mystery and terror by removing gill-man from Amazonian home and placing him in Florida aquarium. Originally in 3-D. Clint Eastwood has his first screen role as lab technician.▼●

Revenge of the Dead (1960) **69m.** BOMB D: Edward D. Wood, Jr. Duke Moore, Kenne Duncan, Paul Marco, Tor Johnson, John Carpenter, Valda Hansen, Jeannie Stevens, Criswell. Long-lost sequel to BRIDE OF THE MONSTER (and to a lesser extent, PLAN 9 FROM OUTER SPACE) doesn't reach the same heights of lunacy, but is still dreadful enough to tickle any bad-movie fan. "Ghosts" have been sighted in East L.A., so cops Moore and Marco are once more shoved into action; the trail leads to phony mystic Dr. Acula (Duncan, who really looks like he's in a trance). The incomparable Criswell again narrates the proceedings, this time from a coffin. Sat unreleased for *23 years* because Wood couldn't pay the lab bill! Retitled NIGHT OF THE GHOULS.▼●

Revenge of the Nerds (1984) **C-90m.** ** D: Jeff Kanew. Robert Carradine, Anthony Edwards, Timothy Busfield, Andrew Cassese, Curtis Armstrong, Larry B. Scott, Julie Montgomery, Michelle Meyrink, Ted McGinley, Matt Salinger, John Goodman, Bernie Casey. Geeky college freshmen, tired of being humiliated by the campus jocks and coed cuties, form their own fraternity, leading to all-out war. As raunchy teen comedies go, not bad, helped by two leads' likable performances. Followed by several sequels. [R]▼●

Revenge of the Nerds II: Nerds in Paradise (1987) **C-92m.** *½ D: Joe Roth. Robert Carradine, Curtis Armstrong, Larry B. Scott, Timothy Busfield, Courtney Thorne-Smith, Andrew Cassese, Donald Gibb, Ed Lauter, Anthony Edwards. Sequel, set at a fraternity gathering in Ft.

Lauderdale, is strictly by-the-numbers; once again the geeky "heroes" manage to triumph over their beefier (but not brainier) college counterparts . . . but this is a lot less fun than the original. Edwards, Carradine's costar in the first picture, makes a token appearance. Followed by 1992 TV sequel. [PG-13]▼●

Revenge of the Ninja (1983) **C-88m.** ** D: Sam Firstenberg. Sho Kosugi, Keith Vitali, Virgil Frye, Arthur Roberts, Mario Gallo. Good ninja Kosugi takes on evil ninja Roberts, a heroin smuggler/kidnapper/killer. Kung fu aficionados should enjoy it, otherwise beware. A follow-up to ENTER THE NINJA, followed by NINJA III—THE DOMINATION. [R]▼

Revenge of the Pink Panther (1978) **C-99m.** ** D: Blake Edwards. Peter Sellers, Herbert Lom, Robert Webber, Dyan Cannon, Burt Kwouk, Robert Loggia, Paul Stewart, Andre Maranne, Graham Stark, Ferdy Mayne. Sellers' final go-round as bumbling Inspector Clouseau is one of the dullest, until a bright wrap-up in Hong Kong with some good sight gags and plenty of spark from Cannon. The "plot" has Clouseau supposedly murdered, allowing him to find "killer" incognito. Followed by TRAIL OF THE PINK PANTHER. Panavision. [PG]▼●◗

Revenge of the Pirates (1951-Italian) **95m.** ** D: Primo Zeglio. Maria Montez, Milly Vitale, Jean-Pierre Aumont, Saro Urzi, Paul Muller, Robert Risso. Aumont and Montez (offscreen husband and wife) try to spark this trite swashbuckler of wicked governor hoarding stolen gold, with Robin Hood of the seas coming to rescue.

Revenge of the Zombies (1943) **61m.** *½ D: Steve Sekely. John Carradine, Robert Lowery, Gale Storm, Veda Ann Borg, Mantan Moreland, Mauritz Hugo. Low-budget mad doctor saga, with Carradine experimenting on human guinea pigs. Moreland's comic relief saves the day.

Revenge of Ukeno-Jo, The SEE: **Actor's Revenge, An**

Revengers, The (1972) **C-112m.** BOMB D: Daniel Mann. William Holden, Ernest Borgnine, Susan Hayward, Woody Strode, Roger Hanin, Rene Koldehoff. Rancher goes after those who massacred his family. Hayward (in her final theatrical feature) is the only good thing about this terrible Western. Panavision. [PG]

Revenge Squad SEE: **Hit and Run** (1982)

Reversal of Fortune (1990) **C-120m.** ***½ D: Barbet Schroeder. Glenn Close, Jeremy Irons, Ron Silver, Annabella Sciorra, Uta Hagen, Fisher Stevens, Jack Gilpin, Christine Baranski, Stephen Mailer. Tantalizing and complex film, embracing drama and very black comedy, sparked by Irons' devastating Oscar-winning performance as the aristocratic, enigmatic Claus von Bülow, who was accused of attempting to murder his socialite wife Sunny. Silver is perfectly cast as real-life Harvard law professor Alan Dershowitz, who agreed to take on the challenge of reversing the jury's decision. Teasingly ambiguous, and one of the most strikingly structured narrative films ever made. Scripted by Nicholas Kazan from Dershowitz's book. Julie Hagerty has small, unbilled role. [R]▼●

Revolt at Fort Laramie (1957) **C-73m.** ** D: Lesley Selander. John Dehner, Frances Helm, Gregg Palmer, Don Gordon, Robert Keys. Grade-B Western of internal rivalries of North-South soldiers at government fort during Civil War. Look for Harry Dean Stanton in his film debut.

Revolt in the Big House (1958) **79m.** **½ D: R. G. Springsteen. Gene Evans, Robert Blake, Timothy Carey, John Qualen. Taut little programmer about convict life.

Revolt of Job, The (1983-Hungarian-German) **C-97m.** ***½ D: Imre Gyongyossy, Barna Kabay. Ferenc Zenthe, Hedi Temessy, Gabor Feher, Peter Rudolf, Leticia Caro. Beautiful tale of a Jewish couple in WW2 Hungary who adopt a non-Jewish boy; their relationship, as he begins to perceive of them as family while the Holocaust hangs over them, is quite touching.▼

Revolt of Mamie Stover, The (1956) **C-92m.** **½ D: Raoul Walsh. Jane Russell, Richard Egan, Joan Leslie, Agnes Moorehead, Jorja Curtright, Jean Willes, Michael Pate. Gorgeous Jane, in glorious color, is Honolulu-based "saloon singer" in 1941. Weak plot; Jane sings "Keep Your Eyes On the Hands." CinemaScope.

Revolt of the Zombies (1936) **65m.** *½ D: Victor Halperin. Dorothy Stone, Dean Jagger, Roy D'Arcy, Robert Noland, George Cleveland. Boring horror film, with weak-willed Jagger discovering secret by which humans can be transformed into zombies.▼

Revolution (1969) **C-90m.** **½ D: Jack O'Connell. Today Malone. Documentary of late-60s hippie life, mostly in San Francisco, has some interesting footage, but directorial technique is sometimes too flashy. Music by Country Joe & the Fish, Quicksilver Messenger Service, Steve Miller Band, Mother Earth.▼

Revolution (1985) **C-123m.** BOMB D: Hugh Hudson. Al Pacino, Donald Sutherland, Nastassja Kinski, Joan Plowright, Dave King, Annie Lennox, Steven Berkoff, Jesse Birdsall, Graham Greene, Robbie Coltrane. Only a half-dozen or so movies have dealt more than superficially with the Revolutionary War; thanks to this megabomb, it'll be 2776 until we get another one. Pacino, two centuries too contemporary to be convincing, is the trapper whose boat and son are conscripted by the Continental Army; Kinski is the headstrong rebel from a family of Tories. Ludicrous script and acting sink some splendid production values. Super 35. [PG]▼●

Revolutionary, The (1970) **C-100m.** *** D: Paul Williams. Jon Voight, Jennifer Salt, Seymour Cassel, Robert Duvall. Tight, well-written study of a college youth who slowly gets drawn into role of political revolutionary with near-tragic results. [PG]▼

Reward, The (1965) **C-92m.** **½ D: Serge Bourguignon. Max von Sydow, Yvette Mimieux, Efrem Zimbalist, Jr., Gilbert Roland, Emilio Fernandez, Henry Silva, Rodolfo Acosta. Promising premise and good cast led astray in static Western: group of bounty hunters turn on each other, as greed for larger share of reward money goads them into conflict. CinemaScope.

Rhapsody (1954) **C-115m.** **½ D: Charles Vidor. Elizabeth Taylor, Vittorio Gassman, John Ericson, Louis Calhern, Michael Chekhov. Three-cornered romance among rich Taylor, violinist Gassman, and pianist Ericson: melodic interludes bolster soaper. Script by Fay and Michael Kanin.▼

Rhapsody in August (1991-Japanese) **C-98m.** **½ D: Akira Kurosawa. Sachiko Murase, Richard Gere, Hisashi Igawa, Narumi Kayashima. Thoughtful but (by his standards) minor Kurosawa, about the painful memories of a Japanese grandmother who recalls the bombing of Nagasaki at the end of WW2. Gere, in a glorified cameo, doesn't seem too out of place as a Japanese-American member of the old woman's extended clan. The director manages a few memorable visual touches, but talky film never quite recovers from its nearly static opening. [PG]▼●

Rhapsody in Blue (1945) **139m.** *** D: Irving Rapper. Robert Alda, Joan Leslie, Alexis Smith, Oscar Levant, Charles Coburn, Julie Bishop, Albert Basserman, Morris Carnovsky, Herbert Rudley, Rosemary DeCamp, Paul Whiteman, Hazel Scott. Hollywood biography of George Gershwin is largely pulp fiction, but comes off more credibly and interestingly than most other composer biopics, capturing Gershwin's enthusiasm for his work, and some of the inner conflicts he faced. Highlight is virtually complete performance of title work.▼●

Rhinestone (1984) **C-111m.** *½ D: Bob Clark. Sylvester Stallone, Dolly Parton, Richard Farnsworth, Ron Leibman, Tim Thomerson. Parton bets that she can turn anyone into a country singer—even N.Y.C. cabdriver Stallone. Contrived, cornball comedy with acres of unfunny dialogue. Panavision. [PG]▼●

Rhino! (1964) **C-91m.** **½ D: Ivan Tors. Robert Culp, Harry Guardino, Shirley Eaton, Harry Mekela. Diverting African gamehunting nonsense, with an enthusiastic cast, good action scenes.

Rhinoceros (1974) **C-101m.** BOMB D: Tom O'Horgan. Zero Mostel, Gene Wilder, Karen Black, Robert Weil, Joe Silver, Marilyn Chris. Eugene Ionesco entry in "Theater of the Absurd" makes sorry transition from stage to screen as clerk Wilder refuses to conform by turning into a pachyderm. The performers try. An American Film Theater Production. [PG]▼

Rhodes (1936-British) **91m.** ** D: Berthold Viertel. Walter Huston, Oscar Homolka, Basil Sydney, Frank Cellier, Peggy Ashcroft, Renne De Vaux, Bernard Lee, Ndanisa Kumalo. Biography of Cecil Rhodes (Huston), who founded Rhodesia and opened up the Transvaal to British exploitation. Huston's performance is big, romantic, and hammy, but the movie is a justification for Rhodes' rape of Africa and the Boer War. Homolka's dour, crafty Kruger is more interesting than Huston's Rhodes. Aka RHODES OF AFRICA ▼

Rhubarb (1951) **95m.** *** D: Arthur Lubin. Ray Milland, Jan Sterling, Gene Lockhart, William Frawley, Elsie Holmes, Taylor Holmes, Leonard Nimoy. Eccentric Lockhart owns the Brooklyn Loons baseball team; he dies and leaves the club to his spunky pet cat. Spirited comedy, based on a famous story by H. Allen Smith.

Rhythm on the Range (1936) **85m.** **½ D: Norman Taurog. Bing Crosby, Frances Farmer, Bob Burns, Martha Raye, Lucille Gleason, Samuel S. Hinds, Louis Prima, Leonid Kinskey. Film noteworthy as Raye's feature-film debut and pleasant excuse for musical nonsense songs, including "I'm an Old Cowhand (from the Rio Grande)." Remade as PARDNERS.▼

Rhythm on the River (1940) **92m.** *** D: Victor Schertzinger. Bing Crosby, Mary Martin, Basil Rathbone, Oscar Levant, Oscar Shaw, Charley Grapewin, William Frawley. Lots of fun, with Crosby and Martin ghost-writing songs for phony Rathbone, trying to break loose on their own. Based on a story coauthored by Billy Wilder.▼●

Rhythm Romance SEE: **Some Like It Hot** (1939)

Rhythm Thief (1995) **88m.** **½ D: Matthew Harrison. Jason Andrews, Eddie Daniels, Kevin Corrigan, Kimberly Flynn, Sean Hagerty, Mark Alfred, Christopher Cooke, Bob McGrath. At once intriguing and pretentious ultra-low-budget portrait of aloof but agonized Andrews, who lives on N.Y.C.'s grimy Lower East Side and earns his keep by selling tapes of illicitly recorded rock music. Original and provocative at times, but too often revels in its artiness. Filmed in 11 days, for $11,000.

Rice Girl (1963-Italian) **C-90m.** **½ D: Raffaello Matarazzo. Elsa Martinelli,

Folco Lulli, Michel Auclair, Rik Battaglia, Susanne Levesy, Liliana Gerace. Atmospheric account of seamy rice workers and Martinelli's past life catching up with her.
Rich and Famous (1981) **C-117m.** ** D: George Cukor. Jacqueline Bisset, Candice Bergen, David Selby, Hart Bochner, Steven Hill, Meg Ryan, Matt Lattanzi, Michael Brandon. Muddled, misguided remake of OLD ACQUAINTANCE, with Bisset and Bergen as women who maintain a stormy friendship for more than 20 years, despite rivalries in love and career. Idiotic dialogue and Bisset's sexual ruminations weaken what should have been a strong contemporary version of John Van Druten's story. Bisset's company produced. Among guests at Malibu party are Marsha Hunt, Christopher Isherwood, and Roger Vadim; later party offers glimpses of Ray Bradbury, Nina Foch, and Frances Bergen (Candice's mother). Cukor's last film; Meg Ryan's first. [R]▼●
Rich and Strange (1932-British) **83m.** **½ D: Alfred Hitchcock. Henry Kendall, Joan Barry, Betty Amann, Percy Marmont, Elsie Randolph. Kendall and Barry, married and bored are given money and travel around the world; he has affair with a "princess," while she becomes romantically attached to an explorer. Fragmented, offbeat drama (until the finale).▼●◗
Richard Pryor Here and Now (1983) **C-83m.** *½ D: Richard Pryor. The comedian's fourth concert film is his least satisfying to date, though hecklers in the audience are as much to blame as any defects in Pryor's material. Some amusing bits on drunks and dopeheads, plus some biting digs at the Reagan White House. Filmed on Bourbon Street in New Orleans. [R]▼●
Richard Pryor Is Back Live in Concert (1979) **C-78m.** ** D: Jeff Margolis. Pryor's still funny, but much of the material is ripped off from RICHARD PRYOR—LIVE IN CONCERT, released earlier that year.
Richard Pryor—Live in Concert (1979) **C-78m.** *** D: Jeff Margolis. Pryor on race, sex, machismo, death, filmed in performance in Long Beach, California. The comedian, uncensored, is at his raunchy best.▼◗
Richard Pryor Live on the Sunset Strip (1982) **C-82m.** **½ D: Joe Layton. Pryor on Africa, sex, lawyers, his wife, sex, Italian mobsters, more sex, and—inevitably—freebasing. Some of it's funny, some isn't, but the audience is always shown doubled over with laughter. [R]▼
Richard's Things (1980-British) **C-104m.** ** D: Anthony Harvey. Liv Ullmann, Amanda Redman, Tim Pigott-Smith, Elizabeth Spriggs, David Markham. Widow Ullmann is seduced by her late husband's girlfriend. Dreary drama, with a catatonic performance by Liv. Screenplay by Frederic Raphael, based on his novel. Made for British TV. [R]▼
Richard III (1955-British) **C-155m.** ***½ D: Laurence Olivier. Laurence Olivier, John Gielgud, Ralph Richardson, Claire Bloom, Alec Clunes, Cedric Hardwicke, Stanley Baker, Pamela Brown, Michael Gough. Elaborate if stagy verson of Shakespeare's chronicle of insane 15th-century British king and his court intrigues. Some prints run 139m. VistaVision.▼●
Richard III (1995-U.S.-British) **C-104m.** *** D: Richard Loncraine. Ian McKellen, Annette Bening, Jim Broadbent, Robert Downey, Jr., Nigel Hawthorne, Kristin Scott Thomas, Maggie Smith, John Wood, Jim Carter, Adrian Dunbar, Edward Hardwicke, Tim McInnerny, Bill Paterson, Donald Sumpter, Dominic West. Ingenious resetting of Shakespeare's drama of multiple murders and political intrigue in 1930s England, during a Fascist coup. McKellen dominates the screen as the devil incarnate, with a persona for every occasion. Visually compelling, often shocking (with glamour, sex, drugs, and violence), and yet doesn't fully capture the power of McKellen's (and Richard Eyre's) stage production, on which it is based. Super 35. [R]▼●◗
Rich Are Always With Us, The (1932) **73m.** ** D: Alfred E. Green. Ruth Chatterton, Adrienne Dore, George Brent, Bette Davis, John Miljan, Robert Warwick, Berton Churchill. Wealthy woman (Chatterton) cannot fall out of love with irresponsible husband (Miljan), even after bitter divorce and new romance with Brent. Silly script.
Richest Girl in the World, The (1934) **76m.** *** D: William A. Seiter. Miriam Hopkins, Joel McCrea, Fay Wray, Reginald Denny, Henry Stephenson. Entertaining romantic comedy by Norman Krasna about millionairess wanting to make sure her next boyfriend loves her for herself, not for her money. Remade as BRIDE BY MISTAKE.
Rich Girl (1991) **C-96m.** **½ D: Joel Bender. Jill Schoelen, Don Michael Paul, Sean Kanan, Ron Karabatsos, Paul Gleason, Bentley Mitchum. Extremely mild time-filler about "poor little rich girl" Schoelen leaving her life of ease in her daddy's Bel-Air mansion and trying to make it on her own, eventually hooking up with a blue-collar rock singer. [R]▼●
Ri¢hie Ri¢h (1994) **C-95m.** **½ D: Donald Petrie. Macaulay Culkin, John Larroquette, Edward Herrmann, Jonathan Hyde, Christine Ebersole, Stephi Lineburg, Michael McShane, Chelcie Ross, Ben Stein. Amusing kids' film with Culkin as the comic-book character Richie Rich, the world's wealthiest boy—which naturally makes him the target of a scheming bad guy

(Larroquette). Hyde is excellent as the boy's very proper valet/companion, and Herrmann and Ebersole are endearing as Richie's parents. Avoids some of the formulaic crudity of John Hughes movies, but weakens during the protracted action finale. Followed by a direct-to-video sequel. [PG]▼●

Rich in Love (1993) **C-105m.** ★★½ D: Bruce Beresford. Albert Finney, Jill Clayburgh, Kathryn Erbe, Kyle MacLachlan, Piper Laurie, Ethan Hawke, Suzy Amis, Alfre Woodard. The people behind DRIVING MISS DAISY have taken Josephine Humphreys' novel and tried hard to weave another evocative Southern tale; they don't really succeed, but there are many fine moments. Film centers on teenager (Erbe, in an award-calibre performance) trying to hold her extended family together; among the members are her idle father (another great Finney portrayal), absent mother, and nutty sister. Beautiful touches both in script and visualization are offset by unfocused, meandering story. [PG-13]▼●

Rich Kids (1979) **C-101m.** ★★★ D: Robert M. Young. Trini Alvarado, Jeremy Levy, John Lithgow, Kathryn Walker, David Selby, Terry Kiser, Paul Dooley, Olympia Dukakis, Jill Eikenberry. Alvarado and Levy are upper class N.Y.C. kids who become best friends as her parents are dissolving their marriage. Effect of divorce is focal point for this fine acting showcase, which also makes good use of N.Y.C. locations. Produced by Robert Altman. [PG]▼

Rich Man, Poor Girl (1938) **70m.** ★★ D: Reinhold Schunzel. Robert Young, Lew Ayres, Ruth Hussey, Lana Turner, Rita Johnson, Don Castle, Guy Kibbee. Good cast, fair film. Title tells story; only noteworthy item is radiant young Turner.

Rich Man's Wife, The (1996) **C-94m.** BOMB D: Amy Holden Jones. Halle Berry, Christopher McDonald, Clive Owen, Peter Greene, Charles Hallahan, Frankie Faison, Clea Lewis. Abandoned Berry somehow gets picked up by a shady character following a vacation tiff with her husband. This leads to a murder-blackmail situation conceived by a filmmaker who's seen STRANGERS ON A TRAIN one too many times. Lots of unintentional yuks, but nothing else to recommend this D.O.A. release. [R]▼●◗

Richthofen and Brown SEE: **Von Richthofen and Brown**

Rich, Young and Pretty (1951) **C-95m.** ★★½ D: Norman Taurog. Jane Powell, Danielle Darrieux, Wendell Corey, Vic Damone, Fernando Lamas, Marcel Dalio, Una Merkel, Richard Anderson. Frivolous MGM musical with Powell in Paris, sightseeing and romancing, meeting mother Darrieux. Cowritten by Sidney Sheldon.▼●

Ricochet (1991) **C-97m.** ★★ D: Russell Mulcahy. Denzel Washington, John Lithgow, Ice T, Kevin Pollak, Lindsay Wagner, Mary Ellen Trainor, Josh Evans, Victoria Dillard, John Amos. Street cop (Washington) becomes a citywide hero when he brings down bad-guy Lithgow—little dreaming that the psycho spends every waking moment in prison planning his revenge. Slick, well-cast, occasionally ugly urban thriller grows more tiresome and predictable as it goes along. Panavision. [R]▼●◗

Ricochet Romance (1954) **80m.** ★★½ D: Charles Lamont. Marjorie Main, Chill Wills, Pedro Gonzalez-Gonzalez, Rudy Vallee, Ruth Hampton. Another Main frolic, with the rambunctious gal hired as ranch cook but putting her two cents' worth into everything.

Ricochets (1986-Israeli) **C-90m.** ★★★ D: Eli Cohen. Roni Pincovich, Shaul Mizrahi, Alon Aboutboul, Dudu Ben-Ze'ev, Boaz Ofri. Gritty, uncompromising look at a group of Israeli soldiers living and dying in occupied Lebanon, focusing on the experiences of one young officer. Made as an Israeli Army training film and shot on location; nevertheless, an eloquent anti-war drama.

Riddle of the Sands, The (1979-British) **C-102m.** ★★ D: Tony Maylam. Simon MacCorkindale, Michael York, Jenny Agutter, Alan Badel, Jurgen Andersen, Olga Lowe, Wolf Kahler. Sailing off the coast of Germany in 1901, yachtsman MacCorkindale stumbles onto what seems to be a plan to invade England, and summons old chum York to help him out. Erskine Childers' novel is considered the prototype of the modern spy thriller, but this adaptation is just too slow and stiff to be really effective. Good to look at, though. Released in the U.S. in 1984. Panavision.▼

Ride a Crooked Trail (1958) **C-87m.** ★★½ D: Jesse Hibbs. Audie Murphy, Gia Scala, Walter Matthau, Henry Silva, Joanna Moore. Murphy plays a thief mistaken for a lawman in this otherwise average Borden Chase–scripted Western. Worth watching for Matthau's zesty performance as a bombastic, alcoholic judge. CinemaScope.

Ride a Violent Mile (1957) **80m.** ★½ D: Charles Marquis Warren. John Agar, Penny Edwards, John Pickard, Sheb Wooley, Eva Novak. Trivial Western set in Civil War times about Southern blockade runners. Regalscope.

Ride a Wild Pony (1976-Australian) **C-91m.** ★★★ D: Don Chaffey. Michael Craig, John Meillon, Robert Bettles, Eva Griffith, Graham Rouse. Genial, atmospheric Disney story about an irresistible pony and the two children—son of poor farm family and crippled rich girl—who vie for its love and ownership. Sentimental tale adapted from James Aldridge's *A Sporting Proposition.* [G]▼

Ride Back, The (1957) **79m.** ★★★ D: Allen H. Miner. Anthony Quinn, Lita Milan, William Conrad, Ellen Hope Monroe, Louis

Towers. Well-handled account of sheriff and prisoner who find they need each other's help to survive elements and Indian attacks.

Ride Beyond Vengeance (1966) **C-100m.** **½ D: Bernard McEveety. Chuck Connors, Michael Rennie, Kathryn Hays, Joan Blondell, Gloria Grahame, Gary Merrill, Bill Bixby, James MacArthur, Claude Akins, Paul Fix, Ruth Warrick, Arthur O'Connell, Frank Gorshin, Jamie Farr. Good supporting cast makes the most of stereotyped roles in flashback account of Connors' sundry encounters with outlaws.

Ride Clear of Diablo (1954) **C-80m.** **½ D: Jesse Hibbs. Audie Murphy, Dan Duryea, Susan Cabot, Abbe Lane, Russell Johnson, Jack Elam, Denver Pyle. Cheerful gunslinger Duryea takes a liking to newly minted deputy Murphy, who is seeking the cattle rustlers who killed his family. Unassuming, intelligent Western is a good showcase for its likable stars.▼

Ride 'Em Cowboy (1942) **86m.** **½ D: Arthur Lubin. Bud Abbott, Lou Costello, Dick Foran, Anne Gwynne, Johnny Mack Brown, Ella Fitzgerald, Douglass Dumbrille. Good combination of Western, comedy, and musical in A&C vehicle, with Ella and the Merry Macs singing tunes including "A Tisket A Tasket," Foran crooning "I'll Remember April."▼●

Ride in the Whirlwind (1965) **C-83m.** **½ D: Monte Hellman. Cameron Mitchell, Jack Nicholson, Tom Filer, Millie Perkins, Katherine Squire, Rupert Crosse, Harry Dean Stanton. Nicholson coproduced and wrote the screenplay for this offbeat Western about three cowboys who find themselves wrongly pursued as outlaws. Neither as arty nor as intriguing as THE SHOOTING, which was filmed simultaneously.▼●

Ride Lonesome (1959) **C-73m.** *** D: Budd Boetticher. Randolph Scott, Karen Steele, Pernell Roberts, James Best, Lee Van Cleef, James Coburn. Typically interesting Boetticher chamber-Western (with a Burt Kennedy script) about a tight-lipped bounty hunter who acquires unwanted companions while bringing in a wanted criminal. Unusually good supporting cast, including Coburn in his film debut. CinemaScope.

Ride Out for Revenge (1957) **79m.** *½ D: Bernard Girard. Rory Calhoun, Gloria Grahame, Lloyd Bridges, Vince Edwards. Tiresome account of gold-hungry men trying to dispossess Indians from their lands.

Rider on the Rain (1970-French) **C-115m.** ***½ D: René Clement. Charles Bronson, Marlene Jobert, Jill Ireland, Annie Cordy. Chilling suspense piece about mysterious man who winds up using Jobert as accomplice when she discovers what he is up to. Best sequence: long, rainy prologue. Story and screenplay by Sebastien Japrisot. [PG]▼

Riders of the Purple Sage (1925) **56m.** *** D: Lynn Reynolds. Tom Mix, Beatrice Burnham, Arthur Morrison, Warner Oland, Fred Kohler, Harold Goodwin, Marion Nixon. Engrossing Zane Grey story filmed on beautiful locations, with Mix a Texas Ranger seeking scoundrel (Oland) who abducted his sister (Burnham). Fascinating twists in this tale, first filmed in 1918, again in 1931, 1941, and 1996. Mix also filmed sequel, THE RAINBOW TRAIL, as done in 1918 and 1932.▼

Riders of the Purple Sage (1996) **C-98m.** **TVM** D: Charles Haid. Ed Harris, Amy Madigan, Henry Thomas, Robin Tunney, Norbert Weisser, G. D. Spradlin. Zane Grey's perennial tale of revenge and redemption, about a frontier woman struggling to hold on to her ranch, a religious cult attempting to spread its often evil influence, and a mysterious drifter dispensing his own justice; rethought for the 90s (by screenwriter Gill Dennis), it's a distinctively photographed, mystically told Western of great appeal. The two stars also produced this film. Made for cable. Above average.▼

Riders of the Storm (1986-British) **C-92m.** *½ D: Maurice Phillips. Dennis Hopper, Michael J. Pollard, Eugene Lipinski, James Aubrey, Nigel Pegram. Unsatisfactory chronicle of Vietnam vets who run a pirate television station and jam right-wing broadcasts; they attempt to sabotage the campaign of a female presidential candidate who is not to their liking. Bright premise, thoroughly stale result. Originally titled THE AMERICAN WAY, at 105m. [R]▼●

Riders of Vengeance SEE: **Raiders, The** (1952)

Riders to the Stars (1954) **C-81m.** **½ D: Richard Carlson. William Lundigan, Herbert Marshall, Richard Carlson, Dawn Addams, Martha Hyer. Labored programmer about early days of space missiles, quite outdated now.

Ride the High Country (1962) **C-94m.** **** D: Sam Peckinpah. Randolph Scott, Joel McCrea, Mariette Hartley, Ronald Starr, Edgar Buchanan, R. G. Armstrong, Warren Oates, John Anderson, L. Q. Jones, James Drury. Literate, magnificent Western about two aged gunfighter pals who reflect on the paths their lives have taken while guarding gold shipment. Considered by some to be Peckinpah's finest film; breathtaking widescreen photography (by Lucien Ballard) and scenery, and flawless performances, with Buchanan notable as a drunken judge. Written by N. B. Stone, Jr. Hartley's first film, Scott's last. CinemaScope.▼●

Ride the High Iron (1956) **74m.** *½ D: Don Weis. Don Taylor, Sally Forrest, Raymond Burr, Lisa Golm, Nestor Paiva, Mae Clarke. Korean veteran Taylor works for slick P.R. man Burr who makes his living keeping people's indiscretions out of the paper. Taylor tries to latch on to rich girl whose family Burr works for. Originally made for TV but shown theatrically.

Ride the Man Down (1952) **C-90m.** ** D: Joseph Kane. Brian Donlevy, Rod Cameron, Ella Raines, Barbara Britton, Chill Wills, Jack LaRue, J. Carrol Naish, Jim Davis. Lumbering account of ranchland feuding in old West.▼

Ride the Pink Horse (1947) **101m.** ***½ D: Robert Montgomery. Robert Montgomery, Wanda Hendrix, Thomas Gomez, Andrea King, Fred Clark, Art Smith, Rita Conde, Grandon Rhodes. Strong film noir of Montgomery coming to small New Mexican town during fiesta to blackmail gangster Clark, but romantic Hendrix and FBI agent Smith keep getting in his way. Taut script by Ben Hecht and Charles Lederer (from the Dorothy B. Hughes novel); super performance by Gomez as friendly carny. Remade for TV as THE HANGED MAN (1964).

Ride the Wild Surf (1964) **C-101m.** **½ D: Don Taylor. Fabian, Tab Hunter, Barbara Eden, Anthony Hayes, James Mitchum, Shelley Fabares. Formula beach boys tale, set in Hawaii; Jan and Dean sing the title song. It's not Shakespeare, but it *is* a cut above the usual BEACH PARTY shenanigans, and the surfing footage is great.▼

Ride to Glory SEE: **Deserter, The**

Ride to Hangman's Tree, The (1967) **C-90m.** **½ D: Al Rafkin. Jack Lord, James Farentino, Don Galloway, Melodie Johnson, Richard Anderson, Robert Yuro. Formula Universal backlot Western, of outlaws in old West.

Ride, Vaquero! (1953) **C-90m.** **½ D: John Farrow. Robert Taylor, Ava Gardner, Howard Keel, Anthony Quinn, Charlita. Oddball casting perks brooding Western set on Mexican border, with sultry Gardner responsible for most of the action.

Ride with the Devil (1999) **C-134m.** **½ D: Ang Lee. Skeet Ulrich, Tobey Maguire, James Caviezel, Jonathan Rhys Meyers, Simon Baker, Jeffrey Wright, Jewel, Tom Wilkinson, Jonathan Brandis. A different take on the Civil War, focusing on the Bushwhackers, Southern guerrilla forces made up largely of young men who stage daring raids on Union farms and towns along the Kansas/Missouri border. Interesting subject matter is diffused by overlong, sometimes unfocused treatment, though the time and place are well drawn. Pop singer Jewel makes an impressive acting debut. 2.35 Research PLC. [R]▼◗

Ridicule (1996-French) **C-102m.** *** D: Patrice Leconte. Charles Berling, Jean Rochefort, Fanny Ardant, Judith Godreche, Bernard Giraudeau. Spirited tale of an earnest young landowner who tries to obtain an audience with King Louis XVI in order to get grant money for swamp drainage. He soon discovers that the only way to be presented at court is to display a ready (and preferably savage) wit—which, to everyone's surprise, he is willing and able to do. Fine performances in this unusual and original period piece. Panavision. [R]▼●

Riding High (1943) **C-89m.** *½ D: George Marshall. Dorothy Lamour, Dick Powell, Victor Moore, Gil Lamb, Cass Daley, Milt Britton and Band, Rod Cameron. Unmemorable songs, flat script, fair performances add up to dubious entertainment; Powell is obsessed with silver mine, while wooing Lamour.

Riding High (1950) **112m.** **½ D: Frank Capra. Bing Crosby, Coleen Gray, Charles Bickford, Margaret Hamilton, Frances Gifford, James Gleason, Raymond Walburn, William Demarest, Ward Bond, Clarence Muse, Percy Kilbride, Gene Lockhart, Douglass Dumbrille, Harry Davenport, Charles Lane, Frankie Darro. Musical remake of BROADWAY BILL follows it so closely that stock footage with some of the actors in their original parts is included from 1934 film. Crosby is racehorse owner whose nag has yet to come through. OK songs, Capra touch make this pleasing if unmemorable entertainment. Oliver Hardy is fun in rare solo appearance. Joe Frisco appears as himself.▼●

Riding on Air (1937) **71m.** ** D: Edward Sedgwick. Joe E. Brown, Guy Kibbee, Florence Rice, Vinton Haworth, Anthony Nace, Harlan Briggs. Average Brown vehicle has him mixed up with smugglers and a wacky invention of a radio beam to control airplanes.▼

Riding Shotgun (1954) **C-74m.** **½ D: Andre de Toth. Randolph Scott, Wayne Morris, Joan Weldon, Joe Sawyer, James Millican, Charles Buchinsky (Bronson), Fritz Feld. Typical, undemanding Scott Western of man seeking to clear his reputation.

Riding the Rails (1997) **C-75m.** ***½ D: Michael Uys, Lexy Lovell. Acclaimed documentary about the thousands of young people who left home to hop freight trains during the Great Depression—some seeking adventure, some hoping to make a living, some with nowhere else to go. Fascinating interviews with octogenarian survivors of that school of hard knocks; debunks most of the "romance" of hobo life.▼

Riffraff (1935) **89m.** **½ D: J. Walter Ruben. Jean Harlow, Spencer Tracy, Una Merkel, Joseph Calleia, Victor Kilian, Mickey Rooney. Comedy-drama doesn't always work, but worth viewing for stars playing married couple in fishing business who end up on wrong side of law.▼

Riffraff (1947) **80m.** *** D: Ted Tetzlaff. Pat O'Brien, Anne Jeffreys, Walter Slezak, Percy Kilbride, Jerome Cowan, George Givot, Jason Robards (Sr.). Fast-paced story of O'Brien foiling villains' attempts to take over oilfield in Panama.▼●

Riff Raff (1991-British) **C-96m.** *** D: Ken Loach. Robert Carlyle, Emer McCourt, Ricky Tomlinson, Jimmy Coleman, George Moss, David Finch. Probing, bitingly funny comedy about the ongoing struggle between the classes in England, examining the plight of a blue-collar type (Carlyle), newly arrived in London, who signs on at a construction site. Some of the regional accents and dialects are so indecipherable that subtitles have been added! Screenplay by Bill Jesse, an ex-construction worker.▼

Riff Raff Girls (1962-French) **97m.** **½ D: Alex Joffe. Nadja Tiller, Robert Hossein, Silvia Monfort, Roger Hanin, Pierre Blanchar. Tiller is quite convincing as club owner whose aim is to be self-sufficient; set on Brussels waterfront.

Rififi (1954-French) **115m.** **** D: Jules Dassin. Jean Servais, Carl Mohner, Magali Noel, Robert Manuel, Perlo Vita (Jules Dassin). The granddaddy of all caper/heist movies, centering on quartet of French jewel thieves who find each other more dangerous than the cops. The burglary sequence itself is famous for being in complete silence. Scripted by director Dassin, Rene Wheeler, and Auguste LeBreton, from LeBreton's novel.▼

Rififi in Tokyo (1963-French) **89m.** ** D: Jacques Deray. Karl Boehm, Michel Vitold, Charles Vanel, Eiji Okada, Keiko Kishi, Barbara Lass, Yanagi. Aging European gangster recruits men for bank heist. Cast is so-so; strictly standard plot line.

Right Approach, The (1961) **92m.** **½ D: David Butler. Frankie Vaughan, Martha Hyer, Juliet Prowse, Gary Crosby, Jane Withers. Plucky minor film of Vaughan, a good-for-nothing who uses anything to get ahead. Adapted by Fay and Michael Kanin from a play by his brother Garson. CinemaScope.

Right Cross (1950) **90m.** **½ D: John Sturges. June Allyson, Dick Powell, Lionel Barrymore, Ricardo Montalban. Fairly compact account of boxing world, with sports-writer Powell and fighter Montalban in love with Allyson. One of Marilyn Monroe's early films.

Right Hand Man, The (1987-Australian) **C-100m.** **½ D: Di Drew. Rupert Everett, Hugo Weaving, Catherine McClements, Arthur Dignam, Jennifer Claire. Well-made but only occasionally involving drama about the various troubles of aristocrat Everett, and what happens when he hires stagecoach driver Weaving. Has its moments, but ultimately peters out. [R]▼

Right Stuff, The (1983) **C-193m.** *** D: Philip Kaufman. Sam Shepard, Scott Glenn, Ed Harris, Dennis Quaid, Fred Ward, Barbara Hershey, Kim Stanley, Veronica Cartwright, Kathy Baker, Pamela Reed, Donald Moffat, Levon Helm, Scott Wilson, David Clennon, William Russ, Jeff Goldblum, Harry Shearer. Offbeat look at the birth of America's space program and the first astronauts, adapted from Tom Wolfe's best-selling book, and tethered to the story of iconoclastic test pilot Chuck Yeager. Writer-director Kaufman draws all his characters as cartoons (including Lyndon Johnson) except for the pilots—and puts thrillingly realistic recreations of space flights against broadly caricatured scenes on Earth. A real curio of a film, with some astonishing performances, exhilarating moments, but a curious overall air of detachment. Long, but never boring. Winner of four Oscars, including Best Editing, Sound, and Original Score (Bill Conti). The real Chuck Yeager has a cameo role as a bartender. [PG]▼●◗

Rikki and Pete (1988-Australian) **C-107m.** **½ D: Nadia Tass. Stephen Kearney, Nina Landis, Tetchie Agbayani, Bill Hunter, Bruno Lawrence, Bruce Spence, Dorothy Allison, Don Reid, Lewis Fitzgerald. Pete is a misfit with a penchant for gimmicky inventions, Rikki is his sister who's still trying to find herself; together they flee to a remote mining village where their lives take some unexpected turns. Follow-up to the delightful MALCOLM by the same writing-directing team (Tass and writer/cinematographer David Parker) hasn't the same sweetness or consistency, but it's admirably quirky, and Parker's Rube Goldberg–ish devices are fun. [R]▼●

Ring, The (1927-British) **73m.** *** D: Alfred Hitchcock. Carl Brisson, Lillian Hall-Davies, Ian Hunter, Harry Terry, Gordon Harker, Billy Wells, Tom Helmore. Boxers Brisson and Hunter battle over their love for the same woman. Standard scenario is uplifted by Hitchcock's keen eye for detail and imaginative use of visuals to communicate feelings and points of view. Written by Hitchcock and Alma Reville.▼◗

Ring, The (1952) **79m.** *** D: Kurt Neumann. Gerald Mohr, Rita Moreno, Lalo Rios, Robert Arthur, Art Aragon, Jack Elam. Neat little boxing yarn with a conscience: under the tutelage of fight manager Mohr, poor Chicano Rios tries his hand in the ring. Film offers a refreshingly nonstereotypical portrait of Mexican-Americans, plus a perceptive view of the fight racket. Scripted by Irving Shulman, based on his novel.▼

Ring-a-Ding Rhythm (1962-British) **78m.** ** D: Richard Lester. Helen Shapiro, Craig Douglas, Felix Felton, Arthur Mullard, John Leyton, Chubby Checker, Del Shannon, Gary "U.S." Bonds, Gene Vincent, Gene McDaniels, Acker Bilk, The Temperance Seven. Shapiro and Douglas—whose characters are called Helen and

Craig—organize a rock 'n' roll and Dixieland jazz show. Of interest only for the appearances of Bonds, Vincent, and company—although there's not one memorable song performed. Lester's first feature. British title: IT'S TRAD, DAD!

Ringer, The (1952-British) **78m.** *** D: Guy Hamilton. Herbert Lom, Mai Zetterling, Donald Wolfit, Greta Gynt, William Hartnell, Norman Wooland. Entertaining mystery from Edgar Wallace novel and play: The Ringer, an arch criminal, gets on the case of an unscrupulous lawyer involved in his sister's death. Filmed previously in 1931, and in 1938 as THE GAUNT STRANGER.

Ringmaster (1998) **C-90m.** *½ D: Neil Abramson. Jerry Springer, Jaime Pressly, William McNamara, Molly Hagan, Michael Dudikoff, Ashley Holbrook, Wendy Raquel Robinson, Michael Jai White. A mom and daughter share a husband/stepfather in a trailer park, but instead of duking it out in secret, they apply to vent their spleens on Springer's TV show, sharing adjacent hotel accommodations with other profiled subjects. Surprisingly well acted under the circumstances, this otherwise listless junk lacks focus and is thoroughly done in by Springer's sanctimoniousness. Tries to do for the host's career what PRIVATE PARTS did for Howard Stern's and can't even pull off that modest feat. [R]▼●◗

Ring of Bright Water (1969-British) **C-107m.** *** D: Jack Couffer. Bill Travers, Virginia McKenna, Peter Jeffrey, Jameson Clark, Helena Gloag. Fine children's film should be a treat for adults, too; modest story of man's love for his pet otter is intelligently and believably told. Nice acting and photography. [G]▼

Ring of Fear (1954) **C-93m.** ** D: James Edward Grant. Clyde Beatty, Pat O'Brien, Mickey Spillane, Sean McClory, Marian Carr, John Bromfield. Offbeat murder-mystery set in a circus; interesting for acting appearance by Spillane, although, curiously, he is *not* one of the credited writers! CinemaScope.

Ring of Fire (1961) **C-91m.** **½ D: Andrew L. Stone. David Janssen, Joyce Taylor, Frank Gorshin, Joel Marston, Doodles Weaver. Assistant sheriff is held hostage by trio of young hoods. Highlight of film is climactic holocaust, including footage of a real Oregon forest fire.

Ring of Terror (1962) **72m.** BOMB D: Clark Paylow. George Mather, Esther Furst, Austin Green, Joseph Conway. A medical student must confront a corpse as a fraternity initiation prank in this low-budget loser.▼

Ring of Treason (1963-British) **90m.** *** D: Robert Tronson. Bernard Lee, William Sylvester, Margaret Tyzack, David Kossoff. Solid spy thriller based on true story of ex-Navy man blackmailed into helping Russian agents. Builds truly exciting atmosphere. British title: RING OF SPIES.

Rings Around the World (1966) **C-79m.** **½ D: Gilbert Cates. Don Ameche introduces world-famous circus acts. OK for those who care; similar to Ameche's TV series, *International Showtime*.▼

Ringside Maisie (1941) **96m.** ** D: Edwin L. Marin. Ann Sothern, George Murphy, Robert Sterling, Virginia O'Brien, Natalie Thompson, Maisie causes romantic complications at a boxer's training camp in this sticky and overlong entry. "Slapsy Maxie" Rosenbloom is fun as a punch-drunk pug. Costars Sothern and Sterling married two years later.

Rings on Her Fingers (1942) **85m.** **½ D: Rouben Mamoulian. Henry Fonda, Gene Tierney, Laird Cregar, Spring Byington, Marjorie Gateson, Iris Adrian, Clara Blandick, Mary Treen. Con-artist Tierney falls for Fonda instead of fleecing him; standard romance with good cast hoping to repeat success of Fonda's THE LADY EVE.

Rio (1939) **75m.** ** D: John Brahm. Basil Rathbone, Victor McLaglen, Sigrid Gurie, Robert Cummings, Leo Carrillo, Billy Gilbert. Rathbone, serving ten-year prison term, suspects his wife (Gurie) is being unfaithful. His performance is sole virtue of this slick potboiler.

Rio Bravo (1959) **C-141m.** ***½ D: Howard Hawks. John Wayne, Dean Martin, Ricky Nelson, Angie Dickinson, Walter Brennan, Ward Bond, John Russell, Claude Akins, Bob Steele. Sheriff Wayne tries to prevent a killer with connections from escaping from the town jail, with only a drunken Dino, leggy Angie, gimpy Brennan and lockjawed Ricky to help him. Quintessential Hawks Western, patronized by reviewers at the time of its release, is now regarded as an American classic; overlong, but great fun. Written by Leigh Brackett and Jules Furthman. Followed by EL DORADO; sort of remade as ASSAULT ON PRECINCT 13.▼●

Rio Conchos (1964) **C-107m.** *** D: Gordon Douglas. Richard Boone, Stuart Whitman, Tony Franciosa, Edmond O'Brien, Jim Brown. Post–Civil War Texas is the setting for this action-filled Western centering around a shipment of stolen rifles, and Boone taking on Franciosa. Brown is notable in his film debut, and there's a zesty performance by O'Brien. CinemaScope.▼

Rio Grande (1950) **105m.** *** D: John Ford. John Wayne, Maureen O'Hara, Ben Johnson, Harry Carey, Jr., Victor McLaglen, Claude Jarman, Jr., Chill Wills, J. Carrol Naish, Grant Withers, Pat Wayne. The last of director Ford's Cavalry trilogy (following FORT APACHE and SHE WORE A YELLOW RIBBON), and the most underrated: a vivid look at the gentlemanly spirit of the Cavalry during post-Civil War days . . . and the difficult relationship between an estranged father (commander Wayne) and his son (new recruit Jarman). Beautifully shot by Bert Glennon and Archie Stout, with lovely theme by Victor Young, songs by Sons of the Pioneers (including Ken Curtis). Also shown in computer-colored version.▼●◗

Rio Lobo (1970) **C-114m.** *** D: Howard Hawks. John Wayne, Jorge Rivero, Jennifer O'Neill, Jack Elam, Chris Mitchum, Mike Henry, Susana Dosamantes, Victor French, Sherry Lansing, Bill Williams, David Huddleston, Jim Davis, Robert Donner. Hawks' final film is a lighthearted Western in the RIO BRAVO mold, with the Duke as ex-Union colonel out to settle some old scores. Youthful costars are weak, but stays on track thanks to snappy dialogue, crisp action, and riotous performance by Elam as shotgun-toting old looney. Future Paramount studio head Lansing's last film as an actress; George Plimpton has a one-line bit that served as the basis of a TV special. [G]▼●

Rio Rita (1929) **B&W/C-103m.** **½ D: Luther Reed. Bebe Daniels, John Boles, Don Alvarado, Dorothy Lee, Bert Wheeler, Robert Woolsey, Georges Renevant. Historically fascinating, but cinematically archaic, version of the Ziegfeld-produced Broadway musical smash, about the bandit called ''Kinkajou'' being pursued in a Mexican border town by merry band of singing Texas Rangers. A straightforward recording of the stage show, the film creaks along, though some of the production numbers are quite lavish for their time, with the last 30m. in early two-strip Technicolor. Film debuts of Wheeler and Woolsey, who played their roles in the Broadway show. Original running time 135m. Loosely remade with Abbott and Costello in 1942.

Rio Rita (1942) **91m.** **½ D: S. Sylvan Simon. Bud Abbott, Lou Costello, Kathryn Grayson, John Carroll, Tom Conway, Barry Nelson. Vintage Broadway musical brought up to date, with Nazis invading Western ranch where Bud and Lou work; some good music helps this one. Previously filmed in 1929 with Wheeler and Woolsey.▼●

Riot (1969) **C-97m.** **½ D: Buzz Kulik. Jim Brown, Gene Hackman, Ben Carruthers, Mike Kellin, Gerald O'Loughlin. Unsurprising but extremely violent prison film; Hackman in stereotyped characterization. Produced by William Castle. [PG—edited from original R rating]▼

Riot in Cell Block 11 (1954) **80m.** *** D: Don Siegel. Neville Brand, Emile Meyer, Frank Faylen, Leo Gordon, Robert Osterloh. Realistic, powerful prison drama still packs a punch. Among the contemporary themes in this 1954 film is ''media manipulation,'' with prisoners trying to use press for leverage.▼

Riot in Juvenile Prison (1959) **71m.** BOMB D: Edward L. Cahn. Jerome Thor, Marcia Henderson, Scott Marlowe, John Hoyt, Dick Tyler, Dorothy Provine, Ann Doran. Programmer fully explained by title.

Riot on Sunset Strip (1967) **C-85m.** *½ D: Arthur Dreifuss. Aldo Ray, Mimsy Farmer, Michael Evans, Laurie Mock, Tim Rooney, Bill Baldwin. Weak exploitation of real-life mid-60s riots on the Strip concerns cop Ray's enraged response when his daughter gets involved with drugs and hippies.

Ripped Off (1971-Italian) **C-83m.** **½ D: Franco Prosperi. Robert Blake, Ernest Borgnine, Gabriele Ferzetti, Catherine Spaak, Tomas Milian. Boxer Blake, framed for the murder of his corrupt manager, is hounded by detective Borgnine and protected by victim's daughter (Spaak). OK of its type; aka THE BOXER, MURDER IN THE RING, and COUNTER PUNCH. [R]▼

Ripper, The (1985) **C-104m.** *½ D: Christopher Lewis. Tom Schreier, Wade Tower, Mona Van Pernis, Andrea Adams, Tom Savini. Extremely gory murders punctuate horror tale of college professor possessed by the evil in Jack the Ripper's ring. Intelligently written, but ultra-cheap and heavily padded. Shot on videotape and released directly to home video.▼

Riptide (1934) **90m.** *** D: Edmund Goulding. Norma Shearer, Robert Montgomery, Herbert Marshall, Mrs. Patrick Campbell, Skeets Gallagher, Ralph Forbes, Lilyan Tashman, Helen Jerome Eddy. Silly but entertaining story of vivacious Shearer marrying stodgy British Lord (Marshall), then becoming involved in scandal with Montgomery. Don't miss opening scene where stars are dressed as giant insects for costume party! That's Walter Brennan as a chauffeur; Bruce Bennett is an extra at the bar at Cannes.▼

Rise and Fall of Legs Diamond, The (1960) **101m.** *** D: Budd Boetticher. Ray Danton, Karen Steele, Elaine Stewart, Jesse White, Simon Oakland, Robert Lowery, Warren Oates. Snappy chronicle of Depression-days gangster, well balanced between action gun battles and Danton's romancing flashy dolls (like young Dyan Cannon). Outstanding photography by Lucien Ballard.▼●

Rise and Shine (1941) **93m.** **½ D: Allan Dwan. Jack Oakie, Linda Darnell, George Murphy, Walter Brennan, Sheldon Leonard, Donald Meek, Ruth Donnelly, Milton Berle, Donald MacBride, Raymond Walburn. Oakie has field day as dumb football player abducted by crooks so team won't win big game. Film is often unconsciously funny. Adapted by Herman J. Mankiewicz from James Thurber's *My Life and Hard Times*.

Rise of Catherine the Great, The SEE: **Catherine the Great**

Rise of Louis XIV, The (1966-French) **C-100m.** *** D: Roberto Rossellini. Jean-Marie Patte, Raymond Jourdan, Silvagni, Katharina Renn, Dominique Vincent, Pierre Barrat. Attractive, but somewhat pedantic effort to show colorful court of not-quite straitlaced Louis XIV. Objective, almost documentary-like, but final effect is uninvolving. Made for French TV.▼

Rising of the Moon, The (1957-Irish) **81m.** **½ D: John Ford. Introduced by Tyrone Power. Cyril Cusack, Maureen Connell, Noel Purcell, Frank Lawton, Jimmy O'Dea. Trio of flavorful stories about Irish life: ''Majesty of the Law,'' ''A Minute's Wait,'' ''1921,'' as performed by Dublin's renowned Abbey Players.

Rising Son (1990) **C-100m. TVM** D: John David Coles. Brian Dennehy, Piper Laurie, Graham Beckel, Emily Longstreth, Matt Damon, Ving Rhames, Jane Adams, Kevin Corrigan. Doting blue-collar dad, who wants the perfect life for his family, learns that he's about to lose his factory job and that his two sons resent him. This type of sturdy drama, written by Bill Phillips, was what put a stamp on TV's Golden Age; Dennehy gives another of his solid performances. Made for cable. Above average. ▼●

Rising Sun (1993) **C-129m.** **½ D: Philip Kaufman. Sean Connery, Wesley Snipes, Harvey Keitel, Cary-Hiroyuki Tagawa, Kevin Anderson, Mako, Ray Wise, Stan Egi, Stan Shaw, Tia Carrere, Steve Buscemi, Tatjana Patitz, Clyde Kusatsu. L.A. cop Snipes and Japan expert Connery investigate a homicide case that implicates a powerful Japanese corporation and a U.S. senator. Stripped-down version of Michael Crichton's detailed and controversial novel (adapted by Crichton and director Kaufman) is alternately compelling, confusing, obvious, and silly, with credibility strained to the breaking point. [R]▼●◗

Risk, The (1960-British) **81m.** *** D: Roy and John Boulting. Tony Britton, Peter Cushing, Ian Bannen, Virginia Maskell, Donald Pleasence. Tense drama of spies chasing scientist who has secret formula to combat plague. Good direction and cast.

Risky Business (1983) **C-96m.** *** D: Paul Brickman. Tom Cruise, Rebecca De Mornay, Curtis Armstrong, Bronson Pinchot, Raphael Sbarge, Joe Pantoliano, Nicholas Pryor, Janet Carroll, Richard Masur, Kevin Anderson. Piquant, original comedy about a reticent teenager who goes a bit wild while his parents are out of town, and becomes involved—in more ways than one—with a prostitute. Brickman's darkly satiric script is balanced by Cruise's utterly likable (and believable) performance in the lead. [R] ▼●◗

Rita, Sue and Bob Too (1986-British) **C-95m.** *** D: Alan Clarke. Siobhan Finneran, Michelle Holmes, George Costigan, Lesley Sharp, Willie Ross, Patti Nicholls, Kulvinder Ghir. Rita and Sue, two plain-looking, slightly overweight working class teens, babysit for Bob and his frigid wife . . . and soon, Rita, Sue and Bob are making three-way whoopee. A shamelessly funny, profane, well-acted sleeper that's definitely not for all tastes. Some of the sex scenes—particularly those in Bob's car—are a riot. [R]▼●

Rite, The (1969-Swedish) **76m.** *** D: Ingmar Bergman. Ingrid Thulin, Gunnar Bjornstrand, Anders Ek, Erik Hell. Penetrating four-character drama, crammed with symbolism, about a trio of actors—a woman, her husband, and her lover—who have been accused of performing a provocative mime act in public, and come before a judge. Strange, disturbing, sexually frank, and uniquely Bergmanesque, with an anti-censorship point of view. Starkly directed and photographed (by Sven Nykvist); a showcase for all four performers. This was Bergman's first film for television.▼

Rites of Summer SEE: **White Water Summer**

Rituals (1978-Canadian) **C-100m.** *½ D: Peter Carter. Hal Holbrook, Lawrence Dane, Robin Gammell, Ken James, Gary Reineke. Ripoff of DELIVERANCE with Holbrook and four fellow M.D.s terrorized during wilderness vacation. Unpleasant, to say the least. Reissued as THE CREEPER. [R]▼

Ritz, The (1976) **C-91m.** **½ D: Richard Lester. Jack Weston, Rita Moreno, Jerry Stiller, Kaye Ballard, F. Murray Abraham, Treat Williams, Paul Price, George Coulouris, Bessie Love, John Ratzenberger. Brisk filming of Terrence McNally's farce about a schnook fleeing his murderous brother-in-law by hiding in gay baths suffers from feeling that it's all a photographed stage performance. Moreno is memorable re-creating her Tony-winning role as no-talent entertainer Googie Gomez. Filmed in England. [R]▼●

Rivals (1972) **C-103m.** **½ D: Krishna Shah. Robert Klein, Joan Hackett, Scott Jacoby. A remarriage forces young child to try and murder the new rival for his mother's affections. Offbeat, to say the least. [R]▼

River, The (1951-Indian) **C-99m.** **** D: Jean Renoir. Patricia Walters, Nora Swinburne, Arthur Shields, Radha, Adrienne Corri, Esmond Knight, narrated by June Hillman. Immensely moving, lyrical adaptation of Rumer Godden novel about English children growing up in Bengal. One of the great color films, a total triumph for cinematographer Claude and director Jean Renoir. Scripted by Godden and Renoir.▼●

River, The (1984) **C-122m.** **½ D: Mark Rydell. Sissy Spacek, Mel Gibson, Shane Bailey, Becky Jo Lynch, Scott Glenn,

Don Hood, Billy Green Bush, James Tolkan. Close-knit family struggles to make good on their farm, which is constantly threatened by river that flows alongside. Spacek's a perfect farm woman (and mother) but Gibson's character is so coldly stubborn that it's hard to empathize. Beautifully shot by Vilmos Zsigmond. [PG-13]▼●◗

River Lady (1948) **C-78m.** ** D: George Sherman. Yvonne De Carlo, Dan Duryea, Rod Cameron, Helena Carter, Lloyd Gough, Florence Bates. Typical De Carlo vehicle about riverboat queen trying to buy her man when she can't win him with love; colorful and empty.

River Niger, The (1976) **C-105m.** *** D: Krishna Shah. James Earl Jones, Cicely Tyson, Glynn Turman, Lou Gossett, Roger E. Mosley, Jonelle Allen. Intelligent, moving story (based on 1972 Tony Award-winning play) of black family trying to come to terms with the world and themselves. Touching and convincing. [R]▼

River of Darkness SEE: **Eureka**

River of Death (1989) **C-111m.** *½ D: Steve Carver. Michael Dudikoff, Donald Pleasence, Herbert Lom, Cynthia Erland, Robert Vaughn, L. Q. Jones, Sarah Maur Thorp. Complicated jungle yarn involving a lost city, mad Nazi scientist Vaughn, vengeful Nazi war criminal Pleasence, hero Dudikoff, and the usual hangers-on. Absurd adventure from Alistair MacLean's novel. [R]▼●

River of No Return (1954) **C-91m.** **½ D: Otto Preminger. Robert Mitchum, Marilyn Monroe, Rory Calhoun, Tommy Rettig, Murvyn Vye, Douglas Spencer. Mitchum rescues Calhoun and Monroe from leaky raft; Calhoun returns the favor by stealing his horse and abandoning them (and Mitchum's young son) to hostile Indians. Dialogue leaves a lot to be desired, but it's worth watching Mitchum and Monroe at her most beautiful—not to mention some gorgeous locations (seen to best advantage in CinemaScope).▼●

River Rat, The (1984) **C-93m.** **½ D: Tom Rickman. Tommy Lee Jones, Nancy Lea Owen, Brian Dennehy, Martha Plimpton. Occasionally perceptive drama about ex-con Jones, falsely imprisoned for murder, and his arrival home after 13 years in the slammer. Works best when focusing on his relationship with his 12-year-old daughter (Plimpton), but spins out of control when dealing with a search for hidden money. Directorial debut for screenwriter Rickman (COAL MINER'S DAUGHTER). [PG]▼●

Riverrun (1970) **C-87m.** ** D: John Korty. John McLiam, Louise Ober, Mark Jenkins, Josephine Nichols. Unmarried couple expecting a baby has its happiness intruded upon by disagreeable visit from her sea-captain father. Mild drama has lovely photography (by Korty), but the leads are bland, story not that interesting. [R]

River Runs Through It, A (1992) **C-123m.** **½ D: Robert Redford. Craig Sheffer, Brad Pitt, Tom Skerritt, Emily Lloyd, Brenda Blethyn, Edie McClurg, Stephen Shellen, Vann Gravage, Nicole Burdette, Susan Traylor, Joseph Gordon-Levitt; narration (uncredited) by Robert Redford. A preacher (Skerritt) teaches his sons about life, grace, and love through the art of fly-fishing in their native Montana, but as the boys grow up and follow very different paths (one straight-and-narrow, the other wild) they find that fishing is the one bond that still draws them together. Respectful adaptation of Norman Maclean's autobiographical novella. Beautifully filmed in Montana, with Oscar-winning cinematography by Philippe Rousselot . . . but the pace is deliberate, the emotions muted, and the result is a bit sleepy at times. [PG]▼●◗

River's Edge, The (1957) **C-87m.** *** D: Allan Dwan. Ray Milland, Anthony Quinn, Debra Paget, Byron Foulger. Melodrama about heel (Milland), his ex-girlfriend (Paget), and her husband (Quinn) trying to cross Mexican border with suitcase of money. Ray has never been nastier. CinemaScope.

River's Edge (1986) **C-99m.** *** D: Tim Hunter. Crispin Glover, Keanu Reeves, Ione Skye Leitch, Roxana Zal, Daniel Roebuck, Tom Bower, Constance Forslund, Leo Rossi, Jim Metzler, Dennis Hopper. Gripping story of teenagers who don't know how to react when one of their friends murders a girl from their clique and leaves her body along the riverbank. Absorbing, if not perfect, study of contemporary kids and their feelings of alienation from grown-ups, from society, and from responsibility . . . with a wild performance by Glover as their self-styled ringleader. Best of all is Hopper, perfectly cast as a leftover biker and druggie who can't relate to the kids' lack of values. Disturbing and thought-provoking—all the more so when you learn that the story was based on a real-life incident! [R]▼●

River Wild, The (1994) **C-108m.** *** D: Curtis Hanson. Meryl Streep, Kevin Bacon, David Strathairn, Joseph Mazzello, John C. Reilly, Elizabeth Hoffman, Victor H. Galloway, Benjamin Bratt. Exciting, well-wrought adventure yarn about a woman taking her young son and nearly estranged husband on a whitewater raft ride—and falling prey to a pair of bad guys on the lam. Streep's complete credibility, as a wife, mom, and rafting expert, keeps this afloat, along with good performances and vivid action scenes. Panavision. [PG-13]▼●◗

RKO 281 (1999-British-U.S.) **C-105m. TVM** D: Benjamin Ross. Liev Schreiber, James Cromwell, Melanie Griffith, John Malkovich, David Suchet, Liam Cunningham, Fiona Shaw, Brenda Blethyn, Roy Scheider. Fascinating speculative drama about the maneuverings by Orson Welles to get CITIZEN KANE made (under the actual production number RKO 281) while William Randolph Hearst tries to blackmail the industry itself to buy up the final print and burn it. The peek at Hollywood history takes a number of liberties, and Schreiber isn't up to playing Welles, but Griffith is an ideal Marion Davies, and the subject matter makes this hard to resist. Made for cable. Average. ▼◗

Road Back, The (1937) **97m.** ** D: James Whale. Richard Cromwell, John King, Slim Summerville, Andy Devine, Barbara Read, Louise Fazenda, Noah Beery, Jr., Lionel Atwill. The German soldiers from ALL QUIET ON THE WESTERN FRONT find postwar life at home full of frustrations. Heavy-handed sequel to the Erich Maria Remarque classic; interesting to watch but unsatisfying. Summerville repeats his role from the 1930 original.

Roadblock (1951) **73m.** **½ D: Harold Daniels. Charles McGraw, Joan Dixon, Lowell Gilmore, Louis Jean Heydt, Milburn Stone. Insurance investigator's growing attachment to a money-hungry woman leads him to crime. Typical film noir formula, smoothly executed.

Road Builder, The SEE: **Night Digger, The**

Roadgames (1981-Australian) **C-100m.** **½ D: Richard Franklin. Stacy Keach, Jamie Lee Curtis, Marion Edward, Grant Page, Bill Stacey. Adequate thriller about truckdriver Keach pursuing a murderer. Curtis is a hitchhiker he picks up. Not bad. Director Franklin, an avowed Hitchcock disciple, went on to make PSYCHO II. Panavision. [PG]▼

Road House (1948) **95m.** *** D: Jean Negulesco. Ida Lupino, Cornel Wilde, Celeste Holm, Richard Widmark, O. Z. Whitehead, Robert Karnes. Psychotic roadhouse owner Widmark deludes himself into thinking he "owns" singer Lupino; when she falls for his childhood friend and employee (Wilde), sparks fly in this entertaining melodrama. Ida even gets to sing, introducing the standard "Again."▼

Road House (1989) **C-114m.** *½ D: Rowdy Herrington. Patrick Swayze, Kelly Lynch, Sam Elliott, Ben Gazzara, Marshall Teague, Kevin Tighe, Kathleen Wilhoite, The Jeff Healey Band. Bouncer Swayze—an N.Y.U. philosophy major, no less—is hired to clean house at a hellhole Midwest saloon, and tangles with local kingpin Gazzara. One broken limb won't suffice when twenty-seven will do; brain-dead yahoo fare is fun for a while. Panavision. [R]▼●

Roadhouse 66 (1984) **C-96m.** *½ D: John Mark Robinson. Willem Dafoe, Judge Reinhold, Kaaren Lee, Kate Vernon, Stephen Elliot, Alan Autry. Predictable, paper-thin nonsense about upper-class Reinhold and hitchhiker Dafoe and their troubles in a small Arizona town after their car breaks down. Pretty boring stuff. [R]▼

Roadie (1980) **C-105m.** *½ D: Alan Rudolph. Meat Loaf, Kaki Hunter, Art Carney, Gailard Sartain, Alice Cooper, Blondie, Roy Orbison, Hank Williams, Jr., Ramblin' Jack Elliot. Fat roadie (Loaf) and skinny aspiring groupie (Hunter) spend nearly two hours of screen time trying to meet Cooper. Talented director Rudolph turns into a Hal Needham clone with loud, excruciatingly dopey comedy. [PG]▼

Road Killers, The (1995) **C-89m.** **½ D: Deran Sarafian. Christopher Lambert, Craig Sheffer, David Arquette, Josh Brolin, Michelle Forbes, Joseph Gordon-Levitt, Adrienne Shelly. HOT RODS TO HELL redux, updated to the dysfunctional 90s: a group of vacationers (led by stone-faced Lambert), on a road trip through the Nevada desert, are terrorized by a gang of psychos (led by Sheffer in a hilarious hippie wig). Enjoyably trashy drive-in fodder—but since there are no more drive-ins, this one went straight to video. Filmed in 1993 under the title ROADFLOWER. Panavision. [R]▼

Roadracers (1994) **C-94m. TVM** D: Robert Rodriguez. David Arquette, John Hawkes, Salma Hayek, Jason Wiles, William Sadler, O'Neal Compton, Christian Klemash, Aaron Vaughn, Tammy Brady Conrad, Mark Lowenthal, Kevin McCarthy. The 1950s: Small-town "wild one" Arquette has problems with his girlfriend Hayek, mean local sheriff Sadler, and the sheriff's hoodlum son. Funny, slightly overstated, well acted, and especially well edited (by the director). Lots of fun, until a grim, violent climax. One of Showtime's "Rebel Highway" entries, based on old American-International pictures; this uses only the title of the 1958 original. Hayek's U.S. feature debut. Above average.▼●

Road Scholar (1993) **C-81m.** *** D: Roger Weisberg. Straightforward, entertaining documentary of humorist/social commentator Andrei Codrescu's journey across America in a '68 Cadillac convertible. An interesting and often wry look at an array of different people in our land, some unique, some eccentric, and some in a world all their own. Codrescu provides perceptive running narration.▼●

Road Show (1941) **87m.** **½ D: Hal Roach, Gordon Douglas, Hal Roach, Jr. Adolphe Menjou, Carole Landis, John Hubbard, Charles Butterworth, Patsy Kelly, George E. Stone. Offbeat comedy of young man, wrongfully committed to an insane asylum, escaping and joining up with traveling carnival; some bright moments in inconsequential film. Cowritten by Harry Langdon.▼

Roadside Prophets (1992) **C-96m.** ***

D: Abbe Wool. John Doe, Adam Horovitz, David Carradine, John Cusack, Bill Cobbs, Jennifer Balgobin, David Anthony Marshall, Stephen Tobolowsky, Timothy Leary, Arlo Guthrie, Ellie Raab. Construction worker Doe, whose best friend is his motorcycle, rides from L.A. to seek the "legendary" city of El Dorado in Nevada. His purpose: to dispose of the ashes of an acquaintance, who died while playing a video game. Along the way he gains a traveling companion (Horovitz) and meets various characters who are leftovers from the 1960s counterculture. A bit too self-consciously hip but a wry, potent look at modern-day alienation and how yesterday's pop culture becomes today's nostalgia. [R]▼●

Road to Bali (1952) **C-90m.** *** D: Hal Walker. Bob Hope, Dorothy Lamour, Bing Crosby, Murvyn Vye, Ralph Moody. Only color ROAD film has lush trappings, many guest stars and good laughs, as Bob and Bing save Dorothy from evil princess and jungle perils. Carolyn Jones has a brief bit.▼

Road to Denver, The (1955) **C-90m.** **½ D: Joseph Kane. John Payne, Lee J. Cobb, Skip Homeier, Mona Freeman, Ray Middleton, Lee Van Cleef, Andy Clyde, Glenn Strange. Fast pacing aids this narrative of Payne and brother Homeier on opposite sides of the law, involved in shoot-out.

Road to El Dorado, The (2000) **C-89m.** ** D: Eric "Bibo" Bergeron, Don Paul. Voices of Kevin Kline, Kenneth Branagh, Rosie Perez, Armand Assante, Edward James Olmos, Jim Cummings. Two con-artist pals in the 16th century find themselves on an accidental journey to the legendary city of gold with a map in their hands. Beautifully designed and staged, but relentlessly mediocre, with one-note humor and forgettable Elton John–Tim Rice songs. Great animation doesn't matter if you don't care about the characters. [PG]▼◗

Road to Galveston, The (1996) **C-100m. TVM** D: Michael Toshiyuki Uno. Cicely Tyson, Piper Laurie, Tess Harper, James McDaniel, Starletta DuPois, Clarence Williams III. Tyson gives heart to this well-written drama about a Texas widow who, to sustain the family farm, provides a home and loving care for several Alzheimer patients and takes them on a trip to see the Galveston seashore. Written by tyro Tony Lee, inspired by his own grandmother's story. Made for cable. Above average. ▼

Road to Glory, The (1936) **95m.** *** D: Howard Hawks. Fredric March, Warner Baxter, Lionel Barrymore, June Lang, Gregory Ratoff, Victor Kilian. Solid production, direction, and acting make more of script (cowritten by William Faulkner) than is really there. Hardened officer Baxter finds his father (Barrymore) serving in his unit in WW1 France. Romantic subplot involves officer March and nurse Lang. Unrelated to same-titled film directed by Hawks in 1926. Remake of 1932 French film LES CROIX DE BOIS, using some of its battle footage.

Road to Hong Kong, The (1962) **91m.** **½ D: Norman Panama. Bob Hope, Bing Crosby, Joan Collins, Dorothy Lamour, Robert Morley, Walter Gotell, Peter Sellers. Final ROAD picture was the first in a decade, and while it's fun it lacks the carefree spirit of its predecessors; Bob and Bing are con men who become involved in international intrigue—and space travel! Sellers has a hilarious cameo; Lamour appears briefly as herself. Look fast for the Bob Crosby Band. Filmed in England.▼●

Road to Morocco (1942) **83m.** *** D: David Butler. Bing Crosby, Dorothy Lamour, Bob Hope, Dona Drake, Anthony Quinn, Vladimir Sokoloff, Monte Blue, Yvonne De Carlo. Typically funny ROAD picture, with Bing selling Bob to slave-trader in mysterious Morocco, both going after princess Lamour. Bing sings "Moonlight Becomes You."▼●◗

Road to Nashville (1967) **C-110m.** *½ D: Robert Patrick. Marty Robbins, Doodles Weaver, Connie Smith, Richard Arlen. Inept promoter tries to line up talent for Country-Western jamboree. The music's not bad when the plot gets out of the way. Techniscope.▼

Road to Rio (1947) **100m.** *** D: Norman Z. McLeod. Bing Crosby, Bob Hope, Dorothy Lamour, Gale Sondergaard, Frank Faylen, The Wiere Brothers. Bob and Bing are musicians trying to wrest Dorothy from sinister aunt Sondergaard. Very funny outing in series. Songs: "But Beautiful," "You Don't Have To Know The Language," sung with guests The Andrews Sisters.▼

Road to Salina (1971-French-Italian) **C-96m.** **½ D: Georges Lautner. Mimsy Farmer, Robert Walker, Rita Hayworth, Ed Begley, Bruce Pecheur. Enjoyably trashy tale about wanderer who returns to his mother's diner, and spends much time making love with a girl who might be his sister. And if that isn't kinky enough for you, Rita does the frug with Ed Begley! Panavision. [R]▼

Road to Singapore (1940) **84m.** **½ D: Victor Schertzinger. Bing Crosby, Dorothy Lamour, Bob Hope, Charles Coburn, Judith Barrett, Anthony Quinn, Jerry Colonna, Monte Blue, Arthur Q. Bryan. Bing and Bob swear off women, hiding out in Singapore; then they meet saronged Lamour. First ROAD film is not the best, but still fun. ▼●

Road to Utopia (1945) **90m.** *** D: Hal Walker. Bing Crosby, Bob Hope, Dorothy Lamour, Hillary Brooke, Douglass Dumbrille, Jack LaRue, Jim Thorpe. Bob and Bing in the Klondike with usual quota of gags, supplemented by talking animals,

Dorothy's song "Personality," Robert Benchley's dry commentary.▼●◗

Road to Wellville, The (1994) **C-117m.** ** D: Alan Parker. Anthony Hopkins, Bridget Fonda, Matthew Broderick, John Cusack, Dana Carvey, Michael Lerner, Colm Meaney, John Neville, Lara Flynn Boyle, Traci Lind, Camryn Manheim, Norbert Weisser, Carole Shelley. Disappointing adaptation of T. Coraghessan Boyle's comic novel, following the plight of a couple (Fonda, Broderick) after they converge on a turn-of-the-century spa operated in Battle Creek, Michigan, by health zealot John W. Kellogg (the real-life inventor of corn flakes). Maddeningly uneven, with plot threads constantly being picked up and dropped. Carvey is especially wasted as Kellogg's oddball son. Only Hopkins' delightful, over-the-top performance as John W. makes this worth watching. [R]▼●

Road to Yesterday, The (1925) **110m.** *** D: Cecil B. DeMille. Joseph Schildkraut, Jetta Goudal, Vera Reynolds, William Boyd, Julia Faye. Criss-crossed couples in romantic tangle are contrasted with 17th century ancestors, who play out similar story against colorful period setting. DeMille at his best: lavish, hokey, always entertaining.▼

Road to Zanzibar (1941) **92m.** **½ D: Victor Schertzinger. Bing Crosby, Bob Hope, Dorothy Lamour, Una Merkel, Eric Blore. Weaker ROAD series entry, still amusing, with Bob and Bing circus performers traveling through jungle with Lamour and Merkel, looking for diamond mine. ▼●

Road Trip (2000) **C-91m.** *** D: Todd Phillips. Breckin Meyer, Seann William Scott, Amy Smart, Paulo Costanzo, DJ Qualls, Rachel Blanchard, Anthony Rapp, Fred Ward, Tom Green, Andy Dick, Horatio Sanz. A college student in upstate N.Y. has to head off an incriminating videotape accidentally sent to his girlfriend in Austin, Texas . . . so he and three others set off on a frantic road trip. Likable teen comedy has the requisite number of gross-out gags and female nudity to please its intended audience . . . but by any standards, it's pretty funny. Hollywood directing debut for Phillips, who made the documentary FRAT HOUSE. [R]

Road Warrior, The (1981-Australian) **C-94m.** ***½ D: George Miller. Mel Gibson, Bruce Spence, Vernon Wells, Mike Preston, Virginia Hey, Emil Minty, Kjell Nilsson. Sequel to MAD MAX finds Max, now a loner, reluctantly helping tiny oil-producing community defend itself against band of depraved crazies thirsty for precious fuel. Far less original script-wise, but trend-setting visual design and some of the most unbelievable car stunts ever filmed make this equal to, if not better than, the first one. Original title: MAD MAX 2; followed by MAD MAX BEYOND THUNDERDOME. Panavision. [R] ▼●◗

Roar (1981) **C-102m.** ** D: Noel Marshall. Tippi Hedren, Noel Marshall, John Marshall, Melanie Griffith, Jerry Marshall, Kyalo Mativo. Accident-ridden production that took 11 years and $17 million for Hedren and husband Marshall to finish. Comedy-adventure about wife and children visiting eccentric scientist husband in jungle after being separated for years is also pro-preservation-of-African-wildlife statement. Nice try, but no cigar. Of additional interest today for early appearance of Hedren's daughter Griffith. Panavision. [PG]

Roaring Timber SEE: **Come and Get It**▼

Roaring Twenties, The (1939) **104m.** *** D: Raoul Walsh. James Cagney, Priscilla Lane, Humphrey Bogart, Gladys George, Jeffrey Lynn, Frank McHugh, Joe Sawyer. Army buddies Cagney, Bogart, and Lynn find their lives intertwining dramatically after WW1 ends. Cagney becomes big-time prohibition racketeer in largely hackneyed script punched across by fine cast, vivid direction. Also shown in computer-colored version.▼●

Roar of the Crowd (1953) **C-71m.** *½ D: William Beaudine. Howard Duff, Helene Stanley, Louise Arthur, Harry Shannon, Minor Watson, Don Haggerty. Hackneyed auto-racing tale done on low budget.

Robber's Roost (1955) **C-82m.** ** D: Sidney Salkow. George Montgomery, Richard Boone, Bruce Bennett, Warren Stevens, Peter Graves, Sylvia Findley. Rugged cast gives zip to this Zane Grey Western of outlaw gangs fighting for control of ranchland. Previously filmed in 1933.

Robbery (1967-British) **C-114m.** *** D: Peter Yates. Stanley Baker, Joanna Pettet, James Booth, Frank Finlay, Barry Foster, William Marlowe. Another study of the British Royal Mail robbery; few surprises, but generally exciting, well-handled.▼

Robbery Under Arms (1957-British) **C-83m.** ** D: Jack Lee. Peter Finch, Ronald Lewis, Laurence Naismith, Maureen Swanson, David McCallum. Quiet account of romance and robbery set in 19th-century Australia.▼

Robbery Under Arms (1985-Australian) **C-141m.** *½ D: Ken Hannam, Donald Crombie. Sam Neill, Steven Vidler, Christopher Cummins, Liz Newman, Deborah Coulls, Susie Lindeman, Tommy Lewis. Tedious adventure about the dashing Captain Starlight (Neill), a fabled 19th-century gentleman-rogue, and two willful young brothers who hook up with his gang. This instantly forgettable actioner originally was a television miniseries. The saga of Starlight was filmed several times before, most famously in 1957.▼

Robe, The (1953) **C-135m.** **½ D: Henry Koster. Richard Burton, Jean Simmons,

Victor Mature, Michael Rennie, Richard Boone, Jay Robinson, Dawn Addams, Dean Jagger, Jeff Morrow, Ernest Thesiger. Earnest but episodic costume drama from Lloyd C. Douglas novel about Roman centurion who presides over Christ's crucifixion. Burton's Oscar-nominated performance seems stiff and superficial today, while Mature (as his slave Demetrius) comes off quite well! Famed as first movie in CinemaScope, though it was simultaneously shot "flat." Sequel: DEMETRIUS AND THE GLADIATORS. ▼●

Roberta (1935) **106m.** *** D: William A. Seiter. Irene Dunne, Fred Astaire, Ginger Rogers, Randolph Scott, Helen Westley, Claire Dodd, Victor Varconi, Candy Candido. The story of this famous Jerome Kern–Otto Harbach musical creaks and groans, but "supporting" characters Astaire and Rogers make up for it in their exuberant dance numbers. You can try counting how many times Scott says "swell," or try to spot young Lucille Ball in fashion-show sequence to get through the rest. Songs include "I Won't Dance," "Lovely to Look At," "Smoke Gets In Your Eyes," and "Yesterdays." Based on the Alice Duer Miller novel *Gowns By Roberta*. Remade as LOVELY TO LOOK AT.▼●

Robert A. Heinlein's The Puppet Masters SEE: **Puppet Masters, The**

Robert et Robert (1978-French) **C-105m.** *** D: Claude Lelouch. Charles Denner, Jacques Villeret, Jean-Claude Brialy, Macha Meril, Germaine Montero, Regine. Winning comedy about a friendship between two lonely bachelors named Robert, one an eccentric, impatient cab driver, the other a shy, indecisive apprentice traffic cop. Villeret really scores as the latter.▼

Robin and Marian (1976-British) **C-112m.** **½ D: Richard Lester. Sean Connery, Audrey Hepburn, Robert Shaw, Richard Harris, Nicol Williamson, Denholm Elliott, Kenneth Haigh, Ian Holm, Ronnie Barker. Middle-aged Robin Hood returns to Sherwood Forest after years in exile, rekindles romance with Maid Marian and faces final challenge against arch-enemy Sheriff of Nottingham. Arid, uninvolving film strips beloved characters of all their magic. "Revisionist" script by James Goldman. [PG]▼●

Robin and the 7 Hoods (1964) **C-123m.** *** D: Gordon Douglas. Frank Sinatra, Dean Martin, Sammy Davis, Jr., Bing Crosby, Peter Falk, Barbara Rush, Victor Buono, Sig Ruman, Allen Jenkins, Hans Conried, Jack LaRue, Edward G. Robinson. Rat Pack's final fling is amusing transposition of the merrie legend to 1928 Chicago, with gangleader Sinatra surprised to find he's something of a local hero. No classic, but good-looking and easy to take; Crosby is adroit as gang's elder statesman. Cahn-Van Heusen songs include "My Kind of Town," "Style," "Mr. Booze." Panavision.▼●

Robin Hood (1973) **C-83m.** **½ D: Wolfgang Reitherman. Voices of Brian Bedford, Phil Harris, Monica Evans, Peter Ustinov, Terry-Thomas, Andy Devine, Roger Miller, Pat Buttram, George Lindsey, Carole Shelley. Undistinguished Disney cartoon feature is pleasant enough for kids, but lacks story strength (and heart). Animals fill traditional Robin Hood roles, with Phil Harris' Little John a virtual reprise of his Baloo the Bear from THE JUNGLE BOOK. Disney's live-action STORY OF ROBIN HOOD was much better. [G]▼●

Robin Hood (1991) **C-150m. TVM** D: John Irvin. Patrick Bergin, Uma Thurman, Jeroen Krabbé, Jürgen Prochnow, Edward Fox, Owen Teale, Jeff Nuttal, David Morrisey. Lengthy but competent retelling of the Robin Hood legend. Bergin plays the title role with a brooding, roguish glint; Thurman plays Maid Marian in a nasty, pouting fashion. Handsomely photographed, although the dark, misty ambience drains virtually *all* color from many scenes. Originally developed as a theatrical feature (which is how it played outside the U.S.), this aired on TV just before the Kevin Costner version debuted. Trimmed to 116m. for video. Average.▼

Robin Hood: Men in Tights (1993) **C-102m.** **½ D: Mel Brooks. Cary Elwes, Richard Lewis, Roger Rees, Amy Yasbeck, David Chappelle, Mark Blankfield, Tracey Ullman, Eric Allan Kramer, Megan Cavanagh, Mel Brooks, Dom DeLuise, Dick Van Patten, Matthew Porretta, Isaac Hayes, Robert Ridgely, Chuck McCann, Clive Revill. Disappointingly mild Brooks parody with Elwes as the hero of Sherwood Forest, and Rees a hilarious Sheriff of Rottingham. (Brooks himself plays Rabbi Tuchman, a variation on Friar Tuck.) Laughs come in fits and starts, but the film has no momentum, and no memorable set-pieces. Cameos by Brooks regulars help a bit; DeLuise is hilarious as The Godfather. [PG-13]▼●

Robin Hood of El Dorado, The (1936) **86m.** **½ D: William Wellman. Warner Baxter, Ann Loring, Margo, Bruce Cabot, J. Carrol Naish. Pseudobiography of Mexican bandit Joaquin Murietta, who turns to crime to avenge his wife's murder. Well made, on beautiful locations, but fools around too much for its dramatic moments to be truly effective.

Robin Hood: Prince of Thieves (1991) **C-138m.** *** D: Kevin Reynolds. Kevin Costner, Morgan Freeman, Mary Elizabeth Mastrantonio, Christian Slater, Alan Rickman, Geraldine McEwan, Michael McShane, Brian Blessed, Michael Wincott, Nick Brimble, Jack Wild. A Robin Hood for the '90s, light years removed from the romantic vision of Errol Flynn . . . but this gritty, pumped-up version can stand on its own, if you're willing to stick with it through a lumpy first hour, and can accept a very American Costner in the lead. Rough, tough, and rousing at times, with Rickman's off-the-wall approach to the Sheriff of Nottingham a real surprise. [PG-13]▼●◗

Robinson Crusoe (1952) SEE: **Adventures of Robinson Crusoe**

Robinson Crusoe on Mars (1964) **C-109m.** **½ D: Byron Haskin. Paul Mantee, Vic Lundin, Adam West. Surprisingly agreeable reworking of the classic Defoe story, with Mantee as stranded astronaut, at first accompanied only by a monkey. "Friday" turns out to be a similarly trapped alien. Beautifully shot in Death Valley by Winton C. Hoch; film's intimate nature helps it play better on TV than most widescreen space films. Techniscope.▼●

RoboCop (1987) **C-103m.** *** D: Paul Verhoeven. Peter Weller, Nancy Allen, Daniel O'Herlihy, Ronny Cox, Kurtwood Smith, Miguel Ferrer, Robert DoQui, Ray Wise, Felton Perry, Paul McCrane, Del Zamora. The setting: Detroit, in the near future. A cop who dies in the line of duty is transformed into an ultrasophisticated cyborg by the corporation which now runs the police department. Only hitch: this "perfect" cop still seeks revenge on the sadistic creeps who killed him. Sharp, slick, slambang action entertainment, with fantastic stop-motion animation supervised by Phil Tippett (ED 209 is a wow!) . . . but its view of life in the future is unremittingly bleak and ugly. Followed by two sequels, an animated and a live-action TV series. Unrated director's cut available on laser disc. [R]▼●◗

RoboCop 2 (1990) **C-118m.** *½ D: Irvin Kershner. Peter Weller, Nancy Allen, Daniel O'Herlihy, Belinda Bauer, Tom Noonan, Gabriel Damon, Felton Perry, Robert DoQui, Willard Pugh, Patricia Charbonneau. Appallingly (and unnecessarily) mean, ugly sequel in which coldblooded corporation czar O'Herlihy and drug kingpin Noonan threaten to end Robo's existence—while the laboratory whizzes cook up a bigger, "better" cyborg cop to take his place. Offensively violent and humorless. Phil Tippett's stop-motion animation is the film's only asset. [R]▼●◗

RoboCop 3 (1993) **C-105m.** ** D: Fred Dekker. Robert John Burke, Nancy Allen, Rip Torn, John Castle, Jill Hennessy, CCH Pounder, Mako, Robert DoQui, Remy Ryan, Bruce Locke. When the evil corporation OCP uses a police-like group to force impoverished Detroit citizens out of their homes, Robocop (Burke) leaves the force and joins the rebellion. The script (by Frank Miller and the director) is smug but crude; though it lacks the first sequel's violence, it's also short on spectacle. Filmed in 1991. [PG-13]▼●◗

Robo Man SEE: **Who?**

Robot Carnival (1987-Japanese) **C-91m.** *** D: Katsuhiro Otomo, Atsuko Fukushima, Kouji Morimoto, Kiroyuki Kitazume, Mao Lamdo, Hidetoshi Ohmori, Yasuomi Umetsu, Hiroyuki Kitakubo, Takashi Nakamura. Nine animators collaborated to create eight short stories on the subject of robots: there's comic book fantasy, romance, comedy, and spectacle. Not all the stories hit the bull's-eye, but the best are quite good: "Presence," about a man falling in love with his female robot, and "Nightmare," in which a drunk awakens to find his city overrun by mechanical creatures.▼●

Robot Monster (1953) **63m.** BOMB D: Phil Tucker. George Nader, Gregory Moffett, Claudia Barrett, Selena Royle, John Mylong. Gorilla in diving helmet wipes out entire Earth population save one family, then spends most of film's running time lumbering around Bronson Canyon trying to find them. One of the genuine legends of Hollywood: embarrassingly, hilariously awful . . . and dig that bubble machine with the TV antenna! Originally in 3-D (except for the dinosaur stock footage from ONE MILLION B.C.).▼●

Rob Roy (1995-U.S.-Scottish) **C-139m.** *** D: Michael Caton-Jones. Liam Neeson, Jessica Lange, John Hurt, Tim Roth, Eric Stoltz, Andrew Keir, Brian Cox, Brian McCardie, Gilbert Martin, Vicki Masson. Absorbing tale of Rob Roy MacGregor, a lowborn man of high ideals in early 1700s Scotland who refuses to sacrifice his integrity to save his skin—or his family's. Beautiful scenery and rugged action (including several sword fights) complement an intelligent script. Deliberately paced, with solid performances from Neeson and Lange, and a delicious, scene-stealing turn by Roth as a smarmy bad-guy. Never quite rousing but always entertaining. J-D-C Scope. [R]▼●◗

Rob Roy, the Highland Rogue (1954) **C-85m.** *½ D: Harold French. Richard Todd, Glynis Johns, James Robertson Justice, Michael Gough, Finlay Currie, Jean Taylor-Smith. Disney's dreariest British film casts Todd as leader of Scottish clan planning uprising against England's King George in 18th century. Turgid and unrewarding. Story told much better in 1995 version. ▼

Rocambole (1962-French) **C-106m.** **½ D: Bernard Borderie. Channing Pollock, Hedy Vessel, Nadia Gray, Guy Delorme, Lilla Brignone. Further adventures of Ponson du Terrail's carefree rogue, played tongue-in-cheek by Pollock, involved in Parisian nightlife.

Rocco and His Brothers (1960-Italian) **180m.** ***½ D: Luchino Visconti. Alain Delon, Renato Salvatori, Annie Girardot, Katina Paxinou, Claudia Cardinale, Roger Hanin, Suzy Delair. Sweeping chronicle of familial loyalty and the tainting of innocence, chronicling the plight of idealistic, saintly Rocco (Delon) after he and his mother and brothers leave their rural southern Italian community and settle in Milan.

Stunningly photographed by Giuseppe Rotunno. Restored to its original running time in 1991; beware many shorter, visually inferior prints and video versions. Aka SAVAGE RUN. ▼●

Rock, The (1996) **C-136m.** ** D: Michael Bay. Sean Connery, Nicolas Cage, Ed Harris, Michael Biehn, William Forsythe, David Morse, John Spencer, John C. McGinley, Tony Todd, Bokeem Woodbine, Danny Nucci, Vanessa Marcil, Anthony Clark. Big, loud, often dumb action/suspense yarn about a disgruntled Marine general who takes over Alcatraz, threatening to obliterate San Francisco with high-tech poison gas. Enter FBI biochemist Cage and long-imprisoned British agent Connery—the only man who ever escaped from The Rock—to lead a rescue team onto the island. Plenty of kinetic action and destruction, as well as contrivances and story holes. David Marshall Grant appears unbilled. Super 35. [R]▼●◗

Rockabye (1932) **67m.** *½ D: George Cukor. Constance Bennett, Joel McCrea, Paul Lukas, Jobyna Howland, Walter Pidgeon, Sterling Holloway. Other than offering a memorable shot of Bennett immersed in balloons, soaper about a morally ambiguous actress's love for her toddler is painful going. A curio for film buffs, but a minor credit for both star and director.

Rock-a-Bye Baby (1958) **C-103m.** *** D: Frank Tashlin. Jerry Lewis, Marilyn Maxwell, Connie Stevens, Baccaloni, Reginald Gardiner, James Gleason, Hans Conried. Good-natured schnook Jerry becomes full-time baby-sitter for movie sex-siren Maxwell, who doesn't want her public to know she's had triplets. Loose remake of Preston Sturges's THE MIRACLE OF MORGAN'S CREEK, with many funny moments. That's Lewis's son Gary playing Jerry as a boy in the musical flashback sequence. VistaVision.

Rock-a-Doodle (1992) **C-77m.** ** D: Don Bluth. Voices of Glen Campbell, Christopher Plummer, Phil Harris, Sandy Duncan, Eddie Deezen, Charles Nelson Reilly, Sorrell Booke, Ellen Greene, Toby Scott Granger. A cocky cock heads for Vegas after suffering a severe blow to his ego, finds success as a nightclub superstar in the Elvis mode. Kiddie cartoon is missing the essential components to make it more than passable entertainment for six-year-olds. [G]▼●◗

Rock All Night (1957) **63m.** ** D: Roger Corman. Dick Miller, Russell Johnson, Jonathan Haze, Abby Dalton, The Platters, Robin Morse. AIP quickie about a pair of killers taking refuge in a bar and terrorizing captive customers. OK Corman potboiler with better-than-average performances, and dig this—Johnson's one of the bad guys and Miller's the hero!▼

Rock & Rule (1983) **C-85m.** **½ D: Clive A. Smith. Voices of Don Francks, Paul Le Mat, Susan Roman, Sam Langevin, Catherine O'Hara. Animated rock fable, with innovative, often dazzling visuals and a solid score (featuring Lou Reed, Debbie Harry, Cheap Trick, Earth, Wind and Fire, Iggy Pop, and others) . . . but story leaves something to be desired. A triumph of technique for Canada's Nelvana animation studio, and certainly worth a look. [PG]▼●

Rock Around the Clock (1956) **77m.** ** D: Fred F. Sears. Bill Haley and His Comets, The Platters, Tony Martinez and His Band, Freddie Bell and His Bellboys, Alan Freed, Johnny Johnston. Premise is slim (unknown band brought to N.Y.C. where they become famous) but picture is now a time-capsule look at the emergence of rock 'n' roll. Bill Haley and the Comets perform "See You Later Alligator," "Razzle Dazzle" and the title song; the Platters chip in with "Only You" and "The Great Pretender." Remade as TWIST AROUND THE CLOCK.▼

Rock Around the World (1957-British) **71m.** *½ D: Gerard Bryant. Tommy Steele, Patrick Westwood, Dennis Price, Tom Littlewood. Humdrum account of Tommy Steele's rise in the singing profession. Originally titled THE TOMMY STEELE STORY.

Rock Baby, Rock It (1957) **84m.** *½ D: Murray Douglas Sporup. Johnny Carroll and His Hot Rocks, Rosco Gordon and The Red Tops, The Five Stars, The Belew Twins, Don Coats and The Bon-Aires, Preacher Smith and The Deacons, The Cell Block Seven, Kay Wheeler. Teens vs. syndicate bookies in this silly period piece that's become a minor cult item, mostly because it was shot in Dallas and highlights performances by regional rock acts. For diehard fans of the genre only.▼

Rockers (1978-Jamaican) **C-100m.** *** D: Theodoros Bafaloukos. Leroy Wallace, Richard Hall, Monica Craig, Marjorie Norman, Jacob Miller. Winningly funky though predictable comedy/drama about Rastafarian drummer Wallace's efforts to earn money and crack open the music establishment. Superior reggae score featuring Peter Tosh, Bunny Wailer, Burning Spear, Third World and Gregory Isaacs.▼

Rocket Attack, U.S.A. (1959) **71m.** BOMB D: Barry Mahon. Monica Davis, John McKay, Daniel Kern, Edward Czerniuk, Arthur Metrano. Spy attempts to uncover Russian missile plans; meanwhile, the dastardly Commies are planning to nuke N.Y.C. Perfectly awful Cold War melodrama with hilarious dialogue, atrocious performances, lots of stock footage.▼

Rocketeer, The (1991) **C-108m.** **½ D: Joe Johnston. Bill Campbell, Jennifer Connelly, Alan Arkin, Timothy Dalton, Paul Sorvino, Terry O'Quinn, Ed Lauter,

James Handy, Tiny Ron, Melora Hardin. Campbell plays a rough-and-ready 1930s pilot who stumbles onto a sought-after secret weapon: an air-pack that turns him into a rocket-man. Film captures the look of the 30s, as well as the gee-whiz innocence of Saturday matinee serials, but it's talky—and takes too much time to get where it's going. Dalton has fun as a villain patterned after Errol Flynn. Film buffs will get a kick out of the Rondo Hatton–esque bad guy (courtesy of makeup whiz Rick Baker). Panavision. [PG]▼●◗

Rocket Gibraltar (1988) **C-100m.** *** D: Daniel Petrie. Burt Lancaster, Suzy Amis, Patricia Clarkson, Frances Conroy, Sinead Cusack, John Glover, George Martin, Bill Pullman, Kevin Spacey, Macaulay Culkin. A family gathers to celebrate patriarch Lancaster's 77th birthday; his grown-up children love him but don't really understand what he's going through, while his grandchildren make a more emotional connection to the old man . . . and vow to carry out his unusual final wish. Lancaster's presence gives the film authority, and a talented ensemble lends credibility to Amos Poe's script. Culkin is wonderful as Lancaster's canny five-year-old grandson. Filmed at beautiful locations on Long Island. [PG]▼

Rocket Man, The (1954) **79m.** ** D: Oscar Rudolph. Charles Coburn, Spring Byington, Anne Francis, John Agar, George "Foghorn" Winslow, Beverly Garland. Campy fantasy of Winslow possessing a space gun that turns crooked people honest. Coscripted by Lenny Bruce—so it's no wonder the villain is a politician, who's portrayed as a drunken, cigar-chomping chiseler.

RocketMan (1997) **C-94m.** BOMB D: Stuart Gillard. Harland Williams, Jessica Lundy, William Sadler, Jeffrey DeMunn, James Pickens, Jr., Beau Bridges, Peter Onorati. Goofball computer expert Williams is the only possible choice to replace an ailing crewman on the first manned expedition to Mars. Predictable "comic" complications ensue, including painfully overstated farting-in-a-spacesuit jokes. Apparently, someone felt Williams was both hilarious and endearing, but we beg to differ. [PG]▼●

Rockets Galore SEE: **Mad Little Island**

Rocketship X-M (1950) **77m.** **½ D: Kurt Neumann. Lloyd Bridges, Osa Massen, Hugh O'Brian, John Emery, Noah Beery, Jr. Slightly better than average production of spaceship to moon that is blown off-course to Mars. Nice photography, good acting. Videocassette version contains new special effects shot in 1976.▼●

Rocket to the Moon SEE: **Cat Women of the Moon**

Rocking Horse Winner, The (1949-British) **91m.** ***½ D: Anthony Pelissier. Valerie Hobson, John Howard Davies, John Mills, Ronald Squire, Hugh Sinclair, Charles Goldner, Susan Richards. Truly unique, fascinating drama based on D. H. Lawrence story; small boy has knack for picking racetrack winners, but complications set in before long. Beautifully done. Screenplay by the director.▼

Rockin' in the Rockies (1945) **63m.** ** D: Vernon Keays. The Three Stooges, Mary Beth Hughes, Jay Kirby, Tim Ryan, Gladys Blake, Vernon Dent. Mediocre grade-B musical comedy actually splits up the Stooges, with Moe playing straight (more or less) and Larry and Curly acting as a team, in a threadbare story of show biz hopefuls on a Western ranch. Only comes to life near the end with some specialty numbers, including one by Spade Cooley and his Western swing band.

Rockin' the Blues (1955) **66m.** ** D: Arthur Rosenblum. Mantan Moreland, F. E. Miller, Connie Carroll, The Wanderers, The Harptones, The Hurricanes, The Five Miller Sisters, Pearl Woods, Linda Hopkins, Hal Jackson. Grade-Z production values hamper this intriguing curio, an all-black rhythm-and-blues show emceed by Jackson, with Moreland along for comic relief. Dance routines are generally awful, but much of the music is priceless; The Hurricanes' army-life number is a real showstopper.▼

Rock 'n' Roll High School (1979) **C-93m.** *** D: Allan Arkush. P. J. Soles, Vincent Van Patten, Clint Howard, Dey Young, The Ramones, Mary Woronov, Paul Bartel, Alix Elias. A 1950's movie gone berserk. A rock-crazy teenager marshals her fellow students to rebel against the repression of new principal Miss Togar. An irresistible, high-energy comedy set to a nonstop soundtrack of Ramones music (and a few oldies). Soles is wonderful as the group's number one fan, Riff Randell. The songs include "Teenage Lobotomy," "Blitzkrieg Bop," "I Wanna Be Sedated," and "Sheena Is a Punk Rocker." Followed by ROCK 'N' ROLL HIGH SCHOOL FOREVER. [PG]▼●◗

Rock 'n' Roll Mom (1988) **C-100m. TVM** D: Michael Schultz. Dyan Cannon, Michael Brandon, Telma Hopkins, Heather Locklear, Nancy Lenehan, Alex Rocco, Nina Blackwood. Amiable Disney comedy about a surburban housewife with teenage kids who becomes an overnight hit as a pop music star. Average.

Rock, Pretty Baby (1956) **89m.** ** D: Richard Bartlett. Sal Mineo, John Saxon, Luana Patten, Edward C. Platt, Fay Wray, Rod McKuen, Shelley Fabares, George Winslow. Prototype of rock 'n' roll entries of 1950s revolving around high school rock group's effort to win big-time musical contest.▼

Rock, Rock, Rock! (1956) **83m.** ** D: Will Price. Tuesday Weld, Teddy Randazzo,

Alan Freed, Frankie Lymon and the Teenagers, The Moonglows, Chuck Berry, The Flamingos, Johnny Burnette Trio, LaVern Baker, Cirino and the Bowties. Weld, in her film debut and barely out of her training bra, must raise $30 to buy a strapless evening dress for a prom! Filmed on a budget of $6.95—and it shows. But the rock 'n' rollers, particularly Chuck Berry, are lively. Lymon and the Teenagers sing "I'm Not a Juvenile Delinquent." Weld's singing voice was dubbed by Connie Francis. One of the teens is young Valerie Harper.▼◗

Rockshow (1980-British) **C-105m.** ★★½ No director credited. Paul McCartney, Linda McCartney, Jimmy McCulloch, Joe English, Denny Laine. Adequate concert film of Paul McCartney and Wings on tour. Effect of Dolby sound recording will be lost on the small screen. [G]▼

Rockula (1990) **C-87m.** ★½ D: Luca Bercovici. Dean Cameron, Tawny Fere, Susan Tyrrell, Bo Diddley, Thomas Dolby, Toni Basil. Teen vampire Cameron is unable to lose his virginity because of a centuries-old curse. Pretty stale stuff; of interest only for—but not redeemed by—the presence of Diddley. [PG-13]▼●

Rocky (1976) **C-119m.** ★★★½ D: John G. Avildsen. Sylvester Stallone, Talia Shire, Burt Young, Carl Weathers, Burgess Meredith, Thayer David. This story of a two-bit fighter who gets his "million-to-one shot" for fame, and self-respect, in a championship bout is impossible to dislike, even though it's just an old B-movie brought up to date. Knowing that the film was a similar do-or-die project for writer-star Stallone added to its good vibes. Oscar winner for Best Picture, Director, Editing (Richard Halsey, Scott Conrad). Followed by four sequels. [PG]▼●◗

Rocky II (1979) **C-119m.** ★★★ D: Sylvester Stallone. Sylvester Stallone, Talia Shire, Burt Young, Carl Weathers, Burgess Meredith. Officially a sequel, this slightly silly film is more of a rehash, but the climactic bout (and buildup to it) hits home. [PG] ▼●◗

Rocky III (1982) **C-99m.** ★★½ D: Sylvester Stallone. Sylvester Stallone, Talia Shire, Burt Young, Burgess Meredith, Carl Weathers, Mr. T. Here, the Italian Stallion is trained by Apollo Creed after being dethroned by obnoxious Clubber Lang (Mr. T). Stallone's got a winning formula, but enough already. [PG]▼●

Rocky IV (1985) **C-91m.** ★★½ D: Sylvester Stallone. Sylvester Stallone, Dolph Lundgren, Carl Weathers, Talia Shire, Burt Young, Brigitte Nielsen, Michael Pataki, James Brown. Totally artificial (and unnecessary) sequel has Rocky doin' what a man's gotta do—avenging a friend's demise and fighting for the U.S.A. (and world peace) against a superhuman Russian champ. Still, Stallone knows how to press all the right buttons, especially in a great training montage. [PG] ▼●◗

Rocky V (1990) **C-104m.** ★★ D: John G. Avildsen. Sylvester Stallone, Talia Shire, Burt Young, Sage Stallone, Burgess Meredith, Tommy Morrison, Richard Gant. The one-time champ has hit rock bottom (again). He winds up in his old neighborhood, broke and ostracized (again). He trains a young boxer who turns ingrate, and in spite of his own brain damage (from the fight in ROCKY IV) is willing to risk everything on another bout. Again. You pays your money, and you gets what you expects in this Stallone screenplay, but the thrill is gone. Stallone's real-life son plays Rocky, Jr. [PG-13]▼●

Rocky Horror Picture Show, The (1975-British) **C-95m.** ★★★ D: Jim Sharman. Tim Curry, Susan Sarandon, Barry Bostwick, Richard O'Brien, Jonathan Adams, Meatloaf, Little Nell (Campbell), Charles Gray, Patricia Quinn. Outrageously kinky horror movie spoof, spiced with sex, transvestism, and rock music, about a straight couple, Janet and Brad (Sarandon, Bostwick), stranded in an old dark house full of weirdos from Transylvania. Music and lyrics by O'Brien; songs include "Time Warp," "Dammit Janet," and "Wild and Untamed Thing." British running time: 100m. Followed by SHOCK TREATMENT. [R]▼●

Rocky Mountain (1950) **83m.** ★★½ D: William Keighley. Errol Flynn, Patrice Wymore, Scott Forbes, Slim Pickens, Sheb Wooley, Yakima Canutt, Dickie Jones. Lumbering Flynn vehicle set in Civil War times, with Rebs and Yankees fighting off an Indian attack.

Rodan (1956-Japanese) **C-70m.** ★★ D: Ishiro Honda. Kenji Sawara, Yumi Shirakawa, Akihiko Hirata, Akio Kobori. Colossal pterodactyl hatches in mine, later goes on destructive rampage in Tokyo. Colorful comic book stuff, all too typical of Toho Studios' monster formula.▼●

Rodeo (1952) **C-70m.** ★½ D: William Beaudine. Jane Nigh, John Archer, Wallace Ford, Frances Rafferty. Tame little account of girl managing a roping show.

Roger & Me (1989) **C-87m.** ★★★½ D: Michael Moore. Inspired, darkly ironic documentary-style film about one man's attempts to track down General Motors chairman Roger Smith, to show him what his factory closing did to the town of Flint, Michigan, where 40,000 jobs were lost. Filmmaker/narrator Moore creates an irresistible blend of documentary and humorous essay in this unique piece of Americana. Followed in 1992 by Moore's 24m. short, PETS OR MEAT: THE RETURN TO FLINT. [R]▼●

Roger Touhy, Gangster (1944) **65m.** ★★½

D: Robert Florey. Preston Foster, Victor McLaglen, Lois Andrews, Anthony Quinn, Kent Taylor, Henry (Harry) Morgan, Trudy Marshall, Kane Richmond. Unexceptional—if mostly factual—account of Chicago bootlegger who waged a turf war with Al Capone, and later masterminded a prison escape.

Rogue Cop (1954) **92m.** *** D: Roy Rowland. Robert Taylor, Janet Leigh, George Raft, Steve Forrest, Anne Francis, Vince Edwards. Dynamic account of policeman Taylor on the underworld payroll, tracking down his brother's killer. Also shown in computer-colored version.

Rogue Male (1976-British) **C-100m. TVM** D: Clive Donner. Peter O'Toole, John Standing, Alastair Sim, Cyd Hayman, Harold Pinter, Hugh Manning. Remake of MAN HUNT with O'Toole as British aristocrat who tries to assassinate Hitler in the 1930s and then is hounded by the Gestapo. First-class BBC production with Frederic Raphael script (from the Geoffrey Household novel). Above average.▼

Rogue River (1950) **C-81m.** ** D: John Rawlins. Rory Calhoun, Peter Graves, Frank Fenton, Ralph Sanford. Talky study of family relationships; little Western action.

Rogues' Gallery (1968) **C-88m.** ** D: Leonard Horn. Roger Smith, Greta Baldwin, Dennis Morgan, Farley Granger, Edgar Bergen, Brian Donlevy, Mala Powers. Private eye comes to aid of beautiful woman attempting suicide, eventually seduced into frameup scheme. Forgettable mystery drama. Never released theatrically. Techniscope.

Rogue's March (1952) **84m.** ** D: Allan Davis. Peter Lawford, Richard Greene, Janice Rule, Leo G. Carroll. Programmer-costumer set in India (via stock footage and rear projection scenes), with Lawford trying to redeem himself with regiment.

Rogues of Sherwood Forest (1950) **C-80m.** ** D: Gordon Douglas. John Derek, Diana Lynn, George Macready, Alan Hale. Despite good production and fair cast, pretty limp; Robin Hood's son (Derek) fights to get the Magna Carta signed.

Rogue's Regiment (1948) **86m.** ** D: Robert Florey. Dick Powell, Marta Toren, Vincent Price, Stephen McNally, Edgar Barrier, Henry Rowland. Contrived actioner about American agent Powell, who joins the French Foreign Legion in Indochina to hunt down Nazi bigwig McNally.

Rollerball (1975) **C-122m.** **½ D: Norman Jewison. James Caan, John Houseman, Maud Adams, John Beck, Moses Gunn, Ralph Richardson. Great-looking but disappointing drama of the 21st century; Caan is the champ at a violent sport in a society where violence has been outlawed. Filmed in Munich and London, adapted by William Harrison from his story *Roller Ball Murders.* [R]▼●◗

Roller Boogie (1979) **C-103m.** BOMB D: Mark L. Lester. Linda Blair, Jim Bray, Beverly Garland, Roger Perry, Mark Goddard, Sean McClory. Blair, Bray, and friends join forces to thwart evil Goddard from closing local roller skating rink. Made to cash in on roller-disco fad, with amateurish script and performances. [PG]▼

Rollercoaster (1977) **C-119m.** ** D: James Goldstone. George Segal, Richard Widmark, Timothy Bottoms, Henry Fonda, Harry Guardino, Susan Strasberg, Helen Hunt, Dorothy Tristan, Craig Wasson, William Prince, Robert Quarry. Silly disaster-type film almost redeemed by Segal's winning performance as civic inspector who tries to nail extortionist (Bottoms) before he sabotages another amusement park. Overlong, but at least TV audiences won't have to watch it in "Sensurround." Hunt's film debut. Panavision. [PG]▼●◗

Rolling Thunder (1977) **C-99m.** ** D: John Flynn. William Devane, Tommy Lee Jones, Linda Haynes, James Best, Dabney Coleman, Lisa Richards, Luke Askew. Devane comes home after eight years as P.O.W. in Vietnam, sees his family murdered, and cold-bloodedly goes for revenge. Intriguing aspects of story (by Paul Schrader) and main characters thrown off-course by graphic violence and vigilante melodramatics. [R]▼●

Rollover (1981) **C-118m.** *½ D: Alan J. Pakula. Jane Fonda, Kris Kristofferson, Hume Cronyn, Josef Sommer, Bob Gunton, Martha Plimpton. Laughably pretentious, barely comprehensible drama about petrochemical heiress (and former film star) Fonda, banker-troubleshooter Kristofferson, and their high-financial dealings. Cronyn excels as a cunning banker. One of the few examples of financial science fiction. [R]▼

Romance (1930) **76m.** ** D: Clarence Brown. Greta Garbo, Lewis Stone, Gavin Gordon, Elliott Nugent, Florence Lake, Clara Blandick. Garbo is miscast in this static, hokey early talkie about an Italian opera star who philosophizes about love and has a relationship with an inexperienced young priest (limply played by Gordon).▼

Romance (1999-French) **C-97m.** *½ D: Catherine Breillat. Caroline Ducey, Sagamore Stévenin, François Berléand, Rocco Siffredi, Reza Habouhossen. Notorious French film from writer-director Breillat about a woman who, rejected by her lover, goes on a sexual odyssey that leads her down some very strange paths. Novelty of a sexual film from a woman's point of view quickly wears off; it's startlingly explicit but strangely unerotic—and, more important, dull. Alternate 84m. video version is rated R. ▼◗

Romance and Riches SEE: **Amazing Adventure**

Romance in Manhattan (1934) **78m.** *** D: Stephen Roberts. Francis Lederer, Ginger Rogers, Arthur Hohl, Jimmy Butler, J. Farrell MacDonald, Helen Ware, Donald Meek, Sidney Toler. Chorus girl Rogers helps illegal alien Lederer, and romance blossoms, in this most enjoyable Capraesque comedy.▼

Romance in the Dark (1938) **80m.** ** D: H. C. Potter. Gladys Swarthout, John Barrymore, John Boles, Claire Dodd, Curt Bois. A womanizing tenor uses a naive young singer (Swarthout) in a scheme to distract his rival, but his plans backfire when he falls in love with her. Stylish treatment of trite material; more a showcase for funny Fritz Feld (as Boles's valet) than for opera star Swarthout.

Romance of a Horsethief (1971-U.S.-Yugoslavian) **C-100m.** *½ D: Abraham Polonsky. Yul Brynner, Eli Wallach, Jane Birkin, Oliver Tobias, Lainie Kazan, David Opatoshu. Wily Jewish horsetraders scheme to outwit Cossack captain Brynner and his men, in a Polish village circa 1904. A heartfelt endeavor for director Polonsky and actor-screenwriter Opatoshu that just doesn't come off. [PG]▼

Romance of Rosy Ridge, The (1947) **105m.** *** D: Roy Rowland. Van Johnson, Thomas Mitchell, Janet Leigh, Marshall Thompson. Selena Royle. Set in post-Civil War days, Missouri farmer Mitchell casts suspicious eye on young Johnson, who is courting his daughter, Leigh (in her film debut).

Romance on the High Seas (1948) **C-99m.** *** D: Michael Curtiz. Jack Carson, Janis Paige, Don DeFore, Doris Day, Oscar Levant, S. Z. Sakall, Fortunio Bonanova, Eric Blore, Franklin Pangborn. Sparkling, trivial romantic musical set on an ocean voyage, with Doris' star-making feature film debut, singing "It's Magic," "Put 'em in a Box." Easygoing fun.▼●

Romancing the Stone (1984) **C-105m.** *** D: Robert Zemeckis. Kathleen Turner, Michael Douglas, Danny DeVito, Zack Norman, Alfonso Arau, Manuel Ojeda. Very likable high-adventure hokum about mousy writer of romantic fiction who finds herself up to her neck in trouble in Colombia, with only a feisty American soldier-of-fortune as her ally. Silly story never stops moving—with some terrific action and stunts—but it's Turner's enormously appealing performance that really makes the film worthwhile. Sequel: THE JEWEL OF THE NILE. Panavision. [PG]▼●◗

Roman Holiday (1953) **119m.** ***½ D: William Wyler. Audrey Hepburn, Gregory Peck, Eddie Albert, Tullio Carminati. Hepburn got first break and an Oscar as princess, yearning for normal life, who runs away from palace, has romance with reporter Peck. Screenplay by John Dighton and Ian McLellan Hunter, from an Oscar-winning story (written by blacklisted Dalton Trumbo and credited for almost 40 years to Hunter, who acted as his "front"). Utterly charming. Remade for TV in 1987 with Catherine Oxenberg and Tom Conti.▼●

Romanoff and Juliet (1961) **C-103m.** *** D: Peter Ustinov. Peter Ustinov, Sandra Dee, John Gavin, Akim Tamiroff, Rik Von Nutter. Ustinov wrote, directed and stars in this cold war satire with offspring of U.S. and Russian ambassadors falling in love. Italian locations substitute for mythical country which Ustinov rules.

Roman Scandals (1933) **92m.** *** D: Frank Tuttle. Eddie Cantor, Ruth Etting, Gloria Stuart, David Manners, Verree Teasdale, Alan Mowbray, Edward Arnold. Old-fashioned, enjoyable musical vehicle for Cantor to romp through as dreamer who is transported back to ancient Rome. Full of funny gags and delightful songs. Big Busby Berkeley production numbers include young Lucille Ball.▼●

Roman Spring of Mrs. Stone, The (1961) **C-104m.** *** D: Jose Quintero. Vivien Leigh, Warren Beatty, Lotte Lenya, Jill St. John, Jeremy Spenser, Coral Browne, Cleo Laine, Bessie Love, Jean Marsh. Middle-aged actress retreats to Rome, buying a fling at romance from gigolo Beatty. Lenya, as Leigh's waspish friend, comes off best. Adapted from Tennessee Williams novella.▼

Romantic Age, The (1949-British) **86m.** ** D: Edmond T. Greville. Mai Zetterling, Hugh Williams, Margot Grahame, Petula Clark, Carol Marsh, Adrienne Corri. Art teacher Williams falls for flirtatious French schoolgirl Zetterling. Trifling; aka NAUGHTY ARLETTE.

Romantic Comedy (1983) **C-103m.** *½ D: Arthur Hiller. Dudley Moore, Mary Steenburgen, Frances Sternhagen, Janet Eilber, Robyn Douglass, Ron Leibman. Faithful adaptation of Bernard Slade's paper-thin play looks even worse on screen, despite a perfect cast. Moore is a playwright who tries to stifle his feelings for his female writing partner over many years' time. Title sounds suspiciously like a generic product—like Canned Peas or Toilet Tissue. Hold out for brand names. [PG]▼

Romantic Englishwoman, The (1975-British) **C-115m.** ***½ D: Joseph Losey. Michael Caine, Glenda Jackson, Helmut Berger, Beatrice Romand, Kate Nelligan, Nathalie Delon, Michel Lonsdale. Caine, a successful novelist married to Jackson, invites Berger into their home to generate material for a screenplay he's writing. Underrated comedy-drama by Tom Stoppard and Thomas Wiseman from Wiseman's novel; stylish and believable. [R]▼

Rome Adventure (1962) **C-119m.** *** D: Delmer Daves. Troy Donahue, Angie Dickinson, Rossano Brazzi, Suzanne Pleshette, Constance Ford, Chad Everett, Al Hirt, Hampton Fancher. Plush soaper with Pleshette as schoolteacher on Roman fling to find romance, torn between roué (Brazzi) and architect (Donahue). As Troy's mistress, Dickinson has some rare repartee. Lush Max Steiner score. Donahue and Pleshette married two years later.▼●

Rome Express, The (1932-British) **94m.** *** D: Walter Forde. Conrad Veidt, Esther Ralston, Harold Huth, Gordon Harker, Donald Calthrop, Joan Barry, Cedric Hardwicke, Frank Vosper, Hugh Williams. Seminal mystery-thriller that spawned many imitations, including THE LADY VANISHES and NIGHT TRAIN TO MUNICH, among others. Entertaining, if slightly talky, tale of assorted group of passengers caught up in criminal activities aboard train. Remade as SLEEPING CAR TO TRIESTE.

Romeo and Juliet (1936) **126m.** ***½ D: George Cukor. Norma Shearer, Leslie Howard, John Barrymore, Edna May Oliver, Basil Rathbone, C. Aubrey Smith, Andy Devine, Reginald Denny, Ralph Forbes. Well-acted, lavish production of Shakespeare's play about ill-fated lovers. Howard and Shearer are so good that one can forget they are too old for the roles. Not the great film it might have been, but a very good one.▼●

Romeo and Juliet (1954-British) **C-140m.** *** D: Renato Castellani. Laurence Harvey, Susan Shentall, Flora Robson, Mervyn Johns, Bill Travers, Sebastian Cabot; introduced by John Gielgud. Sumptuously photographed in Italy, this pleasing version of Shakespeare's tragedy has the virtue of good casting.▼●

Romeo and Juliet (1966-British) **C-126m.** **½ D: Paul Czinner. Margot Fonteyn, Rudolf Nureyev, David Blair, Desmond Doyle, Julia Farron, Michael Somes. Anyone interested in dance will want to see this filmed record of the Royal Ballet production, but actually, it doesn't adapt very well to film; zoom lens is poor substitute for immediacy of live performance.▼

Romeo and Juliet (1968-British-Italian) **C-138m.** ***½ D: Franco Zeffirelli. Leonard Whiting, Olivia Hussey, Milo O'Shea, Michael York, John McEnery, Pat Heywood, Robert Stephens. Narrated by Laurence Olivier. One of the best cinematic versions of Shakespeare's immortal tale of two young lovers kept apart by their families. Unique for its casting leads who were only 17 and 15, respectively, this exquisitely photographed film (by Pasquale de Santis, who won an Oscar) has a hauntingly beautiful musical score by Nino Rota and Oscar-winning costumes by Danilo Donati. [PG—edited from original G rating]▼●◗

Romeo & Juliet (1996) **C-120m.** **½ D: Baz Luhrmann. Claire Danes, Leonardo DiCaprio, Brian Dennehy, John Leguizamo, Pete Postlethwaite, Paul Sorvino, Christina Pickles, Vondie Curtis-Hall, M. Emmet Walsh, Miriam Margolyes, Diane Venora, Harold Perrineau, Paul Rudd. Arrestingly original, post-modern MTV-style '90s version of Shakespeare's tragic love story, set in Miami. The words are all authentic, the images dizzyingly clever, but the conceit wears thin after a while. What keeps it alive is the earnestness of the two youthful leads, whose passion for one another is tangible and appealing. Postlethwaite also scores strongly as Friar Lawrence. Officially titled—with no apparent irony—WILLIAM SHAKESPEARE'S ROMEO & JULIET. Panavision. [PG-13]▼●◗

Romeo Is Bleeding (1993) **C-108m.** **½ D: Peter Medak. Gary Oldman, Lena Olin, Annabella Sciorra, Juliette Lewis, Roy Scheider, David Proval, Will Patton, Larry Joshua, James Cromwell, Julia Migenes, Dennis Farina, Ron Perlman. Nasty, hopped-up contemporary film noir about a crooked cop who's ordered by a crime-family kingpin to bump off a sexy hit woman. Film's standout virtue—and it's a doozy—is Olin's robust performance as a sadistic dominatrix who ends up strangling her assailant between her thighs and tying him down to electrified bedsprings. Outlandish, sometimes funny, but confuses overcooked with hard-boiled. [R]▼●

Romeo Must Die (2000) **C-115m.** **½ D: Andrzej Bartkowiak. Jet Li, Aaliyah, Delroy Lindo, Henry O, Isaiah Washington, Russell Wong, DMX, D.B. Woodside, Anthony Anderson. If there's a Romeo, there must be a Juliet, and this Oakland-set bone-crusher deals with two warring gang families (one African-American, one Chinese) whose straight-and-narrow offspring want no part of the inevitable mayhem. Martial arts star Li's English-language starring debut has toned down the brutality to fashion a movie of slightly broader appeal. OK but overelaborate and overlong. Directorial debut for renowned cinematographer Bartkowiak. Super 35. [R] ▼◗

Rome, Open City SEE: **Open City**

Romero (1989) **C-102m.** *** D: John Duigan. Raul Julia, Richard Jordan, Ana Alicia, Eddie Velez, Alejandro Bracho, Tony Plana, Lucy Reina, Harold Gould, Al Ruscio, Robert Viharo. Absorbing biography of El Salvador's Archbishop Oscar Romero, chronicling his transformation from passive cleric to eloquent defender of his church and people. Thoughtfully directed with a good script by John Sacret Young and a quietly powerful performance by Julia. The initial feature film financed by officials of the United States Roman Catholic Church. [PG-13]▼●

Romper Stomper (1992-Australian) **C-92m.** ★★★ D: Geoffrey Wright. Russell Crowe, Daniel Pollock, Jacqueline McKenzie, Alex Scott, Leigh Russell, Daniel Wyllie, James McKenna. Lashing out at Asians in their neighborhood, a gang of white supremacist Melbourne skinheads is gradually reduced to a handful. Well-observed story is extremely tense, with strong doses of violence and sex. Reminiscent of A CLOCKWORK ORANGE, Wright's feature debut is vividly directed and well acted, but whittling the story down to a sexual triangle is a letdown. Very successful (and controversial) in its native Australia.▼●

Romy and Michele's High School Reunion (1997) **C-91m.** ★★½ D: David Mirkin. Mira Sorvino, Lisa Kudrow, Janeane Garofalo, Alan Cumming, Julia Campbell, Mia Cottet, Kristin Bauer, Camryn Manheim. Best-friend airheads decide to attend their 10-year high school reunion in Tucson . . . then realize that they'd better put on airs if they're going to impress all the A-list snobs who used to make their lives a living hell. Flighty comedy has lulls to match its laughs, but benefits from airtight performances by the two gaudy, likable leads. [R]▼●◗

Rona Jaffe's Mazes and Monsters SEE: **Mazes and Monsters**

Ronin (1998) **C-121m.** ★★ D: John Frankenheimer. Robert De Niro, Jean Reno, Natascha McElhone, Stellan Skarsgård, Jonathan Pryce, Sean Bean, Skipp Sudduth, Michael (Michel) Lonsdale, Jan Triska, Katarina Witt. A group of mercenaries is brought together in France to secure a mysterious package for a high-powered client—but a double-cross leads to a guessing game of whom can be trusted. Great car chases (from the director of GRAND PRIX) are the only draw in this otherwise flat, self-serious espionage yarn. Dialogue about Japanese Ronin doesn't even apply to these characters! Cowriter Richard Weisz is in fact David Mamet. Super 35. [R]▼●◗

Roof, The (1956-Italian) **98m.** ★★½ D: Vittorio De Sica. Gabriella Pallotta, Giorgio Listuzzi, Gastone Renzelli, Maria Di Rollo. Thoughtful neorealist account of a simple young married couple in overcrowded post-WW2 Rome, and their attempt to find a home for themselves. Original title: IL TETTO.▼

Rooftops (1989) **C-95m.** ★½ D: Robert Wise. Jason Gedrick, Troy Beyer, Eddie Velez, Tisha Campbell, Alexis Cruz, Allen Payne. Routine urban B musical about a teenage white male, his forbidden Hispanic girlfriend, drug pushers, and a form of "combat dancing"—the last employing martial-arts footwork, but without the bone crushing. Sole distinction: that it was directed by veteran Wise, who won an Oscar for the thematically similar WEST SIDE STORY. [R]▼●

Roogie's Bump (1954) **71m.** ★½ D: Harold Young. Robert Marriot, Ruth Warrick, Olive Blackeney, Robert Simon, William Harrigan, David Winters. A bump on the arm of young Remington "Roogie" Rigsby (Marriot) results in his getting to pitch for the Brooklyn Dodgers. Slight kiddie fantasy, with more than a passing resemblance to ROOKIE OF THE YEAR. However, fans of Dem Bums will enjoy seeing Roy Campanella, Billy Loes, Carl Erskine, and Russ Meyer as Roogie's teammates.▼

Rookie, The (1959) **86m.** BOMB D: George O'Hanlon. Tommy Noonan, Pete Marshall, Julie Newmar, Jerry Lester, Joe Besser, Vince Barnett, Peter Leeds. Feeble Army comedy of draftee, tough sergeant, movie starlet, and other stereotypes set during 1940s. CinemaScope.

Rookie, The (1990) **C-121m.** ★½ D: Clint Eastwood. Clint Eastwood, Charlie Sheen, Raul Julia, Sonia Braga, Tom Skerritt, Lara Flynn Boyle, Pepe Serna, Mara Corday. Formula filmmaking that even bored its intended audience. Cop Eastwood chews stogies for breakfast, while new partner Sheen is a rich kid who (from evidence supplied here) apparently enjoys collecting facial contusions. Still, there's one good freeway crackup, the you-asked-for-it teaming of Julia and Braga as Germans, and the sight of handcuffed Clint performing under extreme pressure during Braga's bondage rape of him. (Maybe she saw TIGHTROPE.) Panavision. [R]▼●

Rookie of the Year (1993) **C-103m.** ★★★ D: Daniel Stern. Thomas Ian Nicholas, Gary Busey, Albert Hall, Amy Morton, Dan Hedaya, Bruce Altman, Eddie Bracken, Daniel Stern, Robert Gorman. Amiable film for kids about a boy who, after breaking his arm, turns out to have an incredible fastball pitch, which earns him a spot as the new star pitcher for the Chicago Cubs. Benign (almost to a fault), sometimes broad comedy/fantasy has a paper-thin plot, but makes all the right moves to entertain the youthful audience it's aiming for. First-time feature director Stern gives himself the silliest part in the film, as a dimwitted pitching coach. John Candy appears unbilled as an excitable Cubs broadcaster. Similar in premise to a 1954 film, ROOGIE'S BUMP. [PG]▼●

Room at the Top (1959-British) **118m.** ★★★★ D: Jack Clayton. Laurence Harvey, Simone Signoret, Heather Sears, Hermione Baddeley, Donald Wolfit, Ambrosine Philpotts, Donald Houston, Wendy Craig. Brilliant drama of Harvey sacrificing Signoret's love to get ahead by marrying factory boss' daughter. Trenchant and powerful adaptation of John Braine novel won Oscars for Signoret and screenwriter Neil Paterson. Followed by

LIFE AT THE TOP and MAN AT THE TOP.▼●◗

Room for One More (1952) **98m.** *** D: Norman Taurog. Cary Grant, Betsy Drake, Lurene Tuttle, George Winslow, John Ridgely. Grant and Drake are softhearted couple who can't resist adopting needy kids. Sentimental comedy retitled THE EASY WAY; basis for later TV series.

Roommates (1995) **C-108m.** **½ D: Peter Yates. Peter Falk, D. B. Sweeney, Julianne Moore, Ellen Burstyn, Jan Rubes, Frankie Faison, Noah Fleiss, Joyce Reehling, Ernie Sabella. A movie best described as "nice," about a crotchety, working-class Polish immigrant who raises his grandson when the boy is orphaned, and remains a dominant figure in his life even after the young man is married and a father himself. Falk is in fine form in this mildly entertaining story, based on coscreenwriter Max Apple's own experiences. [PG] ▼●

Room Service (1938) **78m.** *** D: William A. Seiter. Groucho, Chico and Harpo Marx, Lucille Ball, Ann Miller, Frank Albertson, Donald MacBride. Broadway farce about destitute producers trying to keep their play afloat—and avoid being evicted from their hotel room—is transformed by scenarist Morrie Ryskind into a vehicle for the Marx Bros. More conventional than their earlier outings, but still has a lot of funny material (and, thankfully, no intrusive songs). Remade as a musical, STEP LIVELY. Also shown in computer-colored version.▼●

Room with a View, A (1986-British) **C-115m.** *** D: James Ivory. Maggie Smith, Helena Bonham Carter, Denholm Elliott, Julian Sands, Daniel Day-Lewis, Simon Callow, Judi Dench, Rosemary Leach, Rupert Graves. Elegant and witty adaptation of E. M. Forster novel about British manners and mores, and a young woman's awakening experiences during a trip (chaperoned, of course) to Florence. Splendid performances, fine attention to detail; only fault is its deliberate pace, which allows interest level to lag from time to time. Won Oscars for screenplay adaptation (Ruth Prawer Jhabvala), art direction, and costume design.▼●

Rooney (1958-British) **88m.** *** D: George Pollock. John Gregson, Muriel Pavlow, Barry Fitzgerald, June Thorburn. Sprightly tale of Irish sanitation worker Gregson with an eye for the girls, trying to avoid marriage; Fitzgerald is bedridden geezer whom Rooney helps.

Rooster Cogburn (1975) **C-107m.** ** D: Stuart Millar. John Wayne, Katharine Hepburn, Anthony Zerbe, Strother Martin, Richard Jordan, John McIntire, Richard Farnsworth. Reprising Wayne's character from TRUE GRIT and teaming him with Hepburn was an obvious attempt to spark an AFRICAN QUEEN-type hit, but starpower is all this film has going for it. Dull story of unlikely duo going after men who murdered Kate's father may play better on TV. Panavision. [PG]▼●◗

Roosters (1993) **C-95m.** *½ D: Robert M. Young. Edward James Olmos, Sonia Braga, Maria Conchita Alonso, Danny Nucci, Sarah Lassez. Leaden-paced drama of irresponsible ex-con Olmos, who's consumed by his machismo, and what happens when he returns to his family in the rural Southwest. Uninvolving and at times downright boring, despite all of the characters' simmering emotions. An *American Playhouse* coproduction. [R]▼

Roots of Heaven, The (1958) **C-131m.** **½ D: John Huston. Errol Flynn, Juliette Greco, Trevor Howard, Eddie Albert, Orson Welles, Herbert Lom, Paul Lukas. Turgid melodramatics set in Africa, with conglomerate cast philosophizing over sanctity of elephants; loosely based on Romain Gary novel. CinemaScope.

Rope (1948) **C-80m.** *** D: Alfred Hitchcock. James Stewart, John Dall, Farley Granger, Cedric Hardwicke, Joan Chandler, Constance Collier, Douglas Dick. Two young men kill prep-school pal, just for the thrill of it, and challenge themselves by inviting friends and family to their apartment afterward—with the body hidden on the premises. Hitchcock's first color film was shot in ten-minute takes to provide a seamless flow of movement, but it remains today what it was then: an interesting, highly theatrical experiment. Inspired by the real-life Leopold-Loeb murder case, which later was depicted in COMPULSION and SWOON. Patrick Hamilton's play was adapted by Hume Cronyn and scripted by Arthur Laurents.▼●

Rope of Sand (1949) **104m.** *** D: William Dieterle. Burt Lancaster, Paul Henreid, Corinne Calvet, Claude Rains, Peter Lorre, Sam Jaffe, John Bromfield, Mike Mazurki. Sturdy cast in adventure tale of smooth thief trying to regain treasure he hid away, with various parties interfering.

Rosalie (1937) **122m.** ** D: W. S. Van Dyke. Eleanor Powell, Nelson Eddy, Frank Morgan, Edna May Oliver, Ray Bolger, Ilona Massey, Billy Gilbert. Elephantine MGM musical about romance between West Point cadet and mythical-kingdom princess. Living proof that money alone can't make a good movie. Cole Porter score includes "In the Still of the Night."▼

Rosalie Goes Shopping (1989-German) **C-94m.** *** D: Percy Adlon. Marianne Sägebrecht, Brad Davis, Judge Reinhold, William Harlander, Erika Blumberger, Patricia Zehentmayr, Alex Winter. Bavarian-born Sägebrecht has settled with American husband Davis in Stuttgart, Arkansas, and they have more children than you can count;

she's become obsessed with spending money and having possessions, and devises an ingenious plan to beat the bill collector. Delightfully loopy comedy (written by the director, Eleanor Adlon and Christopher Dorherty). [PG]▼

Rosa Luxemburg (1986-German) **C-116m.** ★★★½ D: Margarethe von Trotta. Barbara Sukowa, Daniel Olbrychski, Otto Sander, Adelheid Arndt, Jurgen Holtz, Doris Schade. Sukowa offers a towering performance in this compelling, multileveled biography of the dedicated, idealistic democratic socialist/pacifist/humanist who played a prominent role in German politics in the early years of the century. Extremely provocative and well directed.▼

Rosary Murders, The (1987) **C-101m.** ★★ D: Fred Walton. Donald Sutherland, Charles Durning, Belinda Bauer, Josef Sommer, James Murtaugh, John Danelle, Addison Powell, Kathleen Tolan. Mass killer of Motown priests and nuns confesses to Sutherland, who obviously can't inform the cops. Despite an Elmore Leonard script, Sutherland's performance is the sole reward. Starts promisingly but soon fizzles. Filmed on location in Detroit. See I CONFESS instead. [R]▼●

Rose, The (1979) **C-134m.** ★★ D: Mark Rydell. Bette Midler, Alan Bates, Frederic Forrest, Harry Dean Stanton, Barry Primus, David Keith. Spin-off of the Janis Joplin saga equates show biz with hell, then concentrates on giving the audience too much of the latter. Midler (in her starring debut) and Forrest deliver dynamic performances, but film leaves a lot to be desired. Impressive photography by Vilmos Zsigmond. [R]▼●

Rose and the Sword, The SEE: **Flesh + Blood** (1985)

Roseanna McCoy (1949) **100m.** ★★ D: Irving Reis. Farley Granger, Joan Evans, Charles Bickford, Raymond Massey, Richard Basehart, Aline MacMahon. Witless drama of Hatfield-McCoy feud, with young lovers from opposite sides of the fence rekindling old wounds.▼

Rose Bowl Story, The (1952) **C-73m.** ★★ D: William Beaudine. Marshall Thompson, Vera Miles, Natalie Wood, Ann Doran, Jim Backus. Clichéd hogwash about football players, their work and home life.

Rosebud (1975) **C-126m.** BOMB D: Otto Preminger. Peter O'Toole, Richard Attenborough, Cliff Gorman, Claude Dauphin, John V. Lindsay, Peter Lawford, Raf Vallone, Isabelle Huppert, Kim Cattrall. Nadir for director Preminger and usually competent performers. Arab terrorists kill crew of yacht "Rosebud" and kidnap five wealthy young ladies aboard. O'Toole and Attenborough (to say nothing of former N.Y.C. Mayor Lindsay) are embarrassingly bad. Panavision. [PG]▼

Rosebud Beach Hotel, The (1984) **C-87m.** ★½ D: Harry Hurwitz. Colleen Camp, Peter Scolari, Christopher Lee, Fran Drescher, Monique Gabrielle, Eddie Deezen, Chuck McCann. Idiotic, fifth-rate comedy about buffoon Scolari, who with girlfriend Camp operates a resort hotel and hires happy hookers as bellgirls. Camp's bright presence raises the rating of this from BOMB. Originally titled THE BIG LOBBY; aka THE NO-TELL HOTEL. [R]▼

Rose for Everyone, A (1965-Italian) **C-107m.** ★★ D: Franco Rossi. Claudia Cardinale, Nino Manfredi, Mario Adorf, Akim Tamiroff. Brazilian locale with NEVER ON SUNDAY plot. Girl brings happiness to many men and takes active interest in their private lives as well as their sexual lives. Nice locales, banal story.

Rose Garden, The (1989-U.S.-West German) **C-111m.** ★★½ D: Fons Rademakers. Liv Ullmann, Maximilian Schell, Peter Fonda, Jan Niklas, Kurt Hubner. Attorney Ullmann defends Schell on charges of attacking an elderly man whom he recognized as the commandant of a Nazi concentration camp in which his family was killed. Story is earnest and compassionate but uninspired; benefits from fine performances by Ullmann and an almost unrecognizable Schell. [PG-13]▼●

Roseland (1977) **C-103m.** ★★★ D: James Ivory. Teresa Wright, Lou Jacobi, Geraldine Chaplin, Helen Gallagher, Joan Copeland, Christopher Walken, Lilia Skala, David Thomas. Trilogy set in N.Y.C.'s venerable Roseland Ballroom examines bittersweet lives of people who gravitate there. First story is weakest, but other two are absorbing and beautifully performed, with Copeland and Skala as standouts. [PG]▼

Rose-Marie (1936) **110m.** ★★★ D: W. S. Van Dyke II. Jeanette MacDonald, Nelson Eddy, Reginald Owen, Allan Jones, James Stewart, Alan Mowbray, Gilda Gray. Don't expect the original operetta: story has opera star Jeanette searching for fugitive brother Stewart, as mountie Nelson pursues the same man. The two fall in love, sing "Indian Love Call," among others. David Niven appears briefly as Jeanette's unsuccessful suitor. Retitled INDIAN LOVE CALL; previously filmed in 1928, then again in 1954.▼●

Rose Marie (1954) **C-115m.** ★★½ D: Mervyn LeRoy. Ann Blyth, Howard Keel, Fernando Lamas, Bert Lahr, Marjorie Main, Joan Taylor, Ray Collins. More faithful to original operetta than 1936 version, but not as much fun. Mountie Keel tries to "civilize" tomboy Blyth, but falls in love with her instead. Adventurer Lamas completes the triangle. Lahr sings "I'm the Mountie Who Never Got His Man" in comic highlight. CinemaScope.●

Rosemary (1958-German) **99m.** ★★½ D:

Rolf Thiele. Nadja Tiller, Peter Van Eyck, Gert Frobe, Mario Adorf, Carl Raddatz. Convincing study of famed post-WW2 Frankfurt prostitute (Tiller) who blackmailed industrialist; satirically sensational.

Rosemary's Baby (1968) **C-136m.** **** D: Roman Polanski. Mia Farrow, John Cassavetes, Ruth Gordon, Sidney Blackmer, Maurice Evans, Ralph Bellamy, Elisha Cook, Jr., Patsy Kelly, Charles Grodin. Classic modern-day thriller by Ira Levin, perfectly realized by writer-director Polanski: Farrow is unsuspecting young wife whose husband becomes involved with witches' coven and their diabolical plans. Listen closely for Tony Curtis' voice in a phone conversation. Gordon won Best Supporting Actress Oscar. Produced by William Castle; followed by a made-for-TV sequel, LOOK WHAT'S HAPPENED TO ROSEMARY'S BABY (1976, aka ROSEMARY'S BABY II). [R] ▼●

Rosemary's Disciples SEE: **Necromancy**

Rosencrantz and Guildenstern Are Dead (1990) **C-118m.** ** D: Tom Stoppard. Gary Oldman, Tim Roth, Richard Dreyfuss, Joanna Roth, Iain Glen, Donald Sumpter, Joanna Miles, Ian Richardson. Oldman and Roth are engaging as the puckish incidental characters from *Hamlet* who wander into a series of (mostly verbal) adventures in and around the royal castle. Full of delicious wordplay, and some imaginative visual ideas, but there's a basic lifelessness to this film, proving that it should have remained on stage. Playwright Stoppard's feature film directing debut, an adaptation of his own play. [PG]▼●

Rose of Washington Square (1939) **86m.** **½ D: Gregory Ratoff. Tyrone Power, Alice Faye, Al Jolson, William Frawley, Joyce Compton, Hobart Cavanaugh, Louis Prima, Horace McMahon, Moroni Olsen. So-so musical with Faye as a thinly disguised Fanny Brice, who falls head over heels for cocky punk Power (a clone of Nicky Arnstein). Faye gets to sing Brice's signature song, "My Man," but Jolson, essentially playing himself, steals the show performing "Mammy," "California, Here I Come," and other classics.▼

Rose Tattoo, The (1955) **117m.** ***½ D: Daniel Mann. Anna Magnani, Burt Lancaster, Marisa Pavan, Ben Cooper, Virginia Grey, Jo Van Fleet. Magnani shines in Oscar-winning role as earthy, deluded widow in Gulf Coast city who's romanced by rambunctious truck driver Lancaster. Flavorful adaptation of Tennessee Williams play; cinematographer James Wong Howe also won an Oscar. VistaVision.▼●

Rosetta (1999-Belgian-French) **C-95m.** ** D: Luc Dardenne, Jean-Pierre Dardenne. Emilie Dequenne, Fabrizio Rongione, Anne Yernaux, Olivier Gourmet, Florian Delain. Unrelenting, cinema vérité-style portrait of a teenaged girl who is desperate to escape the harshness of her life. She gets a job, but has no idea how to deal with the world around her—except for the desperate survival techniques she has taught herself. With its hand-held camera and fly-on-the-wall storytelling approach, the film paints a vivid picture, but it's tough to watch, and tougher still to pierce the emotional shell of its main character. Top prize-winner at the Cannes Film Festival. [R]▼

Rosewood (1997) **C-142m.** **½ D: John Singleton. Jon Voight, Ving Rhames, Don Cheadle, Bruce McGill, Loren Dean, Esther Rolle, Michael Rooker, Elise Neal, Catherine Kellner. Fact-based story of two neighboring Florida towns, circa 1922–23, and the festering racism that threatens to explode into violence and destroy a law-abiding black community in the process. Rhames (in his biggest role to date) is an outsider who rallies the protest. Well acted and crafted, but turns overly melodramatic. Undoubtedly the most repugnant depiction of Southern "rednecks" since DELIVERANCE. Panavision. [R]▼●◗

Rosie! (1967) **C-98m.** *** D: David Lowell Rich. Rosalind Russell, Sandra Dee, Brian Aherne, Audrey Meadows, James Farentino, Vanessa Brown, Leslie Nielsen, Margaret Hamilton. One of Russell's best late-career performances as madcap grandmother, whose children want her money now. Based on a play by Ruth Gordon. Techniscope.

Rosie the Riveter SEE: **Life and Times of Rosie the Riveter, The**

Roswell (1994) **C-95m. TVM** D: Jeremy Kagan. Kyle MacLachlan, Martin Sheen, Dwight Yoakam, Kim Greist, Peter MacNicol, Bob Gunton, Xander Berkeley. Earnest retelling of real-life army officer Jesse Marcel's thirty-year search for the truth about the government cover-up of his discovery of a UFO landing in the desert near Roswell, New Mexico, in 1947 and the proof taken from him. Playwright Arthur Kopit cowrote the intriguing teleplay, based on the scrupulously documented 1991 book *UFO Crash at Roswell.* Made for cable. Above average.▼●

Rotten to the Core (1965-British) **90m.** *** D: John Boulting. Anton Rodgers, Eric Sykes, Charlotte Rampling, Ian Bannen, Avis Bunnage, Victor Maddern. Well-handled caper of ex-con trio joining forces with crook to carry off large-scale robbery. Panavision.

Rouge Baiser SEE: **Red Kiss**

Rough and the Smooth, The SEE: **Portrait of a Sinner**

Rough Cut (1980) **C-112m.** **½ D: Donald Siegel. Burt Reynolds, Lesley-Anne Down, David Niven, Timothy West, Patrick Magee, Al Matthews, Joss Ackland, Roland Culver. Handsome but uneven romantic caper uses its stars' charm and chemistry to offset weaknesses in script. World-class jewel thief Reynolds falls in love with beautiful woman who's been set up to snag him for Scotland Yard. Filmed in England and Holland. Troubled David Merrick production went through four directors, and scripter Larry Gelbart used a pseudonym; hastily refilmed ending is chief giveaway. [PG]▼●

Roughly Speaking (1945) **117m.** *** D: Michael Curtiz. Rosalind Russell, Jack Carson, Robert Hutton, Jean Sullivan, Alan Hale, Donald Woods. Generally good but long comedy-drama of Russell raising a family while hubby Carson embarks on wild moneymaking schemes; two stars are tops.

Rough Magic (1995-French-British) **C-104m.** ** D: Clare Peploe. Bridget Fonda, Russell Crowe, Jim Broadbent, D. W. Moffett, Kenneth Mars, Paul Rodriguez, Andy Romano, Richard Schiff, Euva Anderson, Michael Ensign. Odd little road movie, with Fonda a magician's assistant in 1950s L.A. who hides out in Mexico with several men in pursuit. Thrust of story concerns "miracle elixirs," a Mayan shaman (female), and farcical situations south of the border. An uneasy mix of genres, faintly reminiscent of OUT OF THE PAST. [PG-13]▼

Rough Night in Jericho (1967) **C-97m.** ** D: Arnold Laven. Dean Martin, George Peppard, Jean Simmons, John McIntire, Slim Pickens, Don Galloway. Gory Western casts Martin as total villain who owns the town. Attractive cast can't fight clichés. Techniscope.▼◗

Rough Riders (1997) **C-120m. TVM** D: John Milius. Tom Berenger, Sam Elliott, Gary Busey, Brad Johnson, Chris Noth, Brian Keith, George Hamilton, Illeana Douglas, R. Lee Ermey, Nick Chinlund, William Katt, Dakin Matthews, Geoffrey Lewis, Francisco Quinn. Full-bodied tale of young Teddy Roosevelt (a nearly unrecognizable Berenger) and how he became an American hero in the Spanish-American War. Keith (terrific in his final role as Pres. William McKinley) played TR in Milius' THE WIND AND THE LION. Busey is also impressive as bigger-than-life Gen. "Fighting Joe" Wheeler. Written by Milius. Made for cable. Above average.▼

Roughshod (1949) **88m.** **½ D: Mark Robson. Robert Sterling, Claude Jarman, Jr., Gloria Grahame, Jeff Donnell, John Ireland, Myrna Dell, Martha Hyer. Intriguing oater in which Sterling and kid brother Jarman head West to start a ranch; they come upon a quartet of stranded saloon-hall dames, and face a trio of murderous escaped cons seeking vengeance.

Rough Shoot SEE: **Shoot First**

Rounders, The (1965) **C-85m.** **½ D: Burt Kennedy. Glenn Ford, Henry Fonda, Sue Ane Langdon, Hope Holiday, Chill Wills, Edgar Buchanan, Kathleen Freeman. Agreeable comedy-Western from Max Evans' novel about two cowboys and an ornery horse was one of the sleepers of its year; nothing much happens, but cast and scenery make it a pleasant way to kill an hour-and-a-half. Panavision.▼

Rounders (1998) **C-121m.** **½ D: John Dahl. Matt Damon, Edward Norton, Gretchen Mol, John Turturro, John Malkovich, Famke Janssen, Martin Landau, Michael Rispoli, Josh Mostel, Tom Aldredge, Michael Lombard, Mal Z. Lawrence. Young poker whiz (Damon) tries to give up the game and focus on being a law student. When his longtime pal—aptly nicknamed Worm (Norton)—is released from prison, he soon finds himself caught up again in the allure of high-stakes games, not because he likes to gamble, but because he knows how good he is. Provocative, interesting, but never entirely engaging—with enough card-playing jargon to last a lifetime. Super 35. [R]▼●◗

Round Midnight (1986-U.S.-French) **C-131m.** ***½ D: Bertrand Tavernier. Dexter Gordon, François Cluzet, Gabrielle Haker, Sandra Reaves-Phillips, Lonette McKee, Herbie Hancock, Bobby Hutcherson, Wayne Shorter, John Berry, Martin Scorsese, Philippe Noiret. A boozy American jazzman working in 1950s Paris is virtually adopted by a fan, and their unusual relationship causes them both to thrive. A loving homage to jazz musicians and their world (inspired by the lives of Bud Powell and Lester Young), with a once-in-a-lifetime performance by real-life tenor-sax great Gordon. Music director—and Oscar winner—Herbie Hancock and his colleagues not only create great jazz right on-screen but also help establish a perfect ambiance. Written by Tavernier and David Rayfiel; designed by premier art director Alexandre Trauner. Panavision. [R]▼●

Roustabout (1964) **C-101m.** **½ D: John Rich. Elvis Presley, Barbara Stanwyck, Leif Erickson, Joan Freeman, Sue Ane Langdon. Elvis is a free-wheeling singer who joins Stanwyck's carnival, learns the meaning of hard work and true love. Stanwyck and supporting cast make this a pleasing Presley songer, with "Little Egypt" his one outstanding tune. Raquel Welch has a bit, and Teri Garr is one of the dancers. Techniscope.▼◗

Rover, The (1967) **C-103m.** *½ D: Terence Young. Anthony Quinn, Rosanna Schiaffino, Rita Hayworth, Richard Johnson, Ivo Garrani, Mino Doro. Quinn stars as 18th-century pirate whose escape from French authorities is sidetracked by relationship with innocent, feeble-minded girl. Plodding film from Joseph Conrad story; made in Italy, barely released here.▼

Rover Dangerfield (1991) **C-74m.** **½

D: Jim George, Bob Seeley. Voices of Rodney Dangerfield, Susan Boyd, Ronnie Schell, Ned Luke, Shawn Southwick, Dana Hill. A wisecracking dog thrives on his life in Las Vegas, until fate sends him to a farm in the middle of nowheresville. The idea of Dangerfield-style one-liners being spoken by a cartoon dog is fun for a while, but the film wavers uneasily between adult and juvenile appeal. Animation fans should check out the incredible opening shot. Dangerfield wrote, produced, and even contributed lyrics to the songs. [G]▼●

Rowdyman, The (1971-Canadian) **C-95m.** **½ D: Peter Carter. Gordon Pinsent, Frank Converse, Will Geer, Linda Gorenson, Ted Henley. Pinsent is the whole show in this occasionally intriguing but ultimately superficial drama about a hard-living womanizer and his fate after accidentally causing the death of a childhood pal. Filmed in Newfoundland; Pinsent also scripted.

Roxanne (1987) **C-107m.** **½ D: Fred Schepisi. Steve Martin, Daryl Hannah, Rick Rossovich, Shelley Duvall, John Kapelos, Fred Willard, Max Alexander, Michael J. Pollard, Damon Wayans, Matt Lattanzi, Kevin Nealon. Martin fashioned this update of *Cyrano de Bergerac* as a vehicle for himself, with Hannah as the object of his affection and Rossovich as the empty-headed hunk for whom he "fronts." Extremely likable and sweet-natured romantic comedy set in a sleepy ski town. Peters out somewhere along the line, unfortunately. Panavision. [PG]▼●◗

Roxie Hart (1942) **75m.** **½ D: William Wellman. Ginger Rogers, Adolphe Menjou, George Montgomery, Lynne Overman, Nigel Bruce, Phil Silvers, Spring Byington, Iris Adrian, George Chandler. Fast-moving spoof of Roaring 20s, with Ginger as publicity-seeking dancer on trial for murder, Menjou her overdramatic lawyer. Hilarious antics make up for dry spells; scripted and produced by Nunnally Johnson. Previously filmed in 1927 as CHICAGO, also the title of the subsequent Broadway musical.▼

Royal Affairs in Versailles (1954-French) **C-152m.** ** D: Sacha Guitry. Claudette Colbert, Orson Welles, Jean-Pierre Aumont, Edith Piaf, Gérard Philipe, Jean Marais, Sacha Guitry, Micheline Presle, Daniel Gelin, Danielle Delorme. Impressive cast in static, leaden-paced chronicle of the Golden Age of the French monarchy. Guitry plays Louis XIV; also seen are D'Artagnan, Mme. de Pompadour, Moliere, Marie Antoinette, etc. Released in U.S. in 1957. Look fast for Brigitte Bardot. Retitled: AFFAIRS IN VERSAILLES.▼

Royal African Rifles, The (1953) **C-75m.** ** D: Lesley Selander. Louis Hayward, Veronica Hurst, Michael Pate, Angela Greene. Adequate actioner set in Africa in 1910, with Hayward the British officer leading mission to recover cache of arms.

Royal Family of Broadway, The (1930) **82m.** ***½ D: George Cukor, Cyril Gardner. Fredric March, Ina Claire, Mary Brian, Henrietta Crosman, Charles Starrett, Arnold Korff, Frank Conroy. Delightful screen version of Edna Ferber-George S. Kaufman play about Barrymore-like theatrical family torn by conflict of show business tradition vs. "normal" private life. March is wickedly funny in his John Barrymore portrayal.

Royal Flash (1975-British) **C-98m.** *** D: Richard Lester. Malcolm McDowell, Alan Bates, Florinda Bolkan, Oliver Reed, Britt Ekland, Lionel Jeffries, Tom Bell, Alastair Sim, Michael Hordern, Joss Ackland, Christopher Cazenove, Bob Hoskins. Comic swashbuckler with McDowell forced to impersonate a Prussian nobleman and marry Ekland. Zippy Lester entry with a fine cast; script by George MacDonald Fraser, from his novel. [PG]▼

Royal Hunt of the Sun, The (1969-British) **C-118m.** *** D: Irving Lerner. Robert Shaw, Christopher Plummer, Nigel Davenport, Michael Craig, Leonard Whiting, James Donald. Colorful tale of Spanish explorer Pizzaro and his quest for gold in South America; from acclaimed stage play by Peter Shaffer, adapted by Philip Yordan. Franscope. [G]◗

Royal Scandal, A (1945) **94m.** **½ D: Ernst Lubitsch, Otto Preminger. Tallulah Bankhead, Charles Coburn, Anne Baxter, William Eythe, Vincent Price, Mischa Auer. Comedy of manners about Catherine the Great of Russia promoting favored soldier Eythe to high rank; started by Lubitsch, "finished" by Preminger. Remake of Lubitsch's 1924 FORBIDDEN PARADISE.

Royal Wedding (1951) **C-93m.** *** D: Stanley Donen. Fred Astaire, Jane Powell, Peter Lawford, Sarah Churchill, Keenan Wynn, Albert Sharpe. Pleasant MGM musical (written by Alan Jay Lerner) about brother and sister team who take their show to London at the time of Queen Elizabeth II's wedding, and find romance of their own. Highlights: Astaire's dancing on the ceiling and partnering with a hatrack, and his dynamite duet with Powell, "How Could You Believe Me When I Said I Loved You (When You Know I've Been a Liar All My Life)?" Burton Lane/Alan Jay Lerner score also includes "Too Late Now." Donen's first solo directing credit.▼●◗

R.P.M. (1970) **C-97m.** *½ D: Stanley Kramer. Anthony Quinn, Ann-Margret, Gary Lockwood, Paul Winfield, Graham Jarvis, Alan Hewitt. Old-fashioned liberal Quinn becomes head of university, then authorizes a police bust of radicals to save institution (*Revolutions* Per Minute, get it?). Inept Erich Segal script, equally bad Kramer direction give film certain camp value, but otherwise, look out. [R]▼

Rubin and Ed (1992) **C-92m.** *½ D: Trent Harris. Crispin Glover, Howard Hesseman, Karen Black, Michael Green, Brittney Lewis. Weird odyssey of two men on a mission to bury a frozen cat. This is one road movie Hope and Crosby never thought of—with good reason. Glover once made an infamous appearance on David Letterman's TV show playing the same character he does here. Letterman kicked him off the show; you can simply eject the video. [PG-13]▼

Ruby (1977) **C-84m.** **½ D: Curtis Harrington. Piper Laurie, Stuart Whitman, Roger Davis, Janit Baldwin, Crystin Sinclaire, Paul Kent. Complex plot has long-dead gangster's spirit possessing deaf-mute girl, sending her on a killing spree at drive-in theater (which specializes in horror movies) run by ex-gang members. A few moments, comic and horrific, stand out in generally uneven supernatural thriller. Some prints run 85m, with a hastily added epilogue. That version is credited to pseudonymous director Allen Smithee. [R]▼

Ruby (1992) **C-110m.** **½ D: John Mackenzie. Danny Aiello, Sherilyn Fenn, Arliss Howard, Tobin Bell, David Duchovny, Richard Sarafian, Joe Cortese, Marc Lawrence. OK speculation about the life and motives of lowlife Jack Ruby, the mob errand boy, FBI informant, and nightclub owner who killed JFK assassin Lee Harvey Oswald. Aiello is good and period recreations are adequate, but film suffers from too many lawyer-dictated characterizations (Frank Sinatra becomes singer "Tony Montana"). [R] ▼●

Ruby Gentry (1952) **82m.** **½ D: King Vidor. Jennifer Jones, Charlton Heston, Karl Malden, Josephine Hutchinson. Turgid, meandering account of easy-virtue Southerner Jones marrying wealthy Malden to spite Heston, the man she loves.▼

Ruby in Paradise (1993) **C-115m.** *** D: Victor Nunez. Ashley Judd, Todd Field, Bentley Mitchum, Allison Dean, Dorothy Lyman. Fine independent effort about a young woman who leaves her Tennessee home for a new life in the beach community of Panama City in West Florida. Though too often self-consciously "poetic," this is a refreshingly low-key character study with none of the easy emotional payoffs of typical Hollywood films. The acting is fine, with Judd (sister of singer Wynonna) outstanding in the lead role. Director Nunez also wrote the screenplay. [R]▼

Ruby Jean and Joe (1996) **C-100m. TVM** D: Geoffrey Sax. Tom Selleck, JoBeth Williams, Ben Johnson, Eileen Seeley, John Diehl, Rebekah Johnson. Easygoing road film, set in the contemporary West, involving a fading rodeo star and the young female hitchhiker he picks up. Selleck executive-produced this offbeat buddy picture. Scripted by James Lee Barrett. Made for cable. Average.▼●

Ruby Ridge: An American Tragedy (1996) **C-200m. TVM** D: Roger Young. Laura Dern, Randy Quaid, Diane Ladd, Kirsten Dunst, Darren Burrows, G. W. Bailey, Bradley Pierce, Bob Gunton, Joe Don Baker. Docudrama about the early '90s standoff between the isolationist Weaver family and the FBI on a remote mountaintop in Idaho. Dern is impressive as a religious extremist protecting her family. Her real-life mom Ladd plays her concerned mother. Originally shown in two parts. Average.

Ruby's Dream SEE: **Dear Mr. Wonderful**

Ruckus (1982) **C-91m.**** D: Max Kleven. Dirk Benedict, Linda Blair, Ben Johnson, Matt Clark, Richard Farnsworth. Slick but ordinary drive-in fare about a shell-shocked Vietnam vet who becomes object of massive manhunt in sleepy Alabama town. Same basic story as later FIRST BLOOD, but less pretentious. [PG]▼

Rude Awakening (1989) **C-100m.** *½ D: Aaron Russo, David Greenwalt. Cheech Marin, Eric Roberts, Julie Hagerty, Robert Carradine, Buck Henry, Louise Lasser, Cindy Williams, Andrea Martin, Cliff DeYoung. "Cheech and Roberts" lacks zing as a comedy-team concept; so does hippie-dippy political farce about a pair of long-haired '60s burnouts who return to N.Y.C. after twenty years in a Central American commune. Henry scrapes up a few chuckles in his only scene. [R]▼●

Rude Boy (1980-British) **C-133m.** *** D: Jack Hazan, David Mingay. The Clash, Ray Gange, John Green, Barry Baker, Terry McQuade, Caroline Coon. Angry young rebel Gange is hired by the punk rock group The Clash as a roadie. Gritty, realistic, documentary-like character study; excellent concert footage. Punk rock fans will not be disappointed: others, beware. Most U.S. prints run 120m. [R]▼

Rudolph the Red-nosed Reindeer: The Movie (1998) **C-83m.** ** D: Bill Kowalchuk. Voices of John Goodman, Eric Idle, Bob Newhart, Debbie Reynolds, Richard Simmons, Whoopi Goldberg. Old-fashioned, innocuous animated feature about that reindeer with the very shiny nose is aimed at very young children and adds some new plot twists and characters to the old story, including a fox (Idle), a polar bear (Newhart) and an evil ice queen (Goldberg). The animation is rudimentary, but the movie is a gentle antidote to the plethora of hyperkinetic contemporary cartoons. [G]▼

Rudy (1993) **C-112m.** *** D: David Anspaugh. Sean Astin, Ned Beatty, Robert Prosky, Charles S. Dutton, Lili Taylor, Jon

Favreau, Jason Miller, Vincent (Vince) Vaughn. Rock-solid, immensely entertaining based-on-fact account of Rudy Ruettiger (Astin), a working-class boy intent on realizing his dream of playing football at old Notre Dame—despite his uninspiring academic record and unimposing athletic ability. Few surprises, but it's well acted (with special kudos to Dutton), and a real crowd-pleaser. Director Anspaugh and screenwriter Angelo Pizzo previously worked together on HOOSIERS. [PG]▼●

Rudyard Kipling's The Jungle Book (1994) **C-110m.** **½ D: Stephen Sommers. Jason Scott Lee, Cary Elwes, Lena Headey, Sam Neill, John Cleese, Jason Flemyng, Stefan Kalipha, Ron Donachie. Agreeably old-fashioned "boys adventure"–style adaptation of Kipling's stories produced under the Disney banner (but with few Disney touches). Lee is simply terrific as Mowgli, the boy raised in the Indian jungle who's brought back to "civilization" by the daughter of a British regiment officer. Sumptuously filmed, with an exciting climax involving a lost city filled with treasure, but somehow never as compelling as it ought to be. Panavision. [PG]▼●

Rudyard Kipling's The Second Jungle Book: Mowgli & Baloo (1997) **C-88m.** *½ D: Duncan McLachlan. James Williams, Bill Campbell, Roddy McDowall, David Paul Francis, Gulshan Grover, Dyrk Ashton. Bland, unimaginative story of a jungle boy pursued by a circus animal procurer, saved again and again by his animal friends. Some stereotypical characters border on racism; a family film that could give "wholesome" a bad name. Hard to believe Kipling would want his name on it. Filmed in Sri Lanka. Technovision. [PG]▼●

Ruggles of Red Gap (1935) **92m.** **** D: Leo McCarey. Charles Laughton, Mary Boland, Charlie Ruggles, ZaSu Pitts, Roland Young, Leila Hyams. Laughton is marvelous as butler won in poker game by uncouth but amiable westerner Ruggles and socially ambitious wife Boland; ZaSu is spinster he falls in love with. A completely winning movie. Harry Leon Wilson's story was filmed before in 1918 and 1923, then remade as FANCY PANTS.▼●

Rugrats Movie, The (1998) **C-79m.** **½ D: Norton Virgien, Igor Kovalyov. Voices of E. G. Daily, Christine Cavanaugh, Kath Soucie, Cheryl Chase, Tara Charendoff, Melanie Chartoff, Jack Riley, Joe Alaskey, Phil Proctor, Michael Bell, Tress MacNeille, Busta Rhymes, Tim Curry, Whoopi Goldberg, David Spade, Margaret Cho. Theatrical spinoff of the popular TV cartoon puts Tommy and his infant friends into a nonstop adventure, which begins with the arrival of a new baby brother and escalates as the kids get lost in the woods. Clever and funny, with some likable songs, though even at 79m. it seems padded . . . and loud. [G]▼●◗

Rulers of the Sea (1939) **96m.** **½ D: Frank Lloyd. Douglas Fairbanks, Jr., Will Fyffe, Margaret Lockwood, George Bancroft, Montagu Love, Alan Ladd, Mary Gordon, Neil Fitzgerald. Well-made drama of problems surrounding first steamship voyage across Atlantic.

Rules of Engagement (2000) **C-128m.** **½ D: William Friedkin. Tommy Lee Jones, Samuel L. Jackson, Guy Pearce, Ben Kingsley, Bruce Greenwood, Blair Underwood, Philip Baker Hall, Anne Archer, Dale Dye. Held responsible for a Middle East embassy massacre in which scores of civilians (and so-called civilians) were killed, Marine officer Jackson calls upon just-retired colleague Jones to defend him in a court-martial after he's left out to dry. Watchable but sometimes silly melodrama finds time for a client-defendant fistfight, and offers a truly novel movie villain: a dastardly government official. Story's punchline has no punch. Panavision. [R]▼●◗

Rules of the Game (1939-French) **113m.** **** D: Jean Renoir. Marcel Dalio, Nora Gregor, Mila Parely, Jean Renoir, Gaston Modot, Roland Toutain, Paulette Dubost, Julien Carette, Odette Talazac. Sublime comedy-drama contrasting *affaires d'amour* of aristocrats and servants during a weekend outing in the country. Poignant, funny, endlessly imitated; perhaps Renoir's best film. Cut to 85m after its commercial failure in Paris; other prints run between 80m. and 110m. Restored to its original length in 1959.▼●

Ruling Class, The (1972-British) **C-154m.** ***½ D: Peter Medak. Peter O'Toole, Alastair Sim, Arthur Lowe, Harry Andrews, Coral Browne, Michael Bryant, Carolyn Seymour, Nigel Green, William Mervyn, James Villiers. Hilarious, irreverent black comedy by Peter Barnes about heir to British lordship (O'Toole) who thinks he's Jesus Christ. Overflowing with crazy ideas, people bursting into song, boisterously funny characterizations, and one-and-only Sim as befuddled bishop. Some prints run 130m; the "uncut" version released in 1983 runs 141m. [PG]▼●

Ruling Voice, The (1931) **71m.** *** D: Rowland V. Lee. Walter Huston, Loretta Young, Doris Kenyon, David Manners, John Halliday, Dudley Digges, Gilbert Emery, Willard Robertson. Gangster Huston rules the nation's underworld, but starts to go soft when his innocent daughter returns from school abroad. Slows down in Loretta's scenes, but when Huston is on screen it really hums.

Rumba (1935) **77m.** ** D: Marion Gering. George Raft, Carole Lombard, Margo, Lynne Overman, Gail Patrick, Akim Tamiroff, Iris Adrian. Weak follow-up to BO-

LERO, with Raft and Lombard in and out of love in silly, contrived story; most of their "dancing" actually done by Veloz and Yolanda.

Rumble Fish (1983) **94m.** ** D: Francis Coppola. Matt Dillon, Mickey Rourke, Diane Lane, Dennis Hopper, Diana Scarwid, Vincent Spano, Nicolas Cage, Christopher Penn, Larry Fishburne, Tom Waits, Sofia Coppola. Ambitious mood piece from S. E. Hinton's young-adult novel about alienated teenager who lives in the shadow of his older brother. Emotionally intense but muddled and aloof; highly stylized, in looks (filmed mostly in black & white) and sounds (with impressionistic music score by Stewart Copeland). Dillon's third Hinton film, Coppola's second (following THE OUTSIDERS). [R]▼●◗

Rumble in the Bronx (1996-U.S.-Hong Kong) **C-89m.** **½ D: Stanley Tong. Jackie Chan, Anita Mui, Bill Tung, Francoise Yip, Marc Akerstream, Garvin Cross, Morgan Lam, Kris Lord. Jackie visits his uncle in America, and agrees to help the woman who's buying the uncle's market to fend off a local gang. Chan's breakthrough film for the U.S. market is slim on story (and even slimmer on credibility). From the 60s-style dubbing to the characterizations, everything is tacky but Jackie; still, he's so engaging he makes up for all the rest, with a nonstop array of eye-popping stunts. The skyline of Vancouver makes a shabby and rather silly substitute for the Bronx. Edited for U.S. release. Technovision. [R]▼●◗

Rumble on the Docks (1956) **82m.** ** D: Fred F. Sears. James Darren, Laurie Carroll, Michael Granger, Jerry Janger, Robert Blake, Edgar Barrier. Low-key waterfront corruption tale, with Darren the street-gang leader aiding racketeers.

Rumor Mill, The SEE: **Malice in Wonderland**

Rumpelstiltskin (1987) **C-84m.** ** D: David Irving. Amy Irving, Billy Barty, Clive Revill, Priscilla Pointer, John Moulder-Brown, Robert Symonds. Threadbare musical adaptation of the Grimms' fairy tale, with Irving and Barty well cast in the leads. Likely to bore even the small-fry. Filmed in Israel, this was a family affair: writer-director Irving is Amy's brother, and Pointer (who plays the Queen) is her mother. For the record, this was the first of Cannon Films' fairy-tale features. [G]▼

Run (1990) **C-91m.** **½ D: Geoff Burrowes. Patrick Dempsey, Kelly Preston, Ken Pogue, Alan C. Peterson, Marc Strange, Christopher Lawford. Law student becomes the object of a citywide chase when he accidentally kills the loutish son of the town's Mr. Hood while blowing time in a gambling club. Sheer speed compensates for lack of distinction. Dempsey's "what-me-worry?" quotient is relatively subdued. Not to be confused with Kurosawa's RAN. [R]▼●

Runaround, The (1946) **86m.** **½ D: Charles Lamont. Rod Cameron, Ella Raines, Broderick Crawford, Frank McHugh, Samuel S. Hinds, George Cleveland. Clever little comedy-drama in which nervy private detective Cameron and bullying rival Crawford clash as they set out on the trail of runaway rich girl Raines.

Runaway (1971) SEE: **Runaway, Runaway**

Runaway (1984) **C-100m.** ** D: Michael Crichton. Tom Selleck, Cynthia Rhodes, Gene Simmons, Kirstie Alley, Stan Shaw, Joey Cramer, G. W. Bailey. Futuristic comic-book nonsense that actually takes itself seriously. Selleck plays a cop who specializes in tracking down robots that have gone "bad." Simmons (from rock group KISS) is ultra-bad-guy who uses robots and other high-tech devices to carry out his evil deeds. Special effects are good, but characters are cold and story is for the birds. Panavision. [PG]▼●

Runaway Bride (1999) **C-116m.** *** D: Garry Marshall. Julia Roberts, Richard Gere, Joan Cusack, Hector Elizondo, Rita Wilson, Paul Dooley, Christopher Meloni, Donal Logue, Sela Ward. Slick romantic comedy about a newspaper columnist who becomes intrigued by a small-town Maryland woman who repeatedly leaves grooms at the altar. Reteaming of the stars and director of PRETTY WOMAN delivers the goods, with Gere in particular more engaging than he's ever been onscreen. Super 35. [PG]▼●◗

Runaway Daughter SEE: **Red Salute**

Runaway Daughters (1956) **92m.** *½ D: Edward L. Cahn. Marla English, Anna Sten, John Litel, Adele Jergens, Lance Fuller, Mary Ellen Kaye, Gloria Castillo, Nicky Blair, Frank Gorshin. Parental angst drives three high-school girls to drift into trouble. Dull, dated, and overlong, this teen exploitation fare boasts a surprisingly geriatric cast. Originally paired in theaters with SHAKE, RATTLE AND ROCK. Remade for TV in 1994.

Runaway Daughters (1994) **C-83m. TVM** D: Joe Dante. Julie Bowen, Holly Fields, Jenny Lewis, Paul Rudd, Chris Young, Dick Miller, Dee Wallace Stone, Christopher Stone, Robert Picardo, Wendy Schaal, Joe Flaherty, Belinda Balaski, Roger Corman, Julie Corman, Fabian, John Astin, Samuel Z. Arkoff. 1957: Teenage Mary is pregnant, so she and her two best friends try to catch her boyfriend before he can enlist in the Navy. Well-made melodrama with comic elements, at once a remake and spoof of the 1956 original. Good cast, with a great role for Miller, and lots of amusing cameos, including an unbilled Cathy Moriarty. One of Showtime's "Rebel Highway" entries, all based on old American-International pictures. Above average.

Runaway, Runaway (1971) **C-85m.** *** D: Bickford Otis Webber. William Smith, Gilda Texter, Rita Murray, Tom Baker, Beach Dickerson. Unsung little gem has young Texter running away from home, taking up with older businessman. Unusually sympathetic role for tough guy Smith, plus a standout performance by Murray as Texter's lesbian roommate. Retitled RUNAWAY. [R]

Runaway Train (1985) **C-111m.** *** D: Andrei Konchalovsky. Jon Voight, Eric Roberts, Rebecca De Mornay, Kyle Heffner, John P. Ryan, T. K. Carter, Kenneth McMillan, Stacey Pickren. A rare bird, this film: an existential action movie! Hardened criminal and young accomplice escape from prison and hide out on a train that's barreling through Alaska without an engineer. Tough, violent, with hair-raising action footage and a superb characterization by Voight in his most atypical role to date. Based on a screenplay by Akira Kurosawa. [R]▼●◗

Runestone, The (1992) **C-105m.** ** D: Willard Carroll. Peter Riegert, Joan Severance, William Hickey, Tim Ryan, Chris Young, Alexander Godunov, Mitchell Laurence, Lawrence Tierney, Dawan Scott. An ancient stone, buried in North America by Norsemen, is unearthed, and promptly turns an archaeologist into an elaborate but unconvincing monster, who slaughters a lot of people with no apparent goal in mind. Handsome production has some interesting moments, but the routine plot weighs it down. Adapted by the director from the novella by Mark E. Rogers. [R]▼●

Run for Cover (1955) **C-93m.** **½ D: Nicholas Ray. James Cagney, Viveca Lindfors, John Derek, Jean Hersholt, Ernest Borgnine. Offbeat Western has ex-con Cagney becoming sheriff, while his embittered young companion (Derek) grows restive and antagonistic. Interesting touches cannot overcome familiar storyline. Retitled: COLORADO. VistaVision.

Run for the Roses (1978) **C-93m.** ** D: Henry Levin. Vera Miles, Stuart Whitman, Sam Groom, Panchito Gomez, Theodore Wilson, Lisa Eilbacher. Formula family film about Puerto Rican boy living with his stepfather in Kentucky, raising a lame colt to run in the Kentucky Derby. Uninspired stuff. Originally titled THOROUGHBRED. [PG]▼

Run for the Sun (1956) **C-99m.** *** D: Roy Boulting. Richard Widmark, Jane Greer, Trevor Howard, Peter Van Eyck, Carlos Henning. Third version of THE MOST DANGEROUS GAME has author Widmark and magazine writer Greer stumbling onto strange plantation run by mysterious Howard and Van Eyck. Engrossing, extremely well-made film. SuperScope 235.

Run for Your Money, A (1949-British) **83m.** *** D: Charles Frend. Donald Houston, Meredith Edwards, Moira Lister, Alec Guinness, Hugh Griffith, Joyce Grenfell. Way-above-par comic study of two Welsh miners having a spree in London.▼

Run Like a Thief (1967-Spanish) **C-92m.** ** D: Harry Spalding. Kieron Moore, Ina Balin, Keenan Wynn, Fernando Rey. Soldier of fortune goes after diamond hijackers with a mobster chief who foils him every step of the way. Techniscope.▼

Run Lola Run (1998-German) **C-88m.** **½ D: Tom Tykwer. Franka Potente, Moritz Bleibtreu, Herbert Knaup, Armin Rohde, Joachim Król, Nina Petri. Hyperkinetic, flashy concept film about a young woman who tries to save her boyfriend, who botched a drug deal, by finding 100,000 marks in twenty minutes' time. Style definitely outranks substance in this visually arresting film, which presents three different scenarios of what might happen, but it's wearying after a while. [R]▼◗

Runner Stumbles, The (1979) **C-99m.** *½ D: Stanley Kramer. Dick Van Dyke, Kathleen Quinlan, Maureen Stapleton, Ray Bolger, Tammy Grimes, Beau Bridges. Sober adaptation of Milan Stitt's Broadway play, based on true story of small-town priest accused of murdering young nun for whom he'd shown unusual affection. Aloof and unconvincing, with Van Dyke unbearably stiff as the clergyman. [PG]▼

Running (1979-Canadian) **C-103m.** *½ D: Steven Hilliard Stern. Michael Douglas, Susan Anspach, Lawrence Dane, Eugene Levy, Charles Shamata. Douglas—32, out of work and father of two daughters—wants to run in the Olympics. A few yocks in this absurdly melodramatic jock drama, but not enough of them. [PG]

Running Brave (1983-Canadian) **C-105m.** **½ D: D. S. Everett (Donald Shebib). Robby Benson, Pat Hingle, Claudia Cron, Jeff McCracken, August Schellenberg, Graham Greene. Story of real-life Olympic champion Billy Mills, who left the Sioux reservation to find his destiny as a runner—and win a gold medal at the 1964 Tokyo Olympics. Modestly entertaining, but too corny and simplistic. [PG]▼●

Running Hot (1984) **C-95m.** ** D: Mark Griffiths. Monica Carrico, Eric Stoltz, Stuart Margolin, Virgil Frye, Richard Bradford, Sorrells Pickard. Downbeat road movie (with nihilistic finish) has teenager Stoltz on the run from the cops, hooking up with older woman Carrico, who's also in deep trouble after her lover Bradford dies in mysterious circumstances. [R]▼

Running Man, The (1963-British) **C-103m.** *** D: Carol Reed. Laurence Harvey, Lee Remick, Alan Bates, Felix Aylmer, Eleanor Summerfield, Allan Cuthbertson. Harvey fakes his death to collect insurance money, but pursuing insurance investigator Bates forces him and wife Remick to go on the lam in Spain. Entertaining but not suspenseful enough. Panavision.

Running Man, The (1987) **C-100m.** ★★½ D: Paul Michael Glaser. Arnold Schwarzenegger, Maria Conchita Alonso, Yaphet Kotto, Jim Brown, Richard Dawson, Jesse Ventura, Mick Fleetwood, Dweezil Zappa. It's 2019, and the U.S. is a totalitarian state; framed mass murderer Arnie is ordered to take part in a *Most Dangerous Game*-type TV show where convicted felons get their one chance for freedom. Relentlessly trashy picture gets big boost from Dawson's sleazy portrayal of the game-show host. Based on a novel by Richard Bachman (Stephen King). [R]▼●◗

Running Mates (1992) **C-110m. TVM** D: Michael Lindsay-Hogg. Diane Keaton, Ed Harris, Ed Begley, Jr., Ben Masters, Robert Harper, Brandon Maggart, Russ Tamblyn. Romantic political comedy has a bachelor presidential candidate falling for a writer with an agenda and a past (who, it turns out, ignored him in high school). Keaton, in her TV-movie acting debut, looks surprisingly like Hillary Rodham Clinton—undoubtedly not by accident—in this amiable film that premiered during the closing days of the 1992 campaign. Writer Carole Eastman chose at the last minute to use the pseudonym of A. L. Appling. Made for cable. Average.▼

Running on Empty (1988) **C-116m.** ★★★½ D: Sidney Lumet. Christine Lahti, River Phoenix, Judd Hirsch, Martha Plimpton, Jonas Arby, Ed Crowley, L.M. Kit Carson, Steven Hill, Augusta Dabney. Intense, moving story of onetime student radicals who are still on the run from the FBI after seventeen years—now with two kids in tow, whose lives are stifled for the sake of sheer survival. Quiet and believable throughout, with superior performances by all. Written by coexecutive producer Naomi Foner. [PG-13]▼●◗

Running Scared (1986) **C-106m.** ★★½ D: Peter Hyams. Gregory Hines, Billy Crystal, Steven Bauer, Darlanne Fluegel, Joe Pantoliano, Dan Hedaya, Jonathan Gries, Tracy Reed, Jimmy Smits. Two longtime Chicago street cops (who act more like Dead End Kids) decide maybe it's time to retire—but there's one more scuzzbag to track down first. Crystal lights up the screen, and there's a great car chase on the Chicago El tracks, but otherwise this is pretty blah. Panavision. [R]▼●

Running Time (1997) **70m.** ★★★ D: Josh Becker. Bruce Campbell, Jeremy Roberts, Anita Barone, Stan Davis, Gordon Jennison, Art LeFleur. Smart, classical heist-gone-wrong thriller made in the all-in-one-take method of ROPE. Shot entirely on real locations in the L.A. area, in gritty black and white. Well acted, suspenseful, both realistic and romantic.▼◗

Running Wild (1927) **68m.** ★★½ D: Gregory La Cava. W.C. Fields, Mary Brian, Claude Buchanan, Marie Shotwell, Barney Raskle, Tom Madden, Frederick Burton. Fields (sporting his silent-film mustache) plays the ultimate milquetoast who undergoes a galvanizing change of personality when he chances to encounter a hypnotist. Fast, funny outing with the surefire satisfaction of seeing the worm turn.▼

Running Wild (1955) **81m.** ★★½ D: Abner Biberman. William Campbell, Mamie Van Doren, Keenan Wynn, Walter Coy. Tawdry, actionful account of young police officer getting the goods on car thief gangs.

Running Wild (1973) **C-103m.** ★★★ D: Robert McCahon. Lloyd Bridges, Dina Merrill, Pat Hingle, Morgan Woodward, Gilbert Roland, Lonny Chapman, R. G. Armstrong. Good family-oriented drama about a news photographer (Merrill) who protests treatment of wild horses while doing a story in Colorado. Beautiful scenery complements solid script. [G]▼

Run of the Arrow (1957) **C-86m.** ★★½ D: Samuel Fuller. Rod Steiger, Sarita Montiel, Brian Keith, Ralph Meeker, Jay C. Flippen, Charles Bronson, Olive Carey, Colonel Tim McCoy. Confederate soldier (played by Steiger with a broad Irish brogue!) cannot accept surrender to the North, aligns himself instead with Sioux Indians after submitting to a grueling test of endurance. Intriguing if not entirely satisfying, with choppy continuity. Angie Dickinson reportedly dubbed Montiel's voice. Video title: HOT LEAD. RKO-Scope.▼

Run of the Country, The (1995-U.S.-British) **C-109m.** ★★ D: Peter Yates. Albert Finney, Matt Keeslar, Victoria Smurfit, Anthony Brophy, David Kelly, Dearbhla Molloy, Carole Nimmons, Vinnie McCabe, Clark Trevor. OK, plot-heavy, Irish family drama about the testy relationship between a widowed cop and his university-aged son who eventually gets involved with a woman who threatens dad's plans. Film takes half its length to decide what it wants to be about. Super 35. [R]▼●

Run Silent Run Deep (1958) **93m.** ★★★ D: Robert Wise. Clark Gable, Burt Lancaster, Jack Warden, Brad Dexter, Nick Cravat, Mary LaRoche, Don Rickles, Eddie Foy III. Battle of wills between officers Gable and Lancaster on WW2 submarine is basis for interesting drama. Script by John Gay, from a novel by Commander Edward L. Beach. One of the great WW2 "sub" pictures.▼◗

Run, Stranger, Run SEE: **Happy Mother's Day, Love, George**

Run Wild, Run Free (1969-British) **C-**

100m. **½ D: Richard C. Sarafian. John Mills, Mark Lester, Sylvia Syms, Gordon Jackson, Bernard Miles, Fiona Fullerton. Good cast helps leisurely, but better-than-usual children's film about young mute and his love for a white colt; nice subdued photography by Wilkie Cooper. [G]

Rush (1991) **C-120m.** ** D: Lili Fini Zanuck. Jason Patric, Jennifer Jason Leigh, Sam Elliott, Max Perlich, Gregg Allman, Tony Frank, William Sadler. Gritty adaptation of Kim Wozencraft's novel about a young woman recruited to be an undercover narc in 1970s Texas, joining a man who's already a bit too strung out to be completely effective. First-time director Zanuck skillfully creates an oppressively seedy atmosphere, but can't compensate for the fact that the story—if not the entire premise—of the film is unconvincing. Patric's performance is a standout, ditto Eric Clapton's striking score. [R]▼●

Rush Hour (1998) **C-98m.** *** D: Brett Ratner. Jackie Chan, Chris Tucker, Elizabeth Peña, Tom Wilkinson, Philip Baker Hall, Mark Rolston, Tzi Ma, Rex Linn, Chris Penn, Ken Leung. Enjoyable action no-brainer with Hong Kong detective Chan coming to L.A. to help his friend, the Chinese consul, rescue his kidnapped daughter. The FBI doesn't want an outsider on the case, however, so they give him to cocky L.A. cop Tucker to baby-sit. Combination of buddy movie, fish-out-of-water comedy, and urban action thriller works well if you don't demand a lot of logic. Panavision. [PG-13]▼●◗

Rushmore (1998) **C-93m.** ***½ D: Wes Anderson. Jason Schwartzman, Bill Murray, Olivia Williams, Seymour Cassel, Brian Cox, Mason Gamble, Sara Tanaka, Stephen McCole, Connie Nielsen, Luke Wilson, Andrew Wilson. The saga of a bona fide oddball who thrives on life at Rushmore prep school in Houston, but complicates his life by falling in love with a first-grade teacher (Williams) and befriending a local tycoon (Murray) who feels a kinship with this young iconoclast. A genuine original, full of keen observational humor and detail, with characters that always ring true. Remarkable debut performance by Schwartzman (son of Talia Shire), and a perfect showcase for Murray. Written by Anderson and Owen Wilson. Panavision. [R] ▼●◗

Russia House, The (1990) **C-123m.** ** D: Fred Schepisi. Sean Connery, Michelle Pfeiffer, Roy Scheider, James Fox, Klaus Maria Brandauer, John Mahoney, Michael Kitchen, J. T. Walsh, Ken Russell, David Threlfall, Ian McNeice, Christopher Lawford. John le Carré yarn (adapted by Tom Stoppard) contends that the business of spying is alive and well—in spite of *glasnost*. Connery plays a British publisher drawn into espionage by a Soviet woman (Pfeiffer), who acts as emissary for a volatile friend. Alternately tedious and intriguing, but it never catches fire. Fox is a standout as a British intelligence officer. Technovision. [R]▼●

Russian Roulette (1975) **C-93m.** **½ D: Lou Lombardo. George Segal, Cristina Raines, Bo Brundin, Denholm Elliott, Gordon Jackson, Peter Donat, Louise Fletcher, Val Avery. Assassins threaten to kill Soviet premier Kosygin during his trip to Vancouver; Segal is assigned to capture elusive troublemaker thought to be the hit-man in this violent, unsatisfying thriller. Filmed in Canada. [PG]▼

Russian Roulette (1993) **C-89m.** *½ D: Greydon Clark. Susan Blakely, Barry Bostwick, E. G. Marshall, Jeff Altman, Victoria Barrett. American teacher Blakely, on vacation in St. Petersburg, Russia, inadvertently becomes involved in a scheme to pilfer a priceless antiquity. One-note thriller is barely entertaining, despite its use of authentic locations. [PG]▼

Russians Are Coming! The Russians Are Coming! The (1966) **C-126m.** **½ D: Norman Jewison. Carl Reiner, Eva Marie Saint, Alan Arkin, Brian Keith, Jonathan Winters, Paul Ford, Theodore Bikel, Tessie O'Shea, John Phillip Law, Ben Blue, Andrea Dromm, Dick Schaal, Parker Fennelly, Doro Merande, Johnnie Whitaker, Michael J. Pollard. Popular comedy about Russian submarine that lands off New England coast was incredibly overrated in 1966; now it's merely a TV sitcom saved by pretty photography and good comic bits by Arkin and Winters. Script by William Rose from Nathaniel Benchley's novel *The Off-Islanders*. Alan Arkin's starring film debut. Panavision. ▼●

Russicum SEE: **Third Solution, The**

Russkies (1987) **C-99m.** *½ D: Rick Rosenthal. Whip Hubley, Leaf Phoenix, Peter Billingsley, Stefan DeSalle, Susan Walters, Patrick Kilpatrick, Vic Polizos, Charles Frank, Susan Blanchard, Carole King, Summer Phoenix. Feeble reworking of THE RUSSIANS ARE COMING! THE RUSSIANS ARE COMING! about Soviet sailor Hubley, washed ashore in Florida, and the trio of youngsters who befriend him. Well-meaning in its message of fellowship, but slight. [PG]▼●

Rustlers' Rhapsody (1985) **C-88m.** ** D: Hugh Wilson. Tom Berenger, G. W. Bailey, Marilu Henner, Andy Griffith, Fernando Rey, Sela Ward, Patrick Wayne. Good-natured but only sporadically funny send-up of Saturday matinee Westerns. If the old cowboy movies were this dull, they never would have survived. [PG]▼●

Rust Never Sleeps (1979) **C-103m.** *** D: Bernard Shakey (Neil Young). Ragged-out but rousing record of Neil Young in concert, with 16 well-performed tunes by rockdom's most lovable downer. My My, Hey, Hey. [PG]▼

Ruthless (1948) **104m.** *** D: Edgar G. Ulmer. Zachary Scott, Louis Hayward, Diana Lynn, Sydney Greenstreet, Lucille Bremer, Martha Vickers, Raymond Burr. Scott steps on everyone to become big shot in this engrossing drama. Greenstreet is especially good as Southern tycoon.

Ruthless Four, The (1968-Italian-German) **C-96m.** *** D: Giorgio Capitani. Van Heflin, Gilbert Roland, George Hilton, Klaus Kinski, Sarah Ross. Good Western explores the complicated relationships of four dubious partners in a Nevada gold mine. Apart from the action, it's a pleasure just to watch Heflin and Roland. Aka EVERY MAN FOR HIMSELF, EACH ONE FOR HIMSELF, and SAM COOPER'S GOLD. Techniscope. [M/PG] ▼

Ruthless People (1986) **C-93m.** **½ D: Jim Abrahams, David Zucker, Jerry Zucker. Danny DeVito, Bette Midler, Judge Reinhold, Helen Slater, Anita Morris, Bill Pullman, William G. Schilling, Art Evans. Wealthy DeVito plans to murder his obnoxious wife—unaware that at that moment she's being kidnapped, and equally unaware that his paramour plans to take *him* for his dough. Clever farce written by Dale Launer has lots of laughs, bright performances, but turns sour: these really *are* unpleasant people! [R]▼●

RX Murder (1958-British) **85m.** ** D: Derek Twist. Rick Jason, Marius Goring, Lisa Gastoni, Mary Merrall. Jason stars as American physician settling in British village to find strange murder. Fair mystery. CinemaScope.

Ryan's Daughter (1970-British) **C-176m.** **½ D: David Lean. Robert Mitchum, Trevor Howard, Sarah Miles, Christopher Jones, John Mills, Leo McKern, Barry Foster. Simple love story blown up to gargantuan proportions in western coastal Ireland, where young girl (Miles) marries simple, plodding schoolteacher (Mitchum) and has affair with British soldier (Jones) stationed in town. Elephantine production overpowers Robert Bolt's thin story, admittedly beautiful scenes dwarfing what plot there is. Mills won Oscar in supporting role as the town idiot, as did—most deservedly—cinematographer Freddie Young. Re-edited after film's debut; original running time 206m. Super Panavision 70. [PG]▼●

Saadia (1953) **C-82m.** *½ D: Albert Lewin. Cornel Wilde, Mel Ferrer, Rita Gam, Cyril Cusack, Richard Johnson. Misfire; intellectual story of modernistic Moroccan ruler and doctor vying for love of superstitious native dancing girl.

Sabaka (1953) **C-81m.** ** D: Frank Ferrin. Nino Marcel, Boris Karloff, Lou Krugman, Reginald Denny, Victor Jory, June Foray, Jay Novello, Lisa Howard, Peter Coe. By-the-numbers adventure with Marcel cast as Gunga Ram, a youthful hero who contends with a cult of devil worshippers in India. GUNGA DIN it ain't. Aka THE HINDU. ▼

Sabata (1969-Italian-Spanish) **C-107m.** ** D: Frank Kramer (Gianfranco Parolini). Lee Van Cleef, William Berger, Franco Ressel, Linda Veras, Pedro Sanchez (Ignazio Spalla). First of three spaghetti Westerns is the best, though that isn't saying much. Van Cleef plays a gambler hired by a trio of nasty businessmen to steal $100,000. Needless to say, the transaction becomes trickier than they expected. Sequel: ADIOS, SABATA. Techniscope. [PG]

Sabotage (1936-British) **76m.** *** D: Alfred Hitchcock. Sylvia Sidney, Oscar Homolka, John Loder, Desmond Tester, Joyce Barbour. Elaborately detailed thriller about woman who suspects that her kindly husband (Homolka), a movie theater manager, is keeping something from her. Full of intriguing Hitchcock touches. Based on Joseph Conrad's *Secret Agent*, originally retitled A WOMAN ALONE for the U.S. ▼●◗

Saboteur (1942) **108m.** *** D: Alfred Hitchcock. Robert Cummings, Priscilla Lane, Norman Lloyd, Otto Kruger, Alan Baxter, Alma Kruger, Dorothy Peterson, Vaughan Glaser. Extremely offbeat wartime Hitchcock yarn about a munitions worker who's falsely accused of sabotage and forced to take it on the lam. Full of quirky touches, unusual supporting characters, and some outstanding set pieces, including famous Statue of Liberty finale . . . though actual story resolution is unfortunately abrupt. Screenplay by Peter Viertel, Joan Harrison, and Dorothy Parker.▼●

Saboteur, Code Name Morituri, The (1965) **123m.** **½ D: Bernhard Wicki. Marlon Brando, Yul Brynner, Janet Margolin, Trevor Howard, Wally Cox, William Redfield, Carl Esmond. Brando highlights great cast in study of anti-Nazi German who helps British capture cargo ship. Cast and Conrad Hall's photography are only assets; script degenerates. Originally released as MORITURI.▼

Sabra (1970-French-Italian) **C-98m.** ** D: Denys de la Patalliere. Akim Tamiroff, Assaf Dayan, Jean Claudio. Simplistic, contrived story of an Arab police inspector who "befriends" a young Israeli spy, in order to gain his confidence. Reissued as DEATH OF A JEW. [PG]

Sabre Jet (1953) **C-96m.** **½ D: Louis King. Robert Stack, Coleen Gray, Richard Arlen, Julie Bishop. Routine Korean War story of lonely wives and fighting husbands.

Sabrina (1954) **113m.** ***½ D: Billy Wilder. Humphrey Bogart, Audrey Hepburn, William Holden, John Williams, Francis X. Bushman, Martha Hyer, Nancy Kulp. Samuel Taylor's play *Sabrina Fair* is good vehicle for Hepburn as chauffeur's daughter romanced by aging tycoon Bogart to keep her from his playboy brother (Holden). Offbeat casting works in this fun film. Screenplay by Ernest Lehman, Billy Wilder, and Taylor. Remade in 1995. ▼●

Sabrina (1995) **C-127m.** *** D: Sydney Pollack. Harrison Ford, Julia Ormond, Greg Kinnear, Nancy Marchand, John Wood, Richard Crenna, Angie Dickinson, Lauren Holly, Dana Ivey, Miriam Colon, Elizabeth Franz, Fanny Ardant. Enjoyable (if overlong) remake of the 1954 movie about a chauffeur's daughter with a lifelong crush on the handsome younger brother in the wealthy household where her father works. When he finally shows some interest in her, his older sibling tries to woo her away—for strictly business reasons. Credible cast (including TV personality Kinnear in an impressive film debut), surehanded direction and a very funny script by Barbara Benedek and David Rayfiel. The Paris scenes are especially lovely. [PG] ▼●

Sabu and the Magic Ring (1957) **C-61m.** *½ D: George Blair. Sabu, Daria Massey, Vladimir Sokoloff, Robin Moore, William Marshall. Low-budget backlot Arabian Nights nonsense, with Sabu chasing thieves to regain stolen girl and priceless gem. Originally shot as two separate TV pilots.

Sacco and Vanzetti (1971-French-Italian) **C-120m.** *½ D: Giuliano Montaldo. Gian Maria Volonte, Riccardo Cucciolla, Milo O'Shea, Cyril Cusack, Rosanna Fratello, Geoffrey Keen. Classic tale of American miscarriage of justice cries for cinematic treatment, but this version makes South Braintree, Massachusetts, look like a town in a Clint Eastwood spaghetti Western. Joan Baez sings title song. [PG]▼◗

Sacketts, The (1979) **C-198m. TVM** D: Robert Totten. Sam Elliott, Tom Selleck, Jeff Osterhage, Glenn Ford, Ben Johnson, Gilbert Roland, Ruth Roman, Jack Elam, Mercedes McCambridge. Rambling sagebrush saga taken from two Louis L'Amour novels following the fortunes of the three Sackett Brothers in the post-Civil War west. Followed by THE SHADOW RIDERS. Average. ▼

Sacred Ground (1983) **C-100m.** **½ D: Charles B. Pierce. Tim McIntire, Jack Elam, Serene Hedin, Mindi Miller, Eloy Phil Casados, L. Q. Jones. Fair drama of turmoil resulting when mountain man McIntire, his Apache wife and baby settle on holy Paiute burial ground. [PG]▼

Sacred Hearts (1985-British) **C-95m.** **½ D: Barbara Rennie. Anna Massey, Katrin Cartlidge, Oona Kirsch, Fiona Shaw, Anne Dyson, Gerard Murphy, Murray Melvin. Repressive, tyrannical Sister Thomas (Massey) ignores the questions, feelings, and fears of her young charges in a convent as the bombs explode around them in WW2 Britain. Sometimes quietly stimulating but also slow and predictable; occasional bits of humor help.

Sacrifice, The (1986-Swedish-French) **C-145m.** **½ D: Andrei Tarkovsky. Erland Josephson, Susan Fleetwood, Valerie Mairesse, Allan Edwall, Gundun Gisladottir. A cataclysmic event occurs during the birthday festivities of intellectual Josephson, who as a result becomes compelled to perform an act of faith. Slow, overly intense, but beautifully filmed (by Sven Nykvist) examination of the need for, and lack of, spirituality in modern society. Decidedly not for all tastes. Tarkovsky's final film. [PG] ▼●

Saddle the Wind (1958) **C-84m.** *** D: Robert Parrish. Robert Taylor, Julie London, John Cassavetes, Donald Crisp, Charles McGraw, Royal Dano. Well-acted Western of turned-good rancher (Taylor) fated to shoot it out with brother (Cassavetes). If you've ever wondered what a Western written by Rod Serling would be like, here's your chance. CinemaScope.

Saddle Tramp (1950) **C-77m.** **½ D: Hugo Fregonese. Joel McCrea, Wanda Hendrix, John McIntire, John Russell, Ed Begley, Jeanette Nolan, Antonio Moreno. Homey Western with McCrea in title role, "adopting" four kids and fighting the good cause.

Sad Horse, The (1959) **C-78m.** ** D: James B. Clark. David Ladd, Chill Wills, Rex Reason, Patrice Wymore. Tender, undemanding tale of a racehorse and a lonely boy (Ladd). CinemaScope.

Sadie McKee (1934) **92m.** *** D: Clarence Brown. Joan Crawford, Franchot Tone, Gene Raymond, Edward Arnold, Esther Ralston, Leo G. Carroll, Akim Tamiroff, Gene Austin. Solidly entertaining film follows serpentine story of working-girl Crawford and the three men in her life: smooth-talking Raymond, tipsy millionaire Arnold, earnest employer Tone. Beautifully paced, handsomely filmed. Song: "All I Do Is Dream of You," plus amusing rendition of "After You've Gone" by Austin, Candy Candido. ▼●

Sadie Thompson (1928) **97m.** *** D: Raoul Walsh. Gloria Swanson, Lionel Barrymore, Raoul Walsh, Blanche Frederici, Charles Lane, James Marcus. Fascinating, frequently high-powered version of W. Somerset Maugham's *Rain,* about a lusty, fun-loving prostitute who arrives in Pago Pago and tangles with stuffy, hypocritical reformer Barrymore while Marine Sgt. Walsh falls for her. Swanson, and especially Barrymore, are well cast. Unseen (except in archival showings) for many years, because the final reel decomposed years ago. Now the footage (about 8m.) has been recreated, using stills and the original title cards. Remade as RAIN, DIRTY GERTIE FROM HARLEM U.S.A., and MISS SADIE THOMPSON. ▼●

Sadist, The (1963) **81m.** **½ D: James Landis. Arch Hall, Jr., Helen Hovey, Richard Alden, Marilyn Manning. Taut little B-picture about a psychotic punk who terrorizes three innocent people at a roadside gas station. Hall is distressingly believable as the psycho. Imaginatively shot by Vilmos (billed as William) Zsigmond. Retitled PROFILE OF TERROR.▼

Sad Sack, The (1957) **98m.** ** D: George Marshall. Jerry Lewis, Phyllis Kirk, David Wayne, Peter Lorre, Gene Evans, Mary Treen. Disjointed comedy vaguely based on George Baker comic strip of Army misfit. Lorre appears as Arab in last part of film. VistaVision▼

Safari (1940) **80m.** ** D: Edward H. Griffith. Douglas Fairbanks, Jr., Madeleine Carroll, Tullio Carminati, Lynne Overman, Muriel Angelus, Billy Gilbert. Standard jungle expedition story, with attractive stars.

Safari (1956-British) **C-91m.** **½ D: Terence Young. Victor Mature, Janet Leigh, John Justin, Roland Culver, Liam Redmond. Fierce jungle drama has Mature leading expedition against Mau Maus. Cast gives good performances. CinemaScope.

Safari Drums (1953) **71m.** *½ D: Ford Beebe. Johnny Sheffield, Douglas Kennedy, Barbara Bestar, Emory Parnell, Smoki Whitfield, Leonard Mudie. Bomba the Jungle Boy enlists his animal friends to capture a murderous guide. Ultra low-budget stereotyped adventure.

Safari 3000 (1982) **C-91m.** *½ D: Harry Hurwitz. David Carradine, Stockard Channing, Christopher Lee, Hamilton Camp, Ian Yule. Ex-Hollywood stuntman is pitted against various adversaries in an international race; third-rate action yarn with tongue-in-cheek. Panavision. [PG]▼

Safe (1995) **C-119m.** **½ D: Todd Haynes. Julianne Moore, Xander Berkeley, Peter Friedman, James Le Gros, Mary Carver, Jessica Harper, Brandon Cruz. Well-to-do L.A. housewife becomes allergic to her own environment when almost overnight everyday household chemicals and substances turn into toxins. Intriguing allegorical approach to society's ills—based on a factual case—never really gels, and second half, set at a New Mexico retreat, grows tiresome. Notable mainly for Moore's terrific performance. [R]▼●

Safe at Home! (1962) **83m.** **½ D: Walter Doniger. Mickey Mantle, Roger Maris, William Frawley, Patricia Barry, Don Collier, Bryan Russell. Kid is pressured into lying to Little League pals about friendship with M&M. The stoic poetry of Jack Webb's acting pales beside that of Maris' in this kiddie time-capsule; leads, cameos by Whitey Ford and Ralph Houk make it a must for Yankee fans . . . if no one else. ▼

Safecracker, The (1958-British) **96m.** ** D: Ray Milland. Ray Milland, Barry Jones, Jeannette Sterke, Ernest Clark, Melissa Stribling, Victor Maddern. Contrived story of burglar who almost goes straight, later forced to use his talents for war effort.

Safe in Hell (1931) **65m.** **½ D: William A. Wellman. Dorothy Mackaill, Donald Cook, Ralf Harolde, John Wray, Ivan Simpson, Victor Varconi, Nina Mae McKinney, Charles Middleton, Clarence Muse, Gustav von Seyffertitz. Remarkably frank and adult pre-Code drama about prostitute Mackaill, who believes she's killed one of her johns and flees to the remote island of Tortuga where she can't be extradited. Unfortunately, the island is populated by every form of slobbering lech and pervert imaginable. Extremely seamy tale pulls no punches, right up to its shocking conclusion . . . but in some ways it's more astonishing than entertaining.

Safe Men (1998) **C-99m.** **½ D: John Hamburg. Sam Rockwell, Steve Zahn, Michael Lerner, Harvey Fierstein, Mark Ruffalo, Josh Pais, Paul Giamatti, Christina Kirk, Allen Swift. Amusing if flyweight low-budget comedy about a couple of guys—who've never made good at anything—who are mistaken for ace safecrackers by small-time hood Lerner, who puts them to work. Colorful characterizations by Lerner, Fierstein, and Giamatti add zip to this offbeat concoction set in Providence, R.I. Feature debut for writer-director Hamburg. [R] ▼●

Safe Passage (1994) **C-98m.** ** D: Robert Allan Ackerman. Susan Sarandon, Sam Shepard, Nick Stahl, Marcia Gay Harden, Robert Sean Leonard, Sean Astin, Matt Keeslar, Jeffrey DeMunn, Philip Bosco, Jason London, Rutanya Alda. Self-consciously predictable, TV movie-ish portrait of a dysfunctional family, with Sarandon (solid as usual) as a woman, estranged from her husband, who's placed her life on hold while raising seven sons. The family pulls together when it learns that one of the boys may have been killed. [PG-13]▼●

Safe Place, A (1971) **C-94m.** ** D: Henry Jaglom. Tuesday Weld, Jack Nicholson, Orson Welles, Philip Proctor, Gwen Welles. Spaced-out, water-logged fantasy of weird girl who lives in dream world where she can never grow up. [PG]

Safety Last (1923) **78m.** *** D: Fred Newmeyer, Sam Taylor. Harold Lloyd, Mildred Davis, Bill Strothers, Noah Young. Crackerjack silent comedy about go-getter Harold determined to make good in the big city includes his justly famous building-climbing sequence—still hair-raising after all these years.▼

Saga of Gosta Berling, The SEE: **Atonement of Gosta Berling, The**

Saga of Hemp Brown, The (1958) **C-80m.** ** D: Richard Carlson. Rory Calhoun, Beverly Garland, John Larch, Russell Johnson. Calhoun is bounced from Army, and seeks to find real crooks in just another Western. CinemaScope.

Sahara (1943) **97m.** ***½ D: Zoltan Korda.

Humphrey Bogart, Bruce Bennett, J. Carrol Naish, Lloyd Bridges, Rex Ingram, Richard Nugent, Dan Duryea, Kurt Krueger. Excellent actioner of British-American unit stranded in Sahara desert in the path of Nazi infantry; Bogie's the sergeant, with fine support by Naish and Ingram. Based on the 1937 Russian film THE THIRTEEN; also made as NINE MEN and LAST OF THE COMANCHES; imitated many other times. Remade for cable-TV in 1995 with James Belushi. ▼●

Sahara (1984) **C-104m.** *½ D: Andrew V. McLaglen. Brooke Shields, Lambert Wilson, Horst Buchholz, John Rhys-Davies, Ronald Lacey, John Mills, Steve Forrest, Perry Lang, Cliff Potts. Tacky modern variation on THE PERILS OF PAULINE with Brooke filling in for her late father in free-for-all auto race across North African desert in the 1920s, being kidnapped by handsome desert sheik. Any resemblance to a good movie is just a mirage. J-D-C Scope. [PG] ▼

Saigon (1948) **94m.** ** D: Leslie Fenton. Alan Ladd, Veronica Lake, Luther Adler, Douglas Dick, Wally Cassell, Morris Carnovsky. Glossy Paramount caper about airmen stationed in Vietnam involved in robbery; only fair.

Sail a Crooked Ship (1962) **88m.** **½ D: Irving S. Brecher. Robert Wagner, Ernie Kovacs, Dolores Hart, Carolyn Jones, Frankie Avalon, Frank Gorshin, Harvey Lembeck. Bungled crime-caper comedy has hilarious moments, but not enough to make it a winner. Based on a Nathaniel Benchley novel. ▼

Sail Into Danger (1957-British) **72m.** ** D: Kenneth Hume. Dennis O'Keefe, Kathleen Ryan, James Hayter, Pedro de Cordoba, John Bull, Felix de Pommes. O'Keefe is ensnared into helping Ryan in smuggling plot; set in Barcelona. Meek actioner.

Sailor Beware (1951) **108m.** *** D: Hal Walker. Dean Martin, Jerry Lewis, Corinne Calvet, Marion Marshall, Robert Strauss, Vince Edwards; guest, Betty Hutton. Hilarious adventures of Martin & Lewis in the Navy. Induction scenes, boxing sequence are highlights in one of the team's funniest outings. James Dean can be glimpsed in the boxing scene. Remake of THE FLEET'S IN.

Sailor Beware! (1957) SEE: **Panic in the Parlor**

Sailor From Gibraltar, The (1967-British) **89m.** ** D: Tony Richardson. Jeanne Moreau, Ian Bannen, Vanessa Redgrave, Zia Mohyeddin, Hugh Griffith, Orson Welles, Umberto Orsini, Eleanor Bron, John Hurt. Uneven adaptation of Marguerite Duras' novel has Moreau (who even gets to warble a song) as the mythical nymphomaniac wandering the seas in search of reunion with her dream sailor. Boasts an intriguing cast, but Richardson's handheld camera and other 1960s techniques have badly dated.

Sailor of the King (1953-U.S.-British) **83m.** *** D: Roy Boulting. Jeffrey Hunter, Michael Rennie, Wendy Hiller, Bernard Lee, Peter Van Eyck. Solid WW2 naval action story, based on C. S. Forester novel *Brown on Resolution*, with Hunter rising to challenge when opportunity arises to attack German raider. British title: SINGLE HANDED. Filmed before in 1935.

Sailor's Lady (1940) **66m.** ** D: Allan Dwan. Nancy Kelly, Jon Hall, Joan Davis, Dana Andrews, Mary Nash, Larry "Buster" Crabbe, Katherine (Kay) Aldridge. Witless comedy of Kelly pretending to have baby to see if sailor-fiance Hall will still marry her.

Sailor's Luck (1933) **78m.** *** D: Raoul Walsh. James Dunn, Sally Eilers, Sammy Cohen, Victor Jory, Frank Moran, Esther Muir. Funny, offbeat film of sailors on leave; Dunn and Eilers carry boy-meets-girl plot while crazy comedy touches surround them, including Jory as oily Baron DeBartolo, who runs dance marathon.

Sailor Takes a Wife, The (1945) **91m.** ** D: Richard Whorf. Robert Walker, June Allyson, Hume Cronyn, Audrey Totter, Eddie "Rochester" Anderson, Reginald Owen. Mild little comedy is summed up by title.

Sailor Who Fell From Grace With the Sea, The (1976-British) **C-104m.** *** D: Lewis John Carlino. Sarah Miles, Kris Kristofferson, Jonathan Kahn, Margo Cunningham, Earl Rhodes. A troubled, impressionable boy tries to deal with his widowed mother's love affair with an amiable sailor, and falls under the influence of a morbid young friend. Passionate love scenes, and a bizarre ending, highlight this unusual film, beautifully shot by Douglas Slocombe on English seacoast locations. Adapted by the director from a novel by Yukio Mishima. Panavision. [R]▼

Saint, The Leslie Charteris' literate, debonair detective has been the subject of an extremely popular British television show, but he never quite made it in the movies. From 1938 to 1942, RKO tried no less than three actors in the leading role. Louis Hayward seemed at home in the role in THE SAINT IN NEW YORK, a smooth underworld saga with a bland leading lady (Kay Sutton) and a fine supporting cast (Sig Rumann as a ganglord, Jack Carson as a thug, etc.). Nevertheless, he didn't repeat the role; it went instead to suave George Sanders, who portrayed The Saint, in five quickly made, entertaining mysteries three of them with Wendy Barrie as leading lady, taking him from Palm Springs to London. The scripts were competent, but it was Sanders' usual offhand manner that kept them alive. In 1941 stage star Hugh Sinclair took a fling in THE SAINT'S VACATION but gave up after a second effort. Sanders left the series only to begin another, The Falcon, at the same studio, although without the main titles to inform viewers which series it was, one could hardly have told the difference. The Falcon continued through the 1940s, while the Saint came to a premature end in 1942. There was one revival attempt with Louis Hayward made in England in 1954, THE SAINT'S GIRL FRIDAY, which was no improvement over the original series. It took British television and Roger Moore to give real life to The Saint at last in the 1960s. Then, in 1997, Val Kilmer assumed the role on the big screen.

THE SAINT

The Saint in New York (1938)
The Saint Strikes Back (1939)
The Saint in London (1939)
The Saint's Double Trouble (1940)
The Saint Takes Over (1940)
The Saint in Palm Springs (1941)
The Saint's Vacation (1941)
The Saint Meets the Tiger (1943)
The Saint's Girl Friday (1954)

Saint, The (1997) **C-116m.** ** D: Phillip Noyce. Val Kilmer, Elisabeth Shue, Rade Serbedzija, Valery Nikolaev, Henry Goodman, Alun Armstrong. Spy for hire and master of disguises Simon Templar agrees to steal a fusion formula for a controversial Russian leader—but falls in love with the beautiful professor who cooked up the recipe. Fanciful, globe-trotting action adventure is fun at first but throws credibility out the window early on, and only gets dumber. And how many endings are we supposed to sit through? Bears little resemblance to Leslie Charteris' hero. Listen for the voice on the radio in the final scene, if you make it that far. Panavision. [PG-13]▼●◗

Sainted Sisters, The (1948) **89m.** **½ D: William Russell. Veronica Lake, Joan Caulfield, Barry Fitzgerald, William Demarest, George Reeves, Beulah Bondi. Fitzgerald's blarney is a bit overdone in this tale of two bad girls who go straight under his guidance.

Saint Ex (1995-British) **C/B&W-86m.** *** D: Anand Tucker. Bruno Ganz, Miranda Richardson, Janet McTeer, Ken Stott, Brid Brennan, Eleanor Bron, Katrin Cartlidge, Anna Calder-Marshall. A self-described "work of imagination," poetic and surreal, freely inspired by the life of Antoine de Saint-Exupéry. Not your standard screen biography, as the dramatic narrative is interspersed with interviews of real people who knew the famed aviator and author of *The Little Prince.* A telling and heartfelt tale of a fascinating man. Richardson plays the spirited and independent-minded woman who is the love of his life. [PG]▼

Saint in London, The (1939) **72m.** **½ D: John Paddy Carstairs. George Sanders, David Burns, Sally Gray, Henry Oscar, Ralph Truman. The Saint travels to England in pursuit of a counterfeiting gang and gets unwanted help from a scatterbrained socialite. Shot on location. ▼

Saint in New York, The (1938) **71m.** *** D: Ben Holmes. Louis Hayward, Kay Sutton, Sig Rumann, Jonathan Hale, Frederick Burton, Jack Carson. First in the series and one of the best, with Hayward the smooth Robin Hood-like avenger hired to bump off six of the Big Apple's most rotten criminals. Extremely faithful adaptation of Leslie Charteris' novel; originally intended as American directorial debut of Alfred Hitchcock. ▼

Saint in Palm Springs, The (1941) **65m.** **½ D: Jack Hively. George Sanders, Wendy Barrie, Jonathan Hale, Paul Guilfoyle, Linda Hayes, Ferris Taylor. Murder follows the Saint as he journeys West to deliver $200,000 worth of rare stamps to an heir. Sanders' last appearance in the series, which was coasting by this point.▼

Saint Jack (1979) **C-112m.** *** D: Peter Bogdanovich. Ben Gazzara, Denholm Elliott, James Villiers, Joss Ackland, Rodney Bewes, George Lazenby, Lisa Lu, Peter Bogdanovich. Absorbing character study of an amiable, ambitious pimp who thrives in Singapore during early 1970s. Fine performances from Gazzara and Elliott, excellent use of location milieu. From a Paul Theroux novel. [R]▼

Saint Joan (1957) **110m.** ** D: Otto Preminger. Jean Seberg, Richard Widmark, Richard Todd, Anton Walbrook, John Gielgud, Felix Aylmer, Harry Andrews, Barry Jones, Finlay Currie, Bernard Miles, Margot Grahame. Big-scale filming of Shaw's play sounded large thud when released; some good acting, but Seberg (who won her first film role after a nationwide search) not suited to film's tempo, throws production askew. Script by Graham Greene. Also shown in computer-colored version. ▼●

Saint Meets the Tiger, The (1943-British) **70m.** ** D: Paul Stein. Hugh Sinclair, Jan Gillie, Clifford Evans, Wylie Watson, Dennis Arundell. The Saint matches wits with the gangster Tiger over a bogus gold mine scheme in this minor entry. Loosely based on Leslie Charteris' first *Saint* story.▼

Saint of Fort Washington, The (1993) **C-108m.** ** D: Tim Hunter. Matt Dillon, Danny Glover, Rick Aviles, Nina Siemaszko, Ving Rhames, Joe Seneca. Sincere but undistinguished portrayal of N.Y.C.'s homeless, with Glover showing the ropes to new friend Dillon, a mentally impaired youth who snaps photographic studies without any film in his camera. Despite impressive location footage and a downbeat conclusion, this (barely released) film seems slick and old-Hollywood. [R]▼●

Saint's Double Trouble, The (1940) **68m.** **½ D: Jack Hively. George Sanders, Helene Whitney, Jonathan Hale, Bela Lugosi, Donald MacBride, John F. Hamilton. The Saint is on the trail of his lookalike, a jewel thief who's smuggled diamonds in a mummy from Cairo to Philadelphia. Passable entry with Sanders in a dual role. Lugosi is wasted as a dull-witted hood.▼

Saint's Girl Friday, The (1954-British) **68m.** ** D: Seymour Friedman. Louis Hayward, Naomi Chance, Sidney Tafler, Charles Victor. Hayward, who played the first Saint in 1938, returns in the last film based on the debonair sleuth, tracking down a gambling syndicate responsible for the death of an ex-girlfriend. Original British title: THE SAINT'S RETURN.

Saint Strikes Back, The (1939) **67m.** *** D: John Farrow. George Sanders, Wendy Barrie, Jonathan Hale, Jerome Cowan, Neil Hamilton, Barry Fitzgerald, Edward Gargan. Sanders takes over the role of the debonair Saint, adding his jaded persona to the character as he helps the daughter of a disgraced San Francisco policeman catch the men who framed him. Superior B mystery, tightly directed. First in the series to use Roy Webb's theme music, which was later carried over to the Roger Moore TV series.▼

Saint's Vacation, The (1941) **60m.** **½ D: Leslie Fenton. Hugh Sinclair, Sally Gray, Arthur Macrae, Cecil Parker, Leueen McGrath, Gordon McLeod. Sinclair picks up the role of The Saint in this decent mystery (cowritten by Leslie Charteris himself) about the search for a music box in Switzerland containing secret codes coveted by Axis spies. Made in England.▼

Saint Takes Over, The (1940) **69m.** **½ D: Jack Hively. George Sanders, Jonathan Hale, Wendy Barrie, Paul Guilfoyle, Morgan Conway, Robert Emmett Keane. Fast-moving entry has The Saint coming to the aid of Inspector Fernack (Hale), who's being framed on bribery charges by some racetrack gambling racketeers.▼

Salaam Bombay! (1988-Indian-British) **C-113m.** *** D: Mira Nair. Shafiq Syed, Sarfuddin Quarrassi, Raju Barnad, Raghubir Yadav, Aneeta Kanwar. Gut-wrenching chronicle of young country boy Syed and his various experiences among the street hustlers, drug peddlers, and prostitutes of Bombay. Unravels as a novel, with a gallery of vividly drawn supporting characters. Fine feature debut for director Nair.▼●

Salamander, The (1981-U.S.-British-Italian) **C-101m.** *½ D: Peter Zinner. Franco Nero, Anthony Quinn, Martin Balsam, Sybil Danning, Christopher Lee, Cleavon Little, Paul Smith, Claudia Cardinale, Eli Wallach. Colonel Nero attempts to prevent a fascist coup d'etat in Italy. A cornball script sinks this potentially intriguing drama, from a Morris West novel.▼

Salem's Lot (1979) **C-200m. TVM** D: Tobe Hooper. David Soul, James Mason, Lance Kerwin, Bonnie Bedelia, Lew Ayres, Reggie Nalder, Ed Flanders, Elisha Cook, Marie Windsor, Clarissa Kaye, Fred Willard, James Gallery, Kenneth McMillan. Well-made hair-raiser based on Stephen King's bestseller about vampirism running rampant in small New England town. Mason is great as sinister antique dealer, and Nalder's vampire is terrifying, but Soul is only so-so as successful writer returning home to strange goings-on. Later cut to 150m.; the 112m. version available on video and shown on cable-TV as SALEM'S LOT: THE MOVIE and BLOOD THIRST is the overseas theatrical version and contains more explicit violence. Followed by A RETURN TO SALEM'S LOT. Above average. [PG]▼●◗

Sallah (1965-Israeli) **C-105m.** *** D: Ephraim Kishon. Haym Topol, Geula Noni, Gila Almagor, Arik Einstein, Shraga Friedman, Esther Greenberg. Topol is amusing as an Oriental Jew who emigrates to Israel with his wife and seven children and who is forever scheming to improve his lot. A modest, lighthearted, thoroughly enjoyable satire.▼

Sally and Saint Anne (1952) **90m.** ** D: Rudolph Maté. Ann Blyth, Edmund Gwenn, John McIntire, Palmer Lee (Gregg Palmer), Hugh O'Brian, Jack Kelly, Frances Bavier, King Donovan. Predictable, overly sentimental comedy about a blarney-filled Irish clan, their feud with an ornery alderman, and daughter Blyth's unwavering faith in the title saint.

Sally, Irene and Mary (1938) **72m.** **½ D: William A. Seiter. Alice Faye, Tony Martin, Fred Allen, Joan Davis, Marjorie Weaver, Gregory Ratoff, Jimmy Durante, Louise Hovick (Gypsy Rose Lee). Predictable story of stage-struck girls trying to break into show business, with good comedy spots by Davis, pleasant songs from Faye and Martin: "I Could Use a Dream," "This Is Where I Came In."

Sally of the Sawdust (1925) **91m.** **½ D: D. W. Griffith. W. C. Fields, Carol Dempster, Alfred Lunt, Erville Alderson, Effie Shannon. Pleasant yarn of sideshow con-man Fields who tries to restore his ward (Dempster) to her rightful place in society, knowing identity of her wealthy grandparents. Interesting to see W. C. in a silent film, particularly since one can compare this to its remake, POPPY.▼●◗

Sally's Irish Rogue SEE: **Poacher's Daughter, The**

Salo, or The 120 Days of Sodom (1975-Italian) **C-117m.** BOMB D: Pier Paolo Pasolini. Paolo Bonacelli, Giorgio Cataldi, Umberto P. Quinavalle, Aldo Valletti, Caterina Boratto. Controversial, disturbing adaptation of de Sade's novel, set during WW2 in Italy, where Fascist rulers brutalize and degrade adolescents. Sadism, scatology, and debauchery galore; Pasolini, whose last film this is, wallows in his own sensationalism.▼●◗

Salome (1953) **C-103m.** **½ D: William Dieterle. Rita Hayworth, Stewart Granger, Charles Laughton, Judith Anderson, Cedric Hardwicke, Maurice Schwartz. Great cast struggles with unintentionally funny script in biblical drama of illustrious dancer who offers herself to spare John the Baptist. Filmed before with Nazimova in 1923.▼

Salome's Last Dance (1988-British) **C-90m.** **½ D: Ken Russell. Glenda Jackson, Stratford Johns, Nickolas Grace, Imogen Millais-Scott, Douglas Hodge. As Oscar Wilde lounges in a brothel (the same one where his subsequent arrest would lead to his downfall), the proprietor stages a production of the playwright's title work, with Salome, Herod, John the Baptist and Co. all strutting their stuff. Typical Russell litmus test for one's tolerance of the outrageous, but wittier and less oppressive than some of the director's other historical pageants. Grace's weak Wilde aside, the actors do remarkably well under the circumstances. [R]▼●◗

Salome, Where She Danced (1945) **C-90m.** BOMB D: Charles Lamont. Yvonne De Carlo, Rod Cameron, David Bruce, Walter Slezak, Albert Dekker, Marjorie Rambeau, J. Edward Bromberg. Ludicrous film provides some laughs while trying to spin tale of exotic dancer becoming Mata Hari-type spy. Nevertheless, this boosted De Carlo to stardom.▼

Salsa (1988) **C-97m.** ** D: Boaz Davidson. Robby Rosa, Rodney Harvey, Magali Alvarado, Miranda Garrison, Moon Orona, Angela Alvarado, Celia Cruz, Tito Puente. All flash and no substance in this DIRTY DANCING-inspired feature-length music video with a Latin beat. Rosa (of the pop group Menudo) stars as a young auto repairman who'd much rather be shaking his body to salsa. Main problem: Where's the script? [PG]▼●

Salt and Pepper (1968-British) **C-101m.** **½ D: Richard Donner. Sammy Davis, Jr., Peter Lawford, Michael Bates, Ilona Rodgers, John LeMesurier. Soho nightclub owners find trouble when two baddies turn up at their club. Contrived, broad comedy. Sequel: ONE MORE TIME. [G]

Salt of the Earth (1953) **94m.** ***½ D: Herbert Biberman. Juan Chacon, Rosaura Revueltas, Will Geer, Mervin Williams, Frank Talavera, Clinton Jencks, Virginia Jencks. Taut drama about striking New Mexico mineworkers, with a refreshingly pro-feminist viewpoint. Director Biberman, actor Geer, producer Paul Jarrico, and screenwriter Michael Wilson were all blacklisted when the film was made.▼●◗

Salty (1973) **C-92m.** ** D: Ricou Browning. Mark Slade, Clint Howard, Nina Foch, Julius W. Harris, Linda Scruggs. Two orphaned brothers adopt a mischievous sea lion in this predictable kiddie film made in Florida. [G]▼

Salty O'Rourke (1945) **99m.** *** D: Raoul Walsh. Alan Ladd, Gail Russell, William Demarest, Stanley Clements, Bruce Cabot, Spring Byington. Lively tale of smooth conman Ladd aiming to clean up with jockey Clements, who turns out to be a large headache. Schoolteacher Russell steps in to foil Ladd's plans.

Salute of the Jugger SEE: **Blood of Heroes, The**

Salute to the Marines (1943) **C-101m.** **½ D: S. Sylvan Simon. Wallace Beery, Fay Bainter, Reginald Owen, Keye Luke, Ray Collins, Marilyn Maxwell. OK Beery vehicle of Marine veteran who reluctantly retires, finds himself caught in surprise attack on Philippines.

Salut l'Artiste (1974-French) **C-102m.** *** D: Yves Robert. Marcello Mastroianni, Jean Rochefort, Françoise Fabian, Carla Gravina. Light comedy about second-rate actors Mastroianni and Rochefort; the former scampers about while going nowhere; the latter opts out for an ad executive job. Amusing, with first-rate cast and performances.▼

Salvador (1986) **C-123m.** **½ D: Oliver Stone. James Woods, James Belushi, Michael Murphy, John Savage, Elpedia Carrillo, Tony Plana, Colby Chester, Cindy (Cynthia) Gibb, John Doe. Uneven but compelling drama based on real experiences of journalist Richard Boyle in strife-ridden El Salvador in 1980–81. Effective propaganda, often potent drama; it takes time to grab hold because lead characters Woods and Belushi are such incredible sleazeballs. Woods's dynamic performance makes up for a lot; his first visit to confession in thirty-two years is a memorably funny scene. Screenplay by Boyle himself and director Stone. [R]▼●

Salvation! (1987) **C-80m.** *½ D: Beth B. Stephen McHattie, Dominique Davalos, Exene Cervenka, Viggo Mortensen, Rockets Redglare, Billy Bastani. Satire of false TV evangelist (McHattie) who gets involved in a sex incident, was released right after the Jim & Tammy Bakker scandal. Unfortunately, underground filmmaker Beth B directs in the manner of an incoherent music video, swamping McHattie's convincing central performance (resembling a young John Carradine). [R]▼

Salvatore Giuliano (1962-Italian) **125m.** ***½ D: Francesco Rosi. Frank Wolff, Salvo Randone, Federico Zardi, Pietro Cammarata, Fernando Cicero. Vivid, documentary-like drama, told in flashback, depicts the career of an infamous post-WW2 Sicilian criminal who rose through the ranks of organized crime, becoming a Mafia chieftain. This fact-based tale intricately weaves a story of political and governmental bureaucracy; it resulted in a real-life investigation of Mafia activities in Italy. Remade as THE SICILIAN.

Salzburg Connection, The (1972) **C-92m.** *½ D: Lee H. Katzin. Barry Newman, Anna Karina, Klaus Maria Brandauer, Karen Jensen, Joe Maross, Wolfgang Preiss. Terrible film version of Helen MacInnes' bestseller about American lawyer on vacation in Salzburg who gets mixed up with spies; irritating use of slow-motion and freeze-frame gimmicks. Brandauer's debut and only film appearance until MEPHISTO. [PG]▼

Samar (1962) **C-89m.** ** D: George Montgomery. George Montgomery, Gilbert Roland, Ziva Rodann, Joan O'Brien, Nico Minardos, Mario Barri. Ordinary actioner has Roland as head of prison compound on a Philippine island who rejects inhumane treatment of prisoners and leads them on escape route.▼

Same Old Song (1997-French-Swiss-British) **C-120m.** *** D: Alain Resnais. Pierre Arditi, Sabine Azema, Jean-Pierre Bacri, Andre Dussollier, Agnes Jaoui, Lambert Wilson, Jane Birkin. Resnais adds a distinctly personal sensibility to this intricately plotted, tongue-in-cheek confection about a group of overindulgent middle-class Parisians who constantly break into lip-synched song as a way of expressing themselves. Bacri and Jaoui scripted this affectionate homage to Dennis Potter (THE SINGING DETECTIVE, PENNIES FROM HEAVEN). Winner of seven César awards.

Same Time, Next Year (1978) **C-117m.** *** D: Robert Mulligan. Ellen Burstyn, Alan Alda. Bernard Slade's two-character Broadway play makes pleasing film, with Alda and Burstyn as adulterous couple who share one weekend a year for 26 years; warm, human comedy-drama reflects changes in American life and attitudes since early '50s in likable fashion. [PG]▼●

Sam Hill: Who Killed Mr. Foster? (1971) **C-100m. TVM** D: Fielder Cook. Ernest Borgnine, Sam Jaffe, J. D. Cannon, Judy Geeson, Will Geer, Bruce Dern, Slim Pickens, John McGiver, Jay C. Flippen. Pending town election jeopardizes security of cynical Western marshal. Uneventful situations, boring dialogue; even somewhat unusual casting doesn't enliven proceedings. A rare misfire from the producing/writing team of Richard Levinson and William Link. Also known as WHO KILLED THE MYSTERIOUS MR. FOSTER? Below average.

Sam Marlowe, Private Eye SEE: **Man with Bogart's Face, The**

Sammy and Rosie Get Laid (1987-British) **C-100m.** ** D: Stephen Frears. Shashi Kapoor, Claire Bloom, Ayub Khan Din, Frances Barber, Roland Gift, Wendy Gazelle, Suzette Llewellyn. The curious lives of a couple with an open sexual relationship are thrown into disarray by the arrival of his father, a powerful reactionary political figure from India who cannot understand their lifestyle—or what has happened to the traditional British way of life he used to enjoy. Disturbing but monotonous look at social and sexual anarchy in England, written by Hanif Kureishi, who previously collaborated with director Frears on MY BEAUTIFUL LAUNDRETTE.▼●

Sammy Going South SEE: **Boy Ten Feet Tall, A**

Sammy Stops the World (1979) **C-104m.** BOMB D: Mel Shapiro. Sammy Davis, Jr., Marian Mercer, Dennis Daniels, Donna Lowe. Pathetic update of *Stop the World, I Want to Get Off* combines nail-your-camera-to-the-ground direction with a stage production that couldn't get by at Three Mile Island Dinner Theatre.

Sammy the Way Out Seal (1962) **C-90m.** **½ D: Norman Tokar. Robert Culp, Jack Carson, Billy Mumy, Patricia Barry. Pretty funny sitcom for the kids about a seal who becomes Mumy's pet and wreaks havoc upon Culp and family. Shown as a feature in Europe, originally made as a two-part Disney TV show.▼

Samson and Delilah (1949) **C-128m.** *** D: Cecil B. DeMille. Victor Mature, Hedy Lamarr, George Sanders, Angela Lansbury, Henry Wilcoxon, Olive Deering, Fay Holden, Russell (Russ) Tamblyn, George Reeves, Tom Tyler, Fritz Leiber, Mike Mazurki. With expected DeMille touches, this remains a tremendously entertaining film. Mature is surprisingly good as Samson, though his famous fight with lion is hopelessly phony; also difficult to swallow idea of Lansbury being Lamarr's *older* sister. Sanders supplies biggest surprise by underplaying his role as the Saran. This won Oscars for its Art Direction-Set Decoration and Costumes. Remade for TV in 1984 (with Mature as Samson's father) and 1996.▼●

Sam's Son (1984) **C-104m.** ** D: Michael Landon. Eli Wallach, Anne Jackson, Timothy Patrick Murphy, Hallie Todd, Alan Hayes, Jonna Lee, Michael Landon. Landon wrote, directed, and appears briefly in this autobiographical saga about an underdog kid, who's a champion javelin thrower, and his loving but frustrated father, who never got to pursue his dreams. Wallach's performance as the father is major asset of this sometimes syrupy film. [PG]▼●

Sam's Song (1969) **C-92m.** *½ D: Jordan Leondopoulos (John Shade, John C. Broderick). Robert De Niro, Jennifer Warren, Jered Mickey, Martin Kelley, Viva. Dreary film about film editor's weekend with friends on Long Island, interesting only for early De Niro performance. Extensive reshooting includes new characters played by Lisa Blount and Sybil Danning; film was reissued in 1979 as THE SWAP. Video title: LINE OF FIRE. [R]▼

Samurai Cowboy (1993-Canadian) **C-101m.** **½ D: Michael Keusch. Hiromigo Go, Catherine Mary Stewart, Matt McCoy, Conchata Ferrell, Robert Conrad. A Japanese businessman, enthralled with classic American Western movies, buys a ranch in Montana and attempts to live his dream of becoming a cowboy. Although the film is hampered by a predictable plot and many formula characters, Japanese pop star Go's ingratiating performance adds a great deal of charm to this likable tale.▼

Sam Whiskey (1969) **C-96m.** ** D: Arnold Laven. Burt Reynolds, Clint Walker, Ossie Davis, Angie Dickinson, Rick Davis, William Schallert, Woodrow Parfrey. Modestly mounted, uninteresting Western wasting talents of good cast. Schemer Whiskey coerced into organizing heist of golden bullion. For Western aficionados and Reynolds addicts only. [M/PG]

San Antone (1953) **90m.** **½ D: Joseph Kane. Rod Cameron, Arleen Whelan, Forrest Tucker, Katy Jurado, Rodolfo Acosta, Bob Steele, Harry Carey, Jr. Offbeat Western tends to ramble, but story of Cameron and friends being victimized by despicable Tucker and bitchy Southern belle Whelan is intriguing.

San Antonio (1945) **C-111m.** *** D: David Butler. Errol Flynn, Alexis Smith, S. Z. Sakall, Victor Francen, Florence Bates, John Litel, Paul Kelly. Elaborate Western has predictable plot but good production as dance-hall girl Smith, working for villain Francen, falls for good-guy Flynn. Screenplay by Alan ("Searchers") LeMay and W. R. Burnett.▼

Sanctuary (1961) **100m.** ** D: Tony Richardson. Lee Remick, Yves Montand, Bradford Dillman, Odetta, Reta Shaw, Howard St. John, Strother Martin. Faulkner's novel of Southern degradation, rape, and murder, filmed before as THE STORY OF TEMPLE DRAKE; much more explicit here. CinemaScope.

Sand (1949) **C-78m.** ** D: Louis King. Mark Stevens, Rory Calhoun, Coleen Gray, Charley Grapewin. Visually picturesque but dull account of show horse who turns wild. Retitled: WILL JAMES' SAND.

Sand Castle, The (1960) **C-67m.** **½ D: Jerome Hill. Barry Cardwell, Laurie Cardwell, George Dunham, Alec Wilder. Imaginative little film of small boy building mud castles on the beach, dreaming of people living in his creation.

Sanders (1963-British) **C-83m.** ** D: Lawrence Huntington. Richard Todd, Marianne Koch, Albert Lieven, Vivi Bach, Jeremy Lloyd. Loose adaptation of Edgar Wallace novel *Sanders of the River* follows police inspector's investigation of murder in an African hospital and discovery of hidden silver mine. British title DEATH DRUMS ALONG THE RIVER. Todd repeated role of Harry Sanders in 1964 COAST OF SKELETONS. Techniscope.

Sanders of the River (1935-British) **98m.** *** D: Zoltan Korda. Paul Robeson, Leslie Banks, Nina Mae McKinney, Robert Cochran, Martin Walker. Dated adventure story (by Edgar Wallace) about river patrol officer maintains interest today, particularly for Robeson's strong presence and African location shooting. A fascinating relic of the sun-never-sets school of British imperialism. Sanders character revived in 1960s' SANDERS (DEATH DRUMS ALONG THE RIVER) and COAST OF SKELETONS.▼●

San Diego, I Love You (1944) **83m.** *** D: Reginald LeBorg. Jon Hall, Louise Allbritton, Edward Everett Horton, Eric Blore, Buster Keaton, Irene Ryan. Whimsical comedy of unconventional family trying to promote father Horton's inventions in San Diego. Allbritton is perky, Keaton memorable in delightful sequence as bored bus driver.

Sandlot, The (1993) **C-101m.** **½ D: David Mickey Evans. Tom Guiry, Mike Vitar, Patrick Renna, Chauncey Leopardi, Marty York, Brandon Adams, Denis Leary, Karen Allen, James Earl Jones, Maury Wills, Art La Fleur. Innocuous film for kids about a 60s sandlot baseball team, their acceptance of the new kid on the block, and their ongoing battle with a ferocious neighboring dog. No real insight or resonance here (and incredibly condescending, heavy handed narration)—but a pleasant enough time-filler for younger viewers. Arliss Howard and Brooke Adams appear unbilled. J-D-C Scope. [PG]▼●

Sandokan Against The Leopard of Sarawak (1964-Italian) **C-94m.** ** D: Luigi Capuano. Ray Danton, Guy Madison, Franca Bettoja, Mario Petri. Danton vs. Madison in this papier mâché, run-of-the-mill epic. Totalscope.

Sandokan Fights Back (1964-Italian) **C-96m.** ** D: Luigi Capuano. Ray Danton, Guy Madison, Franca Bettoja, Mino Doro. Unconvincing, juvenile narrative of princely ruler fighting to regain his throne. Techniscope.▼

Sandokan the Great (1965-Italian) **C-105m.** ** D: Umberto Lenzi. Steve Reeves, Genevieve Grad, Rik Battaglia, Maurice Poli. Reeves actioner in which he rebels against the invading forces of Queen Victoria. At least the time period is different. Techniscope.

Sand Pebbles, The (1966) **C-179m.** *** D: Robert Wise. Steve McQueen, Richard Attenborough, Richard Crenna, Candice Bergen, Mako, Marayat Andriane, Simon Oakland, Larry Gates, Gavin MacLeod.

McQueen gives one of his finest performances as cynical sailor on U.S. gunboat cruising China's Yangtze River in 1926. Long but generally compelling drama mixes traditional action and romance with some pointed notions about American imperialism (and a few parallels to Vietnam). Splendidly photographed by Joseph MacDonald. Panavision.▼●

Sandpiper, The (1965) **C-116m.** **½ D: Vincente Minnelli. Elizabeth Taylor, Richard Burton, Eva Marie Saint, Charles Bronson, Robert Webber, Torin Thatcher, Morgan Mason, Tom Drake. Ordinary triangle love affair. Beatnik Taylor in love with Burton, who is married to Saint. Nothing new, but beautiful California Big Sur settings help; so does Oscar-winning theme, "The Shadow Of Your Smile." Written by Dalton Trumbo and Michael Wilson. Panavision.▼

Sandpit Generals, The SEE: **Wild Pack, The**

Sands of Beersheba (1966) **90m.** ** D: Alexander Ramati. Diane Baker, David Opatoshu, Tom Bell, Paul Stassino. Sluggish account of the Arab-Israeli conflict, involving a non-Jewish American whose fiancé died in the 1948 Palestinian war, an Israeli gunrunner, a Jew-hating Arab terrorist, and the latter's father who's tired of all the bloodshed. The issues remain compelling, but the film is mostly a bore.▼

Sands of Iwo Jima (1949) **110m.** *** D: Allan Dwan. John Wayne, John Agar, Adele Mara, Forrest Tucker, Arthur Franz, Julie Bishop, Richard Jaeckel, Wally Cassell, Richard Webb. Enormously popular WW2 saga, with Wayne in one of his best roles as a tough Marine top-sergeant. Story and characters are pretty two-dimensional, and a bit worn from having been copied so many times since, but it's still good entertainment; use of authentic combat footage is striking. Wayne's first Oscar-nominated performance. The three surviving Marine vets who raised the American flag on Mt. Suribachi have small parts. Also shown in computer-colored version.▼●◗

Sands of the Desert (1960-British) **C-92m.** ** D: John Paddy Carstairs. Charlie Drake, Peter Arne, Sarah Branch, Rebecca Dignam. Heavy-handed comedy set in Arabia, with Drake trying to uncover sabotage attempts at holiday camp.

Sands of the Kalahari (1965-British) **C-119m.** *** D: Cy Endfield. Stuart Whitman, Stanley Baker, Susannah York, Harry Andrews, Theodore Bikel, Nigel Davenport. Well-done story of plane crash survivors struggling through desert and battling simian inhabitants (and each other). Panavision.

Sandy Gets Her Man (1940) **74m.** *½ D: Otis Garrett, Paul Smith. Stuart Erwin, Una Merkel, Baby Sandy, Edgar Kennedy, William Frawley. Precocious Baby Sandy is final arbiter of mama's courters; naive little film kept alive by character actors in cast.

Sandy Is a Lady (1940) **65m.** *½ D: Charles Lamont. Nan Grey, Baby Sandy, Eugene Pallette, Tom Brown, Mischa Auer, Billy Gilbert, Edgar Kennedy, Anne Gwynne. Simplicity-saturated comedy as precocious child helps her family get ahead.

San Francisco (1936) **115m.** ***½ D: W. S. Van Dyke II. Clark Gable, Jeanette MacDonald, Spencer Tracy, Jack Holt, Jessie Ralph, Ted Healy, Shirley Ross, Al Shean. Top-grade entertainment with extremely lavish production. Jeanette overdoes it a bit as the belle of San Francisco, but the music, Tracy's performance, and earthquake climax are still fine. Originally had footage of Golden Gate Bridge under construction; other rhythmically edited shots of S.F. were changed for later reissue. Script by Anita Loos. Also shown in computer-colored version.▼●

San Francisco Story, The (1952) **80m.** ** D: Robert Parrish. Joel McCrea, Yvonne De Carlo, Sidney Blackmer, Richard Erdman, Florence Bates, Onslow Stevens. Tame Western actioner set in gold-rush days, with cleanup of city's criminal elements.

Sangaree (1953) **C-94m.** ** D: Edward Ludwig. Fernando Lamas, Arlene Dahl, Patricia Medina, Francis L. Sullivan, Charles Korvin, Tom Drake, Willard Parker. Lovers of 1950s kitsch will savor this corny, overheated period soaper in which honorable doctor Lamas, the son of a servant, comes to manage a colonel's estate amid much controversy. Lamas utters the word "fabulous," but not "marvelous." Based on a Frank G. Slaughter novel. Filmed in 3-D.

Sanjuro (1962-Japanese) **96m.** *** D: Akira Kurosawa. Toshiro Mifune, Tatsuya Nakadai, Takashi Shimura, Yuzo Kayama, Reiko Dan. Sequel to YOJIMBO has shabby, wandering samurai Mifune aiding nine bumbling younger warriors in exposing corruption among the elders of their clan. Satirical comic-book actioner features a typically deadpan Mifune performance. Tohoscope.▼●

San Quentin (1937) **70m.** **½ D: Lloyd Bacon. Pat O'Brien, Humphrey Bogart, Ann Sheridan, Veda Ann Borg, Barton MacLane. Warner Bros. formula prison film; convict Bogart's sister (Sheridan) loves O'Brien, who's captain of the guards. MacLane is memorable as tough prison guard.

San Quentin (1946) **66m.** **½ D: Gordon Douglas. Lawrence Tierney, Barton MacLane, Marian Carr, Harry Shannon, Carol Forman, Richard Powers (Tom Keene). Ex-con Tierney, organizer of a prison program which straightens out hardened criminals, goes into action when bad-boy MacLane abuses the system. Solid, if somewhat preachy, prison reform-oriented

B film, introduced by Warden Lewis F. Lawes (20,000 YEARS AT SING SING).

Sansho the Bailiff (1954-Japanese) **125m.** **** D: Kenji Mizoguchi. Kinuyo Tanaka, Kisho Hanayagi, Kyoko Kagawa, Eitaro Shindo, Ichiro Sugai. Epic, poetic drama of 11th-century Japan, focusing on the tribulations of a family. Kindly father, a provincial governor, is exiled; children (Hanayagi, Kagawa) become slaves; mother (Tanaka) is sold as a prostitute. Haunting, with stunning direction and cinematography (by Kazuo Miyagawa). Original running-time: 130m. Aka THE BAILIFF. ▼●

Santa Claus (1985) **C-112m.** **½ D: Jeannot Szwarc. Dudley Moore, John Lithgow, David Huddleston, Burgess Meredith, Judy Cornwell, Jeffrey Kramer, Christian Fitzpatrick, Carrie Kei Heim. Story of how Santa came to be starts out so wonderfully—with eye-filling looks at his North Pole toy factory, reindeer, and sleigh—that it's too bad the rest of the film (with contemporary tale of humbug kid and greedy toy magnate) can't measure up. Still entertaining, just a bit less magical than it should have been. Referred to as SANTA CLAUS: THE MOVIE everywhere but on screen! J-D-C Scope. [PG]▼●

Santa Claus Conquers the Martians (1964) **C-80m.** BOMB D: Nicholas Webster. John Call, Leonard Hicks, Vincent Beck, Donna Conforti. Absurd low-budget fantasy (with a Milton Delugg score!) about Santa and two Earth children being abducted to Mars to help solve some of their domestic problems—like kids watching too much TV. One of the Martian tykes is Pia Zadora! Aka SANTA CLAUS DEFEATS THE ALIENS.▼

Santa Clause, The (1994) **C-97m.** *** D: John Pasquin. Tim Allen, Judge Reinhold, Wendy Crewson, Eric Lloyd, David Krumholtz, Peter Boyle, Larry Brandenburg, Mary Gross, Paige Tamada. Neglectful divorced dad inadvertently frightens Santa off his roof and, when he puts on the deceased St. Nick's suit, begins to turn into Santa Claus himself—first on the outside, and then, more significantly, on the inside. Clever script by Steve Rudnick and Leo Benevenuti takes a potential one-joke idea and develops it in interesting and unexpected ways, effectively infusing heart and sentiment into its 1990s sensibility. Impressive screen debut for Allen. [PG]▼●◗

Santa Fe (1951) **C-89m.** ** D: Irving Pichel. Randolph Scott, Janis Carter, Jerome Courtland, Peter Thompson, John Archer, Warner Anderson, Roy Roberts, Jock Mahoney. Routine account of brothers in post-Civil War days, on opposite sides of the law.▼

Santa Fe Passage (1955) **C-90m.** ** D: William Witney. John Payne, Faith Domergue, Rod Cameron, Slim Pickens. Routine wagon train westward; Indian attacks, love among the pioneers, etc.

Santa Fe Satan SEE: **Catch My Soul**

Santa Fe Trail (1940) **110m.** ** D: Michael Curtiz. Errol Flynn, Olivia de Havilland, Raymond Massey, Ronald Reagan, Alan Hale, Guinn Williams, William Lundigan, Ward Bond, Van Heflin, Gene Reynolds, John Litel, Charles Middleton. Lopsided picture can't make up its mind about anything: what side it's taking, what it wants to focus on, etc. Worthless as history, but amid the rubble are some good action scenes as Jeb Stuart (Flynn) and cohorts go after John Brown (Massey). Reagan plays Flynn's West Point classmate and romantic rival, George Armstrong Custer(!). Also shown in computer-colored version.▼●◗

Santa Sangre (1989-Italian-Mexican) **C-121m.** ** D: Alejandro Jodorowsky. Axel Jodorowsky, Blanca Guerra, Sabrina Dennison, Guy Stockwell, Thelma Tixou, Adan Jodorowsky, Faviola Elenka Tapia. Grotesque story about an entertainer whose act consists of performing as the arms for his armless mother; he's also an unwilling murderer. Made in luxurious color with dreamy art direction, this lacks the intellectual charge of Jodorowsky's earlier films. Filmed in English. [Shown both in NC-17 and R-rated versions]▼●

Santee (1973) **C-93m.** ** D: Gary Nelson. Glenn Ford, Michael Burns, Dana Wynter, Jay Silverheels, Harry Townes, John Larch, Robert Wilke, Robert Donner. Bounty hunter Ford, whose boy has been murdered, adopts son of outlaw he has just killed. OK Western. [PG]▼

Santiago (1956) **C-93m.** **½ D: Gordon Douglas. Alan Ladd, Rossana Podesta, Lloyd Nolan, Chill Wills, Paul Fix, L.Q. Jones, Frank DeKova. Ladd and Nolan are involved in gun-running to Cuba during fight with Spain. Ladd becomes humane when he encounters partisan Podesta.

Saphead, The (1921) **78m.** **½ D: Herbert Blaché. Buster Keaton, William H. Crane, Carol Holloway, Edward Connelly, Irving Cummings, Beulah Booker. Buster (in his feature-film debut) is shoehorned into a pleasant but conventional plot about a wealthy boob whose impending marriage is imperiled when he's framed for a stock swindle. Keaton is fine but not allowed to express his unique comic personality. Based on a Broadway play that was filmed once before as THE LAMB (1915) with Douglas Fairbanks. Villain Cummings later became a top director at 20th Century-Fox.▼●◗

Sapphire (1959-British) **C-92m.** *** D: Basil Dearden. Nigel Patrick, Yvonne Mitchell, Michael Craig, Paul Massie, Bernard Miles, Earl Cameron, Rupert Davies, Yvonne Buckingham. When music student is murdered, it is discovered she was passing

as white. Considered daring in its day, still absorbing today—both as entertainment and social comment. Fine performances. Story and screenplay by Janet Green (with additional dialogue by Lukas Heller).▼
Saps At Sea (1940) **57m.** *** D: Gordon Douglas. Stan Laurel, Oliver Hardy, James Finlayson, Ben Turpin, Richard Cramer, Harry Bernard. L&H comedy is short and sweet: Ollie has breakdown working in horn factory, tries to relax on a small boat with Stan . . . and that's impossible. Cramer is a memorable heavy. Harry Langdon was one of the writers.▼●
Saraband (1948-British) **C-95m.** *** D: Basil Dearden. Stewart Granger, Joan Greenwood, Flora Robson, Françoise Rosay, Frederick Valk, Peter Bull, Anthony Quayle, Michael Gough, Megs Jenkins, Christopher Lee. Lavish, tearful romance with Greenwood torn between royal responsibility and love for young rogue. British title: SARABAND FOR DEAD LOVERS.▼
Saracen Blade, The (1954) **C-76m.** *½ D: William Castle. Ricardo Montalban, Betta St. John, Rick Jason, Carolyn Jones, Whitfield Connor. Pretty bad 13th-century stuff, with young man avenging death of father. Unbelievable script traps cast.
Sarafina! (1992-U.S.-British-French) **C-115m.** **½ D: Darrell James Roodt. Whoopi Goldberg, Leleti Khumalo, Miriam Makeba, John Kani, Mbongeni Ngema. Wobbly film version of the anti-Apartheid musical stage hit about a young South African black girl inspired by teacher Goldberg, who's courting trouble by deviating from the curriculum mandated by the white power structure. Arguably the most violent musical ever (taking what was abstract on stage and literalizing it), a key indication of the film's uncertain style. [PG-13]▼●
Sarah and Son (1930) **76m.** ** D: Dorothy Arzner. Ruth Chatterton, Fredric March, Doris Lloyd, Philippe de Lacy. Chatterton, obsessed with finding the son taken from her years ago, enlists aid of lawyer March.
Sarah, Plain and Tall (1991) **C-100m. TVM** D: Glenn Jordan. Glenn Close, Christopher Walken, Lexi Randall, Margaret Sophie Stein, Jon De Vries, Christopher Bell. Sentimental telling of Patricia MacLachlan's gentle children's book (which she and Carol Sobieski adapted) about a Maine schoolteacher who travels to Kansas in 1910 to take charge of a widowed farmer's family. Close shines as an American Mary Poppins. Followed by SKYLARK and WINTER'S END. Above average.▼●◗
Saratoga (1937) **94m.** **½ D: Jack Conway. Clark Gable, Jean Harlow, Lionel Barrymore, Frank Morgan, Walter Pidgeon, Una Merkel, Cliff Edwards, George Zucco, Hattie MacDaniel, Margaret Hamilton. Harlow's last film—she died during production—has stand-in Mary Dees doing many scenes, but comes off pretty well, with Jean as granddaughter of horse-breeder Barrymore, Gable an influential bookie.▼●
Saratoga Trunk (1945) **135m.** *½ D: Sam Wood. Gary Cooper, Ingrid Bergman, Flora Robson, Jerry Austin, John Warburton, Florence Bates. Elaborate but miscast, overlong version of Edna Ferber's novel of New Orleans vixen Bergman and cowboy Cooper. Unbearable at times. Made in 1943.▼
Saskatchewan (1954) **C-87m.** **½ D: Raoul Walsh. Alan Ladd, Shelley Winters, J. Carrol Naish, Hugh O'Brian, Robert Douglas, Richard Long, Jay Silverheels. Cotton-candy Western about Ladd and fellow Canadian mounties trying to prevent Indian uprisings.▼
Sasquatch (1978) **C-102m.** *½ D: Ed Ragozzini. George Lauris, Steve Boergadine, Jim Bradford, Ken Kenzie. Semi-documentary about expedition that goes in search of Bigfoot, including "authentic" if blurry footage of the monster. [G]▼
Satan Bug, The (1965) **C-114m.** ***½ D: John Sturges. George Maharis, Richard Basehart, Anne Francis, Dana Andrews, Edward Asner, Frank Sutton, John Larkin, Henry Beckman. Overlooked little suspense gem, loosely based on Alistair MacLean novel, detailing nerve-racking chase after lunatic who's stolen flasks containing horribly lethal virus from government lab. Taut script (by Edward Anhalt and James Clavell) and direction, stunning photography by Robert Surtees. Panavision.▼●
Satanic Rites of Dracula, The SEE: **Count Dracula and His Vampire Bride**
Satan Met a Lady (1936) **75m.** ** D: William Dieterle. Bette Davis, Warren William, Alison Skipworth, Arthur Treacher, Winifred Shaw, Marie Wilson, Porter Hall. Dashiell Hammett's *Maltese Falcon* incognito; far below 1941 remake. William is private eye, Davis the mysterious client, Skipworth the strange woman searching for priceless artifact (here, a ram's horn). Filmed in 1931 and 1941 as THE MALTESE FALCON.▼
Satan Never Sleeps (1962) **C-126m.** ** D: Leo McCarey. William Holden, Clifton Webb, France Nuyen, Athene Seyler, Martin Benson, Edith Sharpe. Dreary goings-on of two priests holding fast when Communist China invades their territory. McCarey's last film. CinemaScope.
Satan's Cheerleaders (1977) **C-92m.** ** D: Greydon Clark. Kerry Sherman, John Ireland, Yvonne DeCarlo, Jacqueline Cole, Jack Kruschen, John Carradine, Sydney Chaplin. Amusing drive-in fodder about a busload of high school cheerleaders who fall into clutches of a demonic cult. Humor and a cast full of old pros help, but this film is too tame to be really effective. [R]▼
Satan's Claw SEE: **Blood on Satan's Claw**

Satan's Harvest (1970) **C-104m.** ** D: Douglas K. Stone (George Montgomery). George Montgomery, Tippi Hedren, Matt Monro, Davy Kaye, Brian O'Shaughnessy. American detective Montgomery inherits South African ranch and discovers it to be headquarters for a drug smuggling operation. Colorful scenery, tepid story.▼

Satan's Playthings SEE: **In the Devil's Garden**

Satan's Sadists (1970) **C-88m.** BOMB D: Al Adamson. Russ Tamblyn, Scott Brady, Kent Taylor, John Cardos, Greydon Clark, Regina Carrol, William Bonner. Renegade cyclists on the loose down the highway. Change the channel. [R]▼●

Satan's Skin SEE: **Blood on Satan's Claw**

Satellite in the Sky (1956-British) **C-85m.** **½ D: Paul Dickson. Kieron Moore, Lois Maxwell, Donald Wolfit, Bryan Forbes, Jimmy Hanley. Spunky female reporter stows away aboard first British satellite rocket. Complications arise when bomb to be tested sticks to the side of the satellite and ticks away the moments to doom. Elaborate but unexciting. CinemaScope.

Satisfaction (1988) **C-92m.** BOMB D: Joan Freeman. Justine Bateman, Liam Neeson, Trini Alvarado, Britta Phillips, Julia Roberts, Scott Coffey. Bubble-gum theatrical release about a four-girl/one-guy garage band that gets its first break rocking in a wealthy summer resort town. With the entire band shacked up in a single room, figure out where sole male member Coffey sleeps—or *how* he sleeps. Duds like this were more fun in the 1950s. Retitled GIRLS OF SUMMER. [PG-13]▼●

Saturday Night and Sunday Morning (1960-British) **90m.** ***½ D: Karel Reisz. Albert Finney, Shirley Anne Field, Rachel Roberts, Norman Rossington. Grim yet refreshing look at angry young man, who in a burst of nonconformity alters the lives of girlfriends Field and Roberts. Superbly enacted. Script by Alan Sillitoe, from his novel. One of the first and best of Britain's "angry young men" dramas of the 60s. ▼●

Saturday Night Fever (1977) **C-119m.** *** D: John Badham. John Travolta, Karen Lynn Gorney, Barry Miller, Joseph Cali, Paul Pape, Donna Pescow, Julie Bovasso, Denny Dillon, Robert Costanza, Fran Drescher. Travolta's first starring film is thoughtful study of Brooklyn youth who finds only meaning in his life when dancing at local disco. Film pulses to dynamic Bee Gees music score ("Night Fever," "How Deep Is Your Love," "Staying Alive," etc). Plethora of street language may offend some, but not in "alternate" 108m. PG-rated version, where dialogue and certain scenes have been changed or dropped entirely. Sequel: STAYING ALIVE. Reissued in PG version. [R] ▼●

Saturday's Children (1940) **101m.** **½ D: Vincent Sherman. John Garfield, Anne Shirley, Claude Rains, Lee Patrick, George Tobias, Roscoe Karns, Dennis Moore, Elisabeth Risdon. N.Y.C.-based story of poor, hardworking Shirley, her dreamer-boyfriend Garfield, and what happens when they marry. Rains steals film as Shirley's sacrificing father. Based on Maxwell Anderson play previously filmed in 1929 and (as MAYBE IT'S LOVE) in 1935.

Saturday's Hero (1951) **111m.** **½ D: David Miller. John Derek, Donna Reed, Sidney Blackmer, Alexander Knox. Football player Derek wins a college scholarship, then discovers he isn't expected to spend much time in class. Pretty good attack on collegiate sports remains fairly timely; Reed is fine as love interest. Look quickly for Aldo Ray (in film debut).

Saturday's Heroes (1937) **60m.** **½ D: Edward Killy. Van Heflin, Marian Marsh, Richard Lane, Alan Bruce, Minor Watson, Frank Jenks, Al St. John. Zippy little programmer about outspoken college football star's crusade against the hypocrites and bureaucrats who exploit amateur athletes. Biting indictment of the business of college football remains relevant today.

Saturday's Island SEE: **Island of Desire**

Saturday the 14th (1981) **C-75m.** *½ D: Howard R. Cohen. Richard Benjamin, Paula Prentiss, Severn Darden, Jeffrey Tambor, Kari Michaelson, Kevin Brando, Rosemary DeCamp. Limp horror film parody, with Benjamin and Prentiss moving into a weird house and dealing with an assortment of menacing types. A follow-up came along seven years later. [PG]▼

Saturday the 14th Strikes Back (1988) **C-78m.** BOMB D: Howard R. Cohen. Jason Presson, Ray Walston, Avery Schreiber, Patty McCormack, Julianne McNamara, Rhonda Aldrich, Leo V. Gordon. Follow-up to 1981 turkey is even worse, if that seems imaginable: a schlocky, amateurish spoof of horror films with a bevy of monsters attacking Presson on his birthday. [PG]▼

Saturn 3 (1980-British) **C-88m.** ** D: Stanley Donen. Farrah Fawcett, Kirk Douglas, Harvey Keitel, Douglas Lambert. Flashy but empty-headed outer-space opus, with Douglas and Fawcett menaced by Keitel and his sex-starved robot Hector; good-looking package with nothing inside. [R]▼●◗

Savage, The (1952) **C-95m.** **½ D: George Marshall. Charlton Heston, Susan Morrow, Peter Hanson, Joan Taylor, Ted de Corsia. Heston is sincere and energetic as white man raised by the Indians and forced to choose sides when skirmishes break out.

Savage (1973) **C-74m. TVM** D: Steven Spielberg. Martin Landau, Barbara Bain, Will Geer, Paul Richards, Michele Carey, Barry Sullivan, Susan Howard, Dabney Coleman, Pat Harrington. Investigative reporters find a skeleton in the closet of a Supreme Court nominee. Pilot for a prospective Landau-Bain series, and, notably, Spielberg's last TV-movie. Average.▼

Savage Attraction SEE: **Hostage** (1983)

Savage Drums (1951) **73m.** ** D: William Berke. Sabu, Lita Baron, H. B. Warner, Sid Melton, Steve Geray. U. S.-educated Sabu returns to the islands to put down local warfare; fair low-budgeter.

Savage Eye, The (1960) **68m.** *** D: Ben Maddow, Sidney Meyers, Joseph Strick. Barbara Baxley, Herschel Bernardi, Gary Merrill, Jean Hidey. Documentary-style drama of divorcee Baxley trying to start life anew in L.A.; contrived but intriguing.

Savage Harvest (1981) **C-87m.** *½ D: Robert Collins. Tom Skerritt, Michelle Phillips, Shawn Stevens, Anne-Marie Martin, Derek Partridge. Lions prey on Skerritt, Phillips, and children in Kenya. Scary but pointless; enough to turn you into a vegetarian. [PG]

Savage Innocents, The (1960-Italian-French-British) **C-110m.** **½ D: Nicholas Ray. Anthony Quinn, Yoko Tani, Peter O'Toole, Marie Yang, Anna May Wong. Striking but uneven film about conflict of civilization vs. simple ways of Eskimo people. Quinn gives remarkable performance as native Eskimo; beautiful documentary-type location photography combined with studio work. O'Toole's voice is dubbed. Super Technirama 70.

Savage Is Loose, The (1974) **C-114m.** BOMB D: George C. Scott. George C. Scott, Trish Van Devere, John David Carson, Lee H. Montgomery. Scott produced, directed, starred in and even distributed this farrago about the eventual incest between mother and son after they, along with dad, have been stranded on an island for years. Not very stimulating. Panavision. [R]▼

Savage Messiah (1972-British) **C-100m.** *** D: Ken Russell. Dorothy Tutin, Scott Antony, Helen Mirren, Lindsay Kemp, Peter Vaughan. Thoughtful, if intense chronicle of the platonic affair between sculptor Henri Gaudier-Brzeska (Antony), who died in WW1 at age 24, and Sophie Brzeska (Tutin). A convincing, impressive "portrait of an artist as a young man." [R]▼

Savage Mutiny (1953) **73m.** *½ D: Spencer Bennet. Johnny Weissmuller, Angela Stevens, Lester Matthews, Nelson Leigh, Paul Marion. Campy Cold War caper about *Jungle Jim* Weissmuller battling enemy agents while trying to relocate natives from their island to make way for A-bomb testing.

Savage Nights (1992-French) **C-126m.** *** D: Cyril Collard. Cyril Collard, Romane Bohringer, Carlos Lopez, Corine Blue, Claude Winter, Maria Schneider. Rude, socially irresponsible, in-your-face AIDS movie with raw, subjective power. Collard, who in real life succumbed to the disease just three days before his film swept France's César Awards, plays a bisexual moviemaker/musician who reacts to his biological death warrant by sleeping around unprotected with sassy teenager Bohringer and rugby player Lopez, who are both messed up on their own. Occasionally ugly, but can't be dismissed. Imagine these characters taking over the Dean, Wood, and Mineo roles in REBEL WITHOUT A CAUSE.▼

Savage Pampas (1966-Spanish) **C-100m.** ** D: Hugo Fregonese. Robert Taylor, Ron Randell, Ty Hardin, Rosenda Monteros. Remake of 1946 Argentinian film PAMPA BARBARA. Taylor is rugged army captain combating outlaw Randell whose gang is made up of army deserters. Adequate actioner. Superpanorama 70.▼

Savage Run SEE: **Rocco and His Brothers**

Savage Sam (1963) **C-103m.** **½ D: Norman Tokar. Brian Keith, Tommy Kirk, Kevin Corcoran, Dewey Martin, Jeff York, Royal Dano, Marta Kristen. Sequel to Disney's OLD YELLER has Keith and country neighbors trying to rescue children who've been kidnapped by Indians. Savage Sam, canine son of Old Yeller, helps track down the tribe. Colorful but uneven.▼

Savage Seven, The (1968) **C-96m.** *½ D: Richard Rush. Robert Walker, Jr., Larry Bishop, Adam Roarke, Max Julien, Duane Eddy, Joanna Frank, Penny Marshall. Below-par motorcycle melodrama that lives up to its title but nothing else.▼

Savage Streets (1984) **C-93m.** ** D: Danny Steinmann. Linda Blair, John Vernon, Robert Dryer, Johnny Venocur, Sal Landi. Blair, hilariously miscast as a "nice girl," pits her mild-mannered high school gang against a pack of sadistic tramps. Fairly transcendent trash with a hilariously arty bathtub scene, bravura human torch finale . . . but also features an obscene, gratuitously prolonged rape scene. [R]▼●

Savage Wilderness SEE: **Last Frontier, The** (1956)

Savannah Smiles (1982) **C-107m.** **½ D: Pierre DeMoro. Mark Miller, Donovan Scott, Bridgette Andersen, Peter Graves, Chris Robinson, Michael Parks. A rich little girl (Andersen) runs away from home and reforms criminals. Fair morality tale for kids, written by leading actor Miller. [PG]▼●

Save the Children (1973) **123m.** ***½ D: Stan Lathan. Isaac Hayes, Jackson Five, Sammy Davis, Jr., Nancy Wilson, Roberta Flack, Wilson Pickett, Marvin Gaye, The Temptations, Gladys Knight and The Pips, Bill Withers, many others. All-star music documentary filmed at 1972 exposition in Chicago held by Jesse Jackson's Operation PUSH. Fabulous in-concert performances, including Gaye's "What's Going On," The Temptations' "Papa Was a Rolling Stone," and Withers's "Lean On Me." [G]

Save the Tiger (1973) **C-101m.** ** D: John

G. Avildsen. Jack Lemmon, Jack Gilford, Laurie Heineman, Norman Burton, Patricia Smith, Thayer David, Lara Parker. Pretentious Steve Shagan script about dress manufacturer trying to reconcile hero-worship of his childhood with degradations he submits himself to in business world. Film purports to be totally honest, but phoniness comes through; David has best scenes as professional arsonist. Lemmon won Best Actor Oscar. [R]▼●

Saving Grace (1986) **C-112m.** *½ D: Robert M. Young. Tom Conti, Fernando Rey, Erland Josephson, Giancarlo Giannini, Donald Hewlett, Edward James Olmos, Patricia Mauceri. Youthful Pope Conti, overwhelmed by meaningless duties and a general feeling of uselessness, sneaks incognito out of the Vatican and into a small Italian village that has lost its spirit. If you're going to spin a whopper like this, don't pace it so slowly that the audience has too much time to ponder the improbabilities. Technovision. [PG]▼●

Saving Private Ryan (1998) **C-169m.** ***½ D: Steven Spielberg. Tom Hanks, Edward Burns, Tom Sizemore, Jeremy Davies, Vin Diesel, Adam Goldberg, Barry Pepper, Giovanni Ribisi, Matt Damon, Dennis Farina, Ted Danson, Harve Presnell, Dale Dye, Bryan Cranston, David Wohl, Paul Giamatti, Ryan Hurst, Harrison Young. Trenchant WW2 drama about an Army captain (Hanks) assigned to take his squad of seven men into France, locate a private whose three brothers have been killed in combat . . . and give him a ticket home. Conventional elements in the script are balanced by a genuinely complex examination of heroism in the field, and overpowered by the most realistic, relentlessly harrowing battle footage ever committed to a fiction film. Spielberg (aided immeasurably by cameraman Janusz Kaminski and a superb creative team) has created the ultimate vision of war as hell on earth. Oscars include Best Director, Cinematography, Editing (Michael Kahn). [R]▼●◗

Savior, The (1998) **C-103m.** *** D: Peter Antonijevic. Dennis Quaid, Nastassja Kinski, Stellan Skarsgård, Sergej Trifunovic, Natasa Ninkovic. Earnest drama about a man who, after a personal tragedy, joins the Foreign Legion and winds up as a cold-blooded fighting machine. But when he comes upon a young woman about to give birth in Bosnia, he takes care of her and soon becomes emotionally attached to both the mother and infant. Quaid is excellent. Coproduced by Oliver Stone. Super 35. [R] ▼●◗

Saviors of the Forest (1993) **C-75m.** *** D: Bill Day. Amusingly impudent documentary examination of the complexities involved in rescuing Ecuador's tropical rain forest from extinction. This is no boring, preachy pro-ecology tract, but rather an inventive, knowingly funny look at the innumerable ironies which are an integral part of the save-the-environment issue.

Sawdust and Tinsel (1953-Swedish) **92m.** **** D: Ingmar Bergman. Harriet Andersson, Ake Gronberg, Anders Ek, Gudrun Brost, Hasse Ekman, Annika Tretow. Sparks fly in this beautiful, allegorical film set in a small-time circus and focusing on the relationship between circus owner Gronberg and his oversexed mistress (Andersson). A key credit in Bergman's developing maturity as a filmmaker. Aka THE NAKED NIGHT.▼●

Saxon Charm, The (1948) **88m.** *** D: Claude Binyon. Robert Montgomery, Susan Hayward, John Payne, Audrey Totter, Harry Morgan, Cara Williams, Harry Von Zell, Heather Angel. Well-acted but unconvincing study of ruthless producer, with Montgomery miscast in lead role. Still interesting, with fine work from playwright Payne, wife Hayward, and chanteuse Totter.

Say Amen, Somebody (1982) **C-100m.** **** D: George T. Nierenberg. Willie Mae Ford Smith, Thomas A. Dorsey, Sallie Martin, The Barrett Sisters, The O'Neal Brothers. Wonderful documentary about gospel music and two of its shining stars, "Mother" Willie Mae Ford Smith and "Professor" Thomas Dorsey, that brings us into their lives as well as their careers and demonstrates the power of music sung from the heart. A genuine treat. [G]▼●

Say Anything . . . (1989) **C-100m.** *** D: Cameron Crowe. John Cusack, Ione Skye, John Mahoney, Lili Taylor, Amy Brooks, Pamela Segall, Jason Gould, Loren Dean, Bebe Neuwirth, Eric Stoltz, Chynna Phillips, Joanna Frank. Satisfying teenage comedy-drama about a self-assured loner who goes after the Class Brain, and finds her surprisingly human. Amusing, endearing, and refreshingly original; written by first-time director Crowe. Cusack's real-life sister Joan plays his sister here, and Lois Chiles has a cameo as Skye's mother; both appear unbilled. [PG-13]▼●

Say Hello to Yesterday (1971-British) **C-91m.** *½ D: Alvin Rakoff. Jean Simmons, Leonard Whiting, Evelyn Laye, John Lee, Jack Woolgar, Constance Chapman. Ridiculous plot concerning 40-year-old Simmons' affair with 22-year-old Whiting. Symbolic touches by director Rakoff further shroud purpose of film. [PG]▼

Say It in French (1938) **70m.** ** D: Andrew L. Stone. Ray Milland, Olympe Bradna, Irene Hervey, Janet Beecher, Mary Carlisle, Holmes Herbert, Walter Kingsford. Milland goes to great extremes with wife Bradna and ex-fiancee Hervey to pull father out of the red.

Say It With Songs (1929) **85m.** *½ D: Lloyd Bacon. Al Jolson, Davey Lee, Marian Nixon, Holmes Herbert, Kenneth

Thompson, Fred Kohler, Frank Campeau, John Bowers. Poor script hampers this tearjerker about a radio singer (Jolson) who winds up in prison, leaving behind loving wife Nixon and his son, "Little Pal" (Lee).●

Sayonara (1957) **C-147m.** ***½ D: Joshua Logan. Marlon Brando, Ricardo Montalban, Miiko Taka, Miyoshi Umeki, Red Buttons, Martha Scott, James Garner. Romantic James Michener tale of Korean War pilot Brando falling in love with Japanese entertainer Taka; extremely well acted, with Oscar-winning support from Buttons and Umeki, and statuettes also going to the art direction-set decoration. Theme song by Irving Berlin. Paul Osborn wrote the screenplay. Technirama.▼●

Say One for Me (1959) **C-119m.** *½ D: Frank Tashlin. Debbie Reynolds, Bing Crosby, Robert Wagner, Ray Walston, Les Tremayne, Connie Gilchrist, Stella Stevens, Frank McHugh, Joe Besser, Sebastian Cabot. Bing plays a Broadway priest who gets mixed up with a chorus girl (Debbie) and a TV charity show. Terribly contrived; no memorable music. CinemaScope.

Scalawag (1973) **C-93m.** *½ D: Kirk Douglas. Kirk Douglas, Mark Lester, Don Stroud, Neville Brand, Lesley-Anne Down, Phil Brown, Danny DeVito, voice of Mel Blanc. TREASURE ISLAND goes West in this weak adaptation, with a hammy Kirk as one-legged cutthroat; songs turn up when you least expect them. Filmed in Yugoslavia. [G]

Scalpel (1976) **C-96m.** *½ D: John Grissmer. Robert Lansing, Judith Chapman, Arlen Dean Snyder, David Scarroll, Sandy Martin. Plastic surgeon transforms young woman into image of his long-missing daughter, in order to dupe family out of large inheritance. Lurid, violent drama. Originally released as FALSE FACE. [PG—edited from original R rating]▼

Scalphunters, The (1968) **C-102m.** **½ D: Sydney Pollack. Burt Lancaster, Shelley Winters, Ossie Davis, Telly Savalas, Armando Silvestre, Nick Cravat, Dabney Coleman. Western comedy about a fur trapper and his highly educated slave has its moments, but isn't funny enough, nor exciting enough, nor pointed enough to qualify as all-out success. Cast helps. Panavision.▼

Scam (1993) **C-101m.** ** D: John Flynn. Christopher Walken, Lorraine Bracco, Miguel Ferrer, Martin Donovan, Daniel Von Bargen. Con artist Bracco and greedy ex-fed Walken form a stormy alliance to scam a bundle in underworld cash. This would-be erotic thriller was made for theatrical release but premiered on cable. [R]▼

Scandal (1989) **C-106m.** *** D: Michael Caton-Jones. John Hurt, Joanne Whalley-Kilmer, Bridget Fonda, Ian McKellen, Leslie Phillips, Britt Ekland, Daniel Massey, Roland Gift, Jeroen Krabbé. Absorbing look at the people behind Britain's incredible government-sex scandal of the early '60s, with Whalley-Kilmer just right as impressionable showgirl Christine Keeler, and Hurt outstanding as Stephen Ward, the social gadfly and sexual provocateur who introduces Keeler to Cabinet Minister John Profumo (whose wife, incidentally, was a former film star, Valerie Hobson). Fascinating and credible; a good job by first-time director Michael Caton-Jones. Screenplay by Michael Thomas. Original 114m. British version was trimmed to avoid an X-rating in the U.S. Both versions are available on video. [R]▼●

Scandal at Scourie (1953) **C-90m.** **½ D: Jean Negulesco. Greer Garson, Walter Pidgeon, Donna Corcoran, Agnes Moorehead, Arthur Shields. Tepid Garson-Pidgeon entry set in Canada, involving Protestant couple who shock community when they plan to adopt a Catholic child.

Scandal, Inc. (1956) **79m.** *½ D: Edward Mann. Robert Hutton, Patricia Wright, Paul Richards, Robert Knapp. Sensational-style account of scandal magazines.

Scandal in Paris SEE: **Thieves' Holiday**

Scandal in Sorrento (1957-Italian) **C-92m.** *½ D: Dino Risi. Vittorio De Sica, Sophia Loren, Antonio Cifariello, Tina Pica. Listless sex romp of Loren romancing De Sica to make lover jealous. CinemaScope.

Scandalous (1984) **C-94m.** ** D: Rob Cohen. Robert Hays, John Gielgud, Pamela Stephenson, Jim Dale, M. Emmet Walsh, Bow Wow Wow. Featherbrained farce about investigative TV reporter who runs afoul of team of con artists as he tries to extricate himself from murder charge. Alternately stupid and obnoxious, with Gielgud presumably having fun as a disguise-happy sharpster. [PG]▼●

Scandalous John (1971) **C-113m.** *** D: Robert Butler. Brian Keith, Michele Carey, Rick Lenz, Harry Morgan, Simon Oakland, Alfonso Arau, Bill Williams, Bruce Glover, John Ritter, Iris Adrian. Spirited Disney comedy-Western chronicling what happens when elderly, lovably ornery rancher Keith refuses to sell his land to a developer. Keith's crafty performance as a modern-day Don Quixote gives this one a lift. Panavision. [G]▼

Scandal Sheet (1931) **77m.** **½ D: John Cromwell. George Bancroft, Kay Francis, Clive Brook, Lucien Littlefield, Jackie Searl. Usual triangle with good twist. Editor Bancroft has goods on Brook, the man his wife Francis plans to run off with.

Scandal Sheet (1952) **82m.** *** D: Phil Karlson. Broderick Crawford, Donna Reed, John Derek, Rosemary DeCamp, Henry O'Neill, Henry (Harry) Morgan. Engrossing melodrama about an ambitious editor who accidentally kills his ex-wife, then finds his ace reporters investigating the story. Based on a Samuel Fuller novel.

Scanner Cop (1994-Canadian-U.S.) **C-94m.** **½ D: Pierre David. Daniel Quinn, Darlanne Fluegel, Richard Grove, Mark Rolston, Richard Lynch, Hilary Shepard, James Horan, Gary Hudson, Luca Bercovici, Brion James. Rookie Quinn, a powerful telepath (scanner) since childhood, uses his powers, which might destroy him, to track a renegade scientist who's causing ordinary people to kill cops. Despite logic and acting lapses, an entertaining entry—and welcome change of direction—in the SCANNERS series. [R]▼●

Scanner Cop II: Volkin's Revenge SEE: **Scanners: The Showdown**

Scanners (1981-Canadian) **C-102m.** **½ D: David Cronenberg. Jennifer O'Neill, Stephen Lack, Patrick McGoohan, Lawrence Dane, Charles Shamata. Title refers to superbrains who can read minds and cause others' heads to explode; here, a "good" scanner helps doctors track down a bad one. Rather plodding treatment of interesting idea, aided somewhat by great (if yucky) special effects. Followed by several sequels. [R]▼●

Scanners II: The New Order (1991-Canadian) **C-105m.** ** D: Christian Duguay. David Hewlett, Deborah Raffin, Yvan Ponton, Isabelle Mejias, Tom Butler, Raoul Trujillo. Would-be despotic police officer conspires with scientist to trap "scanners" (people with strong ESP abilities), but complications arise when they confront a scanner with principles. OK for what it is. David Cronenberg had no connection with this sequel to his 1981 film. [R]▼●

Scanners III: The Takeover (1992-Canadian) **C-101m.** BOMB D: Christian Duguay. Liliana Komorowska, Valerie Valois, Daniel Pilon, Collin Fox, Claire Cellucci, Michael Copeman, Steve Parrish. A new drug turns good "scanners" bad, and makes Komorowska into yet another telekinetic megalomaniac. Poorly acted, badly written, plodding trifle reduces evil to mere cruelty, and Cronenberg's original ideas to absurdity. Awful. [R]▼●

Scanners: The Showdown (1994) **C-95m.** **½ D: Steve Barnett. Daniel Quinn, Patrick Kilpatrick, Khrystyne Haje, Stephen Mendel, Robert Forster, Brenda Swanson, Jerry Potter, Jewel Shepard. Evil scanner Kilpatrick returns to L.A. with a new power—he can suck the life out of other scanners—and a lust for revenge on scanner cop Quinn, who sent him to prison. Effective, entertaining sequel to SCANNER COP delivers its goods with solid B-movie skill. Aka SCANNER COP II: VOLKIN'S REVENGE. [R]▼●

Scapegoat, The (1959-British) **92m.** **½ D: Robert Hamer. Alec Guinness, Bette Davis, Nicole Maurey, Irene Worth, Peter Bull, Pamela Brown, Geoffrey Keen. Decent acting rescues a fuzzy script. French gentleman murders his wife, tries to involve his British lookalike in scheme. Davis has small but impressive role as the guilty Guinness' dope-ridden mother. Adapted by Hamer and Gore Vidal from a Daphne du Maurier novel.

Scar, The SEE: **Hollow Triumph**

Scaramouche (1952) **C-118m.** ***½ D: George Sidney. Stewart Granger, Eleanor Parker, Janet Leigh, Mel Ferrer, Henry Wilcoxon, Lewis Stone, Nina Foch, Richard Anderson, Robert Coote. Excellent cast in roaring adaptation of Sabatini novel of illustrious cynic who sets out to avenge friend's death, set in 18th-century France. Impeccably done. Highlight is climactic sword duel—the longest in swashbuckling history. Screenplay by Ronald Millar and George Froeschel. Filmed before in 1923. ▼●

Scarecrow (1973) **C-115m.** *** D: Jerry Schatzberg. Gene Hackman, Al Pacino, Dorothy Tristan, Eileen Brennan, Ann Wedgeworth, Richard Lynch. Drifter Hackman, who wants to start car-wash business, meets drifter Pacino, who has abandoned his wife. Moody, not altogether successful tale benefits from top performances and photography (by Vilmos Zsigmond), plus good use of locations. Panavision. [R]▼●

Scarecrow, The (1982-New Zealand) **C-87m.** **½ D: Sam Pillsbury. Jonathan Smith, Daniel McLaren, John Carradine, Tracy Mann, Anne Flannery, Des Kelly. Adequate thriller about a small-town New Zealand teen who must deal with both a rival bully and a crazed killer. Adapted from Ronald Hugh Morrieson's novel. [PG]

Scared Stiff (1945) **65m.** *½ D: Frank McDonald. Jack Haley, Ann Savage, Barton MacLane, Veda Ann Borg, Roger Pryor, George E. Stone, Lucien Littlefield. Inane comedy-chiller with Haley cast as an addle-brained reporter who becomes involved in a murder mystery and search for stolen antique chess pieces. Aka TREASURE OF FEAR.▼

Scared Stiff (1953) **108m.** **½ D: George Marshall. Dean Martin, Jerry Lewis, Lizabeth Scott, Carmen Miranda, Dorothy Malone. Usual Martin and Lewis hijinks with duo on spooky Caribbean island inherited by Scott; Jerry and Carmen make a wild team. Remake of Bob Hope's GHOST BREAKERS.▼●

Scared to Death (1947) **C-65m.** *½ D: Christy Cabanne. Bela Lugosi, Douglas Fowley, Joyce Compton, George Zucco, Nat Pendleton, Angelo Rossitto, Molly Lamont. Lugosi's only color film is a dreadful, cheaply made chiller. Told from the point of view of a beautiful murder victim, chronicling how she came to meet her demise. Lugosi plays Leonide, a hypnotist.▼●◗

Scarf, The (1951) **93m.** **½ D: E. A. Dupont. John Ireland, Mercedes McCambridge, Emlyn Williams, James Barton. Capably handled drama of Ireland trying to prove his innocence of murder charge.

Scarface (1932) **90m.** ***½ D: Howard Hawks. Paul Muni, Ann Dvorak, George Raft, Boris Karloff, Karen Morley, Vince Barnett, Osgood Perkins, C. Henry Gordon. Powerful gangster film is the most potent of the 1930s, with Muni delivering emotionally charged performance as Caponelike mobster with more than just a soft spot for his sister (Dvorak). Raw, harsh, and brimming with unsubtle symbolism; five writers include Ben Hecht and W.R. Burnett. Filmed in 1931, release delayed by censors. The full title is SCARFACE, THE SHAME OF THE NATION. Remade in 1983.▼●

Scarface (1983) **C-170m.** *½ D: Brian De Palma. Al Pacino, Steven Bauer, Michelle Pfeiffer, Mary Elizabeth Mastrantonio, Robert Loggia, Miriam Colon, F. Murray Abraham, Paul Shenar, Harris Yulin. 1932 gangster movie updated by making lead character a Cuban refugee in Miami, and changing profession from bootlegging to drug-dealing . . . but this film wallows in excess and unpleasantness for nearly *three hours,* and offers no new insights except that crime doesn't pay. At least the 1932 movie *moved.* Screenplay by Oliver Stone. Panavision. [R]▼●◗

Scarface Mob, The (1962) **102m.** **½ D: Phil Karlson. Robert Stack, Keenan Wynn, Barbara Nichols, Pat Crowley, Neville Brand, Bruce Gordon. Feature version of a two-part *Desilu Playhouse* from 1959 that led to the hugely popular *Untouchables* TV series with Stack as racket-buster Eliot Ness, who sets out to break Chicago's underworld kingpin Al Capone. Still pretty potent (especially by TV standards) and blessed with the inimitable staccato narration of Walter Winchell.▼

Scarlet Angel (1952) **C-80m.** **½ D: Sidney Salkow. Yvonne De Carlo, Rock Hudson, Richard Denning, Amanda Blake. Neat little drama set in 1860 New Orleans, with De Carlo the dance-hall girl who assumes a dead woman's identity and goes West to stay with wealthy in-laws.

Scarlet Blade, The SEE: **Crimson Blade, The**

Scarlet Claw, The (1944) **74m.** ***½ D: Roy William Neill. Basil Rathbone, Nigel Bruce, Gerald Hamer, Arthur Hohl, Miles Mander, Ian Wolfe, Paul Cavanagh, Kay Harding. The ominous marshes of a French-Canadian village provide the setting for gruesome mutilation murders in this excellent *Sherlock Holmes* mystery, moodily photographed by George Robinson. Clearly the best of the series.▼

Scarlet Clue, The (1945) **65m.** ** D: Phil Rosen. Sidney Toler, Benson Fong, Mantan Moreland, Helen Deveraux, Robert Homans, Virginia Brissac, Jack Norton, Stanford Jolley. One of the more bearable Monogram *Charlie Chan* entries, with Toler after spies who have stolen radar plans.▼●

Scarlet Coat, The (1955) **C-101m.** **½ D: John Sturges. Cornel Wilde, Michael Wilding, George Sanders, Anne Francis, Bobby Driscoll. Plucky costumer livened by cast and bright photography; set in colonial America, dealing with Benedict Arnold spy caper. CinemaScope.

Scarlet Dawn (1932) **76m.** ** D: William Dieterle. Douglas Fairbanks, Jr., Nancy Carroll, Earle Fox, Lilyan Tashman, Sheila Terry, Betty Gillette, Frank Reicher, Arnold Korff, Guy Kibbee, Mae Busch. Fairbanks, a dashing officer in the Czar's army, is forced to flee after the Russian revolution in the company of his former servant (Carroll), whom he tries to seduce—and winds up marrying. Fairly interesting oddity, boosted by its attractive stars and an unusually handsome production.▼

Scarlet Empress, The (1934) **110m.** *** D: Josef von Sternberg. Marlene Dietrich, John Lodge, Louise Dresser, Sam Jaffe, C. Aubrey Smith, Edward Van Sloan. Von Sternberg tells the story of Catherine the Great and her rise to power in uniquely ornate fashion, with stunning lighting and camerawork and fiery Russian music. It's a visual orgy; dramatically uneven, but cinematically fascinating.▼

Scarlet Hour, The (1956) **95m.** ** D: Michael Curtiz. Carol Ohmart, Tom Tryon, Jody Lawrance, James Gregory, Elaine Stritch, E. G. Marshall, Edward Binns. Sluggish study of marital discord leading to murder. VistaVision.

Scarlet Letter, The (1926) **80m.** *** D: Victor Seastrom. Lillian Gish, Lars Hanson, Henry B. Walthall, Karl Dane, William H. Tooker, Marcelle Corday. Excellent, though liberal, adaptation of Hawthorne classic about Hester Prynne (Gish) who bears scar of adultery in Salem, having had clandestine affair with minister Hanson. Filmed several times in the silent era, and in 1934, 1973, 1979 (for TV) and 1995.

Scarlet Letter, The (1934) **70m.** ** D: Robert G. Vignola. Colleen Moore, Hardie Albright, Henry B. Walthall, Cora Sue Collins, Alan Hale, Virginia Howell, William Farnum, Betty Blythe. Slow, poorly directed, though not uninteresting version of the Nathaniel Hawthorne novel. Moore is miscast as Hester Prynne; Walthall repeats his role from the 1926 version as Roger Prynne. A real curio. ▼

Scarlet Letter, The (1973-German) **C-90m.** *** D: Wim Wenders. Senta Berger,

Lou Castel, Hans-Christian Blech, Yella Rottlander, Yelina Samarina, William Layton. Absorbing version of the oft-filmed Hawthorne classic, with Berger as Hester Prynne, Blech as Roger Prynne, and Castel as Rev. Dimmesdale. While it lacks the spontaneity of Wenders' other early films, there is much to ponder and relish here: in particular, Wenders' portrayal of the immigrant New England settlers. Remade in 1995. Filmed in Spain.▼

Scarlet Letter, The (1995) **C-135m.** BOMB D: Roland Joffé. Demi Moore, Gary Oldman, Robert Duvall, Joan Plowright, Robert Prosky, Edward Hardwicke, Roy Dotrice, Dana Ivey, George Aguilar, Amy Wright, Diane Salinger, Eric Schweig, voice of Jodhi May. Hokey adaptation of Nathaniel Hawthorne's classic novel throws in everything from witch hunts to Indian attacks to a controversial happy ending—all to no avail. Moore is woefully miscast as Hester Prynne (though she sure fills a Puritan frock), Oldman gives a histrionic performance, while Duvall is simply incomprehensible. "Erotic" love scenes are especially embarrassing, in soft-focus with phallic candles and a chirpy Disney bird (credited as Rudy the Robin) who sings for sexual freedom! J-D-C Scope. [R]▼●

Scarlet Pimpernel, The (1935-British) **95m.** ***½ D: Harold Young. Leslie Howard, Merle Oberon, Raymond Massey, Nigel Bruce, Bramwell Fletcher, Anthony Bushell, Joan Gardner, Melville Cooper. Excellent costumer with Howard leading double life, aiding innocent victims of French revolution while posing as foppish member of British society. Baroness Orczy's novel was scripted by Robert E. Sherwood, Sam Berman, Arthur Wimperis, and Lajos Biro; produced by Alexander Korda. Remade for TV in 1982. Also shown in computer-colored version. ▼●◗

Scarlet Street (1945) **103m.** *** D: Fritz Lang. Edward G. Robinson, Joan Bennett, Dan Duryea, Margaret Lindsay, Rosalind Ivan. Meek, henpecked Robinson is pulled into world of crime and deception by seductive Bennett and her manipulative boyfriend Duryea. Stars and director of WOMAN IN THE WINDOW keep it interesting, but don't match earlier film. Dudley Nichols adapted this remake of Jean Renoir's LA CHIENNE. Also shown in computer-colored version. ▼

Scars of Dracula (1970-British) **C-94m.** *** D: Roy Ward Baker. Christopher Lee, Dennis Waterman, Jenny Hanley, Christopher Matthews, Wendy Hamilton. Good fang work as young couple tangles with Dracula in search of the young man's missing brother. Last of Hammer's period Draculas; followed by DRACULA A.D. 1972. [R]▼●

Scavenger Hunt (1979) **C-117m.** BOMB D: Michael Schultz. Richard Benjamin, James Coco, Scatman Crothers, Ruth Gordon, Cloris Leachman, Cleavon Little, Roddy McDowall, Robert Morley, Richard Mulligan, Tony Randall, Dirk Benedict, Willie Aames, Stephanie Faracy, Meat Loaf, Carol Wayne, Arnold Schwarzenegger. Vincent Price dies, and his relatives and servants are practically forced to kill each other for his inheritance by collecting commodes, wild animals, etc. in an allotted time. Hard to believe a comedy with so much talent could misfire so greatly, but it does; only Mulligan manages to get some laughs. [PG]▼

Scene of the Crime (1949) **94m.** ** D: Roy Rowland. Van Johnson, Arlene Dahl, Gloria DeHaven, Tom Drake, Leon Ames. Bland detective whodunit, with Johnson a cop trying to solve police murder.

Scene of the Crime (1986-French) **C-90m.** *** D: André Téchiné. Catherine Deneuve, Danielle Darrieux, Wadeck Stanczak, Nicholas Giraudi, Victor Lanoux, Jean Bousquet, Claire Nebout. Stylish, Chabrol–like drama about an unhappy young boy (Giraudi), his equally unhappy mother (Deneuve), and what results when escaped convict Stanczak invades their lives. Entertaining, perceptive, if occasionally uneven examination of repression and desperation.▼

Scenes From a Mall (1991) **C-87m.** ** D: Paul Mazursky. Bette Midler, Woody Allen, Bill Irwin, Daren Firestone, Rebecca Nickels, Paul Mazursky. Affluent L.A. couple, celebrating their anniversary, spend the day together at a mall, where various revelations cause their marriage to unravel. Bette and Woody make a terrific couple, but after a promising start the seriocomic script takes some strange turns and leaves reality behind. Fans of the stars should take a look, but this one ranks as a major disappointment. [R]▼●

Scenes From a Marriage (1973-Swedish) **C-168m.** **** D: Ingmar Bergman. Liv Ullmann, Erland Josephson, Bibi Andersson, Jan Malmsjo, Anita Wall. Passionate, probing and honest look at a marriage, its disintegration, and the relationship that follows. Ullmann and Josephson are remarkable throughout this intimate and often painful portrait, originally made as six TV episodes and edited into feature-length by writer-director Bergman. [PG]▼

Scenes From a Murder (1972-Italian) **C-90m.** ** D: Alberto DeMartino. Telly Savalas, Anne Heywood, Giorgio Piazza, Osvaldo Ruggeri, Rossella Falk. Murder and mayhem in the theater world with Savalas stalking an actress (Heywood) whose lover he has killed. Limp thriller.▼

Scenes From the Class Struggle in Beverly Hills (1989) **C-102m.** *½ D: Paul Bartel. Jacqueline Bisset, Ray Sharkey, Mary Woronov, Robert Beltran, Ed Begley,

Jr., Wallace Shawn, Arnetia Walker, Paul Bartel, Paul Mazursky, Rebecca Schaeffer. Bizarre, scattershot sex romp with various characters of various classes playing musical beds in Beverly Hills. Tries to be outrageous and irreverent while satirizing L.A. types and lifestyles, but mostly inane, veering uncomfortably between drama and farce. The best thing about this is its title. [R]▼●

Scent of a Woman (1974-Italian) **C-104m.** *** D: Dino Risi. Vittorio Gassman, Alessandro Momo, Agostina Belli. Blind, arrogant army captain Gassman galavants through Italy, sensing the presence of attractive women along the way; hapless private Momo is his guide on this fateful trip. Gassman shines in this sharply observed black comedy-drama, based on a novel by Giovanni Arpino. Remade in the U.S. in 1992. Original Italian title: PROFUMO DI DONNA. [R]▼

Scent of a Woman (1992) **C-157m.** **½ D: Martin Brest. Al Pacino, Chris O'Donnell, James Rebhorn, Gabrielle Anwar, Philip S. (Seymour) Hoffman, Richard Venture, Bradley Whitford, Rochelle Oliver, Frances Conroy. Timid prep school student earns much-needed money on a long weekend taking a job as companion to crusty, blind, hard-drinking ex-Army colonel—little dreaming the colonel has his own agenda. Enjoyable (if barely believable) story galvanized by Pacino's bravura, Oscar-winning performance. Bo Goldman's script is seriously weakened by a story appendage that plays like leftover material from DEAD POETS SOCIETY. Based on the 1974 Italian film PROFUMO DI DONNA. [R] ▼●◗

Scent of Green Papaya, The (1993-French-Vietnamese) **C-104m.** *** D: Hung Tran Anh. Tran Nu Yen-Khe, Lu Man San, Truong Thi Loc, Nguyen Anh Hoa, Vuong Hoa Hoi. Thoughtful, carefully observed drama about a ten-year-old servant girl who comes to work in a Saigon household in 1951; the scenario details her relationships with the various household members and concludes a decade later with her growing into a beautiful young woman. Unhurried in its execution and filled with lingering shots, the film is as captivating as its title.▼●

Schindler's List (1993) **C/B&W-195m.** **** D: Steven Spielberg. Liam Neeson, Ben Kingsley, Ralph Fiennes, Caroline Goodall, Jonathan Sagalle, Embeth Davidtz, Malgoscha Gebel, Shmulik Levy, Mark Ivanir, Beatrice Macola. Staggering adaptation of Thomas Keneally's best-seller about the real-life Catholic war profiteer who initially flourished by sucking up to the Nazis, but eventually went broke saving the lives of more than 1,000 Polish Jews by employing them in his factory, manufacturing crockery for the German army. Filmed almost entirely on location in Poland, in gritty b&w, but with a pace to match the most frenzied Spielberg works, this looks and feels like nothing Hollywood has ever made before. The three central characters rate—and receive—unforgettable performances: Neeson, who's towering as Oskar Schindler; Kingsley, superb as his Jewish accountant (and conscience); and Fiennes, who's frightening as the odious Nazi commandant. Outstanding screenplay by Steven Zaillian and cinematography by Janusz Kaminski. Spielberg's most intense and personal film to date. Seven Oscars include Best Picture, Director, Adapted Screenplay, Art Direction, Cinematography, Editing, and Original Score (John Williams). [R] ▼●

Schizoid (1980) **C-91m.** BOMB D: David Paulsen. Klaus Kinski, Marianna Hill, Craig Wasson, Donna Wilkes, Richard Herd, Christopher Lloyd. Kinski's group therapy patients are mysteriously being knocked off. Lurid shocker. [R]▼

Schizopolis (1997) **C-99m.** *** D: Steven Soderbergh. Steven Soderbergh, Betsy Brantley, David Jensen. Giddy mélange of surrealism, satire, silliness, and old-fashioned underground filmmaking written, directed by, and starring Soderbergh. A broad-ranging jab at modern society and its ills, its tone is arch, its technique one of non sequiturs, and its audience likely to be small. But if you latch onto it early enough, you may find (as we did) that it's fun—and funny—to watch.▼

Schlock (1971) **C-80m.** **½ D: John Landis. Saul Kahan, Joseph Piantadosi, Eliza Garrett, John Landis. Landis' first film is enjoyable spoof of B-horror flicks; director (in gorilla suit by Rick Baker) plays missing link on the loose in small town. Many in-jokes for film buffs. Aka THE BANANA MONSTER. [PG]▼

School Daze (1988) **C-114m.** **½ D: Spike Lee. Larry Fishburne, Giancarlo Esposito, Tisha Campbell, Kyme, Joe Seneca, Art Evans, Ellen Holly, Ossie Davis, Bill Nunn, Branford Marsalis, Kadeem Hardison, Spike Lee, Darryl M. Bell, Joie Lee, Tyra Ferrell, Jasmine Guy, Gregg Burge, Kasi Lemmons, Samuel L. Jackson, Phyllis Hyman. Comedy-cum-fantasy about life on a black college campus in the South, where one self-serious student activist fights a lonely battle not only against the administration, but the pervasive mindlessness of his fellow students, most of whom are wrapped up in fraternity and sorority nonsense. Writer-director-costar Lee offers much entertainment and some provocative ideas, though he doesn't follow up on his initial premise until the anticlimactic final scene. [R]▼●

School for Love (1955-French) **72m.** ** D: Marc Allégret. Jean Marais, Brigitte Bardot, Isabelle Pia, Mischa Auer. Occasionally sensual flick with Bardot and Pia competing for Marais' affection. Original title: FUTERES VEDETTES. Retitled: JOY OF LOVING.

School for Scoundrels (1960-British) **94m.** *** D: Robert Hamer. Ian Carmichael, Terry-Thomas, Janette Scott, Alastair Sim, Dennis Price, Peter Jones, Edward Chapman. Wimpy Carmichael, about to lose the girl of his dreams to pushy Thomas, attends the title institute, where he learns "one-upmanship" and "gamesmanship." Clever, funny, veddy British satire.▼

School for Unclaimed Girls (1969-British) **C-95m.** ** D: Robert Hartford-Davis. Madeline Hinde, Renee Asherson, Dennis Waterman, Maureen Lipman, Lesley-Anne Down. Hinde is sent to reform school after killing her mom's boyfriend. Unusual British entry in the cycle of women's prison films features a moving performance by Lipman as a fellow prisoner. U.S. release in 1973. Originally titled THE SMASHING BIRD I USED TO KNOW; aka HOUSE OF UNCLAIMED WOMEN. [R]

School of Flesh, The (1998-French) **C-107m.** **½ D: Benoit Jacquot. Isabelle Huppert, Vincent Martinez, Vincent Lindon, Marthe Keller, François Berléand, Danièle Dubroux, Bernard LeCoq. The always-watchable Huppert plays a well-to-do 40-ish woman who, against her better judgment, falls into an obsessive relationship with a young stud (Martinez) whom she meets at a bar in Paris. Candid examination of relationships is unmemorable, but benefits from star charisma. Based on the novel by Yukio Mishima. Panavision. [R]▼◗

School That Ate My Brain, The SEE: **Zombie High**

School Ties (1992) **C-107m.** **½ D: Robert Mandel. Brendan Fraser, Matt Damon, Chris O'Donnell, Randall Batinkoff, Andrew Lowery, Cole Hauser, Amy Locane, Zeljko Ivanek, Kevin Tighe, Ed Lauter, Peter Donat, Michael Higgins, Ben Affleck, Anthony Rapp. In the 1950s, a Jewish student (well played by Fraser) with working-class roots wins a football scholarship to a snooty prep school, where he's victimized by anti-Semitism. Youth-oriented film tackles an important subject, but it's strained and obvious. [PG-13]▼●◗

Scissors (1991) **C-105m.** ** D: Frank De Felitta. Sharon Stone, Steve Railsback, Ronny Cox, Michelle Phillips. Sexually traumatized Stone is driven mad—à la GASLIGHT—by objects that seemingly come to life in her apartment. Unfortunately, Stone is forced to carry off these histrionics in a generally lifeless, slow-moving production. Interesting idea could have been better executed (no pun intended). [R]▼●

Scorchy (1976) **C-99m.** *½ D: Hikmet Avedis. Connie Stevens, Cesare Danova, William Smith, Marlene Schmidt, Normann Burton, Joyce Jameson, Greg Evigan. Tawdry actioner with Stevens as Seattle undercover cop who sets out to bust high-level drug ring. Plenty of action and gore. [R]▼

Scorpio (1973) **C-114m.** **½ D: Michael Winner. Burt Lancaster, Alain Delon, Gayle Hunnicutt, Paul Scofield, John Colicos, J. D. Cannon, Joanne Linville. Tough espionage film of CIA agent in trouble, and hired killer who wants to go straight but finds himself caught in the system. Good action, dialogue amid familiar trappings. [PG]▼●◗

Scotland Yard Inspector (1952-British) **73m.** ** D: Sam Newfield. Cesar Romero, Lois Maxwell, Bernadette O'Farrell, Geoffrey Keen, Alistair Hunter, Peter Swanwick. Run-of-the-mill actioner with Romero assisting Maxwell in capturing her brother's killer.

Scotland Yard Investigator (1945) **68m.** ** D: George Blair. C. Aubrey Smith, Erich von Stroheim, Stephanie Bachelor, Forrester Harvey, Doris Lloyd, Eva Moore. Low-budget mystery wastes two leading players in routine art-theft tale.

Scott Joplin (1977) **C-96m.** **½ D: Jeremy Paul Kagan. Billy Dee Williams, Clifton Davis, Godfrey Cambridge, Art Carney, Seymour Cassel, Eubie Blake, Margaret Avery, Sam Fuller. Well-made, colorful but down-beat life story of famed ragtime composer. Made for TV, then given fitful theatrical release. Best sequence: the barrel-house piano "duel." [PG]

Scott of the Antarctic (1948-British) **C-110m.** **½ D: Charles Frend. John Mills, Derek Bond, Harold Warrender, James Robertson Justice, Reginald Beckwith, Kenneth More, John Gregson, Christopher Lee. Unrelenting docudrama of determined British explorer Robert Falcon Scott (Mills), highlighting the details of his last expedition to the South Pole. This saga of bravery and endurance features an especially moving finale. Music by Vaughn Williams, who later used part of this score in his seventh symphony. ▼

Scoundrel, The (1935) **78m.** *** D: Ben Hecht, Charles MacArthur. Noel Coward, Julie Haydon, Stanley Ridges, Martha Sleeper, Ernest Cossart, Eduardo Ciannelli, Alexander Woollcott, Lionel Stander. Fascinating Hecht-MacArthur original about a cynical, self-centered N.Y.C. publisher who toys with other people's lives—until his own existence is put on the line. Bizarre, sophisticated, indulgent—and unique. Coward, in his first starring film, puts over a challenging and unusual role. Famed critic/curmudgeon Woollcott plays one of the hangers-on, while Hecht and MacArthur have a funny flop-house cameo. Academy Award winner for Best Original Story.

Scoundrel in White SEE: **High Heels** (1972)

Scout, The (1994) **C-107m.** ** D: Michael Ritchie. Albert Brooks, Brendan Fraser, Dianne Wiest, Anne Twomey, Lane Smith, Michael Rapaport, Tony Bennett, George Steinbrenner, Marcia Rodd. Woefully disappointing baseball yarn, with Brooks as a hard-luck N.Y. Yankees scout who finds a powerhouse pitcher and batter . . . with some serious psychological problems. Funny at first, with Brooks in good form; then takes a sharp left turn toward drama and never recovers. Brooks cowrote the final screenplay (based on an article by Roger Angell) with partner Monica Johnson. Many ball-players and sportscasters appear as themselves. [PG-13]▼●

Scream (1983) **C-81m.** BOMB D: Byron Quisenberry. Pepper Martin, Hank Worden, Alvy Moore, (John) Ethan Wayne, Julie Marine, Gregg Palmer, Woody Strode, Bobby Diamond. Boring tale of a group of people hiking through a Western ghost town, each of whom is killed off. Poor in all departments. Wayne is the son of John. Filmed in 1981. Aka THE OUTING. [R]▼

Scream (1996) **C-110m.** *** D: Wes Craven. Neve Campbell, Skeet Ulrich, Drew Barrymore, Rose McGowan, Matthew Lillard, Jamie Kennedy, Courteney Cox, David Arquette, Liev Schreiber, Linda Blair. Murderer, obsessed with horror movies, begins slaughtering teens in a small city just a year after Campbell's mother was murdered—and the killer seems to be targeting people she knows. Well-drawn characters, suspenseful situations, several plot twists and entertaining movie references highlight this snappy horror thriller, one of Craven's best. Henry Winkler appears unbilled. Followed by two sequels. Panavision. [R]▼●◗

Scream 2 (1997) **C-120m.** **½ D: Wes Craven. David Arquette, Neve Campbell, Courteney Cox, Sarah Michelle Gellar, Jamie Kennedy, Laurie Metcalf, Elise Neal, Jerry O'Connell, Timothy Olyphant, Jada Pinkett, Liev Schreiber, Lewis Arquette, Duane Martin, Rebecca Gayheart, Portia de Rossi, Omar Epps, David Warner, Heather Graham, Kevin Williamson. Valiant survivor Campbell is in college when STAB, a movie based on the murder spree depicted in SCREAM, is released—and more murders begin. As good a sequel as the filmmakers could have done; it's only the climactic showdown that disappoints. As in the first film, there are plenty of slashes and scares, as well as humor. Panavision. [R]▼●◗

Scream 3 (2000) **C-116m.** **½ D: Wes Craven. David Arquette, Neve Campbell, Courteney Cox Arquette, Patrick Dempsey, Scott Foley, Lance Henriksen, Matt Keeslar, Jenny McCarthy, Emily Mortimer, Parker Posey, Deon Richmond, Patrick Warburton, Liev Schreiber, Jamie Kennedy, Kelly Rutherford, Josh Pais, Heather Matarazzo, Roger Corman. ''Finale'' of the SCREAM trilogy, set in Hollywood on the soundstages of STAB 3: RETURN TO WOODSBORO. Several actors (Posey, Keeslar, etc.) play ''stars'' who are portraying your SCREAM favorites. Wonder who's trying to slice them up, one by one? Fun for fans, with some choice cameos. Panavision. [R]▼◗

Scream and Scream Again (1970-British) **C-95m.** **½ D: Gordon Hessler. Vincent Price, Christopher Lee, Peter Cushing, Judy Huxtable, Alfred Marks, Peter Sallis. Distinguished cast does their darnedest to enliven (no pun intended) tired, confusing plot concerning mad scientist's organ/limbs experiments and race of emotionless beings he creates. [M/PG]▼●

Scream, Blacula, Scream! (1973) **C-95m.** ** D: Bob Kelljan. William Marshall, Don Mitchell, Pam Grier, Michael Conrad, Richard Lawson. Poor sequel to BLACULA finds black vampire recalled from eternal rest and forced to go out and nibble again in contemporary black U.S. [PG]▼

Screamers (1995-Canadian) **C-107m.** **½ D: Christian Duguay. Peter Weller, Roy Dupuis, Jennifer Rubin, Andy Lauer, Charles Powell, Ron White, Michael Caloz, Liliana Komorowska. 2078: War has devastated a distant planet; the few human survivors are pitted against ''Screamers,'' self-evolving robots programed to kill. Now the Screamers are able to look exactly like human beings. Intelligent sci-fi action thriller is undermined by a bad ending. Cowritten by Dan O'Bannon; based on the short story ''Second Variety'' by Philip K. Dick. [R]▼●◗

Screaming Eagles (1956) **81m.** ** D: Charles Haas. Tom Tryon, Jan Merlin, Alvy Moore, Martin Milner, Jacqueline Beer. Routine WW2 film focusing on D-Day.

Screaming Mimi (1958) **79m.** ** D: Gerd Oswald. Anita Ekberg, Phil Carey, Harry Townes, Gypsy Rose Lee, Romney Brent, Red Norvo. Lurid low-budget melodrama about a woman who cracks up after being assaulted, takes a job as exotic dancer in Lee's nightclub but remains under the influence of a possessive psychiatrist. Strange, kinky film that sounds more interesting than it really is.

Scream of Fear (1961-British) **81m.** *** D: Seth Holt. Susan Strasberg, Christopher Lee, Ann Todd, Ronald Lewis. Only wheelchair-bound Strasberg sees her father's corpse—while stepmom Todd insists he's on a trip. Good Hammer thriller written by Jimmy Sangster. Original British title: TASTE OF FEAR.▼

Screwed (2000) **C-81m.** BOMB D: Scott Alexander, Larry Karaszewski. Norm Macdonald, Dave Chappelle, Elaine Stritch, Danny DeVito, Daniel Benzali, Sherman Hemsley. Title describes your inevitable state if you waste just two minutes watching this woeful attempt to revive screwball slapstick. Chauffeur Macdonald works for a stingy baking tycoon (Stritch) who won't even buy him a uniform—so he decides to kidnap her attack-mode pet dog and hold it for ransom. Movie tries everything—even making DeVito a mortician who's also vice-president of Jack Lord's fan club—but fizzles for the duration. Directing debut for the writers of ED WOOD and THE PEOPLE VS. LARRY FLYNT. [PG-13]▼◗

Scrooge (1935-British) **78m.** **½ D: Henry Edwards. Sir Seymour Hicks, Donald Calthrop, Robert Cochran, Mary Glynne, Oscar Asche, Maurice Evans. Faithful adaptation of *A Christmas Carol*, with an impressive Sir Seymour (who also cowrote the script) as Scrooge. Dickens' era brought colorfully to life.▼

Scrooge (1970-British) **C-118m.** *** D: Ronald Neame. Albert Finney, Alec Guinness, Edith Evans, Kenneth More, Lawrence Naismith, Michael Medwin, David Collings, Gordon Jackson, Roy Kinnear, Kay Walsh. Handsome musicalization of Dickens' *A Christmas Carol*, with Finney genially hamming it up in the title role and Guinness a surprisingly fey Marley's Ghost. Leslie Bricusse's score is pretty forgettable, save effervescent "Thank You Very Much"; lovely sets by Terry Marsh and evocative title design by Ronald Searle. Panavision. [G]▼●

Scrooged (1988) **C-101m.** ** D: Richard Donner. Bill Murray, Karen Allen, John Forsythe, John Glover, Bobcat Goldthwait, David Johansen (Buster Poindexter), Carol Kane, Robert Mitchum, Nicholas Phillips, Michael J. Pollard, Alfre Woodard, Mabel King, John Murray, Brian Doyle-Murray. Ostensibly a hip, funny rereading of Dickens' *A Christmas Carol*, with Murray as a venal TV executive. The laughs are mild and widely scattered, and toward the end the film seems to want us to take its brotherhood message seriously. Or does it? Features a variety of "guest stars." [PG-13]▼●◗

Scrubbers (1982-British) **C-90m.** ** D: Mai Zetterling. Chrissie Cotterill, Amanda York, Elizabeth Edmonds, Kate Ingram, Kathy Burke. Life in a teenage girls' borstal (reform school), complete with heartbreak, cruelty, lesbianism, suicide. Harrowing but repetitious, and the hows and whys of the girls' anger is never explored. [R]▼

Scudda Hoo! Scudda Hay! (1948) **C-95m.** ** D: F. Hugh Herbert. June Haver, Lon McCallister, Walter Brennan, Anne Revere, Natalie Wood. Any film with a title like that can't be all good, and it isn't; McCallister's life is devoted to two mules. Marilyn Monroe can be glimpsed in a canoe—it's her first film appearance.

Scum (1980-British) **C-98m.** **½ D: Alan Clarke. Ray Winstone, Mick Ford, John Judd, Phil Daniels, John Blundell, Ray Burdis, Julian Firth. The horrors of a borstal (British reform school). Harrowing but familiar; the accents are almost unintelligible. An earlier TV version was commissioned, then banned by the BBC. [R]▼

Sea Around Us, The (1953) **C-61m.** *** Produced by Irwin Allen. Narrated by Don Forbes. Academy Award-winning documentary based on Rachel Carson's study of the history of the ocean, its fauna and life.▼

Sea Chase, The (1955) **C-117m.** **½ D: John Farrow. John Wayne, Lana Turner, Tab Hunter, David Farrar, Lyle Bettger, James Arness, Claude Akins. Strange WW2 film, with Wayne as German (!) captain of fugitive ship with unusual cargo, assorted crew, plus passenger/girlfriend Turner. CinemaScope.▼●

Sea Devils (1937) **88m.** ** D: Ben Stoloff. Victor McLaglen, Preston Foster, Ida Lupino, Donald Woods, Helen Flint, Gordon Jones. One of those brawling-can-be-fun formula films, with McLaglen and Foster as Coast Guard rivals and McLaglen's daughter (Lupino) a focal point of further conflict. Filmed and acted with zest, but script's stupidities all but sink it.▼

Sea Devils (1953-British) **C-91m.** ** D: Raoul Walsh. Yvonne De Carlo, Rock Hudson, Maxwell Reed, Denis O'Dea, Michael Goodliffe, Bryan Forbes. Smuggler Hudson becomes involved in the activities of British spy De Carlo in this unmemorable programmer set in the Napoleonic era. Filmed on and around the Channel Islands.▼

Sea Fury (1958-British) **72m.** ** D: C. Raker Endfield. Stanley Baker, Victor McLaglen, Luciana Paluzzi, Gregoire Aslan, Francis de Wolff, Percy Herbert, Rupert Davies, Robert Shaw. Tug captain McLaglen is set to wed Paluzzi, but she's attracted to first mate Baker. Routine romantic adventure. Original running time: 97m.

Sea Gull, The (1968-British) **C-141m.** **½ D: Sidney Lumet. James Mason, Vanessa Redgrave, Simone Signoret, David Warner, Harry Andrews, Eileen Herlie, Denholm Elliott. Tasteful but reverentially slow-moving transcription of Chekhov play. Signoret's accent becomes rather disconcerting among British players, all trying to be 19th-century Russians. [G]

Sea Gypsies, The (1978) **C-101m.** *** D: Stewart Raffill. Robert Logan, Heather Rattray, Mikki Jamison-Olsen, Shannon Saylor, Cjon Damitri Patterson. Nice family adventure has Logan sailing round the world with daughters, journalist Jamison-Olsen, and little stowaway Patterson, learning to survive when shipwrecked in Alaska. Fine location filming. [G]▼

Sea Hawk, The (1924) **123m.** *** D: Frank Lloyd. Milton Sills, Enid Bennett, Lloyd

Hughes, Wallace MacDonald, Marc MacDermott, Wallace Beery, William Collier, Jr. Grandly entertaining, faithful adaptation of Rafael Sabatini's 1915 novel about an English nobleman who's sold into slavery on a sea galley; in time, he reinvents himself as Sakh-el-Bahr, The Hawk of the Sea. Ship and sea battle footage is vivid and convincing. Sills' stardom peaked with this film. Remade in 1940.
Sea Hawk, The (1940) **127m.** **** D: Michael Curtiz. Errol Flynn, Brenda Marshall, Claude Rains, Donald Crisp, Flora Robson, Alan Hale, Henry Daniell, Una O'Connor, Gilbert Roland. Top-notch combination of classy Warner Bros. costumer and Flynn at his dashing best in adventure on the high seas; lively balance of piracy, romance, and swordplay, handsomely photographed and staged, with rousing Erich Wolfgang Korngold score. Has nothing to do with the Sabatini novel, which was filmed faithfully in 1924. Restored for home video, with additional final scene intended for British audiences, in which Queen Elizabeth I offers morale-building wartime message. Beware of shorter prints. Also shown in computer-colored version.▼●
Sea Hornet, The (1951) **84m.** *½ D: Joseph Kane. Rod Cameron, Adele Mara, Adrian Booth, Chill Wills. Lowjinks about deep-water divers and their women.
Sea Killer SEE: **Beyond the Reef**
Sealed Cargo (1951) **90m.** **½ D: Alfred L. Werker. Dana Andrews, Carla Balenda, Claude Rains, Philip Dorn, Onslow Stevens, Skip Homeier, Arthur Shields. Fishing boat captain Andrews tangles with Nazis attempting to supply war materials to U-boats lurking off the Newfoundland coast. Taut WW2 melodrama.
Sealed Verdict (1948) **83m.** ** D: Lewis Allen. Ray Milland, Florence Marly, Broderick Crawford, John Hoyt, John Ridgely. Far-fetched drama of army lawyer who falls in love with traitorous woman he is supposed to prosecute in court; pretty dismal.
Séance on a Wet Afternoon (1964-British) **115m.** **** D: Bryan Forbes. Kim Stanley, Richard Attenborough, Patrick Magee, Nanette Newman, Judith Donner, Gerald Sim, Maria Kazan, Margaret Lacey. Gripping drama of crazed medium Stanley involving husband Attenborough in shady project. Brilliant acting, direction in this must-see film. Forbes adapted Mark McShane's novel and coproduced the film with Attenborough.▼
Sea of Grass, The (1947) **131m.** **½ D: Elia Kazan. Katharine Hepburn, Spencer Tracy, Melvyn Douglas, Phyllis Thaxter, Robert Walker, Edgar Buchanan, Harry Carey. Plodding drama from Conrad Richter story of farmer-rancher feud over New Mexico grasslands. Walker stands out in hardworking but unsuccessful cast.▼
Sea of Lost Ships (1953) **85m.** ** D: Joseph Kane. John Derek, Wanda Hendrix, Walter Brennan, Richard Jaeckel. Standard fare of two Coast Guard men fighting over Hendrix.
Sea of Love (1989) **C-112m.** ***½ D: Harold Becker. Al Pacino, Ellen Barkin, John Goodman, Michael Rooker, William Hickey, Richard Jenkins, Christine Estabrook, Barbara Baxley, Patricia Barry, Samuel L. Jackson, Jacqueline Brookes, John Spencer. Streetwise cop, going through mid-life crisis, falls in love with a suspect while investigating a serial murder case. Tough, smart, sexy urban thriller with a dynamite script by Richard Price, a perfect role for Pacino, and a steamy showcase for Barkin. Footage added for network TV showing (with Lorraine Bracco as Pacino's ex-wife). [R]▼●◗
Sea of Sand SEE: **Desert Patrol**
Search, The (1948) **105m.** **** D: Fred Zinnemann. Montgomery Clift, Ivan Jandl, Aline MacMahon, Jarmila Novotna, Wendell Corey. Poignant drama of American soldier Clift caring for concentration camp survivor Jandl in postwar Berlin, while the boy's mother desperately searches all Displaced Person's Camps for him. Beautifully acted and directed; won a Best Story Academy Award for Richard Schweitzer and David Wechsler and a special prize for Jandl for outstanding juvenile performance. Also shown in computer-colored version.▼
Search (1972) SEE: **Probe**
Search and Destroy (1981) **C-93m.** ** D: William Fruet. Perry King, Tisa Farrow, Don Stroud, Park Jong Soo, George Kennedy. Undistinguished actioner about former South Vietnamese official Soo seeking revenge against American G.I.s King and Stroud. Filmed in 1978. [PG]▼
Search and Destroy (1995) **C-90m.** *½ D: David Salle. Griffin Dunne, Illeana Douglas, Dennis Hopper, Christopher Walken, John Turturro, Rosanna Arquette, Ethan Hawke, Martin Scorsese. A badly-in-hock worm on the outer limits of show biz schemes to obtain financing for his dream movie project, an adaptation of the pop-psychologist rantings of a men's-movement guru. Despite a black-comedy dream cast and participation by executive producer Scorsese (who directed the thematically comparable THE KING OF COMEDY), this diffuse film grows progressively out of control before collapsing entirely. Directorial debut for N.Y. artist Salle. [R] ▼●
Searchers, The (1956) **C-119m.** **** D: John Ford. John Wayne, Jeffrey Hunter, Vera Miles, Ward Bond, Natalie Wood, John Qualen, Harry Carey, Jr., Olive Carey, Antonio Moreno, Henry Brandon, Hank Worden, Ken Curtis, Lana Wood, Dorothy

Jordan, Pat Wayne. Superb Western saga of Wayne's relentless search for niece (Wood) kidnapped by Indians, spanning many years. Color, scenery, photography all splendid, with moving, insightful Frank Nugent script to match (based on Alan LeMay's novel). And who could ever forget that final shot? Remade and imitated many times since (CARAVANS, WINTERHAWK, GRAYEAGLE, etc.). VistaVision.▼●◗

Search for Bridey Murphy, The (1956) **84m.** **½ D: Noel Langley. Teresa Wright, Louis Hayward, Nancy Gates, Kenneth Tobey, Richard Anderson. Strange account of woman under hypnosis with recollection of prior life; low-key telling to obtain realism makes it slow going. Based on a supposedly true (and then-topical) story. VistaVision.▼

Search for Danger (1949) **62m.** *½ D: Jack Bernhard. John Calvert, Albert Dekker, Myrna Dell, Douglas Fowley, Ben Welden. Low-budget *Falcon* mystery (last in the series), revolves around murderous gamblers who abscond with a fortune.

Search for One-Eyed Jimmy, The (1996) **C-82m.** *½ D: Sam Henry Kass. John Turturro, Samuel L. Jackson, Steve Buscemi, Michael Badalucco, Ray "Boom Boom" Mancini, Anne Meara, Jennifer Beals, Nicholas Turturro, Aida Turturro, Holt McCallany. Oddball story of a documentary filmmaker, fresh out of college, who returns to his old Brooklyn neighborhood and finds cinematic inspiration as his camera follows the trail of a missing local lowlife. Funny premise, fine cast, but never lives up to its promise. A must for Turturro fans, however, as most of the family turns up here. Filmed in 1993. [R]▼●

Search for Signs of Inteligent Life in the Universe, The (1991) **C-120m.** *** D: John Bailey. Clever re-creation of Lily Tomlin's 1985 one-woman Broadway show. Her characterizations run the gamut from bag lady (narrating the proceedings) to teen punk to New Age Woman, with much of the material in a feminist vein. Written by longtime Tomlin collaborator Jane Wagner. (The title is misspelled on purpose.) See also LILY TOMLIN, a 1986 documentary chronicling Tomlin and Wagner's preparation for the show. [PG-13]▼

Search for the Mother Lode: The Last Great Treasure SEE: **Mother Lode**

Searching for Bobby Fischer (1993) **C-110m.** ***½ D: Steven Zaillian. Joe Mantegna, Max Pomeranc, Joan Allen, Ben Kingsley, Laurence Fishburne, Michael Nirenberg, Robert Stephens, David Paymer, William H. Macy, Dan Hedaya, Anthony Heald, Josh Mostel, Tony Shalhoub, Austin Pendleton. Compelling, surefooted drama, based on a true story: A father discovers that his 7-year-old son has a genius for chess, and enters him in competition, losing sight of what this does to the boy's psyche—and his pure enjoyment of the game. Poignant, heart-rending at times (especially for any parent) and exceptionally well done. Screenplay by first-time director Zaillian, from the book by Fred Waitzkin, who's the real-life chess whiz's father. [PG]▼●

Searching Wind, The (1946) **108m.** **½ D: William Dieterle. Robert Young, Sylvia Sidney, Ann Richards, Dudley Digges, Douglas Dick, Albert Basserman. Talky but historically fascinating drama, scripted by Lillian Hellman and based on her play, about a deluded U.S. ambassador (Young) in Europe in the years before WW2. Socialite Richards is his wife, journalist Sydney the woman he really loves. Hellman's scenario mirrors, and condemns, the international politics that allowed Hitler to come to power.

Sea Serpent, The (1986-Spanish) **C-92m.** *½ D: Gregory Greens. Timothy Bottoms, Taryn Power, Jared Martin, Ray Milland, Gerard Tichy, Carole James. In order to clear his name, discredited captain Bottoms searches for sea monster that has been roused from the deep by A-bomb tests. Childish sci-fi with a monster depicted by puppets! Shot in 1984. Milland's last film.▼

Sea Shall Not Have Them, The (1954-British) **91m.** ** D: Lewis Gilbert. Michael Redgrave, Dirk Bogarde, Anthony Steel, Nigel Patrick, Nigel Green, Rachel Kempson. British bomber plane is forced down in the ocean during WW2; a rescue attempt is made.▼

Seaside Swingers (1965-British) **C-94m.** *½ D: James Hill. John Leyton, Mike Sarne, Freddie and The Dreamers, Ron Moody, Liz Fraser. Group of teen-agers working at seaside resort prepare for major talent contest which is to be the highlight of the summer season. Should have given them all the hook. Techniscope.▼

Season of Dreams SEE: **Stacking**

Season of Passion (1959-Australian) **93m.** **½ D: Leslie Norman. Anne Baxter, John Mills, Angela Lansbury, Ernest Borgnine, Janette Craig. Tasteful study of human relationships; Mills and Borgnine are country workers who each year come to the city for their fling with Baxter and Lansbury. Based on Ray Lawlor's play, *Summer of the 17th Doll.*

Sea Wall, The SEE: **This Angry Age**

Sea Wife (1957-British) **C-82m.** *** D: Bob McNaught. Richard Burton, Joan Collins, Basil Sydney, Ronald Squire, Cy Grant. Disarming yarn of Burton and Collins surviving a torpedoed ship. He falls in love with her, not knowing she's a nun. Set during WW2. CinemaScope.▼

Sea Wolf, The (1941) **90m.** ***½ D: Michael Curtiz. Edward G. Robinson, John Garfield, Ida Lupino, Alexander Knox, Gene Lockhart, Barry Fitzgerald, Stanley Ridges. Bristling Jack London tale of brutal but intellectual sea captain Robinson battling wits with accidental passenger Knox, as brash seaman Garfield and fugitive Lupino try to escape. Script by Robert Rossen. Originally released at 100m. Remade many times (BARRICADE, WOLF LARSEN, etc.), as well as several silent versions. Also shown in computer-colored version.▼

Sea Wolf, The (1993) **C-100m. TVM** D: Michael Anderson. Charles Bronson, Christopher Reeve, Catherine Mary Stewart, Marc Singer, Clive Revill, Len Cariou. Tepid remake of Jack London's oft-filmed sea tale with Bronson's defanged Wolf and Reeve's wimpish Humph making one appreciate the Edward G. Robinson version even more. (Some seagoing shots were actually lifted from the 1941 film and colorized.) Made for cable. Average.▼●

Sea Wolves, The (1980-British-U.S.) **C-120m.** *** D: Andrew V. McLaglen. Gregory Peck, Roger Moore, David Niven, Trevor Howard, Barbara Kellerman, Patrick Macnee. You may have to be over 30 to like this true story of a retired British cavalry unit undertaking an espionage operation in WW2, but it's both action-filled and funny. The target: a German radio transmitter on a ship in an Indian port. Moore can't shake his Bond image, and Peck struggles with his British accent, so nothing is to be taken very seriously. Script by Reginald Rose. [PG]▼◗

Sebastian (1968-British) **C-100m.** **½ D: David Greene. Dirk Bogarde, Susannah York, Lilli Palmer, John Gielgud, Margaret Johnston, Nigel Davenport. Flashy but cluttered espionage film of counterintelligence agent Bogarde, who deciphers codes for England, becoming enmeshed in international battle of wits. Intriguing, colorful, but a bit trying; look for Donald Sutherland in a small role.▼

Second Best (1994-British-U.S.) **C-105m.** *** D: Chris Menges. William Hurt, John Hurt, Chris Cleary Miles, Keith Allen, Jane Horrocks, Prunella Scales, Alan Cumming, Jodhi May. Pensive drama with Hurt excellent in an unusual role: an unmarried, terminally shy, 42-year-old postmaster in a small Welsh town who attempts to adopt a deeply troubled 10-year-old boy (Miles). [PG-13]▼●

Second Best Secret Agent in the Whole Wide World (1965-British) **C-96m.** **½ D: Lindsay Shonteff. Tom Adams, Veronica Hurst, Peter Bull, Karel Stepanek, John Arnatt. Snappy James Bondish entry, with virtue of satirical performance by Adams; he prevents the Russians from stealing scientist Stepanek's anti-gravity invention. Original British title: LICENSED TO KILL. Sequel: WHERE THE BULLETS FLY.▼

Second Chance (1953) **C-81m.** **½ D: Rudolph Maté. Robert Mitchum, Linda Darnell, Jack Palance, Reginald Sheffield, Roy Roberts, Dan Seymour, Fortunio Bonanova, Milburn Stone. Two runaways—gambler's girlfriend Darnell and tainted prizefighter Mitchum—fall in love in Mexico. Complications arise when Palance arrives with orders to kill Darnell. OK melodrama, made in 3-D.▼●

Second Chorus (1940) **83m.** ** D: H. C. Potter. Fred Astaire, Paulette Goddard, Artie Shaw and Orchestra, Charles Butterworth, Burgess Meredith. Routine musical of Astaire and Meredith, both musicians with designs on Goddard. Easy to take, but nothing special. Meredith and Goddard later married in real life.▼●

Second Civil War, The (1997) **C-100m. TVM** D: Joe Dante. Beau Bridges, Joanna Cassidy, James Coburn, Kevin Dunn, Phil Hartman, Dan Hedaya, James Earl Jones, Denis Leary, Elizabeth Peña, Ron Perlman, Brian Keith, Kevin McCarthy, William Schallert, Dick Miller, Roger Corman. Black comedy dealing with politics, media manipulation, racism, philandering, and outright war, all started when Idaho governor Bridges decides to close his state borders to a planeload of Pakistani orphans fleeing a nuclear disaster. Comic performances by Hedaya as a network news director, Coburn as a presidential advisor, and Peña as a bombshell TV news reporter add to the satire, which takes a somber wrong turn at the finale. Made for cable. Average.▼●

Second Coming of Suzanne, The (1974) **C-90m.** *½ D: Michael Barry. Sondra Locke, Paul Sand, Jared Martin, Richard Dreyfuss, Gene Barry, Penelope Spheeris. Pretentious time capsule about an egocentric counterculture filmmaker (Martin) who recruits the title character (Locke) to star in his latest epic, a re-creation of the story of Christ! At its very best, this is very bad Fellini; writer-director Barry is the son of Gene (who executive produced). Strictly for Dreyfuss completists. Aka SUZANNE.▼

Second Face, The (1950) **77m.** **½ D: Jack Bernhard. Ella Raines, Bruce Bennett, Rita Johnson, Jane Darwell, John Sutton. Concise study of the effects of plastic surgery on Raines, whose face has been scarred.▼

Second Fiddle (1938) **86m.** **½ D: Sidney Lanfield. Sonja Henie, Tyrone Power, Rudy Vallee, Edna May Oliver, Lyle Talbot, Brian Sisters, Mary Healy, Alan Dinehart, voice of Charles Lane. Contrived Henie musical of Power promoting Hollywood romance for Henie, falling in love himself. Irving Berlin's most uninspired score does include the genuinely strange song—and production number—"Dancing Back to Back."▼

Second Greatest Sex, The (1955) **C-87m.** *½ D: George Marshall. Jeanne Crain, George Nader, Bert Lahr, Mamie Van Doren, Kitty Kallen, Keith Andes, Tommy Rall, Paul Gilbert, Jimmy Boyd. Second-rate musical up-dating of *Lysistrata,* about women out West protesting men's violence by going on sex strike. CinemaScope.

Second-Hand Hearts (1981) **C-102m.** BOMB D: Hal Ashby. Robert Blake, Barbara Harris, Collin Boone, Amber Rose Gold, Bert Remsen, Shirley Stoler. Blake, beer-bellied and jowly, is Loyal Muke (rhymes with Puke), middle-aged drifter, who married Dinette Dusty (Harris) while in a drunken stupor. Pointless, confusing, overblown, a comedy that is embarrassingly unfunny. Even the usually reliable Harris can't salvage this mess. Filmed in 1979 as THE HAMSTER OF HAPPINESS. [PG]

Second Honeymoon (1937) **79m.** **½ D: Walter Lang. Tyrone Power, Loretta Young, Stuart Erwin, Claire Trevor, Lyle Talbot. Power tries to win back ex-wife Young in pat marital farce with attractive cast.

Second Jungle Book: Mowgli & Baloo, The SEE: **Rudyard Kipling's The Second Jungle Book: Mowgli & Baloo**

Seconds (1966) **106m.** ***½ D: John Frankenheimer. Rock Hudson, Salome Jens, John Randolph, Will Geer, Jeff Corey, Murray Hamilton, Wesley Addy. Frustrated middle-aged businessman is transformed into new identity (Hudson) but finds himself at odds with old and new life conflicts. Fascinating from start to finish, with good performances, striking camerawork by James Wong Howe; script by Lewis John Carlino. On video only in the original European version which features just over 1m. of additional footage. ▼●

Second Serve (1986) **C-100m. TVM** D: Anthony Page. Vanessa Redgrave, Martin Balsam, William Russ, Alice Krige, Kerrie Keane, Reni Santoni, Louise Fletcher, Nina Van Pallandt, Jeff Corey. The story of transsexual Renee Richards, the male surgeon turned female tennis luminary. A single-handed triumph for Redgrave as both Richard Raskins (here called Radley) and Renee Richards. Stephanie Liss and Gavin Lambert wrote the absorbing script based on Richards' autobiography. Above average.

Second Sight (1989) **C-84m.** BOMB D: Joel Zwick. John Larroquette, Bronson Pinchot, Bess Armstrong, Stuart Pankin, John Schuck, James Tolkan, William Prince, Christine Estabrook, Cornelia Guest. Superpsychic Pinchot and an otherworldly entity assist ex-cop Larroquette's Second Sight Detective Agency; if that's not enough, there's a cute-'n'-perky nun as love interest! No psychic was needed to gauge how long this one would last in theaters. [PG]▼●

Second Thoughts (1983) **C-98m.** BOMB D: Lawrence Turman. Lucie Arnaz, Craig Wasson, Ken Howard, Anne Schedeen, Arthur Rosenberg, Peggy McCay. Dreary, laughably unrealistic account of lawyer Arnaz divorcing banker Howard and, to her regret, taking up with idealistic Wasson, who is still living in the 1960s. [PG]▼

Second Time Around, The (1961) **C-99m.** **½ D: Vincent Sherman. Debbie Reynolds, Andy Griffith, Steve Forrest, Juliet Prowse, Thelma Ritter, Isobel Elsom. Mild comic Western with widow Debbie moving to Arizona, becoming sheriff, tangling with suitors Griffith and Forrest. CinemaScope.

Second Woman, The (1951) **90m.** **½ D: James V. Kern. Robert Young, Betsy Drake, John Sutton, Florence Bates, Morris Carnovsky, Henry O'Neill, Jean Rogers. Atmospheric psychological drama with architect Young becoming increasingly unstable as a result of his fiancée's death on the eve of their wedding. Is he a danger to himself and his new girlfriend Drake?▼◗

Secret Admirer (1985) **C-98m.** **½ D: David Greenwalt. C. Thomas Howell, Lori Loughlin, Kelly Preston, Dee Wallace Stone, Cliff De Young, Leigh Taylor-Young, Fred Ward, Casey Siemaszko, Corey Haim. Comedy of errors about an unsigned love letter that causes chain of confusion among some teenagers *and* their parents. Cute farce with some appealing performers, but surrenders to the obvious too often. Nice score by Jan Hammer. [R]▼●

Secret Agent, The (1936-British) **86m.** **½ D: Alfred Hitchcock. John Gielgud, Madeleine Carroll, Robert Young, Peter Lorre, Percy Marmont, Lilli Palmer. Strange blend of comedy and thriller elements which don't quite mesh; Carroll and Gielgud are secret agents who pose as man and wife while on assignment in Switzerland to kill enemy spy. One of Hitchcock's oddest films. ▼●◗

Secret Agent, The (1996-British) **C-95m.** BOMB D: Christopher Hampton. Bob Hoskins, Patricia Arquette, Gérard Depardieu, George Spelvin, Jim Broadbent, Christian Bale, Eddie Izzard, Elizabeth Spriggs, Julian Wadham, Peter Vaughan. Stultifying adaptation of the Joseph Conrad novel about Verloc (Hoskins), an anarchist who actually is a secret agent for the Russian government in late 19th-century London; his wife (Arquette) has no idea of his activities. Guaranteed to drive you to slumber land despite its cast (including an unbilled Robin Williams). Aka JOSEPH CONRAD'S THE SECRET AGENT. [R] ▼●

Secret Agent Fireball (1966-Italian) **C-89m.** ** D: Martin Donan (Mario Donen). Richard Harrison, Dominique Boschero, Wandisa Guida. Harrison is American superspy substituted for U.S. scientist in gambit to protect coalition between U.S., Germany, and Russia on new petroleum mechanism project; standard treatment. Techniscope.▼

Secret Agent of Japan (1942) **72m.** ** D: Irving Pichel. Preston Foster, Lynn Bari, Noel Madison, Janis Carter, Sen Yung, Addison Richards, Frank Puglia, Ian Wolfe. Dated espionage film of soldier-of-fortune

Foster working in the Pacific for England before Pearl Harbor.

Secret Agent Super Dragon (1966-French-Italian-W. German) **C-95m.** *½ D: Calvin Jackson Padget (Giorgio Ferroni). Ray Danton, Marisa Mell, Margaret Lee, Jess Hahn. Sloppy foreign spy meller has fair cast but sometimes silly script and atrocious dubbing. Danton repeats role from CODE NAME: JAGUAR. CinemaScope.▼

Secret Agent 00 SEE: **Operation Kid Brother**

Secret Beyond the Door (1948) **98m.** ** D: Fritz Lang. Joan Bennett, Michael Redgrave, Anne Revere, Barbara O'Neil, Natalie Schafer. Tedious Lang misfire along lines of Hitchcock's SUSPICION, with Bennett believing her husband is a demented murderer.▼

Secret Bride, The (1935) **64m.** **½ D: William Dieterle. Barbara Stanwyck, Warren William, Glenda Farrell, Grant Mitchell, Arthur Byron. State Attorney General William secretly weds governor's daughter Stanwyck, and summarily learns that her father may be taking bribes from a convicted embezzler. Tidy, well-acted drama.

Secret Ceremony (1968-British) **C-109m.** ***½ D: Joseph Losey. Elizabeth Taylor, Mia Farrow, Robert Mitchum, Pamela Brown, Peggy Ashcroft. Farrow resembles Taylor's dead daughter, Taylor resembles Farrow's dead mother, and their meeting has strange results. Originally an excellent psychological drama, but then Universal cut footage and shot extra scenes to make film more "acceptable" for TV, at 101m. This rating applies only to original version. [R]▼

Secret Command (1944) **82m.** *** D: A. Edward Sutherland. Pat O'Brien, Carole Landis, Chester Morris, Ruth Warrick, Wallace Ford. No-nonsense O'Brien tries to find source of sabotage in California shipyard during WW2. Good, fast moving espionage story. O'Brien also produced this film.

Secret Diary of Sigmund Freud, The (1984) **C-90m.** *½ D: Danford B. Greene. Bud Cort, Carol Kane, Klaus Kinski, Marisa Berenson, Carroll Baker, Dick Shawn, Ferdinand Mayne. Dreary comedy about the early life of Freud (Cort), with Baker his mother, Kinski a doctor she becomes involved with, and Kane a nurse with a lisp. Pretty boring, even annoying at times. [PG]▼

Secret Friends (1992-U.S.-British) **C-97m.** BOMB D: Dennis Potter. Alan Bates, Gina Bellman, Frances Barber, Tony Doyle, Joanna David, Colin Jeavons, Ian McNeice, Davyd Harries. Amnesiac Bates is a deeply disturbed, guilt-ridden, and jealous man whose young, sexy wife (Bellman) is a constant pain to him. Film, set in part on long train journey, gives new meaning to the term "jumping back and forth in time"; result is appalling, incomprehensible mishmash. Only film to be directed by esteemed writer Dennis Potter, suggested by his novel *Ticket to Ride*. Buffs may enjoy McNeice and Harries as throwbacks to Basil Radford and Naunton Wayne.

Secret Fury, The (1950) **86m.** *** D: Mel Ferrer. Claudette Colbert, Robert Ryan, Jane Cowl, Paul Kelly, Vivian Vance, Philip Ober. Unknown person tries to drive Claudette crazy to prevent her marriage to Ryan. Exciting whodunit with twist ending.

Secret Garden, The (1949) **92m.** *** D: Fred M. Wilcox. Margaret O'Brien, Herbert Marshall, Dean Stockwell, Gladys Cooper, Elsa Lanchester. Young girl who comes to live at run-down Victorian estate finds abandoned garden, devotes herself to it and eventually changes the lives of everyone living there. Vividly atmospheric film with some color sequences. Based on the classic children's book by Frances Hodgson Burnett. Remade as a TV movie in 1987 and as a feature in 1993, as well as a Broadway musical.▼

Secret Garden, The (1993) **C-101m.** *** D: Agnieszka Holland. Kate Maberly, Heydon Prowse, Andrew Knott, Maggie Smith, Laura Crossley, John Lynch, Walter Sparrow, Irène Jacob. Handsome remake of the children's classic, with Maberly as the 10-year-old orphan who restores an abandoned garden in her uncle's eerie Victorian manor. Well-crafted, but doesn't sustain the drama of its story as well as the 1949 version. Francis Ford Coppola was executive producer. [G]▼●◗

Secret Heart, The (1946) **97m.** **½ D: Robert Z. Leonard. Claudette Colbert, Walter Pidgeon, June Allyson, Lionel Barrymore, Robert Sterling, Patricia Medina, Marshall Thompson. Narrated by Hume Cronyn. This is Allyson's film, as young girl obsessed with dead father, unable to accept stepmother Colbert. Film creates eerie mood, and acting is good, but it's offbeat and not for all tastes.

Secret Honor (1984) **C-90m.** ***½ D: Robert Altman. Philip Baker Hall. Richard Nixon, with a Chivas Regal assist, paces around his study in a near-psychotic rail against Hiss, Castro, Ike, Kissinger, and anyone named Kennedy. Hall's one-man stage show is fluidly filmed and outrageously conceived—a titillating one-of-a-kind for anyone who rooted for Khrushchev in the Kitchen Debates. Aka LORDS OF TREASON.▼

Secret Invasion, The (1964) **C-95m.** *** D: Roger Corman. Stewart Granger, Mickey Rooney, Raf Vallone, Henry Silva, Edd Byrnes, Mia Massini. Good action, location photography, and direction in story of British Intelligence using criminals to work behind enemy lines in WW2 Yugoslavia. Panavision.

Secret Land, The (1948) **C-71m.** *** Produced by Orville O. Dull. Narrated by Van Heflin, Robert Montgomery, Robert Taylor. Glossy but penetrating documentary study of Admiral Richard Byrd's exploratory missions to Antarctic.

Secret Life of an American Wife, The (1968) **C-92m.** ** D: George Axelrod. Walter Matthau, Anne Jackson, Patrick O'Neal, Edy Williams, Richard Bull, Paul Napier. Talky, generally unfunny farce about neglected wife who decides to pose as a call girl with one of her husband's clients—a screen lover (Matthau). Disappointing next to the writer-director's hilarious LORD LOVE A DUCK. [R]▼

Secret Life of Walter Mitty, The (1947) **C-110m.** **½ D: Norman Z. McLeod. Danny Kaye, Virginia Mayo, Boris Karloff, Fay Bainter, Ann Rutherford, Florence Bates, Thurston Hall. Formula comedy casts Danny as milquetoast who dreams of manly glory. Not much Thurber here, but daydream sequences are lots of fun, and so is Kaye's famous "Anatole of Paris" patter number. Young Robert Altman, smiling and smoking a cigarette, appears as an extra in a nightclub scene with Kaye.▼●◗

Secret Mission (1942-British) **94m.** **½ D: Harold French. Hugh Williams, James Mason, Michael Wilding, Carla Lehmann, Nancy Price, Roland Culver, Karel Stepanek, Herbert Lom, Stewart Granger. Stiff-upper-lip WW2 drama in which three British spies and a free Frenchman (played by Mason!) sneak into occupied France to gather intelligence for an upcoming invasion. Well paced dramatically, but comical touches seem awkwardly out of place.▼

Secret of Blood Island, The (1965-British) **C-84m.** ** D: Quentin Lawrence. Barbara Shelley, Jack Hedley, Charles Tingwell, Patrick Wymark. Woman agent Shelley parachutes into Malaya during WW2, ends up incognito in a prisoner-of-war camp. Mindless timekiller. Video title: P.O.W.: PRISONERS OF WAR.▼

Secret of Convict Lake, The (1951) **83m.** **½ D: Michael Gordon. Glenn Ford, Gene Tierney, Ethel Barrymore, Zachary Scott, Ann Dvorak, Jeanette Nolan, Ruth Donnelly. Set in 1870s California, escaped prisoners hide out at settlement comprised largely of women; fine cast makes the most of script.

Secret of Dorian Gray, The SEE: **Dorian Gray**

Secret of Dr. Kildare, The (1939) **84m.** **½ D: Harold S. Bucquet. Lew Ayres, Lionel Barrymore, Lionel Atwill, Laraine Day, Helen Gilbert, Nat Pendleton, Sara Haden, Samuel S. Hinds, Emma Dunn, Grant Mitchell, Walter Kingsford, Alma Kruger, Nell Craig, Marie Blake, Martha O'Driscoll, Donald Barry. The good doctor tries to cure a young woman of psychosomatic blindness while working equally hard to get stubborn Dr. Gillespie to take a vacation in this tidy episode.▼

Secret of Dr. Mabuse, The SEE: **Thousand Eyes of Dr. Mabuse, The**

Secret of Madame Blanche, The (1933) **83m.** **½ D: Charles Brabin. Irene Dunne, Lionel Atwill, Phillips Holmes, Douglas Walton, Una Merkel, C. Henry Gordon, Jean Parker. Another MGM tearjerker in the MADAME X vein; Dunne is quite effective as a music-hall singer who loses her son to callous father-in-law Atwill when husband Holmes kills himself. Twenty years later, mother and son meet by accident and are involved in a murder. Contrived but well-made soaper.

Secret of My Success, The (1965-British) **C-112m.** *½ D: Andrew L. Stone. James Booth, Shirley Jones, Stella Stevens, Honor Blackman, Amy Dalby, Lionel Jeffries. Film certainly doesn't succeed. Naive boy is taken in by several crafty females on his road to maturity. Picturesque settings, variety of characterizations by Jeffries. Panavision.

Secret of My Success, The (1987) **C-110m.** **½ D: Herbert Ross. Michael J. Fox, Helen Slater, Richard Jordan, Margaret Whitton, John Pankow, Fred Gwynne, Elizabeth Franz, Christopher Durang, Mercedes Ruehl. Naive but bright, ambitious young man from the sticks hustles his way into the corporate world of N.Y.C., deftly juggling the various complications he encounters. Likable comedy goes on too long, gets most of its juice from Fox's energetic and appealing performance. [PG-13] ▼●◗

Secret of NIMH, The (1982) **C-82m.** **½ D: Don Bluth. Voices of Elizabeth Hartman, Derek Jacobi, Dom DeLuise, John Carradine, Peter Strauss. When her family homestead is threatened, a young widowed mouse seeks help, and comes upon a secret society of superintelligent rats. Well-animated adaptation of Robert C. O'Brien's prize-winning children's book, but not as involving, or as well paced, as it ought to be. First feature from Don Bluth Productions, the studio founded by a group of former Disney artists. Shannen Doherty is the voice of one of the mice children. Followed by a direct-to-video sequel. [G]▼●◗

Secret of Roan Inish, The (1994) **C-102m.** *** D: John Sayles. Jeni Courtney, Eileen Colgan, Mick Lally, Richard Sheridan, John Lynch. Gentle, charming tale of a girl who is sent to live with her grandparents on the west coast of Ireland and discovers the myths and magic that have affected her family. A "small" story to be sure, but it gradually works its spell on you, with an admirably unsentimental tone (perfectly embodied in solemn young Courtney), moody cinematography from Haskell Wexler, and remarkable "performances" from the seals and gulls that populate the film. Adapted from Rosalie Frye's novella *The Secret of Ron Mor Skerry* by director Sayles, who also edited. [PG] ▼●

Secret of Santa Vittoria, The (1969) **C-140m.** **½ D: Stanley Kramer. Anthony Quinn, Anna Magnani, Virna Lisi, Hardy Kruger, Sergio Franchi, Renato Rascel, Eduardo Ciannelli, Giancarlo Giannini, Valentina Cortese. Entertaining comedy from Robert Crichton's novel of Italian town which hides a million bottles of wine from occupying Germans in WW2. Story wanders, however, with needless subplots that make it overlong. Kruger excellent as civilized German officer. Panavision. [M/PG]▼

Secret of the Blue Room (1933) **66m.** **½ D: Kurt Neumann. Lionel Atwill, Gloria Stuart, Paul Lukas, Edward Arnold, Onslow Stevens, William Janney. Atmospheric whodunit set in eerie European castle where Stuart's three suitors accept challenge to sleep in room where several murders took place. Cast makes this one worthwhile; remade as THE MISSING GUEST and MURDER IN THE BLUE ROOM.

Secret of the Incas (1954) **C-101m.** **½ D: Jerry Hopper. Charlton Heston, Robert Young, Nicole Maurey, Thomas Mitchell, Glenda Farrell, Yma Sumac. Good adventure of explorer searching for location of fabled treasure.

Secret of the Purple Reef, The (1960) **C-80m.** ** D: William Witney. Jeff Richards, Margia Dean, Peter Falk, Richard Chamberlain, Robert Earle, Terence DeMarney. Programmer whose capable cast bounces the story along; brothers seek clues to their father's killing in the Caribbean. CinemaScope.

Secret of the Red Orchid, The SEE: **Puzzle of the Red Orchid, The**

Secret of the Whistler (1946) **65m.** *** D: George Sherman. Richard Dix, Leslie Brooks, Mary Currier, Michael Duane, Mona Barrie, Ray Walker. Dix is an insane artist whose second wife suspects him of having killed her predecessor and fears she's his next victim. Nifty *Whistler* entry, with the customary ironic twist.

Secret of Treasure Mountain (1956) **68m.** *½ D: Seymour Friedman. Valerie French, Raymond Burr, William Prince, Lance Fuller, Susan Cummings. Junky trivia about hunt for buried wealth in Indian country. ▼

Secret Partner, The (1961-British) **91m.** *** D: Basil Dearden. Stewart Granger, Haya Harareet, Bernard Lee, Conrad Phillips. Fast-paced, atmospheric mystery about man trying to pull off ingenious scheme whereby he is accused of robbery.

Secret People (1952-British) **87m.** ** D: Thorold Dickinson. Valentina Cortesa, Serge Reggiani, Charles Goldner, Audrey Hepburn, Megs Jenkins, Irene Worth. Heavy-handed drama in which Cortesa and Reggiani attempt to assassinate the dictator responsible for her father's death. Hepburn registers as Cortesa's innocent kid sister.

Secret Places (1985-British) **C-96m.** **½ D: Zelda Barron. Marie-Theres Relin, Tara MacGowran, Claudine Auger, Jenny Agutter, Cassie Stuart, Ann-Marie Gwatkin. Two schoolgirls from very different backgrounds form a friendship that leads to heartbreak on the eve of WW2; set in small English village. Warm, often moving film that somehow falls short. Lead roles are well played by Relin (daughter of Maria Schell) and MacGowran (daughter of Jack MacGowran). [PG]▼

Secret Policeman's Other Ball, The (1982-British) **C-91m.** *** D: Julien Temple, Roger Graef. John Cleese, Peter Cook, Michael Palin, Graham Chapman, Terry Jones, Pete Townshend, Sting, Phil Collins, Eric Clapton, Jeff Beck, Eleanor Bron, Pamela Stephenson, Alexei Sayle. Poorly photographed but entertaining distillation of two concerts (in 1979 and 1981) organized as fund-raisers for Amnesty International. Almost as much music as comedy, but several funny bits by Cook and the Python boys stand out, including hilarious "Cheese Shop" routine. [R]▼●

Secret Rapture (1993-British) **C-96m.** ** D: Howard Davies. Juliet Stevenson, Joanne Whalley-Kilmer, Penelope Wilton, Neil Pearson, Alan Howard, Robert Stephens. Disappointing psychological thriller about vulnerable Stevenson, who was extremely close to her just-deceased father, and who must contend with her shrill, tyrannical sister (Wilton). Good cast flounders in David Hare's one-note script (based on his play); much of its bite regarding greed and business-as-usual amorality in Thatcherite England has been toned down. [R]▼●

Secrets (1971) **C-86m.** *½ D: Philip Saville. Jacqueline Bisset, Per Oscarsson, Shirley Knight Hopkins, Robert Powell, Tarka Kings, Martin C. Thurley. A husband, wife, and daughter all have sexual experiences during the course of a day, which must remain secrets. Dull, somewhat pretentious film notable only for nude Bisset in passionate lovemaking scene. Released in 1978. [R]▼

Secrets & Lies (1996-British) **C-142m.** ***½ D: Mike Leigh. Brenda Blethyn, Marianne Jean-Baptiste, Timothy Spall, Phyllis Logan, Claire Rushbrook, Elizabeth Berrington, Michele Austin, Alison Steadman. Another of filmmaker Leigh's compelling portraits of ordinary people and the sometimes extraordinary circumstances of their lives; here, a young black woman goes in search of her birth parents and discovers that her mother is a working-class white woman. Emotionally wrenching at times, but also endearingly funny. Superlative performances spark this long, deliberately paced, but rewarding slice of life. [R]▼●

Secret Service of the Air (1939) **61m.** ** D: Noel Smith. Ronald Reagan, John Litel, Ila Rhodes, James Stephenson, Eddie Foy, Jr., Rosella Towne. Reagan stars as Lt. Brass Bancroft, a pilot who joins the Secret Service and exposes a smuggling ring. Fast-paced Warner Bros. B entry, the first of a series of four.

Secret Sins of the Father (1994) **C-100m. TVM** D: Beau Bridges. Beau Bridges, Lloyd Bridges, Lee Purcell, Frederick Coffin, Ed Lauter, Victoria Rowell, Bert Remsen. Local police chief Beau suspects his father Lloyd in the death of his mother (real-life mom Dorothy Dean Bridges). Clever use of photos and family home movies of the Bridges in the 1950s, which also include very young Jeff. Beau's son Jordan also has a role as a local teenager. A real family affair that could have used a more riveting mystery. Average.

Secret Six, The (1931) **83m.** **½ D: George Hill. Wallace Beery, Lewis Stone, Clark Gable, Jean Harlow, Johnny Mack Brown, Ralph Bellamy, Marjorie Rambeau, John Miljan. Hard-boiled gangster saga with powerhouse cast; sluggish at times, but worth seeing for milk-drinking racketeer Beery, aristocratic crime-lord Stone, moll-with-a-heart-of-gold Harlow, et al.

Secrets of an Actress (1938) **71m.** ** D: William Keighley. Kay Francis, George Brent, Ian Hunter, Gloria Dickson, Isabel Jeans, Penny Singleton, Dennie Moore. Run-of-the-mill romantic melodrama with actress Francis attracting distraught Brent, an unhappily married architect.

Secrets of a Secretary (1931) **71m.** ** D: George Abbott. Claudette Colbert, Herbert Marshall, George Metaxa, Mary Boland, Berton Churchill. Stiff drawing-room stuff, with Colbert finding ex-hubby Marshall blackmailing her new boss.

Secrets of Life (1956) **C-75m.** *** D: James Algar. Narrated by Winston Hibler. Disney True-Life Adventure features closeup looks at plant life, insect life, sea creatures, and natural wonders like volcanoes. Wonderful footage includes time-lapse photography of plants set to a rousing bolero on the soundtrack.▼

Secrets of the Lone Wolf (1941) **67m.** **½ D: Edward Dmytryk. Warren William, Ruth Ford, Roger Clark, Victor Jory, Eric Blore, Thurston Hall, Fred Kelsey. Sturdy entry with the Lone Wolf's punctilious valet (Blore) thought to be his employer by some crooks who use him as part of a scheme to lift the Napoleon jewels.

Secrets of Women (1952-Swedish) **114m.** *** D: Ingmar Bergman. Anita Bjork, Karl Arne Homsten, Jarl Kulle, Maj-Britt Nilsson, Birger Malmsten, Eva Dahlbeck, Gunnar Bjornstrand. Episodic early Bergman drama about several women in a summer house who confide about their relationships with their men. Final sequence, with Dahlbeck and Bjornstrand trapped in an elevator, is most fascinating.▼

Secret War of Harry Frigg, The (1968) **C-110m.** ** D: Jack Smight. Paul Newman, Sylva Koscina, Andrew Duggan, Tom Bosley, John Williams, Vito Scotti, James Gregory. Noncom soldier selected to free five generals held captive during WW2 in this slick but inane comedy, one of Newman's few real losers. Techniscope.▼

Secret Ways, The (1961) **112m.** **½ D: Phil Karlson. Richard Widmark, Sonja Ziemann, Senta Berger, Charles Regnier. Much on-location shooting helps strengthen caper with Widmark as grim American sent into Communist Hungary to plan escape of pro-West refugee; from an Alistair MacLean novel.

Secret Weapon (1942) SEE: **Sherlock Holmes and The Secret Weapon**

Secret World (1969-French) **C-94m.** ** D: Robert Freeman. Jacqueline Bisset, Giselle Pascal, Pierre Zimmer, Marc Porel, Jean-Francois Maurin. Bisset's presence gives slight boost to pretentiously directed film about young boy's infatuation with his uncle's mistress. [M/PG]

Secret Yearnings SEE: **Good Luck, Miss Wyckoff**

Security Risk (1954) **69m.** ** D: Harold Schuster. John Ireland, Dorothy Malone, Keith Larsen, John Craven, Joe Bassett. Routine F.B.I.-vs-Communist-agent; even Malone isn't diverting in this B thriller.

Seduced and Abandoned (1964-Italian) **118m.** ***½ D: Pietro Germi. Stefania Sandrelli, Saro Urzi, Lando Buzzanca, Leopoldo Trieste. Fast-paced, richly flavorful bedroom romp involving the fate of a Don Juan who manages to impregnate his fiancée's kid sister. A follow-up in spirit to Germi's DIVORCE—ITALIAN STYLE, this very funny film cleverly lampoons sexual tradition. ▼

Seducers, The SEE: **Death Game**

Seduction, The (1982) **C-104m.** BOMB D: David Schmoeller. Morgan Fairchild, Michael Sarrazin, Vince Edwards, Andrew Stevens, Colleen Camp, Wendy Smith Howard. A flashy L.A. TV newswoman is terrorized by a persistent fan. Preposterous, derivative film is neither suspenseful nor titillating, despite its title and sexy star (in her first movie vehicle). [R]▼

Seduction of Joe Tynan, The (1979) **C-107m.** **½ D: Jerry Schatzberg. Alan Alda, Barbara Harris, Meryl Streep, Rip Torn, Charles Kimbrough, Melvyn Douglas. Earnest but shallow drama (written by Alda) about young senator who faces moral dilemmas while climbing political ladder in Washington. Ludicrous resolution really hurts film as a whole. [R]▼●

Seduction of Mimi, The (1972-Italian) **C-89m.** *** D: Lina Wertmuller. Giancarlo Giannini, Mariangela Melato, Agostina Belli, Elena Fiore. Mimi is actually a man (Giannini) whose stubbornness and stupidity get him into trouble politically and sexually. Climactic scene where he tries to make love to an impossibly obese woman is unforgettable. Entertaining film was later Americanized as WHICH WAY IS UP? Released in the U.S. in 1974. [R]▼◗

See Here, Private Hargrove (1944) **100m.** *** D: Wesley Ruggles. Robert Walker, Donna Reed, Keenan Wynn, Robert Benchley, Bob Crosby, Grant Mitchell. Marion Hargrove's anecdotes of army life make an amusing, episodic film; Benchley hilarious as Reed's garrulous dad. Sequel: WHAT NEXT, CORPORAL HARGROVE?

See How She Runs (1978) **C-100m. TVM** D: Richard T. Heffron. Joanne Woodward, John Considine, Lissy Newman, Mary Beth Manning, Barnard Hughes. Breath-of-fresh-air drama about a middle-aged housewife's decision to express herself by entering the grueling 26-mile Boston Marathon. Woodward won an Emmy for her performance (and her run). One of her daughters is played by real-life daughter Lissy Newman in her acting debut. Above average.▼

See How They Run (1964) **C-100m. TVM** D: David Lowell Rich. John Forsythe, Senta Berger, Jane Wyatt, Franchot Tone, Leslie Nielsen, Pamela Franklin, George Kennedy. Pretty fair chase-drama involving three orphans journeying to America, not knowing they carry crucial evidence exposing international organization and that murderers of their father pursue them. Good performances and action, obscuring inadequate motivation and believability. Based on Michael Blankfort's novel *The Widow Makers.* Earns a historical footnote as the first made-for-TV movie. Average.

Seekers, The (1954-British) **C-90m.** **½ D: Ken Annakin. Jack Hawkins, Glynis Johns, Noel Purcell, Inia Te Wiata, Laya Raki. Adequate adventure drama, set in the early 1800s, as British sailor Hawkins, along with his new wife and best friend, settles in New Zealand. The colorful location filming (especially among the Maoris) is a plus. Original U.S. title: LAND OF FURY.▼

Seems Like Old Times (1980) **C-102m.** *** D: Jay Sandrich. Goldie Hawn, Chevy Chase, Charles Grodin, Robert Guillaume, Harold Gould, George Grizzard, Yvonne Wilder, T. K. Carter. Neil Simon's homage to 1930s screwball farces is quite enjoyable, with Goldie as a good-hearted lawyer whose ex-husband (Chase) disrupts her life and threatens the career of her new spouse (Grodin). Funny lines and situations all the way up to pointless finale. Feature debut of TV comedy director Sandrich. [PG]▼●

See My Lawyer (1945) **67m.** ** D: Edward F. Cline. Ole Olsen, Chic Johnson, Alan Curtis, Grace McDonald, Noah Beery, Jr., Franklin Pangborn, Edward S. Brophy. Last and least of Olsen and Johnson's movie vehicles, with the daffy duo at war with nightclub owner Pangborn—and aiding a trio of struggling lawyers. Tissue-thin plot serves only as framework for a variety of specialty acts, including Carmen Amaya and the (Nat) King Cole Trio.

See No Evil (1971-British) **C-89m.** *** D: Richard Fleischer. Mia Farrow, Dorothy Alison, Robin Bailey, Diane Grayson, Lila Kaye. Terrifying chiller by Brian Clemens; blind girl slowly discovers that her uncle's entire family has been murdered and that the killer is silently stalking her. Watch out for the boots. British title: BLIND TERROR. [PG]▼●

See No Evil, Hear No Evil (1989) **C-103m.** ** D: Arthur Hiller. Richard Pryor, Gene Wilder, Joan Severance, Kevin Spacey, Kirsten Childs, Alan North, Anthony Zerbe. Wilder and Pryor are reteamed in this stupid comedy about a deaf man and a blind man who inadvertently become murder suspects and take it on the lam, hoping to catch the real killers. Five writers (including Wilder) are credited for this labored, foul-mouthed comedy; two such talented stars deserve better. [R]▼●

See You in the Morning (1989) **C-119m.** ** D: Alan J. Pakula. Jeff Bridges, Alice Krige, Farrah Fawcett, Linda Lavin, Drew Barrymore, Lukas Haas, David Dukes, Frances Sternhagen, Theodore Bikel, George Hearn, Macaulay Culkin, Robin Bartlett. Bridges and Krige follow a bumpy road to a second marriage (for both of them), trying to erase bad memories and lingering problems . . . and having to win over each other's children. Overall intelligence, warmth, and gentility cannot overcome a certain patness (and forced cuteness) in director Pakula's script—or the greater problem of not knowing when to wrap things up. [PG-13]▼●

Seize the Day (1986) **C-93m.** ***½ D: Fielder Cook. Robin Williams, Joseph Wiseman, Jerry Stiller, Glenne Headly. Williams is outstanding as Tommy Wilhelm, pushing 40 and a failure by society's standards, who's broke, much abused, and desperate for love. Wiseman and Stiller offer fine support as his coldhearted father and a con man he naively trusts. A small masterpiece, like the Saul Bellow novel on which it's based, with a faithful screenplay by Ronald Ribman. Plenty of familiar faces in small roles: Tony Roberts, Richard Shull, John Fiedler, Jo Van Fleet, William Hickey, Eileen Heckart, many others.▼●

Seizure (1974-Canadian) **C-93m.** ** D: Oliver Stone. Jonathan Frid, Martine Beswick, Christina Pickles, Joe Sirola, Herve Villechaize, Mary Woronov, Troy Donahue. Stone's directorial debut is stylish but incoherent shocker in which novelist Frid, his family and friends are forced to play games of death by trio of evil weirdos who may or may not be his nightmares come to life. [PG]▼

Selena (1997) **C-130m.** **½ D: Gregory Nava. Jennifer Lopez, Edward James Olmos, Jon Seda, Constance Marie, Jacob Vargas, Lupe Ontiveros, Jackie Guerra, Rebecca Lee Meza. Glossy, congenially corny biography of the spirited young Tejano singer whose dreams of showbiz fame were cut short by her murder (just as she was about to win success as a cross-over performer). Lopez offers a dynamic, star-making turn as Selena and Olmos also scores as her loving but possessive father. Ironically, the film does more to solidify Selena's celebrity than she was able to accomplish in her short lifetime. Super 35. [PG]▼●◗

Sellout, The (1952) **83m.** **½ D: Gerald Mayer. Walter Pidgeon, John Hodiak, Audrey Totter, Paula Raymond, Cameron Mitchell, Karl Malden, Everett Sloane, Thomas Gomez. Small-town newspaper editor Pidgeon finds himself in over his head when he tries to get the goods on corrupt sheriff Gomez. OK exposé drama.

Seminole (1953) **C-87m.** **½ D: Budd Boetticher. Rock Hudson, Barbara Hale, Anthony Quinn, Richard Carlson, Hugh O'Brian, Russell Johnson, Lee Marvin, James Best. Capable cast in unusual drama about earnest cavalry lieutenant Hudson trying to help Indian tribe's efforts to remain free of white man law.

Seminole Uprising (1955) **C-74m.** *½ D: Earl Bellamy. George Montgomery, Karin Booth, John Pickard, Ed Hinton. Trite handling of Indians vs. cavalry; too little action.

Semi-Tough (1977) **C-108m.** *** D: Michael Ritchie. Burt Reynolds, Kris Kristofferson, Jill Clayburgh, Robert Preston, Bert Convy, Lotte Lenya, Roger E. Mosley, Richard Masur, Carl Weathers, Brian Dennehy, Ron Silver. Easygoing comedy about two football stars and their mutual girlfriend wanders too much to hit any major targets but has some funny moments. Reynolds' charm makes up for film's other deficiencies. Adapted from Dan Jenkins' novel by Ring Lardner, Jr. (who took his name off the credits) and Walter Bernstein. Later a brief TV series. [R]▼●

Senator Was Indiscreet, The (1947) **74m.** *** D: George S. Kaufman. William Powell, Ella Raines, Peter Lind Hayes, Arleen Whelan, Ray Collins, Hans Conried. Wit-playwright Kaufman's only directorial fling turns out quite well, with Powell as Senator whose diary causes embarrassment. Entertaining satire.▼

Sender, The (1982-British) **C-91m.** *** D: Roger Christian. Kathryn Harrold, Zeljko Ivanek, Shirley Knight, Paul Freeman, Sean Hewitt, Harry Ditson. Solid thriller about telepathic, suicidal Ivanek, unable to control his powers, who transfers his nightmares to psychiatrist Harrold and causes havoc in a hospital. Very good of its type. [R]▼●

Send Me No Flowers (1964) **C-100m.** *** D: Norman Jewison. Rock Hudson, Doris Day, Tony Randall, Clint Walker, Paul Lynde, Hal March, Edward Andrews, Patricia Barry. Hypochondriac Rock, convinced he has a short time to live, has Randall find new husband for wife Doris. Funny script by Julius J. Epstein; Lynde is a riot as aggressive cemetery plot salesman.▼●

Senechal the Magnificent (1958-French) **78m.** **½ D: Jacques Boyer. Fernandel, Nadia Gray, Georges Chamarat, Jeanne Aubert, Armontel, Robert Pizani. Fernandel is well cast as buffoon actor who, through mistaken identities and an ability to mimic, becomes a Parisian hit.

Senior Prom (1959) **82m.** *½ D: David Lowell Rich. Jill Corey, Paul Hampton, Barbara Bostock, Jimmy Komack, Tom Laughlin. The title tells all in this flimsy, mostly boring musical. The "guest stars" include Louis Prima, Keely Smith, Mitch Miller, Ed Sullivan, Connee Boswell, Bob Crosby, Les Elgart, and Freddy Martin.

Seniors, The (1978) **C-87m.** ** D: Rod Amateau. Jeffrey Byron, Gary Imhof, Dennis Quaid, Lou Richards, Priscilla Barnes, Alan Reed, Edward Andrews, Robert Emhardt, Alan Hewitt. Four collegians open a bogus sex clinic, which mushrooms into a multimillion-dollar business. Alternately silly and satirical, with some innocuous nudity thrown in. Veteran character actors help a great deal. Written by Stanley (PILLOW TALK) Shapiro. Video title: THE SENIOR. [R]▼

Sensations (1944) **86m.** **½ D: Andrew L. Stone. Eleanor Powell, Dennis O'Keefe. C. Aubrey Smith, Eugene Pallette, W. C. Fields, Cab Calloway, Sophie Tucker. Publicity-wise Powell shows press-agent O'Keefe how to attract attention in this campy musical; one incredible number has her tap-dancing inside giant pinball machine! Fields' skit (his last appearance on film) is only fair. Originally titled SENSATIONS OF 1945.▼

Sense and Sensibility (1995) **C-135m.** ***½ D: Ang Lee. Emma Thompson, Alan Rickman, Kate Winslet, Hugh Grant, James Fleet, Harriet Walter, Gemma Jones, Elizabeth Spriggs, Robert Hardy, Greg Wise, Imelda Staunton, Imogen Stubbs, Hugh Laurie, Emilie Francois. Vivid, contemporary reading of Jane Austen's novel about two newly impoverished sisters—one impulsive and flirtatious, the other repeatedly thwarted and forced to suppress her feelings of love. Perfectly cast and performed, a spirited and moving look at social mores and how disparate personalities dealt with them in early 19th-century England. Thompson won an Oscar for Best Screenplay Adaptation. [PG]▼●◗

Senseless (1998) **C-93m.** ** D: Penelope Spheeris. Marlon Wayans, David Spade, Matthew Lillard, Rip Torn, Brad Dourif, Tamara Taylor, Richard McGonagle. Embroiled in cutthroat competition for a job, college business major gets a dose of one-upmanship when he agrees to take an injection of sense-enhancing "green stuff" as part of a campus lab experiment. Beware those side effects, and beware a comedy in which guinea pig Wayans outmugs even another Marlon (Brando—when he played mad Dr. Moreau). Torn is amusing as the kind of corporate smoothie he can now play in his sleep. [R]▼●◗

Sense of Loss, A (1972-U.S.-Swiss) **C/B&W-135m.** *** D: Marcel Ophuls. Thoughtful documentary about the continuing, never-ending political conflict—and violence—in Northern Ireland. Not up to Ophuls' previous film, THE SORROW AND THE PITY, but still heartbreaking in its most powerful moments.▼

Senso (1954-Italian) **C-115m.** **½ D: Luchino Visconti. Alida Valli, Farley Granger, Massimo Girotti, Heinz Moog. Carefully paced study of human emotions, chronicling the relationship between earthy, materialistic Austrian officer Granger and his aristocratic Italian mistress (Valli). An intriguing union of the neorealism of Visconti's earlier work and the lush romanticism often found in his later films. Retitled WANTON CONTESSA. English-language version, titled THE WANTON COUNTESS, features dialogue by Tennessee Williams and Paul Bowles!▼◗

Sensuous Nurse, The (1976-Italian) **C-78m.** *½ D: Nello Rossati. Ursula Andress, Jack Palance, Duilio Del Prete, Luciana Paluzzi, Lino Toffolo, Mario Pisu. Voluptuous Ursula hires on to help hasten the demise of a wealthy vintner with a heart condition by keeping his pulse racing in this smarmy sex comedy. Ursula does look great in the nude, however. [R]▼

Sentimental Journey (1946) **94m.** ** D: Walter Lang. John Payne, Maureen O'Hara, William Bendix, Cedric Hardwicke, Glenn Langan, Mischa Auer, Connie Marshall. Maudlin yarn of dying actress O'Hara adopting little girl to give husband Payne a companion when she is gone; no holds barred here. Remade as THE GIFT OF LOVE (1958) and as a 1984 TV movie.

Sentinel, The (1977) **C-93m.** ** D: Michael Winner. Cristina Raines, Ava Gardner, Chris Sarandon, Burgess Meredith, Sylvia Miles, Jose Ferrer, Arthur Kennedy, John Carradine, Christopher Walken, Eli Wallach, Jerry Orbach, Jeff Goldblum, Beverly D'Angelo, Martin Balsam, William Hickey, Tom Berenger. Slick but empty-headed shocker about N.Y.C. fashion model who rents Brooklyn Heights brownstone, finds it's full of demons and she's to be the next sentinel guarding the gateway to Hell. Good cast makes it somewhat endurable, but climax is awfully yucky. Freely based on Jeffrey Konvitz' best-seller. [R]▼◗

Senza Pieta SEE: **Without Pity**

Separate but Equal (1991) **C-200m. TVM** D: George Stevens, Jr. Sidney Poitier, Burt Lancaster, Richard Kiley, John McMartin, Graham Beckel, Ed Hall, Lynne Thigpen, Macon McCallman, Albert Hall. Inspiring drama about Thurgood Marshall's arguing the historic Brown vs. Board of Education case before the Supreme Court in 1954. Poitier, in his first TV work in 35 years, is tops, if a tad too old to play a young Marshall, then in his late thirties. Lancaster is eloquent as John W. Davis, his courtroom opponent. Kiley nearly steals it as Chief Justice Earl Warren. Written with heart by director Stevens. Originally shown in two parts. Lancaster's final acting role. Above average. ▼●

Separate Lives (1995) **C-102m.** *½ D: David Madden. Linda Hamilton, James Belushi, Vera Miles, Elisabeth Moss, Drew Snyder. Limp psychosexual thriller has detective (Belushi) on the trail of a murderer who's killing the patients of his sexy group therapist (Hamilton)—while she's convinced she's committing them herself. Predictable and bland. [R]▼

Separate Peace, A (1972) **C-104m.** BOMB D: Larry Peerce. John Heyl, Parker Stevenson, William Roerick, Peter Brush, Victor Bevine, Scott Bradbury. Supposedly sensitive story of two roommates in a 1940s prep school, taken from John Knowles' overrated novel, is enough to make anyone gag. Story is morbid, acting amateurish, and direction has no feeling at all for the period. A total bummer. [PG] ▼

Separate Tables (1958) **99m.** **** D: Delbert Mann. Burt Lancaster, Rita Hayworth, David Niven, Deborah Kerr, Wendy Hiller, Gladys Cooper, Cathleen Nesbitt, Rod Taylor, Felix Aylmer. Terence Rattigan's pair of romantic playlets set at English seaside resort are reworked here into superb drama in the GRAND HOTEL vein; Lancaster and Hayworth are divorced couple trying to make another go of it, Hiller is his timid mistress, Niven a supposed war hero, Kerr a lonely spinster dominated by mother Cooper. Bouquets all around, especially to Oscar winners Niven and Hiller. Screenplay by Rattigan and John Gay.▼●

Separate Ways (1981) **C-92m.** ** D: Howard Avedis. Karen Black, Tony LoBianco, Arlene Golonka, David Naughton, Jack Carter, Sharon Farrell, William Windom, Robert Fuller, Noah Hathaway, Sybil Danning. Low-budget U.S. answer to A MAN AND A WOMAN has former racecar driver LoBianco suffering marital problems with wife Black, exacerbated by her one-night stand with younger man Naughton. Good cast is wasted. [R]▼

September (1987) **C-82m.** ** D: Woody Allen. Denholm Elliott, Mia Farrow, Elaine Stritch, Sam Waterston, Jack Warden, Dianne Wiest. Six people vent their angst during a weekend in the country. Intelligent and well acted, but after a while it dawns on you that there's no earthly reason to be interested in these people and their whining. Stritch is a standout as Mia's flamboyant mom, and it's hard to completely dislike a film that plugs jazz pianist Art Tatum so vigorously. Set in Vermont but filmed completely on a soundstage. Writer-director Allen fared better with his earlier drama, INTERIORS. [PG]▼●

September Affair (1950) **104m.** **½ D: William Dieterle. Joseph Cotten, Joan Fontaine, Françoise Rosay, Jessica Tandy, Robert Arthur, Fortunio Bonanova, Jimmy Lydon. Trim romance of married man Cotten and pianist Fontaine who find that they're listed as dead in plane crash and now have chance to continue their affair. Makes effective use of classical music and Walter Huston's recording of "September Song" (which once again became a hit).▼●

September Storm (1960) **99m.** BOMB D: Byron Haskin. Joanne Dru, Mark Stevens, Robert Strauss, Asher Dann, M. Jean-Pierre Kerien, Vera Valmont. Scheming fashion model joins a group of adventurers searching for buried treasure off the coast of Majorca. Film's only novelty is that it was shot in 3-D CinemaScope.

September 30, 1955 (1978) **C-101m.** **½ D: James Bridges. Richard Thomas, Susan Tyrrell, Deborah Benson, Lisa Blount. Thomas Hulce, Dennis Quaid, Dennis Christopher. Arkansas undergrad, well played by Thomas, goes off his nut when James Dean dies, with tragic results for a girl friend. Original, if excessively uneven drama, is worth consideration for being one of the few films to deal at all seriously with the movie star mystique. Original title: 9/30/55; shown on TV as 24 HOURS OF THE REBEL. [PG]▼●

Sequoia (1934) **73m.** **½ D: Chester Franklin. Jean Parker, Russell Hardie, Samuel S. Hinds, Paul Hurst. Girl living near national forest raises orphaned deer and mountain lion to be friends. Fascinating animal footage burdened by simplistic, often heavy-handed story. Reissued as MALIBU, also the name of book on which it's based.

Serena (1962-British) **62m.** **½ D: Peter Maxwell. Patrick Holt, Emrys Jones, Honor Blackman, Bruce Beeby. Neat mystery programmer with Holt the detective inspector ferreting out the killer of artist Jones' wife.

Serenade (1956) **C-121m.** **½ D: Anthony Mann. Mario Lanza, Joan Fontaine, Sarita Montiel, Vincent Price, Joseph Calleia, Vince Edwards. James M. Cain novel becomes surface soaper of Lanza, the protégé of swank Fontaine, manipulated by manager Price and loved by earthy Montiel; spotty musical interludes.▼

Sergeant, The (1968) **C-107m.** ** D: John Flynn. Rod Steiger, John Phillip Law, Ludmila Mikael, Frank Latimore, Elliott Sullivan. Predictable drama, set in France, about homosexual Army sergeant Steiger and his desire for handsome private Law. Director Flynn has nice eye for detail, but overall, film doesn't make much of an impression. [R]

Sergeant Deadhead (1965) **C-89m.** *½ D: Norman Taurog. Frankie Avalon, Deborah Walley, Eve Arden, Cesar Romero, Fred Clark, Buster Keaton, Gale Gordon, Harvey Lembeck. Bungling Army sergeant goes into space with a chimpanzee and undergoes personality change. Oh, that poor monkey. Also known as SERGEANT DEADHEAD, THE ASTRONUT. Panavision.

Sergeant Madden (1939) **82m.** ** D: Josef von Sternberg. Wallace Beery, Tom Brown, Alan Curtis, Laraine Day, Fay Holden, David Gorcey, Etta McDaniel, Horace McMahon. Director von Sternberg out of his element with standard Beery vehicle of policeman whose son alienates him, marries orphan girl he raised.

Sergeant Murphy (1938) **57m.** ** D: B. Reeves Eason. Ronald Reagan, Mary Maguire, Donald Crisp, Ben Hendricks, William Davidson. Reagan stars in this forgettable programmer as a soldier who loves a talented horse. The sergeant of the title is the animal; Ronnie is a lowly private.

Sergeant Rutledge (1960) **C-118m.** *** D: John Ford. Jeffrey Hunter, Woody Strode, Constance Towers, Billie Burke, Carleton Young, Juano Hernandez, Willis Bouchey, Mae Marsh, Hank Worden, Jack Pennick. Arresting story of a black U.S. Cavalry officer on trial for rape and murder; his story is pieced together in flashback during his court-martial. Unusual subject matter for its time, solidly presented by Ford (with some occasionally awkward comic relief). Strode is commanding in the central role.▼

Sergeant Ryker (1968) **C-85m.** **½ D: Buzz Kulik. Lee Marvin, Bradford Dillman, Vera Miles, Peter Graves, Lloyd Nolan, Murray Hamilton. Adapted from TV film *The Case Against Sergeant Ryker*, story concerns court-martial of Marvin in title role, an Army sergeant during Korean War suspected of being a traitor; Miles is his wife and Dillman the dynamic defense attorney. Aka TORN BETWEEN TWO VALUES. ▼

Sergeant Steiner SEE: **Breakthrough** (1978)

Sergeants 3 (1962) **C-112m.** **½ D: John Sturges. Frank Sinatra, Dean Martin, Sammy Davis, Jr., Peter Lawford, Joey Bishop, Ruta Lee, Henry Silva. Second reworking of GUNGA DIN is amusing, but not up to 1939 original. This time it's out West with the Rat Pack as cavalry sergeants. Davis can't eclipse Sam Jaffe as Gunga Din, though. Panavision.

Sergeant York (1941) **134m.** ***½ D: Howard Hawks. Gary Cooper, Walter Brennan, Joan Leslie, George Tobias, Stanley Ridges, Margaret Wycherly, Ward Bond, Noah Beery, Jr., June Lockhart. Excellent story of pacifist York (Cooper) drafted during WW1, realizing purpose of fighting and becoming hero. Oscar-winning performance by Cooper in fine, intelligent film, balancing segments of rural America with battle scenes. John Huston was one of the writers. Also available in computer-colored version. ▼●

Serial (1980) **C-86m.** *** D: Bill Persky. Martin Mull, Tuesday Weld, Sally Kellerman, Bill Macy, Tom Smothers, Christopher Lee, Peter Bonerz, Jennifer McAlister, Nita Talbot, Stacey Nelkin, Barbara Rhoades, Pamela Bellwood. Trenchant satire on Marin County, Cal., and its residents' obsession with various freakish fads, sexual trends, and psychological mumbo-jumbo, with a Frank Capra-esque finale. Mull (in his first starring role) plays the only sane one in the bunch. Adapted from Cyra McFadden's column and book. [R] ▼●

Serial Mom (1994) **C-93m.** **½ D: John Waters. Kathleen Turner, Sam Waterston, Ricki Lake, Matthew Lillard, Scott Wesley Morgan, Walt MacPherson, Justin Whalin, Patricia Dunnock, Mink Stole, Mary Jo Catlett, Traci Lords, Patricia Hearst, Suzanne Somers. Beaming, cheerful Turner is the perfect mom to her suburban family; she's also a serial killer, bumping off anyone who offends her sense of family values. The main target of this movie's satirical barbs are those who would turn murderers into media heroes, but it takes plenty of other potshots along the way. Blander than most of Waters' films, this works only intermittently, despite a knockout performance from Turner. [R] ▼●◗

Serpent, The SEE: **Night Flight From Moscow**

Serpent and the Rainbow, The (1988) **C-98m.** ** D: Wes Craven. Bill Pullman, Cathy Tyson, Zakes Mokae, Paul Winfield, Brent Jennings, Theresa Merritt, Michael Gough. Ambitious (by Craven standards) but gratuitous chiller about a real-life anthropologist's experiences with black magic and voodoo in Haiti. Well done, but wallows in its atmosphere and special effects; however, Craven fans will boost the rating by a star. Based on the book by Wade Davis. [R] ▼●◗

Serpent of the Nile (1953) **C-81m.** *½ D: William Castle. Rhonda Fleming, William Lundigan, Raymond Burr, Michael Ansara, Julie Newmar. Antony and Cleopatra, B-movie style; good for a few laughs, anyway. Producer Sam Katzman used leftover sets from Rita Hayworth's SALOME.

Serpent's Egg, The (1978-German-U.S.) **C-120m.** *½ D: Ingmar Bergman. Liv Ullmann, David Carradine, Gert Frobe, Heinz Bennent, Glynn Turman, James Whitmore. Smorgasbord of depravities makes story of Jewish trapeze artist in pre-WW2 Germany an overwhelmingly unpleasant movie experience. Sven Nykvist's camerawork is brilliant as usual, but Carradine is fatally miscast. [R] ▼

Serpico (1973) **C-129m.** ***½ D: Sidney Lumet. Al Pacino, John Randolph, Jack Kehoe, Biff McGuire, Barbara Eda-Young, Cornelia Sharpe, Tony Roberts, James Tolkan, Lewis J. Stadlen, M. Emmet Walsh, F. Murray Abraham, Kenneth McMillan. Tough, exciting filmization of Peter Maas book based on true-life accounts of N.Y.C. undercover cop whose nonconformism—and exposure of department corruption—isolate him from the force. Screenplay by Waldo Salt and Norman Wexler. Look for Judd Hirsch as a cop. Followed by a TV movie and short-lived series. [R] ▼●

Servant, The (1963-British) **115m.** ***½ D: Joseph Losey. Dirk Bogarde, James Fox, Sarah Miles, Wendy Craig, Catherine Lacey, Patrick Magee. Insidious story of moral degradation as corrupt manservant Bogarde becomes master of employer Fox; superb study of brooding decadence. Scripted by Harold Pinter. ▼

Service De Luxe (1938) **85m.** ** D: Rowland V. Lee. Constance Bennett, Vincent Price, Charles Ruggles, Mischa Auer, Joy Hodges, Helen Broderick. Easy-to-take but empty-headed froth about a woman who runs a service company that does just about anything its customers require. Price makes his film debut as man who finally breaks through Bennett's "strictly business" facade.

Serving in Silence: The Marguerite Cammermeyer Story (1995) **C-100m. TVM** D: Jeff Bleckner. Glenn Close, Judy Davis, Jan Rubes, Wendy Makkena, Susan Barnes, William Converse-Roberts, Colleen Flynn, William Allan Young, Molly Parker. Close, as a real-life career military officer and combat veteran with a spotless service record and three grown children, casually mentions she's a lesbian during promotion consideration and finds herself being drummed out of the Army. This feminist response to the military's "don't ask, don't tell" policy was coproduced by Close and Barbra Streisand, among others, and drew fire on the eve of its premiere because of a discreet kissing scene between Close and Judy Davis, who plays her lover. Average.▼

Sesame Street Presents Follow That Bird (1985) **C-88m.** **½ D: Ken Kwapis. Carroll Spinney, Jim Henson, Frank Oz, Paul Bartel, Sandra Bernhard, John Candy, Chevy Chase, Joe Flaherty, Waylon Jennings, Dave Thomas. Sweet, simple film about Sesame Street's beloved Big Bird, who's placed in foster home but tries to hitchhike back to Sesame Street. Aimed solely at young children, who should enjoy it—though for adults nothing can top Oscar the Grouch's opening anthem. Cute songs throughout. [G]▼●

Session With the Committee, A (1969) **C-90m.** **½ D: Del Jack. Peter Bonerz, Barbara Bosson, Garry Goodrow, Carl Gottlieb, Jessica Myerson, Christopher Ross, Melvin Stewart, Don Sturdy (Howard Hesseman). Filmed collection of live skits by L.A. comic troupe isn't exactly "pure" cinema, but has the same appeal as a good comedy record album. Plenty of laughs. [PG]▼

Set It Off (1996) **C-121m.** ** D: F. Gary Gray. Jada Pinkett, Queen Latifah, Vivica A. Fox, Kimberly Elise, Blair Underwood, John C. McGinley, Anna Maria Horsford, Ella Joyce, Charlie Robinson, Chaz Lamar Shepard, Dr. Dre. Four black women from the L.A. projects decide to beat the system by robbing banks, and end up testing their friendship to deadly ends. Frustrating, overdirected film wants to be a hard-edged urban drama but relies on pyrotechnics and car chases for impact. Even worse is an unnecessary romantic subplot between Pinkett and suave banker Underwood. Latifah's powerhouse performance as a gun-toting lesbian gives the film a much needed jolt of realism. Super 35. [R] ▼●

Set-Up, The (1949) **72m.** ***½ D: Robert Wise. Robert Ryan, Audrey Totter, George Tobias, Alan Baxter, James Edwards, Wallace Ford. Gutsy account of washed-up fighter refusing to give up or go crooked; Ryan has never been better. Art Cohn's pungent screenplay was inspired by a narrative poem(!) by Joseph Moncure March. Photographed by Milton Krasner. Played out in real time—as you'll see by the clock shown in opening and closing shots.▼●

Seven (1979) **C-100m.** ** D: Andy Sidaris. William Smith, Barbara Leigh, Guich Koock, Art Metrano, Martin Kove, Richard Le Pore, Susan Kiger. Brawny Smith is hired by U.S. intelligence to destroy Hawaiian crime syndicate, which he does with enthusiastic team of "specialists." Violent, sexy, tongue-in-cheek action yarn includes the "shooting the swordsman" gag later immortalized in RAIDERS OF THE LOST ARK. [R]▼

Se7en (1995) **C-127m.** *** D: David Fincher. Brad Pitt, Morgan Freeman, Kevin Spacey, Gwyneth Paltrow, Richard Roundtree, R. Lee Ermey, John C. McGinley, Julie Araskog, Mark Boone Junior, John Cassini, Reginald E. Cathey, Peter Crombie, Hawthorne James, Michael Massee, Leland Orser, Richard Portnow. Dedicated detective (Freeman) breaks in his replacement (Pitt) during his last week before retiring—then stumbles onto the trail of a serial killer who's out to punish perpetrators of the seven deadly sins. Exceptionally well-crafted, intelligently written, and well-acted thriller . . . but also extremely unsettling, almost oppressive at times. Not much violence per se, but the film seems to wallow in the depths of human depravity it so passionately decries. Super 35. [R]▼●◗

Seven Alone (1975) **C-96m.** **½ D: Earl Bellamy. Dewey Martin, Aldo Ray, Anne Collins, Dean Smith, Stewart Peterson. OK family-wilderness picture on true story of seven children who make perilous 2,000 mile trek West during the 1800s after their parents die en route. [G]▼

Seven Angry Men (1955) **90m.** *** D: Charles Marquis Warren. Raymond Massey, Debra Paget, Jeffrey Hunter, James Best, Dennis Weaver, Dabbs Greer, Ann Tyrrell. Good historical drama of John Brown (Massey) and family fighting to free slaves during 1800s. Massey is fine in lead role, which he previously played in SANTA FE TRAIL.

Seven Beauties (1976-Italian) **C-115m.** **** D: Lina Wertmuller. Giancarlo Giannini, Fernando Rey, Shirley Stoler, Elena Fiore, Enzo Vitale. Director-writer Wertmuller's masterpiece follows a small-time Casanova through the horrors of WW2 battle and imprisonment in a concentration camp, where he learns to survive—at any cost. Giannini is superb in this harrowing, unforgettable film. [R]▼◗

Seven Brides for Seven Brothers (1954) **C-103m.** **** D: Stanley Donen. Howard Keel, Jane Powell, Jeff Richards, Russ Tamblyn, Tommy Rall, Virginia Gibson, Julie Newmeyer (Newmar), Ruta Kilmonis (Lee), Matt Mattox. Rollicking musical perfectly integrates song, dance, and story: Keel's decision to get himself a wife (Powell) inspires his rowdy brothers to follow suit. Tuneful Johnny Mercer–Gene DePaul score (with Oscar-winning musical direction by Adolph Deutsch and Saul Chaplin), but it's Michael Kidd's energetic dance numbers that really stand out, with rare screen work by dancers Jacques D'Amboise and Marc Platt. The barn-raising sequence is an absolute knockout. Screenplay by Albert Hackett, Frances Goodrich, and Dorothy Kingsley, from a Stephen

Vincent Benet story. Later a TV series and a Broadway musical. CinemaScope. ▼●◗

Seven Brothers Meet Dracula, The (1974-British-Hong Kong) **C-72m.** ** D: Roy Ward Baker. Peter Cushing, David Chiang, Julie Ege, Robin Stewart, Shih Szu, John Forbes-Robertson. Vampire hunter Van Helsing (Cushing) is in China in the late 19th century to vanquish Dracula with the help of some karate-chopping assistants. Odd blend of Kung Fu action, supernatural, and Dracula themes reportedly worked better in original 89m. version called LEGEND OF THE 7 GOLDEN VAMPIRES. Aka SEVEN GOLDEN VAMPIRES—THE LAST WARNING! Panavision. [R] ▼●◗

7 Capital Sins (1961-French-Italian) **113m.** ** D: Jean-Luc Godard, Roger Vadim, Sylvaine Dhomme, Edouard Molinaro, Philippe De Broca, Claude Chabrol, Jacques Demy. Marie-Jose Nat, Dominique Paturel, Jean-Marc Tennberg, Perrette Pradier. Potpourri of directors and talents play out modern parables concerning anger, envy, gluttony, greed, laziness, lust, and pride. Aka SEVEN DEADLY SINS and LES SEPT PECHES CAPITAUX. Dyaliscope. ▼

Seven Chances (1925) **56m.** ***½ D: Buster Keaton. Buster Keaton, T. Roy Barnes, Snitz Edwards, Ruth Dwyer, Frankie Raymond, Jules Cowles. Buster will inherit a fortune if he's married by 7:00 that evening; a miscommunication with his girlfriend leads to his pursuit by thousands of would-be brides. The highlight: a furious chase down a hill in which Buster dodges dozens of oversized boulders! One of Keaton's silent gems. That's young Jean Arthur as a switchboard operator who turns down Buster's marriage proposal. Remade as THE BACHELOR (1999). ▼●◗

Seven Cities of Gold (1955) **C-103m.** **½ D: Robert D. Webb. Richard Egan, Anthony Quinn, Jeffrey Hunter, Rita Moreno, Michael Rennie. Average spectacle adventure has good cast and fair direction. "Roughneck" learns ways of God in search for fabled Indian treasure in Western U.S. CinemaScope. ▼

Seven Days in May (1964) **118m.** *** D: John Frankenheimer. Burt Lancaster, Kirk Douglas, Fredric March, Ava Gardner, Edmond O'Brien, Martin Balsam, George Macready, Whit Bissell, Hugh Marlowe. Absorbing, believable story of military scheme to overthrow the government. Fine cast includes Lancaster as the general planning the coup and Douglas as the colonel who discovers the plot, March as U.S. President; intelligent suspense in Rod Serling screenplay from Fletcher Knebel and Charles W. Bailey novel. John Houseman made his screen acting debut in small but crucial role. Remade for cable as THE ENEMY WITHIN. ▼●◗

Seven Days' Leave (1942) **87m.** **½ D: Tim Whelan. Lucille Ball, Victor Mature, Harold Peary, Ginny Simms, Peter Lind Hayes, Arnold Stang, Ralph Edwards. Mature is an army private who will inherit $100,000 if he can marry heiress Ball. Sprightly musical comedy, featuring Freddy Martin and Les Brown's bands. ▼

Seven Days to Noon (1950-British) **93m.** **** D: John Boulting. Barry Jones, Olive Sloane, Andre Morell, Sheila Manahan, Hugh Cross, Joan Hickson. Superbly paced thriller (from Paul Dehn and James Bernard's Oscar-winning story) about scientist threatening to explode bomb in London if his demands are not met. Screenplay by Roy Boulting and Frank Harvey.

Seven Deadly Sins, The (1952-Italian-French) **124m.** **½ D: Eduardo De Filippo, Jean Dreville, Yves Allegret, Roberto Rossellini, Carlo Rim, Claude Autant Lara, Georges Lacombe. Gérard Philipe, Michele Morgan, Françoise Rosay, Isa Miranda, Paolo Stoppa, Eduardo De Filippo, Noel Noel, Viviane Romance, Henri Vidal. Episodic potpourri illustrating the seven major vices, with an eighth, "unknown" one thrown in for good measure. The best of the lot are "Gluttony," in which a piece of cheese comes between a man and the willing arms of a woman, and "Envy," in which a woman becomes jealous over her husband's pet cat. Also available in English-dubbed 83m. version. ▼

Seven Different Ways SEE: **Quick, Let's Get Married**

711 Ocean Drive (1950) **102m.** **½ D: Joseph M. Newman. Edmond O'Brien, Joanne Dru, Otto Kruger, Bert Freed. Tidy racketeer yarn of the bookie syndicate in the U.S. with exciting climax at Hoover Dam.

7 Faces of Dr. Lao (1964) **C-100m.** *** D: George Pal. Tony Randall, Barbara Eden, Arthur O'Connell, John Ericson, Kevin Tate, Argentina Brunetti, Noah Beery, Jr., Minerva Urecal, John Qualen, Lee Patrick. Engaging fantasy of Western town brought to its senses by parables performed by mysterious traveling circus; tour de force for Randall, who plays six roles. William Tuttle won special Oscar for makeup creations. Based on Charles G. Finney's novel *The Circus of Dr. Lao*. ▼●

Seven Golden Men (1965-Italian) **C-87m.** **½ D: Marco Vicario. Philippe Leroy, Rossana Podesta, Gastone Moschin, Gabriele Tinti, Jose Suarez. Standard but diverting heist film, with Leroy as mastermind who plans to steal seven tons of gold from Swiss bank. Clumsy dubbing, brassy music track. Released here in 1969. Followed by a sequel.

Seven Golden Men Strike Again (1966-Italian) **C-102m.** ** D: Marco Vicario. Philippe Leroy, Rossana Podesta, Gastone

Moschin, Giampiero Albertini, Gabriele Tinti, Maurice Poli. Espionage expert Leroy is hired under pressure from American agents to spy on Latin American general, but he and Podesta have their eye on gold instead. Complicated cat-and-mouse plot.

Seven Golden Vampires—The Last Warning! SEE: **Seven Brothers Meet Dracula, The**

Seven Graves for Rogan SEE: **Time to Die, A**

Seven Guns for the MacGregors (1968-Italian-Spanish) **C-97m.** *½ D: Frank Garfield (Franco Giraldi). Robert Wood, Manny Zarzo, Nick Anderson, Paul Carter. Standard spaghetti Western about seven brothers unjustly put in jail who escape and go after the crooked sheriff. Sequel: UP THE MACGREGORS. Techniscope.

Seven Hills of Rome (1958) **C-104m.** **½ D: Roy Rowland. Mario Lanza, Peggie Castle, Marisa Allasio, Renato Rascel, Rosella Como. Formula vehicle for Lanza, as a television star who retreats to Rome and falls in love; mellower than usual, with nice scenery and supporting cast. Technirama.▼●

Seven Hours to Judgment (1988) **C-89m.** ** D: Beau Bridges. Beau Bridges, Ron Leibman, Julianne Phillips, Reggie Johnson, Al Freeman, Jr. Bridges directs himself in an earnest but farfetched revenge saga as the hapless judge whom nut case Leibman feels had been too lenient with the minority punks who killed Leibman's wife; Ron retaliates by kidnapping Beau's beautiful spouse (Phillips) and setting Bridges on a survival quest in a tough part of town. [R]▼●

Seven Keys to Baldpate (1947) **66m.** **½ D: Lew Landers. Phillip Terry, Jacqueline White, Eduardo Ciannelli, Margaret Lindsay, Arthur Shields. Mystery writer finds plenty of real-life mystery at the Baldpate Inn, in this sixth go-round for the hardy George M. Cohan stage comedy (based on Earl Derr Biggers' book). Filmed before in 1915, 1917, 1925, 1929, and 1935. Remade as HOUSE OF THE LONG SHADOWS.

Seven Little Foys, The (1955) **C-95m.** *** D: Melville Shavelson. Bob Hope, Milly Vitale, George Tobias, Billy Gray, James Cagney. Pleasant biography of vaudevillian Eddie Foy and his performing family. Hope lively in lead role, Cagney guests as George M. Cohan; their table-top dance duet is the movie's high point. VistaVision.▼

Seven Men From Now (1956) **C-78m.** *** D: Budd Boetticher. Randolph Scott, Gail Russell, Lee Marvin, Walter Reed, John Larch, Donald Barry. Scott tracks down seven bandits who held up Wells Fargo station and killed his wife. Solid Western, first of seven from the Scott-Boetticher team, with a script by Burt Kennedy.

Seven Miles From Alcatraz (1942) **62m.** **½ D: Edward Dmytryk. James Craig, Bonita Granville, Frank Jenks, Cliff Edwards, George Cleveland, Tala Birell, John Banner. Craig and Jenks break out of the "Rock" and hide out at a nearby lighthouse which is being used by Nazi spies. Which, then, is more important: America's freedom, or their own? Medium-grade Hollywood propaganda in this OK B picture.▼

Seven Minutes, The (1971) **C-116m.** **½ D: Russ Meyer. Wayne Maunder, Marianne McAndrew, Philip Carey, Yvonne De Carlo, Jay C. Flippen, Edy Williams, John Carradine, Harold J. Stone. Host of fine character actors fail to save laughable adaptation of Irving Wallace's best-seller about pornography trial; interesting mainly as Meyer's only "straight" film. TV prints run 102m. Look for Tom Selleck as a publisher. [PG—edited from original R rating]

Seven-Per-Cent Solution, The (1976) **C-113m.** *** D: Herbert Ross. Nicol Williamson, Alan Arkin, Vanessa Redgrave, Robert Duvall, Laurence Olivier, Joel Grey, Samantha Eggar, Jeremy Kemp, Charles Gray, Regine. Sherlock Holmes meets Sigmund Freud in this handsome, entertaining film adapted by Nicholas Meyer from his novel. Shifts gears from serious drama to tongue-in-cheek adventure, but stays on target all the way. Nice score by John Addison. [PG]▼●◗

Seven Samurai, The (1954-Japanese) **141m.** **** D: Akira Kurosawa. Toshiro Mifune, Takashi Shimura, Yoshio Inaba, Ko Kimura, Seiji Miyaguchi, Minoru Chiaki. Classic film about 16th-century Japanese village which hires professional warriors to fend off bandits. Kurosawa's "far-east Western" has served as model for many films since, including American remake THE MAGNIFICENT SEVEN (a title once given this film for U.S. release). The complete 208m. version is even *more* impressive for its humanity as well as its powerful action sequences.▼●◗

Seven Seas to Calais (1962-Italian) **C-102m.** **½ D: Rudolph Maté, Primo Zeglio. Rod Taylor, Keith Michell, Irene Worth, Anthony Dawson, Basil Dignam. Minor but entertaining swashbuckler with Taylor as Sir Francis Drake. CinemaScope.

Seven Sinners (1940) **87m.** *** D: Tay Garnett. Marlene Dietrich, John Wayne, Albert Dekker, Broderick Crawford, Anna Lee, Mischa Auer, Billy Gilbert. Alluring Dietrich makes Wayne forget about the Navy for a while in this engaging action-love story with excellent supporting cast. Remade as SOUTH SEA SINNER.▼●

Seven Sweethearts (1942) **98m.** **½ D: Frank Borzage. Kathryn Grayson, Van Heflin, Marsha Hunt, S. Z. Sakall, Cecilia Parker, Peggy Moran, Diana Lewis, Isobel Elsom, Donald Meek, Louise Beavers. Schmaltz about Sakall's brood of daugh-

ters, none of whom can marry until the eldest does.
Seventeen (1940) **78m.** **½ D: Louis King. Jackie Cooper, Betty Field, Otto Kruger, Richard Denning, Peter Lind Hayes, Betty Moran, Ann Shoemaker, Norma Nelson. Cooper is delightful as teen-ager facing adolescent problems, in adaptation of Booth Tarkington story.
Seventeen and Anxious (1970-German) **C-86m.** **½ D: Zbynek Brynych. Anne Koster, Nadja Tiller, Karl Michael Vogler, Peter Kern, Siegfried Rauch. Thoughtful coming-of-age film with excellent Continental supporting cast. Originally titled O HAPPY DAY, making extensive use of the original hit gospel recording of that name. [R]
1776 (1972) **C-141m.** *** D: Peter H. Hunt. William Daniels, Howard da Silva, Ken Howard, Donald Madden, Ron Holgate, David Ford, Blythe Danner, Roy Poole, Virginia Vestoff, John Cullum. America's first Congress in struggle for independence from Britain provides framework for this unique musical by Sherman Edwards and Peter Stone. Almost all of the original Broadway cast remain, with Daniels as John Adams and da Silva as Benjamin Franklin leading the pack. Laserdisc version runs approx. 180m., with many elements director Hunt was forced to cut from theatrical release, including one entire number, "Cool Considerate Men." Panavision. [G]▼●
Seventh Cavalry (1956) **C-75m.** **½ D: Joseph H. Lewis. Randolph Scott, Barbara Hale, Jay C. Flippen, Jeanette Nolan, Frank Faylen. Scott plays an officer who must prove that he didn't desert Custer at the Little Bighorn battle.▼
Seventh Coin, The (1992) **C-95m.** *½ D: Dror Soref. Alexandra Powers, Navin Chowdhry, Peter O'Toole, John Rhys-Davies, Ally Walker, Julius Washington, Nicholas Kallsen. Teen-oriented action-adventure film lacking action and adventure. O'Toole, believing he's King Herod reincarnated, pursues two youths who have a precious coin which belonged to Herod. O'Toole looks and acts waxen. Remember: reading is fun. [PG-13]▼●
Seventh Cross, The (1944) **110m.** *** D: Fred Zinnemann. Spencer Tracy, Signe Hasso, Hume Cronyn, Jessica Tandy, Herbert Rudley, Felix Bressart, Ray Collins, Alexander Granach, Agnes Moorehead, George Macready, Steven Geray, Kaaren Verne, George Zucco. Seven men escape from Nazi concentration camp and are pursued by the Gestapo. Exciting film makes strong statement about a cynic who regains hope when others risk their lives to save him. Tandy and Cronyn's first film together. An early winner for Zinnemann.▼
7th Dawn, The (1964-British) **C-123m.** *½ D: Lewis Gilbert. William Holden, Susannah York, Capucine, Tetsuro Tamba, Michael Goodliffe. Dreary tale of personal and political conflict among WW2 allies—now adversaries—in postwar Malaya.▼
7th Heaven (1927) **119m.** **½ D: Frank Borzage. Janet Gaynor, Charles Farrell, Ben Bard, David Butler, Marie Mosquini, Albert Gran. One of the most famous screen romances of all time does not hold up as perfectly as one would like; Gaynor won first Academy Award as Diane, mistreated Paris waif redeemed and revived by cocky sewer-worker Chico (Farrell). His performance weakens film, as does terrible war subplot and finale. Still interesting, though; beautifully filmed, with lovely theme "Diane." Gaynor received her Oscar for this film, SUNRISE, and STREET ANGEL. Also won Oscars for Screenplay (Benjamin Glazer) and Director. Remade in 1937.▼
Seventh Heaven (1937) **102m.** ** D: Henry King. Simone Simon, James Stewart, Jean Hersholt, Gregory Ratoff, Gale Sondergaard, J. Edward Bromberg, John Qualen. Famous silent film of poignant lovers in France doesn't do as well this time, with Gallic Stewart and soggy script.
Seven Thieves (1960) **102m.** ***½ D: Henry Hathaway. Edward G. Robinson, Rod Steiger, Joan Collins, Eli Wallach, Alexander Scourby, Michael Dante, Berry Kroeger, Sebastian Cabot. Taut caper of well-planned Monte Carlo heist, with excellent cast giving credibility to far-fetched premise. CinemaScope.▼
Seventh Seal, The (1957-Sweden) **96m.** **** D: Ingmar Bergman. Max von Sydow, Gunnar Bjornstrand, Nils Poppe, Bibi Andersson, Bengt Ekerot. Sydow, a disillusioned knight on his way back from the Crusades, tries to solve the mysteries of life while playing chess game with Death, who has offered him a short reprieve. Spellbinding, one-of-a-kind masterpiece helped gain Bergman international acclaim. ▼●◗
Seventh Sign, The (1988) **C-98m.** *½ D: Carl Schultz. Demi Moore, Michael Biehn, Jürgen Prochnow, Peter Friedman, Manny Jacobs, John Taylor, Lee Garlington, Akosua Busia, John Heard, Ian Buchanan. Pregnant Moore is convinced it's apocalypse now and that boarder Prochnow wants her baby for his end-of-the-world machinations. Could be; look out for dead ocean life, icy deserts and rivers running with blood. Supernatural grab bag is directed with all the zeal one brings to a documentary on stock portfolios; result has an extraordinarily high "oh, come on" quotient. Panavision. [R]▼●◗
Seventh Sin, The (1957) **94m.** **½ D: Ronald Neame. Eleanor Parker, Bill Travers, Françoise Rosay, George Sanders, Jean-

Pierre Aumont, Ellen Corby. Remake of W. Somerset Maugham's THE PAINTED VEIL has virtue of Parker's earnest performance as adulterous wife of a doctor who redeems herself during an epidemic; set in Hong Kong and inner China. CinemaScope.

Seventh Veil, The (1945-British) **95m.** ***½ D: Compton Bennett. James Mason, Ann Todd, Herbert Lom, Hugh McDermott, Albert Lieven. Superb psychological drama of pianist Todd, left as ward to her neurotic cousin Mason. Psychiatrist Lom uses hypnosis to enable Todd to regain her professional and personal sanity. All three stars are first-rate in one of the key British films of the forties. Muriel and Sydney Box's screenplay won an Oscar.▼●

Seventh Victim, The (1943) **71m.** *** D: Mark Robson. Tom Conway, Kim Hunter, Jean Brooks, Evelyn Brent, Elizabeth Russell, Hugh Beaumont, Erford Gage, Isabel Jewell, Barbara Hale. Offbeat Val Lewton chiller of innocent Hunter stumbling onto N.Y.C. group of devil-worshipers. Genuinely eerie.▼●

7th Voyage of Sinbad, The (1958) **C-87m.** ***½ D: Nathan Juran. Kerwin Mathews, Kathryn Grant (Crosby), Richard Eyer, Torin Thatcher. Top-notch adventure/fantasy pits hero Sinbad against unscrupulous magician (Thatcher) who has reduced Princess Grant to miniature size. Good pacing, eye-popping special effects by Ray Harryhausen (including famed duel with skeleton), music score by Bernard Herrmann. A winner all the way.▼●◗

Seven Times Seven (1969-Italian) **C-92m.** ** D: Michele Lupo. Terry-Thomas, Lionel Stander, Gastone Moschin, Gordon Mitchell, Adolfo Celi. Middling cops & robbers farce that has a gang of convicts go over the wall, rob the Royal Mint, and then break back into prison. Techniscope.

Seven-Ups, The (1973) **C-103m.** **½ D: Philip D'Antoni. Roy Scheider, Tony LoBianco, Bill Hickman, Richard Lynch, Victor Arnold. THE FRENCH CONNECTION producer directed this unofficial sequel, with Scheider scoring as a tough cop. Action outweighs plot, and car chase is one of the best yet filmed. Shot in N.Y.C. [PG]▼●

Seven Waves Away SEE: **Abandon Ship**

Seven Ways From Sundown (1960) **C-87m.** **½ D: Harry Keller. Audie Murphy, Barry Sullivan, Venetia Stevenson, John McIntire, Kenneth Tobey. Murphy is Texas ranger assigned to bring in seasoned killer Sullivan, with usual results.

7 Women (1966) **C-87m.** ** D: John Ford. Anne Bancroft, Sue Lyon, Margaret Leighton, Flora Robson, Mildred Dunnock, Anna Lee, Betty Field, Eddie Albert, Mike Mazurki, Woody Strode. Flat soaper of dedicated missionaries in China in 1935, menaced by warrior cutthroats. Despite cast and director, a dull film. Ford's last feature. Panavision.●

Seven Women From Hell (1961) **88m.** ** D: Robert D. Webb. Patricia Owens, Denise Darcel, Cesar Romero, John Kerr, Yvonne Craig. Able cast wasted on trite account of female prisoners in Japanese prison, set in WW2 New Guinea. CinemaScope.

Seven Year Itch, The (1955) **C-105m.** *** D: Billy Wilder. Marilyn Monroe, Tommy (Tom) Ewell, Evelyn Keyes, Sonny Tufts, Victor Moore, Oscar Homolka, Carolyn Jones, Doro Merande, Robert Strauss. While Ewell's wife is vacationing in the country, wide-eyed Tom fantasizes about the sexpot who moves in upstairs. This film entered the ranks of pop culture when Marilyn stepped on a subway grating wearing a billowy white skirt . . . but writer-director Wilder had to skirt censorship issues in adapting George Axelrod's Broadway play, and the results are much tamer than the original (though still entertaining). Marilyn is delightful. Clever titles by Saul Bass. CinemaScope.▼●

Seven Years in Tibet (1997) **C-136m.** *** D: Jean-Jacques Annaud. Brad Pitt, David Thewlis, B. D. Wong, Mako, Danny Denzongpa, Victor Wong, Jamyang Jamtsho Wangchuk. Long but absorbing tale of Austrian mountaineer/adventurer Heinrich Harrer, whose attempt to scale a formidable Himalayan mountain peak in 1939 is interrupted by WW2—and whose subsequent adventures bring him to Tibet and the holy city of Llasa, normally closed to outsiders. There he meets and is befriended by the 14-year-old Dalai Lama. Pitt is excellent as Harrer, a difficult character because he is selfish and arrogant—until he learns humility in Tibet. Magnificently filmed. Panavision. [PG-13]▼●◗

Severed Head, A (1971-British) **C-96m.** *** D: Dick Clement. Ian Holm, Lee Remick, Richard Attenborough, Claire Bloom, Clive Revill, Jennie Linden. Sophisticated sex comedy-drama seemed out of step with the youthful 70s, looks better today; vintner Holm is expected to keep a stiff upper lip while wife Remick has an open affair with her shrink (Attenborough). Sharp performances, thoughtful adaptation of the Iris Murdoch novel by Frederic Raphael. [R]

Sex and the Other Man (1996) **C-89m.** *½ D: Karl Slovin. Stanley Tucci, Kari Wuhrer, Ron Eldard. Impotent Eldard discovers his sex-starved girlfriend (Wuhrer) about to hop into bed with her yuppie wimp boss (Tucci), and promptly goes bonkers. Good cast flounders in this poorly scripted and sloppily directed three-character psychodrama. [R]▼●◗

Sex and the Single Girl (1964) **C-114m.** **½ D: Richard Quine. Natalie Wood, Tony Curtis, Lauren Bacall, Henry Fonda,

Mel Ferrer, Fran Jeffries, Edward Everett Horton, Larry Storch, Stubby Kaye, Count Basie and Orchestra. Helen Gurley Brown's book shoved aside, title used to exploit fairly amusing tale of smut-magazine editor Curtis wooing notorious female psychologist Wood. Bacall and Fonda wrap it up as a battling married couple. Coscripted by Joseph Heller.▼●

Sex, Drugs, Rock & Roll (1991) **C-96m.** **½ D: John McNaughton. Eric Bogosian. Industrial-strength performance film of Bogosian's one-man stage show, locking us in a room with ten insufferables it would be a pleasure to avoid. Keenly observed, though, with Bogosian a brilliant mimic; film should benefit from at-home showings, enabling viewers to absorb as much or little as they want in a single sitting. [R]▼

Sex Kittens Go to College (1960) **94m.** BOMB D: Albert Zugsmith. Mamie Van Doren, Tuesday Weld, Mijanou Bardot (Brigitte's sister), Louis Nye, Martin Milner, Mickey Shaughnessy, Pamela Mason, (Norman) "Woo Woo" Grabowski, Jackie Coogan, John Carradine. Priceless title and cast fail to deliver in shockingly unfunny comedy; new head of college science department (Mamie, working very hard to convince us she's a genius) turns out to be an ex-stripper. Finding a movie with worse direction would be almost as impossible as finding another movie with a night club jazz combo fronted by *Conway Twitty!* Don't say you weren't warned. Aka THE BEAUTY AND THE ROBOT.

sex, lies, & videotape (1989) **C-100m.** *** D: Steven Soderbergh. James Spader, Andie MacDowell, Peter Gallagher, Laura San Giacomo. A selfish, successful lawyer—whose wife has turned frigid and whose sister-in-law has become his lover—welcomes an old college friend for a visit, little dreaming the effect he'll have on all of them. This intriguing, exceptionally well-acted first feature for writer-director Soderbergh took top prize at the Cannes Film Festival; its deliberate pace and talky nature are reminiscent of an Eric Rohmer film—and like one of his, it's not to everyone's taste. [R]▼●◗

Sex Play SEE: **Bunny Caper, The**

Sextette (1978) **C-91m.** BOMB D: Ken Hughes. Mae West, Tony Curtis, Ringo Starr, Dom DeLuise, Timothy Dalton, George Hamilton, Alice Cooper, Keith Moon, Rona Barrett, Walter Pidgeon, George Raft. Astonishing is the only word for this comedy about a Hollywood glamor queen whose many ex-husbands keep popping up during her latest honeymoon. Naturally there's curiosity value in seeing octogenarian Mae still strutting her stuff, but it wears out pretty fast. Her last movie, based on her play *Sex.* [PG]▼

Sex Through a Window SEE: **Extreme Close-Up**

Sex With a Smile (1976-Italian) **C-100m.** *½ D: Sergio Martino. Marty Feldman, Edwige Fenech, Sydne Rome, Barbara Bouchet, Dayle Haddon, Enrico Monterrano, Giovanni Ralli. Five episodes that promise a lot in terms of sex and laughter, then (outside of Feldman segment) fail to deliver. Heavy on slapstick, and heavy reliance on knowledge of Italian affairs. [R]▼

S.F.W. (1995) **C-92m.** BOMB D: Jefery Levy. Stephen Dorff, Reese Witherspoon, Jake Busey, Joey Lauren Adams, Pamela Gidley, David Barry Gray, Jack Noseworthy, Richard Portnow, Annie McEnroe, Natasha (Gregson) Wagner, Tobey Maguire, Gary Coleman. Self-described "serio-comedy about terrorism, beer, and talk shows" centers on a surly young rebel who becomes a nationwide hero after being held hostage for 36 days by convenience-store terrorists. Woefully self-deluding in terms of its own importance, strident film at least provides the catch phrase to summarize its worth: title stems from anti-hero Dorff's constant spouting of "S.F.W." (So [expletive] What?). [R]▼

Sgt. Bilko (1996) **C-94m.** *** D: Jonathan Lynn. Steve Martin, Dan Aykroyd, Phil Hartman, Glenne Headly, Daryl Mitchell, Max Casella, Eric Edwards, Dan Ferro, John Marshall Jones, Brian Ortiz, Pamela Segall, Catherine Silvers, Chris Rock, Richard Herd, Travis Tritt. Master Sergeant Ernie Bilko has a moneymaking scheme for every occasion at Fort Baxter, Kansas. His superior, Col. Hall (Aykroyd), looks the other way until the sergeant's long-ago nemesis Major Thorn (Hartman) turns up and seeks revenge. Amiable recycling of the classic 1950s Nat Hiken TV comedy series, which starred Phil Silvers; that's his daughter Catherine as the owlish, uptight Pentagon auditor. Martin remains a first-rate farceur and is surrounded by a highly capable comedy cast. Super 35. [PG]▼●◗

Sgt. Pepper's Lonely Hearts Club Band (1978) **C-111m.** *½ D: Michael Schultz. Peter Frampton, The Bee Gees, George Burns, Frankie Howerd, Donald Pleasence, Sandy Farina, Dianne Steinberg, Billy Preston, Steve Martin, Earth, Wind & Fire. Attempt to link songs from The Beatles' classic album into some sort of storyline just doesn't work; sequences range from tolerable to embarrassing. As to The Bee Gees' acting talent, if you can't say something nice . . . Panavision. [PG]▼●

Shack Out on 101 (1955) **80m.** *** D: Edward Dein. Terry Moore, Frank Lovejoy, Lee Marvin, Keenan Wynn, Whit Bissell. Lee Marvin *is* Slob in this trash classic about the efforts of hash slinger Moore to combat Communism while juggling the lecherous advances of nearly all her co-stars. Absolutely one of a kind, with most of the action taking place on a single shabby set (Wynn's beanery).▼

Shades of Fear (1993-British) **C-92m.** ** D: Beeban Kidron. Rakie Ayola, John Hurt, Jonathan Pryce, Vanessa Redgrave, Dorothy Tutin. Flat, disappointing drama about a young woman (Ayola) who aspires to become a pilot, and the various characters who cross her path as she sails for England. Scripted by Jeanette Winterson, who wrote the far superior ORANGES ARE NOT THE ONLY FRUIT, the British telefilm which helped establish Kidron's reputation. Original title: GREAT MOMENTS IN AVIATION. [R]▼

Shadey (1985-British) **C-106m.** **½ D: Philip Saville. Antony Sher, Billie Whitelaw, Patrick Macnee, Lesley Ash, Larry Lamb, Bernard Hepton, Katherine Helmond. Occasionally funny but mostly uninvolving comedy-fantasy-thriller about the title character (Sher), who is able to transmit to film visions from his mind. He wants to use his ability only for peaceful purposes—yet he also needs money for a sex-change operation. Helmond's role is best, that of a hilariously unpredictable, looney Lady.▼

Shadow, The (1994) **C-108m.** **½ D: Russell Mulcahy. Alec Baldwin, John Lone, Penelope Ann Miller, Peter Boyle, Ian McKellen, Tim Curry, Jonathan Winters, Sab Shimono, Andre Gregory, James Hong, Arsenio "Sonny" Trinidad, Joseph Maher, John Kapelos, Max Wright, Ethan Phillips, Larry Joshua. Lamont Cranston, having lived a life of moral degradation, is "reborn" as a singleminded crimefighter with the ability to cloud men's minds. This adaptation of the venerable pulp novels and beloved radio show (brought to the screen before in the late 1930s, and in a 1940 serial) comes frustratingly close to working, but fails. Cranston is both inscrutable and uninteresting. Great production design and wonderful effects get lost in a movie that keeps the viewer at arm's length throughout. And what a waste of a great supporting cast! [PG-13]▼●◗

Shadow Box, The (1980) **C-100m. TVM** D: Paul Newman. Joanne Woodward, Christopher Plummer, Valerie Harper, James Broderick, Sylvia Sidney, Melinda Dillon, Ben Masters, Curtiss Marlowe, John Considine. Playwright Michael Cristofer adapted his Pulitzer Prize-and Tony Award-winning play about three terminally ill patients and their families during one day at an experimental rustic retreat in California. A powerful and insightful story, well served by this stellar cast. Above average.▼

Shadow Conspiracy (1997) **C-103m.** BOMB D: George P. Cosmatos. Charlie Sheen, Donald Sutherland, Linda Hamilton, Stephen Lang, Ben Gazzara, Nicholas Turturro, Sam Waterston, Charles Cioffi, Theodore Bikel, Gore Vidal, Terry O'Quinn, Paul Gleason, Penny Fuller. White House whiz kid Sheen learns of a sinister conspiracy in the highest levels of the government, but soon becomes a target of the sinister killer himself. Painfully obvious, wearily derivative, and driven by ludicrous coincidences. Panavision. [R]▼●

Shadow in the Sky (1951) **78m.** **½ D: Fred M. Wilcox. Ralph Meeker, Nancy Davis (Reagan), James Whitmore, Jean Hagen, Gladys Hurlbut. Meeker is quite believable as shellshocked ex-G.I. trying to regain his sanity.

Shadowlands (1985-British) **C-90m.** *** D: Norman Stone. Joss Ackland, Claire Bloom, David Waller, Rupert Baderman, Rhys Hopkins. Poignant, wise, quietly rewarding drama about British writer C. S. Lewis (Ackland), a confirmed bachelor, and how he is changed when he falls in love with American divorcée Bloom. Lovely performances by the stars; exceptional award-caliber script by William Nicholson, who later turned this into a stage play. Aka C. S. LEWIS: THROUGH THE SHADOWLANDS. Remade in 1993. ▼

Shadowlands (1993-British) **C-130m.** ***½ D: Richard Attenborough. Anthony Hopkins, Debra Winger, Edward Hardwicke, Michael Denison, Joseph Mazzello, John Wood, Robert Flemyng, Peter Howell, Peter Firth. Absorbing tale of British writer C. S. Lewis (*The Lion, The Witch and the Wardrobe*) whose comfortable if rigid life as an Oxford don in the 1950s is shaken by his meeting with a forthright American poet, Joy Gresham. Intelligent and moving, with Hopkins in peak form, and Winger his match; the supporting actors are equally good. Filmed on location at Oxford. Adapted by William Nicholson from his 1985 television script and subsequent play. Panavision. [PG]▼●◗

Shadow Man, The (1953-British) **75m.** ** D: Richard Vernon. Cesar Romero, Kay Kendall, Victor Maddern. Standard action-programmer with Romero a casino owner in love with Kendall, involved with homicide.

Shadow of a Doubt (1943) **108m.** ***½ D: Alfred Hitchcock. Teresa Wright, Joseph Cotten, Macdonald Carey, Patricia Collinge, Henry Travers, Wallace Ford, Hume Cronyn. Perceptive Americana intertwined with story of young girl who slowly comes to realize her beloved Uncle Charley is really the Merry Widow murderer; Cronyn steals film as nosy pulp-story fan, in his film debut. Scripted by Thornton Wilder, Alma Reville, and Sally Benson from Gordon McDonnell's story. Remade in 1958 (as STEP DOWN TO TERROR) and for TV in 1991.▼●

Shadow of Fear (1956-British) **76m.** ** D: Albert S. Rogell. Mona Freeman, Jean Kent, Maxwell Reed, Hugh Miller, Gretchen Franklin. Flabby suspenser of Freeman realizing that her stepmother is planning to murder her as she did hubby; set in England. Original title: BEFORE I WAKE.

Shadow of the Cat (1961-British) **79m.** ** D: John Gilling. Barbara Shelley, Andre Morell, William Lucas, Richard Warner, Freda Jackson. Engaging horror yarn about feline who avenges her mistress's murder.

Shadow of the Hawk (1976-Canadian) **C-92m.** *½ D: George McCowan. Jan-Michael Vincent, Marilyn Hassett, Chief Dan George, Pea Shandel, Marianne Jones. Formula action meller has Vincent battling supernatural Indian spirits. [PG]

Shadow of the Thin Man (1941) **97m.** *** D: W. S. Van Dyke II. William Powell, Myrna Loy, Barry Nelson, Donna Reed, Sam Levene, Alan Baxter. Nick and Nora probe murder at a race track and run into the usual assortment of shady characters in this agreeable fourth entry in the series, notable for famed future acting teacher Stella Adler in a rare film role (as a gambler's moll).▼●

Shadow of the Wolf (1993-Canadian-French) **C-112m.** ** D: Jacques Dorfman. Lou Diamond Phillips, Toshiro Mifune, Jennifer Tilly, Bernard-Pierre Donnadieu, Donald Sutherland. Overwrought adventure epic set in the Arctic, in which a murder sets the stage for an Eskimo couple's battle against the overwhelming odds of nature and fate. Based on the best-selling Canadian novel *Agaguk*, this film looks expensive—and is—but despite the talent in front of the camera and behind it (including Oscar-winning cinematographer Billy Williams), the scenery easily upstages the drama. Super 35. [PG-13]▼●

Shadow of Zorro, The (1962-Italian) **C-84m.** *½ D: Joaquin Romero Marchent. Frank Latimore, Maria Luz Galicia, Mario Felciani, Marco Tulli. Clumsy film unaided by Latimore in title role of Don Jose who combats outlaws masked as Zorro. Totalscope.▼

Shadow on the Wall (1950) **84m.** *** D: Patrick Jackson. Ann Sothern, Zachary Scott, Nancy Davis (Reagan), Gigi Perreau, Barbara Billingsley, Kristine Miller. Slick mystery of Perreau going into shock when she sees mother murdered, and the eventual trapping of killer.

Shadow on the Window (1957) **73m.** ** D: William Asher. Phil Carey, Betty Garrett, John Barrymore, Jr., Corey Allen, Jerry Mathers. Fair programmer; Garrett is held hostage by robber-killers.

Shadow Play (1986) **C-95m.** *½ D: Susan Shadburne. Dee Wallace Stone, Cloris Leachman, Ron Kuhlman, Barry Laws, Al Strobel. Tepid chiller about playwright Stone, and the psychological problems she's been facing since her lover's demise. Very minor fare. [R]▼

Shadow Riders, The (1982) **C-100m. TVM** D: Andrew V. McLaglen. Tom Selleck, Sam Elliott, Ben Johnson, Katharine Ross, Geoffrey Lewis, Jeffrey Osterhage, Gene Evans, Harry Carey, Jr., Jane Greer, Dominique Dunne. Engrossing Louis L'Amour Western about two brothers' post-Civil War search for their family, kidnapped by Rebel guerrillas during the war. Most of the same players had previously appeared in L'Amour's THE SACKETTS. Scripted by Jim Byrnes. Aka LOUIS L'AMOUR'S THE SHADOW RIDERS. Above average.▼●◗

Shadows (1960) **87m.** *** D: John Cassavetes. Hugh Hurd, Lelia Goldoni, Ben Carruthers, Anthony Ray, Rupert Crosse. Cassavetes' first film as director, an improvisational, groundbreaking, independently made effort about a light-skinned black girl (Goldoni) who becomes involved with a Caucasian (Ray). Formless, crude, but strikingly realistic, with great use of N.Y.C. locations. Look fast for Cassavetes in front of the 42nd Street movie theater. ▼●◗

Shadows and Fog (1992) **86m.** ** D: Woody Allen. Woody Allen, Kathy Bates, John Cusack, Mia Farrow, Jodie Foster, Fred Gwynne, Julie Kavner, Madonna, John Malkovich, Kenneth Mars, Kate Nelligan, Donald Pleasence, Lily Tomlin, Philip Bosco, Robert Joy, Wallace Shawn, Kurtwood Smith, Josef Sommer, David Ogden Stiers. A Kafkaesque nightmare, shrouded in fog, is Woody-ized with only mildly comic results. A strangler who strikes at night terrorizes a city—and a nebbish who's caught between conspiratorial factions in the town. A galaxy of stars pop up in cameo roles, which is more a distraction than an asset. [PG-13] ▼●

Shadows in the Night (1944) **67m.** **½ D: Eugene J. Forde.Warner Baxter, Nina Foch, George Zucco, Minor Watson, Lester Matthews, Ben Welden, Edward Norris. Is Foch really having deadly nightmares or is one of her greedy relatives trying to drive her insane? Dr. Ordway is called in to investigate in one of the better *Crime Doctor* entries.

Shadows of the Peacock SEE: **Echoes of Paradise**

Shadows Over Chinatown (1946) **61m.** *½ D: Terry Morse. Sidney Toler, Mantan Moreland, Victor Sen Yung, Tanis Chandler, Bruce Kellogg, John Gallaudet. More routine sleuthing as Charlie Chan probes an insurance scam in San Francisco. One of the later (and lesser) Chan entries.▼

Shadows Run Black (1986) **C-89m.** *½ D: Howard Heard. William J. Kulzer, Elizabeth Trosper, Shea Porter, George J. Engelson, Dianne Hinkler. Routine slasher film about cop Kulzer tracking down supposed vigilante killer who is preying on a high school ring dealing in drugs and prosti-

tution. An early role for future star Kevin Costner. Filmed in 1981.▼
Shadowzone (1990) **C-89m.** ** D: J. S. Cardone. David Beecroft, Louise Fletcher, Shawn Weatherly, James Hong, Miguel Nunez, Lu Leonard, Frederick Flynn. Experiments in human sleep have unlocked a path to another dimension, and a monster invades an isolated underground government lab in Nevada. Basically just another ALIEN imitation, but it's reasonably suspenseful, well produced on a low budget. Written by the director.▼●
Shadrach (1998) **C-86m.** *** D: Susanna Styron. Andie MacDowell, Harvey Keitel, John Franklin Sawyer, Monica Bugajski, Scott Terra, Darrell Larson, Deborah Hedwall, Daniel Treat; narrated by Martin Sheen. Nicely realized film set in Virginia in 1935. A 99-year-old former slave walks hundreds of miles to the ramshackle property now owned by Keitel and MacDowell so he can die on the land where he was born. Though he's a stranger—and a strange presence indeed—the family feels compelled to help him. Kudos to first-time director Styron; the film is adapted from a short story by her father William. [PG-13]▼●◗
Shaft (1971) **C-100m.** *** D: Gordon Parks. Richard Roundtree, Moses Gunn, Charles Cioffi, Christopher St. John, Drew Bundini Brown, Gwenn Mitchell, Lawrence Pressman, Antonio Fargas. Slick, upbeat entertainment has Ernest Tidyman's black private-eye John Shaft hired to find kidnapped daughter of Harlem ganglord. Heavy doses of sex and violence professionally packaged by director Parks. Isaac Hayes' theme won Oscar. Followed by two sequels and a TV series. [R]▼●◗
Shaft in Africa (1973) **C-112m.** *** D: John Guillermin. Richard Roundtree, Frank Finlay, Vonetta McGee, Neda Arneric, Cy Grant, Jacques Marin. Strong action vehicle for Roundtree finds detective Shaft forced into helping African nation stop latter-day slave trading. Extremely tough and violent. Script by Stirling Silliphant. Panavision. [R] ▼◗
Shaft's Big Score! (1972) **C-104m.** *** D: Gordon Parks. Richard Roundtree, Moses Gunn, Drew Bundini Brown, Joseph Mascolo, Kathy Imrie, Wally Taylor, Joe Santos. Dynamic sequel to SHAFT (reteaming director Parks and writer Ernest Tidyman) has private eye Roundtree running afoul of the underworld as he investigates a friend's murder. Sexy, violent, with hair-raising chase finale; Parks also did the music. Panavision. [R]▼◗
Shag (1988) **C-98m.** **½ D: Zelda Barron. Phoebe Cates, Scott Coffey, Bridget Fonda, Annabeth Gish, Page Hannah, Robert Rusler, Tyrone Power, Jr., Jeff Yagher, Carrie Hamilton, Shirley Anne Field. Southern belle high-school grad Cates is about to get married, so her three girlfriends decide to take her on a "last fling" weekend to Myrtle Beach. Pleasant outing set in 1963 with an unusually appealing and talented young cast. [PG]▼●
Shaggy D.A., The (1976) **C-91m.** *** D: Robert Stevenson. Dean Jones, Suzanne Pleshette, Tim Conway, Keenan Wynn, Jo Anne Worley, Dick Van Patten. Sequel to Disney's SHAGGY DOG is winning slapstick romp, with Jones as helpless victim of transformations. Cast is peppered with a score of movie veterans in supporting and bit parts. Followed by THE RETURN OF THE SHAGGY DOG. [G]▼●
Shaggy Dog, The (1959) **104m.** **½ D: Charles Barton. Fred MacMurray, Jean Hagen, Tommy Kirk, Annette Funicello, Tim Considine, Kevin Corcoran, Cecil Kellaway, Alexander Scourby. Disney's first slapstick comedy has fine fantasy premise (a boy who turns into a sheepdog through ancient spell) but sluggish script. Some good gags, but not up to later Disney standard. Jack Albertson has bit part as reporter. Sequels: THE SHAGGY D.A. and a 1987 TV movie, THE RETURN OF THE SHAGGY DOG. Remade for TV in 1994. Also shown in computer-colored version. ▼●
Shaka Lulu SEE: **Mark of the Hawk, The**
Shakedown (1950) **80m.** **½ D: Joseph Pevney. Howard Duff, Peggy Dow, Brian Donlevy, Bruce Bennett, Peggie Castle, Anne Vernon, Lawrence Tierney. Fast-paced but familiar chronicle of ambitious photographer Duff, who uses any and all means—starting with blackmail—to get ahead. Look for Rock Hudson as a doorman.
Shakedown (1988) **C-90m.** *** D: James Glickenhaus. Peter Weller, Sam Elliott, Patricia Charbonneau, Blanche Baker, Antonio Fargas, Richard Brooks, Tom Waits, Kathryn Rossetter, Paul Bartel, John C. McGinley. Entertaining actioner with public defender Weller and undercover cop Elliott combining forces to rid N.Y.C. of drugs and corruption. Good of its kind, with oodles of sensational stuntwork to compensate for the dearth of originality. [R]▼●◗
Shakedown, The (1959-British) **92m.** *½ D: John Lemont. Terence Morgan, Hazel Court, Donald Pleasence, Bill Owen. Lackluster account of shakedown racket involving a photography school of nudes; good cast but no script.
Shake Hands with the Devil (1959) **110m.** ***½ D: Michael Anderson. James Cagney, Don Murray, Dana Wynter, Glynis Johns, Michael Redgrave, Cyril Cusack, Sybil Thorndike, Richard Harris. Gripping drama of war-torn Ireland in 1920s, with American student trying to stay aloof, but, drawn by circumstances, he joins rebel army led by

iron-willed Cagney. Strikingly filmed on location.▼

Shake, Rattle and Rock (1956) **72m.** ** D: Edward L. Cahn. Touch (Mike) Connors, Lisa Gaye, Sterling Holloway, Fats Domino, Joe Turner, Tommy Charles, Margaret Dumont, Raymond Hatton. Sub-par 1950s rock film with standard plot about adults trying to put the lid on kids' music, benefitting from presences of Domino, Turner, and veteran character actors. Partially remade in 1994.▼

Shake, Rattle and Rock! (1994) **C-84m. TVM** D: Allan Arkush. Renee Zellweger, Howie Mandel, Patricia Childress, Max Perlich, Latanyia Baldwin, Gerrit Graham, John Doe, Nora Dunn, Mary Woronov, P. J. Soles, Jenifer Lewis, Ruth Brown, Stephen Furst, Dick Miller, William Schallert, Paul Anka. The 1950s: Another tale of uptight adults vs. the music their kids like—and the kids themselves. Lots of authentic-sounding rock 'n' roll, good performances (especially Zellweger and Mandel), and a bouncy pace keep this fun throughout, though it turns too serious at the end. One of Showtime's "Rebel Highway" entries, all based on old American-International pictures; partial remake of the 1956 version. Average.

Shaker Run (1985-New Zealand) **C-90m.** ** D: Bruce Morrison. Cliff Robertson, Leif Garrett, Lisa Harrow, Shane Briant, Ian Mune, Peter Rowell, Peter Hayden, Bruce Phillips. Robertson adds character to this otherwise predictable (and implausible) car chase drama. He's a crusty American stunt driver, touring in New Zealand, who unknowingly becomes involved in a plot to transport a stolen virus. ▼●

Shakespeare in Love (1998) **C-122m.** ***½ D: John Madden. Joseph Fiennes, Gwyneth Paltrow, Geoffrey Rush, Judi Dench, Simon Callow, Colin Firth, Imelda Staunton, Ben Affleck, Tom Wilkinson, Martin Clunes, Antony Sher. Spirited, entertaining speculation about a love affair that inspired Will Shakespeare (Fiennes) to write *Romeo and Juliet.* Witty, sensual, and peopled with colorful characters. Climactic performance in the 16th-century theater is as vivid a re-creation of theatergoing in Shakespeare's time as anyone could hope for. Screenplay by Marc Norman and Tom Stoppard. Rupert Everett appears unbilled as Christopher Marlowe. Winner of seven Oscars including Best Picture, Screenplay, Actress (Paltrow), Supporting Actress (Dench), Costumes (Sandy Powell), Score (Stephen Warbeck). Super 35. [R] ▼●◗

Shakespeare Wallah (1965-Indian) **115m.** *** D: James Ivory. Shashi Kapoor, Felicity Kendal, Geoffrey Kendal, Laura Liddell, Madhur Jaffrey, Uptal Dutt. Playboy Kapoor, who has an actress-mistress, romances Felicity Kendal, a member of a two-bit English theatrical company touring Shakespeare in India. Simple, poignant drama.▼

Shakes the Clown (1991) **C-83m.** BOMB D: Bobcat Goldthwait. Bobcat Goldthwait, Julie Brown, Blake Clark, Adam Sandler, Tom Kenny, Sydney Lassick, Paul Dooley, Florence Henderson, Tim Kazurinsky, La Wanda Page, Robin Williams. Excruciating would-be-comic mishmash about an alcoholic clown (Goldthwait) whose slowly disintegrating "career" virtually collapses when he's framed on a murder rap. Aimless, crude, and headache-inducing, not even salvaged by Williams' brief, unbilled appearance as a mime teacher. Not the cultish black comedy one would like it to be. Goldthwait also scripted. [R]▼●◗

Shakiest Gun in the West, The (1968) **C-101m.** **½ D: Alan Rafkin. Don Knotts, Barbara Rhoades, Jackie Coogan, Donald Barry, Ruth McDevitt, Frank McGrath. Remake of Bob Hope's THE PALEFACE provides Knotts with one of his better vehicles, as Philadelphia dentist who finds himself out West, tangled up with gunslingers and beautiful Rhoades. Techniscope. ▼●

Shaking the Tree (1992) **C-97m.** ** D: Duane Clark. Arye Gross, Gale Hansen, Doug Savant, Steven Wilde, Courteney Cox, Christina Haag, Michael Arabian, Nathan Davis. A group of Chicago buddies of similar ages but different backgrounds work at becoming real adults; after overly familiar troubles, they all make it. Earnest and mostly well acted, but very routine. [PG-13]▼

Shalako (1968-British) **C-113m.** *½ D: Edward Dmytryk. Sean Connery, Brigitte Bardot, Stephen Boyd, Jack Hawkins, Peter Van Eyck, Honor Blackman, Woody Strode, Alexander Knox, Valerie French. European aristocrats on hunting tour of New Mexico during 1880s are menaced by Apaches. Supposed potent casting of Connery and Bardot can't revive slow-moving Western, based on a Louis L'Amour novel. Franscope. [M/PG]▼◗

Shalimar (1978-Indian) **C-85m.** *½ D: Krishna Shah. Rex Harrison, Sylvia Miles, John Saxon, Dharmendra, Zenat Aman, Shammi Kapoor. Wily Harrison invites the world's greatest thieves to try and steal the world's most valuable ruby from his custody—at the risk of their lives. This was filmed in both English and Hindi-language versions, but the results were so dull that the English print never made it to theaters. Video title: DEADLY THIEF.▼

Shallow Grave (1994-Scottish) **C-94m.** *** D: Danny Boyle. Kerry Fox, Christopher Eccleston, Ewan McGregor, Ken Stott, Keith Allen, Colin McCredie. Three Edinburgh roommates—a sardonic trio with an iconoclastic worldview—take in a boarder. When they find him dead, and a suitcase full of money in his possession, their worst instincts rise to the surface and involve them in a snowballing scheme to keep the cash. Razor-sharp thriller from screenwriter John Hodge and first-time feature director Boyle is as cold as ice (and too mean-spirited for some tastes) but fascinating at the same time. A Scottish variation on BLOOD SIMPLE with stylistic ties to that flamboyant film. [R]▼●◗

Shall We Dance (1937) **116m.** ***½ D: Mark Sandrich. Fred Astaire, Ginger Rogers, Eric Blore, Edward Everett Horton, Ann Shoemaker, Jerome Cowan, Harriet Hoctor. Lesser Astaire-Rogers is still top musical, with Gershwin's "Let's Call The Whole Thing Off," "They All Laughed," and "They Can't Take That Away From Me" holding together flimsy plot about dance team pretending to be wed.▼●

Shall We Dance? (1996-Japanese) **C-118m.** ***½ D: Masayuki Suo. Koji Yakusho, Tamiyo Kusakari, Naoto Takenaka, Eriko Watanabe, Akira Emoto, Yu Tokui, Hiromasa Taguchi, Reiko Kusamura. Beautifully realized film of middle-aged businessman (Yakusho), who secretly yearns to break out of the rigid conformity of his daily life, encountering the world of ballroom dance. Deliberately paced and laced with humor, with a game cast. Ballerina-turned-actress Kusakari matches Yakusho's fine performance. Written by the director. [PG]▼●

Shame (1961) SEE: **Intruder, The**

Shame (1968-Swedish) **103m.** **** D: Ingmar Bergman. Liv Ullmann, Max von Sydow, Gunnar Bjornstrand, Sigge Furst, Birgitta Valberg, Hans Alfredson. Powerful, brilliantly acted drama (written by the director) examines how married concert violinists are morally challenged by a civil war that rages across their island. One of Bergman's best. [R]▼

Shame (1988-Australian) **C-90m.** ** D: Steve Jodrell. Deborra-Lee Furness, Tony Barry, Simone Buchanan, Gillian Jones, Peter Aanensen, Margaret Ford. Unusual, watchable, but not terribly successful feminist revenge piece, as femme motorcyclist/lawyer takes on a village of goons who look the other way when a gang of teen boys rapes a 16-year-old girl. Strange mix of genres—biker movie, neo-Western, and more—but no MAD MAX. Remade for U.S. TV. [R]▼●

Shameless Old Lady, The (1965-French) **94m.** *** D: Rene Allio. Sylvie, Malka Ribovska, Victor Lanoux, Etienne Bierry. Bertolt Brecht story charmingly brought to the screen. Sylvie is terrific as old woman who lives alone and follows a drab and uneventful routine until there is a strange turnabout in her relationships with others.▼

Shame of the Jungle (1975-French-Belgian) **C-73m.** *½ D: Picha, Boris Szulzinger. Voices of Johnny Weissmuller, Jr., John Belushi, Bill Murray, Brian Doyle-Murray, Christopher Guest, Andrew Duncan. Raunchy cartoon spoof of Tarzan films, created by Belgian cartoonist Picha, then Americanized for U.S. release in 1979 by *Saturday Night Live* writers Anne Beatts and Michael O'Donoghue, with stars of that show providing voices. Crass, unfunny, and unattractive, despite a promising start. Original French-language version ran 85m. [R—edited from original X rating]▼

Shaming, The SEE: **Good Luck, Miss Wyckoff**

Shampoo (1975) **C-109m.** **½ D: Hal Ashby. Warren Beatty, Julie Christie, Goldie Hawn, Lee Grant, Jack Warden, Tony Bill, Carrie Fisher, Howard Hesseman. Muddy satire of morals and mores in Southern California, centered around restless hairdresser and his demanding female customers. Some bright moments lost in dreary comedy-drama by Beatty and Robert Towne. Fisher's film debut; Grant won Best Supporting Actress Oscar. [R]▼●

Shamus (1973) **C-106m.** *** D: Buzz Kulik. Burt Reynolds, Dyan Cannon, Giorgio Tozzi, John Ryan, Joe Santos. Exciting but mindless story of offbeat private-eye trying to crack bizarre case while recovering from numerous beatings, jumpings, and other heroic exploits. [PG]▼●

Shane (1953) **C-118m.** **** D: George Stevens. Alan Ladd, Jean Arthur, Van Heflin, (Walter) Jack Palance, Brandon de Wilde, Ben Johnson, Edgar Buchanan, Emile Meyer, Elisha Cook, Jr. Former gunfighter Ladd comes to defense of homesteaders and is idolized by their son. Palance is unforgettable in role of creepy hired gunslinger. Classic Western is splendid in every way. Breathtaking cinematography by Loyal Griggs won an Oscar. Screenplay by A. B. Guthrie, Jr., from the Jack Schaefer novel. Arthur's final film. Shot in 1951. Later a brief TV series. ▼●

Shanghai (1935) **75m.** *½ D: James Flood. Loretta Young, Charles Boyer, Warner Oland, Fred Keating, Charles Grapewin, Alison Skipworth. Dreary drama of American girl falling in love with mysterious Boyer, who turns out to be (gasp!) Eurasian. Two good stars can't save this turgid outing.

Shanghai Chest, The (1948) **56m.** *½ D: William Beaudine. Roland Winters, Mantan Moreland, Jim Ryan, Victor Sen Yung, Deannie Best, Tristram Coffin, John Alvin, Russell Hicks, Pierre Watkin. An executed criminal appears to have returned from the dead when his fingerprints are found at the scene of several murders. Weak *Charlie Chan* mystery.

Shanghai Cobra, The (1945) **64m.** ** D: Phil Karlson. Sidney Toler, Benson Fong, Mantan Moreland, Walter Fenner, James Cardwell, Joan Barclay, James Flavin, Addison Richards. Charlie Chan is hired by the government to probe a series of murders in which the victims are allegedly killed by a snake bite. Middling entry, although par for the Monogram series.▼●

Shanghai Express (1932) **80m.** *** D: Josef von Sternberg. Marlene Dietrich, Anna May Wong, Warner Oland, Clive Brook, Eugene Pallette, Louise Closser Hale. Dated but prime Dietrich vehicle, grandly photographed by Lee Garmes (who won an Oscar). Marlene is Shanghai Lily, Brook her old flame, Oland a cruel war lord, Wong a spunky partisan, in Jules Furthman–scripted yarn of train ride through China during civil warfare. Remade as PEKING EXPRESS.▼●

Shanghai Gesture, The (1941) **98m.** ** D: Josef von Sternberg. Gene Tierney, Walter Huston, Victor Mature, Ona Munson, Maria Ouspenskaya, Phyllis Brooks, Albert Bassermann, Eric Blore, Mike Mazurki. Slow, overblown drama of Huston discovering daughter Tierney in Oriental gambling setup. Intriguing direction somehow never makes it. The mural is by artist (and actor) Keye Luke!▼●◗

Shanghai Noon (2000) **C-109m.** **½ D: Tom Dey. Jackie Chan, Owen Wilson, Lucy Liu, Brandon Merrill, Roger Yuan, Rafael Baez, Walton Goggins, Xander Berkeley, Jason Connery. In 1881, a faithful servant to Chinese princess follows her from the Forbidden City to Nevada, where she's been taken by kidnappers; along the way he forms a thorny partnership with a slick outlaw who's got the gift of gab. Enjoyable if uneven Western comedy gets better as it goes along and Chan goes into action; still no match for Jackie's Asian starring vehicles. Panavision. [PG-13]

Shanghai Story, The (1954) **99m.** ** D: Frank Lloyd. Ruth Roman, Edmond O'Brien, Richard Jaeckel, Barry Kelley, Whit Bissell. Tawdry yet intriguing little film about Americans trapped by Red Chinese.

Shanghai Surprise (1986) **C-97m.** BOMB D: Jim Goddard. Sean Penn, Madonna, Paul Freeman, Richard Griffiths, Philip Sayer, Clyde Kusatsu, Kay Tong Lim. Missionary Madonna hires adventurer Penn (her then real-life husband) to capture a cache of stolen opium (for medicinal purposes only) in 1937 China. It's all stupefyingly dull. As one critic noted, it's tough for Penn to succeed in the grand adventure movie tradition when the screen legend he most reminds you of here is Ratso Rizzo. Coexecutive producer George Harrison, who appears briefly as a nightclub singer, wrote the songs. [PG-13]▼●

Shanghai Triad (1995-Chinese-French) **C-109m.** *** D: Zhang Yimou. Gong Li, Li Baotian, Li Suejian, Shun Chun, Wang Xiao Xiao. Absorbing tale of Chinese underworld in the 1930s, focusing on a boy who's hired to be the silent servant of a pampered nightclub queen—the mistress of one of Shanghai's gangland bosses. An intriguing companion piece to American gangster movies, and another dazzling showcase for leading lady Gong Li. [R]▼●

Shanks (1974) **C-93m.** *** D: William Castle. Marcel Marceau, Tsilla Chelton, Philippe Clay, Cindy Eilbacher, Helena Kallianiotes, Larry Bishop. One of the strangest movies ever made: mute puppeteer Marceau is given device by dying inventor (also Marceau) which can animate dead bodies. Relatively little dialogue in this bizarre horror-fantasy; alternately amusing and disturbing, with unique performances by three top mimes. A real curio from Castle; his final film as director. [PG]

Shannon's Deal (1989) **C-100m. TVM** D: Lewis Teague. Jamey Sheridan, Elizabeth Pena, Martin Ferrero, Jenny Lewis, Alberta Watson, Miguel Ferrer. Tangy dialogue and sharp characterizations energize this slick thriller about a disillusioned Philadelphia lawyer turned private investigator who becomes embroiled in an international drug-smuggling case. Written with grit by John Sayles; scored by Wynton Marsalis. Pilot to the short-lived TV series. Above average.

Shape of Things to Come, The (1979-Canadian) **C-95m.** *½ D: George McCowan. Jack Palance, Carol Lynley, John Ireland, Barry Morse, Nicholas Campbell, Eddie Benton. Lackluster, low-budget remake of H. G. Wells story has nothing in common with 1936 THINGS TO COME, as few survivors of Earth's destruction are now living in peril on the moon. Diehard sci-fi fans may want to take a look, but it's hardly worth the trouble. [PG]

Share Out, The (1962-British) **62m.** **½ D: Gerard Glaister. Bernard Lee, Patrick Cargill, Alexander Knox, Moira Redmond. Another Edgar Wallace actioner with Lee the Scotland Yard investigator determined to crack a blackmail ring.

Shark! (1969-U.S.-Mexican) **C-92m.** ** D: Samuel Fuller. Burt Reynolds, Barry Sullivan, Arthur Kennedy, Silvia Pinal, Enrique Lucero, Charles Berriochoa. Tired drama of adventurers diving for shark-guarded treasure earned some infamy when a stunt diver was killed by one of the beasts. Fuller disowned this production, which was taken out of his hands and re-edited. Reissued as MAN-EATER. [R—edited from original M rating]▼

Shark Boy of Bora Bora SEE: **Beyond the Reef**

Sharkfighters, The (1956) **C-73m.** *½ D: Jerry Hopper. Victor Mature, Karen Steele, James Olson, Philip Coolidge, Claude Akins. Bland account of Mature et al seeking some way to repel the man-killing fish. CinemaScope.

Sharks' Treasure (1975) **C-95m.** ** D: Cornel Wilde. Cornel Wilde, Yaphet Kotto,

John Nellson, Cliff Osmond, David Canary, David Gilliam. Old-fashioned adventure yarn about diving for sunken treasure in the Caribbean is peppered with physical-fitness messages from director-writer-star Wilde. [PG]▼

Sharky's Machine (1981) **C-119m.** ** D: Burt Reynolds. Burt Reynolds, Rachel Ward, Vittorio Gassman, Brian Keith, Charles Durning, Bernie Casey, Henry Silva, Earl Holliman, Richard Libertini, John Fiedler, Darryl Hickman, Hari Rhodes. Jarring, loud, and extremely bloody actioner; vice cop Reynolds' vendetta against underworld honcho Gassman intensifies after he falls for one of his $1000-a-night hookers (Ward). Action scenes are competently staged, but you'll eventually become numbed by all the sleaze; film's weirdest aspect is its mainstream jazz score. Based on the William Diehl novel, but won't fool anyone who's ever seen LAURA. [R]▼●◗

Shatter SEE: **Call Him Mr. Shatter**

Shattered (1972) SEE: **Something to Hide**

Shattered (1991) **C-98m.** **½ D: Wolfgang Petersen. Tom Berenger, Bob Hoskins, Greta Scacchi, Joanne Whalley-Kilmer, Corbin Bernsen, Theodore Bikel. Man survives catastrophic car accident, but as an amnesiac; trying to piece his life back together, he uncovers growing evidence that things were not quite right even before the crash. Extremely well-made Hitchcock-like thriller comes closer to hitting the mark than most such pretenders, but still falls short. Implausibilities undo a capable cast. [R]▼●

Shawshank Redemption, The (1994) **C-142m.** **½ D: Frank Darabont. Tim Robbins, Morgan Freeman, Bob Gunton, William Sadler, Clancy Brown, Gil Bellows, James Whitmore, Mark Rolston, Jeffrey DeMunn, Paul McCrane. Straight-arrow banker Robbins is railroaded for a double murder and sent to prison for life in the late 1940s. Fellow lifer Freeman and his buddies eventually come to admire Robbins' moral code—and his ability to get things done, in spite of a heinous warden and brutal prison guard. Widely praised film is well crafted but terribly overlong, and (like much of Stephen King's non-horror writing) hollow and predictable. First-time feature director Darabont adapted King's novella *Rita Hayworth and Shawshank Redemption.* [R]▼●◗

She (1935) **95m.** *** D: Irving Pichel, Lansing C. Holden. Helen Gahagan, Randolph Scott, Helen Mack, Nigel Bruce, Gustav von Seyffertitz. Escapist adventure on a grand scale, from H. Rider Haggard's story of expedition seeking Flame of Eternal Life, which has been given to one all-powerful woman. Gahagan's cold personality is major drawback, but film is still fun, with outstanding Max Steiner score. Some prints run 89m. Previously filmed in 1917 and 1926, remade several times. ▼●◗

She (1965-British) **C-106m.** **½ D: Robert Day. Ursula Andress, John Richardson, Peter Cushing, Bernard Cribbins, Christopher Lee, Andre Morell. Effective refilming of H. Rider Haggard's fantasy of love-starved eternal queen, seeking the reincarnation of her long-dead lover. The two leads certainly are attractive. Followed by THE VENGEANCE OF SHE. Hammerscope. ▼●

She (1985-Italian) **C-106m.** BOMB D: Avi Nesher. Sandahl Bergman, David Goss, Quin Kessler, Harrison Muller, Elena Wiedermann, Gordon Mitchell. Bottom-of-the-barrel remake, loosely based on the H. Rider Haggard novel, chronicling the various adventures of the title character (Bergman). Shot in 1982. ▼

Sheba, Baby (1975) **C-89m.** ** D: William Girdler. Pam Grier, Austin Stoker, D'Urville Martin, Rudy Challenger, Dick Merrifield. Middling black action-melodrama with Grier as female private eye trying to help father and friend save their loan business. Less sex and violence than usual, but weak script and amateurish acting. [PG]▼

She-Beast, The (1966-Italian-Yugoslavian) **C-74m.** *½ D: Michael Reeves. Barbara Steele, John Karlsen, Ian Ogilvy, Mel Welles, Jay Riley, Richard Watson. A witch killed by Transylvanian villagers in 18th century comes back to life as modern, attractive English girl on her honeymoon. Really tacky, though it has some laughs. Cromoscope.▼

She Couldn't Say No (1954) **89m.** *½ D: Lloyd Bacon. Robert Mitchum, Jean Simmons, Arthur Hunnicutt, Edgar Buchanan, Wallace Ford, Raymond Walburn, Pinky Tomlin. Silly fluff about wealthy, misguided young Simmons, who shows up in Progress, Arkansas, with a scheme to shower its citizens with free money; Mitchum is out of his element as the town doctor. A real dud. ▼

She Couldn't Take It (1935) **75m.** *** D: Tay Garnett. George Raft, Joan Bennett, Billie Burke, Walter Connolly, Lloyd Nolan, Franklin Pangborn, Alan Mowbray, Donald Meek, Wallace Ford. Fast-paced social comedy of bootlegger Raft impressing his henpecked cell mate Connolly (in stir on an income-tax-evasion rap). Upon release, Connolly appoints Raft his family guardian, causing rivalry with his madcap daughter Bennett.

She Creature, The (1957) **77m.** ** D: Edward L. Cahn. Marla English, Tom Conway, Chester Morris, Ron Randell, Frieda Inescort, Cathy Downs, El Brendel, Jack Mulhall, Frank Jenks. Bizarre blend of CREATURE FROM THE BLACK LAGOON and THE SEARCH FOR BRIDEY

MURPHY. Evil hypnotist uses mesmerized assistant to call back the murderous ghost of the sea creature of which she is a reincarnation. Slow and preposterous but effectively moody, with one of Paul Blaisdell's more memorable monsters, which he also plays. Really odd cast. Remade as CREATURE OF DESTRUCTION.

She Dances Alone (1981-U.S.-Austrian) **C-87m.** *** D: Robert Dornhelm. Kyra Nijinsky, Bud Cort, Patrick Dupond, Sauncey Le Sueur, Max von Sydow. Engrossing blend of reality and fiction, with Cort a director attempting to make a documentary about the late, legendary dancer Vaslav Nijinsky, starring Nijinsky's plump, aging, single-minded daughter Kyra. Her overwhelming presence dominates this strikingly unusual film. Von Sydow appears as himself, and that's his voice reading Nijinsky's diary.

She Demons (1958) **80m.** BOMB D: Richard E. Cunha. Irish McCalla, Tod Griffin, Victor Sen Yung, Rudolph Anders, Gene Roth. Three men and sexy, spoiled McCalla are stranded on an island inhabited by Nazi criminals, a mad scientist, and the title creatures. Too boring to be funny; even McCalla's request to "give me some privacy while I undress" doesn't help.▼

She Devil (1957) **77m.** BOMB D: Kurt Neumann. Mari Blanchard, Jack Kelly, Albert Dekker, John Archer. Blanchard is injected with fruit fly serum in effort to cure her of TB; already rotten, she can now physically adapt to almost anything. Based on a story by Stanley G. Weinbaum. Regalscope.

She-Devil (1989) **C-99m.** ** D: Susan Seidelman. Meryl Streep, Roseanne Barr, Ed Begley, Jr., Linda Hunt, Sylvia Miles, Elizabeth Peters, Bryan Larkin, A Martinez. When her slimeball husband walks out on her, unliberated housewife Barr sets out to methodically destroy his life—while creating one for herself. Extremely disappointing comedy offers no surprises and no irony; what it has is a magnificent comedic performance by Streep as the glamorous, self-absorbed romance novelist who lures Roseanne's husband away. She alone makes the film worth watching. Based on Fay Weldon's novel *The Life and Loves of a She-Devil,* which spawned a British mini-series. [PG-13] ▼●

She Done Him Wrong (1933) **66m.** **** D: Lowell Sherman. Mae West, Cary Grant, Gilbert Roland, Noah Beery, Rochelle Hudson, Rafaela Ottiano, Louise Beavers. West repeats her stage role of Diamond Lil in Gay 90s spoof. Grant is invited by Mae to come up and see her sometime—he does, fireworks result. Mae sings "Frankie and Johnny" and "Easy Rider" in her best film, which she coscripted from her Broadway hit.▼●

She Drives Me Crazy SEE: **Friends, Lovers & Lunatics**

Sheena (1984) **C-117m.** BOMB D: John Guillermin. Tanya Roberts, Ted Wass, Donovan Scott, Elizabeth of Toro. Tanya looks great as the queen of jungle jiggle, but Mother Nature forgot to endow her with a script. Supposed to be campy, but it's just plain awful. Panavision. [PG]▼●

Sheep Has Five Legs, The (1954-French) **95m.** *** D: Henri Verneuil. Fernandel, Delmont, Françoise Arnoul, Paulette Dubost. Fernandel's tour de force, playing an old wine-grower and each of his five sons who have gathered together for a family reunion.▼

Sheepman, The (1958) **C-85m.** *** D: George Marshall. Glenn Ford, Shirley MacLaine, Leslie Nielsen, Mickey Shaughnessy, Edgar Buchanan. Modest, entertaining comedy-Western with Ford battling Nielsen for sheep herds and MacLaine, though not always in that order. Shaughnessy is typically amusing. Written by genre vets William Bowers and James Edward Grant. CinemaScope.

She Gets Her Man (1945) **74m.** *** D: Erle C. Kenton. Joan Davis, Leon Errol, William Gargan, Vivian Austin, Russell Hicks, Donald MacBride. Hilarious slapstick whodunit with daughter of legendary female police chief hired to stop crime wave in city. Davis and Errol make marvelous duo in this fast-moving farce.

She Gods of Shark Reef (1958) **C-63m.** BOMB D: Roger Corman. Bill Cord, Don Durant, Lisa Montell, Carol Lindsay, Jeanne Gerson. Location filming in Hawaii does nothing for this confusing tale of brothers Cord and Durant shipwrecked on an isolated isle inhabited only by women.▼

Sheik, The (1921) **80m.** *** D: George Melford. Rudolph Valentino, Agnes Ayres, Adolphe Menjou, Walter Long, Lucien Littlefield, George Waggner. Ayres, a "civilized" woman, falls completely under the spell of desert chieftain Valentino. The silent film that helped create the Valentino legend is hokey and campy, but still entertaining. It's easy to see why women went crazy for the Latin star. Racist/imperialist angle of the story is equally fascinating. Followed by SON OF THE SHEIK.▼

Sheila Levine Is Dead and Living in New York (1975) **C-113m.** BOMB D: Sidney J. Furie. Jeannie Berlin, Roy Scheider, Rebecca Dianna Smith, Janet Brandt, Sid Melton. Dead is right. Gail Parent's sardonically funny novel about a Jewish American Princess trying to make good in N.Y.C. becomes an unbelievably bad movie, that just goes on and on. Panavision. [PG]

She Learned About Sailors (1934) **76m.** *½ D: George Marshall. Lew Ayres, Alice Faye, Harry Green, Frank Mitchell, Jack

Durant. Silly romantic comedy with complications delaying inevitable final clinch between sailor Ayres and cabaret singer Faye. Much footage devoted to the violent comedy of Mitchell and Durant.

She'll Be Sweet SEE: **Magee and the Lady**

She'll Have to Go (1962-British) **90m.** **½ D: Robert Asher. Bob Monkhouse, Alfred Marks, Hattie Jacques, Anna Karina, Dennis Lotis. Broad farce about two brothers who compete to win the family inheritance left to attractive Corsican cousin (Karina).

Shell Seekers, The (1989-U.S.-British) **C-100m. TVM** D: Waris Hussein. Angela Lansbury, Sam Wanamaker, Christopher Bowen, Michael Gough, Patricia Hodge, Sophie Ward, Denis Quilley, Irene Worth. Lansbury plays a starchy widow battling for independence from her grown-up children following a heart attack in this sudsy adaptation (by playwright John Pielmeier) of Rosemunde Pilcher's novel. Shorn up by a sturdy cast of Britons. Average.▼

She Loves Me Not (1934) **83m.** *** D: Elliott Nugent. Bing Crosby, Miriam Hopkins, Kitty Carlisle, Lynne Overman, Henry Stephenson, George Barbier, Warren Hymer. Hopkins is ebullient (and hilarious) as a nightclub performer running from murder scene who hides out with college man Crosby in his Princeton dorm. Gets funnier as it goes along, and introduces "Love in Bloom" to boot. Based on Howard Lindsay's play. Remade as TRUE TO THE ARMY and HOW TO BE VERY, VERY POPULAR.

Sheltering Sky, The (1990) **C-137m.** ** D: Bernardo Bertolucci. Debra Winger, John Malkovich, Campbell Scott, Jill Bennett, Timothy Spall, Eric Vu-An, Sotigui Koyate, Paul Bowles. Infuriatingly long, dense story of a married American couple who travel to North Africa in the late 1940s, with a friend in tow, hoping for some sort of adventure to spark their odd, repressed relationship. Paul Bowles' novels are often referred to as unfilmable, and this is certainly proof of that. Vividly atmospheric, well acted, and sexually explicit, but this is a journey you may not want to take. Bowles narrates and appears on-screen as mysterious man in bar. [R]▼●

She Married Her Boss (1935) **90m.** **½ D: Gregory La Cava. Claudette Colbert, Melvyn Douglas, Edith Fellows, Michael Bartlett, Raymond Walburn, Jean Dixon. That's what she did, and nothing much happens until tipsy butler Walburn staggers in. Good stars with fair script by usually reliable Sidney Buchman.

Shenandoah (1965) **C-105m.** *** D: Andrew V. McLaglen. James Stewart, Doug McClure, Glenn Corbett, Patrick Wayne, Rosemary Forsyth, Katharine Ross, Tim McIntire, Paul Fix, Denver Pyle, George Kennedy, James Best, Harry Carey, Jr., Dabbs Greer, Strother Martin. Rousing, well-acted saga of Virginia widower indifferent to War between the States until his family is involved. Sentimental drama captures heartbreak of America's Civil War. Basis for later Broadway musical. Ross's film debut.▼●

Shenanigans SEE: **Great Bank Hoax, The**

Shepherd of the Hills (1941) **C-98m.** *** D: Henry Hathaway. John Wayne, Betty Field, Harry Carey, Beulah Bondi, James Barton, Samuel S. Hinds, Marjorie Main, Ward Bond, Marc Lawrence, John Qualen. Beautifully mounted production of Harold Bell Wright story about Ozark mountain folk, and a man who lives his life in the shadow of a curse: the promise to kill the man who abandoned his mother. Wayne is excellent, and surrounded by fine character actors, with unusual roles for Lawrence and Main. Fuzzy Knight sings a sentimental song ("Happy Hunting Ground") as he did in the earlier, not dissimilar TRAIL OF THE LONESOME PINE. Exquisitely shot by Charles Lang, Jr. and W. Howard Greene; filmed before in 1919 and 1928, then remade in 1963.▼

She Played With Fire (1957-British) **95m.** ** D: Sidney Gilliat. Jack Hawkins, Arlene Dahl, Dennis Price, Violet Farebrother, Ian Hunter, Christopher Lee. OK drama of Hawkins, insurance investigator, becoming involved with Dahl, an arsonist.

Sheriff of Fractured Jaw, The (1959-British) **C-103m.** **½ D: Raoul Walsh. Kenneth More, Jayne Mansfield, Henry Hull, William Campbell, Bruce Cabot, Robert Morley. Innocuous Western spoof with Englishman More handed job of sheriff in war-torn town, which he handles surprisingly well. CinemaScope.▼

Sherlock Holmes Sherlock Holmes has been portrayed on film more often—and by more different people—than any other fictional character. The eminent John Barrymore played the detective in a 1922 silent film. Others have included Arthur Wontner (who starred in a series of five modest British films in the 1930s), Reginald Owen (who played Holmes one year after appearing as Watson opposite Clive Brook), Raymond Massey, Christopher Lee, and Peter Cushing. In the 1980s Jeremy Brett starred in a handsome and scrupulously faithful series of Holmes adventures filmed for British television. But there was only one American-made movie series featuring this world-famous sleuth, and it was launched quite inadvertently in 1939 when (by some genius of casting) Basil Rathbone and Nigel Bruce were signed to play Sherlock Holmes and Dr. Watson in an adaptation of Sir Arthur Conan Doyle's

HOUND OF THE BASKERVILLES; its immediate success prompted a follow-up, THE ADVENTURES OF SHERLOCK HOLMES, that same year. These were beautiful, atmospheric productions, faithful to Doyle's stories. Three years later, at a new studio (Universal), the series resumed with SHERLOCK HOLMES AND THE VOICE OF TERROR, updating the Doyle tales to have Holmes battling the Nazis. The twelve "modern" films never captured the flavor of the initial two (THE SCARLET CLAW came closest), but they were always worth seeing for the performances of the two stars: Rathbone—smooth, cunning, seldom caught by surprise; and Bruce—talkative, bumbling, never close to understanding the situation at hand. Mary Gordon made token appearances as Holmes' landlady, Mrs. Hudson, and Dennis Hoey appeared in several films as Scotland Yard Inspector Lestrade, who always managed to get in the way. Holmes was at his best battling wits with Professor Moriarty, played in various episodes by George Zucco, Lionel Atwill, and Henry Daniell. Every episode ended with a stirring ode by Holmes to the glory of England, America, Canada, or some comparable topic, in keeping with the wartime flag-waving nature of Hollywood films. Seldom faithful to Doyle, later episodes like DRESSED TO KILL wearing thin, dialogue often awkward (S. H. IN WASHINGTON, for example), the Sherlock Holmes series relied on Rathbone and Bruce for enjoyment, and they never failed.

SHERLOCK HOLMES

The Hound of the Baskervilles (1939)
The Adventures of Sherlock Holmes (1939)
Sherlock Holmes and the Voice of Terror (1942)
Sherlock Holmes and the Secret Weapon (1942)
Sherlock Holmes in Washington (1943)
Sherlock Holmes Faces Death (1943)
Sherlock Holmes and the Spider Woman (1944)
The Scarlet Claw (1944)
The Pearl of Death (1944)
The House of Fear (1945)
The Woman in Green (1945)
Pursuit to Algiers (1945)
Terror by Night (1946)
Dressed to Kill (1946)

Sherlock Holmes (1932) **68m.** **½ D: William K. Howard. Clive Brook, Ernest Torrence, Miriam Jordan, Alan Mowbray, Herbert Mundin, Reginald Owen. Genteel, stylish approach to Holmes, set in modern-day London; pleasing but subdued. Torrence is a most enjoyable Moriarty.

Sherlock Holmes and the Leading Lady (1990-British-Italian-French-Belgian-Luxembourg) **C-200m. TVM** D: Peter Sasdy. Christopher Lee, Patrick Macnee, Morgan Fairchild, Engelbert Humperdinck, Robert Rietty, John Bennett, Ronald Hines, Jenny Quayle. Holmes comes to the aid of actress friend Irene Adler (Fairchild) once again. Even Sigmund Freud (Bennett) becomes involved. Followed by INCIDENT AT VICTORIA FALLS. Originally shown in two parts. Average.▼

Sherlock Holmes and the Masks of Death (1984-British) **C-75m. TVM** D: Roy Ward Baker. Peter Cushing, John Mills, Gordon Jackson, Anton Diffring, Ray Milland, Anne Baxter, Susan Penhaligon, Jenny Laird. This adventure of Holmes (Cushing) and Watson (Mills) in 1913 involves mysterious deaths in London and the kidnapping of a German prince. Cushing is one of the all-time greatest Sherlocks, though the film is a little flat. Longer version runs 90m. Original title: THE MASKS OF DEATH. Above average.▼

Sherlock Holmes and the Secret Weapon (1942) **68m.** *** D: Roy William Neill. Basil Rathbone, Nigel Bruce, Lionel Atwill, Kaaren Verne, William Post, Jr., Dennis Hoey, Mary Gordon, Holmes Herbert. Holmes is hired to protect the inventor of a new bombsight from the deadly clutches of Moriarty (Atwill). Exciting entry with Hoey scoring as the comically maladroit Inspector Lestrade. Also shown in computer-colored version.▼●

Sherlock Holmes and the Spider Woman SEE: **Spider Woman, The**

Sherlock Holmes and the Voice of Terror (1942) **65m.** **½ D: John Rawlins. Basil Rathbone, Nigel Bruce, Evelyn Ankers, Reginald Denny, Thomas Gomez, Henry Daniell, Montagu Love. First entry in the Universal Rathbone-Bruce series is probably the least impressive, but still enjoyable once you accept the premise of Victorian Holmes (with a particularly risible haircut) battling Nazi saboteurs in WW2 England. Excellent supporting performances by Gomez (in his film debut) and Ankers.▼●

Sherlock Holmes and the Woman in Green SEE: **Woman in Green, The**

Sherlock Holmes Faces Death (1943) **68m.** *** D: Roy William Neill. Basil Rathbone, Nigel Bruce, Hillary Brooke, Milburn Stone, Arthur Margetson, Halliwell Hobbes, Dennis Hoey. The deductive master and his blundering companion check into a mansion for retired officers where a series of murders occurs. Very amusing entry replete with a strange clock tower, a subterranean crypt and a human chessboard. Look for Peter Lawford in a bit as a sailor.▼●

Sherlock Holmes in New York (1976) **C-100m. TVM** D: Boris Sagal. Roger Moore, John Huston, Patrick Macnee, Gig Young, Charlotte Rampling, David Huddleston, Signe Hasso, Leon Ames, Jackie

Coogan. Stylish Holmes original by Alvin Sapinsley that has the sleuth rushing to America after Moriarty has imperiled the world's gold supply and is threatening Holmes' long-time love, Irene Adler. Period valentine for Holmes aficionados. Above average.

Sherlock Holmes in Washington (1943) **71m.** **½ D: Roy William Neill. Basil Rathbone, Nigel Bruce, Marjorie Lord, Henry Daniell, George Zucco, John Archer, Gavin Muir. Holmes and Watson are off to D.C. in search of some hidden microfilm in this cheeky entry notable for its strong WW2 propaganda content and Watson's fascination with American bubble-gum.▼

Sherlock Holmes' Smarter Brother SEE: **Adventure of Sherlock Holmes' Smarter Brother, The**

Sherlock, Jr. (1924) **45m.** **** D: Buster Keaton. Buster Keaton, Kathryn McGuire, Ward Crane, Joseph Keaton, Erwin Connolly. Keaton reached his pinnacle with this brilliant and hilarious story of a hapless projectionist who walks right into the screen and takes part in the imaginary detective drama unfolding. Sublime study of film and fantasy, which has undoubtedly influenced countless filmmakers such as Woody Allen, Jacques Rivette, even Buñuel. ▼●

Sherman's March (1986) **C-157m.** **** D: Ross McElwee. Totally unique documentary odyssey, as romantic sadsack McElwee retraces the title Civil War trek while simultaneously examining the mystique of Southern womanhood. Overlong by a half hour, but the flesh-and-blood subjects end up getting to you the way people in real life do; CRIMES OF THE HEART suffers terribly by comparison. Hilarious subplot involving Burt Reynolds. Followed by sequel, TIME INDEFINITE.▼

She's All That (1999) **C-96m.** **½ D: Robert Iscove. Freddie Prinze, Jr., Rachael Leigh Cook, Matthew Lillard, Paul Walker, Jodi Lyn O'Keefe, Kevin Pollak, Anna Paquin, Kieran Culkin, Elden Henson, Usher Raymond, Kimberly "Lil Kim" Jones, Tim Matheson, Debbi Morgan, Alexis Arquette, Clea DuVall, Chris Owen. High school hunk who's just been dumped by his bitchy but popular girlfriend accepts a bet that he can turn a geeky girl into prom queen. Naturally, he falls in love for real . . . and of course, the geeky girl (Cook) is already quite pretty. Fairly innocuous, predictable teen fare with a likable cast. Sarah Michelle Gellar appears unbilled. [PG-13]▼●◗

She's a Soldier Too (1944) **67m.** ** D: William Castle. Beulah Bondi, Lloyd Bridges, Nina Foch, Percy Kilbride, Shelley Winters, Ida Moore. OK B film with cabdriver Bondi helping out soldier Bridges.

She's Back on Broadway (1953) **C-95m.** **½ D: Gordon Douglas. Virginia Mayo, Steve Cochran, Gene Nelson, Frank Lovejoy, Patrice Wymore. Fading Hollywood star returns to Broadway, finds dealing with director Cochran her biggest challenge. Good cast in slick but predictable musical drama.

She's Gotta Have It (1986) **C/B&W-84m.** *** D: Spike Lee. Tracy Camilla Johns, Tommy Redmond Hicks, John Canada Terrell, Spike Lee, Raye Dowell, Bill Lee. Breezy, funky film about a sexy, independent black woman and the three "macho" men who compete for her undivided attention. The acting is far from smooth; film's streetwise charm compensates. Breakthrough film for writer-director Lee, who also appears as the iconoclastic Mars; his father Bill Lee wrote the music score. One charming sequence is filmed in color. [R]▼●

She's Having a Baby (1988) **C-106m.** **½ D: John Hughes. Kevin Bacon, Elizabeth McGovern, Alec Baldwin, Isabel Lorca, William Windom, Cathryn Damon, Holland Taylor, James Ray, Dennis Dugan, John Ashton, Edie McClurg, Paul Gleason, Lili Taylor. Trials and tribulations of a young couple as they embark on marriage, domestic life, and impending parenthood, as told by the young husband, who feels trapped from the start and questions the meaning of it all. Likable enough comedy-drama grows monotonous after a while; the stars are very appealing, however. Many famous faces appear at the finale. [PG-13]▼●

She's Out of Control (1989) **C-95m.** *½ D: Stan Dragoti. Tony Danza, Catherine Hicks, Wallace Shawn, Dick O'Neill, Ami Dolenz, Laura Mooney, Derek McGrath, Dana Ashbrook, Matthew Perry. Superficial expanded sitcom with Danza offering a one-note performance as a widower suffering anxiety pangs over the budding sexuality of daughter Dolenz (whose real-life dad is ex-Monkee Micky). This one seems as if it was spit out of a computer. [PG]▼●

She's So Lovely (1997-French-U.S.) **C-97m.** *** D: Nick Cassavetes. Sean Penn, Robin Wright Penn, John Travolta, Harry Dean Stanton, Debi Mazar, James Gandolfini, Gena Rowlands, Burt Young, Chloe Webb. An errant husband's latest rage sends him to a mental hospital. Meanwhile, his slightly mad wife remarries, gets her life in order, and raises three children. When husband number one is released ten years later, he sees no reason why he and his ex shouldn't pick up just where they left off. This edgy, extremely well acted comedy-drama could only have been written by John Cassavetes, and it was; his son directed, and his widow (Rowlands) appears in a small role. Executive-produced by Sean Penn, Travolta, and Gérard Depardieu. 2.35 Research PLC. [R]▼●

She's the One (1996) **C-96m.** **½ D: Edward Burns. Edward Burns, Jennifer Aniston, Cameron Diaz, John Mahoney, Maxine Bahns, Mike McGlone, Leslie Mann, Anita Gillette, Frank Vincent. Amusing comedy about a guy, still smarting from catching his fiancée cheating on him three years ago, who marries on impulse, while his cocky married brother turns out to be a philanderer. Winning performances, funny lines and situations abound, though it starts to go flat toward the finale. Writer-director Burns' second film, following THE BROTHERS McMULLEN. Executive-produced by Robert Redford. Original songs written and performed by Tom Petty. [R]▼●

She's Working Her Way Through College (1952) **C-101m.** **½ D: H. Bruce Humberstone. Virginia Mayo, Ronald Reagan, Gene Nelson, Don DeFore, Phyllis Thaxter, Patrice Wymore, Roland Winters. Reworking of THE MALE ANIMAL diminishes the role of the professor (played by Reagan), showcasing Mayo instead, as a burlesque star who tries to bury her past and pursue a college education. Pleasant but minor musical.

She Went to the Races (1945) **86m.** ** D: Willis Goldbeck. James Craig, Frances Gifford, Ava Gardner, Edmund Gwenn, Sig Ruman. Gifford has developed scientific system for beating the horses, but falls in love with horsetrainer; mild comedy.

She-Wolf of London (1946) **61m.** ** D: Jean Yarbrough. Don Porter, June Lockhart, Sara Haden, Jan Wiley, Lloyd Corrigan. Low-grade thriller with nary a werewolf in sight, though killer tries to convince confused Lockhart she is one. No connection to later TV series.▼

She Wore a Yellow Ribbon (1949) **C-103m.** ***½ D: John Ford. John Wayne, Joanne Dru, John Agar, Ben Johnson, Harry Carey, Jr., Victor McLaglen, Mildred Natwick, George O'Brien, Arthur Shields, Francis Ford, Noble Johnson, Tom Tyler. Director Ford's stock company in fine form. Wayne excellent as cavalry officer about to retire, unwilling to walk out on impending war with Indians. Beautifully filmed in color by Oscar-winning Winton C. Hoch, but a bit top-heavy with climaxes. Second of Ford's cavalry trilogy; followed by RIO GRANDE. ▼●

She Wouldn't Say Yes (1945) **87m.** **½ D: Alexander Hall. Rosalind Russell, Lee Bowman, Adele Jergens, Charles Winninger, Harry Davenport, Percy Kilbride. Psychiatrist Russell tests theories on Bowman but finds herself involved with him romantically; predictable but amusing comedy.

She Wrote the Book (1946) **72m.** ** D: Charles Lamont. Joan Davis, Jack Oakie, Mischa Auer, Kirby Grant, John Litel, Jacqueline de Wit, Gloria Stuart. OK comedy about prim professor Davis posing as author of torrid best-seller. Fun for Davis fans, but not one of her best vehicles.

Shield for Murder (1954) **80m.** **½ D: Edmond O'Brien, Howard W. Koch. Edmond O'Brien, John Agar, Marla English, Carolyn Jones, Claude Akins. Tidy, tough yarn of crooked detective involved in theft-murder, trying to keep his loot and avoid capture.

Shillingbury Blowers, The (1980-British) **C-82m.** *½ D: Val Guest. Trevor Howard, Robin Nedwell, Diane Keen, Jack Douglas, Sam Kydd, John LeMesurier. Dated trifle about cantankerous Howard and cronies resisting attempts by young Nedwell to improve the band in an Olde English village.

Shiloh (1997) **C-93m.** ** D: Dale Rosenbloom. Blake Heron, Michael Moriarty, Scott Wilson, Ann Dowd, J. Madison Wright, Rod Steiger, Bonnie Bartlett, Frannie. A beagle, training to be a hunting dog, runs away from its cruel owner and meets up with a lonely preteen. Not your usual boy-and-his-dog tale (no one falls down a mine shaft), it chronicles Heron's attempts to buy the dog from its master. Good cast, solid family values, but lumbering story never picks up. Followed by a sequel. [PG]▼●

Shiloh 2: Shiloh Season (1999) **C-96m.** ** D: Sandy Tung. Michael Moriarty, Zachary Browne, Scott Wilson, Rod Steiger, Bonnie Bartlett, Ann Dowd, Frannie. The boy and his dog return in this sequel which deals with why people are bad and whether they can change. More life lessons explored by a game cast, but the story plods along. [PG] ▼

shinbone alley (1971) **C-86m.** **½ D: John D. Wilson, David Detiege. Voices of Eddie Bracken, Carol Channing, John Carradine, Alan Reed, Sr. Genuinely odd animated feature based on a Broadway musical (by Joe Darion and Mel Brooks) about Don Marquis' famous characters of archy, the lovesick, philosophical cockroach, and mehitabel, the object of his affection, a hedonistic cat. Episodic, to say the least, with some witty and tuneful moments, and great vocal performances by Bracken and Channing. Not really for kids. Aka ARCHY AND MEHITABEL. [G]▼

Shine (1996-Australian) **C-105m.** ***½ D: Scott Hicks. Geoffrey Rush, Armin Mueller-Stahl, Noah Taylor, Alex Rafalowicz, Sonia Todd, Lynn Redgrave, John Gielgud, Nicholas Bell, Googie Withers. Young piano prodigy is pushed to the breaking point by his smothering father. As a dysfunctional adult, he eventually finds peace in the very thing that drove him to the edge: his music. He also finds love for the first time in his life. Arresting film based on the true story of David Helfgott, with vivid performances, led by an astonishing Rush in his Oscar-winning performance. [PG-13]▼●◗

Shine On, Harvest Moon (1944) **112m.** **½ D: David Butler. Ann Sheridan, Jack Carson, Dennis Morgan, Irene Manning, S. Z. Sakall, Marie Wilson, Step Brothers. Lives of great entertainers Nora Bayes and Jack Norworth make for fairly entertaining musical. Finale in color.

Shining, The (1980) **C-142m.** ** D: Stanley Kubrick. Jack Nicholson, Shelley Duvall, Danny Lloyd, Scatman Crothers, Barry Nelson, Joe Turkel, Anne Jackson. Intriguing but ineffectual adaptation of Stephen King's thriller about a man who becomes off-season caretaker at isolated resort hotel—and almost immediately begins to lose his mind. Nicholson goes off the wall so quickly there's no time to get involved in his plight. Some eerie scenes, to be sure, but the film goes on forever. Cut by Kubrick after premiering at 146m. Remade for TV in 1997. [R]▼●◗

Shining Hour, The (1938) **80m.** **½ D: Frank Borzage. Joan Crawford, Margaret Sullavan, Robert Young, Melvyn Douglas, Fay Bainter, Allyn Joslyn. Raging fire burns out all hatred and problems from tangled family in intelligent soap opera. Crawford and Sullavan are a most interesting contrast.▼

Shining Season, A (1979) **C-100m. TVM** D: Stuart Margolin. Timothy Bottoms, Allyn Ann McLerie, Rip Torn, Connie Forslund, Mason Adams. Inspired stricken-athlete story based on that of college track star John Baker who, despite a terminal illness, devoted his final year of life leading an underdog girl's track team to the championship. Above average.▼

Shining Star (1975) **C-100m.** *½ D: Sig Shore. Harvey Keitel, Ed Nelson, Cynthia Bostick, Bert Parks, Jimmy Boyd, Michael Dante. Low key yarn about mob-dominated recording company. Poor sound and photography. Saved—barely—by intriguing look behind the scenes of music business. Music by Earth, Wind and Fire. Originally titled THAT'S THE WAY OF THE WORLD.▼

Shining Through (1992) **C-127m.** **½ D: David Seltzer. Michael Douglas, Melanie Griffith, Liam Neeson, Joely Richardson, John Gielgud, Francis Guinan, Patrick Winczewski, Sylvia Syms. Overlong, overbaked spy drama/romance set in WW2, with a very appealing Griffith as an outspoken young woman who falls in love with her boss (Douglas), and convinces him to let her take a dangerous assignment in Berlin—though she has no espionage experience except what she's seen in movies. Lavish production and empathic performance by Griffith make this palatable—but the story gets more implausible as it reaches its climax. Based on the novel by Susan Isaacs. Panavision. [R]▼●

Shining Victory (1941) **80m.** **½ D: Irving Rapper. James Stephenson, Geraldine Fitzgerald, Donald Crisp, Barbara O'Neil, Montagu Love, Sig Ruman. Handsome production of A. J. Cronin play about ultradedicated research psychologist who can't even see that his new assistant is in love with him. Very watchable but not terribly inspiring. Publicity from the time insists that Bette Davis makes a walk-on appearance as a nurse; just try to find her!

Ship Ahoy (1942) **95m.** **½ D: Edward Buzzell. Eleanor Powell, Red Skelton, Virginia O'Brien, Bert Lahr, John Emery, Tommy Dorsey Orch. with Frank Sinatra and Jo Stafford. Nonsensical plot of Skelton thinking U.S. agent is working for Axis; shipboard yarn has some salty dancing and singing, good Dorsey numbers featuring drummer Buddy Rich.▼●

Shipmates Forever (1935) **124m.** **½ D: Frank Borzage. Dick Powell, Ruby Keeler, Lewis Stone, Ross Alexander, Eddie Acuff, Dick Foran, John Arledge. Cocky Powell takes navy lightly until pressed into action. Usual plot, with songs and dances with Keeler. Reissued at 108m.

Ship of Fools (1965) **149m.** **** D: Stanley Kramer. Vivien Leigh, Oskar Werner, Simone Signoret, Jose Ferrer, Lee Marvin, Jose Greco, George Segal, Elizabeth Ashley, Michael Dunn, Charles Korvin, Lilia Skala. GRAND HOTEL at sea in pre-WW2 days. Superb cast including Leigh, in her last film, as disillusioned divorcée, Werner and Signoret as illicit lovers, Marvin as punchy baseball player. Penetrating drama, when not a soaper. Script by Abby Mann from Katherine Anne Porter's novel; won Oscars for Cinematography (Ernest Laszlo) and Art Direction.▼●

Ships With Wings (1942-British) **89m.** *** D: Sergei Nolbandov. John Clements, Leslie Banks, Jane Baxter, Ann Todd, Basil Sydney, Edward Chapman, Hugh Williams, Michael Wilding, Michael Rennie, Cecil Parker. Sterling, patriotic WW2 drama spotlighting the importance of aircraft carriers in battling the Nazis; romantic subplot has pilot Clements falling for an admiral's daughter.▼

Ship That Died of Shame, The (1955-British) **91m.** *** D: Basil Dearden. Richard Attenborough, George Baker, Bill Owen, Virginia McKenna, Roland Culver, Bernard Lee, Ralph Truman. Crew of British gunboat reteams after WW2 and uses the same vessel for smuggling purposes, until "it" begins to rebel at their increasingly grimy exploits. Fine cast in offbeat drama. Retitled PT RAIDERS and cut to 78m.

Ship Was Loaded, The (1957-British) **81m.** ** D: Val Guest. David Tomlinson, Peggy Cummins, Alfie Bass, Ronald Shiner. Inconsequential zaniness involving impersonations and shenanigans in Her Majesty's Navy. Retitled: CARRY ON ADMIRAL. CinemaScope.▼

Shipwrecked (1990-Norwegian) **C-91m.** *** D: Nils Gaup. Stian Smestad, Gabriel Byrne, Louisa Haigh, Trond Munch, Bjorn Sundquist, Eva Von Hanno, Kjell Stormoen. Young Smestad signs on a South Seas voyage as cabin boy; just before pirate/passenger Byrne is about to take over the ship, a hurricane strands the lad on the very island where Byrne's treasure booty is hidden. Enjoyable pirate yarn with an exciting HOME ALONE–like finish when Smestad booby-traps the island against the invading pirates. A Disney release. Panavision. [PG]▼●

Shiralee, The (1957-British) **99m.** **½ D: Leslie Norman. Peter Finch, Elizabeth Sellars, Dana Wilson, Rosemary Harrys, Tessie O'Shea, Sidney James, George Rose. Rough-hewn Australian swagman takes daughter away from unfaithful wife to accompany him on his wanderings. Moving portrayal of their relationship compensates for diffuse, episodic nature of film. On-location scenery helps, too. Remade as a TV miniseries.
Shirley Valentine (1989-U.S.-British) **C-108m.** *** D: Lewis Gilbert. Pauline Collins, Tom Conti, Alison Steadman, Julia McKenzie, Joanna Lumley, Bernard Hill, Sylvia Syms. Collins repeats her London and Broadway stage triumphs in the role of a saucy, middle-aged, married woman who feels that life has passed her by—until she gets the opportunity to travel to Greece, sans husband. Collins' endearing performance (much of it talking directly to the audience) makes this a must, smoothing over lulls in Willy Russell's adaptation of his own stage play. The same team made EDUCATING RITA. [R]▼●
Shivers SEE: **They Came From Within**
Shoah (1985-French) **C-503m.** **** D: Claude Lanzmann. Remarkable documentary, shown in two parts, each lasting about four and a half hours, chronicling the memories of those who lived through the Holocaust—both victims and oppressors. Lanzmann's persistent interview approach hammers away at details in order to intensify our cumulative response . . . and we begin to see exactly how the unthinkable became a reality. A unique and eloquent film. ▼
Shock (1946) **70m.** ** D: Alfred L. Werker. Vincent Price, Lynn Bari, Frank Latimore, Anabel Shaw, Michael Dunne, Reed Hadley. A woman becomes traumatized after witnessing a murder—and the psychiatrist who takes her case just happens to be the killer. Intriguing premise, so-so result.▼
Shock (1979) SEE: **Beyond the Door II**
Shock Corridor (1963) **101m.** *** D: Samuel Fuller. Peter Breck, Constance Towers, Gene Evans, James Best, Hari Rhodes. Journalist Breck gets admitted to mental institution to unmask murderer, but soon goes crazy himself. Powerful melodrama with raw, emotional impact. Fuller also produced and wrote the script; imaginative photography by Stanley Cortez. Three sequences are in color. ▼●◗
Shocked SEE: **Mesmerized**
Shocker (1989) **C-110m.** BOMB D: Wes Craven. Michael Murphy, Peter Berg, Cami Cooper, Mitch Pileggi, Sam Scarber, Heather Langenkamp, Theodore Raimi, Richard Brooks, Dr. Timothy Leary. Teenager Berg, son of policeman Murphy, is psychically linked to mass murderer, but when the killer is executed, his spirit is free to inhabit a series of victims. Writer-director Craven attempted to create a new Freddy Krueger with this misbegotten farago, a waste of excellent special effects and some good ideas. [R]▼●◗
Shocking Miss Pilgrim, The (1947) **C-85m.** ** D: George Seaton. Betty Grable, Dick Haymes, Anne Revere, Allyn Joslyn, Gene Lockhart, Elizabeth Patterson. Labored story of 1870s Boston woman in business world. Fair Gershwin score includes "For You, For Me, For Evermore."
Shockproof (1949) **79m.** *** D: Douglas Sirk. Cornel Wilde, Patricia Knight, John Baragrey, Esther Minciotti, Howard St. John. Parole officer Wilde is lured into love affair with parolee Knight which threatens to destroy him. Stylish *film noir*, co-written by Samuel Fuller, which unfortunately cops out at the end.
Shock to the System, A (1990) **C-91m.** **½ D: Jan Egleson. Michael Caine, Elizabeth McGovern, Peter Riegert, Swoosie Kurtz, Will Patton, Jenny Wright, John McMartin, Barbara Baxley. Caine adds luster to this so-so black comedy as a harried ad executive who discovers how easy it is to kill anyone in his way after he's passed over for a promotion. Has its moments as a topical look at greed, corporate-style, but could have been far more pointed and involving. [R]▼●
Shock Treatment (1964) **94m.** ** D: Denis Sanders. Stuart Whitman, Carol Lynley, Roddy McDowall, Lauren Bacall, Olive Deering, Ossie Davis, Donald Buka, Bert Freed, Douglass Dumbrille. Out-of-work actor (Whitman) goes undercover at state mental asylum to discover whereabouts of murderer McDowall's supposed million-dollar stash. Odd, unsatisfying melodrama. CinemaScope.
Shock Treatment (1981) **C-94m.** *½ D: Jim Sharman. Jessica Harper, Cliff De Young, Richard O'Brien, Patricia Quinn, Charles Gray, Ruby Wax, Nell Campbell. Dreary, disappointing spin-off from THE ROCKY HORROR PICTURE SHOW, with same director and many cast members. Brad and Janet (played here by De Young and Harper) find themselves contestants (or more appropriately, prisoners) on a TV game show—spoofed far more successfully in MELVIN AND HOWARD. [PG]▼
Shock Waves (1975) **C-86m.** ** D: Ken Wiederhorn. Peter Cushing, Brooke Adams, John Carradine, Fred Buch, Jack Davidson, Luke Halpin. On an island near Florida, pleasure boaters encounter a recluse (Cushing), who turns out to be the creator and guardian of underwater Nazi zombies, left over from WW2. Oddball, partly effective low-budgeter. Adams' film debut. Aka DEATH CORPS. [PG]▼
Shoeshine (1946-Italian) **93m.** **** D: Vittorio De Sica. Rinaldo Smerdoni, Franco Interlenghi, Annielo Mele, Bruno Ortensi, Pacifico Astrologo. A brilliant, haunting

neorealist drama about two youngsters struggling to survive in war-scarred Italy; they become involved with black marketeering and are sent to reform school. This deservedly won a special Oscar—before Best Foreign Film prizes were awarded.▼

Shoes of the Fisherman, The (1968) **C-157m.** ** D: Michael Anderson. Anthony Quinn, Laurence Olivier, Oskar Werner, David Janssen, Vittorio De Sica, Leo McKern, John Gielgud, Barbara Jefford. Pope Quinn, a Russian who spent twenty years as a political prisoner in Siberia, tries to fend off atomic war plus starvation in Red China for half a film while correspondent Janssen tries to patch up his petty marital problems the rest of the time. Fine cast is wasted in slapdash film version of Morris L. West's best-seller, dully directed by Anderson. Panavision. [G]▼●

Shogun (1980) **C-125m. TVM** D: Jerry London. Richard Chamberlain, Toshiro Mifune, Yoko Shimada, Frankie Sakai, Yuri Meguro, John Rhys-Davies, Michael Hordern. Orson Welles (narrator). Colorful, Emmy-winning saga from James Clavell's best-seller about shipwrecked British sailor in feudal Japan, taken under wing of powerful warlord to become the first Western samurai warrior. The flavor of the 10-hour miniseries from which this was chopped down (at least five subplots bit the dust and subtitles were added) remains intact, although it often plays like a movie trailer. (This version, with graphic violence and nudity added, initially was edited specifically for homevideo.) Above average.▼●

Shogun Assassin (1981-Japanese-U.S.) **C-86m.** ***½ D: Kenji Misumi, Robert Houston. Tomisaburo Wakayama, Masahiro Tomikawa, voices of Lamont Johnson, Marshall Efron. Coherent film brilliantly edited out of two different features in Japanese *Sword of Vengeance* series about samurai warrior who travels across countryside pushing his young son in a baby cart, stopping only to get involved in inordinate amounts of combat. Americanized version, narrated by child, is absolutely stunning visual ballet of violence and bloodletting. Sort of a sequel to LIGHTNING SWORDS OF DEATH. Panavision. [R]▼●

Shoot (1976-Canadian) **C-98m.** BOMB D: Harvey Hart. Cliff Robertson, Ernest Borgnine, Henry Silva, James Blendick, Larry Reynolds, Les Carlson, Kate Reid, Helen Shaver. There's a faint echo of DELIVERANCE in this ludicrous tale of gun-happy pals who allow the shooting of one hunter to escalate into warfare. Supposedly anti-gun, the film is also apparently anti-entertainment. [R]▼

Shoot First (1952-British) **88m.** **½ D: Robert Parrish. Joel McCrea, Evelyn Keyes, Herbert Lom, Marius Goring, Roland Culver, Laurence Naismith, Joan Hickson. Routine espionage tale with McCrea as an American colonel in England, who believes he accidentally killed a man, and becomes involved with spies. Screenplay by Eric Ambler. Originally titled: ROUGH SHOOT.

Shooting, The (1967) **C-82m.** *** D: Monte Hellman. Millie Perkins, Jack Nicholson, Will Hutchins, Warren Oates. Cryptic, unconventional Western with deceptively familiar revenge "story." Ultimately powerful film, with offbeat performance by Nicholson as a hired gun . . . and an incredible, unexpected finale. Filmed simultaneously with RIDE IN THE WHIRLWIND.▼●

Shooting Fish (1997-British) **C-93m.** **½ D: Stefan Schwartz. Dan Futterman, Stuart Townsend, Kate Beckinsale, Claire Cox, Dominic Mafham, Nickolas Grace, Peter Capaldi, Annette Crosbie, Jane Lapotaire, Phyllis Logan. Smooth-talking American con artist and British techno-geek team up in London to scam the rich; the catch is they may or may not be "giving to the poor" as they claim. Beckinsale is the innocent but brainy temp who assists them. Amiably frantic farce in the spirit of 1960s Swinging London caper comedies is lightweight fun. Original British running time 112m. Super 35. [PG]▼●◗

Shooting High (1940) **65m.** *½ D: Alfred E. Green. Jane Withers, Gene Autry, Marjorie Weaver, Robert Lowery, Jack Carson. Overhelpful Withers, aided by cowboy Autry, tries to restore peaceful times to her rambunctious family.

Shooting Party, The (1984-British) **C-108m.** ***½ D: Alan Bridges. James Mason, Dorothy Tutin, Edward Fox, Cheryl Campbell, John Gielgud, Gordon Jackson, Aharon Ipale, Rupert Frazer, Robert Hardy, Judi Bowker. Rewarding film about varied personalities, intrigues, and conflicts that crisscross during weekend shooting party in 1913. Mason, the weekend's host, presides over all with grace, wit, and understanding. A telling look at class structure and class consciousness; screenplay by Julian Bond from Isabel Colegate's novel. ▼

Shootist, The (1976) **C-99m.** ***½ D: Don Siegel. John Wayne, Lauren Bacall, Ron Howard, James Stewart, Richard Boone, Hugh O'Brian, Harry Morgan, Rick Lenz, John Carradine, Sheree North, Scatman Crothers. Intelligent story about a legendary gunfighter who learns he has cancer and tries to die in peace, but cannot escape his reputation. A fitting (and poignant) valedictory to Wayne's career. Miles Hood Swarthout and Scott Hale adapted Glendon Swarthout's novel. [PG]▼●

Shoot Loud, Louder . . . I Don't Understand (1966-Italian) **C-100m.** ** D: Eduardo De Filippo. Marcello Mastroianni, Raquel Welch, Guido Alberti, Leopoldo Trieste. Surrealistic but flat film in which Mastroianni plays antique dealer whose life suddenly becomes very complex. Panoramica.▼

Shoot Out (1971) **C-95m.** ** D: Henry Hathaway. Gregory Peck, Pat Quinn, Robert F. Lyons, Susan Tyrrell, Jeff Corey, James Gregory, Rita Gam, Dawn Lyn. Same producer, director and screenwriter of TRUE GRIT in another Western about cowboy and little girl. Formula doesn't work; in spite of title, film has too much talk and not enough action. [PG]◗

Shoot Out at Medicine Bend (1957) **87m.** ** D: Richard L. Bare. Randolph Scott, James Craig, Angie Dickinson, Dani Crayne, James Garner, Gordon Jones. Fair studio Western features Scott as leader of group avenging death of brother at hands of Sioux Indians and men who supplied faulty guns and ammunition.

Shoot the Moon (1982) **C-123m.** *** D: Alan Parker. Albert Finney, Diane Keaton, Karen Allen, Peter Weller, Dana Hill, Viveka Davis, Tracey Gold, Tina Yothers, Leora Dana. Highly charged, emotional drama about the breakup of a marriage. The insights and emotional touchstones of Bo Goldman's script—and superlative acting—help make up for strange gaps of logic and credibility. We learn precious little about what makes the central characters tick; director Parker gives us picture-postcard views of Marin County, California, instead. [R]▼●

Shoot the Piano Player (1960-French) **92m.** **** D: François Truffaut. Charles Aznavour, Marie Dubois, Nicole Berger, Michele Mercier, Albert Remy. Atmospheric early Truffaut gem. Aznavour is marvelous as a former concert pianist who traded in his fame and now plays in rundown Parisian cafe. His ambitious girlfriend wants him to resume his career, but he gets involved with gangsters and murder instead. This film, more than any other, reflects the influence of Hollywood low-budget melodramas on Truffaut and his cinematic style. Dyaliscope. ▼●◗

Shoot to Kill (1988) **C-110m.** **½ D: Roger Spottiswoode. Sidney Poitier, Tom Berenger, Kirstie Alley, Clancy Brown, Richard Masur, Andrew Robinson, Kevin Scannell, Frederick Coffin. Big-city cop (Poitier) is forced to team up with stubborn mountain guide (Berenger) to go into the wilds of the Pacific Northwest in search of a hunting party being led by the guide's girlfriend (Alley)—and infiltrated by a ruthless killer whom Poitier is determined to capture. Slick but highly improbable tale strains credibility, but keeps its grip thanks mostly to a riveting Poitier (his first starring role in ten years). Super 35 [R]▼●

Shop Around the Corner, The (1940) **97m.** ***½ D: Ernst Lubitsch. Margaret Sullavan, James Stewart, Frank Morgan, Joseph Schildkraut, Sara Haden, Felix Bressart, William Tracy, Charles Smith. The ultimate in sheer charm, a graceful period comedy about coworkers in a Budapest notions shop who don't realize that they are lonelyhearts penpals. Superbly scripted by Samson Raphaelson, from Nikolaus Laszlo's play *Parfumerie*. Later musicalized as IN THE GOOD OLD SUMMERTIME, brought to Broadway as *She Loves Me*, remade as YOU'VE GOT MAIL. Also shown in computer-colored version. ▼●

Shop on Main Street, The (1965-Czech) **128m.** **** D: Jan Kadar, Elmar Klos. Josef Kroner, Ida Kaminska, Han Slivkova, Frantisek Holly, Martin Gregor. Potent, poignant drama set in WW2 Czechoslovakia, where an old Jewish woman loses her small button shop, and depends on man who takes it over to shield her from further persecution. Oscar winner as Best Foreign Film. Originally titled THE SHOP ON HIGH STREET.▼●

Shopworn (1932) **72m.** ** D: Nick Grinde. Barbara Stanwyck, Regis Toomey, ZaSu Pitts, Lucien Littlefield, Clara Blandick. Standard Depression soaper with Toomey's rich family rejecting working girl Stanwyck, who shows 'em and becomes famous star.

Shopworn Angel, The (1938) **85m.** *** D: H. C. Potter. Margaret Sullavan, James Stewart, Walter Pidgeon, Hattie McDaniel, Sam Levene, Nat Pendleton. Stewart and Sullavan are always a fine pair, even in this fairly routine soaper. Naive soldier falls in love with loose-moraled actress, who gradually softens under his influence. Beautifully done, including Slavko Vorkapich's masterful opening WW1 montage. Remake of 1929 film with Gary Cooper and Nancy Carroll; filmed again as THAT KIND OF WOMAN.▼

Shore Leave (1925) **74m.** **½ D: John S. Robertson. Richard Barthelmess, Dorothy Mackaill, Ted McNamara, Nick Long, Marie Shotwell, Arthur Metcalf. Appealing if sometimes slow-moving romantic comedy with Barthelmess at his best as reluctant seaman Bilge Smith; Mackaill is a dressmaker, approaching old-maidhood, who's out to make him captain of her schooner. Later musicalized as HIT THE DECK and FOLLOW THE FLEET.▼

Short Circuit (1986) **C-98m.** **½ D: John Badham. Ally Sheedy, Steve Guttenberg, Fisher Stevens, G. W. Bailey, Austin Pendleton, Brian McNamara, voice of Tim Blaney. State-of-the-art robot develops a mind of its own and decides that it doesn't want to go "home" to weapons company from which it escaped. Sheedy is cute as the animal-lover who becomes protective of "No. 5," the equally cute robot. E. T. clone is good fodder for kids but too formula-bound for our taste. Followed by a sequel. Panavision. [PG]▼●

Short Circuit 2 (1988) **C-110m.** ** D:

Kenneth Johnson. Fisher Stevens, Michael McKean, Cynthia Gibb, Jack Weston, Dee McCaffrey, David Hemblen, voice of Tim Blaney. Innocuous (but overlong) sequel has malaprop-prone Stevens and No. 5 (now called Johnny Five) out on their own, falling in with would-be toymaker McKean and bad-guy Weston. Okay for kids, with some chuckles for adults here and there. [PG]▼●

Short Cuts (1993) **C-189m.** **½ D: Robert Altman. Andie MacDowell, Bruce Davison, Jack Lemmon, Julianne Moore, Matthew Modine, Anne Archer, Fred Ward, Jennifer Jason Leigh, Chris Penn, Lili Taylor, Robert Downey, Jr., Madeleine Stowe, Tim Robbins, Lily Tomlin, Tom Waits, Frances McDormand, Peter Gallagher, Annie Ross, Lori Singer, Lyle Lovett, Buck Henry, Huey Lewis, Robert DoQui, Darnell Williams, Michael Beach, Charles Rocket, Dirk Blocker. Mordant mosaic of unpleasant, unhappy lives in Southern California, adapted from the short stories of Raymond Carver. Altman paints on another oversized canvas, with a series of marginally interconnected vignettes about various couples, parents, lovers, and friends (from a phone-sex purveyor who feeds her baby while plying her trade to a children's party clown seized by melancholia) . . . played by a virtual who's who of contemporary talent. As a feat—a directorial achievement—it's something to behold and admire, but as entertainment it's less rewarding. Super 35. [R]▼●

Short Cut to Hell (1957) **87m.** **½ D: James Cagney. Robert Ivers, Georgann Johnson, William Bishop, Murvyn Vye, Yvette Vickers, Roscoe Ates. Generally taut, if uninspired remake of Graham Greene's THIS GUN FOR HIRE, about killer reevaluating his situation. Only fling at directing by Cagney. VistaVision.

Short Eyes (1977) **C-104m.** ***½ D: Robert M. Young. Bruce Davison, Jose Perez, Nathan George, Don Blakely, Shawn Elliott, Curtis Mayfield, Freddy Fender. Raw, uncompromisingly powerful story of men in prison, from Miguel Pinero's highly acclaimed play. Utterly realistic film was shot at N.Y.C.'s now-shuttered Men's House of Detention, known as The Tombs. Title is prison slang for child molester (played by Davison). Scripted by Pinero, who also appears as GoGo. Retitled: SLAMMER. [R]▼

Short Fuse SEE: **Good to Go**

Short Time (1990) **C-97m.** **½ D: Gregg Champion. Dabney Coleman, Matt Frewer, Teri Garr, Barry Corbin, Joe Pantoliano, Xander Berkeley, Rob Roy, Jak-Erik Eriksen. Street-cop Coleman thinks he has a short time to live, and decides to get himself killed on the job so his wife and son will be taken care of financially. Incredible action stunts commingle uneasily with touches of sentiment in this middling comedy; Coleman is so good he almost pulls it off singlehandedly. [PG-13]▼●

Shotgun (1955) **C-81m.** ** D: Lesley Selander. Sterling Hayden, Zachary Scott, Yvonne De Carlo, Guy Prescott, Angela Greene. Unremarkable Western with sheriff Hayden vs. culprit Scott; De Carlo is the half-breed girl they love.▼

Shot in the Dark, A (1964) **C-101m.** **** D: Blake Edwards. Peter Sellers, Elke Sommer, George Sanders, Herbert Lom, Tracy Reed, Burt Kwouk, Graham Stark, Andre Maranne, Turk Thrust (Bryan Forbes). Second Inspector Clouseau comedy is far and away the funniest, with the great detective convinced gorgeous Sommer is innocent of murder despite all evidence to the contrary. Gaspingly hilarious farce never slows down for a second, with memorable scene in a nudist colony. Script by Edwards and William Peter Blatty; fine Henry Mancini score. Series debuts of Lom, Kwouk, Stark, and Maranne; last Clouseau film (excluding 1968's INSPECTOR CLOUSEAU, made by other hands) until THE RETURN OF THE PINK PANTHER in 1975. Panavision.▼●◗

Shout, The (1978-British) **C-87m.** **½ D: Jerzy Skolimowski. Alan Bates, Susannah York, John Hurt, Robert Stephens, Tim Curry. Well-filmed but obscure yarn about an off his-nut wanderer who dominates the household of a young married couple. Title refers to his aboriginal ability to kill by *shouting*. Worth a look on a slow evening. [R]▼

Shout (1991) **C-89m.** BOMB D: Jeffrey Hornaday. John Travolta, James Walters, Heather Graham, Richard Jordan, Linda Fiorentino, Scott Coffey, Glenn Quinn, Frank von Zerneck, Michael Bacall. Preposterous 50s twaddle about the birth of rock 'n' roll, with Travolta as a fugitive hired as music teacher and bandmaster at an ill-defined Texas school for wayward youths. Prisoner Walters and warden's daughter Graham are the kissy-facers who form a forbidden alliance. WHEEZE would have been a better title for this turkey. Film debut of Gwyneth Paltrow. [PG-13]▼●◗

Shout at the Devil (1976-British) **C-119m.** **½ D: Peter R. Hunt. Lee Marvin, Roger Moore, Barbara Parkins, Ian Holm, Rene Kolldehoff. Plot-heavy action nonsense, set in Mozambique, about a poacher, his daughter and an expatriate Englishman who eventually set out to blow up a German battle cruiser at the outset of WW1. Occasionally fun but overlong. Original British running-time: 144m. Panavision. [PG]▼●

Show, The (1995) **C/B&W-90m.** **½ D: Brian Robbins. Craig Mack, Dr. Dre, Naughty by Nature, Run-DMC, Slick Rick, Snoop Doggy Dogg, Tha Dogg Pound.

Spotty concert and backstage documentary still has enough to satisfy fans of rap and hip-hop, contrasting the younger breed—a couple of whom have had serious scrapes with the law—with the wizened old-breed performers like LL Cool J and members of Run-DMC. Film's non-linear structure sometimes comes off as more haphazard than creative. [R]▼●

Show Boat (1936) **113m.** *** D: James Whale. Irene Dunne, Allan Jones, Helen Morgan, Paul Robeson, Charles Winninger, Hattie McDaniel. Entertaining treatment of Jerome Kern–Oscar Hammerstein II musical (filmed before in 1929) mixes music, sentiment, and melodrama, with enough great moments to make up for the rest: Robeson doing "Old Man River," Morgan singing her unforgettable "Bill," etc. Originally an Edna Ferber novel; Hammerstein also wrote the screenplay. Filmed again in 1951.▼●

Show Boat (1951) **C-107m.** *** D: George Sidney. Kathryn Grayson, Ava Gardner, Howard Keel, Joe E. Brown, Marge and Gower Champion, Robert Sterling, Agnes Moorehead, Leif Erickson, William Warfield. MGM's Technicolor valentine to this old-fashioned musical about life on a Mississippi show boat; acted with sincerity, stylishly shot and staged. Gardner makes a beautiful and poignant Julie. Timeless Jerome Kern–Oscar Hammerstein II songs include "Bill" (lyrics by P. G. Wodehouse), "Can't Help Lovin' That Man," "Make Believe," "Old Man River." ▼●◗

Show Business (1944) **92m.** **½ D: Edwin L. Marin. Eddie Cantor, Joan Davis, George Murphy, Nancy Kelly, Constance Moore. If you like Cantor or Davis you'll enjoy this vaudeville musical entirely supported by them. Followed by IF YOU KNEW SUSIE.▼●

Showdown (1963) **79m.** ** D: R. G. Springsteen. Audie Murphy, Kathleen Crowley, Charles Drake, Harold Stone, Skip Homeier, Strother Martin, L.Q. Jones. Unremarkable Western with Murphy and Drake escaped convicts involved in a holdup.

Showdown (1966) SEE: **Tramplers, The**

Showdown (1973) **C-99m.** **½ D: George Seaton. Rock Hudson, Dean Martin, Susan Clark, Donald Moffat, John McLiam, Ed Begley, Jr. Two friends in love with the same woman go their separate ways, until Hudson (now a sheriff) is forced to hunt down Martin (now a robber). Agreeable but unexceptional Western yarn was Seaton's final film. Todd-AO 35. [PG]▼

Showdown at Abilene (1956) **C-80m.** ** D: Charles Haas. Jock Mahoney, Martha Hyer, Lyle Bettger, David Janssen, Grant Williams. Standard Western fare. Mahoney as sheriff returns from Civil War sick of bloodshed.

Showdown at Boot Hill (1958) **72m.** ** D: Gene Fowler, Jr. Charles Bronson, Fintan Meyler, Robert Hutton, John Carradine, Carole Mathews. Unpretentious Western of bounty killer Bronson trying to collect reward money. Regalscope.▼

Showdown at Williams Creek (1991-Canadian) **C-97m.** *** D: Allan Kroeker. Tom Burlinson, Donnelly Rhodes, Michelle Thrush, John Pyper Ferguson, Alex Bruhanski, Raymond Burr. Compelling allegory of racism, exploitation, greed, and survival in the Northwest Territory during the 19th century. The scenario, which unravels in flashback, details the journey of Irishman Burlinson from British army officer to scruffy "squaw man" on trial for murder. Based on actual events. [R]▼

Showdown in Little Tokyo (1991) **C-76m.** BOMB D: Mark L. Lester. Dolph Lundgren, Brandon Lee, Carey-Hiroyuki Tagawa, Tia Carrere, Toshiro Obata. Knuckleheaded martial-arts actioner, with Lundgren and Lee (the son of Bruce Lee) going up against Japanese mobsters. Poorly directed, acted, and (especially) scripted. [R]▼●◗

Show Girl in Hollywood (1930) **77m.** ** D: Mervyn LeRoy. Alice White, Jack Mulhall, Blanche Sweet, Ford Sterling, John Miljan, Virginia Sale, Herman Bing. Routine tale of aspiring Broadway singer (Kewpie-doll White, in her brief fling at movie stardom) who goes West to make it big in pictures. Enlivened by some interesting behind-the-scenes glimpses of the Warner Bros. studio during the very early days of talkies. Al Jolson, Loretta Young, and others have uncredited cameos. Some sequences originally in two-strip Technicolor.

Showgirls (1995) **C-131m.** BOMB D: Paul Verhoeven. Elizabeth Berkley, Kyle MacLachlan, Gina Gershon, Glenn Plummer, Robert Davi, Alan Rachins, Gina Ravera, Lin Tucci, Greg Travis, Patrick Bristow. Stupefyingly awful movie—whose creators swear to have made it with serious intentions—about a young, hotheaded drifter who hitches her way to Vegas, becomes a "lap dancer," and then a full-fledged showgirl, discovering that sex and career moves are hopelessly intertwined. Part soft-core porn, part hokey backstage drama, full of howlingly hilarious dialogue. Berkley sets the tone for her performance in an early scene in which she expresses fury by vigorously spewing ketchup over her french fries. Written by Joe Eszterhas. Released on video in alternate R-rated format with 61 seconds cut, and 20 seconds of footage altered by using different camera angles. Super 35. [NC-17]▼●◗

Show-Off, The (1946) **83m.** **½ D: Harry Beaumont. Red Skelton, Marilyn Maxwell, Marjorie Main, Virginia O'Brien, Eddie "Rochester" Anderson, George Cleveland, Leon Ames, Marshall Thompson, Jacqueline White. Amusing if low-key Skelton vehicle casts the amiable clown as windbag Aubrey Piper, who courts Maxwell—and drives the rest of her family crazy with his reckless braggadocio. Based on the famous play by George Kelly; filmed before in 1926 (with Ford Sterling) and 1934 (with Spencer Tracy).▼

Show of Force, A (1990) **C-93m.** ** D: Bruno Barretto. Amy Irving, Robert Duvall, Andy Garcia, Lou Diamond Phillips, Kevin Spacey, Joe Campanella, Erik Estrada, Priscilla Pointer, Hattie Winston. Oddly stagnant political thriller about Puerto Rico's 1978 version of Watergate. Irving plays a local TV reporter convinced that the F.B.I. set up and killed two political radicals to earn voting support for the current governor. Garcia's role is a glorified cameo; Phillips is surprisingly effective as a flamboyant villain. [R]▼●

Show People (1928) **82m.** ***½ D: King Vidor. Marion Davies, William Haines, Del Henderson, Paul Ralli, Harry Gribbon, Polly Moran. Delightful silent comedy about a girl from the sticks who tries to crash Hollywood—and succeeds, but not as she expected to. Davies' best movie vehicle confirms her comic talent, and offers a lively glimpse behind the scenes of moviemaking. Some amusing guest-star cameos include director Vidor, who plays himself in the closing scene.▼●

Show Them No Mercy! (1935) **76m.** *** D: George Marshall. Rochelle Hudson, Cesar Romero, Bruce Cabot, Edward Norris, Edward Brophy, Warren Hymer. Young couple accidentally stumbles into hideaway of kidnappers who aren't counting on the resourcefulness of the FBI. Solid gangster saga from the G-Men era, well cast, with an unforgettable burst of violence at the finale. Remade in a Western setting as RAWHIDE.▼

Shrieking, The SEE: **Hex**

Shriek in the Night, A (1933) **66m.** **½ D: Albert Ray. Ginger Rogers, Lyle Talbot, Arthur Hoyt, Purnell Pratt, Harvey Clark. Ultra-cheap but interesting B-picture whodunit, reuniting Ginger and Lyle from THE THIRTEENTH GUEST as rival reporters on a murderer's trail; starts with a bang and then simmers down.▼

Shrike, The (1955) **88m.** **½ D: Jose Ferrer. June Allyson, Jose Ferrer, Joy Page, Ed Platt, Mary Bell. Allyson almost succeeds in change of pace title role, playing ultranag who has driven her theater director husband (Ferrer) into a nervous breakdown. Based on Joseph Kramm's play.

Shrimp on the Barbie, The (1990) **C-86m.** *½ D: Alan Smithee. Cheech Marin, Emma Samms, Vernon Wells, Terence Cooper, Jeanette Cronin, Carole Davis. Marin goes Down Under, gets a job as waiter in a Mexican restaurant, winds up posing as the fiancé of a wealthy heiress to thwart her powerful father. Cheech shows some charm, but you know something's up when the director takes his name off the project. Shot in New Zealand. Video version runs 87m., and is rated R. [PG-13]▼●

Shrunken Heads (1994) **C-86m.** **½ D: Richard Elfman. Aeryk Egan, Becky Herbst, A. J. Damato, Bo Sharon, Darris Love, Bodhi Elfman, Meg Foster, Julius Harris. Clever special effects enliven this run-of-the-mill Full Moon horror-comedy in which Haitian voodoo master Harris revives three murdered kids, who seek revenge against the trash responsible for their deaths. Title music composed by the director's brother, Danny Elfman. [R]▼●

Shut My Big Mouth (1942) **71m.** ** D: Charles Barton. Joe E. Brown, Adele Mara, Victor Jory, Fritz Feld, Lloyd Bridges, Forrest Tucker, Pedro de Cordoba. Meek Joe goes West and innocently gets mixed up with gang of outlaws.▼

Shuttered Room, The (1967-British) **C-99m.** **½ D: David Greene. Gig Young, Carol Lynley, Oliver Reed, Flora Robson. Young couple inherit old house in New England, threatened by local toughs and unseen presence. Good cast deserves better material; even revelation is tame. Based on an H. P. Lovecraft story. Video title: BLOOD ISLAND.▼

Shy People (1987) **C-118m.** **½ D: Andrei Konchalovsky. Jill Clayburgh, Barbara Hershey, Martha Plimpton, Mare Winningham, Merritt Butrick, John Philbin, Don Swayze, Pruitt Taylor Vince. N.Y.C. photojournalist Clayburgh ventures into the Louisiana bayous (dragging along rebellious daughter Plimpton and a totally inappropriate wardrobe) to research a *Cosmopolitan* article on a *very* distant branch of her family. Hodgepodge film is implausible, melodramatic, ridiculous—and fascinating. Recommended chiefly for Hershey's riveting performance (as the head of the backwoods clan), and for cinematographer Chris Menges' remarkable opening shot of Manhattan. J-D-C Scope. [R]▼●

Sibling, The SEE: **So Evil, My Sister**

Sibling Rivalry (1990) **C-88m.** ** D: Carl Reiner. Kirstie Alley, Bill Pullman, Carrie Fisher, Jami Gertz, Scott Bakula, Sam Elliott, Ed O'Neill, Frances Sternhagen, John Randolph, Paul Benedict, Bill Macy, Matthew Laurance. Black comedy about a repressed woman, stuck in a tedious marriage; at the urging of her sister, she has a fling with a chance acquaintance—who dies after an afternoon of mad, passionate sex. And that's just the *beginning* of the story. Some clever ideas get bogged down in this heavy-handed film. [PG-13]▼●

Sicilian, The (1987) **C-115m.** BOMB D: Michael Cimino. Christopher Lambert, Terence Stamp, Barbara Sukowa, Giulia Boschi, Joss Ackland, John Turturro, Richard Bauer, Ray McAnally, Barry Miller, Joe Regalbuto, Aldo Ray. Militantly lugubrious bio of Salvatore Giuliano, who took on Church, State, and Mafia in an attempt to promote Sicily's secession from Italy in the late 1940s. Gore Vidal contributed to the screenplay, credited to Steve Shagan. The 146-minute director's cut (**) is available on cassette and actually seems shorter, thanks to more coherency and Sukowa's strengthened role. Neither version, though, can overcome two chief liabilities: Cimino's missing sense of humor and Lambert's laughably stone-faced performance. Title figure was previously the subject of Francesco Rosi's 1962 SALVATORE GIULIANO. J-D-C Scope. [R]▼●

Sicilian Clan, The (1969-French) **C-121m.** *** D: Henri Verneuil. Jean Gabin, Alain Delon, Lino Ventura, Irina Demick, Amedeo Nazzari, Sydney Chaplin. Gangland family's plans for jewel heist grow increasingly complex; crime caper on grandiose scale, totally implausible but great fun. Gabin is smooth head of clan, Delon a young ambitious thief hired for the occasion. Panavision. [PG]

Sid and Nancy (1986) **C-111m.** *** D: Alex Cox. Gary Oldman, Chloe Webb, Drew Schofield, David Hayman, Debby Bishop, Tony London, Perry Benson, Gloria LeRoy, Courtney Love. Harrowing look at the bizarre, self-destructive, and curiously compelling relationship between British punk rock singer Sid Vicious (of The Sex Pistols) and American groupie Nancy Spungen in the 1970s. Director Cox achieves a masterful level of docu-realism, then laces it with allegorical dream images, with striking results. At the core of the film are two remarkable performances, by Oldman and Webb, who don't seem to be performing at all: they *are* Sid and Nancy. A downer, to be sure, but fascinating. [R] ▼●◗

Siddhartha (1973) **C-95m.** **½ D: Conrad Rooks. Shashi Kapoor, Simi Garewal, Romesh Shama, Pinchoo Kapoor, Zul Vellani, Amrik Singh. Uneven version of Hermann Hesse novel follows Indian as he leaves family to find more exciting life. Too arty, but on-location photography by Sven Nykvist (Ingmar Bergman's cinematographer) is often dazzling. Panavision. [R]

Sidecar Racers (1975-Australian) **C-100m.** ** D: Earl Bellamy. Ben Murphy, Wendy Hughes, John Clayton, Peter Graves, John Meillon, John Derum. Murphy becomes a champion sidecar racer; the usual. [PG]

Sidelong Glances of a Pigeon-Kicker SEE: **Pigeons**

Side Out (1990) **C-100m.** *½ D: Peter Israelson. C. Thomas Howell, Peter Horton, Courtney Thorne-Smith, Harley Jane Kozak, Christopher Rydell, Terry Kiser, Randy Stoklos, Sinjin Smith, Kathy Ireland. College kid comes to Southern California for a summer job evicting tenants for his sleazy uncle but instead winds up joining with one of his intended victims for the ultimate beach volleyball match. Sand, surf, and sun are the sole highlights of this no-brainer which purports to be the first major studio film about volleyball. What's next? Badminton? [PG-13]▼●

Side Street (1949) **83m.** *** D: Anthony Mann. Farley Granger, Cathy O'Donnell, James Craig, Paul Kelly, Jean Hagen, Paul Harvey. Grim drama of poor clerk Granger whose minor theft snowballs, affecting his whole life.

Sidewalks of London (1938-British) **84m.** *** D: Tim Whelan. Charles Laughton, Vivien Leigh, Rex Harrison, Tyrone Guthrie, Larry Adler. Laughton is superb as a busker (street entertainer), with Leigh almost matching him as his protegée, who uses and abuses all in her quest for success as a stage star (a character not unlike Scarlett O'Hara!). Top entertainment . . . until that ill-conceived final sequence. Original British title: ST. MARTIN'S LANE.▼

Sidewalks of New York (1931) **74m.** ** D: Jules White, Zion Myers. Buster Keaton, Anita Page, Cliff Edwards, Frank Rowan. Nowhere near Keaton's silent-film classics, but this talkie vehicle has some funny moments as witless young millionaire tries to reform tough street gang.▼●

Sidewalk Stories (1989) **97m.** *** D: Charles Lane. Charles Lane, Nicole Alysia, Sandye Wilson, Darnell Williams, Trula Hoosier. Charming, Chaplinesque fantasy that, in its own modest way, boldly comments on the plight of the homeless in America. Lane stars as a homeless man struggling for survival on the streets of Greenwich Village who finds himself caring for a cute toddler whose father has been stabbed by muggers. There's almost no dialogue; Marc Marder's evocative score adds immeasurably to the film's mood. Don't miss this sweet, gentle sleeper. [R]

Sidewinder 1 (1977) **C-97m.** *½ D: Earl Bellamy. Marjoe Gortner, Michael Parks, Susan Howard, Alex Cord, Charlotte Rae, Bill Vint. Low-grade actioner about motocross (motorcyle) racing; some exciting scenes, lots of nonacting. [PG]▼

Sidney Sheldon's Bloodline SEE: **Bloodline**

Siege, The (1998) **C-116m.** *** D: Edward Zwick. Denzel Washington, Annette Bening, Bruce Willis, Tony Shalhoub, Sami Bouajila, Ahmed Ben Larby, Liana Pai, Mark Valley, Jack Gwaltney, David Proval, Lance Reddick. Terrorists set off bombs all over N.Y.C., crippling the city and leading to the imposition of martial law—including concentration camps for all Arabs, foreigners and citizens alike. Soon the general in charge (a cardboard Willis) is behaving like a tyrant, clashing with FBI man Washington and CIA agent Bening (both excellent). Well made and suspenseful. Super 35. [R]▼●◗

Siege at Red River, The (1954) **C-81m.** ★★½ D: Rudolph Maté. Van Johnson, Joanne Dru, Richard Boone, Milburn Stone, Jeff Morrow. Predictable Western set during Civil War days with an Indian attack finale.

Siege of Pinchgut SEE: **Four Desperate Men**

Siege of Sidney Street, The (1960-British) **94m.** ★★ D: Robert Baker, Monty Berman. Donald Sinden, Nicole Berger, Kieron Moore, Peter Wyngarde. Based on real incident, this film traces account of anarchists in 1910 London, with climactic confrontation between hundreds of cops and battling criminals. Dyaliscope.

Siege of Syracuse (1962-Italian) **C-97m.** ★½ D: Pietro Francisci. Rossano Brazzi, Tina Louise, Enrico Maria Salerno, Gino Cervi. No less than Archimedes defends Syracuse from invading armada by use of giant mirrors that make ships burst into flames. Despite that, it's routine. Dyaliscope.

Siege of the Saxons (1963-British) **C-85m.** ★★½ D: Nathan Juran. Janette Scott, Ronald Lewis, Ronald Howard, John Laurie, Mark Dignam. Colorful escapism about King Arthur's daughter trying to protect her kingdom, and her right to marry the knight she chooses, from takeover by nefarious Edmund of Cornwall.

Siegfried SEE: **Die Nibelungen**

Sierra (1950) **C-83m.** ★★½ D: Alfred E. Green. Audie Murphy, Wanda Hendrix, Dean Jagger, Burl Ives, Sara Allgood, James Arness, Anthony (Tony) Curtis. Capable cast elevates story of son and father on the lam from the law, trying to prove dad's innocence of crime. Remake of 1938 film FORBIDDEN VALLEY.

Sierra Baron (1958) **C-80m.** ★★ D: James B. Clark. Brian Keith, Rick Jason, Rita Gam, Mala Powers, Steve Brodie. Western set in 19th century California and Mexico has virtue of pleasing scenery, marred by usual land-grabbing shoot-out plot. CinemaScope.

Sierra Passage (1951) **81m.** ★½ D: Frank McDonald. Wayne Morris, Lola Albright, Alan Hale, Jr., Roland Winters. Quickie oater with Morris on manhunt for father's murderer.

Sierra Stranger (1957) **74m.** ★½ D: Lee Sholem. Howard Duff, Dick Foran, Barton MacLane, Gloria McGhee. Tame dust-raiser of Duff intervening in a lynching, romancing McGhee.

Siesta (1987) **C-97m.** ★½ D: Mary Lambert. Ellen Barkin, Gabriel Byrne, Jodie Foster, Martin Sheen, Grace Jones, Julian Sands, Isabella Rossellini. Sky diver Barkin ends up disheveled and semi-nude in Spain (by way of Death Valley); her subsequent odyssey has something to do with murder (which may actually be a fantasy) and a taxi driver with rusty teeth who keeps trying to rape her. So-called experimental film is a throwback to some of the more incomprehensible efforts of the 1960s. Music score by Miles Davis. Barkin and Byrne later married in real life. [R]▼●

Signal 7 (1983) **C-92m.** ★★½ D: Rob Nilsson. Bill Ackridge, Dan Leegant, Bob Elross, Hagit Farber, John Tidwell, Herb Mills. Touching and revealing but rambling stream-of-consciousness tale of middle-aged cabdrivers—their camaraderie, illusions, desperation. Ambitious but uneven; dedicated, appropriately, to John Cassavetes. Shot on video then transferred to 16mm for theatrical release. ▼

Sign of Four, The (1983-British) **C-103m. TVM** D: Desmond Davis. Ian Richardson, David Healy, Cherie Lunghi, Terence Rigby, Thorley Walters, John Pedrick, Joe Melia, Clive Merrison. Fine Sherlock Holmes adventure based closely on Conan Doyle's most colorful novel, pitting the great detective against a vengeful one-legged man and a homicidal dwarf. Richardson is an excellent Holmes, delighting in his own brilliance; it's too bad that he made only this and the equally good HOUND OF THE BASKERVILLES (1983). Above average.▼

Sign of the Cross, The (1932) **124m.** ★★½ D: Cecil B. DeMille. Fredric March, Elissa Landi, Claudette Colbert, Charles Laughton, Ian Keith, Vivian Tobin, Nat Pendleton, Joe Bonomo. Well-meaning but heavy-handed account of Christians seeking religious freedom in Rome under Emperor Nero. Very slow going, despite fine work by March as Marcus Superbus, Laughton as Nero, and especially Colbert as alluring Poppaea. Reissued in 1944 at 118m. with many cuts of sexy and sadistic scenes, and a nine-minute WW2 prologue added.▼

Sign of the Gladiator (1959-Italian) **C-84m.** ★½ D: Vittorio Musy Glori. Anita Ekberg, Georges Marchal, Folco Lulli, Chelo Alonso, Jacques Sernas. Gladiator allows himself to be captured by queen of Syria so he can win her confidence. Not so hot. Dyaliscope.

Sign of the Pagan (1954) **C-92m.** ★★½ D: Douglas Sirk. Jeff Chandler, Jack Palance, Ludmilla Tcherina, Rita Gam, Jeff Morrow, Alexander Scourby. Uneven script hampers story of Attila the Hun threatening Rome; Sirk's stylish direction helps somewhat. CinemaScope.

Sign of the Ram (1948) **84m.** ★★½ D: John Sturges. Susan Peters, Alexander Knox, Peggy Ann Garner, Dame May Whitty, Phyllis Thaxter, Ron Randell, Allene Roberts. Well-wrought drama of crippled wife using ailment to hamstring husband and children. Comeback film for wheelchair-bound Peters, who was severely injured in a 1944 hunting accident; sadly this was also her final feature.

Sign of Zorro, The (1960) **91m.** *½ D: Norman Foster, Lewis R. Foster. Guy Williams, Henry Calvin, Gene Sheldon, Britt Lomond, George J. Lewis, Lisa Gaye. Several episodes of Disney's *Zorro* TV show pasted together; clumsy continuity undermines what charm the series had to offer.▼

Sign o' the Times (1987) **C-85m.** *** D: Prince. Prince, Sheila E., Sheena Easton, Dr. Fink, Miko Weaver, Levi Seacer, Jr., Wally Safford, Gregory Allen Brooks, Boni Boyer. Mostly punchy Prince concert film, shot in Rotterdam and Minnesota, features 13 numbers, some overhead photography and lots of bump and grind from both sexes. Stolen to some degree by star drummer Sheila E.; otherwise "live" film features Sheena Easton's rock video "U Got the Look." [PG-13]▼

Signpost to Murder (1965) **74m.** **½ D: George Englund. Stuart Whitman, Joanne Woodward, Edward Mulhare, Alan Napier, Joyce Worsley, Murray Matheson. Escapee from prison for criminally insane seeks shelter in home of woman whose husband is away. Contrived plot mars thriller but strong performances help. Panavision.

Signs of Life (1989) **C-91m.** **½ D: John David Coles. Arthur Kennedy, Kevin J. O'Connor, Vincent Philip D'Onofrio, Michael Lewis, Beau Bridges, Kate Reid, Kathy Bates, Mary-Louise Parker, Georgia Engel. A generations-old boat-building business in Maine closes its doors, and the people, young and old, who've spent their lives working there try to figure out what to do next. An ideal showcase for Kennedy (in his first film in ten years) and a talented cast, but superlative acting cannot completely make up for an air of familiarity in Mark Malone's script. A PBS *American Playhouse* production. [PG-13]▼●

Silas Marner (1985-British) **C-92m.** ***½ D: Giles Foster. Ben Kingsley, Jenny Agutter, Patrick Ryecart, Jonathan Coy, Freddie Jones, Frederick Treves, Angela Pleasence. Solid, marvelously detailed version of the George Eliot novel with Kingsley quite moving as the title character, a weaver who becomes a recluse after he's falsely accused of thievery and sent into exile. Reworked in 1994 as A SIMPLE TWIST OF FATE. ▼

Silence, The (1963-Swedish) **95m.** ***½ D: Ingmar Bergman. Ingrid Thulin, Gunnel Lindblom, Hakan Jahnberb, Birger Malmsten. Stark, forceful symbolic narrative of two sisters who stop at a hotel in a North European city. One sister (Thulin) is a frustrated lesbian with no future, the other (Lindblom) a free-loving mother of a 10-year-old boy. The last in Bergman's trilogy on faith, following THROUGH A GLASS DARKLY and WINTER LIGHT.▼●

Silence (1974) **C-88m.** **½ D: John Korty. Will Geer, Ellen Geer, Richard Kelton, Ian Geer Flanders, Craig Kelly. Outdoor drama of autistic boy Flanders lost in the wilderness is a Geer family affair, interestingly done. Aka CRAZY JACK AND THE BOY. [G]▼

Silence of the Hams, The (1994) **C-81m.** BOMB D: Ezio Greggio. Dom DeLuise, Billy Zane, Joanna Pacula, Charlene Tilton, Martin Balsam, Stuart Pankin, John Astin, Phyllis Diller, Bubba Smith, Larry Storch, Rip Taylor, Shelley Winters. Zane is a rookie FBI agent on the trail of a serial killer; DeLuise is the psychotic criminal he turns to for help. Lame comedy in the AIRPLANE! tradition spoofs THE SILENCE OF THE LAMBS and PSYCHO. Film buffs might want to note cameos by such directors as Joe Dante and John Carpenter. Others might want to avoid the movie altogether. [R]▼●

Silence of the Lambs, The (1991) **C-118m.** ***½ D: Jonathan Demme. Jodie Foster, Anthony Hopkins, Scott Glenn, Ted Levine, Anthony Heald, Brooke Smith, Diane Baker, Kasi Lemmons, Charles Napier, Tracey Walter, Roger Corman, Chris Isaak. FBI trainee Foster is recruited to attempt to get through to a brilliant psychotic criminal, "Hannibal the Cannibal" Lecter (Hopkins), in the hope that he may help catch a serial killer. Almost unbearably intense, brilliantly acted (by Foster and Hopkins), and cannily put together—though the subject material is at times repellent. Based on the Thomas Harris best-seller; the Hannibal character appeared in a previous Harris adaptation, MANHUNTER. Oscar winner for Best Picture, Actor (Hopkins), Actress (Foster), Director, and Adapted Screenplay (Ted Tally). [R]▼●◗

Silence of the North (1981-Canadian) **C-94m.** ** D: Allan Winton King. Ellen Burstyn, Tom Skerritt, Gordon Pinsent, Jennifer McKinney, Donna Dobrijevic, Colin Fox. OK drama of independent-minded Burstyn surviving in the Canadian wilderness. Beautiful scenery; based on a true story. Panavision. [PG]▼

Silencers, The (1966) **C-102m.** **½ D: Phil Karlson. Dean Martin, Stella Stevens, Dahlia Lavi, Victor Buono, Robert Webber, James Gregory, Arthur O'Connell, Cyd Charisse, Roger C. Carmel, Nancy Kovack. Donald Hamilton's secret agent Matt Helm is pulled out of "retirement" to combat Buono's efforts to destroy a U.S. atomic testing site. First of four theatrical Helms is far and away the best, with Stevens just wonderful as well-meaning klutz. Sequel: MURDERERS' ROW.▼●

Silent Assassins (1988) **C-92m.** **½ D: Lee Doo-yong, Scott Thomas. Sam J. Jones, Linda Blair, Jun Chong, Phillip Rhee, Bill Erwin, Gustav Vintas, Mako,

Rebecca Ferratti, Stuart Damon. Well-made actioner has commando Jones whip into action when a scientist is kidnapped by baddies for his secret biological-warfare formula. His helpers, Chong and Rhee, doubled as film's producers and fight choreographers.▼

Silent Call, The (1961) **63m.** BOMB D: John Bushelman. Gail Russell, Roger Mobley. Very mild yarn of a dog traveling cross-country to find his master in L.A. CinemaScope.

Silent Death SEE: **Voodoo Island**

Silent Enemy, The (1958-British) **92m.** **½ D: William Fairchild. Laurence Harvey, Dawn Addams, John Clements, Michael Craig. British Naval frogmen, headed by Harvey, are assigned to combat enemy counterpart during WW2; underwater sequences well handled, with some pre-THUNDERBALL gimmicks.▼

Silent Fall (1994) **C-100m.** *½ D: Bruce Beresford. Richard Dreyfuss, Linda Hamilton, John Lithgow, J.T. Walsh, Ben Faulkner, Liv Tyler. When an autistic youngster (Faulkner) is the only witness to his parents' bloody double murder, controversial shrink Dreyfuss tries to unlock the boy's mind in an attempt to crack the case. Murky all the way, and predictable *nearly* all the way, except for an ill-advised "light" wrap-up that'll make you take a loud fall out of your seat. Barely released. [R]▼●◗

Silent Movie (1976) **C-86m.** **½ D: Mel Brooks. Mel Brooks, Marty Feldman, Dom DeLuise, Bernadette Peters, Sid Caesar, Harold Gould, Ron Carey, guests Burt Reynolds, James Caan, Liza Minnelli, Paul Newman, Anne Bancroft, Marcel Marceau, Harry Ritz. Disappointing attempt to revive silent comedy, with Brooks as movie producer hoping for comeback. Blackout gags range from very funny to misfire. Results are only mild instead of the knockout they should have been. [PG]▼●

Silent Night, Bloody Night (1973) **C-87m.** ** D: Theodore Gershuny. Patrick O'Neal, James Patterson, Mary Woronov, Astrid Heeren, John Carradine, Walter Abel. Uneven low-budgeter about escaped killer from insane asylum terrorizing small New England town, and inhabitants of mysterious old mansion that's up for sale. [R]▼

Silent Night, Deadly Night (1984) **C-79m.** BOMB D: Charles E. Sellier, Jr. Lilyan Chauvan, Gilmer McCormick, Toni Nero, Robert Brian Wilson, Britt Leach. Controversial—and worthless—splatter movie about a psychotic (Wilson), dressed in a Santa suit, who commits brutal ax-murders. Theaters that played this film were picketed; what next—the Easter Bunny as a child molester? Followed by four sequels! [R]▼●

Silent Night, Deadly Night Part II (1987) **C-88m.** BOMB D: Lee Harry. Eric Freeman, James L. Newman, Elizabeth Kaitan. Embarrassing (and unnecessary) follow-up to the Santa Claus-killer film has hero's younger brother continuing the psychotic carnage. About half the footage here is lifted from the original film (including a memorable scene featuring Linnea Quigley); new scenes are perfunctory. [R]▼●

Silent Night, Deadly Night III—Better Watch Out! (1989) **C-91m.** ** D: Monte Hellman. Samantha Scully, Bill Moseley, Richard Beymer, Robert Culp, Eric Da Re, Laura Herring. Shrewdly made sequel pits now grown killer from Part II against young blind woman linked to him by ESP. Well made, with touches of black comedy, but still only a slasher movie, less gruesome than most. Santa Claus is not the heavy this time—he's a victim. [R]▼●

Silent Night, Deadly Night 4 (1990) **C-90m.** *½ D: Brian Yuzna. Maud Adams, Tommy Hinkley, Allyce Beasley, Clint Howard, Neith Hunter, Jeanne Bates, Laurel Lockhart. Investigating a strange death, a young woman would-be reporter becomes involved with witches, large bugs, worms, and Clint Howard. Though intelligent, it's gratuitously gruesome, dull, poorly acted, and bizarrely anti-feminist. Christmas elements are completely superfluous. Actual title onscreen is INITIATION: SILENT NIGHT, DEADLY NIGHT 4. [R]▼

Silent Night, Deadly Night 5: The Toymaker (1991) **C-90m.** ** D: Martin Kitrosser. Jane Higginson, William Thorne, Tracy Fraim, Mickey Rooney, Brian Bremer, Neith Hunter, Clint Howard. Toys are out to kill a little boy at Christmastime, but who's responsible? Drunken toymaker Petto (Rooney) or his odd son Pino? (The names are clumsy clues.) Overplotted but OK horror thriller with a lot of sex. No plot connection to earlier films in series. [R]▼●

Silent Night, Evil Night SEE: **Black Christmas**

Silent Partner, The (1978-Canadian) **C-103m.** *** D: Daryl Duke. Elliott Gould, Christopher Plummer, Susannah York, Celine Lomez, Michael Kirby, Ken Pogue, John Candy. Offbeat film about crafty bank teller Gould playing cat-and-mouse with psychotic robber Plummer. Well directed, with fine eye for detail, but bursts of graphic violence are jarring. Nice score by Oscar Peterson. Screenplay by Curtis Hanson. [R]▼●

Silent Rage (1982) **C-105m.** *½ D: Michael Miller. Chuck Norris, Ron Silver, Steven Keats, Toni Kalem, William Finley, Brian Libby, Stephen Furst. Small-town Texas sheriff Norris versus sickie killer Libby, a Frankenstein-like creation of science. Ho-hum. [R]▼●

Silent Running (1971) **C-89m.** *** D: Douglas Trumbull. Bruce Dern, Cliff Potts, Ron Rifkin, Jesse Vint. Space-age ecology tale of botanist's fight on space station to keep Earth's final vegetation samples from being destroyed. Interesting film marked directorial debut of special effects whiz Trumbull (2001, CLOSE ENCOUNTERS). Script by Deric Washburn, Michael Cimino, and Steven Bochco; unusual score by Peter Schickele. [G]▼●◗

Silent Scream (1980) **C-87m.** *½ D: Denny Harris. Rebecca Balding, Cameron Mitchell, Avery Schreiber, Barbara Steele, Yvonne De Carlo. Another illogical, obvious kids-caught-in-eerie-old-house melodrama. Some scares, but who cares? [R]▼

Silent Tongue (1994) **C-98m.** BOMB D: Sam Shepard. Richard Harris, Alan Bates, River Phoenix, Dermot Mulroney, Sheila Tousey, Jeri Arredondo, Tantoo Cardinal, Bill Irwin, David Shiner, The Red Clay Ramblers. While his son goes delirious in the New Mexico prairie, dragging around the corpse of his halfbreed bride, Harris tries to negotiate a deal for her sister from medicine show proprietor Bates (who sired both girls). If you wonder how a movie with this cast could remain on the shelf for two years, proceed at your own peril. Phoenix's penultimate film (released after his death), though it gives him nothing to do. Shepard also wrote the script. Panavision. [PG-13]▼●

Silent Witness (1932) **73m.** ** D: Marcel Varnel, R. L. Hough. Lionel Atwill, Greta Nissen, Weldon Heyburn, Helen Mack, Bramwell Fletcher. Stagy but pretty interesting courtroom drama with Atwill trying to protect his son from murder charge by taking blame himself.

Silent World, The (1956-French) **C-86m.** *** D: Jacques-Yves Cousteau, Louis Malle. Frederic Duman, Albert Falco, Jacques-Yves Cousteau. Academy Award-winning documentary account of an expedition above and—most memorably—below the sea's surface by Captain Cousteau and his divers and crew. Beautifully photographed; Malle's first film.

Silken Affair, The (1957-British) **96m.** **½ D: Roy Kellino. David Niven, Genevieve Page, Ronald Squire, Wilfrid Hyde-White, Beatrice Straight. Droll little comedy of meek accountant Niven sparked by saucy Page into some fast bookkeeping manipulations.

Silk Road, The (1992-Chinese-Japanese) **C-126m.** **½ D: Junya Sato. Koichi Sato, Toshiyuki Nishida, Tsunehiko Watase, Daijiro Harada, Takahiro Tamura. Extravagant but hokey, overly melodramatic epic set in 11th-century China, about a young man (Koichi Sato) who becomes involved in various adventures and falls in love with a princess. The much-hyped battle scenes are nicely done, but fall short next to those in other films (for example, Kurosawa's KAGEMUSHA and RAN). [PG-13]▼●

Silk Stockings (1957) **C-117m.** *** D: Rouben Mamoulian. Fred Astaire, Cyd Charisse, Janis Paige, Peter Lorre, George Tobias, Jules Munshin, Joseph Buloff, Barrie Chase. Words, music, dance blend perfectly in stylish remake of Garbo's NINOTCHKA. This time Charisse is cold Russian on Paris mission, Astaire the movie producer man-about-town who warms her up. Score by Cole Porter includes "All of You" and "Stereophonic Sound"; Mamoulian's final film. CinemaScope.▼●

Silkwood (1983) **C-128m.** *** D: Mike Nichols. Meryl Streep, Kurt Russell, Cher, Craig T. Nelson, Diana Scarwid, Fred Ward, Ron Silver, Charles Hallahan, Josef Sommer, Sudie Bond, Henderson Forsythe, E. Katherine Kerr, Bruce McGill, David Strathairn, M. Emmet Walsh, Ray Baker, Tess Harper, Anthony Heald. Superb performances, and vivid dramatization of workaday life in an Oklahoma nuclear-parts factory, give strength to a flawed film. Streep is outstanding as real-life Karen Silkwood, but anyone who followed news story knows how this film will end, and that places a special burden on such a long, slowly paced film. Script by Nora Ephron and Alice Arlen. [R]▼●◗

Silverado (1985) **C-132m.** *** D: Lawrence Kasdan. Kevin Kline, Scott Glenn, Kevin Costner, Danny Glover, John Cleese, Rosanna Arquette, Brian Dennehy, Linda Hunt, Jeff Goldblum, Ray Baker, Joe Seneca, Lynn Whitfield, Jeff Fahey. Sprawling, well-made Western about four unlikely comrades who join forces against some very bad guys. First major Hollywood Western in a long time is no classic but offers ample entertainment by throwing in everything but the kitchen sink—and never stops moving. Just don't think about it too hard. Script by Mark and Lawrence Kasdan, fine score by Bruce Broughton. Super Techniscope. [PG-13]▼●◗

Silver Bears (1978) **C-113m.** *** D: Ivan Passer. Michael Caine, Cybill Shepherd, Louis Jourdan, Martin Balsam, Stephane Audran, Tommy Smothers, David Warner, Charles Gray, Jay Leno. Entertaining comedy better suited to TV than theater screens; fine cast in story of high-level chicanery in world silver market. Adapted from Paul Erdman's novel by Peter Stone; filmed in Switzerland and Morocco. [PG]▼

Silver Blaze (1937-British) **71m.** **½ D: Thomas Bentley. Arthur Wontner, Lyn Harding, Ian Fleming, Judy Gunn, Eve Gray, Lawrence Grossmith. It's Sherlock Holmes to the rescue upon the disappearance of a racehorse and murder of its trainer. Moderately entertaining mystery; this was Wontner's final appearance as Sir Arthur Conan Doyle's legendary sleuth. Aka MURDER AT THE BASKERVILLES. ▼

Silver Bullet (1985) **C-95m.** ** D: Daniel Attias. Corey Haim, Gary Busey, Megan Follows, Everett McGill, Terry O'Quinn,

Robin Groves, Leon Russom, Bill Smitrovich, Lawrence Tierney, voice of Tovah Feldshuh. What can it be that's terrorizing a small town by the light of the full moon? The answer is a werewolf, but it takes the folks in this movie a long time to figure that out. Well-acted but often stupid and unbelievable horror tale from Stephen King's novelette, *Cycle of the Werewolf.* J-D-C Scope. [R]▼●

Silver Chalice, The (1954) **C-144m.** ** D: Victor Saville. Virginia Mayo, Pier Angeli, Jack Palance, Paul Newman, Walter Hampden, Joseph Wiseman, Alexander Scourby, Lorne Greene, E. G. Marshall, Natalie Wood. Newman's screen debut is undistinguished in story of Greek who designs framework for cup used at Last Supper. This is the film Newman once apologized for in a famous Hollywood trade ad. From the Thomas Costain novel; Greene's first film, too. CinemaScope.▼●

Silver City (1951) **C-90m.** ** D: Byron Haskin. Edmond O'Brien, Yvonne De Carlo, Richard Arlen, Gladys George, Barry Fitzgerald. Capable cast is above this mishmash set in the mining area of the West, with usual rivalry over gals and ore.

Silver City (1984-Australian) **C-110m.** **½ D: Sophie Turkiewicz. Gosia Dobrowolska, Ivar Kants, Anna Jemison, Steve Bisley, Debra Lawrence. Fair soaper about love affair between Polish immigrants Dobrowolska and Kants in 1940s Australia. The catch: He is married to her close friend. Panavision. [PG]▼

Silver Cord, The (1933) **74m.** **½ D: John Cromwell. Irene Dunne, Joel McCrea, Laura Hope Crews, Frances Dee, Eric Linden. Very much a photographed stage play (by Sidney Howard), but interesting for its look at a self-absorbed woman (Crews) who attempts to dominate her sons' lives completely—not counting on the strength of her new daughter-in-law (Dunne), a career woman with a mind of her own. Both Dunne and Dee are first-rate.

Silver Dollar (1932) **84m.** **½ D: Alfred E. Green. Edward G. Robinson, Bebe Daniels, Aline MacMahon, Robert Warwick, Jobyna Howland. True story (though names are changed) of self-made silver tycoon H. A. W. Tabor, who helped build Denver from mining camp to a thriving city. One of America's great sagas, hampered by unimaginative presentation.

Silver Dream Racer (1980-British) **C-111m.** *½ D: David Wickes. David Essex, Beau Bridges, Cristina Raines, Clarke Peters, Harry H. Corbett, Diane Keen, Lee Montague, Sheila White. Hackneyed drama chronicling the trials of garage-mechanic-turned-motorcyclist Essex as he strives to win the Big Race. Essex wrote and performed music score as well. Panavision. [PG]▼

Silver Lode (1954) **C-80m.** **½ D: Allan Dwan. John Payne, Lizabeth Scott, Dan Duryea, Dolores Moran, Emile Meyer, Harry Carey, Jr., Morris Ankrum, Stuart Whitman, Alan Hale, Jr. A Western town's respected citizen (Payne) is accused of thievery and murder on his wedding day by a slimy U.S. "marshal" (Duryea). So-so melodrama is a fascinating relic of its era as both a HIGH NOON variation and an obvious allegory of HUAC/McCarthyist hypocrisy. The action unfolds on July 4, and the villain is named "McCarty"!▼

Silver Queen (1942) **80m.** ** D: Lloyd Bacon. George Brent, Priscilla Lane, Bruce Cabot, Lynne Overman, Eugene Pallette, Guinn Williams. Post-Civil War tinsel of devoted girl raising money for father; hubby throws it away on "worthless" silver mine.▼

Silver River (1948) **110m.** *½ D: Raoul Walsh. Errol Flynn, Ann Sheridan, Thomas Mitchell, Bruce Bennett, Tom D'Andrea, Barton MacLane, Monte Blue. Mediocre Flynn vehicle: Ann and Errol marry out West, he becomes corrupt.▼

Silver Streak, The (1934) **72m.** *½ D: Thomas Atkins. Sally Blane, Charles Starrett, Hardie Albright, William Farnum, Irving Pichel, Arthur Lake. High-speed train journey is undertaken to deliver iron lungs to epidemic-stricken Nevada town. Derailed by wooden performances and leaden pace although climactic race against time is very exciting; no relation to 1976 film.▼

Silver Streak (1976) **C-113m.** *** D: Arthur Hiller. Gene Wilder, Jill Clayburgh, Richard Pryor, Patrick McGoohan, Ned Beatty, Ray Walston, Scatman Crothers, Clifton James, Richard Kiel, Fred Willard. Nutty blend of comedy, romance, action and suspense as mild-mannered editor Wilder becomes involved in murder plot on cross-country train ride. Switch from comedy to violence is sometimes jarring, but on the whole a highly entertaining picture. One of the best Wilder/Pryor pairings. Imitation Hitchcock written by Colin Higgins. [PG]▼●

Silver Whip, The (1953) **73m.** **½ D: Harmon Jones. Dale Robertson, Rory Calhoun, Robert Wagner, Kathleen Crowley, Lola Albright. Occasionally actionful Western of outlaws vs. stage line.

Simba (1928) **83m.** **½ D: (none credited). Rambling, occasionally interesting "dramatic record" of famed husband-and-wife adventurers Martin and Osa Johnson, and their 15,000-mile trek through the wilds of Africa. Much of the footage now seems overly familiar. The full title is SIMBA, THE KING OF BEASTS.▼●

Simba (1955-British) **C-99m.** ***½ D: Brian Desmond Hurst. Dirk Bogarde, Virginia McKenna, Basil Sydney, Donald Sinden. Fine cast in story of young man arriving in Kenya only to find brother killed by Mau Maus. Some grisly scenes.▼

Simon (1980) **C-97m.** **½ D: Marshall Brickman. Alan Arkin, Madeline Kahn, Austin Pendleton, Judy Graubart, William Finley, Fred Gwynne, Adolph Green. Uneven comedy about psychology professor (Arkin) who's brainwashed by group of think-tank weirdos to believe he's come from another planet. There's a cruel edge to the humor, and signs of a serious film trying to break out, in screenwriter Brickman's directorial debut. [PG]▼

Simon and Laura (1956-British) **C-91m.** **½ D: Muriel Box. Peter Finch, Kay Kendall, Muriel Pavlow, Ian Carmichael, Maurice Denham. Spunky farce involving Finch and Kendall, a married acting couple whose TV image contradicts their violent offscreen battles. VistaVision.

Simon Birch (1998) **C-113m.** *** D: Mark Steven Johnson. Ian Michael Smith, Joseph Mazzello, Ashley Judd, Oliver Platt, David Strathairn, Dana Ivey, Beatrice Winde, Jan Hooks, Jim Carrey. Fable set in the early 1960s about a young boy with arrested growth (real-life 11-year-old Smith) who believes he's part of God's plan, and is destined to be a hero. That destiny is hard to discern in his sad, often frustrated life; the bright spot is his friendship with Mazzello, who's also an outsider as a bastard child in a small town. Well-made tearjerker loosely adapted from John Irving's novel *A Prayer for Owen Meany*; manipulative, borderline mushy at times, but very well done. [PG]▼●◗

Simon of the Desert (1965-Mexican) **45m.** **** D: Luis Buñuel. Claudio Brook, Silvia Pinal, Hortensia Santovena, Enrique Alvarez Felix. Hilarious parable about a bearded ascetic who plops himself atop a pillar to communicate with God better. Could only have been made by one filmmaker; even by Buñuel's standards, the ending of this one is pretty wild.▼

Simon Sez (1999) **C-85m.** BOMB D: Kevin Elders. Dennis Rodman, Xin-Xin Xiong, Dane Cook, Natalia Cigliuti, Filip Nicolic, Emma Sjoberg. Absolutely dreadful actioner with Rodman—the NBA's most famous cross-dressing power forward—playing a James Bond–like Interpol agent who sets out to rescue a kidnapped heiress. Bottom of the barrel in all departments. [PG-13]▼◗

Simpatico (1999) **C-106m.** ** D: Matthew Warchus. Nick Nolte, Jeff Bridges, Sharon Stone, Catherine Keener, Albert Finney, Shawn Hatosy, Kimberly Williams, Liam Waite. Bridges is a Kentucky millionaire horseman whose life comes apart when he hears from a boyhood pal (Nolte) who threatens to expose their dark, longtime secret. Film's overheated tone seems unwarranted by the material itself, but it's great fun watching old-pro Finney. Based on a play by Sam Shepard. [R]▼◗

Simple Men (1992) **C-105m.** *** D: Hal Hartley. Robert Burke, William Sage, Karen Sillas, Elina Löwensohn, Martin Donovan, Mark Chandler Bailey. Original, ingratiating tale of brothers Burke and Sage, who set out in search of their fugitive father, a former Brooklyn Dodgers all-star shortstop who, in the 1960s, became a bomb-throwing anarchist. Infused with a wry sense of humor and consistent offbeat tilt, but the emotions underneath are genuine, and that's what makes the film so endearing. A PBS *American Playhouse* coproduction. [R]▼●

Simple Plan, A (1998) **C-121m.** **½ D: Sam Raimi. Bill Paxton, Billy Bob Thornton, Bridget Fonda, Brent Briscoe, Gary Cole, Chelcie Ross, Jack Walsh, Becky Ann Baker. Wintry tale of three men—a family man, his slow-witted brother, and the latter's redneck pal—who stumble onto a cache of money in a downed airplane. Their decision to keep the cash quickly snowballs into a whirlpool of tension that leads to other crimes. Thornton's exceptional performance makes the film worth seeing, but the story—and its mild-mannered characters' sudden transformation—simply doesn't ring true. Adapted by Scott B. Smith from his novel. [R]▼●◗

Simple Story, A (1978-French) **C-110m.** *** D: Claude Sautet. Romy Schneider, Bruno Cremer, Claude Brasseur, Arlette Bonnard. Fortyish laborer examines her life after aborting a child and dropping her lover. Schneider gives one of her best performances in this graceful drama.▼

Simple Twist of Fate, A (1994) **C-106m.** **½ D: Gillies MacKinnon. Steve Martin, Gabriel Byrne, Catherine O'Hara, Stephen Baldwin, Laura Linney, Byron Jennings, Michael des Barres, Ed Grady, Kristoffer Tabori, Anne Heche. Circumstances drive a man to become a recluse and a miser, until an orphaned toddler wanders into his life. Martin produced, wrote, and starred in this adaptation of George Eliot's novel *Silas Marner,* an odd choice of material that yields an interesting if never quite arresting story. Some of the most entertaining moments are also the most incongruous, when the sober-faced lead character suddenly—and unexpectedly—becomes funny, à la Steve Martin. [PG-13]▼●

Simple Wish, A (1997) **C-89m.** **½ D: Michael Ritchie. Martin Short, Mara Wilson, Kathleen Turner, Robert Pastorelli, Amanda Plummer, Francis Capra, Ruby Dee, Teri Garr. Amusing family film about a bungling male fairy godmother who tries to help a little girl whose wish is to see her father get a part in a new musical play.

Short and Wilson are fun, Turner is over the top as a wicked witch, and the special effects are good . . . though the film never quite takes off. Highlight for grownups is the bogus Andrew Lloyd Webber–ish musical play *Two Cities* which figures in the plot. (Director Ritchie wrote the songs with Lucy Simon.) [PG]▼●◗

Simply Irresistible (1999) **C-96m.** ** D: Mark Tarlov. Sarah Michelle Gellar, Sean Patrick Flanery, Patricia Clarkson, Dylan Baker, Christopher Durang, Larry Gilliard, Jr., Betty Buckley, Amanda Peet. Old-fashioned, overcooked romantic comedy-fantasy about a talentless chef (Gellar) struggling to keep her late mother's restaurant afloat, who is transformed by a magical crab (!) into a master cook whose concoctions seem to have special powers. Along the way, she becomes romantically involved with an executive (Flanery) who is setting up a gourmet restaurant. Occasionally likable, but far too predictable. Super 35. [PG-13] ▼●◗

Sin, The SEE: **Good Luck, Miss Wyckoff**

Sinatra (1992) **C-250m. TVM** D: James Sadwith. Philip Casnoff, Olympia Dukakis, Joe Santos, Gina Gershon, Nina Siemaszko, Marcia Gay Harden, Rod Steiger, Bob Gunton, Jeff Corey, Jay Robinson, Robin Gammell. Surprisingly accurate and relatively well-rounded chronicle of Frank's life and career with its mob, show-biz, and Kennedy connections. Casnoff does an initially on-target impersonation, coming off better in the early days as "The Voice" than as the later "Ol' Blue Eyes." Harden's sexy Ava Gardner is much better than Siemaszko's fey Mia Farrow. Highlights are the dozens of lip-synched Sinatra recordings, although a couple of early ones were redone by Australian actor Tom Burlinson and Frank Jr.; Frank Sr. gave this one his blessing, since it was daughter Tina's personal project. Written by William Mastrosimone. Above average.▼●

Sinbad and the Eye of the Tiger (1977-British) **C-113m.** *½ D: Sam Wanamaker. Patrick Wayne, Jane Seymour, Taryn Power, Margaret Whiting, Patrick Troughton. Dreary followup to GOLDEN VOYAGE OF SINBAD has unusually hackneyed script (even for this kind of film), disappointing Ray Harryhausen effects, and goes on forever. For patient kids only. Taryn is Tyrone Power's daughter. [G]▼●

Sinbad the Sailor (1947) **C-117m.** *** D: Richard Wallace. Douglas Fairbanks Jr., Maureen O'Hara, Anthony Quinn, Walter Slezak, George Tobias, Jane Greer, Mike Mazurki, Sheldon Leonard. Tongue-in-cheek swashbuckler, with lavish color production. Great fun.▼●

Sincerely Yours (1955) **C-115m.** BOMB D: Gordon Douglas. Liberace, Joanne Dru, Dorothy Malone, William Demarest, Richard Eyer, Lurene Tuttle. Remake of George Arliss' MAN WHO PLAYED GOD becomes a ludicrous vehicle for Liberace. Camp classic written by Irving Wallace, with the star's brother George serving as musical adviser.▼●

Since You Went Away (1944) **172m.** ***½ D: John Cromwell. Claudette Colbert, Jennifer Jones, Joseph Cotten, Shirley Temple, Monty Woolley, Hattie McDaniel, Agnes Moorehead, Craig Stevens, Keenan Wynn, Nazimova, Robert Walker, Lionel Barrymore. Tear-jerker supreme with Colbert at her valiant best. Story of family suffering through WW2 with many tragedies and complications dates a bit, but still is very smooth film. Producer David O. Selznick wrote the screenplay, from Margaret Buell Wilder's book. Beautifully photographed by Lee Garmes and Stanley Cortez. Max Steiner's score won an Oscar. Film debuts of Guy Madison (then an actual sailor, in the role of sailor Harold Smith) and John Derek (an extra).▼●

Sinful Davey (1969-British) **C-95m.** **½ D: John Huston. John Hurt, Pamela Franklin, Nigel Davenport, Ronald Fraser, Robert Morley, Fidelma Murphy, Maxine Audley, Brenda Fricker. Tale of 19th-century Scottish highwayman and his love for a "nice" girl is rather ordinary, but does have pleasant performance by Franklin. Based on a true story. Anjelica Huston has a bit part. Panavision. [M/PG]

Sinful Life, A (1989) **C-90m.** ** D: William Schreiner. Anita Morris, Rick Overton, Dennis Christopher, Mark Rolston, Cynthia Szigeti, Blair Tefkin, Cynthia Songe. Very offbeat comedy (filmed on a low, low budget) about a former Sonny and Cher dancer named Claire Vin Blanc who fights to keep her rather *unusual* child, Baby, from being removed to a more "respectable" environment. Not for everyone, but it does give Morris a great vehicle for her comedic talent. Based on the play *Just Like the Pom Pom Girls,* originally presented by L.A.'s Groundlings comedy troupe. [R]▼●

Sing (1989) **C-97m.** BOMB D: Richard Baskin. Lorraine Bracco, Peter Dobson, Jessica Steen, Louise Lasser, George DiCenzo, Patti La Belle. Title refers to a true-life, decades-old tradition—a song-dance competition (or "Sing") between seniors and underclassmen in Brooklyn high schools. Script (by Dean Pitchford) is decades old, too: B-movie clichés about a rebel, a "nice" girl, an understanding teacher, and jelly-spined administrators all locking horns during pageant rehearsals. Threatens to go over the brink throughout . . . and eventually does. [PG-13]▼●

Sing and Swing (1963-British) **75m.** ** D: Lance Comfort. David Hemmings, Veronica Hurst, Jennifer Moss, John Pike. Virtue of modest musical is Hemmings in lead role of messenger boy who joins pals in combo; they record a song, and find their musical career in full sway. Originally titled LIVE IT UP.

Singapore (1947) **79m.** **½ D: John Brahm. Fred MacMurray, Ava Gardner, Roland Culver, Richard Haydn, Spring Byington, Thomas Gomez, Porter Hall. Alluring drama of trader/pearl smuggler MacMurray returning to Singapore after a five-year absence, recalling his previous romantic relationship with Gardner. He thinks she was killed during a Japanese bombing attack, but she really was a victim of amnesia. The characters in this seem to be very loosely modeled after those in CASABLANCA. Remade as ISTANBUL.▼

Singapore, Singapore (1968-French) **C-103m.** ** D: Bernard Toublanc Michel. Sean Flynn, Marika Green, Terry Downes, Marc Michel, Peter Gayford, Denis Berry. So-so espionage tale interesting primarily for Flynn (Errol's son) playing a CIA agent looking into the disappearance of a number of Marines in Singapore. Based on Jean Bruce's novel. Aka FIVE ASHORE IN SINGAPORE.

Singapore Woman (1941) **64m.** ** D: Jean Negulesco. Brenda Marshall, David Bruce, Virginia Field, Jerome Cowan, Rose Hobart, Heather Angel. Sluggish account of young rubber planter set upon helping to remove oriental curse from Marshall. Remake of DANGEROUS.

Sing, Baby, Sing (1936) **87m.** *** D: Sidney Lanfield. Alice Faye, Adolphe Menjou, Gregory Ratoff, Ted Healy, Patsy Kelly, Tony Martin. Pleasant musicomedy stolen by Menjou as John Barrymore prototype involved with publicity-seeking Faye. Songs: "When Did You Leave Heaven?" "You Turned The Tables On Me," title tune. The Ritz Brothers are quite good in their feature-film debut.

Sing Boy Sing (1958) **90m.** ** D: Henry Ephron. Tommy Sands, Lili Gentle, Edmond O'Brien, John McIntire, Nick Adams, Diane Jergens, Josephine Hutchinson, Jerry Paris, Regis Toomey. A teen idol and Elvis Presley clone (Sands) is manipulated by his cold-hearted manager (O'Brien) and kept apart from his roots. Muddled relic of its era, which purports to expose the evils of rock 'n roll and show biz (in between Sands' endless musical numbers). CinemaScope.

Singer Not the Song, The (1961-British) **C-129m.** **½ D: Roy (Ward) Baker. Dirk Bogarde, John Mills, Mylene Demongeot, Eric Pohlmann. Offbeat, sluggish yarn set in Mexico involving conflict of Catholic priest and local bandit to control the town, with Demongeot in love with the clergyman. CinemaScope.▼

Singing Guns (1950) **C-91m.** *½ D: R. G. Springsteen. Vaughn Monroe, Ella Raines, Walter Brennan, Ward Bond, Billy Gray. Minor happenings in the old West with singer Monroe in straight role.

Singing Fool, The (1928) **101m.** **½ D: Lloyd Bacon. Al Jolson, Betty Bronson, Josephine Dunn, Arthur Housman, Davey Lee, Edward Martindel, Helen Lynch, Robert Emmett O'Connor. Part-talkie follow-up to THE JAZZ SINGER is potent melodrama, with Jolson as a songwriter/performer whose domestic life is in turmoil. Jolson's high-energy acting style will either delight or revolt. Songs include "It All Depends on You," "I'm Sitting on Top of the World," "There's a Rainbow 'Round My Shoulder," and "Sonny Boy" (which Jolson sings to Davey Lee).●

Singing Kid, The (1936) **85m.** ** D: William Keighley. Al Jolson, Sybil Jason, Edward Everett Horton, Lyle Talbot, Allen Jenkins, Beverly Roberts, Claire Dodd. Jolson plays a Broadway star who loses his voice and recuperates in the country, where he takes in a young girl—and finds romance. A star vehicle if there ever was one, and recommended only for Jolson fans. Musical appearances by Cab Calloway, Wini Shaw, and The Yacht Club Boys. Highlight of the Harold Arlen-E.Y. Harburg score: "I Love to Singa."●

Singing Nun, The (1966) **C-98m.** ** D: Henry Koster. Debbie Reynolds, Ricardo Montalban, Greer Garson, Agnes Moorehead, Chad Everett, Katharine Ross, Ed Sullivan, Juanita Moore, Tom Drake. Syrupy comic-book stuff based on real-life Belgian nun whose devotion is split between religious work and making hit records. Panavision. ▼●

Singin' in the Rain (1952) **C-102m.** **** D: Gene Kelly, Stanley Donen. Gene Kelly, Debbie Reynolds, Donald O'Connor, Jean Hagen, Cyd Charisse, Millard Mitchell, Douglas Fowley, Madge Blake, Rita Moreno. Perhaps the greatest movie musical of all time, fashioned by Betty Comden and Adolph Green from a catalogue of Arthur Freed-Nacio Herb Brown songs. The setting is Hollywood during the transition to talkies, with Hagen giving the performance of a lifetime as Kelly's silent screen costar, whose voice could shatter glass. Kelly's title number, O'Connor's "Make 'Em Laugh," are just two highlights in a film packed with gems. Later a Broadway musical.▼●◗

Single Girl, A (1995-French) **C-90m.** ***½ D: Benoit Jacquot. Virginie Ledoyen, Benoit Magimel, Dominique Valadie, Vera Briole, Michel Bompoil, Jean-Cretien Sibertin-Blanc. Bright, scintillating slice-of-life, told in real time, about a young woman (Ledoyen) whose personal life is complicated to say the least, and who must contend with additional pressures in her new job as a room-service waitress in a fancy hotel. Exudes the freshness and spontaneity of the early French New Wave; 19-year-old Ledoyen (who seems like Anna Karina reborn) offers a star-making performance.▼

Single Girls, The (1973) **C-85m.** ** D: Ferd and Beverly Sebastian. Claudia Jennings, Jean Marie Ingels, Joan Prather, Cheri Howell, Greg Mullavey, Albert Popwell, Robyn Hilton. Attractive B-movie cast in not bad drive-in thriller about killer on the loose at a Caribbean resort. More sex and comedy than violence, fortunately. [R]

Single Handed SEE: **Sailor of the King**

Single Room Furnished (1968) **C-93m.** *½ D: Matteo Ottaviano (Matt Cimber). Jayne Mansfield, Dorothy Keller, Fabian Dean, Billy M. Greene, Terri Messina, Martin Horsey, Walter Gregg. Pathetic woman, twice impregnated and thrice deserted, decides to become prostitute. Mansfield's last film, released after her death, opens with Walter Winchell tribute and degenerates as she attempts to display serious acting talent.▼

Singles (1992) **C-99m.** **½ D: Cameron Crowe. Bridget Fonda, Matt Dillon, Campbell Scott, Kyra Sedgwick, Sheila Kelley, Jim True, Bill Pullman, James Le Gros, Devon Raymond, Camilo Gallardo, Ally Walker, Tim Burton. Life in the Seattle singles scene; it ain't easy. Lively seriocomedy with some appealing performances (especially by Scott and Sedgwick), but never as solid or as insightful—as you hope it will be. Film has music, setting, and style galore, but also a rather uneven script. Eric Stoltz (who has appeared in all of the director's films), Tom Skerritt, and Peter Horton have amusing cameos. [PG-13] ▼●◗

Single Standard, The (1929) **73m.** ** D: John S. Robertson. Greta Garbo, Nils Asther, John Mack Brown, Dorothy Sebastian, Lane Chandler. Greta is a San Francisco debutante, a free soul who breaks convention and has an affair with artist Asther. Pretty silly stuff, but Garbo is as beautiful as ever. From an Adela Rogers St. Johns novel.▼●

Single White Female (1992) **C-107m.** **½ D: Barbet Schroeder. Bridget Fonda, Jennifer Jason Leigh, Steven Weber, Peter Friedman, Stephen Tobolowsky, Frances Bay, Rene Estevez, Ken Tobey. Self-employed N.Y. career woman (Fonda), her engagement kaput, ends up sharing her dream apartment with the Roommate from Hell. PERSONA meets Roman Polanski's entire oeuvre in well-acted thriller that's terrific for about an hour—until standard slasher-pic silliness sets in. Screendom's first psychological probing to wrap up with a Chrissie Hynde vocal. Based on John Lutz novel *SWF Seeks Same.* [R]▼●◗

Sing Your Way Home (1945) **72m.** *½ D: Anthony Mann. Jack Haley, Anne Jeffreys, Marcy McGuire, Glenn Vernon. RKO Pictures minimusical set on the high seas with youthful entertainers providing modicum of singing talent.

Sing Your Worries Away (1942) **71m.** ** D: A. Edward Sutherland. June Havoc, Bert Lahr, Buddy Ebsen, Patsy Kelly, Sam Levene, Margaret Dumont, King Sisters, Alvino Rey. Mild musical comedy as the theatrical world and racketeers clash.▼

Sing, You Sinners (1938) **88m.** *** D: Wesley Ruggles. Bing Crosby, Fred MacMurray, Donald O'Connor, Elizabeth Patterson, Ellen Drew, John Gallaudet. Gambling gay-blade Crosby can't face responsibility, despite prodding of brother MacMurray. Fine film with "I've Got A Pocketful Of Dreams" and memorable "Small Fry" number featuring young O'Connor.

Sinister Invasion (1971-Mexican-U.S.) **C-90m.** BOMB D: Jack Hill, Juan Ibanez. Boris Karloff, Enrique Guzman, Christa Linder, Maura Monti, Yerye Beirute, Sergio Kleiner. 19th-century scientist Karloff's experiments accidentally summon aliens who dominate a local Ripper-like killer. Cheap, flaccid, ugly film, one of four Karloff worked on simultaneously in 1968; unfortunately this was his last film work. Aka INCREDIBLE INVASION, INVASION SINIESTRA, and ALIEN TERROR. ▼

Sinister Urge, The (1960) **75m.** BOMB D: Edward D. Wood, Jr. Kenne Duncan, Duke Moore, Carl Anthony, Jean Fontaine, Dino Fantini, Jeanne Willardson. Dedicated cops Duncan and Moore set out to smash the "smut picture racket," which is run by a brassy blonde who writes with a four-foot quill pen. One of Wood's least known works demonstrates with complete conviction how photos of plump women in their underwear are the principal cause of juvenile deliquency. Aka THE YOUNG AND THE IMMORAL.▼●

Sink the Bismarck! (1960-British) **97m.** *** D: Lewis Gilbert. Kenneth More, Dana Wynter, Carl Mohner, Laurence Naismith, Geoffrey Keen, Karel Stepanek, Michael Hordern. Good WW2 film based on fact. Exciting sea battles as British navy starts deadly hunt for famed German war vessel. Script by Edmund H. North. CinemaScope. ▼●

Sinner, The SEE: **Desert Desperadoes**

Sinner's Holiday (1930) **60m.** **½ D: John G. Adolfi. Grant Withers, Evalyn Knapp, James Cagney, Joan Blondell, Lucille LaVerne, Noel Madison. Predictable melodrama is interesting to watch, as period piece (with good Coney Island atmosphere) and as film debuts for Cagney and Blondell, recreating stage roles in support of stars Withers and Knapp. Story involves romance, murder, and overprotective mother who runs penny arcade.

Sinner's Holiday (1947) SEE: **Christmas Eve**

Sinners in Paradise (1938) **65m.** ** D: James Whale. John Boles, Madge Evans, Bruce Cabot, Marion Martin, Gene Lockhart, Nana Bryant, Milburn Stone, Donald Barry. Plane crash survivors are stranded on tropic island where mysterious Boles lives as a recluse. Starts great, but peters out.▼

Sinners in the Sun (1932) **70m.** ** D: Alexander Hall. Carole Lombard, Chester Morris, Adrienne Ames, Cary Grant, Walter Byron, Alison Skipworth, Rita La Roy, Ida Lewis. Lovely Lombard learns that money isn't all in this slick, typical triangle; Grant has a bit role.

Sin of Harold Diddlebock, The (1947) **90m.** **½ D: Preston Sturges. Harold Lloyd, Frances Ramsden, Jimmy Conlin, Raymond Walburn, Edgar Kennedy, Arline Judge, Lionel Stander, Rudy Vallee. Fascinating idea of updating Lloyd's 1920s character to show what's happened to that go-getter doesn't fulfill its promise. Aimless comedy can't top opening sequence from THE FRESHMAN (1925), despite enthusiasm of fine cast. Reedited to 79m. and reissued in 1950 as MAD WEDNESDAY.▼

Sin of Madelon Claudet, The (1931) *** **73m.** D: Edgar Selwyn. Helen Hayes, Lewis Stone, Neil Hamilton, Robert Young, Cliff Edwards, Jean Hersholt, Marie Prevost, Karen Morley, Charles Winninger, Alan Hale, Frankie Darro. First-rate, fast-moving soaper in the MADAME X vein, about a woman who sacrifices everything so her illegitimate son will have a good life. Hayes won an Oscar portraying woman who goes from bumpkin to Parisian sophisticate to suffering mother to haggard streetwalker—and she's terrific.▼

Sins of Jezebel (1953) **C-74m.** *½ D: Reginald Le Borg. Paulette Goddard, George Nader, John Hoyt, Eduard Franz. Embarrassing low-budget costumer with Goddard miscast in title role.

Sins of Lola Montes, The SEE: **Lola Montes**

Sins of Rachel Cade, The (1961) **C-124m.** **½ D: Gordon Douglas. Angie Dickinson, Peter Finch, Roger Moore, Woody Strode, Rafer Johnson, Juano Hernandez, Mary Wickes, Scatman Crothers. Turgid melodrama set in Belgian Congo with Dickinson a missionary nurse involved in romance and native conflicts.

Sins of Rome (1954-Italian) **75m.** ** D: Riccardo Freda. Ludmilla Tcherina, Massimo Girotti, Gianna Maria Canale, Yves Vincent. Rebel slave Spartacus incites fellow prisoners to fight Roman republic. Early Italian spectacle doesn't have cheaper look of later grinds.▼

Sin Town (1942) **75m.** **½ D: Ray Enright. Constance Bennett, Broderick Crawford, Anne Gwynne, Ward Bond, Andy Devine, Leo Carrillo, Patric Knowles, Hobart Bosworth. Fast-moving actioner of town in uproar after newspaper editor is killed; good cast in above-average film. Richard Brooks was one of the writers.

Sioux City (1994) **C-102m.** **½ D: Lou Diamond Phillips. Lou Diamond Phillips, Salli Richardson, Melinda Dillon, Lise Cutter, Apesanahkwat, Gary Farmer, Ralph Waite, Tantoo Cardinal, Adam Roarke. Overworked doctor Phillips, Lakota Indian by birth but adopted as a child by an affluent Jewish couple, goes on vacation and returns to the reservation where he was born; there, he learns of the death of his real mother, faces anti-Indian sentiment, and ultimately confronts the mysteries of his past. Sensitively handled drama is engrossing and suspenseful most of the way, until the ridiculous finale. [PG-13]▼

Siren of Atlantis (1948) **75m.** BOMB D: Gregg Tallas. Maria Montez, Jean-Pierre Aumont, Dennis O'Keefe, Henry Daniell, Morris Carnovsky. Ridiculous hokum of soldiers Aumont and O'Keefe stumbling upon famed Lost Continent; Montez is the sultry queen. Despite the title, film takes place in the desert! Based on *L'Atlantide*, previously filmed in 1921 and 1932. Remade as JOURNEY BENEATH THE DESERT.

Siren of Bagdad (1953) **C-77m.** **½ D: Richard Quine. Paul Henreid, Patricia Medina, Hans Conried, Charlie Lung. Comedy-adventure of magician and friend trying to save dancing girls in slave market. Conried provides film's best moments.

Sirens (1994-Australian-British) **C-94m.** *** D: John Duigan. Hugh Grant, Tara Fitzgerald, Sam Neill, Elle Macpherson, Portia de Rossi, Kate Fischer, Pamela Rabe, Ben Mendelsohn, John Polson. Piquant social comedy about a young, liberal British minister and his wife who drop in on scandalous Australian artist Norman Lindsay (Neill), and find themselves seduced (somewhat) by his libertarian ways—and his three gorgeous, free-thinking models, who have no qualms about posing nude. Some may be attracted by the prospect of seeing supermodel Macpherson naked, but she also delivers a good performance. Droll and imaginative work by writer-director Duigan (who also appears onscreen as the earnest minister). Artist Lindsay was portrayed by James Mason in the 1969 film AGE OF CONSENT. [R]▼●◗

Sir Henry at Rawlinson End (1980-British) **72m.** **½ D: Steve Roberts. Trevor Howard, Patrick Magee, Denise Coffey, J. G. Devlin, Sheila Reid, Harry Fowler. Howard is fine as an eccentric, alcoholic aristocrat who attempts to exorcise a family spirit from his domain. Strange but entertaining, and veddy British.

Sirocco (1951) **98m.** **½ D: Curtis Bernhardt. Humphrey Bogart, Marta Toren, Lee J. Cobb, Everett Sloane, Zero Mostel, Ludwig Donath, Harry Guardino. Rugged Bogart perks this yarn of gunrunning set in 1920s Syria.▼●

Sis Hopkins (1941) **98m.** **½ D: Joseph

Santley. Judy Canova, Bob Crosby, Charles Butterworth, Jerry Colonna, Susan Hayward, Katharine Alexander. Fairly amusing comedy of country girl who comes to live with social uncle and attends girls' school. Even Canova is restrained!

Sister Act (1992) **C-100m.** *** D: Emile Ardolino. Whoopi Goldberg, Maggie Smith, Harvey Keitel, Bill Nunn, Kathy Najimy, Wendy Makkena, Mary Wickes, Robert Miranda, Richard Portnow, Joseph Maher. A Reno lounge singer, targeted for murder by her mobster boyfriend, hides out in a convent—where she shakes things up as the new choir director. Crowd-pleasing comedy, cannily written (by Joseph Howard, aka Paul Rudnick) and directed, with a plum part for Whoopi—though veteran character actress Wickes has many of the funniest lines. Followed by a sequel. [PG]▼●

Sister Act 2: Back in the Habit (1993) **C-106m.** **½ D: Bill Duke. Whoopi Goldberg, Maggie Smith, Kathy Najimy, Barnard Hughes, Mary Wickes, James Coburn, Michael Jeter, Wendy Makkena, Sheryl Lee Ralph, Robert Pastorelli, Thomas Gottschalk, Jennifer Love Hewitt. Affable piffle unconvincingly finds Goldberg back with the nuns, coaching students in a choral competition as heavy Coburn plots to close their school. Though someone involved apparently saw THE BELLS OF ST. MARY'S a few too many times, needless sequel does send you out with a smile, thanks to a smashing musical finale and an end-credit sequence that's the best thing in the picture. *Very* slow going at first. [PG]▼●◗

Sister-in-Law, The (1974) **C-85m.** ** D: Joseph Ruben. John Savage, W. G. McMillan, Anne Saxon, Meredith Baer, Jon Oppenheim, Tom Mahoney. Interesting curio has Savage becoming involved with destructive title character as his brother's dupe in drug-smuggling. Hurt by needlessly negative finale. Savage also composed the score and sings several folk ballads pleasantly. [R]▼

Sister Kenny (1946) **116m.** ***½ D: Dudley Nichols. Rosalind Russell, Alexander Knox, Dean Jagger, Philip Merivale, Beulah Bondi, Dorothy Peterson. Russell shines in title role, as Australian nurse who initiated treatment for polio. Engrossing drama is among the better Hollywood biopics. Scripted by Nichols, Knox, and Mary McCarthy, from Mary Kenny's autobiography *And They Shall Walk.*▼●

Sister My Sister (1994-British) **C-102m.** *** D: Nancy Meckler. Julie Walters, Joely Richardson, Jodhi May, Sophie Thursfield. Compelling psychological drama about a dour madame (Walters), obsessed with her respectability, who controls her ungainly daughter (Thursfield) and two maids (Richardson, May); the latter are sisters who share a complicated emotional—and sexual—bond. Strains among the characters build, leading to emotional fireworks. A based-on-fact story that served as the basis of Jean Genet's *The Maids.* [R]▼

Sisters, The (1938) **98m.** *** D: Anatole Litvak. Errol Flynn, Bette Davis, Anita Louise, Ian Hunter, Donald Crisp, Beulah Bondi, Jane Bryan, Lee Patrick, Mayo Methot, Laura Hope Crews, Dick Foran, Henry Travers, Patric Knowles, Alan Hale. Davis, Louise, and Bryan are sisters whose marital problems are traced in this lavish film; Bette's got the most trouble, of course, with unreliable husband Flynn in San Francisco, 1905.▼

Sisters (1973) **C-93m.** *** D: Brian De Palma. Margot Kidder, Jennifer Salt, Charles Durning, Barnard Hughes, William Finley, Mary Davenport, Olympia Dukakis. De Palma's first venture into Hitchcock territory, about separated Siamese twins (Kidder), one of whom is a homicidal maniac, and the reporter (Salt) who—shades of REAR WINDOW—thinks she witnessed one of the slayings. Eerie, gory, tremendously suspenseful, with one of Bernard Herrmann's most chilling scores. [R]▼

Sister, Sister (1982) **C-100m. TVM** D: John Berry. Diahann Carroll, Rosalind Cash, Irene Cara, Paul Winfield, Dick Anthony Williams, Robert Hooks, Christopher St. John, Diana Douglas, Albert Powell. Rewarding drama, written by Maya Angelou, about the uneasy reunion of three sisters that opens up old family wounds. Filmed several years before its initial network showing. Above average.

Sister, Sister (1987) **C-91m.** *½ D: Bill Condon. Eric Stoltz, Jennifer Jason Leigh, Judith Ivey, Dennis Lipscomb, Anne Pitoniak, Benjamin Moulton. Leigh and Ivey are title siblings, two women with myriad problems and repressions. They've converted their parents' mansion into a dreary guest house . . . one which you will not want to visit. Thoroughly unappealing. [R]▼●

Sisters of Nishijin (1952-Japanese) **110m.** ***½ D: Kozaburo Yoshimura. Yumiko Miyagino, Mitsuko Miura, Yuko Tsumura, Chieko Higashiyama. Family of Kyoto silkweavers cannot adapt to industrialization; the father-patriarch kills himself, and his widow, daughters, and assistants try to carry on. Excellent tale of greed and courage.

Sisters, or the Balance of Happiness (1979-German) **C-95m.** **½ D: Margarethe von Trotta. Jutta Lampe, Gudrun Gabriel, Jessica Fruh, Rainer Delventhal, Konstantin Wecker. Slow but not unrewarding psychological study of the complex relationship between two sisters; one, a successful executive secretary, is supporting the other, a graduate student in biology.▼

Sister Streetfighter (1975-Japanese) **C-81m.** *½ D: Kazuhiko Yamaguchi. Etsuko

"Sue" Shiomi, Mie "May" Hayakawa, Hiroshi "Harry" Kondo, Shinichi "Sonny" Chiba, Sanae Obori, Tatsuya Nanjo. Shiomi kicks some major butt when her spy brother is captured by drug runners in Hong Kong. The most outlandishly campy and cartoonish of the STREET FIGHTER series, this is a crudely made concoction of sex and sadism, with Chiba only appearing in a few scenes. Actionscope. [R]▼●

Sitting Bull (1954) **C-105m.** ** D: Sidney Salkow. Dale Robertson, Mary Murphy, J. Carrol Naish, Iron Eyes Cody, John Litel, Bill (William) Hopper. Sluggish Western about cavalry major Robertson, who is compassionate toward the Sioux and clashes with his superiors over their disregard for Indian rights. CinemaScope.▼

Sitting Ducks (1980) **C-90m.** *** D: Henry Jaglom. Michael Emil, Zack Norman, Patrice Townsend, Irene Forrest, Richard Romanus, Henry Jaglom. Energetic, funny sleeper about timid Syndicate accountant Emil and womanizing pal Norman, who take a day's collections and rip off the Mob. Emil and Norman have comedy team potential as the bickering buddies, Townsend (then Mrs. Jaglom) is luscious as a woman they pick up. Lots of belly laughs. [R]▼

Sitting Pretty (1933) **85m.** **½ D: Harry Joe Brown. Ginger Rogers, Jack Oakie, Jack Haley, Thelma Todd, Gregory Ratoff, Lew Cody. First half is bouncy yarn of songwriters Oakie and Haley going Hollywood, meeting homespun Rogers, vamp Todd; remainder bogs down, rescued by finale "Did You Ever See a Dream Walking."▼

Sitting Pretty (1948) **84m.** ***½ D: Walter Lang. Robert Young, Maureen O'Hara, Clifton Webb, Richard Haydn, Louise Allbritton, Ed Begley. Webb is perfect as self-centered genius who accepts job as full-time babysitter in gossip-laden suburban town. Highly entertaining, followed by the MR. BELVEDERE comedies.▼

Sitting Target (1972-British) **C-93m.** *½ D: Douglas Hickox. Oliver Reed, Jill St. John, Ian McShane, Edward Woodward, Frank Finlay, Freddie Jones. Reed breaks out of prison to settle two scores—one of them with his cheating wife (St. John). Violent, generally unpleasant film. [R]

Situation Hopeless—But Not Serious (1965) **97m.** ** D: Gottfried Reinhardt. Alec Guinness, Michael Connors, Robert Redford, Anita Hoefer, Mady Rahl, Paul Dahlke. Odd little comedy, from a Robert Shaw novel, about German clerk Guinness holding two American (Redford, Connors) prisoners for years after WW2 has ended. Interesting characterization by Guinness, but a flat film.

Six Black Horses (1962) **C-80m.** ** D: Harry Keller. Audie Murphy, Dan Duryea, Joan O'Brien, George Wallace. O'Brien pays two men to take her across Indian lands, intending to murder gunman of duo who killed her husband. Mediocre Western with a Burt Kennedy script apparently left over from the Randolph Scott-Budd Boetticher series.

Six Bridges to Cross (1955) **96m.** **½ D: Joseph Pevney. Tony Curtis, Julia (Julie) Adams, George Nader, Sal Mineo, Jay C. Flippen. Entertaining account of Brink's robbery, tracing events leading up to famous heist; on-location filming in Boston. Mineo's film debut.

Six Day Bike Rider (1934) **69m.** **½ D: Lloyd Bacon. Joe E. Brown, Maxine Doyle, Frank McHugh, Lottie Williams. Intriguing gimmick has Brown trying to impress girlfriend by entering marathon race; good little comedy.

Six Days Seven Nights (1998) **C-101m.** *** D: Ivan Reitman. Harrison Ford, Anne Heche, David Schwimmer, Jacqueline Obradors, Temuera Morrison, Allison Janney, Douglas Weston, Danny Trejo, Taj Mahal. Entertaining romantic comedy about a N.Y.C. career woman who's forced to interrupt an idyllic tropical vacation with her boyfriend for a business side trip. Then her charter plane crash-lands, and she's stranded on a deserted island with her pilot—who's not exactly her type (and vice versa). An obvious setup is played out with great verve by the stars. Ford is especially loose and funny. Panavision. [PG-13]▼●◗

Six Degrees of Separation (1993) **C-111m.** *** D: Fred Schepisi. Stockard Channing, Will Smith, Donald Sutherland, Ian McKellen, Mary Beth Hurt, Bruce Davison, Richard Masur, Anthony Michael Hall, Heather Graham, Eric Thal, Anthony Rapp, Osgood Perkins, Catherine Kellner, Jeffrey Abrams, Kitty Carlisle Hart. Stylish, opened-up adaptation by John Guare of his stage success about a handsome con man who convinces well-off, gullible New Yorkers that he is Sidney Poitier's son. Impressively acted film flows smoothly in its first two acts, before the satire gives way to chest-thumping tragedy. Dominant virtue is the wide-screen snap Schepisi gives to the N.Y. settings, both indoors and out. Based on a true incident. Many N.Y.C. society types pop up in cameos. Super 35. [R]▼●

Six Hours to Live (1932) **78m.** ** D: William Dieterle. Warner Baxter, Miriam Jordan, John Boles, George Marion, Beryl Mercer, Irene Ware. Unusual story of diplomat Baxter whose stubbornness at international trade conference leads to his murder; scientist brings him back to life for six hours. Stodgy production spoils interesting idea.

Six Lessons From Madame La Zonga (1941) **62m.** ** D: John Rawlins. Lupe Velez, Leon Errol, Helen Parrish, Charles

Lang, William Frawley, Eddie Quillan, Shemp Howard. Good cast of professional laugh-getters in typical, silly outing; Leon goes Latin, and Lupe goes gold-digging after him in shipboard comedy. Title derived from popular song of the day.

Six of a Kind (1934) **62m.** *** D: Leo McCarey. W. C. Fields, George Burns, Gracie Allen, Charlie Ruggles, Mary Boland, Alison Skipworth. George and Gracie drive Mary and Charlie crazy traveling westward on vacation; Fields as pool-playing sheriff adds to confusion. Zany, wonderful nonsense.▼

Six Pack (1982) **C-110m.** ** D: Daniel Petrie. Kenny Rogers, Diane Lane, Erin Gray, Barry Corbin, Terry Kiser, Bob Hannah, Anthony Michael Hall. Stock car driver more or less inherits six orphans whose idea of good clean fun is stripping down someone else's auto. Not as bad as it sounds, but it won't make your day, either; Rogers' theatrical debut. [PG]▼

Six-Pack Annie (1975) **C-88m.** *** D: Graydon F. David. Lindsay Bloom, Jana Bellan, Ray Danton, Joe Higgins, Stubby Kaye, Louisa Moritz, Richard Kennedy, Doodles Weaver, Bruce Boxleitner, Pedro Gonzalez-Gonzalez, Sid Melton. Minor drive-in classic has busty Bloom as a young girl who goes to Miami to become a hooker to raise money to save her mom's failing diner. Includes a very funny bit by Kennedy as a drunk Texan. [R]

Sixteen (1972) **C-84m.** ** D: Lawrence Dobkin. Mercedes McCambridge, Simone Griffeth, Ford Rainey, Beverly Powers, Parley Baer, Maidie Norman. Sympathetic study of backwoods girl coming of age in the Deep South. Originally titled LIKE A CROW ON A JUNE BUG. [R]▼

Sixteen Candles (1984) **C-93m.** ** D: John Hughes. Molly Ringwald, Anthony Michael Hall, Michael Schoeffling, Paul Dooley, Justin Henry, Gedde Watanabe, Blanche Baker, Carlin Glynn, Edward Andrews, Billie Bird, Carole Cook, Max Showalter, John Cusack, Joan Cusack, Jami Gertz, Beth Ringwald, Haviland Morris. A girl turns 16 and dreams of finding Mr. Right—little dreaming that he's already got his eye on her. Observant, potentially winning comedy cluttered up with cheap jokes and offensive material. Redeemed somewhat by Ringwald's charming performance and Hall's engaging portrayal of a would-be hustler. [PG]▼●◗

16 Days of Glory (1986) **C-145m.** *** D: Bud Greenspan. Narrated by David Perry. Expansive look at the 1984 Los Angeles Olympic Games, with enough natural excitement and irresistible moments to make up for overwritten narration and overbearing score. [G]▼●

Sixteen Fathoms Deep (1934) **57m.** **½ D: Armand Schaefer. Creighton Chaney (Lon Chaney, Jr.), Sally O'Neil, George Regas, Maurice Black, Russell Simpson. Some nicely done underwater cinematography helps this otherwise undistinguished account of sponge fisherman Chaney and loyal girlfriend O'Neil going up against greedy moneylender Regas. Remade in 1948, also with Chaney.▼

16 Fathoms Deep (1948) **C-82m.** ** D: Irving Allen. Lon Chaney, Jr., Lloyd Bridges, Arthur Lake, Eric Feldary, Tanis Chandler, John Qualen, Dickie Moore. Harmless story of sponge fishing in Florida, with a pre-*Sea Hunt* Bridges appropriately cast as a diver. Chaney is the heavy here. In the 1934 version he's the hero.

633 Squadron (1964-British) **C-101m.** **½ D: Walter Grauman. Cliff Robertson, George Chakiris, Maria Perschy, Harry Andrews. Pretentious WW2 aviation film about the group's air mission to bomb German-run factory in Norway. Robertson and Chakiris are stiff-lipped throughout; script by James Clavell and Howard Koch. Panavision. ▼●

Sixth Man, The (1997) **C-107m.** *½ D: Randall Miller. Marlon Wayans, Kadeem Hardison, Kevin Dunn, Michael Michele, David Paymer, Gary Jones. Disney couldn't stop at remaking ANGELS IN THE OUTFIELD and THE ABSENT MINDED PROFESSOR: they had to combine them, in this cloying fantasy about a dead college basketball star who spurs his brother (Wayans) and their team to gravity-defying court feats. Your brain will need a liberal application of Ben-Gay after being pummeled by the idiocy of this foul-mouthed comedy. Wayans mugs outrageously, but with this script, he had to do *something*. [PG-13] ▼●

Sixth Sense, The (1999) **C-107m.** ***½ D: M. Night Shyamalan. Bruce Willis, Toni Collette, Haley Joel Osment, Olivia Williams, Donnie Wahlberg, Glenn Fitzgerald. Exceptional thriller about a dedicated child psychologist who faces his greatest challenge in reaching—and understanding—a young boy who spends his life paralyzed by fear, because he lives in a world of ghosts. Young Osment is extraordinarily good; the film is sinuous and creepy without being manipulative. Writer-director Shyamalan also has a cameo as a doctor. [PG-13] ▼◗

Sixty Glorious Years (1938-British) **C-95m.** *** D: Herbert Wilcox. Anna Neagle, Anton Walbrook, C. Aubrey Smith, Walter Rilla, Charles Carson. Neagle's follow-up to VICTORIA THE GREAT is a repeat of her fine performance as England's legendary queen; good production values. U.S. title: QUEEN OF DESTINY.

Six Weeks (1982) **C-107m.** ** D: Tony Bill. Dudley Moore, Mary Tyler Moore, Katherine Healy, Shannon Wilcox, Bill

Calvert, Joe Regalbuto. Curiously unmoving tearjerker about a politician who meets a precocious young girl who's dying of leukemia, and becomes involved with her mother. Genteel, well acted (Dudley is absolutely charming) but hollow; the characters just don't ring true. Healy, in real life, is an award-winning ballerina. Dudley also composed the score. [PG]▼●

Sizzle Beach, U.S.A. (1986) **C-93m.** BOMB D: Richard Brander. Terry Congie, Leslie Brander, Roselyn Royce, Kevin Costner. Ultra-low-budget beach-bimbo junk, of interest solely as the first film appearance of Costner. Made in 1974. [R]▼●◗

Skateboard (1977) **C-97m.** ** D: George Gage. Allen Garfield, Kathleen Lloyd, Leif Garrett, Richard Van Der Wyk, Tony Alva, Antony Carbone. In trouble with his bookie, Garfield organizes local skateboarders into moneymaking team. Good premise given lackluster treatment. [PG]▼

Skatetown, U.S.A. (1979) **C-98m.** *½ D: William A. Levey. Scott Baio, Flip Wilson, Ron Palillo, Ruth Buzzi, Dave Mason, Greg Bradford, Kelly Lang, Billy Barty, Dorothy Stratten. Comedy-fantasy for the light of heart and slow of brain, with occasionally amusing comedy bits spicing plotless look at the ultimate roller-disco palace. Film's only real distinction is that it's better than ROLLER BOOGIE. Film debut of Patrick Swayze. [PG]

Skeeter (1994) **C-91m.** **½ D: Clark Brandon. Tracy Griffith, Jim Youngs, Charles Napier, Jay Robinson, William Sanderson, Eloy Casados, John Putch, Saxon Trainor, Stacy Edwards, Michael J. Pollard, Buck Flower. Mysterious deaths around a dwindling desert community are traced to toxic waste and the crow-sized mosquitoes it has spawned. Good acting and imaginative, inventive direction result in a funny little thriller that almost overcomes its routine story.▼●

Sketch Artist (1992) **C-100m. TVM** D: Phedon Papamichael. Jeff Fahey, Sean Young, Drew Barrymore, Frank McRae, Tcheky Karyo, James Tolkan, Charlotte Lewis, Ric Young, Stacey Haiduk. A police sketch artist's nightmare: a witness describes the artist's own wife as a murder suspect. Good premise, but the lead character (Fahey) is unappealing, and story unfolds slowly and without conviction. Followed by a sequel. Average. ▼●

Ski Bum, The (1971) **C-136m.** BOMB D: Bruce Clark. Zalman King, Charlotte Rampling, Joseph Mell, Dimitra Arliss, Anna Karen. Deservedly obscure film version of Romain Gary's novel about a ski bum who goes establishment, winds up a pawn in a shady business deal. Aka POINT ZERO. [R]▼

Skidoo (1968) **C-98m.** **½ D: Otto Preminger. Jackie Gleason, Carol Channing, Frankie Avalon, Fred Clark, Michael Constantine, Frank Gorshin, John Phillip Law, Peter Lawford, Burgess Meredith, George Raft, Cesar Romero, Mickey Rooney, Groucho Marx, Austin Pendleton. Avalon plays an up-and-coming gangster, Groucho a mob kingpin named "God," and every single credit to the film is sung. Consequently, about one in a thousand will have the temperament to like this; everyone else will sit there dumbstruck. Music score by Harry Nilsson. Groucho's final film. Panavision. [M]

Ski Fever (1969) **C-98m.** *½ D: Curt Siodmak. Martin Milner, Claudia Martin, Vivi Bach, Dietmar Schoenherr, Toni Sailor, Dorit Dom. American ski instructor giving lessons in Austria to finance his education is unpleasantly surprised to learn his duties include entertaining guests after hours. Why complain when most of them are good-looking girls? Claudia is Dean Martin's daughter. [M]

Skin Deep (1978-New Zealand) **C-103m.** ***½ D: Geoff Steven. Deryn Cooper, Ken Blackburn, Grant Tilly, Alan Jervis, Glenis Leverstam. Small-town civic leaders import a professional masseuse from the big city—all in the name of progress. Subtle, perceptive, well-made examination of hypocrisy and exploitation.

Skin Deep (1989) **C-101m.** **½ D: Blake Edwards. John Ritter, Vincent Gardenia, Alyson Reed, Joel Brooks, Julianne Phillips, Chelsea Field, Nina Foch, Denise Crosby, Michael Kidd, Bryan Genesse, Sheryl Lee Ralph. Successful L.A. writer (Ritter) can't keep his hedonistic life on track—not with diversions around like wine (he's an alcoholic), women (he's insatiable), and song (Cole Porter's a favorite). Spotty, often obvious comedy from writer-director Edwards does have some real laughs—and some unforgettable condoms. Panavision. [R]▼●

Skin Game, The (1931-British) **86m.** ** D: Alfred Hitchcock. Edmund Gwenn, Jill Esmond, John Longden, C. V. France, Helen Haye, Phyllis Konstam. Gwenn adds the only spark of life to this dull adaptation of the Galsworthy play about rivalry between neighboring landowners. Hitchcock claims he didn't make it by choice, and one can believe it considering the many long, static dialogue scenes; very atypical of the Master.▼◗

Skin Game (1971) **C-102m.** ***½ D: Paul Bogart. James Garner, Louis Gossett, Susan Clark, Brenda Sykes, Edward Asner, Andrew Duggan. Exceptional comedy about Garner and Gossett running con-game posing as master and slave in post-Civil War era. Serious undertones enhance this offbeat, entertaining film; Clark delightful as female con-artist who joins duo. Scripter "Pierre Marton" is Peter Stone. Remade for TV by Burt Kennedy as SIDEKICKS in 1974. Panavision. [PG]▼

Ski Party (1965) **C-90m.** ** D: Alan Rafkin. Frankie Avalon, Dwayne Hickman, Deborah Walley, Yvonne Craig, Robert Q. Lewis, Bobbi Shaw, Aron Kincaid. BEACH PARTY gang puts on some clothes in this one, but the shenanigans are the same. Guest star Lesley Gore sings "Sunshine, Lollipops and Rainbows." Panavision.

Skipper Surprised His Wife, The (1950) **85m.** *½ D: Elliott Nugent. Robert Walker, Joan Leslie, Edward Arnold, Spring Byington, Jan Sterling. Unsurprising comedy; weak material about sailor Walker running home like ship. Good cast wasted.

Skippy (1931) **85m.** *** D: Norman Taurog. Jackie Cooper, Robert Coogan, Mitzi Green, Jackie Searl, Willard Robertson, Enid Bennett, Donald Haines. Classic children's film from Percy Crosby's popular comic strip, following misadventures of Cooper, the local health inspector's son, and Coogan, the poor ragamuffin from Shantytown, as they try to scrape up three dollars for a dog license. Simple and dated, but with timeless innocent charm. Taurog (Cooper's uncle) won Best Director Oscar. Followed by a sequel, SOOKY.

Skirts Ahoy! (1952) **C-109m.** **½ D: Sidney Lanfield. Esther Williams, Joan Evans, Vivian Blaine, Barry Sullivan, Keefe Brasselle, Debbie Reynolds, Bobby Van, Billy Eckstine. Chipper cast can't buoy this story of three WAVES and their boyfriends.▼

Ski Troop Attack (1960) **63m.** ** D: Roger Corman. Michael Forest, Frank Wolff, Wally Campo, Richard Sinatra, James Hoffman, Sheila Carol, Roger Corman. Wintry WW2 adventure with five U.S. soldiers on skis behind enemy lines in Germany. OK Corman low-budgeter. ▼

Skokie (1981) **C-125m. TVM** D: Herbert Wise. Danny Kaye, John Rubinstein, Carl Reiner, Kim Hunter, Eli Wallach, Lee Strasberg, Brian Dennehy, Ed Flanders, George Dzundza, James Sutorius, Ruth Nelson. Powerful dramatization by Ernest Kinoy depicting how citizens of Skokie, Ill., became embroiled in a bitter controversy while trying to prevent street demonstrations by neo-Nazis in 1977. Danny Kaye gives a searing performance as a concentration camp survivor in his TV dramatic debut. Above average.▼

Skull, The (1965-British) **C-83m.** **½ D: Freddie Francis. Peter Cushing, Patrick Wymark, Christopher Lee, Nigel Green, Jill Bennett, Michael Gough, George Coulouris, Patrick Magee. Good cast lends needed support to questionable script (based on a Robert Bloch story) of skull of Marquis de Sade that has mysterious powers. Techniscope.▼

Skullduggery (1970) **C-105m.** *½ D: Gordon Douglas. Burt Reynolds, Susan Clark, Roger C. Carmel, Chips Rafferty, Edward Fox, Wilfrid Hyde-White, Pat Suzuki, Rhys Williams. In New Guinea, Reynolds and Clark find gentle ape people called the Tropi; their humanity has to be proved in court to keep them from being slaughtered by developers. Unusual but unsuccessful story whose author had his name removed from the credits. Panavision. [M/PG]▼

Skulls, The (2000) **C-106m.** BOMB D: Rob Cohen. Joshua Jackson, Phil Walker, Hill Harper, Leslie Bibb, Christopher McDonald, William Petersen, Craig T. Nelson, Steve Harris. Quickly termed THE NUMBSKULLS, this Ivy League groaner deals with an unnamed university (it might be Yale because it's not Slippery Rock) and the power-mad chicanery of its secret organization. Insipid acting, dialogue and situations abound, with the film asking us to believe that a treacherous act could be covered up when it's been videotaped and a couple dozen well-connected high-rollers know about it. [PG-13]▼◗

Sky Above The Mud Below, The (1961-French) **C-90m.** *** D: Pierre-Dominique Gaisseau. Narrated by William Peacock. Academy Award-winning documentary showing variety of primitive life found within confines of Dutch New Guinea.▼

Sky Bandits (1986-British) **C-92m.** BOMB D: Zoran Perisic. Scott McGinnis, Jeff Osterhage, Ronald Lacey. McGinnis and Osterhage are a poor man's BUTCH CASSIDY AND THE SUNDANCE KID in this dreary adventure of two Western buddies' aerial exploits during WWI. Touted as the most expensive ($18 million) independent British production ever, film is poorly cast and has nothing to offer but high-flying special effects, designed by director Perisic (who made Chris Reeve "fly" in SUPERMAN). [PG]

Sky Commando (1953) **69m.** *½ D: Fred F. Sears. Dan Duryea, Frances Gifford, Michael Connors, Michael Fox. Limping account of the responsibilities of being an Air Force officer, with usual rash of hackneyed situations.

Sky Devils (1932) **89m.** ** D: A. Edward Sutherland. Spencer Tracy, William "Stage" Boyd, Ann Dvorak, George Cooper, Billy Bevan, Yola D'Avril. Two dumbbells try to avoid WW1 service in this disjointed, low-grade comedy; Dvorak is beautiful; leftover flying scenes from producer Howard Hughes' HELL'S ANGELS are impressive.

Sky Dragon, The (1949) **64m.** BOMB D: Lesley Selander. Roland Winters, Keye Luke, Mantan Moreland, Noel Neill, Tim

Ryan, Iris Adrian, Elena Verdugo, Milburn Stone, Lyle Talbot, John Eldredge. The nadir and, appropriately, the end of the *Charlie Chan* series, an unbearable whodunit set on a plane bound for San Francisco.

Sky Full of Moon (1952) **73m.** ** D: Norman Foster. Carleton Carpenter, Jan Sterling, Keenan Wynn, Elaine Stewart. Unassuming comedy of naive cowpoke falling in love with a not-so-innocent in Las Vegas.

Sky High (1922) **51m.** *** D: Lynn Reynolds. Tom Mix, J. Farrell MacDonald, Eva Novak, Sid Jordan, William Buckley. Tom Mix eschews cowboy garb to play immigration officer out to crack alien-smuggling ring on Mexican border; action packed entertainment.

Skyjacked (1972) **C-100m.** **½ D: John Guillermin. Charlton Heston, Yvette Mimieux, James Brolin, Claude Akins, Jeanne Crain, Susan Dey, Roosevelt Grier, Mariette Hartley, Walter Pidgeon, Ken Swofford, Leslie Uggams, Mike Henry, John Hillerman. Commercial flight hijacked to Russia. Entertaining for first half, even exciting; second half deteriorates. Good cast will distract some from tedium elsewhere. Retitled: SKY TERROR. Panavision. [PG]

Skylark (1941) **94m.** ***½ D: Mark Sandrich. Claudette Colbert, Ray Milland, Brian Aherne, Binnie Barnes, Walter Abel, Ernest Cossart, Grant Mitchell. Sophisticated romance with Aherne trying to take Claudette away from business-minded husband Milland. Stars are at their peak in this smooth adaptation of Samson Raphaelson play.

Skylark (1993) **C-100m. TVM** D: Joseph Sargent. Glenn Close, Christopher Walken, Lexi Randall, Christopher Bell, Margaret Sophie Stein, Jon DeVries, Tresa Hughes, Elizabeth Wilson, Lois Smith, Lee Richardson. Life on the prairie, pre-WW1, is relived by the same sturdy cast of its very popular Emmy-winning predecessor, SARAH, PLAIN AND TALL, although this sequel isn't quite in the same league. Followed by WINTER'S END. Average. ▼●◗

Sky Murder (1940) **72m.** ** D: George B. Seitz. Walter Pidgeon, Donald Meek, Kaaren Verne, Edward Ashley, Joyce Compton, Tom Conway. Pidgeon as detective Nick Carter decides to help refugee Verne in above-average private-eye yarn.

Sky Pirates (1986-Australian) **C-86m.** *½ D: Colin Eggleston. John Hargreaves, Meredith Phillips, Max Phipps, Bill Hunter, Simon Chilvers, Alex Scott. Yet another RAIDERS–INDIANA JONES variation, about an aircraft that crashes through a time warp, a search for a special stone, and other assorted nonsense. Boring and confusing, but Hargreaves earns an *A* for effort. Panavision. [PG-13]▼

Sky Riders (1976) **C-93m.** *** D: Douglas Hickox. James Coburn, Susannah York, Robert Culp, Charles Aznavour, Harry Andrews, John Beck. Lively thriller about a political kidnapping, highlighted by spectacular sequences of hang-gliding. The aerial derring-do and the magnificent Greek scenery make this one worth sitting through. Todd-AO 35. [PG]▼

Skyscraper Souls (1932) **99m.** *** D: Edgar Selwyn. Warren William, Maureen O'Sullivan, Gregory Ratoff, Anita Page, Verree Teasdale, Norman Foster, Jean Hersholt, Wallace Ford, Hedda Hopper, Helen Coburn, Ed Brophy. Entertaining comedy-drama in the GRAND HOTEL mode (released four months earlier, also by MGM) about a ruthless empire-builder (well played by William) who manipulates stock prices and double-crosses lovers in his quest to control a 100-story office building. Potent pre-Code entertainment, much of it still pretty risqué.▼●

Skyscraper Wilderness SEE: **Big City, The** (1937)

Sky's the Limit, The (1943) **89m.** *** D: Edward H. Griffith. Fred Astaire, Joan Leslie, Robert Benchley, Robert Ryan, Elizabeth Patterson, Marjorie Gateson. Fred's a flier on leave who meets photographer Leslie; Benchley's dinner speech, Astaire's "One For My Baby" and "My Shining Hour" make this worthwhile.▼●

Sky Terror SEE: **Skyjacked**

Skyward (1980) **C-100m. TVM** D: Ron Howard. Bette Davis, Howard Hesseman, Suzy Gilstrap, Ben Marley, Clu Gulager, Marion Ross, Lisa Whelchel, Jana Hall. Inspiring story (written by director Ron Howard's *Happy Days* pal and production partner Anson Williams, with a teleplay by Nancy Sackett) about how former stunt pilot Davis and airport watchman Hesseman help a teenaged paraplegic (real-life wheelchair-bound Gilstrap) learn to fly a plane. Above average.

Sky West and Crooked SEE: **Gypsy Girl**

Slacker (1991) **C-97m.** *** D: Richard Linklater. Weird, unique social satire about various contemporary drop-outs in Austin, Texas, who—like the beatniks of the '50s and hippies of the '60s—have formed their own subculture. They're loaded with thoughts and ideas, none of which they seem capable of acting upon. Shot in a free-form style, and featuring a large cast of nonprofessional actors. That's writer-director Linklater as the young man in the taxi. [R]▼●

Slam (1998) **C-100m.** ***½ D: Marc Levin. Saul Williams, Sonja Sohn, Bonz Malone, Beau Sia, Lawrence Wilson. Extraordinary fly-on-the-wall filmmaking technique makes this story of a D.C. ghetto victim seem absolutely real from start to finish. Sent to prison, he has an awakening there and realizes that he cannot endure, or condone, the endless cycle of violence in his community, and uses his gift for poetry as an outlet. Cowritten by its leading actors (Williams, Sohn, Malone) with Levin and Richard Stratton. [R]▼●◗

Slamdance (1987) **C-100m.** BOMB D: Wayne Wang. Tom Hulce, Mary Elizabeth Mastrantonio, Virginia Madsen, Harry Dean Stanton, Millie Perkins, Don Opper, Adam Ant, John Doe. Underground cartoonist/painter Hulce, devoted to his ex-wife and young child, is framed—apparently by the entire population of L.A.—for the murder of party girl Madsen. Weird, without compensating originality. Lifeless melodrama deals only peripherally with the "club" scene; there is as much slamdancing in PYGMALION. [R]▼●

Slam Dunk Ernest (1995) **C-92m.** *½ D: John Cherry. Jim Varney, Cylk Cozart, Miguel A. Nunez, Jr., Lester Barrie, Colin Lawrence, Richard Leacock, Jay Brazeau, Lossen Chambers, Kareem Abdul-Jabbar. Likable dolt Ernest P. Worrell wants to play basketball with his coworkers; they let him play benchwarmer instead, until a pair of magic shoes transforms him into a hoop star. Secondary characters are more interesting than Varney in this direct-to-video release. For Ernest fans only. Followed by ERNEST IN THE ARMY. [PG]▼

Slammer SEE: **Short Eyes**

Slams, The (1973) **C-97m.** ** D: Jonathan Kaplan. Jim Brown, Judy Pace, Roland "Bob" Harris, Frank de Kova, Ted Cassidy. Mindless actioner has Brown in L.A. prison after stashing away a heroin cache and $1.5 million. Halfway through, comedy takes over for a fast pickup. [R]

Slander (1956) **81m.** **½ D: Roy Rowland. Van Johnson, Ann Blyth, Steve Cochran, Marjorie Rambeau, Richard Eyer. Slick, superficial "inside study" of the smut magazines, focusing on their exclusive on a TV personality.

Slappy and the Stinkers (1998) **C-78m.** BOMB D: Barnet Kellman. B. D. Wong, Bronson Pinchot, Jennifer Coolidge, Joseph Ashton, Gary LeRoi Gray, David Dukes, Sam McMurray. Inane story of a group of completely, irresponsibly unsupervised nerdy seven-year-olds rescuing a sea lion against his will. Along the way they torture the head of their boarding school with their antics. A totally unfunny comedy, and a waste of talent on both sides of the camera. [PG]▼

Slap Shot (1977) **C-122m.** *** D: George Roy Hill. Paul Newman, Michael Ontkean, Lindsay Crouse, Jennifer Warren, Melinda Dillon, Strother Martin, Jerry Houser, Swoosie Kurtz, (M.) Emmet Walsh, Kathryn Walker, Paul Dooley. Newman is star of bush-league hockey team that's going nowhere until they decide to play dirty. Uneven but raucously funny at times, with very satisfying wrapup. Andrew Duncan is hilarious as local sports broadcaster; barbed (and very profane) script by Nancy Dowd. [R]▼●◗

Slapstick (Of Another Kind) (1984) **C-82m.** *½ D: Steven Paul. Jerry Lewis, Madeline Kahn, Marty Feldman, Jim Backus, John Abbott, Pat Morita, Samuel Fuller, Merv Griffin, Steven Paul, voice of Orson Welles. Lewis and Kahn give birth to enormous, deformed twins (also Lewis and Kahn) who are in reality alien messengers capable of solving the world's problems—as long as they're not separated. Given that cast and a Kurt Vonnegut novel as source material, you'd think there'd be no way to screw it up, but writer/producer/director/costar Paul manages; some funny things do survive (Fuller and the elder Lewis come off best), but overall, pretty appalling. Filmed in 1982. [PG]▼●

Slate, Wyn & Me (1987-Australian) **C-90m.** ** D: Don McLennan. Sigrid Thornton, Simon Burke, Martin Sacks, Tommy Lewis, Lesley Baker. Meandering drama of brothers Burke and Sacks, who rob a bank, kill a cop . . . and kidnap Thornton, who witnesses their crime. Potentially intriguing tale falls flat after twenty minutes. Panavision. [R]▼

Slattery's Hurricane (1949) **83m.** **½ D: Andre de Toth. Richard Widmark, Linda Darnell, Veronica Lake, John Russell, Gary Merrill. Weather-pilot Widmark, in midst of storm, thinks back on his life, Darnell and Lake are his two loves. Interesting idea; coscripted by Herman Wouk, who later expanded it into a novel.

Slaughter (1972) **C-92m.** ** D: Jack Starrett. Jim Brown, Stella Stevens, Rip Torn, Don Gordon, Cameron Mitchell, Marlene Clark, Robert Phillips. Stevens and Torn are far too good for this violent tripe about ex-Green Beret Brown who goes after syndicate after it kills his parents. Sequel: SLAUGHTER'S BIG RIP-OFF. Todd-AO 35. [R]▼

Slaughter (1976) SEE: **Dogs**

Slaughterhouse-Five (1972) **C-104m.** *** D: George Roy Hill. Michael Sacks, Ron Leibman, Eugene Roche, Sharon Gans, Valerie Perrine, John Dehner, Holly Near, Perry King. Sometimes draggy, sometimes on-target, sprawling view of life through eyes of one Billy Pilgrim, professional nobody who becomes "unstuck" in time. Big-budget adaptation of Kurt Vonnegut's bizarre fantasy novel is hard going for those unfamiliar with author's point of view, gains through repeat viewings. [R]▼●◗

Slaughter in San Francisco (1981-Hong Kong) **C-87m.** BOMB D: William Lowe. Don Wong, Chuck Norris, Sylvia Channing, Robert Jones, Dan Ivan. Former cop Wong seeks vengeance on murderer of his partner; Norris, in a supporting role, is the bad guy. Shoddy production will disappoint chop-socky genre buffs. Filmed in 1973; released to take advantage of Norris's subsequent popularity. Aka KARATE COP and CHUCK NORRIS VS. THE KARATE COP. Widescreen. [R]▼

Slaughter on Tenth Avenue (1957) **103m.** *** D: Arnold Laven. Richard Egan, Jan Sterling, Dan Duryea, Julie Adams, Walter Matthau, Sam Levene, Charles McGraw, Mickey Shaughnessy. Well-handled waterfront racketeer expose, set in N.Y.C. with good supporting cast.

Slaughter's Big Rip-Off (1973) **C-93m.** *½ D: Gordon Douglas. Jim Brown, Ed McMahon, Brock Peters, Don Stroud, Gloria Hendry, Dick Anthony Williams, Art Metrano. Slaughter's still playing cat and mouse with the Mob in this dreary actioner; McMahon gives his role as the Syndicate head better than it deserves. Todd-AO 35. [R]▼

Slaughter Trail (1951) **C-78m.** *½ D: Irving Allen. Brian Donlevy, Gig Young, Virginia Grey, Andy Devine, Robert Hutton, Terry Gilkyson. Cavalry officer Donlevy goes up against bandits who've been terrorizing the title trail. Blah Western, done in by Gilkyson's repetitive, indescribably awful musical narration.▼

Slave, The (1963-Italian) **C-102m.** *½ D: Sergio Corbucci. Steve Reeves, Jacques Sernas, Gianna Maria Canale, Claudio Gora. Interminable Italian spectacle. Son of Spartacus learns story of father, vows vengeance. Good photography only asset. Aka SON OF SPARTACUS. CinemaScope.

Slave Girl (1947) **C-80m.** **½ D: Charles Lamont. Yvonne De Carlo, George Brent, Broderick Crawford, Albert Dekker, Lois Collier, Andy Devine, Arthur Treacher. Tale of adventure with evil potentate holding Americans prisoner; not to be taken seriously (there's even a talking camel), enjoyable on that scale.

Slave Girls SEE: **Prehistoric Women**

Slave of the Cannibal God (1978-Italian) **C-86m.** *½ D: Sergio Martino. Ursula Andress, Stacy Keach, Claudio Cassinelli, Antonio Marsina, Franco Fantasia. Too-glamorous Andress captured by natives and painted in preparation for sacrifice in a scene virtually identical to that directed by ex-husband John Derek for current wife Bo years later in TARZAN, THE APE MAN. Widescreen. [R]▼

Slavers (1978-German) **C-102m.** ** D: Jurgen Goslar. Trevor Howard, Ron Ely, Britt Ekland, Jurgen Goslar, Ray Milland, Ken Gampu, Cameron Mitchell. Pulp-fiction stuff about slave trading in Africa during the 19th century. Good cast saddled with second-rate script. [R]▼

Slaves (1969) **C-110m.** *½ D: Herbert J. Biberman. Stephen Boyd, Dionne Warwick, Ossie Davis, Marilyn Clark, Gale Sondergaard, Shepperd Strudwick, Nancy Coleman, Julius Harris, David Huddleston. Strange cast in revisionist drama about Kentucky slave Davis standing up for his rights; might have meant something in the 60s, but now it's just laughable, with Boyd properly embarrassed as Simon Legree-type "Massa." Notable only as Sondergaard's first film after 20-year blacklist, courtesy director-cowriter (and husband) Biberman.

Slave Ship (1937) **92m.** *** D: Tay Garnett. Warner Baxter, Wallace Beery, Elizabeth Allan, Mickey Rooney, George Sanders, Jane Darwell, Joseph Schildkraut. Rousing drama of slave ship rebellion with fine atmosphere, good Beery-Rooney teaming, plenty of action.

Slaves of Babylon (1953) **C-82m.** ** D: William Castle. Richard Conte, Linda Christian, Maurice Schwartz, Michael Ansara, Julie Newmar. Jumbled biblical adventure mixed with romance. Nebuchadnezzar faces army of Israelites led by shepherd.

Slaves of New York (1989) **C-125m.** *½ D: James Ivory. Bernadette Peters, Adam Coleman Howard, Chris Sarandon, Mary Beth Hurt, Nick Corri, Madeleine Potter, Mercedes Ruehl, Betty Comden, Steve Buscemi, Michael Schoeffling, Tammy Grimes, Charles McCaughan, Anthony LaPaglia. Misguided filming of Tama Janowitz's bestselling collection of stories, set among the too-hip-for-words denizens of N.Y.C.'s downtown art world. As the central character, the talented Peters seems all wrong: too intelligent to spend most of the film being humiliated by her boyfriend (Howard). Overlong and unfocused. Janowitz (who plays Abby) scripted. [R]▼●

Slayground (1984-British) **C-89m.** *½ D: Terry Bedford. Peter Coyote, Billie Whitelaw, Philip Sayer, Bill Luhr, Mel Smith. Dreary actioner about robber Coyote on the lam from a hired killer. Whitelaw in particular is wasted as an amusement park owner. Based on a novel by Donald E. Westlake, writing as Richard Stark. [R]▼

SLC Punk! (1999-U.S.-Australian) **C-97m.** **½ D: James Merendino. Matthew Lillard, Michael Goorjian, Annabeth Gish, Jennifer Lien, Christopher McDonald, Devon Sawa, Adam Pascal, Til Schweiger. Seriocomic coming of ager about punk rocker Stevo and his best pal, Heroin Bob, whose pursuit of "total chaos" is at odds with living in conservative Salt Lake City, Utah, circa 1985. Writer-director Merendino has real affection for the punk scene, but it would've worked better without overused gimmick of having the lead character talk directly to the camera. Charismatic performance from Lillard. Panavision. [R]▼◗

Sleazy Uncle, The (1991-Italian) **C-105m.** **½ D: Franco Brusati. Vittorio Gassman, Giancarlo Giannini, Andrea Ferreol, Stefania Sandrelli, Beatrice Palme. Playfully lecherous uncle (Gassman) is forced to seek temporary asylum with his rich, repressed nephew (Giannini). Predictably, uncle Gassman's outrageous antics—which range from seducing Giannini's mistress and passing out his blood-test certificates to all the ladies (''for your security'') —result in setting Giannini's placid life on its ear. A little too laid back to achieve the farcical comedy attempted here.▼

Sleeper (1973) **C-88m.** ***½ D: Woody Allen. Woody Allen, Diane Keaton, John Beck, Mary Gregory, Don Keefer, John McLiam. Woody turns to slapstick in this engagingly silly tale of a man who's frozen in 1973 and awakened 200 years later. Typical Allen combination of great jokes and duds, with more sight-gags than usual and energetic score by the Preservation Hall Jazz Band. Screenplay by Allen and Marshall Brickman. [PG]▼●

Sleepers (1996) **C-147m.** **½ D: Barry Levinson. Kevin Bacon, Robert De Niro, Dustin Hoffman, Jason Patric, Brad Pitt, Minnie Driver, Brad Renfro, Bruno Kirby, Vittorio Gassman, Billy Crudup, Ron Eldard, Terry Kinney. Absorbing tale of young friends in N.Y.C.'s Hell's Kitchen who wind up in reform school, where they endure a living hell at the hands of sadistic guards. Later in life, one of them (now working for the D.A.) sows the seeds for revenge. Based on Lorenzo Carcaterra's purportedly nonfiction book, the movie grabs and holds you but never quite convinces; the resolution is too pat. Strong performances. Super 35. [R]▼●◗

Sleepers West (1941) **74m.** ** D: Eugene Forde. Lloyd Nolan, Lynn Bari, Mary Beth Hughes, Louis Jean Heydt, Edward Brophy, Don Costello, Ben Carter. Private eye Michael Shayne (Nolan) tries to protect a murder witness on a train to San Francisco in this tolerable suspenser. Remake of SLEEPERS EAST (1934), written by *Torchy Blane* creator Frederick Nebel.

Sleeping Beauty (1959) **C-75m.** *** D: Clyde Geronimi. Voices of Mary Costa, Bill Shirley, Eleanor Audley, Verna Felton, Barbara Jo Allen (Vera Vague), Barbara Luddy. Walt Disney's most expensive and elaborate animated feature (at the time) is actually a simple, straightforward telling of the classic fairy tale, with music adapted from Tchaikovsky, and such memorable characters as Flora, Fauna, and Merryweather (the three good fairies) and the evil witch Maleficent. Highlight: the final, fiery confrontation between Maleficent and Prince Phillip. Bound to lose something on TV, since it was filmed in (and designed for) Super Technirama 70—a widescreen process. ▼●

Sleeping Car, The (1990) **C-87m.** ** D: Douglas Curtis. David Naughton, Judie Aronson, Kevin McCarthy, Jeff Conaway, Ernestine Mercer, John Carl Buechler, Dani Minnick. Good-looking but heavily overstated horror film pitting Naughton and friends against a vicious ghost haunting an old railway sleeping car, now used as an apartment. [R]▼●

Sleeping Car Murder, The (1965-French) **90m.** *** D: Costa-Gavras. Simone Signoret, Yves Montand, Pierre Mondy, Jean-Louis Trintignant, Jacques Perrin, Michel Piccoli, Catherine Allegret, Charles Denner. Quick-paced, atmospheric police-chasing-mad-killer movie. Nice photography by Jean Tournier; original action good but dubbing hurts. Based on a Sebastien Japrisot novel. Costa-Gavras' directorial debut. CinemaScope.

Sleeping Car to Trieste (1948-British) **95m.** *** D: John Paddy Carstairs. Jean Kent, Albert Lieven, Derrick de Marney, Paul Dupuis, Rona Anderson, David Tomlinson. The Orient Express is the setting for fine cat-and-mouse story of espionage agents competing for possession of ''hot'' political diary. Remake of THE ROME EXPRESS. ▼

Sleeping City, The (1950) **85m.** **½ D: George Sherman. Richard Conte, Coleen Gray, Peggy Dow, John Alexander, Alex Nicol, Richard Taber. Earnest depiction of corruption within a medical institution's walls was controversial upon its release. Its hero is a cop (Conte) who goes undercover to ferret out a killer and other evil doings at a N.Y.C. hospital.

Sleeping Dogs (1977-New Zealand) **C-107m.** ** D: Roger Donaldson. Sam Neill, Ian Mune, Warren Oates, Nevan Rowe, Donna Akersten, Ian Watkin, Bill Julliff, Clyde Scott. Muddled thriller about apolitical loner Neill unable to remain aloof from repressive government and revolutionaries during workers' strike. Fascinating concept defeated by confusing direction, illogical plot development, insufficiently defined characters. Michael Seresin's top-notch cinematography helps. The first New Zealand film ever to open in the U.S.▼

Sleeping Tiger, The (1954-British) **89m.** *** D: Victor Hanbury (Joseph Losey). Alexis Smith, Dirk Bogarde, Alexander Knox, Hugh Griffith, Patricia McCarron, Billie Whitelaw. Well-done drama with Knox a psychiatrist who takes low-life criminal Bogarde into his home, much to the consternation of his wife (Smith, in one of her best roles); the result is sexual and emotional fireworks. Losey's first film made outside the U.S., where he was blacklisted; this accounts for the pseudonym.▼

Sleeping With the Enemy (1991) **C-98m.** ** D: Joseph Ruben. Julia Roberts, Patrick Bergin, Kevin Anderson, Elizabeth Lawrence, Kyle Secor, Claudette Nevins. Practically suspense-less thriller about a young woman who flees from her brutal husband and tries to start life anew in Iowa. Unabashed star vehicle for Roberts (complete with ''cute'' montage set to the oldie "Brown-Eyed Girl") is relentlessly predictable. [R]▼●

Sleepless in Seattle (1993) **C-104m.** *** D: Nora Ephron. Tom Hanks, Meg Ryan, Bill Pullman, Ross Malinger, Rosie O'Donnell, Rob Reiner, Gaby Hoffmann, Victor Garber, Rita Wilson, Barbara Garrick, Carey Lowell, Calvin Trillin, Dana Ivey, David Hyde Pierce. Woman who's just gotten engaged hears a widower on a call-in radio show talking about his departed wife and becomes obsessed with meeting him, convinced that he may be her destiny. Sweet romantic comedy, with perfectly cast stars, though its repeated allusions to the old tear-jerker AN AFFAIR TO REMEMBER make you wonder if the only way to generate old-fashioned romance in a '90s movie is to invoke a product of Hollywood's Golden Age. Coscripted by Ephron. [PG] ▼●◗

Sleep My Love (1948) **97m.** *** D: Douglas Sirk. Claudette Colbert, Robert Cummings, Don Ameche, Hazel Brooks, Rita Johnson, George Coulouris, Keye Luke, Raymond Burr, Ralph Morgan. Familiar territory covered by excellent cast as Ameche tries to drive wife Claudette crazy; Cummings saves her. From a Leo Rosten novel.

Sleepwalkers (1992) **C-91m.** **½ D: Mick Garris. Brian Krause, Mädchen Amick, Alice Krige, Jim Haynie, Cindy Pickett, Lyman Ward, Ron Perlman, Dan Martin, Glenn Shadix. A mother-and-son pair of "sleepwalkers" move to a Norman Rockwell–ish Midwestern town, looking for prey. The shape-changing Sleepwalkers live on the life force of teenage virgins, but the target this time (Amick) is one tough cookie. Stephen King's script is thinly plotted and confusing, but the movie is directed with flair and a nicely twisted sense of humor. Excellent effects. Cameos by Joe Dante, John Landis, Clive Barker, Tobe Hooper and King himself, as well as an unbilled one by Mark Hamill. Aka STEPHEN KING'S "SLEEPWALKERS." [R] ▼●

Sleep With Me (1994) **C-86m.** ** D: Rory Kelly. Craig Sheffer, Eric Stoltz, Meg Tilly, Todd Field, Thomas Gibson, Parker Posey, Adrienne Shelly, Susan Traylor, Tegan West, June Lockhart, Quentin Tarantino, Joey Lauren Adams. Forgettable three-sided romance; as Stoltz and Tilly are about to be married, their best friend (Sheffer) declares his love for her. A self-indulgent study of self-absorption. Scripted by six writers, each of whom contributed a different section of the film. The one standout scene has actor/filmmaker Tarantino explaining his unique theory about the subtext of TOP GUN. [R]▼●

Sleepy Hollow (1999) **C-105m.** ** D: Tim Burton. Johnny Depp, Christina Ricci, Miranda Richardson, Michael Gambon, Casper Van Dien, Jeffrey Jones, Richard Griffiths, Ian McDiarmid, Michael Gough, Christopher Walken, Marc Pickering, Lisa Marie, Christopher Lee, Alun Armstrong. Convoluted and unsatisfying script defeats a good-looking revision of the Washington Irving classic. Depp is fun as a bumbling constable who tries to use scientific methods to figure out a series of killings in New York's Hudson Valley. Burton must have had fun figuring out how many different ways he could show beheadings . . . yet the film is anything but scary. Martin Landau appears unbilled. Oscar-winning Art Direction by Rick Heinrichs and Peter Young. [R]▼●◗

Slender Thread, The (1965) **98m.** **½ D: Sydney Pollack. Sidney Poitier, Anne Bancroft, Telly Savalas, Steven Hill, Edward Asner, Dabney Coleman. Interchange between stars is the whole film in an interesting idea that doesn't fulfill potential. Bancroft takes overdose of sleeping pills and calls crisis clinic for help; college student volunteer Poitier tries to keep her on phone while rescue is organized. Filmed on location in Seattle; written by Stirling Silliphant, music by Quincy Jones. Pollack's directorial debut.▼

Sleuth (1972) **C-138m.** **** D: Joseph L. Mankiewicz. Laurence Olivier, Michael Caine. Lighthearted mystery tour de force for two stars, adapted by Anthony Shaffer from his hit play about games-playing mystery writer Olivier leading his wife's lover (Caine) into diabolical trap. But who gets the last laugh on whom? Delicious from start to finish; remarkable production design by Ken Adam. Mankiewicz's last film. [PG] ▼●◗

Sliding Doors (1998-U.S.-British) **C-108m.** **½ D: Peter Howitt. Gwyneth Paltrow, John Hannah, John Lynch, Jeanne Tripplehorn, Zara Turner, Douglas McFerran, Paul Brightwell, Virginia McKenna. Likable romantic comedy explores—in parallel scenes—what happens when Paltrow catches her boyfriend sleeping with another woman, and what would have happened if she'd missed her train and not walked in at that moment. The doltish boyfriend (Lynch) and his extremely bitchy paramour (Tripplehorn) are overstated, unsympathetic characters who bring down the otherwise bright proceedings. Paltrow, sporting a British accent, is delightful; so is Scotsman Hannah. Writing and directing debut for Howitt. [PG-13]▼●◗

Slight Case of Larceny, A (1953) **71m.** ** D: Don Weis. Mickey Rooney, Eddie Bracken, Elaine Stewart, Marilyn Erskine. Low hijinks from Rooney and Bracken as two buddies who open a gas station, siphoning supplies from oil company's pipelines.

Slight Case of Murder, A (1938) **85m.** ***½ D: Lloyd Bacon. Edward G. Robinson, Jane Bryan, Allen Jenkins, Ruth Donnelly, Willard Parker, John Litel, Edward Brophy, Harold Huber. Robinson's in peak comedy form as gangster who goes straight when Prohibition ends. This hilarious adaptation of a play by Damon Runyon and Howard Lindsay has brewer Robinson going bankrupt in a rented summer house filled with characters and corpses. Remake: STOP, YOU'RE KILLING ME.

Slight Case of Murder, A (1999) **C-100m. TVM** D: Steven Schachter. William H. Macy, Adam Arkin, Felicity Huffman, James Cromwell, Julia Campbell, Paul Mazursky. Humorous take on murder in the movie business written by Macy and his partner, director Schachter. A befuddled film critic (Macy) accidentally kills a one-night stand and then concocts a "perfect-crime" cover-up that convinces not only his girlfriend (Huffman, his real-life wife) but also fawning police detective Arkin, who's trying to get his own screenplay produced. Adapted from Donald E. Westlake's novella *A Travesty*. Made for cable. Above average. ▼

Slightly Dangerous (1943) **94m.** ** D: Wesley Ruggles. Lana Turner, Robert Young, Walter Brennan, Dame May Whitty, Eugene Pallette, Florence Bates, Alan Mowbray, Bobby (Robert) Blake. Slightly ridiculous comedy of waitress Turner who claims to be daughter of wealthy industrialist. Good cast in trivial piece of fluff.

Slightly French (1949) **81m.** **½ D: Douglas Sirk. Dorothy Lamour, Don Ameche, Janis Carter, Willard Parker, Adele Jergens. Sassy musical of con-artist director Ameche passing off Lamour as French star.

Slightly Honorable (1940) **83m.** **½ D: Tay Garnett. Pat O'Brien, Edward Arnold, Broderick Crawford, Ruth Terry, Alan Dinehart, Eve Arden, Claire Dodd, Evelyn Keyes, Phyllis Brooks, Janet Beecher. Adequate mystery with lawyers O'Brien and Crawford involved in strange murders with corrupt politician Arnold.▼

Slightly Scarlet (1956) **C-99m.** **½ D: Allan Dwan. John Payne, Arlene Dahl, Rhonda Fleming, Kent Taylor, Ted de Corsia, Lance Fuller. Effective study (from a James M. Cain novel) of big-city corruption; Payne involved with dynamic sister duo (Fleming, Dahl). Arlene steals the show as tipsy ex-con sister. SuperScope.▼

Slim (1937) **80m.** **½ D: Ray Enright. Pat O'Brien, Henry Fonda, Stuart Erwin, Margaret Lindsay, Dick Purcell, John Litel, Jane Wyman. Interesting story of men who string high-voltage wire, with Lindsay the girl who comes between tough veteran O'Brien and novice Fonda. Good performances all around. A semi-remake of TIGER SHARK; remade as MANPOWER.

Slim Carter (1957) **C-82m.** ** D: Richard Bartlett. Jock Mahoney, Julie Adams, Tim Hovey, William Hopper, Ben Johnson, Bill Williams, Barbara Hale. Mild goings-on of Mahoney becoming popular Western star, aided by Adams, who loves him, and Hovey, an orphan who enters their lives.

Slime People, The (1962) **76m.** BOMB D: Robert Hutton. Robert Hutton, Les Tremayne, Susan Hart, Robert Burton. Lumpy, lizardy people from beneath the Earth wall off Los Angeles with curtain of fog. Movie talks itself to death.▼

Sling Blade (1996) **C-134m.** ***½ D: Billy Bob Thornton. Billy Bob Thornton, Dwight Yoakam, J. T. Walsh, John Ritter, Lucas Black, Natalie Canerday, James Hampton, Robert Duvall, Rick Dial, Jim Jarmusch. Fascinating portrait of a mentally deficient man sprung from prison twenty years after killing his mother and her boyfriend; now he attempts to blend into "real life," helped by a boy who befriends him. Incredibly controlled performance by Thornton (who also wrote and directed) anchors this long but rewarding tale, which leads to a somewhat inevitable finale. Young Black is exceptional as Thornton's new friend, country singer Yoakam is first-rate as a short-fused bully, and Ritter is terrific in a most unusual part. Oscar-winner for Best Screenplay Adaptation; based on the short film SOME CALL IT A SLING BLADE. [R]▼●◗

Slingshot, The (1993-Swedish) **C-102m.** **½ D: Ake Sandgren. Jesper Salen, Stellan Skarsgärd, Basia Frydman, Niclas Olund, Ernst-Hugo Jaregard. Odd childhood remembrance, from 78-year-old Roland Schutt's autobiographical novel, about a 10-year-old outcast in 1920s Sweden: Mom's a Russian Jew, Dad's a socialist, and young Roland (Selen) fashions slingshots from the condoms sold by mother on the black market. Perhaps tries to pack too much material into one film, but this was a great success in Sweden. [R] ▼●

Slipper and the Rose, The (1976-British) **C-146m.** *** D: Bryan Forbes. Richard Chamberlain, Gemma Craven, Annette Crosbie, Michael Hordern, Margaret Lockwood, Christopher Gable, Kenneth More, Edith Evans. Bright musical version of Cinderella in which everyone (including veteran British actors) sings and dances; Craven is delightful as Cindy. Songs by the Sherman Brothers. Good fun. Panavision. [G]▼◗

Slip Slide Adventures SEE: **Water Babies, The**

Slipstream (1989-British) **C-92m.** ** D: Steven M. Lisberger. Bill Paxton, Bob Peck, Mark Hamill, Kitty Aldridge, Eleanor David, F. Murray Abraham, Ben Kingsley, Robbie Coltrane. In the future, nature has rebelled, sending people scurrying to live in valleys away from the high-speed slipstream (high winds) that dominates the planet. Unfortunately this unusual setting has little to do with standard story of adventurer Paxton, who swipes a captive from tough bounty hunter Hamill (delivering a top-notch performance). Just as story should be building to a peak, it lurches into clumsy satire. This big-scale production never made it to theaters in the U.S. [PG-13]▼●

Slither (1973) **C-97m.** ★★★ D: Howard Zieff. James Caan, Peter Boyle, Sally Kellerman, Louise Lasser, Allen Garfield, Richard B. Shull. Engaging film is essentially a massive shaggy dog joke; colorful gallery of characters engaged in hunt for elusive cache of money. Perhaps a bit too airy, but perfect TV fare. [PG]▼

Sliver (1993) **C-109m.** ★★ D: Phillip Noyce. Sharon Stone, William Baldwin, Tom Berenger, Polly Walker, Colleen Camp, Amanda Forman, Martin Landau, CCH Pounder, Nina Foch, Keene Curtis, Nicholas Pryor. Lonely Stone moves into a tall, slender, and luxurious Manhattan apartment building with a history of unusual deaths. Writer Berenger pursues her, though she's more interested in Baldwin; however, she soon comes to suspect one of the two is a killer. Robert Evans' handsomely produced sex-and-murder mystery, with emphasis on the sex, was severely damaged by reshooting (which changed the identity of the killer), but Joe Eszterhas' script was already pretentious and exploitive. From Ira Levin's novel. Panavision. [R]▼●

Slow Dancing in the Big City (1978) **C-101m.** ★½ D: John G. Avildsen. Paul Sorvino, Anne Ditchburn, Nicolas Coster, Anita Dangler, Hector Jaime Mercado. Straight-faced romantic absurdity about Jimmy Breslin-like columnist who falls for ailing ballerina who has been told she should no longer dance; he also befriends a little Hispanic orphan/junkie. Shameless climax will fry your brain cells with its bathos. [PG]

Slugger's Wife, The (1985) **C-105m.** ★½ D: Hal Ashby. Michael O'Keefe, Rebecca De Mornay, Martin Ritt, Randy Quaid, Cleavant Derricks, Lisa Langlois, Loudon Wainwright III. Remarkably unappealing Neil Simon original about a boorish baseball star who falls in love with a singer. Dull and disjointed, full of mediocre music—in short, a mess! The team's manager is played by film director (and former actor) Martin Ritt. [PG-13]▼●

Slumber Party '57 (1977) **C-89m.** BOMB D: William A. Levey. Noelle North, Bridget Hollman, Debra Winger, Mary Ann Appleseth, Rainbeaux Smith, Rafael Campos, Will Hutchins, Joyce Jillson, Joe E. Ross. Smutty, sloppily made schlock about a group of girls who swap tales about their sexual initiations, which are recreated in flashback. Of interest only for the appearance of Winger, in her film debut. [R]▼●

Slumber Party Massacre (1982) **C-78m.** ★½ D: Amy Jones. Michele Michaels, Robin Stille, Michael Villela, Andre Honore, Debra Deliso, Gina Mari. Girls have overnight party, boys clown around, crazed killer does them all in. The screenplay, incredibly, is by feminist author Rita Mae Brown. If it's supposed to be a parody, it's about as clever as *Hogan's Heroes.* Followed by two sequels. [R]▼

Slumber Party Massacre II (1987) **C-75m.** BOMB D: Deborah Brock. Crystal Bernard, Kimberly McArthur, Juliette Cummins, Patrick Lowe. Gory, bottom-of-the-barrel sequel, with yet another driller killer doing in the cast one by one. Yecch. [R]▼●

Slums of Beverly Hills (1998) **C-91m.** ★★★ D: Tamara Jenkins. Natasha Lyonne, Alan Arkin, Marisa Tomei, Kevin Corrigan, Jessica Walter, Carl Reiner, Rita Moreno, Eli Marienthal, David Krumholtz, Mena Suvari. Keenly observed, semi-autobiographical slice-of-life from novice director-writer Jenkins, set in the 1970s, about the Abramowitz clan, "Jewish Joads" who move from one low-rent living space to another as the poorest inhabitants of the title municipality. The focus is on Lyonne, the only sane person in a sweetly insane environment, as she attempts to deal with her sexual awakening. Razor-sharp and right on the money. [R]▼●◗

Small Back Room, The (1949-British) **106m.** ★★★½ D: Michael Powell, Emeric Pressburger. David Farrar, Jack Hawkins, Kathleen Byron, Anthony Bushell, Michael Gough, Leslie Banks, Robert Morley, Cyril Cusack, Renee Asherson. Mature, powerful story of crippled munitions expert Farrar, who's frustrated by his infirmity and mindless government bureaucracy during WW2. Beware of edited versions. Original U.S. title: HOUR OF GLORY.▼

Small Change (1976-French) **C-104m.** ★★★★ D: François Truffaut. Geory Desmouceaux, Philippe Goldman, Claudio Deluca, Frank Deluca, Richard Golfier, Laurent Devlaeminck. Thoroughly charming, intelligent film examines the lives of young children—their joys, sorrows, frustrations, adventures—in a small French village. Wise, perceptive, and witty. [PG]▼●

Small Circle of Friends, A (1980) **C-112m.** BOMB D: Rob Cohen. Brad Davis, Karen Allen, Jameson Parker, Shelley Long, John Friedrich, Gary Springer. Cloyingly cute by-the-numbers treatment of '60s campus turmoil as an apparently moronic *ménage à trois* tries to make it through Harvard. Almost makes one long for R.P.M. [R] ▼●

Smallest Show on Earth, The (1957-British) **80m.** ★★★ D: Basil Dearden. Bill Travers, Virginia McKenna, Margaret Rutherford, Peter Sellers, Bernard Miles, Leslie Phillips. Charming, often hilarious comedy about a couple who inherit a run-down movie house and its three equally run-down attendants (Sellers, Rutherford, Miles). Lovely scene in which the three veterans express their love for silent films.▼

Small Faces (1995-Scottish-English) **C-108m.** ***½ D: Gillies MacKinnon. Iain Robertson, Joseph McFadden, J. S. Duffy, Laura Fraser, Garry Sweeney, Clare Higgins, Kevin McKidd, Mark McConnochie. Grim look at a working-class family of three boys in 1968 Glasgow, focusing on the youngest (Robertson), barely a teenager, and his indoctrination into gang warfare. Straightforward and powerful. Written by the director and his brother, Billy MacKinnon. [R]▼●

Small Miracle, The (1973) **C-74m. TVM** D: Jeannot Szwarc. Vittorio De Sica, Raf Vallone, Marco Della Cava, Guidarini Guidi, Jan Larsson. Moving story of young boy who believes St. Francis of Assisi will cure his lame donkey; shot in Assisi and Rome. Paul Gallico's story was filmed before, in 1952, as NEVER TAKE NO FOR AN ANSWER. Average.

Small Sacrifices (1989) **C-200m. TVM** D: David Greene. Farrah Fawcett, Ryan O'Neal, John Shea, Gordon Clapp, Emily Perkins. Fawcett delivers a flamboyant performance as real-life Diane Downs, an Oregon mother accused of shooting her three children. A compelling and emotional story that's very tough to watch; Joyce Eliason based her top-notch script on Ann Rule's bestselling book. Originally shown in two parts. Above average. ▼●

Small Soldiers (1998) **C-99m.** **½ D: Joe Dante. Kirsten Dunst, Gregory Smith, Jay Mohr, Phil Hartman, Kevin Dunn, Denis Leary, David Cross, Ann Magnuson, Wendy Schaal, Dick Miller, Robert Picardo; voices of Tommy Lee Jones, Frank Langella, Ernest Borgnine, Jim Brown, Bruce Dern, George Kennedy, Clint Walker, Christopher Guest, Michael McKean, Harry Shearer, Sarah Michelle Gellar, Christina Ricci. Overeager toy marketer puts military microchips into new combat figures; all hell breaks loose as they declare war on their "enemy" toys. Good premise is weakened by a predictable script. Computer animation is terrific, and director Dante throws in bonuses for film buffs—using cast members from THE DIRTY DOZEN and THIS IS SPINAL TAP as voices, adopting the BRIDE OF FRANKENSTEIN music at a key moment. Hartman's final film. Super 35. [PG-13]▼●◗

Small Time Crooks (2000) **C-94m.** **½ D: Woody Allen. Woody Allen, Tracey Ullman, Hugh Grant, Elaine May, Michael Rapaport, Jon Lovitz, Tony Darrow, Elaine Stritch, George Grizzard. Unusually lightweight comedy from Allen about an ex-con dishwasher who convinces his wife (Ullman) to invest their life's savings in a scheme to rob a bank. Instead, their "front" for the robbery, a cookie store, becomes a success, and wealth goes to her head. Slight, often unfocused, but entertaining, with enjoyable performances and a rare screen appearance by May. [PG]

Small Town Girl (1936) **108m.** *** D: William Wellman. Janet Gaynor, Robert Taylor, Binnie Barnes, Lewis Stone, Andy Devine, James Stewart, Fay Wray. Breezy romance about Gaynor trapping Taylor into marriage while he's drunk, then working to win him over when he's sober. Retitled ONE HORSE TOWN.

Small Town Girl (1953) **C-93m.** **½ D: Leslie Kardos. Jane Powell, Farley Granger, Ann Miller, S. Z. Sakall, Billie Burke, Bobby Van, Robert Keith, Nat King Cole. Bland MGM musical pairing playboy Granger and apple-pie Powell, who meet when he's thrown in jail by her father for speeding through town. Van's human pogo-stick number and Miller's "I've Gotta Hear That Beat," with Busby Berkeley's disembodied orchestra, are highlights.▼●

Small Town in Texas, A (1976) **C-95m.** ** D: Jack Starrett. Timothy Bottoms, Susan George, Bo Hopkins, Art Hindle, Morgan Woodward, John Karlen. Bottoms seeks revenge against heinous sheriff Hopkins, who framed him on a drug charge and has stolen his wife (George). Not bad, but you know what to expect. Widescreen. [PG]▼

Smart Alec (1986) **C-88m.** ** D: Jim Wilson. Ben Glass, Natasha Kautsky, Antony Alda, Lucinda Crosby, Kerry Remsen, Orson Bean, David Hedison, Bill Henderson, Zsa Zsa Gabor. Dull, silly (but not inaccurate) account of pint-sized eccentric Glass, an aspiring filmmaker, and his repeated frustrations as he attempts to finance his movie. Kautsky is most attractive as the model he covets as his leading lady. Aka THE MOVIE MAKER. ▼

Smart Alecks (1942) **60m.** *½ D: Wallace Fox. Leo Gorcey, Huntz Hall, Bobby Jordan, Gabriel Dell, Stanley Clements, Sunshine Sammy Morrison, David Gorcey, Bobby Stone, Maxie Rosenbloom, Gale Storm, Roger Pryor, Walter Woolf King. The East Side Kids indulge in a little larceny to purchase some baseball uniforms in this undernourished entry. Slapsy Maxie gets laughs as a dim-witted hood.▼

Smart Blonde (1936) **59m.** **½ D: Frank McDonald. Glenda Farrell, Barton MacLane, Winifred Shaw, Craig Reynolds, Addison Richards, Charlotte Winters, Jane Wyman. First of nine *Torchy Blane* films sets the pace and tone for the rest, with Farrell and MacLane amusing as the acerbic reporter and her irascible cop boyfriend working together on a murder case. Only series entry adapted directly from story by pulp author Frederick Nebel.

Smartest Girl in Town (1936) **58m.** **½ D: Joseph Santley. Gene Raymond, Ann Sothern, Helen Broderick, Eric Blore, Erik Rhodes. Ann mistakes wealthy Gene for a lowly male model, avoids him as she sets her sights on a rich husband. No surprises, but short and pleasant.▼

Smart Girls Don't Talk (1948) **81m.** ** D: Richard Bare. Virginia Mayo, Bruce Bennett, Helen Westcott, Robert Hutton, Tom D'Andrea. Dull drama of socialite Mayo forced to join up with racketeer.

Smart Money (1931) **90m.** **½ D: Alfred E. Green. Edward G. Robinson, James Cagney, Margaret Livingstone, Evalyn Knapp, Noel Francis. Known as Cagney and Robinson's only costarring film, but Robinson really stars, as lucky barber who becomes big-time gambler. Cagney is fine as Robinson's crony; watch for Boris Karloff in a bit as a shady gambler.

Smart Woman (1948) **93m.** *** D: Edward A. Blatt. Brian Aherne, Constance Bennett, Barry Sullivan, Michael O'Shea, James Gleason, Otto Kruger, Iris Adrian, Isobel Elsom, Selena Royle. Lawyer Aherne doesn't let love interfere with his determined attempt to prosecute crooked D.A. and other officials. Pretty big budget for an Allied Artists film; Alvah Bessie was one of the writers.

Smashing Bird I Used to Know, The SEE: **School for Unclaimed Girls**

Smashing the Crime Syndicate SEE: **Hell's Bloody Devils**

Smashing the Money Ring (1939) **57m.** ** D: Terry Morse. Ronald Reagan, Margot Stevenson, Eddie Foy, Jr., Joe Downing, Charles D. Brown. Reagan, as Lt. Brass Bancroft, again cracks a gang of counterfeiters, as he did in CODE OF THE SECRET SERVICE. Passable programmer.

Smashing Time (1967-British) **96m.** **½ D: Desmond Davis. Rita Tushingham, Lynn Redgrave, Michael York, Anna Quayle, Ian Carmichael. Two girls come to London to crash big-time. Spoof of trendy fashion/show biz world tries to turn Redgrave and Tushingham into Laurel and Hardy, with middling results. Slapstick scenes only mildly funny.▼◗

Smash Palace (1981-New Zealand) **C-100m.** *** D: Roger Donaldson. Bruno Lawrence, Anna Jemison, Greer Robson, Keith Aberdein, Desmond Kelly. Lawrence is more interested in his cars than wife Jemison, who craves attention and affection. Sometimes confusing and overly melodramatic, but still worthwhile—particularly when focusing on their 7-year-old daughter (Robson).▼●

Smash-up Alley (1972) **C-83m.** ** D: Edward J. Lakso. Darren McGavin, Richard Petty, Kathie Browne, Noah Beery, Jr., Pierre Jalbert, L. Q. Jones. Stock-car racer Petty plays himself, McGavin is his father, Lee, in this forgettable chronicle of their careers. Aficionados of the sport may enjoy it, however. Aka 43: THE PETTY STORY. [G]▼

Smash-up, the Story of a Woman (1947) **103m.** *** D: Stuart Heisler. Susan Hayward, Lee Bowman, Marsha Hunt, Eddie Albert, Carl Esmond, Carleton Young. Hayward is excellent as an insecure nightclub singer who gives up her career when she weds soon-to-be radio star Bowman . . . and finds herself helplessly mired in alcoholism. This was Hayward's breakthrough role after a decade in Hollywood, and it deservedly earned her her first Oscar nomination. Taut script by John Howard Lawson, from an original story by Dorothy Parker and Frank Cavett.▼

Smile (1975) **C-113m.** ***½ D: Michael Ritchie. Bruce Dern, Barbara Feldon, Michael Kidd, Geoffrey Lewis, Nicholas Pryor, Colleen Camp, Joan Prather, Annette O'Toole, Melanie Griffith, Maria O'Brien. Hilarious, perceptive satire centering around the behind-the-scenes activity at a California "Young American Miss" beauty pageant, presented as a symbol for the emptiness of American middle-class existence. One of the unsung films of the 1970s, written by Jerry Belson; Kidd is terrific as the contest's career-slumped choreographer. [PG]▼●

Smile Like Yours, A (1997) **C-98m.** BOMB D: Keith Samples. Greg Kinnear, Lauren Holly, Joan Cusack, Jay Thomas, France Nuyen, Christopher McDonald, Donald Moffat, Shirley MacLaine, Ben Stein. He's an engineer, she designs perfumes, and together they cannot conceive a child. The maladroit comic result is so strange that it turns into its year's definitive "what were they thinking of?" movie. That's 60s star Nuyen wielding fertility instruments straight from the Chamber of Horrors. Super 35. [R]▼●

Smile Orange (1976-Jamaican) **C-89m.** *** D: Trevor Rhone. Carl Bradshaw, Glen Morrison, Vaughn Croskill, Stanley Irons. Crudely made but funny comedy about hustling Montego Bay resort-hotel waiter Bradshaw, playing the same role he created in THE HARDER THEY COME. Originally a stage play. [PG]

Smiles of a Summer Night (1955-Swedish) **108m.** **** D: Ingmar Bergman. Ulla Jacobsson, Eva Dahlbeck, Margit Carlquist, Harriet Andersson, Gunnar Bjornstrand, Jarl Kulle. One of the finest romantic comedies ever made, a witty treatise on manners, mores, and sex during a weekend at a country estate in the late 19th century. Inspired the Broadway musical and subsequent film A LITTLE NIGHT MUSIC (as well as Woody Allen's A MIDSUMMER NIGHT'S SEX COMEDY).▼●

Smiley (1956-Australian) **C-97m.** **½ D: Anthony Kimmins. Ralph Richardson, Colin Petersen, John McCallum, Chips Rafferty, Reg Lye. Soft-treading narrative of young boy who wants a bicycle, becoming entangled with drug-smugglers. Sequel: SMILEY GETS A GUN. CinemaScope.

Smiley Gets a Gun (1959-Australian) **C-89m.** ** D: Anthony Kimmins. Sybil Thorndike, Keith Calvert, Bruce Archer, Chips Rafferty, Margaret Christensen. Easy-going account of young boy trying to win the right to have a gun. CinemaScope.

Smiling Lieutenant, The (1931) **88m.** *** D: Ernst Lubitsch. Maurice Chevalier, Claudette Colbert, Miriam Hopkins, Charlie Ruggles, George Barbier, Hugh O'Connell, Elizabeth Patterson. Utterly charming Lubitsch confection about a Viennese lieutenant who's forced to marry the naive, mousy Princess of Flausenthurm (Hopkins) when in fact he's in love with violinist Colbert. Pretty racy for its time. Highlight: the leading ladies singing "Jazz Up Your Lingerie." Based on the operetta *The Waltz Dream,* which was filmed under that title in Germany in 1928.●

Smilin' Through (1932) **97m.** *** D: Sidney Franklin. Norma Shearer, Fredric March, Leslie Howard, O. P. Heggie, Ralph Forbes. Sentimental romantic tale (with fantasy elements) about an embittered old man who lost his love on their wedding day but finds new reason to live when he must raise his orphaned niece (who looks exactly like his long-ago fiancée). Polished MGM production gets a bit pokey midway through but follows through to satisfying finale. Director Franklin originally filmed this with Norma Talmadge in 1922; it was remade in 1941.▼

Smilin' Through (1941) **C-100m.** **½ D: Frank Borzage. Jeanette MacDonald, Gene Raymond, Brian Aherne, Ian Hunter, Francis Robinson, Patrick O'Moore. Glossy remake of sentimental story about romance and rivalry spreading over two generations; lacks conviction of 1932 version, though MacDonald and Raymond are a good match (they married in real life). ▼

Smilla's Sense of Snow (1997-German-Swedish-Danish) **C-121m.** ** D: Bille August. Julia Ormond, Gabriel Byrne, Richard Harris, Robert Loggia, Vanessa Redgrave, Jim Broadbent, Peter Capaldi. Disappointing adaptation of Peter Hoeg's novel, with Ormond as an alienated woman who is devastated by death of neighboring Inuit boy—and obsessed with uncovering details of his possible murder. Part soul-searching saga, action story, romance, and medical thriller . . . and none of it gels. Admittedly a great woman's role, but it gets muddled in the execution. Panavision. [R]▼●

Smith! (1969) **C-112m.** *** D: Michael O'Herlihy. Glenn Ford, Nancy Olson, Dean Jagger, Keenan Wynn, Warren Oates, Chief Dan George. Offbeat Disney drama of stubborn, pro-Indian farmer Ford who steps forward to help Indian accused of murder. Well done, with good characterizations, but low-key qualities soften impact. [G]▼

Smithereens (1982) **C-90m.** ***½ D: Susan Seidelman. Susan Berman, Brad Rinn (Rijn), Richard Hell, Roger Jett, Nada Despotovitch, Kitty Summerall, Christopher Noth. Gritty little character study of selfish, self-assured, rootless hustler Berman, and her vague dreams of success as a punk-rock band manager. Solid characterizations and simple, fluid direction; the sequence with the hooker and her chicken salad sandwich is memorable. [R]▼●

Smoke (1995) **C-112m.** *** D: Wayne Wang. William Hurt, Harvey Keitel, Stockard Channing, Harold Perrineau, Jr., Forest Whitaker, Victor Argo, Erica Gimpel, Clarice Taylor, Giancarlo Esposito, Ashley Judd. A tapestry of lives that intertwine around a Brooklyn smoke shop; key figures include the philosophical manager (Keitel), a burnt-out novelist (Hurt), a worldly wise teenager (Perrineau) whom Hurt more or less adopts, and the boy's actual father (Whitaker), whom he hasn't seen since infancy. Another of Wang's low-key, barely-there narratives that won't enchant every viewer, but does offer considerable pleasure. The actors are compelling and credible; several cast members appear in a second film, BLUE IN THE FACE. Written by Paul Auster. [R]▼●

Smoke Signal (1955) **C-88m.** **½ D: Jerry Hopper. Dana Andrews, Piper Laurie, Rex Reason, Milburn Stone, William Talman. At-times zesty Western involving Indian massacre and survivors' trek downstream to escape.

Smoke Signals (1998) **C-88m.** **½ D: Chris Eyre. Adam Beach, Evan Adams, Irene Bedard, Gary Farmer, Tantoo Cardinal, Cody Lightning, Simon Baker, Michelle St. John, Tom Skerritt, Cynthia Geary. Two Coeur d'Alene Indians—tough, brooding Beach and likable, nerdy Adams—travel from their Idaho reservation to Phoenix to retrieve the remains of the former's dead father, and discover some truths about themselves along the way. Amusing, quirky road movie offers a refreshing Native American point of view, but is too schematic in setting up relationships and themes. However, it does have the memorable chant "John Wayne's Teeth." [PG-13]▼●◗

Smokey and the Bandit (1977) **C-96m.** *** D: Hal Needham. Burt Reynolds, Sally Field, Jackie Gleason, Jerry Reed, Mike Henry, Paul Williams, Pat McCormick. Box-office smash is one long comedy chase, as bootlegger Reynolds outraces Sheriff Gleason for nearly the entire film. Directorial debut of ace stuntman Needham is (expectedly) brimming with stunts. About as subtle as The Three Stooges, but a classic compared to the sequels and countless rip-offs which followed. [PG] ▼●◗

Smokey and the Bandit II (1980) **C-104m.** *½ D: Hal Needham. Burt Reynolds, Jackie Gleason, Jerry Reed, Dom DeLuise, Sally Field, Paul Williams, Pat McCormick, John Anderson. Strange sequel to 1977 hit has Bandit and friends agreeing to truck a pregnant elephant to Texas. Unfortunately, film has hardly any action, and its main character is portrayed as an embittered egomaniac. Some laughs, but not enough to overcome these obstacles. [PG]▼●

Smokey and the Bandit 3 (1983) **C-88m.** BOMB D: Dick Lowry. Jackie Gleason, Jerry Reed, Colleen Camp, Paul Williams, Pat McCormick, Mike Henry, Burt Reynolds. Desperate attempt to ring more laughs from this formula, with Gleason as a flustered red-neck sheriff and Reed as his latest nemesis. Originally filmed as SMOKEY IS THE BANDIT, with Gleason playing *both* roles; when preview audiences were confused, the film was reshot with Reed replacing the "second" Gleason. Panavision. [PG]▼●

Smokey Bites the Dust (1981) **C-85m.** BOMB D: Charles B. Griffith. Jimmy McNichol, Janet Julian, Walter Barnes, Patrick Campbell, Kari Lizer, John Blyth Barrymore. Young McNichol kidnaps homecoming queen, much to the consternation of her sheriff father. Poor excuse for a movie, with all its car-chase action bodily lifted from such earlier films as EAT MY DUST, GRAND THEFT AUTO, THUNDER AND LIGHTNING, and MOVING VIOLATION. [PG]▼

Smoky (1946) **C-87m.** *** D: Louis King. Fred MacMurray, Anne Baxter, Burl Ives, Bruce Cabot, Esther Dale, Roy Roberts. First-rate family film from Will James story of man's devotion to his horse. Previously filmed in 1933, then again in 1966.

Smoky (1966) **C-103m.** ** D: George Sherman. Fess Parker, Diana Hyland, Katy Jurado, Hoyt Axton, Chuck Roberson. Third version of the horse opera about especially independent horse named Smoky who knows what he wants.

Smooth Talk (1985) **C-92m.** **½ D: Joyce Chopra. Treat Williams, Laura Dern, Mary Kay Place, Levon Helm, Elizabeth Berridge. Disarmingly realistic depiction of teenage girl's growing pains and family relations takes sharp left turn when Williams enters as mysterious (and alluring) stranger . . . and all but deadens rest of the film. Worth seeing if only for Dern's fine performance. Impressive feature debut for documentary director Chopra; script by Tom Cole from a Joyce Carol Oates short story. Originally made for PBS' *American Playhouse.* [PG-13]▼●

Smorgasbord SEE: **Cracking Up**

Smugglers' Cove (1948) **66m.** **½ D: William Beaudine. Leo Gorcey, Huntz Hall, Gabriel Dell, Billy Benedict, David Gorcey, Bennie Bartlett, Martin Kosleck, Paul Harvey, Amelita Ward. With Kosleck in the cast, you know there's bound to be some evil Germans, and in this one they're smugglers at a posh Long Island estate, foiled by the Bowery Boys.

Smuggler's Gold (1951) **64m.** ** D: William Berke. Cameron Mitchell, Amanda Blake, Carl Benton Reid, Peter Thompson. Adequate drama about deep-sea diver Mitchell coping with girlfriend's (Blake's) father who's in the smuggling game.

Smuggler's Island (1951) **C-75m.** ** D: Edward Ludwig. Jeff Chandler, Evelyn Keyes, Philip Friend, Marvin Miller. Undemanding adventure story of diver Chandler involved with Keyes and search for sunken gold.

Snafu (1945) **82m.** ** D: Jack Moss. Robert Benchley, Vera Vague (Barbara Jo Allen), Conrad Janis, Nanette Parks, Janis Wilson, Marcia Mae Jones, Kathleen Howard, Jimmy Lloyd, Enid Markey, Eva Puig. Young Conrad Janis is sent home by army because of his age, but he can't get used to civilian life again; mild comedy with Benchley fine as perplexed father.

Snake Eyes (1998) **C-99m.** ** D: Brian De Palma. Nicolas Cage, Gary Sinise, Carla Gugino, Stan Shaw, Kevin Dunn, Mike Starr. Slick, corrupt Atlantic City cop finds himself in the midst of a multi-level conspiracy after a shooting at a heavyweight prizefight. Slick, kinetic filmmaking technique (by De Palma and cinematographer Stephen H. Burum) can only carry this unappealing story so far. By the finale, it's hard to care much about anyone—or anything—in the picture. Panavision. [R] ▼●◗

Snake People (1970-Mexican-U.S.) **C-90m.** BOMB D: Jhon Ibanez (Juan Ibanez and Jack Hill). Boris Karloff, Julissa, Charles (Carlos) East, Ralph Bertrand, Tongolele. Police captain tries to investigate an island where voodoo, LSD, and snake-worshipers run rampant. Ludicrous horror film wastes Karloff's talent. One of the last four films Karloff made; he shot his scenes in 1968. Original title: ISLE OF THE SNAKE PEOPLE. Aka CULT OF THE DEAD. ▼

Snake Pit, The (1948) **108m.** ***½ D: Anatole Litvak. Olivia de Havilland, Mark Stevens, Leo Genn, Celeste Holm, Glenn Langan, Helen Craig, Leif Erickson, Beulah Bondi, Lee Patrick, Natalie Schafer, Ruth Donnelly, Frank Conroy, Minna Gombell, Ann Doran, Betsy Blair, Isabel Jewell. One of the first films to deal intelligently with mental breakdowns and the painstakingly slow recovery process. Gripping film set in mental institution lacks original shock value but still packs a good punch, with de Havilland superb. Screenplay by Frank Partos and Millen Brand, from the Mary Jane Ward novel.▼●

Snapper, The (1993-British) **C-95m.** *** D: Stephen Frears. Colm Meaney, Tina Kellegher, Ruth McCabe, Colm O'Byrne, Eanna Macliam, Ciara Duffy, Joanne Gerrard, Peter Rowen, Fionnula Murphy, Karen Woodley, Pat Laffan, Brendan Gleeson. Wonderful adaptation of Roddy Doyle's novel about a working-class Irish family, and the teenage daughter who finds herself pregnant—with the circumstances too embarrassing to discuss. Vivid, funny, and believable, sparked by good performances—especially Meaney as the bewildered (but basically good-hearted) father; he also appeared earlier in THE COMMITMENTS, the first of Doyle's Barrytown trilogy. Followed by THE VAN. [R]▼●

Sneakers (1992) **C-126m.** **½ D: Phil Alden Robinson. Robert Redford, Dan Aykroyd, Ben Kingsley, Mary McDonnell, River Phoenix, Sidney Poitier, David Strathairn, Timothy Busfield, George Hearn, Stephen Tobolowsky, James Earl Jones. High-tech caper yarn about an offbeat security team that takes on a dangerous assignment to steal a "black box" containing volatile security secrets. Redford is in fine form in a lighthearted leading-man role, and his "team" is fun, but why does this story take so long to unravel—and why does it jettison every shred of believability toward the end? [PG-13]▼●◗

Sniper, The (1952) **87m.** *** D: Edward Dmytryk. Adolphe Menjou, Arthur Franz, Marie Windsor, Richard Kiley, Mabel Paige. Excellent, realistically filmed drama of mentally deranged sniper (Franz) who can't help himself from killing unsuspecting women. Fine performances by all.

Sniper (1975) SEE: **Deadly Tower, The**

Sniper (1993) **C-98m.** ** D: Luis Llosa. Tom Berenger, Billy Zane, J. T. Walsh, Aden Young, Ken Radley, Dale Dye, Richard Lineback. A tough marine sergeant and a green Olympics marksman team up in the Panamanian jungle to eliminate a rebel honcho and his drug lord bankroller. Plodding film is as life-affirming as a broken septic tank, and about as useful; the slow-motion bullet trajectories are a little livelier than the actors. [R]▼●◗

Snoopy, Come Home (1972) **C-70m.** *** D: Bill Melendez. Voices of Chad Webber, David Carey, Stephen Shea, Bill Melendez. Charming *Peanuts* feature (the second) centering around Snoopy, the world's most independent pooch. [G]▼●

Snorkel, The (1958-British) **74m.** **½ D: Guy Green. Peter Van Eyck, Betta St. John, Mandy Miller, Gregoire Aslan. Van Eyck ingeniously murders wife and plots to do away with stepdaughter, when she discovers his gimmick.

Snowball (1960-British) **69m.** ** D: Pat Jackson. Gordon Jackson, Zena Walker, Kenneth Griffith, Daphne Anderson. At times intriguing B film involving small boy's lie which led to the death of a villager.

Snowball Express (1972) **C-99m.** ** D: Norman Tokar. Dean Jones, Nancy Olson, Harry Morgan, Keenan Wynn, Johnny Whitaker, Michael McGreevey. Jones plays N.Y. accountant who inherits battered hotel in Rockies and tries to convert it into ski lodge. Slapstick ski chase is highlight of formula Disney comedy. [G]▼

Snow Creature, The (1954) **70m.** *½ D: W. Lee Wilder. Paul Langton, Leslie Denison, Teru Shimada, Rollin Moriyama. Yeti brought back from Himalayas languishes in customs while officials wrangle over whether it is cargo or a passenger. Dull film at least has virtue of being made for adults, though only kids may like it now.▼

Snow Day (2000) **C-89m.** ** D: Chris Koch. Chris Elliott, Mark Webber, Jean Smart, Schuyler Fisk, Iggy Pop, Pam Grier, Chevy Chase, John Schneider, Zena Grey, Emmanuelle Chriqui, Connor Matheus, J. Adam Brown. A late-season snowstorm closes upstate New York schools, allowing for plot threads spotlighting local weatherman Chase and two of his children: an adolescent boy who is smitten with his dream girl, and his kid sister, who takes on comically sadistic snowplow driver Elliott. Innocuous, predictable family film, a Nickelodeon production. Fisk (who plays Webber's tomboyish pal) is the daughter of Sissy Spacek. [PG]▼●◗

Snow Falling on Cedars (1999) **C-126m.** ** D: Scott Hicks. Ethan Hawke, James Cromwell, Richard Jenkins, James Rebhorn, Sam Shepard, Eric Thal, Max von Sydow, Youki Kudoh, Rick Yune, Jan Rubes, Celia Weston, Max Wright, Željko Ivanek, Daniel von Bargen. Ambitious but unsuccessful adaptation of David Guterson's best-selling novel. Flashback-laden story skips from the 1930s to the 1950s on an island in the Pacific Northwest where a boy falls in love with a Japanese-American girl. Equal parts murder mystery, forbidden romance, history lesson (about racial prejudice), and courtroom drama. Hawke is dull, but von Sydow livens things up as an aged but clever attorney. Self-consciously arty photography by Robert Richardson. Panavision. [PG-13]▼●◗

Snow Job (1972) **C-90m.** *½ D: George Englund. Jean-Claude Killy, Danielle Gaubert, Cliff Potts, Vittorio De Sica. Heist film involving the taking of $250,000 in loot. Although professional skier Killy is appropriate star for film set against the Alps, he can't act; neither can the beautiful Gaubert. Panavision. [PG]

Snow Queen, The (1959) **C-70m.** ** D:

Phil Patton. Art Linkletter, Tammy Marihugh, Jennie Lynn. Voices of Sandra Dee, Tommy Kirk, Patty McCormack, Paul Frees, June Foray. American live-action footage frames a lavish, stately Soviet animated feature from 1955 (directed by Lev Atamanov) based on the Hans Christian Andersen fairy tale about an icy snow queen whose heart is melted by the presence of true love.

Snows of Kilimanjaro, The (1952) **C-117m.** *** D: Henry King. Gregory Peck, Susan Hayward, Ava Gardner, Hildegarde Neff, Leo G. Carroll. Peck finds his forte as renowned writer critically injured while on safari in Africa, trying to decide if he found any meaning to his past; based on Hemingway story. ▼●◗

Snow White and the Seven Dwarfs (1937) **C-83m.** **** D: David Hand. Voices of Adriana Caselotti, Harry Stockwell, Lucille LaVerne, Scotty Mattraw, Roy Atwell, Pinto Colvig, Otis Harlan, Billy Gilbert, Moroni Olsen. Walt Disney's groundbreaking animated feature film—the first of its kind—is still in a class by itself, a warm and joyful rendition of the classic fairy tale, enhanced by the vivid personalities of the seven dwarfs. Only a real-life Grumpy could fail to love it. Songs include "Whistle While You Work," "Heigh Ho," and "Some Day My Prince Will Come."▼●

Snow White and the Three Stooges (1961) **C-107m.** BOMB D: Walter Lang. Three Stooges, Patricia Medina, Carol Heiss, Buddy Baer, Guy Rolfe, Edgar Barrier. Big mistake with skating star Heiss as Snow White, Three Stooges as . . . the Three Stooges. Comics aren't given much to do, despite title; rest of film is rather stodgy. Even kids won't be thrilled with it. CinemaScope.▼

Snow White: A Tale of Terror (1997-U.S.-British) **C-101m. TVM** D: Michael Cohn. Sigourney Weaver, Sam Neill, Gil Bellows, Taryn Davis, Brian Glover, David Conrad, Monica Keena. We're not in Disneyland here, kiddies. Extremely dark, rather bloody, live-action version of the Brothers Grimm fairy tale and an exercise in Gothic horror, with over-the-top Weaver as the evil stepmother. Filmed on location in various castles in the Czech Republic and in Prague Government Park, doubling for the Black Forest. Great (if sadistic) fun. Written by Tom Szollosi and Deborah Serra. Made for theaters; debuted on cable in U.S. Aka THE GRIMM BROTHERS' SNOW WHITE. Above average.▼●◗

Snow White in the Land of Doom SEE: **Happily Ever After**

Soak the Rich (1936) **87m.** BOMB D: Ben Hecht, Charles MacArthur. Walter Connolly, Mary Taylor, John Howard, Alice Duer Miller, Ilka Chase, Lionel Stander. Tycoon's daughter goes to college, falls for the militant anti-capitalist who kidnaps her. Hard to believe that a Hecht–MacArthur collaboration about campus radicals could be thoroughly unwatchable, but it's true. Miller, writer of *The White Cliffs of Dover* and co-member with H&M of the Algonquin Round Table, appears here as Miss Beasely.

Soapdish (1991) **C-95m.** ** D: Michael Hoffman. Sally Field, Kevin Kline, Robert Downey, Jr., Cathy Moriarty, Whoopi Goldberg, Elisabeth Shue, Carrie Fisher, Garry Marshall, Teri Hatcher, Paul Johansson, Costas Mandylor, Stephen Nichols, Kathy Najimy, Ben Stein. Farcical comedy about a soap opera queen who's losing her grip—on the show, and her life. Field and Kline are a treat to watch playing larger-than-life characters, but Whoopi is wasted, Downey is miscast, and the script (by Robert Harling and Andrew Bergman) thinks "frantic" equals "funny." Any one scene in TOOTSIE tops this hands down. Leeza Gibbons' best film work to date; John Tesh also appears. [PG-13]▼●

S.O.B. (1981) **C-121m.** **½ D: Blake Edwards. Julie Andrews, William Holden, Richard Mulligan, Robert Preston, Robert Vaughn, Loretta Swit, Larry Hagman, Marisa Berenson, Robert Webber, Stuart Margolin, Craig Stevens, Shelley Winters, Rosanna Arquette, Jennifer Edwards, Robert Loggia, John Pleshette, Larry Storch, Gene Nelson, Joe Penny, Corbin Bernsen. A producer hatches a scheme to turn his latest turkey into a hit: juice it up with pornography and have his wife-star (Andrews) bare her breasts. A glib satire on modern-day Movieland (and writer-director Edwards' revenge for Hollywood's treatment of him in the early '70s) throws in everything from black humor to slapstick, with wildly uneven results. Holden's last film. Panavision. [R]▼●

So Big (1953) **101m.** *** D: Robert Wise. Jane Wyman, Sterling Hayden, Nancy Olson, Steve Forrest, Martha Hyer, Tommy Rettig. Superficial but engrossing Edna Ferber soaper/saga about teacher who brings up son to be self-sufficient. Filmed before in 1925 and 1932.

Society Doctor (1935) **63m.** ** D: George B. Seitz. Chester Morris, Robert Taylor, Virginia Bruce, Billie Burke, Raymond Walburn, Henry Kolker, Donald Meek. Talky, hokey soaper of the various interactions among doctors, nurses, and patients in a hospital. Morris is the spirited, principled head intern (who even gets to direct his own operation!); Bruce is his nurse-girlfriend, who's loved by intern Taylor; Burke is a pampered patient.

So Dark the Night (1946) **71m.** **½ D: Joseph H. Lewis. Steven Geray, Micheline Cheirel, Eugene Borden, Ann Codee, Egon Brecher, Helen Freeman. Famous Parisian detective is put to work during his holiday

in the French countryside. Impressively made B movie, something of a sleeper in its time, suffers only for lack of charisma on the part of its (mostly unknown) cast.
So Dear to My Heart (1949) **C-84m.** ***½ D: Harold Schuster. Burl Ives, Beulah Bondi, Bobby Driscoll, Luana Patten, Harry Carey. Warm, nostalgic Disney film about young boy's determination to raise a black sheep and bring him to State Fair competition. Brimming with period charm and atmosphere; several animated sequences, too. Songs include "Lavender Blue (Dilly Dilly)." Screenplay by John Tucker Battle, from Sterling North's book *Midnight and Jeremiah*. ▼●
Sodom and Gomorrah (1963-Italian) **C-154m.** **½ D: Robert Aldrich. Stewart Granger, Pier Angeli, Stanley Baker, Anouk Aimée, Rossana Podesta. Lavish retelling of life in biblical twin cities of sin. Strong cast, vivid scenes of vice, gore, and God's wrath, make this overly long tale of ancient Hebrews fairly entertaining.▼●
So Ends Our Night (1941) **117m.** ***½ D: John Cromwell. Fredric March, Margaret Sullavan, Frances Dee, Glenn Ford, Anna Sten, Erich von Stroheim, Allan Brett. Superior filmization of Erich Maria Remarque story of German (March) rejecting Nazi reign, fleeing his country with hot pursuit by Axis agents. Written by Talbot Jennings from Remarque's novel *Flotsam*.▼
So Evil My Love (1948) **109m.** *** D: Lewis Allen. Ray Milland, Ann Todd, Geraldine Fitzgerald, Leo G. Carroll, Raymond Huntley, Martita Hunt, Hugh Griffith. Excellent study of corruption; scoundrel Milland drags innocent Todd into larceny at expense of Fitzgerald.
So Evil, My Sister (1972) **C-76m.** ** D: Reginald LeBorg. Susan Strasberg, Faith Domergue, Sydney Chaplin, Charles Knox Robinson, Steve Mitchell, Kathleen Freeman, John Howard. Gothic B-movie thriller with veteran cast has Strasberg and Domergue as sisters playing cat-and-mouse with the police who are investigating the mysterious death of Strasberg's husband. Several clever twists in the final reel are worth waiting for. Retitled PSYCHO SISTERS. Video title: THE SIBLING. [R]▼
Sofia (1948) **C-82m.** ** D: John Reinhardt. Gene Raymond, Sigrid Gurie, Patricia Morison, Mischa Auer. Acceptable programmer with Raymond helping nuclear scientists escape grip of Russians in Turkey.
Sofie (1992-Danish-Norwegian-Swedish) **C-146m.** **½ D: Liv Ullmann. Karen-Lise Mynster, Erland Josephson, Ghita Norby, Jesper Christensen, Torben Zeller, Stig Hoffmeyer. Ullman's directorial debut (which she also coscripted) is a thoughtful but uneven, Bergmanesque tale of a young Jew in late 19th-century Copenhagen who is unable to break free of family tradition, ruining her one chance at true love. Beautifully detailed but episodic (especially in its second half) and overlong. Mynster offers an effectively subtle performance as Sofie.▼
So Fine (1981) **C-91m.** *** D: Andrew Bergman. Ryan O'Neal, Jack Warden, Mariangela Melato, Richard Kiel, Fred Gwynne, Mike Kellin, David Rounds. Wacky comedy about professor-son of a N.Y.C. garment manufacturer who is dragooned into the business and inadvertently succeeds with an idea for see-through jeans. Film goes off in unexpected directions—some of them surprisingly silly—but remains funny most of the time. Writer Bergman's directorial debut. [R]▼●
Soft Beds, Hard Battles SEE: **Undercovers Hero**
Soft Boiled (1923) **78m.** **½ D: J. G. Blystone. Tom Mix, Joseph Girard, Billie Dove, L. D. Shumway, Tom Wilson, Frank Beal. Tom Mix tries comedy, as young man with challenge to spend 30 days without losing his temper; enjoyable fluff, with typical Mix action finale.
Soft Fruit (2000-Australian-U.S.) **C-101m.** ** D: Christina Andreef. Jeanie Drynan, Linal Haft, Russell Dykstra, Genevieve Lemon, Sacha Horler, Alicia Talbot. Four grown children—three sisters and a brother who's just gotten out of jail—return home to be with their mother, who's dying of liver cancer. Amiable enough mix of comedy and drama about an oddball family doesn't add up to much. Scripted by the director; executive produced by Jane Campion. [R]
Soft Skin, The (1964-French) **120m.** *** D: François Truffaut. Françoise Dorleac, Jean Desailly, Nelly Benedetti. Moody tale of married businessman drawn into tragic affair with beautiful airline stewardess; smooth direction uplifts basic plot.▼●
So Goes My Love (1946) **88m.** **½ D: Frank Ryan. Myrna Loy, Don Ameche, Rhys Williams, Bobby Driscoll, Richard Gaines, Molly Lamont. Amusing period comedy of fortune-hunting Loy marrying oddball inventor Ameche.
So I Married an Axe Murderer (1993) **C-93m.** **½ D: Thomas Schlamme. Mike Myers, Nancy Travis, Anthony LaPaglia, Amanda Plummer, Brenda Fricker, Debi Mazar, Matt Doherty. A guy who's always avoided commitment by finding absurd reasons to break up with his girlfriends finally meets Miss Right—and then comes to believe that she's a notorious axe murderess! Myers is ingratiating and funny (especially in a second role as his own contrary Scottish father) but the film never shifts into high gear. Cameos by such familiar comic personalities as Charles Grodin, Steven Wright, Phil Hartman, and Michael Richards seem mostly gratuitous. Alan Arkin appears unbilled. [PG-13]▼●◗
Solarbabies (1986) **C-94m.** BOMB D:

Alan Johnson. Richard Jordan, Jami Gertz, Jason Patric, Lukas Haas, Charles Durning, Peter DeLuise, Adrian Pasdar, Sarah Douglas, Frank Converse, Terrence Mann, Kelly Bishop. Futuristic teen junk has Gertz and her mostly male cohorts imprisoned by Nazi-like Jordan inside a fortress; the group plots an escape with the help of "Bohdi" —an ancient mystical force. Appallingly bad stinker from (Mel) Brooksfilm that barely got released. J-D-C Scope. [PG-13]▼●

Solar Crisis (1990-U.S.-Japanese) **C-112m.** **½ D: Alan Smithee (Richard Sarafian). Tim Matheson, Charlton Heston, Peter Boyle, Annabel Schofield, Corin Nemec, Jack Palance, Tetsuya Bessho, Dorian Harewood, Brenda Bakke. Futuristic sci-fi thriller with Matheson leading a save-the-planet mission to the sun to prevent a solar flare from destroying the earth. Fine special effects, quality acting, and suspenseful story in space, marred by earth antics of bad boy Boyle who (preposterously) wants to sabotage the mission. Panavision. [PG-13]▼●

Solaris (1972-Russian) **C-165m.** ***½ D: Andrei Tarkovsky. Natalya Bondarchuk, Donatas Banionis, Yuri Yarvet, Anatoly Solonitsin. Mind-bending, metaphysical sci-fi about a psychologist who's sent to a space station to investigate mysterious deaths and discovers supernatural phenomena. Slow-moving and occasionally pretentious, but hypnotic once one adjusts, and an undoubted tour de force by Tarkovsky, who also cowrote the screenplay. Sovscope.▼●◗

Soldier, The (1982) **C-96m.** *½ D: James Glickenhaus. Ken Wahl, Klaus Kinski, William Prince, Alberta Watson, Jeremiah Sullivan. CIA superagent Wahl takes on Russian terrorists who have planted a plutonium bomb in a Saudi Arabian oil field. Clichéd, violent drama. [R]▼

Soldier (1998) **C-98m.** ** D: Paul Anderson. Kurt Russell, Jason Scott Lee, Connie Nielsen, Sean Pertwee, Michael Chiklis, Gary Busey, Jason Isaacs, Jared Thorne, Taylor Thorne. In the near future, Russell, raised to be a soldier, is declared obsolete, thought dead, and dumped on a planet used as a garbage heap. He's befriended by people who crash-landed there some time before; then his old fighting partners show up to "cleanse" the planet. Russell is good, but the movie is derivative, the "science" ludicrous, and the outcome highly predictable. *Please* come back, Shane. Panavision. [R] ▼●◗

Soldier and the Lady, The (1937) **85m.** **½ D: George Nicholls, Jr. Anton Walbrook, Elizabeth Allan, Margot Grahame, Akim Tamiroff, Fay Bainter, Eric Blore. Hollywoodized version of Jules Verne's oft-filmed tale of a Czarist courier sent to deliver critical plans to the army in Siberia. Visually impressive, with sweeping battle scenes, though most exteriors were lifted from previous European version of the film, which also starred Walbrook. Aka MICHAEL STROGOFF.

Soldier Blue (1970) **C-112m.** *½ D: Ralph Nelson. Candice Bergen, Peter Strauss, Donald Pleasence, John Anderson, Jorge Rivero, Dana Elcar, James Hampton. Well-meant attempt to dramatize U.S. mistreatment of the Indians (and perhaps equate it with Vietnam) wasn't very good then and hasn't improved; bulk of the film is still cutesy romance between two survivors of Indian attack, climaxed by cavalry's slaughter of entire village in sequence that remains almost unwatchable. Panavision. [PG—edited from original R rating]▼●

Soldier Girls (1981) **C-87m.** ***½ D: Nicholas Broomfield, Joan Churchill. Hilarious, sometimes maddening and sobering documentary about young women Army recruits in basic training at Fort Gordon, Georgia. Definitely no recruiting poster: accurately advertised as the reality behind PRIVATE BENJAMIN.

Soldier in Skirts SEE: **Triple Echo**

Soldier in the Rain (1963) **88m.** *** D: Ralph Nelson. Jackie Gleason, Steve McQueen, Tuesday Weld, Tony Bill, Tom Poston, Ed Nelson, John Hubbard, Adam West. Strange film wavers from sentimental drama to high comedy. Gleason is swinging sergeant, McQueen his fervent admirer. Script by Blake Edwards and Maurice Richlin from William Goldman's novel.▼

Soldier of Fortune (1955) **C-96m.** *** D: Edward Dmytryk. Clark Gable, Susan Hayward, Michael Rennie, Gene Barry, Tom Tully, Alex D'Arcy, Anna Sten. Gable is hired to find Susan's husband (Barry) held captive in Hong Kong. Rennie is good as police chief. Scripted by Ernest K. Gann, from his novel. CinemaScope.▼

Soldier of Love SEE: **Fan Fan the Tulip**

Soldier of Orange (1979-Dutch) **C-165m.** ***½ D: Paul Verhoeven. Rutger Hauer, Jeroen Krabbé, Peter Faber, Derek De Lint, Eddy Habbema, Susan Penhaligon, Edward Fox. The lives of six wealthy, carefree Dutch university students are irrevocably altered when the Germans occupy their homeland in 1940. Superior drama, with Hauer coming into his own as a handsome aristocrat who becomes involved in the Resistance. Based on autobiographical novel by Erik Hazelhoff. [R]▼●

Soldier's Daughter Never Cries, A (1998) **C-127m.** **½ D: James Ivory. Kris Kristofferson, Barbara Hershey, Leelee Sobieski, Jesse Bradford, Anthony Roth Costanzo, Dominique Blanc, Jane Birkin. Picaresque story of an expatriate American family living in Paris during the '60s and '70s, and what happens when they move back home. Kristofferson is excellent as a macho novelist, and Sobieski and Bradford are equally good as his kids, who are going through various teenage crises, but the film loses its grip when it shifts to America and becomes much more mundane. Based on an autobiographical novel by Kaylie Jones, whose father was author James Jones. [R]▼●

Soldiers of Fortune SEE: **You Can't Win 'Em All**

Soldier's Story, A (1984) **C-101m.** ***½ D: Norman Jewison. Howard E. Rollins, Jr., Adolph Caesar, Dennis Lipscomb, Art Evans, Denzel Washington, Larry Riley, David Alan Grier, Robert Townsend, Patti LaBelle, Wings Hauser, Trey Wilson. Electrifying drama by Charles Fuller from his Pulitzer Prize-winning play (featuring most of original Negro Ensemble Company cast) about murder of a black officer at Southern military post in the 1940s. A solid whodunit plus a probing look at racism within black ranks. It was inspired by Herman Melville's *Billy Budd.* Can't completely escape its stage origins but still a riveting film. [PG]▼●◗

Soldier's Tale, A (1988) **C-94m.** **½ D: Larry Parr. Gabriel Byrne, Marianne Basler, Judge Reinhold, Paul Wyett. Poignant, thought-provoking WW2 story of a beautiful woman accused of being a German collaborator by the French resistance. Byrne plays a British soldier who tries to protect her. Reinhold, who has top billing on the videocassette package, is on screen for all of three minutes. [R]▼●◗

Soldiers Three (1951) **87m.** *** D: Tay Garnett. Stewart Granger, Walter Pidgeon, David Niven, Robert Newton, Cyril Cusack, Greta Gynt, Robert Coote, Dan O'Herlihy. Boisterous action-adventure with light touch; GUNGA DINesque story has three soldiering comrades in and out of spats with each other as they battle in 19th-century India. Loosely based on stories by Rudyard Kipling.

Sole Survivor (1969) **C-100m. TVM** D: Paul Stanley. Vince Edwards, Richard Basehart, William Shatner, Lou Antonio, Larry Casey, Patrick Wayne, Brad Davis, Dennis Cooney, Alan Caillou, Timur Bashtu. Title refers to central character, only person to walk away from suddenly discovered B-25 crash in Libyan desert. Odd drama by Guerdon Trueblood, with Edwards' performance hands-down winner. Above average.

Solid Gold Cadillac, The (1956) **99m.** *** D: Richard Quine. Judy Holliday, Paul Douglas, Fred Clark, John Williams, Arthur O'Connell, Hiram Sherman, Neva Patterson, Ray Collins; narrated by George Burns. Dazzling Judy in entertaining comedy of small stockholder in large company becoming corporate heroine by trying to oust crooked board of directors. George S. Kaufman–Howard Teichman play adapted by Abe Burrows. Jean Louis earned an Oscar for the costumes. Last scene in color. ▼

Sol Madrid (1968) **C-90m.** **½ D: Brian G. Hutton. David McCallum, Stella Stevens, Telly Savalas, Ricardo Montalban, Rip Torn, Pat Hingle, Paul Lukas, Michael Ansara. Old-fashioned but solid thriller about police, Mafia, and running heroin from Mexico. Panavision.

Solo (1996-U.S.-Mexican) **C-94m.** ** D: Norberto Barba. Mario Van Peebles, William Sadler, Adrien Brody, Seidy Lopez, Abraham J. Verduzco, Barry Corbin. Solo is an android who has a crisis of conscience when he directly disobeys an order that would result in the murder of innocent people. This sets him on a collision course with his creators, particularly a sadistic colonel. Standard action for nondiscerning fans of the genre. Van Peebles is actually quite appealing in the lead. Super 35. [PG-13] ▼●◗

Solomon and Sheba (1959) **C-120m.** *** D: King Vidor. Yul Brynner, Gina Lollobrigida, George Sanders, Marisa Pavan, John Crawford, Alejandro Rey, Harry Andrews. Splashy spectacle with alluring Gina and stoic Brynner frolicking in biblical days. Tyrone Power died during filming in Spain, was replaced by Brynner who refilmed his early scenes. Some long shots still show Power, not Brynner. Vidor's final film as director. Restored to 139m. on laserdisc. Super Technirama 70.▼●

Solomon Northrup's Odyssey (1984) **C-113m. TVM** D: Gordon Parks. Avery Brooks, Petronia Paley, Rhetta Greene, John Saxon, Mason Adams, Janet League, Lee Bryant, Joe Seneca, Michael Tolan. Compelling drama about a Northern-born black man (Brooks), a talented fiddler and carpenter, who's kidnapped into slavery during the 1840s. Made with care and conviction and based on a true story. A PBS *American Playhouse* presentation. Retitled HALF-SLAVE, HALF-FREE. Above average.▼

So Long at the Fair (1950-British) **90m.** *** D: Terence Fisher, Anthony Darnborough. Jean Simmons, Dirk Bogarde, David Tomlinson, Honor Blackman, Cathleen Nesbitt, Felix Aylmer, Andre Morell, Betty Warren. Atmospheric drama set during 1889 Paris Exposition with English woman searching for brother who's mysteriously vanished. Worth a look for fans of the offbeat.

Sombrero (1953) **C-103m.** *½ D: Norman Foster. Ricardo Montalban, Pier Angeli, Vittorio Gassman, Yvonne De Carlo, Nina

Foch, Cyd Charisse, Jose Greco, Walter Hampden, Kurt Kasznar, Rick Jason. Strange, overwrought MGM melodrama with music intertwining three love stories in small Mexican village. One good dance number with Charisse.

Somebody Has to Shoot the Picture (1990) **C-105m. TVM** D: Frank Pierson. Roy Scheider, Bonnie Bedelia, Robert Carradine, Andre Braugher, Arliss Howard. Scheider is a photographer hired by a small-time Florida drug dealer, convicted of killing a cop, to document his execution. Strong, no-nonsense drama adapted by photojournalist-writer Doug Magee from his book *Slow Coming Dark.* Made for cable. Above average.▼●◗

Somebody Killed Her Husband (1978) **C-97m.** *½ D: Lamont Johnson. Farrah Fawcett-Majors, Jeff Bridges, John Wood, Tammy Grimes, John Glover, Patricia Elliott. First starring feature for the ex-Charlie's Angel was redubbed "Somebody Killed Her Career" by industry wags, but in any case, this tepid comedy-mystery-romance written by Reginald Rose has little to recommend it. Filmed in Manhattan. [PG]

Somebody Loves Me (1952) **C-97m.** ** D: Irving S. Brecher. Betty Hutton, Ralph Meeker, Adele Jergens, Robert Keith. Schmaltzy vaudeville biography of troupers Blossom Seeley and Benny Fields with no originality and not much entertainment, either.

Somebody to Love (1995-French) **C-103m.** **½ D: Alexandre Rockwell. Rosie Perez, Harvey Keitel, Anthony Quinn, Michael DeLorenzo, Steve Buscemi, Samuel Fuller, Stanley Tucci, Steven Randazzo. Occasionally inspired but mostly meandering slice-of-life with Perez giving her all as a spirited taxi dancer who has moved from Brooklyn to L.A. in the hope of making it big in showbiz. Keitel is her middle-aged has-been actor/lover, DeLorenzo the young man who falls for her and tries to impress her by becoming involved with mobster Quinn. Buscemi is outstanding as a transvestite taxi dancer. Watch for Quentin Tarantino as a bartender, Lelia Goldoni as a waitress. [R]▼●

Somebody Up There Likes Me (1956) **113m.** ***½ D: Robert Wise. Paul Newman, Pier Angeli, Everett Sloane, Eileen Heckart, Sal Mineo, Joseph Buloff, Robert Loggia, Steve McQueen. Top biography of boxer Rocky Graziano's rise from N.Y.C. sidewalks to arena success with fine performance by Newman. Script by Ernest Lehman; cinematographer Joseph Ruttenberg won an Oscar. Film debuts of McQueen and Loggia.▼●

Some Call It Loving (1973) **C-103m.** BOMB D: James B. Harris. Zalman King, Carol White, Tisa Farrow, Richard Pryor. Slow, pretentious fantasy transplanting the story of Sleeping Beauty (played by Farrow, Mia's younger sister) to modern California. As her Prince Charming, King gives a sleepwalking nonperformance. Pryor's vulgar turn as a pathetic graffiti artist/wino clashes with the rest of the picture. [R]▼

Some Came Running (1959) **C-136m.** *** D: Vincente Minnelli. Frank Sinatra, Dean Martin, Shirley MacLaine, Martha Hyer, Arthur Kennedy, Nancy Gates. Slick adaptation of James Jones' novel about disillusionment in a small midwestern town in the late 1940s; more character study than narrative. MacLaine is especially good as luckless floozie who's stuck on Sinatra; Elmer Bernstein's music score also a standout. CinemaScope.▼●

Some Girls (1988) **C-94m.** ** D: Michael Hoffman. Patrick Dempsey, Jennifer Connelly, Sheila Kelley, Andre Gregory, Florinda Bolkan, Lila Kedrova. Odd little comedy about American college student Dempsey and the various complications when he spends Christmas in Quebec City with girlfriend Connelly's family. Gregory rises above the material as Connelly's eccentric father. [R]▼

Some Girls Do (1969-British) **C-93m.** **½ D: Ralph Thomas. Richard Johnson, Daliah Lavi, Beba Loncar, Robert Morley, Sydne Rome, James Villiers. Brisk thriller involving Bulldog Drummond (played with a lack of dash by Johnson) vs. long-time archenemy Carl Peterson (Villiers), who is trying to sabotage Britain's supersonic plane plans. Morley is a delight as an eccentric teacher of high cuisine. Sequel to DEADLIER THAN THE MALE (1967). [G]

Some Kind of a Nut (1969) **C-89m.** BOMB D: Garson Kanin. Dick Van Dyke, Angie Dickinson, Rosemary Forsyth, Zohra Lampert, Elliott Reid, Pippa Scott. Banker Van Dyke loses his job when he grows a beard. Pathetic "contemporary" comedy dates more than Kanin's films of the '30s and '40s. [M/PG]

Some Kind of Hero (1982) **C-97m.** ** D: Michael Pressman. Richard Pryor, Margot Kidder, Ray Sharkey, Ronny Cox, Lynne Moody, Olivia Cole, Paul Benjamin. Pryor rises above uneven, poorly directed comedy-drama about Vietnam veteran who's in for a few surprises when he returns home after six years as a POW. Based on a James Kirkwood novel. [R]▼●

Some Kind of Wonderful (1987) **C-93m.** **½ D: Howard Deutch. Eric Stoltz, Lea Thompson, Mary Stuart Masterson, Craig Sheffer, John Ashton, Elias Koteas, Molly Hagan, Candace Cameron, Chynna Phillips, Scott Coffey. Adorable tomboy Masterson loves Stoltz, but it takes him the entire film to realize she is better for him than the flashier Thompson. Deutch and producer John Hughes have, in effect, done a sex-switch remake of their own PRETTY IN

PINK; the OK result has strong performances by both female leads, and surprises by not making Thompson a snooty bitch. [PG-13]▼●
Some Like It Hot (1939) **64m.** **½ D: George Archainbaud. Bob Hope, Shirley Ross, Una Merkel, Gene Krupa, Richard Denning. Sideshow owner Hope takes advantage of Ross to raise money for show. Airy comedy includes song "The Lady's In Love With You." Retitled RHYTHM ROMANCE; based on a play previously filmed (in 1934) as SHOOT THE WORKS.▼
Some Like It Hot (1959) **119m.** **** D: Billy Wilder. Jack Lemmon, Tony Curtis, Marilyn Monroe, Joe E. Brown, George Raft, Pat O'Brien, Nehemiah Persoff, Joan Shawlee, Mike Mazurki. Legendary comedy by Wilder and I.A.L. Diamond about two musicians who witness the St. Valentine's Day Massacre and try to elude their pursuers by joining an all-girl band heading for Miami. Sensational from start to finish, with dazzling performances by Lemmon and Curtis, a memorably comic turn by Monroe as Sugar Kane, and Oscar-winning costumes by Orry-Kelly. Brown has film's now-classic closing line. Basis for hit Broadway musical *Sugar.*▼●
Some May Live (1967) **105m.** ** D: Vernon Sewell. Joseph Cotten, Martha Hyer, Peter Cushing, John Ronane. Unexciting suspenser set in contemporary Saigon with Cotten a U.S. Intelligence officer setting a trap for the espionage agent within his department. Retitled: IN SAIGON, SOME MAY LIVE.
Some Mother's Son (1996-U.S.-British-Irish) **C-112m.** **½ D: Terry George. Helen Mirren, Fionnula Flanagan, Aidan Gillen, David O'Hara, John Lynch, Tim Woodward. Respectable but muted true-life story about a hunger strike staged by a jailed IRA member in the early 1980s, with Mirren a prisoner's mom who becomes involved in the struggle upon realizing that she doesn't really have a choice. No match for IN THE NAME OF THE FATHER, which treated comparable subject matter far more passionately. Coproduced by Jim Sheridan; associate-produced by Mirren. [R]▼●
Someone Behind the Door (1971-French) **C-97m.** ** D: Nicolas Gessner. Charles Bronson, Anthony Perkins, Jill Ireland, Henri Garcin, Adriano Magestretti. Neuropsychiatrist (Perkins) turns an amnesiac murderer (Bronson) into his tool for revenge on his philandering wife; farfetched melodrama. [PG]▼●
Someone Else's America (1996-British-French) **C-96m.** **½ D: Goran Paskaljevic. Tom Conti, Maria Casares, Miki Manojlovic, Sergei Trifunovic, Zorka Manojlovic. Spanish immigrant moves his blind mother to Brooklyn in hopes of pursuing the American dream. His efforts to make it in the Land of the Free are often amusing, and well observed by Belgrade-born Paskaljevic. Slight but charming character study that speaks a universal language. Casares is well remembered for such earlier films as ORPHEUS and THE TESTAMENT OF ORPHEUS. [R]▼
Someone's Watching Me! (1978) **C-100m. TVM** D: John Carpenter. Lauren Hutton, David Birney, Adrienne Barbeau, Charles Cyphers. Dandy thriller about a career woman who takes things into her own hands after being rebuffed by the police when someone begins stalking her. Carpenter also wrote the script; his first TVM (and first film with Barbeau). Above average.
Someone to Love (1987) **C-111m.** **½ D: Henry Jaglom. Henry Jaglom, Andrea Marcovicci, Sally Kellerman, Orson Welles, Michael Emil, Oja Kodar, Dave Frishberg, Stephen Bishop, Ronee Blakley, Kathryn Harrold, Monte Hellman, Jeremy Kagan, Miles Kreuger. Jaglom is Danny, a filmmaker who's seeking "someone to love." He throws a Valentine's Day party where he questions various friends on the subject . . . and films their responses. Welles, in his last screen appearance, is on hand to offer various insights and profundities, and they're the best thing in this alternately boring and interesting experiment. [R]▼●
Someone to Watch Over Me (1987) **C-106m.** *** D: Ridley Scott. Tom Berenger, Mimi Rogers, Lorraine Bracco, Jerry Orbach, John Rubinstein, Andreas Katsulas, Tony DiBenedetto, James Moriarty. Happily married N.Y.C. cop becomes infatuated with the wealthy and beautiful woman he's assigned to protect from a death threat. Solid romantic thriller, compassionately and believably told; director Scott's warmest film to date (and just as stylish as ever). [R]▼●◗
Something About Amelia (1984) **C-100m. TVM** D: Randa Haines. Ted Danson, Roxana Zal, Glenn Close, Olivia Cole, Kevin Conway, Lane Smith, Jane Kaczmarek. Teenager reveals her father forced her to have sex with him, which throws the family into turmoil. Sensitively handled film about incest, written by William Hanley, received great notoriety and became one of the most watched television movies ever. Zal won an Emmy. Above average.
something big (1971) **C-108m.** BOMB D: Andrew V. McLaglen. Dean Martin, Brian Keith, Honor Blackman, Carol White, Ben Johnson, Albert Salmi, Paul Fix, Denver Pyle. Repellent "comedy"-Western detailing long-running feud between outlaw Martin and cavalry colonel Keith; "happy ending" consists of Dino robbing a stagecoach and mowing down hundreds of Mexi-

cans with a gatling gun—all to a peppy Marvin Hamlisch score. Blecch. [PG]
Something Evil (1972) **C-73m. TVM** D: Steven Spielberg. Sandy Dennis, Darren McGavin, Ralph Bellamy, Jeff Corey, Johnnie Whitaker, John Rubinstein. Worden family buys old house in Pennsylvania, unaware of lurking evil presence. Horror aspect handled matter-of-factly, excellent performances. Above average.
Something for Everyone (1970) **C-112m.** **½ D: Harold Prince. Angela Lansbury, Michael York, Anthony Corlan, Heidelinde Weis, Eva-Maria Meineke, Jane Carr. Very black comedy about amoral, bisexual young man (York) who manipulates staff and family of impoverished Countess (Lansbury) to his advantage. Intriguing but needlessly protracted story; Broadway director Prince's first film, made in Bavaria. [R]▼
Something for the Birds (1952) **81m.** **½ D: Robert Wise. Patricia Neal, Victor Mature, Edmund Gwenn, Larry Keating. Mild romantic froth, with Mature and Neal on opposite sides of issue in lobbying for bird sanctuary protection.
Something for the Boys (1944) **C-85m.** **½ D: Lewis Seiler. Carmen Miranda, Michael O'Shea, Vivian Blaine, Phil Silvers, Sheila Ryan, Perry Como, Glenn Langan, Cara Williams, Thurston Hall. Pleasant musical with diverting Cole Porter score, set in heiress Blaine's Southern plantation, which has been recruited as a home for soldiers' wives. Look for Judy Holliday as a defense-plant welder.
Something in Common (1986) **C-100m. TVM** D: Glenn Jordan. Ellen Burstyn, Tuesday Weld, Patrick Cassidy, Don Murray, Eli Wallach, Amanda Wyss. Breezy romantic comedy about a widowed career woman (Burstyn) whose son falls for a divorcée twice his age—hers. Burstyn and Weld shine in Susan Rice's savvy script. Above average.▼
Something in the Wind (1947) **89m.** **½ D: Irving Pichel. Deanna Durbin, Donald O'Connor, Charles Winninger, Helena Carter. Mild comedy of errors with Durbin as female disk jockey who sings, too. Easy to take, amusing.▼
Something Is Out There (1977) SEE: **Day of the Animals**
Something of Value (1957) **113m.** *** D: Richard Brooks. Rock Hudson, Dana Wynter, Sidney Poitier, Wendy Hiller, Frederick O'Neal. Robert Ruark's novel transformed to screen, sharply detailing brutal Mau Mau warfare in Kenya. Hudson and Poitier are fine as British colonial farmer and his childhood friend; Hiller memorable as widow struggling to retain dignity and spirit.▼
Something Short of Paradise (1979) **C-91m.** ** D: David Helpern, Jr. Susan Sarandon, David Steinberg, Jean-Pierre Aumont, Marilyn Sokol, Joe Grifasi, Robert Hitt. Aptly titled romantic comedy pairs movie theater manager Steinberg and magazine writer Sarandon, but offers little; Steinberg's character is particularly obnoxious in this blatant ANNIE HALL rip-off. Film buffs, however, will enjoy main-title sequence comprised of old movie ads. [PG]▼
Something Special (1986) **C-93m.** *** D: Paul Schneider. Pamela Segall, Patty Duke, Eric Gurry, John Glover, Mary Tanner, Seth Green, Jeb Ellis-Brown, John David Cullum, Corey Parker. Cute, original, generally pleasing little comedy-drama-fantasy about a 14-year-old girl (Segall, in a spunky performance) who wants to become a male—and has her wish granted. Bogs down when the adults are around, but it's still perfect fare for older kids. A shorter version, with tamer language, runs 86m. Original title: WILLY MILLY. Aka I WAS A TEENAGE BOY. [PG-13]▼●
Something to Hide (1972-British) **C-100m.** *½ D: Alastair Reid. Peter Finch, Shelley Winters, Colin Blakely, Linda Hayden, John Stride. All-out marital fighting match between memorably overwrought Winters and Finch deteriorates into unconvincing melodrama concerning pregnant trollop Hayden and Finch's eventual mental breakdown. Unpleasant. Retitled: SHATTERED.▼
Something to Live For (1952) **89m.** **½ D: George Stevens. Joan Fontaine, Ray Milland, Teresa Wright, Douglas Dick, Rudy Lee. Turgid melodrama trying to be another LOST WEEKEND. Fontaine is alcoholic in love with Milland, but he's married.
Something to Shout About (1943) **93m.** ** D: Gregory Ratoff. Don Ameche, Janet Blair, Jack Oakie, Cobina Wright, Jr., William Gaxton, Veda Ann Borg. Hackneyed backstage Broadway musical with good Cole Porter score (including "You'd Be So Nice to Come Home To"), specialty numbers by Hazel Scott, Teddy Wilson and His Orchestra. Look for Cyd Charisse (billed as Lily Norwood) in her feature debut.
Something to Sing About (1937) **93m.** ** D: Victor Schertzinger. James Cagney, Evelyn Daw, William Frawley, Mona Barrie, Gene Lockhart. Low-budget musical doesn't live up to its title, with Cagney the only real asset in this lightweight story of a N.Y. bandleader who goes to Hollywood. Forgettable songs. Reissued at 82m. as BATTLING HOOFER. Also shown in computer-colored version.▼●◗
Something to Talk About (1995) **C-106m.** **½ D: Lasse Hallström. Julia Roberts, Dennis Quaid, Robert Duvall, Gena Rowlands, Kyra Sedgwick, Brett Cullen, Haley Aull, Muse Watson, Anne Shropshire. A somewhat scattered Southern woman dis-

covers her husband is playing around and tries to cut him off, but strong ties—and his involvement in the family business (a prosperous horse-farm)—make it hard to do. The cast is amiable, the film is good looking, but Callie Khouri's screenplay is unfocused and never gives us a handle on Roberts' character or what she's all about. Sedgwick gets a license to steal (scenes, that is), with all the funniest lines in the picture. David Huddleston appears unbilled. [R] ▼●◗

Something Wicked This Way Comes (1983) **C-94m.** **½ D: Jack Clayton. Jason Robards, Jonathan Pryce, Diane Ladd, Pam Grier, Royal Dano, Shawn Carson, Vidal Peterson, Mary Grace Canfield, James Stacy, narrated by Arthur Hill. A mysterious carnival pitches its tent outside an idyllic American town in the early part of the century and fulfills the dreams of its citizens—for a heavy price. Told from a young boy's point of view, film has affecting moments, but never really hits its stride, with the ultimate "revelation" about Mr. Dark and his carnival no surprise at all. Disappointing Disney production of Ray Bradbury's classic story, scripted by the author. [PG]▼●

Something Wild (1961) **112m.** **½ D: Jack Garfein. Carroll Baker, Ralph Meeker, Mildred Dunnock, Martin Kosleck, Jean Stapleton. Bizarre study of rape-victim Baker falling in love with would-be attacker Meeker, coming to rational understanding with mother Dunnock. N.Y.C. location scenes perk melodramatic soaper.

Something Wild (1986) **C-113m.** ** D: Jonathan Demme. Jeff Daniels, Melanie Griffith, Ray Liotta, Margaret Colin, Tracey Walter, Dana Preu, Jack Gilpin. Straight-arrow businessman Daniels goes for a joyride with a flaky, sexy girl he chances to meet, and in the course of a couple of days she turns his life inside out. Many surprising twists and turns as this film veers from kooky comedy to violent melodrama, but end result isn't satisfying, especially with tacked-on happy ending. Filmmakers John Waters and John Sayles have amusing cameos as a used-car salesman and a motorcycle cop, respectively. [R]▼●

Sometimes a Great Notion (1971) **C-114m.** ** D: Paul Newman. Paul Newman, Henry Fonda, Lee Remick, Michael Sarrazin, Richard Jaeckel, Linda Lawson. Disappointing film version of Ken Kesey's mammoth novel about modern-day loggers in Oregon. Jaeckel's performance is outstanding and movie has one great scene involving a drowning, but otherwise film is a letdown. Retitled NEVER GIVE A INCH (the family's motto) for TV. Panavision. [PG]▼●

Somewhere I'll Find You (1942) **108m.** **½ D: Wesley Ruggles. Clark Gable, Lana Turner, Robert Sterling, Patricia Dane, Reginald Owen, Lee Patrick, Charles Dingle, Sara Haden, Rags Ragland, Van Johnson, Leonid Kinskey, Grady Sutton, Keye Luke. Turner and Gable are improbable as WW2 war correspondents, but their love scenes between battles are most convincing. Film debut of Keenan Wynn.▼

Somewhere in the Night (1946) **108m.** **½ D: Joseph L. Mankiewicz. John Hodiak, Nancy Guild, Lloyd Nolan, Richard Conte, Josephine Hutchinson, Fritz Kortner, Sheldon Leonard, Whit Bissell, Jeff Corey, Henry (Harry) Morgan. Satisfactory drama of amnesiac Hodiak trying to discover his true identity; not up to later Mankiewicz efforts.

Somewhere in Time (1980) **C-103m.** *½ D: Jeannot Szwarc. Christopher Reeve, Jane Seymour, Christopher Plummer, Teresa Wright, Bill Erwin, George Voskovec, Tim Kazurinsky. Superficial tearjerker about unhappy playwright Reeve who falls in love with a 70-year-old painting of an actress (Seymour), then wills himself back in time to meet her. Stilted dialogue, corny situations, pretty scenery (on Mackinac Island). Script by Richard Matheson from his novel *Bid Time Return.* [PG]▼●◗

Somewhere Tomorrow (1983) **C-87m.** *** D: Robert Wiemer. Sarah Jessica Parker, Nancy Addison, Tom Shea, Rick Weber, Paul Bates, James Congdon. Offbeat drama about fatherless teen Parker who, after seeing TOPPER on TV and bumping her head, meets the ghost of a boy (Shea) who's been killed in a plane crash. Not without flaws, but still charming and moving. [PG]▼

Sommersby (1993-U.S.-French) **C-113m.** **½ D: Jon Amiel. Richard Gere, Jodie Foster, Bill Pullman, James Earl Jones, William Windom, Brett Kelley, Richard Hamilton, Maury Chaykin, Lanny Flaherty, Frankie Faison, Wendell Wellman, Clarice Taylor, Ronald Lee Ermey. Gere returns to his home in the post-war South, after six years' imprisonment during the Civil War, but his wife can't quite believe he's the same man she married. Sumptuously designed and photographed (in Virginia), this is the kind of film that takes you to another time and place, but despite strong performances, the characters remain aloof—and so does their plight. Executive produced by Gere. Remake of the French hit THE RETURN OF MARTIN GUERRE. Panavision. [PG-13]▼●

Sonatine (1994-Japanese) **C-94m.** *** D: Takeshi Kitano. Beat Takeshi, Tetsu Watanabe, Aya Kokumai, Masanobu Katsumura, Susumu Terashima. Well-observed portrait of a middle-aged gangster who's looking to his future when he's asked to settle a dispute between two warring factions of yakuza on Okinawa. Writer-director-star Kitano (who acts under the name of Beat Takeshi) isn't timid about depicting violence, but he does it with style and a point of view. [R] ▼●

Son-Daughter, The (1932) **79m.** *½ D: Clarence Brown. Helen Hayes, Ramon Novarro, Lewis Stone, Ralph Morgan, Warner Oland. Designed as a tender love story with tragic overtones set in San Francisco's Chinatown, this film plays more like farce, with dialogue that sounds like Chinese Damon Runyon. One of Hayes' most embarrassing performances.

Song Is Born, A (1948) **C-113m.** **½ D: Howard Hawks. Danny Kaye, Virginia Mayo, Hugh Herbert, Steve Cochran, Felix Bressart; guest stars Benny Goodman, Louis Armstrong, Charlie Barnet, Lionel Hampton, Tommy Dorsey. A group of dowdy intellectuals need to learn about jazz to write an intelligent entry for their upcoming encyclopedia. Watered-down remake of BALL OF FIRE (also directed by Hawks) does give Danny some good material, and enables a formidable array of jazz greats to do their stuff (including Benny Goodman, made up as one of the bookish profs). ▼●

Song of Bernadette, The (1943) **156m.** **** D: Henry King. Jennifer Jones, William Eythe, Charles Bickford, Vincent Price, Lee J. Cobb, Anne Revere, Gladys Cooper. Overlong but excellent story of religious French girl in 1800s who sees great vision, incurs local wrath because of it. George Seaton adapted Franz Werfel's best-selling novel. Four Oscars include Best Actress, Cinematography (Arthur Miller), Score (Alfred Newman). That's Linda Darnell, unbilled, as the Virgin Mary. ▼●

Song of Freedom (1936-British) **80m.** **½ D: J. Elder Wills. Paul Robeson, Elizabeth Welch, George Mozart, Esme Percy, Arthur Williams, Robert Adams. Robeson plays stevedore-turned-concert-singer who journeys to Africa in search of his roots. Promising idea doesn't quite work, but Robeson is always worth watching. ▼◗

Song of India (1949) **77m.** ** D: Albert S. Rogell. Sabu, Gail Russell, Turhan Bey, Anthony Caruso, Aminta Dyne. Well-meaning Sabu releases jungle animals callously trapped by royal family; typical jungle escapist adventure. ▼

Song of Love (1947) **119m.** **½ D: Clarence Brown. Katharine Hepburn, Paul Henreid, Robert Walker, Henry Daniell, Leo G. Carroll, Gigi Perreau, Tala Birell, Henry Stephenson, Elsa Janssen. Classy production but slow-moving story of Clara Schuman (Hepburn), her composer husband (Henreid) and good friend Brahms (Walker). ▼

Song of Norway (1970) **C-142m.** BOMB D: Andrew L. Stone. Florence Henderson, Toralv Maurstad, Christina Schollin, Frank Porretta, Edward G. Robinson, Harry Secombe, Robert Morley, Oscar Homolka. A poor biography of composer Edvard Grieg, with weak and abridged versions of his best music. Beautiful to look at in Super Panavision 70, but not likely to impress on TV. [G] ▼

Song of Russia (1943) **107m.** **½ D: Gregory Ratoff. Robert Taylor, Susan Peters, John Hodiak, Robert Benchley, Felix Bressart, Joan Lorring, Darryl Hickman. MGM's war-time attempt to do for Russia what MRS. MINIVER did for England; hokey but effective story of American conductor Taylor falling in love with Russian musician Peters. Then-topical attitude toward U.S.S.R. makes this an interesting period piece.

Song of Scheherazade (1947) **C-106m.** ** D: Walter Reisch. Yvonne De Carlo, Brian Donlevy, Jean-Pierre Aumont, Eve Arden, Philip Reed. Colorful tripe about Rimsky-Korsakov's true inspiration, a dancing girl (De Carlo). ▼

Song of Songs (1933) **90m.** **½ D: Rouben Mamoulian. Marlene Dietrich, Brian Aherne, Lionel Atwill, Alison Skipworth, Hardie Albright, Helen Freeman. Naïve country girl Dietrich falls in love with sculptor Aherne, for whom she poses in the nude . . . but Atwill, a wealthy reprobate, manages to marry her. Humdrum story made worthwhile by good performances, especially Dietrich, who's luminous in her first Hollywood film *not* directed by Josef von Sternberg. ▼

Song of Surrender (1949) **93m.** ** D: Mitchell Leisen. Wanda Hendrix, Claude Rains, Macdonald Carey, Andrea King, Henry O'Neill, Elizabeth Patterson, Eva Gabor. Mild turn-of-the-century tale of young woman (Hendrix) and older husband Rains.

Song of the Islands (1942) **C-75m.** *** D: Walter Lang. Betty Grable, Victor Mature, Jack Oakie, Thomas Mitchell, Hilo Hattie, George Barbier, Billy Gilbert. Mature (with sidekick Oakie) visits idyllic Pacific island and falls in love with Grable, but romance is hindered by feuding between their fathers. Buoyant Technicolor fluff, full of engagingly silly songs by Mack Gordon and Harry Owens. ▼●

Song of the Open Road (1944) **93m.** ** D: S. Sylvan Simon. Charlie McCarthy, Edgar Bergen, Jane Powell, W. C. Fields, Bonita Granville, Peggy O'Neill, Jackie Moran, Reginald Denny, Regis Toomey, Sammy Kaye and His Orchestra. Insipid tale of juvenile film star (Powell, in her screen debut) who rebels, runs away and joins the CCC (Civilian Conservation Corps), picking tomatoes and mingling with "regular" kids. Hard to take, except for specialty numbers and guest appearance by Fields and his longtime wooden nemesis, McCarthy.

Song of the South (1946) **C-94m.** ***½

D: Wilfred Jackson (animation), Harve Foster (live-action). Ruth Warrick, James Baskett, Bobby Driscoll, Luana Patten, Lucile Watson, Hattie McDaniel, Glenn Leedy. Lonely, misunderstood little boy, living on a plantation in the Old South, finds his only happiness in the tales spun by Uncle Remus. Some may find story cloying, but it serves as framework for three terrific Disney cartoon sequences featuring Brer Rabbit, Brer Fox, and Brer Bear (based on writings of Joel Chandler Harris). Superb blend of live-action and animation, sincere performances (Baskett earned a special Academy Award for his), and tuneful songs including Oscar-winning "Zip a Dee Doo Dah" make this a treat. Available only on Japanese import laserdisc.●

Song of the Thin Man (1947) **86m.** **½ D: Edward Buzzell. William Powell, Myrna Loy, Keenan Wynn, Dean Stockwell, Philip Reed, Patricia Morison, Gloria Grahame, Jayne Meadows, Don Taylor, Leon Ames. Nick and Nora search for clues to a murder in the dark and mysterious atmosphere of N.Y. jazz clubs. 11-year-old Stockwell portrays Nick, Jr. in this sixth and final series entry, still amiable and entertaining thanks to the stars' chemistry.▼●

Song o' My Heart (1930) **91m.** ** D: Frank Borzage. John McCormack, Alice Joyce, Maureen O'Sullivan, Tom Clifford, J. M. Kerrigan, John Garrick, J. Farrell MacDonald, Andres De Segurola. Feeble soap opera of Irish villagers and their favorite son, a great singer who gave up his career after a long-ago heartbreak. Designed as a showcase for great Irish tenor McCormack, who proves an engaging personality, and gets to sing many beautiful songs; music is, in fact, the film's only virtue. Screen debut for fresh-faced O'Sullivan, age 19. Grandeur 70mm.▼

Song Remains the Same, The (1976) **C-136m.** ** D: Peter Clifton, Joe Massot. Amateurish mixture of fantasy sequences and documentary footage from Led Zeppelin's 1973 tour is for fans only. Even without the stereo sound, film will still clean out all eight sinus cavities. [PG]▼

Song to Remember, A (1945) **C-113m.** **½ D: Charles Vidor. Cornel Wilde, Paul Muni, Merle Oberon, Stephen Bekassy, Nina Foch, George Coulouris, Sig Arno. Colorful but superficial biography of Chopin (Wilde) with exaggerated Muni as his mentor, lovely Oberon as George Sand; good music, frail plot.▼●

Song Without End (1960) **C-141m.** **½ D: Charles Vidor, George Cukor. Dirk Bogarde, Capucine, Genevieve Page, Patricia Morison, Ivan Desny, Martita Hunt, Lou Jacobi. Beautiful music (scoring won an Oscar) submerged by dramatics of composer Franz Liszt's life. Bogarde tries; settings are lavish. Vidor died during filming, Cukor completed picture. CinemaScope.▼●

Songwriter (1984) **C-94m.** **½ D: Alan Rudolph. Willie Nelson, Kris Kristofferson, Melinda Dillon, Rip Torn, Lesley Ann Warren, Mickey Raphael, Rhonda Dotson, Richard C. Sarafian. Loose, friendly, rambling film about a couple of country singers—one of whom (Nelson) has become an entrepreneur but calls on his old partner Kris to help him outwit a greedy backer (played by film director Sarafian). Doesn't add up to much but certainly pleasant to watch, with top supporting cast and lots of music. [R]▼●

Son In Law (1993) **C-95m.** ** D: Steve Rash. Pauly Shore, Carla Gugino, Lane Smith, Cindy Pickett, Mason Adams, Patrick Renna, Dennis Burkley, Dan Gauthier. Liberated college freshman brings her dorm's biggest goof home to the family farm over Thanksgiving break, passing him off as her fiancé to discourage a hometown lout from proposing. Exactly what you would expect, even more so when Shore teaches square-dancers the funky chicken. Even on his best days Pauly Shore is an acquired taste, but at least the film isn't mean-spirited. Gugino has an infectious cackle. Brendan Fraser appears unbilled. [PG-13]▼●◗

Sonny and Jed (1973-Italian) **C-98m.** ** D: Sergio Corbucci. Tomas Milian, Telly Savalas, Susan George, Rosanna Janni, Laura Betti. Lighthearted spaghetti Western that teams escaped convict, pillaging his way across Mexico, with free-spirited gal who wants to become an outlaw. Shiny-domed Telly is determined lawman dogging their every move. [R]▼

Sonny Boy (1990) **C-98m.** BOMB D: Robert Martin Carroll. David Carradine, Paul L. Smith, Brad Dourif, Conrad Janis, Sydney Lassick, Alexandra Powers, Michael Griffin. Repulsive, socially unredeemable waste of celluloid detailing gruesome upbringing of abused "sonny boy" who's kidnapped by wacko couple Dourif and his "wife" Carradine (who plays the role in full drag). Filmed for no apparent reason except to offend and appall. Panavision. [R]▼

Son of a Gunfighter (1966-Spanish) **C-92m.** *½ D: Paul Landres. Russ Tamblyn, Kieron Moore, James Philbrook, Fernando Rey. Title tells all in oater peppered with Anglo-Saxon actors and bits of the Old West. CinemaScope.

Son of Ali Baba (1952) **C-75m.** ** D: Kurt Neumann. Tony Curtis, Piper Laurie, Susan Cabot, Victor Jory, Hugh O'Brian. Caliph uses princess Laurie to obtain treasure of Ali Baba. After father is captured, son appears and wins hand of princess. Good sets, fair acting.

Son of a Sailor (1933) **73m.** *** D: Lloyd Bacon. Joe E. Brown, Jean Muir, Thelma Todd, Frank McHugh, Johnny Mack Brown, Sheila Terry. Joe blunders into espionage and recovers stolen Navy plans; always-vivacious Todd lends fine support in this entertaining comedy.

Son of Blob SEE: **Beware! The Blob**

Son of Captain Blood, The (1962-U.S.-Italian-Spanish) **C-88m.** *½ D: Tulio Demicheli. Sean Flynn, Ann Todd, Alessandra Panaro, Jose Nieto, John Kitzmiller. Interesting only in that Errol Flynn's 23-year-old son plays the son of the character Errol portrayed in CAPTAIN BLOOD. Ann Todd sparkles as the lad's mother (Olivia de Havilland's character in the original). Otherwise, routine. Filmed in Spain, from a screenplay by Casey Robinson (who also penned the 1935 CAPTAIN BLOOD). CinemaScope.▼

Son of Darkness: To Die For II (1991) **C-95m.** ** D: David F. Price. Rosalind Allen, Michael Praed, Scott Jacoby, Steve Bond, Amanda Wyss, Remy O'Neill, Devin Corrie Sims. Busy plot: Vlad Tepesh is now Dr. Max Schreck, at a hospital in the mountains, in pursuit of heroine who has unknowingly adopted his half-vampire baby. Beautifully shot, and tries to be romantic—but it's routine. [R]▼

Son of Dracula (1943) **78m.** *** D: Robert Siodmak. Lon Chaney, Jr., Robert Paige, Louise Allbritton, Evelyn Ankers, Frank Craven, J. Edward Bromberg, Samuel S. Hinds. Mysterious gentleman named Alucard turns up in the Deep South to sample the local cuisine. One of Universal's most atmospheric chillers, with crisp acting, fine effects . . . and an unexpected finale.▼●

Son of Dracula (1974-British) **C-90m.** *½ D: Freddie Francis. Harry Nilsson, Ringo Starr, Rosanna Lee, Freddie Jones, Dennis Price, Skip Martin. Offbeat but uninspired rock horror pic with seven tunes by Nilsson, who plays the title character. Ringo produced. Retitled: YOUNG DRACULA. [PG]

Son of Dr. Jekyll, The (1951) **77m.** *½ D: Seymour Friedman. Louis Hayward, Jody Lawrance, Alexander Knox, Lester Matthews. Jekyll's son tries to discover and improve upon his father's formula; he never turns into Hyde! Poorly scripted, produced; cast manages to save film from complete ruin.

Son of Flubber (1963) **100m.** **½ D: Robert Stevenson. Fred MacMurray, Nancy Olson, Keenan Wynn, Tommy Kirk, Elliott Reid, Joanna Moore, Leon Ames, Ed Wynn, Charlie Ruggles, Paul Lynde, Jack Albertson. Silly, disjointed sequel to THE ABSENT MINDED PROFESSOR has new inventions—flubbergas, dry rain—and appropriate slapstick highlights, to compensate for uneven script. Helped, too, by cast full of old pros, especially Lynde as smug sportscaster.▼●

Son of Frankenstein (1939) **99m.** *** D: Rowland V. Lee. Basil Rathbone, Boris Karloff, Bela Lugosi, Lionel Atwill, Josephine Hutchinson, Edgar Norton, Donnie Dunagan. Third in the series (after BRIDE) finds late doctor's son attempting to clear family name by making the Monster "good." He should live so long. Lavishly made shocker is gripping and eerie, if a bit talky, with wonderfully bizarre sets by Jack Otterson and Lugosi's finest performance as evil, broken-necked shepherd Ygor. Karloff's last appearance as the Monster. Look fast for Ward Bond(!) as a constable guarding Castle Frankenstein from angry villagers late in film. Sequel: GHOST OF FRANKENSTEIN.▼●

Son of Fury (1942) **98m.** *** D: John Cromwell. Tyrone Power, Gene Tierney, George Sanders, Frances Farmer, Roddy McDowall, Kay Johnson, John Carradine, Elsa Lanchester, Harry Davenport, Dudley Digges, Ethel Griffies. Good costumer about aristocratic Sanders shunning nephew Power, who flees to desert isle to plan revenge; Tierney's on the island, too. Remade as TREASURE OF THE GOLDEN CONDOR.▼

Son of Godzilla (1967-Japanese) **C-86m.** *½ D: Jun Fukuda. Tadao Takashima, Akira Kubo, Bibari Maeda, Akihiko Hirata, Kenji Sahara. Godzilla and son are threatened by giant mantises and a huge spider in this good-natured monster rally, but where's Mrs. Godzilla when you really need her? Some of the same footage later seen in GODZILLA'S REVENGE. Tohoscope.▼

Son of Kong, The (1933) **70m.** **½ D: Ernest B. Schoedsack. Robert Armstrong, Helen Mack, Victor Wong, John Marston, Frank Reicher, Lee Kohlmar. Disappointing sequel to KING KONG, hurriedly put together—and it shows. Armstrong is back as Carl Denham, who discovers Kong's cute li'l offspring. Mostly comedic film has some good moments, and Willis O'Brien's effects are still superb.▼●

Son of Lassie (1945) **C-102m.** **½ D: S. Sylvan Simon. Peter Lawford, Donald Crisp, June Lockhart, Nigel Bruce, William Severn, Leon Ames, Fay Helm, Donald Curtis, Nils Asther, Helen Koford (Terry Moore). War-themed sequel to popular LASSIE COME HOME with Lawford and Lockhart playing adult roles of McDowall and Taylor. Crisp and Bruce are now training dogs for the war effort and Lassie's son (both roles played here by talented collie Pal) accompanies pilot Lawford to Nazi-occupied Norway.▼

Son of Monte Cristo, The (1940) **102m.** *** D: Rowland V. Lee. Louis Hayward, Joan Bennett, George Sanders, Florence Bates, Lionel Royce, Montagu Love. Nothing new in big-scale swashbuckler, but very well done with Hayward battling Sanders and vying for Bennett's hand. Look fast for Clayton Moore in a balcony scene.▼●

Son of Paleface (1952) **C-95m.** ***½ D: Frank Tashlin. Bob Hope, Jane Russell, Roy Rogers, Douglass Dumbrille, Bill Williams, Harry Von Zell, Iron Eyes Cody. One of Hope's best; same basic set-up as THE PALEFACE, but the presence of Rogers gives this one a satirical punch the original doesn't have. Full of director-cowriter Tashlin's cartoon-like gags; the scene where Hope and Trigger share the same bed is an unheralded comedy classic. ▼●

Son of Robin Hood, The (1959-British) **C-81m.** ** D: George Sherman. Al (David) Hedison, June Laverick, David Farrar, Marius Goring, George Coulouris. Bland forest tale continuing the legend of merrie men led by Robin's descendant. CinemaScope.

Son of Sinbad (1955) **C-88m.** *½ D: Ted Tetzlaff. Dale Robertson, Sally Forrest, Lili St. Cyr, Vincent Price. Limp Arabian Nights adventure has Sinbad, captured by caliph, forced to perform wonders to win freedom and save Baghdad from evil Tamerlane. Look fast for Kim Novak as one of the ladies garbed in full-length hooded capes. SuperScope.▼

Son of Spartacus SEE: **Slave, The**

Son of the Gods (1930) **82m.** ** D: Frank Lloyd. Richard Barthelmess, Constance Bennett, Dorothy Matthews, Dickie Moore. Harmless drama. Barthelmess journeys to Europe for college education but finds it no better than home. Fair cast trapped in hokey material.

Son of the Morning Star (1991) **C-186m. TVM** D: Mike Robe. Gary Cole, Rosanna Arquette, Terry O'Quinn, David Strathairn, Dean Stockwell, George American Horse, Rodney A. Grant, Stanley Anderson. Ambitious retelling of the Custer/Little Bighorn saga in epic style—TV's answer to DANCES WITH WOLVES—paced by Cole's vigorous performance, Melissa Mathison's thoughtful, historically accurate script (adapted from the Evan S. Connell historical bestseller), and Kees Van Oostrum's top-notch photography. Originally shown in two parts. Above average. [PG-13]▼●

Son of the Pink Panther (1993) **C-93m.** *½ D: Blake Edwards. Roberto Benigni, Herbert Lom, Claudia Cardinale, Burt Kwouk, Debrah Farentino, Robert Davi, Graham Stark, Jennifer Edwards, Anton Rodgers. Feeble attempt to revive the series, with Benigni as the son of inept Inspector Clouseau, on the trail of a kidnapped princess (Farentino) with plenty of misfired sight gags along the way. Lom, Cardinale, Kwouk and Stark reprise their roles from past entries, and Benigni's enthusiasm helps, but Peter Sellers is sorely missed. Opening animation/live-action credits with Bobby McFerrin's version of the Panther theme is best part of film. Panavision. [PG]▼●

Son of the Shark (1993-French) **C-88m.** ***½ D: Agnes Merlet. Ludovic Vandendaele, Erick Da Silva, Sandrine Blancke, Maxime Leroux. Harrowing, sobering fact-based slice-of-life about two out-of-control pre-teen brothers (Vandendaele and Da Silva, in dazzling performances), who've been abandoned by their mother and abused by their father. One minute they are childlike, the next they are hoodlums who terrorize their hometown. They are neither romanticized nor depicted as villains or victims; the point is that there is no adult around to nurture their good instincts. A grimly realistic film, gutwrenching and heartbreaking. Panavision. ▼

Son of the Sheik, The (1926) **72m.** *** D: George Fitzmaurice. Rudolph Valentino, Vilma Banky, Agnes Ayres, Karl Dane, Bull Montana. Sequel to THE SHEIK contains flavorful account of desert leader who falls in love with dancing-girl Banky. Handsomely mounted silent film is first-rate adventure/romance, with tongue slightly in cheek. Valentino plays a dual role in this, his last film.▼●

Sons and Lovers (1960-British) **103m.** ***½ D: Jack Cardiff. Trevor Howard, Dean Stockwell, Wendy Hiller, Mary Ure, Heather Sears, William Lucas, Donald Pleasence, Ernest Thesiger. Grim D. H. Lawrence story of sensitive youth Stockwell egged on by mother to make something of his life, away from coalmining town and drunken father Howard. Script by Gavin Lambert and T.E.B. Clarke. Freddie Francis' rich cinematography won an Oscar. CinemaScope.

Sons of Katie Elder, The (1965) **C-122m.** *** D: Henry Hathaway. John Wayne, Dean Martin, Martha Hyer, Michael Anderson, Jr., Earl Holliman, Jeremy Slate, James Gregory, George Kennedy, Paul Fix, Dennis Hopper, John Litel, Strother Martin. Typical Western with Duke, Holliman, Anderson, and Martin the rowdy sons of frontier woman Katie Elder, who set out to avenge her death. Film marked return to big screen for Wayne after first highly publicized cancer operation. Lively fun. Music score by Elmer Bernstein. Panavision.▼●

Sons of the Desert (1933) **69m.** ***½ D: William A. Seiter. Stan Laurel, Oliver Hardy, Charley Chase, Mae Busch, Dorothy Christy, Lucien Littlefield. L&H's best feature film; duo sneaks off to fraternal convention without telling the wives; then the fun begins, with Chase as hilariously obnoxious conventioneer. Also shown in computer-colored version. ▼●

Sons o' Guns (1936) **82m.** ** D: Lloyd Bacon. Joe E. Brown, Joan Blondell, Eric Blore, Winifred Shaw, Robert Barrat, Beverly Roberts, Craig Reynolds. So-so comedy with music, with Brown a stage actor humbled into joining the army during WW1; he romances fiery French girl and is accused of being a German spy.

Sooky (1931) **85m.** **½ D: Norman Taurog. Jackie Cooper, Robert Coogan, Jackie Searl, Enid Bennett, Helen Jerome Eddy, Willard Robertson. Middling sequel to SKIPPY with Cooper as Percy Crosby's comic-strip kid and scene-stealing Coogan as his best friend. Lightly comic, with some extra-sentimental scenes.

Sophie's Choice (1982) **C-157m.** **½ D: Alan J. Pakula. Meryl Streep, Kevin Kline, Peter MacNicol, Rita Karin, Stephen D. Newman, Josh Mostel, narrated by Josef Sommer. Streep's Oscar-winning performance is the centerpiece (and raison d'être) for this slavishly faithful, but deadeningly slow-moving, adaptation of William Styron's book about a Polish woman's attempt to justify her existence in America after surviving a living hell during WW2. Nestor Almendros' camera is in love with Streep, but her stunning characterization can't carry the film alone. [R]▼●◗

Sophie's Place SEE: **Crooks and Coronets**

Sophisticated Gents, The (1981) **C-200m. TVM** D: Harry Falk. Bernie Casey, Rosey Grier, Robert Hooks, Ron O'Neal, Thalmus Rasulala, Raymond St. Jacques, Melvin Van Peebles, Dick Anthony Williams, Paul Winfield, Albert Hall, Beah Richards, Janet MacLachlan, Joanna Miles, Denise Nicholas, Marlene Warfield, Harry Guardino, Alfre Woodard. Terrific if overlong multi-character drama focusing on events at the reunion of nine members of a black athletic-social club. Van Peebles wrote the teleplay from John A. Williams' book *The Junior Bachelor Society* and included a pivotal role for himself as a pimp wanted for murder. Above average.▼

So Proudly We Hail! (1943) **126m.** *** D: Mark Sandrich. Claudette Colbert, Paulette Goddard, Veronica Lake, George Reeves, Sonny Tufts, Barbara Britton, Walter Abel. Flag-waving soaper of nurses in WW2 Pacific, headed by Colbert. Versatile cast, action scenes and teary romancing combine well in this woman's service story. Dated but still entertaining.▼

Sorcerer (1977) **C-122m.** **½ D: William Friedkin. Roy Scheider, Bruno Cremer, Francisco Rabal, Amidou, Ramon Bieri, Peter Capell. Four fugitives in seedy Latin American town try to buy freedom by driving trucks of nitroglycerine over bumpy roads to help put out oil fire. Expensive remake of THE WAGES OF FEAR never really catches hold in spite of a few astounding scenes. Strange electronic score by Tangerine Dream. [PG]▼●◗

Sorcerers, The (1967-British) **C-87m.** **½ D: Michael Reeves. Boris Karloff, Catherine Lacey, Ian Ogilvy, Elizabeth Ercy, Susan George. Interesting but flawed low-budgeter. Husband-and-wife scientist team attempt to perfect domination-of-will techniques, persuade young man (Ogilvy) to join experiments. Downhill from there.▼

So Red the Rose (1935) **82m.** **½ D: King Vidor. Margaret Sullavan, Walter Connolly, Randolph Scott, Elizabeth Patterson, Janet Beecher, Robert Cummings, Dickie Moore. Story of Sullavan patiently waiting for Scott to return from Civil War battlefield lacks punch, but is well acted and generally enjoyable; Maxwell Anderson was one of the writers.

Sorority Babes in the Slimeball Bowl-O-Rama (1988) **C-78m.** ** D: David DeCoteau. Linnea Quigley, Michelle Bauer, Andras Jones, Robin Rochelle, Brinke Stevens, Kathi Obrecht, Buck Flower. Wacky fantasy shlocker has sorority girls teaming up with nerds at a shopping mall to do battle with a demonic imp released from a bowling trophy. Good-looking young women in various states of undress are the film's drawing card. [R]▼●

Sorority Girl (1957) **60m.** *½ D: Roger Corman. Susan Cabot, Dick Miller, Barbara Crane, Fay Baker, June Kenney, Barboura O'Neill. Lumbering tale of angst and alienation, 1950s-style. The heroine (Cabot) is a wealthy but warped college coed; she can't fit in with the members of her sorority, so she lashes out at everyone around her. A female version of Calder Willingham's *End as a Man*, filmed that same year as THE STRANGE ONE. Remake: CONFESSIONS OF A SORORITY GIRL (1994). ▼

Sorrento Beach SEE: **Hotel Sorrento**

Sorrow and the Pity, The (1970-Swiss) **260m.** **** D: Marcel Ophuls. Incredibly ambitious documentary about France's performance during WW2 is a total success. Film never becomes dull, in spite of four-and-a-half-hour length, even though bulk of footage is devoted to interviews with those who lived through the Nazi threat. A truly great film. [PG]▼

Sorrowful Jones (1949) **88m.** **½ D: Sidney Lanfield. Bob Hope, Lucille Ball, William Demarest, Mary Jane Saunders, Bruce Cabot, Thomas Gomez. Average racetrack comedy, actually a remake of LITTLE MISS MARKER and hardly as good.▼●

Sorry, Wrong Number (1948) **89m.** ***

D: Anatole Litvak. Barbara Stanwyck, Burt Lancaster, Ann Richards, Wendell Corey, Ed Begley, Leif Erickson, William Conrad. Not up to original radio thriller, movie adaptation is still tense study of woman overhearing murder plan on telephone, discovering she's to be the victim. Stanwyck won an Oscar nomination for her bravura performance; adapted—or rather, expanded—by Lucille Fletcher, from her radio drama (which starred Agnes Moorehead). Remade for cable TV in 1989 with Loni Anderson.▼

S.O.S. Pacific (1960-British) **92m.** **½ D: Guy Green. Eddie Constantine, Pier Angeli, Richard Attenborough, John Gregson, Eva Bartok, Jean Anderson. Middling study of human nature when passengers on plane crash-land on nuclear-test island.

S.O.S. Titanic (1979) **C-105m. TVM** D: William Hale. David Janssen, Cloris Leachman, Susan St. James, David Warner, Ian Holm, Helen Mirren, Harry Andrews. Stylish docu-drama about the oft-told sea disaster, mirroring the fictional elements of the 1953 movie TITANIC and the meticulously detailed facts of the 1958 A NIGHT TO REMEMBER, faithfully recreated here through James Costigan's multicharactered teleplay. Above average.▼

So This Is Africa (1933) **65m.** **½ D: Eddie Cline. Bert Wheeler, Robert Woolsey, Raquel Torres, Esther Muir, Berton Churchill, Clarence Moorehouse, Henry Armetta. Wheeler & Woolsey play vaudevillians who go on a safari to film a jungle movie with the great Mrs. Martini Johnson (Muir). Typical W&W nonsense, though this film was notorious for its censorship problems: Norman Krasna's script is filled to overflowing with sexual double-entendres, even in this version, which was severely cut to satisfy Production Code standards. Some prints run 54m.

So This Is Love (1953) **C-101m.** ** D: Gordon Douglas. Kathryn Grayson, Merv Griffin, Walter Abel, Rosemary DeCamp, Jeff Donnell. Glossy, empty biography of opera star Grace Moore, antiseptically played by Grayson.▼

So This Is New York (1948) **79m.** *** D: Richard Fleischer. Henry Morgan, Rudy Vallee, Bill Goodwin, Hugh Herbert, Leo Gorcey, Virginia Grey, Dona Drake. Cheaply filmed but hilarious adaptation of Ring Lardner's *The Big Town*. Small-towner Morgan's inherits money; they decide to go to N.Y.C., encountering its strange ways. Ingenious, offbeat script; radio/TV star Morgan fares well in screen debut, helped by top supporting cast.

So This Is Paris (1926) **68m.** *** D: Ernst Lubitsch. Monte Blue, Patsy Ruth Miller, Lilyan Tashman, Andre Beranger, Myrna Loy, Sidney D'Albrook. Frothy Lubitsch silent; sophisticated romantic comedy of dancers Tashman and Berenger flirting with Dr. Blue and wife Miller. Entertaining, fast-moving, and funny.▼

So This Is Paris (1954) **C-96m.** **½ D: Richard Quine. Tony Curtis, Gloria DeHaven, Gene Nelson, Corinne Calvet, Paul Gilbert, Allison Hayes, Mara Corday. Perky stars enliven this unmemorable musical of gobs on leave in France. Nelson also served as co-choreographer.

Sotto, Sotto (1984-Italian) **C-105m.** **½ D: Lina Wertmuller. Enrico Montesano, Veronica Lario, Luisa de Santis, Massimo Wertmuller. Obvious, but not unentertaining, tale of Lario, who finds herself attracted to longtime best friend de Santis; her husband (Montesano), a sexist animal with a fragile ego, then goes comically berserk. Incidentally, actor Wertmuller is the director's nephew. [R]▼

Soul Food (1997) **C-114m.** *** D: George Tillman, Jr. Vanessa L. Williams, Vivica A. Fox, Nia Long, Brandon Hammond, Michael Beach, Mekhi Phifer, Irma P. Hall. When Chicago-based black matriarch Hall, the glue that holds her family together, falls ill, grandson Hammond does his best to step in. A rare '90s movie about family values that really works. Excellent ensemble cast in a poignant story that is honest and heartwarming. [R]▼●◗

Soul Man (1986) **C-101m.** ** D: Steve Miner. C. Thomas Howell, Arye Gross, Rae Dawn Chong, James Earl Jones, Melora Hardin, Leslie Nielsen, James B. Sikking, Max Wright, Jeff Altman, Julia Louis-Dreyfus, Ron Reagan. Young man desperate to go to Harvard Law School masquerades as a black in order to get minority scholarship. Slick but distressingly superficial; if this is the 1980s version of social satire, we're all in trouble. [PG-13]▼●

Soul of a Monster, The (1944) **61m.** BOMB D: Will Jason. Rose Hobart, George Macready, Jim Bannon, Jeanne Bates. Other-worldly Hobart has strange control over doctor Macready.

Soul of Nigger Charley, The (1973) **C-104m.** *½ D: Larry Spangler. Fred Williamson, D'Urville Martin, Denise Nicholas, Pedro Armendariz, Jr., Richard Farnsworth. Weak sequel to LEGEND OF NIGGER CHARLEY finds Charley trying to free slaves held captive by former Confederate Army officer in Mexico. Panavision. [R]

Soul of the Game (1996) **C-95m. TVM** D: Kevin Rodney Sullivan. Delroy Lindo, Mykelti Williamson, Blair Underwood, Edward Herrmann, R. Lee Ermey, Gina Ravera, Salli Richardson. Evocative study of baseball greats Satchel Paige, Josh Gibson, and young Jackie Robinson on the eve of integration in the major leagues. The question: Who will be the first to get the call? Lindo is especially riveting as the barnstorming Paige (portrayed in depth only one other time, by Louis Gossett, Jr., in the 1981 TV movie DON'T LOOK BACK). Written with attitude by David Himmelstein from a story by Gary Hoffman. Made for cable. Above average.▼●

Souls at Sea (1937) **92m.** *** D: Henry Hathaway. Gary Cooper, George Raft, Frances Dee, Olympe Bradna, Henry Wilcoxon, Harry Carey, Robert Cummings, Joseph Schildkraut, George Zucco, Virginia Weidler. Fine actioner with Cooper and Raft struggling to save lives during ship tragedy; Cooper wrongly accused of irresponsibility. The stars make a good team here.▼

Souls for Sale SEE: **Confessions of an Opium Eater**

Soul to Soul (1971) **C-95m.** *** D: Denis Sanders. Wilson Pickett, Ike and Tina Turner, Santana, Roberta Flack, Les McCann, Willie Bobo, Eddie Harris, The Staple Singers. Good documentary of American soul, jazz and gospel performers in a concert commemorating the 14th anniversary of Ghanaian independence. Pickett is in top form singing "Funky Broadway" and "Land of 1,000 Dances." [G]▼

Sound and the Fury, The (1959) **C-115m.** **½ D: Martin Ritt. Yul Brynner, Joanne Woodward, Margaret Leighton, Stuart Whitman, Ethel Waters, Jack Warden, Albert Dekker. Strange adaptation of William Faulkner novel becomes plodding tale of girl seeking independence from strict family rule in the South. CinemaScope.

Sound Barrier, The SEE: **Breaking the Sound Barrier**

Sounder (1972) **C-105m.** **** D: Martin Ritt. Cicely Tyson, Paul Winfield, Kevin Hooks, Carmen Mathews, Taj Mahal, James Best, Janet MacLachlan. Beautiful film, romanticizing in a positive sense experiences of black sharecropper family in 1930s —and the maturation of young Hooks. Full of fine performances that make characters utterly real. Mahal also composed the score. Screenplay by Lonnie Elder III from William Armstrong's novel. Sequel: PART 2, SOUNDER. Panavision. [G]▼●

Sounder, Part Two SEE: **Part 2, Sounder**

Sound Off (1952) **C-83m.** ** D: Richard Quine. Mickey Rooney, Anne James, John Archer, Sammy White. Too-often unimaginative Army comedy with Rooney a performer who's drafted and can't stop showing off. Written by Quine and Blake Edwards.

Sound of Fury, The SEE: **Try and Get Me!**

Sound of Music, The (1965) **C-174m.** ***½ D: Robert Wise. Julie Andrews, Christopher Plummer, Eleanor Parker, Peggy Wood, Richard Haydn, Anna Lee, Portia Nelson, Norma Varden, Marni Nixon. The children: Charmian Carr, Nicolas Hammond, Heather Menzies, Duane Chase, Angela Cartwright, Debbie Turner, Kym Karath. Call it corn if you like, but blockbuster Rodgers & Hammerstein musical based on Austria's real-life Von Trapp family, who fled their homeland in 1938 to escape from Nazi rule, pleased more people than practically any other film in history. Fine music, beautiful scenery help offset coy aspects of script. Five Oscars include Best Picture, Director, Score Adaptation (Irwin Kostal), Editing (William Reynolds). Screenplay by Ernest Lehman, based on the Howard Lindsay–Russel Crouse Broadway show. Songs include "Climb Ev'ry Mountain" and title tune. Usually cut for TV to 145m. Todd-AO▼●

Soupçon (1979-French) **C-93m.** **½ D: Jean-Charles Tacchella. Jean Carmet, Marie Dubois, Alain Doutey, Rachel Jenevein, Jose Laccioni. Middle-aged couple (Carmet, Dubois) decide to separate after a quarter-century of marriage. Spirited and attractively played, but still forgettable; a disappointment from the director of COUSIN, COUSINE.

Soup for One (1982) **C-87m.** **½ D: Jonathan Kaufer. Saul Rubinek, Marcia Strassman, Gerrit Graham, Teddy Pendergrass, Richard Libertini, Andrea Martin, Lewis J. Stadlen. Sometimes winning but uneven account of single New Yorker Rubinek searching for his dream girl. The cast is game; solid work by 26-year-old director Kaufer. [R]▼

Soup to Nuts (1930) **71m.** **½ D: Benjamin Stoloff. Ted Healy, Charles Winninger, Frances McCoy, Lucile Browne, Stanley Smith, Hallam Cooley, Roscoe Ates, Billy Barty. Oddball early talkie about a shopkeeper in trouble and some neighborhood firemen; written by cartoonist Rube Goldberg. Its chief point of interest today is the film debut of Healy's sidekicks The Three Stooges, then actually four in number (Moe, Larry, Shemp, and Fred Sanborn). They provide the movie's highlight, doing their vaudeville routine at a firemen's ball.

Source, The (1999) **C-88m.** *** D: Chuck Workman. Pop-style documentary on the Beat movement, drawing on archival footage of Jack Kerouac plus fresh material on William Burroughs and Allen Ginsberg. Audience-friendly rather than scholarly, this lively film serves as an excellent primer on this seminal movement in American culture. Key poems by Kerouac, Burroughs, and Ginsberg are performed on-camera by a well-chosen Johnny Depp, Dennis Hopper, and John Turturro, respectively.▼

Sour Grapes (1998) **C-92m.** **½ D: Larry David. Steven Weber, Craig Bierko, Matt Keeslar, Karen Sillas, Robyn Peterman, Viola Harris, Jennifer Leigh Warren. Bierko hits a $400,000 slot machine jackpot at a casino; Weber, his doctor cousin, thinks he's due half the loot because he loaned him the necessary quarters. Occasionally very funny, the movie is undermined by overemphatic "comedy" acting, unsympathetic characters, and a sitcom approach. Writer-director David cocreated *Seinfeld,* which explains both the good and the bad stuff here. [R]▼●◗

South Central (1992) **C-99m.** **½ D: Steve Anderson. Glenn Plummer, Byron Keith Minns, LaRita Shelby, Carl Lumbly, Lexie D. Bingham, Christian Coleman. Sobering, well-meaning drama of life and desperation in inner-city L.A. is similar in theme to (but not nearly as effective as) BOYZ N THE HOOD. Plummer is aces as an embattled street-gang veteran who undergoes an odyssey of transformation, and determines to spare his young son (Coleman) from the ravages of gang life. Anderson scripted, based on the novel *Crips* by L.A. schoolteacher Donald Bakeer. The executive producer was Oliver Stone. [R]▼●◗

Southern Comfort (1981) **C-106m.** ** D: Walter Hill. Keith Carradine, Powers Boothe, Fred Ward, Franklyn Seales, T. K. Carter, Lewis Smith, Les Lannom, Peter Coyote, Brion James. Macho National Guardsmen patronize Cajuns in the Louisiana swamp, much to their regret. Survival-of-the-fittest yarn is an intellectually muddled, Grade B DELIVERANCE, despite its crisp direction. [R]▼●

Southerner, The (1945) **91m.** **** D: Jean Renoir. Zachary Scott, Betty Field, Beulah Bondi, J. Carrol Naish, Norman Lloyd, Bunny Sunshine, Jay Gilpin, Estelle Taylor, Percy Kilbride, Blanche Yurka. Superb drama of family struggling to make farmland self-supporting against serious odds. Renoir adapted George Sessions Perry's novel *Hold Autumn in Your Hand.*▼◗

Southern Star, The (1969-British-French-U.S.) **C-102m.** **½ D: Sidney Hayers. George Segal, Ursula Andress, Orson Welles, Ian Hendry, Harry Andrews, Michel Constantin. Uneven combination comedy-adventure detailing multiparty chase for possession of unusually large diamond boasts beautiful locations in Senegal, Africa, but not much else. Based on a Jules Verne novel. Techniscope. [M/PG]

Southern Yankee, A (1948) **90m.** *** D: Edward Sedgwick. Red Skelton, Brian Donlevy, Arlene Dahl, George Coulouris, Lloyd Gough, John Ireland, Charles Dingle, Joyce Compton. Hilarious Skelton comedy set during Civil War with Red a bumbling Yankee spy down South. Reminiscent of silent comedies, since Buster Keaton devised many of the film's gags.▼

South of Pago Pago (1940) **98m.** ** D: Alfred E. Green. Victor McLaglen, Jon Hall, Frances Farmer, Olympe Bradna, Gene Lockhart. Juvenile actioner of pirates stealing natives' supply of pearls, encountering local hostility.▼

South of Reno (1987) **C-94m.** **½ D: Mark Rezyka. Jeffrey Osterhage, Lisa Blount, Joe Phelan, Lewis Van Bergen, Julia Montgomery, Billy Bob Thornton. Desert hermit Osterhage discovers that wife Blount has been unfaithful. Well made and visually arresting but convoluted plot-wise; still, an impressive first feature from Rezyka, who also coscripted. [R]▼●

South of St. Louis (1949) **C-88m.** **½ D: Ray Enright. Joel McCrea, Alexis Smith, Zachary Scott, Dorothy Malone, Douglas Kennedy, Alan Hale, Victor Jory. Three ranching partners (McCrea, Scott, Kennedy) fall into dispute over land, money, Civil War gun-running, and women. Unmemorable Western has good cast, fast pacing, and Technicolor on its side.▼

South Pacific (1958) **C-151m.** **½ D: Joshua Logan. Rossano Brazzi, Mitzi Gaynor, John Kerr, Ray Walston, Juanita Hall, France Nuyen, Tom Laughlin, voice of Giorgio Tozzi. Disappointing filmization of great Rodgers & Hammerstein show; adaptation of James Michener's moving vignettes about WW2 life on Pacific island needs dynamic personalities to make it catch fire, and they aren't here. Even location filming is lackluster. Adequate but hardly memorable. Songs include "Some Enchanted Evening," "There Is Nothing Like a Dame." Among the sailors and servicemen you'll spot John Gabriel, Ron Ely, Doug McClure, and James Stacy. Originally shown at 171m. Todd-AO. ▼●◗

South Park: Bigger, Longer & Uncut (1999) **C-81m.** *** D: Trey Parker. Voices of Trey Parker, Matt Stone, Mary Kay Bergman, Isaac Hayes, George Clooney, Brent Spiner, Minnie Driver, Dave Foley, Eric Idle, Mike Judge, Nick Rhodes, Stewart Copeland. The pint-sized, animated kids of South Park, Colorado, are so fond of the new R-rated Terrance and Phillip movie that they start imitating its rude dialogue. This inspires the parents of South Park to mount a campaign against the movie's stars—and homeland, Canada. Sharp, funny (and yes, foul-mouthed) satire, based on the irreverent TV series; sparked by great songs by Parker and Marc Shaiman. [R]▼●◗

South Riding (1938-British) **84m.** *** D: Victor Saville. Ralph Richardson, Edna Best, Edmund Gwenn, Ann Todd, John Clements, Marie Lohr, Milton Rosmer, Glynis Johns. Enjoyable drama from Winifred Holtby's novel about political and personal problems among a group of characters living in Yorkshire. Smoothly made and superbly acted by a flawless cast. Film debut of fifteen-year-old Johns, cast as Richardson's daughter. Original British running time: 90m.▼

South Sea Sinner (1950) **88m.** ** D: H.

Bruce Humberstone. Macdonald Carey, Shelley Winters, Luther Adler, Frank Lovejoy, Liberace. Muddled melodrama involving fugitive from justice being intimidated by those on island who knew his past; Winters is blowsy cafe singer. Remake of 1940 SEVEN SINNERS.

South Sea Woman (1953) **99m.** **½ D: Arthur Lubin. Burt Lancaster, Virginia Mayo, Chuck Connors, Arthur Shields, Paul Burke. Murky tropical isle story of love and deceit with soldier Lancaster sparking with Mayo.

Southside 1-1000 (1950) **73m.** **½ D: Boris Ingster. Don Defore, Andrea King, George Tobias, Barry Kelley. Straightforward narrative of federal agent capturing counterfeiters.▼

Southwest Passage (1954) **C-82m.** ** D: Ray Nazarro. Joanne Dru, Rod Cameron, John Ireland, John Dehner, Guinn Williams, Mark Hanna. Familiar tale of bank robber and gal joining up with settlers heading West, staving off Indian attack.

So Well Remembered (1947-British) **114m.** *** D: Edward Dmytryk. John Mills, Martha Scott, Trevor Howard, Patricia Roc, Richard Carlson, Ivor Barnard. Author James Hilton narrates saga (adapted by John Paxton) of earnest newspaper editor (Mills) determined to improve living conditions in factory town, sidetracked by marriage to blindly ambitious woman (Scott). Very young Juliet Mills has bit part.●

Soylent Green (1973) **C-100m.** ** D: Richard Fleischer. Charlton Heston, Edward G. Robinson, Leigh Taylor-Young, Chuck Connors, Joseph Cotten, Brock Peters, Paula Kelly, Whit Bissell, Mike Henry, Dick Van Patten. Well-intentioned but cardboard adaptation of Harry Harrison's science-fiction classic *Make Room! Make Room!* In the year 2022, Manhattan has become an overcrowded hellhole; cop Heston, investigating murder of bigwig, stumbles onto explosive government secret (which you'll figure out long before he does). Robinson is splendid in his final film; title refers to a precious foodstuff made of soybeans and lentils. Panavision. [PG]▼●

So Young, So Bad (1950) **91m.** **½ D: Bernard Vorhaus. Paul Henreid, Catherine McLeod, Grace Coppin, Cecil Clovelly, Anne Francis, Rosita (Rita) Moreno, Anne Jackson, Enid Pulver. Humane psychiatrist Henreid takes on superintendent Clovelly and sadistic head matron Coppin at a correctional home for girls. Effective study of female juvenile delinquency.

So You Won't Talk (1940) **69m.** ** D: Edward Sedgwick. Joe E. Brown, Frances Robinson, Vivienne Osborne, Bernard Nedell, Tom Dugan. Good, typical mistaken identity comedy with bookworm Brown, a dead ringer for notorious mobster.

Spaceballs (1987) **C-96m.** **½ D: Mel Brooks. Mel Brooks, John Candy, Rick Moranis, Bill Pullman, Daphne Zuniga, Dick Van Patten, George Wyner, Michael Winslow, Lorene Yarnell, John Hurt, Ronny Graham, Rhonda Shear, voices of Joan Rivers, Dom DeLuise. Likably silly parody of STAR WARS (years after the fact) is basically a collection of jokes, both verbal and visual. Enough of them are funny to make for pleasant, if not hilarious, fare. Surprisingly innocuous for Brooks and Co., with Mel tackling two roles, including the diminutive Yogurt. Super 35. [PG] ▼●◗

SpaceCamp (1986) **C-107m.** ** D: Harry Winer. Kate Capshaw, Lea Thompson, Kelly Preston, Larry B. Scott, Leaf Phoenix, Tate Donovan, Tom Skerritt, Barry Primus, Terry O'Quinn, Mitchell Anderson, T. Scott Coffey. Or, BRATS IN SPACE, the story of some kids who wouldn't rate at McDonald's College of Hamburger Knowledge, but somehow get chosen to train at NASA summer camp—and accidentally get launched into space. There's a cute robot, but other special effects are way below par. [PG]▼●

Space Children, The (1958) **69m.** ** D: Jack Arnold. Michel Ray, Peggy Webber, Adam Williams, Jackie Coogan, Johnny Washbrook. Strange force brainwashes children into performing sabotage at Pacific nuclear test site. Anti-war film isn't up to Arnold's other 50s science-fiction classics, but is sufficiently offbeat to warrant a peek. VistaVision.

Spaced Invaders (1990) **C-102m.** *½ D: Patrick Read Johnson. Douglas Barr, Royal Dano, Ariana Richards, J. J. Anderson, Gregg Berger, Kevin Thompson, Jimmy Briscoe. Martians, out to "kick some Earthling butt," fly into a Mayberry-type burg after mistaking a Halloween rebroadcast of Orson Welles' *War of the Worlds* for legitimate invasion orders. Have you ever noticed that Welles couldn't get financing for decades, but movies like this keep getting made? Criminally overlong. [PG]▼●

Spaceflight IC-1 (1965-British) **65m.** *½ D: Bernard Knowles. Bill Williams, Norma West, John Cairney, Linda Marlowe, Jeremy Longhurst. Dreary, talky film with no space thrills and little action, set aboard a spaceship between planets.

Spacehunter: Adventures in the Forbidden Zone (1983-Canadian) **C-90m.** *½ D: Lamont Johnson. Peter Strauss, Molly Ringwald, Ernie Hudson, Andrea Marcovicci. Title character roams a planet's barren wasteland in order to rescue three damsels in distress, who are being held captive by a vicious mutant called Overdog. Boring and obnoxious, even in 3-D. Panavision. [PG]▼●

Space Jam (1996) **C-87m.** *** D: Joe Pytka. Bugs Bunny, Michael Jordan,

Wayne Knight, Theresa Randle, Larry Bird, Charles Barkley, Patrick Ewing, Muggsy Bogues, Larry Johnson; voices of Danny DeVito, Billy West, Dee Bradley Baker, Bob Bergen, Bill Farmer, June Foray. A "high-concept" movie that actually works: basketball superstar Jordan is sucked into Looney Tune Land to help Bugs Bunny, Daffy Duck, Porky Pig and Co. square off against a group of space invaders in a do-or-die basketball game. Jordan is very engaging, the vintage characters perform admirably (although whoever "airbrushed" them had a heavy hand), and the computer-generated special effects are a collective knockout. Bill Murray appears unbilled, and many sports figures appear as themselves. [PG]▼●◗

Space Master X-7 (1958) **71m.** ** D: Edward Bernds. Bill Williams, Robert Ellis, Lyn Thomas, Paul Frees, Joan Barry, Thomas Browne Henry, Moe Howard. A returning satellite brings with it a fast-growing fungus, dubbed "Blood Rust." Williams and Ellis track down the woman who is unknowingly spreading the deadly stuff. Routine but competent. Moe plays a cab driver. Regalscope.

Space Rage (1985) **C-77m.** BOMB D: Conrad Palmisano. Richard Farnsworth, Michael Paré, John Laughlin, Lee Purcell, Lewis Van Bergen, William Windom. Meek space Western is set on a prison planet. Farnsworth is ex-cop who straps on his laser beam six-shooter to teach Paré and the other outlaws a lesson; he should've turned the laser on this bomb instead! [R]▼

Space Raiders (1983) **C-82m.** ** D: Howard R. Cohen. Vince Edwards, David Mendenhall, Patsy Pease, Thom Christopher, Luca Bercovici, Dick Miller. This toothless adventure is another Roger Corman produced space opera using special effects footage and music from BATTLE BEYOND THE STARS. Acceptable genre fare for the undemanding viewer. [PG]▼

Spaceship SEE: **Creature Wasn't Nice, The**

Spaceship to the Unknown (1936) **97m.** **½ D: Frederick Stephani. Buster Crabbe, Jean Rogers, Frank Shannon, Charles Middleton, Priscilla Lawson, John Lipson. Condensed version of FLASH GORDON serial covering first half of original story. With planet Mongo heading toward collision with Earth, Flash, Dale Arden, and Dr. Zarkov fly rocketship to remedy impending disaster. Uninspired handling of footage from this famous serial.

Space Travellers SEE: **Marooned**

Spaceways (1953-British) **76m.** *½ D: Terence Fisher. Howard Duff, Eva Bartok, Andrew Osborn, Alan Wheatley. To prove he hasn't murdered her husband and stuffed him into a just-launched satellite, Duff and Bartok go up to look on the next rocket, but that happens only at the very end of this slow movie. From a novel and radio play by Charles Eric Maine.

Spanish Affair (1958-Spanish) **C-95m.** ** D: Don Siegel. Richard Kiley, Carmen Sevilla, Jose Guardiola, Jesus Tordesillas. Virtually a travelogue pegged on slight plot of Kiley, American architect, traveling in Iberia, falling in love with local girl; nice scenery, but hardly typical Siegel fare. VistaVision.

Spanish Cape Mystery, The (1935) **65m.** **½ D: Lewis D. Collins. Helen Twelvetrees, Donald Cook, Berton Churchill, Frank Sheridan, Guy Usher. First *Ellery Queen* movie finds master sleuth (Cook) investigating murder at seaside resort and falling in love with primary suspect (Twelvetrees). Hokey denouement mars otherwise enjoyable whodunit.

Spanish Gardener, The (1956-British) **C-95m.** *** D: Philip Leacock. Dirk Bogarde, Maureen Swanson, Jon Whiteley, Cyril Cusack, Bernard Lee, Michael Hordern. When gardener befriends employer's young son, diplomat father becomes jealous. Intelligent and beautifully filmed adaptation of A. J. Cronin novel. VistaVision.

Spanish Main, The (1945) **C-100m.** **½ D: Frank Borzage. Paul Henreid, Maureen O'Hara, Walter Slezak, Binnie Barnes, John Emery, Barton MacLane. Colorful escapism with swashbuckling pirate Henreid foiling villain Slezak, winning O'Hara. ●

Spanish Prisoner, The (1998) **C-112m.** **½ D: David Mamet. Campbell Scott, Steve Martin, Rebecca Pidgeon, Ben Gazzara, Ricky Jay, Felicity Huffman, Ed O'Neill. Naive young man, who's developed a secret and highly valuable program for a high-tech company, is concerned that he won't be properly compensated and thus is easy prey for those who would steal the secret. *Too* easy, if you ask us, and that's the problem with this ice-cold but intriguing Mamet screenplay: we didn't buy it at crucial points in its serpentine story. Scott and Martin are excellent; leading lady Pidgeon is Mrs. Mamet. [PG]▼●◗

Spanking the Monkey (1994) **C-106m.** **½ D: David O. Russell. Jeremy Davies, Alberta Watson, Benjamin Hendrickson, Carla Gallo, Matthew Puckett, Judette Jones. Just your average black comedy about masturbation and incest: Bright teenager is told by his traveling-salesman father that he must sacrifice a prestigious summer internship to stay home and tend to his bedridden mother. The intimacy of having to take care of her every need soon leads to unexpected behavior. Debuting writer-director Russell shows assuredness and maintains credibility throughout (thanks, too, to bull's-eye performances), but the tone of the film wavers uncomfortably from comedy to drama. A film festival sleeper and audience favorite.▼●

Spare the Rod (1961-British) **93m.** **½ D: Leslie Norman. Max Bygraves, Donald

Pleasence, Jean Anderson, Betty McDowall, Peter Reynolds, Geoffrey Keen. Bygraves is idealistic teacher in tough London school trying to communicate with pupils and cope with the system; OK drama.

Sparkle (1976) **C-100m.** **½ D: Sam O'Steen. Philip M. (Michael) Thomas, Irene Cara, Lonette McKee, Dwan Smith, Mary Alice, Dorian Harewood, Tony King. Rise of singing group not unlike The Supremes suffers from cliché overdose, but benefits from slick filmmaking, good musical numbers (by Curtis Mayfield), vivid performance by McKee. Worth comparing to later (and similar) Broadway musical *Dreamgirls*. [PG]▼

Sparrows (1926) **84m.** *** D: William Beaudine. Mary Pickford, Gustav von Seyffertitz, Roy Stewart, Mary Louise Miller, Charlotte Mineau, Spec O'Donnell. One of Mary's best silent pictures is a fullblooded melodrama about intrepid girl who struggles to protect band of younger orphans from their wicked captor.▼●◗

Spartacus (1960) **C-184m.** ***½ D: Stanley Kubrick. Kirk Douglas, Laurence Olivier, Jean Simmons, Tony Curtis, Charles Laughton, Peter Ustinov, John Gavin, Nina Foch, Herbert Lom, John Ireland, Charles McGraw, Woody Strode, Joanna Barnes. Epic-scale saga with Douglas as a rebellious slave who leads a crusade for freedom against the forces of the Roman Empire. Overlength (particularly in fully restored version released in 1991) and some dramatic weaknesses are offset by Alex North's magnificent score, staggering battle scenes, and the delicious performances of Olivier, Laughton, and especially Ustinov, who won a Best Supporting Actor Oscar for his scene-stealing work. Oscars also went to Art Direction, Costume Design, and Russell Metty's Cinematography. Screenplay by Dalton Trumbo from the Howard Fast novel. Cut for 1967 reissue. In restored print, Anthony Hopkins dubbed Olivier's voice for notorious bathing scene with Tony Curtis. Super Technirama 70.▼●◗

Spasms (1983-Canadian) **C-87m.** BOMB D: William Fruet. Peter Fonda, Oliver Reed, Kerrie Keane, Al Waxman, Marilyn Lightstone, George Bloomfield. Reed has a telepathic—or, should we say, telepathetic—connection with a deadly serpent. Grade Z junk; filmed in 1981. Aka DEATH BITE. [R]▼

Spawn (1997) **C-97m.** ** D: Mark A. Z. Dippé. John Leguizamo, Michael Jai White, Martin Sheen, Theresa Randle, D. B. Sweeney, Nicol Williamson, Melinda Clarke, Miko Hughes. Government assassin White is killed by evil boss Sheen and goes to Hell, where a demon endows him with great powers and returns him to Earth. Despite the efforts of infernal clown Leguizamo, he becomes a hero. Baroque visual style is film's major virtue, but that can't overcome the many faults, including a boring, familiar, and illogical plot. Love that cape, though. From Todd McFarlane's comic book. Director's cut, rated R, has over a minute of additional footage. [PG-13]▼●◗

Spawn of the North (1938) **110m.** *** D: Henry Hathaway. George Raft, Henry Fonda, Dorothy Lamour, Louise Platt, John Barrymore, Akim Tamiroff, Lynne Overman. Action-packed film of Alaskan fisheries with good cast; Lamour surprisingly good. Barrymore amusing as talky newspaperman. The special photographic and sound effects earned a special Academy Award. Remade as ALASKA SEAS.▼

Speak Easily (1932) **82m.** *** D: Edward Sedgwick. Buster Keaton, Jimmy Durante, Ruth Selwyn, Thelma Todd, Hedda Hopper, Sidney Toler. Dimwitted professor Keaton gets involved with show troupe en route to Broadway. One of Keaton's best talkies, with Durante in good form, Todd a wonderful vamp, Toler an amusing stage manager.▼●

Speaking of Murder (1959-French) **80m.** **½ D: Gilles Grangier. Jean Gabin, Annie Girardot, Paul Frankeur, Lino Ventura. Sensibly handled drama of brothers involved with life of crime.

Speaking Parts (1989-Canadian) **C-92m.** *** D: Atom Egoyan. Michael McManus, Arsinée Khanjian, Gabrielle Rose, Tony Nardi, David Hemblen, Patricia Collins, Gerard Parkes. Fascinating account of laundry worker Khanjian and her fixation on aspiring actor McManus, who finds himself in an unusual relationship with screenwriter Rose. Sinuous story about three lost souls whose lives intersect, in person and on video. Very much of a piece with writer-director Egoyan's other work.▼●

Special Agent (1935) **78m.** **½ D: William Keighley. Bette Davis, George Brent, Ricardo Cortez, Jack LaRue, Henry O'Neill. Programmer about Brent using Davis to get low-down on racketeer Cortez.

Special Bulletin (1983) **C-105m. TVM** D: Edward Zwick. Ed Flanders, Kathryn Walker, Roxanne Hart, Christopher Allport, Rosalind Cash, David Clennon, David Rasche, Michael Madsen. Shattering TV experience, presented on tape as a simulated television newscast, about the threatened nuclear destruction of Charleston, S.C., by quintet of war protesters who demand the dismantling of America's arsenal of warheads; interesting subplot examines how the media react in the face of such incidents. Multi-Emmy winner written by *thirtysomething*'s Zwick and Marshall Herskovitz. Way above average.▼

Special Day, A (1977-Italian-Canadian) **C-106m.** **½ D: Ettore Scola. Sophia Loren, Marcello Mastroianni, John Vernon, Françoise Berd, Nicole Magny. Two lonely people chance to meet on an eventful day in

1938; Loren is frumpy housewife, Mastroianni a troubled homosexual. Fine performances bolster this pleasant but trifling film.▼●
Special Delivery (1955) **86m.** ** D: John Brahm. Joseph Cotten, Eva Bartok, Niall MacGinnis, Rene Deltgen. Mild froth with Cotten on U.S. diplomatic staff posted in Iron Curtain country, dealing with an abandoned baby and curvaceous refugee Bartok.
Special Delivery (1976) **C-99m.** *** D: Paul Wendkos. Bo Svenson, Cybill Shepherd, Michael Gwynne, Tom Atkins, Sorrell Booke, Jeff Goldblum, Vic Tayback, Deidre Hall, Gerrit Graham. Diverting comedy-action caper has Vietnam vets led by Svenson robbing a bank. When only Svenson escapes, he has to contend with nutty artist Shepherd (who's quite good) and killers after he stuffs the loot into a mailbox. Aka DANGEROUS BREAK. [PG]▼
Special Effects (1984) **C-93m.** **½ D: Larry Cohen. Zoe Tamerlis, Eric Bogosian, Brad Rijn, Kevin O'Connor, Bill Oland. Intriguing but uneven tale of a down-on-his-luck director who films the murder of a young actress, and commences making a movie about his deed. He even finds someone to star in his epic who resembles his victim; both are played by Tamerlis. [R]▼
Specialist, The (1975) **C-93m.** ** D: Hikmet Avedis. Ahna Capri, John Anderson, Adam West, Alvy Moore, Christiane Schmidtmer, Marlene Schmidt. Campy exploitation film has Capri well cast as a zaftig female version of usual macho killer-for-hire. Writer-producer Schmidt (director Avedis' wife) plays West's wife. [R]▼
Specialist, The (1994) **C-109m.** ** D: Luis Llosa. Sylvester Stallone, Sharon Stone, James Woods, Rod Steiger, Eric Roberts, Mario Ernesto Sanchez. Explosives expert and freelance hit man Stallone, sullenly suffering angst over his CIA activities, is approached by Stone, who wants him to kill Roberts, the man who murdered her parents years earlier. But Stallone has been targeted by kinetic bad guy Woods and Cuban gangster Steiger, Roberts' father (who sounds like Ricky Ricardo and looks like Fred Mertz). Woods, in a funny, dynamic performance, breezily walks off with the movie. And he's welcome to it. Some good stunts and good work by Stone help keep it watchable. [R]▼●◗
Special Section (1975-French) **C-110m.** ** D: Costa-Gavras. Louis Seigner, Michel Lonsdale, Jacques Perrin, Bruno Cremer, Pierre Dux, Henri Serre. Overlong, excessively wordy drama of true happening in occupied Paris in 1941. Four expendables are tried and ceremonially condemned for the murder of a young German naval cadet. Some interest. [PG]
Special Treatment (1980-Yugoslavian) **C-94m.** *** D: Goran Paskaljevic. Ljuba Tadic, Dusica Zegarac, Danilo Stojkovic, Milena Dravic, Petar Kralj. Fanatical doctor Tadic brings a group of alcoholics he's been treating to a brewery to show off his skills as a healer; of course, his charges don't remain sober for long. Strange, deadpan comedy is occasionally slow but mostly funny.
Species (1995) **C-111m.** **½ D: Roger Donaldson. Ben Kingsley, Michael Madsen, Forest Whitaker, Natasha Henstridge, Alfred Molina, Marg Helgenberger, Whip Hubley, Michelle Williams, Jordan Lund. DNA-tampering scientists at a Utah facility ultimately get theirs after creating a murderous creature, complete with tentacles, who's packaged like a blond centerfold. Fast and not without entertainment value, but don't look at yourself in the mirror too closely if you end up defending it. Direction is somewhat sturdier than the script, which has its share of (we think) unintentional howlers. Followed by a sequel. Panavision. [R]▼●◗
Species II (1998) **C-95m.** BOMB D: Peter Medak. Natasha Henstridge, Michael Madsen, Marg Helgenberger, Mykelti Williamson, Justin Lazard, James Cromwell, George Dzundza, Richard Belzer. The first man on Mars gets infested with alien DNA, and begins raping women who immediately, and fatally, give birth. Elsewhere, scientists have re-created the half-alien woman from the first film, hoping she'll be nice this time. Compared to this clunker, the first looks like a collaboration between Arthur C. Clarke and Ray Bradbury. Peter Boyle appears unbilled. [R]▼●◗
Speckled Band, The (1931-British) **90m.** *½ D: Jack Raymond. Lyn Harding, Raymond Massey, Angela Baddeley, Nancy Price, Athole Stewart. Slow-as-molasses version of the Conan Doyle story, with Sherlock Holmes coming to the aid of a frightened girl (Baddeley), whose sister has been murdered. Interesting to see Massey cast as the sleuth, but this film is really boring. ▼
Specter of the Rose (1946) **90m.** *** D: Ben Hecht. Judith Anderson, Michael Chekhov, Ivan Kirov, Viola Essen, Lionel Stander. Uniquely individual melodrama by Hecht set in the world of ballet, with an unusual cast, including dancers, non-actors, and scene-stealing Chekhov. Fascinating (some might even say strange), though definitely not for all tastes.▼
Speechless (1994) **C-98m.** **½ D: Ron Underwood. Michael Keaton, Geena Davis, Christopher Reeve, Bonnie Bedelia, Ernie Hudson, Charles Martin Smith, Gailard Sartain, Ray Baker, Mitchell Ryan, Harry Shearer, Steven Wright. Keaton and Davis fall in love, unaware that they work as speechwriters for opposing political candidates in a tough Arizona senate race. Cheerful contemporary comedy, with amusing digs at politics and the news media. How well you tolerate the ups and downs of the script and its protracted climax will depend

on your fondness for the two stars: Their engaging personalities carry the film. [PG-13]▼●

Speed (1936) **70m.** ** D: Edwin L. Marin. James Stewart, Wendy Barrie, Una Merkel, Ted Healy, Weldon Heyburn, Ralph Morgan, Patricia Wilder. Stewart enhances this star-building quickie (one of eight features he made in 1936) as a test-car driver who's developed a high-speed carburetor. Most of the racing action consists of blatant rear-projection and stock footage.

Speed (1994) **C-116m.** ***½ D: Jan De Bont. Keanu Reeves, Dennis Hopper, Sandra Bullock, Jeff Daniels, Joe Morton, Alan Ruck, Glenn Plummer, Richard Lineback, Beth Grant, Carlos Carrasco. Incredibly kinetic, supercharged action yarn about an elite SWAT-team cop (Reeves) who's targeted by a psycho/mastermind (Hopper), and led onto an L.A. city bus that's triggered to explode. If you're going to make a nonstop action movie, this is the way to do it—with expert pacing, eye-popping stunts and special effects, and characters who make sense. A bull's-eye! Oscar winner for Best Sound and Sound Effects Editing. Followed by a sequel. Panavision. [R]▼●◗

Speed 2: Cruise Control (1997) **C-121m.** BOMB D: Jan De Bont. Sandra Bullock, Jason Patric, Willem Dafoe, Temuera Morrison, Brian McCardie, Christine Firkins, Colleen Camp, Lois Chiles, Jeremy Hotz, Bo Svenson, Glenn Plummer, Tim Conway. Mind-numbingly stupid action yarn opens with a chase scene that makes no sense, and never improves. Bullock (whose character here is especially annoying) agrees to go on a Caribbean cruise with boyfriend Patric, an L.A.P.D. officer. When madman Dafoe takes control of the ship, Patric feels it's his duty to try and stop him. Did anyone read the script before signing on for this one? Panavision. [PG-13]▼●◗

Speed Crazy (1959) **75m.** BOMB D: William Hole, Jr. Brett Halsey, Yvonne Lime, Charles Willcox, Slick Slavin, Jacqueline Ravell, Baynes Barron, Jackie Joseph. Trashy, campy bottom-of-the-barrel programmer about a psychotic drifter who's "an accident looking for a place to happen." He's obsessed with fast cars, and keeps complaining that "everybody keeps crowding me."▼

Speed to Spare (1948) **57m.** ** D: William Berke. Richard Arlen, Jean Rogers, Richard Travis, Roscoe Karns, Nanette Parks. Arlen is OK as a stunt-car driver who decides to take it easy and become a driver for his friend's trucking company, only to find himself in more trouble. Acceptable programmer from the Paramount "B" factory of Pine-Thomas.

Speedtrap (1977) **C-98m.** ** D: Earl Bellamy. Joe Don Baker, Tyne Daly, Richard Jaeckel, Robert Loggia, Morgan Woodward, Timothy Carey. Private eye Baker is called in by the cops to trap an elusive car thief, and teamed with policewoman Daly. Good cast and predictable screeching tires can't save muddled script. [PG]▼

Speedway (1968) **C-94m.** ** D: Norman Taurog. Elvis Presley, Nancy Sinatra, Bill Bixby, Gale Gordon. Routine Presley tuner with Elvis starring as a bighearted stockcar racer and Sinatra along for the ride as a tax inspector. Richard Petty, Cale Yarborough and other real-life auto racers are featured. Panavision.▼●

Speedy (1928) **86m.** *** D: Ted Wilde. Harold Lloyd, Ann Christy, Bert Woodruff, Brooks Benedict. Contrived but enjoyable comedy has Harold trying to save N.Y.C.'s last horse-drawn trolley, run by his girlfriend's grandfather, from extinction. Vivid N.Y.C. location work includes hair-raising chase scene, and appealing cameo by Babe Ruth as himself.▼

Speed Zone! (1989) **C-95m.** *½ D: Jim Drake. Peter Boyle, Donna Dixon, John Candy, Eugene Levy, Tim Matheson, The Smothers Brothers, Matt Frewer, Joe Flaherty, Shari Belafonte, Art Hindle, John Schneider, Jamie Farr, Lee Van Cleef, Michael Spinks, Brooke Shields, Alyssa Milano, Carl Lewis. Yet another variation on the CANNONBALL RUN cross-country road race, with Boyle as a sheriff who's determined to stop the race before it begins. Pointless, derivative, and unfunny, a particular waste of such talents as Candy, Levy, and Flaherty. You know you're in trouble when Brooke Shields gives the funniest performance in the film! [PG]▼●

Spellbinder (1988) **C-99m.** ** D: Janet Greek. Timothy Daly, Kelly Preston, Rick Rossovich, Diana Bellamy, Audra Lindley, Cary-Hiroyuki Tagawa, Anthony Crivello, Roderick Cook, Stefan Gierasch. L.A. lawyer falls for a mysterious beauty, slowly learns she's a witch, a member of a coven that wants her back as a sacrifice. A why-bother? occult thriller: slick, empty, and extremely predictable. [R]▼

Spellbound (1945) **111m.** ***½ D: Alfred Hitchcock. Ingrid Bergman, Gregory Peck, Leo G. Carroll, John Emery, Michael Chekhov, Wallace Ford, Rhonda Fleming, Bill Goodwin, Regis Toomey. Absorbing tale of psychiatrist Bergman trying to uncover Peck's hangups; Dali dream sequences, innovative (and Oscar-winning) Miklos Rozsa score help Hitchcock create another unique film. Based on novel *The House of Dr. Edwardes* by Francis Beeding; screenplay by Ben Hecht. In original theatrical prints, a key gunshot was shown in color.▼●◗

Spencer's Mountain (1963) **C-119m.** ** D: Delmer Daves. Henry Fonda, Maureen O'Hara, James MacArthur, Donald Crisp, Wally Cox, Veronica Cartwright, Victor French. Mawkish sudser about Wyoming landowner Fonda who keeps promising to build another family house. Good cast stuck with inferior script. Based on the Earl Hamner, Jr. novel; later developed into *The Waltons*. Panavision.▼●

Spetters (1980-Dutch) **C-115m.** *** D: Paul Verhoeven. Hans van Tongeren, Toon Agterberg, Renee Soutendijk, Maarten Spanjer, Marianne Boyer, Rutger Hauer. Adolescent shenanigans and dreams in Holland; teenagers sleep around and race their motorcycles while idolizing race champ Hauer. Graphically sexual, with crisp direction by Verhoeven; luscious Soutendijk scores as an ambitious hash-slinger. [R] ▼●

Sphere (1998) **C-133m.** *½ D: Barry Levinson. Dustin Hoffman, Sharon Stone, Samuel L. Jackson, Peter Coyote, Liev Schreiber, Queen Latifah. Failed sci-fi saga (from Michael Crichton novel) about a group of scientists from different disciplines who are brought to a super-secret underwater site where the U.S. Navy has discovered a mysterious wreckage. What does it signify? Where did it come from and when? Intriguing set-up leads nowhere, with increasingly stupid behavior from the principals and ridiculous chapter headings that lend supposed import to each new sequence. A bust. Super 35. [PG-13]▼●◗

Sphinx, The (1933) **63m.** ** D: Phil Rosen. Lionel Atwill, Sheila Terry, Theodore Newton, Paul Hurst, Luis Alberni, Robert Ellis. Atwill plays a police suspect whose only alibi is his deaf-mute twin brother. Passable low-budgeter. Remade in 1942 as THE PHANTOM KILLER.▼

Sphinx (1981) **C-117m.** *½ D: Franklin J. Schaffner. Lesley-Anne Down, Frank Langella, Maurice Ronet, John Gielgud, Martin Benson, John Rhys-Davies. Harried Egyptologist Down continuously eludes death as she searches for a mystery tomb. Awful script, mummy-like performances, impressive Egyptian scenery. Adapted by John Byrum from Robin Cook novel. Panavision. [PG]▼

Spice World (1997-British) **C-92m.** **½ D: Bob Spiers. The Spice Girls (Mel B, Emma, Mel C, Geri, Victoria), Richard E. Grant, Alan Cumming, Roger Moore, George Wendt, Claire Rushbrook, Mark McKinney, Richard O'Brien, Barry Humphries, Jason Flemyng, Naoki Mori, Meat Loaf, Bill Paterson, Jools Holland, Stephen Fry, Richard Briers. A fantasy look at several days in the lives of the pop phenomenon The Spice Girls and their existence with road manager Grant, leading up to a concert at Albert Hall in London. Amusing, vapid, sometimes silly but lively vignettes featuring the five flashy females who took the pop world by storm in the late '90s. Cameos by Elton John, Bob Hoskins, Bob Geldof, Elvis Costello, The Dream Boys, Jonathan Ross, and Jennifer Saunders. [PG]▼●◗

Spider, The (1945) **62m.** ** D: Robert Webb. Richard Conte, Faye Marlowe, Kurt Kreuger, John Harvey, Martin Kosleck, Mantan Moreland, Walter Sande, Cara Williams, Ann Savage. Humdrum remake of the 1931 thriller, set in the French Quarter of New Orleans, with Conte as a private eye hired to help a carnival mind-reader who fears she may be murdered.

Spider, The (1958) SEE: **Earth vs. the Spider**

Spider and the Fly, The (1949-British) **87m.** **½ D: Robert Hamer. Guy Rolfe, Nadia Gray, Eric Portman, Maurice Denham, James Hayter, Arthur Lowe. Effective drama of Gallic law enforcer and British crook teaming up to retrieve government document; good interplay between cast members.

Spider Baby (1964) **81m.** **½ D: Jack Hill. Lon Chaney, Jr., Sid Haig, Jill Banner, Mantan Moreland, Beverly Washburn, Carol Ohmart. Not bad little chiller about the antics of a very unusual—and very sick—family. At its best it's both scary and funny. Chaney is the clan's chauffeur and sings the title song! The full title is SPIDER BABY OR, THE MADDEST STORY EVER TOLD. Aka THE LIVER EATERS. ▼●

Spiders, The (1919-German) **137m.** *** D: Fritz Lang. Carl de Vogt, Ressel Orla, Lil Dagover, Georg John, Bruno Lettinger. Intrepid explorer/adventurer de Vogt—an early cross between Indiana Jones and James Bond—vies with evil Spider cult for mystic Incan diamond. First two chapters ("The Golden Lake" and "The Diamond Ship") of never completed four-part serial abound with lost civilizations, human sacrifice, pirate treasure, and too many perils to count. Lang's obsession with a diabolical underworld foreshadows his DR. MABUSE films. An exciting curio; the earliest of Lang's films to survive. German title: DIE SPINNEN. ▼●◗

Spider's Stratagem, The (1970-Italian) **C-100m.** *** D: Bernardo Bertolucci. Giulio Brogi, Alida Valli, Tino Scotti, Pippo Campanini, Franco Giovanelli. Young man visits the provincial town where his anti-Fascist father was assassinated 30 years earlier, is rejected by the populace at every turn. Exceedingly atmospheric puzzler, from a Jorge Luis Borges short story, boasts some of the most beautiful color cinematography (by Vittorio Storaro) in memory.▼

Spider Woman, The (1944) **62m.** *** D: Roy William Neill. Basil Rathbone, Nigel Bruce, Gale Sondergaard, Dennis Hoey, Mary Gordon, Arthur Hohl, Alec Craig. A mysterious villainess is responsible for a series of deaths in which the victims are driven to suicide after being bit by poisonous spiders. Rip-roaring entry with thrills to spare; one of the best in the Sherlock Holmes series.▼

Spider Woman Strikes Back, The (1946) **59m.** *½ D: Arthur Lubin. Brenda Joyce, Gale Sondergaard, Kirby Grant, Rondo Hatton, Milburn Stone, Hobart Cavanaugh. Pitiful waste of fine actress Sondergaard in campy thriller with little relation to earlier Sherlock Holmes feature.

Spies (1928-German) **90m.** ***½ D: Fritz Lang. Rudolph Klein-Rogge, Gerda Maurus, Willy Fritsch, Lupu Pick, Fritz Rasp. Silent spy-thriller still packs a wallop as government agent Fritsch determines to thwart seemingly-respectable Klein-Rogge, a wheelchair-bound master-fiend with an uncanny resemblance to Lenin! One of Lang's early masterpieces, aka SPIONE.▼●

Spies à Go Go SEE: **Nasty Rabbit, The**

Spies Like Us (1985) **C-109m.** *** D: John Landis. Chevy Chase, Dan Aykroyd, Steve Forrest, Donna Dixon, Bruce Davison, William Prince, Bernie Casey, Tom Hatten, Matt Frewer. Chase and Aykroyd become government spies—never dreaming that they've been set up as decoys. Engagingly silly comedy patterned after the Hope-Crosby ROAD pictures, with at least one pertinent cameo appearance and minor roles filled by a number of film directors (Michael Apted, Constantin Costa-Gavras, Joel Coen, Sam Raimi, Martin Brest, Bob Swaim, Terry Gilliam, Ray Harryhausen). Written by Aykroyd, Lowell Ganz, and Babaloo Mandel, from a story by Aykroyd and Dave Thomas. [PG]▼●◗

Spike of Bensonhurst (1988) **C-91m.** ** D: Paul Morrissey. Sasha Mitchell, Ernest Borgnine, Anne DeSalvo, Sylvia Miles, Geraldine Smith, Maria Patillo, Talisa Soto, Rick Aviles, Antonia Rey. Blah Mafia comedy with Mitchell as an ambitious Brooklyn street kid who dreams of becoming a boxing champ—and finds himself in trouble when he courts the daughter of the local mob boss (Borgnine). Ethnic stereotypes abound. [R]▼●

Spikes Gang, The (1974) **C-96m.** *½ D: Richard Fleischer. Lee Marvin, Ron Howard, Charlie Martin Smith, Arthur Hunnicutt, Noah Beery, Gary Grimes. Veteran gunfighter turns a trio of runaway boys into bank robbers; old-hat storyline has humor, but not much else. [PG]

Spinal Tap SEE: **This Is Spinal Tap**

Spinout (1966) **C-90m.** **½ D: Norman Taurog. Elvis Presley, Shelley Fabares, Diane McBain, Deborah Walley, Cecil Kellaway, Una Merkel, Warren Berlinger, Carl Betz. Typical Presley vehicle finds the singer racing autos and wooing the girls. Elvis's songs (''Beach Shack,'' ''Adam and Evil,'' ''Smorgasbord'') are far from his best. Panavision.▼●

Spiral Road, The (1962) **C-145m.** *½ D: Robert Mulligan. Rock Hudson, Burl Ives, Gena Rowlands, Geoffrey Keen, Will Kuluva, Neva Patterson. Jan de Hartog's novel about love, leprosy, and lunacy in Java makes for an interminable moviegoing experience. Hudson at his most wooden, Mulligan's direction at its most impersonal.

Spiral Staircase, The (1946) **83m.** ***½ D: Robert Siodmak. Dorothy McGuire, George Brent, Ethel Barrymore, Kent Smith, Rhonda Fleming, Gordon Oliver, Elsa Lanchester, Rhys Williams, Sara Allgood. Superb Hitchcock-like thriller with unforgettable performance by McGuire as mute servant in eerie household which may be harboring a killer. Well scripted by Mel Dinelli, adapting Ethel Lina White's novel *Some Must Watch.* Remade in 1975.▼●

Spiral Staircase, The (1975-British) **C-89m.** ** D: Peter Collinson. Jacqueline Bisset, Christopher Plummer, Sam Wanamaker, Mildred Dunnock, Gayle Hunnicutt, John Phillip Law, Elaine Stritch. Stellar cast gives Ethel Lina White's mystery novel *Some Must Watch* another go in a somewhat mechanical fashion that can't touch the 1946 version.▼

Spirit Is Willing, The (1967) **C-100m.** *½ D: William Castle. Sid Caesar, Vera Miles, Barry Gordon, John McGiver, Cass Daley, Mary Wickes, Jesse White, Harvey Lembeck, Jay C. Flippen, Jill Townsend, John Astin, Doodles Weaver. Some good comedy performers are thrown away in stupid comedy about Caesar and family's summer house that happens to be haunted; based on Nathaniel Benchley's *The Visitors.*

Spirit of Culver (1939) **89m.** ** D: Joseph Santley. Jackie Cooper, Freddie Bartholomew, Tim Holt, Andy Devine, Gene Reynolds, Jackie Moran. All the usual prep-academy clichés adapted for military school setting with Cooper and Bartholomew predictable. Remake of 1932 film TOM BROWN OF CULVER.

Spirit of 76, The (1991) **C-82m.** *½ D: Lucas Reiner. David Cassidy, Olivia d'Abo, Geoff Hoyle, Leif Garrett, Jeff McDonald, Steve McDonald, Barbara Bain, Julie Brown, Tommy Chong, Iron Eyes Cody, Devo, Carl Reiner, Rob Reiner, Moon Zappa. Three time-travelers from 2176 trying to find the true basis of America think they've arrived in 1776, but it's really 1976. Limp spoof of the 1970s simply catalogues the fads, styles, and fashions. Director and cowriter Reiner is Carl's son, Rob's brother. Sofia Coppola did the costumes. [PG-13]▼

Spirit of St. Louis, The (1957) **C-138m.** *** D: Billy Wilder. James Stewart, Patricia Smith, Murray Hamilton, Marc Connelly. Long but inventive presentation of Lindbergh's flight across the Atlantic is mainly a tour de force by Stewart, backed by good Franz Waxman music score. CinemaScope.▼●

Spirit of the Beehive (1973-Spanish)

C-95m. ***½ D: Victor Erice. Fernando Fernan Gomez, Teresa Gimpera, Ana Torrent, Isabel Telleria. Torrent is unforgettable as a lonely little village girl who sees Boris Karloff's FRANKENSTEIN in the town hall and becomes entranced by the monster. Her sister convinces her the monster is still alive, and she treks off into the countryside to find him.▼

Spirit of the Dead SEE: **Asphyx, The**

Spirit of West Point, The (1947) **77m.** ** D: Ralph Murphy. Doc Blanchard, Glenn Davis, Tom Harmon, Robert Shayne, Anne Nagel, Alan Hale, Jr., Bill Stern, Harry Wismer. Comic-book chronicle of "the touchdown twins," all-American football heroes Blanchard and Davis, and their years at West Point. Will they or won't they resign their West Point commissions to play pro ball? The boys (especially Blanchard) are far more believable on the gridiron than reciting lines.▼●

Spirits of the Dead (1968-French-Italian) **C-117m.** ***½ D: Roger Vadim, Louis Malle, Federico Fellini. Brigitte Bardot, Alain Delon, Jane Fonda, Terence Stamp, Peter Fonda, James Robertson Justice. Narrated by Vincent Price. Three separate Poe tales, impossible to describe, delightful to watch, done with skill and flair by three top directors. [R]▼●◗

Spiritualist, The SEE: **Amazing Mr. X, The**

Spite Marriage (1929) **75m.** *** D: Edward Sedgwick. Buster Keaton, Dorothy Sebastian, Edward Earle, Leila Hyams, William Bechtel. Keaton's last silent is also one of his most underrated, a very funny film about a pants-presser who becomes infatuated with a stage actress. Plottier than usual for Buster, but full of great set-pieces. Remade as I DOOD IT.▼●

Spitfire (1934) **88m.** ** D: John Cromwell. Katharine Hepburn, Robert Young, Ralph Bellamy, Martha Sleeper, Sara Haden, Sidney Toler, High Ghere (Bob Burns). Bizarre, boring melodrama with Hepburn sorely miscast in one of her oddest roles: Trigger, a spirited, single-minded but superstition-laden Ozark tomboy who attracts married engineer Young. This one's only for the curious.▼

Spitfire (1942-British) **117m.** *** D: Leslie Howard. Leslie Howard, David Niven, Rosamund John, Roland Culver, Anne Firth, David Horne, J. H. Roberts, Derrick de Marney, Bernard Miles, Patricia Medina. Howard plays R.J. Mitchell, who developed the ace fighting-plane Spitfire which later became one of the Allies' most valuable WW2 assets. Good biographical drama. Howard's last screen appearance. Original title: THE FIRST OF THE FEW. U.S. version cut to 90m.▼

Spitfire Grill, The (1996) **C-116m.** **½ D: Lee David Zlotoff. Alison Elliott, Ellen Burstyn, Marcia Gay Harden, Will Patton, Kieran Mulroney, Gailard Sartain. Ex-convict Elliott arrives in the small, gossip-driven town of Gilead, Maine, and goes to work for Burstyn at the title-named restaurant, hoping to rebuild her life. Sincere, well-acted story goes awry toward the end with contrivance and melodrama; still, Elliott and Burstyn give memorable performances. Written by the director. [PG-13]▼●◗

Splash (1984) **C-111m.** *** D: Ron Howard. Daryl Hannah, Tom Hanks, John Candy, Eugene Levy, Dody Goodman, Richard B. Shull, Shecky Greene, Howard Morris. Entertaining comedy about a man who falls in love with a mermaid, who's played to perfection by Hannah. Buoyant cast, winning gags make this a lot of fun, despite a tendency toward overlength. Script by Lowell Ganz, Babaloo Mandel, and Bruce Jay Friedman. Followed by a TV movie sequel in 1988. [PG] ▼●◗

Splendor (1935) **77m.** **½ D: Elliott Nugent. Miriam Hopkins, Joel McCrea, Paul Cavanagh, Helen Westley, Billie Burke, Katharine Alexander, David Niven. Familiar story of McCrea's family upset when he loves poor-girl Hopkins instead of upper-class young lady; script by Rachel Crothers, from her play.▼

Splendor (1999) **C-93m.** **½ D: Gregg Araki. Kathleen Robertson, Johnathon Schaech, Matt Keeslar, Kelly Macdonald, Eric Mabius. Amusing modern-day romantic comedy with a twist: a willing heroine can't decide between two handsome guys she meets the same evening, so she winds up living with both of them. After such a spiky start, it's too bad it winds up being so conventional . . . but the spirits are high and the cast is engaging. Almost benign for filmmaker Araki. [R]▼

Splendor in the Grass (1961) **C-124m.** *** D: Elia Kazan. Natalie Wood, Warren Beatty, Pat Hingle, Audrey Christie, Sean Garrison, Sandy Dennis, Phyllis Diller, Barbara Loden, Zohra Lampert, Gary Lockwood. Sentimental sudser by William Inge (who won an Oscar) about emotionally broken girl (Wood) rebuilding her life; set in late 1920s Midwest. Film debuts of Beatty, Dennis, and Diller; look for Inge as the minister. Remade for TV in 1981.▼●◗

Split, The (1968) **C-91m.** *½ D: Gordon Flemyng. Jim Brown, Diahann Carroll, Julie Harris, Ernest Borgnine, Gene Hackman, Jack Klugman, Warren Oates, James Whitmore, Donald Sutherland. Cast is good, but it's no match for routine, clichéd story of plot to rob L.A. Coliseum during a Rams game. Only for those who love caper movies. Panavision. [R]

Split Decisions (1988) **C-95m.** ** D: David Drury. Gene Hackman, Craig Sheffer, Jeff Fahey, Jennifer Beals, John McLiam,

Eddie Velez, Carmine Caridi, James Tolkan. Violent family drama set amidst the world of boxing and three generations of prizefighters. Basically just another ROCKY ripoff, but Hackman, in a supporting role, stands out as usual. [R]▼●

Split Image (1982) **C-111m.** *** D: Ted Kotcheff. Michael O'Keefe, Karen Allen, Peter Fonda, James Woods, Elizabeth Ashley, Brian Dennehy, Ronnie Scribner, Pamela Ludwig, Michael Sacks, Peter Horton. Solid drama of nice middle-class boy (superbly played by O'Keefe) who falls for Allen and is brainwashed into joining a cult headed by Fonda. Top performances by Dennehy as O'Keefe's father, Woods as a deprogrammer. Panavision. [R]▼

Split Second (1953) **85m.** **½ D: Dick Powell. Stephen McNally, Alexis Smith, Jan Sterling, Keith Andes, Arthur Hunnicutt, Paul Kelly, Robert Paige, Richard Egan. Capable cast in odd suspenser about escaped convict (McNally) holding several people hostage in Nevada ghost town—though well aware it's a nuclear test site! Script by William Bowers and Irving Wallace. Powell's directorial debut.▼

Split Second (1992-U.S.-British) **C-90m.** *½ D: Tony Maylam. Rutger Hauer, Kim Cattrall, Neil Duncan, Alun Armstrong, Pete Postlethwaite, Ian Drury, Robert Eaton, Michael J. Pollard. In London's near future, tough cop Hauer is after the serial killer who murdered his partner and is saddled with new partner Duncan. The murderer is an ALIEN-like monster, the plot mushes together fantasy and sci-fi elements, and the movie is a derivative, tedious mess. Won't someone rescue Hauer from this kind of junk? [R]▼●

Splitting Heirs (1993-U.S.-British) **C-86m.** ** D: Robert Young. Rick Moranis, Eric Idle, Barbara Hershey, Catherine Zeta Jones, John Cleese, Sadie Frost, Stratford Johns, Brenda Bruce, William Franklyn. A loser (Idle) learns he's really a duke and tries to reclaim his title from the bogus heir (Moranis). Strained comedy in the Monty Python tradition, filled with puns, sight gags, and silliness—only some of which is funny. Idle executive produced and coscripted. [PG-13]▼●

Spoiled Children (1977-French) **C-113m.** *** D: Bertrand Tavernier. Michel Piccoli, Christine Pascal, Michel Aumont, Gerard Jugnot, Arlette Bonnard, Georges Riquier, Gerard Zimmerman. Enticing, penetrating tale which examines, among other issues, the particular problems faced by artists—in this case, a famous but blocked writer-director (Piccoli) who becomes involved with a younger woman (Pascal) and in a tenants' battle with his apartment building's abusive landlord. Fine performances. The semi-autobiographical script was penned by Tavernier with Pascal and Charlotte Dubreuil.▼

Spoilers, The (1942) **87m.** **½ D: Ray Enright. Marlene Dietrich, Randolph Scott, John Wayne, Margaret Lindsay, Harry Carey, Richard Barthelmess. Retelling of famous Yukon tale has good cast but thuds out as average Western, with Dietrich as stereotyped saloon gal. Previously filmed in 1914, 1923 and 1930, then again in 1955.▼●

Spoilers, The (1955) **C-84m.** **½ D: Jesse Hibbs. Anne Baxter, Jeff Chandler, Rory Calhoun, Barbara Britton, Raymond Walburn. Fifth filming of Rex Beach's Klondike actioner; elaborate fight scene intact.

Spoilers of the Forest (1957) **C-68m.** ** D: Joseph Kane. Rod Cameron, Vera Ralston, Ray Collins, Hillary Brooke, Edgar Buchanan. Another timberland Western, with Cameron a tree-cutting foreman, romancing Ralston. Filmed in Naturama.

Spontaneous Combustion (1990) **C-97m.** *½ D: Tobe Hooper. Brad Dourif, Cynthia Bain, Jon Cypher, William Prince, Dey Young, Melinda Dillon, Dale Dye, Dick Butkus, John Landis. Paranoia fuels this misfired horror thriller dealing with spontaneous human combustion, allegedly a reality. Here, however, the blazing deaths are due to the FIRESTARTER-like mental powers of Dourif, the result of yet another evil government experiment. Badly paced and ludicrous. Cowritten by the director. [R]▼●

Spook Busters (1946) **68m.** ** D: William Beaudine. Leo Gorcey, Huntz Hall, Douglass Dumbrille, Tanis Chandler, Bobby Jordan, Gabriel Dell, Billy Benedict, David Gorcey, Charles Middleton, Bernard Gorcey. The Bowery Boys set up shop as ghost exterminators and tangle with a mad scientist. Hmmm . . . wonder if any future comedians caught this one as kids?▼

Spook Chasers (1957) **62m.** *½ D: George Blair. Huntz Hall, Stanley Clements, David Gorcey, Jimmy Murphy, Percy Helton, Darlene Fields, Eddie LeRoy, Bill Henry. Yet another *Bowery Boys* crooks-posing-as-ghosts entry, with a surfeit of wheezy gags.

Spooks Run Wild (1941) **69m.** ** D: Phil Rosen. Bela Lugosi, Leo Gorcey, Huntz Hall, Bobby Jordan, Sunshine Sammy Morrison, Donald Haines, David Gorcey, Dave O'Brien, Dennis Moore, Dorothy Short, Angelo Rossitto. Tongue-in-cheek *East Side Kids* horror-comedy, with the boys encountering Lugosi in a spooky country mansion. Ad libs fly fast and furious, to Lugosi's obvious consternation.▼

Spook Who Sat By the Door, The (1973) **C-102m.** *½ D: Ivan Dixon. Lawrence Cook, Paula Kelly, Janet League, J. A. Preston, Paul Butler. Cook, token black in the CIA, uses his knowledge to organize bands of teenaged guerrillas to bring whitey to his knees. Offbeat but offensive, and way too talky for cheap action fare. [PG]▼

Sporting Blood (1931) **82m.** **½ D: Charles Brabin. Clark Gable, Ernest Torrence, Madge Evans, Lew Cody, Marie Prevost, J. Farrell MacDonald. Minor but likable film about a thoroughbred horse and its various owners; Gable is a tough-guy gambler (''C'mere, woman,'' he says to Evans, grabbing her for a clinch). Beautifully photographed by Harold Rosson.

Sporting Club, The (1971) **C-105m.** BOMB D: Larry Peerce. Robert Fields, Nicolas Coster, Maggie Blye, Jack Warden, Richard Dysart, William Roerick, Logan Ramsey, James Noble, Linda Blair. Badly directed dud about violence and promiscuity among some beautiful people in Northern Michigan has enough gore and ineptitude to offend everyone. [R]▼

Spot SEE: **Dogpound Shuffle**

Spring and Port Wine (1970-British) **C-101m.** *** D: Peter Hammond. James Mason, Susan George, Diana Coupland, Marjorie Rhodes, Arthur Lowe. Unpretentious little gem about the generation gap in a lower-middle-class English family. Mason has one of his better later roles as the strict patriarch.

Spring Break (1983) **C-101m.** BOMB D: Sean S. Cunningham. David Knell, Steve Bassett, Perry Lang, Paul Land, Richard B. Shull, Corinne Alphen. Life among the party-animals who trek to Fort Lauderdale during Easter vacation. Where are Frankie and Annette when you really need them? [R]▼●

Spring Fever (1983-Canadian) **C-100m.** BOMB D: Joseph L. Scanlan. Susan Anton, Frank Converse, Jessica Walter, Stephen Young, Carling Bassett. Young Bassett struggles to be a tennis champ in this bland, feeble tale that is most definitely not the adolescent sex comedy the title implies. [PG]▼

Springfield Rifle (1952) **C-93m.** **½ D: Andre de Toth. Gary Cooper, Phyllis Thaxter, David Brian, Lon Chaney, Jr., Paul Kelly, Phil Carey, Guinn Williams. Unmemorable Cooper fare, with Gary joining up with outlaws to determine who's stealing government arms.▼

Spring in Park Lane (1948-British) **100m.** **½ D: Herbert Wilcox. Anna Neagle, Michael Wilding, Tom Wallis, Marjorie Fielding, Nicholas Phipps, Josephine Fitzgerald. Stylish romance story of Wilding courting Neagle, his employer's niece. This was one of Britain's most popular films of all time.

Spring Madness (1938) **80m.** **½ D: S. Sylvan Simon. Maureen O'Sullivan, Lew Ayres, Ruth Hussey, Burgess Meredith, Ann Morriss, Joyce Compton, Jacqueline Wells (Julie Bishop), Frank Albertson. Collegiate romance between O'Sullivan and brainy Ayres, elevated by strong cast. Enjoyable fluff.

Spring Parade (1940) **89m.** *** D: Henry Koster. Deanna Durbin, Robert Cummings, Mischa Auer, Henry Stephenson, Butch and Buddy, Anne Gwynne. Delightful Austrian fluff with Durbin romancing Cummings, working for baker S. Z. Sakall, dancing with wacky Auer, and singing, of course.

Spring Reunion (1957) **79m.** ** D: Robert Pirosh. Betty Hutton, Dana Andrews, Jean Hagen, James Gleason, Laura LaPlante, George Chandler, Irene Ryan. Potentially good soaper marred by low-budget production: Andrews and Hutton revive old memories at high school reunion and try to plan new future together; Hagen has some fine comic moments. Silent star LaPlante plays Hutton's mother.

Springtime in the Rockies (1942) **C-91m.** *** D: Irving Cummings. Betty Grable, John Payne, Carmen Miranda, Cesar Romero, Charlotte Greenwood, Edward Everett Horton, Jackie Gleason. Near-definitive 1940s Fox musical: Grable at her prettiest, Miranda at her silliest (doing a Brazilian ''Chattanooga Choo Choo''), Technicolor at its lushest, and Harry James and His Band at their best, with Helen Forrest introducing ''I Had the Craziest Dream.'' The ''plot''—about a bickering Broadway duo is neither too tiresome nor too intrusive. Good fun all the way. ▼●

Sprung (1997) **C-105m.** *½ D: Rusty Cundieff. Tisha Campbell, Rusty Cundieff, Paula Jai Parker, Joe Torry, John Witherspoon, Jennifer Lee, Clarence Williams III, Isabel Sanford, Sherman Hemsley. Forgettable and hopelessly predictable plot about a young couple who try planning the perfect wedding for their friends. Unbelievable situations, incredibly hokey sentiment overcome this amateurish attempt at creating a '90s screwball comedy. Preston Sturges is probably spinning in his grave. [R] ▼●◗

Sputnik (1958-French) **85m.** ** D: Jean Dreville. Noel-Noel, Denise Gray, Noel Roquevert, Mischa Auer. Mild Cold War spoof involving Russian missile experiment which has backfired and naive Frenchman caught in the Red trap. Retitled: A DOG, A MOUSE AND A SPUTNIK.▼

Spy Chasers (1955) **66m.** **½ D: Edward Bernds. Leo Gorcey, Huntz Hall, Bernard Gorcey, David (Gorcey) Condon, Bennie Bartlett, Leon Askin, Sig Ruman, Veola Vonn, Richard Benedict. The Bowery Boys help an exiled king and his daughter battle usurpers in this practiced farce.

Spy Hard (1996) **C-72m.** ** D: Rick Friedberg. Leslie Nielsen, Nicollette Sheridan, Charles Durning, Marcia Gay Harden, Barry Bostwick, Andy Griffith, John Ales,

Elya Baskin, Mason Gamble, Carlos Lauchu, Stephanie Romanov, Clyde Kusatsu, Julie Brown, Eddie Deezen, Julie Payne, Thom Sharp. Mild James Bond spoof with Nielsen as Agent WD-40, locking horns with master criminal General Rancor (Griffith). Steady stream of gags (ribbing everything from HOME ALONE to TRUE LIES), mostly silly, sometimes funny, too often sloppy or misfired. Nielsen is much better than the material. Many familiar faces in surprise cameos. Best of all: Weird Al Yankovic's title sequence and song. Nielsen also coexecutive produced. [PG-13]▼●◗

Spy Hunt (1950) **75m.** **½ D: George Sherman. Howard Duff, Marta Toren, Robert Douglas, Philip Dorn, Walter Slezak. Diverting yarn of espionage agent planting micro-film secrets in panthers' collars; when they escape captivity various sides of the law seek the animals. Based on a Victor Canning novel.

Spy in Black, The (1939-British) **82m.** *** D: Michael Powell. Conrad Veidt, Sebastian Shaw, Valerie Hobson, Marius Goring, June Duprez, Helen Haye, Cyril Raymond, Hay Petrie. Intriguing espionage melodrama set in WW1 Scotland with Veidt as German naval officer/spy and Hobson a charming double agent. Nice surprise twists in story, with bittersweet romance worked in. That's Bernard Miles as the desk clerk in the opening scene. Scripted by Emeric Pressburger and Roland Pertwee; first collaboration of Powell and Pressburger (who reteamed with Veidt and Hobson the following year for CONTRABAND). Original U.S. title: U-BOAT 29.▼●

Spy in Your Eye (1966-Italian) **C-88m.** ** D: Vittorio Sala. Brett Halsey, Dana Andrews, Pier Angeli, Gastone Moschin. Hokum has Andrews as scientist with telecamera implanted in eye, Halsey as U.S. agent trying to rescue Andrews' daughter (Angeli) captured by the Russians.

Spymaker SEE: **Secret Life of Ian Fleming, The**

S*P*Y*S (1974) **C-87m.** BOMB D: Irvin Kershner. Donald Sutherland, Elliott Gould, Zouzou, Joss Ackland, Shane Rimmer, Vladek Sheybal. Sutherland-Gould teaming fails to regenerate MASH electricity in a good director's worst film. Laughless CIA spoof about the defection of a Russian dancer is unworthy of anyone's time. [PG]▼

Spy Who Came In from the Cold, The (1965) **112m.** ***½ D: Martin Ritt. Richard Burton, Claire Bloom, Oskar Werner, Peter Van Eyck, George Voskovec, Sam Wanamaker, Cyril Cusack, Michael Hordern, Bernard Lee. John le Carré's potent account of a Cold War spy's existence—minus glamorous trappings of movie cliché. Burton is excellent as embittered agent at the end of his career. Scripted by Paul Dehn and Guy Trosper.▼●

Spy Who Loved Me, The (1977) **C-125m.** ***½ D: Lewis Gilbert. Roger Moore, Barbara Bach, Curt Jurgens, Richard Kiel, Caroline Munro, Bernard Lee, Lois Maxwell, Desmond Llewelyn. Rousing, lavishly produced James Bond adventure with wily 007 joining forces with a seductive Russian agent to quash arch-villain Stromberg's (Jurgens) plans for world destruction. At his best doing battle with a persistent steel-toothed goon, menacingly played by seven-foot-two-inch Kiel. Grand fun for one and all; Carly Simon sings Marvin Hamlisch's theme, "Nobody Does It Better." Panavision. [PG]▼●◗

Spy with a Cold Nose, The (1966-British) **C-93m.** ** D: Daniel Petrie. Laurence Harvey, Daliah Lavi, Lionel Jeffries, Eric Portman, Denholm Elliott, Colin Blakely, Paul Ford. Spoof on secret agent movies. British agents plant bug in bulldog Disraeli, gift to Russian ambassador. Cast tries to keep story afloat.▼

Spy With My Face, The (1966) **C-88m.** **½ D: John Newland. Robert Vaughn, Senta Berger, David McCallum, Leo G. Carroll. Another expanded *Man From U.N.C.L.E.* TV series entry, with Vaughn matching wits with his double (working for foreign powers); Berger is the enemy femme fatale.

Squanto: A Warrior's Tale (1994) **C-101m.** *** D: Xavier Koller. Adam Beach, Mandy Patinkin, Michael Gambon, Nathaniel Parker, Eric Schweig, Donal Donnelly, Stuart Pankin, Alex Norton, Irene Bedard. Thoughtful, painstakingly observed Disney yarn which follows the plight of a 17th-century American Indian (Beach) who is abducted by British traders and taken back to England. At the scenario's core are Squanto's conflicts with (and spiritual similarities to) some reclusive monks. A film to be savored by children and adults alike. [PG]▼●

Square Dance (1987) **C-112m.** **½ D: Daniel Petrie. Jason Robards, Jane Alexander, Winona Ryder, Rob Lowe, Deborah Richter, Guich Koock, Elbert Lewis. Top-notch performances bolster this much too leisurely look at a Texas teenage girl's coming of age, as she leaves her dour grandfather's farm to be with her feisty mom in Fort Worth. Alexander (who coproduced with fellow actor Charles Haid) is a standout as the mother; Lowe effects a real change of pace playing a retarded man befriended by Ryder. Shown on TV as HOME IS WHERE THE HEART IS. [PG-13]▼●

Square Jungle, The (1955) **86m.** **½ D: Jerry Hopper. Tony Curtis, Pat Crowley, Ernest Borgnine, Paul Kelly, Jim Backus.

Overly-familiar boxing yarn with Curtis the fighter on the way up.

Square Ring, The (1953-British) **73m.** ** D: Michael Relph, Basil Dearden. Jack Warner, Kay Kendall, Joan Collins, Robert Beatty, Bill Owen, Maxwell Reed. Uninspired intertwining of events in lives of people involved in the fight game.

Squaw Man, The (1931) **105m.** *** D: Cecil B. DeMille. Warner Baxter, Lupe Velez, Eleanor Boardman, Charles Bickford, Roland Young, Paul Cavanagh, Raymond Hatton, Dickie Moore. DeMille's talkie version of the story he filmed before in 1914 and 1918 is slow to start, but picks up steam after English aristocrat Baxter flees to America and marries Indian Velez. Surprisingly restrained and unsentimental, with a moving finale.

Squeaker, The (1937-British) **77m.** *** D: William K. Howard. Edmund Lowe, Sebastian Shaw, Ann Todd, Tamara Desni, Robert Newton, Alastair Sim. Classy cast in first-rate Edgar Wallace mystery about disgraced inspector Lowe trying to reform and catch infamous jewelry fence known as "the Squeaker." Good, compact Alexander Korda production. Aka MURDER ON DIAMOND ROW. ▼

Squeaker, The (1965-German) **95m.** **½ D: Alfred Vohrer. Heinz Drache, Eddi Arent, Klaus Kinski, Barbara Rutting. Overly complex actioner with a variety of plots spinning from action of underworld selling off proceeds of diamond robbery. From an Edgar Wallace novel previously filmed in 1930 and 1937. Ultrascope.▼

Squeeze, The (1980-Italian) **C-100m.** *½ D: Anthony M. Dawson (Antonio Margheriti). Lee Van Cleef, Karen Black, Edward Albert, Lionel Stander, Robert Alda, Angelo Infanti. Good cast wasted in humdrum caper film about a retired thief (Van Cleef) breaking open one last safe. Filmed in N.Y.C. [R]▼

Squeeze, The (1987) **C-101m.** BOMB D: Roger Young. Michael Keaton, Rae Dawn Chong, Liane Langland, Leslie Bevis, John Davidson, Meat Loaf, Ronald Guttman. Dreadful comedy, almost completely devoid of laughs, with Keaton as a con man who gets involved in murder and mayhem. Davidson plays a slick but corrupt TV lottery host. [PG-13]▼●

Squeeze (1997) **C-89m.** ** D: Robert Patton-Spruill. Tyrone Burton, Eddie Cutanda, Phuong Van Duong, Geoffrey Rhue, Russell G. Jones, Leigh Williams. Three Boston ghetto youths are caught between the violent gang and drug life on the streets and a promise of hope and a better life found in their local youth center. The conflict the teens go through is well played out with terrific performances, especially Burton's, but the dialogue is sometimes stilted and the ending too pat. Great visual style; shot on location in Boston in 1995. [R]▼

Squirm (1976) **C-92m.** *** D: Jeff Lieberman. Don Scardino, Patricia Pearcy, R. A. Dow, Jean Sullivan, Peter MacLean. Above-average horror outing builds to good shock sequences: when power line falls to the ground on rainy Georgia night, it drives large, slimy sandworms from the ground, which terrorize small town. [PG—edited from original R rating]▼

Squizzy Taylor (1982-Australian) **C-89m.** *** D: Kevin Dobson. David Atkins, Jacki Weaver, Alan Cassell, Michael Long, Kim Lewis, Steve Bisley. Atkins shines as the title character, a famous gangster in 1920s Melbourne. Enjoyable, with the era colorfully re-created.▼

Sssssss (1973) **C-99m.** *** D: Bernard L. Kowalski. Strother Martin, Dirk Benedict, Heather Menzies, Richard B. Shull, Tim O'Connor, Jack Ging. Well-done horror tale of doctor who finds a way of transforming man into King Cobra. Exceptional job by makeup master John Chambers. [PG]▼

Stablemates (1938) **89m.** ** D: Sam Wood. Wallace Beery, Mickey Rooney, Arthur Hohl, Margaret Hamilton, Minor Watson, Marjorie Gateson. Sticky story of jockey Rooney and racetrack mentor Beery. All the stops out during the syrupy scenes.

Stacey (1973) **C-79m.** *½ D: Andy Sidaris. Anne Randall, Alan Landers, James Westmoreland, Cristina Raines, Anitra Ford, Marjorie Bennett. Voluptuous former Playmate Randall stars as near-superwoman private eye on absurdly complex case involving murder, blackmail, and a Moonie-like cult. Very sexy and violent, but not very good, with grating, obnoxious score by jazz veteran Don Randi. Aka STACEY AND HER GANGBUSTERS. [R]▼

Stacking (1987) **C-109m.** ** D: Martin Rosen. Christine Lahti, Frederic Forrest, Megan Follows, Jason Gedrick, Ray Baker, Peter Coyote, James Gammon, Kaiulani Lee, Jacqueline Brookes, Irene Daily. Some fine performers (and performances) are wasted in this boring, ever so obvious account of the various experiences and troubles of a young teen (Follows), growing up in the rural West in the early 1950s. More or less a clone of the far superior DESERT BLOOM. Originally titled SEASON OF DREAMS. [PG]▼●

Stacy's Knights (1983) **C-95m.** **½ D: Jim Wilson. Andra Millian, Kevin Costner, Eve Lilith, Mike Reynolds, Garth Howard, Ed Semenza. Millian is Plain Jane struck with blackjack gambling fever who recruits a squad of sharpies to break a casino after her young mentor (Costner) is killed by the casino's goons. Unexciting B-movie offers insight into the world of professional gambling and features a flavorful performance by Costner in his first leading role. (Screenwriter Michael Blake and director Wilson later reteamed with Costner to make DANCES WITH WOLVES.) [PG]▼

Stagecoach (1939) **96m.** **** D: John Ford. Claire Trevor, John Wayne, Andy Devine, John Carradine, Thomas Mitchell, Louise Platt, George Bancroft, Donald Meek, Berton Churchill, Tim Holt, Tom Tyler, Chris-Pin Martin, Francis Ford, Jack Pennick. One of the great American films, and a landmark in the maturing of the Western, balancing character study (as disparate passengers travel together on the same stagecoach) and peerless action (in a lengthy Indian attack, featuring Yakima Canutt's famous stuntwork). Also the film that propelled John Wayne to genuine stardom. Mitchell won an Oscar as the drunken doctor, as did the music score. Script by Dudley Nichols, from Ernest Haycox's story "Stage to Lordsburg" (whose plot is reminiscent of Guy de Maupassant's *Boule de Suif*). Filmed in Ford's beloved Monument Valley on the Arizona-Utah border. Remade in 1966 and as a TVM in 1986. Also shown in computer-colored version.▼●◗

Stagecoach (1966) **C-115m.** **½ D: Gordon Douglas. Ann-Margret, Alex Cord, Red Buttons, Michael Connors, Bing Crosby, Bob Cummings, Van Heflin, Slim Pickens, Stefanie Powers, Keenan Wynn. Colorful, star-studded Western is OK, but can't hold a candle to the 1939 masterpiece. Overlong, with only occasional action scenes to liven it up. Wayne Newton sings the title song! CinemaScope.

Stagecoach (1986) **C-100m. TVM** D: Ted Post. Willie Nelson, Kris Kristofferson, Johnny Cash, Waylon Jennings, John Schneider, Elizabeth Ashley, Tony Franciosa, Anthony Newley, Mary Crosby, June Carter Cash, Jessi Colter, David Allen Coe, Lash Larue. Country music's self-styled "outlaws" team up with wives and pals for a third go at the Ernest Haycox story about a bumpy stagecoach trip through Indian country to Lordsburg, Arizona. The stars made no secret of their disdain for the simple-minded script. Average.▼

Stage Door (1937) **92m.** **** D: Gregory La Cava. Katharine Hepburn, Ginger Rogers, Adolphe Menjou, Andrea Leeds, Gail Patrick, Constance Collier, Lucille Ball, Eve Arden, Ann Miller, Ralph Forbes, Franklin Pangborn, Jack Carson. Theatrical boarding house is setting for wonderful film, from Edna Ferber-George S. Kaufman play. Dynamite cast includes Hepburn as rich girl trying to succeed on her own, Menjou as propositioning producer, Leeds as hypersensitive actress, and several stars-to-be: Lucille Ball, Ann Miller, and Eve Arden. Scripted by Morrie Ryskind and Anthony Veiller.▼●

Stage Door Canteen (1943) **132m.** **½ D: Frank Borzage. Cheryl Walker, William Terry, Marjorie Riordan, Lon McCallister, Margaret Early, Michael Harrison (Sunset Carson). Wartime story of romance between soldier and hostess at N.Y.C.'s fabled canteen is filled with cameos, walk-ons, speeches, and musical numbers by an incredible battery of stars, including Katharine Hepburn, Harpo Marx, Paul Muni, Helen Hayes, Benny Goodman, Count Basie, Edgar Bergen. Many prints run 93m.▼●

Stage Fright (1950) **110m.** **½ D: Alfred Hitchcock. Marlene Dietrich, Jane Wyman, Michael Wilding, Richard Todd, Kay Walsh, Alastair Sim, Joyce Grenfell, Sybil Thorndike, Patricia Hitchcock. Drama student is suspected when actress' husband is murdered; some exciting moments, but the Master misses on this one. Filmed in London with delightful British cast; Marlene sings "The Laziest Gal in Town."▼●

Stage Mother (1933) **87m.** **½ D: Charles Brabin. Alice Brady, Maureen O'Sullivan, Ted Healy, Franchot Tone, Phillips Holmes. Widowed vaudevillian stakes everything on making her daughter a star. Brady is wonderful, and so is seedy backstage atmosphere. Songs include "Beautiful Girl," later immortalized in SINGIN' IN THE RAIN.

Stage Struck (1936) **86m.** **½ D: Busby Berkeley. Dick Powell, Joan Blondell, Warren William, Frank McHugh, Jeanne Madden. Throwaway film with stale plot kept barely alive by energetic cast; backstage musical has no real production numbers. Highlight is The Yacht Club Boys' insane "The Body Beautiful." Leading lady Madden remained obscure after this one.

Stage Struck (1958) **C-95m.** **½ D: Sidney Lumet. Henry Fonda, Susan Strasberg, Joan Greenwood, Christopher Plummer, Herbert Marshall. Faded remake of MORNING GLORY retelling the ascent of Broadway-bound actress. Supporting cast hampered by unconvincing Strasberg in lead role and by unreal theater world atmosphere.▼●

Stage to Thunder Rock (1964) **C-82m.** ** D: William F. Claxton. Barry Sullivan, Marilyn Maxwell, Lon Chaney, Jr., Scott Brady, John Agar, Keenan Wynn, Allan Jones. One of producer A. C. Lyles' humdrum Westerns with veteran stars; this one has Sullivan as a sheriff who's put in the position of having to arrest the outlaw family that raised him. Techniscope.

Staircase (1969-British) **C-100m.** ** D: Stanley Donen. Richard Burton, Rex Harrison, Cathleen Nesbitt, Beatrix Lehmann. Shock value of Burton and Harrison as a gay couple was all this film had going for it in 1969, and nothing has changed since then, except heightened sophistication of audiences. A curio, to be sure. Dudley Moore composed the score. Panavision. [R]

Stairway to Heaven (1946-British) **C-104m.** **** D: Michael Powell, Emeric Pressburger. David Niven, Kim Hunter, Raymond Massey, Roger Livesey, Robert Coote, Marius Goring, Richard Attenborough. Powell and Pressburger manage to straddle reality and fantasy in a most disarming manner in this unusual story of a pilot during WW2 who claims he was accidentally chosen to die, and must now plead for his life in a Heavenly court. Like most films by this writer-director team, an absolute original—and a gem, too. Original British title: A MATTER OF LIFE AND DEATH.▼

Stakeout (1987) **C-115m.** *** D: John Badham. Richard Dreyfuss, Emilio Estevez, Aidan Quinn, Madeleine Stowe, Dan Lauria, Forest Whitaker, Ian Tracey, Earl Billings. While working with his partner on a stakeout, cop Dreyfuss falls in love with the woman he's supposed to be watching. Wildly improbable, and ultimately downright silly, but entertaining throughout, thanks to sharp dialogue and performances, and some big laughs. Dreyfuss and Estevez make a great team. Written by Jim Kouf. Followed by a sequel, ANOTHER STAKEOUT. [R]▼●

Stakeout on Dope Street (1958) **83m.** *½ D: Irvin Kershner. Yale Wexler, Jonathan Haze, Morris Miller, Abby Dalton, Herschel Bernardi. Trio of youths discover cache of heroin, believing their futures will now be uncomplicated; good premise poorly executed.

Stalag 17 (1953) **120m.** **** D: Billy Wilder. William Holden, Don Taylor, Otto Preminger, Robert Strauss, Harvey Lembeck, Richard Erdman, Peter Graves, Neville Brand, Sig Rumann, Ross Bagdasarian, Gil Stratton, Jr. Granddaddy of all WW2 POW films. Holden (in Oscar-winning performance) is super-cynical sergeant suspected of being Nazi spy. Wilder brilliantly blends drama with comedy to show monotonous, anxiety-ridden life of POWs. Wonderful comic relief by Strauss and Lembeck (repeating their Broadway roles), plus superb turn by Preminger as Nazi camp commander. Scripted by Wilder and Edwin Blum, from Donald Bevan and Edmund Trzcinski's play. ▼●◗

Stalin (1992-U.S.-British-Canadian-Russian-Hungarian) **C-170m. TVM** D: Ivan Passer. Robert Duvall, Maximilian Schell, Julia Ormond, Jeroen Krabbe, Joan Plowright, Frank Finlay, Daniel Massey, Joanna Roth. Duvall's stunning portrait of Josef Stalin, along with (nearly unrecognizable) Schell's Lenin, power this strong if episodic drama. Often confusing, because of the myriad of Russian names and not-always-identified characters, spanning the years from 1917 to the dictator's death in 1953. Written by Paul Monash and photographed in Budapest and Moscow by Vilmos Zsigmond. Made for cable. Above average.▼●

Stalker (1979-Russian) **C/B&W-160m.** *** D: Andrei Tarkovsky. Alexander Kaidanovsky, Nikolai Grinko, Anatoli Solonitsin, Alice Friendlich. Stark, eerie, cerebral story of title character, who guides intellectuals Grinko and Solonitsin through the "Zone," a mysterious, forbidden wasteland. Very slow but well acted and rewarding.▼

Stalking Moon, The (1969) **C-109m.** ** D: Robert Mulligan. Gregory Peck, Eva Marie Saint, Robert Forster, Noland Clay, Russell Thorson, Frank Silvera. Army scout helps white woman who has lived with the Apaches to escape with her young half-breed son, while boy's father comes after them. Potentially interesting Western is both slick and dull; nice photography by Charles Lang. Panavision. [G]▼

Stallion Road (1947) **91m.** ** D: James V. Kern. Ronald Reagan, Alexis Smith, Zachary Scott, Peggy Knudsen, Patti Brady, Harry Davenport. Dedicated veterinarian Reagan and novelist friend Scott vie for the affection of horse rancher Smith; low-key drama written by Stephen Longstreet.

Stamboul Quest (1934) **88m.** **½ D: Sam Wood. Myrna Loy, George Brent, Lionel Atwill, C. Henry Gordon, Mischa Auer. Exotic combination of romance and intrigue with German spy Loy falling in love with American student Brent in WW1 Turkey. Herman Mankiewicz's script based on true story also filmed as FRAULEIN DOKTOR.

Stampede (1949) **78m.** **½ D: Lesley Selander. Rod Cameron, Gale Storm, Johnny Mack Brown, Don Castle, John Miljan. Good Western of range war between cattle ranchers.

Stand Alone (1985) **C-90m.** ** D: Alan Beattie. Charles Durning, Pam Grier, James Keach, Bert Remsen, Barbara Sammeth, Lu Leonard, Luis Contreras. Vigilante opus has miscast Durning as a war vet who goes after Latino thugs who are preying on his neighborhood. Grier is wasted in a goody-two-shoes role. Spectacle of overweight Durning running around in action scenes is unintentionally funny. [R]▼

Stand and Deliver (1987) **C-105m.** ***½ D: Ramon Menendez. Edward James Olmos, Lou Diamond Phillips, Rosana de Soto, Andy Garcia, Will Gotay, Ingrid Oliu, Virginia Paris, Mark Eliot. Olmos gives a tour-de-force performance in this outstanding drama as a tough, demanding teacher who inspires his East L.A. barrio students to pass an Advanced Placement Calculus Test . . . and that's only the beginning of the story. Based on fact, with a screenplay by director Menendez and Tom Musca.

This *American Playhouse* feature is a triumph for all concerned. [PG]▼●◗
Stand at Apache River, The (1953) **C-77m.** ** D: Lee Sholem. Stephen McNally, Julia (Julie) Adams, Hugh Marlowe, Jack Kelly, Hugh O'Brian. Title tells all.
Stand by for Action (1942) **109m.** **½ D: Robert Z. Leonard. Robert Taylor, Brian Donlevy, Charles Laughton, Walter Brennan, Marilyn Maxwell, Henry O'Neill, Chill Wills. We're still waiting. Good cast in standard drama-with-comic-touches in which up-by-his-bootstraps Navy officer Donlevy and silver-spoon-fed subordinate Taylor clash in the early days of WW2.
Stand by Me (1986) **C-87m.** *** D: Rob Reiner. Wil Wheaton, River Phoenix, Corey Feldman, Jerry O'Connell, Kiefer Sutherland, Casey Siemaszko, John Cusack, Richard Dreyfuss. Affectionate Americana looking back at boyhood friendship and adventures in the 1950s (and narrated by Dreyfuss, representing author Stephen King, whose novella "The Body" is the basis for this film). Irresistible and wholly believable performances from all four youthful leads. Only complaint: the high volume of four-letter words, decidedly not characteristic of the 1950s. [R]▼●◗
Stand-In (1937) **91m.** *** D: Tay Garnett. Leslie Howard, Humphrey Bogart, Joan Blondell, Alan Mowbray, Marla Shelton, C. Henry Gordon, Jack Carson. Enjoyable spoof of Hollywood, with stuffy banker Howard sent to assess dwindling fortunes of Colossal Pictures, becoming involved with perky stand-in Blondell and mercurial producer Bogart to save company from ruin. Sags in second half.▼
Standing Room Only (1944) **83m.** ** D: Sidney Lanfield. Fred MacMurray, Paulette Goddard, Edward Arnold, Hillary Brooke, Roland Young, Anne Revere. Topical wartime comedy is now dated. MacMurray and Goddard can't find rooms, so they work as servants.
Stand Up and Be Counted (1972) **C-99m.** *½ D: Jackie Cooper. Jacqueline Bisset, Stella Stevens, Steve Lawrence, Gary Lockwood, Lee Purcell, Loretta Swit, Hector Elizondo. Touted as first film about Women's Lib; writer Bisset returns to home town, first becomes aware of abuses women must endure. Cardboard all the way; only standout is Stevens' comic performance. Script by Bernard Slade. [PG]
Stand Up and Cheer (1934) **69m.** ** D: Hamilton MacFadden. Warner Baxter, Madge Evans, James Dunn, Sylvia Froos, John Boles, Shirley Temple, Ralph Morgan, Aunt Jemima, Mitchell and Durant, Nick (Dick) Foran, Nigel Bruce, Stepin Fetchit. Dismal musical fantasy about big-time show producer Baxter being named Secretary of Amusement by the President, to chase the country's Depression blues. Tough sledding until Shirley Temple shows up with Dunn to perform "Baby Take a Bow" (which helped make her a star). Originally released at 80m. Also shown in computer-colored version.▼
Stand Up and Fight (1939) **97m.** ** D: W. S. Van Dyke II. Wallace Beery, Robert Taylor, Florence Rice, Charles Bickford, Charley Grapewin, Selmer Jackson. OK Western with railroading pioneer Taylor meeting crisis after crisis, battling stubborn stage-rider Beery. James M. Cain was one of the writers.
Stanley (1972) **C-106m.** ** D: William Grefe. Chris Robinson, Alex Rocco, Susan Carroll, Steve Alaimo, Mark Harris, Paul Avery. Classic depiction of the Vietnam veteran as a one-dimensional psycho: Robinson cannot relate to any other human being; his only friends are poisonous snakes, which he uses to gain revenge on anyone who mistreats him. WILLARD with snakes instead of rats. [PG]▼
Stanley & Iris (1990) **C-104m.** **½ D: Martin Ritt. Jane Fonda, Robert De Niro, Swoosie Kurtz, Martha Plimpton, Harley Cross, Jamey Sheridan, Feodor Chaliapin, Zohra Lampert, Loretta Devine, Julie Garfield. Beleagured working-class Fonda, still grieving over the loss of her husband eight months before, chances to meet De Niro, a loner who harbors a terrible secret—he can't read. She winds up tutoring him, and they circle each other warily before deciding if they're in love. Story is flat and underdeveloped, but the screen presence and charm of two great stars make it worth watching. Panavision. [PG-13]▼●
Stanley and Livingstone (1939) **101m.** *** D: Henry King. Spencer Tracy, Nancy Kelly, Richard Greene, Walter Brennan, Charles Coburn, Cedric Hardwicke, Henry Hull, Henry Travers, Miles Mander. Elaborate production with Tracy as determined reporter who searches Africa for missing missionary (Hardwicke) at turn of century. Entertaining drama with beautifully understated performance by Tracy.▼
Star, The (1952) **89m.** ***½ D: Stuart Heisler. Bette Davis, Sterling Hayden, Natalie Wood, Warner Anderson, Minor Watson, June Travis. An Oscar-winning actress tries to deal with the fact that her career is over, her money is gone, and she must find some way to put her life together. Modest film, shot on locations all around L.A., has many moments of truth (and a typically compelling performance by Davis) to make up for its moments of excess.▼
Star! (1968) **C-176m.** **½ D: Robert Wise. Julie Andrews, Richard Crenna, Michael Craig, Daniel Massey, Robert Reed, Bruce Forsyth, Beryl Reid, Jenny Agutter, Tony LoBianco, Conrad Bain, Roy Scheider, Bernard Fox. Razzle-dazzle biog-

raphy of stage star Gertrude Lawrence never rings true, but does have mammoth production numbers worth seeing (especially in color). Julie tries, but never comes across; Massey is amusing if affected as Noel Coward (his real-life godfather). After box office flop, film was trimmed to 120m. and retitled THOSE WERE THE HAPPY TIMES. Todd-AO. [G]▼●

Star Chamber, The (1983) **C-109m.** **½ D: Peter Hyams. Michael Douglas, Hal Holbrook, Yaphet Kotto, Sharon Gless, James B. Sikking, Joe Regalbuto, Don Calfa, DeWayne Jessie, Jack Kehoe. Young judge, frustrated by having to turn rapists and murderers free because of legal technicalities, is drawn into a secret judicial society. Well done, but too predictable, and ultimately too unbelievable, to really score. Panavision. [R]▼●

Starcrash (1979-Italian) **C-92m.** *½ D: Lewis Coates (Luigi Cozzi). Marjoe Gortner, Caroline Munro, Christopher Plummer, David Hasselhoff, Robert Tessier, Joe Spinell, voice of Hamilton Camp. Grinning Gortner and sexy Munro are recruited to save the universe from destruction by bad-guy Spinell. Moronic sci-fi movie with variable special effects; unless you're a Munro fan, it's only good for a few laughs, nothing more. Aka FEMALE SPACE INVADERS. [PG]▼

Star Dust (1940) **85m.** **½ D: Walter Lang. Linda Darnell, John Payne, Roland Young, Charlotte Greenwood, William Gargan, Mary Beth Hughes, Mary Healy, Donald Meek. Hokey, entertaining yarn about talent scout Young (from Amalgamated Studios) discovering star-struck Darnell and football player Payne.

Stardust (1975-British) **C-107m.** ***½ D: Michael Apted. David Essex, Adam Faith, Larry Hagman, Keith Moon, Dave Edmunds, Ines Des Longchamps, Edd Byrnes. Powerful sequel to THAT'LL BE THE DAY follows amazing rise and fall of Beatles-like rock group and its lead singer (Essex). Candid, provocative, and utterly believable. [R]

Stardust Memories (1980) **91m.** *** D: Woody Allen. Woody Allen, Charlotte Rampling, Jessica Harper, Marie-Christine Barrault, Tony Roberts, Daniel Stern, Amy Wright. Woody plays a character not unlike himself who's persuaded to attend a film-seminar weekend, at which he's hounded by fans, favor-seekers, groupies, studio executives, relatives, and lovers. Pointed, seriocomic look at fame and success—though many viewers found it simply narcissistic. Look sharp for Sharon Stone on passing train; Louise Lasser and Laraine Newman appear unbilled. [PG] ▼●

Star 80 (1983) **C-102m.** *½ D: Bob Fosse. Mariel Hemingway, Eric Roberts, Cliff Robertson, Carroll Baker, Roger Rees, David Clennon, Josh Mostel, Sidney Miller, Jordan Christopher, Keenen Ivory Wayans, Stuart Damon, Ernest Thompson. Straightforward telling of a lurid tale: innocent Dorothy Stratten's mental seduction by small-time hustler Paul Snider, who promoted her career as a *Playboy* centerfold and movie starlet, then murdered her in a rage of jealousy. Extremely well-crafted, well-acted movie that leaves viewer with nothing but a feeling of voyeurism—and no redeeming insights. Fosse's final film; before his death, he reedited this for network TV. See also TV movie version DEATH OF A CENTERFOLD. [R]▼●◗

Stargate (1994-French-U.S.) **C-119m.** **½ D: Roland Emmerich. Kurt Russell, James Spader, Viveca Lindfors, Jaye Davidson, Alexis Cruz, Mili Avital, Leon Rippy, John Diehl, Carlos Lauchu, Djimon (Hounsou), Erick Avari, French Stewart, Gianin Loffler, Cecil Hoffmann, Rae Allen, Richard Kind. A scholar of ancient languages and hieroglyphics (Spader) is recruited to help the military penetrate the mystery of a stone gateway which, in fact, leads to another universe. Interesting odyssey, impressively mounted and jammed with visual effects, but loses its way dramatically. Davidson (of CRYING GAME fame) is featured as a sort of fey Ming the Merciless. Special edition tape runs 128m. Followed by a made-for-TV movie and TV series. Panavision. [PG-13]▼●◗

Starhops (1978) **C-92m.** ** D: Barbara Peeters. Dorothy Buhrman, Sterling Frazier, Jillian Kesner, Peter Paul Liapis, Paul Ryan, Anthony Mannino, Dick Miller. Ultra-low-budget formula film about three car hops who try to salvage a failing drive-in. Not bad of its type; screenplay by Stephanie Rothman. [R]▼

Star in the Dust (1956) **C-80m.** ** D: Charles Haas. John Agar, Mamie Van Doren, Richard Boone, Leif Erickson, Coleen Gray, James Gleason. Intriguing cast is wasted in this trite tale of sheriff Agar forced to fight his townfolk to retain law and order. Look for Clint Eastwood as a ranch hand.

Star Is Born, A (1937) **C-111m.** ***½ D: William Wellman. Fredric March, Janet Gaynor, Adolphe Menjou, May Robson, Andy Devine, Lionel Stander, Franklin Pangborn. Two remakes haven't dimmed the glow of this drama about a self-destructive actor and the young movie hopeful he marries. March and Gaynor are at their best and 1930s flavor (captured in early Technicolor) is a plus; screenplay by Dorothy Parker, Alan Campbell, and Robert Carson was inspired in part by 1932 film WHAT PRICE HOLLYWOOD? Oscar-winner for original story (by Carson and

director Wellman) and W. Howard Greene's cinematography.▼●◗
Star Is Born, A (1954) **C-170m.** **** D: George Cukor. Judy Garland, James Mason, Charles Bickford, Jack Carson, Tom Noonan. Powerful semi-musical remake of the 1937 classic, with Garland and Mason at their peaks as doomed Hollywood star couple, she on the way up, he down. Incisive script by Moss Hart; great Harold Arlen–Ira Gershwin songs include spellbinding "The Man That Got Away" and the showstopping "Born in a Trunk" sequence by Leonard Gershe. Badly cut to 154m. after premiere engagements of 181m.; restored in 1983 to present length. CinemaScope.▼●◗
Star Is Born, A (1976) **C-140m.** **½ D: Frank Pierson. Barbra Streisand, Kris Kristofferson, Gary Busey, Oliver Clark, Paul Mazursky, Marta Heflin, M.G. Kelly, Sally Kirkland, Robert Englund. By-now familiar story is given an unconvincing treatment, with change of setting to the world of rock music. Only comes to life during Streisand's vibrant numbers, which transcend script and surrounding drama; she and Paul Williams won an Oscar for song "Evergreen." Screenplay by Pierson, Joan Didion, and John Gregory Dunne. ▼●
Star Kid (1998) **C-101m.** ** D: Manny Coto. Joseph Mazzello, Joey Simmrin, Danny Masterson, Richard Gilliland, Corinne Bohrer, Ashlee Levitch. A lonely boy finds a "cyborsuit"—superpowered alien armor—in a junkyard, and has fun trying it out. He makes friends with the suit, which has a mind of its own, but then an evil alien warrior arrives to destroy it. Comic book–like but occasionally entertaining. [PG]▼●◗
Star Knight (1986-Spanish) **C-90m.** *½ D: Fernando Colomo. Klaus Kinski, Harvey Keitel, Fernando Rey, Maria Lamor, Miguel Bosè. Infantile fantasy about a spaceship that lands in a Spanish lake in medieval times and is thought to be a dragon. Keitel (Bronx accent intact) is the only cast member who isn't dubbed. OK special effects. Originally titled: THE KNIGHT OF THE DRAGON.▼●
Starlift (1951) **103m.** ** D: Roy Del Ruth. Janice Rule, Dick Wesson, Ron Hagerthy, Richard Webb. Flimsy account of GI romancing an actress, allowing for scenes of movie stars entertaining troops. Cameos by Warner Bros. people like Cagney, Virginia Mayo, Ruth Roman, Doris Day, Gordon MacRae, etc.
Starlight Hotel (1987-New Zealand) **C-93m.** *** D: Sam Pillsbury. Peter Phelps, Greer Robson, Marshall Napier, The Wizard, Alice Fraser, Patrick Smyth. Nice little film about the exploits of troubled teen Robson and psychologically scarred WW1 vet Phelps. A friendly film about a most unlikely friendship. Warrick Attewell's cinematography is a standout. [PG]▼●
Starlight Slaughter SEE: **Eaten Alive!**
Star Maker, The (1939) **80m.** **½ D: Roy Del Ruth. Bing Crosby, Louise Campbell, Laura Hope Crews, Ned Sparks, Ethel Griffies, Billy Gilbert. Crosby plays Gus Edwards, vaudeville impresario who turned talented youngsters into stars. Pleasant musical doesn't always stick to facts. Originally 94m.
Star Maker, The (1995-Italian) **C-117m.** ** D: Giuseppe Tornatore. Sergio Castellitto, Tiziana Bodato, Franco Scaldati, Leopoldo Trieste, Clelia Rondinella, Tano Cimarosa, Jane Alexander. CINEMA PARADISO's Tornatore offers up the flip side of that beloved film in this period piece about a self-described talent scout who tours Sicily selling screen tests and the pipe dream of a movie career to naive locals who fall prey to his sales pitch. Maybe PARADISO is just too tough an act to follow, but this one doesn't even come close. Tornatore coscripted, from his story. Panavision. [R] ▼●
Starman (1984) **C-115m.** **½ D: John Carpenter. Jeff Bridges, Karen Allen, Charles Martin Smith, Richard Jaeckel. Extremely pleasant, genteel sci-fi about alien who lands on earth, abducts young widow to help him travel cross-country so he can rendezvous with spaceship. Her toughest problem: he's made himself look just like her late husband, and she finds herself attracted to him. Familiar, derivative story line is given solid boost by two lead performances. Later a TV series. Panavision. [PG]▼●◗
Star Maps (1997) **C-95m.** **½ D: Miguel Arteta. Douglas Spain, Efrain Figueroa, Kandeyce Jorden, Martha Velez, Lysa Flores. Occasionally potent but uneven allegorical drama about an 18-year-old with movie-star aspirations who returns from Mexico to L.A. and goes to work for his father as a male prostitute in a ring which is fronted by the selling of "star maps" of celebrity homes. Done in by its preachy tone and lack of depth. [R]▼●
Star of India (1954-British) **C-84m.** **½ D: Arthur Lubin. Cornel Wilde, Jean Wallace, Herbert Lom. So-so costumer, overly earnest. Wilde is Gallic nobleman trying to reestablish his rightful inheritance.
Star of Midnight (1935) **90m.** ** D: Stephen Roberts. William Powell, Ginger Rogers, Paul Kelly, Gene Lockhart, Ralph Morgan, Leslie Fenton, J. Farrell MacDonald. Flip, but not terribly funny, comedy-mystery in the THIN MAN vein, with a convoluted story that doesn't offer much involvement. Powell plays a lawyer who enjoys solving cases more than trying them in court.▼●
Stars and Bars (1988) **C-94m.** BOMB D: Pat O'Connor. Daniel Day-Lewis, Harry

Dean Stanton, Martha Plimpton, Matthew Cowles, Joan Cusack, Maury Chaykin, Dierdre O'Connell, Will Patton, Steven Wright, Keith David, Laurie Metcalf, Glenne Headly, Spalding Gray, Rockets Redglare. A complete misfire, with Day-Lewis thoroughly wasted as a British art expert who treks to America to purchase a Renoir, and instead tangles with hick Stanton and other assorted eccentrics. Overbaked, unfunny, and embarrassing. [R]▼●

Stars and Stripes Forever (1952) **C-89m.** **½ D: Henry Koster. Clifton Webb, Robert Wagner, Ruth Hussey, Debra Paget, Finlay Currie. Diverting, fictionalized biography of bandmaster John Philip Sousa, well-played by Webb, with standard march tunes worked into plot nicely. ▼

Stars Are Singing, The (1953) **C-99m.** **½ D: Norman Taurog. Rosemary Clooney, Anna Maria Alberghetti, Lauritz Melchoir, Fred Clark. Frothy musical with ridiculous plot-line of immigration authorities tracking down Alberghetti as contestant on TV talent show.

Stars Fell on Henrietta, The (1995) **C-110m.** **½ D: James Keach. Robert Duvall, Aidan Quinn, Frances Fisher, Brian Dennehy, Lexi Randall, Kaytlyn Knowles, Billy Bob Thornton, Victor Wong, Paul Lazar, Spencer Garrett, Park Overall, Dylan Baker. Old-fashioned (and a tad contrived) folktale set in the Depression era Texas dust bowl stars Duvall as a wily old oil prospector who charms a cotton farmer and his wife into believing their land is a valuable rig. Suffers mainly from overlength. A real labor of love from the people at Malpaso, Clint Eastwood's production company. Expert casting and superb contributions from cinematographer Bruce Surtees and production designer Henry Bumstead (plus a lush score by David Benoit) keep things enjoyable. That's director Keach's wife Jane Seymour in the opening saloon shot, and Fisher and Eastwood's daughter as Mary. Panavision. [PG]▼●

Starship Invasions (1977-Canadian) **C-87m.** *½ D: Ed Hunt. Robert Vaughn, Christopher Lee, Daniel Pilon, Helen Shaver, Henry Ramer. Abducted by good aliens to help battle bad aliens who are trying to take over earth, UFO expert Vaughn helps save the day with his pocket calculator. Good cast wasted in film boasting the worst special effects since PLAN 9 FROM OUTER SPACE. [PG]▼

Starship Troopers (1997) **C-129m.** *** D: Paul Verhoeven. Casper Van Dien, Dina Meyer, Denise Richards, Jake Busey, Neil Patrick Harris, Clancy Brown, Seth Gilliam, Patrick Muldoon, Michael Ironside, Rue McClanahan, Marshall Bell. A gung-ho WW2 movie transplanted to the future, when high school kids are encouraged to become "citizens" by enlisting in the army and serving the state. Little do they dream that they'll be engaged in a full-scale war against marauding insects. With Verhoeven at the helm, you know this won't be subtle, but it's so sharp, energetic, and (at times) funny that it transcends being a "giant bug" movie. Not for the squeamish, with its graphic dismemberment of humans and insects, but robust entertainment just the same. Based on the novel by Robert A. Heinlein. The incredible creature animation was supervised by Phil Tippett. [R] ▼●◗

Stars in My Crown (1950) **89m.** ***½ D: Jacques Tourneur. Joel McCrea, Ellen Drew, Dean Stockwell, Alan Hale, Lewis Stone, Ed Begley, Amanda Blake, James Arness. Gentle, moving story of a quiet but persuasive minister in rural 19th-century America; episodic film creates warm feeling for characters and setting. Prime Americana from Joe David Brown's popular novel. Also interesting for pre-*Gunsmoke* casting of Arness and Blake.▼

Stars Look Down, The (1939-British) **110m.** **** D: Carol Reed. Michael Redgrave, Margaret Lockwood, Edward Rigby, Emlyn Williams, Nancy Price, Cecil Parker, Linden Travers. Classic adaptation of A.J. Cronin's novel (coscripted by the author) about Welsh coal miners struggling against dangerous working conditions, and Redgrave as a collier's son who intends to run for office. Gripping all the way.▼

Star Spangled Girl (1971) **C-92m.** *½ D: Jerry Paris. Sandy Duncan, Tony Roberts, Todd Susman, Elizabeth Allen. Very unfunny Neil Simon comedy about the saccharine-sweet girl-next-door who falls in with two ultraradical campus newspaper editors. [G]▼

Star Spangled Rhythm (1942) **99m.** *** D: George Marshall. Bing Crosby, Ray Milland, Bob Hope, Veronica Lake, Dorothy Lamour, Susan Hayward, Dick Powell, Mary Martin, Alan Ladd, Paulette Goddard, Cecil B. DeMille, Arthur Treacher, Preston Sturges, Eddie Anderson, Robert Preston, William Bendix, many others. Paramount's silly but agreeable star-packed WW2 extravaganza, filled with songs and sketches. There's a slight plot, about a studio switchboard operator (Betty Hutton) and gate guard (Victor Moore); the latter has told his son (Eddie Bracken), a sailor, that he's the studio's boss. Better numbers include "(That Old) Black Magic," "Time To Hit the Road To Dreamland."▼●

Starstruck (1982-Australian) **C-95m.** *** D: Gillian Armstrong. Jo Kennedy, Ross O'Donovan, Pat Evison, Margo Lee, Max Cullen, John O'May, Geoffrey Rush. Bright little musical comedy about a teenage boy who's determined to promote his cousin to singing stardom as a new-wave rocker . . . no matter what it takes. Amiable tongue-in-cheek outing pokes fun at Hollywood musicals and media hype. Original Australian running time 102m. [PG]▼●

Start Cheering (1938) **78m.** *** D: Albert S. Rogell. Jimmy Durante, Walter Connolly, Joan Perry, Charles Starrett, Gertrude Niesen, Hal LeRoy, The Three Stooges, Broderick Crawford, Louis Prima. Snappy collegiate musical about rugged movie-star Starrett going back to school, with cohorts Connolly and Durante tagging along. Modest, enjoyable film with plenty of specialty numbers, guest stars, songs.▼

Starting Over (1979) **C-106m.** *** D: Alan J. Pakula. Burt Reynolds, Jill Clayburgh, Candice Bergen, Charles Durning, Frances Sternhagen, Austin Pendleton, Mary Kay Place, Wallace Shawn, Daniel Stern, Anne De Salvo, Charles Kimbrough. Likable comedy about divorced man who falls in love but can't erase feelings for his ex-wife; top performances but unfortunately, story goes awry toward conclusion for a lackluster turn of events and denouement. Scripted by James L. Brooks, from the Dan Wakefield novel. Look quickly for Kevin Bacon as a young husband. [R]▼●

Star Trek: First Contact (1996) **C-110m.** *** D: Jonathan Frakes. Patrick Stewart, Jonathan Frakes, Brent Spiner, LeVar Burton, Michael Dorn, Gates McFadden, Marina Sirtis, Alfre Woodard, James Cromwell, Alice Krige, Robert Picardo. Capt. Picard lives his worst nightmare as the villainous Borg (who almost overtook him in a two-part TV episode) land on earth with domination their goal. The solution: the crew travels back in time to 2063 to make sure a cockeyed scientist (Cromwell) fulfills his role in history with a precedent-setting rocket flight. Story goes on a bit, following two concurrent threads, but series fans will have no complaints. Krige is a standout as the seductive Borg Queen. Feature directing debut for Frakes, better known as Riker. Panavision. [PG-13]▼●◗

Star Trek Generations (1994) **C-118m.** *** D: David Carson. Patrick Stewart, William Shatner, Malcolm McDowell, Jonathan Frakes, Brent Spiner, LeVar Burton, Michael Dorn, Gates McFadden, Marina Sirtis, James Doohan, Walter Koenig, Barbara March, Gwyneth Walsh, Alan Ruck. The old guard gives way to the new, as Capt. Kirk (Shatner) passes the baton to a new Starfleet commander, Capt. Picard (Stewart). Episodic adventure yarn plays like an elongated segment of the *Next Generation* TV series; not inspired, perhaps, but entertaining just the same, with some impressive special effects. Oddly enough, the weakest segment is the climactic teaming of Picard and Kirk, which seems like a leftover from an old Saturday matinee serial. Whoopi Goldberg appears unbilled as Guinan. Panavision. [PG] ▼●◗

Star Trek: Insurrection (1998) **C-103m.** *** D: Jonathan Frakes. Patrick Stewart, Jonathan Frakes, Brent Spiner, LeVar Burton, Michael Dorn, Gates McFadden, Marina Sirtis, F. Murray Abraham, Donna Murphy, Anthony Zerbe, Gregg Henry, Daniel Hugh Kelly. Good entry in the long-running series has the crew befriending the eternally youthful residents of a Shangri-La-like planet whose existence is threatened by the vengeful Ru'afo (Abraham). Picard (Stewart) even has a dalliance with one of the women there (Murphy). Reliably entertaining for *Star Trek* fans. Panavision. [PG] ▼●◗

Star Trek—The Motion Picture (1979) **C-132m.** **½ D: Robert Wise. William Shatner, Leonard Nimoy, DeForest Kelley, Stephen Collins, Persis Khambatta, James Doohan, Nichelle Nichols, Walter Koenig, George Takei, Majel Barrett, Grace Lee Whitney, Mark Lenard. The crew of the *Enterprise* is reunited to combat a lethal force field headed toward Earth. Slow, talky, and derivative, somewhat redeemed by terrific special effects and majestic Jerry Goldsmith score; still, mainly for purists. Network and videocassette version—generally considered an improvement—runs 143m. Followed by many sequels—and several new TV series! Panavision. [G]▼●

Star Trek II: The Wrath of Khan (1982) **C-113m.** *** D: Nicholas Meyer. William Shatner, Leonard Nimoy, DeForest Kelley, Ricardo Montalban, James Doohan, Walter Koenig, George Takei, Nichelle Nichols, Kirstie Alley, Bibi Besch, Merritt Butrick, Paul Winfield. Kirk and the *Enterprise* crew must do battle with the nefarious villain of 1967's "Space Seed" episode. A bit hokey and pretentious at times, but a likable adventure overall, with nice touches of warmth and humor. Footage added for network showings. Originally released without the "II" in its title. Panavision. [PG] ▼●

Star Trek III: The Search for Spock (1984) **C-105m.** *** D: Leonard Nimoy. William Shatner, DeForest Kelley, James Doohan, George Takei, Walter Koenig, Nichelle Nichols, Christopher Lloyd, Robin Curtis, Merritt Butrick, Mark Lenard, Dame Judith Anderson, James B. Sikking, John Larroquette, Robert Hooks, Miguel Ferrer, Leonard Nimoy. Picking up where #2 left off, Kirk reassembles his crew and shanghais the *Enterprise* to try and rescue Spock while both he and the rapidly destructing Genesis Planet are endangered by a Klingon warship (led by Lloyd, in an ineffectual performance). Subdued sci-fi outing very much in keeping with tone of the original TV series. Panavision. [PG]▼●◗

Star Trek IV: The Voyage Home (1986) **C-119m.** ***½ D: Leonard Nimoy. William Shatner, Leonard Nimoy, DeForest Kelley, James Doohan, George Takei, Walter Koenig, Nichelle Nichols, Jane Wyatt, Catherine Hicks, Mark Lenard, Robin Curtis, Robert Ellenstein, John Schuck, Brock Peters. The *Enterprise* crew takes a sharp left turn toward comedy in this uncharacteristic—and very entertaining—movie. Story has the familiar characters time-traveling back to the 20th century in order to save the Earth of the future, with the help of some humpback whales. Sheer novelty of the comic tone excuses some forays into the obvious; it's all in fun. Panavision. [PG]▼●◗

Star Trek V: The Final Frontier (1989) **C-106m.** ** D: William Shatner. William Shatner, Leonard Nimoy, DeForest Kelley, James Doohan, Walter Koenig, Nichelle Nichols, George Takei, David Warner, Laurence Luckinbill, Charles Cooper. The *Enterprise* crew takes off on an emergency mission when an apparent madman takes over a distant planet and holds its interstellar ambassadors hostage; his motives, however, turn out to be anything but terroristic. Dramatically shaky trek starts off with a case of the cutes, and gets worse before it (finally) gets better. A weak entry in the series. Shatner's feature-film directing debut; he also shares story credit. Panavision. [PG] ▼●◗

Star Trek VI: The Undiscovered Country (1991) **C-109m.** *** D: Nicholas Meyer. William Shatner, Leonard Nimoy, DeForest Kelley, James Doohan, Walter Koenig, Nichelle Nichols, George Takei, Kim Cattrall, Christopher Plummer, Mark Lenard, Grace Lee Whitney, Brock Peters, Kurtwood Smith, Rosana DeSoto, David Warner, Iman, John Schuck, Michael Dorn, Christian Slater. The *Enterprise* crew is assigned to negotiate truce with Klingon leader, only to fall prey to a trap set by one of his renegade cohorts (Plummer, in a deliciously flamboyant performance). Entertaining saga cowritten by director Meyer. Nimoy helped concoct the story and also executive produced. Video version has 2 minutes of additional footage. Super 35. [PG] ▼●◗

Start the Revolution Without Me (1970) **C-91m.** *** D: Bud Yorkin. Gene Wilder, Donald Sutherland, Hugh Griffith, Jack MacGowran, Billie Whitelaw, Victor Spinetti, Ewa Aulin, Orson Welles. Madcap comedy involving two sets of mismatched twins who meet just before French Revolution. Somewhat ignored in 1970, now has a deserved cult following; the cast, especially Wilder, is hilarious. [PG] ▼

Star Wars (1977) **C-121m.** ***½ D: George Lucas. Mark Hamill, Harrison Ford, Carrie Fisher, Peter Cushing, Alec Guinness, Anthony Daniels, Kenny Baker, voice of James Earl Jones (as Darth Vader). Elaborate, imaginative update of Flash Gordon incredibly became one of the most popular films of all time. It's a hip homage to B-movie ethics and heroism in the space age, as a callow youth (Hamill) becomes an interplanetary hero with the help of some human and robot friends. R2D2 and C-3P0 steal the show. Won seven Oscars for various technical achievements and John Williams' rousing score. Full title onscreen (on re-release prints) is STAR WARS EPISODE IV: A NEW HOPE. Followed by THE EMPIRE STRIKES BACK and RETURN OF THE JEDI. Special Edition released in 1997 features souped-up special effects and about 4m. of new footage. Panavision. [PG]▼●

Star Wars Episode I: The Phantom Menace (1999) **C-133m.** *** D: George Lucas. Liam Neeson, Ewan McGregor, Natalie Portman, Jake Lloyd, Samuel L. Jackson, Frank Oz, Pernilla August, Terence Stamp, Ian McDiarmid, Hugh Quarshie, Ray Park, Ahmed Best, Brian Blessed, Sofia Coppola. Qui-Gon Jinn (Neeson) and his protégé Obi-Wan Kenobi (McGregor) try to negotiate peace but find themselves in the midst of war instead; while attempting to protect the Queen of Naboo (Portman), they stop over on the planet Tatooine, where they encounter young Anakin Skywalker (Lloyd), who clearly has a special gift. The beginning of Lucas' epic saga resembles his first STAR WARS film in both story and tone, with quantum leaps forward in special effects—including computer-generated characters (like comic-relief character Jar Jar Binks) who seem astonishingly real. Not a lot of heart, but certainly a lot of fun in Saturday matinee serial fashion. Arriscope. [PG]▼●

Star Witness (1931) **68m.** *** D: William Wellman. Walter Huston, Sally Blane, Chic Sale, Frances Starr, Grant Mitchell, Edward Nugent, Ralph Ince, Dickie Moore. Gritty, no-nonsense account of a family who witnesses a gangland battle and is terrorized to prevent them from testifying in court. Huston is the idealistic district attorney; Sale steals the film as the crotchety but resourceful grandfather.

State Fair (1933) **96m.** *** D: Henry King. Janet Gaynor, Will Rogers, Lew Ayres, Sally Eilers, Norman Foster, Louise Dresser, Victor Jory, Frank Craven. Not just a Rogers vehicle, but slice of life 30s-style as farm family gets ready for annual outing to state fair: Mom's entering bake-off contest, Dad the pig contest, son and daughter looking for first love. Great atmosphere, good performances. Phil Stong's novel has been remade twice (so far!).

State Fair (1945) **C-100m.** *** D: Walter Lang. Jeanne Crain, Dana Andrews, Dick Haymes, Vivian Blaine, Charles Winninger, Fay Bainter, Donald Meek, Frank McHugh, Percy Kilbride. Remake of the 1933 film is bright, engaging musical of family's adventures at Iowa State Fair; colorful, with fine Rodgers and Hammerstein songs (their only film score), including "That's For Me," "Grand Night for Singing," Oscar-winning "It Might As Well Be Spring." Retitled IT HAPPENED ONE SUMMER for TV. ▼●◗

State Fair (1962) **C-118m.** BOMB D: Jose Ferrer. Pat Boone, Bobby Darin, Pamela Tiffin, Ann-Margret, Alice Faye, Tom Ewell, Wally Cox. Remake of sprightly 1945 musical is pretty bad. Faye came out of retirement to play Tiffin's mother—a bad mistake. Ewell even sings to a pig! Third-rate Americana. CinemaScope.▼

State of Grace (1990) **C-134m.** **½ D: Phil Joanou. Sean Penn, Ed Harris, Gary Oldman, Robin Wright, John Turturro, Burgess Meredith, John C. Reilly. Three strong actors play Irish-American mobsters (inspired by real-life gang, the Westies) contending with the police, the Mafia, and Yuppie gentrification in N.Y.C.'s Hell's Kitchen (a neighborhood now known as Clinton!). Combination of moody stylishness and extreme violence nearly succeeds, but script is more meandering than incisive. This is basically Cagney terrain with a Scorsese-De Niro spin; Oldman and especially Harris sear the screen. [R]▼●

State of Siege (1973-French) **C-120m.** *** D: Costa-Gavras. Yves Montand, Renato Salvatori, O. E. Hasse, Jacques Weber, Jean-Luc Bideau, Evangeline Peterson. Highly controversial film, based on fact, about political assassination in Uruguay; interesting, but way too one-sided to be truly effective.▼

State of the Union (1948) **124m.** ***½ D: Frank Capra. Spencer Tracy, Katharine Hepburn, Angela Lansbury, Van Johnson, Adolphe Menjou, Lewis Stone, Raymond Walburn, Margaret Hamilton, Carl (Alfalfa) Switzer, Charles Lane, Tor Johnson. Contemporary as ever, this literate comedy-drama (adapted from the Howard Lindsay–Russel Crouse play) casts Tracy as an industrialist who struggles to keep his integrity as he's swallowed into the political machinery of running for President. Hepburn is his wife and conscience, Lansbury a power-hungry millionairess backing the campaign, Johnson the sardonic campaign manager. Great entertainment.▼●

State of Things, The (1982-German) **120m.** *** D: Wim Wenders. Allen Goorwitz (Garfield), Samuel Fuller, Paul Getty III, Roger Corman, Patrick Bauchau. Fascinating if uneven mystery from Wenders, centering on what happens as a film crew attempts to complete a remake of Corman's THE DAY THE WORLD ENDED on location in Portugal. Interesting as a peek behind the scenes at the filmmaking process, and as an homage to Corman.▼●

State Penitentiary (1950) **66m.** ** D: Lew Landers. Warner Baxter, Karin Booth, Robert Shayne, Richard Benedict. Programmer with Baxter a prisoner seeking to escape.

State's Attorney (1932) **79m.** *** D: George Archainbaud. John Barrymore, Helen Twelvetrees, William "Stage" Boyd, Ralph Ince, Jill Esmond, Albert Conti, Mary Duncan, C. Henry Gordon, Oscar Apfel, Leon Waycoff (Ames). Barrymore's the whole show as a flamboyant attorney with a flair for women and liquor; not much of a story, but there's some slick dialogue by Rowland Brown and Barrymore crony Gene Fowler.▼

State Secret (1950-British) **104m.** *** D: Sidney Gilliat. Douglas Fairbanks, Jr., Glynis Johns, Herbert Lom, Jack Hawkins, Walter Rilla. American doctor tries to flee Middle European country after he discovers its real leader has been assassinated and replaced with a double. Intelligent and witty suspense yarn; screenplay by Gilliat, from a Roy Huggins novel. Originally released in U.S. as THE GREAT MANHUNT.

Static (1985) **C-93m.** **½ D: Mark Romanek. Keith Gordon, Amanda Plummer, Bob Gunton, Barton Heyman, Lily Knight, Jane Hoffman. Annoyingly uneven comedy-drama about a strange young man (Gordon) and his rather unusual invention, a TV which can supposedly tune in to heaven. Sometimes genuinely touching and funny, but long stretches are deadening and dull. Gunton steals the film with his expert performance as a hilariously paranoid street evangelist. Written by leading actor Gordon and director Romanek. [R]▼●

Station, The (1990-Italian) **C-92m.** *** D: Sergio Rubini. Sergio Rubini, Margherita Buy, Ennio Fantastichini. Engrossing comedy-drama, with director Rubini starring as an unpretentious rural railroad clerk. His peaceful life is disrupted by the arrival of a beautiful woman on the lam from her brutal boyfriend. The manner in which the three characters interrelate forms the crux of this engaging, allegorical sleeper.▼

Stationmaster's Wife, The (1977-German) **C-111m.** **½ D: Rainer Werner Fassbinder. Kurt Raab, Elisabeth Trissenaar, Gustal Bayrhammer, Bernhard Helfrich, Udo Kier, Volker Spengler. Studied, stylized look at a beautiful woman's affairs and manipulation of her husband in pre-Hitler Germany. Some telling moments, and fine performances, but awfully slow going. Made for German television at 200m. Released theatrically in U.S. in 1983.▼

Station Six-Sahara (1964-British) **99m.** *½ D: Seth Holt. Carroll Baker, Peter Van Eyck, Ian Bannen, Denholm Elliott, Biff McGuire. Dreary yarn of five love-starved men who find something new to fight over when sexpot Baker and her estranged husband crash land at their desert oasis. Written by Bryan Forbes and Brian Clemens.

Station West (1948) **80m.** *** D: Sidney Lanfield. Dick Powell, Jane Greer, Tom Powers, Steve Brodie, Gordon Oliver, Raymond Burr, Agnes Moorehead, Burl Ives, Guinn Williams, Regis Toomey. Entertaining adaptation of Luke Short story about undercover military intelligence officer Powell stirring up trouble in Western town to find who's behind series of gold robberies. Script (by Frank Fenton and Winston Miller) has sharp dialogue throughout. Originally released at 92m. Also shown in computer-colored version.▼

Statue, The (1970-British) **C-84m.** BOMB D: Rod Amateau. David Niven, Virna Lisi, Robert Vaughn, Ann Bell, John Cleese, David Mills. Poor comedy concerning 20-foot statue (replica of Niven) with enormous male organ. [R]▼

Statutory Affair SEE: **Lola** (1969)

Stavisky . . . (1974-French-Italian) **C-117m.** ***½ D: Alain Resnais. Jean-Paul Belmondo, Charles Boyer, Francois Perier, Anny Duperey, Michel Lonsdale, Roberto Bisacca, Claude Rich, Gérard Depardieu. Stylish bio of French swindler of the early 1930s; pleasant cast, lavish photography (by Sacha Vierny), fine Stephen Sondheim score. Screenplay by Jorge Semprun. [PG]▼

Stay As You Are (1978-French) **C-95m.** *½ D: Alberto Lattuada. Marcello Mastroianni, Nastassia Kinski, Francisco Rabal, Monica Randal, Giuliana Calandra. Yawner with a twist: Kinski, the teenaged romance of middle-aged Mastroianni, may be his illegitimate daughter. For those who want to see Kinski during her nymphet stage; others beware.▼

Stay Away, Joe (1968) **C-102m.** *½ D: Peter Tewksbury. Elvis Presley, Burgess Meredith, Joan Blondell, Katy Jurado, Thomas Gomez, Henry Jones, L. Q. Jones. Bad film, even for Presley, about contemporary Indians. Reinforces stereotypes, fails to entertain. Panavision. [M/PG]▼●

Stay Hungry (1976) **C-103m.** *** D: Bob Rafelson. Jeff Bridges, Sally Field, Arnold Schwarzenegger, R. G. Armstrong, Robert Englund, Helena Kallianiotes, Roger Mosley, Scatman Crothers, Fannie Flagg, Joanna Cassidy, Richard Gilliland, Ed Begley, Jr., John David Carson, Joe Spinell. Charles Gaines novel about body-building in the "New South" is eccentric mixture of comedy and drama, but many fine scenes; happy performances from Field and Schwarzenegger make it worthwhile. [R]▼●

Staying Alive (1983) **C-96m.** ** D: Sylvester Stallone. John Travolta, Cynthia Rhodes, Finola Hughes, Steve Inwood, Julie Bovasso, Frank Stallone. Sequel to SATURDAY NIGHT FEVER is fashioned by director/cowriter Stallone into a ROCKY-type vehicle for Travolta, who juggles two women in his life while trying to score as a dancer on Broadway. Broadway show finale, *Satan's Alley* (billed, with amazing accuracy, as a musical trip through Hell) may become a camp classic, but neither the script nor the music (mostly by Sly's brother Frank) are in a class with the original 1977 film. [PG]▼●

Staying Together (1989) **C-91m.** **½ D: Lee Grant. Sean Astin, Stockard Channing, Melinda Dillon, Jim Haynie, Levon Helm, Dinah Manoff, Dermot Mulroney, Tim Quill, Keith Szarabajka, Daphne Zuniga. Close-knit small-town family, with three boys on the verge of manhood, gets pulled in all directions. Pat comedy-drama has one too many subplots, though entire cast is good. [R]▼●

Stay Tuned (1992) **C-87m.** *½ D: Peter Hyams. John Ritter, Pam Dawber, Jeffrey Jones, Eugene Levy, David Tom, Heather McComb, Bob Dishy, Joyce Gordon, Erik King, Salt 'n Pepa. Terminal couch potato Ritter unwittingly makes a pact with Devilish Jones, and finds himself and his wife sucked into a TV world in which they're part of the shows, from wrestling to private-eye mysteries. Promising premise goes nowhere in this dismal comedy; the only chuckles come from quick spoofs of TV titles, and the only segment that works is an animated cartoon supervised by the great Chuck Jones. Panavision. [PG]▼●◗

St. Benny the Dip (1951) **80m.** ** D: Edgar G. Ulmer. Dick Haymes, Nina Foch, Roland Young, Lionel Stander, Freddie Bartholomew, Richard Gordon. Silly, rambling account of a trio of con artists and their plight after disguising themselves as priests in order to evade the law. Child star Bartholomew's final film.▼

Steagle, The (1971) **C-90m.** ** D: Paul Sylbert. Richard Benjamin, Chill Wills, Cloris Leachman, Jean Allison, Susan Tyrrell. Missile crisis causes professor to go berserk and try living in lifestyles that previously were mental fantasies. Farfetched. [R]▼

Steal Big, Steal Little (1995) **C-135m.** ** D: Andrew Davis. Andy Garcia, Alan Arkin, Rachel Ticotin, Joe Pantoliano, Holland Taylor, Ally Walker, David Ogden Stiers, Charles Rocket, Richard Bradford, Kevin McCarthy. Amiable mess of a movie with plot strands going in all directions; a real shame, too, because there's a nice feel to this modern fable about twin brothers, separated in childhood, who take different paths in life. One greedily pursues money and power, the other grows up with a free-spirited share-the-wealth ideal. Garcia has never been more engaging. Set and shot in Santa Barbara, California. [PG-13]▼●

Stealing Beauty (1996-French-Italian-British-U.S.) **C-119m.** *** D: Bernardo Bertolucci. Jeremy Irons, Liv Tyler, Joseph Fiennes, Sinead Cusack, Rachel Weisz, Stefania Sandrelli, Jean Marais, D. W. Moffett, Donal McCann, Jason Flemyng. 19-year-old American girl spends the summer at a villa in Tuscany filled with wildly divergent characters and discovers her own independence as she affects the lives of all those around her. Bertolucci returns to his Italian roots for this charming contemporary story. Tyler is a star in the making here, and Irons is touching as a dying man who finds renewed life from this young visitor. Bertolucci co-scripted, from his story. Super 35. [R] ▼●

Stealing Heaven (1988-British-Yugoslavian) **C-115m.** *** D: Clive Donner. Kim Thomson, Derek de Lint, Denholm Elliott, Mark Jax, Bernard Hepton, Kenneth Cranham, Angela Pleasence, Rachel Kempson. Beautifully photographed (if somewhat anachronistic) period piece about the real-life 12th-century lovers Abelard and Héloise. Intelligent treatment even incorporates discussions of theology in the context of this passionate romance. Threatened with an X rating, film was trimmed to 108m. for U.S. release; both versions available on video. [R]▼●

Stealing Home (1988) **C-98m.** **½ D: Steven Kampmann, Will Aldis. Mark Harmon, Jodie Foster, William McNamara, Blair Brown, Harold Ramis, Jonathan Silverman, Richard Jenkins, John Shea, Ted Ross, Helen Hunt, Thatcher Goodwin, Yvette Croskey. Has-been baseball player is summoned home to take care of the ashes of an old friend, who killed herself. Story flashes back to his relationship with her at several ages. Earnest but pat, semi-autobiographical script (by the directors) is helped immeasurably by Foster's wise, outstanding performance as the late friend, a troubled free spirit. [PG-13]▼●◗

Steamboat Bill, Jr. (1928) **71m.** *** D: Charles F. Riesner. Buster Keaton, Ernest Torrence, Marion Byron, Tom Lewis, Tom McGuire. Buster plays a milquetoast who must prove his manhood to steamboat captain father (Torrence). Not one of Keaton's best silents, but there are great moments, and classic, eye-popping cyclone finale.▼●◗

Steamboat 'Round the Bend (1935) **96m.** *** D: John Ford. Will Rogers, Anne Shirley, Irvin S. Cobb, Eugene Pallette, Berton Churchill, John McGuire, Stepin Fetchit, Francis Ford, Pardner Jones, Charles Middleton. Enjoyable Ford/Rogers period-piece of steamboat captain (Rogers) who pilots a ramshackle floating waxworks museum, from which he also dispenses highly alcoholic cure-all medicine. Shirley is particularly good as swamp-girl taken in by Rogers. Churchill shines in comic role of river prophet "The New Moses." Climactic steamboat race is a gem. Released posthumously after Rogers' tragic death.

Steaming (1985-British) **C-95m.** **½ D: Joseph Losey. Vanessa Redgrave, Sarah Miles, Diana Dors, Patti Love, Brenda Bruce, Felicity Dean, Sally Sagoe. Disappointing adaptation of the Nell Dunn play, about the interactions of a group of women in a run-down London steam bath. Not all that bad, really, with collectively above-average performances, but sorely lacks the humor that made it work so well on stage. Director Losey's last film, and Dors' as well. [R]▼

Steel (1980) **C-99m.** **½ D: Steve Carver. Lee Majors, Jennifer O'Neill, Art Carney, George Kennedy, Harris Yulin, Terry Kiser, Richard Lynch, Roger Mosley, Albert Salmi, R. G. Armstrong. Fast-moving, entertaining time-killer about construction workers struggling to complete a skyscraper on schedule. Filmed in Lexington, Ky. Aka LOOK DOWN AND DIE and MEN OF STEEL. [PG]▼

Steel (1997) **C-97m.** *½ D: Kenneth Johnson. Shaquille O'Neal, Annabeth Gish, Judd Nelson, Richard Roundtree, Irma P. Hall, Ray J., Charles Napier. Film version of DC Comics' "Steel" with basketball great Shaq in the title role, as a tall superhero with a heart of gold, wearing a funny metal suit and doing battle with stereotypical enemies of modern civilization. As endearing as Shaq can be, he should definitely *not* give up his day job. [PG-13] ▼●

Steel Bayonet (1957-British) **84m.** ** D: Michael Carreras. Leo Genn, Kieron Moore, Michael Medwin, Robert Brown. Military unit is ordered to defend deserted farmhouse/lookout base at all costs. Tame WW2 film set in Africa; watch for Michael Caine as a German soldier. Hammerscope.

Steel Cage, The (1954) **80m.** ** D: Walter Doniger. Paul Kelly, Maureen O'Sullivan, Walter Slezak, John Ireland, Lawrence Tierney, Alan Mowbray, George E. Stone, Lyle Talbot. Pedestrian telling of life at San Quentin, despite good cast. Sequel to DUFFY OF SAN QUENTIN.

Steel Claw, The (1961) **C-96m.** **½ D: George Montgomery. George Montgomery, Charito Luna, Mario Barri, Paul Sorensen. Montgomery turns partisan leader when he loses hand in WW2, forcing his marine discharge; on-location filming in Philippines and sufficient combat action spark story along.▼

Steel Dawn (1987) **C-100m.** ** D: Lance Hool. Patrick Swayze, Lisa Niemi, Christopher Neame, Brion James, Anthony Zerbe, John Fujioka, Brett Hool. Futuristic rehash of SHANE has Swayze as the mysterious warrior who ends up protecting pretty farmer Niemi (his real-life wife) and her cute son against evil Zerbe and his henchmen. Filmed on attractive desert locations in southern Africa, this failed to extend Swayze's meteoric success in DIRTY DANCING. [R]▼●

Steele Justice (1987) **C-95m.** ** D: Robert Boris. Martin Kove, Sela Ward, Ronny Cox, Bernie Casey, Joseph Campanella, Soon-Teck Oh, Jan Gan Boyd, Robert Kim, Peter Kwong, Shannon Tweed, Sarah Douglas. Howlingly absurd action-revenge yarn with beefy Vietnam vet Kove investigating the murder of a Vietnamese friend and his family in L.A., and going after former Viet general who's now a druglord in America. Nagging doubts persist—do the filmmakers intend this to be so funny? —but Kove's impromptu wound-cauterizing scene makes it all worthwhile. [R]▼●

Steel Fist, The (1952) **73m.** *½ D: Wesley Barry. Roddy McDowall, Kristine Miller,

Harry Lauter, Rand Brooks. Quickie flick with McDowall involved in escape from Iron Curtain country; low production values.

Steel Helmet, The (1951) **84m.** ***½ D: Samuel Fuller. Gene Evans, Robert Hutton, Steve Brodie, James Edwards, Richard Loo, Sid Melton. Evans is a gutsy American sergeant caught in dizzying turn of events in early days of Korean war; solid melodrama written by Fuller, with surprisingly contemporary view of war itself.▼

Steel Jungle, The (1956) **86m.** *½ D: Walter Doniger. Perry Lopez, Beverly Garland, Allison Hayes, Walter Abel, Ted de Corsia, Kenneth Tobey. Lukewarm account of prison life.

Steel Key, The (1953-British) **74m.** **½ D: Robert Baker. Terence Morgan, Joan Rice, Raymond Lovell, Dianne Foster, Esmond Knight. Espionage and homicide abound in this fast-clipping caper about stolen formulas for processing hardened steel.

Steel Lady, The (1953) **84m.** **½ D: E. A. Dupont. Rod Cameron, Tab Hunter, John Dehner, Richard Erdman, Anthony Caruso. Fair adventure of four trapped men in desert who find old German tank.

Steel Magnolias (1989) **C-118m.** *** D: Herbert Ross. Sally Field, Dolly Parton, Shirley MacLaine, Daryl Hannah, Olympia Dukakis, Julia Roberts, Tom Skerritt, Sam Shepard, Dylan McDermott, Kevin J. O'Connor, Bill McCutcheon, Ann Wedgeworth, Janine Turner. Slick comedy-drama about several years in the lives of the women who congregate at Parton's beauty parlor in a small Louisiana town. No TERMS OF ENDEARMENT, but does provide solid entertainment. Written by Robert Harling, who expanded his own one-set play for the screen (and plays the minister here). Super 35. [PG]▼●

Steel Town (1952) **C-85m.** ** D: George Sherman. Ann Sheridan, John Lund, Howard Duff, James Best, Nancy Kulp. Uninspired story of steelmaking and the personal problems of nephew of steel plant owner; Sheridan tries, but can't perk up this programmer.

Steel Trap, The (1952) **85m.** **½ D: Andrew Stone. Joseph Cotten, Teresa Wright, Jonathan Hale, Walter Sande. Trim caper of employee Cotten who steals money from his bank and over the weekend tries to replace it.

Steelyard Blues (1973) **C-93m.** *** D: Alan Myerson. Jane Fonda, Donald Sutherland, Peter Boyle, Garry Goodrow, Howard Hesseman, John Savage. Entertaining comic concoction by David S. Ward about band of misfits who become involved in nutty project of rejuvenating abandoned airplane. Amiably antiestablishment film highlights Boyle as an ingenious fantasist named Eagle. Retitled THE FINAL CRASH for network TV. [PG]▼

Stella (1950) **83m.** **½ D: Claude Binyon. Ann Sheridan, Victor Mature, David Wayne, Frank Fontaine. Screwball comedy and murder don't blend well in tale of nutty family trying to hide a corpse.

Stella (1990) **C-109m.** ** D: John Erman. Bette Midler, John Goodman, Trini Alvarado, Stephen Collins, Marsha Mason, Eileen Brennan, Linda Hart, Ben Stiller, William McNamara. Update of the perennial soaper STELLA DALLAS goes with the times on only one plot element: in this version, Stella *doesn't* marry the father of her child. Tolerable for a while, but hopelessly anachronistic. [PG-13] ▼●

Stella Dallas (1937) **106m.** *** D: King Vidor. Barbara Stanwyck, John Boles, Anne Shirley, Barbara O'Neil, Alan Hale, Tim Holt, Marjorie Main. Definitive soap opera (from Olive Higgins Prouty's novel) of woman who sacrifices everything for her daughter; Stanwyck gives one of her finest performances. Tear-jerking score by Alfred Newman. Filmed before in 1925; remade in 1990 as STELLA. ▼●◗

St. Elmo's Fire (1985) **C-108m.** **½ D: Joel Schumacher. Rob Lowe, Demi Moore, Andrew McCarthy, Judd Nelson, Ally Sheedy, Emilio Estevez, Mare Winningham, Martin Balsam, Jon Cutler, Joyce Van Patten, Andie MacDowell, Blake Clark, Matthew Laurance, Anna Maria Horsford. Slick vehicle for some charismatic young actors, as recent college grads having a hard time coping with Real Life. Invites comparison to THE BREAKFAST CLUB and THE BIG CHILL, but these "young adults" are pretty immature, and so is the film, written by director Schumacher. Panavision. [R]▼●

Step by Step (1946) **62m.** ** D: Phil Rosen. Lawrence Tierney, Anne Jeffreys, Lowell Gilmore, George Cleveland. Patriotic programmer with Tierney a WW2 veteran uncovering Fascist agents in America.

Step Down to Terror (1958) **75m.** ** D: Harry Keller. Colleen Miller, Charles Drake, Rod Taylor, Josephine Hutchinson, Jocelyn Brando. Washed-out remake of Hitchcock's SHADOW OF A DOUBT, retells account of psycho-murderer returning to home town after long absence. Story remade again (for TV) under original title.

Stepfather, The (1987) **C-98m.** *** D: Joseph Ruben. Terry O'Quinn, Jill Schoelen, Shelley Hack, Stephen Shellen, Charles Lanyer. Engrossing thriller has well-cast O'Quinn as a meek-looking guy desperately seeking to have the perfect little family. He turns out to be a psycho who marries widows and eventually erupts into violence. Thoughtful screenplay by Donald E. Westlake and taut direction by Ruben highlight this sleeper. Story by Westlake, Carolyn Lefcourt, and Brian Garfield. Followed by two sequels. [R]▼●

Stepfather II (1989) **C-86m.** *½ D: Jeff Burr. Terry O'Quinn, Meg Foster, Jonathan Brandis, Caroline Williams, Mitchell Laurance, Henry Brown, Leon Martell, Renata Scott. Mad family killer O'Quinn escapes from the booby hatch, sets himself up in suburbia as a marriage counselor, and starts courting a potential new wife (Foster). Inferior sequel is completely devoid of suspense and looks cheap, but O'Quinn still manages to deliver a good performance. [R]▼●

Stepford Wives, The (1975) **C-115m.** *** D: Bryan Forbes. Katharine Ross, Paula Prentiss, Peter Masterson, Nanette Newman, Patrick O'Neal, Tina Louise, Dee Wallace, William Prince. Effective chiller finds suburban housewives Ross and Prentiss trying to understand perpetually blissful state of the women of Stepford, Connecticut. Script by William Goldman from Ira Levin's best-seller. Seven-year-old Mary Stuart Masterson makes her film debut (playing the daughter of real-life dad Peter Masterson). Followed by three inferior TV sequels: REVENGE OF THE STEPFORD WIVES, THE STEPFORD CHILDREN, and THE STEPFORD HUSBANDS. [PG]▼●◗

Stephen King's Cat's Eye SEE: **Cat's Eye**

Stephen King's Graveyard Shift SEE: **Graveyard Shift**

Stephen King's Silver Bullet SEE: **Silver Bullet**

Stephen King's "Sleepwalkers" SEE: **Sleepwalkers**

Stephen King's The Night Flier SEE: **Night Flier, The**

Stephen King's "The Tommyknockers" SEE: **Tommyknockers, The**

Stephen King's Thinner SEE: **Thinner** (1996)

Step Lively (1944) **88m.** *** D: Tim Whelan. Frank Sinatra, George Murphy, Adolphe Menjou, Gloria DeHaven, Eugene Pallette, Anne Jeffreys, Walter Slezak. Brisk musical remake of ROOM SERVICE with producer Murphy wheeling and dealing to get his show produced. Engagingly frantic, with sharp dialogue, funny contribution by Slezak as the hotel manager. If you blink you'll miss (brunette) Dorothy Malone as switchboard operator in lobby.▼

Step Lively, Jeeves! (1937) **69m.** **½ D: Eugene Forde. Arthur Treacher, Patricia Ellis, Robert Kent, Alan Dinehart, George Givot, Franklin Pangborn. Treacher is in top form as P. G. Wodehouse's droll English valet, who comes to America and gets mixed up with gangsters when two con men convince him he's Sir Francis Drake's missing heir. Amusing, if overplotted, follow-up to THANK YOU, JEEVES!, though not based on any Wodehouse story.

Stepmom (1998) **C-125m.** ** D: Chris Columbus. Susan Sarandon, Julia Roberts, Ed Harris, Jena Malone, Liam Aiken, Lynn Whitfield. Slick, big-studio, all-star treatment of life after divorce. Sarandon plays a woman who objects to the presence of her ex's girlfriend in her children's lives. Glossy melodrama with occasional touches of humor; the leads outshine the mawkish material. Panavision. [PG-13]▼●◗

Stepmother, The (1971) **C-94m.** *½ D: Hikmet Avedis. Alejandro Rey, John Anderson, Katherine Justice, John D. Garfield, Marlene Schmidt, Claudia Jennings, Duncan McLeod. Rey is okay as anti-hero of this cheapie murder-suspenser in the Hitchcock mold. John Garfield's son is unimpressive in support. Aka IMPULSION. [R]▼

Steppenwolf (1974) **C-105m.** **½ D: Fred Haines. Max von Sydow, Dominique Sanda, Pierre Clementi, Carla Romanelli, Alfred Bailloux. Literal adaptation of Herman Hesse's unfilmable novel about a misanthropic writer and an enigmatic young woman. Visually jazzy, rarely boring, but a dead end. [R]▼●

Stepping Out (1991) **C-106m.** ** D: Lewis Gilbert. Liza Minnelli, Shelley Winters, Bill Irwin, Ellen Greene, Julie Walters, Robyn Stevan, Jane Krakowski, Sheila McCarthy, Andrea Martin, Carol Woods, Nora Dunn. Harmless blue-haired musical soaper about a smorgasbord group of Buffalo tap-dancing aspirants who bicker under Minnelli's tutelage. Richard Harris (not the actor) adapted his play, glitzed up by director Gilbert. There's a gratuitous show-stopping piece at the end for Liza-watchers, while Winters has some genuinely affecting moments as the piano accompanist. [PG]▼●

Sterile Cuckoo, The (1969) **C-107m.** *** D: Alan J. Pakula. Liza Minnelli, Wendell Burton, Tim McIntire. Lonely Pookie Adams (Minnelli) forces herself on shy freshman Burton, who's impelled to pay attention. Winning look at young love and sensitive feelings gives Liza a stand-out role, with Burton equally fine as naive boy who eventually outgrows her. Dory Previn's song "Come Saturday Morning" is featured. Producer Pakula's directorial debut. Based on a novel by John Nichols. [PG]▼●

Stevie (1978-British) **C-102m.** *** D: Robert Enders. Glenda Jackson, Mona Washbourne, Alec McCowen, Trevor Howard. Film version of Hugh Whitemore's London stage play about British poetess Stevie Smith (Jackson), who lives with her maiden aunt (Washbourne). Finely wrought character study; excellent performances. [PG]▼

Stewardess School (1987) **C-93m.** BOMB D: Ken Blancato. Brett Cullen, Mary Cadorette, Donald Most, Sandahl Bergman, Sherman Hemsley, Vicki Frederick, Judy Landers, Wendie Jo Sperber, Vito Scotti. A major studio financed this low-brow comedy, then kept it on the shelf for a year. It should've stayed. [R]▼●

St. Helens (1981) **C-90m.** **½ D: Ernest Pintoff. Art Carney, David Huffman, Cassie Yates, Ron O'Neal, Bill McKinney,

Albert Salmi. Mount St. Helens is about to erupt, and old codger Carney (named Harry Truman!) refuses to leave his home. Not too bad, with a fine Carney performance; based on a true story. [PG]▼

Stick (1985) **C-109m.** *½ D: Burt Reynolds. Burt Reynolds, Candice Bergen, George Segal, Charles Durning, Jose Perez, Richard Lawson, Alex Rocco, Tricia Leigh Fisher, Dar Robinson. Incredibly boring underworld melodrama about an ex-con who sets out to avenge the death of an old buddy and finds himself knee-deep in ugly drug dealers. Originally set for release in 1984, then pulled back for some reshooting, which apparently didn't help. Based on an Elmore Leonard novel. [R]▼●

Sticky Fingers (1988) **C-97m.** ** D: Catlin Adams. Helen Slater, Melanie Mayron, Danitra Vance, Eileen Brennan, Carol Kane, Loretta Devine, Stephen McHattie, Christopher Guest, Gwen Welles, Shirley Stoler. Dippy roommates find themselves the custodians of a suitcase full of drug money, which they proceed to "borrow" and spend. Earnest attempt at wacky, female-slanted comedy goes completely askew. Likable stars and a high energy level can't keep it afloat. Scripted by director Adams and costar Mayron. [PG-13]▼●

Stiffs SEE: **Out Cold**

Stiff Upper Lips (1998-British) **C-94m.** ** D: Gary Sinyor. Peter Ustinov, Prunella Scales, Georgina Cates, Samuel West, Sean Pertwee, Robert Portal, Brian Glover, Frank Finlay. A high-born young woman falls in love with a handsome peasant. Anemic spoof of Merchant-Ivory films and the type of fodder that turns up on *Masterpiece Theater*. Some easy laughs here and there, but as parodies go this one is strictly second-rate.▼

Stigmata (1999) **C-103m.** *½ D: Rupert Wainwright. Patricia Arquette, Gabriel Byrne, Jonathan Pryce, Nia Long, Thomas Kopache, Rade Sherbedgia (Serbedzija), Enrico Colantoni, Dick Latessa, Portia de Rossi. A lotta *Sturm,* a lotta *Drang,* but not much else in this EXORCIST derivation about a young woman who quite suddenly suffers from bloody attacks (à la stigmata) and hallucinations . . . and the Vatican scientist/priest who comes to investigate. Loud, flamboyant (with meaningless closeups of coffee pouring, an egg frying, etc.), but hopeless. Super 35. [R]▼◗

Stiletto (1969) **C-98m.** *½ D: Bernard Kowalski. Alex Cord, Britt Ekland, Patrick O'Neal, Joseph Wiseman, Barbara McNair, Roy Scheider, Charles Durning, M. Emmett Walsh. Weak Mafia melodrama about handsome killer who lives like a playboy, kills for money. Repercussions abound when he decides to quit his job. From the Harold Robbins novel. Look fast for Raul Julia in a party scene. [R]▼

Still Breathing (1998) **C-108m.** **½ D: James F. Robinson. Brendan Fraser, Joanna Going, Celeste Holm, Ann Magnuson, Lou Rawls, Angus MacFadyen, Toby Huss, Paolo Seganti, Michael McKean, Junior Brown, The Jim Cullum Jazz Band. One of those supposedly "magical" romances, in which two complete opposites (San Antonio puppeteer/dreamer Fraser and L.A. con artist/cynic Going) eventually find each other. Two fine lead performances help lift this above the routine and keep it from being overly syrupy. [PG-13]▼

Still Crazy (1998-U.S.-British) **C-97m.** *** D: Brian Gibson. Stephen Rea, Billy Connolly, Jimmy Nail, Timothy Spall, Bill Nighy, Juliet Aubrey, Helena Bergstrom, Bruce Robinson, Rachael Stirling. Amiable film about the reunion of a 1970s rock band called Strange Fruit and its star-crossed musicians, whose resentments and peccadilloes are still fresh after twenty years. Built on a surefire foundation, the story has just enough twists to keep you guessing where it's going and a gallery of enjoyable performances. Bonus: the music is actually pretty good. [R] ▼●◗

Still of the Night (1982) **C-91m.** ** D: Robert Benton. Roy Scheider, Meryl Streep, Jessica Tandy, Joe Grifasi, Sara Botsford, Josef Sommer, Irving Metzman, Larry Joshua. Yet another disappointing homage to Hitchcock in this tale of a psychiatrist attracted to a woman who may or may not have murdered one of his patients. A cold film with more plot holes than one would care to count. [PG]▼

Still Smokin' (1983) **C-91m.** BOMB D: Thomas Chong. Cheech Marin, Thomas Chong, Hansman In't Veld, Carol Van Herwijnen, Shirleen Stroker, Susan Hahn. Rock bottom. Not even the most forgiving C & C fans can justify this nonmovie that climaxes a scant plot involving an Amsterdam film festival with twenty minutes of laughless concert footage. An unreleaseable film that somehow made it to theaters—for five-day runs. [R]▼●

Sting, The (1973) **C-129m.** ***½ D: George Roy Hill. Paul Newman, Robert Redford, Robert Shaw, Charles Durning, Ray Walston, Eileen Brennan, Harold Gould, Dana Elcar, Jack Kehoe, Dimitra Arliss, Charles Dierkop, Sally Kirkland. Two small-time Chicago con-men try to put "the sting" on a high-roller from N.Y.C. (Shaw) after he has one of their pals killed. This long but entertaining film won seven Oscars, including Best Picture, Director, and Screenplay (David S. Ward), and sparked national revival of Scott Joplin's ragtime music (arranged here by Oscar winner Marvin Hamlisch). Sequel: THE STING II. [PG] ▼●◗

Sting II, The (1983) **C-102m.** *½ D: Jeremy Paul Kagan. Jackie Gleason, Mac Davis, Teri Garr, Karl Malden, Oliver Reed, Bert Remsen. Even as recent sequels go, this tardy follow-up to the Oscar winner is pretty limp. Gleason and Davis (in Newman's and Redford's roles!) rig a boxing match designed to shaft Malden, with Reed (in Shaw's role) as an unknowing cog in the scheme. Despite the male milieu, only Garr delivers a lively performance. Oddly, David S. Ward wrote this one, too. [PG]▼●

Stingray (1978) **C-100m.** *½ D: Richard Taylor. Sherry Jackson, Christopher Mitchum, Bill Watson, Les Lannom, Sondra Theodore, Bert Hinchman. Low-grade mix of action, blood, and comedy as Mitchum and Lannom buy a Stingray, unaware that it's filled with stolen loot and dope, prompting pursuit by murderous Jackson. Filmed in and around St. Louis. Aka ABIGAIL: WANTED. [PG]▼

Stir (1980-Australian) **C-100m.** ***½ D: Stephen Wallace. Bryan Brown, Max Phipps, Dennis Miller, Michael Gow, Phil Motherwell, Gary Waddell. Harrowing tale of life in prison, focusing on the jailors' brutality and culminating in riots and destruction. Excellent performances by all, particularly Brown; a memorable first feature for Wallace. Screenplay by Ben Jewson, based on first-hand experience.

Stir Crazy (1980) **C-111m.** *** D: Sidney Poitier. Gene Wilder, Richard Pryor, Georg Stanford Brown, JoBeth Williams, Miguelangel Suarez, Craig T. Nelson, Barry Corbin, Erland van Lidth de Jeude, Lee Purcell. Broadly funny film about two yoyos who bungle their way into prison. No great shakes in terms of script or direction; just a lot of good laughs. Screenplay by Bruce Jay Friedman; lively score by Tom Scott. Later a brief TV series. [R]▼●◗

Stir of Echoes (1999) **C-99m.** **½ D: David Koepp. Kevin Bacon, Kathryn Erbe, Kevin Dunn, Illeana Douglas, Liza Weil, Conor O'Farrell, Jenny Morrison, Zachary David Cope. Working-class Chicagoan undergoes hypnosis for a lark and suddenly finds himself haunted by visions and premonitions—just like his five-year-old son, who sees ghosts. Intriguing film plays with our emotions and becomes increasingly unpleasant as it goes along. Koepp adapted Richard Matheson's novel. [R]▼●◗

Stitches (1985) **C-89m.** BOMB D: Alan Smithee (Rod Holcomb). Parker Stevenson, Geoffrey Lewis, Brian Tochi, Robin Dearden, Eddie Albert. Derivative comedy about medical students' hijinks is not titillating or funny enough to be diverting. Director Holcomb had his name removed from the credits after film was doctored during postproduction. [R]▼

St. Ives (1976) **C-93m.** ** D: J. Lee Thompson. Charles Bronson, John Houseman, Jacqueline Bisset, Harry Guardino, Maximilian Schell, Harris Yulin, Dana Elcar, Elisha Cook, Michael Lerner, Daniel J. Travanti. Muddled yarn about would-be writer Bronson who becomes a pawn for wealthy conniver Houseman and his beautiful associate (Bisset) and finds himself involved in murder. Glossy but stupid. Look for Jeff Goldblum and Robert Englund as hoods. [PG]▼

St. Louis Blues (1939) **87m.** *** D: Raoul Walsh. Dorothy Lamour, Lloyd Nolan, Tito Guizar, Jerome Cowan, Jessie Ralph, William Frawley. Showgirl Lamour deserts the Great White Way and her manager to appear incognito on a riverboat. Amusing and entertaining Paramount musical-comedy. TV title: BEST OF THE BLUES.

St. Louis Blues (1958) **93m.** ** D: Allen Reisner. Nat "King" Cole, Eartha Kitt, Ruby Dee, Pearl Bailey, Juano Hernandez, Cab Calloway, Ella Fitzgerald, Mahalia Jackson. Treacly dramatics interspersed with outstanding musical performances in this so-called biography of W. C. Handy (Cole, in his lone starring role), who composed the title tune. Billy Preston plays Handy as a boy. VistaVision.

St. Louis Kid (1934) **67m.** **½ D: Ray Enright. James Cagney, Patricia Ellis, Allen Jenkins, Robert Barrat, Addison Richards. Breezy Cagney vehicle casts him and Jenkins as truckdriving buddies who have a knack for getting into trouble—and wind up in the middle of a war between a dairy trust and angry farmers.

St. Martin's Lane SEE: **Sidewalks of London**

Stolen Babies (1993) **C-100m. TVM** D: Eric Laneuville. Lea Thompson, Kathleen Quinlan, Mary Tyler Moore, Mary Nell Santacroce. Thompson plays real-life 1940s Tennessee social worker Anne Beals, who uncovers an illegal adoption ring run by a nearly unrecognizable Moore (in Emmy-winning performance) as the charismatic woman with friends in high places. A pedestrian script compromises the project. Made for cable. Average.

Stolen Children (1992-Italian-French) **C-112m.** ***½ D: Gianni Amelio. Enrico Lo Verso, Valentina Scalici, Giuseppe Ieracitano, Florence Darel, Marina Golovine. A sister and brother are dragged across half of Italy after their no-good mother is arrested; they've been neglected, and the girl knows more about the business of prostitution than any eleven-year-old should. Young military man Lo Verso, charged with transporting these unwanted wards of the state, grows to care about them. Stunning, simple film (a multi-award winner in Europe) harks back to the Italian Neo-realist school, with three unbeatable performances. Scripted by Sandro Petraglia, Stefano Rulli, and the director. Original title: IL LADRO DI BAMBINI. ▼

Stolen Face, A (1952-British) **72m.** **½

D: Terence Fisher. Lizabeth Scott, Paul Henreid, Andre Morell, Susan Stephen, Mary Mackenzie, John Wood. Interesting but far-fetched drama of plastic surgeon Henreid trying to transform female convict into replica of the woman he loves but cannot have.

Stolen Heaven (1938) **88m.** **½ D: Andrew L. Stone. Gene Raymond, Olympe Bradna, Glenda Farrell, Lewis Stone, Porter Hall, Douglass Dumbrille, Joe Sawyer. Offbeat story of jewel thieves posing as musicians on the lam but having change of heart when they meet kindly maestro Stone.

Stolen Hours, The (1963) **C-100m.** **½ D: Daniel Petrie. Susan Hayward, Michael Craig, Diane Baker, Edward Judd, Paul Rogers. Hayward takes Bette Davis' DARK VICTORY, transplants it to contemporary England, in tale of woman with fatal illness trying to get as much out of life as she can. Original is far superior in all departments.▼

Stolen Kisses (1968-French) **C-90m.** **** D: François Truffaut. Jean-Pierre Léaud, Delphine Seyrig, Michel Lonsdale, Claude Jade, Harry Max, Daniel Ceccaldi. This alternately touching and hilarious film about an inept but likable jerk-of-all-trades is possibly Truffaut's best movie and one of the best treatments of young love ever put on the screen. Third in his Antoine Doinel series, followed by BED AND BOARD. [R]▼◗

Stolen Life, A (1946) **107m.** **½ D: Curtis Bernhardt. Bette Davis, Glenn Ford, Dane Clark, Walter Brennan, Charlie Ruggles, Bruce Bennett, Peggy Knudsen. A twin takes her sister's place as wife of the man they both love in this slick but far-fetched soaper with Bette in dual role; remake of 1939 film with Elisabeth Bergner.▼●

Stolen Memories: Secrets From the Rose Garden (1996) **C-100m. TVM** D: Bob Clark. Mary Tyler Moore, Linda Lavin, Shirley Knight, Paul Winfield, Nathan Watt, Wayne Grace. Moore shines as a child-woman sheltered by her two protective sisters, whose lives are altered by their preteen great-nephew (Watt). Period piece set in the 1950s is lovingly realized in the script by first-timer Tim Cagney, recalling his own childhood experiences. Costar Lavin was executive producer. Made for cable. Above average.

Stone Boy, The (1984) **C-93m.** ***½ D: Chris Cain. Robert Duvall, Jason Presson, Glenn Close, Frederic Forrest, Wilford Brimley, Gail Youngs, Cindy Fisher, Linda Hamilton, Dean Cain. Tragedy sends a simple farming family into shock, and leaves the youngest boy to sort out his problems on his own. Perceptive and poignant look at the way people react to serious situations in real life, with a gallery of outstanding performances. May be too slow and introspective for some viewers' taste. Film debut of Cain (the director's stepson). [PG]▼

Stone Cold (1991) **C-90m.** *½ D: Craig R. Baxley. Brian Bosworth, Lance Henriksen, William Forsythe, Arabella Holzbog, Sam McMurray. Football's "Boz" infiltrates a gang of Mississippi bikers whose extortion antics have caught the attention of both the Feds *and* the Mob. Only some amazing stunts save this silliness from the BOMB scrap heap. Written and executive produced by Walter Doniger, who once directed Mantle and Maris in SAFE AT HOME! [R]▼●

Stone Cold Dead (1980-Canadian) **C-97m.** **½ D: George Mendeluk. Richard Crenna, Paul Williams, Linda Sorenson, Belinda J. Montgomery, Charles Shamata, George Chuvalo. Cop Crenna versus mobster Williams. Compact little drama. [R]▼

Stone Killer, The (1973) **C-95m.** **½ D: Michael Winner. Charles Bronson, Martin Balsam, David Sheiner, Norman Fell, Ralph Waite. Good action in thriller about hard-headed cop trying to unravel chain of mystery that leads to elaborate plan using Vietnam vets to stage underworld massacre. Well made but pretty violent. [R]▼●

Stones for Ibarra (1988) **C-100m. TVM** D: Jack Gold. Glenn Close, Keith Carradine, Alfonso Arau, Jorge Cervera, Jr., Trinidad Silva, Angie Porres. Thoughtful, intelligently acted adaptation by veteran Ernest Kinoy of Harriett Doerr's prize-winning novel about an American couple living in a small Mexican village. Aside from the two leads (both hitting all the right chords) the entire cast is Latino. Above average.▼

Stonewall (1995-U.S.-British) **C-99m.** **½ D: Nigel Finch. Guillermo Diaz, Fred Weller, Brendan Corbalis, Bruce MacVittie, Luis Guzman, Duane Boutte, Matthew Faber. Historic look-back at the 1969 Greenwich Village bar riot that sparked the gay rights movement, told as a fictitious personal story about a young Puerto Rican drag queen (the terrific Diaz) who becomes politically conscious when he falls in love with an idealistic midwestern hippie. Important subject matter deserved better, bigger-budgeted film, but this is still an effective portrait of discrimination. Director Finch died of AIDS shortly after the film was completed. Isaiah Washington has a bit part as a cop. [R]▼●

Stony Island (1978) **C-97m.** *** D: Andrew Davis. Richard Davis, Edward Stony Robinson, Ronnie Barron, George Englund, Gene Barge, Susanna Hoffs, Rae Dawn Chong. Independent feature, filmed in Chicago, about an integrated group of youthful rhythm and blues performers and the death of an older black musician, nicely played by Barge. Fine music sequences and use of urban locations make up for lack of character and story development. Aka MY MAIN MAN FROM STONY ISLAND. [PG]

Stooge, The (1953) **100m.** **½ D: Norman Taurog. Dean Martin, Jerry Lewis,

Polly Bergen, Eddie Mayehoff, Marion Marshall. Egocentric singer (Martin) learns the hard way just how important his stooge (Lewis) is to his success. Martin & Lewis go dramatic with middling results. Completed in 1951, not released for two years.▼

Stoogemania (1985) **C-83m.** *½ D: Chuck Workman. Josh Mostel, Melanie Chartoff, Sid Caesar, Josh Miner, Thom Sharp. Well-meaning but completely unfunny tale of one Howard F. Howard, whose passion for The Three Stooges has overtaken his life. Incorporates real footage of the Stooges, and while most of it is far from their best, it's still vastly superior to the new material in this feature. For those who care, some of the Stooge footage is computer-colored. [PG]▼

Stoolie, The (1974) **C-90m.** **½ D: John G. Avildsen. Jackie Mason, Dan Frazer, Marcia Jean Kurtz, Anne Marie. Flawed but interesting little film, with Mason as a paid police informer who absconds to Miami with $7,500 in an attempt to "retire."▼

Stop! Look! and Laugh! (1960) **78m.** **½ D: Jules White. The Three Stooges, Paul Winchell, Jerry Mahoney, Knucklehead Smiff, The Marquis Chimps, Officer Joe Bolton. Original Stooges' funniest sequences strung together by ventriloquist Paul Winchell and dummies is aimed at children. Much of it is familiar, but still amusing.▼

Stop Making Sense (1984) **C-88m.** **** D: Jonathan Demme. Brilliantly conceived, shot, edited, and performed Talking Heads concert film benefits from the presence of a major filmmaker behind the camera, as well as the imagination of lead singer/mastermind David Byrne. One of the greatest rock movies ever made; videocassette version runs 99m. and contains three extra tunes.▼

Stop Me Before I Kill! (1961-British) **109m.** ** D: Val Guest. Claude Dauphin, Diane Cilento, Roland Lewis, Françoise Rosay. Turgid dramatics: mentally unhinged man's new marriage is threatened by his illness and his psychiatrist's yen for his wife. Originally titled THE FULL TREATMENT. Megascope.

Stop! or My Mom Will Shoot (1992) **C-87m.** *½ D: Roger Spottiswoode. Sylvester Stallone, Estelle Getty, JoBeth Williams, Roger Rees, Martin Ferrero, Gailard Sartain, Dennis Burkley, Ving Rhames. Cop Stallone is joined by his loud-mouthed, gun-toting mamma (Getty), and they erase crime from the streets of L.A. One-joke action-comedy which quickly wears thin; Getty's character, meant to be funny, comes off as thoroughly obnoxious. [PG]▼●

Stopover Tokyo (1957) **C-100m.** **½ D: Richard L. Breen. Robert Wagner, Joan Collins, Edmond O'Brien, Ken Scott. Lumbering spy tale, loosely based on John P. Marquand novel. On-location filming in Japan makes a pretty background, but flat characters remain. CinemaScope.▼

Stop the World—I Want to Get Off (1966-British) **C-98m.** **½ D: Philip Saville. Tony Tanner, Millicent Martin, Leila Croft, Valerie Croft. One of producer Bill Sargent's photographed stage presentations, this one preserves Anthony Newley and Leslie Bricusse's allegorical musical about an everyman named Littlechap and his bouts with life and success. A bit heavy-handed, though the score includes "What Kind Of Fool Am I?" Opens in b&w, then changes to color. Remade as SAMMY STOPS THE WORLD. ▼●

Stop Train 349 (1964-German-French) **95m.** ** D: Rolf Haedrich. Jose Ferrer, Sean Flynn, Nicole Courcel, Jess Hahn. Average thriller of Communist manhunt for East German refugee hidden aboard U.S. military train heading from Berlin to west zone.▼

Stop, You're Killing Me (1952) **C-86m.** ** D: Roy Del Ruth. Broderick Crawford, Claire Trevor, Virginia Gibson, Sheldon Leonard, Margaret Dumont. Mild froth based on Damon Runyon story of racketeer Crawford going legitimate. Remake of A SLIGHT CASE OF MURDER.

Stork Club, The (1945) **98m.** **½ D: Hal Walker. Betty Hutton, Barry Fitzgerald, Don Defore, Andy Russell, Iris Adrian, Robert Benchley. Hat-check girl Hutton mysteriously becomes wealthy in fanciful musicomedy, mainly for Betty's fans. She sings "Doctor, Lawyer, Indian Chief."▼

Storm (1987-Canadian) **C-99m.** BOMB D: David Winning. David Palfy, Stan Kane, Harry Freedman, Lawrence Elion, Tom Schioler. Incoherent, interminable psychological drama about two students, one a jerk and the other a prankster, and their fate while on a camping trip. If you make it beyond the first two minutes of this turkey, you deserve a medal. [PG-13]▼

Storm at Daybreak (1933) **80m.** **½ D: Richard Boleslawski. Kay Francis, Nils Asther, Jean Parker, Walter Huston, Phillips Holmes, Eugene Pallette. Lavishly mounted soaper set in Serbia. Francis is wife of mayor Huston, and having affair with convalescing soldier Asther.

Storm Center (1956) **85m.** *½ D: Daniel Taradash. Bette Davis, Brian Keith, Kim Hunter, Paul Kelly. Librarian becomes center of controversy over censorship and Communism. Not even Davis can uplift clichés. An inauspicious directorial debut by veteran screenwriter Taradash.

Storm Fear (1955) **88m.** ** D: Cornel Wilde. Cornel Wilde, Jean Wallace, Dan Duryea, Lee Grant, Dennis Weaver, David Stollery, Steven Hill. Wounded bank robber Wilde and two partners take refuge in farm home of his honest but sickly brother Duryea. Snowstorm increases group tensions and suspense. Well-developed characters in Horton Foote's script are enhanced by good acting. Based on the novel by Clinton Seeley.

Storm in a Teacup (1937-British) **87m.** *** D: Victor Saville, Ian Dalrymple. Vivien Leigh, Rex Harrison, Sara Allgood, Cecil Parker, Arthur Wontner, Ivor Barnard. Witty social comedy, set in a provincial Scottish village, with Harrison a journalist who reports on a pompous politician's cruel treatment of a widow who is unable to afford a dog-license fee. At the same time, he finds himself falling in love with the bureaucrat's daughter (Leigh).▼

Storm in Summer, A (2000) **C-95m. TVM** D: Robert Wise. Peter Falk, Andrew McCarthy, Nastassja Kinski, Ruby Dee, Aaron Meeks. Falk does Ebenezer Scrooge with a Jewish accent, playing a deli owner in upstate N.Y. who finds himself saddled with a black inner-city youngster on a two-week trip to the country. Naturally, each winds up teaching the other a thing or two about life. Veteran director Wise's TV movie debut uses the original Rod Serling script (which was first produced in 1970 with Peter Ustinov). Made for cable. Average. ▼

Storm Over Asia (1928-Russian) **93m.** ***½ D: V. I. Pudovkin. Valeri Inkizhinov, A. Dedinstev, V. Tzoppi, Paulina Belinskaya. Sweeping, visually stunning drama, set in 1920, about a Mongolian trapper, thrust out of his village after a dispute with an American fur trader, who becomes a Soviet partisan. Eventually, he's discovered to be a descendant of Genghis Khan, and is set up as a puppet Mongolian ruler by the British army of occupation. Filmed in Central Asia; especially memorable are the sequence in which the trapper is almost shot and the finale. Aka THE HEIR TO GENGHIS KHAN.▼◗

Storm Over Lisbon (1944) **86m.** ** D: George Sherman. Vera Ralston, Richard Arlen, Erich von Stroheim, Otto Kruger, Eduardo Ciannelli, Mona Barrie. WW2 intrigue in Lisbon with nightclub performer Ralston siding with von Stroheim to get goods on American Arlen; only for those who wonder what CASABLANCA would've been like if it'd been made by Republic.

Storm Over the Nile (1955-British) **C-113m.** **½ D: Zoltan Korda, Terence Young. Anthony Steel, Laurence Harvey, James Robertson Justice, Mary Ure, Christopher Lee. Remake of THE FOUR FEATHERS (by the same director, with stock footage from the original) lacks class and flair, but story is still good; script by R.C. Sherriff. CinemaScope.

Storm Over Tibet (1952) **87m.** ** D: Andrew Marton. Rex Reason, Diana Douglas, Myron Healey, Robert Karnes, Strother Martin, Harold Fong. Reason is an ex-WW2 pilot who journeys to Tibet and gets in plenty of hot water when he purloins a holy mask from a temple. German documentary footage of the Himalayas is used extensively in this Ivan Tors production.

Storm Rider, The (1957) **70m.** *½ D: Edward Bernds. Scott Brady, Mala Powers, Bill Williams, John Goddard. Sagebrush lowjinks of cattle owners vs. ranchers. Regalscope.▼

Storm Rider (1972) SEE: **Grand Duel, The**

Storm Warning (1951) **93m.** **½ D: Stuart Heisler. Ginger Rogers, Ronald Reagan, Doris Day, Steve Cochran, Hugh Sanders, Lloyd Gough, Ned Glass. Feverish but engrossing story of a woman who discovers that her sister (Day) has married a loutish Ku Klux Klansman. Good cast, with Reagan in one of his better roles as a crusading D.A.; cowritten by Richard Brooks.

Stormy Monday (1988-British) **C-93m.** *** D: Mike Figgis. Melanie Griffith, Tommy Lee Jones, Sting, Sean Bean, James Cosmo, Mark Long, Brian Lewis. Extremely stylish film noir about the convergence of four characters in the economically depressed city of Newcastle, where Sting runs a jazz club, and a ruthless American businessman (Jones) hopes to make a killing in redevelopment. More atmosphere than story here, and told at a very deliberate pace, but strong performances by all four leads and striking visual ideas by writer-director Figgis (and cinematographer Roger Deakins) definitely compensate. Figgis is also credited with the music score. [R]▼●

Stormy Weather (1943) **77m.** **½ D: Andrew L. Stone. Lena Horne, Bill (Bojangles) Robinson, Cab Calloway and His Band, Katherine Dunham, Fats Waller, Dooley Wilson, The Nicholas Brothers. This musical offers a legendary lineup of black performers, with Lena singing title song, Fats performing "Ain't Misbehavin'," others doing what they do best. Only problem: a silly storyline that improbably pairs Bojangles and Horne romantically. ▼●

Story Lady, The (1991) **C-100m. TVM** D: Larry Elikann. Jessica Tandy, Tandy Cronyn, Stephanie Zimbalist, Charles Durning, Richard Masur, Ed Begley, Jr., Lisa Jakub, Christopher Gartin. The venerable Jessica delights as a bored widow who finds a new life reading children's stories on a public access TV show and soon finds herself exploited by jaded advertising and network executives. Jessica's real-life daughter Tandy plays her character's daughter. Heartfelt script by Robert Zeschin. Above average.▼◗

Story of Adele H, The (1975-French) **C-97m.** **½ D: François Truffaut. Isabelle Adjani, Bruce Robinson, Sylvia Marriott, Reubin Dorey, Joseph Blatchley, M. White. Understated drama of young woman (the daughter of author Victor Hugo) obsessed with a soldier who does not return her love. Adjani's performance is excellent, but film is curiously unmoving. Shot in simultaneous English and French-language versions. [PG]▼●

Story of Alexander Graham Bell, The (1939) **97m.** *** D: Irving Cummings. Don Ameche, Loretta Young, Henry Fonda, Charles Coburn, Spring Byington, Gene Lockhart, Polly Ann Young. Ameche overacts at times in his famous title role, but entertaining version of inventor is given plush 20th Century-Fox presentation.▼

Story of a Love Story (1973-French) **C-110m.** **½ D: John Frankenheimer. Alan Bates, Dominique Sanda, Evans Evans, Lea Massari, Michel Auclair, Laurence De Monaghan. Writer Bates has an extramarital affair with Sanda—or is it his imagination? Interesting premise, middling result. Originally titled IMPOSSIBLE OBJECT; never released theatrically.▼

Story of a Marriage, The SEE: **On Valentine's Day** and **1918**

Story of a Three Day Pass, The (1967-French) **87m.** *** D: Melvin Van Peebles. Harry Baird, Nicole Berger, Christian Marin, Pierre Doris. Flawed but impressive film about affair between black American soldier and white French girl. Also on tape as LA PERMISSION. ▼

Story of a Woman (1970) **C-90m.** *½ D: Leonardo Bercovici. Bibi Andersson, Robert Stack, James Farentino, Annie Girardot, Didi Perego, Mario Nascimbene. Turgid tale of pianist who tries to remain faithful to her husband, even though she's still hung up on old flame; Bibi is wasted. [R]

Story of Boys and Girls, The (1991-Italian) **C-92m.** *** D: Pupi Avati. Lucretia della Rovere, Davide Bechini, Valeria Bruni Tadeschi, Lina Bernardi, Anna Bonaiuto, Alessandro Haber, Enrico Maria Modungo. A country beauty invites her fiancé's elegant Bolognese family to a 20-course banquet in Italy's Emilia Romagna farmland in 1936. Easygoing, keenly observed comedy of culture clashing, whose subliminal effect isn't completely apparent until the film's conclusion. Have a snack handy.▼

Story of Danny Lester, The SEE: **Bad Boy**

Story of Dr. Wassell, The (1944) **C-140m.** **½ D: Cecil B. DeMille. Gary Cooper, Laraine Day, Signe Hasso, Dennis O'Keefe, Paul Kelly, Philip Ahn, Barbara Britton. Story of real-life dedicated Navy doctor who saved fighting men in Java during WW2; slow-moving adaptation of the James Hilton book. Far from top-grade DeMille or Cooper. ▼

Story of Esther Costello, The (1957-British) **103m.** **½ D: David Miller. Joan Crawford, Rossano Brazzi, Heather Sears, Lee Patterson, Fay Compton, Bessie Love, Ron Randell. Socialite rehabilitates impoverished blind and deaf girl and promotes charity fund in her name. Interesting look at charity huckstering but melodrama is overwrought and often unintentionally funny.▼

Story of G.I. Joe, The (1945) **109m.** ***½ D: William Wellman. Burgess Meredith, Robert Mitchum, Freddie Steele, Wally Cassell, Jimmy Lloyd. Meredith is superb as war correspondent Ernie Pyle living with Yank soldiers on front lines to report their stories; Mitchum's first outstanding film role as soldier.▼◗

Story of Gilbert and Sullivan, The SEE: **Great Gilbert and Sullivan, The**

Story of Gosta Berling, The SEE: **Atonement of Gosta Berling, The**

Story of Louis Pasteur, The (1936) **85m.** ***½ D: William Dieterle. Paul Muni, Josephine Hutchinson, Anita Louise, Donald Woods, Fritz Leiber, Porter Hall, Akim Tamiroff. The achievements of the famous French scientist are chronicled in this engrossing film. Muni gives Oscar-winning performance; writers Sheridan Gibney and Pierre Collings also won.▼●

Story of Mankind, The (1957) **C-100m.** ** D: Irwin Allen. Ronald Colman, Cedric Hardwicke, Vincent Price; guest stars Hedy Lamarr, Groucho, Harpo, Chico Marx, Virginia Mayo, Agnes Moorehead, Francis X. Bushman, Charles Coburn, Marie Windsor, John Carradine, Dennis Hopper. Ambitious in concept, laughable in juvenile results. Henrik Van Loon book of highlights of man's history becomes string of clichéd costume episodes, badly cast and poorly handled; the Marxes don't even appear together!

Story of Molly X, The (1949) **82m.** **½ D: Crane Wilbur. June Havoc, John Russell, Dorothy Hart, Charles McGraw. Havoc is earnest as gangster's widow who goes out to find her husband's killer.

Story of Piera, The (1983-Italian-French) **C-105m.** ** D: Marco Ferreri. Isabelle Huppert, Hanna Schygulla, Marcello Mastroianni, Bettina Gruhn, Tanya Lopert. Odd chronicle of the lifelong relationship between nutty, sensuous Schygulla and her daughter (Gruhn as a pre-teen, then Huppert). Ferreri presents a liberated alternative for relating as a wife, mother, daughter, woman; however, the result is mostly rambling, boring.

Story of Qiu Ju, The (1992-Chinese) **C-100m.** ***½ D: Zhang Yimou. Gong Li, Lei Lao Sheng, Liu Pei Qi, Ge Zhi Jun, Ye Jun, Yang Liu Xia. Exceptional drama about a naive but determined Chinese farm woman (Li), who demands to receive an explanation and simple apology after her husband is beaten up by the obstinate chief of her village. This deft, ironic story of a woman's search for justice examines government bureaucracy and how regulations and rules often have little to do with the real needs of people. [PG]▼●

Story of Robin Hood and His Merrie Men, The (1952) **C-83m.** *** D: Ken Annakin. Richard Todd, Joan Rice, Peter Finch, James Hayter, James Robertson Justice, Martita Hunt, Hubert Gregg, Michael Hordern. Zesty, colorful retelling of the familiar story, filmed in England by Walt Disney with excellent cast. Not as personality-oriented as other versions, but just as good in its own way.▼●

Story of Ruth, The (1960) **C-132m.** **½ D: Henry Koster. Elana Eden, Stuart Whitman, Tom Tryon, Peggy Wood, Viveca Lindfors, Jeff Morrow. Static biblical nonepic retelling story of woman renouncing her "gods" when she discovers true faith. CinemaScope.▼

Story of Seabiscuit, The (1949) **C-93m.** **½ D: David Butler. Shirley Temple, Barry Fitzgerald, Lon McCallister, Rosemary DeCamp. Standard horseracing saga with Fitzgerald supporting most of the film as dedicated trainer of famed thoroughbred.▼

Story of Three Loves, The (1953) **C-122m.** *** D: Vincente Minnelli, Gottfried Reinhardt. Pier Angeli, Moira Shearer, Ethel Barrymore, Kirk Douglas, Farley Granger, Leslie Caron, James Mason, Agnes Moorehead, Zsa Zsa Gabor. Bittersweet trio of love stories, told as flashbacks involving passengers on ocean liner

Story of Us, The (1999) **C-95m.** ** D: Rob Reiner. Bruce Willis, Michelle Pfeiffer, Tim Matheson, Rob Reiner, Rita Wilson, Julie Hagerty, Jayne Meadows, Tom Poston, Betty White, Red Buttons. A couple on the verge of splitting reflect on their 15-year marriage—and try to understand where it went wrong. Sympathetic portrayal of married life has likable performances on its side, but its moments of keen observation are too often undercut by annoying, sitcom-style dialogue that bears no relation to real life. Paul Reiser appears unbilled. [R]▼●◗

Story of Vernon & Irene Castle, The (1939) **93m.** *** D: H. C. Potter. Fred Astaire, Ginger Rogers, Edna May Oliver, Walter Brennan, Lew Fields. Fred and Ginger take an unusual turn, downplaying their usual breezy comedy to portray America's hugely popular early-20th-century husband-and-wife dance team. Many fine period dance numbers and songs. This was the last Astaire–Rogers film until THE BARKLEYS OF BROADWAY ten years later. Incidentally, that's young Marge Champion (then known as Marjorie Belcher) as Irene's girlfriend.▼●

Story of Will Rogers, The (1952) **C-109m.** *** D: Michael Curtiz. Will Rogers, Jr., Jane Wyman, Carl Benton Reid, James Gleason, Mary Wickes, Eddie Cantor. One of few show biz biographies that rings true, with Rogers Jr. faithfully portraying his father, rodeo star turned humorist; Wyman is his loving wife, Cantor appears as himself.

Story of Women, The (1988-French) **C-110m.** *** D: Claude Chabrol. Isabelle Huppert, Francois Cluzet, Marie Trintignant, Nils Tavernier, Louis Ducreux. Huppert gives one of her best performances as a woman who builds a thriving career as an abortionist in Vichy France—and becomes the last of her sex to be guillotined in her country. Ironic, fact-based story provides Chabrol with one of his best subjects; the director is in top form here.▼

Story on Page One, The (1959) **123m.** *** D: Clifford Odets. Rita Hayworth, Anthony Franciosa, Gig Young, Mildred Dunnock, Hugh Griffith, Sanford Meisner, Robert Burton. Lovers Hayworth and Young are accused of killing Rita's husband, hire Franciosa to represent them in court. Odets' stark film has high tension and sincere performances, although Dunnock's Mama portrayal is a bit much. CinemaScope.

Storyville (1992) **C-112m.** *½ D: Mark Frost. James Spader, Joanne Whalley-Kilmer, Jason Robards, Piper Laurie, Charlotte Lewis, Michael Warren, Michael Parks, Chuck McCann, Charles Haid, Chino Fats Williams, Woody Strode, Jeff Perry. Young, obscenely wealthy Louisiana congressional candidate Spader discovers skeletons deeply hidden in his family's closet. Good performances can't save this muddled and obtuse contemporary drama; the murder, mayhem, and mistresses are more than anyone will care about. [R]▼●

Stowaway (1936) **86m.** **½ D: William A. Seiter. Robert Young, Alice Faye, Shirley Temple, Eugene Palette, Helen Westley, Arthur Treacher. Predictable yet engaging shipboard story with Faye and Young romancing, Temple the incurably curious child. Shirley even speaks Chinese! Also shown in computer-colored version.▼

Stowaway Girl (1957-British) **87m.** **½ D: Guy Hamilton. Trevor Howard, Elsa Martinelli, Pedro Armendariz, Donald Pleasence, Warren Mitchell. Trim, sensible romancer of middle-aged captain Howard's infatuation with Martinelli, who hid aboard his ship. Originally titled MANUELA.

Straight on Till Morning (1972-British) **C-96m.** ** D: Peter Collinson. Rita Tushingham, Shane Briant, Tom Bell, Annie Ross, Claire Kelly. Offbeat thriller, but not terribly effective. Naive Tushingham journeys from Liverpool to London to find a willing male to impregnate her, meets ladykiller Briant. The title, if you don't know, is derived from *Peter Pan.* Video titles: TILL DAWN DO US PART and DRESSED FOR DEATH. [R]▼

Straight Out of Brooklyn (1991) **C-91m.** **½ D: Matty Rich. George T. Odom, Ann D. Sanders, Lawrence Gilliard, Jr.,

Barbara Sanon, Reana E. Drummond, Mark Malone. Sobering look at a working-class black family's dead-end existence in the housing projects of Brooklyn, N.Y., and a young man's foolish scheme to turn their lives around. Ambitious and interesting first feature for teenaged writer-director Rich (who also appears on-screen as the talkative Larry). Extremely rough-edged, but redeemed by some fine performances—and searing emotions. [R]▼●

Straight Story, The (1999) **C-111m.** ***½ D: David Lynch. Richard Farnsworth, Sissy Spacek, Harry Dean Stanton, Jane Galloway Heit, Everett McGill, Jennifer Edwards-Hughes. Wonderful, deceptively simple slice of Americana (based on a true story) about a 73-year-old Iowa man who drives a lawnmower some 300 miles to see his ailing brother, with whom he hasn't spoken in a decade. Its measured pace and episodic quality may not appeal to everyone, but its charm and belief in the basic decency of people make it very special indeed. Farnsworth shines in the leading role. Director Lynch's most benign film. Written by Mary Sweeney and John Roach. Panavision. [G]▼◗

Straight Talk (1992) **C-91m.** *½ D: Barnet Kellman. Dolly Parton, James Woods, Griffin Dunne, Michael Madsen, Deirdre O'Connell, John Sayles, Teri Hatcher, Spalding Gray, Jerry Orbach, Philip Bosco, Charles Fleischer, Jay Thomas. New-in-town Dolly is mistaken for the just-hired psychologist at a Chicago radio station, but is a hit on the air with her down-home advice. About as credible as Parton's romance with costar Woods, who despite his billing was completely missing from the film's coming attraction. [PG]▼●

Straight Through the Heart (1983-German) **C-91m.** *** D: Doris Dörrie. Beate Jensen, Sepp Bierbichler, Gabrielle Litty, Nuran Filiz. Highly original, sharply observed tale of a rather peculiar young girl (nicely played by Jensen) and her relationship with divorced, lonely, middle-aged dentist Bierbichler. An impressive initial feature from Dörrie (the director of MEN . . .).

Straight Time (1978) **C-114m.** *** D: Ulu Grosbard. Dustin Hoffman, Theresa Russell, Harry Dean Stanton, Gary Busey, M. Emmet Walsh, Sandy Baron, Kathy Bates, Rita Taggart. Hoffman knocks heads with slimy parole officer Walsh following his release from prison and begins a downward slide. Engrossing if not particularly distinguished melodrama gets a real shot in the arm from terrific supporting performances. Hoffman started directing the film himself, then turned it over to Grosbard. Based on the novel *No Beast So Fierce* by Edward Bunker, who also appears in film as Mickey. [R]▼

Straight to Hell (1987) **C-86m.** BOMB D: Alex Cox. Sy Richardson, Joe Strummer, Dick Rude, Courtney Love, Dennis Hopper, Elvis Costello, Grace Jones, Jim Jarmusch, The Pogues. ''Self-indulgent'' is an understated way of describing this spaghetti Western spoof, written by cult director Cox and costar Rude. Has the insistent air of a hip in-joke, except that it isn't funny. In fact, it's *awful*. [R]▼

Strait-Jacket (1964) **89m.** **½ D: William Castle. Joan Crawford, Diane Baker, Leif Erickson, Anthony Hayes, Howard St. John, Rochelle Hudson, George Kennedy. Crawford served 20 years for axe murders; now, living peacefully with daughter Baker, murders start again and she's suspected. Crawford's strong portrayal makes this one of best in the BABY JANE genre of older-star shockers; script by Robert Bloch.▼●

Stranded (1935) **76m.** ** D: Frank Borzage. Kay Francis, George Brent, Patricia Ellis, Donald Woods, Robert Barrat, Barton MacLane. Francis is a travelers' aid worker solving everybody's problems, tangling with band of racketeers.

Stranded (1987) **C-80m.** ** D: Tex Fuller. Ione Skye, Joe Morton, Maureen O'Sullivan, Susan Barnes, Cameron Dye, Michael Greene, Brendan Hughes. A couple of effective moments cannot uplift this unrewarding sci-fi entry about aliens who come to earth, taking teen Skye and grandmother O'Sullivan hostage. [PG-13] ▼●

Strange Adventure, A (1956) **70m.** *½ D: William Witney. Joan Evans, Ben Cooper, Marla English, Jan Merlin, Nick Adams. Armored-car thieves hold hostages in High Sierras hideout. Familiar but functional melodramatics.

Strange Affair, The (1968-British) **C-106m.** **½ D: David Greene. Michael York, Jeremy Kemp, Susan George, Jack Watson, Nigel Davenport, George A. Cooper, Barry Fantoni. Pretty good police melodrama about young recruit York's dallying with sexy hippie and superior Kemp's failure to get needed conviction; George steals the show in one of her first film appearances. Techniscope. [R]

Strange Affair of Uncle Harry, The (1945) **80m.** *** D: Robert Siodmak. George Sanders, Geraldine Fitzgerald, Ella Raines, Sara Allgood, Moyna MacGill, Samuel S. Hinds. Engrossing melodrama about mild-mannered Sanders falling in love, but unable to break from grip of domineering sister (Fitzgerald). Vivid, if not always believable, with unfortunate ending demanded by 1940s censorship. Produced by longtime Hitchcock associate Joan Harrison. Originally titled UNCLE HARRY.▼●

Strange Affection (1957-British) **84m.** ** D: Wolf Rilla. Richard Attenborough, Colin Petersen, Jill Adams, Terence Morgan. A teacher decides to take in a boy who's been accused of murdering his drunkard

father. Decent British drama. Original British title: THE SCAMP.
Strange Awakening (1958-British) **75m.** *½ D: Montgomery Tully. Lex Barker, Carole Mathews, Nora Swinburne, Richard Molinos, Peter Dyneley. Barker is tourist in France involved in snowballing case of fraud; muddled drama.▼
Strange Bargain (1949) **68m.** **½ D: Will Price. Martha Scott, Jeffrey Lynn, Henry (Harry) Morgan, Katherine Emery, Richard Gaines, Henry O'Neill, Walter Sande. Adequate mystery yarn about a bookkeeper (Lynn), who's framed for murder; Scott is his devoted wife, Morgan the police lieutenant on the case. This star trio reprised their roles 38 years later for a sequel, *Strangest of Bargains*, which aired as an episode of the *Murder, She Wrote* TV series.▼
Strange Bedfellows (1965) **C-98m.** **½ D: Melvin Frank. Rock Hudson, Gina Lollobrigida, Gig Young, Terry-Thomas, Nancy Kulp. Hudson ambles through another marital mix-up comedy, this one with fiery Gina and lots of slapstick. Mild entertainment; filmed in London. ▼
Strange Behavior (1981-New Zealand) **C-98m.** ** D: Michael Laughlin. Michael Murphy, Louise Fletcher, Dan Shor, Fiona Lewis, Arthur Dignam, Scott Brady, Charles Lane. This shocker about grisly murders in a small Midwestern town (shot in New Zealand!) got inexplicably good reviews in many quarters. You may rightly wonder what all the shouting was about. Originally titled DEAD KIDS. Panavision. [R]▼
Strange Brew (1983) **C-90m.** **½ D: Dave Thomas, Rick Moranis. Dave Thomas, Rick Moranis, Max von Sydow, Paul Dooley, Lynne Griffin, voice of Mel Blanc. Uneven but likably goofy film about Bob and Doug, the beer-guzzling McKenzie Brothers introduced on the *SCTV* show. Lags at times, but keeps coming up with funny scenes, especially when playing with the conventions of moviemaking. The stars also directed and cowrote the film, the first in Hoserama. Loosely based on, believe it or not, *Hamlet*. [PG]▼●
Strange Cargo (1940) **113m.** *** D: Frank Borzage. Joan Crawford, Clark Gable, Ian Hunter, Peter Lorre, Albert Dekker, Paul Lukas, Eduardo Ciannelli. Intriguing allegorical film of prisoners escaping from Devil's Island with Christ-like presence of Hunter. Not for all tastes, but there are fine, realistic performances and flavorful Franz Waxman score.▼
Strange Case of Dr. Rx, The (1942) **66m.** ** D: William Nigh. Lionel Atwill, Patric Knowles, Anne Gwynne, Mona Barrie, Shemp Howard, Samuel S. Hinds, Paul Cavanagh, Mantan Moreland. Typical Universal Atwill vehicle, a fast-paced whodunit about hunt for mysterious title character, who murders criminals gotten off by unscrupulous attorney. Not particularly puzzling, but good cast helps.
Strange Case of Madeleine SEE: **Madeleine** (1949)
Strange Confession SEE: **Imposter, The** (1944)
Strange Conquest (1946) **65m.** ** D: John Rawlins. Jane Wyatt, Lowell Gilmore, Julie Bishop, Samuel S. Hinds, Abner Biberman. Inauspicious programmer set in the deep jungles where dedicated men try to conquer native diseases. Remake of THE CRIME OF DR. HALLET.
Strange Days (1995) **C-122m.** **½ D: Kathryn Bigelow. Ralph Fiennes, Angela Bassett, Juliette Lewis, Tom Sizemore, Michael Wincott, Vincent D'Onofrio, Glenn Plummer, Brigitte Bako, Richard Edson, William Fichtner, Josef Sommer, Chris Douridas, Todd Graff. Dazzling but uneasy mixture of futuristic action and social relevance. Fiennes is a hustler selling mental recordings of real-life experiences, to which some become addicted; then he stumbles into a murky murder conspiracy involving his clients. Bombastic and overambitious, but manages to capture, in fits, the addictive thrill of virtual reality. (An interracial romance between Fiennes and Bassett doesn't ring true in the end.) Cowritten by Jay Cocks and James Cameron. Super 35. [R]▼●
Strange Death of Adolf Hitler, The (1943) **72m.** ** D: James Hogan. Ludwig Donath, Fritz Kortner, Gale Sondergaard, George Dolenz, Fred Giermann, William Trenk, Merrill Rodin. Hitler's double helps set trap for his demise. Dated, forgettable melodrama.
Strange Door, The (1951) **81m.** *½ D: Joseph Pevney. Charles Laughton, Boris Karloff, Sally Forrest, Richard Stapley, Michael Pate, Alan Napier, Paul Cavanagh. Laughton camps it up in this heavy-handed, obvious adaptation of a Robert Louis Stevenson story about a sadistic squire and his nefarious schemes. Karloff has a thankless role as a servant named Voltan.▼●
Strange Fascination (1952) **80m.** ** D: Hugo Haas. Hugo Haas, Cleo Moore, Mona Barrie, Rick Vallin, Karen Sharpe. A concert pianist's career—and luck—fall apart because of his obsessive love for a young blonde. Starts interestingly but descends into hollow melodrama. Produced, directed, and written by Haas.
Strange Holiday (1942) **62m.** ** D: Arch Oboler. Claude Rains, Bobbie Stebbins, Barbara Bates, Paul Hilton, Tommy Cook, Martin Kosleck. Adaptation of Oboler's radio play about businessman who returns from vacation to find U.S. democracy overthrown. Unreleased until 1946. This was originally sponsored by General Motors and intended to be shown only to its employees!
Strange Illusion (1945) **80m.** ** D: Edgar G. Ulmer. James Lydon, Sally Eilers, War-

ren William, Regis Toomey. Intriguing but unconvincing melodrama, a B-movie update of *Hamlet*, with teenaged Lydon having doubts about smooth-talker (William) who's wooing his widowed mother (Eilers). Typically bizarre Ulmer touches in this low-budget quickie.▼

Strange Impersonation (1946) **68m.** *** D: Anthony Mann. Brenda Marshall, William Gargan, Hillary Brooke, George Chandler, Ruth Ford, H. B. Warner, Lyle Talbot. Marshall is a chemical research scientist who experiments with her own anesthetic. Ultra-cheap film with almost nonexistent production values is turned into a fairly intriguing little B. Of interest mainly to noir buffs; neat twist ending.

Strange Interlude (1932) **110m.** *** D: Robert Z. Leonard. Norma Shearer, Clark Gable, May Robson, Maureen O'Sullivan, Robert Young, Ralph Morgan, Henry B. Walthall, Mary Alden. Talky Eugene O'Neill play becomes marathon of inner thoughts revealed only to audience in chronicle of Gable, Shearer, et al. growing old without resolving their problems. Engrossing film, with Shearer at her radiant best.▼

Strange Intruder (1956) **82m.** ** D: Irving Rapper. Edmund Purdom, Ida Lupino, Ann Harding, Jacques Bergerac. Purdom promises dying Korean War buddy that he'll visit the man's family; he does, with strange results.

Strange Invaders (1983) **C-94m.** **½ D: Michael Laughlin. Paul LeMat, Nancy Allen, Diana Scarwid, Michael Lerner, Louise Fletcher, Wallace Shawn, Fiona Lewis, Kenneth Tobey, June Lockhart. Affectionate spoof of 50s sci-fi films (with a touch of 80s New Wave), about a midwestern town overtaken by aliens. Has a wonderful feel to it but suffers from weak writing and lethargic pacing. Evocative score by John Addison. Panavision. [PG]▼●

Strange Justice (1999) **C-95m. TVM** D: Ernest Dickerson. Delroy Lindo, Mandy Patinkin, Regina Taylor, Louis Gossett, Jr., Paul Winfield. Strong dramatization of the sometimes circus-like events surrounding Congressional hearings for the 1991 appointment of Clarence Thomas (Lindo) to the Supreme Court. Includes the political and p.r. maneuverings of Kenneth Duberstein (Patinkin) of the Bush administration, and the sexual harassment testimony against Thomas by a reluctant ex-colleague, Anita Hill (Taylor). Adapted and embellished by executive producer Jacob Epstein from the book by Jane Mayer and Jill Abramson. Made for cable. Average.▼

Strange Lady in Town (1955) **C-112m.** **½ D: Mervyn LeRoy. Greer Garson, Dana Andrews, Cameron Mitchell, Lois Smith, Walter Hampden, Nick Adams. Unsuccessful grand-scale soaper-Western. Set in 1880s, Garson is the doctor coming to Santa Fe, involved with Andrews, perplexed by outlaw brother Mitchell. CinemaScope.

Strange Love of Martha Ivers, The (1946) **116m.** *** D: Lewis Milestone. Barbara Stanwyck, Kirk Douglas, Lizabeth Scott, Van Heflin, Judith Anderson, Darryl Hickman. Gripping melodrama, with Stanwyck bound to her husband by crime she committed long ago. Douglas' film debut.▼●◗

Strange Love of Molly Louvain, The (1932) **72m.** **½ D: Michael Curtiz. Ann Dvorak, Lee Tracy, Richard Cromwell, Guy Kibbee, Leslie Fenton, Frank McHugh, Evalyn Knapp, Charles Middleton. Seamy, overplotted pre-Code melodrama about unwed mother Dvorak and the various bad eggs she has a habit of falling for. Typically fast-paced Warner Bros. yarn, though more unpleasant than most.▼

Strange Mr. Gregory, The (1946) **63m.** ** D: Phil Rosen. Edmund Lowe, Jean Rogers, Don Douglas, Marjorie Hoshelle, Robert Emmett Keane. Low-budget drama of magician who goes to any length to win love of married woman.

Strange One, The (1957) **100m.** *** D: Jack Garfein. Ben Gazzara, George Peppard, Pat Hingle, Mark Richman, Geoffrey Horne, James Olson. Bizarre military school account of far-out Gazzara's peculiar hold over various underclassmen. Remarkably frank version of Calder Willingham's *End as a Man*, scripted by the author; also filmed as SORORITY GIRL. Film debuts of Gazzara and Peppard.▼

Stranger, The (1946) **95m.** *** D: Orson Welles. Orson Welles, Loretta Young, Edward G. Robinson, Richard Long, Martha Wentworth. Fine study of escaped Nazi war criminal Welles sedately living in small Connecticut town, about to marry unsuspecting Young. Robinson nicely understates role as federal agent out to get him. Also shown in computer-colored version.▼●◗

Stranger, The (1967-Italian-French) **C-105m.** ***½ D: Luchino Visconti. Marcello Mastroianni, Anna Karina, Bernard Blier, Georges Wilson, Bruno Cremer. Excellent adaptation of Albert Camus' existential novel about a man who feels completely isolated from society. Mastroianni is perfectly cast in lead.

Stranger, The (1987-U.S.-Argentine) **C-88m.** **½ D: Adolfo Aristarain. Bonnie Bedelia, Peter Riegert, Barry Primus, David Spielberg, Marcos Woinski. Clever if occasionally shallow thriller about Bedelia, who observes killings . . . and gets amnesia while the culprits are out to get her. Fairly entertaining most of the way, but could have been much better. Filmed in Buenos Aires. [R]▼

Stranger, The SEE: **Kabloonak**

Stranger Among Us, A (1992) **C-109m.** **½ D: Sidney Lumet. Melanie Griffith,

Eric Thal, John Pankow, Tracy Pollan, Lee Richardson, Mia Sara, Jamey Sheridan, Jake Weber, Burtt Harris. N.Y.C. cop Griffith goes to live among Brooklyn's Hasidic community of religious Jews in order to find the "insider" who murdered one of them. Intriguing at first, but the story gets stalled along the way and never gets back on track, especially in the far-fetched finale. Griffith is surprisingly credible as a policewoman. [PG-13]▼●

Stranger and the Gunfighter, The (1976-Italian-Hong Kong) **C-107m.** **½ D: Anthony Dawson (Antonio Margheriti). Lee Van Cleef, Lo Lieh, Patty Shepard, Julian Ugarte, Karen Yeh. Lively, low-grade tongue-in-cheek actioner has hard-drinking cowboy joining forces with kung fu expert to recover missing fortune, with portions of the map tattooed on the posteriors of assorted lovelies. Amusing mix of spaghetti Western and karate thriller. Panavision. [PG]▼●

Stranger at My Door (1956) **85m.** **½ D: William Witney. Macdonald Carey, Patricia Medina, Skip Homeier, Louis Jean Heydt, Stephen Wootton, Slim Pickens. Offbeat Western about clergyman jeopardizing his family's safety when he tries to reform an outlaw. Solid performances in this original script by Barry Shipman. Highlighted by some truly remarkable scenes with an untamed horse.

Stranger Came Home, A SEE: **Unholy Four, The**

Stranger in Between (1952-British) **84m.** *** D: Charles Crichton. Dirk Bogarde, Elizabeth Sellars, Kay Walsh, Jon Whiteley, Geoffrey Keen. Modest but very entertaining film about orphan boy who grows to understand murderer as both flee police in England. Warm, compassionate performances. Original British title: HUNTED.

Stranger in My Arms, A (1959) **88m.** **½ D: Helmut Kautner. June Allyson, Jeff Chandler, Sandra Dee, Charles Coburn, Mary Astor, Peter Graves, Conrad Nagel. Undemanding old-fashioned weeper, based on Robert Wilder novel. Chandler falls in love with Allyson, wife of Air Force buddy killed in Korean War. Astor is the domineering mother-in-law. Typical Ross Hunter sudser. CinemaScope.

Stranger in Our House (1978) **C-100m. TVM** D: Wes Craven. Linda Blair, Lee Purcell, Jeremy Slate, Carol Lawrence, Macdonald Carey, Jeff McCracken, Jeff East. Teenage witchcraft thriller with always put-upon Linda Blair in constant peril. Based on Lois Duncan's novel *Summer of Fear*. Average.▼

Stranger in the House SEE: **Black Christmas**

Stranger in Town, A (1943) **67m.** *** D: Roy Rowland. Frank Morgan, Richard Carlson, Jean Rogers, Robert Barrat, Porter Hall, Chill Wills, Donald MacBride, John Hodiak. Enjoyable Capra-esque tale about a Supreme Court justice (Morgan) who gets mixed up in a small town's corrupt politics while on a fishing vacation. Highly amusing second feature that skillfully satirizes serious issues and features a gang of crooked politicos worthy of a Preston Sturges film.

Stranger in Town, A (1966-Italian-U.S.) **C-86m.** *½ D: Vance Lewis (Luigi Vanza). Tony Anthony, Frank Wolff, Yolanda Modio, Gia Sandri. Poor imitation of Sergio Leone Western finds Anthony bloodbathing a murderous bandit into submission. Sequel: THE STRANGER RETURNS. [R]

Stranger Is Watching, A (1982) **C-92m.** ** D: Sean S. Cunningham. Kate Mulgrew, Rip Torn, James Naughton, Shawn Von Schreiber, Barbara Baxley, Stephen Joyce. Psychopath Torn kidnaps TV newscaster Mulgrew and young Von Schreiber, holding them hostage in catacombs beneath Grand Central Station. Convoluted thriller from the director of FRIDAY THE 13TH. [R]▼

Stranger on Horseback (1955) **C-66m.** ** D: Jacques Tourneur. Joel McCrea, Kevin McCarthy, Jaclynne Greene, Miroslava, Nancy Gates, John Carradine. McCrea is tight-lipped judge who's forced to kill in order to set justice straight and bring a murderer to trial.

Stranger on My Land (1988) **C-100m. TVM** D: Larry Elikann. Tommy Lee Jones, Dee Wallace Stone, Ben Johnson, Pat Hingle, Terry O'Quinn, Richard Anderson, Ned Romero, Barry Corbin. Vietnam vet fights the Feds, who want his ranch for a missile base. Similar to the earlier FIRE ON THE MOUNTAIN, among others. Average.▼

Stranger on the Prowl (1953-Italian) **82m.** **½ D: Joseph Losey. Paul Muni, Vittorio Manunta, Joan Lorring, Aldo Silvani. Murky drama of Muni a fugitive on the run who tries to set a young would-be-crook straight.

Stranger on the Run (1967) **C-97m. TVM** D: Don Siegel. Henry Fonda, Michael Parks, Anne Baxter, Dan Duryea, Sal Mineo, Lloyd Bochner, Michael Burns, Bernie Hamilton, Zalman King. Solidly conceived, well-executed chase thriller features Fonda as drifter in Banner, New Mexico, trying to deliver message to sister of prison friend, accused of murder, chased by railroad police into desert. Great entertainment with something to say; written by Reginald Rose. Above average.

Stranger on the Third Floor, The (1940) **64m.** *** D: Boris Ingster. Peter Lorre, John McGuire, Margaret Tallichet, Charles Waldron, Elisha Cook, Jr. Reporter's testimony has convicted Cook in brutal murder case, but the newspaperman has second thoughts. Excellent sleeper, with one nightmare montage that's a knockout.▼●

Stranger Returns, The (1968-U.S.-Italian) **C-90m.** BOMB D: Vance Lewis (Luigi Vanza). Tony Anthony, Dan Vadis, Daniele Vargas, Marco Gugielmi, Jill Banner. Sequel to A STRANGER IN TOWN has Anthony chasing solid gold stagecoach full of thieves. Western is worthless; local TV stations may cut the gore. [R]

Strangers (1953-Italian) **97m.** *** D: Roberto Rossellini. Ingrid Bergman, George Sanders, Paul Muller, Maria Mauban, Natalia Ray. Beautiful, meditative tale of married couple Bergman and Sanders trying to reconcile their faltering relationship while driving through Italy. Received dreadful reviews when first released, but was rediscovered (and labelled a masterpiece) by French filmmakers and critics. Video titles: VOYAGE IN ITALY and VOYAGE TO ITALY, running 83m.▼

Strangers (1979) SEE: **Strangers: The Story of a Mother and Daughter**

Strangers at Sunrise (1969) **C-99m.** **½ D: Percival Rubens. George Montgomery, Deana Martin, Brian O'Shaughnessy, Tromp Terreblanche. Turn-of-the-century South African Western with American mining engineer, attracted by the gold rush, trying to clear his name when the British accuse him of spying for the Boers.

Stranger's Hand, The (1954-British) **86m.** *** D: Mario Soldati. Trevor Howard, Alida Valli, Richard Basehart, Eduardo Ciannelli, Richard O'Sullivan, Stephen Murray. British espionage officer, going to Venice to meet schoolboy son, disappears. Intriguing suspense yarn, based on Graham Greene story, with topnotch performances. Filmed in Italy.

Strangers in Good Company (1991-Canadian) **C-100m.** *** D: Cynthia Scott. Alice Diablo, Constance Garneau, Winifred Holden, Cissy Meddings, Mary Meigs, Catherine Roche, Michelle Sweeney, Beth Webber. Slow-paced but rewarding study of a group of women temporarily stuck in the Canadian wilderness when their bus breaks down. All the actresses play themselves in this unusual film from the National Film Board of Canada. It's mainly talk, as we learn about the hopes and sorrows of women who share their feelings during an interlude in their lives. [PG]▼

Strangers in Love (1932) **76m.** ** D: Lothar Mendes. Kay Francis, Fredric March, Stuart Erwin, Juliette Compton, Sidney Toler, George Barbier. Mild comedy; Francis is secretary who loves March, weakling playboy forced to impersonate twin brother to expose family fraud. ▼

Strangers Kiss (1984) **C-94m.** **½ D: Matthew Chapman. Peter Coyote, Victoria Tennant, Blaine Novak, Dan Shor, Richard Romanus, Linda Kerridge. Interesting, offbeat little film about the making of a low-budget movie, circa 1955, and the off-camera relationship between lead actors Novak and Tennant. Novak also cowrote screenplay with director Chapman, inspired by Stanley Kubrick's KILLER'S KISS. [R]▼

Strangers May Kiss (1931) **85m.** ** D: George Fitzmaurice. Norma Shearer, Robert Montgomery, Neil Hamilton, Marjorie Rambeau, Jed Prouty, Hale Hamilton, Henry Armetta, Irene Rich. Polished but ridiculous pre-Code soaper of Shearer in love with—and fooling herself into trusting—unreliable hypocrite Neil Hamilton. Film's conclusion is not to be believed. Montgomery is fine as Shearer's pal; young Ray Milland has a couple of lines as one of her admirers.

Strangers on a Train (1951) **101m.** **** D: Alfred Hitchcock. Farley Granger, Ruth Roman, Robert Walker, Leo G. Carroll, Patricia Hitchcock, Marion Lorne. Walker gives his finest performance as psychopath involved with tennis star Granger in "exchange murders." Lorne is unforgettable as doting mother; so is merry-go-round climax. First-class Hitchcock, based on a Patricia Highsmith novel and coscripted by Raymond Chandler. Remade as ONCE YOU KISS A STRANGER and the inspiration for THROW MOMMA FROM THE TRAIN. British version of film, now available, runs almost two minutes longer, has a different ending and franker dialogue in the first scene where Granger and Walker meet.▼●◗

Stranger's Return, The (1933) **89m.** ***½ D: King Vidor. Lionel Barrymore, Miriam Hopkins, Franchot Tone, Stuart Erwin, Irene Hervey, Beulah Bondi. A young woman, recently separated from her husband, leaves the city to stay at her grandfather's farm. Here she finds her roots, as well as a kindred spirit in neighboring farmer Tone, a college graduate. Why this rich, mature, beautifully made film isn't better known is a mystery. Phil Stong helped adapt his own novel for director Vidor.

Strangers: The Story of a Mother and Daughter (1979) **C-100m. TVM** D: Milton Katselas. Bette Davis, Gena Rowlands, Ford Rainey, Donald Moffat, Royal Dano. Davis at her latter-day best (winning an Emmy Award) and matched scene for scene by Rowlands in this drama about a lonely widow's resentment over her estranged daughter's unexpected homecoming after 20 years. Written by Michael DeGuzman. Aka STRANGERS. Above average. ▼

Strangers When We Meet (1960) **C-117m.** **½ D: Richard Quine. Kirk Douglas, Kim Novak, Ernie Kovacs, Barbara Rush, Walter Matthau, Virginia Bruce, Kent Smith. Expensive soaper with attractive stars; both are married, but fall in love with each other. Script by Evan Hunter, from his novel. CinemaScope.▼

Stranger Than Paradise (1984) **90m.** ★★★ D: Jim Jarmusch. John Lurie, Eszter Balint, Richard Edson, Cecilla Stark. Simple story of a nondescript young man, his doltish best friend, and his 16-year-old female cousin who comes to America from Hungary. Critically acclaimed comedy-road movie is, at its worst, a bit slow; at its best, original, ingratiating, and extremely funny. Independently filmed and developed from a 30m. short. Screenplay by Jarmusch, music by Lurie. [R]▼●

Stranger Wore a Gun, The (1953) **C-83m.** ★★ D: Andre de Toth. Randolph Scott, Claire Trevor, Joan Weldon, George Macready, Lee Marvin, Ernest Borgnine, Alfonso Bedoya. Oddball plot in this Scott Western; Randy is befriended by bandit and becomes involved in a holdup before he can return to normal living. Originally in 3-D.▼

Strange Shadows in An Empty Room (1977) **C-99m.** ★½ D: Martin Herbert (Alberto DeMartino). Stuart Whitman, John Saxon, Martin Landau, Tisa Farrow, Gayle Hunnicutt, Carole Laure. Far-fetched, violent film has police detective Whitman searching for his sister's murderer. Tawdry stuff; filmed in Montreal as BLAZING MAGNUMS (a far more appropriate title). Panavision. [R]▼

Strange Skirts SEE: **When Ladies Meet** (1941)

Strange Vengeance of Rosalie, The (1972) **C-107m.** ★★ D: Jack Starrett. Bonnie Bedelia, Ken Howard, Anthony Zerbe. Offbeat story of Indian girl who holds man captive in rambling house. Far-fetched tale goes way off-base. [PG]

Strange Woman, The (1946) **100m.** ★★½ D: Edgar G. Ulmer. Hedy Lamarr, George Sanders, Louis Hayward, Gene Lockhart, Hillary Brooke. Lamarr offers one of her best performances as a shrewish young woman in 19th-century Maine who affects the lives of three very different men. Nicely directed by Ulmer; a rare instance in which he was allowed a Grade-A cast.▼◗

Strange World of Planet X, The SEE: **Cosmic Monster, The**

Strangler, The (1964) **89m.** ★★★ D: Burt Topper. Victor Buono, David McLean, Ellen Corby, Jeanne Bates, Wally Campo, James (B.) Sikking. Buono gives fine performance as mother-dominated mad killer who strangles women and pitches Boston into frenzy.▼

Strangler's Morgue SEE: **Crimes of Stephen Hawke, The**

Stranglers of Bombay, The (1960-British) **81m.** ★★½ D: Terence Fisher. Andrew Cruickshank, Marne Maitland, Guy Rolfe, Paul Stassino, Jan Holden. Grisly story of fanatical Indian cult attempting to drive British from trading station. Good cast helped by tense direction. Megascope.

Strapless (1989-British) **C-103m.** ★★½ D: David Hare. Blair Brown, Bruno Ganz, Bridget Fonda, Hugh Laurie, Alan Howard, Billy Roch, Camille Coduri, Alexandra Pigg, Michael Gough, Gary O'Brien. American doctor Brown, living and working in London, hits 40 and finds herself at a crossroads, just as her 25-year-old sister arrives for an extended vacation. Brown is fine, and Fonda completely winning in this studied, sometimes ponderous story of the need to face emotions head-on, no matter where they may lead. [R]▼●

Strapped (1993) **C-95m. TVM** D: Forest Whitaker. Bokeem Woodbine, Michael Biehn, Kia Joy Goodwin, Fredro Scruggs, Jermaine Hopkins, Craig Wasson, Monie Love, Starletta Dupois, Tonya Pinkins. Devastating account of an intelligent black teen, who has come of age amid the poverty and desperation of the Brooklyn housing projects. He feels he must do whatever he can to take care of his own, even if it includes selling guns and becoming a police informer. A searing portrait of urban hopelessness. Intelligent, richly textured script by Dena Kleiman, a *New York Times* reporter. Whitaker's directorial debut. Made for cable. Above average. ▼

Strategic Air Command (1955) **C-114m.** ★★½ D: Anthony Mann. James Stewart, June Allyson, Frank Lovejoy, Barry Sullivan, Bruce Bennett, Rosemary DeCamp. Film only gets off the ground when Stewart does, as baseball player recalled to air force duty; Allyson is his sugary wife. VistaVision.▼●

Stratton Story, The (1949) **106m.** ★★★½ D: Sam Wood. James Stewart, June Allyson, Frank Morgan, Agnes Moorehead, Bill Williams, Jimmy Dykes, Bill Dickey. Stewart is fine as Monty Stratton, the baseball player whose loss of one leg did not halt his career; well played by good cast, including ballplayers Dykes and Dickey. Oscar winner for story (Douglas Morrow); screenplay by Morrow and Guy Trosper. Also shown in computer-colored version.▼

Strawberry and Chocolate (1994-Cuban) **C-110m.** ★★½ D: Tomas Gutierrez Alea, Juan Carlos Tabio. Jorge Perugorria, Vladimir Cruz, Mirta Ibarra, Francisco Gattorono, Marilyn Solaya. Entertaining and sympathetic account of the unlikely friendship between David, a heterosexual and devoted Communist who knows nothing of the arts (and is depressed over being dumped by his girlfriend), and homosexual, cultured Diego, who's full of life and doesn't care much for politics. Controversial in its home country, but notable too as the first Cuban film ever nominated for a Best Foreign Film Oscar. [R] ▼●

Strawberry Blonde, The (1941) **97m.** ★★★ D: Raoul Walsh. James Cagney, Olivia de Havilland, Rita Hayworth, Alan Hale,

Jack Carson, George Tobias, Una O'Connor, George Reeves. Cagney's dynamic in entertaining turn-of-the-century story of dentist infatuated with gold-digger Hayworth, and his subsequent marriage to de Havilland. Remade in 1948 as ONE SUNDAY AFTERNOON, the title of the 1933 Gary Cooper film of which *this* is a remake.▼

Strawberry Statement, The (1970) **C-103m.** ** D: Stuart Hagmann. Bruce Davison, Kim Darby, Bob Balaban, James Kunen, Jeannie Berlin, Bud Cort, David Dukes, James Coco, Bert Remsen. Cluttered adaptation of James Kunen's book about Columbia University's riots tries to be too many things at once—comedy, social commentary, musical. Good performances. Script by Israel Horovitz (who also plays Dr. Benton). [R]▼

Straw Dogs (1971) **C-113m.** ***½ D: Sam Peckinpah. Dustin Hoffman, Susan George, Peter Vaughan, T. P. McKenna, Peter Arne, David Warner. One of the most controversial violence-themed films of its day. Hoffman portrays American mathematician whose pacifism is put to supreme test when he and British wife George move to isolated village and are menaced by local hooligans. Screenplay by Peckinpah and David Zelag Goodman from Gordon Williams' novel *Siege at Trenchers Farm*. Filmed in England. Original running time: 118m. [R]▼●◗

Stray Dog (1949-Japanese) **122m.** **** D: Akira Kurosawa. Toshiro Mifune, Takashi Shimura, Keiko Awaji. Classic Japanese film noir, most effective as a look at life in post-WW2 Tokyo. Mifune does well as a detective whose gun is stolen; he sets out on an odyssey to reclaim his weapon, and to seek out a killer. Although not as well known as RASHOMON, this film is just as important to career of Kurosawa and the growth of Japanese cinema.▼●◗

Streamers (1983) **C-118m.** *** D: Robert Altman. Matthew Modine, Michael Wright, Mitchell Lichtenstein, David Alan Grier, Guy Boyd, George Dzundza. A couple of days in an army barracks at the dawn of America's involvement in Vietnam becomes a parable about manhood, death and relationships between the races. Overlong and depressing but still worthwhile, with fine performances in meaty roles. Screenplay by David Rabe, from his play. [R]▼●

Street Angel (1928) **102m.** *** D: Frank Borzage. Janet Gaynor, Charles Farrell, Guido Trento, Natalie Kingston, Henry Armetta. Italian girl fleeing from police joins traveling circus, meets and falls in love with young painter who finds her an inspiration. Follow-up to 7TH HEAVEN is actually much better; a delicate, beautifully photographed silent film. Gaynor won a Best Actress Oscar (shared for her performances in 7TH HEAVEN and SUNRISE).▼

Streetcar Named Desire, A (1951) **122m.** **** D: Elia Kazan. Marlon Brando, Vivien Leigh, Kim Hunter, Karl Malden. Stunning production of Tennessee Williams' play, with Brando as the animalistic Stanley Kowalski and Leigh as his wistful, neurotic sister-in-law, Blanche Dubois, pressed together in a grim New Orleans tenement. Oscars went to Leigh, Hunter, and Malden for their flawless performances, as well as for the art direction-set decoration—but it's Brando who left an indelible mark on audiences. Highly influential jazz score by Alex North. Rereleased in 1993 with 4m. of footage that was censored in 1951, playing up the sexual tension between Blanche and Stanley, and Stella's carnal attraction to her husband. Remade twice for TV.▼●◗

Streetcar Named Desire, A (1984) **C-124m. TVM** D: John Erman. Ann-Margret, Treat Williams, Beverly D'Angelo, Randy Quaid, Rafael Campos, Erica Yohn. Terrific performance by Ann-Margret as Blanche makes this version stand proudly beside its classic predecessor. Above average.▼

Streetcar Named Desire, A (1995) **C-156m. TVM** D: Glenn Jordan. Jessica Lange, Alec Baldwin, Diane Lane, John Goodman. Lange and Baldwin repeat their passionate Blanche and Stanley roles from the lusty 1992 Broadway revival. Much closer to the Williams play than the earlier TV version or even Kazan's Hays-office-emasculated screen version of the '50s. Lange sees Blanche with a feminist bent, and is somewhat less fragile and flighty than Vivien Leigh and Ann-Margret before her. Above average. ▼●

Street Fight SEE: **Coonskin**

Street Fighter, The (1974-Japanese) **C-91m.** **½ D: Shigehiro Ozawa. Sonny Chiba, Gerald Yamada, Doris Nakajima, Tony Cetera, Teijo Shikeharo. Japan's answer to Bruce Lee, Shinichi "Sonny" Chiba, who takes on both the Mafia and the Yakuza in this cult film notable for the level of its bone-crunching, blood-spurting violence. Staged and directed with more skill than most kung fu epics, the plentiful fight scenes required four separate action directors. Title sequence for U.S. version designed by Jack Sholder, who later directed THE HIDDEN. Originally rated X, then rerated R after being cut to 75m. Unrated version released on tape and laserdisc. Followed by RETURN OF THE STREET FIGHTER. Actionscope. [X]▼●

Street Fighter (1994) **C-97m.** BOMB D: Steven E. de Souza. Jean-Claude Van Damme, Raul Julia, Ming-Na Wen, Damian Chapa, Kylie Minogue, Simon Callow, Roshan Seth, Wes Studi, Andrew Bryniarski, Adrian Cronauer. "Allied Nations" commando Van Damme and his action team battle high-tech warlord Julia (looking depressingly gaunt in his final theatrical film) who's holding hostages ransom for $20 billion, and conducting mutation experiments in his mad-scientist lab. Callow, a costar of FOUR WEDDINGS AND A FUNERAL, plays a prissy A.N. undersecretary in the worst movie to date inspired by a video game. Plays more like FOUR HUNDRED FUNERALS AND NO SEX. Followed by STREET FIGHTER II: THE ANIMATED MOVIE. Super 35. [PG-13]▼●◗

Street Fighter's Last Revenge, The (1974-Japanese) **C-79m.** ** D: Shigehiro Ozawa. Shinichi "Sonny" Chiba, Etsuko "Sue" Shiomi, Masafumi Suzuki, Frankie Black, Reiko Ike, Willy Dosey. Chiba swears vengeance on the mob after doing a job for them and getting double-crossed when it's payoff time. Third entry in the ultraviolent series offers more of the same, although Chiba is fashioned as a Bondian secret agent type this time around. Highlight: a character gets knocked into a coffin and sent through a crematory! Followed by SISTER STREETFIGHTER. Actionscope. [R]▼●

Street Gang SEE: **Vigilante**

Street Justice (1989) **C-94m.** *½ D: Richard S. Sarafian. Michael Ontkean, Joanna Kerns, Catherine Bach, J.D. Cannon, Jeanette Nolan, Richard Cox, William Windom, Sandra Currie. Standard Western plot transposed to modern city setting: loner hero cleans up corrupt town dominated by ruthless, wealthy family. Slow, unconvincing, and instantly forgettable. [R]▼

Street Music (1981) **C-92m.** **½ D: Jenny Bowen. Elizabeth Daily, Larry Breeding, Ned Glass, Marjorie Eaton, W. F. Walker, Miriam Phillips, D'Alan Moss. Trifling yet occasionally touching tale of ambitious singer Daily, her irresponsible boyfriend Breeding, and elderly residents of a dilapidated San Francisco hotel who fight the bureaucracy to save their home. Bouncy lead performances. [R]▼

Street of Chance (1942) **74m.** **½ D: Jack Hively. Burgess Meredith, Claire Trevor, Sheldon Leonard, Frieda Inescort, Jerome Cowan, Louise Platt, Adeline De Walt Reynolds. Early, prototypical film noir from a Cornell Woolrich story about a man who suffers from amnesia and tries to find clues to his former identity. The opening sequences are dynamite.

Street of Shame (1956-Japanese) **96m.** ***½ D: Kenji Mizoguchi. Machiko Kyo, Ayako Wakao, Aiko Mimasu, Michiyo Kogure. The stories of various prostitutes in Dreamland, a Tokyo brothel, are sensitively handled in Mizoguchi's last completed film. Kyo is particularly memorable as a tough, cynical lady of the night; her scene with her father is a highlight.▼

Street of Sorrow, The SEE: **Joyless Street, The**

Street People (1976-Italian) **C-92m.** *½ D: Maurizio Lucidi. Roger Moore, Stacy Keach, Ivo Garrani, Fausto Tozzi, Ettore Manni. Insipid though energetic gangster film punctuated by several car chases. San Francisco mafioso dispatches nephew Moore (believe him as a Sicilian?) and his Grand Prix driving buddy Keach to find out which rival Don hid a million-dollar cache of pure heroin in the cross he imported from Italy as a gift for his church. [R]▼

Streets (1990) **C-86m.** **½ D: Katt Shea Ruben. Christina Applegate, David Mendenhall, Eb Lottimer, Patrick Richword, Alan Stock, Alexander Folk, Mel Castelo, Kay Lenz. Serious, well-made story of runaways living in Venice, California, is compromised by concurrent story of psychotic cop who's a serial killer of prostitutes. Applegate is excellent as illiterate heroine. Understated but shockingly violent at times. [R]▼

Street Scene (1931) **80m.** ***½ D: King Vidor. Sylvia Sidney, William Collier, Jr., David Landau, Estelle Taylor, Walter Miller, Beulah Bondi. Heartbreakingly realistic account of life in N.Y. tenements, and younger generation's desperation to get out. Elmer Rice's Pulitzer Prize-winning play (adapted by him) enhanced by fine performances, George Barnes' striking camerawork, Alfred Newman's classic music score.▼

Street Smart (1987) **C-97m.** **½ D: Jerry Schatzberg. Christopher Reeve, Kathy Baker, Mimi Rogers, Morgan Freeman, Jay Patterson, Andre Gregory, Anna Maria Horsford. Out-of-favor writer for a slick Manhattan magazine pitches a high-profile study of N.Y.C pimpdom; unable to find a cooperative subject, he fakes the story, which boomerangs when the D.A. concludes the story is about a real-life murder suspect. Intriguing idea, based on screenwriter David Freeman's own experience at *New York* magazine, but just misses; powerhouse performances by pimp Freeman and hooker Baker make up for Reeve's blandness in the lead. [R]▼●

Streets of Fire (1984) **C-93m.** *** D: Walter Hill. Michael Paré, Diane Lane, Rick Moranis, Amy Madigan, Willem Dafoe, Deborah Van Valkenburgh, Richard Lawson, Rick Rossovich, Bill Paxton, Lee Ving, Robert Townsend, Elizabeth Daily, Marine Jahan, Ed Begley, Jr., Olivia Brown, Matthew Laurance, The Blasters. Female rock star is kidnapped by sadistic bikers, and her embittered ex-boyfriend agrees to bring her back—for a price. This "rock 'n' roll fable" is actually a 1950s B movie brought up to date with pulsating rock score (principally by Ry Cooder), state-of-the-art visuals, and a refusal to take itself too seriously. Unfortunately, near the climax the glitter gives out and we're left with the story—which can't carry film to a really satisfying conclusion. Stunningly photographed (mostly on a soundstage, believe it or not) by Andrew Laszlo. [PG]▼●◗

Streets of Gold (1986) **C-95m.** **½ D: Joe Roth. Klaus Maria Brandauer, Adrian Pasdar, Wesley Snipes, Angela Molina, Elya Baskin, Rainbow Harvest, John Mahoney. Former Russian boxing champ, now a dishwasher in Brooklyn, trains two street kids for U.S. boxing team—hoping to beat his former Russian coach. Well-meaning "feel-good" movie along ROCKY lines; utterly ordinary but for Brandauer's performance. [R]▼●

Streets of Laredo (1949) **C-92m.** ** D: Leslie Fenton. William Holden, Macdonald Carey, Mona Freeman, William Bendix, Stanley Ridges, Alfonso Bedoya. Muddled Western of outlaws Carey, Holden, and Bendix, and how the latter two come to be Texas Rangers; in fact, this is a remake of THE TEXAS RANGERS. Fans of THE TREASURE OF THE SIERRA MADRE will appreciate Bedoya's characterization.

Streets of New York (1939) **73m.** **½ D: William Nigh. Jackie Cooper, Martin Spellman, Marjorie Reynolds, Dick Purcell, George Cleveland, George Irving. Good programmer of an upright young man (Cooper) who admires Abraham Lincoln and must overcome much adversity on the streets of N.Y.C.'s Hell's Kitchen. Aka THE ABE LINCOLN OF NINTH AVENUE.▼

Streetwalkin' (1984) **C-85m.** BOMB D: Joan Freeman. Melissa Leo, Dale Midkiff, Antonio Fargas, Julie Newmar, Leon Robinson, Annie Golden. Ultra-slick, sleazy, hopelessly predictable trash about hooker-with-a-heart-of-gold and her sadistic, unbelievably stupid pimp. [R]▼

Streetwise (1984) **C-92m.** ***½ D: Martin Bell. Sad, gut-wrenching documentary about teen vagrants living—and, in one case, dying—on the mean streets of Seattle. This powerful record of young, lost souls would make a telling double bill with any one of a dozen idiotic adolescent comedies of the 1980s.▼●

Street With No Name, The (1948) **91m.** *** D: William Keighley. Mark Stevens, Richard Widmark, Lloyd Nolan, Barbara Lawrence, Ed Begley, Donald Buka. Fine movie based on actual F.B.I. case of agent uncovering head of city mob. Suspense well handled. Remade as HOUSE OF BAMBOO. ▼

Strictly Ballroom (1992-Australian) **C-94m.** *** D: Baz Luhrmann. Paul Mercurio, Tara Morice, Bill Hunter, Barry Otto, Pat Thompson, Gia Carides, Peter Whitford, John Hannan. Spirited, allegorical musical about a young, competitive ballroom dancer (Mercurio) who outrages his mother, and the "establishment," by insisting on dancing his own provocative steps; he takes on a new ugly-duckling partner (Morice) who blooms under his tutelage. This crowd-pleaser sacrifices credibility for caricature but despite its rough edges emerges a winner. [PG]▼●

Strictly Business (1991) **C-83m.** ** D: Kevin Hooks. Tommy Davidson, Joseph C. Phillips, Anne Marie Johnson, David Marshall Grant, Halle Berry, Jon Cypher, Sam (Samuel L.) Jackson, Kim Coles, James McDaniel, Paul Provenza, Annie Golden. Corporate man-on-the-move with a "yuppie-plus" girlfriend falls for a pretty show-biz hopeful, then enlists the aid of an indolent mailroom employee to loosen up his act, and increase his funk quotient. Silly, simplistic comedy. Director Hooks appears in a small role. [PG-13]▼●

Strictly Dishonorable (1951) **86m.** ** D: Melvin Frank, Norman Panama. Ezio Pinza, Janet Leigh, Millard Mitchell, Gale Robbins. Tame shenanigans of opera star Pinza marrying Leigh to save her reputation. Based on the Preston Sturges play, previously filmed in 1931.

Strike (1924-Russian) **73m.** ***½ D: Sergei Eisenstein. Grigori Alexandrov, Maxim Strauch, Mikhail Gomarov, Alexander Antonov, Judith Glizer. Eisenstein's debut feature is a still-powerful, vivid account of a 1912 factory workers strike in Czarist Russia and its violent suppression. An appropriate prelude to POTEMKIN; some prints run 82m.▼

Strike! SEE: **All I Wanna Do**

Strikebound (1983-Australian) **C-100m.** *** D: Richard Lowenstein. Chris Haywood, Carol Burns, Hugh Keays-Byrne, Rob Steele, Nik Forster. Documentarylike chronicle, based on actual incidents, of a miners' strike in the Australian coal fields during the 1930s, culminating with the workers—many of them Communist Party members—barricading themselves in their mine. Seems a bit romanticized but still taut, perceptive, and extremely well made.

Strike It Rich (1990-British) **C-87m.** *½ D: James Scott. Robert Lindsay, Molly Ringwald, John Gielgud, Max Wall, Simon de la Brosse, Margi Clarke. Second film version of Graham Greene novella *Loser Takes All,* about an obscure conglomerate accountant talked into honeymooning beyond his means in Monte Carlo following a chance encounter with the firm's Grand Old Man. The leads in DRIVING MISS DAISY have more sexual chemistry than postnuptial Lindsay and Ringwald; sole compensations are Gielgud and '50s production design. [PG]▼●

Strike Me Pink (1936) **100m.** *½ D: Norman Taurog. Eddie Cantor, Ethel Merman, Sally Eilers, Parkyakarkus, William

Frawley, Brian Donlevy. One of Cantor's worst films, built around his run-in with racketeers at amusement park which he manages. Good slapstick chase finale, forgettable music numbers.▼●

Strike Up the Band (1940) **120m.** **½ D: Busby Berkeley. Mickey Rooney, Judy Garland, Paul Whiteman, June Preisser, William Tracy, Larry Nunn, Margaret Early, Ann Shoemaker. Rooney is leader of high school band hoping to compete in Paul Whiteman's nationwide radio contest. Typical Mickey-Judy fare, with good songs: "Our Love Affair" and an extended finale featuring the Gershwins' title tune. George Pal contributes a unique segment featuring a symphony performed by animated pieces of fruit (an idea apparently hatched by Vincente Minnelli).▼●

Striking Distance (1993) **C-101m.** ** D: Rowdy Herrington. Bruce Willis, Sarah Jessica Parker, Dennis Farina, Tom Sizemore, Brion James, Robert Pastorelli, Timothy Busfield, John Mahoney, Andre Braugher, Jodi Long. Slick but empty, overly familiar thriller about maverick Pittsburgh river cop Willis, who bucks the status quo within his department, and becomes a pawn in a case involving a serial killer. [R]▼●◗

Strip, The (1951) **85m.** ** D: Leslie Kardos. Mickey Rooney, Sally Forrest, William Demarest, James Craig. Rooney gives sincere, energetic performance as former drummer involved with gangsters, trying to help Forrest get a movie break. Routine film enlivened by great music of Louis Armstrong, Earl Hines, Jack Teagarden and all-star group.

Stripes (1981) **C-105m.** **½ D: Ivan Reitman. Bill Murray, Harold Ramis, Warren Oates, P. J. Soles, Sean Young, John Candy, John Larroquette, Judge Reinhold, Timothy Busfield, Bill Paxton. Loser Murray joins the Army in this predictable service comedy, which somehow pulled in millions at the box office. Sometimes funny, but eminently forgettable. Ramis, who plays Murray's buddy, also coscripted. Brief appearances by Joe Flaherty and Dave Thomas. [R]▼●◗

Stripped to Kill (1987) **C-88m.** **½ D: Katt Shea Ruben. Kay Lenz, Greg Evigan, Norman Fell, Pia Kamakahi, Tracey Crowder, Debby Nassar. Who's killing the classy strippers of L.A.? It's up to policewoman Lenz to find out, by posing as a stripper herself. Stylish, inventive Roger Corman B production hampered by too many strip numbers. Followed by a sequel. [R]▼

Stripped to Kill II (1989) **C-83m.** *½ D: Katt Shea Ruben. Maria Ford, Eb Lottimer, Karen Mayo Chandler, Marjean Holden, Birke Tan, Debra Lamb. More strippers, more murders, and a heroine with slight ESP powers—she dreams of murders as they occur. Followup to STRIPPED TO KILL is inferior in every way—despite same director. [R]▼

Stripper, The (1963) **95m.** **½ D: Franklin Schaffner. Joanne Woodward, Richard Beymer, Claire Trevor, Carol Lynley, Robert Webber, Gypsy Rose Lee, Louis Nye, Michael J. Pollard. Aging stripper falls in love with teen-age boy in this OK filmization of William Inge's play *A Loss of Roses*. Director Schaffner's first movie. CinemaScope.▼

Striptease (1996) **C-115m.** BOMB D: Andrew Bergman. Demi Moore, Armand Assante, Burt Reynolds, Ving Rhames, Robert Patrick, Paul Guilfoyle, Rumer Willis, Frances Fisher. Unspeakably dreary—not to mention dreadful—movie (based on Carl Hiassen's novel) about a woman who's lost custody of her young daughter to her sleazeball ex-husband and becomes a stripper in order to raise money fast for a court appeal. Then she becomes entangled with a horny congressman. Not funny enough, or dramatic enough, or sexy enough, or bad enough, to qualify as entertainment in *any* category. At least SHOWGIRLS had some unintended laughs. That's Moore's real-life daughter playing her little girl. Unrated video version includes 2m. of additional footage. [R] ▼●◗

Stroke of Midnight (1991) **C-91m.** *½ D: Tom Clegg. Rob Lowe, Jennifer Grey, Andrea Ferreol, Elizabeth Vitali, Rebecca Potok, Sacha Brignet. Direct to video dud about completely self-absorbed fashion mogul Lowe's search for a "new face" to represent his line of clothes; of course, he's barely aware of aspiring shoe designer Grey, who works for him. Poorly executed Cinderella yarn—replete with magic shoes. Unfortunately, there's no magic in this movie. [PG]▼●

Stroker Ace (1983) **C-96m.** BOMB D: Hal Needham. Burt Reynolds, Ned Beatty, Jim Nabors, Loni Anderson, Parker Stevenson, Bubba Smith, John Byner, Frank O. Hill. One of Burt's worst has him as champion race-car driver and pea-brain who delights in tormenting his sponsor (Beatty) and leering at buxom Anderson. Lame "good old boy" hijinks, punctuated with TV stock footage of race-car crackups! Note: Jim Nabors sings, too. [PG]▼◗

Stromboli (1949-Italian) **81m.** *½ D: Roberto Rossellini. Ingrid Bergman, Mario Vitale, Renzo Cesana, Mario Sponza. Rambling dreariness with refugee Bergman marrying fisherman Vitale; even an erupting volcano doesn't jar this plodding film, which was boycotted in the U.S. because Bergman had left her husband for Rossellini. Original 107m. version is now available, but is little improvement over U.S. release (which was edited by Alfred Werker and has a different ending).▼

Stronger Than the Sun (1980-British)

C-101m. *** D: Michael Apted. Francesca Annis, Tom Bell. Annis is excellent as a nuclear power plant worker who attempts to expose a radioactive leak. Timely drama bears a striking resemblance to the Karen Silkwood story.

Strongest Man in the World, The (1975) **C-92m.** ** D: Vincent McEveety. Kurt Russell, Joe Flynn, Eve Arden, Cesar Romero, Phil Silvers, Dick Van Patten, Harold Gould, James Gregory. Third of Disney's cookie-cutter student comedies with Russell and pals again discovering a magic formula—this one for super-strength—and battling crooks who want to get their hands on it. Good opening and closing, but even kids may find it draggy midway through. [G]

Stronghold (1951) **82m.** *½ D: Steve Sekely. Veronica Lake, Zachary Scott, Arturo de Cordova, Rita Macedo. Pedestrian costumer set in 1860s, with Lake fleeing U.S. and becoming embroiled in Mexican revolution.

Strong Man, The (1926) **78m.** *** D: Frank Capra. Harry Langdon, Priscilla Bonner, Gertrude Astor, Brooks Benedict, Arthur Thalasso, Robert McKim, William V. Mong. Baby-faced Langdon's best movie (and Capra's feature-film debut) casts him as a WW1 veteran who comes to America in search of the girl he corresponded with during the war. Many fine set-pieces make this a memorable comedy; the star never fared as well again.▼●

Strong Medicine (1979) **C-84m.** **½ D: Richard Foreman. Kate Mannheim, Scotty Snyder, Bill Raymond, Harry Roskolenko, Ron Vawter, Carol Kane, Raul Julia, Buck Henry, Wallace Shawn. Alternately fascinating, boring, surreal chronicle of the various activities and adventures of a mad, manic, eccentric woman. Foreman is an innovative theater director; ultimately, this film is an acquired taste.

Stroszek (1977-German) **C-108m.** *** D: Werner Herzog. Bruno S., Eva Mattes, Clemens Scheitz. Berlin street singer and former mental patient Bruno S. joins with whore (Mattes) and aging eccentric (Scheitz) to travel to the gold-paved streets of America the promised-land—which turns out to be dreary, rural Wisconsin. Most effective as tragicomic, ultimately bitter ridicule of American society.▼

Struggle, The (1931) **77m.** **½ D: D. W. Griffith. Hal Skelly, Zita Johann, Evelyn Baldwin, Edna Hagan, Charlotte Wynters, Jackson Halliday. Griffith's final film as director is a somber drama chronicling the plight and fate of Skelly, an average Joe who is victimized by alcoholism and desperation. A notorious failure in its day, this was the nail in the coffin of Griffith's then-sagging career. Today it's a fascinating curio—and a reminder that THE LOST WEEKEND was not the first film to explore the ravages of alcoholism. Baldwin (who plays Skelly's sister) went on to become Griffith's second wife.▼

Stuart Little (1999) **C-92m.** *** D: Rob Minkoff. Geena Davis, Hugh Laurie, Jonathan Lipnicki, Jeffrey Jones, Julia Sweeney, Allyce Beasley, Brian Doyle-Murray, Dabney Coleman, Estelle Getty; voices of Michael J. Fox, Nathan Lane, Chazz Palminteri, Jennifer Tilly, Bruno Kirby, David Alan Grier, Steve Zahn. Cute family film loosely based on E. B. White's much-loved book about a mouse, adopted by a human family, who falls prey to the plotting of a jealous housecat. Sincere human performances and remarkable computer animation of Stuart make this entertaining for young and old alike. [PG]▼◗

Stuart Saves His Family (1995) **C-95m.** ** D: Harold Ramis. Al Franken, Laura San Giacomo, Vincent D'Onofrio, Shirley Knight, Harris Yulin, Lesley Boone, John Link Graney, Julia Sweeney. Feature-film vehicle for Stuart Smalley, writer-performer Franken's endearingly dippy self-affirmation advocate from *Saturday Night Live* TV skits ("I'm good enough, I'm smart enough, and doggone it, people *like* me"). Unfortunately, this purported comedy about Stuart's attempts to wrest himself from his dysfunctional family (and the blight caused by his alcoholic father) becomes deadly serious! [PG-13] ▼●

Stud, The (1978-British) **C-95m.** BOMB D: Quentin Masters. Joan Collins, Oliver Tobias, Sue Lloyd, Mark Burns, Walter Gottell, Emma Jacobs. A waiter works his way up in the world (so to speak) by sleeping with the boss' wife. Idiotic softcore porn written by Jackie Collins (Joan's sister). Followed by THE BITCH. [R]▼

Student Bodies (1981) **C-86m.** *½ D: Mickey Rose. Kristen Riter, Matthew Goldsby, Richard Brando, Joe Flood, Joe Talarowski. Spoof of HALLOWEEN-type pictures has a promising start, then simply falls apart; ending is particularly bad. Plagued by production problems, as indicated by producing credit for the ubiquitous and nonexistent Allen Smithee (Michael Ritchie here). [R]▼●

Student Confidential (1987) **C-95m.** *½ D: Richard Horian. Eric Douglas, Marlon Jackson, Susan Scott, Richard Horian, Elizabeth Singer, Ronee Blakley. Boring dud about the problems of various students . . . one of whom is a former Playboy bunny. Eric Douglas is the brother of Michael and son of Kirk. Marlon Jackson is the brother of Michael. [R]▼

Student Connection, The (1975-Spanish) **C-92m.** *½ D: Rafael Romero Merchent. Ray Milland, Sylva Koscina, Ramon Oliveros, Maria Silva, Franco Ciacobini. Flat melodrama about a headmaster at a boys' school whose initial crime of passion (killing his mistress' husband) leads to a succession of murders when he learns that one of his students was an eyewitness. Video title: WITNESS TO MURDER.▼

Student Nurses, The (1970) **C-89m.** **½ D: Stephanie Rothman. Elaine Giftos, Karen Carlson, Brioni Farrell, Barbara Leigh, Reni Santoni, Richard Rust. First of five "nurse" movies produced by Roger Corman is easily the best, with good cast, comparatively thoughtful script (cowritten by Rothman), along with expected sex and action; most interesting subplot concerns guilt by young activist nurse after she accidentally shoots a cop. Followed by PRIVATE DUTY NURSES. [R]▼

Student Prince, The (1954) **C-107m.** ** D: Richard Thorpe. Ann Blyth, Edmund Purdom, John Ericson, Louis Calhern, Edmund Gwenn. Romberg music, dubbed voice of Mario Lanza chief assets in venerable operetta about heir to throne sent to Heidelberg for one last fling, where he falls in love with barmaid Blyth. Filmed before (sans music) in 1919 and 1927. CinemaScope.▼●

Student Prince in Old Heidelberg, The (1927) **105m.** **** D: Ernst Lubitsch. Ramon Novarro, Norma Shearer, Jean Hersholt, Gustav von Seyffertitz, Philippe de Lacy, Edgar Norton, George K. Arthur, Edythe Chapman. Silent version of Sigmund Romberg's famed operetta has youthful prince Novarro breaking out of his cloistered life—for the first time—and attending Heidelberg University, where he falls in love with a commoner, pretty barmaid Shearer. This is Lubitsch at his best, an absolute delight from start to finish, and truly the kind of charmer "they just don't make anymore." Also known as OLD HEIDELBERG. Previously filmed in 1919; remade (with music) in 1954.▼●

Student Teachers, The (1973) **C-79m.** **½ D: Jonathan Kaplan. Susan Damante, Brooke Mills, Bob Harris, John Cramer, Dick Miller, Don Steele, Robert Phillips, Charles Dierkop. Antics at Valley High School, with both feminist and "alternate learning center" concepts mixed into the usual sexploitation package. Freewheeling direction by Kaplan; followed by SUMMER SCHOOL TEACHERS. [R]▼

Student Tour (1934) **87m.** *½ D: Charles F. Reisner. Jimmy Durante, Charles Butterworth, Maxine Doyle, Phil Regan, Florine McKinney, Betty Grable, Herman Brix (Bruce Bennett). Deservedly obscure MGM musical about college students on world tour with an incredibly clunky leading lady. Pretty bad, though it's fun to see young Grable, and the sight of coeds swimming in front of the Taj Mahal is nothing to sneeze at. Guest star Nelson Eddy sings silly Bolero-type number "The Carlo."

Studs Lonigan (1960) **95m.** **½ D: Irving Lerner. Christopher Knight, Frank Gorshin, Venetia Stevenson, Carolyn Craig, Jack Nicholson, Dick Foran. Interesting if not altogether successful adaptation of James T. Farrell's "notorious" novel about a restless, sexually active young man in 1920s Chicago. Good period atmosphere, but script makes unfortunate compromises with 1960 taste and censorship. Nicholson is one of Studs' cronies; Foran is impressive as Studs' father. Scripted and produced by Philip Yordan. Basis for a 1979 TV miniseries.▼

Study in Scarlet, A (1933) **70m.** **½ D: Edward L. Marin. Reginald Owen, Anna May Wong, June Clyde, Alan Dinehart, John Warburton, Alan Mowbray, Warburton Gamble. Not-bad low-budget Sherlock Holmes outing (for which Owen wrote much of the dialogue), though it has virtually nothing to do with Conan Doyle story of the same name! Owen played Dr. Watson one year earlier in SHERLOCK HOLMES, while Mowbray, who's Inspector Lestrade here, turned up as villainous Col. Moran in the 1946 TERROR BY NIGHT.▼

Study in Terror, A (1965-British) **C-94m.** *** D: James Hill. John Neville, Donald Houston, Georgia Brown, John Fraser, Anthony Quayle, Barbara Windsor, Robert Morley, Cecil Parker, Frank Finlay, Kay Walsh, Judi Dench. Compact little thriller pits Sherlock Holmes against Jack the Ripper; violent, well paced, and well cast. For another version of Holmes vs. the Ripper, see MURDER BY DECREE.▼●

Stuff, The (1985) **C-93m.** **½ D: Larry Cohen. Michael Moriarty, Andrea Marcovicci, Garrett Morris, Paul Sorvino, Scott Bloom, Danny Aiello, James Dixon, Alexander Scourby, Russell Nype, Brian Bloom, Rutanya Alda. The new dessert sensation that's sweeping the country turns out to be deadly stuff indeed. Typically slapdash Larry Cohen production has some engaging performances, and the spirit of silly '50s science-fiction films, but doesn't always come off—as horror *or* comedy. It *does* have its moments, however—and a bunch of familiar "Commercial Spokespersons." [R]▼

Stunt Man, The (1980) **C-129m.** **** D: Richard Rush. Peter O'Toole, Steve Railsback, Barbara Hershey, Chuck Bail, Allen Goorwitz (Garfield), Adam Roarke, Alex Rocco, Sharon Farrell, Philip Bruns. An outrageous black comedy in which reality and make-believe blur. Fugitive Railsback stumbles onto a movie set, where he accidentally causes the death of their ace stunt man; director O'Toole offers to hide him from the police—if he'll replace the stunt man. Crammed with first-rate action and sly wit, plus a mesmerizing performance by O'Toole as the Christ-like Eli Cross. Attention must be paid, but the rewards are more than ample. Dazzlingly scripted (by

Lawrence B. Marcus from Paul Brodeur's novel) and directed; amusing score by Dominic Frontiere. Filmed in 1978. [R]▼●

Stunt Pilot (1939) **62m.** ** D: George Waggner. John Trent, Marjorie Reynolds, Milburn Stone, Jason Robards, Sr., Pat O'Malley. Not-bad "Tailspin Tommy" tale has him joining a movie studio as a flyer, encountering danger and murder.▼

Stunts (1977) **C-89m.** **½ D: Mark L. Lester. Robert Forster, Fiona Lewis, Joanna Cassidy, Darrell Fetty, Bruce Glover, James Luisi. When a stunt man dies while making a film, his brother (Forster) takes his place in order to probe the "accident." Engaging B movie with terrific action scenes and a wild helicopter-and-car finale. Retitled WHO IS KILLING THE STUNTMEN? [PG]▼

Stupids, The (1996) **C-94m.** **½ D: John Landis. Tom Arnold, Jessica Lundy, Bug Hall, Alex McKenna, Mark Metcalf, Matt Keeslar, Frankie Faison, Christopher Lee, Jenny McCarthy. Likably goofy film for kids about a lunkhead family that somehow gets involved in espionage and an illegal weapons scheme. The cast is ideal, straight-facedly portraying these well-meaning morons (from the children's books by James Marshall and Harry Allard); the tone of the film is admirably consistent and often quite funny. As usual Landis features cameos by other directors, including Robert Wise, Gillo Pontecorvo, Costa-Gavras, Atom Egoyan, Norman Jewison, and David Cronenberg. And yes, that's Captain Kangaroo (Bob Keeshan) as the museum curator. Remember, trust in the Lloyd. [PG]▼●

St. Valentine's Day Massacre, The (1967) **C-100m.** **½ D: Roger Corman. Jason Robards, Jr., George Segal, Ralph Meeker, Jean Hale, Clint Ritchie, Frank Silvera, Joseph Campanella, Bruce Dern. This had the makings of a good film, but they blew it, with Robards (as Al Capone) and Segal (doing a Jimmy Cagney imitation) overacting as they've never done before. So much shooting throughout film that final massacre seems tame by comparison. Many familiar faces appear throughout: Harold Stone, Kurt Krueger, Milton Frome, Mickey Deems, John Agar, Reed Hadley, Alex D'Arcy, etc. Pay close attention and you'll see Jack Nicholson, too! Panavision.▼

Sub-A-Dub-Dub SEE: **Hello Down There**

Subject Was Roses, The (1968) **C-107m.** *** D: Ulu Grosbard. Patricia Neal, Jack Albertson, Martin Sheen, Don Saxon, Elaine Williams, Grant Gordon. Frank D. Gilroy's Pulitzer Prize-winning play about young veteran's strained relationship with his parents makes a generally good film. This was Neal's first film after her near fatal stroke. Sheen and Oscar-winner Albertson recreated their Broadway roles. Gilroy adapted his own play for the screen. [G] ▼

Submarine Alert (1943) **67m.** ** D: Frank McDonald. Richard Arlen, Wendy Barrie, Nils Asther, Roger Pryor, Abner Biberman, Marc Lawrence, Dwight Frye. The old yarn about the fed who's made to look like he is banished by the force so that he can join the gang as a spy. If this is a little better than most of Arlen's quickies, it's because the cast is more interesting than usual, and the plot borrows heavily from THE 39 STEPS.▼

Submarine Command (1951) **87m.** **½ D: John Farrow. William Holden, Nancy Olson, William Bendix, Don Taylor. Predictable but acceptable post-WW2 account of naval military life; Olson is wholesome love interest.

Submarine D-1 (1937) **98m.** **½ D: Lloyd Bacon. Pat O'Brien, George Brent, Wayne Morris, Frank McHugh, Doris Weston, Henry O'Neill, Regis Toomey, Broderick Crawford. Medium-grade Warner Bros. action hokum about loving and fighting among the crew of a new submarine. Well-made documentary-like scenes mix with the contrived plot. Ronald Reagan was originally in the film's cast but wound up on the cutting room floor.

Submarine Patrol (1938) **95m.** **½ D: John Ford. Richard Greene, Nancy Kelly, Preston Foster, George Bancroft, Slim Summerville, John Carradine, J. Farrell McDonald, Maxie Rosenbloom, Jack Pennick, Elisha Cook, Jr. Routine actioner with tough captain Greene revitalizing beat-up Splinter Fleet ship and demoralized crew for duty in WW1.

Submarine X-1 (1968-British) **C-89m.** **½ D: William Graham. James Caan, Rupert Davies, David Summer, William Dysart, Norman Bowler. After losing submarine in battle with German ship, naval officer Caan gets second chance in daring raid with midget subs. Standard WW2 fare. [G]

Subspecies (1991) **C-90m.** ** D: Ted Nicolaou. Michael Watson, Laura Tate, Anders Hove, Michelle McBride, Irina Movila, Ivan J. Rado, Angus Scrimm. Nasty vampire is after some American girls but has to contend with his good-vampire brother. Actually shot in Transylvania on picturesque locations, but the director has no idea how to set up shock scenes. Followed by three sequels. [R]▼●

Substance of Fire, The (1996) **C-101m.** *** D: Daniel Sullivan. Ron Rifkin, Tony Goldwyn, Timothy Hutton, Sarah Jessica Parker, Lee Grant, Eric Bogosian, Elizabeth Franz, Gil Bellows, Roger Rees, Ronny Graham, Adolph Green, George Morfogen, Debra Monk. Literate, intelligent adaptation of Jon Robin Baitz' Off-

Broadway play about a brilliant but inordinately arrogant—and deeply troubled—Holocaust survivor (Rifkin). Now a book publisher, he's obsessed with publishing an extensive history of Nazi medical experiments, rather than a potentially lucrative novel that may save his company from financial ruin. Not surprisingly, he has alienated his three grown children. Extremely well acted, especially by Rifkin (who created his role onstage). Baitz scripted and coproduced. [R]▼●

Substitute, The (1996) **C-114m.** ** D: Robert Mandel. Tom Berenger, Diane Venora, Ernie Hudson, Glenn Plummer, William Forsythe, Richard Brooks, Cliff De Young. The CIA goes to high school in this preposterous but entertaining action story of agent Berenger who substitutes for teacher/girlfriend Venora when her leg is broken by a gang member. When he's not disciplining students, this substitute is busy exposing and fighting drug smugglers. Mindless diversion. Followed by two sequels. [R] ▼●◗

Subterfuge (1968-British) **C-92m.** ** D: Peter Graham Scott. Gene Barry, Joan Collins, Richard Todd, Suzanna Leigh, Michael Rennie. American agent Barry is forced into helping British Intelligence in this routine espionage drama.▼

Subterraneans, The (1960) **C-89m.** **½ D: Ranald MacDougall. Leslie Caron, George Peppard, Janice Rule, Roddy McDowall, Anne Seymour, Jim Hutton, Scott Marlowe. Glossy, superficial study of life and love among the beatniks, with pure cornball stereotype performances; MGM was not the studio for this one. Script by Robert Thom, from the Jack Kerouac novel. Music by Andre Previn, who also appears on screen along with such jazz artists as Gerry Mulligan, Carmen McRae, Art Pepper, Art Farmer, Shelly Manne. CinemaScope.

Suburban Commando (1991) **C-90m.** **½ D: Burt Kennedy. Hulk Hogan (Terry Bollea), Christopher Lloyd, Shelley Duvall, Larry Miller, William Ball, JoAnn Dearing, Jack Elam, Roy Dotrice, Michael Faustino. Engaging film for kids about outer-space warrior who comes to earth for some r&r, and gets involved in the lives of a somewhat stressed-out suburban family. Hogan is surprisingly likable as a vigilante/crusader in this comic vehicle which he coexecutive produced. [PG]▼●

Suburbans, The (1999) **C-90m.** *½ D: Donal Lardner Ward. Donal Lardner Ward, Amy Brenneman, Craig Bierko, Will Ferrell, Jennifer Love Hewitt, Tony Guma, Bridgette Wilson, Ben Stiller, Jerry Stiller, Robert Loggia. Pointless trifle about a one-hit-wonder band from the 1980s attempting to revitalize their career. Not even the Stillers can make it work. [R]▼◗

Suburbia (1983) SEE: **Wild Side, The**

subUrbia (1996) **C-118m.** **½ D: Richard Linklater. Giovanni Ribisi, Steve Zahn, Amie Carey, Samia Shoaib, Ajay Naidu, Nicky Katt, Jayce Bartok, Parker Posey, Dina Spybey. Knowing, laced-in-acid son-of-SLACKER, depicting a group of aimless, alienated 20-year-olds who hang out in a generic suburban parking lot, where various frictions and jealousies emerge—especially upon the appearance of one of their old pals, who has become a rock star. Collectively well acted and pungently scripted by Eric Bogosian (based on his play), though its stage origins weigh it down a bit. [R]▼●

Subway (1985-French) **C-104m.** ** D: Luc Besson. Isabelle Adjani, Christopher Lambert, Richard Bohringer, Michel Galabru, Jean-Hugues Anglade. Dripping in new wave style and attitude, this (literally) underground fable, set in the Paris métro, where various lives intertwine, is utterly aimless and pointless. Intrigues and amuses at first, and then just runs out of steam. Technovision. [R]▼●◗

Subway in the Sky (1959-German) **85m.** *½ D: Muriel Box. Van Johnson, Hildegarde Neff, Katherine Kath, Cec Linder, Albert Lieven, Edward Judd. Flabby caper of soldier Johnson in post-WW2 Berlin, involved in the black market; terrible waste of Neff's talents.

Subway to the Stars (1987-Brazilian) **C-103m.** **½ D: Carlos Diegues. Guilherme Fontes, Milton Goncalves, Taumaturgo Ferreira, Ze Trindade, Ana Beatriz Wiltgen. Gritty, grim account of young sax player Fontes and his experiences as he roams the back streets of Rio in search of his missing girlfriend. Has its moments of insight, but overall too meandering. [R]▼

Success, The (1963-Italian) **103m.** *** D: Dino Risi. Vittorio Gassman, Anouk Aimée, Jean-Louis Trintignant. Intelligent delineation by Gassman as businessman overwhelmed by success urge makes this drama worthy.

Success (1979) SEE: **American Success Company, The**

Success at Any Price (1934) **75m.** *** D: J. Walter Ruben. Douglas Fairbanks, Jr., Genevieve Tobin, Frank Morgan, Colleen Moore, Edward Everett Horton, Allen Vincent. Interesting moral tract tracing the rise and fall of ruthless businessman Fairbanks as he crushes everyone who gets in his way—and loses sight of the one woman who loves him. Surprisingly contemporary, and still potent, though it reveals its stage origins.

Successful Calamity, A (1932) **72m.** **½ D: John G. Adolfi. George Arliss, Mary Astor, Evalyn Knapp, Grant Mitchell, Da-

vid Torrence, William Janney, Hardie Albright, Randolph Scott, Leon Waycoff (Ames). Wealthy world figure returns home after almost a year of traveling, anxious to spend time with his family—only to find them all too concerned with themselves to give him more than a passing nod. Ever-so-slight Arliss comedy hews strictly to formula, but it's a formula that works, and Arliss is charming as always.
Success Is the Best Revenge (1984-British) **C-90m.** **½ D: Jerzy Skolimowski. Michael York, Joanna Szerbic, Michael Lyndon, George Skolimowski, Michel Piccoli, Anouk Aimée, John Hurt. Intriguing if uneven yarn about a Polish director (York) in exile in London and his rebellious teen son (Lyndon), who is anxious to explore his heritage. Skolimowski—himself an exile—explores the meaning of living in a country other than one's own, but he fared better with previous film, MOONLIGHTING.▼●
Such a Gorgeous Kid Like Me (1972-French) **C-98m.** ***½ D: François Truffaut. Bernadette Lafont, Claude Brasseur, Charles Denner, Guy Marchand, Philippe Leotard. Delightful black comedy of female murderer who relates her sordid past to criminology student, gradually entices him just as she did her former "victims." Lafont ideal in leading role. [R]
Such Good Friends (1971) **C-100m.** *** D: Otto Preminger. Dyan Cannon, James Coco, Jennifer O'Neill, Ken Howard, Nina Foch, Laurence Luckinbill, Louise Lasser, Burgess Meredith, Sam Levene. Tart black comedy about man going to hospital, prompting wife (Cannon) to reexamine their relationship and learn about his romantic sideline activities. Fine ensemble acting buoys acidly funny script (by Elaine May, who used a pseudonym); from the Lois Gould novel. [R]
Sudan (1945) **C-76m.** ** D: John Rawlins. Maria Montez, Jon Hall, Turhan Bey, Andy Devine, George Zucco, Robert Warwick. Queen Montez escapes evil prime minister Zucco with help of Hall and Bey in colorful but empty adventure-romance. Montez and Hall's last film together.
Sudden Danger (1955) **85m.** *½ D: Hubert Cornfield. Bill Elliott, Tom Drake, Beverly Garland, Lucien Littlefield, Minerva Urecal, Lyle Talbot, Frank Jenks. Bland hunt-the-murderer-tale.
Sudden Death (1995) **C-110m.** *½ D: Peter Hyams. Jean-Claude Van Damme, Powers Boothe, Raymond J. Barry, Whittni Wright, Ross Malinger, Dorian Harewood, Paul Mochnick, Kate McNeil, Michael Gaston, Audra Lindley. Sardonic mastermind Boothe holds the Vice President hostage in a private box during Stanley Cup hockey playoffs in Pittsburgh, demanding a few billion, or he'll blow up the whole arena. But fire inspector Van Damme is on the job, and Boothe has unwisely captured our hero's daughter . . . DIE HARD clone bludgeons credulity to death early on, and the movie never recovers, despite plenty of action and effects. Panavision. [R]▼●◗
Sudden Fear (1952) **110m.** *** D: David Miller. Joan Crawford, Jack Palance, Gloria Grahame, Bruce Bennett, Touch (Mike) Connors, Virginia Huston. Wealthy playwright Crawford discovers new husband Palance (an actor whom she once fired) is planning to kill her; she uses her writing skills to concoct a scheme to make him trip himself up. Solid suspense thriller with many neat twists.▼●◗
Sudden Impact (1983) **C-117m.** **½ D: Clint Eastwood. Clint Eastwood, Sondra Locke, Pat Hingle, Bradford Dillman, Paul Drake, Jack Thibeau, Albert Popwell. Fourth DIRTY HARRY vehicle relies on durable formula, as maverick cop gives us vicarious pleasure of doing in society's scum, but this entry is longer, and sillier, than need be. Locke plays a woman taking out murderous revenge on men (and one lesbian!) who raped her and her sister years ago. Followed by THE DEAD POOL. Panavision. [R]▼●
Suddenly (1954) **77m.** ***½ D: Lewis Allen. Frank Sinatra, Sterling Hayden, James Gleason, Nancy Gates, Willis Bouchey, Kim Charney, Paul Frees, Christopher Dark, Charles Smith. Sinatra leads trio of paid assassins who take over house in small town where the President will pass on his way to a fishing trip. White-knuckle thriller, written by Richard Sale, with Sinatra excellent in thoroughly detestable role; rest of cast equally fine. "Suddenly," incidentally, is the name of the town. Also shown in computer-colored version.▼●◗
Suddenly, It's Spring (1947) **87m.** ** D: Mitchell Leisen. Paulette Goddard, Fred MacMurray, Macdonald Carey, Arleen Whelan, Lillian Fontaine. Strained comedy about married couple Goddard and MacMurray refusing to divorce each other.
Suddenly, Last Summer (1959) **114m.** ***½ D: Joseph L. Mankiewicz. Elizabeth Taylor, Katharine Hepburn, Montgomery Clift, Mercedes McCambridge, Albert Dekker. Fascinating if talky (though cleaned-up) Tennessee Williams yarn about wealthy Southern matriarch (Hepburn), her supposedly mad niece (Taylor) and a neurosurgeon (Clift); grandly acted. Adaptation by Gore Vidal. Remade for TV.▼●
Suddenly, Last Summer (1992-British) **C-95m. TVM** D: Richard Eyre. Maggie Smith, Rob Lowe, Natasha Richardson, Moira Redmond, Richard E. Grant, Gillian

Raine, Rosaleen Linehan. Simmering redo of Tennessee Williams' 1958 one-acter that's what the whitewashed Taylor-Clift-Hepburn version should have been had screen morals of the time not intervened. Top-flight Maggie. Above average.

Sudden Terror (1970-British) **C-95m.** ** D: John Hough. Mark Lester, Lionel Jeffries, Susan George, Tony Bonner, Jeremy Kemp. Adequate variation on boy-who-cried-wolf theme: prankish youngster witnesses murder of visiting black dignitary, but can't convince others. Almost ruined by self-conscious direction. Originally titled EYEWITNESS. [PG] ▼

Sudie and Simpson (1990) **C-100m. TVM** D: Joan Tewkesbury. Louis Gossett, Jr., Sara Gilbert, John Jackson, Frances Fisher, Paige Danahy, Ken Strong. Poignant tale of relationship between a spirited 12-year-old tomboy and a gentle black man accused of child molestation in rural WW2 Georgia. Stunningly photographed by Mario Di Leo and adapted from Sara Flanigan Carter's autobiographical novel by Carter and Ken Koser. Made for cable. Above average. ▼

Suds (1920) **67m.** **½ D: John Dillon. Mary Pickford, Albert Austin, Harold Goodwin, Rose Dione, Nadyne Montgomery, Darwin Karr. Mostly enjoyable change-of-pace silent-film vehicle for Pickford as a homely cockney laundrywoman who pines for the gentleman who left off a shirt to be cleaned months ago and never returned. Combination of wistfulness, slapstick, and drama doesn't always work.▼●

Suez (1938) **104m.** *** D: Allan Dwan. Tyrone Power, Loretta Young, Annabella, Henry Stephenson, Maurice Moscovich, Joseph Schildkraut, Sidney Blackmer, J. Edward Bromberg, Sig Ruman, Nigel Bruce, Miles Mander, George Zucco, Leon Ames. Power is 19th-century French architect (and dreamer) Ferdinand de Lesseps, who pursues a single-minded goal of building the Suez Canal; his real problem is choosing between aristocratic Loretta and down-to-earth Annabella. Entertaining and elaborate hokum which apparently bears no resemblance to history.

Sugarbaby (1985-German) **C-87m.** **½ D: Percy Adlon. Marianne Sägebrecht, Eisi Gulp. It's love at first sight for chubby mortuary attendant Sägebrecht and subway-train driver Gulp in this droll romantic satire. Players and story are offbeat, but the avant-garde lighting effects and camera movements by cinematographer Johanna Heer become annoying. Remade as BABYCAKES for American TV.▼

Sugar Cane Alley (1984-French) **C-107m.** ***½ D: Euzhan Palcy. Darling Legitimus, Garry Cadenat, Routa Seck, Joby Bernabe, Francisco Charles. Beautifully made, heart-felt drama about an 11-year-old boy and his all-sacrificing grandmother, surviving in a Martinique shantytown during the 1930s. Rich, memorable characterizations; a humanist drama of the highest order. [PG]▼●

Sugarfoot (1951) **C-80m.** **½ D: Edwin L. Marin. Randolph Scott, Adele Jergens, Raymond Massey, S. Z. Sakall, Arthur Hunnicutt. Above-par Scott Western. Randy is ex-Rebel officer who encounters his old adversary in Arizona. Retitled: SWIRL OF GLORY.

Sugar Hill (1974) **C-91m.** ** D: Paul Maslansky. Marki Bey, Robert Quarry, Don Pedro Colley, Richard Lawson, Betty Anne Rees, Zara Cully. Bey stars as "Sugar" Hill, who avenges the mob's rubout of her fiance, conjuring up black zombies from the grave. Outlandish blend of blaxploitation, revenge, and voodoo/horror elements. Cut to 83m. for TV and retitled THE ZOMBIES OF SUGAR HILL. [PG]▼

Sugar Hill (1994) **C-123m.** ** D: Leon Ichaso. Wesley Snipes, Michael Wright, Theresa Randle, Clarence Williams III, Abe Vigoda, Larry Joshua, Ernie Hudson, Leslie Uggams, Khandi Alexander, Raymond Serra, Joe Dallesandro, Vondie Curtis-Hall. So-what crime melodrama featuring Snipes and Wright as Roemello and Raynathan Skuggs, drug-dealing siblings in Harlem. Unlike the more zealous Raynathan, the solitary, soulful Roemello yearns for a career change. Shades of SUPERFLY! Dense and preposterous; you'll be as bored with the film as Roemello is with his life. [R]▼●

Sugarland Express, The (1974) **C-109m.** ***½ D: Steven Spielberg. Goldie Hawn, Ben Johnson, Michael Sacks, William Atherton, Steve Kanaly, Louise Latham. Perfect entertainment, based on fact, about a young fugitive couple fleeing to Sugarland, Texas, to reclaim their son (whom they refuse to give up for adoption), and the cops who pursue them throughout Texas. Spielberg's first theatrical feature, written by Hal Barwood and Matthew Robbins. Panavision. [PG]▼●

Sugartime (1995) **C-110m. TVM** D: John N. Smith. John Turturro, Mary-Louise Parker, Maury Chaykin, Elias Koteas, Louis Del Grande, Deborah Duchene, Larissa Lapchinski. The real-life guns and roses love affair between Chicago mob kingpin Sam Giancana and Phyllis McGuire of the 1950s white-bread singing group The McGuire Sisters. Wired Turturro's swagger and prim Parker's pertness, as mafioso and songbird, mix uneasily, but a chemistry finally evolves, along with their peripheral involvement with such figures as the Kennedys, Sinatra and the Rat Pack, Rowan and Martin, Castro, and J. Edgar Hoover. Intriguing, though whitewashed, film, punctuated by McGuire recordings. Made for cable. Average.▼●

Sugar Town (1999-U.S.-British) **C-92m.** *** D: Allison Anders, Kurt Voss. Ally Sheedy, Rosanna Arquette, John Taylor, Jade Gordon, Michael Des Barres, Larry Klein, Beverly D'Angelo, Vincent Berry, Richmond Arquette, Lucinda Jenney, Martin Kemp. Amusing mosaic of L.A. life featuring a handful of characters whose lives dovetail: a music-world wannabe who'll do anything to get ahead, an uptight single woman who attracts the wrong guys like a magnet, and a band made up of washed-up '80s rock stars, to name a few. Slight, made on a shoestring, but sharp and well observed; good cast includes a number of real-life musicians. Written by the directors. [R]▼

Suicide Battalion (1958) **79m.** BOMB D: Edward L. Cahn. Michael Connors, John Ashley, Jewell Lain, Russ Bender. Static WW2 non-actioner. Army duo goes on mission to destroy government records hidden in building basement at Pearl Harbor.▼

Suicide Kings (1998) **C-106m.** **½ D: Peter O'Fallon. Christopher Walken, Denis Leary, Henry Thomas, Sean Patrick Flanery, Jay Mohr, Jeremy Sisto, Johnny Galecki, Laura San Giacomo, Laura Harris, Cliff De Young, Brad Garrett. Intriguing premise: a group of spoiled rich kids abduct a smooth underworld character and hold him hostage to gain leverage in the kidnaping of Thomas' sister. But during one long night, the mobster (Walken, in fine form) sizes up his captors and plays on their weaknesses. Well-thought-out chamber piece, with some good story twists and first-rate performances; too bad the wrapup isn't as strong as the rest of the film. [R]▼●◗

Suicide Run SEE: **Too Late the Hero**

Suicide Squadron SEE: **Dangerous Moonlight**

Sullivans, The (1944) **111m.** *** D: Lloyd Bacon. Anne Baxter, Thomas Mitchell, Selena Royle, Ward Bond, Bobby Driscoll, Addison Richards. Homey, patriotic but fictionalized story of the real-life Sullivan brothers of Waterloo, Iowa, who fought together in WW2. Knowing the outcome of this story makes it very sad to watch. The Sullivans are played by Edward Ryan, John Campbell, James Cardwell, John Alvin and George Offerman, Jr. Aka THE FIGHTING SULLIVANS. ▼

Sullivan's Empire (1967) **C-91m.** **½ D: Harvey Hart, Thomas Carr. Martin Milner, Clu Gulager, Karen Jensen, Linden Chiles, Don Quine, Arch Johnson. Unconvincing adventure yarn of rich landowner's trio of sons searching for father, whose plane crashed in South American jungle.

Sullivan's Travels (1941) **91m.** **** D: Preston Sturges. Joel McCrea, Veronica Lake, Robert Warwick, William Demarest, Margaret Hayes, Porter Hall, Eric Blore, Robert Greig, Jimmy Conlin, Al Bridge, Franklin Pangborn. Tired of making fluff, movie director McCrea decides to do a "serious" film; to research it, he sets out with 10¢ in his pocket to experience life in "the real world." Slapstick and sorrow blend seamlessly in this landmark Hollywood satire, which grows more pertinent with each passing year. A unique achievement for writer-director Sturges. ▼●

Summer (1986-French) **96m.** ***½ D: Eric Rohmer. Marie Riviere, Lisa Heredia, Vincent Gauthier, Beatrice Romand, Carita. Sensitive but whiny Riviere, abandoned by friends on the eve of a group vacation, goes it alone with initially lonely results. Seemingly more improvised than the other Rohmers, this demands viewer patience and some tolerance of Riviere's "difficult" personality, but patience is rewarded. Finale is quite moving, in what emerges as one of the director's better efforts, from his series "Comedies and Proverbs." [R]▼●◗

Summer and Smoke (1961) **C-118m.** ***½ D: Peter Glenville. Geraldine Page, Laurence Harvey, Una Merkel, John McIntire, Pamela Tiffin, Rita Moreno, Thomas Gomez, Earl Holliman, Casey Adams, Lee Patrick. Spinster Page is in love with young doctor Harvey, but he's understandably not interested; vivid adaptation of Tennessee Williams play, set in 1916 in small Mississippi town, with torrid performances making up for frequent staginess. Atmospheric score by Elmer Bernstein. Panavision.▼●

Summer Camp Nightmare (1987) **C-87m.** *½ D: Bert L. Dragin. Chuck Connors, Charles Stratton, Adam Carl, Harold Pruett, Melissa Brennan, Tom Fridley, Nancy Calabrese. Synthetic update of LORD OF THE FLIES has young Fascist Stratton staging a small-scale revolution by having kids take over two adjoining summer camps, imprisoning the adults. Stratton good in difficult role, but plot gimmicks fail to convince, especially the kids' quickie descent into barbarism. Based on William Butler's novel *The Butterfly Revolution.* [PG-13]▼●

Summer City (1976-Australian) **C-83m.** ** D: Christopher Fraser. John Jarratt, Mel Gibson, Phil Avalon, Steve Bisley, James Elliot, Debbie Forman. Slight, low-budget rock 'n roll road movie detailing the escapades of four buddies who head out of Sydney for a surfing weekend. The shy, quiet one is played by Mel Gibson—it's his screen debut. Aka COAST OF TERROR.▼

Summer Fling SEE: **Last of the High Kings, The**

Summer Heat (1987) **C-90m.** ** D: Michie Gleason. Lori Singer, Anthony Edwards, Bruce Abbott, Kathy Bates, Clu Gulager. How soon will sultry farm wife Singer, neglected by husband Edwards, succumb to the charms of hired hand Abbott? Not long enough for you to want to sit through this bore. Summer Heat, indeed . . . [R]▼●

Summer Holiday (1948) **C-92m.** **½ D: Rouben Mamoulian. Mickey Rooney, Walter Huston, Frank Morgan, Agnes Moorehead, Butch Jenkins, Selena Royle, Marilyn Maxwell, Gloria De Haven, Anne Francis. Lavish musical remake of AH, WILDERNESS! with Rooney (who played the younger brother in 1935) as the young man coming of age. Extremely good-looking film, with exquisite use of Technicolor, but dramatically unexceptional—and not nearly as good as the earlier film. This version was made in 1946. ▼●

Summer Holiday (1963-British) **C-107m.** ** D: Peter Yates. Cliff Richard, Lauri Peters, David Kossoff, Ron Moody, The Shadows, Melvyn Hayes, Una Stubbs, Teddy Green, Jeremy Bulloch. Richard, Hayes, Green, and Bulloch travel through Europe on a bus in this silly but cheerful musical; inauspicious directorial debut by Yates. CinemaScope.

Summer House, The (1993-British) **C-82m.** *** D: Waris Hussein. Jeanne Moreau, Joan Plowright, Julie Walters, Lena Headey, David Threlfall, Maggie Steed, John Wood, Catherine Schell. An actors' field day, as flamboyant Moreau comes to stay with her girlhood friend Walters (now a frumpy housewife in 1950s Croydon) when her strangely reticent daughter is about to be married—to the twit next door. Plowright is wonderful as the idiot-groom's aged mother; her scenes with Moreau are a real treat. Based on the novel *The Clothes in the Wardrobe* by Alice Thomas Ellis. Made for British television.▼●

Summer Interlude SEE: **Illicit Interlude**

Summer Love (1958) **85m.** ** D: Charles Haas. John Saxon, Molly Bee, Rod McKuen, Judi Meredith, Jill St. John, George Winslow, Fay Wray, Edward Platt, Shelley Fabares, Troy Donahue. Sequel to ROCK, PRETTY BABY has Saxon, et al. hired to perform at summer resort camp; perky performances.

Summer Lovers (1982) **C-98m.** ** D: Randal Kleiser. Peter Gallagher, Daryl Hannah, Valerie Quennessen, Barbara Rush, Carole Cook. This one's a matter of tolerance: Any movie that makes you think seriously about having a ménage à trois on a Greek island can't be all bad, but here's a film that's on an even lower intellectual level than you'd *expect* from the director of THE BLUE LAGOON. Bouncy rock soundtrack. Panavision. [R] ▼●

Summer Magic (1963) **C-110m.** **½ D: James Neilson. Hayley Mills, Burl Ives, Dorothy McGuire, Deborah Walley, Eddie Hodges, Una Merkel. Disney's rehash of MOTHER CAREY'S CHICKENS has McGuire as widow who raises family on a shoestring in rambling Maine house. Burl sings "The Ugly Bug Ball." Pleasant but forgettable.▼

Summer Night, with Greek Profile, Almond Eyes and Scent of Basil (1987-Italian) **C-94m.** *½ D: Lina Wertmuller. Mariangela Melato, Michele Placido, Roberto Herlipzka, Massimo Wertmuller. Melato's presence, in a sexual cat-and-mouse tale, might lead one to expect another SWEPT AWAY, but this is light years removed: a relentlessly heavy-handed comedy about a rich, sexy Italian capitalist who abducts a notorious terrorist and tries to give him a taste of his own medicine . . . until she finds herself attracted to him. This "night" seems like it will never end!▼

Summer of Ben Tyler, The (1996) **C-100m. TVM** D: Arthur Allan Seidelman. James Woods, Elizabeth McGovern, Len Cariou, Clifton James, Anita Gillette, Kevin Isola; narrated by Judith Ivey. Woods, in Atticus Finch mode, plays a small-town lawyer in the '40s South who opens his home to a young, mildly retarded black man (newcomer Charles Mattocks) and finds himself at war with the racist, politically corrupt community. A poignant gem, written by Robert Inman. Above average.▼●

Summer of Fear SEE: **Stranger in Our House**

Summer of '42 (1971) **C-102m.** *** D: Robert Mulligan. Jennifer O'Neill, Gary Grimes, Jerry Houser, Oliver Conant, Katherine Allentuck, Christopher Norris, Lou Frizell. Enticing if unprofound nostalgia by Herman Raucher about teenager Grimes with crush on young war bride O'Neill. Captures 1940s flavor, adolescent boyhood, quite nicely. Michel Legrand won an Oscar for the score. Followed by CLASS OF '44. [PG—originally rated R]▼●

Summer of Innocence SEE: **Big Wednesday**

Summer of Sam (1999) **C-142m.** ** D: Spike Lee. John Leguizamo, Adrien Brody, Mira Sorvino, Jennifer Esposito, Anthony LaPaglia, Ben Gazzara, Bebe Neuwirth, Patti LuPone, Mike Starr, Michael Rispoli, John Savage, Michael Badalucco, Jimmy Breslin, Spike Lee. Mosaic of Italian-American characters living in the Bronx during the steamy summer of 1977, when the serial killer known as Son of Sam terrorized N.Y.C., firing both passions and paranoia. Interesting, mostly unpleasant slice of life/period piece goes on much too long . . . and gets pretty sleazy. Cowriters Michael Imperioli and Victor Colicchio appear as Midnight and Chickie, respectively. [R]▼◗

Summer of '64 SEE: **Girls on the Beach, The**

Summer Place, A (1959) **C-130m.** *** D: Delmer Daves. Richard Egan, Dorothy McGuire, Sandra Dee, Arthur Kennedy, Troy

Donahue, Constance Ford, Beulah Bondi. Lushly photographed (by Harry Stradling) soaper of adultery and teenage love at resort house on Maine coast. Excellent Max Steiner score (the theme was a big hit); based on the Sloan Wilson novel.▼●

Summerplay SEE: **Illicit Interlude**

Summer Rental (1985) **C-88m.** **½ D: Carl Reiner. John Candy, Karen Austin, Richard Crenna, Rip Torn, John Larroquette, Richard Herd, Lois Hamilton, Carmine Caridi. Breezy, low-key comedy about a working stiff's refusal to let some arrogant fat cats spoil his family's vacation in Florida. Candy proves he can be endearing in a realistic characterization—and still be funny. [PG]▼●

Summer School (1987) **C-98m.** **½ D: Carl Reiner. Mark Harmon, Kirstie Alley, Robin Thomas, Dean Cameron, Gary Riley, Shawnee Smith, Courtney Thorne-Smith. Harmon is delinquent high school teacher forced to spend his vacation trying to educate group of delinquent students. Not bad as these films go: decent acting, OK pacing, some good laughs . . . with extra chuckles for fans of TEXAS CHAINSAW MASSACRE and those movie-critic TV shows. Director Reiner has a cameo as Harmon's predecessor. [PG-13]▼●

Summer School Teachers (1975) **C-87m.** ** D: Barbara Peeters. Candice Rialson, Pat Anderson, Rhonda Leigh-Hopkins, Dick Miller. Well-paced, episodic film of three girls' romantic adventures while teaching high school. A followup to THE STUDENT TEACHERS. [R]▼

Summer Stock (1950) **C-109m.** *** D: Charles Walters, Judy Garland, Gene Kelly, Eddie Bracken, Marjorie Main, Gloria De Haven, Phil Silvers, Hans Conried. Kelly's theater troupe takes over Judy's farm, she gets show biz bug. Thin plot, breezy Judy, frantic Silvers, chipper De Haven. Judy sings "Get Happy," Kelly dances on newspapers.▼●

Summer Storm (1944) **106m.** *** D: Douglas Sirk. George Sanders, Linda Darnell, Edward Everett Horton, Sig Ruman, Anna Lee, Sarah Padden, Frank Orth. Darnell has one of her best roles as beautiful woman who brings tragedy to all involved with her, including herself; from Chekhov's story "The Shooting Party."

Summer Story, A (1988-British) **C-95m.** *** D: Piers Haggard. Imogen Stubbs, James Wilby, Ken Colley, Sophie Ward, Susannah York, Jerome Flynn. Beautifully made romantic drama, circa 1902, set and filmed entirely in rural southwestern England. Young London lawyer Wilby and farm girl Stubbs fall deeply in love; he soon must make decisions of the mind and heart that could change their lives forever. The two leads are superb. Penelope Mortimer adapted John Galsworthy's story "The Apple Tree." [PG-13]▼

Summertime (1955) **C-99m.** ***½ D: David Lean. Katharine Hepburn, Rossano Brazzi, Isa Miranda, Darren McGavin, Mari Aldon, Andre Morell. Lilting film of spinster vacationing in Venice, falling in love with married man. Hepburn's sensitive portrayal is one of her best. Screenplay by Lean and H.E. Bates, from Arthur Laurents' play *The Time of the Cuckoo*. Beautifully filmed on location by Jack Hildyard.▼●◗

Summertime Killer (1973-French-Italian-Spanish) **C-109m.** ** D: Antonio Isasi. Karl Malden, Christopher Mitchum, Raf Vallone, Claudine Auger, Olivia Hussey. Varied cast in OK revenge meller about a man pursuing his father's murderers. Lots of action, if not much continuity. [PG]▼

Summertree (1971) **C-88m.** ** D: Anthony Newley. Michael Douglas, Jack Warden, Brenda Vaccaro, Barbara Bel Geddes, Kirk Callaway, Bill Vint, Rob Reiner. Highly acclaimed (if overrated) off-Broadway play by Ron Cowen fails as a film; Douglas plays a young music student who clashes with parents over Vietnam War. [PG]▼

Summer Wishes, Winter Dreams (1973) **C-93m.** *** D: Gilbert Cates. Joanne Woodward, Martin Balsam, Sylvia Sidney, Dori Brenner, Ron Rickards. Sensitive character study of frigid woman (Woodward) obsessed by her childhood, upset by her own aloofness towards others; Balsam equally good as understanding husband. [PG]▼

Summer With Monika (1953-Swedish) **96m.** ***½ D: Ingmar Bergman. Harriet Andersson, Lars Ekborg, John Harryson, Georg Skarstedt, Dagmar Ebbesen, Ake Gronberg. A brief affair between two working-class youngsters, aggressive Andersson and boyish Ekborg, results in the birth of their baby and marriage. Simple storyline has been filmed before and since, but rarely with such sensitivity. Video title: MONIKA.▼

Sum of Us, The (1994-Australian) **C/B&W-99m.** **½ D: Kevin Dowling, Geoff Burton. Jack Thompson, Russell Crowe, John Polson, Deborah Kennedy, Mitch Mathews, Joss Moroney, Julie Herbert. Sincere tale about the relationship between a young, gay man (Crowe) and his devoted, widowed father (Thompson), who is refreshingly tolerant of his son's lifestyle. Two solid performances help put this one over, but it's almost undone by the annoying device of having the characters speak to the camera. Scripted by David Stevens, based on his play.▼●

Sun Also Rises, The (1957) **C-129m.** *** D: Henry King. Tyrone Power, Ava Gardner, Mel Ferrer, Errol Flynn, Eddie Albert, Gregory Ratoff, Juliette Greco, Marcel Dalio, Henry Daniell, Bob Cunningham, Danik Patisson, Robert Evans. Hemingway story of expatriates in Parisian 1920s has slow stretches; worthwhile for outstanding cast, especially Flynn as a souse. Mexico City locations add flavor to tale of search for self-identity. Remade (poorly) for TV in 1984. CinemaScope.

Sun and the Moon, The (1987) **C-97m.** *½ D: Kevin Conway. Mila Burnette, Joaquim de Almeida, Maria Norman, Kevin Conway, Jose Ferrer. Chic Manhattanite Burnette, fed up with her lifestyle (and cheating husband), moves in with relatives in the South Bronx (described as "the capital of Puerto Rico"), where she organizes tenants and becomes involved with de Almeida. There's the germ of a serious film here, but the result is slight, silly, frustrating. Originally titled THE VIOLINS CAME WITH THE AMERICANS.

Sunbonnet Sue (1945) **89m.** ** D: Ralph Murphy. Gale Storm, Phil Regan, George Cleveland, Minna Gombell, Edna Holland, Raymond Hatton. Programmer musical of the Gay 90s enhanced by bouncy Storm in title role, as songstress in father's lower N.Y.C. saloon.

Sunburn (1979) **C-94m.** **½ D: Richard C. Sarafian. Farrah Fawcett-Majors, Charles Grodin, Art Carney, Joan Collins, Alejandro Rey, William Daniels. Insurance investigator Grodin has Farrah pose as his wife in order to crack a murder/suicide case in Acapulco. Sloppily made film benefits from appealing performances. Eleanor Parker, Keenan Wynn, and John Hillerman get co-starring billing but barely appear at all. [PG]▼

Sunchaser, The (1996) **C-122m.** *½ D: Michael Cimino. Woody Harrelson, Jon Seda, Anne Bancroft, Alexandra Tydings, Matt Mulhern, Talisa Soto, Richard Bauer, Lawrence Pressman, Harry Carey, Jr., Brett Harrelson. Brilliant but insensitive doctor Harrelson is taken captive by sensitive but dying gang banger Seda, and is forced to drive into the Southwest in search of a lake of spiritual renewal. Misbegotten mess tries to touch all trendy bases, scrambling American Indian mysticism, "New Age" theories and buddy-movie clichés into the format of a road movie. Harrelson and Seda are good, Bancroft is wasted. Panavision. [R]▼●

Sun Comes Up, The (1949) **C-93m.** ** D: Richard Thorpe. Jeanette MacDonald, Lloyd Nolan, Claude Jarman, Jr., Lewis Stone, Dwayne Hickman. Colorful but overly sentimental story of young orphan and embittered widow who blames her son's dog, Lassie, for his death. MacDonald's last film.▼

Sunday (1997) **C-93m.** *** D: Jonathan Nossiter. David Suchet, Lisa Harrow, Jared Harris, Larry Pine, Joe Grifasi, Arnold Barkus. Moving drama of a former corporate executive—now homeless—crossing paths in Queens, N.Y., with an out-of-work actress. What unfolds is essentially a two-character story of middle-aged romance, with harsh reminders of "real life" all around. Suchet and Harrow make flawless leads, though film is admittedly not for all tastes.▼

Sunday, Bloody Sunday (1971-British) **C-110m.** *** D: John Schlesinger. Glenda Jackson, Peter Finch, Murray Head, Peggy Ashcroft, Tony Britton, Maurice Denham, Vivian Pickles, Frank Windsor, Bessie Love, Jon Finch. Glenda loves Murray, but Peter loves Murray, too. Murray loves both, in very good, adult script by Penelope Gilliatt. Schlesinger's direction less forceful than usual, also less effective. Head's bland portrayal offsets brilliant work by Jackson and Finch. A mixed bag. Look for Daniel Day-Lewis as a young vandal. [R]▼●

Sunday Dinner for a Soldier (1944) **86m.** *** D: Lloyd Bacon. Anne Baxter, John Hodiak, Charles Winninger, Anne Revere, Chill Wills, Bobby Driscoll, Jane Darwell. Winning film of family that invites soldier to dinner; they are repaid for their kindness; enjoyable comedy-drama.

Sunday in New York (1963) **C-105m.** *** D: Peter Tewksbury. Cliff Robertson, Jane Fonda, Rod Taylor, Robert Culp, Jim Backus. Entire cast bubbles in this Norman Krasna sex romp of virginal Fonda discovering N.Y.C. and love. Peter Nero's score is perky.

Sunday in the Country, A (1984-French) **C-94m.** ***½ D: Bertrand Tavernier. Louis Ducreux, Sabine Azema, Michel Aumont, Genevieve Mnich, Monique Chaumette, Claude Winter. An elderly widowed French impressionist who never quite made the grade indulges in title gathering with offspring who never quite fulfilled his expectations. Painterly, lovingly acted drama owes not a little to Jean Renoir's A DAY IN THE COUNTRY and is no less affecting for that. Among the best imports of the mid-1980s. [G]▼◗

Sunday Lovers (1980) **C-127m.** *½ D: Bryan Forbes, Edouard Molinaro, Dino Risi, Gene Wilder. Roger Moore, Lynn Redgrave, Priscilla Barnes, Lino Ventura, Robert Webber, Ugo Tognazzi, Sylva Koscina, Gene Wilder, Kathleen Quinlan. Love and sex in four countries. British segment, with Moore, is old-hat farce. French vignette, with Ventura, is intriguing but doesn't go anywhere. Italian skit is broadly funny at times. American contribution, written by, directed by, and starring Wilder, is a pretentious fable of a sanitarium patient, and embarrassingly bad. [R]

Sundays and Cybele (1962-French) **110m.** ***½ D: Serge Bourguignon. Hardy Kruger, Nicole Courcel, Patricia Gozzi, Daniel Ivernel. Intelligently told account of shell-shocked Kruger finding source of communication with the world via orphaned waif Gozzi, with tragic results. Splendidly realized, Oscar winner as Best Foreign Language Film. Filmed in Franscope.▼

Sunday's Children (1992-Swedish) **C-118m.** *** D: Daniel Bergman. Henrik Linnros, Thommy Berggren, Lena Endre, Jakob Leygraf, Malin Ek, Birgitta Valberg, Borje Ahlstedt. Bergman (son of Ingmar) expertly directs his father's evocative, autobiographical script about a young boy called Pu (Linnros) and his connection to his minister father and other family members; also depicted is the adult Pu's disquieting relationship with his elderly dad. A deeply personal film; Bergman's family history also is explored in FANNY AND ALEXANDER, THE BEST INTENTIONS, and PRIVATE CONFESSIONS. ▼

Sunday Too Far Away (1975-Australian) **C-95m.** *** D: Ken Hannam. Jack Thompson, John Ewart, Reg Lyle. The rivalries and problems of macho sheep shearers, focusing on gutsy Thompson, a champion of his trade. Simple and solid.▼

Sunday Woman, The (1976-Italian) **C-110m.** *** D: Luigi Comencini. Marcello Mastroianni, Jacqueline Bisset, Jean-Louis Trintignant, Aldo Reggiani, Pino Caruso. Detective Mastroianni investigates murder among idle rich in Torino, falls in love with wealthy Bisset. Good whodunit makes interesting observation about social structure. [R]

Sundown (1941) **90m.** **½ D: Henry Hathaway. Gene Tierney, Bruce Cabot, George Sanders, Harry Carey, Joseph Calleia, Dorothy Dandridge, Reginald Gardiner. Tierney is surprisingly cast as native girl who assists British troops in Africa during WW2; fairly interesting, lushly photographed by Charles Lang, but it never scores. Also shown in computer-colored version.▼

Sundowners, The (1950) **C-83m.** **½ D: George Templeton. Robert Preston, Cathy Downs, Robert Sterling, John Barrymore, Jr., Jack Elam, Chill Wills. Tightly edited Western about brothers fighting on opposite sides of the law.▼

Sundowners, The (1960) **C-133m.** **** D: Fred Zinnemann. Deborah Kerr, Robert Mitchum, Peter Ustinov, Glynis Johns, Dina Merrill, Chips Rafferty, Michael Anderson, Jr., Lola Brooks, Wylie Watson, Mervyn Johns. First-rate film of Australian family whose lives are devoted to sheepherding. Entire cast excellent, Kerr especially fine. Isobel Lennart adapted Jon Cleary's novel. Wonderfully filmed on location by Jack Hildyard.▼●

Sundown, the Vampire in Retreat (1991) **C-104m.** ** D: Anthony Hickox. David Carradine, Morgan Brittany, Bruce Campbell, Jim Metzler, Maxwell Caulfield, Deborah Foreman, M. Emmet Walsh, John Ireland, John Hancock, Dabbs Greer, Bert Remsen. Overplotted vampire comedy-drama set in present-day American West, as a family happens upon a town populated by bloodsuckers trying—but failing—to "go straight." Unpleasantly smug, with nothing to be smug about. Panavision.▼

Sunflower (1969-Italian) **C-101m.** ** D: Vittorio De Sica. Sophia Loren, Marcello Mastroianni, Ludmilla Savelyeva, Anna Carena. Weak love story of woman who searches for her lost lover. Sophia is wasted in this soppy tale. [G]▼

Sun Never Sets, The (1939) **98m.** **½ D: Rowland V. Lee. Douglas Fairbanks, Jr., Basil Rathbone, Barbara O'Neil, Lionel Atwill, Virginia Field, C. Aubrey Smith. Enjoyable patriotic drama of British brothers trying to prevent outbreak of war in Africa. Well done, with top-notch cast.

Sunny (1941) **98m.** **½ D: Herbert Wilcox. Anna Neagle, Ray Bolger, John Carroll, Edward Everett Horton, Paul & Grace Hartman, Helen Westley. New Orleans society scion Carroll falls in love with circus performer Neagle; pleasant enough musical but nothing special. Bolger's dancing is the real treat. Jerome Kern–Oscar Hammerstein–Otto Harbach score includes "Who?" Filmed before in 1930 with Marilyn Miller.

Sunnyside (1979) **C-100m.** *½ D: Timothy Galfas. Joey Travolta, John Lansing, Stacey Pickren, Andrew Rubin, Michael Tucci, Talia Balsam, Joan Darling. John Travolta's brother made bid for stardom in this cliché-ridden picture about a street kid who wants to end local gang warfare and leave that life behind. Sorry, Joey. [R]▼

Sunny Side of the Street (1951) **C-71m.** *½ D: Richard Quine. Frankie Laine, Terry Moore, Jerome Courtland, Audrey Long. Moore has fickle notions over aspiring Laine in this low-grade musical, with guest stars such as Billy Daniels, Toni Arden.

Sunny Side Up (1929) **122m.** *** D: David Butler. Janet Gaynor, Charles Farrell, El Brendel, Marjorie White, Joe Brown, Frank Richardson, Jackie Cooper. Charming antique, quite impressive for early-talkie musical. Fluffy story of tenement girl Gaynor falling in love with wealthy Farrell sufficient excuse for DeSylva-Brown-Henderson songs: "I'm a Dreamer," "If I Had a Talking Picture of You," title tune, and bizarre production number to "Turn on the Heat."▼

Sunrise (1927) **110m** **** D: F. W. Murnau. George O'Brien, Janet Gaynor, Bodil Rosing, Margaret Livingston, J. Farrell MacDonald. Exquisite silent film is just as powerful today as when it was made, telling simple story of farmer who plans to murder his wife, led on by another woman. Triumph of direction, camerawork, art direction, and performances, all hauntingly beautiful. Screenplay by Carl Mayer, from Hermann Suderman's story. Cinematographers Karl Struss and Charles Rosher won Oscars, as did the film for "artistic quality of production." Gaynor also won Best Actress Oscar (shared for her performances in 7TH HEAVEN and STREET ANGEL). Remade in Germany as THE JOURNEY TO TILSIT. Full title onscreen is SUNRISE—A SONG OF TWO HUMANS. ▼●

Sunrise at Campobello (1960) **C-143m.** *** D: Vincent J. Donehue. Ralph Bellamy, Greer Garson, Hume Cronyn, Jean Hagen, Ann Shoemaker, Alan Bunce, Tim Considine, Zina Bethune, Frank Ferguson, Lyle Talbot. Sincere story of President Franklin Delano Roosevelt, his battles in politics and valiant struggle against polio. Well acted; Bellamy (re-creating his Tony-winning stage role) and Garson *are* the Roosevelts. Script by Dore Schary, from his hit play. ▼●

Sunset (1988) **C-107m.** *½ D: Blake Edwards. Bruce Willis, James Garner, Malcolm McDowell, Mariel Hemingway, Jennifer Edwards, Kathleen Quinlan, Patricia Hodge, Richard Bradford, M. Emmet Walsh, Joe Dallesandro. Cowboy star Tom Mix (Willis) joins forces with legendary marshal Wyatt Earp (Garner) to solve a serpentine whodunit involving the seamier side of Tinseltown. Appallingly abysmal murder-mystery set in late 1920s Hollywood; unpleasant and unbelievable from the word go. Willis registers zero playing one of movie's most magnetic stars, while Garner saves this piece of junk from being a total BOMB with his effortless charisma. Panavision. [R]▼●◗

Sunset Blvd. (1950) **110m.** **** D: Billy Wilder. Gloria Swanson, William Holden, Erich von Stroheim, Nancy Olson, Fred Clark, Jack Webb, Hedda Hopper, Buster Keaton, Cecil B. DeMille, Anna Q. Nilsson. Legendary Hollywood black comedy about faded silent-film star Norma Desmond (Swanson), living in the past with butler (von Stroheim), who shelters hack screenwriter (Holden) as boyfriend. Bitter, funny, fascinating; Gloria's tour de force. Three Oscars include Best Screenplay (Wilder, Charles Brackett, D.M. Marshman, Jr.) and Score (Franz Waxman). Later a Broadway musical.▼●

Sunset Cove (1978) **C-87m.** *½ D: Al Adamson. Jay B. Larson, Karen Fredrik, John Carradine, John Durren, Burr Schmidt. Condominium developers want to build on a strip of beach now inhabited by the usual teen crowd—who decide to fight for their rights in court. Bubbleheaded fare for bikini watchers. [R]

Sunset Park (1996) **C-99m.** **½ D: Steve Gomer. Rhea Perlman, Fredro Starr, Carol Kane, Terrence DaShon Howard, Camille Saviola, De'Aundre Bonds, James Harris, Anthony Hall. Feisty N.Y.C. teacher Perlman, hoping to make enough money to retire to St. Croix, becomes the coach of an all-black high school basketball team. The premise is contrived, and the Great Teacher story is a cliché by now, but the acting is good and the characters well drawn. Perlman's husband Danny DeVito was one of the producers. [R]▼●

Sunshine (1999-Hungarian-British-German-Canadian) **C-182m.** ** D: Istvan Szabo. Ralph Fiennes, Rosemary Harris, Rachel Weisz, Jennifer Ehle, Molly Parker, Deborah (Kara) Unger, James Frain, John Neville, Miriam Margolyes, David De Keyser, William Hurt, Bill Paterson. Ambitious but trite, rambling soap opera chronicling a Hungarian-Jewish family over three generations, beginning in mid-19th century. Fiennes plays three roles; the middle one, a world-champion fencer and self-hating Jew, is the most intriguing. Themes are worthy, but results are obvious and overwrought. Scripted by Szabo and Israel Horovitz. [R]▼

Sunshine Boys, The (1975) **C-111m.** *** D: Herbert Ross. Walter Matthau, George Burns, Richard Benjamin, Lee Meredith, Carol Arthur, Howard Hesseman, Ron Rifkin, Fritz Feld, Jack Bernardi, F. Murray Abraham. Two cranky ex-vaudevillians are persuaded to reteam for a TV special in this popular Neil Simon comedy, from his Broadway play. Some of the "humor" is abrasive, but Matthau and Oscar-winning Burns are masters at work. This was George's first starring film role since HONOLULU in 1939. Remade for TV in 1997. [PG] ▼●

Sun Shines Bright, The (1953) **90m.** *** D: John Ford. Charles Winninger, Arleen Whelan, John Russell, Stepin Fetchit, Milburn Stone, Russell Simpson, Francis Ford, Grant Withers, Slim Pickens, Mae Marsh, Jane Darwell, Clarence Muse, Jack Pennick, Patrick Wayne. This was director Ford's favorite film, a picaresque remake of JUDGE PRIEST with Winninger involved in political contest in small Southern town. Fine array of Ford regulars in character roles. Video and TV version is 100m. print prepared by Ford but never released.▼

Sun Valley Serenade (1941) **86m.** *** D: H. Bruce Humberstone. Sonja Henie, John Payne, Glenn Miller and His Orchestra, Milton Berle, Lynn Bari, Joan Davis, Dorothy Dandridge, The Nicholas Brothers. Light musicomedy with Henie a war refugee, Payne her foster parent, traveling with the Miller band and manager Berle to Sun Valley. Songs: "It Happened In Sun Valley," "In the Mood," "Chattanooga Choo-Choo," "I Know Why (And So Do You)."▼●

Super, The (1991) **C-86m.** *½ D: Rod Daniel. Joe Pesci, Vincent Gardenia, Madolyn Smith-Osborne, Ruben Blades, Stacey Travis, Carole Shelley, Paul Benjamin, Kenny Blank. N.Y.C. slumlord Pesci is forced to move in with his tenants. A worthy idea, and Pesci is watchable as always, but the execution is all wrong: the scenario disastrously veers to comedy when it shouldn't, and the sentimental elements are utterly unbelievable. In dire need of anger and bite. [R]▼●

Superchick (1973) **C-94m.** ** D: Ed Forsyth. Joyce Jillson, Louis Quinn, Thomas Reardon, Tony Young, John Carradine, Uschi Digard, Mary Gavin (Candy Samples). Silly but harmless drive-in fodder has Jillson (better known as an astrologer) as blonde, free-loving stewardess (juggling boyfriends in several cities) who's so desirable she adopts a mousey brunette disguise to get her work done. [R]▼

Supercop SEE: **Police Story III: Supercop**

Super Cops, The (1974) **C-94m.** ***½ D: Gordon Parks. Ron Leibman, David Selby, Sheila Frazier, Pat Hingle, Dan Frazer. Fast, funny, tough telling of the exploits of the Batman and Robin team of David Greenberg (Leibman) and Robert Hantz (Selby) who used unorthodox methods to stop the drug market in Brooklyn's black Bedford-Stuyvesant area. Filmed on location, with Greenberg and Hantz in bits. [PG]

Superdad (1974) **C-96m.** BOMB D: Vincent McEveety. Bob Crane, Kurt Russell, Barbara Rush, Joe Flynn, Kathleen Cody, Dick Van Patten, Joby Baker, B. Kirby, Jr. (Bruno Kirby), Ed Begley, Jr. Disney generation gap comedy is superbad. Crane competes with daughter's fiancé in effort to prove future son-in-law worthy. [G]▼

Superdude SEE: **Hangup**

Superfly (1972) **C-96m.** *** D: Gordon Parks Jr. Ron O'Neal, Carl Lee, Sheila Frazier, Julius W. Harris, Charles McGregor. Morally dubious but undeniably exciting tale of Harlem drug dealer out for the last killing before he quits the business. Film was accused of glorifying drug pushers. Benefits from excellent Curtis Mayfield score. Sequels: SUPERFLY T.N.T. and THE RETURN OF SUPERFLY. [R]▼

Superfly T.N.T. (1973) **C-87m.** BOMB D: Ron O'Neal. Ron O'Neal, Roscoe Lee Browne, Sheila Frazier, Robert Guillaume, Jacques Sernas, William Berger, Roy Bosier. Confused, sloppily constructed and executed B film about black ex-drug pusher, dissatisfied with idyllic existence in Europe, deciding to aid official from African country (Browne). Followed years later by THE RETURN OF SUPERFLY. [R]▼

Super Fuzz (1981-U.S.-Italian) **C-94m.** *½ D: Sergio Corbucci. Terence Hill, Ernest Borgnine, Joanne Dru, Marc Lawrence, Julie Gordon, Lee Sandman. Rookie Miami cop Hill is exposed to radiation, gains superpowers and takes on mobster Lawrence. Pretty poor, including the special effects. Also known as SUPERSNOOPER. Originally 106m. [PG]▼

Supergirl (1984-British) **C-114m.** *½ D: Jeannot Szwarc. Faye Dunaway, Helen Slater, Peter O'Toole, Peter Cook, Brenda Vaccaro, Mia Farrow, Simon Ward, Marc McClure, Hart Bochner, Maureen Teefy, Matt Frewer. This comic-book movie is a superdrag: long, dull, heavy-handed. Slater is cute but bland in title role; Dunaway is a predictably campy villainess. Panavision. [PG]▼●

Supergrass, The (1985-British) **C-105m.** ** D: Peter Richardson. Adrian Edmondson, Jennifer Saunders, Peter Richardson, Dawn French, Keith Allen, Nigel Planer, Robbie Coltrane. To impress a girl, Edmondson innocently brags that he's a big-time drug dealer—much to his regret. Inoffensive comedy. [R]▼

Superman (1978) **C-143m.** ***½ D: Richard Donner. Christopher Reeve, Margot Kidder, Marlon Brando, Gene Hackman, Ned Beatty, Jackie Cooper, Marc McClure, Glenn Ford, Valerie Perrine, Phyllis Thaxter, Jeff East, Trevor Howard, Susannah York, Maria Schell, Terence Stamp, Sarah Douglas, Harry Andrews, Lise Hilboldt, Larry Hagman, John Ratzenberger. Dynamic, grandly entertaining saga of the Man of Steel, tracing his life from Krypton to Smallville to Metropolis, mixing equal parts sincerity, special effects (which earned a special Oscar), and send-up. Great fun. The network TV version added 49m. of outtakes—including cameos by Noel Neill and Kirk Alyn as Lois Lane's parents. Followed by three sequels. Panavision. [PG]▼●

Superman II (1980) **C-127m.** *** D: Richard Lester. Christopher Reeve, Margot Kidder, Gene Hackman, Ned Beatty, Jackie Cooper, Valerie Perrine, Susannah York, Clifton James, E. G. Marshall, Marc McClure, Terence Stamp, Sarah Douglas, Jack O'Halloran. Screw the Superman legend, forget logic, and full speed ahead: that's the attitude of this flashy sequel, wherein three villains from Krypton, with powers just like Superman's, threaten the Earth—while Lois Lane and the Man of Steel fall in love. Full of great effects and entertainingly played, but lacking the sense of awe and wonder of the original film, adding cruelty and violence instead. U.S. release in 1981. Panavision. [PG]▼●

Superman III (1983) **C-123m.** *½ D: Richard Lester. Christopher Reeve, Richard Pryor, Annette O'Toole, Jackie Cooper, Marc McClure, Annie Ross, Pamela Stephenson, Robert Vaughn, Margot Kidder. Appalling sequel trashes everything that Superman is all about for the sake of cheap laughs and a costarring role for Pryor, as computer operator who unwittingly gives villainous Vaughn a chance to conquer the Man of Steel. Director Lester's opening slapstick ballet is a funny set-piece, but doesn't belong in this movie. Network TV added 19m. of footage for its first showing. Panavision. [PG]▼●

Superman IV: The Quest for Peace (1987) **C-90m.** ** D: Sidney J. Furie. Christopher Reeve, Gene Hackman, Jackie Cooper, Marc McClure, Jon Cryer, Sam Wanamaker, Mark Pillow, Mariel Hemingway, Margot Kidder. Superman does his bit for world peace by ridding the globe of nuclear weapons—which inspires Lex Luthor to become a black-market arms profiteer. He also challenges Superman by creating Nuclear Man. Disappointing fantasy adventure is pretty ordinary, with second-rate special effects. Sincere performances help a lot. Reeve receives co-story credit on this one (along with 2nd unit directing). J-D-C Scope. [PG]▼●

Superman and the Mole Men (1951) **58m.** ** D: Lee Sholem. George Reeves, Phyllis Coates, Jeff Corey, Walter Reed, J. Farrell MacDonald, Stanley Andrews. Reporters Clark Kent and Lois Lane go to small town to see the world's deepest oil well; instead, they discover that "mole men" have climbed out of the well, from their home at the center of the earth. This very low-budget feature served as a pilot for the long running TV series, but it's more serious (and less fun) than the subsequent show—and we don't even get to see Superman fly! But it's still great to see Reeves as the Man of Steel. TV title: THE UNKNOWN PEOPLE.▼●

Super Mario Bros. (1993) **C-104m.** *½ D: Rocky Morton, Annabel Jankel. Bob Hoskins, John Leguizamo, Dennis Hopper, Samantha Mathis, Fisher Stevens, Richard Edson, Fiona Shaw, Lance Henriksen. Super, indeed! This overblown, effects-laden turkey chronicles the convoluted story of the title boys from Brooklyn (Hoskins, Leguizamo), plumber-siblings who go up against the villainous King Koopa (Hopper), a semi-human dinosaur who instigates the kidnapping of Daisy (Mathis), a princess who possesses a magical meteorite fragment. This listless film has far less appeal than the video game that inspired it. [PG]▼●

Supernatural (1933) **64m.** **½ D: Victor Halperin. Carole Lombard, Randolph Scott, Vivienne Osborne, H. B. Warner, Alan Dinehart, Beryl Mercer, William Farnum. Interesting little thriller—most unusual for its time—about a doctor's research into paranormal activities, and his fear that a woman on Death Row will transfer her personality to an innocent victim.▼

Supernaturals, The (1986) **C-85m.** BOMB D: Armand Mastroianni. Maxwell Caulfield, Talia Balsam, Bradford Bancroft, LeVar Burton, Bobby DiCicco, Scott Jacoby, Nichelle Nichols. Ludicrous fantasy has butch drill sergeant Nichols (better known as Lt. Uhura on *Star Trek*) leading young troops on maneuvers, accidentally stumbling on Rebel ghosts from the Civil War who are seeking revenge. Boring tale has the production values of a home movie; never released theatrically. [R]▼

Supernova (2000) **C-90m.** *½ D: Thomas Lee. James Spader, Angela Bassett, Lou Diamond Phillips, Robert Forster, Robin Tunney, Peter Facinelli. Alan Smithee gets competition that neither he nor the industry needs; Lee is a pseudonym for director Walter Hill, who took his name off this costly but listlessly derivative space adventure. Story deals with a hospital ship rescuing a battered freighter that has sent out a distress call in "black hole" territory. Spader and Phillips are so pumped up that you wonder where they're getting the celestial weight-room time. Super 35. [PG-13]▼●◗

Super Sleuth (1937) **70m.** *** D: Ben Stoloff. Jack Oakie, Ann Sothern, Edgar Kennedy, Eduardo Ciannelli, Joan Woodbury, Bradley Page. Inconsequential but very funny outing with Oakie as egocentric detective-movie star who tries to solve real-life mystery. Kennedy has plum supporting role as police detective. Remade as GENIUS AT WORK.

Supersnooper SEE: **Super Fuzz**

Superstar (1999) **C-81m.** *½ D: Bruce McCulloch. Molly Shannon, Will Ferrell, Elaine Hendrix, Tom Green, Harland Williams, Mark McKinney, Glynis Johns, Emmy Laybourne. One-note comedy in which Shannon recreates her *Saturday Night Live* character of Mary Katherine Gallagher, a dorky, self-deluded Irish Catholic schoolgirl who wears the unsexiest white underwear, dreams of fame, and pursues the most popular boy in class (Ferrell). Little improvement over such SNL-derived feature films as IT'S PAT and A NIGHT AT THE ROXBURY. [PG-13]▼●◗

Superstar: The Life and Times of Andy Warhol (1991) **C-87m.** *** D: Chuck Workman. Tom Wolfe, Sylvia Miles, David Hockney, Taylor Mead, Dennis Hopper, and a Campbell's Soup spokesman are just some of the many who offer comment on N.Y.C.'s life of the party—and if Workman can't find much old footage of his subject conjugating nouns and verbs, it may not exist. Inevitably entertaining, though Warhol seems no less enigmatic at the conclusion.▼

Support Your Local Gunfighter (1971) **C-92m.** *** D: Burt Kennedy. James Garner, Suzanne Pleshette, Jack Elam, Harry Morgan, John Dehner, Joan Blondell, Dub Taylor, Ellen Corby, Henry Jones, Marie Windsor, Dick Curtis, Chuck Connors, Grady Sutton. Engaging comedy-Western, not a sequel to SHERIFF despite director and cast. Con artist Garner tries to profit from mining dispute by passing off bumbling Elam as notorious gunslinger. Seemingly endless list of character actors adds sparkle, with Elam giving his most side-splitting performance as "Swifty" Morgan; his final line is a gem. [G]▼

Support Your Local Sheriff! (1969) **C-93m.** ***½ D: Burt Kennedy. James Garner, Joan Hackett, Walter Brennan, Harry Morgan, Jack Elam, Bruce Dern, Henry Jones, Gene Evans. Delightful Western parody in which no-fisted Garner tames lawless town by using his wits, breaking all the rules—and kicking virtually every Western cliché in the pants. Brennan is wonderful spoofing his Old Man Clanton character from MY DARLING CLEMENTINE, but Hackett's wealthy klutz, Elam's inept deputy, and Dern's bratty killer are also fine. Written and produced by William Bowers. [G]▼●

Suppose They Gave a War and Nobody Came? (1970) **C-113m.** **½ D: Hy Averback. Tony Curtis, Brian Keith, Ernest Borgnine, Suzanne Pleshette, Ivan Dixon, Bradford Dillman, Tom Ewell, Don Ameche, Arthur O'Connell, John Fiedler. Awful title obscures surprisingly strong satire about strained relations between redneck town and nearby Army base eventually reaching the breaking point. No real "good guys" in this unusual film; not without flaws, but certainly worth a look. Later ripped off by TANK. Retitled WAR GAMES for network TV. [M/PG]▼

Sure Fire (1993) **C-86m.** *** D: Jon Jost. Tom Blair, Kristi Hager, Robert Ernst, Kate Dezina, Philip R. Brown. Provocative tale of smug, hot-shot entrepreneur (Blair), who concocts a scheme to build summer houses in Utah for city-dwelling Californians. Another impressive, visually arresting feature from acclaimed independent filmmaker Jost; most effective as a portrait of a male ego gone haywire. ▼

Sure Thing, The (1985) **C-94m.** **½ D: Rob Reiner. John Cusack, Daphne Zuniga, Anthony Edwards, Boyd Gaines, Tim Robbins, Lisa Jane Persky, Viveca Lindfors, Nicollette Sheridan. Amusing film updates IT HAPPENED ONE NIGHT as two college students who don't get along find themselves traveling cross-country together. Utterly predictable, but cute. [PG-13]▼●

Surf Ninjas (1993) **C-86m.** BOMB D: Neal Israel. Ernie Reyes, Jr., Rob Schneider, Nicolas Cowan, Leslie Nielsen, Tone Loc, Ernie Reyes, Sr., Keone Young, Kelly Hu, John Karlen. Fast-talking Southern California surf dudes travel to a distant Asian kingdom to regain their throne as lost crown princes. Are you following this so far? If you care what happens next, this may be your kind of movie. [PG]▼●

Surf Party (1964) **68m.** BOMB D: Maury Dexter. Bobby Vinton, Jackie De Shannon, Patricia Morrow, Kenny Miller. Teenagers meet and mate in Malibu. Waterlogged.▼

Surf II (1984) **C-91m.** *½ D: Randall Badat. Eddie Deezen, Linda Kerridge, Cleavon Little, Peter Isaacksen, Lyle Waggoner, Eric Stoltz, Morgan Paull, Ruth Buzzi, Carol Wayne, Terry Kiser. Creditable cast washes ashore in 80s spoof of 70s gore films and 60s surfer films (with appropriate oldies on the soundtrack). Deezen's always good for a few laughs, but the film's best joke is its title: there never was a SURF I. [R]▼

Surgeon's Knife, The (1957-British) **75m.** ** D: Gordon Parry. Donald Houston, Adrienne Corri, Lyndon Brook. Tepid drama of doctor Houston implicated in criminal negligence, becoming involved in murder.

Surprise Package (1960-British) **100m.** **½ D: Stanley Donen. Yul Brynner, Mitzi Gaynor, Barry Foster, Eric Pohlmann, Noel Coward, George Coulouris. Versatile Brynner tries screwball comedy, not doing too badly as devil-may-care gambler planning big-time robbery; Gaynor is sprightly leading lady. Script by Harry Kurnitz, from the Art Buchwald novel.▼

Surrender (1950) **90m.** **½ D: Allan Dwan. Vera Ralston, John Carroll, Walter Brennan, Francis Lederer, Jane Darwell, Jeff York. Ralston is exotic if overdramatic playing everyone against each other; Republic Pictures' nicely mounted costumer.

Surrender (1987) **C-95m.** ** D: Jerry Belson. Sally Field, Michael Caine, Steve Guttenberg, Peter Boyle, Jackie Cooper, Julie Kavner, Louise Lasser, Iman. Attractive cast injects little energy into this tired, familiar comedy about confused Field, oft-married Caine, and their complicated courtship. Even Caine's charm cannot save it. Scripted by the director. [PG]▼●

Surrender—Hell! (1959) **85m.** ** D: John Barnwell. Keith Andes, Susan Cabot, Paraluman, Nestor de Villa. Predictable account of Andes rallying partisan forces to combat Japanese control of Philippines.

Surrogate, The (1984-Canadian) **C-95m.** **½ D: Don Carmody. Art Hindle, Carole Laure, Shannon Tweed, Michael Ironside, Jim Bailey, Marilyn Lightstone, Jackie Burroughs. Clever whodunit has handsome couple (Tweed and Hindle) reluctantly turning to sex surrogate Laure to help with their marital problems. Solid Canadian cast punches home contrived script in which nearly every character (including top female impersonator Bailey, as Tweed's best friend) appears to be a psychotic suspect. [R]▼

Survival (1976) **C-85m.** ** D: Michael Campus. Barry Sullivan, Anne Francis, Sheree North, Chuck McCann, Otis Young. Intriguing psychodrama that talks itself to death. Elaborate dinner party evolves into parlor games where each guest must justify his existence, and all but two will be permanently eliminated by the vote of the others.

Survival Run (1980) **C-90m.** ★½ D: Larry Spiegel. Peter Graves, Ray Milland, Vincent Van Patten, Pedro Armendariz, Jr., Alan Conrad. Graves, Milland, and company stalk teenagers stranded in the desert. The object is murder; the film is dreadful. [R]▼

Survive! (1976-Mexican) **C-86m.** ★½ D: Rene Cardona (Sr.). Pablo Ferrel, Hugo Stiglitz, Luz Maria Aguilar, Fernando Larranga, Norma Lazareno. Survivors of a South American plane crash are forced to cannibalize each other in order to stay alive. Based on a true incident, but do you really care? Same story retold in U.S. film ALIVE. [R]

Surviving Picasso (1996) **C-125m.** ★★★ D: James Ivory. Anthony Hopkins, Natascha McElhone, Julianne Moore, Joss Ackland, Joan Plowright, Peter Eyre, Jane Lapotaire, Joseph Maher, Diane Venora, Bob Peck, Peter Gerety, Dominic West, Susannah Harker, Dennis Boutsikaris. Pablo Picasso uses women, then tosses them away, but a young artist ventures into a relationship with him just the same, certain that this time it will be different. McElhone makes an impressive film debut as the willing "victim," but it's Hopkins' charismatic performance as the ego-driven artist that makes this worth seeing. One must be willing to accept a lack of European accents—and the absence of genuine Picasso art. [R]▼●

Surviving the Game (1994) **C-96m.** ★½ D: Ernest Dickerson. Rutger Hauer, Ice-T, Gary Busey, F. Murray Abraham, Charles S. Dutton, John C. McGinley, Jeff Corey. Only the absence of Maria Conchita Alonso keeps this umpteenth variation of THE MOST DANGEROUS GAME from having the definitive schlock action cast, as destitute Ice-T is unwittingly hired to perform vague duties at a secluded woodsy resort, only to learn he's the prey of high-roller hunters. Sub-routine chase pic is Confusion City all the way; it's difficult to believe that the same plot could be recycled less than a year after John Woo's far more stylish HARD TARGET. [R]▼●◗

Survivors, The (1983) **C-102m.** ★★ D: Michael Ritchie. Walter Matthau, Robin Williams, Jerry Reed, James Wainwright, Kristen Vigard, Anne Pitoniak, John Goodman. Two disparate men lose their jobs and find their lives intertwined when they identify a robber and are told that they'll be "fixed." One (Williams) decides to arm himself to the teeth in this combination black comedy and social satire. Likable stars do their best with scattershot script credited to Michael Leeson. [R]▼●

Susana (1951-Mexican) **82m.** ★★½ D: Luis Buñuel. Rosita Quintana, Fernando Soler, Victor Manuel Mendoza, Matilde Palou. A voluptuous orphan of the storm, engagingly played by Quintana, undermines the loving fabric of the family that rescues her. Well handled and staged by Buñuel, until the cop-out finale.▼

Susan and God (1940) **115m.** ★★½ D: George Cukor. Joan Crawford, Fredric March, Ruth Hussey, John Carroll, Rita Hayworth, Nigel Bruce, Bruce Cabot, Rose Hobart, Rita Quigley, Marjorie Main, Gloria De Haven. Crawford is satisfying as woman whose religious devotion loses her the love of her family. Gertrude Lawrence fared better on stage. Screenplay by Anita Loos, based on Rachel Crothers' play.▼

Susan Lenox: Her Fall and Rise (1931) **76m.** ★★½ D: Robert Z. Leonard. Greta Garbo, Clark Gable, Jean Hersholt, John Miljan, Alan Hale. A young woman flees from her loutish father—who wants to marry her off—and finds refuge with Gable, but circumstances keep them apart until the final clinch. Contrived melodrama made compelling by the ever-mesmerizing Garbo.▼

Susannah of the Mounties (1939) **78m.** ★★½ D: William A. Seiter. Shirley Temple, Randolph Scott, Margaret Lockwood, J. Farrell MacDonald, Moroni Olsen, Victor Jory. Mountie Scott raises orphan Shirley in this predictable but entertaining Temple vehicle. Also shown in computer-colored version.▼

Susan Slade (1961) **C-116m.** ★★½ D: Delmer Daves. Troy Donahue, Dorothy McGuire, Connie Stevens, Lloyd Nolan, Brian Aherne, Bert Convy, Kent Smith. Slick soaper, beautifully photographed by Lucien Ballard. McGuire pretends to be mother of daughter's (Stevens) illegitimate child. Donahue is Connie's true love.

Susan Slept Here (1954) **C-98m.** ★★½ D: Frank Tashlin. Dick Powell, Debbie Reynolds, Anne Francis, Glenda Farrell, Alvy Moore. Screenwriter Powell agrees to look after high-spirited delinquent Reynolds in this "cute" sex comedy, which has the distinction of being the only film in history ever narrated by an Oscar statuette!▼●

Suspect, The (1944) **85m.** ★★★½ D: Robert Siodmak. Charles Laughton, Ella Raines, Dean Harens, Molly Lamont, Henry Daniell, Rosalind Ivan. Superb, Hitchcock-like thriller of henpecked Laughton planning to get his wife out of the way so he can pursue lovely Raines.

Suspect (1987) **C-121m.** ★★★ D: Peter Yates. Cher, Dennis Quaid, Liam Neeson, John Mahoney, Joe Mantegna, Philip Bosco, E. Katherine Kerr. Dedicated public defender (Cher) battles a nearly hopeless case, representing a deaf derelict accused of murder, with the unexpected help of one of her jurors (Quaid). Entertaining film manages to override its many implausibilities, with Cher turning in a fine and utterly believable performance. [R]▼●

Suspended Alibi (1956-British) **64m.** *½ D: Alfred Shaughnessy. Patrick Holt, Honor Blackman, Andrew Keir, Valentine Dyall. Holt becomes involved in homicide via circumstantial evidence in this coincidence laden drama. Retitled: SUSPECTED ALIBI.▼

Suspense (1946) **101m.** ** D: Frank Tuttle. Barry Sullivan, Belita, Albert Dekker, Bonita Granville, Eugene Pallette. Completely unsuspenseful story of ambitious heel who makes time with married ice-skating star Belita. Some nice visual touches, but leaden pacing, film noir clichés, and such musical highlights as ''Ice Cuba'' make this heavy going. Opening shot is the best thing in the movie! Script by Philip Yordan.

Suspicion (1941) **99m.** ***½ D: Alfred Hitchcock. Cary Grant, Joan Fontaine, Cedric Hardwicke, Nigel Bruce, Dame May Whitty, Isabel Jeans, Heather Angel, Leo G. Carroll. Fontaine won Oscar for portraying wife who believes husband Grant is trying to kill her. Suspenser is helped by Bruce as Cary's pal, but finale (imposed by the Production Code) leaves viewer flat. Scripted by Samson Raphaelson, Joan Harrison, and Alma Reville (Hitchcock's wife), from *Before the Fact* by Francis Iles (Anthony Berkeley). Remade as a TVM in 1987. Also shown in computer-colored version.▼●

Suspiria (1977-Italian) **C-92m.** *** D: Dario Argento. Jessica Harper, Stefania Casini, Joan Bennett, Alida Valli, Flavio Bucci, Udo Kier. Terrifying tale of American student (Harper) attending European ballet school that turns out to be a witches' coven. Often dumb plot is enriched and overcome by brilliant camerawork, atmosphere, music score and performance (by Argento and rock group Goblin). May lose some of its chilling effectiveness on TV. Also available in more explicit uncut version which runs 107m. Technovision. [R]▼●

Sutter's Gold (1936) **94m.** **½ D: James Cruze. Edward Arnold, Lee Tracy, Binnie Barnes, Katharine Alexander, Addison Richards, Montagu Love, Harry Carey. Biography of John Sutter—initiator of California's gold rush—starts off well, bogs down midway through story. Arnold is always good, but he's fighting a mediocre script here. Look for Billy Gilbert as a Spanish general taken hostage.

Suture (1993) **93m.** *** D: Scott McGehee, David Siegel. Dennis Haysbert, Mel Harris, Dina Merrill, Sab Shimono, Michael Harris, David Graf, Fran Ryan, John Ingle. Unique, off-the-wall tale of Vincent (Michael Harris), who is suspected of murdering his father; he hatches a scheme to fake his own death, substituting the body of his estranged half-brother, Clay (Haysbert), as his corpse. Although these men remark on their uncanny physical resemblance, Vincent is white and Clay is black: a joke which only the audience is in on. A novel and perceptive film about identity. An impressive debut for writer-director-producer duo McGehee and Siegel. Super 35.▼●

Suzanne SEE: **Second Coming of Suzanne, The**

Suzy (1936) **99m.** ** D: George Fitzmaurice. Jean Harlow, Franchot Tone, Cary Grant, Lewis Stone, Benita Hume. Fine cast sinks in this soapy romantic spy drama set in WW1, with Grant as French flier who falls in love with Harlow. Brightest moment has Cary crooning ''Did I Remember?''▼

Svengali (1931) **82m.** *** D: Archie Mayo. John Barrymore, Marian Marsh, Donald Crisp, Carmel Myers, Bramwell Fletcher, Luis Alberni. Absorbing tale of artist's obsession with young girl, Trilby, who becomes singing artist under his hypnotic spell. Prime Barrymore in interesting production with bizarre sets by Anton Grot, memorable visual effects. Followed by THE MAD GENIUS.▼●

Svengali (1955-British) **C-82m.** **½ D: Noel Langley. Hildegarde Neff, Donald Wolfit, Terence Morgan, Noel Purcell, Alfie Bass. Lacks flair of earlier version of du Maurier's novel about mesmerizing teacher and his actress-pupil Trilby.▼

Svengali (1983) **C-100m. TVM** D: Anthony Harvey. Peter O'Toole, Jodie Foster, Elizabeth Ashley, Larry Joshua, Pamela Blair, Barbara Byrne, Holly Hunter. O'Toole's outré performance as a faded musical star who takes young rock singer Foster under his wing makes this new version of the hoary tale watchable. Updated from George du Maurier's nearly one-hundred-year-old *Trilby*. Average.▼

Swamp Diamonds SEE: **Swamp Women**

Swamp Fire (1946) **69m.** ** D: William H. Pine. Johnny Weissmuller, Virginia Grey, Buster Crabbe, Carol Thurston, Pedro De Cordoba, David Janssen. Blah melodrama in which psychologically scarred Weissmuller returns from coast guard service in WW2, and attempts to settle into his old life as a Louisiana river pilot.▼

Swamp Thing (1982) **C-91m.** **½ D: Wes Craven. Louis Jourdan, Adrienne Barbeau, Ray Wise, David Hess, Nicholas Worth. Research scientist continues to love Barbeau from afar even after a chemical turns him into walking vegetation. This was better as a DC comic, though Jourdan's villainous camping in this sweet-natured monster pic is almost on a level with Vincent Price's standard routine. Followed by THE RETURN OF SWAMP THING and a cable TV series. [PG]▼●

Swamp Water (1941) **90m.** **½ D: Jean Renoir. Dana Andrews, Walter Brennan,

Anne Baxter, Walter Huston, Virginia Gilmore, John Carradine, Ward Bond, Guinn Williams, Eugene Pallette, Joe Sawyer, Mary Howard. Renoir's first American film is moody but erratic thriller set in the Okefenokee. Trapper Andrews finds fugitive Brennan hiding in the swamp, tries to clear him of murder rap without letting on that he knows the man's whereabouts. Powerhouse cast, handsome production, weakened by cornball dialogue and miscasting of Brennan. Remade as LURE OF THE WILDERNESS.

Swamp Women (1955) **C-73m.** *½ D: Roger Corman. Carole Mathews, Marie Windsor, Beverly Garland, Touch (Michael) Connors, Jil Jarmyn, Susan Cummings. Heavy-handed nonsense with New Orleans policewoman Mathews going undercover, hooking up with notorious trio of female crooks who escape from jail and head out after stolen diamonds. Fans of Windsor and Garland will not want to miss it. Retitled: SWAMP DIAMONDS, CRUEL SWAMP.▼

Swan, The (1956) **C-112m.** *** D: Charles Vidor. Grace Kelly, Alec Guinness, Louis Jourdan, Agnes Moorehead, Jessie Royce Landis, Brian Aherne, Leo G. Carroll, Estelle Winwood. Mild Molnar comedy of manners has attractive cast but not much sparkle. Jourdan good as Kelly's suitor, but she's promised to prince Guinness. Filmed before in 1925 and (as ONE ROMANTIC NIGHT) in 1930. CinemaScope.▼●

Swanee River (1939) **C-84m.** **½ D: Sidney Lanfield. Don Ameche, Al Jolson, Andrea Leeds, Felix Bressart, Russell Hicks. Bio of Stephen Foster where every song he writes is cued by a line of dialogue; clichés fill the movie, but it's fun on that level. Jolson is terrific as E. P. Christy; minstrel numbers are exceptionally well done. Other Foster bios are HARMONY LANE and I DREAM OF JEANIE.

Swann in Love (1984-French) **C-110m.** **½ D: Volker Schlöndorff. Jeremy Irons, Ornella Muti, Alain Delon, Fanny Ardant, Marie-Christine Barrault, Nathalie Juvet. Lavish but lifeless telescoping of Proust's *Remembrance of Things Past* with Irons surprisingly stiff as French aristocrat obsessed with scandalous, lower-class Muti in 1885 Paris. Redeemed somewhat by the latter and Delon (as a homosexual baron), a sexy under-the-covers love scene, and Sven Nykvist photography. [R]▼

Swan Princess, The (1994) **C-90m.** ** D: Richard Rich. Voices of Jack Palance, Howard McGillin, Michelle Nicastro, Liz Callaway, John Cleese, Steven Wright, Sandy Duncan. Charmless, by-the-numbers animated fantasy about Prince Derek and Princess Odette, who seem fated to wed; barriers arise when they quarrel, and a sorcerer transforms the princess into a swan. Partially based on the fable that inspired *Swan Lake.* Too imitative of Disney's BEAUTY AND THE BEAST for its own good. In fact, the film was made by former Disney animators. Followed by two sequels. [G]▼●

Swan Princess: Escape From Castle Mountain (1997) **C-71m.** BOMB D: Richard Rich. Voices of Michelle Nicastro, Douglas Sills, Jake Williamson, Donald Sage MacKay, Doug Stone. Insipid sequel. Princess Odette and Prince Derek continue incoherently to do battle with an evil sorcerer. No better than a Saturday morning TV cartoon, a waste of time. Followed by direct-to-video sequel. [G]▼

Swap, The SEE: **Sam's Song**

Swarm, The (1978) **C-116m.** BOMB D: Irwin Allen. Michael Caine, Katharine Ross, Richard Widmark, Henry Fonda, Richard Chamberlain, Olivia de Havilland, Fred MacMurray, Ben Johnson, Lee Grant, Jose Ferrer, Patty Duke Astin, Slim Pickens, Bradford Dillman. This formula disaster film from Irwin Allen portrays killer bee invasion with no sting at all; succeeds only in wasting a lot of talented actors. For masochists only: an expanded laserdisc print runs 156m. Panavision. [PG]▼●

Swashbuckler (1976) **C-101m.** BOMB D: James Goldstone. Robert Shaw, James Earl Jones, Peter Boyle, Genevieve Bujold, Beau Bridges, Geoffrey Holder, Avery Schreiber, Anjelica Huston. Poorly constructed, bubble-headed picture—laced with kinky PG sex scenes—would make Errol Flynn turn over in his grave. Incredible waste of talent. Panavision. [PG]▼●◗

Swastika Savages SEE: **Hell's Bloody Devils**

Swedenhielms (1935-Swedish) **88m.** **½ D: Gustaf Molander. Gosta Ekman, Bjorn Berglund, Hakan Westergren, Tutta Rolf, Ingrid Bergman. Slow-moving but not uninteresting tale of poor but honorable scientist Rolf Swedenhielm (well acted by Ekman), who's up for the Nobel Prize, and his careless, childish offspring. Bergman, in her third feature, plays the wealthy fiancee of Swedenhielm's youngest son—and her star appeal is obvious.▼●

Sweeney Todd, The Demon Barber of Fleet Street (1936-British) **68m.** ** D: George King. Tod Slaughter, Bruce Seton, Stella Rho, Eve Lister, Ben Soutten, D.J. Williams. Not many chills in this adaptation of the George Dibdin-Pitt play (later one of the sources for the Broadway musical *Sweeney Todd* by Stephen Sondheim), but it does contain a quintessential eye-rolling performance by Britain's master of grand guignol, Tod Slaughter, playing the sadistic barber who dumps his customers into the cellar and turns them into meat pies. Photographed by Ronald Neame. Not released in the U.S. until 1939.▼

Sweepings (1933) **80m.** ***½ D: John Cromwell. Lionel Barrymore, William Gargan, Gloria Stuart, George Meeker, Eric Linden, Gregory Ratoff, Franklin Pangborn. Compelling Edna Ferberish saga of self-made man who devotes his life to building giant department store, hoping that his four children will carry on his work. Fine acting, inventive direction and camerawork—plus montages by Slavko Vorkapich—make this something special. Remade as THREE SONS in 1939.

Sweet Adeline (1935) **87m.** **½ D: Mervyn LeRoy. Irene Dunne, Donald Woods, Hugh Herbert, Ned Sparks, Joseph Cawthorn, Louis Calhern, Winifred Shaw. Combination of spy chase and operetta isn't always smooth, but Kern-Hammerstein songs like "Why Was I Born" and Dunne's know-how make this enjoyable.▼

Sweet and Low-Down (1944) **75m.** **½ D: Archie Mayo. Benny Goodman and His Band, Linda Darnell, Jack Oakie, Lynn Bari, James Cardwell, Allyn Joslyn, Dickie Moore. Thin story of trombonist Cardwell, a young man with "rough talent" who makes it big in Goodman's orchestra—and with pert deb Darnell. However, the King of Swing and his boys really cook, from the opening credits on; the jam session sequence is especially hot.

Sweet and Lowdown (1999) **C-95m.** **½ D: Woody Allen. Sean Penn, Samantha Morton, Uma Thurman, Brian Markinson, Anthony LaPaglia, James Urbaniak, Gretchen Mol, John Waters, Brad Garrett. A Woody Allen diversion about a fictional jazz guitarist of the 1930s, Emmet Ray (brilliantly played by Penn), who's a musical genius but a rotten human being. Morton is a standout as a naive (and mute) woman with whom he has an unlikely relationship. Music is great, period flavor impeccable, but the story wanders. Howard Alden doubles Penn's guitar playing. Allen appears onscreen as one of the experts recalling Emmet Ray's career. [PG-13]▼◗

Sweet Bird of Youth (1962) **C-120m.** ***½ D: Richard Brooks. Paul Newman, Geraldine Page, Shirley Knight, Ed Begley, Rip Torn, Mildred Dunnock, Madeleine Sherwood, Philip Abbott, Corey Allen. Tennessee Williams' play, cleaned up for the movies, still is powerful drama. Newman returns to Southern town with dissipated movie queen Page, causing corrupt town "boss" Begley (who won an Oscar) to have him fixed proper. Glossy production with cast on top of material. Scripted by Brooks. Remade for TV. CinemaScope.▼●

Sweet Bird of Youth (1989) **C-100m. TVM** D: Nicolas Roeg. Elizabeth Taylor, Mark Harmon, Rip Torn, Valerie Perrine, Ruta Lee, Kevin Geer, Michael Wilding (Jr.). So-so version of Tennessee Williams' play about a faded movie star and her ambitious young lover, rewritten by Gavin Lambert (and reportedly based on Williams' own rethinking of the material). Earnest and watchable but lacks fire. Torn, who played the *lead* on Broadway and Tom Finlay, Jr. in the 1962 film, plays the latter's father, Boss Finlay. Wilding, Taylor's son, has one long phone conversation with her but no face-to-face scenes. Average.▼

Sweet Body of Deborah, The (1969-Italian-French) **C-105m.** BOMB D: Romolo Guerrieri. Carroll Baker, Jean Sorel, Evelyn Stewart, Luigi Pistilli, Michel Bardinet. Convoluted soaper about murder, suicide, blackmail, and other sordid goings-on. This "body" really sags. Techniscope. [R]

Sweet Candy SEE: **Candy Stripe Nurses**

Sweet Charity (1969) **C-133m.** *** D: Bob Fosse. Shirley MacLaine, John McMartin, Ricardo Montalban, Sammy Davis, Jr., Chita Rivera, Paula Kelly, Stubby Kaye, Ben Vereen, Lee Roy Reams. Fine, overlooked adaptation of the Broadway musical written by Neil Simon, and based on Fellini's NIGHTS OF CABIRIA, about prostitute-with-heart-of-gold who falls in love with naive young man who doesn't know about her "work." Cy Coleman-Dorothy Fields score includes "Big Spender," "If They Could See Me Now," rousing "Rhythm of Life." Script by Peter Stone. Fosse's debut as film director. Look for Bud Cort and Kristoffer Tabori as flower children. Home video version runs 20m. longer, and laserdisc edition has an alternate, unused ending for the film. Panavision. [G]▼●

Sweet Country (1986) **C-150m.** BOMB D: Michael Cacoyannis. Jane Alexander, Franco Nero, Carole Laure, Joanna Pettet, Irene Papas, Randy Quaid, Jean-Pierre Aumont. Grueling, heavy-handed drama of a family's reactions to the 1973 Chilean revolution. Notable for idiotic miscasting (Laure and Pettet as Papas' daughters; Quaid as a lip-smacking, lecherous soldier named Raoul). Quite a comedown for ZORBA THE GREEK director Cacoyannis, who includes tasteless sexploitation footage for good measure. Filmed in Greece. [R]▼●

Sweet Dreams (1985) **C-115m.** **½ D: Karel Reisz. Jessica Lange, Ed Harris, Ann Wedgeworth, David Clennon, James Staley, Gary Basaraba, John Goodman, P.J. Soles. Flavorful look at 1950s country singing star Patsy Cline can't escape déjà vu from so many other show-biz biopics. Focuses mainly on Cline's marriage to ne'er-do-well Harris, which also has a too-familiar ring. Made worthwhile by truly fine performances (including Wedgeworth as Patsy's mother) and a lot of wonderful music (Lange lip-syncs to Cline's original recordings). [PG-13]▼●◗

Sweet Ecstasy (1962-French) **75m.** *½ D: Max Pecas. Elke Sommer, Pierre Brice, Christian Pezy, Claire Maurier. Silly soaper about life among the wealthy, beautiful, decadent, selfish young on the Riviera. Sommer is a cynical sexpot with an endless supply of false eyelashes. CinemaScope.▼

Sweetheart of the Campus (1941) **67m.** **½ D: Edward Dmytryk. Ruby Keeler, Ozzie Nelson, Harriet Hilliard, Gordon Oliver, Don Beddoe, The Four Spirits of Rhythm. Dancer Keeler and bandleader Ozzie start a nightclub on a college campus. Modest musical comedy, nothing to write home about, but consistently peppy and surprisingly enjoyable.

Sweethearts (1938) **C-114m.** **½ D: W. S. Van Dyke II. Jeanette MacDonald, Nelson Eddy, Frank Morgan, Florence Rice, Ray Bolger, Mischa Auer. Enjoyable but overlong; Nelson and Jeanette are stage stars of Victor Herbert operetta who are manipulated by their producer (Morgan) into having a marital spat. Handsome color production filled with Herbert melodies. Cinematographer Oliver Marsh won an Oscar.▼●

Sweet Hearts Dance (1988) **C-101m.** **½ D: Robert Greenwald. Don Johnson, Susan Sarandon, Jeff Daniels, Elizabeth Perkins, Kate Reid, Justin Henry, Holly Marie Combs, Heather Coleman. Comedy-drama, set in a small Vermont town, about the breakup of a marriage between two high-school sweethearts—just as their longtime friend is embarking on a serious relationship. Engaging cast, led by Johnson in a very appealing performance, but after a while you wish the two lead characters would just get on with it. Written by Ernest Thompson. [R]▼●

Sweet Hereafter, The (1997-Canadian) **C-110m.** *** D: Atom Egoyan. Ian Holm, Sarah Polley, Bruce Greenwood, Tom McCamus, Arsinée Khanjian, Alberta Watson, Gabrielle Rose, Maury Chaykin, David Hemblen. Tenacious lawyer comes to a Canadian town that's been shattered by a schoolbus accident in which many of its children were killed. He tries to convince the parents to hire him to sue whoever may be responsible—if, indeed, anyone is. Meanwhile, he tries to deal with his fragmented relationship with his own drug-addicted daughter. Egoyan brings his quiet, elliptical approach to Russell Banks' novel and creates a haunting film that's hard to forget . . . though not for every taste. Holm is simply superb. Panavision. [R]▼●◗

Sweetie (1989-Australian) **C-97m.** **½ D: Jane Campion. Genevieve Lemon, Karen Colston, Tom Lycos, Jon Darling, Dorothy Barry. New Zealander Campion's off-beat account of an unbalanced, demanding young woman (Lemon), and her relationship with her weak, obsessive sister (Colston) and her parents. Some brilliant directorial touches, but too many sequences simply don't work. Unsettling, occasionally depressing, and not for all tastes. [R]▼●

Sweet Kill SEE: **Arousers, The**

Sweet Liberty (1986) **C-107m.** ** D: Alan Alda. Alan Alda, Michael Caine, Michelle Pfeiffer, Bob Hoskins, Lise Hilboldt, Lillian Gish, Saul Rubinek, Lois Chiles. Amiable but aimless comedy of college professor who becomes involved with a movie troupe as his historical novel is filmed. Ingratiating cast maintains some level of interest, with funny turns by Caine as a cocky leading man, and Hoskins as an eager-to-please screenwriter. But deep down inside, it's really shallow. [PG]▼●

Sweet Lies (1986) **C-96m.** *½ D: Nathalie Delon. Treat Williams, Joanna Pacula, Julianne Phillips, Laura Manszky, Norbert Weisser, Bernard Fresson. Boring romantic comedy with Williams sorely miscast as an insurance-company detective involved in sexual shenanigans with a trio of women while on assignment in Paris. [R]▼

Sweet Lorraine (1987) **C-91m.** *** D: Steve Gomer. Maureen Stapleton, Trini Alvarado, Lee Richardson, John Bedford Lloyd, Giancarlo Esposito, Edith Falco, Todd Graff, Evan Handler, Freddie Roman. The Lorraine is a cozy little Catskill hotel that's way past its prime; Stapleton is its proprietress, Alvarado her granddaughter who spends a summer working in its kitchen. There's a wealth of atmosphere and some sturdy characterizations in this warm, friendly, very personal slice-of-life sleeper. [PG-13]▼

Sweet Love, Bitter (1967) **92m.** **½ D: Herbert Danska. Dick Gregory, Don Murray, Diane Varsi, Robert Hooks, John Randolph. Intriguing film about the unlikely friendship between a great jazz musician (Gregory) who's seen better days, and a college professor who's hit the skids (Murray). Loosely based on the life of jazz legend Charlie "Bird" Parker; dated in some ways, but also a fascinating artifact of its time. Its comments on race relations are still as potent as ever.▼

Sweet Music (1935) **100m.** **½ D: Alfred E. Green. Rudy Vallee, Ann Dvorak, Helen Morgan, Ned Sparks, Alice White, Allen Jenkins. Genuinely mediocre musical with bandleader Vallee and dancer Dvorak constantly at odds. A few good songs, but the real highlight is the slapstick shenanigans of the Frank & Milt Britton Band, here playing Rudy's musical aggregation.

Sweet Nothing (1996) **C-90m.** ** D: Gary Winick. Michael Imperioli, Mira Sorvino, Paul Calderon, Lisa Langford. Tragic story of a family affected by the horrors of drugs.

Father looking to make a better life for his wife and kids gets in way over his head in the seedy world of crack, becoming both a user and a seller. Grim film offers unappealing characters and story line, showing the harrowing effects of drug addiction on innocent lives. Made in 1993, before Sorvino's Oscar-winning turn in MIGHTY APHRODITE, but released (just barely) after. [R]▼

Sweet November (1968) **C-114m.** **½ D: Robert Ellis Miller. Sandy Dennis, Anthony Newley, Theodore Bikel, Burr DeBenning, Sandy Baron, Marj Dusay, Martin West. Kooky Dennis takes a new lover every month, helping insecure men find confidence, then sending them away; her plans go awry when one of them (Newley) insists on marrying her. Some touching moments in this likable (if implausible) comedy-drama by Herman Raucher.

Sweet Revenge (1977) **C-90m.** BOMB D: Jerry Schatzberg. Stockard Channing, Sam Waterston, Franklin Ajaye, Richard Doughty. Public defender Waterston falls in love with a car thief (Channing) in this turkey, originally called DANDY, THE ALL-AMERICAN GIRL. Panavision. [PG]

Sweet Revenge (1987) **C-78m.** *½ D: Mark Sobel. Nancy Allen, Ted Shackelford, Martin Landau, Sal Landi, Michele Little. Limp programmer with TV journalist Allen kidnapped by a white slavery ring. Plays like a bad TV show. [R]▼

Sweet Ride, The (1968) **C-110m.** *½ D: Harvey Hart. Tony Franciosa, Michael Sarrazin, Jacqueline Bisset, Bob Denver, Michael Wilding, Michele Carey, Warren Stevens. Absurd claptrap about a tennis bum, a surfer and a beautiful girl; some of the Malibu scenery is nice. Panavision. [R]

Sweet Rosie O'Grady (1943) **C-74m.** **½ D: Irving Cummings. Betty Grable, Robert Young, Adolphe Menjou, Reginald Gardiner, Virginia Grey, Phil Regan. Pleasant musical of ex-burlesque star and exposé reporter. Menjou steals film as editor of Police Gazette. Previously filmed as LOVE IS NEWS; remade again as THAT WONDERFUL URGE.

Sweet 16 (1981) **C-90m.** ** D: Jim Sotos. Bo Hopkins, Susan Strasberg, Don Stroud, Dana Kimmell, Aleisa Shirley, Don Shanks, Steve Antin, Logan Clarke, Patrick Macnee, Michael Pataki, Larry Storch, Henry Wilcoxon, Sharon Farrell. Standard terror film (with good cast) set in Texas about a rash of murders occurring as Shirley's 16th birthday approaches. Identity of the vengeful murderer is quite predictable; integration of a racial prejudice (persecuting Indians) subplot doesn't work. Hopkins plays his slightly slow-witted Southern sheriff role for the umpteenth time. [R]▼

Sweet Smell of Success (1957) **96m.** ***½ D: Alexander Mackendrick. Burt Lancaster, Tony Curtis, Marty Milner, Sam Levene, Barbara Nichols, Susan Harrison, Joe Frisco, Chico Hamilton Quintet. Searing Clifford Odets–Ernest Lehman script about ruthless, all-powerful columnist J. J. Hunsecker (Lancaster) and a smarmy press agent (Curtis) who'll do *anything* to curry his favor. Vivid performances, fine jazz score by Elmer Bernstein, outstanding camerawork by James Wong Howe that perfectly captures N.Y.C. nightlife.▼●

Sweet Sweetback's Baad Asssss Song (1971) **C-97m.** *** D: Melvin Van Peebles. Melvin Van Peebles, Rhetta Hughes, Simon Chuckster, John Amos. Van Peebles produced, directed, financed, wrote, scored, and stars in this angry, violent, reverse-racist blaxploitation drama as a superstud who runs, runs, runs from the police. Visually exciting, surprisingly effective. Controversial (and X-rated) when first released. [R]▼●

Sweet Talker (1990-Australian) **C-88m.** **½ D: Michael Jenkins. Bryan Brown, Karen Allen, Chris Haywood, Bill Kerr, Bruce Spence, Bruce Myles, Paul Chubb, Peter Hehir, Justin Rosniak. Amiable if thoroughly familiar tale of a con-man who comes to a remote Australian coastal town to sell his bill of goods, falls in love, and has second thoughts about going through with the con. Pleasant, picturesque, and predictable. Brown cowrote the story. [PG]▼●◗

Sweet Violent Tony SEE: **Cuba Crossing**

Sweet William (1980-British) **C-92m.** **½ D: Claude Whatham. Sam Waterston, Jenny Agutter, Anna Massey, Geraldine James, Daphne Oxenford, Rachel Bell, Arthur Lowe, Tim Pigott-Smith. Waterston is charming as an erratic ALFIE-like bigamist who seduces Agutter in this OK entertainment. [R]▼

Swept Away . . . by an unusual destiny in the blue sea of August (1975-Italian) **C-116m.** **** D: Lina Wertmuller. Giancarlo Giannini, Mariangela Melato. A slovenly sailor is cast adrift on an island with his employer, a rich, selfish woman. Cut off from society, he reverses their roles, stripping her of pride and vanity, and controlling her completely. This fascinating and provocative adult film put writer-director Wertmuller on the map in this country. [R]▼●◗

Swept From the Sea (1998-U.S.-British) **C-114m.** ** D: Beeban Kidron. Rachel Weisz, Vincent Perez, Ian McKellen, Kathy Bates, Joss Ackland, Tony Haygarth, Zoë Wanamaker, Tom Bell. 19th-century melodrama of a silent servant girl who falls in love with the sole survivor of a shipwreck, a Ukrainian emigrant. This tragic romance is the talk of the entire disapproving town. Gorgeous scenery and storms galore can't save this sluggish, shallow film "inspired by" the haunting Joseph Conrad novel *Amy Foster*. Super 35. [PG-13]▼●◗

Swimmer, The (1968) **C-94m.** ***½ D: Frank Perry. Burt Lancaster, Janet Landgard, Janice Rule, Tony Bickley, Marge Champion, Bill Fiore, Kim Hunter, Joan Rivers. Middle-aged man swims from pool to pool on journey home during hot afternoon; each pool evokes past moments and events. Fascinating, vastly underrated film adapted from John Cheever short story; Lancaster is superb, and location filming in Connecticut perfectly captures mood. Script by Eleanor Perry. [M/PG]▼●

Swimming to Cambodia (1987) **C-87m.** *** D: Jonathan Demme. Spalding Gray talks for nearly an hour and a half—about life in general, and about his experiences in Cambodia, where he spent some time while appearing in a minor role in THE KILLING FIELDS. There is no reason why a lengthy monologue should become such a fascinating film—but it does, thanks to Gray's storytelling skills, and Demme's artful (and subtle) direction. An unusual and rewarding experience. Followed by MONSTER IN A BOX.▼●

Swimming With Sharks (1994) **C-93m.** ** D: George Huang. Kevin Spacey, Frank Whaley, Michelle Forbes, Benicio Del Toro, Jerry Levine, T. E. Russell, Roy Dotrice. Young man signs on as the new assistant to venal Hollywood exec Buddy Ackerman and learns new facets of the word "abusive" . . . until the day he exacts revenge on his tormentor. Dark, "inside" comedy is a one-joke idea (written by first-time director Huang, who—not surprisingly—toiled as an underling in the film biz), but Spacey's performance as the modern-day monster is galvanizing. He alone makes the film worth seeing. Incidentally, Spacey also coproduced the picture. [R]▼●◗

Swim Team (1979) **C-92m** *½ D: James Polakoff. James Daughton, Stephen Furst, Richard Young, Jenny Neumann, guest star Buster Crabbe. Can the Whalers reverse their seven-year losing streak as a swim team? Can you sit through this terrible movie to find out? [PG]▼

Swindle, The (1955-Italian) **92m.** **½ D: Federico Fellini. Broderick Crawford, Giulietta Masina, Richard Basehart, Franco Fabrizi. Absorbing Fellini tale, which he coscripted, about a trio of small-time crooks who go about fleecing peasants in Italy, each planning for a better life. The spotlight is on the eldest, a world-weary loser nicely played by Crawford. Not among the director's best; still an intriguing portrait of hope and desperation. Aka THE SWINDLERS. Original title: IL BIDONE. ▼

Swindle, The (1997-French) **C-105m.** *** D: Claude Chabrol. Isabelle Huppert, Michel Serrault, François Cluzet, Jean-François Balmer, Jackie Berroyer. Absorbing comedy/caper film with Huppert and Serrault perfectly cast as a pair of con artists who may or may not be scheming to cheat each other. The crux of the story is set at a Swiss dentists' convention, where Huppert hooks up with enigmatic Cluzet. Slick, engaging entertainment.▼

Swinger, The (1966) **C-81m.** ** D: George Sidney. Ann-Margret, Tony Franciosa, Robert Coote, Horace McMahon, Nydia Westman. Brassy, artificial yarn of good-girl Ann-Margret posing as swinger to impress girlie magazine editor Franciosa.

Swingers (1996) **C-96m.** **½ D: Doug Liman. Jon Favreau, Vince Vaughn, Ron Livingston, Patrick Van Horn, Alex Desert, Deena Martin, Katherine Kendall, Brooke Langton, Heather Graham. Slight but entertaining look at single life in L.A. from a guy's point of view. Main character is a comedian who broke up with his girlfriend six months earlier and hasn't yet gotten over her. Some pointed jabs at L.A. life distinguish this contemporary urban tale, a kind of hip update of AMERICAN GRAFFITI. Leading actor Favreau wrote the script; director Liman also photographed it. [R] ▼●◗

Swing Fever (1944) **80m.** *½ D: Tim Whelan. Kay Kyser, Marilyn Maxwell, William Gargan, Lena Horne, Nat Pendleton. Musical misfire with Kyser a hick with hypnotic powers, who's conned into aiding greedy fight-manager Gargan. Look for Ava Gardner as a receptionist.

Swing High, Swing Low (1937) **95m.** ** D: Mitchell Leisen. Carole Lombard, Fred MacMurray, Charles Butterworth, Jean Dixon, Dorothy Lamour, Harvey Stephens, Anthony Quinn. Musical drama with cornball plot of musician MacMurray's rise and fall. Redeemed somewhat by good cast, glossy production. From the stage play *Burlesque,* made before as THE DANCE OF LIFE and remade as WHEN MY BABY SMILES AT ME.▼

Swingin' Affair, A (1963) **85m.** BOMB D: Jay O. Lawrence. William Wellman, Jr., Arline Judge, Sandra Gale Bettin, Dick Dale and The Deltones. Young Wellman boxes to subsidize his university vacation. Awful drama with surf music. Also known as A SWINGING AFFAIR.

Swingin' Along (1962) **C-74m.** BOMB D: Charles Barton. Tommy Noonan, Peter Marshall, Barbara Eden, Ray Charles, Roger Williams, Bobby Vee. The witless shenanigans of aspiring composer Noonan and manager Marshall—with musical "guest stars" to relieve the tedium. Aka DOUBLE TROUBLE. CinemaScope.

Swinging Barmaids, The (1975) **C-84m.** **½ D: Gus Trikonis. Bruce Watson, Laura Hippe, Katie Saylor, William Smith, Dyanne Thorne, John Alderman. Stylish, engaging psycho-thriller, written by Charles Griffith, has cop Smith tracking down nut who preys on on B-girls. Reissued as EAGER BEAVERS. [R]

Swingin' Summer, A (1965) **C-80m.** *½ D: Robert Sparr. James Stacy, William Wellman, Jr., Quinn O'Hara, Martin West, Allan Jones, Raquel Welch. The Righteous Brothers, The Rip Chords, Gary Lewis and The Playboys, Jody Miller. Typically thin storyline (about three guys who open a dance hall) as an excuse for music numbers by various guest stars. Techniscope.▼

Swing Kids (1993) **C-112m.** ** D: Thomas Carter. Robert Sean Leonard, Christian Bale, Frank Whaley, Barbara Hershey, Tushka Bergen, David Tom, Julia Stemberger, Jayce Bartok, Noah Wyle. This year's NEWSIES, and poor Bale is in both. Transparent Yank actors struggle through a THREE COMRADES kind of yarn about the Nazi persecution of German teens who openly embrace American swing music—taboo, because it employs so many black musicians. Singularly weird enough to carry a mild fascination, but it's the kind of film that needs daring flamboyance to have a prayer of coming off. Eye-massaging production design by Allan Cameron. Kenneth Branagh appears unbilled in a key supporting role as a Nazi. [PG-13]▼●

Swing Parade of 1946 (1946) **74m.** *½ D: Phil Karlson. Gale Storm, Phil Regan, The Three Stooges, Ed Brophy, Will Osborne and His Orchestra, Connee Boswell. Dreary Grade-B musical with enough plot for a 10-minute short. The Stooges add some life, as does Louis Jordan performing "Caledonia," but it's not enough. Auteurists take note: Nicholas Ray is credited with "additional dialogue."▼

Swing Shift (1984) **C-100m.** ** D: Jonathan Demme. Goldie Hawn, Kurt Russell, Christine Lahti, Ed Harris, Fred Ward, Sudie Bond, Holly Hunter, Patty Maloney, Roger Corman, Belinda Carlisle. Misfired attempt to fashion fictional story around real-life situation of housewives who became factory workers during WW2. All the women are interesting (especially Lahti, in a wonderful performance), but the men are shallow and poorly defined—and consequently, so is the film. Pseudonymous screenplay credit for "Rob Morton" masks several top writers, with half-an-hour reportedly shot by another director at producer Hawn's insistence. [PG]▼●

Swing Shift Maisie (1943) **87m.** **½ D: Norman Z. McLeod. Ann Sothern, James Craig, Jean Rogers, Connie Gilchrist, John Qualen, Marta Linden, Donald Curtis, Kay Medford. Patriotic Maisie quits her dog act to help out the war effort at an aircraft factory, only to be accused of sabotage by a jealous "friend" who's trying to steal her beau. Keep an eye out for John Hodiak, Don Taylor, Kirk Alyn, and Jim Davis.

Swing Time (1936) **103m.** **** D: George Stevens. Fred Astaire, Ginger Rogers, Victor Moore, Helen Broderick, Eric Blore, Betty Furness. One of the best Astaire-Rogers films, with stars as dance team whose romance is hampered by Fred's engagement to girl back home (Furness). Fine support by Moore and Broderick, unforgettable Jerome Kern–Dorothy Fields songs "A Fine Romance," "Pick Yourself Up." Oscar-winning "The Way You Look Tonight." Astaire's Bojangles production number is a screen classic.▼●

Swingtime Johnny (1944) **61m.** *½ D: Edward Cline. Andrews Sisters, Harriet Hilliard, Peter Cookson, Tim Ryan. Show biz performers desert the theater for work in munitions factory; lowbrow entertainment.

Swing Your Lady (1938) **79m.** *½ D: Ray Enright. Humphrey Bogart, Frank McHugh, Louise Fazenda, Nat Pendleton, Penny Singleton, Allen Jenkins, Ronald Reagan, Weaver Bros. and Elviry. Bogart promotes wrestler Pendleton; embarrassing comedy is easily his worst starring effort. Reagan appears briefly as a sportswriter.

Swirl of Glory SEE: **Sugarfoot**

Swiss Conspiracy, The (1975-U.S.-German) **C-88m.** ** D: Jack Arnold. David Janssen, Senta Berger, John Ireland, John Saxon, Elke Sommer, Ray Milland, Anton Diffring. Confusing cat-and-mouse intrigue set in Switzerland, where Janssen is hired to protect valued bank customers with large secret accounts. [PG]▼◗

Swiss Family Robinson (1940) **93m.** *** D: Edward Ludwig. Thomas Mitchell, Edna Best, Freddie Bartholomew, Tim Holt, Terry Kilburn. Mitchell decides to move family to Australia for a purer life, but shipwreck strands them on a remote island where his three spoiled sons learn honest values. Excellent adaptation of Johann Wyss book boasts impressive special effects, strong performances, and much darker elements than the later Disney version. Uncredited opening narration by Orson Welles. ▼

Swiss Family Robinson (1960) **C-128m.** ***½ D: Ken Annakin. John Mills, Dorothy McGuire, James MacArthur, Janet Munro, Sessue Hayakawa, Tommy Kirk, Kevin Corcoran. Rollicking entertainment Disney-style, with shipwrecked family building island paradise, neatly dispatching Hayakawa and his pirate band. Pure escapism, larger than life. Panavision.▼●

Swiss Miss (1938) **72m.** ** D: John Blystone. Stan Laurel, Oliver Hardy, Della Lind, Walter Woolf King, Eric Blore, Adia Kuznetzof, Charles Judels. Contrived romantic story with music tries hard to submerge L&H, but Stan and Ollie's scenes save film, especially when Ollie serenades his true love with Stan playing tuba.▼

Switch (1991) **C-104m.** *½ D: Blake Edwards. Ellen Barkin, Jimmy Smits, JoBeth Williams, Lorraine Bracco, Tony Roberts, Perry King, Bruce Martyn Payne. Inferior ripoff of GOODBYE, CHARLIE about a philandering male who's shot by a vindictive conquest and returns to earth as a woman. Old-hat premise with precious few opportunities to exploit Edwards' flair for cartoonish physical humor. Barkin is sole saving grace, far better than anything else in the film. Panavision. [R]▼●

Switchback (1997) **C-121m.** **½ D: Jeb Stuart. Dennis Quaid, Danny Glover, R. Lee Ermey, Jared Leto, Ted Levine. DIE HARD/FUGITIVE screenwriter Stuart debuts as director of this thriller about the kidnapping of an FBI agent's son, and the pursuit of the serial killer who has him. Preposterous plot devices are overshadowed by excellent cast. You really care what happens to these people. Panavision. [R]▼●◗

Switchblade Sisters (1975) **C-91m.** ** D: Jack Hill. Robbie Lee, Joanne Nail, Monica Gayle, Kitty Bruce, Marlene Clark, Michael Miller. Pretty good cheapie about a female gang, although feminism clearly takes a back seat to action. Predates the cycle of gang films by four years; Bruce is Lenny's daughter. Originally released as THE JEZEBELS (the gang's name); reissued as PLAYGIRL GANG. [R]▼●◗

Switching Channels (1988) **C-105m.** *** D: Ted Kotcheff. Kathleen Turner, Burt Reynolds, Christopher Reeve, Ned Beatty, Henry Gibson, George Newbern, Al Waxman, Ken James, Joe Silver, Charles Kimbrough, Tony Rosato. TV reporter Turner tries to quit her job to marry wealthy Reeve, but her boss (and ex-husband) Reynolds isn't going to give her up so easily. Surprisingly good remake of THE FRONT PAGE/HIS GIRL FRIDAY updated to the satellite-television era, but less effective in its use of satire and occasional melodrama than its classic predecessors. All three stars are terrific. [PG]▼●

Swoon (1992) **92m.** *** D: Tom Kalin. Daniel Schlachet, Craig Chester, Ron Vawter, Michael Kirby, Michael Stumm, Valda Z. Drabla, Natalie Stanford. Impressive low-budget stunt of a movie about Chicago's legendary Leopold-Loeb "thrill" killing, with added subtext about the climate of homophobia that figured in the jury's reaction to one of the century's most heinous crimes. Daring and original (though with severe dramatic limitations) and a fascinating companion piece to Hollywood's ROPE and COMPULSION; moody use of black-and-white.▼●

Sword and the Rose, The (1953) **C-93m.** ***½ D: Ken Annakin. Richard Todd, Glynis Johns, James Robertson Justice, Michael Gough, Jane Barrett. Colorful filming of *When Knighthood Was in Flower,* with Johns as Mary Tudor, who uses wiles and power to kindle romance with Todd—but runs afoul of villainous Duke (Gough). Rich period flavor, fine performance by Justice as King Henry VIII. Filmed in England by Walt Disney.▼●

Sword and the Sorcerer, The (1982) **C-100m.** ** D: Albert Pyun. Lee Horsley, Kathleen Beller, Simon MacCorkindale, George Maharis, Richard Lynch, Richard Moll, Robert Tessier, Nina Van Pallandt, Anna Bjorn, Jeff Corey. Aided by resurrected warlock Maharis, nasty Lynch enslaves the kingdom, and it's up to sword-swinging Horsley to save the day. Strictly second-rate in scripting, acting, and production, with just enough bloodletting to please undemanding fans of this kind of stuff. [R]▼●

Sword in the Desert (1949) **100m.** **½ D: George Sherman. Dana Andrews, Marta Toren, Stephen McNally, Jeff Chandler, Philip Friend. Interesting account of underground trail of European refugees during WW2; fairly good suspenser.

Sword in the Stone, The (1963) **C-75m.** **½ D: Wolfgang Reitherman. Voices of Ricky Sorenson, Sebastian Cabot, Karl Swenson, Junius Matthews. One of Disney's weakest animated features follows a young boy named Wart, who is destined to become King Arthur—with the considerable help of Merlin the Magician. Mildly entertaining and fast moving, but dialogue heavy, and full of "modern" references that remove much of the magic and wonder from T. H. White's story. Highlight: wizard's duel between Merlin and Madame Mim. ▼●

Sword of Ali Baba, The (1965) **C-81m.** ** D: Virgil Vogel. Peter Mann, Jocelyn Lane, Peter Whitney, Gavin MacLeod, Frank Puglia. Outrageous remake of ALI BABA AND THE FORTY THIEVES, using a great deal of footage from the 1944 film. Puglia repeats his role as Prince Cassim from '44 version to link old and new footage.

Sword of Gideon (1986-British-Canadian) **C-148m. TVM** D: Michael Anderson. Steven Bauer, Michael York, Rod Steiger, Colleen Dewhurst, Robert Joy, Laurent Malet, Lino Ventura, Leslie Hope. An intelligent and suspenseful thriller with commando Bauer handpicked to head anti-terrorist team and avenge Munich Olympic massacre of Israeli athletes. Dewhurst plays Golda Meir. Adapted by Chris Bryant from George Jonas' book *Vengeance.* Made for cable. Above average.▼

Sword of Lancelot (1963-British) **C-116m.** **½ D: Cornel Wilde. Cornel Wilde, Jean Wallace, Brian Aherne, George Baker. Camelot comes alive, minus music, with profuse action and splendid scenery. Some may find Wilde's approach too juvenile, overly sincere, and Aherne a bit too cavalier. Originally titled LANCELOT AND GUINEVERE. Panavision.▼

Sword of Monte Cristo, The (1951) **C-80m.** ** D: Maurice Geraghty. George Montgomery, Paula Corday, Berry Kroeger, William Conrad, Steve Brodie. Uninspired

adventure of woman who finds legendary sword of Count with key to treasure inscribed on it. Army officer joins her in fight against evil prime minister.▼
Sword of Sherwood Forest (1960-British) **C-80m.** **½ D: Terence Fisher. Richard Greene, Peter Cushing, Niall MacGinnis, Richard Pasco, Jack Gwillim, Sarah Branch, Nigel Green, Oliver Reed. Fair continuation of Robin Hood saga as Earl of Newark plots murder of Archbishop of Canterbury. Megascope. ▼
Sword of the Conqueror (1961-Italian) **C-85m.** *½ D: Carlo Campogalliani. Jack Palance, Eleonora Rossi-Drago, Guy Madison, Carlo D'Angelo. Flabby epic not livened by cast or sets; set in 6th-century Byzantine empire days. CinemaScope.▼
Sword of the Ninja SEE: **Challenge, The** (1982)
Sword of The Valiant (1985-British) **C-101m.** ** D: Stephen Weeks. Miles O'Keeffe, Cyrielle Claire, Leigh Lawson, Sean Connery, Trevor Howard, Peter Cushing, Ronald Lacey, Lila Kedrova, John Rhys-Davies. Connery (as the Green Knight) may only be on screen for a few scenes, but he adds zest to this lumbering account of a chivalrous young squire (a wooden O'Keeffe) who must solve a riddle in one year or die. Remake of GAWAIN AND THE GREEN KNIGHT by the same filmmakers . . . and not much of an improvement! Filmed in 1982. J-D-C Scope. [PG]▼
Swordsman, The (1948) **C-81m.** ** D: Joseph H. Lewis. Larry Parks, Ellen Drew, George Macready, Edgar Buchanan. Parks and Drew have Romeo-Juliet relationship in 18th-century Scotland; OK costumer.
Swordsman of Siena, The (1961-Italian) **C-97m.** ** D: Etienne Perier. Stewart Granger, Sylva Koscina, Christine Kaufmann, Tullio Carminati, Gabriele Ferzetti. Predictable swashbuckler about 16th-century adventurer with mixed loyalties who becomes involved in Spanish underground movement. Good cast saddled with tired script. CinemaScope.
Sybil (1976) **C-198m. TVM** D: Daniel Petrie. Joanne Woodward, Sally Field, Brad Davis, Martine Bartlett, Jane Hoffman, William Prince. Emmy-winning psychological study of a young woman who, disturbed by childhood experiences, has developed seventeen separate personalities. Field is remarkable in title role and Woodward, making a nice turnaround from THE THREE FACES OF EVE, brings special glow to the role of psychiatrist. Fascinating but deeply disturbing drama. Above average.▼
Sylvester (1985) **C-102m.** ** D: Tim Hunter. Richard Farnsworth, Melissa Gilbert, Michael Schoeffling, Constance Towers, Pete Kowanko, Arliss Howard, James Gammon. Seemingly surefire story of a girl and her horse can't clear the hurdles because lead character isn't terribly likable. Some nice riding sequences but uneven narrative (by Carol Sobieski) weighs it down. [PG]▼●
Sylvia (1965) **115m.** **½ D: Gordon Douglas. Carroll Baker, George Maharis, Joanne Dru, Peter Lawford, Viveca Lindfors, Edmond O'Brien, Aldo Ray, Ann Sothern. Baker's prelude to HARLOW is much better, despite overuse of flashbacks and rambling episodes; she plays a bad girl turned good with melodrama unfolding as detective Maharis investigates her life.
Sylvia (1985-New Zealand) **C-98m.** *** D: Michael Firth. Eleanor David, Nigel Terry, Tom Wilkinson, Mary Regan, Joseph George, Eileen Glover. David gives a strong performance as famed educator Sylvia Ashton-Warner, who struggled in the early 1940s to buck New Zealand's educational establishment with innovative reading methods for Maori children. Adapted from her works *Teacher* and *I Passed This Way*. Shirley MacLaine's otherwise unbearable TWO LOVES, based on an Ashton-Warner semiautobiographical story, makes an interesting cross reference. [PG]▼
Sylvia Scarlett (1935) **94m.** *** D: George Cukor. Katharine Hepburn, Cary Grant, Brian Aherne, Edmund Gwenn, Natalie Paley, Dennie Moore. Offbeat, charming comedy-drama; Hepburn and ne'er-do-well father Gwenn take to the road when he gets in trouble. She disguises as a boy as they travel with cockney Grant in touring show. Most unusual film made interesting by performances of Hepburn and Grant in their first film together. Also shown in computer-colored version.▼●
Sympathy for the Devil (1970-French) **C-92m.** ** D: Jean-Luc Godard. Muddled documentary which utilizes the Rolling Stones as a catchall for interspersed study of revolution. Godard's cut, titled ONE PLUS ONE and running somewhat longer, is still extant.▼
Symphony of Six Million (1932) **94m.** **½ D: Gregory La Cava. Irene Dunne, Ricardo Cortez, Anna Appel, Gregory Ratoff, Lita Chevret. Predictable but well-made Fannie Hurst soap opera has young doctor Cortez abandoning his Jewish-ghetto neighborhood, family, friends—and crippled sweetheart Dunne—to join Park Avenue set and make big money.
Synanon (1965) **107m.** **½ D: Richard Quine. Chuck Connors, Stella Stevens, Alex Cord, Richard Conte, Eartha Kitt, Edmond O'Brien, Chanin Hale, Alejandro Rey. Potentially powerful study of dope-addiction treatment via the Synanon House methods bogs down in pat romantic tale with stereotyped performances.
Syncopation (1942) **88m.** ** D: William Dieterle. Adolphe Menjou, Jackie Cooper, Bonita Granville, George Bancroft, Ted North, Todd Duncan, Frank Jenks, Rex

Stewart, Connee Boswell, Hall Johnson Choir. Promising but pedestrian story of early jazz travels from New Orleans to Chicago, focusing on trumpeter Cooper (who's dubbed by Bunny Berigan). Good music throughout; at the very end, there's a jam session featuring Benny Goodman, Charlie Barnet, Gene Krupa, Harry James, Jack Jenny, Joe Venuti, and Alvino Rey.

System, The (1953) **90m.** ** D: Lewis Seiler. Frank Lovejoy, Joan Weldon, Bob Arthur, Jerome Cowan. Uneven scripting spoils this potentially good study of gambling syndicate in large metropolitan city.

System, The (1966) SEE: **Girl-Getters, The**

Table for Five (1983) **C-122m.** *** D: Robert Lieberman. Jon Voight, Richard Crenna, Marie-Christine Barrault, Millie Perkins, Roxana Zal, Robby Kiger, Son Hoang Bui, Kevin Costner. Solid (and unabashed) tearjerker with Voight as a divorced man who tries to make up for being an absentee father by taking his three children on a cruise to Europe—little dreaming how tough an experience it will turn out to be. Curl up and have a good cry. [PG]▼●

Tabu—A Story of the South Seas (1931) **82m.** ***½ D: F.W. Murnau. Anna Chevalier, Matahi, Hitu, Jean, Jules, Kong Ah. Fascinating melding of ethnographic documentary and narrative, about pearl fisherman Matahi and his ill-fated love for young Chevalier, who's been deemed by the gods as taboo to all men. Shot in Tahiti in 1929, produced and scripted by Murnau and Robert Flaherty; the latter left the project in mid-production because of differences in opinion with Murnau—who died in a car accident just prior to the film's premiere. Floyd Crosby's cinematography won an Academy Award.▼●

Taffin (1988-British) **C-96m.** ** D: Francis Megahy. Pierce Brosnan, Ray McAnally, Alison Doody, Jeremy Child, Patrick Bergin. Dull thriller about a bill collector (an uncharismatic Brosnan) and his exploits as he takes on some shady businessmen attempting to build a chemical plant in an Irish village. [R]▼●◗

Taffy and the Jungle Hunter (1965) **C-87m.** ** D: Terry O. Morse. Jacques Bergerac, Manuel Padilla, Shary Marshall, Hari Rhodes. Unassuming tale of son of big game hunter who takes off for jungle adventures with pet elephant and chimp.▼

Tag: The Assassination Game (1982) **C-92m.** ** D: Nick Castle. Robert Carradine, Linda Hamilton, Kristine De Bell, Bruce Abbott, Michael Winslow, Frazer Smith. A role-playing game, played by college students with toy guns, turns deadly when one player (Abbott) becomes unhinged and substitutes real bullets. Short on sense and suspense, with some unintended laughs along the way. Aka EVERYBODY GETS IT IN THE END. [PG]▼

Taggart (1964) **C-85m.** **½ D: R. G. Springsteen. Tony Young, Dan Duryea, Peter Duryea, David Carradine, Jean Hale, Harry Carey, Jr., Bob Steele. Neat little action Western based on a Louis L'Amour novel with Young on a revenge hunt, pursued by gunslingers in Indian territory.

Tailor's Maid, The (1957-Italian) **C-92m.** **½ D: Mario Monicelli. Vittorio De Sica, Marcello Mastroianni, Marisa Merlini, Fiorella Mari, Memmo Carotenuto, Raffaele Pisu. Saucy, inconsequential comedy about an amorous tailor. CinemaScope.

Tail Spin (1939) **84m.** ** D: Roy Del Ruth. Alice Faye, Constance Bennett, Nancy Kelly, Joan Davis, Charles Farrell, Jane Wyman, Kane Richmond, Wally Vernon. Hackneyed saga of female flyers, with Faye (in a change-of-pace role) having to scrounge for pennies and face competition from socialite/aviatrix Bennett. Written by Frank "Spig" Wead.

Tai-Pan (1986) **C-127m.** *½ D: Daryl Duke. Bryan Brown, Joan Chen, John Stanton, Tim Guinee, Bill Leadbitter, Russell Wong, Kyra Sedgwick, Bert Remsen, Janine Turner. Spectacularly silly adventure yarn based on James Clavell's sprawling novel about 19th-century trade baron who establishes his headquarters in Hong Kong. So much story is telescoped, and so many accents are poor and plot points handled with sledgehammer subtlety that there's nothing left to do but treat the whole thing as a goof—or skip it altogether. Actually filmed in China, if that matters. J-D-C Scope. [R]▼●

Take, The (1974) **C-93m.** ** D: Robert Hartford-Davis. Billy Dee Williams, Eddie Albert, Vic Morrow, Frankie Avalon, Albert Salmi. Tepid action pic concerns police lieutenant Williams' efforts to stop syndicate chief Morrow while accepting bribe money on the side. Surprisingly neat cameo by Avalon as a cheap crook. [PG]

Take a Chance (1933) **84m.** *½ D: Laurence Schwab, Monte Brice. James Dunn, Cliff Edwards, June Knight, Charles "Buddy" Rogers, Lillian Roth, Dorothy Lee. Awful adaptation of Broadway musical about carnival hucksters aiming for the big time, redeemed somewhat by fine score and campy number with "Ukulele Ike" Edwards.

Take a Giant Step (1959) **100m.** **½ D: Philip Leacock. Johnny Nash, Estelle Hemsley, Ruby Dee, Frederick O'Neal, Ellen Holly, Beah Richards. Earnest but only partly successful account of black teen Nash's problems in a white world. Stagy adaptation of Louis S. Peterson's play benefits from good performances.

Take a Girl Like You (1970-U.S.-British) **C-101m.** **½ D: Jonathan Miller. Hayley

Mills, Oliver Reed, Noel Harrison, Sheila Hancock, John Bird, Aimi MacDonald, Ronald Lacey, Penelope Keith. Hayley's a young schoolteacher intent on staying virginal until her wedding day. Reed and Harrison are intent on proving otherwise. Pleasant fare with good cast. Based on a Kingsley Amis novel. [R]▼

Take a Hard Ride (1975) **C-109m.** ** D: Anthony Dawson (Antonio Margheriti). Jim Brown, Lee Van Cleef, Fred Williamson, Catherine Spaak, Jim Kelly, Dana Andrews, Barry Sullivan, Harry Carey, Jr. Oddball Western filmed in Canary Islands. Brown must carry large bankroll across Mexican border, attracts a colorful band of "comrades" for his journey, runs afoul of bandit Van Cleef. Good personalities wasted in blah script. [PG]▼

Take a Letter, Darling (1942) **93m.** *** D: Mitchell Leisen. Rosalind Russell, Fred MacMurray, Constance Moore, Robert Benchley, Macdonald Carey, Dooley Wilson, Cecil Kellaway. Witty repartee as advertising exec Roz hires MacMurray as secretary, but relationship doesn't end there. Benchley is wry as Russell's game-playing business partner.

Take Care of My Little Girl (1951) **C-93m.** ** D: Jean Negulesco. Jeanne Crain, Dale Robertson, Mitzi Gaynor, Jean Peters, Jeffrey Hunter, George Nader, Helen Westcott. Overdramatic story of sorority life at college.

Take Down (1978) **C-107m.** *** D: Kieth Merrill. Edward Herrmann, Kathleen Lloyd, Lorenzo Lamas, Maureen McCormick, Nick Beauvy, Kevin Hooks, Stephen Furst. Seriocomic look at high school wrestling, focusing on rebellious student Lamas and reluctant coach Herrmann. Well done.▼

Take Her, She's Mine (1963) **C-98m.** ** D: Henry Koster. James Stewart, Sandra Dee, Audrey Meadows, Robert Morley, Philippe Forquet, John McGiver, Bob Denver, Irene Tsu. Obvious family comedy with Stewart the harried father of wild teen-age daughter Dee. Predictable gags don't help. Script by Nunnally Johnson, from the Broadway hit by Phoebe and Henry Ephron; later ripped-off by THE IMPOSSIBLE YEARS. Look for James Brolin in airport scene. CinemaScope.

Take It or Leave It (1944) **70m.** *½ D: Benjamin Stoloff. Phil Baker, Phil Silvers, Edward Ryan, Marjorie Massow, Stanley Prager, Roy Gordon. Claptrap hinged on lives of contestants on popular quiz show; film uses clips from older pictures to liven proceedings.

Take Me Out to the Ball Game (1949) **C-93m.** *** D: Busby Berkeley. Frank Sinatra, Esther Williams, Gene Kelly, Betty Garrett, Edward Arnold, Jules Munshin, Richard Lane, Tom Dugan. Contrived but colorful turn-of-the-century musical, with Williams taking over Sinatra and Kelly's baseball team. "O'Brien to Ryan to Goldberg" and Kelly's "The Hat My Father Wore on St. Patrick's Day" are musical highlights.▼●

Take Me to Town (1953) **C-81m.** **½ D: Douglas Sirk. Ann Sheridan, Sterling Hayden, Philip Reed, Lee Patrick, Lane Chandler, Lee Aaker. Unpretentious Americana of saloon singer Sheridan on the lam, finding love with widowed preacher Hayden and his three children.

Take One False Step (1949) **94m.** **½ D: Chester Erskine. William Powell, Shelley Winters, Marsha Hunt, James Gleason, Sheldon Leonard, Dorothy Hart, Felix Bressart. Ex-flame Winters attempts to seduce now-married educator Powell, leading to his becoming a wanted man. OK mystery-drama, adapted by Erskine and Irwin Shaw from the novel by Shaw and his brother David.

Take the High Ground (1953) **C-101m.** *** D: Richard Brooks. Richard Widmark, Karl Malden, Elaine Stewart, Steve Forrest, Carleton Carpenter, Russ Tamblyn, Jerome Courtland. Taut account of infantry basic training with on-location filming at Fort Bliss, Texas, helping.

Take the Money and Run (1969) **C-85m.** *** D: Woody Allen. Woody Allen, Janet Margolin, Marcel Hillaire, Jacquelyn Hyde; narrator, Jackson Beck. Woody's first film as director/writer/star is full of funny ideas, telling documentary-style, life story of compulsive thief. Nonstop parade of jokes; some work, some don't, but the ones that *do* are a riot! Louise Lasser seen briefly. [M/PG]▼●◗

Take This Job and Shove It (1981) **C-100m.** **½ D: Gus Trikonis. Robert Hays, Art Carney, Barbara Hershey, David Keith, Tim Thomerson, Martin Mull, Eddie Albert, Penelope Milford. Hays returns to his hometown with orders from his conglomerate to modernize an old-fashioned brewery . . . but being with his old cronies, and one-time girlfriend, effects a change of attitude. Unpretentious film named after 70s hit record by Johnny Paycheck has Capraesque flavor at times, but eventually settles for obvious formula schtick. [PG]▼

Taking Care of Business (1990) **C-107m.** **½ D: Arthur Hiller. James Belushi, Charles Grodin, Anne DeSalvo, Loryn Locklin, Stephen Elliott, Hector Elizondo, Veronica Hamel, Mako, Gates McFadden, John de Lancie, Terrence McNally. At the outset of a weekend business trip, Grodin loses his pocket organizer, which holds the keys to his very existence; escaped convict Belushi finds the combination wallet and appointment book, and assumes Grodin's identity for an eventful weekend. Cute comedy, with Belushi's most appealing role to date . . . but goes on a bit too long. [R]▼●

Taking of Beverly Hills, The (1991) **C-118m.** ** D: Sidney J. Furie. Ken Wahl, Matt Frewer, Harley Jane Kozak, Robert Davi, Lee Ving James, Branscombe Richmond, Lyman Ward, Michael Bowen, William Prince, Ken Swofford, George Wyner. The owner of L.A.'s pro football team masterminds a false toxic spill, which allows his flunkies to loot the estates of Beverly Hills' rich-and-famous while the owners are temporarily whisked away to shelter. Quarterback Wahl ends up *literally* lobbing a few bombs in this speedy stupidity, which languished unreleased for well over a year. Look for Pamela Anderson as a cheerleader. Panavision. [R]▼●

Taking Off (1971) **C-93m.** ***½ D: Milos Forman. Lynn Carlin, Buck Henry, Linnea Heacock, Audra Lindley, Paul Benedict, Georgia Engel. Forman's first American film is beguilingly funny look at American life-styles from two generations' point of view, centering on runaway girl (Heacock) who drives parents (Carlin, Henry) into new experiences of their own. Carly Simon seen as one of auditioning singers. [R]

Taking of Flight 847, The: The Uli Derickson Story (1988) **C-100m. TVM** D: Paul Wendkos. Lindsay Wagner, Eli Danker, Sandy McPeak, Ray Wise, Leslie Easterbrook, Laurie Walters, Joseph Nasser. Taut drama about the real-life 1985 hijacking and the flight attendant credited with saving all but one of the passengers' lives. Wagner is surprisingly good heading a no-name cast, but keep an eye on Danker, chillingly on-target as the unstable leader of the hijackers who speaks no English. A number of Emmy nominations went to this film, but none to writer Norman Morrill. Video title: THE FLIGHT. Above average.▼

Taking of Pelham One Two Three, The (1974) **C-104m.** ***½ D: Joseph Sargent. Walter Matthau, Robert Shaw, Martin Balsam, Hector Elizondo, Earl Hindman, Dick O'Neill, Jerry Stiller, Tony Roberts, Lee Wallace, Doris Roberts, Kenneth McMillan, Julius Harris, James Broderick, Sal Viscuso. Ruthless Shaw and three cohorts hijack N.Y.C. subway train, hold passengers for one million in cash—to be delivered *in one hour!* Outstanding thriller, laced with cynical comedy, bursts with heart-stopping excitement, terrific performances, and first-rate editing. Crackerjack Peter Stone screenplay greatly improves John Godey's bestseller; pulsating score by David Shire. Remade for TV in 1998. Panavision. [R]▼●◗

Talented Mr. Ripley, The (1999) **C-139m.** **½ D: Anthony Minghella. Matt Damon, Gwyneth Paltrow, Jude Law, Cate Blanchett, Philip Seymour Hoffman, Jack Davenport, James Rebhorn, Sergio Rubini, Philip Baker Hall, Celia Weston, Lisa Eichhorn. An unscrupulous (and penniless) young man accepts a job from an American millionaire to find his wastrel son in Italy and convince him to come home. Instead, Tom Ripley (Damon) befriends the young man and aspires to live his carefree life . . . at any price. Two-thirds of a really good movie; Minghella's free adaptation of Patricia Highsmith's novel goes adrift toward the end. Attractive cast and gorgeous views of Italy compensate. Worth comparing to earlier version of same story, PURPLE NOON. Dennis Hopper plays Tom Ripley in THE AMERICAN FRIEND. [R]▼◗

Talent for Loving, A (1969) **C-110m.** ** D: Richard Quine. Richard Widmark, Topol, Cesar Romero, Genevieve Page, Judd Hamilton, Caroline Munro. Rambunctious Western concerning a professional gambler trapped into marrying within rich Mexican family cursed by the Aztecs with a talent for loving. From Richard Condon's novel. Video title: GUN CRAZY. [PG]▼

Talent for the Game (1991) **C-91m.** *½ D: Robert M. Young. Edward James Olmos, Lorraine Bracco, Jamey Sheridan, Terry Kinney, Jeffrey Corbett. Cliché-ridden story of California Angels baseball scout Olmos, who discovers a superior pitching talent on an Idaho farm. Kinney is slimy as a billionaire who buys the team. This struck out in its scant theatrical release and went right to the showers—er, the video shelves. [PG]▼●

Talent Scout (1937) **62m.** *½ D: William Clemens. Donald Woods, Jeanne Madden, Fred Lawrence, Rosalind Marquis, Charles Halton. Tacky B musical about a Hollywood talent scout and the girl he promotes to stardom. The only fun is anticipating the clichéd dialogue scene by scene.

Tale of Africa, A SEE: **Afurika Monogatari**

Tale of a Vampire (1992-British-Japanese) **C-93m.** *½ D: Shimako Sato. Julian Sands, Suzanna Hamilton, Kenneth Cranham, Marian Diamond, Michael Kenton. London: Lonely vampire Sands becomes attracted to librarian Hamilton, who resembles his lost love . . . but mysterious Cranham is keeping an eye on both of them. Horror thriller emphasizes romance; it's good looking and well acted, but ponderous and pretentious. [R]▼

Tale of Five Women, A (1951-British) **86m.** *½ D: Romollo Marcellini, Geza von Cziffra, Wolfgang Staudte, E. E. Reinert, Montgomery Tully. Bonar Colleano, Barbara Kelly, Anne Vernon, Lana Morris, Karen Humbold, Lily Kahn, Eva Bartok, Gina Lollobrigida. Magazine editor Kelly accompanies amnesiac RAF officer to visit lovers in five cities, hoping to jar his memory. Disappointingly dull multi-episode film. Originally titled A TALE OF FIVE CITIES, running 99m.▼

Tale of Springtime, A (1989-French) **C-112m.** *** D: Eric Rohmer. Anne

Teyssedre, Hugues Quester, Florence Darel, Eloise Bennett, Sophie Robin. Typically refreshing, perceptive Rohmer concoction, about high school philosophy teacher Teyssedre; she meets and befriends young Darel, who tries to match her up with her father. Not his best work, but a little Rohmer goes a long way. The first of the filmmaker's "Tales of the Four Seasons," followed by A TALE OF WINTER.▼

Tale of Two Cities, A (1917) **70m.** *** D: Frank Lloyd. William Farnum, Jewel Carmen, Joseph Swickard, Herschell Mayall, Rosita Marstini. Ambitious silent-film version of Dickens story was a big hit in 1917, and it's easy to see why: Farnum is an appealing hero, production is first rate, and battle scenes are reminiscent of Griffith's INTOLERANCE.▼

Tale of Two Cities, A (1935) **128m.** **** D: Jack Conway. Ronald Colman, Elizabeth Allan, Edna May Oliver, Reginald Owen, Basil Rathbone, Blanche Yurka, Isabel Jewell, Walter Catlett, Henry B. Walthall, H.B. Warner, Donald Woods. Dickens' panorama of the 1780s French Revolution becomes an MGM blockbuster, with Colman as carefree lawyer awakened to responsibility, aiding victims of the Reign of Terror. Stage star Blanche Yurka creates a memorable Mme. Defarge in her film debut. Tremendous cast in a truly lavish production. Written for the screen by W.P. Lipscomb and S.N. Behrman. Also shown in computer-colored version.▼●

Tale of Two Cities, A (1958-British) **117m.** *** D: Ralph Thomas. Dirk Bogarde, Dorothy Tutin, Cecil Parker, Stephen Murray, Athene Seyler, Christopher Lee, Donald Pleasence, Ian Bannen. Faithful retelling of Dickens story in this well-made British production, with Bogarde a good Sydney Carton. Remade again for TV in 1980.▼

Tale of Two Cities, A (1980) **C-156m. TVM** D: Jim Goddard. Chris Sarandon, Peter Cushing, Kenneth More, Barry Morse, Flora Robson, Billie Whitelaw, Alice Krige. Seventh filming of the Dickens classic has all the trimmings, but Sarandon can't hold a candle to Ronald Colman as either Sydney Carton or Charles Darnay. John Gay did the script for producer Norman Rosemont, who's been working his way through the literary favorites of the ages for TV. Average.▼

Tale of Winter, A (1992-French) **C-114m.** **½ D: Eric Rohmer. Charlotte Véry, Frédéric Van Den Driessche, Michel Voletti, Hervé Furic, Ava Loraschi, Christiane Desbois. Hairdresser Véry has an affair with an itinerent cook at a beachside resort. They lose touch, and she has his child. She's romanced by two very different suitors, but can't decide upon the one with whom to settle. Bittersweet allegory about not accepting second-best in love; however, it's difficult to sympathize with Véry's flaky character. The second of Rohmer's "Tales of the Four Seasons."▼

Tales From the Crypt (1972-British) **C-92m.** **½ D: Freddie Francis. Ralph Richardson, Peter Cushing, Joan Collins, Richard Greene, Patrick Magee, Ian Hendry, Nigel Patrick. Five stories of terror involving deceit, mayhem, and a few well-timed laughs. Nothing extraordinary, however; based on the old E. C. comics. Followed by VAULT OF HORROR. [PG]▼

Tales From the Crypt, Part II SEE: **Vault of Horror**

Tales From the Crypt Presents Bordello of Blood SEE: **Bordello of Blood**

Tales From the Crypt Presents Demon Knight (1995) **C-92m.** ** D: Ernest Dickerson. Billy Zane, William Sadler, Jada Pinkett, Brenda Bakke, CCH Pounder, Thomas Hayden Church, Charles Fleischer, Dick Miller. Tepid terror tale of a dashing demon and avenging angel vying for the souls of a band of outsiders (town drunkard, lonely prostitute, etc.). Tries for tongue-in-cheek humor but only supplies some gross-out gore and a fair share of t&a. Based on the HBO TV series. [R]▼●◗

Tales From the Darkside: The Movie (1990) **C-93m.** ** D: John Harrison. Deborah Harry, Matthew Lawrence, Christian Slater, Robert Sedgwick, Julianne Moore, David Johansen (Buster Poindexter), William Hickey, James Remar, Rae Dawn Chong, Robert Klein, Steve Buscemi. Boy imprisoned by suburban cannibal Harry tells her three horror stories—about a walking mummy, a supernatural cat, and a vow made to a gargoyle—to stave off being served as a main course. Good production values, but the stories are tepid; only the third one, by Michael McDowell, has a kick (the first two are by Arthur Conan Doyle and Stephen King). Connection to TV series of the same name is tenuous at best. [R]▼●

Tales From the Hood (1995) **C-98m.** *** D: Rusty Cundieff. Corbin Bernsen, Lamont Bentley, De'Aundre Bonds, Rosalind Cash, Rusty Cundieff, Anthony Griffith, David Alan Grier, Brandon Hammond, Wings Hauser, Sam Monroe, Paula Jai Parker, Joe Torry, Clarence Williams III, Tom Wright. Four horror stories with African-American themes are told to three black hoodlums by a bizarre mortician (Williams). The first (a walking corpse) and the third (vengeful dolls) are standard plots with a racial twist, but the second (boy terrorized by monster at his door) and the fourth (gang member subjected to behavior modification) are something different. Good direction, colorful acting, and nifty effects put this above average for horror anthologies of any color. Spike Lee was the executive producer. [R]▼●◗

Tales of Beatrix Potter SEE: **Peter Rabbit and Tales of Beatrix Potter**

Tales of Hoffmann, The (1951-British) **C-118m.** **½ D: Michael Powell, Emeric Pressburger. Moira Shearer, Robert Rounseville, Leonide Massine, Robert Helpmann, Pamela Brown. Jacques Offenbach's fantasy opera of student who engages in bizarre dreams, revealing three states of his life. Striking and offbeat film, not for all tastes. Cut from original 127m.; laserdisc release is restored to the original length. Famous score conducted by Sir Thomas Beecham. ▼●◗

Tales of Manhattan (1942) **118m.** *** D: Julien Duvivier. Charles Boyer, Rita Hayworth, Henry Fonda, Ginger Rogers, Charles Laughton, Edward G. Robinson, Ethel Waters, Paul Robeson, Eddie "Rochester" Anderson, Thomas Mitchell, Cesar Romero, George Sanders. Charming film about the effect a dress tailcoat has on its various owners; five episodes, alternately amusing, poignant, ironic. Our favorite: down and out Robinson attending 25th class reunion. Pictorially stylish throughout; photographed by Joseph Walker. Video has 9m. W. C. Fields episode deleted from original theatrical release.▼

Tales of Ordinary Madness (1983-Italian) **C-107m.** *½ D: Marco Ferreri. Ben Gazzara, Ornella Muti, Susan Tyrrell, Tanya Lopert, Roy Brocksmith. Pretentious swill about poet Gazzara who boozes endlessly and meets the oddest assortment of women. Gazzara, and especially Tyrrell, have never been worse. Based on stories by Charles Bukowski.▼●◗

Tales of Robin Hood (1951) **60m.** *½ D: James Tinling. Robert Clarke, Mary Hatcher, Paul Cavanagh, Wade Crosby. Minor account of folklore hero consisting of episodes of unsold TV series.

Tales of Terror (1962) **C-90m.** *** D: Roger Corman. Vincent Price, Peter Lorre, Basil Rathbone, Debra Paget, Maggie Pierce, Leona Gage, Joyce Jameson. Four Edgar Allan Poe stories distilled by Richard Matheson into three-part film, with Lorre's comic performance as vengeful husband walling up adulterous wife the standout. Price appears in all three segments. Odd widescreen and color effects will suffer on small screen. Panavision.▼●

Tales That Witness Madness (1973-British) **C-90m.** *½ D: Freddie Francis. Kim Novak, Georgia Brown, Joan Collins, Jack Hawkins, Donald Houston, Peter McEnery, Suzy Kendall, Donald Pleasence. Absurd collection of four lame *Twilight Zone*–like stories. A waste of time and talent. [R]▼

Talion SEE: **Eye for an Eye, An** (1966)

Talk About a Stranger (1952) **65m.** *** D: David Bradley. George Murphy, Nancy Davis (Reagan), Billy Gray, Kurt Kasznar, Lewis Stone. A lonely boy tries to prove reclusive neighbor Kasznar killed his dog. Good use of California orchard locations, well-judged direction and John Alton's moody photography result in a fine little B that deserves to be better known.

Talkin' Dirty After Dark (1991) **C-86m.** *½ D: Topper Carew. Martin Lawrence, John Witherspoon, Phyllis Yvonne Stickney, Jedda Jones, "Tiny" Lister, Jr., Darryl Sivad. A night in the life of a black L.A. comedy club, on-stage and off; broad (to say the least), energetically vulgar, and poorly made. Pretty much a waste of film—and time. [R]▼●

Talk of Angels (1998) **C-96m.** **½ D: Nick Hamm. Polly Walker, Frances McDormand, Vincent Perez, Franco Nero, Marisa Paredes, Penelope Cruz, Rossy de Palma, Francisco Rabal, Ariadna Gil, Ruth McCabe. An Irish governess for a wealthy Spanish family falls in love with their married anarchist son. Strong supporting cast and sumptuous period detail can't quite make up for lackluster script and lethargic lead performances from Walker and Perez. McDormand is good in a small role as a repressed lesbian. [PG-13]▼●◗

Talk of the Town, The (1942) **118m.** **** D: George Stevens. Jean Arthur, Ronald Colman, Cary Grant, Glenda Farrell, Edgar Buchanan, Charles Dingle, Rex Ingram, Emma Dunn, Tom Tyler, Lloyd Bridges. Intelligent comedy with brilliant cast; fugitive Grant hides out with unsuspecting professor Colman and landlady Arthur, and tries to convince legal-minded Colman there's a human side to all laws. Splendid film written by Irwin Shaw and Sidney Buchman.▼●

Talk Radio (1988) **C-110m.** **½ D: Oliver Stone. Eric Bogosian, Alec Baldwin, Ellen Greene, Leslie Hope, John C. McGinley, John Pankow, Michael Wincott. Eric Bogosian's one-set play (written with Ted Savinar) is fleshed out for this feature film about an abrasive talk-show host who puts down his many callers but can't get his own life together. Well acted, extremely well shot and directed, but one's enjoyment may depend on one's tolerance for this kind of talk-radio host. Stone and Bogosian collaborated on the screenplay, which also incorporated elements of Steven Singular's book *Talked to Death: The Life and Murder of Alan Berg.* [R]▼●

Tall Blond Man With One Black Shoe, The (1972-French) **C-90m.** *** D: Yves Robert. Pierre Richard, Bernard Blier, Jean Rochefort, Mireille Darc, Jean Carmet. Engaging French farce with rival secret agents making life a shambles for the Tall Blond Man (Richard) who's been innocently pegged a spy. Followed by RETURN OF . . . in 1974 and an American remake (THE MAN WITH ONE RED SHOE) in 1985. [PG]▼

Tall, Dark and Handsome (1941) **78m.**

**½ D: H. Bruce Humberstone. Cesar Romero, Virginia Gilmore, Charlotte Greenwood, Milton Berle, Sheldon Leonard, Stanley Clements, Marc Lawrence, Frank Jenks. Amusing Runyonesque gangster comedy about an underworld bigwig (Romero) who's really a softie, and who falls for naive Gilmore. Leonard is the heavy, a role Romero played in the remake, LOVE THAT BRUTE.

Tall Guy, The (1989-British) **C-90m.** **½ D: Mel Smith. Jeff Goldblum, Emma Thompson, Rowan Atkinson, Emil Wolk, Geraldine James, Kim Thomson, Anna Massey. Quirky comedy of downtrodden American actor Goldblum living in London, playing second banana to a vile star comedian (Atkinson) in a West End revue. Love, allergies, naked strangers, and the lead in a wickedly inspired musical version of *The Elephant Man* ensue. Gawky Goldblum is great in this spotty satire. Atkinson, director Smith, and writer Richard Curtis are British TV comedy veterans. [R]▼●

Tall in the Saddle (1944) **87m.** *** D: Edwin L. Marin. John Wayne, Ella Raines, Ward Bond, Gabby Hayes, Elisabeth Risdon, Raymond Hatton, Paul Fix, Audrey Long. Fast-paced, entertaining Western with Wayne a cowhand who becomes involved in affairs of rancher Raines. Also shown in computer-colored version.▼●

Tall Lie, The SEE: **For Men Only**

Tall Man Riding (1955) **C-83m.** **½ D: Lesley Selander. Randolph Scott, Dorothy Malone, Peggie Castle, John Dehner, Lane Chandler. Sturdy Western with Scott involved in outmaneuvering greedy ranchers during territorial land granting in Montana.

Tall Men, The (1955) **C-122m.** ** D: Raoul Walsh. Clark Gable, Jane Russell, Robert Ryan, Cameron Mitchell, Juan Garcia, Harry Shannon, Emile Meyer, Mae Marsh. Large-scale Western with Gable and Mitchell as ex-Rebels who sign on for Ryan's cattle drive, and in short order all three are fighting Indians, blizzards, and each other (over Russell, of course). Pretty dull, considering stars and director. CinemaScope.▼

Tall Story (1960) **91m.** **½ D: Joshua Logan. Anthony Perkins, Jane Fonda, Ray Walston, Marc Connelly, Anne Jackson, Murray Hamilton, Elizabeth Patterson, Bob Wright, Bart Burns, Gary Lockwood. Fast-moving froth about man-hungry coed Fonda (in film debut) falling in love with college basketball star Perkins. Based on Howard Lindsay-Russel Crouse play.▼●

Tall Stranger, The (1957) **C-81m.** ** D: Thomas Carr. Joel McCrea, Virginia Mayo, Michael Ansara, Michael Pate. Standard fare of McCrea helping wagon convoy cross Colorado territory. Based on a Louis L'Amour novel. CinemaScope.

Tall T, The (1957) **C-78m.** *** D: Budd Boetticher. Randolph Scott, Richard Boone, Maureen O'Sullivan, Henry Silva, Skip Homeier, John Hubbard, Arthur Hunnicutt. Scott becomes involved with kidnapped O'Sullivan, and tries to undermine unity of outlaw gang holding them prisoner. Solid Western all the way, scripted by Burt Kennedy from an Elmore Leonard story.▼

Tall Tale (1995) **C-96m.** ** D: Jeremiah Chechik. Patrick Swayze, Oliver Platt, Roger Aaron Brown, Nick Stahl, Scott Glenn, Stephen Lang, Jared Harris, Catherine O'Hara, Moira Harris, Joseph Grifasi, John P. Ryan, Scott Wilson. Misfired revisionist take on tall-tale heroes Pecos Bill, Paul Bunyan, John Henry, and Calamity Jane, who (in an extended dream sequence) enter the life of an unhappy young boy whose farmer father is being threatened by an evil land developer. Follows a *Wizard of Oz* story structure, but its dark, neurotic tone obliterates the occasional moments of wonder. O'Hara has little more than a cameo as Calamity Jane; Burgess Meredith appears unbilled. Panavision. [PG] ▼●

Tall Target, The (1951) **78m.** *** D: Anthony Mann. Dick Powell, Paula Raymond, Adolphe Menjou, Marshall Thompson, Ruby Dee, Will Geer. Gripping suspense as detective Powell follows tip that Abraham Lincoln is going to be assassinated during 1861 train ride. Interestingly, Powell's character is named John Kennedy!

Tall Texan, The (1953) **82m.** ** D: Elmo Williams. Lloyd Bridges, Lee J. Cobb, Marie Windsor, Luther Adler, Syd Saylor. Good cast cannot uplift this standard Western about a group seeking out a gold deposit in Indian territory. A tale of greed and gold that just doesn't pan out.▼

Tall Women, The (1966-Spanish) **C-101m.** ** D: Sidney Pink. Anne Baxter, Maria Perschy, Rosella Como, John Clarke. Western about seven women making their way through Indian country. Foreign-made movie suffers from bad dubbing and mediocre acting. Techniscope.

Tamahine (1963-British) **C-85m.** ** D: Philip Leacock. Nancy Kwan, John Fraser, Dennis Price, Coral Browne, Dick Dentley, Derek Nimmo, Justin Lord, Michael Gough, James Fox, Allan Cuthbertson. Curious British comedy trifle, about a sheltered but uninhibited Polynesian girl upsetting the order of an upper-crust men's university, might have been retitled *Tamahine, Tell Me True,* since it plays just like a Tammy movie. Cute but forgettable, notable only for its fine British cast. CinemaScope.

Tamango (1957-French) **C-98m.** *** D: John Berry. Dorothy Dandridge, Curt Jurgens, Jean Servais, Roger Hanin, Guy Mairesse, Alex Cressan. Stirring historical drama in which newly enslaved black African Cressan stirs revolt while being transported to Cuba aboard a slave ship. Dandridge is excellent in the complex role of a slave who is ship captain Jurgens' mistress. Way ahead of its time, and ripe for rediscovery. Based on a novelette by Prosper Merimée. CinemaScope.▼

Tamarind Seed, The (1974) **C-123m.** *** D: Blake Edwards. Julie Andrews, Omar Sharif, Anthony Quayle, Daniel O'Herlihy, Sylvia Sims, Oscar Homolka. Well-mounted espionage/romance story set in London, Paris and Barbados; shows what a capable director can do with sappy material. Panavision. [PG]▼

Taming of the Shrew, The (1929) **66m.** ** D: Sam Taylor. Mary Pickford, Douglas Fairbanks, Edwin Maxwell, Joseph Cawthorn, Clyde Cook, Geoffrey Wardell, Dorothy Jordan. Static version of the Shakespeare classic, with wild, shrewish Kate (Pickford) ardently pursued and "tamed" by swaggering, self-confident Petruchio (Fairbanks). Defeated by its lack of pacing and downright embarrassing performances, though it's undeniably fascinating to see Doug and Mary together in their only co-starring appearance. This is the film with the infamous credit, "By William Shakespeare, with additional dialogue by Sam Taylor." Original running time 73m. Newly scored—and shortened—in 1966. Remade in 1967.▼●

Taming of the Shrew, The (1967-U.S.-Italian) **C-126m.** ***½ D: Franco Zeffirelli. Elizabeth Taylor, Richard Burton, Vernon Dobtcheff, Michael Hordern, Natasha Pyne, Michael York, Cyril Cusack, Alan Webb, Victor Spinetti. Colorful version of Shakespeare's romp is well served by Richard and Elizabeth, good supporting cast, lovely photography, and fine musical score by Nino Rota. Shakespeare purists may object, but Zeffirelli has succeeded in making a film instead of a photographed stage play. Scripted by Suso Cecchi d'Amico, Paul Dehn, and Zeffirelli. Filmed before in 1929 with another famous acting couple, Mary Pickford and Douglas Fairbanks. Panavision. ▼●◗

Taming Sutton's Gal (1957) **71m.** *½ D: Lesley Selander. John Lupton, Gloria Talbott, Jack Kelly, May Wynn, Verna Felton. Tedious hokum involving moonshiner's amorous wife. Filmed in Naturama.

T.A.M.I. Show, The (1964) **100m.** *** D: Steve Binder. The Rolling Stones, James Brown, Chuck Berry, Marvin Gaye, The Supremes, Jan and Dean, Gerry & The Pacemakers, Smokey Robinson & The Miracles, Leslie Gore, Billy J. Kramer & The Dakotas. Historic rock and r&b concert at the Santa Monica Civic Auditorium was covered by television cameras and kinescoped onto film by whiz-kid Binder. Invaluable document of music history, with great early Mick Jagger and electrifying footwork by Brown. (Two of those go-go dancers are Teri Garr and Toni Basil!) Originally 113m., with Beach Boys sequence that was later cut (although they're still visible in the finale). Title stands for Teenage Awards Music International. Followed by THE BIG T.N.T. SHOW; see also THAT WAS ROCK.▼

Tam Lin SEE: **Ballad of Tam Lin**

Tammy and the Bachelor (1957) **C-89m.** *** D: Joseph Pevney. Debbie Reynolds, Walter Brennan, Leslie Nielsen, Mala Powers, Fay Wray, Sidney Blackmer, Mildred Natwick, Louise Beavers. Unpretentious if cutesy romantic corn of country girl Reynolds falling in love with pilot Nielsen whom she's nursed back to health after plane crash. Followed by two sequels and a TV series. CinemaScope.▼

Tammy and the Doctor (1963) **C-88m.** **½ D: Harry Keller. Sandra Dee, Peter Fonda, Macdonald Carey, Beulah Bondi, Margaret Lindsay, Reginald Owen, Adam West. Sugary fluff involving homespun Tammy (Dee) courted by a doctor (Fonda, in his film debut); supporting cast adds touching cameos.▼

Tammy and the Millionaire (1967) **C-87m.** ** D: Sidney Miller, Ezra Stone, Leslie Goodwins. Debbie Watson, Frank McGrath, Denver Pyle, George Furth, Donald Woods, Dorothy Green. Four episodes of the TV series spliced into low-grade feature, diluting the fuzzy folksy charm of backwoods girl trying to better the world.

Tammy Tell Me True (1961) **C-97m.** ** D: Harry Keller. Sandra Dee, John Gavin, Virginia Grey, Beulah Bondi, Cecil Kellaway, Edgar Buchanan. Tired romance of girl coming to college for first time, makes name for herself by helping dean of women. Script and acting very uneven.

Tampico (1944) **75m.** ** D: Lothar Mendes. Edward G. Robinson, Lynn Bari, Victor McLaglen, Marc Lawrence, Mona Maris. Robinson uplifts this otherwise obvious WW2 spy yarn, about a supply-ship captain contending with espionage; Bari is the femme fatale who may or may not be the guilty party.

Tampopo (1986-Japanese) **C-114m.** ***½ D: Juzo Itami. Ken Watanabe, Tsutomu Yamakazi, Nobuko Miyamoto, Koji Yakusho. Funny, original comedy-satire about one of everybody's favorite subjects: food. The scenario, which unravels as a series of vignettes, concerns a truck driver who helps a widow make her noodle shop a viable business. A clever, irreverent delight.▼●◗

T&A Academy SEE: **H.O.T.S.**

Tanganyika (1954) **C-81m.** ** D: Andre de Toth. Van Heflin, Ruth Roman, Howard Duff, Jeff Morrow. OK adventure of explorer attempting land claim in East Africa with numerous perils along the way.

Tangier (1946) **76m.** **½ D: George Waggner. Maria Montez, Preston Foster, Robert Paige, Louise Allbritton, Kent Taylor, Sabu, J. Edward Bromberg, Reginald Denny. Limp intrigue in Tangier with vengeful dancer Montez; it isn't even in color.

Tangier Incident (1953) **77m.** *½ D: Lew Landers. George Brent, Mari Aldon, Dorothy Patrick, Bert Freed. Tame actioner with Brent a federal agent hunting an espionage ring.

Tango (1998-Argentinian-Spanish) **C-114m.** *** D: Carlos Saura. Miguel Àngel Solà, Cecilia Narova, Mia Maestro, Juan Carlos Copes, Julio Bocca, Juan Luis Galiardo. Mesmerizing film, not unlike Saura's earlier CARMEN, in which the planning of a performance blurs the line between drama and real life. A middle-aged choreographer plans an ambitious tango piece, which (to the dismay of his backers) will also trace the recent history of Argentina. He also becomes involved with his leading dancer, until now the girlfriend of his principal backer. Long, but full of incredible moments and superlative dance numbers; sinuously photographed by Vittorio Storaro. Univision. [PG-13]▼●◗

Tango & Cash (1989) **C-98m.** ** D: Andrei Konchalovsky. Sylvester Stallone, Kurt Russell, Teri Hatcher, Jack Palance, Brion James, James Hong, Marc Alaimo. Rumored $55 million budget must have gone for male hairstyling in congenitally derivative narc caper about two competitive cops who take on Mr. Big. Surprisingly tolerable, though, with a nifty prison break sequence and a pleasingly relaxed Stallone performance. Panavision. [R] ▼●◗

Tango Bar (1988-Puerto Rican-Argentinian) **C-90m.** *** D: Marcos Zurinaga. Raul Julia, Valeria Lynch, Ruben Juarez. Perceptive, entertaining "political musical" about a tango dancer who left Argentina when the military coup occurred, and is now reunited with her longtime partner Julia after ten years in exile. Serves as both an anthology of the tango, and a tale of Argentina's recent political history. Crammed with clips of film and TV personalities, from Fred Astaire to Fred Flintstone, doing the tango.▼

Tango Lesson, The (1997-U.S.-French-Argentinean) **C/B&W-101m.** *** D: Sally Potter. Sally Potter, Pablo Veron, Carlos Copello, Olga Besio, Caroline Iotti, Gustavo Naveira. A middle-aged British filmmaker named Sally (played by Potter) promises to cast in a movie a distinguished Argentinean tango dancer named Pablo (Veron, who is the same) if he only will give her dance lessons. Film charts their evolving relationship. Striking, provocative (not to mention highly risky and deeply personal) film which blends fiction and reality. Nicely photographed (mostly in black-and-white) by Robby Müller. [PG]▼

Tank (1984) **C-113m.** ** D: Marvin Chomsky. James Garner, G.D. Spradlin, C. Thomas Howell, Shirley Jones, Jenilee Harrison, James Cromwell, Dorian Harewood. One-dimensional rehash of SUPPOSE THEY GAVE A WAR AND NOBODY CAME? turns that film's shades of gray into simplistic good-guy/bad-guy story. Teenage son of career military man is wrongfully jailed by vindictive redneck sheriff; Dad goes to rescue him with the help of his own Sherman tank. Odd to find Garner in such a cornball movie. [PG]▼●◗

Tank Force (1958-British) **C-81m.** *½ D: Terence Young. Victor Mature, Leo Genn, Anthony Newley, Luciana Paluzzi. Clichéd dud of WW2 with assorted British prisoners escaping across Libyan desert. Originally titled NO TIME TO DIE. CinemaScope.

Tank Girl (1995) **C-104m.** ** D: Rachel Talalay. Lori Petty, Ice-T, Naomi Watts, Don Harvey, Jeff Kober, Reg E. Cathey, Scott Coffey, Malcolm McDowell, Stacy Lynn Ramsower, Ann Cusack, Brian Wimmer, Iggy Pop, James Hong. In the waterless future of 2033, tough, smart-mouthed survivor Petty joins forces with mutated kangaroos to combat evil McDowell, who schemes to corner the world's water. Aggressively trendy, self-consciously hip, with animated interludes and attitude enough to spare, this might have worked had it been well directed—but it's not. Petty is a lot of fun, though. Based on the British comic book. Super 35. [R]▼●

Tanks Are Coming, The (1951) **90m.** ** D: Lewis Seiler, D. Ross Lederman. Steve Cochran, Philip Carey, Mari Aldon, Paul Picerni, Harry Bellaver, James Dobson. Moderate WW2 actioner set during Allied capture of Berlin.▼

Tap (1989) **C-110m.** *** D: Nick Castle. Gregory Hines, Suzzanne Douglas, Sammy Davis, Jr., Savion Glover, Joe Morton, Dick Anthony Williams, Terrence McNally, Sandman Sims, Bunny Briggs, Steve Condos, Jimmy Slyde, Pat Rico, Arthur Duncan, Harold Nicholas, Etta James. Slight, old-fashioned but engaging story of a man who shuns his tap-dancing heritage for the good life and easy money he can make pulling jewel robberies . . . until the call of the tap is just too strong. A loving tribute to tap, with some clever contemporary touches by writer-director Castle (whose same-named father was a top choreographer). Hines has never been better; Davis is a standout as Little Mo (in his final feature film), and the challenge dance with old-time hoofers is a special treat. [PG-13]▼●

Tapeheads (1988) **C-97m.** ** D: Bill Fishman. John Cusack, Tim Robbins, Doug McClure, Connie Stevens, Clu Gulager, Mary Crosby, Katy Boyer, Lyle Alzado, Jessica Walter, Susan Tyrrell, Junior Walker, Sam Moore. Energetic but pretentious and silly account of Cusack and Robbins' escapades and adventures as they try to make it in the L.A. music world. Too clever for its own good. Robbins coscripted, and wrote the song "Repave America," which later turned up in his film BOB ROBERTS. [R]▼●

Tap Roots (1948) **C-109m.** **½ D: George Marshall. Van Heflin, Susan Hayward, Boris Karloff, Julie London, Whitfield Connor, Ward Bond, Richard Long, Arthur Shields. Oddball venture into GWTW territory, with Van and Susan as lovers in progressive Mississippi county that says it will secede from the state if the state secedes from the Union! No big deal, but watchable, with Karloff as an Indian medicine man.

Taps (1981) **C-126m.** **½ D: Harold Becker. Timothy Hutton, George C. Scott, Ronny Cox, Sean Penn, Tom Cruise, Brendan Ward. Hutton leads fellow students in armed takeover of their military academy, hoping their "clout" will keep it from being torn down. Earnest performances help carry this film, which plays all its cards too soon, leaving a lot of dead space before its predictable outcome. Penn's film debut. [PG]▼

Tarantula (1955) **80m.** *** D: Jack Arnold. John Agar, Mara Corday, Leo G. Carroll, Nestor Paiva, Ross Elliott, Eddie Parker. Scientist Carroll's new growth formula works a little *too* well, and pretty soon there's a humongous spider chewing up the countryside. One of the best giant-insect films, with fast pacing, convincing special effects, and interesting subplot detailing formula's effect on humans. That's Clint Eastwood as the jet squadron leader in final sequence.▼●

Taras Bulba (1962) **C-122m.** **½ D: J. Lee Thompson. Tony Curtis, Yul Brynner, Christine Kaufmann, Sam Wanamaker, George Macready. Cardboard costumer of 16th-century Ukraine, centering on Cossack life and fighting. Nice photography (on location in Argentina) by Joe MacDonald and fine musical score by Franz Waxman. The Gogol novel was previously filmed in 1936 in France (TARASS BOULBA) and in 1939 in England (THE REBEL SON). Panavision.▼●

Tarawa Beachhead (1958) **77m.** **½ D: Paul Wendkos. Kerwin Mathews, Julie Adams, Ray Danton, Karen Sharpe. Standard account of WW2 military assault with usual focus on problems of troops.

Target (1985) **C-117m.** ** D: Arthur Penn. Gene Hackman, Matt Dillon, Gayle Hunnicutt, Victoria Fyodorova, Josef Sommer, Guy Boyd, Herbert Berghof. Ordinary guy and his teenage son are suddenly plunged into world of international intrigue when wife/mom is kidnapped while vacationing in Paris. Some good action scenes help, but story is so farfetched, key scenes so badly written, and film so overlong that it has to count as a misfire. Reteaming of Hackman and director Penn certainly promised better. [R]▼●

Target (1995-Indian) **C-122m.** *** D: Sandip Ray. Om Puri, Mohan Agashe, Anian Srivastava, Baroon Champa Chakravarty. Intimate story of working-class life in India, directed by the son of Satyajit Ray from his late father's screenplay. A *gangato,* a hunter of the lowest caste (Puri), is hired by a rich and nasty landowner (Agashe) to lead his next safari. The hunter has to live with the landowner's oppressed peasants, and before long he rebels. Stunning countryside locations shot by Barun Raha, who worked on the elder Ray's last three films.

Target Eagle (1984-Spanish-Mexican) **C-99m.** **½ D: Jose Antonio de la Loma. George (Jorge) Rivero, Maud Adams, George Peppard, Max von Sydow, Chuck Connors. Fine cast perks up routine programmer with Rivero as an eagle-tattooed mercenary hired by Spanish police chief von Sydow(!) to infiltrate a drug-smuggling ring. Peppard is excellent in unusual casting as a suave but ruthless villain. ▼

Target Earth (1954) **75m.** **½ D: Sherman Rose. Richard Denning, Virginia Grey, Kathleen Crowley, Richard Reeves, Whit Bissell, Robert Ruark, Steve Pendleton. People in deserted city trapped by invading robot force. Competently acted movie starts off beautifully but bogs down too soon.▼●

Target: Embassy SEE: **Embassy**

Target for Killing (1966-Austrian) **C-93m.** *½ D: Manfred Kohler. Stewart Granger, Curt Jurgens, Adolfo Celi, Klaus Kinski, Rupert Davies, Scilla Gabel, Mollie Peters, Erika Remberg. Run-of-the-mill thriller involving a secret agent trying to thwart the Mob's intended killing of a young heiress.▼

Target: Harry (1969) **C-81m.** *½ D: Henry Neill (Roger Corman). Vic Morrow, Suzanne Pleshette, Victor Buono, Cesar Romero, Stanley Holloway, Charlotte Rampling, Michael Ansara, Ahna Capri. Humdrum redoing of THE MALTESE FALCON, with the three stars mirroring Bogart, Astor, and Greenstreet. Originally shot for TV. Aka HOW TO MAKE IT. [R]

Target of an Assassin (1976-South African) **C-102m.** ** D: Peter Collinson. Anthony Quinn, John Phillip Law, Simon Sabela, Marius Weyers, Sandra Prinsloo. Fairish thriller story about two men who conspire against black African leader—one, a paid assassin, the other a desperate down-and-outer who kidnaps him for ransom. Original title: TIGERS DON'T CRY; aka THE LONG SHOT, AFRICAN RAGE, and FATAL ASSASSIN. [PG]▼

Targets (1968) **C-90m.** ***½ D: Peter Bogdanovich. Boris Karloff, Tim O'Kelly, Nancy Hsueh, James Brown, Sandy Baron, Arthur Peterson, Peter Bogdanovich, Randy Quaid. Karloff (as more or less himself) intends to retire, claiming his films can't compete with the horrors of everyday life; meanwhile, O'Kelly proves it by going out and shooting everybody in sight. Bogdanovich's first feature is incredibly suspenseful, with sweat-inducing climax at drive-in theatre; excellent photography by Laszlo Kovacs. Some prints still have brief gun-control prologue, which was added after Robert Kennedy's assassination. That's Mike Farrell as victim in phone booth. [PG—originally rated R]▼

Target Unknown (1951) **90m.** ** D: George Sherman. Mark Stevens, Alex Nicol, Robert Douglas, Don Taylor, Gig Young, Joyce Holden, James Best. Standard drama of American flyers shot down and becoming POWs in German-occupied France during WW2; Nazis use devious means to interrogate them. Young has interesting role as German-American Nazi officer.

Target Zero (1955) **92m.** ** D: Harmon Jones. Richard Conte, Charles Bronson, Chuck Connors, L.Q. Jones, Peggie Castle, Strother Martin. Unrewarding Korean War film, focusing on plight of Lt. Conte as he leads his platoon behind enemy lines.

Tarnished Angels, The (1958) **91m.** ***½ D: Douglas Sirk. Rock Hudson, Dorothy Malone, Robert Stack, Jack Carson, Robert Middleton, Troy Donahue, William Schallert. Compelling adaptation of William Faulkner's fatalistic drama *Pylon,* set in 1930s, with Hudson as newspaperman drawn to barnstorming pilot Stack—his curious life-style and ethics, his put-upon wife, and his frustrated mechanic. CinemaScope.▼

Tarnished Lady (1931) **83m.** **½ D: George Cukor. Tallulah Bankhead, Clive Brook, Phoebe Foster, Osgood Perkins, Elizabeth Patterson. Bankhead marries Brook for his money but falls in love with him almost too late. Ornate triangle has good performances.

Tars and Spars (1946) **88m.** ** D: Alfred E. Green. Alfred Drake, Janet Blair, Sid Caesar, Marc Platt, Jeff Donnell, Ray Walker. Humdrum musical with Coast Guard backdrop, based very loosely on real-life camp show created by servicemen, one of whom, Sid Caesar, makes his movie debut doing a hilarious war-movie spoof. A rare film appearance for Broadway star Drake.

Tartars, The (1961-Italian) **C-83m.** ** D: Richard Thorpe. Orson Welles, Victor Mature, Folco Lulli, Liana Orfei. Welles' performance as Burundai, head of Tartar invasion of Volga River, plus appearance of Mature, are only distinguishing features of otherwise routine spectacle. Totalscope.

Tartu SEE: **Adventures of Tartu**

Tarzan Several generations of movie buffs have regarded Johnny Weissmuller as the definitive Tarzan, though Edgar Rice Burroughs' jungle king has been portrayed by numerous others since 1918, when beefy Elmo Lincoln first swung onto the screen. There were other silent-film versions of the Tarzan tale, but the next film to make a major impact was the early talkie TARZAN, THE APE MAN (1932), which starred Olympic swimming hero Weissmuller. Though it wasn't particularly faithful to Burroughs' book, it was an entertaining, well-made film that captured the imagination of a Depression-era audience, and led to a string of equally entertaining sequels. Buffs generally cite TARZAN AND HIS MATE (1934) as the best of all. This and the other 1930s entries in this series were "class" films with fine production values, plenty of action, and strong supporting casts, led, of course, by lovely Maureen O'Sullivan as Jane. (The success of these films inspired other producers to try and cash in with their own Tarzan projects, most of which were second-rate endeavors, though they all starred good-looking men who, like Weissmuller, had been Olympic medal winners: Buster Crabbe, Herman Brix—later known as Bruce Bennett—and Glenn Morris.) The later MGM outings such as TARZAN'S NEW YORK ADVENTURE became more contrived, like other series films, with often-excessive comedy relief supplied by Cheetah the chimp, and family interest sparked by the arrival of Johnny Sheffield as Boy. When MGM lost interest in the series, Weissmuller continued making Tarzan movies for producer Sol Lesser at RKO, without O'Sullivan and without that MGM production sheen. Lex Barker took over the role in 1949, and the series became progressively more routine; Barker did his last jungle outing in 1955. Since then a number of people have played Tarzan, including Denny Miller (who starred in a 1959 remake of Weissmuller's 1932 film, filled with tinted stock footage from the original), Jock Mahoney (who also played supporting roles in two other Tarzan films), Mike Henry, and Gordon Scott, the latter faring best in some well-produced British-made adventure stories (including TARZAN'S GREATEST ADVENTURE, an excellent jungle tale shot in color, with young Sean Connery in the cast). Ron Ely took on the role for a Mexican-filmed TV series, and some of these episodes have been strung together into ersatz feature films. But the most recent theatrical ventures involving Tarzan have all been unusual: an unappealing animated spoof called SHAME OF THE JUNGLE featuring the voice of Johnny Weissmuller, Jr.; a live-action farce called TARZAN, THE APE MAN designed as a showcase for sexy Bo Derek; a television update, with tongue in cheek, called TARZAN IN MANHATTAN; and the most ambitious of them all, GREYSTOKE: THE LEGEND OF TARZAN, LORD OF THE APES, which purported to return to Edgar Rice Burroughs' original concept but (for all its dramatic success) deviated from the source in its own way. Compared to a film like GREYSTOKE, the old series films might look simplistic and even quaint—but they're unpretentious and certainly entertaining. And while generations still think of Johnny Weissmuller as the definitive Tarzan, each decade brings new interpretations of the timeless character—the latest in animated form from Disney.

TARZAN

Tarzan of the Apes (1918)
Tarzan, the Ape Man (1932)
Tarzan the Fearless (1933)
Tarzan and His Mate (1934)
New Adventures of Tarzan (1935)
Tarzan Escapes (1936)
Tarzan's Revenge (1938)
Tarzan and the Green Goddess (1938)
Tarzan Finds a Son! (1939)
Tarzan's Secret Treasure (1941)
Tarzan's New York Adventure (1942)
Tarzan Triumphs (1943)
Tarzan's Desert Mystery (1943)
Tarzan and the Amazons (1945)
Tarzan and the Leopard Woman (1946)
Tarzan and the Huntress (1947)
Tarzan and the Mermaids (1948)
Tarzan's Magic Fountain (1949)
Tarzan and the Slave Girl (1950)
Tarzan's Peril (1951)
Tarzan's Savage Fury (1952)
Tarzan and the She-Devil (1953)
Tarzan's Hidden Jungle (1955)
Tarzan and the Lost Safari (1957)
Tarzan's Fight for Life (1958)
Tarzan and the Trappers (1958)
Tarzan's Greatest Adventure (1959)
Tarzan, the Ape Man (1959)
Tarzan the Magnificent (1960)
Tarzan Goes to India (1962)
Tarzan's Three Challenges (1963)
Tarzan and the Valley of Gold (1966)
Tarzan and the Great River (1967)
Tarzan and the Jungle Boy (1968)
Tarzan's Jungle Rebellion (1970)
Tarzan's Deadly Silence (1970)
Tarzan, the Ape Man (1981)
Greystoke: The Legend of Tarzan, Lord of the Apes (1984)
Tarzan in Manhattan (1989)
Tarzan and the Lost City (1998)
Tarzan (1999)

Tarzan (1999) **C-88m.** *** D: Kevin Lima, Chris Buck. Voices of Tony Goldwyn, Minnie Driver, Glenn Close, Rosie O'Donnell, Brian Blessed, Nigel Hawthorne, Lance Henriksen, Wayne Knight. Vibrant animated Disney take on Edgar Rice Burroughs' classic character, with brilliant staging, terrific songs (by Phil Collins), and likable characters (especially Jane, colorfully and amusingly voiced by Driver). Storyline, involving a greedy, hot-headed hunter, almost seems too conventional—and predictable—for all the visual innovations and superior efforts that surround it. Oscar winner for Best Song, "You'll Be in My Heart." [G]▼◗

Tarzan and His Mate (1934) **93m.** ***½ D: Cedric Gibbons, Jack Conway. Johnny Weissmuller, Maureen O'Sullivan, Neil Hamilton, Paul Cavanagh, Forrester Harvey. Jane's jilted fiance (Hamilton) returns to the jungle with a rapacious ivory poacher and tries to get Tarzan to lead them to the elephant graveyard, but the native couple is having too much fun swinging. Opulent, action-packed entry codirected by MGM's famed art director Gibbons, and notable for pre-Code sexual candor and a distinct lack of clothes. Restored version runs 105m. ▼●

Tarzan and the Amazons (1945) **76m.** **½ D: Kurt Neumann. Johnny Weissmuller, Brenda Joyce, Johnny Sheffield, Henry Stephenson, Maria Ouspenskaya, Barton MacLane. Archaeologists seeking to plunder Amazon treasures have to deal with Tarzan first in this amusing nonsense highlighted by the diminutive Ouspenskaya as the Amazon Queen!

Tarzan and the Great River (1967) **C-99m.** *½ D: Robert Day. Mike Henry, Jan Murray, Manuel Padilla, Jr., Diana Millay, Rafer Johnson. Childish entry about an Amazonian despot, although borscht-belt comedian Murray is good for a few (unintentional) laughs. Location filming in South America adds little. Panavision.

Tarzan and the Green Goddess (1938) **72m.** *½ D: Edward Kull. Herman Brix (Bruce Bennett), Ula Holt, Frank Baker, Don Castello, Lewis Sargent. More juvenile jungle escapades, with an educated Ape Man. Derived from 1935's THE NEW ADVENTURES OF TARZAN serial, produced by Edgar Rice Burroughs' own company, and filmed on location in Guatemala. Contains footage not used in serial.▼

Tarzan and the Huntress (1947) **72m.** ** D: Kurt Neumann. Johnny Weissmuller, Brenda Joyce, Johnny Sheffield, Patricia Morison, Barton MacLane. Familiar bungle in the jungle about Tarzan fighting a zoologist (Morison) who's trying to make off with a menagerie. Weissmuller was tired by this time, and so were the plots.

Tarzan and the Jungle Boy (1968) **C-99m.** *½ D: Robert Day. Mike Henry, Alizia Gur, Ronald Gans, Rafer Johnson, Ed Johnson, Steven Bond. A tedious search for the son of a drowned geologist, though Henry isn't bad as the Ape Man. Panavision.

Tarzan and the Leopard Woman (1946) **72m.** ** D: Kurt Neumann. Johnny Weissmuller, Brenda Joyce, Johnny Sheffield, Acquanetta, Edgar Barrier, Tommy Cook. Tarzan and Boy take on a murder cult, and almost pay with their lives. The series was becoming increasingly silly by this time, though it's still fun by Saturday matinee standards.

Tarzan and the Lost City (1998-Australian-U.S.-German) **C-105m.** *½ D: Carl Schenkel. Casper Van Dien, Jane March, Steven Waddington, Winston Ntshona, Rapulana Seiphemo, Ian Roberts. Tarzan returns to Africa on eve of his wedding to Jane; she follows, and together they fight off mercenaries trying to plunder the "mythic city" of Opar. Lousy film—even by jungle adventure standards. Van Dien equates jaw-clenching with acting, and he must be the shortest Lord of the Apes on record. Oddly, the producer of this also made the classy GREYSTOKE. Super 35. [PG]▼●◗

Tarzan and the Lost Safari (1957-British) **C-84m.** ** D: H. Bruce Humberstone. Gordon Scott, Yolande Donlan, Robert Beatty, Betta St. John, Wilfrid Hyde-White, George Coulouris. Color and widescreen spruce up this entry about the passengers of a plane that crashes in the jungle, who are pursued by savage Oparians. But Tarzan still speaks in monosyllables, and the story is pretty slow going. RKO-Scope.

Tarzan and the Mermaids (1948) **68m.** **½ D: Robert Florey. Johnny Weismuller, Brenda Joyce, Linda Christian, John Lanenz, George Zucco, Fernando Wagner. Tarzan comes to the aid of a native (stunning Christian) who's being forced to wed a phony island "God" by evil high-priest Zucco. Outlandish, often campy outing filmed in Mexico. Weismuller hung up his loincloth after this, his 12th Tarzan film.

Tarzan and the She-Devil (1953) **76m.** *½ D: Kurt Neumann. Lex Barker, Joyce MacKenzie, Raymond Burr, Monique Van Vooren, Tom Conway. Boring hokum about ivory poachers led by seductive Van Vooren. Barker's last appearance as Tarzan. Burr is an exceptionally good heavy.

Tarzan and the Slave Girl (1950) **74m.** *½ D: Lee Sholem. Lex Barker, Vanessa Brown, Robert Alda, Hurd Hatfield, Arthur Shields, Anthony Caruso, Denise Darcel. A tribe of lion worshippers kidnaps Jane (Brown), making Tarzan an easy target for alluring half-breed Darcel. Low-grade camp.

Tarzan and the Trappers (1958) **74m.** *½ D: Charles Haas, Sandy Howard. Gordon Scott, Eve Brent, Rickie Sorensen, Leslie Bradley. Cheaply made hokum about evil white hunters on an expedition to find a lost city filled with treasure. Edited together from three half-hour episodes for a Tarzan TV series that never got off the ground.▼

Tarzan and the Valley of Gold (1966) **C-90m.** **½ D: Robert Day. Mike Henry, David Opatoshu, Manuel Padilla, Jr., Nancy Kovack, Don Megowan. Ex-football star Henry takes over the loincloth (after doffing his suit and tie!) in a hunt for kidnapers and jewel thieves. This Tarzan-for-the-60's is pretty good, if you can accept the Ape Man as a jungle James Bond. Excellent location filming in Mexico. Panavision.

Tarzan Escapes (1936) **89m.** *** D: Richard Thorpe. Johnny Weissmuller, Maureen O'Sullivan, John Buckler, Benita Hume, William Henry, Herbert Mundin. Graphically violent (for its time), and energetically directed, this entertaining entry has Tarzan captured by a hunter who wants to put him on exhibition in England. This film was completely reshot and reworked when the original version proved too potent and blood-curdling for preview audiences; as a result there are some plot holes in what might have been the best Tarzan movie of all.▼●

Tarzan Finds a Son! (1939) **90m.** *** D: Richard Thorpe. Johnny Weissmuller, Maureen O'Sullivan, Johnny Sheffield, Ian Hunter, Frieda Inescort, Laraine Day, Henry Wilcoxon. The jungle lovers find a child whose parents were killed in a plane crash and fight his greedy relatives to adopt him in this diverting entry. This was to be O'Sullivan's final appearance as Jane, but the end was reshot so she could return (in TARZAN'S SECRET TREASURE).▼●

Tarzan Goes to India (1962-British) **C-86m.** **½ D: John Guillermin. Jock Mahoney, Mark Dana, Simi, Leo Gordon, Jai. At the request of a dying maharajah, Tarzan tries to save a herd of elephants imperiled by the construction of a dam. Location shooting helps. CinemaScope.

Tarzan in Manhattan (1989) **C-100m. TVM** D: Michael Schultz. Joe Lara, Kim Crosby, Tony Curtis, Jan-Michael Vincent, Jimmy Medina Taggert. Tarzan hits the Big Apple when he finds that some no-good guys have been monkeying around with Cheetah, chimpnapping the little guy in Africa on behalf of nasty vivisectionists. Lighthearted pilot to a prospective new series featuring male model Lara as moviedom's 18th Tarzan and Crosby as a Brooklynese cabbie named Jane. Average.◗

Tarzan of the Apes (1918) **55m.** ★★½ D: Scott Sidney. Elmo Lincoln, Enid Markey, True Boardman, Kathleen Kirkham, Gordon Griffith. The very first Tarzan film is a surprisingly watchable and straightforward telling of the Greystoke tale, though Lincoln looks like he's about fifty years old, with a beer belly to boot.▼

Tarzan's Deadly Silence (1970) **C-99m.** ★½ D: Robert L. Friend, Lawrence Dobkin. Ron Ely, Manuel Padilla, Jr., Jock Mahoney, Woody Strode, Gregorio Acosta. A maniacal soldier plans to capture an African village with his private army; a two-part TV episode released as a feature. [G]

Tarzan's Desert Mystery (1943) **70m.** ★★½ D: William Thiele. Johnny Weissmuller, Nancy Kelly, Johnny Sheffield, Otto Kruger, Joseph Sawyer, Lloyd Corrigan, Robert Lowery. Tarzan vs. Nazis, take two, with some evil Arabs and prehistoric creatures (including a giant spider) thrown in for good measure.

Tarzan's Fight for Life (1958) **C-86m.** ★★ D: H. Bruce Humberstone. Gordon Scott, Eve Brent, Rickie Sorensen, Jil Jarmyn, James Edwards, Woody Strode. The jungle do-gooder helps a medic fight superstitious natives and a conniving witch doctor. Cheesy series entry with the cast stomping around a studio jungle set.

Tarzan's Greatest Adventure (1959-British) **C-88m.** ★★★ D: John Guillermin. Gordon Scott, Anthony Quayle, Sara Shane, Niall MacGinnis, Scilla Gabel, Sean Connery. Honorable attempt to upgrade the series' quality, with Tarzan on the trail of diamond-hunting scoundrels (including a young Connery). A superior action yarn shot on location in Africa, more adult than most of its predecessors. Tarzan has a much expanded vocabulary in this one.

Tarzan's Hidden Jungle (1955) **73m.** ★★ D: Harold Schuster. Gordon Scott, Vera Miles, Peter Van Eyck, Jack Elam, Rex Ingram. Scott's debut as Tarzan is a competent, if unexciting, outing focusing on his battle with evil hunter Elam who tries to butcher half the animal kingdom.

Tarzan's Jungle Rebellion (1970) **C-92m.** ★½ D: William Witney. Ron Ely, Manuel Padilla, Jr., Ulla Stromstedt, Sam Jaffe, William Marshall, Lloyd Haynes. Compilation of a two-part episode from the NBC TV series is substandard in all departments. [G]

Tarzan's Magic Fountain (1949) **73m.** ★★½ D: Lee Sholem. Lex Barker, Brenda Joyce, Evelyn Ankers, Albert Dekker, Alan Napier, Charles Drake, Henry Brandon. Barker's first series entry, and one of his most endurable, as Tarzan finds a secret valley where nobody ages—unless they leave. (Sound a bit like LOST HORIZON?) Too bad the rest of the Barker films weren't as good. Elmo Lincoln, the screen's first Tarzan, has a bit part.

Tarzan's New Adventure SEE: **New Adventures of Tarzan, The**

Tarzan's New York Adventure (1942) **72m.** ★★½ D: Richard Thorpe. Johnny Weissmuller, Maureen O'Sullivan, Johnny Sheffield, Virginia Grey, Charles Bickford, Paul Kelly, Russell Hicks, Chill Wills. When Boy is snatched from the jungle by nasty circus owners, Tarzan swings into action across the seas and over the Brooklyn Bridge to retrieve him. Seems pretty original until you realize that KING KONG was made a decade earlier! Still, an amusing entry; Tarzan's first encounter with indoor plumbing is truly memorable. O'Sullivan's final appearance in the series. ▼●

Tarzan's Peril (1951) **79m.** ★★½ D: Byron Haskin. Lex Barker, Virginia Huston, George Macready, Douglas Fowley, Dorothy Dandridge, Alan Napier. White gunrunners out to get Tarzan try to stir up trouble between warring tribes in this fairly respectable entry with an interesting supporting cast. Dandridge is excellent, if wasted in a small role.

Tarzan's Revenge (1938) **70m.** ★★ D: D. Ross Lederman. Glenn Morris, Eleanor Holm, George Barbier, C. Henry Gordon, Hedda Hopper, George Meeker. Olympic decathlon champ Morris cavorts capably enough in this adventure about an evil African ruler who covets perky Holm (a champion swimmer herself). No other Tarzan film had the Ape Man off screen for such long stretches, however.▼

Tarzan's Savage Fury (1952) **80m.** ★★ D: Cyril Endfield. Lex Barker, Dorothy Hart, Patric Knowles, Charles Korvin, Tommy Carlton. Slackly handled entry about diamond thieves who trick Tarzan into being their guide.

Tarzan's Secret Treasure (1941) **81m.** ★★½ D: Richard Thorpe. Johnny Weissmuller, Maureen O'Sullivan, Johnny Sheffield, Reginald Owen, Barry Fitzgerald, Tom Conway. Melodramatic entry about greedy gold seekers who try to dupe Tarzan into helping them. Tarzan and Jane's treehouse has become pretty elaborate by now.▼●

Tarzan's Three Challenges (1963) **C-92m.** ★★½ D: Robert Day. Jock Mahoney, Woody Strode, Ricky Der, Tsuruko Kobayashi, Earl Cameron. Tarzan protects a young heir to the throne in Thailand from his malevolent uncle in this picturesque entry that includes a wicked machete fight. The athletic Mahoney became deathly ill while filming in India—which is all too obvious from his dramatic weight loss during the course of the picture. Dyaliscope.

Tarzan, the Ape Man (1932) **99m.** ★★★ D: W. S. Van Dyke. Johnny Weissmuller, Maureen O'Sullivan, C. Aubrey Smith,

Neil Hamilton, Doris Lloyd. British gentry meets jungle savagery when the daughter of an English hunter is captured by Tarzan and decides she prefers his primal charms to those of her upper-crust fiance. The original Weissmuller-MGM *Tarzan* entry is a little starchy, but still holds up thanks to a plush production and vivid atmosphere (with jungle footage provided by TRADER HORN). Also shown in a computer-colored version.▼●

Tarzan, the Ape Man (1959) **C-82m.** BOMB D: Joseph Newman. Dennis Miller, Joanna Barnes, Cesare Danova, Robert Douglas, Thomas Yangha. Take one blond UCLA basketball star (Miller), the production values of a pep rally, steal Johnny Weissmuller's famous yell and (tinted) footage of him swinging through the air, add a pseudo African jazz score by Shorty Rogers and what you have is a cheesy and inept effort by MGM to utilize safari footage from KING SOLOMON'S MINES for the umpteenth time.

Tarzan, the Ape Man (1981) **C-112m.** BOMB D: John Derek. Bo Derek, Richard Harris, Miles O'Keeffe, John Phillip Law, Wilfrid Hyde-White. Deranged "remake" of original Tarzan film lacks action, humor, and charm—and nearly forced editors of this book to devise a rating lower than BOMB. Forget about Weissmuller comparisons: O'Keeffe makes *Elmo Lincoln* look like Edwin Booth. If you really want to see Derek unclothed, buy a pinup calendar. [R]▼●

Tarzan the Fearless (1933) **85m.** *½ D: Robert Hill. Buster Crabbe, Jacqueline Wells (Julie Bishop), E. Alyn Warren, Edward Woods, Philo McCullough, Mathew Betz, Frank Lackteen, Mischa Auer. Feature version of a crude serial about a scientific expedition to find the lost city of Zar. Crabbe's Tarzan is even more tight-lipped than Weissmuller's.▼

Tarzan the Magnificent (1960-British) **C-88m.** *** D: Robert Day. Gordon Scott, Jock Mahoney, Betta St. John, John Carradine, Alexandra Stewart, Lionel Jeffries, Earl Cameron. Tarzan captures a murderer and faces numerous perils trying to escort him to the police through the jungle. Similarly mature followup to TARZAN'S GREATEST ADVENTURE, with a strong supporting cast. Ironically, villain Mahoney would take over the lead role from Scott in the next entry.

Tarzan Triumphs (1943) **78m.** *** D: William Thiele. Johnny Weissmuller, Frances Gifford, Johnny Sheffield, Stanley Ridges, Sig Ruman. First of the series made by RKO features stunning Gifford (who earlier starred as Edgar Rice Burroughs' JUNGLE GIRL in a Republic serial) as the princess of a lost city invaded by Nazi paratroopers. WW2 propaganda all the way, with Tarzan an incongruous participant, but still an entertaining and energetic programmer. Cheetah's curtain-closing bit with the Nazis' short-wave radio is not to be missed.

Task Force (1949) **116m.** **½ D: Delmer Daves. Gary Cooper, Jane Wyatt, Wayne Morris, Walter Brennan, Julie London, Bruce Bennett, Stanley Ridges, Jack Holt. Well-made but unremarkable story of a Naval officer's career, tracing aircraft carrier development. Originally shown with some scenes in color.▼

Taste of Fear SEE: **Scream of Fear**

Taste of Honey, A (1961-British) **100m.** ***½ D: Tony Richardson. Rita Tushingham, Robert Stephens, Dora Bryan, Murray Melvin, Paul Danquah. Homely young girl who has affair with black sailor and becomes pregnant is cared for by homosexual friend. Shelagh Delaney's London and Broadway stage hit is poignant and uncompromising film with fine, sensitive performances. Screenplay by Delaney and Richardson. ▼

Taste the Blood of Dracula (1970-British) **C-95m.** **½ D: Peter Sasdy. Christopher Lee, Geoffrey Keen, Gwen Watford, Linda Hayden, Roy Kinnear, Ralph Bates. Fourth in Hammer series (after DRACULA HAS RISEN FROM THE GRAVE) with Lee as famed vampire out to avenge death of Black Magic wizard by affluent thrill seekers in Victorian England. Direction, acting, production not bad, but what was point of having Dracula in film? Beginning and end best parts. Sequel: SCARS OF DRACULA. [PG]▼

Tatie Danielle (1991-French) **C-110m.** *** D: Etienne Chatiliez. Tsilla Chelton, Catherine Jacob, Isabelle Nanty, Neige Dolsky, Eric Prat, Laurence Fevrier. Chelton plays an elderly, extremely unpleasant and manipulative widow who wreaks havoc on the people caring for her as she mourns the loss of her husband. Another delight from the director of LIFE IS A LONG QUIET RIVER, but this time the comedy is a good deal blacker. Renowned stage actress Chelton is wonderful as a woman so mean the movie's ads proclaimed her "the *real* Terminator."▼●

Tattered Dress, The (1957) **93m.** **½ D: Jack Arnold. Jeff Chandler, Jeanne Crain, Jack Carson, Gail Russell, George Tobias. Slowly paced but watchable account of lawyer Chandler defending society couple accused of murder; Crain is his sympathetic wife. CinemaScope.

Tattoo (1981) **C-103m.** *½ D: Bob Brooks. Bruce Dern, Maud Adams, Leonard Frey, Rikke Borge, John Getz, Peter Iachangelo. Mentally ill tattoo-artist Dern kidnaps fashion model Adams so he can use her body as a canvas. Improbable, sleazy melodrama; screenplay by Joyce Buñuel (Luis's daughter-in-law) from a story by director Brooks. [R]▼

Tawny Pipit (1944-British) **85m.** ★★½ D: Bernard Miles, Charles Saunders. Bernard Miles, Rosamund John, Niall MacGinnis, Jean Gillie, George Carney, Christopher Steele, Lucie Mannheim, Wylie Watson, Ian Fleming. Slight but appealing story of some English villagers' fight to save the title rare breed of birds, who have nested in a nearby field. Miles and Saunders also scripted.

Taxi! (1932) **70m.** ★★½ D: Roy Del Ruth. James Cagney, Loretta Young, George E. Stone, Dorothy Burgess, Guy Kibbee, Leila Bennett, Cotton Club Orchestra. Hokey but colorful Depression melodrama of warring N.Y.C. cab drivers, with Cagney fine as a hotheaded hack. Yes, that's George Raft as his dance-contest rival. Nothing can top Jimmy's opening bit in Yiddish!

Taxi (1953) **77m.** ★★ D: Gregory Ratoff. Dan Dailey, Constance Smith, Neva Patterson, Blanche Yurka, Stubby Kaye. Mild little comedy of N.Y.C. cab driver Dailey trying to help an Irish girl find her husband. John Cassavetes' film debut.

Taxi Blues (1990-Russian-French) **C-110m.** ★★★½ D: Pavel Lounguine. Piotr Mamonov, Piotr Zaitchenko, Vladimir Kachpour, Natalia Koliakanova, Hal Singer. Controversial, laced-in-acid tragicomedy chronicling the relationship between a brutish, narrow-minded Moscow cabdriver and an alcoholic Jewish musician: characters who become symbols of the Old and New Russia. The former is desperately out of sync with the changing times; the latter, who embodies the spirit of the oppressed Soviet artist-intellectual, plays his saxophone solos to block out the reality of his existence. Lounguine deservedly earned the best director prize at the Cannes Film Festival for this important and provocative film.▼

Taxi Driver (1976) **C-113m.** ★★ D: Martin Scorsese. Robert De Niro, Cybill Shepherd, Harvey Keitel, Peter Boyle, Jodie Foster, Albert Brooks, Leonard Harris, Joe Spinell, Martin Scorsese. To some, Scorsese and writer Paul Schrader's perception of hell—as a crazed taxi driver's vision of N.Y.C.—was brilliant. To us, this gory, cold-blooded story of sick man's lurid descent into violence is ugly and unredeeming. Judge for yourself. Searing performances and Bernard Herrmann's final music score are among film's few virtues. [R]▼●◗

Taxi for Tobruk (1965-French) **90m.** ★★½ D: Denys De La Patelliere. Lino Ventura, Hardy Kruger, Charles Aznavour, German Cobos. Engaging study of French soldiers and their German prisoner crossing the desert during WW2. Dyaliscope.

Taxing Woman, A (1987-Japanese) **C-126m.** ★★★½ D: Juzo Itami. Nobuko Miyamoto, Tsutomo Yamazaki. Disarming contemporary comedy about a tireless, single-minded investigator for the Japanese Revenue Service, and her confrontation with a hotshot businessman who thinks he knows all the angles when it comes to cheating the government. Somewhat overlong, but delightful, with a winning performance by Miyamoto (writer-director Itami's wife) in the lead. Followed by a sequel.▼●◗

Taxing Woman's Return, A (1988-Japanese) **C-127m.** ★★★ D: Juzo Itami. Nobuko Miyamoto, Rentaro Mikuni, Masahiko Tsugawa, Tetsuro Tamba, Toru Masuoka, Takeya Nakamura, Hosei Komatsu, Mihoko Shibata. Miyamoto "returns" as the dedicated tax investigator; here, she takes on a gaggle of industrialists, politicians, mobsters, and other assorted hypocrites who've conspired to grossly inflate Tokyo's real estate values. On-the-mark satire is as pointed and knowing as it is funny.▼

Taxman, The (1999) **C-100m.** ★★ D: Avi Nesher. Joe Pantoliano, Robert Townsend, Wade Dominguez, Michael Chiklis, Elizabeth Berkley, Fisher Stevens, Casey Siemaszko, Mike Starr. Investigator for the N.Y. state tax office becomes obsessed with a trail he's certain leads to big-time criminal activities involving Russian immigrants in Brighton Beach. Rare leading role for Pantoliano, who's in fine form, but story lags and characters are not fully drawn. Based on a true story written by a former tax investigator. [R]▼◗

Taza, Son of Cochise (1954) **C-79m.** ★★½ D: Douglas Sirk. Rock Hudson, Barbara Rush, Gregg Palmer, Bart Roberts, Morris Ankrum, Joe Sawyer. Actually two sons: one wants to live peacefully with the white man, the other thinks Geronimo has a better idea. Sirk's only Western is uneven followup to BROKEN ARROW—with Jeff Chandler popping in just long enough to die—but sweeping action scenes and sympathetic treatment of Indians help. Originally in 3-D.

Tea and Sympathy (1956) **C-122m.** ★★★ D: Vincente Minnelli. Deborah Kerr, John Kerr, Leif Erickson, Edward Andrews, Darryl Hickman, Dean Jones, Norma Crane. Glossy but well-acted version of Robert Anderson play about prep school boy's affair with a teacher's wife, skirting homosexual issues. Both Kerrs give sensitive portrayals. Scripted by the playwright. All three stars (including Erickson) recreate their Broadway roles. CinemaScope.▼●

Teacher, The (1974) **C-98m.** ★★ D: Hikmet Avedis. Angel Tompkins, Jay North, Anthony James, Marlene Schmidt, Sivi Aberg, Barry Atwater, Med Flory. Trashy but enjoyable film has "older" woman Tompkins introducing North (TV's *Dennis the Menace* all grown up) to sex, while a psychopathic killer (James) threatens both their lives. John

Cassavetes' and Gena Rowlands' mommies have cute cameos as disapproving bystanders in a restaurant scene. [R]▼●

Teacher and the Miracle, The (1961-Italian) **88m.** **½ D: Aldo Fabrizi. Eduardo Nevola, Marco Paolette, Mary Lamar, Jose Calvo. Good tear-jerker of man broken by death of son who had inspired him to start art school. Cast gives adequate performance.

Teachers (1984) **C-106m.** ** D: Arthur Hiller. Nick Nolte, JoBeth Williams, Judd Hirsch, Ralph Macchio, Lee Grant, Richard Mulligan, Allen Garfield, Royal Dano, Laura Dern, Morgan Freeman, William Schallert, Crispin Glover, Zohra Lampert, Art Metrano. "Outrageous" blend of comedy-drama set in urban high school (and filmed in Columbus, Ohio). Seemingly patterned after Paddy Chayefsky's THE HOSPITAL and NETWORK but nowhere near as good. Slick, well cast, but dramatically disjointed and obvious at every turn. [R]▼●

Teacher's Pet (1958) **120m.** *** D: George Seaton. Clark Gable, Doris Day, Gig Young, Mamie Van Doren, Nick Adams, Charles Lane. Self-educated city editor Gable clashes with journalism teacher Day in this airy, amusing comedy. Young is memorable as Doris' intellectual boyfriend. Written by Fay and Michael Kanin. VistaVision. ▼●

Teaching Mrs. Tingle (1999) **C-95m.** *½ D: Kevin Williamson. Helen Mirren, Katie Holmes, Barry Watson, Marisa Coughlan, Liz Stauber, Jeffrey Tambor, Michael McKean, Molly Ringwald, Vivica A. Fox. When they confront a coldhearted teacher who can destroy their college dreams, three high school students accidentally knock her out, then tie her to her bed in order to talk her into changing her ways. Preposterous premise is devoid of story, interest or suspense, with only Mirren's icy, sarcastic performance to recommend it. Williamson (making his directing debut) scripted, but this is a far cry from SCREAM. Lesley Ann Warren appears unbilled. [PG-13]▼◗

Tea for Two (1950) **C-98m.** **½ D: David Butler. Doris Day, Gordon MacRae, Gene Nelson, Patrice Wymore, Eve Arden, Billy De Wolfe, S. Z. Sakall, Bill Goodwin, Virginia Gibson. Pleasant but unexceptional musical very loosely based on the stage play *No, No, Nanette* (which was filmed before in 1930 and 1940). Day bets uncle Sakall she can answer no to every question for the length of a weekend—in order to win her chance to star in a Broadway show.▼●

Teahouse of the August Moon, The (1956) **C-123m.** ***½ D: Daniel Mann. Marlon Brando, Glenn Ford, Machiko Kyo, Eddie Albert, Paul Ford, Henry (Harry) Morgan. Outstanding comedy scripted by John Patrick from his hit play of army officers involved with Americanization of post-WW2 Okinawa. A warm and memorable film. Paul Ford recreates his Broadway role and nearly steals the show. Based on book by Vern J. Sneider. CinemaScope.▼●

Teamster Boss: The Jackie Presser Story (1992) **C-110m. TVM** D: Alastair Reid. Brian Dennehy, Jeff Daniels, Maria Conchita Alonso, Eli Wallach, Robert Prosky, Donald Moffat, Tony Lo Bianco, Kate Reid, Henderson Forsythe, Al Waxman. Another firebrand performance by a padded (!) Dennehy, acting up a storm in the powerful script by veteran Abby Mann, based on James Neff's book, *Mobbed Up*. This one got the jump on Nicholson's HOFFA. Made for cable. Above average.▼

Tea with Mussolini (1999-Italian-British) **C-117m.** *** D: Franco Zeffirelli. Cher, Maggie Smith, Judi Dench, Joan Plowright, Lily Tomlin, Baird Wallace, Charlie Lucas, Massimo Ghini, Paolo Seganti, Paul Checquer. A boy whose mother has died and whose father has all but abandoned him is raised by a group of eccentric British women in 1930s Florence. The coming of war has great impact on the women—known as the Scorpioni—and their flamboyant American counterparts in the artsy expatriate community, but cannot sever ties between the young man and his "surrogate mothers." Entertaining if not always focused comedy-drama based on director Zeffirelli's own experiences as a youth; co-scripted by John Mortimer. [PG]▼◗

Teckman Mystery, The (1954-British) **89m.** ** D: Wendy Toye. Margaret Leighton, John Justin, Meier Tzelniker, Roland Culver, George Coulouris, Michael Medwin. Justin is writer commissioned to do a biography of Medwin, presumably dead war hero, with surprising results. Capably acted.

Ted & Venus (1991) **C-100m.** *½ D: Bud Cort. Bud Cort, James Brolin, Kim Adams, Carol Kane, Rhea Perlman, Woody Harrelson, Martin Mull, Timothy Leary, Cassandra Peterson, Gena Rowlands. Cort's directing debut is a hard-to-take tale of an obnoxious Southern California misfit who relentlessly pursues his "dream woman." Cameos by familiar faces add little to this modest production. [R]▼

Teenage Bad Girl SEE: **Bad Girl**

Teenage Caveman (1958) **66m.** ** D: Roger Corman. Robert Vaughn, Darrah Marshall, Leslie Bradley, Frank De Kova. Vaughn, light years away from THE YOUNG PHILADELPHIANS or S.O.B., is the title character, a prehistoric adolescent hankering for greener pastures, in this AIP quickie with predictable "surprise" ending. Superama.▼

Teen-age Crime Wave (1955) **77m.** BOMB D: Fred F. Sears. Tommy Cook, Sue English, Molly McCart, Frank Griffin, James Bell, Ray Riehl. Adolescent hoodlums terrorize farm family after a robbery and shooting. Bad.▼

Teenage Devil Dolls (1952) **58m.** BOMB D: B. Lawrence Price, Jr. Barbara Marks, Robert A. Sherry, Robert Norman, Elaine Lindenbaum, Joel Climenhaga. Yet another entry in the REEFER MADNESS school of filmmaking, about an insecure, discontented teen girl's descent into drug addiction and crime. Presented as a case history and without dialogue; there's only narration and special effects. Originally titled ONE-WAY TICKET TO HELL.▼

Teenage Doll (1957) **68m.** ** D: Roger Corman. June Kenney, Fay Spain, Richard Devon, Dorothy Neumann. Title dish doesn't want to spend school nights at home in her room, gets involved with punk peers. This above-average sleazy B won't obscure memory of Dreyer and Ozu, but is true to its era.▼

Teenage Dream SEE: **Flying**

Teen-age Millionaire (1961) **84m.** BOMB D: Lawrence Doheny. Jimmy Clanton, ZaSu Pitts, Rocky Graziano, Diane Jergens, Chubby Checker, Jackie Wilson, Dion, Marv Johnson, Bill Black, Jack Larson, Vicki Spencer, Sid Gould, Maurice Gosfield. Deadening musical about teenager Clanton, with a huge inheritance, who becomes a pop star. The rock acts are unusually and annoyingly tame here.

Teenage Mutant Ninja Turtles (1990) **C-93m.** ** D: Steve Barron. Judith Hoag, Elias Koteas, voices of Robbie Rist, Kevin Clash, Brian Tochi, David McCharen, Corey Feldman. Four mutated turtles who live in the sewers of N.Y.C. with their ninja master (an oversized rat from Japan) befriend a plucky TV reporter and help crack an insidious crime wave. The wacked-out comic book creation of Kevin Eastman and Peter Laird (which led to a hit animated TV series) should have inspired a much better movie. Badly written, flatly directed, and murky-looking, it jump-starts every now and then—but not often enough. Strongest asset is the design and articulation of the Turtles by Jim Henson's Creature Shop. Followed by two sequels. [PG] ▼●◗

Teenage Mutant Ninja Turtles II: The Secret of the Ooze (1991) **C-88m.** *½ D: Michael Pressman. Paige Turco, David Warner, Ernie Reyes, Jr., Michelan Sisti, Leif Tilden, Kenn Troum, Mark Caso, Kevin Clash, Francois Chav, Toshishiro Obata, Raymond Serra, Kevin Nash, Vanilla Ice. The evil Shredder finds one remaining container of the ooze that caused the turtles to mutate in the first place. Brainless sequel aims lower than first film, and strips the half-shell heroes of any personality (even having them call each other by nicknames—Raf instead of Raphael, Donny instead of Donatello). Appearance by Vanilla Ice, performing a ninja turtle rap song, is the nadir. [PG]▼●

Teenage Mutant Ninja Turtles III (1993) **C-96m.** ** D: Stuart Gillard. Elias Koteas, Paige Turco, Stuart Wilson, Sab Shimono, Vivian Wu, Mark Caso, Matt Hill, Jim Raposa, David Fraser, James Murray. The guys bolt the sewer for feudal Japan to help rebel villagers conquer an evil lord. SEVEN SAMURAI it ain't (nor Russ Meyer's THE SEVEN MINUTES, either), but those who still care will find a more mellowed-out Turtles saga, complete with a lecture by Raphael on the dangers of violence. Like totally Woodstock, dude! [PG]▼●

Teenage Psycho Meets Bloody Mary, The SEE: **Incredibly Strange Creatures Who Stopped Living and Became Mixed-Up Zombies, The**

Teen-age Rebel (1956) **94m.** **½ D: Edmund Goulding. Ginger Rogers, Michael Rennie, Betty Lou Keim, Mildred Natwick, Rusty Swope, Warren Berlinger, Lilli Gentle, Louise Beavers, Irene Hervey. Pat yet provocative film of divorcée Rogers, now remarried, trying to reestablish understanding with her daughter. CinemaScope.

Teenagers Battle the Thing SEE: **Curse of Bigfoot, The**

Teenagers From Outer Space (1959) **86m.** BOMB D: Tom Graeff. David Love, Dawn Anderson, Harvey B. Dunn, Bryant Grant, Tom Lockyear (Tom Graeff). Ridiculous sci-fi about alien youths who bring monster to Earth, shown as the shadow of a lobster! Very, very cheap; but still a camp classic. Besides directing and starring, Graeff wrote, produced, photographed, and edited!▼

Teenage Zombies (1958) **73m.** BOMB D: Jerry Warren. Don Sullivan, Steve Conte, Katherine Victor, Paul Pepper, Bri Murphy, Mitzi Albertson. Victor captures teenagers snooping around her island, imprisons them for experiments. Typically awful Warren horror film with long stretches in which nothing happens . . . and incidentally, no teenage zombies! Remade as FRANKENSTEIN ISLAND.▼

Teen Witch (1989) **C-105m.** ** D: Dorian Walker. Robyn Lively, Dan Gauthier, Joshua Miller, Dick Sargent, Zelda Rubinstein, Lisa Fuller, Shelley Berman. Teen comedy with a moral, about a girl who, one week before her sixteenth birthday, learns that she's a descendant of some bona fide Salem witches . . . and uses her newfound magical powers to snare a football hero as boyfriend. Some nice ideas, but mostly falls flat. Berman is funny as a stuffy English teacher who becomes a victim of the teenage witch's black magic. [PG-13]▼

Teen Wolf (1985) **C-91m.** ** D: Rod Daniel. Michael J. Fox, James Hampton, Scott Paulin, Susan Ursitti, Jerry Levine, Jim MacKrell. Teenager with usual growing pains discovers that he's also a were wolf—and that this finally makes him popular at school. Pleasant at best, but anemic comedy has nowhere to go. Best moments come from TV comedy writer-producer (and former comic) Jay Tarses as Fox's athletic coach. Followed by an animated TV series and TEEN WOLF TOO. [PG]▼●

Teen Wolf Too (1987) **C-95m.** BOMB D: Christopher Leitch. Jason Bateman, Kim Darby, John Astin, Paul Sand, James Hampton, Mark Holton. Limp comedy, chronicling the adventures of the Teen Wolf's cousin (Bateman), makes the original seem like Preston Sturges in his prime. Excruciating. [PG]▼

Telefon (1977) **C-102m.** *** D: Don Siegel. Charles Bronson, Lee Remick, Donald Pleasence, Tyne Daly, Patrick Magee, Alan Badel, Sheree North. Slick espionage thriller from Walter Wager's ingenious novel; Bronson is Russian agent sent to stop crazy defector from triggering hypnotized spies to commit sabotage throughout U.S. Daly is terrific as wisecracking computer expert. Script by Stirling Silliphant and original director Peter Hyams. [PG]▼

Telephone, The (1988) **C-82m.** BOMB D: Rip Torn. Whoopi Goldberg, Severn Darden, Amy Wright, Elliott Gould, John Heard. Goldberg may have hit rock bottom with this clinker in which she's cast as an out-of-work actress with major psychological problems. The star sued to prevent this version from being released. Terrible script by Harry Nilsson and Terry Southern. Hang up on this wrong number. Actor Torn's directing debut. [R]▼●

Telling Lies in America (1997) **C-101m.** *** D: Guy Ferland. Kevin Bacon, Brad Renfro, Maximilian Schell, Calista Flockhart, Paul Dooley, Jonathan Rhys Myers, Luke Wilson. Evocative and well-done Joe Eszterhas-scripted memoir, set in Cleveland during the early 1960s, about a Hungarian-born teen (Renfro), an outsider trying to find his place in pre-Beatles rock 'n roll America. Bacon is the standout here, offering an award-calibre performance as the boy's mentor, a slick, payola-taking disc jockey. Super 35. [PG-13]▼●◗

Tell It to the Judge (1949) **87m** **½ D: Norman Foster. Rosalind Russell, Robert Cummings, Gig Young, Marie McDonald, Harry Davenport, Douglass Dumbrille. Flyweight marital farce with Russell and Cummings in and out of love every ten minutes; enjoyable if you like the stars.▼

Tell Me a Riddle (1980) **C-90m** **½ D: Lee Grant. Melvyn Douglas, Lila Kedrova, Brooke Adams, Dolores Dorn, Bob Elross, Joan Harris, Zalman King. Thoughtful but static filmization of Tillie Olsen's novella chronicling the relationship between a dying woman and her husband of 40 years. Well acted by Douglas and Kedrova; Grant's first feature as director. That's Peter Coyote as the young Douglas. [PG]▼

Tell Me Lies (1968-British) **C-118m.** ** D: Peter Brook. Glenda Jackson, The Royal Shakespeare Company, Kingsley Amis, Stokely Carmichael, Paul Scofield. Strange, unsuccessful combination of songs, skits, and newsreel footage attacking U.S. involvement in Vietnam wasn't even liked by doves. Interesting now merely as historical document.

Tell Me That You Love Me, Junie Moon (1970) **C-112m.** ***½ D: Otto Preminger. Liza Minnelli, Ken Howard, Robert Moore, James Coco, Kay Thompson, Fred Williamson, Nancy Marchand, Anne Revere. Moving story of three misfits who decide to live together: facially scarred Minnelli, epileptic Howard, wheelchair-bound homosexual Moore. Moments of comedy, melodrama, compassion expertly blended by Preminger in one of his best films; adapted from her novel by Marjorie Kellogg. [PG]

Tell No Tales (1938) **69m.** **½ D: Leslie Fenton. Melvyn Douglas, Louise Platt, Gene Lockhart, Douglass Dumbrille, Sara Haden, Florence George, Zeffie Tilbury. Editor tries to save his dying newspaper by capturing notorious kidnappers himself. Good B picture with some telling vignettes (particularly a black boxer's wake), though it doesn't hold up to the finish.

Tell-Tale Heart, The (1963-British) **81m.** **½ D: Ernest Morris. Laurence Payne, Adrienne Corri, Dermot Walsh, Selma Vaz Dias. Atmospheric Edgar Allan Poe yarn about a meek librarian who becomes obsessed, sexually and otherwise, with his pretty new neighbor—but she shows more of an interest in his charming and good-looking best friend.▼

Tell Them Willie Boy Is Here (1969) **C-96m.** *** D: Abraham Polonsky. Robert Redford, Katharine Ross, Robert Blake, Susan Clark, Barry Sullivan, Charles McGraw, John Vernon. Massive manhunt for Indian who killed in self-defense pretends to be more important than it is, but is so well-crafted the preaching can be overlooked. Moodily photographed by Conrad Hall. The blacklisted Polonsky's first film since FORCE OF EVIL twenty-one years before. Panavision. [PG—originally rated M]▼●

Temp, The (1993) **C-96m.** ** D: Tom Holland. Timothy Hutton, Lara Flynn Boyle, Faye Dunaway, Dwight Schultz, Oliver Platt, Steven Weber, Colleen Flynn, Scott Coffey, Dakin Matthews. Another "(Fill in the blank) From Hell" movie—this one suggesting what Eve Harrington might have been like with a psychotic streak and a penchant for office work instead of backstage-Broadway groupiedom. Surprisingly bearable until office casualties sparked by schemer Boyle's temporary employment become way too silly. [R]▼●

Tempest (1928) **102m.** *** D: Sam Taylor. John Barrymore, Camilla Horn, Louis Wolheim, George Fawcett, Ullrich Haupt, Michael Visaroff. Lushly filmed tale of

Russian Revolution, with peasant Barrymore rising to rank of sergeant, controlling fate of Princess (Horn) who had previously scorned him.▼

Tempest (1959-Italian) **C-125m.** **½ D: Alberto Lattuada. Silvana Mangano, Van Heflin, Viveca Lindfors, Geoffrey Horne, Oscar Homolka, Robert Keith, Agnes Moorehead, Finlay Currie, Vittorio Gassman, Helmut Dantine. Turgid, disjointed costumer set in 18th-century Russia, loosely based on Pushkin novel about peasant uprising to dethrone Catherine the Great (Lindfors). Technirama.

Tempest (1982) **C-140m.** ** D: Paul Mazursky. John Cassavetes, Gena Rowlands, Susan Sarandon, Vittorio Gassman, Raul Julia, Molly Ringwald, Sam Robards, Paul Stewart, Anthony Holland. Aimless comedy, loosely based on Shakespeare's play, has Cassavetes as a N.Y.C. architect who tries to solve his midlife crisis by moving to a Greek island with his teenage daughter. Appealing cast, beautiful scenery, some engaging scenes . . . but they don't quite add up. [PG]▼

Temptation (1946) **98m.** **½ D: Irving Pichel. Merle Oberon, George Brent, Paul Lukas, Charles Korvin, Lenore Ulric, Ludwig Stossel. Woman-with-a-past Oberon marries archeologist Brent, then falls in love with unscrupulous Korvin. Nothing new, but smoothly done.

Tempter, The (1974-Italian) **C-96m.** BOMB D: Alberto de Martino. Carla Gravina, Mel Ferrer, Arthur Kennedy, George Coulouris, Alida Valli, Umberto Orsini. Frenzied but pointless rip-off of THE EXORCIST with Gravina as Ferrer's demonized daughter. Blecch. [R]▼

Temptress, The (1926) **117m.** **½ D: Fred Niblo. Greta Garbo, Antonio Moreno, Roy D'Arcy, Marc MacDermott, Lionel Barrymore, Virginia Brown Faire. Garbo's second American film is dated curio about wicked woman who drives men to death and destruction, only to have her own life ruined by falling in love with Moreno. Adapted from Blasco-Ibanez; some prints run 95m.

Temptress Moon (1996-Hong Kong-Chinese) **C-127m.** ** D: Chen Kaige. Gong Li, Leslie Cheung, Zhou Yemang, Kevin Lin, He Saifei, Zhang Shi. Elaborate epic, set in and around Shanghai in the 1920s, about the long and involved relationship between a boy and girl raised together in an ancestral palace—and their renewed relationship in adult life after the former becomes an underworld character. There's opium, blackmail, implied incest, you name it—but so little cohesion that the U.S. distributor had to affix the equivalent of a baseball scoreboard at the movie's beginning so that audiences would know what was happening. [R]▼

10 (1979) **C-122m.** ** D: Blake Edwards. Dudley Moore, Julie Andrews, Bo Derek, Robert Webber, Dee Wallace, Sam Jones, Brian Dennehy, Max Showalter, Don Calfa, Nedra Volz, James Noble, Doug Sheehan. Middle-aged songwriter finds himself hung up on sex, especially when he sets eyes on beautiful Derek. Blake Edwards' idea of a real sophisticated movie; sporadically funny but tiresome, glib, and pompous. Panavision. [R]▼●◗

Tenant, The (1976-French-U.S.) **C-125m.** ***½ D: Roman Polanski. Roman Polanski, Isabelle Adjani, Melvyn Douglas, Jo Van Fleet, Shelley Winters, Bernard Fresson, Lila Kedrova, Claude Dauphin. Unique, bizarrely cast horror film about a timid clerk who rents an apartment whose previous inhabitant attempted suicide. Critically drubbed upon release but a latter-day cult item. Fine photography by Sven Nykvist. [R]▼

Ten Cents a Dance (1931) **80m.** *½ D: Lionel Barrymore. Barbara Stanwyck, Ricardo Cortez, Monroe Owsley, Sally Blane, Blanche Frederici. Dreary, slow-moving drama about a taxi dancer's unfortunate marriage to a worthless wimp, who turns out to be a crook and a cheat, as well.

Ten Commandments, The (1923) **146m.** *** D: Cecil B. DeMille. Theodore Roberts, Charles de Roche, Estelle Taylor, Richard Dix, Rod La Rocque, Leatrice Joy, Nita Naldi, Agnes Ayres. Biblical story, told in compact form (but on a gargantuan scale—with several scenes in two-color Technicolor) is only first portion of this silent film. The rest is a modern-day parable involving two brothers, one a saint, the other a sinner—and it's anything but subtle. Still, it's good entertainment in the best DeMille style. Remade in 1956.▼

Ten Commandments, The (1956) **C-220m.** **** D: Cecil B. DeMille. Charlton Heston, Yul Brynner, Anne Baxter, Edward G. Robinson, Yvonne De Carlo, Debra Paget, John Derek, Cedric Hardwicke, H.B. Warner, Henry Wilcoxon, Nina Foch, Martha Scott, Judith Anderson, Vincent Price, John Carradine, Woodrow (Woody) Strode. Vivid storytelling at its best. Biblical epic follows Moses' life from birth and abandonment through manhood, slavery, and trials in leading the Jews out of Egypt. Few subtleties in DeMille's second handling of this tale (first filmed in 1923) but few lulls, either. Parting of the Red Sea, writing of the holy tablets are unforgettable highlights. Oscar-winning special effects. VistaVision.▼●◗

Ten Days That Shook the World SEE: **October**

Ten Days to Tulara (1958) **77m.** BOMB D: George Sherman. Sterling Hayden, Grace Raynor, Rodolfo Hoyos, Carlos Muzquiz. Dud adventure account of Hayden at al pursued across Mexico by police for the gold they carry.

Ten Days Wonder (1972-French) **C-101m.** **½ D: Claude Chabrol. Orson Welles, Anthony Perkins, Marlene Jobert, Michel Piccoli, Guido Alberti. Ellery Queen meets Claude Chabrol in erratic but moody mystery concerning Perkins' love affair with stepmother Jobert. Film doesn't work, but is often fascinating to watch. [PG]▼

Tender Comrade (1943) **C-102m.** **½ D: Edward Dmytryk. Ginger Rogers, Robert Ryan, Ruth Hussey, Patricia Collinge, Mady Christians, Kim Hunter, Jane Darwell. Rogers and friends live communally while their men are out fighting the war, a situation that caused this Dmytryk-Dalton Trumbo collaboration to be labeled as Communist propaganda by HUAC in later years. Some unbearable—and ironically, pro-American—speechifying, but occasionally fascinating as social history.▼

Tender Flesh SEE: **Welcome to Arrow Beach**

Tenderfoot, The (1932) **70m.** **½ D: Ray Enright. Joe E. Brown, Ginger Rogers, Lew Cody, George Chandler, Allan Lane, Vivien Oakland. Brown's a naive cowboy who wants to back a Broadway show in the worst way—and does.

Tender Is the Night (1962) **C-146m.** **½ D: Henry King. Jennifer Jones, Jason Robards, Jr., Joan Fontaine, Tom Ewell, Jill St. John, Paul Lukas. Sluggish, unflavorful version of F. Scott Fitzgerald novel with Jones unsatisfactory as mentally unstable wife of psychiatrist Robards; Fontaine is her chic sister; set in 1920s Europe. CinemaScope.

Tender Mercies (1983) **C-89m.** *** D: Bruce Beresford. Robert Duvall, Tess Harper, Allan Hubbard, Betty Buckley, Ellen Barkin, Wilford Brimley, Lenny Von Dohlen, Paul Gleason. Winning but extremely low-key film about a country singer who finds the inspiration to put his life back together when he meets an attractive young widow and her little boy. Duvall's Oscar-winning performance is the real attraction here, though the whole cast is excellent; Horton Foote's screenplay (also an Oscar winner) is not so much a story as a series of vignettes. Incidentally, Duvall wrote his own songs for the film. [PG] ▼●◗

Tender Scoundrel (1966-French-Italian) **C-94m.** *½ D: Jean Becker. Jean-Paul Belmondo, Nadja Tiller, Robert Morley, Genevieve Page. Dumb story of delightful rogue and ladies' man who is constantly on the hustle. Techniscope.

Tender Trap, The (1955) **C-111m.** ***½ D: Charles Walters. Frank Sinatra, Debbie Reynolds, Celeste Holm, David Wayne, Carolyn Jones, Lola Albright, Tom Helmore, James Drury. Delightful romp of swinging bachelor Sinatra who stumbles into marriage with determined Debbie in N.Y.C.; impeccable support from Holm and Wayne, plus memorable Cahn–Van Heusen title tune. Julius J. Epstein adapted Max Shulman's and Robert Paul Smith's play. CinemaScope.▼●

Tender Years, The (1947) **81m.** ** D: Harold Schuster. Joe E. Brown, Richard Lyon, Noreen Nash, Charles Drake, Josephine Hutchinson. Warm drama of minister trying to protect dog his son is attached to; notable mainly for rare dramatic performance by Brown.▼

Tenebrae SEE: **Unsane**

Ten From Your Show of Shows (1973) **92m.** **** D: Max Liebman. Sid Caesar, Imogene Coca, Carl Reiner, Howard Morris, Louis Nye. Incomparable collection from early 50s TV show displaying comic genius of four stars, working with classic material by Mel Brooks, among others. Ten skits include FROM HERE TO ETERNITY spoof, silent-movie sendup, Swiss clock, and final, unbearably funny takeoff on *This Is Your Life.* A must. [G]▼

Ten Gentlemen From West Point (1942) **102m.** *** D: Henry Hathaway. George Montgomery, Maureen O'Hara, John Sutton, Laird Cregar, Victor Francen, Harry Davenport, Ward Bond, Tom Neal, Ralph Byrd, Douglass Dumbrille. Early years of West Point, with focus on vicious commander Cregar and other assorted military film clichés; somehow, it's still entertaining.

Ten Little Indians (1966-British) **92m.** **½ D: George Pollock. Hugh O'Brian, Shirley Eaton, Fabian, Leo Genn, Stanley Holloway, Wilfrid Hyde-White, Daliah Lavi, Dennis Price. Fair remake of Agatha Christie's whodunit AND THEN THERE WERE NONE, with suspects trapped in remote Alpine village. Originally released with gimmick of murder-minute for audience to guess killer. Remade again in 1975 and 1989.▼

Ten Little Indians (1975-British) **C-98m.** *½ D: Peter Collinson. Oliver Reed, Elke Sommer, Herbert Lom, Richard Attenborough, Charles Aznavour, Stephane Audran, Gert Frobe, Adolfo Celi, voice of Orson Welles. Third rendering of Agatha Christie whodunit, set this time in Iran. Great plot cannot survive such tired retelling. [PG]▼

Ten Little Indians (1989) **C-98m.** BOMB D: Alan Birkinshaw. Donald Pleasence, Frank Stallone, Sarah Maur Thorp, Brenda Vaccaro, Herbert Lom, Warren Berlinger, Paul L. Smith, Moira Lister. Producer Harry Alan Towers' *third* redo of the Christie classic is his worst yet. This time he isolates an uninteresting cast in an African safari camp in the 1930s, and boringly plods through this once-intriguing, now-weary plot. Stop Towers before he remakes again! [PG]▼●

Tennessee Champ (1954) **C-73m.** **½ D: Fred M. Wilcox. Shelley Winters, Keenan Wynn, Dewey Martin, Earl Holliman, Dave O'Brien. Good performances highlight average story of boxer who reforms crooked employer. The climactic fight features Charles (Bronson) Buchinsky.

Tennessee Johnson (1942) **103m.** **½ D: William Dieterle. Van Heflin, Lionel Barrymore, Ruth Hussey, Marjorie Main, Charles Dingle, Regis Toomey, Grant Withers, Lynne Carver, Noah Beery, Sr., Morris Ankrum. Sincere historical drama of President Andrew Johnson's rise and subsequent conflicts with Congress, given a glossy MGM production.

Tennessee's Partner (1955) **C-87m.** **½ D: Allan Dwan. John Payne, Rhonda Fleming, Ronald Reagan, Coleen Gray, Morris Ankrum. Offbeat little Western with Payne excellent in an unusual "heel" characterization, Reagan accidentally becoming his pal. Based on a Bret Harte story. Filmed in SuperScope.▼

Ten North Frederick (1958) **102m.** *** D: Philip Dunne. Gary Cooper, Diane Varsi, Suzy Parker, Geraldine Fitzgerald, Tom Tully, Ray Stricklyn, Stuart Whitman, Barbara Nichols. Grasping wife (Fitzgerald) prods her husband (Cooper) into big-time politics, with disastrous results. He finds personal solace in love affair with much younger woman (Parker). Good performances in somewhat soapy adaptation of John O'Hara novel. CinemaScope.▼

10 Rillington Place (1971-British) **C-111m.** *** D: Richard Fleischer. Richard Attenborough, Judy Geeson, John Hurt, Pat Heywood, Andre Morell, Bernard Lee. Low-key presentation of famous John Christie-Timothy Evans murder case that rocked Great Britain in the late 1940s. No overt editorializing but psychological undertone exists; outstanding performances by entire cast and location filming inseparable with film's total effect. [PG]▼●

Ten Seconds to Hell (1959) **93m.** **½ D: Robert Aldrich. Jeff Chandler, Jack Palance, Martine Carol, Robert Cornthwaite, Dave Willock, Wesley Addy. Chandler and Palance are almost believable as Germans involved in defusing bombs in Berlin, while competing for Carol's affection.

Tension (1949) **95m.** **½ D: John Berry. Richard Basehart, Audrey Totter, Cyd Charisse, Barry Sullivan, Tom D'Andrea. Timid Basehart methodically plans to murder his wife's lover, only to have someone beat him to it in this intriguing melodrama.

Tension at Table Rock (1956) **C-93m.** ** D: Charles Marquis Warren. Richard Egan, Dorothy Malone, Cameron Mitchell, Billy Chapin, Angie Dickinson. Soaper Western with Egan on the lam for a murder committed in self-defense.

Tentacles (1977-Italian) **C-90m.** *½ D: Oliver Hellman (Ovidio Assonitis). John Huston, Shelley Winters, Henry Fonda, Bo Hopkins, Delia Boccardo, Cesare Danova. Giant octopus threatens a seaside community in this rip-off of JAWS. Some unexpected casting and the spectacle of having killer whales emerge the heroes save the picture from total decay. Technovision. [PG]▼

Ten Tall Men (1951) **C-97m.** **½ D: Willis Goldbeck. Burt Lancaster, Jody Lawrance, Gilbert Roland, Kieron Moore. Tongue-in-cheek Foreign Legion tale, with dynamic Lancaster pushing the action along.

Tenth Avenue Angel (1948) **74m.** BOMB D: Roy Rowland. Margaret O'Brien, Angela Lansbury, George Murphy, Phyllis Thaxter, Warner Anderson, Rhys Williams, Barry Nelson, Connie Gilchrist. Capable cast is lost in terrible, syrupy script about eight-year-old tenement girl O'Brien, her attachment to ex-con Murphy, and how she learns various, obvious lessons about faith. Filmed in 1946.

10 Things I Hate About You (1999) **C-97m.** **½ D: Gil Junger. Heath Ledger, Julia Stiles, Joseph Gordon-Levitt, Larisa Oleynik, David Krumholtz, Andrew Keegan, Susan May Pratt, Larry Miller, Daryl "Chill" Mitchell, Allison Janney, David Leisure, Letters to Cleo, Save Ferris. Overprotective dad rules that his pretty, popular daughter Bianca can only date when his hostile older daughter Katerina does. Several guys interested in Bianca therefore hire someone to pursue her doggedly unfriendly sister. Cute teen-comedy takeoff of *The Taming of the Shrew* set at Padua High School. Janney is great fun as Ms. Perky. [PG-13] ▼●◗

Tenth Man, The (1988) **C-100m. TVM** D: Jack Gold. Anthony Hopkins, Kristin Scott Thomas, Derek Jacobi, Cyril Cusack, Brenda Bruce, Paul Rogers. A once-prosperous French lawyer becomes a Nazi prisoner during WW2, and gives all his worldly possessions to a fellow captive to take his place in front of a firing squad; after the war, he secures a job as servant in his own villa, now the property of the dead man's family. Slow-moving version of Graham Greene's parable, given the usual first-class Hallmark Hall of Fame treatment. Average.▼●

Ten Thousand Bedrooms (1957) **C-114m.** ** D: Richard Thorpe. Dean Martin, Anna Maria Alberghetti, Eva Bartok, Dewey Martin, Walter Slezak, Paul Henreid, Jules Munshin, Marcel Dalio, Dean Jones. Dean's first film without Jerry Lewis seemed to spell doom for his career; it's a lightweight but overlong musical romance with Dino as a playboy hotel-manager in Rome. CinemaScope.

Tenth Victim, The (1965-Italian) **C-92m.** *** D: Elio Petri. Marcello Mastroianni, Ursula Andress, Elsa Martinelli, Salvo Randone, Massimo Serato. Cult sci-fi of futuristic society where violence is channeled into legalized murder hunts. Here, Ursula hunts Marcello. Intriguing idea, well done. Based on Robert Sheckley's story "The Sixth Victim."▼

Ten to Midnight (1983) **C-100m.** ** D: J. Lee Thompson. Charles Bronson, Andrew Stevens, Gene Davis, Lisa Eilbacher, Wilford Brimley, Geoffrey Lewis. Handsome psycho-killer does his woman-killing in the nude, but runs afoul of police detective Bronson, whose daughter he terrorizes. Kicked off the force for falsifying evidence against the killer, Bronson goes on his usual Death Wish rampage. Ultraviolent, kinkier-than-average Bronson vehicle. [R] ▼●

Ten Wanted Men (1955) **C-80m.** ** D: Bruce Humberstone. Randolph Scott, Jocelyn Brando, Richard Boone, Skip Homeier, Leo Gordon, Donna Martell. Conventional Western programmer with cattleman Scott's dream of law and order smashed by ambitions of ruthless rival Boone.▼●

Ten Who Dared (1960) **C-92m.** BOMB D: William Beaudine. Brian Keith, John Beal, James Drury, R. G. Armstrong, Ben Johnson, L. Q. Jones. Dreadful Disney film based on true story of Major John Wesley Powell's exploration of Colorado River in 1869; cast is drowned in clichés, while action is sparse. Forget it.▼

Teorema (1968-Italian) **C-98m.** ** D: Pier Paolo Pasolini. Terence Stamp, Silvana Mangano, Massimo Girotti, Anna Wiazemsky, Laura Betti, Andres Jose Cruz. Pointed but obvious, occasionally hokey political/sexual fable, with Stamp cast as a young stranger who may be Christ—or Satan. He leaves an irrevocable impression on a bourgeois family by sleeping with its every member. Reworked as DALLAS DOLL, with Sandra Bernhard in the Stamp role!▼

Tequila Sunrise (1988) **C-116m.** **½ D: Robert Towne. Mel Gibson, Michelle Pfeiffer, Kurt Russell, Raul Julia, J.T. Walsh, Arliss Howard, Ann Magnuson, Arye Gross. Lifelong friends, one a supposedly retired drug dealer, the other a fast-rising L.A. cop, are forced to confront each other, both in business and in vying for the affections of a sleek restaurant owner. All three leads exude considerable charisma, but after a snappy start the script leads them nowhere. Veteran director Budd Boetticher plays a judge. Disappointing result for writer-director Towne. [R]▼●◗

Teresa (1951) **102m.** ** D: Fred Zinnemann. Pier Angeli, John Ericson, Patricia Collinge, Richard Bishop, Peggy Ann Garner, Ralph Meeker, Bill Mauldin, Edward Binns, Rod Steiger. Intriguing, but superficially told story of WW2 veteran Ericson who returns to U.S. with his Italian bride, encountering home-town prejudice. Steiger plays psychiatrist in film debut.

Teresa's Tattoo (1993) **C-95m.** BOMB D: Julie Cypher. C. Thomas Howell, Nancy McKeon, Lou Diamond Phillips, Casey Siemaszko, Jonathan Silverman, Adrienne Shelly, Diedrich Bader, Anthony Clark, Tippi Hedren, k.d. lang, Joe Pantoliano, Mary Kay Place, Mare Winningham, Nanette Fabray, Majel Barrett. Moronic kidnappers' equally moronic hostage accidentally drowns, and guess who's her double? A brainy doctoral candidate in applied mathematics. The laughs are nil in this alleged comedy, with a name cast going slumming. Melissa Etheridge (who did the original songs) appears as a hooker. Kiefer Sutherland appears unbilled as a cop. [R]▼

Terminal Bliss (1992) **91m.** **½ D: Jordan Alan. Timothy Owen, Luke Perry, Estee Chandler. Modern teen-angst drama of disaffected rich kids as they betray each other, seduce one another's girlfriends, act self-indulgent, and seem bored by life. Major attraction here is *Beverly Hills 90210* heartthrob Perry—though he poses no major threat to James Dean. Made in 1987. [R]▼●

Terminal Choice (1985-Canadian) **C-97m.** *½ D: Sheldon Larry. Joe Spano, Diane Venora, David McCallum, Robert Joy, Don Francks, Nicholas Campbell, Ellen Barkin. Deadly doings at a hospital; good cast wasted in this unsavory thriller. Also known as DEATHBED. [R]▼

Terminal Island (1973) **C-88m.** *½ D: Stephanie Rothman. Phyllis Elizabeth Davis, Don Marshall, Barbara Leigh, Sean Kenney, Roger Mosley, Tom Selleck, Jo Morrow. Cynical exploitation film about futuristic offshore California penal colony where murderers are sent in lieu of abolished death penalty. Reissued a decade later to capitalize on the presence of several future stars, including *Magnum P.I.*'s Selleck and Mosley. [R]▼

Terminal Man, The (1974) **C-107m.** *** D: Mike Hodges. George Segal, Joan Hackett, Richard A. Dysart, Jill Clayburgh, Donald Moffat, Matt Clark, James (B.) Sikking, Ian Wolfe, Steve Kanaly, Lee DeBroux. Cold but engrossing thriller has computer scientist Segal coming under influence of computers in his brain which cause violence. Well-acted; based on the Michael Crichton novel. [PG]▼

Terminal Station SEE: **Indiscretion of an American Wife**

Terminal Velocity (1994) **C-103m.** *** D: Deran Sarafian. Charlie Sheen, Nastassja

Kinski, James Gandolfini, Christopher McDonald, Gary Bullock, Melvin Van Peebles, Hans R. Howes. Hotshot skydiving instructor Sheen is horrified when, on her first jump, his student Kinski plummets to her death—or does she? While trying to prove what really happened, he's plunged into intrigue, danger, and romance. Fast paced and witty, this is a bright variation on Hitchcock themes that, blessedly, never pretends to take itself very seriously. Sheen is miscast, but Kinski is terrific; so are the action scenes. Panavision. [PG-13]▼●◗

Terminator, The (1984) **C-108m.** ***½ D: James Cameron. Arnold Schwarzenegger, Michael Biehn, Linda Hamilton, Paul Winfield, Lance Henriksen, Rick Rossovich, Earl Boen, Dick Miller, Bill Paxton. A cyborg is sent here from the future to kill a seemingly innocent woman. Schwarzenegger is perfectly cast as violence-prone robot who cannot be stopped. Terrific action picture never lets up for a minute—a model for others to follow. Director Cameron cowrote with producer Gale Anne Hurd (inspired by the works of Harlan Ellison). Followed by a sequel. [R]▼●◗

Terminator 2: Judgment Day (1991) **C-136m.** **½ D: James Cameron. Arnold Schwarzenegger, Linda Hamilton, Edward Furlong, Robert Patrick, Earl Boen, Joe Morton, S. Epatha Merkerson, Castulo Guerra, Danny Cooksey, Jenette Goldstein, Xander Berkeley. A "kinder, gentler" cyborg from the future returns, this time to protect the soon-to-be savior of humanity from destruction by a *rival* terminator. Box-office smash has special effects to knock your socks off (especially the "liquid metal"), and action to spare, but like so many sequels, lacks the freshness of the first film and gives us no one to root for. Oscar winner for Best Makeup, Sound, Sound Effects Editing, and Visual Effects. Some versions feature additional footage. Super 35. [R]▼●◗

Termini Station (1989-Canadian) **C-105m.** ** D: Allan King. Colleen Dewhurst, Megan Follows, Gordon Clapp, Debra McGrath, Leon Pownall, Elliott Smith, Norma Dell'Agnese, Hanna Lee. Dreary, unenlightening portrait of an angst-ridden family: the father was killed in what may have been a suicide, the mother has become an alcoholic, the son a self-absorbed heel, the daughter a grim-faced prostitute. Tennis, anyone?▼

Term of Trial (1962-British) **113m.** **½ D: Peter Glenville. Laurence Olivier, Simone Signoret, Sarah Miles, Terence Stamp, Roland Culver, Hugh Griffith. Talky story of schoolmaster charged with assault by young Miles, and subsequent trial's effect on Olivier's wife, Signoret. Despite fine cast, a wearisome film. Miles' film debut.

Terms of Endearment (1983) **C-132m.** **** D: James L. Brooks. Shirley MacLaine, Debra Winger, Jack Nicholson, John Lithgow, Jeff Daniels, Lisa Hart Carroll, Danny DeVito. Wonderful mix of humor and heartache follows the relationship of a mother and daughter over the years. Consistently offbeat and unpredictable, with exceptional performances by all three stars; first-time director Brooks also wrote the screenplay from Larry McMurtry's novel. Won Oscars for MacLaine, Nicholson, Screenplay, Director, and Best Picture. Sequel: THE EVENING STAR. [PG]▼●

Terrible Beauty, A SEE: **Night Fighters**

Terrible People, The (1960-German) **95m.** ** D: Harald Reinl. Eddi Arent, Karin Dor, Elizabeth Flickenschildt, Fritz Rasp, Joachim Fuchsberger. Fair action story of condemned bank crook vowing to return from dead to punish those who prosecuted him. Retitled: HAND OF THE GALLOWS. ▼

Terror, The (1963) **C-81m.** **½ D: Roger Corman. Boris Karloff, Jack Nicholson, Sandra Knight, Dick Miller. Engaging chiller nonsense with Karloff the mysterious owner of a castle where eerie deeds occur; set on Baltic coast in 1800s. This is the legendary Corman quickie for which all of Karloff's scenes were shot in less than three days as the sets (from THE RAVEN) were being torn down around them! Vistascope ▼●◗

Terror at Midnight (1956) **70m.** ** D: Franklin Adreon. Scott Brady, Joan Vohs, Frank Faylen, John Dehner. Undynamic telling of Vohs being blackmailed and her law-enforcer boyfriend (Brady) helping out.

Terror at Red Wolf Inn SEE: **Terror House**

Terror at the Opera (1987-Italian) **107m.** **½ D: Dario Argento. Cristina Marsillach, Ian Charleson, Urbano Barberini, Daria Nicolodi, Corallina G. Tassoni. Horror opus about a young diva who's being stalked by a madman. As customary with Argento, this is stylish but nonsensical, with some over-the-top gore, backed up by a screeching rock score and insane camera calisthenics. Available in both R and unrated versions. Super 35. [R]▼

Terror Beneath the Sea (1970-Japanese) **C-85m.** *½ D: Hajimo Sato. Peggy Neal, Andrew Hughes, Shinichi (Sonny) Chiba, Mike Daneen, Eric Nielson. Mad scientist creates monsters from human prisoners in an underwater city. The usual.▼

Terror By Night (1946) **60m.** **½ D: Roy William Neill. Basil Rathbone, Nigel Bruce, Alan Mowbray, Dennis Hoey, Renee Godfrey, Mary Forbes. Sherlock Holmes dodges death at every turn while guarding a priceless diamond on a bullet-train en route from London to Edinburgh. Lesser, later entry does give Mowbray a fine sup-

porting role. Also shown in computer-colored version.▼●
Terror Castle SEE: **Horror Castle**
Terror From Under the House SEE: **Inn of the Frightened People**
Terror Hospital SEE: **Beyond the Living**
Terror House (1942) SEE: **Night Has Eyes, The**
Terror House (1972) **C-98m.** *½ D: Bud Townsend. Linda Gillin, Arthur Space, John Neilson, Mary Jackson, Michael Macready. A young woman gets more than she bargained for when she wins a "vacation" trip to an old mansion. Predates other cannibalism efforts, and doesn't take itself that seriously—but still not very good. Aka THE FOLKS AT RED WOLF INN and TERROR AT RED WOLF INN. Some prints run 83m. Video title: TERROR ON THE MENU. [PG—edited from original R rating]▼
Terror in a Texas Town (1958) **80m.** **½ D: Joseph H. Lewis. Sterling Hayden, Sebastian Cabot, Carol Kelly, Eugene Martin, Ned Young, Victor Millan. Offbeat Western drama about Scandinavian whaler (Hayden) who comes to his father's farm in Texas, finds town terrorized by Cabot, who's forcing everyone to sell their oil-rich land. Incredible final shootout.▼
Terror in the Aisles (1984) **C/B&W-85m.** *½ D: Andrew J. Kuehn. Nancy Allen, Donald Pleasence. Endless collage of film clips from almost 75 terror movies, from ALIEN to WAIT UNTIL DARK, with the kitchen sink in between. There's silly commentary from Allen and Pleasence, sitting in a simulated movie house, and just too much footage for it all to make any sense. For diehard genre addicts only. [R]▼
Terror in the Wax Museum (1973) **C-93m.** *½ D: Georg Fenady. Ray Milland, Broderick Crawford, Elsa Lanchester, Maurice Evans, Shani Wallis, John Carradine, Louis Hayward, Patric Knowles, Mark Edwards. Low-budget and low-grade murder mystery takes little advantage of wax museum horror potential; a good cast wasted. If you look closely you can see the "wax figures" moving. [PG]▼
Terror in Toyland SEE: **You Better Watch Out**
Terror Is a Man (1959) **89m.** ** D: Gerry DeLeon. Francis Lederer, Greta Thyssen, Richard Derr, Oscar Keesee. On Blood Island, doctor experiments with panther to turn him into a human. Filmed in the Philippines, this sci-fi horror story comes to life in last third of picture. Clearly inspired by H. G. Wells' *Island of Dr. Moreau.* Aka BLOOD CREATURE.▼◗
Terrorists, The (1975-British) **C-97m.** *½ D: Caspar Wrede. Sean Connery, Ian McShane, Jeffrey Wickham, Isabel Dean, John Quentin. Muddled thriller about political terrorism and airline hijacking is indifferently acted by Connery and McShane, amateurishly directed, and tediously unspooled. Pity, because premise is sound and photography (by Sven Nykvist) is smashing. Filmed in Norway. [PG]▼
Terrornauts, The (1967-British) **C-75m.** *½ D: Montgomery Tully. Simon Oates, Zena Marshall, Charles Hawtrey, Patricia Hayes, Stanley Meadows, Max Adrian. Alien forces kidnap an entire building on Earth, people and all. Based on Murray Leinster's novel *The Wailing Asteroid,* this sci-fi film is hampered by low budget.▼
Terror of Dr. Hichcock SEE: **Horrible Dr. Hichcock, The**
Terror of Frankenstein (1975-Swedish-Irish) **C-91m.** *** D: Calvin Floyd. Leon Vitali, Per Oscarsson, Nicholas Clay, Stacey Dorning, Jan Ohlsson. Literate, well-made adaptation of the classic story, definitely worth a look for horror buffs. This is the most faithful of all film versions of Mary Shelley's novel. Original title: VICTOR FRANKENSTEIN. ▼◗
Terror of Mechagodzilla (1975-Japanese) **C-83m.** *½ D: Ishiro Honda. K. Sasaki, Tomoko Ai, Akihiko Hirata, Kenji Sahara. Mechagodzilla is restored by villains and sent to destroy Godzilla again, aided by the remote-controlled Titanosaurus. Colorful and full of brawling monsters. Tohoscope. ▼●◗
Terror of Sheba, The SEE: **Persecution**
Terror of the Red Mask (1960-Italian) **C-90m.** ** D: Piero Pierotti. Lex Barker, Chelo Alonso, Massimo Serato. Costumer strains to have air of a chiller as hero Barker swordfights his way through castle of horror. ▼
Terror of the Tongs (1961-British) **C-90m.** **½ D: Anthony Bushell. Geoffrey Toone, Burt Kwouk, Brian Worth, Christopher Lee, Richard Leech. Atmospheric British thriller of captain searching for killers of daughter; eventually breaks entire Tong society in Hong Kong. Good acting but may be a little gruesome for some viewers. Released theatrically in b&w.
Terror of Tiny Town, The (1938) **63m.** *½ D: Sam Newfield. Billy Curtis, Yvonne Moray, Little Billy, John Bambury. If you're looking for a midget musical Western, look no further. A typical sagebrush plot is enacted (pretty badly) by a cast of little people, and the indelible impression is that of characters sauntering into the saloon *under* those swinging doors!▼
Terror on a Train (1953-British) **72m.** **½ D: Ted Tetzlaff. Glenn Ford, Anne Vernon, Maurice Denham, Victor Maddern. Tense little film of Ford defusing time bomb placed aboard train full of high explosives.
Terror on the Menu SEE: **Terror House**
Terror Train (1980-Canadian) **C-97m.** ** D: Roger Spottiswoode. Ben Johnson, Jamie

Lee Curtis, Hart Bochner, David Copperfield, Derek Mackinnon, D. D. Winters (Vanity), Bill Maher. Fraternity hires a train for a night-long graduation costume party only to have an ex-member, emotionally scarred by an initiation prank, come aboard, disguised and uninvited, to seek revenge. Stylish photography—by John (A CLOCKWORK ORANGE) Alcott, of all people—and novelty of killer donning the costume of each successive victim lift this above most of the others in this disreputable genre. [R]▼●

TerrorVision (1986) **C-85m.** BOMB D: Ted Nicolaou. Diane Franklin, Mary Woronov, Gerrit Graham, Chad Allen, Bert Remsen, Alejandro Rey, Randi Brooks, Sonny Carl Davis. Inept direction and overacting sink this cartoonish tale of a family and friends' reactions when a monster from outer space emerges from their TV set. Watch the old *Outer Limits* episode instead. [R]▼

Terror Within, The (1988) **C-88m.** ** D: Thierry Notz. Andrew Stevens, Starr Andreeff, Terri Treas, George Kennedy, John LaFayette, Tommy Hinchley. Grim horror/sci-fi concoction set after plague has wiped out 99 percent of humanity. An underground medical center is attacked by hybrid monsters born of human women and bent on creating more of the same. Low budget Roger Corman production is a cross between ALIEN and THE DAY THE WORLD ENDED, with a routine, predictable plot. Followed by a sequel. [R]▼

Terror Within II, The (1992) **C-89m.** *½ D: Andrew Stevens. Andrew Stevens, Stella Stevens, Chick Vennera, R. Lee Ermey, Burton "Bubba" Gilliam, Clare Hoak. More monsters vs. more scientists in underground bunker after catastrophic plague. Debuting director (and star) Stevens, looking like Rambo, fogs the cheap sets and shows a few good ideas, but his own absurd story sinks it all. That's his mom in a costarring part. [R]▼

Tess (1979-French-British) **C-170m.** ***½ D: Roman Polanski. Nastassia Kinski, Peter Firth, John Bett, Tom Chadbon, Rosemary Martin, Leigh Lawson, Sylvia Coleridge. Handsome, evocative adaptation of Thomas Hardy's *Tess of the D'Urbervilles,* with Kinski in her star-making performance as the strong-willed girl from a poor family whose fortunes rise and fall when she is foisted onto polite society. Long but engrossing. Oscar-winner for Cinematography, Costume Design, and Art Direction. Panavision. [PG]▼●

Tess of the Storm Country (1960) **C-84m.** **½ D: Paul Guilfoyle. Diane Baker, Jack Ging, Lee Philips, Wallace Ford, Robert F. Simon, Bert Remsen. Fifth screen version (since 1914) of Grace White's period novel of Scottish girl and uncle coming to America and adjusting to life in Pennsylvania Dutch country; leisurely paced, nicely done. CinemaScope.

Testament (1983) **C-89m.** ***½ D: Lynne Littman. Jane Alexander, William Devane, Roxana Zal, Ross Harris, Lukas Haas, Philip Anglim, Lilia Skala, Leon Ames, Rebecca De Mornay, Mako, Lurene Tuttle, Kevin Costner. Admirably understated drama about a small town contending with nuclear holocaust, focusing on one tight-knit family. Restrained and effective, with a heartrending performance by Alexander. Screenplay by John Sacret Young, from a story by Carol Amen. Originally made for PBS' *American Playhouse.* [PG]▼●

Testament of Dr. Mabuse, The (1932-German) **111m.** ***½ D: Fritz Lang. Rudolf Klein-Rogge, Otto Wernicke, Gustav Diesl, Karl Meixner. Criminal mastermind controls his underworld empire even while confined to an insane asylum! Fabled character from Lang's silent-film epic returns in less stylized but no less entertaining crime story—which even incorporates supernatural elements. Film was a subject of controversy during Nazi era. Lang returned to this character once more for THE THOUSAND EYES OF DR. MABUSE in 1960, but other hands remade this script in 1962. Aka THE LAST WILL OF DR. MABUSE. Many TV prints run 75m. Retitled THE CRIMES OF DR. MABUSE.▼

Testimony (1987-British) **C/B&W 157m.** ** D: Tony Palmer. Ben Kingsley, Terence Rigby, Ronald Pickup, John Shrapnel, Sherry Baines, Robert Stephens, Murray Melvin, Robert Urquhart. Ambitious, overlong biopic of composer Dmitri Shostakovich focuses on his political problems in the Soviet Union. Kingsley brings depth to the leading role, and Nic Knowland provides fabulous widescreen camerawork in b&w (with flashes of color), but these attributes cannot overcome a turgid narrative. Panavision.

Test of Love, A (1984-Australian) **C-93m.** *** D: Gil Brealey. Angela Punch McGregor, Drew Forsythe, Wallas Eaton, Simon Chilvers, Liddy Clark, Tina Arhondis. Moving, inspirational, if a bit too predictable story of a young teacher (Punch McGregor), and her attempts to reach a disabled girl (Arhondis, whose performance is truly wonderful). Based on a true story; originally titled ANNIE'S COMING OUT. [PG]▼

Test Pilot (1938) **118m.** *** D: Victor Fleming. Clark Gable, Myrna Loy, Spencer Tracy, Lionel Barrymore, Samuel S. Hinds, Marjorie Main, Gloria Holden, Louis Jean Heydt. Blend of romantic comedy and drama doesn't always work, but with those stars it's well worth watching. Tracy steals film as Gable's mechanic/pal in story of daredevils who try out new aircraft. Based on a Frank "Spig" Wead story.▼

Tevye (1939) **96m.** ***½ D: Maurice Schwartz. Maurice Schwartz, Rebecca Weintraub, Miriam Riselle, Leon Liebgold. Yiddish stage star Schwartz brightens the screen in his most famous role as Sholom Aleichem's famed Ukrainian dairyman; a crisis comes when one of his daughters wishes to wed a non-Jew. This touching, profound drama was later musicalized as FIDDLER ON THE ROOF. Filmed in Jericho, Long Island. Aka TEVYA.▼

Tex (1982) **C-103m.** *** D: Tim Hunter. Matt Dillon, Jim Metzler, Meg Tilly, Bill McKinney, Frances Lee McCain, Ben Johnson, Emilio Estevez, Jack Thibeau. First of S. E. Hinton's young-adult best sellers to reach the screen (via the Disney company) is an understated but likable tale of a boy whose mother has died, whose father is away, whose brother is trying to raise him with no money and little patience . . . and whose self-esteem is nil. Straightforward little drama. Hinton has a cameo as a teacher. [PG]▼●◗

Texan Meets Calamity Jane, The (1950) **C-71m.** BOMB D: Ande Lamb. Evelyn Ankers, James Ellison, Jack Ingram, Lee "Lasses" White. Ankers is too subdued as famed cowgirl of yesteryear, involved in fight to prove claim to prosperous saloon.

Texans, The (1938) **92m.** **½ D: James Hogan. Randolph Scott, Joan Bennett, May Robson, Walter Brennan, Robert Cummings, Robert Barrat. Post-Civil War Texas is setting for average Western with good cast.▼

Texas (1941) **93m.** *** D: George Marshall. William Holden, Glenn Ford, Claire Trevor, George Bancroft, Edgar Buchanan. High-level Western of two friends, one a rustler, the other a cattleman, competing for Trevor's affection.▼

Texas Across the River (1966) **C-101m.** *** D: Michael Gordon. Dean Martin, Alain Delon, Joey Bishop, Rosemary Forsyth, Peter Graves, Tina Marquand (Aumont), Andrew Prine, Michael Ansara, Dick (Richard) Farnsworth. Diverting takeoff on cowboy-and-Indian films, with Bishop hilarious as a deadpan Indian and Marquand cute as a young squaw. Techniscope.▼●

Texas, Brooklyn and Heaven (1948) **76m.** ** D: William Castle. Guy Madison, Diana Lynn, James Dunn, Lionel Stander, Florence Bates, Roscoe Karns. Stale "comedy" of cowboy who falls in love with city girl who loves horses. Good cast helps a little.▼

Texas Carnival (1951) **C-77m.** ** D: Charles Walters. Esther Williams, Howard Keel, Red Skelton, Ann Miller, Keenan Wynn, Tom Tully, Red Norvo. Emptier than usual, this flabby MGM musical about penniless carny mistaken for millionaire leaves fine cast high and dry with no fresh material.▼●

Texas Chain Saw Massacre, The (1974) **C-83m.** *** D: Tobe Hooper. Marilyn Burns, Gunnar Hansen, Edwin Neal, Allen Danzinger, Paul A. Partain, William Vail. Travelers in rural Texas encounter crazed family of bizarros who have a committed though unusual sense of what cuts of meat you need for good barbecue. Sweat-inducing, claustrophobic, unrelenting suspense-comic-horror film. Classic and influential—and nowhere nearly as violent as it's reputed to be. Narrated by an unbilled John Larroquette. Followed by three sequels. [R]▼●◗

Texas Chainsaw Massacre 2, The (1986) **C-95m.** BOMB D: Tobe Hooper. Dennis Hopper, Caroline Williams, Bill Johnson, Jim Siedow, Bill Moseley. Hooper returns with a mind-numbing, pretentious sequel. Hopper plays a nutty ex-Texas Ranger obsessed with revenge against the crazed family of Texas cannibals, while deejay Williams is simply looking to save her own skin when the cannibals go after her following a broadcast that angers them. Frenetic overacting and unfunny attempts at black humor sink this mess. Followed by LEATHERFACE: TEXAS CHAINSAW MASSACRE III. [R]▼●

Texas Chainsaw Massacre: The Next Generation (1997) **C-84m.** *½ D: Kim Henkel. Renee Zellweger, Matthew McConaughey, Robert Jacks, Tonie Perenski, Lisa Newmyer, Tyler Cone, John Harrison. More Texas teenagers are menaced by a backwoods family of murderous maniacs. Though a semi-remake of the first film, it's nowhere near as interesting or scary—no chainsaws, no cannibalism. Writer-director Henkel tries for profundity at the end, and blows it, but it's clear why Zellweger and the scenery-devouring McConaughey went on to bigger things. Aka RETURN OF THE TEXAS CHAINSAW MASSACRE; that version runs 94m. [R]▼◗

Texas Detour (1978) **C-92m.** ** D: Hikmet Avedis. Patrick Wayne, Mitch Vogel, Lindsay Bloom, R. G. Armstrong, Priscilla Barnes, Cameron Mitchell. Typical low-grade action picture about a macho stunt driver. [R]▼

Texas Guns SEE: **Once Upon a Texas Train**

Texas Lady (1955) **C-86m.** ** D: Tim Whelan. Claudette Colbert, Barry Sullivan, Greg Walcott, Horace McMahon, John Litel. Genteel oater with Colbert lovely as crusading newspaper editor in old West. Mediocre script. SuperScope.▼

Texas Rangers, The (1936) **95m.** *** D: King Vidor. Fred MacMurray, Jack Oakie, Jean Parker, Lloyd Nolan, Edward Ellis. Fine, elaborate Western of three comrades who split up; MacMurray and Oakie become rangers, Nolan an outlaw. Remade as STREETS OF LAREDO; sequel: THE TEXAS RANGERS RIDE AGAIN.▼

Texas Rangers, The (1951) **C-74m.** ** D: Phil Karlson. George Montgomery, Gale Storm, Jerome Courtland, Noah Beery, Jr. Aimless Western involving Texas law enforcers against gang of outlaws.▼

Texas Rangers Ride Again (1940) **68m.** ** D: James Hogan. John Howard, Jack Oakie, Akim Tamiroff, Ellen Drew, May Robson, Robert Ryan, Anthony Quinn. Sequel is standard Western fare of lawmen involved with cattle rustlers in the modern-day West. ▼

Texasville (1990) **C-123m.** **½ D: Peter Bogdanovich. Jeff Bridges, Cybill Shepherd, Annie Potts, Timothy Bottoms, Cloris Leachman, Randy Quaid, Eileen Brennan, William McNamara, Angie Bolling. Mildly diverting sequel to THE LAST PICTURE SHOW, from Larry McMurtry's novel, revealing that time has turned a number of the leading characters into Texas caricatures. No real plot to speak of, just a series of vignettes, some better than others. Potts stands out as Bridges' brassy wife, with Shepherd trying to assert the seriousness of her underwritten role by wearing no makeup and looking as bad (realistic?) as possible in every single shot. [R]▼●

Texican, The (1966) **C-91m.** ** D: Lesley Selander. Audie Murphy, Broderick Crawford, Diana Lorys, Luz Marquez, Antonio Casas, Antonio Perel. Routine Spanish-made Western pits ex-lawman Murphy against ruthless frontier town boss Crawford. Techniscope.▼

Thank God, It's Friday (1978) **C-90m.** BOMB D: Robert Klane. Donna Summer, Valerie Landsburg, Terri Nunn, Chick Vennera, Ray Vitte, Jeff Goldblum, Paul Jabara, Debra Winger, Andrea Howard, The Commodores (with Lionel Richie). Perhaps the worst film ever to have won some kind of Oscar (for Summer's hit song, "Last Dance"), this one-night-in-the-life-of-a-disco comedy is about as monotonous and uninventive as disco music itself. [PG]▼

Thanks a Million (1935) **87m.** *** D: Roy Del Ruth. Dick Powell, Ann Dvorak, Fred Allen, Patsy Kelly, Alan Dinehart, Margaret Irving, Paul Whiteman and Orchestra, Yacht Club Boys. Very entertaining musical of crooner Powell running for governor, with help of wisecracking manager Allen, sweetheart Dvorak, and blustery politician Raymond Walburn. Good fun, with several breezy tunes and specialties by Whiteman and Yacht Club Boys. Script by Nunnally Johnson. Remade as IF I'M LUCKY.

Thanks for the Memory (1938) **77m.** **½ D: George Archainbaud. Bob Hope, Shirley Ross, Charles Butterworth, Otto Kruger, Roscoe Karns, Hedda Hopper, Patricia Wilder, Laura Hope Crews, Eddie Anderson. Paper-thin romantic comedy (from a play by Albert Hackett and Frances Goodrich) reteams Hope and Ross, who sang the title tune in THE BIG BROADCAST OF 1938. Here, they're newlyweds who face a crisis: he's got to stop partying and finish his novel. Song highlight: "Two Sleepy People."▼

Thanksgiving Day (1990) **C-100m. TVM** D: Gino Tanasescu. Mary Tyler Moore, Tony Curtis, Jonathon Brandmeier, Joseph Bologna, Andy Hirsch, Kelly Curtis, Sonny Bono, Morton Downey, Jr. Wacky black comedy about a wealthy family's attempts to cope with life when dad has a heart attack and falls into the Thanksgiving turkey he's carving. Curtis (seen briefly as dad) is a riot and Moore is deliciously flaky as mom. Tony's daughter Kelly plays his misfit daughter in this Steve Zacharias and Jeff Buhai concoction. Above average.

Thanksgiving Promise, The (1986) **C-100m. TVM** D: Beau Bridges. Beau Bridges, Lloyd Bridges, Jordan Bridges, Millie Perkins, Ed Lauter, Jason Bateman, Courtney Thorne-Smith, Dorothy Dean Bridges. Atmospheric Disney charmer about a young boy and the pet goose he is fattening for his neighbor's dinner table. Distinguished for bringing together the entire Bridges family: patriarch Lloyd, wife Dorothy (her belated film debut), son Beau (who directed and coproduced with Mel Ferrer), Beau's son Jordan (in his acting debut), and even—unbilled—Jeff Bridges. Based on the warm novel by Blaine and Brenton Yorgason. Above average.

Thanks of a Grateful Nation (1998) **C-180m. TVM** D: Rod Holcomb. Ted Danson, Brian Dennehy, Marg Helgenberger, Jennifer Jason Leigh, Steven Weber, Matt Keeslar. Drama viewing the painful aftermath of the Persian Gulf War through the eyes of three veterans' families and one investigator (Danson) looking into Gulf War Syndrome, the very existence of which was denied by the U.S. government. Written by the estimable John Sacret Young. Made for cable. Above average.

Thank You All Very Much (1969-British) **C-105m.** *** D: Waris Hussein. Sandy Dennis, Ian McKellen, Eleanor Bron, John Standing. Absorbing study of unwed mother who decides to have her baby. Realistic and touching. [M/PG]

Thank You and Goodnight! (1991) **C-82m.** *** D: Jan Oxenberg. Quirky, funny (and tremendously moving) stylized/fictionalized documentary about a subject that's neither quirky nor funny: the physical decline and death of the filmmaker's Jewish grandmother. Beyond its humor, irony and originality, this *American Playhouse* theatrical film is a tenderhearted look at a grandmother-granddaughter relationship.▼

Thank You, Aunt (1967-Italian) **93m.** ** D: Salvatore Samperi. Lisa Gastoni, Lou Castel, Gabriele Ferzetti. Utterly perverse tale of psychopathic young man (Castel) who comes to live with attractive young aunt (Gastoni) whom he torments with sex games and rituals. Ugh. Released here as GRAZIE, ZIA in 1969.

Thank You, Jeeves (1936) **57m.** **½ D: Arthur Collins. Arthur Treacher, Virginia Field, David Niven, Lester Matthews, Willie Best. Treacher is at peak form playing P.G. Wodehouse's impeccable butler; he and his master (Niven) become immersed in intrigue after crossing paths with mystery woman Field. Retitled: THANK YOU, MR. JEEVES; followed by STEP LIVELY, JEEVES.

Thank You, Mr. Moto (1938) **67m.** *** D: Norman Foster. Peter Lorre, Pauline Frederick, Sidney Blackmer, Sig Rumann, John Carradine, Nedda Harrigan. Second series entry (and possibly the best) involves the Oriental sleuth in a complicated case centering on seven scrolls which hold the key to the hidden treasure of Genghis Khan.

Thank Your Lucky Stars (1943) **127m.** *** D: David Butler. Eddie Cantor, Dennis Morgan, Joan Leslie; guest stars Humphrey Bogart, Bette Davis, Olivia de Havilland, Errol Flynn, John Garfield, Ida Lupino, Ann Sheridan, etc. Very lame plot (Cantor plays both himself and lookalike cabbie) frames all-star Warner Bros. show, with Davis singing "They're Either Too Young Or Too Old," Flynn delightfully performing "That's What You Jolly Well Get," other staid stars breaking loose. ▼●

That Certain Age (1938) **101m.** **½ D: Edward Ludwig. Deanna Durbin, Melvyn Douglas, Jackie Cooper, Irene Rich, Nancy Carroll, John Halliday, Jack Searl. Deanna develops crush on her parents' houseguest, sophisticated Douglas, leaving boyfriend Cooper out in the cold—and saddled with responsibility for putting on amateur show. Silly script made bearable by smooth stars. ▼

That Certain Feeling (1956) **C-103m.** BOMB D: Norman Panama, Melvin Frank. Bob Hope, Eva Marie Saint, George Sanders, Pearl Bailey, Al Capp, Jerry Mathers. Incredibly bad Hope comedy with Bob as neurotic cartoonist; Sanders gives only life to stale film. Pearl sings title song. VistaVision.

That Certain Summer (1972) **C-74m. TVM** D: Lamont Johnson. Hal Holbrook, Hope Lange, Martin Sheen, Joe Don Baker, Scott Jacoby, Marlyn Mason, James McEachin. Divorcé Holbrook must find way to discuss homosexuality with son during one of their usual reunions in San Francisco. Outstanding performances by entire cast in sensibly scripted, carefully crafted film, well done by any medium's standards. A television landmark from the estimable producing/writing team of Richard Levinson and William Link. Above average.

That Certain Woman (1937) **93m.** **½ D: Edmund Goulding. Bette Davis, Henry Fonda, Donald Crisp, Ian Hunter, Minor Watson, Sidney Toler, Anita Louise. Remake of Goulding's early talkie THE TRESPASSER (with Gloria Swanson) features Bette as a gangster's widow who's trying to start life fresh, falling in love for real with Fonda. Well-acted soaper.▼

That Championship Season (1982) **C-110m.** ** D: Jason Miller. Bruce Dern, Stacy Keach, Robert Mitchum, Martin Sheen, Paul Sorvino, Arthur Franz. Disappointing adaptation of Miller's Pulitzer Prize-winning play (which took 10 years to reach the screen), about the 24th annual reunion of a high school basketball squad and their paternalistic coach. Whatever made it work on stage is missing here; the movie never catches fire, and its characters come off more as caricatures. Remade for TV in 1999. [R]▼

That Cold Day in the Park (1969) **C-113m.** *½ D: Robert Altman. Sandy Dennis, Michael Burns, Susanne Benton, John Garfield, Jr., Luana Anders, Michael Murphy. Strange, plodding film with frustrated spinster taking in young man she sees in the park. What follows is bizarre and unmoving; a far cry from Altman's later work. Filmed in Canada. TV print runs 92m. [R]▼

That Dangerous Age SEE: **If This Be Sin**

That Darn Cat! (1965) **C-116m.** *** D: Robert Stevenson. Hayley Mills, Dean Jones, Dorothy Provine, Roddy McDowall, Neville Brand, Elsa Lanchester, William Demarest, Frank Gorshin, Ed Wynn. Long but entertaining suspense comedy from Disney, about a cat that leads FBI man Jones on trail of kidnapped woman. Slapstick scenes and character vignettes highlight this colorful film. Remade in 1997. ▼●

That Darn Cat (1997) **C-89m.** *½ D: Bob Spiers. Christina Ricci, Doug E. Doug, Dean Jones, George Dzundza, Peter Boyle, Michael McKean, Bess Armstrong, Dyan Cannon, John Ratzenberger, Megan Cavanagh, Estelle Parsons, Rebecca Schull. Remake of the 1965 film follows basically the same plot, but without the same results; every change is for the worse. Even the cat is boring. Director Spiers hammers every joke flat, so his talented cast is helpless, though Ricci and McKean have some good moments. Doug is funny, but seems to come from a different, broader movie. [PG]▼●

That Forsyte Woman (1949) **C-114m.** **½ D: Compton Bennett. Errol Flynn,

Greer Garson, Walter Pidgeon, Robert Young, Janet Leigh, Harry Davenport. Rather superficial adaptation of John Galsworthy novel of a faithless woman (Garson) who finds herself attracted to her niece's fiancé; good-looking, but no match for the later BBC-TV series *The Forsyte Saga.*▼

That Funny Feeling (1965) **C-93m.** **½ D: Richard Thorpe. Sandra Dee, Bobby Darin, Donald O'Connor, Nita Talbot, Larry Storch, Leo G. Carroll, Robert Strauss. Funny only if you adore Darin and Dee, and even then story of footloose playboy and maid who pretends she lives with him wears thin.

That Gang of Mine (1940) **62m.** ** D: Joseph H. Lewis. Leo Gorcey, Bobby Jordan, Sunshine Sammy Morrison, Clarence Muse, Dave O'Brien, Joyce Bryant, Donald Haines, David Gorcey. Muggs (Gorcey) trains to be a thoroughbred jockey in this *East Side Kids* entry marked by director Lewis' expertise with galloping racing action.▼

That Girl From Paris (1936) **105m.** **½ D: Leigh Jason. Lily Pons, Jack Oakie, Gene Raymond, Herman Bing, Mischa Auer, Frank Jenks, Lucille Ball. Breezy Pons vehicle. She flees Continental wedding and runs to America. Tuneful songs, fine supporting cast. A remake of STREET GIRL; remade as FOUR JACKS AND A JILL.▼

That Hagen Girl (1947) **83m.** BOMB D: Peter Godfrey. Shirley Temple, Ronald Reagan, Rory Calhoun, Lois Maxwell, Dorothy Peterson, Conrad Janis. The prospect of Reagan and Temple as costars may sound amusing today—but this film is atrocious, with suicidal Shirley believing Ron to be her illegitimate father!

That Hamilton Woman (1941) **128m.** *** D: Alexander Korda. Vivien Leigh, Laurence Olivier, Alan Mowbray, Sara Allgood, Gladys Cooper, Henry Wilcoxon, Heather Angel. Olivier and Leigh—both breathtakingly beautiful—enact ill-fated historical romance of Lord Admiral Nelson and Lady Emma Hamilton in American-made film intended to spur pro-British feelings. P.S.: It was Winston Churchill's favorite movie. Aka LADY HAMILTON. ▼●

That Kind of Woman (1959) **92m.** *** D: Sidney Lumet. Sophia Loren, Tab Hunter, George Sanders, Jack Warden, Keenan Wynn, Barbara Nichols. Soldier Hunter and dishy Loren are attracted to each other on a train, but she's the mistress of elegant fatcat Sanders. Surprisingly adult comedy-drama for its era; excellent performances from all but Hunter, and even he's better than usual. Well shot by Boris Kaufman. Remake of THE SHOPWORN ANGEL, scripted by Walter Bernstein. VistaVision.

That Lady (1955) **C-100m.** **½ D: Terence Young. Olivia de Havilland, Gilbert Roland, Paul Scofield, Dennis Price, Christopher Lee. Unemotional costumer set in 16th-century Spain, with de Havilland a widowed noblewoman involved in court intrigue. Scofield's film debut. CinemaScope.

That Lady From Peking (1970-U.S.-Australian) **C-86m.** *½ D: Eddie Davis. Carl Betz, Nancy Kwan, Bobby Rydell, Sid Melton, Don Reid, Eva von Feilitz. Dull drama of writer Betz on the trail of a murdered Russian diplomat's diary.

That Lady in Ermine (1948) **C-89m.** **½ D: Ernst Lubitsch. Betty Grable, Douglas Fairbanks, Jr., Cesar Romero, Walter Abel, Reginald Gardiner, Harry Davenport. Entertaining if overblown musical of mythical European kingdom where Grable is a just-married princess; her ancestors magically come to life as Fairbanks' conquering army descends on her castle. Lubitsch died during production, which was completed by Otto Preminger. Script by Samson Raphaelson.

That'll Be the Day (1974-British) **C-90m.** *** D: Claude Whatham. David Essex, Ringo Starr, Rosemary Leach, James Booth, Billy Fury, Keith Moon. Compelling story traces British working-class youth (Essex) from adolescence to early adulthood in the 1950's, as his growing frustrations find their eventual outlet in rock music. First half of dynamic story, continued in STARDUST, where character's resemblance to John Lennon crystallizes. [PG]▼●

That Lucky Touch (1975-British) **C-93m.** *½ D: Christopher Miles. Roger Moore, Susannah York, Shelley Winters, Lee J. Cobb, Jean-Pierre Cassel, Raf Vallone, Sydne Rome, Donald Sinden. Tepid romantic farce with Moore cast as an arms dealer; York is the feisty journalist who conflicts with him. Moore sleepwalks through this. Of note only as Cobb's last movie (and he's the best thing in it). [PG]▼

That Man Bolt (1973) **C-105m.** ** D: Henry Levin, David Lowell Rich. Fred Williamson, Byron Webster, Teresa Graves, Jack Ging, Miko Mayama. Scenic actioner, filmed in Hong Kong, Las Vegas and L.A., mixes kung fu, some comedy and two songs by Graves. Plot has Williamson as international courier of syndicate money. [R]▼

That Man From Rio (1964-French) **C-114m.** *** D: Philippe De Broca. Jean-Paul Belmondo. Françoise Dorleac, Jean Servais, Adolfo Celi, Simone Renant. Engaging spoof of Bond-type movies features Belmondo as hero, chasing double-crosser and thief in search for Brazilian treasure. Nice cinematography by Edmond Séchan complements fast-moving script. Enjoyed great international success and spawned many imitations.▼

That Man George (1966-French-Spanish-Italian) **C-90m.** ** D: Jacques Deray.

George Hamilton, Claudine Auger, Alberto De Mendoza, Daniel Ivernel. Routine tale of robbery of armored van transporting bullion from gold mine.

That Man in Istanbul (1966) **C-117m.** **½ D: Anthony (Antonio) Isasi. Horst Buchholz, Sylva Koscina, Mario Adorf, Klaus Kinski. Fairly engaging spy romp featuring Koscina as FBI agent with Buchholz as playboy in search for missing scientist. Techniscope.

That Midnight Kiss (1949) **C-96m.** **½ D: Norman Taurog. Kathryn Grayson, Mario Lanza, Jose Iturbi, Ethel Barrymore, Keenan Wynn, J. Carrol Naish, Jules Munshin. Flimsy musical romance between Lanza and Grayson salvaged by pleasant musical interludes and glossy production.▼●

That Naughty Girl SEE: **Mam'zelle Pigalle**

That Night (1957) **88m.** **½ D: John Newland. John Beal, Augusta Dabney, Malcolm Brodrick, Shepperd Strudwick, Rosemary Murphy. Straightforward account of writer suffering a heart attack, and the effect it has on his family.

That Night (1992) **C-90m.** ** D: Craig Bolotin. Juliette Lewis, C. Thomas Howell, Eliza Dushku, Helen Shaver, J. Smith-Cameron, John Dossett. Young suburban girl (Dushku) worships fiery teen Lewis, who embarks on an ill-fated romance with sensitive bad-boy Howell. Disappointing view of adolescent angst and a child's initial experience with grownup emotions; about as subtle as a blaring boom-box. [PG-13]▼●

That Night in Rio (1941) **C-90m.** **½ D: Irving Cummings. Alice Faye, Don Ameche, Carmen Miranda, S. Z. Sakall, J. Carrol Naish, Curt Bois, Leonid Kinsky, Frank Puglia. Standard 20th Century-Fox musical of mistaken identities, uses Miranda to best advantage; Maria Montez has a tiny role. Filmed before as FOLIES BERGERE, and again as ON THE RIVIERA.

That Night With You (1945) **84m.** ** D: William A. Seiter. Franchot Tone, Susanna Foster, David Bruce, Louise Allbritton, Jacqueline de Wit, Buster Keaton. OK vehicle for soprano Foster who connives her way to show biz break via producer Tone.

That Obscure Object of Desire (1977-Spanish-French) **C-103m.** *** D: Luis Buñuel. Fernando Rey, Carole Bouquet, Angela Molina, Julien Bertheau, Andre Weber. Buñuel's last film is as audacious as any of his classics; wealthy sadomasochist Rey falls hard for a young maid, and she's only too happy to make him "suffer." Buñuel's bizarrest stroke is having Bouquet and Molina alternate playing the girl! Shot in French, with Rey dubbed by Michel Piccoli. Based on a Pierre Louys novel; filmed several times, most notably as THE DEVIL IS A WOMAN (1935). [R]▼●

That Old Feeling (1997) **C-105m.** **½ D: Carl Reiner. Bette Midler, Dennis Farina, Paula Marshall, Gail O'Grady, David Rasche, Jamie Denton, Danny Nucci. Silly but likable comedy about long-feuding ex-spouses who meet after 12 years at their daughter's wedding—and to their own shock and amazement, start having an affair. This seems to have a ricochet effect on everyone around them, in French farce fashion. Not the most believable movie ever made, but it's fun; Midler and Farina make a great couple. [PG-13]▼●◗

That's Dancing! (1985) **C/B&W-105m.** **½ D: Jack Haley, Jr. Narrated and hosted by Gene Kelly, Sammy Davis, Jr., Mikhail Baryshnikov, Liza Minnelli, Ray Bolger. Too many mediocre selections, flat introductions by five guest hosts . . . but there's still much to enjoy in this dance compilation, from Fred and Ginger's "Pick Yourself Up" to WEST SIDE STORY. Added curio: a Bolger number cut from THE WIZARD OF OZ. 1980s selections that end the film seem lumbering and ludicrous compared to the marvels of movement that precede them. Part Widescreen. [G]▼●

That's Entertainment! (1974) **C-132m.** **** D: Jack Haley, Jr. Hosted by Fred Astaire, Bing Crosby, Gene Kelly, Peter Lawford, Liza Minnelli, Donald O'Connor, Debbie Reynolds, Mickey Rooney, Frank Sinatra, James Stewart, Elizabeth Taylor. Stars host nostalgia bash with scenes from nearly 100 MGM musicals. There are many cherished moments with the above-named stars plus unexpectedly delightful numbers with Esther Williams, Clark Gable (singing and dancing!), Jimmy Durante, and Eleanor Powell, whose challenge dance with Astaire is unforgettable. Only complaint: why shorten the final AMERICAN IN PARIS ballet? Followed by two sequels. Part Widescreen. [G]▼●

That's Entertainment, Part 2 (1976) **C-133m.** ***½ D: Gene Kelly. Fred Astaire and Gene Kelly host this inevitable sequel and do some engaging song-and-dance work. Film hasn't cohesion or momentum of its predecessor, but the material is irresistible. This time, comedy and drama are included along with musical numbers—Tracy and Hepburn, Marx Brothers, etc. Most imaginative segment of all is wonderful title sequence by Saul Bass. Cut to 126m. after initial showings. Part Widescreen. [G]▼●

That's Entertainment! III (1994) **C-108m.** ***½ D: Bud Friedgen, Michael J. Sheridan. Hosted by June Allyson, Cyd Charisse, Lena Horne, Howard Keel, Gene Kelly, Ann Miller, Debbie Reynolds, Mickey Rooney, Esther Williams. Yet another collection of marvelous musical moments from the MGM library, spiked by some never-before-seen footage eliminated from the finished films, including a discarded Fred Astaire dance routine (shown in split-screen with its retake), Judy Garland singing Irving Berlin's "Mr. Monotony," Cyd Charisse and Joan Crawford singing and dancing to the same prerecorded number, Lena Horne singing "Ain't It the Truth" from CABIN IN THE SKY, and much, much more. Video release has expanded versions of some numbers cut for the theatrical print. Part Widescreen. [G]▼●

That Sinking Feeling (1979-Scottish) **C-92m.** *** D: Bill Forsyth. Robert Buchanan, John Hughes, Billy Greenlees, Gordon John Sinclair, Janette Rankin. Forsyth's initial feature is a witty little comedy about a gang of bored teens unable to find work in dreary Glasgow. Their leader comes up with a scheme to boost their morale: pilfering sinks from a warehouse. Released in U.S. after the success of Forsyth's subsequent films (GREGORY'S GIRL, LOCAL HERO). [PG]▼●

That's Life! (1986) **C-102m.** *** D: Blake Edwards. Jack Lemmon, Julie Andrews, Sally Kellerman, Robert Loggia, Jennifer Edwards, Rob Knepper, Matt Lattanzi, Chris Lemmon, Cynthia Sikes, Emma Walton, Felicia Farr. Deeply felt observation of an affluent family and its members' personal crises— including Lemmon's anxiety over turning sixty and his loving wife's fear that she may have cancer. Far from perfect, but mostly believable and quite moving. Filmed at Edwards' and wife Andrews' actual Malibu home, with most of their (and Lemmon's) real-life family on-screen . . . including at least one pet! Panavision. [PG-13]▼●

That's My Boy (1951) **98m.** ** D: Hal Walker. Dean Martin, Jerry Lewis, Marion Marshall, Eddie Mayehoff, Ruth Hussey, Polly Bergen, John McIntire. Ex-football star Mayehoff wants klutzy son Lewis to follow in his footsteps, induces Martin to coach him. Supposed comic idea is played straight, with very few laughs, maudlin situations . . . yet it was considered quite funny in 1951 when M&L were in their heyday. Later a TV series.

That's My Man (1947) **99m.** ** D: Frank Borzage. Don Ameche, Catherine McLeod, Roscoe Karns, Joe Frisco, John Ridgely, Kitty Irish, Frankie Darro. Nice-guy accountant Ameche buys a race horse that becomes a champ, but he turns into a heel and neglects his family in the process. Minor Borzage love story is initially lighthearted and offbeat, then turns into a maudlin and clichéd triangle tale about a man, a woman, and a horse.

That's Right—You're Wrong (1939) **93m.** **½ D: David Butler. Kay Kyser, Adolphe Menjou, May Robson, Lucille Ball, Dennis O'Keefe, Edward Everett Horton, Roscoe Karns, Moroni Olsen. Amiable film debut for popular radio band leader Kyser as he and his wacky crew are offered a Hollywood contract and get into all sorts of trouble in Tinseltown. Much of the humor (and music) is dated, but there's plenty to enjoy in the supporting cast, including gossip queens Sheilah Graham and Hedda Hopper as themselves.●

That's the Spirit (1945) **93m.** ** D: Charles Lamont. Peggy Ryan, Jack Oakie, June Vincent, Gene Lockhart, Johnny Coy, Andy Devine, Arthur Treacher, Irene Ryan, Buster Keaton. Whimsy is too studied in this syrupy fantasy of Oakie returning from heaven to make explanations to wife on Earth. Songs include "How Come You Do Me Like You Do?"

That's The Way of the World SEE: **Shining Star**

that thing you do! (1996) **C-110m.** *** D: Tom Hanks. Tom Everett Scott, Johnathon Schaech, Steve Zahn, Ethan Embry, Liv Tyler, Tom Hanks, Charlize Theron, Bill Cobbs, Obba Babatunde, Giovanni Ribisi, Alex Rocco, Chris Isaak, Kevin Pollak, Clint Howard. Likable yarn, set in 1964, about some young people in Erie, Pa., who form a band that, improbably, soars to success with a hit record. Sunny attitude and appealing cast make this hard to resist, even if it turns out to be a "lite" version of THE COMMITMENTS. Hanks also wrote the script and some of the songs. Hanks' wife, Rita Wilson, has an amusing cameo as a cocktail waitress, and his long-ago *Bosom Buddies* TV costar Peter Scolari plays a television host. [PG]▼●

That Touch of Mink (1962) **C-99m.** **½ D: Delbert Mann. Cary Grant, Doris Day, Gig Young, Audrey Meadows, John Astin, Dick Sargent. Attractive cast in silly piece of fluff with wealthy playboy Grant pursuing Day. Amusing at times, but wears thin; Astin is memorable as a creep with designs on poor Doris, and there's a clever sequence featuring Mickey Mantle, Roger Maris, Yogi Berra, and umpire Art Passarella. Panavision.▼●

That Uncertain Feeling (1941) **84m.** *** D: Ernst Lubitsch. Merle Oberon, Melvyn Douglas, Burgess Meredith, Alan Mowbray, Olive Blakeney, Harry Davenport, Sig Rumann, Eve Arden. Chic little Lubitsch comedy about married couple with problems, and their absurd pianist friend. Stolen hands down by Meredith as the musical malcontent. Filmed before (in 1925) by Lubitsch as KISS ME AGAIN. Also shown in computer-colored version.▼◗

That Was Rock (1984) **92m.** ***½ The best rock and R&B numbers from THE T.A.M.I. SHOW (1964) and THE BIG T.N.T. SHOW (1966) with remixed soundtrack and new connecting footage (in color) of Chuck Berry. Of inestimable value as history, and not too shabby as entertainment, either, but who put Ray Charles directly after James Brown?▼

That Was Then, This Is Now (1985) **C-100m.** **½ D: Christopher Cain. Emilio Estevez, Craig Sheffer, Kim Delaney, Barbara Babcock, Jill Schoelen, Frank Howard, Larry B. Scott, Ramon Sheen, Morgan Freeman. Delinquent kid, alienated from society, clings to his relationship with adoptive brother—and freaks out when the older boy takes on a girlfriend, whom he sees as a threat. Estevez wrote the script, from S. E. Hinton's young-adult novel, but its intense emotions probably read better than they play out on screen. A variable film with some strong moments. [R]▼●

That Way With Women (1947) **84m.** ** D: Frederick de Cordova. Dane Clark, Martha Vickers, Sydney Greenstreet, Alan Hale, Craig Stevens. Tired reworking of George Arliss' MILLIONAIRE, with Greenstreet as wealthy man who plays Cupid for Clark and Vickers.

That Woman Opposite SEE: **City After Midnight**

That Wonderful Urge (1948) **82m.** **½ D: Robert B. Sinclair. Tyrone Power, Gene Tierney, Arleen Whelan, Reginald Gardiner, Lucile Watson, Gene Lockhart, Gertrude Michael, Porter Hall. Fairly entertaining remake of LOVE IS NEWS about heiress getting back at nasty reporter. Power repeats his role from the 1937 film.

Theater of Blood (1973-British) **C-104m.** *** D: Douglas Hickox. Vincent Price, Diana Rigg, Robert Morley, Ian Hendry, Harry Andrews, Coral Browne, Robert Coote, Michael Hordern, Jack Hawkins, Diana Dors, Dennis Price, Milo O'Shea. A one-joke film, albeit a great joke: hammy Shakespearean actor Price vows revenge on critics who've blasted him, murders them one by one by recreating famous death scenes from the plays. Somewhat spoiled by incredibly gory killings; great cast has fun with it, though. [R]▼●

Theatre of Death (1967-British) **C-90m.** **½ D: Samuel Gallu. Christopher Lee, Julian Glover, Lelia Goldoni, Jenny Till, Evelyn Laye, Ivor Dean. Vampire-like murders revolving around Paris' Grand Guignol stage sensation and its beautiful young starlet under sinister hypnotic trance. Solid, low-budget mystery-thriller benefits from believable performances. Aka BLOOD FIEND. Techniscope.▼

Thelma & Louise (1991) **C-128m.** *** D: Ridley Scott. Susan Sarandon, Geena Davis, Harvey Keitel, Michael Madsen, Christopher McDonald, Stephen Tobolowsky, Brad Pitt, Timothy Carhart, Lucinda Jenney. Female friends leave responsibilities (as well as husband and boyfriend) behind to take a short trip, but an unexpected incident turns them into fugitives from the law. Dynamic star duo—and Callie Khouri's Oscar-winning feminist script—give this a lot of juice, though it still covers all-too-familiar road-movie territory. Panavision. [R]▼●◗

Thelma Jordon SEE: **File on Thelma Jordon, The**

Thelonious Monk: Straight No Chaser (1988) **C/B&W-90m.** *** D: Charlotte Zwerin. Comprehensive documentary portrait of the legendary, innovative jazz pianist-composer, crammed with footage of Monk in performance. Much of the material was shot during the late 1960s by Christian Blackwood. Executive producer is Clint Eastwood; released the same year as the latter's Charlie Parker biography, BIRD. [PG-13]▼●

Them! (1954) **94m.** ***½ D: Gordon Douglas. James Whitmore, Edmund Gwenn, Joan Weldon, James Arness, Onslow Stevens. First-rate '50s sci-fi about giant ant mutations running wild in the Southwest. Intelligent script (by Ted Sherdeman, from George Worthing Yates' story) extremely well directed, with memorable climax in L.A. sewers. Fess Parker has small but memorable role. Look fast for Leonard Nimoy at a teletype machine.▼●

Then Came Bronson (1969) **C-100m. TVM** D: William Graham. Michael Parks, Bonnie Bedelia, Akim Tamiroff, Martin Sheen, Sheree North, Gary Merrill. Young newspaper reporter (Parks) shaken up after suicide of friend, buys friend's motorcycle and sets out on shore road journey, meeting runaway bride (Bedelia), befriending her. Soft, somber film with a couple of OK episodes, fair performances. Pilot for the series. Above average.

Then There Were Three (1961-Italian) **82m.** ** D: Alex Nicol. Frank Latimore, Alex Nicol, Barry Cahill, Sid Clute. Routine WW2 actioner concerning Nazi officer going behind Allied lines to hunt down Italian partisans.

Theodora Goes Wild (1936) **94m.** ***½ D: Richard Boleslawski. Irene Dunne, Melvyn Douglas, Thomas Mitchell, Thurston Hall, Rosalind Keith, Spring Byington. Dunne's first starring comedy is a delightful story about small-town woman who writes scandalous best-seller and falls in love with sophisticated New Yorker who illustrated the book. Lots of funny twists in this engaging farce, scripted by Sidney Buchman from a Mary McCarthy story.▼

Theodora, Slave Empress (1954-Italian) **88m.** ** D: Riccardo Freda. Gianna Maria Canale, Georges Marchal, Renato Baldini, Henri Guisol, Irene Papas. Better-than-average production values are only asset in standard plot of hero thwarting plan of Roman generals to overthrow empress.

Theodore Rex (1996) **C-91m.** *½ D: Jonathan Betuel. Whoopi Goldberg, Armin Mueller-Stahl, Juliet Landau, Bud Cort, Stephen McHattie, Richard Roundtree, Jack Riley; voices of George Newbern, Carol

Kane. Set in the future, when DNA technology has led to the reanimation of dinosaurs, police officer Goldberg teams up with a talking Tyrannosaurus Rex to solve a murder. Cheesy production and low-key performances hinder this aimless tale. Children may like the cookie-loving dino. Plans for wide theatrical release were (understandably) scrubbed; it went to video instead. [PG]▼●

Theory of Flight, The (1998-British) **C-100m.** ** D: Paul Greengrass. Helena Bonham Carter, Kenneth Branagh, Gemma Jones, Holly Aird, Ray Stevenson. A perpetual screwup who feels he has something to express but no clue how to do it is punished for his last stunt by having to perform community service. His assignment: to spend time with a brilliant but hostile young woman in a wheelchair suffering from motor neuron disease, whose one dream is to have sex. Frightfully contrived from the word go, this forced piece of whimsy never takes off, despite two gifted stars. [R]▼●◗

There Goes My Baby (1994) **C-99m.** *** D: Floyd Mutrux. Dermot Mulroney, Rick Schroder, Kelli Williams, Noah Wyle, Jill Schoelen, Kristin Minter, Lucy Deakins, Seymour Cassel, Paul Gleason, Andrew Robinson; narrated by Anne Archer. It's 1965 and a group of high school seniors pause on the brink of Real Life. If it sounds a lot like AMERICAN GRAFFITI, you're right . . . but this film takes place in 1965, not 1962. In the interim, JFK has been assassinated, the Civil Rights movement is boiling, and Vietnam has become a divisive issue. Writer-director Mutrux effectively blends nostalgia and political awareness in this entertaining film. Made in 1990. [R]▼●

There Goes My Heart (1938) **84m.** *** D: Norman Z. McLeod. Fredric March, Virginia Bruce, Patsy Kelly, Alan Mowbray, Nancy Carroll, Eugene Pallette, Claude Gillingwater, Harry Langdon, Arthur Lake. Typical 30s fluff about runaway heiress Bruce spotted by reporter March; good cast makes one forget trite story-line.

There Goes the Bride (1979-British) **C-88m.** BOMB D: Terence Marcel. Tom Smothers, Twiggy, Martin Balsam, Sylvia Syms, Michael Witney, Hermione Baddeley, Broderick Crawford, Phil Silvers, Jim Backus. Addle-brained father-of-the-bride Smothers throws the wedding party into a tizzy when he has a fling with 1920's-flapper model, Twiggy, whom he has conjured up and only he can see. Unfunny slapstick that comes alive for about 45 seconds when Smothers and Twiggy do an on-target, extravagantly staged Astaire-Rogers routine. Based on Ray Cooney's and John Chapman's 1974 West End farce. [PG]

There Goes the Groom (1937) **65m.** ** D: Joseph Santley. Burgess Meredith, Ann Sothern, Louise Henry, Mary Boland, Onslow Stevens, William Brisbane. Strained screwball comedy about newly rich Meredith suddenly courted by Sothern and her wacky family; a smile or two but little else.

There Goes the Neighborhood (1992) **C-88m.** *½ D: Bill Phillips. Jeff Daniels, Catherine O'Hara, Hector Elizondo, Rhea Perlman, Judith Ivey, Harris Yulin, Jonathan Banks, Dabney Coleman, Chazz Palminteri, Mary Gross. Feeble comedy in which various greedy characters attempt to dig up a fortune buried in the basement of a suburban house. Strong cast deserves better material than this. [PG-13]▼●

Theremin: An Electronic Odyssey (1993) **C/B&W-104m.** *** D: Steven M. Martin. A fascinating chronicle of the life and times of Leon Theremin, the Russian-born genius who invented the first electronic musical instrument (which was adopted by Hollywood for use in movie soundtracks during the 1940s and 50s). Music history meets political and pop-culture history in this endlessly surprising documentary, more interesting for the material it offers than for the brilliance of its presentation. Comic highlight: a passionate if incoherent interview with Beach Boy Brian Wilson, who used the theremin on his hit record "Good Vibrations." [PG]▼●

There's a Girl in My Soup (1970-British) **C-95m.** *½ D: Roy Boulting. Peter Sellers, Goldie Hawn, Tony Britton, Nicky Henson, Diana Dors, Nicola Pagett, Christopher Cazenove. Middle-aged Sellers groping for youth, woos kookie Hawn. Silly story, just a few real laughs. [R]▼

There's Always a Price Tag (1958-French) **102m.** **½ D: Denys de la Patelliere. Michele Morgan, Daniel Gelin, Peter Van Eyck, Bernard Blier. Morgan is excellent in DOUBLE INDEMNITY-type plot about wife who conspires to murder her husband, but film drags and loses credibility after promising start.

There's Always a Woman (1938) **82m.** *** D: Alexander Hall. Joan Blondell, Melvyn Douglas, Mary Astor, Frances Drake, Jerome Cowan, Robert Paige, Thurston Hall. Fine blend of mystery and comedy as D.A. Douglas and detective-wife Blondell try to solve same crime.

There's Always Tomorrow (1956) **84m.** **½ D: Douglas Sirk. Barbara Stanwyck, Fred MacMurray, Joan Bennett, William Reynolds, Pat Crowley, Gigi Perreau, Jane Darwell. MacMurray is in a rut, at work and at home, making him particularly susceptible to old-flame Stanwyck, who comes back into his life. Sudsy but well-acted soap opera, filmed before in 1934.

Therese (1986-French) **C-91m.** *** D: Alain Cavalier. Catherine Mouchet, Aurore Prieto, Sylvie Habault, Ghislane Mona, Helene Alexandridis. Stark, stylistically directed, fact-based story of a dreamy, intense 15-year-old girl (Mouchet) and her desire to become a Carmelite nun, to be wedded to Christ. Winner of six César Awards, including Best Picture. Remake of the 1938 film THERESE MARTIN. ▼

Therese Desqueyroux (1962-French) **107m.** **½ D: Georges Franju. Emmanuele Riva, Philippe Noiret, Edith Scob, Sami Frey. Bored Riva tries to poison rich husband Noiret; she's acquitted in court, but still does not escape punishment. Riva stands out in this otherwise gloomy drama adapted from a Francois Mauriac novel.

There's Magic in Music (1941) **79m.** ** D: Andrew L. Stone. Allan Jones, Susanna Foster, Diana Lynn, Margaret Lindsay, Lynne Overman, Grace Bradley. Adequate showcase for Foster, an ex-burlesque singer who becomes an opera diva at a summer music camp.

There's No Business Like Show Business (1954) **C-117m.** **½ D: Walter Lang. Ethel Merman, Dan Dailey, Donald O'Connor, Marilyn Monroe, Johnnie Ray, Mitzi Gaynor, Hugh O'Brian, Frank McHugh. Gaudy (and seemingly interminable) hokum about a show-biz family, built around catalog of Irving Berlin songs. Entertaining if not inspired, with several expensive numbers designed to fill the wide screen. Merman and Dailey are fine, Marilyn's at her sexiest, and O'Connor is in top form throughout. Then there's Johnnie Ray deciding to become a priest. . . . CinemaScope.▼●

There's One Born Every Minute (1942) **59m.** ** D: Harold Young. Hugh Herbert, Tom Brown, Peggy Moran, Guy Kibbee, Gus Schilling, Edgar Kennedy, Carl "Alfalfa" Switzer, Elizabeth Taylor. Contrived comedy of nutty family whose erstwhile head (Herbert) runs a pudding company. Notable as screen debut of 10-year-old Liz as junior member of the clan.

There's Something About Mary (1998) **C-119m.** ** D: Bobby Farrelly, Peter Farrelly. Cameron Diaz, Matt Dillon, Ben Stiller, Lee Evans, Chris Elliott, Lin Shaye, Jeffrey Tambor, Markie Post, Keith David, Jonathan Richman. Hugely popular comedy about a guy who's never stopped loving the girl he almost got to take to the high school prom—until a painful accident interfered. The ultimate in sophomoric comedy, reveling in politically incorrect gags, but it drags on for two hours. It's only the very appealing Mary (Diaz) who keeps it afloat. [R] ▼●◗

There Was a Crooked Man . . . (1970) **C-125m.** ***½ D: Joseph L. Mankiewicz. Kirk Douglas, Henry Fonda, Hume Cronyn, Warren Oates, Burgess Meredith, John Randolph, Michael Blodgett, Arthur O'Connell, Martin Gabel, Alan Hale, Victor French, Barbara Rhoades, Lee Grant. Bawdy, entertaining Western-comedy-prison-film with Douglas as cocky inmate at territorial prison circa 1883 who matches wits with progressive warden Fonda towards one goal: escape. Powerhouse cast, handsome production. Written by David Newman and Robert Benton. Panavision. [R]▼●

These Are the Damned (1962-British) **96m.** **½ D: Joseph Losey. Macdonald Carey, Shirley Anne Field, Viveca Lindfors, Alexander Knox, Oliver Reed, James Villiers. Odd film chronicling American Carey's confrontation with a Teddy Boy motorcycle gang in Weymouth—after which the scenario becomes a *Twilight Zone*–like sci-fi drama! Original British title: THE DAMNED. Hammerscope.

These Glamour Girls (1939) **80m.** **½ D: S. Sylvan Simon. Lew Ayres, Lana Turner, Richard Carlson, Anita Louise, Marsha Hunt, Ann Rutherford, Mary Beth Hughes, Jane Bryan, Tom Brown. Turner is effective as nonsocialite who turns the tables on sneering girls at swank college weekend; naive but polished gloss.

These Thousand Hills (1959) **C-96m.** *** D: Richard Fleischer. Don Murray, Richard Egan, Lee Remick, Patricia Owens, Stuart Whitman, Albert Dekker, Harold J. Stone. Adult Western with Murray a rancher who learns to accept responsibility and maintain loyalty to dependent friends; sturdy cast. Based on a novel by A.B. Guthrie, Jr. CinemaScope.

These Three (1936) **93m.** **** D: William Wyler. Miriam Hopkins, Merle Oberon, Joel McCrea, Catherine Doucet, Alma Kruger, Bonita Granville, Marcia Mae Jones, Margaret Hamilton, Walter Brennan. Penetrating drama of two young women (Oberon, Hopkins) running school, ruined by lies of malicious student Granville; loosely based on Lillian Hellman's *The Children's Hour*. Superb acting by all, with Granville chillingly impressive; scripted by the playwright. Remade in 1961 by same director as THE CHILDREN'S HOUR. ▼●

These Wilder Years (1956) **91m.** **½ D: Roy Rowland. James Cagney, Barbara Stanwyck, Walter Pidgeon, Betty Lou Keim, Don Dubbins, Edward Andrews, Dean Jones, Tom Laughlin. Unusual to see Cagney in this kind of soap opera, about a man who wants to find his illegitimate son, and becomes involved with teenage unwed mother (Keim) through intervention of foundling home director Stanwyck. Look for young Michael Landon in pool room.

They (1993) **C-99m. TVM** D: John Korty. Patrick Bergin, Vanessa Redgrave, Valerie Mahaffey, Nancy Moore Atchison, Rutanya Alda, Brandlyn Whitaker, Ken Strong, Bill Bender, Benji Wilhoite. Very moving psychological drama–fantasy about workaholic dad Bergin, desperately lacking in good parenting skills, and how he deals with a deeply wounding family tragedy. Redgrave is excellent as usual as a blind seer who has a key role in the proceedings. Based on a short story by Rudyard Kipling. Made for cable. Video title: THEY WATCH. Above average. [PG-13]▼

They All Died Laughing SEE: **Jolly Bad Fellow, A**

They All Kissed the Bride (1942) **85m.** **½ D: Alexander Hall. Joan Crawford, Melvyn Douglas, Roland Young, Billie Burke, Allen Jenkins. Good stars in fairly amusing film of man being arrested for kissing bride at wedding.▼

They All Laughed (1981) **C-115m.** **½ D: Peter Bogdanovich. Audrey Hepburn, Ben Gazzara, John Ritter, Colleen Camp, Dorothy Stratten, Blaine Novak, Patti Hansen, George Morfogen, Sean Ferrer, Glenn Scarpelli, Elizabeth Pena. Quirky romantic comedy, long on style, short on substance, follows the adventures and amours of four private detectives. Spotlights some sharp-looking ladies, makes excellent use of N.Y.C. locations, but personal taste will have to judge its degree of success. Ferrer is the son of Hepburn and Mel Ferrer. Stratten was killed prior to film's release. [PG]▼●

They Call It Sin (1932) **75m.** ** D: Thornton Freeland. Loretta Young, David Manners, George Brent, Louis Calhern, Una Merkel, Elizabeth Patterson. Restless small-town girl is wooed by visiting New Yorker, and follows him to the big city, where she discovers he's engaged to another woman. Interesting at first, then increasingly silly and predictable, but the stars certainly are attractive. Merkel is fun as Loretta's perky pal.▼

They Call Me Bruce? (1982) **C-88m.** *½ D: Elliot Hong. Johnny Yune, Ralph Mauro, Pam Huntington, Margaux Hemingway. Unfunny, frequently obnoxious kung fu parody with Korean comedian Yune a doltish cook who is constantly mistaken for Bruce Lee. About two-thirds of the gags are based on TV commercials. Aka A FISTFUL OF CHOPSTICKS and followed by THEY STILL CALL ME BRUCE. [PG]▼

They Call Me MISTER Tibbs! (1970) **C-108m.** ** D: Gordon Douglas. Sidney Poitier, Barbara McNair, Martin Landau, David Sheiner, Anthony Zerbe, Jeff Corey, Ed Asner. Weak follow-up to IN THE HEAT OF THE NIGHT finds black detective Virgil Tibbs (now married and living in San Francisco) investigating murder of girl, with priest-friend Landau implicated. Followed by THE ORGANIZATION. [PG]▼

They Call Me Trinity (1971-Italian) **C-109m.** **½ D: E. B. Clucher (Enzo Barboni). Terence Hill, Bud Spencer, Farley Granger, Gisela Hahn, Stephen Zacharias, Dan Sturkie. Wild spoof of THE MAGNIFICENT SEVEN made international superstars of Hill and Spencer; they play half-brothers who try to help Mormon settlement protect itself from the inevitable band of Mexican marauders. Virtually nonstop slapstick spiced with gentle ribbing of the spaghetti Western genre; good fun. Sequel: TRINITY IS STILL MY NAME. Techniscope. [G]▼●

They Came From Beyond Space (1967-British) **C-85m.** BOMB D: Freddie Francis. Robert Hutton, Jennifer Jayne, Zia Mohyeddin, Bernard Kay, Michael Gough. Hutton is free to combat spacemen because the silver plate he carries inside his skull makes him immune to their powers. Based on Joseph Millard's *The Gods Hate Kansas.* ▼

They Came From Within (1975-Canadian) **C-87m.** *½ D: David Cronenberg. Paul Hampton, Joe Silver, Lynn Lowry, Allen Magicovsky, Barbara Steele, Susan Petrie. Bizarre, sexually-oriented parasites run rampant through dwellers in high-rise apartment building with plenty of gory violence quick to ensue. First "major" film by cult favorite Cronenberg sets the disgusting pattern for most of his subsequent pictures. Originally titled SHIVERS, then THE PARASITE MURDERS. Cut to 77m. for TV. [R]▼●◗

They Came to Blow Up America (1943) **73m.** ** D: Edward Ludwig. George Sanders, Anna Sten, Ward Bond, Dennis Hoey, Sig Ruman, Ludwig Stossel, Robert Barrat. Overzealous espionage yarn designed for WW2 audiences, dated now. Good cast is only virtue.

They Came to Cordura (1959) **C-123m.** **½ D: Robert Rossen. Gary Cooper, Rita Hayworth, Van Heflin, Tab Hunter, Richard Conte, Michael Callan, Dick York. Soapy oater set in 1916 Mexico. Cooper is Army officer accused of cowardice, sent to find five men worthy of Medal of Honor. Hayworth is shady lady he meets on the way. CinemaScope.▼●

They Came to Rob Las Vegas (1968-Spanish-French-Italian) **C-128m.** ** D: Antonio Isasi. Gary Lockwood, Elke Sommer, Lee J. Cobb, Jack Palance. Big heist is small potatoes as armed robbers plot to intercept Vegas gambling money. Techniscope. [R]

They Dare Not Love (1941) **76m.** *½ D: James Whale. George Brent, Martha Scott, Paul Lukas, Egon Brecher, Roman Bohnen, Edgar Barrier. Good story idea submerged by silly script and Brent's miscasting as dashing Austrian prince, who tries to bargain with Gestapo officer Lukas on behalf of his country. Lloyd Bridges has small role as Nazi seaman.

They Died With Their Boots On (1941) **138m.** *** D: Raoul Walsh. Errol Flynn, Olivia de Havilland, Arthur Kennedy, Charley Grapewin, Gene Lockhart, Anthony Quinn, Stanley Ridges, Sydney Greenstreet, Regis Toomey, Hattie McDaniel, Walter Hampden. Sweeping Hollywood version of

Little Bighorn battle, with Flynn flamboyant as Custer. Fine vignettes amidst episodic buildup to exciting Last Stand climax. This being Errol and Olivia's final film together lends poignance to their farewell scene. Superb score by Max Steiner. Also shown in computer-colored version. ▼●

They Drive by Night (1940) **93m.** ***½ D: Raoul Walsh. George Raft, Ann Sheridan, Ida Lupino, Humphrey Bogart, Gale Page, Alan Hale, Roscoe Karns. Marvelous melodrama of truck-driving brothers, Bogie and Raft, battling the dangers of the open road as well as a murder frame-up by Lupino. Unforgettable dialogue by Jerry Wald and Richard Macaulay. Partial reworking of BORDERTOWN. Also shown in computer-colored version.▼●

They Gave Him a Gun (1937) **94m.** **½ D: W. S. Van Dyke II. Spencer Tracy, Gladys George, Franchot Tone, Edgar Dearing, Charles Trowbridge, Cliff Edwards, Mary Lou Treen. Gun-shy hayseed Tone, who was taught "thou shalt not kill," changes dramatically when he fights in WW1. Tracy is his devoted pal, who later tries to save him from a life of crime. Dramatically obvious, and falls apart with the entrance of nurse George; still, the opening montage is striking, and the war-related scenes exceptional.

They Got Me Covered (1943) **95m.** ** D: David Butler. Bob Hope, Dorothy Lamour, Lenore Aubert, Otto Preminger, Eduardo Ciannelli, Marion Martin, Donald MacBride, Walter Catlett, Donald Meek. Spy yarn (by Harry Kurnitz) set in Washington was topical at the time, awkward now; not up to Hope standards.▼●◗

They Knew What They Wanted (1940) **96m.** *** D: Garson Kanin. Carole Lombard, Charles Laughton, William Gargan, Harry Carey, Frank Fay. Laughton and Lombard are excellent in this flawed adaptation by Robert Ardrey of Sidney Howard's play (filmed twice before). He's an Italian grape-grower in California who conducts correspondence with waitress and asks her to marry him. Fay is too sanctimonious for words as local priest. Watch for Karl Malden and Tom Ewell as rowdy guests at the pre-wedding party.▼

They Learned About Women (1930) **81m.** *** D: Jack Conway, Sam Wood. Joseph T. Schenck, Gus Van, Bessie Love, Mary Doran, J. C. Nugent, Benny Rubin, Tom Dugan, Eddie Gribbon, Francis X. Bushman, Jr. Enjoyable early-talkie musical is a precursor/variation of TAKE ME OUT TO THE BALL GAME. Real-life vaudeville stars Van and Schenck play a pair of baseball-playing vaudevillians; Schenck is set to marry nice-girl Love, but a vamp (Doran) gets in the way.●

They Live (1988) **C-97m.** ** D: John Carpenter. Roddy Piper, Keith David, Meg Foster, George "Buck" Flower, Peter Jason, Raymond St. Jacques, Jason Robards III, Larry Franco. Lonely drifter arrives in L.A., discovers that consumerist society is being dominated by aliens, whose human disguises and subliminal advertising messages are visible only through special glasses. Satiric sci-fi adventure begins well, degenerates into standard urban action piece, not helped by awful alien makeup. Screenwriter "Frank Armitage" (working from a short story by Ray Faraday Nelson) is actually director Carpenter. Panavision. [R]▼●◗

They Live by Night (1949) **95m.** ***½ D: Nicholas Ray. Farley Granger, Cathy O'Donnell, Howard da Silva, Jay C. Flippen, Helen Craig. Director Ray's first film is sensitive, well-made story of young lovers who are fugitives from the law. Set in 1930s, it avoids clichés and builds considerable impact instead. Based on Edward Anderson's *Thieves Like Us*, remade in 1974 under that name. Also shown in computer-colored version.▼●

They Loved Life SEE: **Kanal**

They Made Me a Criminal (1939) **92m.** **½ D: Busby Berkeley. John Garfield, Claude Rains, Gloria Dickson, May Robson, Billy Halop, Huntz Hall, Leo Gorcey, Bobby Jordan, Gabriel Dell, Barbara Pepper, Ward Bond, Ann Sheridan. Garfield takes it on the lam when he thinks he's killed a reporter, stays out West with Robson and Dead End Kids. Enjoyable, with Rains miscast as a Dick Tracy type. Remake of THE LIFE OF JIMMY DOLAN. ▼●◗

They Made Me a Fugitive (1947-British) **103m.** *** D: Cavalcanti. Trevor Howard, Sally Gray, Griffith Jones, Rene Ray, Mary Merrall, Charles Farrell. Dilettante crook is double-crossed by his boss and seeks revenge while on the lam from police. Potent (yet little-known) British film noir packs a real punch, with no holds barred in terms of brutality (and refusal to provide a pat, happy ending). Strikingly photographed by Otto Heller. Look sharp and you'll spot young Peter Bull and Sebastian Cabot. Originally cut when released in U.S. as I BECAME A CRIMINAL; also trimmed for British reissue. Finally restored on video in 1999.▼

They Meet Again (1941) **67m.** *½ D: Erle C. Kenton. Jean Hersholt, Dorothy Lovett, Robert Baldwin, Neil Hamilton, Maude Eburne, Anne Bennett, Barton Yarborough, Arthur Hoyt. Boring entry in Hersholt's *Dr. Christian* series, with the good doctor attempting to prove the innocence of bank teller Yarborough, accused of pilfering $3,000. A real drag, except for little Leon Tyler's jive musical number during a birthday party, a real pip.▼

They Met in Argentina (1941) **77m.** *½

D: Leslie Goodwins, Jack Hively. Maureen O'Hara, James Ellison, Alberto Vila, Buddy Ebsen, Joseph Buloff. Hollywood embraces Pan America in this dismal musical; oil company representative Ellison goes South of the Border, where he mixes business with beautiful O'Hara.

They Met in Bombay (1941) **93m.** **½ D: Clarence Brown. Clark Gable, Rosalind Russell, Peter Lorre, Jessie Ralph, Reginald Owen, Eduardo Ciannelli. Two jewel thieves team up in ordinary romantic comedy-actioner, spiced by Lorre as money-hungry cargo-ship captain. Look for Alan Ladd in a small role.▼

They Might Be Giants (1971) **C-98m.** *** D: Anthony Harvey. Joanne Woodward, George C. Scott, Jack Gilford, Lester Rawlins, Al Lewis, Rue McClanahan, Theresa Merritt, Eugene Roche, James Tolkan, Kitty Winn, Sudie Bond, F. Murray Abraham, Paul Benedict, M. Emmet Walsh. Fun yarn of slightly daffy gentleman (Scott) who believes he is Sherlock Holmes, and his psychiatrist tagalong (Woodward) whose real name is Dr. Watson. Expanded for TV; theatrical version ran only 88m. See also THE RETURN OF THE WORLD'S GREATEST DETECTIVE. [G]▼◗

They Only Kill Their Masters (1972) **C-97m.** **½ D: James Goldstone. James Garner, Katharine Ross, Hal Holbrook, Harry Guardino, June Allyson, Christopher Connelly, Tom Ewell, Peter Lawford, Edmond O'Brien, Arthur O'Connell, Ann Rutherford. Great cast in complicated modern-day whodunit set in coastal California town; tries for Dashiell Hammett feeling, doesn't quite make it. Policeman Garner tries to solve murder of pregnant woman, with formidable Doberman pinscher figuring prominently. Not bad, but a letdown. [PG]▼

They Passed This Way SEE: **Four Faces West**

They Ran for Their Lives (1968) **C-92m.** ** D: Oliver Drake (John Payne). John Payne, Jim Davis, Luana Patten, John Carradine. Fair drama featuring Payne as nobody coming to aid of young woman who's being pursued by thugs after classified documents which once belonged to her father.

They're Playing With Fire (1984) **C-96m.** BOMB D: Howard (Hikmet) Avedis. Eric Brown, Sybil Danning, Andrew Prine, Paul Clemens, K. T. Stevens. What starts off as rehash of Brown's PRIVATE LESSONS quickly turns into sick, ugly slasher film. Danning (as a college English professor!) lures Brown into helping her with a let's-kill-Mom-and-make-off-with-my-inheritance plot—except that someone else is killing everybody in sight. Not even Danning's formidable nude scenes are reason enough to sit through this slop. [R]▼

They Rode West (1954) **C-84m.** **½ D: Phil Karlson. Robert Francis, Donna Reed, May Wynn, Phil Carey, Onslow Stevens. Camp commander prevents army surgeon from attempting to treat Indian epidemic. Good cast in better than average Western.

They Saved Hitler's Brain (1963) **74m.** BOMB D: David Bradley. Walter Stocker, Audrey Caire, Carlos Rivas, John Holland, Dani Lynn, Marshall Reed, Nestor Paiva. Daughter of kidnapped scientist traces him to isle of Mandoras, where Nazis still flourish under the leadership of Hitler's still-living head. Unbelievably muddled plot results from intercutting 1950s studio potboiler, beautifully photographed by Stanley Cortez (MAGNIFICENT AMBERSONS) with super-cheap 1960s footage involving completely different cast. Originally titled MADMEN OF MANDORAS.▼

They Shall Have Music (1939) **101m.** *** D: Archie Mayo. Jascha Heifetz, Joel McCrea, Andrea Leeds, Walter Brennan, Gene Reynolds, Marjorie Main, Porter Hall, Dolly Loehr (Diana Lynn), Terry Kilburn. Cornerstone of Samuel Goldwyn's efforts to bring classical music to the masses. Slum brat Reynolds' interest in the violin is sparked after hearing Heifetz in concert; the boy soon becomes a student at a settlement music school. Heifetz has five violin solos.▼●

They Shoot Horses, Don't They? (1969) **C-121m.** ***½ D: Sydney Pollack. Jane Fonda, Michael Sarrazin, Susannah York, Gig Young, Red Buttons, Bonnie Bedelia, Bruce Dern, Allyn Ann McLerie, Michael Conrad, Al Lewis, Severn Darden, Art Metrano, Paul Mantee. 1930s marathon dance becomes microcosm of life, with myriad of subplots, characters' lives intertwining. Fonda is self-destructive girl who attracts aimless Sarrazin with tragic results; Young won Oscar as oily promoter of grueling "contest." Fascinating. Based on Horace McCoy's novel; script by James Poe and Robert E. Thompson. Panavision. [M/PG]▼●◗

They Still Call Me Bruce (1987) **C-91m.** *½ D: Johnny Yune, James Orr. Johnny Yune, David Mendenhall, Pat Paulsen, Joey Travolta, Robert Guillaume, Bethany Wright, Carl Bensen. In-name-only sequel to THEY CALL ME BRUCE has at least one thing in common with its predecessor: it's awful. This time Yune plays a Korean searching for the American GI who saved him years ago, winding up instead as a big-brother figure for orphan Mendenhall. [PG]▼

They Watch SEE: **They**

They Went That-A-Way and That-A-Way (1978) **C-95m.** *½ D: Edward Montagne, Stuart E. McGowan. Tim Conway, Chuck

McCann, Richard Kiel, Dub Taylor, Reni Santoni. Lame prison escape comedy (with script by Conway) puts Conway and McCann through lackluster routines as a road-company Laurel and Hardy. [PG]▼

They Were Expendable (1945) **135m.** **** D: John Ford. Robert Montgomery, John Wayne, Donna Reed, Jack Holt, Ward Bond, Louis Jean Heydt, Marshall Thompson, Leon Ames, Cameron Mitchell, Russell Simpson, Jack Pennick, Robert Barrat, Tom Tyler. One of the finest (and most underrated) of all WW2 films, based on the true story of America's PT boat squadron in the Philippines during the early days of the war. Moving, exquisitely detailed production (photographed by Joseph August) under Ford's distinctive hand, with real-life Naval officer Montgomery a convincing lead. Screenplay by Frank "Spig" Wead. Also shown in computer-colored version.▼●◗

They Were Sisters (1945-British) **110m.** **½ D: Arthur Crabtree. Phyllis Calvert, James Mason, Hugh Sinclair, Dulcie Gray, Pamela Kellino (Mason). Fresh approach to stock drama of trio of sisters with contrasting marriages and lives.

They Were So Young (1955-German) **80m.** *** D: Kurt Neumann. Scott Brady, Raymond Burr, Johanna Matz, Ingrid Stenn. Nicely produced, grim melodrama of girls sent to South America to be used by crooks. Even without "names" in cast, film would be good. Aka VIOLATED and PARTY GIRLS FOR SALE.▼

They Who Dare (1953-British) **C-101m.** **½ D: Lewis Milestone. Dirk Bogarde, Denholm Elliott, Akim Tamiroff, Eric Pohlmann, David Peel. Effective WW2 actioner with good character delineation, tracing commando raid on German-controlled Aegean air fields.

They Won't Believe Me (1947) **95m.** ***½ D: Irving Pichel. Susan Hayward, Robert Young, Jane Greer, Rita Johnson, Tom Powers, Don Beddoe, Frank Ferguson. Fine James Cain-type melodrama about a philanderer who gets involved with three women, leading to tragedy (and a terrific twist ending). Young excels in his unsympathetic role; Johnson does wonders with her scenes as his wife.▼●

They Won't Forget (1937) **95m.** **** D: Mervyn LeRoy. Claude Rains, Gloria Dickson, Otto Kruger, Allyn Joslyn, Elisha Cook, Jr., Edward Norris. Electrifying drama begins when pretty high school student is murdered in Southern town. A man is arrested, and a big-time Northern lawyer takes the case, but everyone seems more interested in exploiting personal interests than in seeing justice triumph. No punches are pulled in this still-powerful film. Lana Turner plays the unfortunate girl, in her first important role. Script by Robert Rossen and Aben Kandel, from the book *Death in the Deep South* by Ward Greene; based on notorious 1913 incident later dramatized for TV as THE MURDER OF MARY PHAGAN.▼

Thicker Than Water (1993-British) **C-144m. TVM** D: Marc Evans. Theresa Russell, Jonathan Pryce, Robert Pugh, Catherine Neilson, Richard Lynch, Martin Troakes. Russell (in dual role) plays twin sisters with a unique psychic bond caught up in jealousy and (eventually) murder. Russell's low-key performance drains any suspense, and the rest of the cast just goes through the motions. Based on the novel by Dylan Jones. Average.▼

Thief, The (1952) **85m.** **½ D: Russell Rouse. Ray Milland, Rita Gam, Martin Gabel, Harry Bronson. Spy yarn set in N.Y.C. with a difference: no dialogue. Gimmick grows wearisome, script is tame.▼

Thief (1981) **C-122m.** *** D: Michael Mann. James Caan, Tuesday Weld, Willie Nelson, James Belushi, Robert Prosky, Tom Signorelli, Dennis Farina, William L. Petersen. Arresting drama about a professional thief, inventively realized by writer-director Mann (in his feature debut). Caan is excellent as the man with one drive: survival. Stylishly photographed (by Donald Thorin) and scored (by Tangerine Dream). [R]▼●◗

Thief, The (1997-Russian) **C-94m.** *** D: Pavel Chukhrai. Vladimir Mashkov, Ekaterina Rednikova, Misha Philipchuk. Intimate character study set in post WW2 Russia: an abandoned single mother and her adorable 6-year-old son fall for a swarthy military officer, not knowing he's really a petty thief. A powerful tragedy, simply and beautifully told, with superlative performances from its three leads, particularly Mashkov, who exudes the sexy malevolence of a young Robert Mitchum. [R]▼●◗

Thief and the Cobbler, The SEE: **Arabian Knight**

Thief of Bagdad, The (1924) **155m.** ***½ D: Raoul Walsh. Douglas Fairbanks, Julanne Johnston, Anna May Wong, Sojin, Snitz Edwards, Charles Belcher, Brandon Hurst. Fairbanks is unusually balletic (and ingratiating as ever) in this elaborate Arabian Nights pantomime, designed to instill a true sense of wonder. Quite long, but never dull; one of the most imaginative of all silent films, with awesome sets by William Cameron Menzies. Remade three times (so far). ▼●◗

Thief of Bagdad, The (1940-British) **C-106m.** **** D: Ludwig Berger, Tim Whelan, Michael Powell. Sabu, John Justin, June Duprez, Conrad Veidt, Rex Ingram, Miles Malleson, Mary Morris. Remarkable fantasy of native boy Sabu outdoing evil magician Veidt in Arabian Nights fable with incredible Oscar-winning Technicolor photography by Georges Perinal and Osmond Borradaile, special effects and art direction. Ingram gives splendid performance as a genie; vivid score by Miklos Rozsa. ▼●

Thief of Baghdad (1961-Italian) **C-90m.** ** D: Arthur Lubin. Steve Reeves, Giorgia Moll, Arturo Dominici, Edy Vessel. Reeves searches for enchanted blue rose so he can marry Sultan's daughter. Nothing like Sabu version, but occasionally atmospheric. CinemaScope. ▼

Thief of Baghdad, The (1978-British-French) **C-100m. TVM** D: Clive Donner. Roddy McDowall, Peter Ustinov, Kabir Bedi, Frank Finlay, Marina Vlady, Terrence Stamp, Pavla Ustinov, Ian Holm. More flying carpet and genie-in-the-magic-lamp fantasy in this fourth filming of the Arabian Nights adventure that's handsome enough but nowhere near the definitive 1940 version. Average.▼

Thief of Damascus (1952) **C-78m.** ** D: Will Jason. Paul Henreid, John Sutton, Jeff Donnell, Lon Chaney (Jr.), Elena Verdugo. Jumbled costume spectacle featuring Aladdin, Sinbad and Ali Baba out to rescue princess; typical Sam Katzman quickie reuses footage from JOAN OF ARC!

Thief of Hearts (1984) **C-100m.** ** D: Douglas Day Stewart. Steven Bauer, Barbara Williams, John Getz, David Caruso, Christine Ebersole, George Wendt. While ransacking a house Bauer steals woman's diaries, reads them through, and then determines to woo her—using the "secret" knowledge he's learned. Slick but curiously unappealing film written by first-time director Stewart. Reworked slightly for homevideo, with potentially X-rated shots added. [R]▼●

Thief of Paris, The (1967-French) **C-119m.** *** D: Louis Malle. Jean-Paul Belmondo, Genevieve Bujold, Marie Dubois, Francoise Fabian, Julien Guiomar. Solid comedy-drama with personal setbacks turning Belmondo to thievery for revenge on society; soon he finds that robbery has become his whole life.

Thief Who Came to Dinner, The (1973) **C-105m.** ** D: Bud Yorkin. Ryan O'Neal, Jacqueline Bisset, Warren Oates, Jill Clayburgh, Charles Cioffi, Ned Beatty, Austin Pendleton, Gregory Sierra, Michael Murphy, John Hillerman. Disappointing caper comedy (considering cast and director) about a computer expert who becomes a jewel thief in Houston's top social circles. Clayburgh (pre-stardom) has small but telling role as O'Neal's ex-wife; script by Walter Hill. [PG]▼

Thieves (1977) **C-92m.** BOMB D: John Berry. Marlo Thomas, Charles Grodin, Irwin Corey, Hector Elizondo, Mercedes McCambridge, John McMartin, Gary Merrill, Ann Wedgeworth. Pretentious, boring adaptation of Herb Gardner's play about crazy couple trying to recapture their innocence in a corrupt N.Y.C. Corey (as Thomas' cabbie father) adds only life to so-called comedy. Bob Fosse has a brief role. [PG]

Thieves (1996) SEE: **Les Voleurs**

Thieves Fall Out (1941) **72m.** ** D: Ray Enright. Eddie Albert, Joan Leslie, Alan Hale, William T. Orr, John Litel, Anthony Quinn, Edward Brophy. Innocuous drama of rival mattress factory families and their problems.

Thieves' Highway (1949) **94m.** *** D: Jules Dassin. Richard Conte, Valentina Cortese, Lee J. Cobb, Barbara Lawrence, Jack Oakie, Millard Mitchell, Joseph Pevney. Tough postwar drama of a returning vet seeking to avenge his trucker/father's treatment at the hands of a crooked fruit dealer in San Francisco. Masterfully directed; script by A. I. Bezzerides, from his novel. Only the ending seems pat.

Thieves' Holiday (1946) **100m.** *** D: Douglas Sirk. George Sanders, Signe Hasso, Carole Landis, Akim Tamiroff, Gene Lockhart. Famous French thief and rogue, beautifully played by Sanders, works his way into position as prefect of police. Delightful romantic adventure. Originally titled SCANDAL IN PARIS.▼

Thieves Like Us (1974) **C-123m.** ***½ D: Robert Altman. Keith Carradine, Shelley Duvall, John Schuck, Bert Remsen, Louise Fletcher, Ann Latham, Tom Skerritt. Three misfits escape from prison camp in 1930s Midwest, go on a crime spree; the youngest (Carradine) falls in love with a simple, uneducated girl (Duvall). Despite familiar trappings, Altman digs deep into period atmosphere and strong characterizations; this film gets better every time you look at it. Remake of THEY LIVE BY NIGHT. Scripted by Calder Willingham, Joan Tewkesbury, and Altman. [R]▼●

Thin Air (1969-British) **C-91m.** *½ D: Gerry Levy. George Sanders, Maurice Evans, Patrick Allen, Neil Connery, Hilary Dwyer, Robert Flemyng. Parachutists keep disappearing, due to unseen forces; routine sci-fi with little to recommend it. Original British title: THE BODY STEALERS (INVASION OF THE BODY STEALERS). [G]▼

Thin Blue Line, The (1988) **C-96m.** **** D: Errol Morris. Remarkable, perhaps even landmark, documentary, as Morris sets out to prove that a convicted hitchhiker did *not* kill a Dallas policeman in 1976—and that the lowlife who fingered him (and who wound up on Death Row for a subsequent murder) did. Very subjective but totally convincing, so much so that the case was reopened after film's premiere, and the defendant was exonerated. Philip Glass's score adds to hypnotic effect. ▼●

Thing, The (1982) **C-108m.** *½ D: John Carpenter. Kurt Russell, A. Wilford Brimley, Richard Dysart, Richard Masur, Donald Moffat, T.K. Carter, David Clennon. Remake of 1951 film about Antarctic outpost terrorized by an alien organism. More faithful to the original story, but nonstop parade of slimy, repulsive special effects turns this into a freak show and drowns most of the suspense. Panavision. [R]▼●◗

Thing Called Love, The (1993) **C-116m.** **½ D: Peter Bogdanovich. River Phoenix, Samantha Mathis, Dermot Mulroney, Sandra Bullock, K. T. Oslin, Anthony Clark, Webb Wilder, Trisha Yearwood. Ordinary drama about country singer-songwriter Mathis, who yearns to make it in Nashville, and her experiences as she strives for success. At its best when depicting the friendship and rivalry among struggling artists. Of interest mostly as one of Phoenix's last films; he's good as a sulky but talented singer who covers up his emotions. [PG-13]▼●

Thing From Another World, The (1951) **87m.** ***½ D: Christian Nyby. Kenneth Tobey, Margaret Sheridan, Robert Cornthwaite, Douglas Spencer, James Arness, Dewey Martin, William Self, George Fenneman. Classic blend of science-fiction and horror, loosely based on John W. Campbell, Jr.'s *Who Goes There?* Scientists at lonely Arctic outpost dig up alien (Arness) from the permafrost and must fight for their lives when it's accidentally thawed. Tense direction (often credited to producer Howard Hawks), excellent performances, eerie score by Dimitri Tiomkin. Screenplay by Charles Lederer. Watch out for 81m. reissue prints. Remade in 1982. Also shown in computer-colored version. ▼●

Things Are Tough All Over (1982) **C-92m.** ** D: Tom Avildsen. Cheech Marin, Thomas Chong, Shelby Fiddis, Rikki Marin, Evelyn Guerrero. Besides their standard characterizations, the boys play two Arab brothers whose paths cross C & C's as the latter drive a ritzy car to California, one that happens to have $5 million hidden inside. Superb makeup and mimicry give evidence to the team's genuine talent, but the laughs just aren't there most of the time. Panavision. [R]▼●

Things Change (1988) **C-100m.** **½ D: David Mamet. Don Ameche, Joe Mantegna, Robert Prosky, J. J. Johnson, Ricky Jay, Mike Nussbaum, Jack Wallace, Dan Conway, J. T. Walsh. Simple Italian shoemaker (Ameche) agrees to take the rap for a Chicago mob murder for a fee, but the man assigned to baby-sit him for a weekend (Mantegna) decides to take the old man on a final fling before he goes to jail. Slight, sometimes flat comic fable by Mamet and Shel Silverstein is buoyed by some wonderful vignettes and endearing performances by the stars. Ameche is a joy to watch. [PG]▼●◗

Things in Their Season (1974) **C-75m. TVM** D: James Goldstone. Patricia Neal, Ed Flanders, Marc Singer, Meg Foster, Charles Haid, Doreen Lang, Med Flory. Touching, beautifully acted drama of Wisconsin farm family, with wife-mother Neal discovering she is terminally ill with leukemia. Screenplay by John Gay. Above average.

Things to Come (1936-British) **92m.** *** D: William Cameron Menzies. Raymond Massey, Cedric Hardwicke, Ralph Richardson, Maurice Braddell, Edward Chapman, Ann Todd. Stunning visualization of H. G. Wells' depiction of the future. Massey portrays leader of new world, Richardson despotic wartime ruler. Aloof but always interesting, enhanced by Menzies' sets. Vibrant music by Arthur Bliss; Wells himself wrote the screenplay. Originally released at 108m. 1979 movie THE SHAPE OF THINGS TO COME, though taking the actual title of Wells' book, has nothing in common with this film.▼◗

Things To Do in Denver When You're Dead (1995) **C-124m.** ** D: Gary Fleder. Andy Garcia, Gabrielle Anwar, Christopher Walken, Christopher Lloyd, William Forsythe, Treat Williams, Bill Nunn, Steve Buscemi, Jack Warden, Fairuza Balk, Bill Cobbs, Marshall Bell, Glenn Plummer, Sarah Trigger, Jenny McCarthy, Don Cheadle. Another entry in the post-Tarantino, faux-hip crime genre, with Garcia as a reformed crook who agrees to stage an assault to placate his evil, now-wheelchaired mentor Walken. Naturally the plans go horribly wrong. Stylized, violent, and absolutely empty, though Williams' psycho is his best part in years, and Buscemi's hit man has a great name: Mr. Shhh. [R] ▼●◗

Thing That Couldn't Die, The (1958) **69m.** ** D: Will Cowan. Andra Martin, William Reynolds, Robin Hughes, Carolyn Kearney, Jeffrey Stone. You never know what a dowsing rod will find. In this thriller one finds the still living, decapitated head of a Spanish wizard who's looking for his body. Cheap, and looks it, but Hughes is good in title role.

Thing With Two Heads, The (1972) **C-93m.** ** D: Lee Frost. Ray Milland, Rosey Grier, Don Marshall, Roger Perry, Chelsea Brown. Fantastic tale of bigot who finds his head transplanted onto black man's body. Played partially for laughs, which helps a little. [PG]

Thin Ice (1937) **78m.** **½ D: Sidney Lanfield. Sonja Henie, Tyrone Power, Arthur Treacher, Joan Davis, Alan Hale, Raymond

Walburn, Sig Rumann. Satisfactory Henie vehicle, with sly, dashing prince Power romancing commoner Sonja. A highlight: Davis singing "I'm Olga From the Volga."▼

Think Dirty (1970-British) **C-94m.** *½ D: Jim Clark. Marty Feldman, Shelley Berman, Judy Cornwell, Julie Ege, Patrick Cargill, Jack Watson. Leering, obnoxious comedy-fantasy with adman Feldman having to use sex to promote a cereal on TV; meanwhile, his prudish wife is mounting a campaign to purify the airwaves. Original British title: EVERY HOME SHOULD HAVE ONE.▼

Think Fast, Mr. Moto (1937) **66m.** *** D: Norman Foster. Peter Lorre, Virginia Field, Sig Rumann, Murray Kinnell, Lotus Long, J. Carrol Naish. Lorre's first appearance as Moto, the wily Japanese detective, sends him from San Francisco to Shanghai on a worldwide chase after diamond smugglers. Swift, entertaining mystery with Lorre most amusing as the bespectacled master of disguise.

Thin Line Between Love and Hate, A (1996) **C-108m.** ** D: Martin Lawrence. Martin Lawrence, Lynn Whitfield, Regina King, Bobby Brown, Della Reese, Malinda Williams, Daryl M. Mitchell, Roger E. Mosley, Faizon Love. There is a thin line between a movie and a vanity production as director/cowriter/executive producer/star/music supervisor Lawrence plays a young man seemingly irresistible to women. He boasts to a friend that he can bed a beautiful but hard-to-get woman they encounter, leading to a comedic FATAL ATTRACTION: she's harder to get rid of than she ever was to get! Lawrence's first foray behind the scenes is amusing only in spots. Super 35. [R] ▼●◗

The Thin Man One series stands apart from the others; its episodes were filmed two and three years apart, its stars were those of the major rank, and the films were not looked down at as Grade-B efforts. This was THE THIN MAN, a highly successful series launched quite unexpectedly in 1934 with a delightfully unpretentious blend of screwball comedy and murder mystery, from a story by Dashiell Hammett. William Powell and Myrna Loy starred as Nick and Nora Charles, a perfectly happy, sophisticated couple whose marriage never stood in the way of their having fun and going off on detective capers. This blithe, carefree portrayal of a modern American couple was beautifully handled by Loy and Powell, and audiences loved it. Five Thin Man films followed, from 1936 to 1947. None of them fully captured the essence of the original, although they retained much of the charm and had the infallible byplay of the two stars, aided by their dog Asta, who soon became a star in his own right. AFTER THE THIN MAN featured an up-and-coming actor named James Stewart as a suspect, and Sam Levene in the detective role played in the original by Nat Pendleton (and repeated in ANOTHER THIN MAN). ANOTHER THIN MAN also introduced Nick Charles, Jr. as a baby, who grew up in each successive film. SHADOW OF THE THIN MAN was next in the series, and featured Nick and Nora sleuthing at the race track. THE THIN MAN GOES HOME presented Nick's parents (Harry Davenport and Lucile Watson), who never wanted him to be a detective in the first place. The final film, SONG OF THE THIN MAN, had Nick and Nora frequenting many jazz hangouts (à la *Peter Gunn*) for some offbeat sequences. While the original THIN MAN rated above its followups, even the weakest entries were fresh and enjoyable, thanks mainly to the two stars. An attempt to rekindle that magic in the 1991 Broadway musical *Nick and Nora* failed miserably. (A 1957–59 TV series starred Peter Lawford and Phyllis Kirk.) By the way, "The Thin Man" really wasn't Powell—he was a character in the first film, played by Edward Ellis.

THE THIN MAN

The Thin Man (1934)
After the Thin Man (1936)
Another Thin Man (1939)
Shadow of the Thin Man (1941)
The Thin Man Goes Home (1944)
Song of the Thin Man (1947)

Thin Man, The (1934) **93m.** **** D: W. S. Van Dyke. William Powell, Myrna Loy, Maureen O'Sullivan, Nat Pendleton, Minna Gombell, Cesar Romero, Natalie Moorhead, Edward Ellis, Porter Hall. Nick and Nora investigate the death of an inventor in this classic blend of laughs and suspense which marked the first pairing of what was to become one of the movies' great romantic teams. Shot in just two weeks by director Woody "One-Shot" Van Dyke and cinematographer James Wong Howe, this has gone on to become *the* sophisticated comedy-mystery par excellence, inspiring five sequels as well as countless imitations. Frances Goodrich and Albert Hackett adapted Dashiell Hammett's novel.▼●

Thin Man Goes Home, The (1944) **100m.** *** D: Richard Thorpe. William Powell, Myrna Loy, Lucile Watson, Gloria De Haven, Ann Revere, Helen Vinson, Harry Davenport, Leon Ames, Donald Meek, Edward Brophy. Nick takes the family on a vacation to Sycamore Springs to visit his parents, but naturally winds up embroiled in a murder case. Leisurely entry, with even more comedy than usual.▼●

Thinner (1996) **C-92m.** ** D: Tom Holland. Robert John Burke, Joe Mantegna, Lucinda Jenney, Joy Lenz, Michael Constantine, Sam Freed, Kari Wuhrer, John Horton, Daniel Von Bargen. Overweight Maine lawyer Burke accidentally kills an old gypsy woman, so her even older father (Constantine) puts a curse on him; he starts losing weight, and can't stop. Though well made, with good performances and astonishingly convincing makeup by Greg Cannom, the leading characters are unsympathetic and the situation unrelentingly grim. From the novel by Stephen King (writing as "Richard Bachman"), who has his usual cameo. Aka STEPHEN KING'S THINNER (which he is). [R]▼●◗

Thin Red Line, The (1964) **99m.** *** D: Andrew Marton. Keir Dullea, Jack Warden, James Philbrook, Kieron Moore. Gritty adaptation of James Jones' novel about personal conflict during the bloody attack on Guadalcanal during WW2. Dullea is the sensitive, iconoclastic soldier and Warden is the brutal sergeant who won't leave him alone. Remade in 1998. CinemaScope.

Thin Red Line, The (1998) **C-170m.** *** D: Terrence Malick. Sean Penn, Adrien Brody, Jim Caviezel, Ben Chaplin, Nick Nolte, Elias Koteas, John Cusack, Woody Harrelson, Jared Leto, Dash Mihok, Tim Blake Nelson, John C. Reilly, John Savage, George Clooney, John Travolta, Nick Stahl, Shawn Hatosy. Ethereal, moodily philosophical interpretation of James Jones' novel (previously filmed in 1964) about the taking of Guadalcanal during WW2, sparked by intense character studies: a pacifistic soldier (Caviezel), his antagonistic sergeant (Penn), a captain who refuses to sacrifice his men without cause (Koteas), a lieutenant colonel who only wants to see results (Nolte). These powerful portraits are the glue that holds the film together when it begins to wander. Those wanderings turned many viewers off, but the film's strengths outweigh its imperfections. Malick also scripted. Panavision. [R]▼●◗

Third Day, The (1965) **C-119m.** **½ D: Jack Smight. George Peppard, Elizabeth Ashley, Roddy McDowall, Arthur O'Connell, Mona Washbourne, Herbert Marshall, Robert Webber, Charles Drake, Sally Kellerman, Vincent Gardenia, Arte Johnson. Capable cast helps standard amnesia tale about Peppard's inability to remember events that have caused him to be accused of murder. Panavision.

Third Finger, Left Hand (1940) **96m.** ** D: Robert Z. Leonard. Myrna Loy, Melvyn Douglas, Raymond Walburn, Lee Bowman, Bonita Granville. Mediocre comedy with attractive stars. Loy dissuades romance by pretending to be married, so Douglas claims to be her husband!

Third Generation, The (1979-German) **C-111m.** ***½ D: Rainer Werner Fassbinder. Eddie Constantine, Hanna Schygulla, Volker Spengler, Margit Carstensen, Bulle Ogier, Udo Kier, Hark Bohm. Pitch-black comedy about upper-middle-class German terrorists, their cops-and-robbers antics, and how they provide excuse for government oppression. Superb ensemble cast in one of Fassbinder's best films.

Third Key, The (1956-British) **96m.** *** D: Charles Frend. Jack Hawkins, John Stratton, Dorothy Alison, Geoffrey Keen, Ursula Howells. Exciting story of Scotland Yard, as Inspector Hawkins and rookie sergeant (Stratton) diligently pursue safecracking incident to its surprising conclusion. Original British title: THE LONG ARM.▼

Third Man, The (1949-British) **104m.** **** D: Carol Reed. Orson Welles, Joseph Cotten, (Alida) Valli, Trevor Howard, Bernard Lee, Wilfrid Hyde-White. Graham Greene's account of mysterious Harry Lime (Welles) in post-WW2 Vienna is a bona fide classic, with pulp-writer Cotten on a manhunt for Harry. Anton Karas' zither rendition of "The Third Man Theme" adds just the right touch; cinematographer Robert Krasker won an Oscar. Note: there are two versions of this film. The British version features introductory narration by director Reed; the American print is narrated by Cotten, and runs 93m. Little of substance was actually cut, but the film was tightened somewhat by coproducer David O. Selznick. Also shown in computer-colored version.▼●◗

Third Man on the Mountain (1959) **C-105m.** *** D: Ken Annakin. James MacArthur, Michael Rennie, Janet Munro, James Donald, Herbert Lom, Laurence Naismith. Fine Disney adventure about Swiss boy (MacArthur) determined to climb the Matterhorn (here called the Citadel) who learns more than just mountain-climbing in his dogged pursuit. Look quickly to spot MacArthur's mother Helen Hayes in a cameo as tourist.▼●

Third Miracle, The (1999) **C-119m.** *** D: Agnieszka Holland. Ed Harris, Anne Heche, Armin Mueller-Stahl, Michael Rispoli, Charles Haid, James Gallanders, Caterina Scorsone, Barbara Sukowa. A priest who's struggling with his faith is assigned to investigate a statue of the Virgin Mary that's weeping blood; it's a direct link to a beloved woman in a working-class community whom many believe is worthy of nomination for sainthood. Consistently involving and surprising, with fine performances. Based on a novel by Richard Vetere. [R]▼

Third Secret, The (1964-British) **103m.** **½ D: Charles Crichton. Stephen Boyd, Jack Hawkins, Richard Attenborough, Diane

Cilento, Pamela Franklin, Paul Rogers, Alan Webb. Episodic whodunit with Boyd tracking down the murderer of his psychoanalyst; no surprises here. CinemaScope.

Third Solution, The (1989-Italian) **C-113m.** *½ D: Pasquale Squitieri. F. Murray Abraham, Treat Williams, Danny Aiello, Rita Rusic, Robert Balchus, Rossano Brazzi, Nigel Court. Good cast is wasted in this overbaked spy melodrama, with American Williams uncovering a plot to foil the Pope's scheduled visit to the Soviet Union. Original title: RUSSICUM. Panavision.▼●

Third Voice, The (1960) **79m.** *** D: Hubert Cornfield. Edmond O'Brien, Laraine Day, Julie London, Ralph Brooks, Roque Ybarra, Henry Delgado. Neat suspense film involving murder, impersonation and double-crossing. CinemaScope.

Thirst (1949) SEE: **Three Strange Loves**

Thirst (1979-Australian) **C-98m.** *** D: Rod Hardy. Chantal Contouri, David Hemmings, Henry Silva, Max Phipps, Shirley Cameron. Strange, stylish, chilling tale of secret society trying to brainwash Contouri and transform her into a baroness-vampire. Minimum of plot and characterization but maximum suspense in this well-directed shocker. Panavision. [R]▼

Thirsty Dead, The (1975) **C-90m.** BOMB D: Terry Becker. John Considine, Jennifer Billingsley, Judith McConnell, Tani Guthrie. Guide abducts actress and friends to jungle Shangri-La, where strange tribe drinks human blood to regain youth. Boring Philippine-made junk. Aka BLOOD HUNT. [PG]▼

13 SEE: **Eye of the Devil**

Thirteen Chairs, The (1970-French-Italian) **C-95m.** ** D: Nicholas Gessner. Vittorio Gassman, Sharon Tate, Orson Welles, Vittorio De Sica, Terry-Thomas, Mylene Demongeot, Tim Brooke Taylor. Slight comedy about a search for thirteen antique chairs, inside one of which is hidden a fortune. Of interest mainly for its cast, including Tate, who was murdered shortly after this was completed in 1969. Mel Brooks' version of this same, oft-filmed story was called THE TWELVE CHAIRS. Original title: 12 + 1.▼

13 Fighting Men (1960) **69m.** *½ D: Harry Gerstad. Grant Williams, Brad Dexter, Carole Mathews, Robert Dix, Richard Garland, Rayford Barnes, John Erwin. Minor film about Union soldiers fighting off Rebel troops to protect gold shipment. CinemaScope.

13 Frightened Girls (1963) **C-89m.** BOMB D: William Castle. Murray Hamilton, Joyce Taylor, Hugh Marlowe, Khigh Dhiegh. One of Castle's weirdest films (no mean feat), set in Swiss boarding school catering to daughters of diplomats; after trading bits of info they picked up from Daddy during the holidays, the girls decide to go off and do spy stuff. Castle held a worldwide talent search to find his "stars," for whom this was their first—and no doubt last—film. A side-splitting camp classic awaiting rediscovery.

13 Ghosts (1960) **C/B&W-88m.** **½ D: William Castle. Charles Herbert, Donald Woods, Martin Milner, Jo Morrow, Rosemary DeCamp, Margaret Hamilton, John Van Dreelen. Typically tongue-in-cheek Castle spook opera, about nice, all-American family (with children named Buck and Medea!) that inherits a haunted house. Plenty of chills and chuckles, with Hamilton cleverly cast as sinister housekeeper. TV prints run 85m., minus footage of Castle introducing "Illusion-O"—movie patrons were given "ghost viewers" enabling them to see (or not see) the spirits. ▼●

Thirteen Hours by Air (1936) **80m.** **½ D: Mitchell Leisen. Fred MacMurray, Joan Bennett, ZaSu Pitts, John Howard, Bennie Bartlett, Grace Bradley, Alan Baxter, Ruth Donnelly, Dean Jagger. Dated but diverting tale of transcontinental flight, with romance, murder, and intrigue surrounding mysterious passengers.

13 Lead Soldiers (1948) **64m.** ** D: Frank McDonald. Tom Conway, Maria Palmer, Helen Westcott, John Newland, Terry Kilburn, William Stelling. Ancient toy soldiers hold the key to buried treasure in this minor *Bulldog Drummond* yarn.

13 Rue Madeleine (1946) **95m.** **½ D: Henry Hathaway. James Cagney, Annabella, Richard Conte, Frank Latimore, Walter Abel, Melville Cooper, Sam Jaffe. OK documentary-style story of O.S.S. agents' attempt to locate German missile site in France during WW2. Good cast also includes young E. G. Marshall, Karl Malden, Red Buttons.▼

Thirteenth Floor, The (1999-U.S.-German) **C-100m.** **½ D: Josef Rusnak. Craig Bierko, Armin Mueller-Stahl, Gretchen Mol, Vincent D'Onofrio, Dennis Haysbert, Steven Schub. Scientists create a virtual-reality 1937 L.A. so realistic that even the "inhabitants" have their own minds, and don't realize they and everything around them exists only in a computer… then murder links the worlds of the created and the creators. Well-produced sci-fi in film noir style is interesting throughout, but too talky, and the basic idea is familiar. Based on the novel *Simulacron-3* by Daniel F. Galouye. Previously filmed for German TV by Rainer Werner Fassbinder. Super 35. [R].▼●◗

Thirteenth Guest, The (1932) **69m.** **½ D: Albert Ray. Ginger Rogers, Lyle Talbot, J. Farrell MacDonald, Paul Hurst, James C. Eagles. Guests are reassembled from dinner party that took place 13 years earlier—at which the host fell dead—in order to solve mystery of unnamed 13th guest to whom the deceased bequeathed his estate.

Enjoyable antique chiller complete with hooded murderer. Remade as THE MYSTERY OF THE THIRTEENTH GUEST.▼

Thirteenth Hour, The (1947) **65m.** **½ D: William Clemens. Richard Dix, Karen Morley, Mark Dennis, John Kellogg, Bernadene Hayes, Jim Bannon, Regis Toomey. A trucking company owner is suspected of murder when the cop he had a feud with turns up dead. Efficient entry in *The Whistler* series, and Dix's last movie.

13th Letter, The (1951) **85m.** **½ D: Otto Preminger. Linda Darnell, Charles Boyer, Michael Rennie, Constance Smith, Judith Evelyn. Interesting account of effect of series of poison pen letters on townsfolk, set in Canada. Remake of Henri Georges Clouzot's LE CORBEAU.

13th Warrior, The (1999) **C-102m.** *** D: John McTiernan. Antonio Banderas, Diane Venora, Dennis Storhoi, Vladimir Kulich, Omar Sharif. In ancient times, exiled Arabian nobleman Banderas travels with some Norsemen to their homelands, there to face possibly supernatural nighttime marauders, who eat their victims. Sturdy, action-packed adventure with horror overtones, realistic but in the heroic tradition, shot on spectacular Canadian locations. Based on Michael Crichton's novel *Eaters of the Dead,* itself inspired by true travel writings and the medieval tale of *Beowulf.* Panavision. [R]▼◗

13 West Street (1962) **80m.** **½ D: Philip Leacock. Alan Ladd, Rod Steiger, Jeanne Cooper, Michael Callan, Dolores Dorn. Early version of DEATH WISH has Ladd out to get gang of hoodlums; taut actioner with most capable cast. Based on novel *The Tiger Among Us* by Leigh Brackett.

Thirteen Women (1932) **73m.** ** D: George Archainbaud. Irene Dunne, Ricardo Cortez, Myrna Loy, Jill Esmond, Florence Eldridge, Kay Johnson. Silly tripe with Loy as a half-caste with hypnotic powers who has sworn revenge on sorority sisters who rejected her years ago in school.

—30— (1959) **96m.** *½ D: Jack Webb. Jack Webb, William Conrad, David Nelson, Whitney Blake, Louise Lorimer, Joe Flynn, James Bell. Hackneyed, over-written tale of a typical night on a big-city newspaper. Conrad chews the scenery as city editor, but the script's the main villain, abetted by atrocious music score. Title, by the way, is journalists' way of indicating "the end."▼

Thirty Day Princess (1934) **75m.** **½ D: Marion Gering. Sylvia Sidney, Cary Grant, Edward Arnold, Vince Barnett, Lucien Littlefield. Lightly entertaining if formulaic fluff, with Sidney cast in two roles: a princess making a goodwill tour of the U.S. and an unemployed actress hired to impersonate her. Coscripted by Preston Sturges.

35 Up (1991-British) **C/B&W-122m.** *** D: Michael Apted. Still compelling continuation of 28 UP, in which Apted again peeks in on the lives of the subjects he has been filming at seven-year intervals, beginning at age seven. A thoughtful, revealing look at lives lived, and dreams fulfilled and unfulfilled within the British class system. As with all prior entries, this was originally produced for British TV. Followed by 42 UP.▼

30 Foot Bride of Candy Rock, The (1959) **75m.** ** D: Sidney Miller. Lou Costello, Dorothy Provine, Gale Gordon, Charles Lane, Jimmy Conlin, Peter Leeds. Lou Costello's only starring film without Bud Abbott is nothing much, mildly entertaining, with Provine enlarged to gigantic proportions.▼

30 Is a Dangerous Age, Cynthia (1968-British) **C-98m.** **½ D: Joseph McGrath. Dudley Moore, Eddie Foy, Jr., Suzy Kendall, John Bird. Man who has frittered away his life decides that within 6 weeks he wants to be married and famous. Funny, but sometimes falls flat. Dudley also composed the score and cowrote the screenplay.▼

39 Steps, The (1935-British) **87m.** **** D: Alfred Hitchcock. Robert Donat, Madeleine Carroll, Lucie Mannheim, Godfrey Tearle, Peggy Ashcroft, John Laurie, Wylie Watson. Classic Hitchcock mystery with overtones of light comedy and romance, as innocent Donat is pulled into spy-ring activities. Memorable banter between Donat and Carroll, who thinks he's a criminal, set style for sophisticated dialogue for years. John Buchan's novel was adapted by Charles Bennett and Alma Reville; additional dialogue by Ian Hay. Remade twice.▼●◗

39 Steps, The (1959-British) **C-93m.** **½ D: Ralph Thomas. Kenneth More, Taina Elg, Brenda de Banzie, Barry Jones, Reginald Beckwith, Sidney James, James Hayter. Young man is accidentally involved in murder and espionage and ensnares the aid of disbelieving young woman. More and Elg are delightful in this replica of 1935 classic; though not nearly as good, it's still entertaining.▼

Thirty-Nine Steps, The (1978-British) **C-102m.** **½ D: Don Sharp. Robert Powell, David Warner, Eric Porter, Karen Dotrice, John Mills, George Baker. Based more on John Buchan's book than Hitchcock adaptation, remake isn't bad but lacks panache; Powell plays innocent man pursued by villains who believe he's obtained details of their plot to hatch WW1. [PG] ▼●

Thirty Seconds Over Tokyo (1944) **138m.** *** D: Mervyn LeRoy. Van Johnson, Robert Walker, Spencer Tracy, Phyllis Thaxter, Scott McKay, Robert Mitchum, Don DeFore, Stephen McNally, Louis Jean Heydt, Leon Ames, Paul Langton, Bill Williams. Exciting WW2 actioner of first American attack on Japan with sturdy cast, guest appearance by Tracy as General Doolittle. Script by Dalton Trumbo. Oscar-winning special effects.▼●

36 Fillette (1988-French) **C-88m.** **½ D: Catherine Breillat. Delphine Zentout, Etienne Chicot, Olivier Parniere, Jean-Pierre Léaud. Annoyingly uneven account of a restless, amply endowed 14-year-old (well played by Zentout): will she or won't she lose her virginity while on vacation at the beach with her family? Some effective moments, but the film goes nowhere. ▼◗

36 Hours (1964) **115m.** **½ D: George Seaton. James Garner, Eva Marie Saint, Rod Taylor, Werner Peters, Celia Lovsky, Alan Napier. Intriguing WW2 yarn with Garner as captured spy brainwashed into thinking the war is over begins well, but peters out fast. Taylor as German officer is interesting casting. Remade for cable TV as BREAKING POINT in 1989 with Corbin Bernsen. Also shown in computer-colored version. Panavision.▼

Thirty Two Short Films About Glenn Gould (1993-Canadian) **C-93m.** **½ D: Francois Girard. Colm Feore. As the title says . . . and the result is an occasionally illuminating but much too fragmented bio of the famed reclusive concert pianist. People who know Gould talk about him, key scenes from his life are enacted and his works are performed, but it doesn't quite add up, either as documentary or biography. Girard scripted, with Don McKellar.▼

30 Years of Fun (1963) **85m.** **** Compiled by Robert Youngson. Charlie Chaplin, Buster Keaton, Laurel and Hardy, Harry Langdon, Sydney Chaplin, Charley Chase, etc. Without repeating from previous films, Youngson presents hilarious silent comedy footage. Included is rare sequence of Laurel and Hardy performing together for the first time in 1917's LUCKY DOG.

This Above All (1942) **110m.** *** D: Anatole Litvak. Tyrone Power, Joan Fontaine, Thomas Mitchell, Nigel Bruce, Gladys Cooper, Sara Allgood, Phillip Merivale, Alexander Knox. Timely WW2 film shows its age, but is still good, with strong cast in Eric Knight tale of embittered soldier Power finding courage and love with patriotic Britisher Fontaine; adapted by R. C. Sherriff.

This Angry Age (1958-Italian-U.S.) **C-111m.** ** D: René Clement. Silvana Mangano, Anthony Perkins, Alida Valli, Richard Conte, Jo Van Fleet, Nehemiah Persoff. Ludicrous mishmash set in Indo-China with Van Fleet a stereotyped, dominating mother who's convinced that her children (Perkins and Mangano) can make their rice fields a going proposition. Originally titled THE SEA WALL. Technirama.

This Boy's Life (1993) **C-115m.** ***½ D: Michael Caton-Jones. Robert De Niro, Ellen Barkin, Leonardo DiCaprio, Jonah Blechman, Eliza Dushku, Chris Cooper, Carla Gugino, Zack Ansley, Tracey Ellis, Kathy Kinney, Gerrit Graham, Tobey Maguire. Harrowing but utterly absorbing story, set in the 1950s, of a young boy and his footloose mother who wind up living in a remote part of Washington state with a lout who both browbeats the youngster and beats him physically. Searing character study is a showcase for masterful performances (including an eye-opener for young DiCaprio), but what ultimately makes it work is learning that the story is true. Screenplay by Robert Getchell, from Tobias Wolff's memoir. Clairmont-Scope. [R] ▼●

This Can't Be Love (1994) **C-100m. TVM** D: Anthony Harvey. Katharine Hepburn, Anthony Quinn, Jason Bateman, Jami Gertz, Maxine Miller, Michael Feinstein. Lightweight comedy for a couple of heavyweight actors (together for the first time) as battling old-time movie stars rekindling a flame that went out fifty years before. Director Harvey worked with Kate before on THE LION IN WINTER. Average.▼

This Could Be the Night (1957) **103m.** **½ D: Robert Wise. Jean Simmons, Paul Douglas, Anthony Franciosa, Joan Blondell, Neile Adams, ZaSu Pitts, J. Carrol Naish. Forced, frantic comedy of prim teacher Simmons working as secretary to gangster Douglas, who runs a nightclub; Franciosa is the young associate who romances her. CinemaScope.▼●

This Day and Age (1933) **85m.** *** D: Cecil B. DeMille. Charles Bickford, Judith Allen, Richard Cromwell, Harry Green, Eddie Nugent, Ben Alexander, Bradley Page. Fascinating story of high-schoolers taking law into their own hands to pin mobster Bickford for murder of tailor Green. Hardly subtle, yet powerfully effective.

This Earth Is Mine (1959) **C-125m.** **½ D: Henry King. Rock Hudson, Jean Simmons, Dorothy McGuire, Claude Rains, Kent Smith, Anna Lee, Ken Scott. Disjointed soaper set in 1930s California vineyards about intertwining family romances, focusing on Hudson-Simmons love story. CinemaScope.

This Gun for Hire (1942) **80m.** *** D: Frank Tuttle. Alan Ladd, Veronica Lake, Robert Preston, Laird Cregar, Tully Marshall, Marc Lawrence, Pamela Blake. Ladd came into his own as paid gunman seeking revenge on man who double-crossed him, with Lake as a fetching vis-à-vis. Script by W.R. Burnett and Albert Maltz, from Graham Greene's novel *A Gun For Sale*. Remade in 1957 (as SHORT CUT TO HELL) and for cable TV in 1991 (with Robert Wagner).▼●

This Happy Breed (1944-British) **C-114m.** ***½ D: David Lean. Robert Newton, Celia

Johnson, John Mills, Kay Walsh, Stanley Holloway, Amy Veness, Alison Leggatt. Splendidly acted saga follows British family from 1919 to 1939 in this adaptation of Noel Coward play. Scripted by director Lean, cinematographer Ronald Neame and coproducer Anthony Havelock-Allan.▼

This Happy Feeling (1958) **C-92m.** *** D: Blake Edwards. Debbie Reynolds, Curt Jurgens, John Saxon, Alexis Smith, Estelle Winwood, Mary Astor, Troy Donahue, Joe Flynn. Most engaging cast gives zip to simple yarn of Reynolds enthralled by actor Jurgens, but sparked by suitor Saxon; Winwood fine as eccentric housekeeper. CinemaScope.▼

This Is Elvis (1981) **C/B&W-101m.** **½ D: Malcolm Leo, Andrew Solt. David Scott, Paul Boensh III, Johnny Harra, Lawrence Koller, Rhonda Lyn, Debbie Edge, Larry Raspberry, Furry Lewis. Unusual examination of Elvis's life combines documentary footage with sequences of actors playing Presley at various stages of his life. The film is both fascinating and phony, an insightful portrayal of a tragic legend and yet another excuse to rake in profits by trading on his memory. Videocassette version runs 144m. [PG]▼●

This Island Earth (1955) **C-86m.** *** D: Joseph Newman. Jeff Morrow, Rex Reason, Faith Domergue, Russell Johnson, Lance Fuller, Douglas Spencer. Suspenseful, intelligent science fiction about scientists lured to mysterious project, only to find they've been recruited—or more appropriately, shanghaied—by aliens to help them defend their invasion-torn planet. Thoughtful and exciting, with excellent visuals; based on Raymond F. Jones' novel. Film is spoofed in MYSTERY SCIENCE THEATER 3000: THE MOVIE. ▼●◗

This Is My Affair (1937) **101m.** *** D: William A. Seiter. Barbara Stanwyck, Robert Taylor, Victor McLaglen, Brian Donlevy, Sidney Blackmer, John Carradine, Sig Ruman. Exciting film of Taylor joining gang of robbers on order from President McKinley to expose powerful mob; Stanwyck is saloon singer who loves Taylor (they married in real life two years later).

This is my Father (1999-Canadian-Irish) **C-120m.** ** D: Paul Quinn. Aidan Quinn, James Caan, Stephen Rea, John Cusack, Moya Farrelly, Jacob Tierney, Colm Meaney, Donal Donnelly, Brendan Gleeson. Burned-out Chicago schoolteacher (Caan) travels to his ancestral home in Ireland, with his teenage nephew in tow, to unlock the mystery of his father's identity. Played both in present day and flashback, the film aims high but doesn't succeed, despite good performances and period flavor. A labor of love for first-time writer-director Quinn; brother Aidan stars, brother Declan photographed it, and sister Marian appears briefly. All three brothers executive-produced. [R]▼◗

This Is My Life (1992) **C-105m.** **½ D: Nora Ephron. Julie Kavner, Samantha Mathis, Gaby Hoffmann, Carrie Fisher, Dan Aykroyd, Bob Nelson, Caroline Aaron, Danny Zorn, Renee Lippin, Joy Behar, Annie Golden, Kathy Najimy, Valri Bromfield. Single mom with two daughters pursues her dream of becoming a standup comic and, virtually overnight, her career takes off—leaving her girls in second place. Kavner is perfect, the girls are adorable and the story is certainly credible—but somehow the film doesn't quite deliver. Directing debut for writer Ephron (who penned this script with sister Delia), based on Meg Wolitzer's novel *This Is Your Life*. [PG-13]▼●

This Is My Love (1954) **C-91m.** ** D: Stuart Heisler. Linda Darnell, Rick Jason, Dan Duryea, Faith Domergue, Hal Baylor, Jerry Mathers. Darnell and her sister Domergue (who's married to invalid Duryea) compete for affections of Jason in this murky soap-drama.

This Is Spinal Tap (1984) **C-82m.** *** D: Rob Reiner. Michael McKean, Christopher Guest, Harry Shearer, Rob Reiner, Tony Hendra, June Chadwick, R.J. Parnell, David Kaff, Fran Drescher. Admirably precise parody of a rock documentary, with Reiner as director Marty Di Bergi, who chronicles latest American tour of aging British rock group that's a working definition of the term "loser." Collaborative effort improvised by Reiner and his cast of colleagues; cunning satire through and through, though not always terribly funny. Our favorite bit: the amplifier that goes to "11." Many familiar faces appear in cameos. P.S.: In the '90s the "fictitious" group reunited for a series of concerts and a TV special. Laser and video re-release in 1995 features many new scenes. [R]▼●◗

This Is the Army (1943) **C-121m.** *** D: Michael Curtiz. George Murphy, Joan Leslie, Lt. Ronald Reagan, Sgt. Joe Louis, Kate Smith, George Tobias, Alan Hale, Charles Butterworth, Dolores Costello, Una Merkel, Stanley Ridges, Rosemary DeCamp, Frances Langford, Irving Berlin, many others. Soldiers who staged Irving Berlin's WW1 musical *Yip Yip Yaphank* reunite to help mount similar WW2 effort; corny but enjoyable framework (with Warner Bros. cast) for filmed record of legendary 1940s show, a topical melange of songs and skits. P.S.: This is the film where George Murphy plays Ronald Reagan's father!▼

This Is the Life (1944) **87m.** ** D: Felix E. Feist. Donald O'Connor, Peggy Ryan, Susanna Foster, Patric Knowles. Spunky cast of versatile performers with Foster torn between swank Knowles and performer O'Connor. Based on a play by Sinclair Lewis and Fay Wray!

This Is the Night (1932) **78m.** **½ D: Frank Tuttle. Lily Damita, Charlie Ruggles, Roland Young, Thelma Todd, Cary Grant, Irving Bacon. Enjoyable if somewhat strained romantic comedy in the Lubitsch mold, set in Paris and Venice, with Young hiring Damita to pose as his wife to help cover up his amorous pursuit of Todd. Grant has a wonderful entrance (as Todd's athletic husband) in his feature debut.

This Land Is Mine (1943) **103m.** ** D: Jean Renoir. Charles Laughton, Maureen O'Hara, George Sanders, Walter Slezak, Kent Smith, Una O'Connor, Philip Merivale, George Coulouris, Nancy Gates. Meek French teacher Laughton, aroused by Nazi occupation, becomes hero. Patriotic wartime film is dated and disappointing today; written by Dudley Nichols.▼●

This Love of Ours (1945) **90m.** **½ D: William Dieterle. Merle Oberon, Charles Korvin, Claude Rains, Carl Esmond, Sue England, Jess Barker, Harry Davenport, Ralph Morgan. Sudsy soaper of Korvin leaving wife Oberon, meeting twelve years later, falling in love again. Rains steals show in supporting role. Remade in 1956 as NEVER SAY GOODBYE.

This Man Is Mine (1934) **76m.** ** D: John Cromwell. Irene Dunne, Ralph Bellamy, Constance Cummings, Kay Johnson, Sidney Blackmer, Charles Starrett, Vivian Tobin. Lightweight script does in this lesser Dunne vehicle, with Irene vying with Cummings for the love of Bellamy.

This Man Is News (1938-British) **77m.** *** D: David MacDonald. Barry K. Barnes, Valerie Hobson, Alastair Sim, John Warwick, Garry Marsh. Framed newspaperman goes after jewel thieves in this crisp, stylish little comedy-thriller. Sequel: THIS MAN IN PARIS.▼

This Man Must Die (1970-French) **C-115m.** ***½ D: Claude Chabrol. Michel Duchaussoy, Jean Yanne, Caroline Cellier, Lorraine Rainer, Marc DiNapoli, Guy Marly. Outstanding film about man who sets out to find the person who killed his young son in hit-and-run accident and the complications which ensue. This may be the best of many fine Chabrol dramas; Yanne and Cellier are unforgettable, the photography beautiful. [PG]▼

This Man's Navy (1945) **100m.** *** D: William Wellman. Wallace Beery, Tom Drake, James Gleason, Jan Clayton, Selena Royle, Noah Beery, Sr., Steve Brodie. Usual Beery service-story nicely rehashed; Beery treats Drake as a son, gets vicarious pleasure out of his navy career.

This Modern Age (1931) **76m.** ** D: Nick Grinde. Joan Crawford, Neil Hamilton, Marjorie Rambeau, Hobert Bosworth, Emma Dunn. Upper-class Hamilton loves Crawford, but his family doesn't take to the poor working-girl. Standard predictable plot.

This Property Is Condemned (1966) **C-110m.** ** D: Sydney Pollack. Natalie Wood, Robert Redford, Charles Bronson, Kate Reid, Mary Badham, Robert Blake, Alan Baxter, Dabney Coleman, Jon Provost. Often absurd film version of Tennessee Williams' one-act play has doe-eyed Wood falling for Redford, the out-of-towner staying in her mama's boarding house. Except for James Wong Howe's photography, this is trash without the style that often makes trash enjoyable. Francis Ford Coppola was one of the screenwriters.▼●

This Rebel Age SEE: **Beat Generation, The**

This Rebel Breed (1960) **90m.** **½ D: Richard L. Bare. Rita Moreno, Mark Damon, Gerald Mohr, Jay Novello, Eugene Martin, Tom Gilson, Diane (Dyan) Cannon, Al Freeman (Jr.). Above average drama about racial tensions in a multi-ethnic high school, with Moreno well cast as a Latina teen involved with an Anglo boy (which displeases her trouble-prone brother). Cannon is amusingly cast as a gang deb! Retitled THREE SHADES OF LOVE and THE BLACK REBELS, the latter with incongruous R-rated footage added.▼

This Savage Land (1968) **C-98m.** **½ D: Vincent McEveety. Barry Sullivan, Glenn Corbett, Kathryn Hays, Andrew Prine, George C. Scott, John Drew Barrymore. Widower and family sell Ohio spread, head West for new start, ride into town embroiled in vigilante dispute. Excellent performances (especially Scott) in surprisingly believable script. Comprised of episodes of *The Road West* TV series, but given theatrical release. [G]

This Side of the Law (1950) **74m.** ** D: Richard L. Bare. Viveca Lindfors, Kent Smith, Janis Paige, Monte Blue. Hokey script has Smith hired by crooked lawyer to impersonate missing wealthy man.

This Sporting Life (1963-British) **129m.** ***½ D: Lindsay Anderson. Richard Harris, Rachel Roberts, Alan Badel, William Hartnell, Colin Blakely, Arthur Lowe. Yorkshire coal-miner "betters" himself by becoming professional rugby player. Powerful film (written by David Storey) about love, success, and disillusionment; also serves to illustrate what a grueling game rugby is. Film debut of Glenda Jackson. Originally 134m.▼●◗

This Thing Called Love (1941) **98m.** *** D: Alexander Hall. Rosalind Russell, Melvyn Douglas, Binnie Barnes, Allyn Joslyn, Gloria Dickson, Lee J. Cobb. Adult comedy of newlyweds who set up three-month trial run for their marriage. Stars' expertise puts it over.

This Time for Keeps (1947) **C-105m.** **½ D: Richard Thorpe. Esther Williams,

Lauritz Melchior, Jimmy Durante, Johnnie Johnston, Xavier Cugat. Empty-headed, enjoyable Williams bathing-suit musical with Durante around to relieve tedium.▼

This Way Please (1937) **75m.** **½ D: Robert Florey. Charles "Buddy" Rogers, Betty Grable, Mary Livingstone, Ned Sparks, Jim Jordan, Marion Jordan, Porter Hall, Lee Bowman, Rufe Davis. Second-string musical about movie theater usherette with a crush on bandleader Rogers; amusing specialty material by Davis, engaging moments with radio's Fibber McGee and Molly (Jim and Marion Jordan).

This Woman Is Dangerous (1952) **100m.** **½ D: Felix E. Feist. Joan Crawford, Dennis Morgan, David Brian, Richard Webb, Sherry Jackson. In typical tough-girl role, Crawford finds true love after countless mishaps, including an eye operation.

This Woman Is Mine (1941) **91m.** ** D: Frank Lloyd. Franchot Tone, John Carroll, Walter Brennan, Carol Bruce, Nigel Bruce, Leo G. Carroll. Standard love triangle on merchant boat in northern waters plying the fur trade.

This World, Then the Fireworks (1997) **C-100m.** ** D: Michael Oblowitz. Billy Zane, Gina Gershon, Sheryl Lee, Rue McClanahan, Seymour Cassel, Will Patton, Richard Edson. Period noir drama set in the '50s about two devoted siblings, partners in cons and murder, who seemingly find a way out of their miserable lives when a repressed policewoman enters their world. Intriguing title, nice period re-creation, good performances, but we've been down this road too many times before—in better movies. Zane also coexecutive-produced. [R]▼●

This Year's Blonde (1980) **C-100m. TVM** D: John Erman. Constance Forslund, Lloyd Bridges, Norman Fell, Vic Tayback, Michael Lerner, John Marley. The Marilyn Monroe chapter of Garson Kanin's *Moviola* tells of her relationship with her ambitious agent, Johnny Hyde (vividly portrayed by Bridges). Another TV movie, MARILYN: THE UNTOLD STORY, tops this one, as does its star, Catherine Hicks, who's more persuasive as MM than Forslund. Retitled: THE SECRET LOVE OF MARILYN MONROE. Average.

Thomas Crown Affair, The (1968) **C-102m.** *** D: Norman Jewison. Steve McQueen, Faye Dunaway, Paul Burke, Jack Weston, Biff McGuire, Yaphet Kotto. Glittery production complements story of supercool millionaire McQueen who plots perfect bank robbery, as insurance investigator Dunaway coldly determines to nab the gentleman-thief. Perfect nonthink entertainment; use of multi-image screens (designed by Pablo Ferro) may suffer on TV. Oscar-winning song, "The Windmills of Your Mind," by Michel Legrand and Alan and Marilyn Bergman. Remade in 1999. [R]▼●◗

Thomas Crown Affair, The (1999) **C-112m.** **½ D: John McTiernan. Pierce Brosnan, Rene Russo, Denis Leary, Ben Gazzara, Frankie Faison, Fritz Weaver, Charles Keating, Mark Margolis, Faye Dunaway. A handsome, wealthy, jet-setting industrialist moonlights as an art thief, and delights in playing cat-and-mouse with a beautiful insurance investigator. A distant cousin to the 1968 version (despite the presence of Dunaway, as Brosnan's shrink), this is slick and entertaining, but everyone seems to be working a bit too hard to make it look effortless. Brosnan also produced. Panavision. [R]▼●◗

Thomasine & Bushrod (1974) **C-95m.** **½ D: Gordon Parks, Jr. Max Julien, Vonetta McGee, George Murdock, Glynn Turman, Juanita Moore. OK mixture of black exploitation and Western action with comedy, as a black "Bonnie and Clyde" team operate in 1911 Texas. Julien scripted and co-produced, along with the classy-looking McGee. Shot in New Mexico. [PG]

Thoroughbreds Don't Cry (1937) **80m.** **½ D: Alfred E. Green. Judy Garland, Mickey Rooney, Sophie Tucker, C. Aubrey Smith, Frankie Darro, Henry Kolker, Helen Troy. Fairly good racetrack story with jockey Rooney involved in crooked deals, young Garland adding some songs. Mickey and Judy's first film together.▼●

Thoroughly Modern Millie (1967) **C-138m.** **½ D: George Roy Hill. Julie Andrews, James Fox, Mary Tyler Moore, Carol Channing, Beatrice Lillie, John Gavin, Jack Soo, Pat Morita, Philip Ahn. Up to a point this Ross Hunter attempt to recapture some of Andrews' *Boy Friend* magic is successful, but after nearly two and a half hours, one begins to yawn. 1920s farce has a fatal case of the cutes. Elmer Bernstein's score won an Oscar.▼●

Those Calloways (1965) **C-131m.** *** D: Norman Tokar. Brian Keith, Vera Miles, Brandon de Wilde, Walter Brennan, Ed Wynn, Linda Evans, Philip Abbott. Long, episodic but rewarding Disney film about an eccentric New England man (Keith) and his family, focusing on his determined efforts to use nearby lake for bird sanctuary before it's bought up by business interests. Film debut of Linda Evans. Music score by Max Steiner.▼

Those Daring Young Men in their Jaunty Jalopies (1969-British-Italian-French) **C-122m.** **½ D: Ken Annakin. Tony Curtis, Susan Hampshire, Terry-Thomas, Eric Sykes, Gert Frobe, Peter Cook, Dudley Moore, Jack Hawkins. Slapstick adventures of participants in 1,500-mile car race to Monte Carlo during the 1920s. Some funny scenes, but backfires a bit too often. Cut for U.S.

release to 93m. Original British title: MONTE CARLO OR BUST. Panavision. [G]▼

Those Endearing Young Charms (1945) **81m.** **½ D: Lewis Allen. Robert Young, Laraine Day, Bill Williams, Ann Harding, Marc Cramer, Anne Jeffreys, Lawrence Tierney. Surprisingly effective wartime romance finds Day torn between nice-guy Williams and smooth-talking heel Young. Nothing special, but some amusing dialogue, nicely played.

Those Fantastic Flying Fools (1967) **C-95m.** **½ D: Don Sharp. Burl Ives, Troy Donahue, Gert Frobe, Terry-Thomas, Hermione Gingold, Daliah Lavi, Lionel Jeffries. Lightweight tale of Victorian England moon race, loosely adapted from Jules Verne story (previously filmed as FROM THE EARTH TO THE MOON). Original title: BLAST-OFF. Panavision. ▼

Those Lips, Those Eyes (1980) **C-107m.** *** D: Michael Pressman. Frank Langella, Glynnis O'Connor, Thomas Hulce, Kevin McCarthy, Jerry Stiller, Herbert Berghof. Stagestruck adolescent learns about love the hard way while interning in Cleveland summer stock during the early '50s. Hulce is too nerdish in the key role, but Langella as down-on-his-luck actor, O'Connor as company's resident dish, are both quite good. A sleeper, written by David Shaber. [R]▼

Those Magnificent Men in Their Flying Machines (1965) **C-132m.** *** D: Ken Annakin. Stuart Whitman, Sarah Miles, James Fox, Alberto Sordi, Robert Morley, Gert Frobe, Jean-Pierre Cassel, Terry-Thomas, Irina Demick, Benny Hill, Flora Robson, Sam Wanamaker, Gordon Jackson, Millicent Martin, Red Skelton, Tony Hancock; narrated by James Robertson Justice. Long but enjoyable film of great London-to-Paris airplane race involving international conflicts, cheating, and romance. Skelton has funny cameo in amusing prologue, tracing history of aviation. Clever title caricatures and designs by Ronald Searle. Todd-AO.▼●

Those Redheads From Seattle (1953) **C-90m.** ** D: Lewis R. Foster. Rhonda Fleming, Gene Barry, Agnes Moorehead, Teresa Brewer, Guy Mitchell. Modestly produced musical nonsense set in gold-rush era with Moorehead the mother of four girls who takes her brood to Alaska.

Those Were the Days (1940) **76m.** ** D: J. Theodore Reed. William Holden, Bonita Granville, Ezra Stone, Judith Barrett, Vaughan Glaser, Lucien Littlefield, Richard Denning. Light-hearted (and headed) comedy from George Fitch's *Siwash* stories, with Holden as a college hell-raiser (circa 1904) who woos judge's daughter Granville to avoid a jail sentence. We give it a C-minus. Alan Ladd has a small role as a student.

Thousand Acres, A (1997) **C-105m.** ** D: Jocelyn Moorhouse. Michelle Pfeiffer, Jessica Lange, Jason Robards, Jennifer Jason Leigh, Colin Firth, Keith Carradine, Kevin Anderson, Pat Hingle, John Carroll Lynch, Michelle Williams. When a stubborn, single-minded widowed father decides to relinquish ownership of his farm to his three daughters, a family is abruptly torn apart, and long-held secrets come out of the closet. The only thing missing from this melodrama is character motivation, which presumably did exist in Jane Smiley's Pulitzer prizewinning novel, a variation on *King Lear*. A hollow film notable only for the strong performances of the two leading women (whose companies jointly produced the film). [R]▼●◗

Thousand and One Nights, A (1945) **C-93m.** *** D: Alfred E. Green. Cornel Wilde, Evelyn Keyes, Phil Silvers, Adele Jergens, Dusty Anderson, Dennis Hoey, Rex Ingram. Wilde is a genial, singing Aladdin in this slice of Technicolor escapism, with Silvers as his very contemporary sidekick. Keyes is fun as the impish genie who emerges from a magic lamp. Ingram (who played the genie in THE THIEF OF BAGDAD) has a throwaway role here as a giant. Look fast for Shelley Winters.▼

Thousand and One Nights, A (1968-Spanish) **C-86m.** ** D: Joe Lacy (Jose Maria Elorrieta). Jeff Cooper, Raf Vallone, Luciana Paluzzi, Perla Christal, Reuben Rojo. Tongue-in-cheek Arabian Nights fantasy with the familiar tapestry: a flying carpet, a handsome swordsman, a beautiful part-time genie, a sinister vizier. Not to be confused with the similarly titled Cornel Wilde movie of the '40s.

Thousand Clowns, A (1965) **118m.** ***½ D: Fred Coe. Jason Robards, Barbara Harris, Martin Balsam, Barry Gordon, Gene Saks, William Daniels. Faithful adaptation by Herb Gardner of his Broadway comedy about society dropout who's being pressured to drop in again for the sake of young nephew who lives with him. Perfectly cast, filmed in N.Y.C., with Balsam's Oscar-winning performance as Robards' brother.▼●

Thousand Eyes of Dr. Mabuse, The (1960-German) **103m.** **½ D: Fritz Lang. Dawn Addams, Peter Van Eyck, Gert Frobe, Wolfgang Preiss. Fast-moving if unconvincing revival of arch-villain of 1920s, with Frobe the police agent tracking down the reincarnated Mabuse in Berlin; gimmicky, complex plot line. Lang's directorial swan song. Aka THE SECRET OF DR. MABUSE and THE DIABOLICAL DR. MABUSE.▼

Thousand Plane Raid, The (1969) **C-94m.** *½ D: Boris Sagal. Christopher George, Laraine Stephens, J. D. Cannon, Gary Marshall, Michael Evans, Ben Murphy, James Gammon, Gavin MacLeod, Tim

McIntire, Bo Hopkins, Henry Jaglom, Charles Dierkop. Thoroughly routine suspenser about plot to bomb German aircraft factory near end of WW2. [G]
Thousands Cheer (1943) **C-126m.** ★★½ D: George Sidney. Mickey Rooney, Judy Garland, Gene Kelly, Red Skelton, Eleanor Powell, Ann Sothern, Lucille Ball, Virginia O'Brien, Frank Morgan, Kathryn Grayson, Lena Horne, many others. Grayson lives with officer-father John Boles at army base, falls for hotheaded private Kelly and decides to prepare an all-star show for the soldiers. Dubious plot is an excuse for specialty acts by top MGM stars.▼●
Thou Shalt Not Kill (1961-Italian-French-Yugoslavian) **129m.** ★★½ D: Claude Autant-Lara. Laurent Terzieff, Horst Frank, Suzanne Flon, Mica Orlovic. Too-often sterile narrative dealing with trial of French conscientious objector, with side-plot of German priest facing penalty for having killed Frenchman during WW2. Based on a true story, and quite controversial when released. Dyaliscope.
Thrashin' (1986) **C-90m.** ★★ D: David Winters. Josh Brolin, Robert Rusler, Pamela Gilday, Brooke McCarter, Brett Marx, Sherilyn Fenn. Skateboard-riding youth gangs are pitted against each other in this WEST SIDE STORY on wheels . . . minus the spirit and originality, not to mention music. [PG-13]▼
Threads (1984-British) **C-110m.** ★★★ D: Mick Jackson. Karen Meagher, Reece Dinsdale, Rita May, Nicholas Lane, Victoria O'Keefe. Britain's answer to THE DAY AFTER is a powerful, if a bit overlong, drama about effect of nuclear holocaust on working-class town of Sheffield, with the focus on a pair of families whose son and daughter are about to wed. Unrelentingly graphic and grim, sobering, and shattering—as it should be. Originally produced for British television.▼
Threat, The (1949) **65m.** ★★★ D: Felix Feist. Charles McGraw, Michael O'Shea, Virginia Grey, Julie Bishop, Robert Shayne, Anthony Caruso. Thug McGraw escapes prison, kidnaps cop and D.A. who put him away, plus singer he suspects of having squealed. Fast, rugged little "B" keeps action hopping until tough conclusion.▼
Threat, The (1960) **66m.** ★★ D: Charles R. Rondeau. Robert Knapp, Linda Lawson, Lisabeth Hush, James Seay, Mary Castle, Barney Phillips. Standard find-the-real-murderer yarn.
Three Ages (1923) **63m.** ★★★ D: Buster Keaton, Edward F. Cline. Buster Keaton, Margaret Leahy, Wallace Beery, Joe Roberts, Horace Morgan, Lillian Lawrence. Buster's comic observations on the pursuit of a mate in the Stone Age, the Roman Empire, and modern times. Entertaining silent comedy, with Keaton making a memorable entrance atop a dinosaur.▼●◗
¡Three Amigos! (1986) **C-105m.** ★★ D: John Landis. Steve Martin, Chevy Chase, Martin Short, Patrice Martinez, Alfonso Arau, Tony Plana, Joe Mantegna, Jon Lovitz, Phil Hartman. Silent film Western heroes are summoned to Mexico for what they think will be a public appearance, find out they're really supposed to rid a village of its bandit chieftain. Smarmy one-joke comedy has its moments but not too many; buffs may be amused to note that villain Arau was one of the key bad guys in THE WILD BUNCH. Coscripter Randy Newman wrote the songs. [PG]▼●
Three Avengers, The (1964-Italian) **C-97m.** ★½ D: Gianfranco Parolini. Alan Steel, Mimmo Palmara, Lisa Gastoni, Rosalba Neri. Below par Ursus adventure tale, dealing with evil ruler of Atra. Totalscope.▼
3 Bad Men (1926) **92m.** ★★★½ D: John Ford. George O'Brien, Lou Tellegen, J. Farrell MacDonald, Tom Santschi, Frank Campeau. Three gruff outlaws become benevolent protectors of young girl whose father is killed during Western settlement period. Beautiful mixture of action, drama, comedy, and sentiment in one of Ford's best silents.▼
Three Bad Sisters (1956) **76m.** ★½ D: Gilbert L. Kay. Marla English, Kathleen Hughes, Sara Shane, John Bromfield, Jess Barker, Madge Kennedy. Aimless account of title figures fighting among themselves to outdo the others, fighting over their father's estate.
Three Bites of the Apple (1967) **C-105m.** ★½ D: Alvin Ganzer. David McCallum, Sylva Koscina, Tammy Grimes, Harvey Korman, Domenico Modugno, Aldo Fabrizi. Good scenery is only plus of flimsy comedy about McCallum's attempts to avoid heavy taxation of money he's won in a casino on the Riviera. Panavision.
Three Blind Mice (1938) **75m.** ★★½ D: William A. Seiter. Loretta Young, Joel McCrea, David Niven, Stuart Erwin, Marjorie Weaver, Pauline Moore, Jane Darwell, Binnie Barnes. Familiar idea of three fortune-hunting girls going after well-heeled male prospects; slickly done. Remade, reworked many times.
Three Blondes in His Life (1960) **81m.** ★★ D: Leon Chooluck. Jock Mahoney, Greta Thyssen, Anthony Dexter, Jesse White. Occasionally tangy rehash of romances and misconduct of now-deceased insurance investigator.
Three Brave Men (1957) **88m.** ★★½ D: Philip Dunne. Ray Milland, Frank Lovejoy, Ernest Borgnine, Nina Foch, Dean Jagger, Virginia Christine, Edward Andrews, Andrew Duggan, Joseph Wiseman. Navy clerk Borgnine is fired as a security risk because

of alleged Communist leanings; lawyer Milland tries to get him reinstated. Adapted by Dunne from Pulitzer Prize-winning articles by Anthony Lewis, courtroom drama is interesting but unexceptional. CinemaScope.

Three Broadway Girls SEE: **Greeks Had a Word for Them, The**

Three Brothers (1980-Italian-French) **C-113m.** *** D: Francesco Rosi. Philippe Noiret, Charles Vanel, Michele Placido, Vittorio Mezzogiorno, Andrea Ferreol, Maddalena Crippa, Sara Tafuri, Marta Zoffoli. Wise, touching, but slow-moving account of three very different brothers who return to the country village of their youth for their mother's funeral. The recollections of their elderly peasant father (Vanel) and scenes with his young granddaughter (Zoffoli) are particularly moving. Adapted from Platonov's *The Third Son.* [PG]▼

Three Caballeros, The (1945) **C-70m.** *** D: Norman Ferguson. Aurora Miranda, Carmen Molina, Dora Luz, voices of Sterling Holloway, Clarence Nash, Jose Oliveira, Joaquin Garay. Colorful Disney pastiche that followed 1940s Good Neighbor Policy by saluting Latin America, through the eyes of Donald Duck. Filled with infectious music (including "Baia," "You Belong to My Heart"), eye-popping visuals, amusing cartoon sequences, and clever combinations of live-action and animation. Donald, Jose Carioca, and Panchito perform title song in a dazzling display of cartoon wizardry. ▼●◗

Three Came Home (1950) **106m.** ***½ D: Jean Negulesco. Claudette Colbert, Patric Knowles, Florence Desmond, Sessue Hayakawa, Sylvia Andrew, Phyllis Morris. Stunning performances by Colbert and Hayakawa make this a must. British and American families living on Borneo during WW2 are sent to prison camps by Japanese, but cultured officer Hayakawa takes an interest in authoress Colbert. Producer Nunnally Johnson adapted Agnes Newton Keith's autobiographical book.▼

Three Cases of Murder (1955-British) **99m.** **½ D: Wendy Toye, David Eady, George More O'Ferrall. Alan Badel, Hugh Pryse, John Gregson, Elizabeth Sellars, Emrys Jones, Orson Welles, Maxwell Reed, Richard Wattis; introduced by Eammon Andrews. Three offbeat murder stories; opener "In the Picture" is genuinely eerie, closer "Lord Mountdrago" (from Somerset Maugham story) has Welles in absorbing tale of a pompous British government official haunted by a rival.▼●

Three Cheers for the Irish (1940) **100m.** ** D: Lloyd Bacon. Thomas Mitchell, Dennis Morgan, Priscilla Lane, Alan Hale, Virginia Grey, Irene Hervey, Frank Jenks, William Lundigan. Mitchell is the whole show (and chews the scenery) as a stereotypically ornery N.Y.C. Irish beat cop who's forced into retirement. Daughter Lane falls for his replacement (Morgan), who—heaven help him—is a Scotsman.

Three Coins in the Fountain (1954) **C-102m.** *** D: Jean Negulesco. Clifton Webb, Dorothy McGuire, Jean Peters, Louis Jourdan, Maggie McNamara, Rossano Brazzi, Cathleen Nesbitt. Splashy romance yarn made ultra-pleasing by Rome locations. Three women make wishes for romance at Fountain of Trevi, spurring several amorous adventures. Won Oscars for Milton Krasner's photography and the Jule Styne–Sammy Cahn title tune (sung by Frank Sinatra). Remade by same director as THE PLEASURE SEEKERS; reworked for TV in 1990 as COINS IN THE FOUNTAIN. CinemaScope.▼●

Three Comrades (1938) **98m.** ***½ D: Frank Borzage. Robert Taylor, Margaret Sullavan, Franchot Tone, Robert Young, Guy Kibbee, Lionel Atwill. Beautifully poignant film of Erich Maria Remarque's tale of post-WW1 Germany, and three life-long friends who share a love for dying Sullavan. Excellent performances all around; coscripted by F. Scott Fitzgerald.▼

Three-Cornered Moon (1933) **77m.** *** D: Elliott Nugent. Claudette Colbert, Richard Arlen, Mary Boland, Wallace Ford, Hardie Albright, Lyda Roberti. Predates golden age of screwball comedies, but tops many of them; Boland is head of wacky family combating Depression.

Three Daring Daughters (1948) **C-115m.** **½ D: Fred M. Wilcox. Jeanette MacDonald, Jose Iturbi, Elinor Donahue, Ann B. Todd, Jane Powell, Edward Arnold, Harry Davenport. Woman magazine editor tells her daughters that she's remarrying. Despite predictable results, well-acted MGM comedy succeeds.▼

Three Days of the Condor (1975) **C-117m.** *** D: Sydney Pollack. Robert Redford, Faye Dunaway, Cliff Robertson, Max von Sydow, John Houseman, Carlin Glynn. Redford, a reader for U.S. intelligence office, learns more than he should, and suddenly finds himself a hunted man. Dunaway is excellent as innocent woman who shelters him. Good suspense yarn. Panavision. [R]▼●◗

Three Desperate Men (1951) **71m.** *½ D: Sam Newfield. Preston Foster, Virginia Grey, Jim Davis, Ross Latimer. Flabby little oater about three brothers who become outlaws.

Three Faces of Eve, The (1957) **91m.** ***½ D: Nunnally Johnson. Joanne Woodward, David Wayne, Lee J. Cobb, Nancy Kulp, Vince Edwards. Narrated by Alistair Cooke. Academy Award tour de force by Woodward as young woman with multiple personalities and three separate lives. Cobb is psychiatrist who tries to cure her. Johnson

also produced and wrote the screenplay. CinemaScope.▼●
Three Faces West (1940) **79m.** ★★½ D: Bernard Vorhaus. John Wayne, Sigrid Gurie, Charles Coburn, Spencer Charters, Roland Varno, Russell Simpson. Offbeat WW2-era drama about Austrian refugees heading for Oregon under Wayne's sponsorship. Gurie is hardly typical leading lady for the Duke, but film's odd mix of frontier and Nazi elements makes it worth a look.▼
3:15 (1986) **C-95m.** ★★ D: Larry Gross. Adam Baldwin, Deborah Foreman, Rene Auberjonois, Ed Lauter, Scott McGinnis, Danny De La Paz, John Scott Clough, Mario Van Peebles. Good cast in lackluster, low-budget teenage gang film, filmed in 1984. [R]▼
Three for Bedroom C (1952) **C-74m.** ★★ D: Milton Bren. Gloria Swanson, Fred Clark, James Warren, Steve Brodie, Hans Conried, Margaret Dumont. Sadly uneven comedy of romance between movie star and scientist aboard transcontinental train heading to L.A. A derailment for Swanson after her triumph in SUNSET BLVD. ▼
Three for Jamie Dawn (1956) **81m.** ★★ D: Thomas Carr. Laraine Day, Ricardo Montalban, Richard Carlson, June Havoc. Diverting story poorly executed, about jury members being pressured to swing a not-guilty verdict for the defendant.
Three for the Road (1987) **C-88m.** ★½ D: B. W. L. Norton. Charlie Sheen, Kerri Green, Alan Ruck, Sally Kellerman, Blair Tefkin, Raymond J. Barry, Alexa Hamilton. Anachronistic youth movie about the spoiled-brat daughter of a senator who travels to boarding school with Sheen and Ruck—and hits more than a few detours. Dull in the extreme. [PG]▼●
Three for the Show (1955) **C-93m.** ★★ D: H. C. Potter. Betty Grable, Marge and Gower Champion, Jack Lemmon, Myron McCormick. Tuneful music is only thing that holds slight plot together in this dud remake of Maugham's TOO MANY HUSBANDS. Some bright dance numbers staged for widescreen really suffer on TV. CinemaScope. ▼●
Three Fugitives (1989) **C-93m.** ★★½ D: Francis Veber. Nick Nolte, Martin Short, Sarah Rowland Doroff, James Earl Jones, Alan Ruck, Kenneth McMillan, Bruce McGill. Bumbling bank robber—who's only pulling the heist to support his little daughter—takes a hostage with him, little dreaming that the guy is a notorious holdup man who's just finished a long stretch in prison. Fast-paced farce doesn't quite hang together, despite energetic performances; Veber's first American film is a remake of his own French comedy, LES FUGITIFS. [PG-13]▼●
Three Girls About Town (1941) **73m.** ★★½ D: Leigh Jason. Joan Blondell, Binnie Barnes, Janet Blair, John Howard, Robert Benchley, Eric Blore, Hugh O'Connell, Una O'Connor. Wacky but amusing comedy of three sisters encountering a corpse in N.Y.C. hotel and the frantic consequences.
Three Godfathers (1936) **82m.** ★★★ D: Richard Boleslawski. Chester Morris, Lewis Stone, Walter Brennan, Irene Hervey, Willard Robertson, Sidney Toler. Little-seen and underrated version of Peter B. Kyne's story (filmed twice before) about three bad guys who adopt a foundling in the desert. Beautifully shot and warmly acted. Retitled MIRACLE IN THE SAND.
3 Godfathers (1949) **C-105m.** ★★★ D: John Ford. John Wayne, Pedro Armendariz, Harry Carey, Jr., Ward Bond, Mae Marsh, Jane Darwell, Ben Johnson, Mildred Natwick. Sturdy, sentimental, sometimes beautiful rendition of Peter B. Kyne's oft-filmed saga of three bandits who "adopt" a baby born in the desert. Final scene doesn't ring true, but Ford makes up for it in balance of film. Dedicated to the director's first star, Harry Carey, Sr. Remade for TV as THE GODCHILD.▼●
Three Guns for Texas (1968) **C-99m.** ★★ D: David Lowell Rich, Paul Stanley, Earl Bellamy. Neville Brand, Peter Brown, Martin Milner, William Smith, Philip Carey. Boring exploits of three Texas Rangers, strung together from three episodes of *Laredo* TV series. Forgettable action, fair repartee between leads. This actually received theatrical release! [PG]
Three Guys Named Mike (1951) **90m.** ★★ D: Charles Walters. Jane Wyman, Van Johnson, Barry Sullivan, Howard Keel, Phyllis Kirk, Jeff Donnell. Enthusiastic (to the point of nausea) stewardess Wyman has her choice of the title trio of nice, handsome, eligible bachelors. Only in the movies . . . Scripted by Sidney Sheldon. ▼
Three Hearts for Julia (1943) **83m.** ★★ D: Richard Thorpe. Ann Sothern, Melvyn Douglas, Lee Bowman, Richard Ainley, Felix Bressart, Marta Linden, Reginald Owen. Only debonair Douglas could seem right as husband romancing his wife (Sothern) who is divorcing him, but he can't support whole film.
Three Hours to Kill (1954) **C-77m.** ★★★ D: Alfred L. Werker. Dana Andrews, Donna Reed, Dianne Foster, Stephen Elliott, Richard Webb, Carolyn Jones, Whit Bissell. Andrews plays stagecoach driver unjustly accused of killing fiancée's brother; he returns to find real killer. Tight, well done.
365 Nights in Hollywood (1934) **74m.** ★★ D: George Marshall. James Dunn, Alice Faye, Frank Mitchell, Jack Durant, Grant Mitchell, John Bradford. Cheerfully mediocre musical about a girl (Faye, in her Jean Harlow look-alike period) who enrolls at a

phony Hollywood talent school, where ex-big-shot director Dunn now teaches. Songwriter Richard Whiting appears briefly as himself.▼

300 Spartans, The (1962) **C-114m.** *½ D: Rudolph Maté. Richard Egan, Ralph Richardson, Diane Baker, Barry Coe. Events leading up to heroic Greek stand against Persians at Thermopylae; strictly cardboard, except for location filming by Geoffrey Unsworth. CinemaScope.

Three Husbands (1950) **78m.** **½ D: Irving Reis. Eve Arden, Ruth Warrick, Howard da Silva, Vanessa Brown, Shepperd Strudwick, Billie Burke, Emlyn Williams, Jane Darwell. Pleasing comedy of three husbands trying to find out whether or not deceased playboy spent time with their wives. Undoubtedly inspired by the 1949 hit, A LETTER TO THREE WIVES, and cowritten by Vera Caspary, who adapted the earlier film.▼

Three in the Attic (1968) **C-92m.** **½ D: Richard Wilson. Christopher Jones, Judy Pace, Yvette Mimieux, Maggie Thrett. Silly tale of youth with so much style that he works three girls at once until they get wise and decide to lock him in and drain him of his potency. [R]▼

Three in the Cellar SEE: **Up in the Cellar**

Three Into Two Won't Go (1969-British) **C-93m.** ** D: Peter Hall. Rod Steiger, Claire Bloom, Judy Geeson, Peggy Ashcroft, Paul Rogers. Marriage of Steiger and Bloom breaks up when he becomes infatuated with sexy hitchhiker Geeson. Originally an OK drama, but Universal shot extra footage and reedited original film to 100m. for television. [R]

Three Is a Family (1944) **81m.** **½ D: Edward Ludwig. Fay Bainter, Marjorie Reynolds, Charlie Ruggles, Helen Broderick, Arthur Lake, Hattie McDaniel, Jeff Donnell, Walter Catlett, Cheryl Walker. Above-par fluff of hectic homelife in apartment filled with family, friends, and new babies.

Three Kings (1999) **C-115m.** *** D: David O. Russell. George Clooney, Mark Wahlberg, Ice Cube, Spike Jonze, Nora Dunn, Jamie Kennedy, Mykelti Williamson, Cliff Curtis, Said Taghmaoui. At the end of the Persian Gulf War, four renegade U.S. soldiers try to pull off a heist of Kuwaiti gold, but find themselves getting involved with innocent civilians who are being targeted by Saddam Hussein—and being left to fend for themselves by a retreating United States military. A gritty, violent action film with a brain and a point of view. Scripted by the director. Super 35. [R]▼◗

Three Little Girls in Blue (1946) **C-90m.** *** D: H. Bruce Humberstone. June Haver, George Montgomery, Vivian Blaine, Celeste Holm, Vera-Ellen, Frank Latimore, Charles Smith. Colorful tale of three sisters out to trap wealthy husbands; familiar plot with good tunes like "You Make Me Feel So Young." A remake of THREE BLIND MICE and MOON OVER MIAMI, set in turn of the century Atlantic City. Holm's film debut.

Three Little Words (1950) **C-102m.** *** D: Richard Thorpe. Fred Astaire, Vera-Ellen, Red Skelton, Arlene Dahl, Keenan Wynn, Gloria De Haven, Debbie Reynolds, Carleton Carpenter. Standard MGM musical about famous songwriters Kalmar and Ruby and their climb to fame; bouncy cast, fine tunes, including "Who's Sorry Now?" "Thinking of You," title song. Debbie plays Helen Kane, but the real Helen dubbed "I Wanna Be Loved By You."▼●

Three Lives and Only One Death (1996-French-Portuguese) **C-123m.** *** D: Raoul Ruiz. Marcello Mastroianni, Anna Galiena, Marisa Paredes, Melvil Poupaud, Chiara Mastroianni, Arielle Dombasle, Feodor Atkine, Lou Castel. One of Mastroianni's last films casts him in a quartet of roles: a traveling salesman, an anthropology professor, a butler, and a wealthy industrialist. Clever, stimulating film is better seen than described, with plenty of surprises in store. Chiara Mastroianni (daughter of Marcello and Catherine Deneuve) and Poupaud play the young couple who inherit the mansion where Marcello works as a butler.▼

Three Lives of Thomasina, The (1964) **C-97m.** *** D: Don Chaffey. Patrick McGoohan, Susan Hampshire, Karen Dotrice, Matthew Garber, Vincent Winter, Denis Gilmore, Laurence Naismith, Finlay Currie. Charming Disney film made in England from Paul Gallico's story about a heartless veterinarian, his daughter's devotion to her pet cat, and a mystical young woman with life-giving "powers." A winner.▼●

Three Loves Has Nancy (1938) **69m.** **½ D: Richard Thorpe. Janet Gaynor, Robert Montgomery, Franchot Tone, Guy Kibbee, Claire Dodd, Reginald Owen. Naive country girl Gaynor goes to N.Y.C. to find the man who left her at the altar, finds admirers Tone and Montgomery instead.

3 Men and a Baby (1987) **C-102m.** *** D: Leonard Nimoy. Tom Selleck, Steve Guttenberg, Ted Danson, Nancy Travis, Margaret Colin, Philip Bosco, Celeste Holm, Derek de Lint, Cynthia Harris, Lisa & Michelle Blair. Enjoyable remake of France's big hit THREE MEN AND A CRADLE, about a trio of swinging bachelor roommates who suddenly find themselves custodians of an infant. Winning performances all around help keep this buoyant comedy on-track from start to finish. Followed by 3 MEN AND A LITTLE LADY. [PG]▼●

Three Men and a Cradle (1985-French) **C-106m.** *** D: Coline Serreau. Roland

Giraud, Michel Boujenah, Andre Dussolier, Philippine Leroy Beaulieu, Dominique Lavanat, Marthe Villalonga. Very entertaining comedy about three swinging bachelors who find themselves stuck with a baby, which one of them fathered. Compassionate and funny; a real charmer. A box-office sensation in France and winner of three César awards. Remade in U.S. as 3 MEN AND A BABY. [PG-13]▼●

3 Men and a Little Lady (1990) **C-100m.** **½ D: Emile Ardolino. Tom Selleck, Steve Guttenberg, Ted Danson, Nancy Travis, Robin Weisman, Christopher Cazenove, Sheila Hancock, Fiona Shaw, John Boswall, Jonathan Lynn, Sydney Walsh. Pleasant (if unexceptional) followup to hit comedy has the growing tyke's mother (Travis) deciding to marry British actor Cazenove, and move to England . . . forcing the three bachelor fathers to prove that the prospective husband and father is really a rotter before it's too late. [PG]▼●

Three Men in a Boat (1956-British) **C-84m.** *½ D: Ken Annakin. Laurence Harvey, Jimmy Edwards, David Tomlinson, Shirley Eaton, Jill Ireland, Martita Hunt, Adrienne Corri, Lisa Gastoni. Third filming of the Jerome K. Jerome book is a frantic, frequently annoying comedy about womanizer Harvey and bumbling pals Edwards and Tomlinson constantly finding trouble while on a boat trip up the Thames. CinemaScope.▼

Three Men in White (1944) **85m.** ** D: Willis Goldbeck. Lionel Barrymore, Van Johnson, Marilyn Maxwell, Keye Luke, Ava Gardner, Alma Kruger, Rags Ragland, Nell Craig, Walter Kingsford. MGM continued to spot its young starlets in this extension of the *Dr. Kildare* series, revolving around efforts (once again) to decide who should be Dr. Gillespie's assistant.

Three Men on a Horse (1936) **88m.** *** D: Mervyn LeRoy. Frank McHugh, Sam Levene, Joan Blondell, Teddy Hart, Guy Kibbee, Carol Hughes, Allen Jenkins, Edgar Kennedy, Eddie Anderson. First-rate comedy of timid McHugh who always picks winning race-horses; stagy but funny. Blondell's fun as Levene's Brooklynese girlfriend. Adapted from Broadway play by George Abbott and John Cecil Holm. ▼

3 Murderesses (1960-French) **C-96m.** **½ D: Michel Boisrond. Alain Delon, Mylene Demongeot, Pascale Petit, Jacqueline Sassard, Anita Ruf, Simone Renant. Most diverting cast in standard playboy yarn with Delon romancing trio of contrasting females. Originally titled WOMEN ARE WEAK.

Three Musketeers, The (1921) **118m.** *** D: Fred Niblo. Douglas Fairbanks, Marguerite De La Motte, Adolphe Menjou, Barbara La Marr, Leon Barry, George Siegmann, Eugene Pallette, Nigel de Brulier, Boyd Irwin, Mary MacLaren, Sidney Franklin, Charles Stevens. Robust period adventure with Fairbanks a hearty D'Artagnan, Alexandre Dumas' swashbuckling hero who joins the King's Musketeers, becomes pals with Athos, Porthos and Aramis, and battles evil in the court of Louis XIII. De Brulier almost steals the film as Cardinal Richelieu. Great fun! Followed by THE IRON MASK. ▼●◗

Three Musketeers, The (1935) **90m.** ** D: Rowland V. Lee. Walter Abel, Paul Lukas, Ian Keith, Onslow Stevens, Ralph Forbes, Margot Grahame, Heather Angel. Dullest version of Dumas story, with Abel miscast as D'Artagnan.▼●

Three Musketeers, The (1939) **73m.** *** D: Allan Dwan. Don Ameche, Ritz Brothers, Lionel Atwill, Binnie Barnes, Miles Mander, Gloria Stuart, Pauline Moore, John Carradine, Joseph Schildkraut. Spirited musical, generally faithful to Dumas story; Ameche flavorful as D'Artagnan, Barnes lovely as Lady DeWinter, Ritz Brothers funny substitutes for unsuspecting musketeers.▼

Three Musketeers, The (1948) **C-125m.** **½ D: George Sidney. Lana Turner, Gene Kelly, June Allyson, Van Heflin, Angela Lansbury, Robert Coote, Frank Morgan, Vincent Price, Keenan Wynn, Gig Young. Oddball, lavish production of Dumas tale with Kelly as D'Artagnan. Occasional bright moments, but continual change of tone, and Heflin's drowsy characterization as Athos, bog down the action. Lana makes a stunning Lady DeWinter.▼●

Three Musketeers, The (1974-British) **C-105m.** ***½ D: Richard Lester. Oliver Reed, Raquel Welch, Richard Chamberlain, Michael York, Frank Finlay, Christopher Lee, Geraldine Chaplin, Faye Dunaway, Charlton Heston, Jean-Pierre Cassel, Roy Kinnear, Spike Milligan. Delightful tongue-in-cheek version of Dumas classic, mixing swashbuckling adventure and romance with broad slapstick. One of Raquel Welch's finest hours. Followed by THE FOUR MUSKETEERS, which was actually filmed simultaneously, and THE RETURN OF THE MUSKETEERS (1989). [PG]▼●◗

Three Musketeers, The (1993) **C-105m.** *** D: Stephen Herek. Charlie Sheen, Kiefer Sutherland, Chris O'Donnell, Oliver Platt, Tim Curry, Rebecca De Mornay, Gabrielle Anwar, Michael Wincott, Paul McGann, Julie Delpy, Hugh O'Conor. Once again, D'Artagnan (O'Donnell) and the Three Musketeers (Sutherland, Sheen, and Platt) meet for the first time, and cross swords with the lackeys of scheming Cardinal Richelieu. Really just "Young Swords," but it's fast paced and entertaining; lots of action, handsome Austrian locations and attractive costumes. Curry's Richelieu is broad, anachronistic—and absolutely delightful, the highlight of the film. Panavision. [PG] ▼●◗

3 Ninjas (1992) **C-87m.** ** D: Jon Turteltaub. Victor Wong, Michael Treanor, Max Elliott Slade, Chad Power, Rand Kingsley, Alan McRae, Margarita Franco, Patrick Laborteaux. Three young brothers take their hard-earned ninja skills and put them to use against big-time baddies who are out to kidnap them. Harmless Disney release borrows ideas from every kiddie hit of its era. A surprising box-office success. Followed by three sequels. [PG]▼●

3 Ninjas: High Noon at Mega Mountain (1998) **C-93m.** ** D: Sean McNamara. Loni Anderson, Hulk Hogan, Jim Varney, Victor Wong, Mathew Botuchis, Michael J. O'Laskey II, J. P. Roeske II, Chelsey Earlywine, Alan McRae. Latest adventures of the three would-be ninjas (with new cast members) finds them putting their prowess to work unexpectedly when Anderson and a team of commando types take over an amusement park, holding the families inside hostage. Pretty much what you'd expect; OK kids' fare. [PG]▼

3 Ninjas Kick Back (1994) **C-99m.** ** D: Charles T. Kanganis. Victor Wong, Max Elliott Slade, Sean Fox, Evan Bonifant, Caroline Junko King, Dustin Nguyen, Alan McRae, Margarita Franco, Jason Schombing, Angelo Tiffe, Sab Shimono, Joey Travolta. More silliness aimed straight for the sub-teen crowd, as the three brothers (two of them recast from the original film) sacrifice a championship baseball game to fly to Japan to help their grandfather, who's been targeted by an age-old rival. A few moralistic lessons are sprinkled among the slapstick and toilet humor. [PG]▼●

3 Ninjas Knuckle Up (1995) **C-85m.** *½ D: Simon S. Sheen. Victor Wong, Charles Napier, Michael Treanor, Max Elliott Slade, Chad Power, Crystle Lightning, Patrick Kirkpatrick. Rocky, Tum Tum, and Colt join their grandfather to help an Indian tribe whose land is being abused by a corrupt business tycoon (Napier). This artless blend of juvenile slapstick and martial arts was filmed in 1992, *before* 3 NINJAS KICK BACK, with the youthful star trio from the first film intact, but only released (barely, at that) in 1995. Followed by 3 NINJAS: HIGH NOON AT MEGA MOUNTAIN. [PG-13]▼●

Three Nuts in Search of a Bolt (1964) **C/B&W-80m.** *½ D: Tommy Noonan. Mamie Van Doren, Tommy Noonan, Ziva Rodann, Paul Gilbert, John Cronin, Peter Howard, T. C. Jones, Alvy Moore, Marjorie Bennett. Neurotic stripper Mamie and her two pals hire Noonan to act out their personalities for shrink Rodann, so they can receive psychoanalysis at a discount. Because of a couple of scenes in which Mamie plies her trade, this was considered to be quite risqué back in '64; today it's merely idiotic and would be hard-pressed to earn a PG-13 rating. Some stripper and nudie sequences in color although rest of film is b&w. Noonan also coproduced and coscripted.▼

Three O'Clock High (1987) **C-101m.** *½ D: Phil Joanou. Casey Siemaszko, Anne Ryan, Richard Tyson, Jeffrey Tambor, Philip Baker Hall, John P. Ryan, Stacey Glick, Jonathan Wise. High school journalist is assigned to do a welcome-wagon profile on the new psycho in class, finds himself challenged by this behemoth to duke it out in the parking lot after school. Steven Spielberg protégé Joanou is to the camera what James Brown is to shoes, but it's a lot of energy expended over nothing. Siemaszko is underwhelming in the lead. [PG-13]▼●

Three of Hearts (1993) **C-102m.** **½ D: Yurek Bogayevicz. William Baldwin, Kelly Lynch, Sherilyn Fenn, Joe Pantoliano, Gail Strickland, Cec Verrell, Claire Callaway, Marek Johnson, Monique Mannen, Tony Amendola, Tawny Kitaen. Original little film that begins with the end of a relationship between gay couple Lynch and Fenn and goes on to have the former hire a male escort (Baldwin) to try to get her lover back. Effective first half, with a strident Lynch getting to know the cocky gigolo; unfortunately second half of film becomes a more ordinary romantic tale, with the stud falling for his prey. A conventional gangster subplot doesn't help. Still, good use of N.Y.C. locations and excellent performances by Baldwin (who's never been better) and Lynch. [R]▼●

Three on a Couch (1966) **C-109m.** *½ D: Jerry Lewis. Jerry Lewis, Janet Leigh, Mary Ann Mobley, Gila Golan, Leslie Parrish, James Best, Kathleen Freeman. For psychiatrist Leigh to marry him, Lewis has to play five roles; one of them is "straight" but unintentionally funny, the other four zany, but unintentionally unfunny. The women are attractive.

Three on a Match (1932) **64m.** *** D: Mervyn LeRoy. Warren William, Joan Blondell, Bette Davis, Ann Dvorak, Humphrey Bogart, Lyle Talbot, Glenda Farrell, Dawn O'Day (Anne Shirley), Edward Arnold. Fine, fast-moving (and surprisingly potent) pre-Code melodrama of three girls who renew childhood friendship, only to find suspense and tragedy. Dvorak is simply marvelous. Remade as BROADWAY MUSKETEERS. ▼●

Three on a Spree (1961-British) **83m.** *½ D: Sidney J. Furie. Jack Watling, Carole Lesley, Renee Houston, John Slater. Disconcerting, poorly directed comedy of man forced to spend a million pounds in sixty days to inherit eight million, à la BREWSTER'S MILLIONS.

Three on a Ticket (1947) **64m.** ** D: Sam Newfield. Hugh Beaumont, Cheryl Walker, Paul Bryar, Ralph Dunn, Louise

Currie, Gavin Gordon. Efficient low-budget *Michael Shayne* detective entry, revolving around a scramble to piece together a railway locker ticket which has been ripped in three pieces and holds the key to a fortune in bank loot.

3 Penny Opera, The (1931-German) **112m.** ***½ D: G. W. Pabst. Rudolph Forster, Lotte Lenya, Carola Neher, Reinhold Schunzel, Fritz Rasp, Valeska Gert. Fine musical satire chronicling activities of dashing gangster Forster, his cohorts, and antagonists, with Lenya outstanding as Pirate Jenny. From Bertolt Brecht's play, with music by Kurt Weill, adapted from John Gay's *The Beggar's Opera*. Remade many times since.▼●

3 Ring Circus (1954) **C-103m.** ** D: Joseph Pevney. Dean Martin, Jerry Lewis, Joanne Dru, Zsa Zsa Gabor, Wallace Ford, Sig Ruman, Nick Cravat, Elsa Lanchester. So-so Martin and Lewis comedy has them as discharged servicemen up to trouble in a circus. Reissued in shorter version as JERRICO, THE WONDER CLOWN. VistaVision.

Three Sailors and a Girl (1953) **C-95m.** ** D: Roy Del Ruth. Jane Powell, Gordon MacRae, Gene Nelson, Sam Levene, Jack E. Leonard. Bland musical of three gobs who invest ship's surplus funds in a musical show starring Powell. Based on George S. Kaufman's *The Butter and Egg Man*.

Three Seasons (1999) **C-113m.** *** D: Tony Bui. Don Duong, Nguyen Ngoc Hiep, Tran Manh Cuong, Harvey Keitel, Zöe Bui, Nguyen Huu Duoc. Absorbing multi-character story about modern-day Saigon, where a poor boy struggles to survive on the streets, a bicycle-taxi driver falls in love with a prostitute, a young woman who harvests flowers tries to connect with her mysterious employer, and an American soldier (Keitel) returns to make amends for his past. In any other setting these stories might not have the resonance they do. Impressive debut for Vietnamese-American writer-director Bui. [PG-13]▼

Three Secrets (1950) **98m.** *** D: Robert Wise. Eleanor Parker, Patricia Neal, Ruth Roman, Frank Lovejoy, Leif Erickson. Sturdy melodrama; three women wait anxiously for word of which one's child survived plane crash. Remade for TV in 1999.▼

Three Shades of Love SEE: **This Rebel Breed**

Three Sisters, The (1966) **168m.** **½ D: Paul Bogart. Kim Stanley, Geraldine Page, Shelley Winters, Kevin McCarthy, Sandy Dennis. Taped recreation of Actors Studio Broadway production of Chekhov's play about 19th-century Russia and relationships amidst a most unhappy family.▼

Three Sisters (1970-British) **C-165m.** **** D: Laurence Olivier, John Sichel. Laurence Olivier, Joan Plowright, Alan Bates, Jeanne Watts, Louise Purnell, Derek Jacobi. Brilliant rendering of Chekhov play about three daughters of deceased Russian colonel living in provinces, circa 1900. Olivier's vibrant production is definitive screen version of this classic. Released here in 1974 by American Film Theater. [PG]▼

Three Smart Girls (1936) **84m.** ***½ D: Henry Koster. Deanna Durbin, Binnie Barnes, Alice Brady, Ray Milland, Barbara Read, Mischa Auer, Nan Grey, Charles Winninger. Delightful musicomedy with Deanna's feature-film debut as matchmaking girl who brings parents back together. Songs: "Someone To Care For Me," "My Heart Is Singing." Sequel: THREE SMART GIRLS GROW UP.▼●

Three Smart Girls Grow Up (1939) **90m.** *** D: Henry Koster. Deanna Durbin, Charles Winninger, Nan Grey, Helen Parrish, Robert Cummings, William Lundigan. Little Deanna still matchmaking for sisters, warming up stern father, singing "Because," winning over everyone in sight.▼●

Threesome (1994) **C-95m.** *** D: Andrew Fleming. Lara Flynn Boyle, Stephen Baldwin, Josh Charles, Alexis Arquette, Martha Gehman. Through computer error, college student Flynn Boyle is assigned to room with two guys—shy, intellectual Charles, who may be gay, and in-your-face, sex-obsessed Baldwin—resulting in various couplings and emotional complications. Coming-of-age comedy-drama is at once intelligent and impertinent; unlike many other Hollywood films, it does not cop out in its examination of the issue of homosexuality. Fleming also scripted. [R]▼●

Three Sovereigns for Sarah (1985) **C-180m. TVM** D: Philip Leacock. Vanessa Redgrave, Phyllis Thaxter, Kim Hunter, Patrick McGoohan, Shay Duffin, Ronald Hunter, Will Lyman. Riveting, beautifully filmed drama of the Salem witch trials, focusing on a witch-hunt survivor (Redgrave), who attempts to reverse the judgment against herself and her older sisters (Thaxter, Hunter), who have already been hanged. Fine performances all around, with a special nod to Vanessa. Originally presented over several evenings on PBS' *American Playhouse*. Above average.▼

Three Stooges Go Around the World in a Daze, The (1963) **94m.** **½ D: Norman Maurer. Three Stooges, Jay Sheffield, Joan Freeman, Walter Burke, Peter Forster. Even those who dislike the Stooges may enjoy this funny updating of Jules Verne's tale, replete with sight gags and world travel.▼

Three Stooges in Orbit, The (1962) **87m.** **½ D: Edward Bernds. The Three Stooges, Carol Christensen, Edson Stroll, Emil Sitka. Nutty scientist Sitka invents contraption that flies and floats. The Stooges accidentally launch it and run headlong into a few Martian invaders, with usual slapstick results for younger audiences.▼

Three Stooges Meet Hercules, The (1962) **89m.** **½ D: Edward Bernds. The Three Stooges, Vicki Trickett, Quinn Redeker, George N. Neise. Time machine takes the Stooges back to era of Roman legions; they are trapped on galley ship, battle Cyclops, and wind up with chariot chase. Good slapstick for kids and fans.▼

Three Strange Loves (1949-Swedish) **84m.** *** D: Ingmar Bergman. Eva Henning, Birger Malmsten, Birgit Tengroth, Mimi Nelson, Hasse Ekman. Interesting early Bergman drama which foreshadows much of his future work. This one explores the dynamics of a three-cornered love relationship, from a distinctly female perspective, and examines the possibility of two women having the same personality. Bergman can be seen on camera as a train passenger. Aka THIRST.▼

Three Strangers (1946) **92m.** ***½ D: Jean Negulesco. Sydney Greenstreet, Geraldine Fitzgerald, Peter Lorre, Joan Lorring, Robert Shayne, Marjorie Riordan. Greenstreet and Lorre team up with Fitzgerald as partners holding winning sweepstakes ticket under unusual circumstances. Bizarre John Huston–Howard Koch script makes fascinating viewing.

3 Strikes (2000) **C-82m.** *½ D: D. J. Pooh. Brian Hooks, N'Bushe Wright, Faizon Love, Starletta DuPois, George Wallace, David Alan Grier, Antonio Fargas, De'aundre Bonds, Vincent Schiavelli, David Leisure, Gerald S. O'Loughlin. Alleged comedy about a newly minted ex-con (Hooks) with two felony convictions to his name; he knows that a third will land him in jail for 25 years, but he can't seem to avoid trouble. A must for fanciers of flatulence jokes and general idiocy. [R]▼◗

Three Stripes in the Sun (1955) **93m.** **½ D: Richard Murphy. Aldo Ray, Phil Carey, Dick York, Chuck Connors, Mitsuko Kimura. Good film of Japan-hating American soldier Ray, who softens when he becomes involved with Japanese orphans and romances a pretty translator (Kimura). This based-on-fact account effectively mirrors postwar U.S.–Japanese relations. Murphy also scripted.

3:10 to Yuma (1957) **92m.** ***½ D: Delmer Daves. Van Heflin, Glenn Ford, Felicia Farr, Leora Dana, Henry Jones, Richard Jaeckel, Robert Emhardt. Extremely suspenseful Western, one of the best of the 1950s. Farmer Heflin, needing the money, agrees to hold captured outlaw Ford until the train arrives, but Ford starts to psych him out. Gripping every step of the way, with memorable George Duning theme sung by Frankie Laine. Script by Halsted Welles from an Elmore Leonard story.▼●

Three the Hard Way (1974) **C-93m.** **½ D: Gordon Parks, Jr. Jim Brown, Fred Williamson, Jim Kelly, Sheila Frazier, Jay Robinson, Alex Rocco, Corbin Bernsen. Top black action cast in nonstop, nearly bloodless thriller of white supremist Robinson's insane plot to eliminate blacks with a serum in the water supply. Produced by Harry Bernsen (Corbin's father). [R]▼

Three to Tango (1999) **C-103m.** *½ D: Damon Santostefano. Matthew Perry, Neve Campbell, Dylan McDermott, Oliver Platt, Bob Balaban, Cylk Cozart, John C. McGinley, Deborah Rush. Architect Perry is given the job of spying on the mistress of his insanely jealous—and rich—client, who mistakenly thinks he is gay, until they (predictably) fall in love. Glossy comedy of mistaken sexual identity with TV-star cast manages a couple of laughs but tries so hard to get them that it hardly seems worth the effort. [PG-13]▼◗

Three Tough Guys (1974-Italian-U.S.) **C-92m.** **½ D: Duccio Tessari. Lino Ventura, Fred Williamson, Isaac Hayes, Paula Kelly. Oddball but fast-moving actioner, with tough priest Ventura and ex-cop Hayes solving million-dollar bank robbery. Hayes, who also did the music, is nicely subdued as an actor. [PG]

Three Violent People (1956) **C-100m.** **½ D: Rudolph Maté. Charlton Heston, Anne Baxter, Gilbert Roland, Tom Tryon, Forrest Tucker, Elaine Stritch, Bruce Bennett, Barton MacLane. Adequately paced Western set in post-Civil War Texas; Heston, returning home with bride Baxter, is forced to fight carpetbaggers and deal with wife's shady past. VistaVision.▼

Three Wise Fools (1946) **90m.** ** D: Edward Buzzell. Margaret O'Brien, Lionel Barrymore, Lewis Stone, Edward Arnold, Thomas Mitchell, Jane Darwell, Cyd Charisse. Intended as fanciful, this turns out mawkish with adorable O'Brien winning over three crusty old men.

Three Wise Girls (1931) **66m.** ** D: William Beaudine. Jean Harlow, Mae Clarke, Walter Byron, Jameson Thomas, Marie Prevost, Andy Devine, Lucy Beaumont. Harlow plays a small-town girl who moves to N.Y.C. and quickly learns that all men are after just one thing. Strictly so-so, but interesting as Harlow's first starring vehicle, with Clarke giving a typically natural and believable performance as her big city mentor.

Three Wishes (1995) **C-107m.** ** D: Martha Coolidge. Patrick Swayze, Mary Elizabeth Mastrantonio, Joseph Mazzello, Seth Mumy, David Marshall Grant, Jay O. Sanders, Michael O'Keefe, John Diehl, Diane Venora, Colleen Camp, Bill Mumy. A mysterious man and his dog enter the life of a

Korean War widow who's doing her best to raise two sons on her own. Is there more to this stranger than meets the eye? Flashback-framed '50s tale hints at fantasy but doesn't let it flow until the end—by which time it seems like an afterthought. Another purported family film that moves like molasses and dwells on the melancholy. D. B. Sweeney appears unbilled. [PG] ▼●

3 Women (1977) **C-125m.** ***½ D: Robert Altman. Sissy Spacek, Shelley Duvall, Janice Rule, Robert Fortier, Ruth Nelson, John Cromwell. Brilliant, moody, thought-provoking film about a strange young girl (Spacek) who gets a job in an old-age convalescent home and attaches herself to coworker Duvall, who fancies herself a social butterfly. Their interrelationship, and involvement with a quiet, embittered woman (Rule) forms the "plot." Hypnotic film for Altman fans, heavy going for others; a completely unconventional movie. Panavision. [PG]

3 Worlds of Gulliver, The (1960-British) **C-100m.** *** D: Jack Sher. Kerwin Mathews, Jo Morrow, June Thorburn, Lee Patterson, Gregoire Aslan, Basil Sydney, Peter Bull. Hero is washed overboard and finds himself in the Land of Lilliput . . . but that's just the beginning. Well-made adventure/ fantasy designed for kids, fun for older viewers, too. Fine special effects by Ray Harryhausen, charming Bernard Herrmann score.▼●

Three Young Texans (1954) **C-78m.** ** D. Henry Levin. Mitzi Gaynor, Keefe Brasselle, Jeffrey Hunter, Harvey Stephens, Dan Riss. Standard Western has Hunter pulling railroad robbery to prevent crooks from forcing his father to do same job, expected complications.

Threshold (1981-Canadian) **C-97m.** *** D: Richard Pearce. Donald Sutherland, John Marley, Sharon Ackerman, Mare Winningham, Jeff Goldblum, Michael Lerner, Allan Nicholls, Paul Hecht, Robert Joy. Excellent, surprisingly low-key drama about the first artificial heart transplant, with more humanism and offbeat touches than you'd find in typical TV treatment of this sort of thing. Goldblum and Winningham score as, respectively, the biologist who invents the artificial heart and its first recipient. Unreleased in the U.S. until 1983, when Barney Clark's real-life operation made headlines. [PG]▼

Thrill of a Romance (1945) **C-105m.** ** D: Richard Thorpe. Van Johnson, Esther Williams, Frances Gifford, Henry Travers, Spring Byington, Lauritz Melchior, Tommy Dorsey. Typical Williams swim-romance vehicle with one good song, "I Should Care."▼

Thrill of Brazil, The (1946) **91m.** **½ D: S. Sylvan Simon. Evelyn Keyes, Keenan Wynn, Ann Miller, Allyn Joslyn, Tito Guizar. Pleasant South-of-the-border romance with music and spirited cast giving life to ordinary script.

Thrill of It All, The (1963) **C-108m.** *** D: Norman Jewison. Doris Day, James Garner, Arlene Francis, Edward Andrews, Reginald Owen, ZaSu Pitts, Elliott Reid. Enjoyable spoof of TV and commercials by Carl Reiner; good vehicle for Day as housewife-turned-TV-spokeswoman and Garner as her neglected husband. Reiner has a particularly funny series of cameos.▼

Throne of Blood (1957-Japanese) **108m.** **** D: Akira Kurosawa. Toshiro Mifune, Isuzu Yamada, Takashi Shimura, Minoru Chiaki. Graphic, powerful adaptation of *Macbeth* in a samurai setting. Gripping finale, with Taketoki Washizu (the Macbeth character, masterfully played by Mifune) attacked by arrows.▼●

Through a Glass, Darkly (1961-Swedish) **91m.** ***½ D: Ingmar Bergman. Harriet Andersson, Gunnar Bjornstrand, Max von Sydow, Lars Passgard. Four-character drama about just-released mental patient, her husband, her father and her younger brother who spend summer together on secluded island. Moody, evocative story of insanity—well-deserved Oscar winner, one of Bergman's best. The first in the filmmaker's "faith" trilogy, followed by WINTER LIGHT and THE SILENCE.▼●

Throw Momma From the Train (1987) **C-88m.** **½ D: Danny DeVito. Danny DeVito, Billy Crystal, Anne Ramsey, Kim Greist, Kate Mulgrew, Branford Marsalis, Rob Reiner, Bruce Kirby. Black comedy spin-off of Hitchcock's STRANGERS ON A TRAIN, with DeVito (in an excellent performance) as a childish man who tries to persuade his writing professor (Crystal) to "exchange murders" with him so he can bump off his harridan of a mother (Ramsey, who's incredible). Uneven, to be sure, and not as all-out funny as you might expect from the starring duo. Director DeVito has many offbeat ideas, and cinematographer Barry Sonnenfeld (who did those wild gags in RAISING ARIZONA) leaves a distinctive stamp on this film—particularly the runaway car sequence. Written by Stu Silver. [PG-13]▼●

Thumbelina (1994) **C-86m.** **½ D: Don Bluth, Gary Goldman. Voices of Jodi Benson, Gary Imhoff, Gino Conforti, Barbara Cook, Will Ryan, Charo, June Foray, Kenneth Mars, Gilbert Gottfried, John Hurt, Carol Channing. Animated retelling of Hans Christian Andersen's classic fairy tale has the digit-sized heroine evading the clutches of various toads, moles, and beetles before she can proceed with her courtship with her dream lover, Prince Cornelius. Pleasant enough diversion for the small fry, with a handful of sweetly romantic songs from Barry Manilow. [G]▼●

Thumb Tripping (1972) **C-94m.** **½ D:

Quentin Masters. Michael Burns, Meg Foster, Mariana Hill, Bruce Dern, Michael Conrad, Joyce Van Patten. Amusing as a period piece on the hippie era, with Burns and Foster as hitchhikers who decide to travel together and share experiences. [R]▼

Thunder Afloat (1939) **94m.** **½ D: George B. Seitz. Wallace Beery, Chester Morris, Virginia Grey, Clem Bevans, John Qualen, Regis Toomey. Above-average Beery vehicle of old salt pitted against rival (Morris) when he joins the Navy.

Thunder Alley (1967) **C-90m.** *½ D: Richard Rush. Annette Funicello, Fabian, Diane McBain, Warren Berlinger, Jan Murray, Maureen Arthur. Fabian's inept stock-car driving gets him suspended from racing, but unfortunately, the acting profession doesn't have the same rules. Panavision.▼

Thunder and Lightning (1977) **C-95m.** **½ D: Corey Allen. David Carradine, Kate Jackson, Roger C. Carmel, Sterling Holloway, Ed Barth, Ron Feinberg. Amiable moonshine picture with attractive pairing of Carradine and Jackson and lots of expected car smash-ups. [PG]▼

Thunderball (1965-British) **C-129m.** **½ D: Terence Young. Sean Connery, Claudine Auger, Adolfo Celi, Luciana Paluzzi, Rik Van Nutter, Martine Beswick, Bernard Lee, Lois Maxwell, Desmond Llewelyn, Roland Culver. Fourth James Bond film isn't as lively as the others. Plenty of gimmicks, and Oscar-winning special effects, as world is threatened with destruction, but film tends to bog down—especially underwater. Celi makes a formidable Bond villain. Remade eighteen years later—with Connery—as NEVER SAY NEVER AGAIN. Panavision.▼●◗

Thunder Bay (1953) **C-102m.** *** D: Anthony Mann. James Stewart, Joanne Dru, Gilbert Roland, Dan Duryea, Jay C. Flippen, Henry (Harry) Morgan. Action-packed account of oil-drillers vs. Louisiana shrimp fishermen, with peppery cast.▼

Thunder Below (1932) **67m.** **½ D: Richard Wallace. Tallulah Bankhead, Charles Bickford, Paul Lukas, Eugene Pallette, James Finlayson, Edward Van Sloan. Tallulah loves Lukas, but when husband Bickford goes blind, she can't bear to leave him. Melodramatic triangle story, well-acted by all.

Thunder Birds (1942) **C-78m.** ** D: William Wellman. Gene Tierney, Preston Foster, John Sutton, Dame May Whitty, Reginald Denny, Jack Holt, George Barbier. Ultra-patriotic time-capsule is an ode to the WW2 flyer/flying instructor. Freewheeling veteran aviator Foster and intern-turned-trainee Sutton (who's afraid of heights) compete for the affection of flirtatious Tierney.

Thunderbirds (1952) **98m.** **½ D: John H. Auer. John Derek, John Barrymore, Jr., Mona Freeman, Gene Evans. Standard tale of training aviators for WW2, with typical romantic interludes.

Thunderbolt and Lightfoot (1974) **C-114m.** *** D: Michael Cimino. Clint Eastwood, Jeff Bridges, George Kennedy, Geoffrey Lewis, Catherine Bach, Gary Busey, Jack Dodson, Vic Tayback, Dub Taylor, Bill McKinney. Thief Eastwood and drifter Bridges team up with Clint's ex-partners (Kennedy and Lewis) to retrieve loot from previous robbery. Colorful, tough melodrama-comedy with good characterizations; Lewis is particularly fine, but Bridges steals the picture. Cimino's directorial debut. Panavision. [R]▼●

Thundercloud SEE: **Colt .45**

Thunderhead—Son of Flicka (1945) **C-78m.** **½ D: Louis King. Roddy McDowall, Preston Foster, Rita Johnson, James Bell, Diana Hale, Carleton Young. Good, colorful attempt to repeat MY FRIEND FLICKA's success; doesn't match original, but it's enjoyable. Followed by GREEN GRASS OF WYOMING.

Thunderheart (1992) **C-118m.** *** D: Michael Apted. Val Kilmer, Sam Shepard, Graham Greene, Fred Ward, Fred Dalton Thompson, Sheila Tousey, Chief Ted Thin Elk, John Trudell, Dennis Banks, David Crosby. Part-Sioux FBI agent Kilmer is awakened to his heritage when he's assigned to investigate a murder on an Oglala Sioux reservation. Engrossing thriller is notable for its keen attention to detail regarding Sioux customs and spirituality, and its enlightened point of view. Based on events which occurred in the 1970s at Pine Ridge Reservation in South Dakota, where the film was shot. Coproduced by Robert De Niro; before directing this, Apted made a documentary, INCIDENT AT OGLALA, about Indian activist Leonard Peltier. [R]▼●◗

Thunder in Carolina (1960) **C-92m.** ** D: Paul Helmick. Rory Calhoun, Alan Hale, Connie Hines, John Gentry, Ed McGrath, Troyanne Ross. Dull programmer of stock car racing in the South, with Calhoun as a skirt-chasing driver. Video title: HARD DRIVIN'.▼

Thundering Jets (1958) **73m.** *½ D: Helmut Dantine. Rex Reason, Dick Foran, Audrey Dalton, Robert Dix. Still another account of flight officer trying to reevaluate his handling of servicemen. CinemaScope.

Thunder in the City (1937-British) **86m.** *** D: Marion Gering. Edward G. Robinson, Luli Deste, Nigel Bruce, Constance Collier, Ralph Richardson, Arthur Wontner. Amusing film about a go-getting American promoter who visits England and gambles on a long-shot: hitherto unknown mineral known as Magnelite, which he proceeds to "ballyhoo." Tailor-made for an ebullient Robinson.▼

Thunder in the East (1953) **98m.** **½ D: Charles Vidor. Alan Ladd, Deborah Kerr, Charles Boyer, Corinne Calvet, Cecil

Kellaway, John Williams. Adequate, politically loaded adventure with gunrunner Ladd caught amid tension and rebellion in rural India. Kerr and Boyer uplift the proceedings as a refined blind woman who falls for Ladd and a stubbornly pacifistic government official.

Thunder in the Sun (1959) **C-81m.** **½ D: Russell Rouse. Susan Hayward, Jeff Chandler, Jacques Bergerac, Blanche Yurka, Carl Esmond, Fortunio Bonanova. Hayward is romanced by wagon train scout Chandler and Bergerac, head of French Basque immigrants on way to California.

Thunder in the Valley (1947) **C-103m.** **½ D: Louis King. Lon McCallister, Peggy Ann Garner, Edmund Gwenn, Reginald Owen. Usual tale of boy in love with his dog, cruel father who doesn't share his feelings; colorful but standard.

Thunder Island (1963) **65m.** ** D: Jack Leewood. Gene Nelson, Fay Spain, Brian Kelly, Miriam Colon, Art Bedard. A hit man is hired to kill the former dictator of a Latin country who's now living in exile on a nearby island. Unexceptional programmer cowritten by Jack Nicholson. CinemaScope.

Thunder of Drums, A (1961) **C-97m.** **½ D: Joseph M. Newman. George Hamilton, Luana Patten, Richard Boone, Charles Bronson, Richard Chamberlain, Slim Pickens. Better than average cast saves average story of new lieutenant having rough time in cavalry. CinemaScope.

Thunder on the Hill (1951) **84m.** *** D: Douglas Sirk. Claudette Colbert, Ann Blyth, Robert Douglas, Anne Crawford, Gladys Cooper. Nun Colbert can't believe visitor Blyth, about to be hanged, is murderess, sets out to prove her innocent; Cooper fine as Mother Superior. Sincere, interesting drama.

Thunder Over Arizona (1956) **C-75m.** ** D: Joseph Kane. Skip Homeier, Kristine Miller, George Macready, Wallace Ford. Undemanding minor Western showing the corruption and greed of people incited by a rich silver ore discovery. Filmed in widescreen Naturama.▼

Thunder Over Hawaii SEE: **Naked Paradise**

Thunder Over Tangier (1957-British) **66m.** *½ D: Lance Comfort. Robert Hutton, Martin Benson, Derek Sydney, Lisa Gastoni. Flabby account of refugees being conned with phony passports.

Thunder Over the Plains (1953) **C-82m.** ** D: Andre de Toth. Randolph Scott, Lex Barker, Phyllis Kirk, Henry Hull, Elisha Cook, Jr., Richard Benjamin, Charles McGraw, Fess Parker. Routine Western set in post-Civil War Texas, with Scott as army officer sent to prevent carpetbaggers from harassing all.

Thunder Pass (1954) **76m.** ** D: Frank McDonald. Dane Clark, Andy Devine, Dorothy Patrick, John Carradine, Raymond Burr. Usual story of resolute army officer (Clark) pushing settlers onward in face of Indian attack.▼

Thunder Road (1958) **92m.** *** D: Arthur Ripley. Robert Mitchum, Gene Barry, Jacques Aubuchon, Keely Smith, James Mitchum. Rural bootlegger takes on Feds *and* the Mob in cult favorite that even today continues to play in drive-ins; for many this remains the definitive moonshine picture. Jim Mitchum makes screen debut playing Bob's *brother;* the elder Mitchum got a hit record out of the title tune, which he also wrote!▼●◗

Thunder Rock (1942-British) **112m.** *** D: Roy Boulting. Michael Redgrave, Barbara Mullen, Lilli Palmer, James Mason, Frederick Valk. Allegorical fable of discouraged newspaperman given renewed faith by visions of various drowned people. Excellent cast makes this most enjoyable; based on Robert Ardrey's play.

Thunderstorm (1956-Spanish) **81m.** *½ D: John Guillermin. Carlos Thompson, Linda Christian, Charles Korvin, Gary Thorne. Warmed-over trivia concerning Christian's provocative arrival in a small fishing village on the Spanish coast.

Thursday's Child (1943-British) **81m.** **½ D: Rodney Ackland. Sally Ann Howes, Wilfrid Lawson, Kathleen O'Regan, Eileen Bennett, Stewart Granger, Marianne Davis, Gerhardt Kempinski, Felix Aylmer. Melodramatic soap opera of twelve-year-old girl from middle-class family who becomes child film star, to the detriment of all around her. Howes, making her film debut, is excellent as the level-headed youngster. Recommended mainly for buffs, and fans of dashing Granger (in an early supporting role).▼

Thursday's Game (1974) **C-100m. TVM** D: Robert Moore. Gene Wilder, Bob Newhart, Ellen Burstyn, Cloris Leachman, Martha Scott, Nancy Walker, Valerie Harper, Rob Reiner, Norman Fell, Richard Schaal, Dick Gautier, John Archer. Sparkling adult comedy about pokerplaying buddies Wilder and Newhart and their marital and business problems. Absolutely tops with dandy cast and a gloriously intelligent, often hilarious script by James L. Brooks. Filmed in 1971. Above average. ▼●

THX 1138 (1971) **C-88m.** **½ D: George Lucas. Robert Duvall, Donald Pleasence, Maggie McOmie, Don Pedro Colley, Ian Wolfe. Futuristic tale in the *1984* vein about robotlike society where sex is forbidden and everyone looks the same. Dull script, but visually impressive; Lucas' first feature is expanded version of prize-winning featurette he made at USC. Techniscope. [PG]▼●

Thy Kingdom Come . . . Thy Will Be Done (1988-U.S.-British) **C-107m.** ***½

D: Antony Thomas. Provocative documentary about born-again Christianity, which examines everything from the type of person who becomes involved in the movement, to its ties to right-wing politics. A controversial production that almost didn't get seen in this country. Among the highlights: a revealing sequence filmed in Jim and Tammy Bakker's Heritage, USA park.

Tiara Tahiti (1962-British) **C-100m.** ** D: William (Ted) Kotcheff. James Mason, John Mills, Claude Dauphin, Herbert Lom. Mild comedy-drama involving Mason and Mills as former Army officers who have an old grudge to settle; establishment of a Tahiti resort hotel sets wheels in motion.▼

Ticket to Heaven (1981-Canadian) **C-107m.** *** D: Ralph L. Thomas. Nick Mancuso, Saul Rubinek, Meg Foster, Kim Cattrall, R. H. Thomson, Jennifer Dale, Guy Boyd. Mancuso, strung out from bad relationship, is seduced into becoming a "heavenly child" in a Moonie-like cult. Pointed drama is frightening in its relevancy. Mancuso is excellent, Rubinek and Thomson lend fine support as his best friend and a deprogrammer. [PG]▼◗

Ticket to Tomahawk, A (1950) **C-90m.** *** D: Richard Sale. Dan Dailey, Anne Baxter, Rory Calhoun, Walter Brennan, Charles Kemper, Connie Gilchrist, Arthur Hunnicutt, Mauritz Hugo, Chief Yowlachie, Victor Sen Yung. Engaging comedy-Western about stagecoach company that hires gunslinger Calhoun to keep dreaded railroad from running on time. Good fun; one of the chorus girls with Dailey in a musical number is Marilyn Monroe.▼

Tickle Me (1965) **C-90m.** **½ D: Norman Taurog. Elvis Presley, Jocelyn Lane, Julie Adams, Jack Mullaney, Merry Anders, Connie Gilchrist. That's the only way to get any laughs out of this one: Elvis works at all-girl dude ranch singing his usual quota of songs. Written by Elwood Ullman and Edward Bernds, both of whom worked with The Three Stooges in better days. Panavision.▼

Ticklish Affair, A (1963) **C-89m.** ** D: George Sidney. Shirley Jones, Gig Young, Red Buttons, Carolyn Jones, Edgar Buchanan. Amiable film of Navy commander Young falling in love with widow Jones; all it lacks is wit, sparkle and a fresh script. Panavision.

... tick ... tick ... tick ... (1970) **C-100m.** ** D: Ralph Nelson. Jim Brown, George Kennedy, Fredric March, Lynn Carlin, Don Stroud, Clifton James, Janet MacLachlan. Poor man's IN THE HEAT OF THE NIGHT with black man (Brown) replacing white sheriff (Kennedy) in Southern town, flaring local hostilities. March adds film's only spice as aging, cantankerous mayor. Panavision. [PG]

Tidal Wave (1975) **C-82m.** *½ D: Shiro Moriana, Andrew Meyer. Lorne Greene, Kiliu Kobayashi, Rhonda Leigh Hopkins, Hiroshi Fujioka. Laughable Americanization of big-budget (and much superior) Japanese film, SUBMERSION OF JAPAN; epic special effects dwarfed by idiotic new footage with Greene, and horrible dubbing. For diehard disaster buffs only. Panavision. [PG]▼

Tie-Died: Rock 'n Roll's Most Deadicated Fans (1995) **C-80m.** ** D: Andrew Behar. Documentary chronicling the legions of Deadheads, that unique form of fan who make following the rock group The Grateful Dead a way of life. Sporadically interesting look at these groupies, but in the end, we don't know much more than we did when we came in. Released, coincidentally, just after the death of Deadhead guru Jerry Garcia. [R]▼●◗

Tiefland (1954-German) **98m.** **½ D: Leni Riefenstahl. Leni Riefenstahl, Franz Eichberger, Bernard Minetti, Maria Koppenhofer, Luis Rainer. Blonde, dreamy shepherd Eichberger and arrogant marquis Minetti vie for Spanish dancer Riefenstahl. Atmospheric, visually poetic drama, even though the characters lack depth. Filmed between 1942 and 1945; editing wasn't completed until 1954.▼

Tie Me Up! Tie Me Down! (1990-Spanish) **C-101m.** **½ D: Pedro Almodóvar. Victoria Abril, Antonio Banderas, Francisco Rabal, Loles Leon, Julieta Serrano, Maria Barranco. Mental patient kidnaps a former porn star/junkie, slaps her around some, then ties her to a bed; actually, he just wants to get married and have kids. Potential NOW nightmare comes off as surprisingly tame for Almodóvar, though it still has his unpredictable black humor. Thought-provoking and energetically performed. Two scenes (one a loud but fairly explicit sex scene) earned this an X rating, so the distributor decided to release it unrated instead. Later rerated for video. [NC-17]▼●

Tie That Binds, The (1995) **C-98m.** BOMB D: Wesley Strick. Daryl Hannah, Keith Carradine, Moira Kelly, Vincent Spano, Julia Devin, Ray Reinhardt, Barbara Tarbuck. Two psychotic fugitives terrorize the family that's legally adopted their daughter after the youngster was taken into police custody following a foiled robbery attempt. This is what audiences get for having made THE HAND THAT ROCKS THE CRADLE a hit; film (from the same studio) is sleazy, insultingly derivative, and full of dangling plot issues. Directorial debut for screenwriter Strick. [R]▼●◗

Tiger and the Pussycat, The (1967-Italian-U.S.) **C-105m.** **½ D: Dino Risi. Ann-Margret, Vittorio Gassman, Eleanor Parker, Antonella Stani, Fiorenzo Fiorentini. Innocuous sex-comedy of middle-aged businessman Gassman unintentionally getting involved with promiscuous young Ann-Margret. Italian and American players work well together.▼

Tiger Bay (1959-British) **105m.** *** D: J. Lee Thompson. John Mills, Horst Buchholz, Hayley Mills, Yvonne Mitchell, Megs Jenkins, Anthony Dawson. Lonely Cardiff child witnesses a murder and is abducted by the Polish sailor-killer. A poignant, sensitive, and very different police chase story. Hayley steals the film in first major acting role.▼◗

Tiger by the Tail (1968) **C-99m.** ** D: R. G. Springsteen. Christopher George, Tippi Hedren, Dean Jagger, Charo, Glenda Farrell, Lloyd Bochner, Alan Hale, Skip Homeier, R. G. Armstrong. Vietnam war hero is accused of murdering his brother and recruits his socialite girlfriend in hunt for the real killer. Overly talkative thriller. [M/PG]

Tiger Makes Out, The (1967) **C-94m.** **½ D: Arthur Hiller. Eli Wallach, Anne Jackson, Bob Dishy, John Harkins, David Burns, Ruth White, Rae Allen, Charles Nelson Reilly. One-man crusader against society (Wallach) symbolically kidnaps suburban housewife (Jackson). Originally a one-act, two-character play by Murray Schisgal, his expanded screenplay loses focus, relies on vivid N.Y. locations and funny cameos by character actors. Dustin Hoffman's film debut.

Tiger of Eschnapur, The (1958-German) **C-101m.** ** D: Fritz Lang. Debra Paget, Paul Hubschmid, Walther Reyer, Rene Deltman, Luciana Paluzzi. Exotic dancer Paget is desired by dastardly maharajah Reyer, but she loves architect Hubschmid; meanwhile, Reyer's subjects are plotting revolution. Slow-moving, disappointing adventure-romance of interest mostly for Lang's participation. The first of the director's Indian diptych, followed by THE INDIAN TOMB; both were originally edited down to 95m., dubbed and released as JOURNEY TO THE LOST CITY.

Tiger Shark (1932) **80m.** *** D: Howard Hawks. Edward G. Robinson, Richard Arlen, Zita Johann, J. Carrol Naish, Vince Barnett. Robinson gives rich, colorful performance as Portuguese tuna fisherman who marries wayward girl out of pity, then sees her fall in love with his best friend—a plot gambit Warner Bros. reused several times (SLIM, MANPOWER, etc.). Authentically filmed amid fisheries on Monterey coast.

Tigers in Lipstick (1979-Italian) **C-83m.** ** D: Luigi Zampa. Ursula Andress, Laura Antonelli, Sylvia Kristel, Monica Vitti, Michele Placido, Roberto Benigni, Orazio Orlando. Veteran comedy director Zampa pilots a fun but overly tame throwback to '60s sex comedies that spotlights four beautiful actresses (individually) in seven separate segments, emphasizing aggressive women who take advantage of men. Best segment: "The Pickup," in which Antonelli is a frantic businesswoman who disrupts the life of an orchestra conductor. Originally titled: WILD BEDS. [R]▼

Tiger's Tale, A (1987) **C-97m.** *½ D: Peter Douglas. Ann-Margret, C. Thomas Howell, Charles Durning, Kelly Preston, William Zabka, Ann Wedgeworth, James Noble, Tim Thomerson, Steven Kampmann, Angel Tompkins. Unbelievable romantic comedy about a high school senior who gets involved with his girlfriend's mother, a nurse named Rose Butts. Need we say more? Debuting writer-director Douglas (Kirk's son) has bitten off more than he can chew—or we can swallow. Ann-Margret is watchable, as always, but miscast. [R]▼●

Tiger Walks, A (1964) **C-91m.** **½ D: Norman Tokar. Brian Keith, Vera Miles, Pamela Franklin, Sabu, Kevin Corcoran, Peter Brown, Una Merkel, Frank McHugh, Edward Andrews, Jack Albertson. Oddball Disney film about young girl (Franklin) whose compassion for tiger which has broken away from circus stirs controversy and political wheeling-and-dealing. Surprisingly bitter portrait of small-town America. Sabu's last film.▼

Tiger Warsaw (1988) **C-93m.** *½ D: Amin Q. Chaudhri. Patrick Swayze, Piper Laurie, Lee Richardson, Mary McDonnell, Barbara Williams, Bobby DiCicco, Jenny Chrisinger, Kaye Ballard. Muddled melodrama about troubled ex-junkie Swayze and what happens when he comes home and attempts to sort out his life. Hokey and highly improbable. [R]▼●

Tigger Movie, The (2000) **C-77m.** **½ D: Jun Falkenstein. Voices of Jim Cummings, John Fiedler, Nikita Hopkins, Ken Sansom, Peter Cullen, Kath Soucie; narrated by John Hurt. Tigger, who's always boasted that "he's the only one," comes to feel the need for family, and his friends in the Hundred Acre Wood try to help him. Cute movie aimed squarely at young children; not in the same class as major Disney animated features, but serves its purpose well. Best of all are the songs by Disney veterans Richard B. and Robert M. Sherman and their imaginative staging. [G]▼◗

Tight Little Island (1949-British) **82m.** **** D: Alexander Mackendrick. Basil Radford, Joan Greenwood, James Robertson Justice, Jean Cadell, Gordon Jackson, Wylie Watson, John Gregson. Narrated by Finlay Currie. Hilarious, fast-paced comedy about WW2 ship sinking while loaded with whiskey and the antics of local Scottish islanders thirsting for its cargo. A solid hit. Scripted by Compton Mackenzie, the author of the novel, who has a small role as Captain Buncher. British title: WHISKY

GALORE! Followed by MAD LITTLE ISLAND.▼

Tightrope (1984) **C-114m.** **½ D: Richard Tuggle. Clint Eastwood, Genevieve Bujold, Alison Eastwood, Jennifer Beck, Dan Hedaya. New Orleans cop finds he has much in common with the sex murderer he's pursuing. Intriguing Eastwood vehicle undone by sleaziness—and darkness. [R]▼●

Tight Shoes (1941) **68m.** ** D: Albert S. Rogell. Broderick Crawford, Binnie Barnes, John Howard, Anne Gwynne. Cast pushes hard to make this Damon Runyon yarn amusing at times: Crawford is big-shot crook who has big feet.

Tight Spot (1955) **97m.** ***½ D: Phil Karlson. Ginger Rogers, Edward G. Robinson, Brian Keith, Lorne Greene, Katherine Anderson. Solid little film, with Rogers in one of her best performances as a former gangster's moll who's on the spot because she has agreed to testify against him. Tense script by William Bowers.▼

Tigrero: A Film That Was Never Made (1994-Finnish-German-Brazilian) **C-75m.** *** D: Mika Kaurismaki. Absorbing documentary charting director Samuel Fuller's ill-fated attempt to shoot a film in Brazil among the remote Karaja tribe in 1954. Fuller is on hand, returning to the Karaja village where he describes the events to filmmaker Jim Jarmusch and screens footage he shot four decades earlier for villagers. A must for movie-history aficionados, and cultists of Jarmusch, the Kaurismaki brothers, and (especially) Fuller.▼●

Tijuana Story, The (1957) **72m.** BOMB D: Leslie Kardos. James Darren, Jean Willes, Robert McQueeney, Rodolfo Acosta, Robert Blake. Juvenile melodrama of Darren a victim of narcotic addiction, set in Mexico.

Till Dawn Do Us Part SEE: **Straight on Till Morning**

Till Death (1978) **C-89m.** *** D: Walter Stocker. Keith Atkinson, Belinda Balaski, Marshall Reed, Bert Freed, Jonathan Hole. Neat little shocker, virtually a two-character thriller. Atkinson refuses to believe that Balaski was killed on their wedding night, finds her alive in her crypt. Made in 1972.

Tillie and Gus (1933) **58m.** ***½ D: Francis Martin. W.C. Fields, Alison Skipworth, Baby LeRoy, Edgar Kennedy, Jacqueline Wells (Julie Bishop), Clifford Jones, Barton MacLane, Clarence Wilson. Fields and Skipworth are perfectly matched as card hustlers in this very entertaining comedy, which also pits W.C. against Baby LeRoy for the first time. Nominal plot has them helping niece Wells win a crucial riverboat race.

Tillie's Punctured Romance (1914) **73m.** **½ D: Mack Sennett. Charlie Chaplin, Marie Dressler, Mabel Normand, Mack Swain, Charles Bennett, Chester Conklin, Keystone Kops. A comic curio, the first full-length comedy feature film, with Dressler repeating stage role as farm girl fleeced by city-slicker Chaplin (appearing out of his usual character). Not terribly funny, or coherent, but there are good moments; mainly interesting for historical purposes. Dressler starred in a pair of sequels, TILLIE'S TOMATO SURPRISE and TILLIE WAKES UP. ▼●◗

Till Marriage Do Us Part (1974-Italian) **C-97m.** **½ D: Luigi Comencini. Laura Antonelli, Alberto Lionello, Michele Placido, Jean Rochefort, Karin Schubert. A naive young woman unable to consummate her marriage seeks and finds sexual fulfillment elsewhere. Light, forgettable farce featuring Antonelli at her sexiest. [R]▼●

Till the Clouds Roll By (1946) **C-137m.** **½ D: Richard Whorf. Robert Walker, Van Heflin, Lucille Bremer, Dorothy Patrick, many guest stars including Judy Garland, Kathryn Grayson, Lena Horne, Tony Martin, Dinah Shore, Frank Sinatra, June Allyson, Angela Lansbury, Cyd Charisse, Virginia O'Brien. Soggy biography of songwriter Jerome Kern uplifted by song numbers featuring some high-powered MGM talent. Highlights include Lansbury's "How D'Ya Like to Spoon With Me," Lena's "Why Was I Born?," Judy's "Look for the Silver Lining," and mini-production of *Show Boat*.▼●◗

Till the End of Time (1946) **105m.** *** D: Edward Dmytryk. Dorothy McGuire, Guy Madison, Robert Mitchum, Bill Williams, Tom Tully, William Gargan, Jean Porter, Ruth Nelson. Solid, sympathetic drama of three returning WW2 veterans was released months before THE BEST YEARS OF OUR LIVES; the focus is on Madison falling for troubled war widow McGuire. Screenplay by Allen Rivkin, based on Niven Busch's novel *They Dream of Home*. Title song (based on Chopin's Polonaise in A-flat Major) was a big hit.▼●

Till There Was You (1990-U.S.-Australian) **C-94m.** BOMB D: John Seale. Mark Harmon, Deborah Unger, Jeroen Krabbe, Shane Briant. Saxophone player Harmon is summoned to the South Pacific island of Vanuatu by his brother, whose subsequent murder he predictably solves, after bungee jumping with the natives! Pretty scenery can't save this one. [R]▼

Till We Meet Again (1944) **88m.** ** D: Frank Borzage. Ray Milland, Barbara Britton, Walter Slezak, Lucile Watson, Mona Freeman. Fair wartime drama of nun Britton helping pilot Milland return to Allied lines; elements don't always click in this one.

Tilt (1978) **C-111m.** ** D: Rudy Durand. Brooke Shields, Ken Marshall, Charles Durning, John Crawford, Gregory Walcott, Geoffrey Lewis. Meandering tale of pinball wizard Shields and musician Marshall traveling cross-country, eventually challenging champion Durning. Only value of film (aside from Durning) is dazzling point-of-view photography inside pinball machine. Recut by director Durand to 100m. [PG]▼

'Til There Was You (1997) **C-114m.** ** D: Scott Winant. Jeanne Tripplehorn, Dylan McDermott, Sarah Jessica Parker, Jennifer Aniston, Craig Bierko, Nina Foch, Christine Ebersole, Michael Tucker, Steve Antin, Ken Olin, Susan Walters, Karen Allen. A man and a woman's lives mirror each other for over twenty years, and they even have several brief chance encounters. Of course, when they finally do meet, it's love at first sight. Cloying and excruciatingly overlong. It doesn't help that the actors don't really seem to believe in the material. Best moments belong to Parker as a spoiled former TV sitcom teen. [PG-13]▼●

'Til We Meet Again (1940) **99m.** **½ D: Edmund Goulding. Merle Oberon, George Brent, Pat O'Brien, Geraldine Fitzgerald, Binnie Barnes, Frank McHugh, Eric Blore, George Reeves. Overblown remake of ONE WAY PASSAGE recounts romance between suave crook Brent and fatally ill Oberon; McHugh repeats comedy-relief role from 1932 original.

Tim (1979-Australian) **C-108m.** **½ D: Michael Pate. Piper Laurie, Mel Gibson, Alwyn Kurts, Pat Evison, Peter Gwynne, Deborah Kennedy. Lush, well-meaning if a bit schmaltzy chronicle of the relationship between older woman (Laurie) and younger, retarded man (nicely played by Gibson). Pate wrote the screenplay from Colleen McCullough's first novel. Remade for TV in 1996 as MARY & TIM.▼

Timberjack (1955) **C-94m.** ** D: Joseph Kane. Vera Ralston, Sterling Hayden, David Brian, Adolphe Menjou, Hoagy Carmichael. Young man fights crooks taking over lumber mill who also killed his father. Harmless potboiler.

Timber Queen (1943) **66m.** *½ D: Frank McDonald. Richard Arlen, Mary Beth Hughes, June Havoc, Sheldon Leonard. Static programmer with pilot Arlen helping Hughes solve her business problems and romancing her.▼

Timbuktu (1959) **91m.** ** D: Jacques Tourneur. Victor Mature, Yvonne De Carlo, George Dolenz, John Dehner, Marcia Henderson, James Foxx. Mature plays adventurer involved in African story of plot to overthrow government. Script is below average; cast is uneven.

Tim Burton's The Nightmare Before Christmas SEE: **Nightmare Before Christmas, The**

Time After Time (1979) **C-112m.** **½ D: Nicholas Meyer. Malcolm McDowell, David Warner, Mary Steenburgen, Charles Cioffi, Kent Williams, Patti D'Arbanville, Joseph Maher, Corey Feldman, Shelley Hack. Fanciful tale of H. G. Wells following Jack the Ripper from Victorian England to 1979 America in his time machine. Engaging premise eroded by story loopholes, and halfhearted attempts at social comment. Best is Steenburgen in an appealing, star-making performance as Wells' modern American girlfriend. Vivid score by Miklos Rozsa. Panavision. [PG]▼●

Time After Time (1985-British) **C-103m.** *** D: Bill Hays. John Gielgud, Googie Withers, Helen Cherry, Ursula Howells, Brenda Bruce, Freddie Jones, Fiona Walker, Trevor Howard. Very funny comedy about Gielgud, living on an estate with his three elderly sisters (named April, May, and Baby June)—their eccentricities, memories, and what happens when they are visited by their manipulative, long-lost cousin (Withers). Great script by Andrew Davies, from Molly Keane's novel; hampered only by awkward direction.

Time Bandits (1981-British) **C-110m.** **½ D: Terry Gilliam. Sean Connery, Shelley Duvall, John Cleese, Katherine Helmond, Ian Holm, Michael Palin, Ralph Richardson, Peter Vaughan, David Warner, Kenny Baker, David Rappaport. Six dwarfs, pursued by the Supreme Being (Richardson), escort a young English schoolboy through time. They meet Robin Hood (Cleese), Napoleon (Holm), King Agamemnon (Connery). Imaginative, but not as funny or as thrilling as it should be. Written by Gilliam and Palin, of Monty Python fame. British running time 116m. [PG]▼●◗

Time Bomb (1961-French) **92m.** ** D: Yves Ciampi. Curt Jurgens, Mylene Demongeot, Alain Saury, Robert Porte, Jean Durand. So-so story of captain plotting to collect insurance by planting bomb on ship.

Timebomb (1991) **C-96m.** **½ D: Avi Nesher. Michael Biehn, Patsy Kensit, Tracy Scoggins, Robert Culp, Raymond St. Jacques, Richard Jordan, Billy Blanks, Jim Maniaci, Steven J. Oliver, Ray Mancini. When mysterious people try to kill watchmaker Biehn, he finds to his surprise he has the skills to defeat them. He then kidnaps psychologist Kensit to try to find out who he really is. Intriguing premise effectively blends sci-fi and spy elements, with good performances a real plus, but soon the improbable overtakes the unlikely. [R] ▼●

Timecode (2000) **C-97m.** **½ D: Mike Figgis. Saffron Burrows, Stellan Skarsgård, Jeanne Tripplehorn, Salma Hayek, Julian Sands, Holly Hunter, Steven Weber, Danny Huston, Leslie Mann, Alessandro Nivola, Kyle MacLachlan, Glenne Headly. Unique film shot digitally in four concurrent 90-minute takes follows twenty-odd L.A. characters as their unhappy lives crisscross, both personally and professionally. Sound levels direct our attention to the most significant quadrant at any given time. As an experiment it's fresh and exciting; as entertainment it's wildly uneven, although the largely improvised dialogue is at least an improvement over THE BLAIR WITCH PROJECT. [R]▼

Timecop (1994) **C-99m.** **½ D: Peter Hyams. Jean-Claude Van Damme, Mia Sara, Ron Silver, Bruce McGill, Gloria Reuben, Scott Bellis, Jason Schombing. In the year 2004, a new law enforcement agency polices time-tripping criminals; top agent Van Damme is determined to nail the ringleader of these thugs, an evil and ambitious senator (Silver). Thoroughly watchable adaptation of the comic book series, but lacks the energy and imagination to be really satisfying. Panavision. [R]▼●◗

Time for Killing, A (1967) **C-88m.** ** D: Phil Karlson. Glenn Ford, Inger Stevens, George Hamilton, Paul Petersen, Max Baer, Timothy Carey, Kenneth Tobey, Dick Miller, (Harry) Dean Stanton. Civil War drama pits Union Captain Ford against Confederate Major Hamilton, when the latter kidnaps his bride-to-be. Director Karlson has done some good minor films in the past; this isn't one of them. Look for young Harrison Ford. Also known as THE LONG RIDE HOME. Panavision.

Time for Loving, A (1971-British) **C-104m.** **½ D: Christopher Miles. Mel Ferrer, Joanna Shimkus, Britt Ekland, Philippe Noiret, Susan Hampshire, Mark Burns, Lila Kedrova, Robert Dhery, Michel Legrand. Sophisticated Jean Anouilh liaison trilogy in the LA RONDE style. Sometimes called PARIS WAS MADE FOR LOVERS.

Time Guardian, The (1987-Australian) **C-105m.** ** D: Brian Hannant. Tom Burlinson, Nikki Coghill, Dean Stockwell, Carrie Fisher, Tim Robertson, Peter Merrill, Wan Thye Liew, Damon Sanders. Burlinson and Fisher are sent to the 1988 Australian desert, where he teams up with geologist Coghill to battle an army of killer cyborgs from the 41st century. Confusing sci-fi adventure. Panavision. [PG]▼●

Time Indefinite (1993) **C-117m.** ***½ D: Ross McElwee. Revealing, highly personal visual diary in which McElwee offers a glimpse into the dynamics of his family: the relationships between its members, the linking of the generations, and, most poignantly, the way it's affected by marriage and death. McElwee's unique cinematic sensibility adds immeasurably to this impressive follow-up to SHERMAN'S MARCH. ▼

Time Limit (1957) **96m.** *** D: Karl Malden. Richard Widmark, Richard Basehart, Dolores Michaels, June Lockhart, Rip Torn, Martin Balsam, Carl BentonReid, James Douglas. Imaginative direction and acting spark this courtroomer concerning the trial of American military officer suspected of collaborating with enemy while P.O.W. in North Korea. Malden's sole foray behind the camera; Widmark co-produced.

Time Lost and Time Remembered (1966-British) **91m.** *** D: Desmond Davis. Sarah Miles, Cyril Cusack, Julian Glover, Sean Caffrey. Thoughtful study of Miles' unhappy marriage to older man, emphasized by visit home where she discovers new set of values. Original British title: I WAS HAPPY HERE.

Time Machine, The (1960) **C-103m.** *** D: George Pal. Rod Taylor, Alan Young, Yvette Mimieux, Sebastian Cabot, Tom Helmore, Whit Bissell, Doris Lloyd. H. G. Wells' fantasy reduced to comic book level, but still entertaining, with Taylor as single-minded scientist who invents time-travel device and has vivid, frustrating experiences in the future. Oscar-winning special effects. Remade for TV in 1978.▼●

Time of Destiny, A (1988) **C-118m.** ** D: Gregory Nava. William Hurt, Timothy Hutton, Melissa Leo, Stockard Channing, Megan Follows, Francisco Rabal. Major disappointment from the makers of EL NORTE. Plodding soaper, set in the WW2 era, with tragedy and revenge coming between close friends and fellow GIs Hurt and Hutton (whose performances are far from their best). Written and produced by Anna Thomas. [PG-13]▼●

Time of Indifference (1964-Italian) **84m.** ** D: Francesco Maselli. Rod Steiger, Shelley Winters, Claudia Cardinale, Paulette Goddard, Tomas Milian. Turgid melodrama of moral and social decay in Italy during late 1920s, focusing on one nouveau-poor family; from novel by Alberto Moravia.▼

Time of the Gypsies (1989-Yugoslavian) **C-142m.** **½ D: Emir Kusturica. Davor Dujmovic, Bora Todorovic, Ljubica Adzovic, Sinolicka Trpkova, Husnija Hasimovic. Fair chronicle of the coming of age of a naive young gypsy (Dujmovic) and his initiation into the ways of petty crime. Sometimes effective, but way overlong and in no way as magical or memorable as Kusturica's WHEN FATHER WAS AWAY ON BUSINESS. However, he did earn the Best Director prize at the Cannes Film Festival. Shot in a Gypsy language called Romany, this may be the first film ever to require subtitles in every country in which it plays! [R]▼●

Time of Their Lives, The (1946) **82m.** *** D: Charles Barton. Bud Abbott, Lou Costello, Marjorie Reynolds, Binnie Barnes, John Shelton, Gale Sondergaard, Jess Barker. Most unusual film for A&C, and one of their best. Costello and Reynolds are killed during Revolutionary times, and their ghosts haunt a country estate where Abbott and friends come to live. Imaginative, funny, and well done.▼

Time of Your Life, The (1948) **99m.** ** D: H. C. Potter. James Cagney, William Bendix, Wayne Morris, Jeanne Cagney, Broderick Crawford, Ward Bond, James Barton, Paul Draper, James Lydon, Gale Page, Richard Erdman. Uninspired version of William Saroyan's prizewinning morality play about the various characters who populate Nick's Saloon, Restaurant and Entertainment Palace, which is actually a waterfront dive. Interesting cast, but it just doesn't come together.▼◗

Time Out for Love (1961-French-Italian) **91m.** **½ D: Jean Valère. Jean Seberg, Maurice Ronet, Micheline Presle, Françoise Prevost. Sometimes-effective drama chronicling the coming-of-age of young Seberg, an American living in Paris, who falls in love with capricious Ronet.▼

Time Out for Rhythm (1941) **75m.** ** D: Sidney Salkow. Rudy Vallee, Ann Miller, Rosemary Lane, Allen Jenkins, The Three Stooges. Mediocre show-biz musical turns out to be a wonderful showcase for the Stooges, who do some of their best material (including the "Maja? Aha!" routine). One good production number, "Boogie Woogie Man," features Glen Gray and His Casa Loma Orchestra.

Time Out of Mind (1947) **88m.** ** D: Robert Siodmak. Phyllis Calvert, Robert Hutton, Ella Raines, Eddie Albert, Leo G. Carroll. Plodding period-piece of girl in love above her station seeing her lover live unhappy life. From a Rachel Field novel.

Timerider (1983) **C-93m.** ** D: William Dear. Fred Ward, Belinda Bauer, Peter Coyote, Ed Lauter, Richard Masur, Tracey Walter, L. Q. Jones. Motocross bike racer is accidentally sent back in time to the Old West, circa 1875 . . . and that's where the writers fell asleep. Good premise and cast are left hanging as film crawls downhill. Produced and cowritten by Michael Nesmith. [PG]▼●

Time Runner (1993-Canadian-U.S.) **C-90m.** BOMB D: Michael Mazo. Mark Hamill, Rae Dawn Chong, Brion James, Marc Baur, Gordon Tipple, Allen Forget, Barry W. Levy. Fleeing an exploding space station in 2022 when Earth is under attack by aliens, Hamill ends up in 1992, trying to prevent the future war. Silly, poorly plotted, badly presented. [R]▼●

Times of Harvey Milk, The (1984) **C-87m.** ***½ D: Robert Epstein. Narrated by Harvey Fierstein. Extremely moving documentary about Harvey Milk, the first gay supervisor elected in San Francisco; mayor George Moscone; and clean-cut, respectable supervisor Dan White, who assassinated them both. Eerie, fascinating, sad, funny; as dramatic and involving as the most carefully plotted fiction. This deservedly earned a Best Documentary Academy Award.▼●

Times Square (1980) **C-111m.** BOMB D: Alan Moyle. Tim Curry, Trini Alvarado, Robin Johnson, Peter Coffield, Herbert Berghof, Miguel Pinero, Elizabeth Pena. A pair of teenage runaways, one (Alvarado) upper class, the other (Johnson) "of the streets," romp around a curiously unmenacing Times Square. Illogical, unrealistic scenario, frantic direction, music score for the hard of hearing. Script by film critic Jacob Brackman. [R]▼

Timestalkers (1987) **C-100m. TVM** D: Michael Schultz. William Devane, Lauren Hutton, Klaus Kinski, John Ratzenberger, Forrest Tucker, Gail Youngs. Imaginative time-travel adventure with a modern-day college professor falling under the spell of a determined woman from the 26th century, helping track down her scientist dad's villainous associate who has fled back to the 18th century. Adapted by Brian Clemens from Ray Brown's unpublished novel *The Tintype*, it offers the ubiquitous Klaus Kinski in his American TV movie debut and veteran actor Forrest Tucker in his acting swan song. Average.▼

Time Stands Still (1981-Hungarian) **C/B&W-99m.** **½ D: Peter Gothar. Istvan Znamenak, Henrik Pauer, Sandor Soth, Peter Galfy, Aniko Ivan, Agi Kakassy, Lojos Oze, Maria Ronyecz. Budapest's alienated adolescents of the early 1960s, in the aftershock of revolution, focusing on sullen Znamenak and comrades. Downbeat, enigmatic, but intriguing—with American "oldies" on the soundtrack.▼

Timetable (1956) **79m.** ** D: Mark Stevens. Mark Stevens, King Calder, Felicia Farr, Marianne Stewart, Jack Klugman, Wesley Addy. Small-scale account of insurance detective involved in investigation of robbery he engineered. Klugman's film debut.

Time, the Place and the Girl, The (1946) **C-105m.** **½ D: David Butler. Dennis Morgan, Martha Vickers, Jack Carson, Janis Paige, S. Z. Sakall, Alan Hale, Florence Bates, Carmen Cavallero. Best thing about this flimsily plotted put-on-a-show musical is the Arthur Schwartz–Leo Robin score, including "A Gal in Calico" and "Rainy Night in Rio." No relation to 1929 musical of same name.

Time to Die, A (1983) **C-91m.** *½ D: Matt Cimber. Rex Harrison, Rod Taylor, Edward Albert, Jr., Raf Vallone, Linn Stokke. Deadening time-waster with WW2 veteran Albert seeking out the six killers of his wife. Based on a story by Mario Puzo, and filmed in 1979. Originally titled SEVEN GRAVES FOR ROGAN. [R]▼

Time to Die, A (1991) **C-93m.** ** D: Charles Kanganis. Traci Lords, Richard Roundtree, Jeff Conaway, Robert Miano, Jesse Thomas, Nitchie Barrett. By-the-numbers programmer with ex-porn queen Lords cast as a freelance photographer attempting to make a home for her young son. Trouble comes her way when she finds herself and her camera in the right place at the wrong time. [R]▼●

Time to Kill (1942) **61m.** ** D: Herbert I. Leeds. Lloyd Nolan, Ralph Byrd, Heather Angel, Doris Merrick, Richard Lane. Michael Shayne (Nolan) versus counterfeiters of rare coins. Adequate entry in the series, sparked by Nolan's tough-guy performance. Though a Mike Shayne movie, it's based on a Raymond Chandler story; remade as THE BRASHER DOUBLOON.

Time to Kill, A (1996) **C-149m.** *** D: Joel Schumacher. Sandra Bullock, Samuel L. Jackson, Matthew McConaughey, Kevin Spacey, Brenda Fricker, Oliver Platt, Ashley Judd, Donald Sutherland, Kiefer Sutherland, Patrick McGoohan, Kurtwood Smith, Chris Cooper, Joe Seneca, Anthony Heald, Charles S. Dutton, Rae'ven Larrymore Kelly, John Diehl. First-rate adaptation of John Grisham's best-seller about a Mississippi town rocked by a black man's murder of two white-trashers who raped his 10-year-old daughter. Young attorney McConaughey (in a star-making performance) takes the man's case and finds himself in the midst of a firestorm that threatens his life and that of everyone around him. This TIME flies by, thanks to crackerjack storytelling and a well-chosen cast. M. Emmet Walsh appears unbilled. Panavision. [R] ▼●◗

Time to Live, A (1986) **C-100m. TVM** D: Rick Wallace. Liza Minnelli, Jeffrey DeMunn, Swoosie Kurtz, Scott Schwartz, Corey Haim. Liza made her TV-movie debut with a riveting performance as a mother who must cope with her young son's struggles with muscular dystrophy. John McGreevey's sensitive script was adapted from the touching book *Intensive Care* by Mary Lou Weisman (whom Minnelli plays). Above average.▼

Time to Love and a Time to Die, A (1958) **C-132m.** *** D: Douglas Sirk. John Gavin, Lilo Pulver, Jock Mahoney, Don DeFore, Keenan Wynn, Thayer David, Dana (Jim) Hutton, Klaus Kinski. Intensely dramatic love story set against background of WW2. German soldier on furlough from battle falls in love, inevitably must return to the trenches. Well-directed version of Erich Maria Remarque novel (with the author in a small role). Hutton's film debut. CinemaScope.▼

Time to Sing, A (1968) **C-92m.** *½ D: Arthur Dreifuss. Hank Williams, Jr., Ed Begley, Shelley Fabares, Charles Robinson, D'Urville Martin, Donald Woods, Clara Ward. Down-home tale of Williams suppressing love for singing to please uncle-guardian (Begley). Script aimed at 10-year-old mentality, matched by Williams' wooden performance. Panavision. [PG]

Time Trackers (1989) **C-87m.** *½ D: Howard R. Cohen. Ned Beatty, Wil Shriner, Kathleen Beller, Bridget Hoffman, Alex Hyde-White, Lee Bergere, Robert Cornthwaite. Tepid sci-fi tale about group from the future chasing down evil genius determined to use time travel to alter history in his favor. Beatty is a 20th-century cop accidentally picked up along the way. Some laughs at the beginning, but spends far too long (most of the film in fact) in medieval England. [PG]▼

Time Travelers, The (1964) **C-82m.** **½ D: Ib Melchior. Preston Foster, Philip Carey, Merry Anders, John Hoyt, Steve Franken. Spirited flashes of imagination heighten this sci-fi story about scientists who journey into the future and find their actions there will affect the past. Not bad, with downbeat ending; one of the first American films photographed by Vilmos Zsigmond.▼

Time Walker (1982) **C-83m.** BOMB D: Tom Kennedy. Ben Murphy, Nina Axelrod, Kevin Brophy, James Karen, Shari Belafonte-Harper, Antoinette Bower. Alien, buried in King Tut's tomb, is unwrapped and wreaks havoc. Low-budget junk. [PG]▼

Time Warp SEE: **Journey to the Center of Time**

Time Without Pity (1956-British) **88m.** *** D: Joseph Losey. Michael Redgrave, Alec McCowen, Ann Todd, Peter Cushing, Leo McKern, Renee Houston, Lois Maxwell, Joan Plowright. Tense thriller with an anti-capital punishment point of view, as alcoholic Redgrave has twenty-four hours to prove son McCowen's innocence on a murder rap. Scripted by Ben Barzman, from an Emlyn Williams play.▼

Tin Cup (1996) **C-133m.** ** D: Ron Shelton. Kevin Costner, Rene Russo, Don Johnson, Cheech Marin, Linda Hart, Dennis Burkley, Rex Linn. Portrait of a run-down golf pro, now operating a shabby Texas driving range, who's inspired to compete in the U.S. Open in order to impress a woman—the girlfriend of his longtime rival. Problem: he always wants to "go for it" instead of playing it safe. Costner and Russo are appealing, but this long, redundant comedy has alarmingly little to say, and takes its sweet time playing all 18 holes. Cowritten by director Shelton. Panavision. [R]▼●◗

Tin Drum, The (1979-German) **C-142m.** **** D: Volker Schlöndorff. David Bennent, Mario Adorf, Angela Winkler, Daniel Olbrychski, Katharina Thalbach, Heinz Bennent, Andrea Ferreol, Charles Aznavour. Mesmerizing adaptation of the Gunter Grass novel. Three-year-old Oskar (David Bennent) ceases to grow physically as the Nazis take power in Germany and beats out his anger on his drum. A "realistic fantasy" with superb acting, particularly by 12-year-old Bennent. Memorable sequence after memorable sequence; deservedly won a Best Foreign Film Academy Award. [R]▼●◗

Tingler, The (1959) **82m.** **½ D: William Castle. Vincent Price, Judith Evelyn, Darryl Hickman, Philip Coolidge, Patricia Cutts. Preposterous but original shocker: coroner Price discovers that fear causes a creepy-crawly creature to grow on people's spines; it can only be subdued by screaming. This is the infamous picture that got moviegoers into the spirit with electrical buzzers under selected theater seats!—a gimmick director/producer Castle billed as "Percepto." Also noteworthy as likely the earliest film depicting an LSD trip. One critical sequence is in color.▼●◗

Tin Men (1987) **C-112m.** **½ D: Barry Levinson. Richard Dreyfuss, Danny DeVito, Barbara Hershey, John Mahoney, Jackie Gayle, Stanley Brock, Seymour Cassel, Bruno Kirby, J. T. Walsh, Michael Tucker. Writer-director Levinson returns to DINER territory (literally—it's set in 1963 Baltimore) for a melancholy comedy-drama about a hustler (Dreyfuss) and a loser (DeVito), both in the aluminum-siding business, whose lives converge after their cars meet in an accident. Some fine comedy and pointed observations on human nature are undermined by unresolved ideas and inconsistencies in the way the characters behave. Stand-up comic Gayle is hilarious as DeVito's partner, who has *Bonanza* on the brain. [R]▼●

Tin Pan Alley (1940) **94m.** *** D: Walter Lang. Alice Faye, Betty Grable, Jack Oakie, John Payne, Esther Ralston, Allen Jenkins, Nicholas Brothers, John Loder, Elisha Cook, Jr. Predictable plot of struggling pre-WW1 songwriters enlivened by Alfred Newman's Oscar-winning score and colorful numbers including "Sheik of Araby" with Billy Gilbert as sultan. Oakie is in top form. Remade as I'LL GET BY.▼

Tin Star, The (1957) **93m.** *** D: Anthony Mann. Henry Fonda, Anthony Perkins, Betsy Palmer, Neville Brand, Lee Van Cleef, John McIntire, Michel Ray. Fledgling sheriff Perkins turns to bounty hunter Fonda to help combat outlaws preying on his town; solid, well-acted Western. Scripted by Dudley Nichols. VistaVision.▼

Tintorera (1977-British-Mexican) **C-91m.** BOMB D: Rene Cardona, Jr. Susan George, Hugo Stiglitz, Andres Garcia, Fiona Lewis, Jennifer Ashley, Priscilla Barnes, Laura Lyons. Can two Mexican shark hunters find satisfaction with an assortment of vacationing beauties from England and the U.S.? That's the main issue of this listless JAWS rip-off, loaded with gore and nude scenes. [R]▼

Tiny Toon Adventures: How I Spent My Vacation (1991) **C-80m.** **½ D: Rich Arons, Byron Vaughns, Alfred Gimeno, Barry Caldwell, Ken Boyer, Art Leonardi, Kent Butterworth. Voices of Charlie Adler, Tress MacNeille, Joe Alaskey, Don Messick, Jonathan Winters, Edie McClurg, Frank Welker. Direct-to-video feature film spinoff of Steven Spielberg's animated TV series follows the misadventures of Buster and Babs Bunny, Plucky Duck, Hamton Pig, Uncle Stinky, Dizzy Devil, and all the other regulars on their summer vacation. Episodic, to be sure, but with a lot of funny business along the way, a great voice cast, and some good songs, especially the opening number. And pay attention to those closing credits! [G]▼●

Tip Off, The (1931) **75m.** **½ D: Albert Rogell. Eddie Quillan, Robert Armstrong, Ginger Rogers, Joan Peers, Ralf Harolde, Charles Sellon, Mike Donlin. Naive Quillan, with the help of boxer Armstrong and spunky Rogers, manages to avoid trouble after he commences a romance with a gangster's girl. Zippy little programmer.▼

Tip on a Dead Jockey (1957) **99m.** *** D: Richard Thorpe. Dorothy Malone, Robert Taylor, Gia Scala, Martin Gabel, Jack Lord. Neat account of Taylor tied in with smuggling syndicate in Madrid, romancing Malone. Good Charles Lederer adaptation of Irwin Shaw story. CinemaScope.

Titan Find SEE: **Creature**

Titanic (1953) **98m.** *** D: Jean Negulesco. Clifton Webb, Barbara Stanwyck, Robert Wagner, Richard Basehart, Audrey Dalton, Thelma Ritter, Brian Aherne. Hollywoodized version of sea tragedy centers on shipboard story. Not bad, but events better told in A NIGHT TO REMEMBER . . . and more spectacularly in the 1997 film. Oscar-winning script by producer Charles Brackett, Walter Reisch, and Richard Breen.▼●

Titanic (1997) **C-194m.** ***½ D: James Cameron. Leonardo DiCaprio, Kate Winslet, Billy Zane, Frances Fisher, Kathy Bates, David Warner, Danny Nucci, Victor Garber, Gloria Stuart, Bernard Hill, Bernard Fox, Jonathan Hyde, Bill Paxton, Suzy Amis. Sweeping romance set against the backdrop of the R.M.S. *Titanic*'s maiden voyage in 1912—and framed by a modern-day story of a salvager who stumbles onto a heretofore unknown survivor of the sinking (beautifully played by 1930s leading lady Stuart). Spectacular in every way, an eye-filling recreation of the sights and sounds of the grandest ship of its time, but what keeps it afloat are the magnetic performances of the young leads. Storytelling savvy and momentum make up for some banal dialogue. Some footage of the actual *Titanic* wreckage is sprinkled into the opening sequence. Written by the director. Winner of 11 Oscars including Best Picture, Director, Visual Effects, Music (James Horner), Song ("My Heart Will Go On"), Cinematography (Russell Carpenter), Sound, and Costumes (Deborah L. Scott). Super 35. [PG-13]▼●◗

Titan—Story of Michelangelo, The (1950) **68m.** *** D: Richard Lyford. Narrated by Fredric March. Evocative documentary portrait of the great artist, capturing the man through his work. Originally a Swiss film made in 1940, it was reedited for U.S. release by Robert Snyder, and won an Oscar as Best Documentary. ▼

Titfield Thunderbolt, The (1953-British) **C-84m.** *** D: Charles Crichton. Stanley Holloway, George Relph, Naunton Wayne, John Gregson, Godfrey Tearle, Edie Martin, Hugh Griffith, Sid James, Jack MacGowran. Boisterous Ealing comedy about villagers who are attached to their antiquated railway line and run it themselves in competition with the local bus line. Lovely photography by Douglas Slocombe. Script by T.E.B. Clarke.

Tito and Me (1992-Yugoslavian-French) **C-104m.** *** D: Goran Markovic. Dimitrie Vojnov, Lazar Ristovski, Anica Dobra, Pedrag Manojlovic. Sweet, funny comedy-reminiscence about Zoran (Vojnov), a pudgy 10-year-old growing up in Belgrade in 1954. He is obsessed with "Comrade Tito," his nation's leader, just as a lovesick teen pines over a movie or rock star; the heart of the film focuses on how Zoran comes to realize the folly of worshipping false idols. This reportedly is the last film to come out of war-torn Yugoslavia. ▼

Titus (1999) **C-162m.** *** D: Julie Taymor. Anthony Hopkins, Jessica Lange, Alan Cumming, Jonathan Rhys Meyers, Angus Macfadyen, Matthew Rhys, Harry Lennix, James Frain, Colm Feore, Laura Fraser, Geraldine McEwan, Osheen Jones. Potent, time-bending adaptation of Shakespeare's *Titus Andronicus,* with Hopkins as a victorious Roman general whose rigid code of honor and duty proves to be his downfall. Lange is his prisoner, Tamora, queen of the Goths, who plots revenge. Impressive work by innovative theater director Taymor, who also wrote the screenplay as an examination of violence—its cause and effect—as it relates to modern society. Lennix is a standout as Aaron, the Moor. Super 35. [R]▼◗

T-Men (1947) **92m.** *** D: Anthony Mann. Dennis O'Keefe, June Lockhart, Alfred Ryder, Charles McGraw, Wallace Ford, Mary Meade. Semidocumentary-style story of undercover treasury agents trying to get to the bottom of counterfeit ring. Vividly exciting; director Mann and cameraman John Alton went out of their way to use unusual, effective lighting and compositions in this A-1 film. ▼●

T.N.T. Jackson (1974) **C-73m.** ** D: Cirio Santiago. Jeanne Bell, Stan Shaw, Pat Anderson, Ken Metcalf, OK Filipino-shot black actioner with statuesque former Playmate Bell as karate expert searching for her missing brother and kicking the hell out of anyone who gets in her way. A blaxploitation favorite, no doubt for the curious way Bell's shirts get torn off at the start of every fight scene. [R]▼

To All My Friends On Shore (1971) **C-74m. TVM** D: Gilbert Cates. Bill Cosby, Gloria Foster, Dennis Hines, Ray Mason, Dennis Pate. Problems confronted in father-son relationship when they get word that child has incurable disease. Uneven performances, but film's conception and point of view exceptionally strong, refreshing. Above average. ▼

Toast of New Orleans, The (1950) **C-97m.** **½ D: Norman Taurog. Kathryn Grayson, Mario Lanza, David Niven, Rita Moreno, J. Carrol Naish. Lanza plays fisherman transformed into operatic star. Rest of cast good, and Lanza sings "Be My Love." ▼●

Toast of New York, The (1937) **109m.** *** D: Rowland V. Lee. Edward Arnold, Cary Grant, Frances Farmer, Jack Oakie, Donald Meek, Clarence Kolb, Billy Gilbert, Stanley Fields. Arnold is in fine form as rags-to-riches businessman Jim Fisk in late 19th century. Grant is his partner in hokey but entertaining biographical fiction; good showcase for spirited Farmer. ▼●

Tobacco Road (1941) **84m.** **½ D: John Ford. Charley Grapewin, Marjorie Rambeau, Gene Tierney, William Tracy, Elizabeth Patterson, Dana Andrews, Slim Summerville, Ward Bond, Grant Mitchell. Lightly entertaining but genuinely odd seriocomedy about "quaint" Georgia backwoods community; worthwhile mainly to see Grapewin repeating his stage role as cheerful ne'er-do-well Jeeter Lester. Adapted (and sanitized) by Nunnally Johnson from the long-running Broadway play by Jack Kirkland, based on Erskine Caldwell's novel.

To Bed . . . or Not to Bed (1963-Italian) **103m.** **½ D: Gian Luigi Polidoro. Alberto Sordi, Bernhard Tarschys, Inger Sjostrand, Ulf Palme. Saucy sex romp. Sordi expects to find free love on business trip to Stockholm, discovers home sweet home is best. Retitled: THE DEVIL.

To Begin Again (1982-Spanish) **C-93m.** *** D: Jose Luis Garci. Antonio Ferrandis, Encarna Paso, Jose Bodalo, Agustin Gonzalez, Pablo Hoyo. Distinguished—and dying—professor Ferrandis revisits Spain, where he journeys through his past and romances old flame Paso. Sweetly sentimental; Oscar winner for Best Foreign Film. [PG]

To Be or Not to Be (1942) **99m.** ***½ D: Ernst Lubitsch. Jack Benny, Carole Lombard, Robert Stack, Lionel Atwill, Felix Bressart, Sig Ruman, Tom Dugan, Helmut Dantine, Stanley Ridges. Benny has the role of a lifetime as "that great, great actor" Joseph Tura, whose Polish theater troupe is put out of business by invading Nazis—until they become involved in espionage and find their thespian skills being put to the ultimate test. Superb black comedy scripted by Edwin Justus Mayer; the opening gag with Dugan is a gem.

Lombard's final film, released after her death. Remade in 1983.▼●
To Be or Not to Be (1983) **C-108m.** **½ D. Alan Johnson. Mel Brooks, Anne Bancroft, Charles Durning, Tim Matheson, Jose Ferrer, James Haake, Christopher Lloyd, George Gaynes, George Wyner, Jack Riley, Lewis J. Stadlen. Remake of 1942 classic follows the original almost scene for scene, with Brooks and Bancroft—in fine comic form—as stars of Polish theater who become involved with invading Nazis. Offers more laughs than the original film, but less substance; incessant schtick undermines occasional attempts at poignancy. [PG] ▼●
Tobor the Great (1954) **77m.** *½ D: Lee Sholem. Charles Drake, Karin Booth, Billy Chapin, Taylor Holmes, Steven Geray. Scientist allows his genius grandson to become pals with the robot of the title, leading to complications when spies try to glom onto the plans; terrible acting and dialogue. A botched attempt at a heartwarming sci-fi comedy-thriller.▼●
Tobruk (1967) **C-110m.** **½ D: Arthur Hiller. Rock Hudson, George Peppard, Nigel Green, Guy Stockwell, Jack Watson, Leo Gordon, Norman Rossington, Percy Herbert, Liam Redmond. WW2 actioner of Allies trying to destroy Rommel's fuel supply in the Sahara, bogs down in pretentiousness, much social comment, etc. Gordon also wrote the screenplay. Techniscope.▼
Toby Tyler, or Ten Weeks with a Circus (1960) **C-96m.** **½ D: Charles Barton. Kevin Corcoran, Henry Calvin, Gene Sheldon, Bob Sweeney, Richard Eastham, James Drury. Likable Disney fare about a young boy who runs away to join the circus at the turn of the century.▼●
To Catch a Spy (1971-British-French) **C-94m.** *½ D: Dick Clement. Kirk Douglas, Marlene Jobert, Trevor Howard, Tom Courtenay, Patrick Mower, Bernadette Lafont, Bernard Blier. Feeble comedy-mystery of events resulting when Jobert's new husband is arrested by the Russians as a spy; Douglas is a mystery man, Courtenay a bumbling British agent. Also known as CATCH ME A SPY.▼
To Catch a Thief (1955) **C-106m.** *** D: Alfred Hitchcock. Grace Kelly, Cary Grant, Jessie Royce Landis, John Williams, Charles Vanel, Brigitte Auber. The French Riviera serves as picturesque backdrop for this entertaining (if fluffy) Hitchcock caper with Grant as reformed cat burglar suspected in new wave of jewel robberies. Chic and elegant in every way—and Kelly never looked more ravishing. Script (including much-imitated fireworks scene) by John Michael Hayes; Oscar-winning photography by Robert Burks. VistaVision.▼●
To Commit a Murder (1967-French) **C-91m.** *½ D: Edouard Molinaro. Louis Jourdan, Senta Berger, Edmond O'Brien, Bernard Blier, Fabrizzio Capucci. Playboy/writer Jourdan gets involved with a plot to abduct French nuclear scientist; interesting idea poorly handled.▼
To Dance With the White Dog (1993) **C-100m. TVM** D: Glenn Jordan. Hume Cronyn, Jessica Tandy, Christine Baranski, Terry Beaver, Harley Cross, Esther Rolle, Frank Whaley, Amy Wright. Poetic tale of two oldsters. When he suddenly becomes a widower, her spirit inhabits a stray white dog who comes to look after him. Movingly adapted by Susan Cooper from Terry Kay's prize-winning novel. Above average. ▼●
Today We Live (1933) **113m.** ** D: Howard Hawks. Joan Crawford, Gary Cooper, Robert Young, Franchot Tone, Roscoe Karns. Stilted William Faulkner story of WW1 romance and heroism; despite star-studded cast, not much. Faulkner cowrote the screenplay. Torpedo attack scenes were directed by Richard Rosson. ▼
Todd Killings, The (1971) **C-93m.** ** D: Barry Shear. Robert F. Lyons, Richard Thomas, Barbara Bel Geddes, Sherry Miles, Gloria Grahame, Edward Asner, Belinda Montgomery, Meg Foster. Good cast in sleazy story of hip girl-getter Lyons actually involved in series of murders. Retitled A DANGEROUS FRIEND. Panavision. [R]▼
To Die For (1989) **C-90m.** *½ D: Deran Sarafian. Brendan Hughes, Sydney Walsh, Amanda Wyss, Scott Jacoby, Micah Grant, Steve Bond. Dracula legend is updated to modern-day, morally decadent L.A., but the results are strictly second-rate. Vampire ''Vlad Tepish'' sets his sights on sexy real-estate agent Walsh—apparently unaware that realtors in L.A. are a bloodless lot. Followed by SON OF DARKNESS: TO DIE FOR II. [R]▼●
To Die For (1995) **C-103m.** **½ D: Gus Van Sant. Nicole Kidman, Matt Dillon, Joaquin Phoenix, Illeana Douglas, Casey Affleck, Alison Folland, Dan Hedaya, Wayne Knight, Kurtwood Smith, Holland Taylor, Susan Traylor, Maria Tucci, David Cronenberg. Kidman is perfect as a tightly focused sicko who'll stop at nothing, including murder, to reach her goal: a TV career. Based on the real-life case that inspired Joyce Maynard's book, this black comedy seems to make all the right moves, but plays out its story with a surprising lack of irony; by the climax it has nothing more to offer. Douglas is a particular standout as Kidman's sister-in-law, who sees through her artifice from the git-go. George Segal appears unbilled, and the film's screenwriter, Buck Henry, plays a humorless schoolteacher. [R]▼●◗
To Die in Madrid (1963-French) **87m.** **** D: Frederic Rossif. Narrated by John Gielgud and Irene Worth. Masterpiece in documentary filmmaking dealing with

bloody civil war in Spain in which more than a million people died.

To Die of Love (1972-French) **C-110m.** **½ D: André Cayatte. Annie Girardot, Bruno Pradal, François Simon, Monique Melinand, Nathalie Nell, Nicolas Dumayet. Girardot's superb performance carries true story about French schoolteacher who was driven to suicide after she was forced to abandon 16-year-old student she loved. More interesting for subject matter than for actual execution. [PG]

To Each His Own (1946) **122m.** *** D: Mitchell Leisen. Olivia de Havilland, John Lund, Mary Anderson, Roland Culver, Philip Terry, Griff Barnett. Well-turned soaper of unwed mother giving up baby, lavishing love on him as his "aunt" without revealing truth. Fine support by Culver as aging Olivia's beau. De Havilland won Best Actress Oscar. Lund's film debut.▼

To Elvis, With Love SEE: **Touched by Love**

To Find a Man (1972) **C-90m.** *** D: Buzz Kulik. Pamela (Sue) Martin, Darren O'Connor, Lloyd Bridges, Phyllis Newman, Tom Ewell, Tom Bosley. Solid comedy-drama about two high-schoolers' attempts to find an abortionist. Study of friendships is good, and exceedingly fine acting of youthful leads is a definite plus. [PG]

To Forget Venice (1979-Italian) **C-110m.** ** D: Franco Brusati. Erland Josephson, Mariangela Melato, Elenora Giorgi, David Pontremoli. Two pairs of homosexuals (male and female) come to grips with each other at the country estate of a dying opera star. So-so drama managed an Oscar nomination for Best Foreign Film.▼

Together? (1979-Italian) **C-100m.** *½ D: Armenia Balducci. Jacqueline Bisset, Maximilian Schell, Terence Stamp, Monica Guerritore. Bisset and neurotic lover Schell argue, eat, argue, talk about sex, argue, have sex, argue some more. And the viewer gets a migraine. Originally titled I LOVE YOU, I LOVE YOU NOT. [R]▼

Together Again (1944) **100m.** *** D: Charles Vidor. Irene Dunne, Charles Boyer, Charles Coburn, Mona Freeman, Elizabeth Patterson. Little bit of nothing carried off beautifully by Dunne, widow mayor of small town, and Boyer, suave New Yorker whom she hires to sculpt a statue of her late husband; charming comedy.

Together Brothers (1974) **C-94m.** **½ D: William A. Graham. Anthony Wilson, Ahmad Nurradin, Glynn Turman, Richard Yniguez, Lincoln Kilpatrick, Owen Pace. Suspense thriller with five young blacks scouring ghetto for the killer of their policeman friend. Violent treatment balanced by sensitive character studies. [PG]

Togetherness (1970) **C-103m.** ** D: Arthur Marks. George Hamilton, Peter Lawford, John Banner, Olinka Berova, Jesse White. American playboy Hamilton woos Communist athlete Berova in this dated comedy filmed in Greece. [PG]

To Gillian on Her 37th Birthday (1996) **C-92m.** *** D: Michael Pressman. Peter Gallagher, Michelle Pfeiffer, Claire Danes, Bruce Altman, Kathy Baker, Wendy Crewson, Freddie Prinze, Jr., Laurie Fortier. Straightforward tearjerker—with ample comedy leavening—about a man unable and unwilling to let go of his wife's memory two years after her sudden death; his sister-in-law fears that his inertia and melancholy threaten his teenage daughter at a crucial time in her life. Well acted all around. Based on a play by Michael Brady, adapted and coproduced by David E. Kelley (Pfeiffer's husband). [PG-13]▼●

To Have and Have Not (1944) **100m.** ***½ D: Howard Hawks. Humphrey Bogart, Walter Brennan, Lauren Bacall, Hoagy Carmichael, Dan Seymour, Marcel Dalio, Dolores Moran, Sheldon Leonard. Hemingway's "worst novel" forms the basis for Hawks' version of CASABLANCA: tough skipper-for-hire Bogart reluctantly becomes involved with French Resistance, less reluctantly woos even tougher Bacall (in her film debut). Their legendary love scenes make the movie, but there are also solid performances, taut action, and a couple of songs. (Andy Williams was hired to dub Bacall's singing, but that's her voice, after all.) Super dialogue by William Faulkner and Jules Furthman; remade as THE BREAKING POINT and THE GUN RUNNERS. Also shown in computer-colored version. ▼●

To Heal a Nation (1988) **C-100m. TVM** D: Michael Pressman. Eric Roberts, Glynnis O'Connor, Marshall Colt, Scott Paulin, Lee Purcell, Laurence Luckinbill, Linden Chiles, Brock Peters. Earnest drama about Vietnam vet Jan Scruggs, who spearheaded the campaign to build the Vietnam Veterans Memorial in Washington. Talky but powerful script by Lionel Chetwynd (based on the book by Scruggs and Joel L. Swerdlow), with closing scenes that pack a wallop. Above average.▼

To Hell and Back (1955) **C-106m.** *** D: Jesse Hibbs. Audie Murphy, Marshall Thompson, Charles Drake, Jack Kelly, Paul Picerni, Gregg Palmer, Brett Halsey, David Janssen, Art Aragon, Rand Brooks, Denver Pyle, Susan Kohner. Murphy (the most decorated soldier of WW2) stars in very good war film based on his autobiography, with excellent battle sequences depicting Murphy's often breathtaking heroic exploits. Clichés in script are overcome by Murphy and cast's easy-going delivery. CinemaScope.▼

To Joy (1950-Swedish) **95m.** **½ D: Ingmar Bergman. Stig Olin, Maj-Britt Nilsson, John Ekman, Margit Carlquist, Victor Seastrom (Sjöström), Birger Malmsten. Early Bergman drama offers a thematic prelude of what was to come from the filmmaker. Otherwise, it's a modest, occasionally insightful chronicle of Olin and Nilsson's failing marriage.▼

To Kill a Clown (1972) **C-104m.** ★★ D: George Bloomfield. Alan Alda, Blythe Danner, Heath Lamberts, Eric Clavering. Couple whose marriage is on the rocks get trapped on island off New England coast by crippled, deranged Vietnam veteran. Weird mixture of traditional chiller film elements and topical considerations. [R]▼

To Kill a Mockingbird (1962) **129m.** ★★★½ D: Robert Mulligan. Gregory Peck, Mary Badham, Philip Alford, John Megna, Brock Peters, Robert Duvall, Frank Overton, Rosemary Murphy, Paul Fix, Collin Wilcox, Alice Ghostley, William Windom; narrated by Kim Stanley. Peck won Oscar as Southern lawyer who defends a black man (Peters) accused of rape, and tries to explain proceedings to his children and their friend. Leisurely paced, flavorful adaptation of Harper Lee novel; Horton Foote's screenplay also earned an Oscar. Duvall's film debut.▼●◗

To Kill a Priest (1988-U.S.-French) **C-117m.** ★★ D: Agnieszka Holland. Ed Harris, Christopher Lambert, David Suchet, Joss Ackland, Tim Roth, Joanne Whalley, Peter Postlethwaite, Timothy Spall, Cherie Lunghi. Well-intentioned but inept drama about ill-fated Polish priest Lambert (a character based on Father Jerzy Popieluszko, who supported the country's trade unionists and paid for his activism with his life); here he tangles with bullying secret policeman Harris. Director Holland may be a Polish exile, but the film only superficially explores the plight of her country. Panavision. [R]▼●

Tokyo After Dark (1959) **80m.** ★★ D: Norman Herman. Michi Kobi, Richard Long, Lawrence Dobkin, Paul Dubov, Butch Yamaoto. Uninspired account of military cop Long on the lam in Tokyo from unintentional homicide.

Tokyo Decadence (1992-Japanese) **C-112m.** ★★½ D: Ryu Murakami. Miho Nikaido, Tenmei Kano, Yayoi Kusama, Sayoko Amano. So-so account of the various experiences of a young, wide-eyed Tokyo hooker (Nikaido), whose specialty is sadomasochism and whose clients are upperclass businessmen. Initially works as a look at how kinky sexual desires result from take-no-prisoners attitudes in the workplace; it eventually becomes repetitive and muddled. Scripted by Murakami, based on his novel.▼◗

Tokyo Joe (1949) **88m.** ★★½ D: Stuart Heisler. Humphrey Bogart, Florence Marly, Sessue Hayakawa, Alexander Knox, Jerome Courtland. Lesser Bogart film about American in post-war Tokyo pulled into smuggling and blackmail for the sake of his ex-wife and child.▼●

Tokyo Olympiad (1966-Japanese) **C-93m.** ★★½ D: Kon Ichikawa. If you're lucky enough to see the superb original version of this documentary about the 1964 Olympics, shoot this rating to ★★★½. This one was cut down for U.S. release and virtually destroyed by insipid narration; however, the original 170m. print did play the 1984 New York Film Festival and is now available on video. CinemaScope.▼●

Tokyo Pop (1988) **C-99m.** ★★½ D: Fran Rubel Kazui. Carrie Hamilton, Yutaka Tadokoro, Taiji Tonoyama, Tetsuro Tamba, Masumi Harukawa. Trifling if occasionally amusing tale of what happens when punk rocker Hamilton treks off to Japan in search of celebrity. The West-meets-East theme has possibilities, but the result is curiously slight (despite Hamilton's winning performance). By the way, she's the daughter of Carol Burnett. [R]▼●

Tokyo Rose (1945) **69m.** ★★ D: Lew Landers. Byron Barr, Osa Massen, Don Douglas, Richard Loo, Keye Luke, Grace Lem, Leslie Fong, Blake Edwards, Lotus Long. Timid drama of slinky female propagandist for Axis during WW2.

Tokyo Story (1953-Japanese) **134m.** ★★★★ D: Yasujiro Ozu. Chishu Ryu, Chieko Higashiyama, So Yamamura, Haruko Sugimura, Setsuko Hara. An elderly couple (Ryu, Higashiyama) visit their children in Tokyo, who are too busy living their lives and treat them tactlessly. Quietly powerful story of old age, the disappointments parents experience with their children, and the fears the young have of time passing. A masterpiece.▼

Tol'able David (1921) **80m.** ★★★½ D: Henry King. Richard Barthelmess, Gladys Hulette, Ernest Torrence, Warner Richmond, Walter P. Lewis. A mild-mannered boy is forced to take his brother's place delivering the mail—and dealing with a trio of heinous criminals who've moved into their rural community. Beautifully crafted Americana, shot on location in Virginia. The finale is a rip-roaring piece of movie storytelling. Remade in 1930.▼●◗

To Live (1994-Chinese) **C-132m.** ★★★½ D: Zhang Yimou. Ge You, Gong Li, Niu Ben, Guo Tao, Jiang Wu, Ni Dahong, Liu Tianchi, Zhang Lu, Xiao Cong, Dong Fei. Another stirring production from director/actress team of Zhang Yimou and Gong Li, although this time the female role is less powerful, and less pivotal, than the male lead. Film follows married couple as their fortunes rise and fall, through several decades of Chinese life, from 1940's onward. Viewer gets history lesson as time passes, children grow, and freedoms are suppressed. Ge You is outstanding as simple yet unstereotypical patriarch; only flaw is that episodic story eventually develops Edna Ferber–ish soap opera quality. Based on the novel *Lifetimes* by Yu Hua. ▼●

To Live and Die in L.A. (1985) **C-116m.** ★½ D: William Friedkin. William L. Petersen, Willem Dafoe, John Pankow, Debra Feuer, John Turturro, Darlanne Fluegel, Dean

Stockwell, Robert Downey, Dwier Brown. Gritty movie equivalent of TV's *Miami Vice* makes it hard to root for anyone, since the good guys are as sleazy as the bad guys! Petersen plays hotshot Secret Service agent going after slimy counterfeiter—but for a crack federal agent he acts pretty dumb! One spectacular car chase is not enough to counteract bad taste the film leaves behind. [R]▼●

To Love a Vampire SEE: **Lust for a Vampire**

Tollbooth (1994) **C-108m.** *** D: Salome Breziner. Fairuza Balk, Lenny Von Dohlen, Will Patton, Seymour Cassel, James Wilder, William Katt, Louise Fletcher. Clever, humorously macabre sleeper about a young woman (Balk) who for years has been awaiting the return of her missing father. She refuses to sleep with the man she loves (Von Dohlen) until her father shows up; the plot is set into motion when Boyfriend sets out to track down Dad. Cassel appears in two roles and offers a riveting performance as the father.▼●

Toll Gate, The (1920) **59m.** *** D: Lambert Hillyer. William S. Hart, Anna Q. Nilsson, Jack Richardson, Joseph Singleton, Richard Headrick. One of Hart's best films, casting him as fleeing outlaw who stops to save young boy's life, becomes involved with the child's widowed mother. ▼●◗

Toma (1973) **C-74m. TVM** D: Richard Heffron. Tony Musante, Simon Oakland, Susan Strasberg, Nicholas Colasanto, Robert Yuro, Abe Vigoda, Dave Toma, Philip Michael Thomas. Leader of syndicate numbers racket stalked by disguise-master undercover policeman. Excellent lead performance by Musante in challenging role, as he pleads with superiors for less interference and sweats it out when his family becomes syndicate hostages. Written by Edward Hume, Gerald DiPago, based on a true story. Pilot for brief series which later transmogrified into *Baretta.* Above average.

Tomahawk (1951) **C-82m.** **½ D: George Sherman. Yvonne De Carlo, Van Heflin, Preston Foster, Jack Oakie, Alex Nicol, Tom Tully, Rock Hudson. Colorful Western spiked with sufficient action to overcome bland account of friction between Indians and the army.▼

Tom and Huck (1995) **C-92m.** **½ D: Peter Hewitt. Jonathan Taylor Thomas, Brad Renfro, Eric Schweig, Charles Rocket, Amy Wright, Micheal McShane, Marian Seldes, Rachael Leigh Cook, Lanny Flaherty. Umpteenth, by-the-numbers retelling of the Mark Twain classic *The Adventures of Tom Sawyer,* with Taylor Thomas and Renfro both doing well as the title duo. Might amuse kids who are completely unfamiliar with the story. Panavision. [PG]▼●

Tom and Jerry: The Movie (1992) **C-84m.** ** D: Phil Roman. Voices of Richard Kind, Dana Hill, Anndi McAfee, Charlotte Rae, Tony Jay, Henry Gibson, Rip Taylor, Michael Bell, Sydney Lassick, David L. Lander. Tom and Jerry, suddenly homeless, hook up with a little girl who's trying to escape from the clutches of a cruel guardian. Flat attempt to put the lively cat & mouse duo into a feature-length story, with more lulls than highlights, and a score that's not only unmemorable but irrelevant. Released in the U.S. in 1993. [G]▼●

Tom & Viv (1994-British-U.S.) **C-125m.** **½ D: Brian Gilbert. Willem Dafoe, Miranda Richardson, Rosemary Harris, Tim Dutton, Nickolas Grace, Philip Locke. Intriguing (but only partially successful) chronicle of the relationship between poet T. S. Eliot (Dafoe) and his wife, loony socialite Vivienne Haigh-Wood (Richardson), whose psychological affliction was improperly diagnosed. Well acted by the two leads, but the drama comes in fits and starts. Lacks the necessary passion to make you care about the characters and their union. Based on a play by Michael Hastings, who coscripted. Super 35. [R] ▼●

To Mary—With Love (1936) **86m.** **½ D: John Cromwell. Warner Baxter, Myrna Loy, Ian Hunter, Claire Trevor, Jean Dixon, Pat Somerset. Dated drama of Baxter and Loy having stormy period of marriage but ending up loving each other more than ever.

Tomb of Ligeia, The (1964-British) **C-81m.** *** D: Roger Corman. Vincent Price, Elizabeth Shepherd, John Westbrook, Richard Johnson, Derek Francis. Price's late wife seems to be manifesting herself all over the place, both as a cat and in new bride Shepherd. Super-stylish chiller with superb location work. The last of Corman's eight Poe adaptations; screenplay by Robert Towne. Filmed in Widescreen Colorscope.▼●

Tomb of the Living Dead SEE: **Mad Doctor of Blood Island**

Tomboy (1985) **C-92m.** BOMB D: Herb Freed. Betsy Russell, Jerry Dinome (Gerard Christopher), Kristi Somers, Richard Erdman, Cynthia Ann Thompson. Bottom-of-the-barrel formula teenage sex tease film. Role reversal is stressed as Russell is an automotive wiz determined to outrace and win the romantic favor of handsome Dinome. [R]▼

Tomboy and the Champ (1961) **C-92m.** ** D: Francis D. Lyon. Candy Moore, Ben Johnson, Jesse White, Jess Kirkpatrick, Rex Allen. Mild B film about a young girl and her prize cow; strictly for children, who will probably enjoy it, despite standard plot devices.▼

Tom Brown of Culver (1932) **82m.** **½ D: William Wyler. Tom Brown, H. B. Warner, Richard Cromwell, Slim Summerville, Ben Alexander, Sidney Toler, Russell Hopton, Andy Devine. Well-made but corny military-school picture has Tom Brown in namesake role of wayward boy who gets a scholarship to famed Indiana military academy during the Depression. Much of the film was shot on location. Tyrone Power (billed as Jr.) makes his screen debut here, and reportedly, Alan Ladd can be spotted in a bit. Remade as SPIRIT OF CULVER.

Tom Brown's School Days (1940) **86m.** **½ D: Robert Stevenson. Cedric Hardwicke, Freddie Bartholomew, Gale Storm, Jimmy Lydon, Josephine Hutchinson, Billy Halop, Polly Moran. Occasionally overbaked but still entertaining, fast-paced account of life at a Victorian boys' school. Although most of cast is American, British flavor seeps through. Retitled: ADVENTURES AT RUGBY.▼

Tom Brown's Schooldays (1951-British) **93m.** ***½ D: Gordon Parry. John Howard Davies, Robert Newton, Diana Wynyard, Hermione Baddeley, Kathleen Byron, James Hayter, John Charlesworth, John Forrest, Michael Hordern, Max Bygraves. Well-acted film of Victorian England school life with exceptional British cast and good direction. Noel Langley scripted, from Thomas Hughes' novel.▼

Tombstone (1993) **C-128m.** **½ D: George P. Cosmatos. Kurt Russell, Val Kilmer, Michael Biehn, Powers Boothe, Robert Burke, Dana Delany, Sam Elliott, Stephen Lang, Terry O'Quinn, Joanna Pacula, Bill Paxton, Jason Priestley, Michael Rooker, Jon Tenney, Dana Wheeler Nicholson, Billy Zane, Buck Taylor, Harry Carey, Jr., Tomas Arana, Thomas Haden Church, John Corbett, Pedro Armendariz, Jr., Frank Stallone, Billy Bob Thornton, Cecil Hoffmann, Charlton Heston, narrated by Robert Mitchum. Wyatt Earp (Russell) attempts to leave his violent days behind him, moving to Tombstone with his two brothers . . . but the murderous gang called The Cowboys (whose members include the Clantons) dictates otherwise. Not-bad Western saga, with a forceful performance by Russell, and a likably eccentric one by Kilmer as the tubercular Doc Holliday. Delany, however, is positively goofy as Wyatt's love interest, and the story goes on way past the O.K. Corral shootout, with a series of redundant gun battles and showdowns. The real Earp's fifth cousin, Wyatt Earp, plays Billy Claiborne. Panavision. [R]▼●◗

Tom, Dick and Harry (1941) **86m.** ***½ D: Garson Kanin. Ginger Rogers, George Murphy, Alan Marshal, Burgess Meredith, Joe Cunningham, Jane Seymour, Phil Silvers. Spirited comic dilemma as wide-eyed Ginger chooses among three anxious suitors: sincere Murphy, wealthy Marshal, nonconformist Meredith. Silvers has hilarious role as obnoxious ice-cream man. Written by Paul Jarrico. Remade as THE GIRL MOST LIKELY.▼●

Tom Horn (1980) **C-98m.** *½ D: William Wiard. Steve McQueen, Linda Evans, Richard Farnsworth, Billy Green Bush, Slim Pickens, Elisha Cook. McQueen's next-to-last film is beautifully shot, otherwise deadly Western about the final days of real-life Wyoming bounty hunter. See also MR. HORN, a TVM with David Carradine in the title role. Panavision. [R]▼●

Tom Jones (1963-British) **C-129m.** **** D: Tony Richardson. Albert Finney, Susannah York, Hugh Griffith, Edith Evans, Joyce Redman, Diane Cilento, Joan Greenwood, David Tomlinson, Peter Bull, David Warner. Narrated by Michael MacLiammoir. High-spirited adaptation of the Henry Fielding novel about a young man's misadventures and bawdy experiences in 18th-century England; rowdy, randy, and completely disarming. Academy Award winner as Best Picture, it also won Oscars for Richardson, who directed with great flair and imagination, screenwriter John Osborne, who caught the gritty flavor of the period to perfection, and composer John Addison, whose infectious score suits the picture to a tee. Film debuts of Lynn Redgrave and David Warner. Richardson cut the film by seven minutes for its 1989 reissue.▼●◗

Tommy (1975-British) **C-111m.** *** D: Ken Russell. Roger Daltrey, Ann-Margret, Oliver Reed, Elton John, Eric Clapton, Keith Moon, Robert Powell, Tina Turner, Jack Nicholson. Energetic rendering of The Who's best-selling rock opera, with standout musical performances by Clapton, John (who sings "Pinball Wizard") and Turner. Later staged on Broadway. [PG] ▼●

Tommy Boy (1995) **C-96m.** *½ D: Peter Segal. Chris Farley, David Spade, Brian Dennehy, Bo Derek, Dan Aykroyd, Julie Warner, Sean McCann, Zack Grenier. Just out of college, perpetual foul-up Farley returns home to work in his father's factory and witness his dad's marriage to Derek. Dad's sudden death forces Farley to try and save the business—with the help of coworker Spade. Utterly predictable comedy with scattershot laughs; Farley and Spade don't quite have the finesse of Wheeler and Woolsey. Rob Lowe appears unbilled as Derek's "son." [PG-13]▼●◗

Tommyknockers, The (1993) **C-200m. TVM** D: John Power. Jimmy Smits, Marg Helgenberger, John Ashton, Allyce Beasley, Robert Carradine, Joanna Cassidy, Traci Lords, Cliff DeYoung, E. G. Marshall. Stephen King thriller about a mysterious force scaring the bejeebers out of a small Maine town works well in this lengthy, small-screen adaptation by Lawrence D. Cohen. Originally shown in two parts. Above average.▼◗

Tommy Steele Story, The SEE: **Rock Around the World**

Tomorrow (1972) **103m.** ***½ D: Joseph Anthony. Robert Duvall, Olga Bellin, Sudie

Bond, Richard McConnell, Peter Masterson, William Hawley. Overlooked Faulkner story about a handyman who cares for and eventually falls in love with an abandoned pregnant woman. Bellin is excellent, Duvall astonishingly good in best-ever screen presentation of the author's work. Screenplay by Horton Foote. [PG]▼

Tomorrow at Ten (1963-British) **80m.** **½ D: Lance Comfort. John Gregson, Robert Shaw, Alec Clunes, Alan Wheatley. Taut drama involving kidnapper who dies, leaving boy in house (whereabouts unknown) with time bomb set to explode.

Tomorrow Is Another Day (1951) **90m.** **½ D: Felix E. Feist. Ruth Roman, Steve Cochran, Lurene Tuttle, Ray Teal, Morris Ankrum. Frank little film of ex-con Cochran marrying dime-a-dance girl Roman, heading for California, thinking he's killed her old boyfriend.

Tomorrow Is Forever (1946) **105m.** *** D: Irving Pichel. Claudette Colbert, Orson Welles, George Brent, Lucile Watson, Richard Long, Natalie Wood. Weepy rehash of *Enoch Arden*, with Welles as man listed dead in war, returning with new face to find wife Colbert remarried to Brent. Bravura work by Welles with good support by Wood as his adopted daughter.▼

Tomorrow Never Comes (1977-Canadian-British) **C-109m.** ** D: Peter Collinson. Oliver Reed, Susan George, Raymond Burr, John Ireland, Stephen McHattie, Donald Pleasence. Young man goes bananas when he learns his girlfriend has been unfaithful, leading to violent standoff with police in busy resort town. Uninvolving melodrama. [PG]▼

Tomorrow Never Dies (1997) **C-119m.** **½ D: Roger Spottiswoode. Pierce Brosnan, Jonathan Pryce, Michelle Yeoh, Teri Hatcher, Joe Don Baker, Ricky Jay, Götz Otto, Judi Dench, Desmond Llewelyn, Vincent Schiavelli, Geoffrey Palmer, Samantha Bond. James Bond goes after a megalomaniacal media magnate (Pryce) whose tentacles reach around the globe, and whose wife was a former flame of 007. Along the way, he teams up with Asian action-film star Yeoh, who proves a compatible screen companion. The action never flags, though it becomes somewhat mechanical after a while. Panavision. [PG-13]▼●◗

Tomorrow the World (1944) **86m.** ***½ D: Leslie Fenton. Fredric March, Betty Field, Agnes Moorehead, Skippy Homeier, Joan Carroll, Boots Brown. Thoughtful drama based on Broadway play of American couple adopting German boy, trying to undo rigid Nazi influence in him.

Tom Sawyer (1930) **86m.** **½ D: John Cromwell. Jackie Coogan, Mitzi Green, Junior Durkin, Jackie Searle, Clara Blandick, Lucien Littlefield. Enjoyable but slow-moving adaptation of the Mark Twain classic. Coogan, Green, Durkin, and Searle are, respectively, Tom, Becky Thatcher, Huck Finn, and Sid Sawyer; they all repeated their roles the following year in HUCKLEBERRY FINN. Remade in 1938 (as THE ADVENTURES OF TOM SAWYER) and twice in 1973.▼

Tom Sawyer (1973) **C-104m.** *** D: Don Taylor. Johnnie Whitaker, Celeste Holm, Warren Oates, Jeff East, Jodie Foster. Well-crafted musical remake of Tom Sawyer, the boy wonder of Hannibal, Mo., and his friends Huckleberry Finn and Becky Thatcher. Songs by Richard M. and Robert B. Sherman. Panavision. [PG]▼●

Tom Sawyer, Detective (1938) **68m.** **½ D: Louis King. Billy Cook, Donald O'Connor, Porter Hall, Phillip Warren, Janet Waldo, Elizabeth Risdon, William Haade. Pleasant little family film based on Mark Twain's novella that turns Tom (Cook) and Huck (O'Connor) into backwoods detectives investigating a mysterious murder involving a long-lost twin, and attempting to clear the name of local preacher Hall.

tom thumb (1958) **C-98m.** ***½ D: George Pal. Russ Tamblyn, June Thorburn, Peter Sellers, Terry-Thomas, Alan Young, Jessie Matthews, Bernard Miles. Excellent children's picture with Tamblyn as tiny tom thumb, taken in by kindly couple but exploited by villainous Terry-Thomas and henchman Sellers. Charming Puppetoons sequences, Oscar winning special effects, perfect Peggy Lee–Sonny Burke score. Filmed in England.▼●

Toni (1935-French) **90m.** ***½ D: Jean Renoir. Charles Blavette, Celia Montalvan, Jenny Helia, Max Dalban. Italian quarry worker Blavette lives with Montalvan, but falls in love with farm girl Helia—who in turn is wooed away by swaggering foreman Dalban. Renoir coscripted this simple, touching drama, which he filmed in a style that influenced the Italian Neorealist movement of the 1940s.▼

Tonight and Every Night (1945) **C-92m.** *** D: Victor Saville. Rita Hayworth, Janet Blair, Lee Bowman, Marc Platt, Leslie Brooks, Professor Lamberti, Florence Bates. Entertaining wartime musical of British theater that never misses a performance, despite bombings and personal hardships. Try spotting Shelley Winters as one of the chorines.▼

Tonight at 8:30 (1952-British) **C-81m.** *** D: Anthony Pelissier. Valerie Hobson, Nigel Patrick, Jack Warner, Kay Walsh, Ted Ray, Martita Hunt, Stanley Holloway, Betty Ann Davies. Three Noel Coward one-act plays ideally transferred to film. Original British title: MEET ME TONIGHT.

Tonight's the Night (1954) **C-88m.** *** D: Mario Zampi. David Niven, Yvonne De Carlo, Barry Fitzgerald, George Cole,

Robert Urquhart. Good British cast bolsters appealing comedy about house in Ireland which natives claim is haunted.

Tonight We Raid Calais (1943) **70m.** **½ D: John Brahm. Annabella, John Sutton, Lee J. Cobb, Beulah Bondi, Blanche Yurka, Howard da Silva, Marcel Dalio. Fast-paced if undistinguished WW2 tale of sabotage mission in France with good performances; written by Waldo Salt.

Tonight We Sing (1953) **C-109m.** **½ D: Mitchell Leisen. David Wayne, Ezio Pinza, Roberta Peters, Anne Bancroft, Tamara Toumanova, Isaac Stern, Jan Peerce. Hodgepodge supposedly based on impresario Sol Hurok's life, allowing for disjointed string of operatic/musical interludes. Produced by George Jessel.

Tonka (1958) **C-97m.** **½ D: Lewis R. Foster. Sal Mineo, Philip Carey, Jerome Courtland, Rafael Campos, H. M. Wynant, Joy Page. Mineo stands out in this modest Disney film about an Indian brave's attachment to a wild horse, lone "survivor" of Little Bighorn battle, which he captures and tames. Weak resolution and cut-rate version of Custer's Last Stand detract from promising story. Retitled A HORSE NAMED COMANCHE.▼

Tony Draws a Horse (1950-British) **91m.** **½ D: John Paddy Carstairs. Cecil Parker, Anne Crawford, Derek Bond, Mervyn Johns, Barbara Murray, Edward Rigby, Anthony Lang, Sebastian Cabot. Dr. Parker and psychologist Crawford cannot agree on the proper method of rearing their 8-year-old son; his mischief ends up affecting their marriage and entire family. Occasionally funny but overly talky (not to mention outdated) satire.▼

Tony Rome (1967) **C-110m.** **½ D: Gordon Douglas. Frank Sinatra, Jill St. John, Richard Conte, Sue Lyon, Gena Rowlands, Simon Oakland, Jeffrey Lynn, Lloyd Bochner. Good cast in moderately diverting detective caper. Private-eye Rome (Sinatra) hired by millionaire (Oakland) to find out why his daughter would wind up drunk and unconscious in low-class Miami hotel. Sequel: LADY IN CEMENT. Panavision.▼●

Too Bad She's Bad (1955-Italian) **95m.** ** D: Alessandro Blasetti. Sophia Loren, Vittorio De Sica, Marcello Mastroianni, Lina Furia. Unremarkable little comedy about life and love among happy-go-lucky crooks, set in Rome.

Too Beautiful for You (1989-French) **C-91m.** ** D: Bertrand Blier. Gérard Depardieu, Josiane Balasko, Carole Bouquet, Roland Blanche, Francois Cluzet. Car dealer Depardieu cheats on beautiful, cultured wife Bouquet; the object of his affection is his plain, pudgy temporary receptionist (Balasko). Starts off brightly, but then goes absolutely nowhere. Panavision. [R]▼

Too Hot to Handle (1938) **105m.** *** D: Jack Conway. Clark Gable, Myrna Loy, Walter Pidgeon, Leo Carrillo, Johnny Hines, Virginia Weidler. Gable and Pidgeon are rival newsreel photographers vying for aviatrix Loy in this fast-paced action-comedy; Gable's scene faking enemy attack on China is a gem.▼

Too Hot to Handle (1960-British) **C-92m.** ** D: Terence Young. Jayne Mansfield, Leo Genn, Carl Boehm, Christopher Lee, Barbara Windsor. Seamy study of chanteuse Mansfield involved with one man too many in the nightclub circuit. Aka PLAYGIRL AFTER DARK.▼

Too Late Blues (1962) **100m.** ** D: John Cassavetes. Bobby Darin, Stella Stevens, John Cassavetes, Rupert Crosse, Vincent Edwards, Cliff Carnell, Seymour Cassel. Somewhat pretentious drama about jazz musician Darin becoming involved with selfish Stevens. Score by David Raksin, with on-camera performances "doubled" by such jazz greats as Benny Carter, Shelly Manne, and Jimmy Rowles.

Too Late for Tears (1949) **99m.** **½ D: Byron Haskin. Lizabeth Scott, Don DeFore, Dan Duryea, Arthur Kennedy, Kristine Miller. Atmospheric but muddled drama detailing what happens when a bag filled with cash is dropped into the car of greedy bad-girl Scott and nice-guy husband Kennedy. DeFore is a mystery man; Duryea is at his best as a heavy. Aka KILLER BAIT.▼

Too Late the Hero (1970) **C-133m.** *** D: Robert Aldrich. Michael Caine, Cliff Robertson, Henry Fonda, Ian Bannen, Harry Andrews, Denholm Elliott, Ronald Fraser. Two reluctant soldiers (Robertson, Caine) sent on suicide mission on Pacific island during WW2; turns into battle of wits between them and Japanese officer. Action-packed film builds to pulsating finale. Shown on network TV as SUICIDE RUN. Metroscope. [R]▼

Toolbox Murders, The (1978) **C-93m.** *½ D: Dennis Donnelly. Cameron Mitchell, Pamelyn Ferdin, Wesley Eure, Nicholas Beauvy, Aneta Corsaut, Tim Donnelly, Evelyn Guerrero. A film that delivers exactly what its title promises: graphic slayings of young women by means of various pieces of hardware. Yecch. [R]▼

Too Many Crooks (1958-British) **85m.** **½ D: Mario Zampi. Terry-Thomas, George Cole, Brenda De Banzie, Sydney Tafler. OK satire on racketeer films buoyed by Terry-Thomas' presence.▼

Too Many Girls (1940) **85m.** *** D: George Abbott. Lucille Ball, Richard Carlson, Eddie Bracken, Ann Miller, Hal LeRoy, Desi Arnaz, Frances Langford. Engaging Rodgers-Hart musical comedy with winning cast, sharp dialogue. Four boys are hired to keep an eye on footloose Lucy at Pottawatomie College in Stopgap, New Mexico. Stagy presentation of musical numbers seems to work fine here; Van Johnson is very noticeable as one of the chorus boys (it was his film debut, as well as Arnaz and Bracken's). Incidentally, this is where Lucy and Desi met.▼●

Too Many Husbands (1940) **84m.** *** D: Wesley Ruggles. Jean Arthur, Fred MacMurray, Melvyn Douglas, Harry Davenport, Dorothy Peterson, Edgar Buchanan. Jean is married to Douglas when husband #1 (MacMurray), thought dead, turns up. Excellent comedy from W. Somerset Maugham's play *Home and Beauty.* Remade as THREE FOR THE SHOW.

Too Many Thieves (1966) **C-100m.** ** D: Abner Biberman. Peter Falk, Britt Ekland, Joanna Barnes, Nehemiah Persoff, David Carradine, George Coulouris, Elaine Stritch, Ludwig Donath. Falk is lawyer hired to retrieve national treasure stolen from Macedonian shrine. Thieves abound in theatrical feature comprised of two episodes from Falk's *Trials of O'Brien* TV series.

Too Many Winners (1947) **61m.** *½ D: William Beaudine. Hugh Beaumont, Trudy Marshall, Ralph Dunn, Claire Carleton, Charles Mitchell, John Hamilton. Sleuth Michael Shayne tries to take a vacation, but naturally gets entangled in crime solving instead. Final entry in cut-rate series.

Too Much (1987) **C-89m.** BOMB D: Eric Rochat. Bridgette Andersen, Masato Fukazama, Hiroyuki Watanabe, Char Fontana. Threadbare comedy about an adorable (to the point of nausea) little girl (Andersen), her robot friend, and their experiences in Japan. Bottom-of-the-barrel fare. [PG]

Too Much Harmony (1933) **76m.** **½ D: A. Edward Sutherland. Bing Crosby, Jack Oakie, Grace Bradley, Judith Allen, Lilyan Tashman, Ned Sparks. Pleasant, if plotty, backstage musical with some good song numbers, including "Thanks," "The Day You Came Along."

Too Much Sun (1991) **C-110m.** *½ D: Robert Downey. Robert Downey, Jr., Laura Ernst, Jim Haynie, Eric Idle, Ralph Macchio, Andrea Martin, Leo Rossi, Howard Duff, Jennifer Rubin. Farce about competition of brother and sister to have a child first, so as to inherit a fortune from their father; trouble is they're both gay. Few laughs in this dopey comedy that didn't stay long in theaters. [R]▼●

Too Much, Too Soon (1958) **121m.** ** D: Art Napoleon. Dorothy Malone, Errol Flynn, Efrem Zimbalist, Jr., Ray Danton, Neva Patterson, Martin Milner, Murray Hamilton. But not enough, in sensationalistic tale of Diana Barrymore's decline. Flynn steals the show as John Barrymore.

Too Outrageous! (1987-Canadian) **C-100m.** **½ D: Richard Benner. Craig Russell, Hollis McLaren, David McIlwraith, Ron White, Lynne Cormack, Michael J. Reynolds. Russell shines in this disappointing sequel to OUTRAGEOUS! as female impersonator Robin Turner, who's become a smash in N.Y.C.—but will he go mainstream? Unfortunately, the scenario is too hackneyed to make you care. Best moments are his impersonations of Streisand, Mae West, etc. [R]

Too Scared to Scream (1985) **C-104m.** *½ D: Tony Lo Bianco. Mike Connors, Anne Archer, Leon Isaac Kennedy, Ian McShane, Ruth Ford, John Heard, Carrie Nye, Maureen O'Sullivan, Murray Hamilton. Good cast stuck in dreary film about attempts to catch a psycho killer. Filmed in 1982. [R]▼

Too Soon to Love (1960) **85m.** ** D: Richard Rush. Jennifer West, Richard Evans, Warren Parker, Ralph Manza, Jack Nicholson. Mildly interesting period piece about illicit teenage love, pregnancy, and abortion. An early credit for Nicholson and writer-director Rush.

Tootsie (1982) **C-116m.** **** D: Sydney Pollack. Dustin Hoffman, Jessica Lange, Teri Garr, Dabney Coleman, Charles Durning, Bill Murray, Sydney Pollack, George Gaynes, Geena Davis, Estelle Getty, Christine Ebersole. Smashing comedy about an obnoxious N.Y. actor who finally lands a job—disguised as a woman—and soon finds himself a better person female than he ever was male! Farcical premise becomes totally credible thanks to razor-sharp script (credited to Larry Gelbart and Murray Schisgal, from Gelbart and Don McGuire's story), fine direction, and superlative performances all around—including director Pollack's as Hoffman's harried agent. Lange won Best Supporting Actress Oscar. Bill Murray's performance was unbilled in film. Film debut of Geena Davis. Panavision. [PG]▼●

Too Young to Kiss (1951) **91m.** **½ D: Robert Z. Leonard. June Allyson, Van Johnson, Gig Young, Paula Corday, Hans Conried. Allyson is fetching as pianist posing as child prodigy to get her big break falling in love with Johnson.

Too Young to Know (1945) **86m.** ** D: Frederick de Cordova. Joan Leslie, Robert Hutton, Rosemary DeCamp, Dolores Moran. Slick, empty drama of career girl Leslie torn between husband and job.

To Paris With Love (1955-British) **C-78m.** **½ D: Robert Hamer. Alec Guinness, Odile Versois, Vernon Gray, Elina Labourdette, Claude Romain, Jacques Francois, Austin Trevor. Middle-aged widower Guinness and son (Gray) try to marry each other off while on holiday in Paris. So-so comedy should amuse Guinness fans and Francophiles.▼

Topaz (1969) **C-127m.** *** D: Alfred Hitchcock. John Forsythe, Frederick Stafford, Dany Robin, John Vernon, Karin Dor, Michel Piccoli, Philippe Noiret, Claude Jade, Roscoe Lee Browne. French Intelligence agent Stafford works with American official Forsythe to dig out info on Russia's involvement in Cuba. Whirlwind plot circles globe, maintains intrigue level; good, not great Hitchcock, scripted by Samuel Taylor from Leon Uris' best-seller. Video and laserdisc releases include not one but *two* alternate endings Hitchcock shot and then decided not to use! [M/PG]▼●

Topaze (1933) **78m.** *** D: Harry D'Arrast. John Barrymore, Myrna Loy, Albert Conti, Luis Alberni, Reginald Mason, Jobyna Howland. Delightful film adapted from Marcel Pagnol's play about an impeccably honest but naive schoolteacher in France who unwittingly becomes a dupe for wealthy baron's business scheme. Barrymore is perfect. Remade as I LIKE MONEY.▼●

Top Banana (1954) **C-100m.** *** D: Alfred E. Green. Phil Silvers, Rose Marie, Danny Scholl, Judy Lynn, Jack Albertson, Herbie Faye. Literally a filmed version of Silvers' Broadway hit (shot in N.Y.C.'s Winter Garden Theatre) about a Milton Berle-like TV comic. Full of burlesque chestnuts, plus new Johnny Mercer score. Filmed (believe it or not) in 3-D.▼

Top Dog (1995) **C-87m.** *½ D: Aaron Norris. Chuck Norris, Erik Von Detten, Michele Lamar Richards, Carmine Caridi, Herta Ware, Clyde Kusatsu, Peter Savard Moore, Kai Wulff, Francesco Quinn, Timothy Bottoms, Reno the Dog. When terrorists threaten to blow up San Diego, heroic cop Norris is forced to collaborate with a canine partner who seems to outsmart him every step of the way. Not much plot here, and needless to say, the dog steals the show. [PG-13] ▼●◗

Top Gun (1955) **73m.** **½ D: Ray Nazarro. Sterling Hayden, William Bishop, Karin Booth, Regis Toomey, Rod Taylor, Denver Pyle. OK Western about man cleared of murder and elected marshal.

Top Gun (1986) **C-110m.** **½ D: Tony Scott. Tom Cruise, Kelly McGillis, Val Kilmer, Anthony Edwards, Tom Skerritt, Michael Ironside, John Stockwell, Barry Tubb, Rick Rossovich, Tim Robbins, James Tolkan, Meg Ryan, Adrian Pasdar. Young studs vie for glory, on the ground and in the air, at elite naval aviation training school. Contrived beyond belief, with dogfights that play like video games, and total lack of sexual chemistry between the two leads . . . but slickly calculated to please '80s audiences (and fans of ever-smiling Cruise). Edwards, as Cruise's sidekick, steals the show. Giorgio Moroder and Tom Whitlock won an Oscar for the song "Take My Breath Away," performed by Berlin. Super 35. [PG]▼●◗

Top Hat (1935) **99m.** **** D: Mark Sandrich. Fred Astaire, Ginger Rogers, Edward Everett Horton, Helen Broderick, Eric Blore, Erik Rhodes. What can we say? Merely a knock-out of a musical with Astaire and Rogers at their brightest doing "Cheek to Cheek," "Isn't This a Lovely Day to Be Caught in the Rain," "Top Hat, White Tie, and Tails," and the epic "Piccolino," and other Irving Berlin songs, as the duo goes through typical mistaken-identity plot. Wonderful support from rest of cast; that's Lucille Ball as the flower shop clerk. Scripted by Dwight Taylor and Allan Scott, from a play by Alexander Farago and Aladar Laszlo. Originally 101m.; some prints are 93m.▼●

Topkapi (1964) **C-120m.** **** D: Jules Dassin. Melina Mercouri, Peter Ustinov, Maximilian Schell, Robert Morley, Akim Tamiroff, Despo Diamantidou. First-rate entertainment of would-be thieves who plan perfect crime in Constantinople museum; lighthearted caper has inspired many imitations. Filmed in Istanbul, with Ustinov's delightful performance copping an Academy Award. Written by Monja Danischewsky, from Eric Ambler's novel *The Light of Day*; memorable score by Manos Hadjidakis.▼●

To Please a Lady (1950) **91m.** **½ D: Clarence Brown. Clark Gable, Barbara Stanwyck. Adolphe Menjou, Roland Winters, Will Geer, Emory Parnell, Frank Jenks. Unremarkable love story of reporter Stanwyck and race-car driver-heel Gable.▼

Top Man (1943) **74m.** ** D: Charles Lamont. Donald O'Connor, Susanna Foster, Peggy Ryan, Richard Dix, Anne Gwynne, Lillian Gish, Noah Beery, Jr. Youthful O'Connor heads the family when Dad goes off to war; typical assembly-line musical comedy from Universal, with guest spots by Count Basie, Borrah Minnevitch's Harmonica Rascals.

Top of the World (1955) **90m.** ** D: Lewis R. Foster. Dale Robertson, Evelyn Keyes, Frank Lovejoy, Nancy Gates. Set in Alaska, movie revolves around jet pilot Robertson, his ex-wife Keyes and her new boyfriend Lovejoy.

Top o' the Morning (1949) **100m.** **½ D: David Miller. Bing Crosby, Barry Fitzgerald, Ann Blyth, Hume Cronyn, John McIntire, Eileen Crowe. Crosby-Fitzgerald malarkey is wearing thin in this fanciful musical of Bing searching for thief hiding the Blarney Stone.

Topper (1937) **97m.** ***½ D: Norman Z. McLeod. Constance Bennett, Cary Grant, Roland Young, Billie Burke, Alan Mowbray, Eugene Pallette, Arthur Lake, Hedda

Hopper. Delightful gimmick comedy with ghosts Grant and Bennett dominating life of meek Young; sparkling cast in adaptation of Thorne Smith novel, scripted by Jack Jevne, Eddie Moran, and Eric Hatch. Followed by two sequels, a TV series, and a 1979 TV remake starring Kate Jackson and Andrew Stevens. Also shown in computer-colored version (the first b&w film to be "colorized," in 1985).▼●

Topper (1979) **C-100m. TVM** D: Charles S. Dubin. Kate Jackson, Andrew Stevens, Jack Warden, Rue McClanahan, James Karen, Charles Siebert. Breezy updating of the 1937 classic. The two leads (then married) also produced this one, aiming for a new *Topper* TV series. Average.

Topper Returns (1941) **88m.** *** D: Roy Del Ruth. Joan Blondell, Roland Young, Carole Landis, Billie Burke, Dennis O'Keefe, Patsy Kelly, Eddie "Rochester" Anderson. Topper helps ghostly Blondell solve her own murder in the last of this series, with hilarious results. Also shown in computer-colored version. ▼●

Topper Takes a Trip (1939) **85m.** *** D: Norman Z. McLeod. Constance Bennett, Roland Young, Billie Burke, Alan Mowbray, Verree Teasdale, Franklin Pangborn. Cary Grant is missing (except in a flashback), but rest of cast returns for repeat success as Young is frustrated on Riviera vacation by ghostess Bennett. Also shown in computer-colored version.▼

Top Secret! (1984) **C-90m.** **½ D: Jim Abrahams, David Zucker, Jerry Zucker. Val Kilmer, Lucy Gutteridge, Christopher Villiers, Jeremy Kemp, Michael Gough, Omar Sharif, Peter Cushing, Harry Ditson, Jim Carter. Likably silly comedy from the writing-directing team that brought you AIRPLANE!, about an Elvis-like rock star who becomes embroiled in espionage work while touring East Germany—with Nazis as bad guys and French resistance fighters as allies! Lots of laughs but no real momentum—and where's the ending? [PG]▼●

Top Secret Affair (1957) **100m.** **½ D: H. C. Potter. Susan Hayward, Kirk Douglas, Paul Stewart, Jim Backus, John Cromwell. John P. Marquand's *Melville Goodwin, U.S.A.* becomes fair comedy, with most credit going to Hayward as fiery publisher who knows all about the past of Senate appointee (Douglas).

Tops Is the Limit SEE: **Anything Goes** (1936)

Topsy-Turvy (2000-British) **C-160m.** ***½ D: Mike Leigh. Jim Broadbent, Allan Corduner, Lesley Manville, Eleanor David, Ron Cook, Timothy Spall, Kevin McKidd, Martin Savage, Shirley Henderson, Wendy Nottingham, Charles Simon, Alison Steadman. Fascinating, intimate portrait of Gilbert and Sullivan, and the time in which they lived, focusing on their peccadilloes and personalities, and the process of turning their latest ideas into the operetta masterpiece *The Mikado.* Broadbent and Corduner are superb in the leads, and Spall makes a wonderful Mikado. Overflowing with personal and period detail (including Oscar-winning Costume Design and Makeup), this long but rewarding film gets better and better as it goes along. Released in the U.S. in 1999. Their story also told in THE GREAT GILBERT AND SULLIVAN. [R]▼◗

Tora! Tora! Tora! (1970-U.S.-Japanese) **C-143m.** *** D: Richard Fleischer, Toshio Masuda, Kinji Fukasuku. Martin Balsam, Soh Yamamura, Jason Robards, Joseph Cotten, Tatsuya Mihashi, E. G. Marshall, James Whitmore, Wesley Addy, Leon Ames, George Macready. Events leading up to (well-staged) Pearl Harbor attack, from both American and Japanese points of view. Well-documented screenplay shows major and minor blundering on both sides, then recreates attack with frightening realism. Well-made film creates incredible tension. Oscar-winning special effects. Panavision. [PG]▼●◗

Torch, The (1950-Mexican) **90m.** ** D: Emilio Fernandez. Paulette Goddard, Pedro Armendariz, Gilbert Roland, Walter Reed. Mexican revolutionary captures town and falls for daughter of nobility. Rare English-language effort by Mexico's top director; a shame it isn't better. Beautifully photographed by Gabriel Figueroa.▼

Torchlight (1984) **C-90m.** ** D: Tom Wright. Pamela Sue Martin, Steve Railsback, Ian McShane, Al Corley, Rita Taggart. Married couple Martin and Railsback's world is wrecked when he becomes a cocaine addict. Below-average morality tale: its message may be important, but its dramatics are muddled. [R]▼●

Torch Song (1953) **C-90m.** **½ D: Charles Walters. Joan Crawford, Michael Wilding, Marjorie Rambeau, Gig Young, Henry (Harry) Morgan, Dorothy Patrick, Benny Rubin, Nancy Gates. Crawford is hard as nails as a Broadway musical star who chews up people for lunch—until she meets blind pianist Wilding, who isn't cowed by her. Glossy, often hilariously clichéd drama reminds us that It's Lonely At the Top. There's one absurd musical number in which Crawford appears in blackface! Her "clumsy" dance partner in the opening number is director Walters, a former dancer and choreographer. ▼●

Torch Song Trilogy (1988) **C-117m.** **½ D: Paul Bogart. Anne Bancroft, Matthew Broderick, Harvey Fierstein, Brian Kerwin, Karen Young, Charles Pierce. Fierstein rewrote (and considerably compressed) his landmark Broadway play about a drag queen, and lost something in the process. Changing sensibilities in the AIDS era also affect the original material, though there are still fine moments. Fierstein reprises his stage performance as Arnold Beckoff, and Bancroft scores strongly as his mother. [R]▼●

Torchy Blane Glenda Farrell was one of the leading lights of the Warner Bros. stock company; she could always be counted on to add zip and zest to a film, especially if provided with good wisecracks by the screenwriters. Her reward for yeoman service was a series of her own, *Torchy Blane,* which was adapted from a series of pulp magazine stories by the prolific Frederick Nebel. As it happens, Nebel's mystery-solving reporter was a man, and his name was Kennedy, but the gender-switch worked (just as it would a few years later—with spectacular results—when THE FRONT PAGE became HIS GIRL FRIDAY). In every film, Torchy matches wits with police lieutenant Steve McBride, who never quite seems to understand what's going on. It's usually up to Torchy to solve the case at hand, which causes Steve certain embarrassment, since he and Torchy are engaged to be married. Barton MacLane's casting as McBride rescued him from playing the same harsh-mouthed bad guys over and over again, but his part wasn't well written enough to make him terribly endearing. Comic actor Tom Kennedy was cast as Gahagan, McBride's right hand and the dumbest cop ever to hit the screen (though the recurring character of the desk sergeant, played in most cases by George Guhl, just might be his equal). There is nothing to distinguish these quickly made B pictures except for the usual Warner Bros. pizzazz, and the snap of Glenda Farrell. The first film in the series, SMART BLONDE, is easily the best (and the only one to be based directly on a Nebel story); most of the others are quite forgettable. Lola Lane and Paul Kelly replaced Farrell and MacLane for one episode, TORCHY BLANE IN PANAMA; Jane Wyman and Allen Jenkins finished off the series in TORCHY BLANE . . . PLAYING WITH DYNAMITE.

TORCHY BLANE

Smart Blonde (1936)
Fly-Away Baby (1937)
Adventurous Blonde (1937)
Blondes at Work (1938)
Torchy Blane in Panama (1938)
Torchy Gets Her Man (1938)
Torchy Blane in Chinatown (1939)
Torchy Runs for Mayor (1939)
Torchy Blane . . . Playing With Dynamite (1939)

Torchy Blane in Chinatown (1938) **59m.** ★½ D: William Beaudine. Glenda Farrell, Barton MacLane, Tom Kennedy, Patric Knowles, Henry O'Neill, James Stephenson. Torchy and fiancé Steve get mixed up with jade smuggling and murder in this tiresome and confusing series episode. Remake of a 1930 film, MURDER WILL OUT.

Torchy Blane in Panama (1938) **58m.** ★½ D: William Clemens. Lola Lane, Paul Kelly, Tom Kennedy, Anthony Averill, Larry Williams, Betty Compson. Lane and Kelly temporarily replaced Glenda Farrell and Barton MacLane in this indifferent entry about New York bank robbers who flee to Panama on an ocean liner.

Torchy Blane . . . Playing With Dynamite (1939) **59m.** ★★ D: Noel Smith. Jane Wyman, Allen Jenkins, Tom Kennedy, Sheila Bromley, Joe Cunningham, Eddie Marr. Wyman, who had a small part in the first *Torchy Blane* entry, plays the lead in this farcical final episode, in which she goes to jail undercover to get the goods on a crook. Jenkins, replacing Barton MacLane, is very funny.

Torchy Gets Her Man (1938) **62m.** ★★ D: William Beaudine. Glenda Farrell, Barton MacLane, Tom Kennedy, Willard Robertson, George Guhl, John Ridgely, Tommy Jackson. Farrell and MacLane returned for this mostly comical addition to the series, with Torchy in hot pursuit of a counterfeiting gang.

Torchy Runs for Mayor (1939) **58m.** ★★½ D: Ray McCarey. Glenda Farrell, Barton MacLane, Tom Kennedy, John Miljan, Frank Shannon, Joe Cunningham, Irving Bacon. Torchy digs up some dirt on corrupt politicians and you can guess the rest from the title. Pretty good series entry with some very snappy dialogue.

Torment (1944-Swedish) **100m.** ★★★½ D: Alf Sjoberg. Mai Zetterling, Stig Jarrel, Alf Kjellin, Olaf Winnerstrand. Schoolboy Kjellin and girl he falls in love with (Zetterling) are hounded by sadistic teacher Jarrel. Moody and evocative, with a script by Ingmar Bergman. Also known as FRENZY. ▼

Tormented (1960) **75m.** BOMB D: Bert I. Gordon. Richard Carlson, Juli Reding, Susan Gordon, Lugene Sanders, Joe Turkel, Lillian Adams. Low-budget hogwash of guilt-ridden pianist dubious over his forthcoming marriage to society woman. Weak ghost story.▼

Torn Apart (1989) **C-96m.** ★★½ D: Jack Fisher. Adrian Pasdar, Cecilia Peck, Barry Primus, Machram Huri, Arnon Zadok, Margit Polak. Boy and girl grow up together and fall in love—but he's Jewish, she's Arab, and the setting is Israel. A new slant on *Romeo and Juliet* with a topical backdrop, this humanist drama has convincing performances and a timely message. Peck is the daughter of Gregory Peck. [R]▼

Torn Between Two Lovers (1979) **C-100m. TVM** D: Delbert Mann. Lee Remick, Joseph Bologna, George Peppard, Giorgio Tozzi, Molly Cheek. Romantic drama graced by ever-lovely Remick as married socialite who has an affair with a dashing architect she meets on a trip. Title comes from hit song of the late '70s. Average.▼

Torn Between Two Values SEE: **Sergeant Ryker**

Torn Curtain (1966) **C-128m.** **½ D: Alfred Hitchcock. Paul Newman, Julie Andrews, Lila Kedrova, David Opatoshu, Ludwig Donath. Oddly unmoving Hitchcock Cold War thriller about American scientist (Newman) pretending to be defector. Slick but empty film. Some TV prints are cut to 121m., excising violent scenes.▼●

Torpedo Alley (1953) **84m.** ** D: Lew Landers. Dorothy Malone, Mark Stevens, Charles Winninger, Bill Williams. Typical Korean War actioner involving U.S. submarine offensives.▼

Torpedo Bay (1963-Italian-French) **91m.** **½ D: Charles Frend. James Mason, Lilli Palmer, Gabriele Ferzetti, Alberto Lupo, Geoffrey Keen. British and Italian naval crews meet on neutral territory during WW2; modest but fairly interesting drama.

Torpedo Run (1958) **C-98m.** **½ D: Joseph Pevney. Glenn Ford, Ernest Borgnine, Diane Brewster, Dean Jones. Sluggish WW2 revenge narrative of sub-commander Ford whose family was aboard Jap prison ship he had to blow up. CinemaScope▼

Torrent (1926) **87m.** *** D: Monta Bell. Ricardo Cortez, Greta Garbo, Gertrude Olmstead, Edward Connelly, Lucien Littlefield, Martha Mattox, Tully Marshall, Mack Swain, Lucy Bennett. Garbo stars in her first American film as a Spanish peasant girl who becomes a famous prima donna after being deserted by nobleman Cortez, whose life is ruled by his mother. A still entertaining tale of lost love, based on a Blasco-Ibanez novel.

Torrents of Spring (1990-Italian-French) **C-101m.** **½ D: Jerzy Skolimowski. Timothy Hutton, Natassja Kinski, Valeria Golino, William Forsythe, Urbano Barberini, Francesca De Sapio, Jacques Herlin. No disgrace, but an almost inevitably stilted film version of an Ivan Turgenev story. Russian Hutton (!), engaged to German Golino, gets roving glands for married Kinski, who's negotiating to purchase his estate. Nicely shot (with a good duel scene), but Hutton's regal bearing falls apart whenever he's asked to open his mouth. [PG-13]▼●

Torrid Zone (1940) **88m.** ***½ D: William Keighley. James Cagney, Ann Sheridan, Pat O'Brien, Andy Devine, Helen Vinson, Jerome Cowan, George Tobias, George Reeves. South-of-the-border comedy, action and romance with nightclub star Sheridan helping plantation owner O'Brien keep Cagney from leaving. Zesty dialogue (scripted by Richard Macauley and Jerry Wald) in this variation on THE FRONT PAGE.

Torso (1974-Italian) **C-90m.** *½ D: Sergio Martino. Suzy Kendall, Tina Aumont, John Richardson, Luc Merenda. A killer is carving up beautiful co-eds in this bloody potboiler. [R]▼

Tortilla Flat (1942) **105m.** *** D: Victor Fleming. Spencer Tracy, Hedy Lamarr, John Garfield, Frank Morgan, Akim Tamiroff, Sheldon Leonard, Donald Meek, John Qualen, Allen Jenkins. Steinbeck's salty novel of California fishing community vividly portrayed by three top stars, stolen by Morgan as devoted dog lover. Also shown in computer-colored version.▼●

Torture Chamber of Baron Blood, The SEE: **Baron Blood**

Torture Chamber of Dr. Sadism, The (1967-German) **C-90m.** **½ D: Harald Reinl. Christopher Lee, Lex Barker, Karin Dor, Carl Lange, Vladimir Medar. A resurrected Lee seeks revenge on Barker and Dor; after luring them to his castle they are mentally and physically tortured. Based on Poe's *Pit and the Pendulum*. Atmospheric, but not for the squeamish. Aka THE BLOOD DEMON and CASTLE OF THE WALKING DEAD (running 75m.). Techniscope. ▼

Torture Garden (1967-British) **C-93m.** **½ D: Freddie Francis. Jack Palance, Burgess Meredith, Beverly Adams, Peter Cushing, Barbara Ewing, Michael Bryant, Maurice Denham. Anthology horror film revolving around sideshow weirdo Dr. Diabolo (Meredith) with power to let curious visitors see and experience their near-future. Good cast and production, but stories uneven; first and last tales best. Written by Robert Bloch.▼

Torture Zone SEE: **Fear Chamber, The**

To Sir, With Love (1967-British) **C-105m.** ***½ D: James Clavell. Sidney Poitier, Judy Geeson, Christian Roberts, Suzy Kendall, Faith Brook, Geoffrey Bayldon, Patricia Routledge, Adrienne Posta, Lulu, Michael Des Barres. Excellent film of novice teacher Poitier assigned to roughhouse London school, gradually earning respect from his students. Well acted, with nice work by British newcomers; Lulu also sings hit title song. Written and produced by Clavell, from E. R. Braithwaite's novel. Followed by a made-for-TV sequel in 1996.▼●◗

To Sleep With Anger (1990) **C-102m.** *** D: Charles Burnett. Danny Glover, Paul Butler, Mary Alice, Carl Lumbly, Vonetta McGee, Richard Brooks, Sheryl Lee Ralph, Ethel Ayler, Julius Harris, Sy Richardson, Davis Roberts, DeForest Coven, Jimmy Witherspoon. Evocative domestic drama about the effect storyteller/trickster Glover has on the various members of a black family. More than just a portrait of contemporary black society, it's a story of cultural differences between parents and children, of how individuals learn (or don't learn) from experience, and of how there should be no place for those who cause violence and strife. Scripted by Burnett; coexecutive produced by Glover. Screen couple Lumbly and McGee are also married in real life. [PG]▼●

Total Eclipse (1995-U.S.-French) **C-110m.** BOMB D: Agnieszka Holland. Leonardo DiCaprio, David Thewlis, Romane Bohringer, Dominique Blanc, Felicie Pasotti Cabarbaye, Nita Klein, James Thieree, Emmanuelle Oppo, Christopher Hampton. Really bad film about 19th-century French poets Arthur Rimbaud (DiCaprio) and Paul Verlaine (Thewlis) plays like a homosexual version of AMADEUS. Well intentioned and based on fact, but just awful. Hampton adapted the script from his own play. Pick up a couple of poetry books instead. [R] ▼●◗

Totally F*ed Up** (1993) **C-85m.** **½ D: Gregg Araki. James Duval, Roko Belic, Susan Behshid, Jenee Gill, Gilbert Luna, Lance May, Alan Boyce, Craig Gilmore. Jarring, Godardian portrait of a group of bored, alienated L.A. teens. They hang out and talk about sex, relationships, and their parents; their language is littered with such words as ''grossomatic'' and ''gagorama.'' And . . . they're gay, so there is no shortage of venom vented against homophobia. Not bad, but still a come-down from Araki's breakthrough film, THE LIVING END. Araki also scripted, edited, photographed and coproduced.▼

Total Recall (1990) **C-109m.** *** D: Paul Verhoeven. Arnold Schwarzenegger, Rachel Ticotin, Sharon Stone, Ronny Cox, Michael Ironside, Marshall Bell, Mel Johnson, Jr. Schwarzenegger learns he's a victim of mind-tampering in this 21st-century tale—and once he discovers his true identity, journeys to Mars to help fight a power-hungry madman there. Riveting yarn (based on Phillip K. Dick's short story "We Can Remember It for You Wholesale") offers endless twists and intriguing ideas . . . and the kind of over-the-top violence for which director Verhoeven is known. Dazzling, Oscar-winning special effects throughout. Later ''inspired'' a cable TV series. [R]▼●◗

To the Devil—A Daughter (1976-British-German) **C-95m.** **½ D: Peter Sykes. Richard Widmark, Christopher Lee, Honor Blackman, Denholm Elliott, Nastassja Kinski, Michael Goodliffe. Occult novelist Widmark is enlisted to help young girl (Kinski) who's being pursued by defrocked priest Lee for satanic ritual. Hammer Films adaptation of Dennis Wheatley book is well made but lacks punch. Aka CHILD OF SATAN. [R]▼

To the Ends of the Earth (1948) **109m.** ***½ D: Robert Stevenson. Dick Powell, Signe Hasso, Ludwig Donath, Vladimir Sokoloff, Edgar Barrier. Fast-moving thriller of government agent tracking down narcotics smuggling ring has good acting and ironic ending.

To the Shores of Tripoli (1942) **C-86m.** **½ D: H. Bruce Humberstone. John Payne, Maureen O'Hara, Randolph Scott, Nancy Kelly, William Tracy, Maxie Rosenbloom, Iris Adrian. Spoiled rich-boy Payne joins Marines with off-handed attitude, doesn't wake up until film's end. Routine material.▼

To the Victor (1948) **100m.** **½ D: Delmer Daves. Dennis Morgan, Viveca Lindfors, Victor Francen, Bruce Bennett, Dorothy Malone, Eduardo Ciannelli, William Conrad. Story of collaborators standing trial in France for war crimes sadly could have been much better; script by Richard Brooks.

Toto the Hero (1991-Belgian-French-German) **C-90m.** *** D: Jaco van Dormael. Michel Bouquet, Mireille Perrier, Jo De Backer, Gisela Uhlen, Peter Bohlke, Thomas Godet, Sandrine Blancke. Original, immensely clever journey through the life of a character named Thomas, who is shown (through constant cross-cutting) as a child, adult, and elderly man. The young boy imagines that he'll grow up to be Toto the Hero, a secret agent; instead, he'll have to cope with his ultimate ordinariness, his memories, and his dreams. A unique blend of comedy, tragedy, and mystery, especially notable for its discerning—and unflinching—look at childhood. Writer-director van Dormael, a former circus clown, makes his feature directing debut. [PG-13]▼●

To Trap a Spy (1966) **C-90m.** **½ D: Don Medford. Robert Vaughn, David McCallum, Leo G. Carroll, Luciana Paluzzi, Patricia Crowley. Expanded from initial segment of *The Man From U.N.C.L.E.* TV series, this reflects small budget and cast's newness at formula action-espionage type plot.

Touch, The (1971-U.S.-Swedish) **C-112m.** *½ D: Ingmar Bergman. Elliott Gould, Bibi Andersson, Max von Sydow, Sheila Reid. Bergman's first English-language film should be called THE TETCHED, in view of the fact that Andersson leaves doctor-husband von Sydow for boorish Gould. The two Bergman regulars are fine, but Gould is miscast and dialogue embarrassingly awkward. [R]▼

Touch (1997) **C-96m.** **½ D: Paul Schrader. Bridget Fonda, Christopher Walken, Skeet Ulrich, Tom Arnold, Gina Gershon, Lolita Davidovich, Paul Mazursky, Janeane Garofalo, John Doe, Conchata Ferrell, Mason Adams, Anthony Zerbe, LL Cool J, Tamlyn Tomita, Don Novello. Satirical fable about a young ex-monk who has the ability to effect miracle healings—while suffering stigmata: bleeding as Christ did on the cross. This causes no small furor among exploiters like Walken and fanatics like Arnold. Interesting and well cast (with Arnold a standout as the religious zealot), but awfully subdued; it's a film that leaves you wanting. Based on an Elmore Leonard novel, scripted by Schrader. [R]▼●

Touchables, The (1968-British) **C-97m.** BOMB D: Robert Freeman. Judy Huxtable, Esther Anderson, Marilyn Richard, Kathy Simmonds. Dreary tale of four girls and a guy who try to kidnap pop singing idol. Terrible. TV print runs 88m. [PG—edited from original R rating]

Touch and Die (1991) **C-108m.** BOMB D: Piernico Solinas. Renee Estevez, Martin Sheen, David Birney, Franco Nero. The Rome bureau chief of an American newspaper finds lots of bodies with their hands chopped off as he follows the trail of plutonium thieves. Sheen tries to keep real-life daughter Estevez locked in her hotel room, to keep her out of trouble (and off-screen), which may be a wise choice. Extremely confusing globe-trotting thriller. [R]▼

Touch and Go (1955-British) **C-85m.** **½ D: Michael Truman. Jack Hawkins, Margaret Johnston, Roland Culver, June Thorburn. Wry study of sturdy English family trying to overcome obstacles upsetting their planned emigration to Australia.

Touch and Go (1980-Australian) **C-92m.** ** D: Peter Maxwell. Wendy Hughes, Chantal Contouri, Carmen Duncan, Jeanie Drynan, Liddy Clark. Sexy female Robin Hoods steal for worthy causes. A well-meaning comedy-caper film that is slight and forgettable.▼

Touch and Go (1986) **C-101m.** **½ D: Robert Mandel. Michael Keaton, Maria Conchita Alonso, Ajay Naidu, Maria Tucci, Max Wright, Jere Burns, Lara Jill Miller. Self-centered hockey star becomes involved with delinquent kid and his mother. Aptly titled film has persuasive performances but unconvincing story line. [R]▼●

Touched (1983) **C-93m.** ** D: John Flynn. Robert Hays, Kathleen Beller, Ned Beatty, Gilbert Lewis, Lyle Kessler. Uninspired, poorly scripted latter-day DAVID AND LISA with Hays and Beller escaping from mental institution and trying to build a "normal" life for themselves. Good performances, anyway. [R]▼

Touched by Love (1980) **C-95m.** **½ D: Gus Trikonis. Deborah Raffin, Diane Lane, Michael Learned, Cristina Raines, Mary Wickes, Clu Gulager, John Amos, Clive Shalom. Sentimental drama, based on nursing trainee Lena Canada's memoir, of cerebral palsy victim's pen-pal relationship with Elvis Presley. Fine performances by Lane and Raffin. Originally titled TO ELVIS, WITH LOVE. [PG]▼

Touch Me Not (1976-British) **C-84m.** ** D: Douglas Fifthian. Lee Remick, Michael Hinz, Ivan Desny, Ingrid Garbo. Unexciting thriller with industrial spy Hinz using neurotic secretary Remick to gather information on boss Desny. Also known as THE HUNTED. [PG]▼

Touch of a Stranger (1991) **C-87m.** *½ D: Brad Gilbert. Shelley Winters, Anthony Nocerino, Danny Capri, Haley Taylor-Block. Looney recluse (Winters) finds a young stranger on her doorstep (Nocerino) who is carrying a gun and bleeding from a bullet wound. Starved for companionship, she takes him in. Amateurish, and deadly dull. A shame to see Winters overacting with such aimless abandon. [R]

Touch of Class, A (1973) **C-105m.** ** D: Melvin Frank. George Segal, Glenda Jackson, Paul Sorvino, Hildegard Neil, Cec Linder, K Callan, Mary Barclay. Undeniable chemistry of Segal and Jackson can only occasionally breathe life into this stale comedy about married man who intends nothing more than having a carefree affair, only to fall genuinely in love. Jackson won Best Actress Oscar. Panavision. [PG]▼

Touch of Evil (1958) **108m.** **** D: Orson Welles. Charlton Heston, Orson Welles, Janet Leigh, Joseph Calleia, Akim Tamiroff, Marlene Dietrich, Dennis Weaver, Valentin de Vargas, Mort Mills, Victor Milian, Joanna Moore, Zsa Zsa Gabor. Narc Heston and corrupt cop Welles tangle over murder investigation in sleazy Mexican border town, with Heston's bride Leigh the pawn of their struggle. Fantastic, justifiably famous opening shot merely commences stylistic masterpiece, dazzlingly photographed by Russell Metty. Great Latin rock score by Henry Mancini; neat unbilled cameos by Joseph Cotten, Ray Collins, and especially Mercedes McCambridge. Reconstructed according to Welles' notes in 1998, at 111m. Beware 95m. version. ▼●

Touch of Larceny, A (1959-British) **93m.** *** D: Guy Hamilton. James Mason, George Sanders, Vera Miles, Oliver Johnston, William Kendall, Duncan Lamont. Ingenious comedy of officer who uses availability of military secrets to his advantage in off-beat plan.

Tough as They Come (1942) **61m.** ** D: William Nigh. Billy Halop, Huntz Hall, Bernard Punsly, Gabriel Dell, Helen Parrish, Paul Kelly, Ann Gillis. Contrived *Little Tough Guys* tale about law student Halop trying to straighten out a crooked credit union.

Tough Enough (1983) **C-106m.** ** D: Richard Fleischer. Dennis Quaid, Carlene Watkins, Stan Shaw, Pam Grier, Warren Oates, Bruce McGill, Wilford Brimley, Fran Ryan. Numerous problems plagued production of this predictable tale of would-be Country-Western singer Quaid entering Tough Man amateur boxing competitions for exposure. Insipid ROCKY rip-off wastes good cast. Shot in 1981. [PG] ▼

Tougher They Come, The (1950) **69m.** *½ D: Ray Nazarro. Wayne Morris, Preston Foster, William Bishop, Kay Buckley. Trivial study of ruthless operators trying to take over lumber camp.

Toughest Gun in Tombstone (1958) **72m.** *½ D: Earl Bellamy. George Montgomery, Beverly Tyler, Don Beddoe, Jim Davis. Weak shoot-out tale with Montgomery in the title role.

Toughest Man Alive, The (1955) **72m.** ** D: Sidney Salkow. Dane Clark, Lita Milan, Ross Elliott, Myrna Dell, Syd Saylor, Anthony Caruso. Mild caper of tracking down gun-smuggling in South America.

Toughest Man in Arizona, The (1952) **C-90m.** **½ D: R. G. Springsteen. Vaughn Monroe, Joan Leslie, Edgar Buchanan, Victor Jory. While waging war on crime marshal Monroe falls for girl with expected results. Fairly well produced and acted.

Tough Guys (1986) **C-104m.** **½ D: Jeff Kanew. Burt Lancaster, Kirk Douglas, Charles Durning, Alexis Smith, Dana Carvey, Darlanne Fluegel, Eli Wallach, Monty Ash, Billy Barty. A couple of former crooks—who staged America's last train robbery thirty years ago—are finally sprung from prison and gamely try to adjust to 1980s life. Watching Burt and Kirk (in this tailor-made comedy) is a joy, but the film gets more childish and predictable as it goes along. Still watchable but what a shame! Panavision. [PG]▼●

Tough Guys Don't Dance (1987) **C-110m.** **½ D: Norman Mailer. Ryan O'Neal, Isabella Rossellini, Debra Sandlund, Wings Hauser, Lawrence Tierney, Penn Jillette, Frances Fisher, John Bedford Lloyd, Clarence Williams III. Genuinely odd *film noir* cum black-comedy adapted by Mailer from his own novel, with O'Neal as a loser who may have committed murder—but can't remember. Peopled exclusively by weird characters who speak in purple prose . . . but it does have its moments, and a lively performance by Tierney as O'Neal's no-nonsense father who wants to "deep-six the heads." Filmed in Provincetown, Massachusetts. [R]▼●

Tourist Trap (1979) **C-85m.** *½ D: David Schmoeller. Chuck Connors, Jon Van Ness, Jocelyn Jones, Robin Sherwood, Tanya Roberts, Keith McDermott. Here's an original idea for a horror movie: those life-size dummies in Connors' "museum" are strangely lifelike, aren't they? Not so much that the idiots he lures there ever catch on. A couple of genuine scares, but mostly boring thriller. [PG]▼●

Tous les Matins du Monde (1991-French) **C-114m.** ***½ D: Alain Corneau. Jean-Pierre Marielle, Gérard Depardieu, Anne Brochet, Guillaume Depardieu, Caroline Sihol, Carole Richert, Myriam Boyer, Michel Bouquet. Exquisitely detailed historical biography examining the relationship between Sainte Colombe (Marielle), the obsessive, almost mystical 17th-century baroque composer and cellist, and his protegé, Marin Marais (Gérard Depardieu), a man of far less elevated artistic aspirations, who was a celebrated court composer at Versailles. Both stars are excellent, with Depardieu's son Guillaume effectively playing the young Marin Marais. Exemplary use of music on the soundtrack. Screenplay by the director and Pascal Quignard, based on the latter's novel. A smash hit in France, where it won seven César awards. Video title: ALL THE MORNINGS OF THE WORLD.▼●

Tovarich (1937) **98m.** *** D: Anatole Litvak. Claudette Colbert, Charles Boyer, Basil Rathbone, Anita Louise, Melville Cooper, Isabel Jeans, Morris Carnovsky. Boyer and Colbert, royal Russians, flee the Revolution with court treasury but nothing for themselves; they're finally reduced to working as servants. Enjoyable but dated romantic comedy set in Paris. Based on a French play Americanized by Robert E. Sherwood.

Toward the Unknown (1956) **C-115m.** **½ D: Mervyn LeRoy. William Holden, Lloyd Nolan, Virginia Leith, Charles McGraw, James Garner, Murray Hamilton, L.Q. Jones, Paul Fix, Karen Steele. Intelligent narrative about test pilots, focusing on a tarnished air officer (Holden) eager to regain the respect of his men. Garner's film debut.

Towering Inferno, The (1974) **C-165m.** **½ D: John Guillermin, Irwin Allen. Steve McQueen, Paul Newman, William Holden, Faye Dunaway, Fred Astaire, Susan Blakely, Richard Chamberlain, Jennifer Jones, O. J. Simpson, Robert Vaughn, Robert Wagner, Susan Flannery, Gregory Sierra, Dabney Coleman. All-star idiocy about a burning skyscraper. Purports to pay tribute to firemen but spends most of its time devising grisly ways for people to die. The pyrotechnics are gripping, but the movie is just another cold-blooded Hollywood "product." Oscar-winner for Cinematography, Editing and Song ("We May Never Love Like This Again"). Panavision. [PG]▼●◗

Tower of Evil SEE: **Horror on Snape Island**

Tower of London (1939) **92m.** **½ D: Rowland V. Lee. Basil Rathbone, Boris Karloff, Barbara O'Neil, Ian Hunter, Vincent Price, Nan Grey, Leo G. Carroll, John Sutton, Miles Mander. Muddled historical melodrama (not a horror film, as many believe), with Rathbone as unscrupulous, power-hungry Richard III and

Karloff as his dutiful executioner Mord. Court intrigue leads to uninspired battle scenes. Remade in 1962.▼

Tower of London (1962) **79m.** *½ D: Roger Corman. Vincent Price, Michael Pate, Joan Freeman, Robert Brown. Remake of 1939 film has Price, who played Duke of Clarence first time around, tackling role of Richard III in a flat, papier-mâché production.▼●

Tower of Terror SEE: **In the Devil's Garden**

Town Called Hell, A (1971-British-Spanish) **C-95m.** BOMB D: Robert Parrish. Robert Shaw, Telly Savalas, Stella Stevens, Martin Landau, Fernando Rey. A manhunt for Mexican revolutionary Shaw. The pits. Originally titled A TOWN CALLED BASTARD. Franscope. [R]▼

Town Has Turned to Dust, A (1998) **C-100m. TVM** D: Rob Nilsson. Stephen Lang, Ron Perlman, Gabriel Olds, Judy Collins, Barbara Jean Reams. Updated version of Rod Serling's morality play about a small-town mob lynching, written in 1958 for *Playhouse 90*. That version was set in the Old West; the new one is in the 23rd century, when Earth's inhabitants have relocated to the asteroid New Angeles, leaving behind a group of bigoted miners and Native Americans in the Utah desert. Despite this being an update with new script references that were alien to Serling in his day, he was given sole writing credit. Singer Judy Collins has a rare dramatic role here. Made for cable. Average.▼◗

Town Like Alice, A (1956-British) **107m.** **½ D: Jack Lee. Virginia McKenna, Peter Finch, Maureen Swanson, Vincent Ball. Taut WW2 tale, well acted, about Japanese oppression of female British POWS in Malaysia. Based on Nevil Shute's novel, later remade as TV miniseries. Retitled: RAPE OF MALAYA.▼●

Town on Trial (1956-British) **96m.** **½ D: John Guillermin. John Mills, Charles Coburn, Derek Farr, Barbara Bates, Alec McCowen. A murder investigation in a small British town, where there's no shortage of suspects. Low-key drama makes good use of natural locations.

Town Tamer (1965) **C-89m.** ** D: Lesley Selander. Dana Andrews, Terry Moore, Pat O'Brien, Lon Chaney (Jr.), Bruce Cabot, Lyle Bettger, Coleen Gray, Barton MacLane, Richard Arlen, Richard Jaeckel, Sonny Tufts. As title indicates, Andrews cleans up community, and among the rubble are some veteran actors. Routine Western has minor nostalgia value, in light of the cast. Techniscope.

Town That Dreaded Sundown, The (1977) **C-90m.** **½ D: Charles B. Pierce. Ben Johnson, Andrew Prine, Dawn Wells, Christine Ellsworth, Charles B. Pierce. OK thriller made from true story of a hooded killer who terrorized town of Texarkana in the mid-40s. Ben Johnson's presence gives it some stature. Panavision. [R]▼

Town Went Wild, The (1944) **78m.** ** D: Ralph Murphy. Freddie Bartholomew, Jimmy Lydon, Edward Everett Horton, Tom Tully, Jill Browning, Minna Gombell. Fitfully amusing poverty-row comedy concerning two feuding families and the interesting possibility that their children were switched at birth.▼

Town Without Pity (1961) **105m.** **½ D: Gottfried Reinhardt. Kirk Douglas, E. G. Marshall, Christine Kaufmann, Robert Blake, Richard Jaeckel, Frank Sutton, Barbara Rutting. Courtroom drama of G.I.s accused of raping German girl. Decent cast, but could have been better handled. Title song, sung by Gene Pitney, was a big hit. Filmed in Germany.▼

To Wong Foo, Thanks For Everything, Julie Newmar (1995) **C-108m.** *½ D: Beeban Kidron. Patrick Swayze, Wesley Snipes, John Leguizamo, Stockard Channing, Arliss Howard, Chris Penn, Melinda Dillon, Blythe Danner, Beth Grant, RuPaul, Naomi Campbell, Quentin Crisp, Julie Newmar. Incredibly tiresome tale of three self-proclaimed drag queens heading for Hollywood whose car breaks down in a small rural town. There they befriend—and enliven—the local female population. Robin Williams appears in one scene, unbilled, and provides easily the film's funniest moments. [PG-13]▼●

Toxic Avenger, The (1985) **C-100m.** **½ D: Michael Herz, Samuel Weil. Andree Maranda, Mitchell Cohen, Jennifer Baptist, Cindy Manion, Robert Prichard, Mark Torgi, Marisa Tomei. Funny spoof about 90-pound weakling Torgi, who is transformed into a monster who only does good deeds. Not without violence and gore but still entertaining; recommended mostly for fans of the genre. Followed by two sequels. [R]▼●◗

Toxic Avenger, Part II, The (1989) **C-96m.** **½ D: Michael Herz, Lloyd Kaufman. Ron Fazio, John Altamura, Phoebe Legere, Rick Collins, Rikiya Yasuoka, Tsutomu Sekine, Lisa Gaye. Sequel offers more of the same silliness, with Melvin Junko (aka The Toxic Avenger) going after the Japanese conglomerate responsible for destroying a home for the blind in Tromaville in order to build a toxic chemical depot. Exploitation movie spoof has some very funny moments. Shot simultaneously with Part III. [R] ▼●◗

Toxic Avenger Part III, The—The Last Temptation of Toxie (1989) **C-86m.** *½ D: Michael Herz, Lloyd Kaufman. Ron Fazio, Phoebe Legere, Rick Collins, Lisa Gaye, Jessica Dublin, John Altamura. More crossed eyes, comically gruesome deaths, and cheerful vulgarity as Toxie, now an out-of-work superhero, is tempted by evil Apocalypse Inc. into becoming an ambitious yuppie, unaware that the boss (Collins) is the Devil himself. Heavily self-referential and goes on far too long; moronic rather than silly. [R]▼

Toy, The (1982) **C-99m.** *½ D: Richard Donner. Richard Pryor, Jackie Gleason, Scott Schwartz, Teresa Ganzel, Ned Beatty, Wilfrid Hyde-White, Annazette Chase. Stultifying remake of the Pierre Richard comedy LE JOUET with Pryor as penniless writer hired by zillionaire Gleason as plaything for spoiled son Schwartz. A few good gags are lost in a sea of you-can't-buy-friends-you-gotta-earn-them lectures, not to mention dubious taste for an 80's film with a black in such a demeaning part. [PG]▼●

Toys (1992) **C-121m.** *½ D: Barry Levinson. Robin Williams, Michael Gambon, Joan Cusack, Robin Wright, LL Cool J, Donald O'Connor, Arthur Malet, Jack Warden, Debi Mazar, Blake Clark, Art Metrano, Yeardley Smith. Appallingly bad movie about one man's lifelong dream—a whimsical toy factory—turned into a nightmare by his brother, a military martinet with outsized ambitions. This was director-cowriter Levinson's longtime pet project! Aside from Ferdinando Scarfiotti's ingenious production design (worth seeing at least for a few minutes) and some sweet moments at the outset, this is a heavy-handed mess. [PG-13]▼●

Toys in the Attic (1963) **90m.** **½ D: George Roy Hill. Dean Martin, Geraldine Page, Yvette Mimieux, Wendy Hiller, Gene Tierney, Larry Gates, Nan Martin. Timid adaptation (by James Poe) of Lillian Hellman play about man returning home to New Orleans with childlike bride; Page and Hiller are Martin's overprotective sisters. Panavision.▼

Toy Soldiers (1984) **C-91m.** ** D: David Fisher. Jason Miller, Cleavon Little, Rodolfo De Anda, Terri Garber, Tracy Scoggins, Willard Pugh, Mary Beth Evans, Tim Robbins. Fast-paced but forgettable adventure has a plot resembling HIGH RISK (which also starred Little): Miller and Little help kids rescue their young friends from captivity in rebellion-torn Latin American nation. [R]▼

Toy Soldiers (1991) **C-112m.** **½ D: Daniel Petrie, Jr. Sean Astin, Wil Wheaton, Keith Coogan, Andrew Divoff, Louis Gossett, Jr., Denholm Elliott, T. E. Russell, George Perez, Mason Adams, R. Lee Ermey, Tracy Brooks Swope. Prep school populated by wealthy misfit kids is taken over by Colombian terrorists—who haven't counted on the youngsters' ingenuity or determination. Mindless movie takes a seemingly idiotic premise and makes it entertaining, with likable kids and Gibraltar-like Gossett as their father-figure dean. Jerry Orbach appears unbilled. [R]▼●

Toy Story (1995) **C-80m.** *** D: John Lasseter. Voices of Tom Hanks, Tim Allen, Don Rickles, Jim Varney, Wallace Shawn, John Ratzenberger, Annie Potts, John Morris, Erik Von Detten, Laurie Metcalf, R. Lee Ermey. A boy's favorite toy, a cowboy doll named Woody, feels threatened (and rightly so) by the arrival of a new birthday present, a high-tech spaceman model advertised on TV. Clever, incredible-looking animated film, produced entirely on computer. A grownup story masquerading as a kid's film, this story of friendship, fickleness, and the need for acceptance features a colorful cast of characters led by Woody and his rival, Buzz Lightyear. The "acting" of the two leads—their facial expressions and body language—is as good as anything ever seen in a conventional animated cartoon. Presented by Disney, but produced by the innovative Pixar studio. Director Lasseter received a special Oscar for this animation milestone. Followed by a sequel. [G]▼●

Toy Story 2 (1999) **C-92m.** ***½ D: John Lasseter. Voices of Tom Hanks, Tim Allen, Joan Cusack, Kelsey Grammer, Don Rickles, Jim Varney, Wallace Shawn, John Ratzenberger, Annie Potts, Wayne Knight, John Morris, Laurie Metcalf, Estelle Harris, R. Lee Ermey, Jodi Benson. One of the few sequels to live up to—and top—the original: a clever and engaging tale of cowboy doll Woody falling into the hands of a sleazy toy dealer. Shows the relationship of toys and their owners in a canny but heartwarming way, with great gags, a heart-rending song, "When She Loved Me" by Randy Newman (sung by Sarah MacLachlan), and spectacular staging by the computer-animation folks at Pixar. [G]▼◗

Toy Tiger (1956) **C-88m.** **½ D: Jerry Hopper. Jeff Chandler, Laraine Day, Tim Hovey, Cecil Kellaway, Richard Haydn, David Janssen. Pleasant remake of MAD ABOUT MUSIC with Hovey "adopting" Chandler as his father to back up tales to school chums about a real dad.

Toy Wife, The (1938) **95m.** ** D: Richard Thorpe. Luise Rainer, Melvyn Douglas, Robert Young, Barbara O'Neil, H. B. Warner, Alma Kruger, Libby Taylor. Southern belle Rainer is pursued by Young and Douglas, can't decide which one to marry; inconsequential confection.

Traces of Red (1992) **C-105m.** *½ D: Andy Wolk. James Belushi, Lorraine Bracco, Tony Goldwyn, William Russ, Michelle Joyner, Joe Lisi. Tawdry/silly West Palm Beach melodrama with so many suspects that its red herring line has been expanded to include blush, burgundy, and mauve. Belushi and Goldwyn are cops all but tripping over the female corpses, with Bracco a rich widow in an array of unflattering fashions.

Narrated by Belushi's corpse à la SUNSET BLVD., but sorely missing anything resembling Billy Wilder's touch. [R]▼●
Trackdown (1976) **C-98m.** **½ D: Richard T. Heffron. Jim Mitchum, Karen Lamm, Anne Archer, Erik Estrada, Cathy Lee Crosby, Vince Cannon. Montana rancher Mitchum comes to L.A. in search of his runaway sister, who's fallen into seamy street life. Not much depth but lots of action. [R]
Track of the Cat (1954) **C-102m.** ** D: William Wellman. Robert Mitchum, Teresa Wright, Tab Hunter, Diana Lynn, Beulah Bondi, William Hopper, Carl (Alfalfa) Switzer. Slow-moving film of cougar hunt and family difficulties. William H. Clothier's "colorless" color photography is main asset. CinemaScope.▼
Track of the Moon Beast (1976) **C-90m.** BOMB D: Richard Ashe. Chase Cordell, Donna Leigh Drake, Gregorio Sala, Patrick Wright. Young man becomes a hideous monster because of meteor fragment lodged in his body. Good horror makeup, but lousy film.▼
Track of the Vampire SEE: **Blood Bath**
Track of Thunder (1968) **C-83m.** ** D: Joseph Kane. Tom Kirk, Ray Stricklyn, H. M. Wynant. Average melodrama of feuding small-time stock car racers. Techniscope.
Tracks (1976) **C-90m.** *½ D: Henry Jaglom. Dennis Hopper, Taryn Power, Dean Stockwell, Topo Swope, Michael Emil, Zack Norman. Hopper escorts dead Vietnam buddy across the country by train, eventually goes bonkers. We've seen it before and almost always in less muddled fashion. Emil's and Norman's characters later got their own feature, SITTING DUCKS.▼●
Track the Man Down (1955-British) **75m.** ** D: R. G. Springsteen. Kent Taylor, Petula Clark, Renee Houston, George Rose. Dog-tracking background makes this standard Scotland Yard murder hunt above par.
Track 29 (1988-British) **C-90m.** *½ D: Nicolas Roeg. Theresa Russell, Gary Oldman, Christopher Lloyd, Colleen Camp, Sandra Bernhard, Seymour Cassel, Leon Rippy, Vance Colvig. Bizarre black comedy about a love-starved woman, her nerdy husband who's obsessed with model trains, and a stranger who claims to be her long lost son! Even allowing for the usual eccentricities of director Roeg and writer Dennis Potter, this is pretty weird and not terribly entertaining. Filmed in North Carolina. [R]▼
Trader Horn (1931) **120m.** *** D: W. S. Van Dyke II. Harry Carey, Edwina Booth, Duncan Renaldo, Olive Golden (Carey), Mutia Omoolu, C. Aubrey Smith. Early talkie classic filmed largely in African jungles still retains plenty of excitement in tale of veteran native dealer Carey encountering tribal hostility. Remade in 1973.▼
Trader Horn (1973) **C-105m.** *½ D: Reza S. Badiyi. Rod Taylor, Anne Heywood, Jean Sorel, Don Knight, Ed Bernard, Stack Pierce. Laughable remake of 1931 version has Taylor famed explorer and trader of African interior, accompanied by young widow. Obvious use of stock footage and the fact that cast never leaves backlot ruin all notion of believability. [PG]
Trade Winds (1938) **90m.** *** D: Tay Garnett. Fredric March, Joan Bennett, Ralph Bellamy, Ann Sothern, Sidney Blackmer, Thomas Mitchell. Debonair detective March goes after murder-suspect Bennett; by the end of the around-the-world chase, they fall in love and solve mystery. Director Garnett filmed background footage on round-the-world cruise, but the stars never left the studio! This is the film where Bennett went from blonde to brunette—and never went back.
Trading Hearts (1988) **C-88m.** *½ D: Neil Leifer. Raul Julia, Beverly D'Angelo, Jenny Lewis, Parris Buckner. Poor baseball romance in which precocious 11-year-old Lewis tries to manipulate her mother (D'Angelo), a show-biz failure, into marriage with broken-down ballplayer Julia. Look for former N.Y.C. mayor Ed Koch in a bit as a Florida tourist; scripted by Frank DeFord, who can be seen as a bartender. [PG]▼●
Trading Mom (1994) **C-82m.** *½ D: Tia Brelis. Sissy Spacek, Anna Chlumsky, Aaron Michael Metchik, Asher Metchik, Maureen Stapleton, Merritt Yohnka, Andre the Giant. Three siblings who can't stand their mother (Spacek) cast a spell which makes her—and all memory of her—disappear, then go to the Mommy Market to find a replacement mom. A flat and lifeless tale with poor production values. Spacek has a field day as three wildly different moms, but a couple of humiliation scenes made us wince. Brelis adapted the screenplay, based on her mother's story "The Mummy Market." Filmed in 1992. [PG]▼●
Trading Places (1983) **C-116m.** **½ D: John Landis. Dan Aykroyd, Eddie Murphy, Ralph Bellamy, Don Ameche, Denholm Elliott, Jamie Lee Curtis, Paul Gleason, Kristin Holby, Jim Belushi, Alfred Drake, Al Franken, Tom Davis, Bill Cobbs. Fine cast breathes life into time-worn comedy premise (remember those Three Stooges shorts?) testing heredity vs. environment by switching a "have" (preppie Aykroyd) and a "have-not" (street hustler Murphy). Murphy, in his second film, is a comic powerhouse, and makes up for director Landis' indulgences—like a subplot involving a horny gorilla. [R]▼●
Traffic (1972-French) **C-89m.** ** D: Jacques Tati. Jacques Tati, Maria Kimberly, Marcel Fraval, H. Bostel, Tony Kneppers. Initially enjoyable outing with M. Hulot (Tati) trying to transport car from France

to Dutch auto show bogs down in aimless side trips. Bright spots overwhelmed by general lethargy. [PG]▼

Tragedy of a Ridiculous Man (1981-Italian) **C-116m.** ** D: Bernardo Bertolucci. Ugo Tognazzi, Anouk Aimée, Laura Morante, Victor Cavallo, Ricardo Tognazzi. Disappointing drama about cheese manufacturer Tognazzi coping with son's alleged kidnapping by political terrorists. Bertolucci seems to be commenting on modern social and familial stresses and upheavals, but his message is incredibly muddled. [PG]▼

Trail of the Lonesome Pine, The (1936) **C-99m.** *** D: Henry Hathaway. Sylvia Sidney, Henry Fonda, Fred MacMurray, Fred Stone, Fuzzy Knight, Beulah Bondi, Spanky McFarland, Nigel Bruce. Classic story of feuding families and changes that come about when railroad is built on their land. Still strong today, with fine performances, and Fuzzy Knight's rendition of "Melody from the Sky." First outdoor film in full Technicolor. Previously filmed in 1915.▼

Trail of the Pink Panther (1982) **C-97m.** ** D: Blake Edwards. Peter Sellers, David Niven, Herbert Lom, Richard Mulligan, Joanna Lumley, Robert Wagner, Capucine, Robert Loggia, Harvey Korman, Burt Kwouk, Graham Stark, Peter Arne. Attempt to fashion a new Pink Panther film, despite the death of series star Sellers, using previously unseen footage and new linking material. It almost works—until the seams begin to show, as reporter Lumley seeks out people who knew Clouseau for a TV story. Lom *does* have a sidesplitting scene in which he tries to eulogize his long-time nemesis—and can't stop laughing. Filmed at the same time as subsequent CURSE OF THE PINK PANTHER. Panavision. [PG]▼●

Trail of the Vigilantes (1940) **78m.** **½ D: Allan Dwan. Franchot Tone, Warren William, Broderick Crawford, Peggy Moran, Andy Devine, Mischa Auer, Porter Hall. Tone is Eastern law enforcer out West to hunt down outlaw gang; lively comedy-Western.

Trail Street (1947) **84m.** **½ D: Ray Enright. Randolph Scott, Anne Jeffreys, Robert Ryan, George "Gabby" Hayes, Madge Meredith, Steve Brodie. Fast-paced Western in which Bat Masterson (Scott) takes on murderers, robbers, cattle rustlers, and other ornery critters in the town of Liberal, Kansas.▼

Train, The (1964) **133m.** **** D: John Frankenheimer. Burt Lancaster, Paul Scofield, Jeanne Moreau, Michel Simon, Suzanne Flon, Wolfgang Preiss, Albert Remy. Gripping WW2 actioner of French Resistance trying to waylay train carting French art treasures to Germany. High-powered excitement all the way.▼●◗

Train of Life (1998-French-Belgian-Dutch) **C-103m.** *** D: Radu Mihaileanu. Lionel Abelanski, Rufus, Clement Harari, Marie-Jose Nat, Agathe de la Fontaine. Energetic fable set in 1941, in which the inhabitants of a small Central European Jewish village, all too aware of their imminent demise, plot to foil the Nazis by staging their own deportation to Russia. Comedic and dramatic elements occasionally clash, and some of the subplots are inconsequential, but it still works. Released in the U.S. after LIFE IS BEAUTIFUL and JAKOB THE LIAR, but this was actually the first to go into production. Widescreen. [R]▼

Train Robbers, The (1973) **C-92m.** **½ D: Burt Kennedy. John Wayne, Ann-Margret, Rod Taylor, Ben Johnson, Christopher George, Ricardo Montalban, Bobby Vinton, Jerry Gatlin. Interesting little chamber-Western, reminiscent of Kennedy's early Randolph Scott scripts. Outlaw's widow hires Wayne and his pals to locate buried gold so she can return it and clear family name. Low-key film emphasizes character instead of action; relaxed performances, twist ending. Panavision. [PG] ▼●

Trainspotting (1996-British) **C-94m.** *** D: Danny Boyle. Ewan McGregor, Ewen Bremner, Jonny Lee Miller, Kevin McKidd, Robert Carlyle, Kelly Macdonald. Fascinating look at the drug underground in Edinburgh, Scotland, as seen through the eyes of McGregor, who's part of that world but still somehow able to distance himself from his friends' bizarre behavior. Alternately hilarious and harrowing, with some startling surrealistic moments, this was an enormous hit in the U.K. but suffered some backlash in the U.S. for its supposed condoning of drugs—which is simply not true. Adapted by John Hodge from Irvine Welsh's novel. [R]▼●◗

Traitors, The (1963-British) **71m.** **½ D: Robert Tronson. Patrick Allen, James Maxwell, Zena Walker, Harold Goodwin, Sean Lynch. Fair spy meller of U.S. and British agent assigned to catch source of security leak in NATO.

Traitor's Gate (1964-British) **80m.** **½ D: Freddie Francis. Gary Raymond, Albert Lieven, Margot Trooger, Klaus Kinski, Catherina (Catherine) Von Schell. Two brothers are involved at sea in plot to steal crown jewels. Based on Edgar Wallace novel, film has fair acting, good direction.

Tramplers, The (1966-Italian) **C-105m.** ** D: Albert Band. Joseph Cotten, Gordon Scott, James Mitchum, Ilaria Occhini, Franco Nero. Foreign-made Western set in post-Civil War South, with Cotten the domineering father; all just an excuse for gun-play. Aka SHOWDOWN.▼

Tramp, Tramp, Tramp (1926) **62m.** **½ D: Harry Edwards. Harry Langdon, Joan Crawford, Edwards Davis, Carlton Griffin, Alec B. Francis, Brooks Benedict, Tom Murray. Langdon made his feature debut in this tale of a hobo who enters a cross-country walking race to raise money for his father and impress the pretty daughter (Crawford) of a shoe manufacturer. Frank Capra was one of the writers of this cute comedy featuring some impressive stunt sequences.▼

Tramp, Tramp, Tramp (1942) **70m.** *½ D: Charles Barton. Jackie Gleason, Florence Rice, Jack Durant, Bruce Bennett. Meager comedy as Gleason and Durant, 4-F rejects, protect the homefront, becoming involved in murder caper.

Trancers (1985) **C-76m.** *** D: Charles Band. Tim Thomerson, Helen Hunt, Art La Fleur, Biff Manard, Anne Seymour, Richard Herd, Richard Erdman. Comedian Thomerson is cleverly cast as a low-budget version of Harrison Ford from BLADE RUNNER, sent back in time 300 years to 1985 L. A. to inhabit the body of one of his ancestors and change history to prevent a totalitarian state from coming into power. Sci-fi satire is most amusing and visually arresting. Also known as FUTURE COP. Followed by a slew of sequels. [PG-13] ▼●◗

Trancers II (1991) **C-86m.** ** D: Charles Band. Tim Thomerson, Helen Hunt, Megan Ward, Biff Manard, Richard Lynch, Martine Beswicke, Jeffrey Combs, Alyson Croft, Telma Hopkins, Art La Fleur, Barbara Crampton. A cop from the future whose mind wound up in our time in the first film finds that his job isn't through as more zombie-like Trancers are on the loose. What's more, he has to contend with two wives, one from the present, one from the future. Badly structured, but scrupulously faithful to a superior original. Too cheap for its ambitions. [R]▼●

Trancers III (1992) **C-83m.** ** D: C. Courtney Joyner. Tim Thomerson, Melanie Smith, Andrew Robinson, Tony Pierce, Dawn Ann Billings, Helen Hunt, Megan Ward, Stephen Macht, Telma Hopkins, R. A. Mahailoff. Time travel gets a workout here: taken from 1992 to 2352, Jack Deth (Thomerson) is then sent to 2005 to destroy those pesky (and obscurely defined) Trancers at their source. The series continues to be watchable, and Robinson provides a swell villain, but the end is a mess. [R]▼●

Transatlantic Merry-Go-Round (1934) **92m.** ** D: Ben Stoloff. Jack Benny, Nancy Carroll, Gene Raymond, Sidney Blackmer, Patsy Kelly, Mitzi Green, Boswell Sisters. Whodunit set against musical story of ocean-going radio troupe led by Benny. Just fair, with some odd production numbers, and a plot resolution that's for the birds.▼

Transatlantic Tunnel (1935-British) **70m.** **½ D: Maurice Elvey. Richard Dix, Leslie Banks, Madge Evans, Helen Vinson, C. Aubrey Smith, George Arliss, Walter Huston. Disappointing story about building of transatlantic tunnel bogs down in two-dimensional character conflicts. Futuristic sets are main distinction. Originally 94m. and titled THE TUNNEL.▼

Transformers, The (1986) **C-86m.** BOMB D: Nelson Shin. Voices of Orson Welles, Robert Stack, Leonard Nimoy, Eric Idle, Judd Nelson, Lionel Stander. Obnoxious animated feature about the title good guys, who defend the universe against an evil planet (which has a voice of its own . . . provided by Orson Welles). That deafening rock score certainly doesn't help. Little more than a feature-length toy commercial. [PG]▼●

Transmutations SEE: **Underworld**

Transylvania 6-5000 (1985) **C-94m.** BOMB D: Rudy DeLuca. Jeff Goldblum, Joseph Bologna, Ed Begley, Jr., Carol Kane, Jeffrey Jones, John Byner, Geena Davis, Michael Richards, Norman Fell, Teresa Ganzel. Tediously unfunny horror-movie spoof that wastes a lot of talent. Shot in Yugoslavia, and should have stayed there. [PG]▼●

Trap, The (1947) **68m.** *½ D: Howard Bretherton. Sidney Toler, Mantan Moreland, Victor Sen Yung, Tanis Chandler, Larry Blake, Kirk Alyn, Rita Quigley, Anne Nagel. Toler's swan song as Charlie Chan, about a series of murders striking actors at Malibu beach.▼

Trap, The (1959) **C-84m.** **½ D: Norman Panama. Richard Widmark, Lee J. Cobb, Tina Louise, Earl Holliman, Carl Benton Reid, Lorne Greene. Turgid drama set in Southwest desert town, with gangsters on the lam intimidating the few townspeople.▼

Trap, The (1966-British) **C-106m.** *** D: Sidney Hayers. Rita Tushingham, Oliver Reed, Rex Sevenoaks, Barbara Chilcott, Linda Goranson. Fur trapper Reed, having missed annual wife auction after three winters in the snow, settles for orphaned mute Rita. Vivid 1890s tale, well photographed by Robert Krasker. Panavision.▼

Trapeze (1956) **C-105m.** *** D: Carol Reed. Burt Lancaster, Tony Curtis, Gina Lollobrigida, Katy Jurado, Thomas Gomez, Johnny Puleo. Moody love triangle with a European circus background; aerialist Lancaster and Curtis vie in the air and on the ground for Gina's attention. Nice aerial stuntwork by various big top professionals. CinemaScope. ▼●

Trapped (1949) **78m.** **½ D: Richard Fleischer. Lloyd Bridges, Barbara Payton, John Hoyt, James Todd, Russ Conway, Robert Karnes. The FBI's hot on the trail of a gang of counterfeiters in this so-so thriller, done in the semi-documentary style typical of that era.▼

Trapped by Boston Blackie (1948) **67m.** **½ D: Seymour Friedman. Chester Morris, June Vincent, Richard Lane, Patricia White (Barry), Edward Norris, George E.

Stone, Frank Sully. Blackie springs into action to clear himself when an expensive pearl necklace disappears from a party for which he was a security guard.

Trapped in Paradise (1994) **C-112m.** ** D: George Gallo. Nicolas Cage, Jon Lovitz, Dana Carvey, John Ashton, Mädchen Amick, Donald Moffat, Richard Jenkins, Florence Stanley, Angela Paton, Vic Manni, Frank Pesce, Sean McCann, Richard B. Shull. Two larcenous siblings just sprung from jail trick their ambivalent brother into joining them on a trip to the small town of Paradise, Pennsylvania, where there's a bank just waiting to be robbed. Trouble is, the townspeople are so darned nice it seems wrong to take advantage of them . . . especially at Christmastime. Promising story idea is flattened out by vaguely drawn characters and a decided lack of energy. Panavision. [PG-13]▼●

Trauma (1962) **92m.** ** D: Robert Malcolm Young. John Conte, Lynn Bari, Lorrie Richards, David Garner, Warren Kemmerling. Heavy-handed chiller about Richards' attempt to recover lost memory of past horrors in spooky mansion. ▼

Trauma (1993-U.S.-Italian) **C-86m.** **½ D: Dario Argento. Christopher Rydell, Asia Argento, Laura Johnson, James Russo, Brad Dourif, Frederic Forrest, Piper Laurie. Corny theatrics and campy bloodletting effectively blend in this shocker about a traumatized teen (Asia Argento, the director's daughter) and a hooded killer who is sawing off the heads of his victims. Not a typical Argento gorefest, but the filmmaker's fans shouldn't be disappointed. Unrated video version runs 106m. Technovision. [R] ▼●

Traveling Executioner, The (1970) **C-95m.** *½ D: Jack Smight. Stacy Keach, Marianna Hill, Bud Cort, Graham Jarvis, James J. Sloyan. Story of a man's love for an electric chair (spiritual) and love for a woman prisoner (sexual) may or may not be intended for laughs; either way, film is dull and the usually fine Keach gives hammy performance. Panavision. [R]

Traveling Saleslady (1935) **63m.** **½ D: Ray Enright. Joan Blondell, Glenda Farrell, William Gargan, Hugh Herbert, Grant Mitchell. Snappy Warner Bros. programmer, with Blondell helping to put over inventor Herbert's booze-flavored toothpaste—in order to teach her stubborn father (a rival toothpaste manufacturer) a lesson.

Traveling Saleswoman (1950) **75m.** ** D: Charles F. Riesner. Joan Davis, Andy Devine, Adele Jergens, Chief Thundercloud. Davis and Devine mug it up as soap saleswoman and fiancé in stale Western comedy.

Traveller (1997) **C-101m.** **½ D: Jack N. Green. Bill Paxton, Mark Wahlberg, Julianna Margulies, James Gammon, Luke Askew, Nikki Deloach, Danielle Wiener, Michael Shaner, Jo Ann Pflug. Laid-back look at a band of Irish-American gypsy con artists known as "travellers." Paxton takes on the son of an ousted "family" member as his protégé, teaching him various petty scams, and finds himself falling for one of his marks, bartender Margulies. Amiable and well acted, though it doesn't really add up to much. Paxton also coproduced. Directing debut for Clint Eastwood's longtime cinematographer Green. [R]▼●

Travelling North (1987-Australian) **C-98m.** **½ D: Carl Schultz. Leo McKern, Julia Blake, Henri Szeps, Graham Kennedy, Michele Fawdon, Diane Craig. Irascible retiree falls in love with a divorcee, and they move to an idyllic retirement home in North Queensland, Australia . . . but their life together is clouded almost immediately when he learns he has a serious heart condition. Fine performances highlight this simple, straightforward adaptation of David Williamson's play—which, ultimately, may be a bit *too* simple and straightforward. [PG-13]▼

Travels With Anita SEE: **Lovers and Liars**

Travels With My Aunt (1972) **C-109m.** **½ D: George Cukor. Maggie Smith, Alec McCowen, Lou Gossett, Robert Stephens, Cindy Williams. Stylish adaptation of Graham Greene book about strait-laced McCowen being swept into crazy world of his aunt (Smith) who takes him all over Europe on what turns out to be shady scheme. Deliberately paced film never really gets going, leaves viewer in midair like final tossed coin. Anthony Powell earned an Oscar for his costumes. Panavision. [PG]▼●

T. R. Baskin (1971) **C-90m.** **½ D: Herbert Ross. Candice Bergen, Peter Boyle, James Caan, Marcia Rodd, Erin O'Reilly, Howard Platt. Beautiful young small-town girl tries to make it in Chicago, finds problems in the big city. Wildly uneven comedy-drama has a few nice scenes, good acting by Caan in small role. Written and produced by Peter Hyams. [PG]

Treasure Island (1934) **105m.** ***½ D: Victor Fleming. Wallace Beery, Jackie Cooper, Lewis Stone, Lionel Barrymore, Otto Kruger, Nigel Bruce, Douglass Dumbrille. Stirring adaptation of Robert Louis Stevenson pirate yarn of 18th-century England and journey to isle of hidden bounty; Beery is a boisterous Long John Silver in fine film with top production values. Only flaw is a stiff Cooper as Jim Hawkins. Also shown in computer-colored version.▼

Treasure Island (1950) **C-96m.** ***½ D: Byron Haskin. Bobby Driscoll, Robert Newton, Basil Sydney, Walter Fitzgerald, Denis O'Dea, Ralph Truman, Finlay Currie. Vivid Disney version of Robert Louis Stevenson's classic, filmed in England, with

Driscoll a fine Jim Hawkins and Newton *the* definitive Long John Silver. Changes the novel's original ending, but who's quibbling? ''Objectionable'' violence was deleted from 1975 reissue version but restored in 1992 tape/laser reissue.▼●

Treasure Island (1972-British) **C-94m.** ** D: John Hough. Orson Welles, Kim Burfield, Walter Slezak, Lionel Stander. Weak retelling of classic tale finds very hammy Welles (who also coscripted) in the role of Long John Silver. [G]▼

Treasure Island (1990) **C-131m. TVM** D: Fraser Heston. Charlton Heston, Christian Bale, Julian Glover, Richard Johnson, Oliver Reed, Christopher Lee, Clive Wood, Nicholas Amer, Michael Halsey, Peter Postlethwaite. Exciting, realistic, and beautifully photographed version of classic pirate adventure remains faithful in spirit to Robert Louis Stevenson's masterwork. Heston is effectively cast against type as Long John Silver, with Bale as sturdy young Jim Hawkins. Reed and Lee have brief but vivid turns as the doomed Capt. Billy Bones and the hideous Blind Pew. Filmed aboard the H.M.S. *Bounty* (from the 1962 MUTINY ON THE BOUNTY), with a seaworthy score by Paddy Maloney and The Chieftains. Directorial debut for Heston's son who also produced and scripted. Made for cable. Above average.▼●

Treasure of Fear SEE: **Scared Stiff** (1945)

Treasure of Jamaica Reef, The (1974) **C-96m.** *½ D: Virginia Stone. Stephen Boyd, Chuck Woolery, Roosevelt Grier, David Ladd, Cheryl Stoppelmoor (Ladd). A search for gold buried deep in the Caribbean. Of interest only for the presence of Stoppelmoor/Ladd pre-*Charlie's Angels.* Originally titled EVIL IN THE DEEP. Todd-AO 35. [PG]▼

Treasure of Lost Canyon, The (1952) **C-82m.** ** D: Ted Tetzlaff. William Powell, Julia (Julie) Adams, Rosemary DeCamp, Charles Drake, Tommy Ivo. Mild Western, uplifted by Powell as old prospector. Youth uncovers treasure which causes unhappiness to all. From a Robert Louis Stevenson story.

Treasure of Matecumbe (1976) **C-117m.** **½ D: Vincent McEveety. Robert Foxworth, Joan Hackett, Peter Ustinov, Vic Morrow, Jane Wyatt, Johnny Doran, Billy ''Pop'' Attmore. Two boys with treasure map are aided in their quest by Foxworth, Hackett, and Ustinov . . . and pursued by bad-guy Morrow. Ustinov adds life to Disney film, but the ''quest'' seems endless. Filmed in the Florida Keys. [G]▼

Treasure of Monte Cristo (1949) **79m.** ** D: William Berke. Glenn Langan, Adele Jergens, Steve Brodie, Robert Jordan, Michael Whelan, Sid Melton. Jergens marries seaman Langan, a descendant of the Count of Monte Cristo, for his inheritance, then falls in love with him. Adequate programmer.

Treasure of Monte Cristo, The (1960-British) **C-95m.** ** D: Robert S. Baker, Monty Berman. Rory Calhoun, Patricia Bredin, Peter Arne, Gianna Maria Canale. Uninspired variation on Dumas tale, with Calhoun aiding Bredin unearth buried treasure: slow-moving yarn. Dyaliscope.

Treasure of Pancho Villa, The (1955) **C-96m.** *½ D: George Sherman. Rory Calhoun, Shelley Winters, Gilbert Roland, Joseph Calleia. Good cast wasted in plodding account of Calhoun and Roland's search for gold. SuperScope.▼

Treasure of Ruby Hills (1955) **71m.** *½ D: Frank McDonald. Zachary Scott, Carole Matthews, Barton MacLane, Dick Foran, Lola Albright. Uninspired Western of land-grabbing ranchers.

Treasure of San Gennaro, The (1966-Italian-German-French) **C-102m.** ** D: Dino Risi. Nino Manfredi, Senta Berger, Harry Guardino, Claudine Auger, Toto, Mario Adorf. American Guardino and girlfriend Berger plan to rob the treasure of Naples' patron saint, San Gennaro, in typical caper film occasionally redeemed by good comic bits. Poorly dubbed. Filmed in Panoramica.

Treasure of Silver Lake, The (1965-German) **C-88m.** ** D: Harald Reinl. Lex Barker, Gotz George, Pierre Brice, Herbert Lom, Karin Dor, Marianne Hoppe. Dubbed dialogue almost ruins average Western based on Karl May novels with familiar characters Shatterhand and Winnetou. Ultrascope.▼

Treasure of Tayopa (1974) **C-90m.** BOMB D: Bob Cawley. Gilbert Roland, Rena Winters, Bob Corrigan, Phil Trapani, Frank Hernandez, Andrew Farnsworth. Low-grade modern Western about an expedition to find a centuries-lost treasure trove in the Mexican hills. Psycho Trapani turns it into a senseless bloodbath. Only professional connected with the film, Roland, appears in the prologue and epilogue to give credence to the Tayopa legend. [PG]

Treasure of the Amazon, The (1985-Mexican) **C-104m.** ** D: Rene Cardona, Jr. Stuart Whitman, Emilio Fernandez, Donald Pleasence, Bradford Dillman, Ann Sidney, John Ireland, Sonia Infante. Silly adventure film has Whitman leading South American expedition to recover treasure trove of diamonds. Mucho violence. ▼

Treasure of the Four Crowns (1983-Spanish) **C-97m.** BOMB D: Ferdinando Baldi. Tony Anthony, Ana Obregon, Gene Quintano, Francisco Rabal, Jerry Lazarus. Fortune hunters seek ancient prize. It's no accident that the title of this 3-D potboiler sounds suspiciously like RAIDERS OF THE LOST ARK. From the same folks who brought you COMIN AT YA! Widescreen. [PG]▼

Treasure of the Golden Condor (1953) **C-93m.** **½ D: Delmer Daves. Cornel Wilde, Constance Smith, Fay Wray, Anne Bancroft, Leo G. Carroll, Bobby (Robert) Blake. Predictable costumer set in 18th-century Latin America, with noble-born Wilde out to claim his fortune. Remake of SON OF FURY.▼

Treasure of the Sierra Madre, The (1948) **124m.** **** D: John Huston. Humphrey Bogart, Walter Huston, Tim Holt, Bruce Bennett, Barton MacLane, Alfonso Bedoya. Excellent adaptation of B. Traven's tale of gold, greed, and human nature at its worst, with Bogart, Huston, and Holt as unlikely trio of prospectors. John Huston won Oscars for Best Direction and Screenplay, and his father Walter won as Best Supporting Actor. That's John as an American tourist near the beginning, and young Robert Blake selling lottery tickets. Also shown in computer-colored version.▼●

Tree Grows in Brooklyn, A (1945) **128m.** **** D: Elia Kazan. Dorothy McGuire, Joan Blondell, James Dunn, Lloyd Nolan, Peggy Ann Garner, Ted Donaldson, James Gleason, Ruth Nelson, John Alexander. Splendid, sensitive film from Betty Smith's novel about a bright young girl trying to rise above the hardships of her tenement life in turn of the century Brooklyn, New York. Perfect in every detail. Dunn won an Oscar as the father, an incurable pipe dreamer; Garner received a special Academy Award for her performance. Screenplay by Tess Slesinger and Frank Davis. An impressive Hollywood directorial debut by Kazan. Remade for TV in 1974 with Cliff Robertson and Diane Baker.▼●

Tree of Hands SEE: **Innocent Victim**

Tree of Wooden Clogs, The (1978-Italian) **C-185m.** **** D: Ermanno Olmi. Luigi Ornaghi, Francesca Moriggi, Omar Brignoli, Antonio Ferrari. A year in the life of a community of peasants in Northern Italy, just before the turn of the century. Simple, quietly beautiful epic; a work of art.▼●

Trees Lounge (1996) **C-94m.** *** D: Steve Buscemi. Steve Buscemi, Mark Boone Junior, Chloe Sevigny, Michael Buscemi, Anthony LaPaglia, Elizabeth Bracco, Danny Baldwin, Carol Kane, Bronson Dudley, Debi Mazar, Michael Imperioli, Samuel L. Jackson, Seymour Cassel, Mimi Rogers, Steve Randazzo, Rockets Redglare. Colorful, credible slice-of-life set in and around a neighborhood bar in Long Island, N.Y., where a perpetual screw-up (Buscemi) interacts with various family members and fellow barflies. Impressive writing and directing debut for character actor Buscemi, who has a good eye and ear and creates a rich gallery of characters. [R]▼●◗

Trekkies (1999) **C-87m.** *** D: Roger Nygard. Former *Star Trek: The Next Generation* star Denise Crosby conducts this slightly condescending documentary examining the *Trek* fan phenomenon. Many of the actors associated with *Trek* are interviewed, as well as many die-hard Trekkies of varying degrees of obsession. While some are clearly 'round the bend in their fixation on the show, most are shown to be very bright, and live happy, productive lives, even if pointed ears and Klingons figure prominently in them. [PG]▼●◗

Tremors (1990) **C-96m.** *** D: Ron Underwood. Kevin Bacon, Fred Ward, Finn Carter, Michael Gross, Reba McEntire, Bobby Jacoby, Charlotte Stewart, Tony Genaros, Victor Wong. Sharp, funny, and fast-paced, this is an effective updating of 1950s monster-movie themes. Bacon and Ward, amiable handymen, lead a misfit group in a desert valley battling against giant wormlike predators that burrow through the sand. Cast is good, the music appropriate, and special effects outstanding. A small winner all around. Followed by direct-to-video sequel TREMORS II: AFTERSHOCKS. [PG-13] ▼●◗

Trenchcoat (1983) **C-91m.** ** D: Michael Tuchner. Margot Kidder, Robert Hays, Daniel Faraldo, Gila von Weitershausen, David Suchet, Ronald Lacey. Another attempt by the Disney studio to change image finds amateur mystery writer Kidder on vacation in Malta, suddenly involved in real murder and international intrigue with undercover agent Hays. Forced mystery-comedy is reminiscent of the company's juvenile outings of the '50s and '60s, but has no Shaggy Dog to redeem it. [PG]▼

Trent's Last Case (1952-British) **90m.** **½ D: Herbert Wilcox. Michael Wilding, Margaret Lockwood, Orson Welles, Hugh McDermott. Superior cast in lukewarm tale of the investigation of businessman's death. Previously filmed (by Howard Hawks) in 1929.

Trespass (1992) **C-101m.** *** D: Walter Hill. Bill Paxton, Ice T, William Sadler, Ice Cube, Art Evans, De'Voreaux White, Bruce A. Young, Glenn Plummer, Stoney Jackson, John Toles-Bey. Two white firemen get wind that ancient treasure is buried in a slummy building, little knowing that the structure they've invaded is headquarters for a band of very tough drug pushers. Fast, furious, culturally disreputable entertainment filmed in potent cat-and-mouse style by director Hill—his most entertaining movie in years. Executive produced and written by Bob Gale and Robert Zemeckis. [R]▼●◗

Trespasses (1987) **C-100m.** BOMB D: Loren Bivens, Adam Roarke. Robert Kuhn, Van Brooks, Mary Pillot, Adam Roarke, Lou Diamond Phillips, Ben Johnson. A sleep-inducing waste, with cattleman Kuhn and rape victim Pillot becoming involved;

her spineless husband and the pair of rapists are the heavies. Phillips coauthored this. Shot in 1983. [R]▼

Trial (1955) **105m.** *** D: Mark Robson. Glenn Ford, Dorothy McGuire, John Hodiak, Arthur Kennedy, Katy Jurado, Rafael Campos. Intelligent filming of Don Mankiewicz novel, scripted by the author. Courtroomer involves Mexican boy accused of murder, but actually tied in with pro- vs. anti-Communist politics.

Trial, The (1962-French-Italian-German) **118m.** ***½ D: Orson Welles. Anthony Perkins, Jeanne Moreau, Romy Schneider, Elsa Martinelli, Orson Welles, Akim Tamiroff. Gripping, if a bit confusing, adaptation of Kafka novel of man in nameless country arrested for crime that is never explained to him. Not for all tastes.▼●◗

Trial and Error (1962-British) SEE: **Dock Brief, The**

Trial and Error (1997) **C-98m.** *** D: Jonathan Lynn. Michael Richards, Jeff Daniels, Charlize Theron, Rip Torn, Alexandra Wentworth, Austin Pendleton, Lawrence Pressman, Max Casella. When button-down lawyer Daniels can't appear in court (because of a bachelor party hangover), his best friend, wannabe actor Richards, tries to help by taking his place . . . but when the case is ordered to proceed, Richards has to keep up the ruse. Smart, funny farce with terrific performances by the two leads and laugh-out-loud situations; Theron is adorable as the young woman who catches Daniels' eye—even though he's about to marry the boss's daughter. Super 35. [PG-13]▼●◗

Trial by Combat SEE: **Dirty Knight's Work**

Trial by Jury (1994) **C-92m.** **½ D: Heywood Gould. Joanne Whalley-Kilmer, Armand Assante, Gabriel Byrne, William Hurt, Kathleen Quinlan, Margaret Whitton, Ed Lauter, Richard Portnow, Lisa Arrindell Anderson, Jack Gwaltney, Graham Jarvis, William R. Moses, Stuart Whitman. Juror Whalley is terrorized by defendant in a murder case; meanwhile, D.A. Byrne tries to size up the jurors who'll be deciding the fate of this mobster. Improbable but still watchable, with an unusual part for Hurt as a strong-arm man. David Cronenberg appears briefly as a director. Similar premise later utilized in THE JUROR. [R] ▼●

Trial of Billy Jack, The (1974) **C-175m.** BOMB D: Frank Laughlin. Tom Laughlin, Delores Taylor, Victor Izay, Teresa Laughlin, William Wellman, Jr., Sacheen Littlefeather. Further adventures of Mr. Peace-through-Violence prove that Laughlin is the only actor intense enough to risk a hernia from reading lines. Laughable until final, nauseating massacre scene that renders film's constant yammering about "peace" ludicrous. Panavision. [PG]▼

Trial of Lee Harvey Oswald, The (1977) **C-210m. TVM** D: David Greene. Ben Gazzara, Lorne Greene, John Pleshette, Mo Malone, Frances Lee McCain, Lawrence Pressman. Intriguing courtroom drama from the "what if?" school of story-telling. Pleshette is quite good as Oswald, who may or may not have been involved in any of the Kennedy assassination conspiracy theories (some quite bizarre), which are explored here. Originally shown in two parts. Released on video at 192m. Above average.▼

Trials of Oscar Wilde, The (1960-British) **C-123m.** *** D: Ken Hughes. Peter Finch, Yvonne Mitchell, John Fraser, Lionel Jeffries, Nigel Patrick, James Mason. Fascinating, well-acted chronicle of Oscar Wilde's libel suit against the Marquis of Queensberry and the tragic turn his life takes because of it. Finch is superb as the once brilliant wit; stylish widescreen photography by Ted Moore. Released at the same time as OSCAR WILDE with Robert Morley. Super Technirama 70.▼

Tribute (1980-Canadian) **C-121m.** ** D: Bob Clark. Jack Lemmon, Robby Benson, Lee Remick, Colleen Dewhurst, John Marley, Kim Cattrall, Gale Garnett. Mawkish adaptation of Bernard Slade's play about a life-of-the-party type who's dying of cancer and wants to work out a relationship with his estranged son. Badly directed, with sledgehammer approach to sentiment. Worked much better on stage (where Lemmon created the role). Scripted by Slade. [PG]▼●

Tribute to a Bad Man (1956) **C-95m.** *** D: Robert Wise. James Cagney, Don Dubbins, Stephen McNally, Irene Papas, Vic Morrow, Royal Dano, Lee Van Cleef. Cagney is the whole show in this Western about a resourceful, ruthless land baron using any means possible to retain his vast possessions. CinemaScope.▼

Trick (1999) **C-89m.** **½ D: Jim Fall. Christian Campbell, John Paul Pitoc, Tori Spelling, Steve Hayes, Clinton Leupp, Brad Beyer, Lorri Bagley. Shy, aspiring Broadway composer meets the go-go boy of his dreams one night but can't find any place for them to be alone together in all of Manhattan. Lightweight gay comedy-romance set in N.Y.C.'s West Village is sweet but short on plot. Campbell (brother of Neve) is an appealing, boyish lead. [R]▼◗

Trick Baby (1973) **C-89m.** ** D: Larry Yust. Kiel Martin, Mel Stewart, Dallas Edwards Hayes, Beverly Ballard. Con-man who passes for white uses trickery to cash in on society. Usual black exploitation film. Retitled DOUBLE CON. [R]

Trick or Treat (1986) **C-97m.** ** D: Charles Martin Smith. Marc Price, Tony Fields, Lisa Orgolini, Doug Savant, Gene Simmons, Ozzy Osbourne. Hey kids, rock 'n' roll really *is* the Devil's music! Fan of recently killed rocker conjures the dead star by playing his unreleased last album backward—but finds his hero is evil and bent on the world's destruction. Clever and well made, but story becomes terribly trite. Debuting director Smith has a cameo as a high school teacher. [R]▼

Trick or Treats (1982) **C-91m.** BOMB D: Gary Graver. Jackelyn Giroux, David Carradine, Carrie Snodgress, Steve Railsback, Peter Jason, Paul Bartel. Giroux is too old to be convincing as a terrorized babysitter in this cheap horror spoof. Orson Welles is credited as consultant; Graver is better known as the cameraman Welles relied upon in his later film projects. [R]▼

Trigger Effect, The (1996) **C-98m.** **½ D: David Koepp. Kyle MacLachlan, Elisabeth Shue, Dermot Mulroney, Richard T. Jones, Bill Smitrovich, Michael Rooker. Maddeningly uneven apocalyptic thriller about married suburbanites and their plight in the wake of a gigantic, never-ending blackout. Intended as an examination of contemporary insensitivity and alienation, and how society might unravel in the wake of such a catastrophe, but falls apart after a solid start. The finale is especially incongruous. Feature directorial debut for screenwriter Koepp. [R]▼●◗

Trigger Happy SEE: **Mad Dog Time**

Trilogy of Terror (1975) **C-78m. TVM** D: Dan Curtis. Karen Black, Robert Burton, John Karlen, George Gaynes, James Storm, Gregory Harrison, Kathryn Reynolds. Karen plays four tormented women in three exercises in the bizarre by writer Richard Matheson. Best: the third, "Prey," has devil doll hounding her almost to death. This segment alone is worth your time. Followed by a sequel two decades later. Above average.▼◗

Trinity Is STILL My Name! (1972-Italian) **C-117m.** **½ D: E. B. Clucher (Enzo Barboni). Terence Hill, Bud Spencer, Harry Carey, Jr., Jessica Dublin, Yanti Somer. Sequel to THEY CALL ME TRINITY is even funnier, as Trinity and Bambino mosey their way through a clutch of archetypal Western situations with their usual aplomb; scene in a chic French restaurant is a hoot. Later cut to 101m.; original Italian running time 124m. Aka ALL THE WAY TRINITY. Techniscope. [G]▼●◗

Trinity Rides Again SEE: **Boot Hill**

Trinity: Tracking For Trouble SEE: **Knock Out Cop, The**

Trio (1950-British) **88m.** *** D: Ken Annakin, Harold French. James Hayter, Kathleen Harrison, Anne Crawford, Nigel Patrick, Jean Simmons, Michael Rennie. Following the success of QUARTET, three more diverting Somerset Maugham stories, "The Verger," "Mr. Knowall," and "Sanatorium." All beautifully acted.▼

Trip, The (1967) **C-85m.** ** D: Roger Corman. Peter Fonda, Susan Strasberg, Bruce Dern, Dennis Hopper, Salli Sachse, Dick Miller, Luana Anders, Michael Nader, Peter Bogdanovich. TV commercial director Fonda takes his first LSD trip. Definitely a relic of its era, with a screenplay by Jack Nicholson.▼●

Triple Cross (1966-French-British) **C-126m.** ** D: Terence Young. Christopher Plummer, Yul Brynner, Romy Schneider, Trevor Howard, Gert Frobe, Claudine Auger. Adequate WW2 spy yarn features Plummer as real-life British safecracker Eddie Chapman, who works both sides of the fence. A bit too long.▼●

Triple Deception (1956-British) **C-85m.** ** D: Guy Green. Michael Craig, Julia Arnall, Brenda De Banzie, Barbara Bates, David Kosoff, Geoffrey Keen, Gerard Oury, Anton Diffring, Eric Pohlmann. Adequate thriller in which sailor Craig is brought in by British and French authorities to impersonate his double, a member of a gang of counterfeiters who's just been killed in an auto accident. Original British title: HOUSE OF SECRETS. VistaVision. ▼

Triple Echo (1973-British) **C-90m.** *** D: Michael Apted. Glenda Jackson, Oliver Reed, Brian Deacon, Jenny Lee Wright. High-powered talent in sensitive story of transvestite in English countryside during WW2. Young Deacon, an army deserter, is persuaded by lonely farm woman Jackson to pose as her sister, then tough tank Sergeant Reed becomes involved. Retitled SOLDIER IN SKIRTS. [R]▼

Triple Trouble (1950) **66m.** ** D: Jean Yarbrough. Leo Gorcey, Huntz Hall, Gabriel Dell, William Benedict, Pat Collins, Lyn Thomas, Bernard Gorcey, Paul Dubov, David Gorcey. The Bowery Boys are framed for a robbery and try to catch the real culprits from behind prison bars in this wearisome entry.

Tripoli (1950) **C-95m.** ** D: Will Price. John Payne, Maureen O'Hara, Howard da Silva, Philip Reed, Grant Withers, Lowell Gilmore, Connie Gilchrist, Alan Napier. Good cast cannot save average script of U.S. marines battling Barbary pirates in 1805; sole standout is da Silva.

Trippin' (1999) **C-92m.** ** D: David Raynr (Hubbard). Deon Richmond, Maia Campbell, Donald (Adeosun) Faison, Guy Torry, Countess Vaughn, Michael Warren. Goofy teen comedy about a Walter Mitty-esque high school senior who could win his dream girl if he started taking the future seriously. Likable cast can't compensate for clichéd material and gratuitous t&a quotient. Features a pointless cameo by Naomi Campbell. [R]▼◗

Trip to Bountiful, The (1985) **C-106m.** *** D: Peter Masterson. Geraldine Page, John Heard, Carlin Glynn, Richard Bradford, Rebecca De Mornay, Kevin Cooney. Leisurely, richly textured filmization of Horton Foote's 1953 television play (later done on Broadway) about a widow, living unhappily with her son and daughter-in-law, determined to make her way home to Bountiful, Texas, for one last look. Page won well-deserved Oscar for her heartbreaking performance, but entire cast is excellent. Fine filmmaking debut for stage director Masterson. [PG]▼●

Tristana (1970-French-Spanish) **C-98m.** ***½ D: Luis Buñuel. Catherine Deneuve, Fernando Rey, Franco Nero, Jesus Fernandez, Lola Gaos, Vincent Solder. Deneuve plays a young woman who goes to live with her guardian Rey after her mother dies. He falls in love with her but faces competition from Nero. One of Buñuel's most serene, serious yet perverse studies of Catholicism, old age, death, desire, and deformity. Beautifully filmed in Toledo, Spain. Released in Europe at 105m. [PG]▼●

Tristan and Isolde SEE: **Lovespell**

Triumph of Hercules, The (1964-Italian) **C-90m.** ** D: Alberto De Martino. Dan Vadis, Moira Orfei, Pierre Cressoy, Marilu Tolo, Piero Lupi. Average gymnastic runthrough with Vadis more resourceful than most Hercules. Filmed in Cromoscope.▼

Triumph of Sherlock Holmes, The (1935-British) **75m.** **½ D: Leslie Hiscott. Arthur Wontner, Ian Fleming, Lyn Harding, Leslie Perrins, Jane Carr, Charles Mortimer. Wontner and Fleming make a very acceptable team as Holmes and Watson in this minor British series entry about murder and a secret society among coal miners. Based on Conan Doyle's "The Valley of Fear." Original British running time: 84m.▼

Triumph of the Spirit (1989) **C-121m.** *** D: Robert M. Young. Willem Dafoe, Edward James Olmos, Robert Loggia, Wendy Gazelle, Kelly Wolf, Costas Mandylor, Kario Salem. Hard-hitting, heartbreaking, based-on-fact account of Salamo Arouch (Dafoe), Greek-Jewish boxer who is deported with his family to Auschwitz during WW2. Sometimes *too* grim, but it's a story that needs to be told and remembered. Filmed on location. [R]▼●

Triumph of the Ten Gladiators (1964-Italian) **C-94m.** ** D: Nick Nostro. Dan Vadis, Helga Line, Stanley Kent, Gianni Rizzo, Halina Zalewska, John Heston. If not strong on plot, film allows for exuberances of swordplay and knockout brawls; set in ancient Rome. Techniscope.▼

Triumph of the Will (1935-German) **110m.** **** D: Leni Riefenstahl. Riefenstahl's infamous documentary on Hitler's 1934 Nuremberg rallies is rightly regarded as the greatest propaganda film of all time. Fascinating and (of course) frightening to see.▼◗

Triumphs of a Man Called Horse (1983-U.S.-Mexican) **C-86m.** *½ D: John Hough. Richard Harris, Michael Beck, Ana De Sade, Vaughn Armstrong, Anne Seymour, Buck Taylor. Limp sequel to THE RETURN OF A MAN CALLED HORSE with Beck, as Harris' half-breed son, attempting to shelter Sioux from greedy white settlers. Fans of the two earlier HORSES will be disappointed. [PG]▼

Trixie (2000) **C-117m.** *½ D: Alan Rudolph. Emily Watson, Dermot Mulroney, Nick Nolte, Nathan Lane, Brittany Murphy, Lesley Ann Warren, Will Patton, Stephen Lang. A dimwitted young woman given to malapropisms takes a job doing undercover security at a lakeside resort, where she uncovers a shady development deal involving a local bigwig (Patton) and a bombastic senator (Nolte). Seriocomic film noir is stylized to the point where it bears no relation to any recognizable reality. In other words, a fizzle. Widescreen. [R]

Trog (1970-British) **C-91m.** BOMB D: Freddie Francis. Joan Crawford, Michael Gough, Kim Braden, David Griffin, John Hamill. Missing Link discovered by anthropologist Crawford naturally gets loose and does its thing. Do yours—don't watch it. Sadly, Crawford's last film. [PG]▼●

Trojan Eddie (1996-British-Irish) **C-105m.** **½ D: Gillies Mackinnon. Richard Harris, Stephen Rea, Brendan Gleeson, Sean McGinley, Angeline Ball, Brid Brennan. Rea is a spieler who can sell anything to anyone but whose life has otherwise been in shambles; he finds himself caught in the middle when the young wife of his thuggish boss (Harris) runs off with her lover (who is Eddie's assistant). Harris and Rea offer fine, understated performances in this odd, intriguing mood piece.▼

Trojan Horse, The (1962-Italian) **C-105m.** **½ D: Giorgio Ferroni. Steve Reeves, John Drew Barrymore, Hedy Vessel, Juliette Mayniel. Above-average production values and Barrymore's presence in role of Ulysses inflates rating of otherwise stale version of Homer's epic. Techniscope.▼

Trojan Women, The (1972-Greek-U.S.) **C-105m.** ** D: Michael Cacoyannis. Katharine Hepburn, Irene Papas, Genevieve Bujold, Vanessa Redgrave, Patrick Magee, Brian Blessed. Euripides' tragedy about the plight of the women of Troy after its army is defeated gets a surprisingly flat (albeit faithful) rendering here, although any film which brings together four such great actresses can't be totally dismissed. [PG]▼

Troll (1986) **C-86m.** *½ D: John Buechler. Michael Moriarty, Shelley Hack, Noah Hathaway, Jenny Beck, Sonny Bono, June Lockhart, Anne Lockhart, Brad Hall, Julia Louis-Dreyfus. If your idea of entertainment is seeing Sonny Bono metamorphose into an apartment of foliage, this is the movie for you. Angelic tyke is possessed by a troll, who takes over her body and starts turning the neighbors into seed pods that eventually turn into new trolls. Too close to GREMLINS; some viewers may get off on hearing June Lockhart swear. Sequel: TROLL II. [PG-13]▼●

Troll in Central Park, A (1994) **C-76m.** ** D: Don Bluth, Gary Goldman. Voices of Dom DeLuise, Cloris Leachman, Phillip Glasser, Tawney Sunshine Glover, Hayley Mills, Jonathan Pryce, Charles Nelson Reilly. Good-hearted troll falls from favor in Troll Land and is banished to . . . N.Y.C.! There his green thumb helps beautify Central Park and the lives of those around him, including two neglected kids. Amiable and good-looking cartoon feature will appeal mainly to the small fry. DeLuise is fun in the title role. [G]▼●

Tron (1982) **C-96m.** ** D: Steven Lisberger. Jeff Bridges, Bruce Boxleitner, David Warner, Cindy Morgan, Barnard Hughes, Dan Shor. A computer whiz is sucked inside a powerful computer, where he must fight for his life in a giant videogame competition. State-of-the-art special effects are stunning, but the story runs out of steam too soon, with only Bridges' charisma to keep it afloat. Disappointing Disney production. Super Panavision 70. [PG]▼●◗

Troop Beverly Hills (1989) **C-105m.** **½ D: Jeff Kanew. Shelley Long, Craig T. Nelson, Betty Thomas, Mary Gross, Stephanie Beacham, Audra Lindley, Edd Byrnes, Ami Foster, Jenny Lewis. Sometimes-amusing comedy about a spoiled, wealthy Beverly Hills housewife who leads her daughter's Girl Scout troop on unique outings on which everyone learns about self-esteem—and Gucci loafers. Predictable, but undemanding fun. [PG] ▼●

Trooper Hook (1957) **81m.** **½ D: Charles Marquis Warren. Joel McCrea, Barbara Stanwyck, Earl Holliman, Susan Kohner, Sheb Wooley, Celia Lovsky. Woman scorned by whites for having lived with Indians and having child by the chief, begins anew with cavalry sergeant.

Tropic Holiday (1938) **78m.** **½ D: Theodore Reed. Dorothy Lamour, Ray Milland, Martha Raye, Bob Burns, Tito Guizar. Silly musical set in Mexico, with perky performances by all.

Tropic of Cancer (1970) **C-87m.** ***½ D: Joseph Strick. Rip Torn, James Callahan, Ellen Burstyn, David Bauer, Laurence Ligneres, Phil Brown. Director Strick is generally more successful with Henry Miller than he's been with James Joyce, thanks to Torn's earthy portrayal of the loose-living expatriate author amidst a string of amorous adventures in '20s Paris. Slapdash but invigorating; Burstyn makes a strong impression in tiny role as Henry's wife. [X]▼

Tropic Zone (1953) **C-94m.** *½ D: Lewis R. Foster. Ronald Reagan, Rhonda Fleming, Estelita, Noah Beery. Blah actioner set in South America with Reagan fighting the good cause to save a banana plantation from outlaws.

Trottie True SEE: **Gay Lady, The**

Trouble Along the Way (1953) **110m.** **½ D: Michael Curtiz. John Wayne, Donna Reed, Charles Coburn, Sherry Jackson, Marie Windsor, Tom Tully, Leif Erickson, Chuck Connors. Unusually sentimental Wayne vehicle casts him as divorced man trying to maintain custody of his daughter (Jackson); he earns back self-respect by coaching football team for small Catholic school.▼●

Trouble at 16 SEE: **Platinum High School**

Trouble Bound (1993) **C-89m.** *½ D: Jeffrey Reiner. Michael Madsen, Patricia Arquette, Florence Stanley, Seymour Cassel, Billy Bob Thornton. Ex-con Madsen and "college" girl Arquette are on the run in this Mafia mess which features gamblers, drug dealers, hit people, strippers, and a corpse who talks. The two leads save this from being a total loss. [R]▼●

Trouble for Two (1936) **75m.** *** D: J. Walter Ruben. Robert Montgomery, Rosalind Russell, Frank Morgan, Reginald Owen, Louis Hayward. Unique, offbeat black comedy of Montgomery and Russell joining London Suicide Club; based on Robert Louis Stevenson story.

Trouble in Mind (1985) **C-111m.** **½ D: Alan Rudolph. Kris Kristofferson, Keith Carradine, Lori Singer, Genevieve Bujold, Joe Morton, Divine, George Kirby, John Considine. Highly stylized, highly individualistic melodrama set in the near future, with Kristofferson as idealistic ex-cop, fresh from a stretch in jail, who gets involved with some young innocents who've just come to the big city. Odd, unusual, with 1940s film noir feeling but so determinedly vague and unreal that it also comes off rather cold. Still, it's an eyeful, and recommended for fans of the offbeat and Rudolph in particular. Title song sung by Marianne Faithful. [R]▼●

Trouble in Paradise (1932) **83m.** **** D: Ernst Lubitsch. Miriam Hopkins, Kay Francis, Herbert Marshall, Charlie Ruggles, Edward Everett Horton, C. Aubrey Smith, Robert Grieg, Leonid Kinskey. Sparkling Lubitsch confection about two jewel thieves (Marshall and Hopkins) who fall in love, but find their relationship threatened when he turns on the charm to their newest (female) victim. This film is a working definition of the term "sophisticated comedy." Script by Samson Raphaelson and Grover Jones.●

Trouble in Paradise (1988-U.S.-Australian) **C-100m. TVM** D: Di Drew. Raquel Welch, Jack Thompson, Nicholas Hammond, John Gregg. An elegantly tailored widow finds herself marooned on a tropical island with a carousing Aussie seaman and stalked by a gang of drug smugglers. Raquel sashays around seductively (and revealingly) at the head of an all-Australian cast in this harmless comedy that borrows generously from Barrie's THE ADMIRABLE CRICHTON and Wertmuller's SWEPT AWAY. Average.

Trouble in Store (1953-British) **85m.** **½ D: John Paddy Carstairs. Margaret Rutherford, Norman Wisdom, Moira Lister, Megs Jenkins. Full of fun sight gags and good character actors, film traces ups-and-downs of naive department store worker. Wisdom's film debut.▼

Trouble in the Glen (1954-British) **C-91m.** ** D: Herbert Wilcox. Margaret Lockwood, Orson Welles, Forrest Tucker, Victor McLaglen. Scottish-based drama of feud over closing of road that has been used for a long time. Average-to-poor script benefits from Welles.▼

Troublemaker, The (1964) **80m.** ** D: Theodore Flicker. Tom Aldredge, Joan Darling, Theodore Flicker, Buck Henry, Godfrey Cambridge, Al Freeman, Jr. Terribly dated, independently made comedy about a country bumpkin's adventures in N.Y.C.; interesting as an artifact of its time, made by the talented improvisational comedy troupe known as The Premise.

Trouble Makers (1948) **69m.** ** D: Reginald LeBorg. Leo Gorcey, Huntz Hall, Gabriel Dell, Billy Benedict, David Gorcey, Helen Parrish, Fritz Feld, Lionel Stander, Frankie Darro, John Ridgely, Bennie Bartlett, Bernard Gorcey. The Bowery Boys pose as hotel bellboys to probe a murder. This was one of veteran character actor Stander's last films before being blacklisted.

Trouble Man (1972) **C-99m.** ** D: Ivan Dixon. Robert Hooks, Paul Winfield, Ralph Waite, William Smithers, Paula Kelly, Julius W. Harris. Hooks is superslick black troubleshooter caught in gang warfare. Cliché-ridden script includes about four hundred killings, glorifying underworld life. Well-made but tasteless. [R]

Trouble With Angels, The (1966) **C-112m.** **½ D: Ida Lupino. Rosalind Russell, Hayley Mills, June Harding, Binnie Barnes, Mary Wickes, Gypsy Rose Lee, Camilla Sparv. Cutesy study of Pennsylvania convent school, with students Mills and Harding driving mother superior Russell to distraction. Episodic, occasionally touching comedy. Sequel: WHERE ANGELS GO . . . TROUBLE FOLLOWS.▼●

Trouble With Girls (and How to Get Into It), The (1969) **C-104m.** **½ D: Peter Tewksbury. Elvis Presley, Marlyn Mason, Nicole Jaffe, Sheree North, Edward Andrews, John Carradine. Vincent Price, Joyce Van Patten, Dabney Coleman, John Rubinstein, Duke Snider. One of the better Presley vehicles has Elvis as manager of a Chautauqua company (medicine show) in the 1920s; nice feeling for the period. Panavision. [PG] ▼●

Trouble With Harry, The (1955) **C-99m.** *** D: Alfred Hitchcock. Edmund Gwenn, John Forsythe, Shirley MacLaine, Mildred Natwick, Mildred Dunnock, Jerry Mathers, Royal Dano. Offbeat, often hilarious black comedy courtesy Mr. Hitchcock and scripter John Michael Hayes about bothersome corpse causing all sorts of problems for peaceful neighbors in New England community. Gwenn is fine as usual, MacLaine appealing in her first film. Beautiful autumn locations, whimsical score (his first for Hitch) by Bernard Herrmann. VistaVision.▼●

Trouble With Spies, The (1987) **C-91m.** BOMB D: Burt Kennedy. Donald Sutherland, Ned Beatty, Ruth Gordon, Lucy Gutteridge, Michael Hordern, Robert Morley, Gregory Sierra. Awful spy comedy about incompetent British and Soviet secret agents. Good actors wasted; this one's as bad as they come. Filmed in 1984. [PG]▼

Trouble With Women, The (1947) **80m.** ** D: Sidney Lanfield. Ray Milland, Teresa Wright, Brian Donlevy, Rose Hobart, Charles Smith, Lewis Russell, Iris Adrian, Lloyd Bridges. Professor Milland announces that women like to be treated rough; you can guess the rest of this tame comedy.

Trout, The (1982-French) **C-105m.** ** D: Joseph Losey. Isabelle Huppert, Jacques Spiesser, Jeanne Moreau, Jean Pierre Cassel, Daniel Olbrychski, Alexis Smith, Craig Stevens. Elaborate but muddled account of country girl Huppert and her encounters, sexual and otherwise, in the world of high finance. Moreau is wasted as the wife of businessman Cassel; Smith and Stevens appear in cameos. Original title: LA TRUITE. Also released at 116m. [R]▼

Truce, The (1997-Italian-French-Swiss-German-British) **C-117m.** *** D: Francesco Rosi. John Turturro, Massimo Ghini, Rade Serbedzija, Stefano Dionisi, Teco Celio, Roberto Citran. Moving adaptation of Primo Levi's autobiography, which follows the author's liberation from Auschwitz and his emotional reawakening as he struggles to get home to Turin, Italy. Episodic structure dilutes some of the dramatic impact, but there are many powerful, affecting moments, and Turturro is beautifully understated. An interesting companion piece to the documentary THE LONG WAY HOME. [R]▼

Truck Stop Women (1974) **C-88m.** **½ D: Mark Lester. Lieux Dressler, Claudia Jennings, Dennis Fimple, Jennifer Burton. Sloppy but good-natured exploitation fare about women who run truck stop as front for prostitution and truck hijacking activities. Business is so good the Mob tries to move in. Jennings is a standout in this raucous sleaze romp. Techniscope. [R]▼

Truck Turner (1974) **C-91m.** *½ D: Jonathan Kaplan. Isaac Hayes, Yaphet Kotto, Alan Weeks, Annazette Chase, Sam Laws, Nichelle Nichols. Extremely violent black exploiter, with Hayes only distinguishing feature as a skip-tracer (a detective who hunts bail jumpers). His original score is familiar. [R]▼

True Believer (1989) **C-103m.** *** D: Joseph Ruben. James Woods, Robert Downey, Jr., Yuji Okumoto, Margaret Colin, Kurtwood Smith, Tom Bower, Miguel Fernandes, Charles Hallahan. Woods gives his usual dynamic performance as a once-idealistic lawyer, a radical hero of the '60s who's lost his scruples—until his hero-worshipping clerk (Downey) goads him into taking the near-hopeless case of an Asian-American who was apparently railroaded into prison eight years before. Contrived, but entertaining all the way. Followed by a TV series, *Eddie Dodd.* [R]▼●

True Colors (1991) **C-111m.** **½ D: Herbert Ross. John Cusack, James Spader, Imogen Stubbs, Mandy Patinkin, Richard Widmark, Dina Merrill, Philip Bosco, Paul Guilfoyle. Well-acted but thoroughly obvious story of friendship, ethics, and betrayal, following two law-school roommates who take different paths in life: one goes to work for the Justice Department, determined to right wrongs; the other goes into politics, looking for any angle that can get him ahead. No surprises, thus little impact. Stubbs' British accent (in the role of senator Widmark's daughter) also gets in the way. [R]▼●

True Confession (1937) **85m.** *½ D: Wesley Ruggles. Carole Lombard, Fred MacMurray, John Barrymore, Una Merkel, Porter Hall, Edgar Kennedy, Lynne Overman, Irving Bacon, Fritz Feld. Alarmingly unfunny "comedy" about pathological liar Lombard and the trouble she causes for herself and good-natured lawyer husband MacMurray when she confesses to a murder she didn't commit. Remade with Betty Hutton as CROSS MY HEART (1946).

True Confessions (1981) **C-108m.** **½ D: Ulu Grosbard. Robert De Niro, Robert Duvall, Charles Durning, Ed Flanders, Burgess Meredith, Rose Gregorio, Cyril Cusack, Kenneth McMillan, Dan Hedaya, Jeanette Nolan. Methodically slow, complex, and provocative film (adapted by John Gregory Dunne and Joan Didion from Dunne's novel) about the uneasy bond and surprising similarities between two brothers, one a hardened police detective, the other a power-wielding monsignor in the Catholic Church. A meaty but somehow unsatisfying film (based on a true case previously filmed as a TVM, WHO IS THE BLACK DAHLIA?) with two characteristically fine performances by De Niro and Duvall. [R]▼●

True Crime (1999) **C-127m.** *** D: Clint Eastwood. Clint Eastwood, Isaiah Washington, Denis Leary, Lisa Gay Hamilton, James Woods, Bernard Hill, Diane Venora, Michael McKean, Michael Jeter, Mary McCormack, Hattie Winston, Francesca Fisher-Eastwood, Sidney Poitier, Frances Fisher, Christine Ebersole, Anthony Zerbe, William Windom, Lucy Alexis Liu. Formulaic but gripping story about a burnt-out reporter who becomes convinced that a man due to die at San Quentin that night is innocent. Bouncing back and forth between the story of the reporter—who's looking for redemption—and the stoic prisoner doesn't always work, but the suspense is undeniable. Woods is dynamite as Eastwood's sharp-tongued editor. Eastwood's wife, Dina Ruiz, ex-companion (Fisher) and young daughter all appear. [R]▼●◗

True Grit (1969) **C-128m.** *** D: Henry Hathaway. John Wayne, Glen Campbell, Kim Darby, Jeremy Slate, Robert Duvall, Strother Martin, Dennis Hopper, Jeff Corey. Film version of Charles Portis's wonderful novel about an over-the-hill marshal who helps 14-year-old track down her father's killer. Not as good as the book, but Wayne's Oscar-winning performance and rousing last half-hour make it fine screen entertainment. Sequel: ROOSTER COGBURN. Followed by a TV movie in 1978 with Warren Oates and Lisa Pelikan. [G—edited from original M rating]▼●

True Identity (1991) **C-93m.** **½ D: Charles Lane. Lenny Henry, Frank Langella, Charles Lane, Andreas Katsulas, Michael McKenna, James Earl Jones, Melvin Van Peebles. Aspiring black actor recognizes a supposedly dead mob boss on an airplane and disguises himself as an Italian-American hit man in order to save his skin. Familiar premise with a somewhat unfamiliar variation. Serves as a passable showcase for Brit wit Henry and his great gift of mimicry. [R]▼●

True Lies (1994) **C-141m.** *** D: James Cameron. Arnold Schwarzenegger, Jamie Lee Curtis, Tom Arnold, Bill Paxton, Tia Carrere, Art Malik, Charlton Heston, Eliza Dushku, Grant Heslov, Jane Morris. In-your-face entertainment from the Schwarzenegger/Cameron team, with Arnold as a spy in a super-secret, high-tech government agency whose wife thinks he's just a nerdy computer salesman. With humor and action in equal doses, this film makes all the right moves—until it gets bogged down in plot (and a general putdown of women) midway through. A slam-bang action finale brings it back on-course, as credibility is gleefully tossed aside. Cameron also scripted, based on a French film, LA TOTALE. Super 35. [R] ▼●◗

True Love (1989) **C-104m.** *** D: Nancy Savoca. Annabella Sciorra, Ron Eldard, Aida Turturro, Roger Rignack, Star Jasper,

Michael J. Wolfe, Kelly Cinnante. Refreshing, low-budget slice-of-life sleeper about an Italian wedding in the Bronx. There's tons of atmosphere, and the script (by Savoca and her husband, Richard Guay) is never condescending. Fine performances with Sciorra and Eldard perfectly cast as no-nonsense bride and immature groom. [R] ▼●

True Romance (1993) **C-118m.** **½ D: Tony Scott. Christian Slater, Patricia Arquette, Dennis Hopper, Gary Oldman, Brad Pitt, Christopher Walken, Val Kilmer, Bronson Pinchot, Michael Rapaport, Saul Rubinek, Chris Penn, Tom Sizemore, Samuel L. Jackson. A 90s twist on the young-lovers-on-the-lam genre, with hedonism, highly stylized (but potent) violence, and colorful supporting characters the main ingredients. Oldman, as a drug dealer in dreadlocks, is the standout in a first-rate cast. Hopper plays the most ''normal'' person in the movie! Written by Quentin Tarantino. Available in R and unrated (120m.) versions. Panavision. [R]▼●◗

True Stories (1986) **C-111m.** ** D: David Byrne. David Byrne, John Goodman, Swoosie Kurtz, Annie McEnroe, Spalding Gray, Alix Elias, Pops Staples. Smarmy, pseudo-hip tour of modern-day Texas by Talking Heads' Byrne; is there anything easier to satirize than eccentric Lone Star crazies? Photography, likable Goodman performance, and a couple of numbers make this worth a look if you're curious; mostly, though, it's depressing. Playwright Beth Henley had a part in the screenplay. [PG]▼●◗

True Story of Jesse James, The (1957) **C-92m.** **½ D: Nicholas Ray. Robert Wagner, Jeffrey Hunter, Hope Lange, Agnes Moorehead, Alan Hale, John Carradine, Alan Baxter, Frank Gorshin. Remake of 1939 Tyrone Power/Henry Fonda classic (JESSE JAMES) understandably lacks its star power, but there are enough offbeat Ray touches to keep things interesting (along with some stock footage from the original). Screenplay by Walter Newman. CinemaScope.

True Story of Lynn Stuart, The (1958) **78m.** **½ D: Lewis Seiler. Betsy Palmer, Jack Lord, Barry Atwater, Kim Spaulding. Modest, straightforward account of housewife Palmer posing as gun moll to trap gang.

True to Life (1943) **94m.** *** D: George Marshall. Mary Martin, Franchot Tone, Dick Powell, Victor Moore, Mabel Paige, William Demarest, Ernest Truex. Engaging comedy of radio writer going to live with ''typical'' American family to get material for his soap opera. Not a musical, but boasts delightful Hoagy Carmichael–Johnny Mercer song ''The Old Music Master.''

True to the Army (1942) **76m.** ** D: Albert S. Rogell. Allan Jones, Ann Miller, Judy Canova, Jerry Colonna. Zany nonsense erupts when military life and romance clash; loud WW2 escapism. This remake of SHE LOVES ME NOT was remade again as HOW TO BE VERY, VERY POPULAR.

True to the Navy (1930) **71m.** ** D: Frank Tuttle. Clara Bow, Fredric March, Sam Hardy, Eddie Featherstone, Jed Prouty, Rex Bell. Silly early talkie about on-again, off-again romance between sailor March and soda-fountain waitress Bow. Buffs will get a kick out of it; Clara does one sexy dance number.

Truly Madly Deeply (1991-British) **C-107m.** **½ D: Anthony Minghella. Juliet Stevenson, Alan Rickman, Bill Paterson, Michael Maloney, Christopher Rozycki, Keith Bartlett, David Ryall, Stella Maris. Young woman, unable to get over the death of her musician lover, gets the shock of her life when he turns up in her apartment—a ghost, to be sure, but seemingly alive. Minghella conceived this as a vehicle for Stevenson, and that it is (though it also serves as a showcase for Rickman, in an uncharacteristic low-key role); charmingly quirky at times, but unable to sustain its offbeat premise to the very end. ▼●

Truman (1995) **C-135m. TVM** D: Frank Pierson. Gary Sinise, Diana Scarwid, Richard Dysart, Colm Feore, James Gammon, Tony Goldwyn, Pat Hingle, Harris Yulin, Zeljko Ivanek, David Lansbury, Marian Seldes, Lois Smith. Give 'em hell, Gary! Sinise's H.S.T. grabs the 33rd president and shakes the stuffings out of most other interpretations, strutting like the bantam cock Truman was. Adapted by Tom Rickman (COAL MINER'S DAUGHTER) from David McCullough's Pulitzer Prize biography. Incidentally, Dysart, who here plays Secretary of War Henry L. Stimson, earlier portrayed Truman in both DAY ONE and the miniseries *War and Remembrance.* Made for cable. Above average.▼●◗

Truman Show, The (1998) **C-102m.** **½ D: Peter Weir. Jim Carrey, Laura Linney, Ed Harris, Noah Emmerich, Natascha McElhone, Holland Taylor, Brian Delate, Paul Giamatti, Harry Shearer. Truman Burbank lives a seemingly ideal existence in a tranquil seaside community. What he doesn't know is that his life is a giant 24-hour-a-day TV show, orchestrated by electronic mastermind/artist Harris in a completely controlled environment. Satire of our voyeuristic, consumer-driven society scores some points and offers Carrey a change of pace, but after the premise is established it doesn't know where to go. Perhaps that's because it's a short-story idea, not a feature film; *The Twilight Zone* used to do this kind of thing—better—in half-hour segments. [PG]▼●◗

Trumps SEE: **Enormous Changes at the Last Minute**

Trunk, The (1960-British) **72m.** *½ D: Donovan Winter. Phil Carey, Julia Arnall,

Dermot Walsh, Vera Day. Programmer involving trumped-up murder charge and usual dose of red herrings; ill-conceived tale.

Trunk to Cairo (1966-Israeli) **C-80m.** *½ D: Menahem Golan. Audie Murphy, George Sanders, Marianne Koch, Hans Von Bosodi, Joseph Yadin. Murphy, in rare non-Western role, plays still another secret agent in Cairo to investigate Sanders' attempt to build a rocket bound for the moon.

Trust (1991) **C-105m.** *** D: Hal Hartley. Adrienne Shelly, Martin Donovan, Merritt Nelson, John McKay, Edie Falco, Marko Hunt. A pregnant high-school senior is dumped by a football star who fears for his pending college scholarship. When her dad drops dead at the news, she finds a dubious savior: a bookish fellow who can't even clean a bathroom to his own dad's satisfaction. Drollness on screen can sometimes be had cheaply, but a perfect cast is tougher to bankroll; this original has both, enough to defuse the smugness that seems to linger in its soul. [R]▼●

Trusting Beatrice (1991) **C-91m.** ** D: Cindy Lou Johnson. Irène Jacob, Mark Evan Jacobs, Charlotte Moore, Pat McNamara, Leonardo Cimino, Steve Buscemi, Samuel Wright. Offbeat but paper-thin comedy about the unlikely romance between confused, perpetually glum Jacobs, who's just accidentally burned his house down, and confused, vulnerable Jacob, a Frenchwoman with immigration problems. Jacob is especially charming in her American debut. Original title: CLAUDE.▼

Trust Me (1989) **C-104m.** **½ D: Bobby Houston. Adam Ant, David Packer, Talia Balsam, William DeAcutis, Joyce Van Patten, Barbara Bain. Some scattershot laughs cannot sustain this satire of the art scene. Ant plays a gallery owner who will do all he can to see artist Packer dead—so the value of his work will increase. Bright idea, uneven result. [R]▼

Truth About Cats & Dogs, The (1996) **C-97m.** **½ D: Michael Lehmann. Uma Thurman, Janeane Garofalo, Ben Chaplin, Jamie Foxx, James McCaffrey. Cute comedy about a guy who falls in love with a radio talk-show host (Garofalo) before he even meets her; she, on the other hand, is self-conscious about her looks and has her knockout neighbor, a prototypical dumb blonde (Thurman), take her place. Enjoyable romantic comedy with *Cyrano* overtones stays afloat with three engaging performances (plus one terrific dog) but stretches credibility to the limit. [PG-13] ▼●

Truth About Spring, The (1965-British) **C-102m.** *** D: Richard Thorpe. Hayley Mills, John Mills, James MacArthur, Lionel Jeffries, Harry Andrews, Niall MacGinnis, David Tomlinson. Skipper Mills introduces daughter Hayley to first boyfriend, MacArthur, in enjoyable film geared for young viewers.

Truth About Women, The (1958-British) **C-98m.** **½ D: Muriel Box. Laurence Harvey, Julie Harris, Diane Cilento, Mai Zetterling, Eva Gabor, Wilfrid Hyde-White, Christopher Lee, Ernest Thesiger. Multi-episode tale about playboy Harvey's flirtations; well mounted and cast, but slow-going.▼

Truth or Consequences, N.M. (1997) **C-106m.** ** D: Kiefer Sutherland. Vincent Gallo, Mykelti Williamson, Kiefer Sutherland, Kevin Pollak, Kim Dickens, Grace Phillips, Max Perlich, Rod Steiger, Martin Sheen. A robbery goes awry, resulting in murder, and the four criminals take two ordinary people captive to evade Utah police. Well acted, but there's nothing at all new here, and it's pretentious to boot. Sutherland's feature debut as a director. [R] ▼●◗

Truth or Dare (1991) **C/B&W-118m.** *** D: Alek Keshishian. Madonna. Revealing backstage/performance film, very much in the mold of DONT LOOK BACK, examines the phenomenon we know as . . . Madonna. Authorized account, iron-fist commissioned by its subject, is simultaneously candid and manipulated, but the dynamics between Madonna and members of her family (and a couple of hilarious what-me-worry cameos by her then-squeeze Warren Beatty) are compelling. An important film even if you don't care for Madonna; overlength makes the final half-hour a mild ordeal. (The video offers *additional* footage!) Video title: MADONNA TRUTH OR DARE. [R]▼●

Try and Get Me! (1950) **90m.** *** D: Cyril Endfield. Frank Lovejoy, Kathleen Ryan, Richard Carlson, Lloyd Bridges, Katherine Locke, Adele Jergens, Renzo Cesara. Husband and father Lovejoy can't find a job, so he reluctantly helps slick Bridges in a series of robberies . . . but he isn't prepared for kidnapping and murder. Very impressive independent film noir indicts yellow journalism and lynch-mob violence, but doesn't let the criminals off the hook. Based on a true story that took place in California during the 1930s. Deserves to be better known. Originally shown as THE SOUND OF FURY.▼

Trygon Factor, The (1967-British) **C-87m.** *½ D: Cyril Frankel. Stewart Granger, Susan Hampshire, Robert Morley, Cathleen Nesbitt, James Robertson Justice. Impossible-to-follow Scotland Yard whodunit. Centers around bizarre old English family and series of interesting murders.

Tucker: The Man and His Dream (1988) **C-111m.** ***½ D: Francis Ford Coppola. Jeff Bridges, Joan Allen, Martin Landau, Frederic Forrest, Mako, Dean Stockwell, Elias Koteas, Nina Siemaszko, Christian Slater, Corky Nemec, Marshall Bell, Don Novello, Peter Donat, Dean Goodman, Patti Austin. Smart, sassy, stylish film about Preston

Tucker, who tried to build "the car of the future" in the 1940s, only to be crushed by the Big Three automakers and their political cronies. Told with great flair by Coppola (who obviously felt a kinship with the indomitable, family-minded visionary), filled with fine performances, especially Landau in a poignant characterization as Tucker's unlikely partner. Lloyd Bridges (Jeff's dad) appears unbilled as an adversarial senator. Lively score by Joe Jackson. Technovision. [PG]▼●

Tuck Everlasting (1980) **C-100m.** ***½ D: Frederick King Keller. Margaret Chamberlain, Paul Flessa, Fred A. Keller, James McGuire, Sonia Raimi, Bruce D'Auria. Lovely, sweet, entertaining fable about family, invulnerable to pain, aging, and death, and the young girl who learns their secret. Perfect for children who prefer books to video games. Produced independently in upstate New York; based on Natalie Babbitt's award-winning novel.▼

Tuesdays with Morrie (1999) **C-100m. TVM** D: Mick Jackson. Jack Lemmon, Hank Azaria, Wendy Moniz, Caroline Aaron, Bonnie Bartlett. A student-turned-sportswriter and radio personality, Mitch Albom (Azaria), reconnects with a dying professor who was his mentor for a series of loving weekly visits. Lemmon is first-rate as usual in this uplifting (but still four-hanky) Peabody Award–winning drama adapted by Tom Rickman from Albom's hugely successful book. Above average. ▼

Tuff Turf (1985) **C-112m.** *½ D: Fritz Kiersch. James Spader, Kim Richards, Paul Mones, Matt Clark, Claudette Nevins, Robert Downey (Jr.), Olivia Barash, Jack Mack & the Heart Attack. Old-fashioned, unrealistic troubled-teen melodrama with overtones of WEST SIDE STORY, set in a fantasy version of the San Fernando Valley. Pre-SEX, LIES AND VIDEOTAPE Spader, as preppie newcomer, is mannered, but Richards is good. [R]▼

Tugboat Annie (1933) **87m.** **½ D: Mervyn LeRoy. Marie Dressler, Wallace Beery, Robert Young, Maureen O'Sullivan, Willard Robertson, Frankie Darro. Marie is skipper of the tugboat *Narcissus,* Beery her ner'er-do-well husband in this rambling, episodic comedy drama; inimitable stars far outclass their wobbly material. Followed by TUGBOAT ANNIE SAILS AGAIN, and a 1950s TV series.

Tugboat Annie Sails Again (1940) **77m.** ** D: Lewis Seiler. Marjorie Rambeau, Alan Hale, Jane Wyman, Ronald Reagan, Clarence Kolb, Charles Halton. Airy comedy with predictable plot about Annie's job in jeopardy. Rambeau takes up where Marie Dressler left off; Reagan saves the day for her.

Tulips (1981-Canadian) **C-92m.** *½ D: Stan Ferris. Gabe Kaplan, Bernadette Peters, Henry Gibson, Al Waxman, David Boxer. Weak romance, with Kaplan and Peters each attempting to commit suicide, then meeting and falling in love. "Stan Ferris" is a pseudonym for Mark Warren, Rex Bromfield, and Al Waxman—and the lack of directorial cohesion shows. [PG]▼

Tulsa (1949) **C-90m.** *** D: Stuart Heisler. Susan Hayward, Robert Preston, Pedro Armendariz, Lloyd Gough, Chill Wills, Ed Begley, Jimmy Conlin. Bouncy drama of cattlewoman Hayward entering the wildcat oil business to avenge the death of her father, losing her values along the way as she becomes blinded by her success.▼

Tumbleweed (1953) **C-79m.** ** D: Nathan Juran. Audie Murphy, Lori Nelson, Chill Wills, Lee Van Cleef. Bland oater with Murphy trying to prove he didn't desert wagon train under Indian attack.

Tumbleweeds (1925) **81m.** ***½ D: King Baggot. William S. Hart, Barbara Bedford, Lucien Littlefield, J. Gordon Russell, Richard R. Neill. One of the screen's most famous Westerns, with Hart deciding to get in on the opening of the Cherokee Strip in 1889, particularly if pretty Bedford is willing to marry him and settle there. Landrush scene is one of the great spectacles in silent films. Above running time does not include a poignant eight-minute introduction Hart made to accompany 1939 reissue of his classic. ▼●

Tumbleweeds (1999) **C-102m.** *** D: Gavin O'Connor. Janet McTeer, Kimberly J. Brown, Jay O. Sanders, Lois Smith, Laurel Holloman, Michael J. Pollard, Noah Emmerich, Gavin O'Connor. Exceptional performances elevate this somewhat familiar tale of a trailer-trash Southern belle with a penchant for hooking up with crummy men, dragging her young daughter along as she moves from town to town. McTeer is terrific in the lead, matched by Brown as the girl, with cowriter-director O'Connor first rate as a truckdriver who comes into their lives. [PG-13]▼◗

Tuna Clipper (1949) **79m.** *½ D: William Beaudine. Roddy McDowall, Elena Verdugo, Ronald Winters, Rick Vallin, Dickie Moore. Flabby tale of youth (McDowall) who pushes himself into rugged fishing life to prove his worth.

Tune, The (1992) **C-72m.** *** D: Bill Plympton. Offbeat, original cartoon feature from award-winning short-subject animator Plympton follows the trials and tribulations of a songwriter searching for that elusive hit. Maureen McElheron's clever songs provide the tone for a series of imaginative vignettes. Unconventional in every way (including its colored-pencil visuals, executed almost singlehandedly by Plympton) but a quiet treat, especially for animation buffs.▼◗

Tune In Tomorrow . . . (1990) **C-102m.** **½ D: Jon Amiel. Barbara Hershey, Keanu

Reeves, Peter Falk, Bill McCutcheon, Patricia Clarkson, Richard Portnow, Jerome Dempsey, Richard B. Shull. Oddball movie set in 1951 New Orleans. Reeves plays an impressionable young man who falls in love with his sexy aunt (Hershey), while falling under the spell of Falk, a wildly eccentric writer for a radio soap opera who draws on real life in ways his young protégé cannot conceive of. Funny, funky, original; not always on target, but there are inspired moments. Falk is a howl. Familiar faces appear in amusing cameos. Music by Wynton Marsalis, who also appears on camera. Based on Mario Vargas Llosa's novel *Aunt Julia and the Scriptwriter.* [PG-13]▼●

Tunes of Glory (1960-British) **C-106m.** **** D: Ronald Neame. Alec Guinness, John Mills, Susannah York, Kay Walsh, Dennis Price, John Fraser, Duncan Macrae, Gordon Jackson, Allan Cuthbertson. Engrossing clash of wills in peacetime Scottish Highland regiment as popular, easygoing Lt. Col. (Guinness) is replaced by stiff-necked martinet (Mills). Outstanding performances by both men, each in a role more naturally suited to the other! Impressive bagpipe-driven score by Malcolm Arnold. Scripted by James Kennaway, from his novel. York's film debut. ▼●

Tunnel, The SEE: **Transatlantic Tunnel**

Tunnel of Love, The (1958) **98m.** *** D: Gene Kelly. Doris Day, Richard Widmark, Gig Young, Gia Scala. Bright comedy of married couple Widmark and Day enduring endless red tape to adopt a child. Good cast spices adaptation of Joseph Fields-Peter de Vries play. CinemaScope. ▼●

Tunnelvision (1976) **C-67m.** ** D: Neal Israel, Brad Swirnoff. Phil Proctor, Howard Hesseman, Ernie Anderson, Edwina Anderson, James Bacon, Gerrit Graham, Betty Thomas, Chevy Chase, Roger Bowen, Al Franken, Tom Davis, William Schallert, Laraine Newman, Ron Silver. Crude, uneven parody of what TV programming will be like in the future. Of interest only for appearances by now famous performers. [R]▼

Turbo: A Power Rangers Movie (1997-U.S.-Japanese) **C-99m.** *½ D: David Winning. Jason David Frank, Steve Cardenas, Catherine Sutherland, Johnny Yong Bosch, Nakia Burrise, Hilary Shepard Turner, Blake Foster. The Mighty Morphin Power Rangers are back in this cheesy feature, and doing battle against the evil Divatox. Kids may like the gadgets and gimmicks, but few others will. Followed by a direct-to-video sequel. [PG] ▼●

Turbulence (1997) **C-103m.** **½ D: Robert Butler. Ray Liotta, Lauren Holly, Brendan Gleeson, Ben Cross, Rachel Ticotin, Jeffrey DeMunn, John Finn, Catherine Hicks, Hector Elizondo. As a 747 roars through a rising storm, stewardess Holly faces serial killer Liotta—alone. Though undeniably silly (a slasher movie on a plane?), this often delivers the goods through sheer brassiness, and Liotta has a high old time as the nutzoid killer. Super 35. [R]▼●◗

Turkey Shoot SEE: **Escape 2000**

Turk 182! (1985) **C-98m.** ** D: Bob Clark. Timothy Hutton, Robert Urich, Kim Cattrall, Robert Culp, Darren McGavin, Steven Keats, James Tolkan, Peter Boyle, Paul Sorvino, Dick O'Neill. Contrived attempt at Capra-esque comedy. Young Brooklynite turns into super-graffiti artist to protest N.Y.C.'s lack of support for his brother, an injured fireman. Hutton's brooding persona doesn't suit this comic setting. Panavision. [PG-13]▼

Turnabout (1940) **83m.** ** D: Hal Roach. John Hubbard, Carole Landis, Adolphe Menjou, Mary Astor, William Gargan, Joyce Compton, Verree Teasdale, Donald Meek. Unique, but incredibly bad comedy, risqué in its day, about husband and wife switching personalities thanks to magic Buddha; from a story by Thorne Smith, later a short-lived TV series in the 1970s.

Turn Back the Clock (1933) **77m.** *** D: Edgar Selwyn. Lee Tracy, Mae Clarke, Otto Kruger, George Barbier, Peggy Shannon, C. Henry Gordon, Clara Blandick. Fascinating Depression-era sleeper with an intriguing premise. Tracy is ideally cast as a middle-aged working man who gets to relive his life . . . and marry into wealth and power. Snappy script by director Selwyn and Ben Hecht. And watch for The Three Stooges!

Turner & Hooch (1989) **C-97m.** ** D: Roger Spottiswoode. Tom Hanks, Mare Winningham, Craig T. Nelson, Reginald VelJohnson, Scott Paulin, J.C. Quinn, John McIntire, Beasley. Detective Hanks' only means of catching some murderers is by extracting their identity from the sole murder witness: a dog named Hooch. Hanks (who plays a neatness freak) and Hooch (a lovably ugly dog who makes a mess of everything) squeeze all the humor they can out of a paper-thin script—but even they can't make up for a bummer of an ending. [PG] ▼●

Turning, The (1992) **C-91m.** ** D: L. A. Puopolo. Karen Allen, Raymond J. Barry, Michael Dolan, Tess Harper, Gillian Anderson. A disturbed young man arrives in his small Virginia hometown and tries to prevent his parents' divorce, which leads instead to violence. Meant to show how loveless homes can irrevocably scar children, but leaden paced and boring. [R]▼◗

Turning Point, The (1952) **85m.** **½ D: William Dieterle. William Holden, Alexis Smith, Edmond O'Brien, Ed Begley, Tom Tully, Don Porter, Ted de Corsia, Neville Brand, Carolyn Jones. Tough script by

Warren Duff sparks this gritty if familiar drama. O'Brien is a crime-buster investigating big-city corruption; Holden, his boyhood friend, is a cynical reporter. Scenario was inspired by the Kefauver Committee hearings into organized crime.

Turning Point, The (1977) **C-119m.** **½ D: Herbert Ross. Anne Bancroft, Shirley MacLaine, Mikhail Baryshnikov, Leslie Browne, Tom Skerritt, Martha Scott, Marshall Thompson. Two friends who started in ballet are reunited after many years; Bancroft is now a star ballerina, MacLaine a Midwestern housewife/dance teacher whose daughter (Browne) is embarking on her own ballet career. Promising idea bogs down in clichés, with supposedly liberated treatment of women's relationships exemplified by wild catfight. Those few dance sequences presented intact give film its only value. Written by Arthur Laurents; photographed by Robert Surtees. Baryshnikov's film debut. [PG]▼●

Turning to Stone (1985-Canadian) **C-98m.** *** D: Eric Till. Nicky Guadagni, Shirley Douglas, Anne Anglin, Jackie Richardson, Bernard Behrens. Riveting psychological drama about Guadagni, a nice young girl who's busted for smuggling drugs, and her adjustment to unhappy realities of life behind bars. For once, a nonexploitation women's prison drama. Fine performances all around; expert script by Judith Thompson.

Turn of the Screw, The (1992-British-French) **C-95m.** ** D: Rusty Lemorande. Patsy Kensit, Stephane Audran, Julian Sands, Clare Szekores, Joseph England, Marianne Faithfull. Sands hires governess Kensit to look after his deceptively sweet-looking niece and nephew, who reside in a country manor. Wooden adaptation (by director Lemorande) of the Henry James masterpiece. Filmed far more successfully as THE INNOCENTS. ▼●

Turn the Key Softly (1953-British) **83m.** ** D: Jack Lee. Yvonne Mitchell, Terence Morgan, Joan Collins, Kathleen Harrison, Thora Hird, Geoffrey Keen. Film recounts incidents in lives of three women ex-convicts upon leaving prison; contrived dramatics.

Turtle Beach (1992-Australian) **C-85m.** BOMB D: Stephen Wallace. Greta Scacchi, Joan Chen, Jack Thompson, Art Malik, Norman Kaye, Victoria Longley, Martin Jacobs. Photojournalist/mom Scacchi ankles Australia for Malaysia to cover Chen and the Vietnamese boat people, leaving herself open to charges of parental neglect. Not so much edited as patched, and even drably shot by the great Russell Boyd. This unredeemed stinker was barely released in the U.S. [R]

Turtle Diary (1985-British) **C-97m.** *** D: John Irvin. Glenda Jackson, Ben Kingsley, Richard Johnson, Michael Gambon, Harriet Walter, Rosemary Leach, Eleanor Bron, Nigel Hawthorne. Deliciously original (if low-key) fable of two repressed people who are drawn together—and ultimately freed—by an unusual common interest: they both become concerned about the fate of captive giant turtles at the zoo. Witty, decidedly offbeat script by Harold Pinter (who does a cameo as a bookstore customer). Johnson, who plays Jackson's jovial next-door neighbor, also produced the film. [PG]▼●

Tuskegee Airmen, The (1995) **C-106m. TVM** D: Robert Markowitz. Laurence Fishburne, Cuba Gooding, Jr., Andre Braugher, Allen Payne, Malcolm-Jamal Warner, Courtney B. Vance, Christopher McDonald, John Lithgow, Daniel Hugh Kelly, Rosemary Murphy, Graham Jarvis. Well-intentioned celebration of the "Fighting 99th," the first squadron of black combat fighters in WW2, who battled prejudice on the home front, the Axis in Europe, and bigoted officers assigned to oversee them. Rather pedestrian war movie elevated somewhat by a first-rate cast. The proper story of this wartime unit is yet to be told. Made for cable. Average.▼

Tuttles of Tahiti, The (1942) **91m.** *** D: Charles Vidor. Charles Laughton, Jon Hall, Peggy Drake, Florence Bates, Mala, Alma Ross, Victor Francen. Laughton and family lead leisurely life on South Seas island, avoiding any sort of hard labor. That's it . . . but it's good.▼●

Twelfth Night (1996-British) **C-134m.** **½ D: Trevor Nunn. Imogen Stubbs, Helena Bonham Carter, Toby Stephens, Nigel Hawthorne, Ben Kingsley, Richard E. Grant, Mel Smith, Imelda Staunton, Nicholas Farrell, Stephen Mackintosh. Shakespeare's farce gets transported here to the 1890s, with Stubbs donning male disguise in the court of a duke after she's separated from her brother in a shipwreck. For a surprising amount of its long running time, the film plays the story straight, only to loosen up some in the later scenes—particularly those involving Malvolio. Lackluster, but easy to take. Stephens (who plays Orsino) is the son of actors Maggie Smith and Robert Stephens. [PG]▼●

12 Angry Men (1957) **95m.** **** D: Sidney Lumet. Henry Fonda, Lee J. Cobb, Ed Begley, E. G. Marshall, Jack Klugman, Jack Warden, Martin Balsam, John Fiedler, George Voskovec, Robert Webber, Edward Binns, Joseph Sweeney. Brilliant film about one man who tries to convince 11 other jurors that their hasty conviction of a boy on trial should be reconsidered. Formidable cast (including several character-stars-to-be); Lumet's impressive debut film. Script by Reginald Rose, from his television play. Remade for TV in 1997. ▼●

12 Angry Men (1997) **C-95m. TVM** D: William Friedkin. Jack Lemmon, George C. Scott, Hume Cronyn, Ossie Davis, Courtney B. Vance, Armin Mueller-Stahl, Dorian Harewood, Tony Danza, Mykelti Williamson, Edward James Olmos, William Petersen, James Gandolfini. Stellar, contemporized version of the memorable tale of jury haggling on a stuffy afternoon in N.Y.C., with a bunch of cranky men. New to this version are the defendant (who is Latino), a female judge (Mary McDonnell, in a cameo), and a more ethnically diverse jury. Reginald Rose revised his own teleplay and movie script. Made for cable. Above average.▼●

Twelve Chairs, The (1970) **C-94m.** *** D: Mel Brooks. Ron Moody, Frank Langella, Dom DeLuise, Mel Brooks, Bridget Brice, Robert Bernal. Impoverished Russian nobleman Moody seeks one of 12 dining chairs, now scattered, with jewels sewn into seat. DeLuise hilarious as his chief rival. Unsympathetic characters hamper film's success, though mastermind Brooks still provides many laughs. Filmed in Yugoslavia; versions of this same story have been made in Hollywood, Germany, Argentina, England, and Cuba! [G]▼●◗

Twelve Hours to Kill (1960) **83m.** *½ D: Edward L. Cahn. Nico Minardos, Barbara Eden, Grant Richards, Russ Conway, Art Baker, Gavin MacLeod. Poor crime melodrama of gangland murder witnessed by Greek immigrant in N.Y.C. CinemaScope.

Twelve Monkeys (1995) **C-131m.** **½ D: Terry Gilliam. Bruce Willis, Madeleine Stowe, Brad Pitt, Christopher Plummer, Frank Gorshin, David Morse, Jon Seda. In the bleak world of the near-future, a prisoner is sent back in time to the 1990s to discover the source of a plague that killed billions and forced society to move underground. Plays with present/past/future tense in ways both clever and confusing; the kind of movie that leaves you with plenty to talk about afterward. Inspired by Chris Marker's 1962 short film, LA JETÉE. [R]▼●◗

Twelve O'Clock High (1949) **132m.** **** D: Henry King. Gregory Peck, Hugh Marlowe, Gary Merrill, Millard Mitchell, Dean Jagger, Paul Stewart. Taut WW2 story of U.S. flyers in England, an officer replaced for getting too involved with his men (Merrill) and his successor who has same problem (Peck). Jagger won Oscar in supporting role; Peck has never been better. Written by Sy Bartlett and Beirne Lay, Jr., from their novel. Later a TV series.▼●

12:01 (1993) **C-92m. TVM** D: Jack Sholder. Jonathan Silverman, Helen Slater, Martin Landau, Nicolas Surovy, Robin Bartlett, Jeremy Piven. Office worker Silverman is the only one who realizes that the world is caught in a "time bounce," with every day repeating itself. Suspenseful, serious story that might be called the flip side of GROUNDHOG DAY. Based on a Richard Lupoff story that was first filmed as a short subject, "12:01" (1990), which was nominated for an Oscar. Above average.▼

12 + 1 SEE: **Thirteen Chairs, The**

12 to the Moon (1960) **74m.** BOMB D: David Bradley. Ken Clark, Michi Kobi, Tom Conway, Tony Dexter, John Wengraf, Anna-Lisa. International expedition to the moon encounters hostile aliens who freeze North America solid. An ambitious failure.

Twentieth Century (1934) **91m.** **** D: Howard Hawks. John Barrymore, Carole Lombard, Walter Connolly, Roscoe Karns, Etienne Girardot, Ralph Forbes, Charles Levison (Lane), Edgar Kennedy. Super screwball comedy in which egomaniacal Broadway producer Barrymore makes shopgirl Lombard a star; when she leaves him, he does everything he can to woo her back on lengthy train trip. Barrymore has never been funnier, and Connolly and Karns are aces as his long-suffering cronies. Matchless script by Ben Hecht and Charles MacArthur, from their play; later a hit Broadway musical, *On the Twentieth Century*.▼

Twenty Bucks (1993) **C-90m.** ** D: Keva Rosenfeld. Linda Hunt, Brendan Fraser, Elisabeth Shue, Steve Buscemi, Christopher Lloyd, Spalding Gray, David Rasche, George Morfogen, Concetta Tomei, Gladys Knight, William H. Macy, Diane Baker, David Schwimmer, Jeremy Piven, Kevin Kilner, Matt Frewer, Nina Siemaszko, Kamal Holloway. Intriguing concept—a $20 bill passes from hand to hand, and is briefly in the possession of a diverse group of people—but the result is slight and forgettable. Based on an unsold script written by Endre Boehm in 1935; this updated version was scripted by his son Leslie. Chloe Webb appears unbilled. [R]▼

20 Dates (1999) **C-88m.** **½ D: Myles Berkowitz. Wannabe filmmaker Berkowitz concocts the idea of filming twenty dates—as the hook to make a movie and as a means of finding love. Contemporary comedy, told in documentary style, is original and fun to watch, with a resolution neither Berkowitz nor the audience could have foreseen. [R]▼

28 Days (2000) **C-103m.** **½ D: Betty Thomas. Sandra Bullock, Viggo Mortensen, Dominic West, Diane Ladd, Elizabeth Perkins, Steve Buscemi, Alan Tudyk, Azura Skye, Michael O'Malley, Reni Santoni, Marianne Jean-Baptiste, Margo Martindale. Drunken N.Y. writer with an equally boozy boyfriend checks into rehab after an alcohol-induced accident. She gradually conforms to the program after the institution's seen-it-all patients swing their hatchets at the chip on her shoulder. After a strong beginning, film takes a quick nosedive by going for too many cheap belly-laughs. Helping to a point are generally strong performances, including Bullock's best to date. [PG-13]▼◗

28 Up (1985-British) **C/B&W-133m.** *** D: Michael Apted. Unique documentary in which Apted interviews a diverse group of individuals at ages 7, 14, 21, and 28. A one-of-a-kind portrayal of dreams, aspirations, and realities; fascinating to see the subjects literally age before your eyes. Raise this rating to ***½ if viewed in separate installments—the way it was originally made for TV. Followed by 35 UP.▼

25th Hour, The (1967-French-Italian-Yugoslavian) **C-119m.** ** D: Henri Verneuil. Anthony Quinn, Virna Lisi, Michael Redgrave, Gregoire Aslan, Marcel Dalio, Serge Reggiani. Story of Rumanian peasant's Nazi-enforced eight-year separation from his beautiful wife is indifferently done, in spite of capable acting by stars. Franscope.

24 Hours of the Rebel SEE: **September 30, 1955**

Twenty-four Hours to Kill (1965-British) **C-92m.** **½ D: Peter Bezencenet. Mickey Rooney, Lex Barker, Walter Slezak, Michael Medwin, Helga Somerfeld, Wolfgang Lukschy. OK suspenser with Rooney marked for execution by Slezak's smuggling ring when his plane is forced to land in Beirut for 24 hours. Techniscope.▼

24 Hour Woman, The (1999) **C-95m.** ** D: Nancy Savoca. Rosie Perez, Marianne Jean-Baptiste, Patti LuPone, Karen Duffy, Diego Serrano, Wendell Pierce, Aida Turturro, Rosana De Soto, Chris Cooper. Producer of a morning TV show discovers she's pregnant, and begins to deal with the conflicts facing a career woman who's also trying to start a family. Meanwhile, a mother of three returns to the workforce as her new assistant. Credible and energetic, but the "lesson" it teaches is obvious from the start. A disappointment from talented filmmaker Savoca. [R]▼

TwentyFourSeven (1997-British) **96m.** *** D: Shane Meadows. Bob Hoskins, Danny Nussbaum, James Hooton, Darren Campbell, Justin Brady, Jimmy Hynd, Karl Collins, Johann Myers, Anthony Clarke. Poignant, hard-hitting little drama about an idealistic 1980s burnout (Hoskins) who tries to encourage the aimless, angry young men in his working-class town by setting up a boxing club. What might have been a standard, clichéd story is uplifted by a solid script (by Meadows and Paul Fraser), good performances, and plenty of grit. [R]▼●

20 Million Miles to Earth (1957) **82m.** *** D: Nathan Juran. William Hopper, Joan Taylor, Frank Puglia, Thomas Browne Henry, John Zaremba, Tito Vuolo, Bart Bradley. First spaceship to Venus crashes into the sea off Sicily, with two survivors: pilot Hopper and a fast-growing Venusian monster that just wants to be left alone (but fights back when frightened). Climax takes place in the Colosseum in Rome. Intelligent script, fast pace, and exceptional special effects by Ray Harryhausen make this one of the best monster-on-the-loose movies ever. Monster is unnamed in the film, but is known as "the Ymir" to its fans.▼●

Twenty Million Sweethearts (1934) **89m.** **½ D: Ray Enright. Dick Powell, Ginger Rogers, Pat O'Brien, Allen Jenkins, Grant Mitchell, The Mills Brothers. Contrived musical about unscrupulous promoter O'Brien building Powell into radio star, career coming between him and happy marriage to Ginger. Plot soon wears thin, as does constant repetition of Powell's "I'll String Along With You," but bright cast helps out. Two good songs by the Mills Bros. Remade as MY DREAM IS YOURS.

20 Mule Team (1940) **84m.** ** D: Richard Thorpe. Wallace Beery, Leo Carrillo, Marjorie Rambeau, Anne Baxter, Douglas Fowley. Minor Western of borax-miners in Arizona with usual Beery mugging and standard plot. Baxter's first film.

29th Street (1991) **C-101m.** **½ D: George Gallo. Danny Aiello, Anthony LaPaglia, Lainie Kazan, Frank Pesce, Donna Maghani, Rick Aiello, Vic Manni, Ron Karabatsos, Robert Forster, Pete Antico, Joe Franklin. Richly seasoned look at N.Y.C. Italian-Americans through the eyes of Frank Pesce, who sees his life as blessed with luck, even though it presents itself in strange ways; the story is told in flashback on the night of New York State's first lottery drawing. Aiello and LaPaglia are dynamite as father and son, and that's the real Frank Pesce as older brother Vito; he also cowrote the story, based on his life. Directing debut for MIDNIGHT RUN screenwriter Gallo. [R]▼●

Twenty-one (1991-British) **C-101m.** ** D: Don Boyd. Patsy Kensit, Jack Shepherd, Patrick Ryecart, Maynard Eziashi, Rufus Sewell, Sophie Thompson. One Brit's jog around the sexual track before reaching the age of . . . guess. Her array of beaus includes one junkie, and one married jerk who openly hustles her at his own wedding. Inferior to DARLING and THE GRASSHOPPER, of an earlier generation; Kensit's first-person monologues are unusually frank but not as captivating as intended. [R]▼●

21 Days Together (1939-British) **75m.** **½ D: Basil Dean. Vivien Leigh, Laurence Olivier, Hay Petrie, Leslie Banks, Francis L. Sullivan. John Galsworthy's play of lovers with three weeks together before man goes on trial for murder; Olivier and Leigh are fine in worthwhile, but not outstanding, film. Script by Graham Greene. Original title: 21 DAYS.●

Twenty Plus Two (1961) **102m.** ** D: Joseph M. Newman. David Janssen, Jeanne Crain, Dina Merrill, Agnes Moorehead, Brad Dexter. Poor production values detract from potential of yarn with private eye Janssen investigating a murder, encountering a neat assortment of people.

27th Day, The (1957) **75m.** **½ D: William Asher. Gene Barry, Valerie French, Arnold Moss, George Voskovec. Imaginative sci-fi study of human nature with five people given pellets capable of destroying the world. Based on John Mantley's novel.▼

20,000 Eyes (1961) **60m.** *½ D: Jack Leewood. Gene Nelson, Merry Anders, John Banner, James Brown. Flabby robbery caper done on shoestring budget. CinemaScope.

20,000 Leagues Under the Sea (1954) **C-127m.** **** D: Richard Fleischer. Kirk Douglas, James Mason, Paul Lukas, Peter Lorre, Robert J. Wilke, Carleton Young. Superb Disney fantasy-adventure on grand scale, from Jules Verne's novel. Scientist Lukas and sailor Douglas get involved with power-hungry Captain Nemo (Mason) who operates futuristic submarine. Memorable action sequences, fine cast make this a winner. Won Oscars for Art Direction and Special Effects. Too bad its widescreen look is lost on TV. First filmed in 1916. Remade in 1997 as both a miniseries and made-for-TV movie. CinemaScope.▼●◗

20,000 Pound Kiss, The (1963-British) **57m.** **½ D: John Moxey. Dawn Addams, Michael Goodliffe, Richard Thorp, Anthony Newlands. Edgar Wallace tale of blackmail, with a most intricate plot.

20,000 Years in Sing Sing (1933) **81m.** *** D: Michael Curtiz. Spencer Tracy, Bette Davis, Arthur Byron, Lyle Talbot, Warren Hymer, Louis Calhern, Grant Mitchell, Sheila Terry. Still-powerful prison drama has only teaming of Tracy and Davis. He's a hardened criminal, she's his girl. Based on Warden Lewis F. Lawes' book. Remade as CASTLE ON THE HUDSON.

23 Paces to Baker Street (1956) **C-103m.** *** D: Henry Hathaway. Van Johnson, Vera Miles, Cecil Parker, Patricia Laffan, Maurice Denham, Estelle Winwood. Absorbing suspenser filmed in London has blind playwright Johnson determined to thwart crime plans he has overheard. CinemaScope.▼

Twice Dead (1988) **C-85m.** *½ D: Bert Dragin. Tom Breznahan, Jill Whitlow, Jonathan Chapin, Christopher Burgard, Sam Melville, Brooke Bundy, Todd Bridges. Boring horror programmer with an all-too-familiar setting: a mansion, haunted by a dead movie star whose spirit assists its new inhabitants in a battle against some punks. [R]▼●

Twice in a Lifetime (1985) **C-111m.** *** D: Bud Yorkin. Gene Hackman, Ann-Margret, Ellen Burstyn, Amy Madigan, Ally Sheedy, Brian Dennehy, Stephen Lang, Darrell Larson. Middle-aged man falls in love with younger woman and must endure the pain he causes not only his wife but also his children—especially his oldest daughter. Realistic look at the way different people react to situation keeps this film away from cliché and predictability; superior acting, especially by Hackman, Burstyn, and Madigan (as the angry daughter) make it special. Written by Colin Welland. [R]▼●

Twice Round the Daffodils (1962-British) **89m.** ** D: Gerald Thomas. Juliet Mills, Donald Sinden, Donald Houston, Kenneth Williams, Jill Ireland, Nanette Newman. Mills is charming nurse in a male TB ward, trying to avoid romantic inclinations of her patients; expected sex jokes abound.

Twice-Told Tales (1963) **C-119m.** *** D: Sidney Salkow. Vincent Price, Sebastian Cabot, Mari Blanchard, Brett Halsey, Richard Denning. Episodic adaptation of Hawthorne stories has good cast, imaginative direction, and sufficient atmosphere to keep one's interest. One of the TALES is an abbreviated HOUSE OF THE SEVEN GABLES, which also starred Price in the 1940 version.▼●

Twice Upon a Time (1983) **C-75m.** ***½ D: John Korty, Charles Swenson. Voices of Lorenzo Music, Judith Kahan Kampmann, Marshall Efron, James Cranna, Julie Payne, Hamilton Camp, Paul Frees. Captivating, hilarious animated feature done in a pseudo-cut-out style called "Lumage." Evil bosses of the Murkworks intend to blanket the world with perpetual nightmares; only a looney (and indescribable) bunch of would-be heroes can stop them. Too complex and fast-paced for small children, but a real treat for everyone else. Never given a full theatrical release, despite having George Lucas as executive producer. [PG]▼●

Twice Upon a Yesterday (1998-Spanish-British) **C-96m.** ** D: Maria Ripoll. Douglas Henshall, Lena Headey, Penélope Cruz, Gustavo Salmeron, Eusebio Lazaro, Mark Strong, Charlotte Coleman, Elizabeth McGovern. Scotsman Henshall torpedoes his longtime relationship with Headey through his constant philandering. Then two garbage men with magical powers enable him to go back in time and make things right. Odd, undernourished little film doesn't make the most of its premise. [R]▼

Twilight (1998) **C-94m.** **½ D: Robert Benton. Paul Newman, Susan Sarandon, Gene Hackman, Reese Witherspoon, Stockard Channing, James Garner, Giancarlo Esposito, Liev Schreiber, Margo Martindale, John Spencer, M. Emmet Walsh. Newman does a favor for old friend Hackman and finds himself waist-deep in murder and intrigue, as skeletons tumble out of the closet. Old-fashioned private-eye yarn, set in L.A. Newman is in fine form, surrounded by a great cast, but the film lacks spark, momentum, and an original point of view. Benton cowrote this with

Richard Russo, but this is no match for their earlier collaboration (with Newman), NOBODY'S FOOL. [R]▼●◗
Twilight for the Gods (1958) **C-120m.** ★★½ D: Joseph Pevney. Rock Hudson, Cyd Charisse, Arthur Kennedy, Leif Erickson, Charles McGraw, Ernest Truex, Richard Haydn, Wallace Ford. Ernest K. Gann book, adapted by the author, becomes turgid soaper of people on run-down vessel heading for Mexico, their trials and tribulations to survive when ship goes down.
Twilight of Honor (1963) **115m.** ★★½ D: Boris Sagal. Richard Chamberlain, Nick Adams, Joan Blackman, Claude Rains, Joey Heatherton, James Gregory, Pat Buttram, Jeanette Nolan. Routine drama of struggling lawyer who wins murder case with assistance of older expert Rains. Look for Linda Evans in a bit part. Panavision.
Twilight of the Golds (1997) **C-93m.** ★★★ D: Ross Marks. Jennifer Beals, Faye Dunaway, Brendan Fraser, Garry Marshall, Sean O'Bryan, Jon Tenney, Rosie O'Donnell. Reality-based film focuses on the ensuing turmoil after a geneticist's pregnant wife undergoes genetic testing. Thought-provoking drama, outstanding cast; Fraser is particularly captivating as gay Uncle David. Based on an off-Broadway play. Debuted on cable TV before theatrical release. [PG-13]▼●◗
Twilight People (1972-U.S.-Filipino) **C-84m.** BOMB D: Eddie Romero. John Ashley, Pat Woodell, Charles Macaulay, Pam Grier, Jan Merlin, Eddie Garcia. Incredibly inept rip-off of ISLAND OF LOST SOULS has former SS doctor performing hideous experiments resulting in beings half-human, half-creature. Will put insomniacs to sleep. Aka BEASTS. [PG]▼
Twilight's Last Gleaming (1977-U.S.-German) **C-146m.** ★★½ D: Robert Aldrich. Burt Lancaster, Richard Widmark, Charles Durning, Melvyn Douglas, Paul Winfield, Burt Young, Joseph Cotten, Roscoe Lee Browne, Gerald S. O'Loughlin, Richard Jaeckel, Vera Miles, Leif Erickson, Charles McGraw, John Ratzenberger. Unstable Air Force officer seizes missile installation, threatens to start World War 3 unless U.S. comes clean on its former Vietnam policy. OK if overlong; based on Walter Wager's novel *Viper Three.* [R]▼●
Twilight Time (1983-U.S.-Yugoslavian) **C-102m.** ★½ D: Goran Paskaljevic. Karl Malden, Jodi Thelen, Damien Nash, Mia Roth, Pavle Vujisic, Dragon Maksimovic. Sincere but unsuccessful film about an old man saddled with the upbringing of two grandchildren in rural Yugoslavia. Malden's performance is first-rate, but uneasy blend of American and Yugoslav elements and snail's pace all but sink it. [PG]
Twilight Zone—The Movie (1983) **C-102m.** ★★½ D: John Landis, Steven Spielberg, Joe Dante, George Miller. Vic Morrow, Scatman Crothers, Bill Quinn, Selma Diamond, Kathleen Quinlan, Jeremy Licht, Kevin McCarthy, William Schallert, John Lithgow, Abbe Lane, Bill Mumy, John Larroquette, narrated by Burgess Meredith. Dan Aykroyd and Albert Brooks provide entertaining prologue for four unusual tales (three actual remakes from Rod Serling's classic TV series), but none of them provides all-important moment of revelation that made the show so memorable . . . and more tellingly, none improves on the original. Best—final segment, remake of "Nightmare at 20,000 Feet," with Lithgow as terrified airline passenger, though even this episode is more explicit (and therefore less intriguing) than '60s TV version. [PG]▼●
Twin Beds (1942) **85m.** ★★ D: Tim Whelan. Joan Bennett, George Brent, Mischa Auer, Una Merkel, Glenda Farrell, Margaret Hamilton. Life of married couple Bennett and Brent is constantly interrupted by wacky neighbor Auer; and it's his film, too.▼
Twin Dragons (1992-Hong Kong) **C-89m.** ★★★ D: Ringo Lam, Tsui Hark. Jackie Chan, Maggie Cheung, Teddy Robin (Kwan), Nina Li Chi, Alfred Cheung, Lai Ying Chow, Kirk Wong. Separated at birth, twin Jackies unexpectedly meet in Hong Kong; one's a famous conductor, the other a race car mechanic whose best friend has just been kidnapped; the twins are mentally linked, Corsican Brothers–style. Fast-paced action comedy with great stunts is one of Jackie's best vehicles, if silly at times. Reedited and redubbed for 1999 U.S. theatrical release from the 100m. original. Directors Lam and Hark have cameos, as does John Woo. Original title: SEUNG LUNG WUI. Technovision. [PG-13]▼●◗
Twin Falls, Idaho (1999) **C-110m.** ★★½ D: Michael Polish. Michael Polish, Mark Polish, Michele Hicks, Jon Gries, Patrick Bauchau, Lesley Ann Warren, Garrett Morris, William Katt, Holly Woodlawn. Dreamy, oddball tale of Siamese twins, one of whom falls in love with a down-on-her-luck prostitute (Hicks). Surprisingly poignant film about family ties never opts for the grotesque and has a refreshing sense of deadpan humor. Ambitious debut from the Polish brothers, who wrote and costar. Only problem is overlength. [R]▼◗
Twinkle and Shine SEE: **It Happened to Jane**
Twinkle in God's Eye, The (1955) **73m.** ★★ D: George Blair. Mickey Rooney, Coleen Gray, Hugh O'Brian, Joey Forman, Michael Connors. Simple yarn of clergyman Rooney trying to convert wrongdoers in Western town to God's faith via good humor.
Twinkle, Twinkle, Killer Kane SEE: **Ninth Configuration, The**
Twin Peaks: Fire Walk With Me (1992) **C-135m.** ★½ D: David Lynch. Sheryl Lee, Ray Wise, Kyle MacLachlan, Mädchen Amick, Dana Ashbrook, Phoebe Augus-

tine, David Bowie, Eric DaRe, Miguel Ferrer, Pamela Gidley, Heather Graham, Chris Isaak, Moira Kelly, Peggy Lipton, James Marshall, Jürgen Prochnow, Harry Dean Stanton, Kiefer Sutherland, Lenny Von Dohlen, Grace Zabriskie, Frank Silva, Victor Rivers, Calvin Lockhart. Prototypically weird, but also strangely indifferent, prequel to the cult TV series, chronicling the final week in the life of murdered teen Laura Palmer (Lee). Lee is rather affecting under the circumstances, but film was understandably hissed at the Cannes Film Festival and greeted by moviegoer ennui here at home. Two surreal set pieces (one in a bar, the other in a traffic jam) may make it worthwhile for Lynch completists. The director appears as FBI Bureau Chief Gordon Cole. [R]▼●

Twins (1988) **C-112m.** *** D: Ivan Reitman. Arnold Schwarzenegger, Danny DeVito, Kelly Preston, Chloe Webb, Bonnie Bartlett, Marshall Bell, Trey Wilson, Hugh O'Brian, Nehemiah Persoff, David Caruso, Maury Chaykin. Entertaining comedy about genetically designed twins (Schwarzenegger and DeVito!) who discover each other's existence at the age of 35. Effectively blends sentiment and roughhouse humor, with the two mismatched stars packing extra punch in their delightful performances. That's Heather Graham as the mom-to-be in the opening scene. [PG] ▼●◗

Twins of Evil (1971-British) **C-85m.** **½ D: John Hough. Peter Cushing, Madeleine Collinson, Mary Collinson, Luan Peters, Dennis Price, Isobel Black, Harvey Hall. One of the twins is a vampire, but nobody can tell which is which. Engaging Hammer chiller makes inspired use of *Playboy*'s first twin playmates. Follow-up to VAMPIRE LOVERS and LUST FOR A VAMPIRE [R]▼●

Twin Town (1997-British) **C-101m.** ** D: Kevin Allen. Llyr Evans, Rhys Ifans, Dorien Thomas, Dougray Scott, Biddug Williams, Ronnie Williams, Rachel Scorgle. Black comedy—more nasty than funny—about brothers who seek revenge on a bigwig roofing contractor after their handyman father takes a fall. Executive-produced by the makers of TRAINSPOTTING, this features the same brand of cheeky humor, and a rare look at life on the fringe in the U.K. (Swansea, Southwest Wales), but it stalls midway from absurd plotting and never recovers; we're left with irritating characters who have unintelligible dialects. The director cameos as a local TV host. [R]▼●

Twist, The (1976-French) **C-105m.** *½ D: Claude Chabrol. Bruce Dern, Stephane Audran, Ann-Margret, Sydne Rome, Jean-Pierre Cassel, Curt Jurgens, Maria Schell, Charles Aznavour. Undistinguished chronicle of the infidelities of various boring upper-class characters. Lackluster direction, with a superior cast wasted. Originally titled FOLIES BOURGEOISES, and filmed in both English and French versions.▼

Twist (1992-Canadian) **C/B&W-78m.** *** D: Ron Mann. Entertaining documentary about the early years of rock 'n' roll, culminating with the popularity of the Twist, the dance craze which swept the nation during the early 1960s. Interesting as a cultural document (showing how whites co-opted black music and styles), and great fun as a trip down memory lane.▼●

Twist All Night (1961) **78m.** BOMB D: William Hole, Jr. Louis Prima, June Wilkinson, Sam Butera and The Witnesses, Gertrude Michael, David Whorf. Stupid comedy about Prima's attempts to keep his nightclub going; sexy Wilkinson is his girlfriend. Sometimes shown with a nine-minute color prologue, TWIST CRAZE, directed by Allan David. Aka THE CONTINENTAL TWIST.

Twist and Shout (1984-Danish) **C-99m.** *** D: Bille August. Adam Tonsberg, Lars Simonsen, Ulrikke Juul Bondo, Camilla Soeberg, Thomas Nielsen. Funny, endearing, pleasantly nostalgic tale of a pair of teen buddies in the era of The Beatles' heyday. One (Simonsen) is dominated by his stern, manipulative father, while the other (Tonsberg) experiences the joy and pain of love. Sequel to August's earlier ZAPPA. [R]▼

Twist Around the Clock (1961) **86m.** ** D: Oscar Rudolph. Chubby Checker, Dion, The Marcels, Vicki Spencer, Clay Cole, John Cronin, Mary Mitchell. Agent Cronin tries to book Twist performers; of course, by the finale, the dance is the rage of America. Dion performs "The Wanderer" and "Runaround Sue." Remake of ROCK AROUND THE CLOCK.▼

Twisted (1992) **C-82m.** *½ D: Adam Holender. Lois Smith, Christian Slater, Tandy Cronyn, Brooke Tracy, Dina Merrill, Dan Ziskie, Karl Taylor, Noelle Parker, John Cunningham, J. C. Quinn. Sadistic teenage genius Slater, already a murderer, sets his sights on babysitter Smith, a recovering mental patient. Made in 1986. Talky, slow, unconvincing and extremely unpleasant. Aka TWISTED: A STEP BEYOND INSANITY. [R]▼◗

Twisted Brain (1974) **C-85m.** BOMB D: Larry N. Stouffer. Pat Cardi, Rosie Holotik, John Niland, Austin Stoker, Joye Hash. Wimpy high-school kid discovers Jekyll & Hyde formula and kills those who picked on him. Low-budget crud with unbelievably amateurish acting. Aka HORROR HIGH. [PG]▼

Twisted Obsession (1989-Spanish-French) **C-103m.** *½ D: Fernando Trueba. Jeff Goldblum, Miranda Richardson, Anemone, Daniel Ceccaldi, Dexter Fletcher, Liza Walker. Laughable, would-be erotic thriller, with Goldblum a writer in Paris who gets

mixed up with a strange British director and his seductive 16-year-old sister. Pretentious, enervated Eurotrash like this gives "art" movies a bad name . . . but where else could you see Goldblum playing an irresistible stud? Originally titled THE MAD MONKEY. Panavision. [R]▼●
Twister (1988) **C-94m.** *½ D: Michael Almereyda. Harry Dean Stanton, Suzy Amis, Crispin Glover, Dylan McDermott, Jenny Wright, Lois Chiles. Squirrelly clan comedy assembles some unlikely siblings at the old man's mansion; try imagining Stanton as any extended group's patriarch! Film's eccentricity is more off-putting than whimsical; Amis and Glover as siblings would be a challenge to any parent's reproductive tract. Based on Mary Robison's well-regarded novel *OH!*. [PG-13]▼●◗
Twister (1996) **C-114m.** *** D: Jan De Bont. Helen Hunt, Bill Paxton, Cary Elwes, Jami Gertz, Lois Smith, Alan Ruck, Philip Seymour Hoffman, Jeremy Davies, Todd Field, Zach Grenier, Jake Busey. A wild ride of a movie, dealing with storm chasers who want to learn all they can about tornadoes—by getting inside them. The plot and characterizations are best described as lame, but the special effects are so convincing, and the storms so incredible, that they carry you along (no pun intended) from one kinetic burst to another. Great fun. Written by Michael Crichton and his wife, Anne-Marie Martin. Panavision. [PG-13]▼●◗
Twist of Fate (1954-British) **89m.** ** D: David Miller. Ginger Rogers, Herbert Lom, Stanley Baker, Jacques Bergerac, Margaret Rawlings, Coral Browne, Lisa Gastoni, Ferdy Mayne. Turgid thriller in which Rogers is taken in by wealthy Baker, who lavishes her with gifts, which she accepts because she thinks marriage is in the offing. But she's unaware of the true nature of his business, and his marital status. Original British title: BEAUTIFUL STRANGER.▼
Twist of Sand, A (1968-British) **C-90m.** ** D: Don Chaffey. Richard Johnson, Honor Blackman, Jeremy Kemp, Peter Vaughan, Roy Dotrice. Ex-submarine commander Johnson leads crew of smugglers on expedition for diamonds in ordinary programmer.
Twitch of the Death Nerve (1971-Italian) **C-90m.** *** D: Mario Bava. Claudine Auger, Claudio Volonte, Luigi Pistilli, Leopoldo Trieste, Isa Miranda, Laura Betti. The *ne plus ultra* of Bava's colorful horror movies, this influenced such later films as HALLOWEEN and FRIDAY THE 13TH. People in an isolated house are killed one by one in gruesome, imaginative ways. Those who love Bava don't love him for his stories, but for his extraordinary mastery of cinema technique, vividly displayed here. Aka LAST HOUSE ON THE LEFT, PART II (though it has no connection with Part I), BAY OF BLOOD, and CARNAGE—with good reason. Panoramica. [R]▼
Two Against the World (1936) **57m.** ** D: William McGann. Humphrey Bogart, Beverly Roberts, Linda Perry, Carlyle Moore, Jr., Henry O'Neill, Claire Dodd. Remake of FIVE STAR FINAL set in radio station is more contrived, not as effective. Retitled: ONE FATAL HOUR.
Two and Two Make Six (1961-British) **89m.** ** D: Freddie Francis. George Chakiris, Janette Scott, Alfred Lynch, Jackie Lane. Mild romantic yarn of A.W.O.L. soldier Chakiris falling in love with Scott.
Two Bits (1995) **C-93m.** **½ D: James Foley. Mary Elizabeth Mastrantonio, Al Pacino, Jerry Barrone, Patrick Borriello, Andy Romano, Donna Mitchell, Mary Lou Rosato, Joe Grifasi, Joanna Merlin; narrated by Alec Baldwin. Poignant memoir of growing up in South Philadelphia during the Depression, as seen through the eyes of young Gennaro (Barrone, in his movie debut), who lives with his widowed mother and his talkative grandfather (Pacino)—who insists he's going to die any day now. Beautifully acted by the leads, written with feeling by producer Joseph Stefano, but too slow and delicate to realize its full potential. Still worth seeing for a handful of crystalline moments. Panavision. [PG-13]▼●
Two Daughters (1961-Indian) **114m.** ***½ D: Satyajit Ray. Anil Chatterjee, Chandana Bannerjee, Soumitra Chatterjee, Aparna Das Gupta, Sita Mukherji. A pair of episodes, adapted from the writings of Rabindranath Tagore, one good and the other superb. The former concerns the curious relationship between a postmaster and an orphan girl; the latter is the funny, gentle chronicle of what happens when a student rejects the woman his mother has chosen for his wife, deciding instead to marry the local tomboy. Ray scripted both stories. Originally released in India as part of a trilogy, running 171m.▼
2 Days in the Valley (1996) **C-107m.** *** D: John Herzfeld. Danny Aiello, James Spader, Eric Stoltz, Greg Cruttwell, Jeff Daniels, Teri Hatcher, Glenne Headly, Peter Horton, Marsha Mason, Paul Mazursky, Charlize Theron, Keith Carradine, Louise Fletcher, Austin Pendleton, Lawrence Tierney. Wry crime thriller with gnarled plot involving a murder for hire, a betrayed crook, his slick partner, a dogged cop, a deadly wife, and others caroming off each other in L.A.'s San Fernando Valley. Entertaining and stylish, with fine performances, but more than a little contrived. Written by the director. Panavision. [R]▼●◗
Two Deaths (1995-British) **C-102m.** ** D: Nicolas Roeg. Michael Gambon, Sonia Braga, Patrick Malahide, Ion Caramitru, Nickolas Grace. Bizarre drama about a doctor (Gambon) who has various guests in his home for an elegant dinner party while, out-

side, a revolution rages and the streets are filling with blood. Braga is the host's mysterious, silent housekeeper. Potentially intriguing drama is done in by its obvious symbolism and leaden pace. [R]▼●◗

Two Dollar Bettor (1951) **73m.** ** D: Edward L. Cahn. John Litel, Marie Windsor, Steve Brodie, Barbara Logan. Nifty little programmer showing the snowballing of businessman Litel's problems, once he gets racetrack fever.▼

Two English Girls (1971-French) **C-108m.** ***½ D: François Truffaut. Jean-Pierre Léaud, Kika Markham, Stacey Tendeter, Sylvia Marriott, Marie Mansart, Philippe Leotard. Profoundly moving tale of a young writer (Léaud), and his lengthy love affair with two sisters. Fine performances and superb Nestor Almendros cinematography; directed with great feeling by Truffaut. In 1984, he added additional footage, increasing the running time to 132m.—and this version rates ****, one of Truffaut's greatest achievements.▼●◗

Two Evil Eyes (1990-Italian) **C-115m.** *½ D: George Romero, Dario Argento. "The Facts in the Case of Mr. Valdemar": Adrienne Barbeau, Ramy Zada, Bingo O'Malley, Jeff Howell, E. G. Marshall. "The Black Cat": Harvey Keitel, Madeleine Potter, John Amos, Sally Kirkland, Kim Hunter, Holter Ford Graham, Martin Balsam. A pair of Poe stories poorly adapted by two leading horror directors. In the first, by Romero, a greedy wife and unscrupulous doctor leave a man hovering in limbo between life and death. In the second, by Argento, a self-obsessed photographer kills his mistress' black cat, then seals the woman behind a wall with another feline. The second is slightly more successful than the first. [R]▼●

Two-Faced Woman (1941) **94m.** **½ D: George Cukor. Greta Garbo, Melvyn Douglas, Constance Bennett, Roland Young, Robert Sterling, Ruth Gordon, Frances Carson. Garbo's last film, in which MGM tried unsuccessfully to Americanize her personality. Attempted chic comedy of errors is OK, but not what viewer expects from the divine Garbo. Constance Bennett is much more at home in proceedings, stealing the film with her hilarious performance.▼

Two Faces of Dr. Jekyll, The (1960-British) **C-88m.** ** D: Terence Fisher. Paul Massie, Dawn Addams, Christopher Lee, David Kossoff, Francis De Wolff, Norma Marla. Uneven, sometimes unintentionally funny reworking of Stevenson story stresses Mr. and Mrs. relationship, plus fact that doctor himself is a weakling (and Hyde is suave and handsome!). Unfortunately, dialogue and situations are boring. Look for Oliver Reed as a bouncer. Originally shown in U.S. as HOUSE OF FRIGHT. Megascope.▼

Two Flags West (1950) **92m.** ** D: Robert Wise. Joseph Cotten, Linda Darnell, Jeff Chandler, Cornel Wilde, Dale Robertson, Jay C. Flippen, Noah Berry, Jr. Very uneven Civil War Western. Battle scenes of good quality mixed with unappealing script and weak performances.

Two for the Road (1967-British) **C-112m.** *** D: Stanley Donen. Audrey Hepburn, Albert Finney, Eleanor Bron, William Daniels, Claude Dauphin, Nadia Gray, Jacqueline Bisset. Beautifully acted film of bickering couple Hepburn and Finney stopping to reminisce about their twelve years of marriage, trying to work to save their happiness. Perceptive, winning film, well directed by Donen. Lovely theme by Henry Mancini; script by Frederic Raphael. Photographed by Christopher Challis, on luscious French locations. Panavision.▼●

Two for the Seesaw (1962) **120m.** *** D: Robert Wise. Robert Mitchum, Shirley MacLaine, Edmond Ryan, Elisabeth Fraser. Intelligent handling of William Gibson play. Mitchum is Midwest lawyer trying to rebuild life in N.Y.C., involved with eccentric MacLaine. Panavision.▼●

Two for Tonight (1935) **61m.** **½ D: Frank Tuttle. Bing Crosby, Joan Bennett, Mary Boland, Lynne Overman, Thelma Todd, James Blakeley. Songwriter Crosby is forced to write musical play in one week. Entertaining slapstick musical with Boland as his mother, Bennett his girl.

2 Friends (1986-Australian) **C-76m.** **½ D: Jane Campion. Kris Bidenko, Emma Coles, Kris McQuade, Peter Hehir, Kerry Dwyer, Stephen Leeder, Deborah May, Tony Barry, Steve Bisley. Campion's debut feature, produced for Australian television, is the slice-of-life portrait of a friendship between two adolescent girls, and the subtle changes in their relationship. Not without inspired moments, but lacks the assurance of Campion's later work. The scenario unravels in reverse time, a dramatic structure that seems more gimmicky than inspired. Released in the U.S. in 1996.▼

Two Gals and a Guy (1951) **71m.** ** D: Alfred E. Green. Janis Paige, Robert Alda, James Gleason, Lionel Stander. Trials and tribulations of married vocal duo, caught up in the early days of TV performing; standard production.

Two Gentlemen Sharing (1969-British) **C-92m.** ** D: Ted Kotcheff. Robin Phillips, Judy Geeson, Hal Frederick, Esther Anderson, Norman Rossington. Unusual story of mixed racial couples is done more with the sensational in mind than honest portrayal. [R]

Twogether (1994) **C-122m.** *½ D: Andrew Chiaramonte. Nick Cassavetes, Brenda Bakke, Damian London, Jeremy Piven, Jim Beaver. Overlong, uninvolving "relationship drama" in which a couple finds love and fights a lot, in Venice Beach, California. The bodies look good, and there are a couple of hot scenes, but there's nothing much else to recommend in this independently made feature. The leading man is John Cassavetes and Gena Rowlands' son. [R]▼

Two Girls and a Guy (1998) **C-92m.** ** D: James Toback. Robert Downey, Jr., Heather Graham, Natasha Gregson Wagner, Angel David, Frederique Van Der Wal. Two women—each of whom believes she has found the perfect lover—discover that they're both in love with the same man. Virtually a one-set (Downey's N.Y.C. loft) film, it's well played by the three leads but remains more of an actor's dream than a movie. Manages to be fairly funny and scathing in equal parts; also contains one serious though dimly lit sex scene. Wagner is the daughter of Natalie Wood. [R]▼●◗

Two Girls and a Sailor (1944) **124m.** *** D: Richard Thorpe. Van Johnson, June Allyson, Gloria DeHaven, Jose Iturbi, Jimmy Durante, Lena Horne, Donald Meek, Virginia O'Brien, Gracie Allen, Harry James and Xavier Cugat orchestras. Singing sisters Allyson and DeHaven operate a canteen for GIs, and become romantically linked with sailor-with-a-secret Johnson. Breezy entertainment, with many fine musical numbers (from Gracie Allen playing the piano to Lena Horne singing "Paper Doll"). Watch for Ava Gardner as a dancing showgirl and in the dream sequence.▼●

Two Girls on Broadway (1940) **71m.** ** D: S. Sylvan Simon. Lana Turner, George Murphy, Joan Blondell, Kent Taylor, Wallace Ford. Sisters love same man (Murphy) but everything works out in this routine musical, sparked by snappy Blondell. Remake of THE BROADWAY MELODY.

Two Gun Lady (1956) **75m.** ** D: Richard Bartlett. Peggie Castle, Marie Windsor, William Talman. Simple oater of female sure-shot and law enforcer tracking down her father's murderer.

Two Guns and a Badge (1954) **69m.** *½ D: Lewis D. Collins. Wayne Morris, Morris Ankrum, Beverly Garland, Roy Barcroft. Poor script uplifted by competent cast in story of ex-convict who is mistakenly hired as deputy sheriff.

Two Guys From Milwaukee (1946) **90m.** **½ D: David Butler. Dennis Morgan, Jack Carson, Joan Leslie, Janis Paige, S. Z. Sakall, Patti Brady. Silly story of European prince Morgan Americanized by cabdriver Carson; cast is so engaging it doesn't matter. Look for Humphrey Bogart and Lauren Bacall in cameos.

Two Guys From Texas (1948) **C-86m.** **½ D: David Butler. Dennis Morgan, Jack Carson, Dorothy Malone, Penny Edwards, Fred Clark, Forrest Tucker. Average musical about two vaudevillians who find themselves on a Texas ranch. Highlight is an animated sequence with Bugs Bunny and caricatures of Morgan and Carson. Remake of THE COWBOY FROM BROOKLYN.

Two-Headed Spy, The (1958-British) **93m.** *** D: Andre de Toth. Jack Hawkins, Gia Scala, Alexander Knox, Felix Aylmer, Donald Pleasence, Michael Caine, Laurence Naismith. Exciting true story of British spy (Hawkins) who operated in Berlin during WW2 is loaded with heart-stopping tension and suspense. Fine performances all around; one of Caine's earliest roles.

200 Cigarettes (1999) **C-101m.** *½ D: Risa Bramon Garcia. Ben Affleck, Casey Affleck, Jennifer Albano, Dave Chappelle, Guillermo Diaz, Angela Featherstone, Janeane Garofalo, Gaby Hoffmann, Kate Hudson, Catherine Keener, Courtney Love, Brian McCardie, Jay Mohr, Nicole Parker, Martha Plimpton, Christina Ricci, Paul Rudd, David Johansen, Elvis Costello. It's New Year's Eve 1981, in N.Y.C.'s East Village, with an assortment of young people trying (not too hard) to reach a loft party thrown by frantic Plimpton. Merits some sort of prize for Most Obnoxious Ensemble . . . and sorely lacks a coherent script. Hudson is Goldie Hawn's daughter. [R]▼●◗

200 Motels (1971) **C-98m.** **½ D: Frank Zappa, Tony Palmer. Frank Zappa, Mothers of Invention, Theodore Bikel, Ringo Starr, Keith Moon. Visual, aural assault disguised as movie; completely berserk, freeform film (shot on videotape in England) featuring bizarre humor of Zappa and the Mothers. Some of it ingenious, some funny, but not spellbinding enough to maintain entire film. Funny, raunchy animation sequence. [R] ▼●

Two If by Sea (1996) **C-96m.** *½ D: Bill Bennett. Denis Leary, Sandra Bullock, Stephen Dillane, Yaphet Kotto, Wayne Robson, Jonathan Tucker, Mike Starr, Michael Badalucco. Alternately boring and grating comedy about a pair of low-class lovers on the lam after he's stolen a valuable painting. Leary cowrote this unsatisfying "romantic" caper which changes moods with each scene. Bullock's charm emerges unscathed. [R]▼●

Two in a Crowd (1936) **85m.** ** D: Alfred E. Green. Joan Bennett, Joel McCrea, Henry Armetta, Alison Skipworth, Nat Pendleton, Reginald Denny, Andy Clyde, Donald Meek, Elisha Cook, Jr. Down-and-out McCrea and Bennett find a stolen $1,000 note on New Year's Eve. Starts cute, but quickly fizzles.

Two Jakes, The (1990) **C-137m.** ** D: Jack Nicholson. Jack Nicholson, Harvey Keitel, Meg Tilly, Madeleine Stowe, Eli Wallach, Ruben Blades, Frederic Forrest, David Keith, Richard Farnsworth, Tracey Walter, Joe Mantell, James Hong, Perry Lopez, Rebecca Broussard, Luana Anders. Belated sequel to CHINATOWN set in

1948 L.A., with oil having replaced water as the natural resource of choice. Jake Gittes investigates complex case of adultery and shady real estate dealings by Keitel (excellent, as the other Jake) and cheating wife Tilly. Ponderous and convoluted beyond belief (though never boring), film will make no sense to anyone who's never seen CHINATOWN; the old indecipherable plot routine that worked for THE BIG SLEEP (1946) doesn't cut it here. Faye Dunaway makes a brief (and welcome) contribution; Tom Waits appears unbilled as a policeman. Super 35. [R]▼●◗

Two-Lane Blacktop (1971) **C-101m.** ***½ D: Monte Hellman. James Taylor, Warren Oates, Laurie Bird, Dennis Wilson, David Drake, Richard Ruth, Alan Vint. Cult film about race across the Southwest between a '55 Chevy and a new GTO has intense direction to compensate for low-key script; Oates' performance is about as good as you'll ever see and should have had the Oscar. Quintessential movie of its time, with aimless characters who only know one thing: the need to race their cars. Watch for Harry Dean Stanton as a hitchhiker. Techniscope. [R]▼●◗

Two Little Bears, The (1961) **81m.** ** D: Randall Hood. Eddie Albert, Jane Wyatt, Soupy Sales, Nancy Kulp, Brenda Lee. Harmless fable-comedy of Albert confused to discover that his two children turn into bears at night, cavorting around the house. CinemaScope.

Two Lost Worlds (1950) **61m.** *½ D: Norman Dawn. Laura Elliott, James Arness, Bill Kennedy, Gloria Petroff. Draggy story of shipwreck on uncharted island with prehistoric monsters; stock footage courtesy of ONE MILLION B.C. Cast doesn't reach island until last twenty minutes; you may not wait that long.▼◗

Two Loves (1961) **C-100m.** ** D: Charles Walters. Shirley MacLaine, Laurence Harvey, Jack Hawkins, Juano Hernandez, Nobu McCarthy. Plodding sudser set in New Zealand with spinster teacher MacLaine trying to decide between suitors Harvey and Hawkins. CinemaScope.

Two Minute Warning (1976) **C-115m.** *½ D: Larry Peerce. Charlton Heston, John Cassavetes, Martin Balsam, Beau Bridges, Marilyn Hassett, David Janssen, Jack Klugman, Gena Rowlands, Walter Pidgeon, Brock Peters, David Groh, Mitchell Ryan, Pamela Bellwood, Andy Sidaris, Vincent Baggetta, Robert Ginty. Pointless story of attempt to catch sniper in packed football stadium. Usual melange of hackneyed characters in this contrived Hollywood product. Merv Griffin sings the national anthem! (Film heavily doctored for network showing, with nearly one hour added including new cast and subplot; this review applies to original theatrical version.) Panavision. [R]▼●◗

Two-Moon Junction (1988) **C-104m.** **½ D: Zalman King. Sherilyn Fenn, Richard Tyson, Louise Fletcher, Burl Ives, Kristy McNichol, Millie Perkins, Don Galloway, Herve Villechaize, Dabbs Greer, Screamin' Jay Hawkins. Or, *Sorority Girl Goes Nympho.* Well-bred Dixie beauty gets an itch south of the navel to take off with a traveling carny hunk; rich grandma Fletcher and sheriff Ives conspire to halt the union. Camp fest is just funny and sexy enough to maintain interest; McNichol has a lively cameo as a bisexual cowgirl. The title *may* be a pun. Followed by a sequel. [R]▼●◗

Two Mrs. Carrolls, The (1947) **99m.** **½ D: Peter Godfrey. Humphrey Bogart, Barbara Stanwyck, Alexis Smith, Nigel Bruce, Isobel Elsom. Shrill murder drama with Bogie as psychopathic artist who paints wives as Angels of Death, then kills them; Stanwyck registers all degrees of panic as the next marital victim. Filmed in 1945. Also shown in computer-colored version.▼

Two Mrs. Grenvilles, The (1987) **C-200m. TVM** D: John Erman. Ann-Margret, Claudette Colbert, Stephen Collins, Elizabeth Ashley, John Rubinstein, Penny Fuller, Sam Wanamaker. Showgirl marries into socially proper N.Y. family to the dismay of the matriarch and brings scandal when she ''accidentally'' shoots her husband. Derek Marlowe's well-crafted adaptation of Dominick Dunne's novel, loosely based on the 1955 killing of Long Island socialite William Woodward, Jr., provides showy star turns for both leading ladies. Notable mainly for Colbert's return to film after twenty-five years, as well as her swan song. Originally shown in two parts. Above average.

Two Much (1996-U.S.-Spanish) **C-118m.** *½ D: Fernando Trueba. Antonio Banderas, Melanie Griffith, Daryl Hannah, Danny Aiello, Joan Cusack, Eli Wallach, Austin Pendleton, Gabino Diego, Alan Rich, Phil Leeds, Vincent Schiavelli. Miami scam artist Banderas falls for the sister of his new finacée and pretends to be his own twin brother in order to pursue her. Would-be screwball comedy is filled with embarrassing dialogue, which cast struggles to surmount by overacting. A fiasco . . . and an unfortunate English-language debut for the director of the Oscar-winning BELLE EPOQUE. Based on a novel by Donald E. Westlake. Panavision. [PG-13]▼●

Two Mules for Sister Sara (1970) **C-105m.** *** D: Don Siegel. Clint Eastwood, Shirley MacLaine, Manolo Fabregas, Alberto Morin, Armando Silvestre. Engaging story of drifter Eastwood helping nun MacLaine across Mexican desert, becoming wary of her un-pious nature. Beautifully shot (by Gabriel Figueroa), well-acted, good fun, marred by needlessly violent massacre climax. Albert Maltz wrote the screenplay, from a story by Budd Boetticher. Panavision. [M/PG]▼

Twonky, The (1953) **72m.** *½ D. Arch Oboler. Hans Conried, Gloria Blondell, Trilby Conried, Billy Lynn. Satirical sci-fi is misfire entertainment, when Conried's TV set actually takes charge of his life, possessed by a spirit from the future.

Two O'Clock Courage (1945) **68m.** ** D: Anthony Mann. Tom Conway, Ann Rutherford, Richard Lane, Lester Matthews, Roland Drew, Bettejane (Jane) Greer. Conway wakes up on a street corner with amnesia and finds himself the top suspect in a murder case, joins with cabbie Rutherford to solve mystery. Routine effort which looks and sounds like a typical SAINT or FALCON entry, but is actually a remake of a 1936 film, TWO IN THE DARK.

Two of a Kind (1951) **75m.** **½ D: Henry Levin. Edmond O'Brien, Lizabeth Scott, Terry Moore, Alexander Knox. Uninspired suspenser about con-artists plotting to dupe an elderly couple out of their inheritance fund.

Two of a Kind (1983) **C-87m.** BOMB D: John Herzfeld. John Travolta, Olivia Newton-John, Charles Durning, Oliver Reed, Beatrice Straight, Scatman Crothers, Castulo Guerra, Ernie Hudson, Kathy Bates, voice of Gene Hackman. Puerile fantasy-romance with a script that must have been scrawled on a gum wrapper. A quartet of angels try to persuade God to give the human race another chance—using two pretty unappealing subjects (an inventor-turned-bank robber and a not-so-innocent bank teller) as guinea pigs. Just awful. [PG]▼●

Two of Us, The (1968-French) **86m.** ***½ D: Claude Berri. Michel Simon, Alain Cohen, Luce Fabiole, Roger Carel, Paul Preboist, Charles Denner. Charming film about growing relationship between young Jewish boy sent away from WW2 Paris and blustery, anti-Semitic guardian who lives in the country. Warm, funny, beautifully acted.▼

Two on a Guillotine (1965) **107m.** **½ D: William Conrad. Connie Stevens, Dean Jones, Cesar Romero, Parley Baer, Virginia Gregg. To receive inheritance from late father (Romero), Connie must spend night in haunted house. Familiar plot with some scares. Panavision.

Two People (1973) **C-100m.** **½ D: Robert Wise. Peter Fonda, Lindsay Wagner, Estelle Parsons, Alan Fudge, Geoffrey Horne, Frances Sternhagen. Soapy, but oddly affecting drama about Army deserter returning home to face the consequences and fashion model with whom he falls in love. Beautiful photography by Gerald Hirschfeld and likable performance by Wagner in her first major role. [R]

Two Rode Together (1961) **C-109m.** **½ D: John Ford. James Stewart, Richard Widmark, Linda Cristal, Shirley Jones, Andy Devine, John McIntire, Mae Marsh, Henry Brandon, Anna Lee. Fair Western with Stewart as cynical marshal hired to rescue pioneers captured by the Comanches years ago; Widmark is cavalry officer who accompanies him.▼●

Two Seconds (1932) **68m.** **½ D: Mervyn LeRoy. Edward G. Robinson, Vivienne Osborne, Preston Foster, J. Carrol Naish, Guy Kibbee, Berton Churchill. Offbeat and engrossing, if not entirely successful, melodrama tells Robinson's life as he sees it in two seconds it takes for him to die in electric chair. Often overplayed, sometimes unusually effective; a most interesting curio.

Two Sisters From Boston (1946) **112m.** *** D: Henry Koster. Kathryn Grayson, June Allyson, Lauritz Melchior, Jimmy Durante, Peter Lawford, Ben Blue. Grayson and Allyson go to work in Durante's Bowery saloon in this entertaining turn-of-the-century musical; bright score helps.▼

Two Small Bodies (1993) **C-85m.** **½ D: Beth B. Fred Ward, Suzy Amis. Suspicious, neurotic cop Ward investigates the mysterious disappearance of the two children of cocktail waitress Amis, who seems strangely ambivalent over the tragedy. Eerie, effective two-character psychodrama; however, both characters are so unlikable that the film occasionally becomes difficult to watch.▼

Two Smart People (1946) **93m.** ** D: Jules Dassin. Lucille Ball, John Hodiak, Lloyd Nolan, Hugo Haas, Lenore Ulric, Elisha Cook, Jr. Conniving couple involved in art forgery; laughs don't come very often. Cowritten by Leslie Charteris.

2001: A Space Odyssey (1968-British) **C-139m.** **** D: Stanley Kubrick. Keir Dullea, William Sylvester, Gary Lockwood, Daniel Richter; voice of HAL: Douglas Rain. A unique masterpiece, immensely influential; Kubrick starkly depicts several encounters mankind has with never-glimpsed aliens, from the dawn of Man four million years ago to the title year, when an alien artifact is found on the Moon. An expedition tracking its radio signal is launched to Jupiter, with mysterious, haunting results. A visual feast, film also boasts distinction of having put Richard Strauss into the Top 40 with "Also Sprach Zarathustra." Cut by 17 minutes after premiere, by Kubrick himself, to present length. Oscar-winning special effects. Screenplay by Arthur C. Clarke and the director, from Clarke's *The Sentinel*. Followed by **2010** in 1984. Super Panavision 70. [G]▼●◗

2010 (1984) **C-114m.** *** D: Peter Hyams. Roy Scheider, John Lithgow, Helen Mirren, Bob Balaban, Keir Dullea, Madolyn Smith, Dana Elcar, Elya Baskin, Savely Kramarov; voice of Douglas Rain. Ambitious sequel to 2001: A SPACE ODYSSEY written by director Hyams from the follow-up novel by Arthur C. Clarke (who has a cameo on Washington park bench). Scheider is perfect Everyman who journeys into space on joint American-Soviet mission to solve mystery of what went wrong on original *Discovery* flight. More concrete and therefore less mystical than 2001, with an ending that's *much* too literal, but still an entertaining journey, with state-of-the-art visual effects by Richard Edlund. Panavision. [PG]▼●◗

2000 Years Later (1969) **C-80m.** ** D: Bert Tenzer. Terry-Thomas, Edward Everett Horton, John Abbott, Pat Harrington, Lisa Seagram, Monti Rock III, Rudi Gernreich. Amusing story of 20th-century man exploiting a Roman soldier who comes back to life after 2000 years. [R]

Two Tickets to Broadway (1951) **C-106m.** **½ D: James V. Kern. Tony Martin, Janet Leigh, Gloria De Haven, Eddie Bracken, Ann Miller, Barbara Lawrence, Smith and Dale, Bob Crosby. Modest musical involving Martin et al. trying to get on Crosby's TV show. Forget the hackneyed plot and enjoy the Jule Styne–Leo Robin score, along with old standards. Best bit: Crosby's musical spoof of brother Bing, "Let's Make Comparisons" (by Bob C. and Sammy Cahn).▼

Two Tickets to London (1943) **79m.** ** D: Edwin L. Marin. Michele Morgan, Alan Curtis, Barry Fitzgerald, C. Aubrey Smith. Passable drama of Curtis helped by Morgan in hunting down espionage agents.

Two Tickets to Paris (1962) **78m.** BOMB D: Greg Garrison. Joey Dee and The Starlighters, Gary Crosby, Kay Medford, Jeri Lynne Fraser, Lisa James, Charles Nelson Reilly. Engaged to be married teenagers Dee and Fraser sail for France, with each having a meaningless flirtation. Trifling musical comedy; originally released at 90m.

Two Way Stretch (1960-British) **87m.** *** D: Robert Day. Peter Sellers, Wilfrid Hyde-White, Lionel Jeffries, Liz Fraser, Maurice Denham, Bernard Cribbins, David Lodge. Wry shenanigans of Sellers, et al. as prisoners who devise a means of escaping to commit a robbery and then return to safety of their cells.▼

Two Weeks in Another Town (1962) **C-107m.** *** D: Vincente Minnelli. Kirk Douglas, Edward G. Robinson, Cyd Charisse, George Hamilton, Claire Trevor, Daliah Lavi, Rossana Schiaffino, Constance Ford. Overly ambitious attempt to intellectualize Irwin Shaw novel, revolving around problems of people involved in moviemaking in Rome. Reunites much of the talent from THE BAD AND THE BEAUTIFUL, footage from which is used as the film-within-a-film here. CinemaScope. ▼●

Two Weeks in September (1967-French) **C-96m.** **½ D: Serge Bourguignon. Brigitte Bardot, Laurent Terzieff, Michael Sarne, James Robertson Justice. Bardot, mistress to older man, has fling with younger lover, can't decide between the two. Location shooting in London and Scotland enhances OK story. Franscope.▼

Two Weeks With Love (1950) **C-92m.** **½ D: Roy Rowland. Jane Powell, Ricardo Montalban, Louis Calhern, Ann Harding, Debbie Reynolds, Carleton Carpenter. Powell fans will enjoy her role as daughter vacationing in Catskills proving to her parents that she's grown up. Reynolds sings "Abba Dabba Honeymoon" with Carpenter.▼●

Two Wives at One Wedding (1960-British) **66m.** *½ D: Montgomery Tully. Gordon Jackson, Christina Gregg, Lisa Daniely, Andre Maranne. Trite minor film involving Jackson confronted by extortion gang charging him with bigamy.

Two Women (1960-Italian) **99m.** **** D: Vittorio De Sica. Sophia Loren, Raf Vallone, Eleanora Brown, Jean-Paul Belmondo. Loren deservedly won Oscar for heartrending portrayal of Italian mother who, along with young daughter, is raped by Allied Moroccan soldiers during WW2. How they survive is an intensely moving story. Screenplay by Cesare Zavattini from an Alberto Moravia novel. Loren remade this in 1989 as a two-part Italian TVM.▼●◗

Two Yanks in Trinidad (1942) **88m.** ** D: Gregory Ratoff. Brian Donlevy, Pat O'Brien, Janet Blair, Donald MacBride. Donlevy and O'Brien are hoods who join the army, turning their talents to fighting the enemy; flat patriotism.

Two Years Before the Mast (1946) **98m.** *½ D: John Farrow. Alan Ladd, Brian Donlevy, William Bendix, Esther Fernandez, Howard da Silva, Barry Fitzgerald, Albert Dekker, Darryl Hickman. Badly scripted story of Richard Henry Dana's (Donlevy) crusade to expose mistreatment of men at sea. Da Silva is standout as tyrannical captain.▼

Tycoon (1947) **C-128m.** **½ D: Richard Wallace. John Wayne, Laraine Day, Cedric Hardwicke, Judith Anderson, James Gleason, Anthony Quinn, Grant Withers. Wayne plays determined young railroad builder in this over-long, but well-acted drama with fine cast. ▼

Typhoon (1940) **C-70m.** **½ D: Louis King. Dorothy Lamour, Robert Preston, Lynne Overman, J. Carrol Naish, Chief Thundercloud, Jack Carson. Another Lamour sarong epic, typically romantic; Overman provides good comedy support.

Tyrant of the Sea (1950) **70m.** ** D: Lew Landers. Rhys Williams, Ron Randell, Valentine Perkins, Doris Lloyd, Lester Matthews, Terry Kilburn, William Fawcett. Undistinguished melodrama set in 1803. Napoleon is ready to invade England and only retired tough sea captain (Williams) can destroy French landing barges and save the country. Meanwhile, romance blossoms between young Lt. Randell and captain's daughter Perkins.

U-571 (2000) **C-116m.** **½ D: Jonathan Mostow. Matthew McConaughey, Bill Paxton, Harvey Keitel, Jon Bon Jovi, Jake Weber, David Keith, T.C. Carson, Jack Noseworthy, Thomas Guiry, Erik Palladino, Dave Power, Will Estes. WW2 submarine crew has to find a way to board and overtake a German U-boat and bring back a crucial secret-code transmitter. It turns out to be more difficult than they expect. Agreeably old-fashioned WW2 submarine drama starts with a bang and holds interest throughout, but fizzles out at the end. Still pretty entertaining. Super 35. [PG-13] ▼●◗

UFO Incident, The (1975) **C-100m. TVM** D: Richard A. Colla. James Earl Jones, Estelle Parsons, Barnard Hughes, Dick O'Neill, Beeson Carroll, Terrence O'Connor. Absorbing, fact-based, semi-sci-fi drama tracing story of New England couple who claim to have been taken aboard a UFO and examined medically. Long on monologues, skimpy in action, it's kept afloat by two leads and Hughes, the doctor who probes their memories. Above average.

UFOria (1980) **C-100m.** **½ D: John Binder. Cindy Williams, Harry Dean Stanton, Fred Ward, Harry Carey, Jr., Beverly Hope Atkinson. Amiable if sometimes uneasy mix of MELVIN AND HOWARD and CLOSE ENCOUNTERS OF THE THIRD KIND with Williams as a kooky grocery store cashier who believes she has received a message from outer space and will become a female Noah on UFO ark. Long unreleased, this finally found a distributor (and an audience) in 1986. [PG]▼

UFO (Unidentified Flying Objects) (1956) **C/B&W-92m.** ** D: Winston Jones. Documentary-style account of unknown missiles, detailing various reports of unidentified flying objects being spotted. Film lacks excitement.▼

Ugetsu (1953-Japanese) **96m.** ***½ D: Kenji Mizoguchi. Machiko Kyo, Masayuki Mori, Kinuyo Tanaka, Sakae Ozawa. Eerie ghost story set in 16th-century Japan tells of two peasants who leave their families; one seeks wealth in the city and the other wishes to become a samurai warrior. This superbly photographed film was a Venice Film Festival prize winner. Full title UGETSU MONOGATARI.▼●

Ugly American, The (1963) **C-120m.** **½ D: George H. Englund. Marlon Brando, Sandra Church, Pat Hingle, Eiji Okada, Arthur Hill, Kukrit Pramoj, Jocelyn Brando. Brando is American ambassador to Asian country; his arrival stirs up pro-communist elements, leading to havoc. Political revelations of U.S. power struggle aren't meat for exciting film. Adapted by Stewart Stern from the William J. Lederer/Eugene Burdick book.▼

Ugly Dachshund, The (1966) **C-93m.** ** D: Norman Tokar. Dean Jones, Suzanne Pleshette, Charlie Ruggles, Kelly Thordsen, Parley Baer. Silly, featherweight Disney comedy about husband and wife who train their respective dogs for competition at dog show. Fun for kids, but too contrived and silly for anyone else to enjoy.▼

UHF (1989) **C-97m.** ** D: Jay Levey. ''Weird Al'' Yankovic, Victoria Jackson, Kevin McCarthy, Michael Richards, David Bowe, Stanley Brock, Anthony Geary, Trinidad Silva, Gedde Watanabe, Billy Barty, John Paragon, Fran Drescher, Sue Ane Langdon, Emo Philips. Music video parodist Yankovic's starring feature debut casts him as the manager of a small-time TV station who inadvertently hits it big with his unconventional programming ideas. Story is threadbare, but some of the spoofs of commercials, movies, and TV shows are fun. Yankovic scripted with director Levey. [PG-13]▼●

Ulee's Gold (1997) **C-111m.** *** D: Victor Nuñez. Peter Fonda, Patricia Richardson, Jessica Biel, J. Kenneth Campbell, Christine Dunford, Steven Flynn, Dewey Weber, Tom Wood, Vanessa Zima. A small gem from writer-director Nuñez about a taciturn beekeeper in northern Florida whose ordered life is disrupted when his son sends an SOS from prison. His wife is in trouble, and while Fonda has had no use for her since she abandoned her two daughters (whom he is raising) he tries to help—and gets caught in a quagmire involving his son's former partners in crime. Slow and steady, like the leading character, but rewarding, with Fonda a tower of strength in the best part he's ever had. [R]▼●◗

Ultimate Chase, The SEE: **Ultimate Thrill, The**

Ultimate Solution of Grace Quigley, The SEE: **Grace Quigley**

Ultimate Thrill, The (1974) **C-110m.** ** D: Robert Butler. Eric Braeden, Britt Ekland, Barry Brown, Michael Blodgett, John Davis Chandler. Executive is drawn into murder by his paranoiac fears; undistinguished programmer retitled THE ULTIMATE CHASE for network showing. [PG]▼

Ultimate Warrior, The (1975) **C-94m.** **½ D: Robert Clouse. Yul Brynner, Max von Sydow, Joanna Miles, William Smith, Stephen McHattie, Lane Bradbury. Routine acting and directing spoil potentially intriguing futuristic sci-fi. In the 21st century, Brynner and von Sydow control a decreasing band of people fighting for whatever is left in N.Y.C. following ecological disasters. [R]▼

Ulysses (1954-Italian) **C-104m.** ** D: Mario Camerini. Kirk Douglas, Silvana Mangano, Anthony Quinn, Sylvie, Rossana Podesta. Hokey, lumbering costumer with Douglas as Ulysses, on his Odyssey home to Penelope after the Trojan War. Watch Kirk speak in dubbed Italian, then English. Seven writers are credited for this, including Ben Hecht and Irwin Shaw.▼◗

Ulysses (1967) **140m.** **½ D: Joseph Strick. Barbara Jefford, Milo O'Shea, Maurice Roeves, T. P. McKenna, Martin Dempsey, Sheila O'Sullivan. Idea of putting James Joyce's massive novel on the screen seemed daring in 1967, but now seems like a stupid stunt. Lots of good prose makes it to the screen, but end result is interesting curio, not a film. Shot on location in Ireland; Strick far more successfully filmed Joyce's A PORTRAIT OF THE ARTIST AS A YOUNG MAN in 1979. Panavision.▼●

Ulysses Against Hercules (1961-Italian) **C-99m.** *½ D: Mario Caiano. Georges Marchal, Michael Lane, Alessandra Panaro, Gianni Santuccio. Childish blend of myth and muscleman antics with Hercules (Lane) sent to punish Ulysses (Marchal); special effects of bird-men not up to snuff.

Ulzana's Raid (1972) **C-103m.** ***½ D: Robert Aldrich. Burt Lancaster, Bruce Davison, Jorge Luke, Richard Jaeckel, Joaquin Martinez, Lloyd Bochner, Karl Swenson, Richard Farnsworth. Lancaster is a savvy, straight-talking Indian scout who leads cavalry lieutenant Davison (still wet behind the ears) and his company on a discouraging pursuit of an Apache chief. Gritty Western tale written by Alan Sharp, with jarring bursts of violence. [R]▼●◗

Umberto D (1952-Italian) **89m.** **** D: Vittorio De Sica. Carlo Battisti, Maria Pia Casilio, Lina Gennari. Ex-bureaucrat on a meager fixed pension is about to be forced out into Rome streets with only his beloved mongrel to comfort him. De Sica is said to have considered this his greatest work, and he may have been right; subplot about Battisti's relationship with an unmarried, pregnant woman is as touching as predominant story line. Shattering, all the way up to the tear-jerking conclusion.▼●

Umbrellas of Cherbourg, The (1964-French) **C-91m.** ***½ D: Jacques Demy. Catherine Deneuve, Nino Castelnuovo, Anne Vernon, Marc Michel, Ellen Farnen. Haunting music (score by Michel Legrand, lyrics by Demy) and gorgeous photography make this an outstanding romantic drama. All dialogue is sung. Followed by THE YOUNG GIRLS OF ROCHEFORT. ▼●◗

Umbrella Woman, The SEE: **Good Wife, The**

Unbearable Lightness of Being, The (1988) **C-171m.** ***½ D: Philip Kaufman. Daniel Day-Lewis, Juliette Binoche, Lena Olin, Derek de Lint, Erland Josephson, Pavel Landovsky, Donald Moffat. Extraordinarily well-made adaptation of the acclaimed novel by Milan Kundera about a young Czech doctor of the 1960s who has a way with women (lots of women) and an aversion to politics but who finds himself caught up in his country's political turmoil—and a crisis of commitment with the women in his life. Kaufman and Jean-Claude Carrière's adaptation unfolds just like a good book, taking its time but never meandering as it paints a vivid picture of the character's life and times. Sensual, intelligent, and beautifully acted by the three leads; strikingly photographed by Sven Nykvist. [R]▼●

Unbecoming Age (1992) **C-93m.** **½ D: Deborah Ringel, Alfredo Ringel. Diane Salinger, John Calvin, Wallace Shawn, Colleen Camp, George Clooney, Shera Danese, Nicholas Guest, Priscilla Pointer. Salinger turns forty; depressed and bored, she blows ''magic bubbles'' which allow her to forget her age and recapture her youthful vigor. Cute romantic comedy-fantasy works most of the way before it runs out of steam. Video title: THE MAGIC BUBBLE.▼

Unbelievable Truth, The (1990) **C-90m.** ** D: Hal Hartley. Adrienne Shelly, Robert Burke, Christopher Cooke, Julia McNeal, Mark Bailey, Gary Sauer, Katherine Mayfield. Tall, mysterious man returns to his hometown after a stint in prison, causing a variety of reactions from the locals. Small, independently made black comedy may not be to everyone's taste, but it has its moments. Burke went on to replace Peter Weller as Robocop. [R]▼●

Unborn, The (1991) **C-83m.** **½ D: Rodman Flender. Brooke Adams, Jeff Hayenga, James Karen, K Callan, Jane Cameron, Kathy Cameron, Kathy Griffin, Lisa Kudrow. Young wife with a history of miscarriages is convinced that mysterious doctor (Karen) has inseminated her with mutated sperm. The result: a monstrous fetus which is so tough it outlives an attempted abortion. Convincing performances place this horror tale a notch above its exploitive subject matter. 1994 sequel: THE UNBORN II. [R]▼●

Uncanny, The (1977-British-Canadian) **C-85m.** ** D: Denis Heroux. Peter Cushing, Ray Milland, Susan Penhaligon, Joan Greenwood, Alexandra Stewart, Chloe Franks, Donald Pleasence, Samantha Eggar, John Vernon. Lackluster trilogy of ''supernatural'' tales built around author Cushing's assertion that cats are conspiring against mankind.▼

Un Carnet de Bal (1937-French) **109m.** **** D: Julien Duvivier. Marie Bell, Francoise Rosay, Louis Jouvet, Harry Baur, Pierre-Richard Willm, Raimu, Pierre Blanchar, Fernandel, Robert Lynen, Roger

Legris. Wealthy widow travels to various locales, intent on looking up the former beaux who filled her dance card (''carnet de bal''). What she finds surprises her, and viewer is treated to a number of poignant vignettes (some ahead of their time) acted by the cream of 1930's France. Hugely successful, this was the inspiration for all the episodic films that followed. (Duvivier even reworked it in Hollywood in 1941 as LYDIA.) Coscripted by the director, from his story. Music by Maurice Jaubert.

Uncertain Glory (1944) **102m.** ** D: Raoul Walsh. Errol Flynn, Jean Sullivan, Paul Lukas, Lucile Watson, Faye Emerson, Douglass Dumbrille, Dennis Hoey, Sheldon Leonard. Wavering script about French philanderer Flynn deciding to give his life for his country.▼

Unchained (1955) **75m.** ** D: Hall Bartlett. Elroy ''Crazylegs'' Hirsch, Barbara Hale, Chester Morris, Todd Duncan, Johnny Johnston, Peggy Knudsen, Jerry Paris. Fair drama of life at prison farm at Chino, California; highlighted by Alex North–Hy Zarek theme song: ''Unchained Melody.'' Saxophonist Dexter Gordon is seen briefly as a musician (though his playing was dubbed by Georgie Auld).

Uncle Buck (1989) **C-100m.** **½ D: John Hughes. John Candy, Amy Madigan, Jean Louisa Kelly, Gaby Hoffmann, Macaulay Culkin, Elaine Bromka, Garrett M. Brown, Laurie Metcalf, Jay Underwood. Ne'er-do-well bachelor Candy has to look after his brother's kids for a couple of days . . . and surprise! The perpetual foul-up turns out to be a caring and responsible uncle. Comedy with serious and sentimental strains gives Candy one of his better vehicles, though writer-director Hughes' inconsistencies keep it from scoring a bull's-eye. Followed by a TV series. [PG]▼●◗

Uncle Harry SEE: **Strange Affair of Uncle Harry, The**

Uncle Joe Shannon (1978) **C-115m.** BOMB D: Joseph C. Hanwright. Burt Young, Doug McKeon, Madge Sinclair, Jason Bernard, Bert Remsen, Allan Rich. Slobbering, self-indulgent film (written by Young) about down-and-out trumpet player and young boy who tries to resist his ''charm.'' Several hands from ROCKY—including Young—were hoping to duplicate that film's success. Maynard Ferguson dubbed Young's trumpet licks. [PG]

Uncle Moses (1932) **87m.** **½ D: Aubrey Scotto, Sidney Goldin. Maurice Schwartz, Rubin Goldberg, Judith Abarbanel, Zvee Scooler, Mark Schweid, Rebecca Weintraub. Schwartz stars as the title character, a prosperous, patronizing, womanizing sweatshop proprietor who falls for the young daughter of one of his employees, as his workers threaten to go on strike. To say this Yiddish-language film is dramatically overwrought would be an understatement, but it remains intriguing as a mirror of the Jewish immigrant experience and life on N.Y.C.'s Lower East Side. Based on a novel by Sholem Asch; scripted by Schwartz.▼

Uncle Silas SEE: **Inheritance, The** (1947)

Uncle Tom's Cabin (1927) **112m.** *** D: Harry Pollard. James B. Lowe, Virginia Grey, Margarita Fisher, George Siegmann, Eulalie Jensen, Arthur Edmund Carew, Vivien Oakland, Lucien Littlefield, Gertrude Astor. Ingratiatingly heart-tugging (albeit occasionally overwrought) version of Harriet Beecher Stowe's famed abolitionist novel, which charts the plight of various slaves and slave owners in the Deep South prior to and during the Civil War. Sets out to humanize African Americans by depicting the heartlessness of slavery, yet also reflects its era with the worst kind of ''dancin' darkie'' stereotypes.▼◗

Uncle Tom's Cabin (1987) **C-110m. TVM** D: Stan Lathan. Avery Brooks, Kate Burton, Bruce Dern, Paula Kelly, Phylicia Rashad, Kathryn Walker, Edward Woodward, Frank Converse, George Coe, Albert Hall. Ambitious ''contemporary adaptation'' (i.e., slightly revisionist version) of the Harriet Beecher Stowe novel, adapted by John Gay. First American sound version of the classic (following a 1965 German production) doesn't have the Eliza-crossing-the-ice segment but does have a first-rate cast, including a standout Simon Legree in Edward Woodward. Above average.▼

Un Coeur en Hiver (1992-French) **C-105m.** ***½ D: Claude Sautet. Daniel Auteuil, Emmanuelle Béart, André Dussollier. Fascinating study of what happens when two longtime business partners in the classical music world find their ''friendship'' split apart by the appearance of a beautiful young woman. All three stars shine in this talky, offbeat tale of love and music (specifically Ravel). An original film, admittedly not for all tastes.▼

Uncommon Valor (1983) **C-105m.** **½ D: Ted Kotcheff. Gene Hackman, Robert Stack, Fred Ward, Reb Brown, Randall ''Tex'' Cobb, Patrick Swayze, Harold Sylvester, Tim Thomerson, Michael Dudikoff. Formula action film about a retired Army officer who gathers motley crew of Vietnam vets to invade Laos in search of his son, still Missing in Action. Solid performances make this watchable. [R]▼●

Unconquered (1947) **C-146m.** **½ D: Cecil B. DeMille. Gary Cooper, Paulette Goddard, Howard da Silva, Boris Karloff, Cecil Kellaway, Ward Bond, Katherine de Mille, C. Aubrey Smith, Porter Hall, Mike Mazurki. Gargantuan DeMille colonists-vs.-Indians nonsense, one of his most ludicrous films but still fun.▼

Undead, The (1957) **75m.** *** D: Roger Corman. Richard Garland, Pamela Duncan, Allison Hayes, Mel Welles, Billy Barty, Richard Devon, Bruno VeSota. One of Corman's best early films, coscripted by Charles Griffith. A scientist, investigating the possibility of reincarnation, manages to transport himself back into the Dark Ages. Lots of atmosphere and black humor, with a neat twist ending.▼

Undefeated, The (1969) **C-119m.** ** D: Andrew V. McLaglen. John Wayne, Rock Hudson, Tony Aguilar, Roman Gabriel, Bruce Cabot, Lee Meriwether, Ben Johnson, Merlin Olsen, Michael (Jan-Michael) Vincent, Harry Carey, Jr., Royal Dano, Richard Mulligan, James McEachin, Gregg Palmer, Kiel Martin. Aside from interesting Wayne-Hudson teaming and the presence of football stars Gabriel and Olsen, this routine Western has little to offer. Post-Civil War tale casts two stars as Union and Confederate colonels. Best line: "The conversation sorta dried up." Panavision. [G]▼●

Under Capricorn (1949-British) **C-117m.** ** D: Alfred Hitchcock. Ingrid Bergman, Joseph Cotten, Michael Wilding, Margaret Leighton, Cecil Parker. Stuffy costumer set in 19th-century Australia; Bergman is frail wife of hardened husband Cotten; Wilding comes to visit, upsetting everything. Leighton excellent in supporting role. One of Hitchcock's few duds.▼●

Under Cover (1987) **C-94m.** *½ D: John Stockwell. David Neidorf, Jennifer Jason Leigh, Barry Corbin, Kathleen Wilhoite, David Harris. Neidorf is an out-of-town cop operating undercover with female narc Leigh to catch the drug pushers who killed another cop on the case. Best known as the pilot "Cougar" in TOP GUN, Stockwell here makes an uninspired directorial debut. [R]▼

Undercover Blues (1993) **C-89m.** ** D: Herbert Ross. Kathleen Turner, Dennis Quaid, Fiona Shaw, Stanley Tucci, Larry Miller, Obba Babatunde, Tom Arnold, Park Overall, Ralph Brown, Jan Triska, Saul Rubinek. Paper-thin comedy-romance-thriller about supercool married ex-spies Jeff and Jane Blue, parents of a baby girl, who tangle with various heavies in New Orleans. Quaid and Turner are no William Powell and Myrna Loy, and this is no THIN MAN. Tucci, however, is hilarious as thug named Muerte. [PG-13] ▼●

Undercover Girl (1950) **83m.** ** D: Joseph Pevney. Alexis Smith, Scott Brady, Richard Egan, Gladys George, Regis Toomey. Smith in title role joins police to locate her father's killer; George in cameo is outstanding.

Undercover Maisie (1947) **90m.** ** D: Harry Beaumont. Ann Sothern, Barry Nelson, Mark Daniels, Leon Ames, Clinton Sundberg. The brassy chorine joins the police as a special agent in this routine finale to the series.

Under-Cover Man (1932) **70m.** **½ D: James Flood. George Raft, Nancy Carroll, Roscoe Karns, Gregory Ratoff, Lew Cody. Good but familiar tale of Raft devoting his life to finding father's killer. Well acted.

Undercover Man, The (1949) **85m.** *** D: Joseph H. Lewis. Glenn Ford, Nina Foch, James Whitmore, Barry Kelley, Howard St. John. Realistic drama of mob-leader (loosely based on Al Capone) being hunted down by secret service men who hope to nail him on tax-evasion charge. Whitmore's film debut.

Undercovers Hero (1974-British) **C-95m.** BOMB D: Roy Boulting. Peter Sellers, Lila Kedrova, Curt Jurgens, Beatrice Romand, Jenny Hanley, Rex Stallings. Inept WW2 "comedy," with Sellers in six roles, including Hitler; a total dud. Made in 1973, barely released here. British title: SOFT BEDS, HARD BATTLES. [R]

Undercurrent (1946) **116m.** **½ D: Vincente Minnelli. Katharine Hepburn, Robert Taylor, Robert Mitchum, Edmund Gwenn, Marjorie Main, Jayne Meadows. Stale melodramatics of woman realizing her husband is wicked, saved only by fine cast and usual high MGM production quality.▼

Under Fire (1957) **78m.** ** D: James B. Clark. Rex Reason, Steve Brodie, Jon Locke, Harry Morgan, Robert Levin. Bland war tale about soldiers alleged to have deserted under enemy fire. Regalscope.

Under Fire (1983) **C-128m.** ***½ D: Roger Spottiswoode. Nick Nolte, Gene Hackman, Joanna Cassidy, Ed Harris, Jean-Louis Trintignant, Richard Masur, Rene Enriquez, Hamilton Camp. First-rate political thriller about journalists on the line in Managua, Nicaragua, 1979, how their lives intertwine, and how two of them risk their professionalism by becoming involved in the revolutionary conflict. One of those rare films that manages to combine real-life politics and realistic romance with a no-nonsense story. Trio of stars are superb; so is Jerry Goldsmith's music. Only problem: It goes on too long. Screenplay by Ron Shelton and Clayton Frohman. [R]▼●

Underground (1941) **95m.** *** D: Vincent Sherman. Jeffrey Lynn, Philip Dorn, Kaaren Verne, Mona Maris, Frank Reicher, Martin Kosleck. Gripping story of German underground movement, with Dorn shielding his activities from loyal soldier-brother Lynn. Kosleck is definitive Nazi swine.▼

Underground U.S.A. (1980) **C-85m.** *** D: Eric Mitchell. Patti Astor, Eric Mitchell, Rene Ricard, Tom Wright, Cookie Mueller, Jackie Curtis, Taylor Mead. Street hustler Mitchell forces his way into the life of has-been movie star Astor. Rambling but fascinating; a sort of punk rock SUNSET BLVD.

Under Milk Wood (1972-British) **C-90m.** ** D: Andrew Sinclair. Richard Burton, Elizabeth Taylor, Peter O'Toole, Glynis Johns, Sian Phillips, Vivien Merchant. Rather obscure Dylan Thomas, not in terms of his work but in the film's ambitions. Beautiful images, but rather overbearing technique weighs down the acting. [PG]▼

Under My Skin (1950) **86m.** **½ D: Jean Negulesco. John Garfield, Micheline Presle, Luther Adler, Orley Lindgren, Noel Drayton. Pensive study of troubled, crooked jockey Garfield, attempting to reform for the sake of son Lindgren and pretty widow Presle. Based on Ernest Hemingway's *My Old Man*; remade for TV in 1979 under that title.

Underneath (1994) **C-99m.** **½ D: Steven Soderbergh. Peter Gallagher, Alison Elliott, William Fichtner, Adam Trese, Joe Don Baker, Paul Dooley, Elisabeth Shue, Anjanette Comer, Shelley Duvall, Joe Chrest. Ne'er-do-well returns home to Austin to attend his mother's wedding, and foolishly tries to pick up the pieces of his life before he left town. Soon he's pursuing his ex-girlfriend, annoying her gangsterish boyfriend, and cooking up a robbery scheme. Remake of the film noir favorite CRISS CROSS is stylish, intriguing, but awfully low-key. A must for fans of flashbacks. Panavision. [R] ▼●◗

Under-Pup, The (1939) **81m.** **½ D: Richard Wallace. Gloria Jean, Robert Cummings, Nan Grey, Beulah Bondi, Virginia Weidler, Margaret Lindsay, C. Aubrey Smith, Billy Gilbert. Hokey but heartwarming tale of singing tenement child who attends exclusive summer camp as charity guest of a snobbish girls' club. Film debut for Gloria Jean, Universal Pictures' "successor" to Deanna Durbin. Originally released at 88m.

Under Satan's Sun (1987-French) **C-97m.** *** D: Maurice Pialat. Gérard Depardieu, Sandrine Bonnaire, Maurice Pialat, Alain Artur, Yann Dedet. A very demanding and difficult film, not for all tastes but most rewarding to those who can relate to the subject: the questions, conflicts, and torments of rural priest Depardieu. Adapted from a book by Georges Bernanos, author of *Diary of a Country Priest.* Video title: UNDER THE SUN OF SATAN.▼

Undersea Girl (1957) **75m.** BOMB D: John Peyser. Mara Corday, Pat Conway, Dan Seymour, Florence Marly, Myron Healey. Flabby murder yarn with all sides of law hunting for loot buried on ocean bottom.

Undersea Odyssey, An SEE: **Neptune Factor, The**

Under Siege (1992) **C-102m.** **½ D: Andrew Davis. Steven Seagal, Tommy Lee Jones, Gary Busey, Erika Eleniak, Patrick O'Neal, Nick Mancuso, Andy Romano, Colm Meaney. DIE HARD at sea, with cook Seagal playing tiger-and-mouse with thugs plotting to steal nuclear arms from aboard a 900-foot Navy battleship. Seagal's best film to date; Jones and Busey are better villains than film deserves. Worth it just to see Steve in a chef's cap. Followed by a sequel. [R]▼●◗

Under Siege 2: Dark Territory (1995) **C-100m.** ** D: Geoff Murphy. Steven Seagal, Eric Bogosian, Katherine Heigl, Morris Chestnut, Everett McGill, Brenda Bakke, Peter Greene, Andy Romano, Nick Mancuso, Royce D. Applegate, Kurtwood Smith, Afifi. Bad guys take over a cross-continental train to seize control of a satellite particle-beam weapon; then they threaten to blow up the Eastern seaboard. But they didn't reckon with Casey the Cook (Seagal). Elaborately produced and well directed, but still just another connect-the-dots action thriller. [R]▼●◗

Under Suspicion (1992-U.S.-British) **C-99m.** ** D: Simon Moore. Liam Neeson, Laura San Giacomo, Kenneth Cranham, Alphonsia Emmanuel, Maggie O'Neill, Martin Grace, Stephen Moore. Brighton, England, 1959: Ex-cop turned seedy private eye Neeson becomes chief suspect in a murder, and must (surprise!) set out to prove his innocence. Dour-looking and sluggishly paced film is helped by Neeson, good as always, and Cranham—playing his only ally on the police force. San Giacomo is unfortunately miscast as a femme fatale, mistress of a world-renowned artist; she seems absurd in the role and entire production suffers. Panavision. [R]▼●

Under Ten Flags (1960-U.S.-Italian) 92m. **½ D: Duilio Coletti. Van Heflin, Charles Laughton, Mylene Demongeot, John Ericson, Cecil Parker, Liam Redmond, Alex Nicol. German attack-ship during WW2 uses a variety of dodges to elude British pursuers, in naval cat-and-mouse game, told from Axis point of view. Filmed in Italy.

Under the Boardwalk (1989) **C-104m.** *½ D: Fritz Kiersch. Richard Joseph Paul, Danielle Von Zerneck, Steve Monarque, Keith Coogan, Roxana Zal, Hunter Von Leer, Tracey Walter, Dick Miller, Sonny Bono, Elizabeth Kaitan. Surfers from the San Fernando Valley ("Vals") square off against Venice locals ("Lokes"), with Romeo-and-Juliet-like conflict of Val boy who loves Loke girl. Anemic teen picture is a major waste of time. Oddest element: jargon-spouting narrator is 20 years in the future. [R]▼●

Under the Cherry Moon (1986) **98m.** *½ D: Prince. Prince, Jerome Benton, Kristin Scott Thomas, Steven Berkoff, Francesca Annis, Emmanuelle Sallet, Alexandra Stewart, Victor Spinetti. Supremely silly vanity film with Prince self-cast as American gigolo/entertainer in the south of France who has a devastating effect on women (yes, it's a science-fiction story). Stylish-looking fairy-tale/fable, filmed in black & white, is a triumph of self-adoration, and overall embarrassment. Some music throughout, but in fragmented scenes. Kristin Scott Thomas's film debut. [PG-13]▼●

Under the Gun (1950) **83m.** **½ D: Ted Tetzlaff. Richard Conte, Audrey Totter,

Sam Jaffe, John McIntire, Royal Dano. Effective study of gangsters behind bars, played by competent cast.

Under the Gun (1989) **C-89m.** ** D: James Sbardellati. Sam Jones, Vanessa Williams, John Russell, Michael Halsey, Sharon Williams, Bill McKinney, Rockne Tarkington, Don Stark, Nick Cassavetes. Cop Jones teams up with lawyer Williams to go after plutonium thief who ordered the death of Jones' brother. Acceptable but familiar odd-couple crime melodrama; at least it keeps moving. [R]▼●

Under the Hula Moon (1995) **C-96m.** **½ D: Jeff Celentano. Stephen Baldwin, Emily Lloyd, Christopher Penn, Musetta Vander, Pruitt Taylor Vince, Edie McClurg, Carel Stuycken, R. Lee Ermey. An escaped convict holes up with his long-estranged brother, a dreamer/schemer who lives in the desert trying to make his fortune manufacturing a revolutionary sunscreen. Baldwin and Lloyd are an endearingly loopy couple in this off-kilter comedy. Written by the director. [R]▼●

Under the Rainbow (1981) **C-98m.** BOMB D: Steve Rash. Chevy Chase, Carrie Fisher, Eve Arden, Joseph Maher, Adam Arkin, Mako, Pat McCormick, Billy Barty. Even by today's standards this is an astoundingly unfunny and tasteless comedy about spies, undercover agents, and midgets who cross paths in a hotel during filming of THE WIZARD OF OZ. Is this film the Wicked Witch's revenge? [PG]▼

Under the Red Robe (1937-British) **82m.** **½ D: Victor Seastrom. Conrad Veidt, Raymond Massey, Annabella, Romney Brent, Sophie Stewart. Diverting costumer with Veidt as hero, Annabella lovely heroine, and Massey the cruel villain in story of French Cardinal Richelieu's oppression of the Huguenots. Offbeat sense of humor adds to film's enjoyment.▼

Under the Roofs of Paris (1930-French) **92m.** ***½ D: René Clair. Albert Prejean, Pola Illery, Gaston Modot, Edmond Greville, Paul Olivier. Mime and song, with a minimum of dialogue, tell the story in this wonderful film about two ordinary Parisians (Prejean, Greville) involved with the same woman (Illery). A ground-breaking link between silent and sound cinema; Lazare Meerson's sets are outstanding. Written by Clair.▼

Under the Sun of Satan SEE: **Under Satan's Sun**

Under the Volcano (1984) **C-109m.** ***½ D: John Huston. Albert Finney, Jacqueline Bisset, Anthony Andrews, Ignacio Lopez Tarso, Katy Jurado, James Villiers. Somber but striking adaptation of Malcolm Lowry's novel about alcoholic diplomat in Mexico during the late 1930s; rich in atmosphere and texture, with a great performance by Finney. Screenplay by Guy Gallo; music by Alex North. [R]▼●

Under the Yum Yum Tree (1963) **C-110m.** **½ D: David Swift. Jack Lemmon, Carol Lynley, Dean Jones, Edie Adams, Imogene Coca, Paul Lynde, Robert Lansing. Obvious sex comedy owes most of its enjoyment to Lemmon as love-hungry landlord trying to romance tenant Lynley who's living with her fiancé (Jones).▼

Undertow (1949) **71m.** **½ D: William Castle. Scott Brady, John Russell, Dorothy Hart, Peggy Dow, Bruce Bennett, Gregg Martell. Well-done if predictable account of innocent Brady framed on a murder rap, and how he brings the real culprits to justice. Rock Hudson is billed as "Roc" in this, his second film.

Under Two Flags (1936) **96m.** *** D: Frank Lloyd. Ronald Colman, Claudette Colbert, Victor McLaglen, Rosalind Russell, Gregory Ratoff, Nigel Bruce, Herbert Mundin, John Carradine, J. Edward Bromberg. Debonair legionnaire Colman is caught between two women (aristocratic Russell and camp follower Colbert), and the envy of jealous commandant McLaglen in this unbelievable but entertaining Foreign Legion story, from the book by Ouida (filmed before in 1916 and 1922). Originally ran 110m.

Underwater! (1955) **C-99m.** ** D: John Sturges. Jane Russell, Gilbert Roland, Richard Egan, Lori Nelson, Jayne Mansfield. Standard skin-diving fare, with Roland and Egan seeking out treasure in the deep. Russell in a bathing suit is the main attraction. SuperScope.▼●

Underwater City, The (1962) **C-78m.** ** D: Frank McDonald. William Lundigan, Julie Adams, Roy Roberts, Carl Benton Reid, Chet Douglas, Paul Dubov. Mildly diverting sci-fi about engineer who builds experimental underwater city. Released theatrically in b&w.

Underwater Warrior (1958) **91m.** **½ D: Andrew Marton. Dan Dailey, Claire Kelly, James Gregory, Ross Martin. On-location filming in the Philippines adds zest to narrative-style account of frogmen in action during closing days of WW2. CinemaScope.

Under Western Skies (1945) **83m.** *½ D: Jean Yarbrough. Martha O'Driscoll, Noah Beery, Jr., Leon Errol. Uninspired blend of shoot-em-up and musical, with scatter-brained jokes tossed in.

Underworld (1985-British) **C-100m.** **½ D: George Pavlou. Denholm Elliott, Steven Berkoff, Larry Lamb, Miranda Richardson, Art Malik, Nicola Cowper, Ingrid Pitt. Fair thriller about mutants who live underground and who kidnap pretty hooker Cowper in order to obtain from Dr. Elliott the drug that will keep them alive. Retired gunman Lamb is hired by gang boss Berkoff to rescue her. Video title: TRANSMUTATIONS. [R]▼

Underworld After Dark SEE **Big Town After Dark**

Underworld Informers (1965-British) **105m.** *** D: Ken Annakin. Nigel Patrick, Catherine Woodville, Margaret Whiting, Colin Blakely, Harry Andrews, Frank Finlay. Tight, taut crime tale as Scotland Yard inspector Patrick must clear his name by bringing in notorious gangland leaders. Vivid atmosphere, fine acting by all. Original British title: THE INFORMERS.

Underworld Story, The (1950) **90m.** *** D: Cy Endfield. Gale Storm, Dan Duryea, Herbert Marshall, Mary Anderson, Michael O'Shea. Surprisingly effective gangster yarn of reporter joining small town newspaper and uncovering corruption; cast is uniformly good.▼

Underworld U.S.A. (1961) **99m.** **½ D: Samuel Fuller. Cliff Robertson, Dolores Dorn, Beatrice Kay, Robert Emhardt, Larry Gates. Robertson sees his father murdered and develops lifetime obsession to get even with the mob responsible. One of director Fuller's most visually striking films; unfortunately, his script goes astray and doesn't fulfill initial promise.▼

Undying Monster, The (1942) **60m.** **½ D: John Brahm. James Ellison, John Howard, Heather Angel, Bramwell Fletcher. OK chiller of a werewolf on the prowl around an English estate; nothing new, but atmospherically photographed by Lucien Ballard.▼

Unearthly, The (1957) **73m.** *½ D: Brooke L. Peters. John Carradine, Allison Hayes, Myron Healey, Sally Todd. Mad scientist Carradine's experiments in immortality have resulted only in a basement full of deformed morons. Don't you join them.▼

Une Parisienne SEE: **La Parisienne**

Unfaithful, The (1947) **109m.** **½ D: Vincent Sherman. Ann Sheridan, Lew Ayres, Zachary Scott, Eve Arden, Steven Geray, John Hoyt. Title refers to Sheridan, who gets tangled in murder while husband is out of town; good cast in fairly interesting drama. Remake of THE LETTER.

Unfaithfully Yours (1948) **105m.** **** D: Preston Sturges. Rex Harrison, Linda Darnell, Rudy Vallee, Barbara Lawrence, Kurt Kreuger, Lionel Stander, Robert Greig, Edgar Kennedy, Julius Tannen, Al Bridge. Brilliant Sturges comedy of symphony conductor Harrison, who suspects his wife of infidelity and considers three courses of action (including murder) during concert. Great moments from Vallee and Kennedy; often side-splittingly funny. Remade in 1984.▼●

Unfaithfully Yours (1984) **C-96m.** **½ D: Howard Zieff. Dudley Moore, Nastassja Kinski, Armand Assante, Albert Brooks, Cassie Yates, Richard Libertini, Richard B. Shull. Remake of Preston Sturges' wonderful film about an orchestra conductor who suspects his wife of having an affair—and plans to murder her. Pretty funny, with a perfect cast, but loses steam somewhere along the way. Certainly no match for the witty original. [PG]▼●

Unfaithfuls, The (1960-Italian) **89m.** **½ D: Stefano Steno. Mai Britt, Gina Lollobrigida, Pierre Cressoy, Marina Vlady, Anna Maria Ferrero, Tina Lattanzi, Carlo Romano. Multifaceted film of life among rich, corrupt society of Rome.▼

Unfaithful Wife, The SEE: **La Femme Infidele**

Unfinished Business (1941) **96m.** ** D: Gregory La Cava. Irene Dunne, Robert Montgomery, Preston Foster, Eugene Pallette, Dick Foran, Esther Dale, Walter Catlett. Ordinary romance about ambitious singer Dunne, loving Foster, marrying his brother Montgomery for spite—and promptly regretting it. Good cast wasted.

Unfinished Business (1984-Canadian) **C-99m.** *** D: Don Owen. Isabelle Mejias, Peter Spence, Leslie Toth, Peter Kastner, Julie Biggs, Chuck Shamata. Appealing sequel to Owen's NOBODY WAVED GOODBYE. It's twenty years later: Kastner and Biggs, now divorced, have a rebellious offspring of their own, 17-year-old Mejias. Story focuses on her problems and anxieties as she approaches adulthood.

Unfinished Business (1985-Australian) **C-78m.** *** D: Bob Ellis. John Clayton, Michele Fawdon, Norman Kaye, Bob Ellis, Andrew Lesnie. Touching, neatly acted comedy of middle-aged journalist Clayton, who meets up with Fawdon, the woman he once loved. She's married but childless—and proposes that he make her pregnant.

Unfinished Dance, The (1947) **C-101m.** **½ D: Henry Koster. Margaret O'Brien, Cyd Charisse, Karin Booth, Danny Thomas, Esther Dale. Sugar-sweet story of young dancer O'Brien whose idol is ballerina Charisse. Remake of French film BALLERINA (LA MORT DU CYGNE).

Unforgettable (1996) **C-111m.** *½ D: John Dahl. Ray Liotta, Linda Fiorentino, Peter Coyote, Christopher McDonald, Kim Cattrall, Kim Coates, David Paymer, Duncan Fraser, Caroline Elliott. Police department medical examiner who was accused of murdering his wife is obsessed with finding out the truth. When he meets a lab scientist (Fiorentino) who has discovered a way of transferring memory by injection, he experiments on himself, hoping to learn how and why his wife was killed. A solid premise (along the lines of a 50s sci-fi film) is dissipated by plodding treatment and a script that becomes ludicrous. A disappointment from director Dahl. Unendurable is more like it. [R]▼●

Unforgettable Summer, An (1994-French-Rumanian) **C-82m.** **½ D: Lucian Pintilie. Kristin Scott Thomas, Claudiu Bleont, Olga Tudorache, George Constantin, Ion Pavlescu, Marcel Iures, Razvan Vasilescu. Atmospheric 1920s tale of Rumanian military officer's wife, whose devotion to her family and concern for others causes nothing but strife. Ironic and sadly pertinent story set predominately on remote border post where peasant Bulgarians, Macedonians, and Rumanians reside amidst constant tension and turmoil. Scott Thomas is excellent.▼●

Unforgiven, The (1960) **C-125m.** *** D: John Huston. Burt Lancaster, Audrey Hepburn, Audie Murphy, John Saxon, Charles Bickford, Lillian Gish, Doug McClure, Joseph Wiseman, Albert Salmi. Western set in 1850s Texas tells of two families at odds with Indians over Hepburn, whom the latter claim as one of theirs. Gish and Bickford are outstanding in stellar-cast story, with rousing Indian attack climax. Panavision.▼●

Unforgiven (1992) **C-127m.** *** D: Clint Eastwood. Clint Eastwood, Gene Hackman, Morgan Freeman, Richard Harris, Jaimz Woolvett, Saul Rubinek, Frances Fisher, Anna Thomson, Anthony James. Elegiac anti-Western about a one-time mad killer, long since reformed, who comes out of "retirement" to make one more hit because he needs the money for his family. Powerful examination of morality and hypocrisy in the Old West—and the impact of killing (and being killed)—but marred by a midsection that plods. Exquisitely shot by Jack N. Green. Oscar winner for Best Picture, Best Director, Best Supporting Actor (Hackman), Best Film Editing (Joel Cox). Panavision. [R]▼●◗

Unguarded Hour, The (1936) **90m.** **½ D: Sam Wood. Loretta Young, Franchot Tone, Lewis Stone, Roland Young, Jessie Ralph, Dudley Digges, Henry Daniell, Aileen Pringle. Young is being blackmailed and cannot prove an accused murderer's innocence without damaging her own reputation—and embarrassing her prosecutor husband. Intriguing story comes to silly conclusion, but cast maintains interest (though the three leads are not terribly convincing as British subjects).

Unguarded Moment, The (1956) **C-95m.** **½ D: Harry Keller. Esther Williams, George Nader, John Saxon, Edward Andrews, Les Tremayne, Jack Albertson. Mild drama of school teacher whose emotional stability is endangered by lusting pupil. Film noteworthy only for Williams' nonaquatic role; based on a story by Rosalind Russell!

Unholy, The (1988) **C-100m.** ** D: Camilo Vila. Ben Cross, Hal Holbrook, Jill Carroll, William Russ, Trevor Howard, Ned Beatty, Claudia Robinson, Nicole Fortier. Ambitious horror film puts priest Cross to the test when archbishop Holbrook assigns him to cast out the devil from a New Orleans church. Veteran Philip Yordan's script (cowritten by film's designer Fernando Fonseca) is weird but unconvincing. Special effects are arresting, but highlight is Fortier as the supersexy demon. [R]▼●

Unholy Four, The (1954-British) **80m.** *½ D: Terence Fisher. Paulette Goddard, William Sylvester, Patrick Holt, Paul Carpenter, Jeremy Hawk. Muddled drama of amnesiac Sylvester caught up in a murder plot. Original British title: A STRANGER CAME HOME.

Unholy Garden, The (1931) **74m.** **½ D: George Fitzmaurice. Ronald Colman, Fay Wray, Estelle Taylor, Tully Marshall, Warren Hymer, Mischa Auer, Henry Armetta. Forgettable but very entertaining fluff with Colman an adventurer/thief in desert setting; murder, action, romance neatly blended, carried by Colman's effortless charm. Written by Ben Hecht and Charles MacArthur.

Unholy Night, The (1929) **94m.** ** D: Lionel Barrymore. Ernest Torrence, Dorothy Sebastian, Roland Young, Boris Karloff, Natalie Moorhead, Sidney Jarvis, Polly Moran, Sojin. With the murder of several members of their regiment, veterans from the Indian war gather at Young's London home to ferret out the murderer. Stagy Ben Hecht melodrama with much hamming, especially by Karloff.

Unholy Partners (1941) **94m.** *** D: Mervyn LeRoy. Edward G. Robinson, Edward Arnold, Laraine Day, Marsha Hunt, William T. Orr, Don Beddoe, Walter Kingsford. Intriguing premise: Robinson starts sensationalistic newspaper after WWI, is forced to bargain with underworld king Arnold. Day gives fine performance as E.G.'s girl Friday; Hunt sings "After You've Gone."

Unholy Rollers (1972) **C-88m.** **½ D: Vernon Zimmerman. Claudia Jennings, Louis Quinn, Betty Anne Rees, Roberta Collins. Behind-the-scenes life on roller derby circuit, Roger Corman-style; raunchy low-budgeter offers some fun. [R]▼

Unholy Three, The (1925) **86m.** **½ D: Tod Browning. Lon Chaney, Mae Busch, Matt Moore, Victor McLaglen, Harry Earles. In departure from horrific roles, Chaney plays side-show ventriloquist who teams with strongman and midget to form underworld trio. Corny aspects of story can't mar fascination with basic idea, or Chaney's performance. Remade in 1930.▼●

Unholy Three, The (1930) **72m.** **½ D: Jack Conway. Lon Chaney, Lila Lee, Elliott Nugent, Harry Earles, John Miljan, Ivan Linow. Almost scene-for-scene remake of 1925 film was Chaney's only talkie; he's terrific, other players less so. Denouement rewritten for this remake to take advantage of sound. Midget Earles is largely incoherent.▼●

Unholy Wife, The (1957) **C-94m.** *½ D: John Farrow. Rod Steiger, Diana Dors, Tom Tryon, Beulah Bondi, Marie Windsor. Muddled melodrama about farmer's wife attempting to kill husband and mistakenly shooting someone else.▼

Unhook the Stars (1996-French-U.S.) **C-103m.** *** D: Nick Cassavetes. Gena Rowlands, Marisa Tomei, Gérard Depardieu, Moira Kelly, Jake Lloyd, David Thornton, David Sherrill, Clint Howard. Wonderful showcase for Rowlands as a widow with grown children who comes to the rescue of a flaky young neighbor and looks after her little boy one day; soon the two develop a strong bond based on their genuine need for each other. Lovely film cowritten by Cassavetes, son of Rowlands and John Cassavetes. Depardieu (who coproduced the film) has the only underwritten part in the picture. [R]▼●

Unidentified Flying Objects SEE: **UFO: (Unidentified Flying Objects)**

Unidentified Flying Oddball (1979) **C-93m.** **½ D: Russ Mayberry. Dennis Dugan, Jim Dale, Ron Moody, Kenneth More, John LeMesurier, Rodney Bewes, Shelia White. Innocuous Disney update of Mark Twain's CONNECTICUT YANKEE IN KING ARTHUR'S COURT, with young Dugan (and a lookalike robot) catapulted back to medieval times. Retitled A SPACEMAN IN KING ARTHUR'S COURT. [G]▼●◗

Uninhibited, The (1965-Spanish) **C-104m.** ** D: Juan Antonio Bardem. Melina Mercouri, Hardy Kruger, James Mason, Didier Haudepin, Jose Maria Monpin. Good cast can't save muddled drama of troubled souls whose lives intertwine in picturesque seaside village on the Costa Brava.

Uninvited, The (1944) **98m.** ***½ D: Lewis Allen. Ray Milland, Ruth Hussey, Donald Crisp, Gail Russell, Cornelia Otis Skinner, Dorothy Stickney, Barbara Everest, Alan Napier. Eerie ghost suspenser about Russell disturbed by dead mother's spectre; Milland and Hussey, new owners of haunted house, try to solve mystery. No trick ending in this ingenious film, which introduced Victor Young's melody "Stella by Starlight." Spooky cinematography by Charles Lang, Jr. Scripted by Dodie Smith and Frank Partos, from Dorothy Macardle's novel.▼●

Union City (1980) **C-87m.** **½ D: Mark Reichert. Dennis Lipscomb, Deborah Harry, Irina Maleeva, Everett McGill, Pat Benatar, Tony Azito. Harry (of the rock group Blondie) makes her dramatic debut as the wife of neurotic businessman Lipscomb, who beats a vagrant to death. Low-budget film noir is enhanced by Lipscomb performance and moody, quirky direction. [PG]▼●◗

Union Depot (1932) **68m.** *** D: Alfred E. Green. Douglas Fairbanks, Jr., Joan Blondell, Guy Kibbee, Alan Hale, David Landau, Frank McHugh. Fast-paced, eventful yarn that brings sharpie Fairbanks and stranded chorus-girl Blondell together at a bustling train station where a hundred subplots crisscross. Great fun, brimming with early-1930s flavor.

Union Pacific (1939) **135m.** *** D: Cecil B. DeMille. Barbara Stanwyck, Joel McCrea, Robert Preston, Akim Tamiroff, Brian Donlevy, Anthony Quinn, Lynne Overman, Evelyn Keyes, Fuzzy Knight, J. M. Kerrigan, Regis Toomey. Brawling DeMille saga about building the first transcontinental railroad; McCrea the hero, Donlevy the villain, Stanwyck (with Irish brogue!) caught between McCrea and likable troublemaker Preston. Action scenes, including spectacular train wreck, Indian attack, and subsequent cavalry rescue via railroad flat cars are highlights. ▼●

Union Station (1950) **80m.** **½ D: Rudolph Maté. William Holden, Nancy Olson, Barry Fitzgerald, Jan Sterling, Allene Roberts, Lyle Bettger. Dated police techniques, plus general implausibility, detract from well-made film about manhunt for kidnapper (Bettger) of young blind woman (Roberts).▼

Universal Soldier (1992) **C-104m.** ** D: Roland Emmerich. Jean-Claude Van Damme, Dolph Lundgren, Ally Walker, Ed O'Ross, Jerry Orbach, Leon Rippy, Tico Wells, Ralph Moeller. Van Damme and Lundgren—well, it's not exactly Tracy and March in INHERIT THE WIND. Hunks are well cast as rival cyborgs (in a runaway government experiment, natch) whose human components hated each other during Vietnam. Has the requisite number of explosions. The director slyly keeps the grocery store Muzak going during Lundgren's one big emoting scene—right after he eats raw meat from a bin. Followed by a sequel and two cable TV movies. Panavision. [R] ▼●◗

Universal Soldier: The Return (1999) **C-82m.** ** D: Mic Rodgers. Jean-Claude Van Damme, Michael Jai White, Heidi Schanz, Xander Berkeley, Daniel von Bargen, Kiana Tom. The muscles from Brussels is back and must stop an out-of-control super-cyborg from world domination. Derivative but not boring rehash of the original. Features two tough heroines, Schanz and ESPN fitness guru Tom, but if you're threatened by the enlightened sexual politics, there's also a gratuitous brawl at a nudie bar. In his acting debut, WCW superstar Bill Goldberg proves he has all the dramatic range of Foghorn Leghorn. [R]▼●◗

Unknown, The (1927) **50m.** *** D: Tod Browning. Lon Chaney, Joan Crawford, Norman Kerry, Nick De Ruiz, John George. Wild and wooly silent Chaney chiller about a criminal on the lam who hides out in a gypsy circus and pretends he has no arms. Ultra-creepy, even by Browning's bizarre standards, with an unforgettable finale.●

Unknown, The (1946) **70m.** ** D: Henry Levin. Jim Bannon, Barton Yarborough, Karen Morley, Jeff Donnell, Robert Scott, Robert Wilcox. So-so entry in brief *I Love a Mystery* series with Bannon as Jack Packard, Yarborough as Doc Young. This one involves oddball family, with amnesiac daughter Donnell coming home to see her deranged mother (Morley) after twenty years.

Unknown Guest, The (1943) **64m.** **½ D: Kurt Neumann. Victor Jory, Pamela Blake, Veda Ann Borg, Harry Hayden, Emory Parnell. Murder whodunit manages to create suspense and perk interest, largely due to Jory's performance in this programmer.

Unknown Island (1948) **C-76m.** *½ D: Jack Bernhard. Virginia Grey, Philip Reed, Richard Denning, Barton MacLane. Boring story of adventurers searching for prehistoric monsters on strange island has unimaginative special effects, little else.▼●◗

Unknown Man, The (1951) **86m.** **½ D: Richard Thorpe. Walter Pidgeon, Ann Harding, Barry Sullivan, Keefe Brasselle, Lewis Stone, Eduard Franz, Richard Anderson, Dawn Addams. Most capable cast enhances this yarn of lawyer discovering client in murder trial was guilty, and the strange triumph of justice he plots.

Unknown Powers (1979) **C-96m.** *½ D: Don Como. Samantha Eggar, Jack Palance, Will Geer, Roscoe Lee Browne. Inept examination of such phenomena as astrology, mysticism, spiritual healing and psychic surgery, with the "stars" introducing each section. [PG]▼

Unknown Terror, The (1957) **77m.** ** D: Charles Marquis Warren. John Howard, Paul Richards, May Wynn, Mala Powers, Sir Lancelot. Unremarkable chiller supposedly set in South America, involving uncontrollable fungus. Regalscope.

Unknown World (1951) **74m.** ** D: Terrell O. Morse. Bruce Kellogg, Marilyn Nash, Victor Kilian, Jim Bannon. Overbaked relic of its era, with geologist Kilian and colleagues boring to the earth's core in a Cyclotram (mechanical mole). Their purpose: to find a haven from the A-bomb. Nash's character, that of an (at first) icy-cold "feminist" scientist, is alone worth the price of admission. Unabashedly moralistic screenplay by Millard Kaufman.▼

Unlawful Entry (1992) **C-111m.** *** D: Jonathan Kaplan. Kurt Russell, Ray Liotta, Madeleine Stowe, Roger E. Mosley, Ken Lerner, Deborah Offner, Carmen Argenziano, Dick Miller, Djimon (Hounsou). A break-in at the home of Russell and Stowe leads to their befriending lonely LAPD officer Liotta. But the disturbed cop develops a fixation on the wife—and we're into another urban paranoia thriller. It has the genre's usual contrivances and plot holes, but it's tense and exciting, with a terrific performance by Liotta. [R]▼●

Unman, Wittering and Zigo (1971-British) **C-102m.** *** D: John Mackenzie. David Hemmings, Carolyn Seymour, Douglas Wilmer, Hamilton Dyce, Anthony Haygarth, Donald Gee. Nifty little sleeper with Hemmings as new boys' school teacher who is promptly informed by his class that they murdered his predecessor, and that he'd better stay in line . . . or else. Creepy, chilling mystery, loaded with twists and stylishly photographed by Geoffrey Unsworth. Actual killer's identity is not revealed until *after* the closing credits! Title refers to the last three names on the roll . . . but Zigo is always absent. [PG]

Unmarried Woman, An (1978) **C-124m.** **** D: Paul Mazursky. Jill Clayburgh, Alan Bates, Michael Murphy, Cliff Gorman, Pat Quinn, Kelly Bishop, Lisa Lucas, Michael Tucker, Jill Eikenberry. Intelligent, compassionate look at how a woman copes when her husband walks out on her. Mazursky (who also wrote script) pulls no punches and makes no compromises—his characters are living, breathing people and his film is a gem. Clayburgh is magnificent in title role. [R]▼

Unnatural Causes (1986) **C-100m. TVM** D: Lamont Johnson. John Ritter, Alfre Woodard, Patti LaBelle, John Sayles, Sean McCann, John Vargas, Gwen E. Davis. Dynamite drama about a dedicated Veterans Administration benefits counselor and a stricken Vietnam vet who attempt to link the latter's illness to Agent Orange. Woodard mesmerizes as the real-life Maude DeVictor who battled the V.A. power structure; Ritter, as a fictional composite of several of those she attempted to help, is extremely good. Sayles scripted from the heart. Above average.▼●

Unremarkable Life, An (1989) **C-92m.** *½ D: Amin Q. Chaudhri. Patricia Neal, Shelley Winters, Mako, Rochelle Oliver, Charles Dutton, Lily Knight, Jenny Chrisinger. A hokey script does in this dud about two aging, very different sisters who live under the same roof and share memories and disagreements, especially when Mako starts wooing Neal. Neal and Winters try their best, but this is no WHALES OF AUGUST. [PG]▼●

Unsane (1982-Italian) **C-100m.** ** D: Dario Argento. Anthony Franciosa, John Saxon, Daria Nicolodi, Giuliano Gemma, Mirella D'Angelo, John Steiner. Not as interesting as most of horror stylist Argento's thrillers, story is about novelist Franciosa becoming the subject of death threats. Extremely bloody but featuring some arresting camerawork by Luciano Tovoli, who also photographed THE PASSENGER. Originally titled: TENEBRAE. Video version runs 91m. [R]▼●◗

Unseen, The (1945) **81m.** ** D: Lewis Allen. Joel McCrea, Gail Russell, Herbert Marshall, Phyllis Brooks, Isobel Elsom, Norman Lloyd. Man who made THE UNINVITED with Gail Russell tries similar venture but doesn't succeed. Governess Russell haunted again by strange mystery, but film haunted by very weak ending.

Screenplay by Raymond Chandler and Hagar Wilde.

Unseen, The (1981) **C-89m.** BOMB D: Peter Foleg. Barbara Bach, Sydney Lassick, Stephen Furst, Lelia Goldoni, Karen Lamm, Doug Barr, Lois Young. TV reporter Bach and crew—two other women, naturally—are harassed by "Junior" (Furst), product of incestuous affair between Lassick and Goldoni. Moronic horror film is not very horrifying. [R]▼

Unsinkable Molly Brown, The (1964) **C-128m.** *** D: Charles Walters. Debbie Reynolds, Harve Presnell, Ed Begley, Jack Kruschen, Hermione Baddeley, Audrey Christie, Martita Hunt, Harvey Lembeck. Big, splashy, tuneful adaptation of Broadway musical. Debbie is energetically entertaining as backwoods girl who knows what she wants, eventually gets to be wealthiest woman in Denver in the late 1800s. Based on a true story! Meredith Willson score includes "I Ain't Down Yet," "Belly Up to the Bar, Boys." Panavision.▼●

Unstrung Heroes (1995) **C-94m.** **½ D: Diane Keaton. Andie MacDowell, John Turturro, Michael Richards, Maury Chaykin, Nathan Watt, Kendra Krull, Joey Andrews, Celia Weston, Anne DeSalvo, Candice Azzara. A boy's adventures growing up in an off-center Jewish family of the early '60s with a nutty inventor father, a loving mother (who takes ill), and two highly eccentric uncles. The characters are colorful, and the performances are first-rate, but the film never quite gels. Young Watt is a real find. Freely adapted from the autobiographical book by Franz Lidz. [PG]▼●

Unsuitable Job for a Woman, An (1981-British) **C-94m.** *** D: Christopher Petit. Pippa Guard, Billie Whitelaw, Paul Freeman, Dominic Guard, Elizabeth Spriggs. Moody, entertaining film noir thriller about a woman detective (P. Guard) and her investigation of an unusual murder case after her boss commits suicide. Based on a novel by P. D. James.▼

Unsuspected, The (1947) **103m.** **½ D: Michael Curtiz. Claude Rains, Joan Caulfield, Audrey Totter, Constance Bennett, Hurd Hatfield. Predictable melodrama with good cast; superficially charming radio star Rains has murder on his mind, with niece Caulfield the victim.

Untamed (1929) **88m.** ** D: Jack Conway. Joan Crawford, Robert Montgomery, Ernest Torrence, Holmes Herbert, John Miljan, Gwen Lee. Cornball early talkie with Crawford as Bingo, an oil heiress reared in the tropical wilds, who falls in love with poor boy Montgomery.

Untamed (1940) **C-83m.** *½ D: George Archainbaud. Ray Milland, Patricia Morison, Akim Tamiroff, William Frawley, Jane Darwell, Esther Dale. Milland is a brave doctor trying to get serum through a blizzard in this hokey remake of Clara Bow's MANTRAP.

Untamed (1955) **C-111m.** *** D: Henry King. Tyrone Power, Susan Hayward, Agnes Moorehead, Richard Egan, Rita Moreno, John Justin. Quite vivid account of Boer trek through hostile South African country, with Power romancing Hayward. CinemaScope.

Untamed Breed, The (1948) **C-79m.** ** D: Charles Lamont. Sonny Tufts, Barbara Britton, William Bishop, Edgar Buchanan. Routine trials and tribulations of breeding cattle in old Texas, amid romance and gunplay.

Untamed Frontier (1952) **C-75m.** **½ D: Hugo Fregonese. Joseph Cotten, Shelley Winters, Scott Brady, Suzan Ball, Antonio Moreno. Range war between Texan cattle owners is basis for this Western improved by good cast.

Untamed Heart (1993) **C-102m.** **½ D: Tony Bill. Christian Slater, Marisa Tomei, Rosie Perez, Kyle Secor, Willie Carson. Multiple-hankie romantic tale about two troubled adults. Waitress Tomei can't seem to keep a boyfriend, while shy busboy Slater is a well-meaning orphan with a heart ailment. Solid production and good performances (especially from the two stars) go a long way to offset the basically hokey story. Romantics of all ages are sure to enjoy this. [PG-13]▼●

Untamed Heiress (1954) **70m.** *½ D: Charles Lamont. Judy Canova, Donald Barry, Taylor Holmes, George Cleveland. Slight Canova shenanigans involving the search for daughter of woman who financed a now-wealthy man.

Untamed Women (1952) **70m.** *½ D: W. Merle Connell. Mikel Conrad, Doris Merrick, Richard Monahan, Mark Lowell, Midge Ware, Carol Brewster. Campy nonsense about Air Force flyers stranded on Pacific island ruled by strange women, last descendants of the Druids. Caveat emptor!

Untamed Youth (1957) **80m.** BOMB D: Howard W. Koch. Mamie Van Doren, Lori Nelson, John Russell, Don Burnett, Eddie Cochran, Lurene Tuttle, Robert Foulk, Yvonne Lime, Jeanne Carmen, The Hollywood Rock and Rollers. Side-splitting camp masterpiece has sisters Mamie and Lori railroaded onto yucky prison work farm owned by hissably slimy Russell. You know something's wrong when Mamie sings four songs and Cochran only one. Best line: "Don't hit me in the mouth again! You'll break my dental plate!"

Until September (1984) **C-95m.** ** D: Richard Marquand. Karen Allen, Thierry Lhermitte, Christopher Cazenove, Marie-Christina Conti, Nitza Saul, Hutton Cobb. Temporarily stranded in Paris, Allen falls in love with handsome (and married) banker Lhermitte. Utterly predictable romantic drama. [R]▼

Until the End of the World (1991) **C-158m.** ** D: Wim Wenders. William Hurt, Solveig Dommartin, Sam Neill, Max von Sydow, Jeanne Moreau, Rudiger Vogler, Ernie Dingo, Chick Ortega, Eddy Mitchell. In the near future, Dommartin joins Hurt on a mysterious global mission, which leads to the creation of a device that will enable blind people to see. Intended as the "ultimate road movie," but the story doesn't take off until almost halfway through, and the characters and themes remain a jumble. Even the locations (fifteen cities on four continents) can't help. There are some sparks from von Sydow, interesting high-definition TV effects, and an eclectic, all-star soundtrack, but it's still a major disappointment. [R]▼●

Until They Sail (1957) **95m.** **½ D: Robert Wise. Paul Newman, Joan Fontaine, Jean Simmons, Sandra Dee, Piper Laurie, Charles Drake, Patrick Macnee, Dean Jones. Soaper courtroom story set in WW2 New Zealand, with sisters (Fontaine, Simmons, Laurie and Dee) involved in love, misery and murder. From James Michener story. CinemaScope.▼

Untouchables, The (1987) **C-119m.** **** D: Brian De Palma. Kevin Costner, Sean Connery, Charles Martin Smith, Andy Garcia, Robert De Niro, Richard Bradford, Jack Kehoe, Brad Sullivan, Billy Drago, Patricia Clarkson. High-energy entertainment that packs a wallop: writer David Mamet's update of the well-remembered TV series tells how an earnest but naive federal agent named Eliot Ness learns (the hard way) to deal with both underworld crime and police corruption in Prohibition-era Chicago. Fluidly (and often flamboyantly) filmed, with powerhouse performances by Connery (in his Oscar-winning role), as a seasoned street cop, and De Niro, as a grandiose Al Capone. Climactic shoot-out, with echoes of POTEMKIN, will have you on the edge of your seat! Photographed by Stephen H. Burum, with a rich music score by Ennio Morricone. Panavision. [R]▼●

Unvanquished, The SEE: **Aparajito**

Unwed Mother (1958) **74m.** *½ D: Walter Doniger. Norma Moore, Robert Vaughn, Diana Darrin, Billie Bird. Title tells all in this unsensational programmer.

Unzipped (1995) **C/B&W-72m.** *** D: Douglas Keeve. Lively, if selective, documentary about N.Y. fashion designer Isaac Mizrahi, which begins with him mired in a creative slump and ends with a 1994 show that trumpets his "Eskimo line." Benefits from the ceaseless effervescence of its subject, whose oft-demonstrated tastes in movies and television extend to Bette Davis (in BABY JANE mode), Loretta Young, and his beloved Mary Tyler Moore. [R] ▼●

Up at the Villa (2000-U.S.-British) **C-115m.** ** D: Philip Haas. Kristin Scott Thomas, Sean Penn, Anne Bancroft, James Fox, Jeremy Davies, Derek Jacobi, Massimo Ghini. Awkward adaptation of W. Somerset Maugham novella set in 1938 Florence. Thomas takes pity on Austrian immigrant Davies and initiates one night of sex, but the young man shoots himself when she refuses to extend the relationship. Davies' dreadful performance would be enough to sink most movies by itself, but there's also a lack of chemistry between Thomas and Penn (as a roving-eyed American adventurer). As their social circle's resident gossip, Bancroft is broad enough to fit right in with the "Florence set" in the more entertaining TEA WITH MUSSOLINI. [PG-13]▼

Up Close & Personal (1996) **C-124m.** *** D: Jon Avnet. Robert Redford, Michelle Pfeiffer, Stockard Channing, Joe Mantegna, Kate Nelligan, Glenn Plummer, James Rebhorn, Scott Bryce, Raymond Cruz, Dedee Pfeiffer, Miguel Sandoval, Noble Willingham, James Karen. Ambitious young woman goes to work for veteran newsman at a Miami TV station, where he shapes and prods her into a good reporter. As their personal relationship blossoms, they both know it's time for her to move on—and up the television ladder. Paraphrase of A STAR IS BORN has everything but Pfeiffer saying "This is Mrs. Norman Maine" at the end, but it still works because of the thousand-watt charisma of its leads. Screenplay by Joan Didion and John Gregory Dunne of all people. [PG-13]▼●◗

Up From the Beach (1965) **99m.** **½ D: Robert Parrish. Cliff Robertson, Red Buttons, Francoise Rosay, Irina Demick, Marius Goring, Slim Pickens, James Robertson Justice, Broderick Crawford. Static film of American sergeant Robertson involved with French civilians in love and war during Normandy invasion. CinemaScope.

Up Front (1951) **92m.** **½ D: Alexander Hall. David Wayne, Tom Ewell, Marina Berti, Jeffrey Lynn, Richard Egan. Sometimes amusing WW2 comedy based on Bill Mauldin's cartoon characters Willie and Joe, and their military shenanigans. Sequel: BACK AT THE FRONT.

Up Goes Maisie (1946) **89m.** ** D: Harry Beaumont. Ann Sothern, George Murphy, Hillary Brooke, Stephen McNally, Ray Collins, Jeff York, Paul Harvey. Maisie gets a job as secretary to a helicopter inventor and battles crooks who are trying to pilfer the patent. Stock series entry.

Uphill All the Way (1985) **C-86m.** BOMB D: Frank Q. Dobbs. Roy Clark, Mel Tillis, Burl Ives, Glen Campbell, Trish Van Devere, Burt Reynolds, Frank Gorshin, Sheb Wooley. Teaming of singing stars Tillis and Clark as inept robbers in the Old West probably sounded like fun on paper but emerges as a mirthless chase film. Cameo contributions of pals Reynolds and Campbell add little. [PG]▼

Up in Arms (1944) **C-106m.** **½ D: Elliott Nugent. Danny Kaye, Dana Andrews, Constance Dowling, Dinah Shore, Louis Calhern, Lyle Talbot, Margaret Dumont, Elisha Cook, Jr. Danny's first feature film (about a hypochondriac in the Army) doesn't wear well, biggest asset being vivacious Dinah Shore; Virginia Mayo is one of the chorus girls. Only those great patter songs—including "The Lobby Number" and "Melody in 4F"—hold up. Based on *The Nervous Wreck*, filmed before with Eddie Cantor as WHOOPEE!▼

Up in Central Park (1948) **88m.** ** D: William A. Seiter. Deanna Durbin, Dick Haymes, Vincent Price, Albert Sharpe, Tom Powers. Disappointing screen version of Broadway musical hit (minus many of its songs) about an Irish colleen in turn of the century N.Y.C. who helps expose the crooked Tammany Hall tactics of Boss Tweed (Price).▼

Up in Mabel's Room (1944) **76m.** *** D: Allan Dwan. Dennis O'Keefe, Marjorie Reynolds, Gail Patrick, Mischa Auer, Charlotte Greenwood, Lee Bowman. Engaging comedy of innocent O'Keefe embarrassed by presence of old flame (Patrick) in front of his wife (Reynolds). Based on a stage play filmed before in 1926; director and star reteamed in 1945 for GETTING GERTIE'S GARTER.▼

Up in Smoke (1957) **64m.** *½ D: William Beaudine. Huntz Hall, Stanley Clements, Eddie LeRoy, David Gorcey, Judy Bamber, Benny Rubin, Jack Mulhall. The Bowery Boys trash *Faust*, as Sach makes a pact with Satan in exchange for some sure bets at the track.

Up in Smoke (1978) **C-86m.** *** D: Lou Adler. Cheech Marin, Tommy Chong, Stacy Keach, Tom Skerritt, Edie Adams, Strother Martin. This silly pothead comedy breaks down all resistance with its cheerful vignettes about two dummies in search of "good grass." Nothing great, but undeniably funny; this was Cheech and Chong's first movie. Panavision. [R]▼●

Up in the Cellar (1970) **C-92m.** *** D: Theodore J. Flicker. Wes Stern, Joan Collins, Larry Hagman, Judy Pace. Above-average story of alluring youth who knows how to turn women on. Flicker's screenplay is exceptionally sharp. Made to cash in on success of THREE IN THE ATTIC, and was in fact retitled THREE IN THE CELLAR. [R]▼

Up in the World (1956-British) **91m.** **½ D: John Paddy Carstairs. Norman Wisdom, Maureen Swanson, Jerry Desmonde, Colin Gordon, Lionel Jeffries. Typical Wisdom comedy, anticipating Jerry Lewis' solo vehicles. He's a bumbling window cleaner involved with aristocrats and kidnappers, and even gets to sing.

Upper Hand, The (1966-French) **C-86m.** **½ D: Denys de la Patelliere. Jean Gabin, George Raft, Gert Frobe, Nadja Tiller. Labored international underworld yarn, with wooden performances by cast involved in gold smuggling. Franscope.

Up Periscope (1959) **C-111m.** **½ D: Gordon Douglas. James Garner, Edmond O'Brien, Andra Martin, Alan Hale, Carleton Carpenter, Frank Gifford. Garner is Navy Lieutenant transferred to submarine during WW2, with usual interaction among crew as they reconnoiter Japanese held island. WarnerScope.▼●

Upperworld (1934) **72m.** *** D: Roy Del Ruth. Warren William, Mary Astor, Ginger Rogers, Dickie Moore, Andy Devine, J. Carrol Naish, Mickey Rooney, Sidney Toler. Rich businessman William, wed to Astor, becomes involved with burlesque performer Rogers—much to his regret. Entertaining Ben Hecht drama, uplifted by William's charm, Rogers' presence, marred only by an unsatisfying conclusion.

Upstairs and Downstairs (1961-British) **C-100m.** *** D: Ralph Thomas. Mylene Demongeot, Michael Craig, Anne Heywood, James Robertson Justice, Daniel Massey, Claudia Cardinale. Witty study of human nature: Craig married boss' daughter (Heywood) and they must entertain firm's clients. Traces chaos of party-giving, and odd assortment of servants who come and go.

Up the Academy (1980) **C-88m.** ** D: Robert Downey. Ron Leibman, Wendell Brown, Ralph Macchio, Tom Citera, Tom Poston, Stacey Nelkin, Barbara Bach, Leonard Frey, Robert Downey, Jr. Crude, tasteless but occasionally lively comedy about misadventures in a boys' military school. Leibman had his name taken off credits and advertising, but film isn't *that* bad. Aka *MAD MAGAZINE* PRESENTS UP THE ACADEMY, although for cable TV release all references to *Mad* and Alfred E. Neuman were excised. Macchio's film debut. Panavision. [R]▼

Up the Creek (1958-British) **83m.** **½ D: Val Guest. David Tomlinson, Wilfrid Hyde-White, Peter Sellers, Vera Day, Michael Goodliffe. Broad naval spoof à la MR. ROBERTS, which leans too much on slapstick rather than barbs; Hyde-White is best as nonplussed admiral. Previously filmed as OH, MR. PORTER. Hammerscope.▼

Up the Creek (1984) **C-95m.** ** D: Robert Butler. Tim Matheson, Jennifer Runyon, Stephen Furst, Dan Monahan, Sandy Helberg, Jeff East, Blaine Novak, James B. Sikking, John Hillerman. Silly comedy—though far from the worst of its kind—about four college losers (played by graduates of PORKY'S and ANIMAL HOUSE) who battle dastardly preppies and gung-ho military cadets to win a raft race. Plenty of skimpily clad girls, plus a genuinely funny charade scene. [R]▼●

Up the Down Staircase (1967) **C-124m.** *** D: Robert Mulligan. Sandy Dennis, Patrick Bedford, Eileen Heckart, Ruth White, Jean Stapleton, Sorrell Booke, Roy Poole, Ellen O'Mara. Film version of Bel Kaufman's bestseller about N.Y.C. public schools is too slickly handled to be taken seriously, but generally entertaining. Good acting, especially by O'Mara as pathetic student.▼

Up the MacGregors (1967-Italian-Spanish) **C-93m.** *½ D. Frank Garfield. David Bailey, Agata Flori, Leo Anchoriz, Roberto Carmardiel. Sequel to SEVEN GUNS FOR THE MACGREGORS (but released here earlier) is distinguished from a million other Italian Westerns only by its relatively restrained use of violence. Techniscope.

Up the River (1930) **92m.** **½ D: John Ford. Spencer Tracy, Claire Luce, Warren Hymer, Humphrey Bogart, William Collier, Sr. Silly but disarmingly funny comedy about a pair of habitual convicts, played by Tracy (dynamic in his feature-film debut) and Hymer, and their efforts to help fellow inmate Bogart (in his *second* feature), who's fallen in love with female prisoner Luce. Notable for its confluence of great talents at the beginnings of their careers—but it's also fun to watch.

Up the Sandbox (1972) **C-97m.** **½ D: Irvin Kershner. Barbra Streisand, David Selby, Jane Hoffman, John C. Becher, Jacobo Morales, Barbara Rhoades, Stockard Channing, Isabel Sanford, Conrad Bain, Paul Dooley, Anne Ramsey. Uneasy mixture of naturalism and fantasy somewhat redeemed by Streisand's performance, some funny sequences, and genuine feeling for plight of neglected young mother in N.Y.C. [R]▼●

Up Tight (1968) **C-104m.** *** D: Jules Dassin. Raymond St. Jacques, Ruby Dee, Frank Silvera, Julian Mayfield, Roscoe Lee Browne, Max Julien. Tough remake of THE INFORMER, ghetto-style. Black revolutionaries betrayed by one of their own. [PG—originally rated M]

Up to His Ears (1965-French-Italian) **C-94m.** *** D: Philippe De Broca. Jean-Paul Belmondo, Ursula Andress, Maria Pacome, Valerie Lagrange, Jess Hahn. Wealthy young man decides to end his troubles by hiring a killer to do him in, then changes his mind. Energetic comedy runs hot and cold, but has many delicious moments.

Uptown New York (1932) **80m.** **½ D: Victor Schertzinger. Jack Oakie, Shirley Grey, Leon Waycoff (Ames), George Cooper, Raymond Hatton. Modest, occasionally entertaining soaper about young Grey, who's loved by successful but slimy surgeon Waycoff and decent, enterprising bubble-gum salesman Oakie. ▼

Uptown Saturday Night (1974) **C-104m.** **½ D: Sidney Poitier. Sidney Poitier, Bill Cosby, Harry Belafonte, Calvin Lockhart, Flip Wilson, Richard Pryor, Rosalind Cash, Roscoe Lee Browne, Paula Kelly. Undeniably entertaining, this film still looks like an *Amos 'n Andy* script dusted off. Broad, silly comedy about two pals (Poitier, Cosby) who try to retrieve a stolen winning lottery ticket and get involved with an underworld kingpin (Belafonte, in an uproarious Godfather parody). A pair of follow-ups: LET'S DO IT AGAIN and A PIECE OF THE ACTION. [PG]▼

Upturned Glass, The (1947-British) **89m.** *** D: Lawrence Huntington. James Mason, Pamela Kellino (Mason), Rosamund John, Ann Stephens, Henry Oscar, Morland Graham. Mason stars as a doctor who is driven to murder to avenge the death of his lover. Somber psychological thriller that starts slowly but builds suspensefully to a powerful conclusion. Mason also coproduced.

Up Your Alley (1989) **C-88m.** **½ D: Bob Logan. Murray Langston, Linda Blair, Bob Zany, Kevin Benton, Ruth Buzzi, Glen Vincent, Jack Hanrahan, Melissa Shear, Johnny Dark, Yakov Smirnoff. Ambitious low-budget comedy with dramatic underpinnings. Reporter Blair pretends to be homeless to write a story about cynical street person Langston, and his innocent friend Zany. Gags too often undermine sensitive and serious moments. Cowritten by director Logan and star Langston (a.k.a. The Unknown Comic). [R]▼●

Uranium Boom (1956) **67m.** *½ D: William Castle. Dennis Morgan, Patricia Medina, William Talman, Tina Carver. Dull account of two ore prospectors striking it rich, but more concerned with who will win Medina's love.

Uranus (1991-French) **C-100m.** *** D: Claude Berri. Philippe Noiret, Gérard Depardieu, Jean-Pierre Marielle, Michel Blanc, Gérard Desarthe, Michel Galabru, Fabrice Luchini, Daniel Prevost. Communists and anti-communists, collaborators and ex-resisters lobby for power in a French village formerly held by the Nazis. Less politically ambiguous than muddled, and perhaps overplotted—but a potent showcase for some powerhouse French actors.▼

Urban Cowboy (1980) **C-135m.** *** D: James Bridges. John Travolta, Debra Winger, Scott Glenn, Madolyn Smith, Barry Corbin, Brooke Alderson, Mickey Gilley, Charlie Daniels Band, Bonnie Raitt. A young hardhat new to Pasadena, Texas, gravitates to the incredible honky-tonk named Gilley's, with its easy women, macho ambience, and mechanical bull, perfecting an "image" of manhood that doesn't quite work out in real life. An evocative slice of life adapted from Aaron Latham's magazine story by Latham and director Bridges. Panavision. [PG]▼●

Urban Legend (1998) **C-99m.** ** D: Jamie Blanks. Jared Leto, Alicia Witt, Rebecca Gayheart, Natasha Gregson Wagner, Michael Rosenbaum, Loretta Devine, Joshua Jackson, John Neville, Robert Englund, Danielle Harris, Brad Dourif. College friends are stalked by an unknown murderer, who kills them one by one in the style of famous urban legends. Clever premise is undercut by standard presentation and a truly rotten ending. Just another SCREAM clone, but a bit more entertaining than most. Super 35. [R] ▼●◗

Ursus in the Land of Fire (1963-Italian) **C-87m.** *½ D: Giorgio Simonelli. Ed Fury, Claudia Mori, Adriano Micantoni, Luciana Gilli. Stupid muscleman mini-film, with Fury battling all odds to help Gilli regain her throne. Dyaliscope.

Ursus in the Valley of the Lions (1961-Italian) **C-82m.** ** D: Carlo Ludovico Bragaglia. Ed Fury, Moira Orfei, Mary Marlon, Alberto Lupo, Gerard Herter. Routine costumer with Fury teaming with friendly lions to overcome the barbarians. Totalscope.▼

Us (1967) SEE: **Benefit of the Doubt, The**

Used Cars (1980) **C-111m.** *** D: Robert Zemeckis. Kurt Russell, Jack Warden, Gerrit Graham, Frank McRae, Deborah Harmon, Joseph P. Flaherty, David L. Lander, Michael McKean, Andrew Duncan, Wendie Jo Sperber. Outrageous comedy about used car dealer rivalry that leads to spectacular and outlandish customer-getting schemes. Hilarious script by Bob Gale and Bob Zemeckis revels in bad taste, but does it so good-naturedly it's difficult to resist. And remember, $50 never killed anybody. [R]▼●

Used People (1992) **C-115m.** **½ D: Beeban Kidron. Shirley MacLaine, Kathy Bates, Jessica Tandy, Marcello Mastroianni, Marcia Gay Harden, Sylvia Sidney, Joe Pantoliano, Mathew Branton, Bob Dishy, Charles Cioffi, Louis Guss, Doris Roberts. When her husband dies, a middle-aged Jewish woman (MacLaine) finds herself being courted—persistently—by an Italian man (Mastroianni) who's admired her from afar for more than twenty years! Heavily plotted family saga (adapted by actor Todd Graff from a series of his plays) offers many touching and amusing—if never quite convincing—vignettes, with an all-star lineup of actors (again, not terribly convincing, but fun to watch). [PG-13]▼●

U.S. Marshals (1998) **C-133m.** *** D: Stuart Baird. Tommy Lee Jones, Wesley Snipes, Robert Downey, Jr., Kate Nelligan, Joe Pantoliano, Irène Jacob, Daniel Roebuck, Tom Wood, Latanya Richardson, Michael Paul Chan. The take-charge marshal (Jones) from THE FUGITIVE and his team are back on the job when a criminal suspect flees after a plane carrying him and other prisoners crash-lands. The search is helped/hampered by the addition of a Federal agent (Downey, Jr.). Action thriller scarcely takes a breath; falters toward the finale and doesn't know when to quit, but still entertaining. [PG-13]▼●◗

Usual Suspects, The (1995) **C-105m.** **½ D: Bryan Singer. Stephen Baldwin, Gabriel Byrne, Chazz Palminteri, Kevin Pollak, Pete Postlethwaite, Kevin Spacey, Suzy Amis, Benicio Del Toro, Giancarlo Esposito, Dan Hedaya, Paul Bartel. Five criminals of slightly different stripes are busted and put in a police lineup for a crime they didn't commit. They soon discover that fate—and perhaps more earthly forces—brought them together. Terrific cast makes the most of Christopher McQuarrie's intriguing, Oscar-winning, but convoluted script. (If you think about it, the final twist negates the entire film!) Highly praised, but to our minds, too "clever" for its own good. Spacey won an Oscar as Best Supporting Actor. Super 35. [R]▼●◗

Utah Blaine (1957) **75m.** *½ D: Fred F. Sears. Rory Calhoun, Angela Stevens, Max Baer, Paul Langton. Undistinguished Western about Calhoun helping to overcome land-grabbing outlaws.

Utilities (1981-Canadian) **C-91m.** *½ D: Harvey Hart. Robert Hays, Brooke Adams, John Marley, James Blendick, Ben Gordon, Jane Malett, Tony Rosato. Social worker Hays declares war on the gas, electric and phone companies in this undercooked satiric comedy. [PG]▼●

Utopia (1950-French) **80m.** *½ D: Leo Joannon. Stan Laurel, Oliver Hardy, Suzy Delair, Max Elloy. L&H's final film saddles the great comics with poor script and production, despite decent premise of the duo inheriting a uranium-rich island. Aka ATOLL K and ROBINSON CRUSOELAND. ▼◗

Utu (1983-New Zealand) **C-104m.** *½ D: Geoff Murphy. Anzac Wallace, Bruno Lawrence, Tim Elliott, Kelly Johnson, Wi Kuki Kaa. Maori tribesman (and British army subordinate) in New Zealand goes on a ritualistic rampage after his family is wiped out in a senseless raid. Downbeat, dull, and full of stereotypical characters—without the compensating power of Australia's not dissimilar THE CHANT OF JIMMY BLACKSMITH. Originally released in New Zealand at 118m; this review is based on the shorter U.S. version. [R]▼

U Turn (1997) **C-125m.** ** D: Oliver Stone. Sean Penn, Nick Nolte, Jennifer Lopez, Powers Boothe, Claire Danes, Joaquin Phoenix, Billy Bob Thornton, Jon

Voight, Abraham Benrubi, Julie Hagerty, Bo Hopkins, Laurie Metcalf, Liv Tyler. Young punk heading for Vegas is forced to stop in a one-horse Arizona town when his car breaks down; he quickly finds himself in a nightmare world where everything that can go wrong does. You know what you're in for when an animal is killed during the main titles; it only gets worse. A sturdy cast does its best with this predictable, savagely unpleasant pulp nonsense. [R]▼●◗

U2: Rattle and Hum (1988) **C/B&W-99m.** **½ D: Phil Joanou. Title Irish rock band was the late 80s' most celebrated, but scattershot documentary never really explains why to the unknowing or unconverted. Music compensates to some degree, with some of the best numbers fortunately weighted near the end; a side trip to Elvis' Graceland seems out of place. For no apparent reason, first half is in grainy b&w, second is in color. [PG-13]▼●

Utz (1992-British-German-Italian) **C-94m.** ** D: George Sluizer. Armin Mueller-Stahl, Brenda Fricker, Peter Riegert, Paul Scofield, Gaye Brown, Miriam Karlin. Good cast does its best in this overly sedate account of an elderly, dying man (Mueller-Stahl) and his lifelong obsession with collecting porcelain figurines. The point—the ultimate meaninglessness of materialism—is obvious. Scripted by Hugh Whitemore; based on Bruce Chatwin's novel.▼

V (1983) **C-205m. TVM** D: Kenneth Johnson. Marc Singer, Faye Grant, Michael Durrell, Peter Nelson, Jane Badler, Neva Patterson, Andrew Prine, Robert Englund, Richard Herd, Rafael Campos. Legions of alien visitors from space come to Earth on a peace mission and threaten to establish a Fascist dictatorship, singling out the world's scientists as scapegoats. Reportedly one of the most expensive television movies ever, and the great special effects bear it out. Imaginative sci-fi tale written by director-producer Kenneth Johnson. Originally shown in two parts. Followed by V: THE FINAL BATTLE and a series. Above average.▼●

Vacation From Marriage (1945-British) **92m.** *** D: Alexander Korda. Robert Donat, Deborah Kerr, Glynis Johns, Ann Todd, Roland Culver, Elliot Mason. Donat and Kerr sparkle in story of dull couple separated by WW2, each rejuvenated by wartime romance. Johns is perky as Kerr's military friend. Clemence Dane won an Oscar for her original story. British version, titled PERFECT STRANGERS, ran 102m.

Vagabond (1985-French) **C-105m.** ***½ D: Agnés Varda. Sandrine Bonnaire, Macha Meril, Stephane Freiss, Elaine Cortadellas, Marthe Jarnias, Yolande Moreau. Haunting drama about young drifter who wanders about hitching a ride here, sleeping there, and how those she encounters respond to her. A simple, powerful, superbly directed film about chance meetings, missed opportunities, and the price one must pay for one's choices. ▼●◗

Vagabond King, The (1956) **C-86m.** ** D: Michael Curtiz. Kathryn Grayson, Oreste, Rita Moreno, Cedric Hardwicke, Walter Hampden, Leslie Nielsen; narrated by Vincent Price. Bland remake of Rudolf Friml's operetta (filmed before in 1930), about poet-scoundrel François Villon. Oreste was touted as new musical star in 1956, but didn't quite make it. Story, sans music, filmed in 1927 (THE BELOVED ROGUE) and 1938 (IF I WERE KING). VistaVision.

Vagabond Lover, The (1929) **69m.** **½ D: Marshall Neilan. Rudy Vallee, Sally Blane, Marie Dressler, Charles Sellon, Norman Peck. Orchestra leader-crooner Vallee impersonates impresario; rich Dressler hires his band, and he falls for her niece (Blane). Pleasant musical-comedy antique is sparked by Dressler.▼

Vagrant, The (1992-U.S.-French) **C-91m.** *½ D: Chris Walas. Bill Paxton, Michael Ironside, Marshall Bell, Mitzi Kapture, Colleen Camp, Patrika Darbo, Mark McClure, Stuart Pankin, Teddy Wilson, Derek Mark Lochran. A timid, rising executive (Paxton) buys a house where an ugly, diseased hobo has been living, then finds himself terrorized by the bum. Misfired comic satire. Executive produced by Mel Brooks. [R]▼

Valachi Papers, The (1972-Italian) **C-125m.** **½ D: Terence Young. Charles Bronson, Lino Ventura, Jill Ireland, Joseph Wiseman, Walter Chiari, Amedeo Nazzari. Sloppy but engrossing account of Mafia life as seen through eyes of famed informer Joseph Valachi (Bronson). Lots of blood. From the book by Peter Maas. [PG—edited from original R rating]▼

Valdez Horses, The SEE: **Chino**

Valdez Is Coming (1971) **C-90m.** **½ D: Edwin Sherin. Burt Lancaster, Susan Clark, Jon Cypher, Barton Heyman, Richard Jordan, Frank Silvera, Hector Elizondo. OK intellectual Western with Lancaster a Mexican-American deputy sheriff forced to confront ruthless land baron after triggering local hostilities. Shot in Spain; first film for noted Broadway director Sherin. [PG]▼●

Valentino (1951) **C-102m.** *½ D: Lewis Allen. Anthony Dexter, Eleanor Parker, Richard Carlson, Patricia Medina, Joseph Calleia, Lloyd Gough, Otto Kruger. Undistinguished, superficial biography of famed star of American silent films.

Valentino (1977) **C-127m.** *½ D: Ken Russell. Rudolf Nureyev, Leslie Caron, Michelle Phillips, Carol Kane, Felicity Kendal, Seymour Cassel, Peter Vaughan,

Anton Diffring. Typically excessive, visually flamboyant Ken Russell "biography" offers little insight on great screen lover, and suffers further from Nureyev's awkward performance. But any film that casts Huntz Hall as movie mogul Jesse Lasky can't be *all* bad. [R]▼●

Valentino Returns (1987) **C-102m.** **½ D: Peter Hoffman. Frederic Forrest, Veronica Cartwright, Barry Tubb, Jenny Wright, David Packer, Seth Isler, Miguel Ferrer. Meandering drama of young Tubb and his no-account father, frustrated mother, and his desperation to experience sex. Great atmosphere, so-so result. Set in 1950s California. Screenplay by Leonard Gardner (who plays Lyle), based on his short story. [R]▼●

Valerie (1957) **84m.** *½ D: Gerd Oswald. Sterling Hayden, Anita Ekberg, Anthony Steel, Malcolm Atterbury. Unmemorable account (via flashbacks) of facts leading up to the wounding of Hayden's wife, and death of her parents.

Valiant Is the Word for Carrie (1936) **110m.** **½ D: Wesley Ruggles. Gladys George, Arline Judge, John Howard, Dudley Digges, Harry Carey, Isabel Jewell, Jackie Moran. Get out your handkerchief for this one, the epitome of 1930s soapers as selfless Gladys George devotes herself to orphan children. She earned an Oscar nomination for her performance.

Valley Girl (1983) **C-95m.** **½ D: Martha Coolidge. Nicolas Cage, Deborah Foreman, Colleen Camp, Frederic Forrest, Elizabeth Daily, Lee Purcell. Refreshingly nonexploitative punker-suburbanite romance is several cuts above most contemporary teen pics, but the result is still distressingly mild. Attractive leads, amusing performances by Camp and Forrest as Foreman's hippieish parents, but film never really goes anywhere. [R]▼●

Valley of Decision, The (1945) **119m.** *** D: Tay Garnett. Greer Garson, Gregory Peck, Donald Crisp, Lionel Barrymore, Preston Foster, Marsha Hunt, Gladys Cooper, Reginald Owen, Dan Duryea, Jessica Tandy, Barbara Everest, Marshall Thompson, Dean Stockwell. Not overpowering, as intended, but good film of housemaid Garson, master's son Peck. His family owned mine where her father and brother were killed. Romantic tension and workers' strike ensue. Set in 1870 Pittsburgh; from Marcia Davenport's novel.▼

Valley of Gwangi (1969) **C-95m.** **½ D: James O'Connolly. James Franciscus, Gila Golan, Richard Carlson, Laurence Naismith, Dennis Kilbane. Standard reworking of King Kong theme; adventurers in Mexico stumble upon prehistoric monster, hit on idea to display their find in a traveling circus, make money. Script and production have holes, but film is sparked by Ray Harryhausen special effects. Based on a story by Willis O'Brien.▼●

Valley of Head Hunters (1953) **67m.** *½ D: William Berke. Johnny Weissmuller, Christine Larson, Robert C. Foulk, Steven Ritch, Nelson Leigh. Typical *Jungle Jim* entry with our fearless hero fighting bad guys who're trying to steal mineral deposit rights from an African tribe.

Valley of Mystery (1967) **C-94m.** ** D: Josef Leytes. Richard Egan, Peter Graves, Joby Baker, Lois Nettleton, Harry Guardino, Julie Adams, Fernando Lamas, Leonard Nimoy. Lackluster melodrama in which a plane crash-lands in the South American jungle. Expanded from a TV pilot.

Valley of the Dolls (1967) **C-123m.** BOMB D: Mark Robson. Barbara Parkins, Patty Duke, Sharon Tate, Susan Hayward, Paul Burke, Tony Scotti, Martin Milner, Lee Grant, Joey Bishop, George Jessel. Scattered unintentional laughs do not compensate for terribly written, acted, and directed adaptation of Jacqueline Susann novel about three young women in show biz. Author Susann has a bit role as a reporter. Look for Richard Dreyfuss in a quick backstage bit. Remade as a TV movie in 1981. Panavision.▼●

Valley of the Dragons (1961) **79m.** *½ D: Edward Bernds. Cesare Danova, Sean McClory, Joan Staley, Danielle De Metz, Roger Til. A comet carrying a fragment of prehistoric Earth picks up two 19th-century men. Tawdry version of Jules Verne's novel *Off on a Comet*; laden with stock footage. Remade as ON THE COMET.

Valley of the Eagles (1951-British) **85m.** **½ D: Terence Young. Jack Warner, John McCallum, Nadia Gray, Anthony Dawson, Mary Laura Wood, Christopher Lee, Njama Wiwstrand. Above-par chase tale of Swedish scientist tracking down his wife and assistant who stole his research data and headed for the north country.▼

Valley of the Giants (1938) **C-79m.** ** D: William Keighley. Wayne Morris, Claire Trevor, Charles Bickford, Alan Hale, Jack LaRue, Frank McHugh, Donald Crisp, John Litel. Stale actioner of Morris thwarting Bickford's attempt to rape Northern California of its redwoods, with saloon girl Trevor brightening the proceedings. Previously made in 1919 and 1927. Footage and story line were later used in THE BIG TREES.

Valley of the Kings (1954) **C-86m.** ** D: Robert Pirosh. Robert Taylor, Eleanor Parker, Kurt Kasznar, Carlos Thompson. Meandering adventure yarn of excavations in Egypt for tombs of ancient pharaohs.▼

Valley of the Redwoods (1960) **63m.** *½ D: William Witney. John Hudson, Lynn Bernay, Ed Nelson, Michael Forest, Robert Shayne, John Brinkley. Programmer involving payroll theft and escape of robbers to Canada. CinemaScope.

Valley of the Sun (1942) **84m.** *** D: George Marshall. Lucille Ball, Cedric Hardwicke, Dean Jagger, James Craig, Billy Gilbert, Antonio Moreno, Tom Tyler. Intrigue of the old West with crooked white man provoking Indian uprising as he is being hunted by colonial agent.▼

Valley of the Zombies (1946) **56m.** *½ D: Philip Ford. Robert Livingston, Adrian Booth, Ian Keith, Thomas Jackson, LeRoy Mason. Witless horror epic of man-returned-from-dead bent on revenge. No zombies to be found—in a valley or elsewhere.

Valmont (1989-French-British) **C-137m.** **½ D: Milos Forman. Colin Firth, Annette Bening, Meg Tilly, Fairuza Balk, Sian Phillips, Jeffrey Jones, Henry Thomas, Fabia Drake, Ian McNeice. Ah, the bed-hopping of Choderlos de Laclos's *Les Liaisons Dangereuses*! Meticulous retelling—the third on film—of the sexual shenanigans of 18th-century French aristocrats. Youthful cast makes this seem more mischievous than other versions . . . but that playfulness also softens some of its bite. Elderly Drake, who died shortly after film's release, steals every scene she's in. Previously filmed in 1959 (DANGEROUS LIAISONS 1960) and 1988 (DANGEROUS LIAISONS), then again as CRUEL INTENTIONS. Panavision. [R]▼●

Value for Money (1955-British) **C-89m.** *** D: Ken Annakin. John Gregson, Diana Dors, Derek Farr, Donald Pleasence, Cyril Smith, Ernest Thesiger. Funny little comedy about young man inheriting father's money and his enjoyment of same. VistaVision.

Vamp (1986) **C-94m.** *½ D: Richard Wenk. Chris Makepeace, Sandy Baron, Robert Rusler, Dedee Pfeiffer, Gedde Watanabe, Grace Jones, Billy Drago. Fun-loving college guys run afoul of a female vampire in this dreary and distasteful horror outing. Starts out promisingly, with tongue-in-cheek, but soon drops the light touch in favor of the kinky. [R]▼●

Vampira SEE: **Old Dracula**

Vampire, The (1957) **74m.** ** D: Paul Landres. John Beal, Coleen Gray, Dabbs Greer, Raymond Greenleaf. Minor chiller with scientist turned into blood-seeker. Not without some merit; Beal is excellent. Retitled: MARK OF THE VAMPIRE.●

Vampire (1979) **C-100m. TVM** D: E. W. Swackhamer. Jason Miller, E. G. Marshall, Richard Lynch, Jessica Walter, Kathryn Harrold, Barrie Youngfellow, Jonelle Allen, Michael Tucker. Brooding architect and retired cop join forces to destroy a modern-day vampire who's stalking San Francisco taking vengeance on those who despoiled his resting place. Campy, and a pleasant surprise. Script by Steven Bochco and Michael Kozoll. Above average.

Vampire Bat, The (1933) **71m.** **½ D: Frank Strayer. Lionel Atwill, Melvyn Douglas, Fay Wray, Dwight Frye, Maude Eburne, George E. Stone, Lionel Belmore. Good cast helps average story along. Atwill stars as mad doctor forced to kill townsfolk in search of "blood substitute." Beware shorter prints.▼◗

Vampire Circus (1971-British) **C-87m.** **½ D: Robert Young. John Moulder Brown, Adrienne Corri, Laurence Payne, Thorley Walters, Lynne Frederick, David Prowse. Very weird Hammer horror with unique gimmick; 19th-century European circus travels from town to town for good reason: everyone in it is a vampire—including the animals! Last-minute cuts muddled the film considerably, but still well worth a look. [PG]●

Vampire in Brooklyn (1995) **C-102m.** ** D: Wes Craven. Eddie Murphy, Angela Bassett, Allen Payne, Kadeem Hardison, John Witherspoon, Zakes Mokae, Joanna Cassidy, Simbi Khali. Sleek Caribbean vampire Murphy, to perpetuate his race, needs to persuade Brooklyn cop Bassett that she's his soul mate. Oddball film has Murphy cracking jokes, but he's thoroughly evil; on the other hand, it's not scary enough to work as a horror film . . . and it's overlong, to boot. [R]▼●

Vampire Lovers, The (1970-British) **C-88m.** **½ D: Roy Ward Baker. Ingrid Pitt, Pippa Steele, Madeleine Smith, Peter Cushing, George Cole, Dawn Addams, Kate O'Mara. Rather erotic Hammer chiller about lesbian vampires faithfully adapted from Sheridan LeFanu's *Carmilla*, filmed many times before and since. Followed by LUST FOR A VAMPIRE and TWINS OF EVIL. [R]▼●

Vampire Men of the Lost Planet (1970) **C-85m.** BOMB D: Al Adamson. John Carradine, Robert Dix, Vicki Volante, Joey Benson, Jennifer Bishop. Scientist traces epidemic of vampire attacks on earth to strange, distant planet, with the aid of stock footage from other movies. A real mish-mash, released theatrically as HORROR OF THE BLOOD MONSTERS, CREATURES OF THE PREHISTORIC PLANET, HORROR CREATURES OF THE PREHISTORIC PLANET, and SPACE MISSION OF THE LOST PLANET. [PG]▼

Vampire Over London (1952-British) **74m.** ** D: John Gilling. Bela Lugosi, Arthur Lucan, Dora Bryan, Richard Wattis, Philip Leaver, Judith Furse. Overbearing vampire satire with Lugosi cast as Von Housen, crazed criminal who tangles with Old Mother Riley, a comical storekeeper. Last entry in the *Old Mother Riley* series of British farces, with Lucan playing the series title character in drag. Original title: MOTHER RILEY MEETS THE VAMPIRE; aka MY SON, THE VAMPIRE.▼

Vampires (1998) **C-107m.** ** D: John Carpenter. James Woods, Daniel Baldwin, Sheryl Lee, Thomas Ian Griffith, Maximilian Schell, Tim Guinee, Mark Boone, Jr., Gregory Sierra. Under directions from the Vatican, Woods and his team kill pesky vampires in the Southwest, while head vampire Griffith looks for the talisman that will allow his kind to exist in daylight. Like many Carpenter movies, it begins well, then crashes in a heap by the end. Based on the novel *Vampire$* by John Steakley. Aka JOHN CARPENTER'S VAMPIRES. Panavision. [R]▼●▶

Vampire's Kiss (1989) **C-96m.** **½ D: Robert Bierman. Nicolas Cage, Maria Conchita Alonso, Jennifer Beals, Elizabeth Ashley, Kasi Lemmons, Bob Lujan, Jennifer Lundy. N.Y. literary agent, Reagan-era trendy, is convinced that he's been bitten by a you-know-what. Cage's conversation-piece performance is so over the top that it's conceivable the actor was bitten in real life. Amusing at times, also tasteless, with a pointed office-harassment subplot. [R]▼●

Vampyr (1932-French-German) **73m.** *** D: Carl Theodor Dreyer. Julian West (Baron Nicolas de Gunzburg), Sybille Schmitz, Maurice Schutz, Henriette Gerard. Dreyer's stylized use of light, shadow, and camera angles takes precedence over the plot in this chilling vampire-in-a-castle tale. Based on the novella *Carmilla* by Sheridan Le Fanu; filmed several times later. Originally made in French, German and English versions.▼●▶

Van, The (1976) **C-92m.** *½ D: Sam Grossman. Stuart Getz, Deborah White, Danny DeVito, Harry Moses, Marcie Barkin, Bill Adler, Stephen Oliver. Shy Getz uses his fancy new van to seduce pretty girls. Innocuous idiocy of the California youth genre. Aka CHEVY VAN. [R]▼

Van, The (1996-British) **C-105m.** ** D: Stephen Frears. Colm Meaney, Donal O'Kelly, Ger Ryan, Caroline Rothwell, Brendan O'Carroll, Stuart Dunn. Slight, disappointing farce in which unemployed pals attempt to bring in the bucks by operating a hamburger business out of a van. The third (and by far least impressive) of Roddy Doyle's Barrytown Trilogy, following THE COMMITMENTS and THE SNAPPER. [R]▼●

Vanessa, Her Love Story (1935) **74m.** ** D: William K. Howard. Helen Hayes, Robert Montgomery, Otto Kruger, May Robson, Lewis Stone. Soapy story of gypsy love with Hayes attracted to roguish Montgomery. Dated romance doesn't come off too well today. Hayes' last starring role until 1952's MY SON JOHN.

Van Gogh (1991-French) **C-155m.** *** D: Maurice Pialat. Jacques Dutronc, Alexandra London, Gérard Sety, Bernard Le Coq, Corinne Bourdon. Highly subjective chronicle focusing on Van Gogh's final months. Unlike other films, he's clearly depicted as *not* being deranged; the result is a solid, austere work which steers clear of any sort of sensationalism or melodrama. Dutronc offers a thoughtful lead performance. [R]▼

Vanishing, The (1988-French-Dutch) **C-101m.** *** D: George Sluizer. Bernard-Pierre Donnadieu, Gene Bervoets, Johanna Ter Steege. Disturbing psychodrama of a man's obsession with discovering what happened to his girlfriend, who inexplicably vanishes at a vacation rest stop. The viewer, too, becomes involved as the abductor recounts his steps leading up to the crime. A thriller without blood that maintains an uneasy tension from the beginning through its haunting (if implausible) climax. Sluizer also directed the American remake. ▼●▶

Vanishing, The (1993) **C-110m.** ** D: George Sluizer. Jeff Bridges, Kiefer Sutherland, Nancy Travis, Sandra Bullock, Park Overall, Maggie Linderman, Lisa Eichhorn, George Hearn, Lynn Hamilton. Sutherland's girlfriend disappears at a gas station, and after three years of searching for her he's become a man obsessed. Meanwhile, her wily abductor (Bridges) considers revealing himself. Well-performed but unpleasant film can't hold a candle to Sluizer's 1988 original. [R]▼●

Vanishing American, The (1925) **109m.** *** D: George B. Seitz. Richard Dix, Noah Beery, Lois Wilson, Malcolm McGregor, Nocki, Shannon Day. Powerful drama of a valiant early-20th-century Navajo (Dix), and how he and his fellow tribesmen and -women are cruelly manipulated by corrupt government agent Beery. Hampered only by an overlong, boring prologue charting the history of the American West. Based on a novel by Zane Grey, and filmed in Monument Valley. Remade in 1955.▼

Vanishing American, The (1955) **90m.** ** D: Joseph Kane. Scott Brady, Audrey Totter, Forrest Tucker, Gene Lockhart, Jim Davis, Jay Silverheels. Mild, minor film about landgrabbers trying to take Navajo territory; loosely adapted from Zane Grey's novel.

Vanishing Point (1971) **C-107m.** ** D: Richard C. Sarafian. Barry Newman, Cleavon Little, Dean Jagger, Paul Koslo, Robert Donner, Severn Darden, Gilda Texter, Victoria Medlin. Told to drive a Dodge Challenger from Denver to San Francisco, Newman—for no apparent reason—decides to do it in 15 hours. Naturally, the cops are soon in hot pursuit, but Barry gets some help from blind d.j. Super Soul (Little). Existential chase thriller was a big drive-in hit, and remains a cult

favorite, but is pretty much a disappointment. Exceptional rock score. [PG]▼●
Vanishing Prairie, The (1954) **C-75m.** *** D: James Algar. Narrated by Winston Hibler. Disney's second True-Life Adventure feature provides astonishing footage of animal life in the great plains, including the birth of a buffalo calf. Fine presentation with little Disney gimmickry; Academy Award winner.▼
Vanishing Virginian, The (1942) **97m.** *** D: Frank Borzage. Frank Morgan, Kathryn Grayson, Spring Byington, Natalie Thompson, Douglas Newland, Mark Daniels, Juanita Quigley, Scotty Beckett, Dickie Jones, Louise Beavers. Sweet film full of nostalgia for the Old South (though it's set in the 20th century), based on Rebecca Yancey Williams' memoir of her father, a lifelong public servant in Lynchburg, Virginia. Works in elements of suffragette movement, women's rights, and the coming of Prohibition, but focuses mainly on the family, headed by the ever delightful Morgan. Also serves as a musical showcase for young Grayson.
Vanishing Wilderness (1974) **C-93m.** *** D: Arthur Dubs, Heinz Seilmann. Cowboy actor Rex Allen narrates this stunningly photographed wildlife documentary which covers virtually all of North America—from the alligators of the Everglades to the polar bears of the Arctic. Topnotch but for excessive narration and heavenly choirs punctuating each scene. [G]▼
Van Nuys Blvd. (1979) **C-93m.** ** D: William Sachs. Bill Adler, Cynthia Wood, Dennis Bowen, Melissa Prophet, David Hayward. Small-town boy tries to make the Southern California disco-drag-race-hamburger-stand scene. A bit better than average, but that's not saying much. [R]▼
Vanquished, The (1953) **C-84m.** *½ D: Edward Ludwig. John Payne, Jan Sterling, Coleen Gray, Lyle Bettger, Ellen Corby. Bland little Western about corruption within a town's administration.
Vanya on 42nd Street (1994) **C-120m.** ***½ D: Louis Malle. Wallace Shawn, Phoebe Brand, George Gaynes, Jerry Mayer, Andre Gregory, Julianne Moore, Larry Pine, Brooke Smith, Lynn Cohen, Mahdur Jaffrey. Malle's final feature is a riveting, highly cinematic "filmed theater" piece, which examines the illusion that is the theater. Actors come to a crumbling midtown Manhattan stage to rehearse David Mamet's adaptation of Chekhov's *Uncle Vanya*; Gregory is the director, Shawn is taking the leading role (in which he is superb), and all of them remain in street clothes as the rehearsal subtly becomes the play, which intertwines with "real life." As stunningly original as Malle's MY DINNER WITH ANDRE (which also featured Shawn and Gregory). [PG]▼●
Varan, the Unbelievable (1958-Japanese-U.S.) **70m.** *½ D: Ishiro Honda, Jerry Baerwitz. Myron Healy, Tsuruko Kobayashi, Kozo Nomura, Ayumi Sonoda. Typical Japanese rubber monster film except that creature defies clear definition. It's vaguely reptilian, but some insist it's a giant squirrel, since in Japanese prints it flies like a flying squirrel. Regardless, it stomps cities and scares the masses. Unbelievable is key word. Tohoscope. ▼
Variety Girl (1947) **83m.** **½ D: George Marshall. Mary Hatcher, Olga San Juan, DeForest Kelley, William Demarest, Frank Faylen, Frank Ferguson. Hatcher and San Juan head for Hollywood with hopes of stardom; flimsy excuse for countless Paramount guest stars, including Gary Cooper and Ray Milland. Bob Hope and Bing Crosby come off best in amusing golfing scene. Puppetoon segment in color.▼
Variety Lights (1950-Italian) **93m.** **½ D: Federico Fellini, Alberto Lattuada. Peppino De Filippo, Carla Del Poggio, Giulietta Masina, John Kitzmiller, Dante Maggio, Checco Durante. Fellini's first film (though codirected) is a rather ordinary tale of the lovely Del Poggio struggling through small-town music halls to become a star. Some funny and touching scenes featuring the usual Fellini eccentrics.▼●
Varsity Blues (1999) **C-104m.** *½ D: Brian Robbins. James Van Der Beek, Jon Voight, Paul Walker, Ron Lester, Scott Caan, Ali Larter, Amy Smart. Cliché-ridden, MTV-produced high school pigskin drama about a reluctant second-string quarterback (*Dawson's Creek* heartthrob Van Der Beek) and his nefarious steroid-distributing coach (Voight, who seems to think he's doing Eugene O'Neill). Veers between leering low comedy and heavy-handed melodrama. Lester rises above his exploitative role as an overweight lineman. [R]▼●◗
Varsity Show (1937) **81m.** *** D: William Keighley. Dick Powell, Priscilla Lane, Fred Waring, Walter Catlett, Ted Healy, Rosemary Lane. Broadway producer agrees to stage a show at his alma mater; result is a parade of musical numbers, including fine specialties by Buck and Bubbles, and rousing finale staged by Busby Berkeley. Originally released at 121m.
Vasectomy: A Delicate Matter (1986) **C-90m.** BOMB D: Robert Burge. Paul Sorvino, Cassandra Edwards, Abe Vigoda, Ina Balin, June Wilkinson, William Marshall, Lorne Greene, Gary Raff. Bank executive Sorvino is the father of eight. His wife gives him an ultimatum: Get a vasectomy, or it's bye-bye sex life. Utterly inane comedy that's almost (but not quite) too stupid to be offensive. [PG-13]▼
Vatican Affair, The (1969-Italian) **C-94m.** ** D: Emilio Miraglia. Walter Pidgeon, Ira Furstenberg, Klaus Kinski, Tino Carraro.

Pidgeon masterminds Vatican robbery in routine heist film. Colorscope. [M/PG]

Vault of Horror (1973-British) **C-87m.** **½ D: Roy Ward Baker. Daniel Massey, Anna Massey, Terry-Thomas, Glynis Johns, Curt Jurgens, Dawn Addams, Tom Baker, Denholm Elliott, Michael Craig, Edward Judd. Five horror tales interwoven by thin connecting thread, dealing with murder, torture, bloodthirsty vampires, voodoo; adapted from old E. C. Comics. Fine cast with so-so material. Follow-up to TALES FROM THE CRYPT; reissued as TALES FROM THE CRYPT, PART II. [PG]▼

Vegas Vacation (1997) **C-95m.** **½ D: Stephen Kessler. Chevy Chase, Beverly D'Angelo, Randy Quaid, Ethan Embry, Marisol Nichols, Miriam Flynn, Shae D'Lyn, Siegfried & Roy, Wallace Shawn, Sid Caesar, Julia Sweeney, Christie Brinkley. Just what you'd expect, as the Griswold family goes to Las Vegas, where Chase locks horns with a spiteful blackjack dealer (Shawn), D'Angelo is wooed by Wayne Newton, son Embry is mistaken for a high roller, and daughter Nichols is influenced by her cousin, an exotic dancer. Quaid steals every scene he's in. That's producer Jerry Weintraub as slick gambler Jilly from Philly. [PG-13]▼●◗

Veils of Bagdad (1953) **C-82m.** **½ D: George Sherman. Victor Mature, Virginia Field, James Arness, Nick Cravat, Mari Blanchard. Standard Arabian nights costumer, with Mature zestier than most such cardboard heroes.

Velocity of Gary, The (1999) **C-98m.** *½ D: Dan Ireland. Salma Hayek, Vincent D'Onofrio, Thomas Jane, Chad Lindberg, Olivia d'Abo, Shawn Michael Howard, Ethan Hawke. Sloppy, stilted soap opera, set amid the N.Y.C. porno–drag queen subculture, involving a love triangle between bisexual porn actor D'Onofrio, aimless hustler Jane and frenzied waitress Hayek. AIDS (though never named) plays a key role in the story, which labors to be hip but is only affected and muddled. Clairmont-Scope. [R]▼◗

Velvet Goldmine (1998-U.S.-British) **C-117m.** **½ D: Todd Haynes. Ewan McGregor, Jonathan Rhys Meyers, Toni Collette, Christian Bale, Eddie Izzard, Emily Woof, Michael Feast. Opulent, glittery paean to early '70s glam rock (and youth-culture head movies like QUADROPHENIA and PERFORMANCE) is such a triumph of style and excess it's easy to overlook the film's clunky CITIZEN KANE narrative structure and emotionally aloof characters. Rhys Meyers is effectively snotty as a bisexual David Bowie–esque pop star, but Collette is a standout as his neglected party-girl wife. Sandy Powell's inventive, androgynous costumes are great. [R]▼●◗

Velvet Touch, The (1948) **97m.** **½ D: John Gage. Rosalind Russell, Leo Genn, Claire Trevor, Sydney Greenstreet, Leon Ames, Frank McHugh, Martha Hyer. Satisfying murder mystery about a stage actress who commits perfect crime; good Leo Rosten script with a nifty ending. ▼●

Velvet Vampire, The (1971) **C-80m.** ** D: Stephanie Rothman. Michael Blodgett, Celeste Yarnall, Sherry Miles, Jerry Daniels. Stylish transfer of vampire legend to western U.S. with Yarnall as sexy bloodsucker. Later reissued as CEMETERY GIRLS. [R]▼●

Vendetta (1950) **84m.** ** D: Mel Ferrer. Faith Domergue, George Dolenz, Hillary Brooke, Nigel Bruce, Joseph Calleia, Hugo Haas. Florid but uneven costume melodrama about a woman who must avenge her family's honor when her father is murdered. Howard Hughes' expensive showcase for beautiful but inexperienced Domergue. Ferrer was film's fifth director, after Preston Sturges, Max Ophuls, Stuart Heisler, and Hughes.

Venetian Affair, The (1967) **C-92m.** ** D: Jerry Thorpe. Robert Vaughn, Elke Sommer, Felicia Farr, Karl Boehm, Luciana Paluzzi, Boris Karloff, Edward Asner. Limp spy vehicle not far removed from Vaughn's *Man from U.N.C.L.E.* TV series. International intrigue isn't too intriguing in this one; Karloff is good in a supporting role. Panavision.

Venetian Woman, The (1986-Italian) **C-84m.** *** D: Mauro Bolognini. Laura Antonelli, Jason Connery, Monica Guerritore, Claudio Amendola, Annie-Belle. Disarmingly straightforward 16th-century sex comedy-drama of Connery (son of Sean Connery and Diane Cilento) arriving in Venice and juggling affairs with lovely but frustrated older women. Exquisite art direction, gorgeous Antonelli, and clever musical score by Ennio Morricone heighten this little gem. Original Italian title: LA VENEXIANA.

Vengeance (1937) **61m.** ** D: Del Lord. Lyle Talbot, Wendy Barrie, Wally Albright, Marc Lawrence, Eddie Acuff, Lucille Lund, Robert Rideout. Harmless little crime drama about police officer Talbot's act of cowardice during a bank robbery. He resigns from the force in shame and infiltrates the gang of sinister hoodlum Lawrence. Originally titled WHAT PRICE VENGEANCE.▼

Vengeance of Fu Manchu, The (1967-British) **C-91m.** ** D: Jeremy Summers. Christopher Lee, Douglas Wilmer, Tsai Chin, Horst Frank, Maria Rohm, Howard Marion Crawford. Third entry in low-budget series that keeps Sax Rohmer stories in period. This time evil genius is out to destroy world police organization, and discredit arch-nemesis Nayland Smith (Wilmer) with a double. Good cast working below capabilities; lousy script. Followed by BLOOD OF FU MANCHU. ▼

Vengeance of She, The (1968-British) **C-101m.** ** D: Cliff Owen. John Richardson, Olinka Berova, Edward Judd, Colin Blakely. Not a sequel, but more like a remake of Hammer's 1965 version of Haggard's SHE; here, the spirit of Ayesha takes over young Berova. Pretty boring. [G]▼●◗

Vengeance Valley (1951) **C-83m.** ** D: Richard Thorpe. Burt Lancaster, Robert Walker, Joanne Dru, Sally Forrest, John Ireland, Carleton Carpenter, Hugh O'Brian. Sex in the West with Lancaster and Walker as battling brothers, Dru and Forrest their women. Walker plays slimy villain with gusto.▼●

Venice/Venice (1992) **C-108m.** ** D: Henry Jaglom. Nelly Alard, Henry Jaglom, Suzanne Bertish, Melissa Leo, Daphna Kastner, David Duchovny, Diane Salinger, Zack Norman, John Landis. Jaglom pretentiously parodies himself, playing a "maverick" American filmmaker at the Venice Film Festival; Alard is cast as a French journalist who becomes involved with him. Annoyingly self-absorbed, but occasionally effective when depicting the artificial emotion at the festival. The title refers to Venice, Italy, and Venice, California, where the director also is shown to have a coterie of admirers.▼

Venom (1982-British) **C-98m.** *½ D: Piers Haggard. Klaus Kinski, Nicol Williamson, Oliver Reed, Sarah Miles, Sterling Hayden, Cornelia Sharpe, Susan George, Michael Gough. World's deadliest snake terrorizes international terrorist-kidnapper and a houseful of hostages. Half the big-name cast appears to be drunk; the other half looks as though it wishes it were. [R]▼

Venus in Furs (1970-British-Italian-German) **86m.** *½ D: Jess Franco. James Darren, Barbara McNair, Maria Rohm, Klaus Kinski, Dennis Price, Margaret Lee. Musician is baffled to see a woman who had previously washed ashore in a mutilated state; poor mystery. [R]▼

Vera Cruz (1954) **C-94m.** *** D: Robert Aldrich. Gary Cooper, Burt Lancaster, Denise Darcel, Cesar Romero, George Macready, Ernest Borgnine, Charles Bronson. Lumbering yet exciting Western set in 1860s Mexico with Cooper and Lancaster involved in plot to overthrow Emperor Maximilian. SuperScope.▼●

Verboten! (1959) **93m.** **½ D: Samuel Fuller. James Best, Susan Cummings, Tom Pittman, Paul Dubov, Dick Kallman, Steven Geray. American soldier falls in love with embittered German girl in occupied Berlin after WW2. High-pitched drama, flamboyantly directed by Fuller.▼●

Verdict, The (1946) **86m.** **½ D: Don Siegel. Peter Lorre, Sydney Greenstreet, Joan Lorring, George Coulouris, Arthur Shields, Rosalind Ivan, Holmes Herbert. Greenstreet and Lorre make the most of this "perfect crime" yarn, with Greenstreet as Scotland Yard inspector who's "retired" when his methods are thought to be outmoded. Director Siegel's first feature. Remake of THE CRIME DOCTOR (1934).

Verdict, The (1974) SEE: **Jury of One**

Verdict, The (1982) **C-129m.** **** D: Sidney Lumet. Paul Newman, Charlotte Rampling, Jack Warden, James Mason, Milo O'Shea, Edward Binns, Julie Bovasso, Lindsay Crouse, Roxanne Hart, James Handy. Newman gives one of his finest performances as Boston lawyer who's hit bottom, until a medical negligence case gives him a chance to restore his self-esteem—while fighting for the kind of justice he still believes in. Director Lumet uses silence as eloquently as dialogue, and turns a story with more than a few loopholes into an emotionally charged experience. Look carefully for Bruce Willis as a courtroom spectator. Screenplay by David Mamet, from Barry Reed's novel. [R]▼●

Verne Miller (1987) **C-92m.** BOMB D: Rod Hewitt. Scott Glenn, Barbara Stock, Thomas G. Waites, Lucinda Jenney, Sonny Carl Davis, Diane Salinger, Andrew Robinson. Dumb drama with Glenn in a one-note performance as a real-life ex–South Dakota sheriff who became a notorious gangster during the 1920s and '30s. All attitude and posturing. [R]▼●

Vernon Johns Story, The (1994) **C-100m. TVM** D: Kenneth Fink. James Earl Jones, Mary Alice, Tommy Hollis, Cissy Houston, Clifton James, Nicole Leach, Joe Seneca. The spirit of Vernon Johns, a semi-itinerant, forward-looking Southern pastor who inspired the civil rights movement in the 1950s and passed the mantle to a young Martin Luther King (pictured fleetingly at the end), is wonderfully realized in James Earl Jones, alternately low-key and rousing. Kevin Arkadie scripted, from Leslie Lee's story. Above average.

Veronika Voss (1982-German) **105m.** *** D: Rainer Werner Fassbinder. Rosel Zech, Hilmar Thate, Cornelia Froboess, Annemarie Duringer, Doris Schade, Volker Spengler. Interesting saga of faded '40s movie star Zech, allegedly a friend of Goebbels, who ten years after the war's end is a morphine addict. Good, but not great, Fassbinder; the last of his trilogy about post-war Germany, following THE MARRIAGE OF MARIA BRAUN and LOLA. [R]▼

Vertigo (1958) **C-128m.** **** D: Alfred Hitchcock. James Stewart, Kim Novak, Barbara Bel Geddes, Tom Helmore, Henry Jones, Ellen Corby, Raymond Bailey, Lee Patrick. One of Hitchcock's most discussed films. Retired police detective Stewart, who has a fear of heights, is hired by old school chum in San Francisco to keep an eye on his wife (Novak), eventually falls in love with his quarry . . . and that's just the beginning; to reveal more would be unthinkable. Alec Coppel and Samuel Taylor scripted, from the novel *D'entre les morts* by Pierre Boileau and Thomas Narcejac. Haunting, dream-like thriller, with riveting Bernard Herrmann score to match; a genuinely great motion picture that demands multiple viewings. VistaVision.▼●◗

Very Bad Things (1998) **C-100m.** ** D: Peter Berg. Christian Slater, Cameron Diaz, Daniel Stern, Jeanne Tripplehorn, Jon Favreau, Jeremy Piven, Leland Orser. Black—make that *really* black—comedy about a guy who goes to Las Vegas with four pals for a bachelor party. The scene turns ugly very fast, leaving the friends to deal with a couple of crimes and raging guilt as the wedding draws nearer. Extreme, to say the least, but true to its dark mandate, which is awfully grim. Feature writing and directing debut for actor Berg. [R] ▼●◗

Very Brady Sequel, A (1996) **C-89m.** *** D: Arlene Sanford. Shelley Long, Gary Cole, Tim Matheson, Christopher Daniel Barnes, Christine Taylor, Paul Sutera, Jennifer Elise Cox, Henrietta Mantel, Jesse Lee, Olivia Hack, John Hillerman. With a better script than the first BRADY movie, this silly/funny follow-up has the '70s time-warp family thrown asunder when a man claiming to be Carol's first husband shows up. Further problems arise when Greg and Marsha find themselves unsettlingly attracted to one another! Full of the same double-entendre sexual gags as the first film, along with some wonderful musical moments and a handful of gag cameos. [PG-13]▼●

Very Close Quarters (1986) **C-101m.** BOMB D: Vladimir Rif. Shelley Winters, Paul Sorvino, Theodore Bikel, Farley Granger, Lee Taylor Allen. Astonishingly inept, obnoxious comedy about a group of rather vulgar individuals sharing a communal flat in Moscow. THE MORE THE MERRIER this isn't. Interesting cast wasted. Filmed in 1983. [R]▼

Very Edge, The (1962-British) **82m.** ** D: Cyril Frankel. Richard Todd, Anne Heywood, Nicole Maurey, Jack Hedley, Barbara Mullen, Jeremy Brett, Maurice Denham, Patrick Magee. Pregnant Heywood is assaulted by sex pervert Brett, with unfortunate repercussions. Unsavory and unexciting thriller.▼

Very Honorable Guy, A (1934) **62m.** *½ D: Lloyd Bacon. Joe E. Brown, Alice White, Alan Dinehart, Hobart Cavanaugh, Al Dubin. Flat comedy from Damon Runyon story about gambler who sells his body to science—ahead of time—in order to pay off debt.

Very Important Person SEE: **Coming-Out Party** (1961)

Very Private Affair, A (1962-French-Italian) **C-95m.** ** D: Louis Malle. Brigitte Bardot, Marcello Mastroianni, Gregor von Rezzori, Eleonore Hirt, Dirk Sanders. Rather remote romantic drama in which Bardot plays a famous movie star (from Geneva) who is robbed of her privacy and retreats from the world. Mastroianni is her mom's former lover, a theater director now protecting Bardot. Flashy ending filmed against backdrop of the Spoleto Festival. Originally titled: LA VIE PRIVEE. ▼

Very Special Favor, A (1965) **C-104m.** **½ D: Michael Gordon. Rock Hudson, Leslie Caron, Charles Boyer, Walter Slezak, Dick Shawn, Larry Storch, Nita Talbot, Jay Novello. Too-often blah, forced comedy of Boyer asking Hudson to romance daughter Caron.

Very Thought of You, The (1944) **99m.** ** D: Delmer Daves. Dennis Morgan, Eleanor Parker, Dane Clark, Faye Emerson, Beulah Bondi, Henry Travers, William Prince, Andrea King. Flat romance of couple marrying during WW2, encountering family wrath when they return home; unusual Daves backfire.

Very Thought of You, The (1998-British) **C-88m.** *** D: Nick Hamm. Monica Potter, Joseph Fiennes, Rufus Sewell, Tom Hollander, Ray Winstone. Cute romantic comedy about an American woman who impulsively packs up and flies to England, where she simultaneously shakes up the lives of three men. Nicely done. Original British title: MARTHA, MEET FRANK, DANIEL AND LAURENCE. [PG-13]▼◗

Vibes (1988) **C-99m.** ** D: Ken Kwapis. Cyndi Lauper, Jeff Goldblum, Julian Sands, Googy Gress, Peter Falk, Michael Lerner, Ramon Bieri, Elizabeth Pena, Bill McCutcheon, Karen Akers, Park Overall, Steve Buscemi. Unsatisfactory romantic adventure comedy about psychics Lauper (in her first and only starring role) and Goldblum, and their quest for a supposed city of gold in the mountains of Ecuador. Unfortunate misfire from comedy writers Lowell Ganz and Babaloo Mandel. [PG]▼

Vice Raid (1960) **71m.** ** D: Edward L. Cahn. Mamie Van Doren, Richard Coogan, Brad Dexter, Frank Gerstle, Barry Atwater, Carol Nugent. Tawdry vehicle for Van Doren, as a hooker out to frame a cop. Blander than usual, but film does allow for some campy humor.

Vice Squad (1931) **80m.** ** D: John Cromwell. Paul Lukas, Kay Francis, Helen Johnson (Judith Wood), Esther Howard, William B. Davidson. Lukas is excellent in tale of corrupt vice squad, but production needs a shot of adrenalin. Good potential dissipated by slow presentation.▼

Vice Squad (1953) **87m.** **½ D: Arnold Laven. Edward G. Robinson, Paulette Goddard, K. T. Stevens, Porter Hall, Lee Van

Cleef. Well-paced account of events in typical day of police detective department.

Vice Squad (1982) **C-97m.** ** D: Gary A. Sherman. Season Hubley, Gary Swanson, Wings Hauser, Pepe Serna, Beverly Todd. Hooker helps Hollywood cops catch sadistic pimp who sexually mutilates other prostitutes. Both dull and sleazy, but Hauser is undeniably a great movie villain. [R]▼●

Vice Versa (1948-British) **111m.** *** D: Peter Ustinov. Roger Livesey, Kay Walsh, David Hutcheson, Anthony Newley, James Robertson Justice, Petula Clark, Patricia Raine, Joan Young. Entertaining comedy about Victorian stockbroker Livesey and his schoolboy son Newley, who change places after wishing on a magic stone. Parts of it are silly, but much of it is inspired and hilarious. Justice is great as a hypocritical headmaster; Ustinov also wrote the script. Predates the father-son "comedies" of the 1980s.▼

Vice Versa (1988) **C-100m.** *** D: Brian Gilbert. Judge Reinhold, Fred Savage, Corinne Bohrer, Swoosie Kurtz, David Proval, Jane Kaczmarek, William Prince, Gloria Gifford. An ill-gotten mystical Thai skull enables a department store workaholic and his 11-year-old son to become each other. Not up to BIG, but better than it ought to be; Reinhold and Savage appear to be having a whale of a time in their roles. [PG]▼●

Vicious Circle, The SEE: **Circle, The**

Vicki (1953) **85m.** **½ D: Harry Horner. Jeanne Crain, Jean Peters, Elliott Reid, Casey Adams, Richard Boone, Carl Betz, Aaron Spelling. Loose remake of I WAKE UP SCREAMING, with Boone the resolute cop convinced agent Reid killed chanteuse girlfriend Peters. Dramatic flair isn't always evident, but wait till you find out who the killer is.

Victim (1961-British) **100m.** ***½ D: Basil Dearden. Dirk Bogarde, Sylvia Sims, Dennis Price, Nigel Stock, Peter McEnery, Donald Churchill, Anthony Nicholls, Hilton Edwards, Norman Bird. Fine thriller with lawyer Bogarde risking reputation by trying to confront gang of blackmailers who caused death of his onetime lover. Considered daring at the time for treatment of homosexuality. Screenplay by Janet Green and John McCormick. ▼●

Victor Frankenstein SEE: **Terror of Frankenstein**

Victoria the Great (1937-British) **C/B&W-118m.** *** D: Herbert Wilcox. Anna Neagle, Anton Walbrook, H. B. Warner, Walter Rilla, Mary Morris, C. V. France, Charles Carson, Felix Aylmer. Neagle is radiant as Queen Victoria in often-stodgy biopic emphasizing her romance with Prince Albert (Walbrook). Final reel, the jubilee celebration, is in Technicolor. Sequel: SIXTY GLORIOUS YEARS.

Victors, The (1963) **156m.** *** D: Carl Foreman. George Hamilton, George Peppard, Vince Edwards, Eli Wallach, Melina Mercouri, Romy Schneider, Jeanne Moreau, Peter Fonda, Senta Berger, Elke Sommer, Albert Finney. Sprawling WW2 drama of Allied soldiers on the march through Europe, focusing on their loving and fighting. Good cast and direction overcome Foreman's ambling script. Originally released at 175m. Panavision.

Victor/Victoria (1982) **C-133m.** ***½ D: Blake Edwards. Julie Andrews, James Garner, Robert Preston, Lesley Ann Warren, Alex Karras, John Rhys-Davies, Graham Stark, Peter Arne. Down-and-out singer Andrews masquerades as a man and becomes the toast of Paris cabarets in the 1930s, to the delight of her gay mentor (Preston) and the confusion of an American admirer (Garner). Sophisticated, often hilarious comedy, with Henry Mancini and Leslie Bricusse earning Oscars for their song score and adaptation. Edwards' screenplay is based on VIKTOR UND VIKTORIA, a 1933 German film (remade in 1936 as FIRST A GIRL with Jessie Matthews). Later a Broadway musical. Panavision. [PG]▼●

Victory (1940) **78m.** *** D: John Cromwell. Fredric March, Betty Field, Cedric Hardwicke, Jerome Cowan, Rafaela Ottiano, Sig Ruman. March is authentic in tale of loner whose idyllic island life is disrupted by band of cutthroats; flavorful adaptation of Joseph Conrad novel sags at the end. Filmed before in 1919 and in 1930 (as DANGEROUS PARADISE).

Victory (1981) **C-110m.** *½ D: John Huston. Sylvester Stallone, Michael Caine, Max von Sydow, Pele, Daniel Massey, Carole Laure. POWs get a chance to escape German prison camp but stick around to finish soccer game—just as it would have happened in real life. Only Pele's celebrated kicks save this silly bore from a BOMB rating. Panavision. [PG]▼●◗

Victory at Sea (1954) **108m.** *** Produced by Henry Salomon. Narrated by Alexander Scourby. Briskly edited version of popular TV documentary series, highlighting Allied fight during WW2. Excellent photography, rousing Richard Rodgers score.▼

Videodrome (1983-Canadian) **C-90m.** ** D: David Cronenberg. James Woods, Sonja Smits, Deborah Harry, Peter Dvorsky, Les Carlson, Jack Creley, Lynne Gorman. Genuinely intriguing story premise—about pirate cable-TV programmer (Woods, in a dynamic performance) who's mesmerized by bizarre, untraceable transmissions that have hallucinatory power. Unfortunately, story gets slower—and sillier—as it goes along, with icky special effects by Rick Baker. [R]▼●◗

Video Madness SEE: **Joysticks**
View From Pompey's Head, The (1955) **C-97m.** **½ D: Philip Dunne. Richard Egan, Dana Wynter, Cameron Mitchell, Marjorie Rambeau, Sidney Blackmer, Bess Flowers. Superficial gloss from Hamilton Basso novel about social and racial prejudice in small Southern town; Blackmer as aging novelist and Rambeau his wife come off best. CinemaScope.
View From the Bridge, A (1962-French) **110m.** *** D: Sidney Lumet. Raf Vallone, Maureen Stapleton, Carol Lawrence, Jean Sorel, Morris Carnovsky, Harvey Lembeck, Vincent Gardenia. Effective adaptation of Arthur Miller drama set near Brooklyn waterfront, involving dock worker Vallone's rejection of wife Stapleton and suppressed love of niece Lawrence; Sorel is smuggled-in immigrant Lawrence loves.
View to a Kill, A (1985-British) **C-131m.** ** D: John Glen. Roger Moore, Christopher Walken, Tanya Roberts, Grace Jones, Patrick Macnee, Patrick Bauchau, Fiona Fullerton, Alison Doody, Desmond Llewelyn, Robert Brown, Lois Maxwell, Walter Gotell, Dolph Lundgren. One of the weakest James Bond films saddles 007 with a bland villain (Walken, who wants to destroy California's lucrative Silicon Valley), a monotonous villainess (Jones), and a wimpy leading lady (Roberts). And it goes on forever. Only some spectacular stunt sequences keep it alive. (Oh, yes, there's also a gorgeous Russian spy—played by Fullerton—who disappears too soon.) Moore's final appearance as 007. Panavision. [PG]▼●
Vigil (1984-New Zealand) **C-90m.** **½ D: Vincent Ward. Bill Kerr, Fiona Kay, Gordon Shields, Penelope Stewart, Frank Whitten. Ward's first feature is an apt predecessor to his NAVIGATOR. It's a grim, thinly scripted, but visually arresting account of how a young farm girl reacts to the arrival of a stranger upon the death of her father.▼
Vigilante (1982) **C-90m.** BOMB D: William Lustig. Robert Forster, Fred Williamson, Richard Bright, Rutanya Alda, Willie Colon, Joe Spinell, Carol Lynley, Woody Strode. Forster is driven to join DEATH WISH-type vigilantes after his family is viciously attacked by degenerate punks. Script is full of holes, and so is some of the cast after various bloody attacks. Truly distasteful. Also available in unrated director's cut. Originally titled STREET GANG. Panavision. [R]▼●◗
Vigilante Force (1976) **C-89m.** **½ D: George Armitage. Kris Kristofferson, Jan-Michael Vincent, Victoria Principal, Bernadette Peters, Brad Dexter, David Doyle, Andrew Stevens. Vietnam vet Kristofferson, hired to help restore order when small California town is overrun by workers from nearby oilfields, succeeds but then takes over town himself. Minor but interesting, fast-paced film. [PG]
Vigilantes Return, The (1947) **C-67m.** ** D: Ray Taylor. Margaret Lindsay, Jon Hall, Paula Drew, Andy Devine, Robert Wilcox, Jack Lambert. Standard Western with marshal Hall sent to bring law and order to untamed town.
Vigil in the Night (1940) **96m.** *** D: George Stevens. Carole Lombard, Brian Aherne, Anne Shirley, Julien Mitchell, Robert Coote, Brenda Forbes, Rhys Williams, Peter Cushing. Compelling drama of provincial hospital life in England, with outstanding work by Lombard as dedicated nurse, Shirley as her flighty sister, Aherne as doctor. Potentially corny script made credible and exciting by good cast, fine direction pulling viewer into the story.
Viking Queen, The (1967-British) **C-91m.** ** D: Don Chaffey. Don Murray, Carita, Donald Houston, Andrew Keir, Adrienne Corri, Niall MacGinnis, Wilfrid Lawson. Empty-headed Hammer Films costumer of early England under Roman rule, with plenty of gore as anarchists incite a violent uprising among the people. Murray and fine British actors are lost.▼●◗
Vikings, The (1958) **C-114m.** **½ D: Richard Fleischer. Kirk Douglas, Tony Curtis, Ernest Borgnine, Janet Leigh, Alexander Knox, Frank Thring; narrated by Orson Welles. Big name cast and on-location photography in Norway and Brittany are only standouts in routine Viking adventure, sweepingly photographed by Jack Cardiff. Technirama.▼●
Viking Women and the Sea Serpent (1957) **66m.** BOMB D: Roger Corman. Abby Dalton, Susan Cabot, Brad Jackson, Richard Devon, Jonathan Haze. The title ladies are held captive on an island. The original title of this Grade-Z hokum is THE SAGA OF THE VIKING WOMEN AND THEIR VOYAGE TO THE WATERS OF THE GREAT SEA SERPENT(!) By any name, it stinks.▼
Villa! (1958) **C-72m.** *½ D: James B. Clark. Brian Keith, Cesar Romero, Margia Dean, Rodolfo Hoyos. Dull recreation of events in life of Mexican bandit. CinemaScope.
Village of the Damned (1960-British) **78m.** *** D: Wolf Rilla. George Sanders, Barbara Shelley, Michael Gwynne, Laurence Naismith, John Phillips, Richard Vernon. Fine adaptation of John Wyndham novel (*The Midwich Cuckoos*) about blackout in English village followed by birth of strange, emotionless children. Eerie, well-made chiller, followed by CHILDREN OF THE DAMNED. Remade in 1995.▼●
Village of the Damned (1995) **C-98m.** **½ D: John Carpenter. Christopher Reeve, Kirstie Alley, Linda Kozlowski, Michael

Paré, Mark Hamill, Meredith Salenger, Constance Forslund, Buck Flower, Thomas Dekker, Lindsey Haun. A strange mist overcomes an idyllic coastal town, causing ten women to give birth to children who turn out to be mind-controlling demons! Carpenter's remake of the 1960 film is, naturally, more explicit and more violent, with some new characters who don't make much sense (especially Alley), but the premise is still potent enough to pull you in. Panavision. [R] ▼●◗

Village of the Giants (1965) **C-80m.** BOMB D: Bert I. Gordon. Tommy Kirk, Johnny Crawford, Beau Bridges, Ronny Howard, Tisha Sterling, Tim Rooney, Joy Harmon. Poor special effects are just one problem with this silly film about teenagers growing to tremendous heights. Based on H. G. Wells story, refilmed by Gordon in 1976 as FOOD OF THE GODS.▼

Village Tale (1935) **79m.** *** D: John Cromwell. Randolph Scott, Kay Johnson, Arthur Hohl, Robert Barrat, Janet Beecher, Edward Ellis, Dorothy Burgess. Little-known, well-acted adaptation of a Phil Stong novel, focusing on unhappy wife Johnson and her desire for bachelor Scott. Highly unusual (for its time) in its depiction of the underbelly of small-town life, filled with gossip, prejudice, and hypocrisy.

Villain (1971-British) **C-98m.** *½ D: Michael Tuchner. Richard Burton, Ian McShane, Nigel Davenport, Joss Ackland, Fiona Lewis, Donald Sinden, Cathleen Nesbitt. Nasty, stomach-churning melodrama about British underworld, taken from James Barlow's novel *The Burden of Proof.* Burton plays vicious homosexual thug only a mother (Nesbitt) could love. Panavision. [R]

Villain, The (1979) **C-89m.** ** D: Hal Needham. Kirk Douglas, Ann-Margret, Arnold Schwarzenegger, Paul Lynde, Foster Brooks, Ruth Buzzi, Jack Elam, Strother Martin. Lynde plays an Indian chief named Nervous Elk, and so it goes. Combination Western spoof/Road Runner cartoon makes CAT BALLOU look subtle, but may make you laugh if it hits you in a silly frame of mind. [PG]▼●

Villain Still Pursued Her, The (1940) **66m.** ** D: Edward F. Cline. Anita Louise, Richard Cromwell, Hugh Herbert, Alan Mowbray, Buster Keaton, Joyce Compton, Billy Gilbert, Margaret Hamilton. Laughs are few and far between in this full-length spoof of old-time melodramas in which boos and hisses are encouraged. Even pie-throwing sequence is dull. Keaton adds brightest moments.▼

Villa Rides! (1968) **C-125m.** ** D: Buzz Kulik. Yul Brynner, Robert Mitchum, Charles Bronson, Herbert Lom, Jill Ireland, Alexander Knox, Fernando Rey. Witless retelling of Villa's Mexican campaign, with broadened focus on cohort Bronson, captured pilot Mitchum. Rare chance to see Brynner with hair; screenplay by Robert Towne and Sam Peckinpah. John Ireland has an unbilled cameo near the end. Panavision. [R]▼

Vincent (1987-Australian) **C-99m.** *** D: Paul Cox. Engrossing, thoughtfully directed documentary look at the life and letters of Vincent van Gogh. A rare and revealing celluloid examination of an artist and his creativity. The voice of John Hurt is heard as van Gogh. Originally titled VINCENT—THE LIFE AND DEATH OF VINCENT VAN GOGH.▼

Vincent & Theo (1990) **C-138m.** ***½ D: Robert Altman. Tim Roth, Paul Rhys, Johanna Ter Steege, Wladimir Yordanoff, Jip Wijngaarden, Anne Canovas, Hans Kesting, Jean-Pierre Cassel. Evocative, emotionally powerful look at the symbiotic relationship between Vincent van Gogh (Roth) and his brother Theo (Rhys). A far cry from the standard Hollywood bios of tortured artists, with typically unconventional Altman direction and excellent performances by the leads. Beautiful photography by Jean Lepine and art direction by Stephen Altman (the director's son). Originally a four-hour miniseries for European TV. [PG-13]▼●

Vincent, Francois, Paul and the Others (1974-French) **C-118m.** **** D: Claude Sautet. Yves Montand, Michel Piccoli, Serge Reggiani, Gerard Depardieu, Stephane Audran. Melancholy, enormously satisfying life-goes-on drama about longtime male buddies who pursue their respective vocations during the week—medicine, boxing, factory ownership, etc.—then team up for food and drink on idyllic country weekends. Montand stands out in a dream French cast as a going-broke boss in perilous romantic and physical shape.▼●

Vindicator, The (1986-Canadian) **C-88m.** ** D: Jean Claude Lord. Terri Austin, Richard Cox, Pam Grier, Maury Chaykin, David McIlwraith. Updating of FRANKENSTEIN saga concerns infighting among scientists working on cyborg experiments. Highlights: an impressive metallic monster design by Stan Winston plus tough-girl troubleshooter role for guest star Grier. Originally titled: FRANKENSTEIN '88. [R]▼

Vintage, The (1957) **C-92m.** ** D: Jeffrey Hayden. Pier Angeli, Michele Morgan, John Kerr, Mel Ferrer, Theodore Bikel, Leif Erickson. Strangely cast melodrama set in vineyard of France involving two brothers on the lam. CinemaScope.

Violated (1955) SEE: **They Were So Young**

Violated (1984) **C-88m.** BOMB D: Richard Cannistraro. J. C. Quinn, John Heard, D. Balin, April Daisy White, Kaye Dowd. Dreary exploitation film about N.Y.C. businessmen who prey on young party girls. White is a rape victim befriended by cop

Quinn, who goes after the big boys. Contains a brief, standout performance by Heard as a fidgety intermediary who hires Quinn as a hit man. [R]▼

Violent City SEE: **Family, The** (1970)

Violent Enemy, The (1968-British) **C-94m.** *** D: Don Sharp. Tom Bell, Susan Hampshire, Ed Begley, Jon Laurimore, Michael Standing, Noel Purcell. Intense drama of IRA plot to blow up British power plant, and various motives involved.

Violent Four, The (1968-Italian) **C-98m.** ** D: Carlo Lizzani. Gian Maria Volonte, Tomas Milian, Margaret Lee, Carla Gravina, Don Backy. Unexceptional tale of notorious Italian robbery gang which stages massive bank holdup schemes, becoming police's number-one target. Techniscope. [M]

Violent Men, The (1955) **C-96m.** **½ D: Rudolph Maté. Barbara Stanwyck, Glenn Ford, Edward G. Robinson, Dianne Foster, Brian Keith, Richard Jaeckel. Robinson is unscrupulous, wealthy rancher in conflict with good folk of the valley, Stanwyck his wife. Some good action sequences. From a Donald Hamilton novel. CinemaScope.▼●

Violent Ones, The (1967) **C-84m.** *½ D: Fernando Lamas. Fernando Lamas, Aldo Ray, Tommy Sands, David Carradine, Lisa Gaye, Melinda Marx. Junk about lawman Lamas' problems in getting Mexican community to refrain from lynching his prisoners when they are suspected of raping and murdering Marx.▼

Violent Professionals, The (1973-Italian) **C-92m.** ** D: Sergio Martino. Richard Conte, Luc Merenda, Silvana Tranquilli, Steffan Zaccharias. Mezza-mezza Italian action flick about a suspended cop who infiltrates the mob to get the goods on a notorious gang boss. Violent indeed. Techniscope.▼

Violent Road (1958) **86m.** **½ D: Howard W. Koch. Brian Keith, Dick Foran, Efrem Zimbalist, Jr., Merry Anders. Well-done programmer involving men driving explosives over bumpy road, allowing for each to reexamine his way of life.

Violent Saturday (1955) **C-91m.** *** D: Richard Fleischer. Victor Mature, Richard Egan, Stephen McNally, Virginia Leith, Tommy Noonan, Lee Marvin, Margaret (Maggie) Hayes, J. Carrol Naish, Sylvia Sidney, Ernest Borgnine, Brad Dexter. Effective study of repercussion on small Arizona town when bank robbers carry out a bloody holdup. CinemaScope.

Violent Stranger (1957-British) **83m.** **½ D: Montgomery Tully. Zachary Scott, Faith Domergue, Faith Brook, Peter Illing, Gordon Jackson, Kay Callard. Domergue, wife of condemned killer, sets out to find the real culprit. Not bad little crime drama. Originally titled MAN IN THE SHADOW.

Violent Summer (1961-French) **85m.** ** D: Michel Boisrond. Martine Carol, Jean Desailly, Dahlia Lavi, Henri-Jacques Huet. Unconvincing tale of murder of a halfwit girl, with most of the guests at a Riviera resort home prime suspects; too many loose threads.

Violent Years, The (1956) **57m.** BOMB D: William M. Morgan (Franz Eichorn). Jean Moorehead, Barbara Weeks, Arthur Millan, Theresa Hancock, Joanne Cangi, Gloria Farr. Tawdry, preachy juvenile delinquency trash about a rich teen girl, ignored by her parents, who heads up a gang. Wooden acting all around. Scripted by Edward Wood, Jr. Aka FEMALE.▼

Violets Are Blue . . . (1986) **C-88m.** ** D: Jack Fisk. Sissy Spacek, Kevin Kline, Bonnie Bedelia, John Kellogg, Jim Standford, Augusta Dabney. Romantic drama about onetime high school sweethearts, reunited after many years, who try to pick up where they left off—though he's married and settled in their hometown and she's single and a globetrotting photojournalist. Pleasant, attractive, but dull. [PG-13]▼●

Violette (1978-French) **C-122m.** ** D: Claude Chabrol. Isabelle Huppert, Stephane Audran, Jean Carmet, Jean Francoise Garreaud, Bernadette Lafont. Slow-moving account, based on true incident of 14-year-old girl who led double life and poisoned her parents, killing her father. Huppert sleepwalks through the role, and Chabrol lacks his usual directorial flair. Full title VIOLETTE NOZIERE. [R]▼

Violins Came With the Americans, The SEE: **Sun and the Moon, The**

V.I.P.s, The (1963-British) **C-119m.** **½ D: Anthony Asquith. Elizabeth Taylor, Richard Burton, Louis Jourdan, Margaret Rutherford, Rod Taylor, Maggie Smith, Orson Welles, Linda Christian, Elsa Martinelli, Dennis Price, David Frost, Michael Hordern, Robert Coote. Glossy GRAND HOTEL plot, set in London airport. Everyone is terribly rich and beautiful; if you like watching terribly rich, beautiful people, fine. If not, it's all meaningless. Rutherford (who won an Oscar for this) is excellent, and so is Maggie Smith. Written by Terence Rattigan. Panavision.▼●

Virgin and the Gypsy, The (1970-British) **C-92m.** **½ D: Christopher Miles. Joanna Shimkus, Franco Nero, Honor Blackman, Mark Burns, Maurice Denham, Fay Compton, Kay Walsh. D. H. Lawrence's novella comes to screen as interesting, atmospheric, but unbelievable love story. Priest's daughter falls for vagabond gypsy and suffers consequences. Miles later directed Lawrence biopic, PRIEST OF LOVE. [R]▼

Virginia (1941) **C-110m.** ** D: Edward H. Griffith. Madeleine Carroll, Fred MacMurray, Sterling Hayden, Helen Broderick, Marie Wilson, Carolyn Lee. Well-mounted but tedious film of Southern woman (Carroll) who must sacrifice her property and herself in order to raise money to live.▼

Virginia City (1940) **121m.** **½ D: Michael Curtiz. Errol Flynn, Miriam Hopkins, Randolph Scott, Humphrey Bogart, Frank McHugh, Alan Hale, Guinn Williams, John Litel. Followup to DODGE CITY has big cast in lush Civil War Western, but tale of rebel spy Hopkins posing as dance hall girl doesn't live up to expectations; Bogart miscast as slimy Mexican bandido.▼

Virginian, The (1929) **90m.** **½ D: Victor Fleming. Gary Cooper, Richard Arlen, Walter Huston, Mary Brian, Chester Conklin, Eugene Pallette. Owen Wister's novel becomes stiff but interesting Western, salvaged in good climactic shoot-out; Huston is slimy villain, and Cooper has one of his better early roles. Famous line: "If you want to call me that, *smile*." Filmed before in 1914. Remade in 1946, followed by a hit TV series in the 1960s.▼

Virginian, The (1946) **C-90m.** **½ D: Stuart Gilmore. Joel McCrea, Brian Donlevy, Sonny Tufts, Barbara Britton, Fay Bainter, Henry O'Neill, William Frawley, Vince Barnett, Paul Guilfoyle. Remake of '29 classic Western follows story closely. Good, not great, results due to story showing its age. McCrea is hero, Donlevy the villain, Tufts a good-guy-turned-bad.▼

Virgin Island (1958-British) **C-84m.** **½ D: Pat Jackson. John Cassavetes, Virginia Maskell, Sidney Poitier, Colin Gordon. Leisurely study of author Cassavetes and bride Maskell moving to Caribbean isle; film lightly touches on racial issue.

Virgin of Nuremburg, The SEE: **Horror Castle**

Virgin President, The (1968) **71m.** ** D: Graeme Ferguson. Severn Darden, Richard Neuweiler, Andrew Duncan, Richard Schaal, Paul Benedict, Sudie Bond, Peter Boyle. Darden is Fillard Millmore, the 43rd president of the United States. Occasionally funny but mostly silly spoof.

Virgin Queen, The (1955) **C-92m.** *** D: Henry Koster. Bette Davis, Richard Todd, Joan Collins, Herbert Marshall, Jay Robinson, Dan O'Herlihy, Rod Taylor. Davis is in full authority in her second portrayal of Queen Elizabeth I, detailing her conflicts with Walter Raleigh. CinemaScope.▼

Virgin Soldiers, The (1969-British) **C-96m.** *** D: John Dexter. Hywel Bennett, Nigel Patrick, Lynn Redgrave, Nigel Davenport, Rachel Kempson, Tsai Chin, Jack Shepherd, David Bowie. Smooth comedy-drama about British recruits in Singapore; title refers to their lack of experience in battle as well as in bed. Solid Carl Foreman production, adapted by John Hopkins from Leslie Thomas' novel. Followed by STAND UP, VIRGIN SOLDIERS in 1977. [R]▼

Virgin Spring, The (1960-Swedish) **88m.** *** D: Ingmar Bergman. Max von Sydow, Brigitta Valberg, Gunnel Lindblom, Brigitta Pettersson. Brooding medieval fable of a deeply religious farming family whose daughter is raped and murdered by vagrants. Fascinating, beautifully made, an Oscar winner for Best Foreign Film. Remade as—or, more appropriately, ripped off by—LAST HOUSE ON THE LEFT.▼●

Virgin Suicides, The (2000) **C-97m.** **½ D: Sofia Coppola. James Woods, Kathleen Turner, Kirsten Dunst, Hannah Hall, Chelse Swain, A. J. Cook, Leslie Hayman, Josh Hartnett, Michael Paré, Scott Glenn, Danny DeVito, Hayden Christensen; narrated by Giovanni Ribisi. In 1970s suburbia, four lovely sisters head toward a sorry fate as a quartet of neighborhood boys become obsessed with them. First-time writer-director Coppola adapted Jeffrey Eugenides' novel, but for all its atmosphere and good performances (especially Woods and Turner as the girls' uptight, overprotective parents) it never quite comes together. [R]▼

Viridiana (1961-Spanish) **90m.** ***½ D: Luis Buñuel. Francisco Rabal, Silvia Pinal, Fernando Rey, Margarita Lozano. Powerful psychological study of novice nun Pinal, who loses her innocence when forced by Mother Superior to visit nasty uncle Rey. Near-perfect direction by a master filmmaker; solid performances by all.▼

Virtuosity (1995) **C-105m.** *½ D: Brett Leonard. Denzel Washington, Kelly Lynch, Russell Crowe, Stephen Spinella, William Forsythe, Louise Fletcher, William Fichtner, Costas Mandylor, Kevin J. O'Connor, Traci Lords. In the near future, control of the police has unwisely been given over to computer-driven technology, and both the programming nerds and their cold-blooded bosses are out of control. Ex-cop and current convict Washington is the only one who can track down a computer-generated bad guy who's been "sampled" from the world's worst serial killers! Ugly, to say the least, although it's built on a foundation of some interesting ideas. Super 35. [R] ▼●◗

Virtuous Sin, The (1930) **82m.** BOMB D: George Cukor, Louis Gasnier. Walter Huston, Kay Francis, Kenneth MacKenna, Jobyna Howland, Paul Cavanagh. Laughably bad production with alluring Francis giving herself to Russian general Huston so he will exempt her husband from death sentence. A real turkey.

Virus (1980-Japanese) **C-155m.** **½ D: Kinji Fukasaku. Sonny Chiba, Chuck Connors, Glenn Ford, Stephanie Faulkner, Masao Kusakari, Isao Natsuki, Stuart Gillard, Olivia Hussey, George Kennedy, Henry Silva, Bo Svenson, Cecil Linder, Robert Vaughn. Mankind is destroyed by a plague and nuclear war—except for 858 men and eight women. Beautiful sequences filmed in the Antarctic, adequate special effects, but overlong and meandering. Allegedly the biggest budgeted Japanese film to date. [PG]▼

virus (1999-U.S.-Japanese-German) **C-99m.** BOMB D: John Bruno. Jamie Lee

Curtis, William Baldwin, Donald Sutherland, Joanna Pacula, Marshall Bell, Julio Oscar Mechoso, Sherman Augustus, Cliff Curtis. In the eye of a hurricane, the crew of a tugboat boards an abandoned Russian ship possessed by what seems to be living alien electricity. This "creature" apparently considers people just another virus to be wiped out. Drearily routine, with borrowed ideas and stereotyped characters, though Curtis and Pacula try. From the comic book created by Chuck Pfarrer. Super 35. [R]▼●◗

Viscount, The (1967-French-Italian-Spanish) **C-98m.** BOMB D: Maurice Cloche. Kerwin Mathews, Edmond O'Brien, Jane Fleming, Yvelle Lebon, Jean Yanne, Fernando Rey. In spite of the presence of well-known European actors, grade-D spy film is a waste of time. Techniscope.

Vision Quest (1985) **C-105m.** ** D: Harold Becker. Matthew Modine, Linda Fiorentino, Michael Schoeffling, Ronny Cox, Harold Sylvester, Roberts Blossom, Charles Hallahan, Daphne Zuniga, Forest Whitaker, Raphael Sbarge. Muddled, overlong growing-pains movie with too many familiar elements. Modine is a high-school wrestler with a philosophical bent; Fiorentino is a tough-talking older woman who turns him on. Based on a novel by Terry Davis. Madonna appears briefly onscreen singing "Crazy for You." [R]▼●◗

Visions of Eight (1973) **C-110m.** ** D: Juri Ozerov, Mai Zetterling, Arthur Penn, Michael Pfleghar, Kon Ichikawa, Milos Forman, Claude Lelouch, John Schlesinger. Seemingly good idea of having eight different directors give eight different views of 1972 Olympics results in strangely disappointing film, considering all the talent involved; with possible exception of Schlesinger's final chapter on the marathon, none of the episodes is memorable. [G] ▼

Visions of Light: The Art of Cinematography (1993-U.S.-Japanese) **C/B&W-90m.** ***½ D: Arnold Glassman, Todd McCarthy, Stuart Samuels. Contemporary lens masters (E.T.'s Allen Daviau, RAGING BULL's Michael Chapman) discuss their own work and pay tribute to pioneer cinematographers of the past (BIRTH OF A NATION's Billy Bitzer, CITIZEN KANE's Gregg Toland). More than 100 films are excerpted, from critical and commercial hits to offbeat pictures and B movies. Interestingly, many of the most absorbing and amusing anecdotes concern sixties films (IN COLD BLOOD, THE GRADUATE, ROSEMARY'S BABY), a decade full of remarkable innovation and experimentation in filmmaking. Part Widescreen. ▼●◗

Visit, The (1964-German-French-Italian) **100m.** **½ D: Bernhard Wicki. Ingrid Bergman, Anthony Quinn, Irina Demick, Paolo Stoppa, Hans-Christian Blech, Romolo Valli, Valentina Cortese, Eduardo Ciannelli. Intriguing but uneven film parable of greed and evil; wealthy Bergman returns to European home town, offering a fantastic sum to the people there if they will legitimately kill her first seducer (Quinn). Actors struggle with melodramatic script; results are interesting if not always successful. Bowdlerized version of Friedrich Durrenmatt's play. Remade in 1992 as HYÉNES. CinemaScope.

Visiting Hours (1982-Canadian) **C-103m.** BOMB D: Jean Claude Lord. Michael Ironside, Lee Grant, Linda Purl, William Shatner, Harvey Atkin, Helen Hughes. Awful programmer, set in a hospital with demented Ironside stalking TV journalist Grant, who hopefully was well paid for this junk. [R]▼

Visitor, The (1979-Italian) **C-90m.** ** D: Michael J. Paradise (Giulio Paradisi). Mel Ferrer, Glenn Ford, Lance Henriksen, John Huston, Joanne Nail, Shelley Winters, Sam Peckinpah. Filmed Stateside by the BEYOND THE DOOR folks, this passable time-killer wastes a good cast in yet another OMEN rip-off; too bad Huston or Peckinpah couldn't have directed as well. [R]▼

Visitors, The (1972) **C-88m.** BOMB D: Elia Kazan. Patrick McVey, Patricia Joyce, James Woods, Chico Martinez, Steve Railsback. Deplorable story of two Vietnam vets who, upon release from prison for sex crime, invade the house of third vet who testified at their trial. Woods' film debut. [R]▼

Visitors, The (1993-French) **C-106m.** **½ D: Jean-Marie Poiré. Jean Reno, Christian Clavier, Valérie Lemercier, Marie-Anne Chazel, Christian Bujeau, Isabelle Nanty, Gérard Séty, Didier Pain. Rollicking time-travel saga of 12th-century knight (Reno) and his loyal-but-dim squire (Clavier) who find themselves in the contemporary French countryside, trying to make sense of their descendants, indoor plumbing, and the like. Broad hijinks should be a big hit with the kids. A smash in French cinemas, where it played as LES VISITEURS. Followed by THE CORRIDORS OF TIME: THE VISITORS II. Widescreen. [R]▼●

Visit to a Chief's Son (1974) **C-92m.** **½ D: Lamont Johnson. Richard Mulligan, Johnny Sekka, John Philip Hogdon, Jesse Kinaru, Chief Lomoiro, Jock Anderson. OK family drama about a self-centered father and son who become humanized on an African safari. [G]

Visit to a Small Planet (1960) **85m.** **½ D: Norman Taurog. Jerry Lewis, Joan Blackman, Earl Holliman, Fred Clark, John Williams, Jerome Cowan, Lee Patrick, Gale Gordon. Gore Vidal satire becomes talky Lewis vehicle with Jerry the alien who comes to Earth to observe man's strange ways.

Vital Signs (1990) **C-103m.** *½ D: Marisa Silver. Adrian Pasdar, Diane Lane, Jimmy Smits, Norma Aleandro, Jack Gwaltney, Laura San Giacomo, Jane Adams, Tim Ransom, Bradley Whitford, Lisa Jane Persky, William Devane, James Karen, Telma Hopkins. Third-year medical students experience the usual clichés: performing rounds, undercutting rivals, questioning authority, and sneaking an occasional quickie in the hospital linen closet. Watchable, but of absolutely no distinction; stick with THE NEW INTERNS, where you can at least compare the acting styles of Dean Jones and Telly Savalas. Smits effectively projects quiet authority as the surgeon instructor. [R]▼●

Vivacious Lady (1938) **90m.** *** D: George Stevens. James Stewart, Ginger Rogers, James Ellison, Beulah Bondi, Charles Coburn, Frances Mercer, Grady Sutton, Jack Carson, Franklin Pangborn, Hattie McDaniel, Willie Best. Overlong but entertaining comedy of professor Stewart marrying nightclub singer Rogers, trying to break the news to his conservative family and fianceé back home. Bondi is fun in amusing variation on her usual motherly role.▼

Viva Knievel! (1977) **C-106m.** BOMB D: Gordon Douglas. Evel Knievel, Gene Kelly, Lauren Hutton, Marjoe Gortner, Red Buttons, Eric Shea, Leslie Nielsen, Cameron Mitchell, Frank Gifford, Albert Salmi, Dabney Coleman. The senses reel at this hilariously inept attempt to turn the infamous stunt driver into a movie hero. The Bad Guys plan to have Evel "accidentally" killed in Mexico, so they can use his truck to smuggle drugs back into the U.S.! Don't miss opening scene, in which Our Hero sneaks into orphanage at midnight to distribute Evel Knievel plastic model kits—whereupon one little boy miraculously throws away his crutches! Panavision. [PG]▼

Viva Las Vegas (1964) **C-86m.** **½ D: George Sidney. Elvis Presley, Ann-Margret, Cesare Danova, William Demarest, Jack Carter. Elvis and Ann-Margret are well teamed in this popular Presley vehicle, with Elvis a race car driver. Songs include "The Lady Loves Me," "What'd I Say?" "I Need Somebody to Lean On," "Come On, Everybody," "The Yellow Rose of Texas," and classic title tune. Panavision.▼●◗

Viva Maria! (1965-French-Italian) **C-119m.** ***½ D: Louis Malle. Brigitte Bardot, Jeanne Moreau, George Hamilton, Gregor Von Rezzori, Paulette Dubost. Rollicking tale of two beautiful entertainers/revolutionaries in Mexico has inconsistent first half, then takes off for hilarious finish. Lots of fun. Panavision.▼

Viva Max! (1969) **C-92m.** **½ D: Jerry Paris. Peter Ustinov, Pamela Tiffin, Jonathan Winters, John Astin, Keenan Wynn, Harry Morgan, Alice Ghostley, Kenneth Mars, Ann Morgan Guilbert, Paul Sand. Mildly amusing yarn of eccentric Mexican general recapturing Alamo, sending equally inept American militia to rout him out. Forced humor doesn't always work, but not bad; Astin is excellent as Ustinov's loyal sergeant. [G]▼

Viva Villa! (1934) **115m.** ***½ D: Jack Conway. Wallace Beery, Leo Carrillo, Fay Wray, Donald Cook, Stuart Erwin, George E. Stone, Henry B. Walthall, Joseph Schildkraut, Katherine DeMille. Viva Beery, in one of his best films as the rowdy rebel who led the fight for Madera's Mexican Republic. Ben Hecht's script plays with facts, but overall, film is entertaining.▼●

Viva Zapata! (1952) **113m.** **** D: Elia Kazan. Marlon Brando, Jean Peters, Anthony Quinn, Joseph Wiseman, Margo, Mildred Dunnock. Vibrant film about Mexican peasant's rise to power and eventual Presidency. Brando is perfect in title role, Quinn equally fine in Oscar-winning performance as his brother. Script by John Steinbeck.▼●

Vivement Dimanche SEE: **Confidentially Yours**

Vivre Sa Vie SEE: **My Life to Live**

V.I. Warshawski (1991) **C-89m.** BOMB D: Jeff Kanew. Kathleen Turner, Jay O. Sanders, Charles Durning, Angela Goethals, Nancy Paul, Frederick Coffin, Charles McCaughan, Stephen Meadows, Wayne Knight, Stephen Root. Wretchedly scripted, directed, and photographed assemblage of characters taken from Sara Paretsky's series of novels. Turner is a tough Chicago private detective (and closet fashion plate) investigating the murder of a hockey player who'd once caught her fancy. On paper, the star and her character should have melded; slipshod production (for a major star vehicle) helps render this a hall-of-fame boo-boo. [R]▼●

Vogues (1937) **C-108m.** ** D: Irving Cummings. Warner Baxter, Joan Bennett, Helen Vinson, Mischa Auer, Alan Mowbray, Jerome Cowan, Alma Kruger, Marjorie Gateson, Penny Singleton, Polly Rowles, Hedda Hopper, The Wiere Brothers. Minor musical with wealthy Bennett jilting stuffy, high-powered fiancé Mowbray and going to work as model at Baxter's fashion house. One good song, "That Old Feeling," plus an outstanding musical number, "Turn on That Red Hot Heat." Original title: VOGUES OF 1938.▼

Voice in the Mirror (1958) **102m.** **½ D: Harry Keller. Richard Egan, Julie London, Arthur O'Connell, Walter Matthau, Troy Donahue, Mae Clarke. Effective, unpretentious account of Egan trying to combat alcoholism, with help of wife London. CinemaScope.

Voice in the Wind (1944) **85m.** *** D: Arthur Ripley. Francis Lederer, Sigrid Gurie, J. Edward Bromberg, J. Carrol Naish. Low-key drama of pianist Lederer haunted by Nazi oppression, later rekindling old love affair; unusual film, well acted.

Voice of Bugle Ann, The (1936) **70m.** **½ D: Richard Thorpe. Lionel Barrymore, Maureen O'Sullivan, Eric Linden, Dudley Digges, Spring Byington, Charles

Grapewin. Bugle Ann is a very special fox-hunting hound, lovingly raised by Missouri farmer Barrymore. Trouble comes when an antisocial, dog-hating sheepherder becomes his neighbor. Lionel's the whole show in this slight but entertaining tale, based on a MacKinlay Kantor novel.

Voice of Merrill, The SEE: **Murder Will Out**

Voice of Terror SEE: **Sherlock Holmes and the Voice of Terror**

Voice of the Turtle, The (1947) **103m.** ***½ D: Irving Rapper. Ronald Reagan, Eleanor Parker, Eve Arden, Wayne Morris, Kent Smith. Delightful wartime comedy of what happens when dreamy young actress Parker (who's been hurt once too often in love) meets soldier-on-leave Reagan. Arden is at her peak as Parker's flighty friend. John van Druten adapted his own Broadway hit. Retitled ONE FOR THE BOOK.

Voice of the Whistler (1945) **60m.** *** D: William Castle. Richard Dix, Lynn Merrick, Rhys Williams, James Cardwell, Donald Woods, Gigi Perreau. Haunting love story about an avaricious nurse who dumps her fiancé in order to marry a dying millionaire and finds herself a virtual prisoner. Not as suspenseful as the other *Whistler* entries, but just as gripping.

Voices (1979) **C-107m.** ** D: Robert Markowitz. Michael Ontkean, Amy Irving, Alex Rocco, Barry Miller, Herbert Berghof, Viveca Lindfors. Aspiring rock singer falls for deaf woman (well played by Irving) who, never having heard him sing, is able to return his love. Sincerely intentioned drama is ultimately compromised by Hollywood formulas. Musical score by Jimmy Webb. [PG]▼

Voices of Sarafina! (1989) **C-85m.** ***½ D: Nigel Noble. Miriam Makeba, Mbongeni Ngema. Powerful, profound documentary of young, black South African actors performing in the Broadway musical *Sarafina*, which chronicles the involvement of black schoolchildren in the 1976 Soweto uprising. Also details their relationship with Ngema, the show's controversial writer-director. Finale, in which exiled South African singer Makeba appears backstage after a performance, is especially moving. The show itself was filmed with Whoopi Goldberg in 1992.▼

Volcano (1953-Italian) **106m.** ** D: William Dieterle. Anna Magnani, Rossano Brazzi, Geraldine Brooks, Eduardo Ciannelli. Slowly paced dramatics about two sisters involved with unprincipled diver.

Volcano (1969) SEE: **Krakatoa, East of Java**

Volcano (1997) **C-102m.** *** D: Mick Jackson. Tommy Lee Jones, Anne Heche, Gaby Hoffmann, Don Cheadle, Jacqueline Kim, Keith David, John Corbett, Michael Rispoli, John Carroll Lynch. Strange rumblings underground in L.A. attract the attention of the head of the Office of Emergency Management (Jones) and a scientist from Cal Tech (Heche)—who discover a volcanic eruption that can't be stopped. Good, solid disaster movie with credible characters and first-rate special effects. A few sly inside jokes will add to the fun for L.A. viewers—as compensation for seeing their home turf treated so badly. [PG-13]▼●◗

Volere Volare (1991-Italian) **C-92m.** **½ D: Maurizio Nichetti, Guido Manuli. Maurizio Nichetti, Angela Finocchiaro, Mariella Valentini, Patrizio Roversi, Remo Remotti, Renato Scarpa. Italian comedian and cowriter/codirector Nichetti again satirizes the frenzy and soullessness of modern life (as he did in THE ICICLE THIEF), this time playing a naive movie sound-effects technician. When he meets a woman with a hilariously naughty profession, romance blossoms—until this lover of cartoons starts turning into an animated character himself! A decidedly adult tale of childlike love, this comic spree never entirely takes flight, though its title translates as "I Want to Fly." [R]▼●

Volpone (1939-French) **80m.** *** D: Maurice Tourneur. Harry Baur, Louis Jouvet, Fernand Ledoux, Marion Dorian. A rich merchant (Baur) fakes his imminent demise in order to observe the reactions of those set to inherit his wealth. Fine adaptation of famed Ben Jonson comedy, with Baur perfect as Volpone and Jouvet matching him as his servant, Mosca.▼

Voltaire (1933) **72m.** **½ D: John G. Adolfi. George Arliss, Margaret Lindsay, Doris Kenyon, Reginald Owen, Alan Mowbray, Douglass Dumbrille. Arliss offers another crafty, knowing portrayal as the writer, wit and "great humanitarian of the 18th century" who was the conscience of his country in pre-revolutionary France. Arliss is the whole show.

Volunteers (1985) **C-106m.** *½ D: Nicholas Meyer. Tom Hanks, John Candy, Rita Wilson, Tim Thomerson, Gedde Watanabe, George Plimpton. Dismal, grimy-looking comedy about spoiled playboy who accidentally joins Peace Corps and tries running things his way in Thailand. Candy has a few good moments but not enough. Hanks and Wilson later married. [R]▼●◗

Von Richthofen and Brown (1971) **C-97m.** ** D: Roger Corman. John Phillip Law, Barry Primus, Peter Masterson, Karen Huston, Hurd Hatfield, Robert La Tourneaux. Weak historical drama of "Red Baron" of WW1 fame and aerial dogfights with his assorted enemies. Aerial work is excellent; it's the ground work which crashes. Aka BATTLE OF THE ACES. [PG]

Von Ryan's Express (1965) **C-117m.** *** D: Mark Robson. Frank Sinatra, Trevor

Howard, Raffaella Carra, Brad Dexter, Sergio Fantoni, Edward Mulhare, James Brolin, Adolfo Celi, John Leyton, Vito Scotti. Exciting WW2 saga with Sinatra a POW colonel who leads daring escape by taking over freight train that is transporting prisoners. Strong supporting cast helps. CinemaScope.▼●

Voodoo Bloodbath SEE: **I Eat Your Skin**

Voodoo Island (1957) **76m.** ** D: Reginald Le Borg. Boris Karloff, Beverly Tyler, Murvyn Vye, Elisha Cook. Boring horror-thriller has Karloff asked by businessmen to investigate strange doings on potential motel-island resort. Aka SILENT DEATH.

Voodoo Man (1944) **62m.** ** D: William Beaudine. Bela Lugosi, John Carradine, George Zucco, Michael Ames (Tod Andrews), Henry Hall, Wanda McKay, Louise Currie. With touching devotion to zombie-wife, Lugosi performs harrowing experiments with unsuspecting girls to cure her. Campy B film.

Voodoo Tiger (1952) **67m.** *½ D: Spencer Bennet. Johnny Weissmuller, Jean Byron, James Seay, Jeannie Dean, Robert Bray. Absurd *Jungle Jim* hodgepodge featuring gangsters, headhunters, Nazis and a museum curator all in pursuit of stolen art treasures.

Voodoo Woman (1957) **77m.** *½ D: Edward L. Cahn. Marla English, Tom Conway, Michael Connors, Lance Fuller. Cheater-chiller with few scares in lowjinks about deranged scientist changing English into a monster. Incomprehensible film.▼

Voyage, The (1973-Italian) **C-95m.** ** D: Vittorio De Sica. Sophia Loren, Richard Burton, Ian Bannen, Barbara Pilavin, Annabella Incontera, Paolo Lena. Listless adaptation of Pirandello story about star-crossed lovers Burton and Loren, forbidden to marry and shadowed by tragedy. Attractive stars and surroundings, but a draggy film. [PG]

Voyage in Italy SEE: **Strangers** (1953)

Voyage of the Damned (1976-British) **C-134m.** *** D: Stuart Rosenberg. Faye Dunaway, Oskar Werner, Max von Sydow, Orson Welles, Malcolm McDowell, Lynne Frederick, James Mason, Lee Grant, Wendy Hiller, Jose Ferrer, Luther Adler, Katharine Ross, Sam Wanamaker, Denholm Elliott, Nehemiah Persoff, Julie Harris, Maria Schell, Ben Gazzara. Absorbing fact-based drama. In 1939 a ship full of German-Jewish refugees bound for Havana, denied permission to land anywhere, was forced to return to Germany. Picture almost dissolves into separate stories, but von Sydow as ship's captain holds it together. Originally released at 158m. [PG]▼◗

Voyager (1991-German-French-Greek) **C-117m.** *** D: Volker Schlöndorff. Sam Shepard, Julie Delpy, Barbara Sukowa, Dieter Kirchlechner, Traci Lind, Deborah-Lee Furness, August Zirner, Thomas Heinze. In the 1950s, American construction engineer Shepard—an inveterate, nearly rootless traveler—meets a man with a link to his pre-WW2 student days in Europe; soon after, he encounters young German beauty Delpy and they take a romantic journey to her home in Athens. Adult tale is quite leisurely paced but well acted and directed. Long-awaited adaptation of Max Frisch's 1957 Swiss-German best-seller, *Homo Faber*; not without flaws, but more interesting and thought-provoking than most contemporary films. [PG-13]▼●

Voyage to Italy SEE: **Strangers** (1953)

Voyage to the Beginning of the World (1997-Portuguese-French) **C-95m.** *** D: Manoel de Oliveira. Marcello Mastroianni, Jean-Yves Gautier, Leonor Silveira, Diogo Doria, Isabel de Castro, Jose Pinto, Isabel Ruth. Touching, reflective road movie from octogenarian director de Oliveira about an aged filmmaker named Manoel (Mastroianni, in his final screen role) who looks back on his life as he visits various locales from his past in the company of several colleagues. Loaded with insights about life and memory, women and sexual attraction, sinning and confessing sins, and the passage of time. Aka JOURNEY TO THE BEGINNING OF THE WORLD.▼◗

Voyage to the Bottom of the Sea (1961) **C-105m.** *** D: Irwin Allen. Walter Pidgeon, Joan Fontaine, Robert Sterling, Barbara Eden, Michael Ansara, Peter Lorre, Frankie Avalon, Henry Daniell, Regis Toomey. Entertaining, colorful nonsense about conflicts aboard massive atomic submarine, with Pidgeon the domineering admiral trying to keep the Earth from being fried by a burning radiation belt. No deep thinking, just fun. Later a TV series. CinemaScope.▼●

Voyage to the End of the Universe (1963-Czech) **81m.** **½ D: Jack Pollack (Jindrich Polak). Dennis Stephans, Francis Smolen, Dana Meredith, Irene Kova, Rodney Lucas, Otto Lack. Twenty-fifth-century space crew is threatened by mysterious, radioactive dark star. Surprise ending is no surprise. Originally titled IKARIE XB 1, running 90m. CinemaScope.

Voyage to the Planet of Prehistoric Women (1968) **C-80m.** *½ D: Derek Thomas (Peter Bogdanovich). Mamie Van Doren, Mary Marr, Paige Lee, Aldo Roman, Margot Hartman. Astronauts land on Venus and kill the creature worshiped by the planet's gill-women. Actually a 1962 Russian picture, PLANET OF STORMS, framed with new footage conceived (and narrated) by Bogdanovich in 1966. Still an awful movie, but of definite curio interest to film buffs. Also see next entry.▼

Voyage to the Prehistoric Planet (1966) **80m.** *½ D: Jonathan Sebastian (Curtis Harrington). Basil Rathbone, Faith Domergue, Marc Shannon, Christopher Brand. Slow, ponderous saga of an expedition to

Venus in the year 2020; made up mostly of footage from handsome Russian epic PLANET OF STORMS, involving a robot, dinosaurs, other monsters, and hidden, intelligent Venusians. Rathbone's scenes were shot on the sets for PLANET OF BLOOD, made at the same time.▼

Vulture, The (1967-British-Canadian) **C-91m.** *½ D: Lawrence Huntington. Robert Hutton, Akim Tamiroff, Broderick Crawford, Diane Clark, Phillip Friend, Patrick Holt. Disappointing, unsatisfying sci-fi horror with laughable mad scientist (Tamiroff) who becomes half-man, half-bird and avenges death of his ancestor. Released theatrically in b&w.▼

W (1974) **C-95m.** *½ D: Richard Quine. Twiggy, Michael Witney, Dirk Benedict, John Vernon, Eugene Roche, Alfred Ryder. Twiggy struggles through story in which sadistic Benedict, her ex-husband convicted of her supposed murder, menaces her and new husband Witney. Flamboyant but unsuccessful thriller, retitled I WANT HER DEAD. [PG]▼

Wabash Avenue (1950) **C-92m.** *** D: Henry Koster. Betty Grable, Victor Mature, Phil Harris, Reginald Gardiner, James Barton, Margaret Hamilton. Bright, colorful period piece with scoundrel Mature trying to break up romance between saloon-owner Harris and his musical star, Grable. Enjoyable remake of Grable's 1943 vehicle CONEY ISLAND.

WAC From Walla Walla, The (1952) **83m.** *½ D: William Witney. Judy Canova, Stephen Dunne, Allen Jenkins, Irene Ryan, George Cleveland. Lame-brained service adventure of perennial yokel Canova.

Wackiest Ship in the Army, The (1960) **C-99m.** *** D: Richard Murphy. Jack Lemmon, Ricky Nelson, John Lund, Chips Rafferty, Tom Tully, Joby Baker, Warren Berlinger. Comedy-drama sometimes has you wondering if it's serious or not; it succeeds most of the time. Offbeat WW2 story about broken-down sailing ship used as decoy doesn't make fun of the war, for a change, and is entertaining. Later a TV series. CinemaScope.▼●

Wacko (1981) **C-90m.** *½ D: Greydon Clark. Joe Don Baker, Stella Stevens, George Kennedy, Jeff Altman, Anthony James, Andrew (Dice) Clay. A dedicated cop goes after the dreaded "lawnmower killer" who last terrorized a town ten years ago. Heavy-handed spoof of HALLOWEEN-type horror films works hard for laughs but delivers very few. [R—edited from original PG rating]▼●

Waco (1966) **C-85m.** **½ D: R.G. Springsteen. Howard Keel, Jane Russell, Brian Donlevy, Wendell Corey, Terry Moore, John Smith, John Agar, Gene Evans, Richard Arlen, Ben Cooper, Jeff Richards. Gunfighter Keel comes to clean up town, but former girl friend Russell is now married to Reverend Corey. Nice veteran cast, but film is only for Western addicts. Techniscope.

Wages of Fear, The (1952-French-Italian) **156m.** ***½ D: H. G. Clouzot. Yves Montand, Charles Vanel, Peter Van Eyck, Vera Clouzot, Folco Lulli, William Tubbs. Marvelous, gritty and extremely suspenseful epic set in South America, chronicling the personalities of and relationships among four men involved in long-distance driving of trucks filled with nitroglycerine. Beware: many other shorter versions exist. Remade as SORCERER.▼●◗

Wagner (1983-British-Hungarian-Austrian) **C-300m.** ** D: Tony Palmer. Richard Burton, Vanessa Redgrave, Gemma Craven, Laszlo Galffi, John Gielgud, Ralph Richardson, Laurence Olivier, Ronald Pickup, Joan Plowright, Arthur Lowe, Franco Nero. Glossy but uninspired biography of the composer, monotonously acted by Burton. Overlong, to state the obvious. Originally a nine-hour British TV series.▼

Wagon Master (1950) **86m.** *** D: John Ford. Ben Johnson, Joanne Dru, Harry Carey, Jr., Ward Bond, Alan Mowbray, Jane Darwell, James Arness, Jim Thorpe, Russell Simpson, Hank Worden, Francis Ford. Good Ford Western about two roaming cowhands who join a Mormon wagon train heading for Utah frontier. Fine showcase for young stars Johnson and Carey. Beautifully filmed. Inspired the later *Wagon Train* TV series. Also shown in computer-colored version.▼●

Wagons East (1994) **C-106m.** *½ D: Peter Markle. John Candy, Richard Lewis, John C. McGinley, Ellen Greene, Robert Picardo, Ed Lauter, Rodney A. Grant, William Sanderson, Melinda Culea, Russell Means, Charles Rocket. Candy (who died near the end of the film's production) plays an incompetent wagonmaster who leads a group of pioneers who are sick of the wild and woolly West, and have decided to head back East. Astoundingly unfunny, even sad—given knowledge of Candy's fate. [PG-13] ▼●

Wagons Roll at Night, The (1941) **84m.** **½ D: Ray Enright. Humphrey Bogart, Sylvia Sidney, Eddie Albert, Joan Leslie, Sig Ruman, Cliff Clark, Charley Foy, Frank Wilcox. KID GALAHAD in circus trappings is OK, thanks to cast: Bogie's the circus manager, Sidney his star, Albert the hayseed turned lion tamer.▼

Wag the Dog (1997) **C-97m.** *** D: Barry Levinson. Robert De Niro, Dustin Hoffman, Anne Heche, Denis Leary, Willie Nelson, Andrea Martin, Kirsten Dunst, William H. Macy, Suzie Plakson, Woody Harrelson. A desperate White House team, eager to fend off impending negative publicity about the President, hires a political fixer (De Niro) who recruits a hotshot Hollywood producer

(Hoffman) to stage a nonexistent war, simply to distract the public. Pungent (and unexpectedly timely) satire grows a bit self-satisfied after a while, but it's full of funny, clever scenes. Hoffman is a standout in this first-rate cast. Screenplay by David Mamet and Hilary Henkin; based on the novel *American Hero* by Larry Beinhart. Craig T. Nelson appears unbilled. [R]▼●◗

Waikiki Wedding (1937) **89m.** *** D: Frank Tuttle. Bing Crosby, Martha Raye, Shirley Ross, Bob Burns, Leif Erickson, Grady Sutton, Anthony Quinn. Lighthearted musical about a freewheeling "idea man" who finds himself in hot water when the winner of a beauty contest he cooked up, for public relations purposes, shows up in Honolulu—and says she doesn't care for it. Raye's comedy dates badly, and the stars obviously never set foot in the islands, but it's all very pleasant. Score includes Oscar-winning "Sweet Leilani" and "Blue Hawaii," sung first by Bing and then in a delightful duet with Ross.▼

Waiting for Guffman (1997) **C-84m.** **½ D: Christopher Guest. Christopher Guest, Eugene Levy, Fred Willard, Catherine O'Hara, Parker Posey, Lewis Arquette, Matt Keeslar, Bob Balaban, Paul Dooley, Paul Benedict, Larry Miller, Brian Doyle-Murray. Slight but amusing mock documentary about the mounting of a musical show celebrating the 150th anniversary of Blaine, Missouri. Guest plays the outlandish Corky St. Clair, who directs the town's amateur talent in a show he hopes will take him (and them) to Broadway. Engaging performers make this fun. Written by Guest and costar Levy. [R]▼●

Waiting for the Light (1990) **C-94m.** **½ D: Christopher Monger. Shirley MacLaine, Teri Garr, Clancy Brown, Vincent Schiavelli, John Bedford Lloyd, Jeff McCracken, Jack McGee, Colin Baumgartner, Hillary Wolf. Shirley is the whole show in this slimly plotted comic fable as Zena, beloved great-aunt of Wolf and Baumgartner, and what happens when one of her magic tricks causes a "miracle" as Americans are panicking during the 1962 Cuban missile crisis. [PG]▼●

Waiting for the Moon (1987) **C-85m.** *½ D: Jill Godmilow. Linda Hunt, Linda Bassett, Bruce McGill, Jacques Boudet, Andrew McCarthy, Bernadette Lafont. Spiritless, sleep-inducing account of the complex relationship between an ailing Gertrude Stein (Bassett) and her companion, Alice B. Toklas (Hunt). Slow, occasionally confusing, and very disappointing. A PBS *American Playhouse* presentation. [PG]▼

Waiting to Exhale (1995) **C-121m.** ** D: Forest Whitaker. Whitney Houston, Angela Bassett, Loretta Devine, Lela Rochon, Gregory Hines, Dennis Haysbert, Mykelti Williamson, Michael Beach, Leon, Wendell Pierce, Donald Adeosun Faison. Four black women can't seem to find decent men in their lives; this may be because most men are jerks. A cinematic equivalent to easy-listening soul radio, this grows increasingly dreary as it eases along its redundant path. Based on the popular novel by Terry McMillan. Omnipresent music supervised by Kenneth "Babyface" Edmonds. Wesley Snipes and Kelly Preston appear unbilled. [R]▼●◗

Waitress! (1982) **C-93m.** BOMB D: Samuel Weil, Michael Herz. Carol Drake, June Martin, Renata Majer, Jim Harris, David Hunt, Calvert DeForest. If watching a chef spit in soup is your idea of fun, then you might find a couple of laughs in this moronic comedy set in a restaurant. [R]▼

Wait Till the Sun Shines, Nellie (1952) **C-108m.** *** D: Henry King. Jean Peters, David Wayne, Hugh Marlowe, Albert Dekker, Alan Hale, Warren Stevens. Nostalgic film of the hopes and disappointments of small town barber Wayne in the early 1900s. Produced by George Jessel.

Wait Until Dark (1967) **C-108m.** *** D: Terence Young. Audrey Hepburn, Alan Arkin, Richard Crenna, Efrem Zimbalist, Jr., Jack Weston, Samantha Jones. Solid shocker with Hepburn as blind woman left alone in apartment, terrorized by psychotic Arkin and henchmen looking for heroin they think is planted there. Memorable nail-biter, flashy role for Arkin; based on Frederick Knott's Broadway hit.▼●

Wait Until Spring, Bandini (1989-Belgian-Italian-French) **C-100m.** ** D: Dominique Deruddere. Joe Mantegna, Ornella Muti, Faye Dunaway, Michael Bacall, Daniel Wilson, Alex Vincent, Burt Young. A boy recalls turbulent times in 1920s Colorado with his father, an Italian-American bricklayer (who thinks the world owes him a living) and his long-suffering wife. Competent but unremarkable adaptation of John Fante's novel. [PG]▼

Wake in Fright SEE: **Outback**

Wake Island (1942) **87m.** *** D: John Farrow. Brian Donlevy, Robert Preston, Macdonald Carey, Albert Dekker, Walter Abel, Barbara Britton, William Bendix, Rod Cameron. Stirring war film of U.S.'s fight to hold Pacific island at outbreak of WW2. Nothing new here, but exciting and well-done.▼

Wake Me When It's Over (1960) **C-126m.** *** D: Mervyn LeRoy. Dick Shawn, Ernie Kovacs, Margo Moore, Jack Warden, Don Knotts. Entertaining comedy of hustling Shawn making the most of being stationed in the Far East by building a fancy hotel with army supplies. Kovacs lends good support. CinemaScope.

Wake of the Red Witch (1949) **106m.** **½ D: Edward Ludwig. John Wayne, Gail Russell, Luther Adler, Gig Young, Adele Mara, Eduard Franz, Henry Daniell, Paul Fix. Rivalry between East Indies magnate and adventuresome ship's captain over pearls and women. Film is a bit confused, but nicely photographed by Reggie Lanning. Incidentally, Wayne took the name of his production company, Batjac, from this film's shipping firm. Also shown in computer-colored version.▼

Wake Up and Dream (1946) **C-92m.** ** D: Lloyd Bacon. June Haver, John Payne, Charlotte Greenwood, Connie Marshall, John Ireland, Clem Bevans, Lee Patrick. Moody film from Robert Nathan's story about girl determined to find brother missing from WW2.

Wake Up and Live (1937) **91m.** *** D: Sidney Lanfield. Alice Faye, Walter Winchell, Ben Bernie, Jack Haley, Patsy Kelly, Joan Davis, Grace Bradley, Warren Hymer, Ned Sparks, Walter Catlett. Fast-moving spoof of radio with battling Winchell and Bernie, mike-frightened singer Haley, and Faye singing "There's a Lull in My Life."

Waking Ned Devine (1998-British-French) **C-91m.** **½ D: Kirk Jones. Ian Bannen, David Kelly, Fionnula Flanagan, Susan Lynch, James Nesbitt, Maura O'Malley, Robert Hickey, Paddy Ward. Slight comedy about a tiny Irish village (pop. 52) turned asunder when one of its aged residents wins the lottery—and his neighbors try to contrive a way to share the wealth. The whimsy is laid on a bit heavily, to say the least, but it's still fun, especially with old pros like Bannen, Kelly, and Flanagan on hand. Panavision. [PG] ▼●◗

Waking the Dead (2000) **C-103m.** *** D: Keith Gordon. Billy Crudup, Jennifer Connelly, Hal Holbrook, Molly Parker, Janet McTeer, Paul Hipp, Sandra Oh, Lawrence Dane, Ed Harris. Arresting film jumps back and forth in time to tell story of a straight-arrow, blue-collar young man who feels that public service is his destiny . . . but is haunted by his undying love for a free-thinking woman. Uneven but intensely emotional, and beautifully acted by Crudup and Connelly (who's never had such a great part before). Robert Dillon adapted Scott Spencer's novel. [R]▼◗

Walkabout (1971-Australian) **C-95m.** *** D: Nicolas Roeg. Jenny Agutter, Lucien John, David Gulpilil, John Meillon. Lost in the wilderness of Australia, a child (John) and an adolescent (a ravishing Agutter) rely on young aborigine Gulpilil in order to survive. Roeg, in his first solo outing as director, also beautifully photographed this mind-massaging cult favorite; lush score by John Barry. John is Roeg's son and later worked with his father using the name Luc Roeg. Expanded by 5m. for its 1996 rerelease. [PG]▼●◗

Walk a Crooked Mile (1948) **91m.** **½ D: Gordon Douglas. Louis Hayward, Dennis O'Keefe, Louise Allbritton, Carl Esmond, Onslow Stevens, Raymond Burr. Average melodrama about secret service agent who breaks up mob with help of Scotland Yard.

Walk, Don't Run (1966) **C-114m.** *** D: Charles Walters. Cary Grant, Samantha Eggar, Jim Hutton, John Standing, Miiko Taka, Ted Hartley. Enjoyable fluff about Eggar unwittingly agreeing to share her apartment with businessman Grant and athlete Hutton during the Tokyo Olympics. Stars are most agreeable in this remake of THE MORE THE MERRIER. Grant's last film as an actor. Panavision.▼●

Walk East on Beacon (1952) **98m.** **½ D: Alfred L. Werker. George Murphy, Finlay Currie, Virginia Gilmore, George Roy Hill. Good documentary-style drama by Leo Rosten about FBI investigation of espionage; filmed on location in Boston.

Walker (1988) **C-90m.** BOMB D: Alex Cox. Ed Harris, Marlee Matlin, Richard Masur, René Auberjonois, Peter Boyle, Miguel Sandoval, Gerrit Graham. Juvenile, intentionally anachronistic comic history of William Walker, American soldier of fortune (previously played by Marlon Brando in BURN!) who became president of 19th-century Nicaragua thanks to an assist from Cornelius Vanderbilt. Matlin's follow-up to her Oscar is actually an inglorious cameo; the sorry screenplay is by Rudy Wurlitzer. A self-indulgent mess. [R]▼

Walking and Talking (1996) **C-85m.** **½ D: Nicole Holofcener. Catherine Keener, Anne Heche, Todd Field, Liev Schreiber, Kevin Corrigan, Randall Batinkoff, Joseph Siravo, Allison Janney. Two longtime best friends are closing in on thirty; that's bad enough, but when Keener learns of Heche's impending marriage, she feels happy, jealous, panicked, and desolate. Amusing look at the joy and strain of friendship (not to mention dating and therapy), with fine performances all around. [R]▼●

Walking Dead, The (1936) **66m.** *** D: Michael Curtiz. Boris Karloff, Edmund Gwenn, Marguerite Churchill, Ricardo Cortez, Barton MacLane, Warren Hull, Joe Sawyer. Karloff is framed and executed, but professor brings him back to life. As he regains his memory, he seeks out those who framed him. Good horror tale.●

Walking Dead, The (1995) **C-89m.** ** D: Preston A. Whitmore II. Allen Payne, Eddie Griffin, Joe Morton, Vonte Sweet, Roger Floyd. Predominantly black Vietnam Marines have ended up serving for reasons beyond love of the Corps: better housing, lost jobs, legal flight from murder charges, impressing women. Filmmakers try to stylize both the combat and stateside scenes, but their ambitions outpace their abilities. Griffin stands out with his comic commentary throughout the film. [R] ▼●

Walking Hills, The (1949) **78m.** *** D: John Sturges. Randolph Scott, Ella Raines, William Bishop, Edgar Buchanan, Arthur Kennedy. Well-acted oater of Westerners searching for abandoned gold mine.

Walking My Baby Back Home (1953) **C-95m.** **½ D: Lloyd Bacon. Donald O'Connor, Buddy Hackett, Janet Leigh, Scatman Crothers, George Cleveland, Lori Nelson. Confused musical comedy about army buddies forming a Dixieland band; redeemed by Hackett's wacky humor.

Walking Nightmare, A SEE: **Living Ghost, The**

Walking Stick, The (1970-British) **C-101m.** **½ D: Eric Till. Samantha Eggar, David Hemmings, Emlyn Williams, Phyllis Calvert, Ferdy Mayne, Francesca Annis. Potentially interesting story of beautiful polio victim coerced into assisting her worthless lover in a robbery is just too low-key to be consistently absorbing. Eggar's performance helps. Panavision. [PG]

Walking Tall (1973) **C-125m.** ** D: Phil Karlson. Joe Don Baker, Elizabeth Hartman, Gene Evans, Rosemary Murphy, Noah Beery, Felton Perry. Sickeningly violent actioner about determined Southern sheriff's one-man war against corruption. Huge theatrical success, based on real-life exploits of baseball-bat-wielding Buford Pusser; muscular performance by Baker. Followed by a pair of sequels, a 1978 TVM with Brian Dennehy (A REAL AMERICAN HERO) and a series. [R]▼●◗

Walking Tall—Final Chapter SEE: **Final Chapter—Walking Tall**

Walking Tall, Part Two SEE: **Part 2, Walking Tall**

Walk in the Clouds, A (1995) **C-103m.** *** D: Alfonso Arau. Keanu Reeves, Aitana Sanchez-Gijon, Anthony Quinn, Giancarlo Giannini, Angelica Aragon, Evangelina Elizondo, Freddy Rodriguez, Debra Messing. A young man just back from WW2 overseas duty helps out a beautiful woman by pretending to be her husband, in order to smooth over the expected fireworks when her father learns she's pregnant. Of course, he not only falls in love with her but with her family and their idyllic Napa Valley homestead. Blatantly old-fashioned and romantic, even corny, with household scenes reminiscent of the director's LIKE WATER FOR CHOCOLATE. If you're willing to buy into it, it actually works—until the climax. Based on a 1942 Italian film, QUATTRO POASSI FRA LE NUVOLE. [PG-13] ▼●

Walk in the Shadow (1966-British) **93m.** *** D: Basil Dearden. Patrick McGoohan, Janet Munro, Paul Rogers, Megs Jenkins. Fine courtroom melodrama, as emotions flare after a girl's drowning.

Walk in the Spring Rain (1970) **C-100m.** **½ D: Guy Green. Anthony Quinn, Ingrid Bergman, Fritz Weaver, Katherine Crawford. Happily married Bergman has extramarital affair in this low-key romantic drama. One expects more from such a cast. Scripted and produced by Stirling Silliphant. Panavision. [M/PG]▼

Walk in the Sun, A (1945) **117m.** ***½ D: Lewis Milestone. Dana Andrews, Richard Conte, Sterling Holloway, George Tyne, John Ireland, Herbert Rudley, Norman Lloyd, Lloyd Bridges, Huntz Hall. Human aspect of war explored as American battalion attacks Nazi hideout in Italy; good character studies of men in war. Adapted by Robert Rossen from Harry Brown's novel.▼●◗

Walk Into Hell (1957-Australian) **C-93m.** *½ D: Lee Robinson. Chips Rafferty, Francoise Christophe, Reginald Lye, Pierre Cressoy. Lumbering account of civilized Australians vs. native customs, filmed on location in New Guinea.▼

Walk Like a Dragon (1960) **95m.** **½ D: James Clavell. Jack Lord, Nobu McCarthy, James Shigeta, Mel Torme, Josephine Hutchinson, Rodolfo Acosta. Offbeat Western drama of Lord saving McCarthy from life of prostitution, taking her back to San Francisco, overcoming expected obstacles.

Walk Like a Man (1987) **C-86m.** BOMB D: Melvin Frank. Howie Mandel, Christopher Lloyd, Cloris Leachman, Colleen Camp, Amy Steel, Stephen Elliott, George DiCenzo. Mandel is returned to civilization after being raised by wolves, with the expected slapstick results. Puerile comedy with a cast that deserves much better. [PG]▼

Walk on the Moon, A (1999) **C-107m.** **½ D: Tony Goldwyn. Diane Lane, Liev Schreiber, Anna Paquin, Viggo Mortensen, Tovah Feldshuh, Bobby Boriello. A family spends the summer of 1969 at a bungalow colony in the Catskills, where the young wife is drawn into an affair with "the blouse man." Meanwhile, her teenage daughter is on the verge of a first love—and aching to attend a rock concert nearby called Woodstock. Well-observed script by Pamela Gray follows a fairly predictable path, but Lane is miscast as a young Jewish hausfrau. Julie Kavner's distinctive voice is unbilled. Coproduced by Dustin Hoffman. [R] ▼●◗

Walk on the Wild Side (1962) **114m.** **½ D: Edward Dmytryk. Laurence Harvey, Capucine, Jane Fonda, Anne Baxter, Barbara Stanwyck. Lurid hodgepodge set in 1930's New Orleans, loosely based on Nelson Algren novel, of Harvey seeking lost love Capucine, now a member of bordello run by lesbian Stanwyck. Memorable titles by Saul Bass; fine score by Elmer Bernstein.▼

Walk Proud (1979) **C-102m.** ** D: Robert Collins. Robby Benson, Sarah Holcomb, Domingo Ambriz, Pepe Serna, Trinidad Silva. Sincerely intentioned but not very forceful gang picture about a Chicano (Benson) who falls for a WASP beauty who goes to his high school. [PG]

Walk Softly, Stranger (1950) **81m.** *** D: Robert Stevenson. Joseph Cotten, (Alida) Valli, Spring Byington, Paul Stewart, Jack Paar, Jeff Donnell, John McIntire. Small-

time crook Cotten reforms because of the love and faith of crippled girl Valli.▼
Walk Tall (1960) **C-60m.** *½ D: Maury Dexter. Willard Parker, Joyce Meadows, Kent Taylor. Flabby oater about capture of outlaws who killed Indian squaws. CinemaScope.
Walk the Dark Street (1956) **74m.** *½ D: Wyott Ordung. Chuck Connors, Don Ross, Regina Gleason, Eddie Kafafian. Uninspired revenge hunt, set in a metropolitan city, of two men stalking each other with rifles.
Walk the Proud Land (1956) **C-88m.** *** D: Jesse Hibbs. Audie Murphy, Anne Bancroft, Pat Crowley, Charles Drake, Jay Silverheels. Sturdy scripting makes this oater attractive; Murphy is Indian agent trying to quell strife between redskins and settlers, with the capture of Geronimo his major feat. CinemaScope.▼
Walk With Love and Death, A (1969) **C-90m.** ** D: John Huston. Anjelica Huston, Assaf Dayan, Anthony Corlan, John Hallam, Robert Lang, Michael Gough. Fine period flavor but little else of note in story of young love set against turmoil of 14th-century France. Anjelica Huston's film debut; father John has small role. [M/PG]
Wall, The (1982-British) SEE: **Pink Floyd—The Wall**
Wallflower (1948) **77m.** *** D: Frederick de Cordova. Joyce Reynolds, Robert Hutton, Janis Paige, Edward Arnold, Jerome Cowan, Barbara Brown. Amusing comedy based on Broadway success; two stepsisters (Reynolds and Paige) vie for the same love.
Wall of Noise (1963) **112m.** **½ D: Richard Wilson. Suzanne Pleshette, Ty Hardin, Dorothy Provine, Ralph Meeker, Simon Oakland, Murray Matheson. Turgid racetrack drama with adultery, not horses, the focal point.
Walls Came Tumbling Down, The (1946) **82m.** *** D: Lothar Mendes. Lee Bowman, Marguerite Chapman, Edgar Buchanan, Lee Patrick, J. Edward Bromberg. Detective Bowman goes to work when priest is murdered in fast-moving private eye film.
Walls of Glass (1985) **C-86m.** **½ D: Scott Goldstein. Philip Bosco, Geraldine Page, Linda Thorson, Olympia Dukakis, Brian Bloom, Steven Weber, Louis Zorich, William Hickey. Intriguing if uneven character study with Bosco nicely cast as a middle-aged, sonnet-spouting N.Y.C. cab driver who hates his job, and yearns for success as an actor. Occasionally slow, but still effective. [R]▼
Walls of Gold (1933) **74m.** *½ D: Kenneth MacKenna. Sally Eilers, Norman Foster, Ralph Morgan, Rosita Moreno, Rochelle Hudson. Terrible soaper about love conflicts among the well-to-do; Eilers does something to ruffle fiancé Foster, so to spite her he marries her sister, and she marries his uncle. Forget it.
Walls of Hell, The (1964) **88m.** ** D: Gerardo De Leon. Jock Mahoney, Fernando Poe, Jr., Mike Parsons, Paul Edwards, Jr. WW2 actioner set in Manila. Filmed in the Philippines, suffers from amateurish native casting.
Walls of Jericho, The (1948) **106m.** ** D: John M. Stahl. Cornel Wilde, Linda Darnell, Anne Baxter, Kirk Douglas, Ann Dvorak, Marjorie Rambeau, Henry Hull, Colleen Townsend, Barton MacLane. Good cast tries to perk up story of ambitious lawyer in Jericho, Kansas, whose marital problems stand in the way of success; pretty dreary going most of the way.
Wall Street (1987) **C-124m.** *** D: Oliver Stone. Michael Douglas, Charlie Sheen, Daryl Hannah, Hal Holbrook, Martin Sheen, Terence Stamp, Sean Young, Sylvia Miles, James Spader, John McGinley, Saul Rubinek, Franklin Cover, James Karen, Richard Dysart, Josh Mostel, Millie Perkins, Cecilia Peck, Grant Shaud. Young hotshot who's going nowhere in a N.Y. brokerage firm manages to buttonhole the highest roller on Wall Street (Douglas, in an Oscar-winning performance) and win his confidence—but he sells his soul, so to speak, in return for admittance to that high-powered world of wheeling and dealing. Modern-day morality tale by cowriter-director Stone (whose father was a broker, and to whom the film is dedicated) is short on subtlety but completely absorbing, especially in the wake of the real-life "insider trading" scandal of 1986. Stone, Monique Van Vooren, and Liliane Montevecchi can be glimpsed. [R]▼●
Waltz Across Texas (1982) **C-99m.** **½ D: Ernest Day. Terry Jastrow, Anne Archer, Richard Farnsworth, Noah Beery, Mary Kay Place, Josh Taylor, Ben Piazza. Oilman Jastrow and geologist Archer fall in love. Predictable, but far from unpleasant. The leads are husband and wife offscreen; they wrote the story, coproduced the film. [PG]▼
Waltz King, The (1963) **C-95m.** **½ D: Steve Previn. Kerwin Mathews, Brian Aherne, Senta Berger, Peter Kraus, Fritz Eckhardt. Moderately entertaining Disney musical biopic stars Mathews as Johann Strauss, Jr., with lots of good music. Filmed in Germany; shown in the U.S. as two-part TV show.▼
Waltz of the Toreadors (1962-British) **C-105m.** *** D: John Guillermin. Peter Sellers, Dany Robin, Margaret Leighton, John Fraser. Jean Anouilh's saucy sex romp gets top notch handling with Sellers as the retired military officer who still can't keep his eye off the girls.▼●◗
Wanda (1971) **C-101m.** ***½ D: Barbara Loden. Barbara Loden, Michael Higgins,

Charles Dosinan, Frank Jourdano. Touching, original little drama about passive woman (Loden) who takes up with two-bit thief Higgins. Well acted. [PG]

Wanda Nevada (1979) **C-105m.** *½ D: Peter Fonda. Peter Fonda, Brooke Shields, Fiona Lewis, Luke Askew, Ted Markland, Severn Darden, Paul Fix, Henry Fonda. Fonda wins Shields in a poker game, and they set out to prospect for gold in the Grand Canyon. If this film were any more laid-back it would be nonexistent. Peter and Henry's only film together. [PG]▼

Wanderers, The (1979) **C-113m.** ***½ D: Philip Kaufman. Ken Wahl, John Friedrich, Karen Allen, Toni Kalem, Alan Rosenberg, Linda Manz, Erland van Lidth de Jeude, Olympia Dukakis. Impressionistic look at Bronx-Italian high school life in 1963 isn't always consistent in tone, but there are dozens of privileged moments. Understandably, it's become a cult favorite. [R]▼●

Wannsee Conference, The (1984-German-Austrian) **C-87m.** ***½ D: Heinz Schirk. Dietrich Mattausch, Gerd Bockmann, Friedrich Beckhaus, Gunter Spoerrie, Martin Luttge, Peter Fritz. Fascinating, chilling recreation of the infamous meeting, held in a Berlin suburb in January 1942, in which Nazi bigwigs discussed implementation of the Final Solution. Participants plot the destruction of millions with a casual air, which only adds to the terror. Based on minutes taken at the conference; film's length matches the event's actual running time.▼●

Want a Ride, Little Girl? SEE: **Impulse** (1974)

Wanted: Babysitter SEE: **Babysitter, The** (1975)

Wanted: Dead or Alive (1987) **C-104m.** BOMB D: Gary Sherman. Rutger Hauer, Gene Simmons, Robert Guillaume, Mel Harris, William Russ, Susan McDonald, Jerry Hardin. Hauer plays Nick Randall, grandson of fellow bounty hunter Josh, the character Steve McQueen played in the identically named TV series. Link is mentioned, then ignored, in routine cheapo about the CIA's pursuit of an Arab terrorist. Bravura grenade-in-mouth finale. [R]▼●

Wanted for Murder (1946-British) **95m.** **½ D: Lawrence Huntington. Eric Portman, Dulcie Gray, Derek Farr, Roland Culver, Stanley Holloway. Engaging whodunit yarn, effectively underplayed by the cast; coscripted by Emeric Pressburger.

Wanton Countess, The SEE: **Senso**

War, The (1994) **C-125m.** **½ D: Jon Avnet. Elijah Wood, Kevin Costner, Mare Winningham, Lexi Randall, Christine Baranski, Gary Basaraba, Raynor Scheine, Latoya Chisholm, Charlette Julius. Growing up isn't easy for a brother and sister in 1970 Mississippi; their father means well, but hasn't been stable since returning from Vietnam, and his attempts to teach them tolerance and peaceful ways are hard to absorb when they're constantly bullied by a family of mean-spirited kids who live nearby. Well-intentioned message film for young people, diluted by overlength, a lack of focus, and an overabundance of dramatic climaxes. [PG-13]▼●◗

War Against Mrs. Hadley, The (1942) **86m.** ** D: Harold Bucquet. Edward Arnold, Fay Bainter, Richard Ney, Sara Allgood, Spring Byington, Jean Rogers, Frances Rafferty, Dorothy Morris, Rags Ragland, Isobel Elsom, Van Johnson. Mild WW2 human-interest tale by George Oppenheimer about matron Bainter who refuses to participate in war support.

War and Peace (1956-U.S.-Italian) **C-208m.** **½ D: King Vidor. Audrey Hepburn, Henry Fonda, Mel Ferrer, Vittorio Gassman, John Mills, Herbert Lom, Oscar Homolka, Anita Ekberg, Helmut Dantine, Barry Jones, Milly Vitale, Jeremy Brett, Wilfrid Lawson, Mai Britt. Tolstoy's sprawling novel fails to come alive in this overlong, oversimplified adaptation. Star-studded cast and spectacular battle scenes (directed by Mario Soldati) cannot compensate for clumsy script (by six writers, including Vidor) and some profound miscasting. Filmed far more successfully in 1968. VistaVision.▼●

War and Peace (1968-Russian) **C-373m.** **** D: Sergei Bondarchuk. Ludmila Savelyeva, Vyacheslav Tihonov, Hira Ivanov-Golovko, Irina Gubanova, Antonia Shuranova. Sergei Bondarchuk. Even in theaters, poor English dubbing hurt this definitive film version of Tolstoy's novel. Even so, it should be seen for production values alone; a dazzling film. Oscar-winner for Best Foreign Film. Originally shown in U.S. in two parts; released in the USSR in 1966–67 in four parts, totaling 507m. Sovscope 70.▼

War Arrow (1953) **C-78m.** ** D: George Sherman. Maureen O'Hara, Jeff Chandler, Suzan Ball, Charles Drake, Jay Silverheels. Western story of U.S. Cavalry man Chandler coming to Texas to train Seminole Indians to subdue a Kiowa uprising. O'Hara is object of his love.▼

War at Home, The (1996) **C-123m.** ** D: Emilio Estevez. Emilio Estevez, Kathy Bates, Martin Sheen, Kimberly Williams, Corin Nemec, Carla Gugino, Renee Estevez. Stagey adaptation by James Duff of his own play *Homefront,* about recently returned Vietnam vet Estevez trying to move on with his life but haunted by his experience in combat. His family is unable to deal with the fact that the boy they sent off to war never came home. Great acting, especially by Bates, but good intentions outweigh results. Panavision. [R]▼●

War Between Men and Women, The (1972) **C-110m.** **½ D: Melville Shavelson. Jack Lemmon, Barbara Harris, Jason Robards, Herb Edelman, Lisa Gerritsen, Lisa Eilbacher, Severn Darden. Fans of James Thurber won't think much of this mixture of famed writer-cartoonist's material and Hollywood schmaltz, but film occasionally makes for pleasant comedy-romance. Harris comes off best. Material had previously inspired a TV series, *My World—And Welcome To It.* [PG]▼

War Between the Planets (1965-Italian) **C-80m.** BOMB D: Anthony Dawson (Antonio Margheriti). Jack Stuart (Giacomo Rossi-Stuarti), Amber Collins (Ombretta Colli), Peter Martell, Halina Zalewska. Alien planet is on collision course with earth, but valiant efforts by scientific forces snatch victory from the jaws of boredom. Fun only if you like spaghetti sci-fi. Made at same time as other losers such as WAR OF THE PLANETS, WILD WILD PLANET, etc. Aka PLANET ON THE PROWL. ▼

War Drums (1957) **C-75m.** **½ D: Reginald LeBorg. Lex Barker, Joan Taylor, Ben Johnson, Stuart Whitman, Jeanne Carmen. Sufficiently bloody Western set in Civil War days of Indian uprisings against onslaught of gold miners.

War Game, The (1967-British) **47m.** *** D: Peter Watkins. Fascinating, frightening simulated documentary, which vividly projects the aftermath of a nuclear holocaust. Originally produced for television by the BBC and British Film Institute, but deemed to be too incendiary for home audiences. It did open theatrically, and earned a Best Documentary Academy Award.▼

War Games (1970) SEE: **Suppose They Gave a War and Nobody Came?**

WarGames (1983) **C-110m.** **½ D: John Badham. Matthew Broderick, Dabney Coleman, John Wood, Ally Sheedy, Barry Corbin, Juanin Clay, Maury Chaykin, Michael Madsen, John Spencer. FAIL SAFE for the Pac-Man generation: a pop movie about a computer whiz-kid who taps into government early-warning system and nearly starts WW3. Entertaining to a point, but gets more contrived as it goes along, leading to finale straight out of an old B movie. Incidentally, it's easy to see why this was so popular with kids: most of the adults in the film are boobs. [PG]▼●◗

War Gods of the Deep (1965-U.S.-British) **C-85m.** **½ D: Jacques Tourneur. Vincent Price, Tab Hunter, David Tomlinson, Susan Hart, John LeMesurier. Gill-men invade remote seacoast town. Actually, two films in one: establishing menace, first half has odd, almost poetic feel to it, but second half deteriorates, with shoddy underwater city. Tourneur's final feature. British title: THE CITY UNDER THE SEA. Colorscope.

War Hunt (1962) **81m.** **½ D: Denis Sanders. John Saxon, Robert Redford, Charles Aidman, Sydney Pollack. Well-done Korean War story focusing on kill-happy soldier Saxon who tries to help an orphan boy. Redford's film debut.

War Is Hell (1963) **81m.** ** D: Burt Topper. Tony Russel, Baynes Barron, Tony Rich, Burt Topper. Korean War actioner with no new ideas to offer. Introduced by Audie Murphy.

War, Italian Style (1966-Italian) **C-84m.** ** D: Luigi Scattini. Buster Keaton, Franco and Ciccio, Martha Hyer, Fred Clark. Sloppy, meandering spy satire set in WW2 Italy, redeemed barely by Keaton's appearance. Unfortunately, this was his final film. Techniscope.

Warlock (1959) **C-121m.** *** D: Edward Dmytryk. Richard Widmark, Henry Fonda, Anthony Quinn, Dorothy Malone, Dolores Michaels, Wallace Ford, Tom Drake, Richard Arlen, DeForest Kelley, Regis Toomey. Philosophical vigilante "sheriff" Fonda is hired to clean up the crime-infested Western town of Warlock. This sets off a complex storyline involving, among others, crippled Quinn, guilt-ridden Widmark, and embittered Malone. Literate, allegorical adult Western examines the lynch-mob mentality and the meaning of machismo. Forgotten, but worthy of rediscovery. Scripted by Robert Alan Aurthur. CinemaScope.▼

Warlock (1991) **C-102m.** **½ D: Steve Miner. Julian Sands, Lori Singer, Richard E. Grant, Mary Woronov, Richard Kuss, Allan Miller, Kevin O'Brien, Anna Levine, David Carpenter. A warlock escapes from 1691 Boston to 1991 L.A., with a local witch-hunter in full time-warp pursuit; object of their squabble is the Grand Grimoire, or Satan's bible. More fun might have ensued had they ended up on a dusty street with, say, Henry Fonda, but it's worth half-a-star just to see the ever-intense Grant in a rare (for him) heroic role. Followed by two sequels. [R]▼●◗

Warlock: The Armageddon (1993) **C-98m.** *½ D: Anthony Hickox. Julian Sands, Christopher Young, Paula Marshall, Steve Kahan, Charles Hallahan, R. G. Armstrong, Nicole Mercurio, Craig Hurley, Bruce Glover, Zach Galligan, Joanna Pacula. Evil warlock Sands is (literally) reborn, even though there is nothing connecting this entry with the first, other than Sands himself and his role as a wicked, flying sorcerer—this time trying to unleash his father (Satan) upon the world. Weak, jokey film has only Sands' sardonic performance and some good effects to recommend it. Followed by a direct-to-video sequel. [R]▼●◗

War Lord, The (1965) **C-123m.** *** D: Franklin Schaffner. Charlton Heston, Rosemary Forsyth, Richard Boone, Maurice Evans, Guy Stockwell, Niall McGinnis, James Farentino, Henry Wilcoxon, Michael Conrad. Intriguing, generally well-done adaptation of Leslie Stevens' *The Lovers*, with Heston as feudal knight invoking little-known law allowing him to have another man's bride on their wedding night. Title and medieval setting would seem to indicate sweeping spectacle . . . which this certainly isn't. Panavision.▼●◗

Warlords of Atlantis (1978-British) **C-96m.** ★★½ D: Kevin Connor. Doug McClure, Peter Gilmore, Shane Rimmer, Lea Brodie, John Ratzenberger, Cyd Charisse, Daniel Massey. Monsters and mayhem abound in this palatable Saturday matinee item with McClure joining British scientists in search for underwater city.

Warlords of the 21st Century (1982) **C-91m.** ★★ D: Harley Cokliss. Michael Beck, Annie McEnroe, James Wainwright, John Ratzenberger, Bruno Lawrence. Routine action film set after WW3 in time of an oil shortage. Wainwright (as the ruthless, right-wing military villain) virtually repeated his role in the contemporary-set Robin Williams comedy THE SURVIVORS. Filmed in New Zealand; originally titled BATTLETRUCK. [PG]▼

War Lover, The (1962-British) **105m.** ★★½ D: Philip Leacock. Steve McQueen, Robert Wagner, Shirley Anne Field, Gary Cockrell, Michael Crawford, Al Waxman. John Hersey's thoughtful novel becomes superficial account of McQueen and Wagner, two WW2 pilots in England, both in love with Field; aerial photography is above par. Crawford's first film.▼●

Warm December, A (1973) **C-100m.** ★★ D: Sidney Poitier. Sidney Poitier, Esther Anderson, Johnny Sekka, Yvette Curtis. George Baker, Earl Cameron. Story of Poitier's love for Anderson, who is dying of sickle cell anemia, isn't as sappy as it might be, but isn't particularly good, either. Anderson is attractive. Made in England. [PG] ▼

Warning Shot (1967) **C-100m.** ★★★½ D: Buzz Kulik. David Janssen, Ed Begley, Keenan Wynn, Lillian Gish, Eleanor Parker, Sam Wanamaker, Stefanie Powers, George Sanders, George Grizzard, Steve Allen, Carroll O'Connor, Joan Collins, Walter Pidgeon. Exciting action-filled melodrama about cop's attempt to clear his name after killing a supposedly innocent doctor. TV-vet Kulik made this one exciting for theaters; it's even better on TV.

Warning Sign (1985) **C-100m.** ★½ D: Hal Barwood. Sam Waterston, Kathleen Quinlan, Yaphet Kotto, Jeffrey De Munn, Richard Dysart, G. W. Bailey, Jerry Hardin, Rick Rossovich, Cynthia Carle. Self-important, would-be CHINA SYNDROME about disastrous results of chemical spill at research lab that's secretly been working on germ warfare for the government. Unpleasant and ineffectual. Screenwriter Barwood's directing debut. [R]▼

War of the Buttons (1994-British-French-Japanese) **C-90m.** ★★½ D: John Roberts. Gregg Fitzgerald, John Coffey, Liam Cunningham, Johnny Murphy, Colm Meaney, Jim Bartley, Gerard Kearney, Anthony Cunningham. The children of two neighboring Irish towns gradually escalate their quarrels to outright—if painless—warfare. This pleasant comedy-drama tries to say something about war, but the point is obscured as the story begins to focus on two particular boys. Based on the 1912 Louis Pergaud novel *La Guerre des Boutons,* previously filmed in 1938 and 1962. [PG]▼●

War of the Colossal Beast (1958) **68m.** ★½ D: Bert I. Gordon. Sally Fraser, Roger Pace, Dean Parkin, Russ Bender, Charles Stewart. Sequel to THE AMAZING COLOSSAL MAN finds our oversized hero alive but not well; his face is a mess, and so is his mind, leading to the inevitable low-budget rampage. Forget it. Last scene is in color.▼

War of the Gargantuas, The (1966-U.S.-Japanese) **C-93m.** BOMB D: Ishiro Honda. Russ Tamblyn, Kumi Mizuno, Kipp Hamilton, Yu Fujiki. Japan is menaced by a mean, green "gargantua" (humanoid giant), with a friendly brown gargantua trying to make peace. Strange, even by Japanese monster-movie standards. Tohoscope.▼

War of the Planets (1965-Italian) **C-99m.** BOMB D: Anthony Dawson (Antonio Margheriti). Tony Russel, Lisa Gastoni, Massimo Serato, Franco Nero, Carlo Giustini. Light creatures attack earth but are repelled. Cheap sets and plodding script make this a loser.

War of the Roses, The (1989) **C-116m.** ★★½ D: Danny DeVito. Michael Douglas, Kathleen Turner, Danny DeVito, Marianne Sägebrecht, Sean Astin, Heather Fairfield, G. D. Spradlin, Peter Donat, Dan Castellaneta, Danitra Vance. When Douglas and Turner can't agree on a property settlement in their divorce proceedings, war breaks out in (and over) their exquisitely appointed house. As a satire on yuppie materialism, this very black comedy scores a bull's-eye—for about an hour. Then it continues for nearly an hour more as the couple grows increasingly vicious and irrational, literally destroying their home. Some people loved this film (the stars *are* perfect), so obviously it's a matter of taste. DeVito's odd point of view and wild camera angles are an asset throughout. [R]▼●

War of the Satellites (1958) **66m.** ★★ D: Roger Corman. Dick Miller, Susan Cabot, Richard Devon, Robert Shayne, Eric Sinclair. Ruthless combination of THE DAY THE EARTH STOOD STILL and KRONOS has unseen aliens warning Earth to cease their space exploration, brainwashing scientist Devon to make sure it's done. The day after the U.S. Explorer satellite went up, Corman told a studio he could have a film ready in two months . . . and he did. Not so hot, but any movie with Dick Miller as a heroic scientist can't be *all* bad.

War of the Wildcats SEE: **In Old Oklahoma**

War of the Worlds, The (1953) **C-85m.** ***½ D: Byron Haskin. Gene Barry, Les Tremayne, Ann Robinson, Robert Cornthwaite, Henry Brandon, Jack Kruschen; narrated by Sir Cedric Hardwicke. Vivid, frightening adaptation of H. G. Wells' story about a Martian invasion. Dramatically sound and filled with dazzling, Oscar-winning special effects; superior sci-fi, produced by George Pal. Later a TV series. ▼●◗

War of the Zombies (1965-Italian) **C-85m.** ** D: Giuseppe Vari. John Drew Barrymore, Susy Anderson, Ettore Manni, Ida Galli. Rome sends best legionnaire to quell disturbance in Eastern province in clutches of mad priest (Barrymore). Production values somewhat better than usual. Aka NIGHT STAR GODDESS OF ELECTRA. Totalscope.

War Paint (1953) **C-89m.** **½ D: Lesley Selander. Robert Stack, Joan Taylor, Charles McGraw, Peter Graves, Keith Larsen, William Pullen, Richard Cutting, Douglas Kennedy, Walter Reed. Action-packed film of U. S. cavalry detachment overcoming danger and villainous attempts to prevent delivery of peace treaty to an Indian chief.

War Party (1989) **C-97m.** ** D: Franc Roddam. Billy Wirth, Kevin Dillon, Tim Sampson, Jimmie Ray Weeks, M. Emmet Walsh, Dennis Banks, Kevyn Major Howard, Bill McKinney. Reenactment of a hundred-year-old battle between Blackfoot Indian tribe and U.S. Cavalry turns into the real thing once again when one white youth brings a loaded gun to the festivities. Basically an excuse for a cowboys and Indians movie, this intriguing premise becomes just another botched opportunity for Hollywood to shed light on the problems of the American Indian. [R]▼●

Warpath (1951) **C-95m.** **½ D: Byron Haskin. Edmond O'Brien, Dean Jagger, Forrest Tucker, Harry Carey, Jr., Wallace Ford, Polly Bergen. Nifty action Western with O'Brien hunting down outlaws who killed his girlfriend; an Indian attack is thrown in for good measure.

Warrior and the Slave Girl, The (1958-Italian) **C-84m.** ** D: Vittorio Cottafavi. Ettore Manni, Georges Marchal, Gianna Maria Canale, Rafael Calvo. Unsubtle costumer set in ancient Armenia, with Canale the evil princess, subdued by Roman Manni. SuperCinescope.

Warrior and the Sorceress, The (1984) **C-76m.** *½ D: John Broderick. David Carradine, Luke Askew, Maria Socas, Anthony DeLongis, Harry Townes, William Marin. Copycat version of both A FISTFUL OF DOLLARS and YOJIMBO transplants story of a lone fighter playing both ends against the middle to a mythical kingdom on a planet circling two suns. Lovely leading lady Socas plays the entire film topless; you also might note the very convincing makeup effects on a pretty dancer who has four breasts. [R]▼●

Warrior Empress, The (1960-Italian) **C-87m.** ** D: Pietro Francisci. Kerwin Mathews, Tina Louise, Riccardo Garrone, Antonio Batistella, Enrico Maria Salerno. Senseless mixture of fantasy and adventure with Phaon (Mathews) falling in love with Sappho (Louise), overcoming treacherous Salerno. CinemaScope.

Warrior Queen (1987) **C-69m.** BOMB D: Chuck Vincent. Sybil Danning, Donald Pleasence, Richard Hill, Josephine Jacqueline Jones, Tally Chanel, Stasia Micula (Samantha Fox). Ridiculous made-in-Italy exploitation film emphasizes sex in recreating the decadence of ancient Pompeii. Pleasence is at his hammy worst as the mayor whose wife (porn star Fox) has eyes for other men. Relies extensively on footage from the '60 LAST DAYS OF POMPEII for an apocalyptic climax. Unrated 79m. video version has more sex scenes. [R]▼●

Warriors, The (1955-British) **C-85m.** **½ D: Henry Levin. Errol Flynn, Joanne Dru, Peter Finch, Patrick Holt, Yvonne Furneaux, Michael Hordern, Christopher Lee. Flynn's final swashbuckler casts him as British prince protecting French conquests (and lovely Dru) from attacks by Finch and his supporters. Well made but awfully familiar. British title: THE DARK AVENGER. CinemaScope.▼

Warriors, The (1979) **C-90m.** *** D: Walter Hill. Michael Beck, James Remar, Thomas Waites, Dorsey Wright, Brian Tyler, Deborah Van Valkenburgh, Mercedes Ruehl. Comic book plot about N.Y.C. gang crossing rival turfs to get "home" is redeemed by lightning pace, tough action sequences, creative use of color. Notorious for the number of violent incidents it allegedly instigated in theaters, but worthy of some respect. Script by Hill and David Shaber; photographed by Andrew Laszlo. [R]▼●

Warriors of Virtue (1997) **C-103m.** *½ D: Ronny Yu. Angus Macfadyen, Mario Yedidia, Marley Shelton, Jack Tate, Chao-Li Chi, Doug Jones, Michael John Anderson. Incoherent kiddie kung fu movie about an American boy (Yedidia, who's the spitting image of Elijah Wood) who gets hold of a secret Chinese manuscript that transports him to a mystical wonderland where kangaroo warriors fight against evil. Yu's English filmmaking debut is a big disappointment after his fantastical (and very adult) Hong

Kong sword and sorcery epics THE BRIDE WITH WHITE HAIR, Parts 1 and 2. Macfadyen chews scenery as the villain, acting like the errant offspring of Ming the Merciless and Little Richard. Panavision. [PG] ▼●◗

War Room, The (1993) **C-95m.** *** D: D. A. Pennebaker, Chris Hegedus. Compelling documentary which follows the behind-the-scenes machinations of Bill Clinton's 1992 presidential campaign. No great insights or revelations, but still an inherently interesting (and very entertaining) look at political kingmaking, done in classic cinema verité style. Chief political strategist James Carville (the "Ragin' Cajun") has more onscreen charisma than many Hollywood stars.▼●◗

War Wagon, The (1967) **C-101m.** *** D: Burt Kennedy. John Wayne, Kirk Douglas, Howard Keel, Robert Walker, Keenan Wynn, Bruce Cabot, Joanna Barnes, Bruce Dern. Amiable tongue-in-cheek Western, with ex-con Wayne seeking to settle a score with villainous Cabot by plundering his gold-laden stagecoach—with the help of Douglas (who's been hired to kill Wayne on Cabot's behalf) and a motley band of associates. Keel is hilarious as wisecracking Indian. Panavision.▼●◗

War Zone, The (1999-British-Italian) **C-98m.** *** D: Tim Roth. Ray Winstone, Tilda Swinton, Lara Belmont, Freddie Cunliffe. Roth's directorial debut is an ultra-realistic, deeply affecting portrait of incest in a working-class British family. With devastating candor, he charts the unfolding events as 15-year-old Cunliffe suspects that his father (Winstone) is acting inappropriately with his older sister (Belmont). Sometimes difficult to watch, as Roth pulls no punches in his portrayal of this deeply troubled family. Panavision. ▼

Washington Affair, The (1977) **C-86m.** ** D: Victor Stoloff. Barry Sullivan, Carol Lynley, Tom Selleck, Arlene Banas, Kathleen Gaffney. Claustrophobic suspense film (shot almost entirely in just two rooms) has Sullivan as a corrupt businessman who uses a hidden camera and women to entrap government engineer Selleck into getting him an aircraft contract. Unreleased theatrically, it surfaced after Selleck's TV series *Magnum, P.I.,* became a hit. Remake of same director's INTIMACY.▼

Washington B.C. SEE: **Hail to the Chief**

Washington Merry-Go-Round (1932) **79m.** **½ D: James Cruze. Lee Tracy, Constance Cummings, Walter Connolly, Alan Dinehart, Jane Darwell. Dry run for MR. SMITH GOES TO WASHINGTON has idealistic young congressman Tracy out to do good for his Depression-ravaged constituents—only to find it ain't that easy, especially when he opposes an "important" appropriations bill. Remains surprisingly relevant today, with engaging performances and strong feel for the political arena, but peters out after great first half.

Washington Square (1997) **C-115m.** *** D: Agnieszka Holland. Jennifer Jason Leigh, Albert Finney, Ben Chaplin, Maggie Smith, Judith Ivey, Betsy Brantley, Jennifer Garner, Peter Maloney. Spirited adaptation of the Henry James novel about the awkward, plain-Jane daughter of a wealthy, domineering doctor (Finney), who is suddenly courted by a poor but handsome fortune hunter (Chaplin) in 19th-century N.Y.C. Like a number of celebrated period stories filmed in the 1990s, this one features a pointed contemporary feminist sensibility. The stage adaptation of James' novel was filmed before as THE HEIRESS. [PG]▼●

Washington Story (1952) **81m.** ** D: Robert Pirosh. Van Johnson, Patricia Neal, Louis Calhern, Sidney Blackmer, Elizabeth Patterson. Newspaperwoman Neal assigned to harass Congress selects young Congressman Johnson as her target; naturally, she falls in love with him. Romantic angle is better than political one—but neither is particularly interesting.

Wasn't That a Time! SEE: **Weavers, The: Wasn't That a Time!**

Wasp Woman, The (1960) **66m.** **½ D: Roger Corman. Susan Cabot, Fred (Anthony) Eisley, Barboura Morris, Michael Mark, William Roerick. Enjoyable Corman cheapie about cosmetics magnate Cabot, fearful of aging, using royal jelly from wasps to become young and beautiful. She also periodically turns into a wasp-monster that must kill. Minor camp classic; an unauthorized semi-remake, EVIL SPAWN, was made for video in 1987. Remade for TV in 1996.▼

Wasted Lives SEE: **Most Wonderful Moment, The**

Watched! (1972) **C-95m.** *½ D: John Parsons. Stacy Keach, Harris Yulin, Brigid Polk, Denver John Collins. Keach plays a former government lawyer who went underground, befriending dopers. Yulin is chief of the narcotics squad, using lots of surveillance filming in his war of wills with Keach. Haphazard structure of this low-budget film relies upon Keach's nearly one-man show, expressing the personal transition out of 1960s culture. [R]▼

Watcher in the Woods, The (1980) **C-84m.** **½ D: John Hough. Bette Davis, Carroll Baker, David McCallum, Lynn-Holly Johnson, Kyle Richards, Ian Bannen, Richard Pasco. All-American family takes over British country house, where young Johnson is tormented by the spirit of owner Davis's long-missing daughter. Not bad, with atmospheric photography by Alan Hume, but awfully familiar. First shown with an abrupt conclusion, then with special effects sequence that made things worse, then reworked again and improved (by Vincent

McEveety)—for 1981 rerelease! Original running time 100m. [PG]▼

Watchers (1988-U.S.-Canadian) **C-92m.** *½ D: Jon Hess. Corey Haim, Michael Ironside, Barbara Williams, Lala, Duncan Fraser, Dale Wilson, Blu Mankuma. Young Haim is befriended by a super-intelligent dog (the product of military research), but soon both are pursued by a swift, deadly monster. Awful adaptation of Dean R. Koontz's novel, with a ludicrous monster. Followed by three sequels. [R]▼●

Watchers 2 (1990-U.S.-Canadian) **C-97m.** ** D: Thierry Notz. Marc Singer, Tracy Scoggins, Tom Poster, Jonathan Farwell, Mary Woronov. Singer and a super-intelligent dog are pursued by a monster who's the result of the same experimentation that created the canine. More a remake of than a sequel to WATCHERS, and a better movie, though still no world-beater. Followed by two sequels. [R]▼●

Watch It (1993) **C-102m.** *** D: Tom Flynn. Peter Gallagher, Suzy Amis, John C. McGinley, Jon Tenney, Cynthia Stevenson, Lili Taylor, Tom Sizemore, Terri Hawkes, Jordana Capra. Drifter Gallagher returns to Chicago and moves in with smarmy, womanizing cousin Tenney and his crude, immature housemates. He falls for (but cannot make a commitment to) veterinarian Amis, who's had rotten luck with men. Despite some plot implausibilities and a cop-out ending, a perceptive and ingratiating film. Flynn scripted; McGinley coproduced. [R]▼●

Watch It, Sailor! (1961-British) **81m.** ** D: Wolf Rilla. Dennis Price, Liz Fraser, Irene Handl, Graham Stark, Marjorie Rhodes. Mildly amusing stage farce adapted to screen, with Price managing to outdo Fraser's mother (Rhodes), getting to the church on time.

Watch on the Rhine (1943) **114m.** ***½ D: Herman Shumlin. Bette Davis, Paul Lukas, Geraldine Fitzgerald, Lucile Watson, Beulah Bondi, George Coulouris, Donald Woods, Henry Daniell. Fine filmization of Lillian Hellman's timely WW2 play of German Lukas and wife Davis pursued and harried by Nazi agents in Washington. Lukas gives the performance of his career, which won him an Oscar; Bette somewhat overshadowed. Script by Dashiell Hammett. ▼

Watch the Birdie (1950) **70m.** **½ D: Jack Donohue. Red Skelton, Arlene Dahl, Ann Miller, Leon Ames, Pamela Britton, Richard Rober, Mike Mazurki. Average Skelton comedy features him as photographer, silly father and grandfather. Rest of cast is also good with routine material, reworking of Buster Keaton's THE CAMERAMAN.▼

Watch Your Stern (1960-British) **88m.** ** D: Gerald Thomas. Kenneth Connor, Eric Barker, Leslie Phillips, Joan Sims, Hattie Jacques. Amusing, obvious shenanigans on the seas, with Connor impersonating a scientist sent to perfect a torpedo.

Water (1985-British) **C-95m.** BOMB D: Dick Clement. Michael Caine, Brenda Vaccaro, Leonard Rossiter, Valerie Perrine, Jimmie Walker, Billy Connolly, Dennis Dugan. Inept comedy of errors concerns a Caribbean British colony where the local governor (Caine) juggles greedy U.S. oil interests, a comical rebellion, and other assorted looneys as a valuable mineral water is discovered. Rossiter is funny as a diplomat sent from England to calm the situation, and Maureen Lipman is terrific in a nasty caricature of Prime Minister Thatcher; Vaccaro is miscast in strained Carmen Miranda impression. Pointless cameos by Dick Shawn, Fred Gwynne, film's executive producer George Harrison, Eric Clapton, and Ringo Starr. [PG-13]▼

Water Babies, The (1978-British-Polish) **C-92m.** ** D: Lionel Jeffries. James Mason, Billie Whitelaw, Bernard Cribbins, Joan Greenwood, David Tomlinson, Tommy Pender, Samantha Gates. Combination live action and animated film for children, framing its fairy-tale undersea adventure with virtually unrelated story and characters in Dickensian London. Inoffensive for children, but downright boring at times. Aka SLIP SLIDE ADVENTURES.▼

Waterboy, The (1998) **C-88m.** *** D: Frank Coraci. Adam Sandler, Kathy Bates, Fairuza Balk, Henry Winkler, Jerry Reed, Larry Gilliard, Jr., Blake Clark, Clint Howard, Rob Schneider. Dimwitted Cajun boy, sheltered by his smothering mama (Bates), lives only to serve—as a much-abused waterboy for football teams. But when a downtrodden coach (Winkler) discovers that the waterboy can, when properly motivated, run and tackle with great force, he turns him into a football star. Likable, crowd-pleasing comedy with heart. Sandler gets strong support here from Winkler and Bates. Director Coraci plays Roberto in the closing scenes; various sports figures appear as themselves. Sandler coscripted and coexecutive-produced. [PG-13]▼●◗

Waterdance, The (1992) **C-106m.** *** D: Neal Jimenez, Michael Steinberg. Eric Stoltz, Wesley Snipes, William Forsythe, Helen Hunt, Elizabeth Pena, Grace Zabriskie. Fine, affecting story of a young novelist (Stoltz) who becomes paraplegic after a hiking accident and learns to adjust in a multi-ethnic rehabilitation center. Things haven't changed too much since THE MEN, but potentially maudlin situations are handled with directness, grace, and great humor, and the entire cast—particularly Snipes and Forsythe—is excellent. Jimenez, himself paralyzed since an accident in 1984, also wrote the screenplay. [R]▼●

Water Engine, The (1992) **C-110m. TVM** D: Steven Schacter. Charles Durning, Patti LuPone, William H. Macy, John Mahoney, Joe Mantegna, Joanna Miles, Mike Nussbaum, Treat Williams, Andrea Marcovicci, Peter Michael Goetz, David Mamet. Mamet's Kafkaesque original, set in '30s Chicago, finds Macy, as a luckless inventor of a water-powered automobile engine, coming into conflict with big business, represented by Mantegna. Called "An American Fable," it was the admirable maiden production of a cable series of works by noted playwrights produced by Steven Spielberg and Michael Brandman. Above average.▼

Waterfront (1944) **66m.** *½ D: Steve Sekely. John Carradine, J. Carrol Naish, Maris Wrixon, Edwin Maxwell, Terry Frost. Low-grade espionage tale of Nazi agents Carradine and Naish murdering and blackmailing in WW2 San Francisco.▼

Waterhole #3 (1967) **C-95m.** **½ D: William Graham. James Coburn, Carroll O'Connor, Margaret Blye, Claude Akins, Bruce Dern, Joan Blondell, James Whitmore. Amusing Western comedy of three confederates who rob Army of a fortune in gold and bury it in desert waterhole. Produced by Blake Edwards. Techniscope. ▼●

Waterland (1992-British) **C-95m.** *** D: Stephen Gyllenhaal. Jeremy Irons, Sinead Cusack, Ethan Hawke, John Heard, Grant Warnock, Lena Headey, David Morrissey. Arresting film about a desperate, middle-aged high school history teacher who's led a life of emotional upheaval, and seems trapped by his past—all of which affects the way he relates to his students. Peter Prince's screenplay effectively interprets Graham Swift's seemingly unfilmable novel. Irons is ideally cast and offers a peerless performance. Technovision. [R]▼●

Waterloo (1971-Italian-Russian) **C-123m.** ** D: Sergei Bondarchuk. Rod Steiger, Christopher Plummer, Orson Welles, Jack Hawkins, Virginia McKenna, Dan O'Herlihy, Michael Wilding. Cumbersome historical film centering around Napoleon's defeat at Waterloo. Tremendous action but muddled plot. The original Russian version ran nearly four hours. Panavision. [G]▼

Waterloo Bridge (1931) **81m.** *** D: James Whale. Mae Clarke, Kent Douglass (Douglass Montgomery), Doris Lloyd, Frederick Kerr, Enid Bennett, Bette Davis, Ethel Griffies. Excellent early-talkie version of the tearjerker romance made famous in its 1940 remake. Clarke delivers an exceptional performance as an American chorus girl in WW1 London, and the film has a grittiness (missing from the remake) that lenient pre-Code standards allowed. One of Davis' earliest films.

Waterloo Bridge (1940) **103m.** ***½ D: Mervyn LeRoy. Vivien Leigh, Robert Taylor, Lucile Watson, Virginia Field, Maria Ouspenskaya, C. Aubrey Smith. Sentimental love story, well-acted, of soldier and ballet dancer meeting during London air raid, falling in love instantly. Cleaned-up version of the Robert E. Sherwood play, with beautiful performance by lovely Leigh. Screenplay by S.N. Behrman, Hans Rameau, and George Froeschel. First filmed in 1931, remade as GABY. Also shown in computer-colored version. ▼●

Waterloo Road (1944-British) **76m.** *** D: Sidney Gilliat. John Mills, Stewart Granger, Alastair Sim, Joy Shelton, Beatrice Varley, Alison Leggatt, Jean Kent. Enjoyable wartime drama about soldier who goes AWOL when he learns his wife has been seeing another man. Evocative of its period, with spry touches of humor.

Watermelon Man (1970) **C-97m.** **½ D: Melvin Van Peebles. Godfrey Cambridge, Estelle Parsons, Howard Caine, D'Urville Martin, Kay Kimberly, Mantan Moreland, Erin Moran. Provocative serio-comedy about bigoted white man who suddenly turns black and sees his life go upside down. Worth seeing, although Herman Raucher's one-joke script makes its point and then has nowhere to go. TV print edited to 91m. [R]▼●

Watership Down (1978-British) **C-92m.** ***½ D: Martin Rosen. Voices of John Hurt, Richard Briers, Ralph Richardson, Denholm Elliott, Harry Andrews, Joss Ackland; narrated by Michael Hordern. Stylish animated-cartoon from Richard Adams' best-selling book about a family of rabbits seeking a safe place to live, encountering many perils along the way; not a kiddie film by any means. Bird character voiced by Zero Mostel provides only comic relief in this sometimes grim cartoon. Excellent score by Angela Morley and Malcolm Williamson. One of the best non-Disney animated features ever made. [PG]▼●

Waterworld (1995) **C-135m.** *** D: Kevin Reynolds. Kevin Costner, Dennis Hopper, Jeanne Tripplehorn, Tina Majorino, Michael Jeter, Sab Shimono, Robert Joy, R. D. Call, Zakes Mokae, Leonardo Cimino, Gerard Murphy, Neil Giuntoli. Notoriously expensive movie can't live up to its price tag but does offer great action scenes and an interesting futuristic premise. In a world engulfed by water, the drifters and scavengers are pitted against bad guys called Smokers. Costner, known as The Mariner, is a hardened (and remarkably resourceful) survivor who readies himself for the ultimate Smoker showdown with a woman and child in tow. Full of eye-popping stunts and set pieces, and anchored by Costner's forceful and physical performance. Too poky at times and not fully fleshed out at the conclusion, but still solid entertainment. [PG-13]▼●◗

Watts Monster, The SEE: **Dr. Black, Mr. Hyde**

Wattstax (1973) **C-98m.** ***½ D: Mel Stuart. Isaac Hayes, The Staple Singers, Luther Ingram, Rev. Jesse Jackson, Richard Pryor, Rufus Thomas, Carla Thomas, Bar-Kays, Kim Weston, The Emotions, Johnnie Taylor. Exciting, vibrant documentary with music, centering around L.A. community of Watts, and the black experience. Pryor's monologues are exceptionally good. [R]

Watusi (1959) **C-85m.** **½ D: Kurt Neumann. George Montgomery, Taina Elg, David Farrar, Rex Ingram, Dan Seymour. MGM fabricated a sequel to KING SOLOMON'S MINES to utilize leftover footage from its 1950 version of H. Rider Haggard yarn.

Wavelength (1983) **C-87m.** ** D: Mike Gray. Robert Carradine, Cherie Currie, Keenan Wynn. Cheap science-fiction film about aliens on Earth and a government coverup steals liberally from earlier pictures for ideas. Best thing is a varied musical score by Tangerine Dream. [PG]▼●

Waxwork (1988) **C-97m.** *½ D: Anthony Hickox. Zach Galligan, Deborah Foreman, David Warner, Michelle Johnson, Patrick Macnee, Dana Ashbrook, Miles O'Keeffe, John Rhys-Davies. Garbled, peculiar comedy-horror thriller set in evil magician's waxworks exhibit, with apocalyptic battle between humans and most of the famous monsters of history—Dracula (O'Keeffe), Frankenstein, the Mummy, a werewolf, Phantom of the Opera, Audrey II, etc. Followed by WAXWORK II: LOST IN TIME. [R]▼●

Way Ahead, The (1944-British) **91m.** ***½ D: Carol Reed. David Niven, Stanley Holloway, James Donald, John Laurie, Leslie Dwyer, Hugh Burden, Jimmy Hanley, Billy Hartnell, Raymond Huntley, Reginald Tate, Leo Genn, Penelope Dudley Ward, Renée Asherson, Raymond Lovell, Peter Ustinov, Trevor Howard. Exhilarating wartime British film showing how disparate civilians come to work together as a fighting unit; full of spirit and charm, with an outstanding cast, and fine script by Eric Ambler and Peter Ustinov. Film debut of Trevor Howard. Originally released in the U.S. in a shortened, more serious version called THE IMMORTAL BATTALION (with an introduction by journalist Quentin Reynolds). Original British running time 116m.▼

Way Down East (1920) **119m.** *** D: D. W. Griffith. Lillian Gish, Richard Barthelmess, Lowell Sherman, Burr McItosh, Kate Bruce, Mary Hay, Creighton Hale. The ultimate stage melodrama—with a city slicker despoiling the innocence of a virginal heroine, who then must pay the price. Executed with conviction by Griffith and a fine cast, building up to famous climax with Gish drifting away on the ice floes. Often shown in shorter versions; restored to 148m. by the Museum of Modern Art in 1985. Remade in 1935.▼●◗

Way Down East (1935) **80m.** *½ D: Henry King. Rochelle Hudson, Henry Fonda, Russell Simpson, Slim Summerville, Spring Byington. Romantic melodrama set in New England was hokey as a 1920 silent; the remake hasn't improved with age. Ridiculous script conquers all.

Way Down South (1939) **61m.** **½ D: Bernard Vorhaus. Bobby Breen, Alan Mowbray, Clarence Muse, Ralph Morgan, Edwin Maxwell, Steffi Duna, Sally Blane, Charles Middleton, Hall Johnson Choir. Hokey but fascinating musical curio (written by Muse and Langston Hughes!), set in the pre-Civil War South. Boy soprano Breen is the young master of a plantation, whose "happy" slaves are scheduled for sale by crooked lawyer Maxwell.▼

Way for a Sailor (1930) **83m.** ** D: Sam Wood. John Gilbert, Wallace Beery, Leila Hyams, Jim Tully, Polly Moran. Early talkie with silent-star Gilbert as devoted sailor who loses girl for the sea. Mostly a curio for early-talkie film buffs.

Wayne's World (1992) **C-95m.** ** D: Penelope Spheeris. Mike Myers, Dana Carvey, Rob Lowe, Tia Carrere, Brian Doyle-Murray, Lara Flynn Boyle, Kurt Fuller, Colleen Camp, Donna Dixon, Meat Loaf, Ed O'Neill. Hit movie based on silly skit from TV's *Saturday Night Live.* Myers and Carvey are funny as the self-styled party dudes with their own cable TV show, and leading lady Carrere is certainly a "babe," but the story has too many slow spots and muffed jokes. Even casting Lowe as a slimeball doesn't pay off—because he's still so dull. Our advice: party elsewhere. Followed by a sequel. Super 35. [PG-13] ▼●

Wayne's World 2 (1993) **C-94m.** ** D: Stephen Surjik. Mike Myers, Dana Carvey, Tia Carrere, Christopher Walken, Kim Basinger, Ralph Brown, Ed O'Neill, Harry Shearer, James Hong, Drew Barrymore, Chris Farley. The Party Boys return with Wayne organizing a Waynestock music festival, and Garth being seduced by Honey Hornée (Basinger, in a tailor-made role she plays to the hilt). Tired gags from first film run throughout, but occasional bits and cameos (especially from "the better actor") make it worthy. [PG-13]▼●

Way of a Gaucho (1952) **C-91m.** ** D: Jacques Tourneur. Gene Tierney, Rory Calhoun, Richard Boone, Hugh Marlowe, Everett Sloane. Soaper set in 1870's Argentina of Tierney and Calhoun trying to make a go of life on the Pampas.

Way of All Flesh, The (1940) **86m.** ** D: Louis King. Akim Tamiroff, Gladys George,

William Henry, Muriel Angelus, Berton Churchill, Roger Imhof. Overly sentimental tale of poor immigrant who is ''taken'' and must pay for his error; George is superlative as always. Remake of Emil Jannings 1927 silent film.

Way of the Dragon SEE: **Return of the Dragon**

Way of Youth, The (1959-French) **81m.** ** D: Michel Boisrond. Francoise Arnoul, Lino Ventura, Bourvil, Alain Delon. Obvious sensuality fails to arouse sufficient interest in contrived story of adultery and ill-gotten gains.

Way Out, The (1955-British) **90m.** BOMB D: Montgomery Tully. Gene Nelson, Mona Freeman, John Bentley, Michael Goodliffe, Sydney Tafler. Lumbering, sloppily made melodrama in which devoted wife Freeman comes to the aid of duplicitous husband Nelson, who has committed murder while in an alcoholic haze.▼

Way Out West (1937) **65m.** ***½ D: James W. Horne. Stan Laurel, Oliver Hardy, Sharon Lynn, James Finlayson, Rosina Lawrence, Stanley Fields, Vivien Oakland. Stan and Ollie are sent to deliver mine deed to daughter of late prospector, but crooked Finlayson leads them to wrong girl. One of their best features; moves well without resorting to needless romantic subplot. Another bonus: some charming musical interludes, and the boys perform a wonderful soft-shoe dance. Also shown in computer-colored version.▼●

Way to Love, The (1933) **80m.** *** D: Norman Taurog. Maurice Chevalier, Ann Dvorak, Edward Everett Horton, Minna Gombell, Nydia Westman, Douglass Dumbrille, John Miljan, Grace Bradley, Sidney Toler. Chevalier falls in love with Dvorak, who works on the wrong end of a knife throwing act, in this pleasant romantic comedy with music; songs include title tune, ''I'm A Lover of Paris.''

Way to the Gold, The (1957) **94m.** ** D: Robert D. Webb. Jeffrey Hunter, Sheree North, Barry Sullivan, Neville Brand, Walter Brennan. Meandering buried-loot-hunt story. CinemaScope.

Way to the Stars, The (1945-British) **109m.** **** D: Anthony Asquith. John Mills, Michael Redgrave, Douglass Montgomery, Rosamund John, Stanley Holloway, Trevor Howard, Felix Aylmer, Bonar Colleano. Excellent drama about a British airfield and the men stationed there, focusing mainly on personal relationships in wartime. Jean Simmons appears briefly as a singer. Script by Terence Rattigan and Anatole de Grunwald. Originally released in U.S. as JOHNNY IN THE CLOUDS, with a prologue set after the end of WW2.

Wayward Bus, The (1957) **89m.** ** D: Victor Vicas. Joan Collins, Jayne Mansfield, Dan Dailey, Rick Jason. Low-brow version of John Steinbeck novel about interaction of passengers on bus in California. CinemaScope.

Wayward Girl, The (1957) **71m.** *½ D: Lesley Selander. Marcia Henderson, Peter Walker, Whit Bissell, Ray Teal, Barbara Eden. Turgid nonsense about mother and stepdaughter vying for same lover, leading to murder. Filmed in widescreen Naturama.

Wayward Girl, The (1959-Norwegian) **91m.** **½ D: Edith Carlmar. Liv Ullmann, Atle Merton, Rolf Soder, Tore Foss, Nana Stenersen. Moralistic romance tale of young lovers who seek refuge on a deserted farm, becoming involved with the returning owner.

Wayward Wife, The (1955-Italian) **91m.** ** D: Mario Soldati. Gina Lollobrigida, Gabriele Ferzetti, Franco Interlenghi, Renato Baldini. Unimaginative, predictable film of blackmail. Lollobrigida, girl with a past, finds her marriage threatened.

Way ... Way Out (1966) **C-106m.** BOMB D: Gordon Douglas. Jerry Lewis, Connie Stevens, Robert Morley, Dennis Weaver, Howard Morris, Brian Keith, Dick Shawn, Anita Ekberg, James Brolin. One of Jerry's worst. Plot concerns comedian's trip to the moon with sexy astronaut Stevens; hopefully they took the film's negative along. CinemaScope.

Way West, The (1967) **C-122m.** *½ D: Andrew V. McLaglen. Kirk Douglas, Robert Mitchum, Richard Widmark, Lola Albright, Michael Witney, Stubby Kaye, Sally Field, Jack Elam. Despite cast, this version of A. B. Guthrie, Jr.'s epic novel fails completely. McLaglen's lackluster direction partially to blame, but big problem is script, which may hold all-time record for undeveloped sub-plots. Mitchum is good through it all; Sally Field's first feature. Panavision.▼

Way We Were, The (1973) **C-118m.** *** D: Sydney Pollack. Barbra Streisand, Robert Redford, Bradford Dillman, Murray Hamilton, Patrick O'Neal, Viveca Lindfors, Lois Chiles, Allyn Ann McLerie, Herb Edelman, James Woods, Connie Forslund, Sally Kirkland, George Gaynes, Susie Blakely, Dan Seymour. First-class love story about political activist Streisand and her opposite, Waspish Joe College-type Redford, from late 30s to early 50s. Prerelease cutting excised meatiest sequence on blacklist era in Hollywood, alas, leaving Hamilton and Lindfors with bit parts, and some confusion in last portion of plot. Still quite good, with literate Arthur Laurents script from his own novel. Marvin Hamlisch's score and title song (lyrics by Alan and Marilyn Bergman) won Oscars—and look sharp at Beverly Hills movie screening for a Hamlisch cameo. Panavision. [PG]▼●◗

W. C. Fields and Me (1976) **C-111m.** *** D: Arthur Hiller. Rod Steiger, Valerie

Perrine, John Marley, Jack Cassidy, Paul Stewart, Bernadette Peters, Billy Barty. Story of comedian's romance with Carlotta Monti is a cut above most Hollywood bios, thanks to Steiger's excellent performance, authentic atmosphere, good cast. Has little relation to the truth, but still entertaining. [PG]

Weak and the Wicked, The (1953-British) **81m.** **½ D: J. Lee Thompson. Glynis Johns, John Gregson, Diana Dors, Jane Hylton. Frank study of women's prison life, focusing on their rehabilitation.

Weaker Sex, The (1948-British) **89m.** ** D: Roy (Ward) Baker. Ursula Jeans, Cecil Parker, Joan Hopkins, Derek Bond, Thora Hird, Bill Owen. Jeans is staunch English housewife showing her patriotic zest during WW2; modest domestic comedy.

We All Loved Each Other So Much (1974-Italian) **C-124m.** ***½ D: Ettore Scola. Nino Manfredi, Vittorio Gassman, Aldo Fabrizi, Stefania Sandrelli, Stefano Satta Flores, Giovanna Ralli. Spirited, wistful comedy of three friends (Gassman, Manfredi, Satta Flores) who each love Sandrelli over the course of three decades. The latter, an actress, plays a bit role in LA DOLCE VITA; the shooting of Anita Ekberg's Trevi Fountain scene is recreated, complete with Mastroianni and Fellini! A loving homage to Fellini, De Sica, and post-war Italian cinema.▼●

Weapon, The (1956-British) **81m.** **½ D: Val Guest. Steve Cochran, Lizabeth Scott, George Cole, Herbert Marshall, Nicole Maurey, Jon Whiteley. Minor but trim story of youngster who accidentally shoots his pal and runs away. SuperScope 235.

Weapons of Mass Distraction (1997) **C-105m. TVM** D: Steve Surjik. Gabriel Byrne, Ben Kingsley, Mimi Rogers, Jeffrey Tambor, Illeana Douglas, Paul Mazursky, Chris Mulkey, R. Lee Ermey, Caroline Aaron, Jason Lee, Christina Pickles. Larry Gelbart's often profane black satire, loosely based on the no-holds-barred rivalry between media moguls Ted Turner and Rupert Murdoch; here, the competition escalates as they vie for ownership of a football team. Kathy Baker turns up for one telling scene as the outspoken wife of Byrne's Murdoch-like character. Made for cable. Above average. ▼

We Are All Murderers (1952-French) **113m.** *** D: André Cayatte. Marcel Mouloudji, Raymond Pellegrin, Louis Seigner, Antoine Balpetre, Claude Leydu, Georges Poujouly. Powerful, potent anti-capital punishment drama. Mouloudji plays a none-too-bright hood who was praised for killing during WW2, but now is condemned to death for murdering a cop; he, and two other men, await their fates on death row. Released in the U.S. in 1957.

We Are in the Navy Now (1962-British) **C-102m.** ** D: Wendy Toye. Kenneth More, Lloyd Nolan, Joan O'Brien, Mischa Auer. Farcical service comedy without wit or slapstick to see it through. Original title: WE JOINED THE NAVY. CinemaScope.

We Are Not Alone (1939) **112m.** **½ D: Edmund Goulding. Paul Muni, Jane Bryan, Flora Robson, Raymond Severn, Una O'Connor, Henry Daniell, Montagu Love, Cecil Kellaway, Alan Napier. Gentle English country doctor, with a hardened, shrewish wife and an adoring son, innocently takes in a troubled young woman as governess, leading to unforeseen conflicts and crises. Muni is a pleasure to watch, as always, and Bryan is surprisingly effective as the Austrian governess with whom he falls in love, but the story is too pat. More interesting as a cautionary parable for a world on the brink of war, which is what author James Hilton intended; he also co-wrote the script.

Weavers, The: Wasn't That a Time! (1982) **C-78m.** **** D: Jim Brown. Lee Hays, Pete Seeger, Fred Hellerman, Ronnie Gilbert. Simply wonderful documentary about a reunion of the much-loved folk-singing quartet of the 1940s and 50s, climaxed by footage of their Carnegie Hall concert. Irresistible film built on the foundation of Lee Hays' wit and indomitable spirit.▼●

Web, The (1947) **87m.** *** D: Michael Gordon. Ella Raines, Edmond O'Brien, William Bendix, Vincent Price, Maria Palmer. Tough bodyguard engages in murder, then finds himself a patsy for boss' schemes. Exciting melodrama, one of O'Brien's best early roles.

Web of Evidence (1959-British) **88m.** **½ D: Jack Cardiff. Van Johnson, Vera Miles, Emlyn Williams, Bernard Lee, Jean Kent, Ralph Truman, Leo McKern. Sincere drama of Johnson in England finding clues to prove his father innocent of long-standing murder sentence. Original British title: BEYOND THIS PLACE.

Web of Fear (1963-French) **92m.** **½ D: Francois Villiers. Michele Morgan, Dany Saval, Claude Rich, George Rigaud. Morgan is music teacher set up as patsy by Saval and Rich in this moody drama of passion and murder.

Web of Passion (1959-French) **C-101m.** **½ D: Claude Chabrol. Madeleine Robinson, Antonella Lualdi, Jean-Paul Belmondo, Jacques Dacqmine. Non-conformist Belmondo insinuates himself into a family's graces, delighting in breaking down their standards, with murders resulting. Talky but intriguing drama. Retitled: LEDA.

Web of the Spider (1970-Italian) **C-94m.** ** D: Anthony Dawson (Antonio Margheriti). Anthony Franciosa, Michele Mercier, Peter Carsten, Karen Field, Silvano Tranquilli. Overly familiar thriller about the skeptic who accepts a wager that he cannot survive the night alone in a haunted house. Franciosa and associates try vainly to give it a fresh twist. Previously made by the same director as CASTLE OF TERROR. Techniscope.▼

Wedding, A (1978) **C-125m.** ★★½ D: Robert Altman. Carol Burnett, Desi Arnaz, Jr., Amy Stryker, Vittorio Gassman, Geraldine Chaplin, Mia Farrow, Paul Dooley, Lillian Gish, Lauren Hutton, John Cromwell, Pat McCormick, Howard Duff, Pam Dawber, Dennis Christopher, Peggy Ann Garner, Nina Van Pallandt, Dina Merrill, John Considine, Viveca Lindfors, Dennis Franz. Unfocused look at family intrigues surrounding a nouveau riche wedding; some amusing moments and pointed characterizations, but doesn't quite gel. Panavision. [PG]▼

Wedding, The (1998) **C-200m.** TVM D: Charles Burnett. Halle Berry, Eric Thal, Lynn Whitfield, Carl Lumbly, Michael Warren, Marianne Jean-Baptiste, Charlayne Woodard, Shirley Knight. Under Oprah Winfrey's imprimatur, this is a sensitive, multilayered adaptation (by Lisa Jones) of the expansive novel by Dorothy West, one of the last surviving members of the fabled Harlem Renaissance. Set among the upper-class black community of Martha's Vineyard in the mid 1950s, moving back and forth in time, it follows the romantic travails of a beautiful light-skinned black woman (Berry) who is torn between her white fiancé and a divorced black man below her station who comes into her life. Originally shown in two parts. Above average.

Wedding Banquet, The (1993-U.S.-Taiwanese) **C-111m.** ★★★ D: Ang Lee. Winston Chao, May Chin, Mitchell Lichtenstein, Sihung Lung, Ah-Leh Gua, Tien Pien. Gay Taiwanese-American Chao tries to fool his parents via a fake wedding, with unexpected complications. Top-notch comedy which knowingly and poignantly examines the meaning of cultural identity and child-parent relationships. Neatly scripted by Lee, Neil Peng, and James Schamus. [R]▼●

Wedding Bell Blues (1996) **C-100m.** ★★½ D: Dana Lustig. Illeana Douglas, Paulina Porizkova, Julie Warner, John Corbett, Jonathan Penner, Charles Martin Smith, Richard Edson, Joe Urla, Stephanie Beacham, Carla Gugino, Leo Rossi, John Capodice, Victoria Jackson, Debbie Reynolds. A trio of roommates, each about to turn 30 and feeling pressure to marry, splits for Las Vegas to find quickie husbands. Attractive cast helps maintain interest in this somewhat familiar "where-are-all-the-good-men?" saga. [R]▼●

Wedding Gift, The (1993-British) **C-87m.** ★★★ D: Richard Loncraine. Julie Walters, Jim Broadbent, Thora Hird, Sian Thomas, Andrew Lancel, Anastasia Mulroney, Joanna McCallum. Spirited spin on "disease-of-the-week" stories, with marvelous performances by Walters and Broadbent as a loving couple whose sense of humor helps them deal with her mysterious and debilitating ailment. Based on the true story of a woman who decided to find her husband a new mate before she died. Alternately humorous and heart-rending; well worth a look. Based on the memoir by Denis Longden. Made for British TV, where it was shown as WIDE-EYED AND LEGLESS. [PG-13]▼●

Wedding in Blood (1973-French-Italian) **C-98m.** ★★½ D: Claude Chabrol. Stephane Audran, Michel Piccoli, Claude Pieplu, Clothilde Joano, Eliana de Santis. Piccoli and Audran, each married to another, are having an affair. How soon will they murder their spouses? And get caught? Medium Chabrol. [PG]▼

Wedding in White (1972-Canadian) **C-106m.** ★★★ D: William Fruet. Donald Pleasence, Carol Kane, Doris Petrie, Doug McGrath, Leo Phillips. Fine performances in sad tale of girl impregnated by brother's drunken pal during WW2 and her father's efforts to save the family's honor. Panavision. [R]▼

Wedding March, The (1928) **113m.** ★★★★ D: Erich von Stroheim. Erich von Stroheim, Fay Wray, ZaSu Pitts, George Fawcett, Maude George, George Nicholls, Cesare Gravina. A roguish Viennese prince (played to perfection by von Stroheim) agrees to marry for money and position to help his family, then falls in love with a poor but beautiful girl. A masterpiece, blending romance and irony, with an unforgettable finale . . . though what we see is just the first half of the film von Stroheim completed (the second no longer exists). One sequence in two-color Technicolor. ▼

Wedding Night, The (1935) **84m.** ★★½ D: King Vidor. Gary Cooper, Anna Sten, Ralph Bellamy, Walter Brennan, Helen Vinson, Sig Ruman. Study of romance and idealism; unbelievable love yarn but entertaining. Producer Samuel Goldwyn's third and final attempt to make Anna Sten a new Garbo.▼

Wedding Party, The (1969) **92m.** ★½ D: Cynthia Munroe, Brian De Palma, Wilford Leach. Jill Clayburgh, Charles Pfluger, Valda Satterfield, Raymond McNally, Jennifer Salt, John Braswell, Judy Thomas, Robert De Niro, William Finley. Talky, corny, boring comic oddity detailing events preceding marriage of Clayburgh and Pfluger; the bride and her family are boorish, and the groom grows ever more reluctant. Self-consciously directed; of interest only for De Palma's participation, and initial screen appearances of Clayburgh and De Niro (spelled "DeNero" in the credits). Shot in 1963, and barely released.▼

Weddings and Babies (1958) **77m.** ★★½ D: Morris Engel. Viveca Lindfors, John Myhers, Chiarina Barile, Leonard Elliott, Joanna Merlin. Thoughtful observance of human behavior and emotions from always-interesting filmmaker Engel. Photographer who earns his living filming weddings and babies has vague dreams of making "real" movies; his assistant and girlfriend is anxious to have a wedding and babies of her own. ▼

Wedding Singer, The (1998) **C-96m.** *** D: Frank Coraci. Adam Sandler, Drew Barrymore, Angela Featherstone, Allen Covert, Matthew Glave, Christine Taylor, Kevin Nealon, Christina Pickles, Billy Idol. Sandler plays a genuinely sweet guy whose life is shattered when his fiancée stands him up at the altar—but finds consolation in the friendship of a waitress who he discovers is about to marry a real jerk. Sandler has never been more appealing, or Barrymore more adorable. Entertaining romantic comedy set in 1985 marred only by moments of crude dialogue that don't seem absolutely necessary. Steve Buscemi and Jon Lovitz appear unbilled. [PG-13] ▼●◗

We Dive at Dawn (1943-British) **98m.** *** D: Anthony Asquith. John Mills, Eric Portman, Niall MacGinnis, Reginald Purdell, Louis Bradfield, Ronald Millar. First-rate WW2 submarine saga, concentrating on personalities of men in the crew as much as on assignment to sink German battleship. Nicely understated drama. ▼

Wednesday's Child SEE: **Family Life**

Weeds (1987) **C-115m.** **½ D: John Hancock. Nick Nolte, Rita Taggart, Lane Smith, William Forsythe, John Toles-Bey, Joe Mantegna, Ernie Hudson, Anne Ramsey, Charlie Rich. San Quentin lifer/aspiring playwright is near-miraculously sprung from prison when a newspaper critic lobbies for his release, and goes on to form a "Barbed Wire Theatre" acting troupe of ex-cons. Odd, original mix of comedy and drama based on Rick Cluchey's real-life experiences with the San Quentin Drama Group. Earnest and well acted but never quite gels. [R] ▼●

Wee Geordie (1956-British) **C-93m.** ***½ D: Frank Launder. Bill Travers, Alastair Sim, Norah Gorsen, Molly Urquhart, Francis De Wolff. Flavorful romp with Travers a Scottish hammer thrower who goes to the Olympics. Despite predictable sight gags and romance, film makes one relish each situation.

Weekend (1967-French-Italian) **C-103m.** ***½ D: Jean-Luc Godard. Mireille Darc, Jean Yanne, Jean-Pierre Kalfon, Valerie Lagrange, Jean-Pierre Léaud. Mind-expanding anti-Western diatribe about one woman's road to guerrillahood is among Godard's more fully realized works, with a long traffic-jam sequence that is justifiably regarded as one of the great set pieces in screen history. An essential 60s time-capsule entry. ▼

Weekend at Bernie's (1989) **C-97m.** **½ D: Ted Kotcheff. Andrew McCarthy, Jonathan Silverman, Catherine Mary Stewart, Terry Kiser, Don Calfa, Louis Giambalvo. Two young hustlers, far down on the corporate ladder, win an invitation to their boss' sumptuous beach house for the weekend . . . only to find him dead upon arrival. Slim but agreeably silly farce, written by Robert Klane. Followed by a sequel. [PG-13] ▼●◗

Weekend at Bernie's II (1993) **C-89m.** BOMB D: Robert Klane. Andrew McCarthy, Jonathan Silverman, Terry Kiser, Barry Bostwick, Troy Beyer, Tom Wright, Steve James. Witless sequel to a movie that didn't exactly cry out for a followup. Insurance execs McCarthy and Silverman are suspected of embezzlement, and can only save their skins with the help of their "dead body" buddy Bernie (Kiser). After this debacle, let's hope Bernie is allowed to rest in peace. [PG] ▼●

Weekend at Dunkirk (1965-France-Italy) **C-101m.** ** D: Henri Verneuil. Jean-Paul Belmondo, Catherine Spaak, Georges Geret, Jean-Pierre Marielle, Pierre Mondy. Dull war film, based on well-known French novel, about four French soldiers on the Dunkirk Beach around evacuation time early in WW2. Franscope.

Week-end at the Waldorf (1945) **130m.** *** D: Robert Z. Leonard. Ginger Rogers, Lana Turner, Walter Pidgeon, Van Johnson, Edward Arnold, Phyllis Thaxter, Keenan Wynn, Robert Benchley, Leon Ames, Porter Hall, George Zucco, Xavier Cugat. Several "typical" days in the life of the fabled Waldorf-Astoria Hotel. Ultra-glossy MGM remake of GRAND HOTEL weaves disparate characters' lives together. No resonance whatsoever, but good, slick entertainment, with Rogers and Pidgeon standing out in the attractive cast. ▼

Weekend for Three (1941) **61m.** ** D: Tay Garnett. Dennis O'Keefe, Jane Wyatt, Philip Reed, ZaSu Pitts, Edward Everett Horton, Franklin Pangborn, Hans Conried. Hapless O'Keefe and manipulative wife Wyatt entertain her boorish old friend (Reed), who quickly proves to be the houseguest from hell. Considering cast, and writers (Dorothy Parker and Alan Campbell, from a Budd Schulberg story), it's astonishing this isn't better than it is.

Week-end in Havana (1941) **C-80m.** *** D: Walter Lang. Alice Faye, Carmen Miranda, John Payne, Cesar Romero, Cobina Wright, Jr., George Barbier, Leonid Kinskey, Sheldon Leonard, Billy Gilbert. Typically entertaining, Technicolored 20th Century-Fox musical fluff with Payne showing Faye a good time in Havana for business purposes only, but falling in love with her instead. Miranda adds her usual zest. ▼

Week-end Marriage (1932) **66m.** ** D:

Thornton Freeland. Loretta Young, Norman Foster, Aline MacMahon, George Brent, Vivienne Osborne, Roscoe Karns. Comedy courtship leads to drama of money-hungry husband after marriage; nothing special.

Weekend Pass (1984) **C-92m.** BOMB D: Lawrence Bassoff. Patrick Hauser, D. W. Brown, Chip McAllister, Peter Ellenstein, Hilary Shapiro, Pamela G. Kay. Intolerable drive-in comedy lifts its premise from ON THE TOWN: having completed basic training, four stereotypical naval recruits set off for 72 "wild" hours in L.A. 92 minutes of mine sweeping would be more entertaining. [R]▼●

Weekend Warriors (1986) **C-85m.** *½ D: Bert Convy. Chris Lemmon, Vic Tayback, Lloyd Bridges, Graham Jarvis, Daniel Greene, Marty Cohen, Brian Bradley. Low-level, sloppily made comedy about some goof-offs who join the National Guard, and their subsequent hijinks. Convy's debut as director. [R]▼

Weekend With Father (1951) **83m.** **½ D: Douglas Sirk. Van Heflin, Patricia Neal, Virginia Field, Gigi Perreau, Richard Denning. Pleasant frou-frou of widow and widower courting despite their children's interference.

Week's Vacation, A (1980-French) **C-102m.** *** D: Bertrand Tavernier. Nathalie Baye, Gerard Lanvin, Michel Galabru, Philippe Noiret, Philippe Leotard. Subtle drama of schoolteacher Baye briefly escaping her problems by visiting her parents in Lyons. Sensitive depiction of inter-personal relations is director Tavernier's strong suit. Colorful widescreen Panavision photography will suffer on TV. [R]

Wee Willie Winkie (1937) **99m.** *** D: John Ford. Shirley Temple, Victor McLaglen, C. Aubrey Smith, June Lang, Michael Whalen, Cesar Romero, Constance Collier, Douglas Scott. Shirley and her widowed mother come to live at a British Army outpost in India, where the moppet works hard to win over her crusty grandfather, the Colonel (Smith), and is quickly adopted by a soft-hearted sergeant (McLaglen). One of Shirley's best vehicles, "inspired" (it says here) by the Rudyard Kipling story. Beware 77m. prints. Also shown in computer-colored version.▼

Weird Science (1985) **C-94m.** *½ D: John Hughes. Anthony Michael Hall, Kelly LeBrock, Ilan Mitchell-Smith, Bill Paxton, Suzanne Snyder, Judie Aronson, Robert Downey (Jr.), Robert Rusler. Two nerdy teens use computer to conjure up woman of their dreams (sexy LeBrock), but writer-director Hughes doesn't follow through on his own premise! Appalling excuse for comedy; tasteless and endless, unredeemed by Hughes's sharp teenage dialogue and Hall's engaging performance. Later a cable TV series. [PG-13]▼●◗

Weird Woman (1944) **64m.** **½ D: Reginald LeBorg. Lon Chaney, Jr., Anne Gwynne, Evelyn Ankers, Ralph Morgan, Lois Collier, Elizabeth Russell, Phil Brown. Chaney's ex-girlfriend objects to his tropic isle bride, connives to get even. Way-out entry in the *Inner Sanctum* series, based on Fritz Leiber's *Conjure Wife*; good fun, with Ankers' nice change-of-pace villainess. Remade as BURN, WITCH, BURN and WITCHES' BREW.▼

We Joined the Navy SEE: **We Are in the Navy Now**

Welcome Home (1989) **C-96m.** ** D: Franklin J. Schaffner. Kris Kristofferson, JoBeth Williams, Sam Waterston, Brian Keith, Thomas Wilson Brown, Trey Wilson. Please, not again. Presumed dead Air Force officer Kristofferson, 17 years in Cambodia with a new wife and two children, returns home to remarried spouse number one and their teenage son. Tolerably sincere at best, embalmed at worst. Director Schaffner's final film. [R]▼

Welcome Home, Roxy Carmichael (1990) **C-98m.** *½ D: Jim Abrahams. Winona Ryder, Jeff Daniels, Laila Robins, Dinah Manoff, Thomas Wilson Brown, Joan McMurtrey, Frances Fisher, Graham Beckel, Robin Thomas, Robby Kiger, Sachi Parker, Stephen Tobolowsky. Small Ohio town goes berserk anticipating return of sexy and mysterious hometown girl Roxy Carmichael, who's been away in Hollywood living a life of luxury. Teenage beatnik Ryder—moody, brilliant, alienated, intuitive, and adopted—starts fantasizing that Roxy is actually her mother. Flat, disjointed satiric comedy with Ryder the sole bright spot. [PG-13]▼●

Welcome Home, Soldier Boys (1972) **C-91m.** ** D: Richard Compton. Joe Don Baker, Paul Koslo, Alan Vint, Elliott Street, Jennifer Billingsley, Billy "Green" Bush, Geoffrey Lewis, Francine York. Sensationalistic melodrama about four ex-Green Berets who adjust to civilian life by gang-raping a girl and burning down a town. Yet another one-dimensionally violent depiction of Vietnam veterans. [R]

Welcome in Vienna (1986-Austrian) **126m.** *** D: Axel Corti. Gabriel Barylli. Nicolas Brieger, Claudia Messner, Hubert Mann, Liliana Nelska. Intriguing, uncompromising account of Austrian Jew Barylli and German intellectual Brieger, who've fled to America, and return to their homeland as U.S. soldiers during the final months of WW2. A thought-provoking look at the Austrian people's less than honorable response to Nazi aggression. The conclusion of Corti's "Where To and Back" trilogy, preceded by GOD DOESN'T BELIEVE IN US ANYMORE and SANTA FE.

Welcome Stranger (1947) **107m.** *** D: Elliott Nugent. Bing Crosby, Barry Fitzgerald, Joan Caulfield, Wanda Hendrix, Frank Faylen, Elizabeth Patterson. Entertaining musical of Crosby filling in for vacationing doctor in small community, getting involved with local girl and lovely little town. ▼

Welcome to Arrow Beach (1974) **C-99m.** ** D: Laurence Harvey. Laurence Harvey, Joanna Pettet, Stuart Whitman, John Ireland, Meg Foster, Jesse Vint, Gloria LeRoy. Harvey's final film (edited by phone from his deathbed) is strange but watchable shocker. He plays a war veteran who returns to California and kills passersby to feed his newly acquired taste for human flesh (though shortened TV prints seriously alter the story). Good cast helps, especially spellbinding Foster in an early role. Retitled: TENDER FLESH. [R]▼

Welcome to 18 (1987) **C-89m.** ** D: Terry Carr. Courtney Thorne-Smith, Mariska Hargitay, Jo Ann Willette, Cristen Kaufman, John Putch. Tired teen titillation yarn about three girlfriends who spend their first summer out of high school experiencing life in the fast lane in Nevada. Attractive newcomers (including brunette Hargitay, daughter of Jayne Mansfield) muddle through preachy, plot-heavy nonsense. [PG-13]▼

Welcome to Hard Times (1967) **C-105m.** *** D: Burt Kennedy. Henry Fonda, Janice Rule, Keenan Wynn, Janis Paige, John Anderson, Aldo Ray, Warren Oates, Fay Spain, Edgar Buchanan, Lon Chaney, Jr., Elisha Cook, Jr. Intriguing, symbol-laden account of run-down Western town victimized by outlaw Ray, with Fonda finally forced to shoot it out to save what's left. Adapted by Kennedy from E. L. Doctorow novel.

Welcome to L.A. (1977) **C-106m.** **½ D: Alan Rudolph. Keith Carradine, Sally Kellerman, Geraldine Chaplin, Harvey Keitel, Lauren Hutton, Viveca Lindfors, Sissy Spacek, Denver Pyle, John Considine, Richard Baskin. This chronicle of lost, lonely Southern Californians who can only connect for fleeting moments between the sheets is occasionally intriguing, but pales beside some of Rudolph's later, better work. A major debit: Baskin's music, which quickly becomes monotonous. Produced by Robert Altman. [R]▼

Welcome to Sarajevo (1997-British-U.S.) **C-101m.** *** D: Michael Winterbottom. Stephen Dillane, Woody Harrelson, Marisa Tomei, Emira Nusevic, Kerry Fox, Goran Visnjic, Emily Lloyd. Achingly realistic, unsentimental look at reporters covering the Bosnian war in Sarajevo. One British TV reporter becomes especially outraged by the plight of orphaned children and finds his casual promise to a young girl—that he will lead her to safety—being put to the test. Based on a true story, and told with a compelling blend of genuine and staged footage. Difficult to watch at times, but rewarding. Super 35. [R]▼●

Welcome to the Club (1971) **C-88m.** ** D: Walter Shenson. The Warblers, Jack Warden, Brian Foley, Lee Meredith, Andy Jarell. Navy morale officer tries to find quarters for USO entertainers in Japan. Forgettable comedy. [R]

Welcome to the Dollhouse (1996) **C-87m.** ***½ D: Todd Solondz. Heather Matarazzo, Brendan Sexton, Jr., Daria Kalinina, Matthew Faber, Angela Pietropinto, Eric Mabius. The pain of puberty has never been portrayed so unflinchingly; smart-but-ordinary Matarazzo has to deal with her incredibly un-nurturing suburban family (which dotes on her "adorable" younger sister), and worse, the pranks and sexual threats of virtually her entire junior high school. Amid this dire lack of support and warmth is a heroine of enormous pluck and cunning. While viewer may wince as numerous unpleasant situations play out, there is also terrific satire (and guffaws) as life in the Seventh-Grade-From-Hell is depicted with dead-on clarity. Strong performances; sharply scripted by the director. [R]▼●◗

Welcome to Woop Woop (1997-Australian-British) **C-96m.** **½ D: Stephan Elliott. Johnathon Schaech, Rod Taylor, Susie Porter, Dee Smart, Barry Humphries, Richard Moir, Paul Mercurio, Rachel Griffiths, Maggie Kirkpatrick, Tina Louise. American con artist (Schaech) flees to the Outback, where he meets a man-hungry hitchhiker who drags him off to the very remote municipality of Woop Woop. Native Australian Taylor is outrageous as Schaech's dictatorial, unbalanced, Rodgers & Hammerstein–loving father-in-law. Raucous, raunchy farce from the director of THE ADVENTURES OF PRISCILLA, QUEEN OF THE DESERT. 2.35 Research PLC. [R]▼

We Live Again (1934) **82m.** ** D: Rouben Mamoulian. Fredric March, Anna Sten, Sam Jaffe, C. Aubrey Smith, Jane Baxter, Ethel Griffies. Cumbersome costumer with March a Russian nobleman in love with peasant girl Sten. Based on Leo Tolstoy's *Resurrection,* filmed several times before; Preston Sturges and Maxwell Anderson were among the writers.

Well, The (1951) **85m.** *** D: Leo Popkin, Russell Rouse. Richard Rober, Henry (Harry) Morgan, Barry Kelley, Christine Larson, Maidie Norman, Ernest Anderson. Incisive study of crowd psychology, focusing on effects on townfolk when black child becomes lodged in deep well. Fine score by Dimitri Tiomkin.▼

Well-Digger's Daughter, The (1941-French) **142m.** ***½ D: Marcel Pagnol. Raimu, Fernandel, Josette Day, Charpin, George Grey. Naive Day is seduced and abandoned—with child—and peasant father Raimu isn't very pleased. Both touching and hilarious.▼

Well-Groomed Bride, The (1946) **75m.** ** D: Sidney Lanfield. Olivia de Havilland, Ray Milland, Sonny Tufts, James Gleason, Percy Kilbride. Fine cast suffers with ridiculous comedy of stubborn girl insisting on champagne for her wedding.

Wells Fargo (1937) **94m.** *** D: Frank Lloyd. Joel McCrea, Frances Dee, Bob Burns, Lloyd Nolan, Ralph Morgan, Johnny Mack Brown, Porter Hall, Robert Cummings, Harry Davenport. McCrea, struggling to build famous express service, loses love of his wife (Dee) in process. Large-scale Western is long, but filled with action. Originally released at 115m.

We of the Never Never (1983-Australian) **C-132m.** *** D: Igor Auzins. Angela Punch McGregor, Arthur Dignam, Tony Barry, Tommy Lewis, Lewis Fitz-Gerald. True story based on memoirs of first white woman to travel into Australian wilderness known as the Never Never is visually stunning but never develops narrative momentum or dramatic punch. Still, it's a pleasure to look at. Technovision. [G]▼

We're Back: A Dinosaur's Story (1993) **C-72m.** **½ D: Dick Zondag, Ralph Zondag, Phil Nibbelink, Simon Wells. Voices of John Goodman, Charles Fleischer, Felicity Kendal, Rhea Perlman, Martin Short, Walter Cronkite, Julia Child, Kenneth Mars, Jay Leno. Amiable children's animated feature about a quartet of dinosaurs given the opportunity to visit modern-day N.Y.C., where they help two troubled kids—but fall prey to a devilish circus proprietor. Mostly fun, though slow at times, and the freakshow subplot is a bit eerie for younger kids. Executive-produced by Steven Spielberg, the same year he made another well-known film about dinosaurs. [G]▼●

We're Going to Be Rich (1938-British) **78m.** **½ D: Monty Banks. Gracie Fields, Victor McLaglen, Brian Donlevy, Coral Browne, Ted Smith, Gus McNaughton. Entertainer Fields finds herself in the midst of an African oil boom in this OK story with musical numbers; Donlevy and McLaglen in contrived rivalry supply much of the plot.

We're No Angels (1955) **C-106m.** **½ D: Michael Curtiz. Humphrey Bogart, Aldo Ray, Peter Ustinov, Joan Bennett, Basil Rathbone, Leo G. Carroll. Mild entertainment as three escapees from Devil's Island find refuge with French family and extricate them from various predicaments. Remade in 1989. VistaVision.▼●

We're No Angels (1989) **C-106m.** *½ D: Neil Jordan. Robert De Niro, Sean Penn, Demi Moore, Hoyt Axton, Bruno Kirby, Ray McAnally, James Russo, Wallace Shawn, John C. Reilly. Lumbering comedy about a couple of dimwitted convicts who inadvertently escape from prison and find refuge pretending to be priests visiting a nearby shrine. De Niro, who also served as executive producer, mugs as never before, playing Leo Gorcey to Penn's Huntz Hall. Handsome production design is no compensation for a lugubrious script by David Mamet, "suggested by" the play that was filmed before in 1955. Panavision. [PG-13]▼●

We're Not Dressing (1934) **77m.** *** D: Norman Taurog. Bing Crosby, Carole Lombard, George Burns, Gracie Allen, Ethel Merman, Leon Errol, Ray Milland. Musical *Admirable Crichton* with rich-girl Lombard falling in love with sailor Crosby when entourage is ship-wrecked on desert isle. Merman is man-chasing second fiddle, with Burns and Allen on tap as local expeditionists. Great fun; Bing sings "Love Thy Neighbor."▼●

We're Not Married! (1952) **85m.** *** D: Edmund Goulding. Ginger Rogers, Fred Allen, Victor Moore, Marilyn Monroe, Paul Douglas, David Wayne, Eve Arden, Louis Calhern, Zsa Zsa Gabor, James Gleason, Jane Darwell, Eddie Bracken, Mitzi Gaynor. Fine froth served up in several episodes as five married couples discover their weddings weren't legal. Segments vary in quality but the top-notch cast generally delivers the goods. Written and produced by Nunnally Johnson. Lee Marvin has a bit.▼

We're Rich Again (1934) **71m.** ** D: William A. Seiter. Edna May Oliver, Billie Burke, Marian Nixon, Reginald Denny, Joan Marsh, Larry "Buster" Crabbe, Grant Mitchell, Gloria Shea, Edgar Kennedy. Screwball farce with rich Denny about to marry into Marsh's once-wealthy family, having to put up with usual assortment of eccentric relatives, including polo-playing grandma Oliver (who steals the film). Amiable cast defeated by hopelessly silly story.

Werewolf, The (1956) **83m.** **½ D: Fred F. Sears. Steven Ritch, Don Megowan, Joyce Holden, Eleanore Tanin, Harry Lauter. A stranger in a mountain town is revealed to be a werewolf, created by unscrupulous scientists seeking a cure for radiation poisoning. Surprisingly tense, with attractive use of Big Bear Lake locations, and a good performance by Ritch.

Werewolf in a Girl's Dormitory (1961-Italian-Austrian) **84m.** BOMB D: Richard Benson (Paolo Heusch). Carl Schell, Barbara Lass, Curt Lowens, Maurice Marsac. Superintendent at school for problem girls doubles as a werewolf. Strictly bottom-of-the-barrel.▼

Werewolf of London (1935) **75m.** **½ D: Stuart Walker. Henry Hull, Warner Oland, Valerie Hobson, Lester Matthews, Spring Byington. The first film about werewolves is dated but still effective. Scientist Hull stumbles onto curse of lycanthropy and terrorizes London as a mad killer. Oland is fun as mysterious man who warns Hull of impending doom.▼●

Werewolf of Washington, The (1973)

C-90m. *½ D: Milton Moses Ginsberg. Dean Stockwell, Biff McGuire, Clifton James, Beeson Carroll, Thayer David, Jane House, Michael Dunn. Juvenile attempt to mix Watergate horrors with the more traditional kind. For the curious only. [PG]▼

Wes Craven's New Nightmare (1994) **C-112m.** *** D: Wes Craven. Robert Englund, Heather Langenkamp, Miko Hughes, David Newsom, Sara Risher, Robert Shaye, Wes Craven, John Saxon, Jeffrey John Davis. Actress Heather Langenkamp, having nightmares about the fictional murderer Freddy Krueger, gradually learns that the NIGHTMARE movies were protecting the world from a monstrous demon, who has taken on the persona of Freddy and is acting out the events in Wes Craven's new NIGHTMARE script as he writes them. And the script doesn't look like it will have a happy ending. . . . Langenkamp, Wes Craven, and others associated with the NIGHTMARE ON ELM STREET series play themselves in this complex, sophisticated thriller. Scary, intelligent, and witty, but it's also too long, and the last twenty minutes are a bit of a letdown. [R]▼●

Westbound (1959) **C-72m.** **½ D: Budd Boetticher. Randolph Scott, Virginia Mayo, Karen Steele, Michael Dante, Andrew Duggan, Michael Pate. Trim sagebrush tale of Yankee officer Scott organizing a stage coach line to bring in gold from California.

West 11 (1963-British) **93m.** *½ D: Michael Winner. Alfred Lynch, Kathleen Breck, Eric Portman, Diana Dors, Kathleen Harrison. Lumbering account of out-of-work Lynch agreeing to murder Portman's aunt, with the crime bringing about a reformation of his character.

Westerner, The (1940) **100m.** ***½ D: William Wyler. Gary Cooper, Walter Brennan, Fred Stone, Doris Davenport, Forrest Tucker, Chill Wills, Dana Andrews, Tom Tyler, Lillian Bond. Excellent tale of land disputes getting out of hand in the old West, with Brennan's mercurial Judge Roy Bean winning him his third Oscar. Tucker's film debut. Also shown in computer-colored version.▼●◗

Western Union (1941) **C-94m.** *** D: Fritz Lang. Robert Young, Randolph Scott, Dean Jagger, Virginia Gilmore, John Carradine, Slim Summerville, Chill Wills, Barton MacLane. Big-scale Western, in gorgeous Technicolor, focuses on renegade attempts to thwart Western Union on the last leg of its westward expansion in the 1860s. Entertaining, if not terribly inspired.▼

We Still Kill the Old Way (1967-Italian) **C-92m.** ** D: Elio Petri. Irene Papas, Gian Maria Volonte, Luigi Pistilli. Crimes of honor in old Sicily purport to show old-world Mafia methods; actually nothing more than a small revenge film.

West of Shanghai (1937) **64m.** ** D: John Farrow. Boris Karloff, Gordon Oliver, Beverly Roberts, Ricardo Cortez, Sheila Bromley, Vladimir Sokoloff, Richard Loo. Cheap programmer of Chinese warlord Karloff holding Cortez and others prisoner in a remote Chinese outpost.

West of Suez SEE: **Fighting Wildcats**

West of Zanzibar (1928) **63m.** *** D: Tod Browning. Lon Chaney, Lionel Barrymore, Mary Nolan, Warner Baxter, Jacqueline Gadsdon. Crippled Chaney rules a jungle monarchy and lives for one thing: revenge on the man who ruined his life. His scheme: to despoil the man's beautiful young daughter (Nolan). Pat ending nearly mars seamy, bizarre story; remade as KONGO. Originally released at 69m.▼●

West of Zanzibar (1954-British) **C-84m.** ** D: Harry Watt. Anthony Steel, Sheila Sim, Edric Connor, Orlando Martins. Ivory hunters meet up with jungle obstacles and native tribes; Steel and Sim share the adventures.▼

West Point of the Air (1935) **100m.** **½ D: Richard Rosson. Wallace Beery, Robert Young, Maureen O'Sullivan, Lewis Stone, James Gleason, Rosalind Russell, Robert Taylor. Master Sergeant Beery pushes reluctant son Young through army air-training for his own satisfaction. Good cast enlivens standard drama.

West Point Story (1950) **107m.** **½ D: Roy Del Ruth. James Cagney, Virginia Mayo, Doris Day, Gordon MacRae, Gene Nelson, Alan Hale, Jr., Jack Kelly, Roland Winters. Silly but watchable musical about a Broadway director staging a revue at West Point. Wait till you hear "The Military Polka." Cagney hoofs in several numbers with Day and Mayo.▼

West Side Story (1961) **C-151m.** **** D: Robert Wise, Jerome Robbins. Natalie Wood, Richard Beymer, George Chakiris, Rita Moreno, Russ Tamblyn, Tucker Smith, David Winters, Tony Mordente, Simon Oakland, John Astin. Vivid film adaptation of the landmark Broadway musical, updating Romeo and Juliet story to youth-gang atmosphere of late 1950s N.Y.C. Wood and Beymer lack charisma, but everything surrounding them is great: Robbins' choreography, Leonard Bernstein-Stephen Sondheim score (including "Maria," "America," and "Something's Coming"). Script by Ernest Lehman, from Arthur Laurents' play. Winner of 10 Academy Awards including Best Picture, Direction, Supporting Actor and Actress (Chakiris, Moreno), Cinematography, Costumes, Art Direction-Set Decoration, Editing, Scoring; Robbins earned a special award for his choreography. Super Panavision 70.▼●◗

West Side Waltz, The (1995) **C-100m. TVM** D: Ernest Thompson. Shirley

MacLaine, Liza Minnelli, Jennifer Grey, Kathy Bates, Ernest Thompson, Robert Pastorelli, Richard Gilliland, Hal Williams. Eclectic comedy-drama about the bonds uniting three disparate women, neighbors on Manhattan's Upper West Side. Director Thompson's adaptation of his 1981 Broadway play, which starred Katharine Hepburn and Dorothy Loudon, puts MacLaine (with a cane) and Minnelli (with a fat suit) in those roles with gray wigs. Admirable ensemble work by the two stars, plus Grey as the other tenant, and Bates as a bag lady make this interesting viewing. Average.

Westward Ho the Wagons! (1956) **C-90m.** ** D: William Beaudine. Fess Parker, Kathleen Crowley, Jeff York, David Stollery, Sebastian Cabot, George Reeves, Juliette Compton, Iron Eyes Cody. Lackluster pioneer saga has Disney polish but no excitement as wagon train travels West. Four Mouseketeers from the *Mickey Mouse Club* appear—Karen Pendleton, Cubby O'Brien, Tommy Cole, and Doreen Tracy. CinemaScope.▼

Westward Passage (1932) **73m.** ** D: Robert Milton. Ann Harding, Laurence Olivier, Irving Pichel, ZaSu Pitts, Juliette Compton, Irene Purcell, Don Alvarado, Florence Lake, Edgar Kennedy, Ethel Griffies. Acting uplifts clichéd tale of girl who divorces to marry for true love, despite sacrifices. Film debut of child actress Bonita Granville.

Westward the Women (1951) **118m.** *** D: William Wellman. Robert Taylor, Denise Darcel, Beverly Dennis, John McIntire, Hope Emerson, Lenore Lonergan, Julie Bishop, Marilyn Erskine. Intriguing Western with Taylor heading wagon train full of females bound for California to meet mail-order husbands. Based on a story by Frank Capra. Also shown in computer-colored version.▼

Westworld (1973) **C-88m.** *** D: Michael Crichton. Richard Benjamin, Yul Brynner, James Brolin, Norman Bartold, Alan Oppenheimer, Victoria Shaw, Steve Franken. Adult vacation resort of the future offers opportunity to live in various fantasy worlds serviced by robots. Benjamin chooses old-time Western town, but begins to fear when the robots begin malfunctioning. Engaging story by Crichton; followed by FUTUREWORLD. Panavision. [PG]▼●◗

Wetbacks (1956) **C-89m.** *½ D: Hank McCune. Lloyd Bridges, Nancy Gates, John Hoyt, Barton MacLane. Tawdry study of smuggling Mexicans across Texas border.

We the Living (1942-Italian) **174m.** *** D: Goffredo Alessandrini. Alida Valli, Rossano Brazzi, Fosco Giachetti, Giovanni Grasso, Emilio Cigoli, Mario Pisu. Still involving, and now rediscovered, romantic drama of young Russian Valli, an anticommunist who becomes involved with party official Giachetti in order to obtain medical treatment for fugitive lover Brazzi. Based on an Ayn Rand novel and banned soon after its release because its scenario is as antiauthoritarian as it is anticommunist. Originally shown as two separate films (titled NOI VIVI and ADDIO KIRA).▼●

Wetherby (1985-British) **C-97m.** **½ D: David Hare. Vanessa Redgrave, Joely Richardson, Judi Dench, Ian Holm, Tim McInnery, Suzanna Hamilton. Uninvited guest shows up for dinner at a Yorkshire schoolteacher's, then returns the next day to blow his brains out. Writer David Hare's first film as director has some excellent performances and occasionally biting dialogue but is far too self-consciously gloomy. Richardson, radiant as the younger Redgrave in the flashbacks, is real-life daughter of Vanessa and director Tony Richardson. [R]▼

We Think the World of You (1988-British) **C-94m.** *** D: Colin Gregg. Alan Bates, Gary Oldman, Frances Barber, Liz Smith, Max Wall, Kerry Wise. In 1950s London, middle-aged Bates becomes entwined in the lives of imprisoned boyfriend Oldman's working-class family, and Oldman's pet dog in particular. Diverting comedy-drama of unrequited love, adapted by Hugh Stoddart from Joseph R. Ackerley's semi-autobiographical novel. A must for animal lovers . . . and romantics. [PG]▼●

Wet Parade, The (1932) **120m.** **½ D: Victor Fleming. Walter Huston, Myrna Loy, Neil Hamilton, Lewis Stone, Dorothy Jordan, Robert Young, Jimmy Durante, Wallace Ford. Extremely long diatribe about the Devil's Brew which manages to be both anti-liquor and anti-Prohibition. First half features Stone as an alcoholic Southern gentleman; second half moves North to focus on Prohibition agents (including Durante, of all people!). Strange but interesting; script by John Lee Mahin, from the Upton Sinclair novel.

We've Never Been Licked (1943) **103m.** ** D: John Rawlins. Richard Quine, Noah Beery, Jr., Robert Mitchum, Anne Gwynne, Martha O'Driscoll. Jingoistic, melodramatic account of American youth brought up in Japan, and his involvement in WW2.

We Were Dancing (1942) **94m.** ** D: Robert Z. Leonard. Norma Shearer, Melvyn Douglas, Gail Patrick, Marjorie Main, Reginald Owen, Connie Gilchrist, Sig Ruman. Hokey adaptation from Noel Coward's *Tonight at 8:30*, about princess running off with another man at her engagement party. Shearer et al. try, but material defeats them. Ava Gardner's first film.

We Were Strangers (1949) **106m.** *** D: John Huston. Jennifer Jones, John Garfield, Pedro Armendariz, Gilbert Roland, Ramon Novarro. Intense, intriguing political drama of Garfield and Jones joining with the Cuban underground in a plot to overthrow the government. Well directed by Huston; Garfield is fine, but Roland steals the film as one of the revolutionaries. Scripted by Huston and Peter Viertel.

We Who Are Young (1940) **79m.** ** D: Harold S. Bucquet. Lana Turner, John Shelton, Gene Lockhart, Grant Mitchell, Henry Armetta, Jonathan Hale, Clarence Wilson. Turner marries Shelton though his company's policy forbids it; aimless comedy-drama.

We Will All Meet in Paradise (1977-French) **C-110m.** **½ D: Yves Robert. Jean Rochefort, Claude Brasseur, Guy Bedos, Victor Lanoux, Daniele Delorme, Daniel Gelin. The trials and hangups of four boyish middle-aged Frenchmen. Cheerful but slight sex comedy; follow-up to PARDON MON AFFAIRE, and not as good. Aka PARDON MON AFFAIRE, TOO. Panavision. [PG]▼

Whales of August, The (1987) **C-90m.** ***½ D: Lindsay Anderson. Bette Davis, Lillian Gish, Vincent Price, Ann Sothern, Harry Carey, Jr., Margaret Ladd, Tisha Sterling, Mary Steenburgen. Two elderly sisters live together in a cottage in Maine, with ever-patient Gish forced to care for blind and irascible Davis . . . who may be turning senile. Sothern is their ebullient friend and neighbor, Carey their veteran handyman, and Price a courtly Russian émigré who works his charms on the ladies; they're all terrific, but Gish and Davis dominate the film, a lifetime of movie memories in each classic face. An exquisitely delicate film, adapted by David Berry from his play, and beautifully directed by Anderson (in his American debut). Tisha Sterling, Sothern's real-life daughter, plays Sothern as a young woman in opening scene. Gish's last film.▼●

What? (1973-Italian) **C-112m.** **½ D: Roman Polanski. Sydne Rome, Marcello Mastroianni, Hugh Griffith, Romolo Valli, Guido Alberti, Roman Polanski. Ribald comedy about gorgeous innocent who stays at mansion of eccentric millionaire and can't understand all the commotion she causes. Change-of-pace for Polanski is agreeable, if not outstanding; good cast—especially underrated Rome—keeps things bubbling. Later cut to 94m. and reissued as DIARY OF FORBIDDEN DREAMS. Todd-AO 35. [R]▼

What About Bob? (1991) **C-99m.** *** D: Frank Oz. Bill Murray, Richard Dreyfuss, Julie Hagerty, Charlie Korsmo, Kathryn Erbe, Tom Aldredge, Susan Willis, Roger Bowen, Fran Brill, Doris Belack. Phobic patient Murray pursues pompous psychiatrist Dreyfuss to his vacation retreat, where he ingratiates himself with the shrink's family—and drives the doctor crazy. Very funny outing, with Murray and Dreyfuss approaching the relationship of the Road Runner and the Coyote. Only at the very end does it succumb to silliness. [PG] ▼●◗

What a Carve Up! SEE: **No Place Like Homicide**

What a Life (1939) **75m.** **½ D: Jay Theodore Reed. Jackie Cooper, Betty Field, John Howard, Janice Logan, Vaughan Glaser, Lionel Stander, Hedda Hopper, James Corner, Dorothy Stickney, Lucien Littlefield, Sidney Miller. The bittersweet trials and tribulations of Henry Aldrich, the world's biggest patsy and the world's worst student. Mildly likable school-days saga. Billy Wilder and Charles Brackett adapted Clifford Goldsmith's Broadway play, which led to the *Henry Aldrich* series.

What a Way to Go! (1964) **C-111m.** *** D: J. Lee Thompson. Shirley MacLaine, Paul Newman, Robert Mitchum, Dean Martin, Gene Kelly, Bob Cummings, Dick Van Dyke, Reginald Gardiner, Margaret Dumont, Fifi D'Orsay. Lavish, episodic black comedy by Betty Comden and Adolph Green stars MacLaine as jinx who marries succession of men, each of whom promptly dies, leaving her even wealthier than before. Series of movie parodies is amusing, and performances are uniformly charming, especially Newman as obsessed painter and Kelly as egotistical film star. Based on a story by Gwen Davis. One of the dancers on boat deck is Teri Garr. CinemaScope.

What a Woman! (1943) **94m.** **½ D: Irving Cummings. Rosalind Russell, Brian Aherne, Willard Parker, Alan Dinehart, Ann Savage. Literary agent Russell sells film rights to spicy novel, and unwillingly becomes involved with its bookish author (Parker) in this lightweight comedy vehicle.

What a Woman! (1956-Italian) SEE: **Lucky to Be a Woman**

What Became of Jack and Jill? (1972-British) **C-93m.** **½ D: Bill Bain. Vanessa Howard, Paul Nicholas, Mona Washbourne, Peter Copley, Peter Jeffrey. Game attempt at detailing modern day, no-holds-barred love affair twisted by intrusion of grandmother; defeated by smug script, odd point of view. [PG]

What Changed Charley Farthing SEE: **Bananas Boat, The**

What Did You Do in the War, Daddy? (1966) **C-119m.** *** D: Blake Edwards. James Coburn, Dick Shawn, Sergio Fantoni, Aldo Ray, Harry Morgan, Carroll O'Connor, Leon Askin, Giovanna Ralli. A not too funny but quite pleasant film about group of misfit American soldiers trying to tame wacky Italian town into surrender. Written by William Peter Blatty; O'Connor's blustery performance led to his being cast in *All in the Family*. Panavision.▼

What Do You Say to a Naked Lady? (1970) **C-90m.** *** D: Allen Funt. Amusing risqué *Candid Camera* effort. Accent is on sex, and some of the reactions to stunts, and queries, are hilarious. Look for Richard Roundtree! [R—edited from original X rating]▼

What Dreams May Come (1998) **C-113m.** BOMB D: Vincent Ward. Robin Williams, Cuba Gooding, Jr., Annabella Sciorra, Max von Sydow, Rosalind Chao, Matt Salinger, Werner Herzog, Lucinda Jenney. Off-putting gobbledygook about a man who loses his kids in a car accident, then dies himself, and tries to reach out to his loving, grieving wife on earth. Despite its pedigree (a novel by Richard Matheson, a good director and cast), this film fails to evoke any tangible emotions. It just doesn't work. Its elaborate (in fact, overelaborate) special effects won an Oscar. Super 35. [PG-13]▼●◗

Whatever (1998) **C-112m.** *** D: Susan Skoog. Liza Weil, Chad Morgan, Kathryn Rossetter, Frederic Forrest, Gary Wolf, Dan Montano. Sensitive, at times disturbing, portrait of a teenage girl (Weil) coming of age circa 1981, dealing with sex, drugs, and her reckless party-girl best friend (Morgan). Has the texture of a Joyce Carol Oates short story and features a terrific performance by Weil. Written by the director. Good period soundtrack featuring Iggy Pop, Blondie, The Ramones, and The Pretenders. [R] ▼●◗

Whatever Happened to Aunt Alice? (1969) **C-101m.** *** D: Lee H. Katzin. Geraldine Page, Ruth Gordon, Rosemary Forsyth, Robert Fuller, Mildred Dunnock. Eccentric Page stays wealthy by murdering her housekeepers, stealing their savings. Gordon hires on as next "victim," trying to solve missing-persons mystery. Played to the hilt; most enjoyable. [M/PG]▼

What Ever Happened to Baby Jane? (1962) **132m.** ***½ D: Robert Aldrich. Bette Davis, Joan Crawford, Victor Buono, Marjorie Bennett, Anna Lee. Far-fetched, thoroughly engaging black comedy of two former movie stars; Joan's a cripple at the mercy of demented sister Baby Jane Hudson (Davis). Bette has a field day in her macabre characterization, with Buono a perfect match. Triggered a decade-long spate of older female stars in horror films. Script by Lukas Heller, from Henry Farrell's novel. Remade for TV in 1991 with Vanessa and Lynn Redgrave.▼●◗

Whatever It Takes (2000) **C-94m.** ** D: David Raynr (Hubbard). James Franco, Marla Sokoloff, Jodi Lyn O'Keefe, Shane West, Aaron Paul, Richard Schiff, Julia Sweeney. Latest screen variation on *Cyrano de Bergerac* is just one more teen-comedy-of-the-week. When dumb jock Franco can't get to first base with Sokoloff, he asks her platonic next-door neighbor (West) to intervene and supply him romantic "material." As reward, he'll set up his newfound cohort with his school-dish cousin (O'Keefe)—who, in typical bad-movie fashion, is much less attractive than the next-door gal-pal. Movie is a bust down the middle, but director Raynr has some fun around the edges. [PG-13]▼◗

What Every Woman Knows (1934) **92m.** ***½ D: Gregory La Cava. Helen Hayes, Brian Aherne, Madge Evans, Lucile Watson, Dudley Digges, Donald Crisp. Charming, funny adaptation of James Barrie's play about a woman who is "the brains" behind her well-meaning but none-too-bright politician husband. Beautifully acted and surprisingly contemporary. Filmed before in 1921.

What Every Woman Wants (1962-British) **69m.** *½ D: Ernest Morris. William (James) Fox, Hy Hazell, Dennis Lotis, Elizabeth Shepherd. Dull marital comedy of wives trying to reform husbands.

What Happened Was . . . (1993) **C-91m.** *** D: Tom Noonan. Tom Noonan, Karen Sillas. Revealing, extremely well-acted two-character drama follows what happens to two lonely, mismatched coworkers as they experience their first date. Original film is set in real time, on one set; anyone who's ever gone on a first date will surely relate to this material. Actor Noonan also scripted and made his directorial debut with this impressive film. [R]▼●

What Have I Done to Deserve This? (1985-Spanish) **C-100m.** *** D: Pedro Almodóvar. Carmen Maura, Chus Lampreave, Veronica Forque, Kiti Manver. Off-the-wall black comedy about an off-the-wall housewife (delightfully played by Maura) and her various trials and escapades. A fresh, original film, featuring a feminist heroine of classic proportions.▼●

What Next, Corporal Hargrove? (1945) **95m.** **½ D: Richard Thorpe. Robert Walker, Keenan Wynn, Jean Porter, Chill Wills, Hugo Haas, William Phillips, Fred Essler, Cameron Mitchell. Hargrove (Walker) is in France with con-man buddy (Wynn) in OK sequel to SEE HERE, PRIVATE HARGROVE; trivial and episodic.

What! No Beer? (1933) **66m.** ** D: Edward Sedgwick. Buster Keaton, Jimmy Durante, Roscoe Ates, Phyllis Barry, John Miljan, Edward Brophy, Henry Armetta. Mediocre prohibition comedy about dim-witted bootleggers Keaton and Durante; plot makes no sense, Durante is incredibly overbearing. Best scenes involve Buster and leading-lady Barry. Keaton's last starring feature in America.▼

What Planet Are You From? (2000) **C-104m.** **½ D: Mike Nichols. Garry Shandling, Annette Bening, Greg Kinnear, Ben Kingsley, Linda Fiorentino, John Goodman, Richard Jenkins, Caroline Aaron, Judy Greer, Nora Dunn, Ann Cusack, Camryn Manheim, Cathy Ladman. Alien is sent to earth by his planet with the mandate to find a woman who will bear his child. The last thing the interplanetary visitor expects to experience is genuine love and caring. If you're a Shandling fan, you may cut this comedy more slack than others will; it's low-key and somewhat predictable, but surprisingly good-natured. Shandling cowrote the script. Janeane Garofalo appears unbilled. [R]▼◗

What Price Glory? (1926) **120m.** *** D: Raoul Walsh. Victor McLaglen, Edmund Lowe, Dolores Del Rio, William V. Mong, Phyllis Haver, Leslie Fenton, Barry Norton. Boisterous rivalry between Capt. Flagg (McLaglen) and Sgt. Quirt (Lowe) centers on lovely Charmaine (Del Rio) when they go to France during WW1. Zesty comedy, with plenty of fireworks for lip-readers, abruptly turns grim as focus shifts to horrors of war, only to return to Flagg-Quirt hijinks for finale. Fine entertainment, from Laurence Stallings–Maxwell Anderson play; two main characters reappeared in a handful of follow-ups, none of them as good as this. Remade in 1952.▼

What Price Glory? (1952) **C-111m.** **½ D: John Ford. James Cagney, Corinne Calvet, Dan Dailey, Robert Wagner, Marisa Pavan, James Gleason. Classic silent film becomes shallow Cagney-Dailey vehicle of battling Army men Flagg and Quirt in WW1 France.▼

What Price Hollywood? (1932) **88m.** *** D: George Cukor. Constance Bennett, Lowell Sherman, Neil Hamilton, Gregory Ratoff, Brooks Benedict. Soused movie director Sherman helps waitress Bennett fulfill her ambition to become a movie star—while he sinks into alcoholic ruin. Surprisingly sharp-eyed look at Hollywood—both comic and dramatic—that served as inspiration for later A STAR IS BORN. From a story by Adela Rogers St. Johns.▼●

What Price Murder (1958-French) **105m.** **½ D: Henri Verneuil. Henri Vidal, Mylene Demongeot, Isa Miranda, Alfred Adam. Well-turned murder mystery of hubby and secretary planning to do away with wife.

What Price Vengeance SEE: **Vengeance**

What's Eating Gilbert Grape (1993) **C-117m.** **½ D: Lasse Hallström. Johnny Depp, Leonardo DiCaprio, Juliette Lewis, Mary Steenburgen, Darlene Cates, Laura Harrington, Mary Kate Schellhardt, Kevin Tighe, John C. Reilly, Crispin Glover, Penelope Branning. Middling slice-of-life about a young man in a dead-end town saddled with the responsibility of caring for his retarded younger brother, and depressed by his obese mother, who hasn't left the house in seven years. You keep thinking something significant is going to happen, but nothing ever does; still, there are some poignant vignettes and first-rate performances (especially by newcomer Cates, as the mom). [PG-13]▼●

What's Good for the Goose (1969-British) **C-105m.** BOMB D: Menahem Golan. Norman Wisdom, Sally Geeson, Sally Bazely, Sarah Atkinson, Terence Alexander. Weak, unfunny, sex romp wherein the object is to score as often as possible. Skip it. [R]

What's Love Got to Do With It (1993) **C-119m.** *** D: Brian Gibson. Angela Bassett, Laurence Fishburne, Vanessa Bell Calloway, Jenifer Lewis, Rae'ven Kelly, Phyllis Yvonne Stickney, Chi, Khandi Alexander, Penny Johnson, Robert Guy Miranda, Pamela Tyson. Highly charged musical bio of singer Tina Turner, who joined r&b musician Ike Turner as a naive teenager and went on to become a dynamic performer—all the while suffering various forms of abuse at home. Vivid, immediate, and persuasive (though Tina's personality is never explored, and she's painted as something of a saint), but the real attraction here is the phenomenal performances of Bassett and Fishburne as Tina and Ike. Based on *I, Tina* by Turner and Kurt Loder. [R]▼●◗

What's New, Pussycat? (1965) **C-108m.** ** D: Clive Donner. Peter Sellers, Peter O'Toole, Romy Schneider, Capucine, Paula Prentiss, Woody Allen, Ursula Andress. Disturbed fashion editor O'Toole goes to psychiatrist Sellers for help with his romantic problems, but Sellers is even crazier than he. Woody Allen's first feature as actor and writer, and like many of his comedies, one sits through a lot of misfired gags to get to a few undeniable gems. Hit title song by Burt Bacharach and Hal David.▼●

What's So Bad About Feeling Good? (1968) **C-94m.** **½ D: George Seaton. George Peppard, Mary Tyler Moore, Dom DeLuise, John McMartin, Don Stroud, Nathaniel Frey, Susan Saint James, Charles Lane, Thelma Ritter. Amiable attempt at old-fashioned Capraesque comedy, with pixillated toucan spreading good feeling throughout N.Y.C. Doesn't hit bull's-eye, but has its moments. Written by Seaton and Robert Pirosh. Look for Cleavon Little, Moses Gunn. Techniscope.

What's the Matter with Helen? (1971) **C-101m.** *** D: Curtis Harrington. Debbie Reynolds, Shelley Winters, Dennis Weaver, Agnes Moorehead, Michael MacLiammoir. Campy murder tale set in 1930s. Reynolds and Winters try to erase their sordid past, start anew in Hollywood with school for talented kids. Good fun; Debbie ideal in period setting. Written by Henry Farrell. [PG]▼

What's Up, Doc? (1972) **C-94m.** *** D: Peter Bogdanovich. Barbra Streisand, Ryan O'Neal, Kenneth Mars, Austin Pendleton, Madeline Kahn, Sorrell Booke, Michael Murphy, Liam Dunn, John Hillerman, M. Emmet Walsh. Modern-day screwball comedy with impish Streisand making life miserable for stuffy musicologist O'Neal and his fiancée (Kahn, in feature debut), becoming involved in mixup over stolen jewels. Great comic chase scenes highlight overpowering farce, Bogdanovich's bouquet to 1930s

Hollywood (and BRINGING UP BABY in particular). Look for John Byner and Randy Quaid at the hotel banquet. [G]▼●

What's Up, Tiger Lily? (1966) **C-80m.** *** Compiled by Woody Allen. Japanese version directed by Senkichi Taniguchi. Tatsuya Mihashi, Miya Hana, Eiko Wakabayashi, Tadao Nakamura, Woody Allen, China Lee. Slick Japanese imitation James Bond movie (KAGI NO KAG, or KEY OF KEYS, released in 1964) is redubbed by Allen into one long, very funny joke. The object of international intrigue is a valued egg-salad recipe, and the main characters are named Phil Moscowitz, Terri Yaki and Suki Yaki. Music by The Lovin' Spoonful (who also appear in the film). One of the new voices is Louise Lasser. Tohoscope.▼●

What Waits Below (1985) **C-88m.** ** D: Don Sharp. Robert Powell, Lisa Blount, Timothy Bottoms, Richard Johnson, Anne Heywood, Liam Sullivan. Disappointing fantasy thriller of archaeologists stumbling upon a lost race of Lemurians living in South American caves. Effects aren't very special; a good cast is wasted. [PG]▼

Wheeler Dealers, The (1963) **C-106m.** *** D: Arthur Hiller. Lee Remick, James Garner, Jim Backus, Phil Harris, Shelley Berman, Chill Wills, John Astin, Louis Nye. Funny, fast-moving spoof of Texas millionaires who play with investments just for fun. Garner also catches Lee Remick along the way. Panavision.▼

Wheel of Fortune SEE: **Man Betrayed, A**

Wheels of Terror (1987) SEE: **Misfit Brigade, The**

When a Feller Needs a Friend (1932) **67m.** ** D: Harry Pollard. Jackie Cooper, Charles "Chic" Sale, Ralph Graves, Dorothy Peterson, Helen Parrish, Donald Haines. Mediocre tearjerker about a lame boy whose overprotective parents keep him from playing with the neighborhood kids . . . and his rambunctious uncle (Sale) who gives him gumption and shows him a good time.

When a Man Loves a Woman (1994) **C-125m.** **½ D: Luis Mandoki. Andy Garcia, Meg Ryan, Ellen Burstyn, Tina Majorino, Mae Whitman, Lauren Tom, Philip Seymour Hoffman, Eugene Roche, Gail Strickland. Wife and mother of two is forced to deal with the fact that she's an alcoholic . . . but her husband soon learns that he has as much to deal with as she does. Ryan gives a standout performance in this surprisingly frank exploration of the trauma this kind of disease can cause to a family. The film succeeds more as tract than entertainment, however. [R]▼●◗

When a Stranger Calls (1979) **C-97m.** *½ D: Fred Walton. Carol Kane, Charles Durning, Colleen Dewhurst, Tony Beckley, Rachel Roberts, Ron O'Neal. Psycho murders two children after terrorizing their babysitter, returns seven years later to extend his crime. Unpleasant, improbable melodrama falls apart after OK opening 11 minutes. Based on a short subject called THE SITTER. Followed, over a decade later, by a TV sequel. [R]▼●◗

When a Stranger Calls Back (1993) **C-100m. TVM** D: Fred Walton. Carol Kane, Charles Durning, Jill Schoelen, Gene Lythgow, Karen Austin. OK companion piece to writer/director Walton's 1979 bedeviled-babysitter chiller, but like the earlier one it falls apart after a terrific 20-odd minute opening sequence, bringing the viewer back for the wrap-up. Kane and Durning repeat their earlier roles. Made for cable. Average.▼◗

When a Woman Loves (1959-Japanese) **C-97m.** **½ D: Heinosuke Gosho. Ineko Arima, Shin Saburi, Yatsuko Tan-ami, Nobuko Otowa. Utilizing flashbacks, film recalls love affair between Saburi and older man Arima, a war correspondent; sentimental weeper with almost enough class. Grandscope.

When Comedy Was King (1960) **81m.** **** Compiled by Robert Youngson. Charlie Chaplin, Buster Keaton, Laurel and Hardy, Ben Turpin, Fatty Arbuckle, Wallace Beery, Gloria Swanson. Second Youngson compilation of silent comedy clips has many old favorites in classic scenes. Chaplin, Keaton, Laurel & Hardy, Keystone Kops, Charley Chase and others shine in this outstanding film.▼●

When Dinosaurs Ruled the Earth (1970-British) **C-96m.** *** D: Val Guest. Victoria Vetri, Robin Hawdon, Patrick Allen, Drewe Henley, Imogen Hassall, Magda Konopka, Patrick Holt. Fast-paced, enjoyable prehistoric actioner with Vetri and Hawdon lovers ostracized by respective tribes. Beautiful locations, very good special effects by Jim Danforth, and honorable attempt to simulate period, although Vetri (*Playboy*'s 1968 Playmate of the Year—then known as Angela Dorian) seems to have ordered her wardrobe from Frederick's of Bedrock. Story by J.G. Ballard. [G]▼●

When Eight Bells Toll (1971-British) **C-94m.** ** D: Etienne Perier. Anthony Hopkins, Robert Morley, Nathalie Delon, Jack Hawkins, Ferdy Mayne, Corin Redgrave, Derek Bond. Alistair MacLean adapted his best-seller of gold piracy at sea, but the production lacks flash and finesse and Hopkins is too disagreeable a hero. Panavision. [PG]

When Father Was Away on Business (1985-Yugoslavian) **C-135m.** ***½ D: Emir Kusturica. Moreno D'E Bartolli, Miki Manojlovic, Mirjana Karanovic, Mustafa Nadarevic, Mira Furian, Andrew Kopperud. Captivating story about a family's efforts to get along when the head of the household is sent to a labor camp for making an indiscreet remark. Told mostly through the eyes of a six-year-old boy (D'E Bartolli), whose concerns and flights of fancy are irresistible. Set in Sarajevo in the early 1950s. [R]▼

When Harry Met Sally . . . (1989) **C-95m.** ***½ D: Rob Reiner. Billy Crystal, Meg Ryan, Carrie Fisher, Bruno Kirby, Steven Ford, Lisa Jane Persky, Michelle Nicastro, Harley Kozak. Delightful Woody Allen-ish romantic comedy set in N.Y.C. about a man and woman who carve out a genuine friendship, and struggle to keep it from becoming a romantic attachment. Full of great dialogue and knowing remarks about the way men and women view each other. Screenplay by Nora Ephron (with some distinctive Billy Crystalisms throughout). Director Reiner's mother has the movie's single funniest line, at the end of the delicatessen scene. [R]▼●

When Hell Broke Loose (1958) **78m.** ** D: Kenneth G. Crane. Charles Bronson, Violet Rensing, Richard Jaeckel, Arvid Nelson, Eddie Foy III. Tired WW2 melodrama with con artist Bronson joining the army to avoid prison; he romances Rensing, whose brother (Jaeckel) is a Nazi terrorist intent on assassinating Gen. Eisenhower.▼

When I Grow Up (1951) **80m.** *** D: Michael Kanin. Bobby Driscoll, Robert Preston, Martha Scott, Sherry Jackson, Charley Grapewin, Henry (Harry) Morgan. Effective low-key study of the generation gap, with Driscoll most appealing as a boy who finds that he and his grandfather have much in common.

When in Rome (1952) **78m.** **½ D: Clarence Brown. Van Johnson, Paul Douglas, Joseph Calleia, Mimi Aguglia, Tudor Owen. Tasteful yet unrestrained tale of con-artist Douglas disguising himself as priest attending Holy Year pilgrimage in Italy; through American priest Johnson, et al. he finds new faith.

When Ladies Meet (1933) **85m.** *** D: Harry Beaumont. Ann Harding, Robert Montgomery, Myrna Loy, Alice Brady, Frank Morgan. Harding and Loy meet and discuss the characters of a new book, unaware that they both love the same man . . . just like the characters in the novel. Talky but unusual, intelligent film. Remade in 1941.

When Ladies Meet (1941) **108m.** ** D: Robert Z. Leonard. Joan Crawford, Robert Taylor, Greer Garson, Herbert Marshall, Spring Byington. Attractive performers in plodding remake of 1933 movie based on Rachel Crothers' play. Authoress Crawford loves Marshall, who's married to Garson; Taylor loves Joan. Taylor and Garson try to bring life to film, but can't. Retitled STRANGE SKIRTS for TV.▼●

When Lovers Meet SEE: **Lover Come Back** (1946)

When My Baby Smiles at Me (1948) **C-98m.** **½ D: Walter Lang. Betty Grable, Dan Dailey, Jack Oakie, June Havoc, James Gleason, Richard Arlen. Strictly routine musical about burlesque team that breaks up when one member gets job on Broadway. Eventually they're reteamed, of course. Based on famous play *Burlesque*. Filmed before as DANCE OF LIFE and SWING HIGH, SWING LOW.

When Night Is Falling (1995-Canadian) **C-96m.** *** D: Patricia Rozema. Pascale Bussières, Rachael Crawford, Henry Czerny, Don McKellar, Tracy Wright. Though essentially soft-focus lesbian eye-candy, this is also a tremendously entertaining retelling of the myth of Cupid and Psyche. Camille (Bussières), a professor at a Calvinist college engaged to marry a fellow teacher of religion (Czerny), falls for Petra (Crawford), an uninhibited circus performer. The scenes of circus erotica resemble *Red Shoe Diaries* rather than Fellini, but the film's attitude is refreshingly tongue-in-cheek. (Also, both women are stunners and the story's sweet.) [R]▼

When Pigs Fly (1993-German-U.S.-Dutch) **C-94m.** **½ D: Sara Driver. Alfred Molina, Marianne Faithfull, Seymour Cassel, Rachel Bella, Maggie O'Neill, Freddie Brooks. Charming, oddball film about a hipster musician who's visited by a couple of ghostly spirits who need to settle accounts in their lives. With his help, they do, and of course, it helps him get his own act together. Supernatural comedy-drama is vague about where it's set; it was actually shot in Germany. Music by Joe Strummer; coexecutive-produced by Jim Jarmusch.▼

When Strangers Marry (1944) **67m.** *** D: William Castle. Robert Mitchum, Kim Hunter, Dean Jagger, Neil Hamilton, Lou Lubin, Milton Kibbee. Cleverly directed film noir about sweet, innocent Hunter, whose new husband (Jagger) just may be a murderer. Mitchum, as her ex-boyfriend, exudes his trademark cool in his first important role. As good a B picture as you'll ever find. Reissued as BETRAYED.

When's Your Birthday? (1937) **77m.** ** D: Harry Beaumont. Joe E. Brown, Marian Marsh, Edgar Kennedy, Margaret Hamilton, Frank Jenks, Maude Eburne, Fred Keating. Slight, meandering slapstick with Brown trying his best as an astrology-obsessed prizefighter whose prowess depends on the position of the stars.▼

When the Boys Meet the Girls (1965) **C-110m.** ** D: Alvin Ganzer. Connie Francis, Harve Presnell, Herman's Hermits, Louis Armstrong, Liberace, Sue Ane Langdon, Fred Clark, Sam the Sham. Rehash of GIRL CRAZY, turned into a dull guest-star showcase. Panavision. ●

When the Cat's Away (1996-French) **C-91m.** *** D: Cédric Klapisch. Garance Clavel, Zinedine Soualem, Renée Le Calm,

Olivier Py, Romain Duris. Sweet, deft look at a side of Paris rarely seen onscreen as a young woman returns from vacation to discover her cat has disappeared. She takes off on a journey through city streets not only to find her pet but, as it turns out, herself as well. A simple, welcome film about love and loneliness. [R]▼

When the Daltons Rode (1940) **80m.** *** D: George Marshall. Randolph Scott, Kay Francis, Brian Donlevy, Broderick Crawford, Andy Devine, Stuart Erwin, Frank Albertson, George Bancroft, Edgar Buchanan, Mary Gordon. Action-packed (if highly illogical) Western with nice comedic touches, relating how the Dalton brothers were railroaded into becoming desperadoes. Good cast plays to the hilt, with Devine especially amusing as a love object! Also loaded with eye-popping stunt work.

When the Legends Die (1972) **C-105m.** *** D: Stuart Millar. Richard Widmark, Frederic Forrest, Luana Anders, Vito Scotti, Herbert Nelson. Offbeat story of aging rodeo cowboy who cannot accept fact that years are creeping up on him, and young Indian he befriends. [PG]▼

When the North Wind Blows (1974) **C-113m.** **½ D: Stewart Raffill. Henry Brandon, Herbert Nelson, Dan Haggerty. A hermit trapper protects snow tigers in Siberia. Beautiful scenery; OK fare for children. [G]▼

When the Party's Over (1992) **C-114m.** **½ D: Matthew Irmas. Rae Dawn Chong, Fisher Stevens, Sandra Bullock, Elizabeth Berridge, Brian McNamara, Kris Kamm, Michael Landes, Stephen Meadows. Perceptive but seriously flawed, often confusing drama about making it in L.A., focusing on three women and a gay male who share a house and are involved in each other's lives. Chong (as a manipulative yuppie careerist) and Bullock (as a cynical feminist artist) are standouts. [R]▼●

When the Redskins Rode (1951) **C-78m.** *½ D: Lew Landers. Jon Hall, Mary Castle, James Seay, John Ridgley. Lamebrained Western set during French and Indian War of 1750s.

When the Whales Came (1989-British) **C-100m.** ** D: Clive Rees. Paul Scofield, Helen Mirren, Helen Pearce, Max Rennie, David Suchet, David Threlfall, Barbara Jefford, Jeremy Kemp. Dull dud set in 1914 with Scofield, in a performance that's not among his best, cast as a deaf old hermit who loves birds; he lives alone on a remote island and is befriended by youngsters Rennie and Pearce (the latter a nonactor discovered on Britain's Scilly Isles, where film was made). [G]▼●

When Time Ran Out . . . (1980) **C-121m.** BOMB D: James Goldstone. Paul Newman, Jacqueline Bisset, William Holden, James Franciscus, Edward Albert, Red Buttons, Ernest Borgnine, Burgess Meredith, Valentina Cortesa, Veronica Hamel, Alex Karras, Barbara Carrera. WHEN IDEAS RAN OUT, or, THE BLUBBERING INFERNO: Irwin Allen's shameless rehash of all his disaster-movie clichés, set on a Pacific island, is a monumental bore that even a volcanic eruption cannot save. Written by Carl Foreman and Stirling Silliphant—who were presumably well paid. Retitled EARTH'S FINAL FURY for TV. Video version runs 141m. Panavision. [PG]▼

When Tomorrow Comes (1939) **90m.** **½ D: John M. Stahl. Irene Dunne, Charles Boyer, Barbara O'Neil, Nydia Westman, Onslow Stevens. Standard soapy story (by James M. Cain!) enhanced by leading players; Boyer loves Dunne, although he's already married. Remade twice as INTERLUDE.

When We Were Kings (1996) **C-92m.** ***½ D: Leon Gast. Muhammad Ali, George Foreman, Don King, James Brown, B. B. King, Spike Lee, Norman Mailer, George Plimpton. Highly entertaining, Oscar-winning documentary about the classic 1974 "Rumble in the Jungle" matchup in Zaire of heavyweight champions Ali and Foreman. Film chronicles the preparations for the fight, and its postponement, enabling us to learn more about The Greatest in his prime than a more conventional account could ever tell us. Full of fascinating observations from the participants as well as contemporary observers like Mailer, Plimpton, and Lee. Gast spent twenty-three years trying to bring this film to fruition; it was well worth the wait. [PG]▼●◗

When Willie Comes Marching Home (1950) **82m.** **½ D: John Ford. Dan Dailey, Corinne Calvet, Colleen Townsend, William Demarest, Mae Marsh. Schmaltzy WW2 adventures of West Virginia youth Dailey, including interlude with French underground leader Calvet.

When Wolves Cry SEE: **Christmas Tree, The**

When Women Had Tails (1970-Italian) **C-110m.** *½ D: Pasquale Festa Campanile. Senta Berger, Giuliano Gemma, Frank Wolff, Lando Buzzanca, Aldo Giuffre. Cute, harmless but unfunny slapstick comedy with Berger a most attractive cavewoman. Lina Wertmuller co-wrote the screenplay. Sequel: WHEN WOMEN LOST THEIR TAILS. [R]▼

When Worlds Collide (1951) **C-81m.** *** D: Rudolph Maté. Richard Derr, Barbara Rush, Peter Hanson, Larry Keating, John Hoyt. Scientist tries to convince a doubting world that Earth is in path of rogue planet and its sun. Convince yourself this could happen and you'll have fun. Special effects (including submersion of Manhattan) won Oscar for this George Pal production. Based on the novel by Edwin Balmer and Philip Wylie.▼●

When You Comin' Back, Red Ryder? (1979) **C-118m.** *½ D: Milton Katselas. Marjoe Gortner, Hal Linden, Lee Grant, Peter Firth, Candy Clark, Pat Hingle, Stephanie Faracy, Audra Lindley, Bill McKinney. Stagy, unpleasant film of Mark Medoff's play about a psycho terrorizing a disparate group of people in roadside diner. Has its moments, but not enough to justify nearly two hours of viewing. [R]

When You're in Love (1937) **104m.** **½ D: Robert Riskin. Grace Moore, Cary Grant, Aline MacMahon, Thomas Mitchell, Emma Dunn, Louise Brooks. Overlong but enjoyable vehicle for opera star Moore who "hires" Grant as her husband. Most 98m. TV prints are missing film's highlight, where star sings "Minnie the Moocher." Celebrated screenwriter Riskin's only fling at directing.

Where Angels Fear to Tread (1991-British) **C-112m.** **½ D: Charles Sturridge. Helena Bonham Carter, Judy Davis, Rupert Graves, Giovanni Guidelli, Barbara Jefford, Helen Mirren, Thomas Wheatley, Sophie Kullman. Interesting drama of repressed and unleashed sexuality within the British upper class, based on E. M. Forster's first novel. The story follows events after British widow Mirren dallies with and weds a young Tuscan (Guidelli) while vacationing in Italy. Faithful to its source material, and the performances (particularly Bonham Carter's, as Mirren's traveling companion) are first-rate, but the presentation is less inspired than one would like.▼●

Where Angels Go . . . Trouble Follows (1968) **C-95m.** **½ D: James Neilson. Rosalind Russell, Stella Stevens, Binnie Barnes, Mary Wickes, Dolores Sutton, Susan Saint James, Barbara Hunter; guest stars Milton Berle, Arthur Godfrey, Van Johnson, William Lundigan, Robert Taylor. For *Flying Nun* fans only; contrived comedy follow-up to THE TROUBLE WITH ANGELS with Mother Superior Russell pitted against young, progressive nun Stevens. [G]▼

Where Are the Children? (1986) **C-92m.** *½ D: Bruce Malmuth. Jill Clayburgh, Max Gail, Harley Cross, Elisabeth Harnois, Elizabeth Wilson, Barnard Hughes, Frederic Forrest. Clayburgh's two children are kidnapped—just as, nine years before, her first two kids (by a previous marriage) also vanished. Creates some suspense but becomes more ludicrous as it unfolds. Despite a raging storm, the Cape Cod location is the most attractive aspect of the film. Based on Mary Higgins Clark's novel. [R]▼

Where Are Your Children? (1943) **73m.** *½ D: William Nigh. Jackie Cooper, Patricia Morison, Gale Storm, Gertrude Michael, John Litel, Evelynne Eaton. Thoughtless study of juvenile delinquency.

Where Danger Lives (1950) **84m.** ** D: John Farrow. Robert Mitchum, Faith Domergue, Claude Rains, Maureen O'Sullivan. Dr. Mitchum finds himself deep in trouble when he falls hard for manipulative, desperate Domergue. Atmospheric, predictable, and forgettable potboiler.

Where Does It Hurt? (1972) **C-88m.** BOMB D: Rod Amateau. Peter Sellers, Jo Ann Pflug, Rick Lenz, Harold Gould, Hope Summers, Eve Bruce, Kathleen Freeman. Abysmal, tasteless "comedy" about hospital run by corrupt Sellers, staffed by money-hungry incompetents. [R]

Where Do We Go From Here? (1945) **C-77m.** **½ D: Gregory Ratoff. Fred MacMurray, June Haver, Joan Leslie, Gene Sheldon, Anthony Quinn, Carlos Ramirez, Otto Preminger. Engaging but ultimately silly musical comedy about genie enabling MacMurray to travel backwards into American history. Ira Gershwin–Kurt Weill score includes wonderful mini-opera involving Christopher Columbus. Fred and June later married in real life.

Where Eagles Dare (1968) **C-158m.** ***½ D: Brian G. Hutton. Richard Burton, Clint Eastwood, Mary Ure, Michael Hordern, Patrick Wymark, Robert Beatty, Ferdy Mayne, Anton Diffring, Donald Houston, Ingrid Pitt. Modern-day version of Republic serial, with slam-bang cliff-hanger action that never lets up. Burton and company assigned to free American officer held captive in German mountain castle during WW2. Terrific; script by Alistair MacLean, from his best-selling novel. Panavision. [M/PG]▼●

Where It's At (1969) **C-104m.** **½ D: Garson Kanin. David Janssen, Robert Drivas, Rosemary Forsyth, Brenda Vaccaro, Don Rickles, Edy Williams. Pleasant but undistinguished comedy about strained relationship between Las Vegas casino owner and his Princeton-graduate son. [R]

Where Love Has Gone (1964) **C-114m.** **½ D: Edward Dmytryk. Bette Davis, Susan Hayward, Michael Connors, Jane Greer, Joey Heatherton, George Macready. Glossy drama of Heatherton killing mother Hayward's lover; Davis is the domineering grandmother, Greer is a sympathetic probation officer. Script by John Michael Hayes, from Harold Robbins' novel. Techniscope.▼

Where No Vultures Fly SEE: **Ivory Hunter**

Where's Charley? (1952) **C-97m.** *** D: David Butler. Ray Bolger, Allyn Ann McLerie, Robert Shackleton, Mary Germaine, Horace Cooper, Margaretta Scott. Bolger recreates Broadway role in musical adaptation of CHARLEY'S AUNT, as Oxford student whose face-saving impersonation of dowdy dowager leads to endless complications. Frank Loesser score includes "Once in Love with Amy." One of the principal dancers is Jean Marsh. Filmed in England.

Where's Jack? (1969-British) **C-119m.** **½ D: James Clavell. Tommy Steele, Stanley Baker, Fiona Lewis, Alan Badel, Dudley Foster, Sue Lloyd, Noel Purcell. Despite good cast and production values, surprisingly unengrossing historical adventure tale of Britain's most celebrated highwayman and escape artist, Jack Sheppard (Steele), wanted by British government and notorious mercenary (Baker). [G]

Where's Picone? (1984-Italian) **C-122m.** *** D: Nanni Loy. Giancarlo Giannini, Lina Sastri, Aldo Giuffre, Clelia Rondinelli, Carlo Croccolo. Giannini is hilarious in a role tailor-made for his talent: a sleazy, two-bit, ultimately hapless conniver who must live by his wits to survive on the fringes of Neapolitan society. A biting black comedy about bureaucracy and corruption Italian-style.▼

Where's Poppa? (1970) **C-82m.** **½ D: Carl Reiner. George Segal, Ruth Gordon, Trish Van Devere, Ron Leibman, Rae Allen, Vincent Gardenia, Barnard Hughes, Rob Reiner, Garrett Morris, Paul Sorvino. Absurdist comedy has cult following, but grisly subject matter makes it an acquired taste; Segal plays a repressed N.Y.C. lawyer whose senile mother dominates his life. Outlandish gags involve mugging, rape, nursing homes and other ills. Original ending was *too* potent, and changed. Script by Robert Klane, from his novel. Look for Penny Marshall as a courtroom spectator. Reissued as GOING APE. [R]▼●

Where the Boys Are (1960) **C-99m.** **½ D: Henry Levin. Dolores Hart, George Hamilton, Yvette Mimieux, Jim Hutton, Barbara Nichols, Paula Prentiss, Connie Francis, Frank Gorshin, Chill Wills. Not-bad film about teenagers during Easter vacation in Ft. Lauderdale. Connie Francis, in her first film, is pretty good, and sings the hit title tune; other young players seen to good advantage. Nichols is hilarious as usual as a flashy blonde. Ineptly remade in 1984. CinemaScope.▼●

Where the Boys Are '84 (1984) **C-93m.** BOMB D: Hy Averback. Lisa Hartman, Lorna Luft, Wendy Schaal, Lynn-Holly Johnson, Russell Todd, Howard McGillin, Louise Sorel, Alana Stewart. Tacky remake of 1960 film about four college girls (three horny, one virginal) who descend on Ft. Lauderdale, Florida in search of cheap sex. This Allan Carr production has all the appeal of an oil slick. [R]▼

Where the Buffalo Roam (1980) **C-96m.** BOMB D: Art Linson. Peter Boyle, Bill Murray, Bruno Kirby, Rene Auberjonois, R. G. Armstrong, Rafael Campos, Leonard Frey, Mark Metcalf, Craig T. Nelson. Intended celebration of notorious "Gonzo" journalist Hunter S. Thompson will baffle those unfamiliar with his work and insult those who are. Even Neil Young's music can't save dreadful comedy. Reedited (and toned down) for network TV. [R]▼◗

Where the Bullets Fly (1966-British) **C-88m.** **½ D: John Gilling. Tom Adams, Dawn Addams, Tim Barrett, Michael Ripper. Well-paced super spy satire involving Adams tracking down special fuel formula. Sequel to THE SECOND BEST SECRET AGENT IN THE WHOLE WIDE WORLD. ▼

Where the Day Takes You (1992) **C-105m.** **½ D: Marc Rocco. Dermot Mulroney, Robert Knepper, Sean Astin, Balthazar Getty, Will Smith, James Le Gros, Ricki Lake, Lara Flynn Boyle, Peter Dobson, Kyle MacLachlan, Nancy McKeon, Adam Baldwin, Rachel Ticotin, Alyssa Milano, David Arquette, Leo Rossi, Stephen Tobolowsky, Laura San Giacomo. Alternately slick and scuzzy look at homeless L.A. street kids, as related by Mulroney (very good here) to prison psychologist San Giacomo. Wavers in quality from the reasonably compelling to the overwrought; a film that shows us junkie Astin vomiting all over himself can probably do without sappy musical montages. Christian Slater appears unbilled. [R] ▼●

Where the Eagle Flies SEE: **Pickup on 101**

Where the Green Ants Dream (1984-German) **C-100m.** **½ D: Werner Herzog. Bruce Spence, Wandjuk Marika, Roy Marika, Ray Barrett, Norman Kaye, Colleen Clifford. Rambling account of a group of wise, noble Australian aborigines who must go up against a mining company set on bulldozing their sacred land in a quest for uranium. The theme—a clash of civilizations—is characteristic of Herzog, but the result just doesn't gel. [R]▼

Where the Heart Is (1990) **C-94m.** ** D: John Boorman. Dabney Coleman, Uma Thurman, Joanna Cassidy, Crispin Glover, Suzy Amis, Christopher Plummer, Maury Chaykin, David Hewlett. Disappointing farce about wealthy N.Y.C. demolitions expert Coleman, who decides to teach his family humility—and the value of money—by shutting them out and making them homeless. Well-intended hodgepodge that's too outlandish to be taken seriously. Scripted by Boorman and his daughter, Telsche; some saw this as an update of the director's earlier LEO THE LAST. [R]▼●

Where the Heart Is (2000) **C-120m.** *½ D: Matt Williams. Natalie Portman, Ashley Judd, Stockard Channing, Sally Field, Joan Cusack, James Frain, Dylan Bruno. Billie

Letts' novel probably made more sense than this numbingly scattershot script about an abandoned, ill-educated young woman (a miscast Portman) and the circle of friends who nurture her after she gives birth in a Wal-Mart. A near-fatal twister? The baby's kidnapping? The rocky country-western career of the baby's father? Everything here is given equal weight, and the episodic scenes pile up without any cumulative effect. Feature directing debut for the creator/producer of such hit TV sitcoms as *Roseanne* and *Home Improvement*. [PG-13]▼◗

Where the Hot Wind Blows! (1958-French-Italian) **120m.** ** D: Jules Dassin. Gina Lollobrigida, Pierre Brasseur, Marcello Mastroianni, Melina Mercouri, Yves Montand, Paolo Stoppa. Sure-fire cast is wasted in pedestrian drama of hypocrisy in a small Italian town. Lollobrigida is poverty-stricken wench who falls for engineer Mastroianni; Mercouri is judge's wife in love with thug Montand's son.▼◗

Where the Lilies Bloom (1974) **C-96m.** *** D: William A. Graham. Julie Gholson, Jan Smithers, Matthew Burril, Helen Harmon, Harry Dean Stanton, Rance Howard, Sudie Bond. Four Appalachian children carry on by themselves when their father dies—and keep the news of his death a secret, so they won't be taken away by the state. First-rate family drama scripted by Earl Hamner, Jr. and filmed on location in North Carolina. [G]▼

Where the Money Is (2000) **C-89m.** ** D: Marek Kanievska. Paul Newman, Linda Fiorentino, Dermot Mulroney, Susan Barnes, Anne Pitoniak, Bruce MacVittie. Savvy convalescent home nurse Fiorentino senses something about her newest patient, a mute stroke victim who's just been transferred from prison. She becomes convinced that with his bank-robbing background, he can help her and her husband make some easy money. Potentially clever caper goes flat, in spite of charismatic performances by Newman and Fiorentino. A real letdown. [PG-13]▼◗

Where the Red Fern Grows (1974) **C-90m.** *** D: Norman Tokar. James Whitmore, Beverly Garland, Jack Ging, Lonny Chapman, Stewart Peterson. Appealing family drama about a boy's devotion to two hunting dogs, and how his experiences teach him about responsibility and growing up. Set in 1930's Oklahoma. Based on Wilson Rawls' novel. Followed years later by a sequel. [G]▼◗

Where There's Life . . . (1947) **75m.** *** D: Sidney Lanfield. Bob Hope, Signe Hasso, William Bendix, George Coulouris, Vera Marshe, George Zucco, Dennis Hoey, Harry Von Zell. Wacky comedy with fast-talking radio DJ Hope, just about to be married, earmarked as new king of Barovia, and tangling with the country's enemies, along with its top military authority—who happens to be a woman. Bendix is fun as Hope's forever-bellowing brother-in-law-to-be.▼

Where the River Runs Black (1986) **C-100m.** **½ D: Chris Cain. Charles Durning, Alessandro Rabelo, Marcelo Rabelo, Conchata Ferrell, Peter Horton, Dana Delany, Castulo Guerra. Orphaned boy raised in the Amazon jungle is brought to civilization by a well-meaning priest (Durning) who knew his father. Slow-moving story starts well but loses its grip as it leaves behind mystical elements and focuses more on child's-eye view of good guys and bad guys. Nicely filmed on location in Brazil. Super 35. [PG]▼●

Where the Rivers Flow North (1993) **C-106m.** **½ D: Jay Craven. Rip Torn, Tantoo Cardinal, Bill Raymond, Michael J. Fox, John Griesemer, Mark Margolis, Treat Williams, Amy Wright. Thoughtful tale of a man who holds out against authorities determined to buy his Vermont property in order to erect a dam in the late 20s. It turns out that the holdout (Torn) has a hidden agenda, which is one reason this story avoids becoming an idealized good guys vs. bad guys cliché. Fox appears in a supporting role as a heavy. Director Craven also co-scripted. ▼●◗

Where the Sidewalk Ends (1950) **95m.** *** D: Otto Preminger. Dana Andrews, Gene Tierney, Gary Merrill, Karl Malden, Bert Freed, Tom Tully, Ruth Donnelly, Craig Stevens, Neville Brand. While investigating a murder, brutal N.Y.C. cop (Andrews) inadvertently kills a man, then tries to conceal his own guilt while continuing his search for murderer. Moody crime melodrama is a good illustration of film noir. Fine characterizations, pungent script by Ben Hecht from William Stuart's novel *Night Cry*. Oleg Cassini (film's costume designer and Tierney's then-husband) has a cameo.

Where the Spies Are (1966-British) **C-110m.** *** D: Val Guest. David Niven, Françoise Dorleac, John Le Mesurier, Cyril Cusack, Eric Pohlmann, Reginald Beckwith. Well made mixture of dry comedy and suspense in tale of doctor forced into spying. Good cast names enhance already fine movie. Panavision.

Where Time Began (1978-Spanish) **C-86m.** ** D: Piquer Simon. Kenneth More, Pep Munne, Jack Taylor. Mundane retelling of Jules Verne's JOURNEY TO THE CENTER OF THE EARTH, with predictable parade of sea serpents, giant turtles, and dinosaurs. [G]▼

Where Were You When the Lights Went Out? (1968) **C-94m.** *½ D: Hy Averback. Doris Day, Robert Morse, Terry-Thomas, Steve Allen, Lola Albright, Jim Backus, Patrick O'Neal, Pat Paulsen, Ben Blue,

Earl Wilson. Below average Doris Day comedy centering around the massive N.Y.C. blackout on November 9, 1965. Panavision. [M/PG]▼

Which Way Home (1991-Australian) **C-140m. TVM** D: Carl Schultz. Cybill Shepherd, John Waters, Peta Toppana, John Ewart, Ruben Santiago-Hudson, Marc Gray, Andy Tran, Adrian Kwan. Woefully overlong tale of an American nurse's attempts to smuggle seven young orphans out of Cambodia in the late '70s with the help of an Aussie charter-boat captain. Made for cable. Average.▼

Which Way Is Up? (1977) **C-94m.** **½ D: Michael Schultz. Richard Pryor, Lonette McKee, Margaret Avery, Dolph Sweet, Morgan Woodward. Americanization of Lina Wertmuller's very funny THE SEDUCTION OF MIMI doesn't quite make it. Pryor gets to play three roles—a cotton-picking orange picker, a minister, and a dirty old man—and gets the most laughs as the latter. [R]▼

Which Way to the Front? (1970) **C-96m.** BOMB D: Jerry Lewis. Jerry Lewis, John Wood, Jan Murray, Kaye Ballard, Robert Middleton, Paul Winchell, Sidney Miller, Gary Crosby. One of Jerry's worst has him a 4-F millionaire playboy who enlists other 4-Fs to fight Hitler. His last completed film until HARDLY WORKING. Co-scripted by Dick Miller. [G]▼

Whiffs (1975) **C-91m.** *½ D: Ted Post. Elliott Gould, Eddie Albert, Harry Guardino, Godfrey Cambridge, Jennifer O'Neill, Alan Manson. Gould is guinea pig for Army Chemical Corps who has outlived his usefulness . . . but the military isn't rid of him so easily. Another sorry attempt to recapture the lunacy of MASH. Panavision. [PG]▼

While the City Sleeps (1956) **100m.** *** D: Fritz Lang. Dana Andrews, Ida Lupino, Rhonda Fleming, George Sanders, Vincent Price, Thomas Mitchell, Sally Forrest, Howard Duff, James Craig, John Barrymore, Jr., Mae Marsh. Veteran cast and intertwining story-lines keep interest in account of newspaper reporters and police on the track of a berserk killer. SuperScope.▼●

While You Were Sleeping (1995) **C-103m.** **½ D: Jon Turteltaub. Sandra Bullock, Bill Pullman, Peter Gallagher, Peter Boyle, Jack Warden, Glynis Johns, Micole Mercurio, Jason Bernard, Michael Rispoli, Ally Walker, Monica Keena. Lonely Chicago transit worker saves her dream man from muggers, and when he falls into a coma she passes herself off as his fiancée; things get stickier as she's welcomed into his family, and grows close to his brother. Bullock's first starring vehicle showcases her irresistible girl-next-door appeal, but this pleasant, well-cast comedy suffers from anemia. It's a cute story, but it should have been snappier (and shorter). [PG]▼●◗

Whip Hand, The (1951) **82m.** *½ D: William Cameron Menzies. Elliott Reid, Carla Balenda, Raymond Burr, Edgar Barrier, Lurene Tuttle. Communists with germ-warfare intentions have taken over an abandoned resort town, but do these slimes *really* think they can tangle with Elliott Reid? Howard Hughes RKO Special is campy, but not campy enough.

Whiplash (1948) **91m.** ** D: Lewis Seiler. Dane Clark, Alexis Smith, Zachary Scott, Eve Arden, Jeffrey Lynn, S.Z. Sakall, Alan Hale. Unmoving melodrama about artist turning into grim prizefighter. Script is main defect; acting OK.

Whipping Boy, The (1994) **C-99m. TVM** D: Syd Macartney. Truan Munro, Nic Knight, Karen Salt, George C. Scott, Andrew Bicknell, Kevin Conway, Vincent Schiavelli, Mathilda May, Jean Anderson. A spoiled young prince convinces his disinterested dad, the king, to use a street urchin as his whipping boy, to literally take the prince's punishment for him whenever he is disciplined. How the two kids become pals makes for fine family viewing in this Dickensesque Disney movie (based on an award-winning children's book by Sid Fleischman). Script by Max Brindle. Scott is deliciously hammy as a Fagin-like pub-keeping reprobate. Made for cable. Video title: PRINCE BRAT AND THE WHIPPING BOY. Above average. ▼

Whipsaw (1935) **83m.** **½ D: Sam Wood. Myrna Loy, Spencer Tracy, Harvey Stephens, William Harrigan, Clay Clement. Tracy uses bad-girl Loy to lead him to band of thieves; predictable complications follow in familiar but well-done crime drama.

Whirlpool (1934) **73m.** **½ D: Roy William Neill. Jack Holt, Jean Arthur, Donald Cook, Lila Lee, Allen Jenkins, Rita La Roy, John Miljan, Ward Bond. Not-bad vehicle for Holt, who's rock-solid as a carnival proprietor sent to prison for twenty years; upon his release, he does everything he can to protect the daughter he's never met. Script goes flat in second half.

Whirlpool (1949) **97m.** *** D: Otto Preminger. Gene Tierney, Richard Conte, Jose Ferrer, Charles Bickford, Barbara O'Neil, Eduard Franz, Fortunio Bonanova, Constance Collier. Tense melodrama of nefarious hypnotist Ferrer using innocent Tierney to carry out his evil schemes. Script by Ben Hecht (using a pseudonym) and Andrew Solt, from a Guy Endore novel.

Whisky Galore! SEE: **Tight Little Island**

Whisperers, The (1966-British) **106m.** ** D: Bryan Forbes. Edith Evans, Eric

Portman, Nanette Newman, Avis Bunnage, Gerald Sim, Ronald Fraser. Dame Edith is the whole show in this mediocre melodrama about dotty old lady who is sure she is being spied upon; things get worse when her scummy son and husband drop by. Too restrained to be really absorbing, but worth catching just for her performance; moody score by John Barry.▼

Whispering Ghosts (1942) **75m.** ** D: Alfred L. Werker. Brenda Joyce, Milton Berle, John Shelton, John Carradine. Berle is effective as bumbling performer trying to live up to radio role as crackerjack detective.

Whispering Smith (1948) **C-88m.** **½ D: Leslie Fenton. Alan Ladd, Brenda Marshall, Robert Preston, Donald Crisp, William Demarest, Fay Holden, Frank Faylen. Ladd is in his element (in this otherwise ordinary Western) as a soft-spoken but iron-willed railroad agent whose hot-headed best friend (Preston) becomes involved in shady dealings.

Whispering Smith vs. Scotland Yard (1951-British) **77m.** ** D: Francis Searle. Richard Carlson, Greta Gynt, Rona Anderson, Herbert Lom, Dora Bryan. Famed detective proves conclusively that suicide was actually well-staged murder. Good cast in below-average mystery. Stanley Baker has a bit as a reporter and Alan Wheatley appears as an attorney. Original British title: WHISPERING SMITH HITS LONDON.

Whispers (1990-Canadian) **C-96m.** ** D: Douglas Jackson. Victoria Tennant, Chris Sarandon, Jean LeClerc, Peter MacNeill, Linda Sorensen, Eric Christmas. Tennant is forced to kill LeClerc when he attacks her—but he later turns up alive, puzzling police detective Sarandon. Routine, predictable thriller, though LeClerc is amusingly looney. From the best-seller by Dean R. Koontz.▼●

Whispers in the Dark (1992) **C-102m.** **½ D: Christopher Crowe. Annabella Sciorra, Jamey Sheridan, Alan Alda, Jill Clayburgh, Anthony LaPaglia, John Leguizamo, Deborah Unger, Anthony Heald, Jacqueline Brookes. Psychiatrist Sciorra is troubled by her reaction to a female patient, but her failure to respond effectively leads to problems for both of them—and everyone around them. Intriguing, well-cast thriller goes on too long, with more twists and turns than necessary, not all of them plausible. Standout performances by LaPaglia, as a determined cop, and Alda, as Sciorra's psychiatry mentor. [R]▼●

Whistle at Eaton Falls, The (1951) **96m.** **½ D: Robert Siodmak. Lloyd Bridges, Dorothy Gish, Carleton Carpenter, Murray Hamilton, Anne Francis, Ernest Borgnine, Doro Merande, Arthur O'Connell. Set in New Hampshire, this documentary-style film deals with labor relation problems in a small town when new plant manager has to lay off workers. Gish is factory owner in interesting supporting role.

Whistle Blower, The (1986-British) **C-100m.** *** D: Simon Langton. Michael Caine, James Fox, Nigel Havers, Felicity Dean, John Gielgud, Gordon Jackson, Barry Foster. Deftly handled thriller about a middle-aged former intelligence officer (an effectively subtle Caine), whose linguist son has a high-security government position . . . and is a bit too bright and idealistic for his own good. A literate, multileveled story, adapted by Julian Bond from John Hale's novel. [PG]▼●

Whistle Down the Wind (1961-British) **99m.** ***½ D: Bryan Forbes. Hayley Mills, Alan Bates, Bernard Lee, Norman Bird, Elsie Wagstaffe. Fugitive murderer seeking refuge in a North Country barn is discovered by three children who think him to be Christ. Mills and Bates are excellent in this poignant, believable, and well-produced story of childhood innocence. Adapted from novel by Mary Hayley Bell (Hayley's mother). Forbes' directorial debut.▼

The Whistler One of the most unusual—and one of the best—mystery series of the 30s and 40s was based on a popular radio show called "The Whistler." The premise of the show, and at least one of the films, was a mysterious figure who walked along whistling a haunting tune. "I am the Whistler," he would say. "And I know many things." He would introduce the current mystery and reappear from time to time to bridge gaps from one setting to another. Veteran Richard Dix starred in all but one of the eight Whistler films, but he alternated from hero to villain in various entries. The one non-Dix film, THE RETURN OF THE WHISTLER, followed the radio format of the mysterious narrator with excellent results. That entry, and several others, had stories by Cornell Woolrich, while others were written by Eric Taylor; they were all tightly knit, engrossing little mysteries. One of the few series to gain acceptance with the public and critics alike, the Whistler films hold up quite well today.

THE WHISTLER

The Whistler (1944)
Mark of the Whistler (1944)
Power of the Whistler (1945)
Voice of the Whistler (1945)
Mysterious Intruder (1946)
Secret of the Whistler (1946)
The 13th Hour (1947)
The Return of the Whistler (1948)

Whistler, The (1944) **59m.** *** D: William Castle. Richard Dix, Gloria Stuart, Alan Dinehart, Joan Woodbury, J. Carrol

Naish, Byron Foulger. First entry in the series centers on Dix's desperate attempt to cancel the contract he had taken out on his life. Tense and moody tale of fate sets the ironic tone for the rest. Naish shines as the principal hit man.
Whistle Stop (1946) **85m.** ** D: Leonide Moguy. George Raft, Ava Gardner, Victor McLaglen, Tom Conway, Jorja Curtright, Florence Bates, Charles Drake. Unusually stupid Raft vehicle about his on-again, off-again, on-again relationship with Gardner, who wishes he would do something with his life. You may feel the same . . . but Ava *is* stunningly beautiful.▼
Whistling in Brooklyn (1943) **87m.** **½ D: S. Sylvan Simon. Red Skelton, Ann Rutherford, Jean Rogers, "Rags" Ragland, Ray Collins, Henry O'Neill, William Frawley, Sam Levene. Skelton, again as radio sleuth "The Fox," gets mixed up in murder and impersonates the pitcher of a bearded baseball team playing the Dodgers at Ebbets Field. Manager Leo Durocher and his boys appear as themselves.▼
Whistling in Dixie (1942) **74m.** *** D: S. Sylvan Simon. Red Skelton, Ann Rutherford, George Bancroft, Guy Kibbee. Red, as radio's "Fox" marries Ann, but their Southern honeymoon is interrupted by murder and mystery. Funny Skelton vehicle.▼
Whistling in the Dark (1941) **77m.** *** D: S. Sylvan Simon. Red Skelton, Ann Rutherford, Virginia Grey, Conrad Veidt, "Rags" Ragland, Eve Arden. Faithful remake of 1933 film isn't as wacky as subsequent outings with Skelton as radio sleuth "The Fox," but still enjoyable; Red is held by fiendish Veidt and forced to spell out plans for "perfect murder." Followed by two sequels (see above).▼
White (1993-French) **C-92m.** ***½ D: Krzysztof Kieslowski. Zbigniew Zamachowski, Julie Delpy, Janusz Gajos, Jerzy Stuhr. Second of Polish director Kieslowski's "Three Colors" trilogy based on the "liberty, equality, fraternity" symbolism of the blue, white, and red French flag. This story concerns a hapless Pole whose beautiful French wife (Delpy) is divorcing him for no longer being able to perform in bed. Full of irony and subtle wit; the best of the trilogy. Kieslowski wrote the screenplay with frequent collaborator Krzysztof Piesiewicz. Title onscreen is THREE COLORS: WHITE.▼●
White Angel, The (1936) **92m.** ** D: William Dieterle. Kay Francis, Ian Hunter, Donald Woods, Nigel Bruce, Donald Crisp, Henry O'Neill. Lavish but unsuccessful biography of Florence Nightingale with Francis miscast in reworked history of 19th-century British nursing pioneer.
White Balloon, The (1995-Iranian) **C-85m.** *** D: Jafar Panahi. Aïda Mohammadkhani, Mohsen Kafili, Fereshteh Sadr Orfai, Anna Borkowska. It's the Iranian New Year, and a young girl convinces her mother to give her money to buy a goldfish; her trip to make the purchase becomes a mini-odyssey in which she experiences wide-ranging emotions while mixing with characters who run the gamut from greedy to kind. This sweet little film offers an engaging picture of everyday humanity. ▼●
Whiteboyz (1999) **C-97m.** ** D: Marc Levin. Danny Hoch, Dash Mihok, Mark Webber, Piper Perabo, Eugene Byrd, Bonz Malone, Snoop Dogg, Dr. Dre, Fat Joe, Dread Prez, Mic Geronimo, Doug E. Fresh. Hoch is terrific as a young man named Flip who's convinced he's black on the inside, and does his best to talk like an inner-city rapper. This is especially tough for people to understand in the middle of Iowa, where he lives. Fresh and funny for a while, but soon the idea is exhausted; its dramatic climax is all too predictable. [R]▼
White Buffalo, The (1977) **C-97m.** ** D: J. Lee Thompson. Charles Bronson, Jack Warden, Will Sampson, Kim Novak, Clint Walker, Stuart Whitman, Slim Pickens, Cara Williams, John Carradine, Martin Kove. Wild Bill Hickok is haunted by the image of a buffalo that symbolizes his fear of death; strange, murky film, with atypical Bronson role, good support from Warden and Novak. Retitled HUNT TO KILL for network TV. [PG]▼
White Cargo (1942) **90m.** ** D: Richard Thorpe. Hedy Lamarr, Walter Pidgeon, Frank Morgan, Richard Carlson, Reginald Owen. Lamarr, in one of her best-known roles, is the seductive Tondelayo who entrances all at British plantation post in Africa, with Pidgeon the expeditionist who really falls for her. Exotic love scenes, corny plot. Previously filmed in 1929.▼
White Christmas (1954) **C-120m.** ** D: Michael Curtiz. Bing Crosby, Danny Kaye, Rosemary Clooney, Vera-Ellen, Dean Jagger, Mary Wickes, Sig Ruman, Grady Sutton. Nice Irving Berlin score is unfortunately interrupted by limp plot of army buddies Crosby and Kaye boosting popularity of winter resort run by their ex-officer Jagger. "What Can You Do With a General" stands out as Berlin's least memorable tune. Partial reworking of HOLIDAY INN, not half as good. First film released in VistaVision.▼●
White Cliffs of Dover, The (1944) **126m.** *** D: Clarence Brown. Irene Dunne, Alan Marshal, Van Johnson, Frank Morgan, C. Aubrey Smith, Dame May Whitty, Roddy McDowall, Gladys Cooper, Peter Lawford. American Dunne marries Britisher Marshal in patriotic WW1 romancer that boasts wonderful cast (including young Elizabeth Taylor). Slick but shallow.▼
White Comanche (1968-Spanish) **C-90m.** *½ D: Gilbert Kay (Jose Briz). Joseph Cotten, William Shatner, Perla Cristal, Rossana

Yanni. Boring time-killer detailing the conflict between twin boys whose mother is Indian and whose father is white.▼

White Cradle Inn SEE: **High Fury**

White Dawn, The (1974) **C-109m.** **½ D: Philip Kaufman. Warren Oates, Timothy Bottoms, Lou Gossett, Simonie Kopapik. Rambling adventure about three whalers in 1896 who become lost in the Arctic and their subsequent exploitation of the Eskimos who save them. Brilliant photography by Michael Chapman. [PG] ▼●

White Dog (1982) **C-89m.** **½ D: Samuel Fuller. Kristy McNichol, Paul Winfield, Burl Ives, Jameson Parker, Lynn Moody, Marshall Thompson, Paul Bartel, Dick Miller, Parley Baer. Young actress takes in a white dog, unaware that it's been trained to attack black people on sight; professional animal trainer Winfield takes on challenge to *re*train him. Interesting but downbeat drama, undeserving of the controversy and preposterous charges of racism that kept it from being released. Script by director Fuller (who has a cameo as Kristy's agent) and Curtis Hanson, loosely based on the Romain Gary novel. [PG]

White Fang (1972-Italian-Spanish-French) **C-97m.** **½ D: Lucio Fulci. Franco Nero, Vima Lisi, Fernando Rey, Rik Battaglia, Harry Carey, Jr. Scenic but needlessly violent tale of a boy and his dog in the wilds of Alaska, based on the Jack London adventure. Aka WHITE FANG AND THE HUNTER and CHALLENGE TO WHITE FANG. [PG]▼

White Fang (1991) **C-107m.** *** D: Randal Kleiser. Klaus Maria Brandauer, Ethan Hawke, Seymour Cassel, Susan Hogan, James Remar. Winning Disney version of the Jack London perennial, with Hawke a young prospector in Alaska who hooks up with Brandauer and Cassel and befriends the title wolf-dog. Fine fare for kids. Previously filmed in 1936 and 1972. Followed by a sequel. [PG]▼●

White Fang 2: Myth of the White Wolf (1994) **C-106m.** ** D: Ken Olin. Scott Bairstow, Charmaine Craig, Alfred Molina, Geoffrey Lewis, Al Harrington, Anthony Michael Ruivivar, Victoria Racimo, Paul Coeur. Tepid Disney followup to 1991 film, with young prospector Bairstow working the Alaskan gold mine of his predecessor (played in the original by Ethan Hawke) and teaming up with wolf/dog White Fang. Boy and pet then meet Haida Indian princess and become involved with her tribal village. Lumpy blend of mysticism, villainy, romance, and adventure, aimed at kids. Hawke appears unbilled. [PG]▼●

White Feather (1955) **C-102m.** **½ D: Robert D. Webb. Robert Wagner, Jeffrey Hunter, Debra Paget, John Lund, Eduard Franz, Noah Beery, Hugh O'Brian. Pat Western film with some good action scenes of government agent Wagner attempting to convince Indian tribe to move to reservation; Paget and Hunter are members of Cheyenne tribe who resist. CinemaScope.

White Heat (1949) **114m.** ***½ D: Raoul Walsh. James Cagney, Virginia Mayo, Edmond O'Brien, Margaret Wycherly, Steve Cochran. Cagney returned to gangster films, older but forceful as ever, as psychopathic hood with mother obsession; Mayo is his neglected wife, O'Brien the cop out to get him. "Top of the World" finale is now movie legend. Written by Ivan Goff and Ben Roberts, from a Virginia Kellogg story. Also shown in computer-colored version. ▼●

White Hunter, Black Heart (1990) **C-112m.** *** D: Clint Eastwood. Clint Eastwood, Jeff Fahey, George Dzundza, Alun Armstrong, Marisa Berenson, Timothy Spall, Mel Martin. Mature, intelligent (if somewhat one-note) adaptation of Peter Viertel's 1953 novel based on his experiences during the filming of THE AFRICAN QUEEN, and his closeup observations of its macho director, John Huston. Eastwood gives an excellent performance as the contrary, self-destructive (and fictionalized) filmmaker, who becomes obsessed with bagging an elephant while on location in Africa. May not be compelling if you're not already interested in the subject, but convincingly recreates the time and place. Scripted by Viertel, James Bridges, and Burt Kennedy. [PG]▼●

White Lightning (1973) **C-101m.** **½ D: Joseph Sargent. Burt Reynolds, Jennifer Billingsley, Ned Beatty, Bo Hopkins, Matt Clark, Louise Latham, Diane Ladd. Formula melodrama with moonshiner Burt going after crooked sheriff who drowned his brother; pleasant cast helps this OK action pic. Young Laura Dern (Ladd's daughter) is visible throughout; it's her film debut. Sequel: GATOR. [PG]▼●

White Line Fever (1975) **C-92m.** *** D: Jonathan Kaplan. Jan-Michael Vincent, Kay Lenz, Slim Pickens, L. Q. Jones, Leigh French, Don Porter, Martin Kove. A B-picture that hits bull's-eye. Vincent is a young trucker who battles corruption on the road and off, with a diesel truck as his "good buddy." [PG]▼●

White Lions, The (1981) **C-96m.** ** D: Mel Stuart. Michael York, Glynnis O'Connor, Donald Moffat, J. A. Preston, Roger E. Mosley. Slight tale of life in an African wildlife preserve with naturalist York and his family. Mainly for the kids. [PG]

White Man's Burden (1995) **C-96m.** **½ D: Desmond Nakano. John Travolta, Harry Belafonte, Kelly Lynch, Margaret Avery, Tom Bower, Carrie Snodgress, Andrew Lawrence, Sheryl Lee Ralph. Flawed but fascinating, politically loaded allegory, set in a fictitious America in which blacks are the wealthy, white-collar majority and whites comprise the unruly, ill-kempt lower class. Travolta plays a factory worker who is fired due to a misunderstanding and chooses to take desperate action against his former boss (Belafonte). Designed to push the buttons of viewers of both races, but Nakano (who also scripted) tends to generalize a bit too often. [R]▼●◗

White Men Can't Jump (1992) **C-114m.** *** D: Ron Shelton. Wesley Snipes, Woody Harrelson, Rosie Perez, Tyra Ferrell, Cylk Cozart, Kadeem Hardison, Ernest Harden, Jr. Smart, funny, highly profane comedy about urban basketball hustlers Snipes and Harrelson. Writer-director Shelton really knows the territory, and both stars look good on the court, though the film does become slightly redundant after a point. Perez is fun as Woody's girlfriend whose goal is to appear on *Jeopardy!* Some versions run 117m. [R] ▼●

White Mischief (1988-British) **C-106m.** *** D: Michael Radford. Sarah Miles, Joss Ackland, John Hurt, Greta Scacchi, Charles Dance, Susan Fleetwood, Jacqueline Pearce, Murray Head, Geraldine Chaplin, Trevor Howard, Hugh Grant. Elegantly kinky tale based on James Fox's book about the British colony living in Kenya's Happy Valley during early days of WW2, and true story of a husband's response to the local stud stealing his beautiful wife. Sensual and quietly bizarre, with meticulous production detail and a fine cast, headed by Scacchi at her most stunning. [R]▼●

White Nights (1957-Italian) **94m.** *** D: Luchino Visconti. Maria Schell, Jean Marais, Marcello Mastroianni, Clara Calamai. Shy Mastroianni comes upon mysterious Schell, who's been dumped by sailor boyfriend Marais (or so it seems). A captivating, elaborately plotted love story, and a key film in Visconti's transition away from neorealism. Based on a Dostoyevsky story. Original running time 107m.▼

White Nights (1985) **C-135m.** **½ D: Taylor Hackford. Mikhail Baryshnikov, Gregory Hines, Isabella Rossellini, Jerzy Skolimowski, Helen Mirren, Geraldine Page, John Glover. Prominent ballet star who defected from Russia to U.S. finds himself back in the U.S.S.R. after a forced plane landing . . . while American expatriate tap dancer is used as bait to wear down his resistance about fleeing the country again. Baryshnikov's powerful presence (as actor and dancer) almost makes up for contrived story. Nicest surprise is surefooted performance by director Skolimowski as KGB agent. [PG-13]▼●

White of the Eye (1987-British) **C-110m.** *** D: Donald Cammell. David Keith, Cathy Moriarty, Art Evans, Alan Rosenberg, Alberta Watson, Michael Greene, Mark Hayashi. Bizarre thriller set in a small Arizona town about psycho Keith, who's (understandably) having marital squabbles with wife Moriarty. Dazzling technique recalling the experimental films of the 1960s marks this disturbing picture, a smashing return to films for director Cammell (PERFORMANCE, DEMON SEED) and Moriarty. [R]▼

White Palace (1990) **C-103m.** *** D: Luis Mandoki. Susan Sarandon, James Spader, Jason Alexander, Kathy Bates, Eileen Brennan, Spiros Focas, Gina Gershon, Steven Hill, Rachel Levin (Chagall), Corey Parker, Renee Taylor. Superficial but entertaining story of a vulnerable yuppie who's swept away by a sexy older woman . . . and then has to deal with the reality of their enormous social and ethnic differences. Sarandon is ideal in a vivid and believable performance. Reportedly, the improbable conclusion was tacked on at the last minute. Scripted by Ted Tally and Alvin Sargent, from Glenn Savan's novel. [R]▼●◗

White Rose, The (1983-German) **C-108m.** *** D: Michael Verhoeven. Lena Stolze, Martin Benrath, Wulf Kessler, Werner Stocker. Pointed, fascinating account of a group of Munich students who, in 1942, launched an anti-Nazi uprising. Based on fact; Stolze also played her character in Percy Adlon's THE FIVE LAST DAYS and later starred in Verhoeven's not-dissimilar THE NASTY GIRL.▼

White Sands (1992) **C-101m.** ** D: Roger Donaldson. Willem Dafoe, Mary Elizabeth Mastrantonio, Mickey Rourke, Sam (Samuel L.) Jackson, M. Emmet Walsh, James Rebhorn, Maura Tierney. Smalltown lawman finds a corpse, then starts snooping around into what turns out to be some dirty undercover-narc business involving the FBI. Competently performed (even by Rourke), but with little else to distinguish it from dozens of its ilk; Mastrantonio fares best as a complex society type up to her neck in drug-dealing. Mimi Rogers, Fred Dalton Thompson and John P. Ryan appear unbilled. Panavision. [R] ▼●◗

White Savage (1943) **C-75m.** **½ D: Arthur Lubin. Jon Hall, Maria Montez, Sabu, Don Terry, Turhan Bey, Thomas Gomez, Sidney Toler. Standard escapist fare, in glorious Technicolor, with island princess Montez trying to remove obstacles that bar marriage to shark-hunter Hall. Richard Brooks' first screenplay!

White Sheik, The (1951-Italian) **83m.** **½ D: Federico Fellini. Alberto Sordi, Brunella Bova, Leopoldo Trieste, Giulietta Masina. Fellini's first solo film as director is a minor chronicle of the adventures of a provincial couple honeymooning in Rome and the wife's involvement with a cartoon hero, The White Sheik (Sordi). Remade, more or less, as THE WORLD'S GREATEST LOVER.▼

White Sister, The (1933) **110m.** **½ D:

Victor Fleming. Helen Hayes, Clark Gable, Lewis Stone, Louise Closser Hale, May Robson, Edward Arnold. Dated but interesting remake of 1923 silent with Lillian Gish and Ronald Colman. Hayes is woman who enters convent when she thinks her lover has been killed in the war. Fine performances offset predictable story.▼

White Sister (1973-Italian) **C-104m.** **½ D: Alberto Lattuada. Sophia Loren, Adriano Celentano, Fernando Rey. Strange love story of hospital Mother Superior and self-professed young Communist who helps run the wards. [R]

White Slave Ship (1962-Italian) **C-92m.** *½ D: Silvio Amadio. Pier Angeli, Edmund Purdom, Armand Mestral, Ivan Desny. Childish hokum, set in 18th century, of rebellion aboard vessel carrying women to the colonies. Totalscope.

White Squall (1996) **C-127m.** *** D: Ridley Scott. Jeff Bridges, Caroline Goodall, John Savage, Scott Wolf, Jeremy Sisto, Ryan Phillippe, David Lascher, Eric Michael Cole, Jason Marsden, David Selby, Julio Mechoso, Balthazar Getty, Zeljko Ivanek, Ethan (Randall) Embry, James Rebhorn. In 1960, teenage boys—many of them misfits—sign on as shipmates and students with a "floating school" skippered by hard-nosed Bridges, who wants them to learn to rely both on themselves and each other. Put down by some as a paraphrase of DEAD POETS SOCIETY, this is an involving, well-acted coming-of-age drama on its own terms. Climactic storm sequence is genuinely gripping, but the finale seems somehow tacked on. Panavision. [PG-13]▼●◗

White Squaw, The (1956) **75m.** *½ D: Ray Nazarro. David Brian, May Wynn, William Bishop, Nancy Hale. Tedious narrative and a reverse situation; government taking away land from white rancher to give back to the Indians.

White Tie and Tails (1946) **81m.** **½ D: Charles Barton. Dan Duryea, William Bendix, Ella Raines, Clarence Kolb, Frank Jenks, John Miljan, Scotty Beckett. Breezy film with usual-villain Duryea in good comedy form as butler who pretends to be master of house while boss is away.

White Tower, The (1950) **C-98m.** **½ D: Ted Tetzlaff. Glenn Ford, Claude Rains, (Alida) Valli, Oscar Homolka, Cedric Hardwicke, Lloyd Bridges. Stunning location filming in the French Alps helps otherwise ordinary melodrama of various individuals of many nationalities, who attempt to scale a "monstrous, beautiful" mountain peak. Scripted by Paul Jarrico, from James Ramsey Ullman's best-seller.▼

White Voices (1965-Italian) **C-93m.** *** D: Pasquale Festa Campanile, Massimo Franciosa. Paolo Ferrari, Sandra Milo, Anouk Aimée, Graziella Granata, Barbara Steele. Good lusty adventure à la TOM JONES concerns exploits of castrati-singers who have retained high singing voices by means of operation. Techniscope.

White Warrior, The (1961-Italian) **C-86m.** *½ D: Riccardo Freda. Steve Reeves, Giorgia Moll, Renato Baldini, Gerard Herter. Tiring spectacle about tribal chieftain leading rebellion against advancing troops of Czar, set in 19th century. Dyaliscope.▼

White Water Summer (1987) **C-90m.** *½ D: Jeff Bleckner. Kevin Bacon, Sean Astin, Jonathan Ward, K.C. Martel, Matt Adler, Caroline McWilliams, Charles Siebert. Feeble account of Bacon teaching city lad Astin and his pals the ways of the wilderness. Filmed in 1985 and barely released theatrically. Aka RITES OF SUMMER. [PG]▼●

White Wilderness (1958) **C-73m.** *** D: James Algar. Narrated by Winston Hibler. Typically good Disney True-Life feature takes a look at the Arctic region; highlight is extended sequence on lemmings and their yearly suicide ritual.▼

White Witch Doctor (1953) **C-96m.** **½ D: Henry Hathaway. Susan Hayward, Robert Mitchum, Walter Slezak, Timothy Carey. Bakuba territory is scene of diverse interests of nurse Hayward who wants to bring modern medicine to natives and adventurers Mitchum and Slezak bent on finding hidden treasure.

White Zombie (1932) **73m.** *** D: Victor Halperin. Bela Lugosi, Madge Bellamy, Joseph Cawthorn, Robert Frazer, John Harron, Brandon Hurst, Clarence Muse. Zombie master Lugosi menaces newlyweds on Haitian sugar plantation; eerie, unique low-budget chiller. Also shown in a computer-colored version. ▼●◗

Who? (1973-British) **C-93m.** **½ D: Jack Gold. Elliott Gould, Trevor Howard, Joseph Bova, Ed Grover, James Noble, John Lehne. Gould plays FBI agent investigating American scientist's car crash in Russia, and subsequent reappearance with a strangely restructured face. Intriguing if not completely satisfying spy/sci-fi mix. Based on the novel by Algis Budrys. Video title: ROBO MAN. [PG]▼

Who Am I? SEE: **Jackie Chan's Who Am I?**

Who Dares Wins SEE: **Final Option, The**

Who Done It? (1942) **75m.** *** D: Erle C. Kenton. Bud Abbott, Lou Costello, Patric Knowles, Louise Allbritton, William Gargan, William Bendix, Mary Wickes, Don Porter, Thomas Gomez, Jerome Cowan, Ludwig Stossel. One of A&C's best finds the boys as would-be radio writers who pretend to be detectives when the network's president is murdered, and everyone believes them—including the killer! Great supporting cast is topped by Wickes as wise-cracking secretary and Bendix as real cop who's even dumber than Lou.▼●

Who Done It? (1956-British) **85m.** **½ D: Basil Dearden. Benny Hill, Belinda Lee, David Kossoff, Garry Marsh, George Margo, Ernest Thesiger. Hill's only star vehicle movie is a Red Skelton-type comedy about a novice private eye involved with foreign spies. No double-entendre jokes, but lots of slapstick, much of it labored and obvious. Best for kids.▼

Who Fears the Devil SEE: **Legend of Hillbilly John, The**

Who Framed Roger Rabbit (1988) **C-103m.** ***½ D: Robert Zemeckis. Bob Hoskins, Christopher Lloyd, Joanna Cassidy, Stubby Kaye, Alan Tilvern, and the voices of Charles Fleischer, Lou Hirsch, Mel Blanc, Mae Questel, Tony Anselmo, June Foray, Wayne Allwine. Staggering special-effects comedy places down-and-out 1940s detective Hoskins on the trail of a murderer, with cartoon star Roger Rabbit (the chief suspect) at his side. Flaws in story and characterization pale alongside the incredible blend of live-action and animation, but the ultimate feat is making us believe that Roger and his cartoon colleagues actually exist. Extra fun: spotting the many cartoon stars who make cameo appearances. Jessica Rabbit's speaking voice was done by Kathleen Turner (unbilled) and her singing voice by Amy Irving. A coproduction of the Steven Spielberg and Walt Disney companies. Animation director Richard Williams received a special Academy Award; three other Oscars included one for Special Visual Effects. [PG]▼●

Who Goes There? SEE: **Passionate Sentry, The**

Who Has Seen the Wind (1977-Canadian) **C-100m.** **½ D: Allan King. Brian Painchaud, Douglas Junor, Gordon Pinsent, Chapelle Jaffe, Jose Ferrer, Helen Shaver. OK chronicle of young Painchaud and Junor's life in Saskatchewan during the Depression. Ferrer is amusing as a bootlegger.▼

Who Is Harry Kellerman and Why Is He Saying Those Terrible Things About Me? (1971) **C-108m.** ** D: Ulu Grosbard. Dustin Hoffman, Barbara Harris, Jack Warden, David Burns, Gabriel Dell, Dom DeLuise, Betty Walker. Muddled comedy-drama by Herb Gardner casts Dustin as successful rock composer-singer who finds money doesn't answer all of life's questions. Harris comes along late in film to save this debacle with an outstanding performance. [PG]▼

Who Is Killing the Great Chefs of Europe? (1978) **C-112m.** *** D: Ted Kotcheff. George Segal, Jacqueline Bisset, Robert Morley, Jean-Pierre Cassel, Philippe Noiret, Jean Rochefort, Madge Ryan, Joss Ackland, Nigel Havers. Slick comedy whodunit with self-explanatory title has luscious views of European scenery and food, plus a magnificently funny role for Morley as the world's premier gourmet. Script by Peter Stone, based on Nan and Ivan Lyons' novel. [PG]▼

Who Is Killing the Stuntmen? SEE: **Stunts**

Who Killed Doc Robbin? (1948) **C-50m.** ** D: Bernard Carr. Virginia Grey, Don Castle, George Zucco, Whitford Kane, Larry Olsen, Eilene Janssen, Gerard Perreau. Second attempt by producer Hal Roach to rekindle the OUR GANG magic. This time the kids try to rescue a handyman who's accused of murdering a local "mad scientist." Retitled CURLEY AND HIS GANG IN THE HAUNTED MANSION for TV.

Who Killed Gail Preston? (1938) **60m.** **½ D: Leon Barsha. Don Terry, Rita Hayworth, Robert Paige, Wyn Cahoon, Gene Morgan, Marc Lawrence, Arthur Loft. Minor whodunit fairly well played; murder in a nightclub is the premise.

Who Killed Mary What's'ername? (1971) **C-90m.** **½ D: Ernie Pintoff. Red Buttons, Alice Playten, Sylvia Miles, Sam Waterston, Dick Williams, Conrad Bain. Diabetic ex-boxer sets out to find a prostitute's murderer when he becomes angered at everyone's indifference. Whodunit isn't bad, but nothing special; acting is generally good. [PG]▼

Who Killed Teddy Bear? (1965) **91m.** *½ D: Joseph Cates. Juliet Prowse, Sal Mineo, Jan Murray, Elaine Stritch, Dan Travanty (Daniel J. Travanti). Sleazy, leering low-budget suspenser about psychopathic busboy Mineo preying on discotheque hostess Prowse. A waste of talent.

Who Killed the Mysterious Mr. Foster? SEE: **Sam Hill: Who Killed Mr. Foster?**

Whole Nine Yards, The (2000) **C-101m.** **½ D: Jonathan Lynn. Bruce Willis, Matthew Perry, Rosanna Arquette, Michael Clarke Duncan, Amanda Peet, Natasha Henstridge, Kevin Pollak. Perry is broadly funny as a miserably married dentist who learns that his new neighbor is a notorious hit-man. He figures to get something he wants by ratting out the gunman to his former Chicago gang . . . but quickly gets in over his head. Farcical black comedy has enough twists, turns, and laughs to overcome its basic silliness. [PG-13]▼●◗

Whole Town's Talking, The (1935) **95m.** *** D: John Ford. Edward G. Robinson, Jean Arthur, Wallace Ford, Arthur Hohl, Edward Brophy, Arthur Byron, Donald Meek. Entertaining comedy with meek clerk Robinson a lookalike for notorious gangster; fine performances by E. G. and Arthur. Script by Jo Swerling and Robert Riskin, from a W. R. Burnett novel.▼

Whole Truth, The (1958-British) **84m.** **½ D: John Guillermin. Stewart Granger, Donna Reed, George Sanders, Gianna Maria Canale. Good cast lends strength to fair plot of almost perfect attempt to pin murder of movie starlet on producer Granger.

Whole Wide World, The (1996) **C-105m.** *** D: Dan Ireland. Vincent D'Onofrio, Renee Zellweger, Ann Wedgeworth, Harve Presnell, Benjamin Mouton, Michael Corbett. Poignant, based-on-fact drama, set in Texas during the 1930s and charting the complex relationship between two independent-minded souls: pulp novelist Robert E. Howard, the obsessive, overbearing creator of Conan the Barbarian, and schoolteacher/aspiring writer Novalyne Price, upon whose memoir this is based. Their dreams and realities are vividly etched in this extremely well acted film. Clairmont-Scope. [PG]▼●

Who'll Stop the Rain (1978) **C-126m.** *** D: Karel Reisz. Nick Nolte, Tuesday Weld, Michael Moriarty, Anthony Zerbe, Richard Masur, Ray Sharkey, David Opatoshu, Gail Strickland, Charles Haid. Robert Stone's National Book Award-winning *Dog Soldiers* suffers from excessively genteel treatment in telling its truly mean story about the smuggling of heroin from Vietnam to California. Strong performances in virtually every role. Aka DOG SOLDIERS. [R]▼●

Wholly Moses (1980) **C-109m.** *½ D: Gary Weis. Dudley Moore, Laraine Newman, James Coco, Paul Sand, Jack Gilford, Dom DeLuise, John Houseman, Madeline Kahn, David L. Lander, Richard Pryor, John Ritter. Great cast flounders in this stale saga of "savior" Moore, who thinks God has ordained him to lead the Jews out of Egypt. Some amusing bits, notably by DeLuise; otherwise, an appalling waste. Panavision. [PG]▼●

Whoopee! (1930) **C-93m.** *** D: Thornton Freeland. Eddie Cantor, Eleanor Hunt, Paul Gregory, John Rutherford, Ethel Shutta. Antique movie musical sparked by Cantor's performance as a hyper hypochondriac, and Busby Berkeley's wonderful production numbers. Cantor sings "Making Whoopee" and "My Baby Just Cares for Me"; the girl who sings the first chorus of the opening song is a very young Betty Grable. Filmed in two-color Technicolor. Remade as UP IN ARMS.▼●

Whoopee Boys, The (1986) **C-88m.** BOMB D: John Byrum. Michael O'Keefe, Paul Rodriguez, Denholm Elliott, Carole Shelley, Andy Bumatai, Eddie Deezen, Marsha Warfield, Joe Spinell, Dan O' Herlihy. Awful comedy about a couple of wiseguys who try to break into Palm Beach society. Crude, to say the least. [R]▼

Whore (1991) **C-85m.** ** D: Ken Russell. Theresa Russell, Benjamin Mouton, Antonio Fargas, Sanjay, Elizabeth Morehead, Michael Crabtree, John Diehl, Jack Nance, Tom Villard, Ginger Lynn Allen. Reinventing the Wheel: The gist of this melodrama is that streetwalking is a dead-end profession with lots of sordid characters. Russell's performance is so broad—but sometimes so funny—that it's difficult to gauge how good or bad it is. Available on video in a 92m. uncut European release, in the 85m. NC-17 version released in U.S. theaters, in an 85m. "R" version—and in the same 85m. version that's been packaged for title-shy stores as IF YOU CAN'T SAY IT, JUST SEE IT. Hardly worth the trouble. ▼●

Who's Afraid of Virginia Woolf? (1966) **129m.** ***½ D: Mike Nichols. Elizabeth Taylor, Richard Burton, George Segal, Sandy Dennis. Two couples get together for an all-night session of bitter conversation; Burton and Taylor's finest hour (together) in searing Edward Albee drama. Taylor and Dennis won Oscars, as did Haskell Wexler's incisive b&w photography, Richard Sylbert's art direction, and Irene Sharaff's costumes. Film broke Hollywood taboos for adult material, would cause lesser furor today. Script by producer Ernest Lehman. Nichols' first film as director.▼●◗

Who Says I Can't Ride a Rainbow? (1971) **C-85m.** **½ D: Edward Mann. Jack Klugman, Norma French, Reuben Figueroa, David Mann, Morgan Freeman, Esther Rolle. Offbeat story of man who feels it is the children of the world who will determine its future. Freeman's film debut. [G]

Who's Been Sleeping in My Bed? (1963) **C-103m.** **½ D: Daniel Mann. Dean Martin, Elizabeth Montgomery, Carol Burnett, Martin Balsam, Jill St. John, Richard Conte, Louis Nye. Undemanding fluff about TV star Martin being urged altar-ward by fiancée Montgomery. Burnett, in her film debut, is his psychiatrist's nurse. Panavision.

Whose Life Is It Anyway? (1981) **C-118m.** ***½ D: John Badham. Richard Dreyfuss, John Cassavetes, Christine Lahti, Bob Balaban, Kenneth McMillan, Kaki Hunter, Janet Eilber, Thomas Carter. Searing black comedy in which sculptor Dreyfuss is paralyzed from the neck down in an auto accident, argues for his right to die. Remarkable performance by Dreyfuss, excellent ones by hospital chief of staff Cassavetes, doctor Lahti, judge McMillan, nurse trainee Hunter. From Brian Clark's hit play, with a script by the author and Reginald Rose. Panavision. [R]▼

Who's Got the Action? (1962) **C-93m.** **½ D: Daniel Mann. Dean Martin, Lana Turner, Eddie Albert, Nita Talbot, Walter Matthau, Paul Ford, Margo, John McGiver, Jack Albertson. Strained froth of Turner combatting hubby Martin's horse-racing fever by turning bookie. Panavision.▼

Who's Harry Crumb? (1989) **C-98m.** ** D: Paul Flaherty. John Candy, Jeffrey Jones, Annie Potts, Tim Thomerson, Barry Corbin, Shawnee Smith, Valri Bromfield, Renee

Coleman, Joe Flaherty, Lyle Alzado, James Belushi, Stephen Young. Candy is ideally cast as an inept private detective attempting to unearth a kidnapper in this uneven comedy. Has some very funny moments, but too much outright silliness. [PG-13]▼●◗

Who Shot Patakango? (1990) **C-102m.** ** D: Robert Brooks. David Knight, Sandra Bullock, Kevin Otto, Aaron Ingram, Brad Randall. Slight, meandering account of life at a Brooklyn vocational high school in 1957, a time when blacks were moving from the South into Northern inner cities and whites had not yet fled to the suburbs. Brooks coscripted and coedited with wife Halle; he also photographed, and she produced. Aka WHO SHOT PAT? [R]▼●◗

Who Slew Auntie Roo? (1971) **C-89m.** ** D: Curtis Harrington. Shelley Winters, Mark Lester, Chloe Franks, Ralph Richardson, Lionel Jeffries, Hugh Griffith. Sickie about daffy old lady who steers unwitting children into her lair. Made in England; intended to be a travesty of *Hansel and Gretel*! Aka WHOEVER SLEW AUNTIE ROO? [PG]▼

Who's Minding the Mint? (1967) **C-97m.** ***½ D: Howard Morris. Jim Hutton, Dorothy Provine, Milton Berle, Joey Bishop, Bob Denver, Walter Brennan, Victor Buono, Jack Gilford, Jamie Farr, Jackie Joseph. Hilarious comedy, neglected at time of release, is tremendous fun in the classic comedy tradition, with motley gang of thieves helping U.S. Mint worker Hutton replace money he accidentally destroyed. Buono is especially funny as pompous ex-skipper.▼

Who's Minding the Store? (1963) **C-90m.** **½ D: Frank Tashlin. Jerry Lewis, Agnes Moorehead, Jill St. John, John McGiver, Ray Walston, Nancy Kulp, Francesca Bellini. Jerry Lewis vehicle with bumbling idiot (guess who?) set loose in department store. Great supporting cast in stereotyped comic foil roles, plus one good inventive bit.

Who's That Girl? (1987) **C-94m.** BOMB D: James Foley. Madonna, Griffin Dunne, Haviland Morris, John McMartin, Robert Swan, Drew Pillsbury, John Mills. Atrocious attempt at screwball comedy with Dunne as the hapless hero whose life is turned inside out when he's assigned to escort Madonna (just sprung from jail) out of town. Derivative film is missing just two things: charm and humor. [PG]▼●

Who's That Knocking at My Door (1968) **90m.** *** D: Martin Scorsese. Zina Bethune, Harvey Keitel, Anne Collette, Lennard Kuras, Michael Scala, Harry Northup, Bill Minkin. Crude but fascinating autobiographical drama from Scorsese, his first feature, focusing on relationship between streetwise Keitel, hung up by his strict Catholic upbringing, and independent young woman (Bethune). Keitel's film debut. Also released as J.R.▼

Who's the Man? (1993) **C-85m.** ** D: Ted Demme. Ed Lover, Doctor Dre, Badja Djola, Cheryl "Salt" James, Jim Moody, Ice T, Andre B. Blake, Rozwill Young, Colin Quinn, Denis Leary, Kurt Loder, Richard Bright. Nonsensical airhead of a movie in which MTV rap veejays Ed Lover and Doctor Dre play characters named Ed Lover and Doctor Dre, inept Harlem haircutters who somehow become N.Y.C. cops and battle a villainous real estate speculator. Loud, crude, and crammed with cameos by a variety of rap artists (Kriss Kross, B-Real, Humpty Hump, Queen Latifah). Not without laughs, but more valuable as an artifact of the early 90s. [R]▼●

Who Stole the Body? (1962-French) **92m.** ** D: Jean Girault. Francis Blanche, Darry Cowl, Clement Harari, Daniel Ceccaldi, Mario David. Weak farce on horror films, with Blanche and Cowl two dimwits trying to solve a crime.

Who Was That Lady? (1960) **115m.** *** D: George Sidney. Tony Curtis, Dean Martin, Janet Leigh, James Whitmore, John McIntire, Barbara Nichols, Joi Lansing. Spicy shenanigans move along at lively pace as Curtis and Martin pretend to be secret agents to confuse Tony's jealous wife Leigh; script by Norman Krasna, from his play.

Who Will Love My Children? (1983) **C-100m. TVM** D: John Erman. Ann-Margret, Frederic Forrest, Cathryn Damon, Donald Moffat, Lonny Chapman, Patricia Smith, Christopher Allport, Tracey Gold, Soleil Moon Frye, Robbie Kiger. Dying mother strives to have her ten children placed with loving families in this poignant weeper, based by writer Michael Bortman on the true story of Iowa farm wife Lucile Fray. Above average.▼

Why Bother to Knock (1964-British) **88m.** *½ D: Cyril Frankel. Elke Sommer, Richard Todd, Nicole Maurey, Scot Finch. Trashy smut about Todd traipsing around Europe giving out keys to his pals, with the girls all turning up unexpectedly. CinemaScope.

Why Do Fools Fall in Love (1998) **C-112m.** ** D: Gregory Nava. Halle Berry, Vivica A. Fox, Lela Rochon, Larenz Tate, Paul Mazursky, Pamela Reed, Alexis Cruz, David Barry Gray, Miguel A. Nunez, Jr., Clifton Powell, Ben Vereen, Lane Smith. Disappointing account of ill-fated 1950s rock 'n' roller Frankie Lymon (Tate), who ended up a junkie and died of an overdose in 1968 at age 26, and the three very different women he allegedly married. Superficial, to say the least, and sometimes embarrassing. Little Richard (playing himself) enlivens the proceedings whenever he is onscreen. [R] ▼●◗

Why Has Bodhi-Dharma Left for the East? (1989-Korean) **C-135m.** *** D: Bae Yong-kyun. Yi Pan-yong, Sin Won-sop, Huang Hae-jin, Ko Su-myong, Kim Haeyong. Meditative, mind-expanding account of an elderly, dying Zen master and his two disciples, a monk and a boy; they retire to a rural monastery, away from the "turbulence of life," where the master attempts to guide the others toward a state of enlightenment. An unusual film, not for all temperaments, but most rewarding if you can immerse yourself in its flow. Premiered theatrically in the U.S. in 1993.▼●◗

Why Must I Die? (1960) **86m.** ** D: Roy Del Ruth. Terry Moore, Debra Paget, Bert Freed, Julie Reding. Similar to I WANT TO LIVE except in quality. Moore is singer falsely convicted of murder, with expected histrionics.

Why Not! (1979-French) **C-93m.** *** D: Coline Serreau. Sami Frey, Christine Murillo, Mario Gonzalez, Michel Aumont, Nicole Jamet, Mathe Souverbie. Frey, Murillo and Gonzalez, trying to leave their pasts behind, are roommates—and share the same bed. Then Frey becomes involved with Jamet. Sometimes funny and touching, but not as involving as it should be. Original title: POURQUOI PAS!

Why Shoot the Teacher? (1977-Canadian) **C-101m.** *** D: Silvio Narizzano. Bud Cort, Samantha Eggar, Chris Wiggins, Gary Reineke, John Friesen, Michael J. Reynolds. Simple, warm, enjoyable story of Cort's experiences when he takes a teaching job in a small, isolated farming town during the Depression.▼

Why Worry? (1923) **77m.** ***½ D: Fred Newmeyer, Sam Taylor. Harold Lloyd, Jobyna Ralston, John Aasen, Leo White, James Mason. Hilarious story of millionaire playboy Lloyd who stumbles into revolution-ridden country and inadvertently becomes involved. Packed with belly-laugh sight-gags.

Why Would Anyone Want to Kill a Nice Girl Like You? (1969-British) **C-99m.** ** D: Don Sharp. Eva Renzi, David Buck, Peter Vaughan, Paul Hubschmid, Sophie Hardy, Kay Walsh. A young tourist on the French Riviera thinks someone is trying to kill her, but none of the local officials will believe her. Familiar storyline handled in routine fashion.

Why Would I Lie? (1980) **C-105m.** *½ D: Larry Peerce. Treat Williams, Lisa Eichhorn, Gabriel Swann, Susan Heldfond, Anne Byrne, Valerie Curtin, Jocelyn Brando, Nicolas Coster, Severn Darden. Irrational dud about compulsive liar Williams, who tries to unite Swann with ex-con mother Eichhorn. Film is also odiously reactionary; the villainess (Heldfond) is a one-dimensionally manipulative, man-hating feminist. [PG]

Wichita (1955) **C-81m.** **½ D: Jacques Tourneur. Joel McCrea, Vera Miles, Lloyd Bridges, Wallace Ford, Peter Graves, Edgar Buchanan, John Smith, Keith Andes, Jack Elam, Robert Wilke. Action-filled Western; good cast helps Wyatt Earp (McCrea) restore order to Western town overrun with outlaws. CinemaScope.▼

Wicked as They Come (1957-British) **94m.** ** D: Ken Hughes. Arlene Dahl, Phil Carey, Herbert Marshall, David Kossoff. Dahl cavorts nicely in this minor story of a girl from the poor part of town involved with the wrong people.

Wicked City, The (1950-French) **76m.** *½ D: Francois Villiers. Maria Montez, Jean-Pierre Aumont, Lilli Palmer, Marcel Dalio. Even exotic Montez can't spice lazy telling of unscrupulous woman and the gob she involves in her sordid life.

Wicked Dreams of Paula Schultz, The (1968) **C-113m.** BOMB D: George Marshall. Elke Sommer, Bob Crane, Werner Klemperer, Joey Forman, John Banner, Maureen Arthur. Laughless dud about beautiful East German Olympic hopeful who polevaults over Berlin Wall to freedom; unengaging cast was mostly recruited from *Hogan's Heroes.*

Wicked Lady, The (1945-British) **104m.** **½ D: Leslie Arliss. Margaret Lockwood, James Mason, Patricia Roc, Michael Rennie, Martita Hunt, Felix Aylmer. Title refers to Lockwood, in this unconvincing costumer of female outlaw who teams with robber Mason in evil doings. Remade in 1983.▼

Wicked Lady, The (1983-British) **C-98m.** *½ D: Michael Winner. Faye Dunaway, Alan Bates, John Gielgud, Denholm Elliott, Prunella Scales, Oliver Tobias, Glynis Barber, Joan Hickson, Marina Sirtis. Remake of 1945 film about a scheming vixen who becomes a "highwayman" by night; hasn't the panache to turn its campy material into the romp it's intended to be. Heavy-handed stuff—including the periodic nudity. [R] ▼

Wicked Stepmother (1989) **C-92m.** BOMB D: Larry Cohen. Bette Davis, Barbara Carrera, Colleen Camp, David Rasche, Lionel Stander, Tom Bosley, Richard Moll, Evelyn Keyes. Complete mess, pieced together from a troubled (to say the least) production which Davis left after filming for just one week. Resulting patchwork story has Bette as a witch who marries Stander and then, for some reason, turns into Carrera. Notable only as a footnote in Davis' career; this was her final film. [PG-13]▼

Wicked, Wicked (1973) **C-95m.** BOMB D: Richard L. Bare. Tiffany Bolling, Scott Brady, David Bailey, Edd Byrnes. Disastrous mystery-thriller centering around series of hotel murders. Film was released in Duo-vision split-screen process with two things happening at once. Pity there was not enough material for even one. [PG]

Wicked Woman (1954) **77m.** *½ D: Russell Rouse. Richard Egan, Beverly Michaels, Percy Helton, Evelyn Scott. Lumbering drama about no-good waitress leading assorted men astray.

Wicker Man, The (1973-British) **C-103m.** ***½ D: Robin Hardy. Edward Woodward, Christopher Lee, Britt Ekland, Diane Cilento, Ingrid Pitt, Lindsay Kemp. Harrowing, absorbing thriller by Anthony Shaffer; not really a horror film as many believe. Scot police sergeant Woodward comes to small island investigating disappearance of a child, discovers a society of modern pagans. Eerie and erotic, with seemingly authentic local color and folk music; a must-see. Shown only in truncated versions for many years; beware the 87m. and 95m. prints, which may still be in circulation. [R]▼

Wide Awake (1998) **C-90m.** *** D: M. Night Shyamalan. Joseph Cross, Timothy Reifsnyder, Dana Delany, Denis Leary, Robert Loggia, Rosie O'Donnell, Camryn Manheim, Dan Lauria, Julia Stiles. A 10-year-old Catholic school student has loving, affluent parents, but since the recent death of his beloved grandfather, he's been trying to figure out the meaning of life. Warm, quirky, and sensitive comedy/drama/parable. Young lead Cross and costar Loggia (as the deceased grandparent, in flashbacks) stand out in fine cast. Written by the director; shot in 1995. [PG]▼●◗

Wide Blue Road, The (1956-Italian) **100m.** **½ D: Gillo Pontecorvo. Yves Montand, Alida Valli, Francisco Rabal, Peter Carsten, Ronaldino. Montand is non-plussed playboy taking pleasure where he finds it until Valli comes into picture. Performers outshine dialogue.

Wide Open Faces (1938) **67m.** **½ D: Kurt Neumann. Joe E. Brown, Jane Wyman, Alison Skipworth, Lyda Roberti, Alan Baxter, Lucien Littlefield, Sidney Toler. Enjoyable Brown vehicle with top-notch supporting cast; innocent soda jerk mixed up with gangster.

Wide Sargasso Sea (1993-U.S.-Australian) **C-100m.** ** D: John Duigan. Karina Lombard, Nathaniel Parker, Rachel Ward, Michael York, Martine Beswicke, Claudia Robinson, Rowena King. In 1840s Jamaica, free-spirited Creole Antoinette (Lombard), heiress to a declining estate, marries proper Englishman Rochester (Parker); at first entranced by her powerful sensuality, he fears losing control, and coldly turns away from her, which leads to tragedy. Though attractive, a failed attempt to build real drama out of humid tropical passions. Based on Jean Rhys's novel, this is a ''prequel'' to Charlotte Brontë's *Jane Eyre*. Available on video in R and unrated versions. [NC-17] ▼●

Widow, The (1955-Italian) **89m.** ** D: Lewis Milestone. Patricia Roc, Anna Maria Ferrero, Massimo Serrato, Akim Tamiroff. Uneven soaper of Roc involved with lover Serrato, a sports car racer, who falls for Ferrero; film meanders.

Widow From Chicago, The (1930) **64m.** ** D: Edward L. Cline. Alice White, Neil Hamilton, Edward G. Robinson, Frank McHugh, Lee Shumway. Robinson plays a beer baron targeted for revenge by White, whose brother he rubbed out, in this antiquated gangster film, interesting only for Robinson's pre-LITTLE CAESAR performance.

Widows' Peak (1994) **C-101m.** **½ D: John Irvin. Joan Plowright, Mia Farrow, Natasha Richardson, Adrian Dunbar, Jim Broadbent, Britta Smith, Gerard McSorley. Fitfully amusing feminine slant on John Ford's brand of Blarney, with sadsack Farrow butting heads with flashy WW1 widow Richardson, who's moved to an Irish resort village in the mid 1920s. Inconsistent in tone, but three strong leads make it watchable. [PG]▼●

Wife, The (1994) **C-105m.** **½ D: Tom Noonan. Julie Hagerty, Tom Noonan, Wallace Shawn, Karen Young. Married New Age therapists Noonan and Hagerty are visited one evening by one of their patients (Shawn) and his seemingly emotionally disturbed wife (Young). Alternately pretentious and intriguing talkfest gets better as it goes along, but it's nowhere near as impressive as Noonan's previous film, WHAT HAPPENED WAS . . . . [R]▼●◗

Wife, Doctor and Nurse (1937) **85m.** **½ D: Walter Lang. Loretta Young, Warner Baxter, Virginia Bruce, Jane Darwell, Sidney Blackmer, Minna Gombell, Elisha Cook, Jr., Lon Chaney, Jr. Baxter is caught between two women, but seems uninterested in both. Bright comedy with expert cast.

Wife, Husband and Friend (1939) **80m.** *** D: Gregory Ratoff. Loretta Young, Warner Baxter, Binnie Barnes, George Barbier, Cesar Romero, J. Edward Bromberg, Eugene Pallette. Renie Riano. Entertaining comedy about aspiring singer Young whose husband Baxter tries to show her up; fun, but better as EVERYBODY DOES IT. Produced and scripted by Nunnally Johnson, from a story by James M. Cain(!)

Wifemistress (1977-Italian) **C-110m.** **½ D: Marco Vicario. Marcello Mastroianni, Laura Antonelli, Leonard Mann, Annie-Belle, Gastone Moschin, William Berger. Antonelli, repressed by philandering husband Mastroianni, sets out to explore his secret lives after he is forced into hiding and experiences her own sexual awakening. Sometimes erotic but mostly murky comedy-drama. [R]▼

Wife of Monte Cristo, The (1946) **80m.** ** D: Edgar G. Ulmer. John Loder, Lenore Aubert, Charles Dingle, Eduardo Ciannelli, Eva Gabor, Martin Kosleck. Corruption in the medical profession proves a formidable match for the Count; standard low-budget swashbuckler.▼

Wife Takes a Flyer, The (1942) **86m.** **

D: Richard Wallace. Joan Bennett, Franchot Tone, Allyn Joslyn, Cecil Cunningham, Chester Clute. Weak WW2 espionage comedy of Tone pretending to be Bennett's husband to escape from Holland.

Wife vs. Secretary (1936) **88m.** **½ D: Clarence Brown. Clark Gable, Jean Harlow, Myrna Loy, May Robson, George Barbier, James Stewart, Hobart Cavanaugh. Perfect example of Hollywood gloss, with three topnotch stars towering over inferior material. Harlow is particularly good in tale of secretary who becomes invaluable to her boss (Gable), causing complications in both of their lives.▼

Wife Wanted (1946) **73m.** ** D: Phil Karlson. Kay Francis, Paul Cavanagh, Robert Shayne, Veda Ann Borg. In her last film, Francis is film star innocently hooked up with lonely-heart crooks; low production values.

Wigstock: The Movie (1995) **C-85m.** *** D: Barry Shils. Campy documentary record of Wigstock, the drag ball held in N.Y.C. each Labor Day weekend. While famous drag queens like RuPaul appear, the focus is just as much on lesser-known characters such as The Lady Bunny (Wigstock's M.C.), Mistress Formica, and, best of all, the Dueling (Tallulah) Bankheads.▼●

Wilby Conspiracy, The (1975) **C-101m.** *** D: Ralph Nelson. Sidney Poitier, Michael Caine, Nicol Williamson, Prunella Gee, Persis Khambatta, Saeed Jaffrey, Rutger Hauer. Slick chase movie about black African political activist and the reluctant white companion he drags with him on cross-country flight from the law. Memories of Poitier's earlier THE DEFIANT ONES keep focusing throughout, but the two stars maintain a light touch. Sinister Williamson steals it from them both. [PG]▼

Wild America (1997) **C-106m.** ** D: William Dear. Jonathan Taylor Thomas, Devon Sawa, Scott Bairstow, Frances Fisher, Jamey Sheridan, Tracey Walter, Don Stroud. Ho-hum based-on-fact account of the three adventurous Stouffer brothers, who trek across America in 1967 to film wild animals in their natural habitats. The clichéd subplots do this one in, but it's harmless enough fare for kids. The eldest brother, Marty Stouffer (Bairstow), grew up to become a noted wildlife documentary filmmaker. Danny Glover appears unbilled. Clairmont-Scope. [PG] ▼●◗

Wild and the Innocent, The (1959) **C-84m.** **½ D: Jack Sher. Audie Murphy, Joanne Dru, Gilbert Roland, Jim Backus, Sandra Dee, George Mitchell, Peter Breck. Murphy and Dee make an engaging duo as trapper and untamed country girl involved in gunplay in town during July 4th holiday. CinemaScope.

Wild and the Willing, The (1962-British) **112m.** ** D: Ralph Thomas. Virginia Maskell, Paul Rogers, Samantha Eggar, Ian McShane, John Hurt, Richard Warner. Life and love at a provincial university, with over-earnest attempt to be realistic and daring in story of student who seduces professor's wife.

Wild and Wonderful (1964) **C-88m.** **½ D: Michael Anderson. Tony Curtis, Christine Kaufmann, Larry Storch, Marty Ingels, Jacques Aubuchon, Jules Munshin. Empty slapstick froth involving French poodle movie star with Curtis and Kaufmann romancing.

Wild Angels, The (1966) **C-93m.** *½ D: Roger Corman. Peter Fonda, Nancy Sinatra, Bruce Dern, Diane Ladd, Buck Taylor, Norman Alden, Michael J. Pollard, Joan Shawlee, Gayle Hunnicutt, Dick Miller. Predecessor of EASY RIDER without that film's class; Charles Griffith's story of destructive motorcycle gang is OK after about 24 beers. Peter Bogdanovich worked extensively on this film: writing, editing, second unit, etc.; he also can be glimpsed in one of the rumbles. Panavision.▼

Wild at Heart (1990) **C-127m.** ** D: David Lynch. Nicolas Cage, Laura Dern, Diane Ladd, Willem Dafoe, Isabella Rossellini, Harry Dean Stanton, Crispin Glover, Grace Zabriskie, J.E. Freeman, Calvin Lockhart, Marvin Kaplan, W. Morgan Sheppard, David Patrick Kelly, Freddie Jones, John Lurie, Jack Nance, Sherilyn Fenn, Sheryl Lee, Pruitt Taylor Vince. He's Elvis, she's Marilyn, they're madly in love and on the lam: they hop in her convertible and make an odyssey through Hell—or is it Oz? Diehard fans of writer-director Lynch may love this violent Southern Gothic melodrama (and there *are* great moments) but his utter absorption with ugliness makes it tough to take. Formidable performances all around, including real-life mother and daughter Ladd and Dern. Lynch based his screenplay on a novel by Barry Gifford. Rossellini's character went on to get a movie all her own, PERDITA DURANGO (1997). There, the role is played by Rosie Perez. Panavision. [R]▼●

Wild Beds SEE: **Tigers in Lipstick**

Wild Bill (1995) **C-97m.** ** D: Walter Hill. Jeff Bridges, Ellen Barkin, John Hurt, Diane Lane, Keith Carradine, Christina Applegate, Bruce Dern, James Gammon, David Arquette, Marjoe Gortner, James Remar. Odd revisionist take on Wild Bill Hickok, told in episodic form that creates distance from—rather than understanding of—the legendary hell-raiser of the Old West. The title of the film really should be THE ASSASSINATION OF WILD BILL, because that's what it's all about. There *are* those opium dreams to break the monotony . . . Barkin is fun as Calamity Jane, but other characters are superficially drawn at best. [R]▼●

Wild Blue Yonder, The (1951) **98m.**

**½ D: Allan Dwan. Wendell Corey, Vera Ralston, Forrest Tucker, Phil Harris, Walter Brennan, Harry Carey, Jr. Standard WW2 aviation yarn, saluting the B-29 bomber, detailing friendship of Corey and Tucker, rivalry for nurse Ralston, etc. And just for change of pace, Harris sings "The Thing."

Wild Boys of the Road (1933) **68m.** *** D: William A. Wellman. Frankie Darro, Rochelle Hudson, Dorothy Coonan, Edwin Philips, Ann Hovey, Arthur Hohl, Sterling Holloway. Darro, Philips, and Coonan are unable to find work during the Depression, so they ride the rails, panhandle, steal. Dated but still provocative Warner Bros. "social conscience" drama.

Wild Bunch, The (1969) **C-134m.** **** D: Sam Peckinpah. William Holden, Ernest Borgnine, Robert Ryan, Edmond O'Brien, Warren Oates, Ben Johnson, Jaime Sanchez, Strother Martin, L. Q. Jones, Albert Dekker, Bo Hopkins, Emilio Fernandez, Dub Taylor. Peckinpah's best film won instant notoriety for its "beautiful" bloodletting, but seems almost restrained alongside today's films. Aging outlaws with their own code of ethics find themselves passe in 1913 and decide to retire after one final haul. Acting, dialogue, direction, score, photography, and especially editing are world class; an authentic American classic. Reissued in 1981 at 142m., with two deleted sequences restored. European theatrical version running 144m. now available on homevideo. Panavision. [R]▼●◗

Wildcat (1942) **70m.** ** D: Frank McDonald. Richard Arlen, Arline Judge, Buster Crabbe, William Frawley, Arthur Hunnicutt, Elisha Cook, Jr. Crabbe and Arlen are rival oilmen dueling to see who can bring in the first well. Another Pine–Thomas production with the usual quota of thrills and romance.▼

Wildcats (1986) **C-107m.** *** D: Michael Ritchie. Goldie Hawn, Swoosie Kurtz, Robyn Lively, Brandy Gold, James Keach, Jan Hooks, Bruce McGill, Nipsey Russell, Mykel T. Williamson, Wesley Snipes, Woody Harrelson, M. Emmet Walsh, George Wyner, Ann Doran, Gloria Stuart, L.L. Cool J. Football-crazy phys-ed teacher Hawn finally gets her wish—to coach a varsity team—at a rough inner-city high school. Never strays from formula but manages to deliver the laughs. Entertaining. [R]▼●

Wild Cats on the Beach (1959-Italian) **C-96m.** **½ D: Vittorio Sala. Elsa Martinelli, Alberto Sordi, Georges Marchal, Antonio Cifariello. Quartet of love tales set at resort area of Cote D'Azur; varying in quality. Dyaliscope.

Wild Child, The (1970-French) **85m.** *** D: François Truffaut. François Truffaut, Jean-Pierre Cargol, Jean Daste, Paul Ville. Initially absorbing true story of wild boy raised alone in French woods and the doctor who tries to civilize him. Simply told, deliberately old-fashioned in technique; film loses steam half-way through. Truffaut is ideal as the doctor. Set in 1700s. [G]▼●

Wild Company (1930) **73m.** *½ D: Leo McCarey. H. B. Warner, Frank Albertson, Sharon Lynn, Joyce Compton, Claire McDowell, Bela Lugosi. Badly dated melodrama of flaming youth and generation-gap; devil-may-care Albertson ignores parents' warnings about company he keeps, gets into trouble over underworld murder. Lugosi plays nightclub owner.

Wild Country, The (1971) **C-100m.** **½ D: Robert Totten. Steve Forrest, Vera Miles, Ronny Howard, Jack Elam, Frank deKova, Morgan Woodward, Clint Howard. Standard Disney fare, adapted from Ralph Moody's *Little Britches,* about joys and hardships faced by family which moves from Pittsburgh to Wyoming in 1880s. Magnificent scenery. [G]▼

Wild Drifter SEE: **Cockfighter**

Wild Duck, The (1983-Australian) **C-96m.** *½ D: Henri Safran. Liv Ullmann, Jeremy Irons, Lucinda Jones, John Meillon, Arthur Dignam, Michael Pate. Dreary, disappointing adaptation of the Ibsen play, centering on two days in the lives of the Ackland (anglicized from "Ekdal") family members and updating the story by twenty-odd years. The question is: Why? Performances are OK, but it's oh so slow and pretentious. [PG]▼

Wilde (1998-British) **C-115m.** **½ D: Brian Gilbert. Stephen Fry, Jude Law, Tom Wilkinson, Vanessa Redgrave, Jennifer Ehle, Gemma Jones, Judy Parfitt, Zoë Wanamaker. Profile of playwright/author Oscar Wilde is much gamier (to its arguable detriment) than the two 1960 biopics. Begins choppily, drags at the end, but generally compels in a long midsection that deals with events leading up to Wilde's 1895 sodomy trial and conviction. Fry bears a striking resemblance to Wilde, while Wilkinson gives another in a string of rich performances as Wilde's chief adversary, the Marquis of Queensbury. 2.35 Research PLC. [R]▼

Wilder Napalm (1993) **C-109m.** *½ D: Glenn Gordon Caron. Debra Winger, Dennis Quaid, Arliss Howard, M. Emmet Walsh, Jim Varney. Bizarre, almost incomprehensible account of brothers Quaid and Howard, who share a rare talent: when concentrating deeply enough, they can make objects burst into flames. Winger is cast as Howard's spirited wife. It's no wonder that this barely watchable film remained unreleased for quite some time. [PG-13]▼●

Wilderness Family, Part 2 SEE: **Further Adventures of the Wilderness Family**

Wildflower (1991) **C-100m. TVM** D: Diane Keaton. Beau Bridges, Susan Blakely,

William McNamara, Patricia Arquette, Reese Witherspoon, Collin Wilcox Paxton. Delightful tale of a pair of rural '30s teenagers who befriend a "devil-tetched" epileptic (Arquette), living in a cage in the barn behind her abusive father's house. Lovingly adapted by Sara Flanigan from her book, *Alice*. Made for cable. Above average.▼

Wild for Kicks (1960-British) **92m.** ** D: Edmond T. Greville. David Farrar, Noelle Adam, Christopher Lee, Gillian Hills, Adam Faith, Shirley Anne Field, Peter McEnery, Oliver Reed. Sultry teen Hills, with a bad attitude, resents her father's pretty new French-born wife and summarily gets into all sorts of mischief. Not very good; of interest mainly as a period piece. Original British title: BEAT GIRL.▼

Wild Geese, The (1978-British) **C-134m.** **½ D: Andrew V. McLaglen. Richard Burton, Roger Moore, Richard Harris, Hardy Kruger, Stewart Granger, Jack Watson, Frank Finlay, Jeff Corey, Winston Ntshona. Silly but entertaining action yarn by Reginald Rose with Burton miscast as leader of mercenaries who rescue kidnapped African leader. Better (and shorter) script would have helped. Sequel followed in 1985. [R]▼●

Wild Geese II (1985-British) **C-125m.** ** D: Peter Hunt. Scott Glenn, Barbara Carrera, Edward Fox, Laurence Olivier, Robert Webber, Robert Freitag, Kenneth Haigh. Cluttered action-adventure about a much-wanted mercenary hired to spring arch-Nazi Rudolf Hess from Berlin's Spandau prison and the incidents this triggers. Uncomfortable mix of straight action and tongue-in-cheek. [R]▼

Wild Geese Calling (1941) **77m.** ** D: John Brahm. Henry Fonda, Joan Bennett, Warren William, Ona Munson, Barton MacLane, Russell Simpson. Action and romance in 1890s Oregon and Alaska, but not enough of either.

Wild Gold (1934) **75m.** ** D: George Marshall. John Boles, Claire Trevor, Harry Green, Roger Imhof, Monroe Owsley. Strange blend of comedy, melodrama, romance, and music in story of miner Boles infatuated with singer Trevor, facing irate husband, unexpected disaster in remote forest cabin. Uses stock footage from silent film THE JOHNSTOWN FLOOD.

Wild Guitar (1962) **87m.** BOMB D: Ray Dennis Steckler. Arch Hall, Jr., Nancy Czar, William Watters (Arch Hall, Sr.), Cash Flagg (Ray Dennis Steckler). Guitar-playing, motorcycle-riding Hall is exploited by a deceitful record executive. Perfectly awful melodrama.▼

Wild Harvest (1947) **92m.** *½ D: Tay Garnett. Alan Ladd, Dorothy Lamour, Robert Preston, Lloyd Nolan, Richard Erdman, Allen Jenkins. Pretty dismal film of traveling grain-harvesters with Preston and Ladd rivaling for Lamour's love.

Wild Heart, The (1950-British) **C-82m.** ** D: Michael Powell, Emeric Pressburger. Jennifer Jones, David Farrar, Cyril Cusack, Sybil Thorndike, Edward Chapman, George Cole, Hugh Griffith, Esmond Knight. Muddled tale of strange Welsh girl in late 19th century whose life is dominated by superstitions; she marries minister but is stirred by lusty squire. Beautiful location photography by Christopher Challis. Reedited from 110m. British release called GONE TO EARTH, which plays much better.

Wild Hearts Can't Be Broken (1991) **C-88m.** *** D: Steve Miner. Gabrielle Anwar, Michael Schoeffling, Cliff Robertson, Dylan Kussman, Kathleen York, Frank Renzulli. Absorbing Disney picture about real-life Sonora Webster, a strong-willed girl who joins a traveling show in the early 1930s and trains to become a "diving girl"—sitting astride a horse as it dives forty feet into a tank of water. Simply told, and well acted, with Robertson first-rate as a road-company Buffalo Bill. Captures Depression-era flavor (and look) much better than many more ambitious and expensive films. Incidentally, no horses were subjected to high-dives in the making of the film. [G]▼●

Wild Heritage (1958) **C-78m.** **½ D: Charles Haas. Will Rogers, Jr., Maureen O'Sullivan, Rod McKuen, Casey Tibbs, George Winslow, Gigi Perreau, Troy Donahue, John Beradino, Jeanette Nolan. Soaper involving events in the intertwining lives of two westward-bound pioneer families. CinemaScope.

Wild Horse Hank (1979-Canadian) **C-94m.** **½ D: Eric Till. Linda Blair, Michael Wincott, Al Waxman, Pace Bradford, Richard Crenna. Inoffensive adventure of college student Blair trying to save horses from being butchered for dog food. A bit overlong, and Blair walks through her role; still, older children may enjoy it.▼

Wild in the Country (1961) **C-114m.** **½ D: Philip Dunne. Elvis Presley, Hope Lange, Tuesday Weld, Millie Perkins, John Ireland, Gary Lockwood. Can *you* resist Elvis in a Clifford Odets script about a back-country hothead with literary aspirations? Clichéd if earnest, but an undeniable curiosity with some good performances, Elvis' among them. That's young Christina Crawford as Lockwood's girlfriend. CinemaScope.▼

Wild in the Sky (1972) **C-87m.** **½ D: William T. Naud. Georg Stanford Brown, Brandon de Wilde, Keenan Wynn, Tim O'Connor, James Daly, Dick Gautier, Robert Lansing. Zany idea doesn't quite come off in story of three prisoners who hijack a B-52 bomber. Written by Naud and Gautier. Original title: BLACK JACK.

Wild in the Streets (1968) **C-97m.** **½ D: Barry Shear. Christopher Jones, Shelley Winters, Diane Varsi, Hal Holbrook, Millie Perkins, Ed Begley, Richard Pryor, Bert Freed. Dark satire about millionaire singing idol/drug pusher who is elected President after voting age is lowered to 14. Wildly overrated by some critics, film is nonetheless enjoyable on a nonthink level. [PG—originally rated R]▼●

Wild Is the Wind (1957) **114m.** **½ D: George Cukor. Anna Magnani, Anthony Quinn, Anthony Franciosa, Dolores Hart, Joseph Calleia. Turgid soaper set in the West, with Quinn marrying the sister of his dead wife, not able to separate the two. Good acting helps script along. VistaVision.

Wild Life, The (1984) **C-96m.** *½ D: Art Linson. Christopher Penn, Ilan Mitchell-Smith, Eric Stoltz, Jenny Wright, Lea Thompson, Rick Moranis, Hart Bochner, Michael Bowen, Randy Quaid, Sherilyn Fenn, Lee Ving, Nancy Wilson, Laura Dern, Jack Kehoe, Robert Ridgely, Dean Devlin, Ben Stein. Unfunny youth comedy about straight-arrow high school grad Stoltz deciding to leave home and move into "swinging singles" apartment. Meager attempt to clone FAST TIMES AT RIDGEMONT HIGH with same writer and producer (doubling here as director), and Christopher Penn trying to ape brother Sean's flaky character—unsuccessfully. Penn's real-life dad, Leo Penn, plays his father here. [R]▼●

Wild Man Blues (1998) **C-105m.** *** D: Barbara Kopple. Oscar-winning documentarian Kopple follows Woody Allen and his companion (later wife), Soon-Yi Previn, on a 1996 European concert tour given by Allen and his New Orleans–style jazz band. A must for Woodyphiles, surprisingly revealing even in its most mundane moments; others may find it less compelling. It also helps to like the traditional, even primitive, style of music being played. [PG]▼●

Wild Man of Borneo, The (1941) **78m.** ** D: Robert B. Sinclair. Frank Morgan, Mary Howard, Billie Burke, Donald Meek, Marjorie Main, Connie Gilchrist, Bonita Granville, Walter Catlett, Phil Silvers, Dan Dailey. Good cast in weak sideshow comedy; Morgan masquerades as title character in one of his less memorable roles.

Wild McCullochs, The (1975) **C-93m.** ** D: Max Baer. Forrest Tucker, Max Baer, Julie Adams, Janice Heiden, Dennis Redfield, Don Grady, William Demarest. Forgettable QUIET MAN rip-off has Tucker as self-made Texas millionaire who tries to raise his sons in his two-fisted image, with Baer eventually forced to prove he is "a man." Yawn. [PG]▼◗

Wild North, The (1952) **C-97m.** ** D: Andrew Marton. Stewart Granger, Cyd Charisse, Wendell Corey, J. M. Kerrigan, Ray Teal. Undazzling account of accused murderer hunted by Mountie, with the expected proving of innocence before finale; Charisse is love interest.

Wild One, The (1954) **79m.** ***½ D: Laslo Benedek. Marlon Brando, Mary Murphy, Robert Keith, Lee Marvin, Jay C. Flippen, Jerry Paris, Alvy Moore, Gil Stratton, Jr. THE original motorcycle film with Brando's renowned performance as pack-leader terrorizing small town; dated, but well worth viewing. Script by John Paxton, based on a story by Frank Rooney; produced by Stanley Kramer.▼●◗

Wild on the Beach (1965) **77m.** *½ D: Maury Dexter. Frankie Randall, Sherry Jackson, Jackie & Gayle, Sonny & Cher, Sandy Nelson. Randall and Jackson fight over the rights to a beachhouse—and fall in love. Dreary comedy notable only for the appearance of Mr. and Mrs. Bono, and as Cher's screen debut.

Wild Orchid (1990) **C-111m.** BOMB D: Zalman King. Mickey Rourke, Jacqueline Bisset, Carré Otis, Assumpta Serna, Bruce Greenwood, Oleg Vidov, Milton Goncalves. Prim lawyer Otis, employed by banker Bisset, gets assaulted by Rio de Janeiro carny-time temptation: semi-public fornicators, limousine raunch, and the sight of earringed Rourke in deep bronze makeup. Notorious simulated sex scene caused a stir, but it's all for naught; this picture is enough to make any two bananas roll over in Carmen Miranda's grave. Followed by a sequel. European version (unrated here), running 116m., is also available on video. [R] ▼●

Wild Orchid 2: Two Shades of Blue (1992) **C-107m.** BOMB D: Zalman King. Nina Siemaszko, Wendy Hughes, Tom Skerritt, Robert Davi, Brent Fraser, Christopher McDonald, Liane Curtis, Joe Dallesandro, Lydie Denier. For viewers who haven't seen ORCHID 1, the title begs a "what is it?" question. For those who have, it's a "why is it?" question. By day, blond Siemaszko puppy-loves a high school jock—but by night, she dons a black wig in the local brothel to entertain the same unwitting dufus. Standard heavy breathing from director King, but with even more lung congestion than usual. [R]▼●

Wild Orchids (1929) **102m.** **½ D: Sidney Franklin. Greta Garbo, Lewis Stone, Nils Asther. Standard love triangle with married Garbo falling for wealthy, charming Asther on a trip to Java. Garbo's charisma elevates typical soaper. Silent film with music score. ▼

Wild Pack, The (1971) **C-102m.** **½ D: Hall Bartlett. Kent Lane, Tisha Sterling, John Rubinstein, Butch Patrick, Mark de Vries, Peter Nielsen. Fairly interesting drama, set in Brazil, about day-to-day life of a group of black and white orphans who steal food; film won grand prize at Moscow Film Festival. Originally titled THE SANDPIT GENERALS. Video title: THE DEFIANT. Panavision.▼

Wild Pair, The (1987) **C-88m.** *½ D: Beau Bridges. Beau Bridges, Bubba Smith, Lloyd Bridges, Gary Lockwood, Raymond St. Jacques, Danny De La Paz, Lela Rochon, Ellen Geer. Trite police thriller, with cop Smith and FBI agent Beau Bridges teaming up to bring some drug dealing racists to justice. Utterly ordinary in all departments. Bridges' first theatrical film as director. [R]▼●

Wild Party, The (1929) **76m.** **½ D: Dorothy Arzner. Clara Bow, Fredric March, Shirley O'Hara, Marceline Day, Joyce Compton, Jack Oakie. Fascinating antique about dishy new prof at all-girls' school and his on-again, off-again relationship with a sexy student who thinks college is just a lark. Absolutely awful by any objective standards, but great fun to watch.▼

Wild Party, The (1956) **81m.** *½ D: Harry Horner. Anthony Quinn, Carol Ohmart, Arthur Franz, Jay Robinson, Kathryn Grant (Crosby), Nehemiah Persoff, Paul Stewart. Blah attempt at naturalistic drama with Quinn the has-been football star going mildly berserk at a sleazy roadside dance hall.

Wild Party, The (1975) **C-95m.** ** D: James Ivory. James Coco, Raquel Welch, Perry King, Tiffany Bolling, David Dukes, Royal Dano, Dena Dietrich. Uneven evocation of 1920s Hollywood with Coco as a Fatty Arbuckle-type comedian who throws a lavish party to try and save his failing career. Film has definite assets (notably its performances) but just doesn't come off. Based on the narrative poem by Joseph Moncure March; cut by its distributor, later restored by Ivory to 107m. [R]▼

Wild Racers, The (1968) **C-79m.** *½ D: Daniel Haller. Fabian, Mimsy Farmer, Judy Cornwall, David Landers. Dumb racer Fabian loves his work and one-night stands; Farmer is his latest challenge.

Wild Reeds (1994-French) **C-110m.** ***½ D: André Téchiné. Elodie Bouchez, Gael Morel, Staphane Rideau, Frederick Gorny, Michele Moretti. Richly evocative film, set in 1962, about four young people in rural France (where the kids listen to American Top 40 songs!) coming of age and exploring their sexuality. The ideological and emotional turbulence caused by the Algerian war is felt in a quiet boarding school with the arrival of a new French-Algerian student, whose radical politics throw things into disarray. A multilayered story, masterfully directed. Winner of four César Awards including Best Picture. ▼●◗

Wild Ride, The (1960) **63m.** *½ D: Harvey Berman. Jack Nicholson, Georgianna Carter, Robert Bean. Amateurish low-budgeter about a hedonistic hot-rodder who's as casual about killing people as he is about stealing his buddy's girlfriend. Worth seeing only if you're curious about this early Nicholson performance.▼

Wild River (1960) **C-110m.** ***½ D: Elia Kazan. Montgomery Clift, Lee Remick, Jo Van Fleet, Albert Salmi, Jay C. Flippen, James Westerfield. Clift plays Tennessee Valley Authority official trying to convince elderly Van Fleet to sell her property for new projects. Kazan's exquisite evocation of 1930s Tennessee—and moving romance between Clift and Remick—give this film its strength. Bruce Dern makes his film debut in supporting role. CinemaScope.

Wildrose (1984) **C-95m.** ***½ D: John Hanson. Lisa Eichhorn, Tom Bower, Jim Cada, Cinda Jackson, Dan Nemanick, Bill Schoppert. Eichhorn excels in this vivid tale of a female iron pit worker, both strong and insecure, who must deal with the resentment of her male co-workers—as well as a romance. Filmed in Minnesota, with the landscape and its inhabitants carefully, almost lovingly, etched.▼

Wild Rovers (1971) **C-109m.** ***½ D: Blake Edwards. William Holden, Ryan O'Neal, Karl Malden, Lynn Carlin, Tom Skerritt, Joe Don Baker, Rachel Roberts, Moses Gunn. Underrated Western about two cowpokes who become fugitives after they rob a bank on whim. Choppy script seems unimportant in light of Holden's performance, incredibly lyrical scenes. Edwards' original 136m. version has finally been restored and released, which may boost the film's maligned reputation. Panavision. [PG]▼●

Wild Seed, The (1965) **99m.** *** D: Brian Hutton. Michael Parks, Celia Kaye, Ross Elliott, Woodrow Chambliss, Eva Novak. Arty yet gripping story of runaway Kaye traveling to California, guided by road bum Parks.

Wild Side, The (1983) **C-96m.** BOMB D: Penelope Spheeris. Chris Pederson, Bill Coyne, Jennifer Clay, Timothy Eric O'Brien, Andrew Pece, Don Allen. Perfectly awful drama about alienated suburban teenagers, angry kids who cut their hair instead of growing it long and live in abandoned, rat-infested crash pad. Tries to "make a statement" while wallowing in gratuitous violence. Aka SUBURBIA. [R]▼

Wild Stallion (1952) **C-72m.** *½ D: Lewis D. Collins. Martha Hyer, Edgar Buchanan, Hugh Beaumont, Ben Johnson. Shoddy military academy saga interlaced with soapish romance, told via flashbacks.

Wild Strawberries (1957-Swedish) **90m.** **** D: Ingmar Bergman. Victor Sjostrom, Ingrid Thulin, Bibi Andersson, Gunnar Bjornstrand, Folke Sundquist, Bjorn Bjelvenstam. Elderly Stockholm professor reviews the disappointments of his life, while traveling by car to receive an honorary degree. Superb use of flashbacks and brilliant performance by Sjostrom make this Bergman classic an emotional powerhouse. Still a staple of any serious filmgoer's education.▼●

Wild Style (1982) **C-82m.** ** D: Charlie Ahearn. "Lee" Quinones, Sandra "Pink" Fabara, Fred Brathwaite, Patti Astor, Busy Bee, Grand Master Flash. Independent filmmaker's ode to such contemporary street-life phenomena as graffiti art, break dancing, and rap music, centering on Zoro (Quinones), who spray-paints subway cars in the South Bronx. Sociologically interesting, but dramatically naive—and a little "rapping" goes a long way. [R]▼

Wild Thing (1987) **C-92m.** *½ D: Max Reid. Rob Knepper, Kathleen Quinlan, Robert Davi, Maury Chaykin, Betty Buckley. Misguided mishmash about a boy whose parents are murdered and who grows up into a "wild thing" who protects street people from the likes of arch-villain Davi. One would like to think that screenwriter John Sayles had more in mind for this fable than what turned out on screen. [PG-13] ▼

Wild Things (1998) **C-113m.** *** D: John McNaughton. Kevin Bacon, Matt Dillon, Neve Campbell, Theresa Russell, Denise Richards, Daphne Rubin-Vega, Robert Wagner, Bill Murray, Carrie Snodgress. In South Florida, high school counselor Dillon is accused of rape by rich teenage sexpot Richards *and* her tattooed trailer-trash classmate Campbell. Cop Bacon suspects there's a plot behind it, and he's right: this raunchy, entertaining neo-noir has more twists than a pretzel factory. Gorgeously photographed (by Jeffrey L. Kimball) and well played, it never takes itself too seriously. Murray is a hoot as an ambulance-chasing shyster. Panavision. [R]▼●◗

Wild Times (1980) **C-200m. TVM** D: Richard Compton. Sam Elliott, Ben Johnson, Bruce Boxleitner, Penny Peyser, Dennis Hopper, Cameron Mitchell, Pat Hingle, Harry Carey, Jr., Gene Evans, Leif Erickson, Trish Stewart. Engaging version of Brian Garfield's tale about a dime novel hero who becomes America's first Wild West Show impresario. Originally shown in two parts. Average.▼

Wild West (1992-British) **C-85m.** **½ D: David Attwood. Naveen Andrews, Sarita Choudhury, Ronny Jhutti, Ravi Kapoor, Ameet Chana. A Pakistani living in a London suburb encounters typical (and not-so-typical) problems when he tries to put together a country-western band. Funny and colorful film plays on its offbeat characters and backdrop to dodge the fact that the story is actually the same old breaking-into-show-biz warhorse.▼

Wild Westerners, The (1962) **C-70m.** *½ D: Oscar Rudolph. James Philbrook, Nancy Kovack, Duane Eddy, Guy Mitchell. Humdrum account of marshal and new wife overcoming obstacles to bring gold east for Yankee cause.▼

Wild Wheels (1992) **C-64m.** *** D: Harrod Blank. Genuinely funny documentary about the unbelievable crazy custom cars that dot the American highways and auto shows. Must be seen to be truly appreciated—interviews with drivers who own these wild vehicles are a continuing source of entertainment. Highlights include the Grass-Car, the Cowasaki (cowhide-covered motorcycle), the Hippomobile, and a car covered entirely with crucifixes. The director is son of documentary filmmaker Les Blank.▼

Wild, Wild Planet (1965-Italian) **C-93m.** *½ D: Anthony Dawson (Antonio Margheriti). Tony Russel, Lisa Gastoni, Massimo Serato, Franco Nero, Carlo Giustini. Female alien uses robots to gain control of earth scientists by shrinking them. Fairly good ending does not redeem lackluster film. Made at same time as WAR OF THE PLANETS and other losers.●

Wild Wild West (1999) **C-107m.** *½ D: Barry Sonnenfeld. Will Smith, Kevin Kline, Kenneth Branagh, Salma Hayek, Ted Levine, M. Emmett Walsh, Bai Ling, Frederique van der Wal, Musetta Vander, Sofia Eng. Rehash of the 1960s TV series finds special agents James West (Smith) and inventor Artemus Gordon (Kline) on a special mission for President Grant to capture nefarious bad guy Arliss Loveless (Branagh). Overstuffed with visual gimmickry, but leaden in every way. You can hear the banter landing with a thud every few minutes. [PG-13]▼●◗

Wild, Wild Winter (1966) **C-80m.** ** D: Lennie Weinrib. Gary Clarke, Chris Noel, Steve Franken, Don Edmonds. Light-headed ski-slope musical froth, with guest stars Jay and The Americans, The Beau Brummels, Dick and Dee Dee. Techniscope.

Wild Youth SEE: **Naked Youth**

Willard (1971) **C-95m.** ** D: Daniel Mann. Bruce Davison, Elsa Lanchester, Ernest Borgnine, Sondra Locke, Michael Dante, J. Pat O'Malley, Jody Gilbert, Joan Shawlee. Touching story of a boy and his rats captured public's fancy at the box office, but film's lack of style prevents it from being anything more than a second-rate thriller. Sequel: BEN. [PG]▼●

William Shakespeare's A Midsummer Night's Dream SEE: **Midsummer Night's Dream, A**

William Shakespeare's Romeo & Juliet SEE: **Romeo & Juliet** (1996)

Willie and Joe Back at the Front SEE: **Back at the Front**

Willie and Phil (1980) **C-115m.** *** D: Paul Mazursky. Michael Ontkean, Margot Kidder, Ray Sharkey, Jan Miner, Tom Brennan, Julie Bovasso, Louis Guss, Kathleen Maguire, Kaki Hunter, Larry Fishburne, Natalie Wood. Affectionate, perceptive, underrated retelling of JULES AND JIM. Ontkean and Sharkey meet after a screening of the Truffaut classic, become fast pals, then friends and lovers of free-spirited Kidder. A wistful tale of how chance encounters alter lives, how camaraderie between friends is everlasting, how men always do the asking but women do the deciding. [R]▼●

Willie Dynamite (1974) **C-102m.** *** D: Gilbert Moses. Roscoe Orman, Diana Sands, Thalmus Rasulala, Roger Robinson, George Murdock. Good black actioner set in N.Y.C., with Orman as a pimp out to topple big-shot Robinson, an outrageous homosexual. Sands is fine in her last film. [R]

Will James' Sand SEE: **Sand**

Willow (1988) **C-125m.** *** D: Ron Howard. Val Kilmer, Joanne Whalley, Warwick Davis, Jean Marsh, Patricia Hayes, Billy Barty, Pat Roach, Kevin Pollak. Rollicking fantasy-adventure, from a story by George Lucas (not hard to guess, since it follows a definite STAR WARS formula) about a little person (Davis) who takes on the challenge of shepherding an abandoned baby to its place of destiny—where it will destroy the evil powers of Queen Bavmorda (Marsh). Plenty of action, humor, and eye-filling special effects, though a bit intense at times for the youngsters at whom it's targeted. Panavision. [PG]▼●

Will Penny (1968) **C-108m.** ***½ D: Tom Gries. Charlton Heston, Joan Hackett, Donald Pleasence, Lee Majors, Bruce Dern, Ben Johnson, Slim Pickens, Anthony Zerbe, Clifton James. One of the best films on the cowboy/loner ever to come out of Hollywood. Heston's character is one of great strength; supporting actors are exceptional. Written by director Gries. Memorable score by David Raksin.▼●

Will Success Spoil Rock Hunter? (1957) **C-94m.** ***½ D: Frank Tashlin. Tony Randall, Jayne Mansfield, Betsy Drake, Joan Blondell, John Williams, Henry Jones, Mickey Hargitay. Guest star, Groucho Marx. Clever satire uses George Axelrod play about ad man who tries to persuade glamorous star to endorse Stay-Put Lipstick as springboard for scattershot satire on 1950s morals, television, sex, business, et al. Director-writer Tashlin in peak form. CinemaScope.▼●

Willy McBean and His Magic Machine (1965-Japanese) **C-94m.** **½ D: Arthur Rankin, Jr. Voices of Larry Mann, Billie Richards, Alfie Scopp, Paul Ligman. Puppet novelty item about mad professor and his time machine; OK for kids.▼

Willy Milly SEE: **Something Special**

Willy Wonka and the Chocolate Factory (1971) **C-98m.** **½ D: Mel Stuart. Gene Wilder, Jack Albertson, Peter Ostrum, Roy Kinnear, Aubrey Woods, Michael Bollner, Ursula Reit. Adaptation of Roald Dahl's book *Charlie and the Chocolate Factory* has all the ingredients of classic fantasy. Enigmatic Wilder gives kids a tour of his mystery-shrouded candy factory, but cruel edge taints film's enjoyment. Anthony Newley-Leslie Bricusse score includes "Candy Man." Scripted by Dahl, with eye-popping sets by Harper Goff. [G]▼●◗

Wilson (1944) **C-154m.** ***½ D: Henry King. Alexander Knox, Charles Coburn, Geraldine Fitzgerald, Thomas Mitchell, Cedric Hardwicke, Vincent Price, Mary Anderson, Sidney Blackmer, Stanley Ridges, Eddie Foy, Jr., Francis X. Bushman. Superb biography of WW1-era President whose League of Nations idea became an obsession; one of Hollywood's solid films . . . but beware of cutting. Amazingly a notorious box-office flop, even after winning five Oscars (including Lamar Trotti's script and Leon Shamroy's photography). ▼

Winchell (1998) **C-115m. TVM** D: Paul Mazursky. Stanley Tucci, Paul Giamatti, Glenne Headly, Kevin Tighe, Christopher Plummer, Paul Mazursky. Tucci puts on a flamboyant show as complex power-monger Walter Winchell, who as the most-read columnist in America cut an often mean-spirited swath through the late '20s and into the early '50s, only to cross swords with Joe McCarthy. Giamatti plays Winchell's right hand, doormat, and ghostwriter, Herman Klurfeld, on whose biography the film was based. Plummer is especially good as FDR. Written by Scott Abbott. Made for cable. Above average.▼

Winchester '73 (1950) **92m.** ***½ D: Anthony Mann. James Stewart, Shelley Winters, Dan Duryea, Stephen McNally, Charles Drake, Millard Mitchell, John McIntire, Will Geer, Jay C. Flippen, Rock Hudson, Anthony (Tony) Curtis. Exceptional Western story of Stewart tracking down a man—and his stolen gun—through series of interrelated episodes, leading to memorable shootout among rock-strewn hills. First-rate in every way, this landmark film was largely responsible for renewed popularity of Westerns in the 1950s. Script by Robert L. Richards and Borden Chase, from a story by Stuart N. Lake. Beautifully photographed by William Daniels; remade for TV in 1967.▼●

Wind, The (1928) **88m.** **** D: Victor Seastrom. Lillian Gish, Lars Hanson, Montagu Love, Dorothy Cumming, Edward Earle, William Orlamond. Virgin Virginian Gish battles the elements in a barren dustbowl town—marrying on the rebound a man who disgusts her, shooting the lout who rapes her. Probably Gish's greatest vehicle—and one of the last great silents—with a splendidly staged climactic desert storm sequence. Written by Frances Marion, from Dorothy Scarborough's novel. ▼●

Wind, The (1987) **C-92m.** BOMB D: Nico Mastorakis. Meg Foster, Wings Hauser, David McCallum, Robert Morley, Steve Railsback. Good cast is wasted in old-fashioned thriller about mystery writer Foster terrorized by Hauser in her spooky house in Greece. Unconvincing structure has hero Railsback injected artificially into the story in later reels. Released direct to video.▼

Wind (1992) **C-125m.** **½ D: Carroll Ballard. Matthew Modine, Jennifer Grey, Cliff Robertson, Jack Thompson, Stellan Skarsgard, Rebecca Miller, Ned Vaughn. Enjoyable if overly formulaic tale of competitive yacht racing, about young people determined to build their own craft and reclaim the America's Cup from Australia. Story takes a back seat to the sailing sequences, breathtakingly photographed by John Toll. [PG-13]▼●

Wind Across the Everglades (1958) **C-93m.** **½ D: Nicholas Ray. Burl Ives, Christopher Plummer, Gypsy Rose Lee, George Voskovec, Tony Galento, Emmett Kelly, Chana Eden, MacKinlay Kantor. Oddball cast in even odder story of boozy turn-of-the-century Florida game warden (Plummer) who takes it upon himself to rid the area of poachers. Matchup of director Ray and writer-producer Budd Schulberg makes this a genuine curio. Peter Falk makes his film debut in a small role.

Wind and the Lion, The (1975) **C-119m.** **½ D: John Milius. Sean Connery, Candice Bergen, Brian Keith, John Huston, Geoffrey Lewis, Steve Kanaly, Vladek Sheybal. Milius brings modern sensibilities to an old-fashioned adventure-romance, with uneven results. Connery is Moroccan sheik who kidnaps American woman and her son, sparking international incident in which Teddy Roosevelt (Keith) becomes involved. Loosely based on a true incident. Panavision. [PG]▼●

Wind Cannot Read, The (1958-British) **C-110m.** **½ D: Ralph Thomas. Dirk Bogarde, Yoko Tani, Ronald Lewis, John Fraser, Anthony Bushell, Michael Medwin. Tidy tale of Bogarde escaping from Japanese prison camp during WW2 to find his ailing wife Tani.

Wind in the Willows, The (1997-British) **C-83m.** *** D: Terry Jones. Steve Coogan, Eric Idle, Terry Jones, Antony Sher, Nicol Williamson, John Cleese, Michael Palin, Bernard Hill, Julia Sawalha. Charming, veddy British adaptation of Kenneth Grahame's classic children's story in which Rat, Badger, and Mole team up to save their wealthy, reckless friend Toad from losing his estate. Benefits from creative reteaming of many Monty Python members; Jones not only wrote and directed but plays Toad with wild comic abandon. Williamson lends excellent support as the blustery Badger. James Acheson's costumes and production design are wittily on target. Kids and adults alike should enjoy this. Aka MR. TOAD'S WILD RIDE. [G]▼

Windom's Way (1957-British) **C-108m.** *** D: Ronald Neame. Peter Finch, Mary Ure, Natasha Parry, Robert Flemyng, Michael Hordern, Gregoire Aslan. Dedicated doctor (Finch) working in Malayan village tries to en-courage resistance to Communist takeover. Strong performances in this intelligent film.▼

Window, The (1949) **73m.** *** D: Ted Tetzlaff. Bobby Driscoll, Barbara Hale, Arthur Kennedy, Paul Stewart, Ruth Roman. Sleeper film less impressive now than in 1949; still good, with young Driscoll earning a special Academy Award for his performance as a little boy who witnesses a murder and is unable to convince his parents he's not lying. Parents' dialogue weakens credibility, but suspense still mounts; extremely well photographed (by William Steiner) and staged. Based on a story by Cornell Woolrich. Remade as THE BOY CRIED MURDER and CLOAK AND DAGGER (1984).▼

Window in London, A SEE: **Lady in Distress**

Windows (1980) **C-96m.** BOMB D: Gordon Willis. Elizabeth Ashley, Talia Shire, Joseph Cortese, Kay Medford. Homicidal lesbian Ashley is in love with mousy neighbor Shire, who is in turn in love with bland detective Cortese. Reactionary, offensive thriller whose only element of mystery is why it was ever filmed. Directing debut for gifted cinematographer Willis. [R]

Windrider (1986-Australian) **C-92m.** **½ D: Vincent Monton. Tom Burlinson, Nicole Kidman, Charles Tingwell, Jill Perryman, Simon Chilvers. Windsurfer Burlinson and rock star Kidman become romantically involved. Occasionally appealing, but slight and forgettable. [R]▼

Windwalker (1980) **C-108m.** **½ D: Kieth Merrill. Trevor Howard, Nick Ramus, James Remar, Serene Hedin, Dusty Iron Wing McCrea. Indian patriarch Howard returns to life to save his family from the vengeance of his son, a twin who was stolen at birth and raised by an enemy tribe. Curious casting of Howard; however, the Utah scenery is glorious in this unusual Western. Filmed in the Cheyenne and Crow languages, and subtitled. [PG]▼

Windy City (1984) **C-102m.** ** D: Armyan Bernstein. John Shea, Kate Capshaw, Josh Mostel, Jim Borrelli, Jeffrey DeMunn, Lewis J. Stadlen. Promising but uneven film flashes back to last hurrah for some youthful pals whose lives haven't turned out quite as they'd hoped or planned. Writer Bernstein (making directorial debut) invades BIG CHILL/SECAUCUS 7 territory with extremely mixed results. [R]▼●

Wing and a Prayer (1944) **97m.** *** D: Henry Hathaway. Don Ameche, Dana Andrews, William Eythe, Charles Bickford, Cedric Hardwicke, Kevin O'Shea, Richard Jaeckel, Henry (Harry) Morgan, Richard Crane, Glenn Langan, Reed Hadley. Fine WW2 actioner of life aboard a navy aircraft carrier in the South Pacific, just after Pearl Harbor, leading to the Battle of Midway, chronicling the development of U.S. military strategy. Ameche is especially good as the ship's tough flight commander. Excellent use is made of real combat footage.▼

Wing Commander (1999) **C-99m.** *½ D: Chris Roberts. Freddie Prinze, Jr., Saffron Burrows, Matthew Lillard, Tchéky Karyo, Jürgen Prochnow, David Suchet, David Warner. In a 27th-century space war between humans and aliens, the outcome turns out to depend on a single fighter pilot. Well-produced, with lots of CGI effects, but instantly forgettable trifle based on a computer game. Super 35. [PG-13]▼●◗

Winged Serpent, The SEE: **Q**

Winged Victory (1944) **130m.** **½ D: George Cukor. Lon McCallister, Jeanne Crain, Edmond O'Brien, Don Taylor, Judy Holliday, Lee J. Cobb, Peter Lind Hayes, Red Buttons, Barry Nelson, Karl Malden, Gary Merrill, Martin Ritt. WW2 saga is less stirring today than in 1944, but graphic depiction of young men's training for pilot duty is still interesting. So is opportunity of seeing future stars early in their careers. Script by Moss Hart, from his play.

Wings (1927) **139m.** **½ D: William A. Wellman. Clara Bow, Charles "Buddy" Rogers, Richard Arlen, Jobyna Ralston, Gary Cooper, El Brendel. One of the most famous silent films is, alas, not one of the best, despite rose-colored memories. Story of two all-American boys (in love with the same girl) who enlist in the Army Air Corps during WW1 is much too thin to sustain such a long movie. What's important here are the combat flying sequences, among the best in Hollywood history. First Oscar winner as Best Picture.▼●

Wings for the Eagle (1942) **85m.** ** D: Lloyd Bacon. Ann Sheridan, Dennis Morgan, Jack Carson, George Tobias, Don DeFore. Sincere tribute to aircraft workers during WW2 has little meaning today, but Sheridan, et al give good performances.

Wings in the Dark (1935) **77m.** **½ D: James Flood. Cary Grant, Myrna Loy, Dean Jagger, Roscoe Karns, Hobart Cavanaugh, Bert Hanlon. Sky-writing stunt flier Loy falls for flier Grant, who's blinded in a gas explosion. Attractive performers left dangling without a script in this implausible soap opera; fine aerial photography.

Wings of Chance (1961-Canadian) **C-76m.** *½ D: Edward Dew. Frances Rafferty, Jim Brown, Richard Tretter, Patrick Whyte. Tame tale of plane crash in the northern woods and rescue attempts.

Wings of Courage (1995) **C-40m.** ** D: Jean-Jacques Annaud. Craig Sheffer, Elizabeth McGovern, Tom Hulce, Val Kilmer, Ken Pogue, Ron Sauve, Molly Parker. Beautiful scenery aside, this is a lumbering, boring true-life adventure in which pioneer aviator Henri Guillaumet (Sheffer) must fight for survival in the Andes after his plane is forced down while on a mail run circa 1930. Dramatically speaking, it's about as lively as a 1930s Monogram programmer. Of note mostly as the first fiction film made in IMAX 3-D. Annaud co-scripted. [G]▼

Wings of Desire (1988-West German-French) **C/B&W-130m.** ***½ D: Wim Wenders. Bruno Ganz, Solveig Dommartin, Otto Sander, Curt Bois, Peter Falk. Haunting, lyrical, fascinating meditation/fairy tale about a pair of angels who wander through the streets of West Berlin. They observe life around them and ponder what it would be like to be human. Scripted by Wenders and Peter Handke and inspired in part by some Rainer Maria Rilke poems. A must-see. Sequel: FARAWAY, SO CLOSE! Remade as CITY OF ANGELS. [PG-13]▼●

Wings of Eagles, The (1957) **C-110m.** **½ D: John Ford. John Wayne, Maureen O'Hara, Dan Dailey, Ward Bond, Ken Curtis, Edmund Lowe, Kenneth Tobey, Sig Ruman. Biography of Frank "Spig" Wead, pioneer WW1 aviator who later turned to screenwriting (including AIR MAIL and THEY WERE EXPENDABLE for Ford) after an accident; first half is slapstick comedy, with no sense of period detail, then abruptly changes to drama for balance of film. Very mixed bag; film buffs will have fun watching Bond play "John Dodge," spoofing director Ford.▼

Wings of the Dove, The (1997-British-U.S.) **C-101m.** **½ D: Iain Softley. Helena Bonham Carter, Linus Roache, Alison Elliott, Charlotte Rampling, Elizabeth McGovern, Michael Gambon, Alex Jennings. Exquisite but emotionally uneven film (from the Henry James novel) about a young woman torn between her love for a working man (Roache) and her desire for wealth and position . . . complicated by her growing friendship with a rich, guileless American woman (Elliott). Sophisticated and intelligent, but the characters' vacillations and ambiguous feelings make it difficult to empathize with anyone. Venice has never been portrayed so beautifully, or romantically. Gambon and McGovern have thankless roles. Super 35. [R]▼●

Wings of the Hawk (1953) **C-80m.** ** D: Budd Boetticher. Van Heflin, Julia (Julie) Adams, George Dolenz, Pedro Gonzales-Gonzales, Abbe Lane, Antonio Moreno,

Noah Beery. Heflin is hero of thwarted attempt of renegades to overthrow Mexican government; Adams and Lane help him. Originally in 3-D.

Wings of the Morning (1937-British) **C-89m.** **½ D: Harold Schuster. Annabella, Henry Fonda, Leslie Banks, Irene Vanbrugh, Steward Rome, Harry Tate, Helen Haye, Edward Underdown, John McCormack. Trifling story of gypsies, crucial horserace, blossoming love between Fonda and Annabella, initially disguised as a boy. Much ado about nothing. England's first Technicolor film still boasts beautiful pastel hues (by Ray Rennahan and Jack Cardiff) as major attraction, along with famed tenor McCormack doing several songs.▼

Wings of the Navy (1939) **89m.** ** D: Lloyd Bacon. George Brent, Olivia de Havilland, John Payne, Frank McHugh, John Litel, Victor Jory, Henry O'Neill, John Ridgely. Standard semidocumentary of pilots being trained for fighting while de Havilland is vied for by brothers Brent and Payne. Typical Warners prewar propaganda, but watchable.

Winner, The (1997) **C-95m.** **½ D: Alex Cox. Rebecca De Mornay, Vincent D'Onofrio, Michael Madsen, Billy Bob Thornton, Delroy Lindo, Frank Whaley, Richard Edson. When word gets out that a loner (D'Onofrio) wins consistently, every Sunday night at a low-rent Las Vegas casino, the leeches begin to gather around him, including a sexy nightclub singer, an opportunistic thief from out of town, and his own homicidal brother. Interesting fable with a first-rate cast. De Mornay also coexecutive-produced. Debuted on cable TV before theatrical run. ▼●

Winner Take All (1932) **68m.** **½ D: Roy Del Ruth. James Cagney, Virginia Bruce, Marian Nixon, Guy Kibbee, Alan Mowbray, Dickie Moore. Minor but engaging Cagney vehicle with Jimmy as a thick-witted, cocky prizefighter torn between good-girl Nixon and fickle society-girl Bruce. Look fast for George Raft as night club bandleader.

Winning (1969) **C-123m.** *** D: James Goldstone. Paul Newman, Joanne Woodward, Richard Thomas, Robert Wagner, David Sheiner, Clu Gulager. Above average racing story of man who will let nothing stand in the way of track victory. Panavision. [PG]▼●◗

Winning Team, The (1952) **98m.** **½ D: Lewis Seiler. Doris Day, Ronald Reagan, Frank Lovejoy, Eve Miller, James Millican, Rusty Tamblyn. Biography of baseball pitching great Grover Cleveland Alexander focuses on his relationship with supportive wife whose "teamwork" helps Alexander through problems with alcoholism and lack of confidence. Reagan is fine as the Hall of Fame hurler and film boasts good reenactments of Alexander's legendary 1926 World Series heroics. Cameo appearances by real-life big leaguers Bob Lemon, Peanuts Lowrey, Hank Sauer, Gene Mauch, and others.▼●

Win, Place or Steal (1975) **C-81m.** ** D: Richard Bailey. Dean Stockwell, Russ Tamblyn, Alex Karras, McLean Stevenson, Alan Oppenheimer, Kristina Holland. OK racetrack caper comedy, with Tamblyn and Karras doing a Laurel and Hardy. Aka THE BIG PAYOFF. [PG]▼

Winslow Boy, The (1948-British) **117m.** ***½ D: Anthony Asquith. Robert Donat, Margaret Leighton, Cedric Hardwicke, Francis L. Sullivan, Frank Lawton, Basil Radford, Wilfrid Hyde-White, Ernest Thesiger. Superior courtroom melodrama from Terence Rattigan's play, headed by Donat as barrister defending innocent Naval cadet (Neil North) accused of school theft. Script by Rattigan and Anatole de Grunwald. Remade in 1999.▼

Winslow Boy, The (1999) **C-110m.** *** D: David Mamet. Nigel Hawthorne, Rebecca Pidgeon, Jeremy Northam, Gemma Jones, Guy Edwards, Matthew Pidgeon, Colin Stinton, Aden Gillett. Absorbing remake of the Terence Rattigan play about a boy in 1910 England who's expelled from school for a petty theft. His father determines to clear his good name—nearly sacrificing his family in the process. As much about social mores and conventions as the case itself, this even-handed film benefits from a superlative performance by Hawthorne as the head of the Winslow household. Neil North, who plays the First Lord of the Admiralty, was the boy in the 1948 movie. [G]▼◗

Winter à Go-Go (1965) **C-88m.** ** D: Richard Benedict. James Stacy, William Wellman, Jr., Beverly Adams, Jill Donohue, Julie Parrish. Lowbrow shenanigans at a ski resort run by Stacy for the young, affluent set.

Winter Carnival (1939) **105m.** **½ D: Charles F. Riesner. Richard Carlson, Ann Sheridan, Helen Parrish, James Corner, Virginia Gilmore, Robert Walker, Joan Leslie, Peggy Moran. Contrived romance flick (cowritten by Budd Schulberg) set at Dartmouth College during festive weekend; Sheridan is divorcée in love with professor Carlson.

Winter Guest, The (1997-British-U.S.) **C-110m.** *** D: Alan Rickman. Phyllida Law, Emma Thompson, Gary Hollywood, Arlene Cockburn, Sheila Reid, Sandra Voe, Douglas Murphy, Sean Biggerstaff. A Scottish seaside town is frozen over—as is the ocean itself—on a wintry day during which four relationships are explored: a young widow and her mother, who's trying to break through her daughter's defensive shield; the widow's teenage son, who experiences his first sexual encounter; two older women whose hobby is attending funerals; and a couple of boys playing hooky. An incredibly quiet, concentrated film—which, perhaps, goes on too long. Based on a play, coadapted by Rickman (making his feature directing debut). Law and Thompson are real-life mother and daughter. [R]▼●

Winterhawk (1976) **C-98m.** ** D: Charles B. Pierce. Michael Dante, Leif Erickson, Woody Strode, Denver Pyle, Elisha Cook Jr., L. Q. Jones, Arthur Hunnicutt, Dawn Wells. Well-meaning but overly melodramatic story of Blackfoot Indian brave (Dante) who comes to white man for smallpox serum, is attacked instead, and gets revenge by kidnapping two white youngsters. Quite violent at times. Techniscope. [PG]▼

Winter in Lisbon (1990-Spanish-French-Portuguese) **C-100m.** *½ D: Jose Antonio Zorilla. Christian Vadim, Dizzy Gillespie, Helene de Saint-Pere, Eusebio Poncela, Fernando Guillen. Disjointed, turgid account of jazz pianist Vadim and his torrid affair with deceitful de Saint-Pere. Of interest solely for Gillespie's bright presence as an aging, expatriate American jazzman.

Winter Kill (1974) **C-100m. TVM** D: Jud Taylor. Andy Griffith, John Larch, Tim O'Connor, Sheree North, Nick Nolte, Elayne Heilviel, Charles Tyner, Louise Latham. Resort-town sheriff Griffith tracks murderer, who leaves spray-painted messages at the scene. Another Griffith pilot that failed to catch on. Average.

Winter Kills (1979) **C-97m.** **½ D: William Richert. Jeff Bridges, John Huston, Anthony Perkins, Sterling Hayden, Eli Wallach, Belinda Bauer, Richard Boone, Ralph Meeker, Dorothy Malone, Toshiro Mifune, Tomas Milian, Elizabeth Taylor. Younger brother of an assassinated U.S. President tries to solve the case, opens up several cans of political worms. A failure in 1979, it was reedited in 1983 (with original ending restored) and newly appreciated as a black comedy, which not everybody recognized the first time around. Still wildly uneven, but worth a look, if only for Huston's wonderful performance as Bridges' kingpin father. Panavision. [R]▼●

Winter Light (1963-Swedish) **80m.** ***½ D: Ingmar Bergman. Ingrid Thulin, Gunnar Bjornstrand, Max von Sydow, Gunnel Lindblom, Allan Edwall. A difficult film for non-Bergman buffs, this look at a disillusioned priest in a small village is the second of Bergman's trilogy on faith (the first, THROUGH A GLASS DARKLY; the third, THE SILENCE). Powerful, penetrating drama.▼●

Winter Meeting (1948) **104m.** **½ D: Bretaigne Windust. Bette Davis, Janis Paige, James (Jim) Davis, John Hoyt, Florence Bates. Sluggish script of disillusioned poetess who loves embittered war hero, prevents well-acted film from achieving greater heights. Notable as only romantic lead for Jim Davis, better known for his westerns and TV series *Dallas*.▼

Winter of Our Dreams, The (1981-Australian) **C-90m.** **½ D: John Duigan. Judy Davis, Bryan Brown, Cathy Downes, Baz Luhrmann, Peter Mochrie, Mervyn Drake. Davis is fine as a lonely prostitute who becomes involved with dissatisfied bookshop-owner Brown, married to Downes. Intriguing drama is a bit disjointed, particularly near the finale.▼

Winter People (1989) **C-110m.** ** D: Ted Kotcheff. Kurt Russell, Kelly McGillis, Lloyd Bridges, Mitchell Ryan, Amelia Burnette, Eileen Ryan, Jeffrey Meek. Turgid tale of backwoods clans and a blood feud that flares up when McGillis bears a child with the wrong father. Set in the 1930s, but extremely odd by any period's standards; how it came to be made in 1989 is anyone's guess. Overwrought, to say the least. Panavision. [PG-13]▼●

Winter Rates SEE: **Out of Season**

Winterset (1936) **78m.** **½ D: Alfred Santell. Burgess Meredith, Margo, Eduardo Ciannelli, Paul Guilfoyle, John Carradine, Edward Ellis, Stanley Ridges, Myron McCormick, Mischa Auer. Meredith, in his screen debut, plays an idealistic young man determined to find the man responsible for a crime that was pinned on his father years ago. The three stars of Maxwell Anderson's impassioned, allegorical Broadway play recreate their roles in this stagebound but fascinating curio of a film.▼

Winter's Tale, The (1968-British) **C-151m.** ** D: Frank Dunlop. Laurence Harvey, Jane Asher, Diana Churchill, Moira Redmond, Jim Dale. Filmed record of 1966 Edinburgh Festival presentation of Shakespeare's play is as static as a photographed stage play can be; may play better on TV.

Wintertime (1943) **82m.** ** D: John Brahm. Sonja Henie, Jack Oakie, Cesar Romero, Carol Landis, Cornel Wilde, S.Z. Sakall, Woody Herman. Henie gives her all to save uncle's hotel from bankruptcy. Innocuous, below par for her vehicles.▼

Wired (1989) **C-108m.** BOMB D: Larry Peerce. Michael Chiklis, Ray Sharkey, J. T. Walsh, Patti D'Arbanville, Lucinda Jenney, Alex Rocco, Gary Groomes, Jere Burns, Billy Preston. The film fiasco of its year, a numbingly wrongheaded adaptation of Bob Woodward's best-selling cautionary bio of John Belushi—complete with a cab-driving guardian angel (Sharkey). Chiklis looks a little like Belushi but conveys none of his comic genius in some clumsy *Saturday Night Live* recreations. Walsh, as Woodward, is an unintentional howl with the decade's most constipated performance. Sole cast survivor: D'Arbanville as Cathy Smith, the woman who administered the star's fatal drug overdose. [R]▼●

Wisdom (1986) **C-109m.** BOMB D: Emilio Estevez. Emilio Estevez, Demi Moore, Tom Skerritt, Veronica Cartwright, William Allen Young, Richard Minchenberg, Ernie Brown. Recent grad Estevez can't find work because of a long-ago felony on his record; frustration launches him and girlfriend Moore on a cross-country series of bank heists to aid the American farmer's plight. Robert Wise assisted Estevez on the direction, which is certainly more competent than his wretched script; film has one of the most self-defeating wrapups you'll ever see. [R]▼●

Wise Blood (1979) **C-108m.** ***½ D: John Huston. Brad Dourif, Daniel Shor, Amy Wright, Harry Dean Stanton, Ned Beatty, Mary Nell Santacroce. Brilliant translation of Flannery O'Connor's peculiar hell-and-salvation tale. Flawless cast, led by Dourif as obsessed preacher of The Church Without Christ, inhabits Southern Gothic world as though born in it. Huston (who bills himself here as *Jhon* Huston) appears as a preacher. Screenplay by Benedict Fitzgerald. [PG]▼

Wisecracks (1992-Canadian) **C-93m.** *** D: Gail Singer. Affecting, informative tribute to women standup comics, some of whom do feminist routines and a few who don't. Funniest of many: Joy Behar, Pam Stone, Maxine Lapidus, Ellen DeGeneres, Paula Poundstone, Kim Wayans, Whoopi Goldberg, and TV talk-show host Jenny Jones. Added attractions: Archival footage of pioneers in this very tough field, plus a brainy primer by one of them—Phyllis Diller—on working a room. Wisest crack: Nancy Reagan pegged as leader of a group called "Ladies Against Women."▼

Wise Girl (1937) **70m.** **½ D: Leigh Jason. Miriam Hopkins, Ray Milland, Walter Abel, Henry Stephenson, Alec Craig, Guinn Williams, Margaret Dumont. Pleasant screwball comedy about rich girl pretending to be poor in order to track down her late sister's kids, who are living with starving Greenwich Village artist.

Wise Guys (1986) **C-91m.** *½ D: Brian De Palma. Danny DeVito, Joe Piscopo, Harvey Keitel, Ray Sharkey, Dan Hedaya, Captain Lou Albano, Julie Bovasso, Patti LuPone. Whimsical black comedy (that's what we said) about two losers who work for small-time hood in Newark, N.J. When their efforts to double-cross him fail, he sets them up to kill each other. Unsuccessful change of pace for director De Palma is an almost total misfire; buoyed only by DeVito's comic energy. [R]▼

Wishful Thinking (1997) **C-90m.** ** D: Adam Park. Jennifer Beals, James Le Gros, Drew Barrymore, Jon Stewart, Eric Thal, Mel Gorham. A N.Y.C.-based movie about relationships, told in overlapping "chapters," as paranoiacally jealous Le Gros keeps finding ways to drive his lover (Beals) away . . . with a little help from his lovesick friend Barrymore. Makes clever use of footage from an old Vittorio Gassman movie. Never released theatrically. [R]▼

Wishmaster (1997) **C-90m.** *½ D: Robert Kurtzman. Tammy Lauren, Andrew Divoff, Chris Lemmon, Wendy Benson, Tony Crane, Kane Hodder, Tony Todd, Robert Englund, Ted Raimi. An evil djinn (genie to you) is freed from captivity in a gem and sets out to grant (backfiring) wishes while seeking Lauren, because granting *her* wishes will enable him to destroy the world . . . or something. The mythology is too complex, the story too thin, and the plentiful gore mostly gratuitous. Followed by a direct-to-video sequel. [R]▼●◗

Wish You Were Here (1987-British) **C-92m.** *** D: David Leland. Emily Lloyd, Tom Bell, Clare Clifford, Barbara Durkin, Geoffrey Hutchings, Charlotte Barker, Chloe Leland, Jesse Birdsall, Geoffrey Durham, Pat Heywood. A troubled teenage girl expresses herself by being sexually outrageous—without understanding what the consequences might be. Bittersweet film set in early 1950s England with a knockout performance by 16-year-old Lloyd. Strong directing debut for screenwriter Leland, who based his central character on Cynthia Payne, the young madam depicted in PERSONAL SERVICES, which he wrote. [R]▼●

Wistful Widow of Wagon Gap, The (1947) **78m.** **½ D: Charles Barton. Bud Abbott, Lou Costello, Marjorie Main, George Cleveland, Gordon Jones, William Ching, Peter Thompson, Glenn Strange, Audrey Young. Unusual Western spoof for A&C, inspired by real-life law: Lou is accused of killing a man, and is required to take care of his wife (Main) and children (seven). He then becomes sheriff, convinced that no one will dare kill him. Some slow spots, but overall, fun.▼

Witchboard (1985) **C-98m.** ** D: Kevin S. Tenney. Todd Allen, Tawny Kitaen, Stephen Nicholas, Kathleen Wilhoite, Burke Byrnes, Rose Marie, Susan Nickerson. Standard low-budget horror film with a few twists. An evil spirit, contacted by means of a Ouija board (a "witchboard"), impersonates the ghost of a small boy to kill its victims. Well plotted but routinely directed and acted. Followed by a whole bunch of sequels connected only by the Ouija board. [R]▼●

Witchcraft (1964-British) **79m.** ** D: Don Sharp. Lon Chaney (Jr.), Jack Hedley, Jill Dixon, Viola Keats. Standard plot of witch cult happenings in English village after grave of 300-year-old witch is unearthed.

Witch Doctor SEE: **Men of Two Worlds**

Witchery (1989-Italian) **C-96m.** BOMB D: Martin Newlin (Fabrizio Laurenti). Linda Blair, David Hasselhoff, Catherine Hickland, Annie Ross, Hildegard Knef, Leslie Cumming, Rick Farnsworth. Competently made but ponderous, underplotted horror tale of people isolated at old hotel on island, killed one by one by vengeful witch Knef. Horror scenes emphasize torture. Uncomfortable, predictable, and boring. Filmed in Massachusetts.▼

Witches, The (1990-British) **C-91m.** *** D: Nicolas Roeg. Anjelica Huston, Mai Zetterling, Jasen Fisher, Rowan Atkinson, Bill Paterson, Jane Horrocks, Jenny Runacre, Brenda Blethyn. A young boy's seaside vacation turns into a nightmare when he discovers that the hotel is also hosting a convention of witches! Roald Dahl stories can be cruel, and this is no exception, but as a far flung child's-eye fantasy it's pretty good. Zetterling is wonderful as the boy's loving grandmother; Jim Henson's Creature Shop provided the incredible-looking witches—and mice. This was Henson's final feature-film project. [PG]▼●◗

Witches' Brew (1980) **C-99m.** **½ D: Richard Shorr, Herbert L. Strock. Lana Turner, Richard Benjamin, Teri Garr, Kathryn Leigh Scott, Jordan Charney. College prof Benjamin's wife Garr resorts to witchcraft in order to further his career. Turner (in her final film) is good as the veteran witch who has selfish reasons for helping Benjamin's cause. After a dull first half, this comic remake of BURN, WITCH, BURN finally hits its stride. Originally done as WEIRD WOMAN. Based on the book *Conjure Wife* by Fritz Leiber. [PG]▼

Witches' Mountain (1970-Mexican) **98m.** BOMB D: Raul Artigot. Patty Shepard, John Caffari, Monica Randall. A reporter ventures to a "haunted" spot and finds its reputation may not be unearned. Boring.▼

Witches of Eastwick, The (1987) **C-118m.** *** D: George Miller. Jack Nicholson, Cher, Susan Sarandon, Michelle Pfeiffer, Veronica Cartwright, Richard Jenkins, Keith Jochim, Carel Struycken. Lively, colorful fantasy about three man-hungry women in picture-postcard New England town who, unaware of their witchly powers, conjure up the ultimate man: the devil. Magnetic performances and handsome production keep it entertaining throughout, though it careens wildly from sensual fantasy to black-comic farce to full-throttle horror, and ends up not making a lot of sense. Buoyed by an infectious John Williams score. Loosely based on John Updike's novel. Panavision. [R]▼●◗

Witches of Salem, The SEE: **Crucible, The** (1956)

Witchfinder General, The SEE: **Conqueror Worm**

Witching, The SEE: **Necromancy**

Witch Kill SEE: **Witchmaker, The**

Witchmaker, The (1969) **C-99m.** BOMB D: William O. Brown. John Lodge, Alvy Moore, Thordis Brandt, Anthony Eisley, Shelby Grant. Satanism and supernatural elements are behind a series of grisly murders of young women in Louisiana swamp; bloody, and bloody awful. Aka WITCH KILL, WITCHMASTER. Techniscope. [R]▼

Witch Without a Broom, A (1968-Spanish) **C-78m.** *½ D: Joe Lacy (Jose Maria E. Lorrieta). Jeffrey Hunter, Maria Perschy, Perla Cristal, Gustavo Rojo. Jeff finds himself bewitched by a 15th-century apprentice sorceress who takes him on an odyssey from the Stone Age to a futuristic Martian jaunt. Pointless fantasy.▼

With a Song in My Heart (1952) **C-117m.** *** D: Walter Lang. Susan Hayward, Rory Calhoun, David Wayne, Thelma Ritter, Robert Wagner, Una Merkel. Well-intentioned schmaltz based loosely on events in life of singer Jane Froman with Hayward earnest as songstress struggling to make comeback after crippling plane crash. Alfred Newman won an Oscar for Scoring.

With Byrd at the South Pole (1930) **82m.** *** D: (none credited). The title tells all in this fascinating document of U.S. Navy Rear-Admiral Richard E. Byrd, his crew, and their journey by sea from N.Y.C. to the Antarctic, culminating with his Polar flight. Film plays as part historical record, part promotional film hyping Byrd (complete with rah-rah narration in the final sequence). Despite this, it's still a remarkable film. William Van der Veer and Joseph T. Rucker's stunning cinematography earned an Academy Award.▼●◗

With Fire and Sword (1961-Italian) **C-96m.** *½ D: Fernando Cerchio. Jeanne Crain, John Drew Barrymore, Pierre Brice, Akim Tamiroff. Costume spaghetti about Cossacks vs. Poles; embarrassing minor epic. Retitled: DAGGERS OF BLOOD. Filmed in widescreen Euroscope.

With Friends Like These . . . (1999) **C-105m.** *** D: Philip F. Messina. Robert Costanzo, Adam Arkin, Amy Madigan, David Strathairn, Laura San Giacomo, Jon Tenney, Elle Macpherson, Lauren Tom, Beverly D'Angelo, Michael McKean, Jason Alexander, Bill Murray, Martin Scorsese, Garry Marshall. Close friends who are character actors find themselves in a fiercely competitive situation when word gets out that Martin Scorsese is casting a new film on Al Capone. How much does friendship count at a time like this? Affectionate, serio-comic look at working actors, with a fine ensemble. Written by the director. Made for theaters, debuted on cable TV. [R]▼

With Honors (1994) **C-103m.** ** D: Alek Keshishian. Joe Pesci, Brendan Fraser, Moira Kelly, Patrick Dempsey, Josh Hamilton, Gore Vidal, Deborah Fortson, Marshall Hambro. Homeless Pesci trades pages for food after callow Ivy Leaguer Fraser meets him in Irene Dunne screwball style when his thesis falls through a grate into the Harvard boiler room where Pesci resides. Comedy-drama might be insulting if it had just a little more sting, but it's a fizzle almost from the beginning. [PG-13]▼●◗

With Intent to Kill (1984) **C-100m. TVM** D: Mike Robe. Karl Malden, Paul Sorvino, Shirley Knight, Timothy Patrick Murphy, Catherine Mary Stewart, Holly Hunter, Alex McArthur, William Devane. A father vows vengeance on the boyfriend of his murdered daughter following a not-guilty-by-reason-of-insanity verdict. Malden gives another must-watch performance in this script by director Robe. Above average.

Within These Walls (1945) **71m.** ** D: H. Bruce Humberstone. Thomas Mitchell, Mary Anderson, Edward Ryan, Mark Stevens, B. S. Pully. Fairly good but predictable prison drama with warden Mitchell faced with his own son as a prisoner.

Withnail & I (1987-British) **C-105m.** **½ D: Bruce Robinson. Richard E. Grant, Paul McGann, Richard Griffiths, Ralph Brown, Michael Elphick. "I" is a young longhair, living in London in the last months of 1969; Withnail is his eccentric, self-absorbed roommate. Both are unemployed actors, children of their times, who endure a disastrous vacation in the country. Director Robinson wrote this autobiographical film, which has its amusing moments but eventually becomes monotonous. Best laugh: consultant credit for "Richard Starkey, M.B.E." Fellow Beatle George Harrison coexecutive produced the film. [R]▼●

Without a Clue (1988-British) **C-106m.** **½ D: Thom Eberhardt. Michael Caine, Ben Kingsley, Jeffrey Jones, Lysette Anthony, Paul Freeman, Nigel Davenport, Pat Keen, Peter Cook. Mild farce built on the premise that Sherlock Holmes was a fictional creation of wily Dr. John Watson, who is forced to hire a second-rate actor (Caine) to impersonate the now famous and sought-after detective. Scattered laughs, engaging performances by star duo. [PG] ▼●

Without Apparent Motive (1972-French) **C-102m.** ** D: Philippe Labro. Jean-Louis Trintignant, Dominique Sanda, Sacha Distel, Carla Gravina, Paul Crauchet, Laura Antonelli, Jean-Pierre Marielle. Powerhouse European cast can't do much for Ed McBain tale about detective Trintignant's attempts to solve series of unpredictable killings; Erich Segal plays an astrologer. [PG]

Without a Trace (1983) **C-120m.** **½ D: Stanley R. Jaffe. Kate Nelligan, Judd Hirsch, David Dukes, Stockard Channing, Jacqueline Brookes, Kathleen Widdoes. Story of one woman's ordeal when her six-year-old son disappears while walking to school one morning. Genteel, well-made film keeps an arm's-length emotionally, especially in Nelligan's cold portrayal of the mother. Then there's a resolution that's not to be believed. Based on a real-life N.Y.C. incident that had a much different outcome. Directorial debut of producer Jaffe. [PG]▼

Without Honor (1949) **69m.** ** D: Irving Pichel. Laraine Day, Dane Clark, Franchot Tone, Agnes Moorehead, Bruce Bennett. Good cast talks endlessly in melodrama of woman who thinks she's killed a man.

Without Limits (1998) **C-117m.** *** D: Robert Towne. Billy Crudup, Donald Sutherland, Monica Potter, Jeremy Sisto, Matthew Lillard, Billy Burke, Dean Norris, Judith Ivey. Second screen bio of the late University of Oregon runner Steve Prefontaine is more polished than 1997's PREFONTAINE, especially in its recreation of competition scenes. Produced by Tom Cruise, this barely released sleeper benefits from Sutherland's excellent performance as coach Bill Bowerman. Another plus: outstanding—and non-clichéd—use of period music. Super 35. [PG-13]▼●◗

Without Love (1945) **111m.** *** D: Harold S. Bucquet. Spencer Tracy, Katharine Hepburn, Lucille Ball, Keenan Wynn, Carl Esmond, Patricia Morison, Felix Bressart, Gloria Grahame. Tracy and Hepburn have never been livelier, but script (by Donald Ogden Stewart, from Philip Barry's play) lets them down in story of inventor and widow who marry for convenience, later fall in love. Wynn and Ball are excellent second leads.▼●

Without Pity (1948-Italian) **94m.** *** D: Alberto Lattuada. Carla Del Poggio, John Kitzmiller, Giulietta Masina, Folco Lulli, Pierre Luigi. Moving neorealist classic about a black G.I. (Kitzmiller) and his love affair with a prostitute (Del Poggio) in liberated WW2 Italy. Superb supporting performance by Masina; film was cowritten by her husband, Federico Fellini. Originally titled: SENZA PIETA.

Without Reservations (1946) **107m.** *** D: Mervyn LeRoy. Claudette Colbert, John Wayne, Don Defore, Anne Triola, Frank Puglia, Phil Brown, Thurston Hall, Louella Parsons, Dona Drake. Authoress Colbert meets perfect man to play hero in movie version of her new book: soldier Wayne. Engaging comedy-romance, with some amusing swipes at Hollywood, several surprise guest stars. Look fast for Raymond Burr during dance scene. ▼●

Without Warning (1980) **C-89m.** *½ D: Greydon Clark. Jack Palance, Cameron Mitchell, Martin Landau, Ralph Meeker, Tarah Nutter, Sue Ane Langdon, Neville Brand, Larry Storch. Very silly horror film. Alien launches carnivorous disks at various citizens. A few scattered laughs and shudders, some intense acting, and a flagrantly bad job by Landau as a militant ex-sergeant named Fred Dobbs. Aka IT CAME WITHOUT WARNING. [R]

Without You I'm Nothing (1990) **C-94m.** **½ D: John Boskovich. Sandra Bernhard, John Doe, Steve Antin, Lu Leonard, Ken Foree, Cynthia Bailey. Adaptation of Bernhard's one-woman off-Broadway show, in which she takes on a number of roles in order to examine American pop culture, and the challenge of surviving in modern society. She's definitely an acquired taste, but the material does hit its targets more often than not—especially when Sandra does her take on Diana Ross. Video version runs 89m. [R]▼●

With Six You Get Eggroll (1968) **C-95m.** ** D: Howard Morris. Doris Day, Brian Keith, Pat Carroll, Barbara Hershey, George Carlin, Alice Ghostley, Vic Tayback, Jamie Farr, William Christopher. Oft-told tale of a widow and widower who try to move their children under the same roof. Amiable but slow on laughs. Day's last film to date. Panavision. [G]▼

Witness (1985) **C-112m.** *** D: Peter Weir. Harrison Ford, Kelly McGillis, Josef Sommer, Lukas Haas, Jan Rubes, Alexander Godunov, Danny Glover, Patti LuPone, Viggo Mortensen. A big-city cop on the lam hides out on an Amish farm, where he and a young widow are attracted to each other. Entertaining film is marred by jarring shifts in tone, especially toward the end. Oscar winner for writers Earl W. Wallace, William Kelley, Pamela Wallace. [R]▼●◗

Witness Chair, The (1936) **64m.** *½ D: George Nicholls. Ann Harding, Walter Abel, Douglass Dumbrille, Frances Sage, Moroni Olsen, Margaret Hamilton. Faithful secretary tries to take the rap for the boss she's secretly in love with in this unbelievable courtroom/whodunit; polished but dull.

Witness for the Prosecution (1957) **114m.** **** D: Billy Wilder. Marlene Dietrich, Tyrone Power, Charles Laughton, Elsa Lanchester, John Williams, Henry Daniell, Una O'Connor, Ian Wolfe. Fantastically effective London courtroom suspenser from Agatha Christie play. Dietrich is peerless as wife of alleged killer (Power). Laughton at his best as defense attorney, and Lanchester delightful as his long-suffering nurse. Power's last completed film. Scripted by Wilder and Harry Kurnitz. Remade as a TVM.▼●

Witness in the Dark (1959-British) **62m.** *½ D: Wolf Rilla. Patricia Dainton, Conrad Phillips, Madge Ryan, Nigel Green, Enid Lorimer. Uncommonly obvious suspenser with murderer seeking to kill blind girl who was present when crime was committed.

Witness to Murder (1954) **83m.** *** D: Roy Rowland. Barbara Stanwyck, George Sanders, Gary Merrill, Jesse White, Claude Akins. Stanwyck sees ex-Nazi neighbor Sanders strangle a woman, but can't convince detective Merrill. However, *Sanders* believes her. . . . Unconvincing and rather shrill, but suspenseful and well acted, with striking photography (by John Alton).

Witness to Murder (1975-Spanish) SEE: **Student Connection, The**

Wives and Lovers (1963) **103m.** **½ D: John Rich. Janet Leigh, Van Johnson, Shelley Winters, Martha Hyer, Ray Walston, Jeremy Slate. Surface, slick entertainment; newly famous writer Johnson, wife Leigh and child move to suburbia. Literary agent Hyer on the make almost causes divorce; Winters is wise-cracking neighbor. Script by Edward Anhalt, from Jay Presson Allen's play.

Wives Never Know (1936) **75m.** **½ D: Elliott Nugent. Charlie Ruggles, Mary Boland, Adolphe Menjou, Vivienne Osborne, Claude Gillingwater, Fay Holden, Louise Beavers. Flimsy tale of couple trying to awaken each other's love; Ruggles and Boland are always worth watching, and Menjou adds dash.

Wives Under Suspicion (1938) **69m.** **½ D: James Whale. Warren William, Gail Patrick, Constance Moore, William Lundigan, Ralph Morgan. Minor but interesting drama of callous D.A. William waking up when he thinks his wife (Patrick) is seeing another man. Remake of Whale's THE KISS BEFORE THE MIRROR.▼

Wiz, The (1978) **C-133m.** ** D: Sidney Lumet. Diana Ross, Michael Jackson, Nipsey Russell, Ted Ross, Mabel King, Theresa Merritt, Thelma Carpenter, Lena Horne, Richard Pryor. Diana Ross weeps and whines her way through modern black variation on THE WIZARD OF OZ, from the Broadway show by William F. Brown and Charlie Smalls. Some good musical numbers, fine supporting cast, but dreary finale—and drearier performance by Ross—really weigh it down. Music arranged and conducted by Quincy Jones. [G]▼●◗

Wizard, The (1989) **C-99m.** ** D: Todd Holland. Fred Savage, Luke Edwards, Jenny Lewis, Beau Bridges, Christian Slater, Will Seltzer, Jackey Vinson, Wendy Phillips, Sam McMurray. A road movie for kids, with Savage, his traumatized brother Edwards, and Lewis pursued across the Southwest by various relatives and other grown-ups. Limp, overplotted comedy suffers from heavy product plugs. ROCKY-like finish, dealing with Edwards' video-game wizardry, may thrill preteens but few others. [PG]▼●

Wizard of Baghdad, The (1960) **C-92m.** ** D: George Sherman. Dick Shawn, Diane Baker, Barry Coe, John Van Dreelen, Robert F. Simon, Vaughn Taylor. Blah satire on costumers, with Shawn a lazy genie. CinemaScope.

Wizard of Loneliness, The (1988) **C-111m.** ** D: Jenny Bowen. Lukas Haas, Lea Thompson, John Randolph, Anne Pitoniak, Dylan Baker, Lance Guest, Jeremiah Warner. Topnotch acting (especially by precocious young star Haas) fails to save a haphazardly constructed adaptation of John Nichols' novel about a youngster growing up with his grandparents in New England during WW2. His aunt (Thompson in an unusual character role) carries a dark secret that leads to a melodramatic climax. A coproduction of PBS' *American Playhouse*. [PG-13]▼●

Wizard of Oz, The (1939) **C/B&W-101m.** **** D: Victor Fleming. Judy Garland, Ray Bolger, Bert Lahr, Jack Haley, Frank Morgan, Billie Burke, Margaret Hamilton, Charley Grapewin, Clara Blandick, The Singer Midgets. A genuine American classic, based on L. Frank Baum's story of a Kansas girl who goes "Over the Rainbow" to a land of colorful characters and spirited adventure. A perfect cast in the perfect fantasy, with Harold Arlen and E. Y. Harburg's unforgettable score. Just as good the fifteenth time as it is the first time. Won Oscars for "Over the Rainbow" and Herbert Stothart's scoring, plus a special miniature award for Judy. Previously filmed in 1925; remade as THE WIZ (set in N.Y.C.) and OZ (Australia). A pair of sequels: JOURNEY BACK TO OZ and RETURN TO OZ.▼●◗

Wizard of Speed and Time, The (1988) **C-95m.** **½ D: Mike Jittlov. Mike Jittlov, Paige Moore, Richard Kaye, David Conrad, John Massari, Steve Brodie, Frank LaLoggia, Philip Michael Thomas. A young special-effects whiz and his pals buck the Hollywood system and try to make a movie. This completely self-referential low-budget comedy scores big points for gumption and enthusiasm, which helps make up for some amateurish qualities. Best of all are Jittlov's eye-popping, one-of-a-kind visual effects. Expanded from a popular short subject of the same name. [PG]▼●

Wizards (1977) **C-80m.** *½ D: Ralph Bakshi. Voices of Bob Holt, Jesse Wells, Richard Romanus, David Proval, Mark Hamill. Animated sci-fi tale of future world after devastation, with warring factions that conjure up Hitler's armies. Turgid, unappealing film for adults or children. [PG]▼●

Wolf (1994) **C-122m.** *** D: Mike Nichols. Jack Nicholson, Michelle Pfeiffer, James Spader, Kate Nelligan, Christopher Plummer, Richard Jenkins, Eileen Atkins, David Hyde Pierce, Om Puri, Ron Rifkin, Prunella Scales, David Schwimmer. Thoughtful, imaginative werewolf tale in a modern urban setting, with Nicholson as a genteel book editor who's bitten by a wolf—just as he's going through a personal and professional crisis. Literate, intriguing, though perhaps too slowly paced (and genteel) for rabid horror fans. Written by Jim Harrison and Wesley Strick, with makeup effects by Rick Baker. [R]▼●◗

Wolf at the Door (1987-French-Danish) **C-90m.** *** D: Henning Carlsen. Donald Sutherland, Max von Sydow, Valerie Morea, Sofie Grabol, Fanny Bastin, Merete Voldstedlund. Sutherland is more subdued as Gauguin than Anthony Quinn was in LUST FOR LIFE; generally interesting bio covers the middle period of the artist's life, when he returned to Paris from Tahiti—then struggled to raise the money to go back. Arouses your interest in the subject. [R] ▼

Wolf Dog (1958-Canadian) **61m** *½ D: Sam Newfield. Jim Davis, Allison Hayes, Tony Brown, Austin Willis. Low-jinks about farm life in the north country involving land-hungry ranchers. Regalscope.

Wolfen (1981) **C-115m.** *** D: Michael Wadleigh. Albert Finney, Diane Venora, Edward James Olmos, Gregory Hines, Tom Noonan, Dick O'Neill. Detective Finney tracks mysterious beasts (werewolves?) that are terrorizing N.Y.C. Surreal, allegorical mystery is satisfying—and could have been great. Hines stands out as coroner; Gerry Fisher's ingenious cinematography is also noteworthy. Based on the novel by Whitley Streiber. Panavision. [R]▼●

Wolf Lake (1978) **C-87m.** *½ D: Burt Kennedy. Rod Steiger, David Huffman, Robin Mattson, Jerry Hardin, Richard Herd, Paul Mantee. Dull revenge film. Steiger (intense as ever) and four old army buddies stay at hunting lodge run by Huffman, a Vietnam deserter who fled to Canada. Steiger lost his son in the Vietnam war and tries to take out his grief (violently) on Huffman, with tragic results. Also known as THE HONOR GUARD. [R]▼

Wolf Larsen (1958) **83m.** **½ D: Harmon Jones. Barry Sullivan, Peter Graves, Gita Hall, Thayer David. Nicely done version of Jack London's THE SEA WOLF with Sullivan effective as the tyrannical captain of the eerie ship.▼

Wolf Larsen (1975-Italian) **C-92m.** ** D: Giuseppi Vari. Chuck Connors, Barbara Bach, Giuseppi Pambieri. Tired new version of Jack London's SEA WOLF with Connors chewing up scenery as the sadistic sea captain. Video titles: LEGEND OF

SEA WOLF and LARSEN, WOLF OF THE SEVEN SEAS.▼

Wolf Man, The (1941) **70m.** ***½ D: George Waggner. Lon Chaney, Jr., Evelyn Ankers, Claude Rains, Maria Ouspenskaya, Ralph Bellamy, Patric Knowles, Warren William, Bela Lugosi, Fay Helm. One of the finest horror films ever made: Larry Talbot (Chaney) is bitten by werewolf Lugosi, survives to carry the curse himself. Outstanding cast includes Rains as unknowing father, Ankers as perplexed girl friend, Ouspenskaya as wizened gypsy woman who foretells his fate and attempts to care for him. Literate and very engrossing, with superb makeup by Jack Pierce, atmospheric music (re-used in many other Universal chillers) by Charles Previn and Hans J. Salter. Written by Curt Siodmak. Sequel: FRANKENSTEIN MEETS THE WOLF MAN.▼●◗

Woman and the Hunter, The (1957) **79m.** *½ D: George Breakston. Ann Sheridan, David Farrar, John Loder. Tedious love triangle set in the jungles of Kenya; Sheridan tries hard but material defeats all.

Woman-Bait SEE: **Inspector Maigret**

Woman Called Golda, A (1982) **C-200m. TVM** D: Alan Gibson. Ingrid Bergman, Judy Davis, Leonard Nimoy, Anne Jackson, Ned Beatty, Barry Foster, Robert Loggia. Bergman's memorable, Emmy-winning swan song as Golda Meir, following the Israeli prime minister's life and career through her historic meeting with Anwar Sadat in 1977. Written by Harold Gast and Steven Gethers. Originally shown in two parts. Above average.▼

Woman Chases Man (1937) **71m.** **½ D: John G. Blystone. Miriam Hopkins, Joel McCrea, Charles Winninger, Ella Logan, Erik Rhodes, Broderick Crawford. Sometime hilarious, often strained screwball comedy with Hopkins trying to fleece wealthy McCrea, falling in love in the process.

WomanEater (1959-British) **70m.** *½ D: Charles Saunders. George Coulouris, Vera Day, Robert MacKenzie, Norman Claridge, Marpessa Dawn, Jimmy Vaughan. Mad scientist feeds women to a stolen Amazonian tree that he keeps in the dungeon of his British manor, hoping to derive a substance that will revive the dead. And they say that scientific research lacks imagination!▼◗

Woman Hater (1949-British) **70m.** ** D: Terence Young. Stewart Granger, Edwige Feuillere, Ronald Squire, Mary Jerrold. Contrived battle of wits between confirmed bachelor and single girl leads to predictable romance.▼

Woman Hunt (1972-U.S.-Philippine) **C-81m.** BOMB D: Eddie Romero. John Ashley, Sid Haig, Laurie Rose, Lisa Todd, Eddie Garcia, Pat Woodell. Wretched knock-off of THE MOST DANGEROUS GAME, using kidnapped women as prey. Todd's dull performance as a black-leather-clad lesbian sadist wouldn't even amuse her *Hee Haw* fans. [R]▼

Woman Hunter, The (1972) **C-73m. TVM** D: Bernard Kowalski. Barbara Eden, Robert Vaughn, Stuart Whitman, Sydney Chaplin, Larry Storch, Enrique Lucero. Wealthy, unstable Dina Hunter (Eden) on Mexican holiday is fearful that murderer is stalking her and jewels. Unconvincing climax in suspense film that seems excuse for Eden to show off fashions. Average. ▼

Woman in a Dressing Gown (1957-British) **93m.** *** D: J. Lee Thompson. Yvonne Mitchell, Anthony Quayle, Sylvia Syms, Andrew Ray, Carole Lesley. Excellent British drama about middle-aged man lured away from his unkempt wife by an attractive young woman at his office. Mature, intelligent, and moving.

Woman in Green, The (1945) **68m.** *** D: Roy William Neill. Basil Rathbone, Nigel Bruce, Hillary Brooke, Henry Daniell, Paul Cavanagh, Matthew Boulton, Eve Amber. Blackmail, hypnotism, and murdered women with their right forefingers missing are the disparate elements in this solid *Sherlock Holmes* outing, with sleek Brooke and suave Daniell a formidable pair of foes for Holmes and Watson. Also shown in computer-colorized version.▼●

Woman in Hiding (1949) **92m.** ** D: Michael Gordon. Ida Lupino, Howard Duff, Stephen McNally, Peggy Dow, John Litel, Joe Besser. Overdone dramatics do in this soaper about a factory owner (Lupino) whose greedy new husband (McNally) attempts to kill her. She sets out to nail him, and is helped by war-veteran drifter Duff.

Woman in Question, The (1950-British) **89m.** *** D: Anthony Asquith. Jean Kent, Dirk Bogarde, John McCallum, Susan Shaw, Hermione Baddeley, Charles Victor, Duncan Macrae. As a cop investigates the slaying of a fortune teller, the various suspects' conflicting perceptions of the deceased emerge. Nifty whodunit, much of which is told in flashback; Kent is excellent as the murder victim. Retitled: FIVE ANGLES ON MURDER.▼

Woman in Red (1935) **68m.** ** D: Robert Florey. Barbara Stanwyck, Gene Raymond, Genevieve Tobin, John Eldredge, Philip Reed, Dorothy Tree. Routine courtroom drama of Stanwyck and Raymond marriage interrupted by charge that she's been seeing Eldredge.

Woman in Red, The (1984) **C-87m.** *** D: Gene Wilder. Gene Wilder, Kelly LeBrock, Gilda Radner, Joseph Bologna, Charles Grodin, Judith Ivey. Broad remake of French farce PARDON MON AFFAIRE with happily married Wilder going ga-ga over beautiful LeBrock. Stevie

Wonder score includes Oscar-winning "I Just Called to Say I Love You." [PG-13]▼●

Woman Inside, The (1981-Canadian) **C-94m.** BOMB D: Joseph Van Winkle. Gloria Manon, Dane Clark, Joan Blondell, Michael Champion, Marlene Tracy. Vietnam veteran Manon has sex change operation. Flimsy and flaky, with a budget of $32.95. Sadly, Blondell's last screen role, as Manon's aunt. [R]▼

Woman in the Dunes (1964-Japanese) **123m.** ***½ D: Hiroshi Teshigahara. Eiji Okada, Kyoko Kishida, Koji Mitsui, Hiroko Ito, Sen Yano. Entomologist Okada becomes trapped in a sandpit and the prisoner of Kishida. Moving, memorable allegory, with striking direction and cinematography (by Hiroshi Segawa).▼◗

Woman in the Moon (1929-German) **156m.** ** D: Fritz Lang. Klaus Pohl, Willy Fritsch, Gustav von Wangenheim, Gerda Maurus, Fritz Rasp. This lesser Lang effort, his last silent film, is about a spaceship and its trip to the moon. It's slow and way overlong, and it pales beside his brilliant METROPOLIS.▼

Woman in the Window, The (1944) **99m.** ***½ D: Fritz Lang. Joan Bennett, Edward G. Robinson, Dan Duryea, Raymond Massey, Bobby (Robert) Blake, Dorothy Peterson. High-grade melodrama about Robinson meeting subject of alluring painting (Bennett), becoming involved in murder and witnessing his own investigation. Surprise ending tops exciting film. Nunnally Johnson scripted and produced.▼●

Woman in White, The (1948) **109m.** *** D: Peter Godfrey. Eleanor Parker, Alexis Smith, Sydney Greenstreet, Gig Young, Agnes Moorehead, John Emery, John Abbott. Florid gothic thriller from Wilkie Collins book about strange household and tormented Parker.

Woman Is a Woman, A (1961-French) **C-83m.** **½ D: Jean-Luc Godard. Jean-Paul Belmondo, Jean-Claude Brialy, Anna Karina, Noel Pacquin. Pert stripper Karina wants a baby; boyfriend Brialy is not interested in fatherhood, so she approaches his best friend (Belmondo). Occasionally spirited, but mostly a self-indulgent trifle. Franscope.▼◗

Woman Next Door, The (1981-French) **C-106m.** *** D: François Truffaut. Gérard Depardieu, Fanny Ardant, Henri Garcin, Michele Baumgartner, Veronique Silver. Depardieu's new neighbor is ex-lover Ardant. Though now married, they revive their relationship. Somber, compassionate study of human nature and emotions, nicely acted by the two leads. [R]▼●◗

Woman Obsessed (1959) **C-102m.** **½ D: Henry Hathaway. Susan Hayward, Stephen Boyd, Barbara Nichols, Dennis Holmes, Theodore Bikel, Ken Scott. Energetic stars try hard in Canadian ranch-life soaper of widow Hayward who marries Boyd, with predictable clashing and making up. CinemaScope.

Woman of Affairs, A (1928) **96m.** *** D: Clarence Brown. Greta Garbo, John Gilbert, Lewis Stone, John Mack Brown, Douglas Fairbanks, Jr., Hobart Bosworth, Dorothy Sebastian. Smooth, entertaining late-silent with Garbo as reckless socialite who undertakes serious burden of making good her late husband's thefts. Fine cast; story is diluted from Michael Arlen's *The Green Hat.*▼●

Woman of Desire (1993) **C-97m.** ** D: Robert Ginty. Jeff Fahey, Bo Derek, Steven Bauer, Robert Mitchum. Wannabe erotic thriller with down-and-out Fahey being set up for the murder of playgirl Derek's wealthy boyfriend Bauer during a yacht trip—although sly lawyer Mitchum has his doubts in court. This went straight to video with an unrated 99m. version (more Bo nudity). [R]▼●

Woman of Distinction, A (1950) **85m.** *** D: Edward Buzzell. Rosalind Russell, Ray Milland, Edmund Gwenn, Janis Carter, Francis Lederer. Minor but very enjoyable slapstick, as visiting professor Milland causes scandal involving college dean Russell. Energetic cast puts this over; brief guest appearance by Lucille Ball.▼●

Woman of Dolwyn SEE: **Last Days of Dolwyn, The**

Woman of Paris, A (1923) **91m.** *** D: Charles Chaplin. Edna Purviance, Adolphe Menjou, Carl Miller, Lydia Knott, Charles French. French girl Purviance is set to marry her sweetheart (Miller), but a misunderstanding causes her to move to Paris, where she becomes the mistress of wealthy Menjou. Chaplin's one attempt to make a serious film (without himself as star) was quite sophisticated for its time, and remains interesting, even moving, today. It was a box-office flop in 1923; Chaplin reedited it, but waited until 1977 to reissue it, with his newly composed music score. Chaplin does a cameo as a railway porter, but he's virtually unrecognizable.▼●

Woman of Rome (1954-Italian) **93m.** ** D: Luigi Zampa. Gina Lollobrigida, Daniel Gélin, Franco Fabrizi, Raymond Pellegrin, Pina Piovani. Overbaked melodrama of beautiful young Lollobrigida, her complex relationship with her mother, and the varied men with whom she becomes involved in pre-WW2 Rome. Alberto Moravia co-scripted this severely watered-down adaptation of his novel.▼

Woman of Straw (1964-British) **C-117m.** **½ D: Basil Dearden. Sean Connery, Gina Lollobrigida, Ralph Richardson, Johnny Sekka, Alexander Knox. Muddled suspenser of Connery and Lollobrigida plotting the "perfect murder" of old Richardson with ironic results.

Woman of the North Country (1952) **C-90m** ** D: Joseph Kane. Gale Storm, Ruth Hussey, Rod Cameron, Jim Davis,

John Agar, J. Carrol Naish. Predictable love and fight tale set in the mining lands; Storm's last film to date.

Woman of the River (1955-Italian) **C-92m.** ** D: Mario Soldati. Sophia Loren, Gerard Oury, Lise Bourdin, Rik Battaglia. Seamy, gloomy account of Loren involved with passion and criminals. Still, this was the film that really got her career going.

Woman of the Rumor, The (1954-Japanese) **95m.** **½ D: Kenji Mizoguchi. Kinuyo Tanaka, Yoshiko Kuga, Tomoemon Otani, Eitaro Shindo. Melodramatic account of Geisha house operator Tanaka, whose lover really prefers her daughter. Minor Mizoguchi.

Woman of the Town, The (1943) **90m.** *** D: George Archainbaud. Claire Trevor, Albert Dekker, Barry Sullivan, Henry Hull, Marion Martin. First-class Western with Dekker as Bat Masterson, who must choose between love for dance-hall girl Trevor or law and order.▼

Woman of the Year (1942) **112m.** ***½ D: George Stevens. Spencer Tracy, Katharine Hepburn, Fay Bainter, Dan Tobin, Reginald Owen, Roscoe Karns, William Bendix. First teaming of Tracy and Hepburn is a joy; Kate's a world-famed political commentator brought down to earth by sports reporter Tracy, whom she later weds. Unforgettable scene of Hepburn trying to understand her first baseball game. Oscar-winning screenplay by Ring Lardner, Jr. and Michael Kanin; later a hit Broadway musical. Remade for TV in 1976. Also shown in computer-colored version. ▼●◗

Woman on Pier 13 SEE: **I Married a Communist**

Woman on the Beach, The (1947) **71m.** *½ D: Jean Renoir. Robert Ryan, Joan Bennett, Charles Bickford, Nan Leslie, Walter Sande, Irene Ryan. Overheated melodrama wastes clever gimmick: Coast Guard officer isn't completely convinced his lover's husband is really blind. Loaded with laughable dialogue and sledgehammer music cues; easy to see why this was Renoir's American swan song.

Woman on the Run (1950) **77m.** *** D: Norman Foster. Ann Sheridan, Dennis O'Keefe, Robert Keith, Ross Elliott, Frank Jenks. Sheridan is most convincing as wife trying to find husband, witness to gangland murder, before underworld does.▼

Woman Rebels, A (1936) **88m.** *** D: Mark Sandrich. Katharine Hepburn, Herbert Marshall, Elizabeth Allan, Donald Crisp, Doris Dudley, David Manners, Lucile Watson, Van Heflin. Hepburn is marvelous as young girl whose experiences in Victorian England lead to her crusading for Women's Rights. Well-mounted soap opera remains surprisingly timely.

Woman's Devotion, A (1956) **C-88m.** ** D: Paul Henreid. Ralph Meeker, Janice Rule, Paul Henreid, Rosenda Monteros. Choppy mystery of artist Meeker and wife Rule, involved in a murder while in Mexico. Aka BATTLE SHOCK.▼

Woman's Face, A (1941) **105m.** *** D: George Cukor. Joan Crawford, Melvyn Douglas, Conrad Veidt, Osa Massen, Reginald Owen, Albert Bassermann, Marjorie Main, Donald Meek, Connie Gilchrist, Henry Daniell, Richard Nichols. Crawford has one of her most substantial roles in this exciting yarn of a scarred woman whose life changes when she undergoes plastic surgery. Taut climax spotlights villain Veidt. Originally filmed in 1938 in Sweden, as EN KVINNAS ANSIKTE, with Ingrid Bergman; script by Donald Ogden Stewart and Elliot Paul. Also shown in computer-colored version.▼●

Woman's Secret, A (1949) **85m.** **½ D: Nicholas Ray. Maureen O'Hara, Melvyn Douglas, Gloria Grahame, Bill Williams, Victor Jory. Intriguing flashback drama of woman coming to hate singer she built up to success; good performances by two female stars. Just a bit too sloppy. Produced and scripted by Herman J. Mankiewicz, from a Vicki Baum novel.▼

Woman's Tale, A (1991-Australian) **C-93m.** ***½ D: Paul Cox. Sheila Florance, Gosia Dobrowolska, Norman Kaye, Chris Haywood, Ernest Gray, Myrtle Woods, Bruce Myles. 78-year-old woman dying of cancer is determined to live her final days with the same dignity she displayed her entire life. Simple tale—beautifully directed—is heartbreakingly real. Distinguished by the extraordinary and courageous performance of Sheila Florance, whose own illness while making the film paralleled that of her character. (She died two days after receiving Australia's Academy Award as Best Actress.) The kind of movie that, while painful to watch at times, can also illuminate our lives. [PG-13]▼●

Woman's Vengeance, A (1947) **96m.** ***½ D: Zoltan Korda. Charles Boyer, Ann Blyth, Jessica Tandy, Cedric Hardwicke, Mildred Natwick. Outstanding drama of philandering Boyer put on trial when his wife is found dead; brilliant cast gives vivid realistic performances. Script by Aldous Huxley, from his story.

Woman's World (1954) **C-94m.** *** D: Jean Negulesco. Clifton Webb, June Allyson, Van Heflin, Arlene Dahl, Lauren Bacall, Fred MacMurray, Cornel Wilde, Elliott Reid. Sophisticated look at big business, the men and women involved, with arch Webb the corporation boss choosing a new successor. CinemaScope.▼

Woman They Almost Lynched, The (1953) **90m.** ** D: Allan Dwan. John Lund, Joan Leslie, Audrey Totter, Brian Donlevy, Ellen Corby, Minerva Urecal, Jim Davis. Civil War period film about refined young woman Leslie who comes to

Western town and learns to tote gun; title tells the rest.
Woman Times Seven (1967) **C-99m.** *** D: Vittorio De Sica. Shirley MacLaine, Peter Sellers, Rossano Brazzi, Vittorio Gassman, Lex Barker, Elsa Martinelli, Robert Morley, Patrick Wymark, Adrienne Corri, Alan Arkin, Michael Caine, Anita Ekberg, Philippe Noiret. A seven-episode film with MacLaine showing seven types of women; some funny moments, some perceptive comments, but with that cast and director, it should have been much better.▼
Woman Under the Influence, A (1974) **C-155m.** ** D: John Cassavetes. Peter Falk, Gena Rowlands, Katherine Cassavetes, Lady Rowlands, Fred Draper. Typically overlong, overindulgent Cassavetes film, vaguely delineating relationship of woman who's cracking up and her hardhat husband, who can't handle it. Strong performances by Rowlands and Falk are chief virtue of this one. [R]▼●◗
Woman Undone (1996) **C-95m. TVM** D: Evelyn Purcell. Mary McDonnell, Randy Quaid, Sam Elliott, Jim Mercer, Georgann Johnson, Troy Evans, Tara Hartman. Spare, enigmatic drama about a woman accused of her husband's murder when his ashen remains turn up in their four-wheeler in the desert. Made for video; debuted on cable. Average.▼
Woman Wanted (1935) **68m.** ** D: George B. Seitz. Maureen O'Sullivan, Joel McCrea, Lewis Stone, Louis Calhern, Edgar Kennedy, Adrienne Ames, Robert Greig. Unremarkable programmer has O'Sullivan hunt-ed by police and mobsters, McCrea out to prove her innocence.
Woman Who Came Back, The (1945) **68m.** ** D: Walter Colmes. John Loder, Nancy Kelly, Otto Kruger, Ruth Ford, Harry Tyler. Fair yarn of woman (Kelly) who is convinced she has received witches' curse from ancient forebear.▼
Wombling Free (1978-British) **C-96m.** *½ D: Lionel Jeffries. David Tomlinson, Frances De La Tour, Bonnie Langford, Bernard Spear, Yasuko Nagazumi, John Junkin. Silly kiddie pic has the Wombles (actors in creature suits) cleaning up after man's litter and leading a protest against pollution. They're invisible to mankind except for a little girl (Langford) who believes. Objectionable use of stereotypes; best segment has big production-number tributes to Gene Kelly and Fred Astaire. Based on a BBC-TV series and later adapted as a U.S. series with Frank Gorshin.▼
Women, The (1939) **132m.** ***½ D: George Cukor. Joan Crawford, Norma Shearer, Rosalind Russell, Mary Boland, Joan Fontaine, Paulette Goddard, Lucile Watson, Marjorie Main, Virginia Weidler, Phyllis Povah, Ruth Hussey, Mary Beth Hughes, Virginia Grey, Hedda Hopper, Butterfly McQueen. All-star (and all-female) cast shines in this hilarious adaptation of Clare Boothe play about divorce, cattiness, and competition in circle of "friends." Crawford has one of her best roles as bitchy homewrecker. Fashion show sequence is in color; script by Anita Loos and Jane Murfin. Remade as THE OPPOSITE SEX.▼●
Women Are Like That (1938) **78m.** **½ D: Stanley Logan. Kay Francis, Pat O'Brien, Ralph Forbes, Melville Cooper. Smooth fluff: Francis is daughter of ad executive in love with copywriter O'Brien.
Women Are Weak SEE: **3 Murderesses**
Women in Bondage (1943) **70m.** ** D: Steve Sekely. Gail Patrick, Nancy Kelly, Gertrude Michael, Anne Nagel, Tala Birell, Alan Baxter, H. B. Warner. Exploitation patriotism hammering away at Nazi maltreatment of conquered people. Dates badly.
Women in Cages (1972-U.S.-Philippine) **C-78m.** BOMB D: Gerry De Leon. Judy Brown, Pam Grier, Roberta Collins. Lurid prison melodrama, with the emphasis on sadism, has the switcheroo of Grier cast as lesbian guard who tortures prisoners in her gothic chamber, known as "The Playpen." Video title: WOMEN'S PENITENTIARY III. [R]▼
Women in Limbo SEE: **Limbo** (1972)
Women in Love (1969-British) **C-129m.** ***½ D: Ken Russell. Alan Bates, Oliver Reed, Glenda Jackson, Eleanor Bron, Jennie Linden, Alan Webb. Fine adaptation of D. H. Lawrence novel about two interesting love affairs. Tends to bog down toward the end, but acting and direction are really impressive, as is memorable nude wrestling scene. Jackson won her first Oscar for this performance. Followed in 1989 by Russell's THE RAINBOW, a "prequel" in which Jackson plays the mother of her character in this film. [R]▼●
Women of Brewster Place, The (1989) **C-200m. TVM** D: Donna Deitch. Oprah Winfrey, Mary Alice, Olivia Cole, Robin Givens, Moses Gunn, Jackée, Paula Kelly, Lonette McKee, Paul Winfield, Cicely Tyson. Ambitious filming of Gloria Naylor's novel spanning several decades in the lives of seven black women who live in a tenement on a walled-off street and struggle to overcome racism, violence, and poverty. Well-acted ensemble drama with everyone getting at least one star turn, thanks to Karen Hall's multidimensional script. TV acting debut for Winfrey, who was also executive producer. Originally shown in two parts. Later a series, *Brewster Place*. Above average.▼
Women of Devil's Island (1961-Italian) **C-95m.** *½ D: Domenico Paolella. Guy Madison, Michele Mercier, Frederica Ranchi. Humdrum mini-epic with Madison helping aristocratic woman held prisoner on swampy island. CinemaScope. ▼
Women of Pitcairn Island, The (1956)

72m. *½ D: Jean Yarbrough. James Craig, Lynn Bari, John Smith, Arleen Whelan, Sue England, Carol Thurston. Low-budget garbage about families developing from people who remained on island after MUTINY ON THE BOUNTY. Regalscope.

Women of the Prehistoric Planet (1966) **C-87m.** *½ D: Arthur C. Pierce. Wendell Corey, Keith Larsen, John Agar, Irene Tsu, Merry Anders, Adam Roarke, Stuart Margolin. One of many studio-bound sci-fi pix from the '60s, a strange lot indeed. Spaceship crashes on mysterious planet full of prehistoric inhabitants. There's a twist ending, if you stick around for it.▼

Women on the Verge of a Nervous Breakdown (1988-Spanish) **C-88m.** ***½ D: Pedro Almodóvar. Carmen Maura, Antonio Banderas, Julieta Serrano, Maria Barranco, Rossy De Palma. Witty, outrageous, and highly stylized comedy about charmingly off-kilter actress Maura and how she responds when suddenly abandoned by her longtime lover. A real audience-pleaser, with plenty of laughs; crammed with a colorful array of supporting characters (most memorably a taxi driver with a bleached-blond pompadour whose car is a combination drugstore/bar). [R]▼●

Women's Penitentiary I SEE: **Big Doll House, The**

Women's Penitentiary II SEE: **Big Bird Cage, The**

Women's Penitentiary III SEE: **Women in Cages**

Women's Prison (1955) **80m.** ** D: Lewis Seiler. Ida Lupino, Jan Sterling, Cleo Moore, Audrey Totter, Phyllis Thaxter, Howard Duff, Mae Clarke, Gertrude Michael, Juanita Moore. Campy 1950s programmer, with Lupino as a vicious prison superintendent riding herd over a cast that no B movie lover could resist.

Women Without Men SEE: **Blonde Bait**

Wonder Bar (1934) **84m.** **½ D: Lloyd Bacon. Al Jolson, Kay Francis, Dolores Del Rio, Dick Powell, Ricardo Cortez, Louise Fazenda, Hugh Herbert, Hal LeRoy, Guy Kibbee. Very strange, often tasteless musical drama set in Paris nightclub with murder, romance, and Busby Berkeley's incredible "Goin' to Heaven on a Mule" production number, sure to be cut by most TV stations because of its outrageous racial stereotypes.●

Wonder Boys (2000) **C-112m.** *** D: Curtis Hanson. Michael Douglas, Tobey Maguire, Frances McDormand, Robert Downey, Jr., Katie Holmes, Richard Thomas, Rip Torn, Philip Bosco, Jane Adams. Intelligent, low-key comedy about the bond that develops between a college professor (Douglas), whose personal and professional life is floundering, and a strange but gifted student (Maguire), who adds to his chaos. A midlife coming-of-age story that benefits from its freshly observed academic milieu and a strong cast; Douglas is excellent in a change-of-pace role. Steve Kloves adapted Michael Chabon's novel. Super 35. [R]

Wonderful Country, The (1959) **C-96m.** **½ D: Robert Parrish. Robert Mitchum, Julie London, Gary Merrill, Pedro Armendariz, Jack Oakie, Albert Dekker. Brooding Western involving Mitchum running guns along Mexico-Texas line, romancing London; script by Robert Ardrey.

Wonderful, Horrible Life of Leni Riefenstahl, The (1993-German-Belgian British) **C/B&W-182m.** *** D: Ray Muller. Thorough, compelling portrait of Riefenstahl, infamous director of Nazi propaganda films TRIUMPH OF THE WILL and OLYMPIA, that serves as an investigation of her life (traced via film clips, and interviews made with the filmmaker in her early nineties). Was she a woman of evil—an opportunist and a collaborator in her dealings with Adolph Hitler and the Nazi Party? Or was she a feminist pioneer, an apolitical artist who became an innocent victim of circumstance? Riefenstahl would have you believe the latter. Ultimately, the film is most effective as a portrait of denial, and an analysis of any filmmaker's responsibility regarding the power of the moving image.▼●◗

Wonderful Ice Cream Suit, The (1999) **C-77m.** **½ D: Stuart Gordon. Joe Mantegna, Esai Morales, Edward James Olmos, Clifton Gonzales Gonzales, Gregory Sierra, Liz Torres, Sid Caesar, Howard Morris, Lisa Vidal, Pedro Gonzales Gonzales. Well-meaning, upbeat adaptation of Ray Bradbury's short story and play about five L.A. Latinos who share the price of a beautiful white suit which, they believe, will help them realize their dreams. The flavor never seems genuine, and the treatment is heavy-handed, but there is still a magic to the story. Released direct to video. [PG] ▼●

Wonderful World of the Brothers Grimm, The (1962) **C-129m.** *** D: Henry Levin, George Pal. Laurence Harvey, Claire Bloom, Karl Boehm, Oscar Homolka, Martita Hunt, Jim Backus, Yvette Mimieux, Barbara Eden, Walter Slezak, Russ Tamblyn, Buddy Hackett, Beulah Bondi, Terry-Thomas. Fanciful adaptations of Grimm tales offset by OK look at famed brothers' lives. Best of all are Puppetoons sequences in toy shop, Hackett battling fire-breathing dragon. Colorful George Pal entertainment, with Oscar-winning costumes by Mary Wills, was originally shown in Cinerama.▼●

Wonderland (1988) SEE: **Fruit Machine, The**

Wonderland (1999-British) **C-108m.** ** D: Michael Winterbottom. Shirley Henderson, Gina McKee, Molly Parker, Ian Hart, John Simm, Stuart Townsend, Kika Markham, Jack Shepherd. Dreary slice-of-life drama set in London over a long weekend, examining three unhappy generations of a single family. The mise-en-scène is impeccable, the situations completely believable, but the results are less than compelling. Panavision.▼

Wonder Man (1945) **C-98m.** *** D: H. Bruce Humberstone. Danny Kaye, Virginia Mayo, Vera-Ellen, Donald Woods, S. Z. Sakall, Allen Jenkins, Ed Brophy, Steve Cochran, Otto Kruger, Natalie Schafer. Kaye's fun as twins, the serious one forced to take the place of his brash entertainer brother when the latter is killed. Big, colorful production with Oscar-winning special effects.▼●◗

Wonders of Aladdin, The (1961-U.S.-Italian) **C-93m.** ** D: Henry Levin, Mario Bava. Donald O'Connor, Noelle Adam, Vittorio De Sica, Aldo Fabrizi. Few wonders to behold in this mild children's fantasy. CinemaScope.▼

Won Ton Ton, the Dog Who Saved Hollywood (1976) **C-92m.** ** D: Michael Winner. Bruce Dern, Madeline Kahn, Art Carney, Phil Silvers, Teri Garr, Ron Leibman. Fine cast struggles through inept spoof of 1920s Hollywood. Dog comes off better than dozens of veteran stars who make pointless cameo appearances (from Rhonda Fleming to the Ritz Brothers). [PG]

Woo (1998) **C-83m.** BOMB D: Daisy V. S. Mayer. Jada Pinkett Smith, Tommy Davidson, Duane Martin, Dave Chappelle, Michael Ralph, LL Cool J, Foxy Brown, Aida Turturro, Billy Dee Williams. Misbegotten attempt at screwball comedy in which neurotic Manhattanite Pinkett Smith leads dorky law student Davidson on an all-night blind date from hell. Substitutes stupid slapstick and misogynist, homophobic potshots for wit and charm. Wants to be a '90s BRINGING UP BABY but ends up a subpar HOUSE PARTY. [R]▼●

Wood, The (1999) **C-106m.** **½ D: Rick Famuyiwa. Omar Epps, Sean Nelson, Taye Diggs, Trent Cameron, Richard T. Jones, Duane Finley, Malinda Williams, Lisarae. So-so comedy about a reluctant, AWOL bridegroom (Diggs) whose two best pals (Epps, Jones) come to his rescue; in flashbacks we learn how they became friends in their formative years. The predictability of their story is partially offset by the film's charm and humor. [R]▼●◗

Wooden Horse, The (1950-British) **101m.** *** D: Jack Lee. Leo Genn, David Tomlinson, Anthony Steel, Peter Burton, David Greene, Anthony Dawson, Bryan Forbes, Peter Finch. Sturdy, exciting P.O.W. drama of men determined to tunnel their way out of Nazi prison camp using an exercise vaulting horse for cover. Based on Eric Williams' novel *The Tunnel Escape*.▼

Woodstock (1970) **C-184m.** **** D: Michael Wadleigh. Joan Baez, Richie Havens, Crosby, Stills and Nash, Jefferson Airplane, Joe Cocker, Sly and the Family Stone, Ten Years After, Santana, Country Joe and the Fish, John Sebastian, The Who, Jimi Hendrix, Arlo Guthrie. 1970 Oscar-winner as Best Documentary brilliantly captures unique communal experience of outdoor rock festival, along with great performances which highlighted unusual weekend bash. Among highlights: Cocker, Sly Stone, Ten Years After, The Who. Unfortunately, effect of multiscreen images and stereophonic sound may be lost on TV. Martin Scorsese was one of the editors. Forty minutes of previously unseen footage were added in 1994, featuring Janis Joplin, Jimi Hendrix, Canned Heat and Jefferson Airplane, among others. That video title is WOODSTOCK: THREE DAYS OF PEACE & MUSIC (THE DIRECTOR'S CUT). Part Widescreen. [R]▼●◗

Woody Guthrie: Hard Travelin' (1984) **C/B&W-74m.** **** D: Jim Brown. Fascinating, beautifully made documentary about the wiry little drifter who is now recognized as one of the greatest American songwriters. Hosted by his son, Arlo, the film traces Woody's life from birth to his tragically lingering death. Interviewees include friends, like Pete Seeger, Herta Ware and Ramblin' Jack Elliott, and those who were influenced by Woody, such as Joan Baez, Judy Collins and Hoyt Axton. It leaves you singing, and wanting more.▼

Words and Music (1948) **C-119m.** **½ D: Norman Taurog. Mickey Rooney, Tom Drake, June Allyson, Ann Sothern, Judy Garland, Gene Kelly, Lena Horne, Vera-Ellen, Cyd Charisse, Allyn Ann McLerie, Mel Torme, Betty Garrett, Perry Como, Janet Leigh. Sappy, Hollywoodized biography of songwriters Rodgers (Drake) and Hart (Rooney) is salvaged somewhat by their wonderful music, including Kelly and Vera-Ellen's dance to "Slaughter on Tenth Avenue." ▼●

Working Girl (1988) **C-113m.** *** D: Mike Nichols. Harrison Ford, Sigourney Weaver, Melanie Griffith, Alec Baldwin, Joan Cusack, Philip Bosco, Nora Dunn, Oliver Platt, James Lally, Kevin Spacey, Robert Easton, Olympia Dukakis, Ricki Lake, David Duchovny. Cute comedy about a naive but ambitious secretary who tries to outfox her wily boss by closing a big deal—with the help of a man she just happens to fall in love with. Star-making showcase for Griffith also gives Ford an ideal opportunity to play light comedy, and Weaver a sly supporting role as the villainess. Carly Simon's music was scored by Rob Mounsey; her song "Let the River Run" won an Oscar. Later a TV series. [R]▼●

Working Girls, The (1973) **C-81m.** **½

D: Stephanie Rothman. Sarah Kennedy, Laurie Rose, Lynne Guthrie, Solomon Sturges, Mary Beth Hughes, Cassandra Peterson. One of the better drive-in comedies, with three attractive girls struggling to make a success of themselves in a male-oriented world; Kennedy and Sturges (Preston's son) make an endearing couple. A staple of cable-TV because of nifty striptease performed by Peterson (better known as TV's Elvira). [R]▼

Working Girls (1986) **C-90m.** ***½ D: Lizzie Borden. Louise Smith, Ellen McElduff, Amanda Goodwin, Marusia Zach, Janne Peters, Helen Nicholas. Beautifully realized, on-target account of a day in a N.Y.C. brothel; the sex is more humorous and businesslike than erotic, and the profession is depicted as an economic alternative to other traditional "women's" work. First-rate all the way.▼

Working Man, The (1933) **C-74m.** *** D: John G. Adolfi. George Arliss, Bette Davis, Hardie Albright,. Theodore Newton, Gordon Westcott, J. Farrell MacDonald. Charming comedy about a businessman who chances to meet the children of his late arch-rival—and determines to change their wastrel ways, even if it means competing with his own company. A much-improved remake of Arliss' silent film $20 A WEEK (1924); remade with Irvin S. Cobb as EVERYBODY'S OLD MAN (1936).

Work Is a 4-Letter Word (1967 British) **C-93m.** **½ D: Peter Hall. David Warner, Cilla Black, Elizabeth Spriggs, Zia Mohyeddin, Joe Gladwyn. Zany, but hit-and-miss comedy based on the play *Eh?* about young man who raises giant mushrooms that produce euphoria when eaten. Warner is well cast. [M/PG]

World According to Garp, The (1982) **C-136m.** **** D: George Roy Hill. Robin Williams, Mary Beth Hurt, Glenn Close, John Lithgow, Hume Cronyn, Jessica Tandy, Swoosie Kurtz, Amanda Plummer, Warren Berlinger, Brandon Maggart. Dazzling (if somewhat loose) adaptation of John Irving's novel, about an unusual young man's journey through life—an adventure shaped in large part by his unorthodox (and unmarried) mother. Absorbing, surefooted odyssey through vignettes of social observation, absurdist humor, satire, and melodrama; beautifully acted by all, especially Close (in her feature debut) as Garp's mother and Lithgow as a transsexual. Script by Steve Tesich. Director Hill has cameo as pilot who crashes into Garp's house; novelist Irving plays wrestling match referee. [R]▼●

World and the Flesh (1932) **75m.** ** D: John Cromwell. George Bancroft, Miriam Hopkins, Alan Mowbray, George E. Stone. Labored drama of soldier-of-fortune Bancroft asking price of Hopkins to save her wealthy friends from Russian Revolution; moves very slowly.

World Apart, A (1988) **C-112m.** **½ D: Chris Menges. Barbara Hershey, David Suchet, Jeroen Krabbé, Jodhi May, Rosalie Crutchley, Tim Roth, Adrian Dunbar, Paul Freeman. Personal story of South African apartheid as seen through the eyes of a teenage girl whose mother, a Communist activist, is jailed under the notorious 90-day detention act in 1963. Both a story of government abuse and a look at one mother's neglect of her family because of her involvement with a larger cause. Unfortunately, it becomes too diffuse to succeed completely on either count. Young May is remarkable as the girl, however. Autobiographical script was written by Shawn Slovo. Directorial debut for cinematographer Menges. [PG]▼●

World Changes, The (1933) **90m.** *** D: Mervyn LeRoy. Paul Muni, Mary Astor, Aline MacMahon, Donald Cook, Alan Dinehart, Guy Kibbee, Margaret Lindsay, Henry O'Neill, Jean Muir. Extremely watchable Edna Ferber–like saga of farm boy Muni, who pursues his ambitions to Chicago in the late 1800s and becomes a meat-packing baron and multimillionaire—only to see his family life crumble before his very eyes. Astor is excellent as his selfish wife, MacMahon her usual tower of strength as his mother. Cast is brimming with familiar faces, including young Mickey Rooney and pre–*Charlie Chan* Sidney Toler.

World for Ransom (1954) **80m.** ** D: Robert Aldrich. Dan Duryea, Gene Lockhart, Patric Knowles, Reginald Denny, Nigel Bruce, Marian Carr. Deliriously cheesy B movie (made to cash in on Duryea's then-popular *China Smith* TV series) about intrigue and espionage in Singapore. Pretty poor, but some stylish shots and veteran cast are definite assets.

World Gone Mad, The (1932) **74m.** ** D: Christy Cabanne. Pat O'Brien, Evelyn Brent, Neil Hamilton, Mary Brian, Louis Calhern, J. Carrol Naish, Buster Phelps, Richard Tucker. District attorney about to uncover stock swindle is framed and murdered; his intrepid reporter pal (who else but O'Brien) and the new D.A. (Hamilton) investigate. Then-topical programmer has its moments, but is too talky and meandering. Aka PUBLIC BE DAMNED. ▼

World Gone Wild (1988) **C-95m.** ** D: Lee H. Katzin. Bruce Dern, Michael Paré, Catherine Mary Stewart, Adam Ant, Rick Podell, Anthony James. Post-apocalyptic science-fiction saga set in the 21st century, in the desolate village of Lost Wells, which is threatened by evil plunderers (led by Adam Ant). Who will come to the villagers' rescue? THE SEVEN SAMURAI meets MAD MAX in this marginally successful, futuristic action yarn. [R]▼●

World in His Arms, The (1952) **C-104m.** *** D: Raoul Walsh. Gregory Peck, Ann Blyth, John McIntire, Anthony Quinn, Andrea King, Eugenie Leontovich, Sig Ruman. Unlikely but entertaining tale of skipper Peck romancing Russian Blyth, set in 1850s San Francisco.▼

World in My Corner (1956) **82m** **½ D: Jesse Hibbs. Audie Murphy, Barbara Rush, Jeff Morrow, John McIntire, Tommy Rall, Howard St. John. Murphy is poor boy who rises to fame via boxing, almost ruined by rich life with Rush standing by.

World Is Full of Married Men, The (1979-British) **C-107m.** ** D: Robert Young. Anthony Franciosa, Carroll Baker, Sherrie Cronn, Gareth Hunt, Georgina Hale, Anthony Steel. The sexual escapades—and downfall—of advertising executive Franciosa. Slick and sleazy exploitation melodrama that ultimately gives feminism a bad name, from a novel and screenplay by Jackie Collins. [R]▼

World Is Not Enough, The (1999) **C-125m.** **½ D: Michael Apted. Pierce Brosnan, Sophie Marceau, Robert Carlyle, Denise Richards, Robbie Coltrane, Judi Dench, Desmond Llewelyn, John Cleese, Maria Grazia Cucinotta, Samantha Bond, Goldie, Serena Scott Thomas. OK if typically overlong James Bond outing has 007 avenging the murder of an industrialist who was a close friend of M's. Brosnan is fine, as are the action set-pieces, but film allows M (Dench) to look foolish, and absurdly casts Richards as a nuclear physicist (in shorts!) with lots of laughable dialogue. Carlyle is a good villain with an underwritten part; Marceau is delicious as Elektra. Llewelyn's final film as Q. Panavision. [PG-13]▼◗

World Moves On, The (1934) **104m.** **½ D: John Ford. Madeleine Carroll, Franchot Tone, Reginald Denny, Stepin Fetchit, Lumsden Hare, Raul Roulien, Louise Dresser, Sig Ruman. Long but interesting family saga covering 100 years as Louisiana family is split, three sons heading business operations in England, France, Germany, experiencing tremendous changes from peaceful 19th century through WW1.

World of Abbott and Costello, The (1965) **75m.** ** Narrated by Jack E. Leonard. Bud Abbott, Lou Costello, Marjorie Main, Bela Lugosi, Tom Ewell, others. Inept compilation of A&C footage, with curious selection of scenes, senseless narration. Still, there's "Who's on First?" and other fine routines.▼

World of Apu, The (1959-Indian) **103m.** ***½ D: Satyajit Ray. Soumitra Chatterjee, Sharmila Tagore, Alok Chakravarty, Swapan Mukherji. Sadly poetic tale of the shy Apu (Chatterjee) marrying and fathering a child. Magnificently acted; last of the director's "Apu" trilogy.▼

World of Henry Orient, The (1964) **C-106m.** ***½ D: George Roy Hill. Peter Sellers, Tippy Walker, Merrie Spaeth, Paula Prentiss, Angela Lansbury, Phyllis Thaxter, Tom Bosley. Marvelous comedy of two teenage girls who idolize eccentric pianist (Sellers) and follow him around N.Y.C. Bosley and Lansbury are superb as Walker's parents, with Thaxter appealing as Spaeth's understanding mother. Screenplay by Nunnally and Nora Johnson, from her novel. Panavision.▼●

World of Suzie Wong, The (1960) **C-129m.** **½ D: Richard Quine. William Holden, Nancy Kwan, Sylvia Syms, Michael Wilding, Laurence Naismith. Holden's sluggish performance as American artist in love with prostitute Kwan doesn't help this soaper, lavishly filmed in Hong Kong. Script by John Patrick from Paul Osborn's Broadway play.▼●

World of Tomorrow, The (1984) **C/B&W-83m.** *** D: Lance Bird, Tom Johnson. Lovely documentary about 1939 New York World's Fair, a compilation of newsreels, home movies, promotional films, and various other period graphics . . . much of it in color! Occasionally teeters on the edge of pretentiousness, especially in narration spoken by Jason Robards. Cut to one hour for some showings.▼

World Premiere (1941) **70m.** *½ D: Ted Tetzlaff. John Barrymore, Frances Farmer, Eugene Pallette, Virginia Dale, Ricardo Cortez, Sig Ruman, Fritz Feld. Poor excuse for comedy involves idiotic producer Barrymore, jealous movie stars, outlandish publicity stunts, and Nazi saboteurs. A real waste.

World's Greatest Athlete, The (1973) **C-93m.** *** D: Robert Scheerer. John Amos, Jan-Michael Vincent, Tim Conway, Roscoe Lee Browne, Dayle Haddon, Howard Cosell. Hard-luck coach Amos returns to his roots in Africa and discovers super-athlete Vincent; enjoyable Disney comedy with excellent special effects. Conway particularly funny in sequence in which he shrinks to Tom Thumb size. Cosell's classic line: "I've never seen anything like this in my entire illustrious career!" [G]▼

World's Greatest Lover, The (1977) **C-89m.** **½ D: Gene Wilder. Gene Wilder, Carol Kane, Dom DeLuise, Fritz Feld, Carl Ballantine, Michael Huddleston, Matt Collins, Ronny Graham, Danny DeVito. Sporadically funny comedy set in 1920s Hollywood, with Wilder screen-testing as new movie sheik and wife Kane deserting him for real-life Valentino. Wild slapstick combines unevenly with occasional vulgarities and moments of poignancy. Inspired by Fellini's THE WHITE SHEIK. [PG]▼

World, the Flesh, and the Devil, The (1959) **95m.** **½ D: Ranald MacDougall. Harry Belafonte, Inger Stevens, Mel Ferrer. Belafonte and Stevens are only survivors of worldwide nuclear accident; their uneasy relationship is jarred by arrival of Ferrer. Intriguing film starts well, bogs down halfway through, and presents ridiculous conclusion. Best scenes are at beginning, when Belafonte is alone in an impressively deserted Manhattan. CinemaScope.▼●

World Was His Jury, The (1958) **82m.** *½ D: Fred F. Sears. Edmond O'Brien, Mona Freeman, Karin Booth, Robert McQueeney. Routine account of ship's captain proven innocent of negligence in sea disaster.

World Without End (1956) **C-80m.** **½ D: Edward Bernds. Hugh Marlowe, Nancy Gates, Nelson Leigh, Rod Taylor. Space flight headed for Mars breaks the time barrier and ends up on Earth in the 26th century. Pretty good sci-fi owes more than a little to H. G. Wells' *The Time Machine*. CinemaScope.▼

World Without Sun (1964) **C-93m.** **** D: Jacques Cousteau. Excellent, Oscar-winning documentary of Cousteau and his oceanauts, creating an underwater adventure that challenges any fiction.

Worst Woman in Paris?, The (1933) **78m.** **½ D: Monta Bell. Benita Hume, Adolphe Menjou, Harvey Stephens, Helen Chandler. Glossy Lubitsch-like comedy of chic Hume walking out on wealthy husband Menjou, returning to America, falling in love with naive young Stephens.

Worth Winning (1989) **C-102m.** *½ D: Will Mackenzie. Mark Harmon, Madeleine Stowe, Lesley Ann Warren, Maria Holvöe, Mark Blum, Andrea Martin, David Brenner. Smug Harmon bets that he can hustle a trio of women into agreeing to marry him. Occasionally obnoxious (and predictable) comedy. [PG-13]▼●

Woyzeck (1978-German) **C-82m.** **½ D: Werner Herzog. Klaus Kinski, Eva Mattes, Wolfgang Reichmann, Willy Semmelrogge, Josef Bierbichler. Minor Herzog features the usual wide-eyed performance by Kinski as an ostensibly normal man who goes insane and becomes a murderer. Based on Georg Büchner's drama.▼

Wraith, The (1986) **C-92m.** ** D: Mike Marvin. Charlie Sheen, Nick Cassavetes, Randy Quaid, Sherilyn Fenn, Griffin O'Neal, David Sherrill, Jamie Bozian, Clint Howard. A Dodge Turbo Interceptor—it's a car—strangely appears one day and takes on some auto thieves. For those who favor fast cars and lots of noise. [PG-13]▼●

Wrath of God, The (1972) **C-111m.** ** D: Ralph Nelson. Robert Mitchum, Rita Hayworth, Frank Langella, John Colicos, Victor Buono, Ken Hutchison, Paula Pritchett, Gregory Sierra. If you take this film—about a defrocked priest in a revolution-ridden country south of the border—seriously, it's an OK action yarn. Accept it as tongue-in-cheek, it may yield greater enjoyment. Hayworth's final film. Panavision. [PG]

Wrecking Crew, The (1969) **C-105m.** *½ D: Phil Karlson. Dean Martin, Sharon Tate, Elke Sommer, Nancy Kwan, Tina Louise, Nigel Green. Fourth and final theatrical Matt Helm epic, while hardly a good film, is at least a step up from the last two, thanks to a return by the original director and the re-creation (in Tate) of an engaging klutz a la Stella Stevens in THE SILENCERS. Story has Helm after crime ring that's hijacked a train carrying a billion in gold. Chuck Norris has one line with Dino in a bar and Bruce Lee is credited as film's "karate advisor." A TVM and subsequent series (*Matt Helm*) followed in 1975. [M/PG]▼◗

Wreck of the Hesperus, The (1948) **70m.** ** D: John Hoffman. Willard Parker, Edgar Buchanan, Patricia White (Barry). Loosely based on Longfellow poem, this low-budget flick suffers from lack of production values to enhance special effects of storms at sea.

Wreck of the Mary Deare, The (1959-U.S.-British) **C-105m.** **½ D: Michael Anderson. Gary Cooper, Charlton Heston, Michael Redgrave, Emlyn Williams, Cecil Parker, Alexander Knox, Virginia McKenna, Richard Harris. Sticky going: skipper of sunken ship accused of negligence, cleared at inquest by testimony of salvage boat captain. Special effects are real star. Script by Eric Ambler. CinemaScope.▼●

Wrestling Ernest Hemingway (1993) **C-122m.** **½ D: Randa Haines. Robert Duvall, Richard Harris, Shirley MacLaine, Sandra Bullock, Piper Laurie, Nicole Mercurio, Marty Belafsky. A great actor's showcase, if not a great movie, about two older men now living in Florida: a boozy Irish ex-sea captain (Harris) and a retired Cuban barber (Duvall). They have practically nothing in common, but their need for companionship and interaction draws them together in this meandering but easy-to-take character study which was (incredibly) written by a 21-year-old, Steve Conrad. [PG-13] ▼●

Written on the Wind (1957) **C-99m.** *** D: Douglas Sirk. Rock Hudson, Lauren Bacall, Robert Stack, Dorothy Malone, Robert Keith, Grant Williams. Florid melodrama of playboy-millionaire Stack, his nymphomaniac sister Malone, and how they destroy themselves and others around them. Irresistible kitsch. Malone won Oscar for her performance.▼

Wrong Arm of the Law, The (1963-British) **94m.** *** D: Cliff Owen. Peter Sellers, Lionel Jeffries, Bernard Cribbins, Davy Kaye, Nanette Newman, John Le Mesurier, Dennis Price. Wacky comedy spoof has Australian trio being chased by police as well as crooks because they've been dressing as cops and confiscating loot from apprehended robbers. Some very funny moments.▼

Wrong Bet SEE: **Lionheart** (1991)

Wrong Box, The (1966-British) **C-105m.** ***½ D: Bryan Forbes. John Mills, Ralph Richardson, Michael Caine, Peter Cook, Dudley Moore, Nanette Newman, Wilfred Lawson, Tony Hancock, Peter Sellers. Scramble for inheritance is basis for wacky black comedy set in Victorian England; aging Mills attempts to do in brother Richardson (with help from family cohorts) in order to be sole survivor. Sellers has hilarious cameo as oddball doctor. Based on a Robert Louis Stevenson story, scripted by Larry Gelbart and Burt Shevelove.▼●

Wrongfully Accused (1998-U.S.-German) **C-85m.** ** D: Pat Proft. Leslie Nielsen, Richard Crenna, Kelly LeBrock, Sandra Bernhard, Michael York, Melinda McGraw. Silly spoof of THE FUGITIVE is yet another vehicle for Nielsen's deadpan comic shtick. This time, he's on the run for a crime he didn't commit. Amidst the relentless barrage of gags are some that—while entirely obvious—are also pretty funny, if you like this sort of thing. [PG-13]▼●◗

Wrong Guys, The (1988) **C-86m.** *½ D: Danny Bilson. Louie Anderson, Richard Lewis, Richard Belzer, Franklyn Ajaye, Tim Thomerson, Brion James, Biff Maynard, John Goodman, Ernie Hudson, Timothy Van Patten, Rita Rudner. Clumsy and unfunny comedy about a Cub Scout reunion campout that goes awry; cast of stand-up comics do battle with a stupid script. [PG]▼●

Wrong Is Right (1982) **C-117m.** **½ D: Richard Brooks. Sean Connery, George Grizzard, Robert Conrad, Katharine Ross, G. D. Spradlin, John Saxon, Henry Silva, Leslie Nielsen, Robert Webber, Rosalind Cash, Hardy Kruger, Dean Stockwell, Ron Moody, Jennifer Jason Leigh. Broad, bizarre, free-swinging satire of our TV-dominated culture, keyed to superstar reporter Connery's involvement with a terrorist group, and the U.S. government's possible ties to it. Scattershot script manages to hit a few targets, and benefits from Brooks' breathless pace. [R]▼●

Wrong Kind of Girl, The SEE: **Bus Stop**

Wrong Man, The (1957) **105m.** *** D: Alfred Hitchcock. Henry Fonda, Vera Miles, Anthony Quayle, Harold J. Stone, Nehemiah Persoff, Peggy Webber. Unusual Hitchcock film done as semidocumentary, using true story of N.Y.C. musician (Fonda) falsely accused of robbery. Miles is excellent as wife who cracks under strain; offbeat and compelling. Written by Maxwell Anderson and Angus MacPhail.▼●

Wrong Move (1975-German) **C-103m.** **½ D: Wim Wenders. Rudiger Vogler, Hanna Schygulla, Ivan Desny, Marianne Hoppe, Peter Kern, Hans Christian Blech, Nastassja Kinski. Overly metaphorical (but occasionally worthwhile) tale of disgruntled Vogler attempting to understand himself—and his country's past—as he rambles through Germany with various companions. Scripted by Peter Handke, loosely based on Goethe's *Wilhelm Meister.* Kinski's film debut. The second (and least successful) in Wenders' "road movie" trilogy, after ALICE IN THE CITIES and followed by KINGS OF THE ROAD. Original English title: WRONG MOVEMENT.▼

WUSA (1970) **C-115m.** **½ D: Stuart Rosenberg. Paul Newman, Joanne Woodward, Anthony Perkins, Laurence Harvey, Pat Hingle, Cloris Leachman, Don Gordon, Leigh French, Moses Gunn, Bruce Cabot, Lou Gossett, Jr. Newman pet project casts him as cynical drifter who becomes a d.j. for an ultra-right-wing New Orleans radio station and struggles with his own apathy as he grows aware of WUSA's true (and sinister) intentions. Obvious sincerity undercut by simplistic, overwritten script; still, the acting is fine and there are some truly memorable scenes. Panavision. [M/PG]

Wuthering Heights (1939) **103m.** **** D: William Wyler. Merle Oberon, Laurence Olivier, David Niven, Flora Robson, Donald Crisp, Geraldine Fitzgerald, Leo G. Carroll, Cecil Kellaway, Miles Mander, Hugh Williams. Stirring adaptation of Emily Brontë's novel stops at chapter 17, but viewers shouldn't despair: sensitive direction and sweeping performances propel this magnificent story of doomed love in pre-Victorian England. Haunting, a must-see film. Gregg Toland's moody photography won an Oscar; script by Ben Hecht and Charles MacArthur. Remade in 1953, 1970, and 1992.▼●◗

Wuthering Heights (1953-Mexican) **90m.** **½ D: Luis Buñuel. Irasema Dilian, Jorge Mistral, Lilia Prado, Ernesto Alonso, Luis Aceves Castaneda. Strikingly directed but talky, overbaked, ultimately unsuccessful version of the Brontë classic: bitter, cold-hearted former servant Mistral, now rich, returns to disrupt the life of true love Dilian, now married to another.▼

Wuthering Heights (1970-British) **C-105m.** *** D: Robert Fuest. Anna Calder-Marshall, Timothy Dalton, Harry Andrews, Pamela Browne, Judy Cornwell, Ian Ogilvy, Hugh Griffith, Julian Glover. Good, realistic treatment of Brontë's novel with authentic locations and atmosphere, Dalton and Calder-Marshall believable looking as Heathcliff and Cathy, but film's point of view indistinct and pace too fast. [G]▼●

Wuthering Heights (1992-U.S.-British) **C-106m.** *½ D: Peter Kosminsky. Juliette Binoche, Ralph Fiennes, Janet McTeer, Sophie Ward, Simon Shepherd, Jeremy Northam. Excruciating remake of the classic Brontë novel of doomed love. Binoche plays both Cathy and her daughter exactly the same way, with a different hair color. Fiennes' torment is so intense, it's actually a relief when he dies. This was the first film produced by Paramount studio's European production wing but it made its U.S. debut several years after completion, on cable TV. Sinéad O'Connor appears unbilled as Emily Brontë. Title onscreen is EMILY BRONTË'S WUTHERING HEIGHTS. [PG]▼●

W.W. and the Dixie Dancekings (1975) **C-91m.** **½ D: John G. Avildsen. Burt Reynolds, Art Carney, Conny Van Dyke, Jerry Reed, James Hampton, Ned Beatty. Lightly likable film about a conman who hooks up with struggling country-western group and stops at nothing to promote their success; Carney has oddball role as religious lawman pursuing Burt. Script by Thomas Rickman. [PG]

Wyatt Earp (1994) **C-195m.** **½ D: Lawrence Kasdan. Kevin Costner, Dennis Quaid, Gene Hackman, Jeff Fahey, Mark Harmon, Michael Madsen, Catherine O'Hara, Bill Pullman, Isabella Rossellini, Tom Sizemore, JoBeth Williams, Mare Winningham, James Gammon, Annabeth Gish, Betty Buckley, Mackenzie Astin, Karen Grassle, Téa Leoni, Brett Cullen, John Doe, Martin Kove. Epic-length biography shows how fate and circumstance turned the fabled Earp into a hardened and heartless man who killed in the name of law and order. Good storytelling grows ponderous toward the end, as Earp is driven by revenge against his blood enemies from the O.K. Corral. Quaid makes a colorful Doc Holliday, though his equally flashy ladyfriend Big Nosed Kate (Rossellini) disappears just as we get to meet her! Special video edition runs 20m. longer! Panavision. [R]▼●

Wyoming (1940) **89m.** ** D: Richard Thorpe. Wallace Beery, Leo Carrillo, Ann Rutherford, Marjorie Main, Lee Bowman, Joseph Calleia, Bobs Watson. OK oater with Beery and Carrillo fun as on-again, off-again outlaw pals tempted by honesty.

Wyoming (1947) **84m.** **½ D: Joseph Kane. William Elliott, Vera Ralston, John Carroll, "Gabby" Hayes, Albert Dekker, Virginia Grey. Not-bad Wild Bill Elliott Western of ranchers vs. homesteaders in Wyoming territory.▼

Wyoming Kid, The SEE: **Cheyenne**

Wyoming Mail (1950) **C-87m.** **½ D: Reginald LeBorg. Stephen McNally, Alexis Smith, Ed Begley, Richard Egan, James Arness, Frankie Darro, Richard Jaeckel. Postal robbery in old West, with capable cast shining up script's dull spots.

Wyoming Renegades (1955) **C-73m.** *½ D: Fred F. Sears. Phil Carey, Gene Evans, Martha Hyer, William Bishop, Aaron Spelling. Confused Western portraying the story of ex-bandit Carey who wants to go straight.

Xanadu (1980) **C-88m.** *½ D: Robert Greenwald. Olivia Newton-John, Gene Kelly, Michael Beck, James Sloyan, Dimitra Arliss, Katie Hanley, Sandahl Bergman, Marilyn Tokuda, John "Fee" Waybill, voices of Wilfred Hyde-White and Coral Browne. Flashy but empty-headed remake of DOWN TO EARTH, with Olivia as muse who pops in to inspire young roller-boogie artist. Designed as a showcase for the singer, whose screen charisma is nil. Kelly (using his character name from COVER GIRL) tries to perk things up; even a brief animated sequence by Don Bluth doesn't help. Newton-John's future husband, Matt Lattanzi, plays Kelly as a young man. Cable version runs 96m. [PG] ▼●◗

X-15 (1961) **C-106m.** ** D: Richard Donner. David McLean, Charles Bronson, Ralph Taeger, Brad Dexter, Mary Tyler Moore, Patricia Owens. Mild narrative of pilots testing the experimental space plane of the title, and their romantic and family lives. Unusual role for Bronson, even then. Panavision.

X-Files, The (1998) **C-120m.** **½ D: Rob Bowman. David Duchovny, Gillian Anderson, Martin Landau, Armin Mueller-Stahl, Blythe Danner, William B. Davis, John Neville, Mitch Pileggi, Jeffrey DeMunn, Terry O'Quinn, Glenne Headly, Lucas Black. Feature version of popular TV series serves well enough as a conspiracy yarn for newcomers to the exploits of FBI agents Mulder and Scully. After surviving the bombing of a building in Texas, they defy orders and go in search of a new lead about aliens on Earth and the question of who's running what. Overlong by at least one climax, this large-scale thriller will have additional resonance for *X-Files* fans. Video version runs 122m. Super 35. [PG-13]▼●◗

Xica (1978-Brazilian) **C-107m.** **½ D: Carlos Diegues. Zeze Motta, Walmor Chagas, Jose Wilker, Marcus Vinicius, Altair Lima. Saucy, if a bit overspiced, tale of strong-willed black slave Motta who seduces the new Royal Diamond Contractor (Chagas) in corrupt, repressive colonial Brazil. Nicely directed and acted—particularly by Motta—but curiously unmemorable. Filmed in 1976; released in the U.S. in 1982.▼

Xiu Xiu the Sent-down Girl (1999-Chinese-Hong Kong-U.S.) **C-99m.** **½ D: Joan Chen. Lu Lu, Lopsang, Gao Jie, Li Qianqian, Lu Yue. In 1980s China, a bright city girl (16-year-old Lu Lu) is sent to a remote rural area as part of a government cultural program, where she comes under the care of a kind Tibetan herder and horse trainer. Actress Chen's directorial debut is a well-made, richly detailed film with an intriguing story, but the resolution is unsatisfying. Banned in China for its critical stance. Chen also coscripted with Yan Geling, based on the latter's novella. [R]▼◗

X—the Man with X-Ray Eyes (1963) **C-80m.** **½ D: Roger Corman. Ray

Milland, Diana Van Der Vlis, Harold J. Stone, John Hoyt, Don Rickles. Not-bad little film about scientist Milland developing serum that enables him to see through things. He lives to regret it.▼●

X The Unknown (1956-British) **80m.** **½ D: Leslie Norman. Dean Jagger, Leo McKern, William Lucas, Edward Chapman, Anthony Newley. Well-thought-out sci-fi production set in Scotland. Radioactive mud from the earth's center grows and kills anything in its path. Effective chiller written by Jimmy Sangster. ▼●

Xtro (1983-British) **C-82m.** *½ D: Harry Bromley Davenport. Philip Sayer, Bernice Stegers, Danny Brainin, Maryam d'Abo, Simon Nash. Father abducted by aliens returns to Earth three years later to claim his young son, but he's not the man he used to be. Crudely directed sci-fi/horror opus is guided by gruesomeness, not logic. Overwrought but dull, with lots of sexual elements. XTRO II and XTRO: WATCH THE SKIES are sequels in title only. [R]▼

Xtro II: The Second Encounter (1991-Canadian) **C-93m.** *½ D: Harry Bromley Davenport. Jan-Michael Vincent, Paul Koslo, Tara Buckman, Jano Frandsen, Nicholas Lea, W. F. Wadden. Experiments in interdimensional travel loose a fierce monster in an isolated underground lab; things are hampered by interpersonal conflicts. Unimaginative rehash of ALIENS (and others) suffers from an idiotic script and poor acting. No connection to XTRO apart from director. [R]▼

X, Y and Zee (1972-British) **C-110m.** ** D: Brian G. Hutton. Elizabeth Taylor, Michael Caine, Susannah York, Margaret Leighton, John Standing. Contrived, often perverse tale of a woman, her husband, another woman and the way the three are interchangeable in relationships. Original British title: ZEE AND COMPANY. [PG—edited from original R rating]▼

Yakuza, The (1975) **C-112m.** *** D: Sydney Pollack. Robert Mitchum, Takakura Ken, Brian Keith, Herb Edelman, Richard Jordan, Kishi Keiko. Mitchum tries to rescue pal Keith's kidnapped daughter by returning to Japan after several years; he gets more than he bargains for from title organization, a kind of Oriental Mafia. Mitchum and Ken are fine in suspenseful action pic, written by Paul Schrader and Robert Towne. Retitled: BROTHERHOOD OF THE YAKUZA. Originally shown at 123m. Panavision. [R]▼●

Yank at Eton, A (1942) **88m.** ** D: Norman Taurog. Mickey Rooney, Freddie Bartholomew, Tina Thayer, Ian Hunter, Edmund Gwenn, Alan Mowbray, Peter Lawford, Terry Kilburn. Rooney goes to school in England and it's a wonder he's not ejected immediately.

Yank at Oxford, A (1938-U.S.-British) **100m.** *** D: Jack Conway. Robert Taylor, Lionel Barrymore, Maureen O'Sullivan, Vivien Leigh, Edmund Gwenn. Attractive cast, including young Leigh, in familiar story of cocky American trying to adjust to Oxford, and vice versa. Remade in 1984 as OXFORD BLUES.

Yankee Buccaneer (1952) **C-86m.** **½ D: Frederick de Cordova. Jeff Chandler, Scott Brady, Suzan Ball, David Janssen. Standard pirate tale, buoyed by healthy cast.

Yankee Doodle Dandy (1942) **126m.** **** D: Michael Curtiz. James Cagney, Joan Leslie, Walter Huston, Irene Manning, Rosemary DeCamp, Richard Whorf, Jeanne Cagney, S. Z. Sakall, Walter Catlett, Frances Langford, Eddie Foy, Jr., George Tobias. Cagney wraps up film in neat little package all his own with dynamic recreation of George M. Cohan's life and times; he deservedly won Oscar for rare song-and-dance performance, as did music directors Ray Heindorf and Heinz Roemheld. Two computer-colored versions exist—one of which is edited down for TV!▼●

Yankee Pasha (1954) **C-84m.** **½ D: Joseph Pevney. Jeff Chandler, Rhonda Fleming, Mamie Van Doren, Bart Roberts (Rex Reason), Lee J. Cobb, Hal March. Nicely paced costumer set in 1800s with Chandler crossing the ocean to France and beyond to find his true love, captured by pirates.

Yank in Indo-China, A (1952) **67m.** *½ D: Wallace Grissell. John Archer, Douglas Dick, Jean Willes, Don Harvey. Just adequate yarn of American pilots involved in guerilla warfare.

Yank in Korea, A (1951) **73m.** *½ D: Lew Landers. Lon McCallister, William Phillips, Brett King, Larry Stewart. Corny war actioner.

Yank in the RAF, A (1941) **98m.** *** D: Henry King. Tyrone Power, Betty Grable, John Sutton, Reginald Gardiner, Donald Stuart, Richard Fraser. Power's only there so he can see London-based chorine Grable; they make a nice team. Songs: "Another Little Dream Won't Do Us Any Harm," "Hi-Ya Love."▼

Yank in Viet-Nam, A (1964) **80m.** ** D: Marshall Thompson. Marshall Thompson, Enrique Magalona, Mario Barri, Urban Drew. Low-budget topical actioner set in Saigon, with marine Thompson attempting to help the South Vietnamese. Retitled: YEAR OF THE TIGER.

Yanks (1979) **C-139m.** **½ D: John Schlesinger. Richard Gere, Lisa Eichhorn, Vanessa Redgrave, William Devane, Chick Vennera, Wendy Morgan, Rachel Roberts, Joan Hickson, John Ratzenberger, Antony Sher. Lavish production about WW2 romances between U.S. soldiers and British women doesn't deliver the goods, due to choppy structure and flabby direction.

Gere's so-called star power seems to be a casualty of energy crisis cutbacks. [R]▼●

Yaqui Drums (1956) **71m.** *½ D: Jean Yarbrough. Rod Cameron, J. Carrol Naish, Mary Castle, Robert Hutton. Soggy account of rancher vs. criminal saloon owner in old West.

Yearling, The (1946) **C-128m.** ***½ D: Clarence Brown. Gregory Peck, Jane Wyman, Claude Jarman, Jr., Chill Wills, Margaret Wycherly, Henry Travers, Jeff York, Forrest Tucker, June Lockhart. Marjorie Kinnan Rawling's sensitive tale of a boy attached to a young deer was exquisitely filmed in Technicolor on location in Florida, with memorable performances. Oscar-winner for Cinematography and Art Direction, and a special Oscar for newcomer Jarman. Beware 94m. reissue print. Remade as a TV movie in 1994. ▼●

Year My Voice Broke, The (1987-Australian) **C-103m.** *** D: John Duigan. Noah Taylor, Loene Carmen, Ben Mendelsohn, Graeme Blundell, Lynette Curran, Malcolm Robertson, Judi Farr. Affecting story of a teenage boy's friendship and infatuation with a troubled girl; set in a small town in the early 1960s. A cut above the usual coming-of-age film, thanks to director Duigan's touching script and amazingly natural performances by his young actors. Followed by a sequel, FLIRTING. [PG-13]▼●◗

Year of Living Dangerously, The (1983-Australian) **C-115m.** *** D: Peter Weir. Mel Gibson, Sigourney Weaver, Linda Hunt, Michael Murphy, Bill Kerr, Noel Ferrier. Fascinating political drama set in strife-ridden Indonesia just before Sukarno's fall in 1965 . . . much more successful as a mood-piece than as romance, however, with Weaver's flimsy character (and flimsier accent) a detriment. Diminutive Hunt—a woman playing a man—is mesmerizing and most deservedly won an Academy Award. Panavision. [PG]▼●◗

Year of the Comet (1992) **C-89m.** ** D: Peter Yates. Penelope Ann Miller, Tim Daly, Louis Jourdan, Art Malik, Ian Richardson, Ian McNeice, Julia McCarthy. Listless, if not especially painful, variation on ROMANCING THE STONE: Wallflower Miller begins to bloom when her discovery of a priceless wine bottle lands her in the middle of some international intrigue. Agreeably performed, but a pretty slight non-event given William Goldman's first original script since BUTCH CASSIDY AND THE SUNDANCE KID. Panavision. [PG-13] ▼●

Year of the Dragon (1985) **C-136m.** **½ D: Michael Cimino. Mickey Rourke, John Lone, Ariane, Leonard Termo, Ray Barry, Caroline Kava, Eddie Jones. Highly charged, arresting melodrama scripted by Oliver Stone (from Robert Daley's book) about a Vietnam vet who's still fighting his own private war, as a N.Y.C. cop whose current target is corruption in Chinatown, and crime czar Lone in particular. Companion piece to Cimino's THE DEER HUNTER has same intensity but nearly drowns in a sea of excess and self-importance. Still worth watching. Incidentally, virtually all New York settings (including Mott Street) were recreated on location in North Carolina! J-D-C Scope. [R]▼●

Year of the Gun (1991) **C-111m.** ** D: John Frankenheimer. Andrew McCarthy, Valeria Golino, Sharon Stone, John Pankow, Mattia Sbragia, George Murcell. Confused thriller about a young American novelist in Rome who stumbles onto the Red Brigade's plot to kidnap then-Premier Aldo Moro. Frankenheimer (who made such great political thrillers as SEVEN DAYS IN MAY and THE MANCHURIAN CANDIDATE) struggles to keep a wandering story in focus. McCarthy is somewhat blank in the lead role, but Stone is good as an aggressive photojournalist. [R]▼●◗

Year of the Quiet Sun, A (1984-Polish-German) **C-106m.** *** D: Krzysztof Zanussi. Scott Wilson, Maja Komorowska, Hanna Skarzanka, Ewa Dalkowska, Vadim Glowna, Daniel Webb. Stark, haunting drama, set just after WW2, detailing the evolving relationship between two lost souls who don't even speak the same language: hard-luck Polish widow Komorowska and emotionally hungry American GI Wilson. A heartfelt film, loaded with raw emotion and deep feeling. [PG]▼●

Year of the Tiger SEE: **Yank in Viet-Nam, A**

Years Between, The (1946-British) **100m.** **½ D: Compton Bennett. Michael Redgrave, Valerie Hobson, Flora Robson, Felix Aylmer, Dulcie Gray, Edward Rigby, James McKechnie. Sensitively handled drama about war widow Hobson, once a wife, now a career woman and member of Parliament who is about to remarry. Her world is turned upside down when word comes that her husband (Redgrave) is still alive. Based on a play by Daphne du Maurier.▼

Yellow Balloon, The (1952-British) **80m.** **½ D: J. Lee Thompson. Andrew Ray, Kenneth More, Veronica Hurst, William Sylvester, Bernard Lee. Sensible suspenser of small boy who thinks he accidentally killed a chum and is exploited by cheap crook.

Yellowbeard (1983) **C-101m.** BOMB D: Mel Damski. Graham Chapman, Peter Boyle, Richard "Cheech" Marin, Tommy Chong, Peter Cook, Marty Feldman, Martin Hewitt, Michael Hordern, Eric Idle, Madeline Kahn, James Mason, John Cleese, Susannah York, Stacey Nelkin. Appalling waste of talent in a startlingly inept and unfunny pirate comedy. Written by costars Chapman and Cook with Bernard McKenna. They should have walked the plank for this one. This was Feldman's final film. [PG]▼●

Yellow Cab Man, The (1950) **85m.** *** D: Jack Donohue. Red Skelton, Gloria De Haven, Walter Slezak, Edward Arnold, James Gleason, Jay C. Flippen, Polly Moran. Fine Skelton romp with Red as would-be inventor of unbreakable glass, involved with gangsters and crooked businessman; Slezak is perfect as bad-guy. ▼

Yellow Canary, The (1943-British) **98m.** **½ D: Herbert Wilcox. Anna Neagle, Richard Greene, Albert Lieven, Margaret Rutherford, Valentine Dyall. Above average WW2 spy drama with Neagle feigning Nazi loyalty to obtain secrets for the Allies.

Yellow Canary, The (1963) **93m.** BOMB D: Buzz Kulik. Pat Boone, Barbara Eden, Steve Forrest, Jack Klugman, Jesse White, Milton Selzer, John Banner, Jeff Corey, Harold Gould. If you've lain awake nights hoping to see Pat Boone as an obnoxious pop singer in a movie written by Rod Serling, your wish has come true. But don't fret; Pat turns into a nice guy when his infant son is kidnapped and he has to go rescue him. And you thought *The Twilight Zone* was just a TV show! CinemaScope.

Yellow Earth (1984-Chinese) **C-87m.** *** D: Chen Kaige. Xue Bai, Wang Xueqi, Tan Tuo, Liu Qiang. One of the earliest films of the Chinese New Wave is an engrossing, poetic account of a wandering communist soldier who arrives in a rural farming village in 1939 to learn folk songs that he will teach to his regiment; he inspires a 14-year-old girl who is bound by tradition to a life of bitterness and hardship. Photographed by Zhang Yimou; it's interesting to contrast this film's "communism equals freedom" propaganda to the political content of Yimou and Kaige's later work. ▼

Yellow Jack (1938) **83m.** ** D: George B. Seitz. Robert Montgomery, Virginia Bruce, Lewis Stone, Stanley Ridges, Henry Hull, Charles Coburn, Buddy Ebsen, Andy Devine, Henry O'Neill, Sam Levene, Alan Curtis, William Henry. Story of Dr. Walter Reed's determination to find cure for yellow fever is artificial, dramatically stale. Based on Sidney Howard play.

Yellow Mountain, The (1954) **C-78m.** *½ D: Jesse Hibbs. Lex Barker, Mala Powers, Howard Duff, William Demarest. Unremarkable tale of Barker rivaling Duff for gold and love of Powers.

Yellow Rolls-Royce, The (1964-British) **C-122m.** *** D: Anthony Asquith. Rex Harrison, Shirley MacLaine, Ingrid Bergman, Jeanne Moreau, Edmund Purdom, George C. Scott, Omar Sharif, Art Carney, Alain Delon, Roland Culver, Wally Cox. Slick Terence Rattigan drama involving trio of owners of title car, focusing on how romance plays a part in each of their lives; contrived but ever-so-smoothly handled. Panavision. ▼●

Yellow Sky (1948) **98m.** *** D: William Wellman. Gregory Peck, Anne Baxter, Richard Widmark, Robert Arthur, John Russell, Henry (Harry) Morgan, James Barton. Exciting Western with Peck heading a gang of thieves who come to a ghost town, where they confront tough, mysterious Baxter and her grandfather. Similar in atmosphere to Wellman's classic THE OX-BOW INCIDENT. Script by Lamar Trotti from a W. R. Burnett story. Remade as THE JACKALS (1967). ▼

Yellowstone (1936) **65m.** **½ D: Arthur Lubin. Henry Hunter, Judith Barrett, Andy Devine, Alan Hale, Ralph Morgan, Monroe Owsley, Raymond Hatton, Paul Harvey, Paul Fix. Nifty programmer of murder, greed, and stolen money buried in the title park. Ambitious direction and a solid supporting cast elevate this one. ▼

Yellowstone Kelly (1959) **C-91m.** **½ D: Gordon Douglas. Clint Walker, Edward Byrnes, John Russell, Ray Danton, Claude Akins, Rhodes Reason, Warren Oates. Rugged Western involving Indian uprising, with Walker the burly hero trying to keep peace; written by Burt Kennedy.

Yellow Submarine (1968-British) **C-85m.** **** D: George Dunning. Pure delight, a phantasmagorical animated feature with as much to hear as there is to see: Beatles' songs, puns, non sequitur jokes combined with surreal pop-art visions in story of Beatles trying to save Pepperland from the Blue Meanies. Unique, refreshing. Songs include "Lucy in the Sky With Diamonds," "When I'm Sixty-four," "All You Need Is Love." Alternate version runs 90m. and features "Hey Bulldog." [G] ▼●◗

Yellow Ticket, The (1931) **81m.** *** D: Raoul Walsh. Elissa Landi, Laurence Olivier, Lionel Barrymore, Walter Byron, Sarah Padden, Mischa Auer, Boris Karloff. Colorful melodrama set in czarist Russia, with peasant girl Landi coming under lecherous eye of officer Barrymore. Handsome production, lusty storytelling add up nicely; Karloff has good bit as drunken orderly.

Yellow Tomahawk, The (1954) **C-82m.** ** D: Lesley Selander. Rory Calhoun, Peggie Castle, Noah Beery, Warner Anderson, Peter Graves, Lee Van Cleef, Rita Moreno. Calhoun is Indian guide who goes to any length to prevent Indian attack on settlers.

Yellow Winton Flyer, The SEE: **Reivers, The**

Yentl (1983) **C-134m.** **½ D: Barbra Streisand. Barbra Streisand, Mandy Patinkin, Amy Irving, Nehemiah Persoff, Steven Hill. A young woman in Eastern Europe at the turn of the century disguises as a boy in order to fulfill her dream and get an education. Isaac Bashevis Singer's simple short story is handled with love and care by first-time director/producer/cowriter Streisand, but goes on far longer than necessary, with twelve (count 'em) soliloquy songs by Alan and Marilyn Bergman and Michel Legrand (who also earned Oscars for their score) and a finale uncomfortably reminiscent of FUNNY GIRL. A star vehicle if there ever was one; no wonder Streisand fans love it. [PG]▼●

Yes, Giorgio (1982) **C-110m.** *½ D: Franklin J. Schaffner. Luciano Pavarotti, Kathryn Harrold, Eddie Albert, Paolo Borboni, James Hong, Beulah Quo. Opera superstar Pavarotti plays . . . an opera superstar, who pursues an independent-minded lady doctor during American tour. So-called romantic comedy gives the phrase "old fashioned" a bad name; missing ingredient is a parade of character actors like Mischa Auer and Herman Bing to make it palatable. Only saving grace: Pavarotti sings. [PG]▼●

Yes, My Darling Daughter (1939) **86m.** **½ D: William Keighley. Priscilla Lane, Fay Bainter, Roland Young, May Robson, Jeffrey Lynn, Genevieve Tobin, Ian Hunter. Everybody is enthused about young lovers running off together except young man in question (Lynn). Mildly amusing comedy.

Yes, Sir, That's My Baby (1949) **C-82m.** **½ D: George Sherman. Donald O'Connor, Charles Coburn, Gloria De Haven, Joshua Shelley, Barbara Brown. Flimsy musical of football-crazy O'Connor on college campus, rescued by spirit and verve of cast.

Yesterday (1980-Canadian) **C-97m.** *½ D: Larry Kent. Claire Pimpare, Vincent Van Patten, Eddie Albert, Cloris Leachman, Nicholas Campbell. Hackneyed story of love between American Van Patten and French-Canadian Pimpare may appeal to the most undiscriminating adolescent.

Yesterday's Enemy (1959-British) **95m.** *½ D: Val Guest. Stanley Baker, Guy Rolfe, Leo McKern, Gordon Jackson, David Oxley, Philip Ahn, Bryan Forbes. Mild WW2 actioner set in Burma. Megascope.

Yesterday, Today and Tomorrow (1963-Italian) **C-119m.** **** D: Vittorio De Sica. Sophia Loren, Marcello Mastroianni, Tina Pica, Giovanni Ridolfi. Oscar-winner for Best Foreign Film is impeccable trio of comic tales, with Loren never more beautiful than as Italian women who use sex in various ways to get what they want. Striptease for Marcello is among the most famous scenes in her career (and remains pretty steamy). Techniscope.▼

Yidl Mitn Fidl (1936-Polish) **92m.** ***½ D: Joseph Green, Jan-Nowina Przybylski. Molly Picon, Max Bozyk, Leon Liebgold, Simcha Fostel, Dora Fakiel. Splendid, unique Yiddish-language musical comedy, with a storyline not unlike that of YENTL, with Picon (who's charming) posing as a boy, so she can travel the countryside playing her fiddle. English translation: YIDL WITH HIS FIDDLE. Avoid the English-dubbed version, titled CASTLES IN THE SKY.▼

Yojimbo (1961-Japanese) **110m.** **** D: Akira Kurosawa. Toshiro Mifune, Eijiro Tono, Seizaburo Kawazu, Isuzu Yamada, Hiroshi Tachikawa, Kyu Sazanka, Tatsuya Nakadai, Takashi Shimura. Superb tongue-in-cheek samurai picture, the plot of which resembles a Western; Mifune is perfection as samurai up for hire in town with two warring factions, both of whom he teaches a well-deserved lesson. Beautiful on all counts; the inspiration for A FISTFUL OF DOLLARS and many other films. Later remade as LAST MAN STANDING. Sequel: SANJURO. Tohoscope. ▼●

Yokel Boy (1942) **69m.** *½ D: Joseph Santley. Albert Dekker, Joan Davis, Eddie Foy, Jr., Alan Mowbray. Silly slapstick satire on gangster movies.

Yol (1982-Turkish-Swiss) **C-111m.** *** D: Serif Goren. Tarik Akan, Serif Sezer, Halil Ergun, Meral Orhonsoy, Necmettin Cobanoglu. Incisive chronicle of the experiences of a convict who returns home while on "leave" from jail. Screenplay by Yilmaz Guney, written while he was himself in prison. [PG]▼

Yolanda and the Thief (1945) **C-108m.** **½ D: Vincente Minnelli. Fred Astaire, Lucille Bremer, Frank Morgan, Leon Ames, Mildred Natwick, Mary Nash. Opulent musical fantasy about a con-man (Astaire) who tries to convince rich convent-bred girl (Bremer) that he's her guardian angel. Unusual film that you'll either love or hate. Best musical number: "Coffee Time."▼●

Yor, the Hunter from the Future (1983-Italian) **C-88m.** BOMB D: Anthony M. Dawson (Antonio Margheriti). Reb Brown, Corinne Clery, John Steiner, Carole Andre, Alan Collins. Shamelessly idiotic muscleman movie with a nuclear-age twist. Humorously tacky at first, then just plain boring. [PG]▼●

You and Me (1938) **90m.** **½ D: Fritz Lang. Sylvia Sidney, George Raft, Barton MacLane, Harry Carey, Roscoe Karns, George E. Stone, Warren Hymer, Robert Cummings. Genuinely odd but likable film about an ex-con (Raft) who falls in love with Sidney and marries her, unaware that she's a former jailbird herself. Unusual mix of gangsterism, sentiment, Damon Runyonesque comedy, and music (by Kurt Weill)—with even some rhythmic dialogue! Story by Norman Krasna, screenplay by Virginia Van Upp.▼

You Are What You Eat (1968) **C-75m.** ** D: Barry Feinstein. Tiny Tim, Peter Yarrow, Paul Butterfield, Barry McGuire, Father Malcom Boyd, The Electric Flag, Harper's Bizarre, Super Spade. Documentary of the mid-60s does, by the mere appearance of some of the era's luminaries, carry one back; however, film is ill conceived, haphazardly put together.▼

You Belong to Me (1941) **94m.** ** D:

Wesley Ruggles. Barbara Stanwyck, Henry Fonda, Edgar Buchanan, Roger Clark, Ruth Donnelly, Melville Cooper, Maude Eburne. Weak comedy of doctor Stanwyck and hubby Fonda who's wary of her male patients. Looks as though it was made in three days. Coscripted by Dalton Trumbo. Remade as EMERGENCY WEDDING.

You Better Watch Out (1980) **C-100m.** *** D: Lewis Jackson. Brandon Maggart, Dianne Hull, Scott McKay, Joe Jamrog, Peter Friedman, Ray Barry, Bobby Lesser, Sam Gray. Gripping, well-made little thriller about a killer disguised as Santa Claus, with Maggart excellent as the psychopathic Kris Kringle. A sleeper, with cult status possibilities. Video titles: CHRISTMAS EVIL and TERROR IN TOYLAND. [R]▼

You Came Along (1945) **103m.** **½ D: John Farrow. Robert Cummings, Lizabeth Scott, Don DeFore, Charles Drake, Kim Hunter, Julie Bishop, Helen Forrest, Franklin Pangborn, Ruth Roman, Hugh Beaumont. Clowning, womanizing fliers Cummings, DeFore and Drake set out across the U.S. on a bond-selling tour. Their guide is pretty Scott (in her film debut); she falls in love with Cummings, who's harboring a terrible secret. Effective drama captures the essence of its era; Cummings' character shares the same name (Bob Collins) and much the same personality as his character in the later TV sitcom *The Bob Cummings Show*.

You Can't Beat Love (1937) **62m.** ** D: Christy Cabanne. Preston Foster, Joan Fontaine, Herbert Mundin, William Brisbane, Alan Bruce, Paul Hurst. Slow, trivial story of eccentric playboy Foster dabbling in politics and tangling with mayor's daughter Fontaine. Of interest only for the presence of young Fontaine.

You Can't Cheat an Honest Man (1939) **76m.** ***½ D: George Marshall. W. C. Fields, Edgar Bergen, Constance Moore, James Bush, Mary Forbes, Thurston Hall, Edward Brophy, Grady Sutton, Eddie "Rochester" Anderson. Fields (as Larson E. Whipsnade) runs circus with interference from Bergen and Charlie McCarthy in frantic comedy classic with loads of snappy one-liners and memorable ping-pong game. Most of Fields' scenes were directed by Eddie Cline.▼

You Can't Fool Your Wife (1940) **68m.** ** D: Ray McCarey. Lucille Ball, James Ellison, Robert Coote, Emma Dunn, Virginia Vale, Elaine Shepard. Ball and Ellison are dull married couple until hubby takes a fling and wife makes herself glamorous to win him back. Comedy filler, made palatable by Lucy's charms in dual role.▼

You Can't Get Away With Murder (1939) **78m.** **½ D: Lewis Seiler. Humphrey Bogart, Billy Halop, Gale Page, John Litel, Henry Travers, Joe Sawyer. Standard but well-acted crime tale of young Halop (minus the other Dead End Kids) teaming with gangster Bogart, taking rap with him in Sing Sing.

You Can't Have Everything (1937) **99m.** *** D: Norman Taurog. Alice Faye, Ritz Bros., Don Ameche, Charles Winninger, Tony Martin, Louise Hovick (Gypsy Rose Lee), Arthur Treacher, Tip, Tap and Toe. Good show-biz musical as Faye writes drama which only succeeds as musical. Ritz Bros. have good material, Louis Prima adds music.

You Can't Hurry Love (1988) **C-92m.** *½ D: Richard Martini. David Packer, Scott McGinnis, Bridget Fonda, David Leisure, Anthony Geary, Frank Bonner, Lu Leonard, Merete Van Kamp, Sally Kellerman, Charles Grodin, Kristy McNichol. Paper-thin, predictable fare about the adventures of young Packer, who's lost in the L.A. singles scene. [R]▼●

You Can't Run Away From It (1956) **C-95m.** ** D: Dick Powell. June Allyson, Jack Lemmon, Charles Bickford, Paul Gilbert, Jim Backus, Stubby Kaye, Henny Youngman. Slight musical remake of IT HAPPENED ONE NIGHT with Lemmon the reporter, Allyson the madcap heiress. CinemaScope.

You Can't Steal Love SEE: **Live a Little, Steal a Lot**

You Can't Take It With You (1938) **127m.** ***½ D: Frank Capra. Jean Arthur, Lionel Barrymore, James Stewart, Edward Arnold, Mischa Auer, Ann Miller, Spring Byington, Eddie "Rochester" Anderson, Donald Meek, Halliwell Hobbes, Dub Taylor, Samuel S. Hinds, Harry Davenport, Charles Lane. George S. Kaufman-Moss Hart play about eccentric but blissfully happy household becomes prime Capracorn, not quite as compelling today as MR. DEEDS or MR. SMITH (due to Robert Riskin's extensive rewriting), but still highly entertaining. Oscar winner for Best Picture and Director. Followed a half-century later by a TV series.▼●

You Can't Win 'Em All (1970) **C-95m.** *½ D: Peter Collinson. Tony Curtis, Charles Bronson, Michele Mercier, Patrick Magee, Gregoire Aslan. Bronson and Curtis are friendly rivals caught in war-torn Turkey during the early 1920s. Bantering stars make the most of tired script by Leo Gordon (who also has supporting role). Filmed on location. Original title: THE DUBIOUS PATRIOTS. Video title: SOLDIERS OF FORTUNE. Panavision. [PG]▼

You for Me (1952) **71m.** **½ D: Don Weis. Peter Lawford, Jane Greer, Gig Young, Paula Corday, Elaine Stewart. Unpretentious romantic comedy with Greer as well-intentioned nurse involved with a variety of suitors.

You Gotta Stay Happy (1948) **100m.** **½ D: H. C. Potter. Joan Fontaine, James

Stewart, Eddie Albert, Roland Young, Willard Parker, Percy Kilbride, Porter Hall. OK comedy about millionairess who runs off on wedding night to find new marriage. Could have been much better.▼

You Know My Name (1999) **C-94m. TVM** D: John Kent Harrison. Sam Elliott, Arliss Howard, Carolyn McCormick, James Gammon, R. Lee Ermey, James Parks, Walter Olkewicz, Sheila McCarthy. Highly satisfying Western set in 1920s Oklahoma, where retired lawman Bill Tilghman, who captured many legendary outlaws, now appears in his own silent movies. When the citizens of a rowdy town beg for his help, he takes on the job—and a showdown with a corrupt federal agent. Elliott is terrific in the lead. Written by the director. Above average.▼

You Know What Sailors Are (1954-British) **C-89m.** ** D: Ken Annakin. Akim Tamiroff, Donald Sinden, Sarah Lawson, Naunton Wayne. Attempted cold-war spoof of British navy officer, jokingly telling cohorts that salvaged scrap is a new secret weapon.

You Light Up My Life (1977) **C-90m.** **½ D: Joseph Brooks. Didi Conn, Joe Silver, Michael Zaslow, Stephen Nathan, Melanie Mayron. Oscar-winning title song may be best remembered thing about this film, but Conn and Silver are worth watching in loosely structured story of show-business-oriented girl trying to break loose and establish herself while putting her life in order. Produced, directed, written, and musically supervised by Brooks. [PG]▼

You'll Find Out (1940) **97m.** ** D: David Butler. Kay Kyser, Boris Karloff, Peter Lorre, Bela Lugosi, Dennis O'Keefe, Ginny Simms, Helen Parrish, Alma Kruger, Harry Babbitt, Ish Kabibble. Kay and his band spend the night in a debutante's haunted house with three suspicious characters on hand. Obvious and overlong, a real disappointment to anyone anxious to savor the Karloff/Lugosi/Lorre team; more suited for fans of Ish Kabibble. ▼●

You'll Like My Mother (1972) **C-92m.** **½ D: Lamont Johnson. Patty Duke, Rosemary Murphy, Sian Barbara Allen, Richard Thomas, Dennis Rucker. Offbeat thriller with psychological undertones. Duke plays pregnant widow journeying to visit mother-in-law she's never met. Some good moments, but doesn't add up. [PG]

You'll Never Get Rich (1941) **88m.** *** D: Sidney Lanfield. Fred Astaire, Rita Hayworth, John Hubbard, Robert Benchley, Osa Massen, Frieda Inescort, Guinn Williams. Delicious musicomedy has Astaire drafted at inconvenient time, but show he's doing still goes on, and he manages to get Hayworth, too. Cole Porter score includes "So Near and Yet So Far."▼●

You Must Be Joking! (1965-British) **C-100m.** *** D: Michael Winner. Michael Callan, Lionel Jeffries, Terry-Thomas, Denholm Elliott, Wilfrid Hyde-White, James Robertson Justice, Bernard Cribbins, Gabriella Licudi. Engaging poke at British army as zany psychologist (Jeffries) rounds up five weirdos to establish, via special testing, the "complete, quick thinking" exemplary British soldier.

You Never Can Tell (1951) **78m.** *** D: Lou Breslow. Dick Powell, Peggy Dow, Charles Drake, Joyce Holden, Frank Nelson, Albert Sharpe. Amusing fantasy of a murdered dog returning to Earth as a human (Powell) to find his killer. Holden is a delight as his sidekick—who used to be a horse. Storyline reversed in OH, HEAVENLY DOG!

Young Americans (1967) **C-104m.** ** D: Alex Grasshoff. Although this slick documentary about the "Young Americans" singing group won an Academy Award (which it was forced to relinquish when it was discovered that it had played theatrically before the year of its contention), these kids sell America like those guys on TV sell machines that slice carrots 144 different ways.

Young and Dangerous (1957) **78m.** ** D: William Claxton. Mark Damon, Edward Binns, Lili Gentle, Ann Doran, Connie Stevens. Damon, a footloose youth, turns respectable for love of a nice girl. The usual. Regalscope.

Young and Innocent (1937-British) **80m.** *** D: Alfred Hitchcock. Derrick de Marney, Nova Pilbeam, Percy Marmont, Edward Rigby, Mary Clare, Basil Radford. A Hitchcock thriller with charm and humor; young girl helps runaway man innocently accused of murder to find the real culprit. Pleasant echoes of 39 STEPS; nightclub revelation scene is especially memorable. Based on a novel by Josephine Tey; first shown in U.S. as THE GIRL WAS YOUNG.▼●◗

Young and the Damned, The SEE: **Los Olvidados**

Young and the Immoral, The SEE: **Sinister Urge, The**

Young and Wild (1958) **69m.** *½ D: William Witney. Gene Evans, Scott Marlowe, Carolyn Kearney, Robert Arthur. Trashy account of thrill-seeking teenagers on the loose with a stolen car. Naturama.

Young and Willing (1943) **82m.** **½ D: Edward H. Griffith. William Holden, Eddie Bracken, Barbara Britton, James Brown, Martha O'Driscoll, Robert Benchley, Susan Hayward. Perennial summer-stock comedy *Out of the Frying Pan* becomes naive but zany comedy of show biz hopefuls trying to make good.▼

Young at Heart (1954) **C-117m.** *** D: Gordon Douglas. Doris Day, Frank Sinatra, Gig Young, Ethel Barrymore, Dorothy Malone, Alan Hale, Jr. Musical remake of Fannie Hurst's FOUR DAUGHTERS with Sinatra romancing Day amid much tear-shedding. Slickly done.▼

Young Bess (1953) **C-112m.** *** D: George Sidney. Jean Simmons, Stewart Granger, Charles Laughton, Deborah Kerr, Cecil Kellaway, Leo G. Carroll, Kay Walsh. Splashy costumer with Simmons as Elizabeth I, Laughton repeating role of Henry VIII. Fine cast does quite well in historical setting.▼

Young Billy Young (1969) **C-89m.** **½ D: Burt Kennedy. Robert Mitchum, Angie Dickinson, Robert Walker, David Carradine, Jack Kelly, John Anderson, Paul Fix. Sheriff Mitchum, seeking the killer of his son, takes young Walker under his wing as a surrogate. Peculiar Western, adapted by Kennedy from Will Henry's *Who Rides With Wyatt*, is based on the alleged friendship between Wyatt Earp and Billy Clanton; interesting, but nothing special. [G]▼

Youngblood (1986) **C-109m.** *½ D: Peter Markle. Rob Lowe, Cynthia Gibb, Patrick Swayze, Ed Lauter, Eric Nesterenko, George Finn, Fionnula Flanagan. Boring, utterly predictable story of Lowe joining small-time Canadian hockey team, falling in love with the daughter of his no-nonsense coach. This movie has no energy, on the ice or off! Keanu Reeves' screen debut; that's him behind the mask, as the team's goalie. [R]▼●

Youngblood Hawke (1964) **137m.** **½ D: Delmer Daves. James Franciscus, Genevieve Page, Suzanne Pleshette, Eva Gabor, Mary Astor, Lee Bowman, Edward Andrews, Don Porter. Clichéd but somehow compelling trash from Herman Wouk's novel about a naive Southerner who writes a novel and becomes the toast of N.Y.C. literary society—with several women vying for his attention.

Young Captives, The (1959) **61m.** ** D: Irvin Kershner. Steven Marlo, Tom Selden, Luana Patten, Ed Nelson, Joan Granville, Dan Blocker. Lurid melodrama of newlyweds involved with psychopathic killer.

Young Cassidy (1965-British) **C-110m.** *** D: Jack Cardiff, John Ford. Rod Taylor, Julie Christie, Maggie Smith, Flora Robson, Michael Redgrave, Edith Evans, Jack MacGowran. Taylor's best role ever as the earthy intellectual Sean O'Casey, set in 1910 Dublin; filled with rich atmosphere and fine supporting players.

Young Daniel Boone (1950) **C-71m.** *½ D: Reginald LeBorg. David Bruce, Kristine Miller, Mary Treen, Don Beddoe. Programmer adventure involving historical figure in conflict with Indians and settlers.

Young Dillinger (1965) **102m.** **½ D: Terry O. Morse. Nick Adams, Mary Ann Mobley, Robert Conrad, John Ashley, Victor Buono, John Hoyt, Reed Hadley. Adams gives force to chronicle of gangster John Dillinger, his rise and seemingly inevitable fall; sufficient gunplay.▼

Young Doctors, The (1961) **100m.** *** D: Phil Karlson. Fredric March, Ben Gazzara, Dick Clark, Eddie Albert, Ina Balin, Aline MacMahon, Edward Andrews, Arthur Hill, George Segal, Rosemary Murphy, Barnard Hughes, Dick Button, Dolph Sweet; narrated by Ronald Reagan. Sturdy cast uplifts soaper set in large city hospital. Based on an Arthur Hailey novel. Segal's first film.

Young Doctors in Love (1982) **C-95m.** ** D: Garry Marshall. Michael McKean, Sean Young, Harry Dean Stanton, Patrick Macnee, Hector Elizondo, Dabney Coleman, Pamela Reed, Michael Richards, Taylor Negron, Saul Rubinek, Titos Vandis, Ted McGinley, Crystal Bernard. Hospital comedy has plenty of scattershot gags, but not enough laughs—and certainly not enough substance—to maintain a feature film. Many daytime soap opera stars appear in cameos (including Demi Moore and Janine Turner, both then on *General Hospital*). Feature directing debut of TV comedy writer-producer Marshall. [R]▼●

Young Don't Cry, The (1957) **89m.** ** D: Alfred L. Werker. Sal Mineo, James Whitmore, J. Carrol Naish, Paul Carr. OK drama of loner youth Mineo who takes pity on an escaped murderer.

Young Dracula (1974-Italian-French) SEE: **Andy Warhol's Dracula**

Young Dracula (1974-British) SEE: **Son of Dracula**

Young Dr. Kildare (1938) **81m.** **½ D: Harold S. Bucquet. Lew Ayres, Lionel Barrymore, Lynne Carver, Nat Pendleton, Jo Ann Sayers, Samuel S. Hinds, Emma Dunn, Walter Kingsford, Monty Woolley, Phillip Terry, Donald Barry. MGM's first episode in the adventures of Kildare, as he graduates from medical school and must decide between country practice with his father or an offer from the big city's Blair General Hospital.

Young Einstein (1988-Australian) **C-90m.** **½ D: Yahoo Serious. Yahoo Serious, Odile Le Clezio, John Howard, Pee Wee Wilson, Su Cruickshank. Nutty comedy from Down Under based on the premise that Albert Einstein not only developed the theory of relativity, but also invented rock 'n' roll! The silliness continues from there . . . though any movie with "cat pies" can't be all bad. Aptly named Yahoo (born Greg Pead) wrote, produced, directed, and stars in this slapstick epic. [PG]▼●

Younger & Younger (1993-German-French-Canadian) **C-99m.** **½ D: Percy Adlon. Donald Sutherland, Lolita Davidovich, Brendan Fraser, Sally Kellerman, Julie Delpy, Linda Hunt, Nicholas Gunn, Matt

Damon. Likably offbeat modern-day fantasy about a self-styled gay blade and bon vivant who owns a self-storage facility in Glendale, California, and lives in a rarefied world of his own, until reality comes crashing down. This may be your only chance to hear Sutherland sing! Never released theatrically in the U.S. [R]▼

Younger Brothers, The (1949) **C-77m.** ★★½ D: Edwin L. Marin. Wayne Morris, Janis Paige, Bruce Bennett, Geraldine Brooks, Robert Hutton, Alan Hale, Fred Clark, Tom Tyler. OK Western of notorious Younger brothers and the incident that drives them to renewed violence and terror.

Younger Generation, The (1929) **88m.** ★★½ D: Frank Capra. Jean Hersholt, Lina Basquette, Ricardo Cortez, Rosa Rosanova, Rex Lease. Ethnic heart-tugger by Fannie Hurst about a Jewish family that suffers because of one son's determination to abandon his roots and break into N.Y.C. society. (Cortez played a similar role in SYMPHONY OF SIX MILLION.) Director Capra pulls out all the stops in this silent film with talkie sequences.

Youngest Profession, The (1943) **82m.** ★★½ D: Edward Buzzell. Virginia Weidler, Jean Porter, Edward Arnold, John Carroll, Agnes Moorehead, Scotty Beckett. Weidler and Porter are incurable (and obnoxious) autograph hounds in innocent little film with many MGM guest stars (including Lana Turner, William Powell, Robert Taylor, Greer Garson and Walter Pidgeon).

Youngest Spy, The SEE: **My Name Is Ivan**

Young Frankenstein (1974) **105m.** ★★★½ D: Mel Brooks. Gene Wilder, Peter Boyle, Marty Feldman, Teri Garr, Madeline Kahn, Cloris Leachman, Kenneth Mars, Richard Haydn. One of the funniest (and most quotable) movies of all time, a finely tuned parody of old FRANKENSTEIN pictures, scripted by Wilder and Brooks, with appropriate music (by John Morris), sets, laboratory equipment (some of it from the 1930s), and b&w camerawork (by Gerald Hirschfeld). Plus vivid characterizations by mad doctor Wilder, monster Boyle, hunchback assistant Feldman, et al. Spoof of blind-man sequence from BRIDE OF FRANKENSTEIN with Gene Hackman is uproarious. [PG]▼●◗

Young Fury (1965) **C-80m.** ★★½ D: Christian Nyby. Rory Calhoun, Virginia Mayo, Lon Chaney (Jr.), John Agar, Richard Arlen, Linda Foster. Tired gunslinger returns home to discover son leading gang of young hellions. Standard formula plot highlighted by a cast chockfull of old stars. William Bendix's last film. Techniscope.

Young Girls of Rochefort, The (1967-French) **C-124m.** ★★ D: Jacques Demy. Catherine Deneuve, Françoise Dorléac, Gene Kelly, George Chakiris, Danielle Darrieux, Grover Dale, Michel Piccoli. Director Demy's follow-up to THE UMBRELLAS OF CHERBOURG is a homage to the Hollywood musical, but what it has in style it lacks in substance; contrived story and repetitive Michel Legrand music score surely wear thin, and even Gene Kelly can't save it. Franscope. [G]

Young Graduates, The (1971) **C-99m.** BOMB D: Robert Anderson. Patricia Wymer, Tom Stewart, Gary Rist, B. Kirby, Jr. (Bruno Kirby), Jennifer Rist, Dennis Christopher. Idiotic update of 1950's youth films; heroine falls in love with her teacher amid other dumb high school adventures. Christopher's film debut. [PG]▼

Young Guns, The (1956) **84m.** ★★ D: Albert Band. Russ Tamblyn, Gloria Talbott, Perry Lopez, Scott Marlowe. Routine account of Tamblyn trying to erase everyone's memory of gunslinger father so he can live peaceful life.

Young Guns (1988) **C-107m.** ★★½ D: Christopher Cain. Emilio Estevez, Kiefer Sutherland, Lou Diamond Phillips, Charlie Sheen, Dermot Mulroney, Casey Siemaszko, Terence Stamp, Jack Palance, Terry O'Quinn, Sharon Thomas, Brian Keith, Patrick Wayne. Six young punks, taken under the wing of a civilized British gentleman (Stamp), find it hard to retain their equilibrium when they're left on their own, and whipped into a frenzy of violence by their newest recruit—William Bonney, soon to be known as Billy the Kid (Estevez). Contemporary-minded Western adopts 1980s-style language and sensibilities, and has a plot with as many holes as some of Billy's victims. Still watchable, with several strong performances. Try to spot Tom Cruise, in disguise as a bad guy who gets shot. Followed by a sequel. [R] ▼●◗

Young Guns II (1990) **C-103m.** ★★½ D: Geoff Murphy. Emilio Estevez, Kiefer Sutherland, Lou Diamond Phillips, Christian Slater, William Petersen, Alan Ruck, R.D. Call, James Coburn, Balthazar Getty, Jack Kehoe. Not-bad sequel finds Billy Bonney and his gang heading toward the safety of Old Mexico with a band of government men in hot pursuit. Slater is a standout on the trail. Great photography and a sweeping Alan Silvestri score almost make you forget the script ain't so hot. Panavision. [PG-13]▼●◗

Young Guns of Texas (1962) **C-78m.** ★★½ D: Maury Dexter. James Mitchum, Alana Ladd, Jody McCrea, Chill Wills. Second generation of movie stars perform satisfactorily in account of gold and girl hunt in old West, tied in with Indian raid. CinemaScope.

Young Hearts SEE: **Promised Land**

Young Hellions SEE: **High School Confidential**

Young Ideas (1943) **77m.** ★½ D: Jules Dassin. Susan Peters, Herbert Marshall,

Mary Astor, Elliott Reid, Richard Carlson. Dismal comedy in which college students Peters and Reid try to break up the new marriage of mom Astor and serious-minded professor Marshall. Watch for Ava Gardner in a bit.

Young in Heart, The (1938) **90m.** ***½ D: Richard Wallace. Janet Gaynor, Douglas Fairbanks, Jr., Paulette Goddard, Roland Young, Billie Burke, Minnie Dupree, Richard Carlson. Refreshing comedy about wacky family of con artists going straight under influence of unsuspecting Dupree. Written by Paul Osborn and Charles Bennett from an I.A.R. Wylie novel. Also shown in computer-colored version.▼

Young Jesse James (1960) **73m.** *½ D: William Claxton. Ray Stricklyn, Willard Parker, Merry Anders, Robert Dix, Emile Meyer, Jacklyn O'Donnell. Title tells all in this routine oater. CinemaScope.

Young Land, The (1959) **C-89m.** **½ D: Ted Tetzlaff. Pat Wayne, Yvonne Craig, Dennis Hopper, Dan O'Herlihy, Cliff Ketchum. Sincere Western of pre-Mexican war Texas.▼

Young Lions, The (1958) **167m.** ***½ D: Edward Dmytryk. Marlon Brando, Montgomery Clift, Dean Martin, Hope Lange, Barbara Rush, Maximilian Schell, Mai Britt, Lee Van Cleef. One of the all-time best WW2 studies, adapted by Edward Anhalt from the Irwin Shaw novel. Martin and Clift play U.S. soldiers, Brando a confused Nazi officer; effectively photographed by Joe MacDonald, with Hugo Friedhofer's fine score. CinemaScope.▼●

Young Lovers, The (1950) SEE: **Never Fear**

Young Lovers, The (1964) **109m.** ** D: Samuel Goldwyn, Jr. Peter Fonda, Sharon Hugueny, Nick Adams, Deborah Walley, Beatrice Straight, Joseph Campanella, Kent Smith. Amateurish, meandering drama of college youths involved in romance.

Young Man With a Horn (1950) **112m.** *** D: Michael Curtiz. Kirk Douglas, Lauren Bacall, Doris Day, Juano Hernandez, Hoagy Carmichael, Mary Beth Hughes. Effective drama of trumpet-player Douglas compulsively drawn to music, with Bacall the bad girl, Day the wholesome one. Carl Foreman–Edmund H. North script adapted from Dorothy Baker's book, and inspired by Bix Beiderbecke's life; Harry James dubbed Douglas' licks.▼●

Young Man With Ideas (1952) **84m.** **½ D: Mitchell Leisen. Glenn Ford, Ruth Roman, Denise Darcel, Nina Foch, Donna Corcoran, Ray Collins, Sheldon Leonard. Modest comedy-drama about a young Montana lawyer who moves to California with his wife and kids for a fresh start and encounters various problems while studying for the state bar exam.

Young Mr. Lincoln (1939) **100m.** ***½ D: John Ford. Henry Fonda, Alice Brady, Marjorie Weaver, Donald Meek, Richard Cromwell, Eddie Quillan, Milburn Stone, Ward Bond, Francis Ford. Fine Ford Americana with Abraham Lincoln (Fonda) facing years of struggle as a beginning lawyer in the 1800s. Brady lends solid support.▼●

Young Mr. Pitt, The (1942-British) **118m.** **½ D: Carol Reed. Robert Donat, Robert Morley, Phyllis Calvert, John Mills, Max Adrian. Long, only occasionally moving historical drama of young British prime minister during Napoleonic era; thinly veiled WW2 morale-booster. Written by Frank Launder and Sidney Gilliatt.

Young Nurses, The (1973) **C-77m.** ** D: Clinton Kimbrough. Jean Manson, Ashley Porter, Angela Gibbs, Zack Taylor, Jack LaRue, Jr., Dick Miller, Sally Kirkland, Allan Arbus. Fourth of Roger Corman's "nurse" movies is OK, focusing on drug ring working out of the hospital. Neat appearance by director Samuel Fuller as a villain, and a rather sad one by aged Mantan Moreland (in his final film). Followed by CANDY STRIPE NURSES. [R]▼

Young One, The (1961-Mexican) **96m.** *½ D: Luis Buñuel. Zachary Scott, Bernie Hamilton, Key Meersman, Graham Denton, Claudio Brook. Racist Scott, who has violated Lolita-like Meersman on an isolated island, must contend with the presence of on-the-run black jazz musician Hamilton. Turgid, much-too-obvious melodrama is a disappointment from Buñuel.▼

Young People (1940) **78m.** ** D: Allan Dwan. Shirley Temple, Jack Oakie, Charlotte Greenwood, Arleen Whelan, George Montgomery, Kathleen Howard. Show-biz team Oakie and Greenwood raise orphaned Shirley and try to settle down in this weak musical, a later and lesser Temple vehicle. Good dance routine at the finish. Also shown in computer-colored version. ▼

Young Philadelphians, The (1959) **136m.** *** D: Vincent Sherman. Paul Newman, Barbara Rush, Alexis Smith, Brian Keith, Diane Brewster, Billie Burke, John Williams, Robert Vaughn, Otto Kruger, Adam West. Newman and Rush have memorable roles as poor lawyer who schemes to the top, and society girl he hopes to win; Vaughn is army buddy Newman defends on murder charge, Smith quite good as frustrated wife of attorney Kruger.▼

Young Poisoner's Handbook, The (1995-British-French-German) **C-99m.** *** D: Ben Ross. Hugh O'Conor, Antony Sher, Ruth Sheen, Roger Lloyd Pack, Charlotte Coleman. Gleefully gruesome British black comedy about a psychopathic teen (O'Conor) who decides to become "the greatest poisoner the world has ever seen," using his clueless family as guinea pigs. Deliciously mean-spirited film (based on a true story!)

is not for the squeamish. Flavored by a soundtrack of 60s pop oddities.▼●

Young Racers, The (1963) **C-87m.** ** D: Roger Corman. Mark Damon, William Campbell, Patrick Magee, Luana Anders, Robert Campbell. Juvenile nonsense about sports car racing involving ex-racer turned exposé writer, trying to do a book on the sport.

Young Rebel (1967-French-Italian-Spanish) **C-111m.** ** D: Vincent Sherman. Horst Buchholz, Gina Lollobrigida, Jose Ferrer, Louis Jourdan, Francisco Rabal. Despite cast, historical claptrap about Buchholz being sent to Spain by Pope Pius V to obtain help in fighting the Moors. Also known as CERVANTES. Totalscope. [M/PG]

Young Runaways, The (1968) **C-91m.** ** D: Arthur Dreifuss. Brooke Bundy, Kevin Coughlin, Lloyd Bochner, Patty McCormack, Lynn Bari, Norman Fell. Silly B-picture about restless teenagers and how they are swept up into sordid lifestyles. Interesting mainly for early look at Richard Dreyfuss as cocky car thief. Panavision. [R]

Young Savages, The (1961) **103m.** *** D: John Frankenheimer. Burt Lancaster, Dina Merrill, John Davis Chandler, Shelley Winters, Telly Savalas, Edward Andrews, Chris Robinson, Pilar Seurat, Milton Selzer. Lancaster is idealistic D.A. battling all odds to see justice done in street-gang slaying; at times brutal, too often pat. Adapted by Edward Anhalt and JP Miller from Evan Hunter's novel *A Matter of Conviction.* Savalas' film debut.▼●

Young Scarface SEE: **Brighton Rock**

Young Sherlock Holmes (1985) **C-109m.** ** D: Barry Levinson. Nicholas Rowe, Alan Cox, Sophie Ward, Anthony Higgins, Susan Fleetwood, Freddie Jones, Nigel Stock, Michael Hordern. Promising film speculates about Conan Doyle's detective when he was a boy, introduces him to Watson, and involves him in his first great case. Knowing references to Holmes's later life, perfect Victorian atmosphere all give way to jarring 1980s special effects, inappropriate INDIANA JONES-type subplot, and action climax that doesn't make much sense. If you *do* watch it through, be sure to stay through the *very* end. Written by Chris Columbus; Steven Spielberg was an executive producer. [PG-13]▼●

Young Stranger, The (1957) **84m.** *** D: John Frankenheimer. James MacArthur, James Daly, Kim Hunter, James Gregory, Marian Seldes, Whit Bissell. Excellent drama about a teenage boy's brush with delinquency and strained relationship with his wealthy, neglectful father. Surprisingly undated, sincere little film; MacArthur's impressive screen debut (and director Frankenheimer's, too).●

Young Swingers, The (1963) **71m.** BOMB D: Maury Dexter. Molly Bee, Rod Lauren, Gene McDaniels, Jack Larson, Jo Helton. Singer Lauren tries to keep nightclub operating, despite interference of greedy real-estate agent Helton. Grade Z all the way.

Young Tom Edison (1940) **82m.** *** D: Norman Taurog. Mickey Rooney, Fay Bainter, George Bancroft, Virginia Weidler, Eugene Palette, Victor Kilian. Inventor's early life depicted with flair by effective Rooney, who could tone down when he had to; followed by Spencer Tracy's EDISON THE MAN.▼●

Young Warriors, The (1967) **C-93m.** ** D: John Peyser. James Drury, Steve Carlson, Jonathan Daly, Robert Pine, Michael Stanwood. Clichéd WW2 yarn loosely derived from Richard Matheson novel. Panavision.

Young Warriors (1983) **C-103m.** *½ D: Lawrence D. Foldes. Ernest Borgnine, Richard Roundtree, Lynda Day George, James Van Patten, Anne Lockhart, Mike Norris, Dick Shawn, Linnea Quigley. Self-righteous, violent exploitation film has students turning vigilantes to put local criminals out of business. Features several second-generation actors (Van Patten, Lockhart, Norris). Semi-sequel to MALIBU HIGH. [R]▼

Young Widow (1946) **100m.** ** D: Edwin L. Marin. Jane Russell, Marie Wilson, Louis Hayward, Faith Domergue, Kent Taylor, Penny Singleton, Cora Witherspoon. Soap-opera was not Russell's forte and she can't support teary WW2 tale of woman who can't forget her late husband.

Young Winston (1972-British) **C-145m.** *** D: Richard Attenborough. Simon Ward, Anne Bancroft, Robert Shaw, John Mills, Jack Hawkins, Patrick Magee, Ian Holm, Robert Flemyng, Jane Seymour, Edward Woodward, Anthony Hopkins, Laurence Naismith. Entertaining account of Churchill's early life, from school days, through journalistic experience in Africa, up to first election to Parliament. Handsome production, good performances, and rousing battle scenes. Scripted and produced by Carl Foreman. Panavision. [PG]▼

Young Wives' Tale (1951-British) **78m.** **½ D: Henry Cass. Joan Greenwood, Nigel Patrick, Derek Farr, Helen Cherry, Guy Middleton, Athene Seyler, Audrey Hepburn. Slight farce about the housing shortage in post-WW2 England, in which two couples are forced to live under the same roof. Hepburn plays a lodger who also resides in the house.

You Only Live Once (1937) **86m.** *** D: Fritz Lang. Sylvia Sidney, Henry Fonda, William Gargan, Barton MacLane, Jean Dixon, Jerome Cowan, Margaret Hamilton, Ward Bond, Guinn Williams. Beautifully crafted drama about ex-convict Fonda trying to go straight, finding that fate is against him. Loosely based on the Bonnie and Clyde legend, but impressive on its own.▼

You Only Live Twice (1967-British)

C-116m. **½ D: Lewis Gilbert. Sean Connery, Akiko Wakabayashi, Tetsuro Tamba, Mie Hama, Karin Dor, Bernard Lee, Lois Maxwell, Desmond Llewellyn, Donald Pleasence. Big James Bond production with first look at arch-nemesis Blofeld (Pleasence), Japanese locales, but plot (SPECTRE out to cause major powers to declare war on each other) and lack of convincing, clever crisis situations are liabilities film can't shake off. Script by Roald Dahl (!), spectacular sets by Ken Adam. Panavision. [PG]▼●

Your Cheatin' Heart (1964) **99m.** *** D: Gene Nelson. George Hamilton, Susan Oliver, Red Buttons, Arthur O'Connell, Rex Ingram. One of Hamilton's best roles, as legendary country-western singer Hank Williams, who couldn't cope with fame on the ole opry circuit; songs dubbed by Hank Williams, Jr. Oliver most effective as Hank's wife. Also shown in computer-colored version. Panavision.

You're a Big Boy Now (1966) **C-96m.** ***½ D: Francis Ford Coppola. Peter Kastner, Elizabeth Hartman, Geraldine Page, Julie Harris, Rip Torn, Michael Dunn, Tony Bill, Karen Black. Beguiling, way-out film of young man with overprotective parents learning about life from callous young actress Hartman. Will not appeal to everyone, but acting is marvelous, with Dolph Sweet hilarious as tough cop. Location filming in N.Y.C. adds to film, too. Written by Coppola, from the David Benedictus novel. Title song by The Lovin' Spoonful. Film debut of Karen Black. ▼●

You're a Sweetheart (1937) **96m.** ** D: David Butler. Alice Faye, George Murphy, Ken Murray, Andy Devine, William Gargan, Charles Winninger, Donald Meek, Bobby Watson. Routine musical with go-getter Murphy dreaming up publicity stunt for show which stars Faye. Title song became a standard.

You're in the Army Now (1941) **79m.** ** D: Lewis Seiler. Jimmy Durante, Phil Silvers, Donald MacBride, Jane Wyman, Regis Toomey, Joe Sawyer. Rather obvious service comedy, with Durante and Silvers trying hard to rise above their material. Some funny scenes, with finale copied from Chaplin's THE GOLD RUSH. Trivia note: features the longest kiss (between Toomey and Wyman) in screen history, clocked at 3 min., 5 sec.

You're in the Navy Now (1951) **93m.** ** D: Henry Hathaway. Gary Cooper, Jane Greer, Millard Mitchell, Eddie Albert, John McIntire, Ray Collins, Harry Von Zell, Lee Marvin, Jack Webb. Flat naval comedy set in WW2 with Cooper commanding a dumb crew on the U.S.S. *Teakettle* (the ship is outfitted with a steam engine). Film debuts for Marvin and Charles Buchinski (Bronson). Originally screened with the title U.S.S TEAKETTLE.

You're My Everything (1949) **C-94m.** ** D: Walter Lang. Dan Dailey, Anne Baxter, Anne Revere, Stanley Ridges, Alan Mowbray, Selena Royle. Lumpy musical-romance of socialite Baxter and hoofer-husband Dailey, who become movie stars in the 1920s and '30s. Based on a story by George Jessel. Watch for Buster Keaton in Baxter's second "silent film."

You're Never Too Young (1955) **C-102m.** *** D: Norman Taurog. Dean Martin, Jerry Lewis, Diana Lynn, Raymond Burr, Nina Foch, Veda Ann Borg. Fast, funny remake of THE MAJOR AND THE MINOR (which also featured Lynn) with Jerry disguised as 12-year-old at a girls' school, involved in jewel robbery. Script by Sidney Sheldon. VistaVision.

You're Not So Tough (1940) **71m.** **½ D: Joe May. Billy Halop, Huntz Hall, Bobby Jordan, Gabriel Dell, Bernard Punsly, Nan Grey, Henry Armetta. Halop and his pals are drifters who end up working on a California farm beset by the usual villains. One of the better *Little Tough Guys* entries.

You're Only Young Once (1938) **78m.** **½ D: George B. Seitz. Lewis Stone, Cecilia Parker, Mickey Rooney, Fay Holden, Frank Craven, Ann Rutherford. Second *Andy Hardy* film, with Andy (Rooney) and his sister finding romance on a family vacation in Catalina. Energetic Eleanor Lynn makes a peppy partner for Rooney.

You're Telling Me! (1934) **67m.** ***½ D: Erle C. Kenton. W. C. Fields, Joan Marsh, Larry "Buster" Crabbe, Louise Carter, Kathleen Howard, Adrienne Ames. Hilarious remake of Fields' silent film SO'S YOUR OLD MAN, with thin storyline (about a friendly foreign princess giving lowly, browbeaten Fields respectability in his home town) a perfect excuse for some of his funniest routines—including classic golf game.▼

You're Telling Me (1942) **60m.** *½ D: Charles Lamont. Hugh Herbert, Jane Frazee, Robert Paige, Richard Davies, Anne Gwynne, Mischa Auer, Ernest Truex. Tired comedy vehicle for Hugh as bumbler given job with radio advertising agency, involved with matchmaking on the side.

Your Friends & Neighbors (1998) **C-99m.** ** D: Neil LaBute. Amy Brenneman, Jason Patric, Ben Stiller, Aaron Eckhart, Catherine Keener, Nastassja Kinski. Another somewhat smug "let's rip the lid off the hypocrisy of society" tract from writer-director LaBute about two socially and sexually dysfunctional couples and their friends. Some pungent, provocative dialogue, but as in LaBute's IN THE COMPANY OF MEN, it's not clear what the point of it all is. Patric (who also produced) has an especially potent role as a self-styled stud. Super 35. [R]▼●◗

Your Past Is Showing (1957-British) **92m.** *** D: Mario Zampi. Terry-Thomas, Peter Sellers, Peggy Mount, Dennis Price, Shirley Eaton. Droll hijinks of a strange grouping of folks brought together to rid themselves of the editor of a smut-exposé magazine. Original British title: THE NAKED TRUTH.▼

Yours, Mine and Ours (1968) **C-111m.** *** D: Melville Shavelson. Lucille Ball, Henry Fonda, Van Johnson, Tom Bosley, Tim Matheson. For once, a wholesome "family" picture with some intelligent scripting. Based on real situation of widowed mother of eight marrying widower with ten more children. Lucy's drunk scene is a delight in warm, well-made comedy. Among Fonda's brood: Suzanne Cupito (who grew up to be Morgan Brittany) and a very young Tracy Nelson.▼●

Your Three Minutes Are Up (1973) **C-92m.** ***½ D: Douglas N. Schwartz. Beau Bridges, Ron Leibman, Janet Margolin, Kathleen Freeman, David Ketchum, Stu Nisbet. Overlooked comedy with serious undertones vividly captures two American lifestyles in story of ultra-straight Bridges hanging out with swinging buddy Leibman, who's out to beat the system. Unpretentious film says more about our society than many more "important" movies; solid performances. Written by James Dixon. [R]

Your Ticket Is No Longer Valid (1979-Canadian) **C-91m.** BOMB D: George Kaczender. Richard Harris, George Peppard, Jeanne Moreau, Jennifer Dale, Alexandra Stewart, Winston Rekert. Trashy adaptation of a Romain Gary novel is an embarrassment for its cast: Harris is struggling to raise cash for his failed, inherited family business while suffering from impotency and recurring fantasies of a gypsy stud making love to his girlfriend Dale; Peppard is a foulmouthed banker who is also impotent; and Moreau is a Parisian madam who procures the gypsy boy for Harris's and Dale's eventual amusement. Lurid junk. ▼

Your Turn, Darling (1963-French) **93m.** ** D: Bernard Borderie. Eddie Constantine, Elga Andersen, Christine Minazzoli, Gaia Germani, Philippe Lemaire. Lumbering spy tale with Constantine as Lemmy Caution, American secret agent who goes into action when a female spy is murdered and a scientist is kidnapped.▼

You Said a Mouthful (1932) **75m.** *** D: Lloyd Bacon. Joe E. Brown, Ginger Rogers, Preston Foster, Guinn Williams, Sheila Terry. One of Brown's better vehicles, about inventor of unsinkable bathing suit; Rogers is his vivacious leading lady.

You So Crazy (1994) **C-85m.** *½ D: Thomas Schlamme. Martin Lawrence. Embarrassingly crude performance film full of off-color jokes, minus any of the wit or observational insights that made the Richard Pryor films classics of the standup genre. Hard to recall another instance in which a performer labored and sweated so hard for such a minimal payoff. [NC-17]▼●

Youth Runs Wild (1944) **67m.** ** D: Mark Robson. Bonita Granville, Kent Smith, Tessa Brind (Vanessa Brown), Lawrence Tierney, Jean Brooks, Dickie Moore. With parents and older siblings at war or in defense plants, teenagers do just what the title implies. Rare non-horror entry from producer Val Lewton is interesting as time capsule, routine as drama.

You've Got Mail (1998) **C-119m.** *** D: Nora Ephron. Tom Hanks, Meg Ryan, Parker Posey, Greg Kinnear, Jean Stapleton, Steve Zahn, Dave Chappelle, Dabney Coleman, John Randolph. Long but entertaining remake of THE SHOP AROUND THE CORNER, with Ryan as the proud proprietor of a neighborhood bookshop, Hanks as the head of a superstore chain poised to put her out of business. They should be mortal enemies, but they're already e-mail pen-pals, without knowing each other's identity. Pleasant enough fluff with two irresistible stars. The use of old songs (which worked so well in Ephron's SLEEPLESS IN SEATTLE) is overbearing and unnecessary here. [PG-13]▼●◗

You've Got to Walk It Like You Talk It or You'll Lose That Beat (1971) **C-85m.** **½ D: Peter Locke. Zalman King, Richard Pryor, Robert Downey, Sr., Liz Torres, Roz Kelly, Allen Garfield. Uneven, often crude satire focusing on the sorry escapades of a young loser, a product of the 60s. Filmed in 1968.

You Were Meant for Me (1948) **92m.** *** D: Lloyd Bacon. Jeanne Crain, Dan Dailey, Oscar Levant, Barbara Lawrence, Selena Royle. Nice combination of musical score and script of girl who marries band leader; their experiences in Depression are basis of film.

You Were Never Lovelier (1942) **97m.** ***½ D: William A. Seiter. Fred Astaire, Rita Hayworth, Adolphe Menjou, Leslie Brooks, Adele Mara, Xavier Cugat, Gus Schilling, Larry Parks. Astaire pursuing Hayworth via matchmaking father Menjou becomes lilting musical with such lovely Jerome Kern—Johnny Mercer songs as title tune, "Dearly Beloved," "I'm Old-Fashioned." ▼●

Yum-Yum Girls, The (1976) **C-93m.** ** D: Barry Rosen. Judy Landers, Tanya Roberts, Michelle Dawn, Carey Poe, Stan Bernstein. Entertainingly trashy film, made before Landers' and Roberts' TV success, about young girls coming to N.Y.C. to become fashion models. OK cook's tour of the business, marred by unfunny script. [R]▼●

Z (1969-French) **C-127m.** *** D: Costa-Gavras. Yves Montand, Irene Papas, Jean-Louis Trintignant, Charles Denner, Georges Geret, Jacques Perrin, Francois Perier, Marcel Bozzufi. Oscar-winner for Best Foreign Film and Editing, based on true-life incident, concerns political assassination of Montand and chilling aftermath. Talky film praised more for its topicality than cinematics is nonetheless gripping; good acting. [M/PG]▼●◗

Zabriskie Point (1970) **C-112m.** **½ D: Michelangelo Antonioni. Mark Frechette, Daria Halprin, Rod Taylor, Paul Fix, Harrison Ford. Rambling study by a foreigner of the aggressive, materialistic, unflinching American lifestyle. Worth watching but difficult to stay with, though there's a real eye-opening finale. Sam Shepard was one of the scriptwriters. Panavision. [R]▼●

Zachariah (1971) **C-93m.** **½ D: George Englund. John Rubinstein, Pat Quinn, Don Johnson, Country Joe and The Fish, Elvin Jones, New York Rock Ensemble, The James Gang, Dick Van Patten. Audacious rock Western with elements of a morality play and moments of sharp satire; coscripted by members of Firesign Theater. Certainly offbeat, but how much you like it is strictly personal taste. [PG]▼◗

Zamba (1949) **75m.** *½ D: William Berke. Jon Hall, June Vincent, George Cooper, Jane Nigh, George O'Hanlon, Beau Bridges. Juvenile adventure story of boy raised by gorillas; rough going.

Zandalee (1991) **C-100m.** *½ D: Sam Pillsbury. Nicolas Cage, Judge Reinhold, Erika Anderson, Joe Pantoliano, Viveca Lindfors, Aaron Neville, Ian Abercrombie, Marisa Tomei, Zach Galligan. In steamy New Orleans, thrill-seeking Zandalee (Anderson) falls for her now-staid husband's free-spirited friend; their affair leads to tragedy. Routine plot (with liberal doses of sex) gets sillier as it goes along; hampered, too, by unappealing characters. Released direct to video. [R]▼●◗

Zandy's Bride (1974) **C-116m.** *½ D: Jan Troell. Gene Hackman, Liv Ullmann, Eileen Heckart, Harry Dean Stanton, Susan Tyrrell, Sam Bottoms, Joe Santos. Two frequently wasted stars in tepid romance of a mail-order bride and her pioneer husband; no one needs *these* scenes from a marriage. Aka FOR BETTER, FOR WORSE. Panavision. [PG]▼

Zapped! (1982) **C-96m.** *½ D: Robert J. Rosenthal. Scott Baio, Willie Aames, Felice Schachter, Heather Thomas, Robert Mandan, Greg Bradford, Scatman Crothers, Sue Ane Langdon. Attractive cast is wasted in this stupid spoof of CARRIE, in which Baio acquires telekinetic powers . . . which he's most anxious to use in undressing Thomas (or rather, her stand-in). Followed by a sequel.▼●

Zarak (1957-British) **C-99m.** **½ D: Terence Young. Victor Mature, Michael Wilding, Anita Ekberg, Bernard Miles, Finlay Currie. Hokum set in India with Mature the head of native outlaws, Wilding the British officer sent to get him. CinemaScope.

Zardoz (1974-British) **C-105m.** **½ D: John Boorman. Sean Connery, Charlotte Rampling, Sara Kestelman, Sally Anne Newton, John Alderton, Niall Buggy. Weird sci-fi entry, set in 2293, about technology gone wild in society run by group of eternally young intellectuals. Visually striking cult film will probably leave most viewers dissatisfied. Panavision. [R]▼●

Zaza (1939) **83m.** ** D: George Cukor. Claudette Colbert, Herbert Marshall, Bert Lahr, Helen Westley, Constance Collier, Genevieve Tobin, Walter Catlett. Colbert, doing her own singing, is the French music hall performer who falls for married Marshall, playing the role in his sleep. Remake of Gloria Swanson silent vehicle has well-mounted novelty value, but the drama simply never gets into gear.

Zazie dans le Metro (1960-French) **C-88m.** **½ D: Louis Malle. Catherine Demongeot, Philippe Noiret, Vittorio Caprioli, Hubert Deschamps, Carla Marlier. Superficial comedy, coscripted by Malle, about a bright but impish 12-year-old (Demongeot), who visits her female-impersonator uncle (Noiret) in Paris, and is intent on riding in the city's subway.▼

Zebra Force (1977) **C-100m.** ** D: Joe Tornatore. Mike Lane, Richard X. Slattery, Rockne Tarkington, Glenn Wilder, Anthony Caruso. A band of Vietnam vets uses military tactics against the Mob to fatten their own pockets and "rid society of scum." Straightforward low-budgeter suffers from Grade Z performances. Todd-AO 35. [PG]▼

Zebrahead (1992) **C-100m.** *** D: Anthony Drazan. Michael Rapaport, DeShonn Castle, N'Bushe Wright, Ron Johnson, Ray Sharkey, Paul Butler, Candy Ann Brown, Helen Shaver, Luke Reilly, Martin Priest. Refreshing, straightforward drama about a white teen (Rapaport) who attends an integrated Detroit high school. His best friend (Castle) is black, and problems arise when he becomes romantically involved with his pal's cousin (Wright). Benefits from realistic dialogue, and a candid take on the characters' lives and feelings. Drazan also scripted; Oliver Stone was one of the executive producers. [R]▼●

Zebra in the Kitchen (1965) **C-93m.** **½ D: Ivan Tors. Jay North, Martin Milner, Andy Devine, Joyce Meadows, Jim Davis, Dorothy Green. Wholesome family fare of young North involved with wild pets and the city zoo's attempt to keep its inmates locked up.▼

Zed & Two Noughts, A (1985-British-Dutch) **C-115m.** *** D: Peter Greenaway. Andrea Ferreol, Brian Deacon, Eric Deacon, Frances Barber, Joss Ackland. Extremely provocative examination of birth, life, and death, focusing on Ferreol, who has lost a leg in a car crash, and two zoologist brothers (the Deacons) whose wives have been killed in the same accident and who become obsessed with decay. Difficult to watch but well worthwhile for those willing to be challenged. Not so much a film as a visual essay, exquisitely directed and photographed (by Sacha Vierny).▼◗

Zeisters SEE: **Fat Guy Goes Nutzoid**

Zelig (1983) **C/B&W-79m.** *** D: Woody Allen. Woody Allen, Mia Farrow, Garrett Brown, Stephanie Farrow, Will Holt, Sol Lomita, Mary Louise Wilson, Michael Jeter. Pseudo-documentary using remarkable recreations of old newsreels and recordings, about a chameleonlike man named Leonard Zelig (Allen), who became a celebrity in the fad-crazy '20s. A supremely well-executed joke, more clever than funny; it might have worked even better in a shorter format. Gordon Willis's cinematography and Dick Hyman's music are standouts. [PG]▼●

Zelly and Me (1988) **C-87m.** **½ D: Tina Rathborne. Isabella Rossellini, Glynis Johns, Alexandra Johnes, Kaiulani Lee, David Lynch, Joe Morton. Uneven account of the trials and stresses in the life of wealthy, overprotected orphan Johnes. Occasionally insightful but far too introspective—with too much left unexplained. [PG]▼●

Zenobia (1939) **71m.** **½ D: Gordon Douglas. Oliver Hardy, Harry Langdon, Billie Burke, Alice Brady, James Ellison, Jean Parker, June Lang, Chester Conklin, Stepin Fetchit, Hattie McDaniel. Small-town doctor agrees to treat an ailing elephant—and the grateful pachyderm refuses to leave his side! Amiable comedy set in the Old South, with some dated (and mildly tol'able) subplots. This was Hardy's only starring venture without Stan Laurel, and he's quite good, in a fairly straight nonslapsticky performance.▼

Zentropa (1992-Danish-Swedish-French-German) **C/B&W-114m.** ***½ D: Lars von Trier. Barbara Sukowa, Jean-Marc Barr, Udo Kier, Ernst Hugo, Eddie Constantine. Narrated by Max von Sydow. Sukowa plays a railroad magnate's daughter who may be in synch with postwar Nazi sympathizers called "werewolves." Audacious black-comic fantasy utilizes high-tech mixed media, creative use of rear projection, and dramatic shifts in pigment. Though it feels like a stunt, this is a rare contemporary movie that makes one feel privy to the reinvention of cinema. Panavision. ▼●

Zeppelin (1971-British) **C-101m.** *** D: Etienne Perier. Michael York, Elke Sommer, Peter Carsten, Marius Goring, Anton Diffring, Andrew Keir. Colorful cast and atmosphere (including interesting special effects) click in entertaining story of German-born British aviator emotionally torn by duty and homeland during WW1. Panavision. [G]▼

Zero Effect (1998) **C-115m.** **½ D: Jake Kasdan. Bill Pullman, Ben Stiller, Ryan O'Neal, Kim Dickens, Angela Featherstone. Pullman is Daryl Zero, the world's greatest (and most eccentric) private detective, who never meets his clients, but sends emissary Stiller instead. O'Neal hires him to track down a blackmailer, but Pullman finds himself becoming emotionally involved with one of his suspects. Clever, original screenplay by first-time feature director Kasdan (son of Lawrence), but he shoots himself in the foot by deadening the pace and stretching things out too long. Rate this a near miss. [R]▼●◗

Zero for Conduct (1933-French) **44m.** **** D: Jean Vigo. Jean Daste, Robert le Flon, Louis Lefebvre, Constantin Kelber, Gerard de Bedarieux. Life in a French boarding school, where the authorities attempt to regiment the students—unsuccessfully. The kids are all wonderfully spontaneous; one of the best films ever about children among children. The inspiration for IF. . . . Written by the director.▼

Zero Hour (1957) **81m.** **½ D: Hall Bartlett. Dana Andrews, Linda Darnell, Sterling Hayden, Elroy "Crazylegs" Hirsch, Geoffrey Toone, Jerry Paris, Peggy King, John Ashley. Effective suspense story (based on Arthur Hailey teleplay) of potential airplane disaster when pilots are felled by ptomaine poisoning. Remade for TV in 1971 as TERROR IN THE SKY, and then spoofed in 1980 as AIRPLANE!

Zero to Sixty (1978) **C-100m.** *½ D: Don Weis. Darren McGavin, Sylvia Miles, Joan Collins, Denise Nickerson, The Hudson Brothers, Lorraine Gary. McGavin is improbably cast as a schnook who hooks up with a strident, street-smart 16-year-old girl who makes her living repossessing cars. Loud, stupid comedy with more car-chase thrills than humor. [PG]▼

Zeus and Roxanne (1997) **C-98m.** ** D: George Miller. Steve Guttenberg, Kathleen Quinlan, Arnold Vosloo, Dawn McMillan, Miko Hughes, Jessica Howell. Kids' picture paralleling the up and down relationship between two single adults, as well as his dog and her dolphin (you read that right!). Lovely Bahamas locations and exceptional animal work lift this film only slightly above an uninspired script. [PG]▼●◗

Ziegfeld Follies (1946) **C-110m.** *** D:

Vincente Minnelli. William Powell, Judy Garland, Lucille Ball, Fred Astaire, Fanny Brice, Lena Horne, Red Skelton, Victor Moore, Virginia O'Brien, Cyd Charisse, Gene Kelly, Edward Arnold, Esther Williams. Variable all-star film introduced by Powell as Ziegfeld in heaven. Highlights are Brice-Hume Cronyn sketch, Astaire-Kelly dance, Moore-Arnold comedy routine, Skelton's "Guzzler's Gin," Horne's solo, Garland's "The Interview." Various segments directed by George Sidney, Roy Del Ruth, Norman Taurog, Lemuel Ayers, Robert Lewis, Merril Pye. Filmed mostly in 1944.▼●

Ziegfeld Girl (1941) **131m.** *** D: Robert Z. Leonard. James Stewart, Lana Turner, Judy Garland, Hedy Lamarr, Tony Martin, Jackie Cooper, Ian Hunter, Edward Everett Horton, Al Shean, Eve Arden, Dan Dailey, Philip Dorn, Charles Winninger. Large-scale musical drama opens brightly, bogs down into melodrama and preposterous subplots, as the lives of three girls (Turner, Garland, Lamarr) are changed by being recruited as Ziegfeld Follies girls. Busby Berkeley's "You Stepped Out of a Dream" is most famous number, but somewhat overshadowed by Judy's "I'm Always Chasing Rainbows," "Minnie from Trinidad." The MGM glitter has never been brighter. ▼●

Ziggy Stardust and The Spiders From Mars (1983) **C-91m.** *½ D: D. A. Pennebaker. David Bowie. Bowie in concert as Ziggy Stardust, his androgynous alter ego. Practically unwatchable, and unlistenable: cinema verité at its worst. Shot in 1973; of interest to Bowie fans only. [PG]▼●

Zigzag (1970) **105m.** **½ D: Richard A. Colla. George Kennedy, Anne Jackson, Eli Wallach, Steve Ihnat, William Marshall, Joe Maross. Dying insurance investigator (Kennedy) plans a complicated scheme to pin a murder on himself and be executed, so his family will collect a big insurance settlement, but his plans go awry. Good performances in moderately interesting drama. Panavision. [PG]

Zina (1985-British) **C/B&W-90m.** **½ D: Ken McMullen. Domiziana Giordano, Ian McKellen, Philip Madoc, Ron Anderson, Micha Bergese. Extremely (and deliberately) slow exploration of the problems and obsessions of Leon Trotsky's daughter (Giordano) while in psychoanalysis in prewar Berlin. Bryan Loftus' cinematography is exceptional. Not for all tastes.

Zita (1968-French) **C-91m.** *** D: Robert Enrico. Joanna Shimkus, Katina Paxinou, Suzanne Flon, Jose Marie Flotats, Paul Crauchet. Delicate story of young girl who learns about life as her beloved aunt is dying; love blossoms, as she breaks away from mother-figure to become an adult herself. Charming. [M]

Zoltan, Hound of Dracula SEE: **Dracula's Dog**

Zombie (1979-Italian) **C-91m.** BOMB D: Lucio Fulci. Tisa Farrow, Ian McCulloch, Richard Johnson, Al Cliver, Annetta Gay. A zombie epidemic on a small Caribbean island. A poor imitation of George Romero's horror films, and pretty repellent. Techniscope. ▼●◗

Zombie High (1987) **C-93m.** ** D: Ron Link. Virginia Madsen, Richard Cox, James Wilder, Paul Feig, Kay Kuter, Sherilyn Fenn, Paul Williams. This slight, silly horror film is a junior version of THE STEPFORD WIVES. Madsen is newly enrolled at a private school whose preppie students are all suspiciously docile. Aka THE SCHOOL THAT ATE MY BRAIN. [R]▼

Zombie Island Massacre (1984) **C-95m.** BOMB D: John N. Carter. David Broadnax, Rita Jenrette, Tom Cantrell, Diane Clayre Holub. Ex-Abscam Congressional spouse (and *Playboy* subject) Jenrette has three gratuitous nude scenes in the opening 20 minutes—and then they have to ruin everything by going to the stupid island. The corpses keep a-comin' in this cheapo outing. Rita warbles title tune, "Di Reggae Picnic." [R]▼

Zombies of Mora Tau (1957) **70m.** *½ D: Edward L. Cahn. Gregg Palmer, Allison Hayes, Autumn Russell, Joel Ashley. Juvenile hodgepodge about zombies guarding diamonds hidden in a sunken ship.▼

Zombies of Sugar Hill, The SEE: **Sugar Hill** (1974)

Zombies on Broadway (1945) **68m.** ** D: Gordon Douglas. Wally Brown, Alan Carney, Bela Lugosi, Anne Jeffreys, Sheldon Leonard, Frank Jenks. Press agents Brown and Carney (cut-rate version of Abbott and Costello) search for zombie to use in nightclub stunt. Lugosi adds only spice as zombie expert.▼●

Zontar, the Thing from Venus (1968) **C-80m.** BOMB D: Larry Buchanan. John Agar, Anthony Houston, Susan Bjurman, Patricia De Laney, Warren Hammack. Title alien, resembling a bat, arrives to take over with INVASION OF THE BODY SNATCHERS-like methods; it's Agar to the rescue. Crude, Texas-filmed remake of IT CONQUERED THE WORLD.▼

Zoo in Budapest (1933) **85m.** ***½ D: Rowland V. Lee. Loretta Young, Gene Raymond, O. P. Heggie, Paul Fix, Wally Albright. Wonderfully whimsical love story set in famous Budapest zoo where Raymond, who has spent his life there, falls in love with runaway Young, who's hiding inside zoo grounds. Offbeat film bathed in romantic aura; beautifully photographed by Lee Garmes.

Zoot Suit (1981) **C-103m.** *** D: Luis Valdez. Daniel Valdez, Edward James

Olmos, Charles Aidman, Tyne Daly, John Anderson, Tony Plana. Fascinating, powerful, if too theatrical "stylized musical" based on railroading of Chicano gang members to San Quentin for murder in 1942 and efforts to obtain their release; adding commentary is the gang's leader (Valdez) and his zoot-suited alter ego (Olmos). Filmed on stage, with shots of an audience that is presumably watching the performance—a major distraction. Written by Luis Valdez, with music by Daniel Valdez. [R]▼●

Zorba the Greek (1964) **146m.** ***½ D: Michael Cacoyannis. Anthony Quinn, Alan Bates, Irene Papas, Lila Kedrova, George Foundas. Brooding, flavorful rendering of Kazantzakis novel. Quinn is zesty in title role of earthy peasant, Bates his intellectual British cohort. Kedrova won an Oscar as a dying prostitute, as did cinematographer Walter Lassally and the art direction-set decoration. Memorable Mikis Theodorakis score. Scripted by the director, from Nikos Kazantzakis' novel. Later a Broadway musical.▼●

Zorro (1961-Spanish) **C-90m.** **½ D: Joaquin Luis Romero Marchent. Frank Latimore, Mary Anderson, Ralph Marsch, Howard Vernon. Foreign-made Western with salty flavor of old California; Latimore is appropriately zealous as Zorro. SuperScope.▼

Zorro (1975-Italian-French) **C-100m.** *** D: Duccio Tessari. Alain Delon, Stanley Baker, Ottavia Piccolo, Moustache, Enzo Cerusico, Adriana Asti. Zesty retelling of saga of legendary masked rider and hero of the oppressed, not as distinctive as earlier versions (and set in South America rather than old California) but fun. [G]▼

Zorro Rides Again (1937) **68m.** ** D: William Witney, John English. John Carroll, Helen Christian, Reed Howes, Duncan Renaldo, Noah Beery. Edited from vintage Republic serial, recounting adventures of Carroll in old West to help railroad; just fair.▼

Zorro the Avenger SEE: **Shadow of Zorro, The**

Zorro, the Gay Blade (1981) **C-93m.** ** D: Peter Medak. George Hamilton, Lauren Hutton, Brenda Vaccaro, Ron Leibman, Donovan Scott, James Booth. Hamilton is Don Diego Vega, foppish son of the legendary Zorro, and look-alike gay brother Bunny Wigglesworth. So-so, with Leibman overacting outrageously as the villain. Dedicated to Rouben Mamoulian! [PG]▼

Zotz! (1962) **87m.** ** D: William Castle. Tom Poston, Julia Meade, Jim Backus, Fred Clark, Cecil Kellaway, Margaret Dumont. Goofy attempt at humorous chiller with Poston a teacher who finds strange coin that gives him mystical power over others.▼

Zouzou (1934-French) **92m.** **½ D: Marc Allegret. Josephine Baker, Jean Gabin, Pierre Larquey, Yvette Leblon, Illa Meery, Madeleine Guitty. 42ND STREET meets FOOTLIGHT PARADE French-style, with Baker cast as a Creole laundress. In the best backstage musical tradition, she replaces a temperamental performer in a stage revue and captivates the crowd in a star-making turn. Overly familiar story line is helped by fast pace, and engaging musical numbers: how can you top Baker, covered in feathers and perched on a swing? ▼●

Z.P.G. (1972-British) **C-95m.** ** D: Michael Campus. Oliver Reed, Geraldine Chaplin, Don Gordon, Diane Cilento. Sci-fi tale with style but no class. Reproduction becomes crime punishable by death in the future, but some people try to defy the law. Title, of course, stands for Zero Population Growth. [PG]▼

Zulu (1964-British) **C-138m.** *** D: Cy Endfield. Stanley Baker, Jack Hawkins, Ulla Jacobsson, Michael Caine, Nigel Green, James Booth. Narrated by Richard Burton. True story about undermanned British forces trying to defend their African mission from attack by hordes of Zulu warriors. Dramatic elements tend toward cliché, but virtually half the film is taken up by massive battle, which is truly spectacular and exciting. Followed 15 years later by prequel, ZULU DAWN. Technirama.▼●◗

Zulu Dawn (1979-U.S.-Dutch) **C-121m.** *** D: Douglas Hickox. Burt Lancaster, Peter O'Toole, Simon Ward, John Mills, Nigel Davenport, Michael Jayston, Denholm Elliott, Ronald Lacey, Freddie Jones, Christopher Cazenove, Anna Calder-Marshall, Bob Hoskins, Nicholas Clay. A prequel to 1964's ZULU (cowritten by that film's writer-director Cy Endfield), showing the British command's bull-headed and ineffectual handling of the Zulu nation—first in diplomacy, then in battle. Solid war drama of the period, outstanding locations (dwarfed on TV), though there's nothing new here. Released theatrically in U.S. at 98m. Panavision. [PG]▼●

Zuma Beach (1978) **C-100m. TVM** D: Lee H. Katzin. Suzanne Somers, Steven Keats, Michael Biehn, Mark Wheeler, Kimberly Beck, Perry Lang, Rosanna Arquette, Timothy Hutton, Tanya Roberts, P.J. Soles. Fading rock star becomes involved with high schoolers at a beach party. OK if watching Suzanne in a bathing suit is enough to keep you interested for 100m. Cowritten by John Carpenter! Average.

Index of Stars

This index includes *only the films that appear in this book*; therefore what follows doesn't feature a complete list of Mary Pickford's silent films, or John Wayne's B Westerns, or all the films of Gérard Depardieu.

The titles in each entry are in chronological order. Years are indicated in the reviews, and are included here to distinguish between two films of the same title, whether they are remakes (the two *Thomas Crown Affairs*, for example), or have nothing to do with each other (for instance, the two movies named *Where the Heart Is*).

When an actor directs but doesn't act in a movie, this is indicated by "(dir)" after the title; if the actor does appear, the designation is "(also dir)." The only significant exception is Woody Allen, who does it all; he wrote, directed and acted in his movies unless indicated otherwise.

The prefix "co-" means a collaboration as writer, producer, etc. "Cameo" indicates a well-known actor taking a small role, sometimes as a joke; their names almost never appear in the opening credits of a film, though in recent years, they are often listed in the end credits.

adapt	=	screenplay adaptation
app	=	appearance, not a performance (as in a documentary)
dir	=	director
exec prod	=	executive producer
mus	=	composer
narr	=	narrator
prod	=	producer
scr	=	screenplay
sty	=	story
uncred	=	uncredited performance

Alda, Alan: Gone Are the Days!, Paper Lion, The Extraordinary Seaman, The Moonshine War, Jenny, The Mephisto Waltz, To Kill a Clown, California Suite, Same Time, Next Year, The Seduction of Joe Tynan, The Four Seasons (also dir), Sweet Liberty (also dir), A New Life (also dir), Crimes and Misdemeanors, Betsy's Wedding (also dir), Whispers in the Dark, And the Band Played On, Manhattan Murder Mystery, Canadian Bacon, Neil Simon's "Jake's Women," Flirting With Disaster, Everyone Says I Love You, Murder at 1600, Mad City, The Object of My Affection

Allen, Woody: What's New, Pussycat?, What's Up, Tiger Lily?, Casino Royale (act), Take the Money and Run, Bananas, Play It Again, Sam (act), Everything You Always Wanted to Know About Sex (But Were Afraid to Ask), Sleeper, Love and Death, The Front (act), Annie Hall, Interiors (dir, scr), Manhattan, Stardust Memories, A Midsummer Night's Sex Comedy, Zelig, Broadway Danny Rose, The Purple Rose of Cairo (dir, scr), Hannah and Her Sisters, Radio Days, September (dir, scr), King Lear (1987), Another Woman (dir scr), New York Stories, Crimes and Misdemeanors, Alice (dir scr), Scenes From a Mall (act), Shadows and Fog, Husbands and Wives, Manhattan Murder Mystery, Bullets Over Broadway, Don't Drink the Water (1994), Mighty Aphrodite, Everyone Says I Love You, Deconstructing Harry, Wild Man Blues (app), The Impostors (cameo), Antz, Celebrity (dir, scr), Sweet and Lowdown, Small Time Crooks, Picking Up the Pieces

Andrews, Julie: Mary Poppins, The Americanization of Emily, The Sound of Music, Torn Curtain, Hawaii, Thoroughly Modern Millie, Star!, Darling Lili, The Tamarind Seed, 10, Little Miss Marker (1980), S.O.B., Victor/Victoria, The Man Who Loved Women (1983), That's Life!, Duet for One, Our Sons, A Fine Romance

Ann-Margret: Pocketful of Miracles, State Fair (1962), Bye Bye Birdie, Viva Las Vegas, Kitten With a Whip, The Pleasure Seekers, Bus Riley's Back in Town, Once a Thief (1965), The Cincinnati Kid, Made in Paris, Stagecoach (1966), The Swinger, Murderers' Row, The Tiger and the Pussycat, R.P.M., C.C. and Company, Carnal Knowledge, The Train Robbers, The Outside Man, Tommy, The Twist, Joseph Andrews, The Last Remake of Beau Geste, The Cheap Detective, Magic, The Villain, Middle Age Crazy, The Return of the Soldier, I Ought to Be in Pictures, Lookin' to Get Out, Who Will Love My Children?, A Streetcar Named Desire (1984), Twice in a Lifetime, 52 Pick-Up, The Two Mrs. Grenvilles, A Tiger's Tale, A New Life, Our Sons, Newsies, Grumpy Old Men, Nobody's Children, Grumpier Old Men, Any Given Sunday, The Flintstones in Viva Rock Vegas

Arthur, Jean: Seven Chances, Canary Murder Case, The Greene Murder Case, Paramount on Parade, Danger Lights, Whirlpool (1934), The Whole Town's Talking, Public Hero No. 1, Party Wire, Diamond Jim, If You Could Only Cook, Mr. Deeds Goes to Town, The Ex-Mrs. Bradford, Adventure in Manhattan, The Plainsman (1936), More Than a Secretary, History Is Made at Night, Easy Living (1937), You Can't Take It With You, Only Angels Have Wings, Mr. Smith Goes to Washington, Too Many Husbands, Arizona, The Devil and Miss Jones, The Talk of the Town, The More the Merrier, A Lady Takes a Chance, The Impatient Years, A Foreign Affair, Shane

Astaire, Fred: Dancing Lady, Flying Down to Rio, The Gay Divorcee, Roberta, Top Hat, Follow the Fleet, Swing Time, Shall We Dance? (1937), A Damsel in Distress, Carefree, The Story of Vernon & Irene Castle, Broadway Melody of 1940, Second Chorus, You'll Never Get Rich, Holiday Inn, You Were Never Lovelier, The Sky's the Limit, Yolanda and the Thief, Ziegfeld Follies, Blue Skies, Easter Parade, The Barkleys of Broadway, Three Little Words, Let's Dance, Royal Wedding, The Belle of New York, The Band Wagon, Daddy Long Legs, Funny Face, Silk Stockings, On the Beach, The Pleasure of His Company, The Notorious Landlady, Finian's Rainbow, Midas Run, The Towering Inferno, That's Entertainment!, That's Entertainment, Part 2, The Purple Taxi, The Amazing Dobermans, The Man in the Santa Claus Suit, Ghost Story (1981), George Stevens: A Filmmaker's Journey (app)

Aykroyd, Dan: Love at First Sight, 1941, The Blues Brothers, Neighbors, It Came From Hollywood, Doctor Detroit, Trading Places, Twilight Zone—The Movie, Indiana Jones and the Temple of Doom (cameo), Ghostbusters, Nothing Lasts Forever, Into the Night (cameo), Spies Like Us, Dragnet (1987), The Couch Trip, The Great Outdoors, Caddyshack II, My Stepmother Is an Alien, Ghostbusters II, Driving Miss Daisy, Loose Cannons, Nothing but Trouble (1991), My Girl, This Is My Life, Sneakers, Chaplin, Coneheads, My Girl 2, North, Exit to Eden, Tommy Boy, Casper (cameo), Canadian Bacon (cameo), Sgt. Bilko, Getting Away With Murder (1996), Celtic Pride, Feeling Minnesota, My Fellow Americans, Grosse Pointe Blank, Blues Brothers 2000, Antz, Diamonds (1999)

Bacall, Lauren: To Have and Have Not, Confidential Agent, Two Guys From Milwaukee (cameo), The Big Sleep (1946), Dark Passage, Key Largo, Young Man With a Horn, Bright Leaf, How to Marry a Millionaire, Woman's World, The Cobweb, Blood Alley, Written on the Wind, Designing Woman, The Gift of Love, Flame Over India, Shock Treatment (1964), Sex and the Single Girl, Harper, Murder on the Orient Express, The Shootist, Perfect Gentlemen, H.E.A.L.T.H., The Fan (1981), Appointment With Death, Mr. North, Innocent Victim, Misery, All I Want for Christmas, The Portrait, Ready to Wear (Prêt-à-Porter), The Line King (app), The Mirror Has Two Faces (1996), My Fellow Americans, Diamonds (1999)

Bacon, Kevin: National Lampoon's Animal House, Starting Over, Friday the 13th, Hero at Large, Only When I Laugh, Diner, Forty Deuce, Enormous Changes at the Last Minute, Footloose, Quicksilver, White Water Summer, End of the Line, Lemon Sky, Planes, Trains & Automobiles (cameo), She's Having a Baby, Criminal Law, The Big Picture, Tremors, Flatliners, He Said, She Said, Queens Logic, Pyrates, JFK, A Few Good Men, The Air Up There, The River Wild, Murder in the First, Apollo 13, Balto, Losing Chase (dir only), Sleepers, Picture Perfect, Telling Lies in America, Digging to China, Wild Things, Stir of Echoes, My Dog Skip

Baldwin, Alec: The Alamo: 13 Days to Glory, Forever, Lulu, She's Having a Baby, Beetle Juice, Married to the Mob, Talk Radio, Working Girl, Great Balls of Fire!, The Hunt for Red October, Miami Blues, Alice, The Marrying Man, Prelude to a Kiss, Glengarry Glen Ross, Malice, The Getaway (1994), The Shadow, A Streetcar Named Desire (1995), Two Bits, The Juror, Heaven's Prisoners, Ghosts of Mississippi, Looking for Richard, The Edge, Mercury Rising, Notting Hill (cameo), Outside Providence

Barrymore, Drew: Altered States, E.T. The Extra-Terrestrial, Firestarter, Irreconcilable Differences, Cat's Eye, Far from Home (1989), See You in the Morning, Doppelganger: The Evil Within, Guncrazy (1992), Poison Ivy (1992), Sketch Artist, Wayne's World 2, Bad Girls, Batman Forever, Boys on the Side, Mad Love (1995), Scream (1996), Wishful Thinking, Everyone Says I Love You, The Wedding Singer, Ever After, Home Fries, Never Been Kissed

Barrymore, John: Dr. Jekyll and Mr. Hyde (1920), Don Juan, The Beloved Rogue, Tempest (1928), Moby Dick (1930), Svengali (1931), The Mad Genius, Arsene Lupin, Grand Hotel, A Bill of Divorcement (1932), State's Attorney, Rasputin and the Empress, Topaze, Reunion in Vienna, Dinner at Eight, Counsellor-at-Law, Long Lost Father, Twentieth Century, Romeo and Juliet (1936), Maytime, Bulldog Drummond Comes Back, Night Club Scandal, True Confession, Bulldog Drummond's Revenge, Bulldog Drummond's Peril, Romance in the Dark, Spawn of the North, Marie Antoinette (1938), Hold That Co-Ed, The Great Man Votes, Midnight (1939), The Great Profile, The Invisible Woman, World Premiere, Playmates

Basinger, Kim: Hard Country, Mother Lode, The Man Who Loved Women (1983), Never Say Never Again, The Natural, Fool for Love, 9½ Weeks, No Mercy, Blind Date (1987), Nadine, My Stepmother Is an Alien, Batman (1989), The Marrying Man, Final Analysis, Cool World, The Real McCoy, Wayne's World 2 (cameo), The Getaway (1994), Ready to Wear (Prêt-à-Porter), L.A. Confidential, I Dreamed of Africa

Beatty, Warren: Splendor in the Grass, The Roman Spring of Mrs. Stone, All Fall Down, Lilith, Mickey One, Promise Her Anything, Kaleidoscope, Bonnie and Clyde, The Only Game in Town, McCabe & Mrs. Miller, $ (Dollars), The Parallax View, The Fortune, Shampoo, Heaven Can Wait (1978), Reds (also dir), George Stevens: A Filmmaker's Journey (app), Ishtar, Dick Tracy (also dir), Truth or Dare (app), Bugsy, Love Affair (1994), Bulworth (also dir)

Belushi, John: Shame of the Jungle, Goin' South, National Lampoon's Animal House, Old Boyfriends, 1941, The Blues Brothers, Continental Divide, Neighbors

Bening, Annette: The Great Outdoors, Valmont, Postcards From the Edge, The Grifters, Guilty by Suspicion, Regarding Henry, Bugsy, Love Affair (1994), The American President, Richard III (1995), Mars Attacks!, The Siege, In Dreams, American Beauty, What Planet Are You From?

Bergman, Ingrid: Swedenhielms, Intermezzo (1936), Intermezzo (1939), June Night, Rage in Heaven, Adam Had Four Sons, Dr. Jekyll and Mr. Hyde (1941), Casablanca, For Whom the Bell Tolls, Gaslight (1944), The Bells of St. Mary's, Spellbound, Saratoga Trunk, Notorious, Arch of Triumph, Joan of Arc, Under Capricorn, Stromboli, The Greatest Love, Strangers, Paris Does Strange Things, Anastasia (1956), Indiscreet (1958), The Inn of the Sixth Happiness, Goodbye Again, The Yellow Rolls-Royce, The Visit, Cactus Flower, Walk in the Spring Rain, From the Mixed-Up Files of Mrs. Basil E. Frankweiler, Murder on the Orient Express, A Matter of Time, Autumn Sonata, A Woman Called Golda

Bogart, Humphrey: Up the River, Big City Blues, Love Affair (1932), Three on a Match, Midnight (1934), The Petrified Forest, Bullets or Ballots, Two Against the World, China Clipper, Isle of Fury, Black Legion, The Great O'Malley, Marked Woman, Kid Galahad (1937), San Quentin (1937), Dead End, Stand-In, Swing Your Lady, Crime School, Racket Busters, The Amazing Doctor Clitterhouse, Angels with Dirty Faces, King of the Underworld, The Oklahoma Kid, Dark Victory, You Can't

Get Away With Murder, The Roaring Twenties, The Return of Dr. X, Invisible Stripes, Virginia City, It All Came True, Brother Orchid, They Drive By Night, High Sierra, The Wagons Roll at Night, The Maltese Falcon (1941), Across the Pacific, All Through the Night, The Big Shot, Casablanca, Action in the North Atlantic, Thank Your Lucky Stars (cameo), Sahara (1943), Passage to Marseille, To Have and Have Not, Conflict (1945), Two Guys From Milwaukee (cameo), The Big Sleep (1946), Dead Reckoning, The Two Mrs. Carrolls, Dark Passage, Always Together (cameo), The Treasure of the Sierra Madre, Key Largo, Knock on Any Door, Tokyo Joe, Chain Lightning, In a Lonely Place, The Enforcer (1951), Sirocco, The African Queen, Deadline U.S.A., Battle Circus, The Love Lottery (cameo), Beat the Devil, The Caine Mutiny, Sabrina (1954), The Barefoot Contessa, We're No Angels (1955), The Left Hand of God, The Desperate Hours, The Harder They Fall

Boyer, Charles: The Man From Yesterday, Red-Headed Woman, Caravan, Private Worlds, Break of Hearts, Shanghai, Mayerling (1936), The Garden of Allah, Tovarich, Conquest, History Is Made at Night, Algiers, Love Affair (1939), When Tomorrow Comes, All This, and Heaven Too, Back Street (1941), Hold Back the Dawn, Appointment for Love, Tales of Manhattan, The Constant Nymph, Flesh and Fantasy, Gaslight (1944), Together Again, Confidential Agent, Cluny Brown, A Woman's Vengeance, Arch of Triumph, The First Legion, Thunder in the East, The 13th Letter, The Happy Time, The Earrings of Madame de . . ., The Cobweb, Around the World in Eighty Days, La Parisienne, Lucky to Be a Woman, The Buccaneer (1958), Maxime, Fanny (1961), Four Horsemen of the Apocalypse, Adorable Julia, Love Is a Ball, A Very Special Favor, Is Paris Burning?, How to Steal a Million, Casino Royale, Barefoot in the Park, The April Fools, The Madwoman of Chaillot, The Day the Hot Line Got Hot, Lost Horizon (1973), Stavisky . . ., A Matter of Time

Branagh, Kenneth: Coming Through, High Season, A Month in the Country, Henry V (1989; also dir), Dead Again (also dir), Peter's Friends (also dir), Swing Kids, Much Ado About Nothing (also dir), Mary Shelley's Frankenstein (also dir), Othello (1995), A Midwinter's Tale (dir, scr), Anne Frank Remembered, Looking for Richard (app), Hamlet (1996; also dir), The Gingerbread Man, The Proposition, Celebrity, The Theory of Flight, Wild Wild West, The Road to El Dorado, Love's Labour's Lost (also dir)

Brando, Marlon: The Men, A Streetcar Named Desire (1951), Viva Zapata!, Julius Caesar (1953), The Wild One, On the Waterfront, Desiree, Guys and Dolls, The Teahouse of the August Moon, Sayonara, The Young Lions, The Fugitive Kind, One-Eyed Jacks (also dir), Mutiny on the Bounty (1962), The Ugly American, Bedtime Story (1964), The Saboteur, Code Name Morituri, The Chase (1966), The Appaloosa, A Countess From Hong Kong, Reflections in a Golden Eye, Candy, The Night of the Following Day, Burn!, The Nightcomers, The Godfather, Last Tango in Paris, The Missouri Breaks, Superman, Apocalypse Now, The Formula, A Dry White Season, The Freshman (1990), Christopher Columbus: The Discovery, Don Juan DeMarco, The Island of Dr. Moreau (1996), Free Money

Bridges, Jeff: The Company She Keeps, Halls of Anger, The Last Picture Show, Fat City, Bad Company (1972), The Last American Hero, The Iceman Cometh, Lolly Madonna XXX, Thunderbolt and Lightfoot, Rancho Deluxe, Hearts of the West, Stay Hungry, King Kong (1976), Somebody Killed Her Husband, Winter Kills, The American Success Company, Heaven's Gate, Cutter's Way, Kiss Me Goodbye, The Last Unicorn, Tron, Against All Odds (1984), Starman, Jagged Edge, 8 Million Ways to Die, The Morning After, The Thanksgiving Promise (cameo), Nadine, Tucker: The Man and His Dream, Cold Feet (1989; cameo), The Fabulous Baker Boys, See You in the Morning, Texasville, The Fisher King, The Vanishing (1993), American Heart, Fearless, Secret Sins of the Father, Blown Away, Wild Bill, White Squall, Hidden in America, The Mirror Has Two Faces (1996), The Big Lebowski, Arlington Road, The Muse, Simpatico

Bronson, Charles (billed as Charles Buchinski or Buchinsky until Drum Beat): You're in the Navy Now, The People Against O'Hara, The Mob, Red Skies of Montana, My Six Convicts, The Marrying Kind (bit), Pat and Mike, Diplomatic Courier, Bloodhounds of Broadway (1952), House of Wax, The Clown, Miss Sadie Thompson, Crime Wave, Tennessee Champ, Riding Shotgun, Apache, Vera Cruz, Drum Beat, Big House, U.S.A., Target Zero, Jubal, Run of the Arrow, Machine-Gun Kelly, Gang War (1958), Showdown at Boot Hill, When Hell Broke Loose, Ten North Frederick (bit), Never So Few, The Magnificent Seven, Master of the World, A Thunder of Drums, X-15, Kid Galahad (1962), The Great Escape, 4 for Texas, The Sandpiper, Battle of the Bulge, This Property Is Condemned, The Dirty Dozen, Guns for San Sebastian, Farewell, Friend, Villa Rides!, Once Upon a Time in the West, Lola (1969), Rider on the Rain, You Can't Win 'Em All, The Family (1970), Cold Sweat, Someone Behind the Door, Red Sun, The Mechanic, The Valachi Papers, Chato's Land, The Stone Killer, Chino, Mr. Majestyk, Death Wish, Breakout

(1975), Hard Times, From Noon Till Three, Breakheart Pass, St. Ives, Raid on Entebbe, Telefon, The White Buffalo, Love and Bullets, Caboblanco, Borderline (1980), Death Hunt, Death Wish II, Ten to Midnight, The Evil That Men Do, Death Wish 3, Act of Vengeance, Murphy's Law, Assassination, Death Wish 4: The Crackdown, Messenger of Death, Kinjite: Forbidden Subjects, The Indian Runner, Death Wish V: The Face of Death, The Sea Wolf (1993)

Brooks, Albert: Taxi Driver, Real Life (also dir), Private Benjamin, Modern Romance (also dir), Twilight Zone—the Movie, Unfaithfully Yours (1984), Lost in America (also dir), Broadcast News, Defending Your Life (also dir), I'll Do Anything, The Scout, Mother (also dir), Out of Sight (1998), Dr. Dolittle (1998), The Muse (also dir)

Brooks, Louise: A Girl in Every Port (1928), Pandora's Box, Canary Murder Case, Diary of a Lost Girl, Prix de Beauté, The Public Enemy (bit), Other Men's Women (bit), When You're in Love

Bullock, Sandra: A Fool and His Money, Who Shot Patakango?, Love Potion No. 9, When the Party's Over, The Vanishing (1993), Demolition Man, The Thing Called Love, Wrestling Ernest Hemingway, Speed (1994), While You Were Sleeping, The Net, Two If by Sea, Fire on the Amazon, A Time to Kill, In Love and War (1996), Speed 2: Cruise Control, Hope Floats, Practical Magic, The Prince of Egypt, Forces of Nature, Gun Shy, 28 Days

Burns, George, and Gracie Allen: *Together:* The Big Broadcast, International House, College Humor, We're Not Dressing, Six of a Kind, Many Happy Returns, Love in Bloom, The Big Broadcast of 1936, College Holiday, The Big Broadcast of 1937, A Damsel in Distress, College Swing, Honolulu; *George without Gracie:* The Solid Gold Cadillac, The Sunshine Boys, Oh, God!, Sgt. Pepper's Lonely Hearts Club Band, Movie Movie, Just You and Me, Kid, Going in Style, Oh, God! Book II, Oh, God! You Devil, 18 Again!, Radioland Murders (cameo); *Gracie without George:* The Gracie Allen Murder Case, Mr. and Mrs. North, Two Girls and a Sailor

Burton, Richard: The Last Days of Dolwyn, Her Panelled Door, Green Grow the Rushes, My Cousin Rachel, The Desert Rats, The Robe, Demetrius and the Gladiators (cameo), Prince of Players, The Rains of Ranchipur, Alexander the Great, Sea Wife, Bitter Victory, Look Back in Anger, The Bramble Bush, Ice Palace, The Longest Day, Cleopatra (1963), The V.I.P.s, Zulu (narr), Becket, The Night of the Iguana, The Spy Who Came In From the Cold, The Sandpiper, What's New, Pussycat? (cameo), Who's Afraid of Virginia Woolf?, The Taming of the Shrew (1967), Doctor Faustus, The Comedians, Boom!, Candy, Where Eagles Dare, Anne of the Thousand Days, Staircase, Villain, Raid on Rommel, The Assassination of Trotsky, Hammersmith Is Out, Bluebeard (1972), Under Milk Wood (narr), Massacre in Rome, The Voyage, The Klansman, Exorcist II: The Heretic, Equus, The Medusa Touch, The Wild Geese, Lovespell, Breakthrough (1978), Circle of Two, Absolution, Wagner, Nineteen Eighty-Four

Caan, James: Irma la Douce (bit), Lady in a Cage, The Glory Guys, Red Line 7000, El Dorado, Games, Countdown, Journey to Shiloh, Submarine X-1, The Rain People, Rabbit, Run, Brian's Song, T.R. Baskin, The Godfather, Slither, Cinderella Liberty, The Gambler, Freebie and the Bean, The Godfather Part II (cameo), Funny Lady, Rollerball, The Killer Elite, Harry and Walter Go to New York, Silent Movie (cameo), Another Man, Another Chance, A Bridge Too Far, Comes a Horseman, Chapter Two, Hide in Plain Sight, Thief, Bolero (1981), Kiss Me Goodbye, Gardens of Stone, Alien Nation, Dick Tracy (cameo), Misery, The Dark Backward (cameo), For the Boys, Honeymoon in Vegas, The Program, Flesh and Bone, Bottle Rocket, Eraser, Bulletproof (1996), This is my Father, Mickey Blue Eyes

Cage, Nicolas: Fast Times at Ridgemont High, Valley Girl, Rumble Fish, Racing With the Moon, The Cotton Club, Birdy, The Boy in Blue, Peggy Sue Got Married, Raising Arizona, Moonstruck, Vampire's Kiss, Fire Birds, Wild at Heart, Zandalee, Honeymoon in Vegas, Amos & Andrew, Red Rock West, Deadfall (1993), Guarding Tess, It Could Happen to You, Trapped in Paradise, Kiss of Death (1995), Leaving Las Vegas, The Rock, Con Air, Face/Off, City of Angels, Snake Eyes, 8MM, Bringing Out the Dead

Cagney, James: Sinner's Holiday (1930), Doorway to Hell, Other Men's Women, The Millionaire, The Public Enemy, Smart Money, Blonde Crazy, Taxi!, The Crowd Roars (1932), Winner Take All, Hard to Handle, Lady Killer, Picture Snatcher, The Mayor of Hell, Footlight Parade, Jimmy the Gent, He Was Her Man, Here Comes the Navy, St. Louis Kid, Devil Dogs of the Air, "G" Men, The Irish in Us, Frisco Kid, A Midsummer Night's Dream (1935), Ceiling Zero, Great Guy, Something to Sing About, Boy Meets Girl, Angels With Dirty Faces, The Oklahoma Kid, Each Dawn I Die, The Roaring Twenties, The Fighting 69th, Torrid Zone, City for Conquest, The Strawberry Blonde, The Bride Came C.O.D., Captains of the Clouds, Yankee Doodle Dandy, Johnny Come Lately, Blood on the Sun, 13 Rue Madeleine, The Time of Your Life, White Heat, Kiss Tomorrow Goodbye, West Point Story, Come Fill the Cup, Starlift (cameo), What Price Glory? (1952), A

Lion Is in the Streets, Run for Cover, The Seven Little Foys, Love Me or Leave Me, Mister Roberts, Tribute to a Bad Man, These Wilder Years, Man of a Thousand Faces, Short Cut to Hell, Shake Hands With the Devil, Never Steal Anything Small, The Gallant Hours, One, Two, Three, Arizona Bushwhackers, Ragtime

Caine, Michael: Hell in Korea, How to Murder a Rich Uncle, The Key, The Two-Headed Spy, Carve Her Name With Pride, Breakout (1959), Foxhole in Cairo, The Day the Earth Caught Fire, The Wrong Arm of the Law, Zulu, The Ipcress File, Gambit, Alfie, The Wrong Box, Funeral in Berlin, Hurry Sundown, Billion Dollar Brain, Woman Times Seven, Deadfall (1968), Play Dirty, The Magus, The Italian Job, Battle of Britain, Too Late the Hero, Get Carter, The Last Valley, Kidnapped (1971), X, Y and Zee, Pulp, Sleuth, The Destructors (1974), The Black Windmill, The Wilby Conspiracy, The Man Who Would Be King, The Romantic Englishwoman, Peeper, Harry and Walter Go to New York, The Eagle Has Landed, A Bridge Too Far, Silver Bears, The Swarm, California Suite, Ashanti, Beyond the Poseidon Adventure, The Island (1980), Dressed to Kill (1980), The Hand (1981), Victory (1981), Deathtrap, Educating Rita, Beyond the Limit, Blame It on Rio, The Jigsaw Man, Water, The Holcroft Covenant, Hannah and Her Sisters, Sweet Liberty, Mona Lisa, Half Moon Street, The Whistle Blower, Jaws the Revenge, The Fourth Protocol, Surrender (1987), Without a Clue, Dirty Rotten Scoundrels, Jack the Ripper (1988), Bullseye!, A Shock to the System, Mr. Destiny, Jekyll & Hyde, Noises Off, Blue Ice, The Muppet Christmas Carol, On Deadly Ground, Blood and Wine, Mandela and de Klerk, Curtain Call, Little Voice, The Cider House Rules

Candy, John: It Seemed Like a Good Idea at the Time, The Clown Murders, Find the Lady, The Silent Partner, Lost and Found, 1941, The Blues Brothers, Heavy Metal, Stripes, It Came From Hollywood, Going Berserk, National Lampoon's Vacation, Splash, Sesame Street Presents Follow That Bird, Brewster's Millions (1985), Summer Rental, Volunteers, Armed and Dangerous, Little Shop of Horrors, Spaceballs, Planes, Trains & Automobiles, She's Having a Baby (cameo), The Great Outdoors, Hot to Trot, Who's Harry Crumb?, Speed Zone!, Uncle Buck, Home Alone (cameo), The Rescuers Down Under, Nothing but Trouble, Career Opportunities (cameo), Only the Lonely, Delirious, JFK, Boris and Natasha: The Movie (cameo), Once Upon a Crime, Cool Runnings, Rookie of the Year (cameo), Wagons East, Canadian Bacon

Carrey, Jim: Finders Keepers (1984), Once Bitten, Peggy Sue Got Married, The Dead Pool, High Strung (cameo), Earth Girls Are Easy, Pink Cadillac, Ace Ventura: Pet Detective, The Mask (1994), Dumb and Dumber, Batman Forever, Ace Ventura: When Nature Calls, The Cable Guy, Liar Liar, The Truman Show, Simon Birch, Man on the Moon

Chaplin, Charles: (*features only*) Tillie's Punctured Romance, The Kid, A Woman of Paris (cameo), The Gold Rush, The Circus, Show People (cameo), City Lights, Modern Times, The Great Dictator, Monsieur Verdoux, Limelight, A King in New York, A Countess From Hong Kong

Cher: Wild on the Beach, Good Times, Chastity, Come Back to the 5 & Dime, Jimmy Dean, Jimmy Dean, Silkwood, Mask, Moonstruck, Suspect, The Witches of Eastwick, Mermaids, The Player (cameo), Ready to Wear (Prêt-à-Porter), Faithful, If These Walls Could Talk (dir only), Tea with Mussolini

Cleese, John: Interlude (1968), The Bliss of Mrs. Blossom, The Best House in London, The Magic Christian, The Statue, And Now For Something Completely Different, Rentadick, Monty Python and the Holy Grail, Life of Brian, The Great Muppet Caper (cameo), Time Bandits, Monty Python Live at the Hollywood Bowl, The Secret Policeman's Other Ball, Privates on Parade, Monty Python's The Meaning of Life, Yellowbeard, Silverado, Clockwise, A Fish Called Wanda, Erik the Viking, Bullseye! (cameo), The Big Picture (cameo), An American Tail: Fievel Goes West, Splitting Heirs, The Swan Princess, Mary Shelley's Frankenstein, Rudyard Kipling's The Jungle Book, Fierce Creatures, George of the Jungle, The Wind in the Willows, The Out-of-Towners (1999), The World Is Not Enough, Isn't She Great

Clift, Montgomery: The Search, Red River, The Heiress, The Big Lift, A Place in the Sun, I Confess, From Here to Eternity, Indiscretion of an American Wife, Raintree County, The Young Lions, Lonelyhearts, Suddenly Last Summer (1959), Wild River, The Misfits, Judgment at Nuremberg, Freud, The Defector

Close, Glenn: The World According to Garp, The Big Chill, The Stone Boy, The Natural, Greystoke: The Legend of Tarzan, Lord of the Apes, Something About Amelia, Maxie, Jagged Edge, Fatal Attraction (1987), Dangerous Liaisons, Light Years, Stones for Ibarra, Immediate Family, Reversal of Fortune, Hamlet (1990), Sarah, Plain and Tall, Meeting Venus, Hook, Skylark (1994), The House of the Spirits, The Paper, Serving in Silence: The Marguerite Cammermeyer Story, Anne Frank Remembered, Mary Reilly, Mars Attacks!, 101 Dalmatians, Paradise Road, Air Force One, In & Out (cameo), Cookie's Fortune, Tarzan

Coburn, James: Ride Lonesome, Face of a Fugitive, The Magnificent Seven, Hell Is for Heroes, The Man From Galveston, The Great Escape, Charade, The Americanization of Emily, Major Dundee, A High Wind in Jamaica, The Loved One (cameo), Our Man Flint, What Did You Do in the War, Daddy?, Dead Heat on a Merry-Go-Round, In Like Flint, Waterhole #3, The President's Analyst, Duffy, Candy, Hard Contract, Last of the Mobile Hot-Shots, Duck, You Sucker, The Honkers, The Carey Treatment, Pat Garrett & Billy the Kid, The Last of Sheila, Harry in Your Pocket, A Reason to Live, a Reason to Die, The Internecine Project, Hard Times, Bite the Bullet, Sky Riders, The Last Hard Men, Midway, Cross of Iron, California Suite (cameo), The Muppet Movie (cameo), Circle of Iron, Goldengirl, Firepower, The Baltimore Bullet, Mr. Patman, Loving Couples, Looker, High Risk, Martin's Day, Draw!, Death of a Soldier, Young Guns II, Hudson Hawk, The Player (cameo), Sister Act 2: Back in the Habit, Deadfall (1993), Maverick, Avenging Angel, Eraser, The Nutty Professor (1996), The Second Civil War, Keys to Tulsa, Affliction, Payback (uncred)

Colbert, Claudette: The Big Pond, Secrets of a Secretary, His Woman, The Smiling Lieutenant, The Man from Yesterday, The Phantom President, The Sign of the Cross, I Cover the Waterfront, Three-Cornered Moon, Four Frightened People, It Happened One Night, Cleopatra (1934), Imitation of Life (1934), The Gilded Lily, Private Worlds, She Married Her Boss, The Bride Comes Home, Under Two Flags, Maid of Salem, Tovarich, I Met Him in Paris, Bluebeard's Eighth Wife, Zaza, Midnight (1939), Drums Along the Mohawk, It's a Wonderful World, Boom Town, Arise, My Love, Skylark (1941), Remember the Day, The Palm Beach Story, So Proudly We Hail!, No Time for Love, Since You Went Away, Practically Yours, Guest Wife, Tomorrow Is Forever, Without Reservations, The Secret Heart, The Egg and I, Sleep My Love, Family Honeymoon, Bride for Sale, Three Came Home, The Secret Fury, Thunder on the Hill, Let's Make It Legal, Outpost in Malaya, Daughters of Destiny, Royal Affairs in Versailles, Texas Lady, Parrish, The Two Mrs. Grenvilles

Colman, Ronald: Bulldog Drummond, Condemned, Raffles (1930), The Devil to Pay, The Unholy Garden, Arrowsmith, Cynara, The Masquerader, Clive of India, The Man Who Broke the Bank at Monte Carlo, A Tale of Two Cities (1935), Under Two Flags, Lost Horizon (1937), The Prisoner of Zenda (1937), If I Were King, The Light That Failed, Lucky Partners, My Life With Caroline, The Talk of the Town, Random Harvest, Kismet (1944), The Late George Apley, A Double Life, Champagne for Caesar, Around the World in Eighty Days, The Story of Mankind

Connery, Sean: Let's Make Up, No Road Back, Hell Drivers, Action of the Tiger, Another Time, Another Place, Darby O'Gill and the Little People, Tarzan's Greatest Adventure, The Frightened City, Operation Snafu, The Longest Day, Dr. No, From Russia With Love, Marnie, Woman of Straw, Goldfinger, The Hill, Thunderball, A Fine Madness, You Only Live Twice, Shalako, The Molly Maguires, The Red Tent, The Anderson Tapes, Diamonds Are Forever, The Offence, Zardoz, Murder on the Orient Express, The Terrorists, The Wind and the Lion, The Man Who Would Be King, Robin and Marian, The Next Man, A Bridge Too Far, The Great Train Robbery, Meteor, Cuba, Time Bandits, Outland, Wrong Is Right, Five Days One Summer, Never Say Never Again, Sword of the Valiant, Highlander, The Name of the Rose, The Untouchables, The Presidio, Memories of Me (cameo), Indiana Jones and the Last Crusade, Family Business (1989), The Hunt for Red October, The Russia House, Robin Hood: Prince of Thieves (cameo), Highlander II: The Quickening, Medicine Man, Rising Sun, A Good Man in Africa, Just Cause, First Knight, Dragonheart (voice only), The Rock, The Avengers, Playing by Heart, Entrapment

Cooper, Gary: The Eagle (bit), Old Ironsides (bit), Wings, It (1927), The Virginian (1929), Paramount on Parade, Morocco, City Streets (1931), His Woman, The Devil and the Deep, If I Had a Million, A Farewell to Arms (1932), Today We Live, Design for Living, Alice in Wonderland (1933), One Sunday Afternoon (1933), Operator 13, Now and Forever (1934), The Wedding Night, The Lives of a Bengal Lancer, Peter Ibbetson, Desire, Hollywood Boulevard (1936; cameo), Mr. Deeds Goes to Town, The General Died at Dawn, The Plainsman (1936), Souls at Sea, The Adventures of Marco Polo, Bluebeard's Eighth Wife, The Cowboy and the Lady, Beau Geste (1939), The Real Glory, The Westerner, North West Mounted Police, Meet John Doe, Sergeant York, Ball of Fire, The Pride of the Yankees, For Whom the Bell Tolls, The Story of Dr. Wassell, Casanova Brown, Along Came Jones, Saratoga Trunk, Cloak and Dagger, Variety Girl (cameo), Unconquered, Good Sam, The Fountainhead, It's a Great Feeling (cameo), Task Force, Bright Leaf, Dallas, You're in the Navy Now, Starlift (cameo), It's a Big Country, Distant Drums, High Noon, Springfield Rifle, Return to Paradise, Blowing Wild, Vera Cruz, Garden of Evil, The Court-Martial of Billy Mitchell, Friendly Persuasion, Love in the Afternoon, Ten North Frederick, Man of the West, The Hanging Tree, Alias Jesse James (cameo), They Came to Cordura, The Wreck of the Mary Deare, The Naked Edge

Costner, Kevin: Shadows Run Black,

Night Shift, Chasing Dreams, Frances, Stacy's Knights, Table for Five, Testament, The Big Chill, The Gunrunner, American Flyers, Fandango, Silverado, Sizzle Beach, U.S.A., The Untouchables, No Way Out (1987), Bull Durham, Field of Dreams, Revenge (1990), Dances With Wolves, Truth or Dare (app), Robin Hood: Prince of Thieves, JFK, The Bodyguard, A Perfect World, Wyatt Earp, The War, Waterworld, Tin Cup, The Postman (1997), Message in a Bottle, For Love of the Game, Play It to the Bone (cameo)

Crawford, Joan: Tramp, Tramp, Tramp, The Unknown, Our Dancing Daughters, Our Modern Maidens, Untamed (1929), Hollywood Revue of 1929, Montana Moon, Our Blushing Brides, Paid, Dance Fools, Dance, Laughing Sinners, This Modern Age, Possessed (1931), Grand Hotel, Rain, Today We Live, Dancing Lady, Sadie McKee, Forsaking All Others, Chained, No More Ladies, I Live My Life, The Gorgeous Hussy, Love on the Run (1936), The Last of Mrs. Cheyney (1937), The Bride Wore Red, Mannequin (1937), The Shining Hour, Ice Follies of 1939, The Women, Strange Cargo, Susan and God, When Ladies Meet (1941), A Woman's Face, They All Kissed the Bride, Reunion in France, Above Suspicion, Hollywood Canteen, Mildred Pierce, Humoresque, Possessed (1947), Daisy Kenyon, Flamingo Road, It's a Great Feeling (cameo), The Damned Don't Cry, Harriet Craig, Goodbye, My Fancy, This Woman Is Dangerous, Sudden Fear, Torch Song, Johnny Guitar, Female on the Beach, Queen Bee, Autumn Leaves, The Story of Esther Costello, The Best of Everything, What Ever Happened to Baby Jane? (1962), The Caretakers, Strait-Jacket, I Saw What You Did, Berserk, Night Gallery, Trog

Crosby, Bing: King of Jazz, Reaching for the Moon, The Big Broadcast, College Humor, Too Much Harmony, Going Hollywood, We're Not Dressing, Here Is My Heart, She Loves Me Not, Mississippi, Two for Tonight, The Big Broadcast of 1936, Anything Goes (1936), Rhythm on the Range, Pennies From Heaven (1936), Waikiki Wedding, Double or Nothing, Sing, You Sinners, Doctor Rhythm, Paris Honeymoon, The Star Maker (1939), East Side of Heaven, Rhythm on the River (1940), Road to Singapore, If I Had My Way, Birth of the Blues, Road to Zanzibar, My Favorite Blonde (cameo), Holiday Inn, Road to Morocco, Star Spangled Rhythm, Dixie, The Princess and the Pirate (cameo), Going My Way, Here Come the Waves, Out of This World (voice only), Road to Utopia, Duffy's Tavern, The Bells of St. Mary's, Blue Skies, Welcome Stranger, My Favorite Brunette (cameo), Road to Rio, Variety Girl (cameo), The Emperor Waltz, A Connecticut Yankee in King Arthur's Court, The Adventures of Ichabod and Mr. Toad (voice only), Top o' the Morning, Riding High (1950), Mr. Music, Here Comes the Groom, Angels in the Outfield (1951; cameo), The Greatest Show on Earth (cameo), Son of Paleface (cameo), Just for You, Road to Bali, Little Boy Lost, Scared Stiff (1953; cameo), White Christmas, The Country Girl, Anything Goes (1956), High Society (1956), Man on Fire (1957), Alias Jesse James (cameo), Say One for Me, Let's Make Love (cameo), High Time, Pepe (cameo), The Road to Hong Kong, Robin and the Seven Hoods, Stagecoach (1966), Cancel My Reservation (cameo), That's Entertainment!

Cruise, Tom: Endless Love, Taps, All the Right Moves, Risky Business, Losin' It, The Outsiders, Legend, Top Gun (1986), The Color of Money, Cocktail, Young Guns (cameo), Rain Man, Born on the Fourth of July, Days of Thunder, Far and Away, A Few Good Men, The Firm, Interview With the Vampire, Mission: Impossible, Jerry Maguire, Eyes Wide Shut, Magnolia, Mission: Impossible 2

Crystal, Billy: Rabbit Test, Animalympics, This Is Spinal Tap (cameo), Running Scared, The Princess Bride, Throw Momma From the Train, Memories of Me, When Harry Met Sally . . . , City Slickers, Mr. Saturday Night, City Slickers: The Legend of Curly's Gold, Forget Paris, Hamlet (1996), Fathers' Day, Deconstructing Harry, My Giant, Analyze This, Get Bruce (app)

Curtis, Jamie Lee: Halloween, The Fog, Prom Night, Terror Train, Roadgames, Halloween II, Love Letters (1983), Trading Places, Grandview, U.S.A., Perfect, As Summers Die, Amazing Grace and Chuck, A Man in Love, Dominick and Eugene, A Fish Called Wanda, Blue Steel, Queens Logic, My Girl, Forever Young, My Girl 2, Mother's Boys, True Lies, The Heidi Chronicles, House Arrest, Fierce Creatures, Homegrown, Halloween H2O: 20 Years Later, virus (1999), Drowning Mona

Curtis, Tony: Criss Cross, City Across the River, The Lady Gambles, Johnny Stool Pigeon, Francis, I Was a Shoplifter, Winchester '73, Sierra, Kansas Raiders, The Prince Who Was a Thief, Son of Ali Baba, Flesh and Fury, No Room for the Groom, Meet Danny Wilson (cameo), Houdini, All American, Forbidden (1953), Beachhead, Johnny Dark, The Black Shield of Falworth, So This Is Paris (1954), Six Bridges to Cross, The Purple Mask, The Square Jungle, Trapeze, The Rawhide Years, Mister Cory, Sweet Smell of Success, The Midnight Story, The Vikings, Kings Go Forth, The Defiant Ones, The Perfect Furlough, Some Like It Hot (1959), Operation Petticoat, Pepe (cameo), Who Was That Lady?, The Rat Race, Spartacus, The Great Impostor, The Outsider (1961), Taras Bulba, 40 Pounds of Trouble, The List of Adrian Messenger (cameo), Captain Newman, M.D., Wild and Wonderful, Paris—When It Sizzles (cameo), Goodbye Charlie, Sex and the Single Girl, The Great Race, Boeing Boeing, Chamber of Horrors (1966; cameo), Not With My Wife You Don't!, Arrivederci, Baby!, Don't Make Waves, On My Way to the Crusades I Met a Girl Who . . . , Rosemary's Baby (voice only), The Boston Strangler, Those Daring Young Men in Their Jaunty Jalopies, You Can't Win 'Em All, Suppose They Gave a War and Nobody Came?, Lepke, The Count of Monte Cristo (1975), The Last Tycoon, Casanova & Co., The Manitou, Sextette, The Bad News Bears Go to Japan, Little Miss Marker (1980), The Mirror Crack'd, Brainwaves, Insignificance, Balboa, Mafia Princess, Club Life, Midnight (1989), Tarzan in Manhattan, Thanksgiving Day, Christmas in Connecticut, Center of the Web, Naked in New York, The Celluloid Closet (app), Play It to the Bone (cameo)

Cusack, John: Class, Grandview, U.S.A., Sixteen Candles, Better Off Dead (1985), The Journey of Natty Gann, The Sure Thing, One Crazy Summer, Stand By Me, Hot Pursuit, Broadcast News (cameo), Eight Men Out, Tapeheads, Fat Man and Little Boy, Say Anything . . . , The Grifters, True Colors, Shadows and Fog, The Player (cameo), Roadside Prophets, Bob Roberts (cameo), Map of the Human Heart, Money for Nothing, The Road to Wellville, Bullets Over Broadway, Floundering, City Hall, Grosse Pointe Blank, Con Air, Midnight in the Garden of Good and Evil, Anastasia (1997), The Thin Red Line (1998), Pushing Tin, This is my Father, Being John Malkovich, Cradle Will Rock, High Fidelity

Cushing, Peter: The Man in the Iron Mask (1939; bit), A Chump at Oxford, Vigil in the Night, The Howards of Virginia (bit), They Dare Not Love (bit), Hamlet (1948), Moulin Rouge, The Black Knight, The End of the Affair, Magic Fire (bit), Alexander the Great, Time Without Pity, Curse of Frankenstein, The Abominable Snowman of the Himalayas, Horror of Dracula, Revenge of Frankenstein, Mania, John Paul Jones, The Hound of the Baskervilles (1959), The Mummy (1959), The Risk, The Brides of Dracula, Sword of Sherwood Forest, Fury at Smugglers' Bay, The Hellfire Club, The Naked Edge, Night Creatures, The Man Who Finally Died, The Evil of Frankenstein, The Gorgon, Dr. Terror's House of Horrors, She (1965), Dr. Who and the Daleks, The Skull, Island of Terror, Daleks—Invasion Earth 2150 A.D., Frankenstein Created Woman, The Mummy's Shroud, Island of the Burning Doomed, Torture Garden, Some May Live, Corruption, Frankenstein Must Be Destroyed, Scream and Scream Again, The Vampire Lovers, The House That Dripped Blood, One More Time (cameo), Bloodsuckers, I, Monster, Twins of Evil, Fear in the Night (1972), Asylum, Dr. Phibes Rises Again!, Dracula A.D. 1972, Nothing but the Night, Tales From the Crypt, Horror Express, The Creeping Flesh, Count Dracula and His Vampire Bride, And Now the Screaming Starts, From Beyond the Grave, Frankenstein and the Monster From Hell, The Beast Must Die, Legend of the Seven Golden Vampires, Madhouse (1974), Call Him Mr. Shatter, Legend of the Werewolf, The Ghoul (1975), Shock Waves, Land of the Minotaur, At the Earth's Core, Dirty Knight's Work, The Uncanny, Star Wars, An Arabian Adventure, Monster Island, A Tale of Two Cities (1980), House of the Long Shadows, Top Secret!, Sherlock Holmes and the Masks of Death, Sword of The Valiant, Biggles: Adventures in Time

Damon, Matt: The Good Mother (extra), Mystic Pizza, Rising Son, School Ties, Geronimo: An American Legend, The Good Old Boys, Courage Under Fire, Chasing Amy, The Rainmaker (1997), Good Will Hunting, Rounders (1998), Saving Private Ryan, Dogma, The Talented Mr. Ripley

Davis, Bette: Waterloo Bridge (1931), Hell's House, The Dark Horse, The Menace, The Man Who Played God, The Rich Are Always With Us, Cabin in the Cotton, Three on a Match, 20,000 Years in Sing Sing, Parachute Jumper, Ex-Lady, The Working Man, Bureau of Missing Persons, Fashions, The Big Shakedown, Jimmy the Gent, Fog Over Frisco, Housewife, Of Human Bondage (1934), Bordertown, Front Page Woman, Special Agent, Dangerous, The Girl From 10th Avenue, The Golden Arrow, The Petrified Forest, Satan Met a Lady, Kid Galahad (1937), Marked Woman, That Certain Woman, It's Love I'm After, Jezebel, The Sisters, The Private Lives of Elizabeth and Essex, Dark Victory, Juarez, The Old Maid, All This, and Heaven Too, The Letter, The Little Foxes, The Great Lie, Shining Victory (cameo), The Bride Came C.O.D., The Man Who Came to Dinner, In This Our Life, Now, Voyager, Watch on the Rhine, Thank Your Lucky Stars, Old Acquaintance, Mr. Skeffington, Hollywood Canteen, The Corn Is Green (1945), Deception (1946), A Stolen Life, Winter Meeting, June Bride, Beyond the Forest, All About Eve, Another Man's Poison, Payment on Demand, Phone Call From a Stranger, The Star, The Virgin Queen, The Catered Affair, Storm Center, The Scapegoat, John Paul Jones, Pocketful of Miracles (1961), What Ever Happened to Baby Jane?, The Empty Canvas, Dead Ringer, Hush . . . Hush, Sweet Charlotte, Where Love Has Gone, The Nanny, The Anniversary, Connecting Rooms, Bunny O'Hare, Madame Sin, Burnt Offerings, The Disappearance of Aimee, Return From Witch

Mountain, The Dark Secret of Harvest Home, Death on the Nile, Strangers: The Story of a Mother and Daughter, Skyward, The Watcher in the Woods, A Piano for Mrs. Cimino, Little Gloria . . . Happy at Last, Murder With Mirrors, As Summers Die, The Whales of August, Wicked Stepmother

Day, Doris: Romance on the High Seas, My Dream Is Yours, It's a Great Feeling, Young Man With a Horn, West Point Story, Tea for Two, Storm Warning, Lullaby of Broadway, Starlift, On Moonlight Bay, I'll See You in My Dreams, The Winning Team, April in Paris, By the Light of the Silvery Moon, Calamity Jane, Lucky Me, Young at Heart, Love Me or Leave Me, Julie, The Man Who Knew Too Much (1956), The Pajama Game, Teacher's Pet, The Tunnel of Love, It Happened to Jane, Pillow Talk, Midnight Lace, Please Don't Eat the Daisies, Lover Come Back (1961), That Touch of Mink, Billy Rose's Jumbo, The Thrill of It All, Move Over, Darling, Send Me No Flowers, Do Not Disturb, The Glass Bottom Boat, Caprice, The Ballad of Josie, Where Were You When the Lights Went Out?, With Six You Get Egg Roll

Day-Lewis, Daniel: Sunday, Bloody Sunday, Gandhi, The Bounty, The Insurance Man, My Beautiful Laundrette, A Room with a View, Stars and Bars, The Unbearable Lightness of Being, Eversmile, New Jersey, My Left Foot, The Last of the Mohicans (1992), The Age of Innocence (1993), In the Name of the Father, The Crucible (1996), The Boxer (1997)

Dean, James: Sailor Beware, Fixed Bayonets, Has Anybody Seen My Gal?, Trouble Along the Way (bit), East of Eden, Rebel Without a Cause, Giant

de Havilland, Olivia: A Midsummer Night's Dream (1935), Alibi Ike, The Irish in Us, Captain Blood (1935), Anthony Adverse, The Charge of the Light Brigade (1936), Call It a Day, The Great Garrick, It's Love I'm After, Gold Is Where You Find It, The Adventures of Robin Hood, Four's a Crowd, Hard to Get, Wings of the Navy, Dodge City, The Private Lives of Elizabeth and Essex, Gone With the Wind, Raffles (1940), My Love Came Back, Santa Fe Trail, Strawberry Blonde, Hold Back the Dawn, They Died With Their Boots On, The Male Animal, In This Our Life, Thank Your Lucky Stars (cameo), Princess O'Rourke, Government Girl, Devotion, The Well-Groomed Bride, To Each His Own, The Dark Mirror, The Snake Pit, The Heiress, My Cousin Rachel, That Lady, Not As a Stranger, The Ambassador's Daughter, The Proud Rebel, Libel, The Light in the Piazza, Lady in a Cage, Hush . . . Hush, Sweet Charlotte, The Adventurers (1970), Pope Joan, Airport '77, The Swarm, The Fifth Musketeer, Anastasia: The Mystery of Anna

Deneuve, Catherine: The Umbrellas of Cherbourg, Male Hunt, Repulsion, A Matter of Resistance, The Young Girls of Rochefort, Belle de Jour, Benjamin, Mayerling (1968), The April Fools, Mississippi Mermaid, Tristana, Donkey Skin, It Only Happens to Others, Dirty Money, La Grande Bourgeoise, Lovers Like Us, Hustle, March or Die, The Last Metro, Je Vous Aime, Choice of Arms, The Hunger, Fort Saganne, Let's Hope It's a Girl, Love Songs, Scene of the Crime (1986), Indochine, Ma Saison Préférée, The Convent, Les Voleurs, Genealogies of a Crime, East-West

De Niro, Robert: Greetings, The Wedding Party, Sam's Song, Hi, Mom!, Bloody Mama, Jennifer on My Mind, Born to Win, The Gang That Couldn't Shoot Straight, Bang the Drum Slowly, Mean Streets, The Godfather Part II, The Last Tycoon, Taxi Driver, 1900, New York New York, The Deer Hunter, Raging Bull, True Confessions, The King of Comedy, Once Upon a Time in America, Falling in Love, Brazil, The Mission, Angel Heart, Dear America: Letters Home From Vietnam, The Untouchables, Midnight Run, Jacknife, We're No Angels (1989), Stanley & Iris, GoodFellas, Awakenings, Guilty by Suspicion, Backdraft, Cape Fear (1991), Mistress, Night and the City (1992), Mad Dog and Glory, This Boy's Life, A Bronx Tale, Mary Shelley's Frankenstein, Casino, Heat (1995), The Fan (1996), Sleepers, Marvin's Room, Cop Land, Jackie Brown, Wag the Dog, Great Expectations (1998), Ronin, Analyze This, Flawless

Depardieu, Gérard: Going Places (1974), Stavisky . . ., Vincent, François, Paul, and the Others, Maitresse, The Last Woman, 1900, The Left-Handed Woman, Get Out Your Handkerchiefs, Bye Bye Monkey, Buffet Froid, Loulou, Mon Oncle d'Amerique, The Last Metro, Je Vous Aime, Choice of Arms, The Woman Next Door, The Return of Martin Guerre, Danton, The Moon in the Gutter, Les Compères, Police, Fort Saganne, One Woman or Two, Ménage, Jean de Florette, I Hate Actors (cameo), Under Satan's Sun, Camille Claudel, Too Beautiful for You, Cyrano de Bergerac (1990), Green Card, Uranus, Tous les Matins du Monde, 1492: Conquest of Paradise, Hélas Pour Moi, Germinal, My Father, the Hero, The Machine, Colonel Chabert, A Pure Formality, Horseman on the Roof, Bogus, Unhook the Stars, The Secret Agent (1996), Hamlet (1996), The Man in the Iron Mask (1998)

Depp, Johnny: A Nightmare on Elm Street, Private Resort, Platoon, Edward Scissorhands, Cry-Baby, Freddy's Dead: The Final Nightmare (cameo), Benny & Joon, What's Eating Gilbert Grape, Arizona Dream, Ed Wood, Don Juan DeMarco,

Nick of Time, Dead Man, Donnie Brasco, Fear and Loathing in Las Vegas, The Astronaut's Wife, The Ninth Gate, Sleepy Hollow, The Source

Dern, Laura: White Lightning, Alice Doesn't Live Here Anymore, Foxes, Ladies and Gentlemen, the Fabulous Stains, Teachers, Mask, Smooth Talk, Blue Velvet, Sister Sister, Haunted Summer, Fat Man and Little Boy, Wild at Heart, Rambling Rose, Afterburn, Jurassic Park, A Perfect World, Down Came a Blackbird, Ruby Ridge: An American Tragedy, Bastard Out of Carolina, Citizen Ruth, The Baby Dance, October Sky

DeVito, Danny: Lady Liberty, Hurry Up, or I'll Be 30, Scalawag, One Flew Over the Cuckoo's Nest, The Van (1976), The World's Greatest Lover, Goin' South, Going Ape!, Terms of Endearment, Romancing the Stone, The Ratings Game, Johnny Dangerously, Jewel of the Nile, Head Office, My Little Pony, Ruthless People, Wise Guys, Throw Momma From the Train (also dir), Tin Men, Twins, The War of the Roses (also dir), Other People's Money, Batman Returns, Hoffa (also dir), Jack the Bear, Last Action Hero (uncred voice only), Look Who's Talking Now, Renaissance Man, Junior, Get Shorty, Matilda (1996; also dir), Space Jam, Mars Attacks!, Hercules, L.A. Confidential, The Rainmaker (1997), Living Out Loud, Man on the Moon, Drowning Mona, The Big Kahuna, The Virgin Suicides, Screwed

Diaz, Cameron: The Mask (1994), The Last Supper, She's the One, Feeling Minnesota, Head Above Water, My Best Friend's Wedding, Keys to Tulsa, A Life Less Ordinary, Fear and Loathing in Las Vegas (cameo), There's Something About Mary, Very Bad Things, Being John Malkovich, Any Given Sunday

DiCaprio, Leonardo: Critters 3, Poison Ivy (1992), What's Eating Gilbert Grape, This Boy's Life, Total Eclipse, The Quick and the Dead, The Basketball Diaries, Romeo & Juliet, Marvin's Room, Titanic (1997), The Man in the Iron Mask (1998), Celebrity, The Beach

Dietrich, Marlene: The Joyless Street (extra), The Blue Angel (1930), Morocco, Dishonored, Shanghai Express, Blonde Venus, Song of Songs, The Scarlet Empress, The Devil Is a Woman (1935), Desire, The Garden of Allah, Knight Without Armour, Angel (1937), Destry Rides Again, Seven Sinners, The Flame of New Orleans, Manpower, The Lady Is Willing, The Spoilers (1942), Pittsburgh, Follow the Boys (1944), Kismet (1944), Golden Earrings, A Foreign Affair, Jigsaw (1949; cameo), Stage Fright, No Highway in the Sky, Rancho Notorious, Around the World in Eighty Days (cameo), The Monte Carlo Story, Witness for the Prosecution, Touch of Evil (cameo), Judgment at Nuremberg, The Black Fox, Paris—When It Sizzles (cameo), Just a Gigolo, Marlene

Dillon, Matt: Over the Edge, Little Darlings, My Bodyguard, Liar's Moon, Tex, The Outsiders, Rumble Fish, The Flamingo Kid, Rebel (1985), Target (1985), Native Son (1986), The Big Town, Dear America: Letters Home From Vietnam, Kansas, Bloodhounds of Broadway (1989), Drugstore Cowboy, A Kiss Before Dying (1991), Truth or Dare, Singles, Mr. Wonderful, Golden Gate, The Saint of Fort Washington, To Die For (1995), Frankie Starlight, Beautiful Girls, Grace of My Heart, Albino Alligator, In & Out, Wild Things, There's Something About Mary

Douglas, Kirk: The Strange Love of Martha Ivers, I Walk Alone, Out of the Past, Mourning Becomes Electra, My Dear Secretary, The Walls of Jericho, A Letter to Three Wives, Champion, Young Man With a Horn, The Glass Menagerie (1950), Along the Great Divide, The Big Carnival, Detective Story, The Big Sky, The Big Trees, The Bad and the Beautiful, The Story of Three Loves, The Juggler, Act of Love, 20,000 Leagues Under the Sea, Ulysses (1955), The Racers, Man Without a Star, The Indian Fighter, Lust for Life, Top Secret Affair, Gunfight at the O.K. Corral, Paths of Glory, The Vikings, Last Train From Gun Hill, The Devil's Disciple, Strangers When We Meet, Spartacus, The Last Sunset, Town Without Pity, Lonely Are the Brave, Two Weeks in Another Town, The Hook, The List of Adrian Messenger, For Love or Money (1963), Seven Days in May, In Harm's Way, The Heroes of Telemark, Cast a Giant Shadow, Is Paris Burning?, The Way West, The War Wagon, A Lovely Way to Die, The Brotherhood, The Arrangement, There Was a Crooked Man, The Light at the Edge of the World, A Gunfight, To Catch a Spy, The Master Touch, Scalawag, Mousey, Jacqueline Susann's Once Is Not Enough, Posse (1975), The Chosen (1978), The Fury, The Villain, Home Movies, Saturn 3, The Final Countdown, The Man from Snowy River, Remembrance of Love, Eddie Macon's Run, Draw!, Amos, Tough Guys, Queenie, Oscar (cameo), Greedy, Diamonds (1999)

Douglas, Michael: Hail, Hero!, Adam at 6 A.M., Summertree, Napoleon and Samantha, Coma, The China Syndrome, Running, It's My Turn, Tell Me a Riddle, The Star Chamber, Romancing the Stone, A Chorus Line, The Jewel of the Nile, Fatal Attraction, Wall Street, Black Rain (1989), The War of the Roses, Shining Through, Basic Instinct, Falling Down, Disclosure, The American President, The Ghost and the Darkness, The Game, A Perfect Murder, Wonder Boys

Dreyfuss, Richard: Valley of the Dolls, The Graduate (bit), The Young Runaways,

Hello Down There, Dillinger (1973), American Graffiti, The Apprenticeship of Duddy Kravitz, The Second Coming of Suzanne, Jaws, Inserts, Close Encounters of the Third Kind, The Goodbye Girl, The Big Fix, The Competition, Whose Life Is It Anyway?, The Buddy System, Down and Out in Beverly Hills, Stand By Me, Tin Men, Stakeout, Nuts, Moon Over Parador, Let It Ride, Always (1989), Postcards From the Edge, Once Around, Rosencrantz and Guildenstern Are Dead, What About Bob?, Prisoner of Honor, Lost in Yonkers, Another Stakeout, Silent Fall, The American President, Mr. Holland's Opus, James and the Giant Peach, Mad Dog Time, Night Falls on Manhattan, Jack London's Call of the Wild (narr), Krippendorf's Tribe, Lansky

Dunaway, Faye: Hurry Sundown, The Happening, Bonnie and Clyde, The Thomas Crown Affair (1968), The Extraordinary Seaman, A Place for Lovers, The Arrangement, Little Big Man, Puzzle of a Downfall Child, Doc, The Deadly Trap, Oklahoma Crude, The Three Musketeers (1974), The Towering Inferno, Chinatown, The Four Musketeers, Three Days of the Condor, Voyage of the Damned, Network, The Disappearance of Aimee, Eyes of Laura Mars, The Champ (1979), The First Deadly Sin, Evita Peron, Mommie Dearest, The Wicked Lady (1983), Ordeal by Innocence, Supergirl, Barfly, Burning Secret, The Gamble, Midnight Crossing, Cold Sassy Tree, Wait Until Spring, Bandini, The Handmaid's Tale, The Two Jakes, Double Edge, The Temp, Arizona Dream, Don Juan DeMarco, Dunston Checks In, The Chamber, Drunks, Albino Alligator, Twilight of the Golds, The Thomas Crown Affair (1999), The Messenger: The Story of Joan of Arc

Dunne, Irene: Consolation Marriage, Cimarron (1931), Bachelor Apartment, Symphony of Six Million, Thirteen Women, Back Street (1932), The Secret of Madame Blanche, The Silver Cord, Ann Vickers, If I Were Free, This Man Is Mine, The Age of Innocence (1934), Magnificent Obsession (1935), Sweet Adeline, Roberta, Show Boat (1936), Theodora Goes Wild, High, Wide, and Handsome, The Awful Truth, Joy of Living, Invitation to Happiness, Love Affair (1939), When Tomorrow Comes, My Favorite Wife, Penny Serenade, Unfinished Business (1941), Lady in a Jam, A Guy Named Joe, Together Again, The White Cliffs of Dover, Over 21, Anna and the King of Siam, Life With Father, I Remember Mama, Never a Dull Moment (1950), The Mudlark, It Grows on Trees

Durbin, Deanna: Three Smart Girls, One Hundred Men and a Girl, That Certain Age, Mad About Music, Three Smart Girls Grow Up, First Love (1939), Spring Parade, It's a Date, Nice Girl?, It Started With Eve, The Amazing Mrs. Holiday, Hers to Hold, His Butler's Sister, Christmas Holiday, Can't Help Singing, Lady on a Train, Because of Him, I'll Be Yours, Something in the Wind, Up in Central Park, For the Love of Mary

Duvall, Robert: To Kill a Mockingbird, Captain Newman, M.D., Nightmare in the Sun, The Chase (1966), Countdown, The Detective (1968), Bullitt, True Grit, The Rain People, MASH, The Revolutionary, THX 1138, Lawman, The Godfather, Tomorrow, The Great Northfield, Minnesota Raid, Joe Kidd, Badge 373, Lady Ice, The Conversation, The Outfit, The Godfather Part II, Breakout (1975), The Killer Elite, Network, The Seven-Per-Cent Solution, The Eagle Has Landed, The Greatest, The Betsy, Invasion of the Body Snatchers (1978; cameo), Apocalypse Now, The Great Santini, True Confessions, The Pursuit of D. B. Cooper, Angelo, My Love (dir, pro, scr), Tender Mercies, Hotel Colonial, The Stone Boy, The Natural, Belizaire the Cajun, The Lightship, Let's Get Harry, Colors, The Handmaid's Tale, Days of Thunder, A Show of Force, Convicts, Rambling Rose, The Plague, Newsies, Stalin, Falling Down, Geronimo: An American Legend, Wrestling Ernest Hemingway, The Paper, The Stars Fell on Henrietta, Something to Talk About, The Scarlet Letter (1995), A Family Thing, Phenomenon, Sling Blade, The Man Who Captured Eichmann, The Apostle, The Gingerbread Man, Deep Impact, A Civil Action

Eastwood, Clint: Revenge of the Creature, Francis in the Navy, Lady Godiva, Tarantula, Away All Boats, Never Say Goodbye (1956), Star in the Dust, The First Traveling Saleslady, Escapade in Japan, Lafayette Escadrille, Ambush at Cimarron Pass, Fistful of Dollars, For a Few Dollars More, The Good, the Bad and the Ugly, Hang 'Em High, Coogan's Bluff, Where Eagles Dare, Paint Your Wagon, Two Mules for Sister Sara, Kelly's Heroes, The Beguiled, Dirty Harry, Play Misty for Me (also dir), Joe Kidd, High Plains Drifter (also dir), Magnum Force, Breezy (dir), Thunderbolt and Lightfoot, The Eiger Sanction (also dir), The Outlaw—Josey Wales (also dir), The Enforcer (1976), The Gauntlet (also dir), Every Which Way But Loose, Escape From Alcatraz, Bronco Billy (also dir), Any Which Way You Can, Firefox (1982; also dir), Honkytonk Man (also dir), Sudden Impact (also dir), City Heat, Tightrope, Pale Rider (also dir), Heartbreak Ridge (also dir), Bird (dir), The Dead Pool, Pink Cadillac, White Hunter, Black Heart (also dir), The Rookie (1990; also dir), Unforgiven (also dir), In the Line of Fire, A Perfect World (also dir), Casper (cameo), The Bridges of Madison County (also dir), Absolute Power (also dir), Midnight in the Garden of Good and Evil (dir), True Crime (also dir)

Fairbanks, Douglas: Intolerance (cameo),

Robin Hood (1922), The Mark of Zorro (1920), The Thief of Bagdad (1924), Don Q, Son of Zorro, The Black Pirate, The Gaucho, Show People (cameo), The Iron Mask, The Taming of the Shrew (1929), Reaching for the Moon, Mr. Robinson Crusoe, The Private Life of Don Juan, Ali Baba Goes to Town (cameo)

Fairbanks, Douglas, Jr.: A Woman of Affairs, Our Modern Maidens, The Dawn Patrol (1930), Outward Bound, Little Caesar, Chances, I Like Your Nerve, Union Depot, It's Tough to Be Famous, Love Is a Racket, Scarlet Dawn, Parachute Jumper, The Life of Jimmy Dolan, The Narrow Corner, Captured, Morning Glory, Catherine the Great, Success at Any Price, Mimi, The Prisoner of Zenda (1937), The Joy of Living, The Rage of Paris, Having Wonderful Time, The Young in Heart, Gunga Din, The Sun Never Sets, Rulers of the Sea, Green Hell, Safari (1940), Angels Over Broadway, The Corsican Brothers (1941), Sinbad the Sailor, The Exile, That Lady in Ermine, The Fighting O'Flynn, State Secret, Mister Drake's Duck, Ghost Story (1981)

Faye, Alice: George White's Scandals (1934), She Learned About Sailors, 365 Nights in Hollywood, George White's Scandals (1935), Music Is Magic, Every Night at Eight, Poor Little Rich Girl, Sing, Baby, Sing, King of Burlesque, Stowaway, On the Avenue, Wake Up and Live, You Can't Have Everything, You're a Sweetheart, In Old Chicago, Sally, Irene and Mary, Alexander's Ragtime Band, Tail Spin, Hollywood Cavalcade, Barricade (1939), Rose of Washington Square, Lillian Russell, Little Old New York, Tin Pan Alley, That Night in Rio, The Great American Broadcast, Weekend in Havana, Hello Frisco, Hello, The Gang's All Here, Four Jills in a Jeep, Fallen Angel (1945), State Fair (1962), Won Ton Ton, the Dog Who Saved Hollywood, The Magic of Lassie

Field, Sally: The Way West, Maybe I'll Come Home in the Spring, Stay Hungry, Sybil, Smokey and the Bandit, Heroes, Hooper, The End, Norma Rae, Beyond the Poseidon Adventure, Smokey and the Bandit II, Back Roads, Absence of Malice, Kiss Me Goodbye, Places in the Heart, Murphy's Romance, Surrender (1987), Punchline, Steel Magnolias, Not Without My Daughter, Soapdish, Homeward Bound: The Incredible Journey, Mrs. Doubtfire, Forrest Gump, Eye for an Eye, Homeward Bound II: Lost in San Francisco, The Christmas Tree (dir), A Cooler Climate, Where the Heart Is (2000)

Fields, W. C.: Sally of the Sawdust, Running Wild (1927), Her Majesty, Love, If I Had a Million, Million Dollar Legs (1932), International House, Tillie and Gus, Alice in Wonderland (1933), Six of a Kind, You're Telling Me! (1934), The Old Fashioned Way, It's a Gift, Mrs. Wiggs of the Cabbage Patch, David Copperfield (1935), Mississippi, The Man on the Flying Trapeze, Poppy, The Big Broadcast of 1938, You Can't Cheat an Honest Man, My Little Chickadee, The Bank Dick, Never Give a Sucker an Even Break, Tales of Manhattan, Follow the Boys (1944), Song of the Open Road, Sensations of 1945

Finney, Albert: The Entertainer, Saturday Night and Sunday Morning, Tom Jones, The Victors, Night Must Fall (1964), Two for the Road, Charlie Bubbles, The Picasso Summer, Scrooge (1970), Gumshoe, Murder on the Orient Express, The Adventure of Sherlock Holmes' Smarter Brother (cameo), The Duellists, Loophole (1980), Looker, Wolfen, Shoot the Moon, Annie, The Dresser, Pope John Paul II, Under the Volcano, Orphans, The Endless Game, Miller's Crossing, The Playboys, Rich in Love, The Browning Version (1994), A Man of No Importance, The Run of the Country, Washington Square, Breakfast of Champions, Simpatico, Erin Brockovich

Fishburne, Laurence (billed as Larry until 1993): Cornbread, Earl and Me, Apocalypse Now, Willie and Phil, A Rumor of War, Death Wish II, Rumble Fish, For Us, the Living, The Cotton Club, The Color Purple, Quicksilver, Band of the Hand, A Nightmare on Elm Street 3: Dream Warriors, Gardens of Stone, School Daze, Red Heat, King of New York, Decoration Day, Class Action, Cadence, Boyz N the Hood, Deep Cover, What's Love Got to Do With It, Searching for Bobby Fischer, Higher Learning, Bad Company (1995), Just Cause, The Tuskegee Airmen, Othello (1995), Fled, Miss Evers' Boys, Hoodlum, Event Horizon, The Matrix

Flynn, Errol: The Case of the Curious Bride, Captain Blood (1935), The Charge of the Light Brigade (1936), Green Light, The Prince and the Pauper (1937), Another Dawn, The Perfect Specimen, The Adventures of Robin Hood, The Sisters, Four's a Crowd, The Dawn Patrol (1938), Dodge City, The Private Lives of Elizabeth and Essex, Virginia City, The Sea Hawk (1940), Santa Fe Trail, Footsteps in the Dark, Dive Bomber, They Died With Their Boots On, Desperate Journey, Gentleman Jim, Edge of Darkness, Thank Your Lucky Stars (cameo), Northern Pursuit, Uncertain Glory, Objective, Burma!, San Antonio, Never Say Goodbye (1946), Cry Wolf, Escape Me Never, Silver River, Adventures of Don Juan, It's a Great Feeling (cameo), That Forsyte Woman, Montana (1950), Rocky Mountain, Kim (1950), Adventures of Captain Fabian, Mara Maru, Against All Flags, The Master of Ballantrae (1953), Crossed Swords (1954), Let's Make Up, The Warriors (1955), Istanbul (1957), The Big Boodle, The Sun Also Rises, Too Much, Too Soon, The Roots of Heaven, Cuban Rebel Girls

Fonda, Bridget: Aria, You Can't Hurry

Love, Shag, Scandal, Strapless, Frankenstein Unbound, The Godfather Part III, Leather Jackets, Doc Hollywood, Drop Dead Fred (cameo), Iron Maze, Singles, Single White Female, Army of Darkness (cameo), Point of No Return, Bodies, Rest & Motion, It Could Happen to You, Little Buddha, The Road to Wellville, Camilla, Balto, Rough Magic, City Hall, Grace of My Heart, Touch, Jackie Brown, Mr. Jealousy, A Simple Plan, Lake Placid

Fonda, Henry: The Farmer Takes a Wife (1935), Way Down East (1935), I Dream Too Much, The Trail of the Lonesome Pine, The Moon's Our Home, Slim, Wings of the Morning, That Certain Woman, You Only Live Once, Blockade, I Met My Love Again, The Mad Miss Manton, Jezebel, Spawn of the North, Jesse James, The Story of Alexander Graham Bell, Let Us Live, Drums Along the Mohawk, Young Mr. Lincoln, The Grapes of Wrath, The Return of Frank James, Lillian Russell, Chad Hanna, The Lady Eve, Wild Geese Calling, You Belong to Me, Rings on Her Fingers, The Male Animal, The Magnificent Dope, The Big Street, Tales of Manhattan, The Ox-Bow Incident, The Immortal Sergeant, My Darling Clementine, The Fugitive (1947), Daisy Kenyon, The Long Night, Fort Apache, On Our Merry Way, Jigsaw (1949; cameo), Main Street to Broadway Mister Roberts, War and Peace (1956), The Wrong Man, 12 Angry Men (1957), The Tin Star, Stage Struck (1958), Warlock (1959), The Man Who Understood Women, Advise & Consent, The Longest Day, How the West Was Won, Spencer's Mountain, The Best Man, Fail-Safe, Sex and the Single Girl, The Rounders, In Harm's Way, Battle of the Bulge, The Dirty Game, A Big Hand for the Little Lady, Welcome to Hard Times, Stranger on the Run, Firecreek, Madigan, Once Upon a Time in the West, Yours, Mine and Ours, The Boston Strangler, Too Late the Hero, There Was a Crooked Man, The Cheyenne Social Club, Sometimes a Great Notion, Ash Wednesday, The Red Pony (1973), Night Flight From Moscow, My Name Is Nobody, Midway, Tentacles, Rollercoaster, The Great Battle, The Swarm, Fedora (cameo), Wanda Nevada (cameo), City on Fire, Meteor, Gideon's Trumpet, On Golden Pond

Fonda, Jane: Tall Story, The Chapman Report, A Walk on the Wild Side, Period of Adjustment, In the Cool of the Day, Sunday in New York, Joy House, Circle of Love, Cat Ballou, The Chase (1966), The Game Is Over, Any Wednesday, Hurry Sundown, Barefoot in the Park, Spirits of the Dead, Barbarella, They Shoot Horses, Don't They?, Klute, F.T.A., Steelyard Blues, A Doll's House (1973), The Blue Bird (1976), Fun With Dick and Jane, Julia, Coming Home, Comes a Horseman, California Suite, The China Syndrome, The Electric Horseman, 9 to 5, No Nukes, On Golden Pond, Rollover, The Dollmaker, Agnes of God, The Morning After, Old Gringo, Stanley and Iris

Fontaine, Joan: No More Ladies (as Joan Burfield), Quality Street, A Damsel in Distress, You Can't Beat Love, Maid's Night Out, Gunga Din, Man of Conquest, The Women, Rebecca, Suspicion, This Above All, The Constant Nymph, Jane Eyre (1944), Frenchman's Creek, The Affairs of Susan, From This Day Forward, Ivy, Letter From an Unknown Woman, Kiss the Blood Off My Hands, The Emperor Waltz, You Gotta Stay Happy, Born to Be Bad, September Affair, Darling, How Could You!, Othello (1952; cameo), Something to Live For, Ivanhoe (1952), Decameron Nights, Flight to Tangier, The Bigamist, Casanova's Big Night, Serenade, Beyond a Reasonable Doubt, Island in the Sun, Until They Sail, A Certain Smile, Voyage to the Bottom of the Sea, Tender Is the Night, The Devil's Own (1966)

Ford, Glenn: Heaven With a Barbed Wire Fence, Men Without Souls, Blondie Plays Cupid, The Lady in Question, Texas, So Ends Our Night, The Adventures of Martin Eden, Flight Lieutenant, Destroyer, The Desperadoes, Gilda, A Stolen Life, Gallant Journey, Framed (1947), The Mating of Millie, The Loves of Carmen, The Return of October, The Man From Colorado, The Undercover Man, Lust for Gold, Mr. Soft Touch, The Doctor and the Girl, The White Tower, Convicted, The Flying Missile, The Redhead and the Cowboy, Follow the Sun, The Secret of Convict Lake, Young Man with Ideas, The Green Glove, Affair in Trinidad, The Man From the Alamo, Terror on a Train, Plunder of the Sun, The Big Heat, Appointment in Honduras, Human Desire, The Americano, The Violent Men, Interrupted Melody, Blackboard Jungle, Trial, Ransom (1956), Jubal, The Fastest Gun Alive, The Teahouse of the August Moon, 3:10 to Yuma, Don't Go Near the Water, The Sheepman, Cowboy, Torpedo Run, Imitation General, It Started With a Kiss, The Gazebo, Cimarron (1960), Cry for Happy, Pocketful of Miracles, The Four Horsemen of the Apocalypse (1962), Experiment in Terror, The Courtship of Eddie's Father, Love Is a Ball, Advance to the Rear, Fate Is the Hunter, Dear Heart, The Rounders, The Money Trap, Is Paris Burning?, Rage (1966), A Time for Killing, The Last Challenge, Day of the Evil Gun, Heaven With a Gun, Smith!, Santee, Midway, Superman, The Sacketts, The Visitor, Virus, Happy Birthday to Me, Border Shootout

Ford, Harrison: Dead Heat on a Merry-Go-Round, Luv, A Time for Killing, Journey to Shiloh, Getting Straight, American Graffiti, The Conversation, Star Wars, Heroes, Force 10 From Navarone, Hanover Street, Apocalypse Now (cameo), More American Graffiti (cameo), The Frisco Kid, The Empire Strikes

Back, Raiders of the Lost Ark, Blade Runner, Return of the Jedi, Indiana Jones and the Temple of Doom, Witness, The Mosquito Coast, Frantic (1988), Working Girl, Indiana Jones and the Last Crusade, Presumed Innocent, Regarding Henry, Patriot Games, The Fugitive (1993), Jimmy Hollywood (cameo), Clear and Present Danger, Sabrina (1995), The Devil's Own (1997), Air Force One, Six Days Seven Nights, Random Hearts

Foster, Jodie: Napoleon and Samantha, Kansas City Bomber, Tom Sawyer (1973), One Little Indian, Alice Doesn't Live Here Anymore, Echoes of a Summer, Taxi Driver, Bugsy Malone, The Little Girl Who Lives Down the Lane, Freaky Friday, Candleshoe, Carny, Foxes, O'Hara's Wife, Svengali (1983), The Hotel New Hampshire, Mesmerized, Siesta, Five Corners, Stealing Home, The Accused (1988), Backtrack (1989), The Silence of the Lambs, Little Man Tate (also dir), Shadows and Fog, Sommersby, It Was a Wonderful Life, Maverick, Nell, Home for the Holidays (dir, coprod), Contact, Anna and the King

Freeman, Morgan: Who Says I Can't Ride a Rainbow, Attica, Brubaker, Eyewitness (1981), Death of a Prophet, Harry and Son, Teachers, Marie, That Was Then, This Is Now, Resting Place, Street Smart, Clean and Sober, Lean on Me, Driving Miss Daisy, Glory (1989), Johnny Handsome, Bonfire of the Vanities, Robin Hood: Prince of Thieves, The Power of One, Unforgiven, Bopha! (dir), The Shawshank Redemption, Outbreak, Se7en, Moll Flanders, Chain Reaction (1996), Kiss the Girls, The Long Way Home (narr), Amistad, Hard Rain, Deep Impact

Gable, Clark: The Merry Widow (extra), The Johnstown Flood (bit), The Easiest Way, The Painted Desert, Dance, Fools, Dance, The Finger Points, Laughing Sinners, The Secret Six, Night Nurse, A Free Soul, Sporting Blood, Susan Lenox: Her Fall and Rise, Possessed (1931), Hell Divers (1932), Polly of the Circus, Strange Interlude, Red Dust, No Man of Her Own (1932), Hold Your Man, The White Sister, Dancing Lady, Men in White, It Happened One Night, Manhattan Melodrama, Chained, Forsaking All Others, After Office Hours, The Call of the Wild (1935), China Seas, Mutiny on the Bounty (1935), Wife vs. Secretary, San Francisco, Cain and Mabel, Love on the Run (1936), Parnell, Saratoga, Too Hot to Handle (1938), Test Pilot, Idiot's Delight, Gone With the Wind, Strange Cargo, Boom Town, Comrade X, They Met in Bombay, Honky Tonk, Somewhere I'll Find You, Adventure, The Hucksters, Command Decision, Homecoming, Any Number Can Play, Key to the City, To Please a Lady, Across the Wide Missouri, Callaway Went Thataway (cameo), Lone Star (1952), Never Let Me Go, Mogambo, Betrayed (1954), Soldier of Fortune, The Tall Men, The King and Four Queens, Band of Angels, Teacher's Pet, Run Silent, Run Deep, But Not for Me, It Started in Naples, The Misfits

Garbo, Greta: The Atonement of Gosta Berling, The Joyless Street, Torrent, The Temptress, Flesh and the Devil, Love, The Mysterious Lady, A Woman of Affairs, The Kiss (1929), Wild Orchids, The Single Standard, Anna Christie, Romance, Susan Lenox: Her Fall and Rise, Inspiration, Mata Hari (1932), Grand Hotel, As You Desire Me, Queen Christina, The Painted Veil, Anna Karenina (1935), Camille, Conquest, Ninotchka, Two-Faced Woman

Gardner, Ava: We Were Dancing, Joe Smith, American, Kid Glove Killer, Calling Dr. Gillespie, Reunion in France, Pilot #5, Lost Angel, DuBarry Was a Lady (bit), Ghosts on the Loose, Young Ideas, Hitler's Madman, Swing Fever, Two Girls and a Sailor, Three Men in White, Blonde Fever, Maisie Goes to Reno, Music for Millions, She Went to the Races, The Killers (1946), Whistle Stop, The Hucksters, Singapore, One Touch of Venus, The Bribe, East Side, West Side, The Great Sinner, My Forbidden Past, Pandora and the Flying Dutchman, Show Boat (1951), Lone Star (1952), The Snows of Kilimanjaro, Ride, Vaquero!, The Band Wagon (cameo), Mogambo, Knights of the Round Table, The Barefoot Contessa, Bhowani Junction, The Little Hut, The Sun Also Rises, The Naked Maja, On the Beach, The Angel Wore Red, 55 Days at Peking, Seven Days in May, The Night of the Iguana, The Bible, Mayerling (1968), The Ballad of Tam Lin, The Life and Times of Judge Roy Bean, Earthquake, Permission to Kill, The Blue Bird (1976), The Cassandra Crossing, The Sentinel, City on Fire, The Kidnapping of the President, Priest of Love, The Long Hot Summer (1985)

Garfield, John: Footlight Parade (extra?), Four Daughters, Blackwell's Island, Juarez, They Made Me a Criminal, Daughters Courageous, Dust Be My Destiny, Saturday's Children, Flowing Gold, East of the River, Castle on the Hudson, The Sea Wolf (1941), Out of the Fog, Tortilla Flat, Dangerously They Live, Air Force, Destination Tokyo, Thank Your Lucky Stars, The Fallen Sparrow, Between Two Worlds, Hollywood Canteen, Pride of the Marines, The Postman Always Rings Twice (1946), Nobody Lives Forever, Humoresque, Daisy Kenyon (cameo), Body and Soul (1947), Gentleman's Agreement, Force of Evil, We Were Strangers, Jigsaw (1949; cameo), Under My Skin, The Breaking Point, He Ran All the Way

Garland, Judy: Pigskin Parade, Thoroughbreds Don't Cry, Broadway Melody of 1938, Everybody Sing, Listen, Darling, Love Finds Andy Hardy, Babes in Arms, The Wizard of Oz, Andy Hardy Meets Debutante, Little Nellie Kelly, Strike Up the Band, Babes on Broadway, Life Begins for

Andy Hardy, Ziegfeld Girl, For Me and My Gal, Girl Crazy (1943), Presenting Lily Mars, Thousands Cheer, Meet Me in St. Louis, The Clock, The Harvey Girls, Till the Clouds Roll By, Ziegfeld Follies, Easter Parade, The Pirate, Words and Music, In the Good Old Summertime, Summer Stock, A Star Is Born (1954), Pepe (cameo), Judgment at Nuremberg, Gay Purr-ee, A Child Is Waiting, I Could Go on Singing

Garner, James: The Girl He Left Behind, Toward the Unknown, Sayonara, Shoot Out at Medicine Bend, Darby's Rangers, Cash McCall, Up Periscope, The Children's Hour, Boys' Night Out, The Great Escape, Move Over, Darling, The Thrill of It All, The Wheeler Dealers, 36 Hours, The Americanization of Emily, The Art of Love, Mister Buddwing, Duel at Diablo, Grand Prix, A Man Could Get Killed, Hour of the Gun, How Sweet It Is!, The Pink Jungle, Marlowe, Support Your Local Sheriff!, A Man Called Sledge, Skin Game, Support Your Local Gunfighter, They Only Kill Their Masters, One Little Indian, The Castaway Cowboy, H.E.A.L.T.H., The Fan (1981), The Long Summer of George Adams, Victor/Victoria, Tank, Heartsounds, Murphy's Romance, The Promise, Sunset, My Name Is Bill W., Decoration Day, The Distinguished Gentleman, Fire in the Sky, Barbarians at the Gate, Breathing Lessons, Maverick, My Fellow Americans, Dead Silence, Twilight, Legalese

Garson, Greer: Goodbye, Mr. Chips (1939), Remember?, Pride and Prejudice, Blossoms in the Dust, When Ladies Meet (1941), Mrs. Miniver, Random Harvest, Madame Curie, The Youngest Profession, Mrs. Parkington, Adventure, The Valley of Decision, Desire Me, Julia Misbehaves, That Forsyte Woman, The Miniver Story, The Law and the Lady, Julius Caesar (1953), Scandal at Scourie, Her 12 Men, Strange Lady in Town, Pepe (cameo), Sunrise at Campobello, The Singing Nun, The Happiest Millionaire, Little Women (1978)

Gere, Richard: Report to the Commissioner, Baby Blue Marine, Looking for Mr. Goodbar, Bloodbrothers, Days of Heaven, Yanks, American Gigolo, An Officer and a Gentleman, Beyond the Limit, Breathless (1983), The Cotton Club, King David, No Mercy, Power, Miles From Home, Internal Affairs, Pretty Woman, Monster in a Box, Rhapsody in August, Final Analysis, Sommersby, And the Band Played On, Mr. Jones, Intersection, First Knight, Primal Fear, Red Corner, The Jackal, Runaway Bride

Gibson, Mel: Summer City, Tim, Mad Max, Chain Reaction (1980), Attack Force Z, Gallipoli, The Road Warrior, The Year of Living Dangerously, The Bounty, Mrs. Soffel, The River (1984), Mad Max Beyond Thunderdome, Lethal Weapon, Tequila Sunrise, Lethal Weapon 2, Bird on a Wire, Air America, Hamlet (1990), Lethal Weapon 3, Forever Young, The Man Without a Face (also dir), Maverick, Casper (cameo), Braveheart (also dir), Pocahontas, Ransom (1996), Fathers' Day (cameo), Conspiracy Theory, Fairy Tale: A True Story (cameo), Lethal Weapon 4, Payback

Gish, Lillian: The Birth of a Nation, Intolerance, Hearts of the World, Broken Blossoms, Way Down East (1920), Orphans of the Storm, La Boheme, The Scarlet Letter (1926), The Wind (1928), One Romantic Night, His Double Life, The Commandos Strike at Dawn, Top Man, Miss Susie Slagle's, Duel in the Sun, Portrait of Jennie, The Cobweb, Night of the Hunter, Orders to Kill, The Unforgiven, Follow Me, Boys!, Warning Shot, The Comedians, A Wedding (1978), Hambone and Hillie, Adventures of Huckleberry Finn (1985), Sweet Liberty, The Whales of August

Glover, Danny: Escape From Alcatraz, Chu Chu and the Philly Flash, Out, Iceman, Places in the Heart, The Color Purple, Silverado, Witness, Lethal Weapon, Mandela, Bat*21, Dead Man Out, Lethal Weapon 2, Predator 2, To Sleep With Anger, Flight of the Intruder, A Rage in Harlem, Pure Luck, Grand Canyon, Lethal Weapon 3, Bopha!, The Saint of Fort Washington, Maverick (cameo), Angels in the Outfield (1994), Operation Dumbo Drop, Switchback, Wild America (cameo), Buffalo Soldiers, Gone Fishin', The Rainmaker (1997, unbilled), Lethal Weapon 4, Antz, Beloved, The Prince of Egypt, Freedom Song

Goldberg, Whoopi: The Color Purple, Jumpin' Jack Flash, Burglar, Fatal Beauty, The Telephone, Clara's Heart, Kiss Shot, Beverly Hills Brats (cameo), Ghost, Homer and Eddie, The Long Walk Home, House Party 2 (cameo), Soapdish, The Player, Sister Act, Wisecracks, Sarafina!, Made in America, National Lampoon's Loaded Weapon I (cameo), Sister Act 2: Back in the Habit, Naked in New York, The Lion King, The Little Rascals (cameo), Corrina, Corrina, Star Trek: Generations, The Pagemaster, Boys on the Side, Moonlight and Valentino, The Celluloid Closet (app only), Eddie, Theodore Rex, Bordello of Blood (cameo), Bogus, The Associate, Ghosts of Mississippi, In & Out (cameo), An Alan Smithee Film: Burn Hollywood Burn, How Stella Got Her Groove Back, Rudolph the Red-Nosed Reindeer: The Movie, The Deep End of the Ocean, Girl, Interrupted, Get Bruce (app)

Goldblum, Jeff: Death Wish, California Split, Nashville, Next Stop, Greenwich Village, Special Delivery (1976), St. Ives, Annie Hall, Between the Lines, The Sentinel, Invasion of the Body Snatchers (1978), Remember My Name, Thank God, It's Friday, Threshold, The Big Chill, The Right

Stuff, The Adventures of Buckaroo Banzai: Across the Eighth Dimension, Into the Night, Silverado, Transylvania 6-5000, The Fly (1986), Beyond Therapy, Vibes, Earth Girls Are Easy, Twisted Obsession, The Tall Guy, Mister Frost, Fathers and Sons, The Player (cameo), Deep Cover, The Favor, The Watch and the Very Big Fish, Jurassic Park, Lush Life, Hideaway, Nine Months, Powder, The Great White Hype, Independence Day (1996), Mad Dog Time, The Lost World: Jurassic Park, Holy Man, The Prince of Egypt

Goodman, John: C.H.U.D., Revenge of the Nerds, Maria's Lovers, Sweet Dreams, True Stories, Raising Arizona, Burglar, The Big Easy, Punchline, The Wrong Guys, Everybody's All-American, Sea of Love, Always (1989), Stella (1990), Arachnophobia, King Ralph, Barton Fink, The Babe, Matinee, Born Yesterday (1993), We're Back: A Dinosaur's Story, The Flintstones, Kingfish: A Story of Huey P. Long, A Streetcar Named Desire (1995), Mother Night, Pie in the Sky, Fallen, Blues Brothers 2000, The Borrowers, The Big Lebowski, Dirty Work, Rudolph the Red-Nosed Reindeer: The Movie, Bringing Out the Dead, What Planet Are You From?, Ready to Rumble

Grable, Betty: Whoopee!, Palmy Days (bit), The Greeks Had a Word for Them (bit), Hold 'Em Jail, The Kid From Spain, Cavalcade, Melody Cruise, The Gay Divorcee, Student Tour, Hips, Hips, Hooray (bit), The Nitwits, Old Man Rhythm, Pigskin Parade, Follow the Fleet, This Way Please, College Swing, Give Me a Sailor, Man About Town (1939), Million Dollar Legs (1939), Down Argentine Way, Tin Pan Alley, A Yank in the RAF, I Wake Up Screaming, Moon Over Miami, Footlight Serenade, Song of the Islands, Springtime in the Rockies, Coney Island, Sweet Rosie O'Grady, Four Jills in a Jeep, Pin Up Girl, Diamond Horseshoe, The Dolly Sisters, Do You Love Me? (bit), The Shocking Miss Pilgrim, Mother Wore Tights, That Lady in Ermine, When My Baby Smiles at Me, The Beautiful Blonde From Bashful Bend, Wabash Avenue, My Blue Heaven (1950), Call Me Mister, Meet Me After the Show, The Farmer Takes a Wife (1953), How to Marry a Millionaire, Three for the Show, How to Be Very, Very Popular

Grant, Cary: This Is the Night, Sinners in the Sun, Merrily We Go to Hell, Devil and the Deep, Blonde Venus, Madame Butterfly, She Done Him Wrong, The Eagle and the Hawk (1933), I'm No Angel, Alice in Wonderland (1933), Thirty Day Princess, Ladies Should Listen, Enter Madame, Wings in the Dark, The Last Outpost (1935), Sylvia Scarlett, Big Brown Eyes, Suzy, Amazing Adventure, When You're in Love, Topper, The Toast of New York, The Awful Truth, Bringing Up Baby, Holiday (1938), Gunga Din, Only Angels Have Wings, In Name Only, His Girl Friday, My Favorite Wife, The Howards of Virginia, The Philadelphia Story, Penny Serenade, Suspicion, The Talk of the Town, Once Upon a Honeymoon, Mr. Lucky, Destination Tokyo, Once Upon a Time, None But the Lonely Heart, Arsenic and Old Lace, Without Reservations (cameo), Night and Day, Notorious, The Bachelor and the Bobby-Soxer, The Bishop's Wife, Mr. Blandings Builds His Dream House, Every Girl Should Be Married, I Was a Male War Bride, Crisis, People Will Talk (1951), Room for One More, Monkey Business (1952), Dream Wife, To Catch a Thief, The Pride and the Passion, An Affair to Remember, Kiss Them for Me, Indiscreet (1958), Houseboat, North by Northwest, Operation Petticoat, The Grass Is Greener, That Touch of Mink, Charade, Father Goose, Walk, Don't Run, George Stevens: A Filmmaker's Journey (app)

Griffith, Melanie: The Harrad Experiment, Smile, Night Moves, The Drowning Pool, Joyride, One on One, Roar, Body Double, Fear City, Something Wild (1986), Cherry 2000, The Milagro Beanfield War, Stormy Monday, Working Girl, In the Spirit, Pacific Heights, Bonfire of the Vanities, Paradise (1991), Shining Through, A Stranger Among Us, Born Yesterday (1993), Milk Money, Nobody's Fool, Now and Then, Two Much, Mulholland Falls, Lolita (1997), Celebrity, Another Day in Paradise, RKO 281, Crazy in Alabama

Guinness, Sir Alec: Great Expectations (1946), Oliver Twist (1948), Kind Hearts and Coronets, A Run for Your Money, Last Holiday, The Mudlark, The Lavender Hill Mob, The Man in the White Suit, The Promoter, The Captain's Paradise, The Malta Story, The Detective (1954), To Paris With Love, The Prisoner, The Ladykillers, The Swan, All at Sea, The Bridge on the River Kwai, The Horse's Mouth, The Scapegoat, Our Man in Havana, Tunes of Glory, A Majority of One, Damn the Defiant!, Lawrence of Arabia, The Fall of the Roman Empire, Situation Hopeless—But Not Serious, Doctor Zhivago, Hotel Paradiso, The Quiller Memorandum, The Comedians, Cromwell, Scrooge (1970), Brother Sun, Sister Moon, Hitler: The Last Ten Days, Murder by Death, Star Wars, The Empire Strikes Back, Raise the Titanic!, Lovesick, Return of the Jedi, A Passage to India, Monsignor Quixote, Little Dorrit, A Handful of Dust, Kafka, Mute Witness (cameo)

Hackman, Gene: Mad Dog Coll, Lilith, Hawaii, A Covenant With Death, Banning, First To Fight, Bonnie and Clyde, The Split, Riot, Downhill Racer, The Gypsy Moths, Marooned, I Never Sang for My Father, Doctors' Wives, The Hunting Party, The French Connection, Cisco Pike, Prime Cut, The Poseidon Adventure, Scarecrow, The

Conversation, Zandy's Bride, Young Frankenstein (cameo), French Connection II, Bite the Bullet, Night Moves, Lucky Lady, The Domino Principle, March or Die, A Bridge Too Far, Superman, Superman II, All Night Long (1981), Reds, Eureka, Under Fire (1983), Uncommon Valor, Two of a Kind (1983), Misunderstood, Twice in a Lifetime, Target (1985), Power, Hoosiers, No Way Out (1987), Superman IV: The Quest for Peace, Another Woman, Bat*21, Full Moon in Blue Water, Split Decisions, Mississippi Burning, The Package, Loose Cannons, Narrow Margin, Postcards From the Edge, Class Action, Company Business, Unforgiven, The Firm, Geronimo: An American Legend, Wyatt Earp, The Quick and the Dead (1995), Crimson Tide, Get Shorty, The birdcage, The Chamber, Extreme Measures, Absolute Power, Twilight, Antz, Enemy of the State

Hamill, Mark: Star Wars, Wizards, Corvette Summer, The Big Red One, The Empire Strikes Back, The Night the Lights Went Out in Georgia, Britannia Hospital, Return of the Jedi, Slipstream, Sleepwalkers (cameo), The Guyver, Time Runner, Batman: Mask of the Phantasm, Village of the Damned (1995), Wing Commander (uncred voice)

Hanks, Tom: He Knows You're Alone, Mazes and Monsters, Bachelor Party, Splash, The Man With One Red Shoe, Volunteers, Every Time We Say Goodbye, The Money Pit, Nothing in Common, Dragnet (1987), Big, Punchline, The 'burbs, Turner and Hooch, Joe Versus the Volcano, Bonfire of the Vanities, Radio Flyer, A League of Their Own, Sleepless in Seattle, Philadelphia, Forrest Gump, Apollo 13, The Celluloid Closet (app only), Toy Story, that thing you do! (also dir), Saving Private Ryan, You've Got Mail, Toy Story 2, The Green Mile

Harlow, Jean: The Love Parade (bit), Hell's Angels, City Lights (bit), Iron Man (1931), The Public Enemy, Platinum Blonde, The Secret Six, Three Wise Girls, The Beast of the City, Red-Headed Woman, Red Dust, Hold Your Man, Dinner at Eight, Bombshell, The Girl from Missouri, Reckless (1935), China Seas, Riffraff (1935), Wife vs. Secretary, Suzy, Libeled Lady, Personal Property, Saratoga

Harrelson, Woody: Wildcats, She's Having a Baby, Casualties of War, Ted & Venus, L.A. Story (cameo), Doc Hollywood, White Men Can't Jump, Indecent Proposal, The Cowboy Way, I'll Do Anything, Natural Born Killers, Money Train, The Sunchaser, Kingpin, The People vs. Larry Flynt, Welcome to Sarajevo, Wag the Dog (cameo), Palmetto, The Thin Red Line (1998), The Hi-Lo Country, Ed TV, Austin Powers: The Spy Who Shagged Me (cameo), Play It to the Bone

Hawn, Goldie: The One and Only, Genuine, Original Family Band, Cactus Flower, There's a Girl in My Soup, $ (Dollars), Butterflies Are Free, The Sugarland Express, The Girl From Petrovka, Shampoo, The Duchess and the Dirtwater Fox, Foul Play, Lovers and Liars, Private Benjamin, Seems Like Old Times, Best Friends, Swing Shift, Protocol, Wildcats, Overboard, Bird on a Wire, Deceived, CrissCross, HouseSitter, Death Becomes Her, The First Wives Club, Everyone Says I Love You, Hope (dir), The Out-of-Towners (1999)

Hayward, Susan: Hollywood Hotel (bit), The Sisters (bit), Comet Over Broadway (bit), Girls on Probation, The Amazing Doctor Clitterhouse (bit), Beau Geste (1939), Adam Had Four Sons, Sis Hopkins, Among the Living, Reap the Wild Wind, The Forest Rangers, I Married a Witch, Star Spangled Rhythm, Change of Heart, Young and Willing, Jack London, The Fighting Seabees, The Hairy Ape, And Now Tomorrow, Deadline at Dawn, Canyon Passage, Smash-up, the Story of a Woman, They Won't Believe Me, The Lost Moment, Tap Roots, The Saxon Charm, Tulsa, House of Strangers, My Foolish Heart, I'd Climb the Highest Mountain, Rawhide, I Can Get It for You Wholesale, David and Bathsheba, With a Song in My Heart, The Snows of Kilimanjaro, The Lusty Men, The President's Lady, White Witch Doctor, Demetrius and the Gladiators, Garden of Evil, Untamed (1955), Soldier of Fortune, I'll Cry Tomorrow, The Conqueror, Top Secret Affair, I Want to Live!, Woman Obsessed, Thunder in the Sun, The Marriage-Go-Round, Ada, Back Street (1961), I Thank a Fool, The Stolen Hours, Where Love Has Gone, The Honey Pot, Valley of the Dolls, The Revengers

Hayworth, Rita: Charlie Chan in Egypt, In Caliente (bit), Dante's Inferno, Meet Nero Wolfe, Who Killed Gail Preston?, Homicide Bureau, The Lone Wolf Spy Hunt, Only Angels Have Wings, Music in My Heart, Blondie on a Budget, Susan and God, The Lady in Question, Angels Over Broadway, The Strawberry Blonde, Affectionately Yours, Blood and Sand (1941), You'll Never Get Rich, My Gal Sal, Tales of Manhattan, You Were Never Lovelier, Cover Girl, Tonight and Every Night, Gilda, Down to Earth (1947), The Lady From Shanghai, The Loves of Carmen, Affair in Trinidad, Salome, Miss Sadie Thompson, Fire Down Below (1957), Pal Joey, Separate Tables, They Came to Cordura, The Story on Page One, The Happy Thieves, Circus World, The Money Trap, The Poppy Is Also a Flower, The Rover, The Road to Salina, The Wrath of God

Hepburn, Audrey: Laughter in Paradise (bit), Young Wives' Tale, The Lavender Hill Mob, Secret People, Roman Holiday, Sabrina (1954), War and Peace (1956), Funny Face, Love in the Afternoon, Green Mansions, The Nun's Story, The Unforgiven, Breakfast at Tiffany's, The Children's Hour, Charade, Paris—When It Sizzles, My Fair Lady, How to Steal a Million, Two for the Road, Wait Until Dark, Robin and Marian, Bloodline, They All Laughed, Love Among Thieves, Always (1989)

Hepburn, Katharine: A Bill of Divorcement (1932), Christopher Strong, Morning Glory, Little Women (1933), Spitfire (1934), The Little Minister, Break of Hearts, Alice Adams, Sylvia Scarlett, Mary of Scotland, A Woman Rebels, Quality Street, Stage Door, Bringing Up Baby, Holiday (1938), The Philadelphia Story, Woman of the Year, Keeper of the Flame, Stage Door Canteen, Dragon Seed, Without Love, Undercurrent, The Sea of Grass, Song of Love, State of the Union, Adam's Rib, The African Queen, Pat and Mike, Summertime, The Rainmaker (1956), The Iron Petticoat, Desk Set, Suddenly, Last Summer, Long Day's Journey Into Night, Guess Who's Coming to Dinner?, The Lion in Winter, The Madwoman of Chaillot, The Trojan Women, A Delicate Balance, Love Among the Ruins, Rooster Cogburn, Olly, Olly, Oxen Free, On Golden Pond, George Stevens: A Filmmaker's Journey (app), Grace Quigley, Mrs. Delafield Wants to Marry, The Man Upstairs, This Can't Be Love, Love Affair (1994)

Heston, Charlton: Dark City (1950), The Greatest Show on Earth, The Savage, Ruby Gentry, The President's Lady, Pony Express, Arrowhead, Bad for Each Other, The Naked Jungle, Secret of the Incas, The Far Horizons, The Private War of Major Benson, Lucy Gallant, The Ten Commandments (1956), Three Violent People, Touch of Evil, The Big Country, The Buccaneer (1958), The Wreck of the Mary Deare, Ben Hur (1959), El Cid, The Pigeon That Took Rome, Diamond Head, 55 Days at Peking, The Greatest Story Ever Told, Major Dundee, The Agony and the Ecstasy, The War Lord, Khartoum, Counterpoint, Planet of the Apes, Will Penny, Number One, Julius Caesar (1970), Beneath the Planet of the Apes, King: A Filmed Record . . . Montgomery to Memphis (narr), The Hawaiians, The Omega Man, Call of the Wild, Skyjacked, Antony and Cleopatra (also dir), Soylent Green, Airport 1975, The Three Musketeers (1974), Earthquake, The Four Musketeers, The Last Hard Men, Midway, Two Minute Warning, Crossed Swords (1978), Gray Lady Down, The Mountain Men, The Awakening, Mother Lode (also dir), A Man for All Seasons (1988; also dir), Treasure Island (1990), Little Kidnappers (1990), Almost an Angel (cameo), Solar Crisis, The Crucifer of Blood, Wayne's World 2 (cameo), Tombstone, True Lies (cameo), In the Mouth of Madness, Avenging Angel, Alaska, Hamlet (1996), Hercules (1997), Armageddon, Any Given Sunday

Hoffman, Dustin: The Tiger Makes Out, The Graduate, Madigan's Million, Midnight Cowboy, John and Mary, Little Big Man, The Point, Who Is Harry Kellerman and Why Is He Saying Those Terrible Things About Me?, Straw Dogs, The Point, Alfredo, Alfredo, Papillon, Lenny, All the President's Men, Marathon Man, Straight Time, Agatha, Kramer vs. Kramer, Tootsie, Death of a Salesman, Ishtar, Rain Man, Family Business (1989), Common Threads: Stories From the Quilt, Dick Tracy, Billy Bathgate, Hook, Hero, Outbreak, Sleepers, American Buffalo, Mad City, Wag the Dog, Sphere, The Messenger: The Story of Joan of Arc

Holden, William: Million Dollar Legs (1939; bit), Golden Boy, Invisible Stripes, Those Were the Days, Our Town, Arizona, I Wanted Wings, Texas, The Remarkable Andrew, Meet the Stewarts, The Fleet's In, Young and Willing, Variety Girl (cameo), Blaze of Noon, Dear Ruth, Apartment for Peggy, The Man From Colorado, Rachel and the Stranger, The Dark Past, Miss Grant Takes Richmond, Dear Wife, Streets of Laredo, Father Is a Bachelor, Born Yesterday (1950), Sunset Blvd., Union Station, Submarine Command, Force of Arms, Boots Malone, The Turning Point (1952), The Moon Is Blue, Stalag 17, Forever Female, Escape From Fort Bravo, Executive Suite, The Bridges at Toko-Ri, Sabrina (1954), The Country Girl, Love Is a Many-Splendored Thing, Picnic, Toward the Unknown, The Proud and Profane, The Bridge on the River Kwai, The Key (1958), The Horse Soldiers, The World of Suzie Wong, The Counterfeit Traitor, Satan Never Sleeps, The Lion, Paris—When It Sizzles, The 7th Dawn, Alvarez Kelly, Casino Royale (cameo), The Devil's Brigade, The Christmas Tree (1969), The Wild Bunch, Wild Rovers, The Revengers, Breezy, The Towering Inferno, Open Season (1974), Network, Damien—Omen II, Fedora, Escape to Athena, Ashanti, When Time Ran Out . . ., The Earthling, S.O.B.

Hope, Bob: The Big Broadcast of 1938, College Swing, Give Me a Sailor, Thanks for the Memory, Never Say Die, Some Like It Hot (1939), The Cat and the Canary (1939), Road to Singapore, The Ghost Breakers, Road to Zanzibar, Caught in the Draft, Nothing but the Truth, Louisiana Purchase, My Favorite Blonde, Road to Morocco, Star Spangled Rhythm, They Got Me Covered, Let's Face It, The Princess and the Pirate, Road to Utopia, Monsieur Beaucaire, My Favorite Brunette, Where There's Life, Variety Girl (cameo), Road to Rio, The Paleface, Sorrowful Jones, The Great Lover, Fancy Pants, The Lemon Drop Kid, My Favorite Spy (1951), The Greatest Show on Earth (cameo), Son of Paleface, Road to Bali, Off Limits (1953), Scared Stiff (1953; cameo), Here Come the Girls, Casanova's Big Night, The Seven Little Foys, That Certain Feeling, The Iron Petticoat, Beau James, Paris Holiday, The Five Pennies (cameo), Alias Jesse James, The Facts of Life, Bachelor in Paradise, The Road to Hong Kong, Critic's Choice, Call Me Bwana, A Global Affair, I'll Take Sweden, The Oscar (cameo), Not With My Wife You Don't! (cameo), Boy, Did I Get a Wrong Number!, Eight on the Lam, The Private Navy of Sgt. O'Farrell, How to Commit Marriage, Cancel My Reservation, The Muppet Movie (cameo), Spies Like Us (cameo)

Hopkins, Anthony: The Lion in Winter, Hamlet (1969), The Looking Glass War, When Eight Bells Toll, Young Winston, A Doll's House (1973), The Girl From Petrovka, Juggernaut, All Creatures Great and Small, Audrey Rose, A Bridge Too Far, International Velvet, Magic, A Change of Seasons, The Elephant Man, The Bunker, The Hunchback of Notre Dame (1982), A Married Man, The Bounty, Mussolini: The Decline and Fall of Il Duce, The Good Father, 84 Charing Cross Road, The Tenth Man, The Dawning, A Chorus of Disapproval, Desperate Hours, The Silence of the Lambs, Freejack, Howards End, The Efficiency Expert, Bram Stoker's Dracula, Chaplin, The Innocent (1993), The Remains of the Day, Shadowlands (1993), The Road to Wellville, Legends of the Fall, Nixon, August, Surviving Picasso, The Edge, Amistad, The Mask of Zorro, Meet Joe Black, Instinct, Titus, Mission: Impossible 2

Hopper, Dennis: I Died a Thousand Times, Rebel Without a Cause, Giant, Gunfight at the O.K. Corral, The Story of Mankind, From Hell to Texas, The Young Land, Key Witness, Night Tide, The Sons of Katie Elder, Planet of Blood, Cool Hand Luke, The Trip, The Glory Stompers, Panic in the City, Hang 'Em High, Easy Rider (also dir), True Grit, The Last Movie (also dir), Kid Blue, Mad Dog Morgan, Tracks, The American Friend, Apocalypse Now, Out of the Blue (1980; also dir), Wild Times, King of the Mountain, Human Highway, The Osterman Weekend, Rumble Fish, My Science Project, Riders of the Storm, The Texas Chainsaw Massacre 2, Blue Velvet, Hoosiers, Black Widow (1986), River's Edge, Straight to Hell, O.C. and Stiggs, The Pick-up Artist, Colors (dir only), Blood Red, Backtrack (1989; also dir), Flashback, Chattahoochee, The Hot Spot (dir), Superstar: The Life and Times of Andy Warhol, Paris Trout, The Indian Runner, Eye of the Storm, Nails, Boiling Point, Super Mario Bros., The Heart of Justice, Red Rock West, True Romance, Chasers (also dir), Speed (1994), Search and Destroy (1995), Waterworld, Carried Away, Basquiat, The Last Days of Frankie the Fly, Meet the Deedles, Ed TV, Jesus' Son, The Source

Hoskins, Bob: Inserts, Royal Flash, Zulu Dawn, The Long Good Friday, Pink Floyd—The Wall, Beyond the Limit, Lassiter, The Cotton Club, Brazil, The Dunera Boys, Mussolini: The Decline and Fall of Il Duce, Sweet Liberty, Mona Lisa, The Lonely Passion of Judith Hearne, A Prayer for the Dying, Who Framed Roger Rabbit, Heart Condition, Mermaids, Shattered (1991), Hook, The Inner Circle, Passed Away, The Favor, the Watch and the Very Big Fish, Blue Ice, Super Mario Bros., Nixon, Balto, The Secret Agent (1996), Michael, Spice World (cameo), TwentyFourSeven, Cousin Bette, Felicia's Journey

Hudson, Rock: Fighter Squadron, Undertow, I Was a Shoplifter, Winchester '73, One-Way Street, Peggy, The Desert Hawk, Shakedown, Double Crossbones, Tomahawk, Bright Victory, Iron Man (1951), The Fat Man, Air Cadet, Has Anybody Seen My Gal?, Bend of the River, Scarlet Angel, Here Come the Nelsons, Horizons West, The Lawless Breed, Gun Fury, Seminole, The Golden Blade, Back to God's Country, Sea Devils (1953), Taza, Son of Cochise, Bengal Brigade, Magnificent Obsession (1954), Captain Lightfoot, All That Heaven Allows, One Desire, Never Say Goodbye (1956), Written on the Wind, Four Girls in Town (cameo), Giant, Battle Hymn, A Farewell to Arms (1957), Something of Value, The Tarnished Angels, Twilight for the Gods, This Earth Is Mine, Pillow Talk, The Last Sunset, Lover Come Back (1961), Come September, The Spiral Road, A Gathering of Eagles, Marilyn, Send Me No Flowers, Man's Favorite Sport?, Strange Bedfellows, A Very Special Favor, Blindfold, Seconds, Tobruk, Ice Station Zebra, A Fine Pair, The Undefeated, Darling Lili, Hornets' Nest, Pretty Maids All in a Row, Showdown (1973), Embryo, Avalanche (1978), The Mirror Crack'd, The Ambassador

Huston, Anjelica: Sinful Davey, A Walk With Love and Death, Hamlet (1969; bit), Swashbuckler, The Last Tycoon, The Postman Always Rings Twice (1981), Frances, The Ice Pirates, This Is Spinal Tap (cameo), Prizzi's Honor, Good to Go, Gardens of Stone, The Dead, A Handful of Dust, Mr. North, Crimes and Misdemeanors, Enemies, a Love Story, The Witches, The Grifters, The Addams Family, The Player (cameo), Family Pictures, And the Band Played On, Manhattan Murder Mystery, Addams Family Values, The Perez Family, The Crossing Guard, Bastard Out of Carolina (dir), Phoenix, Ever After, Buffalo 66, Agnes Browne (also dir)

Irons, Jeremy: Nijinsky, The French Lieutenant's Woman, Moonlighting, Betrayal, The Wild Duck, Swann in Love, The Mission, Dead Ringers, A Chorus of Disapproval, Reversal of Fortune, Kafka, Damage, Waterland, M. Butterfly, The House of the Spirits, The Lion King, Die Hard With a Vengeance, Stealing Beauty, Chinese Box, Lolita (1997), The Man in the Iron Mask (1998)

Jackson, Samuel L. (formerly billed as Sam): Ragtime, Eddie Murphy Raw (bit), School Daze, Coming to America, Sea of Love, Do the Right Thing, A Shock to the System, The Return of Superfly (cameo), Mo' Better Blues, GoodFellas, The Exorcist III (bit), Def by Temptation, Betsy's Wedding (bit), Strictly Business, Jungle Fever, Johnny Suede, Jumpin at the Boneyard, Patriot Games, Juice, White Sands, National Lampoon's Loaded Weapon I, True Romance, The Meteor Man (cameo), Menace II Society, Jurassic Park, Amos & Andrew, Pulp Fiction, The New Age, Fresh, Against the Wall, Losing Isaiah, Kiss of Death (1995), Die Hard With a Vengeance, Fluke, The Great White Hype, A Time to Kill, The Long Kiss Goodnight, The Search for One-Eyed Jimmy, Trees Lounge, Hard Eight, one eight seven, Eve's Bayou, Jackie Brown, Sphere, The Negotiator, Out of Sight (1998; cameo), Star Wars: Episode I The Phantom Menace, The Red Violin, Deep Blue Sea, Rules of Engagement

Jolson, Al: The Jazz Singer (1927), The Singing Fool, Say It With Songs, Mammy, Big Boy, Show Girl in Hollywood, Hallelujah I'm a Bum, Wonder Bar, Go Into Your Dance, The Singing Kid, Rose of Washington Square, Hollywood Cavalcade, Swanee River, Rhapsody in Blue (cameo), The Jolson Story, Jolson Sings Again (voice only)

Jones, Tommy Lee: Love Story (1970), Jackson County Jail, Rolling Thunder, The Betsy, Eyes of Laura Mars, Coal Miner's Daughter, Back Roads, The Executioner's Song, Nate and Hayes, The River Rat, Black Moon Rising, The Big Town, Stranger on My Land, Stormy Monday, April Morning, The Package, Firebirds (1990), JFK, Under Siege, House of Cards (1993), The Fugitive (1993), Heaven & Earth, Blown Away, Natural Born Killers, The Client, Blue Sky, Cobb, The Good Old Boys, Batman Forever, Volcano (1997), Men in Black, U.S. Marshals, Small Soldiers, Double Jeopardy, Rules of Engagement

Judd, Ashley: Kuffs, Ruby in Paradise, Smoke, Heat (1995), Norma Jean & Marilyn, A Time to Kill (1996), Normal Life, The Locusts, Kiss the Girls, Simon Birch, Eye of the Beholder, Double Jeopardy, Where the Heart Is (2000)

Karloff, Boris: The Last of the Mohicans (1920; bit), Old Ironsides (bit), Behind That Curtain, The Unholy Night, The Criminal Code, Smart Money (bit), I Like Your Nerve, Five Star Final, The Mad Genius, The Yellow Ticket, Frankenstein, Behind the Mask, Scarface (1932), Night World, The Old Dark House (1932), The Mask of Fu Manchu, The Mummy, The Ghoul (1933), The Lost Patrol, House of Rothschild, The Black Cat (1934), Bride of Frankenstein, The Black Room, The Raven (1935), The Invisible Ray, The Walking Dead (1936), The Man Who Lived Again, Charlie Chan at the Opera, Night Key, West of Shanghai, The Invisible Menace, Mr. Wong, Detective, Son of Frankenstein, Mystery of Mr. Wong, Mr. Wong in Chinatown, The Man They Could Not Hang, Tower of London (1939), The Fatal Hour, British Intelligence, Black Friday, The Man With Nine Lives, Devil's Island, Doomed to Die, Before I Hang, The Ape, You'll Find Out, The Devil Commands, The Boogie Man Will Get You, The Climax, House of Frankenstein (1944), The Body Snatcher, Isle of the Dead, Bedlam (1946), The Secret Life of Walter Mitty, Lured, Unconquered, Dick Tracy Meets Gruesome, Tap Roots, Abbott and Costello Meet the Killer, Boris Karloff, The Strange Door, The Black Castle, Abbott and Costello Meet Dr. Jekyll and Mr. Hyde, Sabaka, Voodoo Island, The Haunted Strangler, Frankenstein 1970, Corridors of Blood, The Raven, The Terror, Black Sabbath, The Comedy of Terrors, Bikini Beach (cameo), Die, Monster, Die!, The Ghost in the Invisible Bikini, The Daydreamer, The Venetian Affair, The Sorcerers, Cauldron of Blood, Mad Monster Party?, Targets, Curse of the Crimson Altar, Snake People, The Fear Chamber, House of Evil, Sinister Invasion

Kaye, Danny: Up in Arms, Wonder Man, The Kid From Brooklyn, The Secret Life of Walter Mitty, A Song Is Born, It's a Great Feeling (cameo), The Inspector General, On the Riviera, Hans Christian Andersen, Knock on Wood, White Christmas, The Court Jester, Merry Andrew, Me and the Colonel, The Five Pennies, On the Double, The Man From the Diners' Club, The Madwoman of Chaillot (1969), Skokie

Keaton, Buster: The Saphead, Three Ages, Our Hospitality (also codir), Sherlock Jr., The Navigator (also dir), Seven Chances, Go West (1925; also codir), Battling Butler (also codir), The General (also codir), College, Steamboat Bill, Jr., The Cameraman, The Hollywood Revue of 1929, Spite Marriage, Free and Easy, Doughboys, Parlor, Bedroom and Bath, Sidewalks of New York, The Passionate Plumber, Speak Easily, What! No Beer?, An Old Spanish Custom, Hollywood Cavalcade, The Villain Still Pursued Her, Li'l Abner (1940), Forever and a Day, San Diego I Love You, That's the Spirit, That Night With You, She Went to the Races (bit), God's Country, Boom in the Moon, The Loveable Cheat, In the Good Old Summertime, You're My Everything, Sunset Blvd. (cameo), Limelight, Around the World in Eighty Days (cameo), The Adventures of Huckleberry Finn, It's a Mad, Mad, Mad, Mad World, Pajama Party, Beach Blanket Bingo, How to Stuff a Wild Bikini, Sergeant Deadhead, War, Italian Style, A Funny Thing Happened on the Way to the Forum

Keaton, Diane: Lovers and Other Strangers, The Godfather, Play It Again, Sam, Sleeper, The Godfather, Part II, Love and

Death, I Will, I Will . . . for Now, Harry and Walter Go to New York, Looking for Mr. Goodbar, Annie Hall, Interiors, Manhattan, Reds, Shoot the Moon, The Little Drummer Girl, Mrs. Soffel, Crimes of the Heart, Radio Days, Heaven (1987, dir), Baby Boom, The Good Mother, The Lemon Sisters, The Godfather, Part III, Wildflower (dir), Father of the Bride, Running Mates, Manhattan Murder Mystery, Look Who's Talking Now, Amelia Earhart: The Final Flight, Unstrung Heroes (dir), Father of the Bride Part II, The First Wives Club, Marvin's Room, Northern Lights, The Only Thrill, The Other Sister, Hanging Up (also dir)

Keaton, Michael: Night Shift, Mr. Mom, Johnny Dangerously, Gung Ho, Touch and Go (1986), The Squeeze (1987), Beetle Juice, Clean and Sober, Batman (1989), The Dream Team, Pacific Heights, One Good Cop, Batman Returns, Much Ado About Nothing, My Life, The Paper, Speechless, Multiplicity, Inventing the Abbotts (narr only), Jackie Brown, Desperate Measures, Out of Sight (1998, cameo), Jack Frost

Kelly, Gene: For Me and My Gal, Pilot #5, DuBarry Was a Lady, Thousands Cheer, The Cross of Lorraine, Cover Girl, Christmas Holiday, Anchors Aweigh, Ziegfeld Follies, Living in a Big Way, The Pirate, The Three Musketeers (1948), Words and Music, Take Me Out to the Ball Game, On the Town (also codir), Black Hand, Summer Stock, An American in Paris, It's a Big Country, Love Is Better Than Ever (cameo), Singin' in the Rain (also codir), The Devil Makes Three, Brigadoon, Crest of the Wave, Deep in My Heart (cameo), It's Always Fair Weather (also codir), Invitation to the Dance (also dir), The Happy Road (also dir), Les Girls, The Tunnel of Love (dir), Marjorie Morningstar, Let's Make Love (cameo), Inherit the Wind, Gigot (dir), What a Way to Go!, The Young Girls of Rochefort, A Guide for the Married Man (dir), Hello, Dolly! (dir), The Cheyenne Social Club (dir, prod), 40 Carats, That's Entertainment!, That's Entertainment, Part 2, Viva Knievel!, Xanadu, That's Dancing!, That's Entertainment! III, Cats Don't Dance (choreography consultant)

Kelly, Grace: Fourteen Hours, High Noon, Mogambo, Dial M for Murder, Rear Window, The Country Girl, Green Fire, The Bridges at Toko-Ri, To Catch a Thief, The Swan, High Society (1956), The Children of Theatre Street

Kerr, Deborah: Major Barbara, Love on the Dole, Courageous Mr. Penn, Hatter's Castle, The Day Will Dawn, The Life and Death of Colonel Blimp, Vacation From Marriage, The Adventuress, Black Narcissus, The Hucksters, If Winter Comes, Edward, My Son, Please Believe Me, King Solomon's Mines (1950), Quo Vadis? (1951), The Prisoner of Zenda (1952), Thunder in the East, Young Bess, Julius Caesar (1953), Dream Wife, From Here to Eternity, The End of the Affair, The Proud and Profane, The King and I, Tea and Sympathy, Heaven Knows, Mr. Allison, An Affair to Remember, Bonjour Tristesse, Separate Tables, The Journey, Count Your Blessings, Beloved Infidel, The Sundowners (1960), The Grass Is Greener, The Naked Edge, The Innocents, The Chalk Garden, The Night of the Iguana, Marriage on the Rocks, Eye of the Devil, Casino Royale, Prudence and the Pill, The Gypsy Moths, The Arrangement, The Assam Garden

Kidman, Nicole: Windrider, Dead Calm, Days of Thunder, Flirting, Billy Bathgate, Far and Away, My Life, Malice, To Die For (1995), Batman Forever, The Portrait of a Lady, The Peacemaker (1997), Practical Magic, Eyes Wide Shut

Kline, Kevin: Sophie's Choice, The Pirates of Penzance, The Big Chill, Silverado, Violets Are Blue . . . , Cry Freedom, A Fish Called Wanda, The January Man, I Love You to Death, Soapdish, Grand Canyon, Consenting Adults, Chaplin, Dave, The Nutcracker, Princess Caraboo, French Kiss, The Hunchback of Notre Dame (1996), Looking for Richard (app only), Fierce Creatures, The Ice Storm, In & Out, A Midsummer Night's Dream, Wild Wild West, The Road to El Dorado

Ladd, Alan: Once In a Lifetime (bit), Tom Brown of Culver (bit), Pigskin Parade (bit), The Last Train From Madrid (bit), Hold 'Em Navy (bit), All Over Town (bit), The Goldwyn Follies (bit), Rulers of the Sea, The Howards of Virginia (bit), Those Were the Days, Captain Caution, Brother Rat and a Baby, Great Guns, Citizen Kane, The Black Cat (1941), The Reluctant Dragon, Gangs, Inc., Joan of Paris, This Gun for Hire, The Glass Key (1942), Lucky Jordan, Star Spangled Rhythm (cameo), China, And Now Tomorrow, Salty O'Rourke, Duffy's Tavern (cameo), The Blue Dahlia, O.S.S., Two Years Before the Mast, Calcutta, Variety Girl (cameo), Wild Harvest, My Favorite Brunette (cameo), Saigon, Beyond Glory, Whispering Smith, The Great Gatsby (1949), Chicago Deadline, Captain Carey, U.S.A., Branded, Appointment With Danger, Red Mountain, The Iron Mistress, Thunder in the East, Desert Legion, Shane, Botany Bay, Paratrooper, The Black Knight, Saskatchewan, Hell Below Zero, Drum Beat, The McConnell Story, Hell on Frisco Bay, Santiago, The Big Land, Boy on a Dolphin, The Deep Six, The Proud Rebel, The Badlanders, The Man in the Net, Guns of the Timberland, All the Young Men, One Foot in Hell, Duel of Champions, 13 West Street, The Carpetbaggers

Lancaster, Burt: The Killers (1946), Variety Girl (cameo), Brute Force, Desert Fury, I Walk Alone, All My Sons, Sorry, Wrong Number, Kiss the Blood off My Hands,

Criss Cross, Rope of Sand, The Flame and the Arrow, Mister 880, Vengeance Valley, Jim Thorpe—All American, Ten Tall Men, The Crimson Pirate, Come Back, Little Sheba, South Sea Woman, From Here to Eternity, His Majesty O'Keefe, Apache, Vera Cruz, The Kentuckian, The Rose Tattoo, Trapeze, The Rainmaker (1956), Gunfight at the O.K. Corral, Sweet Smell of Success, Run Silent, Run Deep, Separate Tables, The Devil's Disciple, The Unforgiven, Elmer Gantry, The Young Savages, Judgment at Nuremberg, Birdman of Alcatraz, A Child Is Waiting, The List of Adrian Messenger (cameo), The Leopard, Seven Days in May, The Train, The Hallelujah Trail, The Professionals, The Scalphunters, The Swimmer, Castle Keep, The Gypsy Moths, King: A Filmed Record . . . Montgomery to Memphis (narr), Airport, Lawman, Valdez Is Coming, Ulzana's Raid, Scorpio, Executive Action, The Midnight Man, Conversation Piece, Moses, 1900, Buffalo Bill and the Indians, or Sitting Bull's History Lesson, The Cassandra Crossing, Twilight's Last Gleaming, The Island of Dr. Moreau (1977), Go Tell the Spartans, Zulu Dawn, Cattle Annie and Little Britches, Atlantic City (1980), La Pelle, Local Hero, The Osterman Weekend, Little Treasure, Tough Guys, Rocket Gibraltar, The Jeweller's Shop, Field of Dreams, The Phantom of the Opera (1990), Separate but Equal

Lange, Jessica: King Kong (1976), All That Jazz, How to Beat the High Co$t of Living, The Postman Always Rings Twice (1981), Tootsie, Frances, Country, Sweet Dreams, Crimes of the Heart, Everybody's All-American, Far North, Music Box, Men Don't Leave, Cape Fear (1991), O Pioneers!, Night and the City (1992), Blue Sky, Losing Isaiah, Rob Roy, A Streetcar Named Desire (1995), A Thousand Acres, Hush, Cousin Bette, Titus

Lansbury, Angela: Gaslight (1944), National Velvet, The Picture of Dorian Gray, The Harvey Girls, The Hoodlum Saint, Till the Clouds Roll By, The Private Affairs of Bel Ami, If Winter Comes, Tenth Avenue Angel, State of the Union, The Three Musketeers (1948), The Red Danube, Samson and Delilah (1949), Kind Lady (1951), Mutiny, Remains to Be Seen, A Lawless Street, The Purple Mask, Please Murder Me, The Court Jester, Key Man, The Long Hot Summer (1958), The Reluctant Debutante, Season of Passion, The Dark at the Top of the Stairs, A Breath of Scandal, Blue Hawaii, All Fall Down, The Manchurian Candidate, In the Cool of the Day, The World of Henry Orient, Dear Heart, The Greatest Story Ever Told (cameo), The Amorous Adventures of Moll Flanders, Harlow (Carroll Baker version), Mister Buddwing, Something for Everyone, Bedknobs and Broomsticks, Death on the Nile, The Lady Vanishes (1979), The Mirror Crack'd, The Last Unicorn, Little Gloria . . . Happy at Last, The Pirates of Penzance, The Company of Wolves, The Shell Seekers, The Love She Sought, Beauty and the Beast (1991), Mrs. 'Arris Goes to Paris, Mrs. Santa Claus, Anastasia (1997), Fantasia 2000 (app)

Laughton, Charles: Devil and the Deep, The Old Dark House (1932), Payment Deferred, The Sign of the Cross, If I Had a Million, Island of Lost Souls, The Private Life of Henry VIII, The Barretts of Wimpole Street (1934), Ruggles of Red Gap, Les Miserables (1935), Mutiny on the Bounty (1935), Rembrandt, The Beachcomber (1938), Sidewalks of London, Jamaica Inn, The Hunchback of Notre Dame (1939), They Knew What They Wanted, It Started With Eve, The Tuttles of Tahiti, Tales of Manhattan, Stand By for Action, Forever and a Day, This Land Is Mine, The Man From Down Under, The Canterville Ghost, The Suspect, Captain Kidd, Because of Him, The Paradine Case, Arch of Triumph, The Big Clock, The Girl From Manhattan, The Bribe, The Man on the Eiffel Tower, The Blue Veil, The Strange Door, O. Henry's Full House, Abbott and Costello Meet Captain Kidd, Salome, Young Bess, Hobson's Choice, The Night of the Hunter (dir), Witness for the Prosecution, Under Ten Flags, Spartacus, Advise & Consent

Laurel & Hardy: The Hollywood Revue of 1929 (cameos), Pardon Us, Pack Up Your Troubles (1932), The Devil's Brother, Sons of the Desert, Hollywood Party (cameos), Babes in Toyland (1934), Bonnie Scotland, The Bohemian Girl, Our Relations, Way Out West, Pick a Star (cameos), Swiss Miss, Block-Heads, The Flying Deuces, A Chump at Oxford, Saps at Sea, Great Guns, A-Haunting We Will Go, Air Raid Wardens, Jitterbugs, The Dancing Masters, The Big Noise, Nothing but Trouble (1944), The Bullfighters, Utopia; *features with Oliver Hardy without Stan Laurel:* Zenobia, The Fighting Kentuckian, Riding High (1950)

Lee, Bruce: The Wrecking Crew (karate advisor), Marlowe, Fists of Fury, The Chinese Connection, Enter the Dragon, Return of the Dragon (also dir), Game of Death, Circle of Iron (costy)

Lee, Christopher: Corridor of Mirrors, One Night With You, Hamlet (1948; bit), Saraband, Scott of the Antarctic, The Gay Lady, Captain Horatio Hornblower, Valley of the Eagles, The Crimson Pirate, Babes in Bagdad, Moulin Rouge, Innocents in Paris, That Lady, The Warriors (1955), Storm Over the Nile, The Cockleshell Heroes, Port Afrique, Private's Progress, Beyond Mombasa, Pursuit of the Graf Spee, Night Ambush, She Played With Fire, The Curse of Frankenstein, The Accursed (1957), Bitter

Victory, The Truth About Women, A Tale of Two Cities (1958), Horror of Dracula, Missiles From Hell, The Hound of the Baskervilles (1959), The Man Who Could Cheat Death, The Mummy (1959), Too Hot to Handle, Wild for Kicks, The Two Faces of Dr. Jekyll, Horror Hotel (1960), The Hands of Orlac, The Puzzle of the Red Orchid, The Devil's Daffodil, Scream of Fear, Terror of the Tongs, Hercules in the Haunted World, The Pirates of Blood River, Corridors of Blood, Castle of the Living Dead, Horror Castle, Devil-Ship Pirates, The Gorgon, Dr. Terror's House of Horrors, She (1965), The Skull, The Face of Fu Manchu, Dracula—Prince of Darkness, Rasputin—the Mad Monk, The Brides of Fu Manchu, Psycho-Circus, Theater of Death, The Torture Chamber of Dr. Sadism, The Vengeance of Fu Manchu, Five Golden Dragons, Island of the Burning Doomed, The Devil's Bride, Dracula Has Risen From The Grave, The Crimson Cult, The Blood of Fu Manchu, The Oblong Box, The Magic Christian (cameo), The Castle of Fu Manchu, Scream and Scream Again, Taste the Blood of Dracula, One More Time (cameo), Night of the Blood Monster, Julius Caesar (1970), The Private Life of Sherlock Holmes, Scars of Dracula, The House That Dripped Blood, Count Dracula, Hannie Caulder, I, Monster, Dracula A.D. 1972, Horror Express, Raw Meat (cameo), Nothing but the Night, The Wicker Man, The Creeping Flesh, Count Dracula and His Vampire Bride, The Three Musketeers (1974), The Man With the Golden Gun, Dark Places, Diagnosis: Murder, Killer Force, The Four Musketeers, To the Devil—A Daughter, Dracula and Son, Airport '77, End of the World, Starship Invasions, Return From Witch Mountain, Caravans, The Passage, Jaguar Lives!, An Arabian Adventure, Bear Island, 1941, Circle of Iron, Serial, The Salamander, An Eye for an Eye (1981), Safari 3000, The Last Unicorn, The Return of Captain Invincible, House of the Long Shadows, The Rosebud Beach Hotel, Howling II: Your Sister Is a Werewolf, Jocks, The Return of the Musketeers, Treasure Island (1990), Gremlins 2 The New Batch, Honeymoon Academy, Curse III: Blood Sacrifice, Sherlock Holmes and the Leading Lady, The Rainbow Thief, Incident at Victoria Falls, Police Academy VII: Mission to Moscow, The Stupids, Jinnah, Sleepy Hollow

Leigh, Janet: The Romance of Rosy Ridge, If Winter Comes, Hills of Home, Words and Music, Act of Violence, Little Women (1949), The Doctor and the Girl, That Forsyte Woman, The Red Danube, Holiday Affair, Strictly Dishonorable, Angels in the Outfield (1951), Two Tickets to Broadway, It's a Big Country (cameo), Just This Once, Scaramouche, Fearless Fagan, The Naked Spur, Confidentially Connie, Houdini, Walking My Baby Back Home, Prince Valiant, Living It Up, The Black Shield of Falworth, Rogue Cop, Pete Kelly's Blues, My Sister Eileen (1955), Safari (1956), Jet Pilot, Touch of Evil, The Vikings, The Perfect Furlough, Who Was That Lady?, Psycho, Pepe (cameo), The Manchurian Candidate, Bye Bye Birdie, Wives and Lovers, Kid Rodelo, Harper, Three on a Couch, An American Dream, Grand Slam (1968), Hello Down There, One Is a Lonely Number, Night of the Lepus, Boardwalk, The Fog, Halloween H2O: 20 Years Later

Leigh, Vivien: Fire Over England, Dark Journey, Storm in a Teacup, A Yank at Oxford, Sidewalks of London, 21 Days Together, Gone With the Wind, Waterloo Bridge (1940), That Hamilton Woman, Caesar and Cleopatra, Anna Karenina (1948), A Streetcar Named Desire (1951), The Deep Blue Sea, The Roman Spring of Mrs. Stone, Ship of Fools

Lemmon, Jack: It Should Happen to You, Phffft!, Three for the Show, Mister Roberts, My Sister Eileen (1955), You Can't Run Away From It, Fire Down Below, Operation Mad Ball, Cowboy, Bell, Book and Candle, Some Like It Hot (1959), It Happened to Jane, The Apartment, Pepe (cameo), The Wackiest Ship in the Army, The Notorious Landlady, Days of Wine and Roses, Irma la Douce, Under the Yum Yum Tree, Good Neighbor Sam, How to Murder Your Wife, The Great Race, The Fortune Cookie, Luv, The Odd Couple, The April Fools, The Out of Towners (1970), Kotch (dir), The War Between Men and Women, Avanti!, Save the Tiger, The Front Page (1974), The Prisoner of Second Avenue, Alex and the Gypsy, Airport '77, The China Syndrome, Tribute, Buddy Buddy, Missing, Mass Appeal, Macaroni, That's Life!, Long Day's Journey Into Night, The Murder of Mary Phagan, Dad, JFK, For Richer, For Poorer, The Player (cameo), Glengarry Glen Ross, Short Cuts, A Life in the Theatre, Grumpy Old Men, Grumpier Old Men, Getting Away with Murder, The Grass Harp, My Fellow Americans, Hamlet (1996), Out to Sea, 12 Angry Men (1997), The Odd Couple II, Tuesdays with Morrie

Lewis, Jerry: My Friend Irma, At War With the Army, My Friend Irma Goes West, That's My Boy, Sailor Beware, Road to Bali (cameo), Jumping Jacks, The Stooge, Scared Stiff (1953), The Caddy, Money From Home, Living It Up, Three Ring Circus, You're Never Too Young, Artists and Models, Pardners, Hollywood or Bust, The Delicate Delinquent, The Sad Sack, Rock-a-Bye Baby, The Geisha Boy, Lil'l Abner (1959; cameo), Don't Give Up the Ship, Visit to a Small Planet, Raymie (sings title song), The Bellboy (also dir), Cinderfella, The Ladies Man (1961; also dir), The Errand Boy (also dir), It's Only

Money, It's a Mad, Mad Mad Mad World (cameo), The Nutty Professor (1963; also dir), Who's Minding the Store?, The Patsy (also dir), The Disorderly Orderly, The Family Jewels (also dir), Boeing Boeing, Three on a Couch (also dir), Way . . . Way Out, The Big Mouth (also dir), Don't Raise the Bridge, Lower the River, Hook, Line and Sinker, One More Time (dir), Which Way to the Front? (also dir), Hardly Working (also dir), The King of Comedy, Cracking Up (also dir), Slapstick of Another Kind, Cookie, Mr. Saturday Night (cameo), Arizona Dream, Funny Bones

Lloyd, Harold: Grandma's Boy, Safety Last, Why Worry?, Girl Shy, Hot Water, The Freshman (1925), For Heaven's Sake (1926), The Kid Brother, Speedy, Feet First, Movie Crazy, The Cat's Paw, The Milky Way (1936), Professor Beware, The Sin of Harold Diddlebock

Lombard, Carole: The Johnstown Flood, High Voltage, Fast and Loose (1930), Man of the World, Ladies Man (1931), No One Man, Sinners in the Sun, No Man of Her Own (1932), Supernatural, The Eagle and the Hawk (1933), Bolero (1934), We're Not Dressing, Twentieth Century, Now and Forever (1934), Lady By Choice, The Gay Bride, Rumba, Hands Across the Table, Love Before Breakfast, The Princess Comes Across, My Man Godfrey (1936), Swing High, Swing Low, Nothing Sacred, True Confession, Fools for Scandal, Made For Each Other, In Name Only, Vigil in the Night, They Knew What They Wanted, Mr. & Mrs. Smith, To Be or Not to Be (1942)

Loren, Sophia: Variety Lights (bit), Anna (1951; bit), Quo Vadis? (extra), Aida, Attila, Gold of Naples, Woman of the River, Too Bad She's Bad, Scandal in Sorrento, Lucky to Be a Woman, Boy on a Dolphin, The Pride and the Passion, Legend of the Lost, Desire Under the Elms, The Key (1958), Houseboat, The Black Orchid, That Kind of Woman, Heller in Pink Tights, It Started in Naples, A Breath of Scandal, The Millionairess, Two Women, El Cid, Madame, Boccaccio '70, Five Miles to Midnight, The Condemned of Altona, Yesterday, Today and Tomorrow, The Fall of the Roman Empire, Marriage Italian-Style, Operation Crossbow, Lady L, Judith, Arabesque, A Countess From Hong Kong, More Than a Miracle, Ghosts—Italian Style, Sunflower, The Priest's Wife, Lady Liberty, Man of La Mancha, White Sister, The Voyage, Jury of One, The Cassandra Crossing, A Special Day, Brass Target, Blood Feud, Firepower, Angela (1984), Courage (1986), Mario Puzo's "The Fortunate Pilgrim," Ready to Wear (Prêt-à-Porter), Grumpier Old Men

Lorre, Peter: M, The Man Who Knew Too Much (1934), Mad Love (1935), Crime and Punishment (1935), The Secret Agent (1936), Crack-Up (1937), Nancy Steele Is Missing, Think Fast, Mr. Moto, Lancer Spy, Thank You, Mr. Moto, Mr. Moto's Gamble, Mr. Moto Takes a Chance, I'll Give a Million, Mysterious Mr. Moto, Mr. Moto's Last Warning, Mr. Moto in Danger Island, Mr. Moto Takes a Vacation, Strange Cargo, I Was an Adventuress, Island of Doomed Men, Stranger on the Third Floor, You'll Find Out, The Face Behind the Mask, They Met in Bombay, The Maltese Falcon (1941), All Through the Night, Invisible Agent, The Boogie Man Will Get You, Casablanca, Background to Danger, The Constant Nymph, The Cross of Lorraine, Passage to Marseille, The Mask of Dimitrios, Arsenic and Old Lace, The Conspirators, Hollywood Canteen (cameo), Hotel Berlin, Confidential Agent, Three Strangers, Black Angel, The Chase (1946), The Verdict (1946), The Beast With Five Fingers, My Favorite Brunette, Casbah, Rope of Sand, Quicksand, Double Confession, The Lost One, Beat the Devil, 20,000 Leagues Under the Sea, Meet Me in Las Vegas (cameo), Congo Crossing, Around the World in Eighty Days (cameo), The Buster Keaton Story, Silk Stockings, The Story of Mankind (cameo), Hell Ship Mutiny, The Sad Sack, Big Circus, Voyage to the Bottom of the Sea, Tales of Terror, Five Weeks in a Balloon, The Raven (1963), The Comedy of Terrors, Muscle Beach Party (cameo), The Patsy

Loy, Myrna: Ben-Hur (1926; bit), Don Juan, So This Is Paris (1926), The Jazz Singer (1927), Noah's Ark, Renegades (1930), The Devil to Pay, Consolation Marriage, Arrowsmith, Emma (1932), The Wet Parade, Love Me Tonight, Thirteen Women, The Mask of Fu Manchu, The Animal Kingdom, Topaze, The Barbarian, When Ladies Meet, Penthouse, The Prizefighter and the Lady, Men in White, Manhattan Melodrama, The Thin Man, Stamboul Quest, Evelyn Prentice, Broadway Bill, Wings in the Dark, Whipsaw, Wife vs. Secretary, Petticoat Fever, The Great Ziegfeld, To Mary—with Love, Libeled Lady, After the Thin Man, Parnell, Double Wedding, Man-Proof, Test Pilot, Too Hot to Handle (1938), Lucky Night, The Rains Came, Another Thin Man, I Love You Again, Third Finger Left Hand, Love Crazy, Shadow of the Thin Man, The Thin Man Goes Home, So Goes My Love, The Best Years of Our Lives, The Bachelor and the Bobby-Soxer, The Senator Was Indiscreet (cameo), Song of the Thin Man, Mr. Blandings Builds His Dream House, The Red Pony (1949), If This Be Sin, Cheaper by the Dozen, Belles on Their Toes, The Ambassador's Daughter, Lonelyhearts, From the Terrace, Midnight Lace, The April Fools, Airport 1975, The End, Just Tell Me What You Want

Lugosi, Bela: Wild Company, Renegades

(1930), Dracula (1931), The Black Camel, Broadminded, Murders in the Rue Morgue (1932), White Zombie, Chandu the Magician, Island of Lost Souls, The Death Kiss, International House, Night of Terror, The Devil's in Love, The Black Cat (1934), The Mysterious Mr. Wong, Mark of the Vampire, The Raven (1935), Murder by Television, Phantom Ship, The Invisible Ray, Postal Inspector, Son of Frankenstein, The Gorilla, The Phantom Creeps, Ninotchka, The Human Monster, The Saint's Double Trouble, Black Friday, You'll Find Out, The Devil Bat, The Black Cat (1941), The Invisible Ghost, Spooks Run Wild, The Wolf Man, The Ghost of Frankenstein, Black Dragons, The Corpse Vanishes, Bowery at Midnight, Night Monster, Frankenstein Meets the Wolf Man, The Ape Man, Ghosts on the Loose, Return of the Vampire, Voodoo Man, Return of the Ape Man, One Body Too Many, The Body Snatcher, Zombies on Broadway, Genius at Work, Scared to Death (1947), Abbott and Costello Meet Frankenstein, Bela Lugosi Meets a Brooklyn Gorilla, Vampire Over London, Glen or Glenda?, Bride of the Monster, The Black Sleep, Plan 9 From Outer Space

MacDonald, Jeanette: The Love Parade, Monte Carlo, The Lottery Bride, One Hour With You, Love Me Tonight, The Cat and the Fiddle, The Merry Widow (1934), Naughty Marietta, Rose Marie (1936), San Francisco, Maytime, The Firefly, The Girl of the Golden West, Sweethearts, Broadway Serenade, New Moon, Bitter Sweet (1940), Smilin' Through (1941), I Married an Angel, Cairo (1942), Follow the Boys (1944; cameo), Three Daring Daughters, The Sun Comes Up

MacLaine, Shirley: The Trouble With Harry, Artists and Models, Around the World in Eighty Days, The Sheepman, The Matchmaker, Hot Spell, Some Came Running, Ask Any Girl, Career, Ocean's Eleven (cameo), Can-Can, The Apartment, All in a Night's Work, Two Loves, The Children's Hour, My Geisha, Two for the Seesaw, Irma la Douce, What a Way to Go!, The Yellow Rolls-Royce, John Goldfarb, Please Come Home, Gambit, Woman Times Seven, The Bliss of Mrs. Blossom, Sweet Charity, Two Mules for Sister Sara, Desperate Characters, The Possession of Joel Delaney, The Turning Point (1977), Being There, Loving Couples, A Change of Seasons, Terms of Endearment, Cannonball Run II, Out on a Limb, Madame Sousatzka, Steel Magnolias, Waiting for the Light, Postcards From the Edge, Defending Your Life (cameo), Used People, Wrestling Ernest Hemingway, Guarding Tess, The West Side Waltz, The Celluloid Closet (app only), Mrs. Winterbourne, The Evening Star, Get Bruce (app)

MacMurray, Fred: The Gilded Lily, Alice Adams, Hands Across the Table, The Bride Comes Home, The Trail of the Lonesome Pine, Thirteen Hours by Air, The Princess Comes Across, The Texas Rangers (1936), Champagne Waltz, Maid of Salem, Swing High, Swing Low, Exclusive, True Confession, Cocoanut Grove, Sing, You Sinners, Men With Wings, Cafe Society, Invitation to Happiness, Honeymoon in Bali, Remember the Night, Little Old New York, Too Many Husbands, Rangers of Fortune, Virginia, One Night in Lisbon, Dive Bomber, New York Town, The Lady Is Willing, Take a Letter, Darling, The Forest Rangers, Star Spangled Rhythm, Flight for Freedom, Above Suspicion, No Time for Love, Standing Room Only, And the Angels Sing, Double Indemnity, Practically Yours, Where Do We Go From Here?, Murder, He Says, Captain Eddie, Pardon My Past, Smoky (1946), Suddenly, It's Spring, The Egg and I, Singapore, On Our Merry Way, The Miracle of the Bells, An Innocent Affair, Family Honeymoon, Father Was a Fullback, Borderline (1950), Never a Dull Moment (1950), A Millionaire for Christy, Callaway Went Thataway, Fair Wind to Java, The Moonlighter, The Caine Mutiny, Pushover, Woman's World, The Far Horizons, The Rains of Ranchipur, At Gunpoint, There's Always Tomorrow, Gun for a Coward, Quantez, Day of the Bad Man, Good Day for a Hanging, The Shaggy Dog, Face of a Fugitive, The Oregon Trail, The Apartment, The Absent Minded Professor, Bon Voyage!, Son of Flubber, Kisses for My President, Follow Me, Boys!, The Happiest Millionaire, Charley and the Angel, The Swarm, George Stevens: A Filmmaker's Journey (app)

Malkovich, John: Places in the Heart, The Killing Fields, Eleni, Death of a Salesman (1985), Making Mr. Right, The Glass Menagerie (1987), Empire of the Sun, Miles From Home, Dangerous Liaisons, The Sheltering Sky, Queens Logic, The Object of Beauty, Shadows and Fog, Of Mice and Men (1992), Jennifer Eight, Alive (cameo), In the Line of Fire, Heart of Darkness, The Convent, Mary Reilly, The Ogre, Mulholland Falls, The Portrait of a Lady, Con Air, The Man in the Iron Mask (1998), Rounders (1998), Being John Malkovich, The Messenger: The Story of Joan of Arc, RKO 281

March, Fredric: The Wild Party (1929), Sarah and Son, True to the Navy, Paramount on Parade, Laughter, The Royal Family of Broadway, Dr. Jekyll and Mr. Hyde (1932), Strangers in Love, Merrily We Go to Hell, Smilin' Through (1932), The Sign of the Cross, The Eagle and the Hawk (1933), Design for Living, All of Me (1934), Death Takes a Holiday, Good Dame, Affairs of Cellini, The Barretts of Wimpole Street (1934), We Live Again, Les Miserables (1935), Anna Karenina (1935), The Dark Angel, Mary of Scotland,

The Road to Glory, Anthony Adverse, A Star Is Born (1937), Nothing Sacred, The Buccaneer (1938), There Goes My Heart, Trade Winds, Susan and God, Victory (1940), So Ends Our Night, One Foot in Heaven, I Married a Witch, The Adventures of Mark Twain (1944), Tomorrow the World, The Best Years of Our Lives, Another Part of the Forest, An Act of Murder, Christopher Columbus, The Titan—Story of Michelangelo, Death of a Salesman (1951), It's a Big Country, Man on a Tightrope, Executive Suite, The Bridges at Toko-Ri, The Desperate Hours, Alexander the Great, The Man in the Gray Flannel Suit, Middle of the Night, Inherit the Wind, The Young Doctors, The Condemned of Altona, Seven Days in May, Hombre, . . . tick . . . tick . . . tick . . . , The Iceman Cometh

Martin, Steve: Sgt. Pepper's Lonely Hearts Club Band, The Kids Are Alright, The Muppet Movie (cameo), The Jerk, Pennies From Heaven (1981), Dead Men Don't Wear Plaid, The Man With Two Brains, The Lonely Guy, All of Me (1984), Movers and Shakers, Little Shop of Horrors (1986), ¡Three Amigos!, Roxanne, Planes, Trains & Automobiles, Dirty Rotten Scoundrels, Parenthood, My Blue Heaven (1990), L.A. Story, Father of the Bride (1991), Grand Canyon, HouseSitter, Leap of Faith, And the Band Played On, A Simple Twist of Fate, Mixed Nuts, Father of the Bride Part II, Sgt. Bilko, The Spanish Prisoner, The Prince of Egypt, The Out-of-Towners (1999), Bowfinger, Fantasia 2000 (app)

Marvin, Lee: You're in the Navy Now, Hong Kong, We're Not Married, Diplomatic Courier, The Duel at Silver Creek, Hangman's Knot, Eight Iron Men, Seminole, The Glory Brigade, Down Among the Sheltering Palms, The Stranger Wore a Gun, The Big Heat, Gun Fury, The Wild One, Gorilla at Large, The Caine Mutiny, The Raid, Bad Day at Black Rock, Violent Saturday, Not as a Stranger, A Life in the Balance, Pete Kelly's Blues, I Died a Thousand Times, Shack Out on 101, Seven Men From Now, Pillars of the Sky, The Rack, Attack!, Raintree County, The Missouri Traveler, The Comancheros, The Man Who Shot Liberty Valance, Donovan's Reef, The Killers (1964), Cat Ballou, Ship of Fools, The Professionals, The Dirty Dozen, Point Blank, Sergeant Ryker, Hell in the Pacific, Paint Your Wagon, Monte Walsh, Pocket Money, Prime Cut, Emperor of the North, The Iceman Cometh, The Spikes Gang, The Klansman, Shout at the Devil, Great Scout and Cathouse Thursday, Avalanche Express, The Big Red One, Death Hunt, Gorky Park, Dog Day, The Delta Force

Marx Bros.: *all four:* The Cocoanuts, Animal Crackers, Monkey Business (1931), Horse Feathers, Duck Soup; *Groucho, Harpo, Chico only:* A Night at the Opera, A Day at the Races, Room Service, At the Circus, Go West (1940), The Big Store, A Night in Casablanca, Love Happy, The Story of Mankind; *Groucho only:* The King and the Chorus Girl (sty & scr only), Copacabana, Mr. Music, Double Dynamite, A Girl in Every Port (1952), Will Success Spoil Rock Hunter?, Skidoo

Mason, James: The Mill on the Floss, The High Command, Fire Over England, The Return of the Scarlet Pimpernel, Hatter's Castle, The Night Has Eyes, Secret Mission, Thunder Rock, The Man in Grey, Man of Evil, Hotel Reserve, A Place of One's Own, They Were Sisters, The Seventh Veil, The Wicked Lady (1945), Odd Man Out, The Upturned Glass, Caught (1949), Madame Bovary (1949), The Reckless Moment, East Side, West Side, One-Way Street, The Desert Fox, Pandora and the Flying Dutchman, Lady Possessed, 5 Fingers, The Prisoner of Zenda (1952), Face to Face (1952), The Story of Three Loves, The Desert Rats, Julius Caesar (1953), Botany Bay, The Man Between, Prince Valiant, A Star Is Born (1954), 20,000 Leagues Under the Sea, Forever Darling, Bigger Than Life, Island in the Sun, Cry Terror, The Decks Ran Red, North by Northwest, Journey to the Center of the Earth, A Touch of Larceny, The Trials of Oscar Wilde, The Marriage-Go-Round, Hero's Island, Lolita, Escape From Zahrain, Tiara Tahiti, Torpedo Bay, The Fall of the Roman Empire, The Pumpkin Eater, Lord Jim, The Uninhibited, Genghis Khan, The Blue Max, Georgy Girl, The Deadly Affair, Cop-Out, Duffy, The Sea Gull, Mayerling (1968), Age of Consent, Spring and Port Wine, Cold Sweat, Kill! Kill! Kill!, Bad Man's River, Child's Play (1972), The Last of Sheila, The Mackintosh Man, Frankenstein: The True Story, The Destructors (1974), 11 Harrowhouse, Great Expectations (1974), Inside Out (1975), Autobiography of a Princess, Mandingo, Voyage of the Damned, Cross of Iron, Heaven Can Wait (1978), The Boys From Brazil, The Water Babies, The Passage, Murder by Decree, Bloodline, Salem's Lot, ffolkes, A Dangerous Summer, Evil Under the Sun, Ivanhoe (1982), The Verdict (1982), Dr. Fischer of Geneva, Yellowbeard, The Shooting Party, The Assisi Underground

Mastroianni, Marcello: House of Ricordi, Too Bad She's Bad, White Nights (1957), Lucky to Be a Woman, Big Deal on Madonna Street, Where the Hot Wind Blows!, The Tailor's Maid, The Most Wonderful Moment, Bell'Antonio, La Dolce Vita, Divorce—Italian Style, Ghosts of Rome, La Notte, A Very Private Affair, 8½, The Organizer, Yesterday, Today and Tomorrow, Marriage Italian-Style, Casanova '70, The Man With the Balloons, The Tenth Victim, Shoot Loud, Louder . . . I Don't Understand, The Poppy Is Also a Flower, The

Stranger (1967), Ghosts—Italian Style (cameo), Kiss the Other Sheik, A Place for Lovers, Diamonds for Breakfast, Sunflower, Leo the Last, The Priest's Wife, The Pizza Triangle, Fellini's Roma (cameo), It Only Happens to Others, What?, The Grande Bouffe, Massacre in Rome, Salut l'Artiste, The Sunday Woman, We All Loved Each Other So Much (cameo), A Special Day, Wifemistress, Bye Bye Monkey, Stay As You Are, Blood Feud, City of Women, La Pelle, La Nuit de Varennes, Beyond the Door (1982), Gabriela, The Last Horror Film (cameo), Henry IV, Macaroni, Ginger and Fred, Dark Eyes, Intervista, Everybody's Fine, A Fine Romance, Used People, I Don't Want to Talk About It, Ready to Wear (Prêt-à-Porter), Three Lives and Only One Death, Voyage to the Beginning of the World, Marcello Mastroianni: I Remember, Yes, I Remember

Matthau, Walter: The Kentuckian, The Indian Fighter, Bigger Than Life, A Face in the Crowd, Slaughter on Tenth Avenue, King Creole, Voice in the Mirror, Onionhead, Ride a Crooked Trail, Gangster Story (also dir), Strangers When We Meet, Lonely Are the Brave, Who's Got the Action?, Island of Love, Charade, Ensign Pulver, Fail-Safe, Goodbye Charlie, Mirage, The Fortune Cookie, A Guide for the Married Man, The Odd Couple, The Secret Life of an American Wife, Candy, Hello, Dolly!, Cactus Flower, A New Leaf, Plaza Suite, Kotch, Pete 'n' Tillie, Charley Varrick, The Laughing Policeman, The Taking of Pelham One Two Three, Earthquake, The Front Page (1974), The Sunshine Boys, The Bad News Bears, Casey's Shadow, House Calls, California Suite, Hopscotch, Little Miss Marker (1980), Buddy, Buddy, First Monday in October, I Ought to Be in Pictures, The Survivors, Movers and Shakers, Pirates, The Couch Trip, The Incident (1990), JFK (cameo), Dennis the Menace, Grumpy Old Men, I.Q., Grumpier Old Men, The Grass Harp, I'm Not Rappaport, Out to Sea, The Odd Couple II, Hanging Up

McCrea, Joel: The Single Standard (bit), Dynamite (1929), Girls About Town, The Lost Squadron, Bird of Paradise (1932), The Most Dangerous Game, Rockabye, The Silver Cord, Bed of Roses (1933), Chance at Heaven, Gambling Lady, The Richest Girl in the World (1934), Private Worlds, Our Little Girl, Barbary Coast, Splendor, Woman Wanted, These Three, Two in a Crowd, Adventure in Manhattan, Come and Get It, Banjo on My Knee, Internes Can't Take Money, Woman Chases Man, Dead End, Wells Fargo, Three Blind Mice, Union Pacific, They Shall Have Music, Espionage Agent, He Married His Wife, Primrose Path, Foreign Correspondent, Reaching for the Sun, Sullivan's Travels, The Great Man's Lady, The Palm Beach Story, The More the Merrier, Buffalo Bill, The Great Moment, The Unseen (1945), The Virginian (1946), Ramrod, Four Faces West, South of St. Louis, Colorado Territory, Stars in My Crown, The Outriders, Saddle Tramp, Frenchie, Hollywood Story (cameo), Cattle Drive, The San Francisco Story, Shoot First, Lone Hand, Border River, Black Horse Canyon, Wichita, Stranger on Horseback, The First Texan, The Oklahoman, Trooper Hook, Gunsight Ridge, The Tall Stranger, Cattle Empire, Fort Massacre, The Gunfight at Dodge City, Ride the High Country, Cry Blood, Apache, The Great American Cowboy, Mustang Country, George Stevens: A Filmmaker's Journey (app)

McQueen, Steve: Somebody Up There Likes Me (bit), Never Love a Stranger, The Blob (1958), The Great St. Louis Bank Robbery, Never So Few, The Magnificent Seven, The Honeymoon Machine, Hell Is for Heroes, The War Lover, The Great Escape, Soldier in the Rain, Love With the Proper Stranger, Baby the Rain Must Fall, The Cincinnati Kid, Nevada Smith, The Sand Pebbles, The Thomas Crown Affair (1968), Bullitt, The Reivers, On Any Sunday, Le Mans, Junior Bonner, The Getaway (1972), Papillon, The Towering Inferno, An Enemy of the People (1979), Tom Horn, The Hunter

Midler, Bette: Hawaii (bit), The Rose, Divine Madness, Jinxed, Down and Out in Beverly Hills, Ruthless People, Outrageous Fortune, Big Business, Oliver & Company, Beaches, Stella, Scenes From a Mall, For the Boys, Hocus Pocus, Get Shorty, The First Wives Club, That Old Feeling, Fantasia 2000 (app), Get Bruce (app), Isn't She Great, Drowning Mona

Mifune, Toshiro: Stray Dog, Rashomon, The Idiot (1951), The Life of Oharu, Seven Samurai, Throne of Blood, The Lower Depths (1957), The Hidden Fortress, The Bad Sleep Well, Yojimbo, Sanjuro, Chushingură, High and Low, Red Beard, Grand Prix, Hell in the Pacific, Red Sun, Paper Tiger, Midway, Winter Kills, The Bushido Blade, 1941, Shogun, Inchon!, The Challenge (1982), Shadow of the Wolf, Picture Bride

Mills, Hayley: Tiger Bay, Pollyanna, The Parent Trap, Whistle Down the Wind, In Search of the Castaways, Summer Magic, The Chalk Garden, The Moon-Spinners, The Truth About Spring, That Darn Cat (1965), Gypsy Girl, The Daydreamer, The Trouble With Angels, The Family Way, Africa—Texas Style!, A Matter of Innocence, Take a Girl Like You, Cry of the Penguins, Endless Night, Deadly Strangers, The Bananas Boat, The Kingfisher Caper, Appointment With Death, A Troll in Central Park

Minnelli, Liza: In the Good Old Summertime (as baby), Charlie Bubbles, The Sterile Cuckoo, Tell Me That You Love Me, Junie

Moon, Cabaret, Journey Back to Oz, That's Entertainment!, Lucky Lady, A Matter of Time, Silent Movie, New York New York, Arthur, The Muppets Take Manhattan (cameo), That's Dancing!, A Time to Live, Rent-a-Cop, Arthur 2: On the Rocks, Stepping Out, Parallel Lives, The West Side Waltz

Mitchum, Robert: The Human Comedy, We've Never Been Licked, Corvette K-225, Aerial Gunner, The Dancing Masters, Cry Havoc, Gung Ho!, Johnny Doesn't Live Here Any More, When Strangers Marry, Girl Rush, Thirty Seconds Over Tokyo, Nevada, The Story of G.I. Joe, Till the End of Time, Undercurrent, The Locket, Pursued, Crossfire, Desire Me, Out of the Past, Rachel and the Stranger, Blood on the Moon, The Red Pony (1949), The Big Steal, Holiday Affair, Where Danger Lives, My Forbidden Past, His Kind of Woman, The Racket, Macao, One Minute to Zero, The Lusty Men, Second Chance, Angel Face, White Witch Doctor, She Couldn't Say No, River of No Return, Track of the Cat, Not As a Stranger, Night of the Hunter, Man With the Gun, Foreign Intrigue, Bandido, Heaven Knows, Mr. Allison, Fire Down Below (1957), The Enemy Below, Thunder Road, The Hunters, The Angry Hills, The Wonderful Country, Home From the Hill, The Sundowners (1960), Night Fighters, The Grass Is Greener, The Last Time I Saw Archie, Cape Fear (1962), The Longest Day, Two for the Seesaw, The List of Adrian Messenger, Rampage (1963), Man in the Middle, What a Way to Go!, Mister Moses, The Way West, El Dorado, Villa Rides, Anzio, 5 Card Stud, Secret Ceremony, Young Billy Young, The Good Guys and the Bad Guys, Ryan's Daughter, Going Home, The Wrath of God, The Friends of Eddie Coyle, The Yakuza, Farewell, My Lovely, Midway, The Last Tycoon, The Amsterdam Kill, Matilda (1978), The Big Sleep (1978), Breakthrough (1978), Nightkill, Agency, That Championship Season, Maria's Lovers, The Ambassador, Mr. North, Scrooged, Cape Fear (1991; cameo), Woman of Desire, Tombstone (narr only), Backfire!, Dead Man

Monroe, Marilyn: Scudda Hoo! Scudda Hay!, Ladies of the Chorus, Love Happy, A Ticket to Tomahawk, The Asphalt Jungle, All About Eve, Right Cross, The Fireball, Hometown Story, As Young As You Feel, Love Nest, Let's Make It Legal, Clash by Night, We're Not Married, Don't Bother to Knock, Monkey Business (1952), O. Henry's Full House, Niagara, Gentlemen Prefer Blondes, How to Marry a Millionaire, River of No Return, There's No Business Like Show Business, The Seven Year Itch, Bus Stop, The Prince and the Showgirl, Some Like It Hot (1959), Let's Make Love, The Misfits, Marilyn

Montez, Maria: The Invisible Woman, That Night in Rio, The Mystery of Marie Roget, Arabian Nights (1942), White Savage, Ali Baba and the Forty Thieves, Follow the Boys (1944), Cobra Woman, Gypsy Wildcat, Bowery to Broadway, Sudan, Tangier, The Exile, Pirates of Monterey, Siren of Atlantis, The Wicked City

Moore, Demi: Choices, Parasite, Young Doctors in Love, Blame It on Rio, No Small Affair, St. Elmo's Fire, About Last Night . . . , One Crazy Summer, Wisdom, The Seventh Sign, We're No Angels (1989), Ghost, Nothing but Trouble (1991), Mortal Thoughts, The Butcher's Wife, A Few Good Men, Indecent Proposal, Disclosure, Now and Then, The Scarlet Letter (1995), The Juror, If These Walls Could Talk, Striptease, The Hunchback of Notre Dame (1996), Beavis and Butthead Do America, G.I. Jane, Deconstructing Harry, Passion of Mind

Moore, Julianne: Tales from the Darkside: The Movie, The Hand That Rocks the Cradle, The Gun in Betty Lou's Handbag, Body of Evidence, Benny & Joon, The Fugitive (1993), Short Cuts, Vanya on 42nd Street, Roommates, Safe, Nine Months, Assassins, Surviving Picasso, The Lost World: Jurassic Park, The Myth of Fingerprints, Boogie Nights, The Big Lebowski, Psycho (1998), Cookie's Fortune, An Ideal Husband, A Map of the World, The End of the Affair (1999), Magnolia

Muni, Paul: Scarface (1932), I Am a Fugitive From a Chain Gang, The World Changes, Hi, Nellie!, Bordertown, Black Fury, Dr. Socrates, The Story of Louis Pasteur, The Good Earth, The Life of Emile Zola, Juarez, We Are Not Alone, Hudson's Bay, The Commandos Strike at Dawn, Stage Door Canteen, A Song to Remember, Counter-Attack, Angel on My Shoulder, Stranger on the Prowl, The Last Angry Man

Murphy, Eddie: 48HRS., Trading Places, Best Defense, Beverly Hills Cop, The Golden Child, Beverly Hills Cop II, Eddie Murphy Raw, Coming to America, Harlem Nights, Another 48 HRS, Boomerang, The Distinguished Gentleman, Beverly Hills Cop III, Vampire in Brooklyn, The Nutty Professor (1996), Metro, Mulan, Holy Man, Dr. Dolittle (1998), Life, Bowfinger

Murray, Bill: Shame of the Jungle, Next Stop, Greenwich Village (bit), Meatballs, Caddyshack, Where the Buffalo Roam, Loose Shoes, Stripes, Tootsie, Ghostbusters, The Razor's Edge (1984), Nothing Lasts Forever, Little Shop of Horrors, Scrooged, Ghostbusters II, Quick Change (also codir), What About Bob?, Groundhog Day, Mad Dog and Glory, Ed Wood, Kingpin, Space Jam (uncred), Larger Than Life, The Man Who Knew Too Little, Wild Things, Rushmore, With Friends Like These . . . , Cradle Will Rock, Hamlet (2000)

Neeson, Liam: Excalibur, Krull, The Bounty, Lamb, The Innocent (1985), Arthur the King, The Mission, Suspect, A Prayer for the Dying, Duet for One, Satisfaction, The Dead Pool, The Good Mother, High Spirits, Next of Kin, Darkman, Crossing the Line, Under Suspicion, Shining Through, Leap of Faith, Husbands and Wives, Ethan Frome (1993), Deception (1993), Schindler's List, Nell, Rob Roy, Before and After, Michael Collins, Les Misérables (1998), The Haunting (1999), Star Wars: Episode I The Phantom Menace, Gun Shy

Newman, Paul: The Silver Chalice, Somebody Up There Likes Me, The Rack, The Helen Morgan Story, Until They Sail, The Long Hot Summer, The Left-Handed Gun, Cat on a Hot Tin Roof, Rally 'Round the Flag, Boys!, The Young Philadelphians, From the Terrace, Exodus, The Hustler, Paris Blues, Sweet Bird of Youth (1962), Hemingway's Adventures of a Young Man, Hud, A New Kind of Love, The Prize, What a Way to Go!, The Outrage, Lady L, Harper, Torn Curtain, Hombre, Cool Hand Luke, The Secret War of Harry Frigg, Rachel, Rachel (dir, prod), Winning, Butch Cassidy and the Sundance Kid, King: A Filmed Record . . . Montgomery to Memphis (narr), WUSA, Sometimes a Great Notion, Pocket Money, The Effect of Gamma Rays on Man-in-the-Moon Marigolds (dir, prod), The Life and Times of Judge Roy Bean, The Mackintosh Man, The Sting, The Towering Inferno, The Drowning Pool, Silent Movie (cameo), Buffalo Bill and the Indians, or Sitting Bull's History Lesson, Slap Shot, Quintet, When Time Ran Out . . . , The Shadow Box (dir), Fort Apache, The Bronx, Absence of Malice, The Verdict (1982), Harry and Son, The Color of Money, The Glass Menagerie (1987; dir), Fat Man and Little Boy, Blaze, Mr. & Mrs. Bridge, The Hudsucker Proxy, Nobody's Fool (1994), Twilight, Message in a Bottle, Where the Money Is

Nicholson, Jack: The Cry Baby Killer, Too Soon to Love, The Wild Ride, Studs Lonigan, The Little Shop of Horrors, The Broken Land, The Raven (1963), The Terror, Thunder Island (coscr), Ensign Pulver, Back Door to Hell, Ride in the Whirlwind, Flight to Fury, The Shooting, The St. Valentine's Day Massacre, Hell's Angels on Wheels, The Trip (scr), Head, Psych-Out, Easy Rider, Rebel Rousers, On a Clear Day You Can See Forever, Five Easy Pieces, Carnal Knowledge, A Safe Place, Drive, He Said (dir, coscr, coprod), The King of Marvin Gardens, The Last Detail, Chinatown, Tommy, The Passenger, The Fortune, One Flew Over the Cuckoo's Nest, The Missouri Breaks, The Last Tycoon, Goin' South (also dir), The Shining, The Postman Always Rings Twice (1981), Reds, The Border, Terms of Endearment, Prizzi's Honor, Heartburn, The Witches of Eastwick, Broadcast News, Ironweed, Batman (1989), The Two Jakes (also dir), Man Trouble, A Few Good Men, Hoffa, Wolf, The Crossing Guard, Mars Attacks!, The Evening Star, Blood and Wine, As Good As It Gets

Nolte, Nick: Return to Macon County, The Deep, Who'll Stop the Rain, North Dallas Forty, Heart Beat, 48HRS., Cannery Row, Under Fire (1983), Teachers, Grace Quigley, Down and Out in Beverly Hills, Extreme Prejudice, Weeds, Three Fugitives, Farewell to the King, New York Stories, Q & A, Everybody Wins, Another 48 HRS, Cape Fear (1991), The Prince of Tides, The Player (cameo), Lorenzo's Oil, Blue Chips, I'll Do Anything, I Love Trouble (1994), Jefferson in Paris, Mulholland Falls, Mother Night, U Turn, Afterglow, Nightwatch, Affliction, The Thin Red Line (1998), Breakfast of Champions, Simpatico, Trixie

Norton, Edward: Primal Fear, Everyone Says I Love You, The People vs. Larry Flynt, Rounders (1998), American History X, Fight Club, Keeping the Faith

Novak, Kim: The French Line, Pushover, Phffft!, Son of Sinbad, 5 Against the House, The Man With the Golden Arm, Picnic, The Eddy Duchin Story, Jeanne Eagels, Pal Joey, Vertigo, Bell, Book and Candle, Middle of the Night, Strangers When We Meet, Pepe (cameo), Boys' Night Out, The Notorious Landlady, Of Human Bondage (1964), Kiss Me, Stupid, The Amorous Adventures of Moll Flanders, The Legend of Lylah Clare, The Great Bank Robbery, Tales That Witness Madness, The White Buffalo, Just a Gigolo, The Mirror Crack'd, The Children (1990), Liebestraum

O'Hara, Maureen: Jamaica Inn, The Hunchback of Notre Dame (1939), A Bill of Divorcement (1940), Dance, Girl, Dance, They Met in Argentina, How Green Was My Valley, To the Shores of Tripoli, Ten Gentlemen From West Point, The Black Swan, The Immortal Sergeant, This Land Is Mine, The Fallen Sparrow, Buffalo Bill, The Spanish Main, Sentimental Journey, Do You Love Me?, Sinbad the Sailor, The Homestretch, Miracle on 34th Street (1947), The Foxes of Harrow, Sitting Pretty (1948), The Forbidden Street, A Woman's Secret, Father Was a Fullback, Bagdad, Comanche Territory, Tripoli, Rio Grande, Flame of Araby, At Sword's Point, Kangaroo (1952), The Quiet Man, Against All Flags, The Redhead From Wyoming, War Arrow, Fire Over Africa, The Long Gray Line, The Magnificent Matador, Lady Godiva, Lisbon, Everything but the Truth, The Wings of Eagles, Our Man in Havana, The Parent Trap, The Deadly Companions, Mr. Hobbs Takes a Vacation, Spencer's Mountain, McLintock!, The Battle of the Villa Fiorita, The Rare Breed, How Do I Love Thee?, Big Jake, The Red Pony (1973), Only the Lonely, The Christmas Box

Oldman, Gary: Meantime, Sid and Nancy, Prick Up Your Ears, We Think the World of You, Track 29, Criminal Law, Heading Home, State of Grace, Chattahoochee, Rosencrantz and Guildenstern Are Dead, JFK, Bram Stoker's Dracula, True Romance, Romeo Is Bleeding, The Professional, Immortal Beloved, Murder in the First, The Scarlet Letter (1995), Basquiat, The Fifth Element, Air Force One, Nil by Mouth (dir, scr), Lost in Space, Quest for Camelot

Olivier, Laurence: The Yellow Ticket, Friends and Lovers (1931), Westward Passage, I Stand Condemned, As You Like It, Fire Over England, 21 Days Together, The Divorce of Lady X, Q Planes, Wuthering Heights (1939), Rebecca, Pride and Prejudice, That Hamilton Woman, 49th Parallel, The Demi-Paradise, Henry V (1945; also dir), Hamlet (1948; also dir), The Magic Box (cameo), Carrie (1952), The Beggar's Opera, Richard III (1955; also dir), The Prince and the Showgirl (also dir), The Devil's Disciple, The Entertainer, Spartacus, Term of Trial, Bunny Lake Is Missing, Othello (1965), Khartoum, Romeo and Juliet (1968; narr), The Shoes of the Fisherman, Oh! What a Lovely War, Dance of Death (1969), Battle of Britain, David Copperfield (1970), Three Sisters (also dir), Nicholas and Alexandra, Sleuth, Lady Caroline Lamb, Love Among the Ruins, Marathon Man, The Seven-Per-Cent Solution, A Bridge Too Far, The Betsy, The Boys From Brazil, A Little Romance, Dracula (1979), The Jazz Singer (1980), Clash of the Titans, Inchon!, Wagner, The Jigsaw Man, The Bounty, Wild Geese II

O'Toole, Peter: The Savage Innocents, The Day They Robbed the Bank of England, Kidnapped (1960), Lawrence of Arabia, Becket, Lord Jim, What's New, Pussycat?, The Sandpiper (voice only), How to Steal a Million, The Bible, Night of the Generals, Casino Royale (cameo), The Lion in Winter, Great Catherine, Goodbye, Mr. Chips (1969), Brotherly Love, Murphy's War, Under Milk Wood, The Ruling Class, Man of La Mancha, Rosebud, Man Friday, Foxtrot, Rogue Male, Power Play, Zulu Dawn, The Stunt Man, Caligula, My Favorite Year, Svengali (1983), Supergirl, Kim (1984), Creator, Club Paradise, The Last Emperor, High Spirits, The Nutcracker Prince, The Rainbow Thief, King Ralph, The Seventh Coin, Gulliver's Travels (1996), Fairy Tale: A True Story, Phantoms

Pacino, Al: Me, Natalie, The Panic in Needle Park, The Godfather, Scarecrow, Serpico, The Godfather Part II, Dog Day Afternoon, Bobby Deerfield, . . . And Justice for All, Cruising, Author! Author!, Scarface (1983), Revolution (1985), Sea of Love, Dick Tracy, The Godfather Part III, Truth or Dare (app), Frankie and Johnny (1991), Glengarry Glen Ross, Scent of a Woman (1992), Carlito's Way, Two Bits, Heat (1995), City Hall, Looking for Richard (also dir), Donnie Brasco, The Devil's Advocate, The Insider, Any Given Sunday

Paltrow, Gwyneth: Shout (1991), Hook (1991), Malice, Flesh and Bone, Mrs. Parker and the Vicious Circle, Jefferson in Paris, Moonlight and Valentino, Se7en, Hard Eight, The Pallbearer, Emma (1996), Great Expectations (1998), Hush, Sliding Doors, A Perfect Murder, Shakespeare in Love, The Talented Mr. Ripley

Peck, Gregory: Days of Glory, The Keys of the Kingdom, The Valley of Decision, Spellbound, The Yearling, Duel in the Sun, The Macomber Affair, Gentleman's Agreement, The Paradine Case, Yellow Sky, The Great Sinner, Twelve O'Clock High, The Gunfighter, Only the Valiant, David and Bathsheba, Captain Horatio Hornblower, The Snows of Kilimanjaro, The World in His Arms, Roman Holiday, Man With a Million, The Purple Plain, Night People, The Man in the Gray Flannel Suit, Moby Dick (1956), Designing Woman, The Bravados, The Big Country, Pork Chop Hill, Beloved Infidel, On the Beach, The Guns of Navarone, To Kill a Mockingbird, Cape Fear (1962), How the West Was Won, Captain Newman, M.D., Behold a Pale Horse, John F. Kennedy: Years of Lightning, Day of Drums (narr), Mirage, Arabesque, The Stalking Moon, Mackenna's Gold, The Chairman, Marooned, I Walk the Line, Shoot Out, Billy Two Hats, The Omen, MacArthur, The Boys From Brazil, The Sea Wolves, Amazing Grace and Chuck, Old Gringo, Other People's Money, Cape Fear (1991; cameo), The Portrait

Penn, Sean: Taps, Fast Times at Ridgemont High, Bad Boys (1983), Crackers, Racing With the Moon, The Falcon and the Snowman, At Close Range, Shanghai Surprise, Dear America: Letters Home From Vietnam, Colors, Judgment in Berlin, Casualties of War, We're No Angels (1989), State of Grace, The Indian Runner (dir, scr), The Last Party (app), Carlito's Way, The Crossing Guard (dir, scr), Dead Man Walking, The Game, She's So Lovely, U Turn, Hugo Pool, hurlyburly, The Thin Red Line (1998), Sweet and Lowdown, Up at the Villa

Perkins, Anthony: The Actress, Friendly Persuasion (1956), Fear Strikes Out, The Lonely Man, The Tin Star, Desire Under the Elms, This Angry Age, The Matchmaker, Green Mansions, On the Beach, Tall Story, Psycho, Goodbye Again, Phaedra, Five Miles to Midnight, The Trial (1962), Ravishing Idiot, The Fool Killer, Is Paris Burning?, The Champagne Murders, Pretty Poison, Catch-22, WUSA, Someone Behind the Door, Ten Days Wonder, Play It As It Lays, The Life and Times of Judge Roy Bean,

The Last of Sheila (coscr), Lovin' Molly, Murder on the Orient Express, Mahogany, Remember My Name, First, You Cry, Les Miserables (1978), The Black Hole, Winter Kills, ffolkes, Double Negative, Psycho II, Crimes of Passion, Psycho III (also dir), Lucky Stiff (dir), Edge of Sanity, I'm Dangerous Tonight, Psycho IV: The Beginning

Pfeiffer, Michelle: Falling in Love Again, The Hollywood Knights, Charlie Chan and the Curse of the Dragon Queen, Grease 2, Scarface (1983), Into the Night, Ladyhawke, Sweet Liberty, The Witches of Eastwick, Amazon Women on the Moon, Married to the Mob, Tequila Sunrise, Dangerous Liaisons, The Fabulous Baker Boys, The Russia House, Frankie and Johnny (1991), Batman Returns, Love Field, The Age of Innocence (1993), Wolf, Dangerous Minds, Up Close & Personal, To Gillian on Her 37th Birthday, One Fine Day, A Thousand Acres, The Prince of Egypt, The Deep End of the Ocean, A Midsummer Night's Dream (1999), The Story of Us

Pickford, Mary: Rebecca of Sunnybrook Farm (1917), Pollyanna (1920), Suds, Little Annie Rooney, Sparrows, The Gaucho (cameo), Coquette, The Taming of the Shrew (1929)

Pitt, Brad: Less Than Zero (bit), Cutting Class, Happy Together (1989), Across the Tracks, Thelma & Louise, Cool World, Johnny Suede, A River Runs Through It, True Romance, Kalifornia, The Favor, Interview With the Vampire: The Vampire Chronicles, Legends of the Fall, Se7en, Twelve Monkeys, Sleepers, The Devil's Own (1997), Seven Years in Tibet, The Dark Side of the Sun, Meet Joe Black, Fight Club, Being John Malkovich (uncred)

Poitier, Sidney: No Way Out (1950), Cry, the Beloved Country (1951), Red Ball Express, Go, Man, Go! Blackboard Jungle, Good Bye, My Lady, Edge of the City, Something of Value, Band of Angels, The Mark of the Hawk, Virgin Island, The Defiant Ones, Porgy and Bess, All the Young Men, A Raisin in the Sun, Paris Blues, Pressure Point, Lilies of the Field, The Long Ships, The Greatest Story Ever Told, The Bedford Incident, A Patch of Blue, The Slender Thread, Duel at Diablo, In the Heat of the Night, To Sir, With Love, Guess Who's Coming to Dinner, For Love of Ivy, The Lost Man, King: A Filmed Record . . . Montgomery to Memphis (narr), They Call Me MISTER Tibbs!, The Organization, Brother John, Buck and the Preacher (also dir), A Warm December (also dir), Uptown Saturday Night (also dir), Let's Do It Again (1975; also dir), The Wilby Conspiracy, A Piece of the Action (also dir), Stir Crazy (dir), Hanky Panky (dir), Fast Forward (dir), Shoot to Kill (1988), Little Nikita, Ghost Dad (dir), Separate but Equal, Sneakers, Mandela and de Klerk, The Jackal, Free of Eden

Powell, Dick: Blessed Event, The King's Vacation, 42nd Street, Gold Diggers of 1933, Footlight Parade, College Coach, Wonder Bar, Dames, Twenty Million Sweethearts, Happiness Ahead, Flirtation Walk, Gold Diggers of 1935, Page Miss Glory, Broadway Gondolier, Shipmates Forever, Thanks a Million, A Midsummer Night's Dream (1935), Colleen, Hearts Divided, Stage Struck (1936), Gold Diggers of 1937, On the Avenue, Varsity Show, Hollywood Hotel, The Cowboy From Brooklyn, Hard to Get, Going Places (1938), Naughty but Nice, Christmas in July, I Want a Divorce, In the Navy, Model Wife, Star Spangled Rhythm, Happy Go Lucky, True to Life, Riding High (1943), Meet the People, It Happened Tomorrow, Murder, My Sweet, Cornered, Johnny O'Clock, To the Ends of the Earth, Station West, Pitfall, Rogue's Regiment, Mrs. Mike, The Reformer and the Redhead, Right Cross, The Tall Target, Cry Danger, You Never Can Tell, Callaway Went Thataway (cameo), The Bad and the Beautiful, Split Second (1953; dir, prod), Susan Slept Here, The Conqueror (dir, prod), You Can't Run Away From It (dir, prod), The Enemy Below (dir, prod), The Hunters (dir, prod)

Powell, Eleanor: George White's Scandals (1935), Broadway Melody of 1936, Born to Dance, Broadway Melody of 1938, Rosalie, Honolulu, Broadway Melody of 1940, Lady Be Good, Ship Ahoy, Thousands Cheer, I Dood It, Sensations, Duchess of Idaho (cameo)

Powell, William: The Last Command (1928), Canary Murder Case, Charming Sinners, The Greene Murder Case, Benson Murder Case, Paramount on Parade, Man of the World, Ladies' Man (1931), High Pressure, Jewel Robbery, One Way Passage, Lawyer Man, Man Killer, The Kennel Murder Case, Fashions, Manhattan Melodrama, The Key (1934), The Thin Man, Evelyn Prentice, Star of Midnight, Reckless (1935), Escapade (1935), Rendezvous, The Great Ziegfeld, The Ex-Mrs. Bradford, My Man Godfrey (1936), Libeled Lady, After the Thin Man, The Last of Mrs. Cheyney (1937), The Emperor's Candlesticks, Double Wedding, The Baroness and the Butler, Another Thin Man, I Love You Again, Love Crazy, Shadow of the Thin Man, Crossroads (1942), The Youngest Profession (cameo), The Heavenly Body, The Thin Man Goes Home, Ziegfeld Follies, The Hoodlum Saint, Life With Father, Song of the Thin Man, The Senator Was Indiscreet, Mr. Peabody and the Mermaid, Take One False Step, Dancing in the Dark (1949), It's a Big Country (cameo), The Treasure of Lost Canyon, The Girl Who Had Everything, How to Marry a Millionaire, Mister Roberts

Power, Tyrone: Tom Brown of Culver, Flirtation Walk, Girls' Dormitory, Ladies in Love, Lloyd's of London, Love Is News, Cafe Metropole, Thin Ice, Second Honeymoon, Ali Baba Goes to Town (cameo), In Old Chicago, Alexander's Ragtime Band, Marie Antoinette (1938), Suez, Jesse James, Rose of Washington Square, Second Fiddle, The Rains Came, Day-Time Wife, Johnny Apollo, Brigham Young, The Mark of Zorro (1940), Blood and Sand (1941), A Yank in the RAF, Son of Fury, This Above All, The Black Swan, Crash Dive, The Razor's Edge (1946), Nightmare Alley, Captain From Castile, The Luck of the Irish, That Wonderful Urge, Prince of Foxes, The Black Rose, American Guerilla in the Philippines, Rawhide, I'll Never Forget You, Diplomatic Courier, Pony Soldier, Mississippi Gambler, King of the Khyber Rifles, The Long Gray Line, Untamed (1955), The Eddy Duchin Story, Abandon Ship, The Rising of the Moon, The Sun Also Rises, Witness for the Prosecution

Presley, Elvis: Love Me Tender, Loving You, Jailhouse Rock, King Creole, G.I. Blues, Flaming Star, Wild in the Country, Blue Hawaii, Follow That Dream, Kid Galahad (1962), Girls! Girls! Girls!, It Happened at the World's Fair, Fun in Acapulco, Kissin' Cousins, Viva Las Vegas, Roustabout, Girl Happy, Tickle Me, Harum Scarum, Frankie and Johnny (1966), Paradise, Hawaiian Style, Spinout, Easy Come, Easy Go (1967), Double Trouble (1967), Clambake, Stay Away, Joe, Speedway, Live a Little, Love a Little, Charro!, The Trouble With Girls (and How to Get Into It), Change of Habit, Elvis: That's the Way It Is, Elvis on Tour, This Is Elvis

Preston, Robert: King of Alcatraz, Union Pacific, Beau Geste (1939), Typhoon, North West Mounted Police, Moon Over Burma, Lady From Cheyenne, Parachute Battalion, New York Town, The Night of January 16th, Reap the Wild Wind, This Gun for Hire, Wake Island, Star Spangled Rhythm, Night Plane From Chungking, Variety Girl (cameo), The Macomber Affair, Wild Harvest, The Big City (1948), Blood on the Moon, Whispering Smith, Tulsa, The Lady Gambles, The Sundowners (1950), My Outlaw Brother, When I Grow Up, Best of the Badmen, Cloudburst, Face to Face (1952), The Last Frontier (1956), The Dark at the Top of the Stairs, The Music Man, How the West Was Won, Island of Love, All the Way Home, Junior Bonner, Child's Play (1972), Mame, Semi-Tough, S.O.B., Victor/Victoria, The Last Starfighter, Finnegan Begin Again

Price, Vincent: Service De Luxe, The Private Lives of Elizabeth and Essex, Tower of London (1939), The Invisible Man Returns, The House of the Seven Gables, Green Hell, Brigham Young, Hudson's Bay, The Song of Bernadette, The Eve of St. Mark, Wilson, Laura, The Keys of the Kingdom, A Royal Scandal, Leave Her to Heaven, Shock (1946), Dragonwyck, The Web, Moss Rose, The Long Night, Up in Central Park, Abbott and Costello Meet Frankenstein, The Three Musketeers (1948), Rogue's Regiment, The Bribe, Bagdad, Champagne for Caesar, The Baron of Arizona, Curtain Call at Cactus Creek, His Kind of Woman, Adventures of Captain Fabian, The Las Vegas Story, House of Wax, Dangerous Mission, Casanova's Big Night, The Mad Magician, Son of Sinbad, The Vagabond King, Serenade, While the City Sleeps, The Ten Commandments (1956), The Story of Mankind, The Fly (1958), House on Haunted Hill, Big Circus, The Bat, The Return of the Fly, The Tingler, House of Usher, Master of the World, Pit and the Pendulum, Queen of the Nile, Convicts 4, Confessions of an Opium Eater, The Rage of the Buccaneers, Tales of Terror, Tower of London (1962), The Raven (1963), Diary of a Madman, Beach Party (cameo), Twice-Told Tales, The Comedy of Terrors, The Haunted Palace, The Last Man on Earth, The Masque of the Red Death, The Tomb of Ligeia, War Gods of the Deep, Dr. Goldfoot and the Bikini Machine, Dr. Goldfoot and the Girl Bombs, House of 1,000 Dolls, The Jackals, Conqueror Worm, Spirits of the Dead, More Dead Than Alive, The Oblong Box, The Trouble With Girls (and How to Get Into It), Scream and Scream Again, Cry of the Banshee, The Abominable Dr. Phibes, Dr. Phibes Rises Again!, Theater of Blood, Madhouse (1974), It's Not the Size That Counts, Journey Into Fear (1975), Scavenger Hunt, The Monster Club, House of the Long Shadows, Escapes, The Great Mouse Detective, The Offspring, The Whales of August, Dead Heat, Backtrack (1989), Edward Scissorhands, The Heart of Justice, Arabian Knight

Pryor, Richard: The Busy Body, Wild in the Streets, The Phynx, You've Got to Walk It Like You Talk It or You'll Lose That Beat, Dynamite Chicken, Lady Sings the Blues, Wattstax, The Mack, Hit!, Some Call It Loving, Blazing Saddles (coscr), Uptown Saturday Night, Adios Amigo, The Bingo Long Traveling All-Stars & Motor Kings, Car Wash, Silver Streak, Greased Lightning, Which Way Is Up?, Blue Collar, The Wiz, California Suite, Richard Pryor—Live in Concert, The Muppet Movie (cameo), Richard Pryor Is Back Live in Concert, In God We Tru$t, Wholly Moses, Stir Crazy, Bustin' Loose, Richard Pryor Live on the Sunset Strip, Some Kind of Hero, The Toy, Richard Pryor Here and Now, Superman III, Brewster's Millions (1985), Jo Jo Dancer, Your Life Is Calling, Critical Condition, Moving, See No Evil, Hear No Evil,

Harlem Nights, Another You, Mad Dog Time (cameo), Lost Highway

Quaid, Dennis: Crazy Mama (bit), I Never Promised You a Rose Garden, September 30, 1955, The Seniors, Our Winning Season, G.O.R.P., Breaking Away, The Long Riders, All Night Long (1981), Caveman, The Night the Lights Went Out in Georgia, Johnny Belinda (1982), Tough Enough, Jaws 3-D, The Right Stuff, Dreamscape, Enemy Mine, The Big Easy, Innerspace, Suspect, D.O.A. (1988), Everybody's All-American, Great Balls of Fire!, Postcards From the Edge, Come See The Paradise, Undercover Blues, Wilder Napalm, Flesh and Bone, Wyatt Earp, Something to Talk About, Dragonheart, Switchback, Gang Related, The Savior, The Parent Trap (1998), Playing by Heart, Any Given Sunday, Frequency

Quinn, Anthony: The Plainsman (1936), Swing High, Swing Low, Waikiki Wedding, The Last Train From Madrid, Daughter of Shanghai, The Buccaneer (1938), Dangerous to Know, Bulldog Drummond in Africa, King of Alcatraz, King of Chinatown, Union Pacific, Island of Lost Men, Road to Singapore, The Ghost Breakers, City for Conquest, Texas Rangers Ride Again, Blood and Sand (1941), Knockout, Thieves Fall Out, They Died With Their Boots On, Larceny, Inc., Road to Morocco, The Black Swan, The Ox-Bow Incident, Guadalcanal Diary, Buffalo Bill, Roger Touhy, Gangster, Irish Eyes Are Smiling, China Sky, Where Do We Go From Here?, Back to Bataan, California, Sinbad the Sailor, The Imperfect Lady, Black Gold (1947), Tycoon, The Brave Bulls, Mask of the Avenger, Viva Zapata!, The Brigand, The World in His Arms, Against All Flags, City Beneath the Sea, Seminole, Ride, Vaquero!, East of Sumatra, Blowing Wild, Angels of Darkness, Ulysses (1954), Fatal Desire, Attila, La Strada, The Long Wait, The Magnificent Matador, The Naked Street, Seven Cities of Gold, Lust for Life, Man From Del Rio, The Wild Party (1956), The Hunchback of Notre Dame (1957), The River's Edge, The Ride Back, Wild Is the Wind, Hot Spell, The Buccaneer (1958; dir only), The Black Orchid, Warlock (1959), Last Train From Gun Hill, The Savage Innocents, Heller in Pink Tights, Portrait in Black, The Guns of Navarone, Barabbas, Requiem for a Heavyweight, Lawrence of Arabia, The Visit, Behold a Pale Horse, Zorba the Greek, A High Wind in Jamaica, Marco the Magnificent, Lost Command, The 25th Hour, The Happening, The Rover, Guns for San Sebastian, The Shoes of the Fisherman, The Magus, The Secret of Santa Vittoria, A Dream of Kings, Walk in the Spring Rain, R.P.M., Flap, Arruza, Across 110th Street, Deaf Smith and Johnny Ears, The Don Is Dead, The Destructors (1974), The Inheritance (1976), Target of an Assassin, Mohammad, Messenger of God, The Con Artists, The Greek Tycoon, The Children of Sanchez, Caravans, The Passage, Lion of the Desert, High Risk, The Salamander, Ghosts Can't Do It, Revenge (1990), Only the Lonely, Jungle Fever, Mobsters, Last Action Hero, This Can't Be Love, Somebody to Love, A Walk in the Clouds, Gotti

Rathbone, Basil: The Last of Mrs. Cheyney (1929), Bishop Murder Case, David Copperfield (1935), Anna Karenina (1935), The Last Days of Pompeii (1935), A Tale of Two Cities (1935), Captain Blood (1935), Kind Lady (1936), Private Number, Romeo and Juliet (1936), The Garden of Allah, Confession, Love From a Stranger (1937), Make a Wish, Tovarich, The Adventures of Marco Polo, The Adventures of Robin Hood, If I Were King, The Dawn Patrol (1938), Son of Frankenstein, The Hound of the Baskervilles (1939), The Sun Never Sets, The Adventures of Sherlock Holmes, Rio, Tower of London (1939), Rhythm on the River, The Mark of Zorro (1940), The Mad Doctor, The Black Cat (1941), International Lady, Paris Calling, Fingers at the Window, Crossroads (1942), Sherlock Holmes and the Voice of Terror, Sherlock Holmes and the Secret Weapon, Sherlock Holmes in Washington, Above Suspicion, Sherlock Holmes Faces Death, Crazy House (cameo), The Spider Woman, The Scarlet Claw, Bathing Beauty, The Pearl of Death, Frenchman's Creek, The House of Fear, The Woman in Green, Pursuit to Algiers, Terror by Night, Heartbeat, Dressed to Kill (1946), The Adventures of Ichabod and Mr. Toad, Casanova's Big Night, We're No Angels (1955), The Court Jester, The Black Sleep, The Last Hurrah, Pontius Pilate, The Magic Sword, Tales of Terror, The Comedy of Terrors, Planet of Blood, The Ghost in the Invisible Bikini, Voyage to the Prehistoric Planet, Hillbillys in a Haunted House

Reagan, Ronald: Love Is on the Air, Hollywood Hotel, Sergeant Murphy, Swing Your Lady, The Cowboy From Brooklyn, Boy Meets Girl, Girls on Probation, Brother Rat, Going Places (1938), Accidents Will Happen, Secret Service of the Air, Dark Victory, Code of the Secret Service, Naughty but Nice, Hell's Kitchen, The Angels Wash Their Faces, Smashing the Money Ring, Brother Rat and a Baby, An Angel From Texas, Murder in the Air, Knute Rockne, All American, Tugboat Annie Sails Again, Santa Fe Trail, The Bad Man, Million Dollar Baby, Nine Lives Are Not Enough, International Squadron, Kings Row, Juke Girl, Desperate Journey, This Is the Army, Stallion Road, That Hagen Girl, The Voice of the Turtle, John Loves Mary, Night Unto Night, The Girl From Jones Beach, It's a Great Feeling (cameo), The

Hasty Heart, Louisa, Storm Warning, Bedtime for Bonzo, The Last Outpost (1951), Hong Kong, The Winning Team, She's Working Her Way Through College, Tropic Zone, Law and Order (1953), Prisoner of War, Cattle Queen of Montana, Tennessee's Partner, Hellcats of the Navy, The Young Doctors, The Killers (1964)

Redford, Robert: War Hunt, Situation Hopeless—But Not Serious, Inside Daisy Clover, The Chase (1966), This Property Is Condemned, Barefoot in the Park, Butch Cassidy and the Sundance Kid, Downhill Racer, Tell Them Willie Boy Is Here, Little Fauss and Big Halsy, The Hot Rock, The Candidate, Jeremiah Johnson, The Way We Were, The Sting, The Great Gatsby (1974), The Great Waldo Pepper, Three Days of the Condor, All the President's Men, A Bridge Too Far, The Electric Horseman, Brubaker, Ordinary People (dir), The Natural, Out of Africa, Legal Eagles, The Milagro Beanfield War (dir, prod), Havana, Sneakers, A River Runs Through It (dir, narr), Indecent Proposal, Quiz Show (dir, prod), Up Close & Personal, The Horse Whisperer (also dir)

Redgrave, Vanessa: Morgan!, A Man for All Seasons (1966; cameo), Blowup, The Sailor From Gibraltar, Camelot, The Charge of the Light Brigade (1968), Isadora, The Sea Gull, Oh! What a Lovely War, The Devils, Mary, Queen of Scots, The Trojan Women, Murder on the Orient Express, Out of Season, The Seven-Per-Cent Solution, Julia, Agatha, Yanks, Bear Island, Playing for Time, My Body, My Child, Wagner, The Bostonians, Steaming, Wetherby, Three Sovereigns for Sarah, Second Serve, Prick Up Your Ears, Consuming Passions, A Man for All Seasons (1988), Orpheus Descending, The Ballad of the Sad Cafe, Howards End, Breath of Life, Shades of Fear, They, The House of the Spirits, Mother's Boys, Little Odessa, Down Came a Blackbird, A Month by the Lake, Mission: Impossible, Looking for Richard (app), Smilla's Sense of Snow, Wilde, Déjà Vu (1998), Mrs. Dalloway, Deep Impact, Cradle Will Rock, Girl, Interrupted

Remick, Lee: A Face in the Crowd, The Long Hot Summer (1958), These Thousand Hills, Anatomy of a Murder, Wild River, Sanctuary, Experiment in Terror, Days of Wine and Roses, The Running Man (1963), The Wheeler Dealers, Baby the Rain Must Fall, The Hallelujah Trail, No Way to Treat a Lady, The Detective (1968), Hard Contract, Loot, A Severed Head, Sometimes a Great Notion, A Delicate Balance, Hustling, Hennessy, Touch Me Not, The Omen, Telefon, The Medusa Touch, The Europeans, Tribute, The Competition

Reynolds, Burt: Angel Baby (1961), Armored Command, Operation C.I.A., Navajo Joe, Fade-In, Sam Whiskey, 100 Rifles, Impasse, Shark!, Skullduggery, Run, Simon, Run, Fuzz, Deliverance, Everything You Always Wanted to Know About Sex (But Were Afraid to Ask), Shamus, The Man Who Loved Cat Dancing, White Lightning, The Longest Yard, W.W. and the Dixie Dancekings, At Long Last Love, Lucky Lady, Hustle, Silent Movie (cameo), Gator (also dir), Nickelodeon, Smokey and the Bandit, Semi-Tough, The End (also dir), Hooper, Starting Over, Smokey and the Bandit II, Rough Cut, The Cannonball Run, Sharky's Machine (also dir), Paternity, The Best Little Whorehouse in Texas, Best Friends, The Man Who Loved Women (1983), Stroker Ace, Smokey and the Bandit 3 (cameo), Cannonball Run II, City Heat, Stick (also dir), Uphill All the Way (cameo), Heat (1987), Malone, Rent-a-Cop, Switching Channels, Physical Evidence, Breaking In, All Dogs Go to Heaven, Modern Love, The Player (cameo), Cop & ½, The Maddening, Striptease, Mad Dog Time, Citizen Ruth, Meet Wally Sparks, Bean, Boogie Nights, Mystery, Alaska

Reynolds, Debbie: June Bride, The Daughter of Rosie O'Grady, Three Little Words, Two Weeks With Love, Mr. Imperium, Singin' in the Rain, Skirts Ahoy! (cameo), I Love Melvin, The Affairs of Dobie Gillis, Give a Girl a Break, Susan Slept Here, Athena, Hit the Deck, The Tender Trap, The Catered Affair, Meet Me in Las Vegas (cameo), Bundle of Joy, Tammy and the Bachelor, This Happy Feeling, The Mating Game, Say One for Me, It Started With a Kiss, The Gazebo, The Rat Race, Pepe (cameo), The Pleasure of His Company, The Second Time Around, How the West Was Won, My Six Loves, Mary, Mary, The Unsinkable Molly Brown, Goodbye Charlie, The Singing Nun, Divorce American Style, How Sweet It Is!, What's the Matter with Helen?, Charlotte's Web, That's Entertainment!, The Bodyguard (cameo), Heaven & Earth, That's Entertainment III, Mother, Wedding Bell Blues, In & Out, Rudolph the Red-Nosed Reindeer: The Movie

Roberts, Julia: Blood Red, Baja Oklahoma, Satisfaction, Mystic Pizza, Steel Magnolias, Pretty Woman, Flatliners, Sleeping With the Enemy, Dying Young, Hook, The Player (cameo), The Pelican Brief, I Love Trouble (1994), Ready to Wear (Prêt-à-Porter), Something to Talk About, Mary Reilly, Michael Collins, Everyone Says I Love You, My Best Friend's Wedding, Conspiracy Theory, Stepmom, Notting Hill, Runaway Bride, Erin Brockovich

Robinson, Edward G.: Little Caesar, A Lady to Love, Smart Money, Five Star Final, The Hatchet Man, Two Seconds, Tiger Shark, Silver Dollar, The Little Giant, I Loved a Woman, Dark Hazard, The Man With Two Faces, The Whole Town's Talking, Barbary Coast, Bullets or Ballots, Thunder in the City, Kid Galahad (1937),

The Last Gangster, A Slight Case of Murder, The Amazing Doctor Clitterhouse, I Am the Law, Confessions of a Nazi Spy, Blackmail (1939), Dr. Ehrlich's Magic Bullet, Brother Orchid, A Dispatch From Reuters, The Sea Wolf (1941), Manpower, Unholy Partners, Larceny, Inc., Tales of Manhattan, Destroyer, Flesh and Fantasy, Tampico, Mr. Winkle Goes to War, Double Indemnity, The Woman in the Window, Journey Together, Our Vines Have Tender Grapes, Scarlet Street, The Stranger (1946), The Red House, All My Sons, Key Largo, Night Has a Thousand Eyes, House of Strangers, It's a Great Feeling (cameo), Operation X, Actors and Sin, Vice Squad (1953), Big Leaguer, The Glass Web, Black Tuesday, The Violent Men, Tight Spot, A Bullet for Joey, Illegal, Hell on Frisco Bay, Nightmare (1956), The Ten Commandments (1956), A Hole in the Head, Seven Thieves, Pepe (cameo), My Geisha, Two Weeks in Another Town, A Boy Ten Feet Tall, The Prize, Good Neighbor Sam, Robin and the Seven Hoods (cameo), The Outrage, Cheyenne Autumn, The Cincinnati Kid, Peking Blonde, Grand Slam (1967), It's Your Move, Operation St. Peter's, The Biggest Bundle of Them All, Never a Dull Moment (1968), Mackenna's Gold, Song of Norway, Soylent Green

Rogers, Ginger: The Tip Off, The Thirteenth Guest, You Said a Mouthful, 42nd Street, Broadway Bad, Gold Diggers of 1933, Professional Sweetheart, A Shriek in the Night, Sitting Pretty (1933), Flying Down to Rio, Chance at Heaven, Finishing School, Twenty Million Sweethearts, Upperworld, The Gay Divorcee, Romance in Manhattan, Roberta, Star of Midnight, Top Hat, In Person, Follow the Fleet, Swing Time, Shall We Dance, Stage Door, Having Wonderful Time, Vivacious Lady, Carefree, The Story of Vernon & Irene Castle, Bachelor Mother, 5th Ave. Girl, Primrose Path, Lucky Partners, Kitty Foyle, Tom, Dick and Harry, Roxie Hart, Tales of Manhattan, The Major and the Minor, Once Upon a Honeymoon, Tender Comrade, Lady in the Dark, I'll Be Seeing You, Week-end at the Waldorf, Heartbeat, Magnificent Doll, It Had To Be You, The Barkleys of Broadway, Perfect Strangers (1950), Storm Warning, The Groom Wore Spurs, We're Not Married, Monkey Business (1952), Dreamboat, Forever Female, Black Widow (1954), Twist of Fate, Tight Spot, The First Traveling Saleslady, Teen-age Rebel, Oh, Men! Oh, Women!, Harlow (Carol Lynley version), Quick, Let's Get Married, George Stevens: A Filmmaker's Journey (app)

Rooney, Mickey: The Beast of the City, The Big Cage, The Life of Jimmy Dolan, Broadway to Hollywood, The World Changes, Manhattan Melodrama, Chained, Hide-Out, Blind Date (1934), Upperworld, Death on the Diamond, Reckless (1935), A Midsummer Night's Dream (1935), Ah, Wilderness, Riffraff (1935), Little Lord Fauntleroy (1936), The Devil Is a Sissy, A Family Affair, Captains Courageous, Slave Ship, Hoosier Schoolboy, Live, Love and Learn, Thoroughbreds Don't Cry, You're Only Young Once, Judge Hardy's Children, Lord Jeff, Love Finds Andy Hardy, Boys Town, Stablemates, Out West With the Hardys, Huckleberry Finn (1939), The Hardys Ride High, Andy Hardy Gets Spring Fever, Babes in Arms, Judge Hardy and Son, Young Tom Edison, Andy Hardy Meets Debutante, Strike Up the Band, Andy Hardy's Private Secretary, Men of Boys Town, Life Begins for Andy Hardy, Babes on Broadway, The Courtship of Andy Hardy, A Yank at Eton, Andy Hardy's Double Life, The Human Comedy, Thousands Cheer, Girl Crazy (1943), Andy Hardy's Blonde Trouble, National Velvet, Love Laughs at Andy Hardy, Killer McCoy, Summer Holiday (1948), Words and Music, The Big Wheel, Quicksand, The Fireball, He's a Cockeyed Wonder, My Outlaw Brother, The Strip, Sound Off, All Ashore, Off Limits (1953), A Slight Case of Larceny, Drive a Crooked Road, The Atomic Kid, The Bridges at Toko-Ri, The Twinkle in God's Eye, The Bold and the Brave, Francis in the Haunted House, Magnificent Roughnecks, Operation Mad Ball, Baby Face Nelson, Andy Hardy Comes Home, A Nice Little Bank That Should Be Robbed, The Last Mile (1959), The Big Operator, Platinum High School, The Private Lives of Adam and Eve, King of the Roaring 20's—The Story of Arnold Rothstein, Breakfast at Tiffany's, Everything's Ducky, Requiem for a Heavyweight, It's a Mad Mad Mad Mad World, The Secret Invasion, How to Stuff a Wild Bikini, Twenty-four Hours to Kill, Ambush Bay, The Devil in Love, Skidoo, The Extraordinary Seaman, 80 Steps to Jonah, The Comic, Cockeyed Cowboys of Calico County, Pulp, That's Entertainment!, Journey Back to Oz, Find the Lady, The Domino Principle, Pete's Dragon, The Magic of Lassie, The Black Stallion, An Arabian Adventure, Odyssey of the Pacific, The Fox and the Hound, The Care Bears Movie, Lightning, the White Stallion, Erik the Viking, Little Nemo: Adventures in Slumberland, My Heroes Have Always Been Cowboys, Silent Night, Deadly Night 5: The Toymaker, That's Entertainment! III, Babe: Pig in the City

Russell, Kurt: It Happened at the World's Fair, Follow Me, Boys!, The One and Only, Genuine, Original Family Band, The Horse in the Gray Flannel Suit, The Computer Wore Tennis Shoes, The Barefoot Executive, Fools' Parade, Now You See Him, Now You Don't, Charley and the Angel, Superdad, The Strongest Man in the World,

The Deadly Tower, Elvis, Used Cars, Escape From New York, The Fox and the Hound, The Thing, Silkwood, Swing Shift, The Mean Season, The Best of Times, Big Trouble in Little China, Overboard, Tequila Sunrise, Winter People, Tango & Cash, Backdraft, Unlawful Entry, Captain Ron, Tombstone, Stargate, Executive Decision, Escape From L.A., Breakdown, Soldier

Russell, Rosalind: Evelyn Prentice, Forsaking All Others, West Point of the Air, Casino Murder Case, Reckless (1935), China Seas, Rendezvous, It Had to Happen, Under Two Flags, Trouble for Two, Craig's Wife, Night Must Fall (1937), Live, Love and Learn, Man-Proof, Four's a Crowd, The Citadel, Fast and Loose (1939), The Women, His Girl Friday, Hired Wife, No Time for Comedy, This Thing Called Love, They Met in Bombay, The Feminine Touch (1941), Design for Scandal, Take a Letter, Darling, My Sister Eileen (1942), Flight for Freedom, What a Woman!, Roughly Speaking, She Wouldn't Say Yes, Sister Kenny, The Guilt of Janet Ames, Mourning Becomes Electra, The Velvet Touch, Tell It to the Judge, A Woman of Distinction, Never Wave at a WAC, The Girl Rush, Picnic, Auntie Mame, A Majority of One, Five Finger Exercise, Gypsy, The Trouble With Angels, Oh Dad, Poor Dad, Mama's Hung You in the Closet and I'm Feeling So Sad, Rosie!, Where Angels Go . . . Trouble Follows, Mrs. Pollifax—Spy

Ryan, Meg: Rich and Famous, Amityville 3-D, Top Gun (1986), Armed and Dangerous, Innerspace, Promised Land, D.O.A. (1988), The Presidio, When Harry Met Sally . . . , Joe Versus the Volcano, The Doors, Prelude to a Kiss, Sleepless in Seattle, Flesh and Bone, When a Man Loves a Woman, I.Q., French Kiss, Restoration, Courage Under Fire, Addicted to Love, Anastasia (1997), City of Angels, You've Got Mail, hurlyburly, Hanging Up

Ryder, Winona: Lucas, Square Dance, Beetle Juice, 1969, Great Balls of Fire!, Heathers, Welcome Home, Roxy Carmichael, Mermaids, Edward Scissorhands, Night on Earth, Bram Stoker's Dracula, The Age of Innocence (1993), The House of the Spirits, Reality Bites, Little Women (1994), How to Make an American Quilt, Boys, The Crucible (1996), Looking for Richard (app), Alien Resurrection, Celebrity, Girl, Interrupted

Sarandon, Susan: Joe, Lady Liberty, Lovin' Molly, The Front Page (1974), The Rocky Horror Picture Show, The Great Waldo Pepper, One Summer Love, Checkered Flag or Crash, The Other Side of Midnight, The Great Smokey Roadblock, Pretty Baby (1978), King of the Gypsies, Something Short of Paradise, Loving Couples, Atlantic City (1980), Tempest (1982), The Hunger, In Our Hands, The Buddy System, Mussolini: The Decline and Fall of Il Duce, Compromising Positions, The Witches of Eastwick, Bull Durham, Sweet Hearts Dance, The January Man, A Dry White Season, White Palace, Thelma & Louise, The Player (cameo), Bob Roberts (cameo), Light Sleeper, Lorenzo's Oil, The Client, Safe Passage, Little Women (1994), The Celluloid Closet, Dead Man Walking, James and the Giant Peach, Twilight, Stepmom, Illuminata, Cradle Will Rock, Anywhere But Here, Joe Gould's Secret

Schwarzenegger, Arnold: Hercules in New York (as Arnold Strong), The Long Goodbye (bit), Stay Hungry, Pumping Iron, The Villain, Scavenger Hunt, The Jayne Mansfield Story, Conan the Barbarian, Conan the Destroyer, The Terminator, Red Sonja, Commando (1985), Raw Deal (1986), Predator, The Running Man (1987), Red Heat, Twins, Total Recall, Kindergarten Cop, Terminator 2: Judgment Day, Feed, Christmas in Connecticut (1992; dir), Dave (cameo), Last Action Hero, True Lies, Junior, Eraser, Jingle All the Way, Batman & Robin, End of Days

Scott, George C.: The Hanging Tree, Anatomy of a Murder, The Hustler, The List of Adrian Messenger, Dr. Strangelove or: How I Learned to Stop Worrying and Love the Bomb, The Yellow Rolls-Royce, The Bible, Not With My Wife You Don't!, The Flim Flam Man, Petulia, Patton, Jane Eyre (1971), They Might Be Giants, The Last Run, The Hospital, The New Centurions, Rage (1972; also dir), Oklahoma Crude, The Day of the Dolphin, Bank Shot, The Savage Is Loose (also dir), The Hindenburg, Fear on Trial, Islands in the Stream, Crossed Swords (1978), Movie Movie, Hardcore, The Changeling, The Formula, Taps, Oliver Twist (1982), Firestarter, A Christmas Carol (1984), The Last Days of Patton, The Murders in the Rue Morgue (1986), The Exorcist III, The Rescuers Down Under, Malice, The Whipping Boy, Angus, 12 Angry Men (1998), Gloria (1999)

Seagal, Steven: Above the Law, Hard to Kill, Marked for Death, Out for Justice, Under Siege, On Deadly Ground (also dir), Under Siege 2: Dark Territory, Executive Decision, The Glimmer Man, Fire Down Below, My Giant (cameo), The Patriot (1998), Get Bruce (app)

Sellers, Peter: Down Among the Z Men, Orders Are Orders, The Ladykillers, The Man Who Never Was (voice), The Smallest Show on Earth, Your Past Is Showing, Up the Creek (1958), tom thumb, Man in a Cocked Hat, The Mouse That Roared, I'm All Right Jack, The Battle of the Sexes, Two Way Stretch, Never Let Go, The Millionairess, I Like Money (also dir), Only Two Can Play, Waltz of the Toreadors, The Dock Brief, The Road to Hong Kong (cameo), Lolita, The Wrong Arm of the Law, Heavens Above!, Dr. Strangelove or:

How I Learned to Stop Worrying and Love the Bomb, The Pink Panther, The World of Henry Orient, A Shot in the Dark, What's New, Pussycat?, The Wrong Box, After the Fox, Casino Royale, Woman Times Seven, The Bobo, The Party, I Love You, Alice B. Toklas, The Magic Christian, Hoffman, There's a Girl in My Soup, Where Does It Hurt?, Alice's Adventures in Wonderland, The Optimists, The Blockhouse, Undercovers Hero, The Return of the Pink Panther, Murder by Death, The Pink Panther Strikes Again, Revenge of the Pink Panther, The Prisoner of Zenda (1979), Being There, The Fiendish Plot of Dr. Fu Manchu, Trail of the Pink Panther

Shearer, Norma: Way Down East (1920; bit), He Who Gets Slapped, The Student Prince in Old Heidelberg, The Last of Mrs. Cheyney (1929), The Hollywood Revue of 1929, The Divorcee, Strangers May Kiss, A Free Soul, Private Lives, Strange Interlude, Smilin' Through (1932), Riptide, The Barretts of Wimpole Street (1934), Romeo and Juliet (1936), Marie Antoinette, Idiot's Delight, The Women, Escape (1940), We Were Dancing, Her Cardboard Lover

Sinatra, Frank: Ship Ahoy (singer only), Reveille With Beverly (singer only), Higher and Higher, Step Lively, Anchors Aweigh, Till the Clouds Roll By, It Happened in Brooklyn, The Miracle of the Bells, The Kissing Bandit, Take Me Out to the Ball Game, On the Town, Double Dynamite, Meet Danny Wilson, From Here to Eternity, Suddenly, Three Coins in the Fountain (sings title song), Young at Heart, Not as a Stranger, Guys and Dolls, The Tender Trap, The Man With the Golden Arm, Meet Me in Las Vegas (cameo), High Society (1956), Johnny Concho, Around the World in Eighty Days (cameo), Pal Joey, The Pride and the Passion, The Joker Is Wild, Kings Go Forth, Some Came Running, A Hole in the Head, Never So Few, Can Can, Ocean's Eleven, Pepe (cameo), The Devil at 4 O'Clock, Sergeants 3, The Road to Hong Kong (cameo), The Manchurian Candidate, The List of Adrian Messenger (cameo), Come Blow Your Horn, 4 for Texas, Robin and the Seven Hoods, None but the Brave (also dir), Von Ryan's Express, Marriage on the Rocks, The Oscar (cameo), Cast a Giant Shadow (cameo), Assault on a Queen, The Naked Runner, Tony Rome, The Detective (1968), Lady in Cement, Dirty Dingus Magee, That's Entertainment!, Contract on Cherry Street, The First Deadly Sin, Cannonball Run II (cameo), Listen Up: The Lives of Quincy Jones (app only)

Smith, Will: Where the Day Takes You, Six Degrees of Separation, Made in America, Bad Boys, Independence Day, Men in Black, Enemy of the State, Wild Wild West

Spacek, Sissy: Prime Cut, Ginger in the Morning, Badlands, The Migrants, Phantom of the Paradise (set dec only), Katherine, Carrie (1976), Welcome to L.A., 3 Women, Heart Beat, Coal Miner's Daughter, Raggedy Man, Missing, The Man With Two Brains, The River (1984), Marie, Violets Are Blue . . . , 'Night, Mother, Crimes of the Heart, The Long Walk Home, JFK, Hard Promises, A Private Matter, Trading Mom, The Good Old Boys, Beyond the Call, If These Walls Could Talk, The Grass Harp, Affliction, Blast from the Past, The Straight Story

Spacey, Kevin: Heartburn, Working Girl, Rocket Gibraltar, The Murder of Mary Phagan, See No Evil, Hear No Evil, Dad, A Show of Force, Henry & June, Consenting Adults, Glengarry Glen Ross, The Ref, Iron Will, Swimming with Sharks, Outbreak, The Usual Suspects, Se7en, Looking for Richard, A Time to Kill (1996), L.A. Confidential, Albino Alligator (dir only), Midnight in the Garden of Good and Evil, The Negotiator, hurlyburly, A Bug's Life, American Beauty, The Big Kahuna (also coprod)

Stallone, Sylvester: Bananas (bit), Rebel, The Lord's of Flatbush, The Prisoner of Second Avenue (bit), Capone, Death Race 2000, Farewell, My Lovely, Cannonball, Rocky, F.I.S.T., Paradise Alley (1978), Rocky II, Nighthawks, Victory (1981), First Blood, Rocky III, Staying Alive (dir, coscr, coprod), Rhinestone, Rambo: First Blood Part II, Rocky IV, Cobra (1986), Over the Top, Rambo III, Lock Up, Tango & Cash, Rocky V, Oscar, Stop! or My Mom Will Shoot, Cliffhanger, Demolition Man, The Specialist (1994), Judge Dredd, Assassins, Daylight, Cop Land, An Alan Smithee Film: Burn Hollywood Burn, Antz

Stanwyck, Barbara: Ladies of Leisure, Illicit, Ten Cents a Dance, Night Nurse, The Miracle Woman, Forbidden (1932), Shopworn, The Purchase Price, The Bitter Tea of General Yen, Ladies They Talk About, Baby Face, Ever in My Heart, Gambling Lady, The Secret Bride, Woman in Red, Red Salute, Annie Oakley, A Message to Garcia, The Bride Walks Out, His Brother's Wife, Banjo on My Knee, The Plough and the Stars, Internes Can't Take Money, This Is My Affair, Stella Dallas, Always Goodbye, The Mad Miss Manton, Union Pacific, Golden Boy, Remember the Night, The Lady Eve, Meet John Doe, You Belong to Me, Ball of Fire, The Great Man's Lady, The Gay Sisters, Lady of Burlesque, Flesh and Fantasy, Double Indemnity, Hollywood Canteen, Christmas in Connecticut (1945), My Reputation, The Bride Wore Boots, The Strange Love of Martha Ivers, California, The Two Mrs. Carrolls, Variety Girl (cameo), The Other Love, Cry Wolf, B. F.'s Daughter, Sorry, Wrong Number, The Lady Gambles, East Side, West Side, The File on Thelma Jordon, No Man of Her Own (1950), The Furies, To Please a Lady, The Man With a Cloak, Clash by Night, Jeopardy, Titanic (1953), All I Desire, The Moonlighter, Blowing Wild, Witness to Murder (1954), Executive Suite, Cattle Queen of Montana, The Violent Men, Escape to Burma, There's Always Tomorrow, The Maverick Queen, Crime of Passion, Trooper Hook, Forty Guns, Walk on the Wild Side, Roustabout, The Night Walker

Stewart, James: The Murder Man, Next Time We Love, Rose Marie (1936), Wife Vs. Secretary, Small Town Girl (1936), Speed (1936), The Gorgeous Hussy, Born to Dance, After the Thin Man, Seventh Heaven, The Last Gangster, Navy Blue and Gold, Of Human Hearts, Vivacious Lady, The Shopworn Angel, You Can't Take It With You, Made for Each Other (1939), The Ice Follies of 1939, It's a Wonderful World, Mr. Smith Goes to Washington, Destry Rides Again, The Shop Around the Corner, The Mortal Storm, No Time for Comedy, The Philadelphia Story, Come Live With Me, Pot o' Gold, Ziegfeld Girl, It's a Wonderful Life, Magic Town, On Our Merry Way, Call Northside 777, Rope, You Gotta Stay Happy, The Stratton Story, Malaya, Winchester '73, Broken Arrow (1950), The Jackpot, Harvey, No Highway in the Sky, The Greatest Show on Earth, Bend of the River, Carbine Williams, The Naked Spur, Thunder Bay, The Glenn Miller Story, Rear Window, The Far Country, Strategic Air Command, The Man From Laramie, The Man Who Knew Too Much (1956), The Spirit of St. Louis, Night Passage, Vertigo, Bell, Book and Candle, Anatomy of a Murder, The FBI Story, The Mountain Road, X-15 (narr), Two Rode Together, The Man Who Shot Liberty Valance, Mr. Hobbs Takes a Vacation, How the West Was Won, Take Her, She's Mine, Cheyenne Autumn, Dear Brigitte, Shenandoah, Flight of the Phoenix, The Rare Breed, Firecreek, Bandolero!, The Cheyenne Social Club, Fools' Parade, That's Entertainment!, The Shootist, Airport '77, The Big Sleep (1978), The Magic of Lassie, Afurika Monogatari, An American Tail: Fievel Goes West

Stone, Sharon: Stardust Memories (bit), Deadly Blessing, Bolero (1981), Irreconcilable Differences, King Solomon's Mines (1985), Allan Quatermain and the Lost City of Gold, Police Academy 4: Citizens on Patrol, Cold Steel, Above the Law, Action Jackson, Blood and Sand (1989), Beyond the Stars, Total Recall, He Said, She Said, Scissors, Year of the Gun, Basic Instinct, Diary of a Hitman, Sliver, Last Action Hero (cameo), Intersection, The Specialist (1994), The Quick and the Dead (1995), Casino, Diabolique (1996), Last Dance, Sphere, The Mighty, Antz, Gloria (1999), The Muse, Simpatico, Picking Up the Pieces

Streep, Meryl: Julia, The Deer Hunter, Manhattan, The Seduction of Joe Tynan, Kramer vs. Kramer, The French Lieutenant's Woman, Sophie's Choice, Still of the Night, Silkwood, In Our Hands, Falling in Love, Plenty, Out of Africa, Heartburn, Ironweed, A Cry in the Dark, She-Devil, Postcards From the Edge, Defending Your Life, Death Becomes Her, The House of the Spirits, The River Wild, The Bridges of Madison County, Before and After, Marvin's Room, . . . First Do No Harm, Dancing at Lughnasa, One True Thing, Music of the Heart

Streisand, Barbra: Funny Girl, Hello, Dolly!, On a Clear Day You Can See Forever, The Owl and the Pussycat, What's Up, Doc?, Up the Sandbox, The Way We Were, For Pete's Sake, Funny Lady, A Star Is Born, The Main Event, All Night Long (1981), Yentl (also dir), Nuts, Listen Up: The Lives of Quincy Jones, The Prince of Tides (also dir), The Mirror Has Two Faces (also dir), The King and I (1999)

Sutherland, Donald: Castle of the Living Dead, The Bedford Incident, Dr. Terror's House of Horrors, Die! Die! My Darling!, Promise Her Anything, The Dirty Dozen, Sebastian, Interlude (1968), Oedipus the King, The Split, Joanna, MASH, Start the Revolution Without Me, Kelly's Heroes, Alex in Wonderland, The Act of the Heart, Little Murders, Klute, Johnny Got His Gun, F.T.A., Steelyard Blues, Lady Ice, Don't Look Now, Alien Thunder, S*P*Y*S, The Day of the Locust, End of the Game, Fellini's Casanova, 1900, The Eagle Has Landed, The Kentucky Fried Movie (cameo), The Disappearance, Bethune, National Lampoon's Animal House, Invasion of the Body Snatchers (1978), Blood Relatives, The Great Train Robbery, Murder by Decree, A Man, a Woman and a Bank, Bear Island, Nothing Personal, Ordinary People, Gas, Eye of the Needle, Threshold, Max Dugan Returns, Crackers, Ordeal by Innocence, Heaven Help Us, Revolution (1985), Wolf at the Door, The Rosary Murders, The Trouble With Spies, Apprentice to Murder, Lost Angels, Lock Up, A Dry White Season, Dr. Bethune, Backdraft, Eminent Domain, JFK, The Railway Station Man, Buffy the Vampire Slayer, Shadow of the Wolf, Younger and Younger, Benefit of the Doubt, Six Degrees of Separation, The Puppet Masters, Disclosure, Outbreak, Citizen X, A Time to Kill, Shadow Conspiracy, The Assignment, Fallen, Without Limits, virus (1999), Free Money, Instinct

Taylor, Elizabeth: There's One Born Every Minute, Lassie Come Home, Jane Eyre (1944), The White Cliffs of Dover, National Velvet, Courage of Lassie, Cynthia, Life With Father, A Date With Judy, Julia Misbehaves, Little Women (1949), Conspirator, The Big Hangover, Father of the Bride (1950), Quo Vadis? (1951; cameo), Father's Little Dividend, A Place in the Sun, Callaway Went Thataway (cameo),

Love Is Better Than Ever, Ivanhoe (1952), The Girl Who Had Everything, Rhapsody, Elephant Walk, Beau Brummell, The Last Time I Saw Paris, Giant, Raintree County, Cat on a Hot Tin Roof, Suddenly, Last Summer (1959), Butterfield 8, Cleopatra (1963), The V.I.P.s, The Sandpiper, Who's Afraid of Virginia Woolf?, The Taming of the Shrew (1967), Doctor Faustus, Reflections in a Golden Eye, The Comedians, Boom!, Secret Ceremony, The Only Game in Town, Under Milk Wood, X, Y and Zee, Hammersmith Is Out, Ash Wednesday, The Driver's Seat, Night Watch, That's Entertainment!, The Blue Bird (1976), A Little Night Music, Winter Kills, The Mirror Crack'd, Between Friends, George Stevens: A Filmmaker's Journey (app), Malice in Wonderland, Sweet Bird of Youth (1989), The Flintstones

Taylor, Robert: Society Doctor, West Point of the Air, Broadway Melody of 1936, Magnificent Obsession (1935), Small Town Girl (1936), Private Number, His Brother's Wife, The Gorgeous Hussy, Camille, Personal Property, This Is My Affair, Broadway Melody of 1938, A Yank at Oxford, Three Comrades, The Crowd Roars (1938), Stand Up and Fight, Lucky Night, Lady of the Tropics, Remember?, Waterloo Bridge (1940), Escape (1940), Flight Command, Billy the Kid (1941), When Ladies Meet (1941), Johnny Eager, Her Cardboard Lover, Stand By for Action, Bataan, The Youngest Profession (cameo), Song of Russia, Undercurrent, High Wall, The Bribe, Ambush, Conspirator, Devil's Doorway, Quo Vadis? (1951), Westward the Women, Ivanhoe (1952), Above and Beyond, I Love Melvin (cameo), Ride, Vaquero!, All the Brothers Were Valiant, Knights of the Round Table, Valley of the Kings, Rogue Cop, Many Rivers to Cross, Quentin Durward, The Last Hunt, D-Day the Sixth of June, The Power and the Prize, Tip on a Dead Jockey, Saddle the Wind, The Law and Jake Wade, Party Girl (1958), The Hangman, The House of the Seven Hawks, Killers of Kilimanjaro, Miracle of the White Stallions, Cattle King, The Night Walker, Savage Pampas, Johnny Tiger, The Glass Sphinx, Where Angels Go . . . , Trouble Follows, The Day the Hot Line Got Hot

Temple, Shirley: Out All Night, Stand Up and Cheer, Little Miss Marker (1934), Baby Take a Bow, Now and Forever (1934), Bright Eyes, The Little Colonel, Our Little Girl, Curly Top, The Littlest Rebel, Captain January, Poor Little Rich Girl, Dimples, Stowaway, Wee Willie Winkie, Heidi (1937), Ali Baba Goes to Town (cameo), Rebecca of Sunnybrook Farm (1938), Little Miss Broadway, Just Around the Corner, The Little Princess, Susannah of the Mounties, The Blue Bird (1940), Young People, Kathleen, Miss Annie Rooney, Since You Went Away, I'll Be Seeing You, Kiss and Tell (1945), Honeymoon (1947), The Bachelor and the Bobby-Soxer, That Hagen Girl, Fort Apache, Mr. Belvedere Goes to College, Adventure in Baltimore, The Story of Seabiscuit, A Kiss for Corliss

Thompson, Emma: Henry V (1989), The Tall Guy, Impromptu, Dead Again, Howards End, Peter's Friends, Much Ado About Nothing, The Remains of the Day, In the Name of the Father, My Father, the Hero (cameo), Junior, Carrington, Sense and Sensibility, The Winter Guest, Primary Colors, Judas Kiss

Thurman, Uma: Kiss Daddy Goodnight, Johnny Be Good, Dangerous Liaisons (1988), The Adventures of Baron Munchausen, Where the Heart Is (1990), Henry & June, Robin Hood (TVM, 1991), Jennifer Eight, Final Analysis, Mad Dog and Glory, Even Cowgirls Get the Blues, Pulp Fiction, A Month by the Lake, Beautiful Girls, The Truth About Cats & Dogs, Batman & Robin, Gattaca, Les Misérables (1998), The Avengers, Sweet and Lowdown

Tierney, Gene: The Return of Frank James, Hudson's Bay, Tobacco Road, Belle Starr, Sundown, The Shanghai Gesture, Son of Fury, Rings on Her Fingers, Thunder Birds, China Girl (1942), Heaven Can Wait (1943), Laura, A Bell for Adano, Leave Her to Heaven, Dragonwyck, The Razor's Edge (1946), The Ghost and Mrs. Muir, The Iron Curtain, That Wonderful Urge, Whirlpool (1949), Night and the City (1950), Where the Sidewalk Ends, The Mating Season, On the Riviera, The Secret of Convict Lake, Close to My Heart, Way of a Gaucho, Plymouth Adventure, Never Let Me Go, Personal Affair, Black Widow (1954), The Egyptian, The Left Hand of God, Advise & Consent, Toys in the Attic, The Pleasure Seekers

Tracy, Spencer: Up the River, Quick Millions, Sky Devils, Me and My Gal, 20,000 Years in Sing Sing, The Power and the Glory, Man's Castle, The Murder Man, Dante's Inferno, Whipsaw, Riffraff (1935), Fury, San Francisco, Libeled Lady, They Gave Him a Gun, Captains Courageous, The Big City (1937), Mannequin (1937), Test Pilot, Boys Town, Stanley and Livingstone, I Take This Woman, Northwest Passage (Book I—Roger's Rangers), Edison, the Man, Boom Town, Men of Boys Town, Dr. Jekyll and Mr. Hyde (1941), Woman of the Year, Tortilla Flat, Keeper of the Flame, A Guy Named Joe, The Seventh Cross, Thirty Seconds Over Tokyo, Without Love, The Sea of Grass, Cass Timberlane, State of the Union, Edward, My Son, Adam's Rib, Malaya, Father of the Bride (1950), Father's Little Dividend, The People Against O'Hara, Pat and Mike, Plymouth Adventure, The Actress, Broken Lance, Bad Day at Black Rock, The Mountain, Desk Set, The Old Man and the Sea, The

Last Hurrah, Inherit the Wind, The Devil at 4 O'Clock, Judgment at Nuremberg, It's a Mad Mad Mad Mad World, Guess Who's Coming to Dinner

Travolta, John: The Devil's Rain, Carrie (1976), The Boy in the Plastic Bubble, Saturday Night Fever, Grease, Moment by Moment, Urban Cowboy, Blow Out, Staying Alive, Two of a Kind, Perfect, The Experts, Look Who's Talking, Look Who's Talking Too, Shout, Chains of Gold, Boris and Natasha: The Movie (cameo), Look Who's Talking Now, Pulp Fiction, Eyes of an Angel, Get Shorty, White Man's Burden, Broken Arrow (1996), Phenomenon, Michael, Face/Off, She's So Lovely, Mad City, Primary Colors, A Civil Action, The Thin Red Line (1998), The General's Daughter, Battlefield Earth

Turner, Lana: A Star Is Born (1937; bit), They Won't Forget, The Great Garrick, The Adventures of Marco Polo, Four's a Crowd, Love Finds Andy Hardy, Rich Man, Poor Girl, Dramatic School, Calling Dr. Kildare, These Glamour Girls, Two Girls on Broadway, We Who Are Young, Ziegfeld Girl, Dr. Jekyll and Mr. Hyde (1941), Honky Tonk, Johnny Eager, Somewhere I'll Find You, Slightly Dangerous, The Youngest Profession (cameo), Du Barry Was a Lady (cameo), Marriage Is a Private Affair, Keep Your Powder Dry, Week-end at the Waldorf, The Postman Always Rings Twice (1946), Green Dolphin Street, Cass Timberlane, Homecoming, The Three Musketeers (1948), A Life of Her Own, Mr. Imperium, The Merry Widow (1952), The Bad and the Beautiful, Latin Lovers (1953), The Flame and the Flesh, Betrayed (1954), The Prodigal, The Sea Chase, The Rains of Ranchipur, Diane, Peyton Place, The Lady Takes a Flyer, Another Time, Another Place, Imitation of Life (1959), Portrait in Black, By Love Possessed, Bachelor in Paradise, Who's Got the Action?, Love Has Many Faces, Madame X (1966), The Big Cube, Persecution, Bittersweet Love, Witches' Brew

Valentino, Rudolph: The Four Horsemen of the Apocalypse (1921), The Sheik, Blood and Sand (1922), The Eagle, Cobra (1925), Son of the Sheik

Voight, Jon: Hour of the Gun, Fearless Frank, Out of It, Midnight Cowboy, Catch-22, The Revolutionary, Deliverance, The All-American Boy, Conrack, The Odessa File, End of the Game, Coming Home, The Champ (1979), Lookin' to Get Out, Table for Five, Runaway Train, Desert Bloom, The Last of His Tribe, Rainbow Warrior, Convict Cowboy, Heat (1995), Mission: Impossible, Rosewood, Anaconda, Most Wanted, U Turn, The Rainmaker (1997), The Fixer (1998), Enemy of the State, The General (1998), Varsity Blues, A Dog of Flanders (1999)

Washington, Denzel: Carbon Copy, A Soldier's Story, Power, Cry Freedom, For Queen and Country, The Mighty Quinn, Glory (1989), Mo' Better Blues, Heart Condition, Ricochet, Mississippi Masala, Malcolm X (1992), Much Ado About Nothing, The Pelican Brief, Philadelphia, Crimson Tide, Devil in a Blue Dress, Virtuosity, Courage Under Fire, The Preacher's Wife, Fallen, He Got Game, The Siege, The Bone Collector, The Hurricane (1999)

Wayne, John: Hangman's House (bit), The Big Trail, Central Airport (bit), The Life of Jimmy Dolan, Baby Face, College Coach (bit), California Straight Ahead, I Cover the War, Stagecoach (1939), Allegheny Uprising, Dark Command, Three Faces West, The Long Voyage Home, Seven Sinners, A Man Betrayed, Lady From Louisiana, Shepherd of the Hills, Lady for a Night, Reap the Wild Wind, The Spoilers (1942), In Old California, Flying Tigers, Reunion in France, Pittsburgh, A Lady Takes a Chance, War of the Wildcats, The Fighting Seabees, Tall in the Saddle, Flame of the Barbary Coast, Back to Bataan, They Were Expendable, Dakota (1945), Without Reservations, Angel and the Badman, Tycoon, Fort Apache, Red River, Wake of the Red Witch, 3 Godfathers, The Fighting Kentuckian, She Wore a Yellow Ribbon, Sands of Iwo Jima, Rio Grande, Operation Pacific, Flying Leathernecks, The Quiet Man, Big Jim McLain, Trouble Along the Way, Island in the Sky, Hondo, The High and the Mighty, The Sea Chase, Blood Alley, The Conqueror, The Searchers, The Wings of Eagles, Jet Pilot, Legend of the Lost, I Married a Woman (cameo), The Barbarian and the Geisha, Rio Bravo, The Horse Soldiers, The Alamo, North to Alaska, The Comancheros, The Man Who Shot Liberty Valance, Hatari!, The Longest Day, How the West Was Won, Donovan's Reef, McLintock!, Circus World, The Greatest Story Ever Told (cameo), In Harm's Way, The Sons of Katie Elder, Cast a Giant Shadow (cameo), The War Wagon, El Dorado, The Green Berets, Hellfighters, True Grit, The Undefeated, Chisum, Rio Lobo, Big Jake, The Cowboys, Cancel My Reservation (cameo), The Train Robbers, Cahill—United States Marshal, McQ, Brannigan, Rooster Cogburn, The Shootist

Weaver, Sigourney: Annie Hall (bit), Madman, Alien, Eyewitness (1981), The Year of Living Dangerously, Deal of the Century, Ghostbusters, One Woman or Two, Aliens, Half Moon Street, Gorillas in the Mist, Working Girl, Ghostbusters II, Alien^3, 1492: Conquest of Paradise, Dave, Death and the Maiden, Jeffrey, Copycat, The Ice Storm, Snow White, Alien Resurrection, A Map of the World, Galaxy Quest, Get Bruce (app)

Welles, Orson: *As actor only:* Swiss Family Robinson (1940; narr only), Jane Eyre (1944), Follow the Boys (1944), Tomorrow

Is Forever, Duel in the Sun (narr), Black Magic (1949), Prince of Foxes, The Third Man, The Black Rose, Trent's Last Case, Royal Affairs in Versailles, Trouble in the Glen, Three Cases of Murder, Moby Dick (1956), Man in the Shadow, The Long Hot Summer (1958), The Roots of Heaven, The Vikings (narr), Compulsion, Ferry to Hong Kong, David and Goliath, Crack in the Mirror, The Battle of Austerlitz, The Tartars, King of Kings (1961; narr), Lafayette, The V.I.P.s, Marco the Magnificent, A King's Story (narr), Is Paris Burning?, A Man for All Seasons (1966), Casino Royale, The Sailor From Gibraltar, I'll Never Forget What's 'is Name, Oedipus the King, The Last Roman, The Southern Star, House of Cards (1969), The Thirteen Chairs, The Battle of Neretva, Start the Revolution Without Me, The Kremlin Letter, Catch-22, Waterloo, A Safe Place, Ten Days Wonder, Treasure Island (1972), Get to Know Your Rabbit, Necromancy, Bugs Bunny Superstar (narr), Ten Little Indians (1975), Voyage of the Damned, It Happened One Christmas, The Muppet Movie (cameo), The Double McGuffin, Shogun (narr), Butterfly, History of the World—Part 1, Slapstick (of Another Kind), In Our Hands, The Transformers, Someone to Love

West, Mae: Night After Night, She Done Him Wrong, I'm No Angel, Belle of the Nineties, Goin' to Town, Klondike Annie, Go West, Young Man, Every Day's a Holiday, My Little Chickadee, The Heat's On, Myra Breckinridge, Sextette

Widmark, Richard: Kiss of Death (1947), The Street With No Name, Road House (1948), Yellow Sky, Down to the Sea in Ships (1949), Slattery's Hurricane, Night and the City (1950), Panic in the Streets, No Way Out (1950), Halls of Montezuma, The Frogmen, Red Skies of Montana, Don't Bother to Knock, O. Henry's Full House, My Pal Gus, Destination Gobi, Pickup on South Street, Take the High Ground, Hell and High Water, Garden of Evil, Broken Lance, A Prize of Gold, The Cobweb, Backlash (1956), Run for the Sun, The Last Wagon, Saint Joan, Time Limit, The Law and Jake Wade, The Tunnel of Love, The Trap (1959), Warlock (1959), The Alamo, The Secret Ways, Two Rode Together, Judgment at Nuremberg, How the West Was Won, Flight From Ashiya, The Long Ships, Cheyenne Autumn, The Bedford Incident, Alvarez Kelly, The Way West, Madigan, Death of a Gunfighter, The Moonshine War, A Talent for Loving, When the Legends Die, Murder on the Orient Express, To the Devil—A Daughter, Twilight's Last Gleaming, The Domino Principle, Rollercoaster, Coma, The Swarm, Bear Island, National Lampoon Goes to the Movies, Hanky Panky, The Final Option, Against All Odds (1984), A Gathering of Old Men, Once Upon a Texas Train, Cold Sassy Tree, True Colors

Wilder, Gene: Bonnie and Clyde, The Producers, Start the Revolution Without Me, Quackser Fortune Has a Cousin in the Bronx, Willy Wonka and the Chocolate Factory, Everything You Always Wanted to Know About Sex (But Were Afraid to Ask), Blazing Saddles, Rhinoceros, Thursday's Game, Young Frankenstein, The Little Prince, The Adventure of Sherlock Holmes' Smarter Brother, Silver Streak, The World's Greatest Lover, The Frisco Kid, Stir Crazy, Sunday Lovers, Hanky Panky, The Woman in Red, Haunted Honeymoon (1986), See No Evil, Hear No Evil, Funny About Love, Another You

Williams, Robin: Can I Do It . . . Til I Need Glasses?, Popeye, The World According to Garp, The Survivors, Moscow on the Hudson, The Best of Times, Club Paradise, Seize the Day, Dear America: Letters Home From Vietnam, Good Morning, Vietnam, The Adventures of Baron Munchausen (cameo), Dead Poets Society, Cadillac Man, Awakenings, Dead Again, The Fisher King, Hook, FernGully . . . The Last Rainforest, Aladdin, Toys, Mrs. Doubtfire, Being Human, To Wong Foo, Thanks For Everything, Julie Newmar (cameo), Nine Months, Jumanji, The birdcage, Jack, Aladdin and the King of Thieves, The Secret Agent (1996, cameo), Hamlet (1996), Fathers' Day, Flubber, Deconstructing Harry, Good Will Hunting, What Dreams May Come, Patch Adams, Jakob the Liar, Bicentennial Man, Get Bruce (app)

Willis, Bruce: The First Deadly Sin (bit), The Verdict (1982; bit), Blind Date (1987), Sunset, Die Hard, Look Who's Talking, In Country, Die Hard 2, Look Who's Talking Too, The Bonfire of the Vanities, Mortal Thoughts, Hudson Hawk, Billy Bathgate, The Last Boy Scout, The Player (cameo), Death Becomes Her, National Lampoon's Loaded Weapon I (cameo), Striking Distance, North, Color of Night, Pulp Fiction, Nobody's Fool (1994), Die Hard With a Vengeance, Four Rooms (uncred), Twelve Monkeys, Last Man Standing, Beavis and Butt-head Do America, The Fifth Element, The Jackal, Mercury Rising, Armageddon, The Siege, Breakfast of Champions, The Sixth Sense, The Story of Us, The Whole Nine Yards

Winger, Debra: Slumber Party '57, Thank God, It's Friday, French Postcards, Urban Cowboy, An Officer and a Gentleman, E.T. The Extra-Terrestrial, Cannery Row, Terms of Endearment, Mike's Murder, Legal Eagles, Black Widow (1986), Made in Heaven, Betrayed (1988), Everybody Wins, The Sheltering Sky, Leap of Faith, Wilder Napalm, A Dangerous Woman, Shadowlands (1993), Forget Paris

Wood, Natalie: Happy Land (bit), Tomorrow Is Forever, The Bride Wore Boots, Driftwood, Miracle on 34th Street (1947), The Ghost and Mrs. Muir, Scudda Hoo! Scudda Hay!, Chicken Every Sunday, The Green Promise, Father Was a Fullback, No Sad Songs for Me, Our Very Own, Never a Dull Moment (1950), The Jackpot, Dear Brat (bit), The Blue Veil, Just for You, The Rose Bowl Story, The Star, The Silver Chalice, One Desire, Rebel Without a Cause, The Searchers, The Burning Hills, A Cry in the Night, The Girl He Left Behind, Bombers B-52, Marjorie Morningstar, Kings Go Forth, Cash McCall, All the Fine Young Cannibals, Splendor in the Grass, West Side Story, Gypsy (1962), Love With the Proper Stranger, Sex and the Single Girl, The Great Race, Inside Daisy Clover, This Property Is Condemned, Penelope, Bob & Carol & Ted & Alice, The Candidate (cameo), The Affair (1973), Peeper, Meteor, The Cracker Factory, The Last Married Couple in America, Willie and Phil (cameo), Brainstorm (1983)

Woods, James: The Visitors (1972), Hickey & Boggs, The Way We Were, The Gambler, Distance, Night Moves, Alex and the Gypsy, The Disappearance of Aimee, Raid on Entebbe, The Choirboys, The Onion Field, The Black Marble (cameo), Eyewitness (1981), Fast-Walking, Split Image, Videodrome, Against All Odds (1984), Once Upon a Time in America, Cat's Eye, Joshua Then and Now, Badge of the Assassin, Salvador, Promise, Best Seller, In Love and War (1987), Cop, The Boost, True Believer, My Name Is Bill W., Immediate Family, The Hard Way (1991), The Boys (1991), Straight Talk, Diggstown, Citizen Cohn, Chaplin, The Getaway (1994), Curse of the Starving Class, Next Door, The Specialist (1994), Casino, Nixon, The Summer of Ben Tyler, Killer: A Journal of Murder, Ghosts of Mississippi, Hercules (1997), Contact, Kicked in the Head, Fear and Loathing in Las Vegas, Vampires, Another Day in Paradise, True Crime, The General's Daughter, Any Given Sunday, Play It to the Bone (cameo), The Virgin Suicides

Woodward, Joanne: Count Three and Pray, A Kiss Before Dying (1956), The Three Faces of Eve, No Down Payment, The Long Hot Summer (1958), Rally 'Round the Flag, Boys!, The Sound and the Fury, The Fugitive Kind, From the Terrace, Paris Blues, The Stripper, A New Kind of Love, Signpost to Murder, A Big Hand for the Little Lady, A Fine Madness, Rachel, Rachel, Winning, King: A Filmed Record . . . Montgomery to Memphis (narr), WUSA, They Might Be Giants, The Effect of Gamma Rays on Man-in-the-Moon Marigolds, Summer Wishes, Winter Dreams, The Drowning Pool, Sybil, See How She Runs, The End, A Christmas to Remember, The Shadow Box, Harry and Son, Do You Remember Love, The Glass Menagerie (1987), Mr. & Mrs. Bridge, Blind Spot (1993), The Age of Innocence (1993; narr), Philadelphia, Breathing Lessons

Wyman, Jane: The Kid From Spain (bit), Elmer the Great (bit), All the King's Horses (bit), Rumba (bit), King of Burlesque (bit), Polo Joe (bit), Anything Goes (1936; bit), Cain and Mabel (bit), Gold Diggers of 1937 (bit), My Man Godfrey, Stage Struck (1936; bit), The King and the Chorus Girl, Ready, Willing and Able (bit), Slim, Wide Open Faces, Fools for Scandal (bit), The Crowd Roars (1938), Brother Rat, Tail Spin, Brother Rat and a Baby, An Angel From Texas, My Love Came Back, Tugboat Annie Sails Again, Honeymoon for Three, Bad Men of Missouri, You're in the Army Now, The Body Disappears, Larceny, Inc., My Favorite Spy (1942), Footlight Serenade, Princess O'Rourke, Make Your Own Bed, Crime By Night, The Doughgirls, Hollywood Canteen (cameo), The Lost Weekend, One More Tomorrow, Night and Day, The Yearling, Cheyenne, Magic Town, Johnny Belinda (1948), A Kiss in the Dark, It's a Great Feeling, The Lady Takes a Sailor, Stage Fright, The Glass Menagerie (1950), Three Guys Named Mike, Here Comes the Groom, The Blue Veil, Starlift (cameo), The Story of Will Rogers, Just for You, Let's Do It Again (1953), So Big, Magnificent Obsession (1954), Lucy Gallant, All That Heaven Allows, Miracle in the Rain, Holiday for Lovers, Pollyanna (1960), Bon Voyage!, How to Commit Marriage

Young, Loretta: The Devil to Pay, Show Girl in Hollywood (cameo), Big Business Girl, I Like Your Nerve, Platinum Blonde, The Ruling Voice, Taxi!, The Hatchet Man, Week-end Marriage, Life Begins, They Call It Sin, Employees Entrance, Grand Slam (1933), Zoo in Budapest, The Life of Jimmy Dolan, Midnight Mary, Heroes for Sale, The Devil's in Love, Man's Castle, House of Rothschild, Caravan, Clive of India, Shanghai, The Call of the Wild (1935), The Crusades, The Unguarded Hour, Private Number, Ramona, Ladies in Love, Love Is News, Cafe Metropole, Love Under Fire, Wife, Doctor and Nurse, Second Honeymoon, Four Men and a Prayer, Three Blind Mice, Suez, Kentucky, The Story of Alexander Graham Bell, Wife, Husband and Friend, Eternally Yours, The Doctor Takes a Wife, He Stayed for Breakfast, Lady From Cheyenne, The Men in Her Life, Bedtime Story (1941), A Night to Remember (1943), China, Ladies Courageous, And Now Tomorrow, Along Came Jones, The Stranger (1946), The Perfect Marriage, The Farmer's Daughter (1947), The Bishop's Wife, Rachel and the Stranger, The Accused (1948), Mother Is a Freshman, Come to the Stable, Key to the City, Cause for Alarm, Half Angel, Paula, Because of You, It Happens Every Thursday